California
CIVIL CODE

Mat #42810333

© 2023 Thomson Reuters

ISBN: 978-1-731-98593-4

This publication was created to provide you with accurate and authoritative information concerning the subject matter covered; however, this publication was not necessarily prepared by persons licensed to practice law in a particular jurisdiction. The publisher is not engaged in rendering legal or other professional advice, and this publication is not a substitute for the advice of an attorney. If you require legal or other expert advice, you should seek the services of a competent attorney or other professional.

West's and Westlaw are registered in the U.S. Patent and Trademark Office.
Thomson Reuters Westlaw is a trademark of Thomson Reuters and its affiliates.

PREFACE

California Civil Code contains the complete text of the California Civil Code in one portable volume. Additionally, cross references are included to guide users to related provisions throughout the California Constitution and California Codes.

WHAT'S NEW

Includes all laws through c. 997 of the 2022 portion of the 2021–2022 Regular Session, and propositions voted on at the Nov. 8, 2022 election.

ADDITIONAL INFORMATION

All California legislative enactments in 2022 are effective January 1, 2023, unless indicated otherwise. Additions or changes in statutes affected by 2022 legislation are indicated by underlining; deletions are indicated by asterisks.

Codified legislation which is subject to a governor's veto is followed by an italicized note indicating that fact. For the text of the message, please consult the Historical and Statutory Notes for the provision in *West's Annotated California Codes* or the material pertaining to the legislation affecting the provision in *West's California Legislative Service*.

For official election results, see https://electionresults.sos.ca.gov.

Section captions have been prepared by the publisher, unless specifically indicated otherwise.

CONTACT US

For additional information or research assistance, contact the Reference Attorneys at 1-800-REF-ATTY (1-800-733-2889) or by Live Chat: Access via Westlaw. Contact our U.S. legal editorial department directly with your questions and suggestions by e-mail at editors.us-legal@tr.com.

Thank you for subscribing to this product. Should you have any questions regarding this product, please contact Customer Service at 1-800-328-4880 or by submitting an online request through our Support center on legal.thomsonreuters.com. If you would like to inquire about related publications, or to place an order, please contact us at 1-888-728-7677 or visit us at legal.thomsonreuters.com.

THE PUBLISHER

December 2022

THOMSON REUTERS PROVIEW™

This title is one of many now available on your tablet as an eBook.

Take your research mobile. Powered by the Thomson Reuters ProView™ app, our eBooks deliver the same trusted content as your print resources, but in a compact, on-the-go format.

ProView eBooks are designed for the way you work. You can add your own notes and highlights to the text, and all of your annotations will transfer electronically to every new edition of your eBook.

You can also instantly verify primary authority with built-in links to Westlaw® and KeyCite®, so you can be confident that you're accessing the most current and accurate information.

To find out more about ProView eBooks and available discounts, call 1-800-328-9352.

TABLE OF SECTIONS AFFECTED

This table indicates sections affected by 2022 legislation

Civil Code

Sec.	Effect	Chap.	Sec.
51.7	Amended	48	4
51.14	Added	555	1
51.17	Added	315	1
52	Amended	48	5
52.6	Amended	106	1
52.65	Added	760	1
52.8	Added	26	1
54.3	Amended	48	6
55.32	Amended	897	1
56.05	Amended	690	1
56.06	Amended	690	2
56.10	Amended	968	1
		993	1
			1.5
56.108	Added	628	2
56.109	Added	810	1
prec. § 56.251 Div. 1 Pt. 2.6 ch. 4.1	Added	690	3
56.251	Added	690	3
682.1	Amended	29	1
714.6	Amended	28	20
798.7	Amended	666	1
798.45	Amended	666	2
798.53	Amended	648	1
800.4	Amended	633	1
800.40.5	Added	633	2
815.11	Repealed	131	1
850	Amended	258	2
851	Amended	258	3
853	Amended	258	4
1102.5	Amended	420	9
1632.5	Amended	452	18
1633.3	Amended	39	1
1708.88	Added	504	1
1714.29	Added	586	2
1748.13	Amended	452	19
prec. § 1749.8 Div. 3 Pt. 4 Title 1.4D	Added	857	1
1749.8	Added	857	1
1749.8.1	Added	857	1
1749.8.2	Added	857	1

TABLE OF SECTIONS AFFECTED

Sec.	Effect	Chap.	Sec.
1749.8.3	Added	857	1
1749.8.4	Added	857	1
1749.8.5	Added	857	1
1770	Amended	324	1
prec. § 1784.1 Div. 3 Pt. 4 Title 1.5A	Added	863	1
1784.1	Added	863	1
1788.100	Amended	452	20
1788.103	Amended	452	21
1788.104	Amended	452	22
1789.11	Amended	965	1
1789.12	Amended	452	23
		965	2
1789.13	Amended	965	3
1789.134	Added	965	4
1789.135	Added	965	5
1789.14	Amended	965	6
1789.15	Amended	965	7
1789.16	Amended	965	8
1789.19	Amended	965	9
1789.21	Amended	965	10
1789.25	Amended	965	11
1791	Amended	379	2
1793	Amended	464	1
1793.01	Added	464	2
1798.3	Amended	452	24
			25
1798.24	Amended	28	21
1798.29	Amended	28	22
		419	14
			14.5
1798.82	Amended	28	23
1798.91.04	Amended	785	2
	Repealed	785	4
1798.91.05	Amended	785	3
	Repealed	785	4
1798.91.06	Repealed	785	4
prec. § 1798.97.1 Div. 3 Pt. 4 Title 1.81.35	Added	989	2
1798.97.1	Added	989	2
1798.97.2	Added	989	2
1798.97.3	Added	989	2
1798.97.4	Added	989	2
1798.97.5	Added	989	2
1798.97.6	Added	989	2
1798.99.1	Amended	482	1
prec. § 1798.99.20 Div. 3 Pt. 4 Title 1.81.46	Added	881	1
1798.99.20	Added	881	1
1798.99.21	Added	881	1
1798.99.22	Added	881	1

TABLE OF SECTIONS AFFECTED

Sec.	Effect	Chap.	Sec.
1798.99.23	Added	881	1
prec. § 1798.99.28 Div. 3 Pt. 4 Title 1.81.47	Added	320	2
1798.99.28	Added	320	2
1798.99.29	Added	320	2
1798.99.30	Added	320	2
1798.99.31	Added	320	2
1798.99.32	Added	320	2
1798.99.33	Added	320	2
1798.99.35	Added	320	2
1798.99.40	Added	320	2
1798.99.80	Amended	420	10
1799.91	Amended	149	1
1799.92	Amended	149	2
1799.96	Amended	149	3
1812.201	Amended	452	26
1834.9.3	Added	551	2
1916.5	Amended	452	27
1946.7	Amended	28	24
		558	1
1950.1	Added	288	1
1954.06	Amended	670	1
prec. § 1954.08 Div. 3 Pt. 4 Title 5 ch. 2.4	Added	645	1
1954.08	Added	645	1
1954.09	Added	645	1
1954.091	Added	645	1
1954.092	Added	645	1
1954.093	Added	645	1
2079.7	Amended	258	5
2505	Amended	740	1
2505.5	Added	740	2
2506	Added	740	3
2782.6	Amended	258	6
2923.3	Amended	452	28
2924	Amended	452	29
2924.8	Amended	452	30
2924.12	Amended	452	31
2924.17	Amended	452	32
2924.19	Amended	452	33
2924.20	Amended	452	34
2924c	Amended	452	35
2924d	Amended	642	1
	Added	642	2
2924f	Amended	642	3
			4
2924g	Amended	642	5
			6
2924h	Amended	642	7
			8

TABLE OF SECTIONS AFFECTED

Sec.	Effect	Chap.	Sec.
2924m	Amended	642	9
2924o	Added	642	10
2924p	Added	865	1
2953	Amended	452	36
2981	Amended	283	1
2982	Amended	283	2
2982.2	Amended	283	3
2982.12	Added	283	4
2983.1	Amended	283	5
2983.3	Amended	716	1
prec. § 3273.50 Div. 3 Pt. 4 Title 20	Added	98	3
3273.50	Added	98	3
3273.51	Added	98	3
3273.52	Added	98	3
3273.54	Added	98	3
3273.55	Added	98	3
3333.2	Amended	17	3
3345	Amended	78	1
4041	Amended	632	1
4225	Amended	48	7
4515	Amended	858	2
4739	Added	858	3
5875	Added	858	4
6606	Amended	48	8
6760	Amended	617	2

TABLE OF CONTENTS

	Page
Title of the Act	1
Preliminary Provisions	1
Definitions and Sources of Law	4
Effect of the 1872 Codes	5

DIVISION 1. PERSONS

Part
		Page
1.	Persons With Unsound Mind	7
1.5	Uniform Minor Student Capacity to Borrow Act [Repealed]	8
2.	Personal Rights	9
2.5	Blind and Other Physically Disabled Persons	44
2.52	Construction–Related Accessibility Standards Compliance	55
2.53	Attorney's Fees and Statutory Damages in Construction–Related Accessibility Standards Claims	68
2.55	Small Business Gender Discrimination in Services Compliance Act	71
2.57	Gender Neutral Retail Departments	73
2.6	Confidentiality of Medical Information	74

Chapter
		Page
1.	Definitions	74
2.	Disclosure of Medical Information by Providers	77
2.5	Disclosure of Genetic Test Results by a Health Care Service Plan	88
2.6	Genetic Privacy	89
3.	Use and Disclosure of Medical Information by Employers	92
4.	Relationship of Chapters 2 and 3	94
4.1.	Notifications	94
5.	Use and Disclosure of Medical and Other Information by Third Party Administrators and Others	94
6.	Relationship to Existing Law	95
7.	Violations	96

		Page
2.7	Medical Claims Data Error Correction	100
2.9	California Fair Dealership Law	101
3.	Personal Relations [Repealed]	102
4.	Corporations [Repealed]	105

DIVISION 2. PROPERTY

Part
		Page
1.	Property in General	107

Title
		Page
1.	Nature of Property	107
2.	Ownership	108
3.	General Definitions	127

		Page
2.	Real or Immovable Property	128

IX

TABLE OF CONTENTS

Title		Page
1.	General Provisions	128
2.	Estates in Real Property	128
3.	Rights and Obligations of Owners	206
4.	Uses and Trusts [Repealed]	222
5.	Marketable Record Title	222
6.	Rent Skimming	232
7.	Requirements for Actions for Construction Defects	233
8.	Reconstruction of Homes Lost in Cedar Fire, October 2003 [Repealed]	247

Part
3. Personal or Movable Property ... 248

Title		
1.	Personal Property in General	248
2.	Particular Kinds of Personal Property	248

4. Acquisition of Property ... 255

Title		
1.	Modes in Which Property May Be Acquired	255
2.	Occupancy	256
3.	Accession	258
4.	Transfer	260
5.	Homesteads [Repealed]	311
6.	Common Interest Developments [Repealed]	312
7.	Powers of Appointment [Repealed]	312
8.	Water Rights	313
9.	Hydraulic Mining [Repealed]	314
10.	Mining Claims, Tunnel Rights and Mill Sites [Repealed]	314

DIVISION 3. OBLIGATIONS

Part
1. Obligations in General ... 315

Title		
1.	Definition of Obligations	315
2.	Interpretation of Obligations	315
3.	Transfer of Obligations	318
4.	Extinction of Obligations	321

2. Contracts ... 328

Title		
1.	Nature of a Contract	328
2.	Manner of Creating Contracts	335
2.5	Electronic Transactions	344
3.	Interpretation of Contracts	350
4.	Unlawful Contracts	356
4.5	Liquidated Damages	359
5.	Extinction of Contracts	361

3. Obligations Imposed by Law ... 383
4. Obligations Arising From Particular Transactions ... 413

Title		
1.	Consignment of Fine Art	414
1A.	Independent Wholesale Sales Representatives	415

x

TABLE OF CONTENTS

Title		Page
1.1	Sale and Manufacture of Political Items	416
1.1A	Autographed Memorabilia	417
1.2	Sale of Fine Prints	419
1.2A	Violent Video Games	423
1.3	Credit Cards	425
1.3A	Credit Card Disclosure	435
1.3B	Charge Card Disclosures	439
1.3C	Debit Cards	440
1.3.5	Consumer Refunds	441
1.4	Layaway Practices	442
1.4A	Gift Certificates	442
1.4B	Supermarket Club Cards	444
1.4C	Clarity of Marketplace Terms and Conditions and Dispute Resolution Minimum Fairness	445
1.4D	Online Marketplaces	445
1.5	Consumers Legal Remedies Act	448
1.5A	Vehicle History Reports	456
1.6	Consumer Credit Reporting Agencies Act	456
1.61	Commercial Credit Reports	483
1.6A	Investigative Consumer Reporting Agencies	484
1.6B	Consumer Credit Denial	495
1.6C	Fair Debt Collection Practices	496
1.6C.5	Fair Debt Buying Practices	505
1.6C.7	Educational Debt Collection Practices	509
1.6C.10	Student Loans: Borrower Rights	509
1.6C.15	Private Student Loan Collections Reform Act	517
1.6C.17	Fair Debt Settlement Practices	521
1.6D	Electronic Commerce	525
1.6E	Credit Services	526
1.6F	Check Cashers	534
1.61	Commercial Credit Reports [Editorial Note]	536
1.7	Consumer Warranties	536
1.8	Personal Data	564
1.80	Identification Documents	584
1.807	Domestic Violence, Sexual Assault, and Stalking: Personal Information	585
1.81	Customer Records	586
1.81.1	Confidentiality of Social Security Numbers	597
1.81.15	Reader Privacy Act	599
1.81.2	Confidentiality of Driver's License Information	602
1.81.23	Collection of License Plate Information	602
1.81.25	Consumer Privacy Protection	604
1.81.26	Security of Connected Devices	605
1.81.27	Commercial Use of Booking Photographs	606
1.81.3	Identity Theft	607
1.81.35	Coerced Debt	608
1.81.4	Privacy of Customer Electrical or Natural Gas Usage Data	611

TABLE OF CONTENTS

Title		Page
1.81.45	The Parent's Accountability and Child Protection Act	612
1.81.46	Online Violence Prevention Act	614
1.81.47	The California Age–Appropriate Design Code Act	615
1.81.48	Data Broker Registration	618
1.81.5	California Consumer Privacy Act of 2018	619
1.81.6	Identity Theft in Business Entity Filings	648
1.82	Business Records	649
1.83	Precomputed Interest	652
1.84	Precomputed Finance Charge Contract	652
1.85	Consumer Credit Contracts	653
1.86	Consumer Contract Awareness Act of 1990	657
2.	Credit Sales	659
2.4	Contracts for Dance Studio Lessons and Other Services	690
2.5	Contracts for Health Studio Services	693
2.55	Contracts for the Lease or Rental of Athletic Facilities	697
2.6	Contracts for Discount Buying Services	698
2.7	Contracts for Seller Assisted Marketing Plans	706
2.8	Membership Camping Contracts	717
2.9	Creditor Remedies: Disability Insurance	724
2.91	Employment Agency, Employment Counseling, and Job Listing Services Act	727
2.95	Auctioneer and Auction Companies	749
2.96	California Rental–Purchase Act	754
2.97	Consumer Collection Notice	766
3.	Deposit	766
3.5	Utility Services	789
4.	Loan	790
4.5	Appraisals of Real Property [Repealed]	848
5.	Hiring	848
6.	Service	938
7.	Carriage	951
8.	Involuntary Trusts	961
9.	Agency	964
10.	Recording Artist Contracts	971
10.1	Shared Mobility Devices	971
10A.	Unincorporated Nonprofit Associations and Their Members [Repealed]	974
10.5	Death With Dignity Act [Rejected]	974
11.	Pharmaceutical Services	974
12.	Indemnity	975
13.	Suretyship	984
13.5	Obligation to Defend Action	990
13.7	Obligation to Settle Insurance Claims Fairly [Rejected]	990
14.	Lien	990
15.	Internet Neutrality	1126
16.	General Provisions	1133
17.	Year 2000 Information Disclosures	1133
18.	Providers of Health and Safety Labor or Services	1134

TABLE OF CONTENTS

Title		Page
19.	COVID–19 Small Landlord and Homeowner Relief Act	1134
20.	Firearm Industry Responsibility Act	1136

DIVISION 4. GENERAL PROVISIONS

Part			
1.	Relief		1139
	Title		
	1.	Relief in General	1139
	2.	Compensatory Relief	1139
	3.	Specific and Preventive Relief	1162
	4.	Uniform Single Publication Act	1167
	5.	Uniform Trade Secrets Act	1168
	6.	Interference With Access to Health Care	1170
	7.	Duty of Health Care Service Plans and Managed Care Entities	1171
2.	Special Relations of Debtor and Creditor		1172
	Title		
	1.	General Principles	1172
	2.	Void and Voidable Transfers and Undertakings	1172
	3.	Assignments for the Benefit of Creditors [Repealed]	1179
3.	Nuisance		1180
	Title		
	1.	General Principles	1180
	2.	Public Nuisances	1189
	3.	Private Nuisances	1191
	4.	Motion Pictures	1191
4.	Maxims of Jurisprudence		1194
5.	Common Interest Developments		1196
	Chapter		
	1.	General Provisions	1198
	2.	Application of Act	1205
	3.	Governing Documents	1206
	4.	Ownership and Transfer of Interests	1213
	5.	Property Use and Maintenance	1219
	6.	Association Governance	1231
	7.	Finances	1249
	8.	Assessments and Assessment Collection	1254
	9.	Insurance and Liability	1261
	10.	Dispute Resolution and Enforcement	1262
	11.	Construction Defect Litigation	1267
5.3.	Commercial and Industrial Common Interest Developments		1273
	Chapter		
	1.	General Provisions	1274
	2.	Application of Act	1277
	3.	Governing Documents	1278
	4.	Ownership and Transfer of Interests	1281
	5.	Property Use and Maintenance	1282
	6.	Association Governance	1286
	7.	Assessments and Assessment Collection	1287

TABLE OF CONTENTS

Chapter			Page
	8.	Insurance and Liability	1289
	9.	Dispute Resolution and Enforcement	1290
	10.	Construction Defect Litigation	1291

Part

5.5. Automatic Checkout System 1292
6. Works of Improvement 1294

Title

    1. Works of Improvement Generally 1294
    2. Private Works of Improvement 1306
    3. Public Work of Improvement 1339

7. Uniform Parentage Act [Repealed] 1350
8. Automatic Checkout System [Heading Renumbered] 1350

INDEX
(Page I–1)

XIV

CIVIL CODE

An Act

to

ESTABLISH A CIVIL CODE

[Approved March 21st, 1872.]

The People of the State of California, represented in Senate and Assembly, do enact as follows:

	Section
Title of the Act	1
Preliminary Provisions	2
Definitions and Sources of Law	22
Effect of the 1872 Codes	23

Division		Section
1.	Persons	25
2.	Property	654
3.	Obligations	1427
4.	General Provisions	3274

TITLE OF THE ACT

Section
1. Title and Divisions of Code.

§ 1. Title and Divisions of Code

TITLE AND DIVISIONS OF THIS ACT. This Act shall be known as The Civil Code of the State of California, and is in Four Divisions, as follows:

I. The First Relating to Persons.

II.—The Second to Property.

III.—The Third to Obligations.

IV.—The Fourth Contains General Provisions Relating to the Three Preceding Divisions. *(Enacted in 1872.)*

Cross References

Citation of Code, see Civil Code § 21.
Construction of 1872 Codes, see Civil Code § 23 et seq.
General rules for construction to be as prescribed in preliminary provisions, see Government Code § 9603.
Intent of legislature to be pursued in construing statute, see Code of Civil Procedure § 1859.
Limited partnerships formed prior to adoption of Limited Partnership Act, continuation under former Civil Code provisions, see Corporations Code § 15530.
Maxims of jurisprudence, see Civil Code § 3509.
Operation of statutes and resolutions, see Government Code § 9600 et seq.

Religious corporations formed prior to 3/30/1878, election to continue existence under provisions of Civil Code, see Corporations Code § 10001.
Waiver of code provisions, see Civil Code § 3268.

PRELIMINARY PROVISIONS

Section
2. Effective date of Code.
3. Code provisions not retroactive.
4. Strict construction rule inapplicable; liberal construction.
5. Continuation of similar existing law or common law.
6. Effect on prior proceedings or rights.
7. Holidays.
7.1. Optional bank holidays.
8. Repealed.
9. Business days; optional bank holidays not business days; acts to be performed on optional bank holidays.
9.1. Repealed.
10. Time; computation.
11. Holidays; certain acts performable on next business day.
12. Joint authority construed.
13. Words and phrases; construction.
14. Words and phrases; construction; tense; gender; number.
15, 16. Repealed.
17. Certified mail; compliance with mailing provisions.
18. Notice; actual and constructive.
19. Constructive notice.
20. Repeal or abrogation of prior laws; effect.
21. Citation of act adopting Code.

§ 2. Effective date of Code

This Code takes effect at twelve o'clock noon, on the first day of January, eighteen hundred and seventy-three. *(Enacted in 1872.)*

Cross References

Construction of Code as having been passed on first day of session, see Civil Code § 23.
Effective date of statutes, see Cal. Const. Art. 4, § 8; Government Code § 9600.

Similar provisions, see Code of Civil Procedure § 2; Penal Code § 2.

§ 3. Code provisions not retroactive

No part of it is retroactive, unless expressly so declared. *(Enacted in 1872.)*

Cross References

Conveyances made before code took effect, see Civil Code § 1206.
Legality of instruments made before effective date of code, see Civil Code § 1205.
Nunc pro tunc judgment in marriage dissolution action, see Family Code § 2346.
Similar provisions, see Code of Civil Procedure § 3; Penal Code § 3.

§ 4. Strict construction rule inapplicable; liberal construction

The rule of the common law, that statutes in derogation thereof are to be strictly construed, has no application to this Code. The Code establishes the law of this State respecting the subjects to which it relates, and its provisions are to be liberally construed with a view to effect its objects and to promote justice. *(Enacted in 1872.)*

Cross References

Constitutional construction, see Cal. Const. Art. 1, §§ 24, 26.
Construction of 1872 Codes, see Civil Code § 23 et seq.
Construction of statute in favor of natural right, see Code of Civil Procedure § 1866.
Construction of statutes by judge, see Code of Civil Procedure § 1858; Evidence Code §§ 310, 400.
Intention of legislature to be pursued, see Code of Civil Procedure § 1859.
Similar provisions, see Code of Civil Procedure § 4; Penal Code § 4.
Statutory construction,
 Amended statutes, see Government Code § 9605.
 Amendment of repealed statutes, see Government Code § 9609.
 Duty of judge, see Code of Civil Procedure § 1858; Evidence Code §§ 310, 400.
 General rules, see Code of Civil Procedure §§ 1858, 1859; Government Code § 9603 et seq.
 Giving effect to all provisions, see Code of Civil Procedure § 1858.
 Particular intent controls general, see Code of Civil Procedure § 1859.
 Question of law for court, see Evidence Code § 310.
 Repeal of repealing statute, see Government Code § 9607.
 Temporary suspension of law, see Government Code § 9611.
 Uniform operation of laws of a general nature, see Cal. Const. Art. 4, § 16.
 Words and phrases, see Civil Code §§ 13, 14.

§ 5. Continuation of similar existing law or common law

The provisions of this Code, so far as they are substantially the same as existing statutes or the common law, must be construed as continuations thereof, and not as new enactments. *(Enacted in 1872.)*

Cross References

Repeal of prior laws on same subject, see Civil Code § 20.
Restatements and continuations of statutes, see Government Code § 9604.
Similar provisions, see Code of Civil Procedure § 5; Government Code § 2; Penal Code § 5.

§ 6. Effect on prior proceedings or rights

No action or proceeding commenced before this Code takes effect, and no right accrued, is affected by its provisions. *(Enacted in 1872.)*

Cross References

Similar provisions, see Code of Civil Procedure § 8; Probate Code § 3.

§ 7. Holidays

Holidays within the meaning of this code are every Sunday and such other days as are specified or provided for as holidays in the Government Code of the State of California. *(Enacted in 1872. Amended by Code Am.1880, c. 50, p. 9, § 1; Stats.1889, c. 44, p. 47, § 1; Stats.1893, c. 158, p. 186, § 1; Stats.1897, c. 18, p. 14, § 1; Stats.1907, c. 293, p. 565, § 1; Stats.1907, Ex.Sess., c. 5, p. 5, § 1; Stats.1909, c. 30, p. 23, § 1; Stats.1911, c. 320, p. 520, § 1; Stats.1925, c. 92, p. 224, § 1; Stats.1955, c. 165, p. 613, § 1.)*

Cross References

Admission day, see Government Code § 6703.
Appointed day falling on holiday, see Government Code § 6706.
Cities or districts, Saturday as holiday, see Government Code § 6704.
Courts and judicial business, effect of holidays, see Code of Civil Procedure § 133 et seq.
Document or instrument, last day for filing falling on holiday, see Government Code § 6707.
Election day, see Elections Code §§ 1000 et seq., 1100, 1200 et seq., 1400.
Enumeration of holidays, see Government Code § 6700.
Holidays falling on Sunday, see Government Code § 6701.
Public offices, days on which closed deemed holidays, see Code of Civil Procedure § 12b.
Saturday half-holiday, see Government Code § 6702.
School holidays and observances, see Education Code §§ 37220 et seq., 79020, 79021.
Similar provisions, see Code of Civil Procedure § 10 et seq.; Government Code § 6700 et seq.
Special holidays, optional performance, etc., see Code of Civil Procedure § 13a.
Special or limited holidays, see Government Code § 6705.
State employees, holidays for, see Government Code § 19853.
State offices and institutions, closing on, see Government Code § 6703.
Veterans Day, see Government Code § 6703.

§ 7.1. Optional bank holidays

Optional bank holidays within the meaning of Section 9 are:

(a) Any closing of a bank because of an extraordinary situation, as that term is defined in the Bank Extraordinary Situation Closing Act (Chapter 20 (commencing with Section 3600) of Division 1 of the Financial Code).

(b) Every Saturday.

(c) Every Sunday.

(d) January 1st.

(e) The third Monday in January, known as "Dr. Martin Luther King, Jr. Day."

(f) February 12, known as "Lincoln Day."

(g) The third Monday in February.

(h) The last Monday in May.

(i) July 4th.

(j) The first Monday in September.

(k) September 9th, known as "Admission Day."

(*l*) The second Monday in October, known as "Columbus Day."

(m) November 11th, known as "Veteran's Day."

(n) December 25th.

(o) Good Friday from 12 noon until closing.

(p) The Thursday in November appointed as "Thanksgiving Day."

(q) Any Monday following any Sunday on which January 1st, February 12th, July 4th, September 9th, November 11th, or December 25th falls.

(r) Any Friday preceding any Saturday on which July 4th, September 9th, or December 25th falls. *(Added by Stats. 1994, c. 668 (S.B.1405), § 1.)*

§ 8. Repealed by Stats.1905, c. 17, p. 11, § 1

§ 9. Business days; optional bank holidays not business days; acts to be performed on optional bank holidays

All other days than those mentioned in Section 7 are business days for all purposes; provided, that as to any act appointed by law or contract, or in any other way, to be performed by, at, or through any bank organized under the laws of or doing business in this state, any optional bank holiday as defined in Section 7.1 is not a business day; and provided, that any act appointed by law or contract, or in any other way, to be performed on any day which is an optional bank holiday as defined in Section 7.1, by, at, or through any bank or branch or office thereof, whether acting in its own behalf or in any other capacity whatsoever, may be performed on that optional bank holiday if the bank or branch or office by, at, or through which the act is to be performed is open for the transaction of business on that optional bank holiday, or, at the option of the person obligated to perform the act, it may be performed on the next succeeding business day. *(Enacted in 1872. Amended by Stats.1905, c. 17, p. 11, § 2; Stats.1939, c. 414, p. 1748, § 1; Stats.1955, c. 198, p. 670, § 1; Stats.1955, c. 599, p. 1091, § 1; Stats.1973, c. 285, p. 694, § 1; Stats.1979, c. 159, p. 357, § 1; Stats.1981, c. 67, § 1, eff. June 16, 1981; Stats.1982, c. 1203, p. 4383, § 1, eff. Sept. 22, 1982; Stats.1985, c. 147, § 1, eff. July 8, 1985; Stats.1994, c. 668 (S.B.1405), § 2.)*

Cross References

Judicial days, see Code of Civil Procedure § 133 et seq.
Saturday, public offices, see Government Code §§ 6702, 6704.
Special or limited holiday as holiday applying only to special classes of business, see Government Code § 6705.

§ 9.1. Repealed by Stats.1955, c. 198, p. 671, § 3; Stats. 1955, c. 599, p. 1093, § 3

§ 10. Time; computation

The time in which any act provided by law is to be done is computed by excluding the first day and including the last, unless the last day is a holiday, and then it is also excluded. *(Enacted in 1872.)*

Cross References

Computation of time in general, see Government Code § 6800 et seq.

Document or instrument, last day for filing falling on holiday, see Government Code § 6707.
Similar provisions, see Code of Civil Procedure § 12; Education Code § 9.

§ 11. Holidays; certain acts performable on next business day

Whenever any act of a secular nature, other than a work of necessity or mercy, is appointed by law or contract to be performed upon a particular day, which day falls upon a holiday, it may be performed upon the next business day, with the same effect as if it had been performed upon the day appointed. *(Enacted in 1872.)*

Cross References

Monday following to be observed, see Education Code §§ 37220, 79020; Government Code § 6701.
Similar provision, see Code of Civil Procedure § 13; Government Code § 6706.

§ 12. Joint authority construed

Words giving a joint authority to three or more public officers or other persons are construed as giving such authority to a majority of them, unless it is otherwise expressed in the Act giving the authority. *(Enacted in 1872.)*

Cross References

Similar provision, see Code of Civil Procedure § 15.

§ 13. Words and phrases; construction

Words and phrases are construed according to the context and the approved usage of the language; but technical words and phrases, and such others as may have acquired a peculiar and appropriate meaning in law, or are defined in the succeeding section, are to be construed according to such peculiar and appropriate meaning or definition. *(Enacted in 1872.)*

Cross References

Contracts, interpretation of technical words, see Civil Code § 1645.
Similar provisions, see Code of Civil Procedure § 16; Probate Code § 21122.
Writings, evidence of local, technical or other peculiar signification, see Code of Civil Procedure § 1861.
Written words control printed, see Civil Code § 1651; Code of Civil Procedure § 1862.

§ 14. Words and phrases; construction; tense; gender; number

(a) Words used in this code in the present tense include the future as well as the present; words used in the masculine gender include the feminine and neuter; the singular number includes the plural, and the plural the singular; the word person includes a corporation as well as a natural person; county includes city and county; writing includes printing and typewriting; oath includes affirmation or declaration; and every mode of oral statement, under oath or affirmation, is embraced by the term "testify," and every written one in the term "depose"; signature or subscription includes mark, when the person cannot write, his name being written near it, by a person who writes his own name as a witness; *provided*, that when a signature is by mark it must in order that the same may be acknowledged or may serve as the signature to any sworn statement be witnessed by two persons who must subscribe their own names as witnesses thereto.

(b) The following words have in this code the signification attached to them in this section, unless otherwise apparent from the context:

(1) The word "property" includes property real and personal.

(2) The words "real property" are coextensive with lands, tenements, and hereditaments.

(3) The words "personal property" include money, goods, chattels, things in action, and evidences of debt.

(4) The word "month" means a calendar month, unless otherwise expressed.

(5) The word "will" includes codicil.

(6) The word "section" whenever hereinafter employed refers to a section of this code, unless some other code or statute is expressly mentioned.

(7) The word "spouse" includes a registered domestic partner, as required by Section 297.5 of the Family Code. *(Enacted in 1872. Amended by Code Am.1873–74, c. 612, p. 181, § 1; Stats.1903, c. 281, p. 407, § 1; Stats.2016, c. 50 (S.B.1005), § 3, eff. Jan. 1, 2017.)*

Cross References

Month, definition, see Government Code § 6804.
Personal property, definition, see Civil Code § 663.
Property, definition, see Civil Code §§ 654, 658; Commercial Code § 2105.
Real property defined, see Civil Code § 658.
School month defined, see Education Code § 37201.
Similar provisions, see Penal Code § 7; Code of Civil Procedure § 17.

§§ 15, 16. Repealed by Code Am.1873–74, c. 612, p. 182, § 2

§ 17. Certified mail; compliance with mailing provisions

Wherever any notice or other communication is required by this code to be mailed by registered mail, the mailing of such notice or other communication by certified mail shall be deemed to be a sufficient compliance with the requirements of law. *(Added by Stats.1959, c. 426, p. 2364, § 1.)*

Cross References

Service by mail, see Code of Civil Procedure § 1012 et seq.
Similar provisions, see Code of Civil Procedure § 11; Financial Code § 8.

§ 18. Notice; actual and constructive

Notice is:

1. Actual—which consists in express information of a fact; or,

2. Constructive—which is imputed by law. *(Enacted in 1872.)*

Cross References

Negotiable instruments, notice of dishonor, see Commercial Code § 3503.
Principal, notice to agent as notice to principal, see Civil Code § 2332.
Recorded conveyance as constructive notice, see Civil Code § 1213.
Service of notices upon attorney, see Code of Civil Procedure § 1010.

§ 19. Constructive notice

Every person who has actual notice of circumstances sufficient to put a prudent person upon inquiry as to a particular fact has constructive notice of the fact itself in all cases in which, by prosecuting such inquiry, he or she might have learned that fact. *(Enacted in 1872. Amended by Code Am.1873–74, c. 612, p. 182, § 3; Stats.2017, c. 561 (A.B.1516), § 15, eff. Jan. 1, 2018.)*

Cross References

Action for specific recovery of fine art against museum, gallery, auctioneer, or dealer, statute of limitations, actual discovery defined not to include constructive knowledge, see Code of Civil Procedure § 338.
Conveyance after change of name, constructive notice, see Civil Code § 1096.
Recordation of orders affecting real estate, see Probate Code § 7263.
Recorded conveyance as constructive notice, see Civil Code § 1213.

§ 20. Repeal or abrogation of prior laws; effect

No statute, law, or rule is continued in force because it is consistent with the provisions of this Code on the same subject; but in all cases provided for by this Code, all statutes, laws, and rules heretofore in force in this State, whether consistent or not with the provisions of this Code, unless expressly continued in force by it, are repealed or abrogated.

This repeal or abrogation does not revive any former law heretofore repealed, nor does it affect any right already existing or accrued, or any action or proceeding already taken, except as in this Code provided. *(Enacted in 1872.)*

Cross References

Similar provisions, see Code of Civil Procedure § 18.

§ 21. Citation of act adopting Code

This Act, whenever cited, enumerated, referred to, or amended, may be designated simply as "The Civil Code," adding, when necessary, the number of the section. *(Enacted in 1872.)*

Cross References

Section defined for purposes of this Code, see Civil Code § 14.

DEFINITIONS AND SOURCES OF LAW

Section
22. Law defined.
22.1. Supreme power; expression of will.
22.2. Common law of England; rule of decision.
22.3. Repealed.

§ 22. Law defined

Law is a solemn expression of the will of the supreme power of the State. *(Added by Stats.1951, c. 655, p. 1833, § 1.)*

Cross References

Written laws, see Code of Civil Procedure § 1897.

§ 22.1. Supreme power; expression of will

The will of the supreme power is expressed:

(a) By the Constitution.

(b) By statutes. *(Added by Stats.1951, c. 655, p. 1833, § 1.)*

Cross References

Constitution of United States as supreme law of the land, see Cal. Const. Art. 3, § 1.
Written laws, see Code of Civil Procedure § 1897.

§ 22.2. Common law of England; rule of decision

The common law of England, so far as it is not repugnant to or inconsistent with the Constitution of the United States, or the Constitution or laws of this State, is the rule of decision in all the courts of this State. *(Added by Stats.1951, c. 655, p. 1833, § 1.)*

§ 22.3. Repealed by Stats.1979, c. 373, p. 1264, § 40

EFFECT OF THE 1872 CODES

Section
23. Time of passage of 1872 Codes.
23.1. Inconsistent statutes of 1872 session to prevail over 1872 Codes.
23.2. Construction of 1872 Codes.
23.3. Conflicting provisions of titles of 1872 Codes.
23.4. Conflicting provisions of chapters of 1872 Codes.
23.5. Conflicting provisions of articles of 1872 Codes.
23.6. Conflicting provisions of sections of 1872 Codes.

§ 23. Time of passage of 1872 Codes

With relation to the laws passed at the 1872 Session of the Legislature, the Political Code, Civil Code, Code of Civil Procedure, and Penal Code, shall be construed as though each had been passed on the first day of the session. *(Added by Stats.1951, c. 655, p. 1833, § 2.)*

§ 23.1. Inconsistent statutes of 1872 session to prevail over 1872 Codes

The provisions of any law passed at the 1872 Session of the Legislature which contravene or are inconsistent with the provisions of any of the four codes passed at the 1872 Session prevail. *(Added by Stats.1951, c. 655, p. 1833, § 2.)*

§ 23.2. Construction of 1872 Codes

With relation to each other, the provisions of the four codes shall be construed as though all such codes had been passed at the same moment of time and were parts of the same statute. *(Added by Stats.1951, c. 655, p. 1833, § 2.)*

§ 23.3. Conflicting provisions of titles of 1872 Codes

If the provisions of any title conflict with or contravene the provisions of another title, the provisions of each title shall prevail as to all matters and questions arising out of the subject matter of the title. *(Added by Stats.1951, c. 655, p. 1833, § 2.)*

§ 23.4. Conflicting provisions of chapters of 1872 Codes

If the provisions of any chapter conflict with or contravene the provisions of another chapter of the same title, the provisions of each chapter shall prevail as to all matters and questions arising out of the subject matter of the chapter. *(Added by Stats.1951, c. 655, p. 1833, § 2.)*

§ 23.5. Conflicting provisions of articles of 1872 Codes

If the provisions of any article conflict with or contravene the provisions of another article of the same chapter, the provisions of each article shall prevail as to all matters and questions arising out of the subject matter of the article. *(Added by Stats.1951, c. 655, p. 1833, § 2.)*

§ 23.6. Conflicting provisions of sections of 1872 Codes

If conflicting provisions are found in different sections of the same chapter or article, the provisions of the sections last in numerical order shall prevail, unless such construction is inconsistent with the meaning of the chapter or article. *(Added by Stats.1951, c. 655, p. 1833, § 2.)*

Cross References

Section defined for purposes of this Code, see Civil Code § 14.

Division 1
PERSONS

Part	Section
1. Persons with Unsound Mind	25
1.5. Uniform Minor Student Capacity to Borrow Act [Repealed]	
2. Personal Rights	43
2.5. Blind and Other Physically Disabled Persons	54
2.52. Construction–Related Accessibility Standards Compliance	55.51
2.53. Attorney's Fees and Statutory Damages in Construction–Related Accessibility Standards Claims	55.55
2.55. Small Business Gender Discrimination in Services Compliance Act	55.61
2.57. Gender Neutral Retail Departments	55.7
2.6. Confidentiality of Medical Information	56
2.7. Medical Claims Data Error Correction	57
2.9. California Fair Dealership Law	80
3. Personal Relations [Repealed]	
4. Corporations [Repealed]	

Part 1

PERSONS WITH UNSOUND MIND

Section
25 to 27. Repealed.
28. Repealed.
29. Repealed.
30, 31. Repealed.
32. Repealed.
33 to 37. Repealed.
38. Person without understanding; contract; necessaries; liability.
39. Conveyance or contract; rescission; rebuttable presumption.
40. Judicial determination of incapacity; powers; conservatorship.
41. Civil liability; exemplary damages.
42. Repealed.

§§ 25 to 27. Repealed by Stats.1993, c. 219 (A.B.1500), § 2

§ 28. Repealed by Code Am.1873–74, c. 612, p. 182, § 4

§ 29. Repealed by Stats.1993, c. 219 (A.B.1500), § 2

§§ 30, 31. Repealed by Code Am.1873–74, c. 612, p. 182, § 4

§ 32. Repealed by Stats.1979, c. 730, p. 2465, § 3, operative Jan. 1, 1981

§§ 33 to 37. Repealed by Stats.1993, c. 219 (A.B.1500), § 2

§ 38. Person without understanding; contract; necessaries; liability

A person entirely without understanding has no power to make a contract of any kind, but the person is liable for the reasonable value of things furnished to the person necessary for the support of the person or the person's family. *(Added by Stats.1992, c. 163 (A.B.2641), § 3, operative Jan. 1, 1994.)*

Cross References

Mentally disordered persons, liability of estate for institutional care, see Welfare and Institutions Code § 7275.
Persons capable of contracting, see Civil Code §§ 1556, 1557.

§ 39. Conveyance or contract; rescission; rebuttable presumption

(a) A conveyance or other contract of a person of unsound mind, but not entirely without understanding, made before the incapacity of the person has been judicially determined, is subject to rescission, as provided in Chapter 2 (commencing with Section 1688) of Title 5 of Part 2 of Division 3.

(b) A rebuttable presumption affecting the burden of proof that a person is of unsound mind shall exist for purposes of this section if the person is substantially unable to manage his or her own financial resources or resist fraud or undue influence. Substantial inability may not be proved solely by isolated incidents of negligence or improvidence. *(Added by Stats.1992, c. 163 (A.B.2641), § 3, operative Jan. 1, 1994. Amended by Stats.1995, c. 842 (S.B.730), § 1.)*

Cross References

Burden of proof, generally, see Evidence Code § 500 et seq.
Effect of homicide or abuse of an elder or dependent adult, persons deemed to have predeceased a decedent, see Probate Code § 259.
Persons capable of contracting, see Civil Code §§ 1556, 1557.
Rescission of contracts, see Civil Code § 1688 et seq.

§ 40. Judicial determination of incapacity; powers; conservatorship

(a) Subject to Section 1871 of the Probate Code, and subject to Part 1 (commencing with Section 5000) of Division 5 of the Welfare and Institutions Code, after his or her incapacity has been judicially determined a person of unsound mind can make no conveyance or other contract, nor delegate any power or waive any right, until his or her restoration to capacity.

(b) Subject to Sections 1873 to 1876, inclusive, of the Probate Code, the establishment of a conservatorship under Division 4 (commencing with Section 1400) of the Probate Code is a judicial determination of the incapacity of the conservatee for the purposes of this section. *(Added by Stats.1992, c. 163 (A.B.2641), § 3, operative Jan. 1, 1994.)*

Cross References

Conservatee's power to contract, withdrawal, see Welfare and Institutions Code § 5357.
Conservatorship for gravely disabled persons, see Welfare and Institutions Code § 5350 et seq.
Restoration to capacity of mentally disordered persons,
  Adjudgment by superintendent of state hospital, see Welfare and Institutions Code §§ 7351, 7357.

§ 40

Certificate of superintendent, see Welfare and Institutions Code §§ 7351, 7357.

Discharge from state hospital, see Welfare and Institutions Code § 7357.

§ 41. Civil liability; exemplary damages

A person of unsound mind, of whatever degree, is civilly liable for a wrong done by the person, but is not liable in exemplary damages unless at the time of the act the person was capable of knowing that the act was wrongful. *(Added by Stats.1992, c. 163 (A.B.2641), § 3, operative Jan. 1, 1994.)*

Cross References

Insane persons, cannot commit crime, see Penal Code § 26.

Liability of parent or guardian,
Damages to school property by pupil, see Education Code § 48904.

Failure to return school property by pupil, see Education Code § 48904.

Mentally incompetent persons, trial or punishment prohibited, see Penal Code § 1367.

Willful misconduct of minor, liability of parents and guardians, see Civil Code § 1714.1.

§ 42. Repealed by Stats.1993, c. 219 (A.B.1500), § 2

Part 1.5

UNIFORM MINOR STUDENT CAPACITY TO BORROW ACT [REPEALED]

§§ 42.1 to 42.5. Repealed by Stats.1972, c. 579, p. 993, § 9

Part 2

PERSONAL RIGHTS

Section
43. General personal rights.
43–1 to 43–7. Unconstitutional.
43.1. Unborn child deemed existing person.
43.3. Breastfeeding; location.
43.4. Fraudulent promise to marry or cohabit not actionable.
43.5. Wrongs not actionable.
43.5(a). Renumbered.
43.54. Arrest at courthouse.
43.55. Arrest under warrant regular on face not actionable.
43.56. Foster parents; alienation of child's affection.
43.6. Immunity from liability; actions against parents on childbirth claims; defenses and damages in third party actions.
43.7. Immunity from liability; mental health professional quality assurance committees; professional societies, members or staff; peer review or insurance underwriting committees; hospital governing board.
43.8. Immunity from liability for communication on evaluation of practitioner of healing or veterinary arts.
43.9. Immunity from liability; health care providers; unsolicited referrals from tests by multiphasic screening unit; notice.
43.91. Immunity from liability; members of professional society of persons licensed under the Real Estate Law; peer review committees.
43.92. Psychotherapists; duty to protect from violent behavior of patient; immunity from monetary liability; interpretation of section.
43.93. Psychotherapists; patient's cause of action for sexual contact; definitions.
43.95. Immunity of professional society for referral services or telephone information library; duty to disclose disciplinary actions.
43.96. Information to be provided to a complainant; immunity.
43.97. Medical staff or membership privilege denial or restriction; immunity from liability; unreported or intentional injury exceptions.
43.98. Communications by consultants to Director of Department of Managed Health Care, health care services; monetary liability.
43.99. Immunity from monetary liability; building and other inspectors; independent quality review of plans, specifications or work on residential buildings under the State Housing Law; exceptions.
43.100. Property damage or trespass to motor vehicle resulting from rescue of animal; immunity from civil liability.
43.101. Immunity from liability for damage to unmanned aircraft or unmanned aircraft system; emergency responders.
43.102. Property damage or trespass to motor vehicle while rescuing child; protections.
44. Defamation.
45. Libel.
45a. Libel on its face; other actionable defamatory language.
46. Slander, false and unprivileged publications which constitute.
47. Privileged publication or broadcast.

Section
47.5. Peace officers; defamation action against person filing false complaint alleging misconduct, criminal conduct, or incompetence.
48. Privileged publication or broadcast; malice not inferred.
48a. Libel in daily or weekly news publication; slander by radio broadcast.
48.5. Defamation by radio; non-liability of owner, licensee or operator of broadcasting station or network.
48.7. Child abuse; prohibition against libel or slander action while charges pending; tolling of limitations; pleadings; demurrer; attorney fees and costs.
48.8. Communications to school personnel regarding threats to commit violence on the school grounds involving deadly or dangerous weapons; liability for defamation.
48.9. Anonymous witness program; immunity.
49. Personal relations, acts forbidden by.
50. Force, right to use.
51. Unruh Civil Rights Act; equal rights; business establishments; violations of federal Americans with Disabilities Act.
51.1. Mandatory service on State Solicitor General of each party's brief or petition and brief in causes of action based on violation of civil rights statutes.
51.2. Age discrimination in sale or rental of housing prohibited; housing designed to meet physical and social needs of senior citizens; exceptions; intent; age preferences in federally approved housing programs.
51.3. Housing; age limitations; necessity for senior citizen housing.
51.3.5. Intergenerational housing developments; legislative findings and declarations; conditions for establishment.
51.4. Exemption from special design requirement.
51.5. Discrimination, boycott, blacklist, etc.; business establishments; equal rights.
51.6. Gender Tax Repeal Act of 1995.
51.7. Ralph Civil Rights Act of 1976.
51.8. Discrimination; franchises.
51.9. Sexual harassment; business, service and professional relationships.
51.10. Age discrimination in sale or rental of housing prohibited; construction of Unruh Civil Rights Act; senior housing; intent; age preferences in federally approved housing programs; application of section.
51.11. Riverside County; establishment or preservation of senior housing; legislative findings and declarations; definitions; requirements; qualification of development; application of section.
51.12. Riverside County; senior housing; legislative findings and declarations; right of residency, occupancy, or use; application of section.
51.13. Discounts or other benefits conferred on consumers who have suffered loss or reduction of employment or wages.
51.14. Prohibition against discriminatory pricing based on gender of the consumer; violations; penalties and fines.
51.17. Pilot program recognizing businesses for creating safe and welcoming environments free from discrimination and harassment of customers.
52. Denial of civil rights or discrimination; damages; civil action by persons aggrieved; intervention;

Section

	unlawful practice complaint; waiver of rights by contract.
52.1.	Tom Bane Civil Rights Act.
52.2.	Court of competent jurisdiction; defined; actions.
52.3.	Law enforcement officers; prohibitions against conduct depriving persons of Constitutional rights, privileges, or immunities; civil actions.
52.4.	Civil action for damages arising from gender violence.
52.45.	Civil action for damages arising from sexual orientation violence.
52.5.	Civil action for damages to victims of human trafficking.
52.6.	Notice to be posted at specified businesses and establishments; slavery and human trafficking; location of posting; contents; languages; model notice; employee training; civil penalties; local ordinances.
52.65.	Civil action for hotels in violation of sex trafficking activity.
52.7.	Subcutaneous implanting of identification device; penalties; limitations; restitution; liberal construction; independent action; existing law; definitions.
52.8.	Distribution of unauthorized obscene materials; attorney's fees and costs.
53.	Restrictions upon transfer or use of realty because of characteristics listed or defined in Section 51.
53.5.	Dissemination of guest record or passenger manifest record; court issued subpoena, warrant, or order required; exceptions.
53.7.	Minority groups; political structure equal protection; statutes, ordinances, etc., prohibited from denying; civil actions.

Cross References

California Community Care Facilities Act, misuse of disclosed sex offender registration information, civil action, see Health and Safety Code § 1522.01.

Campaign advertising or communication, application of libel and slander provisions, see Elections Code § 20500.

Sex offenders, misuse of information disclosed to the public, see Penal Code §§ 290.4, 290.46.

§ 43. General personal rights

Besides the personal rights mentioned or recognized in the Government Code, every person has, subject to the qualifications and restrictions provided by law, the right of protection from bodily restraint or harm, from personal insult, from defamation, and from injury to his personal relations. *(Enacted in 1872. Amended by Stats.1953, c. 604, p. 1849, § 1.)*

Cross References

Abstinence from injuring others, see Civil Code § 1708.
Assault and battery, definitions, see Penal Code §§ 240, 242.
Civil Rights Act, see Civil Code § 51 et seq.
Consent to acts, effect, see Civil Code § 3515.
Damages, generally, see Civil Code § 3281 et seq.
Deeds, invalidity of racial restrictions, see Civil Code § 782.
Defamation defined, see Civil Code § 44.
Force, right to use, see Civil Code § 50.
Libel, see Civil Code §§ 44, 45.
Married person, right to sue or be sued without joinder of spouse, see Code of Civil Procedure § 370.
Opportunity to seek, obtain and hold employment without discrimination as civil right, see Government Code § 12920.

Personal relations, act forbidden by, see Civil Code § 49.
Political rights and duties, see Government Code § 270 et seq.
Responsibility for willful acts and negligence, see Civil Code § 1714.
Slander, see Civil Code § 46.
Trade secrets, official proceedings, privileged communication, see Civil Code § 3426.11.
Use of rights, no infringement upon rights of others, see Civil Code § 3514.
Wrongs not actionable, see Civil Code § 43.4 et seq.

§§ 43–1 to 43–7. Unconstitutional

§ 43.1. Unborn child deemed existing person

A child conceived, but not yet born, is deemed an existing person, so far as necessary for the child's interests in the event of the child's subsequent birth. *(Added by Stats.1992, c. 163 (A.B.2641), § 4, operative Jan. 1, 1994.)*

Cross References

Posthumous children, future interests, see Civil Code §§ 698, 739.

§ 43.3. Breastfeeding; location

Notwithstanding any other provision of law, a mother may breastfeed her child in any location, public or private, except the private home or residence of another, where the mother and the child are otherwise authorized to be present. *(Added by Stats.1997, c. 59 (A.B.157), § 1.)*

Cross References

Reasonable accommodations for a lactating student to express breast milk, breast-feed an infant child, or address other needs related to breast-feeding, academic penalty against student for use of reasonable accommodations prohibited, requirement of a sink in new and existing facilities, complaint of noncompliance, implementation of requirements, see Education Code § 66271.9.

Right of applicant or recipient of aid to breastfeed child in county welfare department or other county office, see Welfare and Institutions Code § 11218.

§ 43.4. Fraudulent promise to marry or cohabit not actionable

A fraudulent promise to marry or to cohabit after marriage does not give rise to a cause of action for damages. *(Added by Stats.1959, c. 381, p. 2306, § 1.)*

§ 43.5. Wrongs not actionable

No cause of action arises for:

(a) Alienation of affection.

(b) Criminal conversation.

(c) Seduction of a person over the age of legal consent.

(d) Breach of promise of marriage. *(Added by Stats.1939, c. 128, p. 1245, § 2.)*

Cross References

Inveiglement or enticement of unmarried female under 18, see Penal Code § 266.

§ 43.5(a). Renumbered § 43.55 and amended by Stats. 1986, c. 248, § 15

§ 43.54. Arrest at courthouse

(a) A person shall not be subject to civil arrest in a courthouse while attending a court proceeding or having legal business in the courthouse.

(b) This section does not narrow, or in any way lessen, any existing common law privilege.

(c) This section does not apply to arrests made pursuant to a valid judicial warrant. (Added by Stats.2019, c. 787 (A.B.668), § 2, eff. Jan. 1, 2020.)

§ 43.55. Arrest under warrant regular on face not actionable

(a) There shall be no liability on the part of, and no cause of action shall arise against, any peace officer who makes an arrest pursuant to a warrant of arrest regular upon its face if the peace officer in making the arrest acts without malice and in the reasonable belief that the person arrested is the one referred to in the warrant.

(b) As used in this section, a "warrant of arrest regular upon its face" includes both of the following:

(1) A paper arrest warrant that has been issued pursuant to a judicial order.

(2) A judicial order that is entered into an automated warrant system by law enforcement or court personnel authorized to make those entries at or near the time the judicial order is made. (Formerly § 43.5(a), added by Stats. 1945, c. 1117, p. 2126, § 1. Renumbered § 43.55 and amended by Stats.1986, c. 248, § 15. Amended by Stats.2005, c. 706 (A.B.1742), § 2.)

Application

For application of 2005 amendment, see Stats.2005, c. 706 (A.B.1742), § 41.

Cross References

Arrest, by whom and how made, see Penal Code § 833 et seq.
False imprisonment defined, see Penal Code § 236.
Warrant of arrest,
 Duty of officer making arrest under, see Penal Code § 848.
 Duty when made without, see Penal Code § 849.
 Form of, see Penal Code §§ 814, 1427.

§ 43.56. Foster parents; alienation of child's affection

No cause of action arises against a foster parent for alienation of affection of a foster child. (Formerly § 43.55, added by Stats.1986, c. 1330, § 2, eff. Sept. 29, 1986. Amended by Stats.1988, c. 195, § 1, eff. June 16, 1988. Renumbered § 43.56 and amended by Stats.1990, c. 216 (S.B.2510), § 5.)

§ 43.6. Immunity from liability; actions against parents on childbirth claims; defenses and damages in third party actions

(a) No cause of action arises against a parent of a child based upon the claim that the child should not have been conceived or, if conceived, should not have been allowed to have been born alive.

(b) The failure or refusal of a parent to prevent the live birth of his or her child shall not be a defense in any action against a third party, nor shall the failure or refusal be considered in awarding damages in any such action.

(c) As used in this section "conceived" means the fertilization of a human ovum by a human sperm. (Added by Stats.1981, c. 331, § 1.)

§ 43.7. Immunity from liability; mental health professional quality assurance committees; professional societies, members or staff; peer review or insurance underwriting committees; hospital governing board

(a) There shall be no monetary liability on the part of, and no cause of action for damages shall arise against, any member of a duly appointed mental health professional quality assurance committee that is established in compliance with Section 14725 of the Welfare and Institutions Code, for any act or proceeding undertaken or performed within the scope of the functions of the committee which is formed to review and evaluate the adequacy, appropriateness, or effectiveness of the care and treatment planned for, or provided to, mental health patients in order to improve quality of care by mental health professionals if the committee member acts without malice, has made a reasonable effort to obtain the facts of the matter as to which he or she acts, and acts in reasonable belief that the action taken by him or her is warranted by the facts known to him or her after the reasonable effort to obtain facts.

(b) There shall be no monetary liability on the part of, and no cause of action for damages shall arise against, any professional society, any member of a duly appointed committee of a medical specialty society, or any member of a duly appointed committee of a state or local professional society, or duly appointed member of a committee of a professional staff of a licensed hospital (provided the professional staff operates pursuant to written bylaws that have been approved by the governing board of the hospital), for any act or proceeding undertaken or performed within the scope of the functions of the committee which is formed to maintain the professional standards of the society established by its bylaws, or any member of any peer review committee whose purpose is to review the quality of medical, dental, dietetic, chiropractic, optometric, acupuncture, psychotherapy, midwifery, or veterinary services rendered by physicians and surgeons, dentists, dental hygienists, podiatrists, registered dietitians, chiropractors, optometrists, acupuncturists, veterinarians, marriage and family therapists, professional clinical counselors, licensed midwives, or psychologists, which committee is composed chiefly of physicians and surgeons, dentists, dental hygienists, podiatrists, registered dietitians, chiropractors, optometrists, acupuncturists, veterinarians, marriage and family therapists, professional clinical counselors, licensed midwives or psychologists for any act or proceeding undertaken or performed in reviewing the quality of medical, dental, dietetic, chiropractic, optometric, acupuncture, psychotherapy, midwifery, or veterinary services rendered by physicians and surgeons, dentists, dental hygienists, podiatrists, registered dietitians, chiropractors, optometrists, acupuncturists, veterinarians, marriage and family therapists, professional clinical counselors, midwifery, or psychologists or any member of the governing board of a hospital in reviewing the quality of medical services rendered by members of the staff if the professional society, committee, or board member acts without malice, has made a reasonable effort to obtain the facts of the matter as to which he, she, or it acts, and acts in reasonable belief that the action taken by him, her, or it is warranted by the facts known to him, her, or it after the reasonable effort to obtain facts. "Professional society" includes legal, medical, psychological, dental, dental hygiene, dietetic, accounting, optometric, acupuncture, podiatric, pharmaceutic, chiropractic, physical therapist, veterinary, licensed marriage and family therapy, licensed clinical social work, licensed professional clinical counselor, and engineering organizations having as members at least 25 percent of the eligible persons or licentiates in the geographic area served by the particular society. However, if the society has fewer than 100 members, it shall have as members at least a majority of the eligible persons or licentiates in the geographic area served by the particular society.

"Medical specialty society" means an organization having as members at least 25 percent of the eligible physicians and surgeons within a given professionally recognized medical specialty in the geographic area served by the particular society.

(c) This section does not affect the official immunity of an officer or employee of a public corporation.

(d) There shall be no monetary liability on the part of, and no cause of action for damages shall arise against, any physician and surgeon, podiatrist, or chiropractor who is a member of an underwriting committee of an interindemnity or reciprocal or interinsurance exchange or mutual company for any act or proceeding undertaken or performed in evaluating physicians and surgeons, podiatrists, or chiropractors for the writing of professional liability insurance, or any act or proceeding undertaken or performed in evaluating physicians and surgeons for the writing of an interindemnity, reciprocal, or interinsurance contract as specified in Section 1280.7 of the Insurance Code, if the evaluating physician and surgeon, podiatrist, or chiropractor acts without malice, has made a reasonable effort to obtain the facts of the matter as to which he or she acts, and acts in reasonable belief that the action taken by him or her is warranted by the facts known to him or her after the reasonable effort to obtain the facts.

(e) This section shall not be construed to confer immunity from liability on any quality assurance committee established in compliance with Section 14725 of the Welfare and Institutions Code or hospital. In any case in which, but for the enactment of the preceding provisions of this section, a cause of action would arise against a quality assurance committee established in compliance with Section 14725 of the Welfare and Institutions Code or hospital, the cause of action shall exist as if the preceding provisions of this section had not been enacted. (Added by Stats.1961, c. 623, p. 1780, § 1. Amended by Stats.1963, c. 806, p. 1836, § 1; Stats.1969, c. 264, p. 616, § 1; Stats.1973, c. 191, p. 493, § 1; Stats.1976, c. 532, p. 1287, § 1; Stats.1977, c. 241, p. 1085, § 1; Stats.1977, c. 934, p. 2858, § 1; Stats.1978, c. 268, p. 555, § 1; Stats.1978, c. 503, p. 1647, § 1; Stats.1980, c. 454, § 1, operative Jan. 1, 1990; Stats.1982, c. 234, p. 765, § 2, eff. June 2, 1982; Stats.1982, c. 705, p. 2862, § 1; Stats.1983, c. 289, § 1; Stats.1983, c. 297, § 1; Stats.1983, c. 1081, § 1.8; Stats.1984, c. 515, § 1; Stats.1984, c. 1012, § 1; Stats.1986, c. 669, § 2; Stats.1987, c. 1169, § 2, operative Jan. 1, 1990; Stats.1994, c. 815 (S.B.1279), § 1; Stats.2002, c. 1013 (S.B. 2026), § 72; Stats.2010, c. 82 (A.B.1730), § 1; Stats.2011, c. 381 (S.B.146), § 14; Stats.2012, c. 34 (S.B.1009), § 3, eff. June 27, 2012, operative July 1, 2012; Stats.2017, c. 775 (S.B.798), § 105, eff. Jan. 1, 2018.)

Cross References

Monterey County Special Health Care Authority, persons deemed members of peer review committee, see Health and Safety Code § 101565.

§ 43.8. Immunity from liability for communication on evaluation of practitioner of healing or veterinary arts

(a) In addition to the privilege afforded by Section 47, there shall be no monetary liability on the part of, and no cause of action for damages shall arise against, any person on account of the communication of information in the possession of that person to any hospital, hospital medical staff, veterinary hospital staff, professional society, medical, dental, podiatric, psychology, marriage and family therapy, professional clinical counselor, midwifery, or veterinary school, professional licensing board or division, committee or panel of a licensing board, the Senior Assistant Attorney General of the Health Quality Enforcement Section appointed under Section 12529 of the Government Code, peer review committee, quality assurance committees established in compliance with Sections 4070 and 5624 of the Welfare and Institutions Code, or underwriting committee described in Section 43.7 when the communication is intended to aid in the evaluation of the qualifications, fitness, character, or insurability of a practitioner of the healing or veterinary arts.

(b) The immunities afforded by this section and by Section 43.7 shall not affect the availability of any absolute privilege that may be afforded by Section 47.

(c) Nothing in this section is intended in any way to affect the California Supreme Court's decision in Hassan v. Mercy American River Hospital (2003) 31 Cal.4th 709, holding that subdivision (a) provides a qualified privilege. (Added by Stats.1974, c. 1086, p. 2313, § 1. Amended by Stats.1975, 2nd Ex.Sess., c. 1, p. 3968, § 24.4; Stats.1976, c. 532, p. 1287, § 2; Stats.1977, c. 934, p. 2859, § 2; Stats.1982, c. 234, p. 767, § 3, eff. June 2, 1982; Stats.1982, c. 705, p. 2863, § 2; Stats.1983, c. 1081, § 2; Stats.1984, c. 515, § 4; Stats.1983, c. 1081, § 2, operative Jan. 1, 1990; Stats.1990, c. 1597 (S.B.2375), § 30; Stats.2002, c. 664 (A.B.3034), § 31; Stats.2007, c. 36 (S.B. 822), § 1; Stats.2008, c. 23 (A.B.164), § 1; Stats.2011, c. 381 (S.B.146), § 15; Stats.2017, c. 775 (S.B.798), § 106, eff. Jan. 1, 2018.)

Cross References

Attorney General, generally, see Government Code § 12500 et seq.
Providing information indicating board licensee guilty of unprofessional conduct or impaired because of drug or alcohol abuse or mental illness, additional immunity, see Business and Professions Code § 2318.
Psychiatric technicians, reporting of violations, see Business and Professions Code § 4521.2.
Respiratory Care Practice Act, reporting of violations, see Business and Professions Code § 3759.
Vocational nursing, reporting of violations, see Business and Professions Code § 2878.1.

§ 43.9. Immunity from liability; health care providers; unsolicited referrals from tests by multiphasic screening unit; notice

(a) There shall be no liability on the part of, and no cause of action shall accrue against, any health care provider for professional negligence on account of the receipt by such provider of an unsolicited referral, arising from a test performed by a multiphasic screening unit, for any act or omission, including the failure to examine, treat, or refer for examination or treatment any person concerning whom an unsolicited referral has been received. The immunity from liability granted by this subdivision shall only apply where a health provider meets the obligations established in subdivision (c).

(b) Every multiphasic screening unit shall notify each person it tests that the person should contact the health provider to whom the test results are sent within 10 days and that the health provider may not be obligated to interpret the results or provide further care. The multiphasic screening unit shall include the words "PATIENT TEST RESULTS" on the envelope of any test results sent to a health care provider, and shall include the address of the person tested in the test result material sent to the health care provider.

Nothing contained in this section shall relieve any health care provider from liability, if any, when at the time of receipt of the unsolicited referral there exists a provider-patient relationship, or a contract for health care services, or following receipt of such unsolicited referral there is established or reestablished a provider-patient relationship.

(c) A health care provider who receives unsolicited test results from a multiphasic screening unit shall receive immunity from liability pursuant to subdivision (a) only if the provider who receives such test results and does not wish to evaluate them, or evaluates them and takes no further action, either notifies the multiphasic screening unit of that fact or returns the test results within 21 days. If the health care provider reviews the test results and determines that they indicate a substantial risk of serious illness or death the provider shall make a reasonable effort to notify the person tested of the presumptive finding within 14 days after the provider has received the test results.

(d) For the purposes of this section:

(1) "Health care provider" means any person licensed or certified pursuant to Division 2 (commencing with Section 500) of the Business and Professions Code, or licensed pursuant to the Osteopathic Initiative Act or the Chiropractic Initiative Act, or licensed pursuant to Chapter 2.5 (commencing with Section 1440) of Division 2 of the Health and Safety Code, and any clinic, health dispensary, or health facility licensed pursuant to Division 2 (commencing with Section 1200) of the Health and Safety Code. "Health care provider" also includes the legal representatives of a health care provider.

(2) "Professional negligence" means an action for personal injury or wrongful death proximately caused by a health care provider's negligent act or omission to act in the rendering of professional services, provided that such services are within the scope of services for which the health care provider is licensed and are not within any restriction imposed by the licensing agency or any licensed hospital.

(3) "Unsolicited referral" means any written report regarding the health, physical or mental condition of any person which was forwarded or delivered to a health care provider without prior request by such provider.

(4) A "multiphasic screening unit" means a facility which does not prescribe or treat patients but performs diagnostic testing only. (Added by Stats.1978, c. 1296, p. 4249, § 1. Amended by Stats.1980, c. 676, § 38.)

Cross References

Obligation defined, see Civil Code § 1427.

§ 43.91. Immunity from liability; members of professional society of persons licensed under the Real Estate Law; peer review committees

(a) There shall be no monetary liability on the part of, and no cause of action shall arise against, any member of a duly appointed committee of a professional society which comprises a substantial percentage of the persons licensed pursuant to Part 1 (commencing with Section 10000) of Division 4 of the Business and Professions Code and situated in the geographic area served by the particular society, for any act or proceeding undertaken or performed within the scope of the functions of any such committee which is formed to maintain the professional standards of the society established by its bylaws, if such member acts without malice, has made a reasonable effort to obtain the facts of the matter as to which he acts, and acts in reasonable belief that the action taken by him is warranted by the facts known to him after such reasonable effort to obtain facts.

(b) There shall be no monetary liability on the part of, and no cause of action for damages shall arise against, any person on account of the communication of information in the possession of such person to any committee specified in subdivision (a) when such communication is intended to aid in the evaluation of the qualifications, fitness or character of a member or applicant for membership in any such professional society, and does not represent as true any matter not reasonably believed to be true.

(c) The immunities afforded by this section shall not affect the availability of any absolute privilege which may be afforded by Section 47.

(d) This section shall not be construed to confer immunity from liability on any professional society. In any case in which, but for the enactment of this section, a cause of action would arise against a professional society, such cause of action shall exist as if this section had not been enacted. (Added by Stats.1980, c. 492, § 1.)

§ 43.92. Psychotherapists; duty to protect from violent behavior of patient; immunity from monetary liability; interpretation of section

(a) There shall be no monetary liability on the part of, and no cause of action shall arise against, any person who is a psychotherapist as defined in Section 1010 of the Evidence Code in failing to protect from a patient's threatened violent behavior or failing to predict and protect from a patient's violent behavior except if the patient has communicated to the psychotherapist a serious threat of physical violence against a reasonably identifiable victim or victims.

(b) There shall be no monetary liability on the part of, and no cause of action shall arise against, a psychotherapist who, under the limited circumstances specified in subdivision (a), discharges his or her duty to protect by making reasonable

§ 43.92 PERSONS

efforts to communicate the threat to the victim or victims and to a law enforcement agency.

(c) It is the intent of the Legislature that the amendments made by the act [1] adding this subdivision only change the name of the duty referenced in this section from a duty to warn and protect to a duty to protect. Nothing in this section shall be construed to be a substantive change, and any duty of a psychotherapist shall not be modified as a result of changing the wording in this section.

(d) It is the intent of the Legislature that a court interpret this section, as amended by the act [1] adding this subdivision, in a manner consistent with the interpretation of this section as it read prior to January 1, 2013. *(Added by Stats.1985, c. 737, § 1. Amended by Stats.2006, c. 136 (A.B.733), § 1; Stats.2012, c. 149 (S.B.1134), § 1.)*

[1] Stats.2012, c. 149 (S.B.1134).

Cross References

General acute care hospitals or acute psychiatric hospitals, detention or release, persons exhibiting mental disorders, see Health and Safety Code § 1799.111.

Mediators or evaluators appointed by or connected to the court, limitations upon communication with said persons, exceptions, see Family Code § 216.

Voluntary admissions to mental hospitals and institutions, liability upon release of minor, see Welfare and Institutions Code § 6002.35.

§ 43.93. Psychotherapists; patient's cause of action for sexual contact; definitions

(a) For the purposes of this section the following definitions are applicable:

(1) "Psychotherapy" means the professional treatment, assessment, or counseling of a mental or emotional illness, symptom, or condition.

(2) "Psychotherapist" means a physician and surgeon specializing in the practice of psychiatry, a psychologist, a psychological assistant, a marriage and family therapist, a registered marriage and family therapist intern or trainee, an educational psychologist, an associate clinical social worker, a licensed clinical social worker, a professional clinical counselor, or a registered clinical counselor intern or trainee.

(3) "Sexual contact" means the touching of an intimate part of another person. "Intimate part" and "touching" have the same meanings as defined in subdivisions (f) and (d), respectively, of Section 243.4 of the Penal Code. For the purposes of this section, sexual contact includes sexual intercourse, sodomy, and oral copulation.

(4) "Therapeutic relationship" exists during the time the patient or client is rendered professional service by the psychotherapist.

(5) "Therapeutic deception" means a representation by a psychotherapist that sexual contact with the psychotherapist is consistent with or part of the patient's or former patient's treatment.

(b) A cause of action against a psychotherapist for sexual contact exists for a patient or former patient for injury caused by sexual contact with the psychotherapist, if the sexual contact occurred under any of the following conditions:

(1) During the period the patient was receiving psychotherapy from the psychotherapist.

(2) Within two years following termination of therapy.

(3) By means of therapeutic deception.

(c) The patient or former patient may recover damages from a psychotherapist who is found liable for sexual contact. It is not a defense to the action that sexual contact with a patient occurred outside a therapy or treatment session or that it occurred off the premises regularly used by the psychotherapist for therapy or treatment sessions. No cause of action shall exist between spouses within a marriage.

(d) In an action for sexual contact, evidence of the plaintiff's sexual history is not subject to discovery and is not admissible as evidence except in either of the following situations:

(1) The plaintiff claims damage to sexual functioning.

(2) The defendant requests a hearing prior to conducting discovery and makes an offer of proof of the relevancy of the history, and the court finds that the history is relevant and the probative value of the history outweighs its prejudicial effect.

The court shall allow the discovery or introduction as evidence only of specific information or examples of the plaintiff's conduct that are determined by the court to be relevant. The court's order shall detail the information or conduct that is subject to discovery. *(Added by Stats.1987, c. 1474, § 1. Amended by Stats.1992, c. 890 (S.B.1394), § 5; Stats.1993, c. 589 (A.B.2211), § 19; Stats.2002, c. 1013 (S.B.2026), § 73; Stats.2011, c. 381 (S.B.146), § 16.)*

Cross References

State child welfare services, dependency proceeding, motion to remove social worker, grounds, see Welfare and Institutions Code § 16513.5.

§ 43.95. Immunity of professional society for referral services or telephone information library; duty to disclose disciplinary actions

(a) There shall be no monetary liability on the part of, and no cause of action for damages shall arise against, any professional society or any nonprofit corporation authorized by a professional society to operate a referral service, or their agents, employees, or members, for referring any member of the public to any professional member of the society or service, or for acts of negligence or conduct constituting unprofessional conduct committed by a professional to whom a member of the public was referred, so long as any of the foregoing persons or entities has acted without malice, and the referral was made at no cost added to the initial referral fee as part of a public service referral system organized under the auspices of the professional society. Further, there shall be no monetary liability on the part of, and no cause of action for damages shall arise against, any professional society for providing a telephone information library available for use by the general public without charge, nor against any nonprofit corporation authorized by a professional society for providing a telephone information library available for use by the general public without charge. "Professional society" includes legal, psychological, architectural, medical, dental, dietetic, accounting, optometric, podiatric, pharmaceutic, chiropractic, veterinary, licensed marriage and family therapy, licensed clinical social work, professional clinical counselor, and engineering organizations having as members at least 25 percent of the eligible persons or licentiates in the geographic area served by the particular society. However, if the society has less than 100 members, it shall have as members at least a majority of the eligible persons or licentiates in the geographic area served by the particular society. "Professional society" also includes organizations with referral services that have been authorized by the State Bar of California and operated in accordance with its Minimum Standards for a Lawyer Referral Service in California, and organizations that have been established to provide free assistance or representation to needy patients or clients.

(b) This section shall not apply whenever the professional society, while making a referral to a professional member of the society, fails to disclose the nature of any disciplinary action of which it has actual knowledge taken by a state licensing agency against that professional member. However, there shall be no duty to disclose a disciplinary action in either of the following cases:

(1) Where a disciplinary proceeding results in no disciplinary action being taken against the professional to whom a member of the public was referred.

(2) Where a period of three years has elapsed since the professional to whom a member of the public was referred has satisfied any terms, conditions, or sanctions imposed upon the professional as disciplinary action; except that if the professional is an attorney, there shall be no time limit on the duty to disclose. *(Added by Stats.1987, c. 727, § 4, operative July 1, 1993. Amended by Stats.1988, c. 312, § 2, operative July 1, 1993; Stats.2002, c. 1013 (S.B.2026), § 74; Stats.2011, c. 381 (S.B.146), § 17.)*

Cross References

Attorneys, requirements of referral services, see Business and Professions Code § 6155.

§ 43.96. Information to be provided to a complainant; immunity

(a) Any medical or podiatric society, health facility licensed or certified under Division 2 (commencing with Section 1200) of the Health and Safety Code, state agency as defined in Section 11000 of the Government Code, or local government agency that receives written complaints related to the professional competence or professional conduct of a physician and surgeon or doctor of podiatric medicine from the public shall inform the complainant that the Medical Board of California or the California Board of Podiatric Medicine, as the case may be, is the only authority in the state that may take disciplinary action against the license of the named licensee, and shall provide to the complainant the address and toll-free telephone number of the applicable state board.

(b) The immunity provided in Section 2318 of the Business and Professions Code and in Section 47 shall apply to complaints and information made or provided to a board pursuant to this section. *(Added by Stats.1993, c. 1267 (S.B.916), § 48. Amended by Stats.1994, c. 1206 (S.B.1775), § 26; Stats.1995, c. 708 (S.B.609), § 12.)*

Cross References

Medical board, investigation or commencement of disciplinary actions, see Business and Professions Code § 2220.5.

§ 43.97. Medical staff or membership privilege denial or restriction; immunity from liability; unreported or intentional injury exceptions

There shall be no monetary liability on the part of, and no cause of action for damages, other than economic or pecuniary damages, shall arise against, a hospital for any action taken upon the recommendation of its medical staff, or against any other person or organization for any action taken, or restriction imposed, which is required to be reported pursuant to Section 805 of the Business and Professions Code, if that action or restriction is reported in accordance with Section 805 of the Business and Professions Code. This section shall not apply to an action knowingly and intentionally taken for the purpose of injuring a person affected by the action or infringing upon a person's rights. *(Added by Stats.1981, c. 926, § 1. Amended by Stats.1986, c. 1274, § 5; Stats.2006, c. 538 (S.B.1852), § 36.)*

§ 43.98. Communications by consultants to Director of Department of Managed Health Care; health care services; monetary liability

(a) There shall be no monetary liability on the part of, and no cause of action shall arise against, any consultant on account of any communication by that consultant to the Director of the Department of Managed Health Care or any other officer, employee, agent, contractor, or consultant of the Department of Managed Health Care, when that communication is for the purpose of determining whether health care services have been or are being arranged or provided in accordance with the Knox–Keene Health Care Service Plan Act of 1975 (Chapter 2.2 (commencing with Section 1340) of Division 2 of the Health and Safety Code) and any regulation adopted thereunder and the consultant does all of the following:

(1) Acts without malice.

(2) Makes a reasonable effort to obtain the facts of the matter communicated.

(3) Acts with a reasonable belief that the communication is warranted by the facts actually known to the consultant after a reasonable effort to obtain the facts.

(4) Acts pursuant to a contract entered into on or after January 1, 1998, between the Commissioner of Corporations and a state licensing board or committee, including, but not limited to, the Medical Board of California, or pursuant to a contract entered into on or after January 1, 1998, with the Commissioner of Corporations pursuant to Section 1397.6 of the Health and Safety Code.

(5) Acts pursuant to a contract entered into on or after July 1, 2000, between the Director of the Department of Managed Health Care and a state licensing board or committee, including, but not limited to, the Medical Board of California, or pursuant to a contract entered into on or after July 1, 1999, with the Director of the Department of Managed Health Care pursuant to Section 1397.6 of the Health and Safety Code.

(b) The immunities afforded by this section shall not affect the availability of any other privilege or immunity which may be afforded under this part. Nothing in this section shall be construed to alter the laws regarding the confidentiality of medical records. *(Added by Stats.1997, c. 139 (A.B.564), § 1. Amended by Stats.1999, c. 525 (A.B.78), § 4; Stats.2000, c. 857 (A.B.2903), § 3.)*

Cross References

Contracts with independent medical review organizations, restrictions and requirements, see Health and Safety Code § 1374.32.

Department of Managed Health Care, generally, see Health and Safety Code § 1341 et seq.

Health care service plans, acceptance of premium payments from third party entities, see Health and Safety Code § 1367.016.

Life and disability insurance, acceptance of premium payments from third party entities, see Insurance Code § 10176.11.

Life and disability insurance, contracts with independent medical review organizations, see Insurance Code § 10169.2.

§ 43.99. Immunity from monetary liability; building and other inspectors; independent quality review of plans, specifications or work on residential buildings under the State Housing Law; exceptions

(a) There shall be no monetary liability on the part of, and no cause of action for damages shall arise against, any person or other legal entity that is under contract with an applicant for a residential building permit to provide independent quality review of the plans and specifications provided with the application in order to determine compliance with all applicable requirements imposed pursuant to the State Housing Law (Part 1.5 (commencing with Section 17910) of Division 13 of the Health and Safety Code), or any rules or regulations adopted pursuant to that law, or under contract with that applicant to provide independent quality review of the work of improvement to determine compliance with these plans and specifications, if the person or other legal entity meets the requirements of this section and one of the following applies:

(1) The person, or a person employed by any other legal entity, performing the work as described in this subdivision, has completed not less than five years of verifiable experience in the appropriate field and has obtained certification as a building inspector, combination inspector, or combination dwelling inspector from the International Conference of Building Officials (ICBO) and has successfully passed the technical written examination promulgated by ICBO for those certification categories.

(2) The person, or a person employed by any other legal entity, performing the work as described in this subdivision, has completed not less than five years of verifiable experience in the appropriate field and is a registered professional engineer, licensed general contractor, or a licensed architect rendering independent quality review of the work of improvement or plan examination services within the scope of his or her registration or licensure.

(3) The immunity provided under this section does not apply to any action initiated by the applicant who retained the qualified person.

(4) A "qualified person" for purposes of this section means a person holding a valid certification as one of those inspectors.

(b) Except for qualified persons, this section shall not relieve from, excuse, or lessen in any manner, the responsibility or liability of any person, company, contractor, builder, developer, architect, engineer, designer, or other individual or entity who develops, improves, owns, operates, or manages any residential building for any damages to persons or property caused by construction or design defects. The fact that an inspection by a qualified person has taken place may not be introduced as evidence in a construction defect action, including any reports or other items generated by the qualified person. This subdivision shall not apply in any action initiated by the applicant who retained the qualified person.

(c) Nothing in this section, as it relates to construction inspectors or plans examiners, shall be construed to alter the requirements for licensure, or the jurisdiction, authority, or scope of practice, of architects pursuant to Chapter 3 (commencing with Section 5500) of Division 3 of the Business and Professions Code, professional engineers pursuant to Chapter 7 (commencing with Section 6700) of Division 3 of the Business and Professions Code, or general contractors pursuant to Chapter 9 (commencing with Section 7000) of Division 3 of the Business and Professions Code.

(d) Nothing in this section shall be construed to alter the immunity of employees of the Department of Housing and Community Development under the Government Claims Act (Division 3.6 (commencing with Section 810) of Title 1 of the Government Code) when acting pursuant to Section 17965 of the Health and Safety Code.

(e) The qualifying person shall engage in no other construction, design, planning, supervision, or activities of any kind on the work of improvement, nor provide quality review services for any other party on the work of improvement.

(f) The qualifying person, or other legal entity, shall maintain professional errors and omissions insurance coverage in an amount not less than two million dollars ($2,000,000).

(g) The immunity provided by subdivision (a) does not inure to the benefit of the qualified person for damages caused to the applicant solely by the negligence or willful misconduct of the qualified person resulting from the provision of services under the contract with the applicant. *(Added by Stats.2002, c. 722 (S.B.800), § 2. Amended by Stats.2012, c. 759 (A.B.2690), § 1.)*

Cross References

Construction defects, original construction intended to be sold as an individual dwelling unit, actions to recover for damages, see Civil Code § 900 et seq.

§ 43.100. Property damage or trespass to motor vehicle resulting from rescue of animal; immunity from civil liability

(a) There shall not be any civil liability on the part of, and no cause of action shall accrue against, a person for property damage or trespass to a motor vehicle, if the damage was caused while the person was rescuing an animal in accordance with subdivision (b) of Section 597.7 of the Penal Code.

(b) The immunity from civil liability for property damage to a motor vehicle that is established by subdivision (a) does not affect a person's civil liability or immunity from civil liability for rendering aid to an animal. *(Added by Stats.2016, c. 554 (A.B.797), § 1, eff. Jan. 1, 2017.)*

§ 43.101. Immunity from liability for damage to unmanned aircraft or unmanned aircraft system; emergency responders

(a) An emergency responder shall not be liable for any damage to an unmanned aircraft or unmanned aircraft system, if that damage was caused while the emergency responder was providing, and the unmanned aircraft or unmanned aircraft system was interfering with, the operation, support, or enabling of the emergency services listed in Section 853 of the Government Code.

(b)(1) For purposes of this section, "emergency responder" means either of the following, if acting within the scope of authority implicitly or expressly provided by a local public entity or a public employee of a local public entity to provide emergency services:

(A) A paid or an unpaid volunteer.

(B) A private entity.

(2) All of the following terms shall have the same meaning as the terms as used in Chapter 4.5 (commencing with Section 853) of Part 2 of Division 3.6 of Title 1 of the Government Code:

(A) Local public entity.

(B) Public employee of a local public entity.

(C) Unmanned aircraft.

(D) Unmanned aircraft system. *(Added by Stats.2016, c. 834 (S.B.807), § 1, eff. Jan. 1, 2017.)*

§ 43.102. Property damage or trespass to motor vehicle while rescuing child; protections

There shall not be any civil liability on the part of, and no cause of action shall accrue against, a person for property damage or trespass to a motor vehicle, if the damage was caused while the person was rescuing a child in accordance with subdivision (a) or (b) of Section 1799.101 of the Health and Safety Code. For purposes of this section, "child" means a child who is six years of age or younger. *(Added by Stats.2020, c. 352 (A.B.2717), § 1, eff. Jan. 1, 2021.)*

§ 44. Defamation

Defamation is effected by either of the following:

(a) Libel.

(b) Slander. *(Enacted in 1872. Amended by Stats.1980, c. 676, § 39.)*

Cross References

Defamation by radio, see Civil Code § 48.5.
Slander, false and unprivileged publications which constitute, see Civil Code § 46.
Slander by radio broadcast, see Civil Code § 48a.

Uniform Single Publication Act, see Civil Code § 3425.1 et seq.

§ 45. Libel

Libel is a false and unprivileged publication by writing, printing, picture, effigy, or other fixed representation to the eye, which exposes any person to hatred, contempt, ridicule, or obloquy, or which causes him to be shunned or avoided, or which has a tendency to injure him in his occupation. *(Enacted in 1872.)*

Cross References

Action for libel,
   Answer, see Code of Civil Procedure § 461.
   Complaint, see Code of Civil Procedure § 460.
   Limitation, see Code of Civil Procedure § 340.
   Newspaper, conditions precedent to, see Civil Code § 48a.
Attorney fees, actions for libel or slander not filed in good faith and without reasonable cause, see Code of Civil Procedure § 1021.7.
Criminal prosecution for libel,
   Limitation, see Penal Code § 801.
   Special verdict not permitted, see Penal Code § 1150.
Libel on its face, see Civil Code § 45a.
Malice not inferred, see Civil Code § 48.
Privileged publication or broadcast, see Civil Code § 47.
Uniform single publication act, see Civil Code § 3425.1 et seq.

§ 45a. Libel on its face; other actionable defamatory language

A libel which is defamatory of the plaintiff without the necessity of explanatory matter, such as an inducement, innuendo or other extrinsic fact, is said to be a libel on its face. Defamatory language not libelous on its face is not actionable unless the plaintiff alleges and proves that he has suffered special damage as a proximate result thereof. Special damage is defined in Section 48a of this code. *(Added by Stats.1945, c. 1489, p. 2762, § 1.)*

Cross References

Action for libel,
   Answer, see Code of Civil Procedure § 461.
   Complaint, see Code of Civil Procedure § 460.
   Limitation, see Code of Civil Procedure § 340.
   Newspaper, conditions precedent to, see Civil Code § 48a.
Attorney fees, actions for libel or slander not filed in good faith and without reasonable cause, see Code of Civil Procedure § 1021.7.
Criminal prosecution for libel,
   Limitation, see Penal Code § 801.
   Special verdict not permitted, see Penal Code § 1150.

§ 46. Slander, false and unprivileged publications which constitute

Slander is a false and unprivileged publication, orally uttered, and also communications by radio or any mechanical or other means which:

1. Charges any person with crime, or with having been indicted, convicted, or punished for crime;

2. Imputes in him the present existence of an infectious, contagious, or loathsome disease;

3. Tends directly to injure him in respect to his office, profession, trade or business, either by imputing to him general disqualification in those respects which the office or other occupation peculiarly requires, or by imputing some-

thing with reference to his office, profession, trade, or business that has a natural tendency to lessen its profits;

4. Imputes to him impotence or a want of chastity; or

5. Which, by natural consequence, causes actual damage.

(Enacted in 1872. Amended by Stats.1945, c. 1489, p. 2762, § 2.)

Cross References

Attorney fees, actions for libel or slander not filed in good faith and without reasonable cause, see Code of Civil Procedure § 1021.7.

Attorneys fees, allowance of, see Code of Civil Procedure § 1021.7.

Costs in action for slander, see Code of Civil Procedure § 1021.7.

Non-liability of owner, licensee or operator of broadcasting station or network for defamation by radio, see Civil Code § 48.5.

Pleading and proof in libel and slander actions, see Code of Civil Procedure § 460 et seq.

Special damages for defamation by radio, see Civil Code § 48a.

§ 47. Privileged publication or broadcast

A privileged publication or broadcast is one made:

(a) In the proper discharge of an official duty.

(b) In any (1) legislative proceeding, (2) judicial proceeding, (3) in any other official proceeding authorized by law, or (4) in the initiation or course of any other proceeding authorized by law and reviewable pursuant to Chapter 2 (commencing with Section 1084) of Title 1 of Part 3 of the Code of Civil Procedure, except as follows:

(1) An allegation or averment contained in any pleading or affidavit filed in an action for marital dissolution or legal separation made of or concerning a person by or against whom no affirmative relief is prayed in the action shall not be a privileged publication or broadcast as to the person making the allegation or averment within the meaning of this section unless the pleading is verified or affidavit sworn to, and is made without malice, by one having reasonable and probable cause for believing the truth of the allegation or averment and unless the allegation or averment is material and relevant to the issues in the action.

(2) This subdivision does not make privileged any communication made in furtherance of an act of intentional destruction or alteration of physical evidence undertaken for the purpose of depriving a party to litigation of the use of that evidence, whether or not the content of the communication is the subject of a subsequent publication or broadcast which is privileged pursuant to this section. As used in this paragraph, "physical evidence" means evidence specified in Section 250 of the Evidence Code or evidence that is property of any type specified in Chapter 14 (commencing with Section 2031.010) of Title 4 of Part 4 of the Code of Civil Procedure.

(3) This subdivision does not make privileged any communication made in a judicial proceeding knowingly concealing the existence of an insurance policy or policies.

(4) A recorded lis pendens is not a privileged publication unless it identifies an action previously filed with a court of competent jurisdiction which affects the title or right of possession of real property, as authorized or required by law.

(5) This subdivision does not make privileged any communication between a person and a law enforcement agency in which the person makes a false report that another person has committed, or is in the act of committing, a criminal act or is engaged in an activity requiring law enforcement intervention, knowing that the report is false, or with reckless disregard for the truth or falsity of the report.

(c) In a communication, without malice, to a person interested therein, (1) by one who is also interested, or (2) by one who stands in such a relation to the person interested as to afford a reasonable ground for supposing the motive for the communication to be innocent, or (3) who is requested by the person interested to give the information. This subdivision applies to and includes a communication concerning the job performance or qualifications of an applicant for employment, based upon credible evidence, made without malice, by a current or former employer of the applicant to, and upon request of, one whom the employer reasonably believes is a prospective employer of the applicant. This subdivision applies to and includes a complaint of sexual harassment by an employee, without malice, to an employer based upon credible evidence and communications between the employer and interested persons, without malice, regarding a complaint of sexual harassment. This subdivision authorizes a current or former employer, or the employer's agent, to answer, without malice, whether or not the employer would rehire a current or former employee and whether the decision to not rehire is based upon the employer's determination that the former employee engaged in sexual harassment. This subdivision does not apply to a communication concerning the speech or activities of an applicant for employment if the speech or activities are constitutionally protected, or otherwise protected by Section 527.3 of the Code of Civil Procedure or any other provision of law.

(d)(1) By a fair and true report in, or a communication to, a public journal, of (A) a judicial, (B) legislative, or (C) other public official proceeding, or (D) of anything said in the course thereof, or (E) of a verified charge or complaint made by any person to a public official, upon which complaint a warrant has been issued.

(2) Paragraph (1) does not make privileged any communication to a public journal that does any of the following:

(A) Violates Rule 5–120 of the State Bar Rules of Professional Conduct.

(B) Breaches a court order.

(C) Violates a requirement of confidentiality imposed by law.

(e) By a fair and true report of (1) the proceedings of a public meeting, if the meeting was lawfully convened for a lawful purpose and open to the public, or (2) the publication of the matter complained of was for the public benefit.

(Enacted in 1872. Amended by Code Am.1873–74, c. 612, p. 184, § 11; Stats.1895, c. 163, p. 167, § 1; Stats.1927, c. 866, p. 1881, § 1; Stats.1945, c. 1489, p. 2763, § 3; Stats.1979, c. 184, p. 403, § 1; Stats.1990, c. 1491 (A.B.3765), § 1; Stats.1991, c. 432 (A.B.529), § 1; Stats.1992, c. 615 (S.B.1804), § 1; Stats. 1994, c. 364 (A.B.2778), § 1; Stats.1994, c. 700 (S.B.1457), § 2.5; Stats.1996, c. 1055 (S.B.1540), § 2; Stats.2002, c. 1029 (A.B.2868), § 1, eff. Sept. 28, 2002; Stats.2004, c. 182 (A.B.3081), § 4, operative July 1, 2005; Stats.2018, c. 82 (A.B.2770), § 1, eff. Jan. 1, 2019; Stats.2020, c. 327 (A.B. 1775), § 2, eff. Jan. 1, 2021.)

Cross References

Alameda County Medical Center Hospital Authority, open sessions and peer review proceedings as official proceedings, see Health and Safety Code § 101850.

Arbitration and conciliation of international commercial disputes, immunity of arbitrators from civil liability, see Code of Civil Procedure § 1297.119.

Central Coast Hospital authority, powers of authority, see Health and Safety Code § 101661.

Claims subject to article governing false claims actions, applicability of section, see Government Code § 12654.

Contracts for Medi–Cal services and case management, County of Alameda health authority, open sessions and peer review proceedings as official proceedings, see Welfare and Institutions Code § 14087.35.

Contracts for Medi–Cal services and case management, special commission for Tulare and San Joaquin counties, peer review proceedings as official proceedings, see Welfare and Institutions Code § 14087.31.

Elder Abuse and Dependent Adult Civil Protection Act, mandated reporters of suspected financial abuse, see Welfare and Institutions Code §§ 15630.1, 15630.2.

Evidence of mitigating circumstances, see Code of Civil Procedure § 461.

Expulsion hearings, immunity of pupil witnesses, see Education Code § 48918.6.

Governmental access to financial records, authorized acts, see Government Code § 7480.

Kern County Hospital Authority, meetings, see Health and Safety Code § 101855.

Physician, surgeon, or doctor of podiatric medicine, complaints of professional competence or professional conduct subject to immunity, see Civil Code § 43.96.

Pleading and proof, see Code of Civil Procedure § 460.

Providing information indicating board licensee guilty of unprofessional conduct or impaired because of drug or alcohol abuse or mental illness, additional immunity, see Business and Professions Code § 2318.

Real property defined for purposes of this Code, see Civil Code § 658.

San Luis Obispo County Hospital Authority, open sessions as official proceedings, see Health and Safety Code § 101848.6.

San Luis Obispo County Hospital Authority, peer review proceedings as official proceedings, see Health and Safety Code § 101848.9.

Student expulsion hearings, privileged testimony, see Education Code § 48918.6.

Surplus line advisory organization, communications between interested persons, see Insurance Code § 1780.66.

Trade secrets, disclosure in official proceedings, see Civil Code § 3426.11.

§ 47.5. Peace officers; defamation action against person filing false complaint alleging misconduct, criminal conduct, or incompetence

Notwithstanding Section 47, a peace officer may bring an action for defamation against an individual who has filed a complaint with that officer's employing agency alleging misconduct, criminal conduct, or incompetence, if that complaint is false, the complaint was made with knowledge that it was false and that it was made with spite, hatred, or ill will. Knowledge that the complaint was false may be proved by a showing that the complainant had no reasonable grounds to believe the statement was true and that the complainant exhibited a reckless disregard for ascertaining the truth. *(Added by Stats.1982, c. 1588, p. 6272, § 1.)*

Validity

This section was held unconstitutional on its face, as violative of the right to free speech, in the decision of Walker v. Kiousis (App. 4 Dist. 2001) 114 Cal. Rptr.2d 69, 93 Cal.App.4th 1432.

§ 48. Privileged publication or broadcast; malice not inferred

In the case provided for in subdivision (c) of Section 47, malice is not inferred from the communication. *(Enacted in 1872. Amended by Stats.1895, c. 163, p. 168, § 2; Stats.1945, c. 1489, p. 2763, § 4; Stats.2003, c. 62 (S.B.600), § 11.)*

Cross References

Evidence of mitigating circumstances, see Code of Civil Procedure § 461.

Pleading and proof, see Code of Civil Procedure § 460.

§ 48a. Libel in daily or weekly news publication; slander by radio broadcast

(a) In any action for damages for the publication of a libel in a daily or weekly news publication, or of a slander by radio broadcast, plaintiff shall only recover special damages unless a correction is demanded and is not published or broadcast, as provided in this section. Plaintiff shall serve upon the publisher at the place of publication, or broadcaster at the place of broadcast, a written notice specifying the statements claimed to be libelous and demanding that those statements be corrected. The notice and demand must be served within 20 days after knowledge of the publication or broadcast of the statements claimed to be libelous.

(b) If a correction is demanded within 20 days and is not published or broadcast in substantially as conspicuous a manner in the same daily or weekly news publication, or on the same broadcasting station as were the statements claimed to be libelous, in a regular issue thereof published or broadcast within three weeks after service, plaintiff, if he or she pleads and proves notice, demand and failure to correct, and if his or her cause of action is maintained, may recover general, special, and exemplary damages. Exemplary damages shall not be recovered unless the plaintiff proves that defendant made the publication or broadcast with actual malice and then only in the discretion of the court or jury, and actual malice shall not be inferred or presumed from the publication or broadcast.

(c) A correction published or broadcast in substantially as conspicuous a manner in the daily or weekly news publication, or on the broadcasting station as the statements claimed in the complaint to be libelous, before receipt of a demand for correction, shall be of the same force and effect as though the correction had been published or broadcast within three weeks after a demand for correction.

(d) As used in this section, the following definitions shall apply:

(1) "General damages" means damages for loss of reputation, shame, mortification, and hurt feelings.

(2) "Special damages" means all damages that plaintiff alleges and proves that he or she has suffered in respect to his or her property, business, trade, profession, or occupation, including the amounts of money the plaintiff alleges and

§ 48a   PERSONS

proves he or she has expended as a result of the alleged libel, and no other.

(3) "Exemplary damages" means damages that may in the discretion of the court or jury be recovered in addition to general and special damages for the sake of example and by way of punishing a defendant who has made the publication or broadcast with actual malice.

(4) "Actual malice" means that state of mind arising from hatred or ill will toward the plaintiff; provided, however, that a state of mind occasioned by a good faith belief on the part of the defendant in the truth of the libelous publication or broadcast at the time it is published or broadcast shall not constitute actual malice.

(5) "Daily or weekly news publication" means a publication, either in print or electronic form, that contains news on matters of public concern and that publishes at least once a week. *(Added by Stats.1931, c. 1018, p. 2034, § 1. Amended by Stats.1945, c. 1489, p. 2763, § 5; Stats.2015, c. 343 (A.B.998), § 2, eff. Jan. 1, 2016; Stats.2016, c. 86 (S.B.1171), § 17, eff. Jan. 1, 2017.)*

Cross References

Damages,
  Generally, see Civil Code § 3281 et seq.
  Exemplary damages, see Civil Code § 3294.
Evidence of mitigating circumstances, see Code of Civil Procedure § 461.
Pleading and proof, see Code of Civil Procedure § 460.
Single publication, one cause of action, see Civil Code § 3425.1 et seq.

§ 48.5. Defamation by radio; non-liability of owner, licensee or operator of broadcasting station or network

(1) The owner, licensee or operator of a visual or sound radio broadcasting station or network of stations, and the agents or employees of any such owner, licensee or operator, shall not be liable for any damages for any defamatory statement or matter published or uttered in or as a part of a visual or sound radio broadcast by one other than such owner, licensee or operator, or agent or employee thereof, if it shall be alleged and proved by such owner, licensee or operator, or agent or employee thereof, that such owner, licensee or operator, or such agent or employee, has exercised due care to prevent the publication or utterance of such statement or matter in such broadcast.

(2) If any defamatory statement or matter is published or uttered in or as a part of a broadcast over the facilities of a network of visual or sound radio broadcasting stations, the owner, licensee or operator of any such station, or network of stations, and the agents or employees thereof, other than the owner, licensee or operator of the station, or network of stations, originating such broadcast, and the agents or employees thereof, shall in no event be liable for any damages for any such defamatory statement or matter.

(3) In no event, however, shall any owner, licensee or operator of such station or network of stations, or the agents or employees thereof, be liable for any damages for any defamatory statement or matter published or uttered, by one other than such owner, licensee or operator, or agent or employee thereof, in or as a part of a visual or sound radio broadcast by or on behalf of any candidate for public office, which broadcast cannot be censored by reason of the provisions of federal statute or regulation of the Federal Communications Commission.

(4) As used in this Part 2, the terms "radio," "radio broadcast," and "broadcast," are defined to include both visual and sound radio broadcasting.

(5) Nothing in this section contained shall deprive any such owner, licensee or operator, or the agent or employee thereof, of any rights under any other section of this Part 2. *(Added by Stats.1949, c. 1258, p. 2213, § 1.)*

Cross References

Evidence of mitigating circumstances, see Code of Civil Procedure § 461.
Single publication, one cause of action, see Civil Code § 3425.1 et seq.

§ 48.7. Child abuse; prohibition against libel or slander action while charges pending; tolling of limitations; pleadings; demurrer; attorney fees and costs

(a) No person charged by indictment, information, or other accusatory pleading of child abuse may bring a civil libel or slander action against the minor, the parent or guardian of the minor, or any witness, based upon any statements made by the minor, parent or guardian, or witness which are reasonably believed to be in furtherance of the prosecution of the criminal charges while the charges are pending before a trial court. The charges are not pending within the meaning of this section after dismissal, after pronouncement of judgment, or during an appeal from a judgment.

Any applicable statute of limitations shall be tolled during the period that such charges are pending before a trial court.

(b) Whenever any complaint for libel or slander is filed which is subject to the provisions of this section, no responsive pleading shall be required to be filed until 30 days after the end of the period set forth in subdivision (a).

(c) Every complaint for libel or slander based on a statement that the plaintiff committed an act of child abuse shall state that the complaint is not barred by subdivision (a). A failure to include that statement shall be grounds for a demurrer.

(d) Whenever a demurrer against a complaint for libel or slander is sustained on the basis that the complaint was filed in violation of this section, attorney's fees and costs shall be awarded to the prevailing party.

(e) Whenever a prosecutor is informed by a minor, parent, guardian, or witness that a complaint against one of those persons has been filed which may be subject to the provisions of this section, the prosecutor shall provide that person with a copy of this section.

(f) As used in this section, child abuse has the meaning set forth in Section 11165 of the Penal Code. *(Added by Stats.1981, c. 253, § 1.)*

Cross References

Child abuse, see Penal Code §§ 273a, 273d.
Libel defined, see Civil Code § 45.

Slander defined, see Civil Code § 46.

§ 48.8. Communications to school personnel regarding threats to commit violence on the school grounds involving deadly or dangerous weapons; liability for defamation

(a) A communication by any person to a school principal, or a communication by a student attending the school to the student's teacher or to a school counselor or school nurse and any report of that communication to the school principal, stating that a specific student or other specified person has made a threat to commit violence or potential violence on the school grounds involving the use of a firearm or other deadly or dangerous weapon, is a communication on a matter of public concern and is subject to liability in defamation only upon a showing by clear and convincing evidence that the communication or report was made with knowledge of its falsity or with reckless disregard for the truth or falsity of the communication. Where punitive damages are alleged, the provisions of Section 3294 shall also apply.

(b) As used in this section, "school" means a public or private school providing instruction in kindergarten or grades 1 to 12, inclusive. *(Added by Stats.2001, c. 570 (A.B.1717), § 1.)*

§ 48.9. Anonymous witness program; immunity

(a) An organization which sponsors or conducts an anonymous witness program, and its employees and agents, shall not be liable in a civil action for damages resulting from its receipt of information regarding possible criminal activity or from dissemination of that information to a law enforcement agency.

(b) The immunity provided by this section shall apply to any civil action for damages, including, but not limited to, a defamation action or an action for damages resulting from retaliation against a person who provided information.

(c) The immunity provided by this section shall not apply in any of the following instances:

(1) The information was disseminated with actual knowledge that it was false.

(2) The name of the provider of the information was disseminated without that person's authorization and the dissemination was not required by law.

(3) The name of the provider of information was obtained and the provider was not informed by the organization that the disclosure of his or her name may be required by law.

(d) As used in this section, an "anonymous witness program" means a program whereby information relating to alleged criminal activity is received from persons, whose names are not released without their authorization unless required by law, and disseminated to law enforcement agencies. *(Added by Stats.1983, c. 495, § 1.)*

Cross References
Bribing, influencing, intimidating or threatening witnesses, see Penal Code § 136 et seq.

§ 49. Personal relations, acts forbidden by

The rights of personal relations forbid:

(a) The abduction or enticement of a child from a parent, or from a guardian entitled to its custody;

(b) The seduction of a person under the age of legal consent;

(c) Any injury to a servant which affects his ability to serve his master, other than seduction, abduction or criminal conversation. *(Enacted in 1872. Amended by Stats.1905, c. 70, p. 68, § 1; Stats.1939, c. 128, p. 1245, § 1; Stats.1939, c. 1103, p. 3037, § 5.)*

Cross References
Abduction of minor, purpose of prostitution, see Penal Code § 267.
Custody of child, see Family Code § 3010.
Hormonal chemical treatment, see Penal Code § 645.
Inveiglement or enticement of unmarried female minor for purposes of prostitution, etc., see Penal Code § 266.
Kidnapping,
  Defined, see Penal Code § 207.
  Punishment for, see Penal Code § 208 et seq.
Limitation on action for seduction of person under age of consent, see Code of Civil Procedure § 340.
Wrongs not actionable, see Civil Code § 43.5.

§ 50. Force, right to use

Any necessary force may be used to protect from wrongful injury the person or property of oneself, or of a spouse, child, parent, or other relative, or member of one's family, or of a ward, servant, master, or guest. *(Enacted in 1872. Amended by Code Am.1873–74, c. 612, p. 184, § 12; Stats.2016, c. 50 (S.B.1005), § 4, eff. Jan. 1, 2017.)*

Cross References
Consent, effect of, see Civil Code § 3515.
General personal rights, see Civil Code § 43.
Lawful resistance, see Penal Code § 692 et seq.
Resistance to arrest, see Penal Code § 834a.
Responsibility for agent's negligence or omission, see Civil Code § 2338.
Self-defense, justifiable homicide in, see Penal Code §§ 197, 198.

§ 51. Unruh Civil Rights Act; equal rights; business establishments; violations of federal Americans with Disabilities Act

(a) This section shall be known, and may be cited, as the Unruh Civil Rights Act.

(b) All persons within the jurisdiction of this state are free and equal, and no matter what their sex, race, color, religion, ancestry, national origin, disability, medical condition, genetic information, marital status, sexual orientation, citizenship, primary language, or immigration status are entitled to the full and equal accommodations, advantages, facilities, privileges, or services in all business establishments of every kind whatsoever.

(c) This section shall not be construed to confer any right or privilege on a person that is conditioned or limited by law or that is applicable alike to persons of every sex, color, race, religion, ancestry, national origin, disability, medical condition, marital status, sexual orientation, citizenship, primary language, or immigration status, or to persons regardless of their genetic information.

(d) Nothing in this section shall be construed to require any construction, alteration, repair, structural or otherwise, or modification of any sort whatsoever, beyond that construction, alteration, repair, or modification that is otherwise required by other provisions of law, to any new or existing establishment, facility, building, improvement, or any other structure, nor shall anything in this section be construed to augment, restrict, or alter in any way the authority of the State Architect to require construction, alteration, repair, or modifications that the State Architect otherwise possesses pursuant to other laws.

(e) For purposes of this section:

(1) "Disability" means any mental or physical disability as defined in Sections 12926 and 12926.1 of the Government Code.

(2)(A) "Genetic information" means, with respect to any individual, information about any of the following:

(i) The individual's genetic tests.

(ii) The genetic tests of family members of the individual.

(iii) The manifestation of a disease or disorder in family members of the individual.

(B) "Genetic information" includes any request for, or receipt of, genetic services, or participation in clinical research that includes genetic services, by an individual or any family member of the individual.

(C) "Genetic information" does not include information about the sex or age of any individual.

(3) "Medical condition" has the same meaning as defined in subdivision (i) of Section 12926 of the Government Code.

(4) "Religion" includes all aspects of religious belief, observance, and practice.

(5) "Sex" includes, but is not limited to, pregnancy, childbirth, or medical conditions related to pregnancy or childbirth. "Sex" also includes, but is not limited to, a person's gender. "Gender" means sex, and includes a person's gender identity and gender expression. "Gender expression" means a person's gender-related appearance and behavior whether or not stereotypically associated with the person's assigned sex at birth.

(6) "Sex, race, color, religion, ancestry, national origin, disability, medical condition, genetic information, marital status, sexual orientation, citizenship, primary language, or immigration status" includes a perception that the person has any particular characteristic or characteristics within the listed categories or that the person is associated with a person who has, or is perceived to have, any particular characteristic or characteristics within the listed categories.

(7) "Sexual orientation" has the same meaning as defined in subdivision (s) of Section 12926 of the Government Code.

(f) A violation of the right of any individual under the federal Americans with Disabilities Act of 1990 (Public Law 101–336)[1] shall also constitute a violation of this section.

(g) Verification of immigration status and any discrimination based upon verified immigration status, where required by federal law, shall not constitute a violation of this section.

(h) Nothing in this section shall be construed to require the provision of services or documents in a language other than English, beyond that which is otherwise required by other provisions of federal, state, or local law, including

Section 1632. (Added by Stats.1905, c. 413, p. 553, § 1. Amended by Stats.1919, c. 210, p. 309, § 1; Stats.1923, c. 235, p. 485, § 1; Stats.1959, c. 1866, p. 4424, § 1; Stats.1961, c. 1187, p. 2920, § 1; Stats.1974, c. 1193, p. 2568, § 1; Stats. 1987, c. 159, § 1; Stats.1992, c. 913 (A.B.1077), § 3; Stats. 1998, c. 195 (A.B.2702), § 1; Stats.2000, c. 1049 (A.B.2222), § 2; Stats.2005, c. 420 (A.B.1400), § 3; Stats.2011, c. 261 (S.B.559), § 3; Stats.2011, c. 719 (A.B.887), § 1.5; Stats.2015, c. 303 (A.B.731), § 25, eff. Jan. 1, 2016; Stats.2015, c. 282 (S.B.600), § 1, eff. Jan. 1, 2016.)

[1] For public law sections classified to the U.S.C.A., see USCA–Tables.

Cross References

Alcoholic beverages, club licenses for condominium homeowners' associations, license denied for discriminatory practices, see Business and Professions Code § 23428.20.

Armed forces members, prohibitions and penalties against discrimination, see Military and Veterans Code § 394.

Blind and other physically disabled persons, see Civil Code § 54 et seq.

Bond and loan insurance, occupancy of housing for which a loan is insured, discrimination prohibited, see Health and Safety Code § 51602.

Boycotts, blacklists, etc., by business establishments, see Civil Code § 51.5.

Business of insurance, application of Unruh Civil Rights Act, see Insurance Code § 1861.03.

California Commission on Disability Access, findings and declarations relating to, see Government Code § 14985.

California housing finance agency, equal opportunity without discrimination, see Health and Safety Code § 50955.

Community development and housing, declaration of state antidiscrimination policy, discrimination prohibited, see Health and Safety Code § 33050.

Community development and housing, financial discrimination prohibited, see Health and Safety Code § 35811.

Community redevelopment, property disposition rehabilitation, nondiscrimination and nonsegregation, see Health and Safety Code §§ 33435, 33436.

Construction-related accessibility claims, application for mandatory evaluation conference, see Civil Code § 55.545.

Damages for deprivation of rights, see Civil Code § 52.

Deeds, invalidity of racial restrictions, see Civil Code § 782.

Department of Fair Employment and Housing, construction of provisions with this section, see Government Code § 12993.

Department of Fair Employment and Housing, functions, powers and duties, see Government Code § 12935.

Development of community paramedicine or triage to alternate destination program, duties of local EMS agency, see Health and Safety Code § 1841.

Due process of law, see Cal. Const. Art. 1, § 15, cl. 7.

Employers, labor organizations, employment agencies and other persons, unlawful employment practice, exceptions, see Government Code § 12940.

Floating home residency, private club membership not to be denied on discrimination basis, see Civil Code § 800.25.

Franchises, discrimination, see Civil Code § 51.8.

Historical property rehabilitation, prohibited discrimination, see Health and Safety Code § 37630.

Housing discrimination, unlawful practices, see Government Code § 12955.

Housing discrimination, unlawful practices, business establishment, see Government Code § 12955.8.

Housing without discrimination as a civil right, see Government Code § 12921.

Inalienable rights, see Cal. Const. Art. 1, § 1.

Information regarding patient's rights, duty of hospitals to provide information upon admission of patient, see Health and Safety Code § 1262.6.
Local tenant preference policy, purpose, see Government Code § 7061.
Mobilehome residency, private club membership not to be denied on discrimination basis, see Civil Code § 798.20.
Planning and zoning, prohibition against discrimination, exceptions, see Government Code § 65008.
Pleadings in civil actions, protection of the civil rights of persons with disabilities, high-frequency litigants, see Code of Civil Procedure § 425.55.
Powers and duties of cities and counties, discrimination, community youth athletics and parks and recreation facilities, see Government Code § 53080.
Privileges and immunities, see Cal. Const. Art. 1, § 7.
Provision of housing for homeless youth, age discrimination, see Government Code § 12957.
Real estate licensees, grounds for disciplinary action, induced sale or listing due to adverse impact of persons in neighborhood with certain characteristics, see Business and Professions Code § 10177.
Real property, discriminatory restrictions in deeds, invalidity, see Civil Code §§ 782, 782.5.
Redevelopment construction loans, nondiscrimination in construction and disposition of residences, see Health and Safety Code § 33769.
Residential property rehabilitation, open housing, equal opportunity in employment and contracts, see Health and Safety Code § 37923.
Restrictions on nonprofit lawn bowls club membership prohibited, see Business and Professions Code § 23433.5.
Restrictions upon transfer or use of realty, see Civil Code § 53.
Restroom access for medical conditions, implementation of article, see Health and Safety Code § 118701.
Retaliation prohibited against advocates or employees opposing or filing complaints about practices, fine for violation, see Government Code § 9149.40.
Small business gender discrimination in services compliance act, demand letters, written advisory notice, penalties, application, see Civil Code § 55.62.
Violence or intimidation, see Civil Code § 51.7.

§ 51.1. Mandatory service on State Solicitor General of each party's brief or petition and brief in causes of action based on violation of civil rights statutes

If a violation of Section 51, 51.5, 51.7, 51.9, or 52.1 is alleged or the application or construction of any of these sections is in issue in any proceeding in the Supreme Court of California, a state court of appeal, or the appellate division of a superior court, each party shall serve a copy of the party's brief or petition and brief, on the State Solicitor General at the Office of the Attorney General. No brief may be accepted for filing unless the proof of service shows service on the State Solicitor General. Any party failing to comply with this requirement shall be given a reasonable opportunity to cure the failure before the court imposes any sanction and, in that instance, the court shall allow the Attorney General reasonable additional time to file a brief in the matter. *(Added by Stats.2002, c. 244 (A.B.2524), § 1.)*

Cross References

Attorney General, generally, see Government Code § 12500 et seq.
Business of insurance, application of Unruh Civil Rights Act, see Insurance Code § 1861.03.

Similar provisions, see Civil Code § 55.2; Government Code § 4461; Health and Safety Code §§ 19954.5, 19959.5.

§ 51.2. Age discrimination in sale or rental of housing prohibited; housing designed to meet physical and social needs of senior citizens; exceptions; intent; age preferences in federally approved housing programs

(a) Section 51 shall be construed to prohibit a business establishment from discriminating in the sale or rental of housing based upon age. Where accommodations are designed to meet the physical and social needs of senior citizens, a business establishment may establish and preserve that housing for senior citizens, pursuant to Section 51.3, except housing as to which Section 51.3 is preempted by the prohibition in the federal Fair Housing Amendments Act of 1988 (Public Law 100–430)[1] and implementing regulations against discrimination on the basis of familial status. For accommodations constructed before February 8, 1982, that meet all the criteria for senior citizen housing specified in Section 51.3, a business establishment may establish and preserve that housing development for senior citizens without the housing development being designed to meet physical and social needs of senior citizens.

(b) This section is intended to clarify the holdings in Marina Point, Ltd. v. Wolfson (1982) 30 Cal.3d 72 and O'Connor v. Village Green Owners Association (1983) 33 Cal.3d 790.

(c) This section shall not apply to the County of Riverside.

(d) A housing development for senior citizens constructed on or after January 1, 2001, shall be presumed to be designed to meet the physical and social needs of senior citizens if it includes all of the following elements:

(1) Entryways, walkways, and hallways in the common areas of the development, and doorways and paths of access to and within the housing units, shall be as wide as required by current laws applicable to new multifamily housing construction for provision of access to persons using a standard-width wheelchair.

(2) Walkways and hallways in the common areas of the development shall be equipped with standard height railings or grab bars to assist persons who have difficulty with walking.

(3) Walkways and hallways in the common areas shall have lighting conditions which are of sufficient brightness to assist persons who have difficulty seeing.

(4) Access to all common areas and housing units within the development shall be provided without use of stairs, either by means of an elevator or sloped walking ramps.

(5) The development shall be designed to encourage social contact by providing at least one common room and at least some common open space.

(6) Refuse collection shall be provided in a manner that requires a minimum of physical exertion by residents.

(7) The development shall comply with all other applicable requirements for access and design imposed by law, including, but not limited to, the Fair Housing Act (42 U.S.C. Sec. 3601 et seq.), the Americans with Disabilities Act (42 U.S.C. Sec. 12101 et seq.), and the regulations promulgated at Title 24 of the California Code of Regulations that relate to access for

§ 51.2

persons with disabilities or handicaps. Nothing in this section shall be construed to limit or reduce any right or obligation applicable under those laws.

(e) Selection preferences based on age, imposed in connection with a federally approved housing program, do not constitute age discrimination in housing. *(Added by Stats. 1984, c. 787, § 1. Amended by Stats.1989, c. 501, § 1; Stats.1993, c. 830 (S.B.137), § 1, eff. Oct. 6, 1993; Stats.1996, c. 1147 (S.B.2097), § 2; Stats.1999, c. 324 (S.B.382), § 1; Stats.2000, c. 1004 (S.B.2011), § 2; Stats.2002, c. 726 (A.B. 2787), § 2; Stats.2010, c. 524 (S.B.1252), § 2.)*

[1] Public law sections classified to the U.S.C.A., see USCA–Tables.

Cross References

Alcoholic beverages, club licenses for condominium homeowners' associations, license denied for discriminatory practices, see Business and Professions Code § 23428.20.

Bond and loan insurance, occupancy of housing for which a loan is insured, discrimination prohibited, see Health and Safety Code § 51602.

Business of insurance, application of Unruh Civil Rights Act, see Insurance Code § 1861.03.

California housing finance agency, equal opportunity without discrimination, see Health and Safety Code § 50955.

Community development and housing, declaration of state antidiscrimination policy, discrimination prohibited, see Health and Safety Code § 33050.

Community development and housing, financial discrimination prohibited, see Health and Safety Code § 35811.

Community redevelopment, property disposition rehabilitation, nondiscrimination and nonsegregation, see Health and Safety Code §§ 33435, 33436.

Consideration of proposed universal design guidelines for home construction or home modifications, housing for senior citizens, see Health and Safety Code § 17959.

Facilities offering continuing care contracts, application of this section, see Health and Safety Code § 1775.

Floating home residency, private club membership not to be denied on discrimination basis, see Civil Code § 800.25.

Historical property rehabilitation, prohibited discrimination, see Health and Safety Code § 37630.

Housing discrimination on the basis of familial status, application of prohibitions to housing for older persons, see Government Code § 12955.9.

Mobilehome residency, private club membership not to be denied on discrimination basis, see Civil Code § 798.20.

Obligation defined, see Civil Code § 1427.

Planning and zoning, prohibition against discrimination, exceptions, see Government Code § 65008.

Provision of housing for homeless youth, age discrimination, see Government Code § 12957.

Real estate licensees, grounds for disciplinary action, induced sale or listing due to adverse impact of persons in neighborhood with certain characteristics, see Business and Professions Code § 10177.

Real property, discriminatory restrictions in deeds, invalidity, see Civil Code §§ 782, 782.5.

Redevelopment construction loans, nondiscrimination in construction and disposition of residences, see Health and Safety Code § 33769.

Residential property rehabilitation, open housing, equal opportunity in employment and contracts, see Health and Safety Code § 37923.

§ 51.3. Housing; age limitations; necessity for senior citizen housing

(a) The Legislature finds and declares that this section is essential to establish and preserve specially designed accessible housing for senior citizens. There are senior citizens who need special living environments and services, and find that there is an inadequate supply of this type of housing in the state.

(b) For the purposes of this section, the following definitions apply:

(1) "Qualifying resident" or "senior citizen" means a person 62 years of age or older, or 55 years of age or older in a senior citizen housing development.

(2) "Qualified permanent resident" means a person who meets both of the following requirements:

(A) Was residing with the qualifying resident or senior citizen prior to the death, hospitalization, or other prolonged absence of, or the dissolution of marriage with, the qualifying resident or senior citizen.

(B) Was 45 years of age or older, or was a spouse, cohabitant, or person providing primary physical or economic support to the qualifying resident or senior citizen.

(3) "Qualified permanent resident" also means a disabled person or person with a disabling illness or injury who is a child or grandchild of the senior citizen or a qualified permanent resident as defined in paragraph (2) who needs to live with the senior citizen or qualified permanent resident because of the disabling condition, illness, or injury. For purposes of this section, "disabled" means a person who has a disability as defined in subdivision (b) of Section 54. A "disabling injury or illness" means an illness or injury which results in a condition meeting the definition of disability set forth in subdivision (b) of Section 54.

(A) For any person who is a qualified permanent resident under this paragraph whose disabling condition ends, the owner, board of directors, or other governing body may require the formerly disabled resident to cease residing in the development upon receipt of six months' written notice; provided, however, that the owner, board of directors, or other governing body may allow the person to remain a resident for up to one year after the disabling condition ends.

(B) The owner, board of directors, or other governing body of the senior citizen housing development may take action to prohibit or terminate occupancy by a person who is a qualified permanent resident under this paragraph if the owner, board of directors, or other governing body finds, based on credible and objective evidence, that the person is likely to pose a significant threat to the health or safety of others that cannot be ameliorated by means of a reasonable accommodation; provided, however, that the action to prohibit or terminate the occupancy may be taken only after doing both of the following:

(i) Providing reasonable notice to and an opportunity to be heard for the disabled person whose occupancy is being challenged, and reasonable notice to the coresident parent or grandparent of that person.

(ii) Giving due consideration to the relevant, credible, and objective information provided in the hearing. The evidence shall be taken and held in a confidential manner, pursuant to a closed session, by the owner, board of directors, or other governing body in order to preserve the privacy of the affected persons.

The affected persons shall be entitled to have present at the hearing an attorney or any other person authorized by them to speak on their behalf or to assist them in the matter.

(4) "Senior citizen housing development" means a residential development developed, substantially rehabilitated, or substantially renovated for, senior citizens that has at least 35 dwelling units. Any senior citizen housing development which is required to obtain a public report under Section 11010 of the Business and Professions Code and which submits its application for a public report after July 1, 2001, shall be required to have been issued a public report as a senior citizen housing development under Section 11010.05 of the Business and Professions Code. No housing development constructed prior to January 1, 1985, shall fail to qualify as a senior citizen housing development because it was not originally developed or put to use for occupancy by senior citizens.

(5) "Dwelling unit" or "housing" means any residential accommodation other than a mobilehome.

(6) "Cohabitant" refers to persons who live together as spouses or persons who are domestic partners within the meaning of Section 297 of the Family Code.

(7) "Permitted health care resident" means a person hired to provide live-in, long-term, or terminal health care to a qualifying resident, or a family member of the qualifying resident providing that care. For the purposes of this section, the care provided by a permitted health care resident must be substantial in nature and must provide either assistance with necessary daily activities or medical treatment, or both.

A permitted health care resident shall be entitled to continue his or her occupancy, residency, or use of the dwelling unit as a permitted resident in the absence of the senior citizen from the dwelling unit only if both of the following are applicable:

(A) The senior citizen became absent from the dwelling unit due to hospitalization or other necessary medical treatment and expects to return to his or her residence within 90 days from the date the absence began.

(B) The absent senior citizen or an authorized person acting for the senior citizen submits a written request to the owner, board of directors, or governing board stating that the senior citizen desires that the permitted health care resident be allowed to remain in order to be present when the senior citizen returns to reside in the development.

Upon written request by the senior citizen or an authorized person acting for the senior citizen, the owner, board of directors, or governing board shall have the discretion to allow a permitted health care resident to remain for a time period longer than 90 days from the date that the senior citizen's absence began, if it appears that the senior citizen will return within a period of time not to exceed an additional 90 days.

(c) The covenants, conditions, and restrictions and other documents or written policy shall set forth the limitations on occupancy, residency, or use on the basis of age. Any such limitation shall not be more exclusive than to require that one person in residence in each dwelling unit may be required to be a senior citizen and that each other resident in the same dwelling unit may be required to be a qualified permanent resident, a permitted health care resident, or a person under 55 years of age whose occupancy is permitted under subdivision (h) of this section or under subdivision (b) of Section 51.4. That limitation may be less exclusive, but shall at least require that the persons commencing any occupancy of a dwelling unit include a senior citizen who intends to reside in the unit as his or her primary residence on a permanent basis. The application of the rules set forth in this subdivision regarding limitations on occupancy may result in less than all of the dwellings being actually occupied by a senior citizen.

(d) The covenants, conditions, and restrictions or other documents or written policy shall permit temporary residency, as a guest of a senior citizen or qualified permanent resident, by a person of less than 55 years of age for periods of time, not less than 60 days in any year, that are specified in the covenants, conditions, and restrictions or other documents or written policy.

(e) Upon the death or dissolution of marriage, or upon hospitalization, or other prolonged absence of the qualifying resident, any qualified permanent resident shall be entitled to continue his or her occupancy, residency, or use of the dwelling unit as a permitted resident. This subdivision shall not apply to a permitted health care resident.

(f) The condominium, stock cooperative, limited-equity housing cooperative, planned development, or multiple-family residential rental property shall have been developed for, and initially been put to use as, housing for senior citizens, or shall have been substantially rehabilitated or renovated for, and immediately afterward put to use as, housing for senior citizens, as provided in this section; provided, however, that no housing development constructed prior to January 1, 1985, shall fail to qualify as a senior citizen housing development because it was not originally developed for or originally put to use for occupancy by senior citizens.

(g) The covenants, conditions, and restrictions or other documents or written policies applicable to any condominium, stock cooperative, limited-equity housing cooperative, planned development, or multiple-family residential property that contained age restrictions on January 1, 1984, shall be enforceable only to the extent permitted by this section, notwithstanding lower age restrictions contained in those documents or policies.

(h) Any person who has the right to reside in, occupy, or use the housing or an unimproved lot subject to this section on January 1, 1985, shall not be deprived of the right to continue that residency, occupancy, or use as the result of the enactment of this section.

(i) The covenants, conditions, and restrictions or other documents or written policy of the senior citizen housing development shall permit the occupancy of a dwelling unit by a permitted health care resident during any period that the person is actually providing live-in, long-term, or hospice health care to a qualifying resident for compensation. For purposes of this subdivision, the term "for compensation" shall include provisions of lodging and food in exchange for care.

(j) Notwithstanding any other provision of this section, this section shall not apply to the County of Riverside. *(Added by Stats.1984, c. 1333, § 1. Amended by Stats.1985, c. 1505, § 2; Stats.1989, c. 190, § 1; Stats.1994, c. 464 (S.B.1560), § 1; Stats.1995, c. 147 (S.B.332), § 1; Stats.1996, c. 1147 (S.B. 2097), § 3; Stats.1999, c. 324 (S.B.382), § 2; Stats.2000, c. 1004 (S.B.2011), § 3; Stats.2016, c. 50 (S.B.1005), § 5, eff. Jan. 1, 2017.)*

Cross References

Alcoholic beverages, club licenses for condominium homeowners' associations, license denied for discriminatory practices, see Business and Professions Code § 23428.20.

Application for a public report for a phase of a subdivision as part of a senior citizen housing development, requirements, see Business and Professions Code § 11010.05.

Bond and loan insurance, occupancy of housing for which a loan is insured, discrimination prohibited, see Health and Safety Code § 51602.

Business of insurance, application of Unruh Civil Rights Act, see Insurance Code § 1861.03.

California housing finance agency, equal opportunity without discrimination, see Health and Safety Code § 50955.

Common interest developments, sale or title transfer, provision of specified items to prospective purchasers, see Civil Code § 4525.

Community development and housing, declaration of state antidiscrimination policy, discrimination prohibited, see Health and Safety Code § 33050.

Community development and housing, financial discrimination prohibited, see Health and Safety Code § 35811.

Community redevelopment, property disposition rehabilitation, nondiscrimination and nonsegregation, see Health and Safety Code §§ 33435, 33436.

Density bonuses for senior citizen housing developments, see Government Code § 65915.

Elderly or handicapped households, living together in efficiency, studio or one bedroom units allowed, grounds for prohibiting, see Health and Safety Code § 19904.

Facilities offering continuing care contracts, application of this section, see Health and Safety Code § 1775.

Floating home residency, private club membership not to be denied on discrimination basis, see Civil Code § 800.25.

Historical property rehabilitation, prohibited discrimination, see Health and Safety Code § 37630.

Housing discrimination on the basis of familial status, application of prohibitions to housing for older persons, see Government Code § 12955.9.

Mobilehome residency, private club membership not to be denied on discrimination basis, see Civil Code § 798.20.

Payment of fees, charges, dedications, or other requirements against a development project, senior citizen housing, see Government Code § 65995.1.

Percentage awarded for units restricted to senior citizens, see Health and Safety Code § 50675.1.

Planning and zoning, prohibition against discrimination, exceptions, see Government Code § 65008.

Real estate licensees, grounds for disciplinary action, induced sale or listing due to adverse impact of persons in neighborhood with certain characteristics, see Business and Professions Code § 10177.

Real property, discriminatory restrictions in deeds, invalidity, see Civil Code §§ 782, 782.5.

Redevelopment construction loans, nondiscrimination in construction and disposition of residences, see Health and Safety Code § 33769.

Residential property rehabilitation, open housing, equal opportunity in employment and contracts, see Health and Safety Code § 37923.

§ 51.3.5. Intergenerational housing developments; legislative findings and declarations; conditions for establishment

(a) The Legislature finds and declares that this section is essential to establish and preserve specially designed, accessible, intergenerational housing for senior citizens. There are senior citizens who need special living environments and services and benefit from intergenerational housing environments, and find that there is an inadequate supply of this type of housing in the state.

(b) An intergenerational housing development may be established to provide intergenerational housing consisting of units for senior citizens, caregivers, or transition age youths if all of the following conditions are satisfied:

(1)(A) At least 80 percent of the occupied dwelling units are occupied by at least one senior citizen. This requirement shall commence when at least 25 percent of the units are occupied. A dwelling unit is occupied by at least one senior citizen if, on the date the exemption for housing designed for intergenerational housing is claimed, one of the following conditions is satisfied:

(i) At least one occupant of the dwelling unit is a senior citizen.

(ii) If the dwelling unit is temporarily vacant, at least one of the occupants immediately prior to the date on which the unit was temporarily vacated was a senior citizen.

(B) Up to 20 percent of the occupied dwelling units are occupied by at least one caregiver or transition age youth. A dwelling unit is occupied by at least one caregiver or transition age youth if, on the date the exemption for housing designed for intergenerational housing is claimed, one of the following conditions is satisfied:

(i) At least one occupant of the dwelling unit is a caregiver or transition age youth.

(ii) If the dwelling unit is temporarily vacant, at least one of the occupants immediately prior to the date on which the unit was temporarily vacant was a caregiver or transition age youth.

(2) The development is affordable to lower income households as defined in Section 50079.5 of the Health and Safety Code.

(3)(A) If a unit that is identified for occupancy by a caregiver or transition age youth ceases to house a caregiver or transition age youth, the owner, board of directors, or other governing body may require, at their discretion, the household in that unit to cease residing in the development upon receipt of a minimum of six months written notice, for the sole purpose of ensuring that the unit may be made available to a qualifying caregiver or transition age youth. This action shall not constitute a violation of Section 51 or of Article 2 (commencing with Section 12955) of Chapter 6 of Part 2.8 of Division 3 of Title 2 of the Government Code (California Fair Employment and Housing Act).

(B) The housing facility or community shall not evict or terminate the lease of a family with children in order to comply with the requirement that at least 80 percent of the occupied units be occupied by at least one senior citizen. This provision does not otherwise alter or affect applicable protections for tenants.

(C) The covenants, conditions, and restrictions and other documents or written policy for the development shall set forth the limitations on occupancy, residency, or use consistent with this section.

(4) Housing established pursuant to this section shall comply with all applicable fair housing laws, including, but not limited to, the California Fair Employment and Housing Act (Part 2.8 (commencing with Section 12900) of Division 3 of Title 2 of the Government Code) and the Fair Housing Act (42 U.S.C. Sec. 3601).

(5) Notwithstanding any other law, any occupied dwelling units within an intergenerational housing development established pursuant to this section that are occupied by caregivers or transition age youth as described in subparagraph (B) of paragraph (1) shall not count toward the housing type goal for seniors under the qualified allocation plan adopted by the California Tax Credit Allocation Committee in accordance with Section 50199.14 of the Health and Safety Code.

(c) This section specifically creates a state policy supporting intergenerational housing for senior citizens, caregivers, and transition age youth, as described in Section 42(g)(9) of the Internal Revenue Code,[1] and, further, permits developers in receipt of local or state funds or tax credits designated for affordable rental housing to restrict occupancy to senior citizens, caregivers, and transition age youth, including permitting developers in receipt of tax credits designated for affordable rental housing to retain the right to prioritize and restrict occupancy, so long as that housing does not violate any other applicable laws.

(d) For the purposes of this section, the following terms have the following meanings:

(1) "Caregiver" means a person responsible for meeting the daily care needs of a senior citizen, or a person hired to provide live-in, long-term, or terminal health care to a qualifying resident, or a family member of the qualifying resident providing that care. For purposes of this section, the care provided shall be substantial in nature and shall include either assistance with necessary daily activities or medical treatment, or both.

(2) "Senior citizen" or "resident" means a person 55 years of age or older.

(3) "Transition age youth" means a person who is 18 to 24 years of age, inclusive, and who is either of the following:

(A) A current or former foster youth who has been adjudged a ward or dependent of the juvenile court pursuant to Section 300, 601, or 602 of the Welfare and Institutions Code.

(B) A homeless youth or former homeless youth, who has met the McKinney-Vento Homeless Assistance Act of 1987 definition of "homeless children and youths," as that term is defined in Section 11434a of Title 42 of the United States Code. (Added by Stats.2021, c. 364 (S.B.591), § 3, eff. Jan. 1, 2022.)

[1] Internal Revenue Code sections are in Title 26 of the U.S.C.A.

Cross References

Senior citizen or intergenerational housing developments, public report for subdivision phase, application, see Business and Professions Code § 11010.05.

§ 51.4. Exemption from special design requirement

(a) The Legislature finds and declares that the requirements for senior housing under Sections 51.2 and 51.3 are more stringent than the requirements for that housing under the federal Fair Housing Amendments Act of 1988 (P.L. 100–430) in recognition of the acute shortage of housing for families with children in California. The Legislature further finds and declares that the special design requirements for senior housing under Sections 51.2 and 51.3 may pose a hardship to some housing developments that were constructed before the decision in Marina Point, Ltd. v. Wolfson (1982) 30 Cal.3d 721. The Legislature further finds and declares that the requirement for specially designed accommodations in senior housing under Sections 51.2 and 51.3 provides important benefits to senior citizens and also ensures that housing exempt from the prohibition of age discrimination is carefully tailored to meet the compelling societal interest in providing senior housing.

(b) Any person who resided in, occupied, or used, prior to January 1, 1990, a dwelling in a senior citizen housing development that relied on the exemption to the special design requirement provided by this section prior to January 1, 2001, shall not be deprived of the right to continue that residency, occupancy, or use as the result of the changes made to this section by the enactment of Chapter 1004 of the Statutes of 2000.

(c) This section shall not apply to the County of Riverside. (Added by Stats.1989, c. 501, § 2. Amended by Stats.1991, c. 59 (A.B.125), § 1, eff. June 17, 1991; Stats.1996, c. 1147 (S.B.2097), § 4; Stats.2000, c. 1004 (S.B.2011), § 4; Stats. 2006, c. 538 (S.B.1852), § 37.)

Cross References

Alcoholic beverages, club licenses for condominium homeowners' associations, license denied for discriminatory practices, see Business and Professions Code § 23428.20.

Bond and loan insurance, occupancy of housing for which a loan is insured, discrimination prohibited, see Health and Safety Code § 51602.

Business of insurance, application of Unruh Civil Rights Act, see Insurance Code § 1861.03.

California housing finance agency, equal opportunity without discrimination, see Health and Safety Code § 50955.

Community development and housing, declaration of state antidiscrimination policy, discrimination prohibited, see Health and Safety Code § 33050.

Community development and housing, financial discrimination prohibited, see Health and Safety Code § 35811.

Community redevelopment, property disposition rehabilitation, nondiscrimination and nonsegregation, see Health and Safety Code §§ 33435, 33436.

Floating home residency, private club membership not to be denied on discrimination basis, see Civil Code § 800.25.

Historical property rehabilitation, prohibited discrimination, see Health and Safety Code § 37630.

Housing discrimination on the basis of familial status, application of prohibitions to housing for older persons, see Government Code § 12955.9.

§ 51.4

Mobilehome residency, private club membership not to be denied on discrimination basis, see Civil Code § 798.20.
Planning and zoning, prohibition against discrimination, exceptions, see Government Code § 65008.
Real estate licensees, grounds for disciplinary action, induced sale or listing due to adverse impact of persons in neighborhood with certain characteristics, see Business and Professions Code § 10177.
Real property, discriminatory restrictions in deeds, invalidity, see Civil Code §§ 782, 782.5.
Redevelopment construction loans, nondiscrimination in construction and disposition of residences, see Health and Safety Code § 33769.
Residential property rehabilitation, open housing, equal opportunity in employment and contracts, see Health and Safety Code § 37923.

§ 51.5. Discrimination, boycott, blacklist, etc.; business establishments; equal rights

(a) No business establishment of any kind whatsoever shall discriminate against, boycott or blacklist, or refuse to buy from, contract with, sell to, or trade with any person in this state on account of any characteristic listed or defined in subdivision (b) or (e) of Section 51, or of the person's partners, members, stockholders, directors, officers, managers, superintendents, agents, employees, business associates, suppliers, or customers, because the person is perceived to have one or more of those characteristics, or because the person is associated with a person who has, or is perceived to have, any of those characteristics.

(b) As used in this section, "person" includes any person, firm, association, organization, partnership, business trust, corporation, limited liability company, or company.

(c) This section shall not be construed to require any construction, alteration, repair, structural or otherwise, or modification of any sort whatsoever, beyond that construction, alteration, repair, or modification that is otherwise required by other provisions of law, to any new or existing establishment, facility, building, improvement, or any other structure, nor shall this section be construed to augment, restrict, or alter in any way the authority of the State Architect to require construction, alteration, repair, or modifications that the State Architect otherwise possesses pursuant to other laws. *(Added by Stats.1976, c. 366, p. 1013, § 1. Amended by Stats.1987, c. 159, § 2; Stats.1992, c. 913 (A.B.1077), § 3.2; Stats.1994, c. 1010 (S.B.2053), § 28; Stats. 1998, c. 195 (A.B.2702), § 2; Stats.1999, c. 591 (A.B.1670), § 2; Stats.2000, c. 1049 (A.B.2222), § 3; Stats.2005, c. 420 (A.B.1400), § 4.)*

Cross References

Business of insurance, application of Unruh Civil Rights Act, see Insurance Code § 1861.03.
Department of Fair Employment and Housing, functions, powers and duties, see Government Code § 12935.

§ 51.6. Gender Tax Repeal Act of 1995

(a) This section shall be known, and may be cited, as the Gender Tax Repeal Act of 1995.

(b) No business establishment of any kind whatsoever may discriminate, with respect to the price charged for services of similar or like kind, against a person because of the person's gender.

(c) Nothing in subdivision (b) prohibits price differences based specifically upon the amount of time, difficulty, or cost of providing the services.

(d) Except as provided in subdivision (f), the remedies for a violation of this section are the remedies provided in subdivision (a) of Section 52. However, an action under this section is independent of any other remedy or procedure that may be available to an aggrieved party.

(e) This act does not alter or affect the provisions of the Health and Safety Code, the Insurance Code, or other laws that govern health care service plan or insurer underwriting or rating practices.

(f)(1) The following business establishments shall clearly and conspicuously disclose to the customer in writing the pricing for each standard service provided:

(A) Tailors or businesses providing aftermarket clothing alterations.

(B) Barbers or hair salons.

(C) Dry cleaners and laundries providing services to individuals.

(2) The price list shall be posted in an area conspicuous to customers. Posted price lists shall be in no less than 14–point boldface type and clearly and completely display pricing for every standard service offered by the business under paragraph (1).

(3) The business establishment shall provide the customer with a complete written price list upon request.

(4) The business establishment shall display in a conspicuous place at least one clearly visible sign, printed in no less than 24–point boldface type, which reads: "CALIFORNIA LAW PROHIBITS ANY BUSINESS ESTABLISHMENT FROM DISCRIMINATING, WITH RESPECT TO THE PRICE CHARGED FOR SERVICES OF SIMILAR OR LIKE KIND, AGAINST A PERSON BECAUSE OF THE PERSON'S GENDER. A COMPLETE PRICE LIST IS AVAILABLE UPON REQUEST."

(5) A business establishment that fails to correct a violation of this subdivision within 30 days of receiving written notice of the violation is liable for a civil penalty of one thousand dollars ($1,000).

(6) For the purposes of this subdivision, "standard service" means the 15 most frequently requested services provided by the business.

(g)(1) Commencing January 1, 2021, a city, county, or city and county that issues business licenses shall provide a business, at the time the business is issued the license or when the license is renewed, written notice of these provisions in English, Spanish, Chinese, Tagalog, Vietnamese, and Korean. In order to comply with this paragraph, a city, county, or city and county may provide the business with the notice created by the Department of Consumer Affairs under subdivision (b) of Section 55.63.

(2) A city, county, or city and county that issues business licenses may increase the fee for that license in an amount not to exceed the reasonable costs of providing the written notice above.

(h) The Legislature finds and declares that this section addresses a matter of statewide concern rather than a municipal affair as that term is used in Section 5 of Article XI of the California Constitution. Therefore, this section applies to all cities, including charter cities. *(Added by Stats. 1995, c. 866 (A.B.1100), § 1. Amended by Stats.2001, c. 312 (A.B.1088), § 1; Stats.2019, c. 293 (A.B.1607), § 1, eff. Jan. 1, 2020.)*

Cross References

Business of insurance, application of Unruh Civil Rights Act, see Insurance Code § 1861.03.

Small business gender discrimination in services compliance act, demand letters, written advisory notice, penalties, application, see Civil Code § 55.62.

Small business gender discrimination in services compliance act, pamphlet or informational materials for use by businesses, rights and obligations, provision of pamphlet, see Civil Code § 55.63.

§ 51.7. Ralph Civil Rights Act of 1976

(a) This section shall be known, and may be cited, as the Ralph Civil Rights Act of 1976.

(b)(1) All persons within the jurisdiction of this state have the right to be free from any violence, or intimidation by threat of violence, committed against their persons or property because of political affiliation, or on account of any characteristic listed or defined in subdivision (b) or (e) of Section 51, or position in a labor dispute, or because another person perceives them to have one or more of those characteristics. The identification in this subdivision of particular bases of discrimination is illustrative rather than restrictive.

(2) For purposes of this subdivision, "intimidation by threat of violence" includes, but is not limited to, making or threatening to make a claim or report to a peace officer or law enforcement agency that falsely alleges that another person has engaged in unlawful activity or in an activity that requires law enforcement intervention, knowing that the claim or report is false, or with reckless disregard for the truth or falsity of the claim or report.

(c)(1) A person shall not require another person to waive any legal right, penalty, remedy, forum, or procedure for a violation of this section, as a condition of entering into a contract for goods or services, including the right to file and pursue a civil action or complaint with, or otherwise notify, the Attorney General or any other public prosecutor, or law enforcement agency, the * * * Civil Rights Department, or any court or other governmental entity.

(2) A person shall not refuse to enter into a contract with, or refuse to provide goods or services to, another person on the basis that the other person refuses to waive any legal right, penalty, remedy, forum, or procedure for a violation of this section, including the right to file and pursue a civil action or complaint with, or otherwise notify, the Attorney General or any other public prosecutor, or law enforcement agency, the * * * Civil Rights Department, or any other governmental entity.

(3) Any waiver of any legal right, penalty, remedy, forum, or procedure for a violation of this section, including the right to file and pursue a civil action or complaint with, or otherwise notify, the Attorney General or any other public prosecutor, or law enforcement agency, the * * * Civil Rights Department, or any other governmental entity shall be knowing and voluntary, in writing, and expressly not made as a condition of entering into a contract for goods or services or as a condition of providing or receiving goods and services.

(4) Any waiver of any legal right, penalty, remedy, forum, or procedure for a violation of this section that is required as a condition of entering into a contract for goods or services shall be deemed involuntary, unconscionable, against public policy, and unenforceable. This subdivision does not affect the enforceability or validity of any other provision of the contract.

(5) A person who seeks to enforce a waiver of any legal right, penalty, remedy, forum, or procedure for a violation of this section has the burden of proving that the waiver was knowing and voluntary and not made as a condition of the contract or of providing or receiving the goods or services.

(6) The exercise of a person's right to refuse to waive any legal right, penalty, remedy, forum, or procedure for a violation of this section, including a rejection of a contract requiring a waiver, does not affect any otherwise legal terms of a contract or an agreement.

(7) This subdivision does not apply to an agreement to waive any legal rights, penalties, remedies, forums, or procedures for a violation of this section after a legal claim has arisen.

(8) This subdivision applies to an agreement to waive any legal right, penalty, remedy, forum, or procedure for a violation of this section, including an agreement to accept private arbitration, entered into, altered, modified, renewed, or extended on or after January 1, 2015.

(d) This section does not apply to statements concerning positions in a labor dispute that are made during otherwise lawful labor picketing.

(e) The Legislature finds and declares that this section was enacted as part of the Ralph Civil Rights Act of 1976, in Chapter 1293 of the Statutes of 1976.

(f) This section does not negate or otherwise abrogate the provisions of Sections 1668, 1953, and 3513. *(Added by Stats.1976, c. 1293, p. 5778, § 2. Amended by Stats.1984, c. 1437, § 1; Stats.1985, c. 497, § 1; Stats.1987, c. 1277, § 2; Stats.1994, c. 407 (S.B.1595), § 1; Stats.2005, c. 420 (A.B. 1400), § 5; Stats.2014, c. 910 (A.B.2617), § 2, eff. Jan. 1, 2015; Stats.2018, c. 776 (A.B.3250), § 3, eff. Jan. 1, 2019; Stats.2020, c. 327 (A.B.1775), § 3, eff. Jan. 1, 2021; Stats.2022, c. 48 (S.B.189), § 4, eff. June 30, 2022.)*

Cross References

Additional penalties to be imposed for felony of intimidation because of specified beliefs or characteristics, see Penal Code § 422.7.

Aggravating factors, hate crime, see Penal Code § 422.76.

Assault and battery, see Penal Code § 240 et seq.

Business of insurance, application of Unruh Civil Rights Act, see Insurance Code § 1861.03.

Department of Fair Employment and Housing, construction of provisions with this section, see Government Code § 12993.5.

Department of Fair Employment and Housing, functions, powers and duties, see Government Code § 12935.

Duty on teachers to instruct pupils on morals, manners, and citizenship and to create and foster an environment that is free from discriminatory attitudes, practices, events or activities, in order to prevent acts of hate violence, see Education Code § 233.5.

§ 51.7

Fair employment and housing, enforcement and compliance, written accusation by department, see Government Code § 12965.

Fair employment and housing, enforcement and hearing procedures, prevention and elimination of unlawful employment practices, see Government Code § 12960.

Hate crime training for peace officers, see Penal Code § 13519.6.

Regional training to assist school district personnel in identification and determination of hate violence on school campuses, see Education Code § 233.8.

Time of commencing actions, application of this section, see Code of Civil Procedure § 338.

§ 51.8. Discrimination; franchises

(a) No franchisor shall discriminate in the granting of franchises solely on account of any characteristic listed or defined in subdivision (b) or (e) of Section 51 of the franchisee and the composition of a neighborhood or geographic area reflecting any characteristic listed or defined in subdivision (b) or (e) of Section 51 in which the franchise is located. Nothing in this section shall be interpreted to prohibit a franchisor from granting a franchise to prospective franchisees as part of a program or programs to make franchises available to persons lacking the capital, training, business experience, or other qualifications ordinarily required of franchisees, or any other affirmative action program adopted by the franchisor.

(b) Nothing in this section shall be construed to require any construction, alteration, repair, structural or otherwise, or modification of any sort whatsoever, beyond that construction, alteration, repair, or modification that is otherwise required by other provisions of law, to any new or existing establishment, facility, building, improvement, or any other structure, nor shall anything in this section be construed to augment, restrict, or alter in any way the authority of the State Architect to require construction, alteration, repair, or modifications that the State Architect otherwise possesses pursuant to other laws. (Added by Stats.1980, c. 1303, § 1. Amended by Stats.1987, c. 159, § 3; Stats.1992, c. 913 (A.B.1077), § 3.4; Stats.1998, c. 195 (A.B.2702), § 3; Stats. 2005, c. 420 (A.B.1400), § 6.)

Cross References

Business of insurance, application of Unruh Civil Rights Act, see Insurance Code § 1861.03.

§ 51.9. Sexual harassment; business, service and professional relationships

(a) A person is liable in a cause of action for sexual harassment under this section when the plaintiff proves all of the following elements:

(1) There is a business, service, or professional relationship between the plaintiff and defendant or the defendant holds himself or herself out as being able to help the plaintiff establish a business, service, or professional relationship with the defendant or a third party. Such a relationship may exist between a plaintiff and a person, including, but not limited to, any of the following persons:

(A) Physician, psychotherapist, or dentist. For purposes of this section, "psychotherapist" has the same meaning as set forth in paragraph (1) of subdivision (c) of Section 728 of the Business and Professions Code.

(B) Attorney, holder of a master's degree in social work, real estate agent, real estate appraiser, investor, accountant, banker, trust officer, financial planner loan officer, collection service, building contractor, or escrow loan officer.

(C) Executor, trustee, or administrator.

(D) Landlord or property manager.

(E) Teacher.

(F) Elected official.

(G) Lobbyist.

(H) Director or producer.

(I) A relationship that is substantially similar to any of the above.

(2) The defendant has made sexual advances, solicitations, sexual requests, demands for sexual compliance by the plaintiff, or engaged in other verbal, visual, or physical conduct of a sexual nature or of a hostile nature based on gender, that were unwelcome and pervasive or severe.

(3) The plaintiff has suffered or will suffer economic loss or disadvantage or personal injury, including, but not limited to, emotional distress or the violation of a statutory or constitutional right, as a result of the conduct described in paragraph (2).

(b) In an action pursuant to this section, damages shall be awarded as provided by subdivision (b) of Section 52.

(c) Nothing in this section shall be construed to limit application of any other remedies or rights provided under the law.

(d) The definition of sexual harassment and the standards for determining liability set forth in this section shall be limited to determining liability only with regard to a cause of action brought under this section. (Added by Stats.1994, c. 710 (S.B.612), § 2. Amended by Stats.1996, c. 150 (S.B.195), § 1; Stats.1999, c. 964 (A.B.519), § 1; Stats.2018, c. 951 (S.B.224), § 1, eff. Jan. 1, 2019.)

Cross References

Business of insurance, application of Unruh Civil Rights Act, see Insurance Code § 1861.03.

Retaliation prohibited against advocates or employees opposing or filing complaints about practices, fine for violation, see Government Code § 9149.40.

§ 51.10. Age discrimination in sale or rental of housing prohibited; construction of Unruh Civil Rights Act; senior housing; intent; age preferences in federally approved housing programs; application of section

(a) Section 51 shall be construed to prohibit a business establishment from discriminating in the sale or rental of housing based upon age. A business establishment may establish and preserve housing for senior citizens, pursuant to Section 51.11, except housing as to which Section 51.11 is preempted by the prohibition in the federal Fair Housing Amendments Act of 1988 (Public Law 100–430)[1] and implementing regulations against discrimination on the basis of familial status.

(b) This section is intended to clarify the holdings in Marina Point, Ltd. v. Wolfson (1982) 30 Cal.3d 721, and

O'Connor v. Village Green Owners Association (1983) 33 Cal.3d 790.

(c) Selection preferences based on age, imposed in connection with a federally approved housing program, do not constitute age discrimination in housing.

(d) This section shall only apply to the County of Riverside. *(Added by Stats.1996, c. 1147 (S.B.2097), § 5. Amended by Stats.2004, c. 183 (A.B.3082), § 23; Stats.2010, c. 524 (S.B.1252), § 3.)*

[1] Public law sections classified to the U.S.C.A., see USCA–Tables.

Cross References

Alcoholic beverages, club licenses for condominium homeowners' associations, license denied for discriminatory practices, see Business and Professions Code § 23428.20.

Bond and loan insurance, occupancy of housing for which a loan is insured, discrimination prohibited, see Health and Safety Code § 51602.

Business of insurance, application of Unruh Civil Rights Act, see Insurance Code § 1861.03.

California housing finance agency, equal opportunity without discrimination, see Health and Safety Code § 50955.

Community development and housing, declaration of state antidiscrimination policy, discrimination prohibited, see Health and Safety Code § 33050.

Community development and housing, financial discrimination prohibited, see Health and Safety Code § 35811.

Community redevelopment, property disposition rehabilitation, nondiscrimination and nonsegregation, see Health and Safety Code §§ 33435, 33436.

Floating home residency, private club membership not to be denied on discrimination basis, see Civil Code § 800.25.

Historical property rehabilitation, prohibited discrimination, see Health and Safety Code § 37630.

Mobilehome residency, private club membership not to be denied on discrimination basis, see Civil Code § 798.20.

Planning and zoning, prohibition against discrimination, exceptions, see Government Code § 65008.

Provision of housing for homeless youth, age discrimination, see Government Code § 12957.

Real estate licensees, grounds for disciplinary action, induced sale or listing due to adverse impact of persons in neighborhood with certain characteristics, see Business and Professions Code § 10177.

Real property, discriminatory restrictions in deeds, invalidity, see Civil Code §§ 782, 782.5.

Redevelopment construction loans, nondiscrimination in construction and disposition of residences, see Health and Safety Code § 33769.

Residential property rehabilitation, open housing, equal opportunity in employment and contracts, see Health and Safety Code § 37923.

§ 51.11. Riverside County; establishment or preservation of senior housing; legislative findings and declarations; definitions; requirements; qualification of development; application of section

(a) The Legislature finds and declares that this section is essential to establish and preserve housing for senior citizens. There are senior citizens who need special living environments, and find that there is an inadequate supply of this type of housing in the state.

(b) For the purposes of this section, the following definitions apply:

(1) "Qualifying resident" or "senior citizen" means a person 62 years of age or older, or 55 years of age or older in a senior citizen housing development.

(2) "Qualified permanent resident" means a person who meets both of the following requirements:

(A) Was residing with the qualifying resident or senior citizen prior to the death, hospitalization, or other prolonged absence of, or the dissolution of marriage with, the qualifying resident or senior citizen.

(B) Was 45 years of age or older, or was a spouse, cohabitant, or person providing primary physical or economic support to the qualifying resident or senior citizen.

(3) "Qualified permanent resident" also means a disabled person or person with a disabling illness or injury who is a child or grandchild of the senior citizen or a qualified permanent resident as defined in paragraph (2) who needs to live with the senior citizen or qualified permanent resident because of the disabling condition, illness, or injury. For purposes of this section, "disabled" means a person who has a disability as defined in subdivision (b) of Section 54. A "disabling injury or illness" means an illness or injury which results in a condition meeting the definition of disability set forth in subdivision (b) of Section 54.

(A) For any person who is a qualified permanent resident under paragraph (3) whose disabling condition ends, the owner, board of directors, or other governing body may require the formerly disabled resident to cease residing in the development upon receipt of six months' written notice; provided, however, that the owner, board of directors, or other governing body may allow the person to remain a resident for up to one year, after the disabling condition ends.

(B) The owner, board of directors, or other governing body of the senior citizen housing development may take action to prohibit or terminate occupancy by a person who is a qualified permanent resident under paragraph (3) if the owner, board of directors, or other governing body finds, based on credible and objective evidence, that the person is likely to pose a significant threat to the health or safety of others that cannot be ameliorated by means of a reasonable accommodation; provided, however, that action to prohibit or terminate the occupancy may be taken only after doing both of the following:

(i) Providing reasonable notice to and an opportunity to be heard for the disabled person whose occupancy is being challenged, and reasonable notice to the coresident parent or grandparent of that person.

(ii) Giving due consideration to the relevant, credible, and objective information provided in that hearing. The evidence shall be taken and held in a confidential manner, pursuant to a closed session, by the owner, board of directors, or other governing body in order to preserve the privacy of the affected persons.

The affected persons shall be entitled to have present at the hearing an attorney or any other person authorized by them to speak on their behalf or to assist them in the matter.

(4) "Senior citizen housing development" means a residential development developed with more than 20 units as a senior community by its developer and zoned as a senior community by a local governmental entity, or characterized as

a senior community in its governing documents, as these are defined in Section 4150, or qualified as a senior community under the federal Fair Housing Amendments Act of 1988,[1] as amended. Any senior citizen housing development which is required to obtain a public report under Section 11010 of the Business and Professions Code and which submits its application for a public report after July 1, 2001, shall be required to have been issued a public report as a senior citizen housing development under Section 11010.05 of the Business and Professions Code.

(5) "Dwelling unit" or "housing" means any residential accommodation other than a mobilehome.

(6) "Cohabitant" refers to persons who live together as spouses or persons who are domestic partners within the meaning of Section 297 of the Family Code.

(7) "Permitted health care resident" means a person hired to provide live-in, long-term, or terminal health care to a qualifying resident, or a family member of the qualifying resident providing that care. For the purposes of this section, the care provided by a permitted health care resident must be substantial in nature and must provide either assistance with necessary daily activities or medical treatment, or both.

A permitted health care resident shall be entitled to continue his or her occupancy, residency, or use of the dwelling unit as a permitted resident in the absence of the senior citizen from the dwelling unit only if both of the following are applicable:

(A) The senior citizen became absent from the dwelling unit due to hospitalization or other necessary medical treatment and expects to return to his or her residence within 90 days from the date the absence began.

(B) The absent senior citizen or an authorized person acting for the senior citizen submits a written request to the owner, board of directors, or governing board stating that the senior citizen desires that the permitted health care resident be allowed to remain in order to be present when the senior citizen returns to reside in the development.

Upon written request by the senior citizen or an authorized person acting for the senior citizen, the owner, board of directors, or governing board shall have the discretion to allow a permitted health care resident to remain for a time period longer than 90 days from the date that the senior citizen's absence began, if it appears that the senior citizen will return within a period of time not to exceed an additional 90 days.

(c) The covenants, conditions, and restrictions and other documents or written policy shall set forth the limitations on occupancy, residency, or use on the basis of age. Any limitation shall not be more exclusive than to require that one person in residence in each dwelling unit may be required to be a senior citizen and that each other resident in the same dwelling unit may be required to be a qualified permanent resident, a permitted health care resident, or a person under 55 years of age whose occupancy is permitted under subdivision (g) of this section or subdivision (b) of Section 51.12. That limitation may be less exclusive, but shall at least require that the persons commencing any occupancy of a dwelling unit include a senior citizen who intends to reside in the unit as his or her primary residence on a permanent basis. The application of the rules set forth in this subdivision regarding limitations on occupancy may result in less than all of the dwellings being actually occupied by a senior citizen.

(d) The covenants, conditions, and restrictions or other documents or written policy shall permit temporary residency, as a guest of a senior citizen or qualified permanent resident, by a person of less than 55 years of age for periods of time, not more than 60 days in any year, that are specified in the covenants, conditions, and restrictions or other documents or written policy.

(e) Upon the death or dissolution of marriage, or upon hospitalization, or other prolonged absence of the qualifying resident, any qualified permanent resident shall be entitled to continue his or her occupancy, residency, or use of the dwelling unit as a permitted resident. This subdivision shall not apply to a permitted health care resident.

(f) The covenants, conditions, and restrictions or other documents or written policies applicable to any condominium, stock cooperative, limited-equity housing cooperative, planned development, or multiple-family residential property that contained age restrictions on January 1, 1984, shall be enforceable only to the extent permitted by this section, notwithstanding lower age restrictions contained in those documents or policies.

(g) Any person who has the right to reside in, occupy, or use the housing or an unimproved lot subject to this section on or after January 1, 1985, shall not be deprived of the right to continue that residency, occupancy, or use as the result of the enactment of this section by Chapter 1147 of the Statutes of 1996.

(h) A housing development may qualify as a senior citizen housing development under this section even though, as of January 1, 1997, it does not meet the definition of a senior citizen housing development specified in subdivision (b), if the development complies with that definition for every unit that becomes occupied after January 1, 1997, and if the development was once within that definition, and then became noncompliant with the definition as the result of any one of the following:

(1) The development was ordered by a court or a local, state, or federal enforcement agency to allow persons other than qualifying residents, qualified permanent residents, or permitted health care residents to reside in the development.

(2) The development received a notice of a pending or proposed action in, or by, a court, or a local, state, or federal enforcement agency, which action could have resulted in the development being ordered by a court or a state or federal enforcement agency to allow persons other than qualifying residents, qualified permanent residents, or permitted health care residents to reside in the development.

(3) The development agreed to allow persons other than qualifying residents, qualified permanent residents, or permitted health care residents to reside in the development by entering into a stipulation, conciliation agreement, or settlement agreement with a local, state, or federal enforcement agency or with a private party who had filed, or indicated an intent to file, a complaint against the development with a

local, state, or federal enforcement agency, or file an action in a court.

(4) The development allowed persons other than qualifying residents, qualified permanent residents, or permitted health care residents to reside in the development on the advice of counsel in order to prevent the possibility of an action being filed by a private party or by a local, state, or federal enforcement agency.

(i) The covenants, conditions, and restrictions or other documents or written policy of the senior citizen housing development shall permit the occupancy of a dwelling unit by a permitted health care resident during any period that the person is actually providing live-in, long-term, or hospice health care to a qualifying resident for compensation.

(j) This section shall only apply to the County of Riverside. *(Added by Stats.1996, c. 1147 (S.B.2097), § 6. Amended by Stats.1999, c. 324 (S.B.382), § 3; Stats.2000, c. 1004 (S.B. 2011), § 5; Stats.2012, c. 181 (A.B.806), § 19, operative Jan. 1, 2014; Stats.2016, c. 50 (S.B.1005), § 6, eff. Jan. 1, 2017.)*

[1] See Short Title note under 42 U.S.C.A. § 3601 for classification of the Act to the Code.

Cross References

Alcoholic beverages, club licenses for condominium homeowners' associations, license denied for discriminatory practices, see Business and Professions Code § 23428.20.

Application for a public report for a phase of a subdivision as part of a senior citizen housing development, requirements, see Business and Professions Code § 11010.05.

Bond and loan insurance, occupancy of housing for which a loan is insured, discrimination prohibited, see Health and Safety Code § 51602.

Business of insurance, application of Unruh Civil Rights Act, see Insurance Code § 1861.03.

California housing finance agency, equal opportunity without discrimination, see Health and Safety Code § 50955.

Community development and housing, declaration of state antidiscrimination policy, discrimination prohibited, see Health and Safety Code § 33050.

Community development and housing, financial discrimination prohibited, see Health and Safety Code § 35811.

Community redevelopment, property disposition rehabilitation, nondiscrimination and nonsegregation, see Health and Safety Code §§ 33435, 33436.

Floating home residency, private club membership not to be denied on discrimination basis, see Civil Code § 800.25.

Historical property rehabilitation, prohibited discrimination, see Health and Safety Code § 37630.

Mobilehome residency, private club membership not to be denied on discrimination basis, see Civil Code § 798.20.

Planning and zoning, prohibition against discrimination, exceptions, see Government Code § 65008.

Real estate licensees, grounds for disciplinary action, induced sale or listing due to adverse impact of persons in neighborhood with certain characteristics, see Business and Professions Code § 10177.

Real property, discriminatory restrictions in deeds, invalidity, see Civil Code §§ 782, 782.5.

Redevelopment construction loans, nondiscrimination in construction and disposition of residences, see Health and Safety Code § 33769.

Residential property rehabilitation, open housing, equal opportunity in employment and contracts, see Health and Safety Code § 37923.

§ 51.12. Riverside County; senior housing; legislative findings and declarations; right of residency, occupancy, or use; application of section

(a) The Legislature finds and declares that the requirements for senior housing under Sections 51.10 and 51.11 are more stringent than the requirements for that housing under the federal Fair Housing Amendments Act of 1988 (Public Law 100–430).[1]

(b) Any person who resided in, occupied, or used, prior to January 1, 1990, a dwelling in a senior citizen housing development which relied on the exemption to the special design requirement provided by Section 51.4 as that section read prior to January 1, 2001, shall not be deprived of the right to continue that residency, or occupancy, or use as the result of the changes made to this section by the enactment of Senate Bill 1382 or Senate Bill 2011 at the 1999–2000 Regular Session of the Legislature.

(c) This section shall only apply to the County of Riverside. *(Added by Stats.1996, c. 1147 (S.B.2097), § 7. Amended by Stats.2000, c. 1004 (S.B.2011), § 6.)*

[1] See Short Title note under 42 U.S.C.A. § 3601 for classification of the Act to the Code.

Cross References

Business of insurance, application of Unruh Civil Rights Act, see Insurance Code § 1861.03.

Density bonuses for senior citizen housing developments, see Government Code § 65915.

§ 51.13. Discounts or other benefits conferred on consumers who have suffered loss or reduction of employment or wages

Any discount or other benefit offered to or conferred on a consumer or prospective consumer by a business because the consumer or prospective consumer has suffered the loss or reduction of employment or reduction of wages shall not be considered an arbitrary discrimination in violation of Section 51. *(Added by Stats.2009, c. 641 (S.B.367), § 1, eff. Nov. 2, 2009.)*

§ 51.14. Prohibition against discriminatory pricing based on gender of the consumer; violations; penalties and fines

(a) For the purposes of this section, the following terms apply:

(1) "Business" means any business acting within the State of California that sells goods to any individual or entity, including, but not limited to, retailers, suppliers, manufacturers, and distributors.

(2) "Goods" means any consumer products used, bought, or rendered primarily for personal, family, or household purposes.

(3)(A) "Substantially similar" means two goods that exhibit all of the following characteristics:

(i) No substantial differences in the materials used in production.

(ii) The intended use is similar.

(iii) The functional design and features are similar.

§ 51.14

(iv) The brand is the same or both brands are owned by the same individual or entity.

(B) A difference in coloring among any of the goods shall not be construed as a substantial difference for the purposes of this paragraph.

(b) A person, firm, partnership, company, corporation, or business shall not charge a different price for any two goods that are substantially similar if those goods are priced differently based on the gender of the individuals for whom the goods are marketed and intended.

(c) This section does not prohibit price differences in goods or services based specifically upon any of the following:

(1) The amount of time it took to manufacture those goods.

(2) The difficulty in manufacturing those goods.

(3) The cost incurred in manufacturing those goods.

(4) The labor used in manufacturing those goods.

(5) The materials used in manufacturing those goods.

(6) Any other gender-neutral reason for charging a different price for those goods.

(d)(1) Notwithstanding any other law, whenever the Attorney General has cause to believe that a violation of this section has occurred, the Attorney General may, upon notice to the defendant of not less than five days, seek a court order to enjoin and restrain the continuance of those violations.

(2) If a court finds that the defendant has violated this section, an injunction may be issued by the court enjoining or restraining any violation, without requiring proof that any person has, in fact, been injured or damaged thereby. The court may make direct restitution, if applicable. In connection with the proposed application for an injunction, the Attorney General is authorized to take proof and make a determination of the relevant facts and to issue subpoenas in accordance with the civil practice law and rules.

(3) If a court finds that the defendant has violated this section, a court may impose a civil penalty not to exceed ten thousand dollars ($10,000) for the first violation, and a civil penalty not to exceed one thousand dollars ($1,000) for each subsequent violation. The total civil penalty imposed pursuant to this paragraph shall not exceed one hundred thousand dollars ($100,000).

(4) Notwithstanding paragraph (3), a court may impose additional civil penalties upon a defendant exceeding one hundred thousand dollars ($100,000) if the defendant subsequently violates this section with respect to the same goods for which the maximum civil penalty has been previously imposed under a separate civil action or for any good for which the Attorney General has not brought civil action pursuant to this section.

(e) For the purposes of this section, each instance of charging a different price for two goods that are substantially similar, as specified in subdivision (b), shall constitute a single violation.

(f) This section does not limit liability under the Unruh Civil Rights Act (Section 51). *(Added by Stats.2022, c. 555 (A.B.1287), § 1, eff. Jan. 1, 2023.)*

§ 51.17. Pilot program recognizing businesses for creating safe and welcoming environments free from discrimination and harassment of customers

(a) For purposes of this section, "department" refers to the Civil Rights Department.

(b)(1) On or before January 1, 2025, the department shall establish a pilot program that recognizes businesses for creating safe and welcoming environments free from discrimination and harassment of customers.

(2) To qualify for recognition under the pilot program, a business shall meet the criteria set out by the department, which may include, but not be limited to, the following:

(A) Demonstrating compliance with Section 51.

(B) Offering additional training to educate and inform employees or build skills.

(C) Informing the public of their rights to be free from discrimination and harassment and how to report violations.

(D) Outlining a code of conduct for the public that encourages respectful and civil behavior.

(E) Any other actions designed to prevent and respond to discrimination and harassment regardless of the identity of the perpetrator.

(3) The department shall provide a certificate to qualifying businesses that may be prominently displayed on site and publish on its internet website a database of businesses receiving that certificate.

(4) On or before January 1, 2028, the department shall evaluate whether that recognition is effective, including, at a minimum, whether it affects customer behavior, incentivizes compliance among businesses with Section 51, or reduces the incidence of discrimination and harassment at businesses.

(5) Recognition under the pilot program does not establish and is not relevant to any defense of claims brought under existing law.

(c) This section shall remain in effect only until July 1, 2028, and as of that date is repealed. *(Added by Stats.2022, c. 315 (A.B.2448), § 1, eff. Jan. 1, 2023.)*

Repeal

For repeal of this section, see its terms.

§ 52. Denial of civil rights or discrimination; damages; civil action by persons aggrieved; intervention; unlawful practice complaint; waiver of rights by contract

(a) Whoever denies, aids or incites a denial, or makes any discrimination or distinction contrary to Section 51, 51.5, or 51.6, is liable for each and every offense for the actual damages, and any amount that may be determined by a jury, or a court sitting without a jury, up to a maximum of three times the amount of actual damage but in no case less than four thousand dollars ($4,000), and any attorney's fees that may be determined by the court in addition thereto, suffered by any person denied the rights provided in Section 51, 51.5, or 51.6.

(b) Whoever denies the right provided by Section 51.7 or 51.9, or aids, incites, or conspires in that denial, is liable for each and every offense for the actual damages suffered by any person denied that right and, in addition, the following:

(1) An amount to be determined by a jury, or a court sitting without a jury, for exemplary damages.

(2) A civil penalty of twenty-five thousand dollars ($25,000) to be awarded to the person denied the right provided by Section 51.7 in any action brought by the person denied the right, or by the Attorney General, a district attorney, or a city attorney. An action for that penalty brought pursuant to Section 51.7 shall be commenced within three years of the alleged practice.

(3) Attorney's fees as may be determined by the court.

(c) Whenever there is reasonable cause to believe that any person or group of persons is engaged in conduct of resistance to the full enjoyment of any of the rights described in this section, and that conduct is of that nature and is intended to deny the full exercise of those rights, the Attorney General, any district attorney or city attorney, or any person aggrieved by the conduct may bring a civil action in the appropriate court by filing with it a complaint. The complaint shall contain the following:

(1) The signature of the officer, or, in * * * the officer's absence, the individual acting on behalf of the officer, or the signature of the person aggrieved.

(2) The facts pertaining to the conduct.

(3) A request for preventive relief, including an application for a permanent or temporary injunction, restraining order, or other order against the person or persons responsible for the conduct, as the complainant deems necessary to ensure the full enjoyment of the rights described in this section.

(d) Whenever an action has been commenced in any court seeking relief from the denial of equal protection of the laws under the Fourteenth Amendment to the Constitution of the United States on account of race, color, religion, sex, national origin, or disability, the Attorney General or any district attorney or city attorney for or in the name of the people of the State of California may intervene in the action upon timely application if the Attorney General or any district attorney or city attorney certifies that the case is of general public importance. In that action, the people of the State of California shall be entitled to the same relief as if it had instituted the action.

(e) Actions brought pursuant to this section are independent of any other actions, remedies, or procedures that may be available to an aggrieved party pursuant to any other law.

(f) Any person claiming to be aggrieved by an alleged unlawful practice in violation of Section 51 or 51.7 may also file a verified complaint with the * * * Civil Rights Department pursuant to Section 12948 of the Government Code.

(g) This section does not require any construction, alteration, repair, structural or otherwise, or modification of any sort whatsoever, beyond that construction, alteration, repair, or modification that is otherwise required by other provisions of law, to any new or existing establishment, facility, building, improvement, or any other structure, nor does this section augment, restrict, or alter in any way the authority of the State Architect to require construction, alteration, repair, or modifications that the State Architect otherwise possesses pursuant to other laws.

(h) For the purposes of this section, "actual damages" means special and general damages. This subdivision is declaratory of existing law.

(i) Subdivisions (b) to (f), inclusive, shall not be waived by contract except as provided in Section 51.7. (Added by Stats.1905, c. 413, p. 553, § 2. Amended by Stats.1919, c. 210, p. 309, § 2; Stats.1923, c. 235, p. 485, § 2; Stats.1959, c. 1866, p. 4424, § 2; Stats.1974, c. 1193, p. 2568, § 2; Stats.1976, c. 366, p. 1013, § 2; Stats.1976, c. 1293, p. 5778, § 2.5; Stats.1978, c. 1212, p. 3927, § 1; Stats.1981, c. 521, § 1, eff. Sept. 16, 1981; Stats.1986, c. 244, § 1; Stats.1987, c. 159, § 4; Stats.1989, c. 459, § 1; Stats.1991, c. 607 (S.B.98), § 2; Stats.1991, c. 839 (A.B.1169), § 2; Stats.1992, c. 913 (A.B. 1077), § 3.6; Stats.1994, c. 535 (S.B.1288), § 1; Stats.1998, c. 195 (A.B.2702), § 4; Stats.1999, c. 964 (A.B.519), § 2; Stats.2000, c. 98 (A.B.2719), § 2; Stats.2001, c. 261 (A.B.587), § 1; Stats.2005, c. 123 (A.B.378), § 1; Stats.2014, c. 910 (A.B.2617), § 3, eff. Jan. 1, 2015; Stats.2022, c. 48 (S.B.189), § 5, eff. June 30, 2022.)

Cross References

Armed forces members, prohibitions and penalties against discrimination, see Military and Veterans Code § 394.
Attorney General, generally, see Government Code § 12500 et seq.
Attorney General, prevailing party in enforcement action under this section, award of costs and fees to be made to Attorney General and paid to Public Rights Law Enforcement Special Fund, see Code of Civil Procedure § 1021.8; Government Code § 12530.
Business of insurance, application of Unruh Civil Rights Act, see Insurance Code § 1861.03.
California Fair Employment and Housing Act, see Government Code § 12900 et seq.
Damages,
  Exemplary, see Civil Code § 3294 et seq.
  General principles, see Civil Code § 3281 et seq.
  Interest on damages, see Civil Code § 3287 et seq.
  Measure of, see Civil Code § 3300 et seq.
Deeds, invalidity of racial restrictions, see Civil Code § 782.
Department of Fair Employment and Housing, procedure for prevention and elimination of discrimination in housing, see Government Code § 12980.
Relief in general, see Civil Code § 3274 et seq.
Specific and preventive relief, see Civil Code § 3366 et seq.

§ 52.1. Tom Bane Civil Rights Act

(a) This section shall be known, and may be cited, as the Tom Bane Civil Rights Act.

(b) If a person or persons, whether or not acting under color of law, interferes by threat, intimidation, or coercion, or attempts to interfere by threat, intimidation, or coercion, with the exercise or enjoyment by any individual or individuals of rights secured by the Constitution or laws of the United States, or of the rights secured by the Constitution or laws of this state, the Attorney General, or any district attorney or city attorney may bring a civil action for injunctive and other appropriate equitable relief in the name of the people of the State of California, in order to protect the peaceable exercise or enjoyment of the right or rights secured. An action brought by the Attorney General, any district attorney, or any city attorney may also seek a civil penalty of twenty-five thousand dollars ($25,000). If this civil penalty is requested, it shall be assessed individually against each person who is determined to have violated this section and the penalty shall be awarded to each individual whose rights under this section are determined to have been violated.

(c) Any individual whose exercise or enjoyment of rights secured by the Constitution or laws of the United States, or of rights secured by the Constitution or laws of this state, has been interfered with, or attempted to be interfered with, as described in subdivision (b), may institute and prosecute in their own name and on their own behalf a civil action for damages, including, but not limited to, damages under Section 52, injunctive relief, and other appropriate equitable relief to protect the peaceable exercise or enjoyment of the right or rights secured, including appropriate equitable and declaratory relief to eliminate a pattern or practice of conduct as described in subdivision (b).

(d) An action brought pursuant to subdivision (b) or (c) may be filed either in the superior court for the county in which the conduct complained of occurred or in the superior court for the county in which a person whose conduct complained of resides or has their place of business. An action brought by the Attorney General pursuant to subdivision (b) also may be filed in the superior court for any county wherein the Attorney General has an office, and in that case, the jurisdiction of the court shall extend throughout the state.

(e) If a court issues a temporary restraining order or a preliminary or permanent injunction in an action brought pursuant to subdivision (b) or (c), ordering a defendant to refrain from conduct or activities, the order issued shall include the following statement: VIOLATION OF THIS ORDER IS A CRIME PUNISHABLE UNDER SECTION 422.77 OF THE PENAL CODE.

(f) The court shall order the plaintiff or the attorney for the plaintiff to deliver, or the clerk of the court to mail, two copies of any order, extension, modification, or termination thereof granted pursuant to this section, by the close of the business day on which the order, extension, modification, or termination was granted, to each local law enforcement agency having jurisdiction over the residence of the plaintiff and any other locations where the court determines that acts of violence against the plaintiff are likely to occur. Those local law enforcement agencies shall be designated by the plaintiff or the attorney for the plaintiff. Each appropriate law enforcement agency receiving any order, extension, or modification of any order issued pursuant to this section shall serve forthwith one copy thereof upon the defendant. Each appropriate law enforcement agency shall provide to any law enforcement officer responding to the scene of reported violence, information as to the existence of, terms, and current status of, any order issued pursuant to this section.

(g) A court shall not have jurisdiction to issue an order or injunction under this section, if that order or injunction would be prohibited under Section 527.3 of the Code of Civil Procedure.

(h) An action brought pursuant to this section is independent of any other action, remedy, or procedure that may be available to an aggrieved individual under any other provision of law, including, but not limited to, an action, remedy, or procedure brought pursuant to Section 51.7.

(i) In addition to any damages, injunction, or other equitable relief awarded in an action brought pursuant to subdivision (c), the court may award the petitioner or plaintiff reasonable attorney's fees.

(j) A violation of an order described in subdivision (e) may be punished either by prosecution under Section 422.77 of the Penal Code, or by a proceeding for contempt brought pursuant to Title 5 (commencing with Section 1209) of Part 3 of the Code of Civil Procedure. However, in any proceeding pursuant to the Code of Civil Procedure, if it is determined that the person proceeded against is guilty of the contempt charged, in addition to any other relief, a fine may be imposed not exceeding one thousand dollars ($1,000), or the person may be ordered imprisoned in a county jail not exceeding six months, or the court may order both the imprisonment and fine.

(k) Speech alone is not sufficient to support an action brought pursuant to subdivision (b) or (c), except upon a showing that the speech itself threatens violence against a specific person or group of persons; and the person or group of persons against whom the threat is directed reasonably fears that, because of the speech, violence will be committed against them or their property and that the person threatening violence had the apparent ability to carry out the threat.

(*l*) No order issued in any proceeding brought pursuant to subdivision (b) or (c) shall restrict the content of any person's speech. An order restricting the time, place, or manner of any person's speech shall do so only to the extent reasonably necessary to protect the peaceable exercise or enjoyment of constitutional or statutory rights, consistent with the constitutional rights of the person sought to be enjoined.

(m) The rights, penalties, remedies, forums, and procedures of this section shall not be waived by contract except as provided in Section 51.7.

(n) The state immunity provisions provided in Sections 821.6, 844.6, and 845.6 of the Government Code shall not apply to any cause of action brought against any peace officer or custodial officer, as those terms are defined in Chapter 4.5 (commencing with Section 830) of Title 3 of Part 2 of the Penal Code, or directly against a public entity that employs a peace officer or custodial officer, under this section.

(*o*) Sections 825, 825.2, 825.4, and 825.6 of the Government Code, providing for indemnification of an employee or former employee of a public entity, shall apply to any cause of action brought under this section against an employee or former employee of a public entity. *(Added by Stats.1987, c. 1277, § 3. Amended by Stats.1990, c. 392 (A.B.2683), § 1; Stats.1991, c. 607 (S.B.98), § 3; Stats.2000, c. 98 (A.B.2719), § 3; Stats.2001, c. 261 (A.B.587), § 2; Stats.2002, c. 784 (S.B.1316), § 11; Stats.2004, c. 700 (S.B.1234), § 1; Stats. 2014, c. 296 (A.B.2634), § 1, eff. Jan. 1, 2015; Stats.2014, c. 910 (A.B.2617), § 4.5, eff. Jan. 1, 2015; Stats.2018, c. 776 (A.B.3250), § 4, eff. Jan. 1, 2019; Stats.2021, c. 401 (A.B. 1578), § 1, eff. Jan. 1, 2022; Stats.2021, c. 409 (S.B.2), § 3, eff. Jan. 1, 2022.)*

Cross References

Attorney General, generally, see Government Code § 12500 et seq.
Attorney General, prevailing party in enforcement action under this section, award of costs and fees to be made to Attorney General and paid to Public Rights Law Enforcement Special Fund, see Code of Civil Procedure § 1021.8; Government Code § 12530.

Business of insurance, application of Unruh Civil Rights Act, see Insurance Code § 1861.03.
Reproductive Privacy Act, civil action pursuant to this section, see Health and Safety Code § 123469.
Responsibility for enforcement of orders, see Penal Code §§ 422.77, 422.78.

§ 52.2. Court of competent jurisdiction; defined; actions

An action pursuant to Section 52 or 54.3 may be brought in any court of competent jurisdiction. A "court of competent jurisdiction" shall include small claims court if the amount of the damages sought in the action does not exceed the jurisdictional limits stated in Sections 116.220 and 116.221 of the Code of Civil Procedure. *(Added by Stats.1998, c. 195 (A.B.2702), § 5. Amended by Stats.2006, c. 167 (A.B.2618), § 1.)*

Cross References

Business of insurance, application of Unruh Civil Rights Act, see Insurance Code § 1861.03.

§ 52.3. Law enforcement officers; prohibitions against conduct depriving persons of Constitutional rights, privileges, or immunities; civil actions

(a) No governmental authority, or agent of a governmental authority, or person acting on behalf of a governmental authority, shall engage in a pattern or practice of conduct by law enforcement officers that deprives any person of rights, privileges, or immunities secured or protected by the Constitution or laws of the United States or by the Constitution or laws of California.

(b) The Attorney General may bring a civil action in the name of the people to obtain appropriate equitable and declaratory relief to eliminate the pattern or practice of conduct specified in subdivision (a), whenever the Attorney General has reasonable cause to believe that a violation of subdivision (a) has occurred. *(Added by Stats.2000, c. 622 (A.B.2484), § 1.)*

Cross References

Attorney General, generally, see Government Code § 12500 et seq.
Business of insurance, application of Unruh Civil Rights Act, see Insurance Code § 1861.03.

§ 52.4. Civil action for damages arising from gender violence

(a) Any person who has been subjected to gender violence may bring a civil action for damages against any responsible party. The plaintiff may seek actual damages, compensatory damages, punitive damages, injunctive relief, any combination of those, or any other appropriate relief. A prevailing plaintiff may also be awarded attorney's fees and costs.

(b) An action brought pursuant to this section shall be commenced within three years of the act, or if the victim was a minor when the act occurred, within eight years after the date the plaintiff attains the age of majority or within three years after the date the plaintiff discovers or reasonably should have discovered the psychological injury or illness occurring after the age of majority that was caused by the act, whichever date occurs later.

(c) For purposes of this section, "gender violence" is a form of sex discrimination and means either of the following:

(1) One or more acts that would constitute a criminal offense under state law that has as an element the use, attempted use, or threatened use of physical force against the person or property of another, committed at least in part based on the gender of the victim, whether or not those acts have resulted in criminal complaints, charges, prosecution, or conviction.

(2) A physical intrusion or physical invasion of a sexual nature under coercive conditions, whether or not those acts have resulted in criminal complaints, charges, prosecution, or conviction.

(d) For purposes of this section, "gender" has the meaning set forth in Section 51.

(e) Notwithstanding any other laws that may establish the liability of an employer for the acts of an employee, this section does not establish any civil liability of a person because of his or her status as an employer, unless the employer personally committed an act of gender violence. *(Added by Stats.2002, c. 842 (A.B.1928), § 2. Amended by Stats.2015, c. 202 (A.B.830), § 1, eff. Jan. 1, 2016.)*

Cross References

Business of insurance, application of Unruh Civil Rights Act, see Insurance Code § 1861.03.

§ 52.45. Civil action for damages arising from sexual orientation violence

(a) Any person who has been subjected to sexual orientation violence may bring a civil action for damages against any responsible party. The plaintiff may seek actual damages, compensatory damages, punitive damages, injunctive relief, any combination of those, or any other appropriate relief. A prevailing plaintiff may also be awarded attorney's fees and costs.

(b) An action brought pursuant to this section shall be commenced within three years of the act, or if the victim was a minor when the act occurred, within eight years after the date the plaintiff attains the age of majority or within three years after the date the plaintiff discovers or reasonably should have discovered the psychological injury or illness occurring after the age of majority that was caused by the act, whichever date occurs later.

(c) For purposes of this section, "sexual orientation violence" means one or more acts that would constitute a criminal offense under state law that has as an element the use, attempted use, or threatened use of physical force against the person or property of another, committed at least in part based on the sexual orientation of the victim, whether or not those acts have resulted in criminal complaints, charges, prosecution, or conviction.

(d) Notwithstanding any other laws that may establish the liability of an employer for the acts of an employee, this section does not establish any civil liability of a person because of his or her status as an employer, unless the employer personally committed an act of sexual orientation violence. *(Added by Stats.2015, c. 202 (A.B.830), § 2, eff. Jan. 1, 2016.)*

§ 52.5. Civil action for damages to victims of human trafficking

(a) A victim of human trafficking, as defined in Section 236.1 of the Penal Code, may bring a civil action for actual damages, compensatory damages, punitive damages, injunctive relief, any combination of those, or any other appropriate relief. A prevailing plaintiff may also be awarded attorney's fees and costs.

(b) In addition to the remedies specified in this section, in an action under subdivision (a), the plaintiff may be awarded up to three times his or her actual damages or ten thousand dollars ($10,000), whichever is greater. In addition, punitive damages may be awarded upon proof of the defendant's malice, oppression, fraud, or duress in committing the act of human trafficking.

(c) An action brought pursuant to this section shall be commenced within seven years of the date on which the trafficking victim was freed from the trafficking situation or, if the victim was a minor when the act of human trafficking against the victim occurred, within 10 years after the date the plaintiff attains the age of majority.

(d) If a person entitled to sue is under a disability at the time the cause of action accrues so that it is impossible or impracticable for him or her to bring an action, the time of the disability is not part of the time limited for the commencement of the action. Disability will toll the running of the statute of limitations for this action.

(1) Disability includes being a minor, lacking legal capacity to make decisions, imprisonment, or other incapacity or incompetence.

(2) The statute of limitations shall not run against a plaintiff who is a minor or who lacks the legal competence to make decisions simply because a guardian ad litem has been appointed. A guardian ad litem's failure to bring a plaintiff's action within the applicable limitation period will not prejudice the plaintiff's right to bring an action after his or her disability ceases.

(3) A defendant is estopped from asserting a defense of the statute of limitations when the expiration of the statute is due to conduct by the defendant inducing the plaintiff to delay the filing of the action, or due to threats made by the defendant causing the plaintiff duress.

(4) The suspension of the statute of limitations due to disability, lack of knowledge, or estoppel applies to all other related claims arising out of the trafficking situation.

(5) The running of the statute of limitations is postponed during the pendency of criminal proceedings against the victim.

(e) The running of the statute of limitations may be suspended if a person entitled to sue could not have reasonably discovered the cause of action due to circumstances resulting from the trafficking situation, such as psychological trauma, cultural and linguistic isolation, and the inability to access services.

(f) A prevailing plaintiff may also be awarded reasonable attorney's fees and litigation costs including, but not limited to, expert witness fees and expenses as part of the costs.

(g) Restitution paid by the defendant to the victim shall be credited against a judgment, award, or settlement obtained pursuant to an action under this section. A judgment, award, or settlement obtained pursuant to an action under this section is subject to Section 13963 of the Government Code.

(h) A civil action filed under this section shall be stayed during the pendency of any criminal action arising out of the same occurrence in which the claimant is the victim. As used in this section, a "criminal action" includes investigation and prosecution, and is pending until a final adjudication in the trial court or dismissal. *(Added by Stats.2005, c. 240 (A.B.22), § 2. Amended by Stats.2014, c. 144 (A.B.1847), § 1, eff. Jan. 1, 2015; Stats.2015, c. 474 (A.B.15), § 1, eff. Jan. 1, 2016; Stats.2016, c. 86 (S.B.1171), § 18, eff. Jan. 1, 2017.)*

Cross References

Business of insurance, application of Unruh Civil Rights Act, see Insurance Code § 1861.03.
Department of Fair Employment and Housing functions, powers and duties, see Government Code § 12930.

§ 52.6. Notice to be posted at specified businesses and establishments; slavery and human trafficking; location of posting; contents; languages; model notice; employee training; civil penalties; local ordinances

(a) Each of the following businesses and other establishments shall, upon the availability of the model notice described in subdivision (d), post a notice that complies with the requirements of this section in a conspicuous place near the public entrance of the establishment or in another conspicuous location in clear view of the public and employees where similar notices are customarily posted:

(1) On-sale general public premises licensees under the Alcoholic Beverage Control Act (Division 9 (commencing with Section 23000) of the Business and Professions Code).

(2) Adult or sexually oriented businesses, as defined in subdivision (a) of Section 318.5 of the Penal Code.

(3) Primary airports, as defined in Section 47102(16) of Title 49 of the United States Code.

(4) Intercity passenger rail or light rail stations.

(5) Bus stations.

(6) Truck stops. For purposes of this section, "truck stop" means a privately owned and operated facility that provides food, fuel, shower or other sanitary facilities, and lawful overnight truck parking.

(7) Emergency rooms within general acute care hospitals.

(8) Urgent care centers.

(9) Farm labor contractors, as defined in subdivision (b) of Section 1682 of the Labor Code.

(10) Privately operated job recruitment centers.

(11) Roadside rest areas.

(12) Businesses or establishments that offer massage or bodywork services for compensation and are not described in paragraph (1) of subdivision (b) of Section 4612 of the Business and Professions Code.

(13) Hotels, motels, and bed and breakfast inns, as defined in subdivision (b) of Section 24045.12 of the Business and Professions Code, not including personal residences.

(14) Hair, nail, electrolysis, and skin care, and other related businesses or establishments subject to regulation under Chapter 10 (commencing with Section 7301) of Division 3 of the Business and Professions Code.

(b) The notice to be posted pursuant to subdivision (a) shall be at least 8½ inches by 11 inches in size, written in a 16–point font, and shall state the following:

"If you or someone you know is being forced to engage in any activity and cannot leave-whether it is commercial sex, housework, farm work, construction, factory, retail, or restaurant work, or any other activity-text 233–733 (Be Free) or call the National Human Trafficking Hotline at 1–888–373–7888 or the California Coalition to Abolish Slavery and Trafficking (CAST) at 1–888–KEY–2–FRE(EDOM) or 1–888–539–2373 to access help and services.

Victims of slavery and human trafficking are protected under United States and California law.

The hotlines are:
- Available 24 hours a day, 7 days a week.
- Toll-free.
- Operated by nonprofit, nongovernmental organizations.
- Anonymous and confidential.
- Accessible in more than 160 languages.
- Able to provide help, referral to services, training, and general information."

(c) The notice to be posted pursuant to subdivision (a) shall be printed in English, Spanish, and in one other language that is the most widely spoken language in the county where the establishment is located and for which translation is mandated by the federal Voting Rights Act of 1965 (52 U.S.C. Sec. 10301 et seq.), as applicable. This section does not require a business or other establishment in a county where a language other than English or Spanish is the most widely spoken language to print the notice in more than one language in addition to English and Spanish.

(d)(1) On or before April 1, 2013, the Department of Justice shall develop a model notice that complies with the requirements of this section and make the model notice available for download on the department's internet website.

(2) On or before January 1, 2019, the Department of Justice shall revise and update the model notice to comply with the requirements of this section and make the updated model notice available for download on the department's internet website. A business or establishment required to post the model notice shall not be required to post the updated model notice until on and after January 1, 2019.

(e) On or before January 1, 2021, a business or other establishment that operates a facility described in paragraph (4) or (5) of subdivision (a) shall provide at least 20 minutes of training to its new and existing employees who may interact with, or come into contact with, a victim of human trafficking or who are likely to receive, in the course of their employment, a report from another employee about suspected human trafficking, in recognizing the signs of human trafficking and how to report those signs to the appropriate law enforcement agency.

(f) The employee training pursuant to subdivision (e) shall include, but not be limited to, all of the following:

(1) The definition of human trafficking, including sex trafficking and labor trafficking.

(2) Myths and misconceptions about human trafficking.

(3) Physical and mental signs to be aware of that may indicate that human trafficking is occurring.

(4) Guidance on how to identify individuals who are most at risk for human trafficking.

(5) Guidance on how to report human trafficking, including, but not limited to, national hotlines (1–888-373-7888 and text line 233733) and contact information for local law enforcement agencies that an employee may use to make a confidential report.

(6) Protocols for reporting human trafficking when on the job.

(g)(1) The human trafficking employee training pursuant to subdivision (e) may include, but shall not be limited to, information and material utilized in training Santa Clara County Valley Transportation Authority employees, private nonprofit organizations that represent the interests of human trafficking victims, and the Department of Justice.

(2) The failure to report human trafficking by an employee shall not, by itself, result in the liability of the business or other establishment that operates a facility described in paragraph (4) or (5) of subdivision (a) or of any other person or entity.

(h) A business or establishment that fails to comply with the requirements of this section is liable for a civil penalty of five hundred dollars ($500) for a first offense and one thousand dollars ($1,000) for each subsequent offense. A government entity identified in Section 17204 of the Business and Professions Code may bring an action to impose a civil penalty pursuant to this subdivision against a business or establishment if a local or state agency with authority to regulate that business or establishment has satisfied both of the following:

(1) Provided the business or establishment with reasonable notice of noncompliance, which informs the business or establishment that it is subject to a civil penalty if it does not correct the violation within 30 days from the date the notice is sent to the business or establishment.

(2) Verified that the violation was not corrected within the 30–day period described in paragraph (1).

(i) This section does not prevent a local governing body from adopting and enforcing a local ordinance, rule, or regulation to prevent slavery or human trafficking. If a local ordinance, rule, or regulation duplicates or supplements the requirements that this section imposes upon businesses and other establishments, this section does not supersede or preempt that local ordinance, rule, or regulation. *(Added by Stats.2012, c. 515 (S.B.1193), § 1. Amended by Stats.2017, c. 547 (A.B.260), § 1, eff. Jan. 1, 2018; Stats.2017, c. 565 (S.B.225), § 1.5, eff. Jan. 1, 2018; Stats.2018, c. 812 (A.B. 2034), § 1, eff. Jan. 1, 2019; Stats.2019, c. 57 (S.B.630), § 1, eff. Jan. 1, 2020; Stats.2020, c. 370 (S.B.1371), § 22, eff. Jan. 1, 2021; Stats.2022, c. 106 (A.B.1661), § 1, eff. Jan. 1, 2023.)*

§ 52.65. Civil action for hotels in violation of sex trafficking activity

(a) A hotel is in violation of this section, and subject to civil penalties, if either or both of the following conditions are met:

(1) Sex trafficking activity occurred in the hotel, a supervisory employee of the hotel either knew of the nature of the activity, or acted in reckless disregard of the activity constituting sex trafficking activity within the hotel, and the supervisory employee of the hotel failed to inform law enforcement, the National Human Trafficking Hotline, or another appropriate victim service organization within 24 hours.

(2) An employee of the hotel was acting within the scope of employment and knowingly benefited, financially or by receiving anything of value, by participating in a venture that the employee knew or acted in reckless disregard of the activity constituting sex trafficking within the hotel.

(b) If there is reasonable cause to believe there has been a violation pursuant to subdivision (a), a city, county, or city and county attorney may bring a civil action for injunctive and other equitable relief against a hotel for violation of this section. A city, county, or city and county attorney who brings a civil action under this section may also seek civil penalties in the amount of one thousand dollars ($1,000) for the first violation in a calendar year, three thousand dollars ($3,000) for the second violation within the same calendar year, and five thousand dollars ($5,000) for the third and any subsequent violation within the same calendar year.

(c) The court may exercise its discretion to increase the amount of the civil penalty, not to exceed ten thousand dollars ($10,000), for any fourth or subsequent violation, considering all of the following factors:

(1) The defendant's culpability.

(2) The relationship between the harm and the penalty.

(3) The penalties imposed for similar conduct in similar statutes.

(4) The defendant's ability to pay.

(d) The lack of reporting of a sex trafficking case that occurs in a hotel shall not, by itself, without meeting the conditions in either paragraph (1) or (2) of subdivision (a), result in the liability of an employer of that establishment to the sex trafficking victim or victims in the case in question or to any other party.

(e) No liability for civil penalties shall arise under this section against a hotel employee.

(f) Violation of this section, by itself, shall not result in criminal liability against the hotel.

(g) Nothing in this section affects criminal or civil liability that may arise pursuant to other provisions of law.

(h) For the purposes of this section, the following terms shall have the following definitions:

(1) "Hotel" means a motel, or any other operator or management company that offers and accepts payment for rooms, sleeping accommodations, or board and lodging and retains the right of access to, and control of, a dwelling unit that is required to provide training and education regarding human trafficking awareness pursuant to Section 12950.3 of the Government Code.

(2) "Sex trafficking" means human trafficking for the purposes of engaging in a commercial sex act as set forth in subdivision (c) of Section 236.1 of the Penal Code.

(3) "Supervisory employee" means any individual, regardless of the job description or title, who has each of the following capabilities and qualifications:

(A) Holds authority, in the interest of the employer, to hire, transfer, suspend, lay off, recall, promote, discharge, assign, reward, or discipline other employees, or responsibility to direct them, or to adjust their grievances, or effectively to recommend this action, if, in connection with the foregoing, the exercise of this authority is not of a merely routine or clerical nature, but requires the use of independent judgment.

(B) Holds responsibility for duties that are not substantially similar to those of their subordinates. Employees whose duties are substantially similar to those of their subordinates shall not be considered to be supervisory employees.

(i) An action brought pursuant to this section shall be commenced within five years of the date when the violation of subdivision (a) occurred, or, if the victim of that sex trafficking activity was a minor when the violation occurred, within five years of the date the victim attains the age of majority. *(Added by Stats.2022, c. 760 (A.B.1788), § 1, eff. Jan. 1, 2023.)*

§ 52.7. Subcutaneous implanting of identification device; penalties; limitations; restitution; liberal construction; independent action; existing law; definitions

(a) Except as provided in subdivision (g), a person shall not require, coerce, or compel any other individual to undergo the subcutaneous implanting of an identification device.

(b)(1) Any person who violates subdivision (a) may be assessed an initial civil penalty of no more than ten thousand dollars ($10,000), and no more than one thousand dollars ($1,000) for each day the violation continues until the deficiency is corrected. That civil penalty may be assessed and recovered in a civil action brought in any court of competent jurisdiction. The court may also grant a prevailing plaintiff reasonable attorney's fees and litigation costs, including, but not limited to, expert witness fees and expenses as part of the costs.

(2) A person who is implanted with a subcutaneous identification device in violation of subdivision (a) may bring a civil action for actual damages, compensatory damages, punitive damages, injunctive relief, any combination of those, or any other appropriate relief.

(3) Additionally, punitive damages may also be awarded upon proof of the defendant's malice, oppression, fraud, or duress in requiring, coercing, or compelling the plaintiff to

undergo the subcutaneous implanting of an identification device.

(c)(1) An action brought pursuant to this section shall be commenced within three years of the date upon which the identification device was implanted.

(2) If the victim was a dependent adult or minor when the implantation occurred, actions brought pursuant to this section shall be commenced within three years after the date the plaintiff, or his or her guardian or parent, discovered or reasonably should have discovered the implant, or within eight years after the plaintiff attains the age of majority, whichever date occurs later.

(3) The statute of limitations shall not run against a dependent adult or minor plaintiff simply because a guardian ad litem has been appointed. A guardian ad litem's failure to bring a plaintiff's action within the applicable limitation period will not prejudice the plaintiff's right to do so.

(4) A defendant is estopped to assert a defense of the statute of limitations when the expiration of the statute is due to conduct by the defendant inducing the plaintiff to delay the filing of the action, or due to threats made by the defendant causing duress upon the plaintiff.

(d) Any restitution paid by the defendant to the victim shall be credited against any judgment, award, or settlement obtained pursuant to this section. Any judgment, award, or settlement obtained pursuant to an action under this section shall be subject to the provisions of Section 13963 of the Government Code.

(e) The provisions of this section shall be liberally construed so as to protect privacy and bodily integrity.

(f) Actions brought pursuant to this section are independent of any other actions, remedies, or procedures that may be available to an aggrieved party pursuant to any other law.

(g) This section shall not in any way modify existing statutory or case law regarding the rights of parents or guardians, the rights of children or minors, or the rights of dependent adults.

(h) For purposes of this section:

(1) "Identification device" means any item, application, or product that is passively or actively capable of transmitting personal information, including, but not limited to, devices using radio frequency technology.

(2) "Person" means an individual, business association, partnership, limited partnership, corporation, limited liability company, trust, estate, cooperative association, or other entity.

(3) "Personal information" includes any of the following data elements to the extent they are used alone or in conjunction with any other information used to identify an individual:

(A) First or last name.

(B) Address.

(C) Telephone number.

(D) E-mail, Internet Protocol, or Web site address.

(E) Date of birth.

(F) Driver's license number or California identification card number.

(G) Any unique personal identifier number contained or encoded on a driver's license or identification card issued pursuant to Section 13000 of the Vehicle Code.

(H) Bank, credit card, or other financial institution account number.

(I) Any unique personal identifier contained or encoded on a health insurance, health benefit, or benefit card or record issued in conjunction with any government-supported aid program.

(J) Religion.

(K) Ethnicity or nationality.

(L) Photograph.

(M) Fingerprint or other biometric identifier.

(N) Social security number.

(O) Any unique personal identifier.

(4) "Require, coerce, or compel" includes physical violence, threat, intimidation, retaliation, the conditioning of any private or public benefit or care on consent to implantation, including employment, promotion, or other employment benefit, or by any means that causes a reasonable person of ordinary susceptibilities to acquiesce to implantation when he or she otherwise would not.

(5) "Subcutaneous" means existing, performed, or introduced under or on the skin. *(Added by Stats.2007, c. 538 (S.B.362), § 1.)*

§ 52.8. Distribution of unauthorized obscene materials; attorney's fees and costs

(a) In a civil action seeking damages or equitable relief against any person or entity that distributes, benefits from, promotes, or induces another person to distribute unauthorized obscene materials, including through electronic distribution, a prevailing plaintiff shall be awarded attorney's fees and costs.

(b) For purposes of this section:

(1) "Obscene material" means material, taken as a whole, that to the average person, applying contemporary statewide standards, appeals to the prurient interest, that, taken as a whole, depicts or describes sexual conduct in a patently offensive way, and that, taken as a whole, lacks serious literary, artistic, political, or scientific value.

(2) "Unauthorized" means either of the following:

(A) The obscene material was coerced, made, or obtained by trickery or subterfuge, or stolen, made, obtained, or distributed without the knowledge or without or beyond the express permission, freely given, of the person in the photograph, or the person whose identifiable likeness appears in the photograph.

(B) The obscene material is of a person who was less than 18 years of age at the time the obscene material was created. *(Added by Stats.2022, c. 26 (S.B.1210), § 1, eff. Jan. 1, 2023.)*

§ 53. Restrictions upon transfer or use of realty because of characteristics listed or defined in Section 51

(a) Every provision in a written instrument relating to real property that purports to forbid or restrict the conveyance, encumbrance, leasing, or mortgaging of that real property to any person because of any characteristic listed or defined in subdivision (b) or (e) of Section 51 is void, and every restriction or prohibition as to the use or occupation of real property because of any characteristic listed or defined in subdivision (b) or (e) of Section 51 is void.

(b) Every restriction or prohibition, whether by way of covenant, condition upon use or occupation, or upon transfer of title to real property, which restriction or prohibition directly or indirectly limits the acquisition, use or occupation of that property because of any characteristic listed or defined in subdivision (b) or (e) of Section 51 is void.

(c) In any action to declare that a restriction or prohibition specified in subdivision (a) or (b) is void, the court shall take judicial notice of the recorded instrument or instruments containing the prohibitions or restrictions in the same manner that it takes judicial notice of the matters listed in Section 452 of the Evidence Code. *(Added by Stats.1961, c. 1877, p. 3976, § 1. Amended by Stats.1965, c. 299, p. 1356, § 6, operative Jan. 1, 1967; Stats.1974, c. 1193, p. 2568, § 3; Stats.1987, c. 159, § 5; Stats.1992, c. 913 (A.B.1077), § 3.8; Stats.2005, c. 420 (A.B.1400), § 7.)*

Cross References

Business of insurance, application of Unruh Civil Rights Act, see Insurance Code § 1861.03.
Power of termination, enforceability, see Civil Code § 885.060.
Racial restrictions in deeds, invalidity, see Civil Code § 782.
Real property defined for purposes of this Code, see Civil Code § 658.

§ 53.5. Dissemination of guest record or passenger manifest record; court issued subpoena, warrant, or order required; exceptions

(a) Notwithstanding any other law, except as specified in this section, an innkeeper, hotelkeeper, motelkeeper, lodginghouse keeper, or owner or operator of an inn, hotel, motel, lodginghouse, or other similar accommodations, or any employee or agent thereof, who offers or accepts payment for rooms, sleeping accommodations, or board and lodging, or other similar accommodation, shall not disclose, produce, provide, release, transfer, disseminate, or otherwise communicate, except to a California peace officer, all or any part of a guest record orally, in writing, or by electronic or any other means to a third party without a court-issued subpoena, warrant, or order.

(b) Notwithstanding any other law, except as specified in this section, an owner or operator of a private or charter bus transportation company, or any employee or agent thereof, shall not disclose, produce, provide, release, transfer, disseminate, or otherwise communicate, except to a California peace officer, all or any part of a passenger manifest record orally, in writing, or by electronic or any other means to a third party without a court-issued subpoena, warrant, or order.

(c) "Guest record" for purposes of this section includes any record that identifies an individual guest, boarder, occupant, lodger, customer, or invitee, including, but not limited to, their name, social security number or other unique identifying number, date of birth, location of birth, address, telephone number, driver's license number, other official form of identification, credit card number, or automobile license plate number.

(d) "Passenger manifest record" for purposes of this section includes any record that identifies an individual guest, passenger, customer, or invitee, including, but not limited to, their name, social security number or other unique identifying number, date of birth, location of birth, address, telephone number, driver's license number, other official form of identification, credit card number, or automobile license plate number.

(e) "Court issued subpoena, warrant, or order" for purposes of this section is limited to subpoenas, warrants, or orders issued by a judicial officer. An administrative subpoena, warrant, or order is not sufficient for purposes of this section.

(f) "Third-party service provider," for the purposes of this section, means an entity contracted to provide services outlined in the contract that has no independent right to use or share the data beyond the terms of the contract. Records shared with a third-party service provider shall be subject to limitations on further disclosure as described in subdivisions (a) and (b), except as otherwise permitted by this section.

(g) This section shall not be construed to prevent a government entity from requiring a private business to provide business records, including, but not limited to, guest and passenger manifest records, in a public health, civil rights, or consumer protection investigation, or in an investigation conducted pursuant to Section 308.5 of the Public Utilities Code.

(h) This section shall not be construed to prevent a government entity from requiring a private business to provide business records during an audit or inspection if those records omit the personal information described in subdivisions (c) and (d).

(i) This section shall not be construed to prevent a private business from providing business records containing a guest's or passenger's name, address, credit card number, or driver's license number to a third-party service provider, if required, for the sole purpose of effectuating financial payment, including, approving or processing negotiable instruments, electronic fund transfers, or similar methods of payment, from a guest or passenger to the private business for a good or service, or from providing business records to a third-party service provider that the private business contracts with for business-related services.

(j) This section shall not be construed to prevent a private business from providing, where required, business records to a government entity in order to comply with state and federal laws regarding financial oversight and privacy, including, but not limited to, the federal Gramm–Leach–Bliley Act (15 U.S.C. Sec. 6801). Records shared with a government entity or in compliance with the federal Gramm–Leach–Bliley Act shall be subject to the limitations on further disclosure as described in subdivisions (a) and (b), except as otherwise permitted by this section.

(k) This section shall not be construed to prevent a private business from disclosing records in a criminal investigation if a law enforcement officer in good faith believes that an emergency involving imminent danger of death or serious bodily injury to a person requires a warrantless search, to the extent permitted by law.

(*l*) This section shall not be construed to compel disclosure of a guest record or passenger manifest record by an innkeeper, motelkeeper, lodginghouse keeper, or owner or operator of an inn, hotel, motel, lodginghouse, or other similar accommodation, or an owner or operator of a private or charter bus transportation company, in the absence of a court-issued subpoena, warrant, or order. *(Added by Stats. 2018, c. 853 (S.B.1194), § 2, eff. Jan. 1, 2019. Amended by Stats.2019, c. 2 (A.B.73), § 1, eff. Feb. 13, 2019; Stats.2020, c. 370 (S.B.1371), § 23, eff. Jan. 1, 2021.)*

§ 53.7. Minority groups; political structure equal protection; statutes, ordinances, etc., prohibited from denying; civil actions

(a) A statute, ordinance, or other state or local rule, regulation, or enactment shall not deny a minority group political structure equal protection of the law by altering, restructuring, or reordering the policy decisionmaking process in a manner that burdens the ability of members of the minority group to effect the enactment of future legislation, solely with respect to a matter that inures primarily to the benefit of, or is primarily of interest to, one or more minority groups.

(b)(1) A member of a minority group, as defined in paragraph (2), may bring a civil action challenging the validity of a statute, ordinance, or other state or local rule, regulation, or enactment, pursuant to subdivision (a).

(2) For purposes of this section, "minority group" means a group of persons who share in common any race, ethnicity, nationality, or sexual orientation.

(c) A statute, ordinance, or other state or local rule, regulation, or enactment shall be determined valid in an action brought pursuant to this section, only upon a showing by the government that the burden imposed by the statute, ordinance, or other state or local rule, regulation, or enactment satisfies both of the following criteria:

(1) The burden is necessary to serve a compelling government interest.

(2) The burden is no greater than necessary to serve the compelling government interest. *(Added by Stats.2014, c. 912 (A.B.2646), § 2, eff. Jan. 1, 2015.)*

Part 2.5

BLIND AND OTHER PHYSICALLY DISABLED PERSONS

Section
54. Right to streets, highways, and other public places; disability.
54.1. Access to public conveyances, places of public accommodation, amusement or resort, and housing accommodations.
54.2. Guide, signal or service dogs; right to accompany individuals with a disability and trainers; damages.
54.25. Peace officer or firefighter assigned to canine unit; handler of search and rescue dog; duty away from home jurisdiction; discrimination; civil fine.
54.27. Prelitigation letters and complaints to education entities; requirements; discipline.
54.3. Violations; liability.
54.4. Blind or visually impaired pedestrian; failure to carry cane or use guide dog.
54.5. White cane safety day; proclamation.
54.6. Visually impaired.
54.7. Zoos or wild animal parks; facilities for guide, service or signal dogs accompanying individuals with a disability.
54.8. Individuals who are deaf or hard of hearing; assistive listening systems in civil or criminal proceedings; notice of need; availability; use in proceedings.
54.9. Touch-screen self-service check-in devices at hotels or facilities providing passenger transportation services; manufacturers and distributors to offer devices containing necessary technology.
55. Violations; injunction; action by person actually or potentially aggrieved.
55.1. Violations; injunctions; district or city attorney, attorney general.
55.2. Mandatory service on State Solicitor General of each party's brief or petition and brief in causes of action based on violation of civil rights statutes.
55.3. Written advisory to accompany demand letter or complaint; contents.
55.31. Demand letter alleging construction-related accessibility claim; inclusion of statement of facts; inclusion of prelitigation settlement negotiation offer; prohibition on inclusion of request or demand for money or offer or agreement to accept money; prohibition on issuance of demand for money; violation; application.
55.32. Demand letter or complaint; duties of attorney; violation; report by State Bar; review and report by California Commission on Disability Access; effect of expiration of ground for discipline; application.

§ 54. Right to streets, highways, and other public places; disability

(a) Individuals with disabilities or medical conditions have the same right as the general public to the full and free use of the streets, highways, sidewalks, walkways, public buildings, medical facilities, including hospitals, clinics, and physicians' offices, public facilities, and other public places.

(b) For purposes of this section:

(1) "Disability" means any mental or physical disability as defined in Section 12926 of the Government Code.

(2) "Medical condition" has the same meaning as defined in subdivision (h) of Section 12926 of the Government Code.

(c) A violation of the right of an individual under the Americans with Disabilities Act of 1990 (Public Law 101–336) also constitutes a violation of this section. (*Added by Stats.1968, c. 461, p. 1024, § 1. Amended by Stats.1992, c. 913 (A.B.1077), § 4; Stats.1994, c. 1257 (S.B.1240), § 1; Stats. 1996, c. 498 (S.B.1687), § 1; Stats.2000, c. 1049 (A.B.2222), § 4.*)

Cross References

Construction-related accessibility claims, application for mandatory evaluation conference, see Civil Code § 55.545.
Department of Fair Employment and Housing, functions, powers and duties, see Government Code § 12935.
Injuries to persons, interference or harassment of guide, signal, or service dog or user, see Penal Code § 365.6.

§ 54.1. Access to public conveyances, places of public accommodation, amusement or resort, and housing accommodations

(a)(1) Individuals with disabilities shall be entitled to full and equal access, as other members of the general public, to accommodations, advantages, facilities, medical facilities, including hospitals, clinics, and physicians' offices, and privileges of all common carriers, airplanes, motor vehicles, railroad trains, motorbuses, streetcars, boats, or any other public conveyances or modes of transportation (whether private, public, franchised, licensed, contracted, or otherwise provided), telephone facilities, adoption agencies, private schools, hotels, lodging places, places of public accommodation, amusement, or resort, and other places to which the general public is invited, subject only to the conditions and limitations established by law, or state or federal regulation, and applicable alike to all persons.

(2) As used in this section, "telephone facilities" means tariff items and other equipment and services that have been approved by the Public Utilities Commission to be used by individuals with disabilities in a manner feasible and compatible with the existing telephone network provided by the telephone companies.

(3) "Full and equal access," for purposes of this section in its application to transportation, means access that meets the standards of Titles II and III of the Americans with Disabilities Act of 1990 (Public Law 101–336)[1] and federal regulations adopted pursuant thereto, except that, if the laws of this state prescribe higher standards, it shall mean access that meets those higher standards.

(b)(1) Individuals with disabilities shall be entitled to full and equal access, as other members of the general public, to all housing accommodations offered for rent, lease, or compensation in this state, subject to the conditions and limitations established by law, or state or federal regulation, and applicable alike to all persons.

(2) "Housing accommodations" means any real property, or portion of real property, that is used or occupied, or is intended, arranged, or designed to be used or occupied, as the home, residence, or sleeping place of one or more human beings, but shall not include any accommodations included within subdivision (a) or any single-family residence the

occupants of which rent, lease, or furnish for compensation not more than one room in the residence.

(3)(A) A person renting, leasing, or otherwise providing real property for compensation shall not refuse to permit an individual with a disability, at that person's expense, to make reasonable modifications of the existing rented premises if the modifications are necessary to afford the person full enjoyment of the premises. However, any modifications under this paragraph may be conditioned on the disabled tenant entering into an agreement to restore the interior of the premises to the condition existing before the modifications. No additional security may be required on account of an election to make modifications to the rented premises under this paragraph, but the lessor and tenant may negotiate, as part of the agreement to restore the premises, a provision requiring the disabled tenant to pay an amount into an escrow account, not to exceed a reasonable estimate of the cost of restoring the premises.

(B) A person renting, leasing, or otherwise providing real property for compensation shall not refuse to make reasonable accommodations in rules, policies, practices, or services, when those accommodations may be necessary to afford individuals with a disability equal opportunity to use and enjoy the premises.

(4) This subdivision does not require a person renting, leasing, or providing for compensation real property to modify his or her property in any way or provide a higher degree of care for an individual with a disability than for an individual who is not disabled.

(5) Except as provided in paragraph (6), this part does not require a person renting, leasing, or providing for compensation real property, if that person refuses to accept tenants who have dogs, to accept as a tenant an individual with a disability who has a dog.

(6)(A) It shall be deemed a denial of equal access to housing accommodations within the meaning of this subdivision for a person, firm, or corporation to refuse to lease or rent housing accommodations to an individual who is blind or visually impaired on the basis that the individual uses the services of a guide dog, an individual who is deaf or hard of hearing on the basis that the individual uses the services of a signal dog, or to an individual with any other disability on the basis that the individual uses the services of a service dog, or to refuse to permit such an individual who is blind or visually impaired to keep a guide dog, an individual who is deaf or hard of hearing to keep a signal dog, or an individual with any other disability to keep a service dog on the premises.

(B) Except in the normal performance of duty as a mobility or signal aid, this paragraph does not prevent the owner of a housing accommodation from establishing terms in a lease or rental agreement that reasonably regulate the presence of guide dogs, signal dogs, or service dogs on the premises of a housing accommodation, nor does this paragraph relieve a tenant from any liability otherwise imposed by law for real and personal property damages caused by such a dog when proof of the damage exists.

(C)(i) As used in this subdivision, "guide dog" means a guide dog that was trained by a person licensed under Chapter 9.5 (commencing with Section 7200) of Division 3 of the Business and Professions Code or as defined in the regulations implementing Title III of the Americans with Disabilities Act of 1990 (Public Law 101–336).

(ii) As used in this subdivision, "signal dog" means a dog trained to alert an individual who is deaf or hard of hearing to intruders or sounds.

(iii) As used in this subdivision, "service dog" means a dog individually trained to the requirements of the individual with a disability, including, but not limited to, minimal protection work, rescue work, pulling a wheelchair, or fetching dropped items.

(7) It shall be deemed a denial of equal access to housing accommodations within the meaning of this subdivision for a person, firm, or corporation to refuse to lease or rent housing accommodations to an individual who is blind or visually impaired, an individual who is deaf or hard of hearing, or other individual with a disability on the basis that the individual with a disability is partially or wholly dependent upon the income of his or her spouse, if the spouse is a party to the lease or rental agreement. This subdivision does not prohibit a lessor or landlord from considering the aggregate financial status of an individual with a disability and his or her spouse.

(c) Visually impaired or blind persons and persons licensed to train guide dogs for individuals who are visually impaired or blind pursuant to Chapter 9.5 (commencing with Section 7200) of Division 3 of the Business and Professions Code or guide dogs as defined in the regulations implementing Title III of the Americans with Disabilities Act of 1990 (Public Law 101–336), and persons who are deaf or hard of hearing and persons authorized to train signal dogs for individuals who are deaf or hard of hearing, and other individuals with a disability and persons authorized to train service dogs for individuals with a disability, may take dogs, for the purpose of training them as guide dogs, signal dogs, or service dogs in any of the places specified in subdivisions (a) and (b). These persons shall ensure that the dog is on a leash and tagged as a guide dog, signal dog, or service dog by identification tag issued by the county clerk, animal control department, or other agency, as authorized by Chapter 3.5 (commencing with Section 30850) of Division 14 of the Food and Agricultural Code. In addition, the person shall be liable for any provable damage done to the premises or facilities by his or her dog.

(d) A violation of the right of an individual under the Americans with Disabilities Act of 1990 (Public Law 101–336) also constitutes a violation of this section, and this section does not limit the access of any person in violation of that act.

(e) This section does not preclude the requirement of the showing of a license plate or disabled placard when required by enforcement units enforcing disabled persons parking violations pursuant to Sections 22507.8 and 22511.8 of the Vehicle Code. *(Added by Stats.1968, c. 461, p. 1092, § 1. Amended by Stats.1969, c. 832, p. 1664, § 1; Stats.1972, c. 819, p. 1465, § 1; Stats.1974, c. 108, p. 223, § 1; Stats.1976, c. 971, p. 2269, § 1; Stats.1976, c. 972, p. 2272, § 1.5; Stats.1977, c. 700, p. 2256, § 1; Stats.1978, c. 380, p. 1128, § 12; Stats.1979, c. 293, p. 1092, § 1; Stats.1980, c. 773, § 1; Stats.1988, c. 1595, § 2; Stats.1992, c. 913 (A.B.1077), § 5; Stats.1993, c. 1149 (A.B.1419), § 4; Stats.1993, c. 1214 (A.B.551), § 1.5;*

§ 54.1   PERSONS

Stats.1994, c. 1257 (S.B.1240), § 2; Stats.1996, c. 498 (S.B. 1687), § 1.5; Stats.2016, c. 94 (A.B.1709), § 1, eff. Jan. 1, 2017.)

[1] 42 U.S.C.A. § 12101 et seq.

Cross References

Allowing dog to injure or kill guide, signal or service dog, punishment, see Penal Code § 600.2.

California retail food code, certified farmers' markets, requirements, see Health and Safety Code § 114371.

California retail food code, nonprofit charitable temporary food facilities, live animals, see Health and Safety Code § 114332.3.

Certified farmers' markets, requirements, see Health and Safety Code § 114371.

Construction-related accessibility claims, application for mandatory evaluation conference, see Civil Code § 55.545.

Criminal procedure, authorization for therapy or facility dogs to accompany certain witnesses in criminal or juvenile hearings, see Penal Code § 868.4.

Department of Fair Employment and Housing, functions, powers and duties, see Government Code § 12935.

Donahoe Higher Education Act, provision of instructional materials in electronic format for university or college students with disabilities, see Education Code § 67302.

Guide dogs, signal dogs, and service dogs, application for assistance dog identification tag, affidavit, see Food and Agricultural Code § 30850.

Injuries to persons, interference or harassment of guide, signal, or service dog or user, see Penal Code § 365.6.

Intentional injury to, or death of, guide, signal or service dog, penalty, see Penal Code § 600.5.

Knowing and fraudulent representation as owner or trainer of guide, signal or service dog, penalty, see Penal Code § 365.7.

Public Utilities Act, obligations of public utilities, telephone facilities, see Public Utilities Code § 451.

Real property defined for purposes of this Code, see Civil Code § 658.

"Visually impaired" defined for purposes of this Part, see Civil Code § 54.6.

§ 54.2. Guide, signal or service dogs; right to accompany individuals with a disability and trainers; damages

(a) Every individual with a disability has the right to be accompanied by a guide dog, signal dog, or service dog, especially trained for the purpose, in any of the places specified in Section 54.1 without being required to pay an extra charge or security deposit for the guide dog, signal dog, or service dog. However, the individual shall be liable for any damage done to the premises or facilities by his or her dog.

(b) Individuals who are blind or otherwise visually impaired and persons licensed to train guide dogs for individuals who are blind or visually impaired pursuant to Chapter 9.5 (commencing with Section 7200) of Division 3 of the Business and Professions Code or as defined in regulations implementing Title III of the Americans with Disabilities Act of 1990 (Public Law 101–336),[1] and individuals who are deaf or hard of hearing and persons authorized to train signal dogs for individuals who are deaf or hard of hearing, and individuals with a disability and persons who are authorized to train service dogs for the individuals with a disability may take dogs, for the purpose of training them as guide dogs, signal dogs, or service dogs in any of the places specified in Section 54.1 without being required to pay an extra charge or security deposit for the guide dog, signal dog, or service dog. However, the person shall be liable for any damage done to the premises or facilities by his or her dog. These persons shall ensure the dog is on a leash and tagged as a guide dog, signal dog, or service dog by an identification tag issued by the county clerk, animal control department, or other agency, as authorized by Chapter 3.5 (commencing with Section 30850) of Title 14 of the Food and Agricultural Code.

(c) A violation of the right of an individual under the Americans with Disabilities Act of 1990 (Public Law 101–336) also constitutes a violation of this section, and this section does not limit the access of any person in violation of that act.

(d) As used in this section, the terms "guide dog," "signal dog," and "service dog" have the same meanings as defined in Section 54.1.

(e) This section does not preclude the requirement of the showing of a license plate or disabled placard when required by enforcement units enforcing disabled persons parking violations pursuant to Sections 22507.8 and 22511.8 of the Vehicle Code. (Added by Stats.1968, c. 461, p. 1092, § 1. Amended by Stats.1972, c. 819, p. 1466, § 2; Stats.1979, c. 293, p. 1092, § 2; Stats.1980, c. 773, § 2; Stats.1988, c. 1595, § 3; Stats.1992, c. 913 (A.B.1077), § 6; Stats.1994, c. 1257 (S.B. 1240), § 3; Stats.1996, c. 498 (S.B.1687), § 2; Stats.2016, c. 94 (A.B.1709), § 2, eff. Jan. 1, 2017.)

[1] 42 U.S.C.A. § 12101 et seq.

Cross References

Certified farmers' markets, requirements, guide dogs, signal dogs, or service dogs, see Health and Safety Code § 114371.

Department of Fair Employment and Housing, functions, powers and duties, see Government Code § 12935.

"Visually impaired" defined for purposes of this Part, see Civil Code § 54.6.

§ 54.25. Peace officer or firefighter assigned to canine unit; handler of search and rescue dog; duty away from home jurisdiction; discrimination; civil fine

(a)(1) A peace officer or firefighter assigned to a canine unit or the handler of a search and rescue dog assigned to duty away from his or her home jurisdiction because of a declared federal, state, or local emergency, or an official mutual aid request or training, and in the course and scope of his or her duties shall not be denied service based on the presence of the dog or discriminated against in hotels, lodging establishments, eating establishments, or public transportation by being required to pay an extra charge or security deposit for the dog. However, the peace officer's law enforcement agency, the firefighter's fire agency, or the handler of a search and rescue dog shall be liable for any damages to the premises or facilities caused by the dog.

(2) Any person, firm, association, or corporation, or the agent of any person, firm, association, or corporation that prevents a peace officer or a firefighter assigned to a canine unit and his or her dog or the handler of a search and rescue dog and his or her dog from exercising, or interferes in the exercise of, the rights specified in this section is subject to a civil fine not exceeding one thousand dollars ($1,000).

(b) For purposes of this section, the following definitions apply:

(1) "Declared emergency" is any emergency declared by the President of the United States, the Governor of a state, or local authorities.

(2) "Handler of a search and rescue dog" means a person in possession of a dog that is in training to become registered and approved as a search and rescue dog, or that is currently registered and approved for tasks, including, but not limited to, locating missing persons, discovering controlled substances, explosives, or cadavers, or locating victims in collapsed structures, and assisting with peace officer on-command searches for suspects and victims at crime scenes.

(3) "Peace officer's or firefighter's dog" means a dog owned by a public law enforcement agency or fire department and under the control of a peace officer or firefighter assigned to a canine unit that has been trained in matters, including, but not limited to, discovering controlled substances, explosives, cadavers, victims in collapsed structures, and peace officer on-command searches for suspects and victims at crime scenes.

(4) "Search and rescue dog" means a dog that is officially affiliated with, or sponsored by, a governmental agency and that has been trained and approved as a search and rescue dog, or that is currently registered and approved for search and rescue work with a search and rescue team affiliated with the California Emergency Management Agency. The term also includes a dog that is in training to become registered and approved for that work.

(c) Nothing in this section is intended to affect any civil remedies available for a violation of this section.

(d) This section is intended to provide accessibility without discrimination to a peace officer or firefighter with a peace officer's or firefighter's dog or a handler of a search and rescue dog with a search and rescue dog in hotels, lodging places, eating establishments, and public transportation.

(e) Nothing in this section is intended to prevent the removal of the search and rescue dog in the event the search and rescue dog creates an excessive disturbance to the quiet enjoyment of the property. In the event of an excessive disturbance, the peace officer, firefighter, or handler of the search and rescue dog shall be given a minimum of one warning notice of the excessive disturbance and an opportunity to correct the disturbance. The mere presence of the dog within the hotel, lodging establishment, food establishment, or public transportation shall not be considered an excessive disturbance. (Added by Stats.2008, c. 226 (A.B.2131), § 1. Amended by Stats.2010, c. 92 (A.B.2243), § 1.)

§ 54.27. Prelitigation letters and complaints to education entities; requirements; discipline

(a) An attorney who provides a prelitigation letter to an education entity shall do both of the following:

(1) Include the attorney's State Bar license number in the prelitigation letter.

(2) Within five business days of providing the prelitigation letter, send a copy of the prelitigation letter to the California Commission on Disability Access.

(b) An attorney who sends or serves a complaint against an education entity shall do both of the following:

(1) Send a copy of the complaint and submit information about the complaint in a standard format specified by the California Commission on Disability Access to the commission within five business days of sending or serving the complaint.

(2) Notify the California Commission on Disability Access within five business days of judgment, settlement, or dismissal of the claim or claims alleged in the complaint of the following information in a standard format specified by the commission:

(A) The date of the judgment, settlement, or dismissal.

(B) Whether or not the construction-related accessibility violations alleged in the complaint were remedied in whole or in part after the plaintiff filed a complaint.

(C) If the construction-related accessibility violations alleged in the complaint were not remedied in whole or in part after the plaintiff filed a complaint, whether or not another favorable result was achieved after the plaintiff filed the complaint.

(c) A violation of paragraph (2) of subdivision (a) or subdivision (b) shall constitute cause for the imposition of discipline of an attorney if a copy of the prelitigation letter, complaint, or notification of a case outcome is not sent to the California Commission on Disability Access within five business days. In the event the State Bar of California receives information indicating that an attorney has failed to send a copy of the prelitigation letter, complaint, or notification of a case outcome to the California Commission on Disability Access within five business days, the State Bar of California shall investigate to determine whether paragraph (2) of subdivision (a) or subdivision (b) has been violated.

(d) Notwithstanding subdivisions (a) and (b), an attorney is not required to send to the California Commission on Disability Access a copy of any subsequent prelitigation letter or amended complaint in the same dispute following the initial prelitigation letter or complaint, unless that subsequent prelitigation letter or amended complaint alleges a new construction-related accessibility claim.

(e) A prelitigation letter or notification of a case outcome sent to the California Commission on Disability Access shall be for the informational purposes of Section 8299.08 of the Government Code.

(f) The California Commission on Disability Access shall review and report on the prelitigation letters, complaints, and notifications of case outcomes it receives in the same manner as provided in Section 8299.08 of the Government Code.

(g) Paragraph (2) of subdivision (a) and subdivision (b) does not apply to a prelitigation letter or complaint sent or filed by an attorney employed or retained by a qualified legal services project or a qualified support center, as defined in Section 6213 of the Business and Professions Code, when acting within the scope of employment in asserting a construction-related accessibility claim. The Legislature finds and declares that qualified legal services projects and support centers are extensively regulated by the State Bar of California, and that there is no evidence of any abusive use of demand letters or complaints by these organizations. The Legislature further finds that, in light of the evidence of the extraordinarily small number of construction-related accessi-

§ 54.27

bility cases brought by regulated legal services programs, and given the resources of those programs, exempting regulated legal services programs from the requirements of this section to report to the California Commission on Disability Access will not affect the purpose of the reporting to, and tabulation by, the commission of all other construction-related accessibility claims.

(h) This section does not apply to a claim for money or damages against a public entity governed by Division 3.6 (commencing with Section 810) of Title 1 of the Government Code or make the requirements of this section applicable to such a claim.

(i) For purposes of this section, the following terms have the following meanings:

(1) "Complaint" means a civil complaint that is filed or is to be filed with a court and is sent to or served upon a defendant on the basis of one or more construction-related accessibility claims.

(2) "Construction-related accessibility claim" or "claim" means any claim of a violation of any construction-related accessibility standard, as defined in paragraph (6) of subdivision (a) of Section 55.52, with respect to a public building, public facility, or other public place of an education entity. "Construction-related accessibility claim" does not include a claim of interference with housing within the meaning of paragraph (2) of subdivision (b) of Section 54.1, or any claim of interference caused by something other than the construction-related accessibility condition of the property, including, but not limited to, the conduct of any person.

(3) "Education entity" means the Regents of the University of California, the Trustees of the California State University and the California State University, the office of the Chancellor of the California Community Colleges, a K–12 school district, or any local education agency.

(4) "Prelitigation letter" means a prelitigation written document that alleges the site is in violation of one or more construction-related accessibility standards, as defined in paragraph (6) of subdivision (a) of Section 55.52 and is provided to the education entity whether or not the attorney intends to file a complaint, or eventually files a complaint, in state or federal court. A prelitigation letter does not include a claim for money or damages against a local public entity governed by Division 3.6 (commencing with Section 810) of Title 1 of the Government Code. *(Added by Stats.2016, c. 892 (S.B.1406), § 1, eff. Jan. 1, 2017. Amended by Stats.2017, c. 561 (A.B.1516), § 16, eff. Jan. 1, 2018.)*

Cross References

Compilation and posting of data relating to demand letters or complaints sent to the commission, annual report, see Government Code § 14985.8.

§ 54.3. Violations; liability

(a) Any person or persons, firm or corporation who denies or interferes with admittance to or enjoyment of the public facilities as specified in Sections 54 and 54.1 or otherwise interferes with the rights of an individual with a disability under Sections 54, 54.1 and 54.2 is liable for each offense for the actual damages and any amount as may be determined by a jury, or the court sitting without a jury, up to a maximum of three times the amount of actual damages but in no case less than one thousand dollars ($1,000), and attorney's fees as may be determined by the court in addition thereto, suffered by any person denied any of the rights provided in Sections 54, 54.1, and 54.2. "Interfere," for purposes of this section, includes, but is not limited to, preventing or causing the prevention of a guide dog, signal dog, or service dog from carrying out its functions in assisting a disabled person.

(b) Any person who claims to be aggrieved by an alleged unlawful practice in violation of Section 54, 54.1, or 54.2 may also file a verified complaint with the * * * <u>Civil Rights Department</u> pursuant to Section 12948 of the Government Code. The remedies in this section are nonexclusive and are in addition to any other remedy provided by law, including, but not limited to, any action for injunctive or other equitable relief available to the aggrieved party or brought in the name of the people of this state or of the United States.

(c) A person may not be held liable for damages pursuant to both this section and Section 52 for the same act or failure to act. *(Added by Stats.1968, c. 461, p. 1092, § 1. Amended by Stats.1976, c. 971, p. 2270, § 2; Stats.1976, c. 972, p. 2274, § 2.5; Stats.1977, c. 881, p. 2650, § 1; Stats.1981, c. 395, § 1; Stats.1992, c. 913 (A.B.1077), § 7; Stats.1994, c. 1257 (S.B. 1240), § 4; Stats.1996, c. 498 (S.B.1687), § 2.3; Stats.2022, c. 48 (S.B.189), § 6, eff. June 30, 2022.)*

§ 54.4. Blind or visually impaired pedestrian; failure to carry cane or use guide dog

A blind or otherwise visually impaired pedestrian shall have all of the rights and privileges conferred by law upon other persons in any of the places, accommodations, or conveyances specified in Sections 54 and 54.1, notwithstanding the fact that the person is not carrying a predominantly white cane (with or without a red tip), or using a guide dog. The failure of a blind or otherwise visually impaired person to carry such a cane or to use such a guide dog shall not constitute negligence per se. *(Added by Stats.1968, c. 461, p. 1092, § 1. Amended by Stats.1994, c. 1257 (S.B.1240), § 5.)*

Cross References

Visually handicapped pedestrians, right-of-way, see Vehicle Code § 21963.

"Visually impaired" defined for purposes of this Part, see Civil Code § 54.6.

§ 54.5. White cane safety day; proclamation

Each year, the Governor shall publicly proclaim October 15 as White Cane Safety Day. He or she shall issue a proclamation in which:

(a) Comments shall be made upon the significance of this chapter.

(b) Citizens of the state are called upon to observe the provisions of this chapter and to take precautions necessary to the safety of disabled persons.

(c) Citizens of the state are reminded of the policies with respect to disabled persons declared in this chapter and he urges the citizens to cooperate in giving effect to them.

(d) Emphasis shall be made on the need of the citizenry to be aware of the presence of disabled persons in the community and to keep safe and functional for the disabled the streets, highways, sidewalks, walkways, public buildings, public facilities, other public places, places of public accommodation, amusement and resort, and other places to which the public is invited, and to offer assistance to disabled persons upon appropriate occasions.

(e) It is the policy of this state to encourage and enable disabled persons to participate fully in the social and economic life of the state and to engage in remunerative employment. *(Added by Stats.1968, c. 461, p. 1092, § 1. Amended by Stats.1994, c. 1257 (S.B.1240), § 6.)*

Cross References

Pedestrians' rights and duties, use of white canes in public places, see Vehicle Code § 21964.

§ 54.6. Visually impaired

As used in this part, "visually impaired" includes blindness and means having central visual acuity not to exceed $20/200$ in the better eye, with corrected lenses, as measured by the Snellen test, or visual acuity greater than $20/200$, but with a limitation in the field of vision such that the widest diameter of the visual field subtends an angle not greater than 20 degrees. *(Added by Stats.1968, c. 461, p. 1092, § 1. Amended by Stats.1994, c. 1257 (S.B.1240), § 7; Stats.2006, c. 538 (S.B.1852), § 38.)*

Cross References

Hiring of disabled persons, see Government Code § 19230.

§ 54.7. Zoos or wild animal parks; facilities for guide, service or signal dogs accompanying individuals with a disability

(a) Notwithstanding any other provision of law, the provisions of this part shall not be construed to require zoos or wild animal parks to allow guide dogs, signal dogs, or service dogs to accompany individuals with a disability in areas of the zoo or park where zoo or park animals are not separated from members of the public by a physical barrier. As used in this section, "physical barrier" does not include an automobile or other conveyance.

(b) Any zoo or wild animal park that does not permit guide dogs, signal dogs, or service dogs to accompany individuals with a disability therein shall maintain, free of charge, adequate kennel facilities for the use of guide dogs, signal dogs, or service dogs belonging to these persons. These facilities shall be of a character commensurate with the anticipated daily attendance of individuals with a disability. The facilities shall be in an area not accessible to the general public, shall be equipped with water and utensils for the consumption thereof, and shall otherwise be safe, clean, and comfortable.

(c) Any zoo or wild animal park that does not permit guide dogs to accompany blind or visually impaired persons therein shall provide free transportation to blind or visually impaired persons on any mode of transportation provided for members of the public.

Each zoo or wild animal park that does not permit service dogs to accompany individuals with a disability shall provide free transportation to individuals with a disability on any mode of transportation provided for a member of the public in cases where the person uses a wheelchair and it is readily apparent that the person is unable to maintain complete or independent mobility without the aid of the service dog.

(d) Any zoo or wild animal park that does not permit guide dogs to accompany blind or otherwise visually impaired persons therein shall provide sighted escorts for blind or otherwise visually impaired persons if they are unaccompanied by a sighted person.

(e) As used in this section, "wild animal park" means any entity open to the public on a regular basis, licensed by the United States Department of Agriculture under the Animal Welfare Act as an exhibit, and operating for the primary purposes of conserving, propagating, and exhibiting wild and exotic animals, and any marine, mammal, or aquatic park open to the general public. *(Added by Stats.1979, c. 525, p. 1718, § 1. Amended by Stats.1988, c. 1595, § 4; Stats.1994, c. 1257 (S.B.1240), § 8.)*

Cross References

"Visually impaired" defined for purposes of this Part, see Civil Code § 54.6.

§ 54.8. Individuals who are deaf or hard of hearing; assistive listening systems in civil or criminal proceedings; notice of need; availability; use in proceedings

(a) In any civil or criminal proceeding, including, but not limited to, traffic, small claims court, family court proceedings and services, and juvenile court proceedings, in any court-ordered or court-provided alternative dispute resolution, including mediation and arbitration, or in any administrative hearing of a public agency, where a party, witness, attorney, judicial employee, judge, juror, or other participant who is deaf or hard of hearing, the individual who is deaf or hard of hearing, upon his or her request, shall be provided with a functioning assistive listening system or a computer-aided transcription system. Any individual requiring this equipment shall give advance notice of his or her need to the appropriate court or agency at the time the hearing is set or not later than five days before the hearing.

(b) Assistive listening systems include, but are not limited to, special devices which transmit amplified speech by means of audio-induction loops, radio frequency systems (AM or FM), or infrared transmission. Personal receivers, headphones, and neck loops shall be available upon request by individuals who are deaf or hard of hearing.

(c) If a computer-aided transcription system is requested, sufficient display terminals shall be provided to allow the individual who is deaf or hard of hearing to read the real-time transcript of the proceeding without difficulty.

(d) A sign shall be posted in a prominent place indicating the availability of, and how to request, an assistive listening system and a computer-aided transcription system. Notice of the availability of the systems shall be posted with notice of trials.

(e) Each superior court shall have at least one portable assistive listening system for use in any court facility within the county. When not in use, the system shall be stored in a location determined by the court.

(f) The Judicial Council shall develop and approve official forms for notice of the availability of assistive listening systems and computer-aided transcription systems for individ-

§ 54.8

uals who are deaf or hard of hearing. The Judicial Council shall also develop and maintain a system to record utilization by the courts of these assistive listening systems and computer-aided transcription systems.

(g) If the individual who is deaf or hard of hearing is a juror, the jury deliberation room shall be equipped with an assistive listening system or a computer-aided transcription system upon the request of the juror.

(h) A court reporter may be present in the jury deliberating room during a jury deliberation if the services of a court reporter for the purpose of operating a computer-aided transcription system are required for a juror who is deaf or hard of hearing.

(i) In any of the proceedings referred to in subdivision (a), or in any administrative hearing of a public agency, in which the individual who is deaf or hard of hearing is a party, witness, attorney, judicial employee, judge, juror, or other participant, and has requested use of an assistive listening system or computer-aided transcription system, the proceedings shall not commence until the system is in place and functioning.

(j) As used in this section, "individual who is deaf or hard of hearing" means an individual with a hearing loss, who, with sufficient amplification or a computer-aided transcription system, is able to fully participate in the proceeding.

(k) In no case shall this section be construed to prescribe a lesser standard of accessibility or usability than that provided by Title II of the Americans with Disabilities Act of 1990 (Public Law 101–336)[1] and federal regulations adopted pursuant to that act. *(Added by Stats.1989, c. 1002, § 1. Amended by Stats.1992, c. 913 (A.B.1077), § 8; Stats.1993, c. 1214 (A.B.551), § 2; Stats.2001, c. 824 (A.B.1700), § 1; Stats.2018, c. 776 (A.B.3250), § 5, eff. Jan. 1, 2019.)*

[1] For public law sections classified to the U.S.C.A., see USCA–Tables.

Cross References

Witnesses, deaf or hearing impaired persons, appointment of interpreters, see Evidence Code § 754.

§ 54.9. Touch-screen self-service check-in devices at hotels or facilities providing passenger transportation services; manufacturers and distributors to offer devices containing necessary technology

(a) On and after January 1, 2009, a manufacturer or distributor of touch-screen devices used for the purpose of self-service check-in at a hotel or at a facility providing passenger transportation services shall offer for availability touch-screen self-service check-in devices that contain the necessary technology.

(b) For purposes of this section, "necessary technology" means technology that enables a person with a visual impairment to do the following:

(1) Enter any personal information necessary to process a transaction in a manner that ensures the same degree of personal privacy afforded to those without visual impairments.

(2) Use the device independently and without the assistance of others in the same manner afforded to those without visual impairments.

(c) For purposes of this section, "hotel" means any hotel, motel, bed and breakfast inn, or other similar transient lodging establishment, but it does not include any residential hotel as defined in Section 50519 of the Health and Safety Code.

(d) This section shall not be construed to preclude or limit any other existing right or remedy as it pertains to self-service check-in devices and accessibility. *(Added by Stats.2006, c. 546 (A.B.768), § 2.)*

§ 55. Violations; injunction; action by person actually or potentially aggrieved

Any person who is aggrieved or potentially aggrieved by a violation of Section 54 or 54.1 of this code, Chapter 7 (commencing with Section 4450) of Division 5 of Title 1 of the Government Code, or Part 5.5 (commencing with Section 19955) of Division 13 of the Health and Safety Code may bring an action to enjoin the violation. The prevailing party in the action shall be entitled to recover reasonable attorney's fees. *(Added by Stats.1974, c. 1443, p. 3150, § 1.)*

Cross References

Attorney General, prevailing party in enforcement action under this section, award of costs and fees to be made to Attorney General and paid to Public Rights Law Enforcement Special Fund, see Code of Civil Procedure § 1021.8; Government Code § 12530.

Construction-related accessibility claims, application for mandatory evaluation conference, see Civil Code § 55.545.

§ 55.1. Violations; injunctions; district or city attorney, attorney general

In addition to any remedies available under the federal Americans with Disabilities Act of 1990, Public Law 101-336 (42 U.S.C. Sec. 12102), or other provisions of law, the district attorney, the city attorney, the Department of Rehabilitation acting through the Attorney General, or the Attorney General may bring an action to enjoin any violation of Section 54 or 54.1. *(Added by Stats.1976, c. 869, p. 1979, § 1. Amended by Stats.1994, c. 1257 (S.B.1240), § 9.)*

Cross References

Attorney General, generally, see Government Code § 12500 et seq.

Awarding to Attorney General all costs of investigating and prosecuting the action relating to this section, see Code of Civil Procedure § 1021.8.

§ 55.2. Mandatory service on State Solicitor General of each party's brief or petition and brief in causes of action based on violation of civil rights statutes

If a violation of Section 54, 54.1, 54.2, or 54.3 is alleged or the application or construction of any of these sections is in issue in any proceeding in the Supreme Court of California, a state court of appeal, or the appellate division of a superior court, each party shall serve a copy of the party's brief or petition and brief, on the State Solicitor General at the Office of the Attorney General. No brief may be accepted for filing unless the proof of service shows service on the State Solicitor General. Any party failing to comply with this requirement shall be given a reasonable opportunity to cure the failure before the court imposes any sanction and, in that instance, the court shall allow the Attorney General reasonable additional time to file a brief in the matter. *(Added by Stats.2002, c. 244 (A.B.2524), § 2.)*

Cross References

Attorney General, generally, see Government Code § 12500 et seq.
Similar provisions, see Civil Code § 55.1; Government Code § 4461; Health and Safety Code §§ 19954.5 and 19959.5.

§ 55.3. Written advisory to accompany demand letter or complaint; contents

(a) For purposes of this section, the following apply:

(1) "Complaint" means a civil complaint that is filed or is to be filed with a court and is sent to or served upon a defendant on the basis of one or more construction-related accessibility claims, as defined in this section.

(2) "Construction–related accessibility claim" means any claim of a violation of any construction-related accessibility standard, as defined by paragraph (6) of subdivision (a) of Section 55.52, with respect to a place of public accommodation. "Construction–related accessibility claim" does not include a claim of interference with housing within the meaning of paragraph (2) of subdivision (b) of Section 54.1, or any claim of interference caused by something other than the construction-related accessibility condition of the property, including, but not limited to, the conduct of any person.

(3) "Demand for money" means a prelitigation written document or oral statement that is provided or issued to a building owner or tenant, or the owner's or tenant's agent or employee, that does all of the following:

(A) Alleges that the site is in violation of one or more construction-related accessibility standards, as defined in paragraph (6) of subdivision (a) of Section 55.52, or alleges one or more construction-related accessibility claims, as defined in paragraph (2).

(B) Contains or makes a request or demand for money or an offer or agreement to accept money.

(C) Is provided or issued whether or not the attorney intends to file a complaint, or eventually files a complaint, in state or federal court.

(4) "Demand letter" means a prelitigation written document that is provided to a building owner or tenant, or the owner's or tenant's agent or employee, that alleges the site is in violation of one or more construction-related accessibility standards, as defined in paragraph (6) of subdivision (a) of Section 55.52, or alleges one or more construction-related accessibility claims, as defined in paragraph (2), and is provided whether or not the attorney intends to file a complaint, or eventually files a complaint, in state or federal court.

(b) An attorney shall provide the following items with each demand letter or complaint sent to or served upon a defendant or potential defendant alleging a construction-related accessibility claim:

(1) A written advisory on the form described in subparagraph (B), or, until that form is available, on a separate page or pages that are clearly distinguishable from the demand letter or complaint. The advisory shall not be required in subsequent communications following the initial demand letter or initial complaint unless a new construction-related accessibility claim is asserted in the subsequent demand letter or amended complaint.

(A) The advisory shall state as follows:

STATE LAW REQUIRES THAT YOU GET THIS IMPORTANT ADVISORY INFORMATION FOR BUILDING OWNERS AND TENANTS

This information is available in English, Spanish, Chinese, Vietnamese, and Korean through the Judicial Council of California. Persons with visual impairments can get assistance in viewing this form through the Judicial Council Internet Web site at www.courts.ca.gov.

California law requires that you receive this information because the demand letter or court complaint you received with this document claims that your building or property does not comply with one or more existing construction-related accessibility laws or regulations protecting the civil rights of persons with disabilities to access public places.

YOU HAVE IMPORTANT LEGAL OBLIGATIONS. Compliance with disability access laws is a serious and significant responsibility that applies to all California building owners and tenants with buildings open for business to the public. You may obtain information about your legal obligations and how to comply with disability access laws through the Division of the State Architect at www.dgs.ca.gov. Information is also available from the California Commission on Disability Access at www.ccda.ca.gov/guide.htm.

YOU HAVE IMPORTANT LEGAL RIGHTS. The allegations made in the accompanying demand letter or court complaint do not mean that you are required to pay any money unless and until a court finds you liable. Moreover, RECEIPT OF A DEMAND LETTER OR COURT COMPLAINT AND THIS ADVISORY DOES NOT NECESSARILY MEAN YOU WILL BE FOUND LIABLE FOR ANYTHING. You will have the right if you are later sued to fully present your explanation why you believe you have not in fact violated disability access laws or have corrected the violation or violations giving rise to the claim.

You have the right to seek assistance or advice about this demand letter or court complaint from any person of your choice. If you have insurance, you may also wish to contact your insurance provider. Your best interest may be served by seeking legal advice or representation from an attorney, but you may also represent yourself and file the necessary court papers to protect your interests if you are served with a court complaint. If you have hired an attorney to represent you, you should immediately notify your attorney.

If a court complaint has been served on you, you will get a separate advisory notice with the complaint advising you of special options and procedures available to you under certain conditions.

ADDITIONAL THINGS YOU SHOULD KNOW:

ATTORNEY MISCONDUCT. Except for limited circumstances, state law generally requires that a prelitigation demand letter from an attorney MAY NOT MAKE A REQUEST OR DEMAND FOR MONEY OR AN OFFER

OR AGREEMENT TO ACCEPT MONEY. Moreover, a demand letter from an attorney MUST INCLUDE THE ATTORNEY'S STATE BAR LICENSE NUMBER.

If you believe the attorney who provided you with this notice and prelitigation demand letter is not complying with state law, you may send a copy of the demand letter you received from the attorney to the State Bar of California by facsimile transmission to 1-415-538-2171, or by mail to the State Bar of California, 180 Howard Street, San Francisco, CA, 94105, Attention: Professional Competence.

REDUCING YOUR DAMAGES. If you are a small business owner and correct all of the construction-related violations that are the basis of the complaint against you within 30 days of being served with the complaint, you may qualify for reduced damages. You may wish to consult an attorney to obtain legal advice. You may also wish to contact the California Commission on Disability Access for additional information about the rights and obligations of business owners.

COMMERCIAL TENANT. If you are a commercial tenant, you may not be responsible for ensuring that some or all portions of the premises you lease for your business, including common areas such as parking lots, are accessible to the public because those areas may be the responsibility of your landlord. You may want to refer to your lease agreement and consult with an attorney or contact your landlord, to determine if your landlord is responsible for maintaining and improving some or all of the areas you lease.

(B) On or before July 1, 2016, the Judicial Council shall update the advisory form that may be used by an attorney to comply with the requirements of subparagraph (A). The advisory form shall be in substantially the same format and include all of the text set forth in subparagraph (A). The advisory form shall be available in English, Spanish, Chinese, Vietnamese, and Korean, and shall include a statement that the advisory form is available in additional languages, and the Judicial Council Internet Web site address where the different versions of the advisory form are located. The advisory form shall include Internet Web site information for the Division of the State Architect and the California Commission on Disability Access.

(2) A verified answer form developed by the Judicial Council, which allows a defendant to respond to the complaint in the event a complaint is filed.

(A) The answer form shall be written in plain language and allow the defendant to state any relevant information affecting the defendant's liability or damages including, but not limited to, the following:

(i) Specific denials of the allegations in the complaint, including whether the plaintiff has demonstrated that he or she was denied full and equal access to the place of public accommodation on a particular occasion pursuant to Section 55.56.

(ii) Potential affirmative defenses available to the defendant, including:

(I) An assertion that the defendant's landlord is responsible for ensuring that some or all of the property leased by the defendant, including the areas at issue in the complaint, are accessible to the public. The defendant shall provide facts supporting that assertion, and the name and contact information of the defendant's landlord.

(II) Any other affirmative defense the defendant wishes to assert.

(iii) A request to meet in person at the subject premises, if the defendant qualifies for an early evaluation conference pursuant to Section 55.54.

(iv) Any other information that the defendant believes is relevant to his or her potential liability or damages, including that the defendant qualifies for reduced damages pursuant to paragraph (1) or (2) of subdivision (f) of Section 55.56, and, if so, any facts supporting that assertion.

(B) The answer form shall provide instructions to a defendant who wishes to file the form as an answer to the complaint. The form shall also notify the defendant that he or she may use the completed form as an informal response to a demand letter or for settlement discussion purposes.

(C) On or before July 1, 2016, the Judicial Council shall adopt the answer form that may be used by an attorney to comply with the requirements of this paragraph, and shall post the answer form on the Judicial Council Internet Web site.

(c) Subdivision (b) applies only to a demand letter or complaint made by an attorney. This section does not affect the right to file a civil complaint under any other law or regulation protecting the physical access rights of persons with disabilities. Additionally, this section does not require a party to provide or send a demand letter to another party before proceeding against that party with a civil complaint.

(d) This section does not apply to an action brought by the Attorney General or any district attorney, city attorney, or county counsel. (Added by Stats.2008, c. 549 (S.B.1608), § 2. Amended by Stats.2011, c. 419 (S.B.384), § 2; Stats.2012, c. 162 (S.B.1171), § 9; Stats.2012, c. 383 (S.B.1186), § 3, eff. Sept. 19, 2012; Stats.2015, c. 755 (A.B.1521), § 1, eff. Oct. 10, 2015.)

Cross References

Allegation of construction-related accessibility claim, statement of facts in complaint, verification by plaintiff, amendment of complaint, see Code of Civil Procedure § 425.50.
Violation of Civil Code § 55.3 cause for attorney discipline, see Business and Professions Code § 6106.2.

§ 55.31. Demand letter alleging construction-related accessibility claim; inclusion of statement of facts; inclusion of prelitigation settlement negotiation offer; prohibition on inclusion of request or demand for money or offer or agreement to accept money; prohibition on issuance of demand for money; violation; application

(a) Commencing January 1, 2013, a demand letter alleging a construction-related accessibility claim, as defined in subdivision (a) of Section 55.3, shall state facts sufficient to allow a reasonable person to identify the basis of the violation or violations supporting the claim, including all of the following:

(1) A plain language explanation of the specific access barrier or barriers the individual encountered, or by which the individual alleges he or she was deterred, with sufficient

information about the location of the barrier to enable a reasonable person to identify the access barrier.

(2) The way in which the barrier encountered interfered with the individual's full and equal use or access, or in which it deterred the individual, on each particular occasion.

(3) The date or dates of each particular occasion on which the individual encountered the specific access barrier, or on which he or she was deterred.

(b) A demand letter may offer prelitigation settlement negotiations, but shall not include a request or demand for money or an offer or agreement to accept money.

(1) With respect to potential monetary damages for an alleged construction-related accessibility claim or claims, a demand letter shall not state any specific potential monetary liability for any asserted claim or claims, and may only state: "The property owner or tenant, or both, may be civilly liable for actual and statutory damages for a violation of a construction-related accessibility requirement."

(2) Notwithstanding any other law, a demand letter meeting the requirements of this section shall be deemed to satisfy the requirements for prelitigation notice of a potential claim when prelitigation notice is required by statute or common law for an award of attorney's fees.

(3) This subdivision and subdivision (a) do not apply to a demand for money, which is governed by subdivision (c).

(c) An attorney, or a person acting at the direction of an attorney, shall not issue a demand for money as defined in subdivision (a) of Section 55.3. This subdivision does not apply to a demand letter as defined in subdivision (a) of Section 55.3.

(d)(1) A violation of subdivision (b) or (c) constitutes cause for the imposition of discipline of an attorney. Subdivisions (b) and (c) do not prohibit an attorney from presenting a settlement figure or specification of damages in response to a request from the building owner or tenant, or the owner's or tenant's authorized agent or employee, following a demand letter provided pursuant to Section 55.3.

(2) Any liability for a violation of subdivision (c) is as provided in paragraph (1) of this subdivision. A violation of subdivision (c) does not create a new cause of action.

(e) Subdivision (c) does not prohibit any prelitigation settlement discussion of liability for damages and attorney's fees that occurs after a written or oral agreement is reached between the parties for the repair or correction of the alleged violation or violations of a construction-related accessibility standard.

(f) Subdivision (c) shall not apply to a claim involving physical injury and resulting special damages, but a demand for money relating to that claim that is sent shall otherwise comply with the requirements of subdivision (a) and Section 55.32.

(g) Nothing in this section shall apply to a demand or statement of alleged damages made in a prelitigation claim presented to a governmental entity as required by state or federal law, including, but not limited to, claims made under Part 3 (commencing with Section 900) of Division 3.6 of the Government Code.

(h) If subdivision (c) is not operative or becomes inoperative for any reason, the requirements of subdivision (a) and Section 55.32 shall apply to any written demand for money.
(Added by Stats.2012, c. 383 (S.B.1186), § 4, eff. Sept. 19, 2012.)

§ 55.32. Demand letter or complaint; duties of attorney; violation; report by State Bar; review and report by California Commission on Disability Access; effect of expiration of ground for discipline; application

(a) An attorney who provides a demand letter, as defined in subdivision (a) of Section 55.3, shall do all of the following:

(1) Include the attorney's State Bar license number in the demand letter.

(2) Within five business days of providing the demand letter, send a copy of the demand letter, and submit information about the demand letter in a standard format specified by the California Commission on Disability Access on the commission's internet website pursuant to Section 14985.8 of the Government Code, to the commission.

(b) An attorney who sends or serves a complaint, as defined in subdivision (a) of Section 55.3, <u>or a complaint alleging that an internet website is not accessible,</u> shall do both of the following:

(1) Send a copy of the complaint and submit information about the complaint in a standard format specified by the California Commission on Disability Access on the commission's internet website pursuant to Section 14985.8 of the Government Code to the commission within five business days of sending or serving the complaint.

(2) Notify the California Commission on Disability Access within five business days of judgment, settlement, or dismissal of the claim or claims alleged in the complaint of the following information in a standard format specified by the commission on the commission's internet website pursuant to Section 14985.8 of the Government Code:

(A) The date of the judgment, settlement, or dismissal.

(B) Whether or not the construction-related accessibility violations <u>or accessibility violations related to an internet website</u> alleged in the complaint were remedied in whole or in part after the plaintiff filed a complaint or provided a demand letter, as defined by Section 55.3.

(C) If the construction-related accessibility violations <u>or accessibility violations related to an internet website</u> alleged in the complaint were not remedied in whole or in part after the plaintiff filed a complaint or provided a demand letter, as defined by Section 55.3, whether or not another favorable result was achieved after the plaintiff filed the complaint or provided the demand letter.

(D) Whether or not the defendant submitted an application for an early evaluation conference and stay pursuant to Section 55.54, whether the defendant requested a site inspection <u>of an alleged construction-related accessibility violation,</u> the date of any early evaluation conference, and the date of any site inspection <u>of an alleged construction-related accessibility violation.</u>

(c) A violation of paragraph (2) of subdivision (a) or subdivision (b) shall constitute cause for the imposition of discipline of an attorney if a copy of the demand letter,

§ 55.32

complaint, or notification of a case outcome is not sent to the California Commission on Disability Access in the standard format specified on the commission's internet website pursuant to Section 14985.8 of the Government Code within five business days. In the event the State Bar receives information indicating that an attorney has failed to send a copy of the demand letter, complaint, or notification of a case outcome to the California Commission on Disability Access in the standard format specified on the commission's internet website pursuant to Section 14985.8 of the Government Code within five business days, the State Bar shall investigate to determine whether paragraph (2) of subdivision (a) or subdivision (b) has been violated.

(d) Notwithstanding subdivisions (a) and (b), an attorney is not required to send to the California Commission on Disability Access a copy of any subsequent demand letter or amended complaint in the same dispute following the initial demand letter or complaint, unless that subsequent demand letter or amended complaint alleges a new construction-related accessibility claim.

(e) A demand letter or notification of a case outcome sent to the California Commission on Disability Access shall be for the informational purposes of Section 14985.8 of the Government Code. A demand letter received by the State Bar from the recipient of the demand letter shall be reviewed by the State Bar to determine whether subdivision (b) or (c) of Section 55.31 has been violated.

(f)(1) Notwithstanding Section 10231.5 of the Government Code, on or before April 30, 2019, and annually as part of the Annual Discipline Report, no later than April 30 thereafter, the State Bar shall report to the Legislature and the Chairs of the Senate and Assembly Judiciary Committees, both of the following with respect to demand letters received by the State Bar:

(A) The number of investigations opened to date on a suspected violation of subdivision (b) or (c) of Section 55.31.

(B) Whether any disciplinary action resulted from the investigation, and the results of that disciplinary action.

(2) A report to be submitted pursuant to this subdivision shall be submitted in compliance with Section 9795 of the Government Code.

(g) The California Commission on Disability Access shall review and report on the demand letters, complaints, and notifications of case outcomes it receives as provided in Section 14985.8 of the Government Code.

(h) The expiration of any ground for discipline of an attorney shall not affect the imposition of discipline for any act prior to the expiration. An act or omission that constituted cause for imposition of discipline of an attorney when committed or omitted prior to January 1, 2019, shall continue to constitute cause for the imposition of discipline of that attorney on and after January 1, 2019.

(i) Paragraph (2) of subdivision (a) and subdivision (b) shall not apply to a demand letter or complaint sent or filed by an attorney employed or retained by a qualified legal services project or a qualified support center, as defined in Section 6213 of the Business and Professions Code, when acting within the scope of employment in asserting a construction-related accessibility claim. The Legislature finds and declares that qualified legal services projects and support centers are extensively regulated by the State Bar of California, and that there is no evidence of any abusive use of demand letters or complaints by these organizations. The Legislature further finds that, in light of the evidence of the extraordinarily small number of construction-related accessibility cases brought by regulated legal services programs, and given the resources of those programs, exempting regulated legal services programs from the requirements of this section to report to the California Commission on Disability Access will not affect the purpose of the reporting to, and tabulation by, the commission of all other construction-related accessibility claims. (Added by Stats.2012, c. 383 (S.B.1186), § 6, eff. Sept. 19, 2012, operative Jan. 1, 2016. Amended by Stats.2015, c. 755 (A.B.1521), § 3, eff. Oct. 10, 2015, operative Jan. 1, 2019; Stats.2016, c. 872 (A.B.54), § 2, eff. Jan. 1, 2017, operative Jan. 1, 2019; Stats.2018, c. 659 (A.B.3249), § 147, eff. Jan. 1, 2019; Stats.2020, c. 36 (A.B.3364), § 11, eff. Jan. 1, 2021; Stats.2022, c. 897 (A.B.2917), § 1, eff. Jan. 1, 2023.)

Part 2.52

CONSTRUCTION–RELATED ACCESSIBILITY STANDARDS COMPLIANCE

Section
55.51. Short title; application.
55.52. Definitions.
55.53. Certified access specialists (CASp); post-inspection compliance requirements; conflicting regulations or standards; post-inspection notice to owner or tenant of public accommodation; inspection certificate.
55.54. Service of summons and complaint in construction-related accessibility claim action; simultaneous service of specified notice and application for early evaluation conference; actions following service; construction and application of provisions.
55.545. Mandatory evaluation conference; application; actions following application; construction and application of provisions.

Cross References

Business licenses and building permits for commercial property, informational notice providing additional resources relating to compliance with federal and state disability laws, see Government Code § 4469.5.

§ 55.51. Short title; application

This part shall be known, and may be cited, as the Construction–Related Accessibility Standards Compliance Act. Notwithstanding any other provision of law, the provisions of this part shall apply to any construction-related accessibility claim, as defined in this part, including, but not limited to, any claim brought under Section 51, 54, 54.1, or 55. *(Added by Stats.2008, c. 549 (S.B.1608), § 3.)*

Operative Effect

For operative effect of this section, see Stats.2008, c. 549 (S.B.1608), § 12.

§ 55.52. Definitions

(a) For purposes of this part, the following definitions apply:

(1) "Construction-related accessibility claim" means any civil claim in a civil action with respect to a place of public accommodation, including, but not limited to, a claim brought under Section 51, 54, 54.1, or 55, based wholly or in part on an alleged violation of any construction-related accessibility standard, as defined in paragraph (6).

(2) "Application for stay and early evaluation conference" means an application to be filed with the court that meets the requirements of subdivision (c) of Section 55.54.

(3) "Certified access specialist" or "CASp" means any person who has been certified pursuant to Section 4459.5 of the Government Code.

(4) "Meets applicable standards" means the site was inspected by a CASp and determined to meet all applicable construction-related accessibility standards pursuant to paragraph (1) of subdivision (a) of Section 55.53. A site that is "CASp inspected" on or before the effective date of the amendments made to this section by Senate Bill 1186 of the 2011–12 Regular Session of the Legislature means that the site "meets applicable standards."

(5) "Inspected by a CASp" means the site was inspected by a CASp and is pending a determination by the CASp that the site meets applicable construction-related accessibility standards pursuant to paragraph (2) of subdivision (a) of Section 55.53. A site that is "CASp determination pending" on or before the effective date of the amendments made to this section by Senate Bill 1186 of the 2011–12 Regular Session of the Legislature means that the site was "inspected by a CASp."

(6) "Construction-related accessibility standard" means a provision, standard, or regulation under state or federal law requiring compliance with standards for making new construction and existing facilities accessible to persons with disabilities, including, but not limited to, any provision, standard, or regulation set forth in Section 51, 54, 54.1, or 55 of this code, Section 19955.5 of the Health and Safety Code, the California Building Standards Code (Title 24 of the California Code of Regulations), the federal Americans with Disabilities Act of 1990 (Public Law 101–336; 42 U.S.C. Sec. 12101 et seq.), and the federal Americans with Disabilities Act Accessibility Guidelines (Appendix A to Part 36 of Title 28 of the Code of Federal Regulations).

(7) "Place of public accommodation" has the same meaning as "public accommodation," as set forth in Section 12181(7) of Title 42 of the United States Code and the federal regulations adopted pursuant to that section.

(8) "Qualified defendant" means a defendant in an action that includes a construction-related accessibility claim that is asserted against a place of public accommodation that met the requirements of "meets applicable standards" or "inspected by a CASp" prior to the date the defendant was served with the summons and complaint in that action. To be a qualified defendant, the defendant is not required to have been the party who hired any CASp, so long as the basis of the alleged liability of the defendant is a construction-related accessibility claim. To determine whether a defendant is a qualified defendant, the court need not make a finding that the place of public accommodation complies with all applicable construction-related accessibility standards as a matter of law. The court need only determine that the place of public accommodation has a status of "meets applicable standards" or "inspected by a CASp."

(9) "Site" means a place of public accommodation.

(b) Unless otherwise indicated, terms used in this part relating to civil procedure have the same meanings that those terms have in the Code of Civil Procedure. *(Added by Stats.2008, c. 549 (S.B.1608), § 3. Amended by Stats.2012, c. 383 (S.B.1186), § 7, eff. Sept. 19, 2012.)*

Operative Effect

For operative effect of this section, see Stats.2008, c. 549 (S.B.1608), § 12.

§ 55.53. Certified access specialists (CASp); post-inspection compliance requirements; conflicting regulations or standards; post-inspection notice to owner or tenant of public accommodation; inspection certificate

(a) For purposes of this part, a certified access specialist shall, upon completion of the inspection of a site, comply with the following:

§ 55.53

(1) For a meets applicable standards site, if the CASp determines the site meets all applicable construction-related accessibility standards, the CASp shall provide a written inspection report to the requesting party that includes both of the following:

(A) An identification and description of the inspected structures and areas of the site.

(B) A signed and dated statement that includes both of the following:

(i) A statement that, in the opinion of the CASp, the inspected structures and areas of the site meet construction-related accessibility standards. The statement shall clearly indicate whether the determination of the CASp includes an assessment of readily achievable barrier removal.

(ii) If corrections were made as a result of the CASp inspection, an itemized list of all corrections and dates of completion.

(2) For an inspected by a CASp site, if the CASp determines that corrections are needed to the site in order for the site to meet all applicable construction-related accessibility standards, the CASp shall provide a signed and dated written inspection report to the requesting party that includes all of the following:

(A) An identification and description of the inspected structures and areas of the site.

(B) The date of the inspection.

(C) A statement that, in the opinion of the CASp, the inspected structures and areas of the site need correction to meet construction-related accessibility standards. This statement shall clearly indicate whether the determination of the CASp includes an assessment of readily achievable barrier removal.

(D) An identification and description of the structures or areas of the site that need correction and the correction needed.

(E) A schedule of completion for each of the corrections within a reasonable timeframe.

(3) The CASp shall provide, within 30 days of the date of the inspection of a business that qualifies for the provisions of subparagraph (A) of paragraph (3) of subdivision (g) of Section 55.56, a copy of a report prepared pursuant to that subparagraph to the business.

(4) The CASp shall file, within 10 days of inspecting a business pursuant to subparagraph (A) of paragraph (3) of subdivision (g) of Section 55.56, a notice with the State Architect for listing on the State Architect's Internet Web site, as provided by subdivision (d) of Section 4459.7 of the Government Code, indicating that the CASp has inspected the business, the name and address of the business, the date of the filing, the date of the inspection of the business, the name and license number of the CASp, and a description of the structure or area inspected by the CASp.

(5) The CASp shall post the notice described in paragraph (4), in a form prescribed by the State Architect, in a conspicuous location within five feet of all public entrances to the building on the date of the inspection and instruct the business to keep it in place until the earlier of either of the following:

(A) One hundred twenty days after the date of the inspection.

(B) The date when all of the construction-related violations in the structure or area inspected by the CASp are corrected.

(b) For purposes of this section, in determining whether the site meets applicable construction-related accessibility standards when there is a conflict or difference between a state and federal provision, standard, or regulation, the state provision, standard, or regulation shall apply unless the federal provision, standard, or regulation is more protective of accessibility rights.

(c) Every CASp who conducts an inspection of a place of public accommodation shall, upon completing the inspection of the site, provide the building owner or tenant who requested the inspection with the following notice, which the State Architect shall make available as a form on the State Architect's Internet Web site:

NOTICE TO PRIVATE PROPERTY OWNER/TENANT:

YOU ARE ADVISED TO KEEP IN YOUR RECORDS ANY WRITTEN INSPECTION REPORT AND ANY OTHER DOCUMENTATION CONCERNING YOUR PROPERTY SITE THAT IS GIVEN TO YOU BY A CERTIFIED ACCESS SPECIALIST.

IF YOU BECOME A DEFENDANT IN A LAWSUIT THAT INCLUDES A CLAIM CONCERNING A SITE INSPECTED BY A CERTIFIED ACCESS SPECIALIST, YOU MAY BE ENTITLED TO A COURT STAY (AN ORDER TEMPORARILY STOPPING ANY LAWSUIT) OF THE CLAIM AND AN EARLY EVALUATION CONFERENCE.

IN ORDER TO REQUEST THE STAY AND EARLY EVALUATION CONFERENCE, YOU WILL NEED TO VERIFY THAT A CERTIFIED ACCESS SPECIALIST HAS INSPECTED THE SITE THAT IS THE SUBJECT OF THE CLAIM. YOU WILL ALSO BE REQUIRED TO PROVIDE THE COURT AND THE PLAINTIFF WITH THE COPY OF A WRITTEN INSPECTION REPORT BY THE CERTIFIED ACCESS SPECIALIST, AS SET FORTH IN CIVIL CODE SECTION 55.54. THE APPLICATION FORM AND INFORMATION ON HOW TO REQUEST A STAY AND EARLY EVALUATION CONFERENCE MAY BE OBTAINED AT www.courts.ca.gov/selfhelp–start.htm.

YOU ARE ENTITLED TO REQUEST, FROM A CERTIFIED ACCESS SPECIALIST WHO HAS CONDUCTED AN INSPECTION OF YOUR PROPERTY, A WRITTEN INSPECTION REPORT AND OTHER DOCUMENTATION AS SET FORTH IN CIVIL CODE SECTION 55.53. YOU ARE ALSO ENTITLED TO REQUEST THE ISSUANCE OF A DISABILITY ACCESS INSPECTION CERTIFICATE, WHICH YOU MAY POST ON YOUR PROPERTY.

(d)(1) Commencing July 1, 2010, a local agency shall employ or retain at least one building inspector who is a certified access specialist. The certified access specialist shall provide consultation to the local agency, permit applicants, and members of the public on compliance with state construction-related accessibility standards with respect to inspections of a place of public accommodation that relate to permitting, plan checks, or new construction, including, but not limited to, inspections relating to tenant improvements that may impact access. If a local agency employs or retains two or more certified access specialists to comply with this subdivision, at least one-half of the certified access specialists shall be building inspectors who are certified access specialists.

(2) Commencing January 1, 2014, a local agency shall employ or retain a sufficient number of building inspectors who are certified access specialists to conduct permitting and plan check services to review for compliance with state construction-related accessibility standards by a place of public accommodation with respect to new construction, including, but not limited to, projects relating to tenant improvements that may impact access. If a local agency employs or retains two or more certified access specialists to comply with this subdivision, at least one-half of the certified access specialists shall be building inspectors who are certified access specialists.

(3) If a permit applicant or member of the public requests consultation from a certified access specialist, the local agency may charge an amount limited to a reasonable hourly rate, an estimate of which shall be provided upon request in advance of the consultation. A local government may additionally charge or increase permitting, plan check, or inspection fees to the extent necessary to offset the costs of complying with this subdivision. Any revenues generated from an hourly or other charge or fee increase under this subdivision shall be used solely to offset the costs incurred to comply with this subdivision. A CASp inspection pursuant to subdivision (a) by a building inspector who is a certified access specialist shall be treated equally for legal and evidentiary purposes as an inspection conducted by a private CASp. Nothing in this subdivision shall preclude permit applicants or any other person with a legal interest in the property from retaining a private CASp at any time.

(e)(1) Every CASp who completes an inspection of a place of public accommodation shall, upon a determination that the site meets applicable standards pursuant to paragraph (1) of subdivision (a) or is inspected by a CASp pursuant to paragraph (2) of subdivision (a), provide the building owner or tenant requesting the inspection with a numbered disability access inspection certificate indicating that the site has undergone inspection by a certified access specialist. The disability access inspection certificate shall be dated and signed by the CASp inspector, and shall contain the inspector's name and license number. Upon issuance of a certificate, the CASp shall record the issuance of the numbered certificate, the name and address of the recipient, and the type of report issued pursuant to subdivision (a) in a record book the CASp shall maintain for that purpose.

(2) Beginning March 1, 2009, the State Architect shall make available for purchase by any local building department or CASp sequentially numbered disability access inspection certificates that are printed with a watermark or other feature to deter forgery and that comply with the information requirements specified in subdivision (a).

(3) The disability access inspection certificate may be posted on the premises of the place of public accommodation, unless, following the date of inspection, the inspected site has been modified or construction has commenced to modify the inspected site in a way that may impact compliance with construction-related accessibility standards.

(f) Nothing in this section or any other law is intended to require a property owner or tenant to hire a CASp. A property owner's or tenant's election not to hire a CASp shall not be admissible to prove that person's lack of intent to comply with the law. *(Added by Stats.2008, c. 549 (S.B.1608), § 3. Amended by Stats.2012, c. 383 (S.B.1186), § 8, eff. Sept. 19, 2012; Stats.2016, c. 13 (S.B.269), § 1, eff. May 10, 2016.)*

Operative Effect

For operative effect of this section, see Stats.2008, c. 549 (S.B.1608), § 12.

Cross References

Applicants and renewal applicants for local business license or equivalent instrument or permit, payment of additional fee, retention and use of funds by city, county, or city and county, transfer of funds to Disability Access and Education Revolving Fund, annual report, see Government Code § 4467.

Commercial property lease form or rental agreement, statement regarding Certified Access Specialist (CASp) inspection and construction-related accessibility standards, see Civil Code § 1938.

§ 55.54. Service of summons and complaint in construction-related accessibility claim action; simultaneous service of specified notice and application for early evaluation conference; actions following service; construction and application of provisions

(a)(1) An attorney who causes a summons and complaint to be served in an action that includes a construction-related accessibility claim, including, but not limited to, a claim brought under Section 51, 54, 54.1, or 55, shall, at the same time, cause to be served a copy of the application form specified in subdivision (c) and a copy of the following notice, including, until January 1, 2013, the bracketed text, to the defendant on separate papers that shall be served with the summons and complaint:

ADVISORY NOTICE TO DEFENDANT

YOU MAY BE ENTITLED TO ASK FOR A COURT STAY (AN ORDER TEMPORARILY STOPPING ANY LAWSUIT) AND EARLY EVALUATION CONFERENCE IN THIS LAWSUIT AND MAY BE ASSESSED REDUCED STATUTORY DAMAGES IF YOU MEET CERTAIN CONDITIONS.

If the construction-related accessibility claim pertains to a site that has a Certified Access Specialist (CASp) inspection report for that site, or to a site where new construction or improvement was approved after January 1, 2008, by the local building permit and inspection process, you may make an immediate request for a court stay and early evaluation conference in the construction-related accessibility claim by filing the attached application form with the court. You may be entitled to the court stay and early evaluation conference regarding the accessibility claim only if ALL of the statements in the application form applicable to you are true.

FURTHER, if you are a defendant described above (with a CASp inspection report or with new construction after January 1, 2008), and, to the best of your knowledge, there have been no modifications or alterations completed or commenced since the CASp report or building department approval of the new construction or improvement that impacted compliance with construction-related accessibility standards with respect to the plaintiff's claim, your liability for minimum statutory damages may be reduced to $1,000 for each offense, unless the violation was intentional, and if all construction-related accessibility violations giving rise to the claim are corrected within 60 days of being served with this complaint.

ALSO, if your business has been served with a complaint filed by a high-frequency litigant, as defined in subdivision (b) of Section 425.55 of the Code of Civil Procedure, asserting a construction-related accessibility claim, including, but not limited to, a claim brought under Section 51, 54, 54.1, or 55 of the Civil Code, you may also be entitled to a court stay and an early evaluation conference. If you choose to request a stay and early evaluation conference, you may also request to meet in person with the plaintiff and counsel for both parties, as well as experts if the parties so elect, at the subject premises no later than 30 days after issuance of the court order to jointly inspect the portions of the subject premises and review any conditions that are claimed to constitute a violation of a construction-related accessibility standard.

IN ADDITION, if your business is a small business that, over the previous three years, or the existence of the business if less than three years, employs 25 or fewer employees on average over that time period and meets specified gross receipts criteria, you may also be entitled to the court stay and early evaluation conference and your minimum statutory damages for each claim may be reduced to $2,000 for each offense, unless the violation was intentional, and if all the alleged construction-related accessibility violations are corrected within 30 days of being served with the complaint.

If you plan to correct the violations giving rise to the claim, you should take pictures and measurements or similar action to document the condition of the physical barrier asserted to be the basis for a violation before undertaking any corrective action in case a court needs to see the condition of a barrier before it was corrected.

The court will schedule the conference to be held within 70 days after you file the attached application form. [If you are not a defendant with a CASp inspection report, until a form is adopted by the Judicial Council, you may use the attached form if you modify the form and supplement it with your declaration stating any one of the following:

(1) Until January 1, 2018, that the site's new construction or improvement on or after January 1, 2008, and before January 1, 2016, was approved pursuant to the local building permit and inspection process; that, to the best of your knowledge, there have been no modifications or alterations completed or commenced since the building department approval that impacted compliance with construction-related accessibility standards with respect to the plaintiff's claim; and that all violations giving rise to the claim have been corrected, or will be corrected within 60 days of the complaint being served.

(2) That the site's new construction or improvement passed inspection by a local building department inspector who is a certified access specialist; that, to the best of your knowledge, there have been no modifications or alterations completed or commenced since that inspection approval that impacted compliance with construction-related accessibility standards with respect to the plaintiff's claim; and that all violations giving rise to the claim have been corrected, or will be corrected within 60 days of the complaint being served.

(3) That your business is a small business with 25 or fewer employees and meets the gross receipts criteria set out in Section 55.56 of the Civil Code, and that all violations giving rise to the claim have been corrected, or will be corrected within 30 days of being served with the complaint.]

The court will also issue an immediate stay of the proceedings unless the plaintiff has obtained a temporary restraining order in the construction-related accessibility claim. You may obtain a copy of the application form, filing instructions, and additional information about the stay and early evaluation conference through the Judicial Council Internet Web site at www.courts.ca.gov/selfhelp–start.htm.

You may file the application after you are served with a summons and complaint, but no later than your first court pleading or appearance in this case, which is due within 30 days after you receive the summons and complaint. If you do not file the application, you will still need to file your reply to the lawsuit within 30 days after you receive the summons and complaint to contest it. You may obtain more information about how to represent yourself and how to file a reply without hiring an attorney at www.courts.ca.gov/selfhelp–start.htm.

You may file the application without the assistance of an attorney, but it may be in your best interest to immediately seek the assistance of an attorney experienced in disability access laws when you receive a summons and complaint. You may make an offer to settle the case, and it may be in your interest to put that offer in writing so that it may be considered under Section 55.55 of the Civil Code.

(2) An attorney who files a Notice of Substitution of Counsel to appear as counsel for a plaintiff who, acting in propria persona, had previously filed a complaint in an action that includes a construction-related accessibility claim, including, but not limited to, a claim brought under Section 51, 54, 54.1, or 55, shall, at the same time, cause to be served a copy of the application form specified in subdivision (c) and a copy of the notice specified in paragraph (1) upon the defendant on separate pages that shall be attached to the Notice of Substitution of Counsel.

(b)(1) Notwithstanding any other law, upon being served with a summons and complaint asserting a construction-related accessibility claim, including, but not limited to, a claim brought under Section 51, 54, 54.1, or 55, a qualified defendant, or other defendant as defined in paragraph (2), may file a request for a court stay and early evaluation conference in the proceedings of that claim prior to or simultaneous with that defendant's responsive pleading or other initial appearance in the action that includes the claim. If that defendant filed a timely request for stay and early evaluation conference before a responsive pleading was due, the period for filing a responsive pleading shall be tolled until the stay is lifted. Any responsive pleading filed simultaneously with a request for stay and early evaluation conference may be amended without prejudice, and the period for filing that amendment shall be tolled until the stay is lifted.

(2) This subdivision shall also apply to a defendant if any of the following apply:

(A) Until January 1, 2018, the site's new construction or improvement on or after January 1, 2008, and before January 1, 2016, was approved pursuant to the local building permit and inspection process, and the defendant declares with the application that, to the best of the defendant's knowledge, there have been no modifications or alterations completed or commenced since that approval that impacted compliance with construction-related accessibility standards with respect to the plaintiff's claim, and that all violations have been corrected, or will be corrected within 60 days of being served with the complaint.

(B) The site's new construction or improvement was approved by a local public building department inspector who is a certified access specialist, and the defendant declares with the application that, to the best of the defendant's knowledge, there have been no modifications or alterations completed or commenced since that approval that impacted compliance with construction-related accessibility standards with respect to the plaintiff's claim, and that all violations have been corrected, or will be corrected within 60 days of being served with the complaint.

(C) The defendant is a small business described in subdivision (f) of Section 55.56, and the defendant declares with the application that all violations have been corrected, or will be corrected within 30 days of being served with the complaint.

(D) The defendant is a business that has been served with a complaint filed by a high-frequency litigant, as defined in subdivision (b) of Section 425.55 of the Code of Civil Procedure, asserting a construction-related accessibility claim, including, but not limited to, a claim brought under Section 51, 54, 54.1, or 55.

(3) Notwithstanding any other law, if the plaintiff had acted in propria persona in filing a complaint that includes a construction-related accessibility claim, including, but not limited to, a claim brought under Section 51, 54, 54.1, or 55, a qualified defendant, or a defendant described by paragraph (2), who is served with a Notice of Substitution of Counsel shall have 30 days to file an application for a stay and an early evaluation conference. The application may be filed prior to or after the defendant's filing of a responsive pleading or other initial appearance in the action that includes the claim, except that an application may not be filed in a claim in which an early evaluation conference or settlement conference has already been held on the claim.

(c)(1) An application for an early evaluation conference and stay by a qualified defendant shall include a signed declaration that states both of the following:

(A) The site identified in the complaint has been CASp-inspected or meets applicable standards, or is CASp determination pending or has been inspected by a CASp, and if the site is CASp-inspected or meets applicable standards, there have been no modifications completed or commenced since the date of inspection that may impact compliance with construction-related accessibility standards to the best of the defendant's knowledge.

(B) An inspection report pertaining to the site has been issued by a CASp. The inspection report shall be provided to the court and the plaintiff at least 15 days prior to the court date set for the early evaluation conference.

(2) An application for an early evaluation conference and stay by a defendant described by subparagraph (A) of paragraph (2) of subdivision (b), which may be filed until January 1, 2018, shall include a signed declaration that states all of the following:

(A) The site's new construction or improvement was approved pursuant to the local building permit and inspection process on or after January 1, 2008, and before January 1, 2016.

(B) To the best of the defendant's knowledge there have been no modifications or alterations completed or commenced since that approval that impacted compliance with construction-related accessibility standards with respect to the plaintiff's claim.

(C) All construction-related violations giving rise to the claim have been corrected, or will be corrected within 60 days of the complaint being served upon the defendant.

(3) An application for an early evaluation conference and stay by a defendant described in subparagraph (B) of paragraph (2) of subdivision (b) shall include a signed declaration that states all of the following:

(A) The site's new construction or improvement was approved by a local building department inspector who is a certified access specialist.

(B) To the best of the defendant's knowledge there have been no modifications or alterations completed or commenced since that approval that impacted compliance with construction-related accessibility standards with respect to the plaintiff's claim.

(C) All construction related violations giving rise to the claim have been corrected, or will be corrected within 60 days of the complaint being served upon the defendant.

(4) An application for an early evaluation conference and stay by a defendant described by subparagraph (C) of paragraph (2) of subdivision (b) shall include the materials listed in paragraphs (5) and (6) of this subdivision, and shall include a signed declaration that states both of the following:

(A) The defendant is a small business that employs 25 or fewer employees and meets the gross receipts eligibility criteria provided in paragraph (2) of subdivision (f) of Section 55.56.

(B) All construction-related violations giving rise to the claim have been corrected, or will be corrected within 30 days of the complaint being served upon the defendant.

(5) An application for an early evaluation conference and stay by a small business defendant under paragraph (4) shall

§ 55.54

include evidence showing correction of all violations within 30 days of the service of the complaint and served upon the plaintiff with the reply unless the application is filed prior to completion of the corrections. In that event, the evidence shall be provided to the court and served upon the plaintiff within 10 days of the court order as provided in paragraph (4) of subdivision (d). This paragraph shall not be construed to extend the permissible time under subdivision (f) of Section 55.56 to make the corrections.

(6) An application for an early evaluation conference and stay by a small business defendant under paragraph (4) shall also include both of the following, which shall be confidential documents filed only with the court and not served upon or available to the plaintiff:

(A) Proof of the defendant's number of employees, as shown by wage report forms filed with the Employment Development Department.

(B) Proof of the defendant's average gross receipts for the previous three years, or for the existence of the business if less than three years, as shown by a federal or state tax document.

(7) An application for an early evaluation conference and stay by a defendant described by subparagraph (D) of paragraph (2) of subdivision (b) shall include a signed declaration that the defendant was served with a complaint filed by a high-frequency litigant, as defined in subdivision (b) of Section 425.55 of the Code of Civil Procedure, asserting a construction-related accessibility claim, including, but not limited to, a claim brought under Section 51, 54, 54.1, or 55.

(8) The following provisional request and notice forms may be used and filed by a qualified defendant until forms are adopted by the Judicial Council for those purposes pursuant to subdivision (*l*):

ACCESSIBILITY STANDARDS § 55.54

ATTORNEY OR PARTY WITHOUT ATTORNEY (Name, State Bar number if attorney, and address):	FOR COURT USE ONLY
TELEPHONE NO.: FAX NO. (Optional):	
E-MAIL ADDRESS (Optional):	
ATTORNEY FOR (Name):	

SUPERIOR COURT OF CALIFORNIA, COUNTY OF _____
STREET ADDRESS:
MAILING ADDRESS:
CITY AND ZIP CODE:
BRANCH NAME:

PLAINTIFF:
DEFENDANT:

DEFENDANT'S APPLICATION FOR STAY AND EARLY EVALUATION CONFERENCE PURSUANT TO CIVIL CODE SECTION 55.54 (CONSTRUCTION-RELATED ACCESSIBILITY CLAIM)	**CASE NUMBER:**

(Information about this application and the filing instructions may be obtained at http://www.courtinfo.ca.gov/selfhelp/.)

1. Defendant (name)_____ requests a stay of proceedings and early evaluation conference pursuant to Civil Code Section 55.54.

2. The complaint in this case alleges a construction-related accessibility claim as defined under Civil Code Section 55.52(a)(1).

3. The claim concerns a site that (check the box if the statement is true):
   a. _____ Has been inspected by a Certified Access Specialist (CASp) and determined to be CASp inspected or CASp determination pending and, if CASp inspected, there have been no modifications completed or commenced since the date of inspection that may impact compliance with construction-related accessibility standards to the best of defendant's knowledge; and
   b. _____ An inspection report by a Certified Access Specialist (CASp) relating to the site has been issued.
   (Both (a) and (b) must be met for the court to order a Stay and Early Evaluation Conference.)

4. I am requesting the court to:
   a. Stay the proceedings relating to the construction-related accessibility claim.
   b. Schedule an early evaluation conference.
   c. Order Defendant to file a confidential copy of the Certified Access Specialist (CASp) report with the court and serve a copy of the report on the Plaintiff at least fifteen (15) days before the Early Evaluation Conference date.
   d. Order Plaintiff to file the statement required by Civil Code Section 55.54(d)(6)(A)–(D) with the court and serve a copy of the statement on the Defendant at least fifteen (15) days before the date of the Early Evaluation Conference.

I declare under penalty of perjury under the laws of the State of California that the foregoing is true and correct.

Date:

_____   _____
(TYPE OR PRINT NAME OF DECLARANT)   (SIGNATURE OF DECLARANT)

_____
(TITLE OF DECLARANT)

DEFENDANT'S APPLICATION FOR EARLY EVALUATION CONFERENCE AND STAY OF PROCEEDINGS
(Construction-related Accessibility Claim)   Provisional Form

§ 55.54   PERSONS

ATTORNEY OR PARTY WITHOUT ATTORNEY (Name, State Bar number if attorney, and address):	FOR COURT USE ONLY
TELEPHONE NO.: FAX NO. (Optional):	
E-MAIL ADDRESS (Optional):	
ATTORNEY FOR (Name):	
SUPERIOR COURT OF CALIFORNIA, COUNTY OF _____	
STREET ADDRESS:	
MAILING ADDRESS:	
CITY AND ZIP CODE:	
BRANCH NAME:	
PLAINTIFF:	
DEFENDANT:	
NOTICE OF STAY OR PROCEEDINGS AND EARLY EVALUATION CONFERENCE (CONSTRUCTION-RELATED ACCESSIBILITY CLAIM)	CASE NUMBER:

Stay of Proceedings

For a period of 90 days from the date of the filing of this court notice, unless otherwise ordered by the court, the parties are stayed from taking any further action relating to the construction-related accessibility claim or claims in this case.

This stay does not apply to any construction-related accessibility claim in which the plaintiff has obtained temporary injunctive relief which is still in place.

Notice of Early Evaluation Conference

1. This action includes a construction-related accessibility claim under Civil Code Section 55.52(a)(1) or other provision of law.

2. A defendant has requested an early evaluation conference and a stay of proceedings under Civil Code Section 55.54.

3. The early evaluation conference is scheduled as follows:

   a. Date: Time: Dept.   Room:

   b. The conference will be held at _____ the court address shown above, or _____ at:

4. The plaintiff and defendant shall attend with any other person needed for settlement of the case unless, with court approval, a party's disability requires the party's participation by a telephone appearance or other alternate means or through the personal appearance of an authorized representative.

5. The defendant that requested the conference and stay of proceedings must file with the court and serve on all parties a copy of the CASp report for the site that is the subject of the construction-related accessibility claim at least fifteen (15) days before the date set for the early evaluation conference. The CASp report is confidential and only available as set forth below and in Civil Code Section 55.54(d)(4).

6. The CASp report shall be marked "CONFIDENTIAL" and may be disclosed only to counsel, the parties to the action, the parties' attorneys, those individuals employed or retained by the attorneys to assist in the litigation, and insurance representatives or others involved in the evaluation and settlement of the case.

7. The plaintiff shall file with the court and serve on all parties at least fifteen (15) days before the date set for the early evaluation conference a statement of, to the extent known, all of the following:
   a. An itemized list of specific issues on the subject premises that are the basis of the claimed construction-related accessibility violations in the plaintiff's complaint;
   b. The amount of damages claimed;
   c. The amount of attorney's fees and costs incurred to date, if any, that are being claimed; and
   d. Any demand for settlement of the case in its entirety.

ACCESSIBILITY STANDARDS § 55.54

8. A copy of this Notice and Order and the Defendant's Application shall be served on the plaintiff or plaintiff's attorney by hand delivering it or mailing it to the address listed on the complaint on the same date that the court issues this Notice and Order of Stay of Proceedings and Early Evaluation Conference.

Date: _____   Clerk, by _____, Deputy

More information about this Notice and Order and the defendant's application, and instructions to assist plaintiff and defendants in complying with this Notice and Order, may be obtained at http://www.courtinfo.ca.gov/selfhelp/.

Requests for Accommodation

Assistive listening systems, computer-assisted real-time captioning, or sign language interpreter services are available if you ask at least 5 days before the date on which you are to appear. Contact the clerk's office or go to www.courtinfo.ca.gov/forms for Request for Accommodations by Persons with Disabilities and Order (form MC-410). (Civil Code Section 54.8).

Proof of Service
(Required from Defendant Filing Application for Stay and Early Evaluation Conference)

I served a copy of the defendant's Application For Stay and Early Evaluation Conference Pursuant To Civil Code Section 55.54 and the court Notice and Order of Stay of Proceedings and Early Evaluation Conference (check one):

_____ On the Plaintiff's attorney

_____ On the Plaintiff who is not represented by an attorney

By hand delivering it or mailing it to the address listed on the complaint on the day the court issued this Notice and Order of Stay of Proceedings and Early Evaluation Conference.

I declare under penalty of perjury of the laws of the State of California that the foregoing is true and correct.

Date: _____

_____   _____
Type or Print Name   Signature

_____
Address of named person

NOTICE OF STAY OF PROCEEDINGS AND EARLY EVALUATION CONFERENCE
(Construction-related Accessibility Claim)   Provisional Form

(9) The provisional forms and any replacement Judicial Council forms shall include the defendant's declaration of proof of service of the application, the notice of the court's order, and the court's order pursuant to subdivision (d).

(d) Upon the filing of an application for stay and early evaluation conference by a qualified defendant, or a defendant described by paragraph (2) of subdivision (b), the court shall immediately issue an order that does all of the following:

(1) Grants a 90-day stay of the proceedings with respect to the construction-related accessibility claim, unless the plaintiff has obtained temporary injunctive relief that is still in place for the construction-related accessibility claim.

(2) Schedules a mandatory early evaluation conference for a date as soon as possible from the date of the order, but in no event later than 70 days after issuance of the order, and in no event earlier than 50 days after the filing of the request.

§ 55.54

(3) Directs the parties, and any other person whose authority is required to negotiate and enter into settlement, to appear in person at the time set for the conference. Appearance by counsel shall not satisfy the requirement that the parties or those with negotiation and settlement authority personally appear, provided, however, that the court may allow a party who is unable to attend in person due to his or her disability to participate in the hearing by telephone or other alternative means or through a representative authorized to settle the case.

(4)(A) Directs the qualified defendant to file with the court and serve on the plaintiff a copy of any relevant CASp inspection report at least 15 days before the date of the conference. The CASp inspection report is confidential and is available only as set forth in paragraph (5) of this subdivision and in paragraph (4) of subdivision (e).

(B) Directs a defendant described by subparagraph (A) or (B) of paragraph (2) of subdivision (b) who has filed a declaration stating that the violation or violations have been corrected, or will be corrected within 60 days of service of the complaint to file with the court and serve on the plaintiff evidence showing correction of the violation or violations within 10 calendar days after the completion of the corrections.

(C) Directs a defendant described by subparagraph (C) of paragraph (2) of subdivision (b) who has filed a declaration stating that the violation or violations have been corrected, or will be corrected within 30 days of service of the complaint to file with the court and serve on the plaintiff within 10 days after issuance of the court order evidence of correction of the violation or violations, if that evidence showing correction was not filed previously with the application and served on the plaintiff.

(5) Directs the parties that the CASp inspection report may be disclosed only to the court, the parties to the action, the parties' attorneys, those individuals employed or retained by the attorneys to assist in the litigation, and insurance representatives or others involved in the evaluation and settlement of the case.

(6) If the defendant so requests, directs the parties that no later than 30 days after issuance of the court order the parties and their counsel, accompanied by their experts if the parties so elect, shall meet in person at the subject premises. They shall jointly inspect the portions of the subject premises, and shall review any programmatic or policy issues, that are claimed to constitute a violation of a construction-related accessibility standard. The court may allow a plaintiff who is unable to meet in person at the subject premises to be excused from participating in a site visit or to participate by telephone or other alternative means for good cause. A plaintiff or plaintiff's counsel is not required, but may agree, to attend more than one in-person site meeting. A site inspection pursuant to this paragraph shall not affect the right of the parties to conduct otherwise appropriate discovery.

(7) Directs the plaintiff to file with the court and serve on the defendant at least 15 days before the date of the conference a statement that includes, to the extent reasonably known, for use solely for the purpose of the early evaluation conference, all of the following:

(A) An itemized list of specific conditions on the subject premises that are the basis of the claimed violations of construction-related accessibility standards in the plaintiff's complaint.

(B) The amount of damages claimed.

(C) The amount of attorney's fees and costs incurred to date, if any, that are being claimed.

(D) Any demand for settlement of the case in its entirety.

(e)(1) A party failing to comply with any court order may be subject to court sanction at the court's discretion.

(2)(A) The court shall lift the stay when the defendant has failed to file and serve the CASp inspection report prior to the early evaluation conference and has failed also to produce the report at the time of the early evaluation conference, unless the defendant shows good cause for that failure.

(B) The court shall lift the stay when a defendant described by paragraph (2) of subdivision (b) has failed to file and serve the evidence showing correction of the violation or violations as required by law.

(3) The court may lift the stay at the conclusion of the early evaluation conference upon a showing of good cause by the plaintiff. Good cause may include the defendant's failure to make reasonably timely progress toward completion of corrections noted by a CASp.

(4) The CASp inspection report filed and served pursuant to subdivision (d) shall remain confidential throughout the stay and shall continue to be confidential until the conclusion of the claim, whether by dismissal, settlement, or final judgment, unless there is a showing of good cause by any party. Good cause may include the defendant's failure to make reasonably timely progress toward completion of corrections noted by a CASp. The confidentiality of the inspection report shall terminate upon the conclusion of the claim, unless the owner of the report obtains a court order pursuant to the California Rules of Court to seal the record.

(f) All discussions at the early evaluation conference shall be subject to Section 1152 of the Evidence Code. It is the intent of the Legislature that the purpose of the evaluation conference shall include, but not be limited to, evaluation of all of the following, as applicable:

(1) Whether the defendant is entitled to the 90-day stay for some or all of the identified issues in the case, as a qualified defendant.

(2) The current condition of the site and the status of any plan of corrections, including whether the qualified defendant has corrected or is willing to correct the alleged violations, and the timeline for doing so.

(3) Whether subdivision (f) of Section 55.56 may be applicable to the case, and whether all violations giving rise to the claim have been corrected within the specified time periods.

(4) Whether the case, including any claim for damages or injunctive relief, can be settled in whole or in part.

(5) Whether the parties should share other information that may facilitate early evaluation and resolution of the dispute.

(g) Nothing in this section precludes any party from making an offer to compromise pursuant to Section 998 of the Code of Civil Procedure.

(h) For a claim involving a qualified defendant, as provided in paragraph (1) of subdivision (b), the court may schedule additional conferences and may extend the 90-day stay for good cause shown, but not to exceed one additional 90-day extension.

(i) Early evaluation conferences shall be conducted by a superior court judge or commissioner, or a court early evaluation conference officer. A commissioner shall not be qualified to conduct early evaluation conferences pursuant to this subdivision unless he or she has received training regarding disability access requirements imposed by the federal Americans with Disabilities Act of 1990 (Public Law 101–336; 42 U.S.C. Sec. 12101 et seq.), state laws that govern access to public facilities, and federal and state regulations adopted pursuant to those laws. For purposes of this subdivision, a "court early evaluation conference officer" means an attorney employed by the court who has received training regarding disability access requirements imposed by the federal Americans with Disabilities Act of 1990, state laws that govern access to public facilities, and federal and state regulations adopted pursuant to those laws. Attorneys serving in this capacity may also be utilized by the court for other purposes not related to these proceedings.

(j) Nothing in this part shall be deemed to make any inspection report, opinion, statement, or other finding or conclusion of a CASp binding on the court, or to abrogate in any manner the ultimate authority of the court to make all appropriate findings of fact and law. The CASp inspection report and any opinion, statement, finding, or conclusion therein shall be given the weight the trier of fact finds that it deserves.

(k) Nothing in this part shall be construed to invalidate or limit any California construction-related accessibility standard that provides greater or equal protection for the rights of individuals with disabilities than is afforded by the federal Americans with Disabilities Act (Public Law 101–336; 42 U.S.C. Sec. 12101 et seq.) and the federal regulations adopted pursuant to that act.

(*l*)(1) The Judicial Council shall, by January 1, 2013, prepare and post on its Internet Web site instructions and a form for use by a qualified defendant, or other defendant described by paragraph (2) of subdivision (b), to file an application for stay and early evaluation conference as provided in subdivisions (b) and (c), a form for the court's notice of stay and early evaluation conference, and any other forms appropriate to implement the provisions relating to early evaluation conferences. Until those forms are adopted, the Judicial Council shall post on its Internet Web site the provisional forms set forth in subdivision (c).

(2) Until the adoption of the forms as provided in paragraph (1), the provisional application form may be used by a defendant described by paragraph (2) of subdivision (b).

(3) In lieu of the provisions specified in number 3 of page 1 of the application form set forth in paragraph (7) of subdivision (c), the application shall include one of the following declarations of the defendant as to the basis for the application, as follows:

(A) That all of the following apply to a defendant described by subparagraph (A) of paragraph (2) of subdivision (b):

(i) The site's new construction or improvement was approved pursuant to the local building permit and inspection process on or after January 1, 2008, and before January 1, 2016.

(ii) To the best of the defendant's knowledge there have been no modifications or alterations completed or commenced since that approval that impacted compliance with construction-related accessibility standards with respect to the plaintiff's claim.

(iii) All the violations giving rise to the claim have been corrected, or will be corrected within 60 days of the complaint being served.

(B) That all of the following apply to a defendant described by subparagraph (B) of paragraph (2) of subdivision (b):

(i) The site's new construction or improvement was approved by a local public building department inspector who is a certified access specialist.

(ii) To the best of the defendant's knowledge there have been no modifications or alterations completed or commenced since that approval that impacted compliance with construction-related accessibility standards with respect to the plaintiff's claim.

(iii) All the violations giving rise to the claim have been corrected, or will be corrected within 60 days of the complaint being served.

(C) That both of the following apply to a defendant described by subparagraph (C) of paragraph (2) of subdivision (b):

(i) The defendant is a small business described in paragraph (2) of subdivision (f) of Section 55.56.

(ii) The violation or violations giving rise to the claim have been corrected, or will be corrected within 30 days of the complaint being served.

(4) In lieu of the provision specified in number 4(c) of page 1 of the application form set forth in paragraph (7) of subdivision (c), the application shall include a request that the court order the defendant to do either of the following:

(A) For a defendant who has filed a declaration stating that all violations have been corrected, or will be corrected within 60 days of service of the complaint, file with the court and serve on the plaintiff evidence showing correction of the violation or violations within 10 calendar days of the completion of the corrections.

(B) For a defendant who is a small business that has filed a declaration stating that all the violations have been corrected, or will be corrected within 30 days of the service of the complaint, file with the court and serve on the plaintiff evidence showing correction of the violation or violations within 10 calendar days after issuance of the court order, if that evidence showing correction was not filed previously with the application and served on the plaintiff.

(5) The Judicial Council shall also prepare and post on its Internet Web site instructions and cover pages to assist plaintiffs and defendants, respectively, to comply with their

§ 55.54

filing responsibilities under subdivision (d). The cover pages shall also provide for the party's declaration of proof of service of the pertinent document served under the court order.

(m) The stay provisions shall not apply to any construction-related accessibility claim in which the plaintiff has been granted temporary injunctive relief that remains in place.

(n) This section shall not apply to any action brought by the Attorney General, or by any district attorney, city attorney, or county counsel.

(*o*) The amendments to this section made by Senate Bill 1186 of the 2011–12 Regular Session of the Legislature shall apply only to claims filed on or after the operative date of that act. Nothing in this part is intended to affect any complaint filed before that date.

(p) Nothing in this part is intended to affect existing law regarding class action requirements. *(Added by Stats.2008, c. 549 (S.B.1608), § 3. Amended by Stats.2009, c. 569 (S.B.209), § 1; Stats.2012, c. 383 (S.B.1186), § 9, eff. Sept. 19, 2012; Stats.2015, c. 755 (A.B.1521), § 4, eff. Oct. 10, 2015.)*

Operative Effect

For operative effect of this section, see Stats.2008, c. 549 (S.B.1608), § 12.

Cross References

Pleadings in civil actions, protection of the civil rights of persons with disabilities, high-frequency litigants, see Code of Civil Procedure § 425.55.

§ 55.545. Mandatory evaluation conference; application; actions following application; construction and application of provisions

(a) A defendant who does not qualify for an early evaluation conference pursuant Section 55.54, or who forgoes the provisions of Section 55.54, may request a mandatory evaluation conference. A plaintiff may, if the defendant does not make the request with the filing of the responsive pleadings, request a mandatory evaluation conference by filing an application within 15 days of the defendant's filing of responsive pleadings.

(b) Upon being served with a summons and complaint asserting a construction-related accessibility claim, including, but not limited to, a claim brought under Section 51, 54, 54.1, or 55, a defendant may file an application for a mandatory evaluation conference in the proceedings of that claim simultaneously with the defendant's responsive pleading or other initial appearance in the action that includes the claim. Until the application form for the mandatory evaluation conference is developed by the Judicial Council and posted on its Internet Web site pursuant to subdivision (j), a defendant may request the calendaring of the mandatory evaluation conference in a separate application filed with the defendant's responsive pleadings.

(c) Upon the filing of a request or application for a mandatory evaluation conference by a defendant or plaintiff, the court shall schedule a mandatory evaluation conference for a date as soon as possible from the date of the request or application, but in no event later than 180 days after the date of request or application, or earlier than 120 days after the filing of the request or application. Upon mutual stipulation for an extension of the conference date, the mandatory evaluation conference may be extended for up to 30 days. The court's notice of conference shall also do all of the following:

(1) Direct the parties, and any other person whose authority is required to negotiate and enter into settlement, to appear in person at the time set for the conference. Appearance by counsel shall not satisfy the requirement that the parties, or those with negotiation and settlement authority, personally appear. However, the court may allow a party who is unable to attend in person due to his or her disability to participate in the hearing by telephone or other alternative means, or through a representative authorized to settle the case.

(2) Direct the plaintiff to file with the court and serve on the defendant, at least 30 days before the date of mandatory evaluation conference, a statement that includes, to the extent reasonably known, for use solely for the purpose of the mandatory evaluation conference, all of the following:

(A) An itemized list of specific conditions on the site that are the basis of the claimed violations of construction-related accessibility standards in the plaintiff's complaint.

(B) The amount of damages claimed.

(C) The amount of attorney's fees and costs incurred to date, if any, that are being claimed.

(D) Any demand for settlement of the case in its entirety.

(3) Direct the defendant to file with the court and serve on the plaintiff, at least 30 days before the date of the mandatory evaluation conference, a statement of the defendant detailing any remedial action or remedial correction plan undertaken, or to be undertaken, by the defendant to correct the alleged violations.

(d) A party failing to comply with any court order is subject to court sanction at the court's discretion.

(e) All discussions at the mandatory evaluation conference shall be subject to Section 1152 of the Evidence Code. It is the intent of the Legislature that the purpose of the evaluation conference shall include, but not be limited to, evaluation of all of the following:

(1) The current condition of the site and the status of any plan of correction, including whether the defendant has corrected, or is willing to correct, the alleged violations, and the timeline for doing so.

(2) Whether the case, including any claim for damages or injunctive relief, can be settled in whole or in part.

(3) Whether the parties should share other information that may facilitate evaluation and resolution of the dispute.

(f) Nothing in this section precludes any party from making an offer to compromise pursuant to Section 998 of the Code of Civil Procedure.

(g) The court may schedule additional conferences.

(h) Mandatory evaluation conferences shall be conducted by a superior court judge or commissioner, or by a court early evaluation conference officer as provided in subdivision (i) of Section 55.54.

(i) If an inspection report by a certified access specialist is offered by the defendant, the provisions of Section 55.54

relating to the use and confidentiality of that report shall apply.

(j)(1) The Judicial Council shall prepare and post on its Internet Web site instructions and a form for a party to use to file an application for a mandatory evaluation conference and a form for the court's notice of the mandatory evaluation conference. Until those forms are adopted, a party and the court may use an ad hoc form that complies with the requirements of this section.

(2) The Judicial Council shall also prepare and post on its Internet Web site instructions and cover pages to assist plaintiffs and defendants, respectively, to comply with their filing responsibilities under subdivision (c).

(k) The mandatory evaluation conference may, at the court's discretion, be scheduled or combined with the case management conference within the time period specified in subdivision (c).

(*l*) This section shall not apply to any action brought by the Attorney General, or by any district attorney, city attorney, or county counsel.

(m) This section shall apply only to claims filed on or after January 1, 2013. Nothing in this section is intended to affect any complaint filed before that date. *(Added by Stats.2012, c. 383 (S.B.1186), § 10, eff. Sept. 19, 2012.)*

Part 2.53

ATTORNEY'S FEES AND STATUTORY DAMAGES IN CONSTRUCTION–RELATED ACCESSIBILITY STANDARDS CLAIMS

Section
55.55. Attorney's fees and costs; additional factors to consider.
55.56. Statutory damages awards; grounds; rebuttable presumptions; exemption from liability.
55.57. Application of Part.

§ 55.55. Attorney's fees and costs; additional factors to consider

Notwithstanding subdivision (f) of Section 55.54, in determining an award of reasonable attorney's fees and recoverable costs with respect to any construction-related accessibility claim, the court may consider, along with other relevant information, written settlement offers made and rejected by the parties. Nothing in this section affects or modifies the inadmissibility of evidence regarding offers of compromise pursuant to Section 1152 of the Evidence Code, including, but not limited to, inadmissibility to prove injury or damage. (Added by Stats.2008, c. 549 (S.B.1608), § 4.)

Operative Effect

For operative effect of this section, see Stats.2008, c. 549 (S.B.1608), § 12.

§ 55.56. Statutory damages awards; grounds; rebuttable presumptions; exemption from liability

(a) Statutory damages under either subdivision (a) of Section 52 or subdivision (a) of Section 54.3 may be recovered in a construction-related accessibility claim against a place of public accommodation only if a violation or violations of one or more construction-related accessibility standards denied the plaintiff full and equal access to the place of public accommodation on a particular occasion.

(b) A plaintiff is denied full and equal access only if the plaintiff personally encountered the violation on a particular occasion, or the plaintiff was deterred from accessing a place of public accommodation on a particular occasion.

(c) A violation personally encountered by a plaintiff may be sufficient to cause a denial of full and equal access if the plaintiff experienced difficulty, discomfort, or embarrassment because of the violation.

(d) A plaintiff demonstrates that he or she was deterred from accessing a place of public accommodation on a particular occasion only if both of the following apply:

(1) The plaintiff had actual knowledge of a violation or violations that prevented or reasonably dissuaded the plaintiff from accessing a place of public accommodation that the plaintiff intended to use on a particular occasion.

(2) The violation or violations would have actually denied the plaintiff full and equal access if the plaintiff had accessed the place of public accommodation on that particular occasion.

(e)(1) The following technical violations are presumed to not cause a person difficulty, discomfort, or embarrassment for the purpose of an award of minimum statutory damages in a construction-related accessibility claim, as set forth in subdivision (c), where the defendant is a small business, as described by subparagraph (B) of paragraph (2) of subdivision (g), the defendant has corrected, within 15 days of the service of a summons and complaint asserting a construction-related accessibility claim or receipt of a written notice, whichever is earlier, all of the technical violations that are the basis of the claim, and the claim is based on one or more of the following violations:

(A) Interior signs, other than directional signs or signs that identify the location of accessible elements, facilities, or features, when not all such elements, facilities, or features are accessible.

(B) The lack of exterior signs, other than parking signs and directional signs, including signs that indicate the location of accessible pathways or entrance and exit doors when not all pathways, entrance and exit doors are accessible.

(C) The order in which parking signs are placed or the exact location or wording of parking signs, provided that the parking signs are clearly visible and indicate the location of accessible parking and van-accessible parking.

(D) The color of parking signs, provided that the color of the background contrasts with the color of the information on the sign.

(E) The color of parking lot striping, provided that it exists and provides sufficient contrast with the surface upon which it is applied to be reasonably visible.

(F) Faded, chipped, damaged, or deteriorated paint in otherwise fully compliant parking spaces and passenger access aisles in parking lots, provided that it indicates the required dimensions of a parking space or access aisle in a manner that is reasonably visible.

(G) The presence or condition of detectable warning surfaces on ramps, except where the ramp is part of a pedestrian path of travel that intersects with a vehicular lane or other hazardous area.

(2) The presumption set forth in paragraph (1) affects the plaintiff's burden of proof and is rebuttable by evidence showing, by a preponderance of the evidence, that the plaintiff did, in fact, experience difficulty, discomfort, or embarrassment on the particular occasion as a result of one or more of the technical violations listed in paragraph (1).

(3) This subdivision shall apply only to claims filed on or after the effective date of Senate Bill 269 of the 2015–16 Regular Session.

(f) Statutory damages may be assessed pursuant to subdivision (a) based on each particular occasion that the plaintiff was denied full and equal access, and not upon the number of violations of construction-related accessibility standards identified at the place of public accommodation where the denial of full and equal access occurred. If the place of public accommodation consists of distinct facilities that offer distinct services, statutory damages may be assessed based on each denial of full and equal access to the distinct facility, and not upon the number of violations of construction-related accessibility standards identified at the place of public accommodation where the denial of full and equal access occurred.

(g)(1) Notwithstanding any other law, a defendant's liability for statutory damages in a construction-related accessibility claim against a place of public accommodation is reduced to a minimum of one thousand dollars ($1,000) for each offense if the defendant demonstrates that it has corrected all construction-related violations that are the basis of a claim within 60 days of being served with the complaint, and the defendant demonstrates any of the following:

(A) The structure or area of the alleged violation was determined to be "CASp-inspected" or "meets applicable standards" and, to the best of the defendant's knowledge, there were no modifications or alterations that impacted compliance with construction-related accessibility standards with respect to the plaintiff's claim that were completed or commenced between the date of that determination and the particular occasion on which the plaintiff was allegedly denied full and equal access.

(B) The structure or area of the alleged violation was the subject of an inspection report indicating "CASp determination pending" or "Inspected by a CASp," and the defendant has either implemented reasonable measures to correct the alleged violation before the particular occasion on which the plaintiff was allegedly denied full and equal access, or the defendant was in the process of correcting the alleged violation within a reasonable time and manner before the particular occasion on which the plaintiff was allegedly denied full and equal access.

(C) For a claim alleging a construction-related accessibility violation filed before January 1, 2018, the structure or area of the alleged violation was a new construction or an improvement that was approved by, and passed inspection by, the local building department permit and inspection process on or after January 1, 2008, and before January 1, 2016, and, to the best of the defendant's knowledge, there were no modifications or alterations that impacted compliance with respect to the plaintiff's claim that were completed or commenced between the completion date of the new construction or improvement and the particular occasion on which the plaintiff was allegedly denied full and equal access.

(D) The structure or area of the alleged violation was new construction or an improvement that was approved by, and passed inspection by, a local building department official who is a certified access specialist, and, to the best of the defendant's knowledge, there were no modifications or alterations that affected compliance with respect to the plaintiff's claim that were completed or commenced between the completion date of the new construction or improvement and the particular occasion on which the plaintiff was allegedly denied full and equal access.

(2) Notwithstanding any other law, a defendant's liability for statutory damages in a construction-related accessibility claim against a place of public accommodation is reduced to a minimum of two thousand dollars ($2,000) for each offense if the defendant demonstrates both of the following:

(A) The defendant has corrected all construction-related violations that are the basis of a claim within 30 days of being served with the complaint.

(B) The defendant is a small business that has employed 25 or fewer employees on average over the past three years, or for the years it has been in existence if less than three years, as evidenced by wage report forms filed with the Economic Development Department, and has average annual gross receipts of less than three million five hundred thousand dollars ($3,500,000) over the previous three years, or for the years it has been in existence if less than three years, as evidenced by federal or state income tax returns. The average annual gross receipts dollar amount shall be adjusted biannually by the Department of General Services for changes in the California Consumer Price Index for All Urban Consumers, as compiled by the Department of Industrial Relations. The Department of General Services shall post that adjusted amount on its Internet Web site.

(3)(A) Notwithstanding any other law, a defendant shall not be liable for minimum statutory damages in a construction-related accessibility claim, with respect to a violation noted in a report by a certified access specialist (CASp), for a period of 120 days following the date of the inspection if the defendant demonstrates compliance with each of the following:

(i) The defendant is a business that, as of the date of inspection, has employed 50 or fewer employees on average over the past three years, or for the years it has been in existence if less than three years, as evidenced by wage report forms filed with the Employment Development Department.

(ii) The structure or area of the alleged violation was the subject of an inspection report indicating "CASp determination pending" or "Inspected by a CASp."

(iii) The inspection predates the filing of the claim by, or receipt of a demand letter from, the plaintiff regarding the alleged violation of a construction-related accessibility standard, and the defendant was not on notice of the alleged violation prior to the CASp inspection.

(iv) The defendant has corrected, within 120 days of the date of the inspection, all construction-related violations in the structure or area inspected by the CASp that are noted in the CASp report that are the basis of the claim.

(B) Notwithstanding any other law, a defendant who claims the benefit of the reduction of, or protection from liability for, minimum statutory damages under this subdivision shall disclose the date and findings of any CASp inspection to a plaintiff if relevant to a claim or defense in an action.

(4) A defendant may claim the protection from liability for minimum statutory damages under paragraph (3) only once for each structure or area inspected by a CASp, unless the inspected structure or area has undergone modifications or alterations that affect the compliance with construction-related accessibility standards of those structures or areas after the date of the last inspection, and the defendant obtains an additional CASp inspection within 30 days of final approval by the building department or certificate of occupancy, as appropriate, regarding the modification or alterations.

(5) If the defendant has failed to correct, within 120 days of the date of the inspection, all construction-related violations in the structure or area inspected by the CASp that are

§ 55.56

noted in the CASp report, the defendant shall not receive any protection from liability for minimum statutory damages pursuant to paragraph (3), unless a building permit is required for the repairs which cannot reasonably be completed by the defendant within 120 days and the defendant is in the process of correcting the violations noted in the CASp report, as evidenced by having, at least, an active building permit necessary for the repairs to correct the violation that was noted, but not corrected, in the CASp report and all of the repairs are completed within 180 days of the date of the inspection.

(6) This subdivision shall not be applicable to intentional violations.

(7) Nothing in this subdivision affects the awarding of actual damages, or affects the awarding of treble actual damages.

(8) This subdivision shall apply only to claims filed on or after the effective date of Chapter 383 of the Statutes of 2012, except for paragraphs (3), (4), and (5), which shall apply only to claims filed on or after the effective date of Senate Bill 269 of the 2015–16 Regular Session. Nothing in this subdivision is intended to affect a complaint filed before those dates, as applicable.

(h) This section does not alter the applicable law for the awarding of injunctive or other equitable relief for a violation or violations of one or more construction-related accessibility standards, nor alter any legal obligation of a party to mitigate damages.

(i) In assessing liability under subdivision (d), in an action alleging multiple claims for the same construction-related accessibility violation on different particular occasions, the court shall consider the reasonableness of the plaintiff's conduct in light of the plaintiff's obligation, if any, to mitigate damages.

(j) For purposes of this section, the "structure or area inspected" means one of the following: the interior of the premises, the exterior of the premises, or both the interior and exterior. *(Added by Stats.2008, c. 549 (S.B.1608), § 4. Amended by Stats.2012, c. 383 (S.B.1186), § 11, eff. Sept. 19, 2012; Stats.2013, c. 76 (A.B.383), § 9; Stats.2016, c. 13 (S.B.269), § 2, eff. May 10, 2016.)*

Operative Effect

For operative effect of this section, see Stats.2008, c. 549 (S.B.1608), § 12.

§ 55.57. Application of Part

(a) This part shall apply only to claims filed on or after January 1, 2009. Nothing in this part is intended to affect litigation filed before that date, and no inference shall be drawn from provisions contained in this part concerning the state of the law as it existed prior to January 1, 2009.

(b) Nothing in this part is intended to affect existing law regarding class action requirements. *(Added by Stats.2008, c. 549 (S.B.1608), § 4.)*

Part 2.55

SMALL BUSINESS GENDER DISCRIMINATION IN SERVICES COMPLIANCE ACT

Section
55.61. Short title.
55.62. Definitions; demand letters; written advisory notice; penalties; application.
55.63. Pamphlet or informational materials for use by businesses; rights and obligations; provision of pamphlet.

§ 55.61. Short title

This part shall be known, and may be cited, as the Small Business Gender Discrimination in Services Compliance Act.
(Added by Stats.2017, c. 156 (A.B.1615), § 1, eff. Jan. 1, 2018.)

§ 55.62. Definitions; demand letters; written advisory notice; penalties; application

(a) For purposes of this part, the following definitions apply:

(1) "Gender discrimination in pricing services claim" means any civil claim in a civil action with respect to a business establishment, including, but not limited to, a claim brought under Section 51 or 51.6, based wholly or in part on an alleged price difference charged for services of similar or like kind, against a person because of the person's gender.

(2) "Demand letter" means a prelitigation written document that is provided to a business alleging a gender discrimination in pricing services claim and demanding money, whether or not the attorney intends to file a complaint, or eventually files a complaint, in state court.

(b) An attorney shall provide the following items with each demand letter or complaint sent to or served upon a defendant or potential defendant alleging gender discrimination in pricing services, including, but not limited to, claims brought pursuant to Section 51 or 51.6:

(1) A copy of the written advisory notice as specified in subdivision (c). Until the Judicial Council adopts this notice, the attorney shall provide a written statement that replicates the advisory notice described in subdivision (c).

(2) A copy of the pamphlet or other informational material specified in Section 55.63, after the pamphlet or material is developed by the Department of Consumer Affairs.

(c) On or before January 1, 2019, the Judicial Council shall adopt a written advisory notice that shall be used by a plaintiff's attorney to comply with the requirements of paragraph (1) of subdivision (b). The advisory notice shall be available in English, Spanish, Chinese, Vietnamese, and Korean, and shall include a statement that the advisory notice is available in additional languages, and the Judicial Council Internet Web site address where the different versions of the advisory notice are located. The advisory notice shall state the following:

ADVISORY NOTICE TO DEFENDANT
STATE LAW REQUIRES THAT YOU GET THIS IMPORTANT ADVISORY INFORMATION FOR BUSINESSES

This information is available in English, Spanish, Chinese, Vietnamese, and Korean through the Judicial Council of California. Persons with visual impairments can get assistance in viewing this form through the Judicial Council Internet Web site at www.courts.ca.gov.

California law requires that you receive this information because the demand letter or court complaint you received with this document claims that you have discriminated, with respect to the price charged for services of similar or like kind, against a person because of that person's gender.

YOU HAVE IMPORTANT LEGAL OBLIGATIONS. State law requires that businesses charge the same price for the same services, or services of the same or similar kind, regardless of the customer's gender. In addition, state law requires that certain business establishments clearly and conspicuously disclose to their customers in writing the pricing for each standard service provided. The posting requirement applies to the following businesses:

(1) Tailors or businesses providing aftermarket clothing alterations.

(2) Barbers or hair salons.

(3) Dry cleaners and laundries providing services to individuals.

YOU HAVE IMPORTANT LEGAL RIGHTS. The allegations made in the accompanying demand letter or court complaint do not mean that you are required to pay any money unless and until a court finds you liable. Moreover, RECEIPT OF A DEMAND LETTER OR COURT COMPLAINT AND THIS ADVISORY DOES NOT NECESSARILY MEAN YOU WILL BE FOUND LIABLE FOR ANYTHING.

You have the right to seek assistance or advice about this demand letter or complaint from any person of your choice. If you have insurance, you may also wish to contact your insurance provider. Your best interest may be served by seeking legal advice or representation from an attorney, but you may also represent yourself and file the necessary court papers to protect your interests if you are served with a court complaint. If you have hired an attorney to represent you, you should immediately notify your attorney.

ADDITIONAL THINGS YOU SHOULD KNOW

WHEN YOU CAN AND CANNOT CHARGE DIFFERENT PRICES: The Gender Tax Repeal Act of 1995 (California Civil Code Section 51.6) prohibits a business from charging a different price for the same service because of the gender of the person receiving the service. However, you may charge different prices based specifically upon the amount of time, difficulty, or cost of providing the services.

POSTING PRICES: The Gender Tax Repeal Act of 1995 also requires that certain businesses clearly disclose to the customer in writing the price of each standard service provided. This pricing disclosure is required for the following businesses: tailors or businesses providing aftermarket clothing alterations; barbers or hair salons; dry cleaners and laundries providing service to individuals. The price list must be posted in a place where customers will likely see it and it must be in no less than 14–point boldface font. A business must also provide a written copy of the prices to the customer if one is requested by the customer. Finally, a business must clearly and conspicuously display a sign, in no less than 24–point font, that reads:

"CALIFORNIA LAW PROHIBITS ANY BUSINESS ESTABLISHMENT FROM DISCRIMINATING, WITH RESPECT TO THE PRICE CHARGED FOR SERVICES OF SIMILAR OR LIKE KIND, AGAINST A PERSON BECAUSE OF THE PERSON'S GENDER. A COMPLETE PRICE LIST IS AVAILABLE UPON REQUEST."

RIGHT TO CORRECT A POSTING VIOLATION ONLY: If you receive a written notice claiming that you have failed to properly post any of the above information, you have 30 days to correct the violation. If you fail to correct the violation you will be liable for a civil penalty of $1,000. (Note that the 30–day period to correct applies only to posting violations, not to discriminatory pricing violations.)

(d) This section does not apply to an action brought by the Attorney General or any district attorney, city attorney, or county counsel. *(Added by Stats.2017, c. 156 (A.B.1615), § 1, eff. Jan. 1, 2018.)*

§ 55.63. Pamphlet or informational materials for use by businesses; rights and obligations; provision of pamphlet

(a)(1) On or before January 1, 2019, the Department of Consumer Affairs shall develop a pamphlet or other informational materials for use by the following business establishments: tailors and businesses providing aftermarket clothing alterations; barbers and hair salons; and dry cleaners and laundries providing services to individuals. The pamphlet shall explain the business' rights and obligations under Section 51.6 in clear and concise language. Specifically, the pamphlet shall explain that the business is prohibited from charging different prices for services of similar or like kind based on the customer's gender, unless the price difference is based upon the amount of time, difficulty, or cost of providing the services and that the business shall disclose a price list and sign in the manner prescribed in subdivision (f) of Section 51.6. The pamphlet shall explain that a business has 30 days to correct any violation of the posting requirements in subdivision (f) of Section 51.6 and that a business that fails to correct within 30 days of receiving notice of the violation is liable for a civil penalty of one thousand dollars ($1,000). The department may include any other information that would help the business comply with Section 51.6. The department shall subsequently revise the pamphlet, as necessary.

(2) The department shall provide the pamphlet or other informational materials required by paragraph (1) to an affected business establishment at the time that the business establishment applies for or renews a license, at the time of any inspection, or at both times. The department shall post a copy of the pamphlet or other informational materials on its internet website.

(3) Commencing October 1, 2020, the department shall provide the pamphlet and other informational materials required by paragraph (1) in English, Spanish, Chinese, Tagalog, Vietnamese, and Korean.

(b) By October 1, 2020, the department shall develop a written notice explaining the requirements and obligations specified in Section 51.6. The notice shall be available in English, Spanish, Chinese, Tagalog, Vietnamese, and Korean. The department shall post a copy of the notice in each language on its internet website in a format available for download. The department shall subsequently revise the notice, as necessary. *(Added by Stats.2017, c. 156 (A.B.1615), § 1, eff. Jan. 1, 2018. Amended by Stats.2019, c. 293 (A.B.1607), § 2, eff. Jan. 1, 2020.)*

Part 2.57

GENDER NEUTRAL RETAIL DEPARTMENTS

Section
55.7. Legislative findings and declarations.
55.8. Gender neutral area in retail department stores that offer childcare items or toys for sale; 500 or more employees; penalties and fines.

§ 55.7. Legislative findings and declarations

The Legislature finds and declares both of the following:

(a) Unjustified differences in similar products that are traditionally marketed either for girls or for boys can be more easily identified by the consumer if similar items are displayed closer to one another in one, undivided area of the retail sales floor.

(b) Keeping similar items that are traditionally marketed either for girls or for boys separated makes it more difficult for the consumer to compare the products and incorrectly implies that their use by one gender is inappropriate. *(Added by Stats.2021, c. 750 (A.B.1084), § 1, eff. Jan. 1, 2022.)*

§ 55.8. Gender neutral area in retail department stores that offer childcare items or toys for sale; 500 or more employees; penalties and fines

(a) A retail department store that offers childcare items or toys for sale shall maintain a gender neutral section or area, to be labeled at the discretion of the retailer, in which a reasonable selection of the items and toys for children that it sells shall be displayed, regardless of whether they have been traditionally marketed for either girls or for boys.

(b) This section shall apply only to retail department stores that are physically located in California that have a total of 500 or more employees across all California retail department store locations. This section shall not apply to retail department stores that are physically located outside California.

(c) Beginning on January 1, 2024, a retail department store that fails to comply with this section is liable for a civil penalty, not to exceed two hundred fifty dollars ($250) for a first violation or five hundred dollars ($500) for a subsequent violation, which may be assessed and recovered in a civil action brought in the name of the people of the State of California by the Attorney General, or a district attorney or city attorney, in any court of competent jurisdiction. If the Attorney General, district attorney, or city attorney prevails in an action under this subdivision, the court shall award to the Attorney General, district attorney, or city attorney reasonable attorney's fees and costs.

(d) For purposes of this section:

(1) "Childcare item" means any product designed or intended by the manufacturer to facilitate sleep, relaxation, or the feeding of children, or to help children with sucking or teething.

(2) "Children" means persons 12 years of age or less.

(3) "Toy" means a product designed or intended by the manufacturer to be used by children when they play. *(Added by Stats.2021, c. 750 (A.B.1084), § 1, eff. Jan. 1, 2022.)*

Part 2.6

CONFIDENTIALITY OF MEDICAL INFORMATION

Chapter	Section
1. Definitions	56
2. Disclosure of Medical Information by Providers	56.10
2.5. Disclosure of Genetic Test Results by a Health Care Service Plan	56.17
2.6. Genetic Privacy	56.18
3. Use and Disclosure of Medical Information by Employers	56.20
4. Relationship of Chapters 2 and 3	56.25
4.1. Notifications	56.251
5. Use and Disclosure of Medical and Other Information by Third Party Administrators and Others	56.26
6. Relationship to Existing Law	56.27
7. Violations	56.35

Cross References

California Community Care Facilities Act, home health agency provision of incidental medical services in adult community care facility, conditions, see Health and Safety Code § 1507.1.

California Consumer Privacy Act of 2018, provisions not applicable to information collected by entity governed by the title, see Civil Code § 1798.145.

California Work Opportunity and Responsibility to Kids Act, disclosure between team members of information related to CalWORKs clients, see Welfare and Institutions Code § 11325.93.

Cannabis, confidentiality of patient information, see Business and Professions Code § 26162.

Childhood Lead Poisoning Prevention Act, legislative findings and declarations, posting of information, see Health and Safety Code § 124125.

Confidentiality of personal consumer information, exemption from disclosure requirements, see Health and Safety Code § 127673.81.

County integrated health and human services program, Humboldt, Mendocino, Alameda, and any additional counties, programs for funding and delivery of services, see Welfare and Institutions Code § 18986.86.

Customer records, security procedures, see Civil Code § 1798.81.5.

Death of person in custody, report to Attorney General, confidential medical information, see Government Code § 12525.

Disclosure of Controlled Substance Utilization Review and Evaluation System data, see Health and Safety Code § 11165.1.

Disease management organizations, receipt of medical information, confidentiality and disclosure, see Health and Safety Code § 1399.903.

Emergency medical services, suspension or revocation of licenses or certificates, see Health and Safety Code § 1798.200.

Health care service plans, filing of policies and procedures to protect the security of patient medical information, see Health and Safety Code § 1364.5.

Health care service plans, suspension or revocation of licenses, grounds for disciplinary action, see Health and Safety Code § 1386.

Human Immunodeficiency Virus (HIV) testing, sharing of health records among qualified entities, limited disclosure of information, implementation, see Health and Safety Code § 121026.

Immunization information systems, operation, see Health and Safety Code § 120440.

Patient access to health records, application of confidentiality and information laws, see Health and Safety Code § 123135.

Patient medical information, unlawful or unauthorized access or use, administrative penalty, see Health and Safety Code § 1280.15.

Pharmacy, disciplinary proceedings, unprofessional conduct, see Business and Professions Code § 4301.

Public employees' health benefits, disclosure of cost, utilization, actual claim payments, and contract allowance amounts for health care services rendered, see Government Code § 22854.5

Residential care facilities for persons with chronic life-threatening illness, licensing, see Health and Safety Code § 1568.02.

Residential care facilities for the elderly, incidental medical care, conditions, see Health and Safety Code § 1569.725.

State Ombudsman, access to medical or personal records, conditions, charge for copies, see Welfare and Institutions Code § 9724.

Transfer of inmates, transmission of mental health records, confidentiality, see Penal Code § 5073.

CHAPTER 1. DEFINITIONS

Section
56. Short title.
56.05. Definitions.
56.06. Business organized for the purpose of maintaining medical information in order to supply information to individual or health care provider for specified purposes; business offering hardware or software designed to make medical information available to individuals or health care providers; business licensed under Medicinal and Adult-Use Cannabis Regulation and Safety Act authorized to receive identification cards of information contained in physician's recommendation; confidentiality;
56.07. Medical profile, summary, or information provided; patient's written request; application.
56.1. Repealed.

Cross References

California Consumer Privacy Act of 2018, collection of confidential medical information, protected health information, covered entity or business governed by federal law, see Civil Code § 1798.146.

Forensic medical examination reports, sexual assault investigations, evidence sought from persons in custody, see Penal Code § 11160.1.

§ 56. Short title

This part may be cited as the Confidentiality of Medical Information Act. *(Added by Stats.1981, c. 782, § 2.)*

Cross References

Admission contracts for long-term health care facilities, confidential information, authorization of disclosure of information, see Health and Safety Code § 1599.73.

Medical information defined for purposes of this Part, see Civil Code § 56.05.

Mello–Granlund Older Californians Act, state ombudsman, access to medical or personal records, see Welfare and Institutions Code § 9724.

Professional photocopiers, see Business and Professions Code § 22450 et seq.

§ 56.05. Definitions

For purposes of this part:

(a) "Authorization" means permission granted in accordance with Section 56.11 or 56.21 for the disclosure of medical information.

(b) "Authorized recipient" means a person who is authorized to receive medical information pursuant to Section 56.10 or 56.20.

(c) "Confidential communications request" means a request by a subscriber or enrollee that health care service plan communications containing medical information be communicated to them at a specific mail or email address or specific telephone number, as designated by the subscriber or enrollee.

(d) "Contractor" means a person or entity that is a medical group, independent practice association, pharmaceutical benefits manager, or a medical service organization and is not a health care service plan or provider of health care. "Contractor" does not include insurance institutions as defined in subdivision (k) of Section 791.02 of the Insurance Code or pharmaceutical benefits managers licensed pursuant to the Knox-Keene Health Care Service Plan Act of 1975 (Chapter 2.2 (commencing with Section 1340) of Division 2 of the Health and Safety Code).

(e) "Enrollee" has the same meaning as that term is defined in Section 1345 of the Health and Safety Code.

(f) "Health care service plan" means an entity regulated pursuant to the Knox-Keene Health Care Service Plan Act of 1975 (Chapter 2.2 (commencing with Section 1340) of Division 2 of the Health and Safety Code).

(g) "Licensed health care professional" means a person licensed or certified pursuant to Division 2 (commencing with Section 500) of the Business and Professions Code, the Osteopathic Initiative Act or the Chiropractic Initiative Act, or Division 2.5 (commencing with Section 1797) of the Health and Safety Code.

(h) "Marketing" means to make a communication about a product or service that encourages recipients of the communication to purchase or use the product or service.

"Marketing" does not include any of the following:

(1) Communications made orally or in writing for which the communicator does not receive direct or indirect remuneration, including, but not limited to, gifts, fees, payments, subsidies, or other economic benefits, from a third party for making the communication.

(2) Communications made to current enrollees solely for the purpose of describing a provider's participation in an existing health care provider network or health plan network of a Knox-Keene licensed health plan to which the enrollees already subscribe; communications made to current enrollees solely for the purpose of describing if, and the extent to which, a product or service, or payment for a product or service, is provided by a provider, contractor, or plan or included in a plan of benefits of a Knox-Keene licensed health plan to which the enrollees already subscribe; or communications made to plan enrollees describing the availability of more cost-effective pharmaceuticals.

(3) Communications that are tailored to the circumstances of a particular individual to educate or advise the individual about treatment options, and otherwise maintain the individual's adherence to a prescribed course of medical treatment, as provided in Section 1399.901 of the Health and Safety Code, for a chronic and seriously debilitating or life-threatening condition as defined in subdivisions (d) and (e) of Section 1367.21 of the Health and Safety Code, if the health care provider, contractor, or health plan receives direct or indirect remuneration, including, but not limited to, gifts, fees, payments, subsidies, or other economic benefits, from a third party for making the communication, if all of the following apply:

(A) The individual receiving the communication is notified in the communication in typeface no smaller than 14–point type of the fact that the provider, contractor, or health plan has been remunerated and the source of the remuneration.

(B) The individual is provided the opportunity to opt out of receiving future remunerated communications.

(C) The communication contains instructions in typeface no smaller than 14–point type describing how the individual can opt out of receiving further communications by calling a toll-free number of the health care provider, contractor, or health plan making the remunerated communications. Further communication shall not be made to an individual who has opted out after 30 calendar days from the date the individual makes the opt-out request.

(i) "Medical information" means any individually identifiable information, in electronic or physical form, in possession of or derived from a provider of health care, health care service plan, pharmaceutical company, or contractor regarding a patient's medical history, mental <u>health application information</u>, mental or physical condition, or treatment. "Individually identifiable" means that the medical information includes or contains any element of personal identifying information sufficient to allow identification of the individual, such as the patient's name, address, electronic mail address, telephone number, or social security number, or other information that, alone or in combination with other publicly available information, reveals the identity of the individual.

<u>(j) "Mental health application information" means information related to a consumer's inferred or diagnosed mental health or substance use disorder, as defined in Section 1374.72 of the Health and Safety Code, collected by a mental health digital service.</u>

<u>(k) "Mental health digital service" means a mobile-based application or internet website that collects mental health application information from a consumer, markets itself as facilitating mental health services to a consumer, and uses the information to facilitate mental health services to a consumer.</u>

(*l*) "Patient" means a natural person, whether or not still living, who received health care services from a provider of health care and to whom medical information pertains.

(m) "Pharmaceutical company" means a company or business, or an agent or representative thereof, that manufactures, sells, or distributes pharmaceuticals, medications, or prescription drugs. "Pharmaceutical company" does not include a pharmaceutical benefits manager, as included in subdivision (c), or a provider of health care.

(n) "Protected individual" means any adult covered by the subscriber's health care service plan or a minor who can consent to a health care service without the consent of a parent or legal guardian, pursuant to state or federal law. "Protected individual" does not include an individual that lacks the capacity to give informed consent for health care pursuant to Section 813 of the Probate Code.

(*o*) "Provider of health care" means a person licensed or certified pursuant to Division 2 (commencing with Section

§ 56.05

500) of the Business and Professions Code; a person licensed pursuant to the Osteopathic Initiative Act or the Chiropractic Initiative Act; a person certified pursuant to Division 2.5 (commencing with Section 1797) of the Health and Safety Code; or a clinic, health dispensary, or health facility licensed pursuant to Division 2 (commencing with Section 1200) of the Health and Safety Code. "Provider of health care" does not include insurance institutions as defined in subdivision (k) of Section 791.02 of the Insurance Code.

(p) "Sensitive services" means all health care services related to mental or behavioral health, sexual and reproductive health, sexually transmitted infections, substance use disorder, gender affirming care, and intimate partner violence, and includes services described in Sections 6924, 6925, 6926, 6927, 6928, 6929, and 6930 of the Family Code, and Sections 121020 and 124260 of the Health and Safety Code, obtained by a patient at or above the minimum age specified for consenting to the service specified in the section.

(q) "Subscriber" has the same meaning as that term is defined in Section 1345 of the Health and Safety Code. *(Added by Stats.1981, c. 782, § 2. Amended by Stats.1984, c. 1391, § 3; Stats.1999, c. 526 (S.B.19), § 1; Stats.2000, c. 1067 (S.B.2094), § 1; Stats.2002, c. 853 (A.B.2191), § 1; Stats. 2003, c. 562 (A.B.715), § 1; Stats.2013, c. 444 (S.B.138), § 2; Stats.2021, c. 190 (A.B.1184), § 1, eff. Jan. 1, 2022; Stats.2022, c. 690 (A.B.2089), § 1, eff. Jan. 1, 2023.)*

Cross References

Adoption of unmarried minors, disclosure of information, release of information to providers of health care, see Family Code § 9201.

Attorney General, defense of providers of health care, see Government Code § 12511.5.

Human Immunodeficiency Virus (HIV), mandated blood testing and confidentiality to protect public health, disclosure to subject's providers of health care, see Health and Safety Code §§ 120985, 121010.

Indemnification of providers of health care, see Government Code § 827.

"Medical waste generator" defined to include providers of health care, see Health and Safety Code § 117705.

Patient medical information, unlawful or unauthorized access or use, administrative penalty, see Health and Safety Code § 1280.15.

Small quantity generator requirements, common storage facilities, permits, see Health and Safety Code § 117928.

Workers' compensation and insurance, death of health care worker from HIV-related disease, see Labor Code § 5406.6.

Workers' compensation and insurance, factors affecting employer's premium, disclosures by insurer, medical information, see Labor Code § 3762.

Workers' compensation and insurance, injury arising from provision of bloodborne disease, preventive care to health care worker, see Labor Code § 3208.05.

§ 56.06. Business organized for the purpose of maintaining medical information in order to supply information to individual or health care provider for specified purposes; business offering hardware or software designed to make medical information available to individuals or health care providers; business licensed under Medicinal and Adult-Use Cannabis Regulation and Safety Act authorized to receive identification cards of information contained in physician's recommendation; confidentiality; penalties

(a) Any business organized for the purpose of maintaining medical information * * * in order to make the information available to an individual or to a provider of health care at the request of the individual or a provider of health care, for purposes of allowing the individual to manage * * * their information, or for the diagnosis and treatment of the individual, shall be deemed to be a provider of health care subject to the requirements of this part. However, this section shall not be construed to make a business specified in this subdivision a provider of health care for purposes of any law other than this part, including laws that specifically incorporate by reference the definitions of this part.

(b) Any business that offers software or hardware to consumers, including a mobile application or other related device that is designed to maintain medical information * * * in order to make the information available to an individual or a provider of health care at the request of the individual or a provider of health care, for purposes of allowing the individual to manage * * * their information, or for the diagnosis, treatment, or management of a medical condition of the individual, shall be deemed to be a provider of health care subject to the requirements of this part. However, this section shall not be construed to make a business specified in this subdivision a provider of health care for purposes of any law other than this part, including laws that specifically incorporate by reference the definitions of this part.

(c) Any business that is licensed pursuant to Division 10 (commencing with Section 26000) of the Business and Professions Code that is authorized to receive or receives identification cards issued pursuant to Section 11362.71 of the Health and Safety Code or information contained in a physician's recommendation issued in accordance with Article 25 (commencing with Section 2525) of Chapter 5 of Division 2 of the Business and Professions Code shall be deemed to be a provider of health care subject to the requirements of this part. However, this section shall not be construed to make a business specified in this subdivision a provider of health care for purposes of any law other than this part, including laws that specifically incorporate by reference the definitions of this part.

(d) Any business that offers a mental health digital service to a consumer for the purpose of allowing the individual to manage the individual's information, or for the diagnosis, treatment, or management of a medical condition of the individual, shall be deemed to be a provider of health care subject to the requirements of this part. However, this section shall not be construed to make a business specified in this subdivision a provider of health care for purposes of any law other than this part, including laws that specifically incorporate by reference the definitions of this part.

(e) Any business described in this section shall maintain the same standards of confidentiality required of a provider of health care with respect to medical information disclosed to the business.

(f) Any business described in this section is subject to the penalties for improper use and disclosure of medical information prescribed in this part. *(Added by Stats.1993, c. 1004 (A.B.336), § 1. Amended by Stats.2007, c. 699 (A.B.1298), § 1; Stats.2013, c. 296 (A.B.658), § 1; Stats.2014, c. 913 (A.B.2747), § 2, eff. Jan. 1, 2015; Stats.2017, c. 561 (A.B. 1516), § 17, eff. Jan. 1, 2018; Stats.2018, c. 583 (A.B.2402),*

§ 3, eff. Jan. 1, 2019; Stats.2022, c. 690 (A.B.2089), § 2, eff. Jan. 1, 2023.)

Cross References

Medical information defined for purposes of this Part, see Civil Code § 56.05.

Patient defined for purposes of this Part, see Civil Code § 56.05.

"Provider of health care" defined for purposes of this Part, see Civil Code § 56.05.

§ 56.07. Medical profile, summary, or information provided; patient's written request; application

(a) Except as provided in subdivision (c), upon the patient's written request, any corporation described in Section 56.06, or any other entity that compiles or maintains medical information for any reason, shall provide the patient, at no charge, with a copy of any medical profile, summary, or information maintained by the corporation or entity with respect to the patient.

(b) A request by a patient pursuant to this section shall not be deemed to be an authorization by the patient for the release or disclosure of any information to any person or entity other than the patient.

(c) This section shall not apply to any patient records that are subject to inspection by the patient pursuant to Section 123110 of the Health and Safety Code and shall not be deemed to limit the right of a health care provider to charge a fee for the preparation of a summary of patient records as provided in Section 123130 of the Health and Safety Code. This section shall not apply to a health care service plan licensed pursuant to Chapter 2.2 (commencing with Section 1340) of Division 2 of the Health and Safety Code or a disability insurer licensed pursuant to the Insurance Code. This section shall not apply to medical information compiled or maintained by a fire and casualty insurer or its retained counsel in the regular course of investigating or litigating a claim under a policy of insurance that it has written. For the purposes of this section, a fire and casualty insurer is an insurer writing policies that may be sold by a fire and casualty licensee pursuant to Section 1625 of the Insurance Code. (Added by Stats.2000, c. 1066 (S.B.1903), § 1.)

Cross References

"Authorization" defined for purposes of this Part, see Civil Code § 56.05.

"Health care service plan" defined for purposes of this Part, see Civil Code § 56.05.

Medical information defined for purposes of this Part, see Civil Code § 56.05.

Patient defined for purposes of this Part, see Civil Code § 56.05.

§ 56.1. Repealed by Stats.1969, c. 1608, p. 3313, § 3

CHAPTER 2. DISCLOSURE OF MEDICAL INFORMATION BY PROVIDERS

Section
56.10. Authorization; compelled disclosure; other permitted disclosures.
56.1007. Disclosure of medical information to specified persons involved with patient's care or health care payments; disclosure of medical information for other purposes.

Section
56.101. Medical information; confidentiality; negligence; protection and preservation; patient access.
56.102. Disclosure of medical information by pharmaceutical company; authorizations, releases, consents, or waivers; exceptions.
56.103. Disclosure of a minor's medical information; mental health condition.
56.104. Patient's participation in outpatient treatment with psychotherapist; request for information; application of section.
56.105. Professional negligence actions; settlement or compromise; authorization to disclose medical records to persons or organizations defending professional liability.
56.106. Disclosure of minor's mental health records; minor removed from custody of parent or guardian.
56.107. Health care service plans; protected individual; confidential communications.
56.108. Prohibition on disclosure of medical information related to individual seeking or obtaining an abortion in response to subpoena or request; criteria; disclosure to law enforcement.
56.109. Prohibition on disclosure of medical information related to person or entity allowing a child to receive gender-affirming health care or gender-affirming mental health care in response to subpoena or request; criteria.
56.11. Authorization; form and contents.
56.12. Copy of authorization to patient or signatory on demand.
56.13. Further disclosure by recipient of medical information.
56.14. Communication of limitations of authorization to recipient of medical information.
56.15. Cancellation or modification of authorization; written notice.
56.16. Release of limited information on specific patient; written request by patient to prohibit.

§ 56.10. Authorization; compelled disclosure; other permitted disclosures

(a) A provider of health care, health care service plan, or contractor shall not disclose medical information regarding a patient of the provider of health care or an enrollee or subscriber of a health care service plan without first obtaining an authorization, except as provided in subdivision (b) or (c).

(b) A provider of health care, a health care service plan, or a contractor shall disclose medical information if the disclosure is compelled by any of the following:

(1) * * * A court * * * order * * *.

(2) * * * A board, commission, or administrative agency for purposes of adjudication pursuant to its lawful authority.

(3) * * * A party to a proceeding before a court or administrative agency pursuant to a subpoena, subpoena duces tecum, notice to appear served pursuant to Section 1987 of the Code of Civil Procedure, or any provision authorizing discovery in a proceeding before a court or administrative agency.

(4) * * * A board, commission, or administrative agency pursuant to an investigative subpoena issued under Article 2 (commencing with Section 11180) of Chapter 2 of Part 1 of Division 3 of Title 2 of the Government Code.

§ 56.10 PERSONS

(5) * * * An arbitrator or arbitration panel, when arbitration is lawfully requested by either party, pursuant to a subpoena duces tecum issued under Section 1282.6 of the Code of Civil Procedure, or another provision authorizing discovery in a proceeding before an arbitrator or arbitration panel.

(6) * * * A search warrant lawfully issued to a governmental law enforcement agency.

(7) * * * The patient or the patient's representative pursuant to Chapter 1 (commencing with Section 123100) of Part 1 of Division 106 of the Health and Safety Code.

(8) * * * A medical examiner, forensic pathologist, or coroner, when requested in the course of an investigation by a medical examiner, forensic pathologist, or coroner's office for the purpose of identifying the decedent or locating next of kin, or when investigating deaths that may involve public health concerns, organ or tissue donation, child abuse, elder abuse, suicides, poisonings, accidents, sudden infant deaths, suspicious deaths, unknown deaths, or criminal deaths, or upon notification of, or investigation of, imminent deaths that may involve organ or tissue donation pursuant to Section 7151.15 of the Health and Safety Code, or when otherwise authorized by the decedent's representative. Medical information requested by a medical examiner, forensic pathologist, or coroner under this paragraph shall be limited to information regarding the patient who is the decedent and who is the subject of the investigation or who is the prospective donor and shall be disclosed to a medical examiner, forensic pathologist, or coroner without delay upon request. A medical examiner, forensic pathologist, or coroner shall not disclose the information contained in the medical record obtained pursuant to this paragraph to a third party without a court order or authorization pursuant to paragraph (4) of subdivision (c) of Section 56.11.

(9) When otherwise specifically required by law.

(c) A provider of health care or a health care service plan may disclose medical information as follows:

(1) The information may be disclosed to providers of health care, health care service plans, contractors, or other health care professionals or facilities for purposes of diagnosis or treatment of the patient. This includes, in an emergency situation, the communication of patient information by radio transmission or other means between emergency medical personnel at the scene of an emergency, or in an emergency medical transport vehicle, and emergency medical personnel at a health facility licensed pursuant to Chapter 2 (commencing with Section 1250) of Division 2 of the Health and Safety Code.

(2) The information may be disclosed to an insurer, employer, health care service plan, hospital service plan, employee benefit plan, governmental authority, contractor, or other person or entity responsible for paying for health care services rendered to the patient, to the extent necessary to allow responsibility for payment to be determined and payment to be made. If (A) the patient is, by reason of a comatose or other disabling medical condition, unable to consent to the disclosure of medical information and (B) no other arrangements have been made to pay for the health care services being rendered to the patient, the information may be disclosed to a governmental authority to the extent necessary to determine the patient's eligibility for, and to obtain, payment under a governmental program for health care services provided to the patient. The information may also be disclosed to another provider of health care or health care service plan as necessary to assist the other provider or health care service plan in obtaining payment for health care services rendered by that provider of health care or health care service plan to the patient.

(3) The information may be disclosed to a person or entity that provides billing, claims management, medical data processing, or other administrative services for providers of health care or health care service plans or for any of the persons or entities specified in paragraph (2). However, * * * that disclosed information shall not be further disclosed by the recipient in a way that would violate this part.

(4) The information may be disclosed to organized committees and agents of professional societies or of medical staffs of licensed hospitals, licensed health care service plans, professional standards review organizations, independent medical review organizations and their selected reviewers, utilization and quality control peer review organizations as established by Congress in Public Law 97–248 [1] in 1982, contractors, or persons or organizations insuring, responsible for, or defending professional liability that a provider may incur, if the committees, agents, health care service plans, organizations, reviewers, contractors, or persons are engaged in reviewing the competence or qualifications of health care professionals or in reviewing health care services with respect to medical necessity, level of care, quality of care, or justification of charges.

(5) The information in the possession of a provider of health care or a health care service plan may be reviewed by a private or public body responsible for licensing or accrediting the provider of health care or a health care service plan. However, no patient-identifying medical information may be removed from the premises except as expressly permitted or required elsewhere by law, nor shall that information be further disclosed by the recipient in a way that would violate this part.

(6) The information may be disclosed to a medical examiner, forensic pathologist, or county coroner in the course of an investigation by a medical examiner, forensic pathologist, or coroner's office when requested for all purposes not included in paragraph (8) of subdivision (b). A medical examiner, forensic pathologist, or coroner shall not disclose the information contained in the medical record obtained pursuant to this paragraph to a third party without a court order or authorization pursuant to paragraph (4) of subdivision (c) of Section 56.11.

(7) The information may be disclosed to public agencies, clinical investigators, including investigators conducting epidemiologic studies, health care research organizations, and accredited public or private nonprofit educational or health care institutions for bona fide research purposes. However, no information so disclosed shall be further disclosed by the recipient in a way that would disclose the identity of a patient or violate this part.

(8) A provider of health care or health care service plan that has created medical information as a result of employment-related health care services to an employee conducted

at the specific prior written request and expense of the employer may disclose to the employee's employer that part of the information that:

(A) Is relevant in a lawsuit, arbitration, grievance, or other claim or challenge to which the employer and the employee are parties and in which the patient has placed in issue * * * the patient's medical history, mental or physical condition, or treatment, provided that information may only be used or disclosed in connection with that proceeding.

(B) Describes functional limitations of the patient that may entitle the patient to leave from work for medical reasons or limit the patient's fitness to perform * * * the patient's present employment, provided that no statement of medical cause is included in the information disclosed.

(9) Unless the provider of health care or a health care service plan is notified in writing of an agreement by the sponsor, insurer, or administrator to the contrary, the information may be disclosed to a sponsor, insurer, or administrator of a group or individual insured or uninsured plan or policy that the patient seeks coverage by or benefits from, if the information was created by the provider of health care or health care service plan as the result of services conducted at the specific prior written request and expense of the sponsor, insurer, or administrator for the purpose of evaluating the application for coverage or benefits.

(10) The information may be disclosed to a health care service plan by providers of health care that contract with the health care service plan and may be transferred between providers of health care that contract with the health care service plan, for the purpose of administering the health care service plan. Medical information shall not otherwise be disclosed by a health care service plan except in accordance with this part.

(11) This part does not prevent the disclosure by a provider of health care or a health care service plan to an insurance institution, agent, or support organization, subject to Article 6.6 (commencing with Section 791) of Chapter 1 of Part 2 of Division 1 of the Insurance Code, of medical information if the insurance institution, agent, or support organization has complied with all of the requirements for obtaining the information pursuant to Article 6.6 (commencing with Section 791) of Chapter 1 of Part 2 of Division 1 of the Insurance Code.

(12) The information relevant to the patient's condition, care, and treatment provided may be disclosed to a probate court investigator in the course of an investigation required or authorized in a conservatorship proceeding under the Guardianship-Conservatorship Law as defined in Section 1400 of the Probate Code, or to a probate court investigator, probation officer, or domestic relations investigator engaged in determining the need for an initial guardianship or continuation of an existing guardianship.

(13) The information may be disclosed to an organ procurement organization or a tissue bank processing the tissue of a decedent for transplantation into the body of another person, but only with respect to the donating decedent, for the purpose of aiding the transplant. For the purpose of this paragraph, "tissue bank" and "tissue" have the same meanings as defined in Section 1635 of the Health and Safety Code.

(14) The information may be disclosed when the disclosure is otherwise specifically authorized by law, including, but not limited to, the voluntary reporting, either directly or indirectly, to the federal Food and Drug Administration of adverse events related to drug products or medical device problems, or to disclosures made pursuant to subdivisions (b) and (c) of Section 11167 of the Penal Code by a person making a report pursuant to Sections 11165.9 and 11166 of the Penal Code, provided that those disclosures concern a report made by that person.

(15) Basic information, including the patient's name, city of residence, age, sex, and general condition, may be disclosed to a state-recognized or federally recognized disaster relief organization for the purpose of responding to disaster welfare inquiries.

(16) The information may be disclosed to a third party for purposes of encoding, encrypting, or otherwise anonymizing data. However, no information so disclosed shall be further disclosed by the recipient in a way that would violate this part, including the unauthorized manipulation of coded or encrypted medical information that reveals individually identifiable medical information.

(17) For purposes of disease management programs and services as defined in Section 1399.901 of the Health and Safety Code, information may be disclosed as follows: (A) to an entity contracting with a health care service plan or the health care service plan's contractors to monitor or administer care of enrollees for a covered benefit, if the disease management services and care are authorized by a treating physician, or (B) to a disease management organization, as defined in Section 1399.900 of the Health and Safety Code, that complies fully with the physician authorization requirements of Section 1399.902 of the Health and Safety Code, if the health care service plan or its contractor provides or has provided a description of the disease management services to a treating physician or to the health care service plan's or contractor's network of physicians. This paragraph does not require physician authorization for the care or treatment of the adherents of a well-recognized church or religious denomination who depend solely upon prayer or spiritual means for healing in the practice of the religion of that church or denomination.

(18) The information may be disclosed, as permitted by state and federal law or regulation, to a local health department for the purpose of preventing or controlling disease, injury, or disability, including, but not limited to, the reporting of disease, injury, vital events, including, but not limited to, birth or death, and the conduct of public health surveillance, public health investigations, and public health interventions, as authorized or required by state or federal law or regulation.

(19) The information may be disclosed, consistent with applicable law and standards of ethical conduct, by a psychotherapist, as defined in Section 1010 of the Evidence Code, if the psychotherapist, in good faith, believes the disclosure is necessary to prevent or lessen a serious and imminent threat to the health or safety of a reasonably foreseeable victim or victims, and the disclosure is made to a person or persons reasonably able to prevent or lessen the threat, including the target of the threat.

§ 56.10 PERSONS

(20) The information may be disclosed as described in Section 56.103.

(21)(A) The information may be disclosed to an employee welfare benefit plan, as defined under Section 3(1) of the Employee Retirement Income Security Act of 1974 (29 U.S.C. Sec. 1002(1)), which is formed under Section 302(c)(5) of the Taft-Hartley Act (29 U.S.C. Sec. 186(c)(5)), to the extent that the employee welfare benefit plan provides medical care, and may also be disclosed to an entity contracting with the employee welfare benefit plan for billing, claims management, medical data processing, or other administrative services related to the provision of medical care to persons enrolled in the employee welfare benefit plan for health care coverage, if all of the following conditions are met:

(i) The disclosure is for the purpose of determining eligibility, coordinating benefits, or allowing the employee welfare benefit plan or the contracting entity to advocate on the behalf of a patient or enrollee with a provider, a health care service plan, or a state or federal regulatory agency.

(ii) The request for the information is accompanied by a written authorization for the release of the information submitted in a manner consistent with subdivision (a) and Section 56.11.

(iii) The disclosure is authorized by and made in a manner consistent with the federal Health Insurance Portability and Accountability Act of 1996 (Public Law 104–191).

(iv) Any information disclosed is not further used or disclosed by the recipient in any way that would directly or indirectly violate this part or the restrictions imposed by Part 164 of Title 45 of the Code of Federal Regulations, including the manipulation of the information in any way that might reveal individually identifiable medical information.

(B) For purposes of this paragraph, Section 1374.8 of the Health and Safety Code shall not apply.

(22) Information may be disclosed pursuant to subdivision (a) of Section 15633.5 of the Welfare and Institutions Code by a person required to make a report pursuant to Section 15630 of the Welfare and Institutions Code, provided that the disclosure under subdivision (a) of Section 15633.5 concerns a report made by that person. Covered entities, as they are defined in Section 160.103 of Title 45 of the Code of Federal Regulations, shall comply with the requirements of the federal Health Insurance Portability and Accountability Act of 1996 (HIPAA) privacy rule pursuant to subsection (c) of Section 164.512 of Title 45 of the Code of Federal Regulations if the disclosure is not for the purpose of public health surveillance, investigation, intervention, or reporting an injury or death.

(23) The information may be disclosed to a school-linked services coordinator pursuant to a written authorization between the health provider and the patient or client that complies with the federal Health Insurance Portability and Accountability Act of 1996.

(24) Mental health records, as defined in subdivision (c) of Section 5073 of the Penal Code, may be disclosed by a county correctional facility, county medical facility, state correctional facility, or state hospital, as required by Section 5073 of the Penal Code.

(d) Except to the extent expressly authorized by a patient, enrollee, or subscriber, or as provided by subdivisions (b) and (c), a provider of health care, health care service plan, contractor, or corporation and its subsidiaries and affiliates shall not intentionally share, sell, use for marketing, or otherwise use medical information for a purpose not necessary to provide health care services to the patient.

(e) Except to the extent expressly authorized by a patient or enrollee or subscriber or as provided by subdivisions (b) and (c), a contractor or corporation and its subsidiaries and affiliates shall not further disclose medical information regarding a patient of the provider of health care or an enrollee or subscriber of a health care service plan or insurer or self-insured employer received under this section to a person or entity that is not engaged in providing direct health care services to the patient or * * * the patient's provider of health care or health care service plan or insurer or self-insured employer.

(f) For purposes of this section, * * * the following definitions apply:

(1) "Medical examiner, forensic pathologist, or coroner" means a coroner or deputy coroner, as described in subdivision (c) of Section 830.35 of the Penal Code, or a licensed physician who currently performs official autopsies on behalf of a county coroner's office or a medical examiner's office, whether as a government employee or under contract to that office.

(2) "School-linked services coordinator" means an individual located on a school campus or under contract by a county behavioral health provider agency for the treatment and health care operations and referrals of students and their families that holds any of the following:

(A) A services credential with a specialization in pupil personnel services, as described in Section 44266 of the Education Code.

(B) A services credential with a specialization in health authorizing service as a school nurse, as described in Section 44877 of the Education Code.

(C) A license to engage in the practice of marriage and family therapy issued pursuant to Chapter 13 (commencing with Section 4980) of Division 2 of the Business and Professions Code.

(D) A license to engage in the practice of educational psychology issued pursuant to Chapter 13.5 (commencing with Section 4989.10) of Division 2 of the Business and Professions Code.

(E) A license to engage in the practice of professional clinical counseling issued pursuant to Chapter 16 (commencing with Section 4999.10) of Division 2 of the Business and Professions Code. (Added by Stats.2000, c. 1068 (A.B.1836), § 1.16, operative Jan. 1, 2003. Amended by Stats.2002, c. 123 (A.B.1958), § 1, operative Jan. 1, 2003; Stats.2003, c. 562 (A.B.715), § 2; Stats.2006, c. 874 (S.B.1430), § 2; Stats.2007, c. 506 (A.B.1178), § 1; Stats.2007, c. 552 (A.B.1687), § 2; Stats.2007, c. 553 (A.B.1727), § 1.9; Stats.2008, c. 179 (S.B. 1498), § 27; Stats.2009, c. 493 (A.B.952), § 1; Stats.2010, c. 540 (A.B.2028), § 1; Stats.2013, c. 341 (A.B.1297), § 1; Stats.2016, c. 690 (A.B.2119), § 1, eff. Jan. 1, 2017; Stats.2022,

c. 968 (A.B.2526), § 1, eff. Jan. 1, 2023; Stats.2022, c. 993 (S.B.1184), § 1.5, eff. Jan. 1, 2023.)

[1] For public law sections classified to the U.S.C.A., see USCA-Tables.

Cross References

"Authorization" defined for purposes of this Part, see Civil Code § 56.05.

California Work Opportunity and Responsibility to Kids Act, disclosure between team members of information related to CalWORKs clients, see Welfare and Institutions Code § 11325.93.

Confidential information and records, disclosure, consent, comprehensive assessment, see Welfare and Institutions Code § 4514.

"Contractor" defined for purposes of this Part, see Civil Code § 56.05.

Coroners, duties of county coroners, inquests and autopsies, see Government Code § 27460 et seq.

Coroners, registration of death, responsibilities of coroners, see Health and Safety Code § 102850 et seq.

Department of Health Care Services, generally, see Health and Safety Code § 100100 et seq.

Development of cost, quality, and equity data atlas, included research, agreements to conduct research, see Health and Safety Code § 127670.

Disease management organizations, receipt of medical information, confidentiality and disclosure, see Health and Safety Code § 1399.903.

Domestic violence death review teams, disclosure of medical information, see Penal Code § 11163.3.

Elder death review teams, confidentiality and disclosure of information, see Penal Code § 11174.8.

"Health care service plan" defined for purposes of this Part, see Civil Code § 56.05.

Integrated children's services programs, disclosure of information and records, see Welfare and Institutions Code § 18986.46.

Interagency child death review team, disclosure of records and other information, see Penal Code § 11174.32.

Inventories of medical supplies and drugs, disclosure to local health officials, see Health and Safety Code § 120176.

"Marketing" defined for purposes of this Part, see Civil Code § 56.05.

Medical information defined for purposes of this Part, see Civil Code § 56.05.

Patient defined for purposes of this Part, see Civil Code § 56.05.

Personal health care, administration, reporting and recording of patient test results, see Health and Safety Code § 123148.

"Provider of health care" defined for purposes of this Part, see Civil Code § 56.05.

Response to discharge or release of contagious or communicable biologic agent, authority of first responders to isolate exposed individuals, punishment for noncompliance, see Health and Safety Code § 101080.2.

Search warrants, see Penal Code § 1523 et seq.

§ 56.1007. Disclosure of medical information to specified persons involved with patient's care or health care payments; disclosure of medical information for other purposes

(a) A provider of health care, health care service plan, or contractor may, in accordance with subdivision (c) or (d), disclose to a family member, other relative, domestic partner, or a close personal friend of the patient, or any other person identified by the patient, the medical information directly relevant to that person's involvement with the patient's care or payment related to the patient's health care.

(b) A provider of health care, health care service plan, or contractor may use or disclose medical information to notify, or assist in the notification of, including identifying or locating, a family member, a personal representative of the patient, a domestic partner, or another person responsible for the care of the patient of the patient's location, general condition, or death. Any use or disclosure of medical information for those notification purposes shall be in accordance with the provisions of subdivision (c), (d), or (e), as applicable.

(c)(1) Except as provided in paragraph (2), if the patient is present for, or otherwise available prior to, a use or disclosure permitted by subdivision (a) or (b) and has the capacity to make health care decisions, the provider of health care, health care service plan, or contractor may use or disclose the medical information if it does any of the following:

(A) Obtains the patient's agreement.

(B) Provides the patient with the opportunity to object to the disclosure, and the patient does not express an objection.

(C) Reasonably infers from the circumstances, based on the exercise of professional judgment, that the patient does not object to the disclosure.

(2) A provider of health care who is a psychotherapist, as defined in Section 1010 of the Evidence Code, may use or disclose medical information pursuant to this subdivision only if the psychotherapist complies with subparagraph (A) or (B) of paragraph (1).

(d) If the patient is not present, or the opportunity to agree or object to the use or disclosure cannot practicably be provided because of the patient's incapacity or an emergency circumstance, the provider of health care, health care service plan, or contractor may, in the exercise of professional judgment, determine whether the disclosure is in the best interests of the patient and, if so, disclose only the medical information that is directly relevant to the person's involvement with the patient's health care. A provider of health care, health care service plan, or contractor may use professional judgment and its experience with common practice to make reasonable inferences of the patient's best interest in allowing a person to act on behalf of the patient to pick up filled prescriptions, medical supplies, X-rays, or other similar forms of medical information.

(e) A provider of health care, health care service plan, or contractor may use or disclose medical information to a public or private entity authorized by law or by its charter to assist in disaster relief efforts, for the purpose of coordinating with those entities the uses or disclosures permitted by subdivision (b). The requirements in subdivisions (c) and (d) apply to those uses and disclosures to the extent that the provider of health care, health care service plan, or contractor, in the exercise of professional judgment, determines that the requirements do not interfere with the ability to respond to the emergency circumstances.

(f) Nothing in this section shall be construed to interfere with or limit the access authority of Protection and Advocacy, Inc., the Office of Patients' Rights, or any county patients' rights advocates to access medical information pursuant to

§ 56.1007

any state or federal law. *(Added by Stats.2006, c. 833 (A.B.3013), § 1.)*

Cross References

"Contractor" defined for purposes of this Part, see Civil Code § 56.05.

Emergency services, transfer for nonmedical reasons, conditions, see Health and Safety Code § 1317.2.

"Health care service plan" defined for purposes of this Part, see Civil Code § 56.05.

Medical information defined for purposes of this Part, see Civil Code § 56.05.

Patient defined for purposes of this Part, see Civil Code § 56.05.

"Provider of health care" defined for purposes of this Part, see Civil Code § 56.05.

Release of limited information on specific patient, written request by patient to prohibit, see Civil Code § 56.16.

§ 56.101. Medical information; confidentiality; negligence; protection and preservation; patient access

(a) Every provider of health care, health care service plan, pharmaceutical company, or contractor who creates, maintains, preserves, stores, abandons, destroys, or disposes of medical information shall do so in a manner that preserves the confidentiality of the information contained therein. Any provider of health care, health care service plan, pharmaceutical company, or contractor who negligently creates, maintains, preserves, stores, abandons, destroys, or disposes of medical information shall be subject to the remedies and penalties provided under subdivisions (b) and (c) of Section 56.36.

(b)(1) An electronic health record system or electronic medical record system shall do the following:

(A) Protect and preserve the integrity of electronic medical information.

(B) Automatically record and preserve any change or deletion of any electronically stored medical information. The record of any change or deletion shall include the identity of the person who accessed and changed the medical information, the date and time the medical information was accessed, and the change that was made to the medical information.

(2) A patient's right to access or receive a copy of his or her electronic medical records upon request shall be consistent with applicable state and federal laws governing patient access to, and the use and disclosures of, medical information.

(c) This section shall apply to an "electronic medical record" or "electronic health record" that meets the definition of "electronic health record," as that term is defined in Section 17921(5) of Title 42 of the United States Code. *(Added by Stats.1999, c. 526 (S.B.19), § 3. Amended by Stats.2000, c. 1067 (S.B.2094), § 4; Stats.2002, c. 853 (A.B. 2191), § 2; Stats.2011, c. 714 (S.B.850), § 1.)*

Cross References

"Contractor" defined for purposes of this Part, see Civil Code § 56.05.

"Health care service plan" defined for purposes of this Part, see Civil Code § 56.05.

"Pharmaceutical company" defined for purposes of this Part, see Civil Code § 56.05.

"Provider of health care" defined for purposes of this Part, see Civil Code § 56.05.

§ 56.102. Disclosure of medical information by pharmaceutical company; authorizations, releases, consents, or waivers; exceptions

(a) A pharmaceutical company may not require a patient, as a condition of receiving pharmaceuticals, medications, or prescription drugs, to sign an authorization, release, consent, or waiver that would permit the disclosure of medical information that otherwise may not be disclosed under Section 56.10 or any other provision of law, unless the disclosure is for one of the following purposes:

(1) Enrollment of the patient in a patient assistance program or prescription drug discount program.

(2) Enrollment of the patient in a clinical research project.

(3) Prioritization of distribution to the patient of a prescription medicine in limited supply in the United States.

(4) Response to an inquiry from the patient communicated in writing, by telephone, or by electronic mail.

(b) Except as provided in subdivision (a) or Section 56.10, a pharmaceutical company may not disclose medical information provided to it without first obtaining a valid authorization from the patient. *(Added by Stats.2002, c. 853 (A.B. 2191), § 3.)*

Cross References

"Authorization" defined for purposes of this Part, see Civil Code § 56.05.

Medical information defined for purposes of this Part, see Civil Code § 56.05.

Patient defined for purposes of this Part, see Civil Code § 56.05.

"Pharmaceutical company" defined for purposes of this Part, see Civil Code § 56.05.

§ 56.103. Disclosure of a minor's medical information; mental health condition

(a) A provider of health care may disclose medical information to a county social worker, a probation officer, a foster care public health nurse acting pursuant to Section 16501.3 of the Welfare and Institutions Code, or any other person who is legally authorized to have custody or care of a minor for the purpose of coordinating health care services and medical treatment provided to the minor, including, but not limited to, the sharing of information related to screenings, assessments, and laboratory tests necessary to monitor the administration of psychotropic medications.

(b) For purposes of this section, health care services and medical treatment includes one or more providers of health care providing, coordinating, or managing health care and related services, including, but not limited to, a provider of health care coordinating health care with a third party, consultation between providers of health care and medical treatment relating to a minor, or a provider of health care referring a minor for health care services to another provider of health care.

(c) For purposes of this section, a county social worker, a probation officer, foster care public health nurse, or any other person who is legally authorized to have custody or care of a minor shall be considered a third party who may receive any of the following:

(1) Medical information described in Sections 56.05 and 56.10.

(2) Protected health information described in Section 160.103 of Title 45 of the Code of Federal Regulations.

(d) Medical information disclosed to a county social worker, probation officer, foster care public health nurse, or any other person who is legally authorized to have custody or care of a minor shall not be further disclosed by the recipient unless the disclosure is for the purpose of coordinating health care services and medical treatment of the minor and the disclosure is authorized by law. Medical information disclosed pursuant to this section may not be admitted into evidence in any criminal or delinquency proceeding against the minor. Nothing in this subdivision shall prohibit identical evidence from being admissible in a criminal proceeding if that evidence is derived solely from lawful means other than this section and is permitted by law.

(e)(1) Notwithstanding Section 56.104, if a provider of health care determines that the disclosure of medical information concerning the diagnosis and treatment of a mental health condition of a minor is reasonably necessary for the purpose of assisting in coordinating the treatment and care of the minor, that information may be disclosed to a county social worker, probation officer, foster care public health nurse, or any other person who is legally authorized to have custody or care of the minor. The information shall not be further disclosed by the recipient unless the disclosure is for the purpose of coordinating mental health services and treatment of the minor and the disclosure is authorized by law.

(2) As used in this subdivision, "medical information" does not include psychotherapy notes as defined in Section 164.501 of Title 45 of the Code of Federal Regulations.

(f) The disclosure of information pursuant to this section is not intended to limit the disclosure of information when that disclosure is otherwise required by law.

(g) For purposes of this section, "minor" means a minor taken into temporary custody or as to whom a petition has been filed with the court, or who has been adjudged to be a dependent child or ward of the juvenile court pursuant to Section 300 or 601 of the Welfare and Institutions Code.

(h)(1) Except as described in paragraph (1) of subdivision (e), nothing in this section shall be construed to limit or otherwise affect existing privacy protections provided for in state or federal law.

(2) Nothing in this section shall be construed to expand the authority of a social worker, probation officer, foster care public health nurse, or custodial caregiver beyond the authority provided under existing law to a parent or a patient representative regarding access to medical information. (Added by Stats.2007, c. 552 (A.B.1687), § 3. Amended by Stats.2008, c. 699 (S.B.1241), § 1; Stats.2008, c. 700 (A.B. 2352), § 1; Stats.2015, c. 535 (S.B.319), § 1, eff. Jan. 1, 2016.)

§ 56.104. Patient's participation in outpatient treatment with psychotherapist; request for information; application of section

(a) Notwithstanding subdivision (c) of Section 56.10, except as provided in subdivision (e), no provider of health care, health care service plan, or contractor may release medical information to persons or entities who have requested that information and who are authorized by law to receive that information pursuant to subdivision (c) of Section 56.10, if the requested information specifically relates to the patient's participation in outpatient treatment with a psychotherapist, unless the person or entity requesting that information submits to the patient pursuant to subdivision (b) and to the provider of health care, health care service plan, or contractor a written request, signed by the person requesting the information or an authorized agent of the entity requesting the information, that includes all of the following:

(1) The specific information relating to a patient's participation in outpatient treatment with a psychotherapist being requested and its specific intended use or uses.

(2) The length of time during which the information will be kept before being destroyed or disposed of. A person or entity may extend that timeframe, provided that the person or entity notifies the provider, plan, or contractor of the extension. Any notification of an extension shall include the specific reason for the extension, the intended use or uses of the information during the extended time, and the expected date of the destruction of the information.

(3) A statement that the information will not be used for any purpose other than its intended use.

(4) A statement that the person or entity requesting the information will destroy the information and all copies in the person's or entity's possession or control, will cause it to be destroyed, or will return the information and all copies of it before or immediately after the length of time specified in paragraph (2) has expired.

(b) The person or entity requesting the information shall submit a copy of the written request required by this section to the patient within 30 days of receipt of the information requested, unless the patient has signed a written waiver in the form of a letter signed and submitted by the patient to the provider of health care or health care service plan waiving notification.

(c) For purposes of this section, "psychotherapist" means a person who is both a "psychotherapist" as defined in Section 1010 of the Evidence Code and a "provider of health care" as defined in Section 56.05.

(d) This section does not apply to the disclosure or use of medical information by a law enforcement agency or a regulatory agency when required for an investigation of unlawful activity or for licensing, certification, or regulatory purposes, unless the disclosure is otherwise prohibited by law.

(e) This section shall not apply to any of the following:

(1) Information authorized to be disclosed pursuant to paragraph (1) of subdivision (c) of Section 56.10.

(2) Information requested from a psychotherapist by law enforcement or by the target of the threat subsequent to a disclosure by that psychotherapist authorized by paragraph (19) of subdivision (c) of Section 56.10, in which the additional information is clearly necessary to prevent the serious and imminent threat disclosed under that paragraph.

(3) Information disclosed by a psychotherapist pursuant to paragraphs (14) and (22) of subdivision (c) of Section 56.10

§ 56.104

and requested by an agency investigating the abuse reported pursuant to those paragraphs.

(f) Nothing in this section shall be construed to grant any additional authority to a provider of health care, health care service plan, or contractor to disclose information to a person or entity without the patient's consent. *(Added by Stats.1999, c. 527 (A.B.416), § 3. Amended by Stats.2004, c. 463 (S.B.598), § 1; Stats.2009, c. 464 (A.B.681), § 1; Stats.2010, c. 540 (A.B.2028), § 2; Stats.2013, c. 444 (S.B.138), § 3.)*

§ 56.105. Professional negligence actions; settlement or compromise; authorization to disclose medical records to persons or organizations defending professional liability

Whenever, prior to the service of a complaint upon a defendant in any action arising out of the professional negligence of a person holding a valid physician's and surgeon's certificate issued pursuant to Chapter 5 (commencing with Section 2000) of Division 2 of the Business and Professions Code, a person holding a valid license as a marriage and family therapist issued pursuant to Chapter 13 (commencing with Section 4980) of Division 2 of the Business and Professions Code, a person holding a valid license as a clinical social worker issued pursuant to Chapter 14 (commencing with Section 4991) of Division 2 of the Business and Professions Code, or a person holding a valid license as a professional clinical counselor issued pursuant to Chapter 16 (commencing with Section 4999.10) of Division 2 of the Business and Professions Code, a demand for settlement or offer to compromise is made on a patient's behalf, the demand or offer shall be accompanied by an authorization to disclose medical information to persons or organizations insuring, responsible for, or defending professional liability that the certificate holder may incur. The authorization shall be in accordance with Section 56.11 and shall authorize disclosure of that information that is necessary to investigate issues of liability and extent of potential damages in evaluating the merits of the demand for settlement or offer to compromise.

Notice of any request for medical information made pursuant to an authorization as provided by this section shall be given to the patient or the patient's legal representative. The notice shall describe the inclusive subject matter and dates of the materials requested and shall also authorize the patient or the patient's legal representative to receive, upon request, copies of the information at his or her expense.

Nothing in this section shall be construed to waive or limit any applicable privileges set forth in the Evidence Code except for the disclosure of medical information subject to the patient's authorization. Nothing in this section shall be construed as authorizing a representative of any person from whom settlement has been demanded to communicate in violation of the physician-patient privilege with a treating physician, or to communicate in violation of the psychotherapist-patient privilege with a treating licensed marriage and family therapist, licensed clinical social worker, or licensed professional clinical counselor, except for the medical information request.

The requirements of this section are independent of the requirements of Section 364 of the Code of Civil Procedure. *(Added by Stats.1985, c. 484, § 1. Amended by Stats.2013, c. 58 (S.B.282), § 1; Stats.2018, c. 389 (A.B.2296), § 8, eff. Jan. 1, 2019.)*

Cross References

"Authorization" defined for purposes of this Part, see Civil Code § 56.05.
Medical information defined for purposes of this Part, see Civil Code § 56.05.
Patient defined for purposes of this Part, see Civil Code § 56.05.

§ 56.106. Disclosure of minor's mental health records; minor removed from custody of parent or guardian

(a) Notwithstanding Section 3025 of the Family Code, paragraph (2) of subdivision (c) of Section 56.11, or any other provision of law, a psychotherapist who knows that a minor has been removed from the custody of his or her parent or guardian pursuant to Article 6 (commencing with Section 300) to Article 10 (commencing with Section 360), inclusive, of Chapter 2 of Part 1 of Division 2 of the Welfare and Institutions Code shall not release the mental health records of the minor patient and shall not disclose mental health information about that minor patient based upon an authorization to release those records signed by the minor's parent or guardian. This restriction shall not apply if the juvenile court has issued an order authorizing the parent or guardian to sign an authorization for the release of the mental health records or the information about the minor patient after finding that such an order would not be detrimental to the minor patient.

(b) For purposes of this section, the following definitions apply:

(1) "Mental health records" means mental health records as defined by subdivision (b) of Section 123105 of the Health and Safety Code.

(2) "Psychotherapist" means a provider of health care as defined in Section 1010 of the Evidence Code.

(c) When the juvenile court has issued an order authorizing the parent or guardian to sign an authorization for the release of the mental health records or information about that minor patient under the circumstances described in subdivision (a), the parent or guardian seeking the release of the minor's records or information about the minor shall present a copy of the court order to the psychotherapist before any records or information may be released pursuant to the signed authorization.

(d) Nothing in this section shall be construed to prevent or limit a psychotherapist's authority under subdivision (a) of Section 123115 of the Health and Safety Code to deny a parent's or guardian's written request to inspect or obtain copies of the minor patient's mental health records, notwithstanding the fact that the juvenile court has issued an order authorizing the parent or guardian to sign an authorization for the release of the mental health records or information about that minor patient. Liability for a psychotherapist's decision not to release the mental health records of the minor patient or not to disclose information about the minor patient pursuant to the authority of subdivision (a) of Section 123115 of the Health and Safety Code shall be governed by that section.

(e) Nothing in this section shall be construed to impose upon a psychotherapist a duty to inquire or investigate whether a child has been removed from the physical custody of his or her parent or guardian pursuant to Article 6 (commencing with Section 300) to Article 10 (commencing with Section 360), inclusive, of Chapter 2 of Part 1 of Division 2 of the Welfare and Institutions Code when a parent or guardian presents the minor's psychotherapist with an authorization to release information or the mental health records regarding the minor patient. *(Added by Stats.2012, c. 657 (S.B.1407), § 1.)*

Cross References

Confidential information and records, disclosure to parent or guardian, minor removed from physical custody of parent or guardian, see Welfare and Institutions Code § 5328.03.

Minor removed from physical custody of parent or guardian, mental health records, psychotherapist duty not to permit inspection or obtaining of copies, see Health and Safety Code § 123116.

§ 56.107. Health care service plans; protected individual; confidential communications

Notwithstanding any other law, and to the extent permitted by federal law, a health care service plan shall take the following steps to protect the confidentiality of a subscriber's or enrollee's medical information:

(a)(1) A health care service plan shall not require a protected individual to obtain the policyholder, primary subscriber, or other enrollee's authorization to receive sensitive services or to submit a claim for sensitive services if the protected individual has the right to consent to care.

(2) A health care service plan shall recognize the right of a protected individual to exclusively exercise rights granted under this section regarding medical information related to sensitive services that the protected individual has received.

(3) A health care service plan shall direct all communications regarding a protected individual's receipt of sensitive services directly to the protected individual receiving care as follows:

(A) If the protected individual has designated an alternative mailing address, email address, or telephone number pursuant to subdivision (b), the health care service plan shall send or make all communications related to the protected individual's receipt of sensitive services to the alternative mailing address, email address, or telephone number designated.

(B) If the protected individual has not designated an alternative mailing address, email address, or telephone number pursuant to subdivision (b), the health care service plan shall send or make all communications related to the protected individual's receipt of sensitive services in the name of the protected individual at the address or telephone number on file.

(C) Communications subject to this paragraph shall include the following written, verbal, or electronic communications related to the receipt of sensitive services:

(i) Bills and attempts to collect payment.

(ii) A notice of adverse benefits determinations.

(iii) An explanation of benefits notice.

(iv) A health care service plan's request for additional information regarding a claim.

(v) A notice of a contested claim.

(vi) The name and address of a provider, description of services provided, and other information related to a visit.

(vii) Any written, oral, or electronic communication from a health care service plan that contains protected health information.

(4) A health care service plan shall not disclose medical information related to sensitive health care services provided to a protected individual to the policyholder, primary subscriber, or any plan enrollees other than the protected individual receiving care, absent an express written authorization of the protected individual receiving care.

(b)(1) A health care service plan shall permit subscribers and enrollees to request, and shall accommodate requests for, confidential communication in the form and format requested by the individual, if it is readily producible in the requested form and format, or at alternative locations.

(2) A health care service plan may require the subscriber or enrollee to make a request for a confidential communication described in paragraph (1), in writing or by electronic transmission.

(3) The confidential communication request shall be valid until the subscriber or enrollee submits a revocation of the request or a new confidential communication request is submitted.

(4) The confidential communication request shall apply to all communications that disclose medical information or provider name and address related to receipt of medical services by the individual requesting the confidential communication.

(5) For the purposes of this section, a confidential communications request shall be implemented by the health care service plan within 7 calendar days of receipt of an electronic transmission or telephonic request or within 14 calendar days of receipt by first-class mail. The health care service plan shall acknowledge receipt of the confidential communications request and advise the subscriber or enrollee of the status of implementation of the request if a subscriber or enrollee contacts the health care service plan.

(c)(1) A health care service plan shall notify subscribers and enrollees that they may request a confidential communication pursuant to subdivision (b) and how to make the request.

(2) The information required to be provided pursuant to this subdivision shall be provided to subscribers and enrollees with individual or group coverage upon initial enrollment and annually thereafter upon renewal. The information shall also be provided in the following manner:

(A) In a conspicuously visible location in the evidence of coverage.

(B) On the health care service plan's internet website, accessible through a hyperlink on the internet website's home page and in a manner that allows subscribers, enrollees, prospective subscribers, prospective enrollees, and members of the public to easily locate the information.

§ 56.107

(d) Notwithstanding subdivision (b), the provider of health care may make arrangements with the subscriber or enrollee for the payment of benefit cost sharing and communicate that arrangement with the health care service plan.

(e) A health care service plan shall not condition enrollment or coverage on the waiver of rights provided in this section.

(f) This section shall become operative on July 1, 2022. (Added by Stats.2021, c. 190 (A.B.1184), § 3, eff. Jan. 1, 2022, operative July 1, 2022.)

Cross References

Health care service plans, compliance with provisions of state law, see Health and Safety Code § 1348.5.

§ 56.108. Prohibition on disclosure of medical information related to individual seeking or obtaining an abortion in response to subpoena or request; criteria; disclosure to law enforcement

(a) Notwithstanding subdivisions (b) and (c) of Section 56.10 or subdivision (c) of Section 56.20, a provider of health care, health care service plan, contractor, or employer shall not release medical information related to an individual seeking or obtaining an abortion in response to a subpoena or request if that subpoena or request is based on either another state's laws that interfere with a person's rights under the Reproductive Privacy Act (Article 2.5 (commencing with Section 123460) of Chapter 2 of Part 2 of Division 106 of the Health and Safety Code) or a foreign penal civil action, as defined in Section 2029.200 of the Code of Civil Procedure.

(b) A provider of health care, health care service plan, contractor, or employer shall not release medical information that would identify an individual or that is related to an individual seeking or obtaining an abortion to law enforcement for either of the following purposes, unless that release is pursuant to a subpoena not otherwise prohibited by subdivision (a):

(1) Enforcement of another state's law that would interfere with a person's rights under the Reproductive Privacy Act (Article 2.5 (commencing with Section 123460) of Chapter 2 of Part 2 of Division 106 of the Health and Safety Code).

(2) Enforcement of a foreign penal civil action, as defined in Section 2029.200 of the Code of Civil Procedure. (Added by Stats.2022, c. 628 (A.B.2091), § 2, eff. Sept. 27, 2022.)

§ 56.109. Prohibition on disclosure of medical information related to person or entity allowing a child to receive gender-affirming health care or gender-affirming mental health care in response to subpoena or request; criteria

(a) Notwithstanding subdivision (b) of Section 56.10, a provider of health care, health care service plan, or contractor shall not release medical information related to a person or entity allowing a child to receive gender-affirming health care or gender-affirming mental health care in response to any civil action, including a foreign subpoena, based on another state's law that authorizes a person to bring a civil action against a person or entity that allows a child to receive gender-affirming health care or gender-affirming mental health care.

(b) Notwithstanding subdivision (c) of Section 56.10, a provider of health care, health care service plan, or contractor shall not release medical information to persons or entities who have requested that information and who are authorized by law to receive that information pursuant to subdivision (c) of Section 56.10, if the information is related to a person or entity allowing a child to receive gender-affirming health care or gender-affirming mental health care, and the information is being requested pursuant to another state's law that authorizes a person to bring a civil action against a person or entity who allows a child to receive gender-affirming health care or gender-affirming mental health care.

(c) For the purposes of this section, "person" means an individual or governmental subdivision, agency, or instrumentality.

(d) For the purpose of this section, "gender-affirming health care" and "gender-affirming mental health care" shall have the same meaning as provided in Section 16010.2 of the Welfare and Institutions Code. (Added by Stats.2022, c. 810 (S.B.107), § 1, eff. Jan. 1, 2023.)

§ 56.11. Authorization; form and contents

Any person or entity that wishes to obtain medical information pursuant to subdivision (a) of Section 56.10, other than a person or entity authorized to receive medical information pursuant to subdivision (b) or (c) of Section 56.10, except as provided in paragraph (21) of subdivision (c) of Section 56.10, shall obtain a valid authorization for the release of this information.

An authorization for the release of medical information by a provider of health care, health care service plan, pharmaceutical company, or contractor shall be valid if it:

(a) Is handwritten by the person who signs it or is in a typeface no smaller than 14–point type.

(b) Is clearly separate from any other language present on the same page and is executed by a signature which serves no other purpose than to execute the authorization.

(c) Is signed and dated by one of the following:

(1) The patient. A patient who is a minor may only sign an authorization for the release of medical information obtained by a provider of health care, health care service plan, pharmaceutical company, or contractor in the course of furnishing services to which the minor could lawfully have consented under Part 1 (commencing with Section 25) or Part 2.7 (commencing with Section 60).

(2) The legal representative of the patient, if the patient is a minor or an incompetent. However, authorization may not be given under this subdivision for the disclosure of medical information obtained by the provider of health care, health care service plan, pharmaceutical company, or contractor in the course of furnishing services to which a minor patient could lawfully have consented under Part 1 (commencing with Section 25) or Part 2.7 (commencing with Section 60).

(3) The spouse of the patient or the person financially responsible for the patient, where the medical information is being sought for the sole purpose of processing an application for health insurance or for enrollment in a nonprofit hospital plan, a health care service plan, or an employee benefit plan,

and where the patient is to be an enrolled spouse or dependent under the policy or plan.

(4) The beneficiary or personal representative of a deceased patient.

(d) States the specific uses and limitations on the types of medical information to be disclosed.

(e) States the name or functions of the provider of health care, health care service plan, pharmaceutical company, or contractor that may disclose the medical information.

(f) States the name or functions of the persons or entities authorized to receive the medical information.

(g) States the specific uses and limitations on the use of the medical information by the persons or entities authorized to receive the medical information.

(h) States a specific date after which the provider of health care, health care service plan, pharmaceutical company, or contractor is no longer authorized to disclose the medical information.

(i) Advises the person signing the authorization of the right to receive a copy of the authorization. *(Added by Stats.1981, c. 782, § 2. Amended by Stats.1999, c. 526 (S.B.19), § 4; Stats.2000, c. 1066 (S.B.1903), § 3; Stats.2002, c. 853 (A.B.2191), § 4; Stats.2003, c. 562 (A.B.715), § 3; Stats.2009, c. 493 (A.B.952), § 2.)*

Cross References

"Authorization" defined for purposes of this Part, see Civil Code § 56.05.

Confidential information and records, disclosure, consent, comprehensive assessment, see Welfare and Institutions Code § 4514.

Confidential information and records, disclosure to parent or guardian, minor removed from physical custody of parent or guardian, see Welfare and Institutions Code § 5328.03.

"Contractor" defined for purposes of this Part, see Civil Code § 56.05.

"Health care service plan" defined for purposes of this Part, see Civil Code § 56.05.

Medical information defined for purposes of this Part, see Civil Code § 56.05.

Minor removed from physical custody of parent or guardian, mental health records, psychotherapist duty not to permit inspection or obtaining of copies, see Health and Safety Code § 123116.

Patient defined for purposes of this Part, see Civil Code § 56.05.

Personal health care, administration, reporting and recording of patient test results, see Health and Safety Code § 123148.

"Pharmaceutical company" defined for purposes of this Part, see Civil Code § 56.05.

"Provider of health care" defined for purposes of this Part, see Civil Code § 56.05.

§ 56.12. Copy of authorization to patient or signatory on demand

Upon demand by the patient or the person who signed an authorization, a provider of health care, health care service plan, pharmaceutical company, or contractor possessing the authorization shall furnish a true copy thereof. *(Added by Stats.1981, c. 782, § 2. Amended by Stats.1999, c. 526 (S.B.19), § 5; Stats.2002, c. 853 (A.B.2191), § 5.)*

Cross References

"Authorization" defined for purposes of this Part, see Civil Code § 56.05.

"Contractor" defined for purposes of this Part, see Civil Code § 56.05.

"Health care service plan" defined for purposes of this Part, see Civil Code § 56.05.

Patient defined for purposes of this Part, see Civil Code § 56.05.

"Pharmaceutical company" defined for purposes of this Part, see Civil Code § 56.05.

"Provider of health care" defined for purposes of this Part, see Civil Code § 56.05.

§ 56.13. Further disclosure by recipient of medical information

A recipient of medical information pursuant to an authorization as provided by this chapter or pursuant to the provisions of subdivision (c) of Section 56.10 may not further disclose that medical information except in accordance with a new authorization that meets the requirements of Section 56.11, or as specifically required or permitted by other provisions of this chapter or by law. *(Added by Stats.1981, c. 782, § 2.)*

Cross References

"Authorization" defined for purposes of this Part, see Civil Code § 56.05.

Medical information defined for purposes of this Part, see Civil Code § 56.05.

§ 56.14. Communication of limitations of authorization to recipient of medical information

A provider of health care, health care service plan, or contractor that discloses medical information pursuant to the authorizations required by this chapter shall communicate to the person or entity to which it discloses the medical information any limitations in the authorization regarding the use of the medical information. No provider of health care, health care service plan, or contractor that has attempted in good faith to comply with this provision shall be liable for any unauthorized use of the medical information by the person or entity to which the provider, plan, or contractor disclosed the medical information. *(Added by Stats.1981, c. 782, § 2. Amended by Stats.1999, c. 526 (S.B.19), § 6.)*

Cross References

"Authorization" defined for purposes of this Part, see Civil Code § 56.05.

"Contractor" defined for purposes of this Part, see Civil Code § 56.05.

"Health care service plan" defined for purposes of this Part, see Civil Code § 56.05.

Medical information defined for purposes of this Part, see Civil Code § 56.05.

"Provider of health care" defined for purposes of this Part, see Civil Code § 56.05.

§ 56.15. Cancellation or modification of authorization; written notice

Nothing in this part shall be construed to prevent a person who could sign the authorization pursuant to subdivision (c) of Section 56.11 from cancelling or modifying an authorization. However, the cancellation or modification shall be effective only after the provider of health care actually receives written notice of the cancellation or modification. *(Added by Stats.1981, c. 782, § 2.)*

§ 56.15

Cross References

"Authorization" defined for purposes of this Part, see Civil Code § 56.05.

"Provider of health care" defined for purposes of this Part, see Civil Code § 56.05.

§ 56.16. Release of limited information on specific patient; written request by patient to prohibit

For disclosures not addressed by Section 56.1007, unless there is a specific written request by the patient to the contrary, nothing in this part shall be construed to prevent a general acute care hospital, as defined in subdivision (a) of Section 1250 of the Health and Safety Code, upon an inquiry concerning a specific patient, from releasing at its discretion any of the following information: the patient's name, address, age, and sex; a general description of the reason for treatment (whether an injury, a burn, poisoning, or some unrelated condition); the general nature of the injury, burn, poisoning, or other condition; the general condition of the patient; and any information that is not medical information as defined in Section 56.05. *(Added by Stats.1981, c. 782, § 2. Amended by Stats.2006, c. 833 (A.B.3013), § 2; Stats.2013, c. 76 (A.B.383), § 10; Stats.2013, c. 444 (S.B.138), § 5.)*

Cross References

Disclosure of medical information to specified persons involved with patient's care or health care payments, see Civil Code § 56.1007.

Inspection of public records, other exemptions from disclosure, medical information, see Government Code § 6276.30.

CHAPTER 2.5. DISCLOSURE OF GENETIC TEST RESULTS BY A HEALTH CARE SERVICE PLAN

Section
56.17. Genetic test results; unlawful disclosure; written authorization; penalties.

§ 56.17. Genetic test results; unlawful disclosure; written authorization; penalties

(a) This section shall apply to the disclosure of genetic test results contained in an applicant's or enrollee's medical records by a health care service plan.

(b) Any person who negligently discloses results of a test for a genetic characteristic to any third party in a manner that identifies or provides identifying characteristics of the person to whom the test results apply, except pursuant to a written authorization as described in subdivision (g), shall be assessed a civil penalty in an amount not to exceed one thousand dollars ($1,000) plus court costs, as determined by the court, which penalty and costs shall be paid to the subject of the test.

(c) Any person who willfully discloses the results of a test for a genetic characteristic to any third party in a manner that identifies or provides identifying characteristics of the person to whom the test results apply, except pursuant to a written authorization as described in subdivision (g), shall be assessed a civil penalty in an amount not less than one thousand dollars ($1,000) and no more than five thousand dollars ($5,000) plus court costs, as determined by the court, which penalty and costs shall be paid to the subject of the test.

(d) Any person who willfully or negligently discloses the results of a test for a genetic characteristic to a third party in a manner that identifies or provides identifying characteristics of the person to whom the test results apply, except pursuant to a written authorization as described in subdivision (g), that results in economic, bodily, or emotional harm to the subject of the test, is guilty of a misdemeanor punishable by a fine not to exceed ten thousand dollars ($10,000).

(e) In addition to the penalties listed in subdivisions (b) and (c), any person who commits any act described in subdivision (b) or (c) shall be liable to the subject for all actual damages, including damages for economic, bodily, or emotional harm which is proximately caused by the act.

(f) Each disclosure made in violation of this section is a separate and actionable offense.

(g) The applicant's "written authorization," as used in this section, shall satisfy the following requirements:

(1) Is written in plain language and is in a typeface no smaller than 14–point type.

(2) Is dated and signed by the individual or a person authorized to act on behalf of the individual.

(3) Specifies the types of persons authorized to disclose information about the individual.

(4) Specifies the nature of the information authorized to be disclosed.

(5) States the name or functions of the persons or entities authorized to receive the information.

(6) Specifies the purposes for which the information is collected.

(7) Specifies the length of time the authorization shall remain valid.

(8) Advises the person signing the authorization of the right to receive a copy of the authorization. Written authorization is required for each separate disclosure of the test results.

(h) This section shall not apply to disclosures required by the Department of Health Services necessary to monitor compliance with Chapter 1 (commencing with Section 124975) of Part 5 of Division 106 of the Health and Safety Code, nor to disclosures required by the Department of Managed Care necessary to administer and enforce compliance with Section 1374.7 of the Health and Safety Code.

(i) For purposes of this section, "genetic characteristic" has the same meaning as that set forth in subdivision (d) of Section 1374.7 of the Health and Safety Code. *(Added by Stats.1995, c. 695 (S.B.1020), § 1. Amended by Stats.1996, c. 1023 (S.B.1497), § 25, eff. Sept. 29, 1996; Stats.1996, c. 532 (S.B.1740), § 1; Stats.1999, c. 311 (S.B.1185), § 1; Stats. 1999, c. 525 (A.B.78), § 5; Stats.2000, c. 857 (A.B.2903), § 4; Stats.2000, c. 941 (S.B.1364), § 1; Stats.2003, c. 562 (A.B. 715), § 4.)*

Cross References

"Authorization" defined for purposes of this Part, see Civil Code § 56.05.

Department of Health Care Services, generally, see Health and Safety Code § 100100 et seq.

"Health care service plan" defined for purposes of this Part, see Civil Code § 56.05.

Misdemeanors, definition and penalties, see Penal Code §§ 17, 19 and 19.2.

Public health, transfer of statutory duties, powers, purposes, responsibilities, and jurisdiction to state department of public health, see Health and Safety Code § 131052.

CHAPTER 2.6. GENETIC PRIVACY

Section
56.18. Short title; definitions.
56.181. Duties of direct-to-consumer genetic testing company; provision of privacy practices to consumer; acquisition or revocation of consumer consent; security procedures and practices; discrimination prohibited; disclosure of information.
56.182. Violations; civil penalties; actions; costs.
56.184. Intent, construction, and applicability of chapter.
56.186. Severability.
56.19. Repealed.

§ 56.18. Short title; definitions

(a) This chapter shall be known, and may be cited, as the Genetic Information Privacy Act.

(b) For purposes of this chapter, the following definitions apply:

(1) "Affirmative authorization" means an action that demonstrates an intentional decision by the consumer.

(2) "Biological sample" means any material part of the human, discharge therefrom, or derivative thereof, such as tissue, blood, urine, or saliva, known to contain deoxyribonucleic acid (DNA).

(3) "Consumer" means a natural person who is a California resident.

(4) "Dark pattern" means a user interface designed or manipulated with the substantial effect of subverting or impairing user autonomy, decisionmaking, or choice.

(5) "Direct-to-consumer genetic testing company" means an entity that does any of the following:

(A) Sells, markets, interprets, or otherwise offers consumer-initiated genetic testing products or services directly to consumers.

(B) Analyzes genetic data obtained from a consumer, except to the extent that the analysis is performed by a person licensed in the healing arts for diagnosis or treatment of a medical condition.

(C) Collects, uses, maintains, or discloses genetic data collected or derived from a direct-to-consumer genetic testing product or service, or is directly provided by a consumer.

(6) "Express consent" means a consumer's affirmative authorization to grant permission in response to a clear, meaningful, and prominent notice regarding the collection, use, maintenance, or disclosure of genetic data for a specific purpose. The nature of the data collection, use, maintenance, or disclosure shall be conveyed in clear and prominent terms in such a manner that an ordinary consumer would notice and understand it. Express consent cannot be inferred from inaction. Agreement obtained through use of dark patterns does not constitute consent.

(7)(A) "Genetic data" means any data, regardless of its format, that results from the analysis of a biological sample from a consumer, or from another element enabling equivalent information to be obtained, and concerns genetic material. Genetic material includes, but is not limited to, deoxyribonucleic acids (DNA), ribonucleic acids (RNA), genes, chromosomes, alleles, genomes, alterations or modifications to DNA or RNA, single nucleotide polymorphisms (SNPs), uninterpreted data that results from the analysis of the biological sample, and any information extrapolated, derived, or inferred therefrom.

(B) "Genetic data" does not include deidentified data. For purposes of this subparagraph, "deidentified data" means data that cannot be used to infer information about, or otherwise be linked to, a particular individual, provided that the business that possesses the information does all of the following:

(i) Takes reasonable measures to ensure that the information cannot be associated with a consumer or household.

(ii) Publicly commits to maintain and use the information only in deidentified form and not to attempt to reidentify the information, except that the business may attempt to reidentify the information solely for the purpose of determining whether its deidentification processes satisfy the requirements of this subparagraph, provided that the business does not use or disclose any information reidentified in this process and destroys the reidentified information upon completion of that assessment.

(iii) Contractually obligates any recipients of the information to take reasonable measures to ensure that the information cannot be associated with a consumer or household and to commit to maintaining and using the information only in deidentified form and not to reidentify the information.

(C) "Genetic data" does not include data or a biological sample to the extent that data or a biological sample is collected, used, maintained, and disclosed exclusively for scientific research conducted by an investigator with an institution that holds an assurance with the United States Department of Health and Human Services pursuant to Part 46 (commencing with Section 46.101) of Title 45 of the Code of Federal Regulations, in compliance with all applicable federal and state laws and regulations for the protection of human subjects in research, including, but not limited to, the Common Rule pursuant to Part 46 (commencing with Section 46.101) of Title 45 of the Code of Federal Regulations, United States Food and Drug Administration regulations pursuant to Parts 50 and 56 of Title 21 of the Code of Federal Regulations, the federal Family Educational Rights and Privacy Act (20 U.S.C. Sec. 1232g), and the Protection of Human Subjects in Medical Experimentation Act, Chapter 1.3 (commencing with Section 24170) of Division 20 of the Health and Safety Code.

(8) "Genetic testing" means any laboratory test of a biological sample from a consumer for the purpose of determining information concerning genetic material contained within the biological sample, or any information extrapolated, derived, or inferred therefrom.

(9) "Person" means an individual, partnership, corporation, association, business, business trust, or legal representative of an organization.

(10) "Service provider" means a sole proprietorship, partnership, limited liability company, corporation, association, or other legal entity that is organized or operated for the profit or financial benefit of its shareholders or other owners, that is involved in the collection, transportation, and analysis of the consumer's biological sample or extracted genetic material on behalf of the direct-to-consumer genetic testing company, or on behalf of any other company that collects, uses, maintains, or discloses genetic data collected or derived from a direct-to-consumer genetic testing product or service, or is directly provided by a consumer, or the delivery of the results of the analysis of the biological sample or genetic material. The contract between the company and the service provider shall prohibit the service provider from retaining, using, or disclosing the biological sample, extracted genetic material, genetic data, or any information regarding the identity of the consumer, including whether that consumer has solicited or received genetic testing, as applicable, for any purpose other than for the specific purpose of performing the services specified in the contract for the business, including both of the following:

(A) A provision prohibiting the service provider from retaining, using, or disclosing the biological sample, extracted genetic material, genetic data, or any information regarding the identity of the consumer, including whether that consumer has solicited or received genetic testing, as applicable, for a commercial purpose other than providing the services specified in the contract with the business.

(B) A provision prohibiting the service provider from associating or combining the biological sample, extracted genetic material, genetic data, or any information regarding the identity of the consumer, including whether that consumer has solicited or received genetic testing, as applicable, with information the service provider has received from or on behalf of another person or persons, or has collected from its own interaction with consumers or as required by law.
(Added by Stats.2021, c. 596 (S.B.41), § 2, eff. Jan. 1, 2022.)

§ 56.181. Duties of direct-to-consumer genetic testing company; provision of privacy practices to consumer; acquisition or revocation of consumer consent; security procedures and practices; discrimination prohibited; disclosure of information

(a) To safeguard the privacy, confidentiality, security, and integrity of a consumer's genetic data, a direct-to-consumer genetic testing company shall do both of the following:

(1) Provide clear and complete information regarding the company's policies and procedures for the collection, use, maintenance, and disclosure, as applicable, of genetic data by making available to a consumer all of the following:

(A) A summary of its privacy practices, written in plain language, that includes information about the company's collection, use, maintenance, and disclosure, as applicable, of genetic data.

(B) A prominent and easily accessible privacy notice that includes, at a minimum, complete information about the company's data collection, consent, use, access, disclosure, maintenance, transfer, security, and retention and deletion practices, and information that clearly describes how to file a complaint alleging a violation of this chapter, pursuant to subdivision (c) of Section 56.182.

(C) A notice that the consumer's deidentified genetic or phenotypic information may be shared with or disclosed to third parties for research purposes in accordance with Part 46 (commencing with Section 46.101) of Title 45 of the Code of Federal Regulations.

(2) Obtain a consumer's express consent for collection, use, and disclosure of the consumer's genetic data, including, at a minimum, separate and express consent for each of the following:

(A) The use of the genetic data collected through the genetic testing product or service offered to the consumer, including who has access to genetic data, and how genetic data may be shared, and the specific purposes for which it will be collected, used, and disclosed.

(B) The storage of a consumer's biological sample after the initial testing requested by the consumer has been fulfilled.

(C) Each use of genetic data or the biological sample beyond the primary purpose of the genetic testing or service and inherent contextual uses.

(D) Each transfer or disclosure of the consumer's genetic data or biological sample to a third party other than to a service provider, including the name of the third party to which the consumer's genetic data or biological sample will be transferred or disclosed.

(E)(i) The marketing or facilitation of marketing to a consumer based on the consumer's genetic data or the marketing or facilitation of marketing by a third party based upon the consumer having ordered, purchased, received, or used a genetic testing product or service.

(ii) This subparagraph does not require a direct-to-consumer genetic testing company to obtain a consumer's express consent to market to the consumer on the company's own website or mobile application based upon the consumer having ordered, purchased, received, or used a genetic testing product or service from that company if the content of the advertisement does not depend upon any information specific to that consumer, except for the product or service that the consumer ordered, purchased, received, or used, and the placement of the advertisement is not intended to result in disparate exposure to advertising content on the basis of any characteristic specified in Section 51. Nothing in this subparagraph alters, limits, or negates the requirements of any other antidiscrimination law or targeted advertising law.

(iii) Any advertisement of a third-party product or service presented to a consumer pursuant to either clause (i) or (ii) shall be prominently labeled as advertising content and be accompanied by the name of any third party that has contributed to the placement of the advertising. If applicable, the advertisement also shall clearly indicate that the advertised product or service, and any associated claims, have not been vetted or endorsed by the direct-to-consumer genetic testing company.

(F) For the purpose of this paragraph, "third party" does not include a public or private nonprofit postsecondary educational institution to the extent that the consumer's genetic data or biological sample is disclosed to a public or private nonprofit postsecondary educational institution for the purpose of scientific research or educational activities as described in paragraph (4) of subdivision (b) of Section 56.184.

(b) A company that is subject to the requirements described in paragraph (2) of subdivision (a) shall provide effective mechanisms, without any unnecessary steps, for a consumer to revoke their consent after it is given, at least one of which utilizes the primary medium through which the company communicates with consumers.

(c) If a consumer revokes the consent that they provided pursuant to paragraph (2) of subdivision (a), the company shall honor the consumer's consent revocation as soon as practicable, but not later than 30 days after the individual revokes consent, in accordance with both of the following:

(1) Revocation of consent under this section shall comply with Part 46 of Title 45 of the Code of Federal Regulations.

(2) The company shall destroy a consumer's biological sample within 30 days of receipt of revocation of consent to store the sample.

(d) The direct-to-consumer genetic testing company shall do both of the following:

(1) Implement and maintain reasonable security procedures and practices to protect a consumer's genetic data against unauthorized access, destruction, use, modification, or disclosure.

(2) Develop procedures and practices to enable a consumer to easily do any of the following:

(A) Access the consumer's genetic data.

(B) Delete the consumer's account and genetic data, except for genetic data that is required to be retained by the company to comply with applicable legal and regulatory requirements.

(C) Have the consumer's biological sample destroyed.

(e) A person or public entity shall not discriminate against a consumer because the consumer exercised any of the consumer's rights under this chapter by doing any of the following, including, but not limited to:

(1) Denying goods, services, or benefits to the customer.

(2) Charging different prices or rates for goods or services, including through the use of discounts or other incentives or imposing penalties.

(3) Providing a different level or quality of goods, services, or benefits to the consumer.

(4) Suggesting that the consumer will receive a different price or rate for goods, services, or benefits, or a different level or quality of goods, services, or benefits.

(5) Considering the consumer's exercise of rights under this chapter as a basis for suspicion of criminal wrongdoing or unlawful conduct.

(f)(1) Notwithstanding any other provision in this section, and except as provided in paragraph (2), a direct-to-consumer genetic testing company shall not disclose a consumer's genetic data to any entity that is responsible for administering or making decisions regarding health insurance, life insurance, long-term care insurance, disability insurance, or employment or to any entity that provides advice to an entity that is responsible for performing those functions.

(2) A direct-to-consumer genetic testing company may disclose a consumer's genetic data or biological sample to an entity described in paragraph (1) if all of the following are true:

(A) The entity is not primarily engaged in administering health insurance, life insurance, long-term care insurance, disability insurance, or employment.

(B) The consumer's genetic data or biological sample is not disclosed to the entity in that entity's capacity as a party that is responsible for administering, advising, or making decisions regarding health insurance, life insurance, long-term care insurance, disability insurance, or employment.

(C) Any agent or division of the entity that is involved in administering, advising, or making decisions regarding health insurance, life insurance, long-term care insurance, disability insurance, or employment is prohibited from accessing the consumer's genetic data or biological sample. *(Added by Stats.2021, c. 596 (S.B.41), § 2, eff. Jan. 1, 2022.)*

§ 56.182. Violations; civil penalties; actions; costs

(a) Any person who negligently violates this chapter shall be assessed a civil penalty in an amount not to exceed one thousand dollars ($1,000) plus court costs, as determined by the court.

(b) Any person who willfully violates this chapter shall be assessed a civil penalty in an amount not less than one thousand dollars ($1,000) and not more than ten thousand dollars ($10,000) plus court costs, as determined by the court.

(c) Actions for relief pursuant to this chapter shall be prosecuted exclusively in a court of competent jurisdiction by the Attorney General or a district attorney or by a county counsel authorized by agreement with the district attorney in actions involving violation of a county ordinance, or by a city attorney of a city having a population in excess of 750,000, or by a city attorney in a city and county or, with the consent of the district attorney, by a city prosecutor in a city having a full-time city prosecutor in the name of the people of the State of California upon their own complaint or upon the complaint of a board, officer, person, corporation, or association, or upon a complaint by a person who has suffered injury in fact and has lost money or property as a result of the violation of this chapter.

(d) Court costs recovered pursuant to this section shall be paid to the party or parties that prosecuted the violation. Penalties recovered pursuant to this section shall be paid to the individual to whom the genetic data at issue pertains.

(e) Any provision of a contract or agreement between a consumer and a person governed by this chapter that has, or would have, the effect of delaying or limiting access to a legal remedy for a violation of this chapter shall not apply to the exercise of rights or enforcement pursuant to this chapter.

(f) Each violation of this chapter is a separate and actionable violation. *(Added by Stats.2021, c. 596 (S.B.41), § 2, eff. Jan. 1, 2022.)*

§ 56.184. Intent, construction, and applicability of chapter

(a) The provisions of this chapter shall not reduce a direct-to-consumer genetic testing company's duties, obligations, requirements, or standards under any applicable state and federal laws for the protection of privacy and security.

(b) In the event of a conflict between the provisions of this chapter and any other law, the provisions of the law that afford the greatest protection for the right of privacy for consumers shall control.

(c) This chapter shall not apply to any of the following:

(1) Medical information governed by the Confidentiality of Medical Information Act, Part 2.6 (commencing with Section 56), or to protected health information that is collected, maintained, used, or disclosed by a covered entity or business associate governed by the privacy, security, and breach notification rules issued by the United States Department of Health and Human Services, Parts 160 and 164 of Title 45 of the Code of Federal Regulations established pursuant to the federal Health Insurance Portability and Accountability Act of 1996 (Public Law 104–191) [1] and the federal Health Information Technology for Economic and Clinical Health Act (Public Law 111–5).

(2) A provider of health care governed by the Confidentiality of Medical Information Act (Part 2.6 (commencing with Section 56)) or a covered entity governed by the privacy, security, and breach notification rules issued by the United States Department of Health and Human Services, Parts 160 and 164 of Title 45 of the Code of Federal Regulations, established pursuant to the Health Insurance Portability and Accountability Act of 1996 (Public Law 104–191) and the federal Health Information Technology for Economic and Clinical Health Act, Title XIII of the federal American Recovery and Reinvestment Act of 2009 (Public Law 111–5), to the extent that the provider or covered entity maintains, uses, and discloses genetic information in the same manner as medical information or protected health information, as described in paragraph (1).

(3) A business associate of a covered entity governed by the privacy, security, and data breach notification rules issued by the United States Department of Health and Human Services, Parts 160 and 164 of Title 45 of the Code of Federal Regulations, established pursuant to the federal Health Insurance Portability and Accountability Act of 1996 (Public Law 104–191) and the federal Health Information Technology for Economic and Clinical Health Act, Title XIII of the federal American Recovery and Reinvestment Act of 2009 (Public Law 111–5), to the extent that the business associate maintains, uses, and discloses genetic information in the same manner as medical information or protected health information, as described in paragraph (1).

(4) Scientific research or educational activities conducted by a public or private nonprofit postsecondary educational institution that holds an assurance with the United States Department of Health and Human Services pursuant to Part 46 of Title 45 of the Code of Federal Regulations, to the extent that the scientific research and educational activities conducted by that institution comply with all applicable federal and state laws and regulations for the protection of human subjects in research, including, but not limited to, the Common Rule pursuant to Part 46 (commencing with Section 46.101) of Title 45 of the Code of Federal Regulations, United States Food and Drug Administration regulations pursuant to Parts 50 and 56 of Title 21 of the Code of Federal Regulations, the federal Family Educational Rights and Privacy Act (20 U.S.C. Sec. 1232g), and the Protection of Human Subjects in Medical Experimentation Act, Chapter 1.3 (commencing with Section 24170) of Division 20 of the Health and Safety Code.

(5) The California Newborn Screening Program authorized by Chapter 1 (commencing with Section 124975) of Part 5 of Division 106 of the Health and Safety Code.

(6) Tests conducted exclusively to diagnose whether an individual has a specific disease, to the extent that all persons involved in the conduct of the test maintain, use, and disclose genetic information in the same manner as medical information or protected health information, as described in paragraph (1).

(7) Genetic data used or maintained by an employer, or disclosed by an employee to an employer, to the extent that the use, maintenance, or disclosure of that data is necessary to comply with a local, state, or federal workplace health and safety ordinance, law, or regulation.

(d) Nothing in this chapter shall be construed to affect access to information made available to the public by the consumer. *(Added by Stats.2021, c. 596 (S.B.41), § 2, eff. Jan. 1, 2022.)*

[1] For public law sections classified to the U.S.C.A., see USCA–Tables.

§ 56.186. Severability

The provisions of this chapter are severable. If any provision of this chapter or its application is held invalid, that invalidity shall not affect other provisions or applications that can be given effect without the invalid provision or application. *(Added by Stats.2021, c. 596 (S.B.41), § 2, eff. Jan. 1, 2022.)*

§ 56.19. Repealed by Stats.1981, c. 782, § 1.5

CHAPTER 3. USE AND DISCLOSURE OF MEDICAL INFORMATION BY EMPLOYERS

Section
56.20. Confidentiality; prohibition of discrimination due to refusal to sign authorization; prohibition of disclosure; exceptions.
56.21. Authorization for disclosure by employer.
56.22. Copy of authorization to patient or signatory.
56.23. Communication of limitations of authorization to person to whom disclosure made.
56.24. Cancellation or modification of authorization.
56.245. Further disclosure by recipient of medical information.

§ 56.20. Confidentiality; prohibition of discrimination due to refusal to sign authorization; prohibition of disclosure; exceptions

(a) Each employer who receives medical information shall establish appropriate procedures to ensure the confidentiality and protection from unauthorized use and disclosure of that information. These procedures may include, but are not limited to, instruction regarding confidentiality of employees and agents handling files containing medical information, and security systems restricting access to files containing medical information.

(b) No employee shall be discriminated against in terms or conditions of employment due to that employee's refusal to sign an authorization under this part. However, nothing in this section shall prohibit an employer from taking such action as is necessary in the absence of medical information due to an employee's refusal to sign an authorization under this part.

(c) No employer shall use, disclose, or knowingly permit its employees or agents to use or disclose medical information which the employer possesses pertaining to its employees without the patient having first signed an authorization under Section 56.11 or Section 56.21 permitting such use or disclosure, except as follows:

(1) The information may be disclosed if the disclosure is compelled by judicial or administrative process or by any other specific provision of law.

(2) That part of the information which is relevant in a lawsuit, arbitration, grievance, or other claim or challenge to which the employer and employee are parties and in which the patient has placed in issue his or her medical history, mental or physical condition, or treatment may be used or disclosed in connection with that proceeding.

(3) The information may be used only for the purpose of administering and maintaining employee benefit plans, including health care plans and plans providing short-term and long-term disability income, workers' compensation and for determining eligibility for paid and unpaid leave from work for medical reasons.

(4) The information may be disclosed to a provider of health care or other health care professional or facility to aid the diagnosis or treatment of the patient, where the patient or other person specified in subdivision (c) of Section 56.21 is unable to authorize the disclosure.

(d) If an employer agrees in writing with one or more of its employees or maintains a written policy which provides that particular types of medical information shall not be used or disclosed by the employer in particular ways, the employer shall obtain an authorization for such uses or disclosures even if an authorization would not otherwise be required by subdivision (c). *(Added by Stats.1981, c. 782, § 2.)*

Cross References

"Authorization" defined for purposes of this Part, see Civil Code § 56.05.
Medical information defined for purposes of this Part, see Civil Code § 56.05.
Patient defined for purposes of this Part, see Civil Code § 56.05.
"Provider of health care" defined for purposes of this Part, see Civil Code § 56.05.
Workers' compensation, see Labor Code § 3200 et seq.

§ 56.21. Authorization for disclosure by employer

An authorization for an employer to disclose medical information shall be valid if it complies with all of the following:

(a) Is handwritten by the person who signs it or is in a typeface no smaller than 14–point type.

(b) Is clearly separate from any other language present on the same page and is executed by a signature that serves no purpose other than to execute the authorization.

(c) Is signed and dated by one of the following:

(1) The patient, except that a patient who is a minor may only sign an authorization for the disclosure of medical information obtained by a provider of health care in the course of furnishing services to which the minor could lawfully have consented under Part 1 (commencing with Section 25) or Part 2.7 (commencing with Section 60) of Division 1.

(2) The legal representative of the patient, if the patient is a minor or incompetent. However, authorization may not be given under this subdivision for the disclosure of medical information that pertains to a competent minor and that was created by a provider of health care in the course of furnishing services to which a minor patient could lawfully have consented under Part 1 (commencing with Section 25) or Part 2.7 (commencing with Section 60) of Division 1.

(3) The beneficiary or personal representative of a deceased patient.

(d) States the limitations, if any, on the types of medical information to be disclosed.

(e) States the name or functions of the employer or person authorized to disclose the medical information.

(f) States the names or functions of the persons or entities authorized to receive the medical information.

(g) States the limitations, if any, on the use of the medical information by the persons or entities authorized to receive the medical information.

(h) States a specific date after which the employer is no longer authorized to disclose the medical information.

(i) Advises the person who signed the authorization of the right to receive a copy of the authorization. *(Added by Stats.1981, c. 782, § 2. Amended by Stats.2003, c. 562 (A.B.715), § 5; Stats.2006, c. 538 (S.B.1852), § 39.)*

Cross References

"Authorization" defined for purposes of this Part, see Civil Code § 56.05.
Medical information defined for purposes of this Part, see Civil Code § 56.05.
Patient defined for purposes of this Part, see Civil Code § 56.05.
"Provider of health care" defined for purposes of this Part, see Civil Code § 56.05.

§ 56.22. Copy of authorization to patient or signatory

Upon demand by the patient or the person who signed an authorization, an employer possessing the authorization shall furnish a true copy thereof. *(Added by Stats.1981, c. 782, § 2.)*

Cross References

"Authorization" defined for purposes of this Part, see Civil Code § 56.05.

Patient defined for purposes of this Part, see Civil Code § 56.05.

§ 56.23. Communication of limitations of authorization to person to whom disclosure made

An employer that discloses medical information pursuant to an authorization required by this chapter shall communicate to the person or entity to which it discloses the medical information any limitations in the authorization regarding the use of the medical information. No employer that has attempted in good faith to comply with this provision shall be liable for any unauthorized use of the medical information by the person or entity to which the employer disclosed the medical information. (Added by Stats.1981, c. 782, § 2.)

Cross References

"Authorization" defined for purposes of this Part, see Civil Code § 56.05.

Medical information defined for purposes of this Part, see Civil Code § 56.05.

§ 56.24. Cancellation or modification of authorization

Nothing in this part shall be construed to prevent a person who could sign the authorization pursuant to subdivision (c) of Section 56.21 from cancelling or modifying an authorization. However, the cancellation or modification shall be effective only after the employer actually receives written notice of the cancellation or modification. (Added by Stats.1981, c. 782, § 2.)

Cross References

"Authorization" defined for purposes of this Part, see Civil Code § 56.05.

§ 56.245. Further disclosure by recipient of medical information

A recipient of medical information pursuant to an authorization as provided by this chapter may not further disclose such medical information unless in accordance with a new authorization that meets the requirements of Section 56.21, or as specifically required or permitted by other provisions of this chapter or by law. (Added by Stats.1981, c. 782, § 2.)

Cross References

"Authorization" defined for purposes of this Part, see Civil Code § 56.05.

Medical information defined for purposes of this Part, see Civil Code § 56.05.

CHAPTER 4. RELATIONSHIP OF CHAPTERS 2 AND 3

Section
56.25. Disclosure by employer who is provider of health care.

§ 56.25. Disclosure by employer who is provider of health care

(a) An employer that is a provider of health care shall not be deemed to have violated Section 56.20 by disclosing, in accordance with Chapter 2 (commencing with Section 56.10), medical information possessed in connection with providing health care services to the provider's patients.

(b) An employer shall not be deemed to have violated Section 56.20 because a provider of health care that is an employee or agent of the employer uses or discloses, in accordance with Chapter 2 (commencing with Section 56.10), medical information possessed by the provider in connection with providing health care services to the provider's patients.

(c) A provider of health care that is an employer shall not be deemed to have violated Section 56.10 by disclosing, in accordance with Chapter 3 (commencing with Section 56.20), medical information possessed in connection with employing the provider's employees. Information maintained by a provider of health care in connection with employing the provider's employees shall not be deemed to be medical information for purposes of Chapter 3 (commencing with Section 56.20), unless it would be deemed medical information if received or maintained by an employer that is not a provider of health care. (Added by Stats.1981, c. 782, § 2.)

Cross References

Medical information defined for purposes of this Part, see Civil Code § 56.05.

Patient defined for purposes of this Part, see Civil Code § 56.05.

"Provider of health care" defined for purposes of this Part, see Civil Code § 56.05.

CHAPTER 4.1. NOTIFICATIONS

Section
56.251. Mental health digital service providers; information regarding how to find data breaches.

§ 56.251. Mental health digital service providers; information regarding how to find data breaches

When partnering with a provider of health care to provide a mental health digital service, any business that offers a mental health digital service shall provide to the provider of health care information regarding how to find data breaches reported pursuant to Section 1798.82 on the internet website of the Attorney General. (Added by Stats.2022, c. 690 (A.B.2089), § 3, eff. Jan. 1, 2023.)

CHAPTER 5. USE AND DISCLOSURE OF MEDICAL AND OTHER INFORMATION BY THIRD PARTY ADMINISTRATORS AND OTHERS

Section
56.26. Prohibition; exceptions; inapplicability of section.
56.265. Annuity contracts; disclosure of individually identifiable information concerning health, medical or genetic history; prohibition.

Cross References

Well stimulation treatment fluid information claimed to contain trade secrets, development of timely procedure to provide specified trade secret information, see Public Resources Code § 3160.

§ 56.26. Prohibition; exceptions; inapplicability of section

(a) No person or entity engaged in the business of furnishing administrative services to programs that provide payment for health care services shall knowingly use, disclose, or permit its employees or agents to use or disclose medical information possessed in connection with performing administrative functions for a program, except as reasonably necessary in connection with the administration or maintenance of the program, or as required by law, or with an authorization.

(b) An authorization required by this section shall be in the same form as described in Section 56.21, except that "third party administrator" shall be substituted for "employer" wherever it appears in Section 56.21.

(c) This section shall not apply to any person or entity that is subject to the Insurance Information Privacy Act or to Chapter 2 (commencing with Section 56.10) or Chapter 3 (commencing with Section 56.20). *(Added by Stats.1981, c. 782, § 2. Amended by Stats.2004, c. 183 (A.B.3082), § 24.)*

Cross References

"Authorization" defined for purposes of this Part, see Civil Code § 56.05.

Medical information defined for purposes of this Part, see Civil Code § 56.05.

§ 56.265. Annuity contracts; disclosure of individually identifiable information concerning health, medical or genetic history; prohibition

A person or entity that underwrites or sells annuity contracts or contracts insuring, guaranteeing, or indemnifying against loss, harm, damage, illness, disability, or death, and any affiliate of that person or entity, shall not disclose individually identifiable information concerning the health of, or the medical or genetic history of, a customer, to any affiliated or nonaffiliated depository institution, or to any other affiliated or nonaffiliated third party for use with regard to the granting of credit. *(Added by Stats.2000, c. 278 (A.B.2797), § 2.)*

CHAPTER 6. RELATIONSHIP TO EXISTING LAW

Section
56.27. Employer that is insurance institution, agent or support organization; disclosure not in violation of § 56.20.
56.28. Patient's right to access.
56.29. Information Practices Act of 1977; applicability.
56.30. Exemptions from limitations of this part.
56.31. Disclosure or use of medical information under subdivision (f) of Section 56.30; HIV infection or exposure; employment incident.
56.32. Repealed.

§ 56.27. Employer that is insurance institution, agent or support organization; disclosure not in violation of § 56.20

An employer that is an insurance institution, insurance agent, or insurance support organization subject to the Insurance Information and Privacy Protection Act, Article 6.6 (commencing with Section 791) of Part 2 of Division 1 of the Insurance Code, shall not be deemed to have violated Section 56.20 by disclosing medical information gathered in connection with an insurance transaction in accordance with that act. *(Added by Stats.1981, c. 782, § 2.)*

Cross References

Medical information defined for purposes of this Part, see Civil Code § 56.05.

§ 56.28. Patient's right to access

Nothing in this part shall be deemed to affect existing laws relating to a patient's right of access to his or her own medical information, or relating to disclosures made pursuant to Section 1158 of the Evidence Code, or relating to privileges established under the Evidence Code. *(Added by Stats.1981, c. 782, § 2.)*

Cross References

Medical information defined for purposes of this Part, see Civil Code § 56.05.

Patient defined for purposes of this Part, see Civil Code § 56.05.

§ 56.29. Information Practices Act of 1977; applicability

(a) Nothing in Chapter 1 (commencing with Section 1798) of Title 1.8 of Part 4 of Division 3 shall be construed to permit the acquisition or disclosure of medical information regarding a patient without an authorization, where the authorization is required by this part.

(b) The disclosure of medical information regarding a patient which is subject to subdivision (b) of Section 1798.24 shall be made only with an authorization which complies with the provisions of this part. Such disclosure may be made only within the time limits specified in subdivision (b) of Section 1798.24.

(c) Where the acquisition or disclosure of medical information regarding a patient is prohibited or limited by any provision of Chapter 1 (commencing with Section 1798) of Title 1.8 of Part 4 of Division 3, the prohibition or limit shall be applicable in addition to the requirements of this part. *(Added by Stats.1981, c. 782, § 2.)*

Cross References

"Authorization" defined for purposes of this Part, see Civil Code § 56.05.

Medical information defined for purposes of this Part, see Civil Code § 56.05.

Patient defined for purposes of this Part, see Civil Code § 56.05.

§ 56.30. Exemptions from limitations of this part

The disclosure and use of the following medical information shall not be subject to the limitations of this part:

(a) (Mental health and developmental disabilities) Information and records obtained in the course of providing services under Division 4 (commencing with Section 4000), Division 4.1 (commencing with Section 4400), Division 4.5 (commencing with Section 4500), Division 5 (commencing with Section 5000), Division 6 (commencing with Section 6000), or Division 7 (commencing with Section 7100) of the Welfare and Institutions Code.

(b) (Public social services) Information and records that are subject to Sections 10850, 14124.1, and 14124.2 of the Welfare and Institutions Code.

(c) (State health services, communicable diseases, developmental disabilities) Information and records maintained pursuant to former Chapter 2 (commencing with Section 200) of Part 1 of Division 1 of the Health and Safety Code and pursuant to the Communicable Disease Prevention and Control Act (subdivision (a) of Section 27 of the Health and Safety Code).

(d) (Licensing and statistics) Information and records maintained pursuant to Division 2 (commencing with Section 1200) and Part 1 (commencing with Section 102100) of Division 102 of the Health and Safety Code; pursuant to

§ 56.30

Chapter 3 (commencing with Section 1200) of Division 2 of the Business and Professions Code; and pursuant to Section 8608, 8817, or 8909 of the Family Code.

(e) (Medical survey, workers' safety) Information and records acquired and maintained or disclosed pursuant to Sections 1380 and 1382 of the Health and Safety Code and pursuant to Division 5 (commencing with Section 6300) of the Labor Code.

(f) (Industrial accidents) Information and records acquired, maintained, or disclosed pursuant to Division 1 (commencing with Section 50), Division 4 (commencing with Section 3200), Division 4.5 (commencing with Section 6100), and Division 4.7 (commencing with Section 6200) of the Labor Code.

(g) (Law enforcement) Information and records maintained by a health facility which are sought by a law enforcement agency under Chapter 3.5 (commencing with Section 1543) of Title 12 of Part 2 of the Penal Code.

(h) (Investigations of employment accident or illness) Information and records sought as part of an investigation of an on-the-job accident or illness pursuant to Division 5 (commencing with Section 6300) of the Labor Code or pursuant to Section 105200 of the Health and Safety Code.

(i) (Alcohol or drug abuse) Information and records subject to the federal alcohol and drug abuse regulations (Part 2 (commencing with Section 2.1) of Subchapter A of Chapter 1 of Title 42 of the Code of Federal Regulations) or to Section 11845.5 of the Health and Safety Code dealing with alcohol and drug abuse.

(j) (Patient discharge data) Nothing in this part shall be construed to limit, expand, or otherwise affect the authority of the California Health Facilities Commission to collect patient discharge information from health facilities.

(k) Medical information and records disclosed to, and their use by, the Insurance Commissioner, the Director of the Department of Managed Health Care, the Division of Industrial Accidents, the Workers' Compensation Appeals Board, the Department of Insurance, or the Department of Managed Health Care.

(*l*) Medical information and records related to services provided on and after January 1, 2006, disclosed to, and their use by, the Managed Risk Medical Insurance Board to the same extent that those records are required to be provided to the board related to services provided on and after July 1, 2009, to comply with Section 403 of the federal Children's Health Insurance Program Reauthorization Act of 2009 (Public Law 111–3),[1] applying subdivision (c) of Section 1932 of the federal Social Security Act.[2] *(Added by Stats.1981, c. 782, § 2. Amended by Stats.1990, c. 1363 (A.B.3532), § 1, operative July 1, 1991; Stats.1992, c. 163 (A.B.2641), § 5, operative Jan. 1, 1994; Stats.1993, c. 1004 (A.B.336), § 2; Stats.1996, c. 1023 (S.B.1497), § 26, eff. Sept. 29, 1996; Stats.1999, c. 526 (S.B.19), § 7; Stats.2000, c. 1067 (S.B.2094), § 3; Stats.2010, c. 717 (S.B.853), § 1, eff. Oct. 19, 2010; Stats.2014, c. 71 (S.B.1304), § 14, eff. Jan. 1, 2015.)*

[1] Public law sections classified to the U.S.C.A., see USCA-Tables
[2] 42 U.S.C.A. § 1396u–2.

Cross References

Department of Managed Health Care, generally, see Health and Safety Code § 1341 et seq.
Division of Workers' Compensation, formerly Division of Industrial Accidents, see Labor Code § 110 et seq.
Inspection of public records, other exemptions from disclosure, medical information, see Government Code § 6276.30.
Medical information defined for purposes of this Part, see Civil Code § 56.05.
Patient defined for purposes of this Part, see Civil Code § 56.05.
Workers' compensation, see Labor Code § 3200 et seq.

§ 56.31. Disclosure or use of medical information under subdivision (f) of Section 56.30; HIV infection or exposure; employment incident

Notwithstanding any other provision of law, nothing in subdivision (f) of Section 56.30 shall permit the disclosure or use of medical information regarding whether a patient is infected with or exposed to the human immunodeficiency virus without the prior authorization from the patient unless the patient is an injured worker claiming to be infected with or exposed to the human immunodeficiency virus through an exposure incident arising out of and in the course of employment. *(Added by Stats.1999, c. 766 (A.B.435), § 1.)*

Cross References

"Authorization" defined for purposes of this Part, see Civil Code § 56.05.
Medical information defined for purposes of this Part, see Civil Code § 56.05.
Patient defined for purposes of this Part, see Civil Code § 56.05.

§ 56.32. Repealed by Stats.1981, c. 782, § 1.5

CHAPTER 7. VIOLATIONS

Section
56.35. Compensatory and punitive damages; attorneys' fees and costs.
56.36. Misdemeanors; violations; remedies.
56.37. Authorization, release, consent, or waiver; enforceability.
57. Repealed.
58. Repealed.
59. Repealed.

§ 56.35. Compensatory and punitive damages; attorneys' fees and costs

In addition to any other remedies available at law, a patient whose medical information has been used or disclosed in violation of Section 56.10, 56.104, 56.107, or 56.20 or subdivision (a) of Section 56.26 and who has sustained economic loss or personal injury therefrom may recover compensatory damages, punitive damages not to exceed three thousand dollars ($3,000), attorney's fees not to exceed one thousand dollars ($1,000), and the costs of litigation. *(Added by Stats.1981, c. 782, § 2. Amended by Stats.1999, c. 527 (A.B.416), § 4; Stats.2021, c. 190 (A.B.1184), § 4, eff. Jan. 1, 2022.)*

Cross References

Medical information defined for purposes of this Part, see Civil Code § 56.05.

Patient defined for purposes of this Part, see Civil Code § 56.05.

§ 56.36. Misdemeanors; violations; remedies

(a) A violation of the provisions of this part that results in economic loss or personal injury to a patient is punishable as a misdemeanor.

(b) In addition to any other remedies available at law, an individual may bring an action against a person or entity who has negligently released confidential information or records concerning him or her in violation of this part, for either or both of the following:

(1) Except as provided in subdivision (e), nominal damages of one thousand dollars ($1,000). In order to recover under this paragraph, it is not necessary that the plaintiff suffered or was threatened with actual damages.

(2) The amount of actual damages, if any, sustained by the patient.

(c)(1) In addition, a person or entity that negligently discloses medical information in violation of the provisions of this part shall also be liable, irrespective of the amount of damages suffered by the patient as a result of that violation, for an administrative fine or civil penalty not to exceed two thousand five hundred dollars ($2,500) per violation.

(2)(A) A person or entity, other than a licensed health care professional, who knowingly and willfully obtains, discloses, or uses medical information in violation of this part shall be liable for an administrative fine or civil penalty not to exceed twenty-five thousand dollars ($25,000) per violation.

(B) A licensed health care professional who knowingly and willfully obtains, discloses, or uses medical information in violation of this part shall be liable on a first violation for an administrative fine or civil penalty not to exceed two thousand five hundred dollars ($2,500) per violation, on a second violation for an administrative fine or civil penalty not to exceed ten thousand dollars ($10,000) per violation, or on a third and subsequent violation for an administrative fine or civil penalty not to exceed twenty-five thousand dollars ($25,000) per violation. This subdivision shall not be construed to limit the liability of a health care service plan, a contractor, or a provider of health care that is not a licensed health care professional for a violation of this part.

(3)(A) A person or entity, other than a licensed health care professional, who knowingly or willfully obtains or uses medical information in violation of this part for the purpose of financial gain shall be liable for an administrative fine or civil penalty not to exceed two hundred fifty thousand dollars ($250,000) per violation and shall also be subject to disgorgement of any proceeds or other consideration obtained as a result of the violation.

(B) A licensed health care professional who knowingly and willfully obtains, discloses, or uses medical information in violation of this part for financial gain shall be liable on a first violation for an administrative fine or civil penalty not to exceed five thousand dollars ($5,000) per violation, on a second violation for an administrative fine or civil penalty not to exceed twenty-five thousand dollars ($25,000) per violation, or on a third and subsequent violation for an administrative fine or civil penalty not to exceed two hundred fifty thousand dollars ($250,000) per violation and shall also be subject to disgorgement of any proceeds or other consideration obtained as a result of the violation. This subdivision shall not be construed to limit the liability of a health care service plan, a contractor, or a provider of health care that is not a licensed health care professional for any violation of this part.

(4) This subdivision shall not be construed as authorizing an administrative fine or civil penalty under both paragraphs (2) and (3) for the same violation.

(5) A person or entity who is not permitted to receive medical information pursuant to this part and who knowingly and willfully obtains, discloses, or uses medical information without written authorization from the patient shall be liable for a civil penalty not to exceed two hundred fifty thousand dollars ($250,000) per violation.

(d) In assessing the amount of an administrative fine or civil penalty pursuant to subdivision (c), the State Department of Public Health, licensing agency, or certifying board or court shall consider any of the relevant circumstances presented by any of the parties to the case including, but not limited to, the following:

(1) Whether the defendant has made a reasonable, good faith attempt to comply with this part.

(2) The nature and seriousness of the misconduct.

(3) The harm to the patient, enrollee, or subscriber.

(4) The number of violations.

(5) The persistence of the misconduct.

(6) The length of time over which the misconduct occurred.

(7) The willfulness of the defendant's misconduct.

(8) The defendant's assets, liabilities, and net worth.

(e)(1) In an action brought by an individual pursuant to subdivision (b) on or after January 1, 2013, in which the defendant establishes the affirmative defense in paragraph (2), the court shall award any actual damages and reasonable attorney's fees and costs, but shall not award nominal damages for a violation of this part.

(2) The defendant is entitled to an affirmative defense if all of the following are established, subject to the equitable considerations in paragraph (3):

(A) The defendant is a covered entity or business associate, as defined in Section 160.103 of Title 45 of the Code of Federal Regulations, in effect as of January 1, 2012.

(B) The defendant has complied with any obligations to notify all persons entitled to receive notice regarding the release of the information or records.

(C) The release of confidential information or records was solely to another covered entity or business associate.

(D) The release of confidential information or records was not an incident of medical identity theft. For purposes of this subparagraph, "medical identity theft" means the use of an individual's personal information, as defined in Section 1798.80, without the individual's knowledge or consent, to obtain medical goods or services, or to submit false claims for medical services.

(E) The defendant took appropriate preventive actions to protect the confidential information or records against release consistent with the defendant's obligations under this part or other applicable state law and the Health Insurance Portability and Accountability Act of 1996 (Public Law 104-191) (HIPAA) and all HIPAA Administrative Simplification Regulations in effect on January 1, 2012, contained in Parts 160, 162, and 164 of Title 45 of the Code of Federal Regulations, and Part 2 of Title 42 of the Code of Federal Regulations, including, but not limited to, all of the following:

(i) Developing and implementing security policies and procedures.

(ii) Designating a security official who is responsible for developing and implementing its security policies and procedures, including educating and training the workforce.

(iii) Encrypting the information or records, and protecting against the release or use of the encryption key and passwords, or transmitting the information or records in a manner designed to provide equal or greater protections against improper disclosures.

(F) The defendant took reasonable and appropriate corrective action after the release of the confidential information or records, and the covered entity or business associate that received the confidential information or records destroyed or returned the confidential information or records in the most expedient time possible and without unreasonable delay, consistent with any measures necessary to determine the scope of the breach and restore the reasonable integrity of the data system. A court may consider this subparagraph to be established if the defendant shows in detail that the covered entity or business associate could not destroy or return the confidential information or records because of the technology utilized.

(G) The covered entity or business associate that received the confidential information or records, or any of its agents, independent contractors, or employees, regardless of the scope of the employee's employment, did not retain, use, or release the information or records.

(H) After the release of the confidential information or records, the defendant took reasonable and appropriate action to prevent a future similar release of confidential information or records.

(I) The defendant has not previously established an affirmative defense pursuant to this subdivision, or the court determines, in its discretion, that application of the affirmative defense is compelling and consistent with the purposes of this section to promote reasonable conduct in light of all the facts.

(3)(A) In determining whether the affirmative defense may be established pursuant to paragraph (2), the court shall consider the equity of the situation, including, but not limited to, (i) whether the defendant has previously violated this part, regardless of whether an action has previously been brought, and (ii) the nature of the prior violation.

(B) To the extent the court allows discovery to determine whether there has been any other violation of this part that the court will consider in balancing the equities, the defendant shall not provide any medical information, as defined in Section 56.05. The court, in its discretion, may enter a protective order prohibiting the further use of any personal information, as defined in Section 1798.80, about the individual whose medical information may have been disclosed in a prior violation.

(4) In an action under this subdivision in which the defendant establishes the affirmative defense pursuant to paragraph (2), a plaintiff shall be entitled to recover reasonable attorney's fees and costs without regard to an award of actual or nominal damages or the imposition of administrative fines or civil penalties.

(5) In an action brought by an individual pursuant to subdivision (b) on or after January 1, 2013, in which the defendant establishes the affirmative defense pursuant to paragraph (2), a defendant shall not be liable for more than one judgment on the merits under this subdivision for releases of confidential information or records arising out of the same event, transaction, or occurrence.

(f)(1) The civil penalty pursuant to subdivision (c) shall be assessed and recovered in a civil action brought in the name of the people of the State of California in any court of competent jurisdiction by any of the following:

(A) The Attorney General.

(B) A district attorney.

(C) A county counsel authorized by agreement with the district attorney in actions involving violation of a county ordinance.

(D) A city attorney of a city.

(E) A city attorney of a city and county having a population in excess of 750,000, with the consent of the district attorney.

(F) A city prosecutor in a city having a full-time city prosecutor or, with the consent of the district attorney, by a city attorney in a city and county.

(G) The State Public Health Officer, or his or her designee, may recommend that a person described in subparagraphs (A) to (F), inclusive, bring a civil action under this section.

(2) If the action is brought by the Attorney General, one-half of the penalty collected shall be paid to the treasurer of the county in which the judgment was entered, and one-half to the General Fund. If the action is brought by a district attorney or county counsel, the penalty collected shall be paid to the treasurer of the county in which the judgment was entered. Except as provided in paragraph (3), if the action is brought by a city attorney or city prosecutor, one-half of the penalty collected shall be paid to the treasurer of the city in which the judgment was entered and one-half to the treasurer of the county in which the judgment was entered.

(3) If the action is brought by a city attorney of a city and county, the entire amount of the penalty collected shall be paid to the treasurer of the city and county in which the judgment was entered.

(4) This section shall not be construed as authorizing both an administrative fine and civil penalty for the same violation.

(5) Imposition of a fine or penalty provided for in this section shall not preclude imposition of other sanctions or remedies authorized by law.

(6) Administrative fines or penalties issued pursuant to Section 1280.15 of the Health and Safety Code shall offset any other administrative fine or civil penalty imposed under this section for the same violation.

(g) For purposes of this section, "knowing" and "willful" shall have the same meanings as in Section 7 of the Penal Code.

(h) A person who discloses protected medical information in accordance with the provisions of this part is not subject to the penalty provisions of this part. *(Added by Stats.1981, c. 782, § 2. Amended by Stats.1999, c. 526 (S.B.19), § 8; Stats.2008, c. 602 (A.B.211), § 1; Stats.2012, c. 437 (A.B.439), § 1; Stats.2014, c. 31 (S.B.857), § 1, eff. June 20, 2014; Stats.2015, c. 303 (A.B.731), § 26, eff. Jan. 1, 2016.)*

Cross References

Attorney General, generally, see Government Code § 12500 et seq.
"Authorization" defined for purposes of this Part, see Civil Code § 56.05.
Board of Pharmacy, scope of authority to issue citations containing fines and orders of abatement, see Business and Professions Code § 4314.
"Contractor" defined for purposes of this Part, see Civil Code § 56.05.
Disease management organizations, receipt of medical information, confidentiality and disclosure, see Health and Safety Code § 1399.903.
"Health care service plan" defined for purposes of this Part, see Civil Code § 56.05.
Internal Health Information Integrity Quality Improvement Account, deposit of fines assessed pursuant to this section, see Health and Safety Code § 130204.
"Licensed health care professional" defined for purposes of this Part, see Civil Code § 56.05.
Medical information defined for purposes of this Part, see Civil Code § 56.05.
Misdemeanors, definition and penalties, see Penal Code §§ 17, 19 and 19.2.
Office of Health Information Integrity, administrative fines pursuant to this section, see Health and Safety Code § 130202.
Patient defined for purposes of this Part, see Civil Code § 56.05.
"Provider of health care" defined for purposes of this Part, see Civil Code § 56.05.

§ 56.37. Authorization, release, consent, or waiver; enforceability

(a) No provider of health care, health care service plan, or contractor may require a patient, as a condition of receiving health care services, to sign an authorization, release, consent, or waiver that would permit the disclosure of medical information that otherwise may not be disclosed under Section 56.10 or any other provision of law. However, a health care service plan or disability insurer may require relevant enrollee or subscriber medical information as a condition of the medical underwriting process, provided that Sections 1374.7 and 1389.1 of the Health and Safety Code are strictly observed.

(b) Any waiver by a patient of the provisions of this part, except as authorized by Section 56.11 or 56.21 or subdivision (b) of Section 56.26, shall be deemed contrary to public policy and shall be unenforceable. *(Added by Stats.1981, c. 782, § 2. Amended by Stats.1999, c. 526 (S.B.19), § 9.)*

Cross References

"Authorization" defined for purposes of this Part, see Civil Code § 56.05.
"Contractor" defined for purposes of this Part, see Civil Code § 56.05.
"Health care service plan" defined for purposes of this Part, see Civil Code § 56.05.
Medical information defined for purposes of this Part, see Civil Code § 56.05.
Patient defined for purposes of this Part, see Civil Code § 56.05.
"Provider of health care" defined for purposes of this Part, see Civil Code § 56.05.

§ 57. Repealed by Stats.1969, c. 1608, p. 3313, § 3

§ 58. Repealed by Stats.1905, c. 414, p. 554, § 1

§ 59. Repealed by Stats.1969, c. 1608, p. 3313, § 3

Part 2.7

MEDICAL CLAIMS DATA ERROR CORRECTION

Section
57. Receipt of health care claims data; compliance with requirements for error correction required; definitions.
60 to 63.2. Repealed.
64, 65. Repealed.
66 to 69. Repealed.
69a to 69.5. Repealed.
70. Repealed.
71 to 74. Repealed.
75. Repealed.
76 to 79.1. Repealed.
79½. Renumbered.

§ 57. Receipt of health care claims data; compliance with requirements for error correction required; definitions

(a) A qualified entity, as defined in Section 1395kk(e)(2) of Title 42 of the United States Code, that receives claims data from a health care service plan or health insurer shall comply with the requirements governing provider and supplier requests for error correction established under Section 401.717 of Title 42 of the Code of Federal Regulations for all claims data received, including data from sources other than Medicare.

(b) For purposes of this section, the following definitions apply:

(1) "Provider" means a hospital, a skilled nursing facility, a comprehensive outpatient rehabilitation facility, a home health agency, a hospice, a clinic, or a rehabilitation agency.

(2) "Supplier" means a physician and surgeon or other health care practitioner, or an entity that furnishes health care services other than a provider. *(Added by Stats.2012, c. 869 (S.B.1196), § 1.)*

§§ 60 to 63.2. Repealed by Stats.1992, c. 162 (A.B.2650), § 1, operative Jan. 1, 1994

§§ 64, 65. Repealed by Stats.1993, c. 219 (A.B.1500), §§ 3, 4

§§ 66 to 69. Repealed by Stats.1992, c. 162 (A.B.2650), § 1, operative Jan. 1, 1994

§§ 69a to 69.5. Repealed by Stats.1969, c. 1608, p. 3313, § 3

§ 70. Repealed by Stats.1992, c. 162 (A.B.2650), § 1, operative Jan. 1, 1994

§§ 71 to 74. Repealed by Stats.1969, c. 1608, p. 3313, § 3

§ 75. Repealed by Stats.1895, c. 129, p. 121, § 4

§§ 76 to 79.1. Repealed by Stats.1969, c. 1608, p. 3313, § 3

§ 79½. Renumbered § 79a by Stats.1905, c. 414, p. 555, § 4

Part 2.9

CALIFORNIA FAIR DEALERSHIP LAW

Section
80. Citation.
81. Definitions.
82. Liberal construction; purposes and policies.
83. Refusal to grant dealership; prohibited grounds.
84. Termination, cancellation, or refusal to renew dealership agreement; prohibited grounds.
85. Refusal to make or consent to assignment, sale, transfer, or bequest of dealership; prohibited grounds.
86. Attorney's fees; costs.

§ 80. Citation

This part may be cited as the California Fair Dealership Law. *(Added by Stats.1980, c. 914, § 1.)*

§ 81. Definitions

As used in this part:

(a) "Person" means a natural person, partnership, joint venture, corporation, limited liability company, or other entity.

(b) "Dealership" means a contract or agreement, either express or implied, whether oral or written, between two or more persons, by which a person is granted the right to sell or distribute goods or services, or to use a trade name, trademark, service mark, logotype, or advertising or other commercial symbol, in which there is a community of interest in the business of offering, selling, or distributing goods or services at wholesale, or at retail, by lease, agreement, or otherwise.

(c) "Grantor" means a person who sells, leases, or otherwise transfers a dealership.

(d) "Community of interest" means a continuing financial interest between the grantor and grantee in either the operation of the dealership or the marketing of goods or services.

(e) "Dealer" means a person who is a grantee of a dealership situated in this state.

(f) "Grant" means a sale, lease, or transfer of any kind. *(Added by Stats.1980, c. 914, § 1. Amended by Stats.1994, c. 1010 (S.B.2053), § 29.)*

§ 82. Liberal construction; purposes and policies

This part shall be liberally construed and applied to promote its underlying purposes and policies, which are as follows:

(a) The prohibition of discrimination based upon any characteristic listed or defined in subdivision (b) or (e) of Section 51 in the granting, sale, transfer, bequest, termination, and nonrenewal of dealerships.

(b) The requirements of this part shall not be varied by contract or agreement and any portion of a contract or agreement purporting to do so is void and unenforceable.

(Added by Stats.1980, c. 914, § 1. Amended by Stats.2007, c. 568 (A.B.14), § 10.)

Cross References

"Dealership" defined for purposes of this Part, see Civil Code § 81.

§ 83. Refusal to grant dealership; prohibited grounds

On or after January 1, 1981, no grantor, directly or indirectly, shall refuse to grant a dealership to any person because of any characteristic listed or defined in subdivision (b) or (e) of Section 51. *(Added by Stats.1980, c. 914, § 1. Amended by Stats.2007, c. 568 (A.B.14), § 11.)*

Cross References

"Dealership" defined for purposes of this Part, see Civil Code § 81.
"Grant" defined for purposes of this Part, see Civil Code § 81.
"Grantor" defined for purposes of this Part, see Civil Code § 81.
Person defined for purposes of this Part, see Civil Code § 81.

§ 84. Termination, cancellation, or refusal to renew dealership agreement; prohibited grounds

On or after January 1, 1981, no grantor, directly or indirectly, may terminate, cancel, or refuse to renew a dealership agreement with a dealer because of any characteristic listed or defined in subdivision (b) or (e) of Section 51. *(Added by Stats.1980, c. 914, § 1. Amended by Stats.2007, c. 568 (A.B.14), § 12.)*

Cross References

"Dealer" defined for purposes of this Part, see Civil Code § 81.
"Dealership" defined for purposes of this Part, see Civil Code § 81.
"Grantor" defined for purposes of this Part, see Civil Code § 81.

§ 85. Refusal to make or consent to assignment, sale, transfer, or bequest of dealership; prohibited grounds

On or after January 1, 1981, no grantor or dealer, directly or indirectly, shall refuse to make or to consent to an assignment, sale, transfer, or bequest of a dealership to any person, or to the intestate succession to the dealership by any person, because of any characteristic listed or defined in subdivision (b) or (e) of Section 51. This section shall not be construed to create any right in a dealer to assign, sell, transfer, or bequeath a dealership where the right did not exist prior to January 1, 1981. *(Added by Stats.1980, c. 914, § 1. Amended by Stats.2007, c. 568 (A.B.14), § 13.)*

Cross References

"Dealer" defined for purposes of this Part, see Civil Code § 81.
"Dealership" defined for purposes of this Part, see Civil Code § 81.
"Grantor" defined for purposes of this Part, see Civil Code § 81.
Person defined for purposes of this Part, see Civil Code § 81.

§ 86. Attorney's fees; costs

The prevailing party in any action based on a violation of the provisions of this part shall be entitled to recover reasonable attorney's fees and taxable court costs. *(Added by Stats.1980, c. 914, § 1.)*

Part 3

PERSONAL RELATIONS [REPEALED]

§§ 87, 88. Repealed by Stats.1969, c. 1608, p. 3313, § 3

§ 89. Repealed by Stats.1969, c. 1608, p. 3313, § 3

§§ 90 to 92. Repealed by Stats.1969, c. 1608, p. 3313, § 3

§§ 93 to 108. Repealed by Stats.1969, c. 1608, p. 3313, § 3

§§ 111 to 127. Repealed by Stats.1969, c. 1608, p. 3313, § 3

§§ 128 to 133. Repealed by Stats.1969, c. 1608, p. 3313, § 3

§ 134. Repealed by Stats.1969, c. 1608, p. 3313, § 3

§§ 136 to 138. Repealed by Stats.1969, c. 1608, p. 3313, § 3

§ 138.5. Repealed by Stats.1967, c. 291, p. 1474, § 1

§§ 139 to 148. Repealed by Stats.1969, c. 1608, p. 3313, § 3

§ 149. Repealed by Stats.1969, c. 1608, p. 3313, § 3; Stats.1969, c. 1609, p. 3352, § 1; Stats.1970, c. 269, p. 529, § 2; Stats.1970, c. 962, p. 1725, § 1

§§ 150 to 164.7. Repealed by Stats.1969, c. 1608, p. 3313, § 3

§ 164.8. Repealed by Stats.1969, c. 1608, p. 3313, § 3; Stats.1969, c. 1609, § 34

§§ 165 to 171c. Repealed by Stats.1969, c. 1608, p. 3313, § 3

§ 172. Repealed by Stats.1969, c. 1608, p. 3313, § 3; Stats.1969, c. 1609, § 34

§ 172a. Repealed by Stats.1969, c. 1608, p. 3313, § 3; Stats.1969, c. 1609, § 34

§ 172b. Repealed by Stats.1969, c. 1608, p. 3313, § 3

§§ 172c, 172d. Repealed by Stats.1941, c. 1220, p. 3036, § 3

§§ 173 to 181. Repealed by Stats.1969, c. 1608, p. 3313, § 3

§ 182. Repealed by Stats.1969, c. 1608, p. 3313, § 3; Stats.1969, c. 1609, § 35

§§ 193, 194. Repealed by Stats.1965, c. 299, §§ 8, 9 operative Jan. 1, 1967

§ 195. Repealed by Stats.1975, c. 1244, p. 3195, § 1

§§ 196, 196a. Repealed by Stats.1992, c. 162 (A.B.2650), § 2, operative Jan. 1, 1994

§ 196b. Repealed by Stats.1969, c. 1615, p. 3409, § 1.5

§ 196.5. Repealed by Stats.1993, c. 219 (A.B.1500), § 5

§§ 197, 197.5. Repealed by Stats.1992, c. 162 (A.B.2650), § 2, operative Jan. 1, 1994

§ 198. Repealed by Stats.1976, c. 1399, p. 6312, § 1

§ 199. Repealed by Stats.1984, c. 1671, § 1

§ 200. Repealed by Stats.1975, c. 1244, p. 3195, § 4

§§ 201 to 208.5. Repealed by Stats.1992, c. 162 (A.B.2650), § 2, operative Jan. 1, 1994

§ 209. Repealed by Stats.1979, c. 1170, p. 4561, § 1.3

§§ 210 to 213. Repealed by Stats.1992, c. 162 (A.B.2650), § 2, operative Jan. 1, 1994

§ 214. Repealed by Stats.1969, c. 1608, p. 3314, § 7, operative Jan. 1, 1970

§§ 215, 216. Repealed by Stats.1975, c. 1244, p. 3195, §§ 5, 6

§ 220.10. Repealed by Stats.1992, c. 162 (A.B.2650), § 2, operative Jan. 1, 1994

§§ 220.15, 220.20. Repealed by Stats.1993, c. 219 (A.B.1500), §§ 6, 7

§ 221. Repealed by Stats.1990, c. 1363 (A.B.3532), § 2, operative July 1, 1991

§§ 221.05, 221.07. Repealed by Stats.1993, c. 219 (A.B.1500), §§ 8, 9

§ 221.5. Repealed by Stats.1990, c. 1363 (A.B.3532), § 2, operative July 1, 1991

§§ 221.10 to 221.80. Repealed by Stats.1992, c. 162 (A.B.2650), § 2, operative Jan. 1, 1994

§ 222. Repealed by Stats.1990, c. 1363 (A.B.3532), § 2, operative July 1, 1991

§ 222.10. Repealed by Stats.1993, c. 219 (A.B.1500), § 10

§§ 222.13 to 222.70. Repealed by Stats.1992, c. 162 (A.B.2650), § 2, operative Jan. 1, 1994

§ 222.71. Repealed by Stats.1993, c. 219 (A.B.1500), § 11

§§ 222.72 to 222.90. Repealed by Stats.1992, c. 162 (A.B.2650), § 2, operative Jan. 1, 1994

§ 223. Repealed by Stats.1990, c. 1363 (A.B.3532), § 2, operative July 1, 1991

§§ 224 to 224v. Repealed by Stats.1990, c. 1363 (A.B.3532), § 2, operative July 1, 1991

§ 224.1. Repealed by Stats.1990, c. 1363 (A.B.3532), § 2, operative July 1, 1991

§§ 224.10, 224.20. Repealed by Stats.1992, c. 162 (A.B. 2650), § 2, operative Jan. 1, 1994

§§ 224.21 to 224.30. Repealed by Stats.1993, c. 219 (A.B. 1500), §§ 12 to 15

§ 224.33. Repealed by Stats.1992, c. 162 (A.B.2650), § 2, operative Jan. 1, 1994

§ 224.36. Repealed by Stats.1993, c. 219 (A.B.1500), § 16

§§ 224.37 to 224.42. Repealed by Stats.1992, c. 162 (A.B. 2650), § 2, operative Jan. 1, 1994

§ 224.44. Repealed by Stats.1992, c. 162 (A.B.2650), § 2, operative Jan. 1, 1994

§ 224.45. Repealed by Stats.1991, c. 697 (A.B.1202), § 2, operative Jan. 1, 1993

§ 224.47. Repealed by Stats.1990, c. 1363 (A.B.3532), § 3, operative Jan. 1, 1993

§§ 224.49 to 224.61. Repealed by Stats.1992, c. 162 (A.B. 2650), § 2, operative Jan. 1, 1994

§ 224.62. Repealed by Stats.1992, c. 162 (A.B.2650), § 2, operative Jan. 1, 1994

§ 224.63. Repealed by Stats.1993, c. 219 (A.B.1500), § 19

§ 224.64. Repealed by Stats.1992, c. 162 (A.B.2650), § 2, operative Jan. 1, 1994

§§ 224.66 to 224.95. Repealed by Stats.1992, c. 162 (A.B. 2650), § 2, operative Jan. 1, 1994

§§ 225 to 225q. Repealed by Stats.1990, c. 1363 (A.B.3532), § 2, operative July 1, 1991

§§ 226 to 226m. Repealed by Stats.1990, c. 1363 (A.B.3532), § 2, operative July 1, 1991

§§ 226.1 to 226.4. Repealed by Stats.1990, c. 1363 (A.B. 3532), § 2, operative July 1, 1991

§ 226.5. Repealed by Stats.1990, c. 1363 (A.B.3532), § 2, operative July 1, 1991

§§ 226.6 to 226.9. Repealed by Stats.1990, c. 1363 (A.B. 3532), § 2, operative July 1, 1991

§§ 226.10, 226.11. Repealed by Stats.1992, c. 162 (A.B. 2650), § 2, operative Jan. 1, 1994

§ 226.12. Repealed by Stats.1990, c. 1363 (A.B.3532), § 2, operative July 1, 1991

§§ 226.20, 226.21. Repealed by Stats.1992, c. 162 (A.B. 2650), § 2, operative Jan. 1, 1994

§ 226.23. Repealed by Stats.1993, c. 219 (A.B.1500), § 21

§§ 226.25 to 226.50. Repealed by Stats.1992, c. 162 (A.B. 2650), § 2, operative Jan. 1, 1994

§ 226.51. Repealed by Stats.1990, c. 1363 (A.B.3532), § 2, operative July 1, 1991

§§ 226.52 to 226.66. Repealed by Stats.1992, c. 162 (A.B. 2650), § 2, operative Jan. 1, 1994

§ 226.69. Repealed by Stats.1993, c. 219 (A.B.1500), § 22

§§ 227, 227a. Repealed by Stats.1990, c. 1363 (A.B.3532), § 2, operative July 1, 1991

§ 227aa. Repealed by Stats.1979, c. 373, p. 1264, § 41

§§ 227aaa to 227p. Repealed by Stats.1990, c. 1363 (A.B. 3532), § 2, operative July 1, 1991

§ 227.5. Repealed by Stats.1990, c. 1363 (A.B.3532), § 2, operative July 1, 1991

§ 227.10. Repealed by Stats.1992, c. 162 (A.B.2650), § 2, operative Jan. 1, 1994

§§ 227.20 to 227.40. Repealed by Stats.1993, c. 219 (A.B. 1500), §§ 23 to 25

§ 227.44. Repealed by Stats.1992, c. 162 (A.B.2650), § 2, operative Jan. 1, 1994

§§ 227.46, 227.50. Repealed by Stats.1993, c. 219 (A.B. 1500), §§ 26, 27

§ 227.60. Repealed by Stats.1992, c. 162 (A.B.2650), § 2, operative Jan. 1, 1994

§ 228. Repealed by Stats.1990, c. 1363 (A.B.3532), § 2, operative July 1, 1991

§§ 228.10 to 228.15. Repealed by Stats.1992, c. 162 (A.B. 2650), § 2, operative Jan. 1, 1994

§ 229. Repealed by Stats.1990, c. 1363 (A.B.3532), § 2, operative July 1, 1991

§§ 229.10 to 229.70. Repealed by Stats.1992, c. 162 (A.B. 2650), § 2, operative Jan. 1, 1994

§ 230. Repealed by Stats.1975, c. 1244, p. 3196, § 8

§§ 230.5 to 230.8. Repealed by Stats.1990, c. 1363 (A.B. 3532), § 2, operative July 1, 1991

§§ 230.10 to 230.20. Repealed by Stats.1992, c. 162 (A.B. 2650), § 2, operative Jan. 1, 1994

§ 231. Repealed by Stats.1975, c. 1244, p. 3196, § 9

§ 232. Repealed by Stats.1992, c. 162 (A.B.2650), § 2, operative Jan. 1, 1994

§ 232.1. Repealed by Stats.1981, c. 104, § 18, operative Oct. 1, 1984

§§ 232.3 to 232.9
Repealed

§§ 232.3 to 232.9. Repealed by Stats.1992, c. 162 (A.B. 2650), § 2, operative Jan. 1, 1994

§ 233. Repealed by Stats.1993, c. 219 (A.B.1500), § 28

§§ 233.5 to 239. Repealed by Stats.1992, c. 162 (A.B.2650), § 2, operative Jan. 1, 1994

§ 240. Repealed by Stats.1931, c. 281, p. 687, § 1700

§§ 241, 242. Repealed by Stats.1992, c. 162 (A.B.2650), § 2, operative Jan. 1, 1994

§ 243. Repealed by Stats.1976, c. 130, p. 208, § 3

§§ 244, 245. Repealed by Stats.1992, c. 162 (A.B.2650), § 2, operative Jan. 1, 1994

§ 246. Repealed by Stats.1992, c. 46 (S.B.370), § 1, eff. May 11, 1992, operative July 1, 1992

§§ 247 to 254. Repealed by Stats.1992, c. 162 (A.B.2650), § 2, operative Jan. 1, 1994

§§ 255 to 257. Repealed by Stats.1931, c. 281, p. 687, § 1700

§ 258. Repealed by Stats.1905, c. 562, p. 729, § 9

§§ 264 to 275.4. Repealed by Stats.1992, c. 162 (A.B.2650), § 2, operative Jan. 1, 1994

§§ 276 to 276.3. Repealed by Stats.1990, c. 1581 (A.B.548), § 8, operative July 1, 1991

§ 277. Repealed by Stats.1990, c. 1581 (A.B.548), § 5

Part 4

CORPORATIONS [REPEALED]

§§ 278 to 330.23. Repealed by Stats.1929, c. 711, p. 1287, § 44; Stats.1931, c. 862, p. 1763, § 1; Stats.1933, c. 79, p. 518, § 1; Stats.1947, c. 1038, p. 2439, § 100001; Stats.1951, c. 364, p. 1158, § 50000

§§ 330.24 to 331. Repealed by Stats.1997, c. 598 (S.B.633), § 1

§§ 331a to 413. Repealed by Stats.1907, c. 304, p. 578, § 1; Stats.1929, c. 711, p. 1287, § 44; Stats.1931, c. 862, p. 1763, § 1; Stats.1933, c. 533, p. 1420, § 96; Stats.1947, c. 1038, p. 2439, § 100001

§§ 414 to 453.14. Repealed by Stats.1905, c. 421, p. 571, §§ 1, 2; Stats.1905, c. 470, p. 628, § 1; Stats.1907, c. 119, p. 141, § 1; Stats.1907, c. 486, p. 889, § 1; Stats.1913, c. 270, p. 489, § 4; Stats.1933, c. 97, p. 541, § 1; Stats.1935, c. 145, p. 777, § 13001; Stats.1941, c. 1311, p. 1459, § 15

§§ 454 to 459. Repealed by Stats.1951, c. 764, p. 2258, § 25003

§ 460. Unconstitutional

§§ 465 to 494. Repealed by Code Am.1877–78, c. 621, p. 84, § 1; Stats.1929, c. 711, p. 1287, § 44; Stats.1951, c. 561, p. 1713, § 7; Stats.1951, c. 648, p. 1825, § 3; Stats.1951, c. 764, p. 2258, § 25003

§§ 497 to 511. Repealed by Stats.1951, c. 764, p. 2258, § 25003

§§ 512 to 524. Repealed by Stats.1947, c. 176, p. 737, § 2; Stats.1947, c. 424, p. 1307, § 2

§§ 528 to 536. Repealed by Stats.1997, c. 598 (S.B.633), § 1

§§ 537 to 541. Repealed by Code Am.1873–74, c. 612, p. 216, § 94; Stats.1905, c. 385, p. 491; Stats.1951, c. 764, p. 2258, § 25003

§§ 548, 549. Repealed by Stats.1997, c. 598 (S.B.633), § 1

§ 550. Repealed by Stats.1905, c. 429, p. 580, § 2

§ 551. Repealed by Stats.1943, c. 368, p. 1895, § 150001

§ 552. Repealed by Stats.1997, c. 598 (S.B.633), § 1

§§ 557 to 566. Repealed by Stats.1951, c. 41, p. 167, § 1; Stats.1951, c. 364, p. 1158, § 50000

§§ 571 to 583b. Repealed by Stats.1907, c. 302, p. 576, § 8; Stats.1951, c. 364, p. 1158, § 50000

§§ 584 to 590. Repealed by Code Am.1875–76, c. 608, p. 73, § 2; Stats.1905, c. 432, p. 584, § 1; Stats.1929, c. 711, p. 1287, § 44; Stats.1933, c. 533, p. 1420, § 96; Stats.1939, c. 93, p. 1215, § 10002

§§ 591 to 592e. Repealed by Stats.1947, c. 1038, p. 2439, § 100001

§§ 593 to 606.5. Repealed by Stats.1929, c. 711, p. 1287, § 44; Stats.1931, c. 871, p. 1847, § 1; Stats.1947, c. 850, p. 2019, § 3; Stats.1947, c. 1038, p. 2439, § 100001

§§ 607 to 607c. Repealed by Stats.1947, c. 1038, p. 2439, § 100001

§§ 607d to 607g. Repealed by Stats.1997, c. 598 (S.B.633), § 1

§§ 608, 609. Repealed by Stats.1931, c. 1148, p. 2451, § 32(d)

§§ 610, 611. Repealed by Stats.1997, c. 598 (S.B.633), § 1

§§ 612 to 617. Repealed by Stats.1931, c. 1148, p. 2451, § 32(d)

§§ 620 to 622. Repealed by Stats.1974, c. 370, p. 722, § 6

§§ 628 to 632. Repealed by Stats.1905, c. 435, p. 592, § 1; Stats.1915, c. 91, p. 169, § 86

§§ 633 to 648½. Repealed by Code Am.1873–74, c. 612, p. 181; Stats.1981, c. 174, p. 252, § 1; Stats.1905, c. 565, p. 753, § 2; Stats.1907, c. 502, p. 923, § 1; Stats.1931, c. 269, p. 545, § 14.02

§§ 649 to 651e. Repealed by Stats.1943, c. 71, p. 787, § 40001

§§ 652 to 653. Repealed by Stats.1943, c. 71, p. 787, § 40001

§ 653a. Repealed by Stats.1931, c. 867, p. 1839, § 1

§§ 653b to 653*l*. Repealed by Stats.1931, c. 867, p. 1839, § 1

§§ 653m to 653sc. Repealed by Stats.1931, c. 868, p. 1840, § 1

§§ 653t to 653zd. Repealed by Stats.1931, c. 869, p. 1840, § 1

§ 653aa. Renumbered § 610 and amended by Stats.1980, c. 676, § 47

§§ 653bb to 653dd. Repealed by Stats.1933, c. 25, p. 298, § 1301; Stats.1945, c. 1379, p. 2575, § 13

§ 653ee. Renumbered § 611 and amended by Stats.1980, c. 676, § 48

§§ 653ff to 653yy. Repealed by Stats.1933, c. 25, p. 298, § 1301; Stats.1945, c. 1379, p. 2575, § 13

§§ 653ab to 653ag. Repealed by Stats.1943, c. 71, p. 787, § 40001

§§ 653.1 to 653.16. Repealed by Stats.1947, c. 1038, p. 2439, § 100001; Stats.1947, c. 1091, p. 2503, § 2

Division 2

PROPERTY

Part	Section
1. Property in General	654
2. Real or Immovable Property	755
3. Personal or Movable Property	946
4. Acquisition of Property	1000

Part 1

PROPERTY IN GENERAL

Title	Section
1. Nature of Property	654
2. Ownership	669
3. General Definitions	748

Title 1

NATURE OF PROPERTY

Section
654. Ownership; property defined.
655. Things subject to ownership.
656. Ownership of wild animals.
657. Classification of property.
658. Real property defined.
659. Land defined.
660. Fixtures defined.
661. Repealed.
662. Appurtenances to land.
663. Personal property defined.

§ 654. Ownership; property defined

The ownership of a thing is the right of one or more persons to possess and use it to the exclusion of others. In this Code, the thing of which there may be ownership is called property. *(Enacted in 1872.)*

Cross References

Property as including realty and personalty, see Civil Code § 14.
"Property" defined for purposes of the Code of Civil Procedure, see Code of Civil Procedure § 17.
"Property" defined for purposes of the Penal Code, see Penal Code § 7.
"Property" defined for taxation purposes, see Revenue and Taxation Code § 103; Cal. Const. Art. 13, §§ 1, 3.

§ 655. Things subject to ownership

There may be ownership of all inanimate things which are capable of appropriation or of manual delivery; of all domestic animals; of all obligations; of such products of labor or skill as the composition of an author, the good will of a business, trade marks and signs, and of rights created or granted by statute. *(Enacted in 1872.)*

Cross References

Contingent or expectant interest as not insurable, see Insurance Code § 283.
Dogs as personal property, see Penal Code § 491.
Eminent domain, see Code of Civil Procedure § 1230.010 et seq.
Estates in real property, see Civil Code § 761 et seq.
Good will, see Business and Professions Code § 14100.
Insurable interests, see Insurance Code § 280 et seq.
Obligation defined, see Civil Code § 1427.
Products of the mind, see Civil Code § 980 et seq.
Title deeds, see Civil Code § 994.
Trade names, see Business and Professions Code § 14401 et seq.
Trademarks, see Business and Professions Code § 14200 et seq.

§ 656. Ownership of wild animals

Animals wild by nature are the subjects of ownership, while living, only when on the land of the person claiming them, or when tamed, or taken and held in possession, or disabled and immediately pursued. *(Enacted in 1872.)*

Cross References

Fur bearing animals raised in captivity, ownership, see Civil Code § 996.
Game mammals, see Fish and Game Code § 3950 et seq.
Injury to proprietary animals, see Civil Code § 3340.

§ 657. Classification of property

Property is either:

1. Real or immovable; or,

2. Personal or movable. *(Enacted in 1872.)*

Cross References

Property, construction of words and phrases, see Civil Code § 14.
Real property defined for purposes of the Code of Civil Procedure, see Code of Civil Procedure § 17.

§ 658. Real property defined

Real or immovable property consists of:

1. Land;

2. That which is affixed to land;

3. That which is incidental or appurtenant to land;

4. That which is immovable by law; except that for the purposes of sale, emblements, industrial growing crops and things attached to or forming part of the land, which are agreed to be severed before sale or under the contract of sale, shall be treated as goods and be governed by the provisions of the title of this code regulating the sales of goods. *(Enacted in 1872. Amended by Stats.1931, c. 1070, p. 2259, § 4.)*

Cross References

Fixtures, removal, see Civil Code § 1013.
"Land" defined, see Civil Code § 659.
Real property as coextensive with lands, tenements, and hereditaments, see Civil Code § 14; Code of Civil Procedure § 17; Penal Code § 7.
Savings Association Law, "real estate loan" defined, see Financial Code § 5115.

Servitudes, see Civil Code § 801.

§ 659. Land defined

Land is the material of the earth, whatever may be the ingredients of which it is composed, whether soil, rock, or other substance, and includes free or occupied space for an indefinite distance upwards as well as downwards, subject to limitations upon the use of airspace imposed, and rights in the use of airspace granted, by law. *(Enacted in 1872. Amended by Stats.1963, c. 860, p. 2096, § 5.)*

Cross References

Real property, construction of words and phrases, see Civil Code § 14.

§ 660. Fixtures defined

A thing is deemed to be affixed to land when it is attached to it by roots, as in the case of trees, vines, or shrubs; or imbedded in it, as in the case of walls; or permanently resting upon it, as in the case of buildings; or permanently attached to what is thus permanent, as by means of cement, plaster, nails, bolts, or screws; except that for the purposes of sale, emblements, industrial growing crops and things attached to or forming part of the land, which are agreed to be severed before sale or under the contract of sale, shall be treated as goods and be governed by the provisions of the title of this code regulating the sales of goods. *(Enacted in 1872. Amended by Stats.1931, c. 1070, p. 2259, § 5.)*

Cross References

Affixing to another's land without agreement permitting removal, see Civil Code § 1013.
Eminent domain, damages for improvements, see Code of Civil Procedure § 1263.205.
Mining machinery and tools as fixtures, see Public Resources Code § 3980.
Mobilehomes, foundations, see Health and Safety Code § 18551.
Mortgages, see Civil Code § 2926.
Removal of fixtures, see Civil Code § 1013.5.
Tenant's right to remove fixtures, see Civil Code § 1019.
Theft of fixtures,
    Generally, see Penal Code § 495.
    Removal from encumbered property, see Penal Code § 502.5.

§ 661. Repealed by Stats.1939, c. 93, p. 1215, § 10002

§ 662. Appurtenances to land

APPURTENANCES. A thing is deemed to be incidental or appurtenant to land when it is by right used with the land for its benefit, as in the case of a way, or watercourse, or of a passage for light, air, or heat from or across the land of another. *(Enacted in 1872.)*

Cross References

Easements and servitudes, see Civil Code § 801 et seq.
Water company shares, appurtenant to land, see Corporations Code § 14300.

§ 663. Personal property defined

Every kind of property that is not real is personal. *(Enacted in 1872.)*

Cross References

Accession to personal property, see Civil Code § 1025 et seq.
Acquisition of property, see Civil Code § 1000.
Dogs as personal property, see Penal Code § 491.
Fur-bearing animals, ownership, see Civil Code § 996.
Good will of a business as property, see Business and Professions Code § 14102.
Names other than trade names, see Business and Professions Code § 14492 et seq.
"Personal property" as defined for purposes of taxation, see Revenue and Taxation Code § 106.
Personal property as including money, goods, chattels, things in action, and evidences of debt, see Civil Code § 14; Code of Civil Procedure § 17; Penal Code § 7.
Products of the mind, see Civil Code § 980 et seq.
Trademarks, registration and protection, see Business and Professions Code § 14200 et seq.

Title 2

OWNERSHIP

Chapter		Section
1.	Owners	669
2.	Modification of Ownership	678
2.5.	Principal and Income Law [Repealed]	
2.6.	Legal Estates Principal and Income Law	731
3.	Rights of Owners	732
4.	Termination of Ownership	739

CHAPTER 1. OWNERS

Section
669. Ownership.
670. State property.
671. Persons authorized to own property.
672. Repealed.

§ 669. Ownership

All property has an owner, whether that owner is the State, and the property public, or the owner an individual, and the property private. The State may also hold property as a private proprietor. *(Enacted in 1872.)*

Cross References

"Ownership" defined, see Civil Code § 654.
Ownership rights, see Civil Code § 732 et seq.
Property rights, see Cal. Const. Art. 1, § 1.
Rights and obligations of owners, see Civil Code § 818 et seq.

§ 670. State property

The State is the owner of all land below tide water, and below ordinary high-water mark, bordering upon tide water within the State; of all land below the water of a navigable lake or stream; of all property lawfully appropriated by it to its own use; of all property dedicated to the State; and of all property of which there is no other owner. *(Enacted in 1872. Amended by Code Am.1873–74, c. 612, p. 217, § 99.)*

Cross References

Acquiring property for public use, see Code of Civil Procedure §§ 1240.010, 1240.020.
Coastal boundary, see Government Code § 170.
Inland waters, see Government Code § 171.
Navigable waters, see Government Code § 172.
Public lands, administration and control, see Public Resources Code § 6001 et seq.

Sale of excess land, see Code of Civil Procedure § 1240.120.
State rights over property, see Government Code § 180 et seq.
Unclaimed property, disposition, see Code of Civil Procedure § 1440 et seq.
Unclaimed property, generally, see Code of Civil Procedure § 1300 et seq.

§ 671. Persons authorized to own property

Any person, regardless of their citizenship status, may take, hold, and dispose of property, real or personal, within this state. *(Enacted in 1872. Amended by Code Am.1873–74, c. 612, p. 218, § 100; Stats.2021, c. 296 (A.B.1096), § 12, eff. Jan. 1, 2022.)*

Cross References
Control of property by aliens, see Cal. Const. Art. 1, § 20.
Products of the mind, see Civil Code § 980 et seq.
Property rights, inalienability, see Cal. Const. Art. 1, § 1.
Trade names, see Business and Professions Code § 14401 et seq.
Trademarks, registration and protection, see Business and Professions Code § 14200 et seq.

§ 672. Repealed by Stats.1933, c. 969, p. 2491, § 25

CHAPTER 2. MODIFICATION OF OWNERSHIP

Article	Section
1. Interests in Property	678
2. Conditions of Ownership	707
3. Duration of Leases	715
4. Accumulations	722

ARTICLE 1. INTERESTS IN PROPERTY

Section	
678.	Absolute or qualified ownership.
679.	Absolute ownership defined.
680.	Qualified ownership defined.
681.	Several ownership defined.
682.	Ownership by several persons; types.
682.1.	Community property of spouses; subject to express declaration in transfer documents; application and operation of section.
683.	Joint tenancy; definition; method of creation.
683.1.	Joint tenancy; safe-deposit box.
683.2.	Joint tenancy; severance; right of survivorship; applicable law.
684.	Partnership interest defined.
685.	Interest in common defined.
686.	Interest in common; interests excluded.
687.	Community property defined.
688.	Interests as to time.
689.	Present interest defined.
690.	Future interest defined.
691.	Perpetual interest defined.
692.	Limited interest defined.
693 to 695.	Repealed.
696.	Future interests; alternative.
697.	Future interests; improbability of contingency; validity.
698.	Future interests; posthumous children.
699.	Future interests; transfer of title.
700.	Future interests; possibilities.
701.	Real property; classification of interests.
702.	Personal property; classification of interests.
703.	Future interests; recognition.
704.	Repealed.

Cross References
Estates in real property, see Civil Code § 761 et seq.

§ 678. Absolute or qualified ownership

OWNERSHIP, ABSOLUTE OR QUALIFIED. The ownership of property is either:

1. Absolute; or,
2. Qualified. *(Enacted in 1872.)*

§ 679. Absolute ownership defined

WHEN ABSOLUTE. The ownership of property is absolute when a single person has the absolute dominion over it, and may use it or dispose of it according to his pleasure, subject only to general laws. *(Enacted in 1872.)*

Cross References
Termination of ownership, see Civil Code § 739 et seq.

§ 680. Qualified ownership defined

The ownership of property is qualified:

1. When it is shared with one or more persons;
2. When the time of enjoyment is deferred or limited;
3. When the use is restricted. *(Enacted in 1872.)*

Cross References
"Ownership" defined for purposes of this Code, see Civil Code § 654.

§ 681. Several ownership defined

SEVERAL OWNERSHIP, WHAT. The ownership of property by a single person is designated as a sole or several ownership. *(Enacted in 1872.)*

Cross References
Joinder, see Code of Civil Procedure § 378.
"Ownership" defined for purposes of this Code, see Civil Code § 654.

§ 682. Ownership by several persons; types

The ownership of property by several persons is either:

(a) Of joint interest.
(b) Of partnership interests.
(c) Of interests in common.
(d) Of community interest of spouses. *(Enacted in 1872. Amended by Stats.2016, c. 50 (S.B.1005), § 7, eff. Jan. 1, 2017.)*

Cross References
Community property, presumptions as to property acquired by wife, see Family Code §§ 700, 760, 803.
Delivery,
 Co-owners, see Civil Code § 1827.
 Joint tenancy deposits, see Civil Code § 1828.
Husband and wife, methods of holding property, see Family Code § 750.
Insurance, transfer of interest between partners, see Insurance Code § 304.
Joinder, see Code of Civil Procedure § 378.
Off-highway vehicles, co-ownership, see Vehicle Code § 38045.
"Ownership" defined for purposes of this Code, see Civil Code § 654.

§ 682

Partition, see Code of Civil Procedure § 872.010 et seq.
Partnership property, conveyance of realty, see Corporations Code §§ 16203, 16204.
Registration of vehicles, co-ownership registrations, see Vehicle Code § 4150.5.
Registration of vehicles and certificates of title, transfers of title or interest, co-owners as transferees, see Vehicle Code § 5600.5.
Safe deposit boxes, see Financial Code § 1649.
Waste, actions, see Code of Civil Procedure § 732.

§ 682.1. Community property of spouses; subject to express declaration in transfer documents; application and operation of section

(a)(1) Community property of spouses, when expressly declared in the transfer document to be community property with right of survivorship, and which may be accepted in writing on the face of the document by a statement signed or initialed by the grantees, shall, upon the death of one of the spouses, pass to the survivor, without administration, pursuant to the terms of the instrument, subject to the same procedures, as property held in joint tenancy. Prior to the death of either spouse, the right of survivorship may be terminated pursuant to the same procedures by which a joint tenancy may be severed.

(2) Part 1 (commencing with Section 5000) of Division 5 of the Probate Code and Chapter 2 (commencing with Section 13540), Chapter 3 (commencing with Section 13550), and Chapter 3.5 (commencing with Section 13560) of Part 2 of Division 8 of the Probate Code apply to this property.

(3) For the purposes of Chapter 3 (commencing with Section 13550) of Part 2 of Division 8 of the Probate Code, this property shall be treated as if it had passed without administration under Part 2 (commencing with Section 13500) of Division 8 of the Probate Code.

(b) This section does not apply to a joint account in a financial institution to which Part 2 (commencing with Section 5100) of Division 5 of the Probate Code applies.

(c) This section shall become operative on July 1, 2001, and shall apply to instruments created on or after that date. *(Added by Stats.2000, c. 645 (A.B.2913), § 1, operative July 1, 2001. Amended by Stats.2016, c. 50 (S.B.1005), § 8, eff. Jan. 1, 2017; Stats.2022, c. 29 (A.B.1716), § 1, eff. Jan. 1, 2023.)*

Cross References

Community property, presumptions as to property acquired by wife, see Family Code §§ 700, 760, 803.
Delivery,
  Co-owners, see Civil Code § 1827.
  Joint tenancy deposits, see Civil Code § 1828.
Husband and wife, methods of holding property, see Family Code § 750.
Insurance, transfer of interest between partners, see Insurance Code § 304.
Joinder, see Code of Civil Procedure § 378.
Nonprobate transfers, joint tenancy, severance, see Probate Code § 5601.
Partition, see Code of Civil Procedure § 872.010 et seq.
Partnership property, conveyance of realty, see Corporations Code § 15008.
Safe deposit boxes, see Financial Code § 1649.
Waste, actions, see Code of Civil Procedure § 732.

§ 683. Joint tenancy; definition; method of creation

(a) A joint interest is one owned by two or more persons in equal shares, by a title created by a single will or transfer, when expressly declared in the will or transfer to be a joint tenancy, or by transfer from a sole owner to himself or herself and others, or from tenants in common or joint tenants to themselves or some of them, or to themselves or any of them and others, or from spouses, when holding title as community property or otherwise to themselves or to themselves and others or to one of them and to another or others, when expressly declared in the transfer to be a joint tenancy, or when granted or devised to executors or trustees as joint tenants. A joint tenancy in personal property may be created by a written transfer, instrument, or agreement.

(b) Provisions of this section do not apply to a joint account in a financial institution if Part 2 (commencing with Section 5100) of Division 5 of the Probate Code applies to such account. *(Enacted in 1872. Amended by Stats.1929, c. 93, p. 172, § 1; Stats.1931, c. 1051, p. 2205, § 1; Stats.1935, c. 234, p. 912, § 1; Stats.1955, c. 178, p. 645, § 1; Stats.1983, c. 92, § 1, operative July 1, 1984; Stats.1989, c. 397, § 1, operative July 1, 1990; Stats.1990, c. 79 (A.B.759), § 1, operative July 1, 1991; Stats.2016, c. 50 (S.B.1005), § 9, eff. Jan. 1, 2017.)*

Cross References

Cemetery plots, joint tenants of, see Health and Safety Code § 8625 et seq.
Corporate shares or other securities, transfers, see Corporations Code § 420.
Husband and wife may hold as joint tenants, see Family Code § 750.
Insurance, transfer of interest between partners, see Insurance Code § 304.
Joint tenancy deposits, delivery, see Civil Code § 1828.
Multiple party accounts, see Financial Code § 1402.
Partition, authorized persons, see Code of Civil Procedure § 872.210.
Partnership property, see Corporations Code § 16202 et seq.
Safe deposit boxes, notices, see Financial Code § 1649.
Simultaneous death of joint tenants, see Probate Code § 223.
Waste by joint tenant, see Code of Civil Procedure § 732.

§ 683.1. Joint tenancy; safe-deposit box

No contract or other arrangement made after the effective date of this section between any person, firm, or corporation engaged in the business of renting safe-deposit boxes and the renter or renters of a safe-deposit box, shall create a joint tenancy in or otherwise establish ownership in any of the contents of such safe-deposit box. Any such contract or other arrangement purporting so to do shall be to such extent void and of no effect. *(Added by Stats.1949, c. 1597, p. 2845, § 1.)*

Cross References

Delivery,
  Co-owners, see Civil Code § 1827.
  Joint tenancy, see Civil Code § 1828.
Multiple party accounts, see Financial Code § 1402.
Ownership defined for purposes of this Code, see Civil Code § 654.
Partnership, see Corporations Code § 16101 et seq.

Safe deposit box in multiple names, see Financial Code § 1649.

§ 683.2. Joint tenancy; severance; right of survivorship; applicable law

(a) Subject to the limitations and requirements of this section, in addition to any other means by which a joint tenancy may be severed, a joint tenant may sever a joint tenancy in real property as to the joint tenant's interest without the joinder or consent of the other joint tenants by any of the following means:

(1) Execution and delivery of a deed that conveys legal title to the joint tenant's interest to a third person, whether or not pursuant to an agreement that requires the third person to reconvey legal title to the joint tenant.

(2) Execution of a written instrument that evidences the intent to sever the joint tenancy, including a deed that names the joint tenant as transferee, or of a written declaration that, as to the interest of the joint tenant, the joint tenancy is severed.

(b) Nothing in this section authorizes severance of a joint tenancy contrary to a written agreement of the joint tenants, but a severance contrary to a written agreement does not defeat the rights of a purchaser or encumbrancer for value in good faith and without knowledge of the written agreement.

(c) Severance of a joint tenancy of record by deed, written declaration, or other written instrument pursuant to subdivision (a) is not effective to terminate the right of survivorship of the other joint tenants as to the severing joint tenant's interest unless one of the following requirements is satisfied:

(1) Before the death of the severing joint tenant, the deed, written declaration, or other written instrument effecting the severance is recorded in the county where the real property is located.

(2) The deed, written declaration, or other written instrument effecting the severance is executed and acknowledged before a notary public by the severing joint tenant not earlier than three days before the death of that joint tenant and is recorded in the county where the real property is located not later than seven days after the death of the severing joint tenant.

(d) Nothing in subdivision (c) limits the manner or effect of:

(1) A written instrument executed by all the joint tenants that severs the joint tenancy.

(2) A severance made by or pursuant to a written agreement of all the joint tenants.

(3) A deed from a joint tenant to another joint tenant.

(e) Subdivisions (a) and (b) apply to all joint tenancies in real property, whether the joint tenancy was created before, on, or after January 1, 1985, except that in the case of the death of a joint tenant before January 1, 1985, the validity of a severance under subdivisions (a) and (b) is determined by the law in effect at the time of death. Subdivisions (c) and (d) do not apply to or affect a severance made before January 1, 1986, of a joint tenancy. *(Added by Stats.1984, c. 519, § 1. Amended by Stats.1985, c. 157, § 1.)*

Cross References
Real property defined for purposes of this Code, see Civil Code § 658.

§ 684. Partnership interest defined

PARTNERSHIP INTEREST, WHAT. A partnership interest is one owned by several persons, in partnership, for partnership purposes. *(Enacted in 1872.)*

Cross References
Limited partner's interest, see Corporations Code § 15518.
Partners, transfers of insurable interest, see Insurance Code § 304.
Partners and partnerships, personal income taxes, see Revenue and Taxation Code § 17008.
Partnership formation, see Corporations Code § 16202.
Partnership income tax, see Revenue and Taxation Code § 17851 et seq.
Relations of partners to each other and to partnership, see Corporations Code § 16401 et seq.
Uniform Partnership Act of 1994, see Corporations Code § 16100 et seq.

§ 685. Interest in common defined

INTEREST IN COMMON, WHAT. An interest in common is one owned by several persons, not in joint ownership or partnership. *(Enacted in 1872.)*

Cross References
Compulsory joinder, see Code of Civil Procedure § 389.
Depositary, delivery when owners in common cannot agree, see Civil Code § 1827.
Husband and wife, methods of holding property, see Family Code § 750.
Insurance, transfer of interest in insured property by one owner in common to another, see Insurance Code § 304.
Joinder, see Code of Civil Procedure §§ 378, 379.
Ownership defined for purposes of this Code, see Civil Code § 654.
Partition, see Code of Civil Procedure § 872.010 et seq.
Permissive joinder, see Code of Civil Procedure §§ 378, 379.
Safe deposit boxes, see Financial Code § 1649.
Waste, actions for, see Code of Civil Procedure § 732.

§ 686. Interest in common; interests excluded

WHAT INTERESTS ARE IN COMMON. Every interest created in favor of several persons in their own right is an interest in common, unless acquired by them in partnership, for partnership purposes, or unless declared in its creation to be a joint interest, as provided in Section 683, or unless acquired as community property. *(Enacted in 1872.)*

Cross References
Sale of goods, see Commercial Code § 2105.

§ 687. Community property defined

Community property is property that is community property under Part 2 (commencing with Section 760) of Division 4 of the Family Code. *(Enacted in 1872. Amended by Stats.1992, c. 163 (A.B.2641), § 6, operative Jan. 1, 1994.)*

Cross References
Community property generally, see Family Code §§ 63, 700, 751, 760, 803; Probate Code § 100.
Death of spouse, disposition of community property, see Probate Code § 6401 et seq.
Division of spousal property, see Family Code § 2500 et seq.

Interests of parties in community property, see Family Code § 751.
Separate property of spouse, see Family Code § 770 et seq.
Spousal liability, see Family Code § 910 et seq.

§ 688. Interests as to time

INTERESTS AS TO TIME. In respect to the time of enjoyment, an interest in property is either:

1. Present or future; and,
2. Perpetual or limited. *(Enacted in 1872.)*

Cross References

Conditions precedent and subsequent, see Civil Code § 707 et seq.
Future estates in real property, see Civil Code §§ 767, 773.

§ 689. Present interest defined

PRESENT INTEREST, WHAT. A present interest entitles the owner to the immediate possession of the property. *(Enacted in 1872.)*

§ 690. Future interest defined

FUTURE INTEREST, WHAT. A future interest entitles the owner to the possession of the property only at a future period. *(Enacted in 1872.)*

Cross References

Accumulations, future interests, see Civil Code § 722 et seq.
Conditions of ownership, see Civil Code § 707 et seq.
Termination of ownership, future interests, see Civil Code § 739 et seq.

§ 691. Perpetual interest defined

PERPETUAL INTEREST, WHAT. A perpetual interest has a duration equal to that of the property. *(Enacted in 1872.)*

§ 692. Limited interest defined

LIMITED INTEREST, WHAT. A limited interest has a duration less than that of the property. *(Enacted in 1872.)*

§§ 693 to 695. Repealed by Stats.1963, c. 1455, p. 3009, §§ 1 to 3

§ 696. Future interests; alternative

TWO OR MORE FUTURE INTERESTS. Two or more future interests may be created to take effect in the alternative, so that if the first in order fails to vest, the next in succession shall be substituted for it, and take effect accordingly. *(Enacted in 1872.)*

§ 697. Future interests; improbability of contingency; validity

CERTAIN FUTURE INTERESTS NOT TO BE VOID. A future interest is not void merely because of the improbability of the contingency on which it is limited to take effect. *(Enacted in 1872.)*

Cross References

Defeat of future interests, see Civil Code § 740.

§ 698. Future interests; posthumous children

POSTHUMOUS CHILDREN. When a future interest is limited to successors, heirs, issue, or children, posthumous children are entitled to take in the same manner as if living at the death of their parent. *(Enacted in 1872.)*

Cross References

Decedents estates, posthumous children, see Probate Code § 250.
Defeat of future interests, birth of posthumous child, see Civil Code § 739.
Posthumous children, succession, see Probate Code § 6407.
Unborn child deemed existing person, see Civil Code § 43.1.

§ 699. Future interests; transfer of title

QUALITIES OF EXPECTANT ESTATES. Future interests pass by succession, will, and transfer, in the same manner as present interests. *(Enacted in 1872.)*

§ 700. Future interests; possibilities

SAME. A mere possibility, such as the expectancy of an heir apparent, is not to be deemed an interest of any kind. *(Enacted in 1872.)*

Cross References

Estates in real property, see Civil Code § 761 et seq.
Possibilities, transferability, see Civil Code § 1045.
School bonds, California School Finance Authority, rights and possibilities of participating party, see Education Code § 17199.1.

§ 701. Real property; classification of interests

INTERESTS IN REAL PROPERTY. In respect to real or immovable property, the interests mentioned in this Chapter are denominated estates, and are specially named and classified in Part II of this Division. *(Enacted in 1872.)*

Cross References

Estates in real property, see Civil Code § 761 et seq.
Real property defined for purposes of this Code, see Civil Code § 658.
Real property, words and phrases, see Civil Code § 14.

§ 702. Personal property; classification of interests

SAME. The names and classification of interests in real property have only such application to interests in personal property as is in this Division of the Code expressly provided. *(Enacted in 1872.)*

Cross References

Real property defined for purposes of this Code, see Civil Code § 658.

§ 703. Future interests; recognition

WHAT FUTURE INTERESTS ARE RECOGNIZED. No future interest in property is recognized by the law, except such as is defined in this Division of the Code. *(Enacted in 1872.)*

Cross References

School bonds, California School Finance Authority, rights and possibilities of participating party, see Education Code § 17199.1.

§ 704. Repealed by Stats.1991, c. 1055 (S.B.271), § 1

ARTICLE 2. CONDITIONS OF OWNERSHIP

Section
707. Time of enjoyment of property.
708. Condition precedent or subsequent.
709. Conditions precedent; validity.
710. Conditions in restraint of marriage.
711. Conditions in restraint of alienation.
711.5. Housing purchase or rehabilitation loans by state or local entity directly or indirectly; assumptions; denial; acceleration of principal; change in interest.
712. Conditions restraining right to display sign advertising property for sale, lease or exchange.
713. Local regulations; signs advertising property for sale, lease or exchange.
714. Unenforceability of deeds, contracts or instruments prohibiting or restricting installation or use of solar energy system.
714.1. Solar energy systems; common interest developments; approval; maintenance; indemnification or reimbursement; prohibited association actions.
714.3. Unenforceability of deeds, contracts or instruments prohibiting or unreasonably restricting construction or use of accessory dwelling unit or junior accessory dwelling unit.
714.5. Structures constructed in offsite facility or factory and moved or transported in sections or modules to real property; prohibition of sale, lease, rental or use of real property; management documents.
714.6. Restrictive covenants; enforceability; submission and recording of restrictive covenant modification document; application of section.

§ 707. Time of enjoyment of property

FIXING THE TIME OF ENJOYMENT. The time when the enjoyment of property is to begin or end may be determined by computation, or be made to depend on events. In the latter case, the enjoyment is said to be upon condition. *(Enacted in 1872.)*

Cross References

Conditional dispositions, decedents' estates, see Probate Code § 141.
Conditional obligations, see Civil Code § 1434 et seq.
Grant on condition precedent, effect of performance of condition, see Civil Code § 1110.
Grant on condition subsequent, defeat by nonperformance, see Civil Code § 1109.

§ 708. Condition precedent or subsequent

CONDITIONS. Conditions are precedent or subsequent. The former fix the beginning, the latter the ending, of the right. *(Enacted in 1872.)*

Cross References

Conditional obligations, see Civil Code § 1434 et seq.
Construction of conditions involving forfeiture, see Civil Code § 1442.
Defeated grant upon condition subsequent, reconveyance, see Civil Code § 1109.
Definitions, see Civil Code § 1436 et seq.
Grant on condition precedent, performance of conditions, see Civil Code § 1110.
Remainders, conditional limitations, see Civil Code § 778.

Right of reentry for breach of condition subsequent, transferability, see Civil Code § 1046.

§ 709. Conditions precedent; validity

CERTAIN CONDITIONS PRECEDENT VOID. If a condition precedent requires the performance of an act wrong of itself, the instrument containing it is so far void, and the right cannot exist. If it requires the performance of an act not wrong of itself, but otherwise unlawful, the instrument takes effect and the condition is void. *(Enacted in 1872.)*

Cross References

"Condition precedent" defined, see Civil Code § 1436.

§ 710. Conditions in restraint of marriage

Conditions imposing restraints upon marriage, except upon the marriage of a minor, are void; but this does not affect limitations where the intent was not to forbid marriage, but only to give the use until marriage. *(Enacted in 1872. Amended by Code Am.1873–74, c. 612, p. 218, § 101.)*

Cross References

Contract in restraint of marriage void, see Civil Code § 1669.

§ 711. Conditions in restraint of alienation

CONDITIONS RESTRAINING ALIENATION VOID. Conditions restraining alienation, when repugnant to the interest created, are void. *(Enacted in 1872.)*

Cross References

Assumption of mortgages, housing and infrastructure finance agency, see Health and Safety Code § 51068.
California first-time home buyers, buy-down mortgage plan, acceleration of repayment upon sale or transfer of property to ineligible purchaser or transferee, see Health and Safety Code § 52518.
Cemetery care funds not violative of laws against restraints on alienation or perpetuities, see Health and Safety Code §§ 8737, 8776.
Cemetery plots, establishment of inalienability, see Health and Safety Code § 8680.
Common interest developments, interests included in conveyance, judicial sale or transfer of separate interests, restrictions upon severability of component interests, see Civil Code §§ 4625 et seq., 6662 et seq.
Home financing, acceleration of indebtedness, see Health and Safety Code § 52022.
Home financing program, implementation, see Health and Safety Code § 34312.4.
Income during suspension, see Civil Code § 733.
Local housing finance agencies, acceleration of indebtedness, see Health and Safety Code § 52022.
Residential rehabilitation, loans, amount due on sale or transfer, see Health and Safety Code § 37917.
Shared appreciation loan, validity of "due-on-sale" clause, see Civil Code §§ 1917.062, 1917.162.
Uniform Statutory Rule Against Perpetuities, see Probate Code § 21200 et seq.

§ 711.5. Housing purchase or rehabilitation loans by state or local entity directly or indirectly; assumptions; denial; acceleration of principal; change in interest

(a) Notwithstanding the provisions of Sections 711 and 1916.5, a state or local public entity directly or indirectly providing housing purchase or rehabilitation loans shall have the authority to deny assumptions, or require the denial of

§ 711.5

assumptions, by a subsequent ineligible purchaser or transferee of the prior borrower of the obligation of any such loan made for the purpose of rehabilitating or providing affordable housing. If such a subsequent purchaser or transferee does not meet such an entity's eligibility requirements, that entity may accelerate or may require the acceleration of the principal balance of the loan to be all due and payable upon the sale or transfer of the property.

(b) As a condition of authorizing assumption of a loan pursuant to this section, the entity may recast the repayment schedule for the remainder of the term of the loan by increasing the interest to the current market rate at the time of assumption, or to such lower rate of interest as is the maximum allowed by an entity that provided any insurance or other assistance which results in an assumption being permitted. Any additional increment of interest produced by increasing the rate of interest upon a loan pursuant to this subdivision shall be transmitted or forwarded to the entity for deposit in the specified fund from which the loan was made, or, if no such fund exists, or the public entity has directed otherwise, then to the general fund of such entity.

(c) The state or local public entity providing assistance as specified in this section may implement appropriate measures to assure compliance with this section. (Added by Stats.1979, c. 971, p. 3330, § 1, eff. Sept. 22, 1979.)

Cross References

Assumption of mortgages, housing and infrastructure finance agency, see Health and Safety Code § 51068.
Loans of money, see Civil Code § 1912 et seq.
Obligation defined, see Civil Code § 1427.
Special housing for the developmentally disabled, mentally disordered and physically disabled, assistance to be considered a purchase or rehabilitation loan for purposes of this section, see Health and Safety Code § 50697.

§ 712. Conditions restraining right to display sign advertising property for sale, lease or exchange

(a) Every provision contained in or otherwise affecting a grant of a fee interest in, or purchase money security instrument upon, real property in this state heretofore or hereafter made, which purports to prohibit or restrict the right of the property owner or his or her agent to display or have displayed on the real property, or on real property owned by others with their consent, or both, signs which are reasonably located, in plain view of the public, are of reasonable dimensions and design, and do not adversely affect public safety, including traffic safety, and which advertise the property for sale, lease, or exchange, or advertise directions to the property, by the property owner or his or her agent is void as an unreasonable restraint upon the power of alienation.

(b) This section shall operate retrospectively, as well as prospectively, to the full extent that it may constitutionally operate retrospectively.

(c) A sign that conforms to the ordinance adopted in conformity with Section 713 shall be deemed to be of reasonable dimension and design pursuant to this section. (Added by Stats.1965, c. 1591, p. 3684, § 1. Amended by Stats.1975, c. 147, p. 281, § 1; Stats.1983, c. 51, § 1;

Stats.1990, c. 1282 (A.B.2949), § 1; Stats.1992, c. 773 (S.B. 1474), § 2; Stats.1993, c. 589 (A.B.2211), § 20.)

Cross References

Commercial and industrial common interest developments, application of this section, see Civil Code § 6700.
Commercial and industrial common interest developments, prohibition against association rule or regulation that arbitrarily or unreasonably restricts owner's ability to market his or her interest in common development, application of this section, see Civil Code § 6710.
Common interest developments, application of this section, see Civil Code § 4700.
Common interest developments, prohibition against association rule or regulation that arbitrarily or unreasonably restricts owner's ability to market his or her interest in common development, application of this section, see Civil Code § 4730.
Estates, generally, see Civil Code § 761 et seq.
Property income, right to, see Civil Code § 733.
Real property defined for purposes of this Code, see Civil Code § 658.

§ 713. Local regulations; signs advertising property for sale, lease or exchange

(a) Notwithstanding any provision of any ordinance, an owner of real property or his or her agent may display or have displayed on the owner's real property, and on real property owned by others with their consent, signs which are reasonably located, in plain view of the public, are of reasonable dimensions and design, and do not adversely affect public safety, including traffic safety, as determined by the city, county, or city and county, advertising the following:

(1) That the property is for sale, lease, or exchange by the owner or his or her agent.

(2) Directions to the property.

(3) The owner's or agent's name.

(4) The owner's or agent's address and telephone number.

(b) Nothing in this section limits any authority which a person or local governmental entity may have to limit or regulate the display or placement of a sign on a private or public right-of-way. (Added by Stats.1975, c. 147, p. 281, § 2. Amended by Stats.1983, c. 51, § 2; Stats.1990, c. 1282 (A.B.2949), § 2; Stats.1992, c. 773 (S.B.1474), § 3.)

Cross References

Commercial and industrial common interest developments, application of this section, see Civil Code § 6700.
Commercial and industrial common interest developments, prohibition against association rule or regulation that arbitrarily or unreasonably restricts owner's ability to market his or her interest in common development, application of this section, see Civil Code § 6710.
Common interest developments, application of this section, see Civil Code § 4700.
Common interest developments, prohibition against association rule or regulation that arbitrarily or unreasonably restricts owner's ability to market his or her interest in common development, application of this section, see Civil Code § 4730.
Real property defined for purposes of this Code, see Civil Code § 658.

§ 714. Unenforceability of deeds, contracts or instruments prohibiting or restricting installation or use of solar energy system

(a) Any covenant, restriction, or condition contained in any deed, contract, security instrument, or other instrument affecting the transfer or sale of, or any interest in, real property, and any provision of a governing document, as defined in Section 4150 or 6552, that effectively prohibits or restricts the installation or use of a solar energy system is void and unenforceable.

(b) This section does not apply to provisions that impose reasonable restrictions on solar energy systems. However, it is the policy of the state to promote and encourage the use of solar energy systems and to remove obstacles thereto. Accordingly, reasonable restrictions on a solar energy system are those restrictions that do not significantly increase the cost of the system or significantly decrease its efficiency or specified performance, or that allow for an alternative system of comparable cost, efficiency, and energy conservation benefits.

(c)(1) A solar energy system shall meet applicable health and safety standards and requirements imposed by state and local permitting authorities, consistent with Section 65850.5 of the Government Code.

(2) Solar energy systems used for heating water in single family residences and solar collectors used for heating water in commercial or swimming pool applications shall be certified by an accredited listing agency as defined in the Plumbing and Mechanical Codes.

(3) A solar energy system for producing electricity shall also meet all applicable safety and performance standards established by the California Electrical Code, the Institute of Electrical and Electronics Engineers, and accredited testing laboratories such as Underwriters Laboratories and, where applicable, rules of the Public Utilities Commission regarding safety and reliability.

(d) For the purposes of this section:

(1)(A) For solar domestic water heating systems or solar swimming pool heating systems that comply with state and federal law, "significantly" means an amount exceeding 10 percent of the cost of the system, but in no case more than one thousand dollars ($1,000), or decreasing the efficiency of the solar energy system by an amount exceeding 10 percent, as originally specified and proposed.

(B) For photovoltaic systems that comply with state and federal law, "significantly" means an amount not to exceed one thousand dollars ($1,000) over the system cost as originally specified and proposed, or a decrease in system efficiency of an amount exceeding 10 percent as originally specified and proposed.

(2) "Solar energy system" has the same meaning as defined in paragraphs (1) and (2) of subdivision (a) of Section 801.5.

(e)(1) Whenever approval is required for the installation or use of a solar energy system, the application for approval shall be processed and approved by the appropriate approving entity in the same manner as an application for approval of an architectural modification to the property, and shall not be willfully avoided or delayed.

(2) For an approving entity that is an association, as defined in Section 4080 or 6528, and that is not a public entity, both of the following shall apply:

(A) The approval or denial of an application shall be in writing.

(B) If an application is not denied in writing within 45 days from the date of receipt of the application, the application shall be deemed approved, unless that delay is the result of a reasonable request for additional information.

(f) Any entity, other than a public entity, that willfully violates this section shall be liable to the applicant or other party for actual damages occasioned thereby, and shall pay a civil penalty to the applicant or other party in an amount not to exceed one thousand dollars ($1,000).

(g) In any action to enforce compliance with this section, the prevailing party shall be awarded reasonable attorney's fees.

(h)(1) A public entity that fails to comply with this section may not receive funds from a state-sponsored grant or loan program for solar energy. A public entity shall certify its compliance with the requirements of this section when applying for funds from a state-sponsored grant or loan program.

(2) A local public entity may not exempt residents in its jurisdiction from the requirements of this section. *(Added by Stats.1978, c. 1154, p. 3542, § 3. Amended by Stats.1990, c. 1517 (A.B.3689), § 2, operative July 1, 1991; Stats.1992, c. 1222 (A.B.3554), § 1; Stats.1994, c. 382 (S.B.1553), § 1; Stats.1995, c. 91 (S.B.975), § 16; Stats.2002, c. 570 (S.B.1534), § 1; Stats.2003, c. 290 (A.B.1407), § 1; Stats.2004, c. 789 (A.B.2473), § 2; Stats.2008, c. 40 (A.B.1892), § 1; Stats.2008, c. 539 (A.B.2180), § 2; Stats.2012, c. 181 (A.B.806), § 20, operative Jan. 1, 2014; Stats.2013, c. 605 (S.B.752), § 8; Stats.2014, c. 521 (A.B.2188), § 2, eff. Jan. 1, 2015.)*

Cross References

Commercial and industrial common interest developments, application of this section, see Civil Code § 6700.

Common interest developments, application of this section, see Civil Code § 4700.

Cost of solar energy system, deduction for depreciation, see Revenue and Taxation Code § 17250.

Real property defined for purposes of this Code, see Civil Code § 658.

Regulation of buildings used for human habitation, solar energy systems, approval of applications through issuance of building permits, see Health and Safety Code § 17959.1.

Solar energy system development programs, see Public Utilities Code § 2775.5.

State buildings, solar heating systems, see Public Resources Code § 25498.

Zoning regulations, solar energy systems, limitations on ordinances that create unreasonable barriers to installation, see Government Code § 65850.5.

§ 714.1. Solar energy systems; common interest developments; approval; maintenance; indemnification or reimbursement; prohibited association actions

(a) Notwithstanding Section 714, an association may impose reasonable provisions that:

(1) Restrict the installation of solar energy systems in common areas to those systems approved by the association.

(2) Require the owner of a separate interest to obtain the approval of the association for the installation of a solar energy system in a separate interest owned by another.

§ 714.1

(3) Provide for the maintenance, repair, or replacement of roofs or other building components.

(4) Require installers of solar energy systems to indemnify or reimburse the association or its members for loss or damage caused by the installation, maintenance, or use of the solar energy system.

(b) An association shall not:

(1) Establish a general policy prohibiting the installation or use of a rooftop solar energy system for household purposes on the roof of the building in which the owner resides, or a garage or carport adjacent to the building that has been assigned to the owner for exclusive use.

(2) Require approval by a vote of members owning separate interests in the common interest development, including that specified by Section 4600, for installation of a solar energy system for household purposes on the roof of the building in which the owner resides, or a garage or carport adjacent to the building that has been assigned to the owner for exclusive use.

An action by an association that contravenes paragraph (1) or (2) shall be void and unenforceable.

(c) For purposes of this section:

(1) "Association" has the same meaning as defined in Section 4080 or 6528.

(2) "Common area" has the same meaning as defined in Section 4095 or 6532.

(3) "Separate interest" has the same meaning as defined in Section 4185 or 6564. *(Added by Stats.1992, c. 1222 (A.B. 3554), § 2. Amended by Stats.2012, c. 181 (A.B.806), § 21, operative Jan. 1, 2014; Stats.2013, c. 605 (S.B.752), § 9; Stats.2017, c. 818 (A.B.634), § 1, eff. Jan. 1, 2018.)*

Cross References

Commercial and industrial common interest developments, application of this section, see Civil Code § 6700.

Common interest developments, application of this section, see Civil Code § 4700.

§ 714.3. Unenforceability of deeds, contracts or instruments prohibiting or unreasonably restricting construction or use of accessory dwelling unit or junior accessory dwelling unit

(a) Any covenant, restriction, or condition contained in any deed, contract, security instrument, or other instrument affecting the transfer or sale of any interest in real property that either effectively prohibits or unreasonably restricts the construction or use of an accessory dwelling unit or junior accessory dwelling unit on a lot zoned for single-family residential use that meets the requirements of Section 65852.2 or 65852.22 of the Government Code is void and unenforceable.

(b) This section does not apply to provisions that impose reasonable restrictions on accessory dwelling units or junior accessory dwelling units. For purposes of this subdivision, "reasonable restrictions" means restrictions that do not unreasonably increase the cost to construct, effectively prohibit the construction of, or extinguish the ability to otherwise construct, an accessory dwelling unit or junior accessory dwelling unit consistent with the provisions of Section 65852.2 or 65852.22 of the Government Code. *(Added by Stats.2021, c. 360 (A.B.1584), § 1, eff. Jan. 1, 2022.)*

§ 714.5. Structures constructed in offsite facility or factory and moved or transported in sections or modules to real property; prohibition of sale, lease, rental or use of real property; management documents

The covenants, conditions, and restrictions or other management documents shall not prohibit the sale, lease, rent, or use of real property on the basis that the structure intended for occupancy on the real property is constructed in an offsite facility or factory, and subsequently moved or transported in sections or modules to the real property. Nothing herein shall preclude the governing instruments from being uniformly applied to all structures subject to the covenants, conditions, and restrictions or other management documents.

This section shall apply to covenants, conditions, and restrictions or other management documents adopted on and after the effective date of this section. *(Added by Stats.1987, c. 1339, § 1.)*

Cross References

Commercial and industrial common interest developments, application of this section, see Civil Code § 6700.

Common interest developments, application of this section, see Civil Code § 4700.

Real property defined for purposes of this Code, see Civil Code § 658.

§ 714.6. Restrictive covenants; enforceability; submission and recording of restrictive covenant modification document; application of section

(a) Recorded covenants, conditions, restrictions, or private limits on the use of private or publicly owned land contained in any deed, contract, security instrument, or other instrument affecting the transfer or sale of any interest in real property that restrict the number, size, or location of the residences that may be built on the property, or that restrict the number of persons or families who may reside on the property, shall not be enforceable against the owner of an affordable housing development, if an approved restrictive covenant affordable housing modification document has been recorded in the public record as provided for in this section, except as explicitly provided in this section.

(b)(1) The owner of an affordable housing development shall be entitled to establish that an existing restrictive covenant is unenforceable under subdivision (a) by submitting a restrictive covenant modification document pursuant to Section 12956.2 of the Government Code that modifies or removes any existing restrictive covenant language that restricts the number, size, or location of the residences that may be built on the property, or that restricts the number of persons or families that may reside on the property, to the extent necessary to allow the affordable housing development to proceed under the existing declaration of restrictive covenants.

(2)(A) The owner shall submit to the county recorder a copy of the original restrictive covenant, a copy of any notice the owner believes is required pursuant to paragraph (3) of subdivision (g), and any documents the owner believes necessary to establish that the property qualifies as an affordable housing development under this section prior to, or simultaneously with, the submission of the request for recordation of the restrictive covenant modification document.

(B) Before recording the restrictive covenant modification document, pursuant to subdivision (b) of Section 12956.2 of the Government Code, the county recorder shall, within five business days of receipt, submit the documentation provided to the county recorder by the owner pursuant to subparagraph (A) and the modification document to the county counsel for review. The county counsel shall determine whether the original restrictive covenant document restricts the property in a manner prohibited by subdivision (a), whether the owner has submitted documents sufficient to establish that the property qualifies as an affordable housing development under this section, whether any notice required under this section has been provided, whether any exemption provided in subdivision (g) or (h) applies, and whether the restriction may no longer be enforced against the owner of the affordable housing development and that the owner may record a modification document pursuant to this section.

(C) Pursuant to Section 12956.2 of the Government Code, the county counsel shall return the documents and inform the county recorder of the county counsel's determination within 15 days of submission to the county counsel. If the county counsel is unable to make a determination, the county counsel shall specify the documentation that is needed in order to make the determination. If the county counsel has authorized the county recorder to record the modification document, that authorization shall be noted on the face of the modification or on a cover sheet affixed thereto.

(D) The county recorder shall not record the modification document if the county counsel finds that the original restrictive covenant document does not contain a restriction prohibited by this section or if the county counsel finds that the property does not qualify as an affordable housing development.

(E) A modification document shall be indexed in the same manner as the original restrictive covenant document being modified. It shall contain a recording reference to the original restrictive covenant document, in the form of a book and page or instrument number, and date of the recording. The effective date of the terms and conditions of the modification document shall be the same as the effective date of the original restrictive covenant document, subject to any intervening amendments or modifications, except to the extent modified by the recorded modification document.

(3) If the holder of an ownership interest of record in property causes to be recorded a modification document pursuant to this section that modifies or removes a restrictive covenant that is not authorized by this section, the county shall not incur liability for recording the document. The liability that may result from the unauthorized recordation shall be the sole responsibility of the holder of the ownership interest of record who caused the unauthorized recordation.

(4) A restrictive covenant that was originally invalidated by this section shall become and remain enforceable while the property subject to the restrictive covenant modification is utilized in any manner that violates the terms of the affordability restrictions required by this section.

(5) If the property is utilized in any manner that violates the terms of the affordability restrictions required by this section, the city or county may, after notice and an opportunity to be heard, record a notice of that violation. If the owner complies with the applicable affordability restrictions, the owner may apply to the agency of the city or county that recorded the notice of violation for a release of the notice of violation, and if approved by the city or county, a release of the notice of violation may be recorded.

(6) The county recorder shall charge a standard recording fee to an owner who submits a modification document for recordation pursuant to this section.

(c)(1) Subject to paragraph (2), this section shall only apply to restrictive covenants that restrict the number, size, or location of the residences that may be built on a property or that restrict the number of persons or families who may reside on a property. This section does not apply to any other covenant, including, but not limited to, covenants that:

(A) Relate to purely aesthetic objective design standards, as long as the objective design standards are not applied in a manner that renders the affordable housing development infeasible.

(B) Provide for fees or assessments for the maintenance of common areas.

(C) Provide for limits on the amount of rent that may be charged to tenants.

(2) Paragraph (1) shall not apply to restrictive covenants, fees, and assessments that have not been consistently enforced or assessed prior to the construction of the affordable housing development.

(d) In any suit filed to enforce the rights provided in this section or defend against a suit filed against them, a prevailing owner of an affordable housing development, and any successors or assigns, or a holder of a conservation easement, shall be entitled to recover, as part of any judgment, litigation costs and reasonable attorney's fees, provided that any judgment entered shall be limited to those costs incurred after the modification document was recorded as provided by subdivision (b). This subdivision shall not prevent the court from awarding any prevailing party litigation costs and reasonable attorney's fees otherwise authorized by applicable law, including, but not limited to, subdivision (d) of Section 815.7 of the Civil Code.

(e) Nothing herein shall be interpreted to modify, weaken, or invalidate existing laws protecting affordable and fair housing and prohibiting unlawful discrimination in the provision of housing, including, but not limited to, prohibitions on discrimination in, or resulting from, the enforcement of restrictive covenants.

(f)(1) Provided that the restrictions are otherwise compliant with all applicable laws, this section does not invalidate local building codes or other rules regulating either of the following:

(A) The number of persons who may reside in a dwelling.

(B) The size of a dwelling.

(2) This section shall not be interpreted to authorize any development that is not otherwise consistent with the local general plan, zoning ordinances, and any applicable specific

§ 714.6

plan that apply to the affordable housing development, including any requirements regarding the number of residential units, the size of residential units, and any other zoning restriction relevant to the affordable housing development.

(3) This section does not prevent an affordable housing development from receiving any bonus or incentive pursuant to any statute listed in Section 65582.1 of the Government Code or any related local ordinance.

(g)(1) Subject to paragraph (2), this section does not apply to:

(A) Any conservation easement, as defined in Section 815.1, that is recorded as required by Section 815.5, and held by any of the entities or organizations set forth in Section 815.3.

(B) Any interest in land comparable to a conservation easement that is held by any political subdivision and recorded in the office of the county recorder of the county where the land is situated.

(2) The exclusion from this section of conservation easements held by tax-exempt nonprofit organizations, as provided in subparagraph (A) of paragraph (1), applies only if the conservation easement satisfies one or more of the following:

(A) It was recorded in the office of the county recorder where the property is located before January 1, 2022.

(B) It is, as of the date of recordation of the conservation easement, held by a land trust or other entity that is accredited by the Land Trust Accreditation Commission, or any successor organization, or is a member of the California Council of Land Trusts, or any successor organization, and notice of that ownership is provided in the text of the recorded conservation easement document, or if that notice is not provided in the text of the recorded conservation easement document, the land trust or other entity provides documentation of that accreditation or membership within 30 days of receipt of either of the following:

(i) A written request for that documentation.

(ii) Any written notice of the intended modification of the conservation easement provided pursuant to paragraph (3).

(C) It was funded in whole or in part by a local, state, federal, or tribal government or was required by a local, state, federal, or tribal government as mitigation for, or as a condition of approval of, a project, and notice of that funding or mitigation requirement is provided in the text of the recorded conservation easement document.

(D) It is held by a land trust or other entity whose purpose is to conserve or protect indigenous cultural resources, and that purpose of the land trust or other entity is provided in the text of the recorded conservation easement document.

(E) It, as of the date of recordation of the conservation easement, burdens property that is located entirely outside the boundaries of any urbanized area or urban cluster, as designated by the United States Census Bureau.

(3)(A) At least 60 days before submission of a modification document modifying a conservation easement to a county recorder pursuant to subdivision (b), the owner of an affordable housing development shall provide written notice of the intended modification of any conservation easement to the parties to that conservation easement and any third-party beneficiaries or other entities that are entitled to receive notice of changes to or termination of the conservation easement with the notice being sent to the notice address of those parties as specified in the recorded conservation easement. The notice shall include a return mailing address of the owner of the affordable housing development, the approximate number, size, and location of intended structures to be built on the property for the purposes of affordable housing, and a copy of the intended modification document, and shall specify that it is being provided pursuant to this section.

(B) The county recorder shall not record any restrictive covenant modification document unless the county recorder has received confirmation from the county counsel that any notice required pursuant to subparagraph (A) was provided in accordance with subparagraph (A).

(h) This section shall not apply to any settlement, conservation agreement, or conservation easement, notice of which has been recorded, for which either of the following apply:

(1) It was entered into before January 1, 2022, and limits the density of or precludes development in order to mitigate for the environmental impacts of a proposed project or to resolve a dispute about the level of permitted development on the property.

(2) It was entered into after January 1, 2022, and limits the density of or precludes development where the settlement is approved by a court of competent jurisdiction and the court finds that the density limitation is for the express purpose of protecting the natural resource or open-space value of the property.

(i) The provisions of this section shall not apply to any recorded deed restriction, public access easement, or other similar covenant that was required by a state agency for the purpose of compliance with a state or federal law, provided that the recorded deed restriction, public access easement, or similar covenant contains notice within the recorded document, inclusive of its recorded exhibits, that it was recorded to satisfy a state agency requirement.

(j) For purposes of this section:

(1) "Affordable housing development" means a development located on the property that is the subject of the recorded restrictive covenant and that meets one of the following requirements:

(A) The property is subject to a recorded affordability restriction requiring 100 percent of the units, exclusive of a manager's unit or units, be made available at affordable rent to, and be occupied by, lower income households for 55 years for rental housing, unless a local ordinance or the terms of a federal, state, or local grant, tax credit, or other project financing requires, as a condition of the development of residential units, that the development include a certain percentage of units that are affordable to, and occupied by, low-income, lower income, very low income, or extremely low income households for a term that exceeds 55 years for rental housing units.

(B) The property is owned or controlled by an entity or individual that has submitted a permit application to the relevant jurisdiction to develop a project that complies with subparagraph (A).

(2) "Affordable rent" shall have the same meaning as defined in Section 50053 of the Health and Safety Code.

(3) "Lower income households" shall have the same meaning as defined in Section 50079.5 of the Health and Safety Code.

(4) "Modification document" means a restrictive covenant modification document described in paragraph (1) of subdivision (b).

(5) "Restrictive covenant" means any recorded covenant, condition, restriction, or limit on the use of private or publicly owned land contained in any deed, contract, security instrument, or other instrument affecting the transfer or sale of any interest that restricts the number, size, or location of the residences that may be built on the property or that restricts the number of persons or families who may reside on the property, as described in subdivision (a). *(Added by Stats. 2021, c. 349 (A.B.721), § 2, eff. Jan. 1, 2022. Amended by Stats.2022, c. 28 (S.B.1380), § 20, eff. Jan. 1, 2023.)*

ARTICLE 3. DURATION OF LEASES

Section
715. Execution of certain leases; commencement in possession within 30 years.
715.1. Repealed.
715.2 to 715.7. Repealed.
715.8. Repealed.
716, 716.5. Repealed.
717. Leases of agricultural land; duration.
718. Leases; town or city lots; municipal property; tidelands and submerged lands.
718a. Repealed.
718c. Repealed.
718d. Repealed.
718e. Repealed.
718f. Leases; production of minerals, oil, gas or other hydrocarbons; duration.
719. Leases; city property; maximum term; conditions.

Cross References

Common interest developments, liberal construction of instruments, application of this Article, see Civil Code § 4215.

§ 715. Execution of certain leases; commencement in possession within 30 years

A lease to commence at a time certain or upon the happening of a future event becomes invalid if its term does not actually commence in possession within 30 years after its execution. *(Added by Stats.1991, c. 156 (A.B.1577), § 3.)*

§ 715.1. Repealed by Stats.1959, c. 470, p. 2405, § 1

§§ 715.2 to 715.7. Repealed by Stats.1991, c. 156 (A.B. 1577), §§ 4 to 9

§ 715.8. Repealed by Stats.1970, c. 45, p. 63, § 1

§§ 716, 716.5. Repealed by Stats.1991, c. 156 (A.B.1577), §§ 10, 11

§ 717. Leases of agricultural land; duration

No lease or grant of land for agricultural or horticultural purposes for a longer period than 51 years, in which shall be reserved any rent or service of any kind, shall be valid. *(Enacted in 1872. Amended by Stats.1895, c. 82, p. 75, § 1; Stats.1909, c. 662, p. 1000, § 1; Stats.1915, c. 176, p. 349, § 1; Stats.1963, c. 1906, p. 3897, § 1.)*

Cross References

City land used for agricultural purposes, on which sewage, etc., discharged, see Government Code § 37382.

§ 718. Leases; town or city lots; municipal property; tidelands and submerged lands

No lease or grant of any town or city lot, which reserves any rent or service of any kind, and which provides for a leasing or granting period in excess of 99 years, shall be valid. The property owned by, or that held by, or under the management and control of, any municipality, or any department or board thereof, may be leased for a period not to exceed 55 years. The property of any municipality not acquired for park purposes may, for the purpose of producing, or effecting the production of minerals, oil, gas or other hydrocarbon substances, be leased for a period not to exceed 35 years. Any tidelands or submerged lands, granted to any city by the State of California, may be leased for a period not to exceed 66 years unless the grant from the state of the use thereof provides specifically the term for which said lands may be leased. Tidelands and submerged lands owned or controlled by any city, together with the wharves, docks, piers and other structures or improvements thereon, and so much of the uplands abutting thereon as, in the judgment of the city council, or other governing body, of said city, may be necessary for the proper development and use of its waterfront and harbor facilities, may be leased for a period not to exceed 66 years. Said tidelands, submerged lands and uplands may be so leased only for industrial uses, the improvement and development of any harbor, or harbors, of said city, the construction and maintenance of wharves, docks, piers or bulkhead piers, or any other public use or purpose consistent with the requirements of commerce or navigation at, or in, any such harbor or harbors. *(Enacted in 1872. Amended by Stats.1903, c. 210, p. 247, § 1; Stats.1911, c. 708, p. 1391, § 1; Stats.1915, c. 176, p. 349, § 2; Stats.1917, c. 572, p. 798, § 1; Stats.1927, c. 689, p. 1173, § 1; Stats.1929, c. 170, p. 322, § 1; Stats.1935, c. 695, p. 1893, § 1; Stats.1941, c. 492, p. 1800, § 1; Stats.1961, c. 2010, p. 4220, § 1; Stats.1967, c. 228, p. 1359, § 1.)*

Cross References

Breach of lease, cure or waiver, see Code of Civil Procedure § 1161.5.
City property, leases, dams, reservoirs and appurtenant facilities, see Government Code § 37392.2.
Forcible entry and detainer, see Code of Civil Procedure § 1159.
Lease term where no limit is fixed, see Civil Code § 1943.
Oil and gas and mineral leases by public agencies, authority of city, county or district to enter into agreements for co-operative or unit development of oil and gas, see Public Resources Code § 7058.
Similar provisions as to city-owned property, see Government Code §§ 37380, 37383 et seq.

§ 718a. Repealed by Stats.1949, c. 79, p. 251, § 2

§ 718c. Repealed by Stats.1979, c. 373, p. 1264, § 43

§ 718d
Repealed

§ 718d. Repealed by Stats.1949, c. 79, p. 251, § 2

§ 718e. Repealed by Stats.1949, c. 79, p. 251, § 2

§ 718f. Leases; production of minerals, oil, gas or other hydrocarbons; duration

A lease of land for the purpose of effecting the production of minerals, oil, gas, or other hydrocarbon substances from other lands may be made for a period certain or determinable by any future event prescribed by the parties but no such lease shall be enforceable after 99 years from the commencement of the term thereof. *(Added by Stats.1953, c. 1344, p. 2904, § 1.)*

Cross References

Oil, gas and mineral leases, see Civil Code § 883.130 et seq.; Public Resources Code § 6801 et seq.

Oil and gas conservation, generally, see Public Resources Code § 3000 et seq.

§ 719. Leases; city property; maximum term; conditions

Notwithstanding the 55-year limitation imposed by Section 718, property owned by, or held by, or under the management and control of, any city, or any department or board thereof, may be leased for a period which exceeds 55 years but does not exceed 99 years, if all of the following conditions are met:

(a) The lease shall be subject to periodic review by the city and shall take into consideration the then current market conditions. The local legislative body may, prior to final execution of the lease, establish the lease provisions which will periodically be reviewed, and determine when those provisions are to be reviewed.

(b) Any lease entered into by any city pursuant to this section shall be authorized by an ordinance adopted by the legislative body. The ordinance shall be subject to referendum in the manner prescribed by law for ordinances of cities.

(c) Prior to adopting an ordinance authorizing a lease, the legislative body shall hold a public hearing. Notice of the time and place of the hearing shall be published pursuant to Section 6066 of the Government Code, in one or more newspapers of general circulation within the city and shall be mailed to any person requesting special notice, to any present tenant of the public property, and to all owners of land adjoining the property.

(d) Any lease shall be awarded to the bidder which, in the determination of the legislative body, offers the greatest economic return to the city, after competitive bidding conducted in the manner determined by the legislative body. Notice inviting bids shall be published pursuant to Section 6066 in one or more newspapers of general circulation within the city.

(e) The provisions of subdivisions (b), (c), and (d) of this section do not apply to any charter city, which may utilize a procedure as specified by charter or adopted by ordinance in accordance with its charter.

(f) This section shall not apply to leases of property acquired for park purposes; to leases for the purpose of producing mineral, oil, gas, or other hydrocarbon substances; nor to leases of tidelands or submerged lands or improvements thereon. *(Added by Stats.1983, c. 720, § 1.)*

Cross References

Cities and counties, lease of public property, see Government Code § 50490 et seq.

City property, leases, see Government Code § 37380 et seq.

ARTICLE 4. ACCUMULATIONS

Section
722. Dispositions of income of property; governing rules.
723. Accumulations; validity.
724. Accumulation of income of property; time limit; exception.
725. Accumulations; income of property; directions beyond limit.
726. Accumulations; destitute beneficiaries.

§ 722. Dispositions of income of property; governing rules

Dispositions of the income of property to accrue and to be received at any time subsequent to the execution of the instrument creating such disposition are governed by the rules relating to future interests. *(Enacted in 1872. Amended by Stats.1991, c. 156 (A.B.1577), § 12.)*

Cross References

Revised Uniform Principal and Income Act, see Probate Code § 16320 et seq.

Uniform Statutory Rule Against Perpetuities, see Probate Code § 21201 et seq.

§ 723. Accumulations; validity

ACCUMULATIONS, WHEN VOID. All directions for the accumulation of the income of property, except such as are allowed by this Title, are void. *(Enacted in 1872.)*

Cross References

Revised Uniform Principal and Income Act, see Probate Code § 16320 et seq.

Uniform Statutory Rule Against Perpetuities, see Probate Code § 21201 et seq.

§ 724. Accumulation of income of property; time limit; exception

(a) An accumulation of the income of property may be directed by any will, trust or transfer in writing sufficient to pass the property or create the trust out of which the fund is to arise, for the benefit of one or more persons, objects or purposes, but may not extend beyond the time permitted for the vesting of future interests.

(b) Notwithstanding subdivision (a), the income arising from real or personal property held in a trust forming part of a profit-sharing plan of an employer for the exclusive benefit of its employees or their beneficiaries or forming part of a retirement plan formed primarily for the purpose of providing benefits for employees on or after retirement may be permitted to accumulate until the fund is sufficient, in the opinion of the trustee or trustees, to accomplish the purposes of the trust. *(Enacted in 1872. Amended by Stats.1929, c. 143, p. 276, § 1; Stats.1959, c. 470, p. 2405, § 4; Stats.1991, c. 156 (A.B.1577), § 13.)*

Cross References

Creditors' claims, excess liable for, see Probate Code § 15307.

Income, persons entitled to accumulations in cases of future interests, see Civil Code § 733.
Restraint on transfer of income, see Probate Code § 15300.
Revised Uniform Principal and Income Act, see Probate Code § 16320 et seq.
Trust law, generally, see Probate Code § 15000 et seq.
Uniform Statutory Rule Against Perpetuities, see Probate Code § 21201 et seq.
Wills and intestate succession, generally, see Probate Code § 6100 et seq.

§ 725. Accumulations; income of property; directions beyond limit

If the direction for an accumulation of the income of property is for a longer term than is limited in the last section, the direction only, whether separable or not from the other provisions of the instrument, is void as respects the time beyond the limit prescribed in said last section, and no other part of such instrument is affected by the void portion of such direction. *(Enacted in 1872. Amended by Stats.1929, c. 143, p. 276, § 2.)*

Cross References

Bequest of income, see Probate Code §§ 16340, 16341, 16345, 16346, 16347.
Creditors' claims, excess liable for, see Probate Code § 15307.
Income, persons entitled to accumulations in cases of future interests, see Civil Code § 733.
Restraint on transfer of income, see Probate Code § 15300.
Revised Uniform Principal and Income Act, see Probate Code § 16320 et seq.
Trust law, generally, see Probate Code § 15000 et seq.
Uniform Statutory Rule Against Perpetuities, see Probate Code § 21201 et seq.
Wills and intestate succession, generally, see Probate Code § 6100 et seq.

§ 726. Accumulations; destitute beneficiaries

When one or more persons for whose benefit an accumulation of income has been directed is or are destitute of other sufficient means of support or education, the proper court, upon application, may direct a suitable sum to be applied thereto out of the fund directed to be accumulated for the benefit of such person or persons. *(Enacted in 1872. Amended by Stats.1929, c. 143, p. 276, § 3.)*

Cross References

Bequest of income, see Probate Code §§ 16340, 16341, 16345, 16346, 16347.
Creditors' claims, excess liable for, see Probate Code § 15307.
Income, persons entitled to accumulations in cases of future interests, see Civil Code § 733.
Restraint on transfer of income, see Probate Code § 15300.
Revised Uniform Principal and Income Act, see Probate Code § 16320 et seq.
Trust law, generally, see Probate Code § 15000 et seq.
Uniform Statutory Rule Against Perpetuities, see Probate Code § 21201 et seq.
Wills and intestate succession, generally, see Probate Code § 6100 et seq.

CHAPTER 2.5. PRINCIPAL AND INCOME LAW [REPEALED]

§§ 730 to 730.17. Repealed by Stats.1986, c. 820, § 2, operative July 1, 1987

CHAPTER 2.6. LEGAL ESTATES PRINCIPAL AND INCOME LAW

Section
731. Short title.
731.01. Effect on personal income tax and bank and corporation tax.
731.02. Applicability to transactions by which principal established without interposition of a trust.
731.03. Definitions.
731.04. Law governing ascertainment of income and principal and apportionment of receipts and expenses; exception.
731.05. Principal and income.
731.06. Death of tenant; payments already made; income received after termination of right to income.
731.07. Interests in corporations and distribution of corporate assets.
731.08. Bonds or other obligations for payment of money.
731.09. Use of principal in continuation of business.
731.10. Animals used in business or held as part of principal.
731.11. Timber, mineral, oil or gas, or other natural resources lands.
731.12. Property subject to depletion.
731.13. Delay in change of investment.
731.14. Obligations for payment of money.
731.15. Expenses.

Cross References

Uniform principal and income act, see Probate Code § 16320 et seq.

§ 731. Short title

This chapter may be cited as the Legal Estates Principal and Income Law. *(Added by Stats.1968, c. 193, p. 482, § 1, eff. May 28, 1968, operative July 1, 1968.)*

Cross References

Interest defined for purposes of this Chapter, see Civil Code § 731.03.
Principal defined for purposes of this Chapter, see Civil Code § 731.03.

§ 731.01. Effect on personal income tax and bank and corporation tax

Nothing in this chapter shall affect the provisions of the Personal Income Tax Law and the Bank and Corporation Tax Law. *(Added by Stats.1968, c. 193, p. 482, § 1, eff. May 28, 1968, operative July 1, 1968.)*

Cross References

Corporation Tax Law, see Revenue and Taxation Code § 23001 et seq.
Interest defined for purposes of this Chapter, see Civil Code § 731.03.
Personal Income Tax Law, see Revenue and Taxation Code § 17001 et seq.

§ 731.02. Applicability to transactions by which principal established without interposition of a trust

This chapter shall apply to all transactions by which a principal was established without the interposition of a trust on or after September 13, 1941, or is hereafter so established. Transactions by which a principal is held in trust are governed by Chapter 3 (commencing with Section 16300) of Part 4 of Division 9 of the Probate Code. *(Added by Stats.1968, c. 193,*

§ 731.02

p. 482, § 1, eff. May 28, 1968, operative July 1, 1968. Amended by Stats.1986, c. 820, § 3, operative July 1, 1987.)

Cross References

Principal defined for purposes of this Chapter, see Civil Code § 731.03.

§ 731.03. Definitions

(a) "Principal" as used in this chapter means any realty or personalty which has been so set aside or limited by the owner thereof or a person thereto legally empowered that it and any substitutions for it are eventually to be conveyed, delivered, or paid to a person, while the return therefrom or use thereof or any part of such return or use is in the meantime to be taken or received by or held for accumulation for the same or another person;

(b) "Income" as used in this chapter means the return derived from principal;

(c) "Tenant" as used in this chapter means the person to whom income is presently or currently payable, or for whom it is accumulated or who is entitled to the beneficial use of the principal presently and for a time prior to its distribution;

(d) "Remainderman" as used in this chapter means the person ultimately entitled to the principal, whether named or designated by the terms of the transaction by which the principal was established or determined by operation of law. (Added by Stats.1968, c. 193, p. 482, § 1, eff. May 28, 1968, operative July 1, 1968.)

§ 731.04. Law governing ascertainment of income and principal and apportionment of receipts and expenses; exception

This chapter shall govern the ascertainment of income and principal and the apportionment of receipts and expenses between tenants and remaindermen in all cases where a principal has been established without the interposition of a trust, except that in the establishment of the principal, provision may be made touching all matters covered by this chapter, and the person establishing the principal may himself direct the manner of ascertainment of income and principal and the apportionment of receipts and expenses or grant discretion to the tenant or other person to do so, and such provision and direction, where not otherwise contrary to law shall control notwithstanding this chapter. The exercise by the tenant or other designated person, of such discretionary power if in good faith and according to his best judgment, shall be conclusive, irrespective of whether it may be in accordance with the determination which the court having jurisdiction would have made. (Added by Stats.1968, c. 193, p. 482, § 1, eff. May 28, 1968, operative July 1, 1968.)

Cross References

Interest defined for purposes of this Chapter, see Civil Code § 731.03.
Principal defined for purposes of this Chapter, see Civil Code § 731.03.
"Remainderman" defined for purposes of this Chapter, see Civil Code § 731.03.

PROPERTY

Tenant defined for purposes of this Chapter, see Civil Code § 731.03.

§ 731.05. Principal and income

(a) All receipts of money or other property paid or delivered as rent of realty or hire of personalty, or interest on money loaned, or interest on or the rental or use value of property wrongfully withheld or tortiously damaged or otherwise in return for the use of principal, shall be deemed income unless otherwise expressly provided in this chapter. Dividends on corporate shares, payable in stock or otherwise, shall be deemed income except as provided in Section 731.07.

(b) All receipts of money or other property paid or delivered as the consideration for the sale or other transfer, not a leasing or letting, of property forming a part of principal, or as a repayment of loans, or in liquidation of the assets of a corporation, or as the proceeds of property taken on eminent domain proceedings where separate awards to tenant and remainderman are not made, or as proceeds of insurance upon property forming a part of the principal except where such insurance has been issued for the benefit of either tenant or remainderman alone, or otherwise as a refund or replacement or change in form of principal, shall be deemed principal unless otherwise expressly provided in this chapter. Any profit or loss resulting upon any change in form of principal shall inure to or fall upon principal, except in the case of property referred to and defined by Section 731.14, in which case the provisions of Section 731.14 shall govern.

(c) All income, after payment of expenses properly chargeable to it, shall be paid and delivered to the tenant or retained by him if already in his possession or held for accumulation where legally so directed by the terms of the transaction by which the principal was established; while the principal shall be held for ultimate distribution as determined by the terms of the transaction by which it was established or by law, except in the case of property referred to and defined by Section 731.14, in which case the provisions of Section 731.14 shall govern. (Added by Stats.1968, c. 193, p. 483, § 1, eff. May 28, 1968, operative July 1, 1968.)

Cross References

Interest defined for purposes of this Chapter, see Civil Code § 731.03.
Principal defined for purposes of this Chapter, see Civil Code § 731.03.
"Remainderman" defined for purposes of this Chapter, see Civil Code § 731.03.
Tenant defined for purposes of this Chapter, see Civil Code § 731.03.

§ 731.06. Death of tenant; payments already made; income received after termination of right to income

Whenever a tenant's right to income shall cease by death, or in any other manner, all payments theretofore actually paid to the tenant shall belong to the tenant or to his personal representative; all income actually received after such termination shall be paid to the person next entitled to income by the terms of the transaction by which the principal was established. (Added by Stats.1968, c. 193, p. 483, § 1, eff. May 28, 1968, operative July 1, 1968.)

Cross References

Interest defined for purposes of this Chapter, see Civil Code § 731.03.

Principal defined for purposes of this Chapter, see Civil Code § 731.03.

Tenant defined for purposes of this Chapter, see Civil Code § 731.03.

§ 731.07. Interests in corporations and distribution of corporate assets

(a) All dividends on shares of a corporation forming a part of the principal which are payable

(1) In shares of the declaring corporation of the same kind and rank as the shares on which such dividend is paid; and

(2) In shares of the declaring corporation of a different kind or rank to the extent that they represent a capitalization of surplus not derived from earnings, shall be deemed principal.

Subject to the provisions of this section, all dividends, other than those awarded to principal under (1) and (2) above, including ordinary and extraordinary dividends and dividends payable in shares or other securities or obligations of corporations other than the declaring corporation, shall be deemed income.

Where the tenant shall have the option of receiving a dividend either in cash or in the shares of the declaring corporation, it shall be considered as a cash dividend and deemed income, irrespective of the choice made by the tenant except as provided in subdivision (f) of this section.

(b) All rights to subscribe to the shares or other securities or obligations of a corporation accruing on account of the ownership of shares or other securities in such corporation, and the proceeds of any sale of such rights, shall be deemed principal. All rights to subscribe to the shares or other securities or obligations of a corporation accruing on account of the ownership of shares or other securities in another corporation, and the proceeds of any sale of such rights shall be deemed income.

(c) Where the assets of a corporation are liquidated, amounts paid upon corporate shares as cash dividends declared before such liquidation occurred or as arrears of preferred or guaranteed dividends shall be deemed income; all other amounts paid upon corporate shares on disbursement of the corporate assets to the stockholders shall be deemed principal. All disbursements of corporate assets to the stockholders, whenever made, which are designated by the corporation as a return of capital or division of corporate property shall be deemed principal.

(d) Where a corporation succeeds another by merger, consolidation, or reorganization or otherwise acquires its assets, and the corporate shares of the succeeding corporation are issued to the shareholders of the original corporation in like proportion to, or in substitution for, their shares of the original corporation, the two corporations shall be considered a single corporation in applying the provisions of this section. But, two corporations shall not be considered a single corporation under this section merely because one owns corporate shares of or otherwise controls or directs the other.

(e) In applying this section the date when a dividend accrues to the person who is entitled to it shall be held to be the date specified by the corporation as the one on which the stockholders entitled thereto are determined, or in default thereof the date of declaration of the dividend.

(f) Distributions made from ordinary income by a regulated investment company or by a trust qualifying and electing to be taxed under federal law as a real estate investment trust are income. All other distributions made by the company or trust, including distributions from capital gains, depreciation, or depletion, whether in the form of cash or an option to take new stock or cash or an option to purchase additional shares, are principal.

(g) The tenant may rely upon the statement of the paying corporation as to whether dividends are paid from profits or earnings or are a return of capital or division of corporate property, and as to any other fact, relevant under any provision of this chapter, concerning the source or character of dividends or disbursements of corporate assets. *(Added by Stats.1968, c. 193, p. 484, § 1, eff. May 28, 1968, operative July 1, 1968.)*

Cross References

Corporate reorganization, see Corporations Code § 1200 et seq.

Corporation law generally, dividends, see Corporations Code § 500 et seq.

Interest defined for purposes of this Chapter, see Civil Code § 731.03.

Mergers, see Corporations Code § 1100 et seq.

Obligation defined, see Civil Code § 1427.

Ownership defined for purposes of this Code, see Civil Code § 654.

Principal defined for purposes of this Chapter, see Civil Code § 731.03.

Tenant defined for purposes of this Chapter, see Civil Code § 731.03.

§ 731.08. Bonds or other obligations for payment of money

Where any part of the principal consists of bonds or other obligations for the payment of money, they shall be deemed principal at their inventory value as fixed by the appraiser or appraisers regularly appointed by the court, or, in default thereof, at their market value at the time the principal was established, or at their cost where purchased later, regardless of their par or maturity value; and upon their respective maturities or upon their sale or other disposition any loss or gain realized thereon shall fall upon or inure to the principal, except in the case of property referred to and defined by Section 731.14, in which case the provisions of Section 731.14 shall govern. Where any part of the principal consists of a bond or other obligation for the payment of money, bearing no stated interest but redeemable at maturity or a future time at an amount in excess of the amount in consideration of which it was issued, such accretion, as when realized, shall inure to income. *(Added by Stats.1968, c. 193, p. 485, § 1, eff. May 28, 1968, operative July 1, 1968.)*

Cross References

Interest defined for purposes of this Chapter, see Civil Code § 731.03.

Obligation defined, see Civil Code § 1427.

Principal defined for purposes of this Chapter, see Civil Code § 731.03.

§ 731.09. Use of principal in continuation of business

(a) Whenever a tenant is authorized by the terms of the transaction by which the principal was established or by law,

§ 731.09

to use any part of the principal in the continuance of a business which the original owner of the property comprising the principal had been carrying on, the net profits of such business attributable to such principal shall be deemed income.

(b) Where such business consists of buying and selling property, the net profits for any period shall be ascertained by deducting from the gross returns during, and the inventory value of the property at the end of, such period, the expenses during, and the inventory value of the property at the beginning of, such period.

(c) Where such business does not consist of buying and selling property, the net income shall be computed in accordance with the customary practice of such business, but not in such way as to decrease the principal.

(d) Any increase in the value of the principal used in such business shall be deemed principal, and all losses in any one calendar year, after the income from such business for that year has been exhausted, shall fall upon principal. *(Added by Stats.1968, c. 193, p. 485, § 1, eff. May 28, 1968, operative July 1, 1968.)*

Cross References

Interest defined for purposes of this Chapter, see Civil Code § 731.03.

Principal defined for purposes of this Chapter, see Civil Code § 731.03.

Tenant defined for purposes of this Chapter, see Civil Code § 731.03.

§ 731.10. Animals used in business or held as part of principal

Where any part of the principal consists of animals employed in business, the provisions of Section 731.09 shall apply; and in other cases where the animals are held as a part of the principal partly or wholly because of the offspring or increase which they are expected to produce, all offspring or increase shall be deemed principal to the extent necessary to maintain the original number of such animals and the remainder shall be deemed income; and in all other cases such offspring or increase shall be deemed income. *(Added by Stats.1968, c. 193, p. 486, § 1, eff. May 28, 1968, operative July 1, 1968.)*

Cross References

Interest defined for purposes of this Chapter, see Civil Code § 731.03.

Principal defined for purposes of this Chapter, see Civil Code § 731.03.

§ 731.11. Timber, mineral, oil or gas, or other natural resources lands

(a) Where any part of the principal consists of property in lands from which may be taken timber, minerals, oils, gas, or other natural resources, and the tenant in possession is not under a duty to change the form of the investment of the principal, or (the duty to change the form of the investment being absent) is authorized by law or by the terms of the transaction by which the principal was established, to lease or otherwise develop such natural resources, and no provision is made for the disposition of the net proceeds thereof after the payment of expenses and carrying charges on such property, such proceeds shall be deemed income, whether received as rent or bonus on a lease or as a consideration, by way of royalties or otherwise for the permanent severance of such natural resources from the lands. A duty to change the form of the investment shall be negatived, and authority to develop such natural resources shall be deemed to exist (not excluding other cases where appropriate intent is manifested) where: (1) the resources or the right to exploit them is specifically devised or granted, or (2) where development or exploitation of the resources had begun prior to the transaction by which the principal was established, or (3) where by the terms of that transaction a general authority to lease or otherwise develop is conferred, or (4) where the lands are directed to be retained. The fact that such property received upon creation of the principal does not fall within the category of investments which the tenant or a trustee would be authorized to make under the law or the terms of the particular instrument by which the principal is established, nor the conferring of a mere authority, as distinguished from a direction, to sell such property, shall not be deemed to evidence an intent that the form of the investment shall be changed.

(b) Where any part of the principal consists of property in lands containing such natural resources, and the conditions under which the proceeds thereof become income shall not exist, then in the absence of the expression of contrary intent in the terms of the transaction by which the principal was established, all such proceeds from such resources, not in excess of 5 percent per annum of the inventory value of such resources as fixed by the appraiser or appraisers regularly appointed by the court, or in default thereof their fair market value at the time the principal was established, or their cost if acquired later, shall be deemed income and the remainder principal.

(c) Nothing in this section shall be construed to abrogate or extend any right which may otherwise have accrued by law to a tenant to develop or work such natural resources for his own benefit. *(Added by Stats.1968, c. 193, p. 486, § 1, eff. May 28, 1968, operative July 1, 1968.)*

Cross References

Interest defined for purposes of this Chapter, see Civil Code § 731.03.

Principal defined for purposes of this Chapter, see Civil Code § 731.03.

Tenant defined for purposes of this Chapter, see Civil Code § 731.03.

§ 731.12. Property subject to depletion

Where any part of the principal consists of property subject to depletion, such as leaseholds, patents, copyrights, and royalty rights, and the tenant in possession is not under a duty to change the form of the investment of the principal, the full amount of rents, royalties, or income from the property shall be income to the tenant; but where the tenant is under a duty to change the form of the investment, either at once or as soon as a reasonable price, not representing an undue sacrifice of value, may be obtained, then the rents, royalties or income from such property not in excess of 5 percent per annum of its inventory value as fixed by the appraiser or appraisers regularly appointed by the court, or in default thereof its market value at the time the principal was established or at its cost where purchased later, shall be deemed income and the remainder principal. (Added by Stats.1968, c. 193, p. 487, § 1, eff. May 28, 1968, operative July 1, 1968.)

Cross References

Interest defined for purposes of this Chapter, see Civil Code § 731.03.
Principal defined for purposes of this Chapter, see Civil Code § 731.03.
Tenant defined for purposes of this Chapter, see Civil Code § 731.03.

§ 731.13. Delay in change of investment

(a) Where any part of a principal in the possession of a tenant consists of realty or personalty which for more than a year and until disposed of as hereinafter stated has not produced an average net income of at least 1 percent per annum of its inventory value as fixed by the appraiser or appraisers regularly appointed by the court, or in default thereof its market value at the time the principal was established or of its cost where purchased or otherwise acquired later, and the tenant is under a duty to change the form of the investment as soon as a reasonable price, not representing an undue sacrifice of value, may be obtained and such change is delayed, but is made before the principal is finally distributed, then the tenant shall be entitled to share in the net proceeds received from the property as delayed income to the extent hereinafter stated.

(b) Such income shall be the difference between the net proceeds received from the property and the amount which, had it been placed at simple interest at the rate of 5 percent per annum for the period during which the change was delayed, would have produced the net proceeds at the time of change, but in no event shall such income be more than the amount by which the net proceeds exceed the inventory value of the property as fixed by the appraiser or appraisers regularly appointed by the court, or in default thereof its market value at the time the principal was established or its cost where purchased later. The net proceeds shall consist of the gross proceeds received from the property less any expenses incurred in disposing of it and less all carrying charges which have been paid out of principal during the period while it has been unproductive.

(c) The change shall be taken to have been delayed from the time when the duty to make it first arose, which shall be presumed in the absence of evidence to the contrary, to be one year after the tenant first received the property if then unproductive, otherwise one year after it became unproductive.

(d) If the tenant has received any income from the property or has had any beneficial use thereof during the period while the change has been delayed, his share of the delayed income shall be reduced by the amount of such income received or the value of the use had.

(e) As between successive tenants, or a tenant and a remainderman, delayed income shall be apportioned in the same manner as provided for income by Section 731.06. (Added by Stats.1968, c. 193, p. 487, § 1, eff. May 28, 1968, operative July 1, 1968.)

Cross References

Interest defined for purposes of this Chapter, see Civil Code § 731.03.
Principal defined for purposes of this Chapter, see Civil Code § 731.03.
Remainderman defined for purposes of this Chapter, see Civil Code § 731.03.
Tenant defined for purposes of this Chapter, see Civil Code § 731.03.

§ 731.14. Obligations for payment of money

(a) Where any part of the principal in possession of the tenant consists of an obligation for the payment of money secured by a mortgage or other hypothecation of real or personal property, and by reason of the enforcement of such obligation or by agreement in lieu of enforcement the tenant acquires any property, real or personal, of whatsoever kind, including a money judgment, such property shall be treated as a single substituted asset, and thereafter all income therefrom, expenses incident thereto and proceeds received upon sale, satisfaction, or transfer thereof, not a leasing or letting, excepting gain or profit on such sale, satisfaction or transfer, shall be apportioned in the same manner as provided by this chapter for property of like character acquired by purchase or held as a part of the estate at the time the principal was established.

Gain or profit realized on sale, satisfaction, or transfer, not a leasing or a letting, of property referred to in this section shall be credited to the income in an amount up to, but not exceeding, the accrued unpaid interest on the original obligation secured by such property as of the date of its acquisition by enforcement of the obligation or agreement in lieu thereof, and the balance shall be credited to principal. Such credit to income on account of accrued interest shall be in addition to any and all other credits due income by the terms of any other section of this chapter. Should any portion of such credit to income on account of accrued interest be in a form other than cash, then, and in that event, the full amount of such credit to income shall be paid first out of any sums received from the conversion of such asset into cash whether by payment, sale, or transfer before any sums so received shall be paid to principal.

As between successive tenants or a tenant and a remainderman, all sums paid hereunder on account of accrued interest shall be apportioned in the same manner as provided for income by Section 731.06.

The cost price of the property shall be the unpaid balance of the principal sum of the debt secured by such property, plus all sums whenever paid on any of the following items:

(1) All costs, charges, and expenses incident to the acquisition of such property;

(2) All taxes, bonds, and assessments, or any of them, which were payable at the date of the acquisition of such property by the tenant, excepting, however, interest accruing thereon from the date of the acquisition of such property by the tenant; and all such sums shall be a charge against the principal.

(b) Upon the sale, surrender, or other disposition of a bond, debenture, note, or other evidence of an indebtedness, voluntarily created, or of a certificate of deposit evidencing the deposit of any such instrument with a protective or

§ 731.14   PROPERTY

reorganization committee, or of stock or other security received through participation in the enforcement of such obligation or the foreclosure of the security therefor, upon which bond or other obligation there is overdue unpaid interest which accrued after the establishment of the principal, the proceeds realized upon such sale, surrender, or other disposition, after repayment (1) of expenses incurred in connection therewith and (2) of any sums paid to protect or preserve such security, shall be divided pro rata between income and principal, computing interest at the rate specified in such obligation. The amount allocable to income shall in no case exceed the interest accrued and unpaid on the original obligation up to the time of such sale or other disposition or, where another security has been received in lieu of the original obligation, the income which would have accrued on the latter up to such time, less income received from the original or the substituted security. The terms sale, surrender, or other disposition, as above used, shall include compromise, settlement, accord and satisfaction, and similar arrangements. *(Added by Stats.1968, c. 193, p. 488, § 1, eff. May 28, 1968, operative July 1, 1968.)*

Cross References
Interest defined for purposes of this Chapter, see Civil Code § 731.03.
Obligation defined, see Civil Code § 1427.
Principal defined for purposes of this Chapter, see Civil Code § 731.03.
Remainderman defined for purposes of this Chapter, see Civil Code § 731.03.
Tenant defined for purposes of this Chapter, see Civil Code § 731.03.

§ 731.15. Expenses

(a) All ordinary expenses incurred in connection with the principal or with its administration and management, including regularly recurring taxes assessed against any portion of the principal, water rates, premiums on insurance taken upon the estates of both tenant and remainderman, interest on mortgages on the principal, ordinary repairs, compensation of assistants and court costs on regular accountings, except attorneys' fees, shall be paid out of income. But such expenses where incurred in disposing of, or as carrying charges on, unproductive property as defined in Section 731.13, shall be paid out of principal, subject to the provisions of subdivision (b) of Section 731.13. Attorneys' fees for ordinary or current services shall be paid one-half out of income; one-half out of principal or in such other proportion as the court may direct.

(b) Attorneys' fees and other costs incurred in maintaining or defending any action to protect the property or assure the title thereof, unless due to the fault or cause of the tenant, costs of, or assessments for, improvements to property forming part of the principal, brokers' commissions, title charges, and other costs incurred in connection with purchasing, selling, or leasing property, or investing or reinvesting principal, and all other expenses, except as specified in subdivision (a) of this section, shall be paid out of principal. Any tax levied by any authority, federal, state, or foreign, upon profit or gain defined under the terms of subdivision (b) of Section 731.05 shall be paid out of principal, notwithstanding such tax may be denominated a tax upon income by the taxing authority. *(Added by Stats.1968, c. 193, p. 489, § 1, eff. May 28, 1968, operative July 1, 1968.)*

Cross References
Interest defined for purposes of this Chapter, see Civil Code § 731.03.
Principal defined for purposes of this Chapter, see Civil Code § 731.03.
Remainderman defined for purposes of this Chapter, see Civil Code § 731.03.
Tenant defined for purposes of this Chapter, see Civil Code § 731.03.

CHAPTER 3. RIGHTS OF OWNERS

Section
732. Products and accessions of property.
733. Future interests; income of property.
734. Repealed.

§ 732. Products and accessions of property

INCREASE OF PROPERTY. The owner of a thing owns also all its products and accessions. *(Enacted in 1872.)*

Cross References
Accession to personal property, see Civil Code § 1025 et seq.
Accession to real property, see Civil Code § 1013 et seq.
Acquisition of property by accession, see Civil Code § 1000.
Loan for exchange, title by accession in borrower, see Civil Code § 1904.
Loan for use, title by accession in lender, see Civil Code § 1885.

§ 733. Future interests; income of property

IN CERTAIN CASES, WHO ENTITLED TO INCOME OF PROPERTY. When, in consequence of a valid limitation of a future interest, there is a suspension of the power of alienation or of the ownership during the continuation of which the income is undisposed of, and no valid direction for its accumulation is given, such income belongs to the persons presumptively entitled to the next eventual interest. *(Enacted in 1872.)*

Cross References
"Ownership" defined for purposes of this Code, see Civil Code § 654.

§ 734. Repealed by Stats.1949, c. 79, p. 251, § 2

CHAPTER 4. TERMINATION OF OWNERSHIP

Section
739. Defeat of future interests; birth of posthumous child.
740. Defeat of future interests; condition provided; adjudication.
741. Future interests; alienation or loss of precedent interest.
742. Future interests; premature determination of precedent interest.

§ 739. Defeat of future interests; birth of posthumous child

FUTURE INTERESTS, WHEN DEFEATED. A future interest, depending on the contingency of the death of any person without successors, heirs, issue, or children, is defeated by the birth of a posthumous child of such person, capable of taking by succession. *(Enacted in 1872.)*

Cross References

Posthumous children, see Civil Code § 698.

§ 740. Defeat of future interests; condition provided; adjudication

SAME. A future interest may be defeated in any manner or by any act or means which the party creating such interest provided for or authorized in the creation thereof; nor is a future interest, thus liable to be defeated, to be on that ground adjudged void in its creation. *(Enacted in 1872.)*

§ 741. Future interests; alienation or loss of precedent interest

FUTURE INTERESTS, WHEN NOT DEFEATED. No future interest can be defeated or barred by any alienation or other act of the owner of the intermediate or precedent interest, nor by any destruction of such precedent interest by forfeiture, surrender, merger, or otherwise, except as provided by the next section, or where a forfeiture is imposed by statute as a penalty for the violation thereof. *(Enacted in 1872.)*

Cross References

Future interests, permissible limitation, see Civil Code § 767.

§ 742. Future interests; premature determination of precedent interest

SAME. No future interest, valid in its creation, is defeated by the determination of the precedent interest before the happening of the contingency on which the future interest is limited to take effect; but should such contingency afterwards happen, the future interest takes effect in the same manner and to the same extent as if the precedent interest had continued to the same period. *(Enacted in 1872.)*

Title 3

GENERAL DEFINITIONS

Section
748. Income of property defined.
749. Time of creation of limitation, condition, or interest.

§ 748. Income of property defined

INCOME, WHAT. The income of property, as the term is used in this Part of the Code, includes the rents and profits of real property, the interest of money, dividends upon stock, and other produce of personal property. *(Enacted in 1872.)*

Cross References

Real property defined for purposes of this Code, see Civil Code § 658.

Uniform Principle and Income Act, see Probate Code § 16320 et seq.

§ 749. Time of creation of limitation, condition, or interest

TIME OF CREATION, WHAT. The delivery of the grant, where a limitation, condition, or future interest is created by grant, and the death of the testator, where it is created by will, is to be deemed the time of the creation of the limitation, condition, or interest, within the meaning of this Part of the Code. *(Enacted in 1872.)*

Cross References

Modes of transfer, generally, see Civil Code § 1053 et seq.

Part 2

REAL OR IMMOVABLE PROPERTY

Title	Section
1. General Provisions	755
2. Estates in Real Property	761
3. Rights and Obligations of Owners	818
4. Uses and Trusts [Repealed]	
5. Marketable Record Title	878
6. Rent Skimming	890
7. Requirements for Actions for Construction Defects	895
8. Reconstruction of Homes Lost in Cedar Fire, October 2003 [Repealed]	

Title 1

GENERAL PROVISIONS

Section
755. Real estate; law governing.

Cross References

Accession to real property, see Civil Code § 1013 et seq.
Adverse possession, see Code of Civil Procedure § 321 et seq.
Appurtenances to land, see Civil Code § 662.
Conflicting claims to real property, determination of, see Code of Civil Procedure § 760.010 et seq.
Crimes and offenses, see Penal Code § 450 et seq.
Eminent domain, see Code of Civil Procedure § 1230.010 et seq.
"Fixtures" defined, see Civil Code § 660.
Forcible entry and detainer, see Code of Civil Procedure § 1159 et seq.
Foreclosure of mortgages, see Code of Civil Procedure § 725a et seq.
Hiring of real property, see Civil Code § 1940 et seq.
Homesteads, see Code of Civil Procedure § 704.710 et seq.
Judgment for possession or title, see Civil Code § 3375.
Land defined, see Civil Code § 659.
Limitation of actions for recovery of real property, see Code of Civil Procedure § 315 et seq.
Mechanics liens, enforcement, see Civil Code § 8460 et seq.
Mortgage of real property, see Civil Code § 2920 et seq.
Partition, see Code of Civil Procedure § 872.010 et seq.
Perpetuities, see Probate Code § 21200
Place of trial of real property actions, see Code of Civil Procedure § 392.
Quieting title, see Code of Civil Procedure § 760.010 et seq.
Real property defined, see Civil Code § 658.
Taxation of real property, see Revenue and Taxation Code § 101 et seq.
Transfer of real property, see Civil Code § 1091 et seq.
Trespass, actions for, see Code of Civil Procedure § 733 et seq.
Waste, actions for, see Code of Civil Procedure § 732.

§ 755. Real estate; law governing

Real property within this State is governed by the law of this State, except where the title is in the United States. (Enacted in 1872. Amended by Code Am.1873–74, c. 612, p. 218, § 102.)

Cross References

Accession to real property, see Civil Code § 1013 et seq.
Adverse possession, see Code of Civil Procedure § 321 et seq.
Appurtenances to land, see Civil Code § 662.
Conflicting claims to real property, determination of, see Code of Civil Procedure § 760.010 et seq.
Crimes and offenses, see Penal Code § 450 et seq.
Eminent domain, see Code of Civil Procedure § 1230.010 et seq.
Fixtures defined, see Civil Code § 660.
Forcible entry and detainer, see Code of Civil Procedure § 1159 et seq.
Foreclosure of mortgages, see Code of Civil Procedure § 725a et seq.
Hiring of real property, see Civil Code § 1940 et seq.
Homesteads, see Code of Civil Procedure § 704.710 et seq.
Interests in property, see Civil Code § 678 et seq.
Judgment for possession or title, see Civil Code § 3375.
Land defined, see Civil Code § 659.
Liens, see Civil Code § 2872 et seq.
Limitation of actions for recovery of real property, see Code of Civil Procedure § 315 et seq.
Mechanics liens, enforcement, see Civil Code § 8460 et seq.
Mortgage of real property, see Civil Code § 2920 et seq.
Mortgages, see Civil Code § 2920 et seq.
Partition, see Code of Civil Procedure § 872.010 et seq.
Perpetuities, see Probate Code § 21200
Place of trial of real property actions, see Code of Civil Procedure § 392.
Quieting title, see Code of Civil Procedure § 760.010 et seq.
Real property defined for purposes of this Code, see Civil Code § 658.
Servitude, see Civil Code § 801 et seq.
Taxation of real property, see Revenue and Taxation Code § 101 et seq.
Transfer of real property, see Civil Code § 1091 et seq.
Trespass, actions for, see Code of Civil Procedure § 733 et seq.
Waste, actions for, see Code of Civil Procedure § 732.

Title 2

ESTATES IN REAL PROPERTY

Chapter	Section
1. Estates in General	761
2. Termination of Estates	789
2.5. Mobilehome Residency Law	798
2.6. Recreational Vehicle Park Occupancy Law	799.20
2.7. Floating Home Residency Law	800
3. Servitudes	801
4. Conservation Easements	815
4.5. Greenway Easements	816.50
5. Housing Cooperatives and Housing Cooperative Trusts	817

CHAPTER 1. ESTATES IN GENERAL

Section
761. Estates in real property; kinds.
762. Estate in fee simple defined.
763. Estates tail abolished; fee simple and fee simple absolute.
764. Fee tails as contingent remainders.
765. Freeholds; chattels real; chattel interests.
766. Estate for life of third person; freehold.
767. Future estate; permissible limitation.
768. "Reversion" defined.
769. "Remainder" defined.
770. Repealed.
771. Repealed.
772. Repealed.

Section
773. Authorized future estates and limitations.
774, 775. Repealed.
776. Repealed.
777. Repealed.
778. Remainders; conditional limitation.
779. Heirs of life tenant; taking as purchasers.
780. Remainders; construction of intent.
781. Power of appointment; effect.
782. Discriminatory restrictions in deeds; invalidity; familial status.
782.5. Discriminatory restrictions in deeds or other title-related instruments; deemed revised to omit restrictions; familial status.
783. "Condominium" defined.
783.1. Stock cooperatives; separate and correlative interests.
784. "Restriction" defined.

Cross References

Interests in property, see Civil Code § 678 et seq.
Liens, see Civil Code § 2872 et seq.
Mortgages, see Civil Code § 2920 et seq.
Rights of owner in fee, see Civil Code § 829.
Servitude, see Civil Code § 801 et seq.
Transfer of fee, necessity of words of inheritance, see Civil Code § 1072; Probate Code § 21102.

§ 761. Estates in real property; kinds

ENUMERATION OF ESTATES. Estates in real property, in respect to the duration of their enjoyment, are either:

1. Estates of inheritance or perpetual estates;
2. Estates for life;
3. Estates for years; or,
4. Estates at will. *(Enacted in 1872.)*

Cross References

Hiring of real property, see Civil Code § 1940.
Real property defined for purposes of this Code, see Civil Code § 658.

§ 762. Estate in fee simple defined

Every estate of inheritance is a fee, and every such estate, when not defeasible or conditional, is a fee simple or an absolute fee. *(Enacted in 1872. Amended by Code Am.1873–74, c. 612, p. 218, § 103.)*

Cross References

Words of inheritance or succession, fee transfer, see Civil Code § 1072.

§ 763. Estates tail abolished; fee simple and fee simple absolute

CONDITIONAL FEES AND ESTATES TAIL ABOLISHED. Estates tail are abolished, and every estate which would be at common law adjudged to be a fee tail is a fee simple; and if no valid remainder is limited thereon, is a fee simple absolute. *(Enacted in 1872.)*

Cross References

Uniform Statutory Rule Against Perpetuities, see Probate Code § 21201 et seq.

§ 764. Fee tails as contingent remainders

CERTAIN REMAINDERS VALID. Where a remainder in fee is limited upon any estate, which would by the common law be adjudged a fee tail, such remainder is valid as a contingent limitation upon a fee, and vests in possession on the death of the first taker, without issue living at the time of his death. *(Enacted in 1872.)*

Cross References

Uniform Statutory Rule Against Perpetuities, see Probate Code § 21201 et seq.

§ 765. Freeholds; chattels real; chattel interests

Estates of inheritance and for life are called estates of freehold; estates for years are chattels real; and estates at will are chattel interests, but are not subject to enforcement of a money judgment. *(Enacted in 1872. Amended by Stats.1982, c. 497, p. 2135, § 2, operative July 1, 1983.)*

§ 766. Estate for life of third person; freehold

An estate during the life of a third person, whether limited to heirs or otherwise, is a freehold. *(Enacted in 1872. Amended by Code Am.1873–74, c. 612, p. 218, § 104.)*

§ 767. Future estate; permissible limitation

FUTURE ESTATES, WHAT. A future estate may be limited by the act of the party to commence in possession at a future day, either without the intervention of a precedent estate, or on the termination, by lapse of time or otherwise, of a precedent estate created at the same time. *(Enacted in 1872.)*

Cross References

Uniform Statutory Rule Against Perpetuities, see Probate Code § 21201 et seq.

§ 768. "Reversion" defined

REVERSIONS. A reversion is the residue of an estate left by operation of law in the grantor or his successors, or in the successors of a testator, commencing in possession on the determination of a particular estate granted or devised. *(Enacted in 1872.)*

Cross References

Uniform Statutory Rule Against Perpetuities, see Probate Code § 21201 et seq.

§ 769. "Remainder" defined

REMAINDERS. When a future estate, other than a reversion, is dependent on a precedent estate, it may be called a remainder, and may be created and transferred by that name. *(Enacted in 1872.)*

Cross References

Uniform Statutory Rule Against Perpetuities, see Probate Code § 21201 et seq.

§ 770. Repealed by Stats.1959, c. 470, p. 2405, § 5

§ 771. Repealed by Stats.1986, c. 820, § 4, operative July 1, 1987

§ 772. Repealed by Stats.1951, c. 1463, p. 3443, § 7

§ 773. Authorized future estates and limitations

Subject to the rules of this title, and of Part 1 of this division, a freehold estate, as well as a chattel real, may be created to commence at a future day; an estate for life may be created in a term of years, and a remainder limited thereon; a remainder of a freehold or chattel real, either contingent or vested, may be created, expectant on the determination of a term of years; and a fee may be limited on a fee, upon a contingency, which, if it should occur, must happen within the period prescribed by the statutory rule against perpetuities in Article 2 (commencing with Section 21205) of Chapter 1 of Part 2 of Division 11 of the Probate Code. *(Enacted in 1872. Amended by Stats.1951, c. 1463, p. 3443, § 6; Stats.1991, c. 156 (A.B.1577), § 14.)*

§§ 774, 775. Repealed by Stats.1959, c. 470, p. 2406, § 7

§ 776. Repealed by Stats.1951, c. 1463, p. 3443, § 7

§ 777. Repealed by Stats.1959, c. 470, p. 2406, § 7

§ 778. Remainders; conditional limitation

REMAINDER UPON A CONTINGENCY. A remainder may be limited on a contingency which, in case it should happen, will operate to abridge or determine the precedent estate; and every such remainder is to be deemed a conditional limitation. *(Enacted in 1872.)*

Cross References

Uniform Statutory Rule Against Perpetuities, see Probate Code § 21201.

§ 779. Heirs of life tenant; taking as purchasers

HEIRS OF A TENANT FOR LIFE, WHEN TO TAKE AS PURCHASERS. When a remainder is limited to the heirs, or heirs of the body, of a person to whom a life estate in the same property is given, the persons who, on the termination of the life estate, are the successors or heirs of the body of the owner for life, are entitled to take by virtue of the remainder so limited to them, and not as mere successors of the owner for life. *(Enacted in 1872.)*

Cross References

Uniform Statutory Rule Against Perpetuities, see Probate Code § 21201.

§ 780. Remainders; construction of intent

CONSTRUCTION OF CERTAIN REMAINDERS. When a remainder on an estate for life or for years is not limited on a contingency defeating or avoiding such precedent estate, it is to be deemed intended to take effect only on the death of the first taker, or the expiration, by lapse of time, of such term of years. *(Enacted in 1872.)*

Cross References

Uniform Statutory Rule Against Perpetuities, see Probate Code § 21201.

§ 781. Power of appointment; effect

EFFECT OF POWER OF APPOINTMENT. A general or special power of appointment does not prevent the vesting of a future estate limited to take effect in case such power is not executed. *(Enacted in 1872.)*

Cross References

Powers of appointment,
   Generally, see Probate Code § 600 et seq.
   Release of power, see Probate Code §§ 661, 662.
Uniform Statutory Rule Against Perpetuities, see Probate Code § 21201.

§ 782. Discriminatory restrictions in deeds; invalidity; familial status

(a) Any provision in any deed of real property in California, whether executed before or after the effective date of this section, that purports to restrict the right of any persons to sell, lease, rent, use, or occupy the property to persons having any characteristic listed in subdivision (a) or (d) of Section 12955 of the Government Code, as those bases are defined in Sections 12926, 12926.1, subdivision (m) and paragraph (1) of subdivision (p) of Section 12955 and Section 12955.2 of the Government Code, by providing for payment of a penalty, forfeiture, reverter, or otherwise, is void.

(b) Notwithstanding subdivision (a), with respect to familial status, subdivision (a) shall not be construed to apply to housing for older persons, as defined in Section 12955.9 of the Government Code. With respect to familial status, nothing in subdivision (a) shall be construed to affect Sections 51.2, 51.3, 51.4, 51.10, 51.11, and 799.5 of this code, relating to housing for senior citizens. Subdivision (d) of Section 51, Section 4760, and Section 6714 of this code, and subdivisions (n), (*o*), and (p) of Section 12955 of the Government Code shall apply to subdivision (a). *(Added by Stats.1961, c. 1078, p. 2540, § 1. Amended by Stats.1965, c. 283, p. 1283, § 2; Stats.2006, c. 578 (A.B.2800), § 4; Stats. 2012, c. 181 (A.B.806), § 22, operative Jan. 1, 2014; Stats. 2013, c. 605 (S.B.752), § 10.)*

Cross References

Commercial and industrial common interest developments, application of this section, see Civil Code § 6700.
Common interest developments, application of this section, see Civil Code § 4700.
Real property defined for purposes of this Code, see Civil Code § 658.
Written instruments relating to realty, restrictions because of race, etc., see Civil Code § 53.

§ 782.5. Discriminatory restrictions in deeds or other title-related instruments; deemed revised to omit restrictions; familial status

(a) Any deed or other written instrument that relates to title to real property, or any written covenant, condition, or restriction annexed or made a part of, by reference or otherwise, any deed or instrument that relates to title to real property, which contains any provision that purports to forbid, restrict, or condition the right of any person or persons to sell, buy, lease, rent, use, or occupy the property on account of any basis listed in subdivision (a) or (d) of Section 12955 of the Government Code, as those bases are defined in Sections 12926, 12926.1, subdivision (m) and paragraph (1) of subdivision (p) of Section 12955, and Section 12955.2 of the Government Code, with respect to any person or persons, shall be deemed to be revised to omit that provision.

(b) Notwithstanding subdivision (a), with respect to familial status, subdivision (a) shall not be construed to apply to housing for older persons, as defined in Section 12955.9 of the Government Code. With respect to familial status, nothing in subdivision (a) shall be construed to affect Sections 51.2, 51.3, 51.4, 51.10, 51.11, and 799.5 of this code, relating to housing for senior citizens. Subdivision (d) of Section 51, Section 4760, and Section 6714 of this code, and subdivisions (n), (o), and (p) of Section 12955 of the Government Code shall apply to subdivision (a).

(c) This section shall not be construed to limit or expand the powers of a court to reform a deed or other written instrument. *(Added by Stats.1987, c. 500, § 1. Amended by Stats.2006, c. 578 (A.B.2800), § 5; Stats.2012, c. 181 (A.B. 806), § 23, operative Jan. 1, 2014; Stats.2013, c. 605 (S.B.752), § 11.)*

Cross References

Commercial and industrial common interest developments, application of this section, see Civil Code § 6700.
Common interest developments, application of this section, see Civil Code § 4700.
Real property defined for purposes of this Code, see Civil Code § 658.
Unruh Civil Rights Act, see Civil Code § 51 et seq.

§ 783. "Condominium" defined

A condominium is an estate in real property described in Section 4125 or 6542. A condominium may, with respect to the duration of its enjoyment, be either (1) an estate of inheritance or perpetual estate, (2) an estate for life, (3) an estate for years, such as a leasehold or a subleasehold, or (4) any combination of the foregoing. *(Added by Stats.1985, c. 874, § 9. Amended by Stats.2012, c. 181 (A.B.806), § 24, operative Jan. 1, 2014; Stats.2013, c. 605 (S.B.752), § 12.)*

Cross References

Business and Professions Code, additional subdivisions and interests included in reference to "subdivided lands" and "subdivision", see Business and Professions Code § 11004.5.
Conversion of stock cooperative or community apartment project to condominium, favorable vote of owners, see Government Code § 66452.10.
County or city and county and private person, contract to acquire condominium interest, see Government Code § 25549.20.
Credit against amount of land required to be dedicated or amount of fee imposed, see Government Code § 66477.
Default on real property purchase contract, liquidated damages, newly constructed attached units, see Civil Code § 1675.
Homestead exemption, "dwelling" defined to include a condominium, see Code of Civil Procedure § 704.710.
Improvement Act of 1911, issuance of separate bond for each condominium interest, see Streets and Highways Code § 6422.
Inspections by real estate brokers or seller, see Civil Code § 2079.3.
Property taxation, condominiums, assessment of separate units, see Revenue and Taxation Code § 2188.6.
Real property defined for purposes of this Code, see Civil Code § 658.
Subdivided lands, term of conditional public report for attached residential condominium units, see Business and Professions Code § 11018.12.
Subdivisions, necessity of tentative and final maps, see Government Code § 66426.

Taxation, see Revenue and Taxation Code § 2188.3.

§ 783.1. Stock cooperatives; separate and correlative interests

In a stock cooperative, as defined in Section 4190 or 6566, both the separate interest, as defined in paragraph (4) of subdivision (a) of Section 4185 or in paragraph (3) of subdivision (a) of Section 6564, and the correlative interest in the stock cooperative corporation, however designated, are interests in real property. *(Added by Stats.1985, c. 874, § 10. Amended by Stats.2012, c. 181 (A.B.806), § 25, operative Jan. 1, 2014; Stats.2013, c. 605 (S.B.752), § 13.)*

Cross References

Common interest developments, see Civil Code § 4000 et seq.
Real property defined for purposes of this Code, see Civil Code § 658.

§ 784. "Restriction" defined

"Restriction," when used in a statute that incorporates this section by reference, means a limitation on, or provision affecting, the use of real property in a deed, declaration, or other instrument, whether in the form of a covenant, equitable servitude, condition subsequent, negative easement, or other form of restriction. *(Added by Stats.1998, c. 14 (A.B.707), § 1.)*

Cross References

"Condition subsequent" defined, see Civil Code § 1438.
Real property defined for purposes of this Code, see Civil Code § 658.
Time of commencing action for violation of a restriction, see Code of Civil Procedure § 336.

CHAPTER 2. TERMINATION OF ESTATES

Section
789. Termination of tenancy or other estate at will; written notice to tenant.
789.3. Utility services; prevention of access to property; removal of doors, windows or personalty; intent to terminate occupancy; liability of landlord; injunctive relief.
789.4. Repealed.
789.5 to 789.15. Repealed.
789.16. Renumbered.
790. Right of re-entry or possession.
791. Re-entry, how effected.
792. Summary proceedings for possession.
793. Possessory action, when maintainable.
794. Repealed.

Cross References

Immigration or citizenship status irrelevant to issues of liability or remedy in specified proceedings, discovery, see Civil Code § 3339.10.

§ 789. Termination of tenancy or other estate at will; written notice to tenant

A tenancy or other estate at will, however created, may be terminated by the landlord's giving notice in writing to the tenant, in the manner prescribed by Section 1162 of the Code of Civil Procedure, to remove from the premises within a period of not less than 30 days, to be specified in the notice.

(Enacted in 1872. Amended by Stats.1911, c. 44, p. 61, § 1; Stats.2002, c. 664 (A.B.3034), § 32.)

Cross References

Changing terms of tenancy, see Civil Code § 827.
Estates and tenancy at will, see Civil Code §§ 761, 765, 819.
Notice to terminate tenancy, see Civil Code § 1946.
Tenancy for years, see Civil Code § 819.

§ 789.3. Utility services; prevention of access to property; removal of doors, windows or personalty; intent to terminate occupancy; liability of landlord; injunctive relief

(a) A landlord shall not with intent to terminate the occupancy under any lease or other tenancy or estate at will, however created, of property used by a tenant as his residence willfully cause, directly or indirectly, the interruption or termination of any utility service furnished the tenant, including, but not limited to, water, heat, light, electricity, gas, telephone, elevator, or refrigeration, whether or not the utility service is under the control of the landlord.

(b) In addition, a landlord shall not, with intent to terminate the occupancy under any lease or other tenancy or estate at will, however created, of property used by a tenant as his or her residence, willfully:

(1) Prevent the tenant from gaining reasonable access to the property by changing the locks or using a bootlock or by any other similar method or device;

(2) Remove outside doors or windows; or

(3) Remove from the premises the tenant's personal property, the furnishings, or any other items without the prior written consent of the tenant, except when done pursuant to the procedure set forth in Chapter 5 (commencing with Section 1980) of Title 5 of Part 4 of Division 3.

Nothing in this subdivision shall be construed to prevent the lawful eviction of a tenant by appropriate legal authorities, nor shall anything in this subdivision apply to occupancies defined by subdivision (b) of Section 1940.

(c) Any landlord who violates this section shall be liable to the tenant in a civil action for all of the following:

(1) Actual damages of the tenant.

(2) An amount not to exceed one hundred dollars ($100) for each day or part thereof the landlord remains in violation of this section. In determining the amount of such award, the court shall consider proof of such matters as justice may require; however, in no event shall less than two hundred fifty dollars ($250) be awarded for each separate cause of action. Subsequent or repeated violations, which are not committed contemporaneously with the initial violation, shall be treated as separate causes of action and shall be subject to a separate award of damages.

(d) In any action under subdivision (c) the court shall award reasonable attorney's fees to the prevailing party. In any such action the tenant may seek appropriate injunctive relief to prevent continuing or further violation of the provisions of this section during the pendency of the action. The remedy provided by this section is not exclusive and shall not preclude the tenant from pursuing any other remedy which the tenant may have under any other provision of law.

(Added by Stats.1971, c. 1275, p. 2494, § 1. Amended by Stats.1979, c. 333, p. 1191, § 1.)

Cross References

Prohibitions against termination of public utility services, see Public Utilities Code § 780.
Right of landlord's access to dwelling unit, see Civil Code § 1954.
Termination of public utility services, see Public Utilities Code § 779 et seq.

§ 789.4. Repealed by Stats.2021, c. 27 (A.B.832), § 1, operative Oct. 1, 2021

§§ 789.5 to 789.15. Repealed by Stats.1978, c. 1031, p. 3185, §§ 3 to 17

§ 789.16. Renumbered § 798.26 and amended by Stats. 1978, c. 1033, p. 3188, § 10.5

§ 790. Right of re-entry or possession

EFFECT OF NOTICE. After such notice has been served, and the period specified by such notice has expired, but not before, the landlord may reenter, or proceed according to law to recover possession. *(Enacted in 1872.)*

§ 791. Re-entry, how effected

Whenever the right of re-entry is given to a grantor or a lessor in any grant or lease or otherwise, such reentry may be made at any time after the right has accrued, upon three days' notice, as provided in sections 1161 and 1162, Code of Civil Procedure; provided, however, that the said three days' notice shall not be required in cases where the hiring of real property is for a term not specified by the parties and where such hiring was terminated under and in accordance with the provisions of section 1946 of the Civil Code. *(Enacted in 1872. Amended by Stats.1931, c. 1033, p. 2180, § 1.)*

Cross References

Possessory action, see Civil Code § 793.
Real property defined for purposes of this Code, see Civil Code § 658.
Right of landlord's access to a dwelling unit, see Civil Code § 1954.

§ 792. Summary proceedings for possession

SUMMARY PROCEEDINGS IN CERTAIN CASES PROVIDED FOR. Summary proceedings for obtaining possession of real property forcibly entered, or forcibly and unlawfully detained, are provided for in Sections 1159 to 1175, both inclusive, of the Code of Civil Procedure. *(Enacted in 1872.)*

Cross References

Real property defined for purposes of this Code, see Civil Code § 658.

§ 793. Possessory action, when maintainable

An action for the possession of real property leased or granted, with a right of re-entry, may be maintained at any time, after the right to re-enter has accrued, without the notice prescribed in section seven hundred and ninety-one. *(Enacted in 1872. Amended by Stats.1905, c. 438, p. 599, § 1.)*

REAL OR IMMOVABLE PROPERTY § 798.3

Cross References

Notice to quit leased premises, see Code of Civil Procedure §§ 1161, 1162.

Real property defined for purposes of this Code, see Civil Code § 658.

Recovery of possession of real property, see Civil Code § 3375.

§ 794. Repealed by Stats.1984, c. 240, § 1

CHAPTER 2.5. MOBILEHOME RESIDENCY LAW

Article	Section
1. General	798
2. Rental Agreement	798.15
3. Rules and Regulations	798.23
3.5. Fees and Charges	798.30
4. Utilities	798.40
4.4. Tenant Rental Assistance [Rejected]	
4.5. Rent Control	798.45
5. Homeowner Communications and Meetings	798.50
5.5. Homeowners Meetings with Management	798.53
6. Termination of Tenancy	798.55
7. Transfer of Mobilehome or Mobilehome Park	798.70
8. Actions, Proceedings and Penalties	798.84
9. Subdivisions, Cooperatives and Condominiums	799

Cross References

Housing development approvals, Camp Fire Housing Assistance Act of 2019, see Government Code § 65913.15.

Manufactured homes, installation on lots zoned for single-family dwellings, see Government Code § 65852.3.

Methamphetamine Contaminated Property Cleanup Act of 2005, abatement of nonremediated mobilehome, manufactured home, or recreational vehicle, see Health and Safety Code § 25400.28.

Methamphetamine Contaminated Property Cleanup Act of 2005, vacating affected unit that is determined to be in hazardous zone by local health officer, termination of tenancy by mobilehome park or special occupancy park owner, see Health and Safety Code § 25400.25.

Mobilehome parks, annual permit to operate, penalty fee for late application, see Health and Safety Code § 18506.

Mobilehome Parks Act, see Health and Safety Code § 18200 et seq.

Shelter crisis, emergency housing, homeless shelters, see Government Code § 8698.4.

Special occupancy parks, annual permit to operate, penalty fee for late application, see Health and Safety Code § 18870.7.

ARTICLE 1. GENERAL

Section	
798.	Citation of chapter.
798.1.	Application of definitions.
798.2.	Management.
798.3.	Mobilehome.
798.4.	Mobilehome park.
798.5.	Renumbered.
798.6.	Park.
798.7.	New construction; new mobilehome park construction.
798.8.	Rental agreement.
798.9.	Homeowner.
798.10.	Change of use.
798.11.	Resident.
798.12.	Tenancy.
798.13.	State employee housing.
798.14.	Notices; personal delivery or by mail.

§ 798. Citation of chapter

This chapter shall be known and may be cited as the "Mobilehome Residency Law." *(Added by Stats.1978, c. 1035, p. 3194, § 4. Amended by Stats.1992, c. 958 (S.B.1655), § 1, eff. Sept. 28, 1992.)*

Cross References

Manufactured homes, installation on lots zoned for single-family dwellings, see Government Code § 65852.3.

Methamphetamine Contaminated Property Cleanup Act of 2005, vacating affected unit that is determined to be in hazardous zone by local health officer, termination of tenancy by mobilehome park or special occupancy park owner, see Health and Safety Code § 25400.25.

Mobilehome defined for purposes of this Chapter, see Civil Code § 798.3.

Mobilehome ombudsman, see Health and Safety Code § 18151.

Mobilehome Parks Act, see Health and Safety Code § 18200 et seq.

Writ of possession of real property, see Code of Civil Procedure § 715.050.

§ 798.1. Application of definitions

Unless the provisions or context otherwise requires, the following definitions shall govern the construction of this chapter. *(Added by Stats.1978, c. 1031, p. 3178, § 1.)*

Cross References

Mobilehome defined for purposes of the Health and Safety Code, see Health and Safety Code § 18008.

Mobilehome defined for purposes of the Vehicle Code, see Vehicle Code § 396.

§ 798.2. Management

"Management" means the owner of a mobilehome park or an agent or representative authorized to act on his behalf in connection with matters relating to a tenancy in the park. *(Added by Stats.1978, c. 1031, p. 3178, § 1.)*

Cross References

Mobilehome defined for purposes of this Chapter, see Civil Code § 798.3.

Mobilehome park defined for purposes of this Chapter, see Civil Code § 798.4.

Tenancy defined for purposes of this Chapter, see Civil Code § 798.12.

§ 798.3. Mobilehome

(a) "Mobilehome" is a structure designed for human habitation and for being moved on a street or highway under permit pursuant to Section 35790 of the Vehicle Code. Mobilehome includes a manufactured home, as defined in Section 18007 of the Health and Safety Code, and a mobilehome, as defined in Section 18008 of the Health and Safety Code, but, except as provided in subdivision (b), does not include a recreational vehicle, as defined in Section 799.29 of this code and Section 18010 of the Health and Safety Code or a commercial coach as defined in Section 18001.8 of the Health and Safety Code.

(b) "Mobilehome," for purposes of this chapter, other than Section 798.73, also includes trailers and other recre-

§ 798.3

ational vehicles of all types defined in Section 18010 of the Health and Safety Code, other than motor homes, truck campers, and camping trailers, which are used for human habitation if the occupancy criteria of either paragraph (1) or (2), as follows, are met:

(1) The trailer or other recreational vehicle occupies a mobilehome site in the park, on November 15, 1992, under a rental agreement with a term of one month or longer, and the trailer or other recreational vehicle occupied a mobilehome site in the park prior to January 1, 1991.

(2) The trailer or other recreational vehicle occupies a mobilehome site in the park for nine or more continuous months commencing on or after November 15, 1992.

"Mobilehome" does not include a trailer or other recreational vehicle located in a recreational vehicle park subject to Chapter 2.6 (commencing with Section 799.20). *(Added by Stats.1978, c. 1033, p. 3187, § 2. Amended by Stats.1980, c. 502, § 1; Stats.1982, c. 419, p. 1770, § 1; Stats.1983, c. 1124, § 1, operative July 1, 1984; Stats.1992, c. 958 (S.B.1655), § 2, eff. Sept. 28, 1992; Stats.1993, c. 666 (A.B.503), § 1; Stats. 2005, c. 595 (S.B.253), § 1.)*

Cross References

Mobilehome defined for purposes of the Health and Safety Code, see Health and Safety Code § 18008.

Mobilehome defined for purposes of the Vehicle Code, see Vehicle Code § 396.

Rental agreement defined for purposes of this Chapter, see Civil Code § 798.8.

§ 798.4. Mobilehome park

"Mobilehome park" is an area of land where two or more mobilehome sites are rented, or held out for rent, to accommodate mobilehomes used for human habitation. *(Added by Stats.1978, c. 1031, p. 3178, § 1.)*

Cross References

Methamphetamine Contaminated Property Cleanup Act of 2005, see Health and Safety Code § 25400.10 et seq.

Mobilehome defined for purposes of this Chapter, see Civil Code § 798.3.

Mobilehome defined for purposes of the Health and Safety Code, see Health and Safety Code § 18008.

Mobilehome defined for purposes of the Vehicle Code, see Vehicle Code § 396.

§ 798.5. Renumbered § 798.6 and amended by Stats.1980, c. 502, § 5

§ 798.6. Park

"Park" is a manufactured housing community as defined in Section 18210.7 of the Health and Safety Code, or a mobilehome park. *(Formerly § 798.5, added by Stats.1978, c. 1031, p. 3178, § 1. Renumbered § 798.6 and amended by Stats.1980, c. 502, § 5. Amended by Stats.1993, c. 858 (A.B.2177), § 1; Stats.2007, c. 596 (A.B.382), § 1.)*

Cross References

Methamphetamine Contaminated Property Cleanup Act of 2005, see Health and Safety Code § 25400.10 et seq.

Mobilehome defined for purposes of this Chapter, see Civil Code § 798.3.

Mobilehome park defined for purposes of this Chapter, see Civil Code § 798.4.

§ 798.7. New construction; new mobilehome park construction

(a) "New construction" means any newly constructed spaces initially held out for rent after January 1, 1990. <u>A mobilehome park space shall be considered "initially held out for rent" on the date of issuance of a permit or certificate of occupancy for that space by the enforcement agency in accordance with Section 18551 or 18613 of the Health and Safety Code.</u>

(b) <u>"New mobilehome park construction" means all spaces contained in a newly constructed mobilehome park for which a permit to operate is first issued by the enforcement agency on or after January 1, 2023.</u> *(Added by Stats.1989, c. 412, § 1. Amended by Stats.2022, c. 666 (S.B.940), § 1, eff. Jan. 1, 2023.)*

Cross References

Manufactured housing communities and mobilehome parks, restriction on ordinances, rules, or regulations that prohibit or limit the duration of rental agreements or leases, see Government Code § 65852.11.

§ 798.8. Rental agreement

"Rental agreement" is an agreement between the management and the homeowner establishing the terms and conditions of a park tenancy. A lease is a rental agreement. *(Formerly § 798.6, added by Stats.1978, c. 1031, p. 3178, § 1. Renumbered § 798.8 and amended by Stats.1980, c. 502, § 6. Amended by Stats.1982, c. 1397, p. 5319, § 1.)*

Cross References

Homeowner defined for purposes of this Chapter, see Civil Code § 798.9.

Management defined for purposes of this Chapter, see Civil Code § 798.2.

Tenancy defined for purposes of this Chapter, see Civil Code § 798.12.

§ 798.9. Homeowner

"Homeowner" is a person who has a tenancy in a mobilehome park under a rental agreement. *(Added by Stats.1978, c. 1031, p. 3178, § 1. Amended by Stats.1982, c. 1397, p. 5320, § 2.)*

Cross References

Mobilehome defined for purposes of this Chapter, see Civil Code § 798.3.

Mobilehome park defined for purposes of this Chapter, see Civil Code § 798.4.

Rental agreement defined for purposes of this Chapter, see Civil Code § 798.8.

Tenancy defined for purposes of this Chapter, see Civil Code § 798.12.

§ 798.10. Change of use

"Change of use" means a use of the park for a purpose other than the rental, or the holding out for rent, of two or more mobilehome sites to accommodate mobilehomes used for human habitation, and does not mean the adoption, amendment, or repeal of a park rule or regulation. A change of use may affect an entire park or any portion thereof. "Change of use" includes, but is not limited to, a change of the park or any portion thereof to a condominium, stock cooperative, planned unit development, or any form of ownership wherein spaces within the park are to be sold. (Added by Stats.1979, c. 945, p. 3266, § 1. Amended by Stats.1980, c. 137, § 1.)

Cross References

Mobilehome defined for purposes of this Chapter, see Civil Code § 798.3.
Ownership defined for purposes of this Code, see Civil Code § 654.

§ 798.11. Resident

"Resident" is a homeowner or other person who lawfully occupies a mobilehome. (Formerly § 798.7, added by Stats. 1978, c. 1031, p. 3178, § 1. Renumbered § 748.10 and amended by Stats.1980, c. 502, § 7. Renumbered § 798.11 and amended by Stats.1981, c. 714, § 50. Amended by Stats.1982, c. 1397, p. 5320, § 3.)

Cross References

Homeowner defined for purposes of this Chapter, see Civil Code § 798.9.
Mobilehome defined for purposes of this Chapter, see Civil Code § 798.3.

§ 798.12. Tenancy

"Tenancy" is the right of a homeowner to the use of a site within a mobilehome park on which to locate, maintain, and occupy a mobilehome, site improvements, and accessory structures for human habitation, including the use of the services and facilities of the park. (Formerly § 798.8, added by Stats.1978, c. 1031, p. 3178, § 1. Amended by Stats.1978, c. 1033, p. 3187, § 3. Renumbered § 798.12 and amended by Stats.1980, c. 502, § 8. Amended by Stats.1982, c. 1397, p. 5320, § 4.)

Cross References

Homeowner defined for purposes of this Chapter, see Civil Code § 798.9.
Mobilehome defined for purposes of this Chapter, see Civil Code § 798.3.
Mobilehome park defined for purposes of this Chapter, see Civil Code § 798.4.

§ 798.13. State employee housing

(a) This chapter does not apply to any area owned, operated, or maintained by the state for the purpose of providing employee housing or space for a mobilehome owned or occupied by an employee of the state.

(b) Notwithstanding subdivision (a), a state employer shall provide the occupant of a privately owned mobilehome that is situated in an employee housing area owned, operated, or maintained by the state, and that is occupied by a state employee by agreement with his or her state employer and subject to the terms and conditions of that state employment, with a minimum of 60–days' notice prior to terminating the tenancy for any reason. (Added by Stats.2000, c. 471 (A.B. 2008), § 1.)

Cross References

Mobilehome defined for purposes of this Chapter, see Civil Code § 798.3.
Tenancy defined for purposes of this Chapter, see Civil Code § 798.12.

§ 798.14. Notices; personal delivery or by mail

(a) Unless otherwise provided, all notices required by this chapter shall be either delivered personally to the homeowner or deposited in the United States mail, postage prepaid, addressed to the homeowner at his or her site within the mobilehome park.

(b) All notices required by this chapter to be delivered prior to February 1 of each year may be combined in one notice that contains all the information required by the sections under which the notices are given. (Added by Stats.1988, c. 301, § 1. Amended by Stats.2012, c. 478 (A.B.2150), § 1.)

Cross References

Homeowner defined for purposes of this Chapter, see Civil Code § 798.9.
Mobilehome defined for purposes of this Chapter, see Civil Code § 798.3.
Mobilehome park defined for purposes of this Chapter, see Civil Code § 798.4.

ARTICLE 2. RENTAL AGREEMENT

Section
798.15. Writing; required contents; repair of sudden or unforeseeable breakdown or deterioration of improvements; required notice.
798.16. Inclusion of other provisions; return of executed copy.
798.17. Exemption from local rent control measures; right to inspect agreement; applicability; severability.
798.18. Term; comparable monthly charges for one year as for month-to-month tenancy; automatic extension or renewal.
798.19. Waiver of rights; public policy.
798.19.5. Sale of mobilehome; right of first refusal to management.
798.20. Private club membership not to be denied on discriminatory basis; familial status.
798.21. Rent control measures; space not used as principal residence; exemptions.
798.22. Recreational vehicles in mobilehome parks; designated areas.

§ 798.15. Writing; required contents; repair of sudden or unforeseeable breakdown or deterioration of improvements; required notice

The rental agreement shall be in writing and shall contain, in addition to the provisions otherwise required by law to be included, all of the following:

(a) The term of the tenancy and the rent therefor.

(b) The rules and regulations of the park.

(c) A copy of the text of this chapter shall be provided as an exhibit and shall be incorporated into the rental agreement by reference. Management shall do one of the following prior to February 1 of each year, if a significant

§ 798.15

change was made in this chapter by legislation enacted in the prior year:

(1) Provide all homeowners with a copy of this chapter.

(2) Provide written notice to all homeowners that there has been a change to this chapter and that they may obtain one copy of this chapter from management at no charge. Management shall provide a copy within a reasonable time, not to exceed seven days, upon request.

(d) A provision specifying that (1) it is the responsibility of the management to provide and maintain physical improvements in the common facilities in good working order and condition and (2) with respect to a sudden or unforeseeable breakdown or deterioration of these improvements, the management shall have a reasonable period of time to repair the sudden or unforeseeable breakdown or deterioration and bring the improvements into good working order and condition after management knows or should have known of the breakdown or deterioration. For purposes of this subdivision, a reasonable period of time to repair a sudden or unforeseeable breakdown or deterioration shall be as soon as possible in situations affecting a health or safety condition, and shall not exceed 30 days in any other case except where exigent circumstances justify a delay.

(e) A description of the physical improvements to be provided the homeowner during his or her tenancy.

(f) A provision listing those services which will be provided at the time the rental agreement is executed and will continue to be offered for the term of tenancy and the fees, if any, to be charged for those services.

(g) A provision stating that management may charge a reasonable fee for services relating to the maintenance of the land and premises upon which a mobilehome is situated in the event the homeowner fails to maintain the land or premises in accordance with the rules and regulations of the park after written notification to the homeowner and the failure of the homeowner to comply within 14 days. The written notice shall state the specific condition to be corrected and an estimate of the charges to be imposed by management if the services are performed by management or its agent.

(h) All other provisions governing the tenancy.

(i) A copy of the following notice. Management shall also, prior to February 1 of each year, provide a copy of the following notice to all homeowners:

IMPORTANT NOTICE TO ALL MANUFACTURED
HOME/MOBILEHOME OWNERS: CALIFORNIA LAW
REQUIRES THAT
YOU BE MADE AWARE OF THE FOLLOWING:

The Mobilehome Residency Law (MRL), found in Section 798 et seq. of the Civil Code, establishes the rights and responsibilities of homeowners and park management. The MRL is deemed a part of the terms of any park rental agreement or lease. This notice is intended to provide you with a general awareness of selected parts of the MRL and other important laws. It does not serve as a legal explanation or interpretation. For authoritative information, you must read and understand the laws. These laws change from time to time. In any year in which the law has changed, you may obtain one copy of the full text of the law from management at no charge.

This notice is required by Civil Code Section 798.15(i) and the information provided may not be current.

Homeowners and park management have certain rights and responsibilities under the MRL. These include, but are not limited to:

1. Management must give a homeowner written notice of any increase in his or her rent at least 90 days before the date of the increase. (Civil Code Section 798.30)
2. No rental or sales agreement may contain a provision by which a purchaser or a homeowner waives any of his or her rights under the MRL. (Civil Code Sections 798.19, 798.77)
3. Management may not terminate or refuse to renew a homeowner's tenancy except for one or more of the authorized reasons set forth in the MRL. (Civil Code Sections 798.55, 798.56) Homeowners must pay rent, utility charges, and reasonable incidental service charges in a timely manner. Failure to comply could be grounds for eviction from the park. (Civil Code Section 798.56)
4. Homeowners, residents, and their guests must comply with the rental agreement or lease, including the reasonable rules and regulations of the park and all applicable local ordinances and state laws and regulations relating to mobilehomes. Failure to comply could be grounds for eviction from the park. (Civil Code Section 798.56)
5. Homeowners have a right to peacefully assemble and freely communicate with respect to mobilehome living and for social or educational purposes. Homeowners have a right to meet in the park, at reasonable hours and in a reasonable manner, for any lawful purpose. Homeowners may not be charged a cleaning deposit in order to use the park clubhouse for meetings of resident organizations or for other lawful purposes, such as to hear from political candidates, so long as a homeowner of the park is hosting the meeting and all park residents are allowed to attend. Homeowners may not be required to obtain liability insurance in order to use common facilities unless alcohol is served. (Civil Code Sections 798.50, 798.51)
6. If a home complies with certain standards, the homeowner is entitled to sell it in place in the park. If you sell your home, you are required to provide a manufactured home and mobilehome transfer disclosure statement to the buyer prior to sale. (Civil Code Section 1102.6d) When a home is sold, the owner is required to transfer the title to the buyer. The sale of the home is not complete until you receive the title from the seller. It is the responsibility of the buyer to also file paperwork with the Department of Housing and Community Development to register the home in his or her name. (Civil Code Sections 798.70–798.74)
7. Management has the right to enter the space upon which a mobilehome is situated for maintenance of utilities, trees, and driveways; for inspection and maintenance of the space in accordance with the rules and regulations of the park when the homeowner or resident fails to maintain the space; and for protection and maintenance of the mobilehome park at any reasonable time, but not in a manner or at a time that would interfere with the resident's quiet enjoyment of his or her home. (Civil Code Section 798.26)
8. A homeowner may not make any improvements or alterations to his or her space or home without following the rules and regulations of the park and all applicable local ordinances and state laws and regulations, which may include obtaining a permit to construct, and, if required by park rules or the rental agreement, without prior written approval of management. Failure to com-

ply could be grounds for eviction from the park. (Civil Code Section 798.56)

9. In California, mobilehome owners must pay annual property tax to the county tax collector or an annual fee in lieu of taxes to the Department of Housing and Community Development (HCD). If you are unsure which to pay, contact HCD. Failure to pay taxes or in lieu fees can have serious consequences, including losing your home at a tax sale.

10. For more information on registration, titling, and taxes, contact: the Department of Housing and Community Development www.hcd.ca.gov (800) 952–8356; your County Tax Collector; or call your local county government.

(Added by Stats.1978, c. 1031, p. 3178, § 1. Amended by Stats.1978, c. 1033, p. 3186, § 4; Stats.1980, c. 137, § 2; Stats.1981, c. 667, § 1; Stats.1982, c. 1397, p. 5320, § 5; Stats.1983, c. 519, § 1; Stats.1987, c. 126, § 1; Stats.1993, c. 666 (A.B.503), § 2; Stats.2010, c. 90 (A.B.2120), § 1; Stats. 2012, c. 478 (A.B.2150), § 2; Stats.2016, c. 396 (A.B.587), § 1, eff. Jan. 1, 2017.)

Cross References

Homeowner defined for purposes of this Chapter, see Civil Code § 798.9.
Management defined for purposes of this Chapter, see Civil Code § 798.2.
Mobilehome defined for purposes of this Chapter, see Civil Code § 798.3.
Rental agreement defined for purposes of this Chapter, see Civil Code § 798.8.
Tenancy defined for purposes of this Chapter, see Civil Code § 798.12.

§ 798.16. Inclusion of other provisions; return of executed copy

(a) The rental agreement may include other provisions permitted by law, but need not include specific language contained in state or local laws not a part of this chapter.

(b) Management shall return an executed copy of the rental agreement to the homeowner within 15 business days after management has received the rental agreement signed by the homeowner. (Added by Stats.1978, c. 1031, p. 3178, § 1. Amended by Stats.1978, c. 1033, p. 3188, § 5; Stats.1981, c. 667, § 2; Stats.2004, c. 302 (A.B.2351), § 1.)

Cross References

Homeowner defined for purposes of this Chapter, see Civil Code § 798.9.
Management defined for purposes of this Chapter, see Civil Code § 798.2.
Rental agreement defined for purposes of this Chapter, see Civil Code § 798.8.

§ 798.17. Exemption from local rent control measures; right to inspect agreement; applicability; severability

(a)(1) Except as provided in subdivisions (i), (j), and (k), rental agreements meeting the criteria of subdivision (b) shall be exempt from any ordinance, rule, regulation, or initiative measure adopted by any local governmental entity which establishes a maximum amount that a landlord may charge a tenant for rent. The terms of a rental agreement meeting the criteria of subdivision (b) shall prevail over conflicting provisions of an ordinance, rule, regulation, or initiative measure limiting or restricting rents in mobilehome parks, only during the term of the rental agreement or one or more uninterrupted, continuous extensions thereof. If the rental agreement is not extended and no new rental agreement in excess of 12 months' duration is entered into, then the last rental rate charged for the space under the previous rental agreement shall be the base rent for purposes of applicable provisions of law concerning rent regulation, if any.

(2) In the first sentence of the first paragraph of a rental agreement entered into on or after January 1, 1993, pursuant to this section, there shall be set forth a provision in at least 12–point boldface type if the rental agreement is printed, or in capital letters if the rental agreement is typed, giving notice to the homeowner that the rental agreement will be exempt from any ordinance, rule, regulation, or initiative measure adopted by any local governmental entity which establishes a maximum amount that a landlord may charge a tenant for rent.

(b) Rental agreements subject to this section shall meet all of the following criteria:

(1) The rental agreement shall be in excess of 12 months' duration.

(2) The rental agreement shall be entered into between the management and a homeowner for the personal and actual residence of the homeowner.

(3) The homeowner shall have at least 30 days from the date the rental agreement is first offered to the homeowner to accept or reject the rental agreement.

(4) The homeowner who signs a rental agreement pursuant to this section may void the rental agreement by notifying management in writing within 72 hours of returning the signed rental agreement to management. This paragraph shall only apply if management provides the homeowner a copy of the signed rental agreement at the time the homeowner returns the signed rental agreement.

(5) The homeowner who signs a rental agreement pursuant to this section may void the agreement within 72 hours of receiving an executed copy of the rental agreement pursuant to Section 798.16. This paragraph shall only apply if management does not provide the homeowner with a copy of the signed rental agreement at the time the homeowner returns the signed rental agreement.

(c) If, pursuant to paragraph (3) or (4) of subdivision (b), the homeowner rejects the offered rental agreement or rescinds a signed rental agreement, the homeowner shall be entitled to instead accept, pursuant to Section 798.18, a rental agreement for a term of 12 months or less from the date the offered rental agreement was to have begun. In the event the homeowner elects to have a rental agreement for a term of 12 months or less, including a month-to-month rental agreement, the rental agreement shall contain the same rental charges, terms, and conditions as the rental agreement offered pursuant to subdivision (b), during the first 12 months, except for options, if any, contained in the offered rental agreement to extend or renew the rental agreement.

(d) Nothing in subdivision (c) shall be construed to prohibit the management from offering gifts of value, other than rental rate reductions, to homeowners who execute a rental agreement pursuant to this section.

§ 798.17

(e) With respect to any space in a mobilehome park that is exempt under subdivision (a) from any ordinance, rule, regulation, or initiative measure adopted by any local governmental entity that establishes a maximum amount that a landlord may charge a homeowner for rent, and notwithstanding any ordinance, rule, regulation, or initiative measure, a mobilehome park shall not be assessed any fee or other exaction for a park space that is exempt under subdivision (a) imposed pursuant to any ordinance, rule, regulation, or initiative measure. No other fee or other exaction shall be imposed for a park space that is exempt under subdivision (a) for the purpose of defraying the cost of administration thereof.

(f) At the time the rental agreement is first offered to the homeowner, the management shall provide written notice to the homeowner of the homeowner's right (1) to have at least 30 days to inspect the rental agreement, and (2) to void the rental agreement by notifying management in writing within 72 hours of receipt of an executed copy of the rental agreement. The failure of the management to provide the written notice shall make the rental agreement voidable at the homeowner's option upon the homeowner's discovery of the failure. The receipt of any written notice provided pursuant to this subdivision shall be acknowledged in writing by the homeowner.

(g) No rental agreement subject to subdivision (a) that is first entered into on or after January 1, 1993, shall have a provision which authorizes automatic extension or renewal of, or automatically extends or renews, the rental agreement for a period beyond the initial stated term at the sole option of either the management or the homeowner.

(h) This section does not apply to or supersede other provisions of this part or other state law.

(i) This section shall not apply to any rental agreement entered into on or after January 1, 2021.

(j) This section shall not apply to any rental agreement entered into from February 13, 2020, to December 31, 2020, inclusive.

(k) This section shall remain in effect until January 1, 2025, and as of that date is repealed. As of January 1, 2025, any exemption pursuant to this section shall expire.

(*l*) The provisions of this section are severable. If any provision of this section or its application is held invalid, that invalidity shall not affect other provisions or applications that can be given effect without the invalid provision or application. *(Added by Stats.1985, c. 1084, § 1. Amended by Stats.1986, c. 1416, § 1; Stats.1990, c. 1013 (S.B.2010), § 1; Stats.1990, c. 1046 (S.B.2009), § 2; Stats.1991, c. 24 (S.B.132), § 1, eff. May 7, 1991, operative May 10, 1991; Stats.1991, c. 170 (S.B.360), § 1; Stats.1992, c. 427 (A.B.3355), § 11; Stats.1992, c. 289 (S.B.1454), § 1; Stats.1993, c. 9 (S.B.6), § 1, eff. April 29, 1993; Stats.2012, c. 477 (A.B.1938), § 1; Stats.2020, c. 35 (A.B.2782), § 2, eff. Jan. 1, 2021.)*

Repeal

For repeal of this section, see its terms.

Cross References

Exemption of new construction from local rent control laws, see Civil Code § 798.45.

Fees for use of more than one year, see Civil Code § 798.31.
Homeowner defined for purposes of this Chapter, see Civil Code § 798.9.
Management defined for purposes of this Chapter, see Civil Code § 798.2.
Mobilehome defined for purposes of this Chapter, see Civil Code § 798.3.
Mobilehome park defined for purposes of this Chapter, see Civil Code § 798.4.
Rental agreement defined for purposes of this Chapter, see Civil Code § 798.8.

§ 798.18. Term; comparable monthly charges for one year as for month-to-month tenancy; automatic extension or renewal

(a) A homeowner shall be offered a rental agreement for (1) a term of 12 months, or (2) a lesser period as the homeowner may request, or (3) a longer period as mutually agreed upon by both the homeowner and management.

(b) No rental agreement shall contain any terms or conditions with respect to charges for rent, utilities, or incidental reasonable service charges that would be different during the first 12 months of the rental agreement from the corresponding terms or conditions that would be offered to the homeowners on a month-to-month basis.

(c) No rental agreement for a term of 12 months or less shall include any provision which authorizes automatic extension or renewal of, or automatically extends or renews, the rental agreement beyond the initial term for a term longer than 12 months at the sole option of either the management or the homeowner. *(Added by Stats.1978, c. 1031, p. 3178, § 1. Amended by Stats.1978, c. 1032, p. 3186, § 2; Stats.1978, c. 1033, p. 3188, § 7.5; Stats.1980, c. 206, § 1; Stats.1981, c. 667, § 4; Stats.1982, c. 1397, p. 5320, § 6; Stats.1992, c. 289 (S.B.1454), § 2.)*

Cross References

Homeowner defined for purposes of this Chapter, see Civil Code § 798.9.
Management defined for purposes of this Chapter, see Civil Code § 798.2.
Rental agreement defined for purposes of this Chapter, see Civil Code § 798.8.

§ 798.19. Waiver of rights; public policy

No rental agreement for a mobilehome shall contain a provision by which the homeowner waives his or her rights under the provisions of Articles 1 to 8, inclusive, of this chapter. Any such waiver shall be deemed contrary to public policy and void. *(Added by Stats.1978, c. 1031, p. 3178, § 1. Amended by Stats.1978, c. 1033, p. 3188, § 8; Stats.1982, c. 1397, p. 5320, § 7.)*

Cross References

Hiring of real property, waiver of rights, see Civil Code § 1942.1.
Homeowner defined for purposes of this Chapter, see Civil Code § 798.9.
Mobilehome defined for purposes of this Chapter, see Civil Code § 798.3.
Rental agreement defined for purposes of this Chapter, see Civil Code § 798.8.
Waiver of rights void and unenforceable, see Civil Code § 798.77.

Waiver or modification of lessee's rights void as contrary to public policy, see Civil Code § 1953.

§ 798.19.5. Sale of mobilehome; right of first refusal to management

A rental agreement entered into or renewed on and after January 1, 2006, shall not include a clause, rule, regulation, or any other provision that grants to management the right of first refusal to purchase a homeowner's mobilehome that is in the park and offered for sale to a third party pursuant to Article 7 (commencing with Section 798.70). This section does not preclude a separate agreement for separate consideration granting the park owner or management a right of first refusal to purchase the homeowner's mobilehome that is in the park and offered for sale. *(Added by Stats.2005, c. 35 (S.B.237), § 1.)*

Cross References

Homeowner defined for purposes of this Chapter, see Civil Code § 798.9.
Management defined for purposes of this Chapter, see Civil Code § 798.2.
Mobilehome defined for purposes of this Chapter, see Civil Code § 798.3.
Rental agreement defined for purposes of this Chapter, see Civil Code § 798.8.

§ 798.20. Private club membership not to be denied on discriminatory basis; familial status

(a) Membership in any private club or organization that is a condition for tenancy in a park shall not be denied on any basis listed in subdivision (a) or (d) of Section 12955 of the Government Code, as those bases are defined in Sections 12926, 12926.1, subdivision (m) and paragraph (1) of subdivision (p) of Section 12955, and Section 12955.2 of the Government Code.

(b) Notwithstanding subdivision (a), with respect to familial status, subdivision (a) shall not be construed to apply to housing for older persons, as defined in Section 12955.9 of the Government Code. With respect to familial status, nothing in subdivision (a) shall be construed to affect Sections 51.2, 51.3, 51.4, 51.10, 51.11, and 799.5, relating to housing for senior citizens. Subdivision (d) of Section 51 and Section 4760 of this code and subdivisions (n), (*o*), and (p) of Section 12955 of the Government Code shall apply to subdivision (a). *(Added by Stats.1978, c. 1031, p. 3178, § 1. Amended by Stats.2006, c. 578 (A.B.2800), § 6; Stats.2012, c. 181 (A.B.806), § 26, operative Jan. 1, 2014.)*

Cross References

Tenancy defined for purposes of this Chapter, see Civil Code § 798.12.

§ 798.21. Rent control measures; space not used as principal residence; exemptions

(a) Notwithstanding Section 798.17, if a mobilehome space within a mobilehome park is not the principal residence of the homeowner and the homeowner has not rented the mobilehome to another party, it shall be exempt from any ordinance, rule, regulation, or initiative measure adopted by any city, county, or city and county, which establishes a maximum amount that the landlord may charge a tenant for rent.

(b) Nothing in this section is intended to require any homeowner to disclose information concerning his or her personal finances. Nothing in this section shall be construed to authorize management to gain access to any records which would otherwise be confidential or privileged.

(c) For purposes of this section, a mobilehome shall be deemed to be the principal residence of the homeowner, unless a review of state or county records demonstrates that the homeowner is receiving a homeowner's exemption for another property or mobilehome in this state, or unless a review of public records reasonably demonstrates that the principal residence of the homeowner is out of state.

(d) Before modifying the rent or other terms of tenancy as a result of a review of records, as described in subdivision (c), the management shall notify the homeowner, in writing, of the proposed changes and provide the homeowner with a copy of the documents upon which management relied.

(e) The homeowner shall have 90 days from the date the notice described in subdivision (d) is mailed to review and respond to the notice. Management may not modify the rent or other terms of tenancy prior to the expiration of the 90-day period or prior to responding, in writing, to information provided by the homeowner. Management may not modify the rent or other terms of tenancy if the homeowner provides documentation reasonably establishing that the information provided by management is incorrect or that the homeowner is not the same person identified in the documents. However, nothing in this subdivision shall be construed to authorize the homeowner to change the homeowner's exemption status of the other property or mobilehome owned by the homeowner.

(f) This section does not apply under any of the following conditions:

(1) The homeowner is unable to rent or lease the mobilehome because the owner or management of the mobilehome park in which the mobilehome is located does not permit, or the rental agreement limits or prohibits, the assignment of the mobilehome or the subletting of the park space.

(2) The mobilehome is being actively held available for sale by the homeowner, or pursuant to a listing agreement with a real estate broker licensed pursuant to Chapter 3 (commencing with Section 10130) of Part 1 of Division 4 of the Business and Professions Code, or a mobilehome dealer, as defined in Section 18002.6 of the Health and Safety Code. A homeowner, real estate broker, or mobilehome dealer attempting to sell a mobilehome shall actively market and advertise the mobilehome for sale in good faith to bona fide purchasers for value in order to remain exempt pursuant to this subdivision.

(3) The legal owner has taken possession or ownership, or both, of the mobilehome from a registered owner through either a surrender of ownership interest by the registered owner or a foreclosure proceeding. *(Added by Stats.1996, c. 392 (S.B.1181), § 1. Amended by Stats.2003, c. 132 (A.B. 1173), § 1.)*

Cross References

Homeowner defined for purposes of this Chapter, see Civil Code § 798.9.

§ 798.21

Information for prospective homeowners within a mobilehome park, rent control provisions, see Civil Code § 798.74.5.

Management defined for purposes of this Chapter, see Civil Code § 798.2.

Mobilehome defined for purposes of this Chapter, see Civil Code § 798.3.

Mobilehome park defined for purposes of this Chapter, see Civil Code § 798.4.

Ownership defined for purposes of this Code, see Civil Code § 654.

Rental agreement defined for purposes of this Chapter, see Civil Code § 798.8.

Tenancy defined for purposes of this Chapter, see Civil Code § 798.12.

§ 798.22. Recreational vehicles in mobilehome parks; designated areas

(a) In any new mobilehome park that is developed after January 1, 1982, mobilehome spaces shall not be rented for the accommodation of recreational vehicles as defined by Section 799.29 unless the mobilehome park has a specifically designated area within the park for recreational vehicles, which is separate and apart from the area designated for mobilehomes. Recreational vehicles may be located only in the specifically designated area.

(b) Any new mobilehome park that is developed after January 1, 1982, is not subject to the provisions of this section until 75 percent of the spaces have been rented for the first time. *(Added by Stats.1982, c. 1146, p. 4122, § 1. Amended by Stats.1993, c. 666 (A.B.503), § 3.)*

Cross References

Mobilehome defined for purposes of this Chapter, see Civil Code § 798.3.

Mobilehome park defined for purposes of this Chapter, see Civil Code § 798.4.

ARTICLE 3. RULES AND REGULATIONS

Section
798.23. Park management; compliance; exceptions; mobilehome or mobilehome space.
798.23.5. Rental of homeowner's primary residence, or sublet of space; conditions.
798.24. Common area facilities.
798.25. Amendments to park rules and regulations; written notice; meeting with homeowners.
798.25.5. Void and unenforceable rules or regulations.
798.26. Right of entry by ownership or management; consent; revocation.
798.27. Written notice of nature of zoning permit and duration of lease to homeowners and prospective homeowners.
798.28. Disclosure of mobilehome park owner.
798.285. Renumbered.
798.28.5. Motor vehicles; removal from park; notice of intent to remove.
798.29. Mobilehome Assistance Center signs.
798.29.5. Renumbered.
798.29.6. Installation of accommodations for the disabled.

§ 798.23. Park management; compliance; exceptions; mobilehome or mobilehome space

(a) Management shall be subject to, and comply with, all park rules and regulations to the same extent as residents and their guests.

(b) Subdivision (a) of this section does not apply to either of the following:

(1) Any rule or regulation that governs the age of any resident or guest.

(2) Acts of management that are undertaken to fulfill management's maintenance, management, and business operation responsibilities.

(c)(1) Notwithstanding subdivision (b) and subject to paragraph (2), management shall be subject to, and comply with, all rules and regulations that prohibit a homeowner from renting or subleasing the homeowner's mobilehome or mobilehome space.

(2)(A) If a rule or regulation has been enacted that prohibits either renting or subleasing by a homeowner, management shall not directly rent a mobilehome except as follows:

(i) Management may directly rent up to two mobilehomes within the park for the purpose of housing onsite employees.

(ii) For every 200 mobilehomes in a park, the management may directly rent one more mobilehome within the park, in addition to the mobilehomes authorized for direct rental pursuant to clause (i), for the purpose of housing onsite employees.

(B) For purposes of this paragraph, "the purpose of housing onsite employees" includes directly renting a mobilehome to a person who is not an onsite employee to avoid a vacancy during times when the mobilehome is authorized for direct rental pursuant to subparagraph (A) and not needed for housing onsite employees.

(d) Notwithstanding subdivision (c), management may continue to directly rent a mobilehome to a tenant if both of the following apply:

(1) The tenancy was initially established by a rental agreement executed before January 1, 2022.

(2) A tenant listed on the rental agreement described in paragraph (1) continues to occupy the mobilehome.

(e)(1) A park shall be exempt from the provisions of subdivision (c) if either of the following apply:

(A) The park is owned and operated by an organization that qualifies as an exempt organization under Section 501(c)(3) of the United States Internal Revenue Code of 1986,[1] and the property has been granted an exemption from property taxation pursuant to Section 214 of the Revenue and Taxation Code.

(B) The park is owned by a government agency or an entity controlled by a government agency, and has an affordability covenant in place.

(2) The exemption contained in paragraph (1) applies only to those mobilehomes or mobilehome sites within a park that are restricted for use as affordable housing pursuant to either a written regulatory agreement or the policy or practice of the exempt organization or government agency. *(Added by Stats.1993, c. 520 (A.B.217), § 1. Amended by Stats.1994, c. 340 (S.B.1510), § 1; Stats.2002, c. 672 (S.B.1410), § 1; Stats.2021, c. 706 (A.B.861), § 1, eff. Jan. 1, 2022.)*

[1] Internal Revenue Code sections are in Title 26 of the U.S.C.A.

Cross References

Management defined for purposes of this Chapter, see Civil Code § 798.2.

Resident defined for purposes of this Chapter, see Civil Code § 798.11.

§ 798.23.5. Rental of homeowner's primary residence, or sublet of space; conditions

(a)(1) Management shall permit a homeowner to rent his or her home that serves as the homeowner's primary residence or sublet his or her space, under the circumstances described in paragraph (2) and subject to the requirements of this section.

(2) A homeowner shall be permitted to rent or sublet pursuant to paragraph (1) if a medical emergency or medical treatment requires the homeowner to be absent from his or her home and this is confirmed in writing by an attending physician.

(b) The following provisions shall apply to a rental or sublease pursuant to this section:

(1) The minimum term of the rental or sublease shall be six months, unless the management approves a shorter term, but no greater than 12 months, unless management approves a longer term.

(2) The management may require approval of a prospective renter or sublessee, subject to the process and restrictions provided by subdivision (a) of Section 798.74 for prospective purchasers of mobilehomes. A prospective sublessee shall comply with any rule or regulation limiting residency based on age requirements, pursuant to Section 798.76. The management may charge a prospective sublessee a credit screening fee for the actual cost of any personal reference check or consumer credit report that is provided by a consumer credit reporting agency, as defined in Section 1785.3, if the management or his or her agent requires that personal reference check or consumer credit report.

(3) The renter or sublessee shall comply with all rules and regulations of the park. The failure of a renter or sublessee to comply with the rules and regulations of the park may result in the termination of the homeowner's tenancy in the mobilehome park, in accordance with Section 798.56. A homeowner's tenancy may not be terminated under this paragraph if the homeowner completes an action for unlawful detainer or executes a judgment for possession, pursuant to Chapter 4 (commencing with Section 1159) of Title 3 of Part 3 of the Code of Civil Procedure within 60 days of the homeowner receiving notice of termination of tenancy.

(4) The homeowner shall remain liable for the mobilehome park rent and other park charges.

(5) The management may require the homeowner to reside in the mobilehome park for a term of one year before management permits the renting or subletting of a mobilehome or mobilehome space.

(6) Notwithstanding subdivision (a) of Section 798.39, if a security deposit has been refunded to the homeowner pursuant to subdivision (b) or (c) of Section 798.39, the management may require the homeowner to resubmit a security deposit in an amount or value not to exceed two months' rent in addition to the first month's rent. Management may retain this security deposit for the duration of the term of the rental or sublease.

(7) The homeowner shall keep his or her current address and telephone number on file with the management during the term of rental or sublease. If applicable, the homeowner may provide the name, address, and telephone number of his or her legal representative.

(c) A homeowner may not charge a renter or sublessee more than an amount necessary to cover the cost of space rent, utilities, and scheduled loan payments on the mobilehome, if any. *(Added by Stats.2002, c. 672 (S.B.1410), § 2. Amended by Stats.2011, c. 296 (A.B.1023), § 32.)*

Cross References

Homeowner defined for purposes of this Chapter, see Civil Code § 798.9.

Management defined for purposes of this Chapter, see Civil Code § 798.2.

Mobilehome defined for purposes of this Chapter, see Civil Code § 798.3.

Mobilehome park defined for purposes of this Chapter, see Civil Code § 798.4.

Tenancy defined for purposes of this Chapter, see Civil Code § 798.12.

§ 798.24. Common area facilities

Each common area facility shall be open or available to residents at all reasonable hours and the hours of the common area facility shall be posted at the facility. *(Added by Stats.1983, c. 503, § 1. Amended by Stats.1994, c. 380 (S.B.1508), § 1; Stats.2001, c. 83 (A.B.1202), § 1.)*

Cross References

Resident defined for purposes of this Chapter, see Civil Code § 798.11.

§ 798.25. Amendments to park rules and regulations; written notice; meeting with homeowners

(a) Except as provided in subdivision (d), when the management proposes an amendment to the park's rules and regulations, the management shall meet and consult with the homeowners in the park, their representatives, or both, after written notice has been given to all the homeowners in the park 10 days or more before the meeting. The notice shall set forth the proposed amendment to the park's rules and regulations and shall state the date, time, and location of the meeting.

(b) Except as provided in subdivision (d) following the meeting and consultation with the homeowners, the noticed amendment to the park's rules and regulations may be implemented, as to any homeowner, with the consent of that homeowner, or without the homeowner's consent upon written notice of not less than six months, except for regulations applicable to recreational facilities, which may be amended without homeowner consent upon written notice of not less than 60 days.

(c) Written notice to a homeowner whose tenancy commences within the required period of notice of a proposed amendment to the park's rules and regulations under subdivision (b) or (d) shall constitute compliance with this section where the written notice is given before the inception of the tenancy.

§ 798.25

(d) When the management proposes an amendment to the park's rules and regulations mandated by a change in the law, including, but not limited to, a change in a statute, ordinance, or governmental regulation, the management may implement the amendment to the park's rules and regulations, as to any homeowner, with the consent of that homeowner or without the homeowner's consent upon written notice of not less than 60 days. For purposes of this subdivision, the management shall specify in the notice the citation to the statute, ordinance, or regulation, including the section number, that necessitates the proposed amendment to the park's rules and regulations.

(e) Any amendment to the park's rules and regulations that creates a new fee payable by the homeowner and that has not been expressly agreed upon by the homeowner and management in the written rental agreement or lease, shall be void and unenforceable. (Added by Stats.1978, c. 1033, p. 3186, § 10. Amended by Stats.1982, c. 1397, p. 5321, § 8; Stats.1983, c. 519, § 2; Stats.1993, c. 102 (A.B.285), § 1; Stats.1999, c. 323 (S.B.351), § 1; Stats.2004, c. 622 (S.B.1176), § 1; Stats.2005, c. 22 (S.B.1108), § 11.)

Cross References

Homeowner defined for purposes of this Chapter, see Civil Code § 798.9.

Management defined for purposes of this Chapter, see Civil Code § 798.2.

Rental agreement defined for purposes of this Chapter, see Civil Code § 798.8.

Tenancy defined for purposes of this Chapter, see Civil Code § 798.12.

§ 798.25.5. Void and unenforceable rules or regulations

Any rule or regulation of a mobilehome park that (a) is unilaterally adopted by the management, (b) is implemented without the consent of the homeowners, and (c) by its terms purports to deny homeowners their right to a trial by jury or which would mandate binding arbitration of any dispute between the management and homeowners shall be void and unenforceable. (Added by Stats.1993, c. 889 (A.B.1012), § 1.)

Cross References

Homeowner defined for purposes of this Chapter, see Civil Code § 798.9.

Management defined for purposes of this Chapter, see Civil Code § 798.2.

Mobilehome defined for purposes of this Chapter, see Civil Code § 798.3.

Mobilehome park defined for purposes of this Chapter, see Civil Code § 798.4.

§ 798.26. Right of entry by ownership or management; consent; revocation

(a) Except as provided in subdivision (b), the ownership or management of a park shall have no right of entry to a mobilehome or enclosed accessory structure without the prior written consent of the resident. The consent may be revoked in writing by the resident at any time. The ownership or management shall have a right of entry upon the land upon which a mobilehome is situated for maintenance of utilities, trees, and driveways, for maintenance of the premises in accordance with the rules and regulations of the park when the homeowner or resident fails to so maintain the premises, and protection of the mobilehome park at any reasonable time, but not in a manner or at a time that would interfere with the resident's quiet enjoyment.

(b) The ownership or management of a park may enter a mobilehome or enclosed accessory structure without the prior written consent of the resident in case of an emergency or when the resident has abandoned the mobilehome or accessory structure. (Formerly § 789.16, added by Stats.1978, c. 396, p. 1252, § 1. Renumbered § 798.26 and amended by Stats.1978, c. 1033, p. 3188, § 10.5. Amended by Stats.1981, c. 667, § 5; Stats.1982, c. 1397, p. 5321, § 9; Stats.1983, c. 519, § 3; Stats.2000, c. 423 (A.B.862), § 1; Stats.2004, c. 302 (A.B.2351), § 2; Stats.2008, c. 115 (S.B.1234), § 1.)

Cross References

Homeowner defined for purposes of this Chapter, see Civil Code § 798.9.

Landlord's right of access to a dwelling unit, see Civil Code § 1954.

Management defined for purposes of this Chapter, see Civil Code § 798.2.

Mobilehome defined for purposes of this Chapter, see Civil Code § 798.3.

Mobilehome park defined for purposes of this Chapter, see Civil Code § 798.4.

Ownership defined for purposes of this Code, see Civil Code § 654.

Repair of sudden or unforeseeable breakdown or deterioration of improvements, required contents and notice, see Civil Code § 798.15.

Resident defined for purposes of this Chapter, see Civil Code § 798.11.

§ 798.27. Written notice of nature of zoning permit and duration of lease to homeowners and prospective homeowners

(a) The management shall give written notice to all homeowners and prospective homeowners concerning the following matters: (1) the nature of the zoning or use permit under which the mobilehome park operates. If the mobilehome park is operating pursuant to a permit subject to a renewal or expiration date, the relevant information and dates shall be included in the notice. (2) The duration of any lease of the mobilehome park, or any portion thereof, in which the management is a lessee.

(b) If a change occurs concerning the zoning or use permit under which the park operates or a lease in which the management is a lessee, all homeowners shall be given written notice within 30 days of that change. Notification regarding the change of use of the park, or any portion thereof, shall be governed by subdivision (g) of Section 798.56. A prospective homeowner shall be notified prior to the inception of the tenancy. (Added by Stats.1980, c. 864, § 1. Amended by Stats.1981, c. 667, § 6; Stats.1982, c. 1397, p. 5321, § 10; Stats.1991, c. 190 (A.B.600), § 1.)

Cross References

Change of use defined for purposes of this Chapter, see Civil Code § 798.10.

Homeowner defined for purposes of this Chapter, see Civil Code § 798.9.

Management defined for purposes of this Chapter, see Civil Code § 798.2.

Mobilehome defined for purposes of this Chapter, see Civil Code § 798.3.

Mobilehome park defined for purposes of this Chapter, see Civil Code § 798.4.

Tenancy defined for purposes of this Chapter, see Civil Code § 798.12.

§ 798.28. Disclosure of mobilehome park owner

The management of a mobilehome park shall disclose, in writing, within 10 business days, the name, business address, and business telephone number of the mobilehome park owner upon the receipt of a written request of a homeowner. *(Added by Stats.1981, c. 505, § 1. Amended by Stats.1982, c. 1397, p. 5322, § 11; Stats.1991, c. 62 (A.B.577), § 1; Stats. 2017, c. 31 (A.B.294), § 1, eff. Jan. 1, 2018.)*

Cross References

Homeowner defined for purposes of this Chapter, see Civil Code § 798.9.

Management defined for purposes of this Chapter, see Civil Code § 798.2.

Mobilehome defined for purposes of this Chapter, see Civil Code § 798.3.

Mobilehome park defined for purposes of this Chapter, see Civil Code § 798.4.

§ 798.285. Renumbered § 798.28.5 and amended by Stats. 2004, c. 302 (A.B.2351), § 3

§ 798.28.5. Motor vehicles; removal from park; notice of intent to remove

(a) Except as otherwise provided in this section, the management may cause the removal, pursuant to Section 22658 of the Vehicle Code, of a vehicle other than a mobilehome that is parked in the park when there is displayed a sign at each entrance to the park as provided in paragraph (1) of subdivision (a) of Section 22658 of the Vehicle Code.

(b)(1) Management may not cause the removal of a vehicle from a homeowner's or resident's driveway or a homeowner's or resident's designated parking space except if management has first posted on the windshield of the vehicle a notice stating management's intent to remove the vehicle in seven days and stating the specific park rule that the vehicle has violated that justifies its removal. After the expiration of seven days following the posting of the notice, management may remove a vehicle that remains in violation of a rule for which notice has been posted upon the vehicle. If a vehicle rule violation is corrected within seven days after the rule violation notice is posted on the vehicle, the vehicle may not be removed. If a vehicle upon which a rule violation notice has been posted is removed from the park by a homeowner or resident and subsequently is returned to the park still in violation of the rule stated in the notice, management is not required to post any additional notice on the vehicle, and the vehicle may be removed after the expiration of the seven-day period following the original notice posting.

(2) If a vehicle poses a significant danger to the health or safety of a park resident or guest, or if a homeowner or resident requests to have a vehicle removed from his or her driveway or designated parking space, the requirements of paragraph (1) do not apply, and management may remove the vehicle pursuant to Section 22658 of the Vehicle Code. *(Formerly § 798.285, added by Stats.1993, c. 32 (S.B.209), § 1.*

Renumbered § 798.28.5 and amended by Stats.2004, c. 302 (A.B.2351), § 3.)

Cross References

Homeowner defined for purposes of this Chapter, see Civil Code § 798.9.

Management defined for purposes of this Chapter, see Civil Code § 798.2.

Mobilehome defined for purposes of this Chapter, see Civil Code § 798.3.

Resident defined for purposes of this Chapter, see Civil Code § 798.11.

§ 798.29. Mobilehome Assistance Center signs

The management shall post a Mobilehome Assistance Center sign provided by the Department of Housing and Community Development, as required by Section 18253.5 of the Health and Safety Code. *(Added by Stats.1988, c. 333, § 1. Amended by Stats.1996, c. 402 (S.B.1594), § 1; Stats. 2018, c. 957 (S.B.1078), § 1, eff. Jan. 1, 2019.)*

Cross References

Management defined for purposes of this Chapter, see Civil Code § 798.2.

Mobilehome defined for purposes of this Chapter, see Civil Code § 798.3.

§ 798.29.5. Renumbered § 798.42 and amended by Stats. 2009, c. 558 (S.B.111), § 1

§ 798.29.6. Installation of accommodations for the disabled

The management shall not prohibit a homeowner or resident from installing accommodations for the disabled on the home or the site, lot, or space on which the mobilehome is located, including, but not limited to, ramps or handrails on the outside of the home, as long as the installation of those facilities complies with code, as determined by an enforcement agency, and those facilities are installed pursuant to a permit, if required for the installation, issued by the enforcement agency. The management may require that the accommodations installed pursuant to this section be removed by the current homeowner at the time the mobilehome is removed from the park or pursuant to a written agreement between the current homeowner and the management prior to the completion of the resale of the mobilehome in place in the park. This section is not exclusive and shall not be construed to condition, affect, or supersede any other provision of law or regulation relating to accessibility or accommodations for the disabled. *(Added by Stats.2008, c. 170 (S.B.1107), § 1.)*

ARTICLE 3.5. FEES AND CHARGES

Section
798.30.	Notice of rent increase.
798.30.5.	Limitations on increase of gross rental rate over the course of any 12-month period for a tenancy in a qualified mobile-home; initial rental rate; notice.
798.31.	Authorized fees.
798.32.	Charge for unlisted services; notice; expiration date of fees.
798.33.	Pets.

Section	
798.34.	Guests and live-in health and supportive care or supervision providers.
798.35.	Number of immediate family members.
798.36.	Rule enforcement; removal of personal property; notice; costs; sale or auction of property.
798.37.	Entry, installation or hookup fees; landscaping and maintenance charges.
798.37.5.	Trimming, pruning, or removal of trees; responsibility of mobilehome park management.
798.38.	Lien or security interest by mutual agreement; exception.
798.39.	Security deposit; amount; refund; application.
798.39.5.	Prohibition of charge, fee or increase of rent to reflect cost to management of violations of chapter.

§ 798.30. Notice of rent increase

The management shall give a homeowner written notice of any increase in his or her rent at least 90 days before the date of the increase. *(Added by Stats.1978, c. 1031, p. 3178, § 1. Amended by Stats.1982, c. 1397, p. 5322, § 12; Stats.1993, c. 448 (A.B.870), § 1.)*

Cross References

Delivery of notice, see Civil Code § 798.14.
Homeowner defined for purposes of this Chapter, see Civil Code § 798.9.
Management defined for purposes of this Chapter, see Civil Code § 798.2.
Repair of sudden or unforeseeable breakdown or deterioration of improvements, required contents and notice, see Civil Code § 798.15.

§ 798.30.5. Limitations on increase of gross rental rate over the course of any 12-month period for a tenancy in a qualified mobile-home; initial rental rate; notice

(a)(1) Subject to subdivision (b), management shall not, over the course of any 12–month period, increase the gross rental rate for a tenancy in a qualified mobilehome park more than 3 percent plus the percentage change in the cost of living, or 5 percent, whichever is lower, of the lowest gross rental rate charged for a tenancy at any time during the 12 months prior to the effective date of the increase.

(2) If the same homeowner maintains a tenancy over any 12–month period, the gross rental rate for the tenancy shall not be increased in more than two increments over that 12–month period, subject to the other restrictions of this subdivision governing gross rental rate increase.

(b) For a new tenancy in which no homeowner from the prior tenancy remains in lawful possession of the mobilehome space, management may establish the initial rental rate not subject to subdivision (a), unless the applicable local agency or jurisdiction has adopted an ordinance, rule, regulation, or initiative measure that limits the allowable rental rate for a new tenancy, in which case that ordinance, rule, regulation, or initiative measure shall apply. Subdivision (a) shall be applicable to subsequent increases after that initial rental rate has been established, except as otherwise provided in this section.

(c) A homeowner with a tenancy subject to this section shall not enter into a sublease that results in a total rent for the premises that exceeds the allowable rental rate authorized by subdivision (c) of Section 798.23.5. Nothing in this subdivision authorizes a homeowner to sublet or assign the homeowner's interest where otherwise prohibited.

(d) Management shall provide notice of any increase in the rental rate, pursuant to subdivision (a), to each homeowner in accordance with Section 798.30.

(e) This section shall not apply to a tenancy for any of the following:

(1) A mobilehome space restricted by deed, regulatory restriction contained in an agreement with a government agency, or other recorded document as affordable housing for persons and families of very low, low, or moderate income, as defined in Section 50093 of the Health and Safety Code, or subject to an agreement that provides housing subsidies for affordable housing for persons and families of very low, low, or moderate income, as defined in Section 50093 of the Health and Safety Code or comparable federal statutes.

(2) A mobilehome space constructed and maintained in connection with any higher education institution within the state for use and occupancy by students in attendance at the institution.

(3) A mobilehome space subject to any ordinance, rule, regulation, or initiative measure that restricts annual increases in the rental rate to an amount less than that provided in subdivision (a).

(4) A mobilehome space within a resident-owned mobilehome park, as defined in Section 799.

(f)(1)(A) This section shall apply to all rent increases occurring on or after February 18, 2021.

(B) This section shall become operative January 1, 2022.

(2) In the event that management has increased the rent by more than the amount permissible under subdivision (a) between February 18, 2021, and January 1, 2022, both of the following shall apply:

(A) The applicable rent on January 1, 2022, shall be the rent as of February 18, 2021, plus the maximum permissible increase under subdivision (a).

(B) Management shall not be liable to a homeowner for any corresponding rent overpayment.

(3) Management subject to subdivision (a) who increased the rental rate for a tenancy on or after February 18, 2021, but prior to January 1, 2022, by an amount less than the rental rate increase permitted by subdivision (a) shall be allowed to increase the rental rate twice, as provided in paragraph (2) of subdivision (a), within 12 months of February 18, 2021, but in no event shall that rental rate increase exceed the maximum rental rate increase permitted by subdivision (a).

(g) Any waiver of the rights under this section shall be void as contrary to public policy.

(h) For the purposes of this section:

(1) "Consumer Price Index for All Urban Consumers for All Items" means the following:

(A) The Consumer Price Index for All Urban Consumers for All Items (CPI–U) for the metropolitan area in which the property is located, as published by the United States Bureau of Labor Statistics, which are as follows:

(i) The CPI–U for the Los Angeles–Long Beach–Anaheim metropolitan area covering the Counties of Los Angeles and Orange.

(ii) The CPI–U for the Riverside–San Bernardo–Ontario metropolitan area covering the Counties of Riverside and San Bernardino.

(iii) The CPI–U for the San Diego–Carlsbad metropolitan area covering the County of San Diego.

(iv) The CPI–U for the San Francisco–Oakland–Hayward metropolitan area covering the Counties of Alameda, Contra Costa, Marin, San Francisco, and San Mateo.

(v) Any successor metropolitan area index to any of the indexes listed in clauses (i) to (iv), inclusive.

(B) If the United States Bureau of Labor Statistics does not publish a CPI–U for the metropolitan area in which the property is located, the California Consumer Price Index for All Urban Consumers for All Items as published by the Department of Industrial Relations.

(C) On or after January 1, 2022, if the United States Bureau of Labor Statistics publishes a CPI–U index for one or more metropolitan areas not listed in subparagraph (A), that CPI–U index shall apply in those areas with respect to rent increases that take effect on or after August 1 of the calendar year in which the 12–month change in that CPI–U, as described in subparagraph (B) of paragraph (3), is first published.

(2) "Management" means the management, as defined in Section 798.2, of a qualified mobilehome park.

(3)(A) "Percentage change in the cost of living" means the percentage change in the applicable Consumer Price Index for All Urban Consumers for All Items, as described in paragraph (1) and computed pursuant to subparagraph (B) of this paragraph.

(B)(i) For rent increases that take effect before August 1 of any calendar year, the following shall apply:

(I) The percentage change shall be the percentage change in the amount published for April of the immediately preceding calendar year and April of the year before that.

(II) If there is not an amount published in April for the applicable geographic area, the percentage change shall be the percentage change in the amount published for March of the immediately preceding calendar year and March of the year before that.

(ii) For rent increases that take effect on or after August 1 of any calendar year, the following shall apply:

(I) The percentage change shall be the percentage change in the amount published for April of that calendar year and April of the immediately preceding calendar year.

(II) If there is not an amount published in April for the applicable geographic area, the percentage change shall be the percentage change in the amount published for March of that calendar year and March of the immediately preceding calendar year.

(iii) The percentage change shall be rounded to the nearest one-tenth of 1 percent.

(4) "Qualified mobilehome park" means a mobilehome park, as defined in Section 798.4, that is located within and governed by the jurisdictions of two or more incorporated cities.

(i)(1) Nothing in this section affects the authority of a local government to adopt or maintain an ordinance, rule, regulation, or initiative measure that establishes a maximum amount that may be charged for rent. However, if a local ordinance, rule, regulation, or initiative measure allows for a rental rate increase greater than that provided in subdivision (a), this section shall apply.

(2) Nothing in this section alters the application of Sections 798.17, 798.45, or 798.49 to any ordinance, rule, regulation, or initiative measure that establishes a maximum amount that may be charged for rent.

(3) This section is not intended to express any policy regarding the appropriate, allowable rental rate increase limitations when a local government or jurisdiction adopts an ordinance, rule, regulation, or initiative measure regulating rent increases.

(j) This section shall remain in effect only until January 1, 2030, and as of that date is repealed. *(Added by Stats.2021, c. 125 (A.B.978), § 2, eff. Jan. 1, 2022.)*

Repeal

For repeal of this section, see its terms.

§ 798.31. Authorized fees

A homeowner shall not be charged a fee for other than rent, utilities, and incidental reasonable charges for services actually rendered.

A homeowner shall not be charged a fee for obtaining a lease on a mobilehome lot for (1) a term of 12 months, or (2) a lesser period as the homeowner may request. A fee may be charged for a lease of more than one year if the fee is mutually agreed upon by both the homeowner and management. *(Added by Stats.1978, c. 1031, p. 3178, § 1. Amended by Stats.1982, c. 1397, p. 5322, § 13; Stats.1984, c. 624, § 1.)*

Cross References

Homeowner defined for purposes of this Chapter, see Civil Code § 798.9.
Management defined for purposes of this Chapter, see Civil Code § 798.2.
Mobilehome defined for purposes of this Chapter, see Civil Code § 798.3.
Mobilehome park owners, sale of liquified petroleum gas to mobilehome owners and tenants, limit on price that can be charged, see Civil Code § 798.44.

§ 798.32. Charge for unlisted services; notice; expiration date of fees

(a) A homeowner shall not be charged a fee for services actually rendered which are not listed in the rental agreement unless he or she has been given written notice thereof by the management, at least 60 days before imposition of the charge.

(b) Those fees and charges specified in subdivision (a) shall be separately stated on any monthly or other periodic billing to the homeowner. If the fee or charge has a limited duration or is amortized for a specified period, the expiration date shall be stated on the initial notice and each subsequent billing to the homeowner while the fee or charge is billed to the homeowner. *(Added by Stats.1978, c. 1031, p. 3178, § 1. Amended by Stats.1982, c. 1397, p. 5322, § 14; Stats.1992, c. 338 (S.B.1365), § 1.)*

Cross References

Delivery of notice, see Civil Code § 798.14.

Homeowner defined for purposes of this Chapter, see Civil Code § 798.9.

Management defined for purposes of this Chapter, see Civil Code § 798.2.

Rental agreement defined for purposes of this Chapter, see Civil Code § 798.8.

§ 798.33. Pets

(a) No lease agreement entered into, modified, or renewed on or after January 1, 2001, shall prohibit a homeowner from keeping at least one pet within the park, subject to reasonable rules and regulations of the park. This section may not be construed to affect any other rights provided by law to a homeowner to keep a pet within the park.

(b) A homeowner shall not be charged a fee for keeping a pet in the park unless the management actually provides special facilities or services for pets. If special pet facilities are maintained by the management, the fee charged shall reasonably relate to the cost of maintenance of the facilities or services and the number of pets kept in the park.

(c) For purposes of this section, "pet" means any domesticated bird, cat, dog, aquatic animal kept within an aquarium, or other animal as agreed to between the management and the homeowner. *(Added by Stats.1978, c. 1031, p. 3178, § 1. Amended by Stats.1978, c. 1033, p. 3189, § 11; Stats.1982, c. 1397, p. 5322, § 15; Stats.1989, c. 42, § 1; Stats.2000, c. 551 (A.B.860), § 1.)*

Cross References

Homeowner defined for purposes of this Chapter, see Civil Code § 798.9.

Management defined for purposes of this Chapter, see Civil Code § 798.2.

§ 798.34. Guests and live-in health and supportive care or supervision providers

(a) A homeowner shall not be charged a fee for a guest who does not stay with the homeowner for more than a total of 20 consecutive days or a total of 30 days in a calendar year. A person who is a guest, as described in this subdivision, shall not be required to register with the management.

(b) A homeowner who is living alone in the mobilehome and who wishes to share occupancy of their mobilehome with one other person, to be designated as the homeowner's companion, may do so, and management shall not impose a fee for that person. For purposes of this subdivision, a homeowner may only designate one person at a time as a companion and shall not designate more than three companions in total during any calendar year, unless otherwise authorized by management. Management may refuse to allow a homeowner to share their mobilehome with a companion under this subdivision if park residency is subject to age restrictions and the proposed companion is unable or unwilling to provide documentation that the proposed companion meets those age restrictions.

(c) A homeowner may share their mobilehome with any person over 18 years of age if that person is providing live-in health care, live-in supportive care, or supervision to the homeowner. Management shall not charge a fee for the live-in caregiver but may require written confirmation from a licensed health care professional of the homeowner's need for the care or supervision, if the need is not readily apparent or already known to management.

(d) A senior homeowner who resides in a mobilehome park that has implemented rules or regulations limiting residency based on age requirements for housing for older persons, pursuant to Section 798.76, may share their mobilehome with any person over 18 years of age if this person is a parent, sibling, child, or grandchild of the senior homeowner and requires live-in health care, live-in supportive care, or supervision. Management shall not charge a fee for this parent, sibling, child, or grandchild, but may require written confirmation from a licensed health care professional of the need for the care or supervision, if the need is not readily apparent or already known to management. As used in this section, "senior homeowner" means a homeowner who is 55 years of age or older.

(e) A guest, companion, live-in caregiver, or family member under the care of a senior homeowner, as they are described in this section, shall have no rights of tenancy in the park, and any agreement between the homeowner and the guest, companion, live-in caregiver, or family member under the care of a senior homeowner shall not change the terms and conditions of the rental agreement between management and the homeowner.

(f) A violation of the mobilehome park rules and regulations by a guest, companion, live-in caregiver, or family member under the care of a senior homeowner, as they are described in this section, shall be deemed a violation of the rules and regulations by the homeowner and subject to subdivision (d) of Section 798.56.

(g) Nothing in this section shall be interpreted to create a duty on the part of management to manage, supervise, or provide care for a homeowner's guest, companion, live-in caregiver, or family member under the care of a senior homeowner, during that person's stay in the mobilehome park. *(Added by Stats.1978, c. 1031, p. 3178, § 1. Amended by Stats.1981, c. 240, § 1; Stats.1982, c. 1397, p. 5322, § 16; Stats.1983, c. 128, § 1; Stats.1990, c. 881 (S.B.2547), § 1; Stats.1992, c. 337 (S.B.1314), § 1; Stats.1996, c. 157 (S.B.1624), § 1; Stats.2008, c. 170 (S.B.1107), § 2; Stats.2017, c. 767 (S.B.147), § 1, eff. Jan. 1, 2018; Stats.2019, c. 504 (S.B.274), § 1, eff. Jan. 1, 2020.)*

Cross References

Homeowner defined for purposes of this Chapter, see Civil Code § 798.9.

Management defined for purposes of this Chapter, see Civil Code § 798.2.

Mobilehome defined for purposes of this Chapter, see Civil Code § 798.3.

Mobilehome park defined for purposes of this Chapter, see Civil Code § 798.4.

Rental agreement defined for purposes of this Chapter, see Civil Code § 798.8.

Tenancy defined for purposes of this Chapter, see Civil Code § 798.12.

§ 798.35. Number of immediate family members

A homeowner shall not be charged a fee based on the number of members in his or her immediate family. As used in this section, the "immediate family" shall be limited to the homeowner, his or her spouse, their parents, their children, and their grandchildren under 18 years of age. (Added by Stats.1978, c. 1031, p. 3178, § 1. Amended by Stats.1980, c. 845, § 1; Stats.1982, c. 1397, p. 5322, § 17; Stats.1995, c. 24 (A.B.283), § 1.)

Cross References

Homeowner defined for purposes of this Chapter, see Civil Code § 798.9.

§ 798.36. Rule enforcement; removal of personal property; notice; costs; sale or auction of property

(a) A homeowner shall not be charged a fee for the enforcement of any of the rules and regulations of the park, except a reasonable fee may be charged by management for the maintenance or cleanup, as described in subdivision (b), of the land and premises upon which the mobilehome is situated in the event the homeowner fails to do so in accordance with the rules and regulations of the park after written notification to the homeowner and the failure of the homeowner to comply within 14 days. The written notice shall state the specific condition to be corrected and an estimate of the charges to be imposed by management if the services are performed by management or its agent.

(b)(1) If management determines, in good faith, that the removal of a homeowner's or resident's personal property from the land and premises upon which the mobilehome is situated is necessary to bring the premises into compliance with the reasonable rules and regulations of the park or the provisions of the Mobilehome Parks Act (Part 2.1 (commencing with Section 18200) of Division 13 of the Health and Safety Code) or Title 25 of the California Code of Regulations, management may remove the property to a reasonably secure storage facility. Management shall provide written notice of at least 14 days of its intent to remove the personal property, including a description of the property to be removed. The notice shall include the rule, regulation, or code justifying the removal and shall provide an estimate of the charges to be imposed by management. The property to be removed shall not include the mobilehome or its appurtenances or accessory structures.

(2) The homeowner or resident shall be responsible for reimbursing to management the actual, reasonable costs, if any, of removing and storing the property. These costs incurred by management in correcting the rules violation associated with the removal and storage of the property, are deemed reasonable incidental service charges and may be collected pursuant to subdivision (e) of Section 798.56 if a notice of nonpayment of the removal and storage fees, as described in paragraph (3), is personally served on the homeowner.

(3) Within seven days from the date the property is removed to a storage area, management shall provide the homeowner or resident a written notice that includes an inventory of the property removed, the location where the property may be claimed, and notice that the cost of removal and storage shall be paid by the resident or homeowner. If, within 60 days, the homeowner or resident does not claim the property, the property shall be deemed to be abandoned, and management may dispose of the property in any manner. The homeowner's or resident's liability for storage charges shall not exceed 60 days. If the homeowner or resident claims the property, but has not reimbursed management for storage costs, management may bill those costs in a monthly statement which shall constitute notice of nonpayment, and the costs shall become the obligation of the homeowner or resident. If a resident or homeowner communicates in writing his or her intent to abandon the property before 60 days has expired, management may dispose of the property immediately and no further storage charges shall accrue.

(4) If management elects to dispose of the property by way of sale or auction, and the funds received from the sale or auction exceed the amount owed to management, management shall refund the difference to the homeowner or resident within 15 days from the date of management's receipt of the funds from the sale or auction. The refund shall be delivered to the homeowner or resident by first-class mail postage prepaid to his or her address in the park, or by personal delivery, and shall include an accounting specifying the costs of removal and storage of the property incurred by management in correcting the rules violation and the amount of proceeds realized from any sale or auction. If a sale or auction of the property yields less than the costs incurred by management, the homeowner or resident shall be responsible for the difference, and this amount shall be deemed a reasonable incidental service charge and may be collected pursuant to subdivision (e) of Section 798.56 if a notice of nonpayment of the removal and storage fees, as described in paragraph (3), is personally served on the homeowner. If management elects to proceed under this section, it may not also terminate the tenancy pursuant to subdivision (d) of Section 798.56 based upon the specific violations relied upon to proceed under this section. In any proceeding under this section, management shall bear the burden of proof that enforcement was undertaken in a nondiscriminatory, nonselective fashion. (Added by Stats.1978, c. 1031, p. 3178, § 1. Amended by Stats.1982, c. 1397, p. 5322, § 18; Stats.1983, c. 519, § 4; Stats.2005, c. 24 (S.B.125), § 1.)

Cross References

Burden of proof, generally, see Evidence Code § 500 et seq.
Delivery of notice, see Civil Code § 798.14.
Homeowner defined for purposes of this Chapter, see Civil Code § 798.9.
Landlord duties, effect of tenant violations, see Civil Code § 1941.2.
Management defined for purposes of this Chapter, see Civil Code § 798.2.
Mobilehome defined for purposes of this Chapter, see Civil Code § 798.3.
Mobilehome park defined for purposes of this Chapter, see Civil Code § 798.4.
Obligation defined, see Civil Code § 1427.
Resident defined for purposes of this Chapter, see Civil Code § 798.11.

Tenancy defined for purposes of this Chapter, see Civil Code § 798.12.

§ 798.37. Entry, installation or hookup fees; landscaping and maintenance charges

A homeowner may not be charged a fee for the entry, installation, hookup, or landscaping as a condition of tenancy except for an actual fee or cost imposed by a local governmental ordinance or requirement directly related to the occupancy of the specific site upon which the mobilehome is located and not incurred as a portion of the development of the mobilehome park as a whole. However, reasonable landscaping and maintenance requirements may be included in the park rules and regulations. The management may not require a homeowner or prospective homeowner to purchase, rent, or lease goods or services for landscaping, remodeling, or maintenance from any person, company, or corporation. (Added by Stats.1978, c. 1031, p. 3178, § 1. Amended by Stats.1980, c. 845, § 2; Stats.1982, c. 1397, p. 5322, § 19; Stats.1983, c. 519, § 5; Stats.2004, c. 302 (A.B.2351), § 4.)

Cross References

Homeowner defined for purposes of this Chapter, see Civil Code § 798.9.

Management defined for purposes of this Chapter, see Civil Code § 798.2.

Mobilehome defined for purposes of this Chapter, see Civil Code § 798.3.

Mobilehome park defined for purposes of this Chapter, see Civil Code § 798.4.

Tenancy defined for purposes of this Chapter, see Civil Code § 798.12.

§ 798.37.5. Trimming, pruning, or removal of trees; responsibility of mobilehome park management

(a) With respect to trees on rental spaces in a mobilehome park, park management shall be solely responsible for the trimming, pruning, or removal of any tree, and the costs thereof, upon written notice by a homeowner or a determination by park management that the tree poses a specific hazard or health and safety violation. In the case of a dispute over that assertion, the park management or a homeowner may request an inspection by the Department of Housing and Community Development or a local agency responsible for the enforcement of the Mobilehome Parks Act (Part 2.1 (commencing with Section 18200) of Division 13 of the Health and Safety Code) in order to determine whether a violation of that act exists.

(b) With respect to trees in the common areas of a mobilehome park, park management shall be solely responsible for the trimming, pruning, or removal of any tree, and the costs thereof.

(c) Park management shall be solely responsible for the maintenance, repair, replacement, paving, sealing, and the expenses related to the maintenance of all driveways installed by park management including, but not limited to, repair of root damage to driveways and foundation systems and removal. Homeowners shall be responsible for the maintenance, repair, replacement, paving, sealing, and the expenses related to the maintenance of a homeowner installed driveway. A homeowner may be charged for the cost of any damage to the driveway caused by an act of the homeowner or a breach of the homeowner's responsibilities under the rules and regulations so long as those rules and regulations are not inconsistent with the provisions of this section.

(d) No homeowner may plant a tree within the mobilehome park without first obtaining written permission from the management.

(e) This section shall not apply to alter the terms of any rental agreement in effect prior to January 1, 2001, between the park management and the homeowner regarding the responsibility for the maintenance of trees and driveways within the mobilehome park, except that upon any renewal or extension, the rental agreement shall be subject to this section. This section is not intended to abrogate the content of any existing rental agreement or other written agreements regarding trees or driveways that are in effect prior to January 1, 2001.

(f) This section shall only apply to rental agreements entered into, renewed, or extended on or after January 1, 2001.

(g) Any mobilehome park rule or regulation shall be in compliance with this section. (Added by Stats.2000, c. 423 (A.B.862), § 2. Amended by Stats.2014, c. 298 (A.B.2753), § 1, eff. Jan. 1, 2015.)

Cross References

Homeowner defined for purposes of this Chapter, see Civil Code § 798.9.

Management defined for purposes of this Chapter, see Civil Code § 798.2.

Mobilehome defined for purposes of this Chapter, see Civil Code § 798.3.

Mobilehome park defined for purposes of this Chapter, see Civil Code § 798.4.

Rental agreement defined for purposes of this Chapter, see Civil Code § 798.8.

§ 798.38. Lien or security interest by mutual agreement; exception

The management shall not acquire a lien or security interest, other than an interest arising by reason of process issued to enforce a judgment of any court, in a mobilehome located in the park unless it is mutually agreed upon by both the homeowner and management. Any billing and payment upon the obligation shall be kept separate from current rent. (Formerly § 798.40, added by Stats.1986, c. 390, § 1. Renumbered § 798.38 and amended by Stats.2009, c. 558 (S.B.111), § 5.)

Cross References

Homeowner defined for purposes of this Chapter, see Civil Code § 798.9.

Management defined for purposes of this Chapter, see Civil Code § 798.2.

Mobilehome defined for purposes of this Chapter, see Civil Code § 798.3.

Obligation defined, see Civil Code § 1427.

§ 798.39. Security deposit; amount; refund; application

(a) The management may only demand a security deposit on or before initial occupancy and the security deposit may not be in an amount or value in excess of an amount equal to two months' rent that is charged at the inception of the occupancy, in addition to any rent for the first month. In no event shall additional security deposits be demanded of a homeowner following the initial occupancy.

(b) As to all security deposits collected on or after January 1, 1989, after the homeowner has promptly paid to the management, within five days of the date the amount is due, all of the rent, utilities, and reasonable service charges for any 12-consecutive-month period subsequent to the collection of the security deposit by the management, or upon resale of the mobilehome, whichever occurs earlier, the management shall, upon the receipt of a written request from the homeowner, refund to the homeowner the amount of the security deposit within 30 days following the end of the 12-consecutive-month period of the prompt payment or the date of the resale of the mobilehome.

(c) As to all security deposits collected prior to January 1, 1989, upon the extension or renewal of the rental agreement or lease between the homeowner and the management, and upon the receipt of a written request from the homeowner, if the homeowner has promptly paid to the management, within five days of the date the amount is due, all of the rent, utilities, and reasonable service charges for the 12–consecutive–month period preceding the receipt of the written request, the management shall refund to the homeowner the amount of the security deposit within 60 days.

(d) As to all security deposits collected prior to January 1, 1989, and not disbursed pursuant to subdivision (c), in the event that the mobilehome park is sold or transferred to any other party or entity, the selling park owner shall deposit in escrow an amount equal to all security deposits that the park owner holds. The seller's escrow instructions shall direct that, upon close of escrow, the security deposits therein that were held by the selling park owner (including the period in escrow) for 12 months or more, shall be disbursed to the persons who paid the deposits to the selling park owner and promptly paid, within five days of the date the amount is due, all rent, utilities, and reasonable service charges for the 12–month period preceding the close of escrow.

(e) Any and all security deposits in escrow that were held by the selling park owner that are not required to be disbursed pursuant to subdivision (b), (c), or (d) shall be disbursed to the successors in interest to the selling or transferring park owner, who shall have the same obligations of the park's management and ownership specified in this section with respect to security deposits. The disbursal may be made in escrow by a debit against the selling park owner and a credit to the successors in interest to the selling park owner.

(f) The management shall not be required to place any security deposit collected in an interest-bearing account or to provide a homeowner with any interest on the security deposit collected.

(g) Nothing in this section shall affect the validity of title to real property transferred in violation of this section. (Added by Stats.1988, c. 59, § 1. Amended by Stats.1994, c. 119 (S.B.1386), § 1; Stats.2001, c. 151 (A.B.210), § 1.)

Cross References

Homeowner defined for purposes of this Chapter, see Civil Code § 798.9.

Management defined for purposes of this Chapter, see Civil Code § 798.2.
Mobilehome defined for purposes of this Chapter, see Civil Code § 798.3.
Mobilehome park defined for purposes of this Chapter, see Civil Code § 798.4.
Obligation defined, see Civil Code § 1427.
Ownership defined for purposes of this Code, see Civil Code § 654.
Real property defined for purposes of this Code, see Civil Code § 658.
Rental agreement defined for purposes of this Chapter, see Civil Code § 798.8.

§ 798.39.5. Prohibition of charge, fee or increase of rent to reflect cost to management of violations of chapter

(a)(1) The management shall not charge or impose upon a homeowner any fee or increase in rent which reflects the cost to the management of any fine, forfeiture, penalty, money damages, or fee assessed or awarded by a court of law or an enforcement agency against the management for a violation of this chapter or Part 2.1 (commencing with Section 18200) of Division 13 of the Health and Safety Code, including any attorney's fees and costs incurred by the management in connection therewith.

(2) This section shall not apply to violations for which the registered owner of the mobilehome is initially responsible pursuant to subdivision (b) of Section 18420 of the Health and Safety Code.

(b) A court shall consider the remoteness in time of the assessment or award against the management of any fine, forfeiture, penalty, money damages, or fee in determining whether the homeowner has met the burden of proof that the fee or increase in rent is in violation of this section.

(c) Any provision in a rental agreement entered into, renewed, or modified on or after January 1, 1995, that permits a fee or increase in rent that reflects the cost to the management of any money damages awarded against the management for a violation of this chapter shall be void. (Formerly § 798.42, added by Stats.1990, c. 1374 (S.B.2446), § 1. Amended by Stats.1994, c. 1254 (A.B.3566), § 1. Renumbered § 798.39.5 and amended by Stats.2009, c. 558 (S.B.111), § 6. Amended by Stats.2012, c. 477 (A.B.1938), § 2.)

Cross References

Burden of proof, generally, see Evidence Code § 500 et seq.
Homeowner defined for purposes of this Chapter, see Civil Code § 798.9.
Management defined for purposes of this Chapter, see Civil Code § 798.2.
Rent charges, separate charges for certain fees, assessments, or other costs, exceptions, see Civil Code § 798.49.
Rental agreement defined for purposes of this Chapter, see Civil Code § 798.8.

ARTICLE 4. UTILITIES

Section
798.40. Utility meter service; billing; rate schedule; separate water service bill.
798.41. Utility service fees; separate billing; application; expiration date of fees.

PROPERTY

Section	
798.42.	Interruption in utility service within mobilehome park; written advance notice by ownership or management; liability.
798.43.	Homeowner's meter measuring utility service to common areas; disclosure prior to tenancy.
798.43.1.	California Alternate Rates for Energy (CARE) program; assistance to low-income persons for utility costs; duties of management of master-meter parks; notice; application processes and procedures; discount notice on billing statements.
798.44.	Mobilehome park owners or residents; sale of liquified petroleum gas; limit on price that can be charged.

§ 798.40. Utility meter service; billing; rate schedule; separate water service bill

(a) Where management provides both master-meter and submeter service of utilities to a homeowner, for each billing period the cost of the charges for the period shall be separately stated along with the opening and closing readings for the homeowner's meter. Management shall post, in a conspicuous place, the specific current residential utility rate schedule as published by the serving utility or the internet website address of the specific current residential utility rate schedule. If management elects to post the internet website address where the schedule may be accessed, management shall do both of the following:

(1) Provide a copy of the specific current residential utility rate schedule, upon request, at no cost.

(2) State in the posting that a homeowner may request a copy of the rate schedule from management.

(b) If a third-party billing agent or company prepares utility billing for the park, management shall disclose on each resident's billing, the name, address, and telephone number of the billing agent or company.

(c) Whenever management elects to separately bill water service to a homeowner as a utility service pursuant to Section 798.41, and to provide submetered water service to homeowners as a master-meter customer of the water purveyor, as a part of the regular bill for water service, management shall only bill a homeowner for the following water service:

(1) A charge for volumetric usage, which may be calculated in any of the following ways:

(A) The amount shall be calculated by first determining the proportion of the homeowner's usage, as shown by the submeter, to the total usage as shown by the water purveyor's billing. The dollar amount billed to the homeowner for usage shall be in that same proportion to the dollar amount for usage shown by the water purveyor's billing.

(B) If the water purveyor charges for volumetric usage based on a tiered rate schedule, management may calculate the charge for a homeowner's volumetric usage as described in subparagraph (A) or management may instead divide each tier's volume evenly among the number of mobilehome spaces, and the rate applicable to each block shall be applied to the consumption recorded for each mobilehome space.

(C) If the water purveyor charges the property rates on a per-mobilehome space basis, the homeowners may be charged at those exact per-mobilehome space rates.

(D) In no event shall the charge for volumetric usage under this paragraph include in its calculation water used by or for any common area facility in the park, or water used by any other person or entity, other than the homeowner being billed.

(2) Any recurring fixed charge, however that charge may be designated, for water service billed to the property by the water purveyors that, at management's discretion, shall be calculated by either of the following:

(A) The homeowner's proportion of the total fixed charges charged to management for the park's water use. The homeowner's proportion shall be based on the percentage of the homeowner's volumetric water use in relation to the total volumetric water use of the entire park, as shown on management's water bill during that period.

(B) Dividing the total fixed charges charged to the park equally among the total number of spaces at the park.

(3) A billing, administrative, or other fee representing the combined total of management's and the billing agent's costs, which shall be the lesser of an amount not to exceed four dollars and seventy-five cents ($4.75), as adjusted pursuant to this paragraph, or 25 percent of the amount billed pursuant to paragraph (1). Beginning January 1, 2022, the maximum fee authorized by this paragraph may be adjusted each calendar year by management, no higher than a commensurate increase in the Consumer Price Index based on a California fiscal year average for the previous fiscal year, for all urban consumers, as determined by the Department of Finance.

(d) For the purposes of this section, the following definitions apply:

(1) "Billing agent" means a person or entity that contracts to provide submetering services to management, including billing.

(2) "Submeter" means a device that measures water consumption of an individual mobilehome space within a park, and that is owned and operated by management.

(3) "Water service" includes any charges, whether presented for payment on local water purveyor bills, tax bills, or bills from other entities, related to water treatment, distribution, or usage, including, but not limited to, water, sewer, stormwater, and flood control.

(4) "Water purveyor" means a water purveyor as defined in Section 512 of the Water Code.

(e) Nothing in this section shall be construed to prevent management from recovering its costs to install, maintain, or improve its internal water delivery system, as may otherwise be allowed in any rental agreement or local regulation.
(Formerly § 798.38, added by Stats.1978, c. 1031, p. 3178, § 1. Amended by Stats.1981, c. 714, § 51; Stats.1982, c. 1397, p. 5322, § 20; Stats.2004, c. 728 (S.B.1163), § 1. Renumbered § 798.40 and amended by Stats.2009, c. 558 (S.B.111), § 3. Amended by Stats.2013, c. 201 (S.B.196), § 1; Stats.2021, c. 625 (A.B.1061), § 1, eff. Jan. 1, 2022.)

Cross References

Homeowner defined for purposes of this Chapter, see Civil Code § 798.9.

Management defined for purposes of this Chapter, see Civil Code § 798.2.

Master-meters, see Public Utilities Code §§ 739.5, 12821.5.

Record defined for purposes of this Chapter, see Civil Code § 1798.3.

Resident defined for purposes of this Chapter, see Civil Code § 798.11.

§ 798.41. Utility service fees; separate billing; application; expiration date of fees

(a) Where a rental agreement, including a rental agreement specified in Section 798.17, does not specifically provide otherwise, the park management may elect to bill a homeowner separately for utility service fees and charges assessed by the utility for services provided to or for spaces in the park. Any separately billed utility fees and charges shall not be deemed to be included in the rent charged for those spaces under the rental agreement, and shall not be deemed to be rent or a rent increase for purposes of any ordinance, rule, regulation, or initiative measure adopted or enforced by any local governmental entity which establishes a maximum amount that a landlord may charge a tenant for rent, provided that at the time of the initial separate billing of any utility fees and charges the rent chargeable under the rental agreement or the base rent chargeable under the terms of a local rent control provision is simultaneously reduced by an amount equal to the fees and charges separately billed. The amount of this reduction shall be equal to the average amount charged to the park management for that utility service for that space during the 12 months immediately preceding notice of the commencement of the separate billing for that utility service.

Utility services to which this section applies are natural gas or liquid propane gas, electricity, water, cable television, garbage or refuse service, and sewer service.

(b) This section does not apply to rental agreements entered into prior to January 1, 1991, until extended or renewed on or after that date.

(c) Nothing in this section shall require rental agreements to provide for separate billing to homeowners of fees and charges specified in subdivision (a).

(d) Those fees and charges specified in subdivision (a) shall be separately stated on any monthly or other periodic billing to the homeowner. If the fee or charge has a limited duration or is amortized for a specified period, the expiration date shall be stated on the initial notice and each subsequent billing to the homeowner while the fee or charge is billed to the homeowner. *(Added by Stats.1990, c. 1013 (S.B.2010), § 2. Amended by Stats.1992, c. 160 (S.B.1658), § 1; Stats. 1992, c. 338 (S.B.1365), § 2.)*

Cross References

Homeowner defined for purposes of this Chapter, see Civil Code § 798.9.

Management defined for purposes of this Chapter, see Civil Code § 798.2.

Rental agreement defined for purposes of this Chapter, see Civil Code § 798.8.

§ 798.42. Interruption in utility service within mobilehome park; written advance notice by ownership or management; liability

The management shall provide, by posting notice on the mobilehomes of all affected homeowners and residents, at least 72 hours' written advance notice of an interruption in utility service of more than two hours for the maintenance, repair, or replacement of facilities of utility systems over which the management has control within the park, provided that the interruption is not due to an emergency. The management shall be liable only for actual damages sustained by a homeowner or resident for violation of this section.

"Emergency," for purposes of this section, means the interruption of utility service resulting from an accident or act of nature, or cessation of service caused by other than the management's regular or planned maintenance, repair, or replacement of utility facilities. *(Formerly § 798.29.5, added by Stats.1992, c. 317 (S.B.1389), § 1. Renumbered § 798.42 and amended by Stats.2009, c. 558 (S.B.111), § 1.)*

Cross References

Homeowner defined for purposes of this Chapter, see Civil Code § 798.9.

Management defined for purposes of this Chapter, see Civil Code § 798.2.

Mobilehome defined for purposes of this Chapter, see Civil Code § 798.3.

Resident defined for purposes of this Chapter, see Civil Code § 798.11.

§ 798.43. Homeowner's meter measuring utility service to common areas; disclosure prior to tenancy

(a) Except as provided in subdivision (b), whenever a homeowner is responsible for payment of gas, water, or electric utility service, management shall disclose to the homeowner any condition by which a gas, water, or electric meter on the homeowner's site measures gas, water, or electric service for common area facilities or equipment, including lighting, provided that management has knowledge of the condition.

Management shall disclose this information prior to the inception of the tenancy or upon discovery and shall complete either of the following:

(1) Enter into a mutual written agreement with the homeowner for compensation by management for the cost of the portion of the service measured by the homeowner's meter for the common area facilities or equipment to the extent that this cost accrues on or after January 1, 1991.

(2) Discontinue using the meter on the homeowner's site for the utility service to the common area facilities and equipment.

(b) On and after January 1, 1994, if the electric meter on the homeowner's site measures electricity for lighting mandated by Section 18602 of the Health and Safety Code and this lighting provides lighting for the homeowner's site, management shall be required to comply with subdivision (a). *(Formerly § 798.41, added by Stats.1990, c. 380 (A.B.3259), § 1. Renumbered § 798.43 and amended by Stats.1991, c.*

§ 798.43

1091 (A.B.1487), § 15. Amended by Stats.1993, c. 147 (A.B.1140), § 1.)

Cross References

Homeowner defined for purposes of this Chapter, see Civil Code § 798.9.

Management defined for purposes of this Chapter, see Civil Code § 798.2.

Tenancy defined for purposes of this Chapter, see Civil Code § 798.12.

§ 798.43.1. California Alternate Rates for Energy (CARE) program; assistance to low-income persons for utility costs; duties of management of master-meter parks; notice; application processes and procedures; discount notice on billing statements

(a) The management of a master-meter park shall give written notice to homeowners and residents on or before February 1 of each year in their utility billing statements about assistance to low-income persons for utility costs available under the California Alternate Rates for Energy (CARE) program, established pursuant to Section 739.1 of the Public Utilities Code. The notice shall include CARE information available to master-meter customers from their serving utility, to include, at a minimum: (1) the fact that CARE offers a discount on monthly gas or electric bills for qualifying low-income residents; and (2) the telephone number of the serving utility which provides CARE information and applications. The park shall also post the notice in a conspicuous place in the clubhouse, or if there is no clubhouse, in a conspicuous public place in the park.

(b) The management of a master-meter park may accept and help process CARE program applications from homeowners and residents in the park, fill in the necessary account or other park information required by the serving utility to process the applications, and send the applications to the serving utility. The management shall not deny a homeowner or resident who chooses to submit a CARE application to the utility himself or herself any park information, including a utility account number, the serving utility requires to process a homeowner or resident CARE program application.

(c) The management of a master-meter park shall pass through the full amount of the CARE program discount in monthly utility billings to homeowners and residents who have qualified for the CARE rate schedule, as defined in the serving utility's applicable rate schedule. The management shall notice the discount on the billing statement of any homeowner or resident who has qualified for the CARE rate schedule as either the itemized amount of the discount or a notation on the statement that the homeowner or resident is receiving the CARE discount on the electric bill, the gas bill, or both the electric and gas bills.

(d) "Master-meter park" as used in this section means "master-meter customer" as used in Section 739.5 of the Public Utilities Code. (Added by Stats.2001, c. 437 (S.B.920), § 1.)

Cross References

Homeowner defined for purposes of this Chapter, see Civil Code § 798.9.

Management defined for purposes of this Chapter, see Civil Code § 798.2.

Resident defined for purposes of this Chapter, see Civil Code § 798.11.

§ 798.44. Mobilehome park owners or residents; sale of liquified petroleum gas; limit on price that can be charged

(a) The management of a park that does not permit mobilehome owners or park residents to purchase liquefied petroleum gas for use in the mobilehome park from someone other than the mobilehome park management shall not sell liquefied petroleum gas to mobilehome owners and residents within the park at a cost which exceeds 110 percent of the actual price paid by the management of the park for liquefied petroleum gas.

(b) The management of a park shall post in a visible location the actual price paid by management for liquefied petroleum gas sold pursuant to subdivision (a).

(c) This section shall apply only to mobilehome parks regulated under the Mobilehome Residency Law. This section shall not apply to recreational vehicle parks, as defined in Section 18215 of the Health and Safety Code, which exclusively serve recreational vehicles, as defined in Section 18010 of the Health and Safety Code.

(d) Nothing in this section is intended to abrogate any rights a mobilehome park owner may have under Section 798.31 of the Civil Code.

(e) In addition to a mobilehome park described in subdivision (a), the requirements of subdivisions (a) and (b) shall apply to a mobilehome park where requirements of federal, state, or local law or regulation, including, but not limited to, requirements for setbacks between mobilehomes, prohibit homeowners or residents from installing their own liquefied petroleum gas supply tanks, notwithstanding that the management of the mobilehome park permits mobilehome owners and park residents to buy their own liquefied petroleum gas. (Added by Stats.1999, c. 326 (S.B.476), § 2. Amended by Stats.2000, c. 232 (S.B.1612), § 1; Stats.2009, c. 558 (S.B.111), § 7.)

Cross References

Homeowner defined for purposes of this Chapter, see Civil Code § 798.9.

Management defined for purposes of this Chapter, see Civil Code § 798.2.

Mobilehome defined for purposes of this Chapter, see Civil Code § 798.3.

Mobilehome park defined for purposes of this Chapter, see Civil Code § 798.4.

ARTICLE 4.4. TENANT RENTAL ASSISTANCE [REJECTED]

§§ 798.44.1 to 798.44.7. Rejected March 26, 1996

ARTICLE 4.5. RENT CONTROL

Section
798.45. New construction; new mobilehome park construction; rent control exemption.
798.46.1 to 798.46.4. Rejected.

Section
798.49. Separate charges for certain fees, assessments, or other costs; exceptions.

§ 798.45. New construction; new mobilehome park construction; rent control exemption

(a) Notwithstanding Section 798.17, "new construction," as defined in subdivision (a) of Section 798.7, shall be exempt from any ordinance, rule, regulation, or initiative measure adopted by any city, county, or city and county, that establishes a maximum amount that a landlord may charge a tenant for rent, for a period of 15 years from the date upon which the space is initially held out for rent, as defined in subdivision (a) of Section 798.7.

(b) Notwithstanding Section 798.17, "new mobilehome park construction," as defined in subdivision (b) of Section 798.7, shall be exempt from any ordinance, rule, regulation, or initiative measure adopted by any city, county, or city and county, that establishes a maximum amount that a landlord may charge a tenant for rent for a period of 15 years from the date upon which 50 percent of the spaces in the new mobilehome park are initially held out for rent measured from the date of issuance of a permit or certificate of occupancy for that space by the enforcement agency in accordance with Section 18551 or 18613 of the Health and Safety Code. (Added by Stats.1989, c. 412, § 2. Amended by Stats.2022, c. 666 (S.B.940), § 2, eff. Jan. 1, 2023.)

§§ 798.46.1 to 798.46.4. Rejected March 26, 1996

§ 798.49. Separate charges for certain fees, assessments, or other costs; exceptions

(a) Except as provided in subdivision (d), the local agency of any city, including a charter city, county, or city and county, which administers an ordinance, rule, regulation, or initiative measure that establishes a maximum amount that management may charge a tenant for rent shall permit the management to separately charge a homeowner for any of the following:

(1) The amount of any fee, assessment or other charge first imposed by a city, including a charter city, a county, a city and county, the state, or the federal government on or after January 1, 1995, upon the space rented by the homeowner.

(2) The amount of any increase on or after January 1, 1995, in an existing fee, assessment or other charge imposed by any governmental entity upon the space rented by the homeowner.

(3) The amount of any fee, assessment or other charge upon the space first imposed or increased on or after January 1, 1993, pursuant to any state or locally mandated program relating to housing contained in the Health and Safety Code.

(b) If management has charged the homeowner for a fee, assessment, or other charge specified in subdivision (a) that was increased or first imposed on or after January 1, 1993, and the fee, assessment, or other charge is decreased or eliminated thereafter, the charge to the homeowner shall be decreased or eliminated accordingly.

(c) The amount of the fee, assessment or other charges authorized by subdivision (a) shall be separately stated on any billing to the homeowner. Any change in the amount of the fee, assessment, or other charges that are separately billed pursuant to subdivision (a) shall be considered when determining any rental adjustment under the local ordinance.

(d) This section shall not apply to any of the following:

(1) Those fees, assessments, or charges imposed pursuant to the Mobilehome Parks Act (Part 2.1 (commencing with Section 18200) of Division 13 of the Health and Safety Code), unless specifically authorized by Section 18502 of the Health and Safety Code.

(2) Those costs that are imposed on management by a court pursuant to Section 798.39.5.

(3) Any fee or other exaction imposed upon management for the specific purpose of defraying the cost of administration of any ordinance, rule, regulation, or initiative measure that establishes a maximum amount that management may charge a tenant for rent.

(4) Any tax imposed upon the property by a city, including a charter city, county, or city and county.

(e) Those fees and charges specified in subdivision (a) shall be separately stated on any monthly or other periodic billing to the homeowner. If the fee or charge has a limited duration or is amortized for a specified period, the expiration date shall be stated on the initial notice and each subsequent billing to the homeowner while the fee or charge is billed to the homeowner. (Added by Stats.1992, c. 338 (S.B.1365), § 3. Amended by Stats.1994, c. 340 (S.B.1510), § 2; Stats.2012, c. 770 (A.B.2697), § 1.)

Cross References

Homeowner defined for purposes of this Chapter, see Civil Code § 798.9.
Management defined for purposes of this Chapter, see Civil Code § 798.2.
Mobilehome defined for purposes of this Chapter, see Civil Code § 798.3.
Mobilehome park defined for purposes of this Chapter, see Civil Code § 798.4.

ARTICLE 5. HOMEOWNER COMMUNICATIONS AND MEETINGS

Section
798.50. Legislative intent.
798.51. Homeowner meetings; invitations to public officials to speak; canvassing and petitioning of homeowners; use of park recreation hall or clubhouse; liability insurance; vehicle parking.
798.52. Civil action; abridgment of rights.

§ 798.50. Legislative intent

It is the intent of the Legislature in enacting this article to ensure that homeowners and residents of mobilehome parks have the right to peacefully assemble and freely communicate with one another and with others with respect to mobilehome living or for social or educational purposes. (Added by Stats.1989, c. 198, § 2.)

Cross References

Homeowner defined for purposes of this Chapter, see Civil Code § 798.9.

§ 798.50

Mobilehome defined for purposes of this Chapter, see Civil Code § 798.3.

Mobilehome park defined for purposes of this Chapter, see Civil Code § 798.4.

Repair of sudden or unforeseeable breakdown or deterioration of improvements, required contents and notice, see Civil Code § 798.15.

Resident defined for purposes of this Chapter, see Civil Code § 798.11.

§ 798.51. Homeowner meetings; invitations to public officials to speak; canvassing and petitioning of homeowners; use of park recreation hall or clubhouse; liability insurance; vehicle parking

(a) No provision contained in any mobilehome park rental agreement, rule, or regulation shall deny or prohibit the right of any homeowner or resident in the park to do any of the following:

(1) Peacefully assemble or meet in the park, at reasonable hours and in a reasonable manner, for any lawful purpose. Meetings may be held in the park community or recreation hall or clubhouse when the facility is not otherwise in use, and, with the consent of the homeowner, in any mobilehome within the park.

(2) Invite public officials, candidates for public office, or representatives of mobilehome owner organizations to meet with homeowners and residents and speak upon matters of public interest, in accordance with Section 798.50.

(3) Canvass and petition homeowners and residents for noncommercial purposes relating to mobilehome living, election to public office, or the initiative, referendum, or recall processes, at reasonable hours and in a reasonable manner, including the distribution or circulation of information.

(b) A homeowner or resident may not be charged a cleaning deposit in order to use the park recreation hall or clubhouse for meetings of resident organizations for any of the purposes stated in Section 798.50 and this section, whether or not guests or visitors from outside the park are invited to attend the meeting, if a homeowner or resident of the park is hosting the meeting and all homeowners or residents of the park are allowed to attend.

(c) A homeowner or resident may not be required to obtain liability insurance in order to use common area facilities for the purposes specified in this section and Section 798.50. However, if alcoholic beverages are to be served at any meeting or private function, a liability insurance binder may be required by the park ownership or management. The ownership or management of a mobilehome park may prohibit the consumption of alcoholic beverages in the park common area facilities if the terms of the rental agreement or the rules and regulations of the park prohibit it.

(d) A homeowner, organization, or group of homeowners using a recreation hall or clubhouse pursuant to this section shall be required to adhere to any limitations or restrictions regarding vehicle parking or maximum occupancy for the clubhouse or recreation hall.

(e) A homeowner or resident may not be prohibited from displaying a political campaign sign relating to a candidate for election to public office or to the initiative, referendum, or recall process in the window or on the side of a manufactured home or mobilehome, or within the site on which the home is located or installed. The size of the face of a political sign may not exceed six square feet, and the sign may not be displayed in excess of a period of time from 90 days prior to an election to 15 days following the election, unless a local ordinance within the jurisdiction where the mobilehome park is located imposes a more restrictive period of time for the display of such a sign. (Added by Stats.1989, c. 198, § 2. Amended by Stats.2001, c. 83 (A.B.1202), § 2; Stats.2003, c. 249 (S.B.116), § 1.)

Cross References

Homeowner defined for purposes of this Chapter, see Civil Code § 798.9.

Management defined for purposes of this Chapter, see Civil Code § 798.2.

Mobilehome defined for purposes of this Chapter, see Civil Code § 798.3.

Mobilehome park defined for purposes of this Chapter, see Civil Code § 798.4.

Ownership defined for purposes of this Code, see Civil Code § 654.

Rental agreement defined for purposes of this Chapter, see Civil Code § 798.8.

Repair of sudden or unforeseeable breakdown or deterioration of improvements, required contents and notice, see Civil Code § 798.15.

Resident defined for purposes of this Chapter, see Civil Code § 798.11.

§ 798.52. Civil action; abridgment of rights

Any homeowner or resident who is prevented by management from exercising the rights provided for in Section 798.51 may bring an action in a court of law to enjoin enforcement of any rule, regulation, or other policy which unreasonably deprives a homeowner or resident of those rights. (Added by Stats.1989, c. 198, § 2.)

Cross References

Homeowner defined for purposes of this Chapter, see Civil Code § 798.9.

Management defined for purposes of this Chapter, see Civil Code § 798.2.

Resident defined for purposes of this Chapter, see Civil Code § 798.11.

ARTICLE 5.5. HOMEOWNERS MEETINGS WITH MANAGEMENT

Section
798.53. Meetings and consultation by management with homeowners; notice.

§ 798.53. Meetings and consultation by management with homeowners; notice

(a)(1) The management shall meet and consult with the homeowners, upon written request, within 30 days of the request, either individually, collectively, or with representatives of a group of homeowners who have signed a request to be so represented on the following matters:

(A) Resident concerns regarding <u>interpretation, or enforcement or lack thereof,</u> of existing park rules that are not subject to Section 798.25.

(B) Standards for maintenance of <u>trees, driveways, or</u> physical improvements in the park.

(C) Addition, alteration, or deletion of service, equipment, or physical improvements in the park.

(D) Rental agreements offered to existing residents pursuant to Section 798.17 or 798.18.

(E) Resident concerns regarding utility billing or utility charges.

(F) Common area facility hours and availability.

(2) The meeting may be conducted either in person or virtually using telephone, audio-video, or other audio-only conferencing.

(A) Management shall offer in-person and telephone options. If management allows audio-video conferencing options, management shall provide a list of audio-video conferencing options upon request of the homeowner or homeowners.

(B) Management shall comply with the method of meeting requested by the homeowner or homeowners requesting the meeting provided the method was offered by management pursuant to subparagraph (A).

* * * (b) A collective meeting with a group of homeowners shall be conducted only after notice thereof has been given to all the requesting homeowners 10 days or more before the meeting.

(c) If an individual homeowner or group of homeowners consents to be represented at a meeting, management shall meet with either the designated representative on their behalf, or with both the homeowners and the designated representative, as the homeowners may choose in the written request. If requested by an individual homeowner or group of homeowners, a designated representative may participate in a meeting in person, by telephone, or virtually if management allows audio-video conferencing options pursuant to paragraph (2) of subdivision (a).

(d) Management shall permit the attendance of language interpreters at any meeting pursuant to this section. Interpreters may or may not be the homeowner's designated representative. (Added by Stats.1989, c. 198, § 3. Amended by Stats.1994, c. 340 (S.B.1510), § 3; Stats.2022, c. 648 (A.B.2031), § 1, eff. Jan. 1, 2023.)

Cross References

Homeowner defined for purposes of this Chapter, see Civil Code § 798.9.
Management defined for purposes of this Chapter, see Civil Code § 798.2.
Rental agreement defined for purposes of this Chapter, see Civil Code § 798.8.
Resident defined for purposes of this Chapter, see Civil Code § 798.11.

ARTICLE 6. TERMINATION OF TENANCY

Section
798.55. Protection from actual or constructive eviction; termination or refusal to renew; grounds; notice; title search costs; residents remaining after notice; waiver.
798.56. Authorized reasons for termination.
798.56. Authorized reasons for termination.
798.56a. Notice by legal owner and junior lienholders to management of course of action after receipt of notice to terminate; failure to provide responsive notice.
798.57. Statement of reasons in notice.
798.58. Termination to make site available for buyer or renter of mobilehome from park owner or owner's agent; prohibitions.
798.59. Notice by homeowner; time.
798.60. Application of other laws.
798.61. Abandoned mobilehomes; definitions; notice of belief of abandonment; petition for declaration of abandonment; hearing; judgment; sale; disposal.
798.62. Natural disasters; renewal of tenancy.

§ 798.55. Protection from actual or constructive eviction; termination or refusal to renew; grounds; notice; title search costs; residents remaining after notice; waiver

(a) The Legislature finds and declares that, because of the high cost of moving mobilehomes, the potential for damage resulting therefrom, the requirements relating to the installation of mobilehomes, and the cost of landscaping or lot preparation, it is necessary that the owners of mobilehomes occupied within mobilehome parks be provided with the unique protection from actual or constructive eviction afforded by the provisions of this chapter.

(b)(1) The management may not terminate or refuse to renew a tenancy, except for a reason specified in this article and upon the giving of written notice to the homeowner, in the manner prescribed by Section 1162 of the Code of Civil Procedure, to sell or remove, at the homeowner's election, the mobilehome from the park within a period of not less than 60 days, which period shall be specified in the notice. A copy of this notice shall be sent to the legal owner, as defined in Section 18005.8 of the Health and Safety Code, each junior lienholder, as defined in Section 18005.3 of the Health and Safety Code, and the registered owner of the mobilehome, if other than the homeowner, by United States mail within 10 days after notice to the homeowner. The copy may be sent by regular mail or by certified or registered mail with return receipt requested, at the option of the management.

(2) The homeowner shall pay past due rent and utilities upon the sale of a mobilehome pursuant to paragraph (1).

(c) If the homeowner has not paid the rent due within three days after notice to the homeowner, and if the first notice was not sent by certified or registered mail with return receipt requested, a copy of the notice shall again be sent to the legal owner, each junior lienholder, and the registered owner, if other than the homeowner, by certified or registered mail with return receipt requested within 10 days after notice to the homeowner. Copies of the notice shall be addressed to the legal owner, each junior lienholder, and the registered owner at their addresses, as set forth in the registration card specified in Section 18091.5 of the Health and Safety Code.

(d) If management obtains a court judgment against a homeowner or resident, the cost incurred by management in obtaining a title search for the purpose of complying with the notice requirements of this section shall be recoverable as a cost of suit.

(e) The resident of a mobilehome that remains in the mobilehome park after service of the notice to sell or remove the mobilehome shall continue to be subject to this chapter

§ 798.55

and the rules and regulations of the park, including rules regarding maintenance of the space.

(f) No lawful act by the management to enforce this chapter or the rules and regulations of the park may be deemed or construed to waive or otherwise affect the notice to remove the mobilehome. *(Added by Stats.1978, c. 1031, p. 3178, § 1. Amended by Stats.1978, c. 1033, p. 3189, § 13; Stats.1979, c. 493, p. 1661, § 1; Stats.1980, c. 1149, § 4; Stats.1982, c. 1397, p. 5323, § 24; Stats.1983, c. 519, § 7; Stats.1983, c. 1124, § 2, operative July 1, 1984; Stats.1992, c. 835 (A.B.2715), § 1; Stats.1993, c. 666 (A.B.503), § 4; Stats.1998, c. 542 (S.B.2095), § 1; Stats.2003, c. 561 (A.B. 682), § 1; Stats.2005, c. 24 (S.B.125), § 2.)*

Cross References

Homeowner defined for purposes of this Chapter, see Civil Code § 798.9.
Management defined for purposes of this Chapter, see Civil Code § 798.2.
Mobilehome defined for purposes of this Chapter, see Civil Code § 798.3.
Mobilehome park defined for purposes of this Chapter, see Civil Code § 798.4.
Recreational vehicle park tenants, notice to remove vehicle, see Civil Code § 799.70.
Repair of sudden or unforeseeable breakdown or deterioration of improvements, required contents and notice, see Civil Code § 798.15.
Resident defined for purposes of this Chapter, see Civil Code § 798.11.
Tenancy defined for purposes of this Chapter, see Civil Code § 798.12.

§ 798.56. Authorized reasons for termination

Section operative until Feb. 1, 2025. See, also, § 798.56 operative Feb. 1, 2025.

A tenancy shall be terminated by the management only for one or more of the following reasons:

(a) Failure of the homeowner or resident to comply with a local ordinance or state law or regulation relating to mobilehomes within a reasonable time after the homeowner receives a notice of noncompliance from the appropriate governmental agency.

(b) Conduct by the homeowner or resident, upon the park premises, that constitutes a substantial annoyance to other homeowners or residents.

(c)(1) Conviction of the homeowner or resident for prostitution, for a violation of subdivision (d) of Section 243, paragraph (2) of subdivision (a), or subdivision (b), of Section 245, Section 288, or Section 451, of the Penal Code, or a felony controlled substance offense, if the act resulting in the conviction was committed anywhere on the premises of the mobilehome park, including, but not limited to, within the homeowner's mobilehome.

(2) However, the tenancy may not be terminated for the reason specified in this subdivision if the person convicted of the offense has permanently vacated, and does not subsequently reoccupy, the mobilehome.

(d) Failure of the homeowner or resident to comply with a reasonable rule or regulation of the park that is part of the rental agreement or any amendment thereto.

No act or omission of the homeowner or resident shall constitute a failure to comply with a reasonable rule or regulation unless and until the management has given the homeowner written notice of the alleged rule or regulation violation and the homeowner or resident has failed to adhere to the rule or regulation within seven days. However, if a homeowner has been given a written notice of an alleged violation of the same rule or regulation on three or more occasions within a 12-month period after the homeowner or resident has violated that rule or regulation, no written notice shall be required for a subsequent violation of the same rule or regulation.

Nothing in this subdivision shall relieve the management from its obligation to demonstrate that a rule or regulation has in fact been violated.

(e)(1) Except as provided for in the COVID-19 Tenant Relief Act of 2020 (Chapter 5 (commencing with Section 1179.01) of Title 3 of Part 3 of the Code of Civil Procedure), nonpayment of rent, utility charges, or reasonable incidental service charges; provided that the amount due has been unpaid for a period of at least five days from its due date, and provided that the homeowner shall be given a three-day written notice subsequent to that five-day period to pay the amount due or to vacate the tenancy. For purposes of this subdivision, the five-day period does not include the date the payment is due. The three-day written notice shall be given to the homeowner in the manner prescribed by Section 1162 of the Code of Civil Procedure. A copy of this notice shall be sent to the persons or entities specified in subdivision (b) of Section 798.55 within 10 days after notice is delivered to the homeowner. If the homeowner cures the default, the notice need not be sent. The notice may be given at the same time as the 60 days' notice required for termination of the tenancy. A three-day notice given pursuant to this subdivision shall contain the following provisions printed in at least 12-point boldface type at the top of the notice, with the appropriate number written in the blank:

"Warning: This notice is the (insert number) three-day notice for nonpayment of rent, utility charges, or other reasonable incidental services that has been served upon you in the last 12 months. Pursuant to Civil Code Section 798.56 (e) (5),[1] if you have been given a three-day notice to either pay rent, utility charges, or other reasonable incidental services or to vacate your tenancy on three or more occasions within a 12-month period, management is not required to give you a further three-day period to pay rent or vacate the tenancy before your tenancy can be terminated."

(2) Payment by the homeowner prior to the expiration of the three-day notice period shall cure a default under this subdivision. If the homeowner does not pay prior to the expiration of the three-day notice period, the homeowner shall remain liable for all payments due up until the time the tenancy is vacated.

(3) Payment by the legal owner, as defined in Section 18005.8 of the Health and Safety Code, any junior lienholder, as defined in Section 18005.3 of the Health and Safety Code, or the registered owner, as defined in Section 18009.5 of the Health and Safety Code, if other than the homeowner, on behalf of the homeowner prior to the expiration of 30 calendar days following the mailing of the notice to the legal

owner, each junior lienholder, and the registered owner provided in subdivision (b) of Section 798.55, shall cure a default under this subdivision with respect to that payment.

(4) Cure of a default of rent, utility charges, or reasonable incidental service charges by the legal owner, any junior lienholder, or the registered owner, if other than the homeowner, as provided by this subdivision, may not be exercised more than twice during a 12–month period.

(5) If a homeowner has been given a three-day notice to pay the amount due or to vacate the tenancy on three or more occasions within the preceding 12–month period and each notice includes the provisions specified in paragraph (1), no written three-day notice shall be required in the case of a subsequent nonpayment of rent, utility charges, or reasonable incidental service charges.

In that event, the management shall give written notice to the homeowner in the manner prescribed by Section 1162 of the Code of Civil Procedure to remove the mobilehome from the park within a period of not less than 60 days, which period shall be specified in the notice. A copy of this notice shall be sent to the legal owner, each junior lienholder, and the registered owner of the mobilehome, if other than the homeowner, as specified in paragraph (b) of Section 798.55, by certified or registered mail, return receipt requested, within 10 days after notice is sent to the homeowner.

(6) When a copy of the 60 days' notice described in paragraph (5) is sent to the legal owner, each junior lienholder, and the registered owner of the mobilehome, if other than the homeowner, the default may be cured by any of them on behalf of the homeowner prior to the expiration of 30 calendar days following the mailing of the notice, if all of the following conditions exist:

(A) A copy of a three-day notice sent pursuant to subdivision (b) of Section 798.55 to a homeowner for the nonpayment of rent, utility charges, or reasonable incidental service charges was not sent to the legal owner, junior lienholder, or registered owner, of the mobilehome, if other than the homeowner, during the preceding 12–month period.

(B) The legal owner, junior lienholder, or registered owner of the mobilehome, if other than the homeowner, has not previously cured a default of the homeowner during the preceding 12–month period.

(C) The legal owner, junior lienholder, or registered owner, if other than the homeowner, is not a financial institution or mobilehome dealer.

If the default is cured by the legal owner, junior lienholder, or registered owner within the 30–day period, the notice to remove the mobilehome from the park described in paragraph (5) shall be rescinded.

(f) Condemnation of the park.

(g) Change of use of the park or any portion thereof, provided:

(1) The management gives the homeowners at least 60 days' written notice that the management will be appearing before a local governmental board, commission, or body to request permits for a change of use of the mobilehome park.

(2)(A) After all required permits requesting a change of use have been approved by the local governmental board, commission, or body, the management shall give the homeowners six months' or more written notice of termination of tenancy.

(B) If the change of use requires no local governmental permits, then notice shall be given 12 months or more prior to the management's determination that a change of use will occur. The management in the notice shall disclose and describe in detail the nature of the change of use.

(3) The management gives each proposed homeowner written notice thereof prior to the inception of the proposed homeowner's tenancy that the management is requesting a change of use before local governmental bodies or that a change of use request has been granted.

(4) The notice requirements for termination of tenancy set forth in this section and Section 798.57 shall be followed if the proposed change actually occurs.

(5) A notice of a proposed change of use given prior to January 1, 1980, that conforms to the requirements in effect at that time shall be valid. The requirements for a notice of a proposed change of use imposed by this subdivision shall be governed by the law in effect at the time the notice was given.

(h) The report required pursuant to subdivisions (b) and (i) of Section 65863.7 of the Government Code shall be given to the homeowners or residents at the same time that notice is required pursuant to subdivision (g) of this section.

(i) For purposes of this section, "financial institution" means a state or national bank, state or federal savings and loan association or credit union, or similar organization, and mobilehome dealer as defined in Section 18002.6 of the Health and Safety Code or any other organization that, as part of its usual course of business, originates, owns, or provides loan servicing for loans secured by a mobilehome.

(j) This section remain in effect until February 1, 2025, and as of that date is repealed. *(Added by Stats.1978, c. 1031, p. 3178, § 1. Amended by Stats.1978, c. 1033, p. 3189, § 14; Stats.1979, c. 945, p. 3266, § 2; Stats.1979, c. 1185, p. 4268, § 1.5; Stats.1980, c. 1149, § 5; Stats.1981, c. 714, § 52; Stats.1981, c. 458, § 1; Stats.1982, c. 777, p. 3030, § 1; Stats.1982, c. 1397, p. 5325, § 25.5; Stats.1983, c. 519, § 8; Stats.1983, c. 1124, § 3, operative July 1, 1984; Stats.1987, c. 55, § 1; Stats.1987, c. 883, § 2; Stats.1988, c. 171, § 1; Stats.1988, c. 301, § 2.5; Stats.1990, c. 42 (A.B.1209), § 1; Stats.1990, c. 1357 (A.B.4156), § 1.5; Stats.1998, c. 427 (A.B.1888), § 1; Stats.2003, c. 85 (A.B.805), § 1; Stats.2003, c. 388 (A.B.767), § 1.5; Stats.2020, c. 35 (A.B.2782), § 3, eff. Jan. 1, 2021; Stats.2020, c. 37 (A.B.3088), § 4, eff. Aug. 31, 2020; Stats.2021, c. 360 (A.B.1584), § 2, eff. Jan. 1, 2022.)*

[1] So in enrolled bill.

Repeal

For repeal of this section, see its terms.

Cross References

Application for conversion of mobilehome park to another use, requirement to inform applicant of the provisions of this section, see Government Code § 65863.8.

Change of use defined for the purposes of this Chapter, see Civil Code § 798.10.

Change of use of park or portion of park, notice, see Civil Code § 798.27.

City and county ordinances, resolutions, regulations, or administrative actions adopted in response to the COVID–19 pandemic, requirements, one-year limitation, legislative intent, see Code of Civil Procedure § 1179.05.

Closure or cessation of use of mobilehome park, distribution of impact report to residents, see Government Code § 65863.7.

Failure of registered owner of mobilehome, manufactured home, or recreational vehicle to pay costs of remediation, warehouseman's lien, see Health and Safety Code § 25400.47.

Failure to maintain physical improvements in common facilities, notice of intent to commence action, see Civil Code § 798.84.

Felonies, definition and penalties, see Penal Code §§ 17, 18.

Homeowner defined for purposes of this Chapter, see Civil Code § 798.9.

Management defined for purposes of this Chapter, see Civil Code § 798.2.

Methamphetamine Contaminated Property Cleanup Act of 2005, failure of registered owner of mobilehome, manufactured home, or recreational vehicle to pay costs of remediation, see Health and Safety Code § 25400.47.

Mobilehome defined for purposes of this Chapter, see Civil Code § 798.3.

Mobilehome park defined for purposes of this Chapter, see Civil Code § 798.4.

Notice for residential real property demanding payment of COVID–19 recovery period rental debt, modification, contents, effect of noncompliance, see Code of Civil Procedure § 1179.10.

Notice of termination of utility service, see Public Utilities Code §§ 777 et seq., 12822 et seq.

Obligation defined, see Civil Code § 1427.

Rental agreement defined for purposes of this Chapter, see Civil Code § 798.8.

Repair of sudden or unforeseeable breakdown or deterioration of improvements, required contents and notice, see Civil Code § 798.15.

Requirements for notices that demand payment of COVID–19 rental debts that came due during protected time period and transition time period, delivery of a declaration of COVID–19–related financial distress, filing of declaration with court, see Code of Civil Procedure § 1179.03.

Resident defined for purposes of this Chapter, see Civil Code § 798.11.

Rule enforcement, removal of personal property, see Civil Code § 798.36.

Tenancy defined for purposes of this Chapter, see Civil Code § 798.12.

Tenants who may be found guilty of unlawful detainer, assistance for tenant in relocating, see Code of Civil Procedure § 1179.03.5.

§ 798.56. Authorized reasons for termination

Section operative Feb. 1, 2025. See, also, § 798.56 operative until Feb. 1, 2025.

A tenancy shall be terminated by the management only for one or more of the following reasons:

(a) Failure of the homeowner or resident to comply with a local ordinance or state law or regulation relating to mobilehomes within a reasonable time after the homeowner receives a notice of noncompliance from the appropriate governmental agency.

(b) Conduct by the homeowner or resident, upon the park premises, that constitutes a substantial annoyance to other homeowners or residents.

(c)(1) Conviction of the homeowner or resident for prostitution, for a violation of subdivision (d) of Section 243, paragraph (2) of subdivision (a), or subdivision (b), of Section 245, Section 288, or Section 451, of the Penal Code, or a felony controlled substance offense, if the act resulting in the conviction was committed anywhere on the premises of the mobilehome park, including, but not limited to, within the homeowner's mobilehome.

(2) However, the tenancy may not be terminated for the reason specified in this subdivision if the person convicted of the offense has permanently vacated, and does not subsequently reoccupy, the mobilehome.

(d) Failure of the homeowner or resident to comply with a reasonable rule or regulation of the park that is part of the rental agreement or any amendment thereto.

No act or omission of the homeowner or resident shall constitute a failure to comply with a reasonable rule or regulation unless and until the management has given the homeowner written notice of the alleged rule or regulation violation and the homeowner or resident has failed to adhere to the rule or regulation within seven days. However, if a homeowner has been given a written notice of an alleged violation of the same rule or regulation on three or more occasions within a 12–month period after the homeowner or resident has violated that rule or regulation, no written notice shall be required for a subsequent violation of the same rule or regulation.

Nothing in this subdivision shall relieve the management from its obligation to demonstrate that a rule or regulation has in fact been violated.

(e)(1) Nonpayment of rent, utility charges, or reasonable incidental service charges; provided that the amount due has been unpaid for a period of at least five days from its due date, and provided that the homeowner shall be given a three-day written notice subsequent to that five-day period to pay the amount due or to vacate the tenancy. For purposes of this subdivision, the five-day period does not include the date the payment is due. The three-day written notice shall be given to the homeowner in the manner prescribed by Section 1162 of the Code of Civil Procedure. A copy of this notice shall be sent to the persons or entities specified in subdivision (b) of Section 798.55 within 10 days after notice is delivered to the homeowner. If the homeowner cures the default, the notice need not be sent. The notice may be given at the same time as the 60 days' notice required for termination of the tenancy. A three-day notice given pursuant to this subdivision shall contain the following provisions printed in at least 12–point boldface type at the top of the notice, with the appropriate number written in the blank:

"Warning: This notice is the (insert number) three-day notice for nonpayment of rent, utility charges, or other reasonable incidental services that has been served upon you in the last 12 months. Pursuant to Civil Code Section 798.56 (e) (5),[1] if you have been given a three-day notice to either pay rent, utility charges, or other reasonable incidental services or to vacate your tenancy on three or more occasions within a 12–month period, management is not required to give you a further three-day period to pay rent or vacate the tenancy before your tenancy can be terminated."

(2) Payment by the homeowner prior to the expiration of the three-day notice period shall cure a default under this subdivision. If the homeowner does not pay prior to the expiration of the three-day notice period, the homeowner

shall remain liable for all payments due up until the time the tenancy is vacated.

(3) Payment by the legal owner, as defined in Section 18005.8 of the Health and Safety Code, any junior lienholder, as defined in Section 18005.3 of the Health and Safety Code, or the registered owner, as defined in Section 18009.5 of the Health and Safety Code, if other than the homeowner, on behalf of the homeowner prior to the expiration of 30 calendar days following the mailing of the notice to the legal owner, each junior lienholder, and the registered owner provided in subdivision (b) of Section 798.55, shall cure a default under this subdivision with respect to that payment.

(4) Cure of a default of rent, utility charges, or reasonable incidental service charges by the legal owner, any junior lienholder, or the registered owner, if other than the homeowner, as provided by this subdivision, may not be exercised more than twice during a 12–month period.

(5) If a homeowner has been given a three-day notice to pay the amount due or to vacate the tenancy on three or more occasions within the preceding 12–month period and each notice includes the provisions specified in paragraph (1), no written three-day notice shall be required in the case of a subsequent nonpayment of rent, utility charges, or reasonable incidental service charges.

In that event, the management shall give written notice to the homeowner in the manner prescribed by Section 1162 of the Code of Civil Procedure to remove the mobilehome from the park within a period of not less than 60 days, which period shall be specified in the notice. A copy of this notice shall be sent to the legal owner, each junior lienholder, and the registered owner of the mobilehome, if other than the homeowner, as specified in paragraph (b) of Section 798.55, by certified or registered mail, return receipt requested, within 10 days after notice is sent to the homeowner.

(6) When a copy of the 60 days' notice described in paragraph (5) is sent to the legal owner, each junior lienholder, and the registered owner of the mobilehome, if other than the homeowner, the default may be cured by any of them on behalf of the homeowner prior to the expiration of 30 calendar days following the mailing of the notice, if all of the following conditions exist:

(A) A copy of a three-day notice sent pursuant to subdivision (b) of Section 798.55 to a homeowner for the nonpayment of rent, utility charges, or reasonable incidental service charges was not sent to the legal owner, junior lienholder, or registered owner, of the mobilehome, if other than the homeowner, during the preceding 12–month period.

(B) The legal owner, junior lienholder, or registered owner of the mobilehome, if other than the homeowner, has not previously cured a default of the homeowner during the preceding 12–month period.

(C) The legal owner, junior lienholder, or registered owner, if other than the homeowner, is not a financial institution or mobilehome dealer.

If the default is cured by the legal owner, junior lienholder, or registered owner within the 30–day period, the notice to remove the mobilehome from the park described in paragraph (5) shall be rescinded.

(f) Condemnation of the park.

(g) Change of use of the park or any portion thereof, provided:

(1) The management gives the homeowners at least 60 days' written notice that the management will be appearing before a local governmental board, commission, or body to request permits for a change of use of the mobilehome park.

(2)(A) After all required permits requesting a change of use have been approved by the local governmental board, commission, or body, the management shall give the homeowners six months' or more written notice of termination of tenancy.

(B) If the change of use requires no local governmental permits, then notice shall be given 12 months or more prior to the management's determination that a change of use will occur. The management in the notice shall disclose and describe in detail the nature of the change of use.

(3) The management gives each proposed homeowner written notice thereof prior to the inception of the proposed homeowner's tenancy that the management is requesting a change of use before local governmental bodies or that a change of use request has been granted.

(4) The notice requirements for termination of tenancy set forth in Sections 798.56 and 798.57 shall be followed if the proposed change actually occurs.

(5) A notice of a proposed change of use given prior to January 1, 1980, that conforms to the requirements in effect at that time shall be valid. The requirements for a notice of a proposed change of use imposed by this subdivision shall be governed by the law in effect at the time the notice was given.

(h) The report required pursuant to subdivisions (b) and (i) of Section 65863.7 of the Government Code shall be given to the homeowners or residents at the same time that notice is required pursuant to subdivision (g) of this section.

(i) For purposes of this section, "financial institution" means a state or national bank, state or federal savings and loan association or credit union, or similar organization, and mobilehome dealer as defined in Section 18002.6 of the Health and Safety Code or any other organization that, as part of its usual course of business, originates, owns, or provides loan servicing for loans secured by a mobilehome.

(j) This section shall become operative on February 1, 2025. *(Added by Stats.2020, c. 37 (A.B.3088), § 5, eff. Aug. 31, 2020, operative Feb. 1, 2025. Amended by Stats.2021, c. 360 (A.B.1584), § 3, eff. Jan. 1, 2022, operative Feb. 1, 2025.)*

[1] So in enrolled bill.

Cross References

Application for conversion of mobilehome park to another use, requirement to inform applicant of the provisions of this section, see Government Code § 65863.8.

Change of use defined for the purposes of this Chapter, see Civil Code § 798.10.

Change of use of park or portion of park, notice, see Civil Code § 798.27.

City and county ordinances, resolutions, regulations, or administrative actions adopted in response to the COVID–19 pandemic, requirements, one-year limitation, legislative intent, see Code of Civil Procedure § 1179.05.

Closure or cessation of use of mobilehome park, distribution of impact report to residents, see Government Code § 65863.7.

§ 798.56

Failure of registered owner of mobilehome, manufactured home, or recreational vehicle to pay costs of remediation, warehouseman's lien, see Health and Safety Code § 25400.47.

Failure to maintain physical improvements in common facilities, notice of intent to commence action, see Civil Code § 798.84.

Felonies, definition and penalties, see Penal Code §§ 17, 18.

Homeowner defined for purposes of this Chapter, see Civil Code § 798.9.

Management defined for purposes of this Chapter, see Civil Code § 798.2.

Methamphetamine Contaminated Property Cleanup Act of 2005, failure of registered owner of mobilehome, manufactured home, or recreational vehicle to pay costs of remediation, see Health and Safety Code § 25400.47.

Mobilehome defined for purposes of this Chapter, see Civil Code § 798.3.

Mobilehome park defined for purposes of this Chapter, see Civil Code § 798.4.

Notice for residential real property demanding payment of COVID–19 recovery period rental debt, modification, contents, effect of noncompliance, see Code of Civil Procedure § 1179.10.

Notice of termination of utility service, see Public Utilities Code §§ 777 et seq., 12822 et seq.

Obligation defined, see Civil Code § 1427.

Rental agreement defined for purposes of this Chapter, see Civil Code § 798.8.

Repair of sudden or unforeseeable breakdown or deterioration of improvements, required contents and notice, see Civil Code § 798.15.

Requirements for notices that demand payment of COVID–19 rental debts that came due during protected time period and transition time period, delivery of a declaration of COVID–19–related financial distress, filing of declaration with court, see Code of Civil Procedure § 1179.03.

Resident defined for purposes of this Chapter, see Civil Code § 798.11.

Rule enforcement, removal of personal property, see Civil Code § 798.36.

Tenancy defined for purposes of this Chapter, see Civil Code § 798.12.

Tenants who may be found guilty of unlawful detainer, assistance for tenant in relocating, see Code of Civil Procedure § 1179.03.5.

§ 798.56a. Notice by legal owner and junior lienholders to management of course of action after receipt of notice to terminate; failure to provide responsive notice

(a) Within 60 days after receipt of, or no later than 65 days after the mailing of, the notice of termination of tenancy pursuant to any reason provided in Section 798.56, the legal owner, if any, and each junior lienholder, if any, shall notify the management in writing of at least one of the following:

(1) Its offer to sell the obligation secured by the mobilehome to the management for the amount specified in its written offer. In that event, the management shall have 15 days following receipt of the offer to accept or reject the offer in writing. If the offer is rejected, the person or entity that made the offer shall have 10 days in which to exercise one of the other options contained in this section and shall notify management in writing of its choice.

(2) Its intention to foreclose on its security interest in the mobilehome.

(3) Its request that the management pursue the termination of tenancy against the homeowner and its offer to reimburse management for the reasonable attorney's fees and court costs incurred by the management in that action. If this request and offer are made, the legal owner, if any, or junior lienholder, if any, shall reimburse the management the amount of reasonable attorney's fees and court costs, as agreed upon by the management and the legal owner or junior lienholder, incurred by the management in an action to terminate the homeowner's tenancy, on or before the earlier of (A) the 60th calendar day following receipt of written notice from the management of the aggregate amount of those reasonable attorney's fees and costs or (B) the date the mobilehome is resold.

(b) A legal owner, if any, or junior lienholder, if any, may sell the mobilehome within the park to a third party and keep the mobilehome on the site within the mobilehome park until it is resold only if all of the following requirements are met:

(1) The legal owner, if any, or junior lienholder, if any, notifies management in writing of the intention to exercise either option described in paragraph (2) or (3) of subdivision (a) within 60 days following receipt of, or no later than 65 days after the mailing of, the notice of termination of tenancy and satisfies all of the responsibilities and liabilities of the homeowner owing to the management for the 90 days preceding the mailing of the notice of termination of tenancy and then continues to satisfy these responsibilities and liabilities as they accrue from the date of the mailing of that notice until the date the mobilehome is resold.

(2) Within 60 days following receipt of, or no later than 65 days after the mailing of, the notice of termination of tenancy, the legal owner or junior lienholder commences all repairs and necessary corrective actions so that the mobilehome complies with park rules and regulations in existence at the time the notice of termination of tenancy was given as well as the health and safety standards specified in Sections 18550, 18552, and 18605 of the Health and Safety Code, and completes these repairs and corrective actions within 90 calendar days of that notice, or before the date that the mobilehome is sold, whichever is earlier.

(3) The legal owner, if any, or junior lienholder, if any, complies with the requirements of Article 7 (commencing with Section 798.70) as it relates to the transfer of the mobilehome to a third party.

(c) For purposes of subdivision (b), the "homeowner's responsibilities and liabilities" means all rents, utilities, reasonable maintenance charges of the mobilehome and its premises, and reasonable maintenance of the mobilehome and its premises pursuant to existing park rules and regulations.

(d) If the homeowner files for bankruptcy, the periods set forth in this section are tolled until the mobilehome is released from bankruptcy.

(e)(1) Notwithstanding any other provision of law, including, but not limited to, Section 18099.5 of the Health and Safety Code, if neither the legal owner nor a junior lienholder notifies the management of its decision pursuant to subdivision (a) within the period allowed, or performs as agreed within 30 days, or if a registered owner of a mobilehome, that is not encumbered by a lien held by a legal owner or a junior lienholder, fails to comply with a notice of termination and is either legally evicted or vacates the premises, the management may either remove the mobilehome from the premises and place it in storage or store it on its site. In this case, notwithstanding any other provision of law, the management shall have a warehouse lien in accordance with Section 7209 of the Commercial Code against the mobilehome for the costs of dismantling and moving, if appropriate, as well as storage, that shall be superior to all other liens, except the lien provided for in Section 18116.1 of the Health and Safety Code, and may enforce the lien pursuant to Section 7210 of the Commercial Code either after the date of judgment in an unlawful detainer action or after the date the mobilehome is physically vacated by the resident, whichever occurs earlier. Upon completion of any sale to enforce the warehouse lien in accordance with Section 7210 of the Commercial Code, the management shall provide the purchaser at the sale with evidence of the sale, as shall be specified by the Department of Housing and Community Development, that shall, upon proper request by the purchaser of the mobilehome, register title to the mobilehome to this purchaser, whether or not there existed a legal owner or junior lienholder on this title to the mobilehome.

(2)(A) Notwithstanding any other law, if the management of a mobilehome park acquires a mobilehome after enforcing the warehouse lien and files a notice of disposal pursuant to subparagraph (B) with the Department of Housing and Community Development to designate the mobilehome for disposal, management or any other person enforcing this warehouse lien shall not be required to pay past or current vehicle license fees required by Section 18115 of the Health and Safety Code or obtain a tax clearance certificate, as set forth in Section 5832 of the Revenue and Taxation Code, provided that management notifies the county tax collector in the county in which the mobilehome is located of management's intent to apply to have the mobilehome designated for disposal after a warehouse lien sale. The written notice shall be sent to the county tax collector no less than 30 days after the date of the sale to enforce the lien against the mobilehome by first class mail, postage prepaid.

(B)(i) In order to dispose of a mobilehome after a warehouse lien sale, the management shall file a notice of disposal with the Department of Housing and Community Development in the form and manner as prescribed by the department, no less than 30 days after the date of sale to enforce the lien against the mobilehome.

(ii) After filing a notice of disposal pursuant to clause (i), the management may dispose of the mobilehome after obtaining the information required by applicable laws.

(C)(i) Within 30 days of the date of the disposal of the mobilehome, the management shall submit to the Department of Housing and Community Development all of the following information required for completing the disposal process:

(I) Photographs identifying and demonstrating that the mobilehome was uninhabitable by the removal or destruction of all appliances and fixtures such as ovens, stoves, bathroom fixtures, and heating or cooling appliances prior to its being moved.

(II) A statement of facts as to the condition of the mobilehome when moved, the date it was moved, and the anticipated site of further dismantling or disposal.

(III) The name, address, and license number of the person or entity removing the mobilehome from the mobilehome park.

(ii) The information required pursuant to clause (i) shall be submitted under penalty of perjury.

(D) For purposes of this paragraph, "dispose" or "disposal" shall mean the removal and destruction of an abandoned mobilehome from a mobilehome park, thus making it unusable for any purpose and not subject to, or eligible for, use in the future as a mobilehome.

(f) All written notices required by this section, except the notice in paragraph (2) of subdivision (e), shall be sent to the other party by certified or registered mail with return receipt requested.

(g) Satisfaction, pursuant to this section, of the homeowner's accrued or accruing responsibilities and liabilities shall not cure the default of the homeowner. *(Added by Stats.1990, c. 1357 (A.B.4156), § 2. Amended by Stats.1992, c. 88 (A.B.2548), § 1; Stats.1992, c. 835 (A.B.2715), § 2; Stats.1996, c. 95 (A.B.2781), § 1; Stats.1998, c. 542 (S.B. 2095), § 2; Stats.2010, c. 610 (A.B.2762), § 1.6; Stats.2015, c. 376 (A.B.999), § 1, eff. Jan. 1, 2016; Stats.2016, c. 714 (S.B.944), § 2, eff. Jan. 1, 2017.)*

Cross References

Fee, notice of disposal of mobilehome, see Health and Safety Code § 18080.5.
Homeowner defined for purposes of this Chapter, see Civil Code § 798.9.
Management defined for purposes of this Chapter, see Civil Code § 798.2.
Mobilehome defined for purposes of this Chapter, see Civil Code § 798.3.
Mobilehome park defined for purposes of this Chapter, see Civil Code § 798.4.
Mobilehome park owner, final money judgement for unpaid rent, perfection of lien, see Health and Safety Code § 18080.9.
Obligation defined, see Civil Code § 1427.
Resident defined for purposes of this Chapter, see Civil Code § 798.11.
Tenancy defined for purposes of this Chapter, see Civil Code § 798.12.

§ 798.57. Statement of reasons in notice

The management shall set forth in a notice of termination, the reason relied upon for the termination with specific facts to permit determination of the date, place, witnesses, and circumstances concerning that reason. Neither reference to the section number or a subdivision thereof, nor a recital of the language of this article will constitute compliance with this section. *(Added by Stats.1978, c. 1031, p. 3178, § 1.)*

Cross References

Management defined for purposes of this Chapter, see Civil Code § 798.2.

§ 798.58. Termination to make site available for buyer or renter of mobilehome from park owner or owner's agent; prohibitions

Tenancy may only be terminated for reasons contained in Section 798.56, and a tenancy may not be terminated for the purpose of making a homeowner's site available for a person

§ 798.58

who purchased or proposes to purchase, or rents or proposes to rent, a mobilehome from the owner of the park or the owner's agent. *(Added by Stats.1978, c. 1031, p. 3178, § 1. Amended by Stats.1982, c. 1397, p. 5326, § 26; Stats.2002, c. 672 (S.B.1410), § 3.)*

Cross References

Homeowner defined for purposes of this Chapter, see Civil Code § 798.9.

Mobilehome defined for purposes of this Chapter, see Civil Code § 798.3.

Tenancy defined for purposes of this Chapter, see Civil Code § 798.12.

§ 798.59. Notice by homeowner; time

A homeowner shall give written notice to the management of not less than 60 days before vacating his or her tenancy. *(Added by Stats.1978, c. 1031, p. 3178, § 1. Amended by Stats.1982, c. 1397, p. 5326, § 27.)*

Cross References

Homeowner defined for purposes of this Chapter, see Civil Code § 798.9.

Management defined for purposes of this Chapter, see Civil Code § 798.2.

Repair of sudden or unforeseeable breakdown or deterioration of improvements, required contents and notice, see Civil Code § 798.15.

Tenancy defined for purposes of this Chapter, see Civil Code § 798.12.

§ 798.60. Application of other laws

The provisions of this article shall not affect any rights or proceedings set forth in Chapter 4 (commencing with Section 1159) of Title 3 of Part 3 of the Code of Civil Procedure except as otherwise provided herein. *(Added by Stats.1978, c. 1031, p. 3178, § 1. Amended by Stats.1978, c. 1033, p. 3190, § 15.)*

§ 798.61. Abandoned mobilehomes; definitions; notice of belief of abandonment; petition for declaration of abandonment; hearing; judgment; sale; disposal

(a)(1) As used in this section, "abandoned mobilehome" means a mobilehome about which all of the following are true:

(A) It is located in a mobilehome park on a site for which no rent has been paid to the management for the preceding 60 days.

(B) It is unoccupied.

(C) A reasonable person would believe it to be abandoned.

(D) It is not permanently affixed to the land.

(2) As used in this section:

(A) "Mobilehome" shall include a trailer coach, as defined in Section 635 of the Vehicle Code, or a recreational vehicle, as defined in Section 18010 of the Health and Safety Code, if the trailer coach or recreational vehicle also satisfies the requirements of paragraph (1), including being located on any site within a mobilehome park, even if the site is in a separate designated section pursuant to Section 18215 of the Health and Safety Code.

(B) "Abandoned mobilehome" shall include a mobilehome that is uninhabitable because of its total or partial destruction that cannot be rehabilitated, if the mobilehome also satisfies the requirements of paragraph (1).

(C) "Dispose" or "disposal" shall mean the removal and destruction of an abandoned mobilehome from a mobilehome park, thus making it unusable for any purpose and not subject to, or eligible for, use in the future as a mobilehome.

(b) After determining a mobilehome in a mobilehome park to be an abandoned mobilehome, the management shall post a notice of belief of abandonment on the mobilehome for not less than 30 days, and shall deposit copies of the notice in the United States mail, postage prepaid, addressed to the homeowner at the last known address and to any known registered owner, if different from the homeowner, and to any known holder of a security interest in the abandoned mobilehome. This notice shall be mailed by registered or certified mail with a return receipt requested.

(c)(1) Thirty or more days following posting pursuant to subdivision (b), the management may file a petition in the superior court in the county in which the mobilehome park is located, for a judicial declaration of abandonment of the mobilehome. A proceeding under this subdivision is a limited civil case. Copies of the petition shall be served upon the homeowner, any known registered owner, and any known person having a lien or security interest of record in the mobilehome by posting a copy on the mobilehome and mailing copies to those persons at their last known addresses by registered or certified mail with a return receipt requested in the United States mail, postage prepaid.

(2) To dispose of an abandoned mobilehome pursuant to subdivision (f), the management shall also do all of the following:

(A) Declare in the petition that the management will dispose of the abandoned mobilehome, and therefore will not seek a tax clearance certificate as set forth in Section 5832 of the Revenue and Taxation Code.

(B) Declare in the petition whether the management intends to sell the contents of the abandoned mobilehome before its disposal.

(C) Notify the county tax collector in the county in which the mobilehome park is located of the declaration that management will dispose of the abandoned mobilehome by sending a copy of the petition by first class mail.

(D) Declare in the petition that management intends to file a notice of disposal with the Department of Housing and Community Development and complete the disposal process consistent with the requirements of subdivision (f).

(d)(1) Hearing on the petition shall be given precedence over other matters on the court's calendar.

(2) If, at the hearing, the petitioner shows by a preponderance of the evidence that the criteria for an abandoned mobilehome has been satisfied and no party establishes an interest therein at the hearing and tenders all past due rent and other charges, the court shall enter a judgment of abandonment, determine the amount of charges to which the petitioner is entitled, and award attorney's fees and costs to the petitioner. For purposes of this subdivision, an interest in the mobilehome shall be established by evidence of a right

to possession of the mobilehome or a security or ownership interest in the mobilehome.

(3) A default may be entered by the court clerk upon request of the petitioner, and a default judgment shall be thereupon entered, if no responsive pleading is filed within 15 days after service of the petition by mail.

(e) To sell an abandoned mobilehome, the management shall do all of the following:

(1)(A) Within 10 days following a judgment of abandonment, the management shall enter the abandoned mobilehome and complete an inventory of the contents and submit the inventory to the court.

(B) During this period the management shall post and mail a notice of intent to sell the abandoned mobilehome and its contents under this section, and announcing the date of sale, in the same manner as provided for the notice of determination of abandonment under subdivision (b). The management shall also provide notice to the county tax collector in the county in which the mobilehome park is located.

(C) At any time prior to the sale of an abandoned mobilehome or its contents under this section, any person having a right to possession of the abandoned mobilehome may recover and remove it from the premises upon payment to the management of all rent or other charges due, including reasonable costs of storage and other costs awarded by the court. Upon receipt of this payment and removal of the abandoned mobilehome from the premises pursuant to this paragraph, the management shall immediately file an acknowledgment of satisfaction of judgment pursuant to Section 724.030 of the Code of Civil Procedure.

(2) Following the judgment of abandonment, but not less than 10 days following the notice of sale specified in paragraph (1), the management may conduct a public sale of the abandoned mobilehome, its contents, or both. The management may bid at the sale and shall have the right to offset its bids to the extent of the total amount due it under this section. The proceeds of the sale shall be retained by the management, but any unclaimed amount thus retained over and above the amount to which the management is entitled under this section shall be deemed abandoned property and shall be paid into the treasury of the county in which the sale took place within 30 days of the date of the sale. The former homeowner or any other owner may claim any or all of that unclaimed amount within one year from the date of payment to the county by making application to the county treasurer or other official designated by the county. If the county pays any or all of that unclaimed amount to a claimant, neither the county nor any officer or employee of the county is liable to any other claimant as to the amount paid.

(3) Within 30 days of the date of the sale, the management shall submit to the court an accounting of the moneys received from the sale and the disposition of the money and the items contained in the inventory submitted to the court pursuant to paragraph (1).

(4) The management shall provide the purchaser at the sale of an abandoned mobilehome with a copy of the judgment of abandonment and evidence of the sale, as shall be specified by the Department of Housing and Community Development, which shall register title in the abandoned mobilehome to the purchaser upon presentation thereof within 20 days of purchase. The sale shall pass title to the purchaser free of any prior interest, including any security interest or lien, except the lien provided for in Section 18116.1 of the Health and Safety Code, in the abandoned mobilehome.

(f) To dispose of an abandoned mobilehome, the management shall do all of the following:

(1)(A) Within 10 days following a judgment of abandonment, the management shall enter the abandoned mobilehome and complete an inventory of the contents and submit the inventory to the court.

(B) Within 10 days following a judgment of abandonment, the management shall post and mail a notice of intent to dispose of the abandoned mobilehome and its contents under this section, and announcing the date of disposal, in the same manner as provided for the notice of determination of abandonment under subdivision (b). The management shall also provide notice to the county tax collector in the county in which the mobilehome park is located.

(C)(i) Within 30 days following a judgment of abandonment, the management shall file a notice of disposal with the Department of Housing and Community Development in the form and manner as prescribed by the department.

(ii) Notwithstanding any other law, when filing a notice of disposal pursuant to clause (i), the management shall not be required to pay past or current vehicle license fees required by Section 18115 of the Health and Safety Code or obtain a tax clearance certificated as set forth in Section 5832 of the Revenue and Taxation Code, provided that the management notifies the county tax collector in the county in which the mobilehome is located of the management's intent to apply to have the mobilehome designated for disposal pursuant to this subdivision. The written notice shall be sent to the county tax collector no less than 10 days after the date of the abandonment judgment by first class mail, postage prepaid.

(D) At any time prior to the disposal of an abandoned mobilehome or its contents under this section, any person having a right to possession of the abandoned mobilehome may recover and remove it from the premises upon payment to the management of all rent or other charges due, including reasonable costs of storage and other costs awarded by the court. Upon receipt of this payment and removal of the abandoned mobilehome from the premises pursuant to this subparagraph, the management shall immediately file an acknowledgment of satisfaction of judgment pursuant to Section 724.030 of the Code of Civil Procedure and a cancellation of the notice of disposal with the Department of Housing and Community Development.

(2) Following the judgment of abandonment and approval of the notice of disposal by the Department of Housing and Community Development, but not less than 10 days following the notice of disposal specified in paragraph (1), the management may dispose of the abandoned mobilehome after obtaining the information required in subparagraph (A) of paragraph (3).

§ 798.61

(3)(A) Within 30 days of the date of the disposal of an abandoned mobilehome and its contents, the management shall do both of the following:

(i) Submit to the court and the county tax collector in the county in which the mobilehome park is located a statement that the abandoned mobilehome and its contents were disposed with supporting documentation.

(ii)(I) Submit to the Department of Housing and Community Development all of the following information required for completing the disposal process:

(ia) Photographs identifying and demonstrating that the mobilehome was uninhabitable by the removal or destruction of all appliances and fixtures such as ovens, stoves, bathroom fixtures, and heating or cooling appliances prior to its being moved.

(ib) A statement of facts as to the condition of the mobilehome when moved, the date it was moved, and the anticipated site of further dismantling or disposal.

(ic) The name, address, and license number of the person or entity removing the mobilehome from the mobilehome park.

(II) The information required pursuant to subclause (I) shall be submitted under penalty of perjury.

(B) Within 30 days of the date of the disposal of an abandoned mobilehome or the date of the sale of its contents, whichever date is later, the management shall submit to the court and the county tax collector in the county in which the mobilehome park is located an accounting of the moneys received from the sale and the disposition of the money and the items contained in the inventory submitted to the court pursuant to paragraph (1) and a statement that the abandoned mobilehome was disposed with supporting documentation.

(g) Notwithstanding any other law, the management shall not be required to obtain a tax clearance certificate, as set forth in Section 5832 of the Revenue and Taxation Code, to dispose of an abandoned mobilehome and its contents pursuant to subdivision (f). However, any sale pursuant to this section shall be subject to the registration requirements of Section 18100.5 of the Health and Safety Code and the tax clearance certificate requirements of Section 18092.7 of the Health and Safety Code.

(h) Notwithstanding any other law, forms and procedures made available for the implementation of Chapter 376 of the Statutes of 2015 shall not be subject to Chapter 4.5 (commencing with Section 11400) of Part 1 of Division 3 of Title 2 of the Government Code. (Added by Stats.1986, c. 1153, § 1. Amended by Stats.1988, c. 301, § 3; Stats.1991, c. 564 (A.B.743), § 1; Stats.1995, c. 446 (S.B.69), § 1; Stats.1998, c. 931 (S.B.2139), § 12, eff. Sept. 28, 1998; Stats.2003, c. 449 (A.B.1712), § 2; Stats.2015, c. 376 (A.B.999), § 2, eff. Jan. 1, 2016; Stats.2016, c. 714 (S.B.944), § 3, eff. Jan. 1, 2017.)

Cross References

Actions treated as limited civil case, conditions, see Code of Civil Procedure § 85.
Establishing abandonment of lease property, see Civil Code § 1951.3.
Fee, notice of disposal of mobilehome, see Health and Safety Code § 18080.5.
Homeowner defined for purposes of this Chapter, see Civil Code § 798.9.
Management defined for purposes of this Chapter, see Civil Code § 798.2.
Mobilehome defined for purposes of this Chapter, see Civil Code § 798.3.
Mobilehome park defined for purposes of this Chapter, see Civil Code § 798.4.
Ownership defined for purposes of this Code, see Civil Code § 654.
Right of entry upon abandonment of mobilehome, see Civil Code § 798.26.
Transfer of registration of trailer coach or recreational vehicle after receipt of judgment of abandonment and evidence of sale, see Vehicle Code § 5903.

§ 798.62. Natural disasters; renewal of tenancy

(a) If a mobilehome park is destroyed as a result of a wildfire or other natural disaster, and management elects to rebuild the park at the same location, management shall offer a renewed tenancy in the rebuilt mobilehome park to all previous homeowners in accordance with the following:

(1) The offer of renewed tenancy shall be on substantially the same terms as the previous homeowner's rental agreement that was in existence at the time of the wildfire or other natural disaster. However, management may adjust terms in the previous rental agreement to reflect costs and expenses to rebuild the park that were incurred from the time of the disaster until management received a final certificate of occupancy for all spaces in the park. These costs and expenses may include, but are not limited to, costs associated with demolition, reconstruction, and environmental remediation, as well as taxes and interest expenses.

(2) Management shall provide the previous homeowner, upon request, a statement listing the costs and expenses incurred in rebuilding the park and how the costs and expenses relate to the adjustment of terms in the rental agreement.

(3) The offer shall include an application to accept the renewed tenancy, the terms of the renewed tenancy, the deposit required to secure the renewed tenancy, and a clear statement of when the offer expires.

(4) Management shall send each previous homeowner the offer by certified mail, at least 240 days before the park is reopened, to the last postal address for the previous homeowner known to management, which may be the previous homeowner's former address within the park. If management has an email address or telephone number for the previous homeowner, management shall additionally attempt to notify the homeowner of the offer by those means.

(5) A previous homeowner may accept the offer by submitting, within 60 days from the date the homeowner receives the offer, the application and required deposit to secure the renewed tenancy to management and sign a rental agreement. If the previous homeowner fails to accept the offer within this time period, then the previous homeowner's right to a renewed tenancy under this section is deemed forfeited.

(6) Management shall process applications for renewed tenancy on a first-come-first-served basis.

(7) The previous homeowner shall not transfer the right to a renewed tenancy.

(b) For purposes of this section, "previous homeowner" means a homeowner with a valid tenancy in a mobilehome park at the time of a wildfire or other natural disaster. *(Added by Stats.2019, c. 504 (S.B.274), § 2, eff. Jan. 1, 2020.)*

ARTICLE 7. TRANSFER OF MOBILEHOME OR MOBILEHOME PARK

Section
798.70.   Advertising.
798.71.   Showing or listing a manufactured home or mobilehome for sale by management.
798.72.   Transfer or selling fees; request for service; purchase fees; performance of service.
798.73.   Removal upon sale to third party; conditions; notice.
798.73.5. Sales or transfer of mobilehomes remaining in park; repairs or improvements; conditions; written summary or repairs.
798.74.   Prior approval of prospective purchaser; notice of acceptance or rejection; fee for financial report or credit rating.
798.74.4. Disclosure requirements.
798.74.5. Information for prospective homeowners within a mobilehome park.
798.75.   Sale or transfer of mobilehome to remain in park; required documents; unlawful occupant.
798.75.5. Mobilehome park rental agreement disclosure form; homeowner provided copy.
798.76.   Regulations limiting residency based on age requirements for housing for older persons; compliance with federal act.
798.77.   Waiver of rights; public policy.
798.78.   Rights of heir, joint tenant or personal representative of the estate.
798.79.   Right of legal owner or junior lienholder to sell mobilehome within park.
798.80.   Offer to sell park or entry into listing agreement for sale of park; notice by owner to officers of resident organization.
798.81.   Listing; sales agent; restrictions by management prohibited.
798.82.   School facilities fee; written disclosure; time.
798.83.   Mobilehomes remaining in park; required repairs and improvements.

Cross References

Sale of mobilehome, right of first refusal to management, see Civil Code § 798.19.5.

§ 798.70. Advertising

(a) A homeowner, an heir, joint tenant, or personal representative of the estate who gains ownership of a mobilehome in the mobilehome park through the death of the owner of the mobilehome who was a homeowner at the time of his or her death, or the agent of any such person, may advertise the sale or exchange of his or her mobilehome, or, if not prohibited by the terms of an agreement with the management, may advertise the rental of his or her mobilehome, by displaying one sign in the window of the mobilehome, or by one sign posted on the side of the mobilehome facing the street, or by one sign in front of the mobilehome facing the street, stating that the mobilehome is for sale or exchange or, if not prohibited, for rent by the owner of the mobilehome or his or her agent. Any such person also may display one sign conforming to these requirements indicating that the mobilehome is on display for an "open house," if allowed by the park. The park may allow open houses and may establish reasonable rules or regulations governing how an open house may be conducted, including rules regarding the number of houses allowed to be open at one time, hours, and parking. The sign shall state the name, address, and telephone number of the owner of the mobilehome or his or her agent and the sign face shall not exceed 24 inches in width and 36 inches in height. Signs posted in front of a mobilehome pursuant to this section may be of an H-frame, A-frame, L-frame, or generally accepted yard-arm type design with the sign face perpendicular to, but not extending into, the street. Management may require the use of a step-in L-frame sign. Homeowners may attach to the sign or their mobilehome tubes or holders for leaflets that provide information on the mobilehome for sale, exchange, or rent.

(b) This section shall become operative on July 1, 2016. *(Added by Stats.2015, c. 288 (S.B.419), § 2, eff. Jan. 1, 2016, operative July 1, 2016.)*

Cross References

Advertising, sale, exchange or rental of mobilehome, see Civil Code § 199.1.5.
Homeowner defined for purposes of this Chapter, see Civil Code § 798.9.
Management defined for purposes of this Chapter, see Civil Code § 798.2.
Mobilehome defined for purposes of this Chapter, see Civil Code § 798.3.
Mobilehome park defined for purposes of this Chapter, see Civil Code § 798.4.
Ownership defined for purposes of this Code, see Civil Code § 654.
Repair of sudden or unforeseeable breakdown or deterioration of improvements, required contents and notice, see Civil Code § 798.15.

§ 798.71. Showing or listing a manufactured home or mobilehome for sale by management

(a)(1) The management may not show or list for sale a manufactured home or mobilehome without first obtaining the owner's written authorization. The authorization shall specify the terms and conditions regarding the showing or listing.

(2) Management may require that a homeowner advise management in writing that his or her manufactured home or mobilehome is for sale. If management requires that a homeowner advise management in writing that his or her manufactured home or mobilehome is for sale, failure to comply with this requirement does not invalidate a transfer.

(b) The management shall prohibit neither the listing nor the sale of a manufactured home or mobilehome within the park by the homeowner, an heir, joint tenant, or personal representative of the estate who gains ownership of a manufactured home or mobilehome in the mobilehome park through the death of the owner of the manufactured home or mobilehome who was a homeowner at the time of his or her death, or the agent of any such person other than the management. For purposes of this section, "listing" includes advertising the address of the home to the general public.

(c) The management shall not require the selling homeowner, or an heir, joint tenant, or personal representative of

§ 798.71

the estate who gains ownership of a manufactured home or mobilehome in the mobilehome park through the death of the owner of the manufactured home or mobilehome who was a homeowner at the time of his or her death, to authorize the management or any other specified broker, dealer, or person to act as the agent in the sale of a manufactured home or mobilehome as a condition of resale of the home in the park or of management's approval of the buyer or prospective homeowner for residency in the park.

(d) The management shall not require a homeowner, who is replacing a mobilehome or manufactured home on a space in the park, in which he or she resides, to use a specific broker, dealer, or other person as an agent in the purchase of or installation of the replacement home.

(e) Nothing in this section shall be construed as affecting the provisions of the Health and Safety Code governing the licensing of manufactured home or mobilehome salespersons or dealers.

(f) This section shall become operative on July 1, 2016. *(Added by Stats.2015, c. 288 (S.B.419), § 4, eff. Jan. 1, 2016, operative July 1, 2016.)*

Cross References

Homeowner defined for purposes of this Chapter, see Civil Code § 798.9.
Listing or showing mobilehome by ownership or management, see Civil Code § 799.2.
Management defined for purposes of this Chapter, see Civil Code § 798.2.
Mobilehome dealer violations, see Health and Safety Code § 18062.2.
Mobilehome defined for purposes of this Chapter, see Civil Code § 798.3.
Mobilehome park defined for purposes of this Chapter, see Civil Code § 798.4.
Mobilehome salesperson violations, see Health and Safety Code § 18063.
Ownership defined for purposes of this Code, see Civil Code § 654.

§ 798.72. Transfer or selling fees; request for service; purchase fees; performance of service

(a) The management shall not charge a homeowner, an heir, joint tenant, or personal representative of the estate who gains ownership of a mobilehome in the mobilehome park through the death of the owner of the mobilehome who was a homeowner at the time of his or her death, or the agent of any such person a transfer or selling fee as a condition of a sale of his mobilehome within a park unless the management performs a service in the sale. The management shall not perform any such service in connection with the sale unless so requested, in writing, by the homeowner, an heir, joint tenant, or personal representative of the estate who gains ownership of a mobilehome in the mobilehome park through the death of the owner of the mobilehome who was a homeowner at the time of his or her death, or the agent of any such person.

(b) The management shall not charge a prospective homeowner or his or her agent, upon purchase of a mobilehome, a fee as a condition of approval for residency in a park unless the management performs a specific service in the sale. The management shall not impose a fee, other than for a credit check in accordance with subdivision (b) of Section 798.74, for an interview of a prospective homeowner. *(Added by Stats.1978, c. 1031, p. 3178, § 1. Amended by Stats.1982, c. 1397, p. 5327, § 29; Stats.1988, c. 498, § 2; Stats.1989, c. 745, § 3.)*

Cross References

Homeowner defined for purposes of this Chapter, see Civil Code § 798.9.
Management defined for purposes of this Chapter, see Civil Code § 798.2.
Mobilehome defined for purposes of this Chapter, see Civil Code § 798.3.
Mobilehome park defined for purposes of this Chapter, see Civil Code § 798.4.
Ownership defined for purposes of this Code, see Civil Code § 654.
Unlawful acts of dealer, mobile homes and manufactured housing, see Health and Safety Code § 18062.2.
Unlawful acts of salesperson, mobile homes and manufactured housing, see Health and Safety Code § 18063.

§ 798.73. Removal upon sale to third party; conditions; notice

The management shall not require the removal of a mobilehome from the park in the event of the sale of the mobilehome to a third party during the term of the homeowner's rental agreement or in the 60 days following the initial notice required by paragraph (1) of subdivision (b) of Section 798.55. However, in the event of a sale to a third party, in order to upgrade the quality of the park, the management may require that a mobilehome be removed from the park where:

(a) It is not a "mobilehome" within the meaning of Section 798.3.

(b) It is more than 20 years old, or more than 25 years old if manufactured after September 15, 1971, and is 20 feet wide or more, and the mobilehome does not comply with the health and safety standards provided in Sections 18550, 18552, and 18605 of the Health and Safety Code and the regulations established thereunder, as determined following an inspection by the appropriate enforcement agency, as defined in Section 18207 of the Health and Safety Code.

(c) The mobilehome is more than 17 years old, or more than 25 years old if manufactured after September 15, 1971, and is less than 20 feet wide, and the mobilehome does not comply with the construction and safety standards under Sections 18550, 18552, and 18605 of the Health and Safety Code and the regulations established thereunder, as determined following an inspection by the appropriate enforcement agency, as defined in Section 18207 of the Health and Safety Code.

(d) It is in a significantly rundown condition or in disrepair, as determined by the general condition of the mobilehome and its acceptability to the health and safety of the occupants and to the public, exclusive of its age. The management shall use reasonable discretion in determining the general condition of the mobilehome and its accessory structures. The management shall bear the burden of demonstrating that the mobilehome is in a significantly rundown condition or in disrepair. The management of the park may not require repairs or improvements to the park space or property owned by the management, except for damage caused by the actions or negligence of the homeowner or an agent of the homeowner.

(e) The management shall not require a mobilehome to be removed from the park, pursuant to this section, unless the management has provided to the homeowner notice particularly specifying the condition that permits the removal of the mobilehome. *(Added by Stats.1978, c. 1034, p. 3194, § 2. Amended by Stats.1982, c. 1392, p. 5306, § 1; Stats.1982, c. 1397, p. 5327, § 30.5; Stats.1991, c. 576 (A.B.932), § 1; Stats.1994, c. 729 (A.B.3203), § 1; Stats.1997, c. 367 (A.B. 672), § 1; Stats.2003, c. 561 (A.B.682), § 2; Stats.2007, c. 549 (A.B.446), § 1; Stats.2008, c. 179 (S.B.1498), § 28.)*

Cross References

Homeowner defined for purposes of this Chapter, see Civil Code § 798.9.
Management defined for purposes of this Chapter, see Civil Code § 798.2.
Rental agreement defined for purposes of this Chapter, see Civil Code § 798.8.
Unlawful acts of dealer, mobile homes and manufactured housing, see Health and Safety Code § 18062.2.
Unlawful acts of salesperson, mobile homes and manufactured housing, see Health and Safety Code § 18063.

§ 798.73.5. Sales or transfer of mobilehomes remaining in park; repairs or improvements; conditions; written summary or repairs

(a) In the case of a sale or transfer of a mobilehome that will remain in the park, the management may only require repairs or improvements to the mobilehome, its appurtenances, or an accessory structure that meet all of the following conditions:

(1) Except as provided by Section 798.83, the repair or improvement is to the mobilehome, its appurtenances, or an accessory structure that is not owned and installed by the management.

(2) The repair or improvement is based upon or is required by a local ordinance or state statute or regulation relating to mobilehomes, or a rule or regulation of the mobilehome park that implements or enforces a local ordinance or a state statute or regulation relating to mobilehomes.

(3) The repair or improvement relates to the exterior of the mobilehome, its appurtenances, or an accessory structure that is not owned and installed by the management.

(b) The management, in the case of sale or transfer of a mobilehome that will remain in the park, shall provide a homeowner with a written summary of repairs or improvements that management requires to the mobilehome, its appurtenances, or an accessory structure that is not owned and installed by the management no later than 10 business days following the receipt of a request for this information, as part of the notice required by Section 798.59. This summary shall include specific references to park rules and regulations, local ordinances, and state statutes and regulations relating to mobilehomes upon which the request for repair or improvement is based.

(c) The provisions of this section enacted at the 1999–2000 Regular Session of the Legislature are declarative of existing law as they pertain to allowing park management to enforce park rules and regulations; these provisions specifically limit repairs and improvements that can be required of a homeowner by park management at the time of sale or transfer to the same repairs and improvements that can be required during any other time of a residency. *(Added by Stats.2000, c. 554 (A.B.2239), § 1.)*

Cross References

Homeowner defined for purposes of this Chapter, see Civil Code § 798.9.
Management defined for purposes of this Chapter, see Civil Code § 798.2.
Mobilehome defined for purposes of this Chapter, see Civil Code § 798.3.
Mobilehome park defined for purposes of this Chapter, see Civil Code § 798.4.
Unlawful acts of dealer, mobile homes and manufactured housing, see Health and Safety Code § 18062.2.
Unlawful acts of salesperson, mobile homes and manufactured housing, see Health and Safety Code § 18063.

§ 798.74. Prior approval of prospective purchaser; notice of acceptance or rejection; fee for financial report or credit rating

(a) The management may require the right of prior approval of a prospective purchaser of a mobilehome that will remain in the park.

(b)(1) A selling homeowner or their agent shall give notice of a sale of a mobilehome that will remain in the park to management before the close of the sale.

(2) Management shall, within 15 days, provide the seller and the prospective purchaser both of the following, in writing, upon receiving the notice required in paragraph (1):

(A) The standards that management customarily utilizes to approve a tenancy application, including the minimum reported credit score from a consumer credit reporting agency that management requires for approval.

(B) A list of all documentation that management will require to determine if the prospective purchaser will qualify for tenancy in the park.

(c) Management shall not withhold approval from a prospective purchase of a mobilehome unless any of the following apply:

(1) Management reasonably determines that, based upon the purchaser's prior tenancies, they will not comply with the rules and regulations of the park.

(2) The purchaser does not have the financial ability to pay the rent, estimated utilities, and other charges of the park.

(3) The purchaser has committed fraud, deceit, or concealment of material facts during the application process.

(d) In determining whether the prospective purchaser has the financial ability to pay the rent and charges of the park pursuant to paragraph (2) of subdivision (c), the management may require the prospective purchaser to document the amount and source of their gross monthly income or means of financial support. However, management shall not require the prospective purchaser to submit any of the following:

(1) Documentation beyond that disclosed pursuant to subparagraph (B) of paragraph (2) of subdivision (b).

(2) Copies of any personal income tax returns.

§ 798.74

(e)(1) Within 15 business days of receiving all of the information requested from the prospective purchaser, management shall notify the seller and the prospective purchaser, in writing, of either acceptance or rejection of the application. During this 15–day period, the prospective purchaser shall comply with management's request, if any, for a personal interview.

(2)(A) If management rejects the application, management shall state the reason for the rejection in accordance with subdivision (c). If the rejection is based upon an alleged lack of financial ability to pay the rent, estimated utilities, and other charges of the park, as described in paragraph (2) of subdivision (c), the prospective purchaser may elect to provide additional financial or asset information to management to demonstrate their financial ability to pay the rent, estimated utilities, and other charges of the park. For purposes of this paragraph, "additional financial information" includes, but is not limited to, the following:

(i) Savings accounts.

(ii) Certificates of deposit.

(iii) Stock portfolios.

(iv) Trust interests of which the purchaser is a beneficiary.

(v) Real property.

(vi) Similar financial assets that can be liquidated or sold.

(B) If the prospective purchaser elects to provide additional financial and asset information specified in subparagraph (A), management shall consider the information together with the prospective purchaser's gross monthly income to determine whether the purchaser has the financial ability to pay the rent, estimated utilities, and other charges of the park.

(C) If a prospective purchaser provides additional financial and asset information, management may also consider any liabilities of the prospective purchaser when making a final determination of the prospective purchaser's ability to pay the rent, estimated utilities, and other charges of the park under this subdivision.

(f) If the management collects a fee or charge from a prospective purchaser of a mobilehome in order to obtain a financial report or credit rating, the full amount of the fee or charge shall be credited toward payment of the first month's rent for that mobilehome purchaser. If, for whatever reason, the prospective purchaser is rejected by the management, the management shall refund to the prospective purchaser the full amount of that fee or charge within 30 days from the date of rejection. If the prospective purchaser is approved by the management, but, for whatever reason, the prospective purchaser elects not to purchase the mobilehome, the management may retain the fee, or a portion thereof, to defray its administrative costs under this section.

(g) Management may be held liable by the selling homeowner for any and all damages proximately caused by management's failure to comply with this section.

(h) For purposes of this section:

(1) "Charges" means all charges authorized and imposed by management under Section 798.31.

(2) "Consumer credit reporting agency" has the same meaning as defined in subdivision (d) of Section 1785.3.

(3) "Credit score" has the same meaning as defined in subdivision (b) of Section 1785.15.1. *(Added by Stats.2015, c. 288 (S.B.419), § 6, eff. Jan. 1, 2016, operative July 1, 2016. Amended by Stats.2019, c. 504 (S.B.274), § 3, eff. Jan. 1, 2020.)*

Cross References

Homeowner defined for purposes of this Chapter, see Civil Code § 798.9.
Management defined for purposes of this Chapter, see Civil Code § 798.2.
Mobilehome dealer violations, see Health and Safety Code § 18062.2.
Mobilehome defined for purposes of this Chapter, see Civil Code § 798.3.
Repair of sudden or unforeseeable breakdown or deterioration of improvements, required contents and notice, see Civil Code § 798.15.
Salesperson violations, see Health and Safety Code § 18063.
Tenancy defined for purposes of this Chapter, see Civil Code § 798.12.

§ 798.74.4. Disclosure requirements

The transfer or sale of a manufactured home or mobilehome in a mobilehome park is subject to the transfer disclosure requirements and provisions set forth in Article 1.5 (commencing with Section 1102) of Chapter 2 of Title 4 of Part 4 of the Civil Code. The requirements include, but are not limited to, the use of the Manufactured Home and Mobilehome Transfer Disclosure Statement set forth in Section 1102.6d of the Civil Code. *(Added by Stats.2003, c. 249 (S.B.116), § 2.)*

Cross References

Mobilehome defined for purposes of this Chapter, see Civil Code § 798.3.
Mobilehome park defined for purposes of this Chapter, see Civil Code § 798.4.

§ 798.74.5. Information for prospective homeowners within a mobilehome park

(a) Within two business days of receiving a request from a prospective homeowner for an application for residency for a specific space within a mobilehome park, if the management has been advised that the mobilehome occupying that space is for sale, the management shall give the prospective homeowner a separate document in at least 12–point type entitled "INFORMATION FOR PROSPECTIVE HOMEOWNERS," which includes the following statements:

"As a prospective homeowner you are being provided with certain information you should know prior to applying for tenancy in a mobilehome park. This is not meant to be a complete list of information.

Owning a home in a mobilehome park incorporates the dual role of "homeowner" (the owner of the home) and park resident or tenant (also called a "homeowner" in the Mobilehome Residency Law). As a homeowner under the Mobilehome Residency Law, you will be responsible for paying the amount necessary to rent the space for your home, in addition to other fees and charges described below. You must also follow certain rules and regulations to reside in the park.

If you are approved for tenancy, and your tenancy commences within the next 30 days, your beginning monthly rent will be $____ (must be completed by the management) for space number ____ (must be completed by the management). Additional information regarding future rent or fee increases may also be provided.

In addition to the monthly rent, you will be obligated to pay to the park the following additional fees and charges listed below. Other fees or charges may apply depending upon your specific requests. Metered utility charges are based on use.

_____
_____
(Management shall describe the fee or charge and a good faith estimate of each fee or charge.)

Some spaces are governed by an ordinance, rule, regulation, or initiative measure that limits or restricts rents in mobilehome parks. These laws are commonly known as "rent control." Prospective purchasers who do not occupy the mobilehome as their principal residence may be subject to rent levels which are not governed by these laws. (Civil Code Section 798.21) Long-term leases specify rent increases during the term of the lease. By signing a rental agreement or lease for a term of more than one year, you may be removing your rental space from a local rent control ordinance during the term, or any extension, of the lease if a local rent control ordinance is in effect for the area in which the space is located.

A fully executed lease or rental agreement, or a statement signed by the park's management and by you stating that you and the management have agreed to the terms and conditions of a rental agreement, is required to complete the sale or escrow process of the home. You have no rights to tenancy without a properly executed lease or agreement or that statement. (Civil Code Section 798.75)

If the management collects a fee or charge from you in order to obtain a financial report or credit rating, the full amount of the fee or charge will be either credited toward your first month's rent or, if you are rejected for any reason, refunded to you. However, if you are approved by management, but, for whatever reason, you elect not to purchase the mobilehome, the management may retain the fee to defray its administrative costs. (Civil Code Section 798.74)

We encourage you to request from management a copy of the lease or rental agreement, the park's rules and regulations, and a copy of the Mobilehome Residency Law. Upon request, park management will provide you a copy of each document. We urge you to read these documents before making the decision that you want to become a mobilehome park resident.

Dated: _____
Signature of Park Manager: _____
Acknowledge Receipt by Prospective Homeowner: _____"

(b) Management shall provide a prospective homeowner, upon his or her request, with a copy of the rules and regulations of the park and with a copy of this chapter. *(Added by Stats.2003, c. 767 (A.B.1287), § 2, operative Oct. 1, 2004. Amended by Stats.2012, c. 337 (A.B.317), § 1.)*

Cross References

Homeowner defined for purposes of this Chapter, see Civil Code § 798.9.
Management defined for purposes of this Chapter, see Civil Code § 798.2.
Mobilehome defined for purposes of this Chapter, see Civil Code § 798.3.
Mobilehome park defined for purposes of this Chapter, see Civil Code § 798.4.
Rental agreement defined for purposes of this Chapter, see Civil Code § 798.8.
Resident defined for purposes of this Chapter, see Civil Code § 798.11.
Tenancy defined for purposes of this Chapter, see Civil Code § 798.12.

§ 798.75. Sale or transfer of mobilehome to remain in park; required documents; unlawful occupant

(a) An escrow, sale, or transfer agreement involving a mobilehome located in a park at the time of the sale, where the mobilehome is to remain in the park, shall contain a copy of either a fully executed rental agreement or a statement signed by the park's management and the prospective homeowner that the parties have agreed to the terms and conditions of a rental agreement.

(b) In the event the purchaser fails to execute the rental agreement, the purchaser shall not have any rights of tenancy.

(c) In the event that an occupant of a mobilehome has no rights of tenancy and is not otherwise entitled to occupy the mobilehome pursuant to this chapter, the occupant is considered an unlawful occupant if, after a demand is made for the surrender of the mobilehome park site, for a period of five days, the occupant refuses to surrender the site to the mobilehome park management. In the event the unlawful occupant fails to comply with the demand, the unlawful occupant shall be subject to the proceedings set forth in Chapter 4 (commencing with Section 1159) of Title 3 of Part 3 of the Code of Civil Procedure.

(d) The occupant of the mobilehome shall not be considered an unlawful occupant and shall not be subject to the provisions of subdivision (c) if all of the following conditions are present:

(1) The occupant is the registered owner of the mobilehome.

(2) The management has determined that the occupant has the financial ability to pay the rent and charges of the

§ 798.75

park; will comply with the rules and regulations of the park, based on the occupant's prior tenancies; and will comply with this article.

(3) The management failed or refused to offer the occupant a rental agreement. *(Added by Stats.1978, c. 1031, p. 3178, § 1. Amended by Stats.1981, c. 667, § 8; Stats.1983, c. 519, § 9; Stats.1987, c. 323, § 1; Stats.1989, c. 119, § 1; Stats.1990, c. 645 (S.B.2340), § 2.)*

Cross References

Homeowner defined for purposes of this Chapter, see Civil Code § 798.9.

Management defined for purposes of this Chapter, see Civil Code § 798.2.

Mobilehome defined for purposes of this Chapter, see Civil Code § 798.3.

Mobilehome park defined for purposes of this Chapter, see Civil Code § 798.4.

Rental agreement defined for purposes of this Chapter, see Civil Code § 798.8.

Tenancy defined for purposes of this Chapter, see Civil Code § 798.12.

§ 798.75.5. Mobilehome park rental agreement disclosure form; homeowner provided copy

(a) The management shall provide a prospective homeowner with a completed written disclosure form concerning the park described in subdivision (b) at least three days prior to execution of a rental agreement or statement signed by the park management and the prospective homeowner that the parties have agreed to the terms and conditions of the rental agreement. The management shall update the information on the disclosure form annually, or, in the event of a material change in the condition of the mobilehome park, at the time of the material change in that condition.

(b) The written disclosure form shall read as follows:

REAL OR IMMOVABLE PROPERTY § 798.75.5

Mobilehome Park Rental Agreement Disclosure Form

THIS DISCLOSURE STATEMENT CONCERNS THE MOBILEHOME PARK KNOWN AS

_____ LOCATED AT _____
      park name   park address

IN THE CITY OF _____ COUNTY OF _____
STATE OF CALIFORNIA.
THIS STATEMENT IS A DISCLOSURE OF THE CONDITION OF THE PARK AND PARK COMMON AREAS AS OF _____ IN COMPLIANCE WITH SECTION 798.75.5 OF THE CIVIL CODE.
        date

IT IS NOT A WARRANTY OF ANY KIND BY THE MOBILEHOME PARK OWNER OR PARK MANAGEMENT AND IS NOT A SUBSTITUTE FOR ANY INSPECTION BY THE PROSPECTIVE HOMEOWNER/LESSEE OF THE SPACE TO BE RENTED OR LEASED OR OF THE PARK, INCLUDING ALL COMMON AREAS REFERENCED IN THIS STATEMENT. THIS STATEMENT DOES NOT CREATE ANY NEW DUTY OR NEW LIABILITY ON THE PART OF THE MOBILEHOME PARK OWNER OR MOBILEHOME PARK MANAGEMENT OR AFFECT ANY DUTIES THAT MAY HAVE EXISTED PRIOR TO THE ENACTMENT OF SECTION 798.75.5 OF THE CIVIL CODE, OTHER THAN THE DUTY TO DISCLOSE THE INFORMATION REQUIRED BY THE STATEMENT.

Are you (the mobilehome park owner/mobilehome park manager) aware of any of the following:

A. Park or common area facilities	B. Does the park contain this facility?		C. Is the facility in operation?		D. Does the facility have any known substantial defects?		E. Are there any uncorrected park citations or notices of abatement relating to the facilities issued by a public agency?		F. Is there any substantial, uncorrected damage to the facility from fire, flood, earthquake, or landslides?		G. Are there any pending lawsuits by or against the park affecting the facilities or alleging defects in the facilities?		H. Is there any encroachment, easement, non-conforming use, or violation of setback requirements regarding this park common area facility?	
	Yes	No	Yes	No	Yes	No	Yes	No	Yes	No	Yes	No	Yes	No
Clubhouse														
Walkways														
Streets, roads, and access														
Electric utility system														
Water utility system														
Gas utility system														
Common area lighting system														
Septic or sewer system														
Playground														
RV storage														
Parking areas														
Swimming pool														
Spa pool														
Laundry														
Other common area facilities*														

*If there are other important park or common area facilities, please specify (attach additional sheets if necessary):
_____
_____

If any item in C is checked "no", or any item in D, E, F, G, or H is checked "yes", please explain (attach additional sheets if necessary): _____

171

§ 798.75.5

The mobilehome park owner/park manager states that the information herein has been delivered to the prospective homeowner/lessee a minimum of three days prior to execution of a rental agreement and is true and correct to the best of the park owner/park manager's knowledge as of the date signed by the park owner/manager.

Park Owner/Manager: _____ By: _____ Date: _____
                                    print name   signature

I/WE ACKNOWLEDGE RECEIPT OF A COMPLETED COPY OF THE PARK OWNER/MANAGER STATEMENT.

Prospective Homeowner
Lessee _____ Park Owner/Manager _____
Date: _____   Title

Prospective Homeowner
Lessee _____ Park Owner/Manager _____
Date: _____   Title

(Added by Stats.1999, c. 517 (S.B.534), § 1.)

Cross References

Homeowner defined for purposes of this Chapter, see Civil Code § 798.9.

Management defined for purposes of this Chapter, see Civil Code § 798.2.

Mobilehome defined for purposes of this Chapter, see Civil Code § 798.3.

Mobilehome park defined for purposes of this Chapter, see Civil Code § 798.4.

Rental agreement defined for purposes of this Chapter, see Civil Code § 798.8.

Unlawful acts of dealer, mobile homes and manufactured housing, see Health and Safety Code § 18062.2.

Unlawful acts of salesperson, mobile homes and manufactured housing, see Health and Safety Code § 18063.

§ 798.76. Regulations limiting residency based on age requirements for housing for older persons; compliance with federal act

The management may require that a prospective purchaser comply with any rule or regulation limiting residency based on age requirements for housing for older persons, provided that the rule or regulation complies with the federal Fair Housing Act, as amended by Public Law 104-76, and implementing regulations. (Added by Stats.1978, c. 1031, p. 3178, § 1. Amended by Stats.1992, c. 182 (S.B.1234), § 1.5; Stats.1992, c. 666 (A.B.3453), § 1; Stats.1993, c. 1277 (A.B. 2244), § 1; Stats.1996, c. 61 (S.B.1585), § 1, eff. June 10, 1996.)

Cross References

Applicants seeking density bonus for planning and zoning, incentives or concessions for lower income housing units and child care facilities, see Government Code § 65915.

Density bonuses for mobilehome parks that limit residency based on age requirements pursuant to this section, see Government Code § 65915.

Management defined for purposes of this Chapter, see Civil Code § 798.2.

§ 798.77. Waiver of rights; public policy

No rental or sale agreement shall contain a provision by which the purchaser or homeowner waives his or her rights under this chapter. Any such waiver shall be deemed contrary to public policy and shall be void and unenforceable. (Added by Stats.1978, c. 1031, p. 3178, § 1. Amended by Stats.1978, c. 1033, p. 3191, § 19; Stats.1982, c. 1397, p. 5328, § 32; Stats.1983, c. 519, § 10.)

Cross References

Homeowner defined for purposes of this Chapter, see Civil Code § 798.9.

Repair of sudden or unforeseeable breakdown or deterioration of improvements, required contents and notice, see Civil Code § 798.15.

§ 798.78. Rights of heir, joint tenant or personal representative of the estate

(a) An heir, joint tenant, or personal representative of the estate who gains ownership of a mobilehome in the mobilehome park through the death of the owner of the mobilehome who was a homeowner at the time of his or her death shall have the right to sell the mobilehome to a third party in accordance with the provisions of this article, but only if all the homeowner's responsibilities and liabilities to the management regarding rent, utilities, and reasonable maintenance of the mobilehome and its premises which have arisen since the death of the homeowner have been satisfied as they have accrued pursuant to the rental agreement in effect at the time of the death of the homeowner up until the date the mobilehome is resold.

(b) In the event that the heir, joint tenant, or personal representative of the estate does not satisfy the requirements of subdivision (a) with respect to the satisfaction of the homeowner's responsibilities and liabilities to the management which accrue pursuant to the rental agreement in effect at the time of the death of the homeowner, the management shall have the right to require the removal of the mobilehome from the park.

(c) Prior to the sale of a mobilehome by an heir, joint tenant, or personal representative of the estate, that individual may replace the existing mobilehome with another mobilehome, either new or used, or repair the existing mobilehome so that the mobilehome to be sold complies with health and safety standards provided in Sections 18550, 18552, and 18605 of the Health and Safety Code, and the regulations established thereunder. In the event the mobilehome is to be replaced, the replacement mobilehome shall also meet current standards of the park as contained in the park's most recent written requirements issued to prospective homeowners.

(d) In the event the heir, joint tenant, or personal representative of the estate desires to establish a tenancy in the park, that individual shall comply with those provisions of this article which identify the requirements for a prospective purchaser of a mobilehome that remains in the park. (Added by Stats.1979, c. 198, p. 437, § 1. Amended by Stats.1982, c. 477, p. 2079, § 1; Stats.1982, c. 1397, p. 5328, § 32.5; Stats.1989, c. 745, § 4.)

Cross References

Homeowner defined for purposes of this Chapter, see Civil Code § 798.9.
Management defined for purposes of this Chapter, see Civil Code § 798.2.
Mobilehome defined for purposes of this Chapter, see Civil Code § 798.3.
Mobilehome park defined for purposes of this Chapter, see Civil Code § 798.4.
Ownership defined for purposes of this Code, see Civil Code § 654.
Rental agreement defined for purposes of this Chapter, see Civil Code § 798.8.
Tenancy defined for purposes of this Chapter, see Civil Code § 798.12.

§ 798.79. Right of legal owner or junior lienholder to sell mobilehome within park

(a) Any legal owner or junior lienholder who forecloses on his or her security interest in a mobilehome located in a mobilehome park shall have the right to sell the mobilehome within the park to a third party in accordance with this article, but only if all of the homeowner's responsibilities and liabilities to the management regarding rent, utilities, and reasonable maintenance of a mobilehome and its premises are satisfied by the foreclosing creditor as they accrue through the date the mobilehome is resold.

(b) In the event the legal owner or junior lienholder has received from the management a copy of the notice of termination of tenancy for nonpayment of rent or other charges, the foreclosing creditor's right to sell the mobilehome within the park to a third party shall also be governed by Section 798.56a. (Added by Stats.1979, c. 1185, p. 4629, § 2. Amended by Stats.1982, c. 477, p. 2079, § 2; Stats.1982, c. 1397, p. 5328, § 33.5; Stats.1983, c. 1124, § 4, operative July 1, 1984; Stats.1990, c. 1357 (A.B.4156), § 3; Stats.1991, c. 190 (A.B.600), § 2.)

Cross References

Homeowner defined for purposes of this Chapter, see Civil Code § 798.9.
Management defined for purposes of this Chapter, see Civil Code § 798.2.
Mobilehome defined for purposes of this Chapter, see Civil Code § 798.3.
Mobilehome park defined for purposes of this Chapter, see Civil Code § 798.4.
Tenancy defined for purposes of this Chapter, see Civil Code § 798.12.

§ 798.80. Offer to sell park or entry into listing agreement for sale of park; notice by owner to officers of resident organization

(a) Not less than 30 days nor more than one year prior to an owner of a mobilehome park entering into a written listing agreement with a licensed real estate broker, as defined in Article 1 (commencing with Section 10130) of Chapter 3 of Part 1 of Division 4 of the Business and Professions Code, for the sale of the park, or offering to sell the park to any party, the owner shall provide written notice of his or her intention to sell the mobilehome park by first-class mail or by personal delivery to the president, secretary, and treasurer of any resident organization formed by homeowners in the mobilehome park as a nonprofit corporation, pursuant to Section 23701v of the Revenue and Taxation Code, stock cooperative corporation, or other entity for purposes of converting the mobilehome park to condominium or stock cooperative ownership interests and for purchasing the mobilehome park from the management of the mobilehome park. An offer to sell a park shall not be construed as an offer under this subdivision unless it is initiated by the park owner or agent.

(b) An owner of a mobilehome park shall not be required to comply with subdivision (a) unless the following conditions are met:

(1) The resident organization has first furnished the park owner or park manager a written notice of the name and address of the president, secretary, and treasurer of the resident organization to whom the notice of sale shall be given.

(2) The resident organization has first notified the park owner or manager in writing that the park residents are interested in purchasing the park. The initial notice by the resident organization shall be made prior to a written listing or offer to sell the park by the park owner, and the resident organization shall give subsequent notice once each year thereafter that the park residents are interested in purchasing the park.

(3) The resident organization has furnished the park owner or park manager a written notice, within five days, of any change in the name or address of the officers of the resident organization to whom the notice of sale shall be given.

(c) Nothing in this section affects the validity of title to real property transferred in violation of this section, although a violation shall subject the seller to civil action pursuant to

§ 798.80

Article 8 (commencing with Section 798.84) by homeowner residents of the park or the resident organization.

(d) Nothing in this section affects the ability of a licensed real estate broker, as defined in Article 1 (commencing with Section 10130) of Chapter 3 of Part 1 of Division 4 of the Business and Professions Code, to collect a commission pursuant to an executed contract between the broker and the mobilehome park owner.

(e) Subdivision (a) does not apply to any of the following:

(1) Any sale or other transfer by a park owner who is a natural person to any relation specified in Section 6401 or 6402 of the Probate Code.

(2) Any transfer by gift, devise, or operation of law.

(3) Any transfer by a corporation to an affiliate. As used in this paragraph, "affiliate" means any shareholder of the transferring corporation, any corporation or entity owned or controlled, directly or indirectly, by the transferring corporation, or any other corporation or entity controlled, directly or indirectly, by any shareholder of the transferring corporation.

(4) Any transfer by a partnership to any of its partners.

(5) Any conveyance resulting from the judicial or nonjudicial foreclosure of a mortgage or deed of trust encumbering a mobilehome park or any deed given in lieu of such a foreclosure.

(6) Any sale or transfer between or among joint tenants or tenants in common owning a mobilehome park.

(7) The purchase of a mobilehome park by a governmental entity under its powers of eminent domain. *(Added by Stats.1986, c. 648, § 2. Amended by Stats.1990, c. 421 (A.B.2944), § 1; Stats.1994, c. 219 (S.B.1280), § 1.)*

Cross References

Homeowner defined for purposes of this Chapter, see Civil Code § 798.9.
Management defined for purposes of this Chapter, see Civil Code § 798.2.
Mobilehome defined for purposes of this Chapter, see Civil Code § 798.3.
Mobilehome park defined for purposes of this Chapter, see Civil Code § 798.4.
Ownership defined for purposes of this Code, see Civil Code § 654.
Real property defined for purposes of this Code, see Civil Code § 658.
Resident defined for purposes of this Chapter, see Civil Code § 798.11.

§ 798.81. Listing; sales agent; restrictions by management prohibited

The management (1) shall not prohibit the listing or sale of a used mobilehome within the park by the homeowner, an heir, joint tenant, or personal representative of the estate who gains ownership of a mobilehome in the mobilehome park through the death of the owner of the mobilehome who was a homeowner at the time of his or her death, or the agent of any such person other than the management, (2) nor require the selling homeowner to authorize the management to act as the agent in the sale of a mobilehome as a condition of approval of the buyer or prospective homeowner for residency in the park. *(Added by Stats.1988, c. 1033, § 1. Amended by Stats.1989, c. 745, § 5.)*

Cross References

Homeowner defined for purposes of this Chapter, see Civil Code § 798.9.
Management defined for purposes of this Chapter, see Civil Code § 798.2.
Mobilehome defined for purposes of this Chapter, see Civil Code § 798.3.
Mobilehome park defined for purposes of this Chapter, see Civil Code § 798.4.
Ownership defined for purposes of this Code, see Civil Code § 654.

§ 798.82. School facilities fee; written disclosure; time

The management, at the time of an application for residency, shall disclose in writing to any person who proposes to purchase or install a manufactured home or mobilehome on a space, on which the construction of the pad or foundation system commenced after September 1, 1986, and no other manufactured home or mobilehome was previously located, installed, or occupied, that the manufactured home or mobilehome may be subject to a school facilities fee under Sections 53080 and 53080.4 of, and Chapter 4.9 (commencing with Section 65995) of Division 1 of Title 7 of, the Government Code. *(Added by Stats.1994, c. 983 (S.B.1461), § 1.)*

Cross References

Management defined for purposes of this Chapter, see Civil Code § 798.2.
Mobilehome defined for purposes of this Chapter, see Civil Code § 798.3.

§ 798.83. Mobilehomes remaining in park; required repairs and improvements

In the case of a sale or transfer of a mobilehome that will remain in the park, the management of the park shall not require repairs or improvements to the park space or property owned by the management, except for damage caused by the actions or negligence of the homeowner or an agent of the homeowner. *(Added by Stats.1997, c. 367 (A.B.672), § 2.)*

Cross References

Homeowner defined for purposes of this Chapter, see Civil Code § 798.9.
Management defined for purposes of this Chapter, see Civil Code § 798.2.
Mobilehome defined for purposes of this Chapter, see Civil Code § 798.3.
Unlawful acts of dealer, mobile homes and manufactured housing, see Health and Safety Code § 18062.2.
Unlawful acts of salesperson, mobile homes and manufactured housing, see Health and Safety Code § 18063.

ARTICLE 8. ACTIONS, PROCEEDINGS, AND PENALTIES

Section
798.84. Failure to maintain common facilities or reduction of service; notice of impending action; requisites.
798.85. Attorney's fees and costs.
798.86. Willful violation by management; additional penalty; punitive damages.
798.87. Public nuisances; remedy by civil action or abatement; parties.

Section
798.88. Violation of reasonable rule or regulation of mobilehome park; injunction; temporary restraining order.

§ 798.84. Failure to maintain common facilities or reduction of service; notice of impending action; requisites

(a) No action based upon the management's alleged failure to maintain the physical improvements in the common facilities in good working order or condition or alleged reduction of service may be commenced by a homeowner unless the management has been given at least 30 days' prior notice of the intention to commence the action.

(b) The notice shall be in writing, signed by the homeowner or homeowners making the allegations, and shall notify the management of the basis of the claim, the specific allegations, and the remedies requested. A notice by one homeowner shall be deemed to be sufficient notice of the specific allegation to the management of the park by all of the homeowners in the park.

(c) The notice may be served in the manner prescribed in Chapter 5 (commencing with Section 1010) of Title 14 of Part 2 of the Code of Civil Procedure.

(d) For purposes of this section, management shall be deemed to be notified of an alleged failure to maintain the physical improvements in the common facilities in good working order or condition or of an alleged reduction of services upon substantial compliance by the homeowner or homeowners with the provisions of subdivisions (b) and (c), or when management has been notified of the alleged failure to maintain or the alleged reduction of services by a state or local agency.

(e) If the notice is served within 30 days of the expiration of the applicable statute of limitations, the time for the commencement of the action shall be extended 30 days from the service of the notice.

(f) This section does not apply to actions for personal injury or wrongful death. *(Added by Stats.1988, c. 1592, § 1.)*

Cross References

Homeowner defined for purposes of this Chapter, see Civil Code § 798.9.
Management defined for purposes of this Chapter, see Civil Code § 798.2.

§ 798.85. Attorney's fees and costs

In any action arising out of the provisions of this chapter the prevailing party shall be entitled to reasonable attorney's fees and costs. A party shall be deemed a prevailing party for the purposes of this section if the judgment is rendered in his or her favor or where the litigation is dismissed in his or her favor prior to or during the trial, unless the parties otherwise agree in the settlement or compromise. *(Added by Stats.1978, c. 1031, p. 3178, § 1. Amended by Stats.1978, c. 1033, p. 3191, § 21; Stats.1983, c. 519, § 11.)*

§ 798.86. Willful violation by management; additional penalty; punitive damages

(a) If a homeowner or former homeowner of a park is the prevailing party in a civil action, including a small claims court action, against the management to enforce his or her rights under this chapter, the homeowner, in addition to damages afforded by law, may, in the discretion of the court, be awarded an amount not to exceed two thousand dollars ($2,000) for each willful violation of this chapter by the management.

(b) A homeowner or former homeowner of a park who is the prevailing party in a civil action against management to enforce his or her rights under this chapter may be awarded either punitive damages pursuant to Section 3294 of the Civil Code or the statutory penalty provided by subdivision (a). *(Added by Stats.1978, c. 1031, p. 3178, § 1. Amended by Stats.1978, c. 1033, p. 3191, § 22; Stats.1982, c. 1397, p. 5329, § 34; Stats.1983, c. 519, § 12; Stats.1997, c. 141 (A.B.591), § 1; Stats.2003, c. 98 (A.B.693), § 1.)*

Cross References

Homeowner defined for purposes of this Chapter, see Civil Code § 798.9.
Management defined for purposes of this Chapter, see Civil Code § 798.2.

§ 798.87. Public nuisances; remedy by civil action or abatement; parties

(a) The substantial failure of the management to provide and maintain physical improvements in the common facilities in good working order and condition shall be deemed a public nuisance. Notwithstanding Section 3491, this nuisance may only be remedied by a civil action or abatement.

(b) The substantial violation of a mobilehome park rule shall be deemed a public nuisance. Notwithstanding Section 3491, this nuisance may only be remedied by a civil action or abatement.

(c) A civil action pursuant to this section may be brought by a park resident, the park management, or in the name of the people of the State of California, by any of the following:

(1) The district attorney or the county counsel of the jurisdiction in which the park, or the greater portion of the park, is located.

(2) The city attorney or city prosecutor if the park is located within the jurisdiction of the city.

(3) The Attorney General. *(Added by Stats.1982, c. 1392, p. 5306, § 2. Amended by Stats.1983, c. 187, § 1; Stats.1990, c. 1374 (S.B.2446), § 2; Stats.2002, c. 141 (A.B.2382), § 1.)*

Cross References

Attorney General, generally, see Government Code § 12500 et seq.
Management defined for purposes of this Chapter, see Civil Code § 798.2.
Mobilehome defined for purposes of this Chapter, see Civil Code § 798.3.
Mobilehome park defined for purposes of this Chapter, see Civil Code § 798.4.
Resident defined for purposes of this Chapter, see Civil Code § 798.11.

§ 798.88. Violation of reasonable rule or regulation of mobilehome park; injunction; temporary restraining order

(a) In addition to any right under Article 6 (commencing with Section 798.55) to terminate the tenancy of a homeowner, any person in violation of a reasonable rule or

§ 798.88

regulation of a mobilehome park may be enjoined from the violation as provided in this section.

(b) A petition for an order enjoining a continuing or recurring violation of any reasonable rule or regulation of a mobilehome park may be filed by the management thereof within the limited jurisdiction of the superior court of the county in which the mobilehome park is located. At the time of filing the petition, the petitioner may obtain a temporary restraining order in accordance with subdivision (a) of Section 527 of the Code of Civil Procedure. A temporary order restraining the violation may be granted, with notice, upon the petitioner's affidavit showing to the satisfaction of the court reasonable proof of a continuing or recurring violation of a rule or regulation of the mobilehome park by the named homeowner or resident and that great or irreparable harm would result to the management or other homeowners or residents of the park from continuance or recurrence of the violation.

(c) A temporary restraining order granted pursuant to this subdivision shall be personally served upon the respondent homeowner or resident with the petition for injunction and notice of hearing thereon. The restraining order shall remain in effect for a period not to exceed 15 days, except as modified or sooner terminated by the court.

(d) Within 15 days of filing the petition for an injunction, a hearing shall be held thereon. If the court, by clear and convincing evidence, finds the existence of a continuing or recurring violation of a reasonable rule or regulation of the mobilehome park, the court shall issue an injunction prohibiting the violation. The duration of the injunction shall not exceed three years.

(e) However, not more than three months prior to the expiration of an injunction issued pursuant to this section, the management of the mobilehome park may petition under this section for a new injunction where there has been recurring or continuous violation of the injunction or there is a threat of future violation of the mobilehome park's rules upon termination of the injunction.

(f) Nothing shall preclude a party to an action under this section from appearing through legal counsel or in propria persona.

(g) The remedy provided by this section is nonexclusive and nothing in this section shall be construed to preclude or limit any rights the management of a mobilehome park may have to terminate a tenancy. *(Added by Stats.1991, c. 270 (S.B.459), § 1. Amended by Stats.2012, c. 99 (A.B.2272), § 1; Stats.2015, c. 176 (S.B.244), § 1, eff. Jan. 1, 2016.)*

Cross References

Civil actions, actions treated as a limited civil case, conditions, see Code of Civil Procedure § 85.
Homeowner defined for purposes of this Chapter, see Civil Code § 798.9.
Management defined for purposes of this Chapter, see Civil Code § 798.2.
Mobilehome defined for purposes of this Chapter, see Civil Code § 798.3.
Mobilehome park defined for purposes of this Chapter, see Civil Code § 798.4.
Resident defined for purposes of this Chapter, see Civil Code § 798.11.

Tenancy defined for purposes of this Chapter, see Civil Code § 798.12.

ARTICLE 9. SUBDIVISIONS, COOPERATIVES, AND CONDOMINIUMS

Section
799. Definitions.
799.1. Application of article.
799.1.5. Advertising; sale, exchange or rental of mobilehome; display of signs.
799.2. Listing or showing mobilehome by ownership or management; written authorization.
799.2.5. Right of entry to mobilehome by ownership or management; prior written consent; revocation of consent; emergency.
799.3. Sale to third party; prohibition against required removal.
799.4. Prior approval of purchaser; grounds for withholding.
799.5. Purchaser; compliance with residency based on age requirements for housing for older persons regulations; compliance with federal act.
799.6. Waiver of rights; public policy.
799.7. Interruption in utility service; written advance notice; liability; emergency.
799.8. School facilities fee; written disclosure; time.
799.9. Homeowner sharing mobilehome with others; live-in health care, live-in support care or supervision; relatives requiring care.
799.10. Political campaign signs; right to display; restrictions.
799.11. Installation of accommodations for the disabled.

§ 799. Definitions

As used in this article:

(a) "Ownership or management" means the ownership or management of a subdivision, cooperative, or condominium for mobilehomes, or of a resident-owned mobilehome park.

(b) "Resident" means a person who maintains a residence in a subdivision, cooperative, or condominium for mobilehomes, or a resident-owned mobilehome park.

(c) "Resident–owned mobilehome park" means any entity other than a subdivision, cooperative, or condominium for mobilehomes, through which the residents have an ownership interest in the mobilehome park. *(Added by Stats.1978, c. 1031, p. 3178, § 1. Amended by Stats.1979, c. 198, p. 437, § 2; Stats.1996, c. 61 (S.B.1585), § 2, eff. June 10, 1996; Stats.1997, c. 72 (S.B.484), § 1.)*

Cross References

Management defined for purposes of this Chapter, see Civil Code § 798.2.
Mobilehome defined for purposes of this Chapter, see Civil Code § 798.3.
Mobilehome park defined for purposes of this Chapter, see Civil Code § 798.4.
Ownership defined for purposes of this Code, see Civil Code § 654.
Resident defined for purposes of this Chapter, see Civil Code § 798.11.

§ 799.1. Application of article

(a) Except as provided in subdivision (b), this article shall govern the rights of a resident who has an ownership interest in the subdivision, cooperative, or condominium for mobilehomes, or a resident-owned mobilehome park in which his or her mobilehome is located or installed. In a subdivision, cooperative, or condominium for mobilehomes, or a resident-owned mobilehome park, Article 1 (commencing with Section 798) to Article 8 (commencing with Section 798.84), inclusive, shall apply only to a resident who does not have an ownership interest in the subdivision, cooperative, or condominium for mobilehomes, or the resident-owned mobilehome park, in which his or her mobilehome is located or installed.

(b) Notwithstanding subdivision (a), in a mobilehome park owned and operated by a nonprofit mutual benefit corporation, established pursuant to Section 11010.8 of the Business and Professions Code, whose members consist of park residents where there is no recorded subdivision declaration or condominium plan, Article 1 (commencing with Section 798) to Article 8 (commencing with Section 798.84), inclusive, shall govern the rights of members who are residents that rent their space from the corporation. *(Added by Stats.1995, c. 103 (S.B.110), § 2. Amended by Stats.1996, c. 61 (S.B.1585), § 3, eff. June 10, 1996; Stats.1997, c. 72 (S.B.484), § 2; Stats.2010, c. 175 (S.B.1047), § 1; Stats.2011, c. 296 (A.B. 1023), § 33; Stats.2012, c. 492 (S.B.1421), § 1, eff. Sept. 23, 2012.)*

Cross References

Mobilehome defined for purposes of this Chapter, see Civil Code § 798.3.
Mobilehome park defined for purposes of this Chapter, see Civil Code § 798.4.
Ownership defined for purposes of this Code, see Civil Code § 654.
Ownership defined for the purposes of this Article, see Civil Code § 799.
Resident defined for purposes of this Chapter, see Civil Code § 798.11.
Resident defined for the purposes of this Article, see Civil Code § 799.
Resident-owned mobilehome park defined for the purposes of this Article, see Civil Code § 799.

§ 799.1.5. Advertising; sale, exchange or rental of mobilehome; display of signs

A homeowner or resident, or an heir, joint tenant, or personal representative of the estate who gains ownership of a mobilehome through the death of the resident of the mobilehome who was a resident at the time of his or her death, or the agent of any of those persons, may advertise the sale or exchange of his or her mobilehome or, if not prohibited by the terms of an agreement with the management or ownership, may advertise the rental of his or her mobilehome by displaying a sign in the window of the mobilehome, or by a sign posted on the side of the mobilehome facing the street, or by a sign in front of the mobilehome facing the street, stating that the mobilehome is for sale or exchange or, if not prohibited, for rent by the owner of the mobilehome or his or her agent. Any such person also may display a sign conforming to these requirements indicating that the mobilehome is on display for an "open house," unless the park rules prohibit the display of an open house sign. The sign shall state the name, address, and telephone number of the owner of the mobilehome or his or her agent. The sign face may not exceed 24 inches in width and 36 inches in height. Signs posted in front of a mobilehome pursuant to this section may be of an H-frame or A-frame design with the sign face perpendicular to, but not extending into, the street. A homeowner or resident, or an heir, joint tenant, or personal representative of the estate who gains ownership of a mobilehome through the death of the resident of the mobilehome who was a resident at the time of his or her death, or the agent of any of those persons, may attach to the sign or their mobilehome tubes or holders for leaflets that provide information on the mobilehome for sale, exchange, or rent. *(Formerly § 799.1, added by Stats.1978, c. 1031, p. 3178, § 1. Amended by Stats.1978, c. 1033, p. 3191, § 23; Stats.1979, c. 198, p. 437, § 3; Stats.1983, c. 519, § 13. Renumbered § 799.1.5 and amended by Stats.1995, c. 103 (S.B.110), § 1. Amended by Stats.2004, c. 302 (A.B.2351), § 5; Stats.2005, c. 22 (S.B.1108), § 12.)*

Cross References

Homeowner defined for purposes of this Chapter, see Civil Code § 798.9.
Management defined for purposes of this Chapter, see Civil Code § 798.2.
Mobilehome defined for purposes of this Chapter, see Civil Code § 798.3.
Ownership defined for purposes of this Code, see Civil Code § 654.
Ownership defined for the purposes of this Article, see Civil Code § 799.
Resident defined for purposes of this Chapter, see Civil Code § 798.11.
Resident defined for the purposes of this Article, see Civil Code § 799.

§ 799.2. Listing or showing mobilehome by ownership or management; written authorization

The ownership or management shall not show or list for sale a mobilehome owned by a resident without first obtaining the resident's written authorization. The authorization shall specify the terms and conditions regarding the showing or listing.

Nothing contained in this section shall be construed to affect the provisions of the Health and Safety Code governing the licensing of mobilehome salesmen. *(Added by Stats.1978, c. 1031, p. 3178, § 1. Amended by Stats.1979, c. 198, p. 437, § 4; Stats.1983, c. 519, § 14.)*

Cross References

Management defined for purposes of this Chapter, see Civil Code § 798.2.
Mobilehome defined for purposes of this Chapter, see Civil Code § 798.3.
Ownership defined for purposes of this Code, see Civil Code § 654.
Ownership defined for the purposes of this Article, see Civil Code § 799.
Resident defined for purposes of this Chapter, see Civil Code § 798.11.
Resident defined for the purposes of this Article, see Civil Code § 799.

§ 799.2.5. Right of entry to mobilehome by ownership or management; prior written consent; revocation of consent; emergency

(a) Except as provided in subdivision (b), the ownership or management shall have no right of entry to a mobilehome without the prior written consent of the resident. The consent may be revoked in writing by the resident at any time.

§ 799.2.5

The ownership or management shall have a right of entry upon the land upon which a mobilehome is situated for maintenance of utilities, trees, and driveways, for maintenance of the premises in accordance with the rules and regulations of the subdivision, cooperative, or condominium for mobilehomes, or resident-owned mobilehome park when the homeowner or resident fails to so maintain the premises, and protection of the subdivision, cooperative, or condominium for mobilehomes, or resident-owned mobilehome park at any reasonable time, but not in a manner or at a time that would interfere with the resident's quiet enjoyment.

(b) The ownership or management may enter a mobilehome without the prior written consent of the resident in case of an emergency or when the resident has abandoned the mobilehome. (Added by Stats.2004, c. 302 (A.B.2351), § 6. Amended by Stats.2006, c. 538 (S.B.1852), § 40.)

Cross References

Homeowner defined for purposes of this Chapter, see Civil Code § 798.9.
Management defined for purposes of this Chapter, see Civil Code § 798.2.
Mobilehome defined for purposes of this Chapter, see Civil Code § 798.3.
Mobilehome park defined for purposes of this Chapter, see Civil Code § 798.4.
Ownership defined for purposes of this Code, see Civil Code § 654.
Ownership defined for the purposes of this Article, see Civil Code § 799.
Resident defined for purposes of this Chapter, see Civil Code § 798.11.
Resident defined for the purposes of this Article, see Civil Code § 799.
Resident-owned mobilehome park defined for the purposes of this Article, see Civil Code § 799.

§ 799.3. Sale to third party; prohibition against required removal

The ownership or management shall not require the removal of a mobilehome from a subdivision, cooperative, or condominium for mobilehomes, or resident-owned mobilehome park in the event of its sale to a third party. (Added by Stats.1978, c. 1031, p. 3178, § 1. Amended by Stats.1978, c. 1033, p. 3191, § 24; Stats.1979, c. 198, p. 437, § 5; Stats.1996, c. 61 (S.B.1585), § 4, eff. June 10, 1996; Stats.1997, c. 72 (S.B.484), § 3.)

Cross References

Management defined for purposes of this Chapter, see Civil Code § 798.2.
Mobilehome defined for purposes of this Chapter, see Civil Code § 798.3.
Mobilehome park defined for purposes of this Chapter, see Civil Code § 798.4.
Ownership defined for purposes of this Code, see Civil Code § 654.
Ownership defined for the purposes of this Article, see Civil Code § 799.
Resident defined for purposes of this Chapter, see Civil Code § 798.11.
Resident defined for the purposes of this Article, see Civil Code § 799.
Resident-owned mobilehome park defined for the purposes of this Article, see Civil Code § 799.

§ 799.4. Prior approval of purchaser; grounds for withholding

The ownership or management may require the right to prior approval of the purchaser of a mobilehome that will remain in the subdivision, cooperative, or condominium for mobilehomes, or resident-owned mobilehome park and that the selling resident, or his or her agent give notice of the sale to the ownership or management before the close of the sale. Approval cannot be withheld if the purchaser has the financial ability to pay the fees and charges of the subdivision, cooperative, or condominium for mobilehomes, or resident-owned mobilehome park unless the ownership or management reasonably determines that, based on the purchaser's prior residences, he or she will not comply with the rules and regulations of the subdivision, cooperative, or condominium for mobilehomes, or resident-owned mobilehome park. (Added by Stats.1978, c. 1031, p. 3178, § 1. Amended by Stats.1979, c. 198, p. 437, § 6; Stats.1983, c. 519, § 15; Stats.1996, c. 61 (S.B.1585), § 5, eff. June 10, 1996; Stats.1997, c. 72 (S.B.484), § 4.)

Cross References

Management defined for purposes of this Chapter, see Civil Code § 798.2.
Mobilehome defined for purposes of this Chapter, see Civil Code § 798.3.
Mobilehome park defined for purposes of this Chapter, see Civil Code § 798.4.
Ownership defined for purposes of this Code, see Civil Code § 654.
Ownership defined for the purposes of this Article, see Civil Code § 799.
Resident defined for purposes of this Chapter, see Civil Code § 798.11.
Resident defined for the purposes of this Article, see Civil Code § 799.
Resident-owned mobilehome park defined for the purposes of this Article, see Civil Code § 799.

§ 799.5. Purchaser; compliance with residency based on age requirements for housing for older persons regulations; compliance with federal act

The ownership or management may require that a purchaser of a mobilehome that will remain in the subdivision, cooperative, or condominium for mobilehomes, or resident-owned mobilehome park comply with any rule or regulation limiting residency based on age requirements for housing for older persons, provided that the rule or regulation complies with the provisions of the federal Fair Housing Act, as amended by Public Law 104–76, and implementing regulations. (Added by Stats.1978, c. 1031, p. 3178, § 1. Amended by Stats.1993, c. 1277 (A.B.2244), § 2; Stats.1996, c. 61 (S.B.1585), § 6, eff. June 10, 1996; Stats.1997, c. 72 (S.B.484), § 5.)

Cross References

Alcoholic beverages, club licenses for condominium homeowners' associations, license denied for discriminatory practices, see Business and Professions Code § 23428.20.
Bond and loan insurance, occupancy of housing for which a loan is insured, discrimination prohibited, see Health and Safety Code § 51602.

California housing finance agency, equal opportunity without discrimination, see Health and Safety Code § 50955.
Community development and housing, declaration of state antidiscrimination policy, discrimination prohibited, see Health and Safety Code § 33050.
Community development and housing, financial discrimination prohibited, see Health and Safety Code § 35811.
Community redevelopment, property disposition rehabilitation, nondiscrimination and nonsegregation, see Health and Safety Code §§ 33435 and 33436.
Density bonuses for mobilehome parks that limit residency based on age requirements pursuant to this section, see Government Code § 65915.
Floating home residency, private club membership not to be denied on discrimination basis, see Civil Code § 800.25.
Historical property rehabilitation, prohibited discrimination, see Health and Safety Code § 37630.
Management defined for purposes of this Chapter, see Civil Code § 798.2.
Mobilehome defined for purposes of this Chapter, see Civil Code § 798.3.
Mobilehome park defined for purposes of this Chapter, see Civil Code § 798.4.
Mobilehome residency, private club membership not to be denied on discrimination basis, see Civil Code § 798.20.
Ownership defined for purposes of this Code, see Civil Code § 654.
Ownership defined for the purposes of this Article, see Civil Code § 799.
Planning and zoning, prohibition against discrimination, exceptions, see Government Code § 65008.
Real estate licensees, grounds for disciplinary action, induced sale or listing due to adverse impact of persons in neighborhood with certain characteristics, see Business and Professions Code § 10177.
Real property, discriminatory restrictions in deeds, invalidity, see Civil Code §§ 782 and 782.5.
Redevelopment construction loans, nondiscrimination in construction and disposition of residences, see Health and Safety Code § 33769.
Resident defined for purposes of this Chapter, see Civil Code § 798.11.
Resident defined for the purposes of this Article, see Civil Code § 799.
Residential property rehabilitation, open housing, equal opportunity in employment and contracts, see Health and Safety Code § 37923.
Resident-owned mobilehome park defined for the purposes of this Article, see Civil Code § 799.

§ 799.6. Waiver of rights; public policy

No agreement shall contain any provision by which the purchaser waives his or her rights under the provisions of this article. Any such waiver shall be deemed contrary to public policy and void and unenforceable. *(Formerly § 799.8, added by Stats.1978, c. 1031, p. 3178, § 1. Renumbered § 799.6 and amended by Stats.1978, c. 1033, p. 3192, § 27. Amended by Stats.1983, c. 519, § 16.)*

§ 799.7. Interruption in utility service; written advance notice; liability; emergency

The ownership or management shall provide, by posting notice on the mobilehomes of all affected homeowners and residents, at least 72 hours' written advance notice of an interruption in utility service of more than two hours for the maintenance, repair, or replacement of facilities of utility systems over which the management has control within the subdivision, cooperative, or condominium for mobilehomes, or resident-owned mobilehome park, if the interruption is not due to an emergency. The ownership or management shall be liable only for actual damages sustained by a homeowner or resident for violation of this section.

"Emergency," for purposes of this section, means the interruption of utility service resulting from an accident or act of nature, or cessation of service caused by other than the management's regular or planned maintenance, repair, or replacement of utility facilities. *(Added by Stats.1992, c. 317 (S.B.1389), § 2. Amended by Stats.1996, c. 61 (S.B.1585), § 7, eff. June 10, 1996; Stats.1997, c. 72 (S.B.484), § 6.)*

Cross References

Homeowner defined for purposes of this Chapter, see Civil Code § 798.9.
Management defined for purposes of this Chapter, see Civil Code § 798.2.
Mobilehome defined for purposes of this Chapter, see Civil Code § 798.3.
Mobilehome park defined for purposes of this Chapter, see Civil Code § 798.4.
Ownership defined for purposes of this Code, see Civil Code § 654.
Ownership defined for the purposes of this Article, see Civil Code § 799.
Resident defined for purposes of this Chapter, see Civil Code § 798.11.
Resident defined for the purposes of this Article, see Civil Code § 799.
Resident-owned mobilehome park defined for the purposes of this Article, see Civil Code § 799.

§ 799.8. School facilities fee; written disclosure; time

The management, at the time of an application for residency, shall disclose in writing to any person who proposes to purchase or install a manufactured home or mobilehome on a space or lot, on which the construction of the pad or foundation system commenced after September 1, 1986, and no other manufactured home or mobilehome was previously located, installed, or occupied, that the manufactured home or mobilehome may be subject to a school facilities fee under Sections 53080 and 53080.4 of, and Chapter 4.9 (commencing with Section 65995) of Division 1 of Title 7 of, the Government Code. *(Added by Stats.1994, c. 983 (S.B.1461), § 2.)*

Cross References

Management defined for purposes of this Chapter, see Civil Code § 798.2.
Mobilehome defined for purposes of this Chapter, see Civil Code § 798.3.

§ 799.9. Homeowner sharing mobilehome with others; live-in health care, live-in support care or supervision; relatives requiring care

(a) A homeowner may share his or her mobilehome with any person 18 years of age or older if that person is providing live-in health care, live-in supportive care, or supervision to the homeowner. Management shall not charge a fee for the live-in caregiver, but may require written confirmation from a licensed health care professional of the need for the care or supervision, if the need is not readily apparent or already known to management. That person shall have no rights of tenancy in, and shall comply with the rules and regulations of, the subdivision, cooperative, or condominium for mobilehomes, or resident-owned mobilehome park.

(b) A senior homeowner who resides in a subdivision, cooperative, or condominium for mobilehomes, or a resident-owned mobilehome park, that has implemented rules or regulations limiting residency based on age requirements for housing for older persons, pursuant to Section 799.5, may share his or her mobilehome with any person 18 years of age or older if this person is a parent, sibling, child, or grandchild of the senior homeowner and requires live-in health care, live-in supportive care, or supervision. Management shall not charge a fee for this parent, sibling, child, or grandchild, but may require written confirmation from a licensed health care professional of the need for the care or supervision, if the need is not readily apparent or already known to management. Unless otherwise agreed upon, the management shall not be required to manage, supervise, or provide for this person's care during his or her stay in the subdivision, cooperative, or condominium for mobilehomes, or resident-owned mobilehome park. That person shall have no rights of tenancy in, and shall comply with the rules and regulations of, the subdivision, cooperative, or condominium for mobilehomes, or resident-owned mobilehome park. As used in this subdivision, "senior homeowner" means a homeowner or resident who is 55 years of age or older. (Added by Stats.1997, c. 72 (S.B.484), § 7. Amended by Stats.2008, c. 170 (S.B.1107), § 3; Stats.2017, c. 767 (S.B.147), § 2, eff. Jan. 1, 2018.)

Cross References

Homeowner defined for purposes of this Chapter, see Civil Code § 798.9.
Management defined for purposes of this Chapter, see Civil Code § 798.2.
Mobilehome defined for purposes of this Chapter, see Civil Code § 798.3.
Mobilehome park defined for purposes of this Chapter, see Civil Code § 798.4.
Resident defined for purposes of this Chapter, see Civil Code § 798.11.
Resident defined for the purposes of this Article, see Civil Code § 799.
Resident-owned mobilehome park defined for the purposes of this Article, see Civil Code § 799.
Tenancy defined for purposes of this Chapter, see Civil Code § 798.12.

§ 799.10. Political campaign signs; right to display; restrictions

A resident may not be prohibited from displaying a political campaign sign relating to a candidate for election to public office or to the initiative, referendum, or recall process in the window or on the side of a manufactured home or mobilehome, or within the site on which the home is located or installed. The size of the face of a political sign may not exceed six square feet, and the sign may not be displayed in excess of a period of time from 90 days prior to an election to 15 days following the election, unless a local ordinance within the jurisdiction where the manufactured home or mobilehome subject to this article is located imposes a more restrictive period of time for the display of such a sign. In the event of a conflict between the provisions of this section and the provisions of Part 5 (commencing with Section 4000) of Division 4, relating to the size and display of political campaign signs, the provisions of this section shall prevail. (Added by Stats.2003, c. 249 (S.B.116), § 3. Amended by Stats.2012, c. 181 (A.B.806), § 27, operative Jan. 1, 2014.)

Cross References

Mobilehome defined for purposes of this Chapter, see Civil Code § 798.3.
Resident defined for purposes of this Chapter, see Civil Code § 798.11.
Resident defined for the purposes of this Article, see Civil Code § 799.

§ 799.11. Installation of accommodations for the disabled

The ownership or management shall not prohibit a homeowner or resident from installing accommodations for the disabled on the home or the site, lot, or space on which the mobilehome is located, including, but not limited to, ramps or handrails on the outside of the home, as long as the installation of those facilities complies with code, as determined by an enforcement agency, and those facilities are installed pursuant to a permit, if required for the installation, issued by the enforcement agency. The management may require that the accommodations installed pursuant to this section be removed by the current homeowner at the time the mobilehome is removed from the park or pursuant to a written agreement between the current homeowner and the management prior to the completion of the resale of the mobilehome in place in the park. This section is not exclusive and shall not be construed to condition, affect, or supersede any other provision of law or regulation relating to accessibility or accommodation for the disabled. (Added by Stats.2008, c. 170 (S.B.1107), § 4.)

CHAPTER 2.6. RECREATIONAL VEHICLE PARK OCCUPANCY LAW

Article	Section
1. Definitions	799.20
2. General Provisions	799.40
3. Defaulting Occupants	799.55
4. Defaulting Tenants	799.65
5. Defaulting Residents	799.70
6. Liens for Recreational Vehicles and Abandoned Possessions	799.75
7. Actions and Proceedings	799.78

Cross References

Failure of registered owner of mobilehome, manufactured home, or recreational vehicle to pay costs of remediation, warehouseman's lien, see Health and Safety Code § 25400.47.
Housing development approvals, Camp Fire Housing Assistance Act of 2019, see Government Code § 65913.15.
Methamphetamine Contaminated Property Cleanup Act of 2005, abatement of nonremediated mobilehome, manufactured home, or recreational vehicle, see Health and Safety Code § 25400.28.
Methamphetamine Contaminated Property Cleanup Act of 2005, failure of registered owner of mobilehome, manufactured home, or recreational vehicle to pay costs of remediation, see Health and Safety Code § 25400.47.
Methamphetamine Contaminated Property Cleanup Act of 2005, vacating affected unit that is determined to be in hazardous zone by local health officer, termination of tenancy by mobilehome park or special occupancy park owner, see Health and Safety Code § 25400.25.

Mobilehome parks, annual permit to operate, penalty fee for late application, see Health and Safety Code § 18506.

Shelter crisis, emergency housing, homeless shelters, see Government Code § 8698.4.

Special occupancy parks, annual permit to operate, penalty fee for late application, see Health and Safety Code § 18870.7.

Special occupancy parks, eviction, possession and removal of property, and rights of minors, see Civil Code § 1866.

ARTICLE 1. DEFINITIONS

Section
799.20. Short title.
799.21. Definitions; construction of chapter.
799.22. Defaulting occupant.
799.23. Defaulting resident.
799.24. Defaulting tenant.
799.25. Guest.
799.26. Management.
799.27. Occupancy and occupy.
799.28. Occupant.
799.29. Recreational vehicle.
799.30. Recreational vehicle park or park.
799.31. Resident.
799.32. Tenant.
799.35 to 799.39. Repealed.

§ 799.20. Short title

This chapter shall be known and may be cited as the Recreational Vehicle Park Occupancy Law. *(Added by Stats.1992, c. 310 (A.B.3074), § 2.)*

Cross References

Occupancy defined for purposes of this Chapter, see Civil Code § 799.27.

Recreational vehicle defined for purposes of this Chapter, see Civil Code § 799.29.

§ 799.21. Definitions; construction of chapter

Unless the provisions or context otherwise require, the following definitions shall govern the construction of this chapter. *(Added by Stats.1992, c. 310 (A.B.3074), § 2.)*

§ 799.22. Defaulting occupant

"Defaulting occupant" means an occupant who fails to pay for his or her occupancy in a park or who fails to comply with reasonable written rules and regulations of the park given to the occupant upon registration. *(Added by Stats.1992, c. 310 (A.B.3074), § 2.)*

Cross References

Occupancy defined for purposes of this Chapter, see Civil Code § 799.27.

Occupant defined for purposes of this Chapter, see Civil Code § 799.28.

Registration agreements, form and contents, see Civil Code § 799.43.

§ 799.23. Defaulting resident

"Defaulting resident" means a resident who fails to pay for his or her occupancy in a park, fails to comply with reasonable written rules and regulations of the park given to the resident upon registration or during the term of his or her occupancy in the park, or who violates any of the provisions contained in Article 5 (commencing with Section 799.70). *(Added by Stats.1992, c. 310 (A.B.3074), § 2.)*

Cross References

Occupancy defined for purposes of this Chapter, see Civil Code § 799.27.

Resident defined for purposes of this Chapter, see Civil Code § 799.31.

§ 799.24. Defaulting tenant

"Defaulting tenant" means a tenant who fails to pay for his or her occupancy in a park or fails to comply with reasonable written rules and regulations of the park given to the person upon registration or during the term of his or her occupancy in the park. *(Added by Stats.1992, c. 310 (A.B.3074), § 2.)*

Cross References

Occupancy defined for purposes of this Chapter, see Civil Code § 799.27.

Tenant defined for purposes of this Chapter, see Civil Code § 799.32.

§ 799.25. Guest

"Guest" means a person who is lawfully occupying a recreational vehicle located in a park but who is not an occupant, tenant, or resident. An occupant, tenant, or resident shall be responsible for the actions of his or her guests. *(Added by Stats.1992, c. 310 (A.B.3074), § 2.)*

Cross References

Occupant defined for purposes of this Chapter, see Civil Code § 799.28.

Recreational vehicle defined for purposes of this Chapter, see Civil Code § 799.29.

Resident defined for purposes of this Chapter, see Civil Code § 799.31.

Tenant defined for purposes of this Chapter, see Civil Code § 799.32.

§ 799.26. Management

"Management" means the owner of a recreational vehicle park or an agent or representative authorized to act on his or her behalf in connection with matters relating to the park. *(Added by Stats.1992, c. 310 (A.B.3074), § 2.)*

Cross References

Recreational vehicle defined for purposes of this Chapter, see Civil Code § 799.29.

§ 799.27. Occupancy and occupy

"Occupancy" and "occupy" refer to the use of a recreational vehicle park lot by an occupant, tenant, or resident. *(Added by Stats.1992, c. 310 (A.B.3074), § 2.)*

Cross References

Occupancy defined for purposes of this Chapter, see Civil Code § 799.27.

Occupant defined for purposes of this Chapter, see Civil Code § 799.28.

Recreational vehicle defined for purposes of this Chapter, see Civil Code § 799.29.

Resident defined for purposes of this Chapter, see Civil Code § 799.31.

§ 799.27

Tenant defined for purposes of this Chapter, see Civil Code § 799.32.

§ 799.28. Occupant

"Occupant" means the owner or operator of a recreational vehicle who has occupied a lot in a park for 30 days or less. *(Added by Stats.1992, c. 310 (A.B.3074), § 2.)*

Cross References

California Safe Drinking Water Act, public water system, display of consumer confidence reports, see Health and Safety Code § 116470.

Occupant defined for purposes of this Chapter, see Civil Code § 799.28.

Recreational vehicle defined for purposes of this Chapter, see Civil Code § 799.29.

§ 799.29. Recreational vehicle

"Recreational vehicle" has the same meaning as defined in Section 18010 of the Health and Safety Code. *(Added by Stats.1992, c. 310 (A.B.3074), § 2.)*

Cross References

Mobilehome as defined not to include recreational vehicle as designated in this section, see Civil Code § 798.3.

§ 799.30. Recreational vehicle park or park

"Recreational vehicle park" or "park" has the same meaning as defined in Section 18862.39 of the Health and Safety Code. *(Added by Stats.1992, c. 310 (A.B.3074), § 2. Amended by Stats.2004, c. 530 (A.B.1964), § 1.)*

Cross References

Recreational vehicle defined for purposes of this Chapter, see Civil Code § 799.29.

§ 799.31. Resident

"Resident" means a tenant who has occupied a lot in a park for nine months or more. *(Added by Stats.1992, c. 310 (A.B.3074), § 2.)*

Cross References

Tenant defined for purposes of this Chapter, see Civil Code § 799.32.

§ 799.32. Tenant

"Tenant" means the owner or operator of a recreational vehicle who has occupied a lot in a park for more than 30 consecutive days. *(Added by Stats.1992, c. 310 (A.B.3074), § 2.)*

Cross References

Recreational vehicle defined for purposes of this Chapter, see Civil Code § 799.29.

§§ 799.35 to 799.39. Repealed by Stats.1992, c. 310 (A.B. 3074), § 1

ARTICLE 2. GENERAL PROVISIONS

Section
799.40. Cumulative and additional rights.
799.41. Application to mobilehomes.
799.42. Occupant registration or tenant rental agreements; waiver of rights.
799.43. Registration agreements; form and contents.
799.44. Rules and regulations; copy given at registration.
799.45. Offer of rental agreement.
799.46. Removal of recreational vehicle; display of warning signs.
799.47. Repealed.
799.48. Repealed.
799.49 to 799.51. Repealed.

§ 799.40. Cumulative and additional rights

The rights created by this chapter shall be cumulative and in addition to any other legal rights the management of a park may have against a defaulting occupant, tenant, or resident, or that an occupant, tenant, or resident may have against the management of a park. *(Added by Stats.1992, c. 310 (A.B.3074), § 2.)*

Cross References

Defaulting occupant defined for purposes of this Chapter, see Civil Code § 799.22.

Management defined for purposes of this Chapter, see Civil Code § 799.26.

Occupant defined for purposes of this Chapter, see Civil Code § 799.28.

Resident defined for purposes of this Chapter, see Civil Code § 799.31.

Tenant defined for purposes of this Chapter, see Civil Code § 799.32.

§ 799.41. Application to mobilehomes

Nothing in this chapter shall apply to a mobilehome as defined in Section 18008 of the Health and Safety Code or to a manufactured home as defined in Section 18007 of the Health and Safety Code. *(Added by Stats.1992, c. 310 (A.B.3074), § 2.)*

§ 799.42. Occupant registration or tenant rental agreements; waiver of rights

No occupant registration agreement or tenant rental agreement shall contain a provision by which the occupant or tenant waives his or her rights under the provisions of this chapter, and any waiver of these rights shall be deemed contrary to public policy and void. *(Added by Stats.1992, c. 310 (A.B.3074), § 2.)*

Cross References

Occupant defined for purposes of this Chapter, see Civil Code § 799.28.

Tenant defined for purposes of this Chapter, see Civil Code § 799.32.

§ 799.43. Registration agreements; form and contents

The registration agreement between a park and an occupant thereof shall be in writing and shall contain, in addition to the provisions otherwise required by law to be included, the term of the occupancy and the rent therefor, the fees, if any, to be charged for services which will be provided by the park, and a statement of the grounds for which a defaulting occupant's recreational vehicle may be removed as specified in Section 799.22 without a judicial hearing after the service of a 72-hour notice pursuant to this chapter and the telephone number of the local traffic law enforcement agency. *(Added by Stats.1992, c. 310 (A.B.3074), § 2.)*

Cross References

Occupancy defined for purposes of this Chapter, see Civil Code § 799.27.
Occupant defined for purposes of this Chapter, see Civil Code § 799.28.
Recreational vehicle defined for purposes of this Chapter, see Civil Code § 799.29.

§ 799.44. Rules and regulations; copy given at registration

At the time of registration, an occupant shall be given a copy of the rules and regulations of the park. *(Added by Stats.1992, c. 310 (A.B.3074), § 2.)*

Cross References

Occupant defined for purposes of this Chapter, see Civil Code § 799.28.

§ 799.45. Offer of rental agreement

The management may offer a rental agreement to an occupant of the park who intends to remain in the park for a period in excess of 30 consecutive days. *(Added by Stats. 1992, c. 310 (A.B.3074), § 2.)*

Cross References

Management defined for purposes of this Chapter, see Civil Code § 799.26.
Occupant defined for purposes of this Chapter, see Civil Code § 799.28.

§ 799.46. Removal of recreational vehicle; display of warning signs

At the entry to a recreational vehicle park, or within the separate designated section for recreational vehicles within a mobilehome park, there shall be displayed in plain view on the property a sign indicating that the recreational vehicle may be removed from the premises for the reasons specified in Sections 799.22 and 1866 and containing the telephone number of the local traffic law enforcement agency. Nothing in this section shall prevent management from additionally displaying the sign in other locations within the park. *(Added by Stats.1992, c. 310 (A.B.3074), § 2. Amended by Stats.2004, c. 530 (A.B.1964), § 2.)*

Cross References

Management defined for purposes of this Chapter, see Civil Code § 799.26.
Recreational vehicle defined for purposes of this Chapter, see Civil Code § 799.29.

§ 799.47. Repealed by Stats.1992, c. 310 (A.B.3074), § 1

§ 799.48. Repealed by Stats.1990, c. 317 (A.B.3177), § 4

§§ 799.49 to 799.51. Repealed by Stats.1992, c. 310 (A.B. 3074), § 1

ARTICLE 3. DEFAULTING OCCUPANTS

Section
799.55. Removal of recreational vehicle; notice; correction of payment deficiency.

Section
799.56. Service of notice on defaulting occupant; incapacitated occupants or nonmotorized vehicles; date to quit.
799.57. Authority of management to remove recreational vehicle; statement in notice.
799.58. Removal of persons from recreational vehicle; removal of vehicle; voidance of notice.
799.59. Standard of care in removing vehicles.

§ 799.55. Removal of recreational vehicle; notice; correction of payment deficiency

Except as provided in subdivision (b) of Section 1866, as a prerequisite to the right of management to have a defaulting occupant's recreational vehicle removed from the lot which is the subject of the registration agreement between the park and the occupant pursuant to Section 799.57, the management shall serve a 72–hour written notice as prescribed in Section 799.56. A defaulting occupant may correct his or her payment deficiency within the 72–hour period during normal business hours. *(Added by Stats.1992, c. 310 (A.B.3074), § 2. Amended by Stats.2004, c. 530 (A.B.1964), § 3.)*

Cross References

Defaulting occupant defined for purposes of this Chapter, see Civil Code § 799.22.
Management defined for purposes of this Chapter, see Civil Code § 799.26.
Occupant defined for purposes of this Chapter, see Civil Code § 799.28.
Recreational vehicle defined for purposes of this Chapter, see Civil Code § 799.29.

§ 799.56. Service of notice on defaulting occupant; incapacitated occupants or nonmotorized vehicles; date to quit

(a) The 72-hour written notice shall be served by delivering a copy to the defaulting occupant personally or to a person of suitable age and discretion who is occupying the recreational vehicle located on the lot. In the latter event, a copy of the notice shall also be affixed in a conspicuous place on the recreational vehicle and shall be sent through the mail addressed to the occupant at the place where the property is located and, if available, any other address which the occupant has provided to management in the registration agreement. Delivery of the 72-hour notice to a defaulting occupant who is incapable of removing the occupant's recreational vehicle from the park because of a physical incapacity shall not be sufficient to satisfy the requirements of this section.

(b) In the event that the defaulting occupant is incapable of removing the occupant's recreational vehicle from the park because of a physical incapacity or because the recreational vehicle is not motorized and cannot be moved by the occupant's vehicle, the default shall be cured within 72 hours, but the date to quit shall be no less than seven days after service of the notice.

(c) The management shall also serve a copy of the notice to the city police if the park is located in a city, or, if the park is located in an unincorporated area, to the county sheriff. *(Added by Stats.1992, c. 310 (A.B.3074), § 2.)*

Cross References

Defaulting occupant defined for purposes of this Chapter, see Civil Code § 799.22.

Management defined for purposes of this Chapter, see Civil Code § 799.26.

Occupant defined for purposes of this Chapter, see Civil Code § 799.28.

Recreational vehicle defined for purposes of this Chapter, see Civil Code § 799.29.

§ 799.57. Authority of management to remove recreational vehicle; statement in notice

The written 72-hour notice shall state that if the defaulting occupant does not remove the recreational vehicle from the premises of the park within 72 hours after receipt of the notice, the management has authority pursuant to Section 799.58 to have the recreational vehicle removed from the lot to the nearest secured storage facility. *(Added by Stats.1992, c. 310 (A.B.3074), § 2.)*

Cross References

Defaulting occupant defined for purposes of this Chapter, see Civil Code § 799.22.

Management defined for purposes of this Chapter, see Civil Code § 799.26.

Occupant defined for purposes of this Chapter, see Civil Code § 799.28.

Recreational vehicle defined for purposes of this Chapter, see Civil Code § 799.29.

§ 799.58. Removal of persons from recreational vehicle; removal of vehicle; voidance of notice

Subsequent to serving a copy of the notice specified in this article to the city police or county sheriff, whichever is appropriate, and after the expiration of 72 hours following service of the notice on the defaulting occupant, the police or sheriff, shall remove or cause to be removed any person in the recreational vehicle. The management may then remove or cause the removal of a defaulting occupant's recreational vehicle parked on the premises of the park to the nearest secured storage facility. The notice shall be void seven days after the date of service of the notice. *(Added by Stats.1992, c. 310 (A.B.3074), § 2.)*

Cross References

Defaulting occupant defined for purposes of this Chapter, see Civil Code § 799.22.

Management defined for purposes of this Chapter, see Civil Code § 799.26.

Occupant defined for purposes of this Chapter, see Civil Code § 799.28.

Recreational vehicle defined for purposes of this Chapter, see Civil Code § 799.29.

§ 799.59. Standard of care in removing vehicles

When the management removes or causes the removal of a defaulting occupant's recreational vehicle, the management and the individual or entity that removes the recreational vehicle shall exercise reasonable and ordinary care in removing the recreational vehicle to the storage area. *(Added by Stats.1992, c. 310 (A.B.3074), § 2.)*

Cross References

Defaulting occupant defined for purposes of this Chapter, see Civil Code § 799.22.

Management defined for purposes of this Chapter, see Civil Code § 799.26.

Occupant defined for purposes of this Chapter, see Civil Code § 799.28.

Recreational vehicle defined for purposes of this Chapter, see Civil Code § 799.29.

ARTICLE 4. DEFAULTING TENANTS

Section
799.65. Termination of tenancy for nonpayment of rent, utilities, or service charges; notice; liability of tenant.
799.66. Termination or refusal to renew right of occupancy for other than nonpayment of rent or other charges.
799.67. Evictions.

§ 799.65. Termination of tenancy for nonpayment of rent, utilities, or service charges; notice; liability of tenant

The management may terminate the tenancy of a defaulting tenant for nonpayment of rent, utilities, or reasonable incidental service charges, provided the amount due shall have been unpaid for a period of five days from its due date, and provided the tenant has been given a three-day written notice subsequent to that five-day period to pay the total amount due or to vacate the park. For purposes of this section, the five-day period does not include the date the payment is due. The three-day notice shall be given to the tenant in the manner prescribed by Section 1162 of the Code of Civil Procedure. Any payment of the total charges due, prior to the expiration of the three-day period, shall cure any default of the tenant. In the event the tenant does not pay prior to the expiration of the three-day notice period, the tenant shall remain liable for all payments due up until the time the tenancy is vacated. *(Added by Stats.1992, c. 310 (A.B.3074), § 2.)*

Cross References

Defaulting tenant defined for purposes of this Chapter, see Civil Code § 799.24.

Management defined for purposes of this Chapter, see Civil Code § 799.26.

Tenant defined for purposes of this Chapter, see Civil Code § 799.32.

§ 799.66. Termination or refusal to renew right of occupancy for other than nonpayment of rent or other charges

The management may terminate or refuse to renew the right of occupancy of a tenant for other than nonpayment of rent or other charges upon the giving of a written notice to the tenant in the manner prescribed by Section 1162 of the Code of Civil Procedure to remove the recreational vehicle from the park. The notice need not state the cause for termination but shall provide not less than 30 days' notice of termination of the tenancy. *(Added by Stats.1992, c. 310 (A.B.3074), § 2. Amended by Stats.1994, c. 167 (S.B.1349), § 1.)*

Cross References

Management defined for purposes of this Chapter, see Civil Code § 799.26.
Occupancy defined for purposes of this Chapter, see Civil Code § 799.27.
Recreational vehicle defined for purposes of this Chapter, see Civil Code § 799.29.
Tenant defined for purposes of this Chapter, see Civil Code § 799.32.

§ 799.67. Evictions

Evictions pursuant to this article shall be subject to the requirements set forth in Chapter 4 (commencing with Section 1159) of Title 3 of Part 3 of the Code of Civil Procedure, except as otherwise provided in this article. *(Added by Stats.1992, c. 310 (A.B.3074), § 2.)*

ARTICLE 5. DEFAULTING RESIDENTS

Section
799.70. Notice of termination; reasons for termination.
799.71. Evictions.

§ 799.70. Notice of termination; reasons for termination

The management may terminate or refuse to renew the right of occupancy of a defaulting resident upon the giving of a written notice to the defaulting resident in the manner prescribed by Section 1162 of the Code of Civil Procedure to remove the recreational vehicle from the park. This notice shall provide not less than 60 days' notice of termination of the right of occupancy and shall specify one of the following reasons for the termination of the right of occupancy:

(a) Nonpayment of rent, utilities, or reasonable incidental service charges; provided, that the amount due has been unpaid for a period of five days from its due date, and provided that the resident shall be given a three-day written notice subsequent to that five-day period to pay the total amount due or to vacate the park. For purposes of this subdivision, the five-day period does not include the date the payment is due. The three-day notice shall be given to the resident in the manner prescribed by Section 1162 of the Code of Civil Procedure. The three-day notice may be given at the same time as the 60-day notice required for termination of the right of occupancy; provided, however, that any payment of the total charges due, prior to the expiration of the three-day period, shall cure any default of the resident. In the event the resident does not pay prior to the expiration of the three-day notice period, the resident shall remain liable for all payments due up until the time the tenancy is vacated.

(b) Failure of the resident to comply with a local ordinance or state law or regulation relating to the recreational vehicle park or recreational vehicles within a reasonable time after the resident or the management receives a notice of noncompliance from the appropriate governmental agency and the resident has been provided with a copy of that notice.

(c) Conduct by the resident or guest, upon the park premises, which constitutes a substantial annoyance to other occupants, tenants, or residents.

(d) Conviction of the resident of prostitution, or a felony controlled substance offense, if the act resulting in the conviction was committed anywhere on the premises of the park, including, but not limited to, within the resident's recreational vehicle.

However, the right of occupancy may not be terminated for the reason specified in this subdivision if the person convicted of the offense has permanently vacated, and does not subsequently reoccupy, the recreational vehicle.

(e) Failure of the resident or a guest to comply with a rule or regulation of the park which is part of the rental agreement or any amendment thereto.

No act or omission of the resident or guest shall constitute a failure to comply with a rule or regulation unless the resident has been notified in writing of the violation and has failed to correct the violation within seven days of the issuance of the written notification.

(f) Condemnation of the park.

(g) Change of use of the park or any portion thereof. *(Added by Stats.1992, c. 310 (A.B.3074), § 2.)*

Cross References

Felonies, definition and penalties, see Penal Code §§ 17, 18.
Guest defined for purposes of this Chapter, see Civil Code § 799.25.
Management defined for purposes of this Chapter, see Civil Code § 799.26.
Occupancy defined for purposes of this Chapter, see Civil Code § 799.27.
Occupant defined for purposes of this Chapter, see Civil Code § 799.28.
Recreational vehicle defined for purposes of this Chapter, see Civil Code § 799.29.
Resident defined for purposes of this Chapter, see Civil Code § 799.31.
Tenant defined for purposes of this Chapter, see Civil Code § 799.32.

§ 799.71. Evictions

Evictions pursuant to this article shall be subject to the requirements set forth in Chapter 4 (commencing with Section 1159) of Title 3 of Part 3 of the Code of Civil Procedure, except as otherwise provided in this article. *(Added by Stats.1992, c. 310 (A.B.3074), § 2.)*

ARTICLE 6. LIENS FOR RECREATIONAL VEHICLES AND ABANDONED POSSESSIONS

Section
799.75. Liens; disposition of abandoned possessions.

§ 799.75. Liens; disposition of abandoned possessions

The management shall have a lien upon the recreational vehicle and the contents therein for the proper charges due from a defaulting occupant, tenant, or resident. Such a lien shall be identical to that authorized by Section 1861, and shall be enforced as provided by Sections 1861 to 1861.28, inclusive. Disposition of any possessions abandoned by an occupant, tenant, or resident at a park shall be performed pursuant to Chapter 5 (commencing with Section 1980) of Title 5 of Part 4 of Division 3. *(Added by Stats.1992, c. 310 (A.B.3074), § 2.)*

§ 799.75

Cross References

Defaulting occupant defined for purposes of this Chapter, see Civil Code § 799.22.

Management defined for purposes of this Chapter, see Civil Code § 799.26.

Occupant defined for purposes of this Chapter, see Civil Code § 799.28.

Recreational vehicle defined for purposes of this Chapter, see Civil Code § 799.29.

Resident defined for purposes of this Chapter, see Civil Code § 799.31.

Tenant defined for purposes of this Chapter, see Civil Code § 799.32.

ARTICLE 7. ACTIONS AND PROCEEDINGS

Section
799.78. Attorney's fees and costs.
799.79. Willful violation by management; additional penalty.

§ 799.78. Attorney's fees and costs

In any action arising out of the provisions of this chapter, the prevailing party shall be entitled to reasonable attorney's fees and costs. A party shall be deemed a prevailing party for the purposes of this section if the judgment is rendered in his or her favor or where the litigation is dismissed in his or her favor prior to or during the trial, unless the parties otherwise agree in the settlement or compromise. *(Added by Stats.1992, c. 310 (A.B.3074), § 2.)*

§ 799.79. Willful violation by management; additional penalty

In the event that an occupant, tenant, or resident or a former occupant, tenant, or resident is the prevailing party in a civil action against the management to enforce his or her rights under this chapter, the occupant, tenant, or resident, in addition to damages afforded by law, may, in the discretion of the court, be awarded an amount not to exceed five hundred dollars ($500) for each willful violation of any provision of this chapter by the management. *(Added by Stats.1992, c. 310 (A.B.3074), § 2.)*

Cross References

Management defined for purposes of this Chapter, see Civil Code § 799.26.

Occupant defined for purposes of this Chapter, see Civil Code § 799.28.

Resident defined for purposes of this Chapter, see Civil Code § 799.31.

Tenant defined for purposes of this Chapter, see Civil Code § 799.32.

CHAPTER 2.7. FLOATING HOME RESIDENCY LAW

Article	Section
1. General Provisions	800
2. Rental Agreement	800.20
3. Rules and Regulations	800.30
4. Fees and Charges	800.40
5. Homeowner Meetings	800.60
6. Termination of Tenancy	800.70
7. Transfer of a Floating Home	800.80
8. Transfer of a Floating Home Marina	800.100
9. Actions, Proceedings, and Penalties	800.200
10. Cooperatives and Condominiums	800.300

ARTICLE 1. GENERAL PROVISIONS

Section
800. Short title.
800.1. Construction of chapter.
800.2. Management.
800.3. Floating home.
800.4. Floating home marina.
800.5. Rental agreement.
800.6. Homeowner.
800.7. Change of use.
800.8. Resident.
800.9. Tenancy.

§ 800. Short title

This chapter shall be known and may be cited as the Floating Home Residency Law. *(Added by Stats.1990, c. 1505 (A.B.3139), § 1.)*

§ 800.1. Construction of chapter

Unless the provisions or context otherwise requires, the following definitions shall govern the construction of this chapter. *(Added by Stats.1990, c. 1505 (A.B.3139), § 1.)*

§ 800.2. Management

"Management" means the owner of a floating home marina or an agent or representative authorized to act on his or her behalf in connection with matters relating to a tenancy in the floating home marina. *(Added by Stats.1990, c. 1505 (A.B.3139), § 1.)*

§ 800.3. Floating home

"Floating home" has the same meaning as defined in subdivision (d) of Section 18075.55 of the Health and Safety Code. *(Added by Stats.1990, c. 1505 (A.B.3139), § 1.)*

§ 800.4. Floating home marina

"Floating home marina" means an area where five or more floating home berths are rented, or held out for rent, to accommodate floating homes, but does not include a marina * * * or harbor that satisfies all of the following:

(a) The marina or harbor * * * is managed by a nonprofit organization, the property, assets, and profits of which may not inure to any individual or group of individuals, but only to another nonprofit organization.

(b) <u>The rules and regulations of * * * the marina or harbor</u> are set by majority vote of the berthholders thereof * * *.

(c) * * * <u>The marina or harbor contains berths for fewer than 25 floating homes.</u> *(Added by Stats.1990, c. 1505 (A.B.3139), § 1. Amended by Stats.1991, c. 942 (A.B.628), § 1; Stats.2022, c. 633 (A.B.252), § 1, eff. Jan. 1, 2023.)*

Cross References

Closure, cessation or change of use of floating home marina, filing and distribution of impact report, see Government Code § 65863.12.

§ 800.5. Rental agreement

"Rental agreement" means an agreement between the management and the homeowner establishing the terms and conditions of a tenancy. A lease is a rental agreement. *(Added by Stats.1990, c. 1505 (A.B.3139), § 1.)*

§ 800.6. Homeowner

"Homeowner" means a person who owns or resides in a floating home which is in a floating home marina pursuant to a rental agreement with management. *(Added by Stats.1990, c. 1505 (A.B.3139), § 1.)*

§ 800.7. Change of use

"Change of use" means a use of the floating home marina for a purpose other than the rental, or the holding out for rent, of five or more floating home berths, and does not mean the adoption, amendment, or repeal of a floating home marina rule or regulation. A change of use may affect an entire floating home marina or any portion thereof. "Change of use" includes, but is not limited to, a change of the floating home marina or any portion thereof to a condominium, stock cooperative, or any form of ownership wherein spaces within the floating home marina are to be sold. *(Added by Stats.1990, c. 1505 (A.B.3139), § 1.)*

Cross References

Ownership defined for purposes of this Code, see Civil Code § 654.

§ 800.8. Resident

"Resident" means a homeowner or other person who lawfully occupies a floating home. *(Added by Stats.1990, c. 1505 (A.B.3139), § 1.)*

§ 800.9. Tenancy

"Tenancy" means the right of a homeowner to the use of a berth within a floating home marina on which to locate, maintain, and occupy a floating home, and accessory structures or vessels, including the use of the services and facilities of the floating home marina. *(Added by Stats.1990, c. 1505 (A.B.3139), § 1.)*

ARTICLE 2. RENTAL AGREEMENT

Section
800.20. Copies of notices; availability.
800.21. Written rental agreement; contents.
800.22. Inclusion of other provisions permitted by law.
800.23. Agreements offered to homeowners; contents.
800.24. Waiver of rights prohibited.
800.25. Private club membership not to be denied on discriminatory basis; familial status.
800.26. Copies of chapter; notice of availability.

§ 800.20. Copies of notices; availability

Unless otherwise provided, the management shall make available to floating homeowners, upon request, copies of all notices required by this article and Article 3 (commencing with Section 800.30). *(Added by Stats.1990, c. 1505 (A.B. 3139), § 1.)*

§ 800.21. Written rental agreement; contents

The rental agreement shall be in writing and shall contain, in addition to the provisions otherwise required by law to be included, all of the following:

(a) The term of the tenancy and the rent therefor.

(b) The rules and regulations of the floating home marina.

(c) A reference to this chapter and a statement that a copy of it is available from the marina upon request.

(d) A provision specifying that it is the responsibility of the management to provide and maintain physical improvements in the common facilities in good working order and condition.

(e) A description of the physical improvements to be provided the homeowner during his or her tenancy.

(f) A provision listing those services which will be provided at the time the rental agreement is executed and will continue to be offered for the term of tenancy and the fees, if any, to be charged for those services.

(g) All other provisions governing the tenancy. *(Added by Stats.1990, c. 1505 (A.B.3139), § 1.)*

§ 800.22. Inclusion of other provisions permitted by law

The rental agreement may include other provisions permitted by law, but need not include specific language contained in state or local laws not a part of this chapter. *(Added by Stats.1990, c. 1505 (A.B.3139), § 1.)*

§ 800.23. Agreements offered to homeowners; contents

(a) A homeowner shall be offered a rental agreement for (1) a term of 12 months, (2) a lesser period as mutually agreed upon by both the homeowner and the management, (3) a longer period as mutually agreed upon by both the homeowner and the management, or (4) a longer period as necessary to secure financing from a conventional lending institution.

(b) Rental agreements for a prescribed term shall not contain any terms or conditions with respect to charges for rent, utilities, or incidental reasonable service charges that would be different during the first 12 months of the agreement from the corresponding terms or conditions that would be offered to the homeowner or homeowners on a month-to-month basis. *(Added by Stats.1990, c. 1505 (A.B. 3139), § 1.)*

§ 800.24. Waiver of rights prohibited

No rental agreement for a floating home berth shall contain a provision by which the homeowner waives his or her rights under any of the provisions of this chapter. Any waiver of these rights shall be deemed contrary to public policy and void. *(Added by Stats.1990, c. 1505 (A.B.3139), § 1.)*

§ 800.25. Private club membership not to be denied on discriminatory basis; familial status

(a) Membership in any private club or organization that is a condition for tenancy in a floating home marina shall not be denied on any basis listed in subdivision (a) or (d) of Section 12955 of the Government Code, as those bases are defined in Sections 12926, 12926.1, subdivision (m) and paragraph (1) of subdivision (p) of Section 12955, and Section 12955.2 of the Government Code.

(b) Notwithstanding subdivision (a), with respect to familial status, subdivision (a) shall not be construed to apply to housing for older persons, as defined in Section 12955.9 of the Government Code. With respect to familial status, nothing in subdivision (a) shall be construed to affect

Sections 51.2, 51.3, 51.4, 51.10, 51.11, and 799.5, relating to housing for senior citizens. Subdivision (d) of Section 51 and Section 4760 of this code and subdivisions (n), (o), and (p) of Section 12955 of the Government Code shall apply to subdivision (a). *(Added by Stats.1990, c. 1505 (A.B.3139), § 1. Amended by Stats.2006, c. 578 (A.B.2800), § 7; Stats. 2012, c. 181 (A.B.806), § 28, operative Jan. 1, 2014.)*

§ 800.26. Copies of chapter; notice of availability

On or before March 12, 1991, the management shall notify all floating homeowners, in writing, that a copy of the Floating Home Residency Law is available to them, upon request, from the management. *(Added by Stats.1990, c. 1505 (A.B.3139), § 1.)*

ARTICLE 3. RULES AND REGULATIONS

Section
800.30. Common area facilities; hours.
800.31. Amendment of rules or regulations; written notice.
800.32. Right of entry; written consent required; exceptions.
800.33. Zoning or use permits; duration of lease where management lessee; written notice to homeowners.
800.34. Name and address of floating home marina owner; disclosure.
800.35. Entry in floating home by management of floating home marina; prior written consent; exceptions.
800.36. Abandonment of floating home not owned by marina; notice of belief of abandonment; delivery or mail; form; proof of nonabandonment.
800.37. Abandonment of floating home owned by marina.

§ 800.30. Common area facilities; hours

Each common area facility shall be open or available to residents at all reasonable hours, and the hours of the common area facility shall be posted at the facility. *(Added by Stats.1990, c. 1505 (A.B.3139), § 1.)*

§ 800.31. Amendment of rules or regulations; written notice

A rule or regulation of the floating home marina may be amended at any time with the consent of a homeowner, or without his or her consent upon written notice to him or her of not less than six months. Written notice to a new homeowner, whose tenancy commences within the required period of notice, of a proposed amendment shall constitute compliance with this section where the written notice is given to him or her before the inception of his or her tenancy. *(Added by Stats.1990, c. 1505 (A.B.3139), § 1.)*

§ 800.32. Right of entry; written consent required; exceptions

(a) Except as provided in subdivision (b), and notwithstanding any other provision of law to the contrary, the ownership or management of a floating home marina, cooperative, or condominium for floating homes shall have no right of entry to a floating home without the prior written consent of the resident. This consent may be revoked in writing by the resident at any time. The ownership or management shall have a right of entry into the berth in which a floating home is situated for correction of what management determines to be a hazardous condition at any time, or for maintenance of utilities, docks, and common areas at any reasonable time, but not in a manner or at a time which would interfere with the resident's quiet enjoyment.

(b) The ownership or management of a floating home marina, cooperative, or condominium may enter a floating home without the prior written consent of the resident in case of an emergency or when the resident has abandoned the floating home. *(Added by Stats.1990, c. 1505 (A.B.3139), § 1.)*

Cross References

Ownership defined for purposes of this Code, see Civil Code § 654.

§ 800.33. Zoning or use permits; duration of lease where management lessee; written notice to homeowners

(a) The management shall give written notice to all homeowners and prospective homeowners concerning the following matters: (1) the nature of the zoning or use permit under which the floating home marina operates, (2) if the floating home marina is operating pursuant to a permit subject to a renewal or expiration date, the relevant information and dates shall be included in the notice, and (3) the duration of any lease of the floating home marina, or any portion thereof, in which the management is a lessee.

(b) If a change occurs concerning the zoning or use permit under which the floating home marina operates, a change occurs to the lease under which the management is a lessee and that change could affect the homeowner, including the termination of the lease, litigation occurs regarding termination of the lease, or expiration of a use permit occurs, all homeowners shall be given written notice at least 30 days prior to the effective date of the change. Notification regarding the change of use of the floating home marina, or any portion thereof, shall be governed by subdivision (f) of Section 800.71. A prospective homeowner shall be notified prior to the inception of the tenancy. *(Added by Stats.1990, c. 1505 (A.B.3139), § 1.)*

§ 800.34. Name and address of floating home marina owner; disclosure

The management of a floating home marina shall disclose, in writing, the name and address of the floating home marina owner upon the request of a homeowner. *(Added by Stats.1990, c. 1505 (A.B.3139), § 1.)*

§ 800.35. Entry in floating home by management of floating home marina; prior written consent; exceptions

(a) The management of a floating home marina may enter a floating home, which is owned by the marina, only upon the prior written consent of the renter, except:

(1) In case of an emergency.

(2) Upon reasonable notice and during regular business hours, to make necessary or agreed repairs.

(3) When the homeowner has abandoned the premises.

(4) Pursuant to court order.

(b) The management of a floating home marina may enter a floating home, not owned by the marina, only upon prior written consent, except:

(1) In case of an emergency.

(2) When the homeowner has abandoned the premises.

(3) Pursuant to a court order. *(Added by Stats.1991, c. 942 (A.B.628), § 2.)*

§ 800.36. Abandonment of floating home not owned by marina; notice of belief of abandonment; delivery or mail; form; proof of nonabandonment

(a) A floating home not owned by a floating home marina shall be deemed abandoned by the homeowner, and the lease shall terminate, if the floating home marina gives written notice of its belief of abandonment as provided in this section and the homeowner fails to give the marina written notice, prior to the date of termination specified in the marina's notice, stating that he or she does not intend to abandon the floating home and stating an address at which the homeowner may be served by certified mail in any action for unlawful detainer of the marina.

(b) The marina may give a notice of belief of abandonment to the homeowner pursuant to this section only where the rent on the marina has been due and unpaid for at least 45 consecutive days and the marina management reasonably believes that the homeowner has abandoned the floating home. The date of termination of the lease shall be specified in the marina's notice and shall be not less than 15 days after the notice is served personally or, if mailed, not less than 18 days after the notice is deposited in the mail.

(c) The marina's notice of belief of abandonment shall be personally delivered to the homeowner or sent by first-class mail, postage prepaid, to the homeowner at his or her last known address and, if there is reason to believe that the notice sent to that address will not be received by the homeowner, also to such other address, if any, known to the marina where the homeowner may reasonably be expected to receive the notice.

(d) The notice of belief of abandonment shall be in substantially the following form:

Notice of Belief of Abandonment

To: _____

_____
(Name of homeowner)

_____
(Address of homeowner)

This notice is given pursuant to Section 800.36 of the Civil Code concerning the floating home marina leased by you at _____ (state location of the property by address or other sufficient description). The rent on this marina has been due and unpaid for 45 consecutive days and the marina believes that you have abandoned the floating home.

The floating home will be deemed abandoned within the meaning of Section 1951.2 of the Civil Code and your lease will terminate on _____ (here insert a date not less than 15 days after this notice is served personally or, if mailed, not less than 18 days after this notice is deposited in the mail) unless before that date the undersigned receives at the address indicated below a written notice from you stating both of the following:

(1) Your intent not to abandon the floating home.

(2) An address at which you may be served by certified mail in any action for unlawful detainer of the floating home marina.

You are required to pay the rent due and unpaid on this marina as required by the lease, and your failure to do so can lead to a court proceeding against you.

Dated: _____

_____
(Signature of marina manager/owner)

_____
(Type or print name of marina manager/owner)

_____
(Address to which the homeowner is to send notice)

(e) The floating home shall not be deemed to be abandoned pursuant to this section if the homeowner proves any of the following:

(1) At the time the notice of belief of abandonment was given, the rent was not due and unpaid for 45 consecutive days.

(2) At the time the notice of belief of abandonment was given, it was not reasonable for the marina to believe that the homeowner had abandoned the floating home. The fact that the marina management knew that the homeowner left personal property on the floating home does not, of itself, justify a finding that the marina management did not reasonably believe that the homeowner had abandoned the floating home.

(3) Prior to the date specified in the marina's notice, the homeowner gave written notice to the lessor stating his or her intent not to abandon the floating home and stating an address at which he or she may be served by certified mail in any action for unlawful detainer of the marina.

(4) During the period commencing 45 days before the time the notice of belief of abandonment was given and ending on the date the lease would have terminated pursuant to the notice, the homeowner paid to the marina all or a portion of the rent due and unpaid.

(f) Nothing in this section precludes the marina or the homeowner from otherwise proving that the floating home has been abandoned by the homeowner within the meaning of Section 1951.2.

(g) Nothing in this section precludes the marina from serving a notice requiring the homeowner to pay rent or quit as provided in Section 800.71 at any time permitted by that section, or affects the time and manner of giving any other notice required or permitted by law. The giving of the notice provided by this section does not satisfy the requirements of Sections 1161 and 1162 of the Code of Civil Procedure. *(Added by Stats.1991, c. 942 (A.B.628), § 3.)*

§ 800.37. Abandonment of floating home owned by marina

A floating home which is owned by a floating home marina shall be deemed abandoned according to the procedures and requirements of Section 1951.3. *(Added by Stats.1991, c. 942 (A.B.628), § 4.)*

PROPERTY

ARTICLE 4. FEES AND CHARGES

Section
800.40. Increase in rent; advance written notice.
800.40.5. Rental rates; notice of rent increase; applicability; waivers void; construction with local ordinance, rule, regulation, or initiative measure.
800.41. Prohibited fees; fees for rental agreements in excess of one year.
800.42. Fees for rendered services not listed in rental agreement; written notice.
800.43. Fees for keeping pets; special pet facilities.
800.44. Fees for guests.
800.45. Fee based on number of immediate family members.
800.46. Fees for enforcement of rules and regulations.
800.47. Entry, installation, hookup, or landscaping fees.
800.48. Master meter and submeter utility services; separate billing; posting of rates schedule.
800.49. Security deposits; amount; refund; transfer of management's interests; interest; application of section.
800.50. Liens or security interests.

§ 800.40. Increase in rent; advance written notice

The management shall give a homeowner written notice of any increase in his or her rent at least 30 days before the date of the increase, and the reason for the increase, including the basis for any calculation used in determining the amount of the increase. *(Added by Stats.1990, c. 1505 (A.B.3139), § 1. Amended by Stats.1991, c. 942 (A.B.628), § 5.)*

§ 800.40.5. Rental rates; notice of rent increase; applicability; waivers void; construction with local ordinance, rule, regulation, or initiative measure

(a)(1) Subject to subdivision (b), management shall not, over the course of any 12–month period, increase the gross rental rate for a tenancy for a floating home berth in a floating home marina more than 3 percent plus the percentage change in the cost of living, or 5 percent, whichever is lower, of the lowest gross rental rate charged for a tenancy at any time during the 12 months prior to the effective date of the increase.

(2) If the same homeowner maintains a tenancy over any 12–month period, the gross rental rate for the tenancy shall not be increased in more than two increments over that 12–month period, subject to the other restrictions of this subdivision governing gross rental rate increases.

(b)(1) For a new tenancy in which no homeowner from the prior tenancy remains in lawful possession of the floating home berth, management may establish the initial rental rate not subject to subdivision (a). However, if the applicable local agency or jurisdiction has adopted an ordinance, rule, regulation, or initiative measure that limits the allowable rental rate for a new tenancy, that ordinance, rule, regulation, or initiative measure shall apply. Subdivision (a) shall be applicable to subsequent increases after the initial rental rate has been established, except as otherwise provided in this section.

(2) Notwithstanding paragraph (1), management shall not impose an increase in rent on a homeowner that purchases a floating home if the purchase qualifies as an in-place transfer, and the initial rental rate shall be set at the rental rate of the previous tenancy. Subdivision (a) shall be applicable to subsequent increases after the initial rental rate has been established.

(c) Management shall provide notice of any increase in the rental rate, pursuant to subdivision (a), to each homeowner in accordance with Section 800.40.

(d) Subdivision (a) shall not apply to a tenancy for any of the following:

(1) A floating home berth restricted by deed, regulatory restriction contained in an agreement with a government agency, or other recorded document as affordable housing for persons and families of very low, low, or moderate income, as defined in Section 50093 of the Health and Safety Code, or subject to an agreement that provides housing subsidies for affordable housing for persons and families of very low, low, or moderate income, as defined in Section 50093 of the Health and Safety Code or comparable federal statutes.

(2) A floating home berth subject to any ordinance, rule, regulation, or initiative measure that restricts annual increases in the rental rate to an amount less than that provided in subdivision (a).

(e)(1)(A) This section shall apply to all rent increases occurring on or after January 1, 2022.

(B) This section shall become operative January 1, 2023.

(2) In the event that management has increased the rent by more than the amount permissible under subdivision (a) between January 1, 2022, and January 1, 2023, both of the following shall apply:

(A) The applicable rent on January 1, 2023, shall be the rent as of January 1, 2022, plus the maximum permissible increase under subdivision (a).

(B) Management shall not be liable to a homeowner for any corresponding rent overpayment.

(f) Any waiver of the rights under this section shall be void as contrary to public policy.

(g) For the purposes of this section:

(1) "Consumer Price Index for All Urban Consumers for All Items" means the CPI–U for the San Francisco-Oakland-Hayward metropolitan area, or any successor metropolitan area index.

(2)(A) "Percentage change in the cost of living" means the percentage change in the applicable CPI–U, as described in paragraph (1) and computed pursuant to subparagraph (B) of this paragraph.

(B)(i) For rent increases that take effect before August 1 of any calendar year, the following shall apply:

(I) The percentage change shall be the percentage change in the amount published for April of the immediately preceding calendar year and April of the year before that.

(II) If there is not an amount published in April for the applicable geographic area, the percentage change shall be the percentage change in the amount published for March of the immediately preceding calendar year and March of the year before that.

(ii) For rent increases that take effect on or after August 1 of any calendar year, the following shall apply:

(I) The percentage change shall be the percentage change in the amount published for April of that calendar year and April of the immediately preceding calendar year.

(II) If there is not an amount published in April for the applicable geographic area, the percentage change shall be the percentage change in the amount published for March of that calendar year and March of the immediately preceding calendar year.

(iii) The percentage change shall be rounded to the nearest one-tenth of 1 percent.

(3) "In place transfer" means the sale of a floating home where the floating home is transferred by a homeowner to a subsequent homeowner and remains docked at the same berth.

(h)(1) Nothing in this section affects the authority of a local government to adopt or maintain an ordinance, rule, regulation, or initiative measure that establishes a maximum amount that may be charged for rent or the rental rate for a new tenancy, including any ordinance, rule, regulation, or initiative measure adopted before the effective date of this section. However, if a local ordinance, rule, regulation, or initiative measure allows for the rental rate for a new tenancy or a rental rate increase greater than that provided in subdivision (a), this section shall apply.

(2) This section is not intended to express any policy regarding the appropriate, allowable rental rate increase limitations imposed by ordinance, rule, regulation, or initiative measure regulating rent increases adopted before or after the effective date of this section.

(i) This section shall only apply to floating home marinas in the Counties of Alameda, Contra Costa, and Marin.

(j) This section shall remain in effect only until January 1, 2030, and as of that date is repealed. *(Added by Stats.2022, c. 633 (A.B.252), § 2, eff. Jan. 1, 2023.)*

Repeal

For repeal of this section, see its terms.

§ 800.41. Prohibited fees; fees for rental agreements in excess of one year

A homeowner shall not be charged a fee for other than rent, utilities, and incidental reasonable charges for services actually rendered.

A homeowner shall not be charged a fee for obtaining a rental agreement on a floating home berth for (1) a term of 12 months, or (2) a lesser period as mutually agreed upon by both the homeowner and the management. A fee may be charged for a rental agreement of more than one year if the fee is mutually agreed upon by both the homeowner and management. *(Added by Stats.1990, c. 1505 (A.B.3139), § 1.)*

§ 800.42. Fees for rendered services not listed in rental agreement; written notice

A homeowner shall not be charged a fee for services actually rendered which are not listed in the rental agreement unless he or she has been given written notice thereof by the management, at least 60 days before imposition of the charge. *(Added by Stats.1990, c. 1505 (A.B.3139), § 1.)*

§ 800.43. Fees for keeping pets; special pet facilities

A homeowner shall not be charged a fee for keeping a pet in the floating home marina unless the management actually provides special facilities or services for pets. If special pet facilities are maintained by the management, the fee charged shall reasonably relate to the cost of maintenance of the facilities or services and the number of pets kept in the floating home marina. *(Added by Stats.1990, c. 1505 (A.B. 3139), § 1.)*

§ 800.44. Fees for guests

(a) A homeowner shall not be charged a fee for a guest who does not stay with him or her for more than a total of 20 consecutive days or a total of 30 days in a calendar year. Such a guest shall not be required to register with the management.

(b) A homeowner who is living alone and who wishes to share his or her floating home with one person may do so, and a fee shall not be imposed by management for that person. The person shall be considered a guest of the homeowner and any agreement between the homeowner and the person shall not change the terms and conditions of the rental agreement between management and the homeowner. The guest shall comply with the provisions of the rules and regulations of the floating home marina. *(Added by Stats. 1990, c. 1505 (A.B.3139), § 1.)*

§ 800.45. Fee based on number of immediate family members

A homeowner shall not be charged a fee based on the number of members in his or her immediate family. As used in this section, the "immediate family" includes the homeowner and his or her spouse, their parents, and their children. *(Added by Stats.1990, c. 1505 (A.B.3139), § 1.)*

§ 800.46. Fees for enforcement of rules and regulations

A homeowner shall not be charged a fee for the enforcement of any of the rules and regulations of the floating home marina. *(Added by Stats.1990, c. 1505 (A.B.3139), § 1.)*

§ 800.47. Entry, installation, hookup, or landscaping fees

Unless the homeowner specifically requests the service in writing from the management, a homeowner shall not be charged a fee for the entry, installation, hookup, or landscaping as a condition of tenancy except for an actual fee or cost imposed by a local governmental ordinance or requirement directly related to the occupancy of the specific berth where the floating home is located and not incurred as a portion of the development of the floating home marina as a whole. However, reasonable landscaping and maintenance requirements may be included in the floating home marina rules and regulations. The management shall not require a homeowner or prospective homeowner to purchase, rent, or lease goods or services for landscaping from any person, company, or corporation. *(Added by Stats.1990, c. 1505 (A.B.3139), § 1.)*

§ 800.48. Master meter and submeter utility services; separate billing; posting of rates schedule

Where the management provides both master meter and submeter service of utilities to a homeowner, for each billing period the cost of the charges for the period shall be separately stated along with the opening and closing readings for his or her meter. The management shall post in a conspicuous place, the prevailing residential utilities rate schedule as published by the serving utility. *(Added by Stats.1990, c. 1505 (A.B.3139), § 1.)*

§ 800.49. Security deposits; amount; refund; transfer of management's interests; interest; application of section

(a) The management may only demand a security deposit on or before initial occupancy and the security deposit may not be in an amount or value in excess of an amount equal to two months' rent that is charged at the inception of the tenancy, in addition to any rent for the first month. In no event shall additional security deposits be demanded of a homeowner following initial occupancy.

(b) After the homeowner has promptly paid to the management within five days of the date the amount is due, all of the rent, utilities, and reasonable service charges for any 12-consecutive-month period subsequent to the collection of the security deposit by the management, or upon resale of the floating home, whichever occurs earlier, the management shall, upon the receipt of a written request from the homeowner, refund to the homeowner the amount of the security deposit within 30 days following the end of the 12-consecutive-month period of prompt payment or the date of the resale of the floating home.

(c) In the event that the interest in the floating home marina is transferred to any other party or entity, the successor in interest shall have the same obligations of management contained in this section with respect to the security deposit.

(d) The management shall not be required to place any security deposit collected in an interest-bearing account or to provide a homeowner with any interest on the security deposit collected.

(e) This section applies to all security deposits collected on or after January 1, 1991. *(Added by Stats.1990, c. 1505 (A.B.3139), § 1. Amended by Stats.1991, c. 942 (A.B.628), § 6.)*

Cross References
Obligation defined, see Civil Code § 1427.

§ 800.50. Liens or security interests

The management shall not acquire a lien or security interest, other than an interest arising by reason of process issued to enforce a judgment of any court, in a floating home located in the floating home marina unless it is mutually agreed upon by both the homeowner and management. Any billing and payment upon the obligation shall be kept separate from current rent. *(Added by Stats.1990, c. 1505 (A.B.3139), § 1.)*

Cross References
Obligation defined, see Civil Code § 1427.

ARTICLE 5. HOMEOWNER MEETINGS

Section
800.60. Homeowner or resident meetings.
800.61. Management meetings with homeowners; collective meetings.

§ 800.60. Homeowner or resident meetings

The management shall permit meetings by homeowners or residents of a floating home in the marina, or any or all of them, relating to floating home living or social or educational purposes, including forums for or speeches of public officials or candidates for public office, to be held in any community facility if the meeting is held at reasonable hours and when the facility is not otherwise in use. The management's private office is not to be considered a community facility unless so designated by the management. *(Added by Stats. 1990, c. 1505 (A.B.3139), § 1.)*

§ 800.61. Management meetings with homeowners; collective meetings

The management shall meet and consult with the homeowners, upon written request, within 30 days of the request, either individually, collectively, or with representatives of a group of homeowners who have signed a request to be so represented on the following matters:

(a) Amendments to floating home marina rules and regulations.

(b) Standards for maintenance or physical improvements in the floating home marina.

(c) Addition, alteration, or deletion of services, equipment or physical improvements.

(d) Rental agreements offered pursuant to Article 2 (commencing with Section 800.20).

Any collective meeting shall be conducted only after notice thereof has been given to all the requesting homeowners 10 days or more before the meeting. *(Added by Stats.1990, c. 1505 (A.B.3139), § 1.)*

ARTICLE 6. TERMINATION OF TENANCY

Section
800.70. Legislative findings and declarations; termination or refusal to renew tenancy; notice.
800.71. Termination of tenancy; permitted reasons.
800.72. Notice of termination; contents.
800.73. Termination to make home available for purchaser prohibited.
800.74. Vacation of tenancy; written notice.
800.75. Effect of article on rights relating to summary proceedings for obtaining possession of real property.

§ 800.70. Legislative findings and declarations; termination or refusal to renew tenancy; notice

(a) The Legislature finds and declares that, because of the high cost of moving floating homes, the potential for damage resulting therefrom, the requirements relating to the installation of floating homes, and current government policy limiting the availability of floating home berths, it is necessary that the owners of floating homes within floating home marinas be provided with the unique protection from actual or constructive eviction afforded by the provisions of this chapter.

(b) The management shall not terminate or refuse to renew a tenancy, except for a reason specified in this article and upon the giving of written notice to the homeowner in the manner prescribed by Section 1162 of the Code of Civil Procedure, to remove the floating home from the floating home marina within a period of not less than 60 days, which period shall be specified in the notice. A copy of this notice shall be sent to the legal owner, as defined in Section 18005.8 of the Health and Safety Code, each junior lienholder, as defined in Section 18005.3 of the Health and Safety Code, and the registered owner of the floating home, if other than the homeowner, by United States mail within 10 days after notice to the homeowner, addressed to the legal owner, each junior lienholder, and the registered owner at their addresses, as set forth in the registration card specified in Section 18091.5 of the Health and Safety Code. *(Added by Stats. 1990, c. 1505 (A.B.3139), § 1.)*

§ 800.71. Termination of tenancy; permitted reasons

A tenancy shall be terminated by the management only for one or more of the following reasons:

(a) Failure of the homeowner or resident to comply with a local ordinance or state law or regulation relating to floating homes within a reasonable time after the homeowner receives a notice of noncompliance from the appropriate governmental agency.

(b) Conduct by the homeowner or resident, upon the floating home marina premises, which constitutes a substantial annoyance to other homeowners or residents.

(c) Failure of the homeowner or resident to comply with a reasonable rule or regulation of the floating home marina as set forth in the rental agreement or any amendment thereto. The management may not impose unreasonable restrictions on the right of the homeowner to sublet his or her floating home.

No act or omission of the homeowner or resident shall constitute a failure to comply with a reasonable rule or regulation unless and until the management has given the homeowner written notice of the alleged rule or regulation violation and the homeowner or resident has failed to adhere to the rule or regulation within seven days. However, if a homeowner has been given a written notice of an alleged violation of the same rule or regulation on three or more occasions within a 12-month period after the homeowner or resident has violated that rule or regulation, no written notice shall be required for a subsequent violation of the same rule or regulation.

Nothing in this subdivision shall relieve the management from its obligation to demonstrate that a rule or regulation has in fact been violated.

(d)(1) Nonpayment of rent, utility charges, or reasonable incidental service charges; if the amount due has been unpaid for a period of at least five days from its due date, and provided, that the homeowner shall be given a three-day written notice subsequent to that five-day period to pay the amount due or to vacate the tenancy. The three-day written notice shall be given to the homeowner in the manner prescribed by Section 1162 of the Code of Civil Procedure. The notice may be given at the same time as the 60 days' notice required for termination of the tenancy.

Payment by the homeowner prior to the expiration of the three-day notice period shall cure a default under this subdivision.

(2) However, if a homeowner has been given a three-day notice to pay the amount due or to vacate the tenancy on three or more occasions within the preceding 12-month period, no written three-day notice shall be required for a subsequent nonpayment of rent, utility charges, or reasonable incidental service charges.

(3) Payment by the legal owner, any junior lienholder, or the registered owner, if other than the homeowner, on behalf of the homeowner prior to the expiration of 30 calendar days following the mailing of the notice to the legal owner, each junior lienholder, and the registered owner provided in subdivision (b) of Section 800.70, shall cure a default under this subdivision with respect to that payment.

(4) The homeowner shall remain liable for all payments due up until the time the tenancy is vacated.

(5) Cure of a default of rent, utility charges, or reasonable incidental service charges by the legal owner, any junior lienholder, or the registered owner, if other than the homeowner, as provided by this subdivision, may not be exercised more than twice during a 12-month period.

(e) Condemnation of the floating home marina.

(f) Change of use of the floating home marina or any portion thereof, provided:

(1) The management gives the homeowners at least 60 days' written notice that the management will be appearing before a local governmental board, commission, or body to request permits for a change of use of the floating home marina.

(2) After all required permits requesting a change of use have been approved by the local governmental board, commission, or body, the management shall give the homeowners six months' or more written notice of termination of tenancy.

If the change of use requires no local governmental permits, then notice shall be given 12 months or more prior to the management's determination that a change of use will occur. The management in the notice shall disclose and describe in detail the nature of the change of use.

(3) The management gives each proposed homeowner written notice thereof prior to the inception of his or her tenancy that the management is requesting a change of use before local governmental bodies or that a change of use request has been granted.

(4) The notice requirements for termination of tenancy set forth in this section and Section 800.72 shall be followed if the proposed change actually occurs.

(5) The requirements for a notice of a proposed change of use imposed by this subdivision shall be governed by the law in effect at the time the notice was given. *(Added by Stats.1990, c. 1505 (A.B.3139), § 1.)*

Cross References

Closure, cessation or change of use of floating home marina, filing and distribution of impact report, see Government Code § 65863.12.

§ 800.71

Obligation defined, see Civil Code § 1427.

§ 800.72. Notice of termination; contents

The management shall set forth in a notice of termination the reason relied upon for the termination with specific facts to permit determination of the date, place, witnesses, and circumstances concerning that reason. Neither reference to the section number or a subdivision thereof nor a recital of the language of this article constitutes compliance with this section. *(Added by Stats.1990, c. 1505 (A.B.3139), § 1.)*

§ 800.73. Termination to make home available for purchaser prohibited

No tenancy shall be terminated for the purpose of making a homeowner's berth available for a person who purchases a floating home from the owner of the floating home marina or his or her agent. *(Added by Stats.1990, c. 1505 (A.B.3139), § 1.)*

§ 800.74. Vacation of tenancy; written notice

A homeowner shall give written notice to the management of not less than 60 days before vacating his or her tenancy. *(Added by Stats.1990, c. 1505 (A.B.3139), § 1.)*

§ 800.75. Effect of article on rights relating to summary proceedings for obtaining possession of real property

The provisions of this article shall not affect any rights or proceedings set forth in Chapter 4 (commencing with Section 1159) of Title 3 of Part 3 of the Code of Civil Procedure except as otherwise provided in those sections. *(Added by Stats.1990, c. 1505 (A.B.3139), § 1.)*

ARTICLE 7. TRANSFER OF A FLOATING HOME

Section
- 800.80. Advertisement of sale or rental by owner; sign.
- 800.82. Showing or listing for sale by management; authorization.
- 800.83. Transfer or selling fees; condition of approval for residency fees.
- 800.84. Removal of home upon sale prohibited as term of rental agreement.
- 800.85. Right of prior approval; fees for obtaining financial reports.
- 800.86. Escrow, sale or transfer agreement for home to remain in marina; rental agreement signed by purchaser; unlawful occupant.
- 800.87. Waiver of rights under article prohibited.
- 800.88. Heirs or joint tenants gaining ownership through death of owner; rights to sell.
- 800.89. Legal owners or junior lienholders foreclosing on security interests; rights to sell.
- 800.90. Prohibited acts by management.
- 800.91. Actions for management's alleged failure to maintain physical improvements in common facilities or services; notice.

§ 800.80. Advertisement of sale or rental by owner; sign

A homeowner or his or her agent may advertise the sale or exchange of his or her floating home, or, if not prohibited by the terms of an agreement with the management, may advertise the rental of his or her floating home, by displaying a sign in the window of the floating home, or by a sign posted on the side of the floating home facing the dock or water or both, stating that the floating home is for sale or exchange or, if not prohibited, for rent by the owner of the floating home or his or her agent. The sign shall state the name, address, and telephone number of the owner of the floating home or his or her agent and may be at least 24 inches in width and 18 inches in height. *(Added by Stats.1990, c. 1505 (A.B.3139), § 1.)*

§ 800.82. Showing or listing for sale by management; authorization

(a) The management shall not show or list for sale a floating home without first obtaining the owner's written authorization. The authorization shall specify the terms and conditions regarding the showing or listing.

(b) The management shall prohibit neither the listing nor the sale of a floating home within the floating home marina by the homeowner, or an agent of the homeowner to authorize the management to act as the agent in the sale of a floating home as a condition of management's approval of buyer or prospective homeowner for residency in the floating home marina. *(Added by Stats.1990, c. 1505 (A.B.3139), § 1.)*

§ 800.83. Transfer or selling fees; condition of approval for residency fees

(a) The management shall not charge a homeowner, or his or her agent a transfer or selling fee as a condition of a sale of his or her floating home within a floating home marina unless the management performs a service in the sale. The management shall not perform any such service in connection with the sale unless so requested in writing, by the homeowner or his or her agent.

(b) The management shall not charge a prospective homeowner or his or her agent, upon purchase of a floating home, a fee as a condition of approval for residency in a floating home marina unless the management performs a specific service in the sale. The management shall not impose a fee, other than for a credit check in accordance with subdivision (b) of Section 800.85, for an interview of a prospective homeowner. *(Added by Stats.1990, c. 1505 (A.B.3139), § 1.)*

§ 800.84. Removal of home upon sale prohibited as term of rental agreement

The management shall not require the removal of a floating home from the floating home marina in the event of its sale to a third party during the term of the homeowner's rental agreement. *(Added by Stats.1990, c. 1505 (A.B.3139), § 1.)*

§ 800.85. Right of prior approval; fees for obtaining financial reports

(a) The management may require the right of prior approval of a purchaser of a floating home that will remain in the floating home marina and that the selling homeowner or his or her agent give notice of the sale to the management before the close of the sale. Approval cannot be withheld if the purchaser has the financial ability to pay the rent and charges of the floating home marina unless the management reasonably determines that, based on the purchaser's prior tenancies, he or she will not comply with the rules and regulations of the floating home marina. In determining whether the purchaser has the financial ability to pay the rent and charges of the floating home marina, the management shall not require the purchaser to submit copies of any personal income tax returns in order to obtain approval for residency in the floating home marina. However, management may require the purchaser to document the amount and source of his or her gross monthly income or means of financial support. If the ownership or management rejects a purchaser as a prospective homeowner, the ownership or management shall inform the selling homeowner in writing of its reasons for the rejection. If the approval of a purchaser is withheld for any reason other than those stated in this article, the management or owner may be held liable for all damages proximately resulting therefrom.

(b) If the management collects a fee or charge from a prospective purchaser of a floating home in order to obtain a financial report or credit rating, the full amount of the fee or charge shall be credited toward payment of the first month's rent for that floating home purchaser. If, for whatever reason, the prospective purchaser is rejected by the management, the management shall refund to the prospective purchaser the full amount of that fee or charge within 30 days from the date of rejection. If the prospective purchaser is approved by the management, but, for whatever reason, the prospective purchaser elects not to purchase the floating home, the management may retain the fee, or a portion thereof, to defray its administrative costs under this section. *(Added by Stats.1990, c. 1505 (A.B.3139), § 1.)*

Cross References
Ownership defined for purposes of this Code, see Civil Code § 654.

§ 800.86. Escrow, sale or transfer agreement for home to remain in marina; rental agreement signed by purchaser; unlawful occupant

(a) An escrow, sale, or transfer agreement involving a floating home located in the floating home marina at the time of sale, where the floating home is to remain in the floating home marina, shall contain a provision signed by the purchaser stating that by his or her signature he or she has agreed to the terms of a rental agreement. A copy of a fully executed rental agreement signed by both the purchaser and floating home marina management will satisfy the requirements of this section.

(b) In the event the purchaser fails to execute the rental agreement, the purchaser shall not have any rights of tenancy.

(c) In the event that an occupant of a floating home has no rights of tenancy and is not otherwise entitled to occupy the floating home pursuant to this chapter, the occupant shall be considered an unlawful occupant if, after a demand is made for the surrender of the floating home marina berth, for a period of five days, the occupant has refused to surrender the berth to the floating home marina management. In the event the unlawful occupant fails to comply with the demand, the unlawful occupant shall be subject to the proceedings set forth in Chapter 4 (commencing with Section 1159) of Title 3 of Part 3 of the Code of Civil Procedure.

(d) The occupant of the floating home shall not be considered an unlawful occupant and shall not be subject to the provisions of subdivision (c) if all of the following conditions exist:

(1) The occupant is the registered owner of the floating home.

(2) The management has determined that the occupant has the financial ability to pay the rent and charges of the floating home marina, will comply with the rules and regulations of the floating home marina, based on the occupant's prior tenancies, and will comply with this article.

(3) The management failed or refused to offer the occupant a rental agreement. *(Added by Stats.1990, c. 1505 (A.B.3139), § 1.)*

§ 800.87. Waiver of rights under article prohibited

No rental or sale agreement shall contain a provision by which the purchaser or homeowner waives his or her rights under this article. Any waiver thereof shall be deemed contrary to public policy and shall be void and unenforceable. *(Added by Stats.1990, c. 1505 (A.B.3139), § 1.)*

§ 800.88. Heirs or joint tenants gaining ownership through death of owner; rights to sell

An heir or joint tenant who gains ownership of a floating home in the floating home marina through the death of the owner of the floating home who is a homeowner shall have the right to sell the floating home to a third party in accordance with this article, but only if all the homeowner's responsibilities and liabilities to the management regarding rent, utilities, and reasonable maintenance of the floating home and its premises which have arisen after the transfer of ownership to the heir or joint tenant have been satisfied up until the date the floating home is resold. *(Added by Stats.1990, c. 1505 (A.B.3139), § 1. Amended by Stats.1991, c. 942 (A.B.628), § 7.)*

Cross References
Ownership defined for purposes of this Code, see Civil Code § 654.

§ 800.89. Legal owners or junior lienholders foreclosing on security interests; rights to sell

Any legal owner or junior lienholder who forecloses on his or her security interest in a floating home located in a floating home marina shall have the right to sell the floating home within the floating home marina to a third party in accordance with the provisions of this article, but only if all the homeowner's responsibilities and liabilities to the management regarding rent, utilities, and reasonable maintenance of a floating home and it's premises are satisfied by the foreclosing creditor through the date the floating home is resold. *(Added by Stats.1990, c. 1505 (A.B.3139), § 1.)*

§ 800.90. Prohibited acts by management

The management (1) shall not prohibit the listing or sale of a used floating home within the floating home marina by the homeowner, or an agent of the homeowner other than the management, (2) nor require the selling homeowner to authorize the management to act as the agent in the sale of a floating home as a condition of approval of the buyer or prospective homeowner for residency in the floating home marina. *(Added by Stats.1990, c. 1505 (A.B.3139), § 1.)*

§ 800.91. Actions for management's alleged failure to maintain physical improvements in common facilities or services; notice

(a) No action based upon the management's alleged failure to maintain the physical improvements in the common facilities in good working order or condition or alleged reduction of service may be commenced by a homeowner unless the management has been given at least 30 days' prior notice of the intention to commence the action.

(b) The notice shall be in writing, signed by the homeowner or homeowners making the allegations, and shall notify the management of the basis of the claim, the specific allegations, and the remedies requested. A notice by one homeowner shall be deemed to be sufficient notice of the specific allegation to the management of the floating home marina by all of the homeowners in the floating home marina.

(c) The notice may be served in the manner prescribed in Chapter 5 (commencing with Section 1010) of Title 14 of Part 2 of the Code of Civil Procedure.

(d) For purposes of this section, management shall be deemed to be notified of an alleged failure to maintain the physical improvements in the common facilities in good working order or condition or of an alleged reduction of services upon substantial compliance by the homeowner or homeowners with the provisions of subdivisions (b) and (c), or when management has been notified of the alleged failure to maintain or the alleged reduction of services by a state or local agency.

(e) If the notice is served within 30 days of the expiration of the applicable statute of limitations, the time for the commencement of the action shall be extended 30 days from the service of the notice.

(f) This section does not apply to actions for personal injury or wrongful death. *(Added by Stats.1990, c. 1505 (A.B.3139), § 1.)*

ARTICLE 8. TRANSFER OF A FLOATING HOME MARINA

Section
800.100. Entry into written listing agreement; notice; conditions; application of section.

§ 800.100. Entry into written listing agreement; notice; conditions; application of section

(a) When the owner of a floating home marina enters into a written listing agreement with a licensed real estate broker, as defined in Article 1 (commencing with Section 10130) of Chapter 2 of Part 1 of Division 4 of the Business and Professions Code, for the sale of the marina or offers to sell the marina to any party, the owner shall provide written notice by first-class mail or by personal delivery to the president, secretary, and treasurer of the resident organization, not less than 30 days but no more than one year prior to entering into any written listing agreement for the sale of the marina, or making any offer to sell the marina to any party. An offer to sell a marina shall not be construed as an offer under this subdivision unless it is initiated by the marina owner or his or her agent.

(b) An owner of a floating home marina is not required to comply with subdivision (a) unless the following conditions are met:

(1) The resident organization has first furnished the marina owner or marina manager a written notice of the name and address of the president, secretary, and treasurer of the resident organization to whom the notice of sale shall be given.

(2) The resident organization has first notified the marina owner or manager in writing that the marina residents are interested in purchasing the marina. The initial notice by the resident organization shall be made prior to a written listing or offer to sell the marina by the marina owner, and the resident organization shall give subsequent notice once each year thereafter that the marina residents are interested in purchasing the marina.

(3) The resident organization has furnished the marina owner or marina manager a written notice, within five days, of any change in the name or address of the officers of the resident organization to whom the notice of sale shall be given.

(c) Nothing in this section affects the validity of title to real property transferred in violation of this section, although a violation shall subject the seller to civil action pursuant to Article 9 (commencing with Section 800.200) by homeowner residents of the marina or by the resident organization.

(d) Nothing in this section affects the ability of a licensed real estate broker to collect a commission pursuant to an executed contract between the broker and the floating home marina owner.

(e) This section does not apply to any of the following:

(1) Any sale or other transfer by a marina owner who is a natural person to any relation specified in Section 6401 or 6402 of the Probate Code.

(2) Any transfer by gift, devise, or operation of law.

(3) Any transfer by a corporation to an affiliate. As used in this paragraph, "affiliate" means any shareholder of the transferring corporation, any corporation or entity owned or controlled, directly or indirectly, by the transferring corporation, or any other corporation or entity controlled, directly or indirectly, by any shareholder of the transferring corporation.

(4) Any transfer by a partnership to any of its partners.

(5) Any conveyance resulting from the judicial or nonjudicial foreclosure of a mortgage or deed of trust encumbering a floating home marina or any deed given in lieu of such a foreclosure.

(6) Any sale or transfer between or among joint tenants or tenants in common owning a floating home marina.

(7) The purchase of a floating home marina by a governmental entity under its powers of eminent domain. *(Added by Stats.1990, c. 1505 (A.B.3139), § 1. Amended by Stats. 1991, c. 942 (A.B.628), § 8; Stats.2004, c. 183 (A.B.3082), § 25.)*

Cross References

Real property defined for purposes of this Code, see Civil Code § 658.

ARTICLE 9. ACTIONS, PROCEEDINGS, AND PENALTIES

Section
800.200. Attorney's fees and costs for prevailing party; awards for willful violations.
800.201. Violations deemed public nuisances; remedy.

§ 800.200. Attorney's fees and costs for prevailing party; awards for willful violations

In any action arising out of the provisions of this chapter the prevailing party shall be entitled to reasonable attorney's fees and costs. A party shall be deemed a prevailing party for the purposes of this section if the judgment is rendered in his or her favor or where the litigation is dismissed in his or her favor prior to or during the trial, unless the parties otherwise agree in the settlement or compromise.

In the event a homeowner or former homeowner of a floating home marina is the prevailing party in a civil action against the management to enforce his or her rights under the provisions of this chapter, the homeowner, in addition to damages afforded by law, may, in the discretion of the court, be awarded an amount not to exceed five hundred dollars ($500) for each willful violation of those provisions by the management. *(Added by Stats.1990, c. 1505 (A.B.3139), § 1.)*

§ 800.201. Violations deemed public nuisances; remedy

(a) The substantial failure of the management to provide and maintain physical improvements in the common facilities in good working order and condition shall be deemed a public nuisance. Notwithstanding the provisions of Section 3491, such a nuisance only may be remedied by a civil action or abatement.

(b) The substantial violation of a floating home marina rule shall be deemed a public nuisance. Notwithstanding the provisions of Section 3491, such a nuisance only may be remedied by a civil action or abatement. *(Added by Stats. 1990, c. 1505 (A.B.3139), § 1.)*

ARTICLE 10. COOPERATIVES AND CONDOMINIUMS

Section
800.300. Definitions.
800.301. Advertisement of sale or rental of home; sign.
800.302. Showing or listing for sale by owner or management; resident's written authorization.
800.303. Removal from cooperative or condominium upon sale to third party prohibited.
800.304. Right of prior approval.
800.305. Waiver of rights under article prohibited.
800.306. Application of chapter.

§ 800.300. Definitions

As used in this article:

(a) "Ownership or management" means the ownership or management of a cooperative or condominium for floating homes.

(b) "Resident" means a person who maintains a residence in a cooperative or condominium for floating homes. *(Added by Stats.1990, c. 1505 (A.B.3139), § 1.)*

Cross References

Ownership defined for purposes of this Code, see Civil Code § 654.

§ 800.301. Advertisement of sale or rental of home; sign

A resident may advertise the sale or exchange of his or her floating home or, if not prohibited by the terms of an agreement with the management or ownership, may advertise the rental of his or her floating home by displaying a sign in the window of his or her floating home stating that the floating home is for sale or exchange or, if not prohibited, for rent by the owner of the floating home or his or her agent. The sign shall state the name, address, and telephone number of the owner of the floating home or his or her agent, and shall be 24 inches in width and 18 inches in length. *(Added by Stats.1990, c. 1505 (A.B.3139), § 1. Amended by Stats. 1991, c. 942 (A.B.628), § 9.)*

Cross References

Ownership defined for purposes of this Code, see Civil Code § 654.

§ 800.302. Showing or listing for sale by owner or management; resident's written authorization

The ownership or management shall not show or list for sale a floating home owned by a resident without first obtaining the resident's written authorization. The authorization shall specify the terms and conditions regarding the showing or listing. *(Added by Stats.1990, c. 1505 (A.B.3139), § 1. Amended by Stats.1991, c. 942 (A.B.628), § 10.)*

Cross References

Ownership defined for purposes of this Code, see Civil Code § 654.

§ 800.303. Removal from cooperative or condominium upon sale to third party prohibited

The ownership or management shall not require the removal of a floating home from a cooperative or condominium in the event of its sale to a third party. *(Added by Stats.1990, c. 1505 (A.B.3139), § 1.)*

Cross References

Ownership defined for purposes of this Code, see Civil Code § 654.

§ 800.304. Right of prior approval

The ownership or management may require the right to prior approval of the purchaser of a floating home that will remain in the cooperative or condominium for floating homes and that the selling resident or his or her agent give notice of the sale to the ownership or management before the close of the sale. Approval cannot be withheld if the purchaser has the financial ability to pay the fees and charges of the cooperative or condominium unless the ownership or management reasonably determines that, based on the purchaser's prior residences, he or she will not comply with the rules and regulations of the cooperative or condominium. *(Added by Stats.1990, c. 1505 (A.B.3139), § 1.)*

§ 800.304

Cross References

Ownership defined for purposes of this Code, see Civil Code § 654.

§ 800.305. Waiver of rights under article prohibited

No agreement shall contain any provision by which the purchaser waives his or her rights under this article. Any waiver thereof shall be deemed contrary to public policy and void and unenforceable. *(Added by Stats.1990, c. 1505 (A.B.3139), § 1.)*

§ 800.306. Application of chapter

This chapter applies only to the relationship between the management and the homeowners and residents of floating home marinas. Nothing in this chapter affects residential use of tide and submerged lands, including the public trust doctrine or any legislative grant of tide and submerged lands to a public entity, or the administration of these lands by the State Lands Commission or a legislative grantee. In addition, this chapter does not supplant, lessen, modify, or otherwise affect past or future regulation of floating homes or floating home marinas by the San Francisco Bay Conservation and Development Commission pursuant to the McAteer-Petris Act. *(Added by Stats.1990, c. 1505 (A.B.3139), § 1.)*

CHAPTER 3. SERVITUDES

Section
- 801. Easements; servitudes attached to land.
- 801.5. Solar easement, solar energy system, and electric utility defined; minimum description in instrument.
- 801.7. Extent of railroad right-of-way; railroad corporation defined.
- 802. Servitudes unattached.
- 803. Dominant and servient tenements.
- 804. Persons who may create servitudes.
- 805. Persons who cannot hold servitudes.
- 806. Extent of servitude; determination.
- 807. Partition of dominant tenement; apportionment of servitude.
- 808. Owner of future estate in dominant tenement; use of easement.
- 809. Enforcement of easement; parties plaintiff.
- 810. Owner of servient tenement; possessory action.
- 811. Extinguishment of servitude.
- 812, 812.5. Repealed.
- 813. Consent to use of land; recordation of notice; revocation.

Cross References

Appurtenances to land, see Civil Code § 662.
Covenants for easement, creation, see Government Code § 65871.
Division fences, see Civil Code § 841.
Eminent domain, acquisition of interests in property, see Code of Civil Procedure § 1240.110 et seq.
Guardians, dedication or conveyance of easements, see Probate Code § 2556.
Lateral and subjacent support, see Civil Code § 832.
Maintenance of easements, see Civil Code § 845.
Personal representative may dedicate or convey easements, see Probate Code § 9900.
Prescription, see Civil Code § 1007; Code of Civil Procedure §§ 318, 319, 325.
Requirements for state appraisal review, certified real estate appraiser, see Public Resources Code § 5096.517.
Sewage or drainage easements, abandonment or vacation, see Health and Safety Code § 5400.
State property, grant of easements and rights-of-way across, see Government Code § 14666.
Transfer of real property as passing easements, see Civil Code § 1104.
Vacation of city streets, reservation of easements, see Streets and Highways Code § 8340 et seq.
Water for irrigating, perpetual easement, see Corporations Code § 14452.

§ 801. Easements; servitudes attached to land

The following land burdens, or servitudes upon land, may be attached to other land as incidents or appurtenances, and are then called easements:

1. The right of pasture;
2. The right of fishing;
3. The right of taking game;
4. The right-of-way;
5. The right of taking water, wood, minerals, and other things;
6. The right of transacting business upon land;
7. The right of conducting lawful sports upon land;
8. The right of receiving air, light, or heat from or over, or discharging the same upon or over land;
9. The right of receiving water from or discharging the same upon land;
10. The right of flooding land;
11. The right of having water flow without diminution or disturbance of any kind;
12. The right of using a wall as a party wall;
13. The right of receiving more than natural support from adjacent land or things affixed thereto;
14. The right of having the whole of a division fence maintained by a coterminous owner;
15. The right of having public conveyances stopped, or of stopping the same on land;
16. The right of a seat in church;
17. The right of burial;
18. The right of receiving sunlight upon or over land as specified in Section 801.5. *(Enacted in 1872. Amended by Stats.1978, c. 1154, p. 3542, § 4.)*

Cross References

Acquisition of property by power of eminent domain, see Code of Civil Procedure § 1240.110 et seq.
Adverse possession, elements, see Code of Civil Procedure § 325.
Notice, recordation, consent to use land, see Civil Code § 813.
Recovery of real property, time for commencing action, see Code of Civil Procedure §§ 318, 319.
Vacation order, effect and recordation, see Streets and Highways Code §§ 8325, 8350, 8351.

§ 801.5. Solar easement, solar energy system, and electric utility defined; minimum description in instrument

(a) The right of receiving sunlight as specified in subdivision 18 of Section 801 shall be referred to as a solar easement. "Solar easement" means the right of receiving sunlight across real property of another for any solar energy system.

As used in this section, "solar energy system" means either of the following that is designed to serve one utility retail customer on the same property, more than one utility retail customer on the same property, one utility retail customer on the same, adjacent, or contiguous properties, or more than one utility retail customer on the same, adjacent or contiguous properties, and is not designed for procurement of electricity by an electric utility:

(1) Any solar collector or other solar energy device whose primary purpose is to provide for the collection, storage, and distribution of solar energy for space heating, space cooling, electric generation, or water heating.

(2) A structural design feature, including the following:

(A) Solar racking, solar mounting, and elevated solar support structures, including, but not limited to, solar carports, solar shade structures, solar awnings, solar canopies, and solar patio covers, regardless of whether the feature is on the ground or on a building. Elevated solar support structures include the aboveground superstructure and associated foundation elements that support the solar collectors or other solar energy devices described in paragraph (1).

(B) Any design feature whose primary purpose is to provide for the collection, storage, and distribution of solar energy for electricity generation, space heating or cooling, or for water heating.

(C) Any photovoltaic device or technology that is integrated into a building, including, but not limited to, photovoltaic windows, siding, and roofing shingles or tiles.

(b) Any instrument creating a solar easement shall include, at a minimum, all of the following:

(1) A description of the dimensions of the easement expressed in measurable terms, such as vertical or horizontal angles measured in degrees, or the hours of the day on specified dates during which direct sunlight to a specified surface of a solar collector, device, or structural design feature may not be obstructed, or a combination of these descriptions.

(2) The restrictions placed upon vegetation, structures, and other objects that would impair or obstruct the passage of sunlight through the easement.

(3) The terms or conditions, if any, under which the easement may be revised or terminated.

(c) As used in this section, "electric utility" means an electrical corporation as defined in Section 218 of the Public Utilities Code or a local publicly owned electric utility as defined in Section 224.3 of the Public Utilities Code. *(Added by Stats.1978, c. 1154, p. 3543, § 5. Amended by Stats.2000, c. 537 (S.B.1345), § 2; Stats.2017, c. 849 (A.B.1414), § 1, eff. Jan. 1, 2018; Stats.2021, c. 235 (A.B.1124), § 2, eff. Jan. 1, 2022.)*

Cross References

Real property defined for purposes of this Code, see Civil Code § 658.

Regulation of buildings used for human habitation, solar energy systems, approval of applications through issuance of building permits, see Health and Safety Code § 17959.1.

Zoning regulations, solar energy systems, limitations on ordinances that create unreasonable barriers to installation, see Government Code § 65850.5.

§ 801.7. Extent of railroad right-of-way; railroad corporation defined

(a) When a right-of-way is granted pursuant to Section 801 or 802 to a railroad corporation whose primary business is the transportation of passengers, the grant shall include, but not be limited to, a right-of-way for the location, construction, and maintenance of the railroad corporation's necessary works and for every necessary adjunct thereto.

(b) A "railroad corporation" shall have the same definition as provided in Section 230 of the Public Utilities Code. *(Added by Stats.1982, c. 1553, p. 6061, § 1.)*

§ 802. Servitudes unattached

The following land burdens, or servitudes upon land, may be granted and held, though not attached to land:

One—The right to pasture, and of fishing and taking game.

Two—The right of a seat in church.

Three—The right of burial.

Four—The right of taking rents and tolls.

Five—The right of way.

Six—The right of taking water, wood, minerals, or other things. *(Enacted in 1872. Amended by Code Am.1873–74, c. 612, p. 219, § 108.)*

§ 803. Dominant and servient tenements

DESIGNATION OF ESTATES. The land to which an easement is attached is called the dominant tenement; the land upon which a burden or servitude is laid is called the servient tenement. *(Enacted in 1872.)*

§ 804. Persons who may create servitudes

BY WHOM GRANTABLE. A servitude can be created only by one who has a vested estate in the servient tenement. *(Enacted in 1872.)*

§ 805. Persons who cannot hold servitudes

BY WHOM HELD. A servitude thereon cannot be held by the owner of the servient tenement. *(Enacted in 1872.)*

§ 806. Extent of servitude; determination

EXTENT OF SERVITUDES. The extent of a servitude is determined by the terms of the grant, or the nature of the enjoyment by which it was acquired. *(Enacted in 1872.)*

§ 807. Partition of dominant tenement; apportionment of servitude

APPORTIONING EASEMENTS. In case of partition of the dominant tenement the burden must be apportioned according to the division of the dominant tenement, but not in such a way as to increase the burden upon the servient tenement. *(Enacted in 1872.)*

§ 808. Owner of future estate in dominant tenement; use of easement

RIGHTS OF OWNER OF FUTURE ESTATE. The owner of a future estate in a dominant tenement may use easements attached thereto for the purpose of viewing waste, demanding rent, or removing an obstruction to the enjoyment of such easements, although such tenement is occupied by a tenant. *(Enacted in 1872.)*

§ 809. Enforcement of easement; parties plaintiff

ACTIONS BY OWNER AND OCCUPANT OF DOMINANT TENEMENT. The owner of any estate in a dominant tenement, or the occupant of such tenement, may maintain an action for the enforcement of an easement attached thereto. *(Enacted in 1872.)*

§ 810. Owner of servient tenement; possessory action

ACTIONS BY OWNER OF SERVIENT TENEMENT. The owner in fee of a servient tenement may maintain an action for the possession of the land, against any one unlawfully possessed thereof, though a servitude exists thereon in favor of the public. *(Enacted in 1872.)*

§ 811. Extinguishment of servitude

HOW EXTINGUISHED. A servitude is extinguished:

1. By the vesting of the right to the servitude and the right to the servient tenement in the same person;

2. By the destruction of the servient tenement;

3. By the performance of any act upon either tenement, by the owner of the servitude, or with his assent, which is incompatible with its nature or exercise; or,

4. When the servitude was acquired by enjoyment, by disuse thereof by the owner of the servitude for the period prescribed for acquiring title by enjoyment. *(Enacted in 1872.)*

§§ 812, 812.5. Repealed by Stats.1980, c. 1050, §§ 1, 2

§ 813. Consent to use of land; recordation of notice; revocation

The holder of record title to land may record in the office of the recorder of any county in which any part of the land is situated, a description of said land and a notice reading substantially as follows: "The right of the public or any person to make any use whatsoever of the above described land or any portion thereof (other than any use expressly allowed by a written or recorded map, agreement, deed or dedication) is by permission, and subject to control, of owner: Section 813, Civil Code."

The recorded notice is conclusive evidence that subsequent use of the land during the time such notice is in effect by the public or any user for any purpose (other than any use expressly allowed by a written or recorded map, agreement, deed or dedication) is permissive and with consent in any judicial proceeding involving the issue as to whether all or any portion of such land has been dedicated to public use or whether any user has a prescriptive right in such land or any portion thereof. The notice may be revoked by the holder of record title by recording a notice of revocation in the office of the recorder wherein the notice is recorded. After recording a notice pursuant to this section, and prior to any revocation thereof, the owner shall not prevent any public use appropriate thereto by physical obstruction, notice or otherwise.

In the event of use by other than the general public, any such notices, to be effective, shall also be served by registered mail on the user.

The recording of a notice pursuant to this section shall not be deemed to affect rights vested at the time of recording.

The permission for public use of real property provided for in such a recorded notice may be conditioned upon reasonable restrictions on the time, place, and manner of such public use, and no use in violation of such restrictions shall be considered public use for purposes of a finding of implied dedication. *(Added by Stats.1963, c. 735, p. 1749, § 1. Amended by Stats.1971, c. 941, p. 1845, § 1.)*

Cross References

Real property defined for purposes of this Code, see Civil Code § 658.

CHAPTER 4. CONSERVATION EASEMENTS

Section
815. Legislative findings and declarations.
815.1. Conservation easement.
815.2. Nature.
815.3. Entities authorized to acquire and hold conservation easements.
815.4. Reservation of interests in grantor.
815.5. Recordation.
815.7. Enforcement of easement; injunctive relief; damages; costs.
815.9. Political subdivisions; authority to hold comparable easements.
815.10. Enforceable restrictions for purposes of assessment of land.
815.11. Repealed.
816. Liberal construction of chapter.

Cross References

Agricultural preserves, see Government Code § 51200 et seq.
Community facilities districts, easement or cancellation of contracts prior to release of land from specified liens, see Government Code § 53312.8.
Conveyance of historical property,
  Cities, see Government Code § 37361.1.
  Counties, see Government Code § 25376.
  Districts, see Government Code § 53073.
Easements generally, see Civil Code § 801 et seq.
Land defined, see Civil Code § 659.
Open-space easements, see Government Code § 51050 et seq.
Parcels too small to sustain agricultural use, denial of maps with respect this chapter, see Government Code § 66474.4.
Perpetual duration of conservation easements, see Government Code § 65966.
Wild and scenic rivers, see Public Resources Code § 5093.50 et seq.
Wilderness preservation system, see Public Resources Code § 5093.30 et seq.

§ 815. Legislative findings and declarations

The Legislature finds and declares that the preservation of land in its natural, scenic, agricultural, historical, forested, or open-space condition is among the most important environmental assets of California. The Legislature further finds and declares it to be the public policy and in the public interest of this state to encourage the voluntary conveyance of conservation easements to qualified nonprofit organizations. *(Added by Stats.1979, c. 179, p. 398, § 1.)*

Cross References

Mitigation lands, requirements imposed upon holders of accompanying funds relative to experience, capacity, and knowledge to manage property for mitigation purposes and any accompanying funds, see Government Code § 65965 et seq.

§ 815.1. Conservation easement

For the purposes of this chapter, "conservation easement" means any limitation in a deed, will, or other instrument in the form of an easement, restriction, covenant, or condition, which is or has been executed by or on behalf of the owner of the land subject to such easement and is binding upon successive owners of such land, and the purpose of which is to retain land predominantly in its natural, scenic, historical, agricultural, forested, or open-space condition. *(Added by Stats.1979, c. 179, p. 398, § 1.)*

Cross References

California Wildlife, Coastal, and Park Land Conservation Act, definitions, see Public Resources Code § 5902.
Conservation easement of existing forest lands, see Public Resources Code § 4751.
Eminent domain, acquisition of property subject to conservation easement, proceedings, see Code of Civil Procedure § 1240.055.
Establishment of a central public registry of conservation easements, see Public Resources Code § 5096.520.
Natural Heritage Preservation Tax Credit Act of 2000, definitions, see Public Resources Code § 37002.
Property tax assessments, application of definition, see Revenue and Taxation Code § 421.5.
Property taxation, assessment of land, effect of restrictions on value, see Revenue and Taxation Code § 402.1.
Rangeland, Grazing Land, and Grassland Protection Act, definitions, see Public Resources Code § 10332.
Recording conservation easements, use of index and Notice of Conservation Easements form, see Government Code § 27255.
Restrictive covenants, enforceability, submission and recording of restrictive covenant modification document, application of section, see Civil Code § 714.6.
Servitudes attached to land, see Civil Code § 801.

§ 815.2. Nature

(a) A conservation easement is an interest in real property voluntarily created and freely transferable in whole or in part for the purposes stated in Section 815.1 by any lawful method for the transfer of interests in real property in this state.

(b) A conservation easement shall be perpetual in duration.

(c) A conservation easement shall not be deemed personal in nature and shall constitute an interest in real property notwithstanding the fact that it may be negative in character.

(d) The particular characteristics of a conservation easement shall be those granted or specified in the instrument creating or transferring the easement. *(Added by Stats.1979, c. 179, p. 398, § 1.)*

Cross References

Real property defined for purposes of this Code, see Civil Code § 658.

§ 815.3. Entities authorized to acquire and hold conservation easements

Only the following entities or organizations may acquire and hold conservation easements:

(a) A tax-exempt nonprofit organization qualified under Section 501(c) (3) of the Internal Revenue Code [1] and qualified to do business in this state which has as its primary purpose the preservation, protection, or enhancement of land in its natural, scenic, historical, agricultural, forested, or open-space condition or use.

(b) The state or any city, county, city and county, district, or other state or local governmental entity, if otherwise authorized to acquire and hold title to real property and if the conservation easement is voluntarily conveyed. No local governmental entity may condition the issuance of an entitlement for use on the applicant's granting of a conservation easement pursuant to this chapter.

(c) A federally recognized California Native American tribe or a nonfederally recognized California Native American tribe that is on the contact list maintained by the Native American Heritage Commission to protect a California Native American prehistoric, archaeological, cultural, spiritual, or ceremonial place, if the conservation easement is voluntarily conveyed. *(Added by Stats.1979, c. 179, p. 398, § 1. Amended by Stats.1981, c. 478, § 1; Stats.2004, c. 905 (S.B.18), § 2.)*

[1] 26 U.S.C.A. § 501(c)(3).

Cross References

Agricultural conservation easement, see Public Resources Code § 10211.
Eminent domain, acquisition of property subject to conservation easement, proceedings, see Code of Civil Procedure § 1240.055.
Oak Woodlands Conservation Act, creation of Oak Woodlands Conservation Fund, use of funds, see Fish and Game Code § 1363.
Real property defined for purposes of this Code, see Civil Code § 658.
Restrictive covenants, enforceability, submission and recording of restrictive covenant modification document, application of section, see Civil Code § 714.6.

§ 815.4. Reservation of interests in grantor

All interests not transferred and conveyed by the instrument creating the easement shall remain in the grantor of the easement, including the right to engage in all uses of the land not affected by the easement nor prohibited by the easement or by law. *(Added by Stats.1979, c. 179, p. 398, § 1.)*

§ 815.5. Recordation

Instruments creating, assigning, or otherwise transferring conservation easements shall be recorded in the office of the county recorder of the county where the land is situated, in whole or in part, and such instruments shall be subject in all respects to the recording laws. *(Added by Stats.1979, c. 179, p. 398, § 1.)*

Cross References

Restrictive covenants, enforceability, submission and recording of restrictive covenant modification document, application of section, see Civil Code § 714.6.

§ 815.7. Enforcement of easement; injunctive relief; damages; costs

(a) No conservation easement shall be unenforceable by reason of lack of privity of contract or lack of benefit to

§ 815.7

particular land or because not expressed in the instrument creating it as running with the land.

(b) Actual or threatened injury to or impairment of a conservation easement or actual or threatened violation of its terms may be prohibited or restrained, or the interest intended for protection by such easement may be enforced, by injunctive relief granted by any court of competent jurisdiction in a proceeding initiated by the grantor or by the owner of the easement.

(c) In addition to the remedy of injunctive relief, the holder of a conservation easement shall be entitled to recover money damages for any injury to such easement or to the interest being protected thereby or for the violation of the terms of such easement. In assessing such damages there may be taken into account, in addition to the cost of restoration and other usual rules of the law of damages, the loss of scenic, aesthetic, or environmental value to the real property subject to the easement.

(d) The court may award to the prevailing party in any action authorized by this section the costs of litigation, including reasonable attorney's fees. (Added by Stats.1979, c. 179, p. 398, § 1.)

Cross References

Real property defined for purposes of this Code, see Civil Code § 658.

Restrictive covenants, enforceability, submission and recording of restrictive covenant modification document, application of section, see Civil Code § 714.6.

§ 815.9. Political subdivisions; authority to hold comparable easements

Nothing in this chapter shall be construed to impair or conflict with the operation of any law or statute conferring upon any political subdivision the right or power to hold interests in land comparable to conservation easements, including, but not limited to, Chapter 12 (commencing with Section 6950) of Division 7 of Title 1 of, Chapter 6.5 (commencing with Section 51050), Chapter 6.6 (commencing with Section 51070) and Chapter 7 (commencing with Section 51200) of Part 1 of Division 1 of Title 5 of, and Article 10.5 (commencing with Section 65560) of Chapter 3 of Title 7 of, the Government Code, and Article 1.5 (commencing with Section 421) of Chapter 3 of Part 2 of Division 1 of the Revenue and Taxation Code. (Added by Stats.1979, c. 179, p. 398, § 1.)

§ 815.10. Enforceable restrictions for purposes of assessment of land

A conservation easement granted pursuant to this chapter constitutes an enforceable restriction, for purposes of Section 402.1 of the Revenue and Taxation Code. (Added by Stats.1984, c. 777, § 1.)

Cross References

Land subject to enforceable restrictions, assessment, see Revenue and Taxation Code § 402.1.

§ 815.11. Repealed by Stats.2022, c. 131 (A.B.2966), § 1, eff. Jan. 1, 2023

§ 816. Liberal construction of chapter

The provisions of this chapter shall be liberally construed in order to effectuate the policy and purpose of Section 815. (Added by Stats.1979 c. 179, p. 398, § 1)

CHAPTER 4.5. GREENWAY EASEMENTS

Section
816.50. Legislative findings and declarations regarding development of greenways along urban waterways.
816.52. Definitions.
816.54. Greenway easements; characteristics.
816.56. Entities allowed to hold greenway easements.
816.58. Interests remaining in the grantor of greenway easement.
816.60. Recording of instruments creating, assigning, or transferring greenway easements.
816.62. Reasons that shall not render greenway easements unenforceable; injunctive relief; money damages.
816.64. Chapter does not prevent political subdivisions from holding interests in land comparable to greenway easements.
816.66. Greenway easements as enforceable restrictions.

§ 816.50. Legislative findings and declarations regarding development of greenways along urban waterways

The Legislature finds and declares the following with regard to the development of greenways along urban waterways:

(a) The restoration and preservation of land in its natural, scenic, forested, recreational, or open-space condition is among the most important environmental assets in California.

(b) Greenways have the potential to improve the quality of life in, and connectivity between, communities, and provide important recreational, open-space, wildlife, flood management, greenhouse gas reduction, and urban waterfront revitalization opportunities.

(c) It is the policy of the Legislature and in the best interest in the state to encourage the voluntary conveyance of greenway easements to qualified nonprofit organizations. (Added by Stats.2015, c. 639 (A.B.1251), § 3, eff. Jan. 1, 2016.)

§ 816.52. Definitions

For purposes of this chapter, the following definitions apply:

(a)(1) "Adjacent" means within 400 yards from the property boundary of an existing urban waterway.

(2) This subdivision does not create a new authority to place or extend an easement on private property that is not part of a voluntary agreement.

(b) "Greenway" means a pedestrian and bicycle, nonmotorized vehicle transportation, and recreational travel corridor that meets the following requirements:

(1) Includes landscaping that improves rivers and streams, provides flood protection benefits, and incorporates the significance and value of natural, historical, and cultural resources, as documented in the local agency's applicable planning document, including, but not limited to, a master plan, a general plan, or a specific plan.

(2) Is separated and protected from shared roadways, is adjacent to an urban waterway, and incorporates both ease of access to nearby communities and an array of amenities within an urbanized area and services for the users of the corridor and nearby communities.

(3) Is located on public lands or private lands, or a combination of public and private lands, where public access to those lands for greenway purposes has been legally authorized by, or legally obtained from, the fee owner of the land and, if applicable, the operator of any facility or improvement located on the land, through leases, easements, or other agreements entered into by the fee owner and the operator of any affected facility or improvement on the land.

(4) Reflects design standards regarding appropriate widths, clearances, setbacks from obstructions, and centerlines protecting directional travel, and other considerations, as appropriate, that are applicable for each affected local agency, as documented in the local agency's applicable planning document, including, but not limited to, a master plan, general plan, or specific plan, and that are consistent with plans and facilities for controlling the floodwater of rivers and their tributaries, as applicable.

(5) May incorporate appropriate lighting, public amenities within an urbanized area, art, and other features that are consistent with a local agency's planning document, including, but not limited to, a general plan, master plan, or specific plan.

(c) "Greenway easement" means any limitation in a deed, will, or other instrument in the form of an easement, restriction, covenant, or condition that is or has been executed by or on behalf of the owner of the land subject to the easement and is binding upon successive owners of that land, for either of the following purposes:

(1) Developing greenways adjacent to urban waterways consistent with restoration efforts undertaken at those waterways at the time of the creation of the easement, if any.

(2) Preserving greenways adjacent to urban waterways.

(d) "Local agency" means a city, county, or city and county.

(e) "Urbanized area" has the same meaning as set forth in Section 21071 of the Public Resources Code.

(f) "Urban waterway" means a creek, stream, or river that crosses (1) developed residential, commercial, or industrial property or (2) open space where the land use is designated as residential, commercial, or industrial, as referenced in a local agency's planning document, including, but not limited to, a general plan, master plan, or specific general plan. *(Added by Stats.2015, c. 639 (A.B.1251), § 3, eff. Jan. 1, 2016. Amended by Stats.2016, c. 471 (A.B.2651), § 1, eff. Sept. 22, 2016.)*

Cross References

Local planning, elements required to be included in plan, see Government Code § 65302.

§ 816.54. Greenway easements; characteristics

(a) A greenway easement is an interest in real property voluntarily created and freely transferable in whole or in part for the purposes stated in subdivision (c) of Section 816.52 by any lawful method for the transfer of interests in real property in this state.

(b) A greenway easement shall be perpetual in duration.

(c) Notwithstanding the fact that it may be negative in character, a greenway easement is not personal in nature and shall constitute an interest in real property.

(d) The particular characteristics of a greenway easement shall be those granted or specified in the instrument creating or transferring the easement. *(Added by Stats.2015, c. 639 (A.B.1251), § 3, eff. Jan. 1, 2016.)*

§ 816.56. Entities allowed to hold greenway easements

Only the following entities or organizations may acquire and hold a greenway easement:

(a) A tax-exempt nonprofit organization qualified under Section 501(c)(3) of the Internal Revenue Code [1] and qualified to do business in this state that has as its primary purpose the preservation, protection, or enhancement of land in its natural, scenic, historical, agricultural, forested, or open-space condition or use, or the preservation or development of a greenway.

(b) The state or any city, county, city and county, district, or other state or local governmental entity, if otherwise authorized to acquire and hold title to real property and if the greenway easement is voluntarily conveyed. A local governmental entity shall not condition the issuance of an entitlement for use on the applicant's granting of a greenway easement pursuant to this chapter.

(c) A federally recognized California Native American tribe or a nonfederally recognized California Native American tribe that is on the contact list maintained by the Native American Heritage Commission to protect a California Native American prehistoric, archaeological, cultural, spiritual, or ceremonial place, if the greenway easement is voluntarily conveyed. *(Added by Stats.2015, c. 639 (A.B.1251), § 3, eff. Jan. 1, 2016.)*

[1] Internal Revenue Code sections are in Title 26 of the U.S.C.A.

§ 816.58. Interests remaining in the grantor of greenway easement

All interests not transferred and conveyed by the instrument creating the greenway easement shall remain in the grantor of the greenway easement, including the right to engage in all uses of the land not affected by the greenway easement nor prohibited by the greenway easement or by law. *(Added by Stats.2015, c. 639 (A.B.1251), § 3, eff. Jan. 1, 2016.)*

§ 816.60. Recording of instruments creating, assigning, or transferring greenway easements

Instruments creating, assigning, or otherwise transferring greenway easements shall be recorded in the office of the county recorder of the county where the land is situated, in whole or in part, and those instruments shall be subject in all respects to the recording laws. *(Added by Stats.2015, c. 639 (A.B.1251), § 3, eff. Jan. 1, 2016.)*

§ 816.62. Reasons that shall not render greenway easements unenforceable; injunctive relief; money damages

(a) No greenway easement shall be unenforceable by reason of lack of privity of contract or lack of benefit to

§ 816.62

particular land or because not expressed in the instrument creating it as running with the land.

(b) Actual or threatened injury to or impairment of a greenway easement or actual or threatened violation of its terms may be prohibited or restrained, or the interest intended for protection by that easement may be enforced, by injunctive relief granted by any court of competent jurisdiction in a proceeding initiated by the grantor or by the owner of the greenway easement.

(c) In addition to the remedy of injunctive relief, the holder of a greenway easement shall be entitled to recover money damages for any injury to the greenway easement or to the interest being protected thereby or for the violation of the terms of the greenway easement. In assessing the damages, there may be taken into account, in addition to the cost of restoration and other usual rules of the law of damages, the loss of scenic, aesthetic, or environmental value to the real property subject to the greenway easement.

(d) The court may award to the prevailing party in any action authorized by this section the costs of litigation, including reasonable attorney's fees. *(Added by Stats.2015, c. 639 (A.B.1251), § 3, eff. Jan. 1, 2016.)*

§ 816.64. Chapter does not prevent political subdivisions from holding interests in land comparable to greenway easements

Nothing in this chapter shall be construed to impair or conflict with the operation of any law or statute conferring upon any political subdivision the right or power to hold interests in land comparable to greenway easements, including, but not limited to, Chapter 12 (commencing with Section 6950) of Division 7 of Title 1 of, Chapter 6.5 (commencing with Section 51050), Chapter 6.6 (commencing with Section 51070) and Chapter 7 (commencing with Section 51200) of Part 1 of Division 1 of Title 5 of, and Article 10.5 (commencing with Section 65560) of Chapter 3 of Title 7 of, the Government Code, and Article 1.5 (commencing with Section 421) of Chapter 3 of Part 2 of Division 1 of the Revenue and Taxation Code. *(Added by Stats.2015, c. 639 (A.B.1251), § 3, eff. Jan. 1, 2016.)*

§ 816.66. Greenway easements as enforceable restrictions

A greenway easement granted pursuant to this chapter constitutes an enforceable restriction, for purposes of Section 402.1 of the Revenue and Taxation Code. *(Added by Stats.2015, c. 639 (A.B.1251), § 3, eff. Jan. 1, 2016.)*

CHAPTER 5. HOUSING COOPERATIVES AND HOUSING COOPERATIVE TRUSTS

Section
817. Limited-equity housing cooperative; workforce housing cooperative trust; requirements; purchase and sale of stock or membership interest; application of corporate equity; amendment of bylaws and articles of incorporation.
817.1. Workforce housing cooperative trust; additional requirements; operation at multiple locations; creation.
817.2. Dissolution of limited-equity housing cooperative or workforce housing cooperative trust; procedure.
817.3. Sponsor organizations; legal standing of member.

Section
817.4. Attorney's fees and costs; prohibited use of corporate funds.

§ 817. Limited-equity housing cooperative; workforce housing cooperative trust; requirements; purchase and sale of stock or membership interest; application of corporate equity; amendment of bylaws and articles of incorporation

"Limited-equity housing cooperative" or a "workforce housing cooperative trust" means a corporation organized on a cooperative basis that, in addition to complying with Section 817.1 as may be applicable, meets all of the following requirements:

(a) The corporation is any of the following:

(1) Organized as a nonprofit public benefit corporation pursuant to Part 2 (commencing with Section 5110) of Division 2 of Title 1 of the Corporations Code.

(2) Holds title to real property as the beneficiary of a trust providing for distribution for public or charitable purposes upon termination of the trust.

(3) Holds title to real property subject to conditions that will result in reversion to a public or charitable entity upon dissolution of the corporation.

(4) Holds a leasehold interest, of at least 20 years' duration, conditioned on the corporation's continued qualification under this section, and provides for reversion to a public entity or charitable corporation.

(b)(1) The articles of incorporation or bylaws require the purchase and sale of the stock or membership interest of resident owners who cease to be permanent residents, at no more than a transfer value determined as provided in the articles or bylaws, and that shall not exceed the aggregate of the following:

(A) The consideration paid for the membership or shares by the first occupant of the unit involved, as shown on the books of the corporation.

(B) The value, as determined by the board of directors of the corporation, of any improvements installed at the expense of the member or a prior member with the prior approval of the board of directors.

(C) Accumulated simple interest, an inflation allowance at a rate that may be based on a cost-of-living index, an income index, or market-interest index, or compound interest if specified in the articles of incorporation or bylaws. For newly formed corporations, accumulated simple interest shall apply. Any increment pursuant to this paragraph shall not exceed a 10-percent annual increase on the consideration paid for the membership or share by the first occupant of the unit involved.

(2)(A) Except as provided in subparagraph (B), for purposes of a return of transfer value, both of the following are prohibited:

(i) A board of directors returning transfer value, either full or partial, to a member while he or she still remains a member.

(ii) An existing member accepting the return of his or her transfer value, either full or partial.

(B) A board of directors may return to an existing member and the existing member may accept return of his or her transfer value in the event that the member moves within the cooperative from a category of unit initially valued at a higher price to a different category of unit valued at a lower price.

(c) The articles of incorporation or bylaws require the board of directors to sell the stock or membership interest purchased as provided in subdivision (b) to new member-occupants or resident shareholders at a price that does not exceed the "transfer value" paid for the unit.

(d) The "corporate equity," that is defined as the excess of the current fair market value of the corporation's real property over the sum of the current transfer values of all shares or membership interests, reduced by the principal balance of outstanding encumbrances upon the corporate real property as a whole, shall be applied as follows:

(1) So long as any such encumbrance remains outstanding, the corporate equity shall not be used for distribution to members, but only for the following purposes, and only to the extent authorized by the board, subject to the provisions and limitations of the articles of incorporation and bylaws:

(A) For the benefit of the corporation or the improvement of the real property.

(B) For expansion of the corporation by acquisition of additional real property.

(C) For public benefit or charitable purposes.

(2) Upon sale of the property, dissolution of the corporation, or occurrence of a condition requiring termination of the trust or reversion of title to the real property, the corporate equity is required by the articles, bylaws, or trust or title conditions to be paid out, or title to the property transferred, subject to outstanding encumbrances and liens, for the transfer value of membership interests or shares, for use for a public or charitable purpose.

(e) Amendment of the bylaws and articles of incorporation requires the affirmative vote of at least two-thirds of the resident-owner members or shareholders. *(Added by Stats. 2009, c. 520 (A.B.1246), § 2.)*

Cross References

Place in state housing policy, see Health and Safety Code § 50076.5.
Relocation of persons displaced by community redevelopment projects, preference for limited-equity housing cooperatives, see Health and Safety Code § 33413.7.
Use of "cooperative" as part of corporate name, see Corporations Code § 12311.

§ 817.1. Workforce housing cooperative trust; additional requirements; operation at multiple locations; creation

(a) A "workforce housing cooperative trust" is an entity organized pursuant to this section that complies with Section 817 and with all of the following:

(1) Allows the governing board to be composed of two classes of board members. One class is elected by the residents, and one class is appointed by sponsor organizations, including employer and employee organizations, chambers of commerce, government entities, unions, religious organizations, nonprofit organizations, cooperative organizations, and other forms of organizations. Resident members shall elect a majority of the board members. However, sponsor organizations may appoint up to one less than a majority of the board members. The numerical composition and class of the sponsor and resident board members shall be set in the articles of incorporation and in the bylaws.

(2) Requires the charter board of a workforce housing cooperative trust to be composed of only sponsor board members, to remain in place for one year after the first resident occupancy. One year after the first resident occupancy, the resident members shall elect a single board member. Three years after the first resident occupancy, resident members shall elect a majority of the board members.

(3) Prohibits the removal of the appointees of sponsor organizations, except for cause.

(4) Allows for the issuance of separate classes of shares to sponsor organizations or support organizations. These shares shall be denominated as "workforce housing shares" and shall receive a rate of return of no more than 10 percent simple interest pursuant to subparagraph (C) of paragraph (1) of subdivision (b) of Section 817.

(5) Requires, in order to amend the bylaws or articles of incorporation of a workforce housing cooperative trust, the affirmative vote of at least a majority of the resident-owner members or shareholders and a majority of each class of board members. The rights of the sponsor board members or the sponsors shall not be changed without the affirmative vote of two-thirds of the sponsor board members.

(b) A workforce housing cooperative trust shall be entitled to operate at multiple locations in order to sponsor limited-equity housing cooperatives. A workforce housing cooperative trust may either own or lease land for the purpose of developing limited-equity housing cooperatives.

(c) A workforce housing cooperative trust may be created when at least 51 percent of the occupied units in a multifamily property that is in foreclosure support efforts to buy the building or property. *(Added by Stats.2009, c. 520 (A.B. 1246), § 2.)*

§ 817.2. Dissolution of limited-equity housing cooperative or workforce housing cooperative trust; procedure

The procedure for the dissolution of a limited-equity housing cooperative or workforce housing cooperative trust that receives or has received a public subsidy shall be as follows:

(a) The city, or the county for any unincorporated area, in which the limited-equity housing cooperative or workforce housing cooperative trust is located, shall hold a public hearing. The cooperative or trust shall pay for all costs associated with the public hearing.

(b) The city or county shall provide notice to all interested parties. The notice shall be given at least 120 days prior to the date of the hearing. The city or county shall obtain a list of all other limited-equity housing cooperatives and cooperative development organizations in the state from the California Center for Cooperative Development, if the list exists, and provide notice to all of the entities on the list in an effort to create a merger with an existing limited-equity housing cooperative or workforce housing cooperative trust. The

§ 817.2

notice shall be mailed first class, postage prepaid, in the United States mail.

(c) If the dissolving limited-equity housing cooperative or workforce housing cooperative trust merges with an existing cooperative or trust, to the extent possible, the merger shall be with the geographically closest cooperative or trust.

(d) If the dissolving limited-equity housing cooperative or workforce housing cooperative trust does not merge with an existing cooperative or trust, both of the following shall occur:

(1) Upon completion of the public hearing required pursuant to subdivision (a), the city or county shall adopt a resolution approving of the dissolution and make a finding that the dissolution plan meets the requirements of state and federal law, meets the donative intent standards of the United States Internal Revenue Service, and is free of private inurement, which includes, but is not limited to, a prohibition on any member receiving any payment in excess of the transfer value to which he or she is entitled pursuant to subdivision (b) of Section 817.

(2) The city or county shall forward all of the information and written testimony from the hearing to the Office of the Attorney General for the Attorney General to consider as part of his or her ruling on the dissolution. *(Added by Stats.2009, c. 520 (A.B.1246), § 2.)*

§ 817.3. Sponsor organizations; legal standing of member

Each entity named as a sponsor organization of a workforce housing cooperative trust formed pursuant to Section 817 shall have the legal standing of a member unless it revokes, in writing, its sponsorship. *(Added by Stats.2009, c. 520 (A.B.1246), § 2.)*

§ 817.4. Attorney's fees and costs; prohibited use of corporate funds

(a) In any action instituted on or after January 1, 2010, against a board of directors and its members based upon a breach of corporate or fiduciary duties or a failure to comply with the requirements of this chapter, a prevailing plaintiff may recover reasonable attorney's fees and costs.

(b) If an organization formed under this chapter uses public funds, it shall not use any corporate funds to avoid compliance with this chapter or to pursue dissolution if the intent or outcome is for some or all of the members to receive any payment in excess of the transfer value to which he or she is entitled pursuant to subdivision (b) of Section 817. *(Added by Stats.2009, c. 520 (A.B.1246), § 2.)*

Title 3

RIGHTS AND OBLIGATIONS OF OWNERS

Chapter	Section
1. Rights of Owners	818
2. Obligations of Owners	840
3. Environmental Responsibility Acceptance Act	850

CHAPTER 1. RIGHTS OF OWNERS

Article	Section
1. Incidents of Ownership	818
2. Boundaries	829

ARTICLE 1. INCIDENTS OF OWNERSHIP

Section
818. Life tenant; rights; restriction.
819. Tenant for years or at will; rights.
820. Tenant for years or at will; limitation on rights.
821. Grantees of rents and reversions; rights.
822. Lessor; remedies against assignee of lessee.
823. Lessee and assigns; remedies against lessor and assigns.
824. Lease for life; recovery of rent.
825. Rent dependent upon life; recovery.
826. Remaindermen and reversioners; remedies for injuries to inheritance.
827. Leases; term less than a month; change in terms; notice.

§ 818. Life tenant; rights; restriction

RIGHTS OF TENANT FOR LIFE. The owner of a life estate may use the land in the same manner as the owner of a fee simple, except that he must do no act to the injury of the inheritance. *(Enacted in 1872.)*

Cross References

Duties of tenants for life, see Civil Code § 840.
Treble damages for waste by life tenant, see Code of Civil Procedure § 732.

§ 819. Tenant for years or at will; rights

RIGHTS OF TENANT FOR YEARS, ETC. A tenant for years or at will, unless he is a wrong-doer by holding over, may occupy the buildings, take the annual products of the soil, work mines and quarries open at the commencement of his tenancy. *(Enacted in 1872.)*

Cross References

Determination of tenancy or other estate at will, see Civil Code § 789
Summary proceedings for obtaining possession of real property, see Code of Civil Procedure § 1169 et seq.
Summary proceedings for possession, see Civil Code § 792.

§ 820. Tenant for years or at will; limitation on rights

SAME. A tenant for years or at will has no other rights to the property than such as are given to him by the agreement or instrument by which his tenancy is acquired, or by the last section. *(Enacted in 1872.)*

§ 821. Grantees of rents and reversions; rights

RIGHTS OF GRANTEES OF RENTS AND REVERSION. A person to whom any real property is transferred or devised, upon which rent has been reserved, or to whom any such rent is transferred, is entitled to the same remedies for recovery of rent, for non-performance of any of the terms of the lease, or for any waste or cause of forfeiture, as his grantor or devisor might have had. *(Enacted in 1872.)*

Cross References

Notice to tenant necessary to effectuate grants of rents, reversions and remainders, see Civil Code § 1111.

Real property defined for purposes of this Code, see Civil Code § 658.

§ 822. Lessor; remedies against assignee of lessee

Whatever remedies the lessor of any real property has against his immediate lessee for the breach of any agreement in the lease, or for recovery of the possession, he has against the assignees of the lessee, for any cause of action accruing while they are such assignees, except where the assignment is made by way of security for a loan, and is not accompanied by possession of the premises. *(Enacted in 1872. Amended by Code Am.1873–74, c. 612, p. 219, § 109; Stats.1905, c. 439, p. 599, § 1.)*

Cross References

Real property defined for purposes of this Code, see Civil Code § 658.
Sublease or assignment, unlawful detainer, see Code of Civil Procedure § 1161.

§ 823. Lessee and assigns; remedies against lessor and assigns

RIGHTS OF LESSEES AND THEIR ASSIGNEES, ETC. Whatever remedies the lessee of any real property may have against his immediate lessor, for the breach of any agreement in the lease, he may have against the assigns of the lessor, and the assigns of the lessee may have against the lessor and his assigns, except upon covenants against incumbrances[1] or relating to the title or possession of the premises. *(Enacted in 1872.)*

[1] So in chaptered copy.

Cross References

Real property defined for purposes of this Code, see Civil Code § 658.

§ 824. Lease for life; recovery of rent

REMEDY ON LEASES FOR LIFE. Rent due upon a lease for life may be recovered in the same manner as upon a lease for years. *(Enacted in 1872.)*

§ 825. Rent dependent upon life; recovery

RENT DEPENDENT ON LIFE. Rent dependent on the life of a person may be recovered after as well as before his death. *(Enacted in 1872.)*

§ 826. Remaindermen and reversioners; remedies for injuries to inheritance

REMEDY OF REVERSIONERS, ETC. A person having an estate in fee, in remainder or reversion, may maintain an action for any injury done to the inheritance, notwithstanding an intervening estate for life or years, and although, after its commission, his estate is transferred, and he has no interest in the property at the commencement of the action. *(Enacted in 1872.)*

Cross References

Waste by tenant as terminating lease, see Code of Civil Procedure § 1161.

§ 827. Leases; term less than a month; change in terms; notice

(a) Except as provided in subdivision (b), in all leases of lands or tenements, or of any interest therein, from week to week, month to month, or other period less than a month, the landlord may, upon giving notice in writing to the tenant, in the manner prescribed by Section 1162 of the Code of Civil Procedure, change the terms of the lease to take effect, as to tenancies for less than one month, upon the expiration of a period at least as long as the term of the hiring itself, and, as to tenancies from month to month, to take effect at the expiration of not less than 30 days, but if that change takes effect within a rental term, the rent accruing from the first day of the term to the date of that change shall be computed at the rental rate obtained immediately prior to that change; provided, however, that it shall be competent for the parties to provide by an agreement in writing that a notice changing the terms thereof may be given at any time not less than seven days before the expiration of a term, to be effective upon the expiration of the term.

The notice, when served upon the tenant, shall in and of itself operate and be effectual to create and establish, as a part of the lease, the terms, rents, and conditions specified in the notice, if the tenant shall continue to hold the premises after the notice takes effect.

(b)(1) In all leases of a residential dwelling, or of any interest therein, from week to week, month to month, or other period less than a month, the landlord may increase the rent provided in the lease or rental agreement, upon giving written notice to the tenant, as follows, by either of the following procedures:

(A) By delivering a copy to the tenant personally.

(B) By serving a copy by mail under the procedures prescribed in Section 1013 of the Code of Civil Procedure.

(2) If the proposed rent increase for that tenant is 10 percent or less of the rental amount charged to that tenant at any time during the 12 months before the effective date of the increase, either in and of itself or when combined with any other rent increases for the 12 months before the effective date of the increase, the notice shall be delivered at least 30 days before the effective date of the increase, and subject to Section 1013 of the Code of Civil Procedure if served by mail.

(3)(A) If the proposed rent increase for that tenant is greater than 10 percent of the rental amount charged to that tenant at any time during the 12 months before the effective date of the increase, either in and of itself or when combined with any other rent increases for the 12 months before the effective date of the increase, the notice shall be delivered at least 90 days before the effective date of the increase, and subject to Section 1013 of the Code of Civil Procedure if served by mail.

(B) If the proposed rent increase for that tenant is caused by a change in a tenant's income or family composition as determined by a recertification required by statute or regulation, the notice shall be delivered at least 30 days before the effective date of the increase as described in paragraph (2), and subparagraph (A) of this paragraph shall not apply.

(c) If a state or federal statute, state or federal regulation, recorded regulatory agreement, or contract provides for a longer period of notice regarding a rent increase than that provided in subdivision (a) or (b), the personal service or mailing of the notice shall be in accordance with the longer period. *(Added by Code Am.1873–74, c. 612, p. 220, § 110.*

§ 827

Amended by Stats.1907, c. 39, p. 58, § 1; Stats.1929, c. 138, p. 256, § 1; Stats.1937, c. 356, p. 774, § 1; Stats.1939, c. 1013, p. 2799, § 1; Stats.1947, c. 676, p. 1708, § 1; Stats.2000, c. 680 (S.B.1745), § 2; Stats.2001, c. 593 (A.B.1160), § 1, eff. Oct. 9, 2001; Stats.2002, c. 664 (A.B.3034), § 33; Stats.2004, c. 568 (S.B.1145), § 1; Stats.2019, c. 595 (A.B.1110), § 2, eff. Jan. 1, 2020.)

Cross References

Determination of tenancy or other estate at will, notice, see Civil Code § 789.

Landlord and tenant, cash as exclusive form of rent or security deposit payment, see Civil Code § 1947.3.

Posting or displaying political signs by tenant, landlord not to prohibit, exceptions, notice and enforcement of changes in terms of tenancy, see Civil Code § 1940.4.

Real property, limitation of rent increase, subleases, notice, see Civil Code § 1947.12.

ARTICLE 2. BOUNDARIES

Section
829. Owner in fee; rights.
830. Water as boundary.
831. Way as boundary.
832. Lateral and subjacent support; excavations; degree of care; damages; protection of other structures.
833. Trees; trunks upon land of one owner; ownership.
834. Line trees; common ownership.
835. Electrified security fence; installation and operation requirements.

Cross References

Boundary lines, see Cal. Const. Art. 21, § 1; Government Code § 160.

County boundaries, see Government Code § 23070 et seq.

§ 829. Owner in fee; rights

RIGHTS OF OWNER. The owner of land in fee has the right to the surface and to everything permanently situated beneath or above it. *(Enacted in 1872.)*

§ 830. Water as boundary

Except where the grant under which the land is held indicates a different intent, the owner of the upland, when it borders on tide water, takes to ordinary high-water mark; when it borders upon a navigable lake or stream, where there is no tide, the owner takes to the edge of the lake or stream, at low-water mark; when it borders upon any other water, the owner takes to the middle of the lake or stream. *(Enacted in 1872. Amended by Code Am.1873–74, c. 612, p. 220, § 111.)*

Cross References

Accessions to property,
  Alluvion, see Civil Code § 1014.
  Avulsion, see Civil Code § 1015.
  Islands, see Civil Code § 1016 et seq.
Navigable waters enumerated, see Harbors and Navigation Code § 100 et seq.
Rules for construing description of water boundaries, see Code of Civil Procedure § 2077.

§ 831. Way as boundary

BOUNDARIES BY WAYS. An owner of land bounded by a road or street is presumed to own to the center of the way, but the contrary may be shown. *(Enacted in 1872.)*

Cross References

Highway as boundary, see Civil Code § 1112; Code of Civil Procedure § 2077.

§ 832. Lateral and subjacent support; excavations; degree of care; damages; protection of other structures

Each coterminous owner is entitled to the lateral and subjacent support which his land receives from the adjoining land, subject to the right of the owner of the adjoining land to make proper and usual excavations on the same for purposes of construction or improvement, under the following conditions:

1. Any owner of land or his lessee intending to make or to permit an excavation shall give reasonable notice to the owner or owners of adjoining lands and of buildings or other structures, stating the depth to which such excavation is intended to be made, and when the excavating will begin.

2. In making any excavation, ordinary care and skill shall be used, and reasonable precautions taken to sustain the adjoining land as such, without regard to any building or other structure which may be thereon, and there shall be no liability for damage done to any such building or other structure by reason of the excavation, except as otherwise provided or allowed by law.

3. If at any time it appears that the excavation is to be of a greater depth than are the walls or foundations of any adjoining building or other structure, and is to be so close as to endanger the building or other structure in any way, then the owner of the building or other structure must be allowed at least 30 days, if he so desires, in which to take measures to protect the same from any damage, or in which to extend the foundations thereof, and he must be given for the same purposes reasonable license to enter on the land on which the excavation is to be or is being made.

4. If the excavation is intended to be or is deeper than the standard depth of foundations, which depth is defined to be a depth of nine feet below the adjacent curb level, at the point where the joint property line intersects the curb and if on the land of the coterminous owner there is any building or other structure the wall or foundation of which goes to standard depth or deeper then the owner of the land on which the excavation is being made shall, if given the necessary license to enter on the adjoining land, protect the said adjoining land and any such building or other structure thereon without cost to the owner thereof, from any damage by reason of the excavation, and shall be liable to the owner of such property for any such damage, excepting only for minor settlement cracks in buildings or other structures. *(Enacted in 1872. Amended by Code Am.1873–74, c. 612, p. 221, § 112; Stats. 1931, c. 776, p. 1616, § 1; Stats.1968, c. 835, p. 1606, § 1.)*

§ 833. Trees; trunks upon land of one owner; ownership

TREES WHOSE TRUNKS ARE WHOLLY ON LAND OF ONE. Trees whose trunks stand wholly upon the land of one owner belong exclusively to him, although their roots grow into the land of another. *(Enacted in 1872.)*

§ 834. Line trees; common ownership

LINE TREES. Trees whose trunks stand partly on the land of two or more coterminous owners, belong to them in common. *(Enacted in 1872.)*

§ 835. Electrified security fence; installation and operation requirements

(a) As used in this chapter, "electrified security fence" means any fence, other than an electrified fence as defined in Section 17151 of the Food and Agricultural Code, that meets the following requirements:

(1) The fence is powered by an electrical energizer with both of the following output characteristics:

(A) The impulse repetition rate does not exceed 1 hertz (hz).

(B) The impulse duration does not exceed 10 milliseconds, or $^{10}/_{10000}$ of a second.

(2) The fence is used to protect and secure commercial, manufacturing, or industrial property, or property zoned under another designation, but legally authorized to be used for a commercial, manufacturing, or industrial purpose.

(b) An owner of real property may install and operate an electrified security fence on their property, subject to all of the following:

(1) The property is not located in a residential zone.

(2) The fence meets the 2006 international standards and specifications of the International Electrotechnical Commission for electric fence energizers in "International Standard IEC 60335, Part 2–76."

(3) The fence is identified by prominently placed warning signs that are legible from both sides of the fence. At a minimum, the warning signs shall meet all of the following criteria:

(A) The warning signs are placed at each gate and access point, and at intervals along the fence not exceeding 30 feet.

(B) The warning signs are adjacent to any other signs relating to chemical, radiological, or biological hazards.

(C) The warning signs are marked with a written warning or a commonly recognized symbol for shock, a written warning or a commonly recognized symbol to warn people with pacemakers, and a written warning or commonly recognized symbol about the danger of touching the fence in wet conditions.

(4) The height of the fence does not exceed 10 feet or 2 feet higher than an existing perimeter fence, whichever is greater. The electrified security fence shall be located behind a perimeter fence that is not less than 5 feet in height.

(c) The electrified security fence may interface with a monitored alarm device in a manner that enables the alarm system to transmit a signal intended to summon the business, a monitoring service, or both the business and a monitoring service, in response to an intrusion or burglary.

(d)(1) An owner of real property shall not install or operate an electrified security fence where a local ordinance prohibits the installation or operation of an electrified security fence. A local ordinance that prohibits or regulates only the installation or operation of an electrified fence as defined in Section 17151 of the Food and Agricultural Code does not apply to an electrified security fence.

(2) If a local ordinance allows the installation and operation of an electrified security fence, the installation and operation of the fence shall meet the requirements of that ordinance and the requirements of subdivision (b). *(Added by Stats.2015, c. 273 (S.B.582), § 1, eff. Jan. 1, 2016. Amended by Stats.2021, c. 148 (A.B.358), § 1, eff. Jan. 1, 2022.)*

CHAPTER 2. OBLIGATIONS OF OWNERS

Section
840. Tenant for life; duties.
841. Maintenance of boundaries, monuments, and fences; responsibilities of adjoining landowners; definitions.
841.4. Spite fences.
842. Repealed.
843. Concurrent ownership; ouster; procedure; damages.
844. Repealed.
845. Easements; maintenance; failure to pay owner's share of costs; snow removal.
846. Permission to enter for recreational purposes.
846.1. Public entry for recreational purposes; injury or damage; owner or public entity as defendant; claim for reasonable attorney's fees.
846.2. Invitees on land to glean food for charitable purposes; liability; limited immunity.
846.5. Surveyors; right of entry; use of boundary evidence and performance of surveys; freeways.
846.6. Repealed.
847. Immunity from liability; injuries or death occurring on property during or after the commission of certain felonies.
848. Mineral rights owners; notice of entry on real property to exercise rights; timing; contents; injunctions.
849. Repealed.

§ 840. Tenant for life; duties

DUTIES OF TENANT FOR LIFE. The owner of a life estate must keep the buildings and fences in repair from ordinary waste, and must pay the taxes and other annual charges, and a just proportion of extraordinary assessments benefiting the whole inheritance. *(Enacted in 1872.)*

Cross References

Rights of tenants for life, see Civil Code § 818.
Treble damages for waste by life tenant, see Code of Civil Procedure § 732.

§ 841. Maintenance of boundaries, monuments, and fences; responsibilities of adjoining landowners; definitions

(a) Adjoining landowners shall share equally in the responsibility for maintaining the boundaries and monuments between them.

(b)(1) Adjoining landowners are presumed to share an equal benefit from any fence dividing their properties and, unless otherwise agreed to by the parties in a written agreement, shall be presumed to be equally responsible for the reasonable costs of construction, maintenance, or necessary replacement of the fence.

(2) Where a landowner intends to incur costs for a fence described in paragraph (1), the landowner shall give 30 days' prior written notice to each affected adjoining landowner. The notice shall include notification of the presumption of equal responsibility for the reasonable costs of construction, maintenance, or necessary replacement of the fence. The notice shall include a description of the nature of the problem facing the shared fence, the proposed solution for addressing

the problem, the estimated construction or maintenance costs involved to address the problem, the proposed cost sharing approach, and the proposed timeline for getting the problem addressed.

(3) The presumption in paragraph (1) may be overcome by a preponderance of the evidence demonstrating that imposing equal responsibility for the reasonable costs of construction, maintenance, or necessary replacement of the fence would be unjust. In determining whether equal responsibility for the reasonable costs would be unjust, the court shall consider all of the following:

(A) Whether the financial burden to one landowner is substantially disproportionate to the benefit conferred upon that landowner by the fence in question.

(B) Whether the cost of the fence would exceed the difference in the value of the real property before and after its installation.

(C) Whether the financial burden to one landowner would impose an undue financial hardship given that party's financial circumstances as demonstrated by reasonable proof.

(D) The reasonableness of a particular construction or maintenance project, including all of the following:

(i) The extent to which the costs of the project appear to be unnecessary or excessive.

(ii) The extent to which the costs of the project appear to be the result of the landowner's personal aesthetic, architectural, or other preferences.

(E) Any other equitable factors appropriate under the circumstances.

(4) Where a party rebuts the presumption in paragraph (1) by a preponderance of the evidence, the court shall, in its discretion, consistent with the party's circumstances, order either a contribution of less than an equal share for the costs of construction, maintenance, or necessary replacement of the fence, or order no contribution.

(c) For the purposes of this section, the following terms have the following meanings:

(1) "Landowner" means a private person or entity that lawfully holds any possessory interest in real property, and does not include a city, county, city and county, district, public corporation, or other political subdivision, public body, or public agency.

(2) "Adjoining" means contiguous to or in contact with. *(Added by Stats.2013, c. 86 (A.B.1404), § 3.)*

§ 841.4. Spite fences

Any fence or other structure in the nature of a fence unnecessarily exceeding 10 feet in height maliciously erected or maintained for the purpose of annoying the owner or occupant of adjoining property is a private nuisance. Any owner or occupant of adjoining property injured either in his comfort or the enjoyment of his estate by such nuisance may enforce the remedies against its continuance prescribed in Title 3, Part 3, Division 4 of this code.[1] *(Added by Stats.1953, c. 37, p. 674, § 2.)*

[1] Section 3501 et seq.

§ 842. Repealed by Stats.1943, c. 368, p. 1895, § 150001

§ 843. Concurrent ownership; ouster; procedure; damages

(a) If real property is owned concurrently by two or more persons, a tenant out of possession may establish an ouster from possession by a tenant in possession in the manner provided in this section. This section does not apply to the extent the tenant out of possession is not entitled to possession or an alternative remedy is provided under the terms of an agreement between the cotenants or the instrument creating the cotenancy or another written instrument that indicates the possessory rights or remedies of the cotenants. This section supplements and does not limit any other means by which an ouster may be established.

(b) A tenant out of possession may serve on a tenant in possession a written demand for concurrent possession of the property. The written demand shall make specific reference to this section and to the time within which concurrent possession must be offered under this section. Service of the written demand shall be made in the same manner as service of summons in a civil action. An ouster is established 60 days after service is complete if, within that time, the tenant in possession does not offer and provide unconditional concurrent possession of the property to the tenant out of possession.

(c) A claim for damages for an ouster established pursuant to this section may be asserted by an independent action or in an action for possession or partition of the property or another appropriate action or proceeding, subject to any applicable statute of limitation.

(d) Nothing in this section precludes the cotenants, at any time before or after a demand is served, from seeking partition of the property or from making an agreement as to the right of possession among the cotenants, the payment of reasonable rental value in lieu of possession, or any other terms that may be appropriate. *(Added by Stats.1984, c. 241, § 1.)*

Cross References

Real property defined for purposes of this Code, see Civil Code § 658.

§ 844. Repealed by Stats.1943, c. 368, p. 1895, § 150001

§ 845. Easements; maintenance; failure to pay owner's share of costs; snow removal

(a) The owner of any easement in the nature of a private right-of-way, or of any land to which any such easement is attached, shall maintain it in repair.

(b) If the easement is owned by more than one person, or is attached to parcels of land under different ownership, the cost of maintaining it in repair shall be shared by each owner of the easement or the owners of the parcels of land, as the case may be, pursuant to the terms of any agreement entered into by the parties for that purpose. In the absence of an agreement, the cost shall be shared proportionately to the use made of the easement by each owner.

(c) If any owner refuses to perform, or fails after demand in writing to pay the owner's proportion of the cost, an action to recover that owner's share of the cost, or for specific performance or contribution, may be brought by the other owners, either jointly or severally. The action may be brought before, during, or after performance of the maintenance work, as follows:

(1) The action may be brought in small claims court if the amount claimed to be due as the owner's proportion of the cost does not exceed the jurisdictional limit of the small claims court. A small claims judgment shall not affect apportionment of any future costs that are not requested in the small claims action.

(2) Except as provided in paragraph (1), the action shall be filed in superior court and, notwithstanding Section 1141.13 of the Code of Civil Procedure, the action shall be subject to judicial arbitration pursuant to Chapter 2.5 of Title 3 of Part 3 (commencing with Section 1141.10) of the Code of Civil Procedure. A superior court judgment shall not affect apportionment of any future costs that are not requested in the action, unless otherwise provided in the judgment.

(3) In the absence of an agreement addressing the maintenance of the easement, any action for specific performance or contribution shall be brought in a court in the county in which the easement is located.

(4) Nothing in this section precludes the use of any available alternative dispute resolution program to resolve actions regarding the maintenance of easements in the small claims court or the superior court.

(d) In the event that snow removal is not required under subdivision (a), or under any independent contractual or statutory duty, an agreement entered into pursuant to subdivision (b) to maintain the easement in repair shall be construed to include snow removal within the maintenance obligations of the agreement if all of the following exist:

(1) Snow removal is not expressly precluded by the terms of the agreement.

(2) Snow removal is necessary to provide access to the properties served by the easement.

(3) Snow removal is approved in advance by the property owners or their elected representatives in the same manner as provided by the agreement for repairs to the easement.

(e) This section does not apply to rights-of-way held or used by railroad common carriers subject to the jurisdiction of the Public Utilities Commission. *(Added by Stats.1939, c. 755, p. 2285, § 1. Amended by Stats.1985, c. 985, § 1; Stats.1993, c. 196 (S.B.370), § 1; Stats.2012, c. 244 (A.B. 1927), § 1.)*

Cross References

Obligation defined, see Civil Code § 1427.
Ownership defined for purposes of this Code, see Civil Code § 654.
Servitudes and easements, generally, see Civil Code § 801 et seq.

§ 846. Permission to enter for recreational purposes

(a) An owner of any estate or any other interest in real property, whether possessory or nonpossessory, owes no duty of care to keep the premises safe for entry or use by others for any recreational purpose or to give any warning of hazardous conditions, uses of, structures, or activities on those premises to persons entering for a recreational purpose, except as provided in this section.

(b) A "recreational purpose," as used in this section, includes activities such as fishing, hunting, camping, water sports, hiking, spelunking, sport parachuting, riding, including animal riding, snowmobiling, and all other types of vehicular riding, rock collecting, sightseeing, picnicking, nature study, nature contacting, recreational gardening, gleaning, hang gliding, private noncommercial aviation activities, winter sports, and viewing or enjoying historical, archaeological, scenic, natural, or scientific sites.

(c) An owner of any estate or any other interest in real property, whether possessory or nonpossessory, who gives permission to another for entry or use for the above purpose upon the premises does not thereby do any of the following:

(1) Extend any assurance that the premises are safe for that purpose.

(2) Constitute the person to whom permission has been granted the legal status of an invitee or licensee to whom a duty of care is owed.

(3) Assume responsibility for or incur liability for any injury to person or property caused by any act of the person to whom permission has been granted except as provided in this section.

(d) This section does not limit the liability which otherwise exists for any of the following:

(1) Willful or malicious failure to guard or warn against a dangerous condition, use, structure or activity.

(2) Injury suffered in any case where permission to enter for the above purpose was granted for a consideration other than the consideration, if any, paid to said landowner by the state, or where consideration has been received from others for the same purpose.

(3) Any persons who are expressly invited rather than merely permitted to come upon the premises by the landowner.

(e) This section does not create a duty of care or ground of liability for injury to person or property. *(Added by Stats. 1963, c. 1759, p. 3511, § 1. Amended by Stats.1970, c. 807, p. 1530, § 1; Stats.1971, c. 1028, p. 1975, § 1; Stats.1972, c. 1200, p. 2322, § 1; Stats.1976, c. 1303, p. 5859, § 1; Stats. 1978, c. 86, p. 221, § 1; Stats.1979, c. 150, p. 347, § 1; Stats.1980, c. 408, § 1; Stats.1988, c. 129, § 1; Stats.2014, c. 52 (S.B.1072), § 1, eff. Jan. 1, 2015; Stats.2018, c. 92 (S.B.1289), § 33, eff. Jan. 1, 2019.)*

Cross References

Real property defined for purposes of this Code, see Civil Code § 658.
Shared Habitat Alliance for Recreational Enhancement Program, compensation to private landowners for public use of land, see Fish and Game Code § 1573.
Willful acts of negligence, contributory negligence, liability, see Civil Code § 1714.

§ 846.1. Public entry for recreational purposes; injury or damage; owner or public entity as defendant; claim for reasonable attorney's fees

(a) Except as provided in subdivision (c), an owner of any estate or interest in real property, whether possessory or nonpossessory, who gives permission to the public for entry on or use of the real property pursuant to an agreement with

§ 846.1

a public or nonprofit agency for purposes of recreational trail use, and is a defendant in a civil action brought by, or on behalf of, a person who is allegedly injured or allegedly suffers damages on the real property, may present a claim to the Department of General Services for reasonable attorney's fees incurred in this civil action if any of the following occurs:

(1) The court has dismissed the civil action upon a demurrer or motion for summary judgment made by the owner or upon its own motion for lack of prosecution.

(2) The action was dismissed by the plaintiff without any payment from the owner.

(3) The owner prevails in the civil action.

(b) Except as provided in subdivision (c), a public entity, as defined in Section 831.5 of the Government Code, that gives permission to the public for entry on or use of real property for a recreational purpose, as defined in Section 846, and is a defendant in a civil action brought by, or on behalf of, a person who is allegedly injured or allegedly suffers damages on the real property, may present a claim to the Department of General Services for reasonable attorney's fees incurred in this civil action if any of the following occurs:

(1) The court has dismissed the civil action upon a demurrer or motion for summary judgment made by this public entity or upon its own motion for lack of prosecution.

(2) The action was dismissed by the plaintiff without any payment from the public entity.

(3) The public entity prevails in the civil action.

(c) An owner of any estate or interest in real property, whether possessory or nonpossessory, or a public entity, as defined in Section 831.5 of the Government Code, that gives permission to the public for entry on, or use of, the real property for a recreational purpose, as defined in Section 846, pursuant to an agreement with a public or nonprofit agency, and is a defendant in a civil action brought by, or on behalf of, a person who seeks to restrict, prevent, or delay public use of that property, may present a claim to the Department of General Services for reasonable attorney's fees incurred in the civil action if any of the following occurs:

(1) The court has dismissed the civil action upon a demurrer or motion for summary judgment made by the owner or public entity or upon its own motion for lack of prosecution.

(2) The action was dismissed by the plaintiff without any payment from the owner or public entity.

(3) The owner or public entity prevails in the civil action.

(d) The Department of General Services shall allow the claim if the requirements of this section are met. The claim shall be paid from an appropriation to be made for that purpose. Reasonable attorney's fees, for purposes of this section, may not exceed an hourly rate greater than the rate charged by the Attorney General at the time the award is made, and may not exceed an aggregate amount of twenty-five thousand dollars ($25,000). This subdivision shall not apply if a public entity has provided for the defense of this civil action pursuant to Section 995 of the Government Code. This subdivision shall also not apply if an owner or public entity has been provided a legal defense by the state pursuant to any contract or other legal obligation.

(e) The total of claims allowed by the Department of General Services pursuant to this section shall not exceed two hundred thousand dollars ($200,000) per fiscal year. *(Added by Stats.1996, c. 932 (A.B.2291), § 1. Amended by Stats.1999, c. 775 (S.B.243), § 1; Stats.2006, c. 538 (S.B.1852), § 41; Stats.2016, c. 31 (S.B.836), § 8, eff. June 27, 2016.)*

Cross References

Attorney General, generally, see Government Code § 12500 et seq.

California Victim Compensation and Government Claims Board (formerly State Control Board), see Government Code § 13900 et seq.

Obligation defined, see Civil Code § 1427.

Real property defined for purposes of this Code, see Civil Code § 658.

§ 846.2. Invitees on land to glean food for charitable purposes; liability; limited immunity

No cause of action shall arise against the owner, tenant, or lessee of land or premises for injuries to any person who has been expressly invited on that land or premises to glean agricultural or farm products for charitable purposes, unless that person's injuries were caused by the gross negligence or willful and wanton misconduct of the owner, tenant, or lessee. The immunity provided by this section does not apply if the owner, tenant, or lessee received any consideration for permitting the gleaning activity. *(Added by Stats.1988, c. 1062, § 1.)*

§ 846.5. Surveyors; right of entry; use of boundary evidence and performance of surveys; freeways

(a) The right of entry upon or to real property to investigate and utilize boundary evidence, and to perform surveys, is a right of persons legally authorized to practice land surveying and it shall be the responsibility of the owner or tenant who owns or controls property to provide reasonable access without undue delay. The right of entry is not contingent upon the provision of prior notice to the owner or tenant. However, the owner or tenant shall be notified of the proposed time of entry where practicable.

(b) The requirements of subdivision (a) do not apply to monuments within access-controlled portions of freeways.

(c) When required for a property survey, monuments within a freeway right-of-way shall be referenced to usable points outside the access control line by the agency having jurisdiction over the freeway when requested in writing by the registered civil engineer or licensed land surveyor who is to perform the property survey. The work shall be done within a reasonable time period by the agency in direct cooperation with the engineer or surveyor and at no charge to him. *(Added by Stats.1973, c. 435, p. 903, § 1. Amended by Stats.1982, c. 427, p. 1781, § 1.)*

Cross References

Entry without written permission upon lands under cultivation, enclosed by fence or posted as no entry, violation as an infraction or misdemeanor, exclusion for licensed surveyors, see Penal Code § 602.8.

Real property defined for purposes of this Code, see Civil Code § 658.

§ 846.6. Repealed by Stats.1985, c. 874, § 11

§ 847. Immunity from liability; injuries or death occurring on property during or after the commission of certain felonies

(a) An owner, including, but not limited to, a public entity, as defined in Section 811.2 of the Government Code, of any estate or any other interest in real property, whether possessory or nonpossessory, shall not be liable to any person for any injury or death that occurs upon that property during the course of or after the commission of any of the felonies set forth in subdivision (b) by the injured or deceased person.

(b) The felonies to which the provisions of this section apply are the following: (1) Murder or voluntary manslaughter; (2) mayhem; (3) rape; (4) sodomy by force, violence, duress, menace, or threat of great bodily harm; (5) oral copulation by force, violence, duress, menace, or threat of great bodily harm; (6) lewd acts on a child under the age of 14 years; (7) any felony punishable by death or imprisonment in the state prison for life; (8) any other felony in which the defendant inflicts great bodily injury on any person, other than an accomplice, or any felony in which the defendant uses a firearm; (9) attempted murder; (10) assault with intent to commit rape or robbery; (11) assault with a deadly weapon or instrument on a peace officer; (12) assault by a life prisoner on a noninmate; (13) assault with a deadly weapon by an inmate; (14) arson; (15) exploding a destructive device or any explosive with intent to injure; (16) exploding a destructive device or any explosive causing great bodily injury; (17) exploding a destructive device or any explosive with intent to murder; (18) burglary; (19) robbery; (20) kidnapping; (21) taking of a hostage by an inmate of a state prison; (22) any felony in which the defendant personally used a dangerous or deadly weapon; (23) selling, furnishing, administering, or providing heroin, cocaine, or phencyclidine (PCP) to a minor; (24) grand theft as defined in Sections 487 and 487a of the Penal Code; and (25) any attempt to commit a crime listed in this subdivision other than an assault.

(c) The limitation on liability conferred by this section arises at the moment the injured or deceased person commences the felony or attempted felony and extends to the moment the injured or deceased person is no longer upon the property.

(d) The limitation on liability conferred by this section applies only when the injured or deceased person's conduct in furtherance of the commission of a felony specified in subdivision (b) proximately or legally causes the injury or death.

(e) The limitation on liability conferred by this section arises only upon the charge of a felony listed in subdivision (b) and the subsequent conviction of that felony or a lesser included felony or misdemeanor arising from a charge of a felony listed in subdivision (b). During the pendency of any such criminal action, a civil action alleging this liability shall be abated and the statute of limitations on the civil cause of action shall be tolled.

(f) This section does not limit the liability of an owner or an owner's agent which otherwise exists for willful, wanton, or criminal conduct, or for willful or malicious failure to guard or warn against a dangerous condition, use, structure, or activity.

(g) The limitation on liability provided by this section shall be in addition to any other available defense. *(Added by Stats.1985, c. 1541, § 1.)*

Cross References

Misdemeanors, definition and penalties, see Penal Code §§ 17, 19 and 19.2.

Real property defined for purposes of this Code, see Civil Code § 658.

§ 848. Mineral rights owners; notice of entry on real property to exercise rights; timing; contents; injunctions

(a) Except as provided in subdivision (c), the owner of mineral rights, as defined by Section 883.110, in real property shall give a written notice prior to the first entry to the owner of the real property who is listed as the assessee on the current local assessment roll or to the owner's representative, or to the lessee of the real property if different from the mineral rights owner, and to any public utility that has a recorded interest in the real property if there is to be excavation of the utility interest, under the following circumstances:

(1) If the mineral rights owner or its agent intends to enter real property for the purpose of undertaking non-surface-disrupting activities such as surveying, water and mineral testing, and removal of debris and equipment not involving use of an articulated vehicle on the real property, the owner or agent shall provide a minimum of five days' notice. Reasonable attempts shall be made to deliver the notice by acknowledged personal delivery, but if that cannot occur, the notice shall be delivered by registered letter and be received a minimum of five days prior to the entrance on the property. The notice shall specify all of the following:

(A) Date of entry.

(B) Estimated length of time the property will be occupied.

(C) General nature of the work.

(2) If the mineral rights owner or its agent intends to enter real property for the purpose of excavation or other surface-disrupting activities such as drilling new wells, constructing structures, bringing articulated vehicles or excavation equipment on the real property, or reclamation of the real property after the surface has been disturbed, the owner or agent shall provide a minimum of 30 days' notice. The notice shall specify both of the following:

(A) The extent and location of the prospecting, mining, or extraction operation.

(B) The approximate time or times of entry and exit upon the real property.

(3) If a mineral rights owner's entry to the real property ceases for a period of one year or more, any further entry by the mineral rights owner for the purpose of surface-disturbing activities pursuant to paragraph (2) shall require written notice pursuant to this subdivision.

(b)(1) If a mineral rights owner has been authorized by the Geologic Energy Management Division to drill a relief well or to take other immediate actions in response to an emergency situation, or if the division or its agent is drilling a relief well or taking other immediate actions in response to an emergency situation, the notice provisions under paragraph (2) of subdivision (a) shall be waived.

(2) For purposes of this subdivision, an "emergency" means immediate action is necessary to protect life, health, property, or natural resources.

(c) The notice specified in subdivision (a) shall not be required if the owner of the real property or assessee has a current, already negotiated surface use, access use, or similar agreement with the mineral rights owner, lessee, agent, or operator.

(d) If the mineral rights owner has not complied with the notice requirement specified in subdivision (a), the owner of the real property listed on the current assessment roll or any public utility which has a recorded interest in the real property may request a court to enjoin the prospecting, mining, or extracting operation until the mineral rights owner has complied. The absence of a known owner on the assessment roll or any public utility which has a recorded interest in the real property relieves the mineral rights owner of the obligation to give the written notice to the owner or public utility.

(e) For purposes of this section, an "acknowledged personal delivery" means that the written notice is personally delivered to the owner, the owner's representative, or lessee, and the owner, the owner's representative, or lessee acknowledges, in writing, receipt of the notice. *(Added by Stats.1988, c. 535, § 1. Amended by Stats.2012, c. 542 (A.B.1966), § 1; Stats.2019, c. 771 (A.B.1057), § 1, eff. Jan. 1, 2020.)*

Cross References

Obligation defined, see Civil Code § 1427.
Real property defined for purposes of this Code, see Civil Code § 658.

§ 849. Repealed by Code Am.1873–74, c. 612, p. 221, § 113

CHAPTER 3. ENVIRONMENTAL RESPONSIBILITY ACCEPTANCE ACT

Section
850. Construction of chapter; definitions.
850. Construction of chapter; definitions.
851. Owner with actual awareness of release; notice of potential liability; release report; commitment statement; response; duty to mitigate; application of common law; application of chapter.
851. Owner with actual awareness of release; notice of potential liability; release report; commitment statement; response; duty to mitigate; application of common law; application of chapter.
852. Commitment statement; acceptance or rejection; mediation; effect of accepted commitment statement; construction of chapter; actions; statute of limitations.
853. Commitment statements; admissions; admissibility; construction of chapter; actions; contract rights; application of chapter.
853. Commitment statements; admissions; admissibility; construction of chapter; actions; contract rights; application of chapter.
854. Form of commitment statement.
855. Effective date of § 851 notification requirements.

§ 850. Construction of chapter; definitions

Section operative until Jan. 1, 2024. See, also, § 850 operative Jan. 1, 2024.

The definitions set forth in Section 25260 of the Health and Safety Code govern the construction of this chapter. In addition, the following definitions apply for purposes of this chapter only:

(a) "Actual awareness" means actual knowledge of a fact pertaining to an obligation under this chapter, including actual knowledge of a release exceeding the notification threshold. Only actual awareness possessed by those employees or representatives of an owner of a site who are responsible for monitoring, responding to or otherwise addressing the release shall be attributable to the owner. Only actual awareness possessed by those employees or representatives of a potentially responsible party who are responsible for monitoring, responding to, or otherwise addressing, the release shall be attributable to the potentially responsible party.

(b) "Commitment statement" means a written statement executed by the notice recipient which recites expressly the language specified in Section 854.

(c) "Mediation" means an informal process in which the disputing parties select a neutral third party to assist them in reaching a negotiated settlement in which the neutral third party has no power to impose a solution on the parties, but rather has the power only to assist the parties in shaping solutions to meet their interests and objectives.

(d) "Negative response" means a written response by the recipient of a notice of potential liability indicating that the recipient will not undertake any response action, or a deemed negative response pursuant to subdivision (c) of Section 851 in the event of the recipient's failure to respond.

(e) "Neutral third party" means an experienced professional, such as an attorney, engineer, environmentalist, hydrologist, or retired judge, who has served as a mediator.

(f) "Notice of potential liability" means a notice, sent by the owner of the site, stating that a release that exceeds the notification threshold has occurred at the site and that the owner believes that the recipient of the notice is a responsible party with respect to the release. The notice of potential liability shall describe the location of the site and the nature of the release.

(g) "Notice recipient" means any one of the following:

(1) A person who receives a notice of potential liability pursuant to subdivision (a) of Section 851.

(2) A person who provides a release report pursuant to subdivision (b) of Section 851.

(3) A person who offers a commitment statement to the owner of a site pursuant to subdivision (c) of Section 851.

(h) "Notification threshold" means any release of such a magnitude that:

(1) The release is the subject of a response action which has been ordered by, or is being performed by, an oversight agency; or

(2) The release is impeding the ability of the owner of the site to sell, lease, or otherwise use the site.

(i) "Operation and maintenance" means any activity as defined in subdivision (a) of Section 25318.5 of the Health and Safety Code.

(j) "Oversight agency" means any agency, as defined in subdivision (c) of Section 25260 of the Health and Safety Code, that has jurisdiction over a response action performed in connection with a release that is the subject of a notice of potential liability. Subject to any other limitation imposed by law, an oversight agency retains full discretion as to when it exercises jurisdiction over a site.

(k) "Reasonable steps," as used in subdivision (a) of Section 851, means the least expensive means available to ascertain the potentially responsible parties. If the owner cannot otherwise identify any apparent, potentially responsible parties, then "reasonable steps" includes:

(1) Conducting a title search; and

(2) Reviewing all environmental reports in the owner's possession of which the owner has actual awareness pertaining to the site.

(*l*) "Release" means the release, as defined in Sections 25320 and 25321 of the Health and Safety Code, of a hazardous material or hazardous materials.

(m) "Release report" means a notice sent by a responsible party to the owner of the site stating that a release has occurred on the site which is likely to exceed the notification threshold. The release report shall describe the location of the site and the nature of the release.

(n) "Remedial action" means any action as defined in Section 25322 of the Health and Safety Code.

(o) "Removal action" means any action as defined in subdivision (a) of Section 25323 of the Health and Safety Code.

(p) "Response action" means any removal actions, including, but not limited to, site investigations and remedial actions, including, but not limited to, operation and maintenance measures.

(q) "Responsible party" means any person who is liable under state or local law for taking action in response to a release.

(r) "Site" means any parcel of commercial, industrial, or agricultural real property where a hazardous materials release has occurred.

(s) "Written action" means any official action by any oversight agency where the oversight agency has expressly exercised its cleanup authority in writing, pursuant to the oversight agency's procedures, directing a response action at the site. (Added by Stats.1997, c. 873 (S.B.1081), § 1.)

§ 850. Construction of chapter; definitions

Section operative Jan. 1, 2024. See, also, § 850 operative until Jan. 1, 2024.

The definitions set forth in Section 25260 of the Health and Safety Code govern the construction of this chapter. In addition, the following definitions apply for purposes of this chapter only:

(a) "Actual awareness" means actual knowledge of a fact pertaining to an obligation under this chapter, including actual knowledge of a release exceeding the notification threshold. Only actual awareness possessed by those employees or representatives of an owner of a site who are responsible for monitoring, responding to or otherwise addressing the release shall be attributable to the owner. Only actual awareness possessed by those employees or representatives of a potentially responsible party who are responsible for monitoring, responding to, or otherwise addressing, the release shall be attributable to the potentially responsible party.

(b) "Commitment statement" means a written statement executed by the notice recipient which recites expressly the language specified in Section 854.

(c) "Mediation" means an informal process in which the disputing parties select a neutral third party to assist them in reaching a negotiated settlement in which the neutral third party has no power to impose a solution on the parties, but rather has the power only to assist the parties in shaping solutions to meet their interests and objectives.

(d) "Negative response" means a written response by the recipient of a notice of potential liability indicating that the recipient will not undertake any response action, or a deemed negative response pursuant to subdivision (c) of Section 851 in the event of the recipient's failure to respond.

(e) "Neutral third party" means an experienced professional, such as an attorney, engineer, environmentalist, hydrologist, or retired judge, who has served as a mediator.

(f) "Notice of potential liability" means a notice, sent by the owner of the site, stating that a release that exceeds the notification threshold has occurred at the site and that the owner believes that the recipient of the notice is a responsible party with respect to the release. The notice of potential liability shall describe the location of the site and the nature of the release.

(g) "Notice recipient" means any one of the following:

(1) A person who receives a notice of potential liability pursuant to subdivision (a) of Section 851.

(2) A person who provides a release report pursuant to subdivision (b) of Section 851.

(3) A person who offers a commitment statement to the owner of a site pursuant to subdivision (c) of Section 851.

(h) "Notification threshold" means any release of such a magnitude that:

(1) The release is the subject of a response action which has been ordered by, or is being performed by, an oversight agency; or

(2) The release is impeding the ability of the owner of the site to sell, lease, or otherwise use the site.

(i) "Operation and maintenance" means any activity as defined in * * * Section 78080 of the Health and Safety Code.

(j) "Oversight agency" means any agency, as defined in subdivision (c) of Section 25260 of the Health and Safety Code, that has jurisdiction over a response action performed in connection with a release that is the subject of a notice of potential liability. Subject to any other limitation imposed by law, an oversight agency retains full discretion as to when it exercises jurisdiction over a site.

(k) "Reasonable steps," as used in subdivision (a) of Section 851, means the least expensive means available to ascertain the potentially responsible parties. If the owner cannot otherwise identify any apparent, potentially responsible parties, then "reasonable steps" includes:

(1) Conducting a title search; and

(2) Reviewing all environmental reports in the owner's possession of which the owner has actual awareness pertaining to the site.

(*l*) "Release" means the release, as defined in * * * Section 78105 of the Health and Safety Code, of a hazardous material or hazardous materials.

(m) "Release report" means a notice sent by a responsible party to the owner of the site stating that a release has occurred on the site which is likely to exceed the notification threshold. The release report shall describe the location of the site and the nature of the release.

(n) "Remedial action" means any action as defined in Section 78125 of the Health and Safety Code.

(*o*) "Removal action" means any action as defined in * * * Section 78135 of the Health and Safety Code.

(p) "Response action" means any removal actions, including, but not limited to, site investigations and remedial actions, including, but not limited to, operation and maintenance measures.

(q) "Responsible party" means any person who is liable under state or local law for taking action in response to a release.

(r) "Site" means any parcel of commercial, industrial, or agricultural real property where a hazardous materials release has occurred.

(s) "Written action" means any official action by any oversight agency where the oversight agency has expressly exercised its cleanup authority in writing, pursuant to the oversight agency's procedures, directing a response action at the site. *(Added by Stats.1997, c. 873 (S.B.1081), § 1. Amended by Stats.2022, c. 258 (A.B.2327), § 2, eff. Jan. 1, 2023, operative Jan. 1, 2024.)*

Cross References

Obligation defined, see Civil Code § 1427.
Real property defined for purposes of this Code, see Civil Code § 658.

§ 851. Owner with actual awareness of release; notice of potential liability; release report; commitment statement; response; duty to mitigate; application of common law; application of chapter

Section operative until Jan. 1, 2024. See, also, § 851 operative Jan. 1, 2024.

(a) An owner of a site who has actual awareness of a release exceeding the notification threshold shall take all reasonable steps as defined in subdivision (j) of Section 850 to expeditiously identify the potentially responsible parties. The owner shall, as soon as reasonably possible after obtaining actual awareness of the potentially responsible parties, send a notice of potential liability to the identified potentially responsible parties and the agency, as defined in subdivision (c) of Section 25260 of the Health and Safety Code, that the owner believes to be the appropriate oversight agency. For any release exceeding the notification threshold of which the owner has actual awareness that occurred prior to, but within three years of, the effective date of this section, the notice shall be given on or before December 31, 1998.

(b) A potentially responsible party who has actual awareness of a release which is likely to exceed the notification threshold shall as soon as reasonably possible after obtaining actual awareness of the release provide the owner of the site where the release occurred with a release report. For any release exceeding the notification threshold of which the potentially responsible party has actual awareness that occurred prior to, but within three years of, the effective date of this section, the release report shall be given on or before December 31, 1998. A potentially responsible party may issue, at the potentially responsible party's option, a commitment statement to the owner of the site within 120 days of the potentially responsible party's issuance of a release report. The fact that a release report is issued shall not constitute an admission of liability and may not be admitted as evidence against a potentially responsible party in any litigation.

(c) When a notice of potential liability is issued, a notice recipient shall respond to the owner, in writing, and by certified mail, return receipt requested, within 120 days from the date that the notice of potential liability was mailed. The notice recipient's response shall be either a commitment statement or a negative response. The notice recipient's failure to submit the written response within the 120–day period, or failure to strictly comply with the form of the written response, as provided in Section 854, shall be deemed a negative response. The owner may agree in writing to extend the period during which the notice recipient may respond to the notice of potential liability. An extension of up to 120 days shall be provided if the notice recipient commits to do a site investigation, the results of which shall be provided to the owner and the oversight agency.

(d)(1) The common law duty to mitigate damages shall apply to any failure of the owner of a site to give a timely notice of potential liability when the owner is required to give this notice pursuant to this chapter. Where an owner fails to mitigate damages by not giving a timely notice of potential liability, the owner's damage claim shall be reduced in accordance with common law principles by the amount that the potentially responsible party proves would have likely been mitigated had a timely notice of potential liability been given.

(2) Common law principles shall apply to the failure of the potentially responsible party to issue a timely release report. Where a potentially responsible party fails to give a timely release report, the potentially responsible party, in accordance with common law principles, shall be responsible to the owner of the site, for damages that the owner proves are likely caused by such failure to provide a release report.

(3) Any party who argues the applicability of this subdivision carries the burden of proof in that regard.

(4) Nothing in this section is intended to create a new cause of action or defense beyond that which already exists under common law.

(5) Subdivisions (a) and (b), and paragraphs (1) and (2) of this subdivision, shall not apply when the party to whom a

notice of potential liability or release report is owed already possesses actual awareness of the information required to be transmitted in such notice of potential liability or release report.

(e)(1) Except as provided in paragraph (2), the requirements of this chapter shall not apply to a site listed pursuant to Section 25356 of the Health and Safety Code for response action pursuant to Chapter 6.8 (commencing with Section 25300) of Division 20 of the Health and Safety Code or to a site where an oversight agency has issued an order or entered into an enforceable agreement pursuant to any authority, including, but not limited to, an order or enforceable agreement entered into by a local agency, the Department of Toxic Substance Control, the State Water Resources Control Board, or a regional water quality control board pursuant to Chapter 6.5 (commencing with Section 25100), Chapter 6.7 (commencing with Section 25280), Chapter 6.75 (commencing with Section 25299.10), Chapter 6.8 (commencing with Section 25300), Chapter 6.85 (commencing with Section 25396), or Chapter 6.11 (commencing with Section 25404) of Division 20 of the Health and Safety Code, or pursuant to Division 7 (commencing with Section 13000) of the Water Code.

(2) The requirements of this chapter shall apply if either of the following applies:

(A) The order or enforceable agreement is issued or entered into after the owner accepts a commitment statement.

(B) The Department of Toxic Substance Control, State Water Resources Control Board, or regional water quality control board that issued the order or entered into an enforceable agreement consents in writing to the applicability of this chapter to the site.

(f) It is the intent of the Legislature for this chapter to resolve disputes between, and affect the rights of, private parties only. Nothing in this chapter shall affect the authority of the Department of Toxic Substance Control, the State Water Resources Control Board, a regional water quality control board, or any other oversight agency.

(g) Notwithstanding any other provision of this chapter, any time prior to accepting a commitment statement, the owner may provide the notice to the notice recipient that the provisions of subdivision (c), paragraph (2) of subdivision (e), and Sections 852 and 854, shall not apply to the site, in which case the provisions of subdivision (c), paragraph (2) of subdivision (e), and Sections 852 and 854 shall not apply to the site and the owner and notice recipient shall be entitled to pursue all other legal remedies and defenses authorized by law. *(Added by Stats.1997, c. 873 (S.B.1081), § 1.)*

§ 851. Owner with actual awareness of release; notice of potential liability; release report; commitment statement; response; duty to mitigate; application of common law; application of chapter

Section operative Jan. 1, 2024. See, also, § 851 operative until Jan. 1, 2024.

(a) An owner of a site who has actual awareness of a release exceeding the notification threshold shall take all reasonable steps as defined in subdivision (j) of Section 850 to expeditiously identify the potentially responsible parties. The owner shall, as soon as reasonably possible after obtaining actual awareness of the potentially responsible parties, send a notice of potential liability to the identified potentially responsible parties and the agency, as defined in subdivision (c) of Section 25260 of the Health and Safety Code, that the owner believes to be the appropriate oversight agency. For any release exceeding the notification threshold of which the owner has actual awareness that occurred prior to, but within three years of, the effective date of this section, the notice shall be given on or before December 31, 1998.

(b) A potentially responsible party who has actual awareness of a release which is likely to exceed the notification threshold shall as soon as reasonably possible after obtaining actual awareness of the release provide the owner of the site where the release occurred with a release report. For any release exceeding the notification threshold of which the potentially responsible party has actual awareness that occurred prior to, but within three years of, the effective date of this section, the release report shall be given on or before December 31, 1998. A potentially responsible party may issue, at the potentially responsible party's option, a commitment statement to the owner of the site within 120 days of the potentially responsible party's issuance of a release report. The fact that a release report is issued shall not constitute an admission of liability and may not be admitted as evidence against a potentially responsible party in any litigation.

(c) When a notice of potential liability is issued, a notice recipient shall respond to the owner, in writing, and by certified mail, return receipt requested, within 120 days from the date that the notice of potential liability was mailed. The notice recipient's response shall be either a commitment statement or a negative response. The notice recipient's failure to submit the written response within the 120–day period, or failure to strictly comply with the form of the written response, as provided in Section 854, shall be deemed a negative response. The owner may agree in writing to extend the period during which the notice recipient may respond to the notice of potential liability. An extension of up to 120 days shall be provided if the notice recipient commits to do a site investigation, the results of which shall be provided to the owner and the oversight agency.

(d)(1) The common law duty to mitigate damages shall apply to any failure of the owner of a site to give a timely notice of potential liability when the owner is required to give this notice pursuant to this chapter. Where an owner fails to mitigate damages by not giving a timely notice of potential liability, the owner's damage claim shall be reduced in accordance with common law principles by the amount that the potentially responsible party proves would have likely been mitigated had a timely notice of potential liability been given.

(2) Common law principles shall apply to the failure of the potentially responsible party to issue a timely release report. Where a potentially responsible party fails to give a timely release report, the potentially responsible party, in accordance with common law principles, shall be responsible to the owner of the site, for damages that the owner proves are likely caused by the failure to provide a release report.

(3) Any party who argues the applicability of this subdivision carries the burden of proof in that regard.

§ 851 PROPERTY

(4) Nothing in this section is intended to create a new cause of action or defense beyond that which already exists under common law.

(5) Subdivisions (a) and (b), and paragraphs (1) and (2) of this subdivision, shall not apply when the party to whom a notice of potential liability or release report is owed already possesses actual awareness of the information required to be transmitted in the notice of potential liability or release report.

(e)(1) Except as provided in paragraph (2), the requirements of this chapter shall not apply to a site listed pursuant to Article 5 (commencing with Section * * * 78760) of Chapter 4 of Part 2 of Division 45 of the Health and Safety Code for response action pursuant to * * * Part 2 (commencing with Section 78000) of Division 45 of the Health and Safety Code or to a site where an oversight agency has issued an order or entered into an enforceable agreement pursuant to any authority, including, but not limited to, an order or enforceable agreement entered into by a local agency, the Department of Toxic Substance Control, the State Water Resources Control Board, or a regional water quality control board pursuant to Chapter 6.5 (commencing with Section 25100), Chapter 6.7 (commencing with Section 25280), Chapter 6.75 (commencing with Section 25299.10), Chapter 6.86 (commencing with Section * * * 25396), or Chapter 6.11 (commencing with Section 25404) of Division 20 of, or Part 2 (commencing with Section 78000) of Division 45 of, the Health and Safety Code, or pursuant to Division 7 (commencing with Section 13000) of the Water Code.

(2) The requirements of this chapter shall apply if either of the following applies:

(A) The order or enforceable agreement is issued or entered into after the owner accepts a commitment statement.

(B) The Department of Toxic Substance Control, State Water Resources Control Board, or regional water quality control board that issued the order or entered into an enforceable agreement consents in writing to the applicability of this chapter to the site.

(f) It is the intent of the Legislature for this chapter to resolve disputes between, and affect the rights of, private parties only. Nothing in this chapter shall affect the authority of the Department of Toxic Substance Control, the State Water Resources Control Board, a regional water quality control board, or any other oversight agency.

(g) Notwithstanding any other provision of this chapter, any time prior to accepting a commitment statement, the owner may provide the notice to the notice recipient that the provisions of subdivision (c), paragraph (2) of subdivision (e), and Sections 852 and 854, shall not apply to the site, in which case the provisions of subdivision (c), paragraph (2) of subdivision (e), and Sections 852 and 854 shall not apply to the site and the owner and notice recipient shall be entitled to pursue all other legal remedies and defenses authorized by law. *(Added by Stats.1997, c. 873 (S.B.1081), § 1. Amended by Stats.2022, c. 258 (A.B.2327), § 3, eff. Jan. 1, 2023, operative Jan. 1, 2024.)*

Cross References

Burden of proof, generally, see Evidence Code § 500 et seq.

Effective date of notification requirements of this section, see Civil Code § 855.

§ 852. Commitment statement; acceptance or rejection; mediation; effect of accepted commitment statement; construction of chapter; actions; statute of limitations

(a) Within 45 days after issuance of the commitment statement, the owner may transmit to the notice recipient by certified mail, return receipt requested, an executed copy of the commitment statement, indicating its acceptance. If the owner does not execute the commitment statement, the commitment statement shall be deemed to have been rejected upon expiration of the 45-day period. A notice recipient has no obligation with respect to the provisions of a rejected commitment statement.

(b)(1) Except as otherwise provided in this chapter, or unless the owner or the notice recipient has elected not to proceed with the mediation, if the owner rejects the commitment statement, the owner and notice recipient shall participate in a mediation process prior to the commencement of any litigation which pertains to a release covered by the commitment statement. The mediation process shall be supervised by a neutral third party mutually agreed upon by the owner and the notice recipient in order to mediate a mutually agreeable settlement between the owner and notice recipient of all issues related to the release.

(2) Either the notice recipient or the owner may elect not to proceed further with the mediation process at any time prior to completion of those proceedings.

(3) To the extent a mutually agreeable settlement is reached which allocates the liability and assigns the rights and obligations of the owner and notice recipient in a manner different from or inconsistent with this chapter, the settlement shall supersede the terms of this chapter pursuant to subdivision (f) of Section 853. If a settlement of all issues cannot be reached within 90 days after the owner's rejection of the commitment statement, the neutral third party shall declare the mediation process unsuccessful and terminate the process. The owner and notice recipient may mutually agree to extend the mediation process but shall communicate any such extension in writing to the neutral third party. If the party issuing the commitment statement fails, for any reason, to participate in the mediation within 90 days of the rejection of the commitment statement, the owner may proceed with litigation.

(4) After the termination of an unsuccessful mediation process, the parties shall be free to litigate or otherwise resolve their respective claims. The parties may mutually agree to the terms of the commitment statement at any time after the termination of an unsuccessful mediation process, in which case this chapter shall govern the rights and obligations of the parties.

(5) Any applicable statute of limitations shall be tolled for 90 days following issuance of a notice of potential liability, a release report, or a commitment statement.

(6) Any applicable statute of limitations shall be tolled from the time the owner rejects a commitment statement until the termination of the mediation process. If mediation is not commenced within 90 days after the owner's rejection of the commitment statement, the tolling of the statute of

limitations shall terminate unless otherwise agreed to by the parties.

(7) Unless the owner and notice recipient agree otherwise, the fees and costs of the neutral third party shall be borne equally by the notice recipient and the owner.

(c) Upon taking effect, the commitment statement shall have all of the following results:

(1) The commitment statement shall constitute a binding promise that the notice recipient will undertake any response action as required by an oversight agency through a written action, directed to the owner or notice recipient, in connection with the release that is the subject of the notice of potential liability or release report. The commitment statement shall not create any obligations with respect to releases occurring after the commitment statement is signed, or with respect to any other release that is not the subject of the notice of potential liability.

(2) The commitment statement shall constitute a binding promise that the owner shall provide reasonable site access to the notice recipient to take any action that is reasonably necessary or appropriate to conduct a response action. This grant of access shall not affect the rights of the owner if the notice recipient's activities onsite result in physical damage to the site which the notice recipient fails to repair within a reasonable period after completion of all onsite activities. Unless otherwise ordered by the oversight agency, the notice recipient shall take all reasonable steps to avoid interfering with the owner's use of the site.

(3) Except for civil actions seeking damages for personal injury or wrongful death, once a commitment statement has been accepted, the court shall stay any action brought by the owner of the site against the notice recipient that issued the commitment statement, including, but not limited to, actions in trespass, nuisance, negligence, and strict liability, which arise from or relate to a release for which a commitment statement has been issued. The stay shall be effective for a period of not more than two years from the date of acceptance of the commitment statement, but only so long as the site response action is proceeding to the satisfaction of an oversight agency. The stay shall not apply to any civil action that is based on fraud, failure to disclose, or misrepresentation related to any transaction between the owner of the site and the notice recipient, to any civil action for breach of the commitment statement, or to any civil action which is unrelated to the release. The owner and notice recipient may elect to extend the period of the stay by written agreement.

(4) In an action by an owner who has accepted a commitment statement against the notice recipient who issued the commitment statement, and which arises from or relates to a release for which a commitment statement has been issued, only the following damages shall be recoverable to the extent otherwise authorized by law:

(A) Damages for personal injuries or wrongful death caused by the release.

(B) Damages for breach of a commitment statement.

(C) Damages from the failure of a prospective purchaser to perform under a sales contract because of the release, where such failure to perform occurs prior to the issuance of the commitment statement.

(D) Damages for the lost use of the property prior to the issuance of a commitment statement caused by the release.

(E) Recovery of costs of investigating and responding to the release where such costs are incurred prior to the issuance of the commitment statement.

(F) Remedies for any breach of a preexisting contract entered into prior to the acceptance of a commitment statement.

(G) Damages for lost rents and any other damages recoverable under law associated with lost use of the site caused by any notice recipient during site response action activities.

(5) An owner may obtain rescission of a commitment statement if a notice recipient repudiates its obligations under the commitment statement, in which case Sections 852 and 854 shall no longer apply to the site.

(6) The notice recipient and owner shall copy each other with respect to all correspondence and proposed workplans to and from the oversight agency that relate to the site.

(d) Nothing in this chapter shall affect the authority of an oversight agency under the law to bring an administrative, criminal, or civil action against either a notice recipient or the owner, nor does it compel any action on the part of the oversight agency.

(e) At any time after the commitment statement is accepted, either the owner or the notice recipient may file an action against the other for material breach of rights and obligations associated with the commitment statement. Subject to the stay provided for in paragraph (3) of subdivision (c), the parties may litigate these claims in the same action as any other claims they may have in connection with the release that is the subject of the commitment statement.

(f) Whenever a notice recipient issues a commitment statement, the following notice shall be provided in 14 point boldface type if printed or in boldface capital letters if typed:

"THIS FORM WAS DEVELOPED AS PART OF A PROCESS ENACTED BY THE CALIFORNIA LEGISLATURE TO PROVIDE OWNERS OF PROPERTY AND POTENTIALLY RESPONSIBLE PARTIES AN ALTERNATIVE TO LITIGATING DISPUTES OVER CONTAMINATION. IT IS YOUR OPTION AS TO WHETHER YOU SIGN THIS FORM OR OTHERWISE PARTICIPATE IN THIS PROCESS. IF YOU CHOOSE NOT TO PARTICIPATE IN THE PROCESS, YOU SHOULD NOTIFY THE PARTY WHO SENT YOU THIS FORM. THIS FORM INVOLVES A TRADEOFF WHEREBY EACH PARTY ACQUIRES AND RELINQUISHES CERTAIN RIGHTS. UNDER THIS FORM, THE PROPERTY OWNER GETS THE ASSURANCE THAT THE POTENTIALLY RESPONSIBLE PARTY IS OBLIGATED TO PERFORM INVESTIGATORY AND CLEANUP ACTIONS IN THE EVENT THAT GOVERNMENT AUTHORITIES ELECT TO REQUIRE THESE ACTIONS. ON THE OTHER HAND, THE PROPERTY OWNER FOREGOES CERTAIN CLAIMS ASSOCIATED WITH RESIDUAL CONTAMINATION THAT GOVERNMENTAL AUTHORITIES ALLOW TO REMAIN IN PLACE ON THE PROPERTY. IF YOU ELECT NOT TO SIGN THIS

§ 852   **PROPERTY**

FORM, THE PROCESS DEVELOPED BY THE LEGISLATURE CONTEMPLATES THAT YOU WILL ATTEMPT TO MEDIATE ANY DISPUTES REGARDING THE CONTAMINATION. HOWEVER, MEDIATION IS NEITHER MANDATORY NOR BINDING. IF YOU HAVE QUESTIONS ABOUT THE PROCESS, YOU MAY WISH TO CONSULT AN ATTORNEY."

(g) Any applicable statute of limitations shall be tolled for two and one-half years from the date of acceptance of the commitment statement. If at the end of two years from the date of acceptance of the commitment statement an oversight agency has not issued a written action directed to the owner or notice recipient, the owner has 60 days in which he or she may terminate the commitment statement; and, in this event, it shall have no further force or effect. In the event the owner terminates the commitment statement, subdivision (c) shall no longer apply to the site and shall no longer govern the rights and obligations of the owner or notice recipient. *(Added by Stats.1997, c. 873 (S.B.1081), § 1.)*

Cross References
Obligation defined, see Civil Code § 1427.

§ 853. Commitment statements; admissions; admissibility; construction of chapter; actions; contract rights; application of chapter

Section operative until Jan. 1, 2024. See, also, § 853 operative Jan. 1, 2024.

(a) Neither the failure to issue a commitment statement nor its issuance shall be construed as an admission that the recipient of the notice of potential liability is liable under any federal, state, or local law, including common law, for the release that the party agrees to investigate or respond. Neither the failure to issue a commitment statement nor the contents of the commitment statement shall be admissible evidence in any proceeding, as defined in Section 901 of the Evidence Code, except that the contents of the commitment statement shall be admissible evidence in an action to enforce the commitment statement to the extent that such contents would be admissible under other applicable law.

(b) Nothing in this chapter shall subject a notice recipient to any damages, fines, or penalties for a failure to make a written response, either positive or negative, to a notice of potential liability.

(c) Nothing in this chapter shall subject the owner of a site to any damages, fines, or penalties for a failure to send a notice of potential liability pursuant to Section 851. Failure by the owner of a site to send a notice of potential liability of a release in a timely fashion shall not be deemed to create any liability for the owner under a theory of negligence per se.

(d) Nothing in this chapter imposes an affirmative duty on the owner of a site, or any potentially responsible party, to discover, or determine the nature or extent of, a hazardous materials release at the site. This chapter does not affect such an affirmative duty to the extent it is imposed by any other law.

(e) Subject to the defenses specified in Section 101(35) and 107(b) of the federal Comprehensive Environmental Response, Compensation, and Liability Act of 1980, as amended (42 U.S.C. Secs. 9601(35) and 9607(b)), a cause of action is hereby established whereby a notice recipient may recover from any responsible party any reasonable response costs for conducting a response action as may be approved or overseen by an oversight agency or as incurred pursuant to a commitment statement. Liability among responsible parties shall be allocated based upon the equitable factors specified in subdivision (c) of Section 25356.3 of the Health and Safety Code. No third-party beneficiary rights are created by a commitment statement, except as provided in subdivision (b) of Section 854. This cause of action applies to costs incurred prior to enactment of this subdivision. However, no recovery may be obtained under this subdivision for costs incurred more than three years prior to the filing of litigation to recover those costs. The cause of action established pursuant to this subdivision shall not apply against a current or former owner of a site unless that owner operated a business that caused a release being addressed by a response action at the site and the costs incurred by the notice recipient were in response to a release caused by the owner.

(f) Nothing in this chapter shall affect or limit the rights of an owner under preexisting contract. Nothing in this chapter shall affect or limit the right of a notice recipient and owner to agree to an allocation of liability or to an assignment of rights and obligations that is different from or inconsistent with this chapter. Such agreements shall supersede the terms of this chapter.

(g) Nothing in this chapter shall make a notice recipient a responsible party, beyond the obligations the notice recipient undertakes pursuant to this chapter.

(h) Nothing in this chapter shall apply to causes of action for wrongful death or personal injury. However, the pleading of a cause of action for wrongful death or personal injury shall not affect the applicability of this chapter to other causes of action in the same civil action. *(Added by Stats.1997, c. 873 (S.B.1081), § 1.)*

§ 853. Commitment statements; admissions; admissibility; construction of chapter; actions; contract rights; application of chapter

Section operative Jan. 1, 2024. See, also, § 853 operative until Jan. 1, 2024.

(a) Neither the failure to issue a commitment statement nor its issuance shall be construed as an admission that the recipient of the notice of potential liability is liable under any federal, state, or local law, including common law, for the release that the party agrees to investigate or respond. Neither the failure to issue a commitment statement nor the contents of the commitment statement shall be admissible evidence in any proceeding, as defined in Section 901 of the Evidence Code, except that the contents of the commitment statement shall be admissible evidence in an action to enforce the commitment statement to the extent that the contents would be admissible under other applicable law.

(b) Nothing in this chapter shall subject a notice recipient to any damages, fines, or penalties for a failure to make a written response, either positive or negative, to a notice of potential liability.

(c) Nothing in this chapter shall subject the owner of a site to any damages, fines, or penalties for a failure to send a notice of potential liability pursuant to Section 851. Failure by the owner of a site to send a notice of potential liability of a release in a timely fashion shall not be deemed to create any liability for the owner under a theory of negligence per se.

(d) Nothing in this chapter imposes an affirmative duty on the owner of a site, or any potentially responsible party, to discover, or determine the nature or extent of, a hazardous materials release at the site. This chapter does not affect * * * an affirmative duty described in this subdivision to the extent * * * that duty is imposed by any other law.

(e) Subject to the defenses specified in Sections 101(35) and 107(b) of the federal Comprehensive Environmental Response, Compensation, and Liability Act of 1980, as amended (42 U.S.C. Secs. 9601(35) and 9607(b)), a cause of action is hereby established whereby a notice recipient may recover from any responsible party any reasonable response costs for conducting a response action as may be approved or overseen by an oversight agency or as incurred pursuant to a commitment statement. Liability among responsible parties shall be allocated based upon the equitable factors specified in former subdivision (c) of former Section 25356.3 of the Health and Safety Code, as it existed prior to its repeal by Chapter 39 of the Statutes of 2012. No third-party beneficiary rights are created by a commitment statement, except as provided in subdivision (b) of Section 854. This cause of action applies to costs incurred prior to enactment of this subdivision. However, no recovery may be obtained under this subdivision for costs incurred more than three years prior to the filing of litigation to recover those costs. The cause of action established pursuant to this subdivision shall not apply against a current or former owner of a site unless that owner operated a business that caused a release being addressed by a response action at the site and the costs incurred by the notice recipient were in response to a release caused by the owner.

(f) Nothing in this chapter shall affect or limit the rights of an owner under preexisting contract. Nothing in this chapter shall affect or limit the right of a notice recipient and owner to agree to an allocation of liability or to an assignment of rights and obligations that is different from or inconsistent with this chapter. * * * Agreements allocating liability or assigning rights and obligations shall supersede the terms of this chapter.

(g) Nothing in this chapter shall make a notice recipient a responsible party, beyond the obligations the notice recipient undertakes pursuant to this chapter.

(h) Nothing in this chapter shall apply to causes of action for wrongful death or personal injury. However, the pleading of a cause of action for wrongful death or personal injury shall not affect the applicability of this chapter to other causes of action in the same civil action. (Added by Stats.1997, c. 873 (S.B.1081), § 1. Amended by Stats.2022, c. 258 (A.B.2327), § 4, eff. Jan. 1, 2023, operative Jan. 1, 2024.)

Cross References

Obligation defined, see Civil Code § 1427.

§ 854. Form of commitment statement

A commitment statement shall be executed in substantially the following form:

COUNTY OF _____
STATE OF CALIFORNIA

NOTICE OF ASSUMPTION OF GOVERNMENT IMPOSED SITE INVESTIGATION AND/OR REMEDIAL ACTION ORDERS ("COMMITMENT STATEMENT")

(a) The undersigned notice recipient is aware of, or has received a notice of potential liability pursuant to, Section 851 of the Civil Code ("notice of potential liability") in connection with a release of hazardous materials at a parcel of property ("site") having the following legal description: (Insert description here)

(b) The undersigned notice recipient and the undersigned owner of the site and the owner's successors, heirs, and assigns agree, upon the proper and timely execution and delivery of this commitment statement, to abide by the requirements of Chapter 3 (commencing with Section 850) of Title 3 of Part 2 of Division 2 in connection with the release that is the subject of the notice of potential liability.

(c) The undersigned notice recipient hereby commits to undertake any response action as required by an oversight agency through a written action, directed to the owner or notice recipient, in connection with the release that is the subject of the notice of potential liability or release report. This commitment runs with the land and binds, in addition to the current owner of the site, all of the owner's successors in interest, including current and future lenders having a security interest in the site.

(d) The owner of the site and the owner's successors, heirs, and assigns agree, upon the proper and timely execution and delivery of this commitment statement, to all of the following:

(1) The undersigned notice recipient or the party's designee shall be allowed such access to the site as may be required to perform its obligations under this commitment statement, provided that the undersigned notice recipient shall be liable for any physical damage it causes in conducting a response action, which the notice recipient fails to repair within a reasonable period after completion of all onsite activities.

(2) The parties, their successors, heirs, and assigns shall provide each other with copies of any communication or correspondence with an oversight agency in connection with the release of hazardous materials at the site.

(3) Provided that the undersigned notice recipient performs all of its obligations under this commitment statement, and except as otherwise provided in subdivisions (c) and (e) of Section 852 of the Civil Code, no claim for damages, accruing after the acceptance of the commitment statement, shall be brought against the undersigned notice recipient by the owner of the site or by the owner's successors, heirs, and assigns.

(e) The contents of this commitment statement shall be inadmissible evidence in any proceeding, as defined in Section 901 of the Evidence Code, except in an action to enforce this commitment statement to the extent that such contents would be admissible under other applicable law. This commitment statement may be enforced fully by the owner of the site and all parties identified in paragraph (b). There are no third-party beneficiary rights created by this commitment statement.

§ 854

(f) The owner of the site shall provide a copy of this commitment statement to any prospective purchaser or lessee of the site until this commitment statement is terminated or until all response actions have been completed in accordance with the commitment statement.

(g) If the owner transfers the site, the owner shall notify the undersigned parties to this commitment statement, by mail, within 14 business days of the property transfer.

(h) As provided by law, this commitment statement shall become effective if the owner executes this commitment statement within 45 days from the date of issuance, in which case its terms shall go into effect upon receipt of that acceptance by the issuer of this commitment statement. If the owner rejects this commitment statement, the rejection shall be subject to the mediation provisions of subdivision (b) of Section 852.

(i) If at the end of two years from the date of acceptance of this commitment statement, an oversight agency has not issued a written action directed to the owner or notice recipient, the owner has 60 days in which he or she may terminate the commitment statement; and, in this event, it shall have no further force or effect.

_____   _____
Notice recipient   Date
(Notice recipient's name,
address, and telephone number)
(Notarial affidavit)

_____   _____
Owner   Date
(Owner's name, address,
and telephone number)
(Notarial affidavit)

(Added by Stats.1997, c. 873 (S.B.1081), § 1.)

Cross References

Obligation defined, see Civil Code § 1427.

§ 855. Effective date of § 851 notification requirements

The notification requirements of Section 851 shall not become effective until 180 days after the effective date of this chapter. *(Added by Stats.1997, c. 873 (S.B.1081), § 1.)*

Title 4

USES AND TRUSTS [REPEALED]

§ 856. Repealed by Stats.1986, c. 820, § 5, operative July 1, 1987

§ 857. Repealed by Stats.1929, c. 146, p. 282, § 2

§§ 858 to 860. Repealed by Stats.1986, c. 820, § 5, operative July 1, 1987

§§ 861, 862. Repealed by Code Am.1873–74, c. 612, p. 222, § 119

§§ 863 to 867. Repealed by Stats.1986, c. 820, § 5, operative July 1, 1987

§ 868. Repealed by Code Am.1873–74, c. 612, p. 223, § 121

§§ 869 to 871. Repealed by Stats.1986, c. 820, § 5, operative July 1, 1987

Title 5

MARKETABLE RECORD TITLE

Chapter	Section
1. General Provisions	880.020
2. Ancient Mortgages and Deeds of Trust	882.020
3. Mineral Rights	883.110
4. Unexercised Options	884.010
5. Powers of Termination	885.010
6. Unperformed Contracts for Sale of Real Property	886.010
7. Abandoned Easements	887.010

CHAPTER 1. GENERAL PROVISIONS

Article	Section
1. Construction	880.020
2. Application of Title	880.240
3. Preservation of Interests	880.310

ARTICLE 1. CONSTRUCTION

Section
878 to 880. Repealed.
880.020. Legislative declaration and purpose.
880.030. Construction not to limit or affect equitable principles or recording statutes.

§§ 878 to 880. Repealed by Code Am.1873–74, c. 612, § 123

§ 880.020. Legislative declaration and purpose

(a) The Legislature declares as public policy that:

(1) Real property is a basic resource of the people of the state and should be made freely alienable and marketable to the extent practicable in order to enable and encourage full use and development of the real property, including both surface and subsurface interests.

(2) Interests in real property and defects in titles created at remote times, whether or not of record, often constitute unreasonable restraints on alienation and marketability of real property because the interests are no longer valid or have been abandoned or have otherwise become obsolete.

(3) Such interests and defects produce litigation to clear and quiet titles, cause delays in real property title transactions, and hinder marketability of real property.

(4) Real property title transactions should be possible with economy and expediency. The status and security of recorded real property titles should be determinable to the extent practicable from an examination of recent records only.

(b) It is the purpose of the Legislature in enacting this title to simplify and facilitate real property title transactions in furtherance of public policy by enabling persons to rely on record title to the extent provided in this title, with respect to the property interests specified in this title, subject only to the limitations expressly provided in this title and notwithstanding any provision or implication to the contrary in any other statute or in the common law. This title shall be liberally construed to effect the legislative purpose. *(Added by*

Stats.1982, c. 1268, p. 4671, § 1. Amended by Stats.2011, c. 46 (S.B.284), § 1.)

Cross References

Real property defined for purposes of this Code, see Civil Code § 658.

§ 880.030. Construction not to limit or affect equitable principles or recording statutes

Nothing in this title shall be construed to:

(a) Limit application of the principles of waiver and estoppel, laches, and other equitable principles.

(b) Affect the operation of any statute governing the effect of recording or failure to record, except as specifically provided in this title. *(Added by Stats.1982, c. 1268, p. 4672, § 1.)*

ARTICLE 2. APPLICATION OF TITLE

Section
880.240. Interests not subject to expiration pursuant to title.
880.250. Absolute nature of times prescribed; extending time; revival of interests.
880.260. Action or proceeding tolling expiration or expiration of record.

§ 880.240. Interests not subject to expiration pursuant to title

The following interests are not subject to expiration or expiration of record pursuant to this title:

(a) The interest of a person in possession (including use or occupancy) of real property and the interest of a person under whom a person in possession claims, to the extent the possession would have been revealed by reasonable inspection or inquiry.

(b) An interest of the United States or pursuant to federal law in real property that is not subjected by federal law to the recording requirements of the state and that has not terminated under federal law.

(c) An interest of the state or a local public entity in real property.

(d) A conservation easement pursuant to Chapter 4 (commencing with Section 815) of Title 2. *(Added by Stats.1982, c. 1268, p. 4672, § 1.)*

Cross References

Real property defined for purposes of this Code, see Civil Code § 658.

§ 880.250. Absolute nature of times prescribed; extending time; revival of interests

(a) The times prescribed in this title for expiration or expiration of record of an interest in real property or for enforcement, for bringing an action, or for doing any other required act are absolute and apply notwithstanding any disability or lack of knowledge of any person or any provisions for tolling a statute of limitation and notwithstanding any longer time applicable pursuant to any statute of limitation.

(b) Nothing in this title extends the period for enforcement, for bringing an action, or for doing any other required act, or revives an interest in real property that expires and is unenforceable, pursuant to any applicable statute of limitation. *(Added by Stats.1982, c. 1268, p. 4672, § 1.)*

Cross References

Real property defined for purposes of this Code, see Civil Code § 658.

§ 880.260. Action or proceeding tolling expiration or expiration of record

An interest in real property, as specified in this title, does not expire or expire of record and is not unenforceable pursuant to this title at the time prescribed in this title if within the time an action is commenced to enforce, establish, clear title to, or otherwise affect the interest and a notice of the pendency of the action is recorded as provided by law. For the purpose of this section, action includes special proceeding and arbitration proceeding. *(Added by Stats. 1982, c. 1268, p. 4673, § 1.)*

Cross References

Real property defined for purposes of this Code, see Civil Code § 658.

ARTICLE 3. PRESERVATION OF INTERESTS

Section
880.310. Recordation of notice of intent.
880.320. Persons entitled to record notice of intent.
880.330. Requisites of notice of intent.
880.340. Form of notice of intent.
880.350. County of recording notice of intent.
880.360. Slandering title; recording notice of intent.
880.370. Extension of time for recordation of notice.

§ 880.310. Recordation of notice of intent

(a) If the time within which an interest in real property expires pursuant to this title depends upon recordation of a notice of intent to preserve the interest, a person may preserve the person's interest from expiration by recording a notice of intent to preserve the interest before the interest expires pursuant to this title. Recordation of a notice of intent to preserve an interest in real property after the interest has expired pursuant to this title does not preserve the interest.

(b) Recordation of a notice of intent to preserve an interest in real property does not preclude a court from determining that an interest has been abandoned or is otherwise unenforceable pursuant to other law, whether before or after the notice of intent to preserve the interest is recorded, and does not validate or make enforceable a claim or interest that is otherwise invalid or unenforceable. Recordation of a notice of intent to preserve an interest in real property creates a presumption affecting the burden of proof that the person who claims the interest has not abandoned and does not intend to abandon the interest. *(Added by Stats.1982, c. 1268, p. 4673, § 1.)*

Cross References

Burden of proof, generally, see Evidence Code § 500 et seq.

§ 880.310

Real property defined for purposes of this Code, see Civil Code § 658.

§ 880.320. Persons entitled to record notice of intent

A notice of intent to preserve an interest in real property may be recorded by any of the following persons:

(a) A person who claims the interest.

(b) Another person acting on behalf of a claimant if the person is authorized to act on behalf of the claimant or if the claimant is one of a class whose identity cannot be established or is uncertain at the time of recording the notice of intent to preserve the interest. *(Added by Stats.1982, c. 1268, p. 4673, § 1.)*

Cross References

Real property defined for purposes of this Code, see Civil Code § 658.

§ 880.330. Requisites of notice of intent

Subject to all statutory requirements for recorded documents:

(a) A notice of intent to preserve an interest in real property shall be in writing and signed and verified by or on behalf of the claimant. If the notice is made on behalf of a claimant, the notice shall include a statement of the authority of the person making the notice.

(b) The notice shall contain all of the following information:

(1) The name and mailing address of the claimant. If the notice is made by or on behalf of more than one claimant the notice shall contain the name and mailing address of each claimant.

(2) A statement of the character of interest claimed. The statement shall include a reference by record location to the recorded document that creates or evidences the interest in the claimant.

(3) A legal description of the real property in which the interest is claimed. The description may be the same as that contained in the recorded document that creates or evidences the interest in the claimant. *(Added by Stats.1982, c. 1268, p. 4673, § 1.)*

Cross References

Preserving easements, see Civil Code § 887.060.
Real property defined for purposes of this Code, see Civil Code § 658.

§ 880.340. Form of notice of intent

Subject to all statutory requirements for recorded documents, a notice of intent to preserve an interest in real property shall be in substantially the following form:

RECORDING INFORMATION
Recording requested by: FOR USE OF COUNTY RECORDER

After recording return to:

Indexing instructions.
   This notice must be indexed as follows:
   Grantor and grantee index—each claimant is a grantor.

NOTICE OF INTENT TO PRESERVE INTEREST

This notice is intended to preserve an interest in real property from extinguishment pursuant to Title 5 (commencing with Section 880.020) of Part 2 of Division 2 of the Civil Code (Marketable Record Title).

Claimant   Name:
                Mailing address: (must be given for each claimant)

Interest   Character (e.g., power of termination): Record location of document creating or evidencing interest in claimant:

Real Property   Legal description (may be same as in recorded document creating or evidencing interest in claimant):

I assert under penalty of perjury that this notice is not recorded for the purpose of slandering title to real property and I am informed and believe that the information contained in this notice is true. If this notice is made on behalf of a claimant, I assert under penalty of perjury that I am authorized to act on behalf of the claimant.

Signed: _____   Date: _____
         (claimant)

_____
(person acting on behalf of claimant)

Certificate of acknowledgment required.

(Added by Stats.1982, c. 1268, p. 4674, § 1. Amended by Stats.2012, c. 94 (A.B.1642), § 1.)

Cross References

Preserving easements, see Civil Code § 887.060.
Real property defined for purposes of this Code, see Civil Code § 658.

§ 880.350. County of recording notice of intent

(a) A notice of intent to preserve an interest in real property shall be recorded in the county in which the real property is situated.

(b) The county recorder shall index a notice of intent to preserve an interest in real property in the index of grantors and grantees. The index entry shall be for the grantor, and for the purpose of this index, the claimant under the notice shall be deemed to be the grantor. If a notice of intent to preserve is recorded by or on behalf of more than one claimant, each claimant shall be deemed to be a grantor and a separate index entry shall be made for each claimant. *(Added by Stats.1982, c. 1268, p. 4675, § 1.)*

Cross References

Real property defined for purposes of this Code, see Civil Code § 658.

§ 880.360. Slandering title; recording notice of intent

A person shall not record a notice of intent to preserve an interest in real property for the purpose of slandering title to the real property. If the court in an action or proceeding to establish or quiet title determines that a person recorded a notice of intent to preserve an interest for the purpose of slandering title, the court shall award against the person the cost of the action or proceeding, including a reasonable attorney's fee, and the damages caused by the recording. *(Added by Stats.1982, c. 1268, p. 4675, § 1.)*

Cross References

Real property defined for purposes of this Code, see Civil Code § 658.

§ 880.370. Extension of time for recordation of notice

If the period prescribed by statute during which a notice of intent to preserve an interest in real property must be recorded expires before, on, or within five years after the operative date of the statute, the period is extended until five years after the operative date of the statute. *(Added by Stats.1982, c. 1268, p. 4675, § 1.)*

Cross References

Easements, see Civil Code § 887.090.
Real property defined for purposes of this Code, see Civil Code § 658.

CHAPTER 2. ANCIENT MORTGAGES AND DEEDS OF TRUST

Section
881, 882. Repealed.
882.020. Expiration date; lien of security interest of record; power of sale deemed exercised.
882.030. Effect of expiration of lien of security interest.
882.040. Application of chapter.
883. Repealed.

§§ 881, 882. Repealed by Code Am.1873-74, c. 612, § 123

§ 882.020. Expiration date; lien of security interest of record; power of sale deemed exercised

(a) Unless the lien of a mortgage, deed of trust, or other instrument that creates a security interest of record in real property to secure a debt or other obligation has earlier expired pursuant to Section 2911, the lien expires at, and is not enforceable by action for foreclosure commenced, power of sale exercised, or any other means asserted after, the later of the following times:

(1) If the final maturity date or the last date fixed for payment of the debt or performance of the obligation is ascertainable from the recorded evidence of indebtedness, 10 years after that date.

(2) If the final maturity date or the last date fixed for payment of the debt or performance of the obligation is not ascertainable from the recorded evidence of indebtedness, or if there is no final maturity date or last date fixed for payment of the debt or performance of the obligation, 60 years after the date the instrument that created the security interest was recorded.

(3) If a notice of intent to preserve the security interest is recorded within the time prescribed in paragraph (1) or (2), 10 years after the date the notice is recorded.

(b) For the purpose of this section, a power of sale is deemed to be exercised upon recordation of the deed executed pursuant to the power of sale.

(c) The times prescribed in this section may be extended in the same manner and to the same extent as a waiver made pursuant to Section 360.5 of the Code of Civil Procedure, except that an instrument is effective to extend the prescribed times only if it is recorded before expiration of the prescribed times. *(Added by Stats.1982, c. 1268, p. 4676, § 1. Amended by Stats.2006, c. 575 (A.B.2624), § 1.)*

Cross References

Obligation defined, see Civil Code § 1427.
Real property defined for purposes of this Code, see Civil Code § 658.

§ 882.030. Effect of expiration of lien of security interest

Expiration of the lien of a mortgage, deed of trust, or other security interest pursuant to this chapter or any other statute renders the lien unenforceable by any means commenced or asserted thereafter and is equivalent for all purposes to a certificate of satisfaction, reconveyance, release, or other discharge of the security interest, and execution and recording of a certificate of satisfaction, reconveyance, release, or other discharge is not necessary to terminate or evidence the termination of the security interest. Nothing in this section precludes execution and recording at any time of a certificate of satisfaction, reconveyance, release, or other discharge. *(Added by Stats.1982, c. 1268, p. 4676, § 1.)*

§ 882.040. Application of chapter

(a) Subject to Section 880.370 (grace period for recording notice) and except as otherwise provided in this section, this chapter applies on the operative date to all mortgages, deeds of trust, and other instruments that create a security interest in real property to secure a debt or other obligation, whether executed or recorded before, on, or after the operative date.

(b) This chapter shall not cause the lien of a mortgage, deed of trust, or other security interest in real property to expire or become unenforceable before the passage of five years after the operative date of this chapter. *(Added by Stats.1982, c. 1268, p. 4676, § 1.)*

Cross References

Obligation defined, see Civil Code § 1427.
Real property defined for purposes of this Code, see Civil Code § 658.

§ 883. Repealed by Code Am.1873-74, c. 612, § 123

CHAPTER 3. MINERAL RIGHTS

Article	Section
1. General Provisions	883.110
2. Termination of Dormant Mineral Right	883.210

ARTICLE 1. GENERAL PROVISIONS

Section
883.110. Mineral right defined.

Section
883.120. Application of chapter; mineral rights reserved to United States; mineral rights not subject to expiration.
883.130. Abandoned mineral rights.
883.140. Mineral right lease; expiration or abandonment; quitclaim deed.

Cross References

Entry on real property to exercise mineral rights, notice to owner or owner's representative, see Civil Code § 848.

§ 883.110. Mineral right defined

As used in this chapter, "mineral right" means an interest in minerals, regardless of character, whether fugacious or nonfugacious, organic or inorganic, that is created by grant or reservation, regardless of form, whether a fee or lesser interest, mineral, royalty, or leasehold, absolute or fractional, corporeal or incorporeal, and includes express or implied appurtenant surface rights. *(Added by Stats.1984, c. 240, § 2.)*

§ 883.120. Application of chapter; mineral rights reserved to United States; mineral rights not subject to expiration

(a) This chapter does not apply to a mineral right reserved to the United States (whether in a patent, pursuant to federal law, or otherwise) or to an oil or gas lease, mining claim, or other mineral right of a person entitled pursuant thereto, to the extent provided in Section 880.240.

(b) This chapter does not apply to a mineral right of the state or a local public entity, or of any other person, to the extent provided in Section 880.240. *(Added by Stats.1984, c. 240, § 2.)*

§ 883.130. Abandoned mineral rights

Nothing in this chapter limits or affects the common law governing abandonment of a mineral right or any other procedure provided by statute for clearing an abandoned mineral right from title to real property. *(Added by Stats. 1984, c. 240, § 2.)*

Cross References

Real property defined for purposes of this Code, see Civil Code § 658.

§ 883.140. Mineral right lease; expiration or abandonment; quitclaim deed

(a) As used in this section:

(1) "Lessee" includes an assignee or other successor in interest of the lessee.

(2) "Lessor" includes a successor in interest or heir or grantee of the lessor.

(b) If the term of a mineral right lease has expired or a mineral right lease has been abandoned by the lessee, the lessee shall, within 30 days after demand therefor by the lessor, execute, acknowledge, and deliver, or cause to be recorded, a deed quitclaiming all interest in and to the mineral rights covered by the lease. If the expiration or abandonment covers less than the entire interest of the lessee, the lessee shall execute, acknowledge, and deliver an appropriate instrument or notice of surrender or termination that covers the interest that has expired or been abandoned.

(c) If the lessee fails to comply with the requirements of this section, the lessee is liable for all damages sustained by the lessor as a result of the failure, including, but not limited to, court costs and reasonable attorney's fees in an action to clear title to the lessor's interest. The lessee shall also forfeit to the lessor the sum of one hundred fifty dollars ($150).

(d) Nothing in this section makes a quitclaim deed or other instrument or notice of surrender or termination, or a demand therefor, a condition precedent to an action to clear title to the lessor's interest. *(Added by Stats.1984, c. 240, § 2.)*

Cross References

Condition precedent defined, see Civil Code § 1436.

ARTICLE 2. TERMINATION OF DORMANT MINERAL RIGHT

Section
883.210. Action to terminate dormant mineral right.
883.220. Dormant rights; conditions.
883.230. Notice of intent to preserve mineral right; effect.
883.240. Actions; place; procedure.
883.250. Late notice of intent to preserve mineral right; condition of dismissal of action.
883.260. Termination under article; effect.
883.270. Application of article.

§ 883.210. Action to terminate dormant mineral right

The owner of real property subject to a mineral right may bring an action to terminate the mineral right pursuant to this article if the mineral right is dormant. *(Added by Stats.1984, c. 240, § 2.)*

Cross References

Real property defined for purposes of this Code, see Civil Code § 658.

§ 883.220. Dormant rights; conditions

For the purpose of this article, a mineral right is dormant if all of the following conditions are satisfied for a period of 20 years immediately preceding commencement of the action to terminate the mineral right:

(a) There is no production of the minerals and no exploration, drilling, mining, development, or other operations that affect the minerals, whether on or below the surface of the real property or on other property, whether or not unitized or pooled with the real property.

(b) No separate property tax assessment is made of the mineral right or, if made, no taxes are paid on the assessment.

(c) No instrument creating, reserving, transferring, or otherwise evidencing the mineral right is recorded. *(Added by Stats.1984, c. 240, § 2.)*

Cross References

Real property defined for purposes of this Code, see Civil Code § 658.

§ 883.230. Notice of intent to preserve mineral right; effect

(a) An owner of a mineral right may at any time record a notice of intent to preserve the mineral right.

(b) In lieu of the statement of the character of the interest claimed and the record location of the documents creating or evidencing the mineral rights claimed as otherwise required by paragraph (2) of subdivision (b) of Section 880.330 and in lieu of the legal description of the real property in which the interest is claimed as otherwise required by paragraph (3) of subdivision (b) of Section 880.330 and notwithstanding the provisions of Section 880.340 or any other provision in this title, a notice of intent to preserve a mineral right may refer generally and without specificity to any or all mineral rights claimed by claimant in any real property situated in the county.

(c) A mineral right is not dormant for the purpose of this article if:

(1) A notice of intent to preserve the mineral right is recorded within 20 years immediately preceding commencement of the action to terminate the mineral right.

(2) A notice of intent to preserve the mineral right is recorded pursuant to Section 883.250 after commencement of the action to terminate the mineral right. *(Added by Stats.1984, c. 240, § 2.)*

Cross References

Public notice for projects, see Government Code § 65091.
Real property defined for purposes of this Code, see Civil Code § 658.

§ 883.240. Actions; place; procedure

(a) An action to terminate a mineral right pursuant to this article shall be brought in the superior court of the county in which the real property subject to the mineral right is located.

(b) The action shall be brought in the same manner and shall be subject to the same procedure as an action to quiet title pursuant to Chapter 4 (commencing with Section 760.010) of Title 10 of Part 2 of the Code of Civil Procedure, to the extent applicable. *(Added by Stats.1984, c. 240, § 2.)*

Cross References

Real property defined for purposes of this Code, see Civil Code § 658.

§ 883.250. Late notice of intent to preserve mineral right; condition of dismissal of action

In an action to terminate a mineral right pursuant to this article, the court shall permit the owner of the mineral right to record a late notice of intent to preserve the mineral right as a condition of dismissal of the action, upon payment into court for the benefit of the owner of the real property the litigation expenses attributable to the mineral right or portion thereof as to which the notice is recorded. As used in this section, the term "litigation expenses" means recoverable costs and expenses reasonably and necessarily incurred in preparation for the action, including a reasonable attorney's fee. *(Added by Stats.1984, c. 240, § 2.)*

Cross References

Real property defined for purposes of this Code, see Civil Code § 658.

§ 883.260. Termination under article; effect

A mineral right terminated pursuant to this article is unenforceable and is deemed to have expired. A court order terminating a mineral right pursuant to this article is equivalent for all purposes to a conveyance of the mineral right to the owner of the real property. *(Added by Stats.1984, c. 240, § 2.)*

Cross References

Real property defined for purposes of this Code, see Civil Code § 658.

§ 883.270. Application of article

Subject to Section 880.370 (grace period for recording notice), this article applies to all mineral rights, whether executed or recorded before, on, or after January 1, 1985. *(Added by Stats.1984, c. 240, § 2.)*

CHAPTER 4. UNEXERCISED OPTIONS

Section
884. Repealed.
884.010. Expiration date; recorded instrument.
884.020. Effect of expiration of record.
884.030. Application of chapter.

§ 884. Repealed by Code Am.1873-74, c. 612, § 123

§ 884.010. Expiration date; recorded instrument

If a recorded instrument creates or gives constructive notice of an option to purchase real property, the option expires of record if no conveyance, contract, or other instrument that gives notice of exercise or extends the option is recorded within the following times:

(a) If the expiration date of the option is ascertainable from the recorded instrument, six months after that expiration date.

(b) If the expiration date of the option is not ascertainable from the recorded instrument or the recorded instrument indicates that the option provides no expiration date, six months after the date the instrument that creates or gives constructive notice of the option is recorded.

(c) This section shall become operative on January 1, 2013. *(Added by Stats.2011, c. 46 (S.B.284), § 3, operative Jan. 1, 2013.)*

Cross References

Real property defined for purposes of this Code, see Civil Code § 658.

§ 884.020. Effect of expiration of record

Upon the expiration of record of an option to purchase real property, the recorded instrument that creates or gives constructive notice of the option ceases to be notice to any person or to put any person on inquiry with respect to the exercise or existence of the option or of any contract, conveyance, or other writing that may have been executed pursuant to the option. *(Added by Stats.1982, c. 1268, p. 4677, § 1.)*

§ 884.020

Cross References

Real property defined for purposes of this Code, see Civil Code § 658.

§ 884.030. Application of chapter

(a) Except as otherwise provided in this section, this chapter applies on the operative date to all recorded instruments that create or give constructive notice of options to purchase real property, whether executed or recorded before, on, or after the operative date.

(b) This chapter shall not cause an option that expires according to its terms within one year before, on, or within one year after the operative date of this chapter to expire of record until one year after the operative date.

(c) This chapter shall not cause an option that provides no expiration date and that is recorded before the operative date of this chapter to expire of record until five years after the operative date of this chapter.

(d) Nothing in this chapter affects a recorded instrument that has ceased to be notice to any person or put any person on inquiry with respect to the exercise or existence of an option pursuant to former Section 1213.5 before the operative date of this chapter. *(Added by Stats.1982, c. 1268, p. 4677, § 1.)*

Cross References

Real property defined for purposes of this Code, see Civil Code § 658.

CHAPTER 5. POWERS OF TERMINATION

Section
885.   Repealed.
885.010. Definitions.
885.015. Application of chapter; power of termination.
885.020. Fees simple determinable and possibilities of reverter abolished.
885.030. Expiration dates; recorded instruments; contrary provisions.
885.040. Obsolete powers; expiration; grants to public entities, etc.
885.050. Exercise of power; notice or civil action; record.
885.060. Effect of expiration of power; application to equitable servitude; construction of law.
885.070. Operative date; application of chapter; prior breach of restriction on fee simple estate.

§ 885. Repealed by Code Am.1873-74, c. 612, § 123

§ 885.010. Definitions

(a) As used in this chapter:

(1) "Power of termination" means the power to terminate a fee simple estate in real property to enforce a restriction in the form of a condition subsequent to which the fee simple estate is subject, whether the power is characterized in the instrument that creates or evidences it as a power of termination, right of entry or reentry, right of possession or repossession, reserved power of revocation, or otherwise, and includes a possibility of reverter that is deemed to be and is enforceable as a power of termination pursuant to Section 885.020.

(2) "Power of termination" includes the power created in a transferee to terminate a fee simple estate in real property to enforce a restriction on the use of the real property in the form of a limitation or condition subsequent to which the fee simple estate is subject, whether the power is characterized in the instrument that creates or evidences it as an executory interest, executory limitation, or otherwise, and includes the interest known at common law as an executory interest preceded by a fee simple determinable.

(b) A power of termination is an interest in the real property.

(c) For the purpose of applying this chapter to other statutes relating to powers of termination, the terms "right of reentry," "right of repossession for breach of condition subsequent," and comparable terms used in the other statutes mean "power of termination" as defined in this section. *(Added by Stats.1982, c. 1268, p. 4677, § 1. Amended by Stats.1991, c. 156 (A.B.1577), § 15.)*

Cross References

Condition subsequent defined, see Civil Code § 1438.
Real property defined for purposes of this Code, see Civil Code § 658.

§ 885.015. Application of chapter; power of termination

This chapter does not apply to any of the following:

(a) A power of termination conditioned upon the continued production or removal of oil or gas or other minerals.

(b) A power of termination as to separately owned improvements or fixtures conditioned upon the continued leasehold or possessory interest in the underlying land. *(Added by Stats.1982, c. 1268, p. 4678, § 1. Amended by Stats.1991, c. 156 (A.B.1577), § 16.)*

Cross References

Definitions applicable to this Chapter, see Civil Code § 885.010.

§ 885.020. Fees simple determinable and possibilities of reverter abolished

Fees simple determinable and possibilities of reverter are abolished. Every estate that would be at common law a fee simple determinable is deemed to be a fee simple subject to a restriction in the form of a condition subsequent. Every interest that would be at common law a possibility of reverter is deemed to be and is enforceable as a power of termination. *(Added by Stats.1982, c. 1268, p. 4678, § 1.)*

Cross References

Application of this Chapter, see Civil Code § 885.015.
Condition subsequent defined, see Civil Code § 1438.
Definitions applicable to this Chapter, see Civil Code § 885.010.

§ 885.030. Expiration dates; recorded instruments; contrary provisions

(a) A power of termination of record expires at the later of the following times:

(1) Thirty years after the date the instrument reserving, transferring, or otherwise evidencing the power of termination is recorded.

(2) Thirty years after the date a notice of intent to preserve the power of termination is recorded, if the notice is recorded within the time prescribed in paragraph (1).

(3) Thirty years after the date an instrument reserving, transferring, or otherwise evidencing the power of termination or a notice of intent to preserve the power of termination is recorded, if the instrument or notice is recorded within 30 years after the date such an instrument or notice was last recorded.

(b) This section applies notwithstanding any provision to the contrary in the instrument reserving, transferring, or otherwise evidencing the power of termination or in another recorded document unless the instrument or other recorded document provides an earlier expiration date. *(Added by Stats.1982, c. 1268, p. 4678, § 1.)*

Cross References

Application of this Chapter, see Civil Code § 885.015.
Definitions applicable to this Chapter, see Civil Code § 885.010.

§ 885.040. Obsolete powers; expiration; grants to public entities, etc.

(a) If a power of termination becomes obsolete, the power expires.

(b) As used in this section, a power of termination is obsolete if any of the following circumstances applies:

(1) The restriction to which the fee simple estate is subject is of no actual and substantial benefit to the holder of the power.

(2) Enforcement of the power would not effectuate the purpose of the restriction to which the fee simple estate is subject.

(3) It would be otherwise inequitable to enforce the power because of changed conditions or circumstances.

(c) No power of termination shall expire under this section during the life of the grantor if it arises from a grant by a natural person without consideration to a public entity or to a society, corporation, institution, or association exempt by the laws of this state from taxation. *(Added by Stats.1982, c. 1268, p. 4678, § 1.)*

Cross References

Application of this Chapter, see Civil Code § 885.015.
Definitions applicable to this Chapter, see Civil Code § 885.010.

§ 885.050. Exercise of power; notice or civil action; record

A power of termination shall be exercised only by notice or by civil action and, if the power of termination is of record, the exercise shall be of record. The notice shall be given, and any civil action shall be commenced, within five years after breach of the restriction to which the fee simple estate is subject, or such longer period as may be agreed to by the parties by a waiver or extension recorded before expiration of that period. *(Added by Stats.1982, c. 1268, p. 4678, § 1.)*

Cross References

Application of this Chapter, see Civil Code § 885.015.

Definitions applicable to this Chapter, see Civil Code § 885.010.

§ 885.060. Effect of expiration of power; application to equitable servitude; construction of law

(a) Expiration of a power of termination pursuant to this chapter makes the power unenforceable and is equivalent for all purposes to a termination of the power of record and a quitclaim of the power to the owner of the fee simple estate, and execution and recording of a termination and quitclaim is not necessary to terminate or evidence the termination of the power.

(b) Expiration of a power of termination pursuant to this chapter terminates the restriction to which the fee simple estate is subject and makes the restriction unenforceable by any other means, including, but not limited to, injunction and damages.

(c) However, subdivision (b) does not apply to a restriction for which a power of termination has expired under this chapter if the restriction is also an equitable servitude alternatively enforceable by injunction. Such an equitable servitude shall remain enforceable by injunction and any other available remedies, but shall not be enforceable by a power of termination. This subdivision does not constitute a change in, but is declaratory of, the existing law. However, nothing in this subdivision shall be construed to make enforceable any restriction prohibited or made unenforceable by other provisions of law, including Section 53. *(Added by Stats.1982, c. 1268, p. 4679, § 1. Amended by Stats.1990, c. 1114 (A.B.3220), § 1.)*

Cross References

Application of this Chapter, see Civil Code § 885.015.
Definitions applicable to this Chapter, see Civil Code § 885.010.

§ 885.070. Operative date; application of chapter; prior breach of restriction on fee simple estate

(a) Subject to Section 880.370 (grace period for recording notice) and except as otherwise provided in this section, this chapter applies on the operative date to all powers of termination, whether executed or recorded before, on, or after the operative date.

(b) If breach of the restriction to which the fee simple estate is subject occurred before the operative date of this chapter and the power of termination is not exercised before the operative date of this chapter, the power of termination shall be exercised, or in the case of a power of termination of record, exercised of record, within the earlier of the following times:

(1) The time that would be applicable pursuant to the law in effect immediately prior to the operative date of this chapter.

(2) Five years after the operative date of this chapter.

(c) As used in this section, "operative date" means the operative date of this chapter as enacted or, with respect to any amendment of a section of this chapter, the operative date of the amendment. *(Added by Stats.1982, c. 1268, p. 4679, § 1. Amended by Stats.1991, c. 156 (A.B.1577), § 17.)*

Cross References

Application of this Chapter, see Civil Code § 885.015.

§ 885.070

Definitions applicable to this Chapter, see Civil Code § 885.010.

CHAPTER 6. UNPERFORMED CONTRACTS FOR SALE OF REAL PROPERTY

Section
886. Repealed.
886.010. Definitions.
886.020. Demand; release of unperformed contract; action to clear title.
886.030. Expiration date; recorded extension; waiver.
886.040. Effect of expiration of recorded contract.
886.050. Application of chapter; limitation on expiration of recorded contracts.
887. Repealed.

§ 886. Repealed by Code Am.1873-74, c. 612, § 123

§ 886.010. Definitions

As used in this chapter:

(a) "Contract for sale of real property" means an agreement wherein one party agrees to convey title to real property to another party upon the satisfaction of specified conditions set forth in the contract and which requires conveyance of title within one year from the date of formation of the contract, whether designated in the agreement a "contract for sale of real property," "land sale contract," "deposit receipt," "agreement for sale," "agreement to convey," or otherwise.

(b) "Recorded contract for sale of real property" includes the entire terms of a contract for sale of real property that is recorded in its entirety or is evidenced by a recorded memorandum or short form of the contract. *(Added by Stats.1982, c. 1268, p. 4679, § 1.)*

Cross References

Real property defined for purposes of this Code, see Civil Code § 658.

§ 886.020. Demand; release of unperformed contract; action to clear title

If the party to whom title to real property is to be conveyed pursuant to a recorded contract for the sale of real property fails to satisfy the specified conditions set forth in the contract and does not seek performance of the contract or restitution of amounts paid under the contract, the party shall, upon demand therefor made after the operative date of this chapter, execute a release of the contract, duly acknowledged for record, to the party who agreed to convey title. Willful violation of this section by the party to whom title is to be conveyed without good cause makes the party liable for the damages the party who agreed to convey title sustains by reason of the violation, including but not limited to court costs and reasonable attorney's fees in an action to clear title to the real property. Nothing in this section makes a release or a demand therefor a condition precedent to an action to clear title to the real property. *(Added by Stats.1982, c. 1268, p. 4679, § 1.)*

Cross References

Condition precedent defined, see Civil Code § 1436.
Definitions applicable to this Chapter, see Civil Code § 886.010.

Real property defined for purposes of this Code, see Civil Code § 658.

§ 886.030. Expiration date; recorded extension; waiver

(a) Except as otherwise provided in this section, a recorded contract for sale of real property expires of record at the later of the following times:

(1) Five years after the date for conveyance of title provided in the contract or, if no date for conveyance of title is provided in the contract, five years after the last date provided in the contract for satisfaction of the specified conditions set forth in the contract.

(2) If there is a recorded extension of the contract within the time prescribed in paragraph (1), five years after the date for conveyance of title provided in the extension or, if no date for conveyance of title is provided in the extension, five years after the last date provided in the extension for satisfaction of the specified conditions set forth in the contract.

(b) The time prescribed in this section may be waived or extended only by an instrument that is recorded before expiration of the prescribed times. *(Added by Stats.1982, c. 1268, p. 4680, § 1.)*

Cross References

Definitions applicable to this Chapter, see Civil Code § 886.010.
Real property defined for purposes of this Code, see Civil Code § 658.

§ 886.040. Effect of expiration of recorded contract

Upon the expiration of record of a recorded contract for sale of real property pursuant to this chapter, the contract has no effect, and does not constitute an encumbrance or cloud on the title to the real property as against a person other than a party to the contract. *(Added by Stats.1982, c. 1268, p. 4680, § 1.)*

Cross References

Definitions applicable to this Chapter, see Civil Code § 886.010.
Real property defined for purposes of this Code, see Civil Code § 658.

§ 886.050. Application of chapter; limitation on expiration of recorded contracts

(a) Except as otherwise provided in this section, this chapter applies on the operative date to all recorded contracts for sale of real property, whether recorded before, on, or after the operative date.

(b) This chapter shall not cause a recorded contract for sale of real property to expire of record before the passage of two years after the operative date of this chapter. *(Added by Stats.1982, c. 1268, p. 4680, § 1.)*

Cross References

Definitions applicable to this Chapter, see Civil Code § 886.010.
Real property defined for purposes of this Code, see Civil Code § 658.

§ 887. Repealed by Code Am.1873-74, c. 612, § 123

CHAPTER 7. ABANDONED EASEMENTS

Section
887.010. Definition of "easement".
887.020. Application of chapter.
887.030. Common law.
887.040. Bringing action; venue; procedure.
887.050. Conditions necessary.
887.060. Notice of intent to preserve easement; recording.
887.070. Late notice of intent to preserve easement; recording; litigation expenses.
887.080. Court order; enforceability.
887.090. Application of chapter; exceptions.
888, 889. Repealed.

§ 887.010. Definition of "easement"

As used in this chapter, "easement" means a burden or servitude upon land, whether or not attached to other land as an incident or appurtenance, that allows the holder of the burden or servitude to do acts upon the land. *(Added by Stats.1985, c. 157, § 2.)*

§ 887.020. Application of chapter

This chapter does not apply to an easement that is part of a unified or reciprocal system for the mutual benefit of multiple parties. *(Added by Stats.1985, c. 157, § 2.)*

§ 887.030. Common law

This chapter supplements and does not limit or otherwise affect the common law governing abandonment of an easement or any other procedure provided by statute or otherwise for clearing an abandoned easement from title to real property. *(Added by Stats.1985, c. 157, § 2.)*

Cross References

Real property defined for purposes of this Code, see Civil Code § 658.

§ 887.040. Bringing action; venue; procedure

(a) The owner of real property subject to an easement may bring an action to establish the abandonment of the easement and to clear record title of the easement.

(b) The action shall be brought in the superior court of the county in which the real property subject to the easement is located.

(c) The action shall be brought in the same manner and shall be subject to the same procedure as an action to quiet title pursuant to Chapter 4 (commencing with Section 760.010) of Title 10 of Part 2 of the Code of Civil Procedure, to the extent applicable. *(Added by Stats.1985, c. 157, § 2.)*

§ 887.050. Conditions necessary

(a) For purposes of this chapter, an easement is abandoned if all of the following conditions are satisfied for a period of 20 years immediately preceding commencement of the action to establish abandonment of the easement:

(1) The easement is not used at any time.

(2) No separate property tax assessment is made of the easement or, if made, no taxes are paid on the assessment.

(3) No instrument creating, reserving, transferring, or otherwise evidencing the easement is recorded.

(b) This section applies notwithstanding any provision to the contrary in the instrument creating, reserving, transferring, or otherwise evidencing the easement or in another recorded document, unless the instrument or other document provides an earlier expiration date. *(Added by Stats.1985, c. 157, § 2.)*

§ 887.060. Notice of intent to preserve easement; recording

(a) The owner of an easement may at any time record a notice of intent to preserve the easement.

(b) In lieu of the statement of the character of the interest claimed and the record location of the documents creating or evidencing the easement claimed, as otherwise required by paragraph (2) of subdivision (b) of Section 880.330, and in lieu of the legal description of the real property in which the interest is claimed, as otherwise required by paragraph (3) of subdivision (b) of Section 880.330, and notwithstanding the provisions of Section 880.340, or any other provision in this title, a notice of intent to preserve an easement may refer generally and without specificity to any or all easements claimed by the claimant in any real property situated in the county.

(c) An easement is not abandoned for purposes of this chapter if either of the following occurs:

(1) A notice of intent to preserve the easement is recorded within 20 years immediately preceding commencement of the action to establish the abandonment of the easement.

(2) A notice of intent to preserve the easement is recorded pursuant to Section 887.070 after commencement of the action to establish the abandonment of the easement and before judgment is entered in the action. *(Added by Stats. 1985, c. 157, § 2.)*

§ 887.070. Late notice of intent to preserve easement; recording; litigation expenses

In an action to establish the abandonment of an easement pursuant to this chapter, the court shall permit the owner of the easement to record a late notice of intent to preserve the easement as a condition of dismissal of the action, upon payment into court for the benefit of the owner of the real property the litigation expenses attributable to the easement or portion thereof as to which the notice is recorded. As used in this section, the term "litigation expenses" means recoverable costs and expenses reasonably and necessarily incurred in preparation for the action, including a reasonable attorney's fee. *(Added by Stats.1985, c. 157, § 2.)*

Cross References

Real property defined for purposes of this Code, see Civil Code § 658.

§ 887.080. Court order; enforceability

An abandoned easement is unenforceable and is deemed to have expired. A court order establishing abandonment of an easement pursuant to this chapter is equivalent for all purposes to a conveyance of the easement to the owner of the real property. *(Added by Stats.1985, c. 157, § 2.)*

§ 887.090. Application of chapter; exceptions

Subject to Sections 880.370 (grace period for recording notice) and 887.020, this chapter applies to all easements, whether executed or recorded before, on, or after January 1, 1986. *(Added by Stats.1985, c. 157, § 2.)*

§§ 888, 889. Repealed by Code Am.1873-74, c. 612, § 123

Title 6
RENT SKIMMING

Section
890. Definitions.
891. Civil rights and remedies; invalidity of waiver; applicability of statutes.
892. Criminal penalties; prior convictions; limitations; other remedies or penalties.
893. Affirmative defense; burden of producing evidence, burden of proof.
894. Severability.

§ 890. Definitions

(a)(1) "Rent skimming" means using revenue received from the rental of a parcel of residential real property at any time during the first year period after acquiring that property without first applying the revenue or an equivalent amount to the payments due on all mortgages and deeds of trust encumbering that property.

(2) For purposes of this section, "rent skimming" also means receiving revenue from the rental of a parcel of residential real property where the person receiving that revenue, without the consent of the owner or owner's agent, asserted possession or ownership of the residential property, whether under a false claim of title, by trespass, or any other unauthorized means, rented the property to another, and collected rents from the other person for the rental of the property. This paragraph does not apply to any tenant, subtenant, lessee, sublessee, or assignee, nor to any other hirer having a lawful occupancy interest in the residential dwelling.

(b) "Multiple acts of rent skimming" means knowingly and willfully rent skimming with respect to each of five or more parcels of residential real property acquired within any two-year period.

(c) "Person" means any natural person, any form of business organization, its officers and directors, and any natural person who authorizes rent skimming or who, being in a position of control, fails to prevent another from rent skimming. *(Added by Stats.1986, c. 838, § 1. Amended by Stats.1998, c. 193 (A.B.583), § 1.)*

Cross References

Ownership defined for purposes of this Code, see Civil Code § 654.
Real property defined for purposes of this Code, see Civil Code § 658.

§ 891. Civil rights and remedies; invalidity of waiver; applicability of statutes

(a) A seller of an interest in residential real property who received a promissory note or other evidence of indebtedness for all or a portion of its purchase price secured by a lien on the property may bring an action against any person who has engaged in rent skimming with respect to that property. A seller who prevails in the action shall recover all actual damages and reasonable attorney's fees and costs. The court may award any appropriate equitable relief. The court shall award exemplary damages of not less than three times the actual damages if the defendant has engaged in multiple acts of rent skimming and may award exemplary damages in other cases.

(b) A seller of an interest in residential real property who reacquires the interest from a person who has engaged in rent skimming with respect to that property, or a law enforcement agency, may request the court for an order declaring that the reacquired interest is not encumbered by any lien that is or has the effect of a judgment lien against the person who engaged in rent skimming if the lien is not related to any improvement of the property and does not represent security for loan proceeds made by a bona fide lien holder without knowledge of facts constituting a violation of this title. The motion or application shall be made with at least 30 days' advance written notice to all persons who may be affected by the order, including lienholders, and shall be granted unless the interests of justice would not be served by such an order.

(c) A mortgagee or beneficiary under a deed of trust encumbering residential real property may bring an action against a person who has engaged in rent skimming with respect to that property as one of multiple acts of rent skimming, whether or not the person has become contractually bound by an obligation secured by the mortgage or deed of trust. The mortgagee or beneficiary who prevails in the action shall recover actual damages to the extent of the amount of the rent collected on the encumbered property and attorney's fees and costs. The court also may order any appropriate equitable relief and may award exemplary damages.

(d) A tenant of residential real property may bring an action against a person who has engaged in rent skimming with respect to that property for the recovery of actual damages, including any security, as defined in Section 1950.5, and moving expenses if the property is sold at a foreclosure sale and the tenant was required to move. A prevailing plaintiff in such an action shall be awarded reasonable attorney's fees and costs. The court also may award exemplary damages; it shall award exemplary damages of at least three times the amount of actual damages if the payments due under any deed of trust or mortgage were two or more months delinquent at the time the tenant rented the premises or if the defendant has engaged in multiple acts of rent skimming.

(e) The rights and remedies provided in this section are in addition to any other rights and remedies provided by law.

(f) Rent skimming is unlawful, and any waiver of the provisions of this section are void and unenforceable as contrary to public policy.

(g) Sections 580a, 580b, 580d, and 726 of the Code of Civil Procedure do not apply to any action brought under this title. *(Added by Stats.1986, c. 838, § 1.)*

Cross References

Definitions under Title 6 applicable to this section, see Civil Code § 890.
Obligation defined, see Civil Code § 1427.

Real property defined for purposes of this Code, see Civil Code § 658.

§ 892. Criminal penalties; prior convictions; limitations; other remedies or penalties

(a) Any person who engages in multiple acts of rent skimming is subject to criminal prosecution. Each act of rent skimming comprising the multiple acts of rent skimming shall be separately alleged. A person found guilty of five acts shall be punished by imprisonment pursuant to subdivision (h) of Section 1170 of the Penal Code or by imprisonment in a county jail for not more than one year, by a fine of not more than ten thousand dollars ($10,000), or by both that fine and imprisonment. A person found guilty of additional acts shall be separately punished for each additional act by imprisonment pursuant to subdivision (h) of Section 1170 of the Penal Code or by imprisonment in a county jail for not more than one year, by a fine of not more than ten thousand dollars ($10,000), or by both that fine and imprisonment.

(b) If a defendant has been once previously convicted of a violation of subdivision (a), any subsequent knowing and willful act of rent skimming shall be punishable by imprisonment pursuant to subdivision (h) of Section 1170 of the Penal Code or by imprisonment in a county jail for not more than one year, or by a fine of not more than ten thousand dollars ($10,000), or by both that fine and imprisonment.

(c) A prosecution for a violation of this section shall be commenced within three years after the date of the acquisition of the last parcel of property that was the subject of the conduct for which the defendant is prosecuted.

(d) The penalties under this section are in addition to any other remedies or penalties provided by law for the conduct proscribed by this section. *(Added by Stats.1986, c. 838, § 1. Amended by Stats.2011, c. 15 (A.B.109), § 31, eff. April 4, 2011, operative Oct. 1, 2011.)*

Cross References

Definitions under Title 6 applicable to this section, see Civil Code § 890.

§ 893. Affirmative defense; burden of producing evidence, burden of proof

(a) It is an affirmative defense for a natural person who is a defendant in a civil action brought under Section 891, or a criminal action brought under Section 892, if all of the following occurred:

(1) The defendant used the rental revenue due but not paid to holders of mortgages or deeds of trust to make payments to any of the following:

(A) Health care providers, as defined in paragraph (2) of subdivision (c) of Section 6146 of the Business and Professions Code, for the unforeseen and necessary medical treatment of the defendant or his or her spouse, parents, or children.

(B) Licensed contractors or material suppliers to correct the violation of any statute, ordinance, or regulation relating to the habitability of the premises.

(2) The defendant made the payments within 30 days of receiving the rental revenue.

(3) The defendant had no other source of funds from which to make the payments.

(b) The defendant has the burden of producing evidence of each element of the defense specified in subdivision (a) in a criminal action under Section 892 and the burden of proof of each element of the defense in a civil action under Section 891. *(Added by Stats.1986, c. 838, § 1.)*

Cross References

Burden of proof, generally, see Evidence Code § 500 et seq.
Definitions under Title 6 applicable to this section, see Civil Code § 890.

§ 894. Severability

If any provision of this title or the application thereof to any person or circumstances is held to be unconstitutional, the remainder of the title and the application of its provisions to other persons and circumstances shall not be affected thereby. *(Added by Stats.1986, c. 838, § 1.)*

Cross References

Definitions under Title 6 applicable to this section, see Civil Code § 890.

Title 7

REQUIREMENTS FOR ACTIONS FOR CONSTRUCTION DEFECTS

Chapter	Section
1. Definitions	895
2. Actionable Defects	896
3. Obligations	900
4. Prelitigation Procedure	910
5. Procedure	941

Application

For application of Title 7, see Civil Code § 938.

Cross References

Common interest developments, dispute resolution and enforcement, civil action, authority of board to commence legal proceedings, see Civil Code § 5986.
Indemnification provisions in construction contracts, enforceability, claims arising from or relating to negligence of builder, see Civil Code § 2782.

CHAPTER 1. DEFINITIONS

Section
895. Definitions.

Application

For application of Title 7, see Civil Code § 938.

§ 895. Definitions

(a) "Structure" means any residential dwelling, other building, or improvement located upon a lot or within a common area.

(b) "Designed moisture barrier" means an installed moisture barrier specified in the plans and specifications, contract documents, or manufacturer's recommendations.

§ 895

(c) "Actual moisture barrier" means any component or material, actually installed, that serves to any degree as a barrier against moisture, whether or not intended as a barrier against moisture.

(d) "Unintended water" means water that passes beyond, around, or through a component or the material that is designed to prevent that passage.

(e) "Close of escrow" means the date of the close of escrow between the builder and the original homeowner. With respect to claims by an association, as defined in Section 4080, "close of escrow" means the date of substantial completion, as defined in Section 337.15 of the Code of Civil Procedure, or the date the builder relinquishes control over the association's ability to decide whether to initiate a claim under this title, whichever is later.

(f) "Claimant" or "homeowner" includes the individual owners of single-family homes, individual unit owners of attached dwellings and, in the case of a common interest development, any association as defined in Section 4080. (Added by Stats.2002, c. 722 (S.B.800), § 3. Amended by Stats.2012, c. 181 (A.B.806), § 29, operative Jan. 1, 2014.)

Application

For application of Title 7, see Civil Code § 938.

CHAPTER 2. ACTIONABLE DEFECTS

Section
896. Building standards for original construction intended to be sold as an individual dwelling unit.
897. Function or component of a structure; scope of standards within chapter.
898, 899. Repealed.

Application

For application of Title 7, see Civil Code § 938.

§ 896. Building standards for original construction intended to be sold as an individual dwelling unit

In any action seeking recovery of damages arising out of, or related to deficiencies in, the residential construction, design, specifications, surveying, planning, supervision, testing, or observation of construction, a builder, and to the extent set forth in Chapter 4 (commencing with Section 910), a general contractor, subcontractor, material supplier, individual product manufacturer, or design professional, shall, except as specifically set forth in this title, be liable for, and the claimant's claims or causes of action shall be limited to violation of, the following standards, except as specifically set forth in this title. This title applies to original construction intended to be sold as an individual dwelling unit. As to condominium conversions, this title does not apply to or does not supersede any other statutory or common law.

(a) With respect to water issues:

(1) A door shall not allow unintended water to pass beyond, around, or through the door or its designed or actual moisture barriers, if any.

(2) Windows, patio doors, deck doors, and their systems shall not allow water to pass beyond, around, or through the window, patio door, or deck door or its designed or actual moisture barriers, including, without limitation, internal barriers within the systems themselves. For purposes of this paragraph, "systems" include, without limitation, windows, window assemblies, framing, substrate, flashings, and trim, if any.

(3) Windows, patio doors, deck doors, and their systems shall not allow excessive condensation to enter the structure and cause damage to another component. For purposes of this paragraph, "systems" include, without limitation, windows, window assemblies, framing, substrate, flashings, and trim, if any.

(4) Roofs, roofing systems, chimney caps, and ventilation components shall not allow water to enter the structure or to pass beyond, around, or through the designed or actual moisture barriers, including, without limitation, internal barriers located within the systems themselves. For purposes of this paragraph, "systems" include, without limitation, framing, substrate, and sheathing, if any.

(5) Decks, deck systems, balconies, balcony systems, exterior stairs, and stair systems shall not allow water to pass into the adjacent structure. For purposes of this paragraph, "systems" include, without limitation, framing, substrate, flashing, and sheathing, if any.

(6) Decks, deck systems, balconies, balcony systems, exterior stairs, and stair systems shall not allow unintended water to pass within the systems themselves and cause damage to the systems. For purposes of this paragraph, "systems" include, without limitation, framing, substrate, flashing, and sheathing, if any.

(7) Foundation systems and slabs shall not allow water or vapor to enter into the structure so as to cause damage to another building component.

(8) Foundation systems and slabs shall not allow water or vapor to enter into the structure so as to limit the installation of the type of flooring materials typically used for the particular application.

(9) Hardscape, including paths and patios, irrigation systems, landscaping systems, and drainage systems, that are installed as part of the original construction, shall not be installed in such a way as to cause water or soil erosion to enter into or come in contact with the structure so as to cause damage to another building component.

(10) Stucco, exterior siding, exterior walls, including, without limitation, exterior framing, and other exterior wall finishes and fixtures and the systems of those components and fixtures, including, but not limited to, pot shelves, horizontal surfaces, columns, and plant-ons, shall be installed in such a way so as not to allow unintended water to pass into the structure or to pass beyond, around, or through the designed or actual moisture barriers of the system, including any internal barriers located within the system itself. For purposes of this paragraph, "systems" include, without limitation, framing, substrate, flashings, trim, wall assemblies, and internal wall cavities, if any.

(11) Stucco, exterior siding, and exterior walls shall not allow excessive condensation to enter the structure and cause damage to another component. For purposes of this paragraph, "systems" include, without limitation, framing, sub-

strate, flashings, trim, wall assemblies, and internal wall cavities, if any.

(12) Retaining and site walls and their associated drainage systems shall not allow unintended water to pass beyond, around, or through its designed or actual moisture barriers including, without limitation, any internal barriers, so as to cause damage. This standard does not apply to those portions of any wall or drainage system that are designed to have water flow beyond, around, or through them.

(13) Retaining walls and site walls, and their associated drainage systems, shall only allow water to flow beyond, around, or through the areas designated by design.

(14) The lines and components of the plumbing system, sewer system, and utility systems shall not leak.

(15) Plumbing lines, sewer lines, and utility lines shall not corrode so as to impede the useful life of the systems.

(16) Sewer systems shall be installed in such a way as to allow the designated amount of sewage to flow through the system.

(17) Showers, baths, and related waterproofing systems shall not leak water into the interior of walls, flooring systems, or the interior of other components.

(18) The waterproofing system behind or under ceramic tile and tile countertops shall not allow water into the interior of walls, flooring systems, or other components so as to cause damage. Ceramic tile systems shall be designed and installed so as to deflect intended water to the waterproofing system.

(b) With respect to structural issues:

(1) Foundations, load bearing components, and slabs, shall not contain significant cracks or significant vertical displacement.

(2) Foundations, load bearing components, and slabs shall not cause the structure, in whole or in part, to be structurally unsafe.

(3) Foundations, load bearing components, and slabs, and underlying soils shall be constructed so as to materially comply with the design criteria set by applicable government building codes, regulations, and ordinances for chemical deterioration or corrosion resistance in effect at the time of original construction.

(4) A structure shall be constructed so as to materially comply with the design criteria for earthquake and wind load resistance, as set forth in the applicable government building codes, regulations, and ordinances in effect at the time of original construction.

(c) With respect to soil issues:

(1) Soils and engineered retaining walls shall not cause, in whole or in part, damage to the structure built upon the soil or engineered retaining wall.

(2) Soils and engineered retaining walls shall not cause, in whole or in part, the structure to be structurally unsafe.

(3) Soils shall not cause, in whole or in part, the land upon which no structure is built to become unusable for the purpose represented at the time of original sale by the builder or for the purpose for which that land is commonly used.

(d) With respect to fire protection issues:

(1) A structure shall be constructed so as to materially comply with the design criteria of the applicable government building codes, regulations, and ordinances for fire protection of the occupants in effect at the time of the original construction.

(2) Fireplaces, chimneys, chimney structures, and chimney termination caps shall be constructed and installed in such a way so as not to cause an unreasonable risk of fire outside the fireplace enclosure or chimney.

(3) Electrical and mechanical systems shall be constructed and installed in such a way so as not to cause an unreasonable risk of fire.

(e) With respect to plumbing and sewer issues:

Plumbing and sewer systems shall be installed to operate properly and shall not materially impair the use of the structure by its inhabitants. However, no action may be brought for a violation of this subdivision more than four years after close of escrow.

(f) With respect to electrical system issues:

Electrical systems shall operate properly and shall not materially impair the use of the structure by its inhabitants. However, no action shall be brought pursuant to this subdivision more than four years from close of escrow.

(g) With respect to issues regarding other areas of construction:

(1) Exterior pathways, driveways, hardscape, sidewalls, sidewalks, and patios installed by the original builder shall not contain cracks that display significant vertical displacement or that are excessive. However, no action shall be brought upon a violation of this paragraph more than four years from close of escrow.

(2) Stucco, exterior siding, and other exterior wall finishes and fixtures, including, but not limited to, pot shelves, horizontal surfaces, columns, and plant-ons, shall not contain significant cracks or separations.

(3)(A) To the extent not otherwise covered by these standards, manufactured products, including, but not limited to, windows, doors, roofs, plumbing products and fixtures, fireplaces, electrical fixtures, HVAC units, countertops, cabinets, paint, and appliances shall be installed so as not to interfere with the products' useful life, if any.

(B) For purposes of this paragraph, "useful life" means a representation of how long a product is warranted or represented, through its limited warranty or any written representations, to last by its manufacturer, including recommended or required maintenance. If there is no representation by a manufacturer, a builder shall install manufactured products so as not to interfere with the product's utility.

(C) For purposes of this paragraph, "manufactured product" means a product that is completely manufactured offsite.

(D) If no useful life representation is made, or if the representation is less than one year, the period shall be no less than one year. If a manufactured product is damaged as a result of a violation of these standards, damage to the product is a recoverable element of damages. This subparagraph does not limit recovery if there has been damage to another building component caused by a manufactured product during the manufactured product's useful life.

(E) This title does not apply in any action seeking recovery solely for a defect in a manufactured product located within or adjacent to a structure.

(4) Heating shall be installed so as to be capable of maintaining a room temperature of 70 degrees Fahrenheit at a point three feet above the floor in any living space if the heating was installed pursuant to a building permit application submitted prior to January 1, 2008, or capable of maintaining a room temperature of 68 degrees Fahrenheit at a point three feet above the floor and two feet from exterior walls in all habitable rooms at the design temperature if the heating was installed pursuant to a building permit application submitted on or before January 1, 2008.

(5) Living space air-conditioning, if any, shall be provided in a manner consistent with the size and efficiency design criteria specified in Title 24 of the California Code of Regulations or its successor.

(6) Attached structures shall be constructed to comply with interunit noise transmission standards set by the applicable government building codes, ordinances, or regulations in effect at the time of the original construction. If there is no applicable code, ordinance, or regulation, this paragraph does not apply. However, no action shall be brought pursuant to this paragraph more than one year from the original occupancy of the adjacent unit.

(7) Irrigation systems and drainage shall operate properly so as not to damage landscaping or other external improvements. However, no action shall be brought pursuant to this paragraph more than one year from close of escrow.

(8) Untreated wood posts shall not be installed in contact with soil so as to cause unreasonable decay to the wood based upon the finish grade at the time of original construction. However, no action shall be brought pursuant to this paragraph more than two years from close of escrow.

(9) Untreated steel fences and adjacent components shall be installed so as to prevent unreasonable corrosion. However, no action shall be brought pursuant to this paragraph more than four years from close of escrow.

(10) Paint and stains shall be applied in such a manner so as not to cause deterioration of the building surfaces for the length of time specified by the paint or stain manufacturers' representations, if any. However, no action shall be brought pursuant to this paragraph more than five years from close of escrow.

(11) Roofing materials shall be installed so as to avoid materials falling from the roof.

(12) The landscaping systems shall be installed in such a manner so as to survive for not less than one year. However, no action shall be brought pursuant to this paragraph more than two years from close of escrow.

(13) Ceramic tile and tile backing shall be installed in such a manner that the tile does not detach.

(14) Dryer ducts shall be installed and terminated pursuant to manufacturer installation requirements. However, no action shall be brought pursuant to this paragraph more than two years from close of escrow.

(15) Structures shall be constructed in such a manner so as not to impair the occupants' safety because they contain public health hazards as determined by a duly authorized public health official, health agency, or governmental entity having jurisdiction. This paragraph does not limit recovery for any damages caused by a violation of any other paragraph of this section on the grounds that the damages do not constitute a health hazard. (Added by Stats.2002, c. 722 (S.B.800), § 3. Amended by Stats.2003, c. 762 (A.B.903), § 1; Stats.2006, c. 567 (A.B.2303), § 2; Stats.2012, c. 770 (A.B. 2697), § 2.)

Application

For application of Title 7, see Civil Code § 938.

Cross References

Consumer warranty protection, manufacturers and express warranties, service and repair facilities, see Civil Code § 1793.2.
Definitions under Title 7 applicable to this section, see Civil Code § 895.

§ 897. Function or component of a structure; scope of standards within chapter

The standards set forth in this chapter are intended to address every function or component of a structure. To the extent that a function or component of a structure is not addressed by these standards, it shall be actionable if it causes damage. (Added by Stats.2002, c. 722 (S.B.800), § 3.)

Application

For application of Title 7, see Civil Code § 938.

Cross References

Definitions under Title 7 applicable to this section, see Civil Code § 895.

§§ 898, 899. Repealed by Code Am.1873–74, c. 612, § 123

CHAPTER 3. OBLIGATIONS

Section
900. Fit and finish; limited warranty; scope.
901. Enhanced protection agreement; length of time; minimum standards.
902. Enhanced protection agreement; determination of enforceability.
903. Enhanced protection agreement; time to elect agreement; standards where provisions are unenforceable.
904. Enhanced protection agreement; disputed terms; notice of claim against builder.
905. Enhanced protection agreement; binding determination of applicable building standards; waiver; privity with nonoriginal homeowners.
906. Prelitigation procedures; governing law.
907. Homeowner maintenance obligations, schedules and practices.
908, 909. Repealed.

Application

For application of Title 7, see Civil Code § 938.

§ 900. Fit and finish; limited warranty; scope

As to fit and finish items, a builder shall provide a homebuyer with a minimum one-year express written limited warranty covering the fit and finish of the following building components. Except as otherwise provided by the standards specified in Chapter 2 (commencing with Section 896), this warranty shall cover the fit and finish of cabinets, mirrors, flooring, interior and exterior walls, countertops, paint finishes, and trim, but shall not apply to damage to those components caused by defects in other components governed by the other provisions of this title. Any fit and finish matters covered by this warranty are not subject to the provisions of this title. If a builder fails to provide the express warranty required by this section, the warranty for these items shall be for a period of one year. *(Added by Stats.2002, c. 722 (S.B.800), § 3.)*

Application

For application of Title 7, see Civil Code § 938.

Cross References

Builder defined for purposes of this Title, see Civil Code § 911.
Definitions under Title 7 applicable to this section, see Civil Code § 895.

§ 901. Enhanced protection agreement; length of time; minimum standards

A builder may, but is not required to, offer greater protection or protection for longer time periods in its express contract with the homeowner than that set forth in Chapter 2 (commencing with Section 896). A builder may not limit the application of Chapter 2 (commencing with Section 896) or lower its protection through the express contract with the homeowner. This type of express contract constitutes an "enhanced protection agreement." *(Added by Stats.2002, c. 722 (S.B.800), § 3.)*

Application

For application of Title 7, see Civil Code § 938.

Cross References

Builder defined for purposes of this Title, see Civil Code § 911.
Definitions under Title 7 applicable to this section, see Civil Code § 895.

§ 902. Enhanced protection agreement; determination of enforceability

If a builder offers an enhanced protection agreement, the builder may choose to be subject to its own express contractual provisions in place of the provisions set forth in Chapter 2 (commencing with Section 896). If an enhanced protection agreement is in place, Chapter 2 (commencing with Section 896) no longer applies other than to set forth minimum provisions by which to judge the enforceability of the particular provisions of the enhanced protection agreement. *(Added by Stats.2002, c. 722 (S.B.800), § 3.)*

Application

For application of Title 7, see Civil Code § 938.

Cross References

Builder defined for purposes of this Title, see Civil Code § 911.

Definitions under Title 7 applicable to this section, see Civil Code § 895.

§ 903. Enhanced protection agreement; time to elect agreement; standards where provisions are unenforceable

If a builder offers an enhanced protection agreement in place of the provisions set forth in Chapter 2 (commencing with Section 896), the election to do so shall be made in writing with the homeowner no later than the close of escrow. The builder shall provide the homeowner with a complete copy of Chapter 2 (commencing with Section 896) and advise the homeowner that the builder has elected not to be subject to its provisions. If any provision of an enhanced protection agreement is later found to be unenforceable as not meeting the minimum standards of Chapter 2 (commencing with Section 896), a builder may use this chapter in lieu of those provisions found to be unenforceable. *(Added by Stats.2002, c. 722 (S.B.800), § 3.)*

Application

For application of Title 7, see Civil Code § 938.

Cross References

Builder defined for purposes of this Title, see Civil Code § 911.
Definitions under Title 7 applicable to this section, see Civil Code § 895.

§ 904. Enhanced protection agreement; disputed terms; notice of claim against builder

If a builder has elected to use an enhanced protection agreement, and a homeowner disputes that the particular provision or time periods of the enhanced protection agreement are not greater than, or equal to, the provisions of Chapter 2 (commencing with Section 896) as they apply to the particular deficiency alleged by the homeowner, the homeowner may seek to enforce the application of the standards set forth in this chapter as to those claimed deficiencies. If a homeowner seeks to enforce a particular standard in lieu of a provision of the enhanced protection agreement, the homeowner shall give the builder written notice of that intent at the time the homeowner files a notice of claim pursuant to Chapter 4 (commencing with Section 910). *(Added by Stats.2002, c. 722 (S.B.800), § 3.)*

Application

For application of Title 7, see Civil Code § 938.

Cross References

Builder defined for purposes of this Title, see Civil Code § 911.
Definitions under Title 7 applicable to this section, see Civil Code § 895.

§ 905. Enhanced protection agreement; binding determination of applicable building standards; waiver; privity with nonoriginal homeowners

If a homeowner seeks to enforce Chapter 2 (commencing with Section 896), in lieu of the enhanced protection agreement in a subsequent litigation or other legal action, the builder shall have the right to have the matter bifurcated, and to have an immediately binding determination of his or her responsive pleading within 60 days after the filing of that pleading, but in no event after the commencement of discovery, as to the application of either Chapter 2 (commencing with Section 896) or the enhanced protection agreement as to the deficiencies claimed by the homeowner. If the builder fails to seek that determination in the timeframe specified, the builder waives the right to do so and the standards set forth in this title shall apply. As to any nonoriginal homeowner, that homeowner shall be deemed in privity for purposes of an enhanced protection agreement only to the extent that the builder has recorded the enhanced protection agreement on title or provided actual notice to the nonoriginal homeowner of the enhanced protection agreement. If the enhanced protection agreement is not recorded on title or no actual notice has been provided, the standards set forth in this title apply to any nonoriginal homeowners' claims. *(Added by Stats.2002, c. 722 (S.B.800), § 3.)*

Application

For application of Title 7, see Civil Code § 938.

Cross References

Builder defined for purposes of this Title, see Civil Code § 911.
Definitions under Title 7 applicable to this section, see Civil Code § 895.

§ 906. Prelitigation procedures; governing law

A builder's election to use an enhanced protection agreement addresses only the issues set forth in Chapter 2 (commencing with Section 896) and does not constitute an election to use or not use the provisions of Chapter 4 (commencing with Section 910). The decision to use or not use Chapter 4 (commencing with Section 910) is governed by the provisions of that chapter. *(Added by Stats.2002, c. 722 (S.B.800), § 3.)*

Application

For application of Title 7, see Civil Code § 938.

Cross References

Definitions under Title 7 applicable to this section, see Civil Code § 895.

§ 907. Homeowner maintenance obligations, schedules and practices

A homeowner is obligated to follow all reasonable maintenance obligations and schedules communicated in writing to the homeowner by the builder and product manufacturers, as well as commonly accepted maintenance practices. A failure by a homeowner to follow these obligations, schedules, and practices may subject the homeowner to the affirmative defenses contained in Section 944. *(Added by Stats.2002, c. 722 (S.B.800), § 3.)*

Application

For application of Title 7, see Civil Code § 938.

Cross References

Builder defined for purposes of this Title, see Civil Code § 911.
Definitions under Title 7 applicable to this section, see Civil Code § 895.

Obligation defined, see Civil Code § 1427.

§§ 908, 909. Repealed by Code Am.1873–74, c. 612, § 123

CHAPTER 4. PRELITIGATION PROCEDURE

Section
910. Written notice of claim.
911. "Builder" defined.
912. Document disclosure by builder; designated agent to accept claims and act on builder's behalf; notice to homeowners and purchasers.
913. Written acknowledgement of claim; time to respond; contents.
914. Election to pursue other nonadversarial contractual procedures; affect of Title 7 upon exiting statutory or decisional law.
915. Application of prelitigation provisions upon certain failures to act by builder.
916. Builder election to inspect.
917. Written offer to repair.
918. Homeowner response to repair offer.
919. Mediation by mutual agreement; unresolved disputes; repairs.
920. Claimant right to file action.
921. Repair work; time and date scheduled; completion date.
922. Electronic recordation, video recordation, or photographs during repair work.
923. Documentation relating to repair work; requests for copies.
924. Partial repair of claims; statement of reasons.
925. Failure to repair within time allowed.
926. Release or waiver in exchange for repair work.
927. Claims for violation of statutory process or inadequate repair; limitation of action; extension of time.
928. Mediation after repair completion.
929. Cash offer in lieu of repair; release.
930. Failure to act within mandated timeframes and other requirements; right to file action; motion to stay proceedings.
931. Causes of action or damages exceeding scope of actionable defects; applicability of standards.
932. Subsequently discovered claims of unmet standards.
933. Evidence of repair efforts.
934. Evidence of conduct during enforcement process.
935. Construction of chapter with similar provisions.
936. Parties subject to application of title; determination; defenses available; joint and several liability; strict liability.
937. Construction with professional negligence actions.
938. Application of Title 7 to certain residences.
939, 940. Repealed.

Application

For application of Title 7, see Civil Code § 938.

Cross References

Indemnification provisions in construction contracts, enforceability, claims arising from or relating to negligence of builder, see Civil Code § 2782.

§ 910. Written notice of claim

Prior to filing an action against any party alleged to have contributed to a violation of the standards set forth in Chapter 2 (commencing with Section 896), the claimant shall initiate the following prelitigation procedures:

(a) The claimant or his or her legal representative shall provide written notice via certified mail, overnight mail, or personal delivery to the builder, in the manner prescribed in this section, of the claimant's claim that the construction of his or her residence violates any of the standards set forth in Chapter 2 (commencing with Section 896). That notice shall provide the claimant's name, address, and preferred method of contact, and shall state that the claimant alleges a violation pursuant to this part against the builder, and shall describe the claim in reasonable detail sufficient to determine the nature and location, to the extent known, of the claimed violation. In the case of a group of homeowners or an association, the notice may identify the claimants solely by address or other description sufficient to apprise the builder of the locations of the subject residences. That document shall have the same force and effect as a notice of commencement of a legal proceeding.

(b) The notice requirements of this section do not preclude a homeowner from seeking redress through any applicable normal customer service procedure as set forth in any contractual, warranty, or other builder-generated document; and, if a homeowner seeks to do so, that request shall not satisfy the notice requirements of this section. (Added by Stats.2002, c. 722 (S.B.800), § 3.)

Application

For application of Title 7, see Civil Code § 938.

Cross References

Builder defined for purposes of this Title, see Civil Code § 911.
Construction contracts, indemnity agreements, see Civil Code § 2782 et seq.
Definitions under Title 7 applicable to this section, see Civil Code § 895.
Indemnification provisions in construction contracts, enforceability, claims arising from or relating to negligence of builder, see Civil Code § 2782.

§ 911. "Builder" defined

(a) For purposes of this title, except as provided in subdivision (b), "builder" means any entity or individual, including, but not limited to a builder, developer, general contractor, contractor, or original seller, who, at the time of sale, was also in the business of selling residential units to the public for the property that is the subject of the homeowner's claim or was in the business of building, developing, or constructing residential units for public purchase for the property that is the subject of the homeowner's claim.

(b) For the purposes of this title, "builder" does not include any entity or individual whose involvement with a residential unit that is the subject of the homeowner's claim is limited to his or her capacity as general contractor or contractor and who is not a partner, member of, subsidiary of, or otherwise similarly affiliated with the builder. For purposes of this title, these nonaffiliated general contractors and nonaffiliated contractors shall be treated the same as subcontractors, material suppliers, individual product manufacturers, and design professionals. (Added by Stats.2002, c. 722 (S.B.800), § 3. Amended by Stats.2003, c. 762 (A.B.903), § 2.)

Application

For application of Title 7, see Civil Code § 938.

Cross References

Construction contracts, indemnity agreements, see Civil Code § 2782 et seq.
Definitions under Title 7 applicable to this section, see Civil Code § 895.
Indemnification provisions in construction contracts, enforceability, claims arising from or relating to negligence of builder, see Civil Code § 2782.

§ 912. Document disclosure by builder; designated agent to accept claims and act on builder's behalf; notice to homeowners and purchasers

A builder shall do all of the following:

(a) Within 30 days of a written request by a homeowner or his or her legal representative, the builder shall provide copies of all relevant plans, specifications, mass or rough grading plans, final soils reports, Bureau of Real Estate public reports, and available engineering calculations, that pertain to a homeowner's residence specifically or as part of a larger development tract. The request shall be honored if it states that it is made relative to structural, fire safety, or soils provisions of this title. However, a builder is not obligated to provide a copying service, and reasonable copying costs shall be borne by the requesting party. A builder may require that the documents be copied onsite by the requesting party, except that the homeowner may, at his or her option, use his or her own copying service, which may include an offsite copy facility that is bonded and insured. If a builder can show that the builder maintained the documents, but that they later became unavailable due to loss or destruction that was not the fault of the builder, the builder may be excused from the requirements of this subdivision, in which case the builder shall act with reasonable diligence to assist the homeowner in obtaining those documents from any applicable government authority or from the source that generated the document. However, in that case, the time limits specified by this section do not apply.

(b) At the expense of the homeowner, who may opt to use an offsite copy facility that is bonded and insured, the builder shall provide to the homeowner or his or her legal representative copies of all maintenance and preventative maintenance recommendations that pertain to his or her residence within 30 days of service of a written request for those documents. Those documents shall also be provided to the homeowner in conjunction with the initial sale of the residence.

(c) At the expense of the homeowner, who may opt to use an offsite copy facility that is bonded and insured, a builder shall provide to the homeowner or his or her legal representative copies of all manufactured products maintenance, preventive maintenance, and limited warranty information within 30 days of a written request for those documents. These documents shall also be provided to the homeowner in conjunction with the initial sale of the residence.

(d) At the expense of the homeowner, who may opt to use an offsite copy facility that is bonded and insured, a builder shall provide to the homeowner or his or her legal representative copies of all of the builder's limited contractual warranties in accordance with this part in effect at the time of the original sale of the residence within 30 days of a written request for those documents. Those documents shall also be provided to the homeowner in conjunction with the initial sale of the residence.

(e) A builder shall maintain the name and address of an agent for notice pursuant to this chapter with the Secretary of State or, alternatively, elect to use a third party for that notice if the builder has notified the homeowner in writing of the third party's name and address, to whom claims and requests for information under this section may be mailed. The name and address of the agent for notice or third party shall be included with the original sales documentation and shall be initialed and acknowledged by the purchaser and the builder's sales representative.

This subdivision applies to instances in which a builder contracts with a third party to accept claims and act on the builder's behalf. A builder shall give actual notice to the homeowner that the builder has made such an election, and shall include the name and address of the third party.

(f) A builder shall record on title a notice of the existence of these procedures and a notice that these procedures impact the legal rights of the homeowner. This information shall also be included with the original sales documentation and shall be initialed and acknowledged by the purchaser and the builder's sales representative.

(g) A builder shall provide, with the original sales documentation, a written copy of this title, which shall be initialed and acknowledged by the purchaser and the builder's sales representative.

(h) As to any documents provided in conjunction with the original sale, the builder shall instruct the original purchaser to provide those documents to any subsequent purchaser.

(i) Any builder who fails to comply with any of these requirements within the time specified is not entitled to the protection of this chapter, and the homeowner is released from the requirements of this chapter and may proceed with the filing of an action, in which case the remaining chapters of this part shall continue to apply to the action. *(Added by Stats.2002, c. 722 (S.B.800), § 3. Amended by Stats.2003, c. 762 (A.B.903), § 3; Stats.2013, c. 352 (A.B.1317), § 50, eff. Sept. 26, 2013, operative July 1, 2013.)*

Application

For application of Title 7, see Civil Code § 938.

Cross References

Builder defined for purposes of this Title, see Civil Code § 911.
Definitions under Title 7 applicable to this section, see Civil Code § 895.

§ 913. Written acknowledgement of claim; time to respond; contents

A builder or his or her representative shall acknowledge, in writing, receipt of the notice of the claim within 14 days after receipt of the notice of the claim. If the notice of the claim is served by the claimant's legal representative, or if the builder receives a written representation letter from a homeowner's attorney, the builder shall include the attorney in all subsequent substantive communications, including, without limitation, all written communications occurring pursuant to this chapter, and all substantive and procedural communications, including all written communications, following the commencement of any subsequent complaint or other legal action, except that if the builder has retained or involved legal counsel to assist the builder in this process, all communications by the builder's counsel shall only be with the claimant's legal representative, if any. *(Added by Stats.2002, c. 722 (S.B.800), § 3.)*

Application

For application of Title 7, see Civil Code § 938.

Cross References

Builder defined for purposes of this Title, see Civil Code § 911.
Definitions under Title 7 applicable to this section, see Civil Code § 895.

§ 914. Election to pursue other nonadversarial contractual procedures; affect of Title 7 upon exiting statutory or decisional law

(a) This chapter establishes a nonadversarial procedure, including the remedies available under this chapter which, if the procedure does not resolve the dispute between the parties, may result in a subsequent action to enforce the other chapters of this title. A builder may attempt to commence nonadversarial contractual provisions other than the nonadversarial procedures and remedies set forth in this chapter, but may not, in addition to its own nonadversarial contractual provisions, require adherence to the nonadversarial procedures and remedies set forth in this chapter, regardless of whether the builder's own alternative nonadversarial contractual provisions are successful in resolving the dispute or ultimately deemed enforceable.

At the time the sales agreement is executed, the builder shall notify the homeowner whether the builder intends to engage in the nonadversarial procedure of this section or attempt to enforce alternative nonadversarial contractual provisions. If the builder elects to use alternative nonadversarial contractual provisions in lieu of this chapter, the election is binding, regardless of whether the builder's alternative nonadversarial contractual provisions are successful in resolving the ultimate dispute or are ultimately deemed enforceable.

(b) Nothing in this title is intended to affect existing statutory or decisional law pertaining to the applicability, viability, or enforceability of alternative dispute resolution methods, alternative remedies, or contractual arbitration, judicial reference, or similar procedures requiring a binding resolution to enforce the other chapters of this title or any other disputes between homeowners and builders. Nothing in this title is intended to affect the applicability, viability, or enforceability, if any, of contractual arbitration or judicial reference after a nonadversarial procedure or provision has been completed. *(Added by Stats.2002, c. 722 (S.B.800), § 3.)*

Application

For application of Title 7, see Civil Code § 938.

Cross References

Builder defined for purposes of this Title, see Civil Code § 911.

Definitions under Title 7 applicable to this section, see Civil Code § 895.

§ 915. Application of prelitigation provisions upon certain failures to act by builder

If a builder fails to acknowledge receipt of the notice of a claim within the time specified, elects not to go through the process set forth in this chapter, or fails to request an inspection within the time specified, or at the conclusion or cessation of an alternative nonadversarial proceeding, this chapter does not apply and the homeowner is released from the requirements of this chapter and may proceed with the filing of an action. However, the standards set forth in the other chapters of this title shall continue to apply to the action. *(Added by Stats.2002, c. 722 (S.B.800), § 3.)*

Application

For application of Title 7, see Civil Code § 938.

Cross References

Builder defined for purposes of this Title, see Civil Code § 911.
Definitions under Title 7 applicable to this section, see Civil Code § 895.

§ 916. Builder election to inspect

(a) If a builder elects to inspect the claimed unmet standards, the builder shall complete the initial inspection and testing within 14 days after acknowledgment of receipt of the notice of the claim, at a mutually convenient date and time. If the homeowner has retained legal representation, the inspection shall be scheduled with the legal representative's office at a mutually convenient date and time, unless the legal representative is unavailable during the relevant time periods. All costs of builder inspection and testing, including any damage caused by the builder inspection, shall be borne by the builder. The builder shall also provide written proof that the builder has liability insurance to cover any damages or injuries occurring during inspection and testing. The builder shall restore the property to its pretesting condition within 48 hours of the testing. The builder shall, upon request, allow the inspections to be observed and electronically recorded, video recorded, or photographed by the claimant or his or her legal representative.

(b) Nothing that occurs during a builder's or claimant's inspection or testing may be used or introduced as evidence to support a spoliation defense by any potential party in any subsequent litigation.

(c) If a builder deems a second inspection or testing reasonably necessary, and specifies the reasons therefor in writing within three days following the initial inspection, the builder may conduct a second inspection or testing. A second inspection or testing shall be completed within 40 days of the initial inspection or testing. All requirements concerning the initial inspection or testing shall also apply to the second inspection or testing.

(d) If the builder fails to inspect or test the property within the time specified, the claimant is released from the requirements of this section and may proceed with the filing of an action. However, the standards set forth in the other chapters of this title shall continue to apply to the action.

(e) If a builder intends to hold a subcontractor, design professional, individual product manufacturer, or material supplier, including an insurance carrier, warranty company, or service company, responsible for its contribution to the unmet standard, the builder shall provide notice to that person or entity sufficiently in advance to allow them to attend the initial, or if requested, second inspection of any alleged unmet standard and to participate in the repair process. The claimant and his or her legal representative, if any, shall be advised in a reasonable time prior to the inspection as to the identity of all persons or entities invited to attend. This subdivision does not apply to the builder's insurance company. Except with respect to any claims involving a repair actually conducted under this chapter, nothing in this subdivision shall be construed to relieve a subcontractor, design professional, individual product manufacturer, or material supplier of any liability under an action brought by a claimant. *(Added by Stats.2002, c. 722 (S.B. 800), § 3. Amended by Stats.2003, c. 762 (A.B.903), § 4; Stats.2009, c. 88 (A.B.176), § 12.)*

Application

For application of Title 7, see Civil Code § 938.

Cross References

Builder defined for purposes of this Title, see Civil Code § 911.
Definitions under Title 7 applicable to this section, see Civil Code § 895.

§ 917. Written offer to repair

Within 30 days of the initial or, if requested, second inspection or testing, the builder may offer in writing to repair the violation. The offer to repair shall also compensate the homeowner for all applicable damages recoverable under Section 944, within the timeframe for the repair set forth in this chapter. Any such offer shall be accompanied by a detailed, specific, step-by-step statement identifying the particular violation that is being repaired, explaining the nature, scope, and location of the repair, and setting a reasonable completion date for the repair. The offer shall also include the names, addresses, telephone numbers, and license numbers of the contractors whom the builder intends to have perform the repair. Those contractors shall be fully insured for, and shall be responsible for, all damages or injuries that they may cause to occur during the repair, and evidence of that insurance shall be provided to the homeowner upon request. Upon written request by the homeowner or his or her legal representative, and within the timeframes set forth in this chapter, the builder shall also provide any available technical documentation, including, without limitation, plans and specifications, pertaining to the claimed violation within the particular home or development tract. The offer shall also advise the homeowner in writing of his or her right to request up to three additional contractors from which to select to do the repair pursuant to this chapter. *(Added by Stats.2002, c. 722 (S.B.800), § 3.)*

Application

For application of Title 7, see Civil Code § 938.

Cross References

Builder defined for purposes of this Title, see Civil Code § 911.

Definitions under Title 7 applicable to this section, see Civil Code § 895.

§ 918. Homeowner response to repair offer

Upon receipt of the offer to repair, the homeowner shall have 30 days to authorize the builder to proceed with the repair. The homeowner may alternatively request, at the homeowner's sole option and discretion, that the builder provide the names, addresses, telephone numbers, and license numbers for up to three alternative contractors who are not owned or financially controlled by the builder and who regularly conduct business in the county where the structure is located. If the homeowner so elects, the builder is entitled to an additional noninvasive inspection, to occur at a mutually convenient date and time within 20 days of the election, so as to permit the other proposed contractors to review the proposed site of the repair. Within 35 days after the request of the homeowner for alternative contractors, the builder shall present the homeowner with a choice of contractors. Within 20 days after that presentation, the homeowner shall authorize the builder or one of the alternative contractors to perform the repair. *(Added by Stats.2002, c. 722 (S.B.800), § 3.)*

Application

For application of Title 7, see Civil Code § 938.

Cross References

Builder defined for purposes of this Title, see Civil Code § 911.
Definitions under Title 7 applicable to this section, see Civil Code § 895.

§ 919. Mediation by mutual agreement; unresolved disputes; repairs

The offer to repair shall also be accompanied by an offer to mediate the dispute if the homeowner so chooses. The mediation shall be limited to a four-hour mediation, except as otherwise mutually agreed before a nonaffiliated mediator selected and paid for by the builder. At the homeowner's sole option, the homeowner may agree to split the cost of the mediator, and if he or she does so, the mediator shall be selected jointly. The mediator shall have sufficient availability such that the mediation occurs within 15 days after the request to mediate is received and occurs at a mutually convenient location within the county where the action is pending. If a builder has made an offer to repair a violation, and the mediation has failed to resolve the dispute, the homeowner shall allow the repair to be performed either by the builder, its contractor, or the selected contractor. *(Added by Stats.2002, c. 722 (S.B.800), § 3.)*

Application

For application of Title 7, see Civil Code § 938.

Cross References

Builder defined for purposes of this Title, see Civil Code § 911.
Definitions under Title 7 applicable to this section, see Civil Code § 895.

§ 920. Claimant right to file action

If the builder fails to make an offer to repair or otherwise strictly comply with this chapter within the times specified, the claimant is released from the requirements of this chapter and may proceed with the filing of an action. If the contractor performing the repair does not complete the repair in the time or manner specified, the claimant may file an action. If this occurs, the standards set forth in the other chapters of this part shall continue to apply to the action. *(Added by Stats.2002, c. 722 (S.B.800), § 3.)*

Application

For application of Title 7, see Civil Code § 938.

Cross References

Builder defined for purposes of this Title, see Civil Code § 911.
Definitions under Title 7 applicable to this section, see Civil Code § 895.

§ 921. Repair work; time and date scheduled; completion date

(a) In the event that a resolution under this chapter involves a repair by the builder, the builder shall make an appointment with the claimant, make all appropriate arrangements to effectuate a repair of the claimed unmet standards, and compensate the homeowner for all damages resulting therefrom free of charge to the claimant. The repair shall be scheduled through the claimant's legal representative, if any, unless he or she is unavailable during the relevant time periods. The repair shall be commenced on a mutually convenient date within 14 days of acceptance or, if an alternative contractor is selected by the homeowner, within 14 days of the selection, or, if a mediation occurs, within seven days of the mediation, or within five days after a permit is obtained if one is required. The builder shall act with reasonable diligence in obtaining any such permit.

(b) The builder shall ensure that work done on the repairs is done with the utmost diligence, and that the repairs are completed as soon as reasonably possible, subject to the nature of the repair or some unforeseen event not caused by the builder or the contractor performing the repair. Every effort shall be made to complete the repair within 120 days. *(Added by Stats.2002, c. 722 (S.B.800), § 3.)*

Application

For application of Title 7, see Civil Code § 938.

Cross References

Builder defined for purposes of this Title, see Civil Code § 911.
Definitions under Title 7 applicable to this section, see Civil Code § 895.

§ 922. Electronic recordation, video recordation, or photographs during repair work

The builder shall, upon request, allow the repair to be observed and electronically recorded, video recorded, or photographed by the claimant or his or her legal representative. Nothing that occurs during the repair process may be used or introduced as evidence to support a spoliation defense by any potential party in any subsequent litigation. *(Added by Stats.2002, c. 722 (S.B.800), § 3. Amended by Stats.2009, c. 88 (A.B.176), § 13.)*

Application

For application of Title 7, see Civil Code § 938.

Cross References

Builder defined for purposes of this Title, see Civil Code § 911.
Definitions under Title 7 applicable to this section, see Civil Code § 895.

§ 923. Documentation relating to repair work; requests for copies

The builder shall provide the homeowner or his or her legal representative, upon request, with copies of all correspondence, photographs, and other materials pertaining or relating in any manner to the repairs. *(Added by Stats.2002, c. 722 (S.B.800), § 3.)*

Application

For application of Title 7, see Civil Code § 938.

Cross References

Builder defined for purposes of this Title, see Civil Code § 911.
Definitions under Title 7 applicable to this section, see Civil Code § 895.

§ 924. Partial repair of claims; statement of reasons

If the builder elects to repair some, but not all of, the claimed unmet standards, the builder shall, at the same time it makes its offer, set forth with particularity in writing the reasons, and the support for those reasons, for not repairing all claimed unmet standards. *(Added by Stats.2002, c. 722 (S.B.800), § 3.)*

Application

For application of Title 7, see Civil Code § 938.

Cross References

Builder defined for purposes of this Title, see Civil Code § 911.
Definitions under Title 7 applicable to this section, see Civil Code § 895.

§ 925. Failure to repair within time allowed

If the builder fails to complete the repair within the time specified in the repair plan, the claimant is released from the requirements of this chapter and may proceed with the filing of an action. If this occurs, the standards set forth in the other chapters of this title shall continue to apply to the action. *(Added by Stats.2002, c. 722 (S.B.800), § 3.)*

Application

For application of Title 7, see Civil Code § 938.

Cross References

Builder defined for purposes of this Title, see Civil Code § 911.
Definitions under Title 7 applicable to this section, see Civil Code § 895.

§ 926. Release or waiver in exchange for repair work

The builder may not obtain a release or waiver of any kind in exchange for the repair work mandated by this chapter. At the conclusion of the repair, the claimant may proceed with filing an action for violation of the applicable standard or for a claim of inadequate repair, or both, including all applicable damages available under Section 944. *(Added by Stats.2002, c. 722 (S.B.800), § 3.)*

Application

For application of Title 7, see Civil Code § 938.

Cross References

Builder defined for purposes of this Title, see Civil Code § 911.
Definitions under Title 7 applicable to this section, see Civil Code § 895.

§ 927. Claims for violation of statutory process or inadequate repair; limitation of action; extension of time

If the applicable statute of limitations has otherwise run during this process, the time period for filing a complaint or other legal remedies for violation of any provision of this title, or for a claim of inadequate repair, is extended from the time of the original claim by the claimant to 100 days after the repair is completed, whether or not the particular violation is the one being repaired. If the builder fails to acknowledge the claim within the time specified, elects not to go through this statutory process, or fails to request an inspection within the time specified, the time period for filing a complaint or other legal remedies for violation of any provision of this title is extended from the time of the original claim by the claimant to 45 days after the time for responding to the notice of claim has expired. If the builder elects to attempt to enforce its own nonadversarial procedure in lieu of the procedure set forth in this chapter, the time period for filing a complaint or other legal remedies for violation of any provision of this part is extended from the time of the original claim by the claimant to 100 days after either the completion of the builder's alternative nonadversarial procedure, or 100 days after the builder's alternative nonadversarial procedure is deemed unenforceable, whichever is later. *(Added by Stats.2002, c. 722 (S.B.800), § 3.)*

Application

For application of Title 7, see Civil Code § 938.

Cross References

Builder defined for purposes of this Title, see Civil Code § 911.
Definitions under Title 7 applicable to this section, see Civil Code § 895.

§ 928. Mediation after repair completion

If the builder has invoked this chapter and completed a repair, prior to filing an action, if there has been no previous mediation between the parties, the homeowner or his or her legal representative shall request mediation in writing. The mediation shall be limited to four hours, except as otherwise mutually agreed before a nonaffiliated mediator selected and paid for by the builder. At the homeowner's sole option, the homeowner may agree to split the cost of the mediator and if he or she does so, the mediator shall be selected jointly. The mediator shall have sufficient availability such that the mediation will occur within 15 days after the request for mediation is received and shall occur at a mutually convenient location within the county where the action is pending. In the event that a mediation is used at this point, any applicable statutes of limitations shall be tolled from the date of the request to mediate until the next court day after the

§ 928

mediation is completed, or the 100–day period, whichever is later. *(Added by Stats.2002, c. 722 (S.B.800), § 3.)*

Application

For application of Title 7, see Civil Code § 938.

Cross References

Builder defined for purposes of this Title, see Civil Code § 911.
Definitions under Title 7 applicable to this section, see Civil Code § 895.

§ 929. Cash offer in lieu of repair; release

(a) Nothing in this chapter prohibits the builder from making only a cash offer and no repair. In this situation, the homeowner is free to accept the offer, or he or she may reject the offer and proceed with the filing of an action. If the latter occurs, the standards of the other chapters of this title shall continue to apply to the action.

(b) The builder may obtain a reasonable release in exchange for the cash payment. The builder may negotiate the terms and conditions of any reasonable release in terms of scope and consideration in conjunction with a cash payment under this chapter. *(Added by Stats.2002, c. 722 (S.B.800), § 3.)*

Application

For application of Title 7, see Civil Code § 938.

Cross References

Builder defined for purposes of this Title, see Civil Code § 911.
Definitions under Title 7 applicable to this section, see Civil Code § 895.

§ 930. Failure to act within mandated timeframes and other requirements; right to file action; motion to stay proceedings

(a) The time periods and all other requirements in this chapter are to be strictly construed, and, unless extended by the mutual agreement of the parties in accordance with this chapter, shall govern the rights and obligations under this title. If a builder fails to act in accordance with this section within the timeframes mandated, unless extended by the mutual agreement of the parties as evidenced by a postclaim written confirmation by the affected homeowner demonstrating that he or she has knowingly and voluntarily extended the statutory timeframe, the claimant may proceed with filing an action. If this occurs, the standards of the other chapters of this title shall continue to apply to the action.

(b) If the claimant does not conform with the requirements of this chapter, the builder may bring a motion to stay any subsequent court action or other proceeding until the requirements of this chapter have been satisfied. The court, in its discretion, may award the prevailing party on such a motion, his or her attorney's fees and costs in bringing or opposing the motion. *(Added by Stats.2002, c. 722 (S.B.800), § 3.)*

Application

For application of Title 7, see Civil Code § 938.

Cross References

Builder defined for purposes of this Title, see Civil Code § 911.
Definitions under Title 7 applicable to this section, see Civil Code § 895.
Obligation defined, see Civil Code § 1427.

§ 931. Causes of action or damages exceeding scope of actionable defects; applicability of standards

If a claim combines causes of action or damages not covered by this part, including, without limitation, personal injuries, class actions, other statutory remedies, or fraud-based claims, the claimed unmet standards shall be administered according to this part, although evidence of the property in its unrepaired condition may be introduced to support the respective elements of any such cause of action. As to any fraud-based claim, if the fact that the property has been repaired under this chapter is deemed admissible, the trier of fact shall be informed that the repair was not voluntarily accepted by the homeowner. As to any class action claims that address solely the incorporation of a defective component into a residence, the named and unnamed class members need not comply with this chapter. *(Added by Stats.2002, c. 722 (S.B.800), § 3.)*

Application

For application of Title 7, see Civil Code § 938.

Cross References

Definitions under Title 7 applicable to this section, see Civil Code § 895.

§ 932. Subsequently discovered claims of unmet standards

Subsequently discovered claims of unmet standards shall be administered separately under this chapter, unless otherwise agreed to by the parties. However, in the case of a detached single family residence, in the same home, if the subsequently discovered claim is for a violation of the same standard as that which has already been initiated by the same claimant and the subject of a currently pending action, the claimant need not reinitiate the process as to the same standard. In the case of an attached project, if the subsequently discovered claim is for a violation of the same standard for a connected component system in the same building as has already been initiated by the same claimant, and the subject of a currently pending action, the claimant need not reinitiate this process as to that standard. *(Added by Stats.2002, c. 722 (S.B.800), § 3.)*

Application

For application of Title 7, see Civil Code § 938.

Cross References

Definitions under Title 7 applicable to this section, see Civil Code § 895.

§ 933. Evidence of repair efforts

If any enforcement of these standards is commenced, the fact that a repair effort was made may be introduced to the trier of fact. However, the claimant may use the condition of the property prior to the repair as the basis for contending that the repair work was inappropriate, inadequate, or incomplete, or that the violation still exists. The claimant need not show that the repair work resulted in further damage nor that damage has continued to occur as a result of the violation. (Added by Stats.2002, c. 722 (S.B.800), § 3.)

Application

For application of Title 7, see Civil Code § 938.

Cross References

Definitions under Title 7 applicable to this section, see Civil Code § 895.

§ 934. Evidence of conduct during enforcement process

Evidence of both parties' conduct during this process may be introduced during a subsequent enforcement action, if any, with the exception of any mediation. Any repair efforts undertaken by the builder, shall not be considered settlement communications or offers of settlement and are not inadmissible in evidence on such a basis. (Added by Stats.2002, c. 722 (S.B.800), § 3.)

Application

For application of Title 7, see Civil Code § 938.

Cross References

Builder defined for purposes of this Title, see Civil Code § 911.
Definitions under Title 7 applicable to this section, see Civil Code § 895.

§ 935. Construction of chapter with similar provisions

To the extent that provisions of this chapter are enforced and those provisions are substantially similar to provisions in Section 6000, but an action is subsequently commenced under Section 6000, the parties are excused from performing the substantially similar requirements under Section 6000. (Added by Stats.2002, c. 722 (S.B.800), § 3. Amended by Stats. 2012, c. 181 (A.B.806), § 30, operative Jan. 1, 2014.)

Application

For application of Title 7, see Civil Code § 938.

Cross References

Definitions under Title 7 applicable to this section, see Civil Code § 895.

§ 936. Parties subject to application of title; determination; defenses available; joint and several liability; strict liability

Each and every provision of the other chapters of this title apply to general contractors, subcontractors, material suppliers, individual product manufacturers, and design professionals to the extent that the general contractors, subcontractors, material suppliers, individual product manufacturers, and design professionals caused, in whole or in part, a violation of a particular standard as the result of a negligent act or omission or a breach of contract. In addition to the affirmative defenses set forth in Section 945.5, a general contractor, subcontractor, material supplier, design professional, individual product manufacturer, or other entity may also offer common law and contractual defenses as applicable to any claimed violation of a standard. All actions by a claimant or builder to enforce an express contract, or any provision thereof, against a general contractor, subcontractor, material supplier, individual product manufacturer, or design professional is preserved. Nothing in this title modifies the law pertaining to joint and several liability for builders, general contractors, subcontractors, material suppliers, individual product manufacturer, and design professionals that contribute to any specific violation of this title. However, the negligence standard in this section does not apply to any general contractor, subcontractor, material supplier, individual product manufacturer, or design professional with respect to claims for which strict liability would apply. (Added by Stats.2002, c. 722 (S.B.800), § 3. Amended by Stats.2003, c. 762 (A.B.903), § 5.)

Application

For application of Title 7, see Civil Code § 938.

Cross References

Builder defined for purposes of this Title, see Civil Code § 911.
Definitions under Title 7 applicable to this section, see Civil Code § 895.

§ 937. Construction with professional negligence actions

Nothing in this title shall be interpreted to eliminate or abrogate the requirement to comply with Section 411.35 of the Code of Civil Procedure or to affect the liability of design professionals, including architects and architectural firms, for claims and damages not covered by this title. (Added by Stats.2002, c. 722 (S.B.800), § 3.)

Application

For application of Title 7, see Civil Code § 938.

Cross References

Definitions under Title 7 applicable to this section, see Civil Code § 895.

§ 938. Application of Title 7 to certain residences

This title applies only to new residential units where the purchase agreement with the buyer was signed by the seller on or after January 1, 2003. (Added by Stats.2002, c. 722 (S.B.800), § 3. Amended by Stats.2003, c. 762 (A.B.903), § 6.)

Cross References

Definitions under Title 7 applicable to this section, see Civil Code § 895.

§§ 939, 940. Repealed by Code Am.1873–74, c. 612, § 123

CHAPTER 5. PROCEDURE

Section
941. Limitation of action; tolling.
942. Sufficiency of claim for violation of Chapter 2 standards.
943. Exclusiveness of title; exceptions.
944. Damages; determination of amount.
945. Binding effect upon original purchasers and their successors-in-interest.
945.5. Affirmative defenses.

Application

For application of Title 7, see Civil Code § 938.

§ 941. Limitation of action; tolling

(a) Except as specifically set forth in this title, no action may be brought to recover under this title more than 10 years after substantial completion of the improvement but not later than the date of recordation of a valid notice of completion.

(b) As used in this section, "action" includes an action for indemnity brought against a person arising out of that person's performance or furnishing of services or materials referred to in this title, except that a cross-complaint for indemnity may be filed pursuant to subdivision (b) of Section 428.10 of the Code of Civil Procedure in an action which has been brought within the time period set forth in subdivision (a).

(c) The limitation prescribed by this section may not be asserted by way of defense by any person in actual possession or the control, as owner, tenant or otherwise, of such an improvement, at the time any deficiency in the improvement constitutes the proximate cause for which it is proposed to make a claim or bring an action.

(d) Sections 337.15 and 337.1 of the Code of Civil Procedure do not apply to actions under this title.

(e) Existing statutory and decisional law regarding tolling of the statute of limitations shall apply to the time periods for filing an action or making a claim under this title, except that repairs made pursuant to Chapter 4 (commencing with Section 910), with the exception of the tolling provision contained in Section 927, do not extend the period for filing an action, or restart the time limitations contained in subdivision (a) or (b) of Section 7091 of the Business and Professions Code. If a builder arranges for a contractor to perform a repair pursuant to Chapter 4 (commencing with Section 910), as to the builder the time period for calculating the statute of limitation in subdivision (a) or (b) of Section 7091 of the Business and Professions Code shall pertain to the substantial completion of the original construction and not to the date of repairs under this title. The time limitations established by this title do not apply to any action by a claimant for a contract or express contractual provision. Causes of action and damages to which this chapter does not apply are not limited by this section. *(Added by Stats.2002, c. 722 (S.B.800), § 3. Amended by Stats.2003, c. 62 (S.B.600), § 12; Stats.2003, c. 762 (A.B.903), § 7.)*

Application

For application of Title 7, see Civil Code § 938.

Cross References

Definitions under Title 7 applicable to this section, see Civil Code § 895.

§ 942. Sufficiency of claim for violation of Chapter 2 standards

In order to make a claim for violation of the standards set forth in Chapter 2 (commencing with Section 896), a homeowner need only demonstrate, in accordance with the applicable evidentiary standard, that the home does not meet the applicable standard, subject to the affirmative defenses set forth in Section 945.5. No further showing of causation or damages is required to meet the burden of proof regarding a violation of a standard set forth in Chapter 2 (commencing with Section 896), provided that the violation arises out of, pertains to, or is related to, the original construction. *(Added by Stats.2003, c. 762 (A.B.903), § 9.)*

Application

For application of Title 7, see Civil Code § 938.

Cross References

Burden of proof, generally, see Evidence Code § 500 et seq.
Definitions under Title 7 applicable to this section, see Civil Code § 895.

§ 943. Exclusiveness of title; exceptions

(a) Except as provided in this title, no other cause of action for a claim covered by this title or for damages recoverable under Section 944 is allowed. In addition to the rights under this title, this title does not apply to any action by a claimant to enforce a contract or express contractual provision, or any action for fraud, personal injury, or violation of a statute. Damages awarded for the items set forth in Section 944 in such other cause of action shall be reduced by the amounts recovered pursuant to Section 944 for violation of the standards set forth in this title.

(b) As to any claims involving a detached single-family home, the homeowner's right to the reasonable value of repairing any nonconformity is limited to the repair costs, or the diminution in current value of the home caused by the nonconformity, whichever is less, subject to the personal use exception as developed under common law. *(Formerly § 942, added by Stats.2002, c. 722 (S.B.800), § 3. Renumbered § 943 and amended by Stats.2003, c. 762 (A.B.903), § 8.)*

Application

For application of Title 7, see Civil Code § 938.

Cross References

Definitions under Title 7 applicable to this section, see Civil Code § 895.

§ 944. Damages; determination of amount

If a claim for damages is made under this title, the homeowner is only entitled to damages for the reasonable value of repairing any violation of the standards set forth in this title, the reasonable cost of repairing any damages caused by the repair efforts, the reasonable cost of repairing and rectifying any damages resulting from the failure of the home to meet the standards, the reasonable cost of removing and replacing any improper repair by the builder, reasonable relocation and storage expenses, lost business income if the home was used as a principal place of a business licensed to be operated from the home, reasonable investigative costs for each established violation, and all other costs or fees recoverable by contract or statute. *(Added by Stats.2002, c. 722 (S.B.800), § 3.)*

Application

For application of Title 7, see Civil Code § 938.

Cross References

Builder defined for purposes of this Title, see Civil Code § 911.

Definitions under Title 7 applicable to this section, see Civil Code § 895.

§ 945. Binding effect upon original purchasers and their successors-in-interest

The provisions, standards, rights, and obligations set forth in this title are binding upon all original purchasers and their successors-in-interest. For purposes of this title, associations and others having the rights set forth in Sections 5980 and 5985 shall be considered to be original purchasers and shall have standing to enforce the provisions, standards, rights, and obligations set forth in this title. (Added by Stats.2002, c. 722 (S.B.800), § 3. Amended by Stats.2005, c. 37 (S.B.853), § 1; Stats.2012, c. 181 (A.B.806), § 31, operative Jan. 1, 2014; Stats.2018, c. 92 (S.B.1289), § 34, eff. Jan. 1, 2019.)

Application

For application of Title 7, see Civil Code § 938.

Cross References

Definitions under Title 7 applicable to this section, see Civil Code § 895.
Obligation defined, see Civil Code § 1427.

§ 945.5. Affirmative defenses

A builder, general contractor, subcontractor, material supplier, individual product manufacturer, or design professional, under the principles of comparative fault pertaining to affirmative defenses, may be excused, in whole or in part, from any obligation, damage, loss, or liability if the builder, general contractor, subcontractor, material supplier, individual product manufacturer, or design professional, can demonstrate any of the following affirmative defenses in response to a claimed violation:

(a) To the extent it is caused by an unforeseen act of nature which caused the structure not to meet the standard. For purposes of this section an "unforeseen act of nature" means a weather condition, earthquake, or manmade event such as war, terrorism, or vandalism, in excess of the design criteria expressed by the applicable building codes, regulations, and ordinances in effect at the time of original construction.

(b) To the extent it is caused by a homeowner's unreasonable failure to minimize or prevent those damages in a timely manner, including the failure of the homeowner to allow reasonable and timely access for inspections and repairs under this title. This includes the failure to give timely notice to the builder after discovery of a violation, but does not include damages due to the untimely or inadequate response of a builder to the homeowner's claim.

(c) To the extent it is caused by the homeowner or his or her agent, employee, general contractor, subcontractor, independent contractor, or consultant by virtue of their failure to follow the builder's or manufacturer's recommendations, or commonly accepted homeowner maintenance obligations. In order to rely upon this defense as it relates to a builder's recommended maintenance schedule, the builder shall show that the homeowner had written notice of these schedules and recommendations and that the recommendations and schedules were reasonable at the time they were issued.

(d) To the extent it is caused by the homeowner or his or her agent's or an independent third party's alterations, ordinary wear and tear, misuse, abuse, or neglect, or by the structure's use for something other than its intended purpose.

(e) To the extent that the time period for filing actions bars the claimed violation.

(f) As to a particular violation for which the builder has obtained a valid release.

(g) To the extent that the builder's repair was successful in correcting the particular violation of the applicable standard.

(h) As to any causes of action to which this statute does not apply, all applicable affirmative defenses are preserved. (Added by Stats.2002, c. 722 (S.B.800), § 3. Amended by Stats.2003, c. 762 (A.B.903), § 10.)

Application

For application of Title 7, see Civil Code § 938.

Cross References

Additional affirmative defense, see Civil Code § 936.
Builder defined for purposes of this Title, see Civil Code § 911.
Definitions under Title 7 applicable to this section, see Civil Code § 895.
Obligation defined, see Civil Code § 1427.

Title 8

RECONSTRUCTION OF HOMES LOST IN CEDAR FIRE, OCTOBER 2003 [REPEALED]

§ 945.6. Repealed by Stats.2005, c. 40 (A.B.662), § 2, operative Jan. 1, 2008

Part 3

PERSONAL OR MOVABLE PROPERTY

Title	Section
1. Personal Property in General	946
2. Particular Kinds of Personal Property	953

Title 1

PERSONAL PROPERTY IN GENERAL

Section
946. Personal property; law of domicile.
947. Repealed.

§ 946. Personal property; law of domicile

If there is no law to the contrary, in the place where personal property is situated, it is deemed to follow the person of its owner, and is governed by the law of his domicile. *(Enacted in 1872. Repealed by Code Am.1873–74, c. 612, p. 223, § 123. Reenacted by Code Am.1875–76, c. 167, p. 78, § 1.)*

§ 947. Repealed by Code Am.1873–74, c. 612, p. 223, § 124

Title 2

PARTICULAR KINDS OF PERSONAL PROPERTY

Chapter	Section
1. Things in Action	953
2. Shipping [Repealed]	
3. Products of the Mind	980
4. Other Kinds of Personal Property	994

CHAPTER 1. THINGS IN ACTION

Article	Section
1. Transfer of Things in Action	953
2. Survival of Tort Actions [Repealed]	

ARTICLE 1. TRANSFER OF THINGS IN ACTION

Section
953. Thing in action defined.
954. Transfer of things in action.
954.5. Perfection of transfer of right represented by judgment.
955. Nonnegotiable instruments; transfer; notice.
955.1. Payment intangibles; assignments; priorities; notice to obligor.

§ 953. Thing in action defined

A thing in action is a right to recover money or other personal property by a judicial proceeding. *(Enacted in 1872. Amended by Code Am.1873–74, c. 612, p. 223, § 125.)*

Cross References

Duty of finder of thing in action, see Civil Code § 2080.

Personal property as including thing in action, see Civil Code § 14; Code of Civil Procedure § 17.

§ 954. Transfer of things in action

A thing in action, arising out of the violation of a right of property, or out of an obligation, may be transferred by the owner. *(Enacted in 1872. Amended by Stats.1990, c. 79 (A.B.759), § 2, operative July 1, 1991.)*

Cross References

Burden of obligation, transfer, see Civil Code § 1457.
Cross-demands, assignment as affecting, see Code of Civil Procedure § 431.70.
Defense not prejudiced by assignment, see Code of Civil Procedure § 368.
Estates, sale of choses in action, see Probate Code § 10205.
Execution of writ, collection or sale of things in action, see Code of Civil Procedure § 701.510 et seq.
Industrial loan company may buy or sell choses in action, see Financial Code § 18190.
Insurance tax refund, assignee cannot recover, see Revenue and Taxation Code § 13108.
Liability of thing in action to execution, see Code of Civil Procedure §§ 684.010 et seq., 687.020, 687.030, 695.010 et seq., 697.710, 699.060, 699.520, 699.710, 699.720, 700.010 et seq.
Life or disability insurance policy, transfer, see Insurance Code § 10130.
Mortgage passes by assignment of debt, see Civil Code § 2936.
Motor vehicle fuel tax refund, assignee cannot recover, see Revenue and Taxation Code § 8152.
Obligation defined, see Civil Code § 1427.
Possibility not coupled with interest, transfer, see Civil Code § 1045.
Private railroad car tax refund, assignee cannot recover, see Revenue and Taxation Code § 11577.
Products of the mind, transferability, see Civil Code § 982.
Property subject to transfer, see Civil Code § 1044.
Rights, arising from obligation transferable, see Civil Code § 1458.
Sales or use tax refund, assignee cannot recover, see Revenue and Taxation Code § 6937.
Use fuel tax paid, assignee cannot recover, see Revenue and Taxation Code § 9175.

§ 954.5. Perfection of transfer of right represented by judgment

(a) Subject to subdivisions (b) and (c), a transfer of a right represented by a judgment excluded from coverage of Division 9 of the Commercial Code by paragraph (9) of subdivision (d) of Section 9109 of the Commercial Code shall be deemed perfected as against third persons upon there being executed and delivered to the transferee an assignment thereof in writing.

(b) As between bona fide assignees of the same right for value without notice, the assignee who first becomes an assignee of record, by filing an acknowledgment of assignment of judgment with the court as provided in Section 673 of the Code of Civil Procedure or otherwise becoming an assignee of record, has priority.

(c) The filing of an acknowledgment of assignment of the judgment with the court under Section 673 of the Code of Civil Procedure is not, of itself, notice to the judgment debtor so as to invalidate any payments made by the judgment debtor that would otherwise be applied to the satisfaction of the judgment. *(Added by Stats.1982, c. 497, p. 2135, § 4,* operative July 1, 1983. Amended by Stats.1999, c. 991 (S.B.45), § 1.8, operative July 1, 2001.)

Cross References

Sale of state tobacco assets, pledge of assets, see Government Code § 63049.1.

§ 955. Nonnegotiable instruments; transfer; notice

A transfer other than one intended to create a security interest (paragraph (1) or (3) of subdivision (a) of Section 9109 of the Commercial Code) of a nonnegotiable instrument which is otherwise negotiable within Division 3 of the Commercial Code but which is not payable to order or to bearer and a sale of accounts, chattel paper, payment intangibles, or promissory notes as part of a sale of the business out of which they arose (paragraph (4) of subdivision (d) of Section 9109 of the Commercial Code) shall be deemed perfected against third persons when such property rights have been endorsed or assigned in writing and in the case of such instruments or chattel paper delivered to the transferee, whether or not notice of such transfer or sale has been given to the obligor; but such endorsement, assignment, or delivery is not, of itself, notice to the obligor so as to invalidate any payments made by the obligor to the transferor. (Added by Stats.1941, c. 1025, p. 2655, § 1. Amended by Stats.1953, c. 1242, p. 2806, § 2; Stats.1963, c. 819, p. 1997, § 3, eff. Jan. 1, 1965; Stats.1982, c. 497, p. 2135, § 5, operative July 1, 1983; Stats.1999, c. 991 (S.B.45), § 2, operative July 1, 2001.)

§ 955.1. Payment intangibles; assignments; priorities; notice to obligor

(a) Except as provided in Sections 954.5 and 955 and subject to subdivisions (b) and (c), a transfer other than one intended to create a security interest pursuant to paragraph (1) or (3) of subdivision (a) of Section 9109 of the Commercial Code, of any payment intangible, as defined in Section 9102 of the Commercial Code, and any transfer of accounts, chattel paper, payment intangibles, or promissory notes excluded from the coverage of Division 9 of the Commercial Code by paragraph (4) of subdivision (d) of Section 9109 of the Commercial Code shall be deemed perfected as against third persons upon there being executed and delivered to the transferee an assignment thereof in writing.

(b) As between bona fide assignees of the same right for value without notice, the assignee first giving notice of the right to the obligor in writing has priority.

(c) The assignment is not, of itself, notice to the obligor so as to invalidate any payments made by the obligor to the transferor.

(d) This section does not apply to transfers or assignments of water supply property, as defined in Section 849 of the Public Utilities Code.

(e) This section does not apply to transfers or assignments of recovery property, as defined in Section 848 of the Public Utilities Code. (Added by Stats.1953, c. 1242, p. 2806, § 3. Amended by Stats.1955, c. 741, p. 1238, § 1; Stats.1963, c. 819, p. 1997, § 4, eff. Jan. 1, 1965; Stats.1982, c. 497, p. 2136, § 6, operative July 1, 1983; Stats.1996, c. 854 (A.B.1890), § 2, eff. Sept. 24, 1996; Stats.1999, c. 991 (S.B.45), § 3, operative July 1, 2001; Stats.2004, c. 46 (S.B.772), § 2, eff. June 7, 2004; Stats.2014, c. 482 (S.B.936), § 2, eff. Jan. 1, 2015.)

Cross References

Enforcement of money judgments, assignment order, effect and priority of assignment, see Code of Civil Procedure § 708.530.
Sale of state tobacco assets, pledge of assets, see Government Code § 63049.1.

ARTICLE 2. SURVIVAL OF TORT ACTIONS [REPEALED]

§ 956. Repealed by Stats.1961, c. 657, p. 1867, § 1

CHAPTER 2. SHIPPING [REPEALED]

§§ 960 to 973. Repealed by Stats.1937, c. 368, p. 1002, § 10001

CHAPTER 3. PRODUCTS OF THE MIND

Section
980. Ownership; works not fixed in tangible medium; sound recordings; inventions or designs.
981. Joint ownership; works not fixed in tangible medium; inventions or designs.
982. Transfers of ownership; right of reproduction.
983. Inventions or designs; effect of making public.
984. Inventions or designs; rights of subsequent or original producers.
985. Private writings; ownership; publication.
986. Work of fine art; sale; payment of percentage to artist or deposit for Arts Council; failure to pay; action for damages; exemptions.
987. Preservation of works of art.
988. Ownership of physical work of art; reservation upon conveyance of other ownership rights; resolution of ambiguity.
989. Preservation of cultural and artistic creations.

§ 980. Ownership; works not fixed in tangible medium; sound recordings; inventions or designs

(a)(1) The author of any original work of authorship that is not fixed in any tangible medium of expression has an exclusive ownership in the representation or expression thereof as against all persons except one who orginally [1] and independently creates the same or similar work. A work shall be considered not fixed when it is not embodied in a tangible medium of expression or when its embodiment in a tangible medium of expression is not sufficiently permanent or stable to permit it to be perceived, reproduced, or otherwise communicated for a period of more than transitory duration, either directly or with the aid of a machine or device.

(2) The author of an original work of authorship consisting of a sound recording initially fixed prior to February 15, 1972, has an exclusive ownership therein until February 15, 2047, as against all persons except one who independently makes or duplicates another sound recording that does not directly or indirectly recapture the actual sounds fixed in such prior sound recording, but consists entirely of an independent fixation of other sounds, even though such sounds imitate or simulate the sounds contained in the prior sound recording.

(b) The inventor or proprietor of any invention or design, with or without delineation, or other graphical representation, has an exclusive ownership therein, and in the representation or expression thereof, which continues so long as the invention or design and the representations or expressions thereof made by him remain in his possession. (Enacted in 1872. Amended by Stats.1947, c. 1107, p. 2546, § 1; Stats. 1949, c. 921, p. 1686, § 1; Stats.1982, c. 574, p. 2533, § 2.)

[1] So in chaptered copy.

Cross References

Ownership defined for purposes of this Code, see Civil Code § 654.
Trademarks, see Business and Professions Code § 14200 et seq.

§ 981. Joint ownership; works not fixed in tangible medium; inventions or designs

(a) Unless otherwise agreed, an original work of authorship not fixed in any tangible medium of expression and in the creation of which several persons are jointly concerned, is owned by them in equal proportion.

(b) Unless otherwise agreed, an invention or design in the production of which several persons are jointly concerned is owned by them as follows:

(1) If the invention or design is single, in equal proportions.

(2) If it is not single, in proportion to the contribution of each. (Enacted in 1872. Amended by Stats.1947, c. 1107, p. 2546, § 2; Stats.1949, c. 921, p. 1686, § 2; Stats.1982, c. 574, p. 2533, § 3.)

§ 982. Transfers of ownership; right of reproduction

(a) The owner of any rights in any original works of authorship not fixed in any tangible medium of expression may transfer the ownership therein.

(b) The owner of any invention or design, or of any representation or expression thereof, may transfer his or her proprietary interest in it.

(c) Notwithstanding any other provision in this section, whenever a work of fine art is transferred, whether by sale or on commission or otherwise, by or on behalf of the artist who created it, or that artist's heir, legatee, or personal representative, the right of reproduction thereof is reserved to such artist or such heir, legatee, or personal representative until it passes into the public domain by act or operation of law, unless that right is expressly transferred by a document in writing in which reference is made to the specific right of reproduction, signed by the owner of the rights conveyed or that person's duly authorized agent. If the transfer is pursuant to an employment relationship, the right of reproduction is transferred to the employer, unless it is expressly reserved in writing. If the transfer is pursuant to a legacy or inheritance, the right of reproduction is transferred to the legatee or heir, unless it is expressly reserved by will or codicil. Nothing contained herein, however, shall be construed to prohibit the fair use of such work of fine art.

(d) As used in subdivision (c):

(1) "Fine art" means any work of visual art, including but not limited to, a drawing, painting, sculpture, mosaic, or photograph, a work of calligraphy, work of graphic art (including an etching, lithograph, offset print, silk screen, or a work of graphic art of like nature), crafts (including crafts in clay, textile, fiber, wood, metal, plastic, and like materials), or mixed media (including a collage, assemblage, or any combination of the foregoing art media).

(2) "Artist" means the creator of a work of fine art.

(3) "Right of reproduction", at the present state of commerce and technology shall be interpreted as including, but shall not be limited to, the following: reproduction of works of fine art as prints suitable for framing; facsimile casts of sculpture; reproductions used for greeting cards; reproductions in general books and magazines not devoted primarily to art, and in newspapers in other than art or news sections, when such reproductions in books, magazines, and newspapers are used for purposes similar to those of material for which the publishers customarily pay; art films; television, except from stations operated for educational purposes, or on programs for educational purposes from all stations; and reproductions used in any form of advertising, including magazines, calendars, newspapers, posters, billboards, films or television.

(e) The amendments to this section made at the 1975–76 Regular Session shall only apply to transfers made on or after January 1, 1976. (Enacted in 1872. Amended by Stats.1947, c. 1107, p. 2546, § 3; Stats.1949, c. 921, p. 1686, § 3; Stats.1975, c. 952, p. 2128, § 1; Stats.1982, c. 574, p. 2533, § 4.)

Cross References

Action for specific recovery of fine art against museum, gallery, auctioneer, or dealer, statute of limitations, fine art defined as specified in this section, see Code of Civil Procedure § 338.
Ownership defined for purposes of this Code, see Civil Code § 654.

§ 983. Inventions or designs; effect of making public

If the owner of any invention or design intentionally makes it public, a copy or reproduction may be made public by any person, without responsiblily[1] to the owner, so far as the law of this state is concerned. (Enacted in 1872. Amended by Stats.1947, c. 1107, p. 2546, § 4; Stats.1949, c. 921, p. 1686, § 4; Stats.1982, c. 574, p. 2534, § 5.)

[1] So in chaptered copy.

Cross References

Civil actions, attachment of production to complaint for infringement of rights to a literary, artistic, or intellectual production, see Code of Civil Procedure § 429.30.

§ 984. Inventions or designs; rights of subsequent or original producers

If the owner of an invention or design does not make it public, any other person subsequently and originally producing the same thing has the same right therein as the prior inventor, which is exclusive to the same extent against all persons except the prior inventor, or those claiming under him. (Added by Stats.1949, c. 921, p. 1687, § 5.)

§ 985. Private writings; ownership; publication

PRIVATE WRITINGS. Letters and other private communications in writing belong to the person to whom they are addressed and delivered; but they cannot be published against the will of the writer, except by authority of law. *(Enacted in 1872.)*

§ 986. Work of fine art; sale; payment of percentage to artist or deposit for Arts Council; failure to pay; action for damages; exemptions

(a) Whenever a work of fine art is sold and the seller resides in California or the sale takes place in California, the seller or the seller's agent shall pay to the artist of such work of fine art or to such artist's agent 5 percent of the amount of such sale. The right of the artist to receive an amount equal to 5 percent of the amount of such sale may be waived only by a contract in writing providing for an amount in excess of 5 percent of the amount of such sale. An artist may assign the right to collect the royalty payment provided by this section to another individual or entity. However, the assignment shall not have the effect of creating a waiver prohibited by this subdivision.

(1) When a work of fine art is sold at an auction or by a gallery, dealer, broker, museum, or other person acting as the agent for the seller the agent shall withhold 5 percent of the amount of the sale, locate the artist and pay the artist.

(2) If the seller or agent is unable to locate and pay the artist within 90 days, an amount equal to 5 percent of the amount of the sale shall be tranferred [1] to the Arts Council.

(3) If a seller or the seller's agent fails to pay an artist the amount equal to 5 percent of the sale of a work of fine art by the artist or fails to transfer such amount to the Arts Council, the artist may bring an action for damages within three years after the date of sale or one year after the discovery of the sale, whichever is longer. The prevailing party in any action brought under this paragraph shall be entitled to reasonable attorney fees, in an amount as determined by the court.

(4) Moneys received by the council pursuant to this section shall be deposited in an account in the Special Deposit Fund in the State Treasury.

(5) The Arts Council shall attempt to locate any artist for whom money is received pursuant to this section. If the council is unable to locate the artist and the artist does not file a written claim for the money received by the council within seven years of the date of sale of the work of fine art, the right of the artist terminates and such money shall be transferred to the council for use in acquiring fine art pursuant to the Art in Public Buildings program set forth in Chapter 2.1 (commencing with Section 15813) of Part 10b of Division 3 of Title 2, of the Government Code.

(6) Any amounts of money held by any seller or agent for the payment of artists pursuant to this section shall be exempt from enforcement of a money judgment by the creditors of the seller or agent.

(7) Upon the death of an artist, the rights and duties created under this section shall inure to his or her heirs, legatees, or personal representative, until the 20th anniversary of the death of the artist. The provisions of this paragraph shall be applicable only with respect to an artist who dies after January 1, 1983.

(b) Subdivision (a) shall not apply to any of the following:

(1) To the initial sale of a work of fine art where legal title to such work at the time of such initial sale is vested in the artist thereof.

(2) To the resale of a work of fine art for a gross sales price of less than one thousand dollars ($1,000).

(3) Except as provided in paragraph (7) of subdivision (a), to a resale after the death of such artist.

(4) To the resale of the work of fine art for a gross sales price less than the purchase price paid by the seller.

(5) To a transfer of a work of fine art which is exchanged for one or more works of fine art or for a combination of cash, other property, and one or more works of fine art where the fair market value of the property exchanged is less than one thousand dollars ($1,000).

(6) To the resale of a work of fine art by an art dealer to a purchaser within 10 years of the initial sale of the work of fine art by the artist to an art dealer, provided all intervening resales are between art dealers.

(7) To a sale of a work of stained glass artistry where the work has been permanently attached to real property and is sold as part of the sale of the real property to which it is attached.

(c) For purposes of this section, the following terms have the following meanings:

(1) "Artist" means the person who creates a work of fine art and who, at the time of resale, is a citizen of the United States, or a resident of the state who has resided in the state for a minimum of two years.

(2) "Fine art" means an original painting, sculpture, or drawing, or an original work of art in glass.

(3) "Art dealer" means a person who is actively and principally engaged in or conducting the business of selling works of fine art for which business such person validly holds a sales tax permit.

(d) This section shall become operative on January 1, 1977, and shall apply to works of fine art created before and after its operative date.

(e) If any provision of this section or the application thereof to any person or circumstance is held invalid for any reason, such invalidity shall not affect any other provisions or applications of this section which can be effected, without the invalid provision or application, and to this end the provisions of this section are severable.

(f) The amendments to this section enacted during the 1981–82 Regular Session of the Legislature shall apply to transfers of works of fine art, when created before or after January 1, 1983, that occur on or after that date. *(Added by Stats.1976, c. 1228, p. 5542, § 1. Amended by Stats.1982, c. 497, p. 2136, § 7, operative July 1, 1983; Stats.1982, c. 1609, p. 6433, § 1.5.)*

[1] So in chaptered copy.

Validity

For validity of this section, see Estate of Graham v. Sotheby's Inc., C.D.Cal.2012, 860 F.Supp.2d 1117, 103 U.S.P.Q.2d 1142, remanded 2015 WL 4429309, on remand 178 F.Supp.3d 974 and Sam Francis Foundation v. Christies, Inc., (Cal.)2015, 784 F.3d

1320, on remand 2015 WL 4429309, certiorari denied 136 S.Ct. 795, 193 L.Ed.2d 710.

Cross References

Real property defined for purposes of this Code, see Civil Code § 658.

§ 987. Preservation of works of art

(a) The Legislature hereby finds and declares that the physical alteration or destruction of fine art, which is an expression of the artist's personality, is detrimental to the artist's reputation, and artists therefore have an interest in protecting their works of fine art against any alteration or destruction; and that there is also a public interest in preserving the integrity of cultural and artistic creations.

(b) As used in this section:

(1) "Artist" means the individual or individuals who create a work of fine art.

(2) "Fine art" means an original painting, sculpture, or drawing, or an original work of art in glass, of recognized quality, but shall not include work prepared under contract for commercial use by its purchaser.

(3) "Person" means an individual, partnership, corporation, limited liability company, association or other group, however organized.

(4) "Frame" means to prepare, or cause to be prepared, a work of fine art for display in a manner customarily considered to be appropriate for a work of fine art in the particular medium.

(5) "Restore" means to return, or cause to be returned, a deteriorated or damaged work of fine art as nearly as is feasible to its original state or condition, in accordance with prevailing standards.

(6) "Conserve" means to preserve, or cause to be preserved, a work of fine art by retarding or preventing deterioration or damage through appropriate treatment in accordance with prevailing standards in order to maintain the structural integrity to the fullest extent possible in an unchanging state.

(7) "Commercial use" means fine art created under a work-for-hire arrangement for use in advertising, magazines, newspapers, or other print and electronic media.

(c)(1) No person, except an artist who owns and possesses a work of fine art which the artist has created, shall intentionally commit, or authorize the intentional commission of, any physical defacement, mutilation, alteration, or destruction of a work of fine art.

(2) In addition to the prohibitions contained in paragraph (1), no person who frames, conserves, or restores a work of fine art shall commit, or authorize the commission of, any physical defacement, mutilation, alteration, or destruction of a work of fine art by any act constituting gross negligence. For purposes of this section, the term "gross negligence" shall mean the exercise of so slight a degree of care as to justify the belief that there was an indifference to the particular work of fine art.

(d) The artist shall retain at all times the right to claim authorship, or, for a just and valid reason, to disclaim authorship of his or her work of fine art.

(e) To effectuate the rights created by this section, the artist may commence an action to recover or obtain any of the following:

(1) Injunctive relief.

(2) Actual damages.

(3) Punitive damages. In the event that punitive damages are awarded, the court shall, in its discretion, select an organization or organizations engaged in charitable or educational activities involving the fine arts in California to receive any punitive damages.

(4) Reasonable attorneys' and expert witness fees.

(5) Any other relief which the court deems proper.

(f) In determining whether a work of fine art is of recognized quality, the trier of fact shall rely on the opinions of artists, art dealers, collectors of fine art, curators of art museums, and other persons involved with the creation or marketing of fine art.

(g) The rights and duties created under this section:

(1) Shall, with respect to the artist, or if any artist is deceased, his or her heir, beneficiary, devisee, or personal representative, exist until the 50th anniversary of the death of the artist.

(2) Shall exist in addition to any other rights and duties which may now or in the future be applicable.

(3) Except as provided in paragraph (1) of subdivision (h), may not be waived except by an instrument in writing expressly so providing which is signed by the artist.

(h)(1) If a work of fine art cannot be removed from a building without substantial physical defacement, mutilation, alteration, or destruction of the work, the rights and duties created under this section, unless expressly reserved by an instrument in writing signed by the owner of the building, containing a legal description of the property and properly recorded, shall be deemed waived. The instrument, if properly recorded, shall be binding on subsequent owners of the building.

(2) If the owner of a building wishes to remove a work of fine art which is a part of the building but which can be removed from the building without substantial harm to the fine art, and in the course of or after removal, the owner intends to cause or allow the fine art to suffer physical defacement, mutilation, alteration, or destruction, the rights and duties created under this section shall apply unless the owner has diligently attempted without success to notify the artist, or, if the artist is deceased, his or her heir, beneficiary, devisee, or personal representative, in writing of his or her intended action affecting the work of fine art, or unless he or she did provide notice and that person failed within 90 days either to remove the work or to pay for its removal. If the work is removed at the expense of the artist, his or her heir, beneficiary, devisee, or personal representative, title to the fine art shall pass to that person.

(3) If a work of fine art can be removed from a building scheduled for demolition without substantial physical defacement, mutilation, alteration, or destruction of the work, and the owner of the building has notified the owner of the work of fine art of the scheduled demolition or the owner of the building is the owner of the work of fine art, and the owner of

the work of fine art elects not to remove the work of fine art, the rights and duties created under this section shall apply, unless the owner of the building has diligently attempted without success to notify the artist, or, if the artist is deceased, his or her heir, beneficiary, devisee, or personal representative, in writing of the intended action affecting the work of fine art, or unless he or she did provide notice and that person failed within 90 days either to remove the work or to pay for its removal. If the work is removed at the expense of the artist, his or her heir, beneficiary, devisee, or personal representative, title to the fine art shall pass to that person.

(4) Nothing in this subdivision shall affect the rights of authorship created in subdivision (d) of this section.

(i) No action may be maintained to enforce any liability under this section unless brought within three years of the act complained of or one year after discovery of the act, whichever is longer.

(j) This section shall become operative on January 1, 1980, and shall apply to claims based on proscribed acts occurring on or after that date to works of fine art whenever created.

(k) If any provision of this section or the application thereof to any person or circumstance is held invalid for any reason, the invalidity shall not affect any other provisions or applications of this section which can be effected without the invalid provision or application, and to this end the provisions of this section are severable. *(Added by Stats.1979, c. 409, p. 1501, § 1. Amended by Stats.1982, c. 1517, p. 5882, § 1; Stats.1982, c. 1609, p. 6437, § 2.5; Stats.1989, c. 482, § 1; Stats.1994, c. 1010 (S.B.2053), § 30.)*

§ 988. Ownership of physical work of art; reservation upon conveyance of other ownership rights; resolution of ambiguity

(a) For the purpose of this section:

(1) The term "artist" means the creator of a work of art.

(2) The term "work of art" means any work of visual or graphic art of any media including, but not limited to, a painting, print, drawing, sculpture, craft, photograph, or film.

(b) Whenever an exclusive or nonexclusive conveyance of any right to reproduce, prepare derivative works based on, distribute copies of, publicly perform, or publicly display a work of art is made by or on behalf of the artist who created it or the owner at the time of the conveyance, ownership of the physical work of art shall remain with and be reserved to the artist or owner, as the case may be, unless such right of ownership is expressly transferred by an instrument, note, memorandum, or other writing, signed by the artist, the owner, or their duly authorized agent.

(c) Whenever an exclusive or nonexclusive conveyance of any right to reproduce, prepare derivative works based on, distribute copies of, publicly perform, or publicly display a work of art is made by or on behalf of the artist who created it or the owner at the time of the conveyance, any ambiguity with respect to the nature or extent of the rights conveyed shall be resolved in favor of the reservation of rights by the artist or owner, unless in any given case the federal copyright law provides to the contrary. *(Added by Stats.1982, c. 1319, p. 4873, § 1.)*

Cross References

Ownership defined for purposes of this Code, see Civil Code § 654.

§ 989. Preservation of cultural and artistic creations

(a) The Legislature hereby finds and declares that there is a public interest in preserving the integrity of cultural and artistic creations.

(b) As used in this section:

(1) "Fine art" means an original painting, sculpture, or drawing, or an original work of art in glass, of recognized quality, and of substantial public interest.

(2) "Organization" means a public or private not-for-profit entity or association, in existence at least three years at the time an action is filed pursuant to this section, a major purpose of which is to stage, display, or otherwise present works of art to the public or to promote the interests of the arts or artists.

(3) "Cost of removal" includes reasonable costs, if any, for the repair of damage to the real property caused by the removal of the work of fine art.

(c) An organization acting in the public interest may commence an action for injunctive relief to preserve or restore the integrity of a work of fine art from acts prohibited by subdivision (c) of Section 987.

(d) In determining whether a work of fine art is of recognized quality and of substantial public interest the trier of fact shall rely on the opinions of those described in subdivision (f) of Section 987.

(e)(1) If a work of fine art cannot be removed from real property without substantial physical defacement, mutilation, alteration, or destruction of such work, no action to preserve the integrity of the work of fine art may be brought under this section. However, if an organization offers some evidence giving rise to a reasonable likelihood that a work of art can be removed from the real property without substantial physical defacement, mutilation, alteration, or destruction of the work, and is prepared to pay the cost of removal of the work, it may bring a legal action for a determination of this issue. In that action the organization shall be entitled to injunctive relief to preserve the integrity of the work of fine art, but shall also have the burden of proof. The action shall commence within 30 days after filing. No action may be brought under this paragraph if the organization's interest in preserving the work of art is in conflict with an instrument described in paragraph (1) of subdivision (h) of Section 987.

(2) If the owner of the real property wishes to remove a work of fine art which is part of the real property, but which can be removed from the real property without substantial harm to such fine art, and in the course of or after removal, the owner intends to cause or allow the fine art to suffer physical defacement, mutilation, alteration, or destruction the owner shall do the following:

(A) If the artist or artist's heir, legatee, or personal representative fails to take action to remove the work of fine art after the notice provided by paragraph (2) of subdivision (h) of Section 987, the owner shall provide 30 days' notice of his or her intended action affecting the work of art. The written notice shall be a display advertisement in a newspaper of general circulation in the area where the fine art is located.

§ 989

The notice required by this paragraph may run concurrently with the notice required by subdivision (h) of Section 987.

(i) If within the 30-day period an organization agrees to remove the work of fine art and pay the cost of removal of the work, the payment and removal shall occur within 90 days of the first day of the 30-day notice.

(ii) If the work is removed at the expense of an organization, title to the fine art shall pass to that organization.

(B) If an organization does not agree to remove the work of fine art within the 30-day period or fails to remove and pay the cost of removal of the work of fine art within the 90-day period the owner may take the intended action affecting the work of fine art.

(f) To effectuate the rights created by this section, the court may do the following:

(1) Award reasonable attorney's and expert witness fees to the prevailing party, in an amount as determined by the court.

(2) Require the organization to post a bond in a reasonable amount as determined by the court.

(g) No action may be maintained under this section unless brought within three years of the act complained of or one year after discovery of such act, whichever is longer.

(h) This section shall become operative on January 1, 1983, and shall apply to claims based on acts occurring on or after that date to works of fine art, whenever created.

(i) If any provision of this section or the application thereof to any person or circumstances is held invalid, such invalidity shall not affect other provisions or applications of this section which can be given effect without the invalid provision or application, and to this end the provisions of this section are severable. *(Added by Stats.1982, c. 1517, p. 5888, § 4.)*

Cross References

Burden of proof, generally, see Evidence Code § 500 et seq.
Real property defined for purposes of this Code, see Civil Code § 658.

CHAPTER 4. OTHER KINDS OF PERSONAL PROPERTY

Section
990. Renumbered.
991 to 993. Repealed.
994. Instruments of title, ownership.
995. Repealed.
996. Fur bearing animals raised in captivity; ownership; protection of law.
997. Porcelain painting and stained glass artistry.
998. Electronic data processing or telecommunications goods and services; vendor transactions with private schools.

Cross References

Limited partner's interest as personal property, see Corporations Code § 15518.

§ 990. Renumbered Civil Code § 3344.1 and amended by Stats.1999, c. 998 (S.B.209), § 1; Stats.1999, c. 1000 (S.B.284), § 9.5

§§ 991 to 993. Repealed by Stats.1941, c. 57, p. 703, § 2; Stats.1941, c. 58, p. 709, § 3

§ 994. Instruments of title, ownership

TITLE DEEDS. Instruments essential to the title of real property, and which are not kept in a public office as a record, pursuant to law, belong to the person in whom, for the time being, such title may be vested, and pass with the title. *(Enacted in 1872.)*

Cross References

Real property defined for purposes of this Code, see Civil Code § 658.

§ 995. Repealed by Stats.1943, c. 129, p. 879, § 1

§ 996. Fur bearing animals raised in captivity; ownership; protection of law

Whenever fur bearing animals, which are by their nature known as wild animals, have been brought into, or born in, restraint or captivity upon any farm or ranch for the purpose of cultivating or pelting their furs, such animals, together with their offspring or increase, shall be the subjects of ownership, lien, and all kinds of absolute and other property rights, the same as purely domestic animals, in whatever situation, location, or condition such fur bearing animals may thereafter come or be, and regardless of their remaining in or escaping from such restraint or captivity. Such fur bearing animals shall receive the same protection of law, and in the same way and to the same extent shall be the subject of trespass or larceny as other personal property and shall be considered and classified as domestic animals for the purpose of and within the meaning of any statute or law relating generally to domestic animals, other than dogs and cats or other pets, or relating to farming, to animal husbandry, or to the encouragement of agriculture, unless any such statute or law is impossible of application to such fur bearing animals. *(Added by Stats.1941, c. 404, p. 1689, § 1.)*

Cross References

Ownership defined for purposes of this Code, see Civil Code § 654.
Ownership of wild animals in general, see Civil Code § 656.

§ 997. Porcelain painting and stained glass artistry

In this state, for any purpose, porcelain painting and stained glass artistry shall be considered a fine art and not a craft. *(Added by Stats.1979, c. 202, p. 446, § 1. Amended by Stats.1982, c. 1609, p. 6439, § 3.)*

Cross References

Consignment of fine art, see Civil Code § 1738 et seq.

§ 998. Electronic data processing or telecommunications goods and services; vendor transactions with private schools

Any private vendor of electronic data processing equipment or telecommunications goods and services may sell or lease equipment, goods, or services to a private school for the same price and on similar terms as the vendor sells or leases the equipment, goods, or services to a public school or school district. *(Added by Stats.1988, c. 858, § 1.)*

Part 4

ACQUISITION OF PROPERTY

Title	Section
1. Modes in Which Property May be Acquired	1000
2. Occupancy	1006
3. Accession	1013
4. Transfer	1039
5. Homesteads [Repealed]	
6. Common Interest Developments [Repealed]	
7. Powers of Appointment [Repealed]	
8. Water Rights	1410a
9. Hydraulic Mining [Repealed]	
10. Mining Claims, Tunnel Rights and Mill Sites [Repealed]	

Title 1

MODES IN WHICH PROPERTY MAY BE ACQUIRED

Section
1000. Acquisition of property.
1001. Appurtenant easement; acquisition by eminent domain by private property owner to provide utility service.
1002. Temporary right to enter adjacent or nearby property; exercise of eminent domain by private property owner to repair or reconstruct land or improvements.

§ 1000. Acquisition of property

PROPERTY, HOW ACQUIRED. Property is acquired by:

1. Occupancy;
2. Accession;
3. Transfer;
4. Will; or,
5. Succession. *(Enacted in 1872.)*

Cross References

Accession, see Civil Code § 1013 et seq.
Occupancy, see Civil Code § 1006 et seq.
Succession, see Probate Code § 6400 et seq.
Transfer, see Civil Code § 1039 et seq.
Wills, see Probate Code § 6400 et seq.

§ 1001. Appurtenant easement; acquisition by eminent domain by private property owner to provide utility service

(a) As used in this section, "utility service" means water, gas, electric, drainage, sewer, or telephone service.

(b) Any owner of real property may acquire by eminent domain an appurtenant easement to provide utility service to the owner's property.

(c) In lieu of the requirements of Section 1240.030 of the Code of Civil Procedure, the power of eminent domain may be exercised to acquire an appurtenant easement under this section only if all of the following are established:

(1) There is a great necessity for the taking.

(2) The location of the easement affords the most reasonable service to the property to which it is appurtenant, consistent with the least damage to the burdened property.

(3) The hardship to the owner of the appurtenant property, if the taking is not permitted, clearly outweighs any hardship to the owner of the burdened property. *(Added by Stats.1976, c. 994, p. 2362, § 1.)*

Cross References

Actions against public entities and public employees, special provisions, actions for taking or damaging private property, see Government Code § 955.6.
Acquisition, see Code of Civil Procedure §§ 1235.170, 1240.110, 1240.120; Government Code §§ 15853, 40404, 54340, 54341; Health and Safety Code § 6514; Streets and Highways Code §§ 104, 965, 5101, 5102; Water Code §§ 8304, 8995.
Acquisition of certain interests in property, see Code of Civil Procedure § 1240.110.
Acquisition of property, title by prescription, adverse possession, see Civil Code § 1007.
Actions on claims against the state for taking of property for public use, see Government Code § 905 et seq.
Airports, air space, and air easements, see Government Code §§ 26020, 50470; Public Utilities Code §§ 21633, 21652, 22553.
Claims against public entities, inverse condemnation, claim unnecessary to maintain action, see Government Code § 905.1.
Commencing action for the recovery of real property, adverse possession, occupancy of land, see Code of Civil Procedure § 325.
Constitutional provisions, see Cal. Const. Art. 6, § 10; Cal. Const. Art. 10, § 1; Cal. Const. Art. 12, § 5.
Electric facilities, see Public Resources Code § 25528; Public Utilities Code §§ 612, 6264, 12703, 12771.
Elements of compensation, see Code of Civil Procedure § 1263.310 et seq.
Eminent domain, generally, see Code of Civil Procedure § 1230.010 et seq.
Exercise of power of eminent domain, see Code of Civil Procedure § 1240.010.
Facilities in aid, see Government Code § 39792.
Highways, right of acquisition by eminent domain, see Streets and Highways Code § 102.
Person seeking to acquire an appurtenant easement by eminent domain deemed quasi-public entity, see Code of Civil Procedure § 1245.325.
Public utilities,
  Generally, see Code of Civil Procedure § 1230.010 et seq.; Public Utilities Code §§ 610 et seq., 1206 et seq., 1401 et seq., 1421, 7526, 7533, 7535 et seq., 12703, 12771; Water Code § 259.
  Compensation for properties, see Public Utilities Code § 1401 et seq.
Public utilities act, railroad crossings, apportionment of costs and advancement of money, see Public Utilities Code § 1202.1.
Real property defined for purposes of this Code, see Civil Code § 658.
Rights of way, see Government Code §§ 14662, 14662.5, 39792, 40404; Public Resources Code § 6808; Public Utilities Code § 7533; Public Utilities Code § 7535 et seq.; Streets and Highways Code §§ 104, 820.5, 27165; Water Code § 8996.
Rivers and streams, see Streets and Highways Code § 965; Water Code § 8995.
Sewers and sewerage, see Code of Civil Procedure § 1230.010 et seq.; Government Code §§ 40404, 54340, 54341, 55003; Health and Safety Code §§ 5001, 5008; Public Utilities Code §§ 624, 12703, 12771.
Telegraph and telephone lines, see Public Utilities Code §§ 616, 617.

Time of commencing actions other than for the recovery of real property, three years, see Code of Civil Procedure § 338.

§ 1002. Temporary right to enter adjacent or nearby property; exercise of eminent domain by private property owner to repair or reconstruct land or improvements

(a) Subject to the provisions of Article 3 (commencing with Section 1245.310) of Chapter 4 of Title 7 of Part 3 of the Code of Civil Procedure, the power of eminent domain may be exercised by an owner of real property to acquire a temporary right to enter upon adjacent or nearby property to repair or reconstruct land or improvements, if all of the following conditions are established or met:

(1) There is a necessity to do the repair or reconstruction work and there is a great necessity to enter upon the adjacent or nearby property to do the repair or reconstruction work because (A) the repair or reconstruction work cannot be done safely without entry, or the cost of performing the repair or reconstruction work without entry would be substantially higher; and (B) the property without repair or reconstruction adversely affects the surrounding community.

(2) The right to enter upon the adjacent or nearby land will be exercised in a manner which provides the least damage to the property and the least inconvenience or annoyance to the occupants or owners thereof consistent with satisfactory completion of the repair or reconstruction work.

(3) The hardship to the person seeking to exercise the power of eminent domain, if that power is not exercised, clearly outweighs any hardship to the owner or occupant of the adjacent or nearby property.

(b) No entry shall be made upon the property to be condemned until an eminent domain proceeding has been commenced and then only after a court order permitting entry is issued or after judgment is entered for the plaintiff.

A deposit of security, in the form of cash or a bond, shall be made to the court in an amount the court determines is necessary to permit the owner of the adjacent or nearby property to restore the property to the condition it was in prior to the entry, if the person exercising the power of eminent domain does not do so within a reasonable period of time as determined by the court.

(c) The court may order the person acquiring the temporary right to enter the land of another, pursuant to this section, to pay the owner of the land subject to that temporary right a reasonable amount of rent for the use of the land.

(d) "Adjacent" or "nearby" for purposes of this section shall mean land contiguous with the property needing repair or reconstruction, or land through which the party granted temporary access must pass to reach adjacent land.

(e) The provisions of this section shall not apply to the temporary entry upon lands used primarily for the commercial production of agricultural commodities and forest products. *(Added by Stats.1982, c. 1239, p. 4564, § 1.)*

Cross References

Acquisition of certain interests in property, see Code of Civil Procedure § 1240.110.
Elements of compensation, see Code of Civil Procedure § 1263.310 et seq.
Eminent domain,
　Generally, see Code of Civil Procedure § 1230.010 et seq.
　Constitutional provisions, see Cal. Const. Art. 6, § 10; Cal. Const. Art. 10, § 1; Cal. Const. Art. 12, § 5.
　Exercise of power for public use, see Code of Civil Procedure § 1240.010.
Eminent domain law, temporary right to enter adjacent or nearby property, see Code of Civil Procedure § 1245.326.
Real property defined for purposes of this Code, see Civil Code § 658.
Time of commencing actions other than for the recovery of real property, see Code of Civil Procedure § 338.

Title 2

OCCUPANCY

Section
1006.　Title by occupancy; extent.
1007.　Title by prescription; adverse possession; exemption of public property.
1008.　Title by prescription; permissive use.
1009.　Legislative findings.

Cross References

Requirements for state appraisal review, certified real estate appraiser, see Public Resources Code § 5096.517.

§ 1006. Title by occupancy; extent

Occupancy for any period confers a title sufficient against all except the state and those who have title by prescription, accession, transfer, will, or succession; but the title conferred by occupancy is not a sufficient interest in real property to enable the occupant or the occupant's privies to commence or maintain an action to quiet title, unless the occupancy has ripened into title by prescription. *(Enacted in 1872. Amended by Stats.1915, c. 554, p. 933, § 1; Stats.1980, c. 44, § 1.)*

Cross References

Acquisition of property, title by prescription, adverse possession, see Civil Code § 1007.
Action to redeem mortgage, effect of five years adverse possession, see Code of Civil Procedure § 346.
Actions for the recovery of real property, see Code of Civil Procedure § 315 et seq.
Actions to quiet title, see Code of Civil Procedure § 760.010 et seq.
Boundaries, see Civil Code § 829 et seq.
Claims against public entities, inverse condemnation, claim unnecessary to maintain action, see Government Code § 905.1.
Commencing action for the recovery of real property, adverse possession, occupancy of land, see Code of Civil Procedure § 325.
Easements and servitudes attached to land, see Civil Code § 801.
Five year limitation, mesne profits, see Code of Civil Procedure § 336.
Real estate in adverse possession, transfer of title, see Civil Code § 1047.
Real property defined for purposes of this Code, see Civil Code § 658.

§ 1007. Title by prescription; adverse possession; exemption of public property

Occupancy for the period prescribed by the Code of Civil Procedure as sufficient to bar any action for the recovery of the property confers a title thereto, denominated a title by prescription, which is sufficient against all, but no possession by any person, firm or corporation no matter how long continued of any land, water, water right, easement, or other property whatsoever dedicated to a public use by a public utility, or dedicated to or owned by the state or any public entity, shall ever ripen into any title, interest or right against the owner thereof. *(Enacted in 1872. Amended by Stats. 1935, c. 519, p. 1592, § 1; Stats.1968, c. 1112, p. 2125, § 1.)*

Cross References

Action to redeem mortgage, effect of five years adverse possession, see Code of Civil Procedure § 346.
Boundaries, see Civil Code § 829 et seq.
Easements and servitudes attached to land, see Civil Code § 801.
Five year limitation, mesne profits, see Code of Civil Procedure § 336.
Mortgage of property adversely held, see Civil Code § 2921.
Payment of taxes, necessity of, see Code of Civil Procedure § 325.
Period prescribed by Code of Civil Procedure, see Code of Civil Procedure § 318 et seq.
Quiet title action by adverse possession generally, see Code of Civil Procedure § 760.010 et seq.
Transferability by owner of property in adverse possession of another, see Civil Code § 1047.
Water, appropriation, see Civil Code § 1414 et seq.; Water Code § 1200 et seq.

§ 1008. Title by prescription; permissive use

No use by any person or persons, no matter how long continued, of any land, shall ever ripen into an easement by prescription, if the owner of such property posts at each entrance to the property or at intervals of not more than 200 feet along the boundary a sign reading substantially as follows: "Right to pass by permission, and subject to control, of owner: Section 1008, Civil Code." *(Added by Stats.1965, c. 926, p. 2540, § 1.)*

Cross References

Adverse possession, generally, see Code of Civil Procedure § 325.
Appropriation of water, see Civil Code § 1414 et seq.
Boundaries, see Civil Code § 829 et seq.
Easements and servitudes attached to land, see Civil Code § 801.
Occupancy, see Civil Code §§ 1006, 1007.
Water subject to appropriation, see Water Code § 1200 et seq.

§ 1009. Legislative findings

(a) The Legislature finds that:

(1) It is in the best interests of the state to encourage owners of private real property to continue to make their lands available for public recreational use to supplement opportunities available on tax-supported publicly owned facilities.

(2) Owners of private real property are confronted with the threat of loss of rights in their property if they allow or continue to allow members of the public to use, enjoy or pass over their property for recreational purposes.

(3) The stability and marketability of record titles is clouded by such public use, thereby compelling the owner to exclude the public from his property.

(b) Regardless of whether or not a private owner of real property has recorded a notice of consent to use of any particular property pursuant to Section 813 of the Civil Code or has posted signs on such property pursuant to Section 1008 of the Civil Code, except as otherwise provided in subdivision (d), no use of such property by the public after the effective date of this section shall ever ripen to confer upon the public or any governmental body or unit a vested right to continue to make such use permanently, in the absence of an express written irrevocable offer of dedication of such property to such use, made by the owner thereof in the manner prescribed in subdivision (c) of this section, which has been accepted by the county, city, or other public body to which the offer of dedication was made, in the manner set forth in subdivision (c).

(c) In addition to any procedure authorized by law and not prohibited by this section, an irrevocable offer of dedication may be made in the manner prescribed in Section 7050 of the Government Code to any county, city, or other public body, and may be accepted or terminated, in the manner prescribed in that section, by the county board of supervisors in the case of an offer of dedication to a county, by the city council in the case of an offer of dedication to a city, or by the governing board of any other public body in the case of an offer of dedication to such body.

(d) Where a governmental entity is using private lands by an expenditure of public funds on visible improvements on or across such lands or on the cleaning or maintenance related to the public use of such lands in such a manner so that the owner knows or should know that the public is making such use of his land, such use, including any public use reasonably related to the purposes of such improvement, in the absence of either express permission by the owner to continue such use or the taking by the owner of reasonable steps to enjoin, remove or prohibit such use, shall after five years ripen to confer upon the governmental entity a vested right to continue such use.

(e) Subdivision (b) shall not apply to any coastal property which lies within 1,000 yards inland of the mean high tide line of the Pacific Ocean, and harbors, estuaries, bays and inlets thereof, but not including any property lying inland of the Carquinez Straits bridge, or between the mean high tide line and the nearest public road or highway, whichever distance is less.

(f) No use, subsequent to the effective date of this section, by the public of property described in subdivision (e) shall constitute evidence or be admissible as evidence that the public or any governmental body or unit has any right in such property by implied dedication if the owner does any of the following actions:

(1) Posts signs, as provided in Section 1008, and renews the same, if they are removed, at least once a year, or publishes annually, pursuant to Section 6066 of the Government Code, in a newspaper of general circulation in the county or counties in which the land is located, a statement describing the property and reading substantially as follows: "Right to pass by permission and subject to control of owner: Section 1008, Civil Code."

(2) Records a notice as provided in Section 813.

(3) Enters into a written agreement with any federal, state, or local agency providing for the public use of such land.

After taking any of the actions set forth in paragraph (1), (2), or (3), and during the time such action is effective, the owner shall not prevent any public use which is appropriate under the permission granted pursuant to such paragraphs by physical obstruction, notice, or otherwise.

(g) The permission for public use of real property referred to in subdivision (f) may be conditioned upon reasonable restrictions on the time, place, and manner of such public use, and no use in violation of such restrictions shall be considered public use for purposes of a finding of implied dedication. (Added by Stats.1971, c. 941, p. 1846, § 2.)

Cross References

Real property defined for purposes of this Code, see Civil Code § 658.

Title 3

ACCESSION

Chapter	Section
1. Accession to Real Property	1013
2. Accession to Personal Property	1025

CHAPTER 1. ACCESSION TO REAL PROPERTY

Section
1013. Fixtures; affixing without agreement to remove.
1013.5. Fixtures; removal.
1014. Alluvion.
1015. Avulsion.
1016. Islands; navigable streams state ownership.
1017. Islands; non-navigable streams.
1018. Islands; division of stream.
1019. Tenants; removal of fixtures.

Cross References

Accession, see Civil Code § 1000.
Personal property, definition, see Civil Code §§ 14, 663.
Property defined, see Civil Code §§ 14, 654.
Real property defined, see Civil Code §§ 14, 658.

§ 1013. Fixtures; affixing without agreement to remove

When a person affixes his property to the land of another, without an agreement permitting him to remove it, the thing affixed, except as otherwise provided in this chapter, belongs to the owner of the land, unless he chooses to require the former to remove it or the former elects to exercise the right of removal provided for in Section 1013.5 of this chapter. (Enacted in 1872. Amended by Code Am.1873–74, c. 612, p. 224, § 128; Stats.1953, c. 1175, p. 2674, § 1.)

Cross References

Accession to personal property, see Civil Code § 1025 et seq.
Bulk transferors, see Commercial Code § 6105.
Emblements, see Civil Code §§ 658, 660.
"Fixtures" definition, see Civil Code § 660.
Growing crops, see Civil Code §§ 658, 660.
Injury to fixtures, misdemeanor, see Penal Code §§ 602, 603.
Mining machinery, tools or equipment deemed affixed to mine, see Public Resources Code § 3980.
Removal of fixtures from encumbered property, theft, see Penal Code § 502.5.
Scope of mortgage lien, see Civil Code § 2926.
Severing and removing fixtures, larceny, see Penal Code § 495.
Tenant's right to remove fixtures, see Civil Code § 1019.

Trespass, misdemeanor, see Penal Code § 602.

§ 1013.5. Fixtures; removal

(a) **Right of removal; payment of damages.** When any person, acting in good faith and erroneously believing because of a mistake either of law or fact that he has a right to do so, affixes improvements to the land of another, such person, or his successor in interest, shall have the right to remove such improvements upon payment, as their interests shall appear, to the owner of the land, and any other person having any interest therein who acquired such interest for value after the commencement of the work of improvement and in reliance thereon, of all their damages proximately resulting from the affixing and removal of such improvements.

(b) **Parties; lis pendens; costs and attorney's fee.** In any action brought to enforce such right the owner of the land and encumbrancers of record shall be named as defendants, a notice of pendency of action shall be recorded before trial, and the owner of the land shall recover his costs of suit and a reasonable attorney's fee to be fixed by the court.

(c) **Interlocutory judgment.** If it appears to the court that the total amount of damages cannot readily be ascertained prior to the removal of the improvements, or that it is otherwise in the interests of justice, the court may order an interlocutory judgment authorizing the removal of the improvements upon condition precedent that the plaintiff pay into court the estimated total damages, as found by the court or as stipulated.

(d) **Consent of lienholder.** If the court finds that the holder of any lien upon the property acquired his lien in good faith and for value after the commencement of the work of improvement and in reliance thereon, or that as a result of the making or affixing of the improvements there is any lien against the property under Article XX, Section 15, of the Constitution of this State, judgment authorizing removal, final or interlocutory, shall not be given unless the holder of each such lien shall have consented to the removal of the improvements. Such consent shall be in writing and shall be filed with the court.

(e) **Nature of right created.** The right created by this section is a right to remove improvements from land which may be exercised at the option of one who, acting in good faith and erroneously believing because of a mistake either of law or fact that he has a right to do so, affixes such improvements to the land of another. This section shall not be construed to affect or qualify the law as it existed prior to the 1953 amendment of this section with regard to the circumstances under which a court of equity will refuse to compel removal of an encroachment. (Added by Stats.1953, c. 1175, p. 2674, § 2. Amended by Stats.1955, c. 73, p. 514, § 1.)

Cross References

Condition precedent defined, see Civil Code § 1436.
Fixtures removable by tenant, see Civil Code § 1019.
Good faith improver of property owned by another,
    Court to deny other relief if right to removal under this section would result in substantial justice, see Code of Civil Procedure § 871.4.
    Good faith improver defined, see Code of Civil Procedure § 871.1.

Lis pendens, see Code of Civil Procedure § 405.20 et seq.
Mechanics' liens, see Cal. Const. Art. 14, § 3.
Scope of mortgage lien, see Civil Code § 2926.

§ 1014. Alluvion

ALLUVION. Where, from natural causes, land forms by imperceptible degrees upon the bank of a river or stream, navigable or not navigable, either by accumulation of material or by the recession of the stream, such land belongs to the owner of the bank, subject to any existing right of way over the bank. *(Enacted in 1872.)*

Cross References

Accretions caused by structures, prohibition of fences, see Public Resources Code § 6323.
Boundaries, see Civil Code § 829 et seq.
Islands, see Civil Code § 1016 et seq.
Lands uncovered by recession of inland lakes, see Public Resources Code § 7601 et seq.
Tidelands, state ownership, see Civil Code § 670.

§ 1015. Avulsion

SUDDEN REMOVAL OF BANK. If a river or stream, navigable or not navigable, carries away, by sudden violence, a considerable and distinguishable part of a bank, and bears it to the opposite bank, or to another part of the same bank, the owner of the part carried away may reclaim it within a year after the owner of the land to which it has been united takes possession thereof. *(Enacted in 1872.)*

§ 1016. Islands; navigable streams state ownership

ISLANDS, IN NAVIGABLE STREAMS. Islands and accumulations of land, formed in the beds of streams which are navigable, belong to the State, if there is no title or prescription to the contrary. *(Enacted in 1872.)*

Cross References

Navigable waters, definitions, see Harbors and Navigation Code § 100 et seq.
State property, in general, see Civil Code § 670.

§ 1017. Islands; non-navigable streams

IN UNNAVIGABLE STREAMS. An island, or an accumulation of land, formed in a stream which is not navigable, belongs to the owner of the shore on that side where the island or accumulation is formed; or, if not formed on one side only, to the owners of the shore on the two sides, divided by an imaginary line drawn through the middle of the river. *(Enacted in 1872.)*

§ 1018. Islands; division of stream

ISLANDS FORMED BY DIVISION OF STREAM. If a stream, navigable or not navigable, in forming itself a new arm, divides itself and surrounds land belonging to the owner of the shore, and thereby forms an island, the island belongs to such owner. *(Enacted in 1872.)*

§ 1019. Tenants; removal of fixtures

A tenant may remove from the demised premises, any time during the continuance of his term, anything affixed thereto for purposes of trade, manufacture, ornament, or domestic use, if the removal can be effected without injury to the premises, unless the thing has, by the manner in which it is affixed, become an integral part of the premises. *(Added by Code Am.1873–74, c. 612, p. 224, § 129.)*

Cross References

Fixtures defined, see Civil Code § 660.
Mining machinery, equipment or tools deemed affixed to mine, see Public Resources Code § 3980.
Ownership of property affixed to land, see Civil Code § 1013.

CHAPTER 2. ACCESSION TO PERSONAL PROPERTY

Section
1025. Single thing formed from several things; owner of principal part.
1026. Principal part; separation of lessor but more valuable part.
1027. Principal part; value; bulk.
1028. Ownership of thing made by uniting materials and workmanship.
1029. Ownership of thing made of inseparable materials.
1030. Ownership of thing made from materials of several owners.
1031. Ownership of thing made by willful trespasser.
1032. Election between thing and value.
1033. Damages for wrongful use of materials.

Cross References

Accession to realty, see Civil Code § 1013 et seq.
Damages for wrongful use of materials, see Civil Code § 1033.
Freightage, natural increase in freight, see Civil Code § 2139.
Increase of property loaned, ownership, see Civil Code § 1885.
Increase of property pledged, see Commercial Code § 9207.
Increase of thing lent for exchange, ownership, see Civil Code § 1904.
Ownership of thing made by willful trespasser, see Civil Code § 1031.
Personal property defined, see Civil Code §§ 14, 663.
Products and accessions of property, see Civil Code § 732.
Products of thing hired, ownership, see Civil Code § 1926.

§ 1025. Single thing formed from several things; owner of principal part

ACCESSION BY UNITING SEVERAL THINGS. When things belonging to different owners have been united so as to form a single thing, and cannot be separated without injury, the whole belongs to the owner of the thing which forms the principal part; who must, however, reimburse the value of the residue to the other owner, or surrender the whole to him. *(Enacted in 1872.)*

Cross References

Increase of property loaned, ownership, see Civil Code § 1885.
Increase of property pledged, see Commercial Code § 9207.
Increase of thing lent for exchange, ownership, see Civil Code § 1904.
Products and accessions of property, see Civil Code § 732.

§ 1026. Principal part; separation of lessor but more valuable part

PRINCIPAL PART, WHAT. That part is to be deemed the principal to which the other has been united only for the use, ornament, or completion of the former, unless the latter is the more valuable, and has been united without the knowledge of its owner, who may, in the latter case, require it to be separated and returned to him, although some injury should

§ 1026   PROPERTY

result to the thing to which it has been united. *(Enacted in 1872.)*

Cross References

Increase of property loaned, ownership, see Civil Code § 1885.
Increase of property pledged, see Commercial Code § 9207.
Increase of thing lent for exchange, ownership, see Civil Code § 1904.
Products and accessions of property, see Civil Code § 732.
Products of thing hired, ownership, see Civil Code § 1926.

§ 1027. Principal part; value; bulk

SAME. If neither part can be considered the principal, within the rule prescribed by the last section, the more valuable, or, if the values are nearly equal, the more considerable in bulk, is to be deemed the principal part. *(Enacted in 1872.)*

§ 1028. Ownership of thing made by uniting materials and workmanship

UNITING MATERIALS AND WORKMANSHIP. If one makes a thing from materials belonging to another, the latter may claim the thing on reimbursing the value of the workmanship, unless the value of the workmanship exceeds the value of the materials, in which case the thing belongs to the maker, on reimbursing the value of the materials. *(Enacted in 1872.)*

Cross References

Increase of property loaned, ownership, see Civil Code § 1885.
Increase of property pledged, see Commercial Code § 9207.
Increase of thing lent for exchange, ownership, see Civil Code § 1904.
Ownership of thing made by wilful trespasser, see Civil Code § 1031.

§ 1029. Ownership of thing made of inseparable materials

INSEPARABLE MATERIALS. Where one has made use of materials which in part belong to him and in part to another, in order to form a thing of a new description, without having destroyed any of the materials, but in such a way that they cannot be separated without inconvenience, the thing formed is common to both proprietors; in proportion, as respects the one, of the materials belonging to him, and as respects the other, of the materials belonging to him and the price of his workmanship. *(Enacted in 1872.)*

Cross References

Damages for wrongful use of materials, see Civil Code § 1033.
Increase of property loaned, ownership, see Civil Code § 1885.
Increase of property pledged, see Commercial Code § 9207.
Increase of thing lent for exchange, ownership, see Civil Code § 1904.
Ownership of thing made by wilful trespasser, see Civil Code § 1031.

§ 1030. Ownership of thing made from materials of several owners

MATERIALS OF SEVERAL OWNERS. When a thing has been formed by the admixture of several materials of different owners, and neither can be considered the principal substance, an owner without whose consent the admixture was made may require a separation, if the materials can be separated without inconvenience. If they cannot be thus separated, the owners acquire the thing in common, in proportion to the quantity, quality, and value of their materials; but if the materials of one were far superior to those of the others, both in quantity and value, he may claim the thing on reimbursing to the others the value of their materials. *(Enacted in 1872.)*

Cross References

Damages for wrongful use of materials, see Civil Code § 1033.
Increase of property loaned, ownership, see Civil Code § 1885.
Increase of property pledged, see Commercial Code § 9207.
Increase of thing lent for exchange, ownership, see Civil Code § 1904.
Ownership of thing made by wilful trespasser, see Civil Code § 1031.

§ 1031. Ownership of thing made by willful trespasser

WILLFUL TRESPASSERS. The foregoing sections of this Article are not applicable to cases in which one willfully uses the materials of another without his consent; but, in such cases, the product belongs to the owner of the material, if its identity can be traced. *(Enacted in 1872.)*

Cross References

Restoration of thing wrongfully acquired, see Civil Code §§ 1712, 1713.

§ 1032. Election between thing and value

OWNER MAY ELECT BETWEEN THE THING AND ITS VALUE. In all cases where one whose material has been used without his knowledge, in order to form a product of a different description, can claim an interest in such product, he has an option to demand either restitution of his material in kind, in the same quantity, weight, measure, and quality, or the value thereof; or where he is entitled to the product, the value thereof in place of the product. *(Enacted in 1872.)*

Cross References

Restoration of thing wrongfully acquired, see Civil Code §§ 1712, 1713.

§ 1033. Damages for wrongful use of materials

WRONGDOER LIABLE IN DAMAGES. One who wrongfully employs materials belonging to another is liable to him in damages, as well as under the foregoing provisions of this Chapter. *(Enacted in 1872.)*

Cross References

Damages for wrongful use of materials, see Civil Code § 1033.
Negligence, see Civil Code § 1714.
Ownership of thing made by wilful trespasser, see Civil Code § 1031.
Trespass, wrongful occupation of real property, see Civil Code §§ 3334, 3346.

Title 4

TRANSFER

Chapter	Section
1. Transfers in General	1039
2. Transfer of Real Property	1091
3. Transfer of Personal Property	1135
4. Recording Transfers	1169
5. Unlawful Transfers	1227

CHAPTER 1. TRANSFERS IN GENERAL

Article	Section
1. Definition of Transfer	1039
2. What May be Transferred	1044
3. Mode of Transfer	1052
4. Interpretation of Grants	1066
5. Effect of Transfer	1084
6. Agency Listings for the Transfer of Certain Property	1086
7. Unlawful Influence of Appraisers	1090.5

Cross References

Accumulation of income of property, direction by will, trust or transfer, see Civil Code § 724.
Applicability of chapter to all written contracts, see Civil Code § 1627.
Breach of agreement to transfer realty, presumption of inadequacy of damages, see Civil Code § 3387.
Check of other draft, not an assignment in hands of drawee, see Commercial Code § 3409.
Community personal property, restrictions on disposition, see Family Code § 1100.
Community real property, joinder of spouse in conveyances, see Family Code § 1102.
Covenants running with the land, see Civil Code § 1460 et seq.
Devise of real property, see Probate Code § 120.
Essentials to use of thing granted, inclusion in grant, see Civil Code § 3522.
Forgery of instruments of transfer, see Penal Code § 470 et seq.
Fraudulent conveyances, see Civil Code § 3439 et seq.
Incident follows transfer of principal, see Civil Code § 3540.
Mortgage as transfer, see Civil Code § 2924.
Motor vehicles, transfer of title or interest, see Vehicle Code § 5600 et seq.
Non-negotiable instruments, transfer, see Civil Code § 1459.
Obtaining signature to transfer by threats, see Penal Code § 522.
Ownership, transfers, see Civil Code § 982.
Procuring conveyance by person without right in property, see Penal Code § 531a.
Specific performance, see Civil Code §§ 3387, 3395.
Statute of frauds, see Civil Code § 1624.
Time of creation of limitation, condition, or interest, see Civil Code § 749.

ARTICLE 1. DEFINITION OF TRANSFER

Section
1039. "Transfer" defined.
1040. "Voluntary transfer" defined.

§ 1039. "Transfer" defined

TRANSFER, WHAT. Transfer is an act of the parties, or of the law, by which the title to property is conveyed from one living person to another. *(Enacted in 1872.)*

§ 1040. "Voluntary transfer" defined

VOLUNTARY TRANSFER. A voluntary transfer is an executed contract, subject to all rules of law concerning contracts in general; except that a consideration is not necessary to its validity. *(Enacted in 1872.)*

Cross References

Consideration, see Civil Code § 1605 et seq.
Contracts, see Civil Code § 1549 et seq.
Payment, see Civil Code § 1478.

ARTICLE 2. WHAT MAY BE TRANSFERRED

Section
1044. Property subject to transfer.
1045. Possibility; transferability.
1046. Right of re-entry or repossession; transferability.
1047. Real estate in adverse possession; transfer of title.

Cross References

Animal brands, property right, sale or transfer, see Food and Agricultural Code § 20698.
Apiary brands, transfer, see Food and Agricultural Code § 29052.
Assignment of accounts receivable, secured transactions, see Commercial Code § 9101 et seq.
Authorship of original works, transferability, see Civil Code § 982.
Bills of lading, negotiation and transfer, see Commercial Code § 7501 et seq.
Business name, transferability, see Business and Professions Code § 14103.
Corporate stock, registration of investment security transfer on books, see Commercial Code § 8401 et seq.
Future interests, transfer of title, see Civil Code § 699.
Good will, transferability, see Business and Professions Code § 14102.
Invention or design, transferability, see Civil Code § 982.
Life or disability policies, transfer, see Insurance Code § 10129 et seq.
Old age security benefits, assignability, see Welfare and Institutions Code § 11002.
Partnership property, assignability, see Corporations Code § 16301.
Stock and bond transfers, investment securities, see Commercial Code § 8101 et seq.
Things in action, transferability, see Civil Code § 954; Code of Civil Procedure § 368.5.
Trademarks, transferability, see Business and Professions Code § 14260.
Unemployment insurance benefits, assignability, see Unemployment Insurance Code § 1342.
Veterans' Farm and home purchases, transfer, assignment, see Military and Veterans Code §§ 987.01, 987.1.
Wages, assignability, see Labor Code § 300.

§ 1044. Property subject to transfer

WHAT MAY BE TRANSFERRED. Property of any kind may be transferred, except as otherwise provided by this Article. *(Enacted in 1872.)*

Cross References

Animal brands, property right, sale or transfer, see Food and Agricultural Code § 20698.
Apiary brands, transfer, see Food and Agricultural Code § 29052.
Assignment of accounts receivable, secured transactions, see Commercial Code § 9101 et seq.
Authorship of original works, transferability, see Civil Code § 982.
Bills of lading, negotiation and transfer, see Commercial Code § 7501 et seq.
Business name, transferability, see Business and Professions Code § 14103.
Corporate stock, registration of investment security transfer on books, see Commercial Code § 8401 et seq.
Future interests, transfer of title, see Civil Code § 699.
Good will, transferability, see Business and Professions Code § 14102.
Invention or design, transferability, see Civil Code § 982.

§ 1044   PROPERTY

Life or disability policies, transfer, see Insurance Code § 10129 et seq.
Old age security benefits, assignability, see Welfare and Institutions Code § 11002.
Partnership property, assignability, see Corporations Code § 15009.
Stock and bond transfers, investment securities, see Commercial Code § 8101 et seq.
Things in action, transferability, see Civil Code § 954; Code of Civil Procedure § 368.5.
Trademarks, transferability, see Business and Professions Code § 14260.
Unemployment insurance benefits, assignability, see Unemployment Insurance Code § 1342.
Veterans' Farm and home purchases, transfer, assignment, see Military and Veterans Code §§ 987.01, 987.1.
Wages, assignability, see Labor Code § 300.

§ 1045. Possibility; transferability

POSSIBILITY. A mere possibility, not coupled with an interest, cannot be transferred. *(Enacted in 1872.)*

Cross References

School bonds, California School Finance Authority, rights and possibilities of participating party, see Education Code § 17199.1.
Washoe Project water supply contracts, assignment of rights under contract for water supply by department, see Water Code § 12053.
Washoe Project water supply contracts, assignment of rights under contracts with public agencies by department, see Water Code § 12055.

§ 1046. Right of re-entry or repossession; transferability

RIGHT OF RE-ENTRY CAN BE TRANSFERRED. A right of re-entry, or of repossession for breach of condition subsequent, can be transferred. *(Enacted in 1872.)*

Cross References

Conditions subsequent, see Civil Code § 1109.
Condition subsequent defined, see Civil Code § 1438.

§ 1047. Real estate in adverse possession; transfer of title

OWNER OUSTED OF POSSESSION MAY TRANSFER. Any person claiming title to real property in the adverse possession of another may transfer it with the same effect as if in actual possession. *(Enacted in 1872.)*

Cross References

Adverse possession, see Civil Code § 1007; Code of Civil Procedure §§ 323, 325 and 326.
Real property defined for purposes of this Code, see Civil Code § 658.

ARTICLE 3. MODE OF TRANSFER

Section
1052. Oral transfers; when permissible.
1053. Grant defined.
1054. Necessity of delivery.
1055. Presumption as to date of delivery.
1056. Delivery necessarily absolute.
1057. Delivery in escrow.
1057.3. Release of escrow funds; failure to comply; liability.
1057.5. Escrow agents; prohibited acts; conflicts of interest.
1057.6. Escrow transactions; disclosure statement; title insurance.

Section
1057.7. Escrow instructions; statement of license or authority.
1058. Redelivery or cancellation of grant; effect.
1058.5. Nonacceptance of recorded deed; rescission of invalidated trustee's deed; notice; recordation; effect.
1059. Constructive delivery of grant.
1060. Repealed.

§ 1052. Oral transfers; when permissible

WHEN ORAL. A transfer may be made without writing, in every case in which a writing is not expressly required by statute. *(Enacted in 1872.)*

Cross References

Mortgage, requirement of writing, see Civil Code § 2922.
Ships, transferring interest by writing, see Civil Code § 1135.
Statute of frauds, see Civil Code § 1624.
Wills, requirement of writing, see Probate Code § 6110.

§ 1053. Grant defined

A transfer in writing is called a grant, or conveyance, or bill of sale. The term "grant," in this and the next two Articles, includes all these instruments, unless it is specially applied to real property. *(Enacted in 1872. Amended by Code Am.1873–74, c. 612, p. 225, § 130.)*

Cross References

Conclusiveness of grant, see Civil Code § 1107.
Conveyance defined, see Civil Code § 1215.
Effect of grant, see Civil Code § 1104 et seq.
Form of grant, see Civil Code § 1092.
Interpretation of grants, see Civil Code § 1066 et seq.
Real property defined for purposes of this Code, see Civil Code § 658.
Time of creation of limitation, condition, or interest, delivery of grant, see Civil Code § 749.

§ 1054. Necessity of delivery

DELIVERY NECESSARY. A grant takes effect, so as to vest the interest intended to be transferred, only upon its delivery by the grantor. *(Enacted in 1872.)*

Cross References

Contracts in writing, effective upon delivery, see Civil Code § 1626.
Time of creation of limitation, condition, or interest, delivery of grant, see Civil Code § 749.

§ 1055. Presumption as to date of delivery

DATE. A grant duly executed is presumed to have been delivered at its date. *(Enacted in 1872.)*

§ 1056. Delivery necessarily absolute

DELIVERY TO GRANTEE IS NECESSARILY ABSOLUTE. A grant cannot be delivered to the grantee conditionally. Delivery to him, or to his agent as such, is necessarily absolute, and the instrument takes effect thereupon, discharged of any condition on which the delivery was made. *(Enacted in 1872.)*

§ 1057. Delivery in escrow

DELIVERY IN ESCROW. A grant may be deposited by the grantor with a third person, to be delivered on performance of a condition, and, on delivery by the depositary, it will take effect. While in the possession of the third person, and subject to condition, it is called an escrow. *(Enacted in 1872.)*

Cross References

Escrow defined, see Financial Code § 17003.
Escrow Law, see Financial Code § 17000 et seq.

§ 1057.3. Release of escrow funds; failure to comply; liability

(a) It shall be the obligation of a buyer and seller who enter into a contract to purchase and sell real property to ensure that all funds deposited into an escrow account are returned to the person who deposited the funds or who is otherwise entitled to the funds under the contract, if the purchase of the property is not completed by the date set forth in the contract for the close of escrow or any duly executed extension thereof.

(b) Any buyer or seller who fails to execute any document required by the escrow holder to release funds on deposit in an escrow account as provided in subdivision (a) within 30 days following a written demand for the return of funds deposited in escrow by the other party shall be liable to the person making the deposit for all of the following:

(1) The amount of the funds deposited in escrow not held in good faith to resolve a good faith dispute.

(2) Damages of treble the amount of the funds deposited in escrow not held to resolve a good faith dispute, but liability under this paragraph shall not be less than one hundred dollars ($100) or more than one thousand dollars ($1,000).

(3) Reasonable attorney's fees incurred in any action to enforce this section.

(c) Notwithstanding subdivision (b), there shall be no cause of action under this section, and no party to a contract to purchase and sell real property shall be liable, for failure to return funds deposited in an escrow account by a buyer or seller, if the funds are withheld in order to resolve a good faith dispute between a buyer and seller. A party who is denied the return of the funds deposited in escrow is entitled to damages under this section only upon proving that there was no good faith dispute as to the right to the funds on deposit.

(d) Upon the filing of a cause of action pursuant to this section, the escrow holder shall deposit the sum in dispute, less any cancellation fee and charges incurred, with the court in which the action is filed and be discharged of further responsibility for the funds.

(e) Neither any document required by the escrow holder to release funds deposited in an escrow account nor the acceptance of funds released from escrow, by any principal to the escrow transaction, shall be deemed a cancellation or termination of the underlying contract to purchase and sell real property, unless the cancellation is specifically stated therein. If the escrow instructions constitute the only contract between the buyer and seller, no document required by the escrow holder to release funds deposited in an escrow account shall abrogate a cause of action for breach of a contractual obligation to purchase or sell real property, unless the cancellation is specifically stated therein.

(f) For purposes of this section:

(1) "Close of escrow" means the date, specified event, or performance of prescribed condition upon which the escrow agent is to deliver the subject of the escrow to the person specified in the buyer's instructions to the escrow agent.

(2) "Good faith dispute" means a dispute in which the trier of fact finds that the party refusing to return the deposited funds had a reasonable belief of his or her legal entitlement to withhold the deposited funds. The existence of a "good faith dispute" shall be determined by the trier of fact.

(3) "Property" means real property containing one to four residential units at least one of which at the time the escrow is created is to be occupied by the buyer. The buyer's statement as to his or her intention to occupy one of the units is conclusive for the purposes of this section.

(g) Nothing in this section restricts the ability of an escrow holder to file an interpleader action in the event of a dispute as to the proper distribution of funds deposited in an escrow account. *(Added by Stats.1990, c. 13 (A.B.546), § 1.)*

Cross References

Obligation defined, see Civil Code § 1427.
Real property defined for purposes of this Code, see Civil Code § 658.

§ 1057.5. Escrow agents; prohibited acts; conflicts of interest

Except for the normal compensation of his own employees, no person acting as an escrow agent whether required to be licensed as such or not, shall pay over to any other person any commission, fee, or other consideration as compensation for referring, soliciting, handling, or servicing escrow customers or accounts.

No escrow agent shall enter into any arrangement, either of his own making or of a subsidiary nature, or through any other person having a dual capacity, or through any person having a direct or indirect interest in the escrow, or other device, permitting any fee, commission, or compensation which is contingent upon the performance of any act, condition, or instruction set forth in an escrow, to be drawn or paid, either in whole or in part, or in kind or its equivalent, prior to the actual closing and completion of the escrow.

The provisions of this section shall not be deemed to supersede, negate, or modify any of the provisions of Section 12404 of the Insurance Code. *(Added by Stats.1967, c. 678, p. 2047, § 1.)*

§ 1057.6. Escrow transactions; disclosure statement; title insurance

In an escrow transaction for the purchase or simultaneous exchange of real property, where a policy of title insurance will not be issued to the buyer or to the parties to the exchange, the following notice shall be provided in a separate document to the buyer or parties exchanging real property, which shall be signed and acknowledged by them:

"IMPORTANT: IN A PURCHASE OR EXCHANGE OF REAL PROPERTY, IT MAY BE ADVISABLE TO OBTAIN TITLE INSURANCE IN CONNECTION WITH THE CLOSE OF ESCROW SINCE THERE MAY BE PRIOR RECORDED LIENS AND ENCUMBRANCES

§ 1057.6

WHICH AFFECT YOUR INTEREST IN THE PROPERTY BEING ACQUIRED. A NEW POLICY OF TITLE INSURANCE SHOULD BE OBTAINED IN ORDER TO ENSURE YOUR INTEREST IN THE PROPERTY THAT YOU ARE ACQUIRING." *(Added by Stats.1992, c. 194 (S.B.1738), § 1.)*

Cross References

Real property defined for purposes of this Code, see Civil Code § 658.

§ 1057.7. Escrow instructions; statement of license or authority

All written escrow instructions executed by a buyer or seller, whether prepared by a person subject to Division 6 (commencing with Section 17000) of the Financial Code, or by a person exempt from that division under Section 17006 of the Financial Code, shall contain a statement in not less than 10-point type which shall include the license name and the name of the department issuing the license or authority under which the person is operating. This section shall not apply to supplemental escrow instructions or modifications to escrow instructions.

This section shall become operative on July 1, 1993. *(Added by Stats.1992, c. 861 (A.B.2583), § 2, operative July 1, 1993.)*

Cross References

Cancellation of written instruments, see Civil Code § 3412.

§ 1058. Redelivery or cancellation of grant; effect

SURRENDERING OR CANCELING GRANT DOES NOT RECONVEY. Redelivering a grant of real property to the grantor, or canceling it, does not operate to retransfer the title. *(Enacted in 1872.)*

Cross References

Cancellation of instruments, see Civil Code § 3412.
Real property defined for purposes of this Code, see Civil Code § 658.

§ 1058.5. Nonacceptance of recorded deed; rescission of invalidated trustee's deed; notice; recordation; effect

(a) A notice of nonacceptance of a recorded deed executed by a holder of a security interest, which notice identifies the security interest, contains a legal description of the property, properly identifies the parties to the deed, the date of recordation of the deed, the county in which the project is located, and the county assessor's parcel number of the real property referenced in the deed, may be recorded in the office of the county recorder where the real property is located.

(b) Where a trustee's deed is invalidated by a pending bankruptcy or otherwise, recordation of a notice of rescission of the trustee's deed, which notice properly identifies the deed of trust, the identification numbers used by the recorder or the books and pages at which the trustee's deed and deed of trust are recorded, the names of all trustors and beneficiaries, the location of the property subject to the deed of trust, and the reason for rescission, shall restore the condition of record title to the real property described in the trustee's deed and the existence and priority of all lienholders to the status quo prior to the recordation of the trustee's deed upon sale. Only the trustee or beneficiary who caused the trustee's deed to be recorded, or his or her successor in interest, may record a notice of rescission. *(Added by Stats.1993, c. 724 (A.B.1196), § 1. Amended by Stats.1997, c. 74 (S.B.665), § 1.)*

Cross References

Real property defined for purposes of this Code, see Civil Code § 658.

§ 1059. Constructive delivery of grant

CONSTRUCTIVE DELIVERY. Though a grant be not actually delivered into the possession of the grantee, it is yet to be deemed constructively delivered in the following cases:

1. Where the instrument is, by the agreement of the parties at the time of execution, understood to be delivered, and under such circumstances that the grantee is entitled to immediate delivery; or,

2. Where it is delivered to a stranger for the benefit of the grantee, and his assent is shown, or may be presumed. *(Enacted in 1872.)*

§ 1060. Repealed by Stats.1969, c. 155, p. 409, § 2, operative July 1, 1970

ARTICLE 4. INTERPRETATION OF GRANTS

Section
1066. Interpretation.
1067. Limitations in grant.
1068. Recitals.
1069. Interpretation in favor of grantee; exception.
1070. Irreconcilable parts.
1071. Repealed.
1072. Words of inheritance or succession.
1073. Repealed.

§ 1066. Interpretation

GRANTS, HOW INTERPRETED. Grants are to be interpreted in like manner with contracts in general, except so far as is otherwise provided in this Article. *(Enacted in 1872.)*

Cross References

Construction of written instruments generally, see Code of Civil Procedure § 1857 et seq.
Interpretation of contracts, see Civil Code § 1635 et seq.

§ 1067. Limitations in grant

LIMITATIONS, HOW CONTROLLED. A clear and distinct limitation in a grant is not controlled by other words less clear and distinct. *(Enacted in 1872.)*

§ 1068. Recitals

RECITALS, WHEN RESORTED TO. If the operative words of a grant are doubtful, recourse may be had to its recitals to assist the construction. *(Enacted in 1872.)*

Cross References

Uncertainty resolved against party causing, see Civil Code § 1654.
Whole of contract to be taken together, see Civil Code § 1641.

Words to be understood in usual sense, see Civil Code § 1644.

§ 1069. Interpretation in favor of grantee; exception

INTERPRETATION AGAINST GRANTOR. A grant is to be interpreted in favor of the grantee, except that a reservation in any grant, and every grant by a public officer or body, as such, to a private party, is to be interpreted in favor of the grantor. *(Enacted in 1872.)*

Cross References

Uncertainty resolved against party causing, see Civil Code § 1654.

§ 1070. Irreconcilable parts

IRRECONCILABLE PROVISIONS. If several parts of a grant are absolutely irreconcilable, the former part prevails. *(Enacted in 1872.)*

§ 1071. Repealed by Stats.2002, c. 138 (A.B.1784), § 1

§ 1072. Words of inheritance or succession

WORDS OF INHERITANCE UNNECESSARY. Words of inheritance or succession are not requisite to transfer a fee in real property. *(Enacted in 1872.)*

Cross References

Estate in fee simple defined, see Civil Code § 762.
Heirs of life tenant, taking as purchasers, see Civil Code § 779.
Presumption of transfer of fee simple title, see Civil Code § 1105.
Real property defined for purposes of this Code, see Civil Code § 658.

§ 1073. Repealed by Stats.2002, c. 138 (A.B.1784), § 2

ARTICLE 5. EFFECT OF TRANSFER

Section
1083. Repealed.
1084. Incidents.
1085. Person not a party to grant; acquisition of interest or benefit.

§ 1083. Repealed by Stats.1931, c. 1070, p. 2258, § 2

§ 1084. Incidents

INCIDENTS. The transfer of a thing transfers also all its incidents, unless expressly excepted; but the transfer of an incident to a thing does not transfer the thing itself. *(Enacted in 1872.)*

Cross References

Appurtenances to land, see Civil Code § 662.
Easements pass with title, see Civil Code § 1104.
Servitudes, see Civil Code § 801 et seq.
Subsequently acquired title, passage by operation of law, see Civil Code § 1106.
Trade secrets, disclosure in official proceedings, see Civil Code § 3426.11.
Transfer of land bounded by highway, see Civil Code § 1112.

§ 1085. Person not a party to grant; acquisition of interest or benefit

GRANT MAY INURE TO BENEFIT OF STRANGER. A present interest, and the benefit of a condition or covenant respecting property, may be taken by any natural person under a grant, although not named a party thereto. *(Enacted in 1872.)*

ARTICLE 6. AGENCY LISTINGS FOR THE TRANSFER OF CERTAIN PROPERTY

Section
1086. Definitions.
1087. Multiple listing service (MLS).
1088. Placement of listing; responsibility for accuracy; retention of information.
1089. Application of Section 1102.1 (d).
1089.5. Personal representative contracts; application of article.
1090. Repealed.

§ 1086. Definitions

(a) For purposes of this article, the definitions contained in Chapter 1 (commencing with Section 10000) of Part 1 of Division 4 of the Business and Professions Code apply.

(b) An "agent" is one authorized by law to act in that capacity for that type of property and is licensed as a real estate broker under Chapter 3 (commencing with Section 10130) of Part 1 of Division 4 of the Business and Professions Code, or is a licensee, as defined in Section 18006 of the Health and Safety Code. *(Added by Stats.1982, c. 547, p. 2486, § 1. Amended by Stats.1988, c. 113, § 3, eff. May 25, 1988, operative July 1, 1988; Stats.1993, c. 331 (S.B.914), § 3; Stats.2018, c. 907 (A.B.1289), § 1, eff. Jan. 1, 2019.)*

Cross References

Classes of insurance, home protection company, provision of coverage for a listing period, see Insurance Code § 12761.1.
Obligation defined, see Civil Code § 1427.
Real property defined for purposes of this Code, see Civil Code § 658.

§ 1087. Multiple listing service (MLS)

A multiple listing service (MLS) is a facility of cooperation of agents and appraisers, operating through an intermediary that does not itself act as an agent or appraiser, through which agents establish express or implied contracts for compensation between agents that are MLS participants in accordance with its MLS rules with respect to listed properties in a listing agreement, or that may be used by agents and appraisers, pursuant to the rules of the service, to prepare market evaluations and appraisals of real property. *(Added by Stats.1982, c. 547, p. 2487, § 1. Amended by Stats.1993, c. 331 (S.B.914), § 4; Stats.2018, c. 907 (A.B.1289), § 2, eff. Jan. 1, 2019.)*

Cross References

Definitions applicable to this Article, see Civil Code § 1086.
Estate management contract with licensed real estate broker, use of multiple listing service, see Probate Code § 10150.
Real property defined for purposes of this Code, see Civil Code § 658.
Relocation assistance, offered for sale, defined, see Government Code § 7277.

§ 1088. Placement of listing; responsibility for accuracy; retention of information

(a) A listing may not be placed in a multiple listing service unless authorized or directed by the seller in the listing.

(b) If an agent or appraiser places a listing or other information in the multiple listing service, that agent or appraiser shall be responsible for the truth of all representations and statements made by the agent or appraiser of which that agent or appraiser had knowledge or reasonably should have had knowledge to anyone injured by their falseness or inaccuracy.

(c) A multiple listing service shall retain and make accessible on its computer system, if any, all listing and other information placed in the multiple listing service by an agent or appraiser for no less than three years from the date the listing was placed in the multiple listing service.

(d) This section shall not alter the obligations of a licensed real estate broker to retain documents as specified in subdivision (a) of Section 10148 of the Business and Professions Code. *(Added by Stats.1982, c. 547, p. 2487, § 1. Amended by Stats.1993, c. 331 (S.B.914), § 5; Stats.2018, c. 907 (A.B.1289), § 3, eff. Jan. 1, 2019; Stats.2019, c. 310 (A.B.892), § 1, eff. Jan. 1, 2020.)*

Cross References

Definitions applicable to this Article, see Civil Code § 1086.

§ 1089. Application of Section 1102.1 (d)

The provisions of subdivision (d) of Section 1102.1 shall apply to this article. *(Added by Stats.2018, c. 907 (A.B.1289), § 5, eff. Jan. 1, 2019.)*

§ 1089.5. Personal representative contracts; application of article

Subject to the limitations, conditions, and requirements of Chapter 18 (commencing with Section 10000) of Part 5 of Division 7 of the Probate Code, this article applies to property defined in Section 1086 that is covered by a contract described in Section 10150 of the Probate Code. *(Added by Stats.1988, c. 113, § 4, eff. May 25, 1988, operative July 1, 1988.)*

Cross References

Definitions applicable to this Article, see Civil Code § 1086.

§ 1090. Repealed by Stats.2018, c. 907 (A.B.1289), § 6, eff. Jan. 1, 2019

ARTICLE 7. UNLAWFUL INFLUENCE OF APPRAISERS

Section
1090.5. Valuation of real estate; improper influence; violation.

§ 1090.5. Valuation of real estate; improper influence; violation

(a) No person with an interest in a real estate transaction involving a valuation shall improperly influence or attempt to improperly influence the development, reporting, result, or review of that valuation, through coercion, extortion, bribery, intimidation, compensation, or instruction. For purposes of this section, a valuation is defined as an estimate of the value of real property in written or electronic form, other than one produced solely by an automated valuation model or system. Prohibited acts include, but are not limited to, the following:

(1) Seeking to influence a person who prepares a valuation to report a minimum or maximum value for the property being valued. Such influence may include, but is not limited to:

(A) Requesting that a person provide a preliminary estimate or opinion of value prior to entering into a contract with that person for valuation services.

(B) Conditioning whether to hire a person based on an expectation of the value conclusion likely to be returned by that person.

(C) Conditioning the amount of a person's compensation on the value conclusion returned by that person.

(D) Providing to a person an anticipated, estimated, encouraged, or desired valuation prior to their completion of a valuation.

(2) Withholding or threatening to withhold timely payment to a person or entity that prepares a valuation, or provides valuation management functions, because that person or entity does not return a value at or above a certain amount.

(3) Implying to a person who prepares a valuation that current or future retention of that person depends on the amount at which the person estimates the value of real property.

(4) Excluding a person who prepares a valuation from consideration for future engagement because the person reports a value that does not meet or exceed a predetermined threshold.

(5) Conditioning the compensation paid to a person who prepares a valuation on consummation of the real estate transaction for which the valuation is prepared.

(6) Requesting the payment of compensation to achieve higher priority in the assignment of valuation business.

(b) Subdivision (a) does not prohibit a person with an interest in a real estate transaction from doing any of the following:

(1) Asking a person who performs a valuation to do any of the following:

(A) Consider additional, appropriate property information, including information about comparable properties.

(B) Provide further detail, substantiation, or explanation for the person's value conclusion.

(C) Correct errors in a valuation report.

(2) Obtaining multiple valuations, for purposes of selecting the most reliable valuation.

(3) Withholding compensation due to breach of contract or substandard performance of services.

(4) Providing a copy of the sales contract in connection with a purchase transaction.

(c) If a person who violates this section is licensed or registered under any state licensing or registration law and the violation occurs within the course and scope of the person's duties as a licensee or registrant, the violation shall be deemed a violation of that law.

(d) Nothing in this section shall be construed to authorize communications that are otherwise prohibited under existing law. *(Added by Stats.2007, c. 291 (S.B.223), § 2, eff. Oct. 5, 2007. Amended by Stats.2009, c. 173 (S.B.237), § 21; Stats. 2011, c. 716 (S.B.6), § 5.)*

CHAPTER 2. TRANSFER OF REAL PROPERTY

Article		Section
1.	Mode of Transfer	1091
1.4.	Installation of Water Use Efficiency Improvements	1101.1
1.5.	Disclosures Upon Transfer of Residential Property	1102
1.7.	Disclosure of Natural and Environmental Hazards, Right-to-Farm, and Other Disclosures Upon Transfer of Residential Property	1103
1.8.	Buyer's Choice Act	1103.20
2.	Effect of Transfer	1104

ARTICLE 1. MODE OF TRANSFER

Section
1091. Method of transfer.
1092. Grant; form.
1093. Consolidation of separate and distinct legal descriptions into single instrument of conveyance or security document; effect on separate nature of property.
1094. Repealed.
1095. Attorney in fact; execution of instruments.
1096. Conveyance after change of name; procedure.
1097. Exercise of option or completion of contract for sale of single family residential property; fee of vendor or lessor.
1098. "Transfer fee" defined.
1098.5. Transfer fee documentation; requirements.
1098.6. Prohibition on creation of transfer fees on or after January 1, 2019; exceptions.
1099. Delivery to transferee of structural pest control inspection report and certification.

§ 1091. Method of transfer

REQUISITES FOR TRANSFER OF CERTAIN ESTATES. An estate in real property, other than an estate at will or for a term not exceeding one year, can be transferred only by operation of law, or by an instrument in writing, subscribed by the party disposing of the same, or by his agent thereunto authorized by writing. *(Enacted in 1872.)*

Cross References

Conveyance after name change, see Civil Code § 1096.
Deed as evidence of conveyance, see Evidence Code § 1603.
Discriminatory restrictive deeds and covenants, see Civil Code §§ 53, 782.
Eminent domain, see Code of Civil Procedure § 1230.010 et seq.; Government Code §§ 25350.5, 37350.5.
Interpretation of grants, see Civil Code § 1066 et seq.
Joint tenancy, see Civil Code § 683.
Real property defined for purposes of this Code, see Civil Code § 658.
Revocation of instrument, see Civil Code §§ 1229, 1230.
Sale by operation of law for taxes, see Revenue and Taxation Code § 3436.
Sale of goods, writing required, see Commercial Code § 2201.
Statute of frauds, see Civil Code § 1624.
Transfer of title obtained by adverse possession, see Civil Code § 1047.
Transfers of real property to be in writing, see Code of Civil Procedure §§ 1971, 1972.
Written terms as final expression of agreement, see Code of Civil Procedure § 1856.

§ 1092. Grant; form

A grant of an estate in real property may be made in substance as follows:

"I, A B, grant to C D all that real property situated in (insert name of county) County, State of California, bounded (or described) as follows: (here insert property description, or if the land sought to be conveyed has a descriptive name, it may be described by the name, as for instance, 'The Norris Ranch.')

Witness my hand this (insert day) day of (insert month), 20___.

AB"

(Enacted in 1872. Amended by Stats.1999, c. 608 (A.B. 1342), § 4.)

Cross References

Abandoned or unclaimed property, deeds, see Code of Civil Procedure § 1376.
Construction of instruments, see Code of Civil Procedure § 1858 et seq.
Constructive delivery of grant, see Civil Code § 1059.
Conveyance after name change, see Civil Code § 1096.
Conveyance defined, see Civil Code § 1215.
Description of realty, construction, see Code of Civil Procedure § 2077.
Grant defined, see Civil Code § 1053.
Intention of parties, see Code of Civil Procedure § 1859.
Law governing conveyances prior to code, see Civil Code § 1205.
Necessity of delivery of grant, see Civil Code § 1054.
Preferred construction of two permissible constructions, see Code of Civil Procedure §§ 1864, 1866.
Real property defined for purposes of this Code, see Civil Code § 658.
Rules for construing description of land, see Code of Civil Procedure § 2077.
State's deed conveying tax deeded land, contents, see Revenue and Taxation Code §§ 3710, 3805.
Written words on printed forms, construction, see Code of Civil Procedure § 1862.

§ 1093. Consolidation of separate and distinct legal descriptions into single instrument of conveyance or security document; effect on separate nature of property

Absent the express written statement of the grantor contained therein, the consolidation of separate and distinct legal descriptions of real property contained in one or more deeds, mortgages, patents, deeds of trust, contracts of sale, or other instruments of conveyance or security documents, into a subsequent single deed, mortgage, patent, deed of trust, contract of sale, or other instrument of conveyance or security document (whether by means of an individual listing of the legal descriptions in a subsequent single instrument of conveyance or security document, or by means of a consolidated legal description comprised of more than one previously separate and distinct legal description), does not operate in any manner to alter or affect the separate and distinct nature of the real property so described in the subsequent single

§ 1093

instrument of conveyance or security document containing either the listing of or the consolidated legal description of the parcels so conveyed or secured thereby.

This section does not constitute a change in, but is declaratory of, the existing law. *(Added by Stats.1985, c. 911, § 1.)*

Cross References

Real property defined for purposes of this Code, see Civil Code § 658.

§ 1094. Repealed by Stats.1976, c. 1171, p. 5252, § 3

§ 1095. **Attorney in fact; execution of instruments**

ATTORNEY IN FACT, HOW MUST EXECUTE FOR PRINCIPAL. When an attorney in fact executes an instrument transferring an estate in real property, he must subscribe the name of his principal to it, and his own name as attorney in fact. *(Enacted in 1872.)*

Cross References

Real property defined for purposes of this Code, see Civil Code § 658.

§ 1096. **Conveyance after change of name; procedure**

Any person in whom the title of real estate is vested, who shall afterwards, from any cause, have his or her name changed, must, in any conveyance of said real estate so held, set forth the name in which he or she derived title to said real estate. Any conveyance, though recorded as provided by law, which does not comply with the foregoing provision shall not impart constructive notice of the contents thereof to subsequent purchasers and encumbrancers, but such conveyance is valid as between the parties thereto and those who have notice thereof. *(Added by Stats.1905, c. 443, p. 602, § 1. Amended by Stats.1947, c. 1314, p. 2852, § 1.)*

Cross References

Constructive notice defined, see Civil Code § 19.
Recordation as constructive notice of contents of instrument, see Civil Code § 1213.

§ 1097. **Exercise of option or completion of contract for sale of single family residential property; fee of vendor or lessor**

No vendor or lessor of a single family residential property shall contract for or exact any fee in excess of ten dollars ($10) for the act of signing and delivering a document in connection with the transfer, cancellation or reconveyance of any title or instrument at the time the buyer or lessee exercises an option to buy, or completes performance of the contract for the sale of, the property.

The provisions of this section shall apply prospectively only. *(Added by Stats.1965, c. 352, p. 1458, § 1.)*

§ 1098. **"Transfer fee" defined**

(a) A "transfer fee" is any fee payment requirement imposed within a covenant, restriction, or condition contained in any deed, contract, security instrument, or other document affecting the transfer or sale of, or any interest in, real property that requires a fee be paid as a result of transfer of the real property. A transfer fee does not include any of the following:

(1) Fees or taxes imposed by a governmental entity.

(2) Fees pursuant to mechanics' liens.

(3) Fees pursuant to court-ordered transfers, payments, or judgments.

(4) Fees pursuant to property agreements in connection with a legal separation or dissolution of marriage.

(5) Fees, charges, or payments in connection with the administration of estates or trusts pursuant to Division 7 (commencing with Section 7000), Division 8 (commencing with Section 13000), or Division 9 (commencing with Section 15000) of the Probate Code.

(6) Fees, charges, or payments imposed by lenders or purchasers of loans, as these entities are described in subdivision (c) of Section 10232 of the Business and Professions Code.

(7) Assessments, charges, penalties, or fees authorized by the Davis–Stirling Common Interest Development Act (Part 5 (commencing with Section 4000) of Division 4) or by the Commercial and Industrial Common Interest Development Act (Part 5.3 (commencing with Section 6500) of Division 4).

(8) Fees, charges, or payments for failing to comply with, or for transferring the real property prior to satisfying, an obligation to construct residential improvements on the real property.

(9)(A) Any fee reflected in a document recorded against the property on or before December 31, 2007, that is separate from any covenants, conditions, and restrictions, and that substantially complies with subdivision (a) of Section 1098.5 by providing a prospective transferee notice of the following:

(i) Payment of a transfer fee is required.

(ii) The amount or method of calculation of the fee.

(iii) The date or circumstances under which the transfer fee payment requirement expires, if any.

(iv) The entity to which the fee will be paid.

(v) The general purposes for which the fee will be used.

(B) A fee reflected in a document recorded against the property on or before December 31, 2007, that is not separate from any covenants, conditions, and restrictions, or that incorporates by reference from another document, is a "transfer fee" for purposes of Section 1098.5. A transfer fee recorded against the property on or before December 31, 2007, that complies with subparagraph (A) and incorporates by reference from another document is unenforceable unless recorded against the property on or before December 31, 2016, in a single document that complies with subdivision (b) and with Section 1098.5.

(b) The information in paragraph (9) of subdivision (a) shall be set forth in a single document and shall not be incorporated by reference from any other document. *(Added by Stats.2007, c. 689 (A.B.980), § 1. Amended by Stats.2012, c. 181 (A.B.806), § 32, operative Jan. 1, 2014; Stats.2013, c. 605 (S.B.752), § 14; Stats.2015, c. 634 (A.B.807), § 1, eff. Jan. 1, 2016.)*

Cross References

Transfer fee disclosure statement, requirements, see Civil Code § 1102.6e.

§ 1098.5. Transfer fee documentation; requirements

(a) For transfer fees, as defined in Section 1098, imposed prior to January 1, 2008, the receiver of the fee, as a condition of payment of the fee on or after January 1, 2009, shall record, on or before December 31, 2008, against the real property in the office of the county recorder for the county in which the real property is located a separate document that meets all of the following requirements:

(1) The title of the document shall be "Payment of Transfer Fee Required" in at least 14–point boldface type.

(2) The document shall include all of the following information:

(A) The names of all current owners of the real property subject to the transfer fee, and the legal description and assessor's parcel number for the affected real property.

(B) The amount, if the fee is a flat amount, or the percentage of the sales price constituting the cost of the fee.

(C) If the real property is residential property, actual dollar-cost examples of the fee for a home priced at two hundred fifty thousand dollars ($250,000), five hundred thousand dollars ($500,000), and seven hundred fifty thousand dollars ($750,000).

(D) The date or circumstances under which the transfer fee payment requirement expires, if any.

(E) The purpose for which the funds from the fee will be used.

(F) The entity to which funds from the fee will be paid and specific contact information regarding where the funds are to be sent.

(G) The signature of the authorized representative of the entity to which funds from the fee will be paid.

(b) When a transfer fee, as defined in Section 1098, is imposed upon real property on or after January 1, 2008, the person or entity imposing the transfer fee, as a condition of payment of the fee, shall record in the office of the county recorder for the county in which the real property is located, concurrently with the instrument creating the transfer fee requirement, a separate document that meets all of the following requirements:

(1) The title of the document shall be "Payment of Transfer Fee Required" in at least 14–point boldface type.

(2) The document shall include all of the following information:

(A) The names of all current owners of the real property subject to the transfer fee, and the legal description and assessor's parcel number for the affected real property.

(B) The amount, if the fee is a flat amount, the percentage of the sales price constituting the cost of the fee, or the method for calculating the amount.

(C) If the real property is residential property and the amount of the fee is based on the price of the real property, actual dollar-cost examples of the fee for a home priced at two hundred fifty thousand dollars ($250,000), five hundred thousand dollars ($500,000), and seven hundred fifty thousand dollars ($750,000).

(D) The date or circumstances under which the transfer fee payment requirement expires, if any.

(E) The purpose for which the funds from the fee will be used.

(F) The entity to which funds from the fee will be paid and specific contact information regarding where the funds are to be sent.

(G) The signature of the authorized representative of the entity to which funds from the fee will be paid.

(H) For private transfer fees created on or after February 8, 2011, unless the exception in Section 1228.3 of Title 12 of the Code of Federal Regulations applies, the following notice in at least 14–point boldface type:

The Federal Housing Finance Agency and the Federal Housing Administration are prohibited from dealing in mortgages on properties encumbered by private transfer fee covenants that do not provide a "direct benefit" to the real property encumbered by the covenant. As a result, if you purchase such a property, you or individuals you want to sell the property to may have difficulty obtaining financing.

(c) The recorder shall only be responsible for examining that the document required by subdivision (a) or (b) contains the information required by subparagraphs (A), (F), and (G) of paragraph (2) of subdivision (a) or (b). The recorder shall index the document under the names of the persons and entities identified in subparagraphs (A) and (F) of paragraph (2) of subdivision (a) or (b). The recorder shall not examine any other information contained in the document required by subdivision (a) or (b). *(Added by Stats.2007, c. 689 (A.B.980), § 2. Amended by Stats.2015, c. 634 (A.B.807), § 2, eff. Jan. 1, 2016; Stats.2017, c. 148 (A.B.1139), § 1, eff. Jan. 1, 2018.)*

§ 1098.6. Prohibition on creation of transfer fees on or after January 1, 2019; exceptions

(a)(1) On or after January 1, 2019, a transfer fee shall not be created.

(2) This subdivision does not apply to excepted transfer fee covenants as defined by Section 1228.1 of Title 12 of the Code of Federal Regulations. Excepted transfer fee covenants are not required to comply with subparagraph (H) of paragraph (2) of subdivision (b) of Section 1098.5.

(b) Any transfer fee created in violation of subdivision (a) is void as against public policy.

(c) For purposes of this section, "transfer fee" has the same meaning as that term is defined in Section 1098. *(Added by Stats.2018, c. 306 (A.B.3041), § 1, eff. Jan. 1, 2019.)*

§ 1099. Delivery to transferee of structural pest control inspection report and certification

(a) As soon as practical before transfer of title of any real property or the execution of a real property sales contract as defined in Section 2985, the transferor, fee owner, or his or her agent, shall deliver to the transferee a copy of a structural pest control inspection report prepared pursuant to Section 8516 of the Business and Professions Code upon which any certification in accordance with Section 8519 of the Business and Professions Code may be made, provided that certifica-

§ 1099

tion or preparation of a report is a condition of the contract effecting that transfer, or is a requirement imposed as a condition of financing such transfer.

(b) If a notice of work completed as contemplated by Section 8518 of the Business and Professions Code, indicating action by a structural pest control licensee in response to an inspection report delivered or to be delivered under provisions of subdivision (a), or a certification pursuant to Section 8519 of the Business and Professions Code, has been received by a transferor or his or her agent before transfer of title or execution of a real property sales contract as defined in Section 2985, it shall be furnished to the transferee as soon as practical before transfer of title or the execution of such real property sales contract.

(c) Delivery to a transferee as used in this section means delivery in person or by mail to the transferee himself or herself or any person authorized to act for him or her in the transaction or to such additional transferees who have requested such delivery from the transferor or his or her agent in writing. For the purposes of this section, delivery to either spouse shall be deemed delivery to a transferee, unless the contract affecting the transfer states otherwise.

(d) No transfer of title of real property shall be invalidated solely because of the failure of any person to comply with the provisions of this section unless such failure is an act or omission which would be a valid ground for rescission of such transfer in the absence of this section. *(Added by Stats.1974, c. 649, p. 1512, § 2, operative July 1, 1975. Amended by Stats.2016, c. 50 (S.B.1005), § 10, eff. Jan. 1, 2017.)*

Cross References

Real property defined for purposes of this Code, see Civil Code § 658.

ARTICLE 1.4. INSTALLATION OF WATER USE EFFICIENCY IMPROVEMENTS

Section
1101.1. Legislative findings and declarations regarding water supply.
1101.2. Application of article to specified properties.
1101.3. Definitions.
1101.4. Single-family residential real property; non-compliant plumbing fixtures; replacement with water-conserving plumbing fixtures.
1101.5. Multifamily residential real property and commercial real property; noncompliant plumbing fixtures; replacement with water-conserving plumbing fixtures.
1101.6. Demolition permit; one-year postponement of article requirements.
1101.7. Excluded properties.
1101.8. Local ordinances or policies.
1101.9. Noncompliant plumbing fixture retrofit ordinances; exemption from article requirements.

§ 1101.1. Legislative findings and declarations regarding water supply

The Legislature finds and declares all of the following:

(a) Adequate water supply reliability for all uses is essential to the future economic and environmental health of California.

(b) Environmentally sound strategies to meet future water supply and wastewater treatment needs are key to protecting and restoring aquatic resources in California.

(c) There is a pressing need to address water supply reliability issues raised by growing urban areas.

(d) Economic analysis by urban water agencies has identified urban water conservation as a cost-effective approach to addressing water supply needs.

(e) There are many water conservation practices that produce significant energy and other resource savings that should be encouraged as a matter of state policy.

(f) Since the 1991 signing of the "Memorandum of Understanding Regarding Urban Water Conservation in California," many urban water and wastewater treatment agencies have gained valuable experience that can be applied to produce significant statewide savings of water, energy, and associated infrastructure costs. This experience indicates a need to regularly revise and update water conservation methodologies and practices.

(g) To address these concerns, it is the intent of the Legislature to require that residential and commercial real property built and available for use or occupancy on or before January 1, 1994, be equipped with water-conserving plumbing fixtures.

(h) It is further the intent of the Legislature that retail water suppliers are encouraged to provide incentives, financing mechanisms, and funding to assist property owners with these retrofit obligations. *(Added by Stats.2009, c. 587 (S.B.407), § 1.)*

§ 1101.2. Application of article to specified properties

Except as provided in Section 1101.7, this article shall apply to residential and commercial real property built and available for use on or before January 1, 1994. *(Added by Stats.2009, c. 587 (S.B.407), § 1.)*

§ 1101.3. Definitions

For the purposes of this article:

(a) "Commercial real property" means any real property that is improved with, or consisting of, a building that is intended for commercial use, including hotels and motels, that is not a single-family residential real property or a multifamily residential real property.

(b) "Multifamily residential real property" means any real property that is improved with, or consisting of, a building containing more than one unit that is intended for human habitation, or any mixed residential-commercial buildings or portions thereof that are intended for human habitation. Multifamily residential real property includes residential hotels but does not include hotels and motels that are not residential hotels.

(c) "Noncompliant plumbing fixture" means any of the following:

(1) Any toilet manufactured to use more than 1.6 gallons of water per flush.

(2) Any urinal manufactured to use more than one gallon of water per flush.

(3) Any showerhead manufactured to have a flow capacity of more than 2.5 gallons of water per minute.

(4) Any interior faucet that emits more than 2.2 gallons of water per minute.

(d) "Single-family residential real property" means any real property that is improved with, or consisting of, a building containing not more than one unit that is intended for human habitation.

(e) "Water-conserving plumbing fixture" means any fixture that is in compliance with current building standards applicable to a newly constructed real property of the same type.

(f) "Sale or transfer" means the sale or transfer of an entire real property estate or the fee interest in that real property estate and does not include the sale or transfer of a partial interest, including a leasehold. *(Added by Stats.2009, c. 587 (S.B.407), § 1.)*

Cross References

School modernization project, state funding, see Education Code § 17584.

§ 1101.4. Single-family residential real property; non-compliant plumbing fixtures; replacement with water-conserving plumbing fixtures

(a) For all building alterations or improvements to single-family residential real property, as a condition for issuance of a certificate of final completion and occupancy or final permit approval by the local building department, the permit applicant shall replace all noncompliant plumbing fixtures with water-conserving plumbing fixtures.

(b) On or before January 1, 2017, noncompliant plumbing fixtures in any single-family residential real property shall be replaced by the property owner with water-conserving plumbing fixtures.

(c) A seller or transferor of single-family residential real property shall disclose in writing to the prospective purchaser or transferee the requirements of subdivision (b) and whether the real property includes any noncompliant plumbing fixtures. *(Added by Stats.2009, c. 587 (S.B.407), § 1. Amended by Stats.2019, c. 310 (A.B.892), § 2, eff. Jan. 1, 2020.)*

§ 1101.5. Multifamily residential real property and commercial real property; noncompliant plumbing fixtures; replacement with water-conserving plumbing fixtures

(a) On or before January 1, 2019, all noncompliant plumbing fixtures in any multifamily residential real property and in any commercial real property shall be replaced with water-conserving plumbing fixtures.

(b) An owner or the owner's agent may enter the owner's property for the purpose of installing, repairing, testing, and maintaining water-conserving plumbing fixtures required by this section, consistent with notice requirements of Section 1954.

(c) On and after January 1, 2019, the water-conserving plumbing fixtures required by this section shall be operating at the manufacturer's rated water consumption at the time that the tenant takes possession. A tenant shall be responsible for notifying the owner or owner's agent if the tenant becomes aware that a water-conserving plumbing fixture within his or her unit is not operating at the manufacturer's rated water consumption. The owner or owner's agent shall correct an inoperability in a water-conserving plumbing fixture upon notice by the tenant or if detected by the owner or the owner's agent.

(d)(1) On and after January 1, 2014, all noncompliant plumbing fixtures in any multifamily residential real property and any commercial real property shall be replaced with water-conserving plumbing fixtures in the following circumstances:

(A) For building additions in which the sum of concurrent building permits by the same permit applicant would increase the floor area of the space in a building by more than 10 percent, the building permit applicant shall replace all noncompliant plumbing fixtures in the building.

(B) For building alterations or improvements in which the total construction cost estimated in the building permit is greater than one hundred fifty thousand dollars ($150,000), the building permit applicant shall replace all noncompliant plumbing fixtures that service the specific area of the improvement.

(C) Notwithstanding subparagraph (A) or (B), for any alterations or improvements to a room in a building that require a building permit and that room contains any noncompliant plumbing fixtures, the building permit applicant shall replace all noncompliant plumbing fixtures in that room.

(2) Replacement of all noncompliant plumbing fixtures with water-conserving plumbing fixtures, as described in paragraph (1), shall be a condition for issuance of a certificate of final completion and occupancy or final permit approval by the local building department.

(e) On and after January 1, 2019, a seller or transferor of multifamily residential real property or of commercial real property shall disclose to the prospective purchaser or transferee, in writing, the requirements of subdivision (a) and whether the property includes any noncompliant plumbing fixtures. This disclosure may be included in other transactional documents. *(Added by Stats.2009, c. 587 (S.B.407), § 1. Amended by Stats.2013, c. 183 (S.B.745), § 1.)*

Cross References

Termination of tenancy after continuous and lawful occupation of residential real property for 12 months, just cause required, notice, additional tenants, opportunity to cure violation, relocation assistance or rent waiver, see Civil Code § 1946.2.

§ 1101.6. Demolition permit; one-year postponement of article requirements

The duty of an owner or building permit applicant to comply with the requirements of this article shall be postponed for one year from the date of issuance of a demolition permit for the building. If the building is demolished within the one-year postponement, the requirements of this article shall not apply. If the building is not demolished after the expiration of one year, the provisions of this article shall apply, subject to appeal to the local building department, even though the demolition permit is still in effect or a new demolition permit has been issued. *(Added by Stats.2009, c. 587 (S.B.407), § 1.)*

§ 1101.7. Excluded properties

This article shall not apply to any of the following:

(a) Registered historical sites.

(b) Real property for which a licensed plumber certifies that, due to the age or configuration of the property or its plumbing, installation of water-conserving plumbing fixtures is not technically feasible.

(c) A building for which water service is permanently disconnected. *(Added by Stats.2009, c. 587 (S.B.407), § 1.)*

§ 1101.8. Local ordinances or policies

A city, county, or city and county, or a retail water supplier may do either of the following:

(a) Enact local ordinances or establish policies that promote compliance with this article.

(b) Enact local ordinances or establish policies that will result in a greater amount of water savings than those provided for in this article. *(Added by Stats.2009, c. 587 (S.B.407), § 1.)*

§ 1101.9. Noncompliant plumbing fixture retrofit ordinances; exemption from article requirements

Any city, county, or city and county that has adopted an ordinance requiring retrofit of noncompliant plumbing fixtures prior to July 1, 2009, shall be exempt from the requirements of this article so long as the ordinance remains in effect. *(Added by Stats.2009, c. 587 (S.B.407), § 1.)*

ARTICLE 1.5. DISCLOSURES UPON TRANSFER OF RESIDENTIAL PROPERTY

Section
- 1102. Application of article; definitions; waiver of requirements.
- 1102.1. Legislative intent; effect of 2018 legislation on duties of real estate professionals.
- 1102.2. Nonapplication of article.
- 1102.3. Delivery of required written statement from seller to buyer; indication of compliance with article; disclosures delivered after execution of offer to purchase; time to terminate.
- 1102.3a. Manufactured home or mobilehome; delivery of statement by transferor; termination of offer.
- 1102.4. Errors, inaccuracies, or omissions of information delivered; liability of seller, seller's agent or buyer's agent; delivery of information by public agency; delivery of reports or opinions prepared by experts.
- 1102.5. Information subsequently rendered inaccurate; required information unknown or not available; application of article requirements.
- 1102.6. Disclosure form.
- 1102.6a. Disclosure form.
- 1102.6b. Disclosure to prospective buyer of continuing lien securing special tax levy, fixed lien assessments, or contractual assessment program; satisfaction of disclosure notice requirements.
- 1102.6c. Seller's notice of supplemental property tax bill; requirements.
- 1102.6d. Manufactured home and mobilehome transfer disclosure statement.
- 1102.6e. Transfer fee disclosure statement; requirements.
- 1102.6f. Disclosure to prospective buyer that property is located in high or very high fire hazard severity zone; statement; retrofits; features; final inspection report; building code formulation.
- 1102.6g. Notice of unbiased property appraisal requirement.
- 1102.7. Good faith required.
- 1102.8. Specification of items for disclosure not limitation on other disclosure obligations.
- 1102.9. Amendment of disclosures.
- 1102.10. Delivery of disclosures; personal delivery or mail.
- 1102.11. Escrow agent not deemed agent for purposes of disclosure; exception.
- 1102.12. Licensed real estate brokers as agents in transaction; delivery of disclosure; advising transferee of rights to disclosure; record.
- 1102.13. Failure to comply with article; transfer not invalidated; damages.
- 1102.14. Repealed.
- 1102.15. Former federal or state ordnance locations; definition.
- 1102.155. Water-conserving plumbing fixture requirement; noncompliant plumbing fixtures.
- 1102.16. Window security bars and safety release mechanism; disclosure.
- 1102.17. Sellers of residential real property; written notice of knowledge of property with respect to industrial use.
- 1102.18. Application of Section 1102.1 (d).
- 1102.19. Disclosure of compliance with Section 4291 of Public Resources Code; local vegetation ordinances; property located in high or very high fire hazard severity zone; agreement to obtain documentation of compliance; enforcement of defensible space requirements.

Cross References

Manufactured homes or mobilehomes, transfer or sale subject to disclosure requirements under this Article, see Civil Code § 798.74.4.

Real estate regulations, investigation of alleged violations of certain provisions concerned with disclosures upon certain transfers of real estate, suspension or revocation of license, see Business and Professions Code § 10176.5.

§ 1102. Application of article; definitions; waiver of requirements

(a) Except as provided in Section 1102.2, this article applies to any transfer by sale, exchange, real property sales contract as defined in Section 2985, lease with an option to purchase, any other option to purchase, or ground lease coupled with improvements of any single-family residential property.

(b) For purposes of this article, the definitions contained in Chapter 1 (commencing with Section 10000) of Part 1 of Division 4 of the Business and Professions Code shall apply.

(c) Any waiver of the requirements of this article is void as against public policy. *(Added by Stats.1985, c. 1574, § 2, operative Jan. 1, 1987. Amended by Stats.1986, c. 460, § 1; Stats.1994, c. 817 (S.B.1377), § 1; Stats.1995, c. 335 (A.B. 530), § 1; Stats.1996, c. 677 (S.B.1704), § 1; Stats.1997, c. 71 (S.B.384), § 1, eff. July 14, 1997; Stats.1998, c. 693 (S.B.1988), § 1; Stats.1999, c. 517 (S.B.534), § 2; Stats.2018, c. 907 (A.B.1289), § 7, eff. Jan. 1, 2019; Stats.2019, c. 310 (A.B.892), § 3, eff. Jan. 1, 2020.)*

Cross References

Contracts for sale, required notice, gas and hazardous liquid transmission pipelines, see Civil Code § 2079.10.5.

Real property defined for purposes of this Code, see Civil Code § 658.

Used manufactured homes offered for sale, inspection and disclosure duties, see Health and Safety Code § 18046.

§ 1102.1. Legislative intent; effect of 2018 legislation on duties of real estate professionals

(a) In enacting Chapter 817 of the Statutes of 1994, it was the intent of the Legislature to clarify and facilitate the use of the real estate disclosure statement, as specified in Section 1102.6. The Legislature intended the statement to be used by transferors making disclosures required under this article and by agents making disclosures required by Section 2079 on the agent's portion of the real estate disclosure statement, in transfers subject to this article. In transfers not subject to this article, agents may make required disclosures in a separate writing. The Legislature did not intend to affect the existing obligations of the parties to a real estate contract, or their agents, to disclose any fact materially affecting the value and desirability of the property, including, but not limited to, the physical conditions of the property and previously received reports of physical inspections noted on the disclosure form set forth in Section 1102.6 or 1102.6a, and that nothing in this article shall be construed to change the duty of a real estate broker or salesperson pursuant to Section 2079.

It is also the intent of the Legislature that the delivery of a real estate transfer disclosure statement may not be waived in an "as is" sale, as held in Loughrin v. Superior Court (1993) 15 Cal. App. 4th 1188.

(b) In enacting Chapter 677 of the Statutes of 1996, it was the intent of the Legislature to clarify and facilitate the use of the manufactured home and mobilehome transfer disclosure statement applicable to the resale of a manufactured home or mobilehome pursuant to subdivision (b) of Section 1102. The Legislature intended the statements to be used by transferors making disclosures required under this article and by agents making disclosures required by Section 2079 on the agent's portion of the disclosure statement and as required by Section 18046 of the Health and Safety Code on the dealer's portion of the manufactured home and mobilehome transfer disclosure statement, in transfers subject to this article. In transfers not subject to this article, agents may make required disclosures in a separate writing. The Legislature did not intend to affect the existing obligations of the parties to a real estate contract, or their agents, to disclose any fact materially affecting the value and desirability of the property, including, but not limited to, the physical conditions of the property and previously received reports of physical inspections noted on the disclosure form set forth in Section 1102.6 or 1102.6a or to affect the existing obligations of the parties to a manufactured home or mobilehome purchase contract, and nothing in this article shall be construed to change the duty of a real estate broker or salesperson pursuant to Section 2079 or the duty of a manufactured home or mobilehome dealer or salesperson pursuant to Section 18046 of the Health and Safety Code.

It is also the intent of the Legislature that the delivery of a mobilehome transfer disclosure statement may not be waived in an "as is" sale.

(c) It is the intent of the Legislature that manufactured home and mobilehome dealers and salespersons and real estate brokers and salespersons use the form provided pursuant to Section 1102.6d. It is also the intent of the Legislature for sellers of manufactured homes or mobilehomes who are neither manufactured home dealers or salespersons nor real estate brokers or salespersons to use the Manufactured Home/Mobilehome Transfer Disclosure Statement contained in Section 1102.6d.

(d) Nothing in Assembly Bill 1289 of the 2017–18 Regular Session [1] or Assembly Bill 2884 of the 2017–18 Regular Session [2] shall be construed to affect any of the following:

(1) A real estate broker's duties under existing statutory or common law as an agent of a person who retains that broker to perform acts for which a license is required under this division.

(2) Any fiduciary duties owed by a real estate broker to a person who retains that broker to perform acts for which a license is required under this division.

(3) Any duty of disclosure or any other duties or obligations of a real estate broker, which arise under this division or other existing, applicable California law, including common law.

(4) Any duties or obligations of a salesperson or a broker associate, which arise under this division or existing, applicable California law, including common law, and duties and obligations to the salesperson's or broker associate's responsible broker.

(5) A responsible broker's duty of supervision and oversight for the acts of retained salespersons or broker associates, which arise under this division or other existing, applicable California law, including common law.

For purposes of this subdivision, references to "existing statutory law" and "existing, applicable California law" refer to the law as it read immediately prior to enactment of Assembly Bill 1289 of the 2017–18 Regular Session and Assembly Bill 2884 of the 2017–18 Regular Session. *(Added by Stats.1995, c. 335 (A.B.530), § 2. Amended by Stats.1996, c. 240 (A.B.2383), § 1; Stats.1999, c. 517 (S.B.534), § 3; Stats.2018, c. 907 (A.B.1289), § 8, eff. Jan. 1, 2019.)*

[1] Stats.2018, c. 907.
[2] Stats.2018, c. 285.

Cross References

Obligation defined, see Civil Code § 1427.

§ 1102.2. Nonapplication of article

This article does not apply to the following:

(a) Sales or transfers that are required to be preceded by the furnishing to a prospective buyer of a copy of a public report pursuant to Section 11018.1 of the Business and Professions Code and transfers that can be made without a public report pursuant to Section 11010.4 of the Business and Professions Code.

(b) Sales or transfers pursuant to court order, including, but not limited to, sales ordered by a probate court in the

§ 1102.2

administration of an estate, sales pursuant to a writ of execution, sales by any foreclosure sale, transfers by a trustee in bankruptcy, sales by eminent domain, and sales resulting from a decree for specific performance.

(c) Sales or transfers to a mortgagee by a mortgagor or successor in interest who is in default, sales to a beneficiary of a deed of trust by a trustor or successor in interest who is in default, any foreclosure sale after default, any foreclosure sale after default in an obligation secured by a mortgage, a sale under a power of sale or any foreclosure sale under a decree of foreclosure after default in an obligation secured by a deed of trust or secured by any other instrument containing a power of sale, sales by a mortgagee or a beneficiary under a deed of trust who has acquired the real property at a sale conducted pursuant to a power of sale under a mortgage or deed of trust or a sale pursuant to a decree of foreclosure or has acquired the real property by a deed in lieu of foreclosure, sales to the legal owner or lienholder of a manufactured home or mobilehome by a registered owner or successor in interest who is in default, or sales by reason of any foreclosure of a security interest in a manufactured home or mobilehome.

(d) Sales or transfers by a fiduciary in the course of the administration of a trust, guardianship, conservatorship, or decedent's estate. This exemption shall not apply to a sale if the trustee is a natural person who is a trustee of a revocable trust and is a former owner of the property or was an occupant in possession of the property within the preceding year.

(e) Sales or transfers from one coowner to one or more other coowners.

(f) Sales or transfers made to a spouse, or to a person or persons in the line of consanguinity of one or more of the transferors.

(g) Sales or transfers between spouses resulting from a judgment of dissolution of marriage or of legal separation or from a property settlement agreement incidental to that judgment.

(h) Sales or transfers by the Controller in the course of administering Chapter 7 (commencing with Section 1500) of Title 10 of Part 3 of the Code of Civil Procedure.

(i) Sales or transfers under Chapter 7 (commencing with Section 3691) or Chapter 8 (commencing with Section 3771) of Part 6 of Division 1 of the Revenue and Taxation Code.

(j) Sales or transfers or exchanges to or from any governmental entity.

(k) Sales or transfers of any portion of a property not constituting single-family residential property.

(*l*) The sale, creation, or transfer of any lease of any duration with the exception of a lease with an option to purchase or a ground lease coupled with improvements.

(m) Notwithstanding the definition of sale in Section 10018.10 of the Business and Professions Code and Section 2079.13, the terms "sale" and "transfer," as they are used in this section, shall have their commonly understood meanings. The changes made to this section by Assembly Bill 1289 of the 2017–18 Legislative Session [1] shall not be interpreted to change the application of the law as it read prior to January 1, 2019. *(Formerly § 1102.1, added by Stats.1985, c. 1574, § 2, operative Jan. 1, 1987. Amended by Stats.1986, c. 460, § 2; Stats.1992, c. 163 (A.B.2641), § 7, operative Jan. 1, 1994. Renumbered § 1102.2 and amended by Stats.1995, c. 335 (A.B.530), § 3. Amended by Stats.1999, c. 119 (A.B.594), § 1; Stats.1999, c. 517 (S.B.534), § 4.5; Stats.2000, c. 135 (A.B. 2539), § 11; Stats.2018, c. 907 (A.B.1289), § 9, eff. Jan. 1, 2019; Stats.2019, c. 497 (A.B.991), § 20, eff. Jan. 1, 2020; Stats.2019, c. 310 (A.B.892), § 4, eff. Jan. 1, 2020; Stats.2020, c. 370 (S.B.1371), § 24, eff. Jan. 1, 2021.)*

[1] Stats.2018, c. 907.

Cross References

Common interest developments, rental or leasing of separate interests, provisions in governing documents, see Civil Code § 4740.
Obligation defined, see Civil Code § 1427.
Private works of improvement, recordation of notice of completion or cessation, exclusion for certain persons with a security interest under this section, see Civil Code § 8190.
Real property defined for purposes of this Code, see Civil Code § 658.
State Controller, generally, see Government Code § 12402 et seq.
Used manufactured homes offered for sale, inspection and disclosure duties, see Health and Safety Code § 18046.

§ 1102.3. Delivery of required written statement from seller to buyer; indication of compliance with article; disclosures delivered after execution of offer to purchase; time to terminate

The seller of any single-family real property subject to this article shall deliver to the prospective buyer the completed written statement required by this article, as follows:

(a) In the case of a sale, as soon as practicable before transfer of title.

(b) In the case of sale by a real property sales contract, as defined in Section 2985, or by a lease together with an option to purchase, or a ground lease coupled with improvements, as soon as practicable before execution of the contract. For the purpose of this subdivision, "execution" means the making or acceptance of an offer.

(c) With respect to any sale subject to subdivision (a) or (b), the seller shall indicate compliance with this article on the real property sales contract, the lease, or any addendum attached thereto or on a separate document.

If any disclosure, or any material amendment of any disclosure, required to be made by this article, is delivered after the execution of an offer to purchase, the prospective buyer shall have three days after delivery in person, five days after delivery by deposit in the mail, or five days after delivery of an electronic record in transactions where the parties have agreed to conduct the transaction by electronic means, pursuant to provisions of the Uniform Electronic Transactions Act (Title 2.5 (commencing with Section 1633.1) of Part 2 of Division 3), to terminate the offer by delivery of a written notice of termination to the seller or the seller's agent. The period of time the prospective buyer has in which to terminate the offer commences when Sections I and II, and, if the seller is represented by an agent in the transaction, then also Section III, in the form described in Section 1102.6, are completed and delivered to the buyer or buyer's agent. A real estate agent may complete their own portion of the required disclosure by providing all of the information on the agent's inspection disclosure set forth in Section 1102.6. *(Formerly § 1102.2, added by Stats.1985, c. 1574, § 2, operative Jan. 1, 1987. Amended by Stats.1986, c. 460, § 3. Renumbered § 1102.3 and amended by Stats.1995, c. 335 (A.B.530), § 4. Amended by Stats.2018, c. 907 (A.B.1289), § 10, eff. Jan. 1, 2019; Stats.2019, c. 497 (A.B.991), § 21, eff. Jan. 1, 2020; Stats.2019, c. 310 (A.B.892), § 5, eff. Jan. 1, 2020.)*

Cross References

Methamphetamine Contaminated Property Cleanup Act of 2005, see Health and Safety Code § 25400.10 et seq.

Methamphetamine Contaminated Property Cleanup Act of 2005, site assessment and remediation, duties of property owner while waiting to hear that no further action is required, see Health and Safety Code § 25400.28.

Real property defined for purposes of this Code, see Civil Code § 658.

§ 1102.3a. Manufactured home or mobilehome; delivery of statement by transferor; termination of offer

(a) The transferor of any manufactured home or mobilehome subject to this article shall deliver to the prospective transferee the written statement required by this article, as follows:

(1) In the case of a sale, or a lease with an option to purchase, of a manufactured home or mobilehome, involving an agent, as defined in Section 18046 of the Health and Safety Code, as soon as practicable, but no later than the close of escrow for the purchase of the manufactured home or mobilehome.

(2) In the case of a sale, or lease with an option to purchase, of a manufactured home or mobilehome, not involving an agent, as defined in Section 18046 of the Health and Safety Code, at the time of execution of any document by the prospective transferee with the transferor for the purchase of the manufactured home or mobilehome.

(b) With respect to any transfer subject to this section, the transferor shall indicate compliance with this article either on the transfer disclosure statement, any addendum thereto, or on a separate document.

(c) If any disclosure, or any material amendment of any disclosure, required to be made pursuant to subdivision (b) of Section 1102, is delivered after the execution of an offer to purchase, the transferee shall have three days after delivery in person or five days after delivery by deposit in the mail, to terminate his or her offer by delivery of a written notice of termination to the transferor. *(Added by Stats.1999, c. 517 (S.B.534), § 5.)*

Cross References

Methamphetamine Contaminated Property Cleanup Act of 2005, see Health and Safety Code § 25400.10 et seq.

Methamphetamine Contaminated Property Cleanup Act of 2005, site assessment and remediation, duties of property owner while waiting to hear that no further action is required, see Health and Safety Code § 25400.28.

§ 1102.4. Errors, inaccuracies, or omissions of information delivered; liability of seller, seller's agent or buyer's agent; delivery of information by public agency; delivery of reports or opinions prepared by experts

(a) Neither the seller nor any seller's agent or buyer's agent shall be liable for any error, inaccuracy, or omission of any information delivered pursuant to this article if the error, inaccuracy, or omission was not within the personal knowledge of the seller or that listing or buyer's agent, was based on information timely provided by public agencies or by other persons providing information as specified in subdivision (c) that is required to be disclosed pursuant to this article, and ordinary care was exercised in obtaining and transmitting it.

(b) The delivery of any information required to be disclosed by this article to a prospective buyer by a public agency or other person providing information required to be disclosed pursuant to this article shall be deemed to comply with the requirements of this article and shall relieve the seller or any listing or buyer's agent of any further duty under this article with respect to that item of information.

(c) The delivery of a report or opinion prepared by a licensed engineer, land surveyor, geologist, structural pest control operator, contractor, a C–39 roofing contractor conducting a roof inspection pursuant to subdivision (d) of Section 7197 of the Business and Professions Code, or other expert, dealing with matters within the scope of the professional's license or expertise, shall be sufficient compliance for application of the exemption provided by subdivision (a) if the information is provided to the prospective buyer pursuant to a request therefor, whether written or oral. In responding to such a request, an expert may indicate, in writing, an understanding that the information provided will be used in fulfilling the requirements of Section 1102.6 and, if so, shall indicate the required disclosures, or parts thereof, to which the information being furnished is applicable. Where such a statement is furnished, the expert shall not be responsible for any items of information or parts thereof, other than those expressly set forth in the statement. *(Added by Stats.1985, c. 1574, § 2, operative Jan. 1, 1987. Amended by Stats.1986, c. 460, § 4; Stats.2017, c. 508 (A.B.1357), § 2, eff. Jan. 1, 2018; Stats.2018, c. 907 (A.B.1289), § 11, eff. Jan. 1, 2019.)*

§ 1102.5. Information subsequently rendered inaccurate; required information unknown or not available; application of article requirements

(a) If information disclosed in accordance with this article is subsequently rendered inaccurate as a result of any act, occurrence, or agreement subsequent to the delivery of the required disclosures, any inaccuracy resulting therefrom does not constitute a violation of this article. If at the time the disclosures are required to be made, an item of information required to be disclosed is unknown or not available to the seller, and the seller or * * * the seller's agent has made a

§ 1102.5

reasonable effort to ascertain it, the seller may use an approximation of the information, provided the approximation is clearly identified as such, is reasonable, is based on the best information reasonably available to the seller or * * * the seller's agent, and is not used for the purpose of circumventing or evading this article.

(b) The requirements of this article in effect on the date that all of the parties enter into a contract or agreement subject to this article are the requirements that shall apply to that contract or agreement. An amendment to this article that becomes effective after that date does not alter the requirements under this article that shall apply to that contract or agreement, unless the applicable statute provides otherwise. *(Added by Stats.1985, c. 1574, § 2, operative Jan. 1, 1987. Amended by Stats.2018, c. 907 (A.B.1289), § 12, eff. Jan. 1, 2019; Stats.2022, c. 420 (A.B.2960), § 9, eff. Jan. 1, 2023.)*

§ 1102.6. Disclosure form

(a) The disclosures required by this article pertaining to the property proposed to be transferred are set forth in, and shall be made on a copy of, the following disclosure form:

REAL ESTATE TRANSFER DISCLOSURE STATEMENT

THIS DISCLOSURE STATEMENT CONCERNS THE REAL PROPERTY SITUATED IN THE CITY OF _____, COUNTY OF _____, STATE OF CALIFORNIA, DESCRIBED AS _____
_____. THIS STATEMENT IS A DISCLOSURE OF THE CONDITION OF THE ABOVE DESCRIBED PROPERTY IN COMPLIANCE WITH SECTION 1102 OF THE CIVIL CODE AS OF _____, 20___. IT IS NOT A WARRANTY OF ANY KIND BY THE SELLER(S) OR ANY AGENT(S) REPRESENTING ANY PRINCIPAL(S) IN THIS TRANSACTION, AND IS NOT A SUBSTITUTE FOR ANY INSPECTIONS OR WARRANTIES THE PRINCIPAL(S) MAY WISH TO OBTAIN.

I

COORDINATION WITH OTHER DISCLOSURE FORMS

This Real Estate Transfer Disclosure Statement is made pursuant to Section 1102 of the Civil Code. Other statutes require disclosures, depending upon the details of the particular real estate transaction (for example: special study zone and purchase-money liens on residential property).

Substituted Disclosures: The following disclosures and other disclosures required by law, including the Natural Hazard Disclosure Report/Statement that may include airport annoyances, earthquake, fire, flood, or special assessment information, have or will be made in connection with this real estate transfer, and are intended to satisfy the disclosure obligations on this form, where the subject matter is the same:

☐ Inspection reports completed pursuant to the contract of sale or receipt for deposit.

☐ Additional inspection reports or disclosures:
_____
_____

☐ *No substituted disclosures for this transfer.*

II

SELLER'S INFORMATION

The Seller discloses the following information with the knowledge that even though this is not a warranty, prospective Buyers may rely on this information in deciding whether and on what terms to purchase the subject property. Seller hereby authorizes any agent(s) representing any principal(s) in this transaction to provide a copy of this statement to any person or entity in connection with any actual or anticipated sale of the property.

THE FOLLOWING ARE REPRESENTATIONS MADE BY THE SELLER(S) AND ARE NOT THE REPRESENTATIONS OF THE AGENT(S), IF ANY. THIS INFORMATION IS A DISCLOSURE AND IS NOT INTENDED TO BE PART OF ANY CONTRACT BETWEEN THE BUYER AND SELLER:

ACQUISITION OF PROPERTY § 1102.6

Seller ___is ___is not occupying the property.
A. The subject property has the items checked below (read across):*

___Range
___Dishwasher
___Washer/Dryer Hookups
___Burglar Alarms
___TV Antenna
___Central Heating
___Wall/Window Air Cndtng.
___Septic Tank
___Patio/Decking
___Sauna
___Hot Tub___Locking Safety Cover
___Security Gate(s)

Garage:___Attached
Pool/Spa Heater: ___Gas
Water Heater: ___Gas

Water Supply: ___City
Gas Supply: ___Utility
___Window Screens

___Oven
___Trash Compactor

___Carbon Monoxide Device(s)
___Satellite Dish
___Central Air Cndtng.
___Sprinklers
___Sump Pump
___Built-in Barbecue

___Pool ___Child Resistant Barrier
___Automatic Garage Door Opener(s)
___Not Attached
___Solar

___Well
___Bottled
___Window Security Bars___Quick-Release Mechanism on Bedroom Windows

___Microwave
___Garbage Disposal
___Rain Gutters
___Fire Alarm
___Intercom
___Evaporator Cooler(s)
___Public Sewer System
___Water Softener
___Gazebo

___Spa___Locking Safety Cover
___Number Remote Controls
___Carport
___Electric
___Private Utility or Other_____

___Water-conserving plumbing fixtures

Exhaust Fan(s) in _____ 220 Volt Wiring in _____ Fireplace(s) in _____
Gas Starter _____ Roof(s): Type: _____ Age: _____ (approx.)
Other:_____
Are there, to the best of your (Seller's) knowledge, any of the above that are not in operating condition? ___Yes ___No. If yes, then describe.
(Attach additional sheets if necessary): _____
_____
_____

B. Are you (Seller) aware of any significant defects/malfunctions in any of the following?
___Yes ___No. If yes, check appropriate space(s) below.
___Interior Walls ___Ceilings ___Floors ___Exterior Walls ___Insulation ___Roof(s)
___Windows ___Doors ___Foundation ___Slab(s) ___Driveways ___Sidewalks
___Walls/Fences ___Electrical Systems ___Plumbing/Sewers/Septics ___Other Structural Components (Describe: _____
_____)
If any of the above is checked, explain. (Attach additional sheets if necessary):_____
_____
_____

* Installation of a listed appliance, device, or amenity is not a precondition of sale or transfer of the dwelling. The carbon monoxide device, garage door opener, or child-resistant pool barrier may not be in compliance with the safety standards relating to, respectively, carbon monoxide device standards of Chapter 8 (commencing with Section 13260) of Part 2 of Division 12 of, automatic reversing device standards of Chapter 12.5 (commencing with Section 19890) of Part 3 of Division 13 of, or the pool safety standards of Article 2.5 (commencing with Section 115920) of Chapter 5 of Part 10 of Division 104 of, the Health and Safety Code. Window security bars may not have quick-release mechanisms in compliance with the 1995 edition of the California Building Standards Code. Section 1101.4 of the Civil Code requires all single-family residences built on or before January 1, 1994, to be equipped with water-conserving plumbing fixtures after January 1, 2017. Additionally, on and after January 1, 2014, a single-family residence built on or before January 1, 1994, that is altered or improved is required to be equipped with water-conserving plumbing fixtures as a condition of final approval. Fixtures in this dwelling may not comply with Section 1101.4 of the Civil Code.

§ 1102.6   PROPERTY

C. Are you (Seller) aware of any of the following:
1. Substances, materials, or products which may be an environmental hazard such as, but not limited to, asbestos, formaldehyde, radon gas, lead-based paint, mold, fuel or chemical storage tanks, and contaminated soil or water on the subject property .... __Yes __No
2. Features of the property shared in common with adjoining landowners, such as walls, fences, and driveways, whose use or responsibility for maintenance may have an effect on the subject property .... __Yes __No
3. Any encroachments, easements or similar matters that may affect your interest in the subject property .... __Yes __No
4. Room additions, structural modifications, or other alterations or repairs made without necessary permits.. __Yes __No
5. Room additions, structural modifications, or other alterations or repairs not in compliance with building codes... __Yes __No
6. Fill (compacted or otherwise) on the property or any portion thereof .... __Yes __No
7. Any settling from any cause, or slippage, sliding, or other soil problems .... __Yes __No
8. Flooding, drainage or grading problems .... __Yes __No
9. Major damage to the property or any of the structures from fire, earthquake, floods, or landslides .... __Yes __No
10. Any zoning violations, nonconforming uses, violations of "setback" requirements .... __Yes __No
11. Neighborhood noise problems or other nuisances .... __Yes __No
12. CC&Rs or other deed restrictions or obligations .... __Yes __No
13. Homeowners' Association which has any authority over the subject property .... __Yes __No
14. Any "common area" (facilities such as pools, tennis courts, walkways, or other areas co-owned in undivided interest with others)... __Yes __No
15. Any notices of abatement or citations against the property... __Yes __No
16. Any lawsuits by or against the Seller threatening to or affecting this real property, claims for damages by the Seller pursuant to Section 910 or 914 of the Civil Code threatening to or affecting this real property, claims for breach of warranty pursuant to Section 900 of the Civil Code threatening to or affecting this real property, or claims for breach of an enhanced protection agreement pursuant to Section 903 of the Civil Code threatening to or affecting this real property, including any lawsuits or claims for damages pursuant to Section 910 or 914 of the Civil Code alleging a defect or deficiency in this real property or "common areas" (facilities such as pools, tennis courts, walkways, or other areas co-owned in undivided interest with others)................... __Yes __No

If the answer to any of these is yes, explain. (Attach additional sheets if necessary.): _____
_____

D. 1. The Seller certifies that the property, as of the close of escrow, will be in compliance with Section 13113.8 of the Health and Safety Code by having

278

ACQUISITION OF PROPERTY § 1102.6

  operable smoke detectors(s) which are approved, listed, and installed in accordance with the State Fire Marshal's regulations and applicable local standards.
 2. The Seller certifies that the property, as of the close of escrow, will be in compliance with Section 19211 of the Health and Safety Code by having the water heater tank(s) braced, anchored, or strapped in place in accordance with applicable law.

Seller certifies that the information herein is true and correct to the best of the Seller's knowledge as of the date signed by the Seller.

Seller _____ Date _____
Seller _____ Date _____

III

AGENT'S INSPECTION DISCLOSURE

(To be completed only if the Seller is represented by an agent in this transaction.)

THE UNDERSIGNED, BASED ON THE ABOVE INQUIRY OF THE SELLER(S) AS TO THE CONDITION OF THE PROPERTY AND BASED ON A REASONABLY COMPETENT AND DILIGENT VISUAL INSPECTION OF THE ACCESSIBLE AREAS OF THE PROPERTY IN CONJUNCTION WITH THAT INQUIRY, STATES THE FOLLOWING:

☐ Agent notes no items for disclosure.

☐ Agent notes the following items:
_____
_____
_____
_____

Agent (Broker
Representing Seller) _____ By _____ Date _____
         (Please Print)   (Associate Licensee
                or Broker Signature)

IV
AGENT'S INSPECTION DISCLOSURE

(To be completed only if the agent who has obtained the offer is other than the agent above.)

THE UNDERSIGNED, BASED ON A REASONABLY COMPETENT AND DILIGENT VISUAL INSPECTION OF THE ACCESSIBLE AREAS OF THE PROPERTY, STATES THE FOLLOWING:

☐ Agent notes no items for disclosure.

☐ Agent notes the following items:
_____
_____
_____

Agent (Broker
Obtaining the Offer) _____ By _____ Date _____
                 (Please Print)   (Associate Licensee
                                   or Broker Signature)

V

BUYER(S) AND SELLER(S) MAY WISH TO OBTAIN PROFESSIONAL ADVICE AND/OR INSPECTIONS OF THE PROPERTY AND TO PROVIDE FOR APPROPRIATE PROVISIONS IN A CONTRACT BETWEEN BUYER(S) AND SELLER(S) WITH RESPECT TO ANY ADVICE/INSPECTIONS/DEFECTS.

I/WE ACKNOWLEDGE RECEIPT OF A COPY OF THIS STATEMENT.

Seller _____ Date _____ Buyer _____ Date _____
Seller _____ Date _____ Buyer _____ Date _____

Agent (Broker
Representing Seller) _____ By _____ Date _____
                (Please Print)   (Associate Licensee
                                  or Broker Signature)

Agent (Broker
Obtaining the Offer) _____ By _____ Date _____
                 (Please Print)   (Associate Licensee
                                   or Broker Signature)

SECTION 1102.3 OF THE CIVIL CODE PROVIDES A BUYER WITH THE RIGHT TO RESCIND A PURCHASE CONTRACT FOR AT LEAST THREE DAYS AFTER THE DELIVERY OF THIS DISCLOSURE IF DELIVERY OCCURS AFTER THE SIGNING OF AN OFFER TO PURCHASE. IF YOU WISH TO RESCIND THE CONTRACT, YOU MUST ACT WITHIN THE PRESCRIBED PERIOD.

A REAL ESTATE BROKER IS QUALIFIED TO ADVISE ON REAL ESTATE. IF YOU DESIRE LEGAL ADVICE, CONSULT YOUR ATTORNEY.

(b) The amendments to this section by the act adding this subdivision [1] shall become operative on July 1, 2014. (Added by Stats.1985, c. 1574, § 2, operative Jan. 1, 1987. Amended by Stats.1986, c. 460, § 5; Stats.1989, c. 171, § 1; Stats.1990, c. 1336 (A.B.3600), § 2, operative July 1, 1991; Stats.1994, c. 817 (S.B.1377), § 2; Stats.1996, c. 240 (A.B.2383), § 2; Stats.1996, c. 925 (A.B.3305), § 1; Stats.1996, c. 926 (A.B. 3026), § 1.5, operative July 1, 1997; Stats.2001, c. 584 (S.B.732), § 1; Stats.2002, c. 664 (A.B.3034), § 35; Stats. 2002, c. 496 (A.B.2776), § 3, operative Jan. 1, 2004; Stats. 2003, c. 62 (S.B.600), § 13; Stats.2010, c. 19 (S.B.183), § 1; Stats.2011, c. 61 (S.B.837), § 1; Stats.2013, c. 431 (S.B.652), § 1, operative July 1, 2014; Stats.2014, c. 71 (S.B.1304), § 15, eff. Jan. 1, 2015; Stats.2019, c. 310 (A.B.892), § 6, eff. Jan. 1, 2020; Stats.2020, c. 370 (S.B.1371), § 25, eff. Jan. 1, 2021.)

[1] Stats.2013, c. 431 (S.B.652).

Cross References

Automatic garage door openers, violations, civil penalties, see Health and Safety Code § 19891.

Common interest developments, rental or leasing of separate interests, provisions in governing documents, see Civil Code § 4740.

Financial affairs, preparation of current tax roll of assessment obligations, see Government Code § 53754.

Mello–Roos Community Facilities Act of 1982, special tax levies, notice of special tax, see Government Code § 53340.2.

Obligation defined, see Civil Code § 1427.

Real property defined for purposes of this Code, see Civil Code § 658.

Toxic mold, disclosures, see Health and Safety Code § 26150.

Toxic Mold Protection Act of 2001, see Health and Safety Code § 26100 et seq.

Water heater strapping, certification of earthquake resistance, see Health and Safety Code § 19211.

Window security bars, safety release mechanisms, disclosure, see Health and Safety Code § 17958.4.

§ 1102.6a. Disclosure form

(a) On and after July 1, 1990, any city or county may elect to require disclosures on the form set forth in subdivision (b) in addition to those disclosures required by Section 1102.6. However, this section does not affect or limit the authority of a city or county to require disclosures on a different disclosure form in connection with transactions subject to this article pursuant to an ordinance adopted prior to July 1, 1990. An ordinance like this adopted prior to July 1, 1990, may be amended thereafter to revise the disclosure requirements of the ordinance, in the discretion of the city council or county board of supervisors.

(b) Disclosures required pursuant to this section pertaining to the property proposed to be sold, shall be set forth in, and shall be made on a copy of, the following disclosure form:

§ 1102.6a   **PROPERTY**

LOCAL OPTION

REAL ESTATE TRANSFER DISCLOSURE STATEMENT

THIS DISCLOSURE STATEMENT CONCERNS THE REAL PROPERTY SITUATED IN THE CITY OF _____, COUNTY OF _____, STATE OF CALIFORNIA, DESCRIBED AS _____. THIS STATEMENT IS A DISCLOSURE OF THE CONDITION OF THE ABOVE-DESCRIBED PROPERTY IN COMPLIANCE WITH ORDINANCE NO. _____ OF THE _____ CITY OR COUNTY CODE AS OF _____, 20 _____. IT IS NOT A WARRANTY OF ANY KIND BY THE SELLER(S) OR ANY REAL ESTATE LICENSEE(S) REPRESENTING ANY PRINCIPAL(S) IN THIS TRANSACTION, AND IS NOT A SUBSTITUTE FOR ANY INSPECTIONS OR WARRANTIES THE PRINCIPAL(S) MAY WISH TO OBTAIN.

I

SELLER'S INFORMATION

The Seller discloses the following information with the knowledge that even though this is not a warranty, prospective Buyers may rely on this information in deciding whether and on what terms to purchase the subject property. Seller hereby authorizes any real estate licensee(s) representing any principal(s) in this transaction to provide a copy of this statement to any person or entity in connection with any actual or anticipated sale of the property.

ACQUISITION OF PROPERTY § 1102.6a

THE FOLLOWING ARE REPRESENTATIONS MADE BY THE SELLER(S) AS REQUIRED BY THE CITY OR COUNTY OF _____, AND ARE NOT THE REPRESENTATIONS OF THE REAL ESTATE LICENSEE(S), IF ANY. THIS INFORMATION IS A DISCLOSURE AND IS NOT INTENDED TO BE PART OF ANY CONTRACT BETWEEN THE BUYER AND SELLER.

1. _____
_____
_____
_____

2. _____
_____
_____
_____

(Example: Adjacent land is zoned for timber production which may be subject to harvest.)

Seller certifies that the information herein is true and correct to the best of the Seller's knowledge as of the date signed by the Seller.

Seller _____ Date _____
Seller _____ Date _____

II

BUYER(S) MAY WISH TO OBTAIN PROFESSIONAL ADVICE AND/OR INSPECTIONS OF THE PROPERTY AND TO PROVIDE FOR APPROPRIATE PROVISIONS IN A CONTRACT BETWEEN BUYER AND SELLER(S) WITH RESPECT TO ANY ADVICE/INSPECTIONS/DEFECTS.

I/WE ACKNOWLEDGE RECEIPT OF A COPY OF THIS STATEMENT.

Buyer_____ Date_____
Buyer_____ Date_____

A REAL ESTATE BROKER IS QUALIFIED TO ADVISE ON REAL ESTATE. IF YOU DESIRE LEGAL ADVICE, CONSULT YOUR ATTORNEY.

(c) This section does not preclude the use of addenda to the form specified in subdivision (b) to facilitate the required disclosures. This section does not preclude a city or county from using the disclosure form specified in subdivision (b) for a purpose other than that specified in this section.

(d)(1) On and after January 1, 2005, if a city or county adopts a different or additional disclosure form pursuant to this section regarding the proximity or effects of an airport, the statement in that form shall contain, at a minimum, the information in the statement "Notice of Airport in Vicinity" found in Section 11010 of the Business and Professions Code, or Section 1103.4 or 4255.

(2) On and after January 1, 2006, if a city or county does not adopt a different or additional disclosure form pursuant

§ 1102.6a

to this section, then the provision of an "airport influence area" disclosure pursuant to Section 11010 of the Business and Professions Code, or Section 1103.4 or 4255, or if there is not a current airport influence map, a written disclosure of an airport within two statute miles, shall be deemed to satisfy any city or county requirements for the disclosure of airports in connection with sales of real property. *(Added by Stats. 1989, c. 171, § 2. Amended by Stats.2004, c. 66 (A.B.920), § 1; Stats.2012, c. 181 (A.B.806), § 33, operative Jan. 1, 2014; Stats.2018, c. 907 (A.B.1289), § 13, eff. Jan. 1, 2019.)*

Cross References

California Emergency Services Act, flooding, disclosure to potential transferee, see Government Code § 8589.4.

California Emergency Services Act, property within special flood hazard area, disclosure to prospective transferee, see Government Code § 8589.3.

Earthquake fault zoning, disclosure of property location by transferor or agent, see Public Resources Code § 2621.9.

Forest fires, responsibility for fire protection, real property located within state responsibility area, disclosures, see Public Resources Code § 4136.

Property within a very high fire hazard severity zone, disclosure to prospective transferee, see Government Code § 51183.5.

Real property defined for purposes of this Code, see Civil Code § 658.

Seismic hazards mapping, disclosure of property location by transferor or agent, see Public Resources Code § 2694.

Toxic mold, disclosures, see Health and Safety Code § 26150.

Water heater strapping, certification of earthquake resistance, see Health and Safety Code § 19211.

§ 1102.6b. Disclosure to prospective buyer of continuing lien securing special tax levy, fixed lien assessments, or contractual assessment program; satisfaction of disclosure notice requirements

(a) This section applies to all sales of real property for which all of the following apply:

(1) The sale is subject to this article.

(2) The property being sold is subject to a continuing lien securing the levy of special taxes pursuant to the Mello–Roos Community Facilities Act (Chapter 2.5 (commencing with Section 53311) of Part 1 of Division 2 of Title 5 of the Government Code), to a fixed lien assessment collected in installments to secure bonds issued pursuant to the Improvement Bond Act of 1915 (Division 10 (commencing with Section 8500) of the Streets and Highways Code), or to a contractual assessment program authorized pursuant to Chapter 29 (commencing with Section 5898.10) of Part 3 of Division 7 of the Streets and Highway Code.

(3) A notice is not required pursuant to Section 53341.5 of the Government Code.

(b) In addition to any other disclosure required pursuant to this article, the seller of any real property subject to this section shall make a good faith effort to obtain a disclosure notice concerning the special tax as provided for in Section 53340.2 of the Government Code, or a disclosure notice concerning an assessment installment as provided in Section 53754 of the Government Code, from each local agency that levies a special tax pursuant to the Mello–Roos Community Facilities Act, or that collects assessment installments to secure bonds issued pursuant to the Improvement Bond Act of 1915 (Division 10 (commencing with Section 8500) of the Streets and Highways Code), or a disclosure notice concerning the contractual assessment as provided in Section 5898.24 of the Streets and Highways Code, on the property being sold, and shall deliver that notice or those notices to the prospective buyer, as long as the notices are made available by the local agency.

(c)(1) The seller of real property subject to this section may satisfy the disclosure notice requirements in regard to the bonds issued pursuant to the Improvement Bond Act of 1915 (Division 10 (commencing with Section 8500) of the Streets and Highways Code) by delivering a disclosure notice that is substantially equivalent and obtained from another source until December 31, 2004.

(2) The seller of real property subject to this section may satisfy the disclosure notice requirements in regard to the assessments collected under the contractual assessment program authorized pursuant to Chapter 29 (commencing with Section 5898.10) of Part 3 of Division 7 of the Streets and Highway Code by delivering a disclosure notice that is substantially equivalent and obtained from another source.

(3) For the purposes of this section, a substantially equivalent disclosure notice includes, but is not limited to, a copy of the most recent year's property tax bill or an itemization of current assessment amounts applicable to the property.

(d)(1) Notwithstanding subdivision (c), the seller of real property subject to this section may satisfy the disclosure notice requirements of this section by delivering a disclosure notice obtained from a nongovernmental source that satisfies the requirements of paragraph (2).

(2) A notice provided by a private entity other than a designated office, department, or bureau of the levying entity may be modified as needed to clearly and accurately describe a special tax pursuant to the Mello–Roos Community Facilities Act levied against the property or to clearly and accurately consolidate information about two or more districts that levy or are authorized to levy a special tax pursuant to the Mello–Roos Community Facilities Act against the property, and shall include the name of the Mello–Roos entity levying taxes against the property, the annual tax due for the Mello–Roos entity for the current tax year, the maximum tax that may be levied against the property in any year, the percentage by which the maximum tax for the Mello–Roos entity may increase per year, and the date until the tax may be levied against the property for the Mello–Roos entity and a contact telephone number, if available, for further information about the Mello–Roos entity. A notice provided by a private entity other than a designated office, department, or bureau of the levying entity may be modified as needed to clearly and accurately describe special assessments and bonds pursuant to the Improvement Bond Act of 1915 levied against the property, or to clearly and accurately consolidate information about two or more districts that levy or are authorized to levy special assessments and bonds pursuant to the Improvement Bond Act of 1915 against the property, and shall include the name of the special assessments and bonds issued pursuant to the Improvement Bond Act of 1915, the current annual tax on the property for the special assessments and bonds issued pursuant to the Improvement Bond Act of 1915 and a contact telephone

number, if available, for further information about the special assessments and bonds issued pursuant to the Improvement Bond Act of 1915.

(3) This section does not change the ability to make disclosures pursuant to Section 1102.4 of the Civil Code.

(e) If a disclosure received pursuant to subdivision (b), (c), or (d) has been delivered to the buyer, a seller or his or her agent is not required to provide additional information concerning, and information in the disclosure shall be deemed to satisfy the responsibility of the seller or his or her agent to inform the buyer regarding the special tax or assessment installments and the district. Notwithstanding subdivision (b), (c), or (d), nothing in this section imposes a duty to discover a special tax or assessment installments or the existence of any levying district not actually known to the agents. *(Added by Stats.1992, c. 772 (S.B.1464), § 1.3, operative July 1, 1993. Amended by Stats.2001, c. 673 (S.B.1122), § 1; Stats.2002, c. 770 (S.B.1879), § 1, eff. Sept. 21, 2002; Stats.2002, c. 771 (A.B.337), § 1; Stats.2003, c. 62 (S.B.600), § 14; Stats.2009, c. 444 (A.B.474), § 1; Stats.2018, c. 907 (A.B.1289), § 14, eff. Jan. 1, 2019.)*

Cross References

Real estate regulations, investigation of alleged violations of certain provisions concerned with disclosures upon certain transfers of real estate, suspension or revocation of license, see Business and Professions Code § 10176.5.

Real property defined for purposes of this Code, see Civil Code § 658.

§ 1102.6c. Seller's notice of supplemental property tax bill; requirements

(a) In addition to any other disclosure required pursuant to this article, it shall be the sole responsibility of the seller of any real property subject to this article, or his or her agent, to deliver to the prospective buyer a disclosure notice that includes both of the following:

(1) A notice, in at least 12–point type or a contrasting color, as follows:

"California property tax law requires the Assessor to revalue real property at the time the ownership of the property changes. Because of this law, you may receive one or two supplemental tax bills, depending on when your loan closes.

The supplemental tax bills are not mailed to your lender. If you have arranged for your property tax payments to be paid through an impound account, the supplemental tax bills will not be paid by your lender. It is your responsibility to pay these supplemental bills directly to the tax collector. If you have any question concerning this matter, please call your local tax collector's office."

(2) A title, in at least 14–point type or a contrasting color, that reads as follows: "Notice of Your 'Supplemental' Property Tax Bill."

(b) The disclosure notice requirements of this section may be satisfied by delivering a disclosure notice pursuant to Section 1102.6b that satisfies the requirements of subdivision (a). *(Added by Stats.2005, c. 392 (A.B.459), § 2. Amended by Stats.2018, c. 907 (A.B.1289), § 15, eff. Jan. 1, 2019.)*

Cross References

Ownership defined for purposes of this Code, see Civil Code § 654.
Real property defined for purposes of this Code, see Civil Code § 658.
Subdivided lands, notice of intention to sell or lease, see Business and Professions Code § 11010.

§ 1102.6d. Manufactured home and mobilehome transfer disclosure statement

Except for manufactured homes and mobilehomes located in a common interest development governed by Part 5 (commencing with Section 4000) of Division 4, the disclosures applicable to the resale of a manufactured home or mobilehome pursuant to subdivision (b) of Section 1102 are set forth in, and shall be made on a copy of, the following disclosure form:

MANUFACTURED HOME AND MOBILEHOME: TRANSFER DISCLOSURE STATEMENT

THIS DISCLOSURE STATEMENT CONCERNS THE MANUFACTURED HOME OR MOBILEHOME (HEREAFTER REFERRED TO AS "HOME") LOCATED AT _____ IN THE CITY OF _____, COUNTY OF _____, STATE OF CALIFORNIA, DESCRIBED AS

YEAR   MAKE   SERIAL #(s)   HCD DECAL # or Equivalent

THIS STATEMENT IS A DISCLOSURE OF THE CONDITION OF THE ABOVE–DESCRIBED HOME IN COMPLIANCE WITH SUBDIVISION (b) OF SECTION 1102 OF THE CIVIL CODE AND SECTIONS 18025 AND 18046 OF THE HEALTH AND SAFETY CODE AS OF _____

DATE

IT IS NOT A WARRANTY OF ANY KIND BY THE LAWFUL OWNER OF THE MANUFACTURED HOME OR MOBILEHOME WHO OFFERS THE HOME FOR SALE (HEREAFTER THE SELLER), OR ANY AGENT(S) REPRESENTING ANY PRINCIPAL(S) IN THIS TRANSACTION, AND IS NOT A SUBSTITUTE FOR ANY INSPECTIONS OR WARRANTIES THE PRINCIPAL(S) MAY WISH TO OBTAIN, AN "AGENT" MEANS ANY DEALER OR SALESPERSON LICENSED PURSUANT TO PART 2 (COMMENCING WITH SECTION 18000) OF THE HEALTH AND SAFETY CODE, OR A REAL ESTATE BROKER OR SALESPERSON LICENSED PURSUANT TO DIVISION 4 (COMMENCING WITH SECTION 10000) OF DIVISION 13 OF THE BUSINESS AND PROFESSIONS CODE.

I

COORDINATION WITH OTHER DISCLOSURE & INFORMATION

This Manufactured Home and Mobilehome Transfer Disclosure Statement is made pursuant to Article 1.5 (commencing with Section 1102) of Chapter 2 of Title 4 of Part 4 of Division 2 of the Civil Code. Other statutes require disclosures, or other information may be important to the prospective buyer, depending upon the details of the particular transaction (including, but not limited to, the condition of the park in which the manufactured home or mobilehome will be located;

§ 1102.6d PROPERTY

disclosures required or information provided by the Mobilehome Residency Law. Section 798 of the Civil Code et seq.; the mobilehome park rental agreement or lease: the mobilehome park rules and regulations; and park and lot inspection reports, if any, completed by the state or a local enforcement agency). Substituted Disclosures: The following disclosures have or will be made in connection with this transfer, and are intended to satisfy the disclosure obligations of this form, where the subject matter is the same:

☐ Home inspection reports completed pursuant to the contract of sale or receipt for deposit.

☐ Additional inspection reports or disclosures: _____

II

SELLER'S INFORMATION

The Seller discloses the following information with the knowledge that even though this is not a warranty, prospective buyers may rely on this information in deciding whether, and on what terms, to purchase the subject Home. Seller hereby authorizes any agent(s), as defined in Section 18046 of the Health and Safety Code, representing any principal(s) in this transaction to provide a copy of this statement to any person or entity in connection with any actual or anticipated sale of the Home.

THE FOLLOWING ARE REPRESENTATIONS MADE BY THE SELLER(S) AND ARE NOT THE REPRESENTATIONS OF THE AGENT(S), IF ANY, AS DEFINED IN SECTION 18046 OF THE HEALTH AND SAFETY CODE. THIS INFORMATION IS A DISCLOSURE AND IS NOT INTENDED TO BE PART OF ANY CONTRACT BETWEEN THE BUYER AND THE SELLER.

Seller ___ is ___ is not occupying the Home.

A. The subject Home includes the items checked below which are being sold with the Home (read across):*

___Range	___Oven	___Microwave
___Dishwasher	___Trash Compactor	___Garbage Disposal
___Burglar Alarm		___Fire Alarm
___TV Antenna	___Carbon Monoxide Device(s)	___Intercom
___Central Heating		___Wall/Window Air Cndtng.
___Evaporative Cooler(s)	___Satellite Dish	___Water Softener
___Porch Decking	___Central Air Cndtng.	___Gazebo
___Private Sauna	___Sump Pump	___Spa Locking Safety Cvr
___Private Hot Tub	___Porch Awning	___Gas/Spa Heater
___Solar/Spa Heater	___Private Spa	___Solar Water Heater
___Electric Water Heater	___Hot Tub Locking Cvr	___Bottled Propane
	___Gas Water Heater	
___Carport Awning		
___Automatic Garage Door Opener(s)	___Attached Garage	___Detached Garage

___Window Secure Bars	___# Remote Controls	___Window Screens
___Earthquake Resistant Bracing System	___Bedroom Window Quick Release Mechanism	
	___Washer/Dryer Hookups	___Rain Gutters

Exhaust Fan(s) in _____ 220 Volt Wiring in _____

Fireplace(s) in _____ Gas Starter(s) _____

Roof(s) and type(s) _____ Roof age (Approximate) _____
Other _____

* Installation of a listed appliance, device, or amenity is not a precondition of sale or transfer of the home. The carbon monoxide device, garage door opener, or child-resistant pool barrier may not be in compliance with the safety standards relating to, respectively, carbon monoxide device standards of Chapter 8 (commencing with Section 13260) of Part 2 of Division 12 of, automatic reversing device standards of Chapter 12.5 (commencing with Section 19890) of Part 3 of Division 13 of, or the pool safety standards of Article 2.5 (commencing with Section 115920) of Chapter 5 of Part 10 of Division 104 of the Health and Safety Code. Window security bars may not have quick-release mechanisms in compliance with the 1995 edition of the California Building Standards Code.

Are there, to the best of your (Seller's) knowledge, any of the above that are not in operating condition? ___ Yes ___No. If yes, then describe. (Attach additional sheets if necessary):
_____
_____

B. Are you (the Seller) aware of any significant defects/malfunctions in any of the following in connection with the Home?

___Yes ___No If yes, check appropriate space(s) below:

___Interior Walls, ___Ceilings, ___Floors, ___Exterior Walls, ___Insulation,
___Roof(s), ___Windows, ___Doors, ___Home Electrical Systems, ___Plumbing,
___Porch or Deck, ___Porch Steps & Railings, ___Other Steps & Railings,
___Porch Awning, ___Carport Awning, ___Other Awnings, ___Skirting,
___Home Foundation or Support System,
___Other Structural Components (Describe: _____)

If any of the above is checked, explain. (Attach additional sheets if necessary): _____
_____

C. Are you (the Seller) aware of any of the following:

1. Substances, materials, or products which may be an environmental hazard, such as, but not limited to, asbestos, formaldehyde, radon gas, lead-based paint, or chemical storage tanks on the subject home interior or exterior .... ___Yes ___No

2. Room additions, structural modifications, or other alterations or repairs made without necessary permits ..... ___Yes ___No

3. Room additions, structural modifications, or other alterations or repairs not in compliance with applicable codes . ___Yes ___No

ACQUISITION OF PROPERTY § 1102.6d

4. Any settling from slippage, sliding or problems with leveling of the home or the foundation or support system ... ___Yes ___No

5. Drainage or grading problems with the home, space or lot .... ___Yes ___No

6. Damage to the home or accessory structures being sold with the home from fire, flood, earthquake, or landslides . ___Yes ___No

7. Any notices of abatement or citations against the home or accessory structures being sold with the home .... ___Yes ___No

8. Any lawsuits by or against the seller threatening to or affecting the home or the accessory structures being sold with the home, including any lawsuits alleging any defect or deficiency in the home or accessories sold with the home ..... ___Yes ___No

9. Neighborhood noise problems or other nuisances .... ___Yes ___No

10. Any encroachment, easement, non-conforming use or violation of setback requirements with the home, accessory structures being sold with the home, or space .... ___Yes ___No

If the answer to any of these is yes, explain. (Attach additional sheets if necessary.): _____
_____
_____

D. 1. The Seller certifies that the home, as of the close of escrow, will be in compliance with Section 13113.8 of the Health and Safety Code by having operable smoke detectors(s) which are approved, listed, and installed in accordance with the State Fire Marshal's regulations and applicable local standards.

2. The Seller certifies that the home, as of the close of escrow, will be in compliance Section 19211 of the Health and Safety Code by having the water heater tank(s) braced, anchored, or strapped in place in accordance with applicable law.

Seller certifies that the information herein is true and correct to the best of the Seller's knowledge as of the date signed by the Seller.

Seller _____ Date _____
Seller _____ Date _____

III

AGENT'S INSPECTION DISCLOSURE

(To be completed only if the Seller is represented by an Agent in this transaction)

THE UNDERSIGNED, BASED ON THE ABOVE INQUIRY OF THE SELLER(S) AS TO THE CONDITION OF THE HOME AND BASED ON A REASONABLY COMPETENT AND DILIGENT VISUAL INSPECTION OF THE ACCESSIBLE AREAS OF THE HOME IN CONJUNCTION WITH THAT INQUIRY, STATES THE FOLLOWING:

☐ Agent notes no items for disclosure.
☐ Agent notes the following items:
_____
_____
_____

Agent Representing Seller _____ By _____ Date _____
(Please Print) (Signature)

IV

AGENT'S INSPECTION DISCLOSURE

(To be completed only if the Agent who has obtained the offer is other than the Agent above.)

THE UNDERSIGNED, BASED ON A REASONABLY COMPETENT AND DILIGENT VISUAL INSPECTION OF THE ACCESSIBLE AREAS OF THE HOME, STATES THE FOLLOWING:

☐ Agent notes no items for disclosure.
☐ Agent notes the following items:
_____
_____
_____

Agent Representing Buyer _____ By _____ Date _____
(Please Print) (Signature)

V

BUYER(S) AND SELLER(S) MAY WISH TO OBTAIN PROFESSIONAL ADVICE AND/ OR INSPECTIONS OF THE HOME AND TO PROVIDE FOR APPROPRIATE PROVISIONS IN A CONTRACT BETWEEN THE BUYER(S) AND SELLER(S) WITH RESPECT TO ANY ADVICE/ INSPECTIONS/DEFECTS.

I/WE ACKNOWLEDGE RECEIPT OF A COPY OF THIS STATEMENT.

Seller _____ Date _____ Buyer _____ Date _____
Seller _____ Date _____ Buyer _____ Date _____

Agent Representing Seller _____ By _____ Date _____
(Please Print) (Signature)

Agent Representing Buyer _____ By _____ Date _____
(Please Print) (Signature)

VI

SECTION 1102.3a OF THE CIVIL CODE PROVIDES A PROSPECTIVE BUYER WITH THE RIGHT TO RESCIND THE PURCHASE OF THE MANUFACTURED HOME OR MOBILEHOME FOR AT LEAST THREE DAYS AFTER DELIVERY OF THIS DISCLOSURE. IF DELIVERY OCCURS AFTER THE SIGNING OF AN OFFER TO PURCHASE. IF YOU WISH TO RESCIND THE CONTRACT, YOU MUST ACT WITHIN THE PRESCRIBED PERIOD.

§ 1102.6d

A MANUFACTURED HOME OR MOBILEHOME DEALER OR A REAL ESTATE BROKER IS QUALIFIED TO PROVIDE ADVICE ON THE SALE OF A MANUFACTURED HOME OR MOBILEHOME. IF YOU DESIRE LEGAL ADVICE, CONSULT YOUR ATTORNEY.

(Added by Stats.1999, c. 517 (S.B.534), § 6. Amended by Stats.2010, c. 19 (S.B.183), § 2; Stats.2012, c. 181 (A.B.806), § 34, operative Jan. 1, 2014.)

Cross References

Manufactured homes or mobilehomes, transfer or sale subject to disclosure requirements under this section, see Civil Code § 798.74.4.

§ 1102.6e. Transfer fee disclosure statement; requirements

If a property being transferred on or after January 1, 2008, is subject to a transfer fee, as defined in Section 1098, the transferor shall provide, at the same time as the transfer disclosure statement required pursuant to Section 1102.6 is provided if the document required by subdivision (b) of Section 1098.5 has not already been provided, an additional disclosure statement containing all of the following:

(a) Notice that payment of a transfer fee is required as a result of transfer of the property.

(b) The amount of the fee required for the asking price of the real property, if the amount of the fee is based on the price of the real property, and a description of how the fee is calculated.

(c) Notice that the final amount of the fee may be different if the fee is based upon a percentage of the final sale price.

(d) The entity to which funds from the fee will be paid.

(e) The purposes for which funds from the fee will be used.

(f) The date or circumstances under which the obligation to pay the transfer fee expires, if any. *(Added by Stats.2007, c. 689 (A.B.980), § 3. Amended by Stats.2015, c. 634 (A.B.807), § 3, eff. Jan. 1, 2016.)*

§ 1102.6f. Disclosure to prospective buyer that property is located in high or very high fire hazard severity zone; statement; retrofits; features; final inspection report; building code formulation

(a) On or after January 1, 2021, in addition to any other disclosure required pursuant to this article, the seller of any real property subject to this article that is located in a high or very high fire hazard severity zone, as identified by the Director of Forestry and Fire Protection pursuant to Section 51178 of the Government Code or Article 9 (commencing with Section 4201) of Chapter 1 of Part 2 of Division 4 of the Public Resources Code, shall provide a disclosure notice to the buyer, if the home was constructed before January 1, 2010, that includes the following information:

(1) A statement as follows: "This home is located in a high or very high fire hazard severity zone and this home was built before the implementation of the Wildfire Urban Interface building codes which help to fire harden a home. To better protect your home from wildfire, you might need to consider improvements. Information on fire hardening, including current building standards and information on minimum annual vegetation management standards to protect homes from wildfires, can be obtained on the internet website http://www.readyforwildfire.org."

(2) On or after July 1, 2025, a list of low-cost retrofits developed and listed pursuant to Section 51189 of the Government Code. The notice shall disclose which listed retrofits, if any, have been completed during the time that the seller has owned the property.

(3) A list of the following features that may make the home vulnerable to wildfire and flying embers. The notice shall disclose which of the listed features, if any, that exist on the home of which the seller is aware:

(A) Eave, soffit, and roof ventilation where the vents have openings in excess of one-eighth of an inch or are not flame and ember resistant.

(B) Roof coverings made of untreated wood shingles or shakes.

(C) Combustible landscaping or other materials within five feet of the home and under the footprint of any attached deck.

(D) Single pane or nontempered glass windows.

(E) Loose or missing bird stopping or roof flashing.

(F) Rain gutters without metal or noncombustible gutter covers.

(b) If, pursuant to Section 51182 of the Government Code, a seller has obtained a final inspection report described in that section, the seller shall provide to the buyer a copy of that report or information on where a copy of the report may be obtained.

(c) This section shall not be construed as a requirement, instruction, or consideration for present or future building code formulation, including, but not limited to, the Wildland Urban Interface building standards (Chapter 7A (commencing with Section 701A.1) of Part 2 of Title 24 of the California Code of Regulations). *(Added by Stats.2019, c. 391 (A.B.38), § 2, eff. Jan. 1, 2020. Amended by Stats.2020, c. 370 (S.B.1371), § 26, eff. Jan. 1, 2021.)*

§ 1102.6g. Notice of unbiased property appraisal requirement

(a) After July 1, 2022, every contract for the sale of real property shall contain, in no less than 8–point type, the following notice:

"Any appraisal of the property is required to be unbiased, objective, and not influenced by improper or illegal considerations, including, but not limited to, any of the following: race, color, religion (including religious dress, grooming practices, or both), gender (including, but not limited to, pregnancy, childbirth, breastfeeding, and related conditions, and gender identity and gender expression), sexual orientation, marital status, medical condition, military or veteran status, national origin (including language use and possession of a driver's license issued to persons unable to provide their presence in the United States is authorized under federal law), source of income, ancestry, disability (mental and physical, including, but not limited to, HIV/AIDS status, cancer diagnosis, and genetic characteristics), genetic information, or age. If a buyer or seller believes that the appraisal has been influenced by any of the above factors, the seller or buyer can report this information to the lender or mortgage broker that retained the appraiser and may also file a complaint with the Bureau of Real Estate Appraisers at https://www2.brea.ca.gov/complaint/ or call (916) 552–9000 for further information on how to file a complaint."

(b) The notice described in subdivision (a) shall also be delivered by a licensed person refinancing a first lien purchase money loan secured by residential real property containing no more than four dwelling units, either prior to, or with, the loan estimate as required by the federal Truth in Lending Act, as amended (15 U.S.C. Sec. 1601 et seq.), or the mortgage loan disclosure statement as required pursuant to Section 10240 of the Business and Professions Code. The notice described in subdivision (a) may be included as part of the disclosure required under Section 1002.14(a)(2) of the federal Equal Credit Opportunity Act (Regulation B) (12 C.F.R. Sec. 1002 et seq.).

(c) For purposes of this section, a "licensed person" means a depository institution chartered under federal or state law, a person covered by the licensing requirements of Division 9 (commencing with Section 22000) or Division 20 (commencing with Section 50000) of the Financial Code, or a person licensed pursuant to Part 1 (commencing with Section 10000) of Division 4 of the Business and Professions Code. *(Added by Stats.2021, c. 352 (A.B.948), § 6, eff. Jan. 1, 2022.)*

Cross References

Real estate valuation, legislative intent, complaint form, collection of demographic information, report to Legislature, see Business and Professions Code § 11310.3.

§ 1102.7. Good faith required

Each disclosure required by this article and each act which may be performed in making the disclosure, shall be made in good faith. For purposes of this article, "good faith" means honesty in fact in the conduct of the transaction. *(Added by Stats.1985, c. 1574, § 2, operative Jan. 1, 1987.)*

§ 1102.8. Specification of items for disclosure not limitation on other disclosure obligations

The specification of items for disclosure in this article does not limit or abridge any obligation for disclosure created by any other provision of law or which may exist in order to avoid fraud, misrepresentation, or deceit in the transfer transaction. *(Added by Stats.1985, c. 1574, § 2, operative Jan. 1, 1987.)*

Cross References

Obligation defined, see Civil Code § 1427.

§ 1102.9. Amendment of disclosures

Any disclosure made pursuant to this article may be amended in writing by the seller or his or her agent, but the amendment shall be subject to Section 1102.3 or 1102.3a. *(Added by Stats.1985, c. 1574, § 2, operative Jan. 1, 1987. Amended by Stats.1996, c. 240 (A.B.2383), § 3; Stats.1999, c. 517 (S.B.534), § 7; Stats.2018, c. 907 (A.B.1289), § 16, eff. Jan. 1, 2019.)*

§ 1102.10. Delivery of disclosures; personal delivery or mail

Delivery of disclosures required by this article shall be by personal delivery to the tranferee [1] or by mail to the prospective transferee. For the purposes of this article, delivery to the spouse of a transferee shall be deemed delivery to the transferee, unless provided otherwise by contract. *(Added by Stats.1985, c. 1574, § 2, operative Jan. 1, 1987.)*

[1] So in chaptered copy.

§ 1102.11. Escrow agent not deemed agent for purposes of disclosure; exception

Any person or entity, other than a real estate licensee licensed pursuant to Part 1 (commencing with Section 10000) of Division 4 of the Business and Professions Code, acting in the capacity of an escrow agent for the transfer of real property subject to this article shall not be deemed the agent of the transferor or transferee for purposes of the disclosure requirements of this article, unless the person or entity is empowered to so act by an express written agreement to that effect. The extent of such an agency shall be governed by the written agreement. *(Added by Stats.1985, c. 1574, § 2, operative Jan. 1, 1987.)*

Cross References

Real property defined for purposes of this Code, see Civil Code § 658.

§ 1102.12. Licensed real estate brokers as agents in transaction; delivery of disclosure; advising transferee of rights to disclosure; record

(a) If more than one licensed real estate broker is acting as an agent in a transaction subject to this article, the broker who has obtained the offer made by the transferee shall, except as otherwise provided in this article, deliver the disclosure required by this article to the transferee, unless the transferor has given other written instructions for delivery.

(b) If a licensed real estate broker responsible for delivering the disclosures under this section cannot obtain the disclosure document required and does not have written assurance from the transferee that the disclosure has been received, the broker shall advise the transferee in writing of his or her rights to the disclosure. A licensed real estate broker responsible for delivering disclosures under this section shall maintain a record of the action taken to effect compliance in accordance with Section 10148 of the Business and Professions Code. *(Added by Stats.1985, c. 1574, § 2, operative Jan. 1, 1987. Amended by Stats.1986, c. 460, § 6.)*

§ 1102.13. Failure to comply with article; transfer not invalidated; damages

No transfer subject to this article shall be invalidated solely because of the failure of any person to comply with any provision of this article. However, any person who willfully or negligently violates or fails to perform any duty prescribed by any provision of this article shall be liable in the amount of actual damages suffered by a transferee. *(Added by Stats. 1985, c. 1574, § 2, operative Jan. 1, 1987.)*

§ 1102.14
Repealed

§ 1102.14. Repealed by Stats.2018, c. 907 (A.B.1289), § 17, eff. Jan. 1, 2019

§ 1102.15. Former federal or state ordnance locations; definition

The seller of residential real property subject to this article who has actual knowledge of any former federal or state ordnance locations within the neighborhood area shall give written notice of that knowledge as soon as practicable before transfer of title.

For purposes of this section, "former federal or state ordnance locations" means an area identified by an agency or instrumentality of the federal or state government as an area once used for military training purposes which may contain potentially explosive munitions. "Neighborhood area" means within one mile of the residential real property.

The disclosure required by this section does not limit or abridge any obligation for disclosure created by any other law or that may exist in order to avoid fraud, misrepresentation, or deceit in the transfer transaction. *(Added by Stats.1989, c. 294, § 1.)*

Cross References

Disclosure of former federal or state ordnance locations, see Civil Code § 1940.7.
Obligation defined, see Civil Code § 1427.
Real property defined for purposes of this Code, see Civil Code § 658.

§ 1102.155. Water-conserving plumbing fixture requirement; noncompliant plumbing fixtures

(a)(1) The seller of single-family residential real property subject to this article shall disclose, in writing, that Section 1101.4 requires that California single-family residences be equipped with water-conserving plumbing fixtures on or after January 1, 2017, and shall disclose whether the property includes any noncompliant plumbing fixtures as defined in subdivision (c) of Section 1101.3.

(2) The seller shall affirm that this representation is that of the seller and not a representation of any agent, and that this disclosure is not intended to be part of any contract between the buyer and the seller. The seller shall further affirm that this disclosure is not a warranty of any kind by the seller or any agent representing any principal in the transaction and is not a substitute for any inspections or warranties that any principal may wish to obtain.

(b) This section shall become operative on January 1, 2017. *(Added by Stats.2009, c. 587 (S.B.407), § 2, operative Jan. 1, 2017. Amended by Stats.2018, c. 907 (A.B.1289), § 18, eff. Jan. 1, 2019.)*

§ 1102.16. Window security bars and safety release mechanism; disclosure

The disclosure of the existence of any window security bars and any safety release mechanism on those window security bars shall be made pursuant to Section 1102.6 or 1102.6a of the Civil Code. *(Added by Stats.1996, c. 926 (A.B.3026), § 2, operative July 1, 1997. Amended by Stats.2004, c. 183 (A.B.3082), § 26.)*

§ 1102.17. Sellers of residential real property; written notice of knowledge of property with respect to industrial use

The seller of residential real property subject to this article who has actual knowledge that the property is adjacent to, or zoned to allow, an industrial use described in Section 731a of the Code of Civil Procedure, or affected by a nuisance created by such a use, shall give written notice of that knowledge as soon as practicable before transfer of title. *(Added by Stats.1999, c. 876 (A.B.248), § 2. Amended by Stats.2004, c. 66 (A.B.920), § 2.)*

Cross References

Real property defined for purposes of this Code, see Civil Code § 658.

§ 1102.18. Application of Section 1102.1 (d)

The provisions of subdivision (d) of Section 1102.1 shall apply to this article. *(Added by Stats.2018, c. 907 (A.B.1289), § 19, eff. Jan. 1, 2019.)*

§ 1102.19. Disclosure of compliance with Section 4291 of Public Resources Code; local vegetation ordinances; property located in high or very high fire hazard severity zone; agreement to obtain documentation of compliance; enforcement of defensible space requirements

(a) On and after July 1, 2021, a seller of a real property subject to this article that is located in a high or very high fire hazard severity zone, as identified by the Director of Forestry and Fire Protection pursuant to Section 51178 of the Government Code or Article 9 (commencing with Section 4201) of Chapter 1 of Part 2 of Division 4 of the Public Resources Code, shall provide to the buyer documentation stating that the property is in compliance with Section 4291 of the Public Resources Code or local vegetation management ordinances, as follows:

(1) In a local jurisdiction that has enacted an ordinance requiring an owner of real property to obtain documentation that the property is in compliance with Section 4291 of the Public Resources Code or a local vegetation management ordinance, the seller shall provide the buyer with a copy of the documentation that complies with the requirements of that local ordinance and information on the local agency from which a copy of that documentation may be obtained.

(2) In a local jurisdiction that has not enacted an ordinance for an owner of real property to obtain documentation that a property is in compliance with Section 4291 of the Public Resources Code or a local vegetation management ordinance, and if a state or local agency, or other government entity, or other qualified nonprofit entity, provides an inspection with documentation for the jurisdiction in which the property is located, the seller shall provide the buyer with the documentation obtained in the six-month period preceding the date the seller enters into a transaction to sell that real property and provide information on the local agency from which a copy of that documentation may be obtained.

(b) On and after July 1, 2021, if the seller of a real property described in subdivision (a) has not obtained documentation of compliance in accordance with paragraph (1) or (2) of subdivision (a), the seller and the buyer shall enter into a written agreement pursuant to which the buyer agrees to obtain documentation of compliance with Section 4291 of the Public Resources Code or a local vegetation management ordinance as follows:

(1) In a local jurisdiction that has enacted an ordinance requiring an owner or buyer to obtain documentation of compliance with Section 4291 of the Public Resources Code or a local vegetation management ordinance, the buyer shall comply with that ordinance.

(2) In a local jurisdiction that has not enacted an ordinance requiring an owner or buyer to obtain documentation of compliance, and if a state or local agency, or other government entity, or other qualified nonprofit entity, provides an inspection with documentation for the jurisdiction in which the property is located, the buyer shall obtain documentation of compliance within one year of the date of the close of escrow.

(c) Nothing in this section, including the existence of an agreement between a buyer and seller pursuant to subdivision (b), shall limit the ability of a state or local agency to enforce defensible space requirements pursuant to Section 51182 of the Government Code, Section 4291 of the Public Resources Code, or other applicable statutes, regulations, and local ordinances. *(Added by Stats.2019, c. 391 (A.B.38), § 3, eff. Jan. 1, 2020. Amended by Stats.2020, c. 36 (A.B.3364), § 12, eff. Jan. 1, 2021.)*

ARTICLE 1.7. DISCLOSURE OF NATURAL AND ENVIRONMENTAL HAZARDS, RIGHT–TO–FARM, AND OTHER DISCLOSURES UPON TRANSFER OF RESIDENTIAL PROPERTY

Section
1103. Definitions; application of article; waiver of requirements.
1103.1. Application of article; exclusions.
1103.2. Natural Hazard Disclosure Statement.
1103.3. Seller's delivery of written statement to prospective buyer.
1103.4. Errors, inaccuracies, or omissions in any information delivered under article; liability; notice of airport in vicinity; notice of San Francisco Bay Conservation and Development Commission; notice of right to farm; notice of mining operations.
1103.5. Seller's and seller's agent's relief from duty regarding items of information.
1103.7. Acts of disclosure made in good faith.
1103.8. Obligations for disclosure created under other laws.
1103.9. Amendments to disclosures.
1103.10. Delivery of disclosures; personal delivery by mail.
1103.11. Escrow agents for transfer of real property; not agent of transferor or transferee.
1103.12. Licensed real estate broker obtaining offer from transferee; duty of delivery.
1103.13. Invalidation of transfer; effect of noncompliance with article.
1103.14. Repealed.
1103.15. Application of Section 1102.1 (d).

§ 1103. Definitions; application of article; waiver of requirements

(a) For purpose of this article, the definitions in Chapter 1 (commencing with Section 10000) of Part 1 of Division 4 of the Business and Professions Code shall apply.

(b) Except as provided in Section 1103.1, this article applies to a sale, exchange, real property sales contract, as defined in Section 2985, lease with an option to purchase, any other option to purchase, or ground lease coupled with improvements, of any single-family residential real property.

(c) This article shall apply to the transactions described in subdivision (b) only if the seller or his or her agent is required by one or more of the following to disclose the property's location within a hazard zone:

(1) A seller's agent for a seller of real property that is located within a special flood hazard area (any type Zone "A" or "V") designated by the Federal Emergency Management Agency, or the seller if the seller is acting without a seller's agent, shall disclose to any prospective buyer the fact that the property is located within a special flood hazard area if either:

(A) The seller, or the seller's agent, has actual knowledge that the property is within a special flood hazard area.

(B) The local jurisdiction has compiled a list, by parcel, of properties that are within the special flood hazard area and a notice has been posted at the offices of the county recorder, county assessor, and county planning agency that identifies the location of the parcel list.

(2) A seller's agent for a seller of real property that is located within an area of potential flooding designated pursuant to Section 6161 of the Water Code, or the seller if the seller is acting without a seller's agent, shall disclose to any prospective buyer the fact that the property is located within an area of potential flooding if either:

(A) The seller, or the seller's agent, has actual knowledge that the property is within an inundation area.

(B) The local jurisdiction has compiled a list, by parcel, of properties that are within the inundation area and a notice has been posted at the offices of the county recorder, county assessor, and county planning agency that identifies the location of the parcel list.

(3) A seller of real property that is located within a very high fire hazard severity zone, designated pursuant to Section 51178 of the Government Code, or the seller's agent, shall disclose to any prospective buyer the fact that the property is located within a very high fire hazard severity zone and is subject to the requirements of Section 51182 of the Government Code if either:

(A) The seller or the seller's agent, has actual knowledge that the property is within a very high fire hazard severity zone.

(B) A map that includes the property has been provided to the local agency pursuant to Section 51178 of the Government Code and a notice has been posted at the offices of the county recorder, county assessor, and county planning agency that identifies the location of the map and any information regarding changes to the map received by the local agency.

(4) A seller's agent for a seller of real property that is located within an earthquake fault zone, designated pursuant to Section 2622 of the Public Resources Code, or the seller, if the seller is acting without an agent, shall disclose to any prospective buyer the fact that the property is located within a delineated earthquake fault zone if either:

(A) The seller, or the seller's agent, has actual knowledge that the property is within a delineated earthquake fault zone.

(B) A map that includes the property has been provided to the city or county pursuant to Section 2622 of the Public Resources Code and a notice has been posted at the offices of the county recorder, county assessor, and county planning agency that identifies the location of the map and any information regarding changes to the map received by the county.

(5) A seller's agent for a seller of real property that is located within a seismic hazard zone, designated pursuant to Section 2696 of the Public Resources Code, or the seller if the seller is acting without an agent, shall disclose to any prospective buyer the fact that the property is located within a seismic hazard zone if either:

(A) The seller, or the seller's agent, has actual knowledge that the property is within a seismic hazard zone.

(B) A map that includes the property has been provided to the city or county pursuant to Section 2696 of the Public Resources Code and a notice has been posted at the offices of the county recorder, county assessor, and county planning agency that identifies the location of the map and any information regarding changes to the map received by the county.

(6) A seller of real property that is located within a state responsibility area determined by the board, pursuant to Section 4125 of the Public Resources Code, or the seller's agent, shall disclose to any prospective buyer the fact that the property is located within a wildland area that may contain substantial forest fire risks and hazards and is subject to the requirements of Section 4291 of the Public Resources Code if either:

(A) The seller, or the seller's agent, has actual knowledge that the property is within a wildland fire zone.

(B) A map that includes the property has been provided to the city or county pursuant to Section 4125 of the Public Resources Code and a notice has been posted at the offices of the county recorder, county assessor, and county planning agency that identifies the location of the map and any information regarding changes to the map received by the county.

(d) Any waiver of the requirements of this article is void as against public policy. *(Added by Stats.1999, c. 876 (A.B.248), § 3. Amended by Stats.2000, c. 135 (A.B.2539), § 12; Stats. 2003–2004, 1st Ex.Sess., c. 8 (S.B.25), § 1, eff. May 5, 2003; Stats.2003, c. 741 (S.B.1049), § 2; Stats.2004, c. 183 (A.B. 3082), § 27; Stats.2017, c. 26 (S.B.92), § 1, eff. June 27, 2017; Stats.2018, c. 907 (A.B.1289), § 20, eff. Jan. 1, 2019.)*

Cross References

California Emergency Services Act, flooding, disclosure to potential transferee, see Government Code § 8589.4.
California Emergency Services Act, property within special flood hazard area, disclosure to prospective transferee, see Government Code § 8589.3.
Earthquake fault zoning, disclosure of property location by transferor or agent, see Public Resources Code § 2621.9.
Forest fires, responsibility for fire protection, real property located within state responsibility area, disclosures, see Public Resources Code § 4136.
Property within a very high fire hazard severity zone, disclosure to prospective transferee, see Government Code § 51183.5.
Real property defined for purposes of this Code, see Civil Code § 658.
Seismic hazards mapping, disclosure of property location by transferor or agent, see Public Resources Code § 2694.

§ 1103.1. Application of article; exclusions

(a) This article does not apply to the following sales:

(1) Sales or transfers pursuant to court order, including, but not limited to, sales ordered by a probate court in administration of an estate, sales pursuant to a writ of execution, sales by any foreclosure sale, sales by a trustee in bankruptcy, sales by eminent domain, and sales resulting from a decree for specific performance.

(2) Sales or transfers to a mortgagee by a mortgagor or successor in interest who is in default, sales to a beneficiary of a deed of trust by a trustor or successor in interest who is in default, transfers by any foreclosure sale after default, any foreclosure sale after default in an obligation secured by a mortgage, sale under a power of sale or any foreclosure sale under a decree of foreclosure after default in an obligation secured by a deed of trust or secured by any other instrument containing a power of sale, or sales by a mortgagee or a beneficiary under a deed of trust who has acquired the real property at a sale conducted pursuant to a power of sale under a mortgage or deed of trust or a sale pursuant to a decree of foreclosure or has acquired the real property by a deed in lieu of foreclosure.

(3) Sales or transfers by a fiduciary in the course of the administration of a trust, guardianship, conservatorship, or decedent's estate. This exemption shall not apply to a sale if the trustee is a natural person who is a trustee of a revocable trust and the seller is a former owner of the property or an occupant in possession of the property within the preceding year.

(4) Sales or transfers from one coowner to one or more other coowners.

(5) Sales or transfers made to a spouse, or to a person or persons in the line of consanguinity of one or more of the sellers.

(6) Sales or transfers between spouses resulting from a judgment of dissolution of marriage or of legal separation of the parties or from a property settlement agreement incidental to that judgment.

(7) Sales or transfers by the Controller in the course of administering Chapter 7 (commencing with Section 1500) of Title 10 of Part 3 of the Code of Civil Procedure.

(8) Sales or transfers under Chapter 7 (commencing with Section 3691) or Chapter 8 (commencing with Section 3771) of Part 6 of Division 1 of the Revenue and Taxation Code.

(9) Sales, transfers, or exchanges to or from any governmental entity.

(10) The sale, creation, or transfer of any lease of any duration except a lease with an option to purchase or a ground lease coupled with improvements.

(b) Sales and transfers not subject to this article may be subject to other disclosure requirements, including those under Sections 8589.3, 8589.4, and 51183.5 of the Government Code and Sections 2621.9, 2694, and 4136 of the Public Resources Code. In sales not subject to this article, agents may make required disclosures in a separate writing.

(c) Notwithstanding the definition of sale in Section 10018.5 of the Business and Professions Code and Section 2079.13, the terms "sale" and "transfer," as they are used in this section, shall have their commonly understood meanings. The changes made to this section by Assembly Bill 1289 of the 2017–18 Legislative Session [1] shall not be interpreted to change the application of the law as it read prior to January 1, 2019. *(Added by Stats.1999, c. 876 (A.B.248), § 3. Amended by Stats.2018, c. 907 (A.B.1289), § 21, eff. Jan. 1, 2019; Stats.2019, c. 497 (A.B.991), § 22, eff. Jan. 1, 2020; Stats.2019, c. 310 (A.B.892), § 7, eff. Jan. 1, 2020; Stats.2020, c. 370 (S.B.1371), § 27, eff. Jan. 1, 2021.)*

[1] Stats.2018, c. 907.

Cross References

Obligation defined, see Civil Code § 1427.
Real property defined for purposes of this Code, see Civil Code § 658.
State Controller, generally, see Government Code § 12402 et seq.

§ 1103.2. Natural Hazard Disclosure Statement

(a) The disclosures required by this article are set forth in, and shall be made on a copy of, the following Natural Hazard Disclosure Statement:

NATURAL HAZARD DISCLOSURE STATEMENT

This statement applies to the following property: _____

The seller and the seller's agent(s) or a third-party consultant disclose the following information with the knowledge that even though this is not a warranty, prospective buyers may rely on this information in deciding whether and on what terms to purchase the subject property. Seller hereby authorizes any agent(s) representing any principal(s) in this action to provide a copy of this statement to any person or entity in connection with any actual or anticipated sale of the property.

The following are representations made by the seller and the seller's agent(s) based on their knowledge and maps drawn by the state and federal governments. This information is a disclosure and is not intended to be part of any contract between the seller and buyer.

THIS REAL PROPERTY LIES WITHIN THE FOLLOWING HAZARDOUS AREA(S):

A SPECIAL FLOOD HAZARD AREA (Any type Zone "A" or "V") designated by the Federal Emergency Management Agency.

Yes _____ No _____   Do not know and information not available from local jurisdiction _____

AN AREA OF POTENTIAL FLOODING shown on a dam failure inundation map pursuant to Section 8589.5 of the Government Code.

Yes _____ No _____   Do not know and information not available from local jurisdiction _____

A VERY HIGH FIRE HAZARD SEVERITY ZONE pursuant to Section 51178 or 51179 of the Government Code. The owner of this property is subject to the maintenance requirements of Section 51182 of the Government Code.

Yes _____ No _____

A WILDLAND AREA THAT MAY CONTAIN SUBSTANTIAL FOREST FIRE RISKS AND HAZARDS pursuant to Section 4125 of the Public Resources Code. The owner of this property is subject to the maintenance requirements of Section 4291 of the Public Resources Code. Additionally, it is not the state's responsibility to provide fire protection services to any building or structure located within the wildlands unless the Department of Forestry and Fire Protection has entered into a cooperative agreement with a local agency for those purposes pursuant to Section 4142 of the Public Resources Code.

Yes _____ No _____

AN EARTHQUAKE FAULT ZONE pursuant to Section 2622 of the Public Resources Code.

Yes _____ No _____

A SEISMIC HAZARD ZONE pursuant to Section 2696 of the Public Resources Code.

Yes (Landslide Zone) _____   Yes (Liquefaction Zone) _____
No _____   Map not yet released by state _____

THESE HAZARDS MAY LIMIT YOUR ABILITY TO DEVELOP THE REAL PROPERTY, TO OBTAIN INSURANCE, OR TO RECEIVE ASSISTANCE AFTER A DISASTER.

THE MAPS ON WHICH THESE DISCLOSURES ARE BASED ESTIMATE WHERE NATURAL HAZARDS EXIST. THEY ARE NOT DEFINITIVE INDICATORS OF WHETHER OR NOT A PROPERTY WILL BE AFFECTED BY A NATURAL DISASTER. SELLER(S) AND BUYER(S) MAY WISH TO OBTAIN PROFESSIONAL ADVICE REGARDING THOSE HAZARDS AND OTHER HAZARDS THAT MAY AFFECT THE PROPERTY.

Signature of Seller(s) _____ Date _____
Signature of Seller(s) _____ Date _____

Seller's Agent(s) _____ Date _____
Seller's Agent(s) _____ Date _____

Check only one of the following:

☐ Seller(s) and their agent(s) represent that the information herein is true and correct to the best of their knowledge as of the date signed by the transferor(s) and agent(s).

☐ Seller(s) and their agent(s) acknowledge that they have exercised good faith in the selection of a third-party report provider as required in Section 1103.7 of the Civil Code, and that the representations made in this Natural Hazard Disclosure Statement are based upon information provided by the independent third-party disclosure provider as a substituted disclosure pursuant to Section 1103.4 of the Civil

Code. Neither seller(s) nor their agent(s) (1) has independently verified the information contained in this statement and report or (2) is personally aware of any errors or inaccuracies in the information contained on the statement. This statement was prepared by the provider below:

Third–Party
Disclosure Provider(s) ____ Date _____

Buyer represents that Buyer has read and understands this document. Pursuant to Section 1103.8 of the Civil Code, the representations made in this Natural Hazard Disclosure Statement do not constitute all of the seller's or agent's disclosure obligations in this transaction.

Signature of Buyer(s) ____ Date _____
Signature of Buyer(s) ____ Date _____

(b) If an earthquake fault zone, seismic hazard zone, very high fire hazard severity zone, or wildland fire area map or accompanying information is not of sufficient accuracy or scale that a reasonable person can determine if the subject real property is included in a natural hazard area, the seller or seller's agent shall mark "Yes" on the Natural Hazard Disclosure Statement. The seller's agent may mark "No" on the Natural Hazard Disclosure Statement if the seller attaches a report prepared pursuant to subdivision (c) of Section 1103.4 that verifies the property is not in the hazard zone. This subdivision is not intended to limit or abridge any existing duty of the seller or the seller's agent to exercise reasonable care in making a determination under this subdivision.

(c) If the Federal Emergency Management Agency has issued a Letter of Map Revision confirming that a property is no longer within a special flood hazard area, then the seller or seller's agent may mark "No" on the Natural Hazard Disclosure Statement, even if the map has not yet been updated. The seller or seller's agent shall attach a copy of the Letter of Map Revision to the disclosure statement.

(d) If the Federal Emergency Management Agency has issued a Letter of Map Revision confirming that a property is within a special flood hazard area and the location of the letter has been posted pursuant to subdivision (g) of Section 8589.3 of the Government Code, then the seller or seller's agent shall mark "Yes" on the Natural Hazard Disclosure Statement, even if the map has not yet been updated. The seller or seller's agent shall attach a copy of the Letter of Map Revision to the disclosure statement.

(e) The disclosure required pursuant to this article may be provided by the seller and the seller's agent in the Local Option Real Estate Disclosure Statement described in Section 1102.6a, provided that the Local Option Real Estate Disclosure Statement includes substantially the same information and substantially the same warnings that are required by this section.

(f)(1) The legal effect of a consultant's report delivered to satisfy the exemption provided by Section 1103.4 is not changed when it is accompanied by a Natural Hazard Disclosure Statement.

(2) A consultant's report shall always be accompanied by a completed and signed Natural Hazard Disclosure Statement.

(3) In a disclosure statement required by this section, an agent and third-party provider may cause the agent and third-party provider's name to be preprinted in lieu of an original signature in the portions of the form reserved for signatures. The use of a preprinted name shall not change the legal effect of the acknowledgment.

(g) The disclosure required by this article is only a disclosure between the seller, the seller's agent, and the prospective buyer, and shall not be used by any other party, including, but not limited to, insurance companies, lenders, or governmental agencies, for any purpose.

(h) In any transaction in which a seller has accepted, prior to June 1, 1998, an offer to purchase, the seller, or the seller's agent shall be deemed to have complied with the requirement of subdivision (a) if the seller or agent delivers to the prospective buyer a statement that includes substantially the same information and warning as the Natural Hazard Disclosure Statement. (Added by Stats.1999, c. 876 (A.B.248), § 3. Amended by Stats.2003–2004, 1st Ex.Sess., c. 8 (S.B.25), § 2, eff. May 5, 2003; Stats.2003, c. 741 (S.B.1049), § 3; Stats. 2004, c. 66 (A.B.920), § 3; Stats.2018, c. 907 (A.B.1289), § 22, eff. Jan. 1, 2019; Stats.2019, c. 497 (A.B.991), § 23, eff. Jan. 1, 2020.)

Cross References

California Emergency Services Act, flooding, disclosure to potential transferee, see Government Code § 8589.4.
California Emergency Services Act, property within special flood hazard area, disclosure to prospective transferee, see Government Code § 8589.3.
Earthquake fault zoning, disclosure of property location by transferor or agent, see Public Resources Code § 2621.9.
Forest fires, responsibility for fire protection, real property located within state responsibility area, disclosures, see Public Resources Code § 4136.
Obligation defined, see Civil Code § 1427.
Property within a very high fire hazard severity zone, disclosure to prospective transferee, see Government Code § 51183.5.
Real property defined for purposes of this Code, see Civil Code § 658.
Seismic hazards mapping, disclosure of property location by transferor or agent, see Public Resources Code § 2694.

§ 1103.3. Seller's delivery of written statement to prospective buyer

(a) The seller of any real property subject to this article shall deliver to the prospective buyer the written statement required by this article, as follows:

(1) In the case of a sale, as soon as practicable before transfer of title.

(2) In the case of a sale by a real property sales contract, as defined in Section 2985, or by a lease together with an option to purchase, or a ground lease coupled with improvements, as soon as practicable before the prospective buyer's execution of the contract. For the purpose of this subdivision, "execution" means the making or acceptance of an offer.

(b) The seller shall indicate compliance with this article either on the real property sales contract, the lease, any addendum attached thereto, or on a separate document.

(c) If any disclosure, or any material amendment of any disclosure, required to be made pursuant to this article is delivered after the execution of an offer to purchase, the prospective buyer shall have three days after delivery in person, five days after delivery by deposit in the mail, or five days after delivery of an electronic record in transactions where the parties have agreed to conduct the transaction by electronic means, pursuant to provisions of the Uniform Electronic Transactions Act (Title 2.5 (commencing with Section 1633.1) of Part 2 of Division 3), to terminate his or her offer by delivery of a written notice of termination to the seller or the seller's agent. *(Added by Stats.1999, c. 876 (A.B.248), § 3. Amended by Stats.2018, c. 907 (A.B.1289), § 23, eff. Jan. 1, 2019.)*

Cross References

Real property defined for purposes of this Code, see Civil Code § 658.

§ 1103.4. Errors, inaccuracies, or omissions in any information delivered under article; liability; notice of airport in vicinity; notice of San Francisco Bay Conservation and Development Commission; notice of right to farm; notice of mining operations

(a) Neither the seller nor any seller's agent or buyer's agent shall be liable for any error, inaccuracy, or omission of any information delivered pursuant to this article if the error, inaccuracy, or omission was not within the personal knowledge of the seller or the seller's agent or buyer's agent and was based on information timely provided by public agencies or by other persons providing information as specified in subdivision (c) that is required to be disclosed pursuant to this article, and ordinary care was exercised in obtaining and transmitting the information.

(b) The delivery of any information required to be disclosed by this article to a prospective buyer by a public agency or other person providing information required to be disclosed pursuant to this article shall be deemed to comply with the requirements of this article and shall relieve the seller, seller's agent, and buyer's agent of any further duty under this article with respect to that item of information.

(c) The delivery of a report or opinion prepared by a licensed engineer, land surveyor, geologist, or expert in natural hazard discovery dealing with matters within the scope of the professional's license or expertise shall be sufficient compliance for application of the exemption provided by subdivision (a) if the information is provided to the prospective buyer pursuant to a request therefor, whether written or oral. In responding to that request, an expert may indicate, in writing, an understanding that the information provided will be used in fulfilling the requirements of Section 1103.2 and, if so, shall indicate the required disclosures, or parts thereof, to which the information being furnished is applicable. Where such a statement is furnished, the expert shall not be responsible for any items of information or parts thereof, other than those expressly set forth in the statement.

(1) In responding to the request, the expert shall determine whether the property is within an airport influence area as defined in subdivision (b) of Section 11010 of the Business and Professions Code. If the property is within an airport influence area, the report shall contain the following statement:

NOTICE OF AIRPORT IN VICINITY

This property is presently located in the vicinity of an airport, within what is known as an airport influence area. For that reason, the property may be subject to some of the annoyances or inconveniences associated with proximity to airport operations (for example: noise, vibration, or odors). Individual sensitivities to those annoyances can vary from person to person. You may wish to consider what airport annoyances, if any, are associated with the property before you complete your purchase and determine whether they are acceptable to you.

(2) In responding to the request, the expert shall determine whether the property is within the jurisdiction of the San Francisco Bay Conservation and Development Commission, as defined in Section 66620 of the Government Code. If the property is within the commission's jurisdiction, the report shall contain the following notice:

NOTICE OF SAN FRANCISCO BAY CONSERVATION AND DEVELOPMENT COMMISSION JURISDICTION

This property is located within the jurisdiction of the San Francisco Bay Conservation and Development Commission. Use and development of property within the commission's jurisdiction may be subject to special regulations, restrictions, and permit requirements. You may wish to investigate and determine whether they are acceptable to you and your intended use of the property before you complete your transaction.

(3) In responding to the request, the expert shall determine whether the property is presently located within one mile of a parcel of real property designated as "Prime Farmland," "Farmland of Statewide Importance," "Unique Farmland," "Farmland of Local Importance," or "Grazing Land" on the most current "Important Farmland Map" issued by the California Department of Conservation, Division of Land Resource Protection, utilizing solely the county-level GIS map data, if any, available on the Farmland Mapping and Monitoring Program Web site. If the residential property is within one mile of a designated farmland area, the report shall contain the following notice:

NOTICE OF RIGHT TO FARM

This property is located within one mile of a farm or ranch land designated on the current county-level GIS "Important Farmland Map," issued by the California Department of Conservation, Division of Land Resource Protection. Accordingly, the property may be subject to inconveniences or discomforts resulting from agricultural operations that are a normal and necessary aspect of living in a community with a strong rural character and a healthy agricultural sector. Customary agricultural practices in farm operations may include, but are not limited to, noise, odors, dust, light, insects, the operation of pumps and machinery, the storage and disposal of manure, bee pollination, and the ground or aerial application of fertilizers, pesticides, and herbicides. These agricultural practices may occur at any time during the 24–hour day. Individual sensitivities to those practices can vary from person to person. You may wish to consider the impacts of such agricultural practices before you complete your purchase. Please be advised that you may be barred from obtaining legal remedies against agricultural practices conducted in a manner consistent with proper and accepted

§ 1103.4 PROPERTY

customs and standards pursuant to Section 3482.5 of the Civil Code or any pertinent local ordinance.

(4) In responding to the request, the expert shall determine, utilizing map coordinate data made available by the Office of Mine Reclamation, whether the property is presently located within one mile of a mine operation for which map coordinate data has been reported to the director pursuant to Section 2207 of the Public Resources Code. If the expert determines, from the available map coordinate data, that the residential property is located within one mile of a mine operation, the report shall contain the following notice:

NOTICE OF MINING OPERATIONS:

This property is located within one mile of a mine operation for which the mine owner or operator has reported mine location data to the Department of Conservation pursuant to Section 2207 of the Public Resources Code. Accordingly, the property may be subject to inconveniences resulting from mining operations. You may wish to consider the impacts of these practices before you complete your transaction. *(Added by Stats.1999, c. 876 (A.B.248), § 3. Amended by Stats.2002, c. 496 (A.B.2776), § 4, operative Jan. 1, 2004; Stats.2004, c. 618 (S.B.1568), § 2; Stats.2008, c. 686 (A.B.2881), § 3; Stats.2011, c. 253 (S.B.110), § 1; Stats.2018, c. 907 (A.B.1289), § 24, eff. Jan. 1, 2019.)*

Cross References

Earthquake fault zoning, disclosure of property location by transferor or agent, see Public Resources Code § 2621.9.

Forest fires, responsibility for fire protection, real property located within state responsibility area, disclosures, see Public Resources Code § 4136.

Property within a very high fire hazard severity zone, disclosure to prospective transferee, see Government Code § 51183.5.

Seismic hazards mapping, disclosure of property location by transferor or agent, see Public Resources Code § 2694.

§ 1103.5. Seller's and seller's agent's relief from duty regarding items of information

(a) After a seller and his or her agent comply with Section 1103.2, they shall be relieved of further duty under this article with respect to those items of information. The seller and the seller's agent shall not be required to provide notice to the prospective buyer if the information provided subsequently becomes inaccurate as a result of any governmental action, map revision, changed information, or other act or occurrence, unless the seller or agent has actual knowledge that the information has become inaccurate.

(b) If information disclosed in accordance with this article is subsequently rendered inaccurate as a result of any governmental action, map revision, changed information, or other act or occurrence subsequent to the delivery of the required disclosures, the inaccuracy resulting therefrom does not constitute a violation of this article. *(Added by Stats. 1999, c. 876 (A.B.248), § 3. Amended by Stats.2018, c. 907 (A.B.1289), § 25, eff. Jan. 1, 2019.)*

§ 1103.7. Acts of disclosure made in good faith

Each disclosure required by this article and each act that may be performed in making the disclosure shall be made in good faith. For purposes of this article, "good faith" means honesty in fact in the conduct of the transaction. *(Added by Stats.1999, c. 876 (A.B.248), § 3.)*

§ 1103.8. Obligations for disclosure created under other laws

(a) The specification of items for disclosure in this article does not limit or abridge any obligation for disclosure created by any other provision of law or that may exist in order to avoid fraud, misrepresentation, or deceit in the sale transaction. The Legislature does not intend to affect the existing obligations of the parties to a real estate contract, or their agents, to disclose any fact materially affecting the value and desirability of the property, including, but not limited to, the physical condition of the property and previously received reports of physical inspection noted on the disclosure form provided pursuant to Section 1102.6 or 1102.6a.

(b) Nothing in this article shall be construed to change the duty of a real estate broker or salesperson pursuant to Section 2079. *(Added by Stats.1999, c. 876 (A.B.248), § 3. Amended by Stats.2018, c. 907 (A.B.1289), § 26, eff. Jan. 1, 2019.)*

Cross References

Obligation defined, see Civil Code § 1427.

§ 1103.9. Amendments to disclosures

Any disclosure made pursuant to this article may be amended in writing by the seller or the seller's agent, but the amendment shall be subject to Section 1103.3. *(Added by Stats.1999, c. 876 (A.B.248), § 3. Amended by Stats.2018, c. 907 (A.B.1289), § 27, eff. Jan. 1, 2019.)*

§ 1103.10. Delivery of disclosures; personal delivery by mail

Delivery of disclosures required by this article shall be by personal delivery to the transferee or by mail to the prospective transferee. For the purposes of this article, delivery to the spouse of a transferee shall be deemed delivery to the transferee, unless provided otherwise by contract. *(Added by Stats.1999, c. 876 (A.B.248), § 3.)*

§ 1103.11. Escrow agents for transfer of real property; not agent of transferor or transferee

Any person or entity, other than a real estate licensee licensed pursuant to Part 1 (commencing with Section 10000) of Division 4 of the Business and Professions Code, acting in the capacity of an escrow agent for the transfer of real property subject to this article shall not be deemed the agent of the transferor or transferee for purposes of the disclosure requirements of this article, unless the person or entity is empowered to so act by an express written agreement to that effect. The extent of that agency shall be governed by the written agreement. *(Added by Stats.1999, c. 876 (A.B.248), § 3.)*

Cross References

California Emergency Services Act, flooding, disclosure to potential transferee, see Government Code § 8589.4.

California Emergency Services Act, property within special flood hazard area, disclosure to prospective transferee, see Government Code § 8589.3.

Earthquake fault zoning, disclosure of property location by transferor or agent, see Public Resources Code § 2621.9.

Real property defined for purposes of this Code, see Civil Code § 658.

Seismic hazards mapping, disclosure of property location by transferor or agent, see Public Resources Code § 2694.

§ 1103.12. Licensed real estate broker obtaining offer from transferee; duty of delivery

(a) If more than one licensed real estate broker is acting as an agent in a transaction subject to this article, the broker who has obtained the offer made by the transferee shall, except as otherwise provided in this article, deliver the disclosure required by this article to the transferee, unless the transferor has given other written instructions for delivery.

(b) If a licensed real estate broker responsible for delivering the disclosures under this section cannot obtain the disclosure document required and does not have written assurance from the transferee that the disclosure has been received, the broker shall advise the transferee in writing of his or her rights to the disclosure. A licensed real estate broker responsible for delivering disclosures under this section shall maintain a record of the action taken to effect compliance in accordance with Section 10148 of the Business and Professions Code. *(Added by Stats.1999, c. 876 (A.B. 248), § 3.)*

§ 1103.13. Invalidation of transfer; effect of noncompliance with article

No transfer subject to this article shall be invalidated solely because of the failure of any person to comply with any provision of this article. However, any person who willfully or negligently violates or fails to perform any duty prescribed by any provision of this article shall be liable in the amount of actual damages suffered by a transferee. *(Added by Stats. 1999, c. 876 (A.B.248), § 3.)*

Cross References

California Emergency Services Act, flooding, disclosure to potential transferee, see Government Code § 8589.4.

California Emergency Services Act, property within special flood hazard area, disclosure to prospective transferee, see Government Code § 8589.3.

Earthquake fault zoning, disclosure of property location by transferor or agent, see Public Resources Code § 2621.9.

Forest fires, responsibility for fire protection, real property located within state responsibility area, disclosures, see Public Resources Code § 4136.

Property within a very high fire hazard severity zone, disclosure to prospective transferee, see Government Code § 51183.5.

Seismic hazards mapping, disclosure of property location by transferor or agent, see Public Resources Code § 2694.

§ 1103.14. Repealed by Stats.2018, c. 907 (A.B.1289), § 28, eff. Jan. 1, 2019

§ 1103.15. Application of Section 1102.1 (d)

The provisions of subdivision (d) of Section 1102.1 shall apply to this article. *(Added by Stats.2018, c. 907 (A.B.1289), § 29, eff. Jan. 1, 2019.)*

ARTICLE 1.8. BUYER'S CHOICE ACT

Section
1103.20. Short title.
1103.21. Legislative findings and declarations; sales of foreclosed properties.
1103.22. Seller of residential real properties; requiring purchase of title insurance or escrow service from particular insurer or agent prohibited; violations.
1103.23. Repealed.

§ 1103.20. Short title

This article shall be known, and may be cited, as the Buyer's Choice Act. *(Added by Stats.2009, c. 264 (A.B.957), § 1, eff. Oct. 11, 2009.)*

§ 1103.21. Legislative findings and declarations; sales of foreclosed properties

(a) The Legislature finds and declares:

(1) Sales of foreclosed properties have become a dominant portion of homes on the resale real estate market.

(2) The recent troubled real estate market has resulted in a concentration of the majority of homes available for resale within the hands of foreclosing lenders and has dramatically changed the market dynamics affecting ordinary home buyers.

(3) Preserving the fair negotiability of contract terms is an important policy goal to be preserved in real estate transactions.

(4) The potential for unfairness occasioned by the resale of large numbers of foreclosed homes on the market requires that protections against abuses be made effective immediately.

(5) The federal Real Estate Settlement Procedures Act (RESPA) creates general rules for fair negotiation of settlement services, prohibits kickbacks and specifically prohibits a seller in a federally related transaction from requiring a buyer to purchase title insurance from a particular insurer.

(6) California law does not specifically prohibit a seller from imposing, as a condition of sale of a foreclosed home, the purchase of title insurance or escrow services from a particular insurer or provider.

(7) Therefore it is necessary to add this act to California law to provide to a home buyer protection that follows the RESPA model and applies to, and prevents, the conditioning of a sale of a foreclosed home on the buyer's purchase of title insurance from a particular insurer or title company and/or the buyer's purchase of escrow services from a particular provider.

(b) It is the intent of the Legislature that, for the purpose of this act, the sale of a residential real property is deemed to include the receipt of an offer to purchase that residential real property. *(Added by Stats.2009, c. 264 (A.B.957), § 1, eff. Oct. 11, 2009.)*

§ 1103.22. Seller of residential real properties; requiring purchase of title insurance or escrow service from particular insurer or agent prohibited; violations

(a) A seller of residential real property improved by four or fewer dwelling units shall not require directly or indirectly,

§ 1103.22

as a condition of selling the property, that title insurance covering the property or escrow service provided in connection with the sale of the property be purchased by the buyer from a particular title insurer or escrow agent. This section does not prohibit a buyer from agreeing to accept the services of a title insurer or an escrow agent recommended by the seller if written notice of the right to make an independent selection of those services is first provided by the seller to the buyer.

(b) For purposes of this section:

(1) [1]"Escrow service" means service provided by a person licensed pursuant to Division 6 (commencing with Section 17000) of the Financial Code, or exempt from licensing pursuant to Section 17006 of the Financial Code.

(2) "Seller" means a mortgagee or beneficiary under a deed of trust who acquired title to residential real property improved by four or fewer dwelling units at a foreclosure sale, including a trustee, agent, officer, or other employee of any such mortgagee or beneficiary.

(3) "Title insurance" means insurance offered by an insurer admitted in this state to transact title insurance pursuant to Chapter 1 (commencing with Section 12340) of Part 6 of the Insurance Code.

(c) A seller who violates this section shall be liable to a buyer in an amount equal to three times all charges made for the title insurance or escrow service. In addition, any person who violates this section shall be deemed to have violated his or her license law and shall be subject to discipline by his or her licensing entity.

(d) A transaction subject to this section shall not be invalidated solely because of the failure of any person to comply with any provision of this act. *(Added by Stats.2009, c. 264 (A.B.957), § 1, eff. Oct. 11, 2009.)*

[1] So in enrolled bill.

§ 1103.23. Repealed by Stats.2014, c. 198 (S.B.1051), § 1, eff. Jan. 1, 2015

ARTICLE 2. EFFECT OF TRANSFER

Section
1104. Easements passing with property.
1105. Fee simple title; presumption.
1106. Subsequently acquired title; passage by operation of law.
1107. Conclusiveness of grant; exception.
1108. Estate for life or years; purported transfer of greater estate than that owned.
1109. Defeated grant upon condition subsequent; reconveyance.
1110. Grant on condition precedent; performance of condition; effect.
1111. Grants of rents, reversions and remainders.
1112. Grant of land bounded by highway.
1113. Grant; implied covenants.
1114. Incumbrances defined.
1115. Lineal and collateral warranties abolished; covenants; effect upon heirs and devisees.
1133. Property subject to blanket encumbrance but exempt from compliance with § 11013.2; notice to prospective purchaser or lessee; civil and criminal liability.

Section
1134. Statement of defects or disclaimer; termination of purchase agreement; definitions.
1134.5. Repealed.

§ 1104. Easements passing with property

WHAT EASEMENTS PASS WITH PROPERTY. A transfer of real property passes all easements attached thereto, and creates in favor thereof an easement to use other real property of the person whose estate is transferred in the same manner and to the same extent as such property was obviously and permanently used by the person whose estate is transferred, for the benefit thereof, at the time when the transfer was agreed upon or completed. *(Enacted in 1872.)*

Cross References

Covenants for easement, creation, see Government Code § 65871.
Easements and servitudes generally, see Civil Code § 801 et seq.
Real property defined for purposes of this Code, see Civil Code § 658.
Transfer of a thing carries its incidents, see Civil Code §§ 1084, 3540.

§ 1105. Fee simple title; presumption

WHEN FEE SIMPLE TITLE IS PRESUMED TO PASS. A fee simple title is presumed to be intended to pass by a grant of real property, unless it appears from the grant that a lesser estate was intended. *(Enacted in 1872.)*

Cross References

Construction of instruments, see Code of Civil Procedure § 1858 et seq.
Easements pass with property, see Civil Code § 1104.
Real property defined for purposes of this Code, see Civil Code § 658.
Transfer of title obtained by adverse possession, see Civil Code § 1000 et seq.

§ 1106. Subsequently acquired title; passage by operation of law

SUBSEQUENTLY ACQUIRED TITLE PASSES BY OPERATION OF LAW. Where a person purports by proper instrument to grant real property in fee simple, and subsequently acquires any title, or claim of title thereto, the same passes by operation of law to the grantee, or his successors. *(Enacted in 1872.)*

Cross References

Acquisition of title by prescription, see Civil Code § 1007.
Mortgagee, subsequently acquired title as inuring to, see Civil Code § 2930.
Real property defined for purposes of this Code, see Civil Code § 658.

§ 1107. Conclusiveness of grant; exception

GRANT, HOW FAR CONCLUSIVE ON PURCHASERS. Every grant of an estate in real property is conclusive against the grantor, also against every one subsequently claiming under him, except a purchaser or incumbrancer who in good faith and for a valuable consideration acquires a title or lien by an instrument that is first duly recorded. *(Enacted in 1872.)*

Cross References

Good faith purchasers or incumbrancers,
  Mortgagee as against unrecorded conveyance, see Civil Code § 1214.
Protection against unlawful transfers, see Civil Code § 1227 et seq.
Real property defined for purposes of this Code, see Civil Code § 658.
Recording of transfers, effect of or of want thereof in general, see Civil Code § 1213 et seq.

§ 1108. Estate for life or years; purported transfer of greater estate than that owned

CONVEYANCES BY OWNER FOR LIFE OR FOR YEARS. A grant made by the owner of an estate for life or years, purporting to transfer a greater estate than he could lawfully transfer, does not work a forfeiture of his estate, but passes to the grantee all the estate which the grantor could lawfully transfer. *(Enacted in 1872.)*

§ 1109. Defeated grant upon condition subsequent; reconveyance

GRANT MADE ON CONDITION SUBSEQUENT. Where a grant is made upon condition subsequent, and is subsequently defeated by the non-performance of the condition, the person otherwise entitled to hold under the grant must reconvey the property to the grantor or his successors, by grant, duly acknowledged for record. *(Enacted in 1872.)*

Cross References

Condition subsequent defined, see Civil Code § 1438.
Conditional obligations, see Civil Code § 1434 et seq.
Conditions of ownership, see Civil Code § 707 et seq.
Construction of conditions involving forfeiture, see Civil Code § 1442.
Discriminatory restrictive deeds and covenants, see Civil Code §§ 53, 782.
Impossible or unlawful conditions, see Civil Code § 1441.
Reentry for breach of condition subsequent, transferability, see Civil Code § 1046.
Restraints on alienation, see Civil Code § 712.

§ 1110. Grant on condition precedent; performance of condition; effect

An instrument purporting to be a grant of real property, to take effect upon condition precedent, passes the estate upon the performance of the condition. *(Enacted in 1872. Amended by Code Am.1873–74, c. 612, p. 225, § 132.)*

Cross References

Condition precedent defined, see Civil Code § 1436.
Real property defined for purposes of this Code, see Civil Code § 658.

§ 1111. Grants of rents, reversions and remainders

GRANT OF RENTS, REVERSIONS, AND REMAINDERS. Grants of rents or of reversions or of remainders are good and effectual without attornments of the tenants; but no tenant who, before notice of the grant, shall have paid rent to the grantor, must suffer any damage thereby. *(Enacted in 1872.)*

Cross References

Rights of grantees of rents and reversions, see Civil Code § 821.

§ 1112. Grant of land bounded by highway

A transfer of land, bounded by a highway, passes the title of the person whose estate is transferred to the soil of the highway in front to the center thereof, unless a different intent appears from the grant. *(Enacted in 1872. Amended by Code Am.1873–74, c. 612, p. 225, § 133.)*

Cross References

Road or street as boundary, see Civil Code § 831; Code of Civil Procedure § 2077.

§ 1113. Grant; implied covenants

IMPLIED COVENANTS. From the use of the word "grant" in any conveyance by which an estate of inheritance or fee simple is to be passed, the following covenants, and none other, on the part of the grantor for himself and his heirs to the grantee, his heirs, and assigns, are implied, unless restrained by express terms contained in such conveyance:

1. That previous to the time of the execution of such conveyance, the grantor has not conveyed the same estate, or any right, title, or interest therein, to any person other than the grantee;

2. That such estate is at the time of the execution of such conveyance free from encumbrances done, made, or suffered by the grantor, or any person claiming under him.

Such covenants may be sued upon in the same manner as if they had been expressly inserted in the conveyance. *(Enacted in 1872.)*

Cross References

Damages for breach of covenant, see Civil Code § 3304.

§ 1114. Incumbrances defined

The term "incumbrances" includes taxes, assessments, and all liens upon real property. *(Enacted in 1872. Amended by Code Am.1873–74, c. 612, p. 225, § 134.)*

Cross References

Covenants running with the land, see Civil Code § 1460 et seq.
Implied warranties of title, sale of goods, see Commercial Code § 2312.
Real property defined for purposes of this Code, see Civil Code § 658.

§ 1115. Lineal and collateral warranties abolished; covenants; effect upon heirs and devisees

LINEAL AND COLLATERAL WARRANTIES ABOLISHED. Lineal and collateral warranties, with all their incidents, are abolished; but the heirs and devisees of every person who has made any covenant or agreement in reference to the title of, in, or to any real property, are answerable upon such covenant or agreement to the extent of the land descended or devised to them, in the cases and in the manner prescribed by law. *(Enacted in 1872.)*

§ 1115

Cross References

Real property defined for purposes of this Code, see Civil Code § 658.

§ 1133. Property subject to blanket encumbrance but exempt from compliance with § 11013.2; notice to prospective purchaser or lessee; civil and criminal liability

(a) If a lot, parcel, or unit of a subdivision is subject to a blanket encumbrance, as defined in Section 11013 of the Business and Professions Code, but is exempt from a requirement of compliance with Section 11013.2 of the Business and Professions Code, the subdivider, his or her agent, or representative, shall not sell, or lease for a term exceeding five years, the lot, parcel, or unit, nor cause it to be sold, or leased for a term exceeding five years, until the prospective purchaser or lessee of the lot, parcel, or unit has been furnished with and has signed a true copy of the following notice:

BUYER/LESSEE IS AWARE OF THE FACT THAT THE LOT, PARCEL, OR UNIT WHICH HE OR SHE IS PROPOSING TO PURCHASE OR LEASE IS SUBJECT TO A DEED OF TRUST, MORTGAGE, OR OTHER LIEN KNOWN AS A "BLANKET ENCUMBRANCE."

IF BUYER/LESSEE PURCHASES OR LEASES THIS LOT, PARCEL, OR UNIT, HE OR SHE COULD LOSE THAT INTEREST THROUGH FORECLOSURE OF THE BLANKET ENCUMBRANCE OR OTHER LEGAL PROCESS EVEN THOUGH BUYER/LESSEE IS NOT DELINQUENT IN HIS OR HER PAYMENTS OR OTHER OBLIGATIONS UNDER THE MORTGAGE, DEED OF TRUST, OR LEASE.

_____   _____
Date   Signature of Buyer or Lessee

(b) "Subdivision," as used in subdivision (a), means improved or unimproved land that is divided or proposed to be divided for the purpose of sale, lease, or financing, whether immediate or future, into two or more lots, parcels, or units and includes a condominium project, as defined in Section 4125 or 6542, a community apartment project, as defined in Section 4105, a stock cooperative, as defined in Section 4190 or 6566, and a limited equity housing cooperative, as defined in Section 4190.

(c) The failure of the buyer or lessee to sign the notice shall not invalidate any grant, conveyance, lease, or encumbrance.

(d) Any person or entity who willfully violates the provisions of this section shall be liable to the purchaser of a lot or unit which is subject to the provisions of this section for actual damages, and, in addition thereto, shall be guilty of a public offense punishable by a fine in an amount not to exceed five hundred dollars ($500). In an action to enforce the liability or fine, the prevailing party shall be awarded reasonable attorney's fees. (Added by Stats.1982, c. 148, § 3, eff. April 5, 1982. Amended by Stats.1985, c. 874, § 12; Stats.2012, c. 181 (A.B.806), § 35, operative Jan. 1, 2014; Stats.2013, c. 605 (S.B.752), § 15.)

Cross References

Common interest developments, application of this section, see Civil Code § 4535.

Individual interest in stock cooperative or a limited equity housing cooperative, sale or lease subject to blanket encumbrance, conditions, see Business and Professions Code § 11013.6.

Obligation defined, see Civil Code § 1427.

§ 1134. Statement of defects or disclaimer; termination of purchase agreement; definitions

(a) As soon as practicable before transfer of title for the first sale of a unit in a residential condominium, community apartment project, or stock cooperative which was converted from an existing dwelling to a condominium project, community apartment project, or stock cooperative, the owner or subdivider, or agent of the owner or subdivider, shall deliver to a prospective buyer a written statement listing all substantial defects or malfunctions in the major systems in the unit and common areas of the premises, or a written statement disclaiming knowledge of any such substantial defects or malfunctions. The disclaimer may be delivered only after the owner or subdivider has inspected the unit and the common areas and has not discovered a substantial defect or malfunction which a reasonable inspection would have disclosed.

(b) If any disclosure required to be made by this section is delivered after the execution of an agreement to purchase, the buyer shall have three days after delivery in person or five days after delivery by deposit in the mail, to terminate his or her agreement by delivery of written notice of that termination to the owner, subdivider, or agent. Any disclosure delivered after the execution of an agreement to purchase shall contain a statement describing the buyer's right, method and time to rescind as prescribed by this subdivision.

(c) For the purposes of this section:

(1) "Major systems" includes, but is not limited to, the roof, walls, floors, heating, air conditioning, plumbing, electrical systems or components of a similar or comparable nature, and recreational facilities.

(2) Delivery to a prospective buyer of the written statement required by this section shall be deemed effected when delivered personally or by mail to the prospective buyer or to an agent thereof, or to a spouse unless the agreement provides to the contrary. Delivery shall also be made to additional prospective buyers who have made a request therefor in writing.

(3) "Prospective buyer" includes any person who makes an offer to purchase a unit in the condominium, community apartment project, or stock cooperative.

(d) Any person who willfully fails to carry out the requirements of this section shall be liable in the amount of actual damages suffered by the buyer.

(e) Nothing in this section shall preclude the injured party from pursuing any remedy available under any other provision of law.

(f) No transfer of title to a unit subject to the provisions of this chapter shall be invalid solely because of the failure of any person to comply with the requirements of this section.

(g) The written statement required by this section shall not abridge or limit any other obligation of disclosure created by any other provision of law or which is or may be required to avoid fraud, deceit, or misrepresentation in the transaction. *(Added by Stats.1981, c. 811, § 1, operative July 1, 1982.)*

Cross References

Common interest developments, application of this section, see Civil Code § 4535.
Obligation defined, see Civil Code § 1427.
Regulation of buildings used for human habitation, inspection of exterior elevated elements, see Health and Safety Code § 17973.

§ 1134.5. Repealed by Stats.1986, c. 460, § 8

CHAPTER 3. TRANSFER OF PERSONAL PROPERTY

Article	Section
1. Mode of Transfer	1135
2. What Operates as a Transfer [Repealed]	
3. Gifts	1146
4. California Uniform Gifts to Minors Act [Repealed]	

ARTICLE 1. MODE OF TRANSFER

Section
1135. Ship; method of transfer.
1136. Repealed.
1140. Dies, molds and forms; transfer of rights and title to molder by operation of law; notice; disposition by molder; rights under patent, copyright and unfair competition laws.

§ 1135. Ship; method of transfer

An interest in a ship can be transferred only by operation of law, or by written instrument, subscribed by the person making the transfer, or by his agent. *(Enacted in 1872. Amended by Stats.1931, c. 1070, p. 2259, § 6.)*

Cross References

Recording transfers of ships, see Civil Code § 1173.
Transfer of and liens without delivery, see Civil Code § 3440.

§ 1136. Repealed by Stats.1931, c. 1070, p. 2258, § 2

§ 1140. Dies, molds and forms; transfer of rights and title to molder by operation of law; notice; disposition by molder; rights under patent, copyright and unfair competition laws

(a) For purposes of this section:

(1) The term "customer" means any individual or entity who causes or caused a molder to fabricate, cast, or otherwise make a die, mold, or form.

(2) The term "molder" means any individual or entity, including, but not limited to, a tool or die maker, who fabricates, casts, or otherwise makes a die, mold, or form.

(3) For purposes of this section, the term "within three years following the last prior use" shall be construed to include any period following the last prior use of a die, mold, or form regardless of whether or not that period precedes the effective date of this section.

(b) In the absence of any agreement to the contrary, the customer shall have all rights and title to any die, mold, or form in the possession of the molder.

(c) If a customer does not claim possession from a molder of a die, mold, or form within three years following the last prior use thereof, all rights and title to any die, mold, or form may be transferred by operation of law to the molder for the purpose of destroying or otherwise disposing of such die, mold, or form, consistent with this section.

(d) If a molder chooses to have all rights and title to any die, mold, or form transferred to the molder by operation of law, the molder shall send written notice by registered mail to the chief executive officer of the customer or, if the customer is not a business entity, to the customer himself or herself at the customer's last known address indicating that the molder intends to terminate the customer's rights and title by having all such rights and title transferred to the molder by operation of law pursuant to this section.

(e) If a customer does not respond in person or by mail to claim possession of the particular die, mold, or form within 120 days following the date the notice was sent, or does not make other contractual arrangements with the molder for storage thereof, all rights and title of the customer shall transfer by operation of law to the molder. Thereafter, the molder may destroy or otherwise dispose of the particular mold, tool, or die as the molder's own property without any risk of liability to the customer, except that this section shall not be construed in any manner to affect any right of the customer, under federal patent or copyright law or any state or federal law pertaining to unfair competition. *(Added by Stats.1979, c. 180, p. 400, § 1. Amended by Stats.1981, c. 290, § 1.)*

ARTICLE 2. WHAT OPERATES AS A TRANSFER [REPEALED]

§§ 1141, 1142. Repealed by Stats.1931, c. 1070, p. 2258, § 2

ARTICLE 3. GIFTS

Section
1146. Gift defined.
1147. Verbal gift; requisites.
1148. Revocability.
1149 to 1153. Repealed.

Cross References

Birds, mammals and fish, donations to state for propagating, etc., see Fish and Game Code §§ 1525, 10503.
California Uniform Transfers to Minors Act, see Probate Code § 3900 et seq.
Capri figs, gifts to counties for control of, see Food and Agricultural Code § 6133.
Cemetery endowment care fund, see Health and Safety Code §§ 8735 et seq., 9000.
Community personal property, see Family Code § 1100.
Department of Education, gifts to, see Education Code §§ 33332, 71046.
Forests, gifts to state for, see Public Resources Code § 4701.
Interpretation of testamentary bequest, see Code of Civil Procedure § 764.020.
Liability of marital property, division of property, see Family Code § 916.
Liability of marital property, injury or damage caused by spouse, see Family Code § 1000.
Loan or gift of public credit or funds, see Cal. Const. Art. 16, § 6.

Marriage, recovery of gifts made in contemplation of, see Civil Code § 1590.
Mines, gifts to division of, see Public Resources Code § 2204.
Physically handicapped children, gifts to aid state treatment of, see Health and Safety Code § 123910.
Quiet title, action to, property passing by gift, see Code of Civil Procedure § 764.020.
School district, gifts to, see Education Code §§ 8766, 41030, 41032.
Unsolicited goods, see Civil Code § 1584.5.

§ 1146. Gift defined

GIFTS DEFINED. A gift is a transfer of personal property, made voluntarily, and without consideration. *(Enacted in 1872.)*

Cross References

Authority of Board of Governors to accept gifts to community colleges, see Education Code § 71046.
Bank and corporation taxes, basis for determining gain or loss, see Revenue and Taxation Code § 24914.
Fraudulent conveyances, see Civil Code § 3439 et seq.
Gifts causa mortis, see Probate Code § 5702 et seq.
Recovery of gift causa mortis, see Probate Code § 9653.
Revocation of gift, see Civil Code § 1148; Probate Code § 5704.
Voluntary transfers, see Civil Code § 1040.

§ 1147. Verbal gift; requisites

GIFT, HOW MADE. A verbal gift is not valid, unless the means of obtaining possession and control of the thing are given, nor, if it is capable of delivery, unless there is an actual or symbolical delivery of the thing to the donee. *(Enacted in 1872.)*

§ 1148. Revocability

A gift, other than a gift in view of impending death, cannot be revoked by the giver. *(Enacted in 1872. Amended by Stats.1991, c. 1055 (S.B.271), § 2.)*

Cross References

Revocation of gifts in view of death, see Probate Code § 5704.

§§ 1149 to 1153. Repealed by Stats.1991, c. 1055 (S.B.271), §§ 3 to 7

ARTICLE 4. CALIFORNIA UNIFORM GIFTS TO MINORS ACT [REPEALED]

§§ 1154 to 1165. Repealed by Stats.1984, c. 243, § 1

CHAPTER 4. RECORDING TRANSFERS

Article	Section
1. What May be Recorded [Repealed]	
2. Mode of Recording	1169
3. Proof and Acknowledgment of Instruments	1180
4. Effect of Recording, or the Want Thereof	1213

ARTICLE 1. WHAT MAY BE RECORDED [REPEALED]

ARTICLE 2. MODE OF RECORDING

Section	
1169.	Place of recordation.
1170.	Time instrument deemed recorded.
1171.	Grants and mortgages; separate sets of books.
1172.	Recorder; duties.
1173.	Vessels; mode of recording.
1179.04.5.	Renumbered.

Cross References

Recording of instruments or judgments relating to real property, see Government Code § 27280 et seq.

§ 1169. Place of recordation

IN WHAT OFFICE. Instruments entitled to be recorded must be recorded by the County Recorder of the county in which the real property affected thereby is situated. *(Enacted in 1872.)*

Cross References

Constructive notice, recording as, see Civil Code § 1213.
Instruments or judgments which may be recorded, see Government Code § 27280 et seq.
Real property defined for purposes of this Code, see Civil Code § 658.

§ 1170. Time instrument deemed recorded

An instrument is deemed to be recorded when, being duly acknowledged or proved and certified, it is deposited in the Recorder's office, with the proper officer, for record. *(Enacted in 1872. Amended by Code Am.1873–74, c. 612, p. 226, § 138.)*

Cross References

Acknowledgment, necessity of, see Government Code § 27287.
Documents to be recorded, see Government Code § 27280 et seq.
Documents which may be recorded without acknowledgments, see Government Code §§ 27282, 27283, 27285.
Fee for recording instruments, see Government Code § 27361.
Foreign language, recording of instruments in, see Government Code § 27293.
Manner of recording, see Government Code § 27320.
Payment of recording fees, see Government Code § 27201.

§ 1171. Grants and mortgages; separate sets of books

BOOKS OF RECORD. Grants, absolute in terms, are to be recorded in one set of books, and mortgages in another. *(Enacted in 1872.)*

Cross References

Acceptance of instruments for recording, see Government Code § 27201.
Acknowledgment of execution prior to recording, see Government Code § 27287.
Additional indexing, see Government Code § 27328.
Documents recordable without acknowledgment, see Government Code §§ 27282, 27285.
Execution, acknowledgment and proof of agreements affecting realty, see Government Code § 27288.
Manner of recording, see Government Code §§ 27320, 27322.
Record lost or destroyed, see Government Code § 27329.
Recording and indexing fees, see Government Code § 27361.
Recording in improper book and indexing in proper book, effect, see Government Code § 27327.
Recording in "Official Records" in lieu of in separate books, see Government Code § 27323.
Recording instruments in foreign language, see Government Code § 27293.

Selection and recording of declared homestead, see Code of Civil Procedure §§ 704.920, 704.930.

§ 1172. Recorder; duties

The duties of county recorders, in respect to recording instruments, are prescribed by the Government Code. *(Enacted in 1872. Amended by Stats.1959, c. 593, p. 2564, § 1.)*

Cross References

Books, acquisition and custody by recorders, see Government Code §§ 27230, 27231.
Duties of recorder, see Government Code § 27201 et seq.
Microphotography of records, see Government Code § 27322.2.

§ 1173. Vessels; mode of recording

TRANSFER OF VESSELS. The mode of recording transfers of ships registered under the laws of the United States is regulated by Acts of Congress. *(Enacted in 1872.)*

Cross References

Transfer of vessels, see Civil Code § 1135.

§ 1179.04.5. Renumbered Code of Civil Procedure § 1179.04.5 and amended by Stats.2021, c. 124 (A.B. 938), § 3, eff. Jan. 1, 2022; Stats.2021, c. 5 (A.B.81), § 2, eff. Feb. 23, 2021

ARTICLE 3. PROOF AND ACKNOWLEDGMENT OF INSTRUMENTS

Section
1180. Persons before whom proof or acknowledgment may be made.
1181. Notaries public; officers before whom proof or acknowledgment may be made.
1182. Proof or acknowledgment of instrument; out of state.
1183. Officers outside country.
1183.5. Notarial acts.
1184. Proof or acknowledgment of instruments; deputies.
1185. Acknowledgments; requisites; civil penalties.
1186. Repealed.
1187. Repealed.
1188. Certificate of acknowledgment.
1189. Certificate of acknowledgment; sufficiency of out-of-state acknowledgment; force and effect of acknowledgment under prior laws; civil penalties.
1190. Certificate of acknowledgment as prima facie evidence; duly authorized person.
1190a to 1192. Repealed.
1193. Certificate of acknowledgment; authentication.
1194. Repealed.
1195. Proof of execution; methods; certificate form.
1196. Subscribing witness; proof.
1197. Subscribing witness; items to be proved.
1198. Proof of handwriting; when authorized.
1199. Proof of handwriting; scope.
1200. Proof of execution; certificate; contents.
1201. Authority of officers taking proof.
1202. Defective certificate; action for correction.
1203. Action for judgment proving instrument.
1204. Judgment proving instrument; effect.
1205. Conveyances prior to code; law governing.
1206. Conveyances prior to code; evidence; recording.
1207. Defectively executed instruments; validity.

Cross References

Acknowledged writings, prima facie evidence of facts, see Evidence Code § 1451.
Recording of instruments or judgments relating to real property, see Government Code § 27280 et seq.

§ 1180. Persons before whom proof or acknowledgment may be made

The proof or acknowledgment of an instrument may be made at any place within this state before a justice, retired justice, or Clerk/Executive Officer of the Supreme Court, a justice, retired justice, or clerk of any court of appeal or judge or retired judge of a superior court, or the Secretary of the Senate or Chief Clerk of the Assembly. *(Enacted in 1872. Amended by Code Am.1880, c. 39, p. 2, § 1; Stats.1953, c. 457, p. 1701, § 1; Stats.1967, c. 17, p. 826, § 3; Stats.1986, c. 1417, § 1; Stats.1999, c. 20 (S.B.301), § 1; Stats.2017, c. 36 (A.B.452), § 3, eff. Jan. 1, 2018.)*

Cross References

Acknowledged defined for purposes of general corporation law, see Corporations Code § 149.
Articles of incorporation, see Corporations Code § 200.
Deputies authorized to take acknowledgments, see Civil Code § 1184.
Documents that may be recorded without acknowledgments, see Government Code §§ 27282, 27283, 27285.
Instruments which must be acknowledged to be recorded, see Government Code § 27287.
Military personnel authorized to take acknowledgments, see Civil Code § 1183.5.
Party by whom agreement affecting realty must be acknowledged, see Government Code § 27288.
Power of judge or justice to take and certify the proof and acknowledgment of a conveyance or other written instrument, see Code of Civil Procedure § 179.

§ 1181. Notaries public; officers before whom proof or acknowledgment may be made

The proof or acknowledgment of an instrument may be made before a notary public at any place within this state, or within the county or city and county in this state in which the officer specified below was elected or appointed, before either:

(a) A clerk of a superior court.

(b) A county clerk.

(c) A court commissioner.

(d) A retired judge of a municipal or justice court.

(e) A district attorney.

(f) A clerk of a board of supervisors.

(g) A city clerk.

(h) A county counsel.

(i) A city attorney.

(j) Secretary of the Senate.

(k) Chief Clerk of the Assembly. *(Enacted in 1872. Amended by Code Am.1880, c. 39, p. 2, § 2; Stats.1891, c. 150, p. 214, § 1; Stats.1911, c. 247, p. 429, § 1; Stats.1941, c. 1096, p. 2789, § 1; Stats.1945, c. 240, p. 705, § 2; Stats.1951, c. 1676, p. 3861, § 3; Stats.1953, c. 457, p. 1701, § 2; Stats.1959, c. 1162, p. 2352, § 1; Stats.1961, c. 49, p. 988, § 1; Stats.1963,*

c. 200, p. 938, § 1; Stats.1968, c. 576, p. 1244, § 1; Stats.1971, c. 27, p. 38, § 1; Stats.1981, c. 390, § 1; Stats.1986, c. 1417, § 2; Stats.1992, c. 876 (A.B.3296), § 3; Stats.1998, c. 931 (S.B.2139), § 13, eff. Sept. 28, 1998; Stats.1999, c. 20 (S.B. 301), § 2; Stats.2002, c. 784 (S.B.1316), § 12.)

Cross References

Court commissioners, see Code of Civil Procedure § 259.
Deputies authorized to take acknowledgments, see Civil Code § 1184.
Fee of county clerk, see Government Code § 26855.
Fee of recorder, see Government Code § 27375.
Judge or justice, power to take acknowledgments, see Code of Civil Procedure § 179.
Notary public, duties of, see Government Code § 8205.
Property taxation, acknowledgment of documents pursuant to this section, see Revenue and Taxation Code § 168.5.

§ 1182. Proof or acknowledgment of instrument; out of state

The proof or acknowledgment of an instrument may be made without this state, but within the United States, and within the jurisdiction of the officer, before any of the following:

(1) A justice, judge, or clerk of any court of record of the United States.

(2) A justice, judge, or clerk of any court of record of any state.

(3) A commissioner appointed by the Governor or Secretary of State for that purpose.

(4) A notary public.

(5) Any other officer of the state where the acknowledgment is made authorized by its laws to take such proof or acknowledgment. *(Enacted in 1872. Amended by Stats.1971, c. 1611, p. 3469, § 1.)*

Cross References

Deputies' authority to take acknowledgments, see Civil Code § 1184.

§ 1183. Officers outside country

The proof or acknowledgment of an instrument may be made without the United States, before any of the following:

(a) A minister, commissioner, or chargè d'affaires of the United States, resident and accredited in the country where the proof or acknowledgment is made.

(b) A consul, vice consul, or consular agent of the United States, resident in the country where the proof or acknowledgment is made.

(c) A judge of a court of record of the country where the proof or acknowledgment is made.

(d) Commissioners appointed by the Governor or Secretary of State for that purpose.

(e) A notary public.

If the proof or acknowledgment is made before a notary public, the signature of the notary public shall be proved or acknowledged (1) before a judge of a court of record of the country where the proof or acknowledgment is made, or (2) by any American diplomatic officer, consul general, consul, vice consul, or consular agent, or (3) by an apostille (certification) affixed to the instrument pursuant to the terms of The Hague Convention Abolishing the Requirement of Legalization for Foreign Public Documents. *(Enacted in 1872. Amended by Code Am.1873–74, c. 612, p. 227, § 139; Stats.1939, c. 249, p. 1505, § 1; Stats.1943, c. 28, p. 156, § 1; Stats.1963, c. 144, p. 816, § 1; Stats.1971, c. 1611, p. 3469, § 2; Stats.1982, c. 520, § 13; Stats.1984, c. 1017, § 1.)*

Cross References

Adoption agreement, execution, see Family Code § 8612.
In absentia acknowledgment of adoption agreement by adopting party, see Family Code § 8613.
Waiver of personal appearance of prospective adoptive parent, see Family Code § 8613.5.

§ 1183.5. Notarial acts

Any officer on active duty or performing inactive-duty training in the armed forces having the general powers of a notary public pursuant to Section 936 or 1044a of Title 10 of the United States Code (Public Law 90–632 and 101-510) and any successor statutes may perform all notarial acts for any person serving in the armed forces of the United States, wherever he or she may be, or for any spouse of a person serving in the armed forces, wherever he or she may be, or for any person eligible for legal assistance under laws and regulations of the United States, wherever he or she may be, for any person serving with, employed by, or accompanying such armed forces outside the United States and outside the Canal Zone, Puerto Rico, Guam and the Virgin Islands, and any person subject to the Uniform Code of Military Justice outside of the United States.

Any instrument acknowledged by any such officer or any oath or affirmation made before such officer shall not be rendered invalid by the failure to state therein the place of execution or acknowledgment. No seal or authentication of the officer's certificate of acknowledgment or of any jurat signed by him or her shall be required but the officer taking the acknowledgment shall endorse thereon or attach thereto a certificate substantially in a form authorized by the laws of this state or in the following form:

On this the _____ day of _____, 19___, before me _____, the undersigned officer, personally appeared _____ known to me (or satisfactorily proven) to be (a) serving in the armed forces of the United States, (b) a spouse of a person serving in the armed forces of the United States, or (c) a person serving with, employed by, or accompanying the armed forces of the United States outside the United States and outside the Canal Zone, Puerto Rico, Guam, and the Virgin Islands, and to be the person whose name is subscribed to the within instrument and acknowledged that he or she executed the same. And the undersigned does further certify that he or she is at the date of this certificate a commissioned officer of the armed forces of the United States having the general powers of a notary public under the provisions of Section 936 or 1044a of Title 10 of the United States Code (Public Law 90–632 and 101-510).

_____
Signature of officer, rank,
branch of service and capacity
in which signed.

To any affidavit subscribed and sworn to before such officer there shall be attached a jurat substantially in the following form:

Subscribed and sworn to before me on this _____ day of _____, 19___.

```
         _____
         Signature of officer, rank,
         branch of service and capacity
         in which signed.
```

The recitals contained in any such certificate or jurat shall be prima facie evidence of the truth thereof, and any certificate of acknowledgment, oath or affirmation purporting to have been made by any commissioned officer of the Army, Air Force, Navy, Marine Corps or Coast Guard shall, notwithstanding the omission of any specific recitals therein, constitute presumptive evidence of the existence of the facts necessary to authorize such acknowledgment, oath or affirmation to be taken by the certifying officer pursuant to this section. *(Added by Stats.1943, c. 28, p. 156, § 2. Amended by Stats.1943, c. 365, p. 1600, § 1; Stats.1945, c. 106, p. 414, § 1; Stats.1947, c. 10, p. 483, § 1; Stats.1949, c. 1186, p. 2106, § 2; Stats.1951, c. 386, p. 1185, § 1; Stats.1953, c. 603, p. 1848, § 1; Stats.1957, c. 898, p. 2109, § 1; Stats.1974, c. 91, p. 186, § 1; Stats.1992, c. 77 (S.B.208), § 1; Stats.1994, c. 587 (A.B.3600), § 1.)*

Cross References

Adoption agreement, execution, see Family Code § 8612.
In absentia acknowledgment of adoption agreement by adopting party, see Family Code § 8613.
Prima facie evidence, see Evidence Code § 602.
Waiver of personal appearance of prospective adoptive parent, see Family Code § 8613.5.

§ 1184. Proof or acknowledgment of instruments; deputies

When any of the officers mentioned in Sections 1180, 1181, 1182, and 1183 are authorized by law to appoint a deputy, the acknowledgment or proof may be taken by such deputy, in the name of his principal. *(Enacted in 1872. Amended by Stats.1953, c. 457, p. 1701, § 3.)*

Cross References

Deputies, powers and duties, see Government Code § 1194.

§ 1185. Acknowledgments; requisites; civil penalties

(a) The acknowledgment of an instrument shall not be taken unless the officer taking it has satisfactory evidence that the person making the acknowledgment is the individual who is described in and who executed the instrument.

(b) For purposes of this section, "satisfactory evidence" means the absence of information, evidence, or other circumstances that would lead a reasonable person to believe that the person making the acknowledgment is not the individual he or she claims to be and any one of the following:

(1)(A) The oath or affirmation of a credible witness personally known to the officer, whose identity is proven to the officer upon presentation of a document satisfying the requirements of paragraph (3) or (4), that the person making the acknowledgment is personally known to the witness and that each of the following are true:

(i) The person making the acknowledgment is the person named in the document.

(ii) The person making the acknowledgment is personally known to the witness.

(iii) That it is the reasonable belief of the witness that the circumstances of the person making the acknowledgment are such that it would be very difficult or impossible for that person to obtain another form of identification.

(iv) The person making the acknowledgment does not possess any of the identification documents named in paragraphs (3) and (4).

(v) The witness does not have a financial interest in the document being acknowledged and is not named in the document.

(B) A notary public who violates this section by failing to obtain the satisfactory evidence required by subparagraph (A) shall be subject to a civil penalty not exceeding ten thousand dollars ($10,000). An action to impose this civil penalty may be brought by the Secretary of State in an administrative proceeding or a public prosecutor in superior court, and shall be enforced as a civil judgment. A public prosecutor shall inform the secretary of any civil penalty imposed under this subparagraph.

(2) The oath or affirmation under penalty of perjury of two credible witnesses, whose identities are proven to the officer upon the presentation of a document satisfying the requirements of paragraph (3) or (4), that each statement in paragraph (1) is true.

(3) Reasonable reliance on the presentation to the officer of any one of the following, if the document or other form of identification is current or has been issued within five years:

(A) An identification card or driver's license issued by the Department of Motor Vehicles.

(B) A passport issued by the Department of State of the United States.

(C) An inmate identification card issued by the Department of Corrections and Rehabilitation, if the inmate is in custody in prison.

(D) Any form of inmate identification issued by a sheriff's department, if the inmate is in custody in a local detention facility.

(4) Reasonable reliance on the presentation of any one of the following, provided that a document specified in subparagraphs (A) to (F), inclusive, shall either be current or have been issued within five years and shall contain a photograph and description of the person named on it, shall be signed by the person, and shall bear a serial or other identifying number:

(A) A valid consular identification document issued by a consulate from the applicant's country of citizenship, or a valid passport from the applicant's country of citizenship.

(B) A driver's license issued by a state other than California or by a Canadian or Mexican public agency authorized to issue driver's licenses.

§ 1185

(C) An identification card issued by a state other than California.

(D) An identification card issued by any branch of the Armed Forces of the United States.

(E) An employee identification card issued by an agency or office of the State of California, or by an agency or office of a city, county, or city and county in this state.

(F) An identification card issued by a federally recognized tribal government.

(c) An officer who has taken an acknowledgment pursuant to this section shall be presumed to have operated in accordance with the provisions of law.

(d) A party who files an action for damages based on the failure of the officer to establish the proper identity of the person making the acknowledgment shall have the burden of proof in establishing the negligence or misconduct of the officer.

(e) A person convicted of perjury under this section shall forfeit any financial interest in the document. (Enacted in 1872. Amended by Stats.1905, c. 445, p. 603, § 2; Stats.1982, c. 197, § 1, eff. May 12, 1982; Stats.1987, c. 307, § 1; Stats.1988, c. 842, § 1; Stats.1993, c. 1044 (A.B.1090), § 1; Stats.2007, c. 399 (A.B.886), § 1; Stats.2008, c. 179 (S.B. 1498), § 29; Stats.2008, c. 67 (A.B.2452), § 1; Stats.2010, c. 328 (S.B.1330), § 28; Stats.2013, c. 159 (A.B.625), § 2; Stats.2015, c. 42 (A.B.1036), § 1, eff. Jan. 1, 2016; Stats.2016, c. 491 (S.B.997), § 1, eff. Jan. 1, 2017; Stats.2016, c. 762 (A.B.2566), § 1.5, eff. Jan. 1, 2017.)

Cross References

Authentication of signature, see Civil Code § 1193.
Burden of proof, generally, see Evidence Code § 500 et seq.
Defective certificate, correction, see Civil Code § 1202.
Department of Corrections, generally, see Penal Code § 5000 et seq.
Notaries public, generally, see Government Code § 8200 et seq.

§ 1186. Repealed by Stats.1891, c. 125, p. 137, § 1

§ 1187. Repealed by Stats.1976, c. 1171, p. 5252, § 4

§ 1188. Certificate of acknowledgment

An officer taking the acknowledgment of an instrument shall endorse thereon or attach thereto a certificate pursuant to Section 1189. (Enacted in 1872. Amended by Code Am.1873–74, c. 612, p. 227, § 140; Stats.1990, c. 1070 (S.B.2251), § 1; Stats.2013, c. 78 (A.B.464), § 1.)

§ 1189. Certificate of acknowledgment; sufficiency of out-of-state acknowledgment; force and effect of acknowledgment under prior laws; civil penalties

(a)(1) Any certificate of acknowledgment taken within this state shall include a notice at the top of the certificate of acknowledgment in an enclosed box stating: "A notary public or other officer completing this certificate verifies only the identity of the individual who signed the document to which this certificate is attached, and not the truthfulness, accuracy, or validity of that document." This notice shall be legible.

(2) The physical format of the boxed notice at the top of the certificate of acknowledgment required pursuant to paragraph (3) is an example, for purposes of illustration and not limitation, of the physical format of a boxed notice fulfilling the requirements of paragraph (1).

(3) A certificate of acknowledgment taken within this state shall be in the following form:

A notary public or other officer completing this certificate verifies only the identity of the individual who signed the document to which this certificate is attached, and not the truthfulness, accuracy, or validity of that document.

State of California   )
County of _____)

On _____ before me, (here insert name and title of the officer), personally appeared, _____, who proved to me on the basis of satisfactory evidence to be the person(s) whose name(s) is/are subscribed to the within instrument and acknowledged to me that he/she/they executed the same in his/her/their authorized capacity(ies), and that by his/her/their signature(s) on the instrument the person(s), or the entity upon behalf of which the person(s) acted, executed the instrument.

I certify under PENALTY OF PERJURY under the laws of the State of California that the foregoing paragraph is true and correct.

WITNESS my hand and official seal.

Signature _____ (Seal)

---

(4) A notary public who willfully states as true any material fact that he or she knows to be false shall be subject to a civil penalty not exceeding ten thousand dollars ($10,000). An action to impose a civil penalty under this subdivision may be brought by the Secretary of State in an administrative proceeding or any public prosecutor in superior court, and shall be enforced as a civil judgment. A public prosecutor shall inform the secretary of any civil penalty imposed under this section.

(b) Any certificate of acknowledgment taken in another place shall be sufficient in this state if it is taken in accordance with the laws of the place where the acknowledgment is made.

(c) On documents to be filed in another state or jurisdiction of the United States, a California notary public may complete any acknowledgment form as may be required in that other state or jurisdiction on a document, provided the form does not require the notary to determine or certify that the signer holds a particular representative capacity or to make other determinations and certifications not allowed by California law.

(d) An acknowledgment provided prior to January 1, 1993, and conforming to applicable provisions of former Sections 1189, 1190, 1190a, 1190.1, 1191, and 1192, as repealed by Chapter 335 of the Statutes of 1990, shall have the same force and effect as if those sections had not been repealed. (Added by Stats.1990, c. 335 (A.B.2581), § 2. Amended by Stats.1990, c. 1070 (S.B.2251), § 2; Stats.1991, c. 157 (A.B.1750), § 1; Stats.1996, c. 97 (A.B.3304), § 1; Stats.2005, c. 295 (A.B.361),

§ 1; Stats.2007, c. 399 (A.B.886), § 2; Stats.2014, c. 197 (S.B.1050), § 1, eff. Jan. 1, 2015.)

Cross References

Forgery of signatures or seals, corruption of records, falsifying or issuing acknowledgments, see Penal Code § 470.
Revocation of notary commission upon certain convictions, see Government Code § 8214.8.
Solicitation of improper notarial act as misdemeanor, and other remedies, see Government Code § 8225.
Uniform statutory form power of attorney, see Probate Code § 4401.
Willful failure to perform duty or control notarial seal, see Government Code § 8228.1.

§ 1190. Certificate of acknowledgment as prima facie evidence; duly authorized person

The certificate of acknowledgment of an instrument executed on behalf of an incorporated or unincorporated entity by a duly authorized person in the form specified in Section 1189 shall be prima facie evidence that the instrument is the duly authorized act of the entity named in the instrument and shall be conclusive evidence thereof in favor of any good faith purchaser, lessee, or encumbrancer. "Duly authorized person," with respect to a domestic or foreign corporation, includes the president, vice president, secretary, and assistant secretary of the corporation. *(Added by Stats.1990, c. 1070 (S.B.2251), § 3.)*

Cross References

Prima facie evidence, see Evidence Code § 602.

§§ 1190a to 1192. Repealed by Stats.1990, c. 335 (A.B. 2581), §§ 4 to 7

§ 1193. Certificate of acknowledgment; authentication

OFFICERS MUST AFFIX THEIR SIGNATURES. Officers taking and certifying acknowledgments or proof of instruments for record, must authenticate their certificates by affixing thereto their signatures, followed by the names of their offices; also, their seals of office, if by the laws of the State or country where the acknowledgment or proof is taken, or by authority of which they are acting, they are required to have official seals. *(Enacted in 1872.)*

§ 1194. Repealed by Stats.1939, c. 824, p. 2397, § 1

§ 1195. Proof of execution; methods; certificate form

(a) Proof of the execution of an instrument, when not acknowledged, may be made by any of the following:

(1) By the party executing it, or either of them.

(2) By a subscribing witness.

(3) By other witnesses, in cases mentioned in Section 1198.

(b)(1) Proof of the execution of a power of attorney, grant deed, mortgage, deed of trust, quitclaim deed, security agreement, or any instrument affecting real property is not permitted pursuant to Section 27287 of the Government Code, though proof of the execution of a trustee's deed or deed of reconveyance is permitted.

(2) Proof of the execution for any instrument requiring a notary public to obtain a thumbprint from the party signing the document in the notary public's journal is not permitted.

(c) Any certificate for proof of execution taken within this state shall include a notice at the top of the certificate for proof of execution in an enclosed box stating: "A notary public or other officer completing this certificate verifies only the identity of the individual who signed the document to which this certificate is attached, and not the truthfulness, accuracy, or validity of that document." This notice shall be legible.

(d) The physical format of the boxed notice at the top of the certificate for proof of execution required pursuant to subdivision (e) is an example, for purposes of illustration and not limitation, of the physical format of a boxed notice fulfilling the requirements of subdivision (c).

(e) A certificate for proof of execution taken within this state shall be in the following form:

> A notary public or other officer completing this certificate verifies only the identity of the individual who signed the document to which this certificate is attached, and not the truthfulness, accuracy, or validity of that document.

State of California _____) ss.
County of _____)
On ____ (date), before me, ____ (name and title of officer), personally appeared ____ (name of subscribing witness), proved to me to be the person whose name is subscribed to the within instrument, as a witness thereto, on the oath of (name of credible witness), a credible witness who is known to me and provided a satisfactory identifying document. ____ (name of subscribing witness), being by me duly sworn, said that he/she was present and saw/heard ____ (name[s] of principal[s]), the same person(s) described in and whose name(s) is/are subscribed to the within or attached instrument in his/her/their authorized capacity(ies) as (a) party(ies) thereto, execute or acknowledge executing the same, and that said affiant subscribed his/her name to the within or attached instrument as a witness at the request of ____ (name[s] of principal[s]).

WITNESS my hand and official seal.
Signature _____ (Seal)

(Enacted in 1872. Amended by Stats.1997, c. 319 (S.B.618), § 1; Stats.2011, c. 296 (A.B.1023), § 34; Stats.2011, c. 269 (A.B.75), § 3; Stats.2012, c. 202 (A.B.2326), § 1; Stats.2013, c. 76 (A.B.383), § 11; Stats.2013, c. 78 (A.B.464), § 2; Stats.2014, c. 197 (S.B.1050), § 2, eff. Jan. 1, 2015.)

Cross References

Acknowledged writings as evidence, see Evidence Code § 1451.
False verification or acknowledgment of instrument, see Penal Code § 529.
Official records as evidence, see Evidence Code §§ 1532, 1600.
Proof of handwriting, when authorized, see Civil Code § 1198.
Writings, proof, see Evidence Code § 1412 et seq.

§ 1196. Subscribing witness; proof

A witness shall be proved to be a subscribing witness by the oath of a credible witness who provides the officer with any document satisfying the requirements of paragraph (3) or (4) of subdivision (b) of Section 1185. *(Enacted in 1872. Amended by Stats.1982, c. 197, § 7, eff. May 12, 1982; Stats.2008, c. 67 (A.B.2452), § 2.)*

§ 1197. Subscribing witness; items to be proved

WITNESS MUST PROVE, WHAT. The subscribing witness must prove that the person whose name is subscribed to the instrument as a party is the person described in it, and that such person executed it, and that the witness subscribed his name thereto as a witness. *(Enacted in 1872.)*

§ 1198. Proof of handwriting; when authorized

HANDWRITING MAY BE PROVED, WHEN. The execution of an instrument may be established by proof of the handwriting of the party and of a subscribing witness, if there is one, in the following cases:

1. When the parties and all the subscribing witnesses are dead; or,

2. When the parties and all the subscribing witnesses are non-residents of the State; or,

3. When the place of their residence is unknown to the party desiring the proof, and cannot be ascertained by the exercise of due diligence; or,

4. When the subscribing witness conceals himself, or cannot be found by the officer by the exercise of due diligence in attempting to serve the subpoena or attachment; or,

5. In case of the continued failure or refusal of the witness to testify, for the space of one hour, after his appearance. *(Enacted in 1872.)*

Cross References

Acknowledgment of execution of certain instruments or proof by subscribing witness required before recording, see Government Code § 27287.
Evidence, proof of handwriting, see Evidence Code § 1416 et seq.
Forgery or counterfeiting, see Penal Code § 470 et seq.
Necessity of depositing original instrument in proper office where proved and certified, see Government Code § 27290.
Opinion evidence, handwriting, see Evidence Code § 1416.
Proof of execution of will, see Probate Code § 8253.
Proof of will by proof of handwriting, see Probate Code § 8221.

§ 1199. Proof of handwriting; scope

The evidence taken under the preceding section must satisfactorily prove to the officer the following facts:

One. The existence of one or more of the conditions mentioned therein; and,

Two. That the witness testifying knew the person whose name purports to be subscribed to the instrument as a party, and is well acquainted with his signature, and that it is genuine; and,

Three. That the witness testifying personally knew the person who subscribed the instrument as a witness, and is well acquainted with his signature, and that it is genuine; and,

Four. The place of residence of the witness. *(Enacted in 1872. Amended by Code Am.1873–74, c. 612, p. 227, § 141.)*

Cross References

Acknowledgment of execution of certain instruments or proof by subscribing witness required before recording, see Government Code § 27287.
Evidence of handwriting, see Evidence Code § 1416 et seq.
Necessity of depositing original instrument in proper office where proved and certified, see Government Code § 27290.
Proof of will, generally, see Probate Code § 8253.
Proof of will by proof of handwriting, see Probate Code § 8221.

§ 1200. Proof of execution; certificate; contents

CERTIFICATE OF PROOF. An officer taking proof of the execution of any instrument must, in his certificate indorsed thereon or attached thereto, set forth all the matters required by law to be done or known by him, or proved before him on the proceeding, together with the names of all the witnesses examined before him, their places of residence respectively, and the substance of their testimony. *(Enacted in 1872.)*

§ 1201. Authority of officers taking proof

OFFICERS AUTHORIZED TO DO CERTAIN THINGS. Officers authorized to take the proof of instruments are authorized in such proceedings:

1. To administer oaths or affirmations, as prescribed in Section 2093, Code of Civil Procedure;

2. To employ and swear interpreters;

3. To issue subpoena, as prescribed in Section 1986, Code of Civil Procedure;

4. To punish for contempt, as prescribed in Sections 1991, 1993, 1994, Code of Civil Procedure.

The civil damages and forfeiture to the party aggrieved are prescribed in Section 1992, Code of Civil Procedure. *(Enacted in 1872.)*

Cross References

Disobedience to subpoena, see Code of Civil Procedure § 1991 et seq.
Officers authorized to administer oaths and affirmations, see Code of Civil Procedure § 2093.
Penalty for disobedience to subpoena, see Code of Civil Procedure § 1992.
Subpoena, when obtainable, see Code of Civil Procedure § 1986.
Warrant for absent witness, contempt, see Code of Civil Procedure §§ 1993, 1994.

§ 1202. Defective certificate; action for correction

When the acknowledgment or proof of the execution of an instrument is properly made, but defectively certified, any party interested may have an action in the superior court to obtain a judgment correcting the certificate. *(Enacted in 1872. Amended by Stats.1905, c. 445, p. 604, § 4.)*

Cross References

Acknowledgment of execution of certain instruments or proof by subscribing witness required before recording, see Government Code § 27287.

§ 1203. Action for judgment proving instrument

Any person interested under an instrument entitled to be proved for record, may institute an action in the superior court against the proper parties to obtain a judgment proving such instrument. *(Enacted in 1872. Amended by Stats.1905, c. 445, p. 604, § 5.)*

Cross References

Acknowledgment of execution of certain instruments or proof by subscribing witness or otherwise required before recording, see Government Code § 27287.

§ 1204. Judgment proving instrument; effect

EFFECT OF JUDGMENT IN SUCH ACTION. A certified copy of the judgment in a proceeding instituted under either of the two preceding sections, showing the proof of the instrument, and attached thereto, entitles such instrument to record, with like effect as if acknowledged. *(Enacted in 1872.)*

§ 1205. Conveyances prior to code; law governing

CONVEYANCES HERETOFORE MADE TO BE GOVERNED BY THEN EXISTING LAWS. The legality of the execution, acknowledgment, proof, form, or record of any conveyance or other instrument made before this Code goes into effect, executed, acknowledged, proved, or recorded is not affected by anything contained in this Chapter, but depends for its validity and legality upon the laws in force when the act was performed. *(Enacted in 1872.)*

§ 1206. Conveyances prior to code; evidence; recording

RECORDING, AND AS EVIDENCE, TO BE GOVERNED BY THEN EXISTING LAWS. All conveyances of real property made before this Code goes into effect, and acknowledged or proved according to the laws in force at the time of such making and acknowledgment or proof, have the same force as evidence, and may be recorded in the same manner and with the like effect, as conveyances executed and acknowledged in pursuance of this Chapter. *(Enacted in 1872.)*

Cross References

Real property defined for purposes of this Code, see Civil Code § 658.
Retroactivity of Civil Code, see Civil Code § 3.

§ 1207. Defectively executed instruments; validity

Any instrument affecting the title to real property, one year after the same has been copied into the proper book of record, kept in the office of any county recorder, imparts notice of its contents to subsequent purchasers and encumbrancers, notwithstanding any defect, omission, or informality in the execution of the instrument, or in the certificate of acknowledgment thereof, or the absence of any such certificate; but nothing herein affects the rights of purchasers or encumbrancers previous to the taking effect of this act. Duly certified copies of the record of any such instrument may be read in evidence with like effect as copies of an instrument duly acknowledged and recorded; provided, when such copying in the proper book of record occurred within five years prior to the trial of the action, it is first shown that the original instrument was genuine. *(Added by Code Am.1983–74, c. 612, p. 228, § 142. Amended by Stats.1897, c. 74, p. 64, § 1; Stats.1903, c. 97, p. 108, § 1; Stats.1909, c. 54, p. 45, § 1; Stats.1913, c. 71, p. 75, § 1; Stats.1915, c. 626, p. 1211, § 1; Stats.1919, c. 163, p. 244, § 1; Stats.1921, c. 97, p. 94, § 1; Stats.1927, c. 489, p. 828, § 1.)*

Cross References

Real property defined for purposes of this Code, see Civil Code § 658.

ARTICLE 4. EFFECT OF RECORDING, OR THE WANT THEREOF

Section
1213. Record of conveyances; constructive notice; recording certified copies; effect.
1213.5. Repealed.
1214. Prior recording of subsequent conveyances, mortgages, judgments.
1215. "Conveyance" defined.
1216. Power of attorney, revocation.
1217. Unrecorded instrument; validity between parties.
1218. Recording certified copies of instrument or certified copy of record; effect.
1219. Oil and gas leases; manner of recording and giving constructive notice; fictitious oil and gas leases.
1220. Standing timber or trees; recordation of instruments.

§ 1213. Record of conveyances; constructive notice; recording certified copies; effect

Every conveyance of real property or an estate for years therein acknowledged or proved and certified and recorded as prescribed by law from the time it is filed with the recorder for record is constructive notice of the contents thereof to subsequent purchasers and mortgagees; and a certified copy of such a recorded conveyance may be recorded in any other county and when so recorded the record thereof shall have the same force and effect as though it was of the original conveyance and where the original conveyance has been recorded in any county wherein the property therein mentioned is not situated a certified copy of the recorded conveyance may be recorded in the county where such property is situated with the same force and effect as if the original conveyance had been recorded in that county. *(Enacted in 1872. Amended by Stats.1897, c. 68, p. 59, § 1; Stats.1909, c. 179, p. 278, § 1; Stats.1989, c. 698, § 1.)*

Cross References

Certified copies, recordation, see Civil Code § 1218.
Certified copy of record, prima facie evidence of conveyance, see Evidence Code § 1603.
Conclusiveness of grant, exception, see Civil Code § 1107.
Constructive notice, see Civil Code § 19.
Conveyance defined for purposes of this section, see Civil Code § 1215.
Instrument of defeasance, necessity of recording, see Civil Code § 2950.
Real property defined for purposes of this Code, see Civil Code § 658.
When instrument is deemed recorded, see Civil Code § 1170.

§ 1213.5. Repealed by Stats.1982, c. 1268, § 2

§ 1214. Prior recording of subsequent conveyances, mortgages, judgments

Every conveyance of real property or an estate for years therein, other than a lease for a term not exceeding one year, is void as against any subsequent purchaser or mortgagee of the same property, or any part thereof, in good faith and for a valuable consideration, whose conveyance is first duly record-

§ 1214

ed, and as against any judgment affecting the title, unless the conveyance shall have been duly recorded prior to the record of notice of action. *(Enacted in 1872. Amended by Stats. 1895, c. 48, p. 50, § 1; Stats.1989, c. 698, § 2.)*

Cross References

Conclusiveness of grant, see Civil Code § 1107.
Enforcement of money judgments, assignment order, effect and priority of assignment, see Code of Civil Procedure § 708.530.
Instruments made with intent to defraud, invalidity as to bona fide purchasers or incumbrances, see Civil Code § 1227.
Obligations of third person dealing with trustee, see Probate Code § 18100.
Real property defined for purposes of this Code, see Civil Code § 658.

§ 1215. "Conveyance" defined

CONVEYANCE DEFINED. The term "conveyance," as used in Sections 1213 and 1214, embraces every instrument in writing by which any estate or interest in real property is created, aliened, mortgaged, or incumbered, or by which the title to any real property may be affected, except wills. *(Enacted in 1872.)*

Cross References

Real property defined for purposes of this Code, see Civil Code § 658.

§ 1216. Power of attorney, revocation

No power contained in an instrument to convey or execute instruments affecting real property which has been recorded is revoked by any act of the party by whom it was executed, unless the instrument containing such revocation is also acknowledged or proved, certified and recorded, in the same office in which the instrument containing the power was recorded. *(Enacted in 1872. Amended by Stats.1970, c. 323, p. 717, § 1.)*

Cross References

Real property defined for purposes of this Code, see Civil Code § 658.
This section unaffected by provision for termination of agency not coupled with an interest, see Civil Code § 2356.

§ 1217. Unrecorded instrument; validity between parties

UNRECORDED INSTRUMENT VALID BETWEEN THE PARTIES. An unrecorded instrument is valid as between the parties thereto and those who have notice thereof. *(Enacted in 1872.)*

§ 1218. Recording certified copies of instrument or certified copy of record; effect

A certified copy of an instrument affecting the title to real property, once recorded, or a certified copy of the record of such instrument may be recorded in any other county, and, when so recorded, the record thereof has the same force and effect as though it was of the original instrument. *(Added by Stats.1905, c. 446, p. 604, § 1. Amended by Stats.1913, c. 191, p. 335, § 1.)*

Cross References

Real property defined for purposes of this Code, see Civil Code § 658.

Recordation of certified copies, see Civil Code § 1213.

§ 1219. Oil and gas leases; manner of recording and giving constructive notice; fictitious oil and gas leases

Oil and gas leases may be acknowledged or proved, certified and recorded in like manner and with like effect, as grants of real property. However, an oil and gas lease may be recorded and constructive notice of the same and the contents of that lease given in the following manner:

Any person may record in the office of county recorder of any county fictitious oil and gas leases. Those fictitious oil and gas leases need not be acknowledged, or proved, or certified, to be recorded or entitled to record. Oil and gas leases shall have noted upon the face thereof that they are fictitious. The county recorder shall index and record fictitious oil and gas leases in the same manner as other oil and gas leases are recorded, and shall note on all indices and records of the same that they are fictitious. Thereafter, any of the provisions of any recorded fictitious oil and gas lease may be included for any and all purposes in any oil and gas lease by reference therein to those provisions, without setting the same forth in full, if the fictitious oil and gas lease is of record in the county in which the oil and gas lease adopting or including by reference any of the provisions of the lease is recorded. The reference shall contain a statement, as to each county in which the oil and gas lease containing such a reference is recorded, of the date the fictitious oil and gas lease was recorded, the county recorder's office in which it is recorded, and the book or volume and the first page of the records or the recorder's instrument number in the recorder's office in which the fictitious oil and gas lease was recorded, and a statement by paragraph numbers or any other method that will definitely identify the same, of the specific provisions of any fictitious oil and gas lease that are being adopted and included therein. The recording of any oil and gas lease which has included any provisions by reference shall operate as constructive notice of the whole including the terms, as a part of the written contents of any oil and gas lease, of any provisions so included by reference as though the same were written in full therein. The parties bound or to be bound by provisions so adopted and included by reference shall be bound thereby in the same manner and with like effect for all purposes as though the provisions had been and were set forth in full in the oil and gas lease. *(Added by Stats.1955, c. 1541, p. 2824, § 1. Amended by Stats.2009, c. 54 (S.B.544), § 4.)*

Cross References

Acknowledgment as condition of recordation, see Government Code § 27287.
Oil and gas leases, see Public Resources Code § 6826 et seq.
Proof and acknowledgment of instruments, see Civil Code § 1180 et seq.
Real property defined for purposes of this Code, see Civil Code § 658.

§ 1220. Standing timber or trees; recordation of instruments

Contracts for the purchase or sale of standing timber or trees, for severance or otherwise, and all instruments in writing by which any estate or interest in, or right to cut, standing timber or trees is created, aliened, mortgaged or encumbered or by which the title to any standing timber or trees may be affected, may be acknowledged or proved, certified and recorded in like manner and with like effect, as grants of real property, and all statutory provisions relating to the recordation or nonrecordation of conveyances of real property and to the effect thereof shall apply to such contracts and instruments with like effect.

Any such contracts for purchase and sale or instruments in writing affecting the title to standing timber or trees, executed and delivered before the effective date of the amendment of this section at the 1959 Regular Session of the Legislature but unrecorded before such date, shall become subject to all statutory provisions relating to the recordation or nonrecordation of conveyances of real property and to the effect thereof one year from said effective date. *(Added by Stats.1957, c. 1937, p. 3467, § 1. Amended by Stats.1959, c. 1795, p. 4276, § 1.)*

Cross References

Bulk sales, see Commercial Code § 6101 et seq.
Proof and acknowledgment of instruments, see Civil Code § 1180 et seq.
Real property defined for purposes of this Code, see Civil Code § 658.
Transfers and liens without delivery, see Civil Code § 3440.

CHAPTER 5. UNLAWFUL TRANSFERS

Section
1227. Instruments made with intent to defraud; invalidity as to bona fide purchasers or incumbrancers.
1228. Instruments made with intent to defraud; subsequent purchasers or incumbrancers with notice, effect.
1229. Power to revoke; execution by subsequent grant or charge.
1230. Power to revoke; when deemed executed.
1231. Other provisions concerning unlawful transfers.

§ 1227. Instruments made with intent to defraud; invalidity as to bona fide purchasers or incumbrancers

CERTAIN INSTRUMENTS VOID AGAINST PURCHASERS, ETC. Every instrument, other than a will, affecting an estate in real property, including every charge upon real property, or upon its rents or profits, made with intent to defraud prior or subsequent purchasers thereof, or incumbrancers thereon, is void as against every purchaser or incumbrancer, for value, of the same property, or the rents or profits thereof. *(Enacted in 1872.)*

Cross References

Real property defined for purposes of this Code, see Civil Code § 658.
Uniform Voidable Transactions Act, see Civil Code § 3439 et seq.

§ 1228. Instruments made with intent to defraud; subsequent purchasers or incumbrancers with notice, effect

NOT VOID AGAINST PURCHASER HAVING NOTICE, UNLESS FRAUD IS MUTUAL. No instrument is to be avoided under the last section, in favor of a subsequent purchaser or incumbrancer having notice thereof at the time his purchase was made, or his lien acquired, unless the person in whose favor the instrument was made was privy to the fraud intended. *(Enacted in 1872.)*

§ 1229. Power to revoke; execution by subsequent grant or charge

POWER TO REVOKE, WHEN DEEMED EXECUTED. Where a power to revoke or modify an instrument affecting the title to, or the enjoyment of, an estate in real property, is reserved to the grantor, or given to any other person, a subsequent grant of, or charge upon, the estate, by the person having the power of revocation, in favor of a purchaser or incumbrancer for value, operates as a revocation of the original instrument, to the extent of the power, in favor of such purchaser or incumbrancer. *(Enacted in 1872.)*

Cross References

Conclusiveness of grant, see Civil Code § 1107.
Real property defined for purposes of this Code, see Civil Code § 658.
Relief against parties claiming under person bound to perform, see Civil Code § 3395.

§ 1230. Power to revoke; when deemed executed

SAME. Where a person having a power of revocation, within the provisions of the last section, is not entitled to execute it until after the time at which he makes such a grant or charge as is described in that section, the power is deemed to be executed as soon as he is entitled to execute it. *(Enacted in 1872.)*

§ 1231. Other provisions concerning unlawful transfers

OTHER PROVISIONS. Other provisions concerning unlawful transfers are contained in Part II, Division Fourth, of this Code,[1] concerning the Special Relations of Debtor and Creditor. *(Enacted in 1872.)*

[1] Section 3429 et seq.

Title 5

HOMESTEADS [REPEALED]

§ 1237. Repealed by Stats.1982, c. 497, § 8, operative July 1, 1983

§§ 1237a, 1237b. Unconstitutional

§§ 1237.5, 1238. Repealed by Stats.1982, c. 497, § 8, operative July 1, 1983

§ 1239. Repealed by Stats.1976, c. 463, p. 1200, § 2

§§ 1240 to 1269. Repealed by Stats.1982, c. 497, § 8, operative July 1, 1983

§§ 1269a to 1269c. Repealed by Stats.1941, c. 1220, p. 3036, § 3

§ 1270. Repealed by Stats.1931, c. 281, p. 687, § 1700

§ 1271. Repealed by Code Am.1873–74, c. 612, pp. 232, § 160

§§ 1272 to 1283. Repealed by Stats.1931, c. 281, p. 687, § 1700

§ 1284. Repealed by Code Am.1873–74, c. 612, p. 232, § 164

§ 1285. Repealed by Stats.1931, c. 281, p. 687, § 1700

§ 1286. Repealed by Code Am.1873–74, c. 612, p. 233, § 166

§§ 1287 to 1293. Repealed by Stats.1931, c. 281, p. 687, § 1700

§ 1294. Repealed by Code Am.1873–74, c. 612, p. 233, § 168

§§ 1295 to 1299. Repealed by Stats.1931, c. 281, p. 687, § 1700

§ 1300. Repealed by Stats.1982, c. 497, § 8, operative July 1, 1983

§ 1300a. Repealed by Stats.1931, c. 281, p. 687, § 1700

§§ 1301 to 1304. Repealed by Stats.1982, c. 497, § 8, operative July 1, 1983

§§ 1305 to 1349. Repealed by Stats.1931, c. 281, p. 687, § 1700

Title 6

COMMON INTEREST DEVELOPMENTS [REPEALED]

§§ 1350 to 1351. Repealed by Stats.2012, c. 180 (A.B.805), § 1, operative Jan. 1, 2014

§§ 1352 to 1357.150. Repealed by Stats.2012, c. 180 (A.B.805), § 1, operative Jan. 1, 2014

§§ 1358 to 1362. Repealed by Stats.2012, c. 180 (A.B.805), § 1, operative Jan. 1, 2014

§§ 1363 to 1363.04. Repealed by Stats.2012, c. 180 (A.B.805), § 1, operative Jan. 1, 2014

§ 1363.05. Repealed by Stats.2012, c. 180 (A.B.805), § 1, operative Jan. 1, 2014; Stats.2013, c. 183 (S.B.745), § 2

§§ 1363.07 to 1363.850. Repealed by Stats.2012, c. 180 (A.B.805), § 1, operative Jan. 1, 2014

§§ 1364 to 1366.2. Repealed by Stats.2012, c. 180 (A.B.805), § 1, operative Jan. 1, 2014

§ 1366.3. Repealed by Stats.2005, c. 452 (S.B.137), § 3

§§ 1366.4 to 1367.6. Repealed by Stats.2012, c. 180 (A.B.805), § 1, operative Jan. 1, 2014

§ 1368. Repealed by Stats.2012, c. 180 (A.B.805), § 1, operative Jan. 1, 2014; Stats.2013, c. 183 (S.B.745), § 3

§ 1368.1. Repealed by Stats.2012, c. 180 (A.B.805), § 1, operative Jan. 1, 2014

§ 1368.2. Repealed by Stats.2012, c. 180 (A.B.805), § 1, operative Jan. 1, 2014; Stats.2013, c. 183 (S.B.745), § 4

§§ 1368.3 to 1369.590. Repealed by Stats.2012, c. 180 (A.B.805), § 1, operative Jan. 1, 2014

§§ 1370 to 1375. Repealed by Stats.2012, c. 180 (A.B.805), § 1, operative Jan. 1, 2014

§ 1375.05. Repealed by Stats.2002, c. 664 (A.B.3034), § 37, operative Jan. 1, 2011

§§ 1375.1, 1376. Repealed by Stats.2012, c. 180 (A.B.805), § 1, operative Jan. 1, 2014

§ 1377. Repealed by Stats.1931, c. 281, § 1700

§ 1378. Repealed by Stats.2012, c. 180 (A.B.805), § 1, operative Jan. 1, 2014

Title 7

POWERS OF APPOINTMENT [REPEALED]

§§ 1380.1 to 1382.1. Repealed by Stats.1992, c. 30 (A.B.1722), § 1

§§ 1383, 1384. Repealed by Stats.1931, c. 281, p. 687, § 1700

§ 1384.1. Repealed by Stats.1992, c. 30 (A.B.1722), § 1

§ 1385. Repealed by Code Am.1873–74, c. 612, p. 236, § 179

§§ 1385.1 to 1385.5. Repealed by Stats.1992, c. 30 (A.B.1722), § 1

§ 1386. Repealed by Stats.1931, c. 281, p. 687, § 1700

§§ 1386.1 to 1386.3. Repealed by Stats.1992, c. 30 (A.B.1722), § 1

§ 1387. Repealed by Stats.1931, c. 281, p. 687, § 1700

§§ 1387.1 to 1387.3. Repealed by Stats.1992, c. 30 (A.B.1722), § 1

§ 1388. Repealed by Stats.1931, c. 281, p. 687, § 1700

§§ 1388.1 to 1388.3. Repealed by Stats.1992, c. 30 (A.B.1722), § 1

§ 1389. Repealed by Stats.1931, c. 281, p. 687, § 1700

§§ 1389.1 to 1389.5. Repealed by Stats.1992, c. 30 (A.B.1722), § 1

§ 1390. Repealed by Stats.1931, c. 281, p. 687, § 1700

§§ 1390.1 to 1390.5. Repealed by Stats.1992, c. 30 (A.B. 1722), § 1

§ 1391. Repealed by Stats.1992, c. 30 (A.B.1722), § 1

§§ 1391.1, 1391.2. Repealed by Stats.1991, c. 156 (A.B. 1577), § 19

§ 1392. Repealed by Stats.1931, c. 281, p. 687, § 1700

§ 1392.1. Repealed by Stats.1992, c. 30 (A.B.1722), § 1

§§ 1393 to 1409. Repealed by Stats.1931, c. 281, p. 687, § 1700

Title 8

WATER RIGHTS

Section
1410. Repealed.
1410a. Repealed.
1410b to 1413. Repealed.
1414. Appropriation of waters; priority.
1415. Appropriation of waters; notice; contents; posting; recordation.
1416. Appropriation of waters; construction of works; dams; county or municipal works.
1417. Appropriation of waters; completion defined.
1418. Appropriation of waters; right of use, relation back to time of notice.
1419. Appropriation of waters; forfeiture.
1420. Appropriation of waters; rights of existing claimants.
1421. Book for recording notices.
1422. Appropriation of waters; time to commence works on public reservations.

Cross References

Appropriation of water, see Water Code § 1200 et seq.
Appurtenances to land, see Civil Code § 662.
Completion defined for purposes of this Title, see Civil Code § 1417.
Conservation of water resources, restriction on riparian rights, see Cal. Const. Art. 10, § 2.
Forfeiture defined for purposes of this Title, see Civil Code § 1419.
Rights in streams and watercourses generally, see Water Code § 101 et seq.

§ 1410. Repealed by Stats.1943, c. 368, p. 1604, § 150001

§ 1410a. Repealed by Stats.2014, c. 274 (A.B.2759), § 1, eff. Jan. 1, 2015

§§ 1410b to 1413. Repealed by Stats.1943, c. 368, p. 1895, § 150001

§ 1414. Appropriation of waters; priority

FIRST IN TIME, FIRST IN RIGHT. As between appropriators, the one first in time is the first in right. *(Enacted in 1872.)*

Cross References

Changes in use of water, persons entitled to make, see Water Code § 1706.
Priorities, appropriation of waters, see Water Code § 1450 et seq.
Purpose of appropriation, cessation of right, see Water Code § 1240.

Relation back of water right, see Civil Code § 1418.

§ 1415. Appropriation of waters; notice; contents; posting; recordation

A person desiring to appropriate water must post a notice, in writing, in a conspicuous place at the point of intended diversion, stating therein:

1. That he claims the water there flowing to the extent of (giving the number) inches, measured under a four-inch pressure;

2. The purposes for which he claims it, and the place of intended use;

3. The means by which he intends to divert it, and the size of the flume, ditch, pipe, or aqueduct in which he intends to divert it.

A copy of the notice must, within ten days after it is posted, be recorded in the office of the recorder of the county in which it is posted. After filing such copy for record, the place of intended diversion or the place of intended use or the means by which it is intended to divert the water, may be changed by the person posting said notice or his assigns, if others are not injured by such change. This provision applies to notices already filed as well as to notices hereafter filed. *(Enacted in 1872. Amended by Stats.1903, c. 262, p. 361, § 1.)*

Cross References

Applications to appropriate water, see Water Code § 1250 et seq.
Appropriation of waters, time to commence works on public reservations, see Civil Code § 1422.
Changes in diversion of water, persons entitled to make, see Water Code § 1706.

§ 1416. Appropriation of waters; construction of works; dams; county or municipal works

Within sixty days after the notice is posted, the claimant must commence the excavation or construction of the works in which he intends to divert the water, or the survey, road or trail building, necessarily incident thereto, and must prosecute the work diligently and uninterruptedly to completion, unless temporarily interrupted by snows or rain; provided, that if the erection of a dam has been recommended by the California débris [1] commission at or near the place where it is intended to divert the water, the claimant shall have sixty days after the completion of such dam in which to commence the excavation or construction of the works in which he intends to divert the water; provided, that whenever any city and county, or any incorporated city or town within this state makes, or has made, or acquires, or has acquired any appropriation of any of the waters of this state in accordance with the provisions of section 1415 of this code, it shall not be necessary for such city and county, city or town to commence the work for development of more of the water so claimed than is actually necessary for the immediate needs of such city and county, city or town and it shall be held to be a sufficient compliance with the requirements of this chapter, to the full amount of water stated in the notice posted and recorded, for such city and county, city or town to within sixty days make the necessary surveys, or within six months to authorize the issuance of municipal bonds, for the construction of the necessary works designed to supply such city and county, city or town with the water required for immediate use. Any appropriation heretofore made by any such city and county, city or town in connection with which surveys were at any time made, or an issue of bonds authorized for the construction of any portion of the works necessary for a diversion of any part of the water appropriated, is hereby confirmed to the full amount of water stated in the original notice or notices. *(Enacted in 1872. Amended by Stats.1895, c. 74, p. 70, § 1; Stats.1903, c. 272, p. 396, § 1; Stats.1907, c. 429, p. 780, § 1; Stats.1911, c. 730, p. 1419, § 1.)*

[1] So in chaptered copy.

Cross References

Failure to construct works, see Civil Code § 1420.
Joint use and development of appropriated waters, see Water Code § 1750 et seq.
Relation back of water rights, see Civil Code § 1418.
Statutory adjudications for determination of water rights, time for completion of appropriation initiated prior to December 19, 1914, see Water Code § 2802.
Time to commence works on public reservations, see Civil Code § 1422.

§ 1417. Appropriation of waters; completion defined

COMPLETION DEFINED. By "completion" is meant conducting the waters to the place of intended use. *(Enacted in 1872.)*

§ 1418. Appropriation of waters; right of use, relation back to time of notice

DOCTRINE OF RELATION APPLIED. By a compliance with the above rules the claimant's right to the use of the water relates back to the time the notice was posted. *(Enacted in 1872.)*

§ 1419. Appropriation of waters; forfeiture

FORFEITURE. A failure to comply with such rules deprives the claimants of the right to the use of the water as against a subsequent claimant who complies therewith. *(Enacted in 1872.)*

§ 1420. Appropriation of waters; rights of existing claimants

RIGHTS OF PRESENT CLAIMANT. Persons who have heretofore claimed the right to water, and who have not constructed works in which to divert it, and who have not diverted nor applied it to some useful purpose, must, after this Title takes effect, and within twenty days thereafter, proceed as in this Title provided, or their right ceases. *(Enacted in 1872.)*

§ 1421. Book for recording notices

RECORDER TO KEEP BOOK IN WHICH TO RECORD NOTICES. The Recorder of each county must keep a book, in which he must record the notices provided for in this Title. *(Enacted in 1872.)*

§ 1422. Appropriation of waters; time to commence works on public reservations

If the place of intended diversion or any part of the route of intended conveyance of water so claimed, be within, and a part of, any national park, forest reservation, or other public reservation, and be so shown in the notice of appropriation of said water, then the claimant shall have sixty days, after the grant of authority to occupy and use such park or reservation for such intended purpose, within which to commence the excavation or construction of said works; provided that within sixty days after the posting of said notice of appropriation, as provided in section 1415 of the Civil Code, the claimant shall in good faith commence (and thereafter diligently and continuously, except when temporarily interrupted by snow or rain, prosecute to completion) such surveys and other work as under the regulations governing such park or reservations, may be required as preliminary to, or for use with, an application for such authority; and provided also that the claimant shall in good faith on completion of said survey and preliminary work, apply to the officer, board, or body, having charge of such park or reservation, for such authority, and shall thereafter, prosecute said application with reasonable diligence. *(Added by Stats.1903, c. 272, p. 397, § 2.)*

Title 9

HYDRAULIC MINING [REPEALED]

§§ 1424, 1425. Repealed by Stats.1939, c. 93, p. 1215, § 10002

Title 10

MINING CLAIMS, TUNNEL RIGHTS AND MILL SITES [REPEALED]

§§ 1426 to 1426s. Repealed by Stats.1939, c. 93, p. 1215, § 10002

Division 3

OBLIGATIONS

Part	Section
1. Obligations in General	1427
2. Contracts	1549
3. Obligations Imposed by Law	1708
4. Obligations Arising from Particular Transactions	1738

Part 1

OBLIGATIONS IN GENERAL

Title	Section
1. Definition of Obligations	1427
2. Interpretation of Obligations	1429
3. Transfer of Obligations	1457
4. Extinction of Obligations	1473

Title 1

DEFINITION OF OBLIGATIONS

Section
1427. Obligation defined.
1428. Creation and enforcement.

Cross References

Contracts, for purposes of this Division, see Civil Code § 1549 et seq.
Extinction of obligations, see Civil Code § 1473 et seq.
Interpretation of obligations, see Civil Code § 1429 et seq.
Obligations imposed by law, see Civil Code § 1708 et seq.
Transfer of obligations, see Civil Code § 1457 et seq.

§ 1427. Obligation defined

OBLIGATION, WHAT. An obligation is a legal duty, by which a person is bound to do or not to do a certain thing. *(Enacted in 1872.)*

Cross References

Similar provision, see Code of Civil Procedure § 26.

§ 1428. Creation and enforcement

An obligation arises either from:

One—The contract of the parties; or,

Two—The operation of law. An obligation arising from operation of law may be enforced in the manner provided by law, or by civil action or proceeding. *(Enacted in 1872. Amended by Code Am.1873–74, c. 612, p. 239, § 181½.)*

Cross References

Contracts, generally, see Civil Code § 1549 et seq.

Title 2

INTERPRETATION OF OBLIGATIONS

Chapter	Section
1. General Rules of Interpretation	1429
2. Joint or Several Obligations	1430
3. Conditional Obligations	1434
4. Alternative Obligations	1448

Cross References

Contracts, for purposes of this Division, see Civil Code § 1549 et seq.
Definition of obligations, see Civil Code § 1427 et seq.
Extinction of obligations, see Civil Code § 1473 et seq.
Obligation defined for purposes of this Division, see Civil Code § 1427.
Obligations imposed by law, see Civil Code § 1708 et seq.
Transfer of obligations, see Civil Code § 1457 et seq.

CHAPTER 1. GENERAL RULES OF INTERPRETATION

Section
1429. General rules of interpretation.

Cross References

Obligation defined for purposes of this Division, see Civil Code § 1427.

§ 1429. General rules of interpretation

GENERAL RULES. The rules which govern the interpretation of contracts are prescribed by Part II of this Division.[1] Other obligations are interpreted by the same rules by which statutes of a similar nature are interpreted. *(Enacted in 1872.)*

[1] Section 1549 et seq.

Cross References

Contracts, generally, see Civil Code § 1549 et seq.
Interpretation of contracts, see Civil Code § 1635 et seq.

CHAPTER 2. JOINT OR SEVERAL OBLIGATIONS

Section
1430. Classification of obligations.
1431. Joint liability.
1431.1. Findings and declaration of purpose.
1431.2. Several liability for non-economic damages.
1431.3. Law of immunity.
1431.4. Amendment or repeal of measure.
1431.5. Severability.
1432. Contribution among joint obligors.

Cross References

Alternative obligations, see Civil Code § 1448 et seq.
Conditional obligations, see Civil Code § 1434 et seq.
General rules of contract interpretation, see Civil Code § 1429.
Obligation defined for purposes of this Division, see Civil Code § 1427.

§ 1430. Classification of obligations

OBLIGATIONS, JOINT OR SEVERAL, ETC. An obligation imposed upon several persons, or a right created in favor of several persons, may be:

§ 1430

1. Joint;
2. Several; or,
3. Joint and several. *(Enacted in 1872.)*

Cross References

Contribution among joint tortfeasors, see Code of Civil Procedure § 875 et seq.
Extinguishment of obligation in favor of several persons, see Civil Code § 1475.
Indemnity, joint or separate liability, see Civil Code § 2777.
Negotiable instruments,
 Indorsements jointly and severally, see Commercial Code § 3416.
 Notice of dishonor to joint parties, see Commercial Code § 3503.
 Presentment where several persons primarily liable, see Commercial Code § 3501.
Partnerships, joint obligations and joint and several obligations, see Corporations Code § 16306.
Presumption of joint and several promise, see Civil Code §§ 1659, 1660.

§ 1431. Joint liability

An obligation imposed upon several persons, or a right created in favor of several persons, is presumed to be joint, and not several, except as provided in Section 1431.2, and except in the special cases mentioned in the title on the interpretation of contracts. This presumption, in the case of a right, can be overcome only by express words to the contrary. *(Enacted in 1872. Amended by § 2 of Initiative Measure, approved by the People, June 3, 1986.)*

Cross References

Common interest developments, reduction of damages awarded, comparative fault of association, see Civil Code § 5985.
Contracts, generally, see Civil Code § 1549 et seq.
Interpretation of contracts, Title 3, see Civil Code § 1635 et seq.
Judgments for periodic payment against a public entity, modification of installment payments pursuant to this section, see Government Code § 984.
Presumption of joint and several promise, see Civil Code §§ 1659, 1660.

§ 1431.1. Findings and declaration of purpose

The People of the State of California find and declare as follows:

a) The legal doctrine of joint and several liability, also known as "the deep pocket rule", has resulted in a system of inequity and injustice that has threatened financial bankruptcy of local governments, other public agencies, private individuals and businesses and has resulted in higher prices for goods and services to the public and in higher taxes to the taxpayers.

b) Some governmental and private defendants are perceived to have substantial financial resources or insurance coverage and have thus been included in lawsuits even though there was little or no basis for finding them at fault. Under joint and several liability, if they are found to share even a fraction of the fault, they often are held financially liable for all the damage. The People—taxpayers and consumers alike—ultimately pay for these lawsuits in the form of higher taxes, higher prices and higher insurance premiums.

c) Local governments have been forced to curtail some essential police, fire and other protections because of the soaring costs of lawsuits and insurance premiums.

Therefore, the People of the State of California declare that to remedy these inequities, defendants in tort actions shall be held financially liable in closer proportion to their degree of fault. To treat them differently is unfair and inequitable.

The People of the State of California further declare that reforms in the liability laws in tort actions are necessary and proper to avoid catastrophic economic consequences for state and local governmental bodies as well as private individuals and businesses. *(Added by § 3 of Initiative Measure, approved by the People, June 3, 1986.)*

Cross References

Judgments for periodic payment against a public entity, modification of installment payments pursuant to this section, see Government Code § 984.

§ 1431.2. Several liability for non-economic damages

(a) In any action for personal injury, property damage, or wrongful death, based upon principles of comparative fault, the liability of each defendant for non-economic damages shall be several only and shall not be joint. Each defendant shall be liable only for the amount of non-economic damages allocated to that defendant in direct proportion to that defendant's percentage of fault, and a separate judgment shall be rendered against that defendant for that amount.

(b)(1) For purposes of this section, the term "economic damages" means objectively verifiable monetary losses including medical expenses, loss of earnings, burial costs, loss of use of property, costs of repair or replacement, costs of obtaining substitute domestic services, loss of employment and loss of business or employment opportunities.

(2) For the purposes of this section, the term "non-economic damages" means subjective, non-monetary losses including, but not limited to, pain, suffering, inconvenience, mental suffering, emotional distress, loss of society and companionship, loss of consortium, injury to reputation and humiliation. *(Added by § 4 of Initiative Measure, approved by the People, June 3, 1986.)*

Cross References

Judgments for periodic payment against a public entity, modification of installment payments pursuant to this section, see Government Code § 984.
Oil spill response and contingency planning, liability of responsible party, see Government Code § 8670.56.5.

§ 1431.3. Law of immunity

Nothing contained in this measure is intended, in any way, to alter the law of immunity. *(Added by § 5 of Initiative Measure, approved by the People, June 3, 1986.)*

Cross References

Judgments for periodic payment against a public entity, modification of installment payments pursuant to this section, see Government Code § 984.

§ 1431.4. Amendment or repeal of measure

This measure may be amended or repealed by either of the procedures set forth in this section. If any portion of subsection (a) is declared invalid, then subsection (b) shall be the exclusive means of amending or repealing this measure.

(a) This measure may be amended to further its purposes by statute, passed in each house by rollcall vote entered in the journal, two-thirds of the membership concurring and signed by the Governor, if at least 20 days prior to passage in each house the bill in its final form has been delivered to the Secretary of State for distribution to the news media.

(b) This measure may be amended or repealed by a statute that becomes effective only when approved by the electors. *(Added by § 6 of Initiative Measure, approved by the People, June 3, 1986.)*

Cross References

Judgments for periodic payment against a public entity, modification of installment payments pursuant to this section, see Government Code § 984.

§ 1431.5. Severability

If any provision of this measure, or the application of any such provision to any person or circumstances, shall be held invalid, the remainder of this measure to the extent it can be given effect, or the application of such provision to persons or circumstances other than those as to which it is held invalid, shall not be affected thereby, and to this end the provisions of this measure are severable. *(Added by § 7 of Initiative Measure, approved by the People, June 3, 1986.)*

Cross References

Judgments for periodic payment against a public entity, modification of installment payments pursuant to this section, see Government Code § 984.

§ 1432. Contribution among joint obligors

Except as provided in Section 877 of the Code of Civil Procedure, a party to a joint, or joint and several obligation, who satisfies more than his share of the claim against all, may require a proportionate contribution from all the parties joined with him. *(Enacted in 1872. Amended by Stats.1987, c. 677, § 1.)*

Cross References

Contribution among joint tortfeasors, see Code of Civil Procedure § 875 et seq.
Contribution between sureties on several bonds, see Code of Civil Procedure § 996.250.
Surety entitled to benefit of securities held by creditor, see Civil Code § 2849.
Surety's right of contribution from co-sureties, see Civil Code § 2848.

CHAPTER 3. CONDITIONAL OBLIGATIONS

Section
1434. Conditional obligation defined.
1435. Kinds of conditions.
1436. Condition precedent defined.
1437. Condition concurrent defined.
1438. Condition subsequent defined.
1439. Performance; necessity.
1440. Performance; excuse.
1441. Impossible or unlawful conditions.
1442. Forfeiture; strict construction.

Cross References

Obligation defined for purposes of this Division, see Civil Code § 1427.

§ 1434. Conditional obligation defined

OBLIGATION, WHEN CONDITIONAL. An obligation is conditional, when the rights or duties of any party thereto depend upon the occurrence of an uncertain event. *(Enacted in 1872.)*

Cross References

Condition precedent or subsequent, see Civil Code § 708.
Conditional ownership, see Civil Code § 707 et seq.
Conditions imposing restraints on marriage, see Civil Code § 710.
Conditions in restraint of alienation, see Civil Code § 711.
Illegality of condition precedent affecting instrument, see Civil Code § 709.
Offer dependent upon performance of condition precedent or concurrent, see Civil Code § 1498.
Performance of condition precedent as affecting specific performance, see Civil Code § 3392.

§ 1435. Kinds of conditions

CONDITIONS, KINDS OF. Conditions may be precedent, concurrent, or subsequent. *(Enacted in 1872.)*

Cross References

Conditions of property ownership, see Civil Code § 707 et seq.

§ 1436. Condition precedent defined

CONDITIONS PRECEDENT. A condition precedent is one which is to be performed before some right dependent thereon accrues, or some act dependent thereon is performed. *(Enacted in 1872.)*

Cross References

Conditions precedent, see Civil Code §§ 707, 708.
Necessity of performance of conditions, see Civil Code § 1439.
Offer dependent on performance of conditions, see Civil Code § 1498.
Performance of conditions precedent, pleading and proof, see Code of Civil Procedure § 457.
Time of performance not specified, see Civil Code § 1657.
Void conditions precedent, see Civil Code § 709.

§ 1437. Condition concurrent defined

CONDITIONS CONCURRENT. Conditions concurrent are those which are mutually dependent, and are to be performed at the same time. *(Enacted in 1872.)*

Cross References

Offer dependent on performance of conditions, see Civil Code § 1498.

§ 1438. Condition subsequent defined

CONDITION SUBSEQUENT. A condition subsequent is one referring to a future event, upon the happening of which the obligation becomes no longer binding upon the other party, if he chooses to avail himself of the condition. *(Enacted in 1872.)*

§ 1438 OBLIGATIONS

Cross References
Conditions subsequent, see Civil Code § 708.

§ 1439. Performance; necessity

PERFORMANCE, ETC. OF CONDITIONS, WHEN ESSENTIAL. Before any party to an obligation can require another party to perform any act under it, he must fulfill all conditions precedent thereto imposed upon himself; and must be able and offer to fulfill all conditions concurrent so imposed upon him on the like fulfillment by the other party, except as provided by the next section. *(Enacted in 1872.)*

Cross References
Impossible or unlawful conditions, see Civil Code § 1441.
Offer dependent on performance of conditions, see Civil Code § 1498.
Performance of conditions precedent, pleading and proof, see Code of Civil Procedure § 457.

§ 1440. Performance; excuse

WHEN PERFORMANCE, ETC., EXCUSED. If a party to an obligation gives notice to another, before the latter is in default, that he will not perform the same upon his part, and does not retract such notice before the time at which performance upon his part is due, such other party is entitled to enforce the obligation without previously performing or offering to perform any conditions upon his part in favor of the former party. *(Enacted in 1872.)*

Cross References
Causes excusing performance, see Civil Code § 1511.
Refusal to accept performance, see Civil Code § 1515.
Unlawful detainer actions, new causes of action on same rental agreement not barred because of appeal, see Code of Civil Procedure § 1176.

§ 1441. Impossible or unlawful conditions

IMPOSSIBLE OR UNLAWFUL CONDITIONS VOID. A condition in a contract, the fulfillment of which is impossible or unlawful, within the meaning of the Article on the Object of Contracts, or which is repugnant to the nature of the interest created by the contract, is void. *(Enacted in 1872.)*

Cross References
Contracts,
  Generally, see Civil Code § 1549 et seq.
  Interpretation, see Civil Code § 1635 et seq.
Impossibility, see Civil Code § 1596 et seq.
Nullity of alternative obligations, effect, see Civil Code § 1451.
Object of contracts, see Civil Code § 1595 et seq.
Void conditions precedent, see Civil Code § 709.

§ 1442. Forfeiture; strict construction

CONDITIONS INVOLVING FORFEITURE, HOW CONSTRUED. A condition involving a forfeiture must be strictly interpreted against the party for whose benefit it is created. *(Enacted in 1872.)*

Cross References
Appropriation of waters, forfeiture of, see Civil Code § 1419.
Contracts for forfeiture, property subject to lien, void, see Civil Code § 2889.
Corporate directors or shareholders, action against, see Code of Civil Procedure § 359.

Enforcement of penalties or forfeitures, see Civil Code § 3369.
Grant in excess of title does not work forfeiture, see Civil Code § 1108.
Hiring contract, forfeiture of rights under, see Civil Code §§ 1930, 1931.
Limitation of actions on forfeiture, see Code of Civil Procedure § 340.
Relief in case of forfeiture, see Civil Code § 3275.
Servitude, extinguishment, see Civil Code § 811.

CHAPTER 4. ALTERNATIVE OBLIGATIONS

Section
1448. Right of selection.
1449. Loss of right.
1450. Indivisibility of alternatives.
1451. Nullity of one or more alternatives.

Cross References
Conditional obligations, see Civil Code § 1434 et seq.
General rules of contract interpretation, see Civil Code § 1429.
Joint or several obligations, see Civil Code § 1430 et seq.
Obligation defined for purposes of this Division, see Civil Code § 1427.

§ 1448. Right of selection

WHO HAS THE RIGHT OF SELECTION. If an obligation requires the performance of one of two acts, in the alternative, the party required to perform has the right of selection, unless it is otherwise provided by the terms of the obligation. *(Enacted in 1872.)*

§ 1449. Loss of right

RIGHT OF SELECTION, HOW LOST. If the party having the right of selection between alternative acts does not give notice of his selection to the other party within the time, if any, fixed by the obligation for that purpose, or, if none is so fixed, before the time at which the obligation ought to be performed, the right of selection passes to the other party. *(Enacted in 1872.)*

§ 1450. Indivisibility of alternatives

ALTERNATIVES INDIVISIBLE. The party having the right of selection between alternative acts must select one of them in its entirety, and cannot select part of one and part of another without the consent of the other party. *(Enacted in 1872.)*

§ 1451. Nullity of one or more alternatives

NULLITY OF ONE OR MORE ALTERNATIVE OBLIGATIONS. If one of the alternative acts required by an obligation is such as the law will not enforce, or becomes unlawful, or impossible of performance, the obligation is to be interpreted as though the other stood alone. *(Enacted in 1872.)*

Title 3

TRANSFER OF OBLIGATIONS

Section
1457. Burden of obligation; consent.
1458. Right arising from obligation.
1459. Non-negotiable instruments; indorsement.
1459.5. Attorney's fees, costs, and expenses.
1460. Covenants running with land defined.

Section
1461. Covenants running with land.
1462. Covenants running with land; direct benefit of existing property.
1463. Covenants running with land; direct benefit of existing property; list.
1464. Repealed.
1465. Covenants running with land; persons bound.
1466. Covenants running with land; persons not bound.
1467. Covenants running with land; apportionment.
1468. Covenants running with land of both covenantor and covenantee; successive owners.
1469. Lessor's affirmative covenants as to contiguous land; successive owners.
1470. Lessor's negative covenants as to contiguous land; successive owners.
1471. Covenants to do or refrain from doing; persons bound; successive owners; requirements; apportionment of burden; certified copies to California Environmental Protection Agency.

Cross References

Business name, transfer of right to use, see Business and Professions Code § 14103.
Good will of business transferable, see Business and Professions Code § 14102.
Insurance, transfer of life or disability policies, see Insurance Code § 10129 et seq.
Mere possibility not transferable, see Civil Code § 1045.
Obligation defined for purposes of this Division, see Civil Code § 1427.
Products of the mind, ownership, see Civil Code § 980 et seq.
Products of the mind, transferability, see Civil Code § 982.
Property of any kind transferable, see Civil Code § 1044.
Rents, reversions and remainders, transfer of, see Civil Code § 1111.
Things in action, transferability, see Civil Code § 954.
Transfer of a thing carries its incidents, but not vice versa, see Civil Code § 1084.

§ 1457. Burden of obligation; consent

BURDEN OF OBLIGATION NOT TRANSFERABLE. The burden of an obligation may be transferred with the consent of the party entitled to its benefit, but not otherwise, except as provided by Section 1466. (Enacted in 1872.)

§ 1458. Right arising from obligation

RIGHTS ARISING OUT OF OBLIGATION TRANSFERABLE. A right arising out of an obligation is the property of the person to whom it is due, and may be transferred as such. (Enacted in 1872.)

§ 1459. Non-negotiable instruments; indorsement

NON-NEGOTIABLE INSTRUMENTS MAY BE TRANSFERRED. A non-negotiable written contract for the payment of money or personal property may be transferred by indorsement, in like manner with negotiable instruments. Such indorsement shall transfer all the rights of the assignor under the instrument to the assignee, subject to all equities and defenses existing in favor of the maker at the time of the indorsement. (Enacted in 1872.)

Cross References

Assignment of retail installment sale contract, effect on rights, equities or defenses, see Civil Code § 1804.2.
Commercial paper, transfer and negotiation, see Commercial Code § 3201 et seq.
Warehouse receipts and bills of lading, negotiation and transfer, see Commercial Code § 7501 et seq.

§ 1459.5. Attorney's fees, costs, and expenses

A plaintiff who prevails on a cause of action against a defendant named pursuant to Part 433 of Title 16 of the Code of Federal Regulations or any successor thereto, or pursuant to the contractual language required by that part or any successor thereto, may claim attorney's fees, costs, and expenses from that defendant to the fullest extent permissible if the plaintiff had prevailed on that cause of action against the seller. (Added by Stats.2019, c. 116 (A.B.1821), § 1, eff. Jan. 1, 2020. Amended by Stats.2020, c. 370 (S.B.1371), § 28, eff. Jan. 1, 2021.)

Validity

For validity of this section, see Spikener v. Ally Financial, Inc. (App. 1 Dist. 2020), 263 Cal.Rptr.3d 726, review denied.

§ 1460. Covenants running with land defined

COVENANTS RUNNING WITH LAND, WHAT. Certain covenants, contained in grants of estates in real property, are appurtenant to such estates, and pass with them, so as to bind the assigns of the covenantor and to vest in the assigns of the covenantee, in the same manner as if they had personally entered into them. Such covenants are said to run with the land. (Enacted in 1872.)

Cross References

Implied covenants, see Civil Code § 1113.
Real property defined for purposes of this Code, see Civil Code § 658.

§ 1461. Covenants running with land

WHAT COVENANTS RUN WITH LAND. The only covenants which run with the land are those specified in this Title, and those which are incidental thereto. (Enacted in 1872.)

§ 1462. Covenants running with land; direct benefit of existing property

SAME. Every covenant contained in a grant of an estate in real property, which is made for the direct benefit of the property, or some part of it then in existence, runs with the land. (Enacted in 1872.)

Cross References

Effect of transfers in general, see Civil Code §§ 1084, 1085.
Real property defined for purposes of this Code, see Civil Code § 658.

§ 1463. Covenants running with land; direct benefit of existing property; list

SAME. The last section includes covenants "of warranty," "for quiet enjoyment," or for further assurance on the part of a grantor, and covenants for the payment of rent, or of taxes or assessments upon the land, on the part of a grantee. (Enacted in 1872.)

Cross References

Damages for breach of covenants of warranty, etc., see Civil Code § 3304.

Lessor required to secure quiet possession to hirer, see Civil Code § 1927.

§ 1464. Repealed by Stats.1998, c. 14 (A.B.707), § 2

§ 1465. Covenants running with land; persons bound

WHO ARE BOUND BY COVENANTS. A covenant running with the land binds those only who acquire the whole estate of the covenantor in some part of the property. *(Enacted in 1872.)*

§ 1466. Covenants running with land; persons not bound

WHO ARE NOT. No one, merely by reason of having acquired an estate subject to a covenant running with the land, is liable for a breach of the covenant before he acquired the estate, or after he has parted with it or ceased to enjoy its benefits. *(Enacted in 1872.)*

§ 1467. Covenants running with land; apportionment

APPORTIONMENT OF COVENANTS. Where several persons, holding by several titles, are subject to the burden or entitled to the benefit of a covenant running with the land, it must be apportioned among them according to the value of the property subject to it held by them respectively, if such value can be ascertained, and if not, then according to their respective interests in point of quantity. *(Enacted in 1872.)*

§ 1468. Covenants running with land of both covenantor and covenantee; successive owners

Each covenant, made by an owner of land with the owner of other land or made by a grantor of land with the grantee of land conveyed, or made by the grantee of land conveyed with the grantor thereof, to do or refrain from doing some act on his own land, which doing or refraining is expressed to be for the benefit of the land of the covenantee, runs with both the land owned by or granted to the covenantor and the land owned by or granted to the covenantee and shall, except as provided by Section 1466, or as specifically provided in the instrument creating such covenant, and notwithstanding the provisions of Section 1465, benefit or be binding upon each successive owner, during his ownership, of any portion of such land affected thereby and upon each person having any interest therein derived through any owner thereof where all of the following requirements are met:

(a) The land of the covenantor which is to be affected by such covenants, and the land of covenantee to be benefited, are particularly described in the instrument containing such covenants;

(b) Such successive owners of the land are in such instrument expressed to be bound thereby for the benefit of the land owned by, granted by, or granted to the covenantee;

(c) Each such act relates to the use, repair, maintenance or improvement of, or payment of taxes and assessments on, such land or some part thereof, or if the land owned by or granted to each consists of undivided interests in the same parcel or parcels, the suspension of the right of partition or sale in lieu of partition for a period which is reasonable in relation to the purpose of the covenant;

(d) The instrument containing such covenants is recorded in the office of the recorder of each county in which such land or some part thereof is situated.

Where several persons are subject to the burden of any such covenant, it shall be apportioned among them pursuant to Section 1467, except that where only a portion of such land is so affected thereby, such apportionment shall be only among the several owners of such portion. This section shall apply to the mortgagee, trustee or beneficiary of a mortgage or deed of trust upon such land or any part thereof while but only while he, in such capacity, is in possession thereof. *(Added by Stats.1905, c. 450, p. 610, § 1. Amended by Stats.1968, c. 680, p. 1377, § 1; Stats.1969, c. 245, p. 594, § 1; Stats.1973, c. 474, p. 948, § 1, eff. Sept. 11, 1973.)*

§ 1469. Lessor's affirmative covenants as to contiguous land; successive owners

Each covenant made by the lessor in a lease of real property to do any act or acts on other real property which is owned by the lessor and is contiguous (except for intervening public streets, alleys or sidewalks) to the real property demised to the lessee shall, except as provided by Section 1466, be binding upon each successive owner, during his ownership, of any portion of such contiguous real property affected thereby where all of the following requirements are met:

(a) Such contiguous real property is particularly described in the lease;

(b) Such successive owners are in the lease expressed to be bound thereby for the benefit of the demised real property;

(c) Each such act relates to the use, repair, maintenance or improvement of, or payment of taxes and assessments on, such contiguous real property or some part thereof;

(d) The lease is recorded in the same manner as grants of real property, in the office of the recorder of each county in which such contiguous real property or some part thereof is situate. Such lease shall include the description of any such contiguous land described in any unrecorded instrument, the contents of which unrecorded instrument are incorporated by reference in such recorded lease.

Where several persons are subject to the burden of any such covenant, it shall be apportioned among them pursuant to Section 1467, except that where only a portion of such contiguous real property is so affected thereby, such apportionment shall be only among the several owners of such portion. This section shall apply to the mortgagee, trustee or beneficiary of a mortgage or deed of trust upon such contiguous real property or any part thereof while but only while he, in such capacity, is in possession thereof. *(Added by Stats.1953, c. 652, p. 1903, § 1. Amended by Stats.1965, c. 1502, p. 3527, § 1.)*

Cross References

Real property defined for purposes of this Code, see Civil Code § 658.

§ 1470. Lessor's negative covenants as to contiguous land; successive owners

Each covenant made by the lessor in a lease of real property not to use or permit to be used contrary to the terms of such lease any other real property which is owned by the lessor and is contiguous (except for intervening public streets, alleys or sidewalks) to the real property demised to the lessee shall, except as provided by Section 1466, be binding upon each successive owner, during his ownership, of any portion of such contiguous real property affected thereby and upon each person having any interest therein derived through any owner thereof where all of the following requirements are met:

(a) Such contiguous real property is particularly described in the lease;

(b) Such successive owners and persons having any such interest are in the lease expressed to be bound thereby for the benefit of the demised real property;

(c) The lease is recorded in the same manner as grants of real property, in the office of the recorder of each county in which such contiguous real property or some part thereof is situate. Such lease shall include therein the description of any such contiguous land described in any unrecorded instrument, the contents of which unrecorded instrument are incorporated by reference in such recorded lease.

Where several persons are subject to the burden of any such covenant, it shall be apportioned among them pursuant to Section 1467, except that where only a portion of such contiguous real property is so affected thereby, such apportionment shall be only among the several owners of, and persons having any such interest in, such portion. This section shall apply to the mortgagee, trustee or beneficiary of a mortgage or deed of trust upon such contiguous real property or any part thereof while and only while he, in such capacity, is in possession thereof. (Added by Stats.1953, c. 652, p. 1904, § 2. Amended by Stats.1963, c. 2054, p. 4297, § 1.)

Cross References

Real property defined for purposes of this Code, see Civil Code § 658.

§ 1471. Covenants to do or refrain from doing; persons bound; successive owners; requirements; apportionment of burden; certified copies to California Environmental Protection Agency

(a) Notwithstanding Section 1468 or any other provision of law, a covenant made by an owner of land or by the grantee of land to do or refrain from doing some act on his or her own land, which doing or refraining is expressed to be for the benefit of the covenantee, regardless of whether or not it is for the benefit of land owned by the covenantee, shall run with the land owned by or granted to the covenantor if all the following requirements are met:

(1) The land of the covenantor that is to be affected by the covenant is particularly described in the instrument containing the covenant.

(2) The successive owners of the land are expressed to be bound thereby for the benefit of the covenantee in the instrument containing the covenant.

(3) Each act that the owner or grantee will do or refrain from doing relates to the use of land and each act is reasonably necessary to protect present or future human health or safety or the environment as a result of the presence on the land of hazardous materials, as defined in Section 25260 of the Health and Safety Code.

(4) The instrument containing the covenant is recorded in the office of the recorder of each county in which the land or some portion thereof is situated and the instrument includes in its title the words: "Environmental Restriction."

(b) Except as provided by Section 1466 or as specifically provided in the instrument creating a covenant made pursuant to this section, the covenant shall be binding upon each successive owner, during his or her ownership, of any portion of the land affected thereby and upon each person having any interest therein derived through any owner thereof.

(c) If several persons are subject to the burden of a covenant recorded pursuant to this section, it shall be apportioned among them pursuant to Section 1467, except if only a portion of the land is so affected thereby, the apportionment shall be only among the several owners of that portion.

(d) This section shall apply to the mortgagee, trustee, or beneficiary of a mortgage or deed of trust upon the land or any part thereof while, but only while, he or she, in that capacity, is in possession thereof.

(e)(1) If an instrument containing a covenant is recorded pursuant to paragraph (4) of subdivision (a) as an "Environmental Restriction," in accordance with this section, the office of the recorder of the county may send a certified copy of the instrument to the California Environmental Protection Agency, for posting on its Web site, for informational purposes only, pursuant to Section 57012 of the Health and Safety Code, unless the instrument indicates that it is required by a board or department specified in paragraphs (1) to (3), inclusive, of subdivision (d) of Section 57012 of the Health and Safety Code.

(2) Notwithstanding any provision of law, the office of the recorder of the county and any of its employees shall not be subject to any liability under any state law or in any action for damages if the office of the recorder does not send a certified copy of the instrument pursuant to paragraph (1).

(f) The office of the recorder of the county may assess a reasonable fee, as determined by resolution of its governing body, to cover the costs of taking the action authorized by subdivision (e). (Added by Stats.1995, c. 188 (A.B.1120), § 1. Amended by Stats.2002, c. 592 (A.B.2436), § 1.)

Cross References

Bona fide ground tenant immunity, enumerated immunities, extent and effect of thereof, see Health and Safety Code § 25395.104.
California Land Reuse and Revitalization Act, definitions, land use control, see Health and Safety Code § 25395.76.
Regulation of environmental protection, restricted land uses, see Health and Safety Code § 57012.
Water quality enforcement and implementation, cleanup or site closure proposals, property not suitable for unrestricted use, see Water Code § 13307.1.

Title 4

EXTINCTION OF OBLIGATIONS

Chapter	Section
1. Performance	1473
2. Offer of Performance	1485
3. Prevention of Performance or Offer	1511

OBLIGATIONS

Chapter	Section
4. Accord and Satisfaction	1521
5. Novation	1530
6. Release	1541

Cross References

Obligation defined for purposes of this Division, see Civil Code § 1427.

CHAPTER 1. PERFORMANCE

Section
1473. Performance.
1474. Performance by one of several joint obligors.
1475. Performance to one of joint obligees; exception.
1476. Performance in manner directed by creditors.
1477. Partial performance; effect.
1478. Payment defined.
1479. Act of performance applicable to two or more obligations; application to specific obligation.

Cross References

Obligation defined for purposes of this Division, see Civil Code § 1427.

§ 1473. Performance

OBLIGATION EXTINGUISHED BY PERFORMANCE. Full performance of an obligation, by the party whose duty it is to perform it, or by any other person on his behalf, and with his assent, if accepted by the creditor, extinguishes it. *(Enacted in 1872.)*

Cross References

Causes excusing performance, see Civil Code § 1511.
Extinction of contracts, see Civil Code § 1682 et seq.
Obligation defined, see Civil Code § 1427; Code of Civil Procedure § 26.
Partial performance, see Civil Code §§ 1477, 1524.
Right to receipt for payment or delivery, see Code of Civil Procedure § 2075.
Specific performance, see Civil Code § 3384 et seq.
Time of performance, see Civil Code § 1657.
Transfer of obligations, consent of party entitled to benefit necessary, see Civil Code § 1457.

§ 1474. Performance by one of several joint obligors

PERFORMANCE BY ONE OF SEVERAL JOINT DEBTORS. Performance of an obligation, by one of several persons who are jointly liable under it, extinguishes the liability of all. *(Enacted in 1872.)*

Cross References

Contribution among joint obligors, debtors, see Civil Code § 1432; Code of Civil Procedure §§ 882, 883.
Obligations presumed to be joint, see Civil Code § 1431.
Release of a joint debtor, see Civil Code § 1543.

§ 1475. Performance to one of joint obligees; exception

PERFORMANCE TO ONE OF JOINT CREDITORS. An obligation in favor of several persons is extinguished by performance rendered to any of them, except in the case of a deposit made by owners in common, or in joint ownership, which is regulated by the Title on Deposit. *(Enacted in 1872.)*

Cross References

Deposits by joint tenants, see Civil Code § 1828.

§ 1476. Performance in manner directed by creditors

EFFECT OF DIRECTIONS BY CREDITORS. If a creditor, or any one of two or more joint creditors, at any time directs the debtor to perform his obligation in a particular manner, the obligation is extinguished by performance in that manner, even though the creditor does not receive the benefit of such performance. *(Enacted in 1872.)*

§ 1477. Partial performance; effect

PARTIAL PERFORMANCE. A partial performance of an indivisible obligation extinguishes a corresponding proportion thereof, if the benefit of such performance is voluntarily retained by the creditor, but not otherwise. If such partial performance is of such a nature that the creditor cannot avoid retaining it without injuring his own property, his retention thereof is not presumed to be voluntary. *(Enacted in 1872.)*

Cross References

Offer of part performance, see Civil Code § 1486.
Partial satisfaction of obligation, see Civil Code § 2822.
Satisfaction by part performance, see Civil Code § 1524.

§ 1478. Payment defined

PAYMENT, WHAT. Performance of an obligation for the delivery of money only, is called payment. *(Enacted in 1872.)*

Cross References

Offer of payment and deposit in bank or savings and loan association extinguishes debt, see Civil Code § 1500.
Right to receipt for payment, see Code of Civil Procedure § 2075.
Transfer of property, see Civil Code § 1039 et seq.
Written offer to pay as tender, see Code of Civil Procedure § 2074.

§ 1479. Act of performance applicable to two or more obligations; application to specific obligation

Where a debtor, under several obligations to another, does an act, by way of performance, in whole or in part, which is equally applicable to two or more of such obligations, such performance must be applied as follows:

One—If, at the time of performance, the intention or desire of the debtor that such performance should be applied to the extinction of any particular obligation, be manifested to the creditor, it must be so applied.

Two—If no such application be then made, the creditor, within a reasonable time after such performance, may apply it toward the extinction of any obligation, performance of which was due to him from the debtor at the time of such performance; except that if similar obligations were due to him both individually and as a trustee, he must, unless otherwise directed by the debtor, apply the performance to the extinction of all such obligations in equal proportion; and an application once made by the creditor cannot be rescinded without the consent of [the] debtor.

Three—If neither party makes such application within the time prescribed herein, the performance must be applied to the extinction of obligations in the following order; and, if there be more than one obligation of a particular class, to the extinction of all in that class, ratably:

1. Of interest due at the time of the performance.
2. Of principal due at that time.
3. Of the obligation earliest in date of maturity.
4. Of an obligation not secured by a lien or collateral undertaking.
5. Of an obligation secured by a lien or collateral undertaking. *(Enacted in 1872. Amended by Code 1873–74, c. 612, p. 239, § 182.)*

CHAPTER 2. OFFER OF PERFORMANCE

Section
1485. Extinction of obligation.
1486. Partial performance.
1487. Person required to make offer.
1488. Procedure in making offer.
1489. Place of offer.
1490. Time of offer.
1491. Time of offer; performance time not fixed.
1492. Offer of compensation for delay.
1493. Good faith.
1494. Conditions.
1495. Ability and willingness to perform.
1496. Production of thing to be delivered.
1497. Separation of thing offered.
1498. Offer dependent upon performance of conditions.
1499. Receipt for property delivered in performance.
1500. Offer of payment; deposit; notice.
1501. Time for objection to mode of offer.
1502. Title to thing offered in performance.
1503. Deposit of thing offered.
1504. Effect of offer on interest and incidents of obligation.
1505. Refusal of thing offered; retention.

Cross References

Obligation defined for purposes of this Division, see Civil Code § 1427.

§ 1485. Extinction of obligation

OBLIGATION EXTINGUISHED BY OFFER OF PERFORMANCE. An obligation is extinguished by an offer of performance, made in conformity to the rules herein prescribed, and with intent to extinguish the obligation. *(Enacted in 1872.)*

Cross References

Full performance extinguishes obligation, see Civil Code § 1473.
Objection to tender must be specified, see Code of Civil Procedure § 2076.
Offer of payment and deposit of money in bank or savings and loan association extinguishes debt, see Civil Code § 1500.
Offer to perform act in redemption from lien, see Civil Code § 2905.
Part performance extinguishes obligation, see Civil Code § 1524.
Transfer of title to thing offered, see Civil Code § 1502.
Written offer to perform as equivalent to performance, see Code of Civil Procedure § 2074.

§ 1486. Partial performance

OFFER OF PARTIAL PERFORMANCE. An offer of partial performance is of no effect. *(Enacted in 1872.)*

Cross References

Part performance extinguishes obligation, see Civil Code § 1524.
Partial performance of indivisible obligation, see Civil Code § 1477.

Partial satisfaction of obligation, see Civil Code § 2822.

§ 1487. Person required to make offer

BY WHOM TO BE MADE. An offer of performance must be made by the debtor, or by some person on his behalf and with his assent. *(Enacted in 1872.)*

Cross References

Full performance of obligation by a third party extinguishes obligation, see Civil Code § 1473.

§ 1488. Procedure in making offer

An offer of performance must be made to the creditor, or to any one of two or more joint creditors, or to a person authorized by one or more of them to receive or collect what is due under the obligation, if such creditor or authorized person is present at the place where the offer may be made; and if not, wherever the creditor may be found. *(Enacted in 1872. Amended by Code Am.1873–74, c. 612, p. 240, § 183.)*

Cross References

Rendition of performance to any joint obligee, see Civil Code § 1475.

§ 1489. Place of offer

WHERE OFFER MAY BE MADE. In the absence of an express provision to the contrary, an offer of performance may be made, at the option of the debtor:

1. At any place appointed by the creditor; or,
2. Wherever the person to whom the offer ought to be made can be found; or,
3. If such person cannot, with reasonable diligence, be found within this State, and within a reasonable distance from his residence or place of business, or if he evades the debtor, then at his residence or place of business, if the same can, with reasonable diligence, be found within the State; or,
4. If this cannot be done, then at any place within this State. *(Enacted in 1872.)*

Cross References

Offer of performance, excused, see Civil Code § 1511.

§ 1490. Time of offer

WHEN OFFER MUST BE MADE. Where an obligation fixes a time for its performance, an offer of performance must be made at that time, within reasonable hours, and not before nor afterwards. *(Enacted in 1872.)*

§ 1491. Time of offer; performance time not fixed

SAME. Where an obligation does not fix the time for its performance, an offer of performance may be made at any time before the debtor, upon a reasonable demand, has refused to perform. *(Enacted in 1872.)*

§ 1492. Offer of compensation for delay

COMPENSATION AFTER DELAY IN PERFORMANCE. Where delay in performance is capable of exact and entire compensation, and time has not been expressly declared to be of the essence of the obligation, an offer of performance, accompanied with an offer of such compensation, may be made at any time after it is due, but without prejudice to any rights acquired by the

§ 1492

creditor, or by any other person, in the meantime. *(Enacted in 1872.)*

Cross References

Relief from forfeiture upon making compensation, see Civil Code § 3275.
When offer must be made, see Civil Code § 1490.

§ 1493. Good faith

OFFER TO BE MADE IN GOOD FAITH. An offer of performance must be made in good faith, and in such manner as is most likely, under the circumstances, to benefit the creditor. *(Enacted in 1872.)*

Cross References

"Good faith" defined, see Commercial Code § 1201.

§ 1494. Conditions

CONDITIONAL OFFER. An offer of performance must be free from any conditions which the creditor is not bound, on his part, to perform. *(Enacted in 1872.)*

Cross References

Offer dependent on performance of conditions, see Civil Code § 1498.
Receipt for property delivered in performance, see Civil Code § 1499.

§ 1495. Ability and willingness to perform

ABILITY AND WILLINGNESS ESSENTIAL. An offer of performance is of no effect if the person making it is not able and willing to perform according to the offer. *(Enacted in 1872.)*

§ 1496. Production of thing to be delivered

PRODUCTION OF THING TO BE DELIVERED NOT NECESSARY. The thing to be delivered, if any, need not in any case be actually produced, upon an offer of performance, unless the offer is accepted. *(Enacted in 1872.)*

Cross References

Offer in writing to deliver personal property equivalent to tender, see Code of Civil Procedure § 2074.

§ 1497. Separation of thing offered

THING OFFERED TO BE KEPT SEPARATE. A thing, when offered by way of performance, must not be mixed with other things from which it cannot be separated immediately and without difficulty. *(Enacted in 1872.)*

Cross References

Buyer's option concerning delivery of mixed goods, see Commercial Code § 2601.
Buyer's option on improper delivery, see Commercial Code § 2601.
Deposit of thing offered, see Civil Code § 1503.
Manner of seller's tender, see Commercial Code § 2503.

§ 1498. Offer dependent upon performance of conditions

PERFORMANCE OF CONDITION PRECEDENT. When a debtor is entitled to the performance of a condition precedent to, or concurrent with, performance on his part, he may make his offer to depend upon the due performance of such condition. *(Enacted in 1872.)*

Cross References

Condition concurrent, defined, see Civil Code § 1437.
Condition precedent, defined, see Civil Code §§ 708, 1436.
Conditions subsequent, defined, see Civil Code §§ 708, 1438.
Excuse for performance of conditions, see Civil Code § 1440.
Impossible, wrong or unlawful conditions, see Civil Code §§ 709, 1441.
Party must fulfill conditions imposed upon himself before requiring another party to perform, see Civil Code § 1439.

§ 1499. Receipt for property delivered in performance

WRITTEN RECEIPTS. A debtor has a right to require from his creditor a written receipt for any property delivered in performance of his obligation. *(Enacted in 1872.)*

Cross References

Similar provision, see Code of Civil Procedure § 2075.

§ 1500. Offer of payment; deposit; notice

An obligation for the payment of money is extinguished by a due offer of payment, if the amount is immediately deposited in the name of the creditor, with some bank or savings and loan association within this state, of good repute, and notice thereof is given to the creditor. *(Enacted in 1872. Amended by Stats.1981, c. 632, § 1, eff. Sept. 23, 1981.)*

Cross References

Effect of offer on interest and incidents of obligation, see Civil Code § 1504.
Rejected offer equivalent to production and tender, see Code of Civil Procedure § 2074.

§ 1501. Time for objection to mode of offer

OBJECTIONS TO MODE OF OFFER. All objections to the mode of an offer of performance, which the creditor has an opportunity to state at the time to the person making the offer, and which could be then obviated by him, are waived by the creditor, if not then stated. *(Enacted in 1872.)*

Cross References

Similar provision with respect to objections to tenders, see Code of Civil Procedure § 2076.

§ 1502. Title to thing offered in performance

TITLE TO THING OFFERED. The title to a thing duly offered in performance of an obligation passes to the creditor, if the debtor at the time signifies his intention to that effect. *(Enacted in 1872.)*

Cross References

Fee simple title, presumption as to title passing, see Civil Code § 1105.
Transfer of property and title upon a sale of goods, see Commercial Code § 2401 et seq.

§ 1503. Deposit of thing offered

CUSTODY OF THING OFFERED. The person offering a thing, other than money, by way of performance, must, if he means to treat it as belonging to the creditor, retain it as a depositary for hire, until the creditor accepts it, or until he has given reasonable notice to the creditor that he will retain it no longer, and, if with reasonable diligence he can find a suitable depositary therefor, until he has deposited it with such person. *(Enacted in 1872.)*

Cross References

Depositories, for hire, degree of care, see Civil Code § 1852.
Deposits in general, see Civil Code § 1813 et seq.
Separation of thing offered, see Civil Code § 1497.

§ 1504. Effect of offer on interest and incidents of obligation

EFFECT OF OFFER ON ACCESSORIES OF OBLIGATION. An offer of payment or other performance, duly made, though the title to the thing offered be not transferred to the creditor, stops the running of interest on the obligation, and has the same effect upon all its incidents as a performance thereof. *(Enacted in 1872.)*

Cross References

Costs, effect of tender, see Code of Civil Procedure § 1025.
Offer in writing equivalent to payment, see Code of Civil Procedure § 2074.
Transfer of title to thing offered, see Civil Code § 1502.

§ 1505. Refusal of thing offered; retention

CREDITOR'S RETENTION OF THING WHICH HE REFUSES TO ACCEPT. If anything is given to a creditor by way of performance, which he refuses to accept as such, he is not bound to return it without demand; but if he retains it, he is a gratuitous depositary thereof. *(Enacted in 1872.)*

Cross References

Costs, effect of tender before action, see Code of Civil Procedure § 1025.
Gratuitous deposit, see Civil Code § 1844 et seq.

CHAPTER 3. PREVENTION OF PERFORMANCE OR OFFER

Section
1511. Causes excusing performance.
1512. Performance prevented by creditor.
1513. Repealed.
1514. Performance prevented by cause excusing performance.
1515. Refusal to accept performance before offer.

Cross References

Obligation defined for purposes of this Division, see Civil Code § 1427.

§ 1511. Causes excusing performance

The want of performance of an obligation, or of an offer of performance, in whole or in part, or any delay therein, is excused by the following causes, to the extent to which they operate:

1. When such performance or offer is prevented or delayed by the act of the creditor, or by the operation of law, even though there may have been a stipulation that this shall not be an excuse; however, the parties may expressly require in a contract that the party relying on the provisions of this paragraph give written notice to the other party or parties, within a reasonable time after the occurrence of the event excusing performance, of an intention to claim an extension of time or of an intention to bring suit or of any other similar or related intent, provided the requirement of such notice is reasonable and just;

2. When it is prevented or delayed by an irresistible, superhuman cause, or by the act of public enemies of this state or of the United States, unless the parties have expressly agreed to the contrary; or,

3. When the debtor is induced not to make it, by any act of the creditor intended or naturally tending to have that effect, done at or before the time at which such performance or offer may be made, and not rescinded before that time. *(Enacted in 1872. Amended by Stats.1965, c. 1730, p. 3888, § 1.)*

Cross References

Compensation and performance after delay, see Civil Code § 1492.
Part performance accepted in writing, in satisfaction, extinguishes obligation, see Civil Code § 1524.
Performance of conditions excused, see Civil Code § 1440.

§ 1512. Performance prevented by creditor

If the performance of an obligation be prevented by the creditor, the debtor is entitled to all the benefits which he would have obtained if it had been performed by both parties. *(Enacted in 1872. Amended by Code Am.1873–74, c. 612, p. 240, § 184.)*

§ 1513. Repealed by Code Am.1873–74, c. 612, p. 240, § 185

§ 1514. Performance prevented by cause excusing performance

SAME. If performance of an obligation is prevented by any cause excusing performance, other than the act of the creditor, the debtor is entitled to a ratable proportion of the consideration to which he would have been entitled upon full performance, according to the benefit which the creditor receives from the actual performance. *(Enacted in 1872.)*

§ 1515. Refusal to accept performance before offer

EFFECT OF REFUSAL TO ACCEPT PERFORMANCE BEFORE OFFER. A refusal by a creditor to accept performance, made before an offer thereof, is equivalent to an offer and refusal, unless, before performance is actually due, he gives notice to the debtor of his willingness to accept it. *(Enacted in 1872.)*

Cross References

Notice of nonperformance excuses performance of conditions imposed upon other party, see Civil Code § 1440.

CHAPTER 4. ACCORD AND SATISFACTION

Section
1521. "Accord" defined.
1522. Accord; necessity of execution.
1523. Satisfaction defined.
1524. Satisfaction; part performance.
1525. Part payment of disputed sum.
1526. Check or draft tendered in full discharge of claim; acceptance; protest; composition or extension agreement between debtor and creditors; release of claim.

OBLIGATIONS

Cross References

Obligation defined for purposes of this Division, see Civil Code § 1427.

§ 1521. "Accord" defined

An accord is an agreement to accept, in extinction of an obligation, something different from or less than that to which the person agreeing to accept is entitled. *(Enacted in 1872. Amended by Code Am.1873–74, c. 612, p. 240, § 186.)*

Cross References

Consideration, see Civil Code §§ 1550, 1605 et seq.
Novation, see Civil Code § 1530 et seq.
Release, see Civil Code § 1541 et seq.
Third persons, acceptance of obligations or orders on, see Civil Code § 1533.

§ 1522. Accord; necessity of execution

EFFECT OF ACCORD. Though the parties to an accord are bound to execute it, yet it does not extinguish the obligation until it is fully executed. *(Enacted in 1872.)*

§ 1523. Satisfaction defined

SATISFACTION, WHAT. Acceptance, by the creditor, of the consideration of an accord extinguishes the obligation, and is called satisfaction. *(Enacted in 1872.)*

§ 1524. Satisfaction; part performance

Part performance of an obligation, either before or after a breach thereof, when expressly accepted by the creditor in writing, in satisfaction, or rendered in pursuance of an agreement in writing for that purpose, though without any new consideration, extinguishes the obligation. *(Enacted in 1872. Amended by Code Am.1873–74, c. 612, p. 241, § 187.)*

Cross References

Obligation defined, see Civil Code § 1427.
Obligation extinguished by release in writing with or without new consideration, see Civil Code § 1541.
Partial performance, see Civil Code §§ 1477, 1486.
Performance, extinction of obligation by, see Civil Code § 1473.
Written instrument, presumption of consideration, see Civil Code § 1614.

§ 1525. Part payment of disputed sum

It is the public policy of this State, in the best interests of the taxpayer and of the litigant, to encourage fair dealing and to promote justice by reducing litigated matters to the lowest level of jurisdiction.

In case of a dispute over total money due on a contract and it is conceded by the parties that part of the money is due, the debtor may pay, without condition, the amount conceded to be due, leaving to the other party all remedies to which he might otherwise be entitled as to any balance claimed.

If any conditions are attached to the payment, this section shall not be deemed to have limited the remedies available to the other party under other provisions of law on the original amount claimed. *(Added by Stats.1963, c. 1495, p. 3074, § 1.)*

§ 1526. Check or draft tendered in full discharge of claim; acceptance; protest; composition or extension agreement between debtor and creditors; release of claim

(a) Where a claim is disputed or unliquidated and a check or draft is tendered by the debtor in settlement thereof in full discharge of the claim, and the words "payment in full" or other words of similar meaning are notated on the check or draft, the acceptance of the check or draft does not constitute an accord and satisfaction if the creditor protests against accepting the tender in full payment by striking out or otherwise deleting that notation or if the acceptance of the check or draft was inadvertent or without knowledge of the notation.

(b) Notwithstanding subdivision (a), the acceptance of a check or draft constitutes an accord and satisfaction if a check or draft is tendered pursuant to a composition or extension agreement between a debtor and its creditors, and pursuant to that composition or extension agreement, all creditors of the same class are accorded similar treatment, and the creditor receives the check or draft with knowledge of the restriction.

A creditor shall be conclusively presumed to have knowledge of the restriction if a creditor either:

(1) Has, previous to the receipt of the check or draft, executed a written consent to the composition or extension agreement.

(2) Has been given, not less than 15 days nor more than 90 days prior to receipt of the check or draft, notice, in writing, that a check or draft will be tendered with a restrictive endorsement and that acceptance and cashing of the check or draft will constitute an accord and satisfaction.

(c) Notwithstanding subdivision (a), the acceptance of a check or draft by a creditor constitutes an accord and satisfaction when the check or draft is issued pursuant to or in conjunction with a release of a claim.

(d) For the purposes of paragraph (2) of subdivision (b), mailing the notice by first-class mail, postage prepaid, addressed to the address shown for the creditor on the debtor's books or such other address as the creditor may designate in writing constitutes notice. *(Added by Stats.1987, c. 1268, § 1.)*

Validity

This section was held to be superceded, as to discharge of an unliquidated claim or a claim subject to a bona fide dispute by tendering a negotiable instrument as full satisfaction of the claim, by Commercial Code § 3311, in the decision of Woolridge v. J.F.L. Electric, Inc., 2002, 117 Cal.Rptr.2d 771, 96 Cal.App.4th Supp. 52.

Cross References

Performance or acceptance under reservation of rights, see Commercial Code § 1207.
Satisfaction of claim by use of instrument, see Commercial Code § 3311.

CHAPTER 5. NOVATION

Section
1530. "Novation" defined.

Section
1531. Methods.
1532. Applicability of contract rules.
1533. Rescission.

Cross References

Obligation defined for purposes of this Division, see Civil Code § 1427.

§ 1530. "Novation" defined

NOVATION, WHAT. Novation is the substitution of a new obligation for an existing one. *(Enacted in 1872.)*

Cross References

Applicability of contract rules, see Civil Code § 1532.
Enforcement by third party beneficiary, see Civil Code § 1559.
Transfer of obligations, see Civil Code § 1457 et seq.

§ 1531. Methods

MODES OF NOVATION. Novation is made:

1. By the substitution of a new obligation between the same parties, with intent to extinguish the old obligation;

2. By the substitution of a new debtor in place of the old one, with intent to release the latter; or,

3. By the substitution of a new creditor in place of the old one, with intent to transfer the rights of the latter to the former. *(Enacted in 1872.)*

§ 1532. Applicability of contract rules

NOVATION A CONTRACT. Novation is made by contract, and is subject to all the rules concerning contracts in general. *(Enacted in 1872.)*

§ 1533. Rescission

When the obligation of a third person, or an order upon such person is accepted in satisfaction, the creditor may rescind such acceptance if the debtor prevents such person from complying with the order, or from fulfilling the obligation; or if, at the time the obligation or order is received, such person is insolvent, and this fact is unknown to the creditor, or if, before the creditor can with reasonable diligence present the order to the person upon whom it is given, he becomes insolvent. *(Enacted in 1872. Amended by Code Am.1873–74, c. 612, p. 241, § 188.)*

CHAPTER 6. RELEASE

Section
1541. Extinction of obligations.
1542. General release; extent.
1542.1. Defense of health care providers by Attorney General or other legal counsel provided by state; scope of release.
1543. One or more joint debtors.

Cross References

Obligation defined for purposes of this Division, see Civil Code § 1427.

§ 1541. Extinction of obligations

An obligation is extinguished by a release therefrom given to the debtor or the released party by the creditor or releasing party, upon a new consideration, or in writing, with or without new consideration. *(Enacted in 1872. Amended by Stats. 2018, c. 157 (S.B.1431), § 1, eff. Jan. 1, 2019.)*

Cross References

Written instrument, consideration presumed, see Civil Code § 1614.

§ 1542. General release; extent

A general release does not extend to claims that the creditor or releasing party does not know or suspect to exist in his or her favor at the time of executing the release and that, if known by him or her, would have materially affected his or her settlement with the debtor or released party. *(Enacted in 1872. Amended by Code Am.1873–74, c. 612, p. 241, § 189; Stats.2004, c. 183 (A.B.3082), § 28; Stats.2018, c. 157 (S.B.1431), § 2, eff. Jan. 1, 2019.)*

§ 1542.1. Defense of health care providers by Attorney General or other legal counsel provided by state; scope of release

Notwithstanding Section 1542, a provider of health care, as defined in Section 56.05, or its officers, employees, agents, or subcontractors, shall release the state and its officers, employees, and agents, from any claim arising from the defense of the provider of health care by the Attorney General, or other legal counsel provided by the state pursuant to Section 12511.5 of the Government Code. *(Added by Stats.1995, c. 749 (A.B.1177), § 2, eff. Oct. 10, 1995.)*

§ 1543. One or more joint debtors

A release of one of two or more joint debtors does not extinguish the obligations of any of the others, unless they are mere guarantors; nor does it affect their right to contribution from him or her, except as provided in Section 877 of the Code of Civil Procedure. *(Enacted in 1872. Amended by Stats.1987, c. 677, § 1.5.)*

Cross References

Discharge of sureties' liability, see Civil Code § 2819.
Rights of surety, see Civil Code § 2845.

Part 2

CONTRACTS

Title		Section
1.	Nature of a Contract	1549
2.	Manner of Creating Contracts	1619
2.5.	Electronic Transactions	1633.1
3.	Interpretation of Contracts	1635
4.	Unlawful Contracts	1667
4.5.	Liquidated Damages	1671
5.	Extinction of Contracts	1682

Cross References

Arbitration agreements, see Code of Civil Procedure § 1280 et seq.
Attachment, see Code of Civil Procedure § 484.010 et seq.
Commissions, rate agreed to in writing, presumption, see Insurance Code § 769.1.
Conditional sales contracts, motor vehicles, see Civil Code § 2981 et seq.
Estoppel, see Evidence Code § 623.
Forgery of contract, see Penal Code § 470.
Holidays, performance of obligation arising from contract, see Civil Code § 11; Code of Civil Procedure § 13 et seq.
Injunction, breach of contract, see Code of Civil Procedure § 526.
Joinder of actions, see Code of Civil Procedure §§ 427.10, 428.10.
Limitation of actions, contracts, see Code of Civil Procedure §§ 337, 339.
Marriage settlement contracts, see Family Code §§ 1500, 1610 et seq.
Obligations,
   Generally, see Civil Code § 1427 et seq.
   Arising from contract, see Civil Code § 1428; Code of Civil Procedure § 26.
   Imposed by law, see Civil Code § 1708 et seq.
Pledge, contract transferring personalty as security, see Commercial Code § 9102.
Restraint of trade, contracts, see Business and Professions Code § 16600 et seq.
Sales, see Commercial Code § 2204 et seq.
Separation agreements, see Family Code § 3580.
Specific performance, see Civil Code § 3384 et seq.
Statute of frauds, see Civil Code §§ 1623, 1624; Commercial Code § 2201.
Successive actions on same contract, see Code of Civil Procedure § 1047.
Transfer,
   Obligations, see Civil Code § 1457 et seq.
   Property, see Civil Code § 1044.
Waiver,
   Generally, see Civil Code §§ 3268, 3513, 3516.
   Offer of performance of obligation, see Civil Code § 1501.

Title 1

NATURE OF A CONTRACT

Chapter		Section
1.	Definition	1549
2.	Parties	1556
3.	Consent	1565
4.	Object of a Contract	1595
5.	Consideration	1605

CHAPTER 1. DEFINITION

Section	
1549.	"Contract" defined.
1550.	Essential elements.
1550.5.	Cannabis legislation; legislative intent; lawfulness of specified cannabis–related activities.

§ 1549. "Contract" defined

CONTRACT, WHAT. A contract is an agreement to do or not to do a certain thing. *(Enacted in 1872.)*

Cross References

"Conditional obligations" defined, see Civil Code § 1434.
Contract for sale of goods, definition and formation, see Commercial Code §§ 2106, 2204 et seq.
"Contract of carriage" defined, see Civil Code § 2085.
Employment contract, definition, see Labor Code § 2750.
"Executed and executory contracts" defined, see Civil Code § 1661.
"Express contract" defined, see Civil Code § 1620.
"Implied contract" defined, see Civil Code § 1621.
Object of contract, definition, see Civil Code § 1595.
Obligation defined see Civil Code § 1427; Code of Civil Procedure § 26.
Parties to contracts, see Civil Code § 1556 et seq.
Unlawful contracts, see Civil Code § 1667 et seq.

§ 1550. Essential elements

ESSENTIAL ELEMENTS OF CONTRACT. It is essential to the existence of a contract that there should be:

1. Parties capable of contracting;
2. Their consent;
3. A lawful object; and,
4. A sufficient cause or consideration. *(Enacted in 1872.)*

Cross References

Consent,
   Generally, see Civil Code § 1565 et seq.
   Mutuality, see Civil Code § 1580.
Consideration in general, see Civil Code § 1605 et seq.
Failure as ground for rescission, see Civil Code § 1689.
Gifts, see Civil Code § 1146.
Inadequacy as bar to specific performance, see Civil Code § 3391.
Object of contract,
   Definition, see Civil Code § 1595.
   Legality, see Civil Code §§ 1596, 1599, 1667 et seq.
Parties, see Civil Code § 1556 et seq.
Presumptions, see Civil Code § 1614; Evidence Code § 620.
Separation agreements, see Family Code § 3580.
Statute of frauds, see Civil Code § 1624; Commercial Code § 2201.
Voluntary transfers, see Civil Code § 1040.
Written instrument, consideration presumed, see Civil Code § 1614.

§ 1550.5. Cannabis legislation; legislative intent; lawfulness of specified cannabis–related activities

(a) The Legislature finds and declares all of the following:

(1) The Compassionate Use Act of 1996, an initiative measure enacted by the approval of Proposition 215 at the November 5, 1996, statewide general election, authorized the use of marijuana for medical purposes in this state.

(2) The Legislature passed the Medical Cannabis Regulation and Safety Act, formerly Chapter 3.5 (commencing with

Section 19300) of Division 8 of the Business and Professions Code, to regulate and license medical cannabis in the state.

(3) The Control, Regulate and Tax Adult Use of Marijuana Act (AUMA), an initiative measure enacted by the approval of Proposition 64 at the November 8, 2016, statewide general election, authorized the consumption of nonmedical marijuana by persons over 21 years of age and provided for the licensure and regulation of certain commercial nonmedical marijuana activities in this state.

(4) The Legislature passed the Medicinal and Adult–Use Cannabis Regulation and Safety Act (Division 10 (commencing with Section 26000) of the Business and Professions Code) to consolidate the licensure and regulation of certain commercial activities with respect to medicinal cannabis and nonmedical marijuana, now known as adult-use cannabis.

(b) Notwithstanding any law, including, but not limited to, Sections 1550, 1667, and 1668 and federal law, commercial activity relating to medicinal cannabis or adult-use cannabis conducted in compliance with California law and any applicable local standards, requirements, and regulations shall be deemed to be all of the following:

(1) A lawful object of a contract.

(2) Not contrary to, an express provision of law, any policy of express law, or good morals.

(3) Not against public policy. *(Added by Stats.2017, c. 530 (A.B.1159), § 1, eff. Jan. 1, 2018. Amended by Stats.2018, c. 92 (S.B.1289), § 35, eff. Jan. 1, 2019.)*

CHAPTER 2. PARTIES

Section
1556. Persons capable of contracting.
1557. Capacity of minors and persons of unsound mind.
1558. Identification of parties; necessity.
1559. Enforcement by third party beneficiary.

Cross References

Contribution among joint obligors, see Civil Code § 1432.
Joint or several obligations, see Civil Code § 1430 et seq.
Public officials, interest in public contracts, see Government Code § 1090 et seq.
State agencies, interagency contracts, see Government Code § 11256.

§ 1556. Persons capable of contracting

WHO MAY CONTRACT. All persons are capable of contracting, except minors, persons of unsound mind, and persons deprived of civil rights. *(Enacted in 1872.)*

Cross References

Civil rights, suspension, see Penal Code § 2600.
Contracts for necessaries by persons incapable of contracting, see Family Code § 6712.
Husband and wife, contracts with each other and third persons, see Family Code §§ 721, 1620.
Minors' contracts, see Family Code § 6700 et seq.
Minors' contracts with artists' managers, see Labor Code § 1700.37.
Persons of unsound mind, contracts, see Civil Code § 39.

Persons without understanding, contracts, see Civil Code § 38.

§ 1557. Capacity of minors and persons of unsound mind

(a) The capacity of a minor to contract is governed by Division 11 (commencing with Section 6500) of the Family Code.

(b) The capacity of a person of unsound mind to contract is governed by Part 1 (commencing with Section 38) of Division 1. *(Added by Stats.1992, c. 163 (A.B.2641), § 9, operative Jan. 1, 1994.)*

Cross References

Minors, incapacities, see Family Code § 6701.

§ 1558. Identification of parties; necessity

IDENTIFICATION OF PARTIES NECESSARY. It is essential to the validity of a contract, not only that the parties should exist, but that it should be possible to identify them. *(Enacted in 1872.)*

§ 1559. Enforcement by third party beneficiary

WHEN CONTRACT FOR BENEFIT OF THIRD PERSON MAY BE ENFORCED. A contract, made expressly for the benefit of a third person, may be enforced by him at any time before the parties thereto rescind it. *(Enacted in 1872.)*

CHAPTER 3. CONSENT

Section
1565. Essentials of consent.
1566. Consent not free; rescission.
1567. Reality or freedom of consent; causes for defeating.
1568. Consent obtained by cause defeating reality or freedom.
1568.5. Minors; representation of consent by parent or guardian.
1569. Duress.
1570. Menace.
1571. Kinds of fraud.
1572. Actual fraud.
1573. Constructive fraud.
1574. Actual fraud; question of fact.
1575. Undue influence.
1576. Kinds of mistake.
1577. Mistake of fact.
1578. Mistake of law.
1579. Mistake of foreign law.
1580. Mutuality of consent.
1581. Communication; consent.
1582. Communication; acceptance of proposal.
1583. Communication; completion.
1584. Acceptance of proposal; performing conditions or acceptance of consideration.
1584.5. Voluntary and unsolicited sending of goods, wares, merchandise or services; receipt deemed unconditional gift; action to enjoin billing.
1584.6. Membership in organization making retail sales to members; notification of termination; receipt of unordered goods, wares or merchandise deemed unconditional gift.
1585. Acceptance of proposal; absolute acceptance; qualified acceptance.
1586. Revocation of proposal; time.
1587. Revocation of proposal; method.
1588. Ratification of voidable contract.

Section
1589. Consent by acceptance of benefits.
1590. Gifts in contemplation of marriage; recovery.

Cross References

Acquiescence in error as consent, see Civil Code § 3516.
Essential elements of contract, see Civil Code § 1550.

§ 1565. Essentials of consent

ESSENTIALS OF CONSENT. The consent of the parties to a contract must be:

1. Free;

2. Mutual; and,

3. Communicated by each to the other. *(Enacted in 1872.)*

Cross References

Communication of consent, see Civil Code § 1581 et seq.
Mutuality of consent, see Civil Code § 1580.

§ 1566. Consent not free; rescission

CONSENT, WHEN VOIDABLE. A consent which is not free is nevertheless not absolutely void, but may be rescinded by the parties, in the manner prescribed by the Chapter on Rescission. *(Enacted in 1872.)*

Cross References

Partially void contracts, one of several objects unlawful, see Civil Code § 1599.
Rescission, see Civil Code § 1688 et seq.
Void contracts, unlawful object, see Civil Code § 1598.

§ 1567. Reality or freedom of consent; causes for defeating

APPARENT CONSENT, WHEN NOT FREE. An apparent consent is not real or free when obtained through:

1. Duress;

2. Menace;

3. Fraud;

4. Undue influence; or,

5. Mistake. *(Enacted in 1872.)*

Cross References

"Duress" defined, see Civil Code § 1569.
"Fraud" defined, see Civil Code § 1571 et seq.
"Menace" defined, see Civil Code § 1570.
Mistake, see Civil Code § 1576 et seq.
Mistake as grounds for rescission, see Civil Code § 1689.
Undue influence, see Civil Code § 1575.

§ 1568. Consent obtained by cause defeating reality or freedom

WHEN DEEMED TO HAVE BEEN OBTAINED BY FRAUD, ETC. Consent is deemed to have been obtained through one of the causes mentioned in the last section only when it would not have been given had such cause not existed. *(Enacted in 1872.)*

§ 1568.5. Minors; representation of consent by parent or guardian

A representation by a minor that the minor's parent or legal guardian has consented shall not be considered to be consent for purposes of this chapter. *(Added by Stats.2021, c. 28 (A.B.891), § 1, eff. Jan. 1, 2022.)*

§ 1569. Duress

Duress consists in any of the following:

(a) Unlawful confinement of the person of the party, or of the spouse of such party, or of an ancestor, descendant, or adopted child of such party or spouse.

(b) Unlawful detention of the property of any such person.

(c) Confinement of such person, lawful in form, but fraudulently obtained, or fraudulently made unjustly harassing or oppressive. *(Enacted in 1872. Amended by Stats.2016, c. 50 (S.B.1005), § 11, eff. Jan. 1, 2017.)*

Cross References

Annulment of marriage, causes for, see Family Code § 2210.
Bill of lading obtained through duress, see Commercial Code § 7502.
Negotiable document of title obtained through duress, see Commercial Code § 7502.
Negotiable instruments, defense of duress, see Commercial Code § 3305.
Rescission of contract obtained through duress, see Civil Code § 1689.
Wills made under duress, see Probate Code § 6104.

§ 1570. Menace

MENACE, WHAT. Menace consists in a threat:

1. Of such duress as is specified in Subdivisions 1 and 3 of the last section;

2. Of unlawful and violent injury to the person or property of any such person as is specified in the last section; or,

3. Of injury to the character of any such person. *(Enacted in 1872.)*

Cross References

Annulment of marriage, causes for, see Family Code § 2210.
Extortion, see Penal Code § 518 et seq.
Negotiable paper, obtained through force or fear, see Commercial Code §§ 3304, 3305.
Rescission of contract obtained through menace, see Civil Code § 1689.
Wills executed through menace, see Probate Code § 6104.

§ 1571. Kinds of fraud

FRAUD, ACTUAL OR CONSTRUCTIVE. Fraud is either actual or constructive. *(Enacted in 1872.)*

Cross References

Rescission of contract, fraud or grounds, see Civil Code § 1689.

§ 1572. Actual fraud

ACTUAL FRAUD, WHAT. Actual fraud, within the meaning of this Chapter, consists in any of the following acts, committed by a party to the contract, or with his connivance, with intent to deceive another party thereto, or to induce him to enter into the contract:

1. The suggestion, as a fact, of that which is not true, by one who does not believe it to be true;

2. The positive assertion, in a manner not warranted by the information of the person making it, of that which is not true, though he believes it to be true;

3. The suppression of that which is true, by one having knowledge or belief of the fact;

4. A promise made without any intention of performing it; or,

5. Any other act fitted to deceive. *(Enacted in 1872.)*

Cross References

Actions by state or nationally chartered banks or their subsidiaries for recovery of damages from borrowers who fraudulently induced original lender to make real estate loans, see Financial Code § 1301.
Actions taken by associations or federal associations for recovery of damages from borrowers who fraudulently induced original lender to make real estate loans, see Financial Code § 7460.
Attachment, see Code of Civil Procedure § 484.010 et seq.
Bill of lading obtained through fraud, see Commercial Code § 7502.
Contracts exempting responsibility for fraud, contrary to policy of law, see Civil Code § 1668.
Damages for deceit,
  Generally, see Civil Code § 1709.
  Exemplary damages, see Civil Code § 3294.
  Interest, see Civil Code § 3288.
  Purchase, sale, or exchange of property, see Civil Code § 3343.
Deceit, see Civil Code § 1709 et seq.
Fraudulent conveyances, offense, see Penal Code § 531.
Fraudulent instruments and conveyances, see Civil Code § 3439 et seq.
Impeaching judgment for fraud, see Code of Civil Procedure § 1916.
Insurance contracts, concealment, see Insurance Code § 330 et seq.
Intent to defraud, see Penal Code § 8.
Interpretation of contract failing to express intent through fraud, see Civil Code § 1640.
Limitation of actions for relief on ground of fraud, see Code of Civil Procedure § 338.
Loan secured by mortgage or deed of trust on real property, action under this section against borrower, see Code of Civil Procedure § 726.
Mobilehomes—manufactured housing, fraud, see Health and Safety Code § 18004.6.
Motor vehicle dealers, actions against for fraud, see Vehicle Code § 11711.
Negotiable documents of title obtained through fraud, see Commercial Code § 7502.
Negotiable instruments, defense of fraud, see Commercial Code § 3305.
Parol evidence to establish fraud, see Code of Civil Procedure § 1856.
Presumption against fraud in private transactions, see Civil Code § 3545.
Rescission of contract for fraud,
  Generally, see Civil Code § 1689.
  Stipulations against right, see Civil Code § 1690.
Restoration of thing wrongfully acquired, see Civil Code §§ 1712, 1713.
Revision of contracts for fraud, see Civil Code § 3399.
Specific performance barred by fraud, see Civil Code § 3391.
Statute of frauds, see Civil Code §§ 1623, 1624; Commercial Code § 2201.
Wills procured by fraud, see Probate Code § 6104.

§ 1573. Constructive fraud

CONSTRUCTIVE FRAUD. Constructive fraud consists:

1. In any breach of duty which, without an actually fraudulent intent, gains an advantage to the person in fault, or any one claiming under him, by misleading another to his prejudice, or to the prejudice of any one claiming under him; or,

2. In any such act or omission as the law specially declares to be fraudulent, without respect to actual fraud. *(Enacted in 1872.)*

Cross References

Deceit defined, see Civil Code § 1710.
Defects in form of pleading, effect, see Penal Code §§ 960, 1404.
Mobilehomes—manufactured housing, fraud, see Health and Safety Code § 18004.6.
Rescission of contract for fraud, see Civil Code § 1689.
Restoration of thing wrongfully acquired, see Civil Code §§ 1712, 1713.
Technical defects, effect on judgment, see Penal Code § 1258.

§ 1574. Actual fraud; question of fact

ACTUAL FRAUD A QUESTION OF FACT. Actual fraud is always a question of fact. *(Enacted in 1872.)*

Cross References

Fraudulent conveyances, see Civil Code § 3439 et seq.

§ 1575. Undue influence

UNDUE INFLUENCE, WHAT. Undue influence consists:

1. In the use, by one in whom a confidence is reposed by another, or who holds a real or apparent authority over him, of such confidence or authority for the purpose of obtaining an unfair advantage over him;

2. In taking an unfair advantage of another's weakness of mind; or,

3. In taking a grossly oppressive and unfair advantage of another's necessities or distress. *(Enacted in 1872.)*

Cross References

Consent obtained by undue influence, see Civil Code § 1567.
Presumption of undue influence in transactions between trustee and beneficiary, see Probate Code §§ 16002, 16004.
Rescission of contract, undue influence as ground, see Civil Code § 1689.
Wills procured by undue influence, see Probate Code § 6104.

§ 1576. Kinds of mistake

MISTAKE, WHAT. Mistake may be either of fact or law. *(Enacted in 1872.)*

Cross References

Interpretation of contracts, mistake obscuring intent, see Civil Code § 1640.
Judgments and orders, clerical mistakes, see Code of Civil Procedure § 473.
Liens, effect of mistakes, see Civil Code § 8422.
Limitation of actions for relief on ground of mistake, see Code of Civil Procedure § 338.
Negotiable documents obtained through mistake, see Commercial Code § 7502.
Negotiable instruments, cancellation or renunciation, see Commercial Code § 3604.
Parol evidence to correct mistake in written agreement, see Code of Civil Procedure § 1856.

Pleadings, immaterial errors, see Penal Code §§ 960, 1258, 1404.
Proceedings, immaterial errors, see Penal Code §§ 1258, 1404.
Property wrongfully acquired, restoration, see Civil Code §§ 1712, 1713.
Rescission, procedure,
  Generally, see Civil Code § 1689.
  Restoration of benefits, see Civil Code § 1691.
  Stipulations against right, see Civil Code § 1690.
Revision of contracts for mistake, see Civil Code § 3399.
Specific performance barred by mistake, see Civil Code § 3391.
Wills, correction of mistakes, see Probate Code § 105.

§ 1577. Mistake of fact

MISTAKE OF FACT. Mistake of fact is a mistake, not caused by the neglect of a legal duty on the part of the person making the mistake, and consisting in:

1. An unconscious ignorance or forgetfulness of a fact past or present, material to the contract; or,

2. Belief in the present existence of a thing material to the contract, which does not exist, or in the past existence of such a thing, which has not existed. *(Enacted in 1872.)*

Cross References

Mistake as grounds for rescission, see Civil Code § 1689.

§ 1578. Mistake of law

MISTAKE OF LAW. Mistake of law constitutes a mistake, within the meaning of this Article, only when it arises from:

1. A misapprehension of the law by all parties, all supposing that they knew and understood it, and all making substantially the same mistake as to the law; or,

2. A misapprehension of the law by one party, of which the others are aware at the time of contracting, but which they do not rectify. *(Enacted in 1872.)*

§ 1579. Mistake of foreign law

MISTAKE OF FOREIGN LAWS. Mistake of foreign laws is a mistake of fact. *(Enacted in 1872.)*

§ 1580. Mutuality of consent

MUTUALITY OF CONSENT. Consent is not mutual, unless the parties all agree upon the same thing in the same sense. But in certain cases defined by the Chapter on Interpretation, they are to be deemed so to agree without regard to the fact. *(Enacted in 1872.)*

Cross References

Essential element of contracts, necessity of consent, see Civil Code § 1550.
Essentials of consent, see Civil Code § 1565.
Interpretation of contracts, giving effect to mutual intention, see Civil Code § 1636.
Specific performance, mutuality of remedy, see Civil Code § 3386.

§ 1581. Communication; consent

COMMUNICATION OF CONSENT. Consent can be communicated with effect, only by some act or omission of the party contracting, by which he intends to communicate it, or which necessarily tends to such communication. *(Enacted in 1872.)*

§ 1582. Communication; acceptance of proposal

MODE OF COMMUNICATING ACCEPTANCE OF PROPOSAL. If a proposal prescribes any conditions concerning the communication of its acceptance, the proposer is not bound unless they are conformed to; but in other cases any reasonable and usual mode may be adopted. *(Enacted in 1872.)*

§ 1583. Communication; completion

WHEN COMMUNICATION DEEMED COMPLETE. Consent is deemed to be fully communicated between the parties as soon as the party accepting a proposal has put his acceptance in the course of transmission to the proposer, in conformity to the last section. *(Enacted in 1872.)*

§ 1584. Acceptance of proposal; performing conditions or acceptance of consideration

ACCEPTANCE BY PERFORMANCE OF CONDITIONS. Performance of the conditions of a proposal, or the acceptance of the consideration offered with a proposal, is an acceptance of the proposal. *(Enacted in 1872.)*

§ 1584.5. Voluntary and unsolicited sending of goods, wares, merchandise or services; receipt deemed unconditional gift; action to enjoin billing

No person, firm, partnership, association, or corporation, or agent or employee thereof, shall, in any manner, or by any means, offer for sale goods, wares, merchandise, or services, where the offer includes the voluntary and unsolicited sending or providing of goods, wares, merchandise, or services not actually ordered or requested by the recipient, either orally or in writing. The receipt of any goods, wares, merchandise, or services shall for all purposes be deemed an unconditional gift to the recipient who may use or dispose of the goods, wares, merchandise, or services in any manner he or she sees fit without any obligation on his or her part to the sender or provider.

If, after any receipt deemed to be an unconditional gift under this section, the sender or provider continues to send bill statements or requests for payment with respect to the gift, an action may be brought by the recipient to enjoin the conduct, in which action there may also be awarded reasonable attorney's fees and costs to the prevailing party.

For the purposes of this section and limited to merchandise or services offered for sale through the mails, the "voluntary and unsolicited sending or providing of goods, wares, merchandise, or services not actually ordered or requested by the recipient, either orally or in writing," includes any merchandise or services selected by the company and offered to the consumer which will be mailed to him or her for sale or on approval or provided to him or her unless he or she exercises an option to reject the offer of sale or receipt on approval. Merchandise or services selected by the seller and offered for sale on a periodic basis must be affirmatively ordered by a statement or card signed by the consumer as to each periodic offer of merchandise or services. This paragraph shall not apply to any of the following:

(a) Contractual plans or arrangements complying with this subdivision under which the seller periodically provides the consumer with a form or announcement card which the consumer may use to instruct the seller not to ship the offered merchandise. Any instructions not to ship merchandise included on the form or card shall be printed in type as large as all other instructions and terms stated on the form or card. The form or card shall specify a date by which it shall be mailed by the consumer (the "mailing date") or received by the seller (the "return date") to prevent shipment of the offered merchandise. The seller shall mail the form or card either at least 25 days prior to the return date or at least 20 days prior to the mailing date, or provide a mailing date of at least 10 days after receipt by the consumer, except that whichever system the seller chooses for mailing the form or card, the system must be calculated to afford the consumer at least 10 days in which to mail his or her form or card. The form or card shall be preaddressed to the seller so that it may serve as a postal reply card or, alternatively, the form or card shall be accompanied by a return envelope addressed to seller. Upon the membership contract or application form or on the same page and immediately adjacent to the contract or form, and in clear and conspicuous language, there shall be disclosed the material terms of the plan or arrangement including all of the following:

(1) That aspect of the plan under which the subscriber must notify the seller, in the manner provided for by the seller, if he or she does not wish to purchase or receive the selection.

(2) Any obligation assumed by the subscriber to purchase a minimum quantity of merchandise.

(3) The right of a contract-complete subscriber to cancel his or her membership at any time.

(4) Whether billing charges will include an amount for postage and handling.

(b) Other contractual plans or arrangements not covered under subdivision (a), such as continuity plans, subscription arrangements, standing order arrangements, supplements and series arrangements under which the seller periodically ships merchandise to a consumer who has consented in advance to receive the merchandise on a periodic basis. *(Added by Stats.1969, c. 400, p. 931, § 1. Amended by Stats.1971, c. 1623, p. 3494, § 1, operative July 1, 1972; Stats.1973, c. 916, p. 1697, § 1, operative Jan. 1, 1975; Stats.1985, c. 80, § 1.)*

§ 1584.6. Membership in organization making retail sales to members; notification of termination; receipt of unordered goods, wares or merchandise deemed unconditional gift

If a person is a member of an organization which makes retail sales of any goods, wares, or merchandise to its members, and the person notifies the organization of his termination of membership by certified mail, return receipt requested, any unordered goods, wares, or merchandise which are sent to the person after 30 days following execution of the return receipt for the certified letter by the organization, shall for all purposes be deemed unconditional gifts to the person, who may use or dispose of the goods, wares, or merchandise in any manner he sees fit without any obligation on his part to the organization.

If the termination of a person's membership in such organization breaches any agreement with the organization, nothing in this section shall relieve the person from liability for damages to which he might be otherwise subjected to pursuant to law, but he shall not be subject to any damages with respect to any goods, wares, or merchandise which are deemed unconditional gifts to him under this section.

If after any receipt deemed to be an unconditional gift under this section, the sender continues to send bill statements or requests for payment with respect thereto, an action may be brought by the recipient to enjoin such conduct, in which action there may also be awarded reasonable attorneys' fees and costs to the prevailing party. *(Added by Stats.1969, c. 400, p. 931, § 2.)*

§ 1585. Acceptance of proposal; absolute acceptance; qualified acceptance

ACCEPTANCE MUST BE ABSOLUTE. An acceptance must be absolute and unqualified, or must include in itself an acceptance of that character which the proposer can separate from the rest, and which will conclude the person accepting. A qualified acceptance is a new proposal. *(Enacted in 1872.)*

Cross References

Additional terms in acceptance or confirmation, see Commercial Code § 2207.

§ 1586. Revocation of proposal; time

REVOCATION OF PROPOSAL. A proposal may be revoked at any time before its acceptance is communicated to the proposer, but not afterwards. *(Enacted in 1872.)*

§ 1587. Revocation of proposal; method

A proposal is revoked by any of the following:

(a) By the communication of notice of revocation by the proposer to the other party, in the manner prescribed by Sections 1581 and 1583, before his or her acceptance has been communicated to the former.

(b) By the lapse of the time prescribed in the proposal for its acceptance or, if no time is prescribed, the lapse of a reasonable time without communication of the acceptance.

(c) By the failure of the acceptor to fulfill a condition precedent to acceptance.

(d) By the death or legal incapacity to make decisions of the proposer. *(Enacted in 1872. Amended by Stats.2014, c. 144 (A.B.1847), § 2, eff. Jan. 1, 2015.)*

Cross References

Communication of consent, see Civil Code § 1581.
Completion of communication of consent, see Civil Code § 1583.

§ 1588. Ratification of voidable contract

RATIFICATION OF CONTRACT, VOID FOR WANT OF CONSENT. A contract which is voidable solely for want of due consent, may be ratified by a subsequent consent. *(Enacted in 1872.)*

§ 1589. Consent by acceptance of benefits

ASSUMPTION OF OBLIGATION BY ACCEPTANCE OF BENEFITS. A voluntary acceptance of the benefit of a transaction is equivalent to a consent to all the obligations arising from it, so far as the facts are known, or ought to be known, to the person accepting. *(Enacted in 1872.)*

Cross References

Acceptance of burden with benefit, see Civil Code § 3521.

§ 1589

Bailment contracts, acceptance of benefits, see Civil Code § 1630.

§ 1590. Gifts in contemplation of marriage; recovery

Where either party to a contemplated marriage in this State makes a gift of money or property to the other on the basis or assumption that the marriage will take place, in the event that the donee refuses to enter into the marriage as contemplated or that it is given up by mutual consent, the donor may recover such gift or such part of its value as may, under all of the circumstances of the case, be found by a court or jury to be just. *(Added by Stats.1939, c. 128, p. 1245, § 3.)*

CHAPTER 4. OBJECT OF A CONTRACT

Section
1595. Object defined.
1596. Object; elements.
1597. Impossibility defined.
1598. Object unlawful, impossible or unascertainable.
1599. One of several objects unlawful; effect.

Cross References

Consideration in general, see Civil Code § 1605 et seq.
Essential element of contracts, lawful object, see Civil Code § 1550.
Executory consideration, applicability of this chapter, see Civil Code § 1609.
Interpretation of contracts, see Civil Code § 1635 et seq.
Performance of obligations, see Civil Code § 1473 et seq.
Unlawful contracts, see Civil Code § 1667 et seq.

§ 1595. Object defined

OBJECT, WHAT. The object of a contract is the thing which it is agreed, on the part of the party receiving the consideration, to do or not to do. *(Enacted in 1872.)*

Cross References

Impossible or unlawful conditions, see Civil Code § 1441.

§ 1596. Object; elements

REQUISITES OF OBJECT. The object of a contract must be lawful when the contract is made, and possible and ascertainable by the time the contract is to be performed. *(Enacted in 1872.)*

Cross References

Essential element of contracts, lawful object, see Civil Code § 1550.
Unlawful contracts, see Civil Code § 1667 et seq.

§ 1597. Impossibility defined

IMPOSSIBILITY, WHAT. Everything is deemed possible except that which is impossible in the nature of things. *(Enacted in 1872.)*

§ 1598. Object unlawful, impossible or unascertainable

WHEN CONTRACT WHOLLY VOID. Where a contract has but a single object, and such object is unlawful, whether in whole or in part, or wholly impossible of performance, or so vaguely expressed as to be wholly unascertainable, the entire contract is void. *(Enacted in 1872.)*

Cross References

Essential element of contracts, lawful object, see Civil Code § 1550.
Illegal consideration, see Civil Code § 1608.
Impossibilities never required by law, see Civil Code § 3531.
Unlawful contracts, see Civil Code § 1667 et seq.

§ 1599. One of several objects unlawful; effect

WHEN CONTRACT PARTIALLY VOID. Where a contract has several distinct objects, of which one at least is lawful, and one at least is unlawful, in whole or in part, the contract is void as to the latter and valid as to the rest. *(Enacted in 1872.)*

Cross References

Contract providing apparently possible method of ascertainment, see Civil Code § 1613.
Essential element of contracts, lawful object, see Civil Code § 1550.
Illegal consideration, effect, see Civil Code § 1608.
Unlawful contracts, see Civil Code § 1667 et seq.

CHAPTER 5. CONSIDERATION

Section
1605. Good consideration defined.
1606. Good consideration; legal or moral obligation.
1607. Lawfulness of consideration.
1608. Illegal consideration; effect.
1609. Executed and executory consideration.
1610. Executory consideration; specification of amount or means of ascertainment.
1611. Ascertainment of consideration.
1612. Contract providing impossible method of ascertainment; invalidity.
1613. Contract providing apparently possible method of ascertainment.
1614. Written instrument; presumption of consideration.
1615. Want of consideration; burden of proof.

§ 1605. Good consideration defined

GOOD CONSIDERATION, WHAT. Any benefit conferred, or agreed to be conferred, upon the promisor, by any other person, to which the promisor is not lawfully entitled, or any prejudice suffered, or agreed to be suffered, by such person, other than such as he is at the time of consent lawfully bound to suffer, as an inducement to the promisor, is a good consideration for a promise. *(Enacted in 1872.)*

Cross References

Acceptance of proposal, accepting consideration offered, see Civil Code § 1584.
Agency, consideration unnecessary, see Civil Code § 2308.
Failure to consideration as ground for rescission, see Civil Code § 1689.
Inadequacy as barring specific performance, see Civil Code § 3391.
Joint and several consideration, see Civil Code §§ 1659, 1660.
Necessity of consideration, see Civil Code § 1550.
Negotiable instruments, consideration for, see Commercial Code § 3303.
Release of discretionary power, consideration, see Probate Code § 661.
Releases, necessity of consideration, see Civil Code § 1541.
Separation agreements, consideration, see Family Code § 3580.
Suretyship, consideration, see Civil Code § 2792.
Voluntary transfers, consideration not necessary, see Civil Code § 1040.

§ 1606. Good consideration; legal or moral obligation

HOW FAR LEGAL OR MORAL OBLIGATION IS A GOOD CONSIDERATION. An existing legal obligation resting upon the promisor, or a moral obligation originating in some benefit conferred upon the promisor, or prejudice suffered by the promisee, is also a good consideration for a promise, to an extent corresponding with the extent of the obligation, but no further or otherwise. *(Enacted in 1872.)*

§ 1607. Lawfulness of consideration

CONSIDERATION LAWFUL. The consideration of a contract must be lawful within the meaning of Section 1667. *(Enacted in 1872.)*

Cross References

Unlawful contracts, see Civil Code § 1667 et seq.

§ 1608. Illegal consideration; effect

EFFECT OF ITS ILLEGALITY. If any part of a single consideration for one or more objects, or of several considerations for a single object, is unlawful, the entire contract is void. *(Enacted in 1872.)*

Cross References

Unlawful contracts, see Civil Code § 1667 et seq.
Unlawful in part, effect, see Civil Code §§ 1598, 1599.

§ 1609. Executed and executory consideration

CONSIDERATION EXECUTED OR EXECUTORY. A consideration may be executed or executory, in whole or in part. In so far as it is executory, it is subject to the provisions of Chapter IV [1] of this Title. *(Enacted in 1872.)*

[1] So in chaptered copy.

§ 1610. Executory consideration; specification of amount or means of ascertainment

EXECUTORY CONSIDERATION. When a consideration is executory, it is not indispensable that the contract should specify its amount or the means of ascertaining it. It may be left to the decision of a third person, or regulated by any specified standard. *(Enacted in 1872.)*

§ 1611. Ascertainment of consideration

HOW ASCERTAINED. When a contract does not determine the amount of the consideration, nor the method by which it is to be ascertained, or when it leaves the amount thereof to the discretion of an interested party, the consideration must be so much money as the object of the contract is reasonably worth. *(Enacted in 1872.)*

Cross References

Presumption of consideration, written instruments, see Civil Code § 1614.
Reasonable price when consideration not fixed, see Commercial Code § 2305.

§ 1612. Contract providing impossible method of ascertainment; invalidity

Where a contract provides an exclusive method by which its consideration is to be ascertained, which method is on its face impossible of execution, the entire contract is void; but this section shall not apply to the cases provided for in sections 1729 and 1730 of this code. *(Enacted in 1872. Amended by Stats.1931, c. 1070, p. 2259, § 7.)*

§ 1613. Contract providing apparently possible method of ascertainment

Where a contract provides an exclusive method by which its consideration is to be ascertained, which method appears possible on its face, but in fact is, or becomes, impossible of execution, such provision only is void; but this section shall not apply to the cases provided for in sections 1729 and 1730 of this code. *(Enacted in 1872. Amended by Stats.1931, c. 1070, p. 2260, § 8.)*

Cross References

Partial invalidity of contract, effect, see Civil Code §§ 1598, 1599.

§ 1614. Written instrument; presumption of consideration

WRITTEN INSTRUMENT PRESUMPTIVE EVIDENCE OF CONSIDERATION. A written instrument is presumptive evidence of a consideration. *(Enacted in 1872.)*

Cross References

Negotiable instruments, consideration, see Commercial Code § 3303.
Production of evidence, burden of proof, see Evidence Code §§ 500, 550.
Sealed and unsealed instruments, distinction between abolished, see Civil Code § 1629.

§ 1615. Want of consideration; burden of proof

BURDEN OF PROOF TO INVALIDATE SUFFICIENT CONSIDERATION. The burden of showing a want of consideration sufficient to support an instrument lies with the party seeking to invalidate or avoid it. *(Enacted in 1872.)*

Cross References

Burden of proof in general, see Evidence Code §§ 500, 550.

Title 2

MANNER OF CREATING CONTRACTS

Section
1619. Express or implied contracts.
1620. Express contract defined.
1621. Implied contract defined.
1622. Oral contracts; authorization.
1623. Statute of frauds; enforcement of contract oral by reason of fraud.
1624. Statute of frauds.
1624.5. Written contract; sale of personal property exceeding $5000; exceptions.
1624a. Repealed.
1625. Written contracts; effect on negotiations or stipulations.
1626. Written contracts; effective upon delivery.
1627. Written contracts; law governing.
1628. Seals; method of affixing.
1629. Sealed and unsealed instruments; distinctions abolished.
1630. Bailment contracts with automobile parking lots; requirements.
1630.5. Automobile parking lots; liability for theft.
1631. Sale of mining machinery; bill of sale; record; contents.
1632. Translation of contracts negotiated in language other than English; necessity; exceptions.

Section	
1632.5.	Supervised financial organizations negotiating primarily in Spanish, Chinese, Tagalog, Vietnamese, or Korean; contracts for loans or extensions of credit secured by residential real property; delivery in foreign language prior to execution; version executed in English to govern rights and responsibilities; exceptions.
1633.	Electronically transmitted application to enter into brokerage agreement.

§ 1619. Express or implied contracts

A contract is either express or implied. *(Enacted in 1872.)*

Cross References

Attachment in actions upon express or implied contracts, see Code of Civil Procedure § 483.010.
Express or implied consumer warranties, see Civil Code § 1791.1 et seq.
Express or implied warranties in insurance policies, see Insurance Code § 440 et seq.
Form and formation of sales contract, see Commercial Code § 2201 et seq.
Implied incidents to contract, see Civil Code § 1656.
Implied stipulations, see Civil Code § 1655.
Implied warranties, see Commercial Code §§ 2314, 2315.
Joinder of causes of action, see Code of Civil Procedure §§ 427.10, 428.10.
Obligation defined, see Code of Civil Procedure § 26.
Obligation from contract or operation of law, see Civil Code § 1428.
Promise or order in commercial paper unconditional even if subject to implied or constructive conditions, see Commercial Code § 3106.

§ 1620. Express contract defined

An express contract is one, the terms of which are stated in words. *(Enacted in 1872.)*

Cross References

Ascertaining intention of parties to contract, see Civil Code § 1637 et seq.
Execution of instrument defined, see Code of Civil Procedure § 1933.
Intent of parties in construction of instruments, see Code of Civil Procedure § 1859.

§ 1621. Implied contract defined

An implied contract is one, the existence and terms of which are manifested by conduct. *(Enacted in 1872.)*

Cross References

Conduct defined, see Evidence Code § 125.
Formation of contract for sale of goods by conduct of parties, see Commercial Code §§ 2204, 2207.
Obligations imposed by law, see Civil Code § 1708 et seq.

§ 1622. Oral contracts; authorization

All contracts may be oral, except such as are specially required by statute to be in writing. *(Enacted in 1872.)*

Cross References

Demurrer to complaint or answer due to inability to ascertain of whether the pleaded contract is written or oral, see Code of Civil Procedure § 430.10.
Limitation of actions on oral contract, see Code of Civil Procedure § 339.

Writing, necessity as to contracts, see Civil Code §§ 1623, 1624; Commercial Code §§ 1206, 2201.

§ 1623. Statute of frauds; enforcement of contract oral by reason of fraud

Where a contract, which is required by law to be in writing, is prevented from being put into writing by the fraud of a party thereto, any other party who is by such fraud led to believe that it is in writing, and acts upon such belief to his prejudice, may enforce it against the fraudulent party. *(Enacted in 1872.)*

Cross References

Disregard of parts of contract which fail to express real intentions of parties due to fraud, mistake or accident, see Civil Code § 1640.
Limitation of action for relief on ground of fraud or mistake, see Code of Civil Procedure § 338.
Remedies for fraud in sales contract, see Commercial Code § 2721.
Statute of frauds, see Commercial Code § 2201.

§ 1624. Statute of frauds

(a) The following contracts are invalid, unless they, or some note or memorandum thereof, are in writing and subscribed by the party to be charged or by the party's agent:

(1) An agreement that by its terms is not to be performed within a year from the making thereof.

(2) A special promise to answer for the debt, default, or miscarriage of another, except in the cases provided for in Section 2794.

(3) An agreement for the leasing for a longer period than one year, or for the sale of real property, or of an interest therein; such an agreement, if made by an agent of the party sought to be charged, is invalid, unless the authority of the agent is in writing, subscribed by the party sought to be charged.

(4) An agreement authorizing or employing an agent, broker, or any other person to purchase or sell real estate, or to lease real estate for a longer period than one year, or to procure, introduce, or find a purchaser or seller of real estate or a lessee or lessor of real estate where the lease is for a longer period than one year, for compensation or a commission.

(5) An agreement that by its terms is not to be performed during the lifetime of the promisor.

(6) An agreement by a purchaser of real property to pay an indebtedness secured by a mortgage or deed of trust upon the property purchased, unless assumption of the indebtedness by the purchaser is specifically provided for in the conveyance of the property.

(7) A contract, promise, undertaking, or commitment to loan money or to grant or extend credit, in an amount greater than one hundred thousand dollars ($100,000), not primarily for personal, family, or household purposes, made by a person engaged in the business of lending or arranging for the lending of money or extending credit. For purposes of this section, a contract, promise, undertaking, or commitment to loan money secured solely by residential property consisting of one to four dwelling units shall be deemed to be for personal, family, or household purposes.

(b) Notwithstanding paragraph (1) of subdivision (a):

(1) An agreement or contract that is valid in other respects and is otherwise enforceable is not invalid for lack of a note, memorandum, or other writing and is enforceable by way of action or defense, provided that the agreement or contract is a qualified financial contract as defined in paragraph (2) and one of the following apply:

(A) There is, as provided in paragraph (3), sufficient evidence to indicate that a contract has been made.

(B) The parties thereto by means of a prior or subsequent written contract, have agreed to be bound by the terms of the qualified financial contract from the time they reached agreement (by telephone, by exchange of electronic messages, or otherwise) on those terms.

(2) For purposes of this subdivision, a "qualified financial contract" means an agreement as to which each party thereto is other than a natural person and that is any of the following:

(A) For the purchase and sale of foreign exchange, foreign currency, bullion, coin, or precious metals on a forward, spot, next-day value or other basis.

(B) A contract (other than a contract for the purchase of a commodity for future delivery on, or subject to the rules of, a contract market or board of trade) for the purchase, sale, or transfer of any commodity or any similar good, article, service, right, or interest that is presently or in the future becomes the subject of a dealing in the forward contract trade, or any product or byproduct thereof, with a maturity date more than two days after the date the contract is entered into.

(C) For the purchase and sale of currency, or interbank deposits denominated in United States dollars.

(D) For a currency option, currency swap, or cross-currency rate swap.

(E) For a commodity swap or a commodity option (other than an option contract traded on, or subject to the rules of, a contract market or board of trade).

(F) For a rate swap, basis swap, forward rate transaction, or an interest rate option.

(G) For a security-index swap or option, or a security or securities price swap or option.

(H) An agreement that involves any other similar transaction relating to a price or index (including, without limitation, any transaction or agreement involving any combination of the foregoing, any cap, floor, collar, or similar transaction with respect to a rate, commodity price, commodity index, security or securities price, security index, other price index, or loan price).

(I) An option with respect to any of the foregoing.

(3) There is sufficient evidence that a contract has been made in any of the following circumstances:

(A) There is evidence of an electronic communication (including, without limitation, the recording of a telephone call or the tangible written text produced by computer retrieval), admissible in evidence under the laws of this state, sufficient to indicate that in the communication a contract was made between the parties.

(B) A confirmation in writing sufficient to indicate that a contract has been made between the parties and sufficient against the sender is received by the party against whom enforcement is sought no later than the fifth business day after the contract is made (or any other period of time that the parties may agree in writing) and the sender does not receive, on or before the third business day after receipt (or the other period of time that the parties may agree in writing), written objection to a material term of the confirmation. For purposes of this subparagraph, a confirmation or an objection thereto is received at the time there has been an actual receipt by an individual responsible for the transaction or, if earlier, at the time there has been constructive receipt, which is the time actual receipt by that individual would have occurred if the receiving party, as an organization, had exercised reasonable diligence. For the purposes of this subparagraph, a "business day" is a day on which both parties are open and transacting business of the kind involved in that qualified financial contract that is the subject of confirmation.

(C) The party against whom enforcement is sought admits in its pleading, testimony, or otherwise in court that a contract was made.

(D) There is a note, memorandum, or other writing sufficient to indicate that a contract has been made, signed by the party against whom enforcement is sought or by its authorized agent or broker.

For purposes of this paragraph, evidence of an electronic communication indicating the making in that communication of a contract, or a confirmation, admission, note, memorandum, or writing is not insufficient because it omits or incorrectly states one or more material terms agreed upon, as long as the evidence provides a reasonable basis for concluding that a contract was made.

(4) For purposes of this subdivision, the tangible written text produced by telex, telefacsimile, computer retrieval, or other process by which electronic signals are transmitted by telephone or otherwise shall constitute a writing, and any symbol executed or adopted by a party with the present intention to authenticate a writing shall constitute a signing. The confirmation and notice of objection referred to in subparagraph (B) of paragraph (3) may be communicated by means of telex, telefacsimile, computer, or other similar process by which electronic signals are transmitted by telephone or otherwise, provided that a party claiming to have communicated in that manner shall, unless the parties have otherwise agreed in writing, have the burden of establishing actual or constructive receipt by the other party as set forth in subparagraph (B) of paragraph (3).

(c) This section does not apply to leases subject to Division 10 (commencing with Section 10101) of the Commercial Code.

(d) An electronic message of an ephemeral nature that is not designed to be retained or to create a permanent record, including, but not limited to, a text message or instant message format communication, is insufficient under this title to constitute a contract to convey real property, in the absence of a written confirmation that conforms to the requirements of subparagraph (B) of paragraph (3) of subdivision (b). *(Enacted in 1872. Amended by Code Am.1873–74, c. 612, p. 241, § 190; Code Am.1877–78, c. 165, p. 86, § 1; Stats.1905, c. 451, p. 610, § 1; Stats.1931, c. 1070, p. 2260, § 9; Stats.1937, c. 316, p. 695, § 2; Stats.1963, c. 814,*

§ 1624

p. 1843, § 1; Stats.1967, c. 52, p. 953, § 1; Stats.1983, c. 842, § 6, operative Jan. 1, 1985; Stats.1985, c. 1315, § 1; Stats. 1988, c. 1096, § 1; Stats.1988, c. 1368, § 1.5, operative Jan. 1, 1990; Stats.1998, c. 78 (S.B.1865), § 1; Stats.2014, c. 107 (A.B.2136), § 2, eff. Jan. 1, 2015.)

Cross References

Admissibility of evidence to charge a person upon representation as to credit of third person, see Code of Civil Procedure § 1974.
Agent defined, see Civil Code § 2295.
Assignment of wages, see Labor Code § 300.
Authentication and proof of writings, see Evidence Code § 1400 et seq.
Authority of agent to enter into contract required to be in writing must be in writing, see Civil Code § 2309.
Bond of employee in cash, see Labor Code § 403.
Broker defined, Real Estate Law, see Business and Professions Code § 10012.
Bulk sales, see Commercial Code § 6101 et seq.
Cancellation of written instrument, see Civil Code § 3412 et seq.
Contract for sale of goods for $500 or more, see Commercial Code § 2201.
Contract for sale of personal property over $5,000, see Commercial Code § 1206.
Deed of trust defined, see Business and Professions Code § 10028.
Destruction or concealment of instrument in writing about to be produced in evidence upon any trial, see Penal Code § 135.
Execution of instrument defined, see Code of Civil Procedure § 1933.
Fraudulent conveyances, see Civil Code § 3439 et seq.
Interpretation of language of a writing, see Code of Civil Procedure § 1857.
Letters of credit, see Commercial Code § 5104.
Marriage defined, see Family Code § 300.
Modification of sales contract, see Commercial Code § 2209.
Mortgage defined, see Civil Code § 2920.
Mortgages, see Civil Code § 2922.
Offer by merchant to buy or sell goods, see Commercial Code § 2205.
Offering in evidence any forged, fraudulently altered or ante-dated written instrument, see Penal Code § 132.
Oral and written authorizations, see Civil Code § 2309.
Original obligations not requiring a writing, see Civil Code § 2794.
Personal representative, promise to answer for decedent's debts, etc., see Probate Code § 9604.
Power of attorney to execute mortgage, see Civil Code § 2933.
Property, permissible oral transfers, see Civil Code § 1052.
Real estate brokers and salesmen, regulation and licensing, see Business and Professions Code § 10130 et seq.
Real property, transfer, see Civil Code § 1091; Code of Civil Procedure § 1971.
Representation as to credit of third person, writing required, see Code of Civil Procedure § 1974.
Retention of documents, inspection and audit, costs of audit, suspension, revocation, or denial of license, recovery and determination of costs, see Business and Professions Code § 10148.
Sale of goods, see Commercial Code § 2201.
Secured transactions, see Commercial Code § 9203.
Ship, transfer by operation of law or written instrument only, see Civil Code § 1135.
Subscription defined for purposes of this Code, see Civil Code § 14.
Suretyship, see Civil Code § 2793 et seq.
Swimming pool construction contracts, necessity of writing, see Business and Professions Code § 7167.
Transfer of non-negotiable written contract for payment of money or personal property by indorsement, see Civil Code § 1459.
Trusts relating to real property, see Probate Code § 15206.
Workers' compensation, release or compromise agreement, see Labor Code § 5003.
Writing defined for purposes of this Code, see Civil Code § 14; Commercial Code § 1201; Evidence Code § 250.

§ 1624.5. Written contract; sale of personal property exceeding $5000; exceptions

(a) Except in the cases described in subdivision (b), a contract for the sale of personal property is not enforceable by way of action or defense beyond five thousand dollars ($5,000) in amount or value of remedy unless there is some record, as defined in subdivision (m) of Section 1633.2, but solely to the extent permitted by applicable law, that indicates that a contract for sale has been made between the parties at a defined or stated price, reasonably identifies the subject matter, and is signed, including by way of electronic signature, as defined in subdivision (h) of Section 1633.2, but solely to the extent permitted by applicable law, by the party against whom enforcement is sought or by his or her authorized agent.

(b) Subdivision (a) does not apply to contracts governed by the Commercial Code, including contracts for the sale of goods (Section 2201 of the Commercial Code), contracts for the sale of securities (Section 8113 of the Commercial Code), and security agreements (Sections 9201 and 9203 of the Commercial Code).

(c) Subdivision (a) does not apply to a qualified financial contract as that term is defined in paragraph (2) of subdivision (b) of Section 1624 if either of the following exists:

(1) There is, as provided in paragraph (3) of subdivision (b) of Section 1624, sufficient evidence to indicate that a contract has been made.

(2) The parties thereto, by means of a prior or subsequent written contract, have agreed to be bound by the terms of the qualified financial contract from the time they reach agreement (by telephone, by exchange of electronic messages, or otherwise) on those terms. *(Added by Stats.2006, c. 254 (S.B.1481), § 1.)*

Application

For provision relating to application of Stats.2006, c. 254 (S.B.1481) to documents of title that are issued or bailments that arise before Jan. 1, 2007, see § 81 of that act.

§ 1624a. Repealed by Stats.1963, c. 819, p. 1998, § 5, eff. Jan. 1, 1965

§ 1625. Written contracts; effect on negotiations or stipulations

The execution of a contract in writing, whether the law requires it to be written or not, supersedes all the negotiations or stipulations concerning its matter which preceded or accompanied the execution of the instrument. *(Enacted in 1872. Amended by Stats.1905, c. 451, p. 611, § 2.)*

Cross References

Best evidence rule, see Evidence Code § 1520 et seq.
Execution of instrument defined, see Code of Civil Procedure § 1933.

Intent of parties to be ascertained from writing alone, if possible, see Civil Code § 1639.
Parol evidence as to terms in writing, exclusion, see Code of Civil Procedure § 1856.
Revision of contracts in general, see Civil Code § 3399 et seq.
Sales contracts, parol or extrinsic evidence, see Commercial Code § 2202.
Written instrument, presumption of consideration, see Civil Code § 1614.
Written words control on printed form, see Code of Civil Procedure § 1862.

§ 1626. Written contracts; effective upon delivery

A contract in writing takes effect upon its delivery to the party in whose favor it is made, or to his agent. *(Enacted in 1872.)*

Cross References

Constructive delivery, see Civil Code § 1059.
Delivery defined, see Commercial Code § 1201.
Delivery for purposes of transaction taxes, see Revenue and Taxation Code § 7261.
Delivery of grant, see Civil Code § 1054.
Mode of transfer of grant, see Civil Code § 1053 et seq.
Presumption of delivery on date of duly executed grant, see Civil Code § 1055.
Presumptions as to delivery, see Evidence Code § 631 et seq.
Sales, passing of title, see Commercial Code § 2401.
Time of performance of contract, see Civil Code § 1657.

§ 1627. Written contracts; law governing

The provisions of the Chapter on Transfers in General, concerning the delivery of grants, absolute and conditional, apply to all written contracts. *(Enacted in 1872.)*

Cross References

Grant defined, see Civil Code § 1053.
Mode of transfer, see Civil Code § 1052 et seq.
Transfers in general, see Civil Code § 1039 et seq.

§ 1628. Seals; method of affixing

A corporate or official seal may be affixed to an instrument by a mere impression upon the paper or other material on which such instrument is written. *(Enacted in 1872.)*

Cross References

Failure to affix corporate seal, effect, see Corporations Code § 207.
Manner of affixation of official seal by controller, see Government Code § 12421.
Notary public, seals, see Government Code § 8207.
Presumption of genuineness of official seal, see Evidence Code § 1452.
Seal defined, see Code of Civil Procedure §§ 14, 1930, 1931; Penal Code § 7.
Seals generally, see Code of Civil Procedure § 1930 et seq.

§ 1629. Sealed and unsealed instruments; distinctions abolished

All distinctions between sealed and unsealed instruments are abolished. *(Enacted in 1872.)*

Cross References

Compromise of debt by unsealed agreement, validity, see Code of Civil Procedure § 1934.
Negotiable instrument subject to division of Commercial Code on commercial paper even though under seal, see Commercial Code § 3113.
Public and private seals, see Code of Civil Procedure § 1931.
Similar provision, see Code of Civil Procedure § 1932.

§ 1630. Bailment contracts with automobile parking lots; requirements

Except as provided in Section 1630.5, a printed contract of bailment providing for the parking or storage of a motor vehicle shall not be binding, either in whole or in part, on the vehicle owner or on the person who leaves the vehicle with another, unless the contract conforms to the following:

(a) "This contract limits our liability—read it" is printed at the top in capital letters of 10-point type or larger.

(b) All the provisions of the contract are printed legibly in eight-point type or larger.

(c) Acceptance of benefits under a contract included within the provisions of this section shall not be construed a waiver of this section, and it shall be unlawful to issue such a contract on condition that provisions of this section are waived.

A copy of the contract printed in large type, in an area at least 17 by 22 inches, shall be posted in a conspicuous place at each entrance of the parking lot.

Nothing in this section shall be construed to prohibit the enactment of city ordinances on this subject that are not less restrictive, and such enactments are expressly authorized. (Added by Stats.1957, c. 1472, p. 2794, § 1. Amended by Stats.1970, c. 1277, p. 2311, § 1.)

Cross References

Consent by acceptance of benefits, see Civil Code § 1589.
Hiring,
    Generally, see Civil Code § 1925 et seq.
    Personal property, see Civil Code § 1955 et seq.
Loan for use, see Civil Code § 1884 et seq.
Motor vehicle defined, see Vehicle Code § 415.
Possessory liens for motor vehicle storage or parking charges over $300, see Civil Code § 3051a.
Possessory liens for safekeeping of personal property, see Civil Code §§ 1856, 3051.
Storage, deposit for hire, see Civil Code § 1851 et seq.
Unlawful use or tampering with vehicle by bailee, see Vehicle Code § 10854.
Warehouse receipts, contractual limitation of liability, see Commercial Code § 7204.

§ 1630.5. Automobile parking lots; liability for theft

The provisions of any contract of bailment for the parking or storage of a motor vehicle shall not exempt the bailee from liability, either in whole or in part, for the theft of any motor vehicle, when such motor vehicle is parked or stored with such bailee, and the keys are required by such bailee to be left in the parked or stored vehicle. (Added by Stats.1970, c. 1277, p. 2311, § 2.)

Cross References

Embezzlement by bailee, see Penal Code § 507.
Liability of bailee for death or injury to person or property due to operation of motor vehicle, see Vehicle Code § 17151.
Storage, deposit for hire, see Civil Code § 1851 et seq.
Theft defined, see Penal Code § 484.

§ 1630.5

Unlawful use or tampering with vehicle by bailee, see Vehicle Code § 10854.

§ 1631. Sale of mining machinery; bill of sale; record; contents

Every person in this State who sells machinery used or to be used for mining purposes shall, at the time of sale, give to the buyer a bill of sale for the machinery. The seller shall keep a written record of the sale, giving the date thereof, describing the machinery, and showing the name and address of the buyer, and the buyer, if in this State, shall keep a record of his purchase, giving the name and address of the seller, describing the machinery, and showing the date of the purchase. *(Added by Stats.1959, c. 222, p. 2130, § 1.)*

Cross References

Bill of sale as grant or transfer in writing, see Civil Code § 1053.
Failure to give bill of sale or keep record as misdemeanor, see Penal Code § 653d.

§ 1632. Translation of contracts negotiated in language other than English; necessity; exceptions

(a) The Legislature hereby finds and declares all of the following:

(1) This section was enacted in 1976 to increase consumer information and protections for the state's sizeable and growing Spanish-speaking population.

(2) Since 1976, the state's population has become increasingly diverse and the number of Californians who speak languages other than English as their primary language at home has increased dramatically.

(3) According to data from the American Community Survey, which has replaced the decennial census for detailed socioeconomic information about United States residents, approximately 15.2 million Californians speak a language other than English at home, based on data from combined years 2009 through 2011. This compares to approximately 19.6 million people who speak only English at home. Among the Californians who speak a language other than English at home, approximately 8.4 million speak English very well, and another 3 million speak English well. The remaining 3.8 million Californians surveyed do not speak English well or do not speak English at all. Among this group, the five languages other than English that are most widely spoken at home are Spanish, Chinese, Tagalog, Vietnamese, and Korean. These five languages are spoken at home by approximately 3.5 million of the 3.8 million Californians with limited or no English proficiency, who speak a language other than English at home.

(b) Any person engaged in a trade or business who negotiates primarily in Spanish, Chinese, Tagalog, Vietnamese, or Korean, orally or in writing, in the course of entering into any of the following, shall deliver to the other party to the contract or agreement, and any other person who will be signing the contract or agreement, and before the execution thereof, a translation of the contract or agreement in the language in which the contract or agreement was negotiated, that includes a translation of every term and condition in that contract or agreement:

(1) A contract or agreement subject to the provisions of Title 2 (commencing with Section 1801) of, and Chapter 2b

OBLIGATIONS

(commencing with Section 2981) and Chapter 2d (commencing with Section 2985.7) of Title 14 of, Part 4 of Division 3.

(2) A loan or extension of credit secured other than by real property, or unsecured, for use primarily for personal, family, or household purposes.

(3) A lease, sublease, rental contract or agreement, or other term of tenancy contract or agreement, for a period of longer than one month, covering a dwelling, an apartment, or mobilehome, or other dwelling unit normally occupied as a residence.

(4) Notwithstanding paragraph (2), a loan or extension of credit for use primarily for personal, family, or household purposes in which the loan or extension of credit is subject to the provisions of Article 7 (commencing with Section 10240) of Chapter 3 of Part 1 of Division 4 of the Business and Professions Code, or Division 7 (commencing with Section 18000), or Division 9 (commencing with Section 22000) of the Financial Code.

(5) Notwithstanding paragraph (2), a reverse mortgage as described in Chapter 8 (commencing with Section 1923) of Title 4 of Part 4 of Division 3.

(6) A contract or agreement, containing a statement of fees or charges, entered into for the purpose of obtaining legal services, when the person who is engaged in business is currently licensed to practice law pursuant to Chapter 4 (commencing with Section 6000) of Division 3 of the Business and Professions Code.

(7) A foreclosure consulting contract subject to Article 1.5 (commencing with Section 2945) of Chapter 2 of Title 14 of Part 4 of Division 3.

(c) Notwithstanding subdivision (b), for a loan subject to this part and to Article 7 (commencing with Section 10240) of Chapter 3 of Part 1 of Division 4 of the Business and Professions Code, the delivery of a translation of the statement to the borrower required by Section 10240 of the Business and Professions Code in any of the languages specified in subdivision (b) in which the contract or agreement was negotiated, is in compliance with subdivision (b).

(d) At the time and place where a lease, sublease, or rental contract or agreement described in subdivision (b) is executed, notice in any of the languages specified in subdivision (b) in which the contract or agreement was negotiated shall be provided to the lessee or tenant.

(e) Provision by a supervised financial organization of a translation of the disclosures required by Regulation M or Regulation Z, and, if applicable, Division 7 (commencing with Section 18000) or Division 9 (commencing with Section 22000) of the Financial Code in any of the languages specified in subdivision (b) in which the contract or agreement was negotiated, prior to the execution of the contract or agreement, shall also be deemed in compliance with the requirements of subdivision (b) with regard to the original contract or agreement.

(1) "Regulation M" and "Regulation Z" mean any rule, regulation, or interpretation promulgated by the Board of Governors of the Federal Reserve System and any interpretation or approval issued by an official or employee duly authorized by the board to issue interpretations or approvals dealing with, respectively, consumer leasing or consumer

lending, pursuant to the Federal Truth in Lending Act, as amended (15 U.S.C. Sec. 1601 et seq.).

(2) As used in this section, "supervised financial organization" means a bank, savings association as defined in Section 5102 of the Financial Code, credit union, or holding company, affiliate, or subsidiary thereof, or any person subject to Article 7 (commencing with Section 10240) of Chapter 3 of Part 1 of Division 4 of the Business and Professions Code, or Division 7 (commencing with Section 18000) or Division 9 (commencing with Section 22000) of the Financial Code.

(f) At the time and place where a contract or agreement described in paragraph (1) or (2) of subdivision (b) is executed, a notice in any of the languages specified in subdivision (b) in which the contract or agreement was negotiated shall be conspicuously displayed to the effect that the person described in subdivision (b) is required to provide a contract or agreement in the language in which the contract or agreement was negotiated, or a translation of the disclosures required by law in the language in which the contract or agreement was negotiated, as the case may be. If a person described in subdivision (b) does business at more than one location or branch, the requirements of this section shall apply only with respect to the location or branch at which the language in which the contract or agreement was negotiated is used.

(g) The term "contract" or "agreement," as used in this section, means the document creating the rights and obligations of the parties and includes any subsequent document making substantial changes in the rights and obligations of the parties. The term "contract" or "agreement" does not include any subsequent documents authorized or contemplated by the original document such as periodic statements, sales slips or invoices representing purchases made pursuant to a credit card agreement, a retail installment contract or account or other revolving sales or loan account, memoranda of purchases in an add-on sale, or refinancing of a purchase as provided by, or pursuant to, the original document.

The term "contract" or "agreement" does not include a home improvement contract as defined in Sections 7151.2 and 7159 of the Business and Professions Code, nor does it include plans, specifications, description of work to be done and materials to be used, or collateral security taken or to be taken for the retail buyer's obligation contained in a contract for the installation of goods by a contractor licensed pursuant to Chapter 9 (commencing with Section 7000) of Division 3 of the Business and Professions Code, if the home improvement contract or installation contract is otherwise a part of a contract described in subdivision (b).

Matters ordinarily incorporated by reference in contracts or agreements as described in paragraph (3) of subdivision (b), including, but not limited to, rules and regulations governing a tenancy and inventories of furnishings to be provided by the person described in subdivision (b), are not included in the term "contract" or "agreement."

(h)(1) This section does not apply to any person engaged in a trade or business who negotiates primarily in a language other than English, as described by subdivision (b), if the party with whom that person is negotiating is a buyer of goods or services, or receives a loan or extension of credit, or enters an agreement obligating that party as a tenant, lessee, or sublessee, or similarly obligates the party by contract or lease, and the party negotiates the terms of the contract, lease, or other obligation through the party's own interpreter.

(2) As used in this subdivision, "the party's own interpreter" means a person who is not a minor and who is able to speak fluently and read with full understanding both the English language and any of the languages specified in subdivision (b) in which the contract, lease, or other obligation was negotiated, and who is not employed by, or whose service is not made available through, the person engaged in the trade or business.

(i) Notwithstanding subdivision (b), a translation may retain the following elements of the executed English-language contract or agreement without translation: names and titles of individuals and other persons, addresses, brand names, trade names, trademarks, registered service marks, full or abbreviated designations of the make and model of goods or services, alphanumeric codes, numerals, dollar amounts expressed in numerals, dates, and individual words or expressions having no generally accepted non-English translation. It is permissible, but not required, that this translation be signed.

(j) The terms of the contract or agreement that is executed in the English language shall determine the rights and obligations of the parties. However, the translation of the contract or the disclosures required by subdivision (e) in any of the languages specified in subdivision (b) in which the contract or agreement was negotiated shall be admissible in evidence only to show that no contract was entered into because of a substantial difference in the material terms and conditions of the contract and the translation.

(k) Upon a failure to comply with the provisions of this section, the person aggrieved may rescind the contract or agreement in the manner provided by this chapter. If the contract for a consumer credit sale or consumer lease that has been sold and assigned to a financial institution is rescinded pursuant to this subdivision, the consumer shall make restitution to and have restitution made by the person with whom the consumer made the contract and shall give notice of rescission to the assignee. Notwithstanding that the contract was assigned without recourse, the assignment shall be deemed rescinded, and the assignor shall promptly repurchase the contract from the assignee. (Added by Stats.1974, c. 1446, p. 3156, § 1. Amended by Stats.1975, c. 892, p. 1972, § 1; Stats.1976, c. 312, p. 624, § 1, eff. July 2, 1976, operative July 1, 1976; Stats.1981, c. 724, p. 2833, § 3; Stats.1988, c. 1531, § 1; Stats.2001, c. 306 (A.B.446), § 35; Stats.2002, c. 664 (A.B.3034), § 38; Stats.2003, c. 330 (A.B.309), § 1, operative July 1, 2004; Stats.2003, c. 589 (S.B.146), § 1; Stats.2003, c. 589 (S.B.146), § 1.5, operative July 1, 2004; Stats.2006, c. 202 (S.B.1609), § 1; Stats.2008, c. 278 (A.B. 180), § 1, operative July 1, 2009; Stats.2014, c. 117 (S.B.245), § 1, eff. Jan. 1, 2015; Stats.2020, c. 161 (A.B.3254), § 1, eff. Jan. 1, 2021.)

Cross References

Business licenses and building permits for commercial property, informational notice providing additional resources relating to compliance with federal and state disability laws, see Government Code § 4469.5.

§ 1632   OBLIGATIONS

Clean energy assessment contracts, oral confirmation before property owner executes assessment contract, duties of program administrator, see Streets and Highways Code § 5913.
Contracts for legal services, reporting complaints, notice, see Business and Professions Code § 6243.
Discontinuation of residential water service for nonpayment, availability of written notices and policies in specified languages, see Health and Safety Code §§ 116906, 116922.
District utility services, notices of termination, contents, see Government Code § 60371.
False, deceptive, or misleading acts or practices prohibited when providing debt settlement services, unfair, abusive, or deceptive acts or practices prohibited, see Civil Code § 1788.302.
Individually metered residential service, written notice of termination for nonpayment, use of language other than English,
  Municipal corporations, see Public Utilities Code § 10009.
  Municipal utility districts, see Public Utilities Code § 12822.
  Public utilities, see Public Utilities Code § 777.
Licensee who negotiates or offers to perform mortgage loan modifications for compensation, violations, see Business and Professions Code § 10147.6.
Master-metered residential service, written notice of termination for nonpayment, use of language other than English,
  Municipal corporations, see Public Utilities Code § 10009.1.
  Municipal utility districts, see Public Utilities Code § 12822.1.
  Public utilities, see Public Utilities Code § 777.1.
  Public utility districts, see Public Utilities Code § 16481.1.
Mobilehome park, water service to tenants, commission jurisdiction, notice of right to file complaint, failure to provide notice, penalties, reimbursement of unjust or unreasonable rate, see Public Utilities Code § 2705.6.
Notice for residential real property demanding payment of COVID–19 recovery period rental debt, modification, contents, effect of noncompliance, see Code of Civil Procedure § 1179.10.
Person who offers to perform mortgage loan modifications for fee, violations, see Civil Code § 2944.6.
Public utility districts, see Public Utilities Code § 16481.
Refund anticipation loans, see Business and Professions Code § 22253.1.
Requirements for notices that demand payment of COVID–19 rental debts that came due during protected time period and transition time period, delivery of a declaration of COVID–19–related financial distress, filing of declaration with court, see Code of Civil Procedure § 1179.03.
Termination of tenancy after continuous and lawful occupation of residential real property for 12 months, just cause required, notice, additional tenants, opportunity to cure violation, relocation assistance or rent waiver, see Civil Code § 1946.2.
Unlawful detainer actions to abate nuisance caused by illegal conduct, notice provided in translated languages,
  Controlled substances, see Civil Code § 3486.
  Unlawful weapons or ammunition, see Civil Code § 3485.

§ 1632.5. Supervised financial organizations negotiating primarily in Spanish, Chinese, Tagalog, Vietnamese, or Korean; contracts for loans or extensions of credit secured by residential real property; delivery in foreign language prior to execution; version executed in English to govern rights and responsibilities; exceptions

(a)(1) A supervised financial organization that negotiates primarily in Spanish, Chinese, Tagalog, Vietnamese, or Korean, whether orally or in writing, in the course of entering into a contract or agreement for a loan or extension of credit secured by residential real property, shall deliver to the other party to that contract or agreement prior to the execution of the contract or agreement the applicable form or forms described in subdivision (i) for that language.

(2) A supervised financial organization that negotiates the modification of any of the terms of a loan or extension of credit secured by residential real property primarily in Spanish, Chinese, Tagalog, Vietnamese, or Korean, and that offers a borrower a final loan modification in writing, shall deliver to that borrower, at the time the final loan modification offer is made, one of the forms described in paragraph (4) of subdivision (i) summarizing the modified terms of the loan in the same language as the negotiation.

(b) For purposes of this section:

(1) "Contract" or "agreement" has the same meaning as defined in subdivision (g) of Section 1632.

(2) "Supervised financial organization" means a bank, savings association, as defined in Section 5102 of the Financial Code, credit union, or holding company, affiliate, or subsidiary thereof, or any person subject to Division 7 (commencing with Section 18000), Division 9 (commencing with Section 22000), or Division 20 (commencing with Section 50000) of the Financial Code.

(c)(1) With respect to a contract or agreement for a loan or extension of credit secured by residential real property as described in subdivision (a), a supervised financial organization that complies with this section shall be deemed in compliance with Section 1632.

(2) Except with respect to a loan or extension of credit described in paragraph (2) of subdivision (a), a supervised financial organization that complies with Section 1632, with respect to a contract or agreement for a loan or extension of credit secured by residential real property as described in subdivision (a), shall be deemed in compliance with this section.

(d)(1) Except as provided in paragraphs (2) and (3), the supervised financial organization shall provide the Good Faith Estimate disclosure form described in paragraph (1) of subdivision (i) to the borrower no later than three business days after receipt of the written application, and if any of the loan terms summarized materially change after provision of the translated form but prior to consummation of the loan, the supervised financial organization shall provide an updated version of the translated form prior to consummation of the loan.

(2) For a transaction subject to subsection (e) of Section 1026.19 of Title 12 of the Code of Federal Regulations, the supervised financial organization shall provide the Loan Estimate form described in paragraph (2) of subdivision (i) translated in the applicable language no later than three business days after receipt of the written application. If any of the summarized loan terms materially change after provision of the Loan Estimate form but prior to consummation of the loan, the supervised financial organization shall provide an updated version of the translated form prior to consummation of the loan.

(3) For a transaction subject to subsection (f) of Section 1026.19 of Title 12 of the Code of Federal Regulations, the supervised financial organization shall provide the Closing Disclosure form described in paragraph (3) of subdivision (i) translated in the applicable language at least three business days prior to consummation of the loan.

(e)(1) This section does not apply to a supervised financial organization that negotiates primarily in a language other than English, as described by subdivision (a), if the party with whom the supervised financial organization is negotiating, negotiates the terms of the contract through the party's own interpreter.

(2) For purposes of this subdivision, "the party's own interpreter" means a person, not a minor, who is able to speak fluently and read with full understanding both the English language and one of the languages specified in subdivision (a) that is the language in which the contract was negotiated, who is not employed by, and whose services are not made available through, the person engaged in the trade or business.

(f) Notwithstanding subdivision (a), a translated form may retain any of the following elements of the executed English language contract or agreement without translation:

(1) Names and titles of individuals and other persons.

(2) Addresses, brand names, trade names, trademarks, or registered service marks.

(3) Full or abbreviated designations of the make and model of goods or services.

(4) Alphanumeric codes.

(5) Individual words or expressions having no generally accepted non-English translation.

(g) The terms of the contract or agreement that is executed in the English language shall determine the rights and obligations of the parties. However, the translation of the forms described in subdivision (i) and required by subdivision (a) shall be admissible in evidence only to show that no contract or agreement was entered into because of a substantial difference in the material terms and conditions of the contract or agreement and the prior translated forms provided to the borrower.

(h)(1) A licensing agency may, by order, after appropriate notice and opportunity for hearing, levy administrative penalties against a supervised financial organization that violates any provision of this section, and the supervised financial organization may be liable for administrative penalties, up to the amounts of two thousand five hundred dollars ($2,500) for the first violation, five thousand dollars ($5,000) for the second violation, and ten thousand dollars ($10,000) for each subsequent violation. Except for licensing agencies exempt from the provisions of the Administrative Procedure Act, any hearing shall be held in accordance with the Administrative Procedure Act (Chapter 5 (commencing with Section 11500) of Part 1 of Division 3 of Title 2 of the Government Code), and the licensing agency shall have all the powers granted under that act.

(2) A licensing agency may exercise any and all authority and powers available to it under any other provisions of law to administer and enforce this section, including, but not limited to, investigating and examining the licensed person's books and records, and charging and collecting the reasonable costs for these activities. The licensing agency shall not charge a licensed person twice for the same service. Any civil, criminal, and administrative authority and remedies available to the licensing agency pursuant to its licensing law may be sought and employed in any combination deemed advisable by the licensing agency to enforce the provisions of this section.

(3) Any supervised financial organization that violates this section shall be deemed to have violated its licensing law.

(4) This section shall not be construed to impair or impede the Attorney General from bringing an action to enforce this division.

(i) The Department of * * * <u>Financial Protection and Innovation</u> shall make available each of the following forms based on existing forms in each of the languages set forth in subdivision (a) for use by a supervised financial organization to summarize the terms of a mortgage loan pursuant to subdivision (a). In making available the forms, the Department of * * * <u>Financial Protection and Innovation</u> may use as guidance the following existing forms:

(1) The Good Faith Estimate disclosure form from the United States Department of Housing and Urban Development.

(2) The Loan Estimate form from the Consumer Financial Protection Bureau.

(3) The Closing Disclosure form from the Consumer Financial Protection Bureau.

(4) The Agreement for Modification, Re-Amortization, or Extension of a Mortgage (Form 181), the Loan Modification Agreement (Providing for Fixed Interest Rate) (Form 3179), and the Loan Modification Agreement (Providing for Adjustable Interest Rate) (Form 3161) from the Federal National Mortgage Association.

(j) This section does not apply to federally chartered banks, credit unions, savings banks, or thrifts.

(k) Except as otherwise provided in subdivision (h), this section shall not be construed to create or enhance any claim, right of action, or civil liability that did not previously exist under state law, or limit any claim, right of action, or civil liability that otherwise exists under state law.

(*l*) An action against a supervised financial organization for a violation of this section may only be brought by a licensing agency or by the Attorney General. (Added by Stats.2009, c. 274 (A.B.1160), § 1, operative Sept. 26, 2010. Amended by Stats.2015, c. 190 (A.B.1517), § 2, eff. Jan. 1, 2016; Stats.2018, c. 356 (S.B.1201), § 1, eff. Jan. 1, 2019, operative contingent; Stats.2019, c. 497 (A.B.991), § 24, eff. Jan. 1, 2020; Stats.2022, c. 452 (S.B.1498), § 18, eff. Jan. 1, 2023.)

Cross References

Attorney General, generally, see Government Code § 12500 et seq.

§ 1633. Electronically transmitted application to enter into brokerage agreement

(a) Notwithstanding any other provision of law, an application by a prospective customer to enter into a brokerage agreement with a broker-dealer, which application is transmitted electronically and is accompanied by the prospective customer's electronic signature or digital signature as described in subdivisions (d), (e), (f), and (g), shall be deemed, upon acceptance by the broker-dealer, to be a fully executed, valid, enforceable, and irrevocable written contract, unless grounds exist which would render any other contract invalid, unenforceable, or revocable.

(b) Nothing in this section abrogates or limits any existing law that would otherwise apply to contracts governed by this section, or any theory of liability or any remedy otherwise available at law.

(c) "Broker–dealer," for purposes of this section, means any broker-dealer licensed pursuant to Part 3 (commencing with Section 25200) of Division 1 of Title 4 of the Corporations Code or exempted from licensing pursuant thereto.

(d) "Electronic" means relating to technology having electrical, digital, magnetic, wireless, optical, electromagnetic, or similar capabilities.

(e) "Electronic record" means a record created, generated, sent, communicated, received, or stored electronically.

(f) "Electronic signature" means an electronic sound, symbol, or process attached to or logically associated with an electronic record and executed or adopted by a person with the intent to sign the electronic record.

(g) "Digital signature," for the purposes of this section, means an electronic identifier, created by a computer, that is intended by the party using it to have the same force and effect as the use of a manual signature. The use of a digital signature shall have the same force or effect as a manual signature if it embodies all of the following attributes:

(1) It is unique to the person using it.

(2) It is capable of verification.

(3) It is under the sole control of the person using it.

(4) It is linked to data in a manner that if the data is changed, the digital signature is invalidated.

(h) The use of an electronic signature or digital signature shall have the same force or effect as a manual signature.

(i) The application that is transmitted electronically pursuant to subdivision (a) shall comply with all applicable federal and state securities laws and regulations relating to disclosures to prospective customers. Unless those laws and regulations currently require disclosures to be displayed or printed in bold, to be of specific type or print size, and to be placed prominently at specified locations within the application, the disclosures shall be displayed prominently and printed in capital letters, in bold type and displayed or printed immediately above the signature line. Disclosures shall be written in plain English. The full text of the disclosures shall be contained in the application as required by this subdivision.

(j) Whenever a disclosure to a prospective customer is required under federal or state law or regulation to be confirmed as having been made, the application that is transmitted electronically pursuant to subdivision (a) shall provide a means by which the prospective customer shall confirm that he or she has read the disclosure. *(Added by Stats.1999, c. 213 (S.B.1124), § 1, eff. July 28, 1999.)*

Title 2.5

ELECTRONIC TRANSACTIONS

Section
1633.1. Short title.

Section
1633.2. Definitions.
1633.3. Application of title.
1633.4. Further application of title.
1633.5. Record or signature requirement; agreement to transact electronically.
1633.6. Construction and application of title.
1633.7. Legal effect or enforceability of electronic record, signature, or contract.
1633.8. Requirement to provide, send, or deliver information in writing; electronic satisfaction.
1633.9. Attribution of electronic record or signature.
1633.10. Change or error in electronic record; rules.
1633.11. Notarization and signature under penalty of perjury requirements.
1633.12. Retaining records; electronic satisfaction.
1633.13. Evidence in electronic form; admissibility.
1633.14. Automated transaction rules.
1633.15. Sending and receiving records; timing.
1633.16. Notice of right to cancel.
1633.17. Regulation of electronic signature.

Cross References

Electrical or gas consumption data, electrical and gas corporations prohibited from sharing, disclosing, or making accessible to third party, see Public Utilities Code § 8380.

Income tax returns, disclosure of information, separate consent document as electronic record executed by electronic signature, see Business and Professions Code § 17530.5; Civil Code § 1799.1a.

Life insurance, written records required to be provided by a licensee, authorization to provide by electronic transmission, see Insurance Code § 38.6.

Local building permits, properly executed declarations construed as records, see Health and Safety Code § 19826.

Progress report on reduction of solid waste, electronic reporting format system, applicability of Uniform Electronic Transactions Act, see Public Resources Code § 41821.

Treaties, statutes, tariffs, classifications, and regulations, conflicts with Uniform Electronic Transactions Act, see Commercial Code § 7103.

Yacht and ship brokers, electronically generated or transmitted records, see Harbors and Navigation Code § 702.5.

§ 1633.1. Short title

This title may be cited as the Uniform Electronic Transactions Act. *(Added by Stats.1999, c. 428 (S.B.820), § 1.)*

Cross References

Electronic defined for purposes of this Title, see Civil Code § 1633.2.

Income tax returns, disclosure of information, separate consent document as electronic record executed by electronic signature, see Business and Professions Code § 17530.5; Civil Code § 1799.1a.

Local building permits, properly executed declarations construed as records, see Health and Safety Code § 19826.

Progress report on reduction of solid waste, electronic reporting format system, applicability of Uniform Electronic Transactions Act, see Public Resources Code § 41821.

Transaction defined for purposes of this Title, see Civil Code § 1633.2.

Treaties, statutes, tariffs, classifications, and regulations, conflicts with Uniform Electronic Transactions Act, see Commercial Code § 7103.

Yacht and ship brokers, electronically generated or transmitted records, see Harbors and Navigation Code § 702.5.

§ 1633.2. Definitions

In this title the following terms have the following definitions:

(a) "Agreement" means the bargain of the parties in fact, as found in their language or inferred from other circumstances and from rules, regulations, and procedures given the effect of agreements under laws otherwise applicable to a particular transaction.

(b) "Automated transaction" means a transaction conducted or performed, in whole or in part, by electronic means or electronic records, in which the acts or records of one or both parties are not reviewed by an individual in the ordinary course in forming a contract, performing under an existing contract, or fulfilling an obligation required by the transaction.

(c) "Computer program" means a set of statements or instructions to be used directly or indirectly in an information processing system in order to bring about a certain result.

(d) "Contract" means the total legal obligation resulting from the parties' agreement as affected by this title and other applicable law.

(e) "Electronic" means relating to technology having electrical, digital, magnetic, wireless, optical, electromagnetic, or similar capabilities.

(f) "Electronic agent" means a computer program or an electronic or other automated means used independently to initiate an action or respond to electronic records or performances in whole or in part, without review by an individual.

(g) "Electronic record" means a record created, generated, sent, communicated, received, or stored by electronic means.

(h) "Electronic signature" means an electronic sound, symbol, or process attached to or logically associated with an electronic record and executed or adopted by a person with the intent to sign the electronic record. For purposes of this title, a "digital signature" as defined in subdivision (d) of Section 16.5 of the Government Code is a type of electronic signature.

(i) "Governmental agency" means an executive, legislative, or judicial agency, department, board, commission, authority, institution, or instrumentality of the federal government or of a state or of a county, municipality, or other political subdivision of a state.

(j) "Information" means data, text, images, sounds, codes, computer programs, software, databases, or the like.

(k) "Information processing system" means an electronic system for creating, generating, sending, receiving, storing, displaying, or processing information.

(*l*) "Person" means an individual, corporation, business trust, estate, trust, partnership, limited liability company, association, joint venture, governmental agency, public corporation, or any other legal or commercial entity.

(m) "Record" means information that is inscribed on a tangible medium or that is stored in an electronic or other medium and is retrievable in perceivable form.

(n) "Security procedure" means a procedure employed for the purpose of verifying that an electronic signature, record, or performance is that of a specific person or for detecting changes or errors in the information in an electronic record. The term includes a procedure that requires the use of algorithms or other codes, identifying words or numbers, encryption, or callback or other acknowledgment procedures.

(*o*) "Transaction" means an action or set of actions occurring between two or more persons relating to the conduct of business, commercial, or governmental affairs. (Added by Stats.1999, c. 428 (S.B.820), § 1. Amended by Stats.2016, c. 144 (A.B.2296), § 2, eff. Jan. 1, 2017.)

Cross References

Cooperation with securities agencies or administrators, electronic record defined, see Corporations Code § 25612.5.

Privileged character of electronic communications, electronic defined, see Evidence Code § 917.

§ 1633.3. Application of title

(a) Except as otherwise provided in subdivisions (b) and (c), this title applies to electronic records and electronic signatures relating to a transaction.

(b) This title does not apply to transactions subject to <u>any</u> of the following laws:

(1) A law governing the creation and execution of wills, codicils, or testamentary trusts.

(2) Division 1 (commencing with Section 1101) of the Uniform Commercial Code, except Sections 1206 and 1306.

(3) Divisions 3 (commencing with Section 3101), 4 (commencing with Section 4101), 5 (commencing with Section 5101), 8 (commencing with Section 8101), 9 (commencing with Section 9101), and 11 (commencing with Section 11101) of the Uniform Commercial Code.

(4) A law that requires that specifically identifiable text or disclosures in a record or a portion of a record be separately signed, including initialed, from the record. However, this paragraph does not apply to Section 1677 or 1678 of this code or Section 1298 of the Code of Civil Procedure.

(c) This title does not apply to any specific transaction described in Section 17511.5 of the Business and Professions Code, Section 56.11, 56.17, 798.14, 1133, or 1134 of, Section 1689.6, 1689.7, or 1689.13 of, Chapter 2.5 (commencing with Section 1695) of Title 5 of Part 2 of Division 3 of, Section 1720, 1785.15, 1789.14, 1789.16, or 1793.23 of, Chapter 1 (commencing with Section 1801) of Title 2 of Part 4 of Division 3 of, Section 1861.24, 1862.5, 1917.712, 1917.713, 1950.6, 1983, 2924b, 2924c, 2924f, 2924i, 2924j, 2924.3, or 2937 of, Article 1.5 (commencing with Section 2945) of Chapter 2 of Title 14 of Part 4 of Division 3 of, Section 2954.5 or 2963 of, Chapter 2b (commencing with Section 2981) or 2d (commencing with Section 2985.7) of Title 14 of Part 4 of Division 3 of, Section 3071.5 of, Part 5 (commencing with Section 4000) of Division 4 of, or Part 5.3 (commencing with Section 6500) of Division 4 of, this code, subdivision (b) of Section 18608 or Section 22328 of the Financial Code, Section 1358.15, 1365, 1368.01, 1368.1, 1371, or 18035.5 of the Health and Safety Code, Section 786 as it applies to individual and group disability policies, * * * 10199.44, 10199.46, 10235.16, 10235.40, 11624.09, or 11624.1 of the

§ 1633.3

Insurance Code, Section 779.1, 10010.1, or 16482 of the Public Utilities Code, or Section 9975 or 11738 of the Vehicle Code. An electronic record may not be substituted for any notice that is required to be sent pursuant to Section 1162 of the Code of Civil Procedure. * * * This subdivision * * * does not prohibit the recordation of any document with a county recorder by electronic means.

(d) This title applies to an electronic record or electronic signature otherwise excluded from the application of this title under subdivision (b) when used for a transaction subject to a law other than those specified in subdivision (b).

(e) A transaction subject to this title is also subject to other applicable substantive law.

(f) The exclusion of a transaction from the application of this title under subdivision (b) or (c) shall be construed only to exclude the transaction from the application of this title, but shall not be construed to prohibit the transaction from being conducted by electronic means if the transaction may be conducted by electronic means under any other applicable law.

(g) Notwithstanding subdivisions (b) and (c), this title shall apply to electronic records and electronic signatures relating to transactions conducted by a person licensed, certified, or registered pursuant to the Alarm Company Act (Chapter 11.6 (commencing with Section 7590) of Division 3 of the Business and Professions Code) for purposes of activities authorized by Section 7599.54 of the Business and Professions Code. *(Added by Stats.2013, c. 369 (S.B.251), § 3, operative Jan. 1, 2019. Amended by Stats.2014, c. 913 (A.B.2747), § 4, eff. Jan. 1, 2015, operative Jan. 1, 2019; Stats.2015, c. 439 (A.B.1097), § 4, eff. Jan. 1, 2016, operative Jan. 1, 2019; Stats.2015, c. 638 (A.B.1131), § 2.5, eff. Jan. 1, 2016, operative Jan. 1, 2019; Stats.2016, c. 617 (A.B.2591), § 2, eff. Jan. 1, 2017; Stats.2019, c. 235 (A.B.1065), § 1, eff. Jan. 1, 2020; Stats.2022, c. 39 (S.B.1179), § 1, eff. Jan. 1, 2023.)*

Cross References

Cancellation of insurance contract, notice of reason for cancellation, electronic delivery, see Insurance Code § 666.
Consumer Automotive Recall Safety Act, electronic authorization for repair of manufacturer recall, see Vehicle Code § 11755.
Electronic defined for purposes of this Title, see Civil Code § 1633.2.
Electronic record defined for purposes of this Title, see Civil Code § 1633.2.
Electronic signature defined for purposes of this Title, see Civil Code § 1633.2.
Good driver discount policy, refusal to issue, electronic delivery of statement of reasons to applicant, see Insurance Code § 658.
Record defined for purposes of this Title, see Civil Code § 1633.2.
Transaction defined for purposes of this Title, see Civil Code § 1633.2.

§ 1633.4. Further application of title

This title applies to any electronic record or electronic signature created, generated, sent, communicated, received, or stored on or after January 1, 2000. *(Added by Stats.1999, c. 428 (S.B.820), § 1.)*

Cross References

Electronic defined for purposes of this Title, see Civil Code § 1633.2.
Electronic record defined for purposes of this Title, see Civil Code § 1633.2.
Electronic signature defined for purposes of this Title, see Civil Code § 1633.2.
Record defined for purposes of this Title, see Civil Code § 1633.2.

§ 1633.5. Record or signature requirement; agreement to transact electronically

(a) This title does not require a record or signature to be created, generated, sent, communicated, received, stored, or otherwise processed or used by electronic means or in electronic form.

(b) This title applies only to a transaction between parties each of which has agreed to conduct the transaction by electronic means. Whether the parties agree to conduct a transaction by electronic means is determined from the context and surrounding circumstances, including the parties' conduct. Except for a separate and optional agreement the primary purpose of which is to authorize a transaction to be conducted by electronic means, an agreement to conduct a transaction by electronic means may not be contained in a standard form contract that is not an electronic record. An agreement in such a standard form contract may not be conditioned upon an agreement to conduct transactions by electronic means. An agreement to conduct a transaction by electronic means may not be inferred solely from the fact that a party has used electronic means to pay an account or register a purchase or warranty. This subdivision may not be varied by agreement.

(c) A party that agrees to conduct a transaction by electronic means may refuse to conduct other transactions by electronic means. If a seller sells goods or services by both electronic and nonelectronic means and a buyer purchases the goods or services by conducting the transaction by electronic means, the buyer may refuse to conduct further transactions regarding the goods or services by electronic means. This subdivision may not be varied by agreement.

(d) Except as otherwise provided in this title, the effect of any of its provisions may be varied by agreement. The presence in certain provisions of this title of the words "unless otherwise agreed," or words of similar import, does not imply that the effect of other provisions may not be varied by agreement. *(Added by Stats.1999, c. 428 (S.B.820), § 1.)*

Cross References

Agreement defined for purposes of this Title, see Civil Code § 1633.2.
Agreement to conduct business electronically with insurer, allowance of policyholder to electronically opt out of agreement, see Insurance Code § 38.8.
Contract defined for purposes of this Title, see Civil Code § 1633.2.
Electronic defined for purposes of this Title, see Civil Code § 1633.2.
Electronic record defined for purposes of this Title, see Civil Code § 1633.2.
Record defined for purposes of this Title, see Civil Code § 1633.2.
Transaction defined for purposes of this Title, see Civil Code § 1633.2.

§ 1633.6. Construction and application of title

This title shall be construed and applied according to all of the following:

(1) To facilitate electronic transactions consistent with other applicable law.

(2) To be consistent with reasonable practices concerning electronic transactions and with the continued expansion of those practices.

(3) To effectuate its general purpose to make uniform the law with respect to the subject of this title among states enacting it. *(Added by Stats.1999, c. 428 (S.B.820), § 1.)*

Cross References

Electronic defined for purposes of this Title, see Civil Code § 1633.2.
Transaction defined for purposes of this Title, see Civil Code § 1633.2.

§ 1633.7. Legal effect or enforceability of electronic record, signature, or contract

(a) A record or signature may not be denied legal effect or enforceability solely because it is in electronic form.

(b) A contract may not be denied legal effect or enforceability solely because an electronic record was used in its formation.

(c) If a law requires a record to be in writing, an electronic record satisfies the law.

(d) If a law requires a signature, an electronic signature satisfies the law. *(Added by Stats.1999, c. 428 (S.B.820), § 1.)*

Cross References

Contract defined for purposes of this Title, see Civil Code § 1633.2.
Electronic defined for purposes of this Title, see Civil Code § 1633.2.
Electronic record defined for purposes of this Title, see Civil Code § 1633.2.
Electronic signature defined for purposes of this Title, see Civil Code § 1633.2.
Record defined for purposes of this Title, see Civil Code § 1633.2.

§ 1633.8. Requirement to provide, send, or deliver information in writing; electronic satisfaction

(a) If parties have agreed to conduct a transaction by electronic means and a law requires a person to provide, send, or deliver information in writing to another person, that requirement is satisfied if the information is provided, sent, or delivered, as the case may be, in an electronic record capable of retention by the recipient at the time of receipt. An electronic record is not capable of retention by the recipient if the sender or its information processing system inhibits the ability of the recipient to print or store the electronic record.

(b) If a law other than this title requires a record to be posted or displayed in a certain manner, to be sent, communicated, or transmitted by a specified method, or to contain information that is formatted in a certain manner, all of the following rules apply:

(1) The record shall be posted or displayed in the manner specified in the other law.

(2) Except as otherwise provided in paragraph (2) of subdivision (d), the record shall be sent, communicated, or transmitted by the method specified in the other law.

(3) The record shall contain the information formatted in the manner specified in the other law.

(c) If a sender inhibits the ability of a recipient to store or print an electronic record, the electronic record is not enforceable against the recipient.

(d) The requirements of this section may not be varied by agreement, except as follows:

(1) To the extent a law other than this title requires information to be provided, sent, or delivered in writing but permits that requirement to be varied by agreement, the requirement under subdivision (a) that the information be in the form of an electronic record capable of retention may also be varied by agreement.

(2) A requirement under a law other than this title to send, communicate, or transmit a record by first-class mail may be varied by agreement to the extent permitted by the other law. *(Added by Stats.1999, c. 428 (S.B.820), § 1.)*

Cross References

Agreement defined for purposes of this Title, see Civil Code § 1633.2.
Electronic defined for purposes of this Title, see Civil Code § 1633.2.
Electronic record defined for purposes of this Title, see Civil Code § 1633.2.
Information defined for purposes of this Title, see Civil Code § 1633.2.
Information processing system defined for purposes of this Title, see Civil Code § 1633.2.
Person defined for purposes of this Title, see Civil Code § 1633.2.
Record defined for purposes of this Title, see Civil Code § 1633.2.
Transaction defined for purposes of this Title, see Civil Code § 1633.2.

§ 1633.9. Attribution of electronic record or signature

(a) An electronic record or electronic signature is attributable to a person if it was the act of the person. The act of the person may be shown in any manner, including a showing of the efficacy of any security procedure applied to determine the person to which the electronic record or electronic signature was attributable.

(b) The effect of an electronic record or electronic signature attributed to a person under subdivision (a) is determined from the context and surrounding circumstances at the time of its creation, execution, or adoption, including the parties' agreement, if any, and otherwise as provided by law. *(Added by Stats.1999, c. 428 (S.B.820), § 1.)*

Cross References

Agreement defined for purposes of this Title, see Civil Code § 1633.2.
Electronic defined for purposes of this Title, see Civil Code § 1633.2.
Electronic record defined for purposes of this Title, see Civil Code § 1633.2.
Electronic signature defined for purposes of this Title, see Civil Code § 1633.2.
Person defined for purposes of this Title, see Civil Code § 1633.2.
Record defined for purposes of this Title, see Civil Code § 1633.2.
Security procedure defined for purposes of this Title, see Civil Code § 1633.2.

§ 1633.10. Change or error in electronic record; rules

If a change or error in an electronic record occurs in a transmission between parties to a transaction, the following rules apply:

(1) If the parties have agreed to use a security procedure to detect changes or errors and one party has conformed to the procedure, but the other party has not, and the nonconforming party would have detected the change or error had

§ 1633.10   OBLIGATIONS

that party also conformed, the conforming party may avoid the effect of the changed or erroneous electronic record.

(2) In an automated transaction involving an individual, the individual may avoid the effect of an electronic record that resulted from an error made by the individual in dealing with the electronic agent of another person if the electronic agent did not provide an opportunity for the prevention or correction of the error and, at the time the individual learns of the error, all of the following conditions are met:

(i) The individual promptly notifies the other person of the error and that the individual did not intend to be bound by the electronic record received by the other person.

(ii) The individual takes reasonable steps, including steps that conform to the other person's reasonable instructions, to return to the other person or, if instructed by the other person, to destroy the consideration received, if any, as a result of the erroneous electronic record.

(iii) The individual has not used or received any benefit or value from the consideration, if any, received from the other person.

(3) If neither paragraph (1) nor (2) applies, the change or error has the effect provided by other law, including the law of mistake, and the parties' contract, if any.

(4) Paragraphs (2) and (3) may not be varied by agreement. (Added by Stats.1999, c. 428 (S.B.820), § 1.)

Cross References

Agreement defined for purposes of this Title, see Civil Code § 1633.2.
Automated transaction defined for purposes of this Title, see Civil Code § 1633.2.
Contract defined for purposes of this Title, see Civil Code § 1633.2.
Electronic agent defined for purposes of this Title, see Civil Code § 1633.2.
Electronic defined for purposes of this Title, see Civil Code § 1633.2.
Electronic record defined for purposes of this Title, see Civil Code § 1633.2.
Person defined for purposes of this Title, see Civil Code § 1633.2.
Record defined for purposes of this Title, see Civil Code § 1633.2.
Security procedure defined for purposes of this Title, see Civil Code § 1633.2.
Transaction defined for purposes of this Title, see Civil Code § 1633.2.

§ 1633.11. Notarization and signature under penalty of perjury requirements

(a) If a law requires that a signature be notarized, the requirement is satisfied with respect to an electronic signature if an electronic record includes, in addition to the electronic signature to be notarized, the electronic signature of a notary public together with all other information required to be included in a notarization by other applicable law.

(b) In a transaction, if a law requires that a statement be signed under penalty of perjury, the requirement is satisfied with respect to an electronic signature, if an electronic record includes, in addition to the electronic signature, all of the information as to which the declaration pertains together with a declaration under penalty of perjury by the person who submits the electronic signature that the information is true and correct. (Added by Stats.1999, c. 428 (S.B.820), § 1.)

Cross References

Electronic defined for purposes of this Title, see Civil Code § 1633.2.
Electronic filing of statement of economic interests, requirements of agency's proposed electronic filing system, see Government Code § 87500.2.
Electronic record defined for purposes of this Title, see Civil Code § 1633.2.
Electronic signature defined for purposes of this Title, see Civil Code § 1633.2.
Information defined for purposes of this Title, see Civil Code § 1633.2.
Online system for filing statements of economic interests, requirements, electronic confirmation, public hearings, training and assistance programs, public access to information, redaction of private information, see Government Code § 87500.3.
Person defined for purposes of this Title, see Civil Code § 1633.2.
Record defined for purposes of this Title, see Civil Code § 1633.2.
Transaction defined for purposes of this Title, see Civil Code § 1633.2.

§ 1633.12. Retaining records; electronic satisfaction

(a) If a law requires that a record be retained, the requirement is satisfied by retaining an electronic record of the information in the record, if the electronic record reflects accurately the information set forth in the record at the time it was first generated in its final form as an electronic record or otherwise, and the electronic record remains accessible for later reference.

(b) A requirement to retain a record in accordance with subdivision (a) does not apply to any information the sole purpose of which is to enable the record to be sent, communicated, or received.

(c) A person may satisfy subdivision (a) by using the services of another person if the requirements of subdivision (a) are satisfied.

(d) If a law requires a record to be retained in its original form, or provides consequences if the record is not retained in its original form, that law is satisfied by an electronic record retained in accordance with subdivision (a).

(e) If a law requires retention of a check, that requirement is satisfied by retention of an electronic record of the information on the front and back of the check in accordance with subdivision (a).

(f) A record retained as an electronic record in accordance with subdivision (a) satisfies a law requiring a person to retain a record for evidentiary, audit, or like purposes, unless a law enacted after the effective date of this title specifically prohibits the use of an electronic record for a specified purpose.

(g) This section does not preclude a governmental agency from specifying additional requirements for the retention of a record subject to the agency's jurisdiction. (Added by Stats.1999, c. 428 (S.B.820), § 1.)

Cross References

Electronic defined for purposes of this Title, see Civil Code § 1633.2.
Electronic record defined for purposes of this Title, see Civil Code § 1633.2.
Governmental agency defined for purposes of this Title, see Civil Code § 1633.2.
Information defined for purposes of this Title, see Civil Code § 1633.2.

Person defined for purposes of this Title, see Civil Code § 1633.2.
Record defined for purposes of this Title, see Civil Code § 1633.2.

§ 1633.13. Evidence in electronic form; admissibility

In a proceeding, evidence of a record or signature may not be excluded solely because it is in electronic form. *(Added by Stats.1999, c. 428 (S.B.820), § 1.)*

Cross References

Electronic defined for purposes of this Title, see Civil Code § 1633.2.
Record defined for purposes of this Title, see Civil Code § 1633.2.

§ 1633.14. Automated transaction rules

(a) In an automated transaction, the following rules apply:

(1) A contract may be formed by the interaction of electronic agents of the parties, even if no individual was aware of or reviewed the electronic agents' actions or the resulting terms and agreements.

(2) A contract may be formed by the interaction of an electronic agent and an individual, acting on the individual's own behalf or for another person, including by an interaction in which the individual performs actions that the individual is free to refuse to perform and which the individual knows or has reason to know will cause the electronic agent to complete the transaction or performance.

(b) The terms of the contract are determined by the substantive law applicable to it. *(Added by Stats.1999, c. 428 (S.B.820), § 1.)*

Cross References

Agreement defined for purposes of this Title, see Civil Code § 1633.2.
Automated transaction defined for purposes of this Title, see Civil Code § 1633.2.
Contract defined for purposes of this Title, see Civil Code § 1633.2.
Electronic agent defined for purposes of this Title, see Civil Code § 1633.2.
Electronic defined for purposes of this Title, see Civil Code § 1633.2.
Person defined for purposes of this Title, see Civil Code § 1633.2.
Transaction defined for purposes of this Title, see Civil Code § 1633.2.

§ 1633.15. Sending and receiving records; timing

(a) Unless the sender and the recipient agree to a different method of sending that is reasonable under the circumstances, an electronic record is sent when the information is addressed properly or otherwise directed properly to the recipient and either (1) enters an information processing system outside the control of the sender or of a person that sent the electronic record on behalf of the sender, or (2) enters a region of an information processing system that is under the control of the recipient.

(b) Unless the sender and the recipient agree to a different method of receiving that is reasonable under the circumstances, an electronic record is received when the electronic record enters an information processing system that the recipient has designated or uses for the purpose of receiving electronic records or information of the type sent, in a form capable of being processed by that system, and from which the recipient is able to retrieve the electronic record.

(c) Subdivision (b) applies even if the place the information processing system is located is different from the place the electronic record is deemed to be received under subdivision (d).

(d) Unless otherwise expressly provided in the electronic record or agreed between the sender and the recipient, an electronic record is deemed to be sent from the sender's place of business and to be received at the recipient's place of business or, if the recipient is an individual acting on his or her own behalf, at the recipient's place of residence. For purposes of this subdivision, the following rules apply:

(1) If the sender or recipient has more than one place of business, the place of business of that person is the place having the closest relationship to the underlying transaction.

(2) If the sender or the recipient does not have a place of business, the place of business is the sender's or recipient's residence, as the case may be.

(e) An electronic record is received under subdivision (b) even if no individual is aware of its receipt.

(f) Receipt of an electronic acknowledgment from an information processing system described in subdivision (b) establishes that a record was received but, by itself, does not establish that the content sent corresponds to the content received.

(g) If a person is aware that an electronic record purportedly sent under subdivision (a), or purportedly received under subdivision (b), was not actually sent or received, the legal effect of the sending or receipt is determined by other applicable law. Except to the extent permitted by the other law, this subdivision may not be varied by agreement. *(Added by Stats.1999, c. 428 (S.B.820), § 1.)*

Cross References

Agreement defined for purposes of this Title, see Civil Code § 1633.2.
Electronic defined for purposes of this Title, see Civil Code § 1633.2.
Electronic record defined for purposes of this Title, see Civil Code § 1633.2.
Information defined for purposes of this Title, see Civil Code § 1633.2.
Information processing system defined for purposes of this Title, see Civil Code § 1633.2.
Life insurance, written records required to be provided by a licensee, authorization to provide by electronic transmission, see Insurance Code § 38.6.
Person defined for purposes of this Title, see Civil Code § 1633.2.
Record defined for purposes of this Title, see Civil Code § 1633.2.
Transaction defined for purposes of this Title, see Civil Code § 1633.2.

§ 1633.16. Notice of right to cancel

If a law other than this title requires that a notice of the right to cancel be provided or sent, an electronic record may not substitute for a writing under that other law unless, in addition to satisfying the requirements of that other law and this title, the notice of cancellation may be returned by electronic means. This section may not be varied by agreement. *(Added by Stats.1999, c. 428 (S.B.820), § 1.)*

Cross References

Agreement defined for purposes of this Title, see Civil Code § 1633.2.
Electronic defined for purposes of this Title, see Civil Code § 1633.2.

§ 1633.16

Electronic record defined for purposes of this Title, see Civil Code § 1633.2.

Life insurance, written records required to be provided by a licensee, authorization to provide by electronic transmission, see Insurance Code § 38.6.

Record defined for purposes of this Title, see Civil Code § 1633.2.

§ 1633.17. Regulation of electronic signature

No state agency, board, or commission may require, prohibit, or regulate the use of an electronic signature in a transaction in which the agency, board, or commission is not a party unless a law other than this title expressly authorizes the requirement, prohibition, or regulation. *(Added by Stats.1999, c. 428 (S.B.820), § 1.)*

Cross References

Electronic defined for purposes of this Title, see Civil Code § 1633.2.

Electronic signature defined for purposes of this Title, see Civil Code § 1633.2.

Transaction defined for purposes of this Title, see Civil Code § 1633.2.

Title 3
INTERPRETATION OF CONTRACTS

Section
- 1635. Public and private contracts; uniformity of interpretation.
- 1636. Mutual intention to be given effect.
- 1637. Ascertainment of intention.
- 1638. Ascertainment of intention; language.
- 1639. Ascertainment of intention; written contracts.
- 1640. Writing disregarded; unexpressed intention.
- 1641. Whole contract, effect to be given.
- 1642. Several contracts as parts of one transaction.
- 1643. Interpretation in favor of contract.
- 1644. Sense of words.
- 1645. Sense of words; technical words.
- 1646. Law and usage of place.
- 1646.5. Law governing rights and duties of parties; agreement; exceptions; application.
- 1647. Circumstances.
- 1648. Restriction to object.
- 1649. Ambiguity or uncertainty; promise.
- 1650. Particular clauses; general intent.
- 1651. Printed forms; insertions under special directions; written parts.
- 1652. Reconcilement of repugnancies.
- 1653. Inconsistent words.
- 1654. Uncertainty; interpretation against person causing.
- 1655. Implied stipulations.
- 1656. Implied incidents.
- 1656.1. Sales tax reimbursement to retailer; addition to sales price; rebuttable presumptions; schedule.
- 1656.2. Repealed.
- 1656.5. Addition of estimated personal property tax reimbursement to the rental price of heavy equipment property to a lessee; presumptions.
- 1657. Performance; time.
- 1657.1. Contract of adhesion; time for performance shall be reasonable.
- 1658. Repealed.
- 1659. Joint and several promise; presumption; promisors benefiting from consideration.
- 1660. Joint and several promise; presumption; several persons executing promise in singular number.

Section
- 1661. Executed and executory contracts defined.
- 1662. Uniform Vendor and Purchaser Risk Act.
- 1663. Introduction of the euro as a medium of payment.

Cross References

Construction of agreement reduced to writing, see Code of Civil Procedure § 1856 et seq.

Construction of instruments, duty of judge, see Code of Civil Procedure § 1858; Evidence Code §§ 310, 400 et seq., 457.

Indemnity contracts, interpretation, see Civil Code § 2778.

Interpretation of obligations, see Civil Code § 1429.

§ 1635. Public and private contracts; uniformity of interpretation

All contracts, whether public or private, are to be interpreted by the same rules, except as otherwise provided by this Code. *(Enacted in 1872.)*

Cross References

Impairment of obligation of contract, see Cal. Const. Art. 1, § 9.

§ 1636. Mutual intention to be given effect

A contract must be so interpreted as to give effect to the mutual intention of the parties as it existed at the time of contracting, so far as the same is ascertainable and lawful. *(Enacted in 1872.)*

Cross References

Best evidence rule, see Evidence Code § 1520 et seq.

Construction of instrument, duty of judge, see Code of Civil Procedure § 1858; Evidence Code §§ 310, 400 et seq., 457.

Contract restricted to its evident object, see Civil Code § 1648.

Interpretation to make contract operative, see Civil Code § 1643.

Parole evidence to explain ambiguity etc., see Code of Civil Procedure § 1856.

Particular clauses subordinate to general intent, see Civil Code § 1650.

Terms in writing intended as final agreement, see Code of Civil Procedure § 1856.

§ 1637. Ascertainment of intention

For the purpose of ascertaining the intention of the parties to a contract, if otherwise doubtful, the rules given in this Chapter are to be applied. *(Enacted in 1872.)*

Cross References

Construction of instruments, intent, see Code of Civil Procedure § 1859.

Parol evidence, when admissible to contradict writing, see Code of Civil Procedure § 1856.

Party causing uncertainty, interpretation against, see Civil Code § 1654.

Proof of writings, see Evidence Code §§ 1520 et seq., 1601.

§ 1638. Ascertainment of intention; language

The language of a contract is to govern its interpretation, if the language is clear and explicit, and does not involve an absurdity. *(Enacted in 1872.)*

Cross References

Language of writing, interpretation according to meaning in place of execution, see Code of Civil Procedure § 1857.

Proof of writings, see Code of Civil Procedure § 1856; Evidence Code § 1520 et seq.

Terms of writing, presumption as to use, see Code of Civil Procedure § 1861.

§ 1639. Ascertainment of intention; written contracts

When a contract is reduced to writing, the intention of the parties is to be ascertained from the writing alone, if possible; subject, however, to the other provisions of this Title. *(Enacted in 1872.)*

Cross References

Best evidence rule, see Code of Civil Procedure § 1856; Evidence Code §§ 1520 et seq., 1601.
Circumstances explaining contracts, see Civil Code § 1647.
Evidence of terms of writing, other than writing itself, see Code of Civil Procedure § 1856.
Statute of frauds, see Civil Code § 1624.
Written contract supersedes prior agreements, see Civil Code § 1625.
Written words control on printed form, see Code of Civil Procedure § 1862.

§ 1640. Writing disregarded; unexpressed intention

When, through fraud, mistake, or accident, a written contract fails to express the real intention of the parties, such intention is to be regarded, and the erroneous parts of the writing disregarded. *(Enacted in 1872.)*

Cross References

Consent in formation of contract, see Civil Code § 1565 et seq.
Deceit defined, see Civil Code § 1710.
Enforcement of contract oral by reason of fraud, see Civil Code § 1623.
Fraud defined, see Civil Code § 1571 et seq.
Mistake, see Civil Code § 1576 et seq.
Parol evidence to show mistake or invalidity of agreement, see Code of Civil Procedure § 1856.
Remedies for fraud in sales contract, see Commercial Code § 2721.
Rescission for lack of consent, see Civil Code § 1689.
Revision of contracts due to fraud or mistake, see Civil Code § 3399 et seq.
Validity of contracts exempting one from responsibility for fraud, see Civil Code § 1668.

§ 1641. Whole contract, effect to be given

The whole of a contract is to be taken together, so as to give effect to every part, if reasonably practicable, each clause helping to interpret the other. *(Enacted in 1872.)*

Cross References

Conveyances, construction, see Code of Civil Procedure § 2077.
Inconsistent words in contract, see Civil Code § 1653.
Preference accorded interpretation which gives effect, see Civil Code § 3541.
Repugnancies in contract, see Civil Code § 1652.
Similar provision, see Code of Civil Procedure § 1858.

§ 1642. Several contracts as parts of one transaction

Several contracts relating to the same matters, between the same parties, and made as parts of substantially one transaction, are to be taken together. *(Enacted in 1872.)*

§ 1643. Interpretation in favor of contract

A contract must receive such an interpretation as will make it lawful, operative, definite, reasonable, and capable of being carried into effect, if it can be done without violating the intention of the parties. *(Enacted in 1872.)*

Cross References

Interpretation which gives effect preferred, see Civil Code § 3541.
Invalidity of contract with unlawful, impossible or unascertainable object, see Civil Code § 1598.
Validity of contract with one of several objects unlawful, see Civil Code § 1599.

§ 1644. Sense of words

The words of a contract are to be understood in their ordinary and popular sense, rather than according to their strict legal meaning; unless used by the parties in a technical sense, or unless a special meaning is given to them by usage, in which case the latter must be followed. *(Enacted in 1872.)*

Cross References

Course of dealing and usage of trade, see Commercial Code § 1205.
Judicial notice of signification of English words and phrases, see Evidence Code § 451.
Similar provisions, see Civil Code § 13; Code of Civil Procedure § 16; Probate Code § 21122.

§ 1645. Sense of words; technical words

Technical words are to be interpreted as usually understood by persons in the profession or business to which they relate, unless clearly used in a different sense. *(Enacted in 1872.)*

Cross References

Construction of technical words and phrases, see Civil Code § 13; Code of Civil Procedure §§ 16, 1861; Probate Code § 21122.

§ 1646. Law and usage of place

A contract is to be interpreted according to the law and usage of the place where it is to be performed; or, if it does not indicate a place of performance, according to the law and usage of the place where it is made. *(Enacted in 1872.)*

Cross References

Admissibility of evidence on local or peculiar meaning of terms of writing, see Code of Civil Procedure § 1861.
Course of dealing and usage of trade, see Commercial Code § 1205.
Interpretation of language of writing according to meaning at place of its execution, see Code of Civil Procedure § 1857.

§ 1646.5. Law governing rights and duties of parties; agreement; exceptions; application

Notwithstanding Section 1646, the parties to any contract, agreement, or undertaking, contingent or otherwise, relating to a transaction involving in the aggregate not less than two hundred fifty thousand dollars ($250,000), including a transaction otherwise covered by subdivision (a) of Section 1301 of the Commercial Code, may agree that the law of this state shall govern their rights and duties in whole or in part, whether or not the contract, agreement, or undertaking or transaction bears a reasonable relation to this state. This section does not apply to any contract, agreement, or undertaking (a) for labor or personal services, (b) relating to any transaction primarily for personal, family, or household purposes, or (c) to the extent provided to the contrary in subdivision (c) of Section 1301 of the Commercial Code.

§ 1646.5

This section applies to contracts, agreements, and undertakings entered into before, on, or after its effective date; it shall be fully retroactive. Contracts, agreements, and undertakings selecting California law entered into before the effective date of this section shall be valid, enforceable, and effective as if this section had been in effect on the date they were entered into; and actions and proceedings commencing in a court of this state before the effective date of this section may be maintained as if this section were in effect on the date they were commenced. *(Added by Stats.1992, c. 615 (S.B. 1804), § 2. Amended by Stats.2006, c. 254 (S.B.1481), § 1.5.)*

Application

For provision relating to application of Stats.2006, c. 254 (S.B.1481) to documents of title that are issued or bailments that arise before Jan. 1, 2007, see § 81 of that act.

§ 1647. Circumstances

A contract may be explained by reference to the circumstances under which it was made, and the matter to which it relates. *(Enacted in 1872.)*

Cross References

Construction of instruments, consideration of circumstances, see Code of Civil Procedure § 1860.
Manner of creating contracts, see Civil Code § 1619 et seq.
Object of a contract, see Civil Code § 1595 et seq.
Parole evidence, see Code of Civil Procedure § 1856.

§ 1648. Restriction to object

However broad may be the terms of a contract, it extends only to those things concerning which it appears that the parties intended to contract. *(Enacted in 1872.)*

Cross References

Ascertainment of intention, see Civil Code § 1638.
Intention controls, see Civil Code § 1636.
Object of a contract, see Civil Code § 1595 et seq.
Rejection of words inconsistent with main intention of parties, see Civil Code § 1653.

§ 1649. Ambiguity or uncertainty; promise

If the terms of a promise are in any respect ambiguous or uncertain, it must be interpreted in the sense in which the promisor believed, at the time of making it, that the promisee understood it. *(Enacted in 1872.)*

Cross References

Interpretation of grant in favor of grantee, see Civil Code § 1069.
Interpretation of language against person causing uncertainty, see Civil Code § 1654.
Similar provision, see Code of Civil Procedure § 1864.

§ 1650. Particular clauses; general intent

Particular clauses of a contract are subordinate to its general intent. *(Enacted in 1872.)*

Cross References

Whole of contract to be taken together, see Civil Code § 1641.

§ 1651. Printed forms; insertions under special directions; written parts

Where a contract is partly written and partly printed, or where part of it is written or printed under the special directions of the parties, and with a special view to their intention, and the remainder is copied from a form originally prepared without special reference to the particular parties and the particular contract in question, the written parts control the printed parts, and the parts which are purely original control those which are copied from a form. And if the two are absolutely repugnant, the latter must be so far disregarded. *(Enacted in 1872.)*

Cross References

Control of written words over printed words, see Code of Civil Procedure § 1862.
Rules of construction of commercial paper, see Commercial Code § 3118.

§ 1652. Reconcilement of repugnancies

Repugnancy in a contract must be reconciled, if possible, by such an interpretation as will give some effect to the repugnant clauses, subordinate to the general intent and purpose of the whole contract. *(Enacted in 1872.)*

Cross References

Prevalence of former part if several parts of grant are irreconcilable, see Civil Code § 1070.
Whole of contract to be taken together, see Civil Code § 1641.

§ 1653. Inconsistent words

Words in a contract which are wholly inconsistent with its nature, or with the main intention of the parties, are to be rejected. *(Enacted in 1872.)*

Cross References

Mutual intention to be given effect, see Civil Code § 1636.

§ 1654. Uncertainty; interpretation against person causing

In cases of uncertainty not removed by the preceding rules, the language of a contract should be interpreted most strongly against the party who caused the uncertainty to exist. *(Enacted in 1872. Amended by Stats.1982, c. 1120, p. 4045, § 1.)*

Cross References

Interpretation in sense promisor believed promisee to rely, see Civil Code § 1649.
Interpretation of grant in favor of grantee, see Civil Code § 1069.
Preference between two permissible constructions, see Code of Civil Procedure § 1864.

§ 1655. Implied stipulations

Stipulations which are necessary to make a contract reasonable, or conformable to usage, are implied, in respect to matters concerning which the contract manifests no contrary intention. *(Enacted in 1872.)*

Cross References

California Finance Lenders Law,
   Exemption for program-related investment by private foundation, tax-exempt organization and loan, guaranty, or investment made by public charity, tax-exempt organization, see Financial Code § 22064.
   Loans by franchisor to franchisee or subfranchisor, or by subfranchisor to franchisee, compliance with these provisions, see Financial Code § 22063.

Venture capital companies and operating companies, application, see Financial Code § 22062.
Interpretation of contract to make it reasonable and operable, see Civil Code § 1643.

§ 1656. Implied incidents

All things that in law or usage are considered as incidental to a contract, or as necessary to carry it into effect, are implied therefrom, unless some of them are expressly mentioned therein, when all other things of the same class are deemed to be excluded. *(Enacted in 1872.)*

Cross References

Award of attorney's fees and costs, see Civil Code § 1717.
Course of dealing and usage of trade, see Commercial Code § 1205.
Easements that pass with property, see Civil Code § 1104.
Incident follows principal, see Civil Code § 3540.
Incidents of ownership of real property, see Civil Code § 818 et seq.
Incidents pass with transfer of thing, see Civil Code § 1084.

§ 1656.1. Sales tax reimbursement to retailer; addition to sales price; rebuttable presumptions; schedule

(a) Whether a retailer may add sales tax reimbursement to the sales price of the tangible personal property sold at retail to a purchaser depends solely upon the terms of the agreement of sale. It shall be presumed that the parties agreed to the addition of sales tax reimbursement to the sales price of tangible personal property sold at retail to a purchaser if:

(1) The agreement of sale expressly provides for such addition of sales tax reimbursement;

(2) Sales tax reimbursement is shown on the sales check or other proof of sale; or

(3) The retailer posts in his or her premises in a location visible to purchasers, or includes on a price tag or in an advertisement or other printed material directed to purchasers, a notice to the effect that reimbursement for sales tax will be added to the sales price of all items or certain items, whichever is applicable.

(b) It shall be presumed that the property, the gross receipts from the sale of which is subject to the sales tax, is sold at a price which includes tax reimbursement if the retailer posts in his or her premises, or includes on a price tag or in an advertisement (whichever is applicable) one of the following notices:

(1) "All prices of taxable items include sales tax reimbursement computed to the nearest mill."

(2) "The price of this item includes sales tax reimbursement computed to the nearest mill."

(c)(1) The State Board of Equalization shall prepare and make available for inspection and duplication or reproduction a sales tax reimbursement schedule which shall be identical with the following tables up to the amounts specified therein:

4¾ percent

Price	Tax
.01– .10	.00
.11– .31	.01
.32– .52	.02
.53– .73	.03
.74– .94	.04
.95–1.15	.05

5 percent

Price	Tax
.01– .09	.00
.10– .29	.01
.30– .49	.02
.50– .69	.03
.70– .89	.04
.90–1.09	.05

5¼ percent

Price	Tax
.01– .09	.00
.10– .28	.01
.29– .47	.02
.48– .66	.03
.67– .85	.04
.86–1.04	.05

5½ percent

Price	Tax
.01– .09	.00
.10– .27	.01
.28– .45	.02
.46– .63	.03
.64– .81	.04
.82– .99	.05
1.00–1.18	.06

5¾ percent

Price	Tax
.01– .08	.00
.09– .26	.01
.27– .43	.02
.44– .60	.03
.61– .78	.04
.79– .95	.05
.96–1.13	.06

6 percent

Price	Tax
.01– .08	.00
.09– .24	.01
.25– .41	.02
.42– .58	.03
.59– .74	.04
.75– .91	.05
.92–1.08	.06

6¼ percent

Price	Tax
.01– .07	.00
.08– .23	.01
.24– .39	.02
.40– .55	.03
.56– .71	.04
.72– .87	.05
.88–1.03	.06

6½ percent

Price	Tax
.01– .07	.00
.08– .23	.01
.24– .38	.02
.39– .53	.03
.54– .69	.04

§ 1656.1

Price	Tax
.70– .84	.05
.85– .99	.06
1.00–1.15	.07

6¾ percent

Price	Tax
.01– .07	.00
.08– .22	.01
.23– .37	.02
.38– .51	.03
.52– .66	.04
.67– .81	.05
.82– .96	.06
.97–1.11	.07

7 percent

Price	Tax
.01– .07	.00
.08– .21	.01
.22– .35	.02
.36– .49	.03
.50– .64	.04
.65– .78	.05
.79– .92	.06
.93–1.07	.07

7¼ percent

Price	Tax
.01– .06	.00
.07– .20	.01
.21– .34	.02
.35– .48	.03
.49– .62	.04
.63– .75	.05
.76– .89	.06
.90–1.03	.07

7½ percent

Price	Tax
.01– .06	.00
.07– .19	.01
.20– .33	.02
.34– .46	.03
.47– .59	.04
.60– .73	.05
.74– .86	.06
.87– .99	.07
1.00–1.13	.08

(2) Reimbursement on sales prices in excess of those shown in the schedules may be computed by applying the applicable tax rate to the sales price, rounded off to the nearest cent by eliminating any fraction less than one-half cent and increasing any fraction of one-half cent or over to the next higher cent.

(3) If sales tax reimbursement is added to the sales price of tangible personal property sold at retail, the retailer shall use a schedule provided by the board, or a schedule approved by the board.

(d) The presumptions created by this section are rebuttable presumptions. (Added by Stats.1978, c. 1211, p. 3915, § 1. Amended by Stats.1985, c. 20, § 1, eff. March 29, 1985, operative April 1, 1985; Stats.1990, c. 1528 (S.B.2196), § 1.)

Cross References

Collection of sales tax reimbursement or use tax, failure to timely remit to board, see Revenue and Taxation Code § 6597.
Gross receipts under sales tax, application of this section in determining whether retailers absorb sales tax, see Revenue and Taxation Code § 6012.
Refund of unconstitutional taxes, claim of credit against total state and county sales and use taxes, see Revenue and Taxation Code § 7276.

§ 1656.2. Repealed by Stats.1990, c. 1528 (S.B.2196), § 2

§ 1656.5. Addition of estimated personal property tax reimbursement to the rental price of heavy equipment property to a lessee; presumptions

(a) Whether a qualified heavy equipment renter may add estimated personal property tax reimbursement to the rental price of heavy equipment property to a lessee depends solely upon the terms of the rental agreement. It shall be presumed that the parties agreed to the addition of estimated personal property tax reimbursement to the rental price of heavy equipment property to a lessee if all of the following conditions occur:

(1) The rental agreement expressly provides for the addition of estimated personal property tax reimbursement.

(2) Estimated personal property tax reimbursement is separately stated and charged on the rental agreement.

(3) The estimated personal property tax reimbursement amount shall not exceed 0.75 percent of the rental price of the heavy equipment property.

(b) The presumptions created by this section are rebuttable presumptions.

(c) For purposes of this section:

(1) "Qualified heavy equipment renter" shall have the same meaning as provided in Section 31202 of the Revenue and Taxation Code.

(2) "Rental price" means the total amount of the charge for renting the heavy equipment property, excluding any separately stated charges that are not rental charges, including, but not limited to, separately stated charges for delivery and pickup fees, damage waivers, environmental mitigation fees, sales tax reimbursement, or use taxes. (Added by Stats.2017, c. 505 (A.B.1130), § 1, eff. Jan. 1, 2018.)

Cross References

Heavy equipment renter, collection of property tax reimbursement, see Revenue and Taxation Code § 31203.

§ 1657. Performance; time

If no time is specified for the performance of an act required to be performed, a reasonable time is allowed. If the act is in its nature capable of being done instantly—as, for example, if it consists in the payment of money only—it must be performed immediately upon the thing to be done being exactly ascertained. (Enacted in 1872.)

Cross References

Delivery of goods sold, time for, see Commercial Code § 2309.
Effective date of contract, see Civil Code § 1626.
Offer of performance when time is not of essence, see Civil Code § 1492.

Time of offer of performance, see Civil Code § 1491.
Time of performance of sales contract, see Commercial Code §§ 2309, 2503.

§ 1657.1. Contract of adhesion; time for performance shall be reasonable

Any time specified in a contract of adhesion for the performance of an act required to be performed shall be reasonable. *(Added by Stats.2021, c. 222 (S.B.762), § 1, eff. Jan. 1, 2022.)*

§ 1658. Repealed by Code Am.1873–74, c. 612, p. 242, § 191

§ 1659. Joint and several promise; presumption; promisors benefiting from consideration

Where all the parties who unite in a promise receive some benefit from the consideration, whether past or present, their promise is presumed to be joint and several. *(Enacted in 1872.)*

Cross References

Joint and several liability by persons indemnifying with person indemnified, see Civil Code § 2777.
Joint and several liability on commercial paper, see Commercial Code § 3116.
Joint and several obligations, see Civil Code § 1430 et seq.
Performance by one of several joint obligors, extinguishing liability of all, see Civil Code § 1474.
Presumptions, generally, see Evidence Code § 600 et seq.

§ 1660. Joint and several promise; presumption; several persons executing promise in singular number

A promise, made in the singular number, but executed by several persons, is presumed to be joint and several. *(Enacted in 1872.)*

Cross References

Extinguishment of liability of joint obligors by performance of one, see Civil Code § 1474.
Presumptions, generally, see Evidence Code § 600 et seq.

§ 1661. Executed and executory contracts defined

An executed contract is one, the object of which is fully performed. All others are executory. *(Enacted in 1872.)*

§ 1662. Uniform Vendor and Purchaser Risk Act

Any contract hereafter made in this State for the purchase and sale of real property shall be interpreted as including an agreement that the parties shall have the following rights and duties, unless the contract expressly provides otherwise:

(a) If, when neither the legal title nor the possession of the subject matter of the contract has been transferred, all or a material part thereof is destroyed without fault of the purchaser or is taken by eminent domain, the vendor cannot enforce the contract, and the purchaser is entitled to recover any portion of the price that he has paid;

(b) If, when either the legal title or the possession of the subject matter of the contract has been transferred, all or any part thereof is destroyed without fault of the vendor or is taken by eminent domain, the purchaser is not thereby relieved from a duty to pay the price, nor is he entitled to recover any portion thereof that he has paid.

This section shall be so interpreted and construed as to effectuate its general purpose to make uniform the law of those states which enact it.

This section may be cited as the Uniform Vendor and Purchaser Risk Act. *(Added by Stats.1947, c. 497, p. 1486, § 1.)*

Cross References

Transfers of real property, see Civil Code § 1091 et seq.

§ 1663. Introduction of the euro as a medium of payment

(a) As used in this section, the following terms shall have the following meanings:

(1) "Euro" means the currency of participating member states of the European Union that adopt a single currency in accordance with the Treaty on European Union signed February 7, 1992, as amended from time to time.

(2) "Introduction of the euro" includes, but is not limited to, the implementation from time to time of economic and monetary union in member states of the European Union in accordance with the Treaty on European Union signed February 7, 1992, as amended from time to time.

(3) "ECU" or "European Currency Unit" means the currency basket that is from time to time used as the unit of account of the European community, as defined in European Council Regulation No. 3320/94.

(b) If a subject or medium of payment of a contract, security, or instrument is the ECU or a currency that has been substituted or replaced by the euro, the euro shall be a commercially reasonable substitute and substantial equivalent that may be either tendered or used in determining the value of the ECU or currency, in each case at the conversion rate specified in, and otherwise calculated in accordance with, the regulations adopted by the Council of the European Union.

(c) The introduction of the euro, the tendering of euros in connection with any obligation in compliance with subdivision (b), the determining of the value of any obligation in compliance with subdivision (b), or the calculating or determining of the value of the subject or medium of payment of a contract, security, or instrument with reference to an interest rate or other basis that has been substituted or replaced due to the introduction of the euro and that is a commercially reasonable substitute and substantial equivalent, shall neither have the effect of discharging or excusing performance under any contract, security, or instrument, nor give a party the right unilaterally to alter or terminate any contract, security, or instrument.

(d) This section shall be subject to any agreements between parties with specific reference to, or agreement regarding, the introduction of the euro.

(e) Notwithstanding the Commercial Code or any other law of this state, this section shall apply to all contracts, securities, and instruments, including contracts with respect to commercial transactions, and shall not be deemed to be displaced by any other law of this state.

(f) In the event of other currency changes, the provisions of this section with respect to the euro shall not be interpreted as creating any negative inference or negative presumption regarding the validity or enforceability of con-

Title 4

UNLAWFUL CONTRACTS

Section	
1667.	"Unlawfulness" defined.
1668.	Contracts contrary to policy of law.
1669.	Restraint of marriage.
1669.5.	Minor victim of unlawful sex act; payment of money or other consideration; application; district attorney enforcement; deposit to State Children's Trust Fund.
1669.7.	Contract for consideration for providing information obtained as a result of witnessing a crime; validity; civil actions.
1670.	Construction contract with public agency; disputes; resolution.
1670.5.	Unconscionable contract or clause of contract; finding as matter of law; remedies.
1670.6.	Telemarketing sales; unlawful contracts.
1670.7.	Provision deducting from wages for cost of emigrating and transporting; void.
1670.8.	Contracts for sale or lease of consumer goods or services; prohibited provisions waiving consumer's right to make statements regarding seller, lessor, employees or agents, or the goods or services; unlawful acts; waiver; civil penalties; other relief or remedies; lawful removal of online consumer statements.
1670.8.5.	Contracts for provision of a consumer service; provisions limiting right to file complaint with licensing board prohibited; waiver; violation.
1670.9.	Civil immigration custody; prohibition of contracts with federal government, federal agency, or private corporation to house or detain in locked detention facility noncitizens on or after January 1, 2018; prohibition of renewal or modification of contracts entered into before January 1, 2018; conveyance of land for facility.
1670.10.	Sale of dogs and cats; retail installment contracts prohibited; remedies.
1670.11.	Contract or settlement agreement waiving right to testify concerning alleged criminal conduct or sexual harassment; void and unenforceable.

§ 1667. "Unlawfulness" defined

That is not lawful which is:

1. Contrary to an express provision of law;

2. Contrary to the policy of express law, though not expressly prohibited; or,

3. Otherwise contrary to good morals. *(Enacted in 1872.)*

Cross References

Cannabis legislation, legislative intent, lawfulness of specified cannabis–related activities, see Civil Code § 1550.5.
Conditions to ownership of property, see Civil Code § 707 et seq.
Consent, element of contract, see Civil Code § 1565 et seq.
Consideration for contract, see Civil Code § 1605 et seq.
Contracts in restraint of trade, see Business and Professions Code § 16600 et seq.
Effect of illegal consideration, see Civil Code § 1608.
Grounds for rescission of contract, see Civil Code § 1689.
Illegal contracts,
  Between husband and wife, see Family Code § 1620.
  Capacity, see Civil Code §§ 1556, 1557.
  Construction of swimming pools, see Business and Professions Code § 7167 et seq.
  Dance studio lessons, see Civil Code § 1812.53.
  Franchise investments, see Corporations Code § 31000 et seq.
  Health studio services, see Civil Code § 1812.84.
  Persons in violation of pollution laws, see Government Code § 4477.
  Sale or lease of lots in subdivisions without report, see Business and Professions Code § 11018.2.
Impossible or unlawful conditions, see Civil Code § 1441.
Necessity of lawful consideration, see Civil Code § 1607.
Object of contract, see Civil Code § 1595 et seq.
Public educational employment, meeting and negotiating defined, see Government Code § 3540.1.
Retail installment sales, see Civil Code § 1801 et seq.
Rule against perpetuities, see Probate Code § 21200
Usury law,
  Generally, see Civil Code § 1916–1 et seq.
  Real property loans, see Business and Professions Code § 10242.

§ 1668. Contracts contrary to policy of law

All contracts which have for their object, directly or indirectly, to exempt anyone from responsibility for his own fraud, or willful injury to the person or property of another, or violation of law, whether willful or negligent, are against the policy of the law. *(Enacted in 1872.)*

Cross References

Cannabis legislation, legislative intent, lawfulness of specified cannabis–related activities, see Civil Code § 1550.5.
Enforcement of oral contract by reason of fraud, see Civil Code § 1623.
Essential elements of contract, see Civil Code § 1550.
Freedom from violence or intimidation, waiver of civil rights by contract, provisions of this section not abrogated, see Civil Code § 51.7.
Insurance contracts, claims against local public entities and employees, see Government Code § 990.
Invalid agreements of exoneration by common carrier, see Civil Code § 2175.
Kinds of fraud, see Civil Code § 1571 et seq.
Object of contract, see Civil Code § 1595 et seq.

§ 1669. Restraint of marriage

Every contract in restraint of the marriage of any person, other than a minor, is void. *(Added by Stats.1977, c. 198, p. 718, § 1, operative July 1, 1978.)*

Cross References

Action to determine validity of marriage, see Family Code § 309.
Conditions in restraint of marriage, see Civil Code § 710.
Lack of cause of action for fraudulent promise to marry, see Civil Code § 43.4.
Marriage,
  Contract, see Family Code § 300 et seq.
  Minor, see Family Code § 302.
Minor defined, see Family Code § 6500.
Statute of frauds, see Civil Code § 1624.

§ 1669.5. Minor victim of unlawful sex act; payment of money or other consideration; application; district attorney enforcement; deposit to State Children's Trust Fund

(a) Any contract for the payment of money or other consideration to a minor who has been alleged to be the victim of an unlawful sex act, or to his or her legal representative, by the alleged perpetrator of that unlawful sex act, or his or her legal representative, entered into on or after the time of the alleged unlawful sex act, and providing for any payments to be made more than one year after the date of the execution of the contract, is void as contrary to public policy. A district attorney may bring an action or intervene in any action to enjoin enforcement of any contract which is in violation of this section.

(b) This section does not apply after the date of the final judgment in a criminal case against the alleged perpetrator for the unlawful sex act described in subdivision (a).

(c) This section does not apply to a contract for the payment of money or other consideration made from a nonrevocable trust established for the benefit of the minor if the alleged perpetrator has no direct or indirect access to, or control over, the trust.

(d) This section does not apply to an alleged perpetrator of an unlawful sex act against a minor to the extent he or she agrees to pay, or is required by court order to pay, child support for that minor upon a dissolution or legal separation.

(e) For purposes of this section, "unlawful sex act," means a felony sex offense committed against a minor.

(f) Notwithstanding subdivision (a), any contract declared void as contrary to public policy under this section may still be enforced by a district attorney against the payor, and the proceeds thereof shall be deposited in the State Children's Trust Fund pursuant to Section 18969 of the Welfare and Institutions Code. *(Added by Stats.1993–94, 1st Ex.Sess., c. 54 (S.B.35), § 1, eff. Nov. 30, 1994.)*

Cross References

Felonies, definition and penalties, see Penal Code §§ 17, 18.
Minor victim of unlawful sex act, parent and perpetrator contract, misdemeanor, see Penal Code § 310.5.

§ 1669.7. Contract for consideration for providing information obtained as a result of witnessing a crime; validity; civil actions

A contract for the payment of money or other consideration in violation of Section 132.5 of the Penal Code is void as contrary to public policy. The Attorney General or the district attorney of the county in which a violation of Section 132.5 of the Penal Code occurs may bring a civil action, or intervene in any civil action, to enjoin the enforcement of a contract that violates that section. *(Added by Stats.1994, c. 869 (S.B.1999), § 1.)*

Cross References

Attorney General, generally, see Government Code § 12500 et seq.

§ 1670. Construction contract with public agency; disputes; resolution

Any dispute arising from a construction contract with a public agency, which contract contains a provision that one party to the contract or one party's agent or employee shall decide any disputes arising under that contract, shall be resolved by submitting the dispute to independent arbitration, if mutually agreeable, otherwise by litigation in a court of competent jurisdiction. *(Added by Stats.1978, c. 1374, p. 4556, § 1.)*

§ 1670.5. Unconscionable contract or clause of contract; finding as matter of law; remedies

(a) If the court as a matter of law finds the contract or any clause of the contract to have been unconscionable at the time it was made the court may refuse to enforce the contract, or it may enforce the remainder of the contract without the unconscionable clause, or it may so limit the application of any unconscionable clause as to avoid any unconscionable result.

(b) When it is claimed or appears to the court that the contract or any clause thereof may be unconscionable the parties shall be afforded a reasonable opportunity to present evidence as to its commercial setting, purpose, and effect to aid the court in making the determination. *(Added by Stats.1979, c. 819, p. 2827, § 3, eff. Sept. 19, 1979.)*

Cross References

Unconscionable loan contracts, violations and remedies, see Financial Code § 22302.

§ 1670.6. Telemarketing sales; unlawful contracts

A contract with a consumer located in California for the purchase of a good or service that is made in connection with a telephone solicitation made in or from outside of California and is primarily for personal, family, or household use, is unlawful if, with respect to that telephone solicitation, the telemarketer is in violation of Section 310.4(a)(6)(i) of, or has not complied with Section 310.5(a)(5) of, the Federal Trade Commission's Telemarketing Sales Rule (16 C.F.R. Part 310), as published in the Federal Register, Volume 68, Number 19, on January 29, 2003. This section shall apply only to those entities subject to, and does not apply to any transaction exempted under Section 310.6 of, the Telemarketing Sales Rule (16 C.F.R. Part 310), as published in the Federal Register, Volume 68, Number 19, on January 29, 2003. *(Added by Stats.2003, c. 77 (A.B.88), § 1.)*

§ 1670.7. Provision deducting from wages for cost of emigrating and transporting; void

Any provision of a contract that purports to allow a deduction from a person's wages for the cost of emigrating and transporting that person to the United States is void as against public policy. *(Added by Stats.2008, c. 258 (A.B. 1278), § 1. Amended by Stats.2009, c. 35 (S.B.174), § 2.)*

§ 1670.8. Contracts for sale or lease of consumer goods or services; prohibited provisions waiving consumer's right to make statements regarding seller, lessor, employees or agents, or the goods or services; unlawful acts; waiver; civil penalties; other relief or remedies; lawful removal of online consumer statements

(a)(1) A contract or proposed contract for the sale or lease of consumer goods or services may not include a provision waiving the consumer's right to make any statement regarding the seller or lessor or its employees or agents, or concerning the goods or services.

(2) It shall be unlawful to threaten or to seek to enforce a provision made unlawful under this section, or to otherwise penalize a consumer for making any statement protected under this section.

§ 1670.8

(b) Any waiver of the provisions of this section is contrary to public policy, and is void and unenforceable.

(c) Any person who violates this section shall be subject to a civil penalty not to exceed two thousand five hundred dollars ($2,500) for the first violation, and five thousand dollars ($5,000) for the second and for each subsequent violation, to be assessed and collected in a civil action brought by the consumer, by the Attorney General, or by the district attorney or city attorney of the county or city in which the violation occurred. When collected, the civil penalty shall be payable, as appropriate, to the consumer or to the general fund of whichever governmental entity brought the action to assess the civil penalty.

(d) In addition, for a willful, intentional, or reckless violation of this section, a consumer or public prosecutor may recover a civil penalty not to exceed ten thousand dollars ($10,000).

(e) The penalty provided by this section is not an exclusive remedy, and does not affect any other relief or remedy provided by law. This section shall not be construed to prohibit or limit a person or business that hosts online consumer reviews or comments from removing a statement that is otherwise lawful to remove. (Added by Stats.2014, c. 308 (A.B.2365), § 1, eff. Jan. 1, 2015.)

§ 1670.8.5. Contracts for provision of a consumer service; provisions limiting right to file complaint with licensing board prohibited; waiver; violation

(a) A contract or proposed contract for the provision of a consumer service by a licensee regulated by a licensing board shall not include a provision limiting the consumer's ability to file a complaint with that board or to participate in the board's investigation into the licensee.

(b) Any waiver of the provisions of this section is contrary to public policy, and is void and unenforceable.

(c) For purposes of this section, the following terms apply:

(1) "Consumer service" means any service that is obtained for use primarily for personal, family, or household purposes.

(2) "Licensing board" means any entity described in Section 101 of the Business and Professions Code, the State Bar of California, the Department of Real Estate, or any other state agency that issues a license, certificate, or registration authorizing a person to engage in a business or profession.

(d) Violation of this section by a licensee shall constitute unprofessional conduct subject to discipline by the licensee's licensing board. (Added by Stats.2020, c. 312 (S.B.1474), § 98, eff. Jan. 1, 2021.)

§ 1670.9. Civil immigration custody; prohibition of contracts with federal government, federal agency, or private corporation to house or detain in locked detention facility noncitizens on or after January 1, 2018; prohibition of renewal or modification of contracts entered into before January 1, 2018; conveyance of land for facility

(a) A city, county, city and county, or local law enforcement agency that does not, as of January 1, 2018, have a contract with the federal government or any federal agency or a private corporation to house or detain noncitizens for purposes of civil immigration custody, shall not, on and after January 1, 2018, enter into a contract with the federal government or any federal agency or a private corporation, to house or detain in a locked detention facility noncitizens for purposes of civil immigration custody.

(b) A city, county, city and county, or local law enforcement agency that, as of January 1, 2018, has an existing contract with the federal government or any federal agency or a private corporation to detain noncitizens for purposes of civil immigration custody, shall not, on and after January 1, 2018, renew or modify that contract in a manner that would expand the maximum number of contract beds that may be utilized to house or detain in a locked detention facility noncitizens for purposes of civil immigration custody.

(c) Any facility that detains a noncitizen pursuant to a contract with a city, county, city and county, or a local law enforcement agency is subject to the California Public Records Act (Division 10 (commencing with Section 7920.000) of Title 1 of the Government Code).

(d) A city, county, city and county, or public agency shall not, on and after January 1, 2018, approve or sign a deed, instrument, or other document related to a conveyance of land or issue a permit for the building or reuse of existing buildings by any private corporation, contractor, or vendor to house or detain noncitizens for purposes of civil immigration proceedings unless the city, county, city and county, or public agency has done both of the following:

(1) Provided notice to the public of the proposed conveyance or permitting action at least 180 days before execution of the conveyance or permit.

(2) Solicited and heard public comments on the proposed conveyance or permit action in at least two separate meetings open to the public. (Added by Stats.2017, c. 494 (S.B.29), § 2, eff. Jan. 1, 2018. Amended by Stats.2021, c. 615 (A.B.474), § 42, eff. Jan. 1, 2022, operative Jan. 1, 2023.)

§ 1670.10. Sale of dogs and cats; retail installment contracts prohibited; remedies

(a)(1) Except as provided in paragraph (2), a contract entered into on or after January 1, 2018, to transfer ownership of a dog or cat in which ownership is contingent upon the making of payments over a period of time subsequent to the transfer of possession of the dog or cat is void as against public policy.

(2) Paragraph (1) shall not apply to payments to repay an unsecured loan for the purchase of the dog or cat.

(b) A contract entered into on or after January 1, 2018, for the lease of a dog or cat that provides for or offers the option of transferring ownership of the dog or cat at the end of the lease term is void as against public policy.

(c) In addition to any other remedies provided by law, the consumer taking possession of a dog or cat transferred under a contract described in paragraph (1) of subdivision (a) or in subdivision (b) shall be deemed the owner of the dog or cat and shall also be entitled to the return of all amounts the consumer paid under the contract. (Added by Stats.2017, c. 761 (A.B.1491), § 1, eff. Jan. 1, 2018.)

§ 1670.11. Contract or settlement agreement waiving right to testify concerning alleged criminal conduct or sexual harassment; void and unenforceable

Notwithstanding any other law, a provision in a contract or settlement agreement entered into on or after January 1, 2019, that waives a party's right to testify in an administrative, legislative, or judicial proceeding concerning alleged criminal conduct or alleged sexual harassment on the part of the other party to the contract or settlement agreement, or on the part of the agents or employees of the other party, when the party has been required or requested to attend the proceeding pursuant to a court order, subpoena, or written request from an administrative agency or the Legislature, is void and unenforceable. *(Added by Stats.2018, c. 949 (A.B.3109), § 1, eff. Jan. 1, 2019. Amended by Stats.2019, c. 497 (A.B.991), § 25, eff. Jan. 1, 2020.)*

Title 4.5

LIQUIDATED DAMAGES

Chapter	Section
1. General Provisions	1671
2. Default on Real Property Purchase Contract	1675

CHAPTER 1. GENERAL PROVISIONS

Section
1671. Validity; standards for determination; applicability of section.
1672. Repealed.
1673. Repealed.
1674. Repealed.

§ 1671. Validity; standards for determination; applicability of section

(a) This section does not apply in any case where another statute expressly applicable to the contract prescribes the rules or standard for determining the validity of a provision in the contract liquidating the damages for the breach of the contract.

(b) Except as provided in subdivision (c), a provision in a contract liquidating the damages for the breach of the contract is valid unless the party seeking to invalidate the provision establishes that the provision was unreasonable under the circumstances existing at the time the contract was made.

(c) The validity of a liquidated damages provision shall be determined under subdivision (d) and not under subdivision (b) where the liquidated damages are sought to be recovered from either:

(1) A party to a contract for the retail purchase, or rental, by such party of personal property or services, primarily for the party's personal, family, or household purposes; or

(2) A party to a lease of real property for use as a dwelling by the party or those dependent upon the party for support.

(d) In the cases described in subdivision (c), a provision in a contract liquidating damages for the breach of the contract is void except that the parties to such a contract may agree therein upon an amount which shall be presumed to be the amount of damage sustained by a breach thereof, when, from the nature of the case, it would be impracticable or extremely difficult to fix the actual damage. *(Enacted in 1872. Amended by Stats.1977, c. 198, p. 718, § 5, operative July 1, 1978.)*

Cross References

Application of this section to leases of real property, see Civil Code § 1951.5.
Damages for breach of contract, see Civil Code § 3300 et seq.
Fish marketing contracts, authority to provide for liquidated damages, see Corporations Code § 13353.
Fraudulent sale of real estate by personal representative, see Probate Code § 10381.
Liquidated damages against contractor, delay in completion of project, public agency, see Government Code § 4215.
Liquidated damages by public officer, failure to comply with publication requirements, see Government Code § 6044.
Marketing association's agreements, see Food and Agricultural Code § 54264.
Personal property leases, liquidation of damages, see Commercial Code § 10504.
Sales contracts, liquidation or limitation of damages, see Commercial Code § 2718.
Specific performance, see Civil Code § 3389.

§ 1672. Repealed by Code Am.1873–74, c. 304, p. 242, § 191

§ 1673. Repealed by Stats.1941, c. 526, p. 1847, § 2

§ 1674. Repealed by Stats.1941, c. 526, p. 1847, § 2

CHAPTER 2. DEFAULT ON REAL PROPERTY PURCHASE CONTRACT

Section
1675. Residential property; failure of buyer to complete the purchase; validity of contract provisions; newly constructed attached condominium units.
1676. General validity of contract provisions.
1677. Requirements; validity of contract provisions.
1678. Multiple payments; liquidated damages under § 1675; requirements.
1679. Applicability of chapter; specified provisions.
1680. Specific performance; applicability of chapter.
1681. Real property sales contracts; applicability of chapter.

§ 1675. Residential property; failure of buyer to complete the purchase; validity of contract provisions; newly constructed attached condominium units

(a) As used in this section, "residential property" means real property primarily consisting of a dwelling that meets both of the following requirements:

(1) The dwelling contains not more than four residential units.

(2) At the time the contract to purchase and sell the property is made, the buyer intends to occupy the dwelling or one of its units as his or her residence.

(b) A provision in a contract to purchase and sell residential property that provides that all or any part of a payment made by the buyer shall constitute liquidated damages to the seller upon the buyer's failure to complete the purchase of the property is valid to the extent that payment in the form of cash or check, including a postdated check, is actually made if

§ 1675

the provision satisfies the requirements of Sections 1677 and 1678 and either subdivision (c) or (d) of this section.

(c) If the amount actually paid pursuant to the liquidated damages provision does not exceed 3 percent of the purchase price, the provision is valid to the extent that payment is actually made unless the buyer establishes that the amount is unreasonable as liquidated damages.

(d) If the amount actually paid pursuant to the liquidated damages provision exceeds 3 percent of the purchase price, the provision is invalid unless the party seeking to uphold the provision establishes that the amount actually paid is reasonable as liquidated damages.

(e) For the purposes of subdivisions (c) and (d), the reasonableness of an amount actually paid as liquidated damages shall be determined by taking into account both of the following:

(1) The circumstances existing at the time the contract was made.

(2) The price and other terms and circumstances of any subsequent sale or contract to sell and purchase the same property if the sale or contract is made within six months of the buyer's default.

(f)(1) Notwithstanding either subdivision (c) or (d), for the initial sale of newly constructed attached condominium units, as defined pursuant to Section 783, that involves the sale of an attached residential condominium unit located within a structure of 10 or more residential condominium units and the amount actually paid to the seller pursuant to the liquidated damages provision exceeds 3 percent of the purchase price of the residential unit in the transaction both of the following shall occur in the event of a buyer's default:

(A) The seller shall perform an accounting of its costs and revenues related to and fairly allocable to the construction and sale of the residential unit within 60 calendar days after the final close of escrow of the sale of the unit within the structure.

(B) The accounting shall include any and all costs and revenues related to the construction and sale of the residential property and any delay caused by the buyer's default. The seller shall make reasonable efforts to mitigate any damages arising from the default. The seller shall refund to the buyer any amounts previously retained as liquidated damages in excess of the greater of either 3 percent of the originally agreed-upon purchase price of the residential property or the amount of the seller's losses resulting from the buyer's default, as calculated by the accounting.

(2) The refund shall be sent to the buyer's last known address within 90 days after the final close of escrow of the sale or lease of all the residential condominium units within the structure.

(3) If the amount retained by the seller after the accounting does not exceed 3 percent of the purchase price, the amount is valid unless the buyer establishes that the amount is unreasonable as liquidated damages pursuant to subdivision (e).

(4) Subdivision (d) shall not apply to any dispute regarding the reasonableness of any amount retained as liquidated damages pursuant to this subdivision.

(5) Notwithstanding the time periods regarding the performance of the accounting set forth in paragraph (1), if a new qualified buyer has entered into a contract to purchase the residential property in question, the seller shall perform the accounting within 60 calendar days after a new qualified buyer has entered into a contract to purchase.

(6) As used in this subdivision, "structure" means either of the following:

(A) Improvements constructed on a common foundation.

(B) Improvements constructed by the same owner that must be constructed concurrently due to the design characteristics of the improvements or physical characteristics of the property on which the improvements are located.

(7) As used in this subdivision, "new qualified buyer" means a buyer who either:

(A) Has been issued a loan commitment, which satisfies the purchase agreement loan contingency requirement, by an institutional lender to obtain a loan for an amount equal to the purchase price less any downpayment possessed by the buyer.

(B) Has contracted to pay a purchase price that is greater than or equal to the purchase price to be paid by the original buyer.

(g) This section shall become operative on July 1, 2014. (Added by Stats.2008, c. 665 (A.B.2020), § 2, operative July 1, 2014.)

Cross References

Real estate, regulation of vacation ownership and time-shares, refund of money from prospective purchaser if escrow does not close, see Business and Professions Code § 11256.

§ 1676. General validity of contract provisions

Except as provided in Section 1675, a provision in a contract to purchase and sell real property liquidating the damages to the seller if the buyer fails to complete the purchase of the property is valid if it satisfies the requirements of Section 1677 and the requirements of subdivision (b) of Section 1671. (Added by Stats.1977, c. 198, p. 719, § 7, operative July 1, 1978.)

Cross References

Real estate, regulation of vacation ownership and time-shares, refund of money from prospective purchaser if escrow does not close, see Business and Professions Code § 11256.

§ 1677. Requirements; validity of contract provisions

A provision in a contract to purchase and sell real property liquidating the damages to the seller if the buyer fails to complete the purchase of the property is invalid unless:

(a) The provision is separately signed or initialed by each party to the contract; and

(b) If the provision is included in a printed contract, it is set out either in at least 10-point bold type or in contrasting red print in at least eight-point bold type. (Added by Stats.1977, c. 198, p. 719, § 7, operative July 1, 1978.)

Cross References

Real estate, regulation of vacation ownership and time-shares, refund of money from prospective purchaser if escrow does not close, see Business and Professions Code § 11256.

§ 1678. Multiple payments; liquidated damages under § 1675; requirements

If more than one payment made by the buyer is to constitute liquidated damages under Section 1675, the amount of any payment after the first payment is valid as liquidated damages only if (1) the total of all such payments satisfies the requirements of Section 1675 and (2) a separate liquidated damages provision satisfying the requirements of Section 1677 is separately signed or initialed by each party to the contract for each such subsequent payment. *(Added by Stats.1977, c. 198, p. 719, § 7, operative July 1, 1978.)*

Cross References

Real estate, regulation of vacation ownership and time-shares, refund of money from prospective purchaser if escrow does not close, see Business and Professions Code § 11256.

§ 1679. Applicability of chapter; specified provisions

This chapter applies only to a provision for liquidated damages to the seller if the buyer fails to complete the purchase of real property. The validity of any other provision for liquidated damages in a contract to purchase and sell real property shall be determined under Section 1671. *(Added by Stats.1977, c. 198, p. 719, § 7, operative July 1, 1978.)*

§ 1680. Specific performance; applicability of chapter

Nothing in this chapter affects any right a party to a contract for the purchase and sale of real property may have to obtain specific performance. *(Added by Stats.1977, c. 198, p. 719, § 7, operative July 1, 1978.)*

§ 1681. Real property sales contracts; applicability of chapter

This chapter does not apply to real property sales contracts as defined in Section 2985. *(Added by Stats.1977, c. 198, p. 719, § 7, operative July 1, 1978.)*

Title 5

EXTINCTION OF CONTRACTS

Chapter		Section
1.	Contracts, How Extinguished	1682
2.	Rescission	1688
2.1.	Dating Service Contracts	1694
2.2.	Weight Loss Contracts	1694.5
2.5.	Home Equity Sales Contracts	1695
3.	Modification and Cancellation	1697

CHAPTER 1. CONTRACTS, HOW EXTINGUISHED

Section
1682. Contract, extinguishment.

§ 1682. Contract, extinguishment

A contract may be extinguished in like manner with any other obligation, and also in the manner prescribed by this Title. *(Enacted in 1872.)*

Cross References

Cancellation of instruments, see Civil Code § 3412 et seq.
Jurisdiction of municipal and justice courts, see Code of Civil Procedure § 86.
Manner of creating contracts, see Civil Code § 1619 et seq.
Rejected offer in writing as equivalent to actual tender of money, instrument or property, see Code of Civil Procedure § 2074.
Substitution of obligations,
  By accord and satisfaction, see Civil Code § 1521 et seq.
  By novation, see Civil Code § 1530 et seq.
  By performance, see Civil Code § 1473 et seq.
  By release, see Civil Code § 1541 et seq.
Offer of performance, see Civil Code § 1485.

CHAPTER 2. RESCISSION

Section	
1688.	Extinguishment.
1689.	Grounds.
1689.2.	Endless chain scheme.
1689.3.	Dental services; contracts directly with office or plan; right to compensation.
1689.5.	Definitions.
1689.6.	Right to cancel home solicitation contracts or offers; "personal emergency response unit" defined.
1689.7.	Home solicitation contract or offer for purchase of personal emergency response unit; required statements relating to cancellation.
1689.8.	Liens on real property; home solicitation contracts; offers for home improvement goods or services; retail installment sales.
1689.9.	Goods affixed to realty; effect of subsequent sale or encumbrance of realty.
1689.10.	Tender by seller to buyer of payments or goods traded in; retention of and lien on goods delivered.
1689.11.	Tender by buyer to seller of goods delivered by seller pursuant to contract or offer.
1689.12.	Waiver or confession of judgment of provisions; voidness.
1689.13.	Conditions making §§ 1689.5, 1689.6, 1689.7, 1689.10, 1689.12 and 1689.14 not apply to a contract.
1689.14.	Repairs or restoration of residential premises damaged by a disaster.
1689.15.	Right of contractor to commence work on a service and repair project; necessary conditions; right of cancellation.
1689.20.	Seminar sales solicitation contracts or offers; cancellation rights and procedures.
1689.21.	Seminar sales contracts or offers; notice of cancellation; language and contents; copy to buyer.
1689.22.	Seller's tender of payments or evidence of indebtedness upon cancellation; buyer's rights in goods delivered by seller.
1689.23.	Buyer's tender of goods upon cancellation; duty of care; compensation of seller for services.
1689.24.	Definitions.
1690.	Stipulations against right; effect.
1691.	Procedure.
1692.	Relief based on rescission.

Section	
1693.	Effect upon relief of delay in notice of rescission or in restoration of benefits.

Cross References

Structural pest control operators, subcontracting, see Business and Professions Code § 8514.

§ 1688. Extinguishment

A contract is extinguished by its rescission. *(Enacted in 1872.)*

Cross References

Enforcement of contract by third party beneficiary prior to rescission, see Civil Code § 1559.
Insurance contracts,
    Cancellation, see Insurance Code § 660 et seq.
    Rescission, see Insurance Code §§ 650, 651 et seq.
Interior design contracts, see Business and Professions Code § 5807.
Jurisdiction of municipal and justice court, see Code of Civil Procedure § 86.

§ 1689. Grounds

(a) A contract may be rescinded if all the parties thereto consent.

(b) A party to a contract may rescind the contract in the following cases:

(1) If the consent of the party rescinding, or of any party jointly contracting with him, was given by mistake, or obtained through duress, menace, fraud, or undue influence, exercised by or with the connivance of the party as to whom he rescinds, or of any other party to the contract jointly interested with such party.

(2) If the consideration for the obligation of the rescinding party fails, in whole or in part, through the fault of the party as to whom he rescinds.

(3) If the consideration for the obligation of the rescinding party becomes entirely void from any cause.

(4) If the consideration for the obligation of the rescinding party, before it is rendered to him, fails in a material respect from any cause.

(5) If the contract is unlawful for causes which do not appear in its terms or conditions, and the parties are not equally at fault.

(6) If the public interest will be prejudiced by permitting the contract to stand.

(7) Under the circumstances provided for in Sections 39, 1533, 1566, 1785,[1] 1789,[2] 1930 and 2314 of this code, Section 2470 of the Corporations Code,[3] Sections 331, 338, 359, 447, 1904 and 2030 of the Insurance Code or any other statute providing for rescission. *(Enacted in 1872. Amended by Stats.1931, c. 1070, p. 2260, § 10; Stats.1961, c. 589, p. 1733, § 1.)*

[1] Repealed. See, now, Commercial Code § 2610.

[2] Former section repealed. See, now, Commercial Code §§ 2106, 2507, 2601, 2607, 2608, 2711, 2714, 2715, 2717.

[3] Repealed. See, now, Commercial Code §§ 8301, 8315.

Cross References

Anticipatory repudiation, see Commercial Code § 2610.
Buyer's cancellation of sales contract for breach, see Commercial Code § 2711.
Consent, see Civil Code § 1565 et seq.
Consent not real when obtained through duress, menace, fraud, undue influence or mistake, see Civil Code §§ 1567, 1568.
Consideration, see Civil Code § 1605 et seq.
Duress defined, see Civil Code § 1569.
Fraud defined,
    Generally, see Civil Code §§ 1572, 1573.
    Deceit, see Civil Code § 1710.
Grey market goods, grounds for rescission, see Civil Code § 1797.86.
Grounds for cancellation, see Civil Code § 3412.
Hiring of property, see Civil Code § 1930.
Insurance, rescission,
    Generally, see Insurance Code § 650 et seq.
    Alteration of use or condition of insured property, see Insurance Code § 2030.
    Concealment, see Insurance Code §§ 331, 338.
    Misrepresentations, see Insurance Code §§ 359, 1904.
    Warranty violations, see Insurance Code § 447.
Insurance contracts,
    Cancellation, see Insurance Code § 660 et seq.
    Rescission, see Insurance Code §§ 650, 651 et seq.
Joint or several promise or consideration,
    Generally, see Civil Code § 1430 et seq.
    Presumptions, see Civil Code §§ 1659, 1660.
Limitations period, see Code of Civil Procedure § 337 et seq.
Menace defined, see Civil Code § 1570.
Mistake, see Civil Code § 1576 et seq.
Novation, grounds for rescission, see Civil Code § 1533.
Person of unsound mind, see Civil Code § 39.
Purchase or obtaining vehicle subject to prior credit or lease, payment of prior obligation before sale, consignment or transfer, prior good faith notice, see Vehicle Code § 11709.4.
Rescission of ratification of act of agent, see Civil Code § 2314.
Restoration of benefits upon rescission, see Civil Code § 1691.
Revision of contracts due to fraud or mistake, see Civil Code § 3399 et seq.
Sales,
    Breach, repudiation and excuse, see Commercial Code § 2601 et seq.
    Modification, rescission and waiver, see Commercial Code § 2209.
    Remedies, see Commercial Code § 2701 et seq.
Seller's cancellation of sales contract for breach, see Commercial Code § 2703.
Stipulations against right to rescind, effect, see Civil Code § 1690.
Undue influence defined, see Civil Code § 1575.
Unlawful contracts, see Civil Code § 1667 et seq.
Writing disregarded for mistake, see Civil Code § 1640.

§ 1689.2. Endless chain scheme

A participant in an endless chain scheme, as defined in Section 327 of the Penal Code, may rescind the contract upon which the scheme is based, and may recover all consideration paid pursuant to the scheme, less any amounts paid or consideration provided to the participant pursuant to the scheme. In addition, the court may, upon motion, award reasonable attorney's fees to a prevailing plaintiff. *(Added by Stats.1989, c. 436, § 1.)*

§ 1689.3. Dental services; contracts directly with office or plan; right to compensation

Any patient who contracts directly with a dental office or plan for services may rescind the contract or plan until midnight of the third business day after the day on which the patient signs the contract or plan. If services have been provided to the patient, the dental office shall be entitled to compensation for those services. *(Added by Stats.1991, c. 596 (A.B.1283), § 2.)*

§ 1689.5. Definitions

As used in Sections 1689.6 to 1689.11, inclusive, and in Section 1689.14, all of the following definitions apply:

(a) "Home solicitation contract or offer" means any contract, whether single or multiple, or any offer which is subject to approval, for the sale, lease, or rental of goods or services or both, made at other than appropriate trade premises in an amount of twenty-five dollars ($25) or more, including any interest or service charges. "Home solicitation contract" does not include any contract under which the buyer has the right to rescind pursuant to Title 1, Chapter 2, Section 125 of the Federal Consumer Credit Protection Act (P.L. 90–321)[1] and the regulations promulgated pursuant thereto.

(b) "Appropriate trade premises," means premises where either the owner or seller normally carries on a business, or where goods are normally offered or exposed for sale in the course of a business carried on at those premises.

(c) "Goods" means tangible chattels bought for use primarily for personal, family, or household purposes, including certificates or coupons exchangeable for these goods, and including goods that, at the time of the sale or subsequently, are to be so affixed to real property as to become a part of the real property whether or not severable therefrom, but does not include any vehicle required to be registered under the Vehicle Code, nor any goods sold with this vehicle if sold under a contract governed by Section 2982, and does not include any mobilehome, as defined in Section 18008 of the Health and Safety Code, nor any goods sold with this mobilehome if either are sold under a contract subject to Section 18036.5 of the Health and Safety Code.

(d) "Services" means work, labor and services, including, but not limited to, services furnished in connection with the repair, restoration, alteration, or improvement of residential premises, or services furnished in connection with the sale or repair of goods as defined in Section 1802.1, and courses of instruction, regardless of the purpose for which they are taken, but does not include the services of attorneys, real estate brokers and salesmen, securities dealers or investment counselors, physicians, optometrists, or dentists, nor financial services offered by banks, savings institutions, credit unions, industrial loan companies, personal property brokers, consumer finance lenders, or commercial finance lenders, organized pursuant to state or federal law, that are not connected with the sale of goods or services, as defined herein, nor the sale of insurance that is not connected with the sale of goods or services as defined herein, nor services in connection with the sale or installation of mobilehomes or of goods sold with a mobilehome if either are sold or installed under a contract subject to Section 18036.5 of the Health and Safety Code, nor services for which the tariffs, rates, charges, costs, or expenses, including in each instance the time sale price, is required by law to be filed with and approved by the federal government or any official, department, division, commission, or agency of the United States or of the state.

(e) "Business day" means any calendar day except Sunday, or the following business holidays: New Year's Day, Washington's Birthday, Memorial Day, Independence Day, Labor Day, Columbus Day, Veterans' Day, Thanksgiving Day, and Christmas Day.

(f) "Senior citizen" means an individual who is 65 years of age or older. *(Added by Stats.1971, c. 375, p. 739, § 1. Amended by Stats.1972, c. 1415, p. 3078, § 2; Stats.1973, c. 554, p. 1076, § 1; Stats.1981, c. 975, p. 3721, § 1.5; Stats. 1985, c. 660, § 1; Stats.1986, c. 1229, § 2; Stats.1988, c. 1104, § 1; Stats.1993–94, 1st Ex.Sess., c. 51 (A.B.57), § 1; Stats. 2004, c. 566 (S.B.30), § 15, operative July 1, 2005; Stats.2005, c. 48 (S.B.1113), § 23, eff. July 18, 2005, operative Jan. 1, 2006; Stats.2020, c. 158 (A.B.2471), § 4, eff. Jan. 1, 2021.)*

[1] For public law sections classified to the U.S.C.A., see USCA–Tables.

Cross References

Committing crime substantially related to qualifications, functions or duties of a contractor, rehabilitation, see Business and Professions Code § 7073.
Conditions making this section not apply to a contract with respect to rescission, see Civil Code § 1689.13.
Contract defined, see Civil Code § 1549; Commercial Code § 1201.
Contract or offer subject to approval for the sale, lease, or rental of a water treatment device, see Business and Professions Code § 17577.3.
Emergencies and major disasters, unfair advantage of consumers, price controls and penalties, goods defined, see Penal Code § 396.
Emergency repairs or services exempt from this section, see Civil Code § 1689.13.
Employment of minors, door-to-door sales defined, minimum monetary limitation, see Labor Code § 1286.
Fire alarm sold in conjunction with an alarm system, see Business and Professions Code § 7159.9.
Goods, see Civil Code § 1802.1; Commercial Code § 2105.
Home improvement contracts,
    Alarm company licensees, see Business and Professions Code § 7159.
    Buyer's receipt of contract and rights to cancel, see Business and Professions Code § 7159.
    Goods or service defined, see Business and Professions Code § 7151.
Home solicitation contract or offer,
    Telephone sellers, information provided to prospective purchaser, see Business and Professions Code § 17511.5.
    Water treatment devices, expiration of rescission period, see Business and Professions Code § 17577.3.
Insurance contracts, solicitation, form of contract and notice of cancellation, business day defined, see Insurance Code § 15027.
Mortgage foreclosure consultants, owner's right to cancel contract with consultant until midnight of third "business day" as defined by provision of this section, see Civil Code § 2945.2.
Real estate, regulation of vacation ownership and time-share transactions, exemption from home solicitation sales requirements, see Business and Professions Code § 11211.7.
Service and repair contracts, application to home improvement contracts with alarm company operators, see Business and Professions Code § 7159.10.
Waiver of this section prohibited, see Civil Code § 1689.12.
Willful or deliberate disregard and violation of building laws, contractor disciplinary actions, see Business and Professions Code § 7110.

§ 1689.6. Right to cancel home solicitation contracts or offers; "personal emergency response unit" defined

(a)(1) Except for a contract written pursuant to Section 7151.2 or 7159.10 of the Business and Professions Code, in addition to any other right to revoke an offer, the buyer has the right to cancel a home solicitation contract or offer until midnight of the third business day, or until midnight of the fifth business day if the buyer is a senior citizen, after the day on which the buyer signs an agreement or offer to purchase which complies with Section 1689.7.

(2) In addition to any other right to revoke an offer, the buyer has the right to cancel a home solicitation contract written pursuant to Section 7151.2 of the Business and Professions Code until midnight of the third business day, or until midnight of the fifth business day if the buyer is a senior citizen, after the buyer receives a signed and dated copy of the contract or offer to purchase that complies with Section 1689.7 of this code.

(3)(A) In addition to any other right to revoke an offer, the buyer has the right to cancel a home solicitation contract or offer to purchase written pursuant to Section 7159.10 of the Business and Professions Code, until the buyer receives a signed and dated copy of a service and repair contract that complies with the contract requirements specified in Section 7159.10 of the Business and Professions Code and the work commences.

(B) For any contract written pursuant to Section 7159.10 of the Business and Professions Code, or otherwise presented to the buyer as a service and repair contract, unless all of the conforming requirements listed under subdivision (a) of that section are met, the requirements set forth under Section 7159 of the Business and Professions Code shall be applicable, regardless of the aggregate contract price, including the right to cancel as set forth under this section.

(4) The five-day right to cancel added by the act that amended paragraphs (1) and (2)[1] shall apply to contracts entered into, or offers to purchase conveyed, on or after January 1, 2021.

(b) In addition to any other right to revoke an offer, any buyer has the right to cancel a home solicitation contract or offer for the purchase of a personal emergency response unit until midnight of the seventh business day after the day on which the buyer signs an agreement or offer to purchase which complies with Section 1689.7. This subdivision shall not apply to a personal emergency response unit installed with, and as part of, a home security alarm system subject to the Alarm Company Act (Chapter 11.6 (commencing with Section 7590) of Division 3 of the Business and Professions Code) which has two or more stationary protective devices used to enunciate an intrusion or fire and is installed by an alarm company operator operating under a current license issued pursuant to the Alarm Company Act, which shall instead be subject to subdivision (a).

(c) In addition to any other right to revoke an offer, a buyer has the right to cancel a home solicitation contract or offer for the repair or restoration of residential premises damaged by a disaster that was not void pursuant to Section 1689.14, until midnight of the seventh business day after the buyer signs and dates the contract unless the provisions of Section 1689.15 are applicable.

(d) Cancellation occurs when the buyer gives written notice of cancellation to the seller at the address specified in the agreement or offer.

(e) Notice of cancellation, if given by mail, is effective when deposited in the mail properly addressed with postage prepaid.

(f) Notice of cancellation given by the buyer need not take the particular form as provided with the contract or offer to purchase and, however expressed, is effective if it indicates the intention of the buyer not to be bound by the home solicitation contract or offer.

(g) "Personal emergency response unit," for purposes of this section, means an in-home radio transmitter device or two-way radio device generally, but not exclusively, worn on a neckchain, wrist strap, or clipped to clothing, and connected to a telephone line through which a monitoring station is alerted of an emergency and emergency assistance is summoned. (Added by Stats.1971, c. 375, p. 740, § 2. Amended by Stats.1973, c. 554, p. 1077, § 2; Stats.1991, c. 394 (A.B. 585), § 1; Stats.1992, c. 145 (A.B.2378), § 1; Stats.1993–94, 1st Ex.Sess., c. 51 (A.B.57), § 2; Stats.2004, c. 566 (S.B.30), § 16, operative July 1, 2005; Stats.2005, c. 48 (S.B.1113), § 25, eff. July 18, 2005, operative Jan. 1, 2006; Stats.2005, c. 385 (A.B.316), § 11; Stats.2020, c. 158 (A.B.2471), § 5, eff. Jan. 1, 2021.)

[1] Stats.2020, c. 158 (A.B.2471), § 5, eff. Jan. 1, 2021.

Cross References

Business day defined for purposes of this section, see Civil Code § 1689.5.
Buyer, see Commercial Code § 2103.
Committing crime substantially related to qualifications, functions or duties of a contractor, rehabilitation, see Business and Professions Code § 7073.
Conditions making this section not apply to a contract with respect to rescission, see Civil Code § 1689.13.
Discount buying services, see Civil Code § 1812.100 et seq.
Emergency repairs or services exempt from this section, see Civil Code § 1689.13.
Fire alarm sold in conjunction with an alarm system, see Business and Professions Code § 7159.9.
Fixtures exempt from this section after sale or encumbrance of realty, see Civil Code § 1689.9.
Home improvement contracts, buyer's receipt of contract and rights to cancel, see Business and Professions Code § 7159.
Home solicitation contract or offer defined for purposes of this section, see Civil Code § 1689.5.
Private cemetery contracts, right of cancellation, see Health and Safety Code § 8278.
Real estate, regulation of vacation ownership and time-share transactions, exemption from home solicitation sales requirements, see Business and Professions Code § 11211.7.
Seller, see Commercial Code § 2103.
Service and repair contracts,
  Application to home improvement contracts with alarm company operators, see Business and Professions Code § 7159.10.
  Rights to rescind, see Business and Professions Code § 7159.10.
Speech-language pathologists and audiologists, unprofessional conduct based on violation of this section, see Business and Professions Code § 2533.
Tender required of buyer on cancellation, exceptions under this section, see Civil Code § 1689.11.
Tender required of seller on cancellation, exceptions under this section, see Civil Code § 1689.10.

Waiver of this section prohibited, see Civil Code § 1689.12.

Water treatment devices, home solicitation contract or offer, expiration of rescission period, see Business and Professions Code § 17577.3.

Willful or deliberate disregard and violation of building laws, contractor disciplinary actions, see Business and Professions Code § 7110.

§ 1689.7. Home solicitation contract or offer for purchase of personal emergency response unit; required statements relating to cancellation

(a)(1) Except for contracts written pursuant to Sections 7151.2 and 7159.10 of the Business and Professions Code, in a home solicitation contract or offer, the buyer's agreement or offer to purchase shall be written in the same language, e.g., Spanish, as principally used in the oral sales presentation, shall be dated, shall be signed by the buyer, and except as provided in paragraph (2), shall contain in immediate proximity to the space reserved for the buyer's signature, a conspicuous statement in a size equal to at least 10–point boldface type, as follows:

(A) For a buyer who is a senior citizen: "You, the buyer, may cancel this transaction at any time prior to midnight of the fifth business day after the date of this transaction. See the attached notice of cancellation form for an explanation of this right."

(B) For all other buyers: "You, the buyer, may cancel this transaction at any time prior to midnight of the third business day after the date of this transaction. See the attached notice of cancellation form for an explanation of this right."

(2) The statement required pursuant to this subdivision for a home solicitation contract or offer for the purchase of a personal emergency response unit, as defined in Section 1689.6, that is not installed with and as part of a home security alarm system subject to the Alarm Company Act (Chapter 11.6 (commencing with Section 7590) of Division 3 of the Business and Professions Code) that has two or more stationary protective devices used to enunciate an intrusion or fire and is installed by an alarm company operator operating under a current license issued pursuant to the Alarm Company Act, is as follows: "You, the buyer, may cancel this transaction at any time prior to midnight of the seventh business day after the date of this transaction. See the attached notice of cancellation form for an explanation of this right."

(3) Except for contracts written pursuant to Sections 7151.2 and 7159.10 of the Business and Professions Code, the statement required pursuant to this subdivision for the repair or restoration of residential premises damaged by a disaster pursuant to subdivision (c) of Section 1689.6 is as follows: "You, the buyer, may cancel this transaction at any time prior to midnight of the seventh business day after the date of this transaction. See the attached notice of cancellation form for an explanation of this right."

(4)(A) A home solicitation contract written pursuant to Section 7151.2 of the Business and Professions Code shall be written in the same language, e.g., Spanish, as principally used in the oral sales presentation. The contract, or an attachment to the contract that is subject to Section 7159 of the Business and Professions Code shall include in immediate proximity to the space reserved for the buyer's signature, the following statement in a size equal to at least 12–point boldface type, which shall be dated and signed by the buyer:

"Three-Day Right to Cancel

You, the buyer, have the right to cancel this contract within three business days. You may cancel by e-mailing, mailing, faxing, or delivering a written notice to the contractor at the contractor's place of business by midnight of the third business day after you received a signed and dated copy of the contract that includes this notice. Include your name, your address, and the date you received the signed copy of the contract and this notice.

If you cancel, the contractor must return to you anything you paid within 10 days of receiving the notice of cancellation. For your part, you must make available to the contractor at your residence, in substantially as good condition as you received it, any goods delivered to you under this contract or sale. Or, you may, if you wish, comply with the contractor's instructions on how to return the goods at the contractor's expense and risk. If you do make the goods available to the contractor and the contractor does not pick them up within 20 days of the date of your notice of cancellation, you may keep them without any further obligation. If you fail to make the goods available to the contractor, or if you agree to return the goods to the contractor and fail to do so, then you remain liable for performance of all obligations under the contract."

(B) References to "three" and "third" in the statement set forth in subparagraph (A) shall be changed to "five" and "fifth," respectively, for a buyer who is a senior citizen.

(b) The agreement or offer to purchase shall contain on the first page, in a type size no smaller than that generally used in the body of the document, the following: (1) the name and address of the seller to which the notice is to be mailed, and (2) the date the buyer signed the agreement or offer to purchase.

(c)(1) Except for contracts written pursuant to Sections 7151.2 and 7159.10 of the Business and Professions Code, or except as provided in subdivision (d), the agreement or offer to purchase shall be accompanied by a completed form in duplicate, captioned "Notice of Cancellation" which shall be attached to the agreement or offer to purchase and be easily detachable, and which shall contain in type of at least 10–point the following statement written in the same language, e.g., Spanish, as used in the contract:

"Notice of Cancellation"
/enter date of transaction/
_____
(Date)

"You may cancel this transaction, without any penalty or obligation, within three business days from the above date.

If you cancel, any property traded in, any payments made by you under the contract or sale, and any negotiable instrument executed by you will be returned within 10 days following receipt by the seller of your cancellation notice, and any security interest arising out of the transaction will be canceled.

If you cancel, you must make available to the seller at your residence, in substantially as good condition as when received, any goods delivered to you under this contract or sale,

§ 1689.7

or you may, if you wish, comply with the instructions of the seller regarding the return shipment of the goods at the seller's expense and risk.

If you do make the goods available to the seller and the seller does not pick them up within 20 days of the date of your notice of cancellation, you may retain or dispose of the goods without any further obligation. If you fail to make the goods available to the seller, or if you agree to return the goods to the seller and fail to do so, then you remain liable for performance of all obligations under the contract."

To cancel this transaction, mail or deliver a signed and dated copy of this cancellation notice, or any other written notice, or send a telegram

to _____
/name of seller/

at _____
/address of seller's place of business/

not later than midnight of _____
(Date)

I hereby cancel this transaction. _____
(Date)

_____
(Buyer's signature)

(2) The reference to "three" in the statement set forth in paragraph (1) shall be changed to "five" for a buyer who is a senior citizen.

(d) Any agreement or offer to purchase a personal emergency response unit, as defined in Section 1689.6, which is not installed with and as part of a home security alarm system subject to the Alarm Company Act which has two or more stationary protective devices used to enunciate an intrusion or fire and is installed by an alarm company operator operating under a current license issued pursuant to the Alarm Company Act, shall be subject to the requirements of subdivision (c), and shall be accompanied by the "Notice of Cancellation" required by subdivision (c), except that the first paragraph of that notice shall be deleted and replaced with the following paragraph:

You may cancel this transaction, without any penalty or obligation, within seven business days from the above date.

(e) A home solicitation contract written pursuant to Section 7151.2 of the Business and Professions Code for the repair or restoration of residential premises damaged by a disaster that is subject to subdivision (c) of Section 1689.6, shall be written in the same language, e.g., Spanish, as principally used in the oral sales presentation. The contract, or an attachment to the contract that is subject to Section 7159 of the Business and Professions Code shall include, in immediate proximity to the space reserved for the buyer's signature, the following statement in a size equal to at least 12–point boldface type, which shall be signed and dated by the buyer:

"Seven-Day Right to Cancel"

You, the buyer, have the right to cancel this contract within seven business days. You may cancel by e-mailing, mailing, faxing, or delivering a written notice to the contractor at the contractor's place of business by midnight of the seventh business day after you received a signed and dated copy of the contract that includes this notice. Include your name, your address, and the date you received the signed copy of the contract and this notice.

If you cancel, the contractor must return to you anything you paid within 10 days of receiving the notice of cancellation. For your part, you must make available to the contractor at your residence, in substantially as good condition as you received it, any goods delivered to you under this contract or sale. Or, you may, if you wish, comply with the contractor's instructions on how to return the goods at the contractor's expense and risk. If you do make the goods available to the contractor and the contractor does not pick them up within 20 days of the date of your notice of cancellation, you may keep them without any further obligation. If you fail to make the goods available to the contractor, or if you agree to return the goods to the contractor and fail to do so, then you remain liable for performance of all obligations under the contract."

(f) The seller shall provide the buyer with a copy of the contract or offer to purchase and the attached notice of cancellation, and shall inform the buyer orally of the buyer's right to cancel and the requirement that cancellation be in writing, at the time the home solicitation contract or offer is executed.

(g) Until the seller has complied with this section the buyer may cancel the home solicitation contract or offer.

(h) "Contract or sale" as used in subdivision (c) means "home solicitation contract or offer" as defined by Section 1689.5.

(i) The five-day right to cancel added by the act that added subparagraph (A) to paragraph (1) and subparagraph (B) to paragraph (4) of subdivision (a), and paragraph (2) to subdivision (c)[1] applies to contracts, or offers to purchase conveyed, entered into, on or after January 1, 2021. *(Added by Stats.1971, c. 375, p. 741, § 3. Amended by Stats.1973, c. 554, p. 1078, § 3; Stats.1974, c. 175, p. 348, § 1, eff. April 17, 1974; Stats.1991, c. 394 (A.B.585), § 2; Stats.1992, c. 145 (A.B.2378), § 2; Stats.1993, c. 589 (A.B.2211), § 22; Stats. 1993–94, 1st Ex.Sess., c. 51 (A.B.57), § 3; Stats.2004, c. 566 (S.B.30), § 17, operative July 1, 2005; Stats.2005, c. 48 (S.B.1113), § 27, eff. July 1, 2005, operative Jan. 1, 2006; Stats.2005, c. 385 (A.B.316), § 12; Stats.2020, c. 158 (A.B. 2471), § 6, eff. Jan. 1, 2021; Stats.2021, c. 124 (A.B.938), § 4, eff. Jan. 1, 2022.)*

[1] Stats.2020, c. 158 (A.B.2471), § 6, eff. Jan. 1, 2021.

Cross References

Buyer, see Commercial Code § 2103.
Committing crime substantially related to qualifications, functions or duties of a contractor, rehabilitation, see Business and Professions Code § 7073.
Conditions making this section not apply to a contract with respect to rescission, see Civil Code § 1689.13.
Discount buying services, see Civil Code § 1812.100 et seq.
Emergency repairs or services exempt from this section, see Civil Code § 1689.13.
Fire alarm sold in conjunction with an alarm system, see Business and Professions Code § 7159.9.
Fixtures exempt from this section after sale or encumbrance of realty, see Civil Code § 1689.9.
Home improvement contracts, buyer's receipt of contract and rights to cancel, see Business and Professions Code § 7159.
Home solicitation contract or offer defined, see Civil Code § 1689.5.
Private cemetery contracts, right of cancellation, see Health and Safety Code § 8278.

Real estate, regulation of vacation ownership and time-share transactions, exemption from home solicitation sales requirements, see Business and Professions Code § 11211.7.
Seller, see Commercial Code § 2103.
Service and repair contracts,
  Application to home improvement contracts with alarm company operators, see Business and Professions Code § 7159.10.
  Costs, charges, payments, and cancellation, see Civil Code § 1759.13.
  Rights to rescind, see Business and Professions Code § 7159.10.
Tender required of buyer or cancellation, exception under this section, see Civil Code § 1689.11.
Tender required of seller on cancellation, exceptions under this section, see Civil Code § 1689.10.
Waiver of this section prohibited, see Civil Code § 1689.12.
Water treatment devices, home solicitation contract or offer, expiration of rescission period, see Business and Professions Code § 17577.3.

§ 1689.8. Liens on real property; home solicitation contracts; offers for home improvement goods or services; retail installment sales

(a) Every home solicitation contract or offer for home improvement goods or services which provides for a lien on real property is subject to the provisions of Chapter 1 (commencing with Section 1801) of Title 2 of Part 4 of Division 3.

(b) For purposes of this section, "home improvement goods or services" means goods and services, as defined in Section 1689.5, which are bought in connection with the improvement of real property. Such home improvement goods and services include, but are not limited to, burglar alarms, carpeting, texture coating, fencing, air conditioning or heating equipment, and termite extermination. Home improvement goods include goods which, at the time of sale or subsequently, are to be so affixed to real property as to become a part of real property whether or not severable therefrom. *(Added by Stats.1979, c. 1012, p. 3439, § 6.)*

Cross References

Home improvement contracts for specified transactions, buyer's receipt of contract and rights to cancel, see Business and Professions Code § 7159.
Private cemetery contracts, right of cancellation, see Health and Safety Code § 8278.
Real estate, regulation of vacation ownership and time-share transactions, exemption from home solicitation sales requirements, see Business and Professions Code § 11211.7.
Tender required of buyer on cancellation, exceptions under this section, see Civil Code § 1689.11.
Tender required of seller on cancellation, exceptions under this section, see Civil Code § 1689.10.
Waiver of this section prohibited, see Civil Code § 1689.12.
Water treatment devices, home solicitation contract or offer, expiration of rescission period, see Business and Professions Code § 17577.3.
Willful or deliberate disregard and violation of building laws, contractor disciplinary actions, see Business and Professions Code § 7110.

§ 1689.9. Goods affixed to realty; effect of subsequent sale or encumbrance of realty

Where the goods sold under any home solicitation contract are so affixed to real property as to become a part thereof, whether or not severable therefrom, the buyer shall not have the right to cancel as provided in Section 1689.6 or Section 1689.7 if, subsequent to his signing such contract, he has sold or encumbered such real property to a bona fide purchaser or encumbrancer who was not a party to such sale of goods or to any loan agreement in connection therewith. *(Added by Stats.1971, c. 375, p. 741, § 5.)*

Cross References

Buyer, see Commercial Code § 2103.
Fixtures defined, see Civil Code § 660.
Goods, see Civil Code §§ 1689.5, 1802.1; Commercial Code § 2105.
Home improvement contracts for specified transactions, buyer's receipt of contract and rights to cancel, see Business and Professions Code § 7159.
Home solicitation contract or offer defined, see Civil Code § 1689.5.
Incumbrances defined, see Civil Code § 1114.
Lien defined, see Civil Code § 2872; Code of Civil Procedure § 1180.
Private cemetery contracts, right of cancellation, see Health and Safety Code § 8278.
Real estate, regulation of vacation ownership and time-share transactions, exemption from home solicitation sales requirements, see Business and Professions Code § 11211.7.
Seller, see Commercial Code § 2103.
Tender required of buyer on cancellation, exceptions under this section, see Civil Code § 1689.11.
Waiver of this section prohibited, see Civil Code § 1689.12.
Water treatment devices, home solicitation contract or offer, expiration of rescission period, see Business and Professions Code § 17577.3.
Willful or deliberate disregard and violation of building laws, contractor disciplinary actions, see Business and Professions Code § 7110.

§ 1689.10. Tender by seller to buyer of payments or goods traded in; retention of and lien on goods delivered

(a) Except as provided in Sections 1689.6 to 1689.11, inclusive, within 10 days after a home solicitation contract or offer has been canceled, the seller must tender to the buyer any payments made by the buyer and any note or other evidence of indebtedness.

(b) If the downpayment includes goods traded in, the goods must be tendered in substantially as good condition as when received.

(c) Until the seller has complied with the obligations imposed by Sections 1689.7 to 1689.11, inclusive, the buyer may retain possession of goods delivered to him by the seller and has a lien on the goods for any recovery to which he is entitled. *(Added by Stats.1971, c. 375, p. 742, § 6. Amended by Stats.1973, c. 554, p. 1079, § 5.)*

Cross References

Conditions making this section not apply to a contract with respect to rescission, see Civil Code § 1689.13.
Home improvement contracts for specified transactions, buyer's receipt of contract and rights to cancel, see Business and Professions Code § 7159.
Home solicitation contract or offer defined, see Civil Code § 1689.5.
Objection to tender, see Code of Civil Procedure § 2076.
Private cemetery contracts, right of cancellation, see Health and Safety Code § 8278.
Real estate, regulation of vacation ownership and time-share transactions, exemption from home solicitation sales requirements, see Business and Professions Code § 11211.7.

§ 1689.10 OBLIGATIONS

Rejected offer as equivalent to tender of property, see Code of Civil Procedure § 2074.
Waiver of this section prohibited, see Civil Code § 1689.12.
Water treatment devices, home solicitation contract or offer, expiration of rescission period, see Business and Professions Code § 17577.3.
Willful or deliberate disregard and violation of building laws, contractor disciplinary actions, see Business and Professions Code § 7110.

§ 1689.11. Tender by buyer to seller of goods delivered by seller pursuant to contract or offer

(a) Except as provided in subdivision (c) of Section 1689.10, within 20 days after a home solicitation contract or offer has been canceled, the buyer, upon demand, must tender to the seller any goods delivered by the seller pursuant to the sale or offer, but he is not obligated to tender at any place other than his own address. If the seller fails to demand possession of goods within 20 days after cancellation, the goods become the property of the buyer without obligation to pay for them.

(b) The buyer has a duty to take reasonable care of the goods in his possession both prior to cancellation and during the 20-day period following. During the 20-day period after cancellation, except for the buyer's duty of care, the goods are at the seller's risk.

(c) If the seller has performed any services pursuant to a home solicitation contract or offer prior to its cancellation, the seller is entitled to no compensation. If the seller's services result in the alteration of property of the buyer, the seller shall restore the property to substantially as good condition as it was at the time the services were rendered. *(Added by Stats.1971, c. 375, p. 742, § 7. Amended by Stats.1973, c. 554, p. 1079, § 6.)*

Cross References

Goods, see Civil Code §§ 1689.5, 1802.1; Commercial Code § 2105.
Home improvement contracts for specified transactions, buyer's receipt of contract and rights to cancel, see Business and Professions Code § 7159.
Home solicitation contract or offer defined, see Civil Code § 1689.5.
Private cemetery contracts, right of cancellation, see Health and Safety Code § 8278.
Real estate, regulation of vacation ownership and time-share transactions, exemption from home solicitation sales requirements, see Business and Professions Code § 11211.7.
Rejected offer as equivalent to tender of property, see Code of Civil Procedure § 2074.
Services, see Civil Code § 1689.5.
Time for objection to tender, see Code of Civil Procedure § 2076.
Water treatment devices, home solicitation contract or offer, expiration of rescission period, see Business and Professions Code § 17577.3.
Willful or deliberate disregard and violation of building laws, contractor disciplinary actions, see Business and Professions Code § 7110.

§ 1689.12. Waiver or confession of judgment of provisions; voidness

Any waiver or confession of judgment of the provisions of Sections 1689.5 to 1689.11, inclusive, shall be deemed contrary to public policy and shall be void and unenforceable. *(Added by Stats.1971, c. 375, p. 743, § 8. Amended by Stats.1973, c. 554, p. 1080, § 7.)*

Cross References

Conditions making this section not apply to a contract with respect to rescission, see Civil Code § 1689.13.
Effect of certain stipulations against right to rescind, see Civil Code § 1690.
Home improvement contracts for specified transactions, buyer's receipt of contract and rights to cancel, see Business and Professions Code § 7159.
Partial nullity of contract with void provision, see Civil Code § 1599.
Real estate, regulation of vacation ownership and time-share transactions, exemption from home solicitation sales requirements, see Business and Professions Code § 11211.7.
Waiver of code provisions, see Civil Code § 3268.
Water treatment devices, home solicitation contract or offer, expiration of rescission period, see Business and Professions Code § 17577.3.
Willful or deliberate disregard and violation of building laws, contractor disciplinary actions, see Business and Professions Code § 7110.

§ 1689.13. Conditions making §§ 1689.5, 1689.6, 1689.7, 1689.10, 1689.12 and 1689.14 not apply to a contract

Sections 1689.5, 1689.6, 1689.7, 1689.10, 1689.12, and 1689.14 do not apply to a contract that meets all of the following requirements:

(a) The contract is initiated by the buyer or the buyer's agent or insurance representative.

(b) The contract is executed in connection with making of emergency or immediately necessary repairs that are necessary for the immediate protection of persons or real or personal property.

(c)(1) The buyer gives the seller a separate statement that is dated and signed that describes the situation that requires immediate remedy, and expressly acknowledges and waives the right to cancel the sale within three, five, or seven business days, whichever applies.

(2) The waiver of the five-day right to cancel added by the act that amended paragraph (1) shall apply to contracts entered into, or offers to purchase conveyed, on or after January 1, 2021. *(Added by Stats.2004, c. 566 (S.B.30), § 19, operative July 1, 2005. Amended by Stats.2005, c. 48 (S.B. 1113), § 29, eff. July 18, 2005, operative Jan. 1, 2006; Stats.2020, c. 158 (A.B.2471), § 7, eff. Jan. 1, 2021.)*

Cross References

Committing crime substantially related to qualifications, functions or duties of a contractor, rehabilitation, see Business and Professions Code § 7073.
Home improvement contracts for specified transactions, buyer's receipt of contract and rights to cancel, see Business and Professions Code § 7159.
Real estate, regulation of vacation ownership and time-share transactions, exemption from home solicitation sales requirements, see Business and Professions Code § 11211.7.
Water treatment devices, home solicitation contract or offer, expiration of rescission period, see Business and Professions Code § 17577.3.
Willful or deliberate disregard and violation of building laws, contractor disciplinary actions, see Business and Professions Code § 7110.

§ 1689.14. Repairs or restoration of residential premises damaged by a disaster

(a) Any home solicitation contract or offer for the repair or restoration of residential premises signed by the buyer on or after the date on which a disaster causes damage to the residential premises, but not later than midnight of the seventh business day after this date, shall be void, unless the buyer or his or her agent or insurance representative solicited the contract or offer at the appropriate trade premises of the seller. Any contract covered by this subdivision shall not be void if solicited by the buyer or his or her agent or insurance representative regardless of where the contract is made. For purposes of this section, buyer solicitation includes a telephone call from the buyer to the appropriate trade premises of the seller whether or not the call is in response to a prior home solicitation.

(b) As used in this section and Section 1689.6, "disaster" means an earthquake, flood, fire, hurricane, riot, storm, tidal wave, or other similar sudden or catastrophic occurrence for which a state of emergency has been declared by the President of the United States or the Governor or for which a local emergency has been declared by the executive officer or governing body of any city, county, or city and county. (Added by Stats.1993–94, 1st Ex.Sess., c. 51 (A.B.57), § 5. Amended by Stats.1995, c. 123 (A.B.1610), § 1, eff. July 18, 1995.)

Cross References

Appropriate trade premises defined for purposes of this section, see Civil Code § 1689.5.
Business day defined for purposes of this section, see Civil Code § 1689.5.
Conditions making this section not apply to a contract with respect to rescission, see Civil Code § 1689.13.
Home improvement contracts for specified transactions, buyer's receipt of contract and rights to cancel, see Business and Professions Code § 7159.
Home solicitation contract or offer defined for purposes of this section, see Civil Code § 1689.5.
Real estate, regulation of vacation ownership and time-share transactions, exemption from home solicitation sales requirements, see Business and Professions Code § 11211.7.
Solicitation of contract of engagement after a disaster, see Insurance Code § 15027.1.
Total loss to primary insured structure under a residential policy, disasters, see Insurance Code § 675.1.
Willful or deliberate disregard and violation of building laws, contractor disciplinary actions, see Business and Professions Code § 7110.

§ 1689.15. Right of contractor to commence work on a service and repair project; necessary conditions; right of cancellation

Notwithstanding any other provision of law, a contractor who is duly licensed pursuant to Chapter 9 (commencing with Section 7000) of Division 3 of the Business and Professions Code may commence work on a service and repair project as soon as the buyer receives a signed and dated copy of a service and repair contract that meets all of the contract requirements specified in Section 7159.10 of the Business and Professions Code. The buyer retains any right of cancellation applicable to home solicitations under Sections 1689.5 to 1689.14, inclusive, until such time as the buyer receives a signed and dated copy of a service and repair contract that meets all of the contract requirements specified in Section 7159.10 of the Business and Professions Code and the licensee in fact commences that project, at which time any cancellation rights provided in Sections 1689.5 to 1689.14, inclusive, are extinguished by operation of law. (Added by Stats.2004, c. 566 (S.B.30), § 20, operative July 1, 2005. Amended by Stats.2005, c. 48 (S.B.1113), § 30, eff. July 18, 2005, operative Jan. 1, 2006; Stats.2005, c. 385 (A.B.316), § 13.)

Operative Effect

Stats.2005, c. 48 (S.B.1113), was enacted and immediately effective on July 18, 2005. Stats.2004, c. 566 (S.B.30), became operative on July 1, 2005, by terms of § 21 of that act. Section 31 of c. 48 repealed Stats.2004, c. 566, § 21. The general effective date for 2004 regular session laws is Jan. 1, 2005.

Cross References

Committing crime substantially related to qualifications, functions or duties of a contractor, rehabilitation, see Business and Professions Code § 7073.
Willful or deliberate disregard and violation of building laws, contractor disciplinary actions, see Business and Professions Code § 7110.

§ 1689.20. Seminar sales solicitation contracts or offers; cancellation rights and procedures

(a)(1) In addition to any other right to revoke an offer, the buyer has the right to cancel a seminar sales solicitation contract or offer until midnight of the third business day, or until midnight of the fifth business day if the buyer is a senior citizen, after the day on which the buyer signs an agreement or offer to purchase which complies with Section 1689.21.

(2) The five-day right to cancel added by the act that amended paragraph (1)[1] shall apply to contracts entered into, or offers to purchase conveyed, on or after January 1, 2021.

(b) Cancellation occurs when the buyer gives written notice of cancellation to the seller at the address specified in the agreement or offer.

(c) Notice of cancellation, if given by mail, is effective when deposited in the mail properly addressed with postage prepaid.

(d) Notice of cancellation given by the buyer need not take the particular form as provided with the contract or offer to purchase and, however expressed, is effective if it indicates the intention of the buyer not to be bound by the seminar sales solicitation contract or offer. (Added by Stats.1989, c. 724, § 1. Amended by Stats.2020, c. 158 (A.B.2471), § 8, eff. Jan. 1, 2021.)

[1] Stats.2020, c. 158 (A.B.2471), § 8, eff. Jan. 1, 2021.

Cross References

Real estate, regulation of vacation ownership and time-share transactions, exemption from home seminar sales requirements, see Business and Professions Code § 11211.7.

§ 1689.21. Seminar sales contracts or offers; notice of cancellation; language and contents; copy to buyer

(a) In a seminar sales solicitation contract or offer, the buyer's agreement or offer to purchase shall be written in the

§ 1689.21

same language, e.g., Spanish, as principally used in the oral sales presentation, shall be dated, signed by the buyer, and shall contain in immediate proximity to the space reserved for the buyer's signature, a conspicuous statement in a size equal to at least 10–point bold type, as follows:

(1) For a buyer who is a senior citizen: "You, the buyer, may cancel this transaction at any time prior to midnight of the fifth business day after the date of this transaction. See the attached notice of cancellation form for an explanation of this right."

(2) For all other buyers: "You, the buyer, may cancel this transaction at any time prior to midnight of the third business day after the date of this transaction. See the attached notice of cancellation form for an explanation of this right."

(b) The agreement or offer to purchase shall contain on the first page, in a type size no smaller than that generally used in the body of the document, each of the following:

(1) The name and address of the seller to which the notice is to be mailed.

(2) The date the buyer signed the agreement or offer to purchase.

(c)(1) The agreement or offer to purchase shall be accompanied by a completed form in duplicate, captioned "Notice of Cancellation," which shall be attached to the agreement or offer to purchase and be easily detachable, and which shall contain in type of at least 10–point, the following statement written in the same language, e.g., Spanish, as used in the contract:

"Notice of Cancellation"

/enter date of transaction/
_____
(Date)

You may cancel this transaction, without any penalty or obligation, within three business days from the above date.

If you cancel, any property traded in, any payments made by you under the contract or sale, and any negotiable instrument executed by you will be returned within 10 days following receipt by the seller of your cancellation notice, and any security interest arising out of the transaction will be canceled.

If you cancel, you must make available to the seller at your residence, in substantially as good condition as when received, any goods delivered to you under this contract or sale, or you may, if you wish, comply with the instructions of the seller regarding the return shipment of the goods at the seller's expense and risk.

If you do make the goods available to the seller and the seller does not pick them up within 20 days of the date of your notice of cancellation, you may retain or dispose of the goods without any further obligation. If you fail to make the goods available to the seller, or if you agree to return the goods to the seller and fail to do so, then you remain liable for performance of all obligations under the contract.

To cancel this transaction, mail or deliver a signed and dated copy of this cancellation notice, or any other written notice, or send a telegram to

_____ at _____
/name of seller/   /Address of sellers place of business/

OBLIGATIONS

not later than midnight of _____
                                (Date)

I hereby cancel this transaction _____
                                      (Date)

_____
(Buyer's signature)

(2) The reference to "three" in the statement set forth in paragraph (1) shall be changed to "five" for a buyer who is a senior citizen.

(d) The seller shall provide the buyer with a copy of the contract or offer to purchase and the attached notice of cancellation, and shall inform the buyer orally of the buyer's right to cancel at the time the seminar sales solicitation contract or offer is executed.

(e) Until the seller has complied with this section, the buyer may cancel the seminar sales solicitation contract or offer.

(f) "Contract or sale" as used in subdivision (c), means "seminar sales solicitation contract or offer" as defined by Section 1689.24.

(g) The five-day right to cancel added by the act that added paragraph (1) to subdivision (a) and added paragraph (2) to subdivision (c)[1] shall apply to contracts entered into or offers to purchase conveyed on or after January 1, 2021. *(Added by Stats.1989, c. 724, § 2. Amended by Stats.2020, c. 158 (A.B.2471), § 9, eff. Jan. 1, 2021.)*

[1] Stats.2020, c. 158 (A.B.2471), § 9, eff. Jan. 1, 2021.

Cross References

Real estate, regulation of vacation ownership and time-share transactions, exemption from home seminar sales requirements, see Business and Professions Code § 11211.7.

§ 1689.22. Seller's tender of payments or evidence of indebtedness upon cancellation; buyer's rights in goods delivered by seller

(a) Except as provided in Sections 1689.20 and 1689.21, within 10 days after a seminar sales solicitation contract or offer has been cancelled, the seller must tender to the buyer any payments made by the buyer and any note or other evidence of indebtedness.

(b) If the downpayment includes goods traded in, the goods must be tendered in substantially as good condition as when received.

(c) Until the seller has complied with the obligations imposed by Sections 1689.20 and 1689.21, the buyer may retain possession of goods delivered to him or her by the seller and has a lien on the goods for any recovery to which he or she is entitled. *(Added by Stats.1989, c. 724, § 3.)*

Cross References

Real estate, regulation of vacation ownership and time-share transactions, exemption from home seminar sales requirements, see Business and Professions Code § 11211.7.

§ 1689.23. Buyer's tender of goods upon cancellation; duty of care; compensation of seller for services

(a) Except as provided in subdivision (c) of Section 1689.22, within 20 days after a seminar sales solicitation contract or offer has been canceled, the buyer, upon demand, must tender to the seller any goods delivered by the seller pursuant to the sale or offer, but he or she is not obligated to tender at any place other than his or her own address. If the seller fails to demand possession of goods within 20 days after cancellation, the goods become the property of the buyer without obligation to pay for them.

(b) The buyer has a duty to take reasonable care of the goods in his or her possession, both prior to cancellation and during the 20-day period following. During the 20-day period after cancellation, except for the buyer's duty of care, the goods are at the seller's risk.

(c) If the seller has performed any services pursuant to a seminar sales solicitation contract or offer prior to its cancellation, the seller is entitled to no compensation. If the seller's services result in the alteration of property of the buyer, the seller shall restore the property to substantially as good condition as it was at the time the services were rendered. *(Added by Stats.1989, c. 724, § 4.)*

Cross References

Real estate, regulation of vacation ownership and time-share transactions, exemption from home seminar sales requirements, see Business and Professions Code § 11211.7.

§ 1689.24. Definitions

As used in Sections 1689.20 to 1689.23, inclusive:

(a) "Seminar sales solicitation contract or offer" means any contract, whether single or multiple, or any offer which is subject to approval, for the sale, lease, or rental of goods or services or both, made using selling techniques in a seminar setting in an amount of twenty-five dollars ($25) or more, including any interest or service charges. "Seminar sales solicitation contract" does not include any contract under which the buyer has the right to rescind pursuant to Title 1, Chapter 2, Section 125 of the Federal Consumer Credit Protection Act (Public Law 90–321)[1] and the regulations promulgated pursuant thereto or any contract which contains a written and dated statement signed by the prospective buyer stating that the negotiation between the parties was initiated by the prospective buyer.

(b) "Seminar setting" means premises other than the residence of the buyer.

(c) "Goods" means tangible chattels bought for use primarily for personal, family, or household purposes, including certificates or coupons exchangeable for these goods, and including goods which, at the time of the sale or subsequently, are to be so affixed to real property as to become a part of the real property whether or not severable therefrom, but does not include any vehicle required to be registered under the Vehicle Code, nor any goods sold with a vehicle if sold under a contract governed by Section 2982, and does not include any mobilehome, as defined in Section 18008 of the Health and Safety Code, nor any goods sold with a mobilehome if either are sold under a contract subject to Section 18036.5 of the Health and Safety Code.

(d) "Services" means work, labor and services, including, but not limited to, services furnished in connection with the repair, alteration, or improvement of residential premises, or services furnished in connection with the sale or repair of goods as defined in Section 1802.1, and courses of instruction, regardless of the purpose for which they are taken, but does not include the services of attorneys, real estate brokers and salesmen, securities dealers or investment counselors, physicians, optometrists, or dentists, nor financial services offered by banks, savings institutions, credit unions, industrial loan companies, personal property brokers, consumer finance lenders, or commercial finance lenders, organized pursuant to state or federal law, which are not connected with the sale of goods or services, as defined herein, nor the sale of insurance which is not connected with the sale of goods or services as defined herein, nor services in connection with the sale or installation of mobilehomes or of goods sold with a mobilehome if either are sold or installed under a contract subject to Section 18036.5 of the Health and Safety Code, nor services for which the tariffs, rates, charges, costs, or expenses, including in each instance the time sale price, is required by law to be filed with and approved by the federal government or any official, department, division, commission, or agency of the United States or of the State of California.

(e) "Business day" means any calendar day except Sunday, or the following business holidays: New Year's Day, Washington's Birthday, Memorial Day, Independence Day, Labor Day, Columbus Day, Veterans' Day, Thanksgiving Day, and Christmas Day.

(f) "Senior citizen" means an individual who is 65 years of age or older. *(Added by Stats.1989, c. 724, § 5. Amended by Stats.2020, c. 158 (A.B.2471), § 10, eff. Jan. 1, 2021.)*

[1] 15 U.S.C.A. § 1635.

Cross References

Real estate, regulation of vacation ownership and time-share transactions, exemption from home seminar sales requirements, see Business and Professions Code § 11211.7.

§ 1690. Stipulations against right; effect

A stipulation that errors of description shall not avoid a contract, or shall be the subject of compensation, or both, does not take away the right of rescission for fraud, nor for mistake, where such mistake is in a matter essential to the inducement of the contract, and is not capable of exact and entire compensation. *(Enacted in 1872.)*

Cross References

Effect of consent, see Civil Code § 3515.
Prohibited waivers, see Civil Code § 1689.12.
Waiver of Code provisions, see Civil Code § 3268.

§ 1691. Procedure

Subject to Section 1693, to effect a rescission a party to the contract must, promptly upon discovering the facts which entitle him to rescind if he is free from duress, menace, undue influence or disability and is aware of his right to rescind:

(a) Give notice of rescission to the party as to whom he rescinds; and

(b) Restore to the other party everything of value which he has received from him under the contract or offer to restore the same upon condition that the other party do likewise, unless the latter is unable or positively refuses to do so.

When notice of rescission has not otherwise been given or an offer to restore the benefits received under the contract

§ 1691

has not otherwise been made, the service of a pleading in an action or proceeding that seeks relief based on rescission shall be deemed to be such notice or offer or both. *(Enacted in 1872. Amended by Stats.1961, c. 589, p. 1734, § 2.)*

Cross References

Cancellation of written instruments, see Civil Code § 3412.
Constructive notice of particular facts, see Civil Code § 19.
Delay in giving notice of rescission or in tendering restoration, see Civil Code § 1693.
Disability of persons of unsound mind, see Civil Code § 40.
Duress defined, see Civil Code § 1569.
Insurance contracts,
   Cancellation, see Insurance Code § 660 et seq.
   Rescission, see Insurance Code §§ 650, 651 et seq.
Limitation of actions, see Code of Civil Procedure §§ 337, 339.
Menace defined, see Civil Code § 1570.
Nonperformance, right of other party to enforce contract without performing conditions, see Civil Code § 1440.
Notice defined, see Commercial Code § 1201.
Recovery of possession of,
   Personal property, see Civil Code § 3379 et seq.
   Real property, see Civil Code § 3375.
Relief from forfeiture, see Civil Code § 3275.
Restrictions of minors, see Family Code § 6701.
Undue influence defined, see Civil Code § 1575.

§ 1692. Relief based on rescission

When a contract has been rescinded in whole or in part, any party to the contract may seek relief based upon such rescission by (a) bringing an action to recover any money or thing owing to him by any other party to the contract as a consequence of such rescission or for any other relief to which he may be entitled under the circumstances or (b) asserting such rescission by way of defense or cross-complaint.

If in an action or proceeding a party seeks relief based upon rescission and the court determines that the contract has not been rescinded, the court may grant any party to the action any other relief to which he may be entitled under the circumstances.

A claim for damages is not inconsistent with a claim for relief based upon rescission. The aggrieved party shall be awarded complete relief, including restitution of benefits, if any, conferred by him as a result of the transaction and any consequential damages to which he is entitled; but such relief shall not include duplicate or inconsistent items of recovery.

If in an action or proceeding a party seeks relief based upon rescission, the court may require the party to whom such relief is granted to make any compensation to the other which justice may require and may otherwise in its judgment adjust the equities between the parties. *(Added by Stats.1961, c. 589, p. 1734, § 3. Amended by Stats.1971, c. 244, p. 373, § 1, operative July 1, 1972.)*

Cross References

Counterclaim treated as cross-complaint, see Code of Civil Procedure § 428.80.
Purchaser's lien for amount paid, see Civil Code § 3050.

Transfer of obligations, see Civil Code § 1457 et seq.

§ 1693. Effect upon relief of delay in notice of rescission or in restoration of benefits

When relief based upon rescission is claimed in an action or proceeding, such relief shall not be denied because of delay in giving notice of rescission unless such delay has been substantially prejudicial to the other party.

A party who has received benefits by reason of a contract that is subject to rescission and who in an action or proceeding seeks relief based upon rescission shall not be denied relief because of a delay in restoring or in tendering restoration of such benefits before judgment unless such delay has been substantially prejudicial to the other party; but the court may make a tender of restoration a condition of its judgment. *(Added by Stats.1961, c. 589, p. 1735, § 4.)*

Cross References

Notice of rescission, see Civil Code § 1691.

CHAPTER 2.1. DATING SERVICE CONTRACTS

Section
1694. Dating service contract; definition.
1694.1. Cancellation; notice; refund.
1694.2. Contract form and content.
1694.3. Death, disability, or relocation.
1694.4. Noncompliance with chapter; fraud; civil action; installment contracts; refund; waiver.

§ 1694. Dating service contract; definition

(a) As used in this chapter, a dating service contract is any contract with any organization that offers dating, matrimonial, or social referral services by any of the following means:

(1) An exchange of names, telephone numbers, addresses, and statistics.

(2) A photograph or video selection process.

(3) Personal introductions provided by the organization at its place of business.

(4) A social environment provided by the organization intended primarily as an alternative to other singles' bars or club-type environments.

(b) As used in this chapter, an "online dating service" means any person or organization engaged in the business of offering dating, matrimonial, or social referral services online, where the services are offered primarily online, such as by means of an Internet Web site or a mobile application. *(Added by Stats.1989, c. 138, § 1. Amended by Stats.2017, c. 578 (A.B.314), § 1, eff. Jan. 1, 2018.)*

§ 1694.1. Cancellation; notice; refund

(a) In addition to any other right to revoke an offer, the buyer has the right to cancel a dating service contract or offer, until midnight of the third business day after the day on which the buyer signs an agreement or offer to purchase those services.

(b)(1) Cancellation occurs when the buyer gives written notice of cancellation by mail, telegram, or delivery to the seller at the address specified in the agreement or offer.

(2) In the case of a dating service contract with an online dating service, cancellation occurs when the buyer gives written notice of cancellation by email to an email address provided by the seller. Additional electronic means of cancellation may be provided by the agreement or offer.

(c) Notice of cancellation, if given by mail, is effective when deposited in the mail properly addressed with postage prepaid.

(d) Notice of cancellation given by the buyer need not take the particular form as provided in the contract or offer to purchase and, however expressed, is effective if it indicates the intention of the buyer not to be bound by the dating service contract.

(e) All moneys paid pursuant to any contract for dating services shall be refunded within 10 days of receipt of the notice of cancellation.

(f) The buyer may notify the dating service of his or her intent to cancel the contract within the three-day period specified in this section and stop the processing of a credit card voucher or check by telephone notification to the dating service. However, this does not negate the obligation of the buyer to cancel the contract by mail, email or other electronic means, telegram, or delivery as required pursuant to this section. (Added by Stats.1989, c. 138, § 1. Amended by Stats.1993, c. 359 (A.B.1323), § 1; Stats.2017, c. 578 (A.B. 314), § 2, eff. Jan. 1, 2018.)

§ 1694.2. Contract form and content

(a) A dating service contract shall be in writing, which, in the case of an online dating service contract, may be an electronic writing made available for viewing online. A copy of the contract shall be provided to the buyer at the time he or she signs the contract, except that an online dating service shall not be required to provide a copy of the contract where (1) the contract is available through a direct link that is provided in a clear and conspicuous manner on the Internet Web site page where the buyer provides consent to the agreement and, (2) upon request by the buyer, the online dating service provides a PDF format or retainable digital copy of the contract.

(b)(1) Every dating service contract shall contain on its face, and in close proximity to the space reserved for the signature of the buyer, a conspicuous statement in a size equal to at least 10–point boldface type, as follows:

"You, the buyer, may cancel this agreement, without any penalty or obligation, at any time prior to midnight of the original contract seller's third business day following the date of this contract, excluding Sundays and holidays. To cancel this agreement, mail or deliver a signed and dated notice, or send a telegram which states that you, the buyer, are canceling this agreement, or words of similar effect. This notice shall be sent to:

_____
(Name of the business that sold you the contract)
_____ ,"
(Address of the business that sold you the contract)

(2) Paragraph (1) shall not otherwise apply to an online dating service if the online dating service contract includes the statement in paragraph (1) in a clear and conspicuous manner in a stand-alone first paragraph of the contract.

(c)(1) The dating service contract shall contain on the first page, in a type size no smaller than that generally used in the body of the document, the name and address of the dating service operator to which the notice of cancellation is to be mailed, and the date the buyer signed the contract.

(2) In the case of an online dating service contract, if the name of the dating service operator and the email address that can be used for cancellation appears in the first paragraph of the contract, in a type size no smaller than that generally used in the body of the document, the other requirements of paragraph (1) shall not apply.

(d)(1) No dating service contract shall require payments or financing by the buyer over a period in excess of two years from the date the contract is entered into, nor shall the term of any such contract be measured by the life of the buyer. However, the services to be rendered to the buyer under the contract may extend over a period beginning within six months and ending within three years of the date the contract is entered into.

(2) In the case of an online dating service contract, if the initial term is one year or less, and subsequent terms are one year or less, paragraph (1) shall not apply.

(e) If a dating service contract is not in compliance with this chapter, the buyer may, at any time, cancel the contract. (Added by Stats.1989, c. 138, § 1. Amended by Stats.1993, c. 359 (A.B.1323), § 2; Stats.2017, c. 578 (A.B.314), § 3, eff. Jan. 1, 2018.)

§ 1694.3. Death, disability, or relocation

(a) Every dating service contract shall contain language providing that:

(1) If by reason of death or disability the buyer is unable to receive all services for which the buyer has contracted, the buyer and the buyer's estate may elect to be relieved of the obligation to make payments for services other than those received before death or the onset of disability, except as provided in paragraph (4).

(2) If the buyer has prepaid any amount for services, so much of the amount prepaid that is allocable to services that the buyer has not received shall be promptly refunded to the buyer or his or her representative.

(3) "Disability" means a condition which precludes the buyer from physically using the services specified in the contract during the term of disability and the condition is verified in writing by a physician designated and remunerated by the buyer. The written verification of the physician shall be presented to the seller.

(4) If the physician determines that the duration of the disability will be less than six months, the seller may extend the term of the contract for a period of six months at no additional charge to the buyer in lieu of cancellation.

(b)(1) If the buyer relocates his or her primary residence further than 50 miles from the dating service office and is unable to transfer the contract to a comparable facility, the buyer may elect to be relieved of the obligation to make payment for services other than those received prior to that relocation, and if the buyer has prepaid any amount for

§ 1694.3

dating services, so much of the amount prepaid that is allocable to services that the buyer has not received shall be promptly refunded to the buyer. A buyer who elects to be relieved of further obligation pursuant to this subdivision may be charged a predetermined fee not to exceed one hundred dollars ($100) or, if more than half the life of the contract has expired, a predetermined fee not to exceed fifty dollars ($50).

(2) Paragraph (1) shall not apply to online dating services that are generally available to users on a regional, national, or global basis.

(c) In addition to any other requirements, online dating services shall also maintain both of the following features:

(1) A reference or link to dating safety awareness information that includes, at a minimum, a list or descriptions of safety measures reasonably aimed at increasing awareness of safer dating practices.

(2) A means to report issues or concerns relating to the behavior of other users of the online dating service arising out of their use of the service. *(Added by Stats.1989, c. 138, § 1. Amended by Stats.2017, c. 578 (A.B.314), § 4, eff. Jan. 1, 2018.)*

§ 1694.4. Noncompliance with chapter; fraud; civil action; installment contracts; refund; waiver

(a) Any contract for dating services which does not comply with this chapter is void and unenforceable.

(b) Any contract for dating services entered into under willful and fraudulent or misleading information or advertisements of the seller is void and unenforceable.

(c) Any buyer injured by a violation of this chapter may bring an action for the recovery of damages in a court of competent jurisdiction. Judgment may be entered for three times the amount at which the actual damages are assessed. Reasonable attorney fees may be awarded to the prevailing party.

(d) Notwithstanding the provisions of any contract to the contrary, whenever the contract price is payable in installments and the buyer is relieved from making further payments or entitled to a refund under this chapter, the buyer shall be entitled to receive a refund or refund credit of that portion of the cash price as is allocable to the services not actually received by the buyer. The refund of any finance charge shall be computed according to the "sum of the balance method," also known as the "Rule of 78."

(e) Any waiver by the buyer of this chapter is void and unenforceable. *(Added by Stats.1989, c. 138, § 1.)*

CHAPTER 2.2. WEIGHT LOSS CONTRACTS

Section
1694.5. Weight loss contract; definition.
1694.6. Cancellation; notice; refund.
1694.7. Contract form and content.
1694.8. Death, disability, or relocation.
1694.9. Noncompliance with chapter; fraud; civil action; installment contracts; waiver.

§ 1694.5. Weight loss contract; definition

(a) As used in this chapter, a weight loss contract is a contract with any weight loss program or center that offers any of the following:

(1) Instruction, counseling, supervision, or assistance in weight reduction, body shaping, diet, and eating habits, by persons who are not licensed health care professionals.

(2) Use of facilities of a weight loss center for any of the purposes specified in paragraph (1).

(3) Membership in any group, club, association, or organization formed for any of the purposes specified in paragraph (1).

(4) Prepackaged, or premeasured "diet foods" provided by the weight loss program or center.

(b) This chapter does not apply to any contract for health studio services as defined in Section 1812.81. *(Added by Stats.1989, c. 138, § 2.)*

§ 1694.6. Cancellation; notice; refund

(a) In addition to any other right to revoke an offer, the buyer has the right to cancel a weight loss contract or offer until midnight of the third business day after the day on which the buyer signs an agreement or offer to purchase those services.

(b) Cancellation occurs when the buyer gives written notice of cancellation by mail, telegram, or delivery to the seller at the address specified in the agreement or offer.

(c) Notice of cancellation, if given by mail, is effective when deposited in the mail properly addressed with postage prepaid.

(d) Notice of cancellation given by the buyer need not take the particular form as provided in the contract or offer to purchase and, however expressed, is effective if it indicates the intention of the buyer not to be bound by the weight loss contract.

(e) All moneys paid pursuant to any weight loss contract shall be refunded within 10 days of receipt of the notice of cancellation.

(f) The buyer may notify the weight loss program of his or her intent to cancel the contract within the three-day period specified in this section and stop the processing of a credit card voucher or check by telephone notification to the weight loss program. However, this does not negate the obligation of the buyer to cancel the contract by mail, telegram, or delivery as required pursuant to this section. *(Added by Stats.1989, c. 138, § 2. Amended by Stats.1993, c. 359 (A.B.1323), § 3.)*

§ 1694.7. Contract form and content

(a) A weight loss contract shall be in writing. A copy of the contract shall be provided to the buyer at the time he or she signs the contract.

(b) Every weight loss contract shall contain on its face, and in close proximity to the space reserved for the signature of the buyer, a conspicuous statement in a size equal to at least 10-point boldface type, as follows:

"You, the buyer, may cancel this agreement, without any penalty or obligation, at any time prior to midnight of the original contract seller's third business day following the date of this contract, excluding Sundays and holidays. To cancel this agreement, mail or deliver a signed and dated notice, or send a telegram which states that you, the buyer, are canceling this agreement, or words of similar effect. This notice shall be sent to:

_____
(Name of the business that sold you the contract)
_____ ."
(Address of the business that sold you the contract)

(c) The weight loss contract shall contain on the first page, in a type size no smaller than that generally used in the body of the document, the name and address of the weight loss program operator to which the notice of cancellation is to be mailed; and the date the buyer signed the contract.

(d) No weight loss contract shall require payments or financing by the buyer over a period in excess of two years from the date the contract is entered into, nor shall the term of any such contract be measured by the life of the buyer. The services to be rendered to the buyer under the contract shall not extend for more than three years after the date the contract is entered into.

(e) If a weight loss contract is not in compliance with this chapter, the buyer may, at any time, cancel the contract. *(Added by Stats.1989, c. 138, § 2. Amended by Stats.1993, c. 359 (A.B.1323), § 4.)*

§ 1694.8. Death, disability, or relocation

Every weight loss contract shall contain language providing that:

(a) If by reason of death or disability the buyer is unable to receive all services for which the buyer has contracted, the buyer and the buyer's estate may elect to be relieved of the obligation to make payments for services other than those received before death or the onset of disability, except as provided in paragraph (3).

(1) If the buyer has prepaid any amount for services, so much of the amount prepaid that is allocable to services that the buyer has not received shall be promptly refunded to the buyer or his or her representative.

(2) "Disability" means a condition which precludes the buyer from physically using the services specified in the contract during the term of disability and the condition is verified in writing by a physician designated and remunerated by the buyer. The written verification of the physician shall be presented to the seller.

(3) If the physician determines that the duration of the disability will be less than six months, the seller may extend the term of the contract for a period of six months at no additional charge to the buyer in lieu of cancellation.

(b) If the buyer relocates his or her primary residence further than 50 miles from the weight loss center and is unable to transfer the contract to a comparable facility, the buyer may elect to be relieved of the obligation to make payment for services other than those received prior to that relocation, and if the buyer has prepaid any amount for weight loss services, so much of the amount prepaid that is allocable to services that the buyer has not received shall be promptly refunded to the buyer. A buyer who elects to be relieved of further obligation pursuant to this subdivision may be charged a predetermined fee not to exceed one hundred dollars ($100) or, if more than half the life of the contract has expired, a predetermined fee not to exceed fifty dollars ($50). *(Added by Stats.1989, c. 138, § 2.)*

§ 1694.9. Noncompliance with chapter; fraud; civil action; installment contracts; waiver

(a) Any contract for weight loss services which does not comply with this chapter is void and unenforceable.

(b) Any contract for weight loss services entered into under willful and fraudulent or misleading information or advertisements of the seller is void and unenforceable.

(c) Any buyer injured by a violation of this chapter may bring an action for the recovery of damages in a court of competent jurisdiction. Judgment may be entered for three times the amount at which the actual damages are assessed if the violation is willful. Reasonable attorney fees may be awarded to the prevailing party.

(d) Notwithstanding the provisions of any contract to the contrary, whenever the contract price is payable in installments and the buyer is relieved from making further payments or entitled to a refund under this chapter, the buyer shall be entitled to receive a refund or refund credit of that portion of the cash price as is allocable to the services not actually received by the buyer. The refund of any finance charge shall be computed according to the "sum of the balance method," also known as the "Rule of 78."

(e) Any waiver by the buyer of this chapter is void and unenforceable. *(Added by Stats.1989, c. 138, § 2.)*

CHAPTER 2.5. HOME EQUITY SALES CONTRACTS

Section
1695. Legislative findings and declarations.
1695.1. Definitions.
1695.2. Written contract; size of type; language; signature and date.
1695.3. Contents; survival of contract.
1695.4. Right of cancellation; time and manner of exercise.
1695.5. Right of cancellation; notice of right; form.
1695.6. Contract requirements; responsibility of equity purchaser; prohibited transactions; bona fide purchasers and encumbrancers; cancellation; return of original documents; untrue or misleading statements; encumbrances.
1695.7. Actions by equity seller for recovery of damages or other equitable relief against equity purchaser for violation of enumerated sections.
1695.8. Violations by equity purchaser; criminal penalties.
1695.9. Nonexclusivity of chapter.
1695.10. Waiver.
1695.11. Severability.
1695.12. Absolute conveyance with repurchase option deemed loan transaction; rights of bona fide purchasers or encumbrancers.
1695.13. Prohibited acts.
1695.14. Rescission.
1695.15. Liability of equity purchaser for statements or acts committed by representative.
1695.16. Limitation of liability under section 1695.15; voiding provision or contract; arbitration.

Section
1695.17. Representative of equity purchaser; statements to be provided to seller; remedies.

§ 1695. Legislative findings and declarations

(a) The Legislature finds and declares that homeowners whose residences are in foreclosure have been subjected to fraud, deception, and unfair dealing by home equity purchasers. The recent rapid escalation of home values, particularly in the urban areas, has resulted in a significant increase in home equities which are usually the greatest financial asset held by the homeowners of this state. During the time period between the commencement of foreclosure proceedings and the scheduled foreclosure sale date, homeowners in financial distress, especially the poor, elderly, and financially unsophisticated, are vulnerable to the importunities of equity purchasers who induce homeowners to sell their homes for a small fraction of their fair market values through the use of schemes which often involve oral and written misrepresentations, deceit, intimidation, and other unreasonable commercial practices.

(b) The Legislature declares that it is the express policy of the state to preserve and guard the precious asset of home equity, and the social as well as the economic value of homeownership.

(c) The Legislature further finds that equity purchasers have a significant impact upon the economy and well-being of this state and its local communities, and therefore the provisions of this chapter are necessary to promote the public welfare.

(d) The intent and purposes of this chapter are the following:

(1) To provide each homeowner with information necessary to make an informed and intelligent decision regarding the sale of his or her home to an equity purchaser; to require that the sales agreement be expressed in writing; to safeguard the public against deceit and financial hardship; to insure, foster, and encourage fair dealing in the sale and purchase of homes in foreclosure; to prohibit representations that tend to mislead; to prohibit or restrict unfair contract terms; to afford homeowners a reasonable and meaningful opportunity to rescind sales to equity purchasers; and to preserve and protect home equities for the homeowners of this state.

(2) This chapter shall be liberally construed to effectuate this intent and to achieve these purposes. *(Added by Stats.1979, c. 1029, p. 3536, § 1.)*

Cross References

Contract defined for purposes of this Chapter, see Civil Code § 1695.1.
Equity purchaser defined for purposes of this Chapter, see Civil Code § 1695.1.
Forfeitures and restraints upon redemption invalid, see Civil Code § 2889.
Mortgage foreclosure consultants, similar findings and declarations, see Civil Code § 2945.

§ 1695.1. Definitions

The following definitions apply to this chapter:

(a) "Equity purchaser" means any person who acquires title to any residence in foreclosure, except a person who acquires such title as follows:

(1) For the purpose of using such property as a personal residence.

(2) By a deed in lieu of foreclosure of any voluntary lien or encumbrance of record.

(3) By a deed from a trustee acting under the power of sale contained in a deed of trust or mortgage at a foreclosure sale conducted pursuant to Article 1 (commencing with Section 2920) of Chapter 2 of Title 14 of Part 4 of Division 3.

(4) At any sale of property authorized by statute.

(5) By order or judgment of any court.

(6) From a spouse, blood relative, or blood relative of a spouse.

(b) "Residence in foreclosure" and "residential real property in foreclosure" means residential real property consisting of one- to four-family dwelling units, one of which the owner occupies as his or her principal place of residence, and against which there is an outstanding notice of default, recorded pursuant to Article 1 (commencing with Section 2920) of Chapter 2 of Title 14 of Part 4 of Division 3.

(c) "Equity seller" means any seller of a residence in foreclosure.

(d) "Business day" means any calendar day except Sunday, or the following business holidays: New Year's Day, Washington's Birthday, Memorial Day, Independence Day, Labor Day, Columbus Day, Veterans' Day, Thanksgiving Day, and Christmas Day.

(e) "Contract" means any offer or any contract, agreement, or arrangement, or any term thereof, between an equity purchaser and equity seller incident to the sale of a residence in foreclosure.

(f) "Property owner" means the record title owner of the residential real property in foreclosure at the time the notice of default was recorded. *(Added by Stats.1979, c. 1029, p. 3536, § 1. Amended by Stats.1980, c. 423, p. 835, § 4, eff. July 11, 1980.)*

Cross References

Actions for foreclosure of mortgages, see Code of Civil Procedure § 725a et seq.
Lien defined, see Civil Code § 2872.
Mortgage defined, see Civil Code § 2920.
Mortgage foreclosure consultants, residence in foreclosure defined, see Civil Code § 2945.1.
Mortgage not a conveyance, see Code of Civil Procedure § 744.
Real Estate Fraud Prosecution Trust Fund, distribution and purpose, fraud against individuals, residences in danger of or in foreclosure, see Government Code § 27388.

§ 1695.2. Written contract; size of type; language; signature and date

Every contract shall be written in letters of a size equal to 10-point bold type, in the same language principally used by the equity purchaser and equity seller to negotiate the sale of the residence in foreclosure and shall be fully completed and signed and dated by the equity seller and equity purchaser prior to the execution of any instrument of conveyance of the residence in foreclosure. *(Added by Stats.1979, c. 1029, p. 3536, § 1.)*

Cross References

Contract defined for purposes of this Chapter, see Civil Code § 1695.1.
Contracts partly written and partly printed, see Civil Code § 1651.
Equity purchaser defined for purposes of this Chapter, see Civil Code § 1695.1.
Equity seller defined for purposes of this Chapter, see Civil Code § 1695.1.
Requirements of this section to be provided by equity purchaser, see Civil Code § 1695.6.
Residence in foreclosure and residential real property in foreclosure defined for purposes of this Chapter, see Civil Code § 1695.1.
Right of cancellation, see Civil Code § 1695.5.
Written words on printed form as controlling, see Code of Civil Procedure § 1862.

§ 1695.3. Contents; survival of contract

Every contract shall contain the entire agreement of the parties and shall include the following terms:

(a) The name, business address, and the telephone number of the equity purchaser.

(b) The address of the residence in foreclosure.

(c) The total consideration to be given by the equity purchaser in connection with or incident to the sale.

(d) A complete description of the terms of payment or other consideration including, but not limited to, any services of any nature which the equity purchaser represents he will perform for the equity seller before or after the sale.

(e) The time at which possession is to be transferred to the equity purchaser.

(f) The terms of any rental agreement.

(g) A notice of cancellation as provided in subdivision (b) of Section 1695.5.

(h) The following notice in at least 14-point boldface type, if the contract is printed or in capital letters if the contract is typed, and completed with the name of the equity purchaser, immediately above the statement required by Section 1695.5(a):

"NOTICE REQUIRED BY CALIFORNIA LAW

Until your right to cancel this contract has ended, _____
(Name)
or anyone working for_____
(Name)

CANNOT ask you to sign or have you sign any deed or any other document."

The contract required by this section shall survive delivery of any instrument of conveyance of the residence in foreclosure, and shall have no effect on persons other than the parties to the contract. *(Added by Stats.1979, c. 1029, p. 3536, § 1. Amended by Stats.1980, c. 423, p. 835, § 5, eff. July 11, 1980.)*

Cross References

Consideration, see Civil Code § 1605 et seq.

Contract defined for purposes of this Chapter, see Civil Code § 1695.1.
Contracts partly written and partly printed, see Civil Code § 1651.
Equity purchaser defined for purposes of this Chapter, see Civil Code § 1695.1.
Equity seller defined for purposes of this Chapter, see Civil Code § 1695.1.
Mortgage foreclosure consultants, see Civil Code § 2945 et seq.
Requirements of this section to be provided by equity purchaser, see Civil Code § 1695.6.
Residence in foreclosure and residential real property in foreclosure defined for purposes of this Chapter, see Civil Code § 1695.1.
Right of cancellation, see Civil Code § 1695.5.
Whole contract, effect to be given, see Civil Code § 1641.
Written contract supersedes prior agreements, see Civil Code § 1625.
Written words on printed form as controlling, see Code of Civil Procedure § 1862.

§ 1695.4. Right of cancellation; time and manner of exercise

(a) In addition to any other right of rescission, the equity seller has the right to cancel any contract with an equity purchaser until midnight of the fifth business day following the day on which the equity seller signs a contract that complies with this chapter or until 8 a.m. on the day scheduled for the sale of the property pursuant to a power of sale conferred in a deed of trust, whichever occurs first.

(b) Cancellation occurs when the equity seller personally delivers written notice of cancellation to the address specified in the contract or sends a telegram indicating cancellation to that address.

(c) A notice of cancellation given by the equity seller need not take the particular form as provided with the contract and, however expressed, is effective if it indicates the intention of the equity seller not to be bound by the contract. *(Added by Stats.1979, c. 1029, p. 3536, § 1. Amended by Stats.1997, c. 50 (A.B.669), § 1.)*

Cross References

Business day defined for purposes of this Chapter, see Civil Code § 1695.1.
Cancellation of instruments, see Civil Code § 3412 et seq.
Contract defined for purposes of this Chapter, see Civil Code § 1695.1.
Equity purchaser defined for purposes of this Chapter, see Civil Code § 1695.1.
Equity seller defined for purposes of this Chapter, see Civil Code § 1695.1.
Mortgage foreclosure consultants, see Civil Code § 2945 et seq.
Return of original contract and other documents upon cancellation, see Civil Code § 1695.6.

§ 1695.5. Right of cancellation; notice of right; form

(a) The contract shall contain in immediate proximity to the space reserved for the equity seller's signature a conspicuous statement in a size equal to at least 12-point bold type, if the contract is printed or in capital letters if the contract is typed, as follows:

"You may cancel this contract for the sale of your house without any penalty or obligation at any time before

_____
(Date and time of day)

See the attached notice of cancellation form for an explanation of this right."

The equity purchaser shall accurately enter the date and time of day on which the rescission right ends.

§ 1695.5

(b) The contract shall be accompanied by a completed form in duplicate, captioned "notice of cancellation" in a size equal to 12–point bold type, if the contract is printed or in capital letters if the contract is typed, followed by a space in which the equity purchaser shall enter the date on which the equity seller executes any contract. This form shall be attached to the contract, shall be easily detachable, and shall contain in type of at least 10–point, if the contract is printed or in capital letters if the contract is typed, the following statement written in the same language as used in the contract:

"NOTICE OF CANCELLATION

_____
(Enter date contract signed)

You may cancel this contract for the sale of your house, without any penalty or obligation, at any time before

_____
(Enter date and time of day)

To cancel this transaction, personally deliver a signed and dated copy of this cancellation notice, or send a telegram to _____,
(Name of purchaser)

at _____
(Street address of purchaser's place of business)

NOT LATER THAN _____
(Enter date and time of day)

I hereby cancel this transaction _____.

_____"
(Seller's signature)

(c) The equity purchaser shall provide the equity seller with a copy of the contract and the attached notice of cancellation.

(d) Until the equity purchaser has complied with this section, the equity seller may cancel the contract. *(Added by Stats.1979, c. 1029, p. 3536, § 1. Amended by Stats.1980, c. 423, p. 836, § 6, eff. July 11, 1980; Stats.1997, c. 50 (A.B.669), § 2.)*

Cross References

Cancellation of instruments, see Civil Code § 3412 et seq.
Contract defined for purposes of this Chapter, see Civil Code § 1695.1.
Contracts partly written and partly printed, see Civil Code § 1651.
Equity purchaser defined for purposes of this Chapter, see Civil Code § 1695.1.
Equity seller defined for purposes of this Chapter, see Civil Code § 1695.1.
Mortgage foreclosure consultants, owner's right to cancel contract, see Civil Code § 2945.2.
Written contract supersedes prior agreements, see Civil Code § 1625.
Written words on printed form as controlling, see Code of Civil Procedure § 1862.

§ 1695.6. Contract requirements; responsibility of equity purchaser; prohibited transactions; bona fide purchasers and encumbrancers; cancellation; return of original documents; untrue or misleading statements; encumbrances

(a) The contract as required by Sections 1695.2, 1695.3, and 1695.5, shall be provided and completed in conformity with those sections by the equity purchaser.

(b) Until the time within which the equity seller may cancel the transaction has fully elapsed, the equity purchaser shall not do any of the following:

(1) Accept from any equity seller an execution of, or induce any equity seller to execute, any instrument of conveyance of any interest in the residence in foreclosure.

(2) Record with the county recorder any document, including, but not limited to, any instrument of conveyance, signed by the equity seller.

(3) Transfer or encumber or purport to transfer or encumber any interest in the residence in foreclosure to any third party, provided no grant of any interest or encumbrance shall be defeated or affected as against a bona fide purchaser or encumbrancer for value and without notice of a violation of this chapter, and knowledge on the part of any such person or entity that the property was "residential real property in foreclosure" shall not constitute notice of a violation of this chapter. This section shall not be deemed to abrogate any duty of inquiry which exists as to rights or interests of persons in possession of the residential real property in foreclosure.

(4) Pay the equity seller any consideration.

(c) Within 10 days following receipt of a notice of cancellation given in accordance with Sections 1695.4 and 1695.5, the equity purchaser shall return without condition any original contract and any other documents signed by the equity seller.

(d) An equity purchaser shall make no untrue or misleading statements regarding the value of the residence in foreclosure, the amount of proceeds the equity seller will receive after a foreclosure sale, any contract term, the equity seller's rights or obligations incident to or arising out of the sale transaction, the nature of any document which the equity purchaser induces the equity seller to sign, or any other untrue or misleading statement concerning the sale of the residence in foreclosure to the equity purchaser.

(e) Whenever any equity purchaser purports to hold title as a result of any transaction in which the equity seller grants the residence in foreclosure by any instrument which purports to be an absolute conveyance and reserves or is given by the equity purchaser an option to repurchase such residence, the equity purchaser shall not cause any encumbrance or encumbrances to be placed on such property or grant any interest in such property to any other person without the written consent of the equity seller. Nothing in this subdivision shall preclude the application of paragraph (3) of subdivision (b). *(Added by Stats.1979, c. 1029, p. 3536, § 1. Amended by Stats.1980, c. 423, p. 837, § 7, eff. July 11, 1980; Stats.1997, c. 50 (A.B.669), § 3.)*

Cross References

Actual fraud, see Civil Code § 1572.
Cancellation of instruments, see Civil Code § 3412 et seq.
Constructive fraud, see Civil Code § 1573.
Contract defined for purposes of this Chapter, see Civil Code § 1695.1.
Deceit defined, see Civil Code § 1710.
Equity purchaser defined for purposes of this Chapter, see Civil Code § 1695.1.
Equity seller defined for purposes of this Chapter, see Civil Code § 1695.1.
Fraud in purchase, sale or exchange of property, see Civil Code § 3343.

Kinds of fraud, see Civil Code § 1571 et seq.
Mortgage foreclosure consultants, see Civil Code § 2945 et seq.
Residence in foreclosure and residential real property in foreclosure defined for purposes of this Chapter, see Civil Code § 1695.1.

§ 1695.7. Actions by equity seller for recovery of damages or other equitable relief against equity purchaser for violation of enumerated sections

An equity seller may bring an action for the recovery of damages or other equitable relief against an equity purchaser for a violation of any subdivision of Section 1695.6 or Section 1695.13. The equity seller shall recover actual damages plus reasonable attorneys' fees and costs. In addition, the court may award exemplary damages or equitable relief, or both, if the court deems such award proper, but in any event shall award exemplary damages in an amount not less than three times the equity seller's actual damages for any violation of paragraph (3) of subdivision (b) of Section 1695.6 or Section 1695.13; or the court may award a civil penalty of up to two thousand five hundred dollars ($2,500), but it may not award both exemplary damages and a civil penalty. Any action brought pursuant to this section shall be commenced within four years after the date of the alleged violation. *(Added by Stats.1979, c. 1029, p. 3536, § 1. Amended by Stats.1980, c. 423, p. 838, § 8, eff. July 11, 1980; Stats.2003, c. 74 (S.B.455), § 1.)*

Cross References

Compensatory relief, see Civil Code § 3281 et seq.
Damages, see Civil Code §§ 3281, 3301 et seq.
Equity purchaser defined for purposes of this Chapter, see Civil Code § 1695.1.
Equity seller defined for purposes of this Chapter, see Civil Code § 1695.1.
Exemplary damages, see Civil Code §§ 3294, 3295.
Injunction, see Civil Code § 3420 et seq.
Relief in general, see Civil Code § 3274 et seq.
Specific relief, see Civil Code §§ 3366, 3367, 3375.

§ 1695.8. Violations by equity purchaser; criminal penalties

Any equity purchaser who violates any subdivision of Section 1695.6 or who engages in any practice which would operate as a fraud or deceit upon an equity seller shall, upon conviction, be punished by a fine of not more than twenty-five thousand dollars ($25,000), by imprisonment in the county jail for not more than one year, or pursuant to subdivision (h) of Section 1170 of the Penal Code, or by both that fine and imprisonment for each violation. *(Added by Stats.1979, c. 1029, p. 3536, § 1. Amended by Stats.1985, c. 270, § 1; Stats.2003, c. 74 (S.B.455), § 2; Stats.2011, c. 15 (A.B.109), § 32, eff. April 4, 2011, operative Oct. 1, 2011.)*

Cross References

Actual fraud, see Civil Code § 1572.
Constructive fraud, see Civil Code § 1573.
Deceit defined, see Civil Code § 1710.
Equity purchaser defined for purposes of this Chapter, see Civil Code § 1695.1.
Equity seller defined for purposes of this Chapter, see Civil Code § 1695.1.
Fraud in purchase, sale or exchange of property, see Civil Code § 3343.

Kinds of fraud, see Civil Code § 1571 et seq.

§ 1695.9. Nonexclusivity of chapter

The provisions of this chapter are not exclusive and are in addition to any other requirements, rights, remedies, and penalties provided by law. *(Added by Stats.1979, c. 1029, p. 3536, § 1.)*

§ 1695.10. Waiver

Any waiver of the provisions of this chapter shall be void and unenforceable as contrary to the public policy. *(Added by Stats.1979, c. 1029, p. 3536, § 1.)*

§ 1695.11. Severability

If any provision of this chapter, or if any application thereof to any person or circumstance is held unconstitutional, the remainder of this chapter and the application of its provisions to other persons and circumstances shall not be affected thereby. *(Added by Stats.1979, c. 1029, p. 3536, § 1.)*

§ 1695.12. Absolute conveyance with repurchase option deemed loan transaction; rights of bona fide purchasers or encumbrancers

In any transaction in which an equity seller purports to grant a residence in foreclosure to an equity purchaser by any instrument which appears to be an absolute conveyance and reserves to himself or herself or is given by the equity purchaser an option to repurchase, such transaction shall create a presumption affecting the burden of proof, which may be overcome by clear and convincing evidence to the contrary that the transaction is a loan transaction, and the purported absolute conveyance is a mortgage; however, such presumption shall not apply to a bona fide purchaser or encumbrancer for value without notice of a violation of this chapter, and knowledge on the part of any such person or entity that the property was "residential real property in foreclosure" shall not constitute notice of a violation of this chapter. This section shall not be deemed to abrogate any duty of inquiry which exists as to rights or interests of persons in possession of the residential real property in foreclosure. *(Added by Stats.1979, c. 1029, p. 3536, § 1. Amended by Stats.1980, c. 423, p. 838, § 9, eff. July 11, 1980.)*

Cross References

Burden of proof, generally, see Evidence Code § 500 et seq.
Equity purchaser defined for purposes of this Chapter, see Civil Code § 1695.1.
Equity seller defined for purposes of this Chapter, see Civil Code § 1695.1.
Loan of money in general, see Civil Code § 1912 et seq.
Mortgage of realty in general, see Civil Code § 2947 et seq.
Presumptions in general, see Evidence Code § 600 et seq.
Residence in foreclosure and residential real property in foreclosure defined for purposes of this Chapter, see Civil Code § 1695.1.
Residence in foreclosure defined, mortgage foreclosure consultants, see Civil Code § 2945.1.
Terms of writing presumed used in their general acceptation, see Code of Civil Procedure § 1861.
Uncertainty in writing, interpretation against person causing, see Civil Code § 1654.

§ 1695.13. Prohibited acts

It is unlawful for any person to initiate, enter into, negotiate, or consummate any transaction involving residen-

§ 1695.13 OBLIGATIONS

tial real property in foreclosure, as defined in Section 1695.1, if such person, by the terms of such transaction, takes unconscionable advantage of the property owner in foreclosure. *(Added by Stats.1980, c. 423, p. 839, § 10, eff. July 11, 1980.)*

Cross References

Actions for foreclosure of mortgages, see Code of Civil Procedure § 725a et seq.
Actual fraud, see Civil Code § 1572.
California Residential Mortgage Lending Act, licensee prohibited acts, see Financial Code § 50204.
Cancellation of instruments, see Civil Code § 3412 et seq.
Consideration, see Civil Code § 1605 et seq.
Constructive fraud, see Civil Code § 1573.
Deceit defined, see Civil Code § 1710.
Exempt persons and firms, see Business and Professions Code § 10133.1.
Financial lenders, prohibited conduct, fraudulent or misleading conduct or statements, see Financial Code § 22161.
Fraud in purchase, sale or exchange of property, see Civil Code § 3343.
Kinds of fraud, see Civil Code § 1571 et seq.
Mortgage defined, see Civil Code § 2920.
Mortgage foreclosure consultants, see Civil Code § 2945 et seq.
Object of contract, see Civil Code § 1595 et seq.
Residence in foreclosure defined, mortgage foreclosure consultants, see Civil Code § 2945.1.
Residential mortgage lender or servicer, acts under authority of license, application of this section, see Business and Professions Code § 10133.1.
Unconscionable contracts, see Civil Code § 1670.5.

§ 1695.14. Rescission

(a) In any transaction involving residential real property in foreclosure, as defined in Section 1695.1, which is in violation of Section 1695.13 is voidable and the transaction may be rescinded by the property owner within two years of the date of the recordation of the conveyance of the residential real property in foreclosure.

(b) Such rescission shall be effected by giving written notice as provided in Section 1691 to the equity purchaser and his successor in interest, if the successor is not a bona fide purchaser or encumbrancer for value as set forth in subdivision (c), and by recording such notice with the county recorder of the county in which the property is located, within two years of the date of the recordation of the conveyance to the equity purchaser. The notice of rescission shall contain the names of the property owner and the name of the equity purchaser in addition to any successor in interest holding record title to the real property and shall particularly describe such real property. The equity purchaser and his successor in interest if the successor is not a bona fide purchaser or encumbrancer for value as set forth in subdivision (c), shall have 20 days after the delivery of the notice in which to reconvey title to the property free and clear of encumbrances created subsequent to the rescinded transaction. Upon failure to reconvey title within such time, the rescinding party may bring an action to enforce the rescission and for cancellation of the deed.

(c) The provisions of this section shall not affect the interest of a bona fide purchaser or encumbrancer for value if such purchase or encumbrance occurred prior to the recordation of the notice of rescission pursuant to subdivision (b).

Knowledge that the property was residential real property in foreclosure shall not impair the status of such persons or entities as bona fide purchasers or encumbrancers for value. This subdivision shall not be deemed to abrogate any duty of inquiry which exists as to rights or interests of persons in possession of the residential real property in foreclosure.

(d) In any action brought to enforce a rescission pursuant to this section, the prevailing party shall be entitled to costs and reasonable attorneys fees.

(e) The remedies provided by this section shall be in addition to any other remedies provided by law. *(Added by Stats.1980, c. 423, p. 839, § 11, eff. July 11, 1980.)*

Cross References

Consent not free, see Civil Code § 1566.
Consideration in general, see Civil Code § 1605 et seq.
Extinguishment of contract, see Civil Code § 1688 et seq.
Failure of consideration, see Civil Code § 1689.
Fraud in purchase, sale or exchange of property, see Civil Code § 3343.
Limitation of actions, see Code of Civil Procedure § 337.
Modification of contract, see Civil Code § 1698.
Notice, see Civil Code §§ 1691, 1693.
Procedure, see Civil Code § 1691.

§ 1695.15. Liability of equity purchaser for statements or acts committed by representative

(a) An equity purchaser is liable for all damages resulting from any statement made or act committed by the equity purchaser's representative in any manner connected with the equity purchaser's acquisition of a residence in foreclosure, receipt of any consideration or property from or on behalf of the equity seller, or the performance of any act prohibited by this chapter.

(b) "Representative" for the purposes of this section means a person who in any manner solicits, induces, or causes any property owner to transfer title or solicits any member of the property owner's family or household to induce or cause any property owner to transfer title to the residence in foreclosure to the equity purchaser. *(Added by Stats.1990, c. 1537 (S.B.2641), § 1.)*

Cross References

Equity purchaser defined for purposes of this Chapter, see Civil Code § 1695.1.
Equity seller defined for purposes of this Chapter, see Civil Code § 1695.1.
Property owner defined for purposes of this Chapter, see Civil Code § 1695.1.
Residence in foreclosure and residential real property in foreclosure defined for purposes of this Chapter, see Civil Code § 1695.1.

§ 1695.16. Limitation of liability under section 1695.15; voiding provision or contract; arbitration

(a) Any provision of a contract which attempts or purports to limit the liability of the equity purchaser under Section 1695.15 shall be void and shall at the option of the equity seller render the equity purchase contract void. The equity purchaser shall be liable to the equity seller for all damages proximately caused by that provision. Any provision in a contract which attempts or purports to require arbitration of any dispute arising under this chapter shall be void at the option of the equity seller only upon grounds as exist for the revocation of any contract.

(b) This section shall apply to any contract entered into on or after January 1, 1991. *(Added by Stats.1990, c. 1537 (S.B.2641), § 2.)*

Cross References

Contract defined for purposes of this Chapter, see Civil Code § 1695.1.
Equity purchaser defined for purposes of this Chapter, see Civil Code § 1695.1.
Equity seller defined for purposes of this Chapter, see Civil Code § 1695.1.

§ 1695.17. Representative of equity purchaser; statements to be provided to seller; remedies

(a) Any representative, as defined in subdivision (b) of Section 1695.15, deemed to be the agent or employee, or both the agent and the employee of the equity purchaser shall be required to provide both of the following:

(1) Written proof to the equity seller that the representative has a valid current California Real Estate Sales License and that the representative is bonded by an admitted surety insurer in an amount equal to twice the fair market value of the real property which is the subject of the contract.

(2) A statement in writing, under penalty of perjury, that the representative has a valid current California Real Estate Sales License, is bonded by an admitted surety insurer in an amount equal to at least twice the value of the real property which is the subject of the contract and has complied with paragraph (1). The written statement required by this paragraph shall be provided to all parties to the contract prior to the transfer of any interest in the real property which is the subject of the contract.

(b) The failure to comply with subdivision (a) shall at the option of the equity seller render the equity purchase contract void and the equity purchaser shall be liable to the equity seller for all damages proximately caused by the failure to comply. *(Added by Stats.1990, c. 1537 (S.B.2641), § 3.)*

Validity

This section was held unconstitutional as a violation of the void-for-vagueness doctrine of the due process clause in the decision of Schweitzer v. Westminster Investments, Inc. (App. 4 Dist. 2007) 69 Cal.Rptr.3d 472, 157 Cal.App.4th 1195, review denied.

Cross References

Contract defined for purposes of this Chapter, see Civil Code § 1695.1.
Equity purchaser defined for purposes of this Chapter, see Civil Code § 1695.1.
Equity seller defined for purposes of this Chapter, see Civil Code § 1695.1.

CHAPTER 3. MODIFICATION AND CANCELLATION

Section
1697. Oral contract.
1698. Written contract; oral agreement; rules of law.
1699. Written contract; extinction by destruction or cancellation.

Section
1700. Written contract; extinction by destruction, cancellation or material alteration by beneficiary.
1701. Destruction or alteration of duplicate.

Cross References

Adjudication of cancellation, see Civil Code § 3412 et seq.
Authentication of altered writing, see Evidence Code § 1402.
Investment securities, completion or alteration, see Commercial Code § 8206.
Negotiable instruments,
    Alteration of instruments, see Commercial Code § 3407.
    Incomplete instruments, see Commercial Code § 3115.

§ 1697. Oral contract

A contract not in writing may be modified in any respect by consent of the parties, in writing, without a new consideration, and is extinguished thereby to the extent of the modification. *(Enacted in 1872. Amended by Code Am.1873–74, c. 612, p. 242, § 192; Stats.1976, c. 109, p. 170, § 2.)*

Cross References

Alteration of writing produced as evidence, see Evidence Code § 1402.
Authorization for oral contracts, see Civil Code § 1622.
Consideration in general, see Civil Code § 1605 et seq.
Enforcement of contract oral by reason of fraud, see Civil Code § 1623.
Several contracts as parts of one transaction, see Civil Code § 1642.
Statute of frauds, see Civil Code § 1624.

§ 1698. Written contract; oral agreement; rules of law

(a) A contract in writing may be modified by a contract in writing.

(b) A contract in writing may be modified by an oral agreement to the extent that the oral agreement is executed by the parties.

(c) Unless the contract otherwise expressly provides, a contract in writing may be modified by an oral agreement supported by new consideration. The statute of frauds (Section 1624) is required to be satisfied if the contract as modified is within its provisions.

(d) Nothing in this section precludes in an appropriate case the application of rules of law concerning estoppel, oral novation and substitution of a new agreement, rescission of a written contract by an oral agreement, waiver of a provision of a written contract, or oral independent collateral contracts. *(Added by Stats.1976, c. 109, p. 171, § 4.)*

Cross References

Accord and satisfaction, extinction of obligation, see Civil Code § 1521 et seq.
Ascertainment of intention of contracting parties, see Civil Code § 1639; Code of Civil Procedure § 1856.
Cancellation of instruments, see Civil Code § 3412 et seq.
Circumstances explaining contract, see Civil Code § 1647.
Consideration in general, see Civil Code § 1605 et seq.
Creation of voluntary trust, see Probate Code § 15200 et seq.
Executed and executory contracts defined, see Civil Code § 1661.
Manner of creating contracts, see Civil Code § 1619 et seq.
Means of extinguishment, see Civil Code § 1682.
Modification of contract for sale, see Commercial Code § 2209.
Negotiations superseded by written contract, see Civil Code § 1625.

§ 1698

OBLIGATIONS

Novation, see Civil Code § 1530 et seq.
Offer of performance, extinction of obligation, see Civil Code § 1485.
Performance excused, see Civil Code §§ 1440, 1511.
Performance in general, see Civil Code § 1473 et seq.
Release, see Civil Code § 1541 et seq.
Rescission, see Civil Code § 1688 et seq.
Several contracts as parts of one transaction, see Civil Code § 1642.
Trusts, see Civil Code § 82 et seq.
Waiver,
  Attorney fees, see Civil Code § 1717.
  Code provisions, see Civil Code § 3268.
Written contract supersedes prior agreements, see Civil Code § 1625.

§ 1699. Written contract; extinction by destruction or cancellation

The destruction or cancellation of a written contract, or of the signature of the parties liable thereon, with intent to extinguish the obligation thereof, extinguishes it as to all the parties consenting to the act. *(Enacted in 1872.)*

Cross References

Cancellation of instruments, see Civil Code § 3412 et seq.
Effect of written contract on negotiations or stipulations, see Civil Code § 1625.
Extinction of obligations, see Civil Code § 1473 et seq.
Letter of credit, wrongful cancellation, see Commercial Code § 5115.
Specific enforcement of contract signed by one party only, see Civil Code § 3388.

§ 1700. Written contract; extinction by destruction, cancellation or material alteration by beneficiary

The intentional destruction, cancellation, or material alteration of a written contract, by a party entitled to any benefit under it, or with his consent, extinguishes all the executory obligations of the contract in his favor, against parties who do not consent to the act. *(Enacted in 1872.)*

Cross References

Alteration as defense, see Commercial Code §§ 3406, 3407.
Alteration of negotiable instruments, effect, see Commercial Code § 3407.
Altered bills of lading, see Commercial Code § 7306.
Altered investment security, see Commercial Code § 8206.
Altered warehouse receipts, see Commercial Code § 7208.
Authentication of altered writing, see Evidence Code § 1402.
Bank customer's duty to report altered items, see Commercial Code § 4406.
Cancellation of indorsement, see Commercial Code § 3207.
Claim for antecedent breach, effect of cancellation, see Commercial Code § 2720.
Consent required to contract, see Civil Code § 1565 et seq.
Effect of cancellation, see Commercial Code § 2106.
Executed contracts defined, see Civil Code § 1661.
Extinction of obligations, see Civil Code § 1473 et seq.
Forgery or false alteration of contract, see Penal Code § 470.
Investment securities, completion or alteration, see Commercial Code § 8206.
Letter of credit, wrongful cancellation, see Commercial Code § 5115.
Negligence contributing to alteration, see Commercial Code § 3406.
Novation, see Civil Code § 1530 et seq.
Warranty against alteration,
  Investment security, see Commercial Code § 8306.
  Negotiable instruments, see Commercial Code § 3417.

§ 1701. Destruction or alteration of duplicate

Where a contract is executed in duplicate, an alteration or destruction of one copy, while the other exists, is not within the provisions of the last section. *(Enacted in 1872.)*

Cross References

Best evidence rule, see Evidence Code § 1500 et seq.

Part 3

OBLIGATIONS IMPOSED BY LAW

Section
1708. Injuring person or property of another, or infringing upon any of his or her rights.
1708.5. Sexual battery; damages; equitable relief.
1708.5.5. Sexual battery by adult in position of authority over minor; consent as defense.
1708.5.6. Misusing sperm, ova, or embryos; damages.
1708.6. Liability for tort of domestic violence.
1708.7. Liability for tort of stalking; damages and equitable remedies.
1708.8. Physical or constructive invasion of privacy; personal or familial activities; damages and equitable remedies; employee-employer relationships; defenses; proceedings to recover civil fines.
1708.85. Distribution of sexually explicit materials; private cause of action; use of pseudonym.
1708.86. Distribution of sexually explicitly material depicting an individual using digital or electronic technology; cause of action; exemption from liability; defenses; damages; limitations; severability.
1708.88. Knowingly sending unsolicited image depicting obscene material by electronic means; private cause of action; damages; exemptions.
1708.9. Interference with persons attempting to enter or exit school grounds or health facility prohibited; exception for parents or guardians; injunctive relief, damages, and civil penalties; constitutionally protected activities.
1709. Deceit; damages.
1710. Deceit defined.
1710.1. Removal of manufacturer's distinguishing number or identification mark from mechanical or electrical devices or appliances; liability.
1710.2. Occupant of property afflicted with or who died from AIDS; disclosures to transferee not required; state preemption of AIDS disclosure.
1711. Deceit to defraud public or particular class.
1712. Restoration of thing wrongfully acquired; exceptions.
1713. Restoration of thing wrongfully acquired; demand.
1714. Responsibility for willful acts and negligence; furnishing alcoholic beverages; legislative intent; liability of social hosts; liability of parents, guardians, or adults who furnish alcoholic beverages to minors.
1714¼, 1714½. Repealed.
1714.01. Domestic partners; negligent infliction of emotional distress; damages.
1714.1. Liability of parents and guardians for willful misconduct of minor.
1714.2. Cardiopulmonary resuscitation; emergency care; immunity from civil liability.
1714.21. Defibrillators; CPR; immunity from civil liability.
1714.22. Opioid antagonist; prescription and dispensing permitted by authorized licensed health care providers to persons at risk of opioid-related overdose or persons in position to assist person at risk; standing distribution orders; overdose prevention and treatment training; immunity from liability.
1714.23. Administration of epinephrine auto-injector; liability for civil damages; requirements for immunity.

Section
1714.24. Collector maintaining secure drug take-back bin; civil or criminal liability; requirements for immunity.
1714.25. Donations by persons, gleaners, or food facilities to nonprofit charitable organizations; immunity.
1714.26. Vision screenings and eyeglasses provided by nonprofit charitable organizations and licensed optometrists, ophthalmologists, or trained volunteers working with such organizations; limitation of liability; exceptions.
1714.29. Trauma kits; contents; application of Good Samaritan Law; liability limitation for training and certification.
1714.3. Liability of parent or guardian for injury to person or property caused by discharge of firearm by minor under 18.
1714.4. Knowingly assisting child support obligor escape, evade, or avoid paying court-ordered or court-approved child support; application to financial institutions.
1714.41. Knowingly assisting a child support obligor to escape, evade, or avoid paying child support; included actions.
1714.43. Retailers to disclose efforts to eradicate slavery and human trafficking from direct supply chain for tangible goods; definitions; posting on Internet Website; contents; injunctive relief for violation.
1714.45. Products liability; consumer products known by consumers to be inherently unsafe.
1714.5. Defense shelters or other necessary facility for emergency purposes.
1714.55. Retail or wholesale telecommunications service provider of 9–1–1 service; liability for civil claim, damage, or loss; definitions.
1714.6. Compliance with military orders or regulations under Emergency Services Act; suspension of civil and criminal liability.
1714.7. Injury while getting on, riding on, or getting off, moving locomotive or railroad car without authority; exemption of owner or operator from liability; exception.
1714.8. Health care providers; professional negligence or malpractice; exemption from liability; definition.
1714.85. Rejected,.
1714.9. Responsibility for willful acts or want of ordinary care causing injury to peace officers, firefighters or emergency service personnel; circumstances; comparative fault; subrogation; exception.
1714.10. Attorney client civil conspiracy; proof and court determination prior to pleading; defense; limitations; appeal.
1714.11. Donation of fire protection apparatus or equipment; immunity from liability for damage or injury resulting from use; conditions.
1715. Other obligations.
1716. Solicitations for orders; notice or disclaimer; penalties.
1717. Action on contract; award of attorney's fees and costs; prevailing party; deposit of amounts in insured, interest-bearing account; damages not based on contract.
1717.5. Action on contract based on book account; award of attorney's fees for the prevailing party; effect of written agreement; scope of application.
1718. Farm machinery repair shops; invoices; estimates; definitions.

Section	
1719.	Dishonored checks; liability; demands for payment; stop payments; notice; penalties, damages and service charges; assignees.
1720.	Failure of obligee to give timely response to inquiry concerning debit or credit applicable to obligation.
1721.	Vandalism at construction site; treble damages and attorney fees.
1722.	Retail sale and delivery, and service or repair transactions; time of delivery, service or repair; delay or inability to deliver; notification; damages for failure to deliver or to commence service or repair; cable television; utilities; void contracts.
1723.	Retail sellers; policies of no refund or no exchange; notice; exceptions; violations.
1724.	Unauthorized sale, purchase, or use of data.
1725.	Negotiable instruments; identification; credit card as condition of acceptance prohibited.
1726 to 1729.	Repealed.
1730.	Repealed.
1730.5 to 1736.	Repealed.
1737.	Repealed.

§ 1708. Injuring person or property of another, or infringing upon any of his or her rights

Every person is bound, without contract, to abstain from injuring the person or property of another, or infringing upon any of his or her rights. *(Enacted in 1872. Amended by Stats.2002, c. 664 (A.B.3034), § 38.5.)*

Cross References

Actions by unmarried minor children, see Code of Civil Procedure § 376.
Acts forbidden by personal relations, see Civil Code § 49.
Civil actions arising out of obligations, or injuries, see Code of Civil Procedure § 25.
Creation and enforcement of obligation by operation of law, see Civil Code § 1428.
Damages, see Civil Code § 3281 et seq.
Force, right to use, see Civil Code § 50.
General personal rights, see Civil Code § 43.
Immunity from liability, see Civil Code § 43.6 et seq.
Indemnity for victims of crime, see Government Code § 29631 et seq.
Judicial remedies, see Code of Civil Procedure § 20 et seq.
Lack of cause of action for arrest under warrant regular on its face, see Civil Code § 43.55.
Parties to civil actions, see Code of Civil Procedure § 367 et seq.
Person suffering detriment may recover damages, see Civil Code § 3281.
Personal rights, see Civil Code § 43.
Remedy for every wrong, see Civil Code § 3523.
Rights, use so as not to infringe on rights of another, see Civil Code § 3514.
Suffering from act of another, see Civil Code § 3520.
Taking advantage of own wrong prohibited, see Civil Code § 3517.
Unlawful contracts, see Civil Code § 1667 et seq.
Wrongs not actionable, see Civil Code § 43.5.

§ 1708.5. Sexual battery; damages; equitable relief

(a) A person commits a sexual battery who does any of the following:

(1) Acts with the intent to cause a harmful or offensive contact with an intimate part of another, and a sexually offensive contact with that person directly or indirectly results.

(2) Acts with the intent to cause a harmful or offensive contact with another by use of the person's intimate part, and a sexually offensive contact with that person directly or indirectly results.

(3) Acts to cause an imminent apprehension of the conduct described in paragraph (1) or (2), and a sexually offensive contact with that person directly or indirectly results.

(4) Causes contact between a sexual organ, from which a condom has been removed, and the intimate part of another who did not verbally consent to the condom being removed.

(5) Causes contact between an intimate part of the person and a sexual organ of another from which the person removed a condom without verbal consent.

(b) A person who commits a sexual battery upon another is liable to that person for damages, including, but not limited to, general damages, special damages, and punitive damages.

(c) The court in an action pursuant to this section may award equitable relief, including, but not limited to, an injunction, costs, and any other relief the court deems proper.

(d) For the purposes of this section:

(1) "Intimate part" means the sexual organ, anus, groin, or buttocks of any person, or the breast of a female.

(2) "Offensive contact" means contact that offends a reasonable sense of personal dignity.

(e) The rights and remedies provided in this section are in addition to any other rights and remedies provided by law. *(Added by Stats.1990, c. 1531 (S.B.2336), § 1. Amended by Stats.2021, c. 613 (A.B.453), § 1, eff. Jan. 1, 2022.)*

Cross References

Sexual battery defined, see Penal Code § 243.4.
Victims of domestic violence, rape, and sexual battery, conditions of issuance of new and different license plates, see Vehicle Code § 4467.

§ 1708.5.5. Sexual battery by adult in position of authority over minor; consent as defense

(a) Notwithstanding Section 3515, consent shall not be a defense in any civil action under Section 1708.5 if the person who commits the sexual battery is an adult who is in a position of authority over the minor.

(b) For purposes of this section, an adult is in a "position of authority" if he or she, by reason of that position, is able to exercise undue influence over a minor. A "position of authority" includes, but is not limited to, a natural parent, stepparent, foster parent, relative, partner of any such parent or relative, caretaker, youth leader, recreational director, athletic manager, coach, teacher, counselor, therapist, religious leader, doctor, employee of one of those aforementioned persons, or coworker.

(c) For purposes of this section, "undue influence" has the same meaning as in Section 15610.70 of the Welfare and Institutions Code. *(Added by Stats.2015, c. 128 (S.B.14), § 1, eff. Jan. 1, 2016.)*

§ 1708.5.6. Misusing sperm, ova, or embryos; damages

(a) A private cause of action for damages lies against a person who misuses sperm, ova, or embryos in violation of Section 367g of the Penal Code.

(b) A prevailing plaintiff who suffers harm as a result of a violation of Section 367g of the Penal Code may be awarded actual damages or statutory damages of not less than fifty thousand dollars ($50,000), whichever is greater. *(Added by Stats.2021, c. 170 (A.B.556), § 1, eff. Jan. 1, 2022.)*

§ 1708.6. Liability for tort of domestic violence

(a) A person is liable for the tort of domestic violence if the plaintiff proves both of the following elements:

(1) The infliction of injury upon the plaintiff resulting from abuse, as defined in subdivision (a) of Section 13700 of the Penal Code.

(2) The abuse was committed by the defendant, a person having a relationship with the plaintiff as defined in subdivision (b) of Section 13700 of the Penal Code.

(b) A person who commits an act of domestic violence upon another is liable to that person for damages, including, but not limited to, general damages, special damages, and punitive damages pursuant to Section 3294.

(c) The court, in an action pursuant to this section, may grant to a prevailing plaintiff equitable relief, an injunction, costs, and any other relief that the court deems proper, including reasonable attorney's fees.

(d) The rights and remedies provided in this section are in addition to any other rights and remedies provided by law.

(e) The time for commencement of an action under this section is governed by Section 340.15 of the Code of Civil Procedure. *(Added by Stats.2002, c. 193 (A.B.1933), § 2.)*

Cross References

Domestic violence victims, application for new and different license plates, see Vehicle Code § 4467.

§ 1708.7. Liability for tort of stalking; damages and equitable remedies

(a) A person is liable for the tort of stalking when the plaintiff proves all of the following elements of the tort:

(1) The defendant engaged in a pattern of conduct the intent of which was to follow, alarm, place under surveillance, or harass the plaintiff. In order to establish this element, the plaintiff shall be required to support his or her allegations with independent corroborating evidence.

(2) As a result of that pattern of conduct, either of the following occurred:

(A) The plaintiff reasonably feared for his or her safety, or the safety of an immediate family member. For purposes of this subparagraph, "immediate family" means a spouse, parent, child, any person related by consanguinity or affinity within the second degree, or any person who regularly resides, or, within the six months preceding any portion of the pattern of conduct, regularly resided, in the plaintiff's household.

(B) The plaintiff suffered substantial emotional distress, and the pattern of conduct would cause a reasonable person to suffer substantial emotional distress.

(3) One of the following:

(A) The defendant, as a part of the pattern of conduct specified in paragraph (1), made a credible threat with either (i) the intent to place the plaintiff in reasonable fear for his or her safety, or the safety of an immediate family member, or (ii) reckless disregard for the safety of the plaintiff or that of an immediate family member. In addition, the plaintiff must have, on at least one occasion, clearly and definitively demanded that the defendant cease and abate his or her pattern of conduct and the defendant persisted in his or her pattern of conduct unless exigent circumstances make the plaintiff's communication of the demand impractical or unsafe.

(B) The defendant violated a restraining order, including, but not limited to, any order issued pursuant to Section 527.6 of the Code of Civil Procedure, prohibiting any act described in subdivision (a).

(b) For the purposes of this section:

(1) "Pattern of conduct" means conduct composed of a series of acts over a period of time, however short, evidencing a continuity of purpose. Constitutionally protected activity is not included within the meaning of "pattern of conduct."

(2) "Credible threat" means a verbal or written threat, including that communicated by means of an electronic communication device, or a threat implied by a pattern of conduct, including, but not limited to, acts in which a defendant directly, indirectly, or through third parties, by any action, method, device, or means, follows, harasses, monitors, surveils, threatens, or interferes with or damages the plaintiff's property, or a combination of verbal, written, or electronically communicated statements and conduct, made with the intent and apparent ability to carry out the threat so as to cause the person who is the target of the threat to reasonably fear for his or her safety or the safety of his or her immediate family.

(3) "Electronic communication device" includes, but is not limited to, telephones, cellular telephones, computers, video recorders, fax machines, or pagers. "Electronic communication" has the same meaning as the term defined in Subsection 12 of Section 2510 of Title 18 of the United States Code.

(4) "Follows" means to move in relative proximity to a person as that person moves from place to place or to remain in relative proximity to a person who is stationary or whose movements are confined to a small area but does not include following the plaintiff within the residence of the defendant. For purposes of the liability created by subdivision (a), "follows" does not include any lawful activity of private investigators licensed pursuant to Article 3 (commencing with Section 7520) of Chapter 11.3 of Division 3 of the Business and Professions Code, or of law enforcement personnel or employees of agencies, either public or private, who, in the course and scope of their employment, encourage or attempt to engage in any conduct or activity to obtain evidence of suspected illegal activity or other misconduct, suspected violation of any administrative rule or regulation, suspected fraudulent conduct, or any suspected activity involving a

violation of law or business practice or conduct of a public official that adversely affects public welfare, health, or safety. For purposes of the liability created by subdivision (a), "follows" also does not include any newsgathering conduct connected to a newsworthy event.

(5) "Harass" means a knowing and willful course of conduct directed at a specific person which seriously alarms, annoys, torments, or terrorizes the person, and which serves no legitimate purpose. The course of conduct must be such as would cause a reasonable person to suffer substantial emotional distress, and must actually cause substantial emotional distress to the person.

(6) "Place under surveillance" means remaining present outside of the plaintiff's school, place of employment, vehicle, residence, other than the residence of the defendant, or other place occupied by the plaintiff. For purposes of the liability created by subdivision (a), "place under surveillance" does not include any lawful activity of private investigators licensed pursuant to Article 3 (commencing with Section 7520) of Chapter 11.3 of Division 3 of the Business and Professions Code, or of law enforcement personnel or employees of agencies, either public or private, who, in the course and scope of their employment, encourage or attempt to engage in any conduct or activity to obtain evidence of suspected illegal activity or other misconduct, suspected violation of any administrative rule or regulation, suspected fraudulent conduct, or any suspected activity involving a violation of law or business practice or conduct of a public official that adversely affects public welfare, health, or safety. For purposes of the liability created by subdivision (a), "place under surveillance" also does not include any newsgathering conduct connected to a newsworthy event.

(7) "Substantial emotional distress" shall not be construed to have the same meaning as the "severe emotional distress" requirement for intentional infliction of emotional distress. "Substantial emotional distress" does not require a showing of physical manifestations of emotional distress; rather, it requires the evaluation of the totality of the circumstances to determine whether the defendant reasonably caused the plaintiff substantial fear, anxiety, or emotional torment.

(c) A person who commits the tort of stalking upon another is liable to that person for damages, including, but not limited to, general damages, special damages, and punitive damages pursuant to Section 3294.

(d) In an action pursuant to this section, the court may grant equitable relief, including, but not limited to, an injunction.

(e) The rights and remedies provided in this section are cumulative and in addition to any other rights and remedies provided by law.

(f) This section shall not be construed to impair any constitutionally protected activity, including, but not limited to, speech, protest, and assembly.

(g) This act is an exercise of the police power of the state for the protection of the health, safety, and welfare of the people of the State of California, and shall be liberally construed to effectuate those purposes. (Added by Stats. 1993, c. 582 (A.B.1548), § 1. Amended by Stats.1994, c. 509 (A.B.2676), § 1; Stats.1998, c. 825 (S.B.1796), § 2; Stats. 2014, c. 853 (A.B.1356), § 1, eff. Jan. 1, 2015.)

Cross References

Domestic violence victims, application for new and different license plates, see Vehicle Code § 4467.
Employers with 25 or more employees, victims of domestic violence, sexual assault, or stalking, employer prohibited from discharging or discriminating against employee for taking time off for specific purposes, see Labor Code § 230.1.
Lease not to be terminated based on domestic or sexual assault against tenant, landlord's liability for compliance, form for affirmative defense to unlawful detainer action, see Code of Civil Procedure § 1161.3.
Legal actions by victims of domestic violence, sexual assault, or stalking, employer prohibited from discharging or discriminating against employee for taking time off or due to employee's status as a victim, see Labor Code § 230.
Records of Department of Motor Vehicles, confidential records, residence or mailing address, grounds for suppression, see Vehicle Code § 1808.21.
Summoning law enforcement assistance or emergency assistance, lease or rental agreement provisions prohibiting or limiting right void, see Civil Code § 1946.8.
Summoning law enforcement assistance or emergency assistance by victim of abuse, victim of crime, or individual in emergency, local agency ordinance, etc. limiting right prohibited, see Government Code § 53165.
Unlawful detainer, commission of nuisance upon premises, see Code of Civil Procedure § 1161.
Victims of domestic violence, sexual assault, or stalking, written notice to terminate tenancy, requirements, see Civil Code § 1946.7.

§ 1708.8. Physical or constructive invasion of privacy; personal or familial activities; damages and equitable remedies; employee-employer relationships; defenses; proceedings to recover civil fines

(a) A person is liable for physical invasion of privacy when the person knowingly enters onto the land or into the airspace above the land of another person without permission or otherwise commits a trespass in order to capture any type of visual image, sound recording, or other physical impression of the plaintiff engaging in a private, personal, or familial activity and the invasion occurs in a manner that is offensive to a reasonable person.

(b) A person is liable for constructive invasion of privacy when the person attempts to capture, in a manner that is offensive to a reasonable person, any type of visual image, sound recording, or other physical impression of the plaintiff engaging in a private, personal, or familial activity, through the use of any device, regardless of whether there is a physical trespass, if this image, sound recording, or other physical impression could not have been achieved without a trespass unless the device was used.

(c) An assault or false imprisonment committed with the intent to capture any type of visual image, sound recording, or other physical impression of the plaintiff is subject to subdivisions (d), (e), and (h).

(d) A person who commits any act described in subdivision (a), (b), or (c) is liable for up to three times the amount of any general and special damages that are proximately caused by the violation of this section. This person may also be liable for punitive damages, subject to proof according to

Section 3294. If the plaintiff proves that the invasion of privacy was committed for a commercial purpose, the person shall also be subject to disgorgement to the plaintiff of any proceeds or other consideration obtained as a result of the violation of this section. A person who comes within the description of this subdivision is also subject to a civil fine of not less than five thousand dollars ($5,000) and not more than fifty thousand dollars ($50,000).

(e) A person who directs, solicits, actually induces, or actually causes another person, regardless of whether there is an employer-employee relationship, to violate any provision of subdivision (a), (b), or (c) is liable for any general, special, and consequential damages resulting from each said violation. In addition, the person that directs, solicits, actually induces, or actually causes another person, regardless of whether there is an employer-employee relationship, to violate this section shall be liable for punitive damages to the extent that an employer would be subject to punitive damages pursuant to subdivision (b) of Section 3294. A person who comes within the description of this subdivision is also subject to a civil fine of not less than five thousand dollars ($5,000) and not more than fifty thousand dollars ($50,000).

(f)(1) The transmission, publication, broadcast, sale, offer for sale, or other use of any visual image, sound recording, or other physical impression that was taken or captured in violation of subdivision (a), (b), or (c) shall not constitute a violation of this section unless the person, in the first transaction following the taking or capture of the visual image, sound recording, or other physical impression, publicly transmitted, published, broadcast, sold, or offered for sale the visual image, sound recording, or other physical impression with actual knowledge that it was taken or captured in violation of subdivision (a), (b), or (c), and provided compensation, consideration, or remuneration, monetary or otherwise, for the rights to the unlawfully obtained visual image, sound recording, or other physical impression.

(2) For the purposes of paragraph (1), "actual knowledge" means actual awareness, understanding, and recognition, obtained prior to the time at which the person purchased or acquired the visual image, sound recording, or other physical impression, that the visual image, sound recording, or other physical impression was taken or captured in violation of subdivision (a), (b), or (c). The plaintiff shall establish actual knowledge by clear and convincing evidence.

(3) Any person that publicly transmits, publishes, broadcasts, sells, or offers for sale, in any form, medium, format, or work, a visual image, sound recording, or other physical impression that was previously publicly transmitted, published, broadcast, sold, or offered for sale by another person, is exempt from liability under this section.

(4) If a person's first public transmission, publication, broadcast, or sale or offer for sale of a visual image, sound recording, or other physical impression that was taken or captured in violation of subdivision (a), (b), or (c) does not constitute a violation of this section, that person's subsequent public transmission, publication, broadcast, sale, or offer for sale, in any form, medium, format, or work, of the visual image, sound recording, or other physical impression, does not constitute a violation of this section.

(5) This section applies only to a visual image, sound recording, or other physical impression that is captured or taken in California in violation of subdivision (a), (b), or (c) after January 1, 2010, and shall not apply to any visual image, sound recording, or other physical impression taken or captured outside of California.

(6) Nothing in this subdivision shall be construed to impair or limit a special motion to strike pursuant to Section 425.16, 425.17, or 425.18 of the Code of Civil Procedure.

(7) This section shall not be construed to limit all other rights or remedies of the plaintiff in law or equity, including, but not limited to, the publication of private facts.

(g) This section shall not be construed to impair or limit any otherwise lawful activities of law enforcement personnel or employees of governmental agencies or other entities, either public or private, who, in the course and scope of their employment, and supported by an articulable suspicion, attempt to capture any type of visual image, sound recording, or other physical impression of a person during an investigation, surveillance, or monitoring of any conduct to obtain evidence of suspected illegal activity or other misconduct, the suspected violation of any administrative rule or regulation, a suspected fraudulent conduct, or any activity involving a violation of law or business practices or conduct of public officials adversely affecting the public welfare, health, or safety.

(h) In any action pursuant to this section, the court may grant equitable relief, including, but not limited to, an injunction and restraining order against further violations of subdivision (a), (b), or (c).

(i) The rights and remedies provided in this section are cumulative and in addition to any other rights and remedies provided by law.

(j) It is not a defense to a violation of this section that no image, recording, or physical impression was captured or sold.

(k) For the purposes of this section, "for a commercial purpose" means any act done with the expectation of a sale, financial gain, or other consideration. A visual image, sound recording, or other physical impression shall not be found to have been, or intended to have been, captured for a commercial purpose unless it is intended to be, or was in fact, sold, published, or transmitted.

(*l*)(1) For the purposes of this section, "private, personal, and familial activity" includes, but is not limited to:

(A) Intimate details of the plaintiff's personal life under circumstances in which the plaintiff has a reasonable expectation of privacy.

(B) Interaction with the plaintiff's family or significant others under circumstances in which the plaintiff has a reasonable expectation of privacy.

(C) If and only after the person has been convicted of violating Section 626.8 of the Penal Code, any activity that occurs when minors are present at any location set forth in subdivision (a) of Section 626.8 of the Penal Code.

(D) Any activity that occurs on a residential property under circumstances in which the plaintiff has a reasonable expectation of privacy.

§ 1708.8

(E) Other aspects of the plaintiff's private affairs or concerns under circumstances in which the plaintiff has a reasonable expectation of privacy.

(2) "Private, personal, and familial activity" does not include illegal or otherwise criminal activity as delineated in subdivision (g). However, "private, personal, and familial activity" shall include the activities of victims of crime in circumstances under which subdivision (a), (b), or (c) would apply.

(m)(1) A proceeding to recover the civil fines specified in subdivision (d) or (e) may be brought in any court of competent jurisdiction by a county counsel or city attorney.

(2) Fines collected pursuant to this subdivision shall be allocated, as follows:

(A) One-half shall be allocated to the prosecuting agency.

(B) One-half shall be deposited in the Arts and Entertainment Fund, which is hereby created in the State Treasury.

(3) Funds in the Arts and Entertainment Fund created pursuant to paragraph (2) may be expended by the California Arts Council, upon appropriation by the Legislature, to issue grants pursuant to the Dixon–Zenovich–Maddy California Arts Act of 1975 (Chapter 9 (commencing with Section 8750) of Division 1 of Title 2 of the Government Code).

(4) The rights and remedies provided in this subdivision are cumulative and in addition to any other rights and remedies provided by law.

(n) The provisions of this section are severable. If any provision of this section or its application is held invalid, that invalidity shall not affect other provisions or applications that can be given effect without the invalid provision or application. *(Added by Stats.1998, c. 1000 (S.B.262), § 1. Amended by Stats.2005, c. 424 (A.B.381), § 1; Stats.2009, c. 449 (A.B.524), § 2; Stats.2010, c. 685 (A.B.2479), § 1; Stats.2014, c. 852 (A.B.1256), § 1, eff. Jan. 1, 2015; Stats.2014, c. 858 (A.B.2306), § 1.5, eff. Jan. 1, 2015; Stats.2015, c. 521 (A.B. 856), § 1, eff. Jan. 1, 2016.)*

§ 1708.85. Distribution of sexually explicit materials; private cause of action; use of pseudonym

(a) A private cause of action lies against a person who intentionally distributes by any means a photograph, film, videotape, recording, or any other reproduction of another, without the other's consent, if (1) the person knew, or reasonably should have known, that the other person had a reasonable expectation that the material would remain private, (2) the distributed material exposes an intimate body part of the other person, or shows the other person engaging in an act of intercourse, oral copulation, sodomy, or other act of sexual penetration, and (3) the other person suffers general or special damages as described in Section 48a.

(b) As used in this section, "intimate body part" means any portion of the genitals, and, in the case of a female, also includes any portion of the breast below the top of the areola, that is uncovered or visible through less than fully opaque clothing.

(c) There shall be no liability on the part of the person distributing material under subdivision (a) under any of the following circumstances:

(1) The distributed material was created under an agreement by the person appearing in the material for its public use and distribution or otherwise intended by that person for public use and distribution.

(2) The person possessing or viewing the distributed material has permission from the person appearing in the material to publish by any means or post the material on an internet website.

(3) The person appearing in the material waived any reasonable expectation of privacy in the distributed material by making it accessible to the general public.

(4) The distributed material constitutes a matter of public concern.

(5) The distributed material was photographed, filmed, videotaped, recorded, or otherwise reproduced in a public place and under circumstances in which the person depicted had no reasonable expectation of privacy.

(6) The distributed material was previously distributed by another person, unless the plaintiff served on the defendant, by certified mail, a notice to cease distribution of the material, and the defendant failed to cease distribution within 20 days of receiving the notice.

(d) In addition to any other relief available at law, the court may order equitable relief against the person violating subdivision (a), including a temporary restraining order, or a preliminary injunction or a permanent injunction ordering the defendant to cease distribution of material. The court may grant injunctive relief maintaining the confidentiality of a plaintiff using a pseudonym as provided in subdivision (f).

(e) The court may also grant, after holding a properly noticed hearing, reasonable attorney's fees and costs to the prevailing plaintiff.

(f)(1) A plaintiff in a civil proceeding pursuant to subdivision (a), may proceed using a pseudonym, either John Doe, Jane Doe, or Doe, for the true name of the plaintiff and may exclude or redact from all pleadings and documents filed in the action other identifying characteristics of the plaintiff. A plaintiff who proceeds using a pseudonym and excluding or redacting identifying characteristics as provided in this section shall file with the court and serve upon the defendant a confidential information form for this purpose that includes the plaintiff's name and other identifying characteristics excluded or redacted. The court shall keep the plaintiff's name and excluded or redacted characteristics confidential.

(2) In cases where a plaintiff proceeds using a pseudonym under this section, the following provisions shall apply:

(A) All other parties and their agents and attorneys shall use this pseudonym in all pleadings, discovery documents, and other documents filed or served in the action, and at hearings, trial, and other court proceedings that are open to the public.

(B)(i) Any party filing a pleading, discovery document, or other document in the action shall exclude or redact any identifying characteristics of the plaintiff from the pleading, discovery document, or other document, except for a confidential information form filed pursuant to this subdivision.

(ii) A party excluding or redacting identifying characteristics as provided in this section shall file with the court and serve upon all other parties a confidential information form that includes the plaintiff's name and other identifying characteristics excluded or redacted. The court shall keep the plaintiff's name and excluded or redacted characteristics confidential.

(C) All court decisions, orders, petitions, discovery documents, and other documents shall be worded so as to protect the name or other identifying characteristics of the plaintiff from public revelation.

(3) The following definitions apply to this subdivision:

(A) "Identifying characteristics" means name or any part thereof, address or any part thereof, city or unincorporated area of residence, age, marital status, relationship to defendant, and race or ethnic background, telephone number, email address, social media profiles, online identifiers, contact information, or any other information, including images of the plaintiff, from which the plaintiff's identity can be discerned.

(B) "Online identifiers" means any personally identifying information or signifiers that would tie an individual to a particular electronic service, device, or Internet application, website, or platform account, including, but not limited to, access names, access codes, account names, aliases, avatars, credentials, gamer tags, display names, handles, login names, member names, online identities, pseudonyms, screen names, user accounts, user identifications, usernames, Uniform Resource Locators (URLs), domain names, Internet Protocol (IP) addresses, and media access control (MAC) addresses.

(4) The responsibility for excluding or redacting the name or identifying characteristics of the plaintiff from all documents filed with the court rests solely with the parties and their attorneys. Nothing in this section requires the court to review pleadings or other papers for compliance with this provision.

(5) Upon request of the plaintiff, the clerk shall allow access to the court file in an action filed under this section only as follows:

(A) To a party to the action, including a party's attorney.

(B) To a person by order of the court on a showing of good cause for access.

(C) To any person 60 days after judgment is entered unless the court grants a plaintiff's motion to seal records pursuant to Chapter 3 of Division 4 of Title 2 of the California Rules of Court.

(g) In an action pursuant to this section, the plaintiff shall state in the caption of the complaint "ACTION BASED ON CIVIL CODE SECTION 1708.85."

(h) Nothing in this section shall be construed to alter or negate any rights, obligations, or immunities of an interactive service provider under Section 230 of Title 47 of the United States Code. Nothing in this section shall be construed to limit or preclude a plaintiff from securing or recovering any other available remedy.

(i) The provisions of this section are severable. If any provision of this section or its application is held invalid, that invalidity shall not affect other provisions or applications that can be given effect without the invalid provision or application.

(j) The Judicial Council shall, on or before January 1, 2019, adopt or revise as appropriate rules and forms in order to implement subdivision (f). *(Added by Stats.2014, c. 859 (A.B.2643), § 1, eff. Jan. 1, 2015, operative July 1, 2015. Amended by Stats.2017, c. 233 (S.B.157), § 1, eff. Jan. 1, 2018; Stats.2021, c. 518 (A.B.514), § 1, eff. Jan. 1, 2022.)*

§ 1708.86. Distribution of sexually explicitly material depicting an individual using digital or electronic technology; cause of action; exemption from liability; defenses; damages; limitations; severability

(a) For purposes of this section:

(1) "Altered depiction" means a performance that was actually performed by the depicted individual but was subsequently altered to be in violation of this section.

(2) "Authorized Representative" means an attorney, talent agent, or personal manager authorized to represent a depicted individual if the depicted individual is represented.

(3)(A) "Consent" means an agreement written in plain language signed knowingly and voluntarily by the depicted individual that includes a general description of the sexually explicit material and the audiovisual work in which it will be incorporated.

(B) A depicted individual may rescind consent by delivering written notice within three business days from the date consent was given to the person in whose favor consent was made, unless one of the following requirements is satisfied:

(i) The depicted individual is given at least 72 hours to review the terms of the agreement before signing it.

(ii) The depicted individual's authorized representative provides written approval of the signed agreement.

(4) "Depicted individual" means an individual who appears, as a result of digitization, to be giving a performance they did not actually perform or to be performing in an altered depiction.

(5) "Despicable conduct" means conduct that is so vile, base, or contemptible that it would be looked down on and despised by a reasonable person.

(6) "Digitization" means to realistically depict any of the following:

(A) The nude body parts of another human being as the nude body parts of the depicted individual.

(B) Computer-generated nude body parts as the nude body parts of the depicted individual.

(C) The depicted individual engaging in sexual conduct in which the depicted individual did not engage.

(7) "Disclose" means to publish, make available, or distribute to the public.

(8) "Individual" means a natural person.

(9) "Malice" means that the defendant acted with intent to cause harm to the plaintiff or despicable conduct that was done with a willful and knowing disregard of the rights of the plaintiff. A person acts with knowing disregard within the meaning of this paragraph when they are aware of the probable harmful consequences of their conduct and deliberately fail to avoid those consequences.

(10) "Nude" means visible genitals, pubic area, anus, or a female's postpubescent nipple or areola.

(11) "Person" means a human being or legal entity.

(12) "Plaintiff" includes cross-plaintiff.

(13) "Sexual conduct" means any of the following:

(A) Masturbation.

(B) Sexual intercourse, including genital, oral, or anal, whether between persons regardless of sex or gender or between humans and animals.

(C) Sexual penetration of the vagina or rectum by, or with, an object.

(D) The transfer of semen by means of sexual conduct from the penis directly onto the depicted individual as a result of ejaculation.

(E) Sadomasochistic abuse involving the depicted individual.

(14) "Sexually explicit material" means any portion of an audiovisual work that shows the depicted individual performing in the nude or appearing to engage in, or being subjected to, sexual conduct.

(b) A depicted individual has a cause of action against a person who does either of the following:

(1) Creates and intentionally discloses sexually explicit material and the person knows or reasonably should have known the depicted individual in that material did not consent to its creation or disclosure.

(2) Intentionally discloses sexually explicit material that the person did not create and the person knows the depicted individual in that material did not consent to the creation of the sexually explicit material.

(c)(1) A person is not liable under this section in either of the following circumstances:

(A) The person discloses the sexually explicit material in the course of any of the following:

(i) Reporting unlawful activity.

(ii) Exercising the person's law enforcement duties.

(iii) Hearings, trials, or other legal proceedings.

(B) The material is any of the following:

(i) A matter of legitimate public concern.

(ii) A work of political or newsworthy value or similar work.

(iii) Commentary, criticism, or disclosure that is otherwise protected by the California Constitution or the United States Constitution.

(2) For purposes of this subdivision, sexually explicit material is not of newsworthy value solely because the depicted individual is a public figure.

(d) It shall not be a defense to an action under this section that there is a disclaimer included in the sexually explicit material that communicates that the inclusion of the depicted individual in the sexually explicit material was unauthorized or that the depicted individual did not participate in the creation or development of the material.

(e)(1) A prevailing plaintiff who suffers harm as a result of the violation of subdivision (b) may recover any of the following:

(A) An amount equal to the monetary gain made by the defendant from the creation, development, or disclosure of the sexually explicit material.

(B) One of the following:

(i) Economic and noneconomic damages proximately caused by the disclosure of the sexually explicit material, including damages for emotional distress.

(ii) Upon request of the plaintiff at any time before the final judgment is rendered, the plaintiff may instead recover an award of statutory damages for all unauthorized acts involved in the action, with respect to any one work, as follows:

(I) A sum of not less than one thousand five hundred dollars ($1,500) but not more than thirty thousand dollars ($30,000).

(II) If the unlawful act was committed with malice, the award of statutory damages may be increased to a maximum of one hundred fifty thousand dollars ($150,000).

(C) Punitive damages.

(D) Reasonable attorney's fees and costs.

(E) Any other available relief, including injunctive relief.

(2) The remedies provided by this section are cumulative and shall not be construed as restricting a remedy that is available under any other law.

(f) An action under this section shall be commenced no later than three years from the date the unauthorized creation, development, or disclosure was discovered or should have been discovered with the exercise of reasonable diligence.

(g) The provisions of this section are severable. If any provision of this section or its application is held invalid, that invalidity shall not affect other provisions. *(Added by Stats. 2019, c. 491 (A.B.602), § 1, eff. Jan. 1, 2020.)*

§ 1708.88. Knowingly sending unsolicited image depicting obscene material by electronic means; private cause of action; damages; exemptions

(a) A private cause of action lies against a person 18 years of age or older who knowingly sends an image, that the person knows or reasonably should know is unsolicited, by electronic means, depicting obscene material.

(b) For purposes of this section, the following terms have the following meanings:

(1) An "image" includes, but is not limited to, a moving visual image.

(2) "Obscene material" means material, including, but not limited to, images depicting a person engaging in an act of sexual intercourse, sodomy, oral copulation, sexual penetration, or masturbation, or depicting the exposed genitals or anus of any person, taken as a whole, that to the average person, applying contemporary statewide standards, appeals to the prurient interest, that, taken as a whole, depicts or describes sexual conduct in a patently offensive way, and that,

taken as a whole, lacks serious literary, artistic, political, or scientific value.

(3) An image is "unsolicited" if the recipient has not consented to or has expressly forbidden the receipt of the image.

(c)(1) A prevailing plaintiff who suffers harm as a result of receiving an image in violation of subdivision (a) may recover economic and noneconomic damages proximately caused by the receipt of the image, including damages for emotional distress.

(2) A prevailing plaintiff who suffers harm as a result of receiving an image, the receipt of which had been expressly forbidden by the plaintiff, in violation of subdivision (a), may recover the following:

(A) Economic and noneconomic damages proximately caused by the receipt of the image, including damages for emotional distress.

(B) Upon request of the plaintiff at any time before the final judgment is rendered, the plaintiff may, in lieu of those damages specified in subparagraph (A), recover an award of statutory damages of a sum of not less than one thousand five hundred dollars ($1,500) but not more than thirty thousand dollars ($30,000).

(C) Punitive damages.

(3) A prevailing plaintiff described in paragraph (1) or (2) may recover the following:

(A) Reasonable attorney's fees and costs.

(B) Any other available relief, including injunctive relief.

(4) The remedies provided by this section are cumulative and shall not be construed as restricting a remedy that is available under any other law.

(d) This section does not apply to any of the following:

(1) An internet service provider, mobile data provider, or operator of an online or mobile application, to the extent that the entity is transmitting, routing, or providing connections for electronic communications initiated by or at the direction of another person.

(2) Any service that transmits images or audiovisual works, including, without limitation, an on-demand, subscription, or advertising-supported service.

(3) A health care provider transmitting an image for a legitimate medical purpose.

(4) An individual who has not expressly opted-out of receiving sexually explicit images on the service in which the image is transmitted, where such an option is available. (Added by Stats.2022, c. 504 (S.B.53), § 1, eff. Jan. 1, 2023.)

§ 1708.9. Interference with persons attempting to enter or exit school grounds or health facility prohibited; exception for parents or guardians; injunctive relief, damages, and civil penalties; constitutionally protected activities

(a) It is unlawful for any person, except a parent or guardian acting toward his or her minor child, to commit any of the following acts:

(1) By force, threat of force, or physical obstruction that is a crime of violence, to intentionally injure, intimidate, interfere with, or attempt to injure, intimidate, or interfere with, any person attempting to enter or exit a facility.

(2) By nonviolent physical obstruction, to intentionally injure, intimidate, interfere with, or attempt to injure, intimidate, or interfere with, any person attempting to enter or exit a facility.

(b) For purposes of this section:

(1) "Facility" means any public or private school grounds, as described in subdivision (a) of Section 626.8 of the Penal Code, or any health facility, as described in Section 1250 of the Health and Safety Code.

(2) To "interfere" means to restrict a person's freedom of movement.

(3) To "intimidate" means to place a person in reasonable apprehension of bodily harm to himself, herself, or another person.

(4) "Nonviolent" means conduct that would not constitute a crime of violence.

(5) "Physical obstruction" means rendering ingress to or egress from a facility impassable to another person, or rendering passage to or from a facility unreasonably difficult or hazardous to another person.

(c) A person aggrieved by a violation of subdivision (a) may bring a civil action to enjoin the violation, for compensatory and punitive damages, for injunctive relief, and for the cost of suit and reasonable attorney's and expert witness' fees. With respect to compensatory damages, the plaintiff may elect, at any time prior to the rendering of a final judgment, to recover, in lieu of actual damages, an award of statutory damages in the amount of five thousand dollars ($5,000) per violation of paragraph (1) of subdivision (a), and one thousand dollars ($1,000) per violation of paragraph (2) of subdivision (a).

(d) The Attorney General, a district attorney, or a city attorney may bring a civil action to enjoin a violation of subdivision (a), for compensatory damages to persons or entities aggrieved by the violation, and for the imposition of a civil penalty against each respondent. The civil penalty for a violation of paragraph (1) of subdivision (a) shall not exceed fifteen thousand dollars ($15,000), or twenty-five thousand dollars ($25,000) for a second or subsequent violation. The civil penalty for a violation of paragraph (2) of subdivision (a) shall not exceed five thousand dollars ($5,000), or twenty-five thousand dollars ($25,000) for a second or subsequent violation.

(e) This section shall not be construed to impair the right to engage in any constitutionally protected activity, including, but not limited to, speech, protest, or assembly.

(f) The adoption of the act that added this section is an exercise of the police power of the state for purposes of protecting the health, safety, and welfare of the people of California, and this section shall be liberally construed to effectuate that purpose.

(g) This section shall not be construed to restrict, inhibit, prevent, or bring a chilling effect upon any actions by a person that are reasonable under the circumstances to protect, secure, provide safety to, or prevent illness in any child or adult in a facility. *(Added by Stats.2014, c. 852 (A.B.1256), § 2, eff. Jan. 1, 2015.)*

§ 1709. Deceit; damages

One who willfully deceives another with intent to induce him to alter his position to his injury or risk, is liable for any damage which he thereby suffers. *(Enacted in 1872.)*

Cross References

Actual fraud, see Civil Code § 1572.
Attorney-client privilege, exception in cases of fraud, see Evidence Code § 956.
Contract exempting one from fraud, see Civil Code § 1668.
Damages for fraud in purchase, sale or exchange of property, see Civil Code § 3343.
Damages for wrongs, see Civil Code § 3333 et seq.
Disregard of provisions of written contract which fail to express the real intention of the parties due to fraud, see Civil Code § 1640.
Exemplary damages for fraud, see Civil Code § 3294.
Fraud, see Civil Code § 1571 et seq.
Interest in cases of fraud in an action, see Civil Code § 3288.
Misrepresentation of solvency by buyer, see Commercial Code § 2702.
Remedies for fraud or material misrepresentation in sales contract, see Commercial Code § 2721.
Rescission for fraud, see Civil Code § 1689.
Rescission of contract due to fraud in obtaining consent, see Civil Code § 1567 et seq.
Revision of contracts, see Civil Code § 3399.
Solicitation of money, false invoices or statements, see Civil Code § 1716.
Statute of limitations for fraud, see Code of Civil Procedure §§ 337, 338.

§ 1710. Deceit defined

A deceit, within the meaning of the last section, is either:

1. The suggestion, as a fact, of that which is not true, by one who does not believe it to be true;

2. The assertion, as a fact, of that which is not true, by one who has no reasonable ground for believing it to be true;

3. The suppression of a fact, by one who is bound to disclose it, or who gives information of other facts which are likely to mislead for want of communication of that fact; or,

4. A promise, made without any intention of performing it. *(Enacted in 1872.)*

Cross References

Actual fraud defined, see Civil Code § 1572.
Damages, recovery by person suffering detriment, see Civil Code § 3281.
Lessor-retailers, suspension or revocation of license, see Vehicle Code § 11613.
Manufacturers, transporters, and dealers, suspension or revocation of license, see Vehicle Code § 11705.
Measure of damages, see Civil Code §§ 3300, 3333.
Mobilehomes-manufactured housing, deceit, see Health and Safety Code § 18004.6.
Purchase, sale or exchange of property, fraud in, see Civil Code § 3343.

§ 1710.1. Removal of manufacturer's distinguishing number or identification mark from mechanical or electrical devices or appliances; liability

Any person who, with intent to defraud, sells or disposes of a radio, piano, phonograph, sewing machine, washing machine, typewriter, adding machine, comptometer, bicycle, firearm, safe, vacuum cleaner, dictaphone, watch, watch movement, watchcase, or any other mechanical or electrical device, appliance, contrivance, material, piece of apparatus or equipment, from which the manufacturer's nameplate, serial number or any other distinguishing number or identification mark has been removed, defaced, covered, altered or destroyed, is civilly liable to the manufacturer in the sum of five hundred dollars ($500) per transaction and civilly liable to the purchaser for treble the actual damages sustained by the purchaser.

This section does not apply to those cases or instances where any of the changes or alterations enumerated in this section have been customarily made or done as an established practice in the ordinary and regular conduct of business by the original manufacturer or his duly appointed direct representative or under specific authorization from the original manufacturer. *(Added by Stats.1971, c. 1713, p. 3654, § 1.)*

Cross References

Consumers Legal Remedies Act, see Civil Code § 1750 et seq.
Obliterating or concealing brand on equipment, see Business and Professions Code § 14430.
Purchase, sale or possession of mechanical or electrical device from which manufacturer's identification mark removed, see Penal Code § 537e.

§ 1710.2. Occupant of property afflicted with or who died from AIDS; disclosures to transferee not required; state preemption of AIDS disclosure

(a) (1) Subject to subdivision (d), an owner of real property or his or her agent, or any agent of a transferee of real property, is not required to disclose either of the following to the transferee, as these are not material facts that require disclosure:

(A) The occurrence of an occupant's death upon the real property or the manner of death where the death has occurred more than three years prior to the date the transferee offers to purchase, lease, or rent the real property.

(B) That an occupant of that property was living with human immunodeficiency virus (HIV) or died from AIDS-related complications.

(2) As used in this section:

(A) "Agent" includes any person licensed pursuant to Part 1 (commencing with Section 10000) of Division 4 of the Business and Professions Code.

(B) "Transferee" includes a purchaser, lessee, or renter of real property.

(3) No cause of action shall arise against an owner or his or her agent or any agent of a transferee for not disclosing facts pursuant to paragraph (1).

(b) It is the intent of the Legislature to occupy the field of regulation of disclosure related to either of the following:

(1) Deaths occurring upon real property.

(2) The HIV-positive status of a prior occupant in situations affecting the transfer of real property or any estate or interest in real property.

(c) This section shall not be construed to alter the law relating to disclosure pertaining to any other physical or mental condition or disease, and this section shall not relieve any owner or agent of any obligation to disclose the physical condition of the premises.

(d) This section shall not be construed to immunize an owner or his or her agent from making an intentional misrepresentation in response to a direct inquiry from a transferee or a prospective transferee of real property, concerning deaths on the real property. *(Added by Stats. 1986, c. 498, § 2. Amended by Stats.1987, c. 494, § 1; Stats.2016, c. 548 (A.B.73), § 1, eff. Sept. 24, 2016.)*

§ 1711. Deceit to defraud public or particular class

One who practices a deceit with intent to defraud the public, or a particular class of persons, is deemed to have intended to defraud every individual in that class, who is actually misled by the deceit. *(Enacted in 1872.)*

§ 1712. Restoration of thing wrongfully acquired; exceptions

One who obtains a thing without the consent of its owner, or by a consent afterwards rescinded, or by an unlawful exaction which the owner could not at the time prudently refuse, must restore it to the person from whom it was thus obtained, unless he has acquired a title thereto superior to that of such other person, or unless the transaction was corrupt and unlawful on both sides. *(Enacted in 1872.)*

Cross References

Claim and delivery of personal property, see Code of Civil Procedure § 511.010 et seq.
Damages for conversion, see Civil Code § 3336 et seq.
Election between the thing and its value, see Civil Code § 1032.
Embezzlement by bailee, see Penal Code § 507.
Joinder of causes of action, see Code of Civil Procedure § 427.10.
Ownership of property, see Civil Code §§ 654, 669 et seq.
Personal property, judgment for possession or value, see Code of Civil Procedure § 667.
Present interest as entitle to immediate possession, see Civil Code § 689.
Right of person suffering detriment to recover damages, see Civil Code § 3281.
Specific personal property, verdict in action for recovery, see Code of Civil Procedure § 627.
Theft or larceny, see Penal Code § 484 et seq.
Things in action, see Civil Code § 953 et seq.
Vehicle, unlawful use or tampering by bailee, see Vehicle Code § 10854.

§ 1713. Restoration of thing wrongfully acquired; demand

The restoration required by the last section must be made without demand, except where a thing is obtained by mutual mistake, in which case the party obtaining the thing is not bound to return it until he has notice of the mistake. *(Enacted in 1872.)*

Cross References

Measure of damages, see Civil Code §§ 3300, 3333.
Mistake of fact or law defined, see Civil Code §§ 1577, 1578.

Notice defined, see Commercial Code § 1201.

§ 1714. Responsibility for willful acts and negligence; furnishing alcoholic beverages; legislative intent; liability of social hosts; liability of parents, guardians, or adults who furnish alcoholic beverages to minors

(a) Everyone is responsible, not only for the result of his or her willful acts, but also for an injury occasioned to another by his or her want of ordinary care or skill in the management of his or her property or person, except so far as the latter has, willfully or by want of ordinary care, brought the injury upon himself or herself. The design, distribution, or marketing of firearms and ammunition is not exempt from the duty to use ordinary care and skill that is required by this section. The extent of liability in these cases is defined by the Title on Compensatory Relief.

(b) It is the intent of the Legislature to abrogate the holdings in cases such as Vesely v. Sager (1971) 5 Cal.3d 153, Bernhard v. Harrah's Club (1976) 16 Cal.3d 313, and Coulter v. Superior Court (1978) 21 Cal.3d 144 and to reinstate the prior judicial interpretation of this section as it relates to proximate cause for injuries incurred as a result of furnishing alcoholic beverages to an intoxicated person, namely that the furnishing of alcoholic beverages is not the proximate cause of injuries resulting from intoxication, but rather the consumption of alcoholic beverages is the proximate cause of injuries inflicted upon another by an intoxicated person.

(c) Except as provided in subdivision (d), no social host who furnishes alcoholic beverages to any person may be held legally accountable for damages suffered by that person, or for injury to the person or property of, or death of, any third person, resulting from the consumption of those beverages.

(d)(1) Nothing in subdivision (c) shall preclude a claim against a parent, guardian, or another adult who knowingly furnishes alcoholic beverages at his or her residence to a person whom he or she knows, or should have known, to be under 21 years of age, in which case, notwithstanding subdivision (b), the furnishing of the alcoholic beverage may be found to be the proximate cause of resulting injuries or death.

(2) A claim under this subdivision may be brought by, or on behalf of, the person under 21 years of age or by a person who was harmed by the person under 21 years of age. *(Enacted in 1872. Amended by Stats.1978, c. 929, p. 2904, § 2; Stats.2002, c. 906 (A.B.496), § 1; Stats.2002, c. 913 (S.B.682), § 1; Stats.2003, c. 62 (S.B.600), § 15; Stats.2010, c. 154 (A.B.2486), § 1; Stats.2011, c. 410 (A.B.1407), § 1.)*

Cross References

Action by parents for injury to child, see Code of Civil Procedure § 376.
Agent, conformity to limits of authority, see Civil Code § 2019.
Baggage, limitation of railroad's liability, see Civil Code § 2178.
Blind pedestrian, failure to carry white cane, see Civil Code § 54.4.
Boats or vessels,
  Liability of owner of undocumented vessel, see Harbors and Navigation Code § 661.
  Negligent operation, see Harbors and Navigation Code § 655.
Boilers, criminal penalty for negligent operation, see Labor Code §§ 7770, 7771.

§ 1714 OBLIGATIONS

Borrower,
    Degree of care required, see Civil Code § 1886.
    Repair of injuries due to negligence, see Civil Code § 1889.
Breach of obligation other than contract, damages for, see Civil Code § 3333.
Care required of carriers of passengers, see Civil Code § 2100 et seq.
Carriage of property, degree of care and diligence required, see Civil Code § 2114.
Civil action out of obligation or injury, see Code of Civil Procedure § 25 et seq.
Common carriers of persons, liability for luggage, see Civil Code § 2182.
Common carriers of property, liability for delay, see Civil Code § 2196.
Compensatory relief, see Civil Code § 3281 et seq.
Contracts exempting one from negligence, invalidity, see Civil Code § 1668.
Depository, liability for damages or negligence, see Civil Code §§ 1836, 1838 et seq., 1852.
Dog bites, liability of owner, see Civil Code § 3342.
Employee's liability to employer for losses due to negligence, see Labor Code § 2865.
Employer's liability for losses of employee, see Labor Code § 2800.
Evidence,
    Admissibility of existence of insurance for negligence, see Evidence Code § 1155.
    Admissibility of subsequent remedial conduct, see Evidence Code § 1151.
    Boat accident reports, see Harbors and Navigation Code § 656.
    Fires, prima facie evidence of negligence from escape of campfire or origination from device kindling fire, see Public Resources Code §§ 4434, 4435.
    Motor vehicle accidents, see Vehicle Code § 40830 et seq.
    Presumptions of failure to exercise due care, see Evidence Code § 669.
    Res ipsa loquitur, see Evidence Code § 646.
Excavations by owner of adjoining land, see Civil Code § 832.
Fires, liabilities, see Health and Safety Code § 13000 et seq.
Force, right to use, see Civil Code § 50.
Good Samaritan Law, see Business and Professions Code §§ 2058, 2060, 2395, 2398, 2727.5.
Gratuitous carriage of persons, degree of care, see Civil Code § 2096.
Gratuitous depositary, degree of care required, see Civil Code § 1846.
Hiring, degree of care on part of hirer, see Civil Code § 1928 et seq.
Husband and wife, concurring negligence of spouse as defense by third party, see Family Code § 783.
Inland carrier's liability for negligence, see Civil Code § 2195.
Innkeepers' liability, see Civil Code §§ 1859, 1860.
Intoxicants, sales to drunkard or intoxicated person, see Business and Professions Code § 25602.
Joint tortfeasors, releases and contribution, see Code of Civil Procedure § 875 et seq.
Lender's liability for concealed defects, see Civil Code § 1893.
Liability of lender financing design, manufacture, construction, repair, modification or improvement of real or personal property, see Civil Code § 3434.
Messages,
    Care and diligence in transmission and delivery, see Civil Code § 2162.
    Damages for refusing or postponing, see Civil Code § 2209.
Military personnel, immunity from liability, see Military and Veterans Code § 392.
Minors, liability, wrongs, see Family Code § 6600.
Misuse of thing lent for particular purpose, see Civil Code § 1930.
Negligence defined, see Penal Code § 7.
Parental liability limits, liability of parents and guardians for willful misconduct of minor, see Civil Code § 1714.1.
Personal rights, see Civil Code § 43.
Persons of unsound mind, liability for wrongs, see Civil Code § 41.
Principal's responsibility for negligence and wrongs of agent, see Civil Code §§ 2338, 2339.
Public employees, liability, see Government Code § 820 et seq.
Public entities and public employees, claims and actions against, see Government Code § 810 et seq.
Real property owners, duty of care of easements and for entry or use by others for recreational purposes, see Civil Code § 846.
Remedy for every wrong, see Civil Code § 3523.
Repairs by hirer, see Civil Code § 1929.
Right of person suffering detriment to recover damages, see Civil Code § 3281.
Trial of issue of liability preceding trial of other issues, see Code of Civil Procedure § 598.
Trustees, care and diligence required, see Probate Code § 16041.
Unclaimed property, liability for negligence of warehouseman, see Civil Code § 2081.4.
Unlawful act of another, damages for, see Civil Code § 3281.
Vehicles, civil liability of owners and operators, see Vehicle Code § 17000 et seq.
Voluntary interference with property, care required, see Civil Code § 2078.
Warehousemen, duty of care, see Commercial Code § 7204.
Wrongful death, see Code of Civil Procedure § 377.60 et seq.

§§ 1714¼, 1714½. Repealed by Stats.1935, c. 27, p. 246, § 802

§ 1714.01. Domestic partners; negligent infliction of emotional distress; damages

(a) Domestic partners shall be entitled to recover damages for negligent infliction of emotional distress to the same extent that spouses are entitled to do so under California law.

(b) For the purpose of this section, "domestic partners" has the meaning provided in Section 297 of the Family Code. (Added by Stats.2001, c. 893 (A.B.25), § 1.)

Cross References

California Domestic Partner Rights and Responsibilities Act, sections included, see Family Code §§ 297 to 299.3; Government Code § 14771.

§ 1714.1. Liability of parents and guardians for willful misconduct of minor

(a) Any act of willful misconduct of a minor that results in injury or death to another person or in any injury to the property of another shall be imputed to the parent or guardian having custody and control of the minor for all purposes of civil damages, and the parent or guardian having custody and control shall be jointly and severally liable with the minor for any damages resulting from the willful misconduct.

Subject to the provisions of subdivision (c), the joint and several liability of the parent or guardian having custody and control of a minor under this subdivision shall not exceed twenty-five thousand dollars ($25,000) for each tort of the minor, and in the case of injury to a person, imputed liability shall be further limited to medical, dental and hospital expenses incurred by the injured person, not to exceed twenty-five thousand dollars ($25,000). The liability imposed by this section is in addition to any liability now imposed by law.

(b) Any act of willful misconduct of a minor that results in the defacement of property of another with paint or a similar substance shall be imputed to the parent or guardian having custody and control of the minor for all purposes of civil damages, including court costs, and attorney's fees, to the prevailing party, and the parent or guardian having custody and control shall be jointly and severally liable with the minor for any damages resulting from the willful misconduct, not to exceed twenty-five thousand dollars ($25,000), except as provided in subdivision (c), for each tort of the minor.

(c) The amounts listed in subdivisions (a) and (b) shall be adjusted every two years by the Judicial Council to reflect any increases in the cost of living in California, as indicated by the annual average of the California Consumer Price Index. The Judicial Council shall round this adjusted amount up or down to the nearest hundred dollars. On or before July 1 of each odd-numbered year, the Judicial Council shall compute and publish the amounts listed in subdivisions (a) and (b), as adjusted according to this subdivision.

(d) The maximum liability imposed by this section is the maximum liability authorized under this section at the time that the act of willful misconduct by a minor was committed.

(e) Nothing in this section shall impose liability on an insurer for a loss caused by the willful act of the insured for purposes of Section 533 of the Insurance Code. An insurer shall not be liable for the conduct imputed to a parent or guardian by this section for any amount in excess of ten thousand dollars ($10,000). *(Added by Stats.1955, c. 820, p. 1438, § 1. Amended by Stats.1965, c. 407, p. 1719, § 1; Stats.1970, c. 640, p. 1258, § 1; Stats.1972, c. 442, p. 811, § 1; Stats.1974, c. 340, p. 670, § 1; Stats.1979, c. 127, p. 314, § 1; Stats.1983, c. 981, § 1; Stats.1994, c. 568 (A.B.308), § 1; Stats.1994, c. 909 (S.B.1779), § 1; Stats.2007, c. 738 (A.B. 1248), § 2.)*

Cross References

Child abuse, prohibition against libel or slander action while charges pending, see Civil Code § 48.7.
Computer data access and fraud, offense of minor imputed to parent or legal guardian pursuant to this section, see Penal Code § 502.
Joint and several obligations, see Civil Code § 1430 et seq.
Juvenile court law,
   Criminal violation by minor, restitution hearing, citation ordering appearance by parents or guardians, see Welfare and Institutions Code § 739.5.
   Graffiti Removal and Damage Recovery Program, clean up, repair or replacement of property, restitution, see Welfare and Institutions Code § 742.16.
   Restitution, fine, or penalty assessment order, liability of parent or guardian, see Welfare and Institutions Code § 730.7.
Liability of parent or guardian for damage to school property by minor, see Education Code § 48904.
Minor defined, see Family Code § 6500.
Minor's liability for wrongs, see Family Code § 6600.
Motor vehicle accident, liability of parent, guardian or person signing application, see Vehicle Code §§ 17707, 17708.
Offenses against libraries by minors, liability of parents, see Education Code §§ 19910, 19911.
Petty theft of retail merchandise, inapplicability of this section, see Penal Code § 490.5.

§ 1714.2. Cardiopulmonary resuscitation; emergency care; immunity from civil liability

(a) In order to encourage citizens to participate in emergency medical services training programs and to render emergency medical services to fellow citizens, no person who has completed a basic cardiopulmonary resuscitation course which complies with the standards adopted by the American Heart Association or the American Red Cross for cardiopulmonary resuscitation and emergency cardiac care, and who, in good faith, renders emergency cardiopulmonary resuscitation at the scene of an emergency, shall be liable for any civil damages as a result of any acts or omissions by such person rendering the emergency care.

(b) This section shall not be construed to grant immunity from civil damages to any person whose conduct in rendering such emergency care constitutes gross negligence.

(c) In order to encourage local agencies and other organizations to train citizens in cardiopulmonary resuscitation techniques, no local agency, entity of state or local government, or other public or private organization which sponsors, authorizes, supports, finances, or supervises the training of citizens in cardiopulmonary resuscitation shall be liable for any civil damages alleged to result from such training programs.

(d) In order to encourage qualified individuals to instruct citizens in cardiopulmonary resuscitation, no person who is certified to instruct in cardiopulmonary resuscitation by either the American Heart Association or the American Red Cross shall be liable for any civil damages alleged to result from the acts or omissions of an individual who received instruction on cardiopulmonary resuscitation by that certified instructor.

(e) This section shall not be construed to grant immunity from civil damages to any person who renders such emergency care to an individual with the expectation of receiving compensation from the individual for providing the emergency care. *(Added by Stats.1977, c. 595, p. 1970, § 1.)*

Cross References

Emergency medical services,
   Immunity from liability, see Health and Safety Code § 1799.100 et seq.
   Liability limitation, firefighters, law enforcement officers, emergency medical technicians and employing agencies, see Health and Safety Code § 1799.106.
Emergency services, immunity from civil damages, see Government Code § 50086.

§ 1714.21. Defibrillators; CPR; immunity from civil liability

(a) For purposes of this section, the following definitions shall apply:

(1) "AED" or "defibrillator" means an automated external defibrillator.

(2) "CPR" means cardiopulmonary resuscitation.

(b) Any person who, in good faith and not for compensation, renders emergency care or treatment by the use of an AED at the scene of an emergency is not liable for any civil damages resulting from any acts or omissions in rendering the emergency care.

(c) A person or entity who provides CPR and AED training to a person who renders emergency care pursuant to subdivision (b) is not liable for any civil damages resulting

§ 1714.21 OBLIGATIONS

from any acts or omissions of the person rendering the emergency care.

(d)(1) A person or entity that acquires an AED for emergency use pursuant to this section is not liable for any civil damages resulting from any acts or omissions in the rendering of the emergency care by use of an AED if that person or entity has complied with subdivision (b) of Section 1797.196 of the Health and Safety Code.

(2) A physician and surgeon or other health care professional that is involved in the selection, placement, or installation of an AED pursuant to Section 1797.196 of the Health and Safety Code is not liable for civil damages resulting from acts or omissions in the rendering of emergency care by use of that AED.

(e) The protections specified in this section do not apply in the case of personal injury or wrongful death that results from the gross negligence or willful or wanton misconduct of the person who renders emergency care or treatment by the use of an AED.

(f) This section does not relieve a manufacturer, designer, developer, distributor, installer, or supplier of an AED or defibrillator of any liability under any applicable statute or rule of law. (Added by Stats.1999, c. 163 (S.B.911), § 2. Amended by Stats.2002, c. 718 (A.B.2041), § 1; Stats.2015, c. 264 (S.B.658), § 1, eff. Jan. 1, 2016.)

Cross References

Automated external defibrillators (AEDs), employee, public school or school district liability, see Education Code § 49417.

Interscholastic athletic programs, availability of automated external defibrillators, civil liability, gross negligence or misconduct, testing, see Education Code § 35179.6.

Lifeguard services, defibrillators, see Health and Safety Code § 116045.

Requirements for persons acquiring automatic external defibrillator, see Health and Safety Code § 1797.196.

§ 1714.22. Opioid antagonist; prescription and dispensing permitted by authorized licensed health care providers to persons at risk of opioid-related overdose or persons in position to assist person at risk; standing distribution orders; overdose prevention and treatment training; immunity from liability

(a) For purposes of this section, the following definitions apply:

(1) "Opioid antagonist" means naloxone hydrochloride or any other opioid antagonist that is approved by the United States Food and Drug Administration for the treatment of an opioid overdose.

(2) "Opioid overdose prevention and treatment training program" means any program operated by a local health jurisdiction or that is registered by a local health jurisdiction to train individuals to prevent, recognize, and respond to an opiate overdose, and that provides, at a minimum, training in all of the following:

(A) The causes of an opiate overdose.

(B) Mouth to mouth resuscitation.

(C) How to contact appropriate emergency medical services.

(D) How to administer an opioid antagonist.

(b) A licensed health care provider who is authorized by law to prescribe an opioid antagonist may, if acting with reasonable care, prescribe and subsequently dispense or distribute an opioid antagonist to a person at risk of an opioid-related overdose or to a family member, friend, or other person in a position to assist a person at risk of an opioid-related overdose.

(c)(1) A licensed health care provider who is authorized by law to prescribe an opioid antagonist may issue standing orders for the distribution of an opioid antagonist to a person at risk of an opioid-related overdose or to a family member, friend, or other person in a position to assist a person at risk of an opioid-related overdose.

(2) A licensed health care provider who is authorized by law to prescribe an opioid antagonist may issue standing orders for the administration of an opioid antagonist to a person at risk of an opioid-related overdose by a family member, friend, or other person in a position to assist a person experiencing or reasonably suspected of experiencing an opioid overdose.

(d)(1) A person who is prescribed or possesses an opioid antagonist pursuant to a standing order shall receive the training provided by an opioid overdose prevention and treatment training program.

(2) A person who is prescribed an opioid antagonist directly from a licensed prescriber shall not be required to receive training from an opioid prevention and treatment training program.

(e) A licensed health care provider who acts with reasonable care shall not be subject to professional review, be liable in a civil action, or be subject to criminal prosecution for issuing a prescription or order pursuant to subdivision (b) or (c).

(f) Notwithstanding any other law, a person who possesses or distributes an opioid antagonist pursuant to a prescription or standing order shall not be subject to professional review, be liable in a civil action, or be subject to criminal prosecution for this possession or distribution. Notwithstanding any other law, a person not otherwise licensed to administer an opioid antagonist, but trained as required under paragraph (1) of subdivision (d), who acts with reasonable care in administering an opioid antagonist, in good faith and not for compensation, to a person who is experiencing or is suspected of experiencing an overdose shall not be subject to professional review, be liable in a civil action, or be subject to criminal prosecution for this administration. (Added by Stats.2007, c. 477 (S.B.767), § 2. Amended by Stats.2010, c. 545 (A.B.2145), § 1; Stats.2013, c. 707 (A.B.635), § 1; Stats.2021, c. 554 (S.B.823), § 1, eff. Jan. 1, 2022.)

Cross References

Training and standards for prehospital emergency medical care personnel, see Health and Safety Code § 1797.197.

§ 1714.23. Administration of epinephrine auto-injector; liability for civil damages; requirements for immunity

(a) For purposes of this section, the following definitions shall apply:

(1) "Anaphylaxis" means a potentially life-threatening hypersensitivity or allergic reaction to a substance.

(A) Symptoms of anaphylaxis may include shortness of breath, wheezing, difficulty breathing, difficulty talking or swallowing, hives, itching, swelling, shock, or asthma.

(B) Causes of anaphylaxis may include, but are not limited to, insect stings or bites, foods, drugs, and other allergens, as well as idiopathic or exercise-induced anaphylaxis.

(2) "Epinephrine auto-injector" means a disposable delivery device designed for the automatic injection of a premeasured dose of epinephrine into the human body to prevent or treat a life-threatening allergic reaction.

(b)(1) Any person described in subdivision (b) of Section 1797.197a of the Health and Safety Code who administers an epinephrine auto-injector, in good faith and not for compensation, to another person who appears to be experiencing anaphylaxis at the scene of an emergency situation is not liable for any civil damages resulting from his or her acts or omissions in administering the epinephrine auto-injector, if that person has complied with the requirements and standards of Section 1797.197a of the Health and Safety Code.

(2)(A) An authorized entity shall not be liable for any civil damages resulting from any act or omission other than an act or omission constituting gross negligence or willful or wanton misconduct connected to the administration of an epinephrine auto-injector by any one of its employees, volunteers, or agents who is a lay rescuer, as defined by paragraph (4) of subdivision (a) of Section 1797.197a of the Health and Safety Code, if the entity has complied with all applicable requirements of Section 1797.197a of the Health and Safety Code.

(B) The failure of an authorized entity to possess or administer an epinephrine auto-injector shall not result in civil liability.

(3) This subdivision does not affect any other immunity or defense that is available under law.

(c) The protection specified in paragraph (1) of subdivision (b) shall not apply in a case of personal injury or wrongful death that results from the gross negligence or willful or wanton misconduct of the person who renders emergency care treatment by the use of an epinephrine auto-injector.

(d) Nothing in this section relieves a manufacturer, designer, developer, distributor, or supplier of an epinephrine auto-injector of liability under any other applicable law.

(e) An authorizing physician and surgeon is not subject to professional review, liable in a civil action, or subject to criminal prosecution for the issuance of a prescription or order in accordance with Section 1797.197a of the Health and Safety Code unless the physician and surgeon's issuance of the prescription or order constitutes gross negligence or willful or malicious conduct. *(Added by Stats.2013, c. 725 (S.B.669), § 2. Amended by Stats.2016, c. 374 (A.B.1386), § 2, eff. Jan. 1, 2017.)*

§ 1714.24. Collector maintaining secure drug take-back bin; civil or criminal liability; requirements for immunity

(a) For purposes of this section, the following definitions shall apply:

(1) "Collector" includes only those entities authorized by and registered with the federal Drug Enforcement Administration to receive a controlled substance for the purpose of destruction, if the entity is in good standing with any applicable licensing authority.

(2) "Compensation" means reimbursement or funds received from a customer to compensate for the cost incurred in obtaining, installing, or maintaining a secure drug take-back bin. "Compensation" does not include reimbursement or funds received from any other person or entity, other than a customer, to compensate for the costs incurred in obtaining, installing, or maintaining a secure drug take-back bin.

(3) "Home-generated pharmaceutical waste" means a pharmaceutical that is no longer wanted or needed by the consumer and includes any delivery system, such as pills, liquids, and inhalers.

(4) "Maintains" includes owning, leasing, operating, or otherwise hosting a secure drug take-back bin on the collector's premises.

(5) "Pharmaceutical" means a prescription or over-the-counter human or veterinary drug, including, but not limited to, a drug as defined in Section 109925 of the Health and Safety Code and Section 321(g)(1) of Title 21 of the United States Code. "Pharmaceutical" includes controlled substances included in Schedule II, III, IV, or V of the California Uniform Controlled Substances Act (Division 10 (commencing with Section 11000) of the Health and Safety Code), but does not include a controlled substance included in Schedule I.

(6) "Secure drug take-back bin" means a collection receptacle as described in Section 1317.75 of Title 21 of the Code of Federal Regulations.

(b) Any collector that maintains a secure drug take-back bin shall not be liable in a civil action, or be subject to criminal prosecution, for any injury or harm that results from the collector maintaining a secure drug take-back bin on its premises provided that the collector, not for compensation, acts in good faith to take all of the following steps to ensure the health and safety of consumers and employees and the proper disposal in the waste stream of the home-generated pharmaceutical waste contained in a secure drug take-back bin, unless the injury or harm results from the collector's gross negligence or willful and wanton misconduct:

(1) Complies with all applicable state and federal laws and regulations relating to the collection of home-generated pharmaceutical waste for disposal in secure drug take-back bins, including, but not limited to, the federal Secure and Responsible Drug Disposal Act of 2010 (Public Law 111–273).[1]

(2) Notifies local law enforcement and any local environmental health department as to the existence and location of any secure drug take-back bin on the collector's premises and the status of the collector's registration as a collector with the federal Drug Enforcement Administration.

(3) Ensures that the secure drug take-back bin is placed in a location that is regularly monitored by employees of the registered collector.

(4) Ensures that conspicuous signage is posted on the secure drug take-back bin that clearly notifies customers as to what controlled and noncontrolled substances are and are not

§ 1714.24

acceptable for deposit into the bin, as well as the hours during which collection is allowed.

(5) Ensures that public access to the secure drug take-back bin is limited to hours in which employees of the registered collector are present and able to monitor the operation of the secure drug take-back bin.

(6) Regularly inspects the area surrounding the secure drug take-back bin for potential tampering or diversion. Record logs of those inspections shall be maintained and retained for two years, reflecting the date and time of the inspection, and the initials of the employee inspecting the area. The logs shall be maintained in writing or electronically and may be combined with logs required by state or federal regulations. The logs may be used to demonstrate regular inspection of the area. Other records or reports mandated by federal or state regulations shall also be retained for a minimum of two years unless regulations mandate a longer period.

(7) Notifies local law enforcement authorities of any suspected or known tampering, theft, or significant loss of controlled substances, within one business day of discovery. If the collector maintains daily business hours, this notification shall be made within one calendar day.

(8) Notify local law enforcement as to any decision to discontinue its voluntary collection of controlled substances and provide documentation of its written notification to the federal Drug Enforcement Administration's Registration Unit as otherwise required under federal laws and regulations.

(c) Nothing in this section shall be construed to require entities that may qualify as a collector to acquire, maintain, or make available to the public a secure drug take-back bin on its premises. *(Added by Stats.2016, c. 238 (S.B.1229), § 2, eff. Jan. 1, 2017.)*

[1] For public law sections classified to the U.S.C.A., see USCA–Tables.

§ 1714.25. Donations by persons, gleaners, or food facilities to nonprofit charitable organizations; immunity

(a) Except for injury resulting from gross negligence or intentional misconduct in the preparation or handling of donated food, no person, gleaner, or food facility that donates food that is fit for human consumption at the time it was donated to a nonprofit charitable organization or food bank shall be liable for any damage or injury resulting from the consumption of the donated food. Food facilities may donate food directly to end recipients for consumption.

The immunity from civil liability provided by this subdivision applies regardless of compliance with any laws, regulations, or ordinances regulating the packaging or labeling of food, and regardless of compliance with any laws, regulations, or ordinances regulating the storage or handling of the food by the donee after the donation of the food. The donation of nonperishable food that is fit for human consumption but that has exceeded the labeled shelf life date recommended by the manufacturer is protected under the California Good Samaritan Food Donation Act. The donation of perishable food that is fit for human consumption but that has exceeded the labeled shelf life date recommended by the manufacturer is protected under the California Good Samaritan Food Donation Act if the person that distributes the food to the end recipient makes a good faith evaluation that the food to be donated is wholesome.

(b) A nonprofit charitable organization or a food bank that, in good faith, receives and distributes food without charge that is fit for human consumption at the time it was distributed is not liable for an injury or death due to the food unless the injury or death is a direct result of the gross negligence or intentional misconduct of the organization.

(c) Nothing in this chapter shall be construed to limit the ability of a person, gleaner, or food facility to donate food.

(d) For the purposes of this section:

(1) "Food bank" has the same meaning as defined in Section 113783 of the Health and Safety Code.

(2) "Food facility" has the same meaning as defined in Section 113789 of the Health and Safety Code.

(3) "Gleaner" means a person who harvests for free distribution to the needy, or for donation to a nonprofit organization for ultimate distribution to the needy, an agricultural crop that has been donated by the owner.

(4) "Nonprofit charitable organization" has the same meaning as defined in Section 113841 of the Health and Safety Code.

(5) "Person" means an individual, school, local educational agency as defined in Section 421 of the Education Code, corporation, partnership, limited liability company, organization, association, or governmental entity, including a retail grocer, wholesaler, hotel, motel, manufacturer, restaurant, caterer, farmer, and nonprofit food distributor or hospital. In the case of a corporation, partnership, organization, association, or governmental entity, the term includes an officer, director, partner, manager or managing member, deacon, trustee, council member, or other elected or appointed individual responsible for the governance of the entity. *(Added by Stats.1988, c. 735, § 1. Amended by Stats.1996, c. 1023 (S.B.1497), § 27, eff. Sept. 29, 1996; Stats.2017, c. 619 (A.B.1219), § 3, eff. Jan. 1, 2018.)*

§ 1714.26. Vision screenings and eyeglasses provided by nonprofit charitable organizations and licensed optometrists, ophthalmologists, or trained volunteers working with such organizations; limitation of liability; exceptions

(a) Except for damage or injury resulting from gross negligence or a willful act, there is no liability for any damage or injury on the part of a nonprofit charitable organization that provides vision screenings and, if applicable, provides donated or recycled eyeglasses, or a participating licensed optometrist, ophthalmologist, or trained volunteer who works with such a nonprofit charitable organization in the performance of vision screenings, if all of the following conditions are met:

(1) The vision screening is provided to address ocular health concerns and, if applicable, to provide a temporary solution in the form of donated or recycled eyeglasses until the patient can get a full examination and eyeglasses.

(2) The vision screening is not intended to replace a full ocular health examination provided by a licensed optometrist or ophthalmologist.

(3) The patient signs a waiver acknowledging that the services provided are a temporary solution until the patient can get a full examination by a licensed optometrist or ophthalmologist.

(4) Each vision screening is supervised by an attending licensed optometrist or ophthalmologist.

(5) The eyeglass prescription determinations and ocular health recommendations are provided by an attending licensed optometrist or ophthalmologist.

(6) A written prescription is not provided to the patient.

(7) The eyeglasses provided to the patients are a close or approximate match, within tolerances allowed by the attending licensed optometrist or ophthalmologist, to the prescription determined during the vision screening.

(8) The vision screening and eyeglasses are provided without a charge.

(9) The optometrist, ophthalmologist, or volunteer is authorized by the nonprofit organization to provide the vision screening and eyeglasses on behalf of the nonprofit organization and is acting within the scope of his or her authorized responsibilities and the guidelines of the nonprofit charitable organization when providing the vision screening or eyeglasses.

(10) The nonprofit charitable organization provides procedural, risk management, and quality control training, as applicable, to the participating optometrist, ophthalmologist, or volunteer who provides the vision screening or eyeglasses.

(b) The limitation of liability provided in subdivision (a) is not applicable if an action is brought by an officer of a state or local government pursuant to state or local law.

(c) The limitation of liability provided in subdivision (a) is not applicable if the conduct of the nonprofit charitable organization, optometrist, ophthalmologist, or volunteer includes any of the following types of misconduct:

(1) A crime of violence.

(2) A hate crime.

(3) An act involving a sexual offense.

(4) An act involving misconduct in violation of federal or state civil rights laws.

(5) An act performed while the defendant was under the influence of drugs or alcohol.

(d) For the purposes of this section:

(1) "Nonprofit charitable organization" means an organization exempt from federal income tax as an organization described in Section 501(c)(3) of the Internal Revenue Code.[1]

(2) "Vision screening" means a test or examination of an individual using a portion of the usual examination procedures in a comprehensive eye examination and refraction, that are selected or directed by an attending licensed optometrist or ophthalmologist, and are within the guidelines of the nonprofit charitable organization. *(Added by Stats. 2013, c. 68 (S.B.724), § 1.)*

[1] Internal Revenue Code sections are in Title 26 of the U.S.C.A.

§ 1714.29. Trauma kits; contents; application of Good Samaritan Law; liability limitation for training and certification

(a) For purposes of this section, "trauma kit" means a first aid response kit that contains at least all of the following:

(1) One tourniquet endorsed by the Committee on Tactical Combat Casualty Care.

(2) One bleeding control bandage.

(3) One pair of nonlatex protective gloves and a marker.

(4) One pair of scissors.

(5) Instructional documents developed by the Stop the Bleed national awareness campaign of the United States Department of Homeland Security or the American College of Surgeons Committee on Trauma, the American Red Cross, the Committee for Tactical Emergency Casualty Care, or any other partner of the United States Department of Defense.

(b) Medical materials and equipment similar to those described in paragraphs (1) to (4), inclusive, of subdivision (a) and any additional items that are approved by the medical director of the local emergency medical services agency may be included as supplements in addition to the items described in paragraphs (1) to (4), inclusive, of subdivision (a) if they adequately treat a traumatic injury and can be stored in a readily available kit.

(c) Subdivision (b) of Section 1799.102 of the Health and Safety Code, the "Good Samaritan Law," applies to any lay rescuer or person who, in good faith and not for compensation, renders emergency care or treatment by the use of a trauma kit at the scene of an emergency.

(d) A person who renders emergency care or treatment by the use of a trauma kit at the scene of an emergency and who receives compensation as a result of their employment by a property managing entity, a tenant of a building, or any other private or public employer, but is not compensated to provide emergency medical care, is not providing emergency medical care "for compensation" for purposes of Section 1799.102 of the Health and Safety Code.

(e) Section 1799.100 of the Health and Safety Code applies to a person or entity that voluntarily, and without expectation and receipt of compensation, does either of the following:

(1) Provides training in the use of a trauma kit to provide emergency medical treatment to victims of trauma, including, but not limited to, training in the use of the trauma kit in emergency first care response to an active shooter.

(2) Certifies persons, other than physicians and surgeons, registered nurses, and licensed vocational nurses, who are trained in the use of a trauma kit to provide emergency medical treatment to victims of trauma.

(f) This section does not require a property manager or person employed by a property managing entity to respond to an emergency with the use of trauma kits. *(Added by Stats.2022, c. 586 (A.B.2260), § 2, eff. Jan. 1, 2023.)*

§ 1714.3. Liability of parent or guardian for injury to person or property caused by discharge of firearm by minor under 18

Civil liability for any injury to the person or property of another proximately caused by the discharge of a firearm by a minor under the age of 18 years shall be imputed to a parent or guardian having custody and control of the minor for all purposes of civil damages, and such parent or guardian shall be jointly and severally liable with such minor for any damages resulting from such act, if such parent or guardian either permitted the minor to have the firearm or left the firearm in a place accessible to the minor.

The liability imposed by this section is in addition to any liability otherwise imposed by law. However, no person, or group of persons collectively, shall incur liability under this section in any amount exceeding thirty thousand dollars ($30,000) for injury to or death of one person as a result of any one occurrence or, subject to the limit as to one person, exceeding sixty thousand dollars ($60,000) for injury to or death of all persons as a result of any one such occurrence. *(Added by Stats.1970, c. 843, p. 1576, § 1. Amended by Stats.1977, c. 87, p. 505, § 1; Stats.1986, c. 1099, § 1.)*

Cross References

Firearm capable of being concealed upon the person defined, see Penal Code § 12001.
Joint and several obligations, see Civil Code § 1430 et seq.
Juvenile court law,
    Criminal violation by minor, restitution hearing, citation ordering appearance by parents or guardians, see Welfare and Institutions Code § 739.5.
    Restitution, fine, or penalty assessment order, liability of parent or guardian, see Welfare and Institutions Code § 730.7.
Minor's liability for wrongs, see Family Code § 6600.

§ 1714.4. Knowingly assisting child support obligor escape, evade, or avoid paying court-ordered or court-approved child support; application to financial institutions

(a) Any person or business entity that knowingly assists a child support obligor who has an unpaid child support obligation to escape, evade, or avoid paying court-ordered or court-approved child support shall be liable for three times the value of the assistance provided, such as the fair market value of the obligor's assets transferred or hidden. The maximum liability imposed by this section shall not exceed the entire child support obligation due. Any funds or assets collected pursuant to this section shall be paid to the child support obligee, and shall not reduce the amount of the unpaid child support obligation. Upon the satisfaction of the unpaid child support obligation, this section shall not apply.

(b) For purposes of this section, actions taken to knowingly assist a child support obligor to escape, evade, or avoid paying court-ordered or court-approved child support include, with actual knowledge of the child support obligation, helping to hide or transfer assets of the child support obligor.

(c) This section shall not apply to a financial institution unless the financial institution has actual knowledge of the child support obligation and, with that knowledge, knowingly assists the obligor to escape, evade, or avoid paying the child support obligation. However, a financial institution with knowledge of an asset transfer has no duty to inquire into the rightfulness of the transaction, nor shall it be deemed to have knowingly assisted an obligor to escape, evade, or avoid paying the child support obligation if that assistance is provided by an employee or agent of the financial institution acting outside the terms and conditions of employment or agency without the actual knowledge of the financial institution. *(Added by Stats.2006, c. 820 (A.B.2440), § 2.)*

§ 1714.41. Knowingly assisting a child support obligor to escape, evade, or avoid paying child support; included actions

(a) Any person or business entity that knowingly assists a child support obligor who has an unpaid child support obligation to escape, evade, or avoid paying court-ordered or court-approved child support shall be liable for three times the value of the assistance provided, such as the fair market value of the assets transferred or hidden, or the amount of the wages or other compensation paid to the child support obligor but not reported. The maximum liability imposed by this section shall not exceed the entire child support obligation due. Any funds or assets collected pursuant to this section shall be paid to the child support obligee, and shall not reduce the amount of the unpaid child support obligation. Upon the satisfaction of the unpaid child support obligation, this section shall not apply.

(b) For purposes of this section, actions taken to knowingly assist a child support obligor to escape, evade, or avoid paying court-ordered or court-approved child support include, but are not limited to, any of the following actions taken when the individual or entity knew or should have known of the child support obligation:

(1) Hiring or employing the child support obligor as an employee in a trade or business and failing to timely file a report of new employees with the California New Employee Registry maintained by the Employment Development Department.

(2) Engaging the child support obligor as a service provider and failing to timely file a report with the Employment Development Department as required by Section 1088.8 of the Unemployment Insurance Code.

(3) When engaged in a trade or business, paying wages or other forms of compensation for services rendered by a child support obligor that are not reported to the Employment Development Department as required, including, but not limited to, payment in cash or via barter or trade. *(Added by Stats.2006, c. 820 (A.B.2440), § 3.)*

§ 1714.43. Retailers to disclose efforts to eradicate slavery and human trafficking from direct supply chain for tangible goods; definitions; posting on Internet Website; contents; injunctive relief for violation

(a)(1) Every retail seller and manufacturer doing business in this state and having annual worldwide gross receipts that exceed one hundred million dollars ($100,000,000) shall disclose, as set forth in subdivision (c), its efforts to eradicate slavery and human trafficking from its direct supply chain for tangible goods offered for sale.

(2) For the purposes of this section, the following definitions shall apply:

(A) "Doing business in this state" shall have the same meaning as set forth in Section 23101 of the Revenue and Taxation Code.

(B) "Gross receipts" shall have the same meaning as set forth in Section 25120 of the Revenue and Taxation Code.

(C) "Manufacturer" means a business entity with manufacturing as its principal business activity code, as reported on the entity's tax return filed under Part 10.2 (commencing with Section 18401) of Division 2 of the Revenue and Taxation Code.

(D) "Retail seller" means a business entity with retail trade as its principal business activity code, as reported on the entity's tax return filed under Part 10.2 (commencing with Section 18401) of Division 2 of the Revenue and Taxation Code.

(b) The disclosure described in subdivision (a) shall be posted on the retail seller's or manufacturer's Internet Web site with a conspicuous and easily understood link to the required information placed on the business' homepage. In the event the retail seller or manufacturer does not have an Internet Web site, consumers shall be provided the written disclosure within 30 days of receiving a written request for the disclosure from a consumer.

(c) The disclosure described in subdivision (a) shall, at a minimum, disclose to what extent, if any, that the retail seller or manufacturer does each of the following:

(1) Engages in verification of product supply chains to evaluate and address risks of human trafficking and slavery. The disclosure shall specify if the verification was not conducted by a third party.

(2) Conducts audits of suppliers to evaluate supplier compliance with company standards for trafficking and slavery in supply chains. The disclosure shall specify if the verification was not an independent, unannounced audit.

(3) Requires direct suppliers to certify that materials incorporated into the product comply with the laws regarding slavery and human trafficking of the country or countries in which they are doing business.

(4) Maintains internal accountability standards and procedures for employees or contractors failing to meet company standards regarding slavery and trafficking.

(5) Provides company employees and management, who have direct responsibility for supply chain management, training on human trafficking and slavery, particularly with respect to mitigating risks within the supply chains of products.

(d) The exclusive remedy for a violation of this section shall be an action brought by the Attorney General for injunctive relief. Nothing in this section shall limit remedies available for a violation of any other state or federal law.

(e) The provisions of this section shall take effect on January 1, 2012. *(Added by Stats.2010, c. 556 (S.B.657), § 3, operative Jan. 1, 2012.)*

Cross References

List of retail sellers and manufactures required to disclose efforts to eradicate slavery and human trafficking to be provided to Attorney General annually, contents, see Revenue and Taxation Code § 19547.5.

§ 1714.45. Products liability; consumer products known by consumers to be inherently unsafe

(a) In a product liability action, a manufacturer or seller shall not be liable if both of the following apply:

(1) The product is inherently unsafe and the product is known to be unsafe by the ordinary consumer who consumes the product with the ordinary knowledge common to the community.

(2) The product is a common consumer product intended for personal consumption, such as sugar, castor oil, alcohol, and butter, as identified in comment i to Section 402A of the Restatement (Second) of Torts.

(b) This section does not exempt the manufacture or sale of tobacco products by tobacco manufacturers and their successors in interest from product liability actions, but does exempt the sale or distribution of tobacco products by any other person, including, but not limited to, retailers or distributors.

(c) For purposes of this section, the term "product liability action" means any action for injury or death caused by a product, except that the term does not include an action based on a manufacturing defect or breach of an express warranty.

(d) This section is intended to be declarative of and does not alter or amend existing California law, including Cronin v. J.B.E. Olson Corp. (1972), 8 Cal.3d 121, and shall apply to all product liability actions pending on, or commenced after, January 1, 1988.

(e) This section does not apply to, and never applied to, an action brought by a public entity to recover the value of benefits provided to individuals injured by a tobacco-related illness caused by the tortious conduct of a tobacco company or its successor in interest, including, but not limited to, an action brought pursuant to Section 14124.71 of the Welfare and Institutions Code. In the action brought by a public entity, the fact that the injured individual's claim against the defendant may be barred by a prior version of this section shall not be a defense. This subdivision does not constitute a change in, but is declaratory of, existing law relating to tobacco products.

(f) It is the intention of the Legislature in enacting the amendments to subdivisions (a) and (b) of this section adopted at the 1997–98 Regular Session to declare that there exists no statutory bar to tobacco-related personal injury, wrongful death, or other tort claims against tobacco manufacturers and their successors in interest by California smokers or others who have suffered or incurred injuries, damages, or costs arising from the promotion, marketing, sale, or consumption of tobacco products. It is also the intention of the Legislature to clarify that those claims that were or are brought shall be determined on their merits, without the imposition of any claim of statutory bar or categorical defense.

(g) This section shall not be construed to grant immunity to a tobacco industry research organization. *(Added by Stats.1987, c. 1498, § 3. Amended by Stats.1997, c. 25 (A.B.1603), § 2, eff. June 12, 1997; Stats.1997, c. 570 (S.B.67), § 1; Stats.1998, c. 485 (A.B.2803), § 38.)*

Cross References

Admissibility of subsequent remedial conduct, see Evidence Code § 1151.

§ 1714.5. Defense shelters or other necessary facility for emergency purposes

(a) There shall be no liability on the part of one, including the State of California, county, city and county, city or any other political subdivision of the State of California, who owns or maintains any building or premises which have been designated as a shelter from destructive operations or attacks by enemies of the United States by any disaster council or any public office, body, or officer of this state or of the United States, or which have been designated or are used as mass care centers, first aid stations, temporary hospital annexes, or as other necessary facilities for mitigating the effects of a natural, manmade, or war-caused emergency, for any injuries arising out of the use thereof for such purposes sustained by any person while in or upon said building or premises as a result of the condition of said building or premises or as a result of any act or omission, or in any way arising from the designation of such premises as a shelter, or the designation or use thereof as a mass care center, first aid station, temporary hospital annex, or other necessary facility for emergency purposes, except a willful act, of such owner or occupant or his or her servants, agents or employees when such person has entered or gone upon or into said building or premises for the purpose of seeking refuge, treatment, care, or assistance therein during destructive operations or attacks by enemies of the United States or during tests ordered by lawful authority or during a natural or manmade emergency.

(b) Notwithstanding any other provision of law, no disaster service worker who is performing disaster services during a state of war emergency, a state of emergency, or a local emergency, as such emergencies are defined in Section 8558 of the Government Code, shall be liable for civil damages on account of personal injury to or death of any person or damage to property resulting from any act or omission while performing disaster services anywhere within any jurisdiction covered by such emergency, except one that is willful.

(c) For purposes of this subdivision, a disaster service worker shall be performing disaster services when acting within the scope of the disaster service worker's responsibilities under the authority of the governmental emergency organization.

(d) For purposes of this subdivision, "governmental emergency organization" shall mean the emergency organization of any state, city, city and county, county, district, or other local governmental agency or public agency, which is authorized pursuant to the California Emergency Services Act (Chapter 7 (commencing with Section 8550) of Division 1 of Title 2 of the Government Code).

(e) Nothing in this section shall be construed to alter any existing legal duties or obligations. The amendments to this section made by the act amending this section shall apply exclusively to any legal action filed on or after the effective date of the act. *(Added by Stats.1943, c. 463, p. 1998, § 1. Amended by Stats.1951, c. 247, p. 507, § 1; Stats.1955, c. 1777, p. 3283, § 1; Stats.1971, c. 38, p. 48, § 1; Stats.1974, c. 1158, p. 2464, § 1; Stats.2009, c. 27 (S.B.39), § 1, eff. Aug. 6, 2009.)*

Cross References

California Emergency Services Act, see Government Code § 8550 et seq.

Persons rendering emergency medical or nonmedical care at emergency scene for no compensation, see Health and Safety Code § 1799.102.

§ 1714.55. Retail or wholesale telecommunications service provider of 9–1–1 service; liability for civil claim, damage, or loss; definitions

(a) A retail or wholesale service provider of telecommunications service, or other service, involved in providing 9–1–1 service in accordance with the Warren–911–Emergency Assistance Act (Article 6 (commencing with Section 53100) of Chapter 1 of Part 1 of Division 2 of Title 5 of the Government Code), shall not be liable for any civil claim, damage, or loss caused by an act or omission in the design, development, installation, maintenance, or provision of 9–1–1 service, unless the act or omission that proximately caused the claim, damage, or loss constituted gross negligence, wanton or willful misconduct, or intentional misconduct.

(b) For purposes of this section:

(1) "Public safety agency" means a public safety agency as defined in accordance with the Warren–911–Emergency Assistance Act (Article 6 (commencing with Section 53100) of Chapter 1 of Part 1 of Division 2 of Title 5 of the Government Code).

(2) "9–1–1 service" means a telecommunications service, or other wireline or wireless service, that provides to the user of the public telephone system the ability to reach a public safety agency by utilizing the digits 9–1–1 or otherwise facilitates the provision of emergency services pursuant to the Warren–911–Emergency Assistance Act (Article 6 (commencing with Section 53100) of Chapter 1 of Part 1 of Division 2 of Title 5 of the Government Code). "9–1–1 service" includes a 9–1–1 service that utilizes in whole or in part an Internet Protocol.

(c) This section shall not apply to services provided under tariff.

(d) This section shall not be construed to modify the liability of a manufacturer, distributor, or other person arising from a claim, damage, or loss, related to the operation or performance of an end-user device that is not related to the provision of 9–1–1 service. *(Added by Stats.2011, c. 297 (A.B.1074), § 1, eff. Sept. 21, 2011.)*

§ 1714.6. Compliance with military orders or regulations under Emergency Services Act; suspension of civil and criminal liability

The violation of any statute or ordinance shall not establish negligence as a matter of law where the act or omission involved was required in order to comply with an order or proclamation of any military commander who is authorized to issue such orders or proclamations; nor when the act or omission involved is required in order to comply with any regulation, directive, or order of the Governor promulgated under the California Emergency Services Act.[1] No person shall be prosecuted for a violation of any statute or ordinance when violation of such statute or ordinance is required in order to comply with an order or proclamation of any military commander who is authorized to issue such orders or proclamations; nor shall any person be prosecuted for a violation of any statute or ordinance when violation of such statute or ordinance is required in order to comply with any regulation, directive, or order of the Governor promulgated under the California Emergency Services Act. The provisions of this section shall apply to such acts or omissions whether occurring prior to or after the effective date of this section. *(Formerly § 1714.5, added by Stats.1943, c. 895, p. 2741, § 1. Renumbered § 1714.6 and amended by Stats.1951, c. 514, p. 1661, § 1. Amended by Stats.1971, c. 438, p. 857, § 15.)*

[1] Government Code § 8550 et seq.

§ 1714.7. Injury while getting on, riding on, or getting off, moving locomotive or railroad car without authority; exemption of owner or operator from liability; exception

No person who is injured while getting on, or attempting to get on, a moving locomotive or railroad car, without authority from the owner or operator of the railroad, or who, having gotten on a locomotive or railroad car while in motion without such authority, is injured while so riding or getting off, shall recover any damages from the owner or operator thereof for such injuries unless proximately caused by an intentional act of such owner or operator with knowledge that serious injury is the probable result of such act, or with a wanton and reckless disregard of the probable result of such act. *(Added by Stats.1971, c. 1554, p. 3067, § 1.)*

Cross References

Ejection of passengers, see Civil Code § 2188.
Railroads, liability for injuries to passengers, see Public Utilities Code § 7654.

§ 1714.8. Health care providers; professional negligence or malpractice; exemption from liability; definition

(a) No health care provider shall be liable for professional negligence or malpractice for any occurrence or result solely on the basis that the occurrence or result was caused by the natural course of a disease or condition, or was the natural or expected result of reasonable treatment rendered for the disease or condition. This section shall not be construed so as to limit liability for the failure to inform of the risks of treatment or failure to accept treatment, or for negligent diagnosis or treatment or the negligent failure to diagnose or treat.

(b) As used in this section, "health care provider" means any person licensed or certified pursuant to Division 2 (commencing with Section 500) of the Business and Professions Code, or licensed pursuant to the Osteopathic Initiative Act or the Chiropractic Initiative Act, or certified pursuant to Chapter 2.5 (commencing with Section 1440) of Division 2 of the Health and Safety Code, and any clinic, health dispensary, or health facility licensed pursuant to Division 2 (commencing with Section 1200) of the Health and Safety Code. *(Added by Stats.1978, c. 1358, p. 4510, § 1.)*

Cross References

Professional negligence by health care provider, liability, see Civil Code §§ 3333.1, 3333.2.
Time of commencing civil actions, see Code of Civil Procedure §§ 340.5, 364, 597.5.
Unsolicited referrals from tests by multiphasic screening unit, immunity from liability, see Civil Code § 43.9.

§ 1714.85. Rejected, eff. Nov. 4, 2014

§ 1714.9. Responsibility for willful acts or want of ordinary care causing injury to peace officers, firefighters or emergency service personnel; circumstances; comparative fault; subrogation; exception

(a) Notwithstanding statutory or decisional law to the contrary, any person is responsible not only for the results of that person's willful acts causing injury to a peace officer, firefighter, or any emergency medical personnel employed by a public entity, but also for any injury occasioned to that person by the want of ordinary care or skill in the management of the person's property or person, in any of the following situations:

(1) Where the conduct causing the injury occurs after the person knows or should have known of the presence of the peace officer, firefighter, or emergency medical personnel.

(2) Where the conduct causing injury violates a statute, ordinance, or regulation, and the conduct causing injury was itself not the event that precipitated either the response or presence of the peace officer, firefighter, or emergency medical personnel.

(3) Where the conduct causing the injury was intended to injure the peace officer, firefighter, or emergency medical personnel.

(4) Where the conduct causing the injury is arson as defined in Section 451 of the Penal Code.

(b) This section does not preclude the reduction of an award of damages because of the comparative fault of the peace officer, firefighter, or emergency medical personnel in causing the injury.

(c) The employer of a firefighter, peace officer or emergency medical personnel may be subrogated to the rights granted by this section to the extent of the worker's compensation benefits, and other liabilities of the employer, including all salary, wage, pension, or other emolument paid to the employee or the employee's dependents.

(d) The liability imposed by this section shall not apply to an employer of a peace officer, firefighter, or emergency medical personnel.

(e) This section is not intended to change or modify the common law independent cause exception to the firefighter's rule as set forth in Donohue v. San Francisco Housing Authority (1993) 16 Cal.App.4th 658. *(Added by Stats.1982, c. 258, p. 836, § 1. Amended by Stats.1983, c. 136, § 1; Stats.2001, c. 140 (S.B.448), § 2.)*

Cross References

Assault on peace officer or firefighter, see Penal Code §§ 240, 241, 241.4, 245.
Battery on peace officer or firefighter, see Penal Code § 243.
Illegal conduct at burning of building, see Penal Code § 148.2.

§ 1714.9   OBLIGATIONS

Resisting, delaying or obstructing officer, see Penal Code § 148.

§ 1714.10. Attorney client civil conspiracy; proof and court determination prior to pleading; defense; limitations; appeal

(a) No cause of action against an attorney for a civil conspiracy with his or her client arising from any attempt to contest or compromise a claim or dispute, and which is based upon the attorney's representation of the client, shall be included in a complaint or other pleading unless the court enters an order allowing the pleading that includes the claim for civil conspiracy to be filed after the court determines that the party seeking to file the pleading has established that there is a reasonable probability that the party will prevail in the action. The court may allow the filing of a pleading claiming liability based upon such a civil conspiracy following the filing of a verified petition therefor accompanied by the proposed pleading and supporting affidavits stating the facts upon which the liability is based. The court shall order service of the petition upon the party against whom the action is proposed to be filed and permit that party to submit opposing affidavits prior to making its determination. The filing of the petition, proposed pleading, and accompanying affidavits shall toll the running of any applicable statute of limitations until the final determination of the matter, which ruling, if favorable to the petitioning party, shall permit the proposed pleading to be filed.

(b) Failure to obtain a court order where required by subdivision (a) shall be a defense to any action for civil conspiracy filed in violation thereof. The defense shall be raised by the attorney charged with civil conspiracy upon that attorney's first appearance by demurrer, motion to strike, or such other motion or application as may be appropriate. Failure to timely raise the defense shall constitute a waiver thereof.

(c) This section shall not apply to a cause of action against an attorney for a civil conspiracy with his or her client, where (1) the attorney has an independent legal duty to the plaintiff, or (2) the attorney's acts go beyond the performance of a professional duty to serve the client and involve a conspiracy to violate a legal duty in furtherance of the attorney's financial gain.

(d) This section establishes a special proceeding of a civil nature. Any order made under subdivision (a), (b), or (c) which determines the rights of a petitioner or an attorney against whom a pleading has been or is proposed to be filed, shall be appealable as a final judgment in a civil action.

(e) Subdivision (d) does not constitute a change in, but is declaratory of, the existing law. *(Added by Stats.1988, c. 1052, § 1. Amended by Stats.1991, c. 916 (S.B.820), § 1; Stats.1992, c. 427 (A.B.3355), § 12; Stats.1993, c. 645 (S.B. 764), § 1; Stats.2000, c. 472 (A.B.2069), § 2.)*

§ 1714.11. Donation of fire protection apparatus or equipment; immunity from liability for damage or injury resulting from use; conditions

(a) Except for damage or injury proximately caused by a grossly negligent act or omission or willful or wanton misconduct of the donor, no public employee or public entity, including, but not limited to, a fire department, a fire protection district, or the Department of Forestry and Fire Protection, that donates fire protection apparatus or equipment to a volunteer fire department, volunteer fire protection district, or volunteer fire company is liable for any damage or injury that results from the use of that apparatus or equipment by the recipient fire department, fire protection district, or fire company.

(b)(1) The immunity provided by this section only shall apply if the donor of the fire protection apparatus or equipment discloses in writing to the recipient fire department, fire protection district, or fire company any known damage to, or deficiencies in, the apparatus and equipment.

(2) A volunteer fire department, volunteer fire protection district, or volunteer fire company that receives donated fire protection apparatus or equipment shall inspect and repair the apparatus and equipment prior to use for public safety purposes. *(Added by Stats.2002, c. 388 (A.B.1821), § 1.)*

§ 1715. Other obligations

Other obligations are prescribed by Divisions I [1] and II [2] of this Code. *(Enacted in 1872.)*

[1] Civil Code § 38 et seq.
[2] Civil Code § 654 et seq.

§ 1716. Solicitations for orders; notice or disclaimer; penalties

(a) It is unlawful for a person to solicit payment of money by another by means of a written statement or invoice, or any writing that reasonably could be considered a bill, invoice, or statement of account due, but is in fact a solicitation for an order, unless the solicitation conforms to subdivisions (b) to (f), inclusive.

(b) A solicitation described in subdivision (a) shall bear on its face either the disclaimer prescribed by subparagraph (A) of paragraph (2) of subsection (d) of Section 3001 of Title 39 of the United States Code or the following notice:

"THIS IS NOT A BILL. THIS IS A SOLICITATION. YOU ARE UNDER NO OBLIGATION TO PAY THE AMOUNT STATED ABOVE UNLESS YOU ACCEPT THIS OFFER."

The statutory disclaimer or the alternative notice shall be displayed in conspicuous boldface capital letters of a color prominently contrasting with the background against which they appear, including all other print on the face of the solicitation and shall be at least as large, bold, and conspicuous as any other print on the face of the solicitation but no smaller than 30–point type.

(c) The notice or disclaimer required by this section shall be displayed conspicuously apart from other print on the page and immediately below each portion of the solicitation that reasonably could be construed to specify a monetary amount due and payable by the recipient. The notice or disclaimer shall not be preceded, followed, or surrounded by words, symbols, or other matter that reduces its conspicuousness or that introduces, modifies, qualifies, or explains the required text, such as "legal notice required by law."

(d) The notice or disclaimer may not, by folding or any other device, be rendered unintelligible or less prominent than any other information on the face of the solicitation.

(e) If a solicitation consists of more than one page or if any page is designed to be separated into portions, such as by tearing along a perforated line, the notice or disclaimer shall be displayed in its entirety on the face of each page or portion of a page that reasonably might be considered a bill, invoice, or statement of account due as required by subdivisions (b) and (c).

(f) For the purposes of this section, "color" includes black and "color prominently contrasting" excludes any color, or any intensity of an otherwise included color, that does not permit legible reproduction by ordinary office photocopying equipment used under normal operating conditions, and that is not at least as vivid as any other color on the face of the solicitation.

(g) Any person damaged by noncompliance with this section, in addition to other remedies, is entitled to damages in an amount equal to three times the sum solicited.

(h) Any person who violates this section shall be liable for a civil penalty not to exceed ten thousand dollars ($10,000) for each violation, which shall be assessed and recovered in a civil action brought in the name of the people of the State of California by the Attorney General or by any district attorney, county counsel, or city attorney in any court of competent jurisdiction. If the action is brought by the Attorney General, one-half of the penalty collected shall be paid to the treasurer of the county in which the judgment was entered and one-half to the State Treasurer. If brought by a district attorney or county counsel, the entire amount of the penalty collected shall be paid to the treasurer of the county in which the judgment was entered. If brought by a city attorney or city prosecutor, one-half of the penalty shall be paid to the treasurer of the county and one-half to the city.

(i) A violation of this section is a misdemeanor punishable by imprisonment in a county jail not exceeding six months, by a fine not exceeding two thousand five hundred dollars ($2,500), or by both that fine and imprisonment. *(Added by Stats.1967, c. 346, p. 1545, § 1. Amended by Stats.1978, c. 492, p. 1624, § 1; Stats.1996, c. 397 (S.B.1530), § 1.)*

Cross References

Attorney General, generally, see Government Code § 12500 et seq.
Fraudulent claims against public entity or officer, see Penal Code § 72.
Misdemeanors, definition and penalties, see Penal Code §§ 17, 19, 19.2.
State Treasurer, generally, see Government Code § 12302 et seq.

§ 1717. Action on contract; award of attorney's fees and costs; prevailing party; deposit of amounts in insured, interest-bearing account; damages not based on contract

(a) In any action on a contract, where the contract specifically provides that attorney's fees and costs, which are incurred to enforce that contract, shall be awarded either to one of the parties or to the prevailing party, then the party who is determined to be the party prevailing on the contract, whether he or she is the party specified in the contract or not, shall be entitled to reasonable attorney's fees in addition to other costs.

Where a contract provides for attorney's fees, as set forth above, that provision shall be construed as applying to the entire contract, unless each party was represented by counsel in the negotiation and execution of the contract, and the fact of that representation is specified in the contract.

Reasonable attorney's fees shall be fixed by the court, and shall be an element of the costs of suit.

Attorney's fees provided for by this section shall not be subject to waiver by the parties to any contract which is entered into after the effective date of this section. Any provision in any such contract which provides for a waiver of attorney's fees is void.

(b)(1) The court, upon notice and motion by a party, shall determine who is the party prevailing on the contract for purposes of this section, whether or not the suit proceeds to final judgment. Except as provided in paragraph (2), the party prevailing on the contract shall be the party who recovered a greater relief in the action on the contract. The court may also determine that there is no party prevailing on the contract for purposes of this section.

(2) Where an action has been voluntarily dismissed or dismissed pursuant to a settlement of the case, there shall be no prevailing party for purposes of this section.

Where the defendant alleges in his or her answer that he or she tendered to the plaintiff the full amount to which he or she was entitled, and thereupon deposits in court for the plaintiff, the amount so tendered, and the allegation is found to be true, then the defendant is deemed to be a party prevailing on the contract within the meaning of this section.

Where a deposit has been made pursuant to this section, the court shall, on the application of any party to the action, order the deposit to be invested in an insured, interest-bearing account. Interest on the amount shall be allocated to the parties in the same proportion as the original funds are allocated.

(c) In an action which seeks relief in addition to that based on a contract, if the party prevailing on the contract has damages awarded against it on causes of action not on the contract, the amounts awarded to the party prevailing on the contract under this section shall be deducted from any damages awarded in favor of the party who did not prevail on the contract. If the amount awarded under this section exceeds the amount of damages awarded the party not prevailing on the contract, the net amount shall be awarded the party prevailing on the contract and judgment may be entered in favor of the party prevailing on the contract for that net amount. *(Added by Stats.1968, c. 266, p. 578, § 1. Amended by Stats.1981, c. 888, p. 3399, § 1; Stats.1983, c. 1073, § 1; Stats.1986, c. 377, § 1; Stats.1986, c. 785, § 1; Stats.1987, c. 1080, § 1.)*

Cross References

Arbitration of attorneys' fees, see Business and Professions Code § 6200 et seq.
Automobile contract or purchase order, attorney's fees and costs, see Civil Code § 2983.4.
Civil actions, cost, items allowable, see Code of Civil Procedure § 1033.5.
Costs, see Code of Civil Procedure §§ 585, 1034.
Credit card holder, award of attorney's fees against issuer or retailer, see Civil Code § 1747.50 et seq.
Dance studio lessons, contracts, see Civil Code § 1812.62.

§ 1717

Default judgment, contracts with provisions for attorney fees, see Code of Civil Procedure § 585.
Discount buying services, contracts, see Civil Code § 1812.123.
Health studio services, contracts, see Civil Code § 1812.94.
Home equity sales contracts, see Civil Code § 1695.7.
Invention development services contract, civil action for damages, see Business and Professions Code § 22386.
Membership camping contracts, see Civil Code § 1812.306.
Mortgage foreclosure or trustee's sale, liability for attorney's fees, see Code of Civil Procedure §§ 580c, 726, 730.
Retail installment sales, attorney's fees, agreements, see Civil Code §§ 1810.4, 1811.1.
State Contract Act, resolution of claims, see Public Contract Code § 10240.13.
Swimming pool construction contracts, award of attorney's fees, see Business and Professions Code § 7168.

§ 1717.5. Action on contract based on book account; award of attorney's fees for the prevailing party; effect of written agreement; scope of application

(a) Except as otherwise provided by law or where waived by the parties to an agreement, in any action on a contract based on a book account, as defined in Section 337a of the Code of Civil Procedure, entered into on or after January 1, 1987, which does not provide for attorney's fees and costs, as provided in Section 1717, the party who is determined to be the party prevailing on the contract shall be entitled to reasonable attorney's fees, as provided below, in addition to other costs. The prevailing party on the contract shall be the party who recovered a greater relief in the action on the contract. The court may determine that there is no party prevailing on the contract for purposes of this section.

Reasonable attorney's fees awarded pursuant to this section for the prevailing party bringing the action on the book account shall be fixed by the court in an amount that shall not exceed the lesser of: (1) nine hundred sixty dollars ($960) for book accounts based upon an obligation owing by a natural person for goods, moneys, or services which were primarily for personal, family, or household purposes; and one thousand two hundred dollars ($1,200) for all other book accounts to which this section applies; or (2) 25 percent of the principal obligation owing under the contract.

For the party against whom the obligation on the book account was asserted in the action subject to this section, if that party is found to have no obligation owing on a book account, the court shall award that prevailing party reasonable attorney's fees not to exceed nine hundred sixty dollars ($960) for book accounts based upon an obligation owing by a natural person for goods, moneys, or services which were primarily for personal, family, or household purposes, and one thousand two hundred dollars ($1,200) for all other book accounts to which this section applies. These attorney's fees shall be an element of the costs of the suit.

If there is a written agreement between the parties signed by the person to be charged, the fees provided by this section may not be imposed unless that agreement contains a statement that the prevailing party in any action between the parties is entitled to the fees provided by this section.

(b) The attorney's fees allowed pursuant to this section shall be the lesser of either the maximum amount allowed by this section, the amount provided by any default attorney's fee schedule adopted by the court applicable to the suit, or an amount as otherwise provided by the court. Any claim for attorney's fees pursuant to this section in excess of the amounts set forth in the default attorney's fee schedule shall be reasonable attorney's fees, as proved by the party, as actual and necessary for the claim that is subject to this section.

(c) This section does not apply to any action in which an insurance company is a party nor shall an insurance company, surety, or guarantor be liable under this section, in the absence of a specific contractual provision, for the attorney's fees and costs awarded a prevailing party against its insured.

This section does not apply to any action in which a bank, a savings association, a federal association, a state or federal credit union, or a subsidiary, affiliate, or holding company of any of those entities, or an authorized industrial loan company, a licensed consumer finance lender, or a licensed commercial finance lender, is a party. (Added by Stats.1986, c. 884, § 1. Amended by Stats.1987, c. 764, § 4; Stats.1991, c. 406 (S.B.182), § 1; Stats.1992, c. 530 (A.B.2516), § 2; Stats. 2004, c. 328 (A.B.2347), § 1; Stats.2015, c. 80 (S.B.363), § 1, eff. Jan. 1, 2016.)

§ 1718. Farm machinery repair shops; invoices; estimates; definitions

(a) As used in this section:

(1) "Farm machinery" means all tools and equipment used in relation to the operation of a farm.

(2) "Farm machinery repair shop" means a business which, for compensation, engages in the operation, on or off its premises, of repairing farm machinery.

(3) "Per-job basis" means each act of maintenance or repair which is performed on farm machinery.

(b) All work done by a farm machinery repair shop, including all warranty work, shall be recorded on an invoice, which shall describe all service work done and parts supplied. If more than one act of maintenance or repair is performed by a farm machinery repair shop, the invoice shall be written in such a way that the labor cost per hour and total labor cost, as well as the specific parts used and their cost, shall be recorded on a per-job basis.

However, where work is done on an agreed total-cost-per-job basis, or the work includes an agreed total cost for component unit replacement, the invoice shall describe the work done on such basis and the total cost for such work.

(c) Each farm machinery repair shop shall give to each customer, upon request, a written estimated price for labor and parts necessary, on a per-job basis. It shall not charge for work done or parts supplied in excess of the estimated price without the consent of the customer, which shall be obtained at some time after it is determined that the estimated price is insufficient and before the work not included in the estimate is done, or the parts not included in the estimate are supplied. Nothing in this section shall be construed to require a farm machinery repair shop to give a written estimated price if the shop does not agree to perform the requested repair.

(d) Any violation of this section is a misdemeanor. (Added by Stats.1972, c. 302, p. 573, § 1. Amended by Stats.1973, c. 235, p. 621, § 1.)

Cross References

Automotive Repair Act,
   Generally, see Business and Professions Code § 9880 et seq.
   Estimates, see Business and Professions Code § 9884.9.
Misdemeanor,
   Definition, see Penal Code § 17.
   Punishment, see Penal Code § 19.
Repair shop, defined, see Vehicle Code § 510.

§ 1719. Dishonored checks; liability; demands for payment; stop payments; notice; penalties, damages and service charges; assignees

(a)(1) Notwithstanding any penal sanctions that may apply, any person who passes a check on insufficient funds shall be liable to the payee for the amount of the check and a service charge payable to the payee for an amount not to exceed twenty-five dollars ($25) for the first check passed on insufficient funds and an amount not to exceed thirty-five dollars ($35) for each subsequent check to that payee passed on insufficient funds.

(2) Notwithstanding any penal sanctions that may apply, any person who passes a check on insufficient funds shall be liable to the payee for damages equal to treble the amount of the check if a written demand for payment is mailed by certified mail to the person who had passed a check on insufficient funds and the written demand informs this person of (A) the provisions of this section, (B) the amount of the check, and (C) the amount of the service charge payable to the payee. The person who had passed a check on insufficient funds shall have 30 days from the date the written demand was mailed to pay the amount of the check, the amount of the service charge payable to the payee, and the costs to mail the written demand for payment. If this person fails to pay in full the amount of the check, the service charge payable to the payee, and the costs to mail the written demand within this period, this person shall then be liable instead for the amount of the check, minus any partial payments made toward the amount of the check or the service charge within 30 days of the written demand, and damages equal to treble that amount, which shall not be less than one hundred dollars ($100) nor more than one thousand five hundred dollars ($1,500). When a person becomes liable for treble damages for a check that is the subject of a written demand, that person shall no longer be liable for any service charge for that check and any costs to mail the written demand.

(3) Notwithstanding paragraphs (1) and (2), a person shall not be liable for the service charge, costs to mail the written demand, or treble damages if he or she stops payment in order to resolve a good faith dispute with the payee. The payee is entitled to the service charge, costs to mail the written demand, or treble damages only upon proving by clear and convincing evidence that there was no good faith dispute, as defined in subdivision (b).

(4) Notwithstanding paragraph (1), a person shall not be liable under that paragraph for the service charge if, at any time, he or she presents the payee with written confirmation by his or her financial institution that the check was returned to the payee by the financial institution due to an error on the part of the financial institution.

(5) Notwithstanding paragraph (1), a person shall not be liable under that paragraph for the service charge if the person presents the payee with written confirmation that his or her account had insufficient funds as a result of a delay in the regularly scheduled transfer of, or the posting of, a direct deposit of a social security or government benefit assistance payment.

(6) As used in this subdivision, to "pass a check on insufficient funds" means to make, utter, draw, or deliver any check, draft, or order for the payment of money upon any bank, depository, person, firm, or corporation that refuses to honor the check, draft, or order for any of the following reasons:

(A) Lack of funds or credit in the account to pay the check.

(B) The person who wrote the check does not have an account with the drawee.

(C) The person who wrote the check instructed the drawee to stop payment on the check.

(b) For purposes of this section, in the case of a stop payment, the existence of a "good faith dispute" shall be determined by the trier of fact. A "good faith dispute" is one in which the court finds that the drawer had a reasonable belief of his or her legal entitlement to withhold payment. Grounds for the entitlement include, but are not limited to, the following: services were not rendered, goods were not delivered, goods or services purchased are faulty, not as promised, or otherwise unsatisfactory, or there was an overcharge.

(c) In the case of a stop payment, the notice to the drawer required by this section shall be in substantially the following form:

NOTICE

To: _____
   (name of drawer)

_____ is the payee of a check you wrote
(name of payee)

for $ _____. The check was not paid because
   (amount)

you stopped payment, and the payee demands payment. You may have a good faith dispute as to whether you owe the full amount. If you do not have a good faith dispute with the payee and fail to pay the payee the full amount of the check in cash, a service charge of an amount not to exceed twenty-five dollars ($25) for the first check passed on insufficient funds and an amount not to exceed thirty-five dollars ($35) for each subsequent check passed on insufficient funds, and the costs to mail this notice within 30 days after this notice was mailed, you could be sued and held responsible to pay at least both of the following:

(1) The amount of the check.

(2) Damages of at least one hundred dollars ($100) or, if higher, three times the amount of the check up to one thousand five hundred dollars ($1,500).

If the court determines that you do have a good faith dispute with the payee, you will not have to pay the service charge, treble damages, or mailing cost. If you stopped payment because you have a good faith dispute with the payee, you should try to work out your dispute with the payee. You can contact the payee at:

_____

§ 1719

_____
(name of payee)

_____
(street address)

_____
(telephone number)

You may wish to contact a lawyer to discuss your legal rights and responsibilities.

_____
(name of sender of notice)

(d) In the case of a stop payment, a court may not award damages or costs under this section unless the court receives into evidence a copy of the written demand that, in that case, shall have been sent to the drawer and a signed certified mail receipt showing delivery, or attempted delivery if refused, of the written demand to the drawer's last known address.

(e) A cause of action under this section may be brought in small claims court by the original payee, if it does not exceed the jurisdiction of that court, or in any other appropriate court. The payee shall, in order to recover damages because the drawer instructed the drawee to stop payment, show to the satisfaction of the trier of fact that there was a reasonable effort on the part of the payee to reconcile and resolve the dispute prior to pursuing the dispute through the courts.

(f) A cause of action under this section may be brought by a holder of the check or an assignee of the payee. A proceeding under this section is a limited civil case. However, if the assignee is acting on behalf of the payee, for a flat fee or a percentage fee, the assignee may not charge the payee a greater flat fee or percentage fee for that portion of the amount collected that represents treble damages than is charged the payee for collecting the face amount of the check, draft, or order. This subdivision shall not apply to an action brought in small claims court.

(g) Notwithstanding subdivision (a), if the payee is the court, the written demand for payment described in subdivision (a) may be mailed to the drawer by the court clerk. Notwithstanding subdivision (d), in the case of a stop payment where the demand is mailed by the court clerk, a court may not award damages or costs pursuant to subdivision (d), unless the court receives into evidence a copy of the written demand, and a certificate of mailing by the court clerk in the form provided for in subdivision (4) of Section 1013a of the Code of Civil Procedure for service in civil actions. For purposes of this subdivision, in courts where a single court clerk serves more than one court, the clerk shall be deemed the court clerk of each court.

(h) The requirements of this section in regard to remedies are mandatory upon a court.

(i) The assignee of the payee or a holder of the check may demand, recover, or enforce the service charge, damages, and costs specified in this section to the same extent as the original payee.

(j)(1) A drawer is liable for damages and costs only if all of the requirements of this section have been satisfied.

(2) The drawer shall in no event be liable more than once under this section on each check for a service charge, damages, or costs.

(k) Nothing in this section is intended to condition, curtail, or otherwise prejudice the rights, claims, remedies, and defenses under Division 3 (commencing with Section 3101) of the Commercial Code of a drawer, payee, assignee, or holder, including a holder in due course as defined in Section 3302 of the Commercial Code, in connection with the enforcement of this section. (Added by Stats.1983, c. 522, § 1. Amended by Stats.1985, c. 196, § 1; Stats.1986, c. 225, § 1; Stats.1986, c. 708, § 1; Stats.1987, c. 4, § 1, eff. March 17, 1987; Stats.1990, c. 599 (S.B.2130), § 1; Stats.1994, c. 926 (A.B.2533), § 1; Stats.1995, c. 134 (A.B.522), § 1; Stats.1996, c. 1000 (A.B. 2643), § 1; Stats.1998, c. 931 (S.B.2139), § 14, eff. Sept. 28, 1998.)

Cross References

Deferred deposit transactions,
  Fees, extension of time and payment plans for repayment, see Financial Code § 23036.
  Limitation on recovery of damages, see Financial Code § 23036.
  Personal checks, agreement and notice to customers, see Financial Code § 23035.
Fictitious instruments, see Penal Code § 476.
Governmental units, payments by bad personal check, charges, see Government Code § 6157.
Honor defined, see Commercial Code § 1201.
Issuance of check or other paper to circulate as money, see Penal Code § 648.
Jurisdiction in limited civil cases, actions treated as limited civil case, see Code of Civil Procedure § 85.
Negotiable instruments, protest, see Commercial Code § 3505.
Passing worthless checks, see Penal Code § 476a.
Payment of wages or fringe benefits with bad check, penalty, application, see Labor Code § 203.1.
Small Claims Act jurisdiction, see Code of Civil Procedure § 116.110 et seq.

§ 1720. Failure of obligee to give timely response to inquiry concerning debit or credit applicable to obligation

(a) If an obligee fails to give a timely response to an inquiry of an obligor concerning any debit or credit applicable to an obligation, he shall not be entitled to interest, financing charges, service charges, or any other similar charges thereon, from the date of mailing of the inquiry to the date of mailing of the response.

(b) For the purpose of subdivision (a):

(1) An "inquiry" is a writing which is posted by certified mail to the address of the obligee to which payments are normally tendered, unless another address is specifically indicated on the statement for such purpose, then to such address.

(2) A "response" is a writing which is responsive to an inquiry and mailed to the last known address of the obligor.

(3) A response is "timely" if it is mailed within 60 days from the date on which the inquiry was mailed.

(c) This section shall only apply to an obligation created pursuant to a retail installment account as defined by Section 1802.7. (Added by Stats.1970, c. 191, p. 446, § 1. Amended by Stats.1971, c. 1019, p. 1958, § 3.)

§ 1721. Vandalism at construction site; treble damages and attorney fees

In an action for the intentional and malicious destruction of real or personal property at a site where substantial improvements to real property are under construction, upon judgment in favor of the plaintiff, the court may, in its discretion, award the plaintiff an amount not to exceed three times the amount of actual damages, and may award reasonable attorney's fees. *(Added by Stats.1983, c. 474, § 1.)*

§ 1722. Retail sale and delivery, and service or repair transactions; time of delivery, service or repair; delay or inability to deliver; notification; damages for failure to deliver or to commence service or repair; cable television; utilities; void contracts

(a)(1) Whenever a contract is entered into between a consumer and a retailer with 25 or more employees relating to the sale of merchandise which is to be delivered by the retailer or the retailer's agent to the consumer at a later date, and the parties have agreed that the presence of the consumer is required at the time of delivery, the retailer and the consumer shall agree, either at the time of the sale or at a later date prior to the delivery date, on a four-hour time period within which any delivery shall be made. Whenever a contract is entered into between a consumer and a retailer with 25 or more employees for service or repair of merchandise, whether or not the merchandise was sold by the retailer to the consumer, and the parties have agreed that the presence of the consumer is required at the time of service or repair, upon receipt of a request for service or repair under the contract, the retailer and the consumer shall agree, prior to the date of service or repair, on a four-hour period within which the service or repair shall be commenced. Once a delivery, service, or repair time is established, the retailer or the retailer's agent shall deliver the merchandise to the consumer, or commence service or repair of the merchandise, within that four-hour period.

(2) If the merchandise is not delivered, or service or repair are not commenced, within the specified four-hour period, except for delays caused by unforeseen or unavoidable occurrences beyond the control of the retailer, the consumer may bring an action in small claims court against the retailer for lost wages, expenses actually incurred, or other actual damages not exceeding a total of six hundred dollars ($600).

(3) No action shall be considered valid if the consumer was not present at the time, within the specified period, when the retailer or the retailer's agent attempted to make the delivery, service, or repairs or made a diligent attempt to notify the consumer by telephone or in person of its inability to do so because of unforeseen or unavoidable occurrences beyond its control. If notification is by telephone, the retailer or the retailer's agent shall leave a telephone number for a return telephone call by the consumer to the retailer or its agent, to enable the consumer to arrange a new two-hour period for delivery, service, or repair with the retailer or the retailer's agent.

(4) In any small claims action, logs and other business records maintained by the retailer or the retailer's agent in the ordinary course of business shall be prima facie evidence of the time period specified for the delivery, service, or repairs and of the time when the merchandise was delivered, or of a diligent attempt by the retailer or the retailer's agent to notify the consumer of delay caused by unforeseen or unavoidable occurrences.

(5) It shall be a defense to the action if a diligent attempt was made to notify the consumer of the delay caused by unforeseen or unavoidable occurrences beyond the control of the retailer or the retailer's agent, or the retailer or the retailer's agent was unable to notify the consumer of the delay because of the consumer's absence or unavailability during the four-hour period, and, in either instance, the retailer or the retailer's agent makes the delivery, service, or repairs within two hours of a newly agreed upon time or, if the consumer unreasonably declines to arrange a new time for the delivery, service, or repairs.

(b)(1) Cable television companies shall inform their subscribers of their right to service connection or repair within a four-hour period, if the presence of the subscriber is required, by offering the four-hour period at the time the subscriber calls for service connection or repair. Whenever a subscriber contracts with a cable television company for a service connection or repair which is to take place at a later date, and the parties have agreed that the presence of the subscriber is required, the cable company and the subscriber shall agree, prior to the date of service connection or repair, on the time for the commencement of the four-hour period for the service connection or repair.

(2) If the service connection or repair is not commenced within the specified four-hour period, except for delays caused by unforeseen or unavoidable occurrences beyond the control of the company, the subscriber may bring an action in small claims court against the company for lost wages, expenses actually incurred or other actual damages not exceeding a total of six hundred dollars ($600).

(3) No action shall be considered valid if the subscriber was not present at the time, within the specified period, that the company attempted to make the service connection or repair or made a diligent attempt to notify the subscriber by telephone or in person of its inability to do so because of unforeseen or unavoidable occurrences beyond its control. If notification is by telephone, the cable television company or its agent shall leave a telephone number for a return telephone call by the subscriber to the company or its agent, to enable the consumer to arrange a new two-hour period for service connection or repair.

(4) In any small claims action, logs and other business records maintained by the company or its agents in the ordinary course of business shall be prima facie evidence of the time period specified for the commencement of the service connection or repair and the time that the company or its agents attempted to make the service connection or repair, or of a diligent attempt by the company to notify the subscriber in person or by telephone of a delay caused by unforeseen or unavoidable occurrences.

(5) It shall be a defense to the action if a diligent attempt was made to notify the subscriber of a delay caused by unforeseen or unavoidable occurrences beyond the control of the company or its agents, or the company or its agents were unable to notify the subscriber because of the subscriber's absence or unavailability during the four-hour period, and, in either instance, the cable television company commenced service or repairs within a newly agreed upon two-hour period.

(6) No action shall be considered valid against a cable television company pursuant to this section when the franchise or any local ordinance provides the subscriber with a

§ 1722

remedy for a delay in commencement of a service connection or repair and the subscriber has elected to pursue that remedy. If a subscriber elects to pursue his or her remedies against a cable television company under this section, the franchising or state or local licensing authority shall be barred from imposing any fine, penalty, or other sanction against the company, arising out of the same incident.

(c)(1) Utilities shall inform their subscribers of their right to service connection or repair within a four-hour period, if the presence of the subscriber is required, by offering the four-hour period at the time the subscriber calls for service connection or repair. Whenever a subscriber contracts with the utility for a service connection or repair, and the parties have agreed that the presence of the subscriber is required, and the subscriber has requested a four-hour appointment, the utility and the subscriber shall agree, prior to the date of service connection or repair, on the time for the commencement of the four-hour period for the service connection or repair.

(2) If the service connection or repair is not commenced within the four-hour period provided under paragraph (1) or another period otherwise agreed to by the utility and the subscriber, except for delays caused by unforeseen or unavoidable circumstances beyond the control of the utility, the subscriber may bring an action in small claims court against the utility for lost wages, expenses actually incurred, or other actual damages not exceeding a total of six hundred dollars ($600).

(3) No action shall be considered valid if the subscriber was not present at the time, within the specified period, that the utility attempted to make the service connection or repair or made a diligent attempt to notify the subscriber by telephone or in person of its inability to do so because of unforeseen or unavoidable occurrences beyond its control. If notification is by telephone, the utility or its agent shall leave a telephone number for a return telephone call by the subscriber to the utility or its agent, to enable the consumer to arrange a new two-hour period for service connection or repair.

(4) In any small claims action, logs and other business records maintained by the utility or its agents in the ordinary course of business shall be prima facie evidence of the time period specified for the commencement of the service connection or repair and of the time that the utility attempted to make the service connection or repair, or of a diligent attempt by a utility to notify the subscriber in person or by telephone of a delay caused by unforeseen or unavoidable occurrences.

(5) It shall be a defense to the action if a diligent attempt was made by the utility to notify the subscriber of a delay caused by unforeseen or unavoidable occurrences beyond the control of the utility, and the utility commenced service within a newly agreed upon two-hour period.

(d) Any provision of a delivery, service, or repair contract in which the consumer or subscriber agrees to modify or waive any of the rights afforded by this section is void as contrary to public policy. *(Added by Stats.1989, c. 1075, § 1. Amended by Stats.1990, c. 193 (S.B.1968), § 1; Stats.1991, c. 394 (A.B.585), § 3; Stats.1992, c. 427 (A.B.3355), § 13;* *Stats.1992, c. 693 (S.B.1387), § 1; Stats.1993, c. 28 (S.B.47), § 1; Stats.2002, c. 279 (S.B.500), § 1.)*

Cross References

Cable Television and Video Provider Customer Service and Information Act, see Government Code § 53054 et seq.
Prima facie evidence, see Evidence Code § 602.
Video Customer Service Act, see Government Code § 53088 et seq.

§ 1723. Retail sellers; policies of no refund or no exchange; notice; exceptions; violations

(a) Every retail seller which sells goods to the public in this state that has a policy as to any of those goods of not giving full cash or credit refunds, or of not allowing equal exchanges, or any combination thereof, for at least seven days following purchase of the goods if they are returned and proof of their purchase is presented, shall conspicuously display that policy either on signs posted at each cash register and sales counter, at each public entrance, on tags attached to each item sold under that policy, or on the retail seller's order forms, if any. This display shall state the store's policy, including, but not limited to, whether cash refund, store credit, or exchanges will be given for the full amount of the purchase price; the applicable time period; the types of merchandise which are covered by the policy; and any other conditions which govern the refund, credit, or exchange of merchandise.

(b) This section does not apply to food, plants, flowers, perishable goods, goods marked "as is," "no returns accepted," "all sales final," or with similar language, goods used or damaged after purchase, customized goods received as ordered, goods not returned with their original package, and goods which cannot be resold due to health considerations.

(c)(1) Any retail store which violates this section shall be liable to the buyer for the amount of the purchase if the buyer returns, or attempts to return, the purchased goods on or before the 30th day after their purchase.

(2) Violations of this section shall be subject to the remedies provided in the Consumers Legal Remedies Act (Title 1.5 (commencing with Section 1750) of Part 4).

(3) The duties, rights, and remedies provided in this section are in addition to any other duties, rights, and remedies provided by state law. *(Added by Stats.1990, c. 422 (A.B.3047), § 2.)*

§ 1724. Unauthorized sale, purchase, or use of data

(a) As used in this section:

(1) "Authorized person" means a person who has come to possess or access the data lawfully and who continues to maintain the legal authority to possess, access, or use that data, under state or federal law, as applicable.

(2) "Data" has the same meaning as defined in Section 502 of the Penal Code.

(b) It is unlawful for a person to sell data, or sell access to data, that the person has obtained or accessed pursuant to the commission of a crime.

(c) It is unlawful for a person, who is not an authorized person, to purchase or use data from a source that the person knows or reasonably should know has obtained or accessed that data through the commission of a crime.

(d) This section shall not be construed to limit the constitutional rights of the public, the rights of whistleblowers, and the press regarding matters of public concern, including, but not limited to, those described in Bartnicki v. Vopper, (2001) 532 U.S. 514.

(e) This section does not limit providing or obtaining data in an otherwise lawful manner for the purpose of protecting a computer system or data stored in a computer system or protecting an individual from risk of identity theft or fraud.

(f) The court in an action pursuant to this section may award equitable relief, including, but not limited to, an injunction, costs, and any other relief the court deems proper.

(g) Liability under this section shall not limit or preclude liability under any other law.

(h) A violation of this section shall not constitute a crime. (Added by Stats.2021, c. 594 (A.B.1391), § 1, eff. Jan. 1, 2022.)

§ 1725. Negotiable instruments; identification; credit card as condition of acceptance prohibited

(a) Unless permitted under subdivision (c), no person accepting a negotiable instrument as payment in full or in part for goods or services sold or leased at retail shall do any of the following:

(1) Require the person paying with a negotiable instrument to provide a credit card as a condition of acceptance of the negotiable instrument, or record the number of the credit card.

(2) Require, as a condition of acceptance of the negotiable instrument, or cause the person paying with a negotiable instrument to sign a statement agreeing to allow his or her credit card to be charged to cover the negotiable instrument if returned as no good.

(3) Record a credit card number in connection with any part of the transaction described in this subdivision.

(4) Contact a credit card issuer to determine if the amount of any credit available to the person paying with a negotiable instrument will cover the amount of the negotiable instrument.

(b) For the purposes of this section, the following terms have the following meanings:

(1) "Check guarantee card" means a card issued by a financial institution, evidencing an agreement under which the financial institution will not dishonor a check drawn upon itself, under the terms and conditions of the agreement.

(2) "Credit card" has the meaning specified in Section 1747.02, and does not include a check guarantee card or a card that is both a credit card and a check guarantee card.

(3) "Negotiable instrument" has the meaning specified in Section 3104 of the Commercial Code.

(4) "Retail" means a transaction involving the sale or lease of goods or services or both, between an individual, corporation, or other entity regularly engaged in business and a consumer, for use by the consumer and not for resale.

(c) This section does not prohibit any person from doing any of the following:

(1) Requiring the production of reasonable forms of positive identification, other than a credit card, which may include a driver's license or a California state identification card, or where one of these is not available, another form of photo identification, as a condition of acceptance of a negotiable instrument.

(2) Requesting, but not requiring, a purchaser to voluntarily display a credit card as an indicia of creditworthiness or financial responsibility, or as an additional identification, provided the only information concerning the credit card which is recorded is the type of credit card displayed, the issuer of the card, and the expiration date of the card. All retailers that request the display of a credit card pursuant to this paragraph shall inform the customer, by either of the following methods, that displaying the credit card is not a requirement for check writing:

(A) By posting the following notice in a conspicuous location in the unobstructed view of the public within the premises where the check is being written, clearly and legibly: "Check writing ID: credit card may be requested but not required for purchases."

(B) By training and requiring the sales clerks or retail employees requesting the credit card to inform all check writing customers that they are not required to display a credit card to write a check.

(3) Requesting production of, or recording, a credit card number as a condition for cashing a negotiable instrument that is being used solely to receive cash back from the person.

(4) Requesting, receiving, or recording a credit card number in lieu of requiring a deposit to secure payment in event of default, loss, damage, or other occurrence.

(5) Requiring, verifying, and recording the purchaser's name, address, and telephone number.

(6) Requesting or recording a credit card number on a negotiable instrument used to make a payment on that credit card account.

(d) This section does not require acceptance of a negotiable instrument whether or not a credit card is presented.

(e) Any person who violates this section is subject to a civil penalty not to exceed two hundred fifty dollars ($250) for a first violation, and to a civil penalty not to exceed one thousand dollars ($1,000) for a second or subsequent violation, to be assessed and collected in a civil action brought by the person paying with a negotiable instrument, by the Attorney General, or by the district attorney or city attorney of the county or city in which the violation occurred. However, no civil penalty shall be assessed for a violation of this section if the defendant shows by a preponderance of the evidence that the violation was not intentional and resulted from a bona fide error made notwithstanding the defendant's maintenance of procedures reasonably adopted to avoid such an error. When collected, the civil penalty shall be payable, as appropriate, to the person paying with a negotiable instrument who brought the action or to the general fund of whichever governmental entity brought the action to assess the civil penalty.

(f) The Attorney General, or any district attorney or city attorney within his or her respective jurisdiction, may bring an action in the superior court in the name of the people of the State of California to enjoin violation of subdivision (a)

§ 1725 OBLIGATIONS

and, upon notice to the defendant of not less than five days, to temporarily restrain and enjoin the violation. If it appears to the satisfaction of the court that the defendant has, in fact, violated subdivision (a), the court may issue an injunction restraining further violations, without requiring proof that any person has been damaged by the violation. In these proceedings, if the court finds that the defendant has violated subdivision (a), the court may direct the defendant to pay any or all costs incurred by the Attorney General, district attorney, or city attorney in seeking or obtaining injunctive relief pursuant to this subdivision.

(g) Actions for collection of civil penalties under subdivision (e) and for injunctive relief under subdivision (f) may be consolidated. *(Added by Stats.1990, c. 637 (A.B.2880), § 1.*

Amended by Stats.1991, c. 1089 (A.B.1477), § 1, eff. Oct. 14, 1991; Stats.1995, c. 458 (A.B.1316), § 1.)

Cross References

Attorney General, generally, see Government Code § 12500 et seq.

§§ 1726 to 1729. Repealed by Stats.1979, c. 747, p. 2598, § 3

§ 1730. Repealed by Stats.1985, c. 874, § 16

§§ 1730.5 to 1736. Repealed by Stats.1979, c. 747, p. 2598, § 3

§ 1737. Repealed by Stats.1963, c. 819, p. 1997, § 2, eff. Jan. 1, 1965

Part 4

OBLIGATIONS ARISING FROM PARTICULAR TRANSACTIONS

Title		Section
1.	Consignment of Fine Art	1738
1A.	Independent Wholesale Sales Representatives	1738.10
1.1.	Sale and Manufacture of Political Items	1739
1.1A.	Autographed Memorabilia	1739.7
1.2.	Sale of Fine Prints	1740
1.2A.	Violent Video Games	1746
1.3.	Credit Cards	1747
1.3A.	Credit Card Disclosure	1748.10
1.3B.	Charge Card Disclosures	1748.20
1.3C.	Debit Cards	1748.30
1.3.5.	Consumer Refunds	1748.40
1.4.	Layaway Practices	1749
1.4A.	Gift Certificates	1749.45
1.4B.	Supermarket Club Cards	1749.60
1.4C.	Clarity of Marketplace Terms and Conditions and Dispute Resolution Minimum Fairness	1749.7
1.4D.	Online Marketplaces	1749.8
1.5.	Consumers Legal Remedies Act	1750
1.5A.	Vehicle History Reports	1784.1
1.6.	Consumer Credit Reporting Agencies Act	1785.1
1.61.	Commercial Credit Reports	1785.41
1.6A.	Investigative Consumer Reporting Agencies	1786
1.6B.	Consumer Credit Denial	1787.1
1.6C.	Fair Debt Collection Practices	1788
1.6C.5.	Fair Debt Buying Practices	1788.50
1.6C.7.	Educational Debt Collection Practices	1788.90
1.6C.10.	Student Loans: Borrower Rights	1788.100
1.6C.15.	Private Student Loan Collections Reform Act	1788.200
1.6C.17.	Fair Debt Settlement Practices	1788.300
1.6D.	Electronic Commerce	1789
1.6E.	Credit Services	1789.10
1.6F.	Check Cashers	1789.30
1.61.	Commercial Credit Reports [Editorial Note]	
1.7.	Consumer Warranties	1790
1.8.	Personal Data	1798
1.80.	Identification Documents	1798.79
1.807.	Domestic Violence, Sexual Assault, and Stalking: Personal Information	1798.79.8
1.81.	Customer Records	1798.80
1.81.1.	Confidentiality of Social Security Numbers	1798.85
1.81.15.	Reader Privacy Act	1798.90
1.81.2.	Confidentiality of Driver's License Information	1798.90.1
1.81.23.	Collection of License Plate Information	1798.90.5
1.81.25.	Consumer Privacy Protection	1798.91
1.81.26.	Security of Connected Devices	1798.91.04
1.81.27.	Commercial Use of Booking Photographs	1798.91.1
1.81.3.	Identity Theft	1798.92
1.81.35.	Coerced Debt	1798.97.1
1.81.4.	Privacy of Customer Electrical or Natural Gas Usage Data	1798.98
1.81.45.	The Parent's Accountability and Child Protection Act	1798.99.1
1.81.46.	Online Violence Prevention Act	1798.99.20
1.81.47.	The California Age–Appropriate Design Code Act	1798.99.28
1.81.48.	Data Broker Registration	1798.99.80
1.81.5.	California Consumer Privacy Act of 2018	1798.100
1.81.6.	Identity Theft in Business Entity Filings	1798.200
1.82.	Business Records	1799
1.83.	Precomputed Interest	1799.5
1.84.	Precomputed Finance Charge Contract	1799.8
1.85.	Consumer Credit Contracts	1799.90
1.86.	Consumer Contract Awareness Act of 1990	1799.200
2.	Credit Sales	1801
2.4.	Contracts for Dance Studio Lessons and Other Services	1812.50
2.5.	Contracts for Health Studio Services	1812.80
2.55.	Contracts for the Lease or Rental of Athletic Facilities	1812.97
2.6.	Contracts for Discount Buying Services	1812.100
2.7.	Contracts for Seller Assisted Marketing Plans	1812.200
2.8.	Membership Camping Contracts	1812.300
2.9.	Creditor Remedies: Disability Insurance	1812.400
2.91.	Employment Agency, Employment Counseling, and Job Listing Services Act	1812.500
2.95.	Auctioneer and Auction Companies	1812.600
2.96.	California Rental-Purchase Act	1812.620
2.97.	Consumer Collection Notice	1812.700
3.	Deposit	1813
3.5.	Utility Services	1882
4.	Loan	1884
4.5.	Appraisals of Real Property [Repealed]	
5.	Hiring	1925
6.	Service	2019
7.	Carriage	2085
8.	Involuntary Trusts	2223
9.	Agency	2295
10.	Recording Artist Contracts	2500
10.1.	Shared Mobility Devices	2505
10A.	Unincorporated Nonprofit Associations and Their Members [Repealed]	
10.5.	Death with Dignity Act [Rejected]	
11.	Pharmaceutical Services	2527
12.	Indemnity	2772
13.	Suretyship	2787
13.5.	Obligation to Defend Action	2860
13.7.	Obligation to Settle Insurance Claims Fairly [Rejected]	
14.	Lien	2872
15.	Internet Neutrality	3082
16.	General Provisions	3268
17.	Year 2000 Information Disclosures	3269
18.	Providers of Health and Safety Labor or Services	3273

Title		Section
19.	COVID–19 Small Landlord and Homeowner Relief Act	3273.01
20.	Firearm Industry Responsibility Act	3273.50

Cross References

Personal property leases, see Commercial Code § 10101 et seq.

Privacy or confidentiality of information or material provided to Nationwide Multistate Licensing System & Registry, debt collector licensing, see Financial Code § 100016.

Secured transactions, general effectiveness of security agreement, see Commercial Code § 9201.

Title 1

CONSIGNMENT OF FINE ART

Chapter	Section
1. Definitions	1738
2. General Provisions	1738.5

CHAPTER 1. DEFINITIONS

Section
1738. Definitions.

§ 1738. Definitions

As used in this title:

(a) "Artist" means the person who creates a work of fine art or, if that person is deceased, that person's heir, legatee, or personal representative.

(b) "Fine art" means a painting, sculpture, drawing, work of graphic art (including an etching, lithograph, offset print, silk screen, or a work of graphic art of like nature), a work of calligraphy, or a work in mixed media (including a collage, assemblage, or any combination of the foregoing art media).

(c) "Art dealer" means a person engaged in the business of selling works of fine art, other than a person exclusively engaged in the business of selling goods at public auction.

(d) "Person" means an individual, partnership, corporation, limited liability company, association or other group, however organized.

(e) "Consignment" means that no title to, estate in, or right to possession of, fine art, superior to that of the consignor shall vest in the consignee, notwithstanding the consignee's power or authority to transfer and convey to a third person all of the right, title and interest of the consignor in and to such fine art. *(Added by Stats.1975, c. 953, p. 2130, § 1. Amended by Stats.1994, c. 1010 (S.B.2053), § 31.)*

CHAPTER 2. GENERAL PROVISIONS

Section
1738.5. Delivery to and acceptance by art dealer; effect.
1738.6. Results of consignment; agency, property in trust, liability and proceeds.
1738.7. Trust property.
1738.8. Waiver by consignor as void.
1738.9. Application of title.

§ 1738.5. Delivery to and acceptance by art dealer; effect

Notwithstanding any custom, practice or usage of the trade to the contrary, whenever an artist delivers or causes to be delivered a work of fine art of the artist's own creation to an art dealer in this state for the purpose of exhibition or sale, or both, on a commission, fee or other basis of compensation, the delivery to and acceptance of such work of fine art by the art dealer shall constitute a consignment, unless the delivery to the art dealer is pursuant to an outright sale for which the artist receives or has received full compensation for the work of fine art upon delivery. *(Added by Stats.1975, c. 953, p. 2130, § 1.)*

Cross References

Art dealer defined for purposes of this Title, see Civil Code § 1738.
Artist defined for purposes of this Title, see Civil Code § 1738.
The California Art Preservation Act, see Civil Code § 987.
Consignment defined for purposes of this Title, see Civil Code § 1738.
Fine art defined for purposes of this Title, see Civil Code § 1738.
Written statement of sales, consignees, false statements, see Penal Code §§ 536, 536a.

§ 1738.6. Results of consignment; agency, property in trust, liability and proceeds

A consignment of a work of fine art shall result in all of the following:

(a) The art dealer, after delivery of the work of fine art, shall constitute an agent of the artist for the purpose of sale or exhibition of the consigned work of fine art within the State of California.

(b) The work of fine art shall constitute property held in trust by the consignee for the benefit of the consignor, and shall not be subject to claim by a creditor of the consignee.

(c) The consignee shall be responsible for the loss of, or damage to, the work of fine art.

(d) The proceeds from the sale of the work of fine art shall constitute funds held in trust by the consignee for the benefit of the consignor. Such proceeds shall first be applied to pay any balance due to the consignor, unless the consignor expressly agrees otherwise in writing. *(Added by Stats.1975, c. 953, p. 2130, § 1.)*

Cross References

Art dealer defined for purposes of this Title, see Civil Code § 1738.
Artist defined for purposes of this Title, see Civil Code § 1738.
California Art Preservation Act, see Civil Code § 987.
Consignment defined for purposes of this Title, see Civil Code § 1738.
Fine art defined for purposes of this Title, see Civil Code § 1738.

§ 1738.7. Trust property

A work of fine art received as a consignment shall remain trust property, notwithstanding the subsequent purchase thereof by the consignee directly or indirectly for the consignee's own account until the price is paid in full to the consignor. If such work is thereafter resold to a bona fide purchaser before the consignor has been paid in full, the proceeds of the resale received by the consignee shall constitute funds held in trust for the benefit of the consignor to the extent necessary to pay any balance still due to the consignor and such trusteeship shall continue until the fiduciary obligation of the consignee with respect to such transaction is discharged in full. *(Added by Stats.1975, c. 953, p. 2131, § 1.)*

Cross References

The California Art Preservation Act, see Civil Code § 987.
Consignment defined for purposes of this Title, see Civil Code § 1738.
Fine art defined for purposes of this Title, see Civil Code § 1738.

§ 1738.8. Waiver by consignor as void

Any provision of a contract or agreement whereby the consignor waives any provision of this title is void. *(Added by Stats.1975, c. 953, p. 2131, § 1.)*

Cross References

The California Art Preservation Act, see Civil Code § 987.

§ 1738.9. Application of title

This title shall not apply to a written contract executed prior to the effective date of this title, unless either the parties agree by mutual written consent that this title shall apply or such contract is extended or renewed after the effective date of this title.

The provisions of this title shall prevail over any conflicting or inconsistent provisions of the Commercial Code affecting the subject matter of this title. *(Added by Stats.1975, c. 953, p. 2131, § 1.)*

Cross References

Secured transactions, see Commercial Code § 9101 et seq.

Title 1A

INDEPENDENT WHOLESALE SALES REPRESENTATIVES

Section
1738.10. Legislative findings, declarations and intent.
1738.11. Title of chapter.
1738.12. Definitions.
1738.13. Written contracts required; contents; copies and receipts; information and documentation; waiver.
1738.14. Nonresident manufacturers, jobbers or distributors; personal jurisdiction.
1738.15. Willful failure to enter contract or pay commissions; treble damages to sales representative.
1738.16. Attorney's fees and costs.
1738.17. Application of chapter.

§ 1738.10. Legislative findings, declarations and intent

The Legislature finds and declares that independent wholesale sales representatives are a key ingredient to the California economy. The Legislature further finds and declares the wholesale sales representatives spend many hours developing their territory in order to properly market their products, and therefore should be provided unique protection from unjust termination of the territorial market areas. Therefore, it is the intent of the Legislature, in enacting this act to provide security and clarify the contractual relations between manufacturers and their nonemployee sales representatives. *(Added by Stats.1990, c. 964 (A.B.3456), § 1.)*

Cross References

Manufacturer defined, see Civil Code § 1738.12.
Wholesale sales representative defined, see Civil Code § 1738.12.

§ 1738.11. Title of chapter

This chapter shall be known and cited as the Independent Wholesale Sales Representatives Contractual Relations Act of 1990. *(Added by Stats.1990, c. 964 (A.B.3456), § 1.)*

Cross References

Wholesale sales representative defined, see Civil Code § 1738.12.

§ 1738.12. Definitions

For purposes of this chapter the following terms have the following meaning:

(a) "Manufacturer" means any organization engaged in the business of producing, assembling, mining, weaving, importing or by any other method of fabrication, a product tangible or intangible, intended for resale to, or use by the consumers of this state.

(b) "Jobber" means any business organization engaged in the business of purchasing products intended for resale and invoicing to purchasers for resale to, or use by, the consumers of this state.

(c) "Distributor" means any business organization engaged in offering for sale products which are shipped from its inventory, or from goods in transit to its inventory, to purchasers and intended for resale to, or use by, the consumers of this state.

(d) "Chargeback" means any deduction taken against the commissions earned by the sales representative which are not required by state or federal law.

(e) "Wholesale sales representative" means any person who contracts with a manufacturer, jobber, or distributor for the purpose of soliciting wholesale orders, is compensated, in whole or part, by commission, but shall not include one who places orders or purchases exclusively for his own account for resale and shall not include one who sells or takes orders for the direct sale of products to the ultimate consumer. *(Added by Stats.1990, c. 964 (A.B.3456), § 1.)*

§ 1738.13. Written contracts required; contents; copies and receipts; information and documentation; waiver

(a) Whenever a manufacturer, jobber, or distributor is engaged in business within this state and uses the services of a wholesale sales representative, who is not an employee of the manufacturer, jobber, or distributor, to solicit wholesale orders at least partially within this state, and the contemplated method of payment involves commissions, the manufacturer, jobber, or distributor shall enter into a written contract with the sales representative.

(b) The written contract shall include all of the following:

(1) The rate and method by which the commission is computed.

(2) The time when commissions will be paid.

(3) The territory assigned to the sales representative.

(4) All exceptions to the assigned territory and customers therein.

§ 1738.13

(5) What chargebacks will be made against the commissions, if any.

(c) The sales representative and the manufacturer, jobber, or distributor shall each be provided with a signed copy of the written contract and the sales representative shall sign a receipt acknowledging receipt of the signed contract.

(d) The sales representative shall be provided with the following written information and documentation with payment of the commission:

(1) An accounting of the orders for which payment is made, including the customer's name and invoice number.

(2) The rate of commission on each order.

(3) Information relating to any chargebacks included in the accounting.

(e) No contract shall contain any provision which waives any rights established pursuant to this chapter. Any such waiver is deemed contrary to public policy and void. *(Added by Stats.1990, c. 964 (A.B.3456), § 1.)*

Cross References

Chargeback defined, see Civil Code § 1738.12.
Distributor defined, see Civil Code § 1738.12.
Jobber defined, see Civil Code § 1738.12.
Manufacturer defined, see Civil Code § 1738.12.
Wholesale sales representative defined, see Civil Code § 1738.12.

§ 1738.14. Nonresident manufacturers, jobbers or distributors; personal jurisdiction

A manufacturer, jobber, or distributor who is not a resident of this state, and who enters into a contract regulated by this chapter is deemed to be doing business in this state for purposes of personal jurisdiction. *(Added by Stats.1990, c. 964 (A.B.3456), § 1.)*

Cross References

Distributor defined, see Civil Code § 1738.12.
Jobber defined, see Civil Code § 1738.12.
Manufacturer defined, see Civil Code § 1738.12.

§ 1738.15. Willful failure to enter contract or pay commissions; treble damages to sales representative

A manufacturer, jobber, or distributor who willfully fails to enter into a written contract as required by this chapter or willfully fails to pay commissions as provided in the written contract shall be liable to the sales representative in a civil action for treble the damages proved at trial. *(Added by Stats.1990, c. 964 (A.B.3456), § 1.)*

Cross References

Distributor defined, see Civil Code § 1738.12.
Jobber defined, see Civil Code § 1738.12.
Manufacturer defined, see Civil Code § 1738.12.

§ 1738.16. Attorney's fees and costs

In a civil action brought by the sales representative pursuant to this chapter, the prevailing party shall be entitled to reasonable attorney's fees and costs in addition to any other recovery. *(Added by Stats.1990, c. 964 (A.B.3456), § 1.)*

§ 1738.17. Application of chapter

This chapter shall not apply to any person licensed pursuant to Division 9 (commencing with Section 23000) of the Business and Professions Code. *(Added by Stats.1990, c. 964 (A.B.3456), § 1.)*

Title 1.1

SALE AND MANUFACTURE OF POLITICAL ITEMS

Section
1739. Prohibited offers, advertisements or sales.
1739.1. Political item.
1739.2. Original political item.
1739.3. Copies or reproductions; labeling.
1739.4. Civil actions; treble damages; limitation of actions.

§ 1739. Prohibited offers, advertisements or sales

No person shall sell, advertise for sale, or offer for sale any political item which is purported to be an original political item but which is not in fact an original political item. *(Added by Stats.1977, c. 69, p. 472, § 1.)*

§ 1739.1. Political item

For purposes of this title, a "political item" is any button, ribbon, poster, sticker, literature, or advertising concerning any candidate or ballot proposition in any electoral campaign. *(Added by Stats.1977, c. 69, p. 472, § 1.)*

§ 1739.2. Original political item

For purposes of this title, an "original political item" is any political item produced during any electoral campaign for use in support of or in opposition to any candidate or ballot proposition before the voters in that campaign. *(Added by Stats.1977, c. 69, p. 472, § 1.)*

§ 1739.3. Copies or reproductions; labeling

No political item which is labeled "copy" or "reproduction" at the time of sale, advertising for sale, or offering for sale shall violate Section 1739. *(Added by Stats.1977, c. 69, p. 472, § 1.)*

§ 1739.4. Civil actions; treble damages; limitation of actions

(a) A person who offers or sells any political item in violation of this title shall be liable to the person purchasing such political item from him, who may sue to recover the consideration paid for the political item, with interest at the legal rate thereon, upon the tender of the political item.

(b) In any case in which a person knowingly offers or sells a political item in violation of this title, the person purchasing such political item may recover from the person who offers or sells such political item an amount equal to three times the amount required under subdivision (a).

(c) No action shall be maintained to enforce any liability under this section unless brought within one year after discovery of the violation upon which it is based and in no event more than three years after the political item was sold. *(Added by Stats.1977, c. 69, p. 472, § 1.)*

Title 1.1A

AUTOGRAPHED MEMORABILIA

Section
1739.7. Express warranties; representations; cancellation of sale; displays or offers; disclosures; civil actions and penalties.

§ 1739.7. Express warranties; representations; cancellation of sale; displays or offers; disclosures; civil actions and penalties

(a) As used in this section:

(1) "Autographed collectible" means an item bearing the signature of a particular person that is sold or offered for sale for fifty dollars ($50) or more, excluding sales tax and shipping fees, when the dealer offers the signed item at a higher price than the dealer would charge for a comparable item without the signature.

(2) For purposes of this section, an autographed collectible shall be limited to the following items:

(A) Sports items, including, but not limited to, a photograph, ticket, plaque, sports program, trading card, item of sports equipment or clothing, or other sports memorabilia.

(B) Entertainment media items related to music, television, and films, including, but not limited to, a picture, photo, record, compact disc, digital video disc, ticket, program, playbill, clothing, hat, poster, toy, plaque, trading card, musical instrument, or other entertainment memorabilia.

(3) For purposes of this section, and notwithstanding paragraph (2), an autographed collectible does not include the following items:

(A) Works of fine art, as defined by paragraph (1) of subdivision (d) of Section 982 that are originals or numbered multiples, and signed by the artist or maker.

(B) Furniture and decorative objects, including works of pottery, jewelry, and design that are signed by the artist or maker.

(C) Signed books, manuscripts, and correspondence, as well as ephemera not related to sports or entertainment media.

(D) Signed numismatic items or bullion.

(4) "Consumer" means any natural person who purchases an autographed collectible from a dealer for personal, family, or household purposes. "Consumer" also includes a prospective purchaser meeting these criteria.

(5)(A) "Dealer" means a person who is in the business of selling or offering for sale autographed collectibles exclusively or nonexclusively, and sells three or more autographed collectibles in a period of 12 months. "Dealer" includes an auctioneer or auction company that sells autographed collectibles at a public auction. "Dealer" includes a person engaged in a mail-order, telephone-order, online, or television business for the sale of autographed collectibles.

(B) "Dealer" does not include any of the following:

(i) A pawnbroker licensed pursuant to Chapter 3 (commencing with Section 21300) of Division 8 of the Financial Code, if the autographed collectible was acquired through a foreclosure on a collateral loan, provided that the pawnbroker does not hold himself or herself out as having knowledge or skill peculiar to autographed collectibles.

(ii) The person who autographed the collectible.

(6) "Limited edition" means any autographed collectible that meets all of the following requirements:

(A) A company has produced a specific quantity of an autographed collectible and placed it on the open market.

(B) The producer of the autographed collectible has posted a notice, at its primary place of business, that it will provide any consumer, upon request, with a copy of a notice that states the exact number of an autographed collectible produced in that series of limited editions.

(C) The producer makes available, upon request of a consumer, evidence that the electronic encoding, films, molds, or plates used to create the autographed collectible have been destroyed after the specified number of autographed collectibles have been produced.

(D) The sequence number of the autographed collectible and the number of the total quantity produced in the limited edition are printed on the autographed collectible.

(7) "Person" means any natural person, partnership, corporation, limited liability company, company, trust, association, or other entity, however organized.

(8) "Representation" means any oral or written representation, including, but not limited to, a representation in an advertisement, brochure, catalog, flyer, invoice, sign, radio or television broadcast, online communication, Internet Web page, email, or other commercial or promotional material.

(9) "Auctioneer" means an auctioneer as defined in subdivision (d) of Section 1812.601, or a representative or agent of an auctioneer.

(10) "Auction company" means an auction company as defined in subdivision (c) of Section 1812.601, or a representative or agent of an auction company.

(b) A dealer who, in selling or offering to sell to a consumer an autographed collectible, makes a representation to a consumer that the signature on the autographed collectible is the authentic signature of a particular person in that person's own hand, shall furnish an express warranty to the consumer at the time of sale. The dealer shall retain a copy of the express warranty for not less than seven years. The express warranty, which may be included in the bill of sale or invoice, shall meet all of the following criteria:

(1) Is written in at least 10-point type.

(2) Is signed by the dealer or his or her authorized agent, and contains the dealer's true legal name, business street address, and the last four digits of the dealer's seller's permit account number from the California Department of Tax and Fee Administration, if applicable.

(3) Specifies the date of sale and the purchase price.

(4) Describes the autographed collectible and specifies the name of the person who autographed it.

(5) Expressly warrants the autographed collectible as authentic, and that the warranty is conclusively presumed to be part of the bargain. The warranty shall not be negated or limited by reason of the lack of words such as "warranty" or

"guarantee" or because the dealer does not have a specific intent or authorization to make the warranty or because any statement relevant to the autographed collectible is or purports to be, or is capable of being, merely the dealer's opinion.

(6) If the autographed collectible is offered as one of a limited edition, specifies (A) how the autographed collectible and edition are numbered and (B) the size of the edition and the size of any prior or anticipated future edition, if known by the dealer. If the size of the edition and the size of any prior or anticipated future edition is not known, the warranty shall contain an explicit statement to that effect.

(7) Indicates whether the dealer is surety bonded or is otherwise insured to protect the consumer against errors and omissions of the dealer and, if bonded or insured, provides proof thereof.

(8) Indicates if the autographed collectible was autographed in the presence of the dealer, and any proof thereof. Specify the date and location of, and the name of a witness to, the autograph signing, if known, and applicable.

(9) Identifies all information upon which the dealer relied when making the representation that the autographed collectible is authentic.

(10) Indicates an identifying serial number that corresponds to an identifying number printed on the autographed collectible item, if any.

(11) Indicates whether the item was obtained or purchased from a third party.

(c) The dealer shall retain, after January 1, 2018, a record of the name and address of the third party, as described in paragraph (11) of subdivision (b). This third-party information may be discoverable during a civil dispute. However, nothing in this subdivision prohibits a party from objecting to a discovery request on the grounds of a right to privacy. This third-party information shall be kept on file for seven years.

(d)(1) In addition to any other right or remedy provided under existing law, including, but not limited to, any rights and remedies provided under contract law, a consumer shall have the right to cancel the contract for the purchase of an autographed collectible represented by a dealer as authentic until midnight of the third day after the day on which the consumer purchased the autographed collectible. Notice of the cancellation may be provided in person or in a written or electronic form, and is deemed effective once communicated or sent. The autographed collectible shall be returned to the dealer within 30 days of the sale in the same condition in which it was sold, the cost of which shall be borne by the consumer. The price paid by the consumer shall be refunded within 10 days of receipt of the returned autographed collectible. Nothing in this section prevents the parties from agreeing to cancel a contract after midnight of the third day after the day on which the consumer purchases the autographed collectible.

(2) This subdivision does not apply to the following:

(A) Autographed collectibles sold by an auctioneer or auction company at auction.

(B) Autographed collectibles purchased by barter or trade of other items.

(C) Autographed collectibles sold at a trade show.

(D) Autographed collectibles sold by one dealer to another dealer.

(e)(1) No dealer shall display or offer for sale an autographed collectible unless, at the location where the autographed collectible is offered for sale and in close proximity to the autographed collectible merchandise, there is a conspicuous sign that reads as follows:

"SALE OF AUTOGRAPHED COLLECTIBLES: AS REQUIRED BY LAW, A DEALER WHO SELLS TO A CONSUMER ANY COLLECTIBLE DESCRIBED AS BEING AUTOGRAPHED MUST PROVIDE A WRITTEN EXPRESS WARRANTY AT THE TIME OF SALE AND A THREE–DAY RIGHT OF RETURN. THIS DEALER MAY BE SURETY BONDED OR OTHERWISE INSURED TO ENSURE THE AUTHENTICITY OF ANY AUTOGRAPHED COLLECTIBLE SOLD BY THIS DEALER."

(2) This subdivision does not apply to an autographed collectible sold by an auctioneer or auction company at auction or an autographed collectible sold at a trade show.

(f) No dealer selling at a trade show, nor an auctioneer or auction company shall display or offer for sale an autographed collectible unless, at the location where the autographed collectible is offered for sale and in close proximity to the autographed collectible merchandise, there is a conspicuous sign that reads as follows:

"SALE OF AUTOGRAPHED COLLECTIBLES: AS REQUIRED BY LAW, A DEALER WHO SELLS TO A CONSUMER ANY COLLECTIBLE DESCRIBED AS BEING AUTOGRAPHED MUST PROVIDE A WRITTEN EXPRESS WARRANTY AT THE TIME OF SALE. THIS DEALER MAY BE SURETY BONDED OR OTHERWISE INSURED TO ENSURE THE AUTHENTICITY OF ANY AUTOGRAPHED COLLECTIBLE SOLD BY THIS DEALER."

(g) Any dealer engaged in a mail-order, telephone-order, or online business for the sale of autographed collectibles:

(1) Shall include the disclosure specified in subdivision (e), in type of conspicuous size, in any written advertisement relating to an autographed collectible.

(2) Shall include in each television or online advertisement relating to an autographed collectible the following written onscreen message, which shall be prominently displayed, easily readable, and clearly visible for no less than five seconds, and which shall be repeated for five seconds once during each four-minute segment of the advertisement following the initial four minutes:

"A written express warranty is provided with each autographed collectible, as required by law. This dealer may be surety bonded or otherwise insured to ensure the authenticity of any autographed collectible sold by this dealer."

(3) Shall include as part of the oral message of each radio advertisement for an autographed collectible the disclosure specified in subdivision (e).

(h) In a civil action brought by a consumer against a dealer, the following shall apply:

(1) A dealer who fails to provide an express warranty, or provides an express warranty that does not comply with all of the requirements of subdivision (b), shall be subject to a civil penalty of up to one thousand dollars ($1,000), payable to the consumer.

(2) A dealer who provides a false express warranty that injures the consumer shall be subject to a civil penalty of up to one thousand dollars ($1,000) payable to the consumer.

(3) A dealer who provides a false express warranty and whose act or omission amounts to gross negligence that injures the consumer, shall be subject to a civil penalty of three thousand dollars ($3,000), or an amount equal to three times actual damages, whichever is greater, payable to the consumer.

(4) A dealer who knowingly provides a false express warranty, or knowingly fails to provide an express warranty required by this section, and whose act or omission results in an injury to a consumer shall be subject to a civil penalty of five thousand dollars ($5,000), or an amount equal to five times actual damages, whichever is greater, payable to the consumer.

(5) A consumer may recover court costs, reasonable attorney's fees, interest, and expert witness fees, if applicable, pursuant to an action described in paragraphs (2) to (4), inclusive.

(6) The remedies specified in this section are in addition to, and not in lieu of, any other remedy that may be provided by law. The court, in its discretion, may award punitive damages based on the egregiousness of the dealer's conduct.

(i) A dealer may be surety bonded or otherwise insured for purposes of indemnification against errors and omissions arising from the authentication, sale, or resale of autographed collectibles.

(j) It is the intent of the Legislature that neither the amendment to this section by Assembly Bill 1570 of the 2015–2016 Regular Session, adding an exclusion of a provider or operator of an online marketplace to the definition of a dealer, nor the amendment to this section by Assembly Bill 228 of the 2017–2018 Regular Session, removing that exclusion from the definition of a dealer, be construed to affect the decision of the Court of Appeal in Gentry v. eBay, Inc. (2002) 99 Cal.App.4th 816. *(Added by Stats.1992, c. 656 (A.B.3113), § 1. Amended by Stats.1994, c. 1010 (S.B.2053), § 32; Stats.1995, c. 360 (A.B.434), § 3; Stats.1998, c. 494 (S.B. 2024), § 1; Stats.1999, c. 83 (S.B.966), § 20; Stats.2016, c. 258 (A.B.1570), § 2, eff. Jan. 1, 2017; Stats.2017, c. 696 (A.B.228), § 1, eff. Oct. 12, 2017.)*

Title 1.2

SALE OF FINE PRINTS

Chapter	Section
1. General Provisions	1740
2. Full Disclosure in the Sale of Fine Prints	1742
3. Remedies and Penalties	1745

Cross References

California Art Preservation Act, see Civil Code § 987 et seq.

CHAPTER 1. GENERAL PROVISIONS

Section
1740. Definitions.
1741. Application of title.

§ 1740. Definitions

As used in this title:

(a) "Fine art multiple" or "multiple" for the purposes of this title means any fine print, photograph (positive or negative), sculpture cast, collage, or similar art object produced in more than one copy. Pages or sheets taken from books and magazines and offered for sale or sold as art objects shall be included, but books and magazines shall be excluded.

(b) "Fine print" or "print" means a multiple produced by, but not limited to, engraving, etching, woodcutting, lithography, and serigraphy, and means multiples produced or developed from photographic negatives, or any combination thereof.

(c) "Master" is used in lieu of and has the same meaning as a printing plate, stone, block, screen, photographic negative, or mold or other process as to a sculpture, which contains an image used to produce fine art objects in multiples.

(d) "Artist" means the person who created the image which is contained in, or constitutes, the master or conceived of, and approved the image which is contained in, or constitutes, the master.

(e) Whether a multiple is "signed" or "unsigned" as these terms are used in this title relating to prints and photographs, depends upon whether or not the multiple was autographed by the artist's own hand, and not by mechanical means, after the multiple was produced, irrespective of whether it was signed or unsigned in the plate.

(f) "Impression" means each individual fine art multiple made by printing, stamping, casting, or any other process.

(g) "Art dealer" means a person who is in the business of dealing, exclusively or nonexclusively, in the fine art multiples to which this title is applicable, or a person who by his or her occupation holds himself or herself out as having knowledge or skill peculiar to these works, or to whom that knowledge or skill may be attributed by his or her employment of an agent or other intermediary who by his or her occupation holds himself or herself out as having that knowledge or skill. The term "art dealer" includes an auctioneer who sells these works at public auction, but excludes persons, not otherwise defined or treated as art dealers herein, who are consignors or principals of auctioneers.

(h) "Limited edition" means fine art multiples produced from a master, all of which are the same image and bear numbers or other markings to denote the limited production thereof to a stated maximum number of multiples, or are otherwise held out as limited to a maximum number of multiples.

(i) "Proofs" means multiples which are the same as, and which are produced from the same master as, the multiples in a limited edition, but which, whether so designated or not, are set aside from and are in addition to the limited edition to which they relate.

(j) "Certificate of authenticity" means a written or printed description of the multiple which is to be sold, exchanged, or consigned by an art dealer. Every certificate shall contain the following statement:

"This is to certify that all information and the statements contained herein are true and correct."

(k) "Person" means an individual, partnership, corporation, limited liability company, association, or other entity, however organized. *(Added by Stats.1970, c. 1223, p. 2141, § 1, operative July 1, 1971. Amended by Stats.1982, c. 1320, p. 4873, § 1; Stats.1988, c. 819, § 1; Stats.1994, c. 1010 (S.B.2053), § 33.)*

§ 1741. Application of title

This title shall apply to any fine art multiple when offered for sale or sold at wholesale or retail for one hundred dollars ($100) or more, exclusive of any frame. *(Added by Stats.1970, c. 1223, p. 2141, § 1, operative July 1, 1971. Amended by Stats.1982, c. 1320, p. 4875, § 2.)*

Cross References

Fine art multiple or multiple defined for purposes of this Title, see Civil Code § 1740.

CHAPTER 2. FULL DISCLOSURE IN THE SALE OF FINE PRINTS

Section
1742. Certificate of authenticity to be furnished to buyer or consignee; auctions; materials soliciting a direct sale; disclosures.
1742.6. Charitable organizations; exemptions.
1743. Repealed.
1744. Informational detail.
1744.7. Express warranties.
1744.9. Liability; consignor to purchaser from consignee; art dealer who sells for consignor not art dealer or artist as agent.

§ 1742. Certificate of authenticity to be furnished to buyer or consignee; auctions; materials soliciting a direct sale; disclosures

(a) An art dealer shall not sell or consign a multiple into or from this state unless a certificate of authenticity is furnished to the purchaser or consignee, at his or her request, or in any event prior to a sale or consignment, which sets forth as to each multiple, the descriptive information required by Section 1744 for any period. If a prospective purchaser so requests, the certificate shall be transmitted to him or her prior to the payment or placing of an order for a multiple. If payment is made by a purchaser prior to delivery of such a multiple, this certificate shall be supplied at the time of or prior to delivery. With respect to auctions, this information may be furnished in catalogues or other written materials which are made readily available for consultation and purchase prior to sale, provided that a bill of sale, receipt, or invoice describing the transaction is then provided which makes reference to the catalogue and lot number in which this information is supplied. Information supplied pursuant to this subdivision shall be clearly, specifically and distinctly addressed to each of the items listed in Section 1744 unless the required data is not applicable. This section is applicable to transactions by and between art dealers and others considered to be art dealers for the purposes of this title.

(b) An art dealer shall not cause a catalogue, prospectus, flyer, or other written material or advertisement to be distributed in, into, or from this state which solicits a direct sale, by inviting transmittal of payment for a specific multiple, unless it clearly sets forth, in close physical proximity to the place in such material where the multiple is described, the descriptive information required by Section 1744 for any time period. In lieu of this required information, the written material or advertising may set forth the material contained in the following quoted passage, or the passage itself, if the art dealer then supplies the required information prior to or with delivery of the multiple. The nonobservance of the terms within the following passage shall constitute a violation of this title:

"California law provides for disclosure in writing of information concerning certain fine prints, photographs, and sculptures prior to effecting a sale of them. This law requires disclosure of such matters as the identity of the artist, the artist's signature, the medium, whether the multiple is a reproduction, the time when the multiple was produced, use of the plate which produced the multiple, and the number of multiples in a "limited edition." If a prospective purchaser so requests, the information shall be transmitted to him or her prior to payment, or the placing of an order for a multiple. If payment is made by a purchaser prior to delivery of the multiple, this information will be supplied at the time of or prior to delivery, in which case the purchaser is entitled to a refund if, for reasons related to matter contained in such information, he or she returns the multiple in the condition in which received, within 30 days of receiving it. In addition, if after payment and delivery, it is ascertained that the information provided is incorrect, the purchaser may be entitled to certain remedies, including refund upon return of the multiple in the condition in which received."

This requirement is not applicable to general written material or advertising which does not constitute an offer to effect a specific sale.

(c) In each place of business in the state where an art dealer is regularly engaged in sales of multiples, the art dealer shall post in a conspicuous place, a sign which, in a legible format, contains the information included in the following passage:

"California law provides for the disclosure in writing of certain information concerning prints, photographs, and sculpture casts. This information is available to you, and you may request to receive it prior to purchase."

(d) If an art dealer offering multiples by means of a catalogue, prospectus, flyer or other written material or advertisement distributed in, into or from this state disclaims knowledge as to any relevant detail referred to in Section 1744, he or she shall so state specifically and categorically with regard to each such detail to the end that the purchaser shall be enabled to judge the degree of uniqueness or scarcity of each multiple contained in the edition so offered. Describing the edition as an edition of "reproductions" eliminates the need to furnish further informational details unless the edition was allegedly published in a signed, numbered, or limited edition, or any combination thereof, in which case all of the informational details are required to be furnished.

(e) Whenever an artist sells or consigns a multiple of his or her own creation or conception, the artist shall disclose the information required by Section 1744, but an artist shall not otherwise be regarded as an art dealer. *(Added by Stats.1970, c. 1223, p. 2141, § 1, operative July 1, 1971. Amended by Stats.1982, c. 1320, p. 4875, § 3; Stats.1988, c. 819, § 2.)*

Cross References

Art dealer defined for purposes of this Title, see Civil Code § 1740.
Artist defined for purposes of this Title, see Civil Code § 1740.
Certificate of authenticity defined for purposes of this Title, see Civil Code § 1740.
Fine print or print defined for purposes of this Title, see Civil Code § 1740.
Limited edition defined for purposes of this Title, see Civil Code § 1740.
Signed or unsigned defined for purposes of this Title, see Civil Code § 1740.

§ 1742.6. Charitable organizations; exemptions

Any charitable organization which conducts a sale or auction of fine art multiples shall be exempt from the disclosure requirements of this title if it posts in a conspicuous place, at the site of the sale or auction, a disclaimer of any knowledge of the information specified in Section 1744, and includes such a disclaimer in a catalogue, if any, distributed by the organization with respect to the sale or auction of fine art multiples. If a charitable organization uses or employs an art dealer to conduct a sale or auction of fine art multiples, the art dealer shall be subject to all disclosure requirements otherwise required of an art dealer under this title. *(Added by Stats.1982, c. 1320, p. 4876, § 4.)*

Cross References

Art dealer defined for purposes of this Title, see Civil Code § 1740.
Fine art multiple or multiple defined for purposes of this Title, see Civil Code § 1740.

§ 1743. Repealed by Stats.1982, c. 1320, p. 4876, § 4.2

§ 1744. Informational detail

(a) Except as provided in subdivisions (c), (d), (e), and otherwise in this title, a certificate of authenticity containing the following informational details shall be required to be supplied in all transactions covered by subdivisions (a), (b), and (e) of Section 1742:

(1) The name of the artist.

(2) If the artist's name appears on the multiple, a statement whether the multiple was signed by the artist.

If the multiple was not signed by the artist, a statement of the source of the artist's name on the multiple, such as whether the artist placed his signature on the multiple or on the master, whether his name was stamped or estate stamped on the multiple or on the master, or was from some other source or in some other manner placed on the multiple or on the master.

(3) A description of the medium or process, and where pertinent to photographic processes, the material used in producing the multiple, such as whether the multiple was produced through the etching, engraving, lithographic, serigraphic, or a particular method or material used in photographic developing processes. If an established term, in accordance with the usage of the trade, cannot be employed accurately to describe the medium or process, a brief, clear description shall be made.

(4) If the multiple or the image on or in the master constitutes, as to prints and photographs, a photomechanical or photographic type of reproduction, or as to sculptures a surmoulage or other form of reproduction of sculpture cases, of an image produced in a different medium, for a purpose other than the creation of the multiple being described, a statement of this information and the respective mediums.

(5) If paragraph (4) is applicable, and the multiple is not signed, a statement whether the artist authorized or approved in writing the multiple or the edition of which the multiple being described is one.

(6) If the purported artist was deceased at the time the master was made which produced the multiple, this shall be stated.

(7) If the multiple is a "posthumous" multiple, that is, if the master was created during the life of the artist but the multiple was produced after the artist's death, this shall be stated.

(8) If the multiple was made from a master which produced a prior limited edition, or from a master which constitutes or was made from a reproduction or surmoulage of a prior multiple or the master which produced the prior limited edition, this shall be stated as shall the total number of multiples, including proofs, of all other editions produced from that master.

(9) As to multiples produced after 1949, the year, or approximate year, the multiple was produced shall be stated. As to multiples produced prior to 1950, state the year, approximate year or period when the master was made which produced the multiple and when the particular multiple being described was produced. The requirements of this subdivision shall be satisfied when the year stated is approximately accurate.

(10) Whether the edition is being offered as a limited edition, and if so: (i) the authorized maximum number of signed or numbered impressions, or both, in the edition; (ii) the authorized maximum number of unsigned or unnumbered impressions, or both, in the edition; (iii) the authorized maximum number of artist's, publisher's or other proofs, if any, outside of the regular edition; and (iv) the total size of the edition.

(11) Whether or not the master has been destroyed, effaced, altered, defaced, or canceled after the current edition.

(b) If the multiple is part of a limited edition, and was printed after January 1, 1983, the statement of the size of the limited edition, as stated pursuant to paragraph (10) of subdivision (a) of Section 1744 shall also constitute an express warranty that no additional multiples of the same image,

§ 1744 OBLIGATIONS

including proofs, have been produced in this or in any other limited edition.

(c) If the multiple was produced in the period from 1950 to the effective date of this section, the information required to be supplied need not include the information required by paragraphs (5) and (8) of subdivision (a).

(d) If the multiple was produced in the period from 1900 to 1949, the information required to be supplied need only consist of the information required by paragraphs (1), (2), (3), and (9) of subdivision (a).

(e) If the multiple was produced before the year 1900, the information to be supplied need only consist of the information required by paragraphs (1), (3), and (9) of subdivision (a). *(Added by Stats.1982, c. 1320, p. 4877, § 5. Amended by Stats.1988, c. 819, § 3.)*

Cross References

Artist defined for purposes of this Title, see Civil Code § 1740.
Certificate of authenticity defined for purposes of this Title, see Civil Code § 1740.
Fine print or print defined for purposes of this Title, see Civil Code § 1740.
Impression defined for purposes of this Title, see Civil Code § 1740.
Limited edition defined for purposes of this Title, see Civil Code § 1740.
Master defined for purposes of this Title, see Civil Code § 1740.
Proofs defined for purposes of this Title, see Civil Code § 1740.
Signed or unsigned defined for purposes of this Title, see Civil Code § 1740.

§ 1744.7. Express warranties

Whenever an art dealer furnishes the name of the artist pursuant to Section 1744 for any time period after 1949, and otherwise furnishes information required by any of the subdivisions of Section 1744 for any time period, as to transactions including offers, sales, or consignments made to other than art dealers, and to other art dealers, such information shall be a part of the basis of the bargain and shall create express warranties as to the information provided. Such warranties shall not be negated or limited because the art dealer in the written instrument did not use formal words such as "warrant" or "guarantee" or because the art dealer did not have a specific intention or authorization to make a warranty or because any required statement is, or purports to be, or is capable of being merely the seller's opinion. The existence of a basis in fact for information warranted by virtue of this subdivision shall not be a defense in an action to enforce such warranty. However, with respect to photographs and sculptures produced prior to 1950, and other multiples produced prior to 1900, as to information required by paragraphs (3), (4), (5), and (6) of subdivision (a) of Section 1744, the art dealer shall be deemed to have satisfied this section if a reasonable basis in fact existed for the information provided. When information is not supplied as to any subdivision or paragraph of Section 1744 because not applicable, this shall constitute the express warranty that the paragraph is not applicable.

Whenever an art dealer disclaims knowledge as to a particular item about which information is required, such disclaimer shall be ineffective unless clearly, specifically, and categorically stated as to the particular item and contained in the physical context of other language setting forth the required information as to a specific multiple. *(Added by Stats.1982, c. 1320, p. 4878, § 6.)*

Cross References

Art dealer defined for purposes of this Title, see Civil Code § 1740.
Artist defined for purposes of this Title, see Civil Code § 1740.

§ 1744.9. Liability; consignor to purchaser from consignee; art dealer who sells for consignor not art dealer or artist as agent

(a) An artist or art dealer who consigns a multiple to an art dealer for the purpose of effecting a sale of the multiple, shall have no liability to a purchaser under this article if the consignor, as to the consignee, has complied with the provisions of this title.

(b) When an art dealer has agreed to sell a multiple on behalf of a consignor, who is not an art dealer, or an artist has not consigned a multiple to an art dealer but the art dealer has agreed to act as the agent for an artist for the purpose of supplying the information required by this title, the art dealer shall incur the liabilities of other art dealers prescribed by this title, as to a purchaser. *(Added by Stats.1982, c. 1320, p. 4879, § 7.)*

Cross References

Art dealer defined for purposes of this Title, see Civil Code § 1740.
Artist defined for purposes of this Title, see Civil Code § 1740.

CHAPTER 3. REMEDIES AND PENALTIES

Section
1745. Violations by art dealer; liability; limitations of actions; costs, and attorneys' and expert witnesses' fees.
1745.5. Injunctions; civil penalty; penalty surcharge.

§ 1745. Violations by art dealer; liability; limitations of actions; costs, and attorneys' and expert witnesses' fees

(a) An art dealer, including a dealer consignee, who offers or sells a multiple in, into or from this state without providing the certificate of authenticity required in Sections 1742 and 1744 of this title for any time period, or who provides information which is mistaken, erroneous or untrue, except for harmless errors, such as typographical errors, shall be liable to the purchaser of the multiple. The art dealer's liability shall consist of the consideration paid by the purchaser for the multiple, with interest at the legal rate thereon, upon the return of the multiple in the condition in which received by the purchaser.

(b) In any case in which an art dealer, including a dealer consignee, willfully offers or sells a multiple in violation of this title, the person purchasing such multiple may recover from the art dealer, including a dealer consignee, who offers or sells such multiple an amount equal to three times the amount required under subdivision (a).

(c) No action shall be maintained to enforce any liability under this section unless brought within one year after discovery of the violation upon which it is based and in no event more than three years after the multiple was sold.

(d) In any action to enforce any provision of this title, the court may allow the prevailing purchaser the costs of the action together with reasonable attorneys' and expert witnesses' fees. In the event, however, the court determines that an action to enforce was brought in bad faith, it may allow such expenses to the seller as it deems appropriate.

(e) These remedies shall not bar or be deemed inconsistent with a claim for damages or with the exercise of additional remedies otherwise available to the purchaser.

(f) In any proceeding in which an art dealer relies upon a disclaimer of knowledge as to any relevant information set forth in Section 1744 for any time period, such disclaimer shall be effective unless the claimant is able to establish that the art dealer failed to make reasonable inquiries, according to the custom and usage of the trade, to ascertain the relevant information or that such relevant information would have been ascertained as a result of such reasonable inquiries. (Added by Stats.1970, c. 1223, p. 2142, § 1, operative July 1, 1971. Amended by Stats.1982, c. 1320, p. 4879, § 8; Stats. 1988, c. 819, § 4.)

Cross References

Art dealer defined for purposes of this Title, see Civil Code § 1740.
Certificate of authenticity defined for purposes of this Title, see Civil Code § 1740.
Damages, generally, see Civil Code §§ 3274, 3281 et seq.
One year limitation of actions, generally, see Code of Civil Procedure § 340.
Person defined for purposes of this Title, see Civil Code § 1740.

§ 1745.5. Injunctions; civil penalty; penalty surcharge

(a) Any person performing or proposing to perform an act in violation of this title within this state may be enjoined in any court of competent jurisdiction.

(b) Actions for injunction pursuant to this title may be prosecuted by the following persons:

(1) The Attorney General.

(2) Any district attorney.

(3) Any city attorney.

(4) With the consent of the district attorney, a city prosecutor in any city or city and county having a full-time city prosecutor in the name of the people of the State of California upon their own complaint, or upon the complaint of any board, officer, person, corporation, or association.

(5) Any person acting in his or her own interests, or in the interests of the members of a corporation or association, or in the interests of the general public.

(c) Any person who violates any provision of this title may also be liable for a civil penalty not to exceed one thousand dollars ($1,000) for each violation, which may be assessed and recovered in a civil action brought in the name of the people of the State of California by the Attorney General or by any district attorney or any city attorney, and, with the consent of the district attorney, by a city prosecutor in any city or city and county having a full-time city prosecutor in any court of competent jurisdiction.

If the action is brought by the Attorney General, one-half of the penalty collected shall be paid to the treasurer of the county in which the judgment was entered, and one-half to the General Fund. If brought by a district attorney, the penalty collected shall be paid to the treasurer of the county in which the judgment was entered. If brought by a city attorney or city prosecutor, one-half of the penalty collected shall be paid to the treasurer of the city in which the judgment was entered, and one-half to the treasurer of the county in which the judgment was entered.

(d) Any person who violates any provision of this title may also be liable for a civil penalty surcharge not to exceed one thousand dollars ($1,000) for each violation which shall be assessed and recovered in the manner provided in subdivision (c). Any penalty surcharge collected shall be applied to the costs of enforcing this title by the prosecuting officer. (Added by Stats.1982, c. 1320, p. 4880, § 9. Amended by Stats.1988, c. 819, § 5.)

Cross References

Attorney General, generally, see Government Code § 12500 et seq.
Injunction in general, see Civil Code § 3420 et seq.; Code of Civil Procedure § 525 et seq.
Person defined for purposes of this Title, see Civil Code § 1740.

Title 1.2A

VIOLENT VIDEO GAMES

Section
1746. Definitions.
1746.1. Sale and rental to minors prohibited; affirmative defenses; non-application of prohibition to enumerated relatives or legal guardian.
1746.2. Package labels.
1746.3. Penalties.
1746.4. Violations; reporting.
1746.5. Severability.

Validity

The sections under Title 1.2A were held unconstitutional in the decision of Video Software Dealers Ass'n v. Schwarzenegger, C.A.9 (Cal.)2009, 556 F.3d 950, certiorari granted 130 S.Ct. 2398, 559 U.S. 1092, 176 L.Ed.2d 784, affirmed 131 S.Ct. 2729, 564 U.S. 786, 180 L.Ed.2d 708.

The sections under Title 1.2A were held unconstitutional in the decision of Brown v. Entertainment Merchants Ass'n, 2011, 131 S.Ct. 2729, 564 U.S. 786, 180 L.Ed.2d 708.

§ 1746. Definitions

For purposes of this title, the following definitions shall apply:

(a) "Minor" means any natural person who is under 18 years of age.

(b) "Person" means any natural person, partnership, firm, association, corporation, limited liability company, or other legal entity.

(c) "Video game" means any electronic amusement device that utilizes a computer, microprocessor, or similar electronic circuitry and its own monitor, or is designed to be used with a television set or a computer monitor, that interacts with the user of the device.

(d)(1) "Violent video game" means a video game in which the range of options available to a player includes killing, maiming, dismembering, or sexually assaulting an image of a human being, if those acts are depicted in the game in a manner that does either of the following:

(A) Comes within all of the following descriptions:

(i) A reasonable person, considering the game as a whole, would find appeals to a deviant or morbid interest of minors.

(ii) It is patently offensive to prevailing standards in the community as to what is suitable for minors.

(iii) It causes the game, as a whole, to lack serious literary, artistic, political, or scientific value for minors.

(B) Enables the player to virtually inflict serious injury upon images of human beings or characters with substantially human characteristics in a manner which is especially heinous, cruel, or depraved in that it involves torture or serious physical abuse to the victim.

(2) For purposes of this subdivision, the following definitions apply:

(A) "Cruel" means that the player intends to virtually inflict a high degree of pain by torture or serious physical abuse of the victim in addition to killing the victim.

(B) "Depraved" means that the player relishes the virtual killing or shows indifference to the suffering of the victim, as evidenced by torture or serious physical abuse of the victim.

(C) "Heinous" means shockingly atrocious. For the killing depicted in a video game to be heinous, it must involve additional acts of torture or serious physical abuse of the victim as set apart from other killings.

(D) "Serious physical abuse" means a significant or considerable amount of injury or damage to the victim's body which involves a substantial risk of death, unconsciousness, extreme physical pain, substantial disfigurement, or substantial impairment of the function of a bodily member, organ, or mental faculty. Serious physical abuse, unlike torture, does not require that the victim be conscious of the abuse at the time it is inflicted. However, the player must specifically intend the abuse apart from the killing.

(E) "Torture" includes mental as well as physical abuse of the victim. In either case, the virtual victim must be conscious of the abuse at the time it is inflicted; and the player must specifically intend to virtually inflict severe mental or physical pain or suffering upon the victim, apart from killing the victim.

(3) Pertinent factors in determining whether a killing depicted in a video game is especially heinous, cruel, or depraved include infliction of gratuitous violence upon the victim beyond that necessary to commit the killing, needless mutilation of the victim's body, and helplessness of the victim. (Added by Stats.2005, c. 638 (A.B.1179), § 2.)

Validity

This section was held unconstitutional in the decision of Video Software Dealers Ass'n v. Schwarzenegger, C.A.9 (Cal.)2009, 556 F.3d 950, certiorari granted 130 S.Ct. 2398, 559 U.S. 1092, 176 L.Ed.2d 784, affirmed 131 S.Ct. 2729, 564 U.S. 786, 180 L.Ed.2d 708.

This section was held unconstitutional in the decision of Brown v. Entertainment Merchants Ass'n, 2011, 131 S.Ct. 2729, 564 U.S. 786, 180 L.Ed.2d 708.

§ 1746.1. Sale and rental to minors prohibited; affirmative defenses; non-application of prohibition to enumerated relatives or legal guardian

(a) A person may not sell or rent a video game that has been labeled as a violent video game to a minor.

(b) Proof that a defendant, or his or her employee or agent, demanded, was shown, and reasonably relied upon evidence that a purchaser or renter of a violent video game was not a minor or that the manufacturer failed to label a violent video game as required pursuant to Section 1746.2 shall be an affirmative defense to any action brought pursuant to this title. That evidence may include, but is not limited to, a driver's license or an identification card issued to the purchaser or renter by a state or by the Armed Forces of the United States.

(c) This section shall not apply if the violent video game is sold or rented to a minor by the minor's parent, grandparent, aunt, uncle, or legal guardian. (Added by Stats.2005, c. 638 (A.B.1179), § 2.)

Validity

This section was held unconstitutional in the decision of Video Software Dealers Ass'n v. Schwarzenegger, C.A.9 (Cal.)2009, 556 F.3d 950, certiorari granted 130 S.Ct. 2398, 559 U.S. 1092, 176 L.Ed.2d 784, affirmed 131 S.Ct. 2729, 564 U.S. 786, 180 L.Ed.2d 708.

This section was held unconstitutional in the decision of Brown v. Entertainment Merchants Ass'n, 2011, 131 S.Ct. 2729, 564 U.S. 786, 180 L.Ed.2d 708.

Cross References

Minor defined for purposes of this Title, see Civil Code § 1746.
Person defined for purposes of this Title, see Civil Code § 1746.
Video game defined for purposes of this Title, see Civil Code § 1746.
Violent video game defined for purposes of this Title, see Civil Code § 1746.

§ 1746.2. Package labels

Each violent video game that is imported into or distributed in California for retail sale shall be labeled with a solid white "18" outlined in black. The "18" shall have dimensions of no less than 2 inches by 2 inches. The "18" shall be displayed on the front face of the video game package. (Added by Stats.2005, c. 638 (A.B.1179), § 2.)

Validity

This section was held unconstitutional in the decision of Video Software Dealers Ass'n v. Schwarzenegger, C.A.9 (Cal.)2009, 556 F.3d 950, certiorari granted 130 S.Ct. 2398, 559 U.S. 1092, 176 L.Ed.2d 784, affirmed 131 S.Ct. 2729, 564 U.S. 786, 180 L.Ed.2d 708.

This section was held unconstitutional in the decision of Brown v. Entertainment Merchants Ass'n, 2011, 131 S.Ct. 2729, 564 U.S. 786, 180 L.Ed.2d 708.

ARISING FROM PARTICULAR TRANSACTIONS

Cross References

Video game defined for purposes of this Title, see Civil Code § 1746.
Violent video game defined for purposes of this Title, see Civil Code § 1746.

§ 1746.3. Penalties

Any person who violates any provision of this title shall be liable in an amount of up to one thousand dollars ($1,000), or a lesser amount as determined by the court. However, this liability shall not apply to any person who violates those provisions if he or she is employed solely in the capacity of a salesclerk or other, similar position and he or she does not have an ownership interest in the business in which the violation occurred and is not employed as a manager in that business. *(Added by Stats.2005, c. 638 (A.B.1179), § 2.)*

Validity

This section was held unconstitutional in the decision of Video Software Dealers Ass'n v. Schwarzenegger, C.A.9 (Cal.)2009, 556 F.3d 950, certiorari granted 130 S.Ct. 2398, 559 U.S. 1092, 176 L.Ed.2d 784, affirmed 131 S.Ct. 2729, 564 U.S. 786, 180 L.Ed.2d 708.

This section was held unconstitutional in the decision of Brown v. Entertainment Merchants Ass'n, 2011, 131 S.Ct. 2729, 564 U.S. 786, 180 L.Ed.2d 708.

Cross References

Person defined for purposes of this Title, see Civil Code § 1746.

§ 1746.4. Violations; reporting

A suspected violation of this title may be reported to a city attorney, county counsel, or district attorney by a parent, legal guardian, or other adult acting on behalf of a minor to whom a violent video game has been sold or rented. A violation of this title may be prosecuted by any city attorney, county counsel, or district attorney. *(Added by Stats.2005, c. 638 (A.B.1179), § 2.)*

Validity

This section was held unconstitutional in the decision of Video Software Dealers Ass'n v. Schwarzenegger, C.A.9 (Cal.)2009, 556 F.3d 950, certiorari granted 130 S.Ct. 2398, 559 U.S. 1092, 176 L.Ed.2d 784, affirmed 131 S.Ct. 2729, 564 U.S. 786, 180 L.Ed.2d 708.

This section was held unconstitutional in the decision of Brown v. Entertainment Merchants Ass'n, 2011, 131 S.Ct. 2729, 564 U.S. 786, 180 L.Ed.2d 708.

Cross References

Minor defined for purposes of this Title, see Civil Code § 1746.
Violent video game defined for purposes of this Title, see Civil Code § 1746.

§ 1746.5. Severability

The provisions of this title are severable. If any provision of this title or its application is held to be invalid, that invalidity shall not affect other provisions or applications that can be given effect without the invalid provision or application. *(Added by Stats.2005, c. 638 (A.B.1179), § 2.)*

Validity

This section was held unconstitutional in the decision of Video Software Dealers Ass'n v. Schwarzenegger, C.A.9 (Cal.)2009, 556 F.3d 950, certiorari granted 130 S.Ct. 2398, 559 U.S. 1092, 176 L.Ed.2d 784, affirmed 131 S.Ct. 2729, 564 U.S. 786, 180 L.Ed.2d 708.

This section was held unconstitutional in the decision of Brown v. Entertainment Merchants Ass'n, 2011, 131 S.Ct. 2729, 564 U.S. 786, 180 L.Ed.2d 708.

Title 1.3

CREDIT CARDS

Section	
1747.	Short title.
1747.01.	Legislative intent; conformance with federal law.
1747.02.	Definitions.
1747.03.	Electronic fund transfer and purchases of petroleum products by key or card key at automated dispensing outlet; inapplicability of title; exception.
1747.04.	Public policy; waiver of rights.
1747.05.	Limitations on issuance.
1747.06.	Offer or solicitation to receive card; completed application returned with different address; verification; liability; address change.
1747.08.	Personal identification information; prohibition upon collection of data upon credit card transaction form; exemptions; civil penalties and injunctive relief.
1747.09.	Printing credit or debit card receipts; restrictions.
1747.8.	Renumbered.
1747.9.	Renumbered.
1747.10.	Limitations on liability for unauthorized credit card use.
1747.20.	Multiple cards issued for use by employees of an organization; liability for unauthorized use; agreements.
1747.30.	Repealed.
1747.40.	Failure of card issuer to give timely response to inquiry concerning debit or credit applicable to obligation.
1747.50.	Correction of billing errors by card issuer; penalty for failure to correct; action.
1747.60.	Correction of billing errors by retailer; penalty for failure to correct; action.
1747.65.	Card issuer or retailer not liable for billing error made by the other.
1747.70.	Giving of untrue or unfavorable credit information by card issuer; unlawful cancellation or refusal to renew credit card; penalty.
1747.80.	Refusal to issue credit card for discriminatory reasons; penalty.
1747.81.	Married women; name on card.
1747.85.	Cancellation of credit card; notice; exceptions; inactive status; updating information to verify current creditworthiness.
1747.90.	Cardholders' claims and defenses arising from card transactions; assertion against issuer; conditions; amount of claims or defenses.
1747.94.	Secured credit card disclosures; statement in deed of trust executed in connection with card; applicability of section; violation.
1748.	Agreements to prohibit discounts for cash payment; invalidity.

OBLIGATIONS

Section
1748.1. Surcharges; violations.
1748.5. Finance charges; cardholder information request; frequency; form; application.
1748.7. Credit card transactions through retailer's account with financial institution or credit card issuer without furnishing of goods or services; exemptions; violations; remedies; penalties.
1748.9. Preprinted checks or drafts; required disclosures.
1748.95. Identity theft; credit card application filed by unauthorized person; right of victim to receive copies of specified documents from credit card company.

Cross References

Animal control officers, acceptance of credit cards, payment of licenses, fees, etc., see Food and Agricultural Code § 31255.

Civil actions, filing of papers by facsimile transmission, payment of fees with credit cards, surcharge, see Code of Civil Procedure § 1010.5.

Credit cards, debit cards, and electronic funds transfers, acceptance by courts, cities, counties, or other public agencies, surcharges additional fee, see Government Code § 6159.

Credit sales, membership fees, see Civil Code § 1810.4

Crimes and offenses, credit cards, see Penal Code § 484d et seq.

Department of Fish and Game, general license provisions, credit card charges, surcharge, see Fish and Game Code § 1050.5.

Finance lenders law, application of law to credit cards, see Financial Code § 22052.

Franchise and income tax laws, payment to franchise tax board, see Revenue and Taxation Code § 19005.

Public agency obligations, payments with credit cards, see Government Code § 6159.

Regulation and licensing of dogs, fees for impounding, credit cards, surcharge, see Food and Agricultural Code § 31255.

State park system, charge for use of state parks, surcharge, see Public Resources Code § 5010.

§ 1747. Short title

This title may be cited as the "Song-Beverly Credit Card Act of 1971." *(Added by Stats.1971, c. 1019, p. 1958, § 4.)*

§ 1747.01. Legislative intent; conformance with federal law

It is the intent of the Legislature that the provisions of this title as to which there are similar provisions in the federal Truth in Lending Act, as amended (15 U.S.C. 1601, et seq.), essentially conform, and be interpreted by anyone construing the provisions of this title to so conform, to the Truth in Lending Act and any rule, regulation, or interpretation promulgated thereunder by the Board of Governors of the Federal Reserve System, and any interpretation issued by an official or employee of the Federal Reserve System duly authorized to issue such interpretation. *(Added by Stats. 1982, c. 545, p. 2480, § 1.)*

§ 1747.02. Definitions

As used in this title:

(a) "Credit card" means any card, plate, coupon book, or other single credit device existing for the purpose of being used from time to time upon presentation to obtain money, property, labor, or services on credit. "Credit card" does not mean any of the following:

(1) Any single credit device used to obtain telephone property, labor, or services in any transaction under public utility tariffs.

(2) Any device that may be used to obtain credit pursuant to an electronic fund transfer, but only if the credit is obtained under an agreement between a consumer and a financial institution to extend credit when the consumer's asset account is overdrawn or to maintain a specified minimum balance in the consumer's asset account.

(3) Any key or card key used at an automated dispensing outlet to obtain or purchase petroleum products, as defined in subdivision (c) of Section 13401 of the Business and Professions Code, that will be used primarily for business rather than personal or family purposes.

(b) "Accepted credit card" means any credit card that the cardholder has requested or applied for and received or has signed, or has used, or has authorized another person to use, for the purpose of obtaining money, property, labor, or services on credit. Any credit card issued in renewal of, or in substitution for, an accepted credit card becomes an accepted credit card when received by the cardholder, whether the credit card is issued by the same or a successor card issuer.

(c) "Card issuer" means any person who issues a credit card or the agent of that person for that purpose with respect to the credit card.

(d) "Cardholder" means a natural person to whom a credit card is issued for consumer credit purposes, or a natural person who has agreed with the card issuer to pay consumer credit obligations arising from the issuance of a credit card to another natural person. For purposes of Sections 1747.05, 1747.10, and 1747.20, the term includes any person to whom a credit card is issued for any purpose, including business, commercial, or agricultural use, or a person who has agreed with the card issuer to pay obligations arising from the issuance of that credit card to another person.

(e) "Retailer" means every person other than a card issuer who furnishes money, goods, services, or anything else of value upon presentation of a credit card by a cardholder. "Retailer" shall not mean the state, a county, city, city and county, or any other public agency.

(f) "Unauthorized use" means the use of a credit card by a person, other than the cardholder, (1) who does not have actual, implied, or apparent authority for that use and (2) from which the cardholder receives no benefit. "Unauthorized use" does not include the use of a credit card by a person who has been given authority by the cardholder to use the credit card. Any attempted termination by the cardholder of the person's authority is ineffective as against the card issuer until the cardholder complies with the procedures required by the card issuer to terminate that authority. Notwithstanding the above, following the card issuer's receipt of oral or written notice from a cardholder indicating that it wishes to terminate the authority of a previously authorized user of a credit card, the card issuer shall follow its usual procedures for precluding any further use of a credit card by an unauthorized person.

(g) An "inquiry" is a writing that is posted by mail to the address of the card issuer to which payments are normally tendered, unless another address is specifically indicated on the statement for that purpose, then to that other address, and that is received by the card issuer no later than 60 days after the card issuer transmitted the first periodic statement that reflects the alleged billing error, and that does all of the following:

(1) Sets forth sufficient information to enable the card issuer to identify the cardholder and the account.

(2) Sufficiently identifies the billing error.

(3) Sets forth information providing the basis for the cardholder's belief that the billing error exists.

(h) A "response" is a writing that is responsive to an inquiry and mailed to the cardholder's address last known to the card issuer.

(i) A "timely response" is a response that is mailed within two complete billing cycles, but in no event later than 90 days, after the card issuer receives an inquiry.

(j) A "billing error" means an error by omission or commission in (1) posting any debit or credit, or (2) in computation or similar error of an accounting nature contained in a statement given to the cardholder by the card issuer. A "billing error" does not mean any dispute with respect to value, quality, or quantity of goods, services, or other benefit obtained through use of a credit card.

(k) "Adequate notice" means a printed notice to a cardholder that sets forth the pertinent facts clearly and conspicuously so that a person against whom it is to operate could reasonably be expected to have noticed it and understood its meaning.

(*l*) "Secured credit card" means any credit card issued under an agreement or other instrument that pledges, hypothecates, or places a lien on real property or money or other personal property to secure the cardholder's obligations to the card issuer.

(m) "Student credit card" means any credit card that is provided to a student at a public or private college or university and is provided to that student solely based on his or her enrollment in a public or private university, or is provided to a student who would not otherwise qualify for that credit card on the basis of his or her income. A "student credit card" does not include a credit card issued to a student who has a cocardholder or cosigner who would otherwise qualify for a credit card other than a student credit card.

(n) "Retail motor fuel dispenser" means a device that dispenses fuel that is used to power internal combustion engines, including motor vehicle engines, that processes the sale of fuel through a remote electronic payment system, and that is in a location where an employee or other agent of the seller is not present.

(*o*) "Retail motor fuel payment island automated cashier" means a remote electronic payment processing station that processes the retail sale of fuel that is used to power internal combustion engines, including motor vehicle engines, that is in a location where an employee or other agent of the seller is not present, and that is located in close proximity to a retail motor fuel dispenser. *(Added by Stats.1971, c. 1019, p. 1958, § 4. Amended by Stats.1979, c. 574, p. 1802, § 1, eff. Sept. 12, 1979; Stats.1982, c. 545, p. 2480, § 2; Stats.1982, c. 646, p. 2659, § 1.5; Stats.1991, c. 608 (A.B.998), § 1; Stats.1992, c. 523 (S.B.1683), § 1; Stats.2001, c. 294 (A.B.521), § 1; Stats. 2011, c. 690 (A.B.1219), § 1, eff. Oct. 9, 2011.)*

Cross References

Adoption of policies to regulate marketing practices used on college campuses by credit card companies, see Education Code § 99030.
Credit card holders and telephone accountholders change of address requests and notifications, requirements and restrictions for credit card issuers and business entities providing telephone accounts, see Civil Code § 1799.1b.
Credit card offenses, see Penal Code § 484d et seq.
Franchise investment law, application to bank credit card plans, see Corporations Code § 31103.
Impoundment of vehicle, driving without a license or while privilege suspended, revoked, or restricted, see Vehicle Code § 14602.6.
Impoundment of vehicle, fleeing or evading a peace officer, reckless driving, see Vehicle Code § 14602.7.
Impoundment of vehicle, repeat offenders, vehicle owner's rights and responsibilities, see Vehicle Code § 14602.8.
Impoundment of vehicle illegally operated as taxi, towing and storage charges, release, see Vehicle Code § 21100.4.
Inquiry, additional definition, see Civil Code § 1747.60.
Military Families Financial Relief Act, see Military and Veterans Code § 800 et seq.
Removal of vehicle from private property by property owner, acceptance of credit card by person or in charge of storage facility, see Vehicle Code § 22658.
Towing and service charges, credit card or cash payment, see Vehicle Code § 22651.1.
Vehicle used in violation of code governing repossessors, seizure, release and liability, including fees, see Vehicle Code § 23118.

§ 1747.03. Electronic fund transfer and purchases of petroleum products by key or card key at automated dispensing outlet; inapplicability of title; exception

(a) Any rights or responsibilities created by this title that are based on the use of a credit card shall have no effect with respect to:

(1) Those transactions that constitute an electronic fund transfer as defined by Regulation E of the Federal Reserve Board (12 CFR, Part 205).

(2) Those transactions involving the use of any key or a card key used at an automated dispensing outlet to obtain or purchase petroleum products, as defined in subdivision (c) of Section 13401 of the Business and Professions Code, which will be used primarily for business rather than personal or family purposes.

(b) Notwithstanding subdivision (a), a person, company, or corporation that has been issued a key or card key described in paragraph (2) of subdivision (a) shall not be liable for losses due to the loss or theft of the key or card key incurred after receipt by the issuer of the key or card key of written or oral notification of the loss or theft. *(Added by Stats.1979, c. 574, p. 1803, § 2, eff. Sept. 12, 1979. Amended by Stats.1982, c. 646, p. 2661, § 2.)*

Cross References

Credit card defined for purposes of this Title, see Civil Code § 1747.02.

§ 1747.04. Public policy; waiver of rights

Any waiver of the provisions of this title is contrary to public policy, and is void and unenforceable. *(Added by Stats.2002, c. 815 (A.B.2331), § 2.)*

§ 1747.05. Limitations on issuance

(a) No credit card shall be issued except:

(1) In response to an oral or written request or application therefor.

(2) As a renewal of, or in substitution for, an accepted credit card whether that card is issued by the same or a successor card issuer.

(b) A credit card issued in substitution for an accepted credit card may be issued only if the card issuer provides an activation process whereby the cardholder is required to contact the card issuer to activate the credit card prior to the first use of the credit card in a credit transaction.

(c) This section does not prohibit the completion of an overdraft protection advance or recurring-charge transaction that a cardholder has previously authorized on an accepted credit card. (Added by Stats.1971, c. 1019, p. 1960, § 4. Amended by Stats.1982, c. 545, p. 2482, § 3; Stats.2002, c. 862 (S.B.1617), § 1.)

Cross References

Accepted credit card defined for purposes of this Title, see Civil Code § 1747.02.
Card issuer defined for purposes of this Title, see Civil Code § 1747.02.
Cardholder defined for purposes of this Title, see Civil Code § 1747.02.
Credit card defined for purposes of this Title, see Civil Code § 1747.02.
Response defined for purposes of this Title, see Civil Code § 1747.02.

§ 1747.06. Offer or solicitation to receive card; completed application returned with different address; verification; liability; address change

(a) A credit card issuer that mails an offer or solicitation to receive a credit card and, in response, receives a completed application for a credit card that lists an address that is different from the address on the offer or solicitation shall verify the change of address by contacting the person to whom the solicitation or offer was mailed.

(b) Notwithstanding any other provision of law, a person to whom an offer or solicitation to receive a credit card is made shall not be liable for the unauthorized use of a credit card issued in response to that offer or solicitation if the credit card issuer does not verify the change of address pursuant to subdivision (a) prior to the issuance of the credit card, unless the credit card issuer proves that this person actually incurred the charge on the credit card.

(c) When a credit card issuer receives a written or oral request for a change of the cardholder's billing address and then receives a written or oral request for an additional credit card within 10 days after the requested address change, the credit card issuer shall not mail the requested additional credit card to the new address or, alternatively, activate the requested additional credit card, unless the credit card issuer has verified the change of address.

(d) This section shall become operative on July 1, 2000. (Added by Stats.1999, c. 423 (S.B.930), § 1, operative July 1, 2000.)

Cross References

Card issuer defined for purposes of this Title, see Civil Code § 1747.02.
Cardholder defined for purposes of this Title, see Civil Code § 1747.02.
Credit card defined for purposes of this Title, see Civil Code § 1747.02.
Response defined for purposes of this Title, see Civil Code § 1747.02.
Unauthorized use defined for purposes of this Title, see Civil Code § 1747.02.

§ 1747.08. Personal identification information; prohibition upon collection of data upon credit card transaction form; exemptions; civil penalties and injunctive relief

(a) Except as provided in subdivision (c), no person, firm, partnership, association, or corporation that accepts credit cards for the transaction of business shall do any of the following:

(1) Request, or require as a condition to accepting the credit card as payment in full or in part for goods or services, the cardholder to write any personal identification information upon the credit card transaction form or otherwise.

(2) Request, or require as a condition to accepting the credit card as payment in full or in part for goods or services, the cardholder to provide personal identification information, which the person, firm, partnership, association, or corporation accepting the credit card writes, causes to be written, or otherwise records upon the credit card transaction form or otherwise.

(3) Utilize, in any credit card transaction, a credit card form which contains preprinted spaces specifically designated for filling in any personal identification information of the cardholder.

(b) For purposes of this section "personal identification information," means information concerning the cardholder, other than information set forth on the credit card, and including, but not limited to, the cardholder's address and telephone number.

(c) Subdivision (a) does not apply in the following instances:

(1) If the credit card is being used as a deposit to secure payment in the event of default, loss, damage, or other similar occurrence.

(2) Cash advance transactions.

(3) If any of the following applies:

(A) The person, firm, partnership, association, or corporation accepting the credit card is contractually obligated to provide personal identification information in order to complete the credit card transaction.

(B) The person, firm, partnership, association, or corporation accepting the credit card in a sales transaction at a retail motor fuel dispenser or retail motor fuel payment island automated cashier uses the Zip Code information solely for prevention of fraud, theft, or identity theft.

(C) The person, firm, partnership, association, or corporation accepting the credit card is obligated to collect and record the personal identification information by federal or state law or regulation.

(4) If personal identification information is required for a special purpose incidental but related to the individual credit card transaction, including, but not limited to, information relating to shipping, delivery, servicing, or installation of the purchased merchandise, or for special orders.

(d) This section does not prohibit any person, firm, partnership, association, or corporation from requiring the cardholder, as a condition to accepting the credit card as payment in full or in part for goods or services, to provide reasonable forms of positive identification, which may include a driver's license or a California state identification card, or where one of these is not available, another form of photo identification, provided that none of the information contained thereon is written or recorded on the credit card transaction form or otherwise. If the cardholder pays for the transaction with a credit card number and does not make the credit card available upon request to verify the number, the cardholder's driver's license number or identification card number may be recorded on the credit card transaction form or otherwise.

(e) Any person who violates this section shall be subject to a civil penalty not to exceed two hundred fifty dollars ($250) for the first violation and one thousand dollars ($1,000) for each subsequent violation, to be assessed and collected in a civil action brought by the person paying with a credit card, by the Attorney General, or by the district attorney or city attorney of the county or city in which the violation occurred. However, no civil penalty shall be assessed for a violation of this section if the defendant shows by a preponderance of the evidence that the violation was not intentional and resulted from a bona fide error made notwithstanding the defendant's maintenance of procedures reasonably adopted to avoid that error. When collected, the civil penalty shall be payable, as appropriate, to the person paying with a credit card who brought the action, or to the general fund of whichever governmental entity brought the action to assess the civil penalty.

(f) The Attorney General, or any district attorney or city attorney within his or her respective jurisdiction, may bring an action in the superior court in the name of the people of the State of California to enjoin violation of subdivision (a) and, upon notice to the defendant of not less than five days, to temporarily restrain and enjoin the violation. If it appears to the satisfaction of the court that the defendant has, in fact, violated subdivision (a), the court may issue an injunction restraining further violations, without requiring proof that any person has been damaged by the violation. In these proceedings, if the court finds that the defendant has violated subdivision (a), the court may direct the defendant to pay any or all costs incurred by the Attorney General, district attorney, or city attorney in seeking or obtaining injunctive relief pursuant to this subdivision.

(g) Actions for collection of civil penalties under subdivision (e) and for injunctive relief under subdivision (f) may be consolidated.

(h) The changes made to this section by Chapter 458 of the Statutes of 1995 apply only to credit card transactions entered into on and after January 1, 1996. Nothing in those changes shall be construed to affect any civil action which was filed before January 1, 1996. (Formerly § 1747.8, added by Stats.1990, c. 999 (A.B.2920), § 1. Amended by Stats.1991, c. 1089 (A.B.1477), § 2, eff. Oct. 14, 1991; Stats.1995, c. 458 (A.B.1316), § 2. Renumbered § 1747.08 and amended by Stats.2004, c. 183 (A.B.3082), § 29. Amended by Stats.2005, c. 22 (S.B.1108), § 14; Stats.2011, c. 690 (A.B.1219), § 2, eff. Oct. 9, 2011.)

Cross References

Attorney General, generally, see Government Code § 12500 et seq.
Businesses that own or license personal identification information, duty to provide reasonable security to protect, see Civil Code § 1798.81.5.
Cardholder defined for purposes of this Title, see Civil Code § 1747.02.
Credit card defined for purposes of this Title, see Civil Code § 1747.02.
Disclosure of a customer's personal information by business with an established business relationship within the preceding calendar year, customer's right to receive additional information relating to disclosure, see Civil Code § 1798.83.

§ 1747.09. Printing credit or debit card receipts; restrictions

(a) Except as provided in this section, no person, firm, partnership, association, corporation, or limited liability company that accepts credit or debit cards for the transaction of business shall print more than the last five digits of the credit or debit card account number or the expiration date upon any of the following:

(1) Any receipt provided to the cardholder.

(2) Any receipt retained by the person, firm, partnership, association, corporation, or limited liability company, which is printed at the time of the purchase, exchange, refund, or return, and is signed by the cardholder.

(3) Any receipt retained by the person, firm, partnership, association, corporation, or limited liability company, which is printed at the time of the purchase, exchange, refund, or return, but is not signed by the cardholder, because the cardholder used a personal identification number to complete the transaction.

(b) This section shall apply only to receipts that include a credit or debit card account number that are electronically printed and shall not apply to transactions in which the sole means of recording the person's credit or debit card account number is by handwriting or by an imprint or copy of the credit or debit card.

(c) This section shall not apply to documents, other than the receipts described in paragraphs (1) to (3), inclusive, of subdivision (a), used for internal administrative purposes.

(d) Paragraphs (2) and (3) of subdivision (a) shall become operative on January 1, 2009. (Formerly § 1747.9, added by Stats.1999, c. 423 (S.B.930), § 2. Renumbered § 1747.09 and amended by Stats.2004, c. 183 (A.B.3082), § 30. Amended by Stats.2005, c. 445 (S.B.802), § 1; Stats.2006, c. 682 (S.B.1699), § 1.)

Cross References

Cardholder defined for purposes of this Title, see Civil Code § 1747.02.

§ 1747.8. Renumbered § 1747.08 and amended by Stats. 2004, c. 183 (A.B.3082), § 29

§ 1747.9. Renumbered § 1747.09 and amended by Stats. 2004, c. 183 (A.B.3082), § 30

§ 1747.10. Limitations on liability for unauthorized credit card use

A cardholder shall be liable for the unauthorized use of a credit card only if all of the following conditions are met:

(a) The card is an accepted credit card.

(b) The liability is not in excess of fifty dollars ($50).

(c) The card issuer gives adequate notice to the cardholder of the potential liability.

(d) The card issuer has provided the cardholder with a description of a means by which the card issuer may be notified of loss or theft of the card.

(e) The unauthorized use occurs before the card issuer has been notified that an unauthorized use of the credit card has occurred or may occur as the result of loss, theft, or otherwise.

(f) The card issuer has provided a method whereby the user of such card can be identified as the person authorized to use it. *(Added by Stats.1982, c. 545, p. 2482, § 5.)*

Cross References

Accepted credit card defined for purposes of this Title, see Civil Code § 1747.02.
Adequate notice defined for purposes of this Title, see Civil Code § 1747.02.
Card issuer defined for purposes of this Title, see Civil Code § 1747.02.
Cardholder defined for purposes of this Title, see Civil Code § 1747.02.
Credit card defined for purposes of this Title, see Civil Code § 1747.02.
Limits on application of identity theft actions to transactions subject to this section, see Civil Code § 1798.97.
Unauthorized use defined for purposes of this Title, see Civil Code § 1747.02.

§ 1747.20. Multiple cards issued for use by employees of an organization; liability for unauthorized use; agreements

If 10 or more credit cards are issued by one card issuer for use by the employees of an organization, Section 1747.10 does not prohibit the card issuer and the organization from agreeing to liability for unauthorized use without regard to Section 1747.10. However, liability for unauthorized use may be imposed on an employee of the organization, by either the card issuer or the organization, only in accordance with Section 1747.10. *(Added by Stats.1982, c. 545, p. 2482, § 7.)*

Cross References

Card issuer defined for purposes of this Title, see Civil Code § 1747.02.
Credit card defined for purposes of this Title, see Civil Code § 1747.02.
Unauthorized use defined for purposes of this Title, see Civil Code § 1747.02.

§ 1747.30. Repealed by Stats.1982, c. 545, p. 2483, § 8

§ 1747.40. Failure of card issuer to give timely response to inquiry concerning debit or credit applicable to obligation

If a card issuer fails to give a timely response to an inquiry of a cardholder concerning any debit or credit applicable to an obligation incurred through the use of a credit card, he shall not be entitled to interest, finance charges, service charges, or any other charges thereon, from the date of mailing of the inquiry to the date of mailing of the response. *(Added by Stats.1971, c. 1019, p. 1960, § 4.)*

Cross References

Card issuer defined for purposes of this Title, see Civil Code § 1747.02.
Cardholder defined for purposes of this Title, see Civil Code § 1747.02.
Credit card defined for purposes of this Title, see Civil Code § 1747.02.
Inquiry defined for purposes of this Title, see Civil Code § 1747.02.
Response defined for purposes of this Title, see Civil Code § 1747.02.
Timely response defined for purposes of this Title, see Civil Code § 1747.02.

§ 1747.50. Correction of billing errors by card issuer; penalty for failure to correct; action

(a) Every card issuer shall correct any billing error made by the card issuer within two complete billing cycles, but in no event later than 90 days, after receiving an inquiry.

(b) Any card issuer who fails to correct a billing error made by the card issuer within the period prescribed by subdivision (a) shall not be entitled to the amount by which the outstanding balance of the cardholder's account is greater than the correct balance, nor any interest, finance charges, service charges, or other charges on the obligation giving rise to the billing error.

(c) Any cardholder who is injured by a willful violation of this section may bring an action for the recovery of damages. Judgment may be entered for three times the amount at which actual damages are assessed. The cardholder shall be entitled to recover reasonable attorney's fees and costs incurred in the action. *(Added by Stats.1971, c. 1019, p. 1960, § 4. Amended by Stats.1982, c. 545, p. 2483, § 9.)*

Cross References

Action on contract, award of attorney's fees and costs, see Civil Code § 1717.
Attorney's fees and costs, see Civil Code §§ 1717, 1811.1.
Automobile conditional sales contract, attorney's fees, see Civil Code § 2983.4.
Breach of warranty, award of attorney's fees, see Civil Code §§ 1794, 1794.1.
Commercial paper, provision for attorney's fees and collection costs, see Commercial Code § 3106.
Damages, generally, see Civil Code §§ 3274, 3281 et seq.
Penalty for imposing sanctions on cardholder obtaining relief under this section, see Civil Code § 1747.70.
Retail installment accounts, provision for attorney's fees, see Civil Code § 1810.4.
Swimming pool construction contracts, award of attorney's fees, see Business and Professions Code § 7168.

§ 1747.60. Correction of billing errors by retailer; penalty for failure to correct; action

(a) Every retailer shall correct any billing error made by the retailer within 60 days from the date on which an inquiry concerning a billing error was mailed.

(b) Any retailer who fails to correct a billing error made by the retailer within the period prescribed by subdivision (a) shall be liable to the cardholder in the amount by which the outstanding balance of the cardholder's account is greater than the correct balance, and any interest, finance charges, service charges, or other charges on the obligation giving rise to the billing error.

(c) Any cardholder who is injured by a willful violation of this section may bring an action for the recovery of damages. Judgment may be entered for three times the amount at which actual damages are assessed. The cardholder shall be entitled to recover reasonable attorney's fees and costs incurred in the action.

(d) As used in this section, an "inquiry" is a writing which is posted by mail to the address of the retailer, unless another address is specifically indicated by the retailer for the purpose of mailing inquiries with respect to billing errors, then to such address. (Added by Stats.1971, c. 1019, p. 1960, § 4.)

Cross References

Action on contract, award of attorney's fees and costs, see Civil Code § 1717.
Attorney's fees and costs, see Civil Code §§ 1717, 1811.1.
Automobile conditional sales contract, attorney's fees, see Civil Code § 2983.4.
Billing error defined for purposes of this Title, see Civil Code § 1747.02.
Breach of warranty, award of attorney's fees, see Civil Code §§ 1794, 1794.1.
Cardholder defined for purposes of this Title, see Civil Code § 1747.02.
Commercial paper, provision for attorney's fees and collection costs, see Commercial Code § 3106.
Damages, generally, see Civil Code §§ 3274, 3281 et seq.
Inquiry defined for purposes of this Title, see Civil Code § 1747.02.
Retail installment accounts, provision for attorney's fees, see Civil Code § 1810.4.
Retailer defined for purposes of this Title, see Civil Code § 1747.02.
Swimming pool construction contracts, award of attorney's fees, see Business and Professions Code § 7168.

§ 1747.65. Card issuer or retailer not liable for billing error made by the other

(a) A card issuer shall not be liable for a billing error made by the retailer.

(b) A retailer shall not be liable for a billing error made by a card issuer. (Added by Stats.1971, c. 1019, p. 1961, § 4.)

Cross References

Billing error defined for purposes of this Title, see Civil Code § 1747.02.
Card issuer defined for purposes of this Title, see Civil Code § 1747.02.
Retailer defined for purposes of this Title, see Civil Code § 1747.02.

§ 1747.70. Giving of untrue or unfavorable credit information by card issuer; unlawful cancellation or refusal to renew credit card; penalty

(a) No card issuer shall knowingly give any untrue credit information to any other person concerning a cardholder.

(b) No card issuer, after receiving an inquiry from a cardholder regarding a billing error and prior to satisfying the requirements of Section 1747.50, shall communicate unfavorable credit information concerning the cardholder to any person solely because of the cardholder's failure to pay the amount by which the outstanding balance of the cardholder's account is greater than the correct balance.

(c) No card issuer shall cancel or refuse to renew a credit card for the reason that the cardholder has obtained relief under Section 1747.50.

(d) Any cardholder who is injured by a willful violation of this section may bring an action for the recovery of damages. Judgment may be entered for three times the amount at which actual damages are assessed. The cardholder shall be entitled to recover reasonable attorney's fees and costs incurred in the action. (Added by Stats.1971, c. 1019, p. 1961, § 4.)

Cross References

Action on contract, award of attorney's fees and costs, see Civil Code § 1717.
Attorney's fees and costs, see Civil Code §§ 1717, 1811.1.
Automobile conditional sales contract, attorney's fees, see Civil Code § 2983.4.
Billing error defined for purposes of this Title, see Civil Code § 1747.02.
Breach of warranty, award of attorney's fees, see Civil Code §§ 1794, 1794.1.
Card issuer defined for purposes of this Title, see Civil Code § 1747.02.
Cardholder defined for purposes of this Title, see Civil Code § 1747.02.
Commercial paper, provision for attorney's fees and collection costs, see Commercial Code § 3106.
Consumer credit reporting, see Civil Code § 1785.1 et seq.
Credit card defined for purposes of this Title, see Civil Code § 1747.02.
Damages, generally, see Civil Code §§ 3274, 3281 et seq.
Inquiry defined for purposes of this Title, see Civil Code § 1747.02.
Retail installment accounts, provision for attorney's fees, see Civil Code § 1810.4.
Swimming pool construction contracts, award of attorney's fees, see Business and Professions Code § 7168.

§ 1747.80. Refusal to issue credit card for discriminatory reasons; penalty

(a) No card issuer shall refuse to issue a credit card to any person solely because of any characteristic listed or defined in subdivision (b) or (e) of Section 51.

(b) Any card issuer who willfully violates this section is liable for each and every offense for the actual damages, and two hundred fifty dollars ($250) in addition thereto, suffered by any person denied a credit card solely for the reasons set forth in subdivision (a). In addition, that person may petition the court to order the card issuer to issue him or her a credit card upon the terms, conditions, and standards as the

---

Travel Consumer Restitution Corporation, see Business and Professions Code § 17550.38.

§ 1747.80

card issuer normally utilizes in granting credit to other individuals. *(Added by Stats.1971, c. 1019, p. 1961, § 4. Amended by Stats.2007, c. 568 (A.B.14), § 14.)*

Cross References

Card issuer defined for purposes of this Title, see Civil Code § 1747.02.
Credit card defined for purposes of this Title, see Civil Code § 1747.02.
Damages, generally, see Civil Code §§ 3274, 3281 et seq.
Damages for discrimination, see Civil Code § 52.

§ 1747.81. Married women; name on card

(a) If a card issuer has determined in the normal course of business that it will issue a card to a married woman, the card shall be issued bearing either the maiden name or married name of the woman, as the woman may direct.

(b) Card issuers may require that a married woman requesting a card in her maiden name open a new account in that name. *(Added by Stats.1974, c. 1252, p. 2712, § 1.)*

Cross References

Card issuer defined for purposes of this Title, see Civil Code § 1747.02.

§ 1747.85. Cancellation of credit card; notice; exceptions; inactive status; updating information to verify current creditworthiness

Unless requested by the cardholder, no card issuer shall cancel a credit card without having first given the cardholder 30 days' written notice of its intention to do so unless the cardholder is or has been within the last 90 days in default of payment or otherwise in violation of any provision of the agreement between the card issuer and the cardholder governing the cardholder's use of the credit card or unless the card issuer has evidence or reasonable belief that the cardholder is unable or unwilling to repay obligations incurred under the agreement or that an unauthorized use of the card may be made.

Nothing provided herein shall be construed to prohibit a card issuer from placing the account of a cardholder on inactive status if the cardholder has not used the card for a period in excess of 18 months or from requiring that cardholder, upon subsequent reuse of a card, to provide to the card issuer such updated information as will enable the card issuer to verify the current creditworthiness of the cardholder. *(Added by Stats.1976, c. 34, p. 60, § 1. Amended by Stats.1983, c. 1247, § 1.)*

Cross References

Card issuer defined for purposes of this Title, see Civil Code § 1747.02.
Cardholder defined for purposes of this Title, see Civil Code § 1747.02.
Credit card defined for purposes of this Title, see Civil Code § 1747.02.
Unauthorized use defined for purposes of this Title, see Civil Code § 1747.02.

§ 1747.90. Cardholders' claims and defenses arising from card transactions; assertion against issuer; conditions; amount of claims or defenses

(a)(1) Subject to the limitation contained in subdivision (b), a card issuer who has issued a credit card to a cardholder pursuant to an open-end consumer credit plan shall be subject to all claims and defenses, other than tort claims, arising out of any transaction in which the credit card is used as a method of payment or extension of credit if the following conditions are met:

(A) The cardholder has made a good faith attempt to obtain satisfactory resolution of a disagreement or problem relative to the transaction from the person honoring the credit card.

(B) The amount of the initial transaction exceeds fifty dollars ($50).

(C) The place where the initial transaction occurred was in California, or, if not within California, then within 100 miles from the cardholder's current designated address in California.

(2) The limitations set forth in subparagraphs (B) and (C) of paragraph (1) with respect to a cardholder's right to assert claims and defenses against a card issuer shall not be applicable to any transaction in which the person honoring the credit card satisfies any of the following requirements:

(A) Is the same person as the card issuer.

(B) Is controlled by the card issuer.

(C) Is under direct or indirect common control with the card issuer.

(D) Is a franchised dealer in the card issuer's products or services.

(E) Has obtained the order for such transaction through a mail solicitation made by or participated in by the card issuer in which the cardholder is solicited to enter into such transaction by using the credit card issued by the card issuer.

(b) The amount of claims or defenses asserted by the cardholder may not exceed the amount of credit outstanding with respect to such transaction at the time the cardholder first notifies the card issuer or the person honoring the credit card of such claim or defense. For the purpose of determining the amount of credit outstanding, payments and credits to the cardholder's account are deemed to have been applied, in the order indicated, to the payment of the following:

(1) Late charges in the order of their entry to the account.

(2) Finance charges in order of their entry to the account.

(3) Debits to the account other than those set forth above, in the order in which each debit entry to the account was made.

(c) This section does not apply to the use of a check guarantee card or a debit card in connection with an overdraft credit plan, or to a check guarantee card used in connection with cash advance checks. *(Added by Stats.1982, c. 545, p. 2483, § 11.)*

Cross References

Card issuer defined for purposes of this Title, see Civil Code § 1747.02.
Cardholder defined for purposes of this Title, see Civil Code § 1747.02.
Credit card defined for purposes of this Title, see Civil Code § 1747.02.
Finance charge, see Civil Code § 1802.10.

Travel Consumer Restitution Corporation, see Business and Professions Code § 17550.38.

§ 1747.94. Secured credit card disclosures; statement in deed of trust executed in connection with card; applicability of section; violation

(a) In addition to any other disclosures required by law, a card issuer of a secured credit card shall, in every advertisement or solicitation to prospective cardholders, expressly identify the credit instrument offered as a "secured credit card" and prominently disclose that credit extended under the secured credit card is secured, and shall describe the security by item or type.

(b) Any deed of trust executed in connection with a secured credit card shall contain a statement that it is security for a secured credit card obligation. However, failure to include the statement shall not invalidate the deed of trust.

(c) This section does not apply to either of the following:

(1) Any credit card which is issued under an agreement or other instrument creating a purchase money security interest in property purchased with the credit card, but which does not pledge, hypothecate, or place a lien on other property of the cardholder or any co-obligor.

(2) Loans or extensions of credit subject to the Federal Home Equity Loan Consumer Protection Act of 1988 (P.L. 100-709).

(d) Any violation of this section shall constitute unfair competition within the meaning of Section 17200 of the Business and Professions Code. *(Added by Stats.1991, c. 608 (A.B.998), § 2.)*

Cross References

Card issuer defined for purposes of this Title, see Civil Code § 1747.02.
Cardholder defined for purposes of this Title, see Civil Code § 1747.02.
Credit card defined for purposes of this Title, see Civil Code § 1747.02.
Secured credit card defined for purposes of this Title, see Civil Code § 1747.02.

§ 1748. Agreements to prohibit discounts for cash payment; invalidity

Any provision in a contract between a card issuer and a retailer which has the effect of prohibiting the retailer from offering price discounts or from charging a different and lower price to customers who pay for goods or services by cash instead of by credit card is contrary to public policy and void. *(Added by Stats.1974, c. 1520, p. 3402, § 1.)*

Cross References

Card issuer defined for purposes of this Title, see Civil Code § 1747.02.
Credit card defined for purposes of this Title, see Civil Code § 1747.02.
Retailer defined for purposes of this Title, see Civil Code § 1747.02.

§ 1748.1. Surcharges; violations

(a) No retailer in any sales, service, or lease transaction with a consumer may impose a surcharge on a cardholder who elects to use a credit card in lieu of payment by cash, check, or similar means. A retailer may, however, offer discounts for the purpose of inducing payment by cash, check, or other means not involving the use of a credit card, provided that the discount is offered to all prospective buyers.

(b) Any retailer who willfully violates this section by imposing a surcharge on a cardholder who elects to use a credit card and who fails to pay that amount to the cardholder within 30 days of a written demand by the cardholder to the retailer by certified mail, shall be liable to the cardholder for three times the amount at which actual damages are assessed. The cardholder shall also be entitled to recover reasonable attorney's fees and costs incurred in the action.

A cause of action under this section may be brought in small claims court, if it does not exceed the jurisdiction of that court, or in any other appropriate court.

(c) A consumer shall not be deemed to have elected to use a credit card in lieu of another means of payment for purposes of this section in a transaction with a retailer if only credit cards are accepted by that retailer in payment for an order made by a consumer over a telephone, and only cash is accepted at a public store or other facility of the same retailer.

(d) Charges for third-party credit card guarantee services, when added to the price charged by the retailer if cash were to be paid, shall be deemed surcharges for purposes of this section even if they are payable directly to the third party or are charged separately.

(e) It is the intent of the Legislature to promote the effective operation of the free market and protect consumers from deceptive price increases for goods and services by prohibiting credit card surcharges and encouraging the availability of discounts by those retailers who wish to offer a lower price for goods and services purchased by some form of payment other than credit card.

(f) This section does not apply to charges for payment by credit card or debit card that are made by an electrical, gas, or water corporation and approved by the Public Utilities Commission pursuant to Section 755 of the Public Utilities Code. *(Added by Stats.1985, c. 913, § 1. Amended by Stats.1990, c. 309 (S.B.1763), § 1; Stats.2005, c. 426 (A.B. 746), § 1.)*

Validity

For validity of this section, see Italian Colors Restaurant v. Harris, E.D.Cal.2015, 99 F.Supp.3d 1199, affirmed 878 F.3d 1165.

Cross References

Cardholder defined for purposes of this Title, see Civil Code § 1747.02.
Credit card defined for purposes of this Title, see Civil Code § 1747.02.
Credit charges for towing and storage services, compliance with this section, see Vehicle Code § 22651.07.
Credit or debit card payment options for public utility payments, see Public Utilities Code § 755.
Impoundment of vehicle, driving without a license or while privilege suspended, revoked, or restricted, see Vehicle Code § 14602.6.
Impoundment of vehicle, fleeing or evading a peace officer, reckless driving, see Vehicle Code § 14602.7.
Impoundment of vehicle, repeat offenders, vehicle owner's rights and responsibilities, see Vehicle Code § 14602.8.

§ 1748.1

Impoundment of vehicle illegally operated as taxi, towing and storage charges, release, see Vehicle Code § 21100.4.

Removal of parked and abandoned vehicles, towing and service charges, credit card or cash payment, see Vehicle Code § 22651.1.

Removal of vehicle from private property by property owner, towing companies and charges, see Vehicle Code § 22658.

Retailer defined for purposes of this Title, see Civil Code § 1747.02.

Vehicle used in commission of specified offenses, public nuisance, see Vehicle Code § 22659.5.

§ 1748.5. Finance charges; cardholder information request; frequency; form; application

(a) A cardholder may request, not more frequently than once a year, that the card issuer inform the cardholder of the total amount of finance charges assessed on the account during the preceding calendar year and the card issuer shall provide that information to the cardholder within 30 days of receiving the request, without charge.

If the cardholder's request for the information is made in writing, the card issuer shall provide the information in writing. However, if the card issuer is required to furnish the cardholder with a periodic billing or periodic statement of account or furnishes the billing or statement of account, the requested statement of finance charges may be furnished along with the periodic billing or periodic statement of account.

(b) This section shall not apply to card issuers or cardholders who issue or use credit cards in connection with a retail installment account, as defined by Section 1802.7. *(Added by Stats.1996, c. 180 (S.B.1871), § 2.)*

Cross References

Card issuer defined for purposes of this Title, see Civil Code § 1747.02.

Cardholder defined for purposes of this Title, see Civil Code § 1747.02.

Credit card defined for purposes of this Title, see Civil Code § 1747.02.

§ 1748.7. Credit card transactions through retailer's account with financial institution or credit card issuer without furnishing of goods or services; exemptions; violations; remedies; penalties

(a) No person shall process, deposit, negotiate, or obtain payment of a credit card charge through a retailer's account with a financial institution or through a retailer's agreement with a financial institution, card issuer, or organization of financial institutions or card issuers if that retailer did not furnish or agree to furnish the goods or services which are the subject of the charge.

(b) No retailer shall permit any person to process, deposit, negotiate, or obtain payment of a credit card charge through the retailer's account with a financial institution or the retailer's agreement with a financial institution, card issuer, or organization of financial institutions or card issuers if that retailer did not furnish or agree to furnish the goods or services which are the subject of the charge.

(c) Subdivisions (a) and (b) do not apply to any of the following:

(1) A person who furnishes goods or services on the business premises of a general merchandise retailer and who processes, deposits, negotiates, or obtains payment of a credit card charge through that general merchandise retailer's account or agreement.

(2) A general merchandise retailer who permits a person described in paragraph (1) to process, deposit, negotiate, or obtain payment of a credit card charge through that general merchandise retailer's account or agreement.

(3) A franchisee who furnishes the cardholder with goods or services that are provided in whole or in part by the franchisor and who processes, deposits, negotiates, or obtains payment of a credit card charge through that franchisor's account or agreement.

(4) A franchisor who permits a franchisee described in paragraph (3) to process, deposit, negotiate, or obtain payment of a credit card charge through that franchisor's account or agreement.

(5) The credit card issuer or a financial institution or a parent, subsidiary, or affiliate of the card issuer or a financial institution.

(6) A person who processes, deposits, negotiates, or obtains payment of less than five hundred dollars ($500) of credit card charges in any one year period through a retailer's account or agreement. The person shall have the burden of producing evidence that the person transacted less than five hundred dollars ($500) in credit card charges during any one year period.

(d) Any person injured by a violation of this section may bring an action for the recovery of damages, equitable relief, and reasonable attorney's fees and costs.

(e) Any person who violates this section shall be guilty of a misdemeanor. Each occurrence in which a person processes, deposits, negotiates, or otherwise seeks to obtain payment of a credit card charge in violation of subdivision (a) constitutes a separate offense.

(f) The penalties and remedies provided in this section are in addition to any other remedies or penalties provided by law.

(g) The exemptions from this title specified in Section 1747.03 do not apply to this section.

(h) As used in this section:

(1) "General merchandise retailer" means any person or entity, regardless of the form of organization, that has continuously offered for sale or lease more than 100 different types of goods or services to the public in this state throughout a period which includes the immediately preceding five years.

(2) "Franchisor" has the same meaning as defined in Section 31007 of the Corporations Code.

(3) "Franchisee" has the same meaning as defined in Section 31006 of the Corporations Code. *(Added by Stats. 1989, c. 855, § 1.)*

Cross References

Card issuer defined for purposes of this Title, see Civil Code § 1747.02.

Cardholder defined for purposes of this Title, see Civil Code § 1747.02.

Credit card defined for purposes of this Title, see Civil Code § 1747.02.

Misdemeanors, definition and penalties, see Penal Code §§ 17, 19, 19.2.

Retailer defined for purposes of this Title, see Civil Code § 1747.02.

§ 1748.9. Preprinted checks or drafts; required disclosures

(a)[1] A credit card issuer that extends credit to a cardholder through the use of a preprinted check or draft shall disclose on the front of an attachment that is affixed by perforation or other means to the preprinted check or draft, in clear and conspicuous language, all of the following information:

(1) That "use of the attached check or draft will constitute a charge against your credit account."

(2) The annual percentage rate and the calculation of finance charges, as required by Section 226.16 of Regulation Z of the Code of Federal Regulations, associated with the use of the attached check or draft.

(3) Whether the finance charges are triggered immediately upon the use of the check or draft. *(Added by Stats.1999, c. 171 (S.B.545), § 1, operative July 1, 2000.)*

[1] So in enrolled bill.

Validity

This section was held preempted by the National Bank Act in the decision of Parks v. MBNA America Bank, N.A., (2012) 142 Cal.Rptr.3d 837, 54 Cal.4th 376, 278 P.3d 1193, certiorari denied 133 S.Ct. 653, 568 U.S. 1028, 184 L.Ed.2d 460, on remand 2012 WL 6016741, unpublished.

Cross References

Card issuer defined for purposes of this Title, see Civil Code § 1747.02.

Cardholder defined for purposes of this Title, see Civil Code § 1747.02.

Credit card defined for purposes of this Title, see Civil Code § 1747.02.

§ 1748.95. Identity theft; credit card application filed by unauthorized person; right of victim to receive copies of specified documents from credit card company

(a)(1) Upon the request of a person who has obtained a police report pursuant to Section 530.6 of the Penal Code, a credit card issuer shall provide to the person, or to a law enforcement officer specified by the person, copies of all application forms or application information containing the person's name, address, or other identifying information pertaining to the application filed with the credit card issuer by an unauthorized person in violation of Section 530.5 of the Penal Code.

(2) Before providing copies pursuant to paragraph (1), the credit card issuer shall inform the requesting person of the categories of identifying information that the unauthorized person used to complete the application and shall require the requesting person to provide identifying information in those categories and a copy of the police report.

(3) The credit card issuer shall provide copies of all forms and information required by this section, without charge, within 10 business days of receipt of the person's request and submission of the required copy of the police report and identifying information.

(b)(1) Before a credit card issuer provides copies to a law enforcement officer pursuant to paragraph (1) of subdivision (a), the credit card issuer may require the requesting person to provide them with a signed and dated statement by which the person does all of the following:

(A) Authorizes disclosure for a stated period.

(B) Specifies the name of the agency or department to which the disclosure is authorized.

(C) Identifies the type of records that the person authorizes to be disclosed.

(2) The credit card issuer shall include in the statement to be signed by the requesting person a notice that the person has the right at any time to revoke the authorization.

(c) As used in this section, "law enforcement officer" means a peace officer as defined by Section 830.1 of the Penal Code. *(Added by Stats.2001, c. 493 (S.B.125), § 1.)*

Cross References

Card issuer defined for purposes of this Title, see Civil Code § 1747.02.

Credit card defined for purposes of this Title, see Civil Code § 1747.02.

Governmental access to financial records, exceptions, authorized acts, see Government Code § 7480.

Title 1.3A

CREDIT CARD DISCLOSURE

Section
1748.10. Short title.
1748.11. Disclosures to accompany application form; manner of disclosure; "Regulation Z"; additional terms, etc.; federal disclosure requirement; establishment of equal requirements; open-end credit card account application form; application of title.
1748.12. Marketing information disclosure; notice to cardholder of right to prohibit information release; federal requirements.
1748.13. Statements to be provided by credit card issuer to cardholder in each billing statement; definitions; limitations on application.
1748.14. Public policy; waiver of rights.

§ 1748.10. Short title

This act shall be known and may be cited as the "Areias Credit Card Full Disclosure Act of 1986." *(Added by Stats.1986, c. 1397, § 2. Amended by Stats.2000, c. 375 (A.B.1331), § 2; Stats.2000, c. 977 (A.B.2869), § 1; Stats.2001, c. 159 (S.B.662), § 32.)*

§ 1748.11. Disclosures to accompany application form; manner of disclosure; "Regulation Z"; additional terms, etc.; federal disclosure requirement; establishment of equal requirements; open-end credit card account application form; application of title

(a) Any application form or preapproved written solicitation for an open-end credit card account to be used for personal, family, or household purposes that is mailed on or after October 1, 1987, to a consumer residing in this state by or on behalf of a creditor, whether or not the creditor is located in this state, other than an application form or solicitation included in a magazine, newspaper, or other publication distributed by someone other than the creditor, shall contain or be accompanied by either of the following disclosures:

(1) A disclosure of each of the following, if applicable:

(A) Any periodic rate or rates that may be applied to the account, expressed as an annual percentage rate or rates. If the account is subject to a variable rate, the creditor may instead either disclose the rate as of a specific date and indicate that the rate may vary, or identify the index and any

§ 1748.11

amount or percentage added to, or subtracted from, that index and used to determine the rate. For purposes of this section, that amount or percentage shall be referred to as the "spread."

(B) Any membership or participation fee that may be imposed for availability of a credit card account, expressed as an annualized amount.

(C) Any per transaction fee that may be imposed on purchases, expressed as an amount or as a percentage of the transaction, as applicable.

(D) If the creditor provides a period during which the consumer may repay the full balance reflected on a billing statement that is attributable to purchases of goods or services from the creditor or from merchants participating in the credit card plan, without the imposition of additional finance charges, the creditor shall either disclose the number of days of that period, calculated from the closing date of the prior billing cycle to the date designated in the billing statement sent to the consumer as the date by which that payment must be received to avoid additional finance charges, or describe the manner in which the period is calculated. For purposes of this section, the period shall be referred to as the "free period" or "free-ride period." If the creditor does not provide this period for purchases, the disclosure shall so indicate.

(2) A disclosure that satisfies the initial disclosure statement requirements of Regulation Z.

(b) A creditor need not present the disclosures required by paragraph (1) of subdivision (a) in chart form or use any specific terminology, except as expressly provided in this section. The following chart shall not be construed in any way as a standard by which to determine whether a creditor who elects not to use such a chart has provided the required disclosures in a manner that satisfies paragraph (1) of subdivision (a). However, disclosures shall be conclusively presumed to satisfy the requirements of paragraph (1) of subdivision (a) if a chart with captions substantially as follows is completed with the applicable terms offered by the creditor, or if the creditor presents the applicable terms in tabular, list, or narrative format using terminology substantially similar to the captions included in the following chart:

THE FOLLOWING INFORMATION IS PROVIDED PURSUANT TO THE AREIAS CREDIT CARD FULL DISCLOSURE ACT OF 1986:

INTEREST RATES, FEES, AND FREE-RIDE PERIOD FOR PURCHASES UNDER THIS CREDIT CARD ACCOUNT

ANNUAL PERCENTAGE RATE(1)	VARIABLE RATE INDEX AND SPREAD(2)	ANNUALIZED MEMBERSHIP OR PARTICIPATION FEE	TRANSACTION FEE	FREE-RIDE PERIOD(3)

(1) For fixed interest rates. If variable rate, creditor may elect to disclose a rate as of a specified date and indicate that the rate may vary.

(2) For variable interest rates. If fixed rate, creditor may eliminate the column, leave the column blank, or indicate "No" or "None" or "Does not apply."

(3) For example, "30 days" or "Yes, if full payment is received by next billing date" or "Yes, if full new balance is paid by due date."

(c) For purposes of this section, "Regulation Z" has the meaning attributed to it under Section 1802.18, and all of the terms used in this section have the same meaning as attributed to them in federal Regulation Z (12 C.F.R. 226.1 et seq.). For the purposes of this section, "open-end credit card account" does not include an account accessed by a device described in paragraph (2) of subdivision (a) of Section 1747.02.

(d) Nothing in this section shall be deemed or construed to prohibit a creditor from disclosing additional terms, conditions, or information, whether or not relating to the disclosures required under this section, in conjunction with the disclosures required by this section.

(e) If a creditor is required under federal law to make any disclosure of the terms applicable to a credit card account in connection with application forms or solicitations, the creditor shall be deemed to have complied with the requirements of paragraph (1) of subdivision (a) with respect to those application forms or solicitations if the creditor complies with the federal disclosure requirement. For example, in lieu of complying with the requirements of paragraph (1) of subdivision (a), a creditor has the option of disclosing the specific terms required to be disclosed in an advertisement under Regulation Z, if the application forms or solicitations constitute advertisements in which specific terms must be disclosed under Regulation Z.

(f) If for any reason the requirements of this section do not apply equally to creditors located in this state and creditors not located in this state, then the requirements applicable to creditors located in this state shall automatically be reduced to the extent necessary to establish equal requirements for both categories of creditors, until it is otherwise determined by a court of law in a proceeding to which the creditor located in this state is a party.

(g) All application forms for an open-end credit card account distributed in this state on or after October 1, 1987, other than by mail, shall contain a statement in substantially the following form:

"If you wish to receive disclosure of the terms of this credit card, pursuant to the Areias Credit Card Full Disclosure Act of 1986, check here and return to the address on this application."

A box shall be printed in or next to this statement for placement of such a checkmark.

However, this subdivision does not apply if the application contains the disclosures provided for in this title.

(h) This title does not apply to any application form or written advertisement or an open-end credit card account where the credit to be extended will be secured by a lien on real or personal property or both real and personal property.

(i) This title does not apply to any person who is subject to Article 10.5 (commencing with Section 1810.20) of Chapter 1 of Title 2. *(Added by Stats.1986, c. 1397, § 2. Amended by Stats.2000, c. 375 (A.B.1331), § 3; Stats.2001, c. 159 (S.B. 662), § 33.)*

Cross References

Disclosures, credit card applications, see Civil Code §§ 1748.22, 1810.21.

§ 1748.12. Marketing information disclosure; notice to cardholder of right to prohibit information release; federal requirements

(a) For purposes of this section:

(1) "Cardholder" means any consumer to whom a credit card is issued, provided that, when more than one credit card has been issued for the same account, all persons holding those credit cards may be treated as a single cardholder.

(2) "Credit card" means any card, plate, coupon book, or other single credit device existing for the purpose of being used from time to time upon presentation to obtain money, property, labor, or services on credit. "Credit card" does not mean any of the following:

(A) Any single credit device used to obtain telephone property, labor, or services in any transaction under public utility tariffs.

(B) Any device that may be used to obtain credit pursuant to an electronic fund transfer but only if the credit is obtained under an agreement between a consumer and a financial institution to extend credit when the consumer's asset account is overdrawn or to maintain a specified minimum balance in the consumer's asset account.

(C) Any key or card key used at an automated dispensing outlet to obtain or purchase petroleum products, as defined in subdivision (c) of Section 13401 of the Business and Professions Code, which will be used primarily for business rather than personal or family purposes.

(3) "Marketing information" means the categorization of cardholders compiled by a credit card issuer, based on a cardholder's shopping patterns, spending history, or behavioral characteristics derived from account activity which is provided to a marketer of goods or services or a subsidiary or affiliate organization of the company that collects the information for consideration. "Marketing information" does not include aggregate data that does not identify a cardholder based on the cardholder's shopping patterns, spending history, or behavioral characteristics derived from account activity or any communications to any person in connection with any transfer, processing, billing, collection, chargeback, fraud prevention, credit card recovery, or acquisition of or for credit card accounts.

(b) If the credit card issuer discloses marketing information concerning a cardholder to any person, the credit card issuer shall provide a written notice to the cardholder that clearly and conspicuously describes the cardholder's right to prohibit the disclosure of marketing information concerning the cardholder which discloses the cardholder's identity. The notice shall be in 10–point type and shall advise the cardholder of his or her ability to respond either by completing a preprinted form or a toll-free telephone number that the cardholder may call to exercise this right.

(c) The requirements of subdivision (b) shall be satisfied by furnishing the notice to the cardholder:

(1) At least 60 days prior to the initial disclosure of marketing information concerning the cardholder by the credit card issuer.

(2) For all new credit cards issued on or after April 1, 2002, on the form containing the new credit card when the credit card is delivered to the cardholder.

(3) At least once per calendar year, to every cardholder entitled to receive an annual statement of billings rights pursuant to 12 C.F.R. 226.9 (Regulation Z). The notice required by this paragraph may be included on or with any periodic statement or with the delivery of the renewal card.

(d)(1) The cardholder's election to prohibit disclosure of marketing information shall be effective only with respect to marketing information that is disclosed to any party beginning 30 days after the credit card issuer has received, at the designated address on the form containing the new credit card or on the preprinted form, or by telephone, the cardholder's election to prohibit disclosure. This does not apply to the disclosure of marketing information prior to the cardholder's notification to the credit card issuer of the cardholder's election.

(2) An election to prohibit disclosure of marketing information shall terminate upon receipt by the credit card issuer of notice from the cardholder that the cardholder's election to prohibit disclosure is no longer effective.

(e) The requirements of this section do not apply to any of the following communications of marketing information by a credit card issuer:

(1) Communications to any party to, or merchant specified in, the credit card agreement, or to any person whose name appears on the credit card or on whose behalf the credit card is issued.

(2) Communications to consumer credit reporting agencies, as defined in subdivision (d) of Section 1785.3.

(3) To the extent that the Fair Credit Reporting Act preempts the requirements of this section as to communication by a credit card issuer to a corporate subsidiary or affiliate, the credit card issuer may communicate information about a cardholder to a corporate subsidiary or affiliate to the extent and in the manner permitted under that act.

(4) Communications to a third party when the third party is responsible for conveying information from the card issuer to any of its cardholders.

(f) If the laws of the United States require disclosure to cardholders regarding the use of personal information, compliance with the federal requirements shall be deemed to be compliance with this section.

(g) This section shall become operative on April 1, 2002. *(Added by Stats.2000, c. 977 (A.B.2869), § 3, operative April 1, 2002.)*

§ 1748.13. **Statements to be provided by credit card issuer to cardholder in each billing statement; definitions; limitations on application**

(a) A credit card issuer shall, with each billing statement provided to a cardholder in this state, provide the following on the front of the first page of the billing statement in type no smaller than that required for any other required disclosure, but in no case in less than 8–point capitalized type:

(1) A written statement in the following form: "Minimum Payment Warning: Making only the minimum payment will increase the interest you pay and the time it takes to repay your balance."

(2) Either of the following:

(A) A written statement in the form of and containing the information described in clause (i) or (ii), as applicable, as follows:

(i) A written three-line statement, as follows:

"A one thousand dollar ($1,000) balance will take 17 years and three months to pay off at a total cost of two thousand five hundred ninety dollars and thirty-five cents ($2,590.35).

A two thousand five hundred dollar ($2,500) balance will take 30 years and three months to pay off at a total cost of seven thousand seven hundred thirty-three dollars and forty-nine cents ($7,733.49).

A five thousand dollar ($5,000) balance will take 40 years and two months to pay off at a total cost of sixteen thousand three hundred five dollars and thirty-four cents ($16,305.34).

This information is based on an annual percentage rate of 17 percent and a minimum payment of 2 percent or ten dollars ($10), whichever is greater."

In the alternative, a credit card issuer may provide this information for the three specified amounts at the annual percentage rate and required minimum payment which are applicable to the cardholder's account. The statement provided shall be immediately preceded by the statement required by paragraph (1).

(ii) Instead of the information required by clause (i), retail credit card issuers shall provide a written three-line statement to read, as follows:

"A two hundred fifty dollar ($250) balance will take two years and eight months to pay off a total cost of three hundred twenty-five dollars and twenty-four cents ($325.24).

A five hundred dollar ($500) balance will take four years and five months to pay off at a total cost of seven hundred nine dollars and ninety cents ($709.90).

A seven hundred fifty dollar ($750) balance will take five years and five months to pay off at a total cost of one thousand ninety-four dollars and forty-nine cents ($1,094.49).

This information is based on an annual percentage rate of 21 percent and a minimum payment of 5 percent or ten dollars ($10), whichever is greater."

In the alternative, a retail credit card issuer may provide this information for the three specified amounts at the annual percentage rate and required minimum payment which are applicable to the cardholder's account. The statement provided shall be immediately preceded by the statement required by paragraph (1). A retail credit card issuer is not required to provide this statement if the cardholder has a balance of less than five hundred dollars ($500).

(B) A written statement providing individualized information indicating an estimate of the number of years and months and the approximate total cost to pay off the entire balance due on an open-end credit card account if the cardholder were to pay only the minimum amount due on the open-ended account based upon the terms of the credit agreement. For purposes of this subparagraph only, if the account is subject to a variable rate, the creditor may make disclosures based on the rate for the entire balance as of the date of the disclosure and indicate that the rate may vary. In addition, the cardholder shall be provided with referrals or, in the alternative, with the "800" telephone number of the National Foundation for Credit Counseling through which the cardholder can be referred, to credit counseling services in, or closest to, the cardholder's county of residence. The credit counseling service shall be in good standing with the National Foundation for Credit Counseling or accredited by the Council on Accreditation for Children and Family Services. The creditor is required to provide, or continue to provide, the information required by this paragraph only if the cardholder has not paid more than the minimum payment for six consecutive months, after July 1, 2002.

(3)(A) A written statement in the following form: "For an estimate of the time it would take to repay your balance, making only minimum payments, and the total amount of those payments, call this toll-free telephone number: (Insert toll-free telephone number)." This statement shall be provided immediately following the statement required by subparagraph (A) of paragraph (2). A credit card issuer is not required to provide this statement if the disclosure required by subparagraph (B) of paragraph (2) has been provided.

(B) The toll-free telephone number shall be available between the hours of 8 a.m. and 9 p.m., Pacific standard time, seven days a week, and shall provide consumers with the opportunity to speak with a person, rather than a recording, from whom the information described in subparagraph (A) may be obtained.

(C) The Department of * * * <u>Financial Protection and Innovation</u> shall establish a detailed table illustrating the approximate number of months that it would take and the approximate total cost to repay an outstanding balance if the consumer pays only the required minimum monthly payments and if no other additional charges or fees are incurred on the account, such as additional extension of credit, voluntary credit insurance, late fees, or dishonored check fees by assuming all of the following:

(i) A significant number of different annual percentage rates.

(ii) A significant number of different account balances, with the difference between sequential examples of balances being no greater than one hundred dollars ($100).

(iii) A significant number of different minimum payment amounts.

(iv) That only minimum monthly payments are made and no additional charges or fees are incurred on the account, such as additional extensions of credit, voluntary credit insurance, late fees, or dishonored check fees.

(D) A creditor that receives a request for information described in subparagraph (A) from a cardholder through the toll-free telephone number disclosed under subparagraph (A), or who is required to provide the information required by subparagraph (B) of paragraph (2), may satisfy its obligation to disclose an estimate of the time it would take and the approximate total cost to repay the cardholder's balance by disclosing only the information set forth in the table described in subparagraph (C). Including the full chart along with a billing statement does not satisfy the obligation under this section.

(b) For purposes of this section:

(1) "Credit card" has the same meaning as in paragraph (2) of subdivision (a) of Section 1748.12.

(2) "Open-end credit card account" means an account in which consumer credit is granted by a creditor under a plan in which the creditor reasonably contemplates repeated transactions, the creditor may impose a finance charge from time to time on an unpaid balance, and the amount of credit that may be extended to the consumer during the term of the plan is generally made available to the extent that any outstanding balance is repaid and up to any limit set by the creditor.

(3) "Retail credit card" means a credit card issued by or on behalf of a retailer, or a private label credit card that is limited to customers of a specific retailer.

(c)(1) This section shall not apply in any billing cycle in which the account agreement requires a minimum payment of at least 10 percent of the outstanding balance.

(2) This section shall not apply in any billing cycle in which finance charges are not imposed. *(Added by Stats.2001, c. 711 (A.B.865), § 1. Amended by Stats.2002, c. 664 (A.B. 3034), § 39; Stats.2015, c. 190 (A.B.1517), § 3, eff. Jan. 1, 2016; Stats.2022, c. 452 (S.B.1498), § 19, eff. Jan. 1, 2023.)*

§ 1748.14. Public policy; waiver of rights

Any waiver of the provisions of this title is contrary to public policy, and is void and unenforceable. *(Added by Stats.2002, c. 815 (A.B.2331), § 3.)*

Title 1.3B

CHARGE CARD DISCLOSURES

Section
1748.20. Short title.
1748.21. Definitions.
1748.22. Disclosures in application form; table of interest rate; additional terms; "Regulation Z".
1748.23. Public policy; waiver of rights.

Cross References

Consumers Legal Remedies Act, see Civil Code § 1750 et seq.
Credit card disclosure, see Civil Code § 1748.10 et seq.
Credit cards, see Civil Code § 1747 et seq.

§ 1748.20. Short title

This title may be cited as the "Areias-Robbins Charge Card Full Disclosure Act of 1986." *(Added by Stats.1986, c. 1397, § 3.)*

§ 1748.21. Definitions

For the purposes of this title:

(a) "Charge card" means any card, plate, or other credit device pursuant to which the charge card issuer extends credit to the charge cardholder, primarily for personal, family, or household purposes where (1) the credit extended does not subject the charge cardholder to a finance charge and (2) the charge cardholder cannot automatically access credit that is repayable in installments.

(b) "Charge cardholder" means the person to whom a charge card is issued.

(c) "Charge card issuer" means any person that issues a charge card or that person's agent with respect to the card. *(Added by Stats.1986, c. 1397, § 3.)*

§ 1748.22. Disclosures in application form; table of interest rate; additional terms; "Regulation Z"

(a) On and after October 1, 1987, issuers of charge cards shall clearly and conspicuously disclose in any charge card application form or preapproved written solicitation for a charge card mailed to a consumer who resides in this state to apply for a charge card, whether or not the charge card issuer is located in this state, other than an application form or solicitation included in a magazine, newspaper, or other publication distributed by someone other than the charge card issuer, the following information:

(1) Any fee or charge assessed for or which may be assessed for the issuance or renewal of the charge card, expressed as an annualized amount. The fee or charge required to be disclosed pursuant to this paragraph shall be denominated as an "annual fee."

(2) The charge card does not permit the charge cardholder to defer payment of charges incurred by the use of the charge card upon receipt of a periodic statement of charges from the charge card issuer.

(3) Any fee that may be assessed for an extension of credit to a charge cardholder where the extension of credit is made by the charge card issuer, and is not a credit sale and where the charge cardholder receives the extension of credit in the form of cash or where the charge cardholder obtains the extension of credit through the use of a preprinted check, draft, or similar credit device provided by the charge card issuer to obtain an extension of credit. This fee shall be denominated as a "cash advance fee" in the disclosure required by this paragraph.

(b) A charge card issuer shall be conclusively presumed to have complied with the disclosure requirements of subdivision (a) if the table set out in subdivision (b) of Section 1748.11 is completed with the applicable terms offered by the charge card issuer in a clear and conspicuous manner and the completed table in subdivision (b) of Section 1748.11 is then provided to the person invited to apply for the charge card as a part of or in material which accompanies the charge card application or written advertisement which invites a person to apply for a charge card.

The charge card issuer shall include as part of table set out in subdivision (b) of Section 1748.11 the following sentences in the boxes or in a footnote outside of the boxes that relate to the interest rate disclosure: "This is a charge card which

§ 1748.22

does not permit the charge cardholder to pay for purchases made using this charge card in installments. All charges made by a person to whom the charge card is issued are due and payable upon the receipt of a periodic statement of charges by the charge cardholder."

The inclusion or exclusion of an expiration date with table set out in subdivision (b) of Section 1748.11 or the use of footnotes in the boxes of the table to set out the information required to be disclosed by this section outside of the boxes of the table set out in subdivision (b) of Section 1748.11 shall not affect the conclusive presumption of compliance pursuant to this subdivision. If a charge card issuer does not offer or require one of the selected attributes of credit cards in the table set out in subdivision (b) of Section 1748.11 the charge card issuer shall employ the phrase in the appropriate box or in the appropriate footnote "Not offered" or "Not required" or a substantially similar phrase without losing the conclusive presumption of compliance with the requirements of subdivision (a). If one of the selected attributes of charge cards required to be disclosed pursuant to subdivision (a) is not applicable to the charge card issuer, the charge card issuer may employ in the appropriate box or in the appropriate footnote outside of the box in the table set out in subdivision (b) of Section 1748.11 the phrase "Not applicable" or a substantially similar phrase without losing the conclusive presumption of compliance with the requirements of subdivision (a).

(c) Nothing in this section shall be deemed or construed to prohibit a charge card issuer from disclosing additional terms, conditions, or information, whether or not relating to the disclosures required under this section by subdivision (a) or in connection with the disclosure provided in subdivision (b), in conjunction with the disclosures required by this section.

(d) If the charge card issuer offers to the charge cardholder any program or service under which the charge cardholder may elect to access open-end credit, the charge card issuer shall provide to the charge cardholder, before the charge cardholder has the right to access that credit, the initial disclosure statement required by Regulation Z, as defined in subdivision (c) of Section 1748.10.

(e) All charge card application forms distributed in this state on or after October 1, 1987, other than by mail, shall contain a statement in substantially the following form:

"If you wish to receive disclosure of the terms of this credit card, pursuant to the Areias Charge Card Full Disclosure Act of 1986, check here and return to the address on this application."

A box shall be printed in or next to this statement for placing such a checkmark.

However, this subdivision does not apply if the application contains the disclosures provided for in this title. *(Added by Stats.1986, c. 1397, § 3. Amended by Stats.2000, c. 375 (A.B.1331), § 4.)*

Cross References

Charge card defined for purposes of this Title, see Civil Code § 1748.21.

Charge card issuer defined for purposes of this Title, see Civil Code § 1748.21.

Charge cardholder defined for purposes of this Title, see Civil Code § 1748.21.

Disclosures, credit card applications, see Civil Code §§ 1748.11, 1810.21.

§ 1748.23. Public policy; waiver of rights

Any waiver of the provisions of this title is contrary to public policy, and is void and unenforceable. *(Added by Stats.2002, c. 815 (A.B.2331), § 4.)*

Title 1.3C

DEBIT CARDS

Section
1748.30. Definitions.
1748.31. Liability for unauthorized use.
1748.32. Public policy; waiver of rights.

§ 1748.30. Definitions

For purposes of this title, the following definitions shall apply:

(a) "Accepted debit card" means any debit card which the debit cardholder has requested and received or has signed, or has used, or has authorized another person to use, for the purpose of obtaining money, property, labor, or services. Any debit card issued in renewal of, or in substitution for, an accepted debit card becomes an accepted debit card when received by the debit cardholder, whether the debit card is issued by the same or by a successor card issuer.

(b) "Account" means a demand deposit (checking), savings, or other consumer asset account, other than an occasional or incidental credit balance in a credit plan, established primarily for personal, family, or household purposes.

(c) "Adequate notice" has the same meaning as found in subdivision (k) of Section 1747.02.

(d) "Debit card" means an accepted debit card or other means of access to a debit cardholder's account that may be used to initiate electronic funds transfers and may be used without unique identifying information such as a personal identification number to initiate access to the debit cardholder's account.

(e) "Debit card issuer" means any person who issues a debit card or the agent of that person for that purpose.

(f) "Debit cardholder" means a natural person to whom a debit card is issued.

(g) "Unauthorized use" means the use of a debit card by a person, other than the debit cardholder, to initiate an electronic fund transfer from the debit cardholder's account without actual authority to initiate the transfer and from which the debit cardholder receives no benefit. The term does not include an electronic fund transfer initiated in any of the following manners:

(1) By a person who was furnished the debit card to the debit cardholder's account by the debit cardholder, unless the debit cardholder has notified the debit card issuer that transfers by that person are no longer authorized.

(2) With fraudulent intent by the debit cardholder or any person acting in concert with the debit cardholder.

(3) By the debit card issuer or its employee. *(Added by Stats.1999, c. 244 (S.B.313), § 1.)*

§ 1748.31. Liability for unauthorized use

(a) A debit cardholder shall be liable for an unauthorized use of a debit card only if all of the following conditions are met:

(1) The card is an accepted debit card.

(2) Except as provided in subdivision (b), the liability is not in excess of fifty dollars ($50).

(3) The debit card issuer has given adequate notice to the debit cardholder of the potential liability.

(4) The debit card issuer has provided the debit cardholder with a description of the means by which the debit card issuer may be notified of loss or theft of the card.

(5) The unauthorized use occurs before the debit card issuer has been notified by the debit cardholder that an unauthorized use of the debit card has occurred or may occur as a result of loss, theft, or otherwise.

(6) The debit card issuer has provided a means to identify the debit cardholder to whom the debit card was issued.

(b) Notwithstanding subdivision (a), if the debit cardholder fails to report an unauthorized use that appears on a periodic statement within 60 days of the debit card issuer's transmittal of the statement, and if the issuer establishes that an unauthorized use would not have occurred had the debit cardholder notified the issuer within the 60-day period, the debit cardholder shall be liable for the amount of each unauthorized transfer that occurs after the close of the 60 days and before notice to the issuer. If the debit cardholder's delay in notifying the debit card issuer was due to extenuating circumstances beyond the debit cardholder's reasonable control, the time specified above shall be extended by a reasonable period. For the purposes of this subdivision, examples of extenuating circumstances include, but are not limited to, extended travel, the death or serious illness of the debit cardholder or a member of the debit cardholder's family, hospitalization, permanent mental impairment, or serious physical impairment, unless the circumstance did not reasonably contribute to the cardholder's delay in notifying the debit card issuer within the 60-day period.

(c) A debit cardholder shall have no liability for erroneous or fraudulent transfers initiated by a debit card issuer, its agent, or employee. *(Added by Stats.1999, c. 244 (S.B.313), § 1.)*

Cross References

Adequate notice defined for purposes of this Title, see Civil Code § 1748.30.
Debit card defined for purposes of this Title, see Civil Code § 1748.30.
Debit card issuer defined for purposes of this Title, see Civil Code § 1748.30.
Debit cardholder defined for purposes of this Title, see Civil Code § 1748.30.
Limitations on liability for unauthorized credit card use, see Civil Code § 1747.10.

Unauthorized use defined for purposes of this Title, see Civil Code § 1748.30.

§ 1748.32. Public policy; waiver of rights

Any waiver of the provisions of this title is contrary to public policy, and is void and unenforceable. *(Added by Stats.2002, c. 815 (A.B.2331), § 5.)*

Title 1.3.5

CONSUMER REFUNDS

Section
1748.40. Definitions.
1748.41. Refunds via prepaid debit card; alternate method of receiving refund required.

§ 1748.40. Definitions

For purposes of this title:

(a) "Accepted debit card" means any debit card which the debit cardholder has requested and received or has signed, or has used, or has authorized another person to use, for the purpose of obtaining money, property, labor, or services. Any debit card issued in renewal of, or in substitution for, an accepted debit card becomes an accepted debit card when received by the debit cardholder, whether the debit card is issued by the same or by a successor card issuer.

(b) "Business" means a proprietorship, partnership, corporation, or other form of commercial enterprise. "Business" does not include a restaurant.

(c) "Cardholder" means a natural person to whom a prepaid debit card is issued.

(d) "Debit card" means an accepted debit card or other means of access to a debit cardholder's account that may be used to initiate electronic funds transfers and may be used without unique identifying information such as a personal identification number to initiate access to the debit cardholder's account.

(e) "Prepaid debit card" means a debit card that meets either of the following:

(1) A card, code, or other means of access to funds of a recipient that is usable at multiple, unaffiliated merchants for goods or services, or usable at automated teller machines.

(2) The same as those terms or related terms are defined in the regulations adopted under the Electronic Fund Transfer Act regarding general use reloadable cards.

(f) "Refund" means a return of a sum of money to a customer who has overpaid for services or property or is otherwise owed money by the business. *(Added by Stats. 2019, c. 130 (A.B.1428), § 1, eff. Jan. 1, 2020.)*

§ 1748.41. Refunds via prepaid debit card; alternate method of receiving refund required

If a business offers a refund to a customer via a prepaid debit card for a purchase initiated by the customer in California, the business shall provide the customer with at least one other method of receiving the refund other than a prepaid debit card. *(Added by Stats.2019, c. 130 (A.B.1428), § 1, eff. Jan. 1, 2020.)*

OBLIGATIONS

Title 1.4

LAYAWAY PRACTICES

Section
1749. Written statement of terms and conditions of agreement; furnishing by retail seller; contents.
1749.1. Definitions.
1749.2. Waiver of provisions of title; unenforceability.
1749.3. Cumulative remedies.
1749.4. Nonapplicability to credit sales or other legal obligations.

§ 1749. Written statement of terms and conditions of agreement; furnishing by retail seller; contents

Any retail seller which permits consumers to lay away consumer goods shall provide to any consumer entering into a layaway agreement with the seller a written statement of the terms and conditions of the agreement, including the following information:

(1) The amount of the deposit received.

(2) The length of time the goods will be held on layaway which may be expressed as a period of time or as a date when final payment for the goods is due.

(3) A specific description of the goods.

(4) The total purchase price of the goods including a separate listing of any handling or processing charges.

(5) Any other terms and conditions of the layaway agreement.

(6) That the seller will refund any layaway deposit and subsequent payments, if any, when, before the end of the stated layaway period, the goods have for any reason become no longer available in the same condition as at the time of the sale to the consumer. *(Added by Stats.1975, c. 825, p. 1879, § 1.)*

Cross References

Consumer good defined for purposes of this Title, see Civil Code § 1749.1.
Layaway defined for purposes of this Title, see Civil Code § 1749.1.
Retail seller defined for purposes of this Title, see Civil Code § 1749.1.

§ 1749.1. Definitions

For purposes of this title, the following terms have the following meanings:

(a) "Consumer good" means any article which is used or bought for use primarily for personal, family, or household purposes.

(b) "Retail seller" means an individual, firm, partnership, corporation, joint stock company, association, organization, or other legal entity which engages in the business of selling consumer goods to retail buyers.

(c) "Layaway" means an agreement by a retail seller with a consumer to retain specified consumer goods for sale to the consumer at a specified price, in earnest of which sale the consumer has deposited with the retail seller an agreed upon sum of money, and any other terms and conditions not contrary to law which are mutually agreed upon. *(Added by Stats.1975, c. 825, p. 1879, § 1.)*

§ 1749.2. Waiver of provisions of title; unenforceability

Any waiver by the buyer of consumer goods of the provisions of this title, except as expressly provided in this title, shall be deemed contrary to public policy and shall be unenforceable and void. *(Added by Stats.1975, c. 825, p. 1879, § 1.)*

Cross References

Consumer good defined for purposes of this Title, see Civil Code § 1749.1.

§ 1749.3. Cumulative remedies

The remedies provided by this title are cumulative and shall not be construed as restricting any remedy that is otherwise available. *(Added by Stats.1975, c. 825, p. 1880, § 1.)*

§ 1749.4. Nonapplicability to credit sales or other legal obligations

Nothing in this title shall be construed to limit or reduce any legal obligations imposed under Title 2 (commencing with Section 1801) of Part 4 of Division 3 or under any other applicable law. *(Added by Stats.1975, c. 825, p. 1880, § 1.)*

Title 1.4A

GIFT CERTIFICATES

Section
1749.45. Definitions; exemption for prepaid calling cards.
1749.5. Prohibited transactions; redemption or replacement; expiration dates; application of section; full refund.
1749.51. Public policy; waiver of rights.
1749.6. Gift certificates; value held in trust; bankruptcy of issuer; limitations of section.

Cross References

Application of Code of Civil Procedure § 1520 to gift certificates subject to this title, see Code of Civil Procedure § 1520.5.

§ 1749.45. Definitions; exemption for prepaid calling cards

(a) As used in this title, "gift certificate" includes gift cards, but does not include any gift card usable with multiple sellers of goods or services, provided the expiration date, if any, is printed on the card. This exemption does not apply to a gift card usable only with affiliated sellers of goods or services.

(b) Nothing in this title prohibits those fees or practices expressly permitted by Section 17538.9 of the Business and Professions Code with respect to a prepaid calling card, as defined in that section, that is issued solely to provide an access number and authorization code for prepaid calling services. *(Added by Stats.2003, c. 116 (A.B.1092), § 1.)*

§ 1749.5. Prohibited transactions; redemption or replacement; expiration dates; application of section; full refund

(a) It is unlawful for any person or entity to sell a gift certificate to a purchaser that contains any of the following:

(1) An expiration date.

(2) A service fee, including, but not limited to, a service fee for dormancy, except as provided in subdivision (e).

(b)(1) Any gift certificate sold after January 1, 1997, is redeemable in cash for its cash value, or subject to replacement with a new gift certificate at no cost to the purchaser or holder.

(2) Notwithstanding paragraph (1), any gift certificate with a cash value of less than ten dollars ($10) is redeemable in cash for its cash value.

(c) A gift certificate sold without an expiration date is valid until redeemed or replaced.

(d) This section does not apply to any of the following gift certificates issued on or after January 1, 1998, provided the expiration date appears in capital letters in at least 10–point font on the front of the gift certificate:

(1) Gift certificates that are distributed by the issuer to a consumer pursuant to an awards, loyalty, or promotional program without any money or other thing of value being given in exchange for the gift certificate by the consumer.

(2) Gift certificates that are donated or sold below face value at a volume discount to employers or to nonprofit and charitable organizations for fundraising purposes if the expiration date on those gift certificates is not more than 30 days after the date of sale.

(3) Gift certificates that are issued for perishable food products.

(e) Paragraph (2) of subdivision (a) does not apply to a dormancy fee on a gift card that meets all of the following criteria:

(1) The remaining value of the gift card is five dollars ($5) or less each time the fee is assessed.

(2) The fee does not exceed one dollar ($1) per month.

(3) There has been no activity on the gift card for 24 consecutive months, including, but not limited to, purchases, the adding of value, or balance inquiries.

(4) The holder may reload or add value to the gift card.

(5) A statement is printed on the gift card in at least 10–point font stating the amount of the fee, how often the fee will occur, that the fee is triggered by inactivity of the gift card, and at what point the fee will be charged. The statement may appear on the front or back of the gift card, but shall appear in a location where it is visible to any purchaser prior to the purchase thereof.

(f) An issuer of gift certificates may accept funds from one or more contributors toward the purchase of a gift certificate intended to be a gift for a recipient, provided that each contributor is provided with a full refund of the amount that he or she paid toward the purchase of the gift certificate upon the occurrence of all of the following:

(1) The funds are contributed for the purpose of being redeemed by the recipient by purchasing a gift certificate.

(2) The time in which the recipient may redeem the funds by purchasing a gift certificate is clearly disclosed in writing to the contributors and the recipient.

(3) The recipient does not redeem the funds within the time described in paragraph (2).

(g) The changes made to this section by the act adding this subdivision shall apply only to gift certificates issued on or after January 1, 2004.

(h) For purposes of this section, "cash" includes, but is not limited to, currency or check. If accepted by both parties, an electronic funds transfer or an application of the balance to a subscriber's wireless telecommunications account is permissible. *(Added by Stats.1996, c. 933 (A.B.2466), § 1. Amended by Stats.1997, c. 472 (A.B.1054), § 1; Stats.2003, c. 116 (A.B.1092), § 2; Stats.2004, c. 319 (A.B.656), § 1; Stats.2007, c. 640 (S.B.250), § 1.)*

Cross References

Application of unclaimed property law, see Code of Civil Procedure § 1520.5.
Gift certificate defined for purposes of this Title, see Civil Code § 1749.45.

§ 1749.51. Public policy; waiver of rights

Any waiver of the provisions of this title is contrary to public policy, and is void and unenforceable. *(Added by Stats.2002, c. 815 (A.B.2331), § 6.)*

§ 1749.6. Gift certificates; value held in trust; bankruptcy of issuer; limitations of section

(a) A gift certificate constitutes value held in trust by the issuer of the gift certificate on behalf of the beneficiary of the gift certificate. The value represented by the gift certificate belongs to the beneficiary, or to the legal representative of the beneficiary to the extent provided by law, and not to the issuer.

(b) An issuer of a gift certificate who is in bankruptcy shall continue to honor a gift certificate issued prior to the date of the bankruptcy filing on the grounds that the value of the gift certificate constitutes trust property of the beneficiary.

(c)(1) This section does not alter the terms of a gift certificate. The terms of a gift certificate may not make its redemption or other use invalid in the event of a bankruptcy.

(2) This section does not require, unless otherwise required by law, the issuer of a gift certificate to:

(A) Redeem a gift certificate for cash.

(B) Replace a gift certificate that has been lost or stolen.

(C) Maintain a separate account for the funds used to purchase the gift certificate.

(d)(1) This section does not create an interest in favor of the beneficiary of the gift certificate in any specific property of the issuer.

(2) This section does not create a fiduciary or quasi-fiduciary relationship between the beneficiary of the gift certificates and the issuer, unless otherwise provided by law.

(3) The issuer of a gift certificate has no obligation to pay interest on the value of the gift certificate held in trust under this section, unless otherwise provided by law. *(Added by Stats.2002, c. 997 (A.B.2473), § 1.)*

Cross References

Escheat of unclaimed personal property, application to gift certificates, see Civil Code § 1520.5.

§ 1749.6

Gift certificate defined for purposes of this Title, see Civil Code § 1749.45.

Title 1.4B

SUPERMARKET CLUB CARDS

Section
1749.60. Short title.
1749.61. Definitions.
1749.63. Violation of title; unfair competition.
1749.64. Club card issuer; prohibited from requesting driver's license number or social security number.
1749.65. Club card issuer; prohibited from selling or sharing cardholders' personal identification information.
1749.66. Public policy; waiver of rights.

§ 1749.60. Short title

This title shall be known and may be cited as the "Supermarket Club Card Disclosure Act of 1999." *(Added by Stats.1999, c. 586 (S.B.926), § 1, operative July 1, 2000.)*

Cross References

Supermarket club card defined for purposes of this Title, see Civil Code § 1749.61.

Supermarket defined for purposes of this Title, see Civil Code § 1749.61.

§ 1749.61. Definitions

For purposes of this title:

(a) "Cardholder" means any consumer to whom a supermarket club card is issued, provided that in cases where more than one supermarket club card has been issued for the same account, all persons holding those supermarket club cards may be treated as a single cardholder.

(b) "Supermarket" means any retailer that sells food items.

(c) "Supermarket club card" means any card, plate, coupon book, or other single device existing for the purpose of being used from time to time upon presentation for price discounts on retail products offered by the club card issuer. "Supermarket club card" does not include any credit card that is subject to Section 1748.12.

(d) "Club card issuer" means a supermarket that provides supermarket club cards to consumers, and includes a supermarket's contract information services provider.

(e) "Marketing information" means the categorization of cardholders compiled by a club card issuer, based on a cardholder's shopping patterns, spending history, or behavioral characteristics derived from account activity which is provided to any person or entity for consideration. "Marketing information" does not include aggregate data which does not identify a cardholder based on the cardholder's shopping patterns, spending history, or behavioral characteristics derived from account activity. *(Added by Stats.1999, c. 586 (S.B.926), § 1, operative July 1, 2000.)*

§ 1749.63. Violation of title; unfair competition

A violation of this title constitutes "unfair competition" as defined in Section 17200 of the Business and Professions Code and is punishable as prescribed in Chapter 5 (commencing with Section 17200) of Part 2 of Division 7 of the Business and Professions Code. *(Added by Stats.1999, c. 586 (S.B.926), § 1, operative July 1, 2000.)*

§ 1749.64. Club card issuer; prohibited from requesting driver's license number or social security number

Notwithstanding any other provision of law, no club card issuer shall request in a supermarket club card application, or require as a condition of obtaining a supermarket club card, that an applicant provide a driver's license number or a social security account number. This section shall not be construed to prohibit a club card issuer from requesting a driver's license number or a social security account number for a supermarket club card that can also be used as identification for check cashing purposes or to debit the checking or savings account of the cardholder. However, no club card issuer shall, as a condition of obtaining a supermarket club card, require a cardholder to obtain a supermarket club card that can also be used as identification for check cashing purposes or to debit the checking or savings account of the cardholder. *(Added by Stats.1999, c. 586 (S.B.926), § 1, operative July 1, 2000.)*

Cross References

Cardholder defined for purposes of this Title, see Civil Code § 1749.61.

Club card issuer defined for purposes of this Title, see Civil Code § 1749.61.

Supermarket club card defined for purposes of this Title, see Civil Code § 1749.61.

Supermarket defined for purposes of this Title, see Civil Code § 1749.61.

§ 1749.65. Club card issuer; prohibited from selling or sharing cardholders' personal identification information

(a) Notwithstanding any other provision of law, no club card issuer may sell or share a cardholder's name, address, telephone number, or other personal identification information.

(b) Nothing in this section is intended to prevent a club card issuer from providing names and addresses of cardholders to a third party for purposes of mailing supermarket club card information to cardholders on behalf of the club card issuer. However, that third party shall not use the information for any other purpose.

(c) Notwithstanding subdivision (a), this section does not prohibit a club card issuer from sharing marketing information that includes cardholder names and addresses if the club card issuer complies with all of the following:

(1) The club card issuer charges an annual fee for its supermarket club card.

(2) The club card issuer requires cardholders to renew supermarket club cards annually and to pay an annual renewal fee.

(3) The club card issuer allows only cardholders, and not members of the public, to make purchases in the supermarket.

(4) The club card issuer provides a privacy statement to the cardholder in the supermarket club card application and in the club card issuer's annual renewal material notifying cardholders that outside companies will be receiving market-

ing information including names and addresses of cardholders, and the cardholder has agreed to allow the club card issuer to share this information.

(5) Prior to selling or transferring names and addresses of cardholders to an outside company, the club card issuer has obtained a written confidentiality agreement from the outside company that the outside company will not sell or share the information with any other entity. *(Added by Stats.1999, c. 586 (S.B.926), § 1, operative July 1, 2000.)*

Cross References

Age verification when selling products that are illegal to sell to minor, reasonable steps, products requiring age verification, penalties, see Civil Code § 1798.99.1.
Cardholder defined for purposes of this Title, see Civil Code § 1749.61.
Club card issuer defined for purposes of this Title, see Civil Code § 1749.61.
Marketing information defined for purposes of this Title, see Civil Code § 1749.61.
Supermarket club card defined for purposes of this Title, see Civil Code § 1749.61.
Supermarket defined for purposes of this Title, see Civil Code § 1749.61.

§ 1749.66. Public policy; waiver of rights

Any waiver of the provisions of this title is contrary to public policy, and is void and unenforceable. *(Added by Stats.2002, c. 815 (A.B.2331), § 7.)*

Title 1.4C

CLARITY OF MARKETPLACE TERMS AND CONDITIONS AND DISPUTE RESOLUTION MINIMUM FAIRNESS

Section
1749.7. Marketplace commercial relationship terms and conditions; requirements; payments to influence search results; suspension or termination of seller.

§ 1749.7. Marketplace commercial relationship terms and conditions; requirements; payments to influence search results; suspension or termination of seller

(a) Every marketplace shall ensure that their terms and conditions regarding commercial relationships with marketplace sellers meet all of the following requirements:

(1) Are drafted in plain and intelligible language.

(2) Are easily available online for marketplace sellers at all stages of their commercial relationship with the marketplace, including, but not limited to, during the stage prior to the formation of a contract.

(3) Set out the grounds for decisions to retain, or refuse to disburse, funds in its possession belonging to a marketplace seller pending investigation or resolution of a dispute between the marketplace and the marketplace seller and the grounds for suspending or terminating a marketplace seller from participating in the marketplace.

(b) If a marketplace permits a marketplace seller to pay the marketplace to influence search results through ranking or preferential placement within the marketplace of tangible personal property or services sold by marketplace sellers through the marketplace, the marketplace, in its terms and conditions or policies, shall describe those possibilities and the effects of such payment on the ranking or preferential placement, and either (1) the price of that ranking or preferential placement or (2) how a marketplace seller may obtain written price information for such ranking or preferential placement.

(c) If a marketplace decides to suspend or terminate a marketplace seller based upon an alleged violation of law or a term, condition, or policy of the marketplace, the marketplace shall provide the marketplace seller, without undue delay, with a written statement of reasons for that decision. The written statement of reasons shall, at a minimum, do all of the following:

(1) Without disclosing information that would result in the disclosure of any proprietary, confidential, or trade secret information, or disclosing information that would hinder any investigation or prevention of deceptive, fraudulent, or illegal activity, describe the facts and circumstances that led to the decision unless the marketplace reasonably believes that giving a written statement of reasons could negatively impact the safety or property of another user or the marketplace itself.

(2) Identify the term, condition, or policy that serves as the basis for the suspension or termination.

(3) Explain whether or not the decision may be appealed, and, if so, the procedure for such an appeal.

(d) For purposes of this section, the following definitions shall apply:

(1) "Marketplace" means a physical or electronic place, including, but not limited to, a store, booth, internet website, catalog, television or radio broadcast, or a dedicated sales software application, that sells or offers for retail sale services or tangible personal property for delivery in this state and has an agreement with a marketplace seller to make retail sales of services or tangible personal property through that marketplace, regardless of whether the tangible personal property or the marketplace has a physical presence in the state.

(2) "Marketplace seller" means a person residing in the state who has an agreement with a marketplace and makes retail sales of services or tangible personal property through a marketplace owned, operated, or controlled by that marketplace.

(3) "Ranking" means the relative prominence given to the tangible personal property or services offered to consumers through a marketplace, as organized or communicated to those consumers by the marketplace, irrespective of the technological means used for that organization or communication. *(Added by Stats.2019, c. 635 (A.B.1790), § 1, eff. Jan. 1, 2020.)*

Title 1.4D

ONLINE MARKETPLACES

Section
1749.8. Definitions.

OBLIGATIONS

Section
1749.8.1. Online marketplace; high-volume third-party seller; required information; verification; updates.
1749.8.2. Online marketplace; high volume third-party seller; additional information; disclosure to consumers; suspension of future sales activity.
1749.8.3. Online marketplace; information maintenance.
1749.8.4. Violation of title.
1749.8.5. Scope of title.

Operative Effect

For operative effect of this title, see Civil Code § 1749.8.5.

§ 1749.8. Definitions

Section operative July 1, 2023.

For purposes of this chapter:

(a) "Consumer product" means tangible personal property that is distributed in commerce and normally used for personal, family, or household purposes, including property intended to be attached to or installed in real property regardless of whether it is actually attached or installed.

(b)(1) "High-volume third-party seller" means a third-party seller who, in any continuous 12–month period during the previous 24 months, has entered into 200 or more discrete transactions through an online marketplace for the sale of new or unused consumer products to buyers located in California resulting in the accumulation of an aggregate total of five thousand dollars ($5,000) or more in gross revenues.

(2) The number of discrete transactions referenced in paragraph (1) includes only those transactions through the online marketplace for which payment is processed by the online marketplace directly or through its payment processor.

(c) "Online marketplace" means a consumer-directed, electronically accessed platform for which all of the following are true:

(1) The platform includes features that allow for, facilitate, or enable third-party sellers to engage in the sale, purchase, payment, storage, shipping, or delivery of a consumer product in this state.

(2) The features described in paragraph (1) are used by third-party sellers.

(3) The platform has a contractual relationship with consumers governing their use of the platform to purchase consumer products.

(d) "Third-party seller" means a person or entity, independent of an online marketplace, who sells, offers to sell, or contracts with an online marketplace to sell a consumer product in the state by or through an online marketplace.

(e) "Verify" means to confirm that information provided to an online marketplace pursuant to this section is accurate. Methods of confirmation include the use of one or more methods that enable the online marketplace to reliably determine that the information and documents are valid, correspond to the seller or an individual acting on the seller's behalf, are not misappropriated, and are not falsified. *(Added by Stats.2022, c. 857 (S.B.301), § 1, eff. Jan. 1, 2023, operative July 1, 2023.)*

Operative Effect

For operative effect of this title, see Civil Code § 1749.8.5.

§ 1749.8.1. Online marketplace; high-volume third-party seller; required information; verification; updates

Section operative July 1, 2023.

(a) An online marketplace shall require each high-volume third-party seller on the online marketplace to provide, not later than 10 days after qualifying as a high-volume third-party seller, all of the following information to the online marketplace:

(1)(A) A bank account number, or, if the high-volume third-party seller does not have a bank account, the name of the payee for payments issued by the online marketplace to the seller.

(B) The high-volume third-party seller shall provide the information required by this paragraph to one of the following as specified by the online marketplace:

(i) The online marketplace.

(ii) A payment processor or other third party designated by the online marketplace that is required, pursuant to a contract with the online marketplace, to maintain the information in a confidential manner and disclose the information only in response to a court order or to the online marketplace upon its request.

(2) If the high-volume third-party seller is an individual, the individual's name.

(3) If the high-volume third-party seller is not an individual, one of the following:

(A) A copy of a valid government-issued identification for an individual who has the legal authority to act on behalf of the high-volume third-party seller that includes the individual's name.

(B) A copy of a valid government record or tax document dated within the past 24 months that includes the business name and physical address of the high-volume third-party seller.

(4) A business tax identification number, or, if the high-volume third-party seller does not have a business tax identification number, a taxpayer identification number.

(5) A valid email address and telephone number for the high-volume third-party seller.

(b) An online marketplace shall verify the information provided pursuant to subdivision (a) within 10 days and shall verify within 10 days any changes to the information that is provided to the marketplace by a high-volume third-party seller. If a high-volume third-party seller provides a copy of a valid government-issued tax document, information contained within the tax document shall be presumed to be verified as of the date of issuance of the record or document.

(c)(1) The online marketplace shall, on at least an annual basis, notify each high-volume third-party seller operating on the online marketplace of the requirement to inform the online marketplace of any changes to the information provided by the seller pursuant to subdivision (a) within 10 days of receiving the notification and shall instruct each high-volume third-party seller, as part of the notification, to electronically certify that the information is accurate and that either that the seller's information is unchanged or that the seller is providing updated information.

(2) If a high-volume third-party seller does not provide the information or certification required under this section,,[1] the online marketplace shall, after providing the seller with written or electronic notice and opportunity to provide the information or certification not later than 10 days after the issuance of the notice, suspend any future sales activity of the seller until the seller provides the information or certification. *(Added by Stats.2022, c. 857 (S.B.301), § 1, eff. Jan. 1, 2023, operative July 1, 2023.)*

[1] Punctuation so in enrolled bill.

Operative Effect

For operative effect of this title, see Civil Code § 1749.8.5.

§ 1749.8.2. Online marketplace; high volume third-party seller; additional information; disclosure to consumers; suspension of future sales activity

Section operative July 1, 2023.

(a) An online marketplace shall require a high-volume third-party seller with at least twenty thousand dollars ($20,000) of gross annual revenues from transactions with buyers in California through the online marketplace in either of the two prior calendar years to provide, in addition to the information required by 1749.8.1, the following information to the online marketplace and to disclose the information about the high-volume third-party seller to consumers in a clear and conspicuous manner in the order confirmation message, or other communication made to a consumer after a purchase is finalized, and in the consumer's account transaction history:

(1)(A) Except as provided in subparagraph (B), the high-volume third-party seller shall provide all of the following identifying information:

(i) The full name of the high-volume third-party seller, which may include the seller's name or company name, or the name by which the seller or company operates on the online marketplace.

(ii) The high-volume third-party seller's physical address.

(iii) Contact information for the high-volume third-party seller, including a current working telephone number, email address, or any other means of direct electronic messaging, to allow users of the online marketplace to have direct and unhindered communication with the seller.

(B) A high-volume third-party seller may request that the online marketplace accept the following partial disclosures of information in lieu of the disclosures required pursuant to subparagraph (A):

(i) If the high-volume third-party seller certifies to the online marketplace that they do not have a physical address other than a residential physical address, or a combined business and residential physical address, the online marketplace may disclose only the country and state, if applicable, in which the seller resides and inform consumers that inquiries should be submitted to the seller by telephone, email, or electronic means provided by the online marketplace.

(ii) If the high-volume third-party seller certifies to the online marketplace that they do not have a telephone number other than a personal telephone number, the online marketplace shall inform consumers that no telephone number is available for the seller, and inquiries should be submitted to the seller's email address or electronic means provided by the online marketplace.

(2)(A) Whether or not another party is responsible for supplying the product to the consumer upon purchase.

(B) If requested by an authenticated purchaser, the contact information described in paragraph (1) for the party who is responsible for supplying the product to the consumer upon purchase.

(b) An online marketplace shall disclose to consumers, in a clear and conspicuous manner on the product listing of a high-volume third-party seller, a reporting mechanism that allows for electronic and telephonic reporting of suspicious activity by the high-volume third-party seller to the online marketplace.

(c)(1)(A) An online marketplace shall suspend future sales activity of a high-volume third-party seller that meets any of the following criteria:

(i) The high-volume third-party seller is not in compliance with the requirements of this section.

(ii) The high-volume third-party seller made a false representation to the online marketplace about the applicability of subparagraph (B) of paragraph (1) of subdivision (a).

(iii) The high-volume third-party seller made a false representation to consumers.

(B) An online marketplace may suspend future sales activity of a high-volume third-party seller that has not answered consumer inquiries within a reasonable timeframe.

(2)(A) An online marketplace shall provide notice of an impending suspension pursuant to clause (i) of subparagraph (A) of paragraph (1) and shall not suspend the high-volume third-party seller if the seller becomes in compliance with this section within 10 days of the date on which the notice was issued.

(B) If the high-volume third-party seller provides the information required by subdivision (a) more than 10 days after the date of the notice, the online marketplace shall restore the ability of the seller to have transactions facilitated by or through the online marketplace within 10 days of receiving all of the information. *(Added by Stats.2022, c. 857 (S.B.301), § 1, eff. Jan. 1, 2023, operative July 1, 2023.)*

Operative Effect

For operative effect of this title, see Civil Code § 1749.8.5.

§ 1749.8.3. Online marketplace; information maintenance

Section operative July 1, 2023.

(a)(1) An online marketplace shall keep the information provided to comply with the requirements of this title for no less than two years.

(2) Information provided solely to comply with the requirements of this title shall not be used for any other purpose unless required by law.

§ 1749.8.3 OBLIGATIONS

(3) An online marketplace shall implement and maintain reasonable security procedures and practices, including administrative, physical, and technical safeguards, appropriate to the nature of the information and the purposes for which the information will be used, to protect the information provided to comply with the requirements of this title from unauthorized use, disclosure, access, destruction, and modification.

(b) A high-volume third-party seller may redact from a document provided solely to comply with a requirement of this title any information that is not necessary for either of the following:

(1) To comply with a requirement of this title.

(2) To verify the authenticity of the document as a copy of a valid government-issued identification, government record, or tax document, as applicable. *(Added by Stats.2022, c. 857 (S.B.301), § 1, eff. Jan. 1, 2023, operative July 1, 2023.)*

Operative Effect

For operative effect of this title, see Civil Code § 1749.8.5.

§ 1749.8.4. Violation of title

Section operative July 1, 2023.

(a) A person or entity who violates any provision of this title shall be liable for a civil penalty not to exceed ten thousand dollars ($10,000) for each violation, which may be assessed and recovered only in a civil action brought in the name of the people of the State of California by the Attorney General.

(b) In addition to the civil penalty provided by subdivision (a), the Attorney General who prevails in an action to enforce this title shall be entitled to the following relief:

(1) Reasonable attorney's fees and costs, including expert witness fees and other litigation expenses.

(2) Preventive relief, including a permanent or temporary injunction, restraining order, or other order against any person responsible for the conduct. *(Added by Stats.2022, c. 857 (S.B.301), § 1, eff. Jan. 1, 2023, operative July 1, 2023.)*

Operative Effect

For operative effect of this title, see Civil Code § 1749.8.5.

§ 1749.8.5. Scope of title

Section operative July 1, 2023.

(a) This title does not apply to or affect the liability of an entity, including an entity that meets the definition of a high-volume third-party seller under this title, for damages caused by a consumer product that is sold online.

(b) This title shall become operative July 1, 2023. *(Added by Stats.2022, c. 857 (S.B.301), § 1, eff. Jan. 1, 2023, operative July 1, 2023.)*

Title 1.5

CONSUMERS LEGAL REMEDIES ACT

Chapter	Section
1. General Provisions	1750
2. Construction and Definitions	1760
3. Deceptive Practices	1770
4. Remedies and Procedures	1780

Cross References

Advertisement of used vehicle as certified, see Vehicle Code § 11713.18.

Made in California Program, enforcement, see Government Code § 12098.11.

CHAPTER 1. GENERAL PROVISIONS

Section
1750. Citation.
1751. Waiver; public policy.
1752. Cumulative remedies; class actions.
1753. Partial invalidity.
1754. Exemptions; structures.
1755. Exemptions; advertising media.
1756. Time of application of title.
1757. Renumbered.
1758, 1759. Repealed.

§ 1750. Citation

This title may be cited as the Consumers Legal Remedies Act. *(Added by Stats.1970, c. 1550, p. 3157, § 1.)*

Validity

This section was held preempted by the federal Food, Drug, and Cosmetic Act in the decision of Perez v. Nidek Co. Ltd., S.D.Cal.2009, 657 F.Supp.2d 1156, affirmed 711 F.3d 1109.

This section was held preempted by the Federal Communications Act of 1934 with respect to rates and market entry of commercial mobile service providers in the decision of In re Apple iPhone 3G Products Liability Litigation, N.D.Cal.2010, 728 F.Supp.2d 1065, leave to file for reconsideration denied 2010 WL 3119789.

Cross References

Consumer affairs, see Business and Professions Code § 300 et seq.

Consumer defined for purposes of this Title, see Civil Code § 1761.

Display of logo of public agency, contractors of public agency's, disclosure requirements, remedies, see Civil Code § 3273.

§ 1751. Waiver; public policy

Any waiver by a consumer of the provisions of this title is contrary to public policy and shall be unenforceable and void. *(Added by Stats.1970, c. 1550, p. 3157, § 1.)*

Cross References

Consumer defined for purposes of this Title, see Civil Code § 1761.

§ 1752. Cumulative remedies; class actions

The provisions of this title are not exclusive. The remedies provided herein for violation of any section of this title or for conduct proscribed by any section of this title shall be in addition to any other procedures or remedies for any violation or conduct provided for in any other law.

Nothing in this title shall limit any other statutory or any common law rights of the Attorney General or any other person to bring class actions. Class actions by consumers brought under the specific provisions of Chapter 3 (commencing with Section 1770) of this title shall be governed exclusively by the provisions of Chapter 4 (commencing with Section 1780); however, this shall not be construed so as to deprive a consumer of any statutory or common law right to bring a class action without resort to this title. If any act or practice proscribed under this title also constitutes a cause of action in common law or a violation of another statute, the consumer may assert such common law or statutory cause of action under the procedures and with the remedies provided for in such law. (Added by Stats.1970, c. 1550, p. 3157, § 1. Amended by Stats.1975, c. 615, p. 1344, § 1.)

Cross References

Attorney General, generally, see Government Code § 12500 et seq.
Attorney General, powers and duties, see Government Code § 12510 et seq.
Class action, see Code of Civil Procedure § 382.
Consumer affairs, see Business and Professions Code § 300 et seq.
Consumer defined for purposes of this Title, see Civil Code § 1761.
Person defined for purposes of this Title, see Civil Code § 1761.

§ 1753. Partial invalidity

If any provision of this title or the application thereof to any person or circumstance is held to be unconstitutional, the remainder of the title and the application of such provision to other persons or circumstances shall not be affected thereby. (Added by Stats.1970, c. 1550, p. 3157, § 1.)

Cross References

Person defined for purposes of this Title, see Civil Code § 1761.

§ 1754. Exemptions; structures

The provisions of this title shall not apply to any transaction which provides for the construction, sale, or construction and sale of an entire residence or all or part of a structure designed for commercial or industrial occupancy, with or without a parcel of real property or an interest therein, or for the sale of a lot or parcel of real property, including any site preparation incidental to such sale. (Added by Stats.1970, c. 1550, p. 3157, § 1.)

Cross References

Transaction defined for purposes of this Title, see Civil Code § 1761.

§ 1755. Exemptions; advertising media

Nothing in this title shall apply to the owners or employees of any advertising medium, including, but not limited to, newspapers, magazines, broadcast stations, billboards and transit ads, by whom any advertisement in violation of this title is published or disseminated, unless it is established that such owners or employees had knowledge of the deceptive methods, acts or practices declared to be unlawful by Section 1770. (Added by Stats.1970, c. 1550, p. 3157, § 1.)

Cross References

False advertising, broadcasters and publishers acting in good faith, see Business and Professions Code § 17502.

§ 1756. Time of application of title

The substantive and procedural provisions of this title shall only apply to actions filed on or after January 1, 1971. (Added by Stats.1970, c. 1550, p. 3158, § 1.)

§ 1757. Renumbered § 1785.8 and amended by Stats.1973, c. 167, p. 467, § 9.

§§ 1758, 1759. Repealed by Stats.1963, c. 819, p. 1997, § 2, eff. Jan. 1, 1965

CHAPTER 2. CONSTRUCTION AND DEFINITIONS

Section
1760. Construction and application.
1761. Definitions.
1762 to 1769. Repealed.

§ 1760. Construction and application

This title shall be liberally construed and applied to promote its underlying purposes, which are to protect consumers against unfair and deceptive business practices and to provide efficient and economical procedures to secure such protection. (Added by Stats.1970, c. 1550, p. 3158, § 1.)

Cross References

Consumer affairs, see Business and Professions Code § 300 et seq.
Consumer defined for purposes of this Title, see Civil Code § 1761.

§ 1761. Definitions

As used in this title:

(a) "Goods" means tangible chattels bought or leased for use primarily for personal, family, or household purposes, including certificates or coupons exchangeable for these goods, and including goods that, at the time of the sale or subsequently, are to be so affixed to real property as to become a part of real property, whether or not they are severable from the real property.

(b) "Services" means work, labor, and services for other than a commercial or business use, including services furnished in connection with the sale or repair of goods.

(c) "Person" means an individual, partnership, corporation, limited liability company, association, or other group, however organized.

(d) "Consumer" means an individual who seeks or acquires, by purchase or lease, any goods or services for personal, family, or household purposes.

(e) "Transaction" means an agreement between a consumer and another person, whether or not the agreement is a contract enforceable by action, and includes the making of, and the performance pursuant to, that agreement.

(f) "Senior citizen" means a person who is 65 years of age or older.

(g) "Disabled person" means a person who has a physical or mental impairment that substantially limits one or more major life activities.

(1) As used in this subdivision, "physical or mental impairment" means any of the following:

(A) A physiological disorder or condition, cosmetic disfigurement, or anatomical loss substantially affecting one or more of the following body systems: neurological; musculoskeletal; special sense organs; respiratory, including speech organs; cardiovascular; reproductive; digestive; genitourinary; hemic and lymphatic; skin; or endocrine.

(B) A mental or psychological disorder, including intellectual disability, organic brain syndrome, emotional or mental illness, and specific learning disabilities. "Physical or mental impairment" includes, but is not limited to, diseases and conditions that include orthopedic, visual, speech, and hearing impairment, cerebral palsy, epilepsy, muscular dystrophy, multiple sclerosis, cancer, heart disease, diabetes, intellectual disability, and emotional illness.

(2) "Major life activities" means functions that include caring for one's self, performing manual tasks, walking, seeing, hearing, speaking, breathing, learning, and working.

(h) "Home solicitation" means a transaction made at the consumer's primary residence, except those transactions initiated by the consumer. A consumer response to an advertisement is not a home solicitation. (Added by Stats. 1970, c. 1550, p. 3157, § 1. Amended by Stats.1988, c. 823, § 2; Stats.1994, c. 1010 (S.B.2053), § 34; Stats.1995, c. 255 (S.B.320), § 1; Stats.2006, c. 538 (S.B.1852), § 44; Stats. 2012, c. 448 (A.B.2370), § 4; Stats.2012, c. 457 (S.B.1381), § 4.)

Cross References

Contracts for sale of home improvement goods or services, real property lien to secure small contracts, action for damages, by senior citizen or disabled person, see Business and Professions Code § 7159.2.

§§ 1762 to 1769. Repealed by Stats.1963, c. 819, p. 1997, § 2, eff. Jan. 1, 1965

CHAPTER 3. DECEPTIVE PRACTICES

Section
1770. List of proscribed practices.
1771 to 1779. Repealed.

Cross References

Law governing class actions under this chapter, see Civil Code § 1752.

§ 1770. List of proscribed practices

(a) The unfair methods of competition and unfair or deceptive acts or practices listed in this subdivision undertaken by any person in a transaction intended to result or that results in the sale or lease of goods or services to any consumer are unlawful:

(1) Passing off goods or services as those of another.

(2) Misrepresenting the source, sponsorship, approval, or certification of goods or services.

(3) Misrepresenting the affiliation, connection, or association with, or certification by, another.

(4) Using deceptive representations or designations of geographic origin in connection with goods or services.

(5) Representing that goods or services have sponsorship, approval, characteristics, ingredients, uses, benefits, or quantities that they do not have or that a person has a sponsorship, approval, status, affiliation, or connection that the person does not have.

(6) Representing that goods are original or new if they have deteriorated unreasonably or are altered, reconditioned, reclaimed, used, or secondhand.

(7) Representing that goods or services are of a particular standard, quality, or grade, or that goods are of a particular style or model, if they are of another.

(8) Disparaging the goods, services, or business of another by false or misleading representation of fact.

(9) Advertising goods or services with intent not to sell them as advertised.

(10) Advertising goods or services with intent not to supply reasonably expectable demand, unless the advertisement discloses a limitation of quantity.

(11) Advertising furniture without clearly indicating that it is unassembled if that is the case.

(12) Advertising the price of unassembled furniture without clearly indicating the assembled price of that furniture if the same furniture is available assembled from the seller.

(13) Making false or misleading statements of fact concerning reasons for, existence of, or amounts of, price reductions.

(14) Representing that a transaction confers or involves rights, remedies, or obligations that it does not have or involve, or that are prohibited by law.

(15) Representing that a part, replacement, or repair service is needed when it is not.

(16) Representing that the subject of a transaction has been supplied in accordance with a previous representation when it has not.

(17) Representing that the consumer will receive a rebate, discount, or other economic benefit, if the earning of the benefit is contingent on an event to occur subsequent to the consummation of the transaction.

(18) Misrepresenting the authority of a salesperson, representative, or agent to negotiate the final terms of a transaction with a consumer.

(19) Inserting an unconscionable provision in the contract.

(20) Advertising that a product is being offered at a specific price plus a specific percentage of that price unless (A) the total price is set forth in the advertisement, which may include, but is not limited to, shelf tags, displays, and media advertising, in a size larger than any other price in that advertisement, and (B) the specific price plus a specific percentage of that price represents a markup from the seller's costs or from the wholesale price of the product. This subdivision shall not apply to in-store advertising by businesses that are open only to members or cooperative organizations organized pursuant to Division 3 (commencing with Section 12000) of Title 1 of the Corporations Code if more than 50 percent of purchases are made at the specific price set forth in the advertisement.

(21) Selling or leasing goods in violation of Chapter 4 (commencing with Section 1797.8) of Title 1.7.

(22)(A) Disseminating an unsolicited prerecorded message by telephone without an unrecorded, natural voice first informing the person answering the telephone of the name of the caller or the organization being represented, and either the address or the telephone number of the caller, and without obtaining the consent of that person to listen to the prerecorded message.

(B) This subdivision does not apply to a message disseminated to a business associate, customer, or other person having an established relationship with the person or organization making the call, to a call for the purpose of collecting an existing obligation, or to any call generated at the request of the recipient.

(23)(A) The home solicitation, as defined in subdivision (h) of Section 1761, of a consumer who is a senior citizen where a loan or assessment is made encumbering the primary residence of that consumer for purposes of paying for home improvements and where the transaction is part of a pattern or practice in violation any of the following:

(i) Subsection (h) or (i) of Section 1639 of Title 15 of the United States Code.

(ii) Paragraph (1), (2), or (4) of subdivision (a) of Section 226.34 of Title 12 of the Code of Federal Regulations.

(iii) Section 22684, 22685, 22686, or 22687 of the Financial Code.

(iv) Section 5898.16, 5898.17, 5913, 5922, 5923, 5924, 5925, 5926, or 5940 of the Streets and Highways Code.

(B) A third party shall not be liable under this subdivision unless (i) there was an agency relationship between the party who engaged in home solicitation and the third party, or (ii) the third party had actual knowledge of, or participated in, the unfair or deceptive transaction. A third party who is a holder in due course under a home solicitation transaction shall not be liable under this subdivision.

(24)(A) Charging or receiving an unreasonable fee to prepare, aid, or advise any prospective applicant, applicant, or recipient in the procurement, maintenance, or securing of public social services.

(B) For purposes of this paragraph * * *:

(i) "Public social services" means those activities and functions of state and local government administered or supervised by the State Department of Health Care Services, the State Department of Public Health, or the State Department of Social Services, and involved in providing aid or services, or both, including health care services, and medical assistance, to those persons who, because of their economic circumstances or social condition, are in need of that aid or those services and may benefit from them.

(ii) "Public social services" also includes activities and functions administered or supervised by the United States Department of Veterans Affairs or the California Department of Veterans Affairs involved in providing aid or services, or both, to veterans, including pension benefits.

(iii) "Unreasonable fee" means a fee that is exorbitant and disproportionate to the services performed. Factors to be considered, if appropriate, in determining the reasonableness of a fee, are based on the circumstances existing at the time of the service and shall include, but not be limited to, all of the following:

(I) The time and effort required.

(II) The novelty and difficulty of the services.

(III) The skill required to perform the services.

(IV) The nature and length of the professional relationship.

(V) The experience, reputation, and ability of the person providing the services.

(C) This paragraph shall not apply to attorneys licensed to practice law in California, who are subject to the California Rules of Professional Conduct and to the mandatory fee arbitration provisions of Article 13 (commencing with Section 6200) of Chapter 4 of Division 3 of the Business and Professions Code, when the fees charged or received are for providing representation in administrative agency appeal proceedings or court proceedings for purposes of procuring, maintaining, or securing public social services on behalf of a person or group of persons.

(25)(A) Advertising or promoting any event, presentation, seminar, workshop, or other public gathering regarding veterans' benefits or entitlements that does not include the following statement in the same type size and font as the term "veteran" or any variation of that term:

(i) "I am not authorized to file an initial application for Veterans' Aid and Attendance benefits on your behalf, or to represent you before the Board of Veterans' Appeals within the United States Department of Veterans Affairs in any proceeding on any matter, including an application for those benefits. It would be illegal for me to accept a fee for preparing that application on your behalf." The requirements of this clause do not apply to a person licensed to act as an agent or attorney in proceedings before the Agency of Original Jurisdiction and the Board of Veterans' Appeals within the United States Department of Veterans Affairs when that person is offering those services at the advertised event.

(ii) The statement in clause (i) shall also be disseminated, both orally and in writing, at the beginning of any event, presentation, seminar, workshop, or public gathering regarding veterans' benefits or entitlements.

(B) Advertising or promoting any event, presentation, seminar, workshop, or other public gathering regarding veterans' benefits or entitlements that is not sponsored by, or affiliated with, the United States Department of Veterans Affairs, the California Department of Veterans Affairs, or any other congressionally chartered or recognized organization of honorably discharged members of the Armed Forces of the United States, or any of their auxiliaries that does not include the following statement, in the same type size and font as the term "veteran" or the variation of that term:

"This event is not sponsored by, or affiliated with, the United States Department of Veterans Affairs, the California Department of Veterans Affairs, or any other congressionally chartered or recognized organization of honorably discharged members of the Armed Forces of the United States, or any of their auxiliaries. None of the insurance products promoted at this sales event are endorsed by those organizations, all of which offer free advice to veterans about how to qualify and apply for benefits."

(i) The statement in this subparagraph shall be disseminated, both orally and in writing, at the beginning of any event, presentation, seminar, workshop, or public gathering regarding veterans' benefits or entitlements.

(ii) The requirements of this subparagraph shall not apply in a case where the United States Department of Veterans Affairs, the California Department of Veterans Affairs, or other congressionally chartered or recognized organization of honorably discharged members of the Armed Forces of the United States, or any of their auxiliaries have granted written permission to the advertiser or promoter for the use of its name, symbol, or insignia to advertise or promote the event, presentation, seminar, workshop, or other public gathering.

(26) Advertising, offering for sale, or selling a financial product that is illegal under state or federal law, including any cash payment for the assignment to a third party of the consumer's right to receive future pension or veteran's benefits.

(27) Representing that a product is made in California by using a Made in California label created pursuant to Section 12098.10 of the Government Code, unless the product complies with Section 12098.10 of the Government Code.

(28)(A) Failing to include either of the following in a solicitation by a covered person, or an entity acting on behalf of a covered person, to a consumer for a consumer financial product or service:

(i) The name of the covered person, and, if applicable, the entity acting on behalf of the covered person, and relevant contact information, including a mailing address and telephone number.

(ii) The following disclosure statement in at least 18-point bold type and in the language in which the solicitation is drafted: "THIS IS AN ADVERTISEMENT. YOU ARE NOT REQUIRED TO MAKE ANY PAYMENT OR TAKE ANY OTHER ACTION IN RESPONSE TO THIS OFFER."

(B) For purposes of this paragraph:

(i) "Consumer financial product or service" has the same meaning as defined in Section 90005 of the Financial Code.

(ii)(I) "Covered person" has the same meaning as defined in Section 90005 of the Financial Code.

(II) "Covered person" does not mean an entity exempt from Division 24 (commencing with Section 90000) of the Financial Code pursuant to Section 90002 of the Financial Code.

(iii) "Solicitation" means an advertisement or marketing communication through writing or graphics that is directed to, or likely to give the impression of being directed to, an individually identified person, residence, or business location. "Solicitation" does not include any of the following:

(I) Communication through a mass advertisement, including in a catalog, on a radio or television broadcast, or on a publicly accessible internet website, if that communication is not directed to, or is not likely to give the impression of being directed to, an individually identified person, residence, or business location.

(II) Communication via a telephone, mail, or electronic communication that was initiated by a consumer.

(III) A written credit or insurance solicitation that is subject to the disclosure requirements of subsection (d) of Section 1681m of Title 15 of the United States Code.

(b)(1) It is an unfair or deceptive act or practice for a mortgage broker or lender, directly or indirectly, to use a home improvement contractor to negotiate the terms of any loan that is secured, whether in whole or in part, by the residence of the borrower and that is used to finance a home improvement contract or any portion of a home improvement contract. For purposes of this subdivision, "mortgage broker or lender" includes a finance lender licensed pursuant to the California Financing Law (Division 9 (commencing with Section 22000) of the Financial Code), a residential mortgage lender licensed pursuant to the California Residential Mortgage Lending Act (Division 20 (commencing with Section 50000) of the Financial Code), or a real estate broker licensed under the Real Estate Law (Division 4 (commencing with Section 10000) of the Business and Professions Code).

(2) This section shall not be construed to either authorize or prohibit a home improvement contractor from referring a consumer to a mortgage broker or lender by this subdivision. However, a home improvement contractor may refer a consumer to a mortgage lender or broker if that referral does not violate Section 7157 of the Business and Professions Code or any other law. A mortgage lender or broker may purchase an executed home improvement contract if that purchase does not violate Section 7157 of the Business and Professions Code or any other law. Nothing in this paragraph shall have any effect on the application of Chapter 1 (commencing with Section 1801) of Title 2 to a home improvement transaction or the financing of a home improvement transaction. (Added by Stats.1970, c. 1550, p. 3157, § 1. Amended by Stats.1975, c. 379, p. 853, § 1; Stats.1979, c. 819, p. 2827, § 4, eff. Sept. 19, 1979; Stats.1984, c. 1171, § 1; Stats.1986, c. 1497, § 1; Stats.1990, c. 1641 (A.B.4084), § 1; Stats.1995, c. 255 (S.B.320), § 2; Stats.1996, c. 684 (S.B.2045), § 1; Stats.2008, c. 479 (S.B.1136), § 1; Stats.2009, c. 140 (A.B.1164), § 26; Stats.2011, c. 79 (S.B.180), § 1; Stats.2012, c. 653 (S.B.1170), § 1; Stats.2013, c. 541 (S.B.12), § 1; Stats.2015, c. 246 (S.B.386), § 1, eff. Jan. 1, 2016; Stats.2016, c. 86 (S.B.1171), § 19, eff. Jan. 1, 2017; Stats.2019, c. 143 (S.B.251), § 14, eff. Jan. 1, 2020; Stats.2021, c. 589 (A.B.790), § 1, eff. Jan. 1, 2022; Stats.2022, c. 324 (A.B.1904), § 1, eff. Jan. 1, 2023.)

Validity

This section was held preempted by the Federal Communications Act of 1934 with respect to rates and market entry of commercial mobile service providers in the decision of In re Apple iPhone 3G Products Liability Litigation, N.D.Cal.2010, 728 F.Supp.2d 1065, leave to file for reconsideration denied 2010 WL 3119789.

Cross References

Advertisement defined, see Health and Safety Code § 109885.

Advertising secondhand, used, defective, second grade or blemished merchandise, see Business and Professions Code § 17531.

American Indian made articles, see Business and Professions Code § 17569 et seq.

Butter substitutes, passing off as butter, see Food and Agricultural Code §§ 39431, 39432.

Canneries, mislabeling and false advertising, see Health and Safety Code § 112680.
Check sellers, bill payers and proraters, false advertising, see Financial Code § 12311.
Circulation of newspapers or periodicals, misrepresentation, see Business and Professions Code § 17533.
Coal, sale of one kind as another kind, see Business and Professions Code § 17532.
Consumer defined for purposes of this Title, see Civil Code § 1761.
Contracts with rebate contingent upon happening of future event, see Civil Code § 1803.10.
Dance studio lesson contracts, invalidity for fraud, see Civil Code § 1812.60.
Deceit, see Civil Code § 1710.
Defense of good faith, see Civil Code § 1784.
Department of Health Care Services, generally, see Health and Safety Code § 100100 et seq.
Exemption of advertising media without knowledge of practices listed in this section, see Civil Code § 1755.
Explosives, deceptive marking, see Health and Safety Code § 12088.
Fair packaging and labeling, see Business and Professions Code § 12601 et seq.; Health and Safety Code § 110340 et seq.
False advertising,
   Generally, see Business and Professions Code § 17500 et seq.; Health and Safety Code §§ 110290, 110390 et seq.
   Private investigators, see Business and Professions Code § 7561.3.
Firearm industry standard of conduct, compliance, violations, see Civil Code § 3273.51.
Fraud, see Civil Code § 1571 et seq.
Goods defined for purposes of this Title, see Civil Code § 1761.
Health care service plans, deceptive advertising, see Health and Safety Code §§ 1360, 1361.
Health studio service contracts, invalidity for fraud, see Civil Code § 1812.92.
Label requirements, etc., see Health and Safety Code § 110295 et seq.
Liability of agents, see Business and Professions Code § 17095 et seq.
Limitation of actions, see Civil Code § 1783.
Made in U.S.A. label on goods made elsewhere, see Business and Professions Code § 17533.7.
Milk containers, deceptive advertising, see Food and Agricultural Code § 36061.
Misbranded cosmetics, see Health and Safety Code § 111730 et seq.
Misrepresentation of products as made by blind persons, see Business and Professions Code § 17522.
Motel and motor court rate signs, see Business and Professions Code § 17560 et seq.
Outdoor advertising, see Business and Professions Code § 5200 et seq.
Pasteurized, use of word in advertising, see Food and Agricultural Code § 34091.
Penalties for unfair trade practices, see Business and Professions Code § 17100 et seq.
Person defined for purposes of this Title, see Civil Code § 1761.
Preliminary notices and demands, see Civil Code § 1782.
Price of articles purchased at forced closeout or bankrupt sale, etc., advertising, see Business and Professions Code § 17027.
Removal of manufacturer's distinguishing identification mark from mechanical or electrical devices, see Civil Code § 1710.1.
Secret rebates, refunds, etc., see Business and Professions Code § 17045.
Senior citizen defined for purposes of this Title, see Civil Code § 1761.
Senior insurance, advertisements and other lead generating devices, presentations regarding veterans' benefits, compliance with this section, see Insurance Code § 787.
Services defined for purposes of this Title, see Civil Code § 1761.
Television picture tube labeling, see Business and Professions Code § 17531.6 et seq.
Transaction defined for purposes of this Title, see Civil Code § 1761.
Unadvertised restrictions on quantity of articles advertised, see Business and Professions Code § 17500.5.
Unfair trade practices, see Business and Professions Code § 17000 et seq.

§§ 1771 to 1779. Repealed by Stats.1963, c. 819, p. 1997, § 2, eff. Jan. 1, 1965

CHAPTER 4. REMEDIES AND PROCEDURES

Section
1780. Consumer's action; relief; senior citizens or disabled persons; venue; court costs and attorney's fees.
1781. Consumer's class action; conditions; notices; judgment.
1782. Preliminary notices and demands; defenses; injunctive relief; evidence.
1783. Limitation of actions.
1784. Damages, defense.

Cross References
Application of chapter to class actions, see Civil Code § 1752.
Dentists, prohibited charges to open-end credit extended by third parties, damages, see Business and Professions Code § 654.3.

§ 1780. Consumer's action; relief; senior citizens or disabled persons; venue; court costs and attorney's fees

(a) Any consumer who suffers any damage as a result of the use or employment by any person of a method, act, or practice declared to be unlawful by Section 1770 may bring an action against that person to recover or obtain any of the following:

(1) Actual damages, but in no case shall the total award of damages in a class action be less than one thousand dollars ($1,000).

(2) An order enjoining the methods, acts, or practices.

(3) Restitution of property.

(4) Punitive damages.

(5) Any other relief that the court deems proper.

(b)(1) Any consumer who is a senior citizen or a disabled person, as defined in subdivisions (f) and (g) of Section 1761, as part of an action under subdivision (a), may seek and be awarded, in addition to the remedies specified therein, up to five thousand dollars ($5,000) where the trier of fact does all of the following:

(A) Finds that the consumer has suffered substantial physical, emotional, or economic damage resulting from the defendant's conduct.

(B) Makes an affirmative finding in regard to one or more of the factors set forth in subdivision (b) of Section 3345.

(C) Finds that an additional award is appropriate.

(2) Judgment in a class action by senior citizens or disabled persons under Section 1781 may award each class member that additional award if the trier of fact has made the foregoing findings.

(c) Whenever it is proven by a preponderance of the evidence that a defendant has engaged in conduct in violation of paragraph (24) of subdivision (a) of Section 1770, in addition to all other remedies otherwise provided in this section, the court shall award treble actual damages to the plaintiff. This subdivision shall not apply to attorneys licensed to practice law in California, who are subject to the California Rules of Professional Conduct and to the mandatory fee arbitration provisions of Article 13 (commencing with Section 6200) of Chapter 4 of Division 3 of the Business and Professions Code, when the fees charged or received are for providing representation in administrative agency appeal proceedings or court proceedings for purposes of procuring, maintaining, or securing public social services on behalf of a person or group of persons.

(d) An action under subdivision (a) or (b) may be commenced in the county in which the person against whom it is brought resides, has his or her principal place of business, or is doing business, or in the county where the transaction or any substantial portion thereof occurred.

In any action subject to this section, concurrently with the filing of the complaint, the plaintiff shall file an affidavit stating facts showing that the action has been commenced in a county described in this section as a proper place for the trial of the action. If a plaintiff fails to file the affidavit required by this section, the court shall, upon its own motion or upon motion of any party, dismiss the action without prejudice.

(e) The court shall award court costs and attorney's fees to a prevailing plaintiff in litigation filed pursuant to this section. Reasonable attorney's fees may be awarded to a prevailing defendant upon a finding by the court that the plaintiff's prosecution of the action was not in good faith. (Added by Stats.1970, c. 1550, p. 3157, § 1. Amended by Stats.1988, c. 823, § 3; Stats.1988, c. 1343, § 2; Stats.1998, c. 931 (S.B. 2139), § 15, eff. Sept. 28, 1998; Stats.2003, c. 449 (A.B.1712), § 3; Stats.2008, c. 479 (S.B.1136), § 2; Stats.2009, c. 140 (A.B.1164), § 27.)

Validity

This section was held preempted by the Federal Communications Act of 1934 with respect to rates and market entry of commercial mobile service providers in the decision of In re Apple iPhone 3G Products Liability Litigation, N.D.Cal.2010, 728 F.Supp.2d 1065, leave to file for reconsideration denied 2010 WL 3119789.

Cross References

Actions subject to title, time, see Civil Code § 1756.
Consumer affairs, see Business and Professions Code § 300 et seq.
Consumer defined for purposes of this Title, see Civil Code § 1761.
Contracts for sale of home improvement goods or services, real property lien to secure small contracts, action for damages, by senior citizen or disabled person, see Business and Professions Code § 7159.2.
Corrective steps as bar to action, see Civil Code § 1782.
Damages for fraudulent deceit, see Civil Code § 1709.
Dance studio lesson contracts, invalidity for fraud, see Civil Code § 1812.60.
Exemplary damages, see Civil Code § 3294.
False corporate financial statements, liability, see Corporations Code § 1507.
Health studio service contracts, invalidity for fraud, see Civil Code § 1812.92.
Injunction, generally, see Civil Code § 3420 et seq.
Injunction against unfair trade practices, see Business and Professions Code §§ 17070, 17078 et seq.
Injunction against violation of television picture tube labeling requirements, see Business and Professions Code § 17531.9.
Liability of agents, see Business and Professions Code § 17095 et seq.
Penal damages, see Civil Code § 3345.
Penalties for unfair trade practices, see Business and Professions Code § 17100 et seq.
Person defined for purposes of this Title, see Civil Code § 1761.
Representation of consumers, see Business and Professions Code §§ 320, 321.
Services defined for purposes of this Title, see Civil Code § 1761.
Transaction defined for purposes of this Title, see Civil Code § 1761.

§ 1781. Consumer's class action; conditions; notices; judgment

(a) Any consumer entitled to bring an action under Section 1780 may, if the unlawful method, act, or practice has caused damage to other consumers similarly situated, bring an action on behalf of himself and such other consumers to recover damages or obtain other relief as provided for in Section 1780.

(b) The court shall permit the suit to be maintained on behalf of all members of the represented class if all of the following conditions exist:

(1) It is impracticable to bring all members of the class before the court.

(2) The questions of law or fact common to the class are substantially similar and predominate over the questions affecting the individual members.

(3) The claims or defenses of the representative plaintiffs are typical of the claims or defenses of the class.

(4) The representative plaintiffs will fairly and adequately protect the interests of the class.

(c) If notice of the time and place of the hearing is served upon the other parties at least 10 days prior thereto, the court shall hold a hearing, upon motion of any party to the action which is supported by affidavit of any person or persons having knowledge of the facts, to determine if any of the following apply to the action:

(1) A class action pursuant to subdivision (b) is proper.

(2) Published notice pursuant to subdivision (d) is necessary to adjudicate the claims of the class.

(3) The action is without merit or there is no defense to the action.

A motion based upon Section 437c of the Code of Civil Procedure shall not be granted in any action commenced as a class action pursuant to subdivision (a).

(d) If the action is permitted as a class action, the court may direct either party to notify each member of the class of the action. The party required to serve notice may, with the consent of the court, if personal notification is unreasonably expensive or it appears that all members of the class cannot be notified personally, give notice as prescribed herein by publication in accordance with Section 6064 of the Government Code in a newspaper of general circulation in the county in which the transaction occurred.

(e) The notice required by subdivision (d) shall include the following:

(1) The court will exclude the member notified from the class if he so requests by a specified date.

(2) The judgment, whether favorable or not, will include all members who do not request exclusion.

(3) Any member who does not request exclusion, may, if he desires, enter an appearance through counsel.

(f) A class action shall not be dismissed, settled, or compromised without the approval of the court, and notice of the proposed dismissal, settlement, or compromise shall be given in such manner as the court directs to each member who was given notice pursuant to subdivision (d) and did not request exclusion.

(g) The judgment in a class action shall describe those to whom the notice was directed and who have not requested exclusion and those the court finds to be members of the class. The best possible notice of the judgment shall be given in such manner as the court directs to each member who was personally served with notice pursuant to subdivision (d) and did not request exclusion. *(Added by Stats.1970, c. 1550, p. 3157, § 1.)*

Validity

This section was held preempted by the Federal Communications Act of 1934 with respect to rates and market entry of commercial mobile service providers in the decision of In re Apple iPhone 3G Products Liability Litigation, N.D.Cal.2010, 728 F.Supp.2d 1065, leave to file for reconsideration denied 2010 WL 3119789.

Cross References

Actions subject to title, time, see Civil Code § 1756.
Arbitration, submission of at-issue civil actions, inapplicability to this section, see Code of Civil Procedure § 1141.11.
Class action, see Code of Civil Procedure § 382.
Consumer complaints, see Business and Professions Code § 325 et seq.
Consumer defined for purposes of this Title, see Civil Code § 1761.
Liability of agents, see Business and Professions Code § 17095 et seq.
Person defined for purposes of this Title, see Civil Code § 1761.
Representation of consumers, see Business and Professions Code § 320.
Solicitation at residence of prospect, statement of purpose, penalties, remedies and defenses for violation, see Business and Professions Code § 17500.3.
Transaction defined for purposes of this Title, see Civil Code § 1761.

§ 1782. Preliminary notices and demands; defenses; injunctive relief; evidence

(a) Thirty days or more prior to the commencement of an action for damages pursuant to this title, the consumer shall do the following:

(1) Notify the person alleged to have employed or committed methods, acts, or practices declared unlawful by Section 1770 of the particular alleged violations of Section 1770.

(2) Demand that the person correct, repair, replace, or otherwise rectify the goods or services alleged to be in violation of Section 1770.

The notice shall be in writing and shall be sent by certified or registered mail, return receipt requested, to the place where the transaction occurred or to the person's principal place of business within California.

(b) Except as provided in subdivision (c), no action for damages may be maintained under Section 1780 if an appropriate correction, repair, replacement, or other remedy is given, or agreed to be given within a reasonable time, to the consumer within 30 days after receipt of the notice.

(c) No action for damages may be maintained under Section 1781 upon a showing by a person alleged to have employed or committed methods, acts, or practices declared unlawful by Section 1770 that all of the following exist:

(1) All consumers similarly situated have been identified, or a reasonable effort to identify such other consumers has been made.

(2) All consumers so identified have been notified that upon their request the person shall make the appropriate correction, repair, replacement, or other remedy of the goods and services.

(3) The correction, repair, replacement, or other remedy requested by the consumers has been, or, in a reasonable time, shall be, given.

(4) The person has ceased from engaging, or if immediate cessation is impossible or unreasonably expensive under the circumstances, the person will, within a reasonable time, cease to engage, in the methods, act, or practices.

(d) An action for injunctive relief brought under the specific provisions of Section 1770 may be commenced without compliance with subdivision (a). Not less than 30 days after the commencement of an action for injunctive relief, and after compliance with subdivision (a), the consumer may amend his or her complaint without leave of court to include a request for damages. The appropriate provisions of subdivision (b) or (c) shall be applicable if the complaint for injunctive relief is amended to request damages.

(e) Attempts to comply with this section by a person receiving a demand shall be construed to be an offer to compromise and shall be inadmissible as evidence pursuant to Section 1152 of the Evidence Code. Furthermore, these attempts to comply with a demand shall not be considered an admission of engaging in an act or practice declared unlawful by Section 1770. Evidence of compliance or attempts to comply with this section may be introduced by a defendant for the purpose of establishing good faith or to show compliance with this section. *(Added by Stats.1970, c. 1550, p. 3157, § 1. Amended by Stats.1999, c. 1000 (S.B.284), § 10.)*

Cross References

Actions subject to title, time, see Civil Code § 1756.
Consumer defined for purposes of this Title, see Civil Code § 1761.
Goods defined for purposes of this Title, see Civil Code § 1761.
Injunction against unfair trade practices, see Business and Professions Code §§ 17070, 17078 et seq.
Injunction against violation of television picture tube labeling requirements, see Business and Professions Code § 17531.9.
Person defined for purposes of this Title, see Civil Code § 1761.
Services defined for purposes of this Title, see Civil Code § 1761.

§ 1782

Transaction defined for purposes of this Title, see Civil Code § 1761.

§ 1783. Limitation of actions

Any action brought under the specific provisions of Section 1770 shall be commenced not more than three years from the date of the commission of such method, act, or practice. *(Added by Stats.1970, c. 1550, p. 3157, § 1.)*

Cross References

Actions subject to title, time, see Civil Code § 1756.
Damages, generally, see Civil Code §§ 3274, 3281 et seq.
Three year statute of limitations, see Code of Civil Procedure § 338.

§ 1784. Damages, defense

No award of damages may be given in any action based on a method, act, or practice declared to be unlawful by Section 1770 if the person alleged to have employed or committed such method, act, or practice (a) proves that such violation was not intentional and resulted from a bona fide error notwithstanding the use of reasonable procedures adopted to avoid any such error and (b) makes an appropriate correction, repair or replacement or other remedy of the goods and services according to the provisions of subdivisions (b) and (c) of Section 1782. *(Added by Stats.1970, c. 1550, p. 3157, § 1.)*

Cross References

Actions subject to title, time, see Civil Code § 1756.
Goods defined for purposes of this Title, see Civil Code § 1761.
Person defined for purposes of this Title, see Civil Code § 1761.
Services defined for purposes of this Title, see Civil Code § 1761.

Title 1.5A

VEHICLE HISTORY REPORTS

Section
1784.1. Definitions; disclosure of contact information of vehicle history report provider; procedures for confirmation and response to inquiries; waiver; construction with Vehicle Code provisions.
1785. Repealed.

§ 1784.1. Definitions; disclosure of contact information of vehicle history report provider; procedures for confirmation and response to inquiries; waiver; construction with Vehicle Code provisions

(a) For purposes of this section, the following definitions apply:

(1) "Affiliate" means any person or persons controlling, controlled by, or under common control with, other persons.

(2) "Dealer" has the same meaning as in Section 285 of the Vehicle Code.

(3) "Vehicle" has the same meaning as in Section 670 of the Vehicle Code.

(4) "Vehicle history database" means a database from which a person may obtain vehicle history information specific to a vehicle identification number (VIN).

(5) "Vehicle history report provider" means an entity that generates vehicle history reports from a vehicle history database that are provided directly to consumers for the purpose of selling or purchasing a vehicle. "Vehicle history report provider" does not include a dealer that obtains a vehicle history report from a third party that is not an affiliate of the dealer and who then communicates the vehicle history report without altering the vehicle history information therein.

(6) "Vehicle history information" includes, but is not limited to, any of the following related to a vehicle:

(A) Accident or damage information.

(B) The number of previous owners.

(C) Information regarding service or maintenance history.

(D) Odometer reading.

(7) "Vehicle history report" means any written or electronic communication of vehicle history information made by a vehicle history report provider that is made available to consumers.

(b)(1) Every vehicle history report shall clearly and conspicuously disclose the vehicle history report provider's contact information by which an owner can submit an inquiry regarding the vehicle history information contained in a vehicle history report, including a request for a vehicle history report provider to research and address any potential discrepancies found within the vehicle history report.

(2) A vehicle history report provider shall confirm receipt of a California resident's inquiry under paragraph (1) promptly, within three days of receipt. The confirmation shall include a means to obtain regular updates until the request is completed.

(3) A vehicle history report provider shall use reasonable efforts to complete the inquiry within 14 days from the date it was received. If there is a delay in completing the inquiry that is beyond the reasonable control of the vehicle history report provider, the 14-day requirement is waived and the vehicle history report provider shall promptly notify the consumer of the delay no later than the 15th day from the date the inquiry was received and shall provide the requester weekly updates thereafter until the inquiry is completed.

(c) Any attempted waiver of the provisions of this section is contrary to public policy, and is void and unenforceable.

(d) This section does not relieve any party of its responsibilities under Section 11713.26 of the Vehicle Code. To the extent that a provision of this section conflicts with Section 11713.26 of the Vehicle Code, Section 11713.26 of the Vehicle Code shall control. *(Added by Stats.2022, c. 863 (A.B.1871), § 1, eff. Jan. 1, 2023.)*

§ 1785. Repealed by Stats.1963, c. 819, p. 1997, § 2, eff. Jan. 1, 1965

Title 1.6

CONSUMER CREDIT REPORTING AGENCIES ACT

Chapter	Section
1. General Provisions	1785.1
2. Obligations of Consumer Credit Reporting Agencies	1785.10

Chapter	Section
3. Requirements on Users of Consumer Credit Reports	1785.20
3.5. Obligations of Furnishers of Credit Information	1785.25
3.6. Escrow Agent Rating Service	1785.28
4. Remedies	1785.30

Cross References

Electrical and gas corporations, which participate in centralize credit check system as subject to this act, see Public Utilities Code § 761.5.

Fair debt collection practices, see Civil Code § 1788 et seq.

Investigative consumer reporting agencies, see Civil Code § 1786 et seq.

CHAPTER 1. GENERAL PROVISIONS

Section
1785.1. Legislative findings and declaration.
1785.2. Short title.
1785.3. Definitions.
1785.4. Inapplicability to repossessors; exception.
1785.5. Assembly, evaluation or dissemination of information on checking account experiences of financial institution customers.
1785.6. Consumer notice or disclosure; California addresses.
1785.7, 1785.8. Repealed.

Cross References

Electrical and gas corporations, participation in centralized credit check system, applicability of Consumer Credit Reporting Agencies Act, see Public Utilities Code § 761.5.

§ 1785.1. Legislative findings and declaration

The Legislature finds and declares as follows:

(a) An elaborate mechanism has been developed for investigating and evaluating the credit worthiness, credit standing, credit capacity, and general reputation of consumers.

(b) Consumer credit reporting agencies have assumed a vital role in assembling and evaluating consumer credit and other information on consumers.

(c) There is a need to insure that consumer credit reporting agencies exercise their grave responsibilities with fairness, impartiality, and a respect for the consumer's right to privacy.

(d) It is the purpose of this title to require that consumer credit reporting agencies adopt reasonable procedures for meeting the needs of commerce for consumer credit, personnel, insurance, hiring of a dwelling unit, and other information in a manner which is fair and equitable to the consumer, with regard to the confidentiality, accuracy, relevancy, and proper utilization of such information in accordance with the requirements of this title.

(e) The Legislature hereby intends to regulate consumer credit reporting agencies pursuant to this title in a manner which will best protect the interests of the people of the State of California.

(f) The extension of credit is a privilege and not a right. Nothing in this title shall preclude a creditor from denying credit to any applicant providing such denial is based on factors not inconsistent with present law.

(g) Any clauses in contracts which prohibit any action required by this title are not in the public interest and shall be considered unenforceable. This shall not invalidate the other terms of such a contract. *(Added by Stats.1975, c. 1271, p. 3369, § 1. Amended by Stats.1976, c. 666, p. 1638, § 1; Stats.1982, c. 1127, p. 4062, § 1.)*

Cross References

Consumer credit reporting agency defined for purposes of this Title, see Civil Code § 1785.3.

Consumer defined for purposes of this Title, see Civil Code § 1785.3.

Electrical and gas corporations, participation in centralized credit check system, applicability of Consumer Credit Reporting Agencies Act, see Public Utilities Code § 761.5.

§ 1785.2. Short title

This act may be referred to as the Consumer Credit Reporting Agencies Act. *(Added by Stats.1975, c. 1271, p. 3369, § 1.)*

Cross References

Consumer credit reporting agency defined for purposes of this Title, see Civil Code § 1785.3.

Consumer defined for purposes of this Title, see Civil Code § 1785.3.

§ 1785.3. Definitions

The following terms as used in this title have the meaning expressed in this section:

(a) "Adverse action" means a denial or revocation of credit, a change in the terms of an existing credit arrangement which is adverse to the interests of the consumer, or a refusal to grant credit in substantially the amount or on substantially the terms requested. "Adverse action" includes all of the following:

(1) Any denial of, increase in any charge for, or reduction in the amount of, insurance for personal, family, or household purposes made in connection with the underwriting of insurance.

(2) Any denial of employment or any other decision made for employment purposes which adversely affects any current or prospective employee.

(3) Any action taken, or determination made, with respect to a consumer (A) for an application for an extension of credit, or an application for the hiring of a dwelling unit, and (B) that is adverse to the interests of the consumer.

"Adverse action" does not include (A) a refusal to extend additional credit to a consumer under an existing credit arrangement if (i) the applicant is delinquent or otherwise in default under that credit arrangement or (ii) the additional credit would exceed a credit limit previously established for the consumer or (B) a refusal or failure to authorize an account transaction at a point of sale.

(b) "Consumer" means a natural individual.

(c) "Consumer credit report" means any written, oral, or other communication of any information by a consumer credit reporting agency bearing on a consumer's credit worthiness, credit standing, or credit capacity, which is used or is expected to be used, or collected in whole or in part, for the purpose of serving as a factor in establishing the consumer's eligibility for: (1) credit to be used primarily for personal, family, or household purposes, or (2) employment

§ 1785.3 OBLIGATIONS

purposes, or (3) hiring of a dwelling unit, as defined in subdivision (c) of Section 1940, or (4) other purposes authorized in Section 1785.11.

The term does not include (1) any report containing information solely as to transactions or experiences between the consumer and the person making the report, (2) any communication of that information or information from a credit application by a consumer that is internal within the organization that is the person making the report or that is made to an entity owned by, or affiliated by corporate control with, that person; provided that the consumer is informed by means of a clear and conspicuous written disclosure that information contained in the credit application may be provided to these persons; however, where a credit application is taken by telephone, disclosure shall initially be given orally at the time the application is taken, and a clear and conspicuous written disclosure shall be made to the consumer in the first written communication to that consumer after the application is taken, (3) any authorization or approval of a specific extension of credit directly or indirectly by the issuer of a credit card or similar device, (4) any report by a person conveying a decision whether to make a specific extension of credit directly or indirectly to a consumer in response to a request by a third party, if the third party advises the consumer of the name and address of the person to whom the request was made and the person makes the disclosures to the consumer required under Section 1785.20, (5) any report containing information solely on a consumer's character, general reputation, personal characteristics, or mode of living which is obtained through personal interviews with neighbors, friends, or associates of the consumer reported on, or others with whom he is acquainted or who may have knowledge concerning those items of information, (6) any communication about a consumer in connection with a credit transaction which is not initiated by the consumer, between persons who are affiliated (as defined in Section 150 of the Corporations Code) by common ownership or common corporate control (as defined by Section 160 of the Corporations Code), if either of those persons has complied with paragraph (2) of subdivision (b) of Section 1785.20.1 with respect to a prequalifying report from which the information communicated is taken and provided the consumer has consented to the provision and use of the prequalifying report in writing, or (7) any consumer credit report furnished for use in connection with a transaction which consists of an extension of credit to be used solely for a commercial purpose.

(d) "Consumer credit reporting agency" means any person who, for monetary fees, dues, or on a cooperative nonprofit basis, regularly engages in whole or in part in the business of assembling or evaluating consumer credit information or other information on consumers for the purpose of furnishing consumer credit reports to third parties, but does not include any governmental agency whose records are maintained primarily for traffic safety, law enforcement, or licensing purposes.

(e) "Credit transaction that is not initiated by the consumer" does not include the use of a consumer credit report by an assignee for collection or by a person with which the consumer has an account for purposes of (1) reviewing the account or (2) collecting the account. For purposes of this subdivision, "reviewing the account" includes activities related to account maintenance and monitoring, credit line increases, and account upgrades and enhancements.

(f) "Employment purposes," when used in connection with a consumer credit report, means a report used for the purpose of evaluating a consumer for employment, promotion, reassignment, or retention as an employee.

(g) "File," when used in connection with information on any consumer, means all of the information on that consumer recorded and retained by a consumer credit reporting agency, regardless of how the information is stored.

(h) "Firm offer of credit" means any offer of credit to a consumer that will be honored if, based on information in a consumer credit report on the consumer and other information bearing on the creditworthiness of the consumer, the consumer is determined to meet the criteria used to select the consumer for the offer and the consumer is able to provide any real property collateral specified in the offer. For purposes of this subdivision, the phrase "other information bearing on the creditworthiness of the consumer" means information that the person making the offer is permitted to consider pursuant to any rule, regulation, or formal written policy statement relating to the federal Fair Credit Reporting Act, as amended (15 U.S.C. Sec. 1681 et seq.), promulgated by the Federal Trade Commission or any federal bank regulatory agency.

(i) "Item of information" means any of one or more informative entries in a credit report which causes a creditor to deny credit to an applicant or increase the cost of credit to an applicant or deny an applicant a checking account with a bank or other financial institution.

(j) "Person" means any individual, partnership, corporation, trust, estate, cooperative, association, government or governmental subdivision or agency, or other entity.

(k) "Prequalifying report" means a report containing the limited information permitted under paragraph (2) of subdivision (b) of Section 1785.11.

(*l*) "State or local child support enforcement agency" means the Department of Child Support Services or local child support agency acting pursuant to Division 17 (commencing with Section 17000) of the Family Code to establish, enforce or modify child support obligations, and any state or local agency or official that succeeds to these responsibilities under a successor statute. (Added by Stats.1975, c. 1271, p. 3369, § 1. Amended by Stats.1976, c. 666, p. 1638, § 2; Stats.1982, c. 1127, p. 4062, § 2; Stats.1990, c. 1144 (S.B. 2751), § 1; Stats.1992, c. 1194 (A.B.1629), § 1, operative July 1, 1993; Stats.1993, c. 285 (A.B.1340), § 1, eff. Aug. 2, 1993; Stats.1994, c. 225 (S.B.1483), § 1; Stats.1994, c. 1010 (S.B. 2053), § 35; Stats.2000, c. 808 (A.B.1358), § 3, eff. Sept. 28, 2000.)

Cross References

Liens, conditional sales contracts, maintenance of documents, see Civil Code § 2984.5.
Notice to vehicle credit applicant of consumer credit score, see Vehicle Code § 11713.20.
Use of change-of-address data from consumer credit reporting agency, disclosure and use, notice, see Elections Code § 2227.
Vital records and health statistics, preservation of certificates, indices, see Health and Safety Code § 102230.

Waiver of advantage, law established for public reason, see Civil Code § 3513.

Waiver of code provisions unless against public policy, see Civil Code § 3268.

§ 1785.4. Inapplicability to repossessors; exception

Nothing in this title shall apply to any person licensed pursuant to the provisions of Chapter 11 (commencing with Section 7500) of Division 3 of the Business and Professions Code, or to any employee of such person, unless such person is employed directly by a consumer credit reporting agency. *(Added by Stats.1975, c. 1271, p. 3370, § 1.)*

Cross References

Consumer credit reporting agency defined for purposes of this Title, see Civil Code § 1785.3.

Consumer defined for purposes of this Title, see Civil Code § 1785.3.

Person defined for purposes of this Title, see Civil Code § 1785.3.

§ 1785.5. Assembly, evaluation or dissemination of information on checking account experiences of financial institution customers

Any person who, for monetary fees, dues, or on a cooperative nonprofit basis, regularly engages in whole or in part in the practice of assembling, evaluating, or disseminating information on the checking account experiences of consumer customers of banks or other financial institutions is, with the exception of compliance with the requirements of Section 1785.10, subdivisions (c), (d), and (e), only with regard to the provision of the address and telephone number, subject to the same laws which govern consumer credit reporting agencies. *(Added by Stats.1990, c. 1144 (S.B.2751), § 2. Amended by Stats.2001, c. 236 (A.B.488), § 1, operative Jan. 1, 2003.)*

Cross References

Consumer credit reporting agency defined for purposes of this Title, see Civil Code § 1785.3.

Consumer defined for purposes of this Title, see Civil Code § 1785.3.

Person defined for purposes of this Title, see Civil Code § 1785.3.

§ 1785.6. Consumer notice or disclosure; California addresses

The notices and disclosures to consumers provided for in this title shall be required to be made only to those consumers who have a mailing address in California. *(Added by Stats.1993, c. 285 (A.B.1340), § 2, eff. Aug. 2, 1993.)*

Cross References

Consumer defined for purposes of this Title, see Civil Code § 1785.3.

§§ 1785.7, 1785.8. Repealed by Stats.1975, c. 1271, p. 3369, § 2

CHAPTER 2. OBLIGATIONS OF CONSUMER CREDIT REPORTING AGENCIES

Section	
1785.10.	Inspection of files by consumer; advice to consumer; coded files; availability of information; disclosure of recipients of credit reports and inquiries; reselling report or information; exemptions.
1785.10.1.	Consumer credit report; adverse action taken by user against consumer; unlawful for agency to prohibit or to dissuade or attempt to dissuade user from furnishing copy of report to consumer; civil penalty.
1785.11.	Furnishing consumer report; circumstances.
1785.11.1.	Security alerts in credit reports.
1785.11.2.	Security freeze on credit report.
1785.11.3.	Official information in consumer credit report requiring written confirmation where there is a security freeze on the report; security alerts and copies.
1785.11.4.	Application of specified provisions to consumer credit reporting agency that acts only as a reseller of credit information; honoring security freezes.
1785.11.6.	Entities not required to place in credit report either a security alert or security freeze.
1785.11.8.	Election by consumer to remove name from list that consumer credit reporting agency furnishes for credit card solicitations.
1785.11.9.	Terms defined for purposes of Sections 1785.11.10 and 1785.11.11.
1785.11.10.	Application of provisions to use of protected consumer's consumer credit report by particular persons and agencies.
1785.11.11.	Security freezes for protected consumers; events requiring security freeze; disclosure and notification; removal of freeze.
1785.12.	Report to governmental agency.
1785.13.	Items of information prohibited; exceptions.
1785.135.	Consumer credit reports; documents acting as lien or encumbrance.
1785.14.	Agency procedures; record of purposes; disclosure to consumer; notice to supplier of information regarding obligations under title.
1785.15.	Supplying files and information; right to information.
1785.15.1.	Credit scores supplied upon request by consumer; key factors.
1785.15.2.	Credit scoring model.
1785.15.3.	Statement of rights; monthly credit reports.
1785.16.	Disputes as to completeness or accuracy of information in file; reinvestigation and recording of current status; notice of results; deletion and reinsertion of information; statement of dispute; agency procedures; block of information appearing as a result of Penal Code § 530.5; unblocking information.
1785.16.1.	Deletion of inquiries for credit reports from consumer credit report with respect to identity theft.
1785.16.2.	Sale of consumer debt to debt collector; identity theft; subsidiaries or affiliates; interstate commerce requirement.
1785.16.3.	Consumer reporting agencies acting as resellers of credit information.
1785.17.	Charges to consumer; exceptions.
1785.18.	Matters of public record; source; reports for employment purposes; prohibited information.
1785.19.	Civil penalties; improperly obtaining or misusing file data; costs; attorney fees.
1785.19.5.	Procedures to prevent report or file data from being provided for marketing purposes or offers of credit.

§ 1785.10. Inspection of files by consumer; advice to consumer; coded files; availability of information; disclosure of recipients of credit reports and inquiries; reselling report or information; exemptions

(a) Every consumer credit reporting agency shall, upon request and proper identification of any consumer, allow the consumer to visually inspect all files maintained regarding that consumer at the time of the request.

(b) Every consumer reporting agency, upon contact by a consumer by telephone, mail, or in person regarding information which may be contained in the agency files regarding that consumer, shall promptly advise the consumer of his or her rights under Sections 1785.11.8, 1785.19, and 1785.19.5, and of the obligation of the agency to provide disclosure of the files in person, by mail, or by telephone pursuant to Section 1785,15, including the obligation of the agency to provide a decoded written version of the file or a written copy of the file with an explanation of any code, including any credit score used, and the key factors, as defined in Section 1785.15.1, if the consumer so requests that copy. The disclosure shall be provided in the manner selected by the consumer, chosen from among any reasonable means available to the consumer credit reporting agency.

The agency shall determine the applicability of subdivision (1) of Section 1785.17 and, where applicable, the agency shall inform the consumer of the rights under that section.

(c) All information on a consumer in the files of a consumer credit reporting agency at the time of a request for inspection under subdivision (a), shall be available for inspection, including the names, addresses and, if provided by the sources of information, the telephone numbers identified for customer service for the sources of information.

(d)(1) The consumer credit reporting agency shall also disclose the recipients of any consumer credit report on the consumer which the consumer credit reporting agency has furnished:

(A) For employment purposes within the two-year period preceding the request.

(B) For any other purpose within the 12–month period preceding the request.

(2) Disclosure of recipients of consumer credit reports for purposes of this subdivision shall include the name of the recipient or, if applicable, the fictitious business name under which the recipient does business disclosed in full. The identification shall also include the address and, if provided by the recipient, the telephone number identified for customer service for the recipient.

(e) The consumer credit reporting agency shall also disclose a record of all inquiries received by the agency in the 12–month period preceding the request that identified the consumer in connection with a credit transaction which is not initiated by the consumer. This record of inquiries shall include the name, address and, if provided by the recipient, the telephone number identified for customer service for each recipient making an inquiry.

(f) Any consumer credit reporting agency when it is subject to the provisions of Section 1785.22 is exempted from the requirements of subdivisions (c), (d), and (e), only with regard to the provision of the address and telephone number.

(g) Any consumer credit reporting agency, that provides a consumer credit report to another consumer credit reporting agency that procures the consumer credit report for the purpose of resale and is subject to Section 1785.22, is exempted from the requirements of subdivisions (d) and (e), only with regard to the provision of the address and telephone number regarding each prospective user to which the consumer credit report was sold.

(h) This section shall become operative on January 1, 2003. *(Added by Stats.2002, c. 9 (A.B.1531), § 2, eff. Feb. 19, 2002, operative Jan. 1, 2003.)*

Cross References

California Consumer Financial Protection Law, provision of information to consumers, see Financial Code § 90008.
Consumer credit report defined for purposes of this Title, see Civil Code § 1785.3.
Consumer credit reporting agency defined for purposes of this Title, see Civil Code § 1785.3.
Consumer defined for purposes of this Title, see Civil Code § 1785.3.
Credit transaction that is not initiated by the consumer defined for purposes of this Title, see Civil Code § 1785.3.
Employment purposes defined for purposes of this Title, see Civil Code § 1785.3.
Escrow agent rating service, compliance with provisions of this section, see Civil Code § 1785.28.
File defined for purposes of this Title, see Civil Code § 1785.3.
Identity theft civil actions, see Civil Code § 1798.92 et seq.
Person defined for purposes of this Title, see Civil Code § 1785.3.
Similar provisions, see Civil Code § 1786.10.

§ 1785.10.1. Consumer credit report; adverse action taken by user against consumer; unlawful for agency to prohibit or to dissuade or attempt to dissuade user from furnishing copy of report to consumer; civil penalty

(a) It is unlawful for a consumer credit reporting agency to prohibit in any manner, including, but not limited to, in the terms of a contract enforceable in the state, or to dissuade or attempt to dissuade, a user of a consumer credit report furnished by the credit reporting agency from providing a copy of the consumer's credit report to the consumer, upon the consumer's request, if the user has taken adverse action against the consumer based in whole or in part upon information in the report.

(b) The Attorney General, any district attorney or city attorney, or a city prosecutor in any city or city and county having a full-time city prosecutor, may bring a civil action in any court of competent jurisdiction against any credit reporting agency violating this section for a civil penalty not to exceed five thousand dollars ($5,000) which may be assessed and recovered in a civil action brought in the name of the people of the State of California. *(Added by Stats.2013, c. 433 (A.B.1220), § 1.)*

§ 1785.11. Furnishing consumer report; circumstances

(a) A consumer credit reporting agency shall furnish a consumer credit report only under the following circumstances:

(1) In response to the order of a court having jurisdiction to issue an order.

(2) In accordance with the written instructions of the consumer to whom it relates.

(3) To a person whom it has reason to believe:

(A) Intends to use the information in connection with a credit transaction, or entering or enforcing an order of a court of competent jurisdiction for support, involving the consumer as to whom the information is to be furnished and involving the extension of credit to, or review or collection of an account of, the consumer; or

(B) Intends to use the information for employment purposes; or

(C) Intends to use the information in connection with the underwriting of insurance involving the consumer, or for insurance claims settlements; or

(D) Intends to use the information in connection with a determination of the consumer's eligibility for a license or other benefit granted by a governmental instrumentality required by law to consider the applicant's financial responsibility or status; or

(E) Intends to use the information in connection with the hiring of a dwelling unit, as defined in subdivision (c) of Section 1940; or

(F) Otherwise has a legitimate business need for the information in connection with a business transaction involving the consumer.

(b) A consumer credit reporting agency may furnish information for purposes of a credit transaction specified in subparagraph (A) of paragraph (3) of subdivision (a), where it is a credit transaction that is not initiated by the consumer, only under the circumstances specified in paragraph (1) or (2), as follows:

(1) The consumer authorizes the consumer credit reporting agency to furnish the consumer credit report to the person.

(2) The proposed transaction involves a firm offer of credit to the consumer, the consumer credit reporting agency has complied with subdivision (d), and the consumer has not elected pursuant to paragraph (1) of subdivision (d) to have the consumer's name excluded from lists of names provided by the consumer credit reporting agency for purposes of reporting in connection with the potential issuance of firm offers of credit. A consumer credit reporting agency may provide only the following information pursuant to this paragraph:

(A) The name and address of the consumer.

(B) Information pertaining to a consumer that is not identified or identifiable with a particular consumer.

(c) Except as provided in paragraph (3) of subdivision (a) of Section 1785.15, a consumer credit reporting agency shall not furnish to any person a record of inquiries solely resulting from credit transactions that are not initiated by the consumer.

(d)(1) A consumer may elect to have his or her name and address excluded from any list provided by a consumer credit reporting agency pursuant to paragraph (2) of subdivision (b) by notifying the consumer credit reporting agency, by telephone or in writing, through the notification system maintained by the consumer credit reporting agency pursuant to subdivision (e), that the consumer does not consent to any use of consumer credit reports relating to the consumer in connection with any transaction that is not initiated by the consumer.

(2) An election of a consumer under paragraph (1) shall be effective with respect to a consumer credit reporting agency, and any affiliate of the consumer credit reporting agency, on the date on which the consumer notifies the consumer credit reporting agency.

(3) An election of a consumer under paragraph (1) shall terminate and be of no force or effect following notice from the consumer to the consumer credit reporting agency, through the system established pursuant to subdivision (e), that the election is no longer effective.

(e) Each consumer credit reporting agency that furnishes a prequalifying report pursuant to subdivision (b) in connection with a credit transaction not initiated by the consumer shall establish and maintain a notification system, including a toll-free telephone number, that permits any consumer, with appropriate identification and for which the consumer credit reporting agency has a file, to notify the consumer credit reporting agency of the consumer's election to have the consumer's name removed from any list of names and addresses provided by the consumer credit reporting agency, and by any affiliated consumer credit reporting agency, pursuant to paragraph (2) of subdivision (b). Compliance with the requirements of this subdivision by a consumer credit reporting agency shall constitute compliance with those requirements by any affiliate of that consumer credit reporting agency.

(f) Each consumer credit reporting agency that compiles and maintains files on consumers on a nationwide basis shall establish and maintain a notification system under paragraph (1) of subdivision (e) jointly with its affiliated consumer credit reporting agencies. (Added by Stats.1975, c. 1271, p. 3371, § 1. Amended by Stats.1982, c. 1127, p. 4063, § 3; Stats.1992, c. 1194 (A.B.1629), § 3, operative July 1, 1993; Stats.1993, c. 285 (A.B.1340), § 4, eff. Aug. 2, 1993; Stats.1994, c. 146 (A.B.3601), § 11; Stats.2000, c. 1012 (S.B.2166), § 1; Stats. 2002, c. 664 (A.B.3034), § 40.)

Cross References

Consumer credit report defined for purposes of this Title, see Civil Code § 1785.3.

Consumer credit reporting agency defined for purposes of this Title, see Civil Code § 1785.3.

Consumer defined for purposes of this Title, see Civil Code § 1785.3.

Credit transaction that is not initiated by the consumer defined for purposes of this Title, see Civil Code § 1785.3.

Employment purposes defined for purposes of this Title, see Civil Code § 1785.3.

Escrow agent rating service, compliance with provisions of this section, see Civil Code § 1785.28.

File defined for purposes of this Title, see Civil Code § 1785.3.

Firm offer of credit defined for purposes of this Title, see Civil Code § 1785.3.

Immigration or citizenship status, prohibited landlord actions, rebuttable presumptions, see Code of Civil Procedure § 1161.4.

Person defined for purposes of this Title, see Civil Code § 1785.3.

Prequalifying report defined for purposes of this Title, see Civil Code § 1785.3.

§ 1785.11

Similar provisions, see Civil Code § 1786.12.

§ 1785.11.1. Security alerts in credit reports

(a) A consumer may elect to place a security alert in his or her credit report by making a request in writing or by telephone to a consumer credit reporting agency. "Security alert" means a notice placed in a consumer's credit report, at the request of the consumer, that notifies a recipient of the credit report that the consumer's identity may have been used without the consumer's consent to fraudulently obtain goods or services in the consumer's name.

(b) A consumer credit reporting agency shall notify each person requesting consumer credit information with respect to a consumer of the existence of a security alert in the credit report of that consumer, regardless of whether a full credit report, credit score, or summary report is requested.

(c) Each consumer credit reporting agency shall maintain a toll-free telephone number to accept security alert requests from consumers 24 hours a day, seven days a week.

(d) The toll-free telephone number shall be included in any written disclosure by a consumer credit reporting agency to any consumer pursuant to Section 1785.15 and shall be printed in a clear and conspicuous manner.

(e) A consumer credit reporting agency shall place a security alert on a consumer's credit report no later than five business days after receiving a request from the consumer.

(f) The security alert shall remain in place for at least 90 days, and a consumer shall have the right to request a renewal of the security alert.

(g) Any person who uses a consumer credit report in connection with the approval of credit based on an application for an extension of credit, or with the purchase, lease, or rental of goods or non-credit-related services and who receives notification of a security alert pursuant to subdivision (a) may not lend money, extend credit, or complete the purchase, lease, or rental of goods or non-credit-related services without taking reasonable steps to verify the consumer's identity, in order to ensure that the application for an extension of credit or for the purchase, lease, or rental of goods or non-credit-related services is not the result of identity theft. If the consumer has placed a statement with the security alert in his or her file requesting that identity be verified by calling a specified telephone number, any person who receives that statement with the security alert in a consumer's file pursuant to subdivision (a) shall take reasonable steps to verify the identity of the consumer by contacting the consumer using the specified telephone number prior to lending money, extending credit, or completing the purchase, lease, or rental of goods or non-credit-related services. If a person uses a consumer credit report to facilitate the extension of credit or for another permissible purpose on behalf of a subsidiary, affiliate, agent, assignee, or prospective assignee, that person may verify a consumer's identity under this section in lieu of the subsidiary, affiliate, agent, assignee, or prospective assignee.

(h) For purposes of this section, "extension of credit" does not include an increase in the dollar limit of an existing open-end credit plan, as defined in Regulation Z issued by the Board of Governors of the Federal Reserve System (12 C.F.R. 226.2), or any change to, or review of, an existing credit account.

(i) If reasonable steps are taken to verify the identity of the consumer pursuant to subdivision (b) of Section 1785.20.3, those steps constitute compliance with the requirements of this section, except that if a consumer has placed a statement including a telephone number with the security alert in his or her file, his or her identity shall be verified by contacting the consumer using that telephone number as specified pursuant to subdivision (g).

(j) A consumer credit reporting agency shall notify each consumer who has requested that a security alert be placed on his or her consumer credit report of the expiration date of the alert.

(k) Notwithstanding Section 1785.19, any consumer credit reporting agency that recklessly, willfully, or intentionally fails to place a security alert pursuant to this section shall be liable for a penalty in an amount of up to two thousand five hundred dollars ($2,500) and reasonable attorneys' fees. *(Added by Stats.2001, c. 720 (S.B.168), § 1, operative July 1, 2002. Amended by Stats.2003, c. 533 (S.B.602), § 2; Stats. 2003, c. 907 (S.B.25), § 1.5, operative July 1, 2004.)*

Cross References

Consumer credit report defined for purposes of this Title, see Civil Code § 1785.3.
Consumer credit reporting agency defined for purposes of this Title, see Civil Code § 1785.3.
Consumer defined for purposes of this Title, see Civil Code § 1785.3.
File defined for purposes of this Title, see Civil Code § 1785.3.
Person defined for purposes of this Title, see Civil Code § 1785.3.
Telephone corporations, customer right of privacy, restrictions on availability of information, see Public Utilities Code § 2891.

§ 1785.11.2. Security freeze on credit report

(a) A consumer may elect to place a security freeze on his or her credit report by making a request in writing by mail to a consumer credit reporting agency. "Security freeze" means a notice placed in a consumer's credit report, at the request of the consumer, and subject to certain exceptions, that prohibits the consumer credit reporting agency from releasing the consumer's credit report or any information from it without the express authorization of the consumer. If a security freeze is in place, information from a consumer's credit report may not be released to a third party without prior express authorization from the consumer. This subdivision does not prevent a consumer credit reporting agency from advising a third party that a security freeze is in effect with respect to the consumer's credit report.

(b) A consumer credit reporting agency shall place a security freeze on a consumer's credit report no later than three business days after receiving a written request from the consumer.

(c) The consumer credit reporting agency shall send a written confirmation of the security freeze to the consumer within 10 business days and shall provide the consumer with a unique personal identification number or password to be used by the consumer when providing authorization for the release of his or her credit for a specific party or period of time.

(d) If the consumer wishes to allow his or her credit report to be accessed for a specific party or period of time while a freeze is in place, he or she shall contact the consumer credit reporting agency, request that the freeze be temporarily lifted, and provide the following:

(1) Proper identification, as defined in subdivision (c) of Section 1785.15.

(2) The unique personal identification number or password provided by the credit reporting agency pursuant to subdivision (c).

(3) The proper information regarding the third party who is to receive the credit report or the time period for which the report shall be available to users of the credit report.

(e) A consumer credit reporting agency that receives a request from a consumer to temporarily lift a freeze on a credit report pursuant to subdivision (d) shall comply with the request no later than three business days after receiving the request.

(f) A consumer credit reporting agency may develop procedures involving the use of telephone, fax, the Internet, or other electronic media to receive and process a request from a consumer to temporarily lift a freeze on a credit report pursuant to subdivision (d) in an expedited manner.

(g) A consumer credit reporting agency shall remove or temporarily lift a freeze placed on a consumer's credit report only in the following cases:

(1) Upon consumer request, pursuant to subdivision (d) or (j).

(2) If the consumer's credit report was frozen due to a material misrepresentation of fact by the consumer. If a consumer credit reporting agency intends to remove a freeze upon a consumer's credit report pursuant to this paragraph, the consumer credit reporting agency shall notify the consumer in writing prior to removing the freeze on the consumer's credit report.

(h) A third party who requests access to a consumer credit report in connection with an application for credit or any other use may treat the application as incomplete if a security freeze is in effect and the consumer does not allow his or her credit report to be accessed for that specific party or period of time.

(i) If a consumer requests a security freeze, the consumer credit reporting agency shall disclose the process of placing and temporarily lifting a freeze and the process for allowing access to information from the consumer's credit report for a specific party or period of time while the freeze is in place.

(j) A security freeze shall remain in place until the consumer requests that the security freeze be removed. A consumer credit reporting agency shall remove a security freeze within three business days of receiving a request for removal from the consumer if the consumer provides both of the following:

(1) Proper identification, as defined in subdivision (c) of Section 1785.15.

(2) The unique personal identification number or password provided by the credit reporting agency pursuant to subdivision (c).

(k) A consumer credit reporting agency shall require proper identification, as defined in subdivision (c) of Section 1785.15, of the person making a request to place or remove a security freeze.

(*l*) The provisions of this section do not apply to the use of a consumer credit report by any of the following:

(1)(A)(i) A person or entity with which the consumer has or had, prior to any assignment, an account or contract, including a demand deposit account, or to which the consumer issued a negotiable instrument, for the purpose of reviewing the account or collecting the financial obligation owing for the account, contract, or negotiable instrument.

(ii) A subsidiary, affiliate, or agent of a person or entity described in clause (i), an assignee of a financial obligation owing by the consumer to such a person or entity, or a prospective assignee of a financial obligation owing by the consumer to such a person or entity in conjunction with the proposed purchase of the financial obligation, for the purpose of reviewing the account or collecting the financial obligation owing for the account, contract, or negotiable instrument.

(B) For purposes of this paragraph, "reviewing the account" includes activities related to account maintenance, monitoring, credit line increases, and account upgrades and enhancements.

(2) A subsidiary, affiliate, agent, assignee, or prospective assignee of a person to whom access has been granted under subdivision (d) for purposes of facilitating the extension of credit or other permissible use.

(3) Any state or local agency, law enforcement agency, trial court, or private collection agency acting pursuant to a court order, warrant, or subpoena.

(4) A child support agency acting pursuant to Chapter 2 (commencing with Section 17400) of Division 17 of the Family Code or Title IV–D of the Social Security Act (42 U.S.C. et seq.).

(5) The State Department of Health Care Services or its agents or assigns acting to investigate Medi–Cal fraud.

(6) The Franchise Tax Board or its agents or assigns acting to investigate or collect delinquent taxes or unpaid court orders or to fulfill any of its other statutory responsibilities.

(7) The use of credit information for the purposes of prescreening as provided for by the federal Fair Credit Reporting Act.

(8) Any person or entity administering a credit file monitoring subscription service to which the consumer has subscribed.

(9) Any person or entity for the purpose of providing a consumer with a copy of his or her credit report upon the consumer's request.

(m)(1) Except as provided in paragraph (2), this title does not prevent a consumer credit reporting agency from charging a fee of no more than ten dollars ($10) to a consumer for the placement of each freeze, the removal of the freeze, the temporary lift of the freeze for a period of time, or the temporary lift of the freeze for a specific party, regarding access to a consumer credit report, except that a consumer credit reporting agency may not charge a fee to a victim of identity theft who has submitted a valid police report or valid

§ 1785.11.2 OBLIGATIONS

Department of Motor Vehicles investigative report that alleges a violation of Section 530.5 of the Penal Code.

(2) With respect to a consumer who is 65 years of age or older and who has provided identification confirming his or her age, a consumer credit reporting agency shall not charge a fee for the placement of an initial security freeze, but may charge a fee not to exceed five dollars ($5) for the removal of the freeze, the temporary lift of the freeze for a period of time, the temporary lift of the freeze for a specific party, or replacing the freeze.

(n) Regardless of the existence of a security freeze, a consumer reporting agency may disclose public record information lawfully obtained by, or for, the consumer reporting agency from an open public record to the extent otherwise permitted by law. This subdivision does not prohibit a consumer reporting agency from electing to apply a valid security freeze to the entire contents of a credit report. (Added by Stats.2001, c. 720 (S.B.168), § 2, operative Jan. 1, 2003. Amended by Stats.2002, c. 664 (A.B.3034), § 41; Stats.2002, c. 786 (S.B.1730), § 1; Stats.2003, c. 533 (S.B.602), § 3; Stats.2007, c. 699 (A.B.1298), § 2; Stats.2008, c. 151 (A.B.372), § 1; Stats.2012, c. 645 (A.B.2374), § 1.)

Validity

A prior version of this section was held unconstitutional as violating free speech in the decision of U.D. Registry, Inc. v. State (App. 2 Dist. 2006) 50 Cal. Rptr.3d 647, 144 Cal.App.4th 405, modified on denial of rehearing, review denied.

Cross References

Consumer credit report defined for purposes of this Title, see Civil Code § 1785.3.
Consumer credit reporting agency defined for purposes of this Title, see Civil Code § 1785.3.
Consumer defined for purposes of this Title, see Civil Code § 1785.3.
File defined for purposes of this Title, see Civil Code § 1785.3.
Person defined for purposes of this Title, see Civil Code § 1785.3.
Telephone corporations, customer right of privacy, restrictions on availability of information, see Public Utilities Code § 2891.
Unlawful use of personal identifying information by another, issuance of law enforcement investigation, determination of factual innocence of victim, see Penal Code § 530.5.

§ 1785.11.3. Official information in consumer credit report requiring written confirmation where there is a security freeze on the report; security alerts and copies

(a) If a security freeze is in place, a consumer credit reporting agency shall not change any of the following official information in a consumer credit report without sending a written confirmation of the change to the consumer within 30 days of the change being posted to the consumer's file: name, date of birth, social security number, and address. Written confirmation is not required for technical modifications of a consumer's official information, including name and street abbreviations, complete spellings, or transposition of numbers or letters. In the case of an address change, the written confirmation shall be sent to both the new address and to the former address.

(b) If a consumer has placed a security alert, a consumer credit reporting agency shall provide the consumer, upon request, with a free copy of his or her credit report at the time the 90-day security alert period expires. (Added by Stats. 2001, c. 720 (S.B.168), § 3, operative Jan. 1, 2003.)

Cross References

Consumer credit report defined for purposes of this Title, see Civil Code § 1785.3.
Consumer credit reporting agency defined for purposes of this Title, see Civil Code § 1785.3.
Consumer defined for purposes of this Title, see Civil Code § 1785.3.
File defined for purposes of this Title, see Civil Code § 1785.3.

§ 1785.11.4. Application of specified provisions to consumer credit reporting agency that acts only as a reseller of credit information; honoring security freezes

The provisions of Sections 1785.11.1, 1785.11.2, and 1785.11.3 do not apply to a consumer credit reporting agency that acts only as a reseller of credit information pursuant to Section 1785.22 by assembling and merging information contained in the data base of another consumer credit reporting agency or multiple consumer credit reporting agencies, and does not maintain a permanent data base of credit information from which new consumer credit reports are produced. However, a consumer credit reporting agency acting pursuant to Section 1785.22 shall honor any security freeze placed on a consumer credit report by another consumer credit reporting agency. (Added by Stats.2001, c. 720 (S.B.168), § 4.)

Cross References

Consumer credit report defined for purposes of this Title, see Civil Code § 1785.3.
Consumer credit reporting agency defined for purposes of this Title, see Civil Code § 1785.3.
Consumer defined for purposes of this Title, see Civil Code § 1785.3.

§ 1785.11.6. Entities not required to place in credit report either a security alert or security freeze

The following entities are not required to place in a credit report either a security alert, pursuant to Section 1785.11.1, or a security freeze, pursuant to Section 1785.11.2:

(a) A check services or fraud prevention services company, which issues reports on incidents of fraud or authorizations for the purpose of approving or processing negotiable instruments, electronic funds transfers, or similar methods of payments.

(b) A deposit account information service company, which issues reports regarding account closures due to fraud, substantial overdrafts, ATM abuse, or similar negative information regarding a consumer, to inquiring banks or other financial institutions for use only in reviewing a consumer request for a deposit account at the inquiring bank or financial institution. (Added by Stats.2001, c. 720 (S.B.168), § 5. Amended by Stats.2002, c. 786 (S.B.1730), § 2; Stats. 2003, c. 907 (S.B.25), § 2.)

Cross References

Consumer defined for purposes of this Title, see Civil Code § 1785.3.

§ 1785.11.8. Election by consumer to remove name from list that consumer credit reporting agency furnishes for credit card solicitations

A consumer may elect that his or her name shall be removed from any list that a consumer credit reporting agency furnishes for credit card solicitations, by notifying the consumer credit reporting agency, by telephone or in writing, pursuant to the notification system maintained by the consumer credit reporting agency pursuant to subdivision (d) of Section 1785.11. The election shall be effective for a minimum of two years, unless otherwise specified by the consumer. *(Added by Stats.2001, c. 354 (A.B.655), § 2.)*

Cross References

Consumer credit reporting agency defined for purposes of this Title, see Civil Code § 1785.3.

Consumer defined for purposes of this Title, see Civil Code § 1785.3.

§ 1785.11.9. Terms defined for purposes of Sections 1785.11.10 and 1785.11.11

For purposes of Sections 1785.11.10 and 1785.11.11, the following terms shall have the following meanings:

(a) "Protected consumer" means an individual who is any of the following:

(1) Under 16 years of age at the time a request for the placement of a security freeze is made.

(2) An incapacitated person or a protected person for whom a guardian or conservator has been appointed.

(3) Under the jurisdiction of a county welfare department or county probation department, has been placed in a foster care setting, and is under 16 years of age at the time a request for placement of a security freeze is made.

(b) "Record" means a compilation of information that:

(1) Identifies a protected consumer.

(2) Was created by a consumer credit reporting agency solely for the purpose of complying with this section.

(3) Is not otherwise authorized to be created or used to consider the protected consumer's creditworthiness, credit standing, credit capacity, character, general reputation, personal characteristics, or mode of living.

(c)(1) "Representative" means a person who provides to a consumer credit reporting agency sufficient proof of authority to act on behalf of a protected consumer.

(2) For a protected consumer who has been placed in a foster care setting, "representative" means either of the following:

(A) A county welfare department or its agent or designee.

(B) A county probation department or its agent or designee.

(3) For a protected consumer who has been placed in a foster care setting, "representative" does not mean a foster parent.

(d) "Security freeze" means:

(1) If a consumer credit reporting agency does not have a file pertaining to a protected consumer, a restriction that:

(A) Is placed on the protected consumer's record in accordance with this section.

(B) Prohibits the consumer credit reporting agency from releasing the protected consumer's record except as authorized in this section.

(2) If a consumer credit reporting agency has a file pertaining to a protected consumer, a restriction that:

(A) Is placed on the protected consumer's consumer credit report in accordance with this section.

(B) Prohibits the consumer credit reporting agency from releasing the protected consumer's consumer credit report or any information derived from the protected consumer's consumer credit report except as authorized in this section.

(e) "Sufficient proof of authority" means documentation that shows that a representative has authority to act on behalf of a protected consumer in a financial matter. This documentation includes, but is not limited to:

(1) A court order or relevant enabling document issued by a court.

(2) A legally sufficient and valid power of attorney, or a durable power of attorney.

(3) A written, notarized statement signed by a representative that expressly describes the authority of the representative to act on behalf of a protected consumer, including a temporary conservator or temporary guardian.

(4) A written communication from a county welfare department or its agent or designee or a county probation department or its agent or designee certifying that the protected consumer is a foster youth under its jurisdiction.

(f) "Sufficient proof of identification" means information or documentation that identifies a protected consumer or a representative of a protected consumer. This information or documentation includes, but is not limited to:

(1) A social security number or a copy of a social security card issued by the Social Security Administration.

(2) A certified copy or official copy of a birth certificate issued by the entity authorized to issue the birth certificate.

(3) A copy of a driver's license, an identification issued by the Department of Motor Vehicles, or any other government-issued identification.

(4) A copy of a bill for telephone, sewer, septic tank, water, electric, oil, or natural gas services that shows a name and a home address.

(5) A written communication from a county welfare department or its agent or designee or a county probation department or its agent or designee certifying that the protected consumer is a foster youth under its jurisdiction. *(Added by Stats.2016, c. 494 (A.B.1580), § 1, eff. Jan. 1, 2017.)*

§ 1785.11.10. Application of provisions to use of protected consumer's consumer credit report by particular persons and agencies

Sections 1785.11.9 to 1785.11.11, inclusive, do not apply to the use of a protected consumer's consumer credit report or record by any of the following:

(a) A person or entity listed in paragraph (1) or (2) of subdivision (*l*) of Section 1785.11.2, or Section 1785.11.4 or 1785.11.6.

(b) A person administering a credit file monitoring subscription service to which the representative of the protected consumer has subscribed on behalf of the protected consumer.

(c) A person who provides the protected consumer or the protected consumer's representative with a copy of the

§ 1785.11.10

protected consumer's consumer credit report at the request of the protected consumer or at the request of the protected consumer's representative.

(d) Any state or local agency, law enforcement agency, trial court, or private collection agency acting pursuant to a court order, warrant, or subpoena.

(e) A child support agency acting pursuant to Chapter 2 (commencing with Section 17400) of Division 17 of the Family Code and Title IV–D of the Social Security Act (42 U.S.C. Sec. 651 et seq.).

(f) The State Department of Health Care Services or its agents or assigns acting to investigate Medi–Cal fraud.

(g) The Franchise Tax Board or its agents or assigns acting to investigate or collect delinquent taxes or unpaid court orders or to fulfill any of its other statutory responsibilities.
(Added by Stats.2016, c. 494 (A.B.1580), § 2, eff. Jan. 1, 2017.)

§ 1785.11.11. Security freezes for protected consumers; events requiring security freeze; disclosure and notification; removal of freeze

(a) A consumer credit reporting agency shall place a security freeze for a protected consumer if both of the following occur:

(1) The consumer credit reporting agency receives a request from the protected consumer's representative for the placement of the security freeze pursuant to this section.

(2) The protected consumer's representative does all of the following:

(A) Submits the request to the consumer credit reporting agency at the address or other point of contact and in the manner specified by the consumer credit reporting agency.

(B) Provides to the consumer credit reporting agency sufficient proof of identification of the protected consumer and the representative.

(C) Provides to the consumer credit reporting agency sufficient proof of authority to act on behalf of the protected consumer.

(D) Pays to the consumer credit reporting agency a fee as authorized by subdivision (i).

(b) If a consumer credit reporting agency does not have a file pertaining to a protected consumer when the consumer credit reporting agency receives a request pursuant to paragraph (1) of subdivision (a), the consumer credit reporting agency shall create a record for the protected consumer.

(c) If a protected consumer's representative requests a security freeze, the consumer credit reporting agency shall disclose the process for placing and removing a security freeze.

(d) Within 30 days after receiving a request that meets the requirements of subdivision (a), a consumer credit reporting agency shall place a security freeze for the protected consumer. The consumer credit reporting agency shall send written confirmation of the security freeze to the address on file within 10 days of the placement of the security freeze.

(e) Unless a security freeze for a protected consumer is removed pursuant to subdivision (h) or (j), a consumer credit reporting agency shall not release the protected consumer's consumer credit report, any information derived from the protected consumer's consumer credit report, or any record created for the protected consumer.

(f) A security freeze for a protected consumer placed pursuant to this section shall remain in effect until either of the following occurs:

(1) The protected consumer or the protected consumer's representative requests that the consumer credit reporting agency remove the security freeze in accordance with subdivision (h).

(2) The security freeze is removed in accordance with subdivision (j).

(g) To remove a security freeze, a protected consumer or a protected consumer's representative shall do all of the following:

(1) Submit a request for removal of the security freeze to the consumer credit reporting agency at the address or other point of contact and in the manner specified by the consumer credit reporting agency.

(2) Provide to the consumer credit reporting agency:

(A) If the request is made by the protected consumer:

(i) Proof that the sufficient proof of authority for the protected consumer's representative to act on behalf of the protected consumer is no longer valid, he or she has been emancipated, or he or she is 16 years of age or older.

(ii) Sufficient proof of identification of the protected consumer.

(B) If the request is made by the representative of a protected consumer:

(i) Sufficient proof of identification of the protected consumer and the representative.

(ii) Sufficient proof of authority to act on behalf of the protected consumer.

(3) Pay to the consumer credit reporting agency a fee as authorized by subdivision (i).

(h) Within 30 days after receiving a request that meets the requirements of subdivision (g), a consumer credit reporting agency shall remove a security freeze for a protected consumer.

(i)(1) Except as provided in paragraph (2), a consumer credit reporting agency may not charge a fee for any service performed pursuant to this section.

(2) A consumer credit reporting agency is authorized to charge a reasonable fee, not exceeding ten dollars ($10), for each placement or removal of a security freeze for a protected consumer.

(3) Notwithstanding paragraph (2), a consumer credit reporting agency shall not charge any fee pursuant to this section under any of the following circumstances:

(A) The protected consumer's representative has received a report of alleged identity theft against the protected consumer under Section 530.5 of the Penal Code and has provided copy of the report to the consumer credit reporting agency.

(B) The request for the placement or removal of a security freeze is for a protected consumer who is under 16 years of age at the time of the request and the consumer credit reporting agency has a report pertaining to the protected consumer.

(C) The request for the placement or removal of a security freeze is for a protected consumer who has been placed in a foster care setting.

(j) A consumer credit reporting agency is authorized to remove a security freeze for a protected consumer or to delete a record of a protected consumer if the security freeze was placed or the record was created based upon a material misrepresentation of fact by the protected consumer or the protected consumer's representative.

(k) A consumer credit reporting agency may develop procedures involving the use of telephone, mail, fax, the Internet, or other electronic media to receive and process a request for a protected consumer's security freeze to be placed or removed. *(Added by Stats.2016, c. 494 (A.B.1580), § 3, eff. Jan. 1, 2017.)*

§ 1785.12. Report to governmental agency

Notwithstanding the provisions of Section 1785.11, a consumer credit reporting agency may furnish to a governmental agency a consumer's name, address, former address, places of employment, or former places of employment. *(Added by Stats.1975, c. 1271, p. 3371, § 1.)*

Cross References

Consumer credit reporting agency defined for purposes of this Title, see Civil Code § 1785.3.
Consumer defined for purposes of this Title, see Civil Code § 1785.3.
Similar provisions, see Civil Code § 1786.14.

§ 1785.13. Items of information prohibited; exceptions

(a) No consumer credit reporting agency shall make any consumer credit report containing any of the following items of information:

(1) Bankruptcies that, from the date of the order for relief, antedate the report by more than 10 years.

(2) Suits and judgments that, from the date of entry or renewal, antedate the report by more than seven years or until the governing statute of limitations has expired, whichever is the longer period.

(3) Unlawful detainer actions, unless the lessor was the prevailing party. For purposes of this paragraph, the lessor shall be deemed to be the prevailing party only if (A) final judgment was awarded to the lessor (i) upon entry of the tenant's default, (ii) upon the granting of the lessor's motion for summary judgment, or (iii) following trial, or (B) the action was resolved by a written settlement agreement between the parties that states that the unlawful detainer action may be reported. In any other instance in which the action is resolved by settlement agreement, the lessor shall not be deemed to be the prevailing party for purposes of this paragraph.

(4) Paid tax liens that, from the date of payment, antedate the report by more than seven years.

(5) Accounts placed for collection or charged to profit and loss that antedate the report by more than seven years.

(6) Records of arrest, indictment, information, misdemeanor complaint, or conviction of a crime that, from the date of disposition, release, or parole, antedate the report by more than seven years. These items of information shall no longer be reported if at any time it is learned that in the case of a conviction a full pardon has been granted, or in the case of an arrest, indictment, information, or misdemeanor complaint a conviction did not result.

(7) Any other adverse information that antedates the report by more than seven years.

(b) The seven-year period specified in paragraphs (5) and (7) of subdivision (a) shall commence to run, with respect to any account that is placed for collection (internally or by referral to a third party, whichever is earlier), charged to profit and loss, or subjected to any similar action, upon the expiration of the 180–day period beginning on the date of the commencement of the delinquency that immediately preceded the collection activity, charge to profit and loss, or similar action. Where more than one of these actions is taken with respect to a particular account, the seven-year period specified in paragraphs (5) and (7) shall commence concurrently for all these actions on the date of the first of these actions.

(c) Any consumer credit reporting agency that furnishes a consumer credit report containing information regarding any case involving a consumer arising under the bankruptcy provisions of Title 11 of the United States Code shall include an identification of the chapter of Title 11 of the United States Code under which the case arose if that can be ascertained from what was provided to the consumer credit reporting agency by the source of the information.

(d) A consumer credit report shall not include any adverse information concerning a consumer antedating the report by more than 10 years or that otherwise is prohibited from being included in a consumer credit report.

(e) If a consumer credit reporting agency is notified by a furnisher of credit information that an open-end credit account of the consumer has been closed by the consumer, any consumer credit report thereafter issued by the consumer credit reporting agency with respect to that consumer, and that includes information respecting that account, shall indicate the fact that the consumer has closed the account. For purposes of this subdivision, "open-end credit account" does not include any demand deposit account, such as a checking account, money market account, or share draft account.

(f) Consumer credit reporting agencies shall not include medical information in their files on consumers or furnish medical information for employment, insurance, or credit purposes in a consumer credit report without the consent of the consumer.

(g) A consumer credit reporting agency shall include in any consumer credit report information, if any, on the failure of the consumer to pay overdue child or spousal support, where the information either was provided to the consumer credit reporting agency pursuant to Section 4752 or has been provided to the consumer credit reporting agency and verified by another federal, state, or local governmental agency. *(Added by Stats.1975, c. 1271, p. 3371, § 1. Amended by Stats.1982, c. 1127, p. 4064, § 4; Stats.1988, c. 900, § 1; Stats.1991, c. 965 (A.B.1796), § 1; Stats.1991, c. 1145 (A.B. 2032), § 1.1; Stats.1992, c. 1194 (A.B.1629), § 4, operative July 1, 1993; Stats.1993, c. 285 (A.B.1340), § 5, eff. Aug. 2,*

§ 1785.13

1993; Stats.1994, c. 146 (A.B.3601), § 12; Stats.2000, c. 1012 (S.B.2166), § 2; Stats.2009, c. 500 (A.B.1059), § 10.)

Validity

A prior version of this section was held unconstitutional as a violation of the First Amendment in the decision of U.D. Registry, Inc. v. State of California (App. 2 Dist. 1995) 40 Cal.Rptr.2d 228, 34 Cal. App.4th 107.

Cross References

Consumer credit report defined for purposes of this Title, see Civil Code § 1785.3.
Consumer credit reporting agency defined for purposes of this Title, see Civil Code § 1785.3.
Consumer defined for purposes of this Title, see Civil Code § 1785.3.
Escrow agent rating service, compliance with provisions of this section, see Civil Code § 1785.28.
File defined for purposes of this Title, see Civil Code § 1785.3.
Item of information defined for purposes of this Title, see Civil Code § 1785.3.
Similar provisions, see Civil Code § 1786.18.

§ 1785.135. Consumer credit reports; documents acting as lien or encumbrance

No consumer credit reporting agency shall make any consumer credit report with respect to a document which acts as a lien or other encumbrance, including, but not limited to, a notice of lis pendens, but which has together with it a court order striking or releasing the lien or other encumbrance pursuant to Section 765.030 of the Code of Civil Procedure. *(Added by Stats.1998, c. 779 (S.B.1759), § 1.)*

Cross References

Consumer credit report defined for purposes of this Title, see Civil Code § 1785.3.
Consumer credit reporting agency defined for purposes of this Title, see Civil Code § 1785.3.
Consumer defined for purposes of this Title, see Civil Code § 1785.3.

§ 1785.14. Agency procedures; record of purposes; disclosure to consumer; notice to supplier of information regarding obligations under title

(a) Every consumer credit reporting agency shall maintain reasonable procedures designed to avoid violations of Section 1785.13 and to limit furnishing of consumer credit reports to the purposes listed under Section 1785.11. These procedures shall require that prospective users of the information identify themselves, certify the purposes for which the information is sought and certify that the information will be used for no other purposes. From the effective date of this act the consumer credit reporting agency shall keep a record of the purposes as stated by the user. Every consumer credit reporting agency shall make a reasonable effort to verify the identity of a new prospective user and the uses certified by the prospective user prior to furnishing the user a consumer report. No consumer credit reporting agency may furnish a consumer credit report to any person unless the consumer credit reporting agency has reasonable grounds for believing that the consumer credit report will be used by the person for the purposes listed in Section 1785.11. A consumer credit reporting agency does not have reasonable grounds for believing that a consumer credit report will be used by the person for the purposes listed in Section 1785.11 unless all of the following requirements are met:

(1) If the prospective user is a retail seller, as defined in Section 1802.3, and intends to issue credit to a consumer who appears in person on the basis of an application for credit submitted in person, the consumer credit reporting agency shall, with a reasonable degree of certainty, match at least three categories of identifying information within the file maintained by the consumer credit reporting agency on the consumer with the information provided to the consumer credit reporting agency by the retail seller. The categories of identifying information may include, but are not limited to, first and last name, month and date of birth, driver's license number, place of employment, current residence address, previous residence address, or social security number. The categories of information shall not include mother's maiden name.

(2) If the prospective user is a retail seller, as defined in Section 1802.3, and intends to issue credit to a consumer who appears in person on the basis of an application for credit submitted in person, the retail seller certifies, in writing, to the consumer credit reporting agency that it instructs its employees and agents to inspect a photo identification of the consumer at the time the application was submitted in person. This paragraph does not apply to an application for credit submitted by mail.

(3) If the prospective user intends to extend credit by mail pursuant to a solicitation by mail, the extension of credit shall be mailed to the same address as on the solicitation unless the prospective user verifies any address change by, among other methods, contacting the person to whom the extension of credit will be mailed.

(b) Whenever a consumer credit reporting agency prepares a consumer credit report, it shall follow reasonable procedures to assure maximum possible accuracy of the information concerning the individual about whom the report relates. These reasonable procedures shall include, but not be limited to, permanent retention by the consumer credit reporting agency in the consumer's file, or a separately individualized file, of that portion of the data in the file that is used by the consumer credit reporting agency to identify the individual consumer pursuant to paragraph (1) of subdivision (a). This permanently retained data shall be available for use in either a reinvestigation pursuant to subdivision (a) of Section 1785.16, an investigation where the consumer has filed a police report pursuant to subdivision (k) of Section 1785.16, or a restoration of a file involving the consumer. If the permanently retained identifying information is retained in a consumer's file, it shall be clearly identified in the file in order for an individual who reviews the file to easily distinguish between the permanently stored identifying information and any other identifying information that may be a part of the file. This retention requirement shall not apply to data that is reported in error, that is obsolete, or that is found to be inaccurate through the results of a reinvestigation initiated by a consumer pursuant to subdivision (a) of Section 1785.16.

(c) No consumer credit reporting agency may prohibit any user of any consumer credit report furnished by the consumer credit reporting agency from disclosing the contents of the consumer credit report to the consumer who is the subject of the report if adverse action may be taken by the user based in whole or in part on the consumer credit report. The act of disclosure to the consumer by the user of the contents of a consumer credit report shall not be a basis for liability of the consumer credit reporting agency or the user under Section 1785.31.

(d) A consumer credit reporting agency shall provide a written notice to any person who regularly and in the ordinary course of business supplies information to the consumer credit reporting agency concerning any consumer or to whom a consumer credit report is provided by the consumer credit reporting agency. The notice shall specify the person's obligations under this title. Copies of the appropriate code sections shall satisfy the requirement of this subdivision. *(Added by Stats.1975, c. 1271, p. 3372, § 1. Amended by Stats.1992, c. 1194 (A.B.1629), § 5, operative July 1, 1993; Stats.1993, c. 285 (A.B.1340), § 6, eff. Aug. 2, 1993; Stats. 1997, c. 768 (A.B.156), § 1, operative July 1, 1998.)*

Cross References

Adverse action defined for purposes of this Title, see Civil Code § 1785.3.
Consumer credit report defined for purposes of this Title, see Civil Code § 1785.3.
Consumer credit reporting agency defined for purposes of this Title, see Civil Code § 1785.3.
Consumer defined for purposes of this Title, see Civil Code § 1785.3.
Escrow agent rating service, compliance with provisions of this section, see Civil Code § 1785.28.
File defined for purposes of this Title, see Civil Code § 1785.3.
Person defined for purposes of this Title, see Civil Code § 1785.3.
Similar provisions, see Civil Code § 1786.20.

§ 1785.15. Supplying files and information; right to information

(a) A consumer credit reporting agency shall supply files and information required under Section 1785.10 during normal business hours and on reasonable notice. In addition to the disclosure provided by this chapter and any disclosures received by the consumer, the consumer has the right to request and receive all of the following:

(1) Either a decoded written version of the file or a written copy of the file, including all information in the file at the time of the request, with an explanation of any code used.

(2) A credit score for the consumer, the key factors, and the related information, as defined in and required by Section 1785.15.1.

(3) A record of all inquiries, by recipient, that result in the provision of information concerning the consumer in connection with a credit transaction not initiated by the consumer and that were received by the consumer credit reporting agency in the 12–month period immediately preceding the request for disclosure under this section.

(4) The recipients, including end users specified in Section 1785.22, of any consumer credit report on the consumer which the consumer credit reporting agency has furnished:

(A) For employment purposes within the two-year period preceding the request.

(B) For any other purpose within the 12–month period preceding the request.

Identification for purposes of this paragraph shall include the name of the recipient or, if applicable, the fictitious business name under which the recipient does business disclosed in full. If requested by the consumer, the identification shall also include the address of the recipient.

(b) Files maintained on a consumer shall be disclosed promptly as follows:

(1) In person, at the location where the consumer credit reporting agency maintains the trained personnel required by subdivision (d), if he or she appears in person and furnishes proper identification.

(2) By mail, if the consumer makes a written request with proper identification for a copy of the file or a decoded written version of that file to be sent to the consumer at a specified address. A disclosure pursuant to this paragraph shall be deposited in the United States mail, postage prepaid, within five business days after the consumer's written request for the disclosure is received by the consumer credit reporting agency. Consumer credit reporting agencies complying with requests for mailings under this section shall not be liable for disclosures to third parties caused by mishandling of mail after the mailings leave the consumer credit reporting agencies.

(3) A summary of all information contained in files on a consumer and required to be provided by Section 1785.10 shall be provided by telephone, if the consumer has made a written request, with proper identification for telephone disclosure.

(4) Information in a consumer's file required to be provided in writing under this section may also be disclosed in another form if authorized by the consumer and if available from the consumer credit reporting agency. For this purpose, a consumer may request disclosure in person pursuant to Section 1785.10, by telephone upon disclosure of proper identification by the consumer, by electronic means if available from the consumer credit reporting agency, or by any other reasonable means that is available from the consumer credit reporting agency.

(c) "Proper identification," as used in subdivision (b) means that information generally deemed sufficient to identify a person. Only if the consumer is unable to reasonably identify himself or herself with the information described above may a consumer credit reporting agency require additional information concerning the consumer's employment and personal or family history in order to verify his or her identity.

(d) The consumer credit reporting agency shall provide trained personnel to explain to the consumer any information furnished him or her pursuant to Section 1785.10.

(e) The consumer shall be permitted to be accompanied by one other person of his or her choosing, who shall furnish reasonable identification. A consumer credit reporting agency may require the consumer to furnish a written statement granting permission to the consumer credit reporting agency to discuss the consumer's file in that person's presence.

(f) Any written disclosure by a consumer credit reporting agency to any consumer pursuant to this section shall include a written summary of all rights the consumer has under this title and, in the case of a consumer credit reporting agency

§ 1785.15

that compiles and maintains consumer credit reports on a nationwide basis, a toll-free telephone number that the consumer can use to communicate with the consumer credit reporting agency. The written summary of rights required under this subdivision is sufficient if in substantially the following form:

"You have a right to obtain a copy of your credit file from a consumer credit reporting agency. You may be charged a reasonable fee not exceeding eight dollars ($8). There is no fee, however, if you have been turned down for credit, employment, insurance, or a rental dwelling because of information in your credit report within the preceding 60 days. The consumer credit reporting agency must provide someone to help you interpret the information in your credit file.

You have a right to dispute inaccurate information by contacting the consumer credit reporting agency directly. However, neither you nor any credit repair company or credit service organization has the right to have accurate, current, and verifiable information removed from your credit report. Under the Federal Fair Credit Reporting Act, the consumer credit reporting agency must remove accurate, negative information from your report only if it is over seven years old. Bankruptcy information can be reported for 10 years.

If you have notified a consumer credit reporting agency in writing that you dispute the accuracy of information in your file, the consumer credit reporting agency must then, within 30 business days, reinvestigate and modify or remove inaccurate information. The consumer credit reporting agency may not charge a fee for this service. Any pertinent information and copies of all documents you have concerning an error should be given to the consumer credit reporting agency.

If reinvestigation does not resolve the dispute to your satisfaction, you may send a brief statement to the consumer credit reporting agency to keep in your file, explaining why you think the record is inaccurate. The consumer credit reporting agency must include your statement about disputed information in a report it issues about you.

You have a right to receive a record of all inquiries relating to a credit transaction initiated in 12 months preceding your request. This record shall include the recipients of any consumer credit report.

You may request in writing that the information contained in your file not be provided to a third party for marketing purposes.

You have a right to place a "security alert" in your credit report, which will warn anyone who receives information in your credit report that your identity may have been used without your consent. Recipients of your credit report are required to take reasonable steps, including contacting you at the telephone number you may provide with your security alert, to verify your identity prior to lending money, extending credit, or completing the purchase, lease, or rental of goods or services. The security alert may prevent credit, loans, and services from being approved in your name without your consent. However, you should be aware that taking advantage of this right may delay or interfere with the timely approval of any subsequent request or application you make regarding a new loan, credit, mortgage, or cellular phone or other new account, including an extension of credit at point of sale. If you place a security alert on your credit report, you have a right to obtain a free copy of your credit report at the time the 90-day security alert period expires. A security alert may be requested by calling the following toll-free telephone number: (Insert applicable toll-free telephone number). California consumers also have the right to obtain a "security freeze."

You have a right to place a "security freeze" on your credit report, which will prohibit a consumer credit reporting agency from releasing any information in your credit report without your express authorization. A security freeze must be requested in writing by mail. The security freeze is designed to prevent credit, loans, and services from being approved in your name without your consent. However, you should be aware that using a security freeze to take control over who gets access to the personal and financial information in your credit report may delay, interfere with, or prohibit the timely approval of any subsequent request or application you make regarding a new loan, credit, mortgage, or cellular phone or other new account, including an extension of credit at point of sale. When you place a security freeze on your credit report, you will be provided a personal identification number or password to use if you choose to remove the freeze on your credit report or authorize the release of your credit report for a specific party or period of time after the freeze is in place. To provide that authorization you must contact the consumer credit reporting agency and provide all of the following:

(1) The personal identification number or password.

(2) Proper identification to verify your identity.

(3) The proper information regarding the third party who is to receive the credit report or the period of time for which the report shall be available to users of the credit report.

A consumer credit reporting agency must authorize the release of your credit report no later than three business days after receiving the above information.

A security freeze does not apply when you have an existing account and a copy of your report is requested by your existing creditor or its agents or affiliates for certain types of account review, collection, fraud control, or similar activities.

If you are actively seeking credit, you should understand that the procedures involved in lifting a security freeze may slow your application for credit. You should plan ahead and lift a freeze, either completely if you are shopping around, or specifically for a certain creditor, before applying for new credit.

A consumer credit reporting agency may not charge a fee to a consumer for placing or removing a security freeze if the consumer is a victim of identity theft and submits a copy of a valid police report or valid Department of Motor Vehicles investigative report. A person 65 years of age or older with proper identification shall not be charged a fee for placing an initial security freeze, but may be charged a fee of no more than five dollars ($5) for lifting, removing, or replacing a security freeze. All other consumers may be charged a fee of no more than ten dollars ($10) for each of these steps.

You have a right to bring civil action against anyone, including a consumer credit reporting agency, who improperly obtains access to a file, knowingly or willfully misuses file data, or fails to correct inaccurate file data.

If you are a victim of identity theft and provide to a consumer credit reporting agency a copy of a valid police report or a valid investigative report made by a Department of Motor Vehicles investigator with peace officer status describing your circumstances, the following shall apply:

(1) You have a right to have any information you list on the report as allegedly fraudulent promptly blocked so that the information cannot be reported. The information will be unblocked only if (A) the information you provide is a material misrepresentation of the facts, (B) you agree that the information is blocked in error, or (C) you knowingly obtained possession of goods, services, or moneys as a result of the blocked transactions. If blocked information is unblocked, you will be promptly notified.

(2) You have a right to receive, free of charge and upon request, one copy of your credit report each month for up to 12 consecutive months." (Added by Stats.1975, c. 1271, p. 3373, § 1. Amended by Stats.1976, c. 666, p. 1639, § 3; Stats.1980, c. 1113, p. 3580, § 2; Stats.1992, c. 1194 (A.B. 1629), § 6, operative July 1, 1993; Stats.2000, c. 978 (S.B. 1607), § 2, operative July 1, 2001; Stats.2001, c. 720 (S.B.168), § 6; Stats.2002, c. 860 (S.B.1239), § 1; Stats.2003, c. 907 (S.B.25), § 3; Stats.2008, c. 151 (A.B.372), § 2; Stats.2012, c. 645 (A.B.2374), § 2.)

Cross References

Consumer credit report defined for purposes of this Title, see Civil Code § 1785.3.
Consumer credit reporting agency defined for purposes of this Title, see Civil Code § 1785.3.
Consumer defined for purposes of this Title, see Civil Code § 1785.3.
Employment purposes defined for purposes of this Title, see Civil Code § 1785.3.
Escrow agent rating service, compliance with provisions of this section, see Civil Code § 1785.28.
File defined for purposes of this Title, see Civil Code § 1785.3.
Person defined for purposes of this Title, see Civil Code § 1785.3.
Similar provisions, see Civil Code § 1786.22.

§ 1785.15.1. Credit scores supplied upon request by consumer; key factors

(a) Upon the consumer's request for a credit score, a consumer credit reporting agency shall supply to a consumer a notice which shall include the information described in paragraphs (1) to (5), inclusive, and a statement indicating that the information and credit scoring model may be different than the credit score that may be used by the lender. However, if the consumer requests the credit file and not the credit score, then the consumer shall receive the credit file and a statement that he or she may request and obtain a credit score.

(1) The consumer's current credit score or the consumer's most recent credit score that was previously calculated by the credit reporting agency for a purpose related to the extension of credit.

(2) The range of possible credit scores under the model used.

(3) All the key factors that adversely affected the consumer's credit score in the model used, the total number of which shall not exceed four.

(4) The date the credit score was created.

(5) The name of the person or entity that provided the credit score or credit file upon which the credit score was created.

(b) For purposes of this act, "credit score" means a numerical value or a categorization derived from a statistical tool or modeling system used by a person who makes or arranges a loan to predict the likelihood of certain credit behaviors, including default. The numerical value or the categorization derived from this analysis may also be referred to as a "risk predictor" or "risk score." "Credit score" does not include any mortgage score or rating of an automated underwriting system that considers one or more factors in addition to credit information, including, but not limited to, the loan to value ratio, the amount of down payment, or a consumer's financial assets. "Credit score" does not include other elements of the underwriting process or underwriting decision.

(c) For the purposes of this section, "key factors" means all relevant elements or reasons adversely affecting the credit score for the particular individual listed in the order of their importance based on their effect on the credit score.

(d) The information required by this section shall be provided in the same timeframe and manner as the information described in Section 1785.15.

(e) This section shall not be construed to compel a consumer reporting agency to develop or disclose a score if the agency does not (1) distribute scores that are used in connection with residential real property loans, or (2) develop scores that assist credit providers in understanding a consumer's general credit behavior and predicting his or her future credit behavior.

(f) This section shall not be construed to require a consumer credit reporting agency that distributes credit scores developed by another person or entity to provide a further explanation of them, or to process a dispute arising pursuant to subdivision (a) of Section 1785.16, except that the consumer credit reporting agency shall provide the consumer with the name and address and website for contacting the person or entity who developed the score or developed the methodology of the score. This subdivision does not apply to a consumer credit reporting agency that develops or modifies scores that are developed by another person or entity.

(g) This section shall not be construed to require a consumer reporting agency to maintain credit scores in its files. (Added by Stats.2000, c. 978 (S.B.1607), § 3, operative July 1, 2001.)

Cross References

Consumer credit reporting agency defined for purposes of this Title, see Civil Code § 1785.3.
Consumer defined for purposes of this Title, see Civil Code § 1785.3.
File defined for purposes of this Title, see Civil Code § 1785.3.
Liens, conditional sales contracts, maintenance of documents, see Civil Code § 2984.5.
Notice to vehicle credit applicant of consumer credit score, see Vehicle Code § 11713.20.
Person defined for purposes of this Title, see Civil Code § 1785.3.

§ 1785.15.2. Credit scoring model

(a) In complying with Section 1785.15.1, a consumer credit reporting agency shall supply the consumer with a credit

§ 1785.15.2

score that is derived from a credit scoring model that is widely distributed to users by that consumer credit reporting agency in connection with residential real property loans or with a credit score that assists the consumer in understanding the credit scoring assessment of his or her credit behavior and predictions about his or her future credit behavior, and a statement indicating that the information and credit scoring model may be different than that used by the lender.

(b) A consumer credit reporting agency may charge a reasonable fee for providing the information required under Section 1785.15.1. *(Added by Stats.2000, c. 978 (S.B.1607), § 4, operative July 1, 2001.)*

Cross References

Consumer credit reporting agency defined for purposes of this Title, see Civil Code § 1785.3.
Consumer defined for purposes of this Title, see Civil Code § 1785.3.

§ 1785.15.3. Statement of rights; monthly credit reports

(a) In addition to any other rights the consumer may have under this title, every consumer credit reporting agency, after being contacted by telephone, mail, or in person by any consumer who has reason to believe he or she may be a victim of identity theft, shall promptly provide to that consumer a statement, written in a clear and conspicuous manner, describing the statutory rights of victims of identity theft under this title.

(b) Every consumer credit reporting agency shall, upon the receipt from a victim of identity theft of a police report prepared pursuant to Section 530.6 of the Penal Code, or a valid investigative report made by a Department of Motor Vehicles investigator with peace officer status regarding the public offenses described in Section 530.5 of the Penal Code, provide the victim, free of charge and upon request, with up to 12 copies of his or her file during a consecutive 12-month period, not to exceed one copy per month, following the date of the police report. Notwithstanding any other provision of this title, the maximum number of free reports a victim of identity theft is entitled to obtain under this title is 12 per year, as provided by this subdivision.

(c) Subdivision (a) does not apply to a consumer reporting agency that acts only as a reseller of credit information by assembling and merging information contained in the database of another consumer reporting agency or agencies and that does not maintain a permanent database of credit information from which new credit reports are produced.

(d) The provisions of this section shall become effective July 1, 2003. *(Added by Stats.2002, c. 860 (S.B.1239), § 2, operative July 1, 2003.)*

Cross References

Consumer credit reporting agency defined for purposes of this Title, see Civil Code § 1785.3.
Consumer defined for purposes of this Title, see Civil Code § 1785.3.
File defined for purposes of this Title, see Civil Code § 1785.3.
Person defined for purposes of this Title, see Civil Code § 1785.3.

§ 1785.16. Disputes as to completeness or accuracy of information in file; reinvestigation and recording of current status; notice of results; deletion and reinsertion of information; statement of dispute; agency procedures; block of information appearing as a result of Penal Code § 530.5; unblocking information

(a) If the completeness or accuracy of any item of information contained in his or her file is disputed by a consumer, and the dispute is conveyed directly to the consumer credit reporting agency by the consumer or user on behalf of the consumer, the consumer credit reporting agency shall within a reasonable period of time and without charge, reinvestigate and record the current status of the disputed information before the end of the 30-business-day period beginning on the date the agency receives notice of the dispute from the consumer or user, unless the consumer credit reporting agency has reasonable grounds to believe and determines that the dispute by the consumer is frivolous or irrelevant, including by reason of a failure of the consumer to provide sufficient information, as requested by the consumer credit reporting agency, to investigate the dispute. Unless the consumer credit reporting agency determines that the dispute is frivolous or irrelevant, before the end of the five-business-day period beginning on the date the consumer credit reporting agency receives notice of dispute under this section, the agency shall notify any person who provided information in dispute at the address and in the manner specified by the person. A consumer credit reporting agency may require that disputes by consumers be in writing.

(b) In conducting that reinvestigation the consumer credit reporting agency shall review and consider all relevant information submitted by the consumer with respect to the disputed item of information. If the consumer credit reporting agency determines that the dispute is frivolous or irrelevant, it shall notify the consumer by mail or, if authorized by the consumer for that purpose, by any other means available to the consumer credit reporting agency, within five business days after that determination is made that it is terminating its reinvestigation of the item of information. In this notification, the consumer credit reporting agency shall state the specific reasons why it has determined that the consumer's dispute is frivolous or irrelevant. If the disputed item of information is found to be inaccurate, missing, or can no longer be verified by the evidence submitted, the consumer credit reporting agency shall promptly add, correct, or delete that information from the consumer's file.

(c) No information may be reinserted in a consumer's file after having been deleted pursuant to this section unless the person who furnished the information certifies that the information is accurate. If any information deleted from a consumer's file is reinserted in the file, the consumer credit reporting agency shall promptly notify the consumer of the reinsertion in writing or, if authorized by the consumer for that purpose, by any other means available to the consumer credit reporting agency. As part of, or in addition to, this notice the consumer credit reporting agency shall, within five business days of reinserting the information, provide the consumer in writing (1) a statement that the disputed information has been reinserted, (2) a notice that the agency will provide to the consumer, within 15 days following a request, the name, address, and telephone number of any furnisher of information contacted or which contacted the consumer credit reporting agency in connection with the reinsertion, (3) the toll-free telephone number of the consumer credit reporting agency that the consumer can use to obtain this name, address, and telephone number, and (4) a notice that the consumer has the right to a reinvestigation of the information reinserted by the consumer credit reporting agency and to add a statement to his or her file disputing the accuracy or completeness of the information.

(d) A consumer credit reporting agency shall provide written notice to the consumer of the results of any reinvestigation under this subdivision, within five days of completion of the reinvestigation. The notice shall include (1) a statement that the reinvestigation is completed, (2) a consumer credit report that is based on the consumer's file as that file is revised as a result of the reinvestigation, (3) a description or indication of any changes made in the consumer credit report as a result of those revisions to the consumer's file and a description of any changes made or sought by the consumer that were not made and an explanation why they were not made, (4) a notice that, if requested by the consumer, a description of the procedure used to determine the accuracy and completeness of the information shall be provided to the consumer by the consumer credit reporting agency, including the name, business address, and telephone number of any furnisher of information contacted in connection with that information, (5) a notice that the consumer has the right to add a statement to the consumer's file disputing the accuracy or completeness of the information, (6) a notice that the consumer has the right to request that the consumer credit reporting agency furnish notifications under subdivision (h), (7) a notice that the dispute will remain on file with the agency as long as the credit information is used, and (8) a statement about the details of the dispute will be furnished to any recipient as long as the credit information is retained in the agency's data base. A consumer credit reporting agency shall provide the notice pursuant to this subdivision respecting the procedure used to determine the accuracy and completeness of information, not later than 15 days after receiving a request from the consumer.

(e) The presence of information in the consumer's file that contradicts the contention of the consumer shall not, in and of itself, constitute reasonable grounds for believing the dispute is frivolous or irrelevant.

(f) If the consumer credit reporting agency determines that the dispute is frivolous or irrelevant, or if the reinvestigation does not resolve the dispute, or if the information is reinserted into the consumer's file pursuant to subdivision (c), the consumer may file a brief statement setting forth the nature of the dispute. The consumer credit reporting agency may limit these statements to not more than 100 words if it provides the consumer with assistance in writing a clear summary of the dispute.

(g) Whenever a statement of dispute is filed, the consumer credit reporting agency shall, in any subsequent consumer credit report containing the information in question, clearly note that the information is disputed by the consumer and shall include in the report either the consumer's statement or a clear and accurate summary thereof.

(h) Following the deletion of information from a consumer's file pursuant to this section, or following the filing of a statement of dispute pursuant to subdivision (f), the consumer credit reporting agency, at the request of the consumer, shall furnish notification that the item of information has been deleted or that the item of information is disputed. In the case of disputed information, the notification shall include the statement or summary of the dispute filed pursuant to subdivision (f). This notification shall be furnished to any person designated by the consumer who has, within two years prior to the deletion or the filing of the dispute, received a consumer credit report concerning the consumer for employment purposes, or who has, within 12 months of the deletion or the filing of the dispute, received a consumer credit report concerning the consumer for any other purpose, if these consumer credit reports contained the deleted or disputed information. The consumer credit reporting agency shall clearly and conspicuously disclose to the consumer his or her rights to make a request for this notification. The disclosure shall be made at or prior to the time the information is deleted pursuant to this section or the consumer's statement regarding the disputed information is received pursuant to subdivision (f).

(i) A consumer credit reporting agency shall maintain reasonable procedures to prevent the reappearance in a consumer's file and in consumer credit reports of information that has been deleted pursuant to this section and not reinserted pursuant to subdivision (c).

(j) If the consumer's dispute is resolved by deletion of the disputed information within three business days, beginning with the day the consumer credit reporting agency receives notice of the dispute in accordance with subdivision (a), and provided that verification thereof is provided to the consumer in writing within five business days following the deletion, then the consumer credit reporting agency shall be exempt from requirements for further action under subdivisions (d), (f), and (g).

(k) If a consumer submits to a credit reporting agency a copy of a valid police report, or a valid investigative report made by a Department of Motor Vehicles investigator with peace officer status, filed pursuant to Section 530.5 of the Penal Code, the consumer credit reporting agency shall promptly and permanently block reporting any information that the consumer alleges appears on his or her credit report as a result of a violation of Section 530.5 of the Penal Code so that the information cannot be reported. The consumer credit reporting agency shall promptly notify the furnisher of the information that the information has been so blocked. Furnishers of information and consumer credit reporting agencies shall ensure that information is unblocked only upon a preponderance of the evidence establishing the facts required under paragraph (1), (2), or (3). The permanently blocked information shall be unblocked only if: (1) the information was blocked due to a material misrepresentation of fact by the consumer or fraud, or (2) the consumer agrees that the blocked information, or portions of the blocked information, were blocked in error, or (3) the consumer knowingly obtained possession of goods, services, or moneys as a result of the blocked transaction or transactions or the consumer should have known that he or she obtained possession of goods, services, or moneys as a result of the blocked transaction or transactions. If blocked information is unblocked pursuant to this subdivision, the consumer shall be promptly notified in the same manner as consumers are notified of the reinsertion of information pursuant to subdivision (c). The prior presence of the blocked information in the consumer credit reporting agency's file on the consumer is not evidence of whether the consumer knew or should have

§ 1785.16 OBLIGATIONS

known that he or she obtained possession of any goods, services, or moneys. For the purposes of this subdivision, fraud may be demonstrated by circumstantial evidence. In unblocking information pursuant to this subdivision, furnishers and consumer credit reporting agencies shall be subject to their respective requirements pursuant to this title regarding the completeness and accuracy of information.

(*l*) In unblocking information as described in subdivision (k), a consumer reporting agency shall comply with all requirements of this section and 15 U.S.C. Sec. 1681i relating to reinvestigating disputed information. In addition, a consumer reporting agency shall accept the consumer's version of the disputed information and correct or delete the disputed item when the consumer submits to the consumer reporting agency documentation obtained from the source of the item in dispute or from public records confirming that the report was inaccurate or incomplete, unless the consumer reporting agency, in the exercise of good faith and reasonable judgment, has substantial reason based on specific, verifiable facts to doubt the authenticity of the documentation submitted and notifies the consumer in writing of that decision, explaining its reasons for unblocking the information and setting forth the specific, verifiable facts on which the decision was based.

(m) Any provision in a contract that prohibits the disclosure of a credit score by a person who makes or arranges loans or a consumer credit reporting agency is void. A lender shall not have liability under any contractual provision for disclosure of a credit score. *(Added by Stats.1975, c. 1271, p. 3373, § 1. Amended by Stats.1976, c. 666, p. 1640, § 4; Stats.1980, c. 1113, p. 3581, § 3; Stats.1990, c. 1315 (S.B. 2750), § 1; Stats.1992, c. 1194 (A.B.1629), § 7, operative July 1, 1993; Stats.1993, c. 285 (A.B.1340), § 7, eff. Aug. 2, 1993; Stats.1997, c. 768 (A.B.156), § 2, operative July 1, 1998; Stats.2000, c. 978 (S.B.1607), § 5, operative July 1, 2001; Stats.2001, c. 354 (A.B.655), § 3.)*

Cross References

Consumer credit report defined for purposes of this Title, see Civil Code § 1785.3.
Consumer credit reporting agency defined for purposes of this Title, see Civil Code § 1785.3.
Consumer defined for purposes of this Title, see Civil Code § 1785.3.
Employment purposes defined for purposes of this Title, see Civil Code § 1785.3.
Escrow agent rating service, compliance with provisions of this section, see Civil Code § 1785.28.
File defined for purposes of this Title, see Civil Code § 1785.3.
Identity theft civil actions, see Civil Code § 1798.92 et seq.
Item of information defined for purposes of this Title, see Civil Code § 1785.3.
Person defined for purposes of this Title, see Civil Code § 1785.3.
Similar provisions, see Civil Code § 1786.24.

§ 1785.16.1. Deletion of inquiries for credit reports from consumer credit report with respect to identity theft

A consumer credit reporting agency shall delete from a consumer credit report inquiries for credit reports based upon credit requests that the consumer credit reporting agency verifies were initiated as the result of identity theft, as defined in Section 1798.92. *(Added by Stats.2001, c. 354 (A.B.655), § 4.)*

Cross References

Consumer credit report defined for purposes of this Title, see Civil Code § 1785.3.
Consumer credit reporting agency defined for purposes of this Title, see Civil Code § 1785.3.
Consumer defined for purposes of this Title, see Civil Code § 1785.3.
Identity theft civil actions, see Civil Code § 1798.92 et seq.

§ 1785.16.2. Sale of consumer debt to debt collector; identity theft; subsidiaries or affiliates; interstate commerce requirement

(a) No creditor may sell a consumer debt to a debt collector, as defined in 15 U.S.C. Sec. 1692a, if the consumer is a victim of identity theft, as defined in Section 1798.2, and with respect to that debt, the creditor has received notice pursuant to subdivision (k) of Section 1785.16 or paragraph (2) of subdivision (g) of Section 1788.18.

(b) Subdivision (a) does not apply to a creditor's sale of a debt to a subsidiary or affiliate of the creditor, if, with respect to that debt, the subsidiary or affiliate does not take any action to collect the debt.

(c) For the purposes of this section, the requirement in 15 U.S.C. Sec. 1692a, that a person must use an instrumentality of interstate commerce or the mails in the collection of any debt to be considered a debt collector, does not apply. *(Added by Stats.2001, c. 354 (A.B.655), § 4.5. Amended by Stats.2002, c. 1030 (A.B.1068), § 1, eff. Sept. 28, 2002; Stats.2016, c. 376 (A.B.1723), § 2, eff. Jan. 1, 2017.)*

Cross References

Consumer defined for purposes of this Title, see Civil Code § 1785.3.
Identity theft civil actions, see Civil Code § 1798.92 et seq.
Person defined for purposes of this Title, see Civil Code § 1785.3.

§ 1785.16.3. Consumer reporting agencies acting as resellers of credit information

The provisions of subdivisions (k) and (*l*) of Section 1785.16 do not apply to a consumer reporting agency that acts only as a reseller of credit information by assembling and merging information contained in the database of another consumer reporting agency or agencies, and that does not maintain a permanent database of credit information from which new credit reports are produced. *(Added by Stats. 2002, c. 1029 (A.B.2868), § 2, eff. Sept. 28, 2002.)*

Cross References

Consumer defined for purposes of this Title, see Civil Code § 1785.3.

§ 1785.17. Charges to consumer; exceptions

(a) Except as otherwise provided, a consumer credit reporting agency may impose a reasonable charge upon a consumer, as follows:

(1) For making a disclosure pursuant to Section 1785.10 or 1785.15, the consumer credit reporting agency may charge a fee not exceeding eight dollars ($8).

(2) For furnishing a notification, statement, or summary, to any person pursuant to subdivision (h) of Section 1785.16, the consumer credit reporting agency may charge a fee not exceeding the charge that it would impose on each designated recipient for a consumer credit report, and the amount of the

charge shall be indicated to the consumer before furnishing the notification, statement, or summary.

(b) A consumer credit reporting agency shall make all disclosures pursuant to Sections 1785.10 and 1785.15 and furnish all consumer reports pursuant to Section 1785.16 without charge, if requested by the consumer within 60 days after receipt by the consumer of a notification of adverse action pursuant to Section 1785.20 or of a notification from a debt collection agency affiliated with the consumer credit reporting agency stating that the consumer's credit rating may be or has been adversely affected.

(c) A consumer credit reporting agency shall not impose any charge for (1) providing notice to a consumer required under Section 1785.16 or (2) notifying a person pursuant to subdivision (h) of Section 1785.16 of the deletion of any information which is found to be inaccurate or which can no longer be verified, if the consumer designates that person to the consumer credit reporting agency before the end of the 30-day period beginning on that date of notice under subdivision (d) of Section 1785.16. *(Added by Stats.1975, c. 1271, p. 3374, § 1. Amended by Stats.1976, c. 666, p. 1641, § 5; Stats.1980, c. 1113, p. 3582, § 4; Stats.1992, c. 651 (A.B.2999), § 1; Stats.1992, c. 1194 (A.B.1629), § 8, operative July 1, 1993.)*

Cross References

Adverse action defined for purposes of this Title, see Civil Code § 1785.3.
Consumer credit report defined for purposes of this Title, see Civil Code § 1785.3.
Consumer credit reporting agency defined for purposes of this Title, see Civil Code § 1785.3.
Consumer defined for purposes of this Title, see Civil Code § 1785.3.
Person defined for purposes of this Title, see Civil Code § 1785.3.
Similar provisions, see Civil Code § 1786.26.

§ 1785.18. Matters of public record; source; reports for employment purposes; prohibited information

(a) Each consumer credit reporting agency which compiles and reports items of information concerning consumers which are matters of public record, shall specify in any report containing public record information the source from which that information was obtained, including the particular court, if there be such, and the date that the information was initially reported or publicized.

(b) A consumer credit reporting agency which furnishes a consumer credit report for employment purposes, and which for that purpose compiles and reports items of information on consumers which are matters of public record and are likely to have an adverse effect upon a consumer's ability to obtain employment shall, in addition, maintain strict procedures designed to ensure that whenever public record information which is likely to have an adverse effect on a consumer's ability to obtain employment is reported it is complete and up to date. For purposes of this paragraph, items of public record relating to arrests, indictments, convictions, suits, tax liens, and outstanding judgments shall be considered up to date if the current public record status of the item at the time of the report is reported.

(c) No consumer credit reporting agency which furnishes a consumer credit report for employment purposes shall report information on the age, marital status, race, color, or creed of any consumer. *(Added by Stats.1975, c. 1271, p. 3375, § 1. Amended by Stats.1991, c. 971 (A.B.1102), § 1.)*

Cross References

Consumer credit report defined for purposes of this Title, see Civil Code § 1785.3.
Consumer credit reporting agency defined for purposes of this Title, see Civil Code § 1785.3.
Consumer defined for purposes of this Title, see Civil Code § 1785.3.
Employment purposes defined for purposes of this Title, see Civil Code § 1785.3.
Escrow agent rating service, compliance with provisions of this section, see Civil Code § 1785.28.
Inspection of public records, other exemptions from disclosure, see Government Code § 6276.12.
Item of information defined for purposes of this Title, see Civil Code § 1785.3.
Similar provisions, see Civil Code § 1786.28.

§ 1785.19. Civil penalties; improperly obtaining or misusing file data; costs; attorney fees

(a) In addition to any other remedy provided by law, a consumer may bring an action for a civil penalty, not to exceed two thousand five hundred dollars ($2,500), against any of the following:

(1) A person who knowingly and willfully obtains access to a file other than as provided in Section 1785.11.

(2) Any person who knowingly and willfully obtains data from a file other than as provided in Section 1785.11.

(3) A person who uses the data received from a file in a manner contrary to an agreement with the consumer credit reporting agency.

Such an action may also be brought by the person or entity responsible for the file accessed. This remedy is in addition to any other remedy which may exist.

(b) If a plaintiff prevails in an action under subdivision (a) he or she shall be awarded the civil penalty, costs, and reasonable attorney fees. *(Added by Stats.1990, c. 842 (A.B.2908), § 2.)*

Cross References

Consumer credit reporting agency defined for purposes of this Title, see Civil Code § 1785.3.
Consumer defined for purposes of this Title, see Civil Code § 1785.3.
File defined for purposes of this Title, see Civil Code § 1785.3.
Person defined for purposes of this Title, see Civil Code § 1785.3.

§ 1785.19.5. Procedures to prevent report or file data from being provided for marketing purposes or offers of credit

Every consumer credit reporting agency, upon written request and the furnishing of sufficient identification to identify the consumer and the subject file, shall create reasonable procedures to prevent a consumer credit report or information from a consumer's file from being provided to any third party for marketing purposes or for any offer of credit not requested by the consumer. This section does not apply to the use of information by a credit grantor for purposes related to an existing credit relationship. *(Added by Stats.1990, c. 842 (A.B.2908), § 3.)*

§ 1785.19.5 OBLIGATIONS

Cross References

Consumer credit report defined for purposes of this Title, see Civil Code § 1785.3.
Consumer credit reporting agency defined for purposes of this Title, see Civil Code § 1785.3.
Consumer defined for purposes of this Title, see Civil Code § 1785.3.
File defined for purposes of this Title, see Civil Code § 1785.3.

CHAPTER 3. REQUIREMENTS ON USERS OF CONSUMER CREDIT REPORTS

Section

1785.20. Adverse action based on consumer credit report information; notice and disclosure to consumer; denial of credit or insurance or increase in charge because of information from one other than agency; liability.

1785.20.1. Credit transactions not initiated by consumer; solicitation to consumer; required statement; prequalifying reports; consumer's consent.

1785.20.2. Loans to consumers; use of consumer credit score; information to be provided to consumer; notice and form.

1785.20.3. Consumer credit reports with approval of credit based on application for credit extension; consumer address error with respect to identity theft; verification safeguard; violations.

1785.20.4. Tenant evaluation; COVID–19 rental debt.

1785.20.5. Report for employment purposes; prior notice to person involved; contemporaneous copies for user and subject; denial of employment; identity of reporter; notice by user to consumer; liability.

1785.21. Contact of reporter by user at request of consumer; investigation of disputed item of information; report by reporter to user and consumer.

1785.22. Reselling report or information; disclosure to agency; requirements.

§ 1785.20. Adverse action based on consumer credit report information; notice and disclosure to consumer; denial of credit or insurance or increase in charge because of information from one other than agency; liability

(a) If any person takes any adverse action with respect to any consumer, and the adverse action is based, in whole or in part, on any information contained in a consumer credit report, that person shall do all of the following:

(1) Provide written notice of the adverse action to the consumer.

(2) Provide the consumer with the name, address, and telephone number of the consumer credit reporting agency which furnished the report to the person.

(3) Provide a statement that the credit grantor's decision to take adverse action was based in whole or in part upon information contained in a consumer credit report.

(4) Provide the consumer with a written notice of the following rights of the consumer:

(A) The right of the consumer to obtain within 60 days a free copy of the consumer's consumer credit report from the consumer credit reporting agency identified pursuant to paragraph (2) and from any other consumer credit reporting agency which compiles and maintains files on consumers on a nationwide basis.

(B) The right of the consumer under Section 1785.16 to dispute the accuracy or completeness of any information in a consumer credit report furnished by the consumer credit reporting agency.

(b) Whenever credit or insurance for personal, family, or household purposes involving a consumer is denied or the charge for such credit is increased either wholly or in part because of information obtained from a person other than a consumer credit reporting agency bearing upon consumer's credit worthiness or credit standing, the user of that information shall, within a reasonable period of time, and upon the consumer's written request for the reasons for that adverse action received within 60 days after learning of the adverse action, disclose the nature and substance of the information to the consumer. The user of the information shall clearly and accurately disclose to the consumer his or her right to make such a written request at the time the adverse action is communicated to the consumer.

(c) No person shall be held liable for any violation of this section if he or she shows by a preponderance of the evidence that at the time of the alleged violation he or she maintained reasonable procedures to assure compliance with this section.

(d) Nothing in this chapter shall excuse compliance with the requirements of Section 1787.2. (Added by Stats.1975, c. 1271, p. 3375, § 1. Amended by Stats.1980, c. 1113, p. 3582, § 5; Stats.1982, c. 1127, p. 4065, § 5; Stats.1992, c. 1194 (A.B.1629), § 9, operative July 1, 1993.)

Cross References

Adverse action defined for purposes of this Title, see Civil Code § 1785.3.
Consumer credit report defined for purposes of this Title, see Civil Code § 1785.3.
Consumer credit reporting agency defined for purposes of this Title, see Civil Code § 1785.3.
Consumer defined for purposes of this Title, see Civil Code § 1785.3.
File defined for purposes of this Title, see Civil Code § 1785.3.
Insurance Information and Privacy Protection Act, insurance institutions, agents, insurance support organizations or any insurance transaction subject to Act as exempt from this section, see Insurance Code § 791.01.
Person defined for purposes of this Title, see Civil Code § 1785.3.
Similar provisions, see Civil Code § 1786.40.

§ 1785.20.1. Credit transactions not initiated by consumer; solicitation to consumer; required statement; prequalifying reports; consumer's consent

(a) Except as provided in subdivision (b), any person who uses a consumer credit report in connection with any credit transaction not initiated by the consumer and which consists of a firm offer of credit shall provide with any solicitation made to the consumer a clear and conspicuous statement as to all of the following:

(1) Information contained in the consumer's prequalifying report was used in connection with the transaction.

(2) The consumer received the offer of credit, because the consumer satisfied the criteria for creditworthiness under which the consumer was selected for the offer.

(3) Where applicable, the credit may not be extended if, after the consumer responds to the offer, the consumer does

not meet the criteria used to select the consumer for the offer.

(4) The consumer has a right to prohibit use of information contained in the consumer's file with any consumer credit reporting agency in connection with any credit transaction that is not initiated by the consumer. The consumer may exercise this right by notifying the notification system or joint notification system established under subdivision (d) or (e) of Section 1785.11.

(b) Subdivision (a) does not apply to any person using a prequalifying report if all of the following conditions are met:

(1) The person using the prequalifying report is affiliated by common ownership or common corporate control with the person who procured the report.

(2) The person who procures the prequalifying report from the consumer credit reporting agency clearly and conspicuously discloses to the consumer to whom the report relates, before the prequalifying report is provided to the person who uses the report, that the prequalifying report might be provided to, and used by, persons affiliated in the manner specified in paragraph (1) with the person that procured the report.

(3) The consumer consents in writing to this provision and use of the prequalifying report.

(c) No person shall be denied credit on the basis of the consumer's refusal to provide consent pursuant to paragraph (3) of subdivision (b), unless that consent is necessary for the extension of credit, related to that transaction, by an affiliate. (Added by Stats.1992, c. 1194 (A.B.1629), § 9.5, operative July 1, 1993.)

Cross References

Consumer credit report defined for purposes of this Title, see Civil Code § 1785.3.
Consumer credit reporting agency defined for purposes of this Title, see Civil Code § 1785.3.
Consumer defined for purposes of this Title, see Civil Code § 1785.3.
Credit transaction that is not initiated by the consumer defined for purposes of this Title, see Civil Code § 1785.3.
File defined for purposes of this Title, see Civil Code § 1785.3.
Firm offer of credit defined for purposes of this Title, see Civil Code § 1785.3.
Person defined for purposes of this Title, see Civil Code § 1785.3.
Prequalifying report defined for purposes of this Title, see Civil Code § 1785.3.

§ 1785.20.2. Loans to consumers; use of consumer credit score; information to be provided to consumer; notice and form

Any person who makes or arranges loans and who uses a consumer credit score as defined in Section 1785.15.1 in connection with an application initiated or sought by a consumer for a closed end loan or establishment of an open end loan for a consumer purpose that is secured by one to four units of residential real property shall provide the following to the consumer as soon as reasonably practicable:

(a) A copy of the information identified in subdivision (a) of Section 1785.15.1 that was obtained from a credit reporting agency or was developed and used by the user of the information. In addition to the information provided to it by a third party that provided the credit score or scores, a lender is only required to provide the notice contained in subdivision (d).

(b) If a person who is subject to this section uses an automated underwriting system to underwrite a loan, that person may satisfy the obligation to provide a credit score by disclosing a credit score and associated key factors supplied by a consumer credit reporting agency. However, if a numerical credit score is generated by an automated underwriting system used by an enterprise, and that score is disclosed to the person, it shall be disclosed to the consumer consistent with subdivision (c). For purposes of this subdivision, the term "enterprise" shall have the meaning provided in paragraph (6) of Section 4502 of Title 12 of the United States Code.

(c) A person subject to the provisions of this section who uses a credit score other than a credit score provided by a consumer reporting agency may satisfy the obligation to provide a credit score by disclosing a credit score and associated key factors supplied by a consumer credit reporting agency.

(d) A copy of the following notice, which shall include the name, address, and telephone number of each credit bureau providing a credit score that was used:

NOTICE TO THE HOME LOAN APPLICANT

In connection with your application for a home loan, the lender must disclose to you the score that a credit bureau distributed to users and the lender used in connection with your home loan, and the key factors affecting your credit scores.

The credit score is a computer generated summary calculated at the time of the request and based on information a credit bureau or lender has on file. The scores are based on data about your credit history and payment patterns. Credit scores are important because they are used to assist the lender in determining whether you will obtain a loan. They may also be used to determine what interest rate you may be offered on the mortgage. Credit scores can change over time, depending on your conduct, how your credit history and payment patterns change, and how credit scoring technologies change.

Because the score is based on information in your credit history, it is very important that you review the credit-related information that is being furnished to make sure it is accurate. Credit records may vary from one company to another.

If you have questions about your credit score or the credit information that is furnished to you, contact the credit bureau at the address and telephone number provided with this notice, or contact the lender, if the lender developed or generated the credit score. The credit bureau plays no part in the decision to take any action on the loan application and is unable to provide you with specific reasons for the decision on a loan application.

If you have questions concerning the terms of the loan, contact the lender.

(e) This section shall not require any person to do the following:

§ 1785.20.2

(1) Explain the information provided pursuant to Section 1785.15.1.

(2) Disclose any information other than a credit score or key factor, as defined in Section 1785.15.1.

(3) Disclose any credit score or related information obtained by the user after a loan has closed.

(4) Provide more than one disclosure per loan transaction.

(5) Provide the disclosure required by this section when another person has made the disclosure to the consumer for that loan transaction.

(f) Any person's obligation pursuant to this section shall be limited solely to providing a copy of the information that was received from the consumer credit reporting agency. No person has liability under this section for the content of that information or for the omission of any information within the report provided by the consumer credit reporting agency.

(g) As used in this section, the term "person" does not include an "enterprise" as defined in paragraph (6) of Section 4502 of Title 12 of the United States Code. *(Added by Stats.2000, c. 978 (S.B.1607), § 6, operative July 1, 2001.)*

Cross References

Consumer credit reporting agency defined for purposes of this Title, see Civil Code § 1785.3.
Consumer defined for purposes of this Title, see Civil Code § 1785.3.
File defined for purposes of this Title, see Civil Code § 1785.3.
Person defined for purposes of this Title, see Civil Code § 1785.3.

§ 1785.20.3. Consumer credit reports with approval of credit based on application for credit extension; consumer address error with respect to identity theft; verification safeguard; violations

(a) Any person who uses a consumer credit report in connection with the approval of credit based on an application for an extension of credit, and who discovers that the consumer's first and last name, address, or social security number, on the credit application does not match, within a reasonable degree of certainty, the consumer's first and last name, address or addresses, or social security number listed, if any, on the consumer credit report, shall take reasonable steps to verify the accuracy of the consumer's first and last name, address, or social security number provided on the application to confirm that the extension of credit is not the result of identity theft, as defined in Section 1798.92.

(b) Any person who uses a consumer credit report in connection with the approval of credit based on an application for an extension of credit, and who has received notification pursuant to subdivision (k) of Section 1785.16 that the applicant has been a victim of identity theft, as defined in Section 1798.92, may not lend money or extend credit without taking reasonable steps to verify the consumer's identity and confirm that the application for an extension of credit is not the result of identity theft.

(c) Any consumer who suffers damages as a result of a violation of this section by any person may bring an action in a court of appropriate jurisdiction against that person to recover actual damages, court costs, attorney's fees, and punitive damages of not more than thirty thousand dollars ($30,000) for each violation, as the court deems proper.

(d) As used in this section, "identity theft" has the meaning given in subdivision (b) of Section 1798.92.

(e) For the purposes of this section, "extension of credit" does not include an increase in an existing open-end credit plan, as defined in Regulation Z of the Federal Reserve System (12 C.F.R. 226.2), or any change to or review of an existing credit account.

(f) If a consumer provides initial written notice to a creditor that he or she is a victim of identity theft, as defined in subdivision (d) of Section 1798.92, the creditor shall provide written notice to the consumer of his or her rights under subdivision (k) of Section 1785.16.

(g) The provisions of subdivisions (k) and (*l*) of Section 1785.16 do not apply to a consumer credit reporting agency that acts only as a reseller of credit information by assembling and merging information contained in the database of another consumer credit reporting agency or the databases of multiple consumer credit reporting agencies, and does not maintain a permanent database of credit information from which new credit reports are produced.

(h) This section does not apply if one of the addresses at issue is a United States Army or Air Force post office address or a United States Fleet post office address. *(Added by Stats.2001, c. 354 (A.B.655), § 5. Amended by Stats.2002, c. 1030 (A.B.1068), § 2, eff. Sept. 28, 2002; Stats.2003, c. 41 (A.B.1610), § 1.)*

Cross References

Consumer credit report defined for purposes of this Title, see Civil Code § 1785.3.
Consumer credit reporting agency defined for purposes of this Title, see Civil Code § 1785.3.
Consumer defined for purposes of this Title, see Civil Code § 1785.3.
Identity theft civil actions, see Civil Code § 1798.92 et seq.
Person defined for purposes of this Title, see Civil Code § 1785.3.

§ 1785.20.4. Tenant evaluation; COVID–19 rental debt

A housing provider, tenant screening company, or other entity that evaluates tenants on behalf of a housing provider shall not use an alleged COVID–19 rental debt, as defined in Section 1179.02 of the Code of Civil Procedure, as a negative factor for the purpose of evaluating a prospective housing application or as the basis for refusing to rent a dwelling unit to an otherwise qualified prospective tenant. *(Added by Stats.2021, c. 2 (S.B.91), § 2, eff. Jan. 29, 2021. Amended by Stats.2021, c. 5 (A.B.81), § 3, eff. Feb. 23, 2021.)*

§ 1785.20.5. Report for employment purposes; prior notice to person involved; contemporaneous copies for user and subject; denial of employment; identity of reporter; notice by user to consumer; liability

(a) Prior to requesting a consumer credit report for employment purposes, the user of the report shall provide written notice to the person involved. The notice shall inform the person that a report will be used, and shall identify the specific basis under subdivision (a) of Section 1024.5 of the Labor Code for use of the report. The notice shall also inform the person of the source of the report, and shall contain a box that the person may check off to receive a copy of the credit report. If the consumer indicates that he or she wishes to receive a copy of the report, the user shall request that a copy be provided to the person when the user requests its copy from the credit reporting agency. The report to the user and to the subject person shall be provided contemporaneously and at no charge to the subject person.

(b) Whenever employment involving a consumer is denied either wholly or partly because of information contained in a consumer credit report from a consumer credit reporting agency, the user of the consumer credit report shall so advise the consumer against whom the adverse action has been taken and supply the name and address or addresses of the consumer credit reporting agency making the report. No person shall be held liable for any violation of this section if he or she shows by a preponderance of the evidence that, at the time of the alleged violation, he or she maintained reasonable procedures to assure compliance with this section. *(Added by Stats.1976, c. 666, p. 1643, § 7.5. Amended by Stats.1991, c. 971 (A.B.1102), § 2; Stats.2011, c. 724 (A.B.22), § 1.)*

Cross References

Adverse action defined for purposes of this Title, see Civil Code § 1785.3.
Consumer credit report defined for purposes of this Title, see Civil Code § 1785.3.
Consumer credit reporting agency defined for purposes of this Title, see Civil Code § 1785.3.
Consumer defined for purposes of this Title, see Civil Code § 1785.3.
Employment purposes defined for purposes of this Title, see Civil Code § 1785.3.
Person defined for purposes of this Title, see Civil Code § 1785.3.

§ 1785.21. Contact of reporter by user at request of consumer; investigation of disputed item of information; report by reporter to user and consumer

(a) A user in its discretion may notify the consumer that upon request the user may contact the consumer reporting agency and request that the consumer reporting agency investigate the current status of an item or items of information contained in the consumer report if the consumer disputes the completeness or accuracy of an item or items of information as provided to the user.

(b) The consumer credit reporting agency may require identification from the user to insure the validity of the request and, in that regard, may require that the request be put in writing with proper identification.

(c) In the event that any such request is made and identification given in the form or manner demanded by the consumer credit reporting agency, such agency shall review the file of the consumer and report the current status of the disputed information to the user and the consumer by the most expeditious means possible.

(d) No user who furnishes information pursuant to this section shall be liable to any person for furnishing such information. *(Added by Stats.1976, c. 666, p. 1643, § 8.)*

Cross References

Consumer credit reporting agency defined for purposes of this Title, see Civil Code § 1785.3.
Consumer defined for purposes of this Title, see Civil Code § 1785.3.
File defined for purposes of this Title, see Civil Code § 1785.3.
Item of information defined for purposes of this Title, see Civil Code § 1785.3.
Person defined for purposes of this Title, see Civil Code § 1785.3.

§ 1785.22. Reselling report or information; disclosure to agency; requirements

(a) A person may not procure a consumer credit report for the purpose of reselling the report or any information therein unless the person discloses to the consumer credit reporting agency which issues the report the identity of the ultimate end user and each permissible purpose for which the report is furnished to the end user of the consumer credit report or information therein.

(b) A person that procures a consumer credit report for the purpose of reselling the report or any information therein shall do all of the following:

(1) Establish and comply with reasonable procedures designed to ensure that the consumer credit report or information is resold by the person only for a purpose for which the report may be furnished under this title. These procedures shall include all of the following:

(A) Identification of each prospective user of the resold consumer credit report or information.

(B) Certification of each purpose for which the consumer credit report or information will be used.

(C) Certification that the consumer credit report or information will be used for no other purpose.

(2) Before reselling the consumer credit report or information, the person shall make reasonable efforts to verify the identities and certifications made under paragraph (1). *(Added by Stats.1992, c. 1194 (A.B.1629), § 10, operative July 1, 1993.)*

Cross References

Consumer credit report defined for purposes of this Title, see Civil Code § 1785.3.
Consumer credit reporting agency defined for purposes of this Title, see Civil Code § 1785.3.
Consumer defined for purposes of this Title, see Civil Code § 1785.3.
Disclosure of information contained in agency files to consumers, limited exemptions from disclosure requirements for consumer credit reporting agencies subject to the provisions of this section, see Civil Code § 1785.10.
Person defined for purposes of this Title, see Civil Code § 1785.3.

CHAPTER 3.5. OBLIGATIONS OF FURNISHERS OF CREDIT INFORMATION

Section
1785.25. Incomplete or inaccurate information; knowledge; notification to agency; dispute as to completeness or accuracy; notice; closing of open-end credit account; delinquent accounts; investigation of dispute; liability of furnisher.
1785.26. Creditor; negative credit information; notification to consumer; form and service of notice; liability of creditor.

§ 1785.25. Incomplete or inaccurate information; knowledge; notification to agency; dispute as to completeness or accuracy; notice; closing of open-end credit account; delinquent accounts; investigation of dispute; liability of furnisher

(a) A person shall not furnish information on a specific transaction or experience to any consumer credit reporting

§ 1785.25

agency if the person knows or should know the information is incomplete or inaccurate.

(b) A person who (1) in the ordinary course of business regularly and on a routine basis furnishes information to one or more consumer credit reporting agencies about the person's own transactions or experiences with one or more consumers and (2) determines that information on a specific transaction or experience so provided to a consumer credit reporting agency is not complete or accurate, shall promptly notify the consumer credit reporting agency of that determination and provide to the consumer credit reporting agency any corrections to that information, or any additional information, that is necessary to make the information provided by the person to the consumer credit reporting agency complete and accurate.

(c) So long as the completeness or accuracy of any information on a specific transaction or experience furnished by any person to a consumer credit reporting agency is subject to a continuing dispute between the affected consumer and that person, the person may not furnish the information to any consumer credit reporting agency without also including a notice that the information is disputed by the consumer.

(d) A person who regularly furnishes information to a consumer credit reporting agency regarding a consumer who has an open-end credit account with that person, and which is closed by the consumer, shall notify the consumer credit reporting agency of the closure of that account by the consumer, in the information regularly furnished for the period in which the account is closed.

(e) A person who places a delinquent account for collection (internally or by referral to a third party), charges the delinquent account to profit or loss, or takes similar action, and subsequently furnishes information to a credit reporting agency regarding that action, shall include within the information furnished the approximate commencement date of the delinquency which gave rise to that action, unless that date was previously reported to the credit reporting agency. Nothing in this provision shall require that a delinquency must be reported to a credit reporting agency.

(f) Upon receiving notice of a dispute noticed pursuant to subdivision (a) of Section 1785.16 with regard to the completeness or accuracy of any information provided to a consumer credit reporting agency, the person that provided the information shall (1) complete an investigation with respect to the disputed information and report to the consumer credit reporting agency the results of that investigation before the end of the 30-business-day period beginning on the date the consumer credit reporting agency receives the notice of dispute from the consumer in accordance with subdivision (a) of Section 1785.16 and (2) review relevant information submitted to it.

(g) A person who furnishes information to a consumer credit reporting agency is liable for failure to comply with this section, unless the furnisher establishes by a preponderance of the evidence that, at the time of the failure to comply with this section, the furnisher maintained reasonable procedures to comply with those provisions. (Added by Stats.1992, c. 1194 (A.B.1629), § 11, operative July 1, 1993. Amended by Stats.1993, c. 285 (A.B.1340), § 8, eff. Aug. 2, 1993.)

Validity

This section is recognized as preempted by the federal Fair Credit Reporting Act, in the decision of Buraye v. Equifax, C.D.Cal.2008, 625 F.Supp.2d 894.

This section is recognized as preempted by the federal Fair Credit Reporting Act, in Howard v. Blue Ridge Bank, N.D.Cal.2005, 371 F.Supp.2d 1139.

The investigation provisions contained in subd. (f) of this section were held preempted in the decision of Carvalho v. Equifax Information Services, LLC, C.A.9 (Cal.)2010, 615 F.3d 1217, amended and superseded on denial of rehearing en banc 629 F.3d 876.

Cross References

Consumer credit reporting agency defined for purposes of this Title, see Civil Code § 1785.3.
Consumer defined for purposes of this Title, see Civil Code § 1785.3.
Consumer loans, instant loan checks and live checks, identity theft, see Financial Code § 22342.
Person defined for purposes of this Title, see Civil Code § 1785.3.

§ 1785.26. Creditor; negative credit information; notification to consumer; form and service of notice; liability of creditor

(a) As used in this section:

(1) "Creditor" includes an agent or assignee of a creditor, including an agent engaged in administering or collecting the creditor's accounts.

(2) "Negative credit information" means information concerning the credit history of a consumer that, because of the consumer's past delinquencies, late or irregular payment history, insolvency, or any form of default, would reasonably be expected to affect adversely the consumer's ability to obtain or maintain credit. "Negative credit information" does not include information or credit histories arising from a nonconsumer transaction or any other credit transaction outside the scope of this title, nor does it include inquiries about a consumer's credit record.

(b) A creditor may submit negative credit information concerning a consumer to a consumer credit reporting agency, only if the creditor notifies the consumer affected. After providing this notice, a creditor may submit additional information to a credit reporting agency respecting the same transaction or extension of credit that gave rise to the original negative credit information without providing additional notice.

(c) The notice shall be in writing and shall be delivered in person or mailed first class, postage prepaid, to the party's last known address, prior to or within 30 days after the transmission of the negative credit information.

(1) The notice may be part of any notice of default, billing statement, or other correspondence, and may be included as preprinted or standard form language in any of these from the creditor to the consumer.

(2) The notice is sufficient if it is in substantially the following form:

"As required by law, you are hereby notified that a negative credit report reflecting on your credit record may be submitted to a credit reporting agency if you fail to fulfill the terms of your credit obligations."

(3) The notice may, in the creditor's discretion, be more specific than the form given in paragraph (2). The notice may include, but shall not be limited to, particular information regarding an account or information respecting the approximate date on which the creditor submitted or intends to submit a negative credit report.

(4) The giving of notice by a creditor as provided in this subdivision does not create any requirement for the creditor to actually submit negative credit information to a consumer credit reporting agency. However, this section shall not be construed to authorize the use of notice as provided in this subdivision in violation of the federal Fair Debt Collection Practices Act (15 U.S.C., Sec. 1592 et seq.).

(d) A creditor is liable for failure to provide notice pursuant to this section, unless the creditor establishes, by a preponderance of the evidence, that at the time of that failure to give notice the creditor maintained reasonable procedures to comply with this section. *(Added by Stats.1992, c. 1194 (A.B.1629), § 11, operative July 1, 1993.)*

Cross References

Consumer credit reporting agency defined for purposes of this Title, see Civil Code § 1785.3.
Consumer defined for purposes of this Title, see Civil Code § 1785.3.
Consumer loans, instant loan checks and live checks, identity theft, see Financial Code § 22342.
Person defined for purposes of this Title, see Civil Code § 1785.3.

CHAPTER 3.6. ESCROW AGENT RATING SERVICE

Section
1785.28.   Definitions; compliance with provisions applicable to consumer credit agencies.
1785.28.6. Duration of chapter.

Repeal

For repeal of Chapter 3.6, see Civil Code § 1785.28.6.

§ 1785.28. Definitions; compliance with provisions applicable to consumer credit agencies

(a) For the purposes of this section, the following definitions shall apply:

(1) Escrow means any transaction in which one person, for the purpose of effecting the sale, transfer, encumbering, or leasing of real or personal property to another person, delivers any written instrument, money, evidence of title to real or personal property, or other thing of value to a third person to be held by that third person until the happening of a specified event or the performance of a prescribed condition, when it is then to be delivered by that third person to a grantee, grantor, promisee, promisor, obligee, obligor, bailee, bailor, or any agent or employee of any of the latter.

(2) An escrow agent is any of the following:

(A) A natural person who performs escrow services for an entity licensed pursuant to the Escrow Law contained in Division 6 (commencing with Section 17000) of the Financial Code.

(B) A natural person performing escrow services for a title insurer admitted pursuant to Article 3 (commencing with Section 699) of Chapter 1 of Part 2 of Division 1 of the Insurance Code or an underwritten title company licensed pursuant to Article 3.7 (commencing with Section 12389) of Chapter 1 of Part 6 of Division 2 of the Insurance Code.

(C) A natural person performing escrow services for a controlled escrow company, as defined in Section 12340.6 of the Insurance Code.

(D) A natural person licensed pursuant to Division 4 (commencing with Section 10000) of the Business and Professions Code, who performs escrow services, in accordance with Section 17006 of the Financial Code.

(3) An escrow agent rating service is a person or entity that prepares a report, for compensation or in expectation of compensation, for use by a creditor in evaluating the capacity of an escrow agent to perform escrow services in connection with an extension of credit. An escrow agent rating service does not include either of the following:

(A) A creditor or an employee of a creditor evaluating an escrow agent in connection with an extension of credit by that creditor.

(B) An entity described in paragraph (2) for which a natural person performs escrow services as an employee or an independent contractor.

(4) An escrow agent rating service shall be considered a reseller of credit information within the meaning of Section 1785.22 if it assembles and merges information contained in the database or databases maintained by a consumer credit reporting agency.

(5) "Consumer" also means escrow agent.

(b) An escrow agent rating service shall comply with and be subject to the following sections of this title applicable to a consumer credit reporting agency:

(1) Subdivision (a) of Section 1785.10.

(2) Subdivision (b) of Section 1785.10, limited to the obligation to advise a consumer of his or her right to a decoded written version of a file.

(3) Subdivision (d) of Section 1785.10.

(4) Paragraph (2) of subdivision (a) of Section 1785.11.

(5) Section 1785.13.

(6) Section 1785.14.

(7) Paragraph (1) of subdivision (a) of Section 1785.15, limited to the right to request and receive a decoded written version of the file.

(8) Section 1785.16.

(9) Section 1785.18.

(c) An escrow agent rating service that acts as a reseller of credit information as described in paragraph (4) of subdivision (a) shall comply with and be subject to Section 1785.22.

(d) An escrow agent rating service shall establish policies and procedures reasonably intended to safeguard from theft or misuse any personally identifiable information it obtains from an escrow agent.

(e) An escrow agent who suffers damages as a result of the failure of an escrow agent rating service to comply with

§ 1785.28

subdivision (b), (c), or (d) may bring an action in a court of competent jurisdiction pursuant to Section 1785.31 of the Civil Code.

(f) If an escrow agent rating service is also a consumer credit reporting agency as defined in subdivision (d) of Section 1785.3, nothing in this section shall be construed to suggest that an escrow agent reporting service that is also a consumer credit reporting agency is not otherwise required to comply with other provisions of this title applicable to consumer credit reporting agencies.

(g) Nothing in this section shall be construed to authorize a person, who was not otherwise legally authorized to perform escrow services prior to the effective date of this section, to legally perform escrow services.

(h) Nothing in this section is intended to alter the provisions of Section 17420 of the Financial Code, including the legal authority of an escrow agent to compensate an escrow agent rating service for a report prepared pursuant to paragraph (3) of subdivision (a). *(Added by Stats.2013, c. 380 (A.B.1169), § 1.)*

Repeal

For repeal of Chapter 3.6, see Civil Code § 1785.28.6.

§ 1785.28.6. Duration of chapter

This chapter shall remain in effect only until January 1, 2027, and as of that date is repealed. *(Added by Stats.2013, c. 380 (A.B.1169), § 1. Amended by Stats.2016, c. 135 (A.B. 2416), § 1, eff. Jan. 1, 2017; Stats.2021, c. 105 (S.B.360), § 1, eff. Jan. 1, 2022.)*

CHAPTER 4. REMEDIES

Section
1785.30. Consumer's written demand to correct; correction or deletion.
1785.31. Actions for actual and punitive damages; remedies available; class actions; court costs and attorney fees.
1785.32. Actions for defamation, invasion of privacy or negligence; malice or wilful intent to injure.
1785.33. Limitations on action; discovery of misrepresentation.
1785.34. Action pending under federal law; effect of federal judgment.
1785.35. Application of title.
1785.36. Public policy; waiver of rights.

§ 1785.30. Consumer's written demand to correct; correction or deletion

Upon notification of the results of a consumer credit reporting agency's reinvestigation pursuant to Section 1785.16, a consumer may make a written demand on any person furnishing information to the consumer credit reporting agency to correct any information that the consumer believes to be inaccurate. The person upon whom the written demand is made shall acknowledge the demand within 30 days. The consumer may require the consumer credit reporting agency to indicate on any subsequent reports issued during the dispute that the item or items of information are in dispute. If upon investigation the information is found to be inaccurate or incorrect, the consumer may require the consumer credit reporting agency to delete or correct the item or items of information within a reasonable time. If within 90 days the consumer credit reporting agency does not receive any information from the person requested to furnish the same or any communication relative to this information from this person, the consumer credit reporting agency shall delete the information from the report. *(Added by Stats.1976, c. 666, p. 1643, § 10. Amended by Stats.1997, c. 768 (A.B.156), § 3, operative July 1, 1998; Stats.2004, c. 183 (A.B.3082), § 31.)*

Cross References

Consumer credit reporting agency defined for purposes of this Title, see Civil Code § 1785.3.
Consumer defined for purposes of this Title, see Civil Code § 1785.3.
Item of information defined for purposes of this Title, see Civil Code § 1785.3.
Person defined for purposes of this Title, see Civil Code § 1785.3.

§ 1785.31. Actions for actual and punitive damages; remedies available; class actions; court costs and attorney fees

(a) Any consumer who suffers damages as a result of a violation of this title by any person may bring an action in a court of appropriate jurisdiction against that person to recover the following:

(1) In the case of a negligent violation, actual damages, including court costs, loss of wages, attorney's fees and, when applicable, pain and suffering.

(2) In the case of a willful violation:

(A) Actual damages as set forth in paragraph (1) above:

(B) Punitive damages of not less than one hundred dollars ($100) nor more than five thousand dollars ($5,000) for each violation as the court deems proper;

(C) Any other relief that the court deems proper.

(3) In the case of liability of a natural person for obtaining a consumer credit report under false pretenses or knowingly without a permissible purpose, an award of actual damages pursuant to paragraph (1) or subparagraph (A) of paragraph (2) shall be in an amount of not less than two thousand five hundred dollars ($2,500).

(b) Injunctive relief shall be available to any consumer aggrieved by a violation or a threatened violation of this title whether or not the consumer seeks any other remedy under this section.

(c) Notwithstanding any other provision of this section, any person who willfully violates any requirement imposed under this title may be liable for punitive damages in the case of a class action, in an amount that the court may allow. In determining the amount of award in any class action, the court shall consider among relevant factors the amount of any actual damages awarded, the frequency of the violations, the resources of the violator and the number of persons adversely affected.

(d) Except as provided in subdivision (e), the prevailing plaintiffs in any action commenced under this section shall be entitled to recover court costs and reasonable attorney's fees.

(e) If a plaintiff brings an action pursuant to this section against a debt collector, as defined in subdivision (c) of

Section 1788.2, and the basis for the action is related to the collection of a debt, whether issues relating to the debt collection are raised in the same or another proceeding, the debt collector shall be entitled to recover reasonable attorney's fees upon a finding by the court that the action was not brought in good faith.

(f) If a plaintiff only seeks and obtains injunctive relief to compel compliance with this title, court costs and attorney's fees shall be awarded pursuant to Section 1021.5 of the Code of Civil Procedure.

(g) Nothing in this section is intended to affect remedies available under Section 128.5 of the Code of Civil Procedure. *(Added by Stats.1976, c. 666, p. 1644, § 12. Amended by Stats.1992, c. 1194 (A.B.1629), § 12, operative July 1, 1993; Stats.1997, c. 768 (A.B.156), § 4, operative July 1, 1998; Stats.1999, c. 836 (A.B.758), § 1.)*

Validity

This section is recognized as preempted by the federal Fair Credit Reporting Act, in the decision of Buraye v. Equifax, C.D.Cal.2008, 625 F.Supp.2d 894.

This section is recognized as preempted by the federal Fair Credit Reporting Act, in Howard v. Blue Ridge Bank, N.D.Cal.2005, 371 F.Supp.2d 1139.

Cross References

Consumer credit report defined for purposes of this Title, see Civil Code § 1785.3.
Consumer defined for purposes of this Title, see Civil Code § 1785.3.
Person defined for purposes of this Title, see Civil Code § 1785.3.

§ 1785.32. Actions for defamation, invasion of privacy or negligence; malice or wilful intent to injure

Except as provided in Section 1785.31, no consumer may bring any action or proceeding in the nature of defamation, invasion of privacy or negligence with respect to the reporting of information against any consumer reporting agency, any user of information, or any person who furnishes information to a consumer reporting agency, based on information disclosed pursuant to Section 1785.10, 1785.15 or 1785.20 of this title, except as to false information furnished with malice or willful intent to injure such consumer. *(Formerly § 1785.31, added by Stats.1975, c. 1271, p. 3377, § 1. Renumbered § 1785.32 and amended by Stats.1976, c. 666, p. 1644, § 11.)*

Cross References

Consumer defined for purposes of this Title, see Civil Code § 1785.3.
Person defined for purposes of this Title, see Civil Code § 1785.3.

§ 1785.33. Limitations on action; discovery of misrepresentation

An action to enforce any liability created under this chapter may be brought in any appropriate court of competent jurisdiction within two years from the date the plaintiff knew of, or should have known of, the violation of this title, but not more than seven years from the earliest date on which liability could have arisen, except that where a defendant has materially and willfully misrepresented any information required under this chapter to be disclosed to a consumer and the information so misrepresented is material to the establishment of the defendant's liability to the consumer under this chapter, the action may be brought at any time within two years after the discovery by the consumer of the misrepresentation. *(Formerly § 1785.32, added by Stats.1975, c. 1271, p. 3377, § 1. Renumbered § 1785.33 and amended by Stats.1976, c. 666, p. 1645, § 13. Amended by Stats.1997, c. 768 (A.B.156), § 5, operative July 1, 1998.)*

Cross References

Consumer defined for purposes of this Title, see Civil Code § 1785.3.

§ 1785.34. Action pending under federal law; effect of federal judgment

(a) Any consumer credit reporting agency or user of information against whom an action brought pursuant to Section 1681n or 1681o of Title 15 of the United States Code is pending shall not be subject to suit for the same act or omission under Section 1785.31.

(b) The entry of a final judgment against a consumer credit reporting agency or user of information in an action brought pursuant to the provisions of Section 1681n or 1681o of Title 15 of the United States Code shall be a bar to the maintenance of any action based on the same act or omission which might be brought under this chapter. *(Formerly § 1785.33, added by Stats.1975, c. 1271, p. 3377, § 1. Renumbered § 1785.34 and amended by Stats.1976, c. 666, p. 1645, § 14.)*

Cross References

Consumer credit reporting agency defined for purposes of this Title, see Civil Code § 1785.3.
Consumer defined for purposes of this Title, see Civil Code § 1785.3.

§ 1785.35. Application of title

This title does not apply to any consumer credit report that by its terms is limited to disclosures from public records relating to land and land titles and does not apply to any person whose records and files are maintained for the primary purpose of reporting those portions of the public records that impart constructive notice under the law of matters relating to land and land titles. *(Formerly § 1785.34, added by Stats.1975, c. 1271, p. 3377, § 1. Renumbered § 1785.35 and amended by Stats.1976, c. 666, p. 1645, § 15. Amended by Stats.1999, c. 836 (A.B.758), § 2.)*

Cross References

Consumer credit report defined for purposes of this Title, see Civil Code § 1785.3.
Consumer defined for purposes of this Title, see Civil Code § 1785.3.
File defined for purposes of this Title, see Civil Code § 1785.3.
Person defined for purposes of this Title, see Civil Code § 1785.3.
Similar provisions, see Civil Code § 1786.54.

§ 1785.36. Public policy; waiver of rights

Any waiver of the provisions of this title is contrary to public policy, and is void and unenforceable. *(Added by Stats.2002, c. 815 (A.B.2331), § 8.)*

Title 1.61

COMMERCIAL CREDIT REPORTS

Section
1785.41. Application of Consumer Credit Reporting Agencies Act.

Section
1785.42. Definitions.
1785.43. Protection of identity of sources of information; copy to subject of report upon request; procedure for correction of inaccuracies.
1785.44. Public policy; waiver of rights.

§ 1785.41. Application of Consumer Credit Reporting Agencies Act

Consumer credit reporting is subject to the regulations of the Consumer Credit Reporting Agencies Act.[1] Commercial credit reports, which differ significantly, are not subject to that act. The circumstances, business practices, and reports themselves differ sufficiently to make it impractical to include commercial credit reports under the Consumer Credit Reporting Agencies Act. *(Added by Stats.1992, c. 101 (S.B.652), § 1.)*

[1] See Civil Code § 1785.1 et seq.

Cross References

Commercial credit report defined, see Civil Code § 1785.42.

§ 1785.42. Definitions

(a) "Commercial credit report" means any report provided to a commercial enterprise for a legitimate business purpose, relating to the financial status or payment habits of a commercial enterprise which is the subject of the report. It does not include a report subject to Title 1.6 (commencing with Section 1785.1), Title 1.6A (commencing with Section 1786), or a report prepared for commercial insurance underwriting, claims, or auditing purposes.

The term does not include (1) any report containing information related to transactions or experiences between the subject and the person making the report; (2) any authorization or approval of a specific extension of credit directly or indirectly by the issuer of a credit card or similar device; or (3) any report in which a person who has been requested by a third party to make a specific extension of credit directly or indirectly to the subject conveys its decision with respect to that request.

(b) "Commercial credit reporting agency" means any person who, for monetary fees, dues, or on a cooperative nonprofit basis, provides commercial credit reports to third parties.

(c) "Subject" means the commercial enterprise about which a commercial credit report has been compiled. *(Added by Stats.1992, c. 101 (S.B.652), § 1. Amended by Stats. 1993, c. 285 (A.B.1340), § 9, eff. Aug. 2, 1993.)*

§ 1785.43. Protection of identity of sources of information; copy to subject of report upon request; procedure for correction of inaccuracies

(a) Commercial credit reporting agencies may protect the identity of sources of information to be used in commercial credit reports.

(b) Upon the request of a representative of the subject of a report, the commercial credit reporting agency shall provide one printed copy of the subject's commercial credit report in a format routinely made available to third parties, at a cost no greater than the cost usually charged to third parties.

(c) In the event that the subject of a commercial credit report believes the report contains an inaccurate statement of fact, a representative of the subject of the report may, within 30 days of receipt of the report pursuant to subdivision (b), file with the commercial credit reporting agency a written summary statement of not more than 50 words identifying the particular statement of fact that is disputed, and indicating the nature of the disagreement with the statement in the report. Within 30 days of receipt of a subject's summary statement of disagreement, the commercial credit reporting agency shall either delete the disputed item of information from the report, or include in the report an indication that the subject's summary statement of disagreement will be provided upon request. *(Added by Stats.1992, c. 101 (S.B. 652), § 1.)*

Cross References

Commercial credit report defined, see Civil Code § 1785.42.
Commercial credit reporting agency defined, see Civil Code § 1785.42.
Subject defined, see Civil Code § 1785.42.

§ 1785.44. Public policy; waiver of rights

Any waiver of the provisions of this title is contrary to public policy, and is void and unenforceable. *(Added by Stats.2002, c. 815 (A.B.2331), § 9.)*

Title 1.6A

INVESTIGATIVE CONSUMER REPORTING AGENCIES

Article	Section
1. General Provisions	1786
2. Obligations of Investigative Consumer Reporting Agencies	1786.10
3. Requirements on Users of Investigative Consumer Reports [Repealed]	
4. Remedies	1786.50

Cross References

Consumer Credit Reporting Agencies Act, see Civil Code § 1785.1 et seq.
Credit Services Act, see Civil Code § 1789.10.
Fair debt collection practices, see Civil Code § 1788 et seq.

ARTICLE 1. GENERAL PROVISIONS

Section
1786. Legislative findings and declarations.
1786.1. Short title.
1786.2. Definitions.

§ 1786. Legislative findings and declarations

The Legislature finds and declares as follows:

(a) Investigative consumer reporting agencies have assumed a vital role in collecting, assembling, evaluating, compiling, reporting, transmitting, transferring, or communicating information on consumers for employment and insurance purposes, and for purposes relating to the hiring of dwelling units, subpoenas and court orders, licensure, and other lawful purposes.

(b) There is a need to insure that investigative consumer reporting agencies exercise their grave responsibilities with fairness, impartiality, and a respect for the consumer's right to privacy.

(c) The crime of identity theft in this new computer era has exploded to become the fastest growing white collar crime in America.

(d) The unique nature of this crime means it can often go undetected for years without the victim being aware his identity has been misused.

(e) Because notice of identity theft is critical before the victim can take steps to stop and prosecute this crime, consumers are best protected if they are automatically given copies of any investigative consumer reports made on them.

(f) It is the purpose of this title to require that investigative consumer reporting agencies adopt reasonable procedures for meeting the needs of commerce for employment, insurance information, and information relating to the hiring of dwelling units in a manner which is fair and equitable to the consumer, with regard to the confidentiality, accuracy, relevancy, and proper utilization of the information in accordance with the requirements of this title.

(g) The Legislature hereby intends to regulate investigative consumer reporting agencies pursuant to this title in a manner which will best protect the interests of the people of the State of California. *(Added by Stats.1975, c. 1272, p. 3378, § 1. Amended by Stats.1982, c. 1127, p. 4065, § 6; Stats.2001, c. 354 (A.B.655), § 6.)*

Cross References

Consumer defined for purposes of this Title, see Civil Code § 1786.2.
Identity theft civil actions, see Civil Code § 1798.92 et seq.
Investigative consumer report defined for purposes of this Title, see Civil Code § 1786.2.
Investigative consumer reporting agency defined for purposes of this Title, see Civil Code § 1786.2.
Personal information obtained regarding consumer in lieu of using services of an investigative consumer reporting agency, disclosure, see Civil Code § 1786.53.

§ 1786.1. Short title

This title may be referred to as the Investigative Consumer Reporting Agencies Act. *(Added by Stats.1975, c. 1272, p. 3378, § 1.)*

Cross References

Consumer defined for purposes of this Title, see Civil Code § 1786.2.
Investigative consumer reporting agency defined for purposes of this Title, see Civil Code § 1786.2.

§ 1786.2. Definitions

The following terms as used in this title have the meaning expressed in this section:

(a) The term "person" means any individual, partnership, corporation, limited liability company, trust, estate, cooperative, association, government or governmental subdivision or agency, or other entity. The term "person" as used in this title shall not be construed to require duplicative reporting by any individual, corporation, trust, estate, cooperative, association, government, or governmental subdivision or agency, or other entity involved in the same transaction.

(b) The term "consumer" means a natural individual who has made application to a person for employment purposes, for insurance for personal, family, or household purposes, or the hiring of a dwelling unit, as defined in subdivision (c) of Section 1940.

(c) The term "investigative consumer report" means a consumer report in which information on a consumer's character, general reputation, personal characteristics, or mode of living is obtained through any means. The term does not include a consumer report or other compilation of information that is limited to specific factual information relating to a consumer's credit record or manner of obtaining credit obtained directly from a creditor of the consumer or from a consumer reporting agency when that information was obtained directly from a potential or existing creditor of the consumer or from the consumer. Notwithstanding the foregoing, for transactions between investigative consumer reporting agencies and insurance institutions, agents, or insurance-support organizations subject to Article 6.6 (commencing with Section 791) of Chapter 1 of Part 2 of Division 1 of the Insurance Code, the term "investigative consumer report" shall have the meaning set forth in Section 791.02 of the Insurance Code.

(d) The term "investigative consumer reporting agency" means any person who, for monetary fees or dues, engages in whole or in part in the practice of collecting, assembling, evaluating, compiling, reporting, transmitting, transferring, or communicating information concerning consumers for the purposes of furnishing investigative consumer reports to third parties, but does not include any governmental agency whose records are maintained primarily for traffic safety, law enforcement, or licensing purposes, or any licensed insurance agent, insurance broker, or solicitor, insurer, or life insurance agent.

(e) The term "file," when used in connection with information on any consumer, means all of the information on that consumer recorded and retained by an investigative consumer reporting agency regardless of how the information is stored.

(f) The term "employment purposes," when used in connection with an investigative consumer report, means a report used for the purpose of evaluating a consumer for employment, promotion, reassignment, or retention as an employee.

(g) The term "medical information" means information on a person's medical history or condition obtained directly or indirectly from a licensed physician, medical practitioner, hospital, clinic, or other medical or medically related facility. *(Added by Stats.1975, c. 1272, p. 3378, § 1. Amended by Stats.1976, c. 1150, p. 5209, § 1; Stats.1982, c. 1127, p. 4066, § 7; Stats.1994, c. 1010 (S.B.2053), § 36; Stats.1998, c. 988 (S.B.1454), § 1; Stats.2001, c. 354 (A.B.655), § 7; Stats.2013, c. 444 (S.B.138), § 6.)*

ARTICLE 2. OBLIGATIONS OF INVESTIGATIVE CONSUMER REPORTING AGENCIES

Section
1786.10. Inspection of files by consumer; availability; sources; discovery; identification of recipients; disclosure.

OBLIGATIONS

Section
1786.11. Availability of report to consumer.
1786.12. Furnishing consumer report; circumstances.
1786.14. Report to governmental agency.
1786.16. Procurement or preparation of report; conditions; insurance; employment; dwelling unit hiring; disclosure of nature and scope of investigation.
1786.18. Items of information prohibited.
1786.20. Agency reporting procedures; records; identity of user and uses to be made of reports.
1786.22. Supplying files and information; time; methods.
1786.24. Disputes as to completeness and accuracy of file; reinvestigation; notice to sources; contents; frivolous or irrelevant dispute; deletion and reinsertion of information; notice to consumer; statement of dispute.
1786.26. Allowable fees charged to consumer by an investigative consumer reporting agency for making disclosures to consumer; other disclosures without charge.
1786.28. Matters of public record; source; reports for employment purposes.
1786.29. Notices to be provided by investigative consumer-reporting agency.
1786.30. Subsequent reports; verification.
1786.40. Consumer insurance request denied; notice to consumer of adverse action.

§ 1786.10. Inspection of files by consumer; availability; sources; discovery; identification of recipients; disclosure

(a) Every investigative consumer reporting agency shall, upon request and proper identification of any consumer, allow the consumer to visually inspect all files maintained regarding the consumer at the time of the request.

(b)(1) All items of information shall be available for inspection, except that the sources of information, other than public records and records from databases available for sale, acquired solely for use in preparing an investigative consumer report and actually used for no other purpose need not be disclosed. However, if an action is brought under this title, those sources shall be available to the consumer under appropriate discovery procedures in the court in which the action is brought.

(2) This title shall not be interpreted to mean that investigative consumer reporting agencies are required to divulge to consumers the sources of investigative consumer reports, except in appropriate discovery procedures as outlined in this title.

(c) The investigative consumer reporting agency shall also identify the recipients of any investigative consumer report on the consumer that the investigative consumer reporting agency has furnished for either of the following purposes:

(1) For employment or insurance purposes within the three-year period preceding the request.

(2) For any other purpose within the three-year period preceding the request.

(d) The identification of a recipient under subdivision (c) shall include the name of the recipient or, if applicable, the trade name (written in full) under which the recipient conducts business and, upon request of the consumer, the address and telephone number of the recipient.

(e) The investigative consumer reporting agency shall also disclose the dates, original payees, and amounts of any checks or charges upon which is based any adverse characterization of the consumer, included in the file at the time of the disclosure. *(Added by Stats.1975, c. 1272, p. 3379, § 1. Amended by Stats.1998, c. 988 (S.B.1454), § 2; Stats.2001, c. 354 (A.B.655), § 8; Stats.2006, c. 538 (S.B.1852), § 45.)*

Cross References

Consumer defined for purposes of this Title, see Civil Code § 1786.2.
File defined for purposes of this Title, see Civil Code § 1786.2.
Investigative consumer report defined for purposes of this Title, see Civil Code § 1786.2.
Investigative consumer reporting agency defined for purposes of this Title, see Civil Code § 1786.2.

§ 1786.11. Availability of report to consumer

Every investigative consumer reporting agency that provides an investigative consumer report to a person other than the consumer shall make a copy of that report available, upon request and proper identification, to the consumer for at least two years after the date that the report is provided to the other person. *(Added by Stats.1998, c. 988 (S.B.1454), § 3. Amended by Stats.2001, c. 354 (A.B.655), § 9; Stats.2002, c. 1029 (A.B.2868), § 3, eff. Sept. 28, 2002.)*

Cross References

Consumer defined for purposes of this Title, see Civil Code § 1786.2.
Investigative consumer report defined for purposes of this Title, see Civil Code § 1786.2.
Investigative consumer reporting agency defined for purposes of this Title, see Civil Code § 1786.2.
Person defined for purposes of this Title, see Civil Code § 1786.2.

§ 1786.12. Furnishing consumer report; circumstances

An investigative consumer reporting agency shall only furnish an investigative consumer report under the following circumstances:

(a) In response to the order of a court having jurisdiction to issue the order.

(b) In compliance with a lawful subpoena issued by a court of competent jurisdiction.

(c) In accordance with the written instructions of the consumer to whom it relates.

(d) To a person that it has reason to believe:

(1) Intends to use the information for employment purposes; or

(2) Intends to use the information serving as a factor in determining a consumer's eligibility for insurance or the rate for any insurance; or

(3) Intends to use the information in connection with a determination of the consumer's eligibility for a license or other benefit granted by a governmental instrumentality required by law to consider the applicant's financial responsibility or status; or

(4) Intends to use the information in connection with an order of a court of competent jurisdiction to provide support where the imposition or enforcement of the order involves the consumer; or

(5) Intends to use the information in connection with the hiring of a dwelling unit, as defined in subdivision (c) of Section 1940.

(e) An investigative consumer reporting agency shall not prepare or furnish an investigative consumer report to a person described in subdivision (d) unless the agency has received the certification under paragraph (4) of subdivision (a) of Section 1786.16 from the person requesting the report.

(f) An investigative consumer reporting agency shall not furnish an investigative consumer report to a person described in subdivision (d) if that report contains medical information about a consumer, unless the consumer consents to the furnishing of the report. *(Added by Stats.1975, c. 1272, p. 3380, § 1. Amended by Stats.1976, c. 1150, p. 5210, § 2; Stats.1982, c. 1127, p. 4067, § 8; Stats.1998, c. 988 (S.B.1454), § 4.)*

Cross References

Consumer defined for purposes of this Title, see Civil Code § 1786.2.
Employment purposes defined for purposes of this Title, see Civil Code § 1786.2.
Inspection of public records, other exemptions from disclosure, see Government Code § 6276.26.
Investigative consumer report defined for purposes of this Title, see Civil Code § 1786.2.
Investigative consumer reporting agency defined for purposes of this Title, see Civil Code § 1786.2.
Medical information defined for purposes of this Title, see Civil Code § 1786.2.
Person defined for purposes of this Title, see Civil Code § 1786.2.

§ 1786.14. Report to governmental agency

Notwithstanding the provisions of Section 1786.12 an investigative consumer reporting agency may furnish to a governmental agency a consumer's name, address, former address, places of employment, or former places of employment. *(Added by Stats.1975, c. 1272, p. 3380, § 1.)*

Cross References

Consumer defined for purposes of this Title, see Civil Code § 1786.2.
Investigative consumer reporting agency defined for purposes of this Title, see Civil Code § 1786.2.

§ 1786.16. Procurement or preparation of report; conditions; insurance; employment; dwelling unit hiring; disclosure of nature and scope of investigation

(a) Any person described in subdivision (d) of Section 1786.12 shall not procure or cause to be prepared an investigative consumer report unless the following applicable conditions are met:

(1) If an investigative consumer report is sought in connection with the underwriting of insurance, it shall be clearly and accurately disclosed in writing at the time the application form, medical form, binder, or similar document is signed by the consumer that an investigative consumer report regarding the consumer's character, general reputation, personal characteristics, and mode of living may be made. If no signed application form, medical form, binder, or similar document is involved in the underwriting transaction, the disclosure shall be made to the consumer in writing and mailed or otherwise delivered to the consumer not later than three days after the report was first requested. The disclosure shall include the name and address of any investigative consumer reporting agency conducting an investigation, plus the nature and scope of the investigation requested, and a summary of the provisions of Section 1786.22.

(2) If, at any time, an investigative consumer report is sought for employment purposes other than suspicion of wrongdoing or misconduct by the subject of the investigation, the person seeking the investigative consumer report may procure the report, or cause the report to be made, only if all of the following apply:

(A) The person procuring or causing the report to be made has a permissible purpose, as defined in Section 1786.12.

(B) The person procuring or causing the report to be made provides a clear and conspicuous disclosure in writing to the consumer at any time before the report is procured or caused to be made in a document that consists solely of the disclosure, that:

(i) An investigative consumer report may be obtained.

(ii) The permissible purpose of the report is identified.

(iii) The disclosure may include information on the consumer's character, general reputation, personal characteristics, and mode of living.

(iv) Identifies the name, address, and telephone number of the investigative consumer reporting agency conducting the investigation.

(v) Notifies the consumer in writing of the nature and scope of the investigation requested, including a summary of the provisions of Section 1786.22.

(vi) Notifies the consumer of the Internet Web site address of the investigative consumer reporting agency identified in clause (iv), or, if the agency has no Internet Web site address, the telephone number of the agency, where the consumer may find information about the investigative reporting agency's privacy practices, including whether the consumer's personal information will be sent outside the United States or its territories and information that complies with subdivision (d) of Section 1786.20. This clause shall become operative on January 1, 2012.

(C) The consumer has authorized in writing the procurement of the report.

(3) If an investigative consumer report is sought in connection with the hiring of a dwelling unit, as defined in subdivision (c) of Section 1940, the person procuring or causing the request to be made shall, not later than three days after the date on which the report was first requested, notify the consumer in writing that an investigative consumer report will be made regarding the consumer's character, general reputation, personal characteristics, and mode of living. The notification shall also include the name and address of the investigative consumer reporting agency that will prepare the report and a summary of the provisions of Section 1786.22.

(4) The person procuring or causing the request to be made shall certify to the investigative consumer reporting agency that the person has made the applicable disclosures to the consumer required by this subdivision and that the person will comply with subdivision (b).

§ 1786.16

(5) The person procuring the report or causing it to be prepared agrees to provide a copy of the report to the subject of the investigation, as provided in subdivision (b).

(b) Any person described in subdivision (d) of Section 1786.12 who requests an investigative consumer report, in accordance with subdivision (a) regarding that consumer, shall do the following:

(1) Provide the consumer a means by which the consumer may indicate on a written form, by means of a box to check, that the consumer wishes to receive a copy of any report that is prepared. If the consumer wishes to receive a copy of the report, the recipient of the report shall send a copy of the report to the consumer within three business days of the date that the report is provided to the recipient, who may contract with any other entity to send a copy to the consumer. The notice to request the report may be contained on either the disclosure form, as required by subdivision (a), or a separate consent form. The copy of the report shall contain the name, address, and telephone number of the person who issued the report and how to contact them.

(2) Comply with Section 1786.40, if the taking of adverse action is a consideration.

(c) Subdivisions (a) and (b) do not apply to an investigative consumer report procured or caused to be prepared by an employer, if the report is sought for employment purposes due to suspicion held by an employer of wrongdoing or misconduct by the subject of the investigation.

(d) Those persons described in subdivision (d) of Section 1786.12 constitute the sole and exclusive class of persons who may cause an investigative consumer report to be prepared. (Added by Stats.1975, c. 1272, p. 3380, § 1. Amended by Stats.1976, c. 1150, p. 5210, § 3; Stats.1982, c. 1127, p. 4067, § 9; Stats.1998, c. 988 (S.B.1454), § 5; Stats.2001, c. 354 (A.B.655), § 10; Stats.2002, c. 1030 (A.B.1068), § 3, eff. Sept. 28, 2002; Stats.2010, c. 481 (S.B.909), § 1.)

Cross References

Consumer defined for purposes of this Title, see Civil Code § 1786.2.
Employment purposes defined for purposes of this Title, see Civil Code § 1786.2.
Identity theft civil actions, see Civil Code § 1798.92 et seq.
Investigative consumer report defined for purposes of this Title, see Civil Code § 1786.2.
Investigative consumer reporting agency defined for purposes of this Title, see Civil Code § 1786.2.
Person defined for purposes of this Title, see Civil Code § 1786.2.

§ 1786.18. Items of information prohibited

(a) Except as authorized under subdivision (b), an investigative consumer reporting agency may not make or furnish any investigative consumer report containing any of the following items of information:

(1) Bankruptcies that, from the date of the order for relief, antedate the report by more than 10 years.

(2) Suits that, from the date of filing, and satisfied judgments that, from the date of entry, antedate the report by more than seven years.

(3) Unsatisfied judgments that, from the date of entry, antedate the report by more than seven years.

(4) Unlawful detainer actions where the defendant was the prevailing party or where the action is resolved by settlement agreement.

(5) Paid tax liens that, from the date of payment, antedate the report by more than seven years.

(6) Accounts placed for collection or charged to profit and loss that antedate the report by more than seven years.

(7) Records of arrest, indictment, information, misdemeanor complaint, or conviction of a crime that, from the date of disposition, release, or parole, antedate the report by more than seven years. These items of information shall no longer be reported if at any time it is learned that, in the case of a conviction, a full pardon has been granted or, in the case of an arrest, indictment, information, or misdemeanor complaint, a conviction did not result; except that records of arrest, indictment, information, or misdemeanor complaints may be reported pending pronouncement of judgment on the particular subject matter of those records.

(8) Any other adverse information that antedates the report by more than seven years.

(b) The provisions of subdivision (a) are not applicable in either of the following circumstances:

(1) If the investigative consumer report is to be used in the underwriting of life insurance involving, or that may reasonably be expected to involve, an amount of two hundred fifty thousand dollars ($250,000) or more.

(2) If the investigative consumer report is to be used by an employer who is explicitly required by a governmental regulatory agency to check for records that are prohibited by subdivision (a) when the employer is reviewing a consumer's qualification for employment.

(c) Except as otherwise provided in Section 1786.28, an investigative consumer reporting agency shall not furnish an investigative consumer report that includes information that is a matter of public record and that relates to an arrest, indictment, conviction, civil judicial action, tax lien, or outstanding judgment, unless the agency has verified the accuracy of the information during the 30–day period ending on the date on which the report is furnished.

(d) An investigative consumer reporting agency shall not prepare or furnish an investigative consumer report on a consumer that contains information that is adverse to the interest of the consumer and that is obtained through a personal interview with a neighbor, friend, or associate of the consumer or with another person with whom the consumer is acquainted or who has knowledge of the item of information, unless either (1) the investigative consumer reporting agency has followed reasonable procedures to obtain confirmation of the information, from an additional source that has independent and direct knowledge of the information, or (2) the person interviewed is the best possible source of the information. (Added by Stats.1975, c. 1272, p. 3381, § 1. Amended by Stats.1982, c. 1127, p. 4068, § 10; Stats.1991, c. 965 (A.B.1796), § 2; Stats.1998, c. 988 (S.B.1454), § 6; Stats. 2001, c. 354 (A.B.655), § 11; Stats.2002, c. 1029 (A.B.2868), § 4, eff. Sept. 28, 2002; Stats.2009, c. 500 (A.B.1059), § 11.)

Cross References

Consumer defined for purposes of this Title, see Civil Code § 1786.2.

Investigative consumer report defined for purposes of this Title, see Civil Code § 1786.2.
Investigative consumer reporting agency defined for purposes of this Title, see Civil Code § 1786.2.
Misdemeanors, definition and penalties, see Penal Code §§ 17, 19, 19.2.
Person defined for purposes of this Title, see Civil Code § 1786.2.

§ 1786.20. Agency reporting procedures; records; identity of user and uses to be made of reports

(a) An investigative consumer reporting agency shall maintain reasonable procedures designed to avoid violations of Section 1786.18 and to limit furnishing of investigative consumer reports for the purposes listed under Section 1786.12. These procedures shall require that prospective users of the information identify themselves, certify the purposes for which the information is sought and that the information will be used for no other purposes, and make the certifications described in paragraph (4) of subdivision (a) of Section 1786.16. From the effective date of this title, the investigative consumer reporting agency shall keep a record of the purposes for which information is sought, as stated by the user. The investigative consumer reporting agency may assume that the purpose for which a user seeks information remains the same as that which a user has previously stated. The investigative consumer reporting agency shall inform the user that the user is obligated to notify the agency of any change in the purpose for which information will be used. An investigative consumer reporting agency shall make a reasonable effort to verify the identity of a new prospective user and the uses certified by the prospective user prior to furnishing the user any investigative consumer reports. An investigative consumer reporting agency may not furnish an investigative consumer report to a person unless it has a written agreement that the investigative consumer reports will be used by that person only for purposes listed in Section 1786.12.

(b) Whenever an investigative consumer reporting agency prepares an investigative consumer report, it shall follow reasonable procedures to assure maximum possible accuracy of the information concerning the individual about whom the report relates. An investigative consumer reporting agency shall retain the investigative consumer report for two years after the report is provided.

(c) An investigative consumer reporting agency may not make an inquiry for the purpose of preparing an investigative consumer report on a consumer for employment purposes if the making of the inquiry by an employer or prospective employer of the consumer would violate applicable federal or state equal employment opportunity law or regulation.

(d)(1) An investigative consumer reporting agency doing business in this state shall conspicuously post, as defined in subdivision (b) of Section 22577 of the Business and Professions Code, on its primary Internet Web site information describing its privacy practices with respect to its preparation and processing of investigative consumer reports. If the investigative consumer reporting agency does not have an Internet Web site, it shall, upon request, mail a written copy of the privacy statement to consumers. The privacy statement shall conspicuously include, but not be limited to, both of the following:

(A) A statement entitled "Personal Information Disclosure: United States or Overseas," that indicates whether the personal information will be transferred to third parties outside the United States or its territories.

(B) A separate section that includes the name, mailing address, e-mail address, and telephone number of the investigative consumer reporting agency representatives who can assist a consumer with additional information regarding the investigative consumer reporting agency's privacy practices or policies in the event of a compromise of his or her information.

(2) For purposes of this subdivision, "third party" shall include, but not be limited to, a contractor, foreign affiliate, wholly owned entity, or an employee of the investigative consumer reporting agency.

(e) An investigative consumer reporting agency shall be liable to a consumer who is the subject of a report if the consumer is harmed by any unauthorized access of the consumer's personally identifiable information, act, or omission that occurs outside the United States or its territories as a result of the investigative consumer reporting agency negligently preparing or processing an investigative consumer report, or portion thereof, outside of the United States or its territories. Liability shall be in an amount equal to the sum of (1) any actual damages sustained by the consumer as a result of the unauthorized access, and (2) in the case of any successful action to enforce any liability under this section, the costs of the action together with reasonable attorney's fees, as determined by the court. *(Added by Stats.1975, c. 1272, p. 3381, § 1. Amended by Stats.1998, c. 988 (S.B.1454), § 7; Stats.2001, c. 354 (A.B.655), § 12; Stats.2002, c. 1029 (A.B.2868), § 5, eff. Sept. 28, 2002; Stats.2003, c. 146 (A.B.1399), § 1; Stats.2010, c. 481 (S.B.909), § 2.)*

Cross References

Consumer defined for purposes of this Title, see Civil Code § 1786.2.
Employment purposes defined for purposes of this Title, see Civil Code § 1786.2.
Identity theft civil actions, see Civil Code § 1798.92 et seq.
Investigative consumer report defined for purposes of this Title, see Civil Code § 1786.2.
Investigative consumer reporting agency defined for purposes of this Title, see Civil Code § 1786.2.
Liability of reporter or user to consumer, see Civil Code § 1786.50.
Person defined for purposes of this Title, see Civil Code § 1786.2.

§ 1786.22. Supplying files and information; time; methods

(a) An investigative consumer reporting agency shall supply files and information required under Section 1786.10 during normal business hours and on reasonable notice.

(b) Files maintained on a consumer shall be made available for the consumer's visual inspection, as follows:

(1) In person, if he appears in person and furnishes proper identification. A copy of his file shall also be available to the consumer for a fee not to exceed the actual costs of duplication services provided.

(2) By certified mail, if he makes a written request, with proper identification, for copies to be sent to a specified addressee. Investigative consumer reporting agencies complying with requests for certified mailings under this section shall not be liable for disclosures to third parties caused by

§ 1786.22

mishandling of mail after such mailings leave the investigative consumer reporting agencies.

(3) A summary of all information contained in files on a consumer and required to be provided by Section 1786.10 shall be provided by telephone, if the consumer has made a written request, with proper identification for telephone disclosure, and the toll charge, if any, for the telephone call is prepaid by or charged directly to the consumer.

(c) The term "proper identification" as used in subdivision (b) shall mean that information generally deemed sufficient to identify a person. Such information includes documents such as a valid driver's license, social security account number, military identification card, and credit cards. Only if the consumer is unable to reasonably identify himself with the information described above, may an investigative consumer reporting agency require additional information concerning the consumer's employment and personal or family history in order to verify his identity.

(d) The investigative consumer reporting agency shall provide trained personnel to explain to the consumer any information furnished him pursuant to Section 1786.10.

(e) The investigative consumer reporting agency shall provide a written explanation of any coded information contained in files maintained on a consumer. This written explanation shall be distributed whenever a file is provided to a consumer for visual inspection as required under Section 1786.22.

(f) The consumer shall be permitted to be accompanied by one other person of his choosing, who shall furnish reasonable identification. An investigative consumer reporting agency may require the consumer to furnish a written statement granting permission to the consumer reporting agency to discuss the consumer's file in such person's presence. (Added by Stats.1975, c. 1272, p. 3382, § 1. Amended by Stats.1976, c. 666, p. 1645, § 16.)

Cross References

Consumer defined for purposes of this Title, see Civil Code § 1786.2.
File defined for purposes of this Title, see Civil Code § 1786.2.
Investigative consumer reporting agency defined for purposes of this Title, see Civil Code § 1786.2.
Person defined for purposes of this Title, see Civil Code § 1786.2.

§ 1786.24. Disputes as to completeness and accuracy of file; reinvestigation; notice to sources; contents; frivolous or irrelevant dispute; deletion and reinsertion of information; notice to consumer; statement of dispute

(a) If the completeness or accuracy of any item of information contained in his or her file is disputed by a consumer, and the dispute is conveyed directly to the investigative consumer reporting agency by the consumer, the investigative consumer reporting agency shall, without charge, reinvestigate and record the current status of the disputed information or delete the item from the file in accordance with subdivision (c), before the end of the 30-day period beginning on the date on which the agency receives the notice of the dispute from the consumer.

(b) The agency shall notify any person who provided information in dispute at the address and in the manner specified by that person. The notice shall include all relevant information regarding the dispute that the investigative consumer reporting agency has received from the consumer. The agency shall also promptly provide to the person who provided the information in dispute all relevant information regarding the dispute that is received by the agency from the consumer during the reinvestigation.

(c) In conducting a reinvestigation, the investigative consumer reporting agency shall review and consider all relevant information submitted by the consumer with respect to the disputed item of information.

(d) Notwithstanding subdivision (a), an investigative consumer reporting agency may terminate a reinvestigation of information disputed by a consumer if the investigative consumer reporting agency reasonably determines that the dispute is frivolous or irrelevant, including by reason of a failure by a consumer to provide sufficient information to investigate the disputed information. Upon making a determination that a dispute is frivolous or irrelevant, the investigative consumer reporting agency shall notify the consumer, by mail or, if authorized by the consumer for that purpose, by any other means available to the agency. In this notification, the investigative consumer reporting agency shall state the specific reasons why it has determined that the consumer's dispute is frivolous or irrelevant and provide a description of any information required to investigate the disputed information, that may consist of a standardized form describing the general nature of the required information.

(e) If a reinvestigation is made and, after reinvestigation, the disputed item of information is found to be inaccurate, incomplete, or cannot be verified by the evidence submitted, the investigative consumer reporting agency shall promptly delete that information from the consumer's file or modify the information, as appropriate, based on the results of the reinvestigation, and shall notify the consumer that the information has been deleted or modified. The consumer reporting agency shall also notify any and all sources from which the disputed information was obtained and inform them in writing of the reasons and results of the reinvestigation, and send a copy of this notification to the consumer. In accordance with subdivision (b) of Section 1786.10, the copy of the notification sent to the consumer need not reveal the identity of the source of information, unless otherwise required by law.

(f) No information may be reinserted in the file of a consumer after having been deleted pursuant to this section, unless the person who furnished the information verifies that the information is complete and accurate. If any information deleted from the file of a consumer is reinserted in the file, the investigative consumer reporting agency shall promptly notify the consumer of the reinsertion in writing or, if authorized by the consumer for that purpose, by any other means available to the agency. As part of, or in addition to, this notice, the investigative consumer reporting agency shall provide to the consumer in writing (1) a statement that the disputed information has been reinserted, (2) the name, address, and telephone number of any furnisher of information contacted or that contacted the investigative consumer reporting agency in connection with the reinsertion, and the telephone number of the furnisher, if reasonably available, and (3) a notice that the consumer has the right to a reinvestigation of the information reinserted by the investigative consumer reporting agency and to add a statement to his or her file disputing the accuracy or completeness of the information.

(g) An investigative consumer reporting agency shall provide notice to the consumer of the results of any reinvestigation under this section by mail or, if authorized by the consumer for that purpose, by other means available to the agency. The notice shall include (1) a statement that the reinvestigation is completed, (2) an investigative consumer report that is based on the consumer's file as that file is revised as a result of the reinvestigation, (3) a description or indication of any changes made in the investigative consumer report as a result of those revisions to the consumer's file, (4) a notice that, if requested by the consumer, a description of the procedure used to determine the accuracy and completeness of the information shall be provided to the consumer by the investigative consumer reporting agency, including the name, business address, and telephone number of any furnisher of information contacted in connection with that information, (5) a notice that the consumer has the right to add a statement to the consumer's file disputing the accuracy or completeness of the information, and (6) a notice that the consumer has the right to request that the investigative consumer reporting agency furnish notifications under subdivision (k).

(h) The presence of information in the consumer's file that contradicts the contention of the consumer shall not, in and of itself, constitute reasonable grounds for believing the dispute is frivolous or irrelevant.

(i) If the investigative consumer reporting agency determines that the dispute is frivolous or irrelevant, or if the reinvestigation does not resolve the dispute, or if the information is reinserted into the file of a consumer pursuant to subdivision (f), the consumer may file a brief statement setting forth the nature of the dispute. The investigative consumer reporting agency may limit these statements to not more than 500 words if it provides the consumer with assistance in writing a clear summary of the dispute.

(j) If a statement of dispute is filed, the investigative consumer reporting agency shall, in any subsequent investigative consumer report containing the information in question, clearly note that the information is disputed by the consumer and shall include in the report either the statement of the consumer or a clear and accurate summary thereof.

(k) Following the deletion of information from the file of a consumer pursuant to this section, or following the filing of a dispute pursuant to subdivision (i), the investigative consumer reporting agency shall, at the request of the consumer, furnish notification that the item of information has been deleted or that the item of information is disputed. In the case of disputed information, the notification shall include the statement or summary of the dispute filed pursuant to subdivision (i). This notification shall be furnished to any person who has, within two years prior to the deletion or the filing of the dispute, received an investigative consumer report concerning the consumer for employment purposes, or who has, within one year of the deletion or the filing of the dispute, received an investigative consumer report concerning the consumer for any other purpose, if these investigative consumer reports contained the deleted or disputed information, unless the consumer specifically requests in writing that this notification not be given to all persons or to any specified persons. The investigative consumer reporting agency shall clearly and conspicuously disclose to the consumer his or her rights to make a request that this notification not be made.

(*l*) An investigative consumer reporting agency shall maintain reasonable procedures designed to prevent the reappearance in the file of a consumer and in investigative consumer reports information that has been deleted pursuant to this section and not reinserted pursuant to subdivision (f).

(m) If the dispute of a consumer is resolved by deletion of the disputed information within three business days, beginning with the day the investigative consumer reporting agency receives notice of the dispute in accordance with subdivision (a), the investigative consumer reporting agency is exempt from requirements for further action under subdivisions (g), (i), and (j), if the agency: (1) provides prompt notice of the deletion to the consumer by telephone, (2) provides written confirmation of the deletion and a copy of an investigative consumer report of the consumer that is based on the file of a consumer after the deletion, and (3) includes, in the telephone notice or in a written notice that accompanies the confirmation and report, a statement of the consumer's right to request under subdivision (k) that the agency not furnish notifications under that subdivision.

(n) Any investigative consumer reporting agency that compiles and maintains files on consumers on a nationwide basis, as defined in the federal Fair Credit Reporting Act, as amended (15 U.S.C. Sec. 1681 et seq.), shall implement an automated system through which furnishers of information to that agency may report the results of a reinvestigation that finds incomplete or inaccurate information in the file of a consumer to other investigative consumer reporting agencies.

(*o*) All actions to be taken by an investigative consumer reporting agency under this section are governed by the applicable time periods specified in Section 611 of the federal Fair Credit Reporting Act, as amended (15 U.S.C. Sec. 1681i). *(Added by Stats.1975, c. 1272, p. 3383, § 1. Amended by Stats.1998, c. 988 (S.B.1454), § 8; Stats.2001, c. 354 (A.B.655), § 13; Stats.2002, c. 1029 (A.B.2868), § 6, eff. Sept. 28, 2002; Stats.2002, c. 1030 (A.B.1068), § 4, eff. Sept. 28, 2002; Stats.2004, c. 183 (A.B.3082), § 32.)*

Cross References

Consumer defined for purposes of this Title, see Civil Code § 1786.2.
Employment purposes defined for purposes of this Title, see Civil Code § 1786.2.
File defined for purposes of this Title, see Civil Code § 1786.2.
Investigative consumer report defined for purposes of this Title, see Civil Code § 1786.2.
Investigative consumer reporting agency defined for purposes of this Title, see Civil Code § 1786.2.
Person defined for purposes of this Title, see Civil Code § 1786.2.

§ 1786.26. Allowable fees charged to consumer by an investigative consumer reporting agency for making disclosures to consumer; other disclosures without charge

(a) Except as otherwise provided in subdivision (c), an investigative consumer reporting agency may charge a consumer a fee not exceeding eight dollars ($8) for making

§ 1786.26

disclosures to the consumer pursuant to Sections 1786.10, 1786.11, and 1786.22. Any charges shall be indicated to the consumer prior to disclosure.

(b) An investigative consumer reporting agency shall not impose any charge for providing notice to a consumer required under Section 1786.24, furnishing an investigative consumer report pursuant to Section 1786.24, or notifying a person pursuant to subdivision (k) of Section 1786.24 of the deletion of information that is found to be inaccurate or that cannot be verified.

(c) Upon the request of the consumer, an investigative consumer reporting agency shall make all disclosures pursuant to Section 1786.10 and 1786.22 once during any 12–month period without charge to that consumer if the consumer certifies in writing that he or she (1) is unemployed and intends to apply for employment in the 60–day period beginning on the date the certification is made, (2) is a recipient of public welfare assistance, or (3) has reason to believe that the file on the consumer at the investigative consumer reporting agency contains inaccurate information due to fraud.

(d) An investigative consumer reporting agency shall not impose any charge on a consumer for providing any notification or making any disclosure required by this title, except as authorized by this section. (Added by Stats.1975, c. 1272, p. 3384, § 1. Amended by Stats.1976, c. 666, p. 1646, § 17; Stats.1977, c. 579, p. 1838, § 31; Stats.1998, c. 988 (S.B.1454), § 9; Stats.2001, c. 354 (A.B.655), § 14.)

Cross References

Consumer defined for purposes of this Title, see Civil Code § 1786.2.
File defined for purposes of this Title, see Civil Code § 1786.2.
Investigative consumer report defined for purposes of this Title, see Civil Code § 1786.2.
Investigative consumer reporting agency defined for purposes of this Title, see Civil Code § 1786.2.
Person defined for purposes of this Title, see Civil Code § 1786.2.

§ 1786.28. Matters of public record; source; reports for employment purposes

(a) Each investigative consumer reporting agency that collects, assembles, evaluates, compiles, reports, transmits, transfers, or communicates items of information concerning consumers which are matters of public record shall specify in any report containing public record information the source from which this information was obtained, including the particular court, if applicable, and the date that this information was initially reported or publicized.

(b) A consumer reporting agency which furnishes a consumer report for employment purposes and which for that purpose compiles, collects, assembles, evaluates, reports, transmits, transfers, or communicates items of information on consumers which are matters of public record and are likely to have an adverse effect upon a consumer's ability to obtain employment shall in addition maintain strict procedures designed to insure that whenever public record information which is likely to have an adverse effect on a consumer's ability to obtain employment is reported it is complete and up to date. For purposes of this paragraph, items of public record relating to arrests, indictments, convictions, suits, tax liens, and outstanding judgments shall be considered up to date if the current public record status of the item at the time of the report is reported. (Added by Stats.1975, c. 1272, p. 3384, § 1. Amended by Stats.2001, c. 354 (A.B.655), § 15.)

Cross References

Consumer defined for purposes of this Title, see Civil Code § 1786.2.
Employment purposes defined for purposes of this Title, see Civil Code § 1786.2.
Investigative consumer reporting agency defined for purposes of this Title, see Civil Code § 1786.2.

§ 1786.29. Notices to be provided by investigative consumer-reporting agency

An investigative consumer reporting agency shall provide the following notices on the first page of an investigative consumer report:

(a) A notice in at least 12–point boldface type setting forth that the report does not guarantee the accuracy or truthfulness of the information as to the subject of the investigation, but only that it is accurately copied from public records, and information generated as a result of identity theft, including evidence of criminal activity, may be inaccurately associated with the consumer who is the subject of the report.

(b) An investigative consumer reporting agency shall provide a consumer seeking to obtain a copy of a report or making a request to review a file, a written notice in simple, plain English and Spanish setting forth the terms and conditions of his or her right to receive all disclosures, as provided in Section 1786.26. (Added by Stats.2001, c. 354 (A.B.655), § 16. Amended by Stats.2002, c. 1030 (A.B.1068), § 5, eff. Sept. 28, 2002.)

Cross References

Consumer defined for purposes of this Title, see Civil Code § 1786.2.
File defined for purposes of this Title, see Civil Code § 1786.2.
Investigative consumer report defined for purposes of this Title, see Civil Code § 1786.2.
Investigative consumer reporting agency defined for purposes of this Title, see Civil Code § 1786.2.

§ 1786.30. Subsequent reports; verification

Whenever an investigative consumer reporting agency prepares an investigative consumer report, no adverse information in the report (other than information that is a matter of public record, the status of which has been updated pursuant to Section 1786.28) may be included in a subsequent investigative consumer report unless that adverse information has been verified in the process of making the subsequent investigative consumer report, or the adverse information was received within the three-month period preceding the date the subsequent report is furnished. (Added by Stats.1975, c. 1272, p. 3385, § 1. Amended by Stats.1998, c. 988 (S.B.1454), § 10.)

Cross References

Consumer defined for purposes of this Title, see Civil Code § 1786.2.
Investigative consumer report defined for purposes of this Title, see Civil Code § 1786.2.

Investigative consumer reporting agency defined for purposes of this Title, see Civil Code § 1786.2.

§ 1786.40. Consumer insurance request denied; notice to consumer of adverse action

(a) Whenever insurance for personal, family, or household purposes, employment, or the hiring of a dwelling unit involving a consumer is denied, or the charge for that insurance or the hiring of a dwelling unit is increased, under circumstances in which a report regarding the consumer was obtained from an investigative consumer reporting agency, the user of the investigative consumer report shall so advise the consumer against whom the adverse action has been taken and supply the name and address of the investigative consumer reporting agency making the report.

(b) Whenever insurance for personal, family, or household purposes involving a consumer is denied or the charge for that insurance is increased, either wholly or in part because of information bearing upon the consumer's general reputation, personal characteristics, or mode of living, that was obtained from a person other than an investigative consumer reporting agency, the consumer, or another person related to the consumer and acting on the consumer's behalf, the user of the information shall, within a reasonable period of time, and upon the consumer's written request for the reasons for the adverse action received within 60 days after learning of the adverse action, disclose the nature and substance of the information to the consumer. The user of the information shall clearly and accurately disclose to the consumer his or her right to make this written request at the time the adverse action is communicated to the consumer. *(Added by Stats. 2002, c. 1030 (A.B.1068), § 6, eff. Sept. 28, 2002.)*

Cross References

Consumer defined for purposes of this Title, see Civil Code § 1786.2.

Insurance Information and Privacy Protection Act, insurance institutions, agents, insurance support organizations or any insurance transaction subject to Act as exempt from this section, see Insurance Code § 791.01.

Investigative consumer report defined for purposes of this Title, see Civil Code § 1786.2.

Investigative consumer reporting agency defined for purposes of this Title, see Civil Code § 1786.2.

Person defined for purposes of this Title, see Civil Code § 1786.2.

ARTICLE 3. REQUIREMENTS ON USERS OF INVESTIGATIVE CONSUMER REPORTS [REPEALED]

ARTICLE 4. REMEDIES

Section
1786.50. Liability of consumer reporting agency or user of information to consumer; actual and punitive damages; costs.
1786.52. Actions for invasion of privacy or defamation; limitations; discovery of misrepresentation.
1786.53. Personal information obtained regarding consumer without use of services of an investigative consumer reporting agency; disclosure; definitions; copy of information to consumer.
1786.54. Application of title.
1786.55. Information obtained by an employer or employment agency without use of investigative consumer reporting agency; attorney-client communications or attorney work product.
1786.56. Severability.
1786.57. Public policy; waiver of rights.
1786.60. Permitted printing of social security numbers on account statements.
1787. Repealed.

Cross References

Obligations of Investigative Consumer Reporting Agencies, see Civil Code § 1786.10 et seq.

§ 1786.50. Liability of consumer reporting agency or user of information to consumer; actual and punitive damages; costs

(a) An investigative consumer reporting agency or user of information that fails to comply with any requirement under this title with respect to an investigative consumer report is liable to the consumer who is the subject of the report in an amount equal to the sum of all the following:

(1) Any actual damages sustained by the consumer as a result of the failure or, except in the case of class actions, ten thousand dollars ($10,000), whichever sum is greater.

(2) In the case of any successful action to enforce any liability under this chapter, the costs of the action together with reasonable attorney's fees as determined by the court.

(b) If the court determines that the violation was grossly negligent or willful, the court may, in addition, assess, and the consumer may recover, punitive damages.

(c) Notwithstanding subdivision (a), an investigative consumer reporting agency or user of information that fails to comply with any requirement under this title with respect to an investigative consumer report shall not be liable to a consumer who is the subject of the report where the failure to comply results in a more favorable investigative consumer report than if there had not been a failure to comply. *(Added by Stats.1975, c. 1272, p. 3386, § 1. Amended by Stats.1998, c. 988 (S.B.1454), § 12; Stats.2001, c. 354 (A.B.655), § 18; Stats.2002, c. 1029 (A.B.2868), § 7, eff. Sept. 28, 2002; Stats.2003, c. 146 (A.B.1399), § 2.)*

Cross References

Consumer defined for purposes of this Title, see Civil Code § 1786.2.

Investigative consumer report defined for purposes of this Title, see Civil Code § 1786.2.

Investigative consumer reporting agency defined for purposes of this Title, see Civil Code § 1786.2.

Notices to be provided by investigative consumer-reporting agency, see Civil Code § 1786.29.

§ 1786.52. Actions for invasion of privacy or defamation; limitations; discovery of misrepresentation

Nothing in this chapter shall in any way affect the right of any consumer to maintain an action against an investigative consumer reporting agency, a user of an investigative consumer report, or an informant for invasion of privacy or defamation.

An action to enforce any liability created under this title may be brought in any appropriate court of competent jurisdiction within two years from the date of discovery.

§ 1786.52

(a) Any investigative consumer reporting agency or user of information against whom an action brought pursuant to Section 1681n or 1681o of Title 15 of the United States Code is pending shall not be subject to suit for the same act or omission under Section 1786.50.

(b) The entry of a final judgment against the investigative consumer reporting agency or user of information in an action brought pursuant to the provisions of Section 1681n or 1681o of Title 15 of the United States Code shall be a bar to the maintenance of any action based on the same act or omission which might be brought under this title. *(Added by Stats.1975, c. 1272, p. 3386, § 1. Amended by Stats.2001, c. 354 (A.B.655), § 19.)*

Cross References

Consumer defined for purposes of this Title, see Civil Code § 1786.2.
Investigative consumer report defined for purposes of this Title, see Civil Code § 1786.2.
Investigative consumer reporting agency defined for purposes of this Title, see Civil Code § 1786.2.

§ 1786.53. Personal information obtained regarding consumer without use of services of an investigative consumer reporting agency; disclosure; definitions; copy of information to consumer

(a) Any person who collects, assembles, evaluates, compiles, reports, transmits, transfers, or communicates information on a consumer's character, general reputation, personnel characteristics, or mode of living, for employment purposes, which are matters of public record, and does not use the services of an investigative consumer reporting agency, shall provide that information to the consumer pursuant to subdivision (b). For purposes of this section:

(1) "Adverse action," as relating to employment, means a denial of employment or any decision made for an employment purpose that adversely affects any current or prospective employee.

(2) The term "person" does not include an agency subject to the Information Practices Act of 1977 (Chapter 1 (commencing with Section 1798) of Title 1.8).

(3) "Public records" means records documenting an arrest, indictment, conviction, civil judicial action, tax lien, or outstanding judgment.

(b)(1) Any person described in subdivision (a), or any person who receives information pursuant to subdivision (a), shall provide a copy of the related public record to the consumer within seven days after receipt of the information, regardless of whether the information is received in a written or oral form.

(2) Any person shall provide on any job application form, or any other written form, a box that, if checked by the consumer, permits the consumer to waive his or her right to receive a copy of any public record obtained pursuant to this section.

(3) If any person obtains a public record pursuant to this section for the purpose of conducting an investigation for suspicion of wrongdoing or misconduct by the subject of the investigation, the person may withhold the information until the completion of the investigation. Upon completion, the person shall provide a copy of the public record pursuant to paragraph (1), unless the consumer waived his or her rights pursuant to paragraph (2).

(4) If any person takes any adverse action as a result of receiving information pursuant to subdivision (a), the person shall provide to the consumer a copy of the public record, regardless of whether the consumer waived his or her rights pursuant to paragraph (2).

(c) Nothing in subdivision (a) or (b) requires any person to provide the same information to any consumer on more than one occasion. *(Added by Stats.2001, c. 354 (A.B.655), § 20. Amended by Stats.2002, c. 1030 (A.B.1068), § 7, eff. Sept. 28, 2002.)*

Cross References

Consumer defined for purposes of this Title, see Civil Code § 1786.2.
Employment purposes defined for purposes of this Title, see Civil Code § 1786.2.
Investigative consumer reporting agency defined for purposes of this Title, see Civil Code § 1786.2.
Person defined for purposes of this Title, see Civil Code § 1786.2.

§ 1786.54. Application of title

This title does not apply to any investigative consumer report which by its terms is limited to disclosures from public records relating to land and land titles or which is a report issued preliminary to the issuance of a policy of title insurance, and it does not apply to any person whose records are maintained for the primary purpose of reporting those portions of public records which impart constructive notice under the law of matters relating to land and land titles and which may be issued as the basis for the issuance of a policy of title insurance. *(Added by Stats.1975, c. 1272, p. 3387, § 1.)*

Cross References

Consumer defined for purposes of this Title, see Civil Code § 1786.2.
Investigative consumer report defined for purposes of this Title, see Civil Code § 1786.2.
Person defined for purposes of this Title, see Civil Code § 1786.2.

§ 1786.55. Information obtained by an employer or employment agency without use of investigative consumer reporting agency; attorney-client communications or attorney work product

Nothing in this chapter is intended to modify Section 1198.5 of the Labor Code or existing law concerning information obtained by an employer or employment agency without the use of the services of an investigative consumer reporting agency for employment reference checks, background investigations, credential verifications, or employee investigations, except as provided in Section 1786.53. Nothing in this chapter is intended to change or supersede existing law related to privileged attorney-client communications or attorney work product, or require the production or disclosure of that information. *(Added by Stats.2002, c. 1030 (A.B.1068), § 8, eff. Sept. 28, 2002.)*

Cross References

Consumer defined for purposes of this Title, see Civil Code § 1786.2.

Investigative consumer reporting agency defined for purposes of this Title, see Civil Code § 1786.2.

§ 1786.56. Severability

If any provision of this act or the application thereof to any person or circumstances is held invalid, such invalidity shall not affect other provisions or applications of the act which can be given effect without the invalid provision or application, and to this end the provisions of this act are severable. *(Added by Stats.1975, c. 1272, p. 3387, § 1.)*

Cross References

Person defined for purposes of this Title, see Civil Code § 1786.2.

§ 1786.57. Public policy; waiver of rights

Any waiver of the provisions of this title is contrary to public policy, and is void and unenforceable. *(Added by Stats.2002, c. 815 (A.B.2331), § 10.)*

§ 1786.60. Permitted printing of social security numbers on account statements

Notwithstanding subdivision (a) of Section 1798.85, prior to July 1, 2004, any financial institution may print the social security number of an individual on any account statement or similar document mailed to that individual, if the social security number is provided in connection with a transaction governed by the rules of the National Automated Clearing House Association, or a transaction initiated by a federal governmental entity through an automated clearing house network. *(Added by Stats.2002, c. 1030 (A.B.1068), § 9, eff. Sept. 28, 2002. Amended by Stats.2003, c. 907 (S.B.25), § 4.)*

§ 1787. Repealed by Stats.1963, c. 819, p. 1997, § 2, eff. Jan. 1, 1965

Title 1.6B

CONSUMER CREDIT DENIAL

Article	Section
1. General Provisions	1787.1
2. Remedies	1787.3

Cross References

Areias Credit Card Full Disclosure Act, see Civil Code § 1748.10 et seq.
Areias-Robbins Charge Card Full Disclosure Act, see Civil Code § 1748.20 et seq.
Consumers Legal Remedies Act, see Civil Code § 1750 et seq.
Temporary restraining order and injunction for harassment, see Code of Civil Procedure § 527.6.

ARTICLE 1. GENERAL PROVISIONS

Section
1787.1. Short title.
1787.2. Notice to applicant of disposition; statement of reasons for denial; definitions.

§ 1787.1. Short title

This title may be cited as "The Holden Credit Denial Disclosure Act of 1976." *(Added by Stats.1976, c. 1072, p. 4834, § 1, operative March 31, 1977.)*

§ 1787.2. Notice to applicant of disposition; statement of reasons for denial; definitions

(a) Within 30 days, or at a later reasonable time as specified in federal law or regulations, after receipt of a completed written application for credit, a creditor shall notify the applicant of its action on the application.

(b) Each applicant denied credit shall be entitled to a statement of reasons for such action from the creditor. A creditor satisfies this obligation by:

(1) Providing statements of reasons in writing as a matter of course to applicants denied credit; or

(2) Giving written notification of credit denial which discloses:

(i) The applicant's right to a statement of reasons within 30 days after receipt by the creditor of a request made within 60 days after such notification; and

(ii) The identity and address of the person or office from which the statement of reasons may be obtained.

(3) The statement of reasons may be given orally if the written notification advises the applicant of the right to have the statement of reasons confirmed in writing on written request.

(c) A statement of reasons meets the requirements of this section only if it contains the specific reasons for the credit denial.

(d) Where a creditor has been requested by a third party to make a specific extension of credit directly or indirectly to an applicant, the notification and statement of reasons required by this section may be made directly by such creditor, or indirectly through the third party, provided in either case that the identity of the creditor is disclosed.

(e) For purposes of this section:

(1) The term "applicant" means a natural person who applies for credit primarily for personal, family or household purposes.

(2) The term "credit denial" means a denial or revocation of credit, a change in the terms of an existing credit arrangement, or a refusal to grant credit in substantially the amount or on substantially the terms requested. Such term does not include a refusal to extend additional credit under an existing credit arrangement where the applicant is delinquent or otherwise in default, or where such additional credit would exceed a previously established credit limit without a specific written application or written request for an increase in the credit limit.

(3) The term "creditor" refers only to creditors who regularly extend, or arrange for the extension of, credit whether in connection with loans, sales of property or services, or otherwise.

(f) Nothing in this section shall be construed to limit any authority, derived from other provisions of law, of any state department or agency. *(Added by Stats.1976, c. 1072, p. 4834, § 1, operative March 31, 1977.)*

ARTICLE 2. REMEDIES

Section
1787.3. Failure of creditor to comply; liability for actual or punitive damages; costs; attorney's fee; inapplicability to act in good faith under federal rule; limitation of actions.
1787.4. Public policy; waiver of rights.

§ 1787.3. Failure of creditor to comply; liability for actual or punitive damages; costs; attorney's fee; inapplicability to act in good faith under federal rule; limitation of actions

(a) Any creditor who fails to comply with any requirement of Section 1787.2 shall be liable for any actual damages sustained by an applicant as a result of such failure.

(b) Any creditor, other than a government or governmental subdivision or agency, who fails to comply with any requirement imposed under this title shall be liable to the aggrieved applicant for punitive damages in an amount not greater than ten thousand dollars ($10,000), in addition to any actual damages provided in subdivision (a), except that in the case of a class action the total recovery under this subdivision shall not exceed the lesser of five hundred thousand dollars ($500,000) or 1 percent of the net worth of the creditor. In determining the amount of such damages in any action, the court shall consider, among other relevant factors, the amount of any actual damages awarded, the frequency and persistence of failures of compliance by the creditor, the resources of the creditor, the number of persons adversely affected, and the extent to which the creditor's failure of compliance was intentional.

(c) In the case of any action brought by an aggrieved applicant under subdivision (a) or (b), the costs of the action, together with a reasonable attorney's fee as determined by the court, shall be added to any damages awarded by the court.

(d) No provision of this title imposing liability shall apply to any act done or omitted in good faith in conformity with any official rule, regulation, or interpretation thereby by the Board of Governors of the Federal Reserve System or in conformity with any interpretation or approval by an official or employee of the Federal Reserve System duly authorized by the board to issue such interpretations or approvals under such procedures as the board may prescribe therefor, notwithstanding that after such act or omission has occurred, such rule, regulation, interpretation, or approval is amended, rescinded, or determined by judicial or other authority to be invalid for any reason.

(e) Actions alleging a failure to comply with any requirement of Section 1787.2 shall be brought within two years from the date of the occurrence of the violation. (Added by Stats.1976, c. 1072, p. 4834, § 1, operative March 31, 1977.)

§ 1787.4. Public policy; waiver of rights

Any waiver of the provisions of this title is contrary to public policy, and is void and unenforceable. (Added by Stats.2002, c. 815 (A.B.2331), § 11.)

Title 1.6C

FAIR DEBT COLLECTION PRACTICES

Article	Section
1. General Provisions	1788
2. Debt Collector Responsibilities	1788.10
3. Debtor Responsibilities	1788.20
4. Enforcement	1788.30

Cross References

Civil actions, harassment, temporary restraining order and injunction, application to this time, see Code of Civil Procedure § 527.6.

Consumer collection notice, violations, application of this act, see Civil Code § 1812.702.

Consumers Legal Remedies Act, see Civil Code § 1750 et seq.

Debt collector license, violation of division, notice and opportunity for hearing, ancillary relief, see Financial Code § 100005.

Deferred deposit transactions, fees, extension of time and payment plans for repayment, see Financial Code § 23036.

Elder Abuse and Dependent Adult Civil Protection Act, civil actions for abuse of elderly or dependent adults, protective orders, application to the title, see Welfare and Institutions Code § 15657.03

Emergency physician fair pricing policies, written notice required before a report of adverse information to a consumer credit reporting agency or commencement of a civil action for nonpayment, inclusion of summary of patient rights pursuant to Rosenthal Fair Debt Collection Practices Act, see Health and Safety Code § 127457.

Hospital fair pricing policies, notice required prior to commencing collection activities, see Health and Safety Code § 127430.

Powers and duties of Commissioner on Business Oversight, debt collector licensing, see Financial Code § 100003.

Private child support collectors, prohibited acts, see Family Code § 5614.

Proceedings for revocation of license, debt collector licensing, see Financial Code § 100003.3.

Repossessors, demands for payment, compliance with this act, see Business and Professions Code § 7507.4.

ARTICLE 1. GENERAL PROVISIONS

Section
1788. Short title.
1788.1. Legislative findings.
1788.2. Definitions.
1788.3. Credit union; information to employer who is an employee, officer, etc. of credit union.

§ 1788. Short title

This title may be cited as the Rosenthal Fair Debt Collection Practices Act. (Added by Stats.1977, c. 907, p. 2771, § 1. Amended by Stats.1999, c. 319 (A.B.969), § 1; Stats.2000, c. 375 (A.B.1331), § 5.)

Cross References

Debt collection defined for purposes of this Title, see Civil Code § 1788.2.

Debt defined for purposes of this Title, see Civil Code § 1788.2.

Violations of title by debt buyer, actions to enforce liability, limitations to recovery, see Civil Code § 1788.62.

§ 1788.1. Legislative findings

(a) The Legislature makes the following findings:

(1) The banking and credit system and grantors of credit to consumers are dependent upon the collection of just and owing debts. Unfair or deceptive collection practices undermine the public confidence which is essential to the continued functioning of the banking and credit system and sound extensions of credit to consumers.

(2) There is need to ensure that debt collectors and debtors exercise their responsibilities to one another with fairness, honesty and due regard for the rights of the other.

(b) It is the purpose of this title to prohibit debt collectors from engaging in unfair or deceptive acts or practices in the collection of consumer debts and to require debtors to act fairly in entering into and honoring such debts, as specified in this title. (Added by Stats.1977, c. 907, p. 2771, § 1.)

Validity

This section was held to be preempted by the Fair Credit Reporting Act in the decision of Nelson v. Equifax Information Services, LLC, C.D.Cal.2007, 522 F.Supp.2d 1222.

Cross References

Consumer debt and consumer credit defined for purposes of this Title, see Civil Code § 1788.2.

Debt collector defined for purposes of this Title, see Civil Code § 1788.2.

Debt defined for purposes of this Title, see Civil Code § 1788.2.

Debtor defined for purposes of this Title, see Civil Code § 1788.2.

§ 1788.2. Definitions

(a) Definitions and rules of construction set forth in this section are applicable for the purpose of this title.

(b) The term "debt collection" means any act or practice in connection with the collection of consumer debts.

(c) The term "debt collector" means any person who, in the ordinary course of business, regularly, on behalf of that person or others, engages in debt collection. The term includes any person who composes and sells, or offers to compose and sell, forms, letters, and other collection media used or intended to be used for debt collection.

(d) The term "debt" means money, property, or their equivalent that is due or owing or alleged to be due or owing from a natural person to another person.

(e) The term "consumer credit transaction" means a transaction between a natural person and another person in which property, services, or money is acquired on credit by that natural person from the other person primarily for personal, family, or household purposes.

(f) The terms "consumer debt" and "consumer credit" mean money, property, or their equivalent, due or owing or alleged to be due or owing from a natural person by reason of a consumer credit transaction. The term "consumer debt" includes a mortgage debt.

(g) The term "person" means a natural person, partnership, corporation, limited liability company, trust, estate, cooperative, association, or other similar entity.

(h) Except as provided in Section 1788.18, the term "debtor" means a natural person from whom a debt collector seeks to collect a consumer debt that is due and owing or alleged to be due and owing from such person.

(i) The term "creditor" means a person who extends consumer credit to a debtor.

(j) The term "consumer credit report" means any written, oral, or other communication of any information by a consumer reporting agency bearing on a consumer's creditworthiness, credit standing, credit capacity, character, general reputation, personal characteristics, or mode of living that is used or expected to be used or collected in whole or in part for the purpose of serving as a factor in establishing the consumer's eligibility for (1) credit or insurance to be used primarily for personal, family, or household purposes, or (2) employment purposes, or (3) other purposes authorized under any applicable federal or state law or regulation. The term does not include (a) any report containing information solely as to transactions or experiences between the consumer and the person making the report; (b) any authorization or approval of a specific extension of credit directly or indirectly by the issuer of a credit card or similar device; or (c) any report in which a person who has been requested by a third party to make a specific extension of credit directly or indirectly to a consumer conveys that person's decision with respect to that request, if the third party advises the consumer of the name and address of the person to whom the request was made, and the person makes the disclosures to the consumer required under any applicable federal or state law or regulation.

(k) The term "consumer reporting agency" means any person that, for monetary fees, dues, or on a cooperative nonprofit basis, regularly engages, in whole or in part, in the practice of assembling or evaluating consumer credit information or other information on consumers for the purpose of furnishing consumer credit reports to third parties and uses any means or facility for the purpose of preparing or furnishing consumer credit reports. (Added by Stats.1977, c. 907, p. 2771, § 1. Amended by Stats.1994, c. 1010 (S.B.2053), § 37; Stats.2006, c. 538 (S.B.1852), § 46; Stats.2006, c. 521 (A.B.2043), § 1; Stats.2019, c. 545 (S.B.187), § 2, eff. Jan. 1, 2020.)

Cross References

Collection of consumer debt, attorneys and employees, compliance with requirements, see Business and Professions Code § 6077.5.

§ 1788.3. Credit union; information to employer who is an employee, officer, etc. of credit union

Nothing contained in this title shall be construed to prohibit a credit union chartered under Division 5 (commencing with Section 14000) of the Financial Code or under the Federal Credit Union Act (Chapter 14 (commencing with Section 1751) of Title 12 of the United States Code) from providing information to an employer when the employer is ordinarily and necessarily entitled to receive such information because he is an employee, officer, committee member, or agent of such credit union. (Added by Stats.1977, c. 907, p. 2771, § 1.)

ARTICLE 2. DEBT COLLECTOR RESPONSIBILITIES

Section
1788.10. Threats; unlawful conduct.
1788.11. Obscene or profane language; use of telephones; unlawful practices.

Section

1788.12. Communications with third parties; unlawful practices.

1788.13. Misrepresentations in communications; unlawful practices.

1788.14. Unlawful practices; affirmation from debtor; collection of collector's fee and expenses from debtor; communication with debtor instead of debtor's attorney; written communication to collect time-barred debt without providing written notice.

1788.14.5. Debt collectors; statements to be provided on debtor's request; proof of debt; time for production of information; provision of debt collector address; notice.

1788.15. Judicial proceedings where service of process defective; venue.

1788.16. Communications simulating legal or judicial process or governmental authorization; unlawful practice in consumer debt collection; misdemeanor; punishment.

1788.17. Compliance with federal provisions.

1788.18. Debtor as an alleged victim of identity theft; sworn statement; inferences and presumptions; duties after collection terminated.

1788.185. Complaint for action by debt collector for debt that originated with a general acute care hospital license; attachments to complaint; default judgment.

§ 1788.10. Threats; unlawful conduct

No debt collector shall collect or attempt to collect a consumer debt by means of the following conduct:

(a) The use, or threat of use, of physical force or violence or any criminal means to cause harm to the person, or the reputation, or the property of any person;

(b) The threat that the failure to pay a consumer debt will result in an accusation that the debtor has committed a crime where such accusation, if made, would be false;

(c) The communication of, or threat to communicate to any person the fact that a debtor has engaged in conduct, other than the failure to pay a consumer debt, which the debt collector knows or has reason to believe will defame the debtor;

(d) The threat to the debtor to sell or assign to another person the obligation of the debtor to pay a consumer debt, with an accompanying false representation that the result of such sale or assignment would be that the debtor would lose any defense to the consumer debt;

(e) The threat to any person that nonpayment of the consumer debt may result in the arrest of the debtor or the seizure, garnishment, attachment or sale of any property or the garnishment or attachment of wages of the debtor, unless such action is in fact contemplated by the debt collector and permitted by the law; or

(f) The threat to take any action against the debtor which is prohibited by this title. *(Added by Stats.1977, c. 907, p. 2771, § 1.)*

Cross References

Consumer debt and consumer credit defined for purposes of this Title, see Civil Code § 1788.2.

Debt collector defined for purposes of this Title, see Civil Code § 1788.2.

Debt defined for purposes of this Title, see Civil Code § 1788.2.

Debtor defined for purposes of this Title, see Civil Code § 1788.2.

Person defined for purposes of this Title, see Civil Code § 1788.2.

Private child support collectors, prohibited acts, see Family Code § 5614.

§ 1788.11. Obscene or profane language; use of telephones; unlawful practices

No debt collector shall collect or attempt to collect a consumer debt by means of the following practices:

(a) Using obscene or profane language.

(b) Placing a telephone call without disclosing the caller's identity, provided that an employee of a licensed collection agency may identify oneself by using their registered alias name if they correctly identify the agency that they represent. A debt collector shall provide its California debt collector license number upon the consumer's request.

(c) Causing expense to any person for long distance telephone calls, telegram fees, or charges for other similar communications, by misrepresenting to the person the purpose of the telephone call, telegram or similar communication.

(d) Causing a telephone to ring repeatedly or continuously to annoy the person called.

(e) Communicating, by telephone or in person, with the debtor with such frequency as to be unreasonable, and to constitute harassment of the debtor under the circumstances.

(f) Sending written or digital communication to the person that does not display the California license number of the collector in at least 12–point type. *(Added by Stats.1977, c. 907, p. 2771, § 1. Amended by Stats.2020, c. 163 (S.B.908), § 1, eff. Jan. 1, 2021.)*

Cross References

Consumer debt and consumer credit defined for purposes of this Title, see Civil Code § 1788.2.

Debt collector defined for purposes of this Title, see Civil Code § 1788.2.

Debt defined for purposes of this Title, see Civil Code § 1788.2.

Debtor defined for purposes of this Title, see Civil Code § 1788.2.

Person defined for purposes of this Title, see Civil Code § 1788.2.

Private child support collectors, prohibited acts, see Family Code § 5614.

§ 1788.12. Communications with third parties; unlawful practices

No debt collector shall collect or attempt to collect a consumer debt by means of the following practices:

(a) Communicating with the debtor's employer regarding the debtor's consumer debt unless such a communication is necessary to the collection of the debt, or unless the debtor or his attorney has consented in writing to such communication. A communication is necessary to the collection of the debt only if it is made for the purposes of verifying the debtor's employment, locating the debtor, or effecting garnishment, after judgment, of the debtor's wages, or in the case of a medical debt for the purpose of discovering the existence of medical insurance. Any such communication, other than a communication in the case of a medical debt by a health care provider or its agent for the purpose of discovering the existence of medical insurance, shall be in writing unless such written communication receives no response within 15 days and shall be made only as many times as is necessary to the collection of the debt. Communications to a debtor's employer regarding a debt shall not contain language that would be improper if the communication were made to the debtor. One communication solely for the purpose of verifying the debtor's employment may be oral without prior written contact.

(b) Communicating information regarding a consumer debt to any member of the debtor's family, other than the debtor's spouse or the parents or guardians of the debtor who is either a minor or who resides in the same household with such parent or guardian, prior to obtaining a judgment against the debtor, except where the purpose of the communication is to locate the debtor, or where the debtor or his attorney has consented in writing to such communication;

(c) Communicating to any person any list of debtors which discloses the nature or existence of a consumer debt, commonly known as "deadbeat lists", or advertising any consumer debt for sale, by naming the debtor; or

(d) Communicating with the debtor by means of a written communication that displays or conveys any information about the consumer debt or the debtor other than the name, address and telephone number of the debtor and the debt collector and which is intended both to be seen by any other person and also to embarrass the debtor.

(e) Notwithstanding the foregoing provisions of this section, the disclosure, publication or communication by a debt collector of information relating to a consumer debt or the debtor to a consumer reporting agency or to any other person reasonably believed to have a legitimate business need for such information shall not be deemed to violate this title. *(Added by Stats.1977, c. 907, p. 2771, § 1. Amended by Stats.1978, c. 390, p. 1238, § 1, eff. July 11, 1978.)*

Cross References

Consumer debt and consumer credit defined for purposes of this Title, see Civil Code § 1788.2.
Consumer reporting agency defined for purposes of this Title, see Civil Code § 1788.2.
Debt collector defined for purposes of this Title, see Civil Code § 1788.2.
Debt defined for purposes of this Title, see Civil Code § 1788.2.
Debtor defined for purposes of this Title, see Civil Code § 1788.2.
Person defined for purposes of this Title, see Civil Code § 1788.2.
Private child support collectors, prohibited acts, see Family Code § 5614.

§ 1788.13. Misrepresentations in communications; unlawful practices

No debt collector shall collect or attempt to collect a consumer debt by means of the following practices:

(a) Any communication with the debtor other than in the name either of the debt collector or the person on whose behalf the debt collector is acting;

(b) Any false representation that any person is an attorney or counselor at law;

(c) Any communication with a debtor in the name of an attorney or counselor at law or upon stationery or like written instruments bearing the name of the attorney or counselor at law, unless such communication is by an attorney or counselor at law or shall have been approved or authorized by such attorney or counselor at law;

(d) The representation that any debt collector is vouched for, bonded by, affiliated with, or is an instrumentality, agent or official of any federal, state or local government or any agency of federal, state or local government, unless the collector is actually employed by the particular governmental agency in question and is acting on behalf of such agency in the debt collection matter;

(e) The false representation that the consumer debt may be increased by the addition of attorney's fees, investigation fees, service fees, finance charges, or other charges if, in fact, such fees or charges may not legally be added to the existing obligation;

(f) The false representation that information concerning a debtor's failure or alleged failure to pay a consumer debt has been or is about to be referred to a consumer reporting agency;

(g) The false representation that a debt collector is a consumer reporting agency;

(h) The false representation that collection letters, notices or other printed forms are being sent by or on behalf of a claim, credit, audit or legal department;

(i) The false representation of the true nature of the business or services being rendered by the debt collector;

(j) The false representation that a legal proceeding has been, is about to be, or will be instituted unless payment of a consumer debt is made;

(k) The false representation that a consumer debt has been, is about to be, or will be sold, assigned, or referred to a debt collector for collection; or

(*l*) Any communication by a licensed collection agency to a debtor demanding money unless the claim is actually assigned to the collection agency. *(Added by Stats.1977, c. 907, p. 2771, § 1. Amended by Stats.1980, c. 1126, p. 3626, § 7.)*

Cross References

Consumer debt and consumer credit defined for purposes of this Title, see Civil Code § 1788.2.
Consumer reporting agency defined for purposes of this Title, see Civil Code § 1788.2.
Debt collection defined for purposes of this Title, see Civil Code § 1788.2.
Debt collector defined for purposes of this Title, see Civil Code § 1788.2.
Debt defined for purposes of this Title, see Civil Code § 1788.2.
Debtor defined for purposes of this Title, see Civil Code § 1788.2.
Person defined for purposes of this Title, see Civil Code § 1788.2.
Private child support collectors, prohibited acts, see Family Code § 5614.

§ 1788.14. Unlawful practices; affirmation from debtor; collection of collector's fee and expenses from debtor; communication with debtor instead of debtor's attorney; written communication to collect time-barred debt without providing written notice

No debt collector shall collect or attempt to collect a consumer debt by means of the following practices:

§ 1788.14

(a) Obtaining an affirmation from a debtor of a consumer debt that has been discharged in bankruptcy, without clearly and conspicuously disclosing to the debtor, in writing, at the time the affirmation is sought, the fact that the debtor is not legally obligated to make an affirmation.

(b) Collecting or attempting to collect from the debtor the whole or any part of the debt collector's fee or charge for services rendered, or other expense incurred by the debt collector in the collection of the consumer debt, except as permitted by law.

(c) Initiating communications, other than statements of account, with the debtor with regard to the consumer debt, when the debt collector has been previously notified in writing by the debtor's attorney that the debtor is represented by the attorney with respect to the consumer debt and the notice includes the attorney's name and address and a request by the attorney that all communications regarding the consumer debt be addressed to the attorney, unless the attorney fails to answer correspondence, return telephone calls, or discuss the obligation in question. This subdivision shall not apply if prior approval has been obtained from the debtor's attorney, or if the communication is a response in the ordinary course of business to a debtor's inquiry.

(d) Sending a written communication to a debtor in an attempt to collect a time-barred debt without providing the debtor with one of the following written notices:

(1) If the debt is not past the date for obsolescence set forth in Section 605(a) of the federal Fair Credit Reporting Act (15 U.S.C. Sec. 1681c), the following notice shall be included in the first written communication provided to the debtor after the debt has become time-barred:

"The law limits how long you can be sued on a debt. Because of the age of your debt, we will not sue you for it. If you do not pay the debt, [insert name of debt collector] may [continue to] report it to the credit reporting agencies as unpaid for as long as the law permits this reporting."

(2) If the debt is past the date for obsolescence set forth in Section 605(a) of the federal Fair Credit Reporting Act (15 U.S.C. Sec. 1681c), the following notice shall be included in the first written communication provided to the debtor after the date for obsolescence:

"The law limits how long you can be sued on a debt. Because of the age of your debt, we will not sue you for it, and we will not report it to any credit reporting agency."

(e) Collecting consumer debt that originated with a hospital licensed pursuant to subdivision (a) of Section 1250 of the Health and Safety Code without including in the first written communication to the debtor a copy of the notice required pursuant to subdivision (e) of Section 127425 of the Health and Safety Code and a statement that the debt collector will wait at least 180 days from the date the debtor was initially billed for the hospital services that are the basis of the debt before reporting adverse information to a credit reporting agency or filing a lawsuit against the debtor.

(f) For purposes of this section, "first written communication" means the first communication sent to the debtor in writing or by facsimile, email, or other similar means. (Added by Stats.1977, c. 907, p. 2771, § 1. Amended by Stats.2009, c. 500 (A.B.1059), § 12; Stats.2018, c. 247 (A.B. 1526), § 1, eff. Jan. 1, 2019; Stats.2021, c. 473 (A.B.1020), § 1, eff. Jan. 1, 2022.)

Cross References

Consumer debt and consumer credit defined for purposes of this Title, see Civil Code § 1788.2.
Debt collector defined for purposes of this Title, see Civil Code § 1788.2.
Debt defined for purposes of this Title, see Civil Code § 1788.2.
Debtor defined for purposes of this Title, see Civil Code § 1788.2.
Private child support collectors, prohibited acts, see Family Code § 5614.

§ 1788.14.5. Debt collectors; statements to be provided on debtor's request; proof of debt; time for production of information; provision of debt collector address; notice

(a) A debt collector to which delinquent debt has been assigned shall provide to the debtor, upon the debtor's written request, a statement that includes all of the following information pursuant to subdivision (c):

(1) That the debt collector has authority to assert the rights of the creditor to collect the debt.

(2)(A) The debt balance and an explanation of the amount, nature, and reason for all interest and fees, if any, imposed by the creditor or any subsequent entities to which the debt was assigned.

(B) The explanation required by subparagraph (A) shall identify separately the balance, the total of any interest, and the total of any fees.

(3) The date the debt became delinquent or the date of the last payment.

(4) The name and an address of the creditor and the creditor's account number associated with the debt. The creditor's name and address shall be in sufficient form so as to reasonably identify the creditor.

(5) The name and last known address of the debtor as they appeared in the creditor's records before the assignment of the debt to the debt collector.

(6) The names and addresses of all persons or entities other than the debt collector to which the debt was assigned. The names and addresses shall be in sufficient form so as to reasonably identify each assignee.

(7) The California license number of the debt collector.

(b) A debt collector to which delinquent debt has been assigned shall not make a written statement to a debtor in an attempt to collect a delinquent debt unless the debt collector has access to a copy of a contract or other document evidencing the debtor's agreement to the debt, except in the following circumstances:

(1) If the claim is based on debt for which no signed contract or agreement exists, the debt collector shall have access to a copy of a document provided to the debtor while the account was active, demonstrating that the debt was incurred by the debtor.

(2) For a revolving credit account, the most recent monthly statement recording a purchase transaction, last payment, or balance transfer shall be deemed sufficient to satisfy the requirements of this subparagraph.

(c)(1) A debt collector to which delinquent debt has been assigned shall provide the information or documents identified in subdivisions (a) and (b) to the debtor without charge within 30 calendar days of receipt of a debtor's written request for information regarding the debt or proof of the debt.

(2) If the debt collector cannot provide the information or documents within 30 calendar days, the debt collector shall cease all collection of the debt until the debt collector provides the debtor the information or documents described in subdivisions (a) and (b).

(d)(1) A debt collector shall provide a debtor with whom it has contact an active postal address to which a debtor may send a request for the information described in this section.

(2) A debt collector may also provide an active email address to which these requests can be sent and through which information and documents can be delivered if the parties agree.

(e)(1) A debt collector to which delinquent debt has been assigned shall include in its first written communication with the debtor in no smaller than 12–point type, a separate prominent notice that contains the following statement:

"You may request records showing the following: (1) that [insert name of debt collector] has the right to seek collection of the debt; (2) the debt balance, including an explanation of any interest charges and additional fees; (3) the date the debt became delinquent or the date of the last payment; (4) the name of the creditor and the account number associated with the debt; (5) the name and last known address of the debtor as it appeared in the creditor's records prior to assignment of the debt; and (6) the names of all persons or entities other than the debt collector to which the debt has been assigned, if applicable. You may also request from us a copy of the contract or other document evidencing your agreement to the debt.

A request for these records may be addressed to: [insert debt collector's active mailing address and email address, if applicable]."

(2) If a language other than English is principally used by the debt collector in the initial oral contact with the debtor, the notice required by this subdivision shall be provided to the debtor in that language within five business days.

(f)(1) A debt buyer that complies with the requirements of Section 1788.52 shall be deemed to be in compliance with this section.

(2) For purposes of this subdivision, "debt buyer" shall have the same meaning as in Section 1788.50.

(g) For the purposes of this section, the term "delinquent debt" means a consumer debt, other than a mortgage debt, that is past due at least 90 days and has not been charged off.

(h) This section shall apply to all delinquent debt sold or assigned on or after July 1, 2022.

(i) This section shall become operative on July 1, 2022. *(Added by Stats.2021, c. 455 (S.B.531), § 1, eff. Jan. 1, 2022, operative July 1, 2022.)*

§ 1788.15. Judicial proceedings where service of process defective; venue

(a) No debt collector shall collect or attempt to collect a consumer debt by means of judicial proceedings when the debt collector knows that service of process, where essential to jurisdiction over the debtor or his property, has not been legally effected.

(b) No debt collector shall collect or attempt to collect a consumer debt, other than one reduced to judgment, by means of judicial proceedings in a county other than the county in which the debtor has incurred the consumer debt or the county in which the debtor resides at the time such proceedings are instituted, or resided at the time the debt was incurred. *(Added by Stats.1977, c. 907, p. 2771, § 1.)*

Cross References

Consumer debt and consumer credit defined for purposes of this Title, see Civil Code § 1788.2.
Debt collector defined for purposes of this Title, see Civil Code § 1788.2.
Debt defined for purposes of this Title, see Civil Code § 1788.2.
Debtor defined for purposes of this Title, see Civil Code § 1788.2.
Private child support collectors, prohibited acts, see Family Code § 5614.

§ 1788.16. Communications simulating legal or judicial process or governmental authorization; unlawful practice in consumer debt collection; misdemeanor; punishment

It is unlawful, with respect to attempted collection of a consumer debt, for a debt collector, creditor, or an attorney, to send a communication which simulates legal or judicial process or which gives the appearance of being authorized, issued, or approved by a governmental agency or attorney when it is not. Any violation of the provisions of this section is a misdemeanor punishable by imprisonment in the county jail not exceeding six months, or by a fine not exceeding two thousand five hundred dollars ($2,500) or by both. *(Added by Stats.1980, c. 1126, p. 3627, § 8.)*

Cross References

Consumer debt and consumer credit defined for purposes of this Title, see Civil Code § 1788.2.
Creditor defined for purposes of this Title, see Civil Code § 1788.2.
Debt collector defined for purposes of this Title, see Civil Code § 1788.2.
Debt defined for purposes of this Title, see Civil Code § 1788.2.
Misdemeanors, definition and penalties, see Penal Code §§ 17, 19, 19.2.
Private child support collectors, prohibited acts, see Family Code § 5614.

§ 1788.17. Compliance with federal provisions

Notwithstanding any other provision of this title, every debt collector collecting or attempting to collect a consumer debt shall comply with the provisions of Sections 1692b to 1692j, inclusive, of, and shall be subject to the remedies in Section 1692k of, Title 15 of the United States Code. However, subsection (11) of Section 1692e and Section 1692g shall not apply to any person specified in paragraphs (A) and (B) of subsection (6) of Section 1692a of Title 15 of the United States Code or that person's principal. The references to federal codes in this section refer to those codes as they read

§ 1788.17

January 1, 2001. *(Added by Stats.1999, c. 319 (A.B.969), § 2. Amended by Stats.2000, c. 688 (A.B.1669), § 1.)*

Cross References

Consumer debt and consumer credit defined for purposes of this Title, see Civil Code § 1788.2.
Debt collector defined for purposes of this Title, see Civil Code § 1788.2.
Debt defined for purposes of this Title, see Civil Code § 1788.2.
Person defined for purposes of this Title, see Civil Code § 1788.2.

§ 1788.18. Debtor as an alleged victim of identity theft; sworn statement; inferences and presumptions; duties after collection terminated

(a) Upon receipt from a debtor of all of the following, a debt collector shall cease collection activities until completion of the review provided in subdivision (d):

(1) A copy of a Federal Trade Commission (FTC) identity theft report, completed and signed by the debtor. The debtor may choose, instead, to send a copy of a police report filed by the debtor alleging that the debtor is the victim of an identity theft crime, including, but not limited to, a violation of Section 530.5 of the Penal Code, for the specific debt being collected by the debt collector; however, the debt collector shall not also require a police report if the debtor submits an FTC identity theft report.

(2) The debtor's written statement that the debtor claims to be the victim of identity theft with respect to the specific debt being collected by the debt collector.

(b) The written statement described in paragraph (2) of subdivision (a) shall consist of any of the following:

(1) A written statement that contains the content of the Identity Theft Victim's Fraudulent Account Information Request offered to the public by the California Office of Privacy Protection.

(2) A written statement that certifies that the representations are true, correct, and contain no material omissions of fact to the best knowledge and belief of the person submitting the certification. A person submitting the certification who declares as true any material matter pursuant to this subdivision that they know to be false is guilty of a misdemeanor. The statement shall contain or be accompanied by the following, to the extent that an item listed below is relevant to the debtor's allegation of identity theft with respect to the debt in question:

(A) A statement that the debtor is a victim of identity theft.

(B) A copy of the debtor's driver's license or identification card, as issued by the state.

(C) Any other identification document that supports the statement of identity theft.

(D) Specific facts supporting the claim of identity theft, if available.

(E) Any explanation showing that the debtor did not incur the debt.

(F) Any available correspondence disputing the debt after transaction information has been provided to the debtor.

(G) Documentation of the residence of the debtor at the time of the alleged debt. This may include copies of bills and statements, such as utility bills, tax statements, or other statements from businesses sent to the debtor, showing that the debtor lived at another residence at the time the debt was incurred.

(H) A telephone number for contacting the debtor concerning any additional information or questions, or direction that further communications to the debtor be in writing only, with the mailing address specified in the statement.

(I) To the extent the debtor has information concerning who may have incurred the debt, the identification of any person whom the debtor believes is responsible.

(J) An express statement that the debtor did not authorize the use of the debtor's name or personal information for incurring the debt.

(K) The certification required pursuant to this paragraph shall be sufficient if it is in substantially the following form:

"I certify the representations made are true, correct, and contain no material omissions of fact.

———————————————— ————————————————"
(Date and Place)   (Signature)

(c) If a debtor notifies a debt collector orally that they are a victim of identity theft, the debt collector shall notify the debtor, orally or in writing, that the debtor's claim must be in writing. If a debtor notifies a debt collector in writing that they are a victim of identity theft, but omits information required pursuant to subdivision (a) or, if applicable, the certification required pursuant to paragraph (3) of subdivision (b), if the debt collector does not cease collection activities, the debt collector shall provide written notice to the debtor of the additional information that is required, or the certification required pursuant to paragraph (3) of subdivision (b), as applicable, or send the debtor a copy of the Federal Trade Commission's identity theft form.

(d) Within 10 business days of receiving the complete statement and information described in subdivision (a), the debt collector shall, if it furnished adverse information about the debtor to a consumer credit reporting agency, notify the consumer credit reporting agency that the account is disputed, and initiate a review considering all of the information provided by the debtor and other information available to the debt collector in its file or from the creditor. The debt collector shall send notice of its determination to the debtor no later than 10 business days after concluding the review. The debt collector may recommence debt collection activities only upon making a good faith determination that the information does not establish that the debtor is not responsible for the specific debt in question. The debt collector's determination shall be made in a manner consistent with the provisions of subsection (1) of Section 1692 of Title 15 of the United States Code, as incorporated by Section 1788.17 of this code. The debt collector shall notify the debtor in writing of that determination and the basis for that determination before proceeding with any further collection activities. The debt collector's determination shall be based on all of the information provided by the debtor and other information available to the debt collector in its file or from the creditor.

(e) No inference or presumption that the debt is valid or invalid, or that the debtor is liable or not liable for the debt, shall arise if the debt collector decides after the review described in subdivision (d) to cease or recommence the debt collection activities. The exercise or nonexercise of rights under this section is not a waiver of any other right or defense of the debtor or debt collector.

(f) The statement and supporting documents that comply with subdivision (a) may also satisfy, to the extent those documents meet the requirements of, the notice requirement of paragraph (5) of subdivision (c) of Section 1798.93.

(g) A debt collector who ceases collection activities under this section and does not recommence those collection activities shall do all of the following:

(1) If the debt collector has furnished adverse information to a consumer credit reporting agency, notify the agency to delete that information no later than 10 business days after making its determination.

(2) Notify the creditor no later than 10 business days after making its determination that debt collection activities have been terminated based upon the debtor's claim of identity theft.

(h) A debt collector who has possession of documents that the debtor is entitled to request from a creditor pursuant to Section 530.8 of the Penal Code is authorized to provide those documents to the debtor.

(i) Notwithstanding subdivision (h) of Section 1788.2, for the purposes of this section, "debtor" means a natural person, firm, association, organization, partnership, business trust, company, corporation, or limited liability company from which a debt collector seeks to collect a debt that is due and owing or alleged to be due and owing from the person or entity. The remedies provided by this title shall apply equally to violations of this section. *(Added by Stats.2003, c. 287 (A.B.1294), § 1. Amended by Stats.2006, c. 521 (A.B.2043), § 2; Stats.2007, c. 130 (A.B.299), § 34; Stats.2016, c. 376 (A.B.1723), § 3, eff. Jan. 1, 2017; Stats.2020, c. 36 (A.B.3364), § 13, eff. Jan. 1, 2021; Stats.2021, c. 265 (A.B.430), § 1, eff. Jan. 1, 2022.)*

Cross References

Consumer debt and consumer credit defined for purposes of this Title, see Civil Code § 1788.2.
Creditor defined for purposes of this Title, see Civil Code § 1788.2.
Debt collector defined for purposes of this Title, see Civil Code § 1788.2.
Debt defined for purposes of this Title, see Civil Code § 1788.2.
Debtor defined for purposes of this Title, see Civil Code § 1788.2.
Misdemeanors, definition and penalties, see Penal Code §§ 17, 19, 19.2.
Person defined for purposes of this Title, see Civil Code § 1788.2.
Sale of consumer debt to debt collector, identity theft, subsidiaries or affiliates, interstate commerce requirement, see Civil Code § 1785.16.12.

§ 1788.185. Complaint for action by debt collector for debt that originated with a general acute care hospital license; attachments to complaint; default judgment

(a) The complaint in an action brought by a debt collector for debt that originated with a general acute care hospital licensed pursuant to subdivision (a) of Section 1250 of the Health and Safety Code shall allege all of the following:

(1) That the plaintiff is a debt collector.

(2) That the underlying debt originated with a general acute care hospital.

(3) The information contained in paragraph (6) of subdivision (e) of Section 127425 of the Health and Safety Code and a statement identifying the language in which that information was sent to the debtor.

(4) The balance of the debt upon assignment to the debt collector and an explanation of the amount, nature, and reason for any interest and fees that are added to the debt balance by the debt collector after the assignment of the debt. This paragraph shall not be deemed to require a specific itemization, but the explanation shall identify separately the charge-off balance of the debt upon assignment to the debt collector, the total of any interest, and the total of any fees added to the debt balance by the debt collector after the assignment of the debt.

(5) The date of default or the date of the last payment, and the date the debt was assigned.

(6) The name and address of the hospital at the time of assignment.

(7) The hospital's account number associated with the debt.

(b) Copies of the application for financial assistance that was provided to the debtor by the hospital and the notice that was provided to the debtor by the hospital about applying for financial assistance shall be attached to the complaint. If the notice was provided as part of the hospital bill that cannot be separated, the bill shall be redacted to remove confidential information or a sample hospital bill with the substance of the notice regarding financial assistance in the format in use at the time the patient was billed may be provided.

(c) This title does not require the disclosure in public records of personal, financial, or medical information, the confidentiality of which is protected by state or federal law. The plaintiff shall redact protected information filed with the complaint.

(d) A default or other judgment shall not be entered against a debtor for debt pursuant to this section unless business records, authenticated through a sworn declaration, are submitted by the debt collector to the court to establish the facts required to be alleged pursuant to subdivision (a).

(e) If a debt collector plaintiff seeks a default judgment and has not complied with this title, the court shall not enter a default judgment for the plaintiff and may, in its discretion, dismiss the action.

(f) Except as provided in this title, this section does not modify or otherwise amend the procedures established in Section 585 of the Code of Civil Procedure. *(Added by Stats.2021, c. 473 (A.B.1020), § 2, eff. Jan. 1, 2022.)*

ARTICLE 3. DEBTOR RESPONSIBILITIES

Section
1788.20. Request or application for credit; inability or lack of intention to pay obligation; falsity of or concealment of information.
1788.21. Notice of change in name, address or employment; disclosure by creditor of debtor's responsibility.

Section
1788.22. Credit extended under an account; duties of debtor disclosure by creditor of debtor's responsibility.

§ 1788.20. Request or application for credit; inability or lack of intention to pay obligation; falsity of or concealment of information

In connection with any request or application for consumer credit, no person shall:

(a) Request or apply for such credit at a time when such person knows there is no reasonable probability of such person's being able, or such person then lacks the intention, to pay the obligation created thereby in accordance with the terms and conditions of the credit extension; or

(b) Knowingly submit false or inaccurate information or willfully conceal adverse information bearing upon such person's credit worthiness, credit standing, or credit capacity. *(Added by Stats.1977, c. 907, p. 2771, § 1.)*

Cross References

Consumer debt and consumer credit defined for purposes of this Title, see Civil Code § 1788.2.
Person defined for purposes of this Title, see Civil Code § 1788.2.

§ 1788.21. Notice of change in name, address or employment; disclosure by creditor of debtor's responsibility

(a) In connection with any consumer credit existing or requested to be extended to a person, such person shall within a reasonable time notify the creditor or prospective creditor of any change in such person's name, address, or employment.

(b) Each responsibility set forth in subdivision (a) shall apply only if and after the creditor clearly and conspicuously in writing discloses such responsibility to such person. *(Added by Stats.1977, c. 907, p. 2771, § 1.)*

Cross References

Consumer debt and consumer credit defined for purposes of this Title, see Civil Code § 1788.2.
Creditor defined for purposes of this Title, see Civil Code § 1788.2.
Person defined for purposes of this Title, see Civil Code § 1788.2.

§ 1788.22. Credit extended under an account; duties of debtor disclosure by creditor of debtor's responsibility

(a) In connection with any consumer credit extended to a person under an account:

(1) No such person shall attempt to consummate any consumer credit transaction thereunder knowing that credit privileges under the account have been terminated or suspended.

(2) Each such person shall notify the creditor by telephone, telegraph, letter, or any other reasonable means that an unauthorized use of the account has occurred or may occur as the result of loss or theft of a credit card, or other instrument identifying the account, within a reasonable time after such person's discovery thereof, and shall reasonably assist the creditor in determining the facts and circumstances relating to any unauthorized use of the account.

(b) Each responsibility set forth in subdivision (a) shall apply only if and after the creditor clearly and conspicuously in writing discloses such responsibility to such person. *(Added by Stats.1977, c. 907, p. 2771, § 1.)*

Cross References

Consumer credit transaction defined for purposes of this Title, see Civil Code § 1788.2.
Consumer debt and consumer credit defined for purposes of this Title, see Civil Code § 1788.2.
Creditor defined for purposes of this Title, see Civil Code § 1788.2.
Person defined for purposes of this Title, see Civil Code § 1788.2.

ARTICLE 4. ENFORCEMENT

Section
1788.30. Liability of debt collector; individual action; actual and punitive damages; costs; cure of violation; venue; defenses.
1788.31. Severability.
1788.32. Cumulative remedies; effect on existing regulations.
1788.33. Public policy; waiver of rights.

Cross References

Unlawful conduct for collection of debts, see Civil Code § 1788.10 et seq.

§ 1788.30. Liability of debt collector; individual action; actual and punitive damages; costs; cure of violation; venue; defenses

(a) Any debt collector who violates this title with respect to any debtor shall be liable to that debtor only in an individual action, and his liability therein to that debtor shall be in an amount equal to the sum of any actual damages sustained by the debtor as a result of the violation.

(b) Any debt collector who willfully and knowingly violates this title with respect to any debtor shall, in addition to actual damages sustained by the debtor as a result of the violation, also be liable to the debtor only in an individual action, and his additional liability therein to that debtor shall be for a penalty in such amount as the court may allow, which shall not be less than one hundred dollars ($100) nor greater than one thousand dollars ($1,000).

(c) In the case of any action to enforce any liability under this title, the prevailing party shall be entitled to costs of the action. Reasonable attorney's fees, which shall be based on time necessarily expended to enforce the liability, shall be awarded to a prevailing debtor; reasonable attorney's fees may be awarded to a prevailing creditor upon a finding by the court that the debtor's prosecution or defense of the action was not in good faith.

(d) A debt collector shall have no civil liability under this title if, within 15 days either after discovering a violation which is able to be cured, or after the receipt of a written notice of such violation, the debt collector notifies the debtor of the violation, and makes whatever adjustments or corrections are necessary to cure the violation with respect to the debtor.

(e) A debt collector shall have no civil liability to which such debt collector might otherwise be subject for a violation of this title, if the debt collector shows by a preponderance of evidence that the violation was not intentional and resulted notwithstanding the maintenance of procedures reasonably adapted to avoid any such violation.

(f) Any action under this section may be brought in any appropriate court of competent jurisdiction in an individual capacity only, within one year from the date of the occurrence of the violation.

(g) Any intentional violation of the provisions of this title by the debtor may be raised as a defense by the debt collector, if such violation is pertinent or relevant to any claim or action brought against the debt collector by or on behalf of the debtor. *(Added by Stats.1977, c. 907, p. 2771, § 1.)*

Cross References

Creditor defined for purposes of this Title, see Civil Code § 1788.2.
Debt collector defined for purposes of this Title, see Civil Code § 1788.2.
Debt defined for purposes of this Title, see Civil Code § 1788.2.
Debtor defined for purposes of this Title, see Civil Code § 1788.2.
Private child support collectors, civil liability, see Family Code § 5615.

§ 1788.31. Severability

If any provision of this title, or the application thereof to any person or circumstances, is held invalid, the remaining provisions of this title, or the application of such provisions to other persons or circumstances, shall not be affected thereby. *(Added by Stats.1977, c. 907, p. 2771, § 1.)*

Cross References

Person defined for purposes of this Title, see Civil Code § 1788.2.

§ 1788.32. Cumulative remedies; effect on existing regulations

The remedies provided herein are intended to be cumulative and are in addition to any other procedures, rights, or remedies under any other provision of law. The enactment of this title shall not supersede existing administrative regulations of the Director of Consumer Affairs except to the extent that those regulations are inconsistent with the provisions of this title. *(Added by Stats.1977, c. 907, p. 2771, § 1.)*

§ 1788.33. Public policy; waiver of rights

Any waiver of the provisions of this title is contrary to public policy, and is void and unenforceable. *(Added by Stats.2002, c. 815 (A.B.2331), § 12.)*

Title 1.6C.5

FAIR DEBT BUYING PRACTICES

Section
1788.50. Definitions; application of title.
1788.52. Debt buyer written statements to debtor to attempt debt collection; information that must be provided to debtor; timing requirements; written notice; form; conflict of laws.
1788.54. Settlement agreements; requirement of written agreement or documentation in open court; monthly and final statement requirements for payments by debtor.
1788.56. Statute of limitations bar to actions.
1788.58. Actions brought by debt buyer; contents of complaint; requirements.
1788.60. Default or other judgment; submissions to establish facts alleged in complaint; dismissal of action.

Section
1788.61. Motion to set aside default or default judgment entered on or after Jan. 1, 2010; time for bringing motion; notice of motion; other remedies; cases of identity theft or mistaken identity.
1788.62. Violations of title by debt buyer; liability; damages; court considerations; limitation of actions.
1788.64. Waiver of provisions void.
1788.65. Repealed.
1788.66. COVID–19 rental debt; persons qualifying for federal rental assistance funding; restrictions on sale or assignment.

Cross References

Debt collector license, violation of division, notice and opportunity for hearing, ancillary relief, see Financial Code § 100005.
Powers and duties of Commissioner on Business Oversight, debt collector licensing, see Financial Code § 100003.
Proceedings for revocation of license, debt collector licensing, see Financial Code § 100003.3.

§ 1788.50. Definitions; application of title

(a) As used in this title:

(1) "Debt buyer" means a person or entity that is regularly engaged in the business of purchasing charged-off consumer debt for collection purposes, whether it collects the debt itself, hires a third party for collection, or hires an attorney-at-law for collection litigation. "Debt buyer" does not mean a person or entity that acquires a charged-off consumer debt incidental to the purchase of a portfolio predominantly consisting of consumer debt that has not been charged off.

(2) "Charged-off consumer debt" means a consumer debt that has been removed from a creditor's books as an asset and treated as a loss or expense.

(b) The acquisition by a check services company of the right to collect on a paper or electronic check instrument, including an Automated Clearing House item, that has been returned unpaid to a merchant does not constitute a purchase of delinquent consumer debt under this title.

(c) Terms defined in Title 1.6C (commencing with Section 1788) shall apply to this title.

(d) This title shall apply to debt buyers with respect to all consumer debt sold or resold on or after January 1, 2014. *(Added by Stats.2013, c. 64 (S.B.233), § 2.)*

Cross References

Consumer debt buyer collection actions, debt buyer plaintiff failure to appear, dismissal and award of costs, see Code of Civil Procedure § 581.5.

§ 1788.52. Debt buyer written statements to debtor to attempt debt collection; information that must be provided to debtor; timing requirements; written notice; form; conflict of laws

(a) A debt buyer shall not make any written statement to a debtor in an attempt to collect a consumer debt unless the debt buyer possesses the following information:

(1) That the debt buyer is the sole owner of the debt at issue or has authority to assert the rights of all owners of the debt.

(2) The debt balance at charge off and an explanation of the amount, nature, and reason for all post-charge-off

interest and fees, if any, imposed by the charge-off creditor or any subsequent purchasers of the debt. This paragraph shall not be deemed to require a specific itemization, but the explanation shall identify separately the charge-off balance, the total of any post-charge-off interest, and the total of any post-charge-off fees.

(3) The date of default or the date of the last payment.

(4) The name and an address of the charge-off creditor at the time of charge off, and the charge-off creditor's account number associated with the debt. The charge-off creditor's name and address shall be in sufficient form so as to reasonably identify the charge-off creditor.

(5) The name and last known address of the debtor as they appeared in the charge-off creditor's records prior to the sale of the debt. If the debt was sold prior to January 1, 2014, the name and last known address of the debtor as they appeared in the debt owner's records on December 31, 2013, shall be sufficient.

(6) The names and addresses of all persons or entities that purchased the debt after charge off, including the debt buyer making the written statement. The names and addresses shall be in sufficient form so as to reasonably identify each such purchaser.

(7) The California license number of the debt buyer.

(b) A debt buyer shall not make any written statement to a debtor in an attempt to collect a consumer debt unless the debt buyer has access to a copy of a contract or other document evidencing the debtor's agreement to the debt. If the claim is based on debt for which no signed contract or agreement exists, the debt buyer shall have access to a copy of a document provided to the debtor while the account was active, demonstrating that the debt was incurred by the debtor. For a revolving credit account, the most recent monthly statement recording a purchase transaction, last payment, or balance transfer shall be deemed sufficient to satisfy this requirement.

(c) A debt buyer shall provide the information or documents identified in subdivisions (a) and (b) to the debtor without charge within 15 calendar days of receipt of a debtor's written request for information regarding the debt or proof of the debt. If the debt buyer cannot provide the information or documents within 15 calendar days, the debt buyer shall cease all collection of the debt until the debt buyer provides the debtor the information or documents described in subdivisions (a) and (b). Except as provided otherwise in this title, the request by the debtor shall be consistent with the validation requirements contained in Section 1692g of Title 15 of the United States Code. A debt buyer shall provide all debtors with whom it has contact an active postal address to which these requests can be sent. A debt buyer may also provide an active email address to which these requests can be sent and through which information and documents can be delivered, if the parties agree.

(d)(1) A debt buyer shall include with its first written communication with the debtor in no smaller than 12–point type, a separate prominent notice that provides:

"You may request records showing the following: (1) that [insert name of debt buyer] has the right to seek collection of the debt; (2) the debt balance, including an explanation of any interest charges and additional fees; (3) the date of default or the date of the last payment; (4) the name of the charge-off creditor and the account number associated with the debt; (5) the name and last known address of the debtor as it appeared in the charge-off creditor's or debt buyer's records prior to the sale of the debt, as appropriate; and (6) the names of all persons or entities that have purchased the debt. You may also request from us a copy of the contract or other document evidencing your agreement to the debt.

"A request for these records may be addressed to: [insert debt buyer's active mailing address and email address, if applicable]."

(2) When collecting on a time-barred debt where the debt is not past the date for obsolescence provided for in Section 605(a) of the federal Fair Credit Reporting Act (15 U.S.C. Sec. 1681c):

"The law limits how long you can be sued on a debt. Because of the age of your debt, we will not sue you for it. If you do not pay the debt, [insert name of debt buyer] may [continue to] report it to the credit reporting agencies as unpaid for as long as the law permits this reporting."

(3) When collecting on a time-barred debt where the debt is past the date for obsolescence provided for in Section 605(a) of the federal Fair Credit Reporting Act (15 U.S.C. Sec. 1681c):

"The law limits how long you can be sued on a debt. Because of the age of your debt, we will not sue you for it, and we will not report it to any credit reporting agency."

(e) If a language other than English is principally used by the debt buyer in the initial oral contact with the debtor, the notice required by subdivision (d) shall be provided to the debtor in that language within five working days.

(f) A debt buyer shall not collect, or make any attempt to collect consumer debt that originated with a hospital licensed pursuant to subdivision (a) of Section 1250 of the Health and Safety Code without including in the first written communication to the debtor a copy of the notice required pursuant to subdivision (e) of Section 127425 of the Health and Safety Code.

(g) In the event of a conflict between the requirements of subdivision (d) and federal law, so that it is impracticable to comply with both, the requirements of federal law shall prevail. *(Added by Stats.2013, c. 64 (S.B.233), § 2. Amended by Stats.2020, c. 163 (S.B.908), § 2, eff. Jan. 1, 2021; Stats. 2021, c. 473 (A.B.1020), § 3, eff. Jan. 1, 2022.)*

Cross References

Statement upon debtor's written request to debt collector with assigned delinquent debt, see Civil Code § 1788.14.5.

§ 1788.54. Settlement agreements; requirement of written agreement or documentation in open court; monthly and final statement requirements for payments by debtor

(a) All settlement agreements between a debt buyer and a debtor shall be documented in open court or otherwise reduced to writing. The debt buyer shall ensure that a copy of the written agreement is provided to the debtor.

(b) A debt buyer that receives payment on a debt shall provide, within 30 calendar days, a receipt or monthly statement, to the debtor. The receipt or statement shall clearly and conspicuously show the amount and date paid, the name of the entity paid, the current account number, the name of the charge-off creditor, the account number issued by the charge-off creditor, and the remaining balance owing, if any. The receipt or statement may be provided electronically if the parties agree.

(c) A debt buyer that accepts a payment as payment in full, or as a full and final compromise of the debt, shall provide, within 30 calendar days, a final statement that complies with subdivision (b). A debt buyer shall not sell an interest in a resolved debt, or any personal or financial information related to the resolved debt. *(Added by Stats.2013, c. 64 (S.B.233), § 2.)*

§ 1788.56. Statute of limitations bar to actions

A debt buyer shall not bring suit or initiate an arbitration or other legal proceeding to collect a consumer debt if the applicable statute of limitations on the debt buyer's claim has expired. *(Added by Stats.2013, c. 64 (S.B.233), § 2.)*

§ 1788.58. Actions brought by debt buyer; contents of complaint; requirements

In an action brought by a debt buyer on a consumer debt:

(a) The complaint shall allege all of the following:

(1) That the plaintiff is a debt buyer.

(2) The nature of the underlying debt and the consumer transaction or transactions from which it is derived, in a short and plain statement.

(3) That the debt buyer is the sole owner of the debt at issue, or has authority to assert the rights of all owners of the debt.

(4) The debt balance at charge off and an explanation of the amount, nature, and reason for all post-charge-off interest and fees, if any, imposed by the charge-off creditor or any subsequent purchasers of the debt. This paragraph shall not be deemed to require a specific itemization, but the explanation shall identify separately the charge-off balance, the total of any post-charge-off interest, and the total of any post-charge-off fees.

(5) The date of default or the date of the last payment.

(6) The name and an address of the charge-off creditor at the time of charge off and the charge-off creditor's account number associated with the debt. The charge-off creditor's name and address shall be in sufficient form so as to reasonably identify the charge-off creditor.

(7) The name and last known address of the debtor as they appeared in the charge-off creditor's records prior to the sale of the debt. If the debt was sold prior to January 1, 2014, the debtor's name and last known address as they appeared in the debt owner's records on December 31, 2013, shall be sufficient.

(8) The names and addresses of all persons or entities that purchased the debt after charge off, including the plaintiff debt buyer. The names and addresses shall be in sufficient form so as to reasonably identify each such purchaser.

(9) That the debt buyer has complied with Section 1788.52.

(b) A copy of the contract or other document described in subdivision (b) of Section 1788.52 shall be attached to the complaint.

(c) The complaint in an action brought by a debt buyer for debt that originated with a general acute care hospital licensed pursuant to subdivision (a) of Section 1250 of the Health and Safety Code shall also contain both of the following:

(1) The information contained in paragraph (6) of subdivision (e) of Section 127425 of the Health and Safety Code and a statement identifying the language in which that information was sent to the debtor.

(2) Copies of the application for financial assistance that was provided to the debtor by the hospital and the notice that was provided to the debtor by the hospital about applying for financial assistance, attached to the complaint. If the notice was provided as part of the hospital bill that cannot be separated, the bill shall be redacted to remove confidential information, or a sample hospital bill with the substance of the notice regarding financial assistance in the format in use at the time the patient was billed may be provided.

(d) The requirements of this title shall not be deemed to require the disclosure in public records of personal, financial, or medical information, the confidentiality of which is protected by any state or federal law. *(Added by Stats.2013, c. 64 (S.B.233), § 2. Amended by Stats.2014, c. 71 (S.B.1304), § 16, eff. Jan. 1, 2015; Stats.2021, c. 473 (A.B.1020), § 4, eff. Jan. 1, 2022.)*

§ 1788.60. Default or other judgment; submissions to establish facts alleged in complaint; dismissal of action

(a) In an action initiated by a debt buyer, no default or other judgment may be entered against a debtor unless business records, authenticated through a sworn declaration, are submitted by the debt buyer to the court to establish the facts required to be alleged by paragraphs (3) to (8), inclusive, of subdivision (a) of Section 1788.58.

(b) No default or other judgment may be entered against a debtor unless a copy of the contract or other document described in subdivision (b) of Section 1788.52, authenticated through a sworn declaration, has been submitted by the debt buyer to the court.

(c) In any action on a consumer debt, if a debt buyer plaintiff seeks a default judgment and has not complied with the requirements of this title, the court shall not enter a default judgment for the plaintiff and may, in its discretion, dismiss the action.

(d) Except as provided in this title, this section is not intended to modify or otherwise amend the procedures established in Section 585 of the Code of Civil Procedure. *(Added by Stats.2013, c. 64 (S.B.233), § 2.)*

§ 1788.61. Motion to set aside default or default judgment entered on or after Jan. 1, 2010; time for bringing motion; notice of motion; other remedies; cases of identity theft or mistaken identity

(a)(1) Notwithstanding Section 473.5 of the Code of Civil Procedure, if service of a summons has not resulted in actual notice to a person in time to defend an action brought by a debt buyer and a default or default judgment has been entered against the person in the action, the person may serve and file a notice of motion and motion to set aside the default or default judgment and for leave to defend the action.

(2) Except as provided in paragraph (3), the notice of motion shall be served and filed within a reasonable time, but in no event exceeding the earlier of:

(A) Six years after entry of the default or default judgment against the person.

(B) One hundred eighty days of the first actual notice of the action.

(3)(A) Notwithstanding paragraph (2), in the case of identity theft or mistaken identity, the notice of motion shall be served and filed within a reasonable time, but in no event exceeding 180 days of the first actual notice of the action.

(B)(i) In the case of identity theft, the person alleging that they are a victim of identity theft shall provide the court with either a copy of a Federal Trade Commission identity theft report or a copy of a police report filed by the person alleging that they are the victim of an identity theft crime, including, but not limited to, a violation of Section 530.5 of the Penal Code, for the specific debt associated with the judgment.

(ii) In the case of mistaken identity, the moving party shall provide relevant information or documentation to support the claim that they are not the party named in the judgment or is not the person who incurred or owes the debt.

(b) A notice of motion to set aside a default or default judgment and for leave to defend the action shall designate as the time for making the motion a date prescribed by Section 1005 of the Code of Civil Procedure, and it shall be accompanied by an affidavit stating under oath that the person's lack of actual notice in time to defend the action was not caused by their avoidance of service or inexcusable neglect. The person shall serve and file with the notice a copy of the answer, motion, or other pleading proposed to be filed in the action. Either party may introduce, and the court may consider, evidence in support of its motion or opposition, including evidence relating to the process server who appears on the proof of service of the summons and complaint.

(c) Upon a finding by the court that the motion was made within the period permitted by subdivision (a) and that the person's lack of actual notice in time to defend the action was not caused by their avoidance of service or inexcusable neglect, the court may set aside the default or default judgment on whatever terms as may be just and allow the party to defend the action. If the validity of the judgment is not challenged, the court may select an appropriate remedy other than setting aside the default or default judgment.

(d) This section shall apply to a default or default judgment entered on or after January 1, 2010, except in the case of identity theft or mistaken identity, in which case this section shall apply regardless of the date of the default or default judgment.

(e) This section shall not limit the equitable authority of the court or other available remedies under law. *(Added by Stats.2015, c. 804 (S.B.641), § 1, eff. Jan. 1, 2016. Amended by Stats.2021, c. 265 (A.B.430), § 2, eff. Jan. 1, 2022.)*

Cross References

Private student loans, motion to set aside default judgment, see Civil Code § 1788.207.

§ 1788.62. Violations of title by debt buyer; liability; damages; court considerations; limitation of actions

(a) In the case of an action brought by an individual or individuals, a debt buyer that violates any provision of this title with respect to any person shall be liable to that person in an amount equal to the sum of the following:

(1) Any actual damages sustained by that person as a result of the violation, including, but not limited to, the amount of any judgment obtained by the debt buyer as a result of a time-barred suit to collect a debt from that person.

(2) Statutory damages in an amount as the court may allow, which shall not be less than one hundred dollars ($100) nor greater than one thousand dollars ($1,000).

(b) In the case of a class action, a debt buyer that violates any provision of this title shall be liable for any statutory damages for each named plaintiff as provided in paragraph (2) of subdivision (a). If the court finds that the debt buyer engaged in a pattern and practice of violating any provision of this title, the court may award additional damages to the class in an amount not to exceed the lesser of five hundred thousand dollars ($500,000) or 1 percent of the net worth of the debt buyer.

(c)(1) In the case of any successful action to enforce liability under this section, the court shall award costs of the action, together with reasonable attorney's fees as determined by the court.

(2) Reasonable attorney's fees may be awarded to a prevailing debt buyer upon a finding by the court that the plaintiff's prosecution of the action was not in good faith.

(d) In determining the amount of liability under subdivision (b), the court shall consider, among other relevant factors, the frequency and persistence of noncompliance by the debt buyer, the nature of the noncompliance, the resources of the debt buyer, and the number of persons adversely affected.

(e) A debt buyer shall have no civil liability under this section if the debt buyer shows by a preponderance of evidence that the violation was not intentional and resulted from a bona fide error, and occurred notwithstanding the maintenance of procedures reasonably adopted to avoid any error.

(f) An action to enforce any liability created by this title shall be brought within one year from the date of the last violation.

(g) Recovery in an action brought under the Rosenthal Fair Debt Collection Practices Act (Title 1.6C (commencing with Section 1788)) or the federal Fair Debt Collection Practices Act (15 U.S.C. Sec. 1692 et seq.) shall preclude recovery for the same acts in an action brought under this title. *(Added by Stats.2013, c. 64 (S.B.233), § 2.)*

§ 1788.64. Waiver of provisions void

Any waiver of the provisions of this title is contrary to public policy, and is void and unenforceable. *(Added by Stats.2013, c. 64 (S.B.233), § 2.)*

§ 1788.65. Repealed by Stats.2021, c. 27 (A.B.832), § 2, operative Oct. 1, 2021

§ 1788.66. COVID–19 rental debt; persons qualifying for federal rental assistance funding; restrictions on sale or assignment

Notwithstanding any other law, a person shall not sell or assign any unpaid COVID–19 rental debt, as defined in Section 1179.02 of the Code of Civil Procedure, for the time period between March 1, 2020, and September 30, 2021, of any person who would have qualified for rental assistance funding provided by the Secretary of the Treasury pursuant to Section 501 of Subtitle A of Title V of Division N of the federal Consolidated Appropriations Act, 2021 (Public Law 116–260)[1] or Section 3201 of Subtitle B of Title III of the federal American Rescue Plan Act of 2021 (Public Law 117–2), if the person's household income is at or below 80 percent of the area median income for the 2020 or 2021 calendar year. *(Added by Stats.2021, c. 2 (S.B.91), § 4, eff. Jan. 29, 2021. Amended by Stats.2021, c. 5 (A.B.81), § 5, eff. Feb. 23, 2021; Stats.2021, c. 27 (A.B.832), § 3, eff. June 28, 2021.)*

[1] For public law sections classified to the U.S.C.A., see USCA–Tables.

Title 1.6C.7

EDUCATIONAL DEBT COLLECTION PRACTICES

Section
1788.90. Short title.
1788.91. Legislative findings and declarations; withholding of transcripts interferes with student educational and career opportunities.
1788.92. Definitions.
1788.93. Use of transcript issuance as tool for debt collection prohibited.

§ 1788.90. Short title

This title shall be known, and may be cited, as the Educational Debt Collection Practices Act. *(Added by Stats.2019, c. 518 (A.B.1313), § 1, eff. Jan. 1, 2020.)*

§ 1788.91. Legislative findings and declarations; withholding of transcripts interferes with student educational and career opportunities

The Legislature finds and declares all of the following:

(a) Schools and colleges have threatened to withhold transcripts from students as a debt collection tactic. The practice can cause severe hardship by preventing students from pursuing educational and career opportunities, and it is therefore unfair and contrary to public policy. Moreover, the practice is counterproductive as it may further delay the payment of the debt by creating obstacles to student employment.

(b) It is the purpose of this title to prohibit schools from interfering with student educational and career opportunity by the withholding of transcripts. *(Added by Stats.2019, c. 518 (A.B.1313), § 1, eff. Jan. 1, 2020.)*

§ 1788.92. Definitions

For purposes of this title, the following terms shall have the following meanings:

(a) "School" means any public or private postsecondary school, or any public or private entity, responsible for providing transcripts to current or former students of a school.

(b) "Debt" means any money, obligation, claim, or sum, due or owing, or alleged to be due or owing, from a student, but does not include the fee, if any, charged to all students for the actual costs of providing the transcripts. *(Added by Stats.2019, c. 518 (A.B.1313), § 1, eff. Jan. 1, 2020.)*

§ 1788.93. Use of transcript issuance as tool for debt collection prohibited

Notwithstanding any provision of law, a school shall not do any of the following:

(a) Refuse to provide a transcript for a current or former student on the grounds that the student owes a debt.

(b) Condition the provision of a transcript on the payment of a debt, other than a fee charged to provide the transcript.

(c) Charge a higher fee for obtaining a transcript, or provide less favorable treatment of a transcript request because a student owes a debt.

(d) Use transcript issuance as a tool for debt collection. *(Added by Stats.2019, c. 518 (A.B.1313), § 1, eff. Jan. 1, 2020.)*

Cross References

Prohibited practices, see Education Code § 94897.

Title 1.6C.10

STUDENT LOANS: BORROWER RIGHTS

Chapter	Section
1. Student Borrower Bill of Rights	1788.100
2. Setting Clear "Rules of the Road" for the Student Loan Industry	1788.102
3. Enforcement of the Student Borrower Bill of Rights	1788.103
4. Establishment of the California Student Loan Ombudsman	1788.104
5. Shining a Spotlight on Student Loan Industry Practices	1788.105

CHAPTER 1. STUDENT BORROWER BILL OF RIGHTS

Section
1788.100. Definitions.
1788.101. Prohibited acts by student loan servicers; abusive acts or practices defined.

§ 1788.100. Definitions

For purposes of this title, the following definitions apply:

(a) "Borrower" means either of the following:

(1) A person who has received or agreed to pay a student loan.

(2) A person who shares responsibility for repaying a student loan with a person described in paragraph (1).

(b) "Borrower with disabilities" means a borrower who a student loan servicer knows, or reasonably should know, is a person who has a disability, as defined in Section 54.

(c) "Borrower working in public service" means a borrower who a student loan servicer knows, or reasonably should know, is employed in a public service job, as defined in the Higher Education Act (20 U.S.C. Sec. 1087e(m)) and its implementing regulations.

(d) "Commissioner" means the Commissioner of * * * Financial Protection and Innovation.

(e) "Department" means the Department of * * * Financial Protection and Innovation.

(f) "Engage in the business" means, without limitation, servicing student loans.

(g) "In this state" means any activity of a person relating to servicing student loans that originates from this state and is directed to persons outside this state, that originates from outside this state and is directed to persons inside this state, or that originates inside this state and is directed to persons inside this state.

(h) "Licensee" means a person licensed pursuant to the Student Loan Servicing Act (Division 12.5 (commencing with Section 28100) of the Financial Code).

(i) "Military borrower" means any of the following:

(1) A borrower who is one of the following:

(A) A servicemember as defined in the Servicemember Civil Relief Act (50 U.S.C. Sec. 3911).

(B) Self-identifies as a service member when interacting with a student loan servicer.

(C) Is a service member as defined in Section 400 of the Military and Veterans Code.

(2) A borrower who is a veteran of a branch of the Armed Forces as defined in Section 101 of Title 38 of the United States Code.

(3) An authorized representative of a borrower described in paragraph (1) or (2).

(j) "Older borrower" means a borrower who a student loan servicer knows, or reasonably should know, is a senior citizen, as defined in Section 51.3.

(k) "Overpayment" means a payment on a student loan account in excess of the monthly amount due from a borrower on a student loan, also commonly referred to as a prepayment.

(*l*) "Partial payment" means a payment on a student loan account in an amount less than the current amount due from a borrower on the student loan account, also commonly referred to as an underpayment.

(m) "Person" means an individual, a corporation, a partnership, a limited liability company, an association, a trust, an unincorporated organization, a government, or a political subdivision of a government, and any other entity.

(n) "Qualified request" means any inbound telephone call, the subject of which cannot be resolved in a single phone call, made by a borrower to a student loan servicer in which either the borrower requests specific information from the student loan servicer or reports what the borrower believes to be an error regarding the borrower's account.

(*o*) "Qualified written request" means a written correspondence made by a borrower, other than notice on a payment medium supplied by a student loan servicer, that is transmitted by mail, facsimile, or electronically through an email address or internet website designated by the student loan servicer to receive communications from a borrower that does all of the following:

(1) Enables the student loan servicer to identify the name and account of the borrower.

(2) Includes a statement of the reasons for the belief by the borrower, to the extent applicable, that the account is in error or that provides sufficient detail to the servicer regarding information sought by the borrower, such as requesting a complete payment history for the loan or the borrower's account, a copy of the borrower's student loan promissory note, or the contact information for the creditor to whom the borrower's student loan is owed.

(p) "Servicing" means any of the following activities related to a student loan of a borrower:

(1) Performing both of the following:

(A) Receiving any scheduled periodic payments from a borrower or any notification that a borrower made a scheduled periodic payment.

(B) Applying payments to the borrower's account pursuant to the terms of the student loan or the contract governing the servicing.

(2) During a period when no payment is required on a student loan, performing both of the following:

(A) Maintaining account records for the student loan.

(B) Communicating with the borrower regarding the student loan on behalf of the owner of the student loan promissory note.

(3) Interacting with a borrower related to that borrower's student loan, with the goal of helping the borrower avoid default on their student loan or facilitating the activities described in paragraph (1) or (2).

(q)(1) "Student loan" means any loan made solely for use to finance a postsecondary education and costs of attendance at a postsecondary institution, including, but not limited to, tuition, fees, books and supplies, room and board, transportation, and miscellaneous personal expenses. A "student loan" includes a loan made to refinance a student loan.

(2)(A) A "student loan" shall not include an extension of credit under an open-end consumer credit plan, a reverse mortgage transaction, a residential mortgage transaction, or any other loan that is secured by real property or a dwelling.

(B) A "student loan" shall not include an extension of credit made by a postsecondary educational institution to a borrower if one of the following applies:

(i) The term of the extension of credit is no longer than the borrower's education program.

(ii) The remaining, unpaid principal balance of the extension of credit is less than one thousand five hundred dollars ($1,500) at the time of the borrower's graduation or completion of the program.

(iii) The borrower fails to graduate or successfully complete their education program and has a balance due at the time of their disenrollment from the postsecondary institution.

(r) "Student loan account" means student loans owed by a borrower grouped together for billing purposes by a student loan servicer.

(s) "Student loan servicer" means any person engaged in the business of servicing student loans in this state. A "student loan servicer" does not include any of the following:

(1) A debt collector, as defined in subdivision (c) of Section 1788.2, whose student loan debt collection business, and business operations, involve collecting, or attempting to collect, on defaulted student loans, that is, federal student loans for which no payment has been received for 270 days or more, or private student loans, in default, according to the terms of the loan documents. Debt collectors who also service nondefaulted student loans as part of their business and business operations are "student loan servicers."

(2) In connection with its responsibilities as a guaranty agency engaged in default aversion, a state or nonprofit private institution or organization having an agreement with the United States Secretary of Education under the Higher Education Act of 1965 (20 U.S.C. Sec. 1078(b)).

(3) A federally chartered credit union. *(Added by Stats. 2020, c. 154 (A.B.376), § 2, eff. Jan. 1, 2021. Amended by Stats.2022, c. 452 (S.B.1498), § 20, eff. Jan. 1, 2023.)*

§ 1788.101. Prohibited acts by student loan servicers; abusive acts or practices defined

(a)(1) A person shall not engage in abusive acts or practices when servicing a student loan in this state.

(2) An act or practice is abusive in connection with the servicing of a student loan, if the act or practice does either of the following:

(A) Materially interferes with the ability of a borrower to understand a term or condition of a student loan.

(B) Takes unreasonable advantage of any of the following:

(i) A lack of understanding on the part of a borrower of the material risks, costs, or conditions of the student loan.

(ii) The inability of a borrower to protect the interests of the borrower when selecting or using either of the following:

(I) A student loan.

(II) A feature, term, or condition of a student loan.

(iii) The reasonable reliance by the borrower on a person engaged in servicing a student loan to act in the interests of the borrower.

(3) Abusive acts and practices include, but are not limited to, those described in paragraph (2).

(b) A student loan servicer shall not do any of the following:

(1) Directly or indirectly employ a scheme, device, or artifice to defraud or mislead a borrower.

(2) Engage in an unfair or deceptive practice toward a borrower or misrepresent or omit material information in connection with the servicing of a student loan, including, but not limited to, misrepresenting the amount, nature, or terms of a fee or payment due or claimed to be due on a student loan, the terms and conditions of the student loan agreement, or the borrower's obligations under the student loan.

(3) Misapply payments made by a borrower to the outstanding balance of a student loan.

(4)(A) If the student loan servicer is required to or voluntarily reports to a consumer reporting agency, fail to accurately report each borrower's payment performance to at least one consumer reporting agency that compiles and maintains files on consumers on a nationwide basis, upon acceptance as a data furnisher by that consumer reporting agency.

(B) For purposes of this paragraph, "consumer reporting agency that compiles and maintains files on consumers on a nationwide basis" has the same meaning as defined in the federal Fair Credit Reporting Act (15 U.S.C. Sec. 1681a(p)).

(5) Refuse to communicate with an authorized representative of the borrower who provides a written authorization signed by the borrower, provided the student loan servicer may adopt reasonable procedures for verifying that the representative is in fact authorized to act on behalf of the borrower and for protecting the borrower from fraud or abusive practices.

(6) Negligently or intentionally make a false statement or knowingly and willfully make an omission of a material fact in connection with information or reports filed with the department or another governmental agency.

(7) Engage in an unfair or deceptive practice toward a military borrower or misrepresent or omit material information in connection with the servicing of a student loan owed by a military borrower. For purposes of this paragraph, "misrepresent or omit material information" includes, but is not limited to:

(A) Misrepresenting or omitting the availability of a program or protection specific to military borrowers or applicable to military borrowers.

(B) A misrepresentation or omission in violation of paragraph (2) of this subdivision.

(8) Engage in an unfair or deceptive practice toward any borrower working in public service or misrepresent or omit material information in connection with the servicing of a student loan owed by a borrower working in public service. For purposes of this paragraph, "misrepresent or omit material information" includes, but is not limited to:

(A) Misrepresenting or omitting the availability of a program or protection specific to borrowers working in public service or applicable to those borrowers.

§ 1788.101

(B) A misrepresentation or omission in violation of paragraph (2).

(9) Engage in an unfair or deceptive practice toward an older borrower or older cosigner or misrepresent or omit material information in connection with the servicing of a student loan owed or cosigned by an older borrower. For purposes of this paragraph, "misrepresent or omit material information" includes, but is not limited to:

(A) Misrepresenting or omitting the availability of a program or protection specific to older borrowers or older cosigners or applicable to those borrowers or cosigners.

(B) Misrepresenting or omitting the older borrower's or older cosigner's obligations under the student loan.

(C) A misrepresentation or omission in violation of paragraph (2).

(10) Engage in an unfair or deceptive practice toward a borrower with a disability or misrepresent or omit material information in connection with the servicing of a student loan owed by a borrower with a disability. For purposes of this paragraph, "misrepresent or omit material information" includes, but is not limited to:

(A) Misrepresenting or omitting the availability of a program or protection specific to borrowers with disabilities or applicable to those borrowers.

(B) A misrepresentation or omission in violation of paragraph (2) of this subdivision. *(Added by Stats.2020, c. 154 (A.B.376), § 2, eff. Jan. 1, 2021.)*

CHAPTER 2. SETTING CLEAR "RULES OF THE ROAD" FOR THE STUDENT LOAN INDUSTRY

Section
1788.102. Duties of student loan servicer; processing and allocation of student loan payments; imposition of fees; response to and handling of borrower qualified requests; transfer of servicing of student loans; customer service personnel training.

§ 1788.102. Duties of student loan servicer; processing and allocation of student loan payments; imposition of fees; response to and handling of borrower qualified requests; transfer of servicing of student loans; customer service personnel training

Except to the extent that this section is inconsistent with any provision of federal law or regulation, and then only to the extent of the inconsistency, a student loan servicer shall do all of the following:

(a) Post and process student loan payments in a timely manner pursuant to the servicer's established payment processing policies that shall be disclosed to and readily accessible by borrowers and credit student loan payments in a timely manner in accordance with the following:

(1) A payment received on or before 11:59 p.m. on the date on which that payment is due, in the amount, manner, and location indicated by the person engaged in student loan servicing, shall be credited as effective on the date on which the payment was received by the person engaged in student loan servicing in this state. A person engaged in student loan servicing in this state shall treat a payment received from the borrower on the borrower's due date as an "on-time" payment.

(2) If a payment is made by check, credit the payment on the date the check was received by the student loan servicer regardless of the date of processing. A borrower's online account shall reflect payments made within three business days of the date of payment unless payment is made by check and contains no information identifying to which account or loan the payment should be credited. In the event the student loan servicer receives a paper check with no information identifying to which account or loan the payment should be credited, the student loan servicer shall determine, within 10 business days, to which account and loan the payment should be credited. When the servicer determines to which account and loan the payment should be credited, the servicer shall credit the payment as of the date the payment was received by the servicer and update the borrower's online account within one business day.

(b) If a person engaged in servicing a student loan makes a material change in the mailing address, office, or procedures for handling borrower payments, and that change causes a material delay in the crediting of a borrower payment made during the 60–day period following the date on which that change took effect, the person engaged in servicing the student loan shall not impose on the borrower any negative consequences related to that material change, including negative credit reporting, lost eligibility for a borrower benefit, late fees, interest capitalization, or other financial injury.

(c)(1) Inquire of a borrower how to apply an overpayment to a student loan. A borrower's direction on how to apply an overpayment to a student loan shall be effective with respect to future overpayments during the term of a student loan until the borrower provides a different direction.

(2)(A) In the absence of a direction provided by a borrower pursuant to paragraph (1), allocate an overpayment on a student loan account in a manner that is in the best financial interest of a student loan borrower.

(B) As used in this paragraph, "best financial interest of a student loan borrower" means reducing the total cost of the student loan, including principal balance, interest, and fees.

(3) A student loan servicer shall be considered to meet the requirements of paragraph (2) if the servicer allocates the overpayment to the loan with the highest interest rate on the borrower's student loan account, unless the borrower specifies otherwise.

(d)(1) Except as provided in federal law or required by a student loan agreement, comply with a direction provided by a borrower as to how to allocate a partial payment to a student loan.

(2) In the absence of a direction provided by a borrower pursuant to paragraph (1) of this subdivision, allocate a partial payment in a manner that minimizes late fees and negative credit reporting.

(3) A student loan servicer shall be considered to have satisfied paragraph (2) if, when there are multiple loans on a borrower's student loan account at an equal stage of delinquency, the student loan servicer allocates partial payments

to satisfy as many loans as possible on a borrower's student loan account.

(e)(1) If a student loan servicer imposes a fee on a borrower for a past due student loan payment, that fee shall be reasonable and proportional to the total costs incurred as a result of the late payment by a borrower, and shall not exceed 6 percent of any amount past due.

(2) A student loan servicer shall not impose a minimum late fee. For purposes of this paragraph, "minimum late fee" includes any fee that is not assessed as a percentage of any amount past due.

(f) Diligently oversee its service providers. For purposes of this subdivision, "diligently oversee its service providers" includes maintaining policies and procedures to oversee compliance by third-party service providers engaged in any aspect of student loan servicing. Student loan servicers have joint and several liability for the conduct of their service providers for any act or practice that violates this title.

(g)(1) Timely process its paperwork, consistent with existing federal requirements, including, but not limited to, ensuring that customer service personnel have received both of the following:

(A) Appropriate training about the handling of paperwork.

(B) Access to necessary information about forms and applications that are in process, have been approved, or have been denied.

(2) The requirements of this subdivision include ensuring that customer service personnel have access to applications for income-driven repayment plans and other forms required to access benefits and protections for federal student loans, as described in Section 1070 and following of Title 20 of the United States Code.

(h) Except as required by a student loan agreement, all records about a borrower's account shall be maintained for the period of time during which a person performs student loan servicing for a borrower's account and for a minimum of three years after the loan serviced has been paid in full, assigned to collection, or the servicing rights have been transferred.

(i) Treat a qualified request as if it were a qualified written request and comply with subdivision (t) with respect to that qualified request.

(j) Maintain policies and procedures permitting a borrower who is dissatisfied with the outcome of an initial qualified request to escalate the borrower's concern to a supervisor.

(k)(1) Protect borrowers from any negative consequences that are directly related to the issue identified in a borrower's qualified request or qualified written request until that request has been resolved. For purposes of this subdivision, "negative consequences" include, but are not limited to, negative credit reporting, lost eligibility for a borrower benefit, late fees, interest capitalization, or other financial injury.

(2) Notwithstanding paragraph (1), after receipt of a qualified request or qualified written request related to a dispute on a borrower's payment on a student loan, a student loan servicer shall not, for 60 days, furnish information to a consumer reporting agency regarding a payment that is the subject of the qualified request or the qualified written request.

(*l*) Protect borrowers from any negative consequences stemming from a sale, assignment, transfer, system conversion, or payment made by the borrower to the original student loan servicer consistent with the original student loan servicer's policy. For purposes of this subdivision, "negative consequences" include, but are not limited to, any of the following:

(1) Negative credit reporting.

(2) The imposition of late fees not required by the promissory note.

(3) Loss of or denial of eligibility for any benefit or protection established under federal law or included in a loan contract.

(m) If the sale, assignment, or other transfer of the servicing of a student loan results in a change in the identity of the party to whom the borrower is required to send payments or direct any communications concerning the student loan, the student loan servicer shall notify the borrower in writing at least 15 days before the borrower is required to send a payment on the student loan of all of the following:

(1) The identity of the new student loan servicer and the number of the license, issued by the commissioner, of the new student loan servicer.

(2) The name and address of the new student loan servicer to whom subsequent payments or communications are required to be sent.

(3) The telephone numbers and internet websites of the new student loan servicer.

(4) The effective date of the sale, assignment, or transfer.

(5) The date on which the current student loan servicer will stop accepting payments on the borrower's student loan.

(6) The date on which the new student loan servicer will begin accepting payments on the borrower's student loan.

(n) Ensure all necessary information regarding a borrower, a borrower's account, and a borrower's student loan accompanies a loan when it transfers to a new student loan servicer within 45 calendar days of the effective date of the sale, assignment, or transfer. For purposes of this subdivision, "necessary information" shall include, at minimum, all of the following:

(1) A schedule of all transactions credited or debited to the student loan account.

(2) A copy of the promissory note for the student loan.

(3) Any notes created by the student loan servicer's personnel reflecting communications with the borrower about the student loan account.

(4) A report of the data fields relating to the borrower's student loan account created by the student loan servicer's electronic systems in connection with servicing practices.

(5) Copies or electronic records of any information or documents provided by the borrower to the student loan servicer.

§ 1788.102 OBLIGATIONS

(6) Usable data fields with information necessary to assess qualification for forgiveness, including public service loan forgiveness, if applicable.

(7) Any information necessary to compile a payment history.

(*o*) Provide specialized training for any customer service personnel that advises military borrowers about student loan repayment benefits and protections.

(p) Provide specialized training for any customer service personnel that advises borrowers working in public service about student loan repayment benefits and protections.

(q) Provide specialized training for any customer service personnel that advises older borrowers about risks specifically applicable to older borrowers to ensure that, once identified, older borrowers are informed about student loan repayment benefits and protections, including disability discharge programs for private and federal loans, if applicable, and, to the extent an older borrower serves as cosigner, about cosigner release provisions in private student loan contracts.

(r) Provide specialized training for any customer service personnel that advises borrowers with disabilities about student loan repayment benefits and protections, including disability discharge programs for private and federal loans. Under no circumstances shall a person engage in any unfair or deceptive practice toward any borrower with a disability or misrepresent or omit any material information in connection with the servicing of a student loan owed by a borrower with a disability. For purposes of this subdivision, "misrepresent or omit any material information" includes, but is not limited to, misrepresenting or omitting any of the following:

(1) The availability of any program or protection specific to borrowers with disabilities or applicable to those borrowers.

(2) The amount, nature, or terms of any fee or payment due or claimed to be due on a student loan.

(3) The terms and conditions of the student loan agreement.

(4) The borrower's obligations under the student loan.

(s) Respond within 10 business days to communications from the Student Loan Ombudsman, established pursuant to Chapter 4 (commencing with Section 1788.104), or within a shorter, reasonable time as the Student Loan Ombudsman may request in that person's communication.

(t)(1) Respond to a qualified written request by acknowledging receipt of the request within 10 business days and within 30 business days, provide information relating to the request and, if applicable, either the action the student loan servicer will take to correct the account or an explanation for the position that the borrower's account is correct.

(2) The 30–day period described in paragraph (1) may be extended for not more than 15 days if, before the end of the 30–day period, the student loan servicer notifies the borrower of the extension and the reason for the delay in responding.
(Added by Stats.2020, c. 154 (A.B.376), § 2, eff. Jan. 1, 2021. Amended by Stats.2021, c. 124 (A.B.938), § 5, eff. Jan. 1, 2022.)

CHAPTER 3. ENFORCEMENT OF THE STUDENT BORROWER BILL OF RIGHTS

Section
1788.103. Compliance by student loan servicer; action for damages; penalties; duties of consumer bringing action; compliance with demand not deemed admission of unlawful acts; correction and remedies.

§ 1788.103. Compliance by student loan servicer; action for damages; penalties; duties of consumer bringing action; compliance with demand not deemed admission of unlawful acts; correction and remedies

(a) A student loan servicer shall do both of the following:

(1) Comply with this title.

(2) Comply with all applicable federal laws relating to student loan servicing, as from time to time amended, and the regulations promulgated thereunder.

(b) Any consumer who suffers damage as a result of the failure of a student loan servicer to comply with paragraph (1) or (2) of subdivision (a) may, subject to the requirements of subdivisions (d) to (g), inclusive, bring an action on that consumer's behalf and on behalf of a similarly situated class of consumers against that student loan servicer to recover or obtain any of the following:

(1) Actual damages, but in no case, shall the total award of damages be less than five hundred dollars ($500) per plaintiff, per violation.

(2) An order enjoining the methods, acts, or practices.

(3) Restitution of property.

(4) Punitive damages.

(5) Attorney's fees.

(6) Any other relief that the court deems proper.

(c) In addition to any other remedies provided by this subdivision or otherwise provided by law, whenever it is proven by a preponderance of the evidence that a student loan servicer has engaged in conduct that substantially interferes with a borrower's right to an alternative payment arrangement; loan forgiveness, cancellation, or discharge; or any other financial benefit as established under the terms of a borrower's promissory note or under the Higher Education Act of 1965 (20 U.S.C. Sec. 1070a et seq.), as from time to time amended, and the regulations promulgated thereunder, the court shall award treble actual damages to the plaintiff, but in no case shall the award of damages be less than one thousand five hundred dollars ($1,500) per plaintiff, per violation.

(d)(1) At least 45 days before bringing an action for damages or injunctive relief pursuant to this chapter, a consumer shall do all of the following:

(A) Provide written notice to the person alleged to have violated subdivision (a) regarding the nature of the alleged violations.

(B) Demand that the person correct and remedy the method, acts, or practices to which the notice required by subparagraph (A) refers.

(2) The notice required by this subdivision shall be sent by certified or registered mail, return receipt requested, to the person's address on file with the Department of * * * Financial Protection and Innovation or to the person's principal place of business within California.

(e) An action for damages or injunctive relief brought by a consumer only on that consumer's behalf may not be maintained under subdivision (b) upon a showing by a person that an appropriate correction and remedy is given, or agreed to be given within a reasonable time, to the consumer within 30 days after receipt of the notice.

(f) An action for damages brought by a consumer on both the consumer's behalf and on behalf of a similarly situated class of consumers may not be maintained under subdivision (b) upon a showing by a person alleged to have employed or committed methods, acts, or practices declared unlawful that all of the following are true:

(1) All consumers similarly situated have been identified, or a reasonable effort to identify those other consumers has been made.

(2) All consumers so identified have been notified that, upon their request, the person shall make the appropriate correction and remedy.

(3) The correction and remedy requested by the consumers has been, or, in a reasonable time, will be, given.

(4) The person has ceased from engaging, or if immediate cessation is impossible or unreasonably expensive under the circumstances, the person will, within a reasonable time, cease to engage, in the methods, act, or practices.

(g) Attempts to comply with a demand described in paragraph (2) of subdivision (d) by a person receiving that demand shall be construed to be an offer to compromise and shall be inadmissible as evidence pursuant to Section 1152 of the Evidence Code. Furthermore, these attempts to comply with a demand shall not be considered an admission of engaging in an act or practice declared unlawful by subdivision (a). Evidence of compliance or attempts to comply with this section may be introduced by a defendant for the purpose of establishing good faith or to show compliance with subdivision (a).

(h) An award of damages shall not be given in an action based on a method, act, or practice in violation of subdivision (a) if the person alleged to have employed or committed that method, act, or practice does both of the following:

(1) Proves by a preponderance of the evidence that the violation was not intentional and resulted from a bona fide error notwithstanding the use of reasonable procedures adopted to avoid that error.

(2) Makes an appropriate correction, repair, replacement, or other remedy according to the provisions of subdivisions (d) and (e) as required by law.

(i) The commissioner shall administer and enforce the provisions of this title and may promulgate rules and regulations and issue orders consistent with that authority.

(1) The commissioner shall have the authority to carry over any regulations issued pursuant to the Student Loan Servicing Act in order to implement equivalent provisions of this act.

(2) Any rules issued pursuant to the Student Loan Servicing Act in effect at the time of enactment of this act shall remain in effect until the commissioner repeals or reissues those regulations. (Added by Stats.2020, c. 154 (A.B.376), § 2, eff. Jan. 1, 2021. Amended by Stats.2022, c. 452 (S.B.1498), § 21, eff. Jan. 1, 2023.)

CHAPTER 4. ESTABLISHMENT OF THE CALIFORNIA STUDENT LOAN OMBUDSMAN

Section
1788.104. Student Loan Ombudsman; appointment; review and referral of complaints; duties.

§ 1788.104. Student Loan Ombudsman; appointment; review and referral of complaints; duties

(a) Not later than 180 days following the operative date of this chapter, the commissioner shall designate a Student Loan Ombudsman to work within the department. The Student Loan Ombudsman shall hire additional staff as necessary to implement this section.

(b) The Student Loan Ombudsman shall receive and review complaints from student loan borrowers.

(c) Any complaint regarding a student loan servicer licensed or subject to licensing under the Student Loan Servicing Act (Division 12.5 (commencing with Section 28100) of the Financial Code) shall be referred to the appropriate unit within the department. This unit may investigate complaints referred by the Student Loan Ombudsman, and from the public, who may also submit complaints directly to the department.

(d) Complaints regarding student loans not subject to the Student Loan Servicing Act (Division 12.5 (commencing with Section 28100) of the Financial Code) shall be referred to the Department of Justice. The Department of Justice may investigate complaints regarding student loans referred by the Student Loan Ombudsman, and from the public, who may also submit complaints directly to the Department of Justice.

(e) Complaints regarding any private postsecondary educational institution licensed by the Bureau for Private Postsecondary Education shall be referred to the Bureau for Private Postsecondary Education's Office of Student Assistance and Relief.

(f) The Student Loan Ombudsman shall confer with the Department of Justice and the Office of Student Assistance and Relief regarding the student loan complaints, the proper referral processes for those complaints, and the reporting requirements of the Student Loan Ombudsman under this title.

(g) The Student Loan Ombudsman has all of the following duties:

(1) Compiling and analyzing data on the number of student loan borrower complaints received by the Department of * * * Financial Protection and Innovation and referred to the Department of Justice.

(2) Providing information to the public, agencies, legislators, and others regarding the problems and concerns of student loan borrowers and making recommendations for resolving those problems and concerns.

§ 1788.104

(3) Analyzing and monitoring the development and implementation of federal and state laws, rules, regulations, and policies relating to student loan borrowers.

(4) Disseminating information concerning the availability of the Department of * * * Financial Protection and Innovation, the Department of Justice, and the Bureau of Private Postsecondary Education to accept complaints from individual student loan borrowers and potential student loan borrowers.

(5) Requesting and compiling information provided by any student loan servicer if reasonably determined by the Student Loan Ombudsman to be necessary to effectuate the duties described in this subdivision, except if that student loan servicer is a national bank, as defined in Section 25b of Title 12 of the United States Code, and only to the extent that the requirements of this paragraph are preempted with respect to national banks pursuant to Section 25b and following of Title 12 of the United States Code.

(6) Not later than 18 months after the operative date of this chapter, and not less frequently than once per year thereafter, the Student Loan Ombudsman shall submit a report to the appropriate committees of the Legislature having jurisdiction over higher education and financial institutions. The Student Loan Ombudsman shall report on all of the following:

(A) The implementation of this section.

(B) The types of complaints received regarding student loan borrowing, student loan repayment and servicing, and how these complaints are resolved.

(C) Other data and analysis on outstanding student loan issues faced by borrowers.

(h) Notwithstanding subdivision (*l*) of Section 1788.100, for purposes of this chapter, "student loan servicer" includes a state or nonprofit private institution or organization having an agreement with the United States Secretary of Education under the Higher Education Act of 1965 (20 U.S.C. Sec. 1078(b)) in connection with its responsibilities as a guaranty agency engaged in default aversion.

(i) The operation of this chapter is contingent upon the enactment of an appropriation in the annual Budget Act for its purposes.

(j) This chapter shall become operative on July 1, 2021. (Added by Stats.2020, c. 154 (A.B.376), § 2, eff. Jan. 1, 2021, operative July 1, 2021. Amended by Stats.2022, c. 452 (S.B.1498), § 22, eff. Jan. 1, 2023.)

CHAPTER 5. SHINING A SPOTLIGHT ON STUDENT LOAN INDUSTRY PRACTICES

Section
1788.105. Monitoring and assessment of student loan servicing by commissioner; factors considered; gathering and compilation of information; publication of student loan servicer metrics.

§ 1788.105. Monitoring and assessment of student loan servicing by commissioner; factors considered; gathering and compilation of information; publication of student loan servicer metrics

(a) The commissioner may monitor for risks to consumers in the provision of student loan servicing in this state, including developments in the market for those services, by compiling and analyzing data and other information based on any of the following considerations:

(1) The likely risks and costs to consumers associated with using or repaying a student loan or with the servicing of a student loan.

(2) The understanding by consumers of the risks of a student loan or the servicing of a student loan.

(3) The legal protections applicable to the offering or provision of a student loan or the servicing of a student loan, including the extent to which the law is likely to adequately protect consumers.

(4) The rates of growth in the offering or provision of a student loan or the servicing of that loan.

(5) The extent, if any, to which the risks of a student loan or the servicing of a student loan disproportionately affect traditionally underserved consumers.

(6) The type, number, and other pertinent characteristics of student loan servicers in this state.

(b) In conducting any monitoring or assessment authorized by this section, the commissioner may gather information regarding the organization, business conduct, markets, and activities of student loan servicers in this state, except if that student loan servicer is a national bank, as defined in Section 25b of Title 12 of the United States Code, and only to the extent that the requirements of this paragraph are preempted with respect to national banks pursuant to Section 25b and following of Title 12 of the United States Code. The commissioner may enter into contracts to perform the duties required in this section, as necessary.

(c) In order to gather information described in subdivision (b), the commissioner may do both of the following:

(1) Gather and compile information from a variety of sources, including consumer complaints, voluntary surveys and voluntary interviews of consumers, surveys and interviews with student loan servicers and service providers, and review of available databases.

(2) Require persons engaged in student loan servicing and licensed or subject to the licensing requirements of the Student Loan Servicing Act (Division 12.5 (commencing with Section 28100) of the Financial Code) to file, under oath or otherwise, in the form and within a reasonable period of time as the commissioner may prescribe, annual or special reports, or answers in writing to specific questions, as necessary for the commissioner to fulfill the monitoring, assessment, and reporting responsibilities required in this title.

(d)(1) In addition to any other market monitoring activities deemed necessary by the commissioner, pursuant to subdivision (a), the department may gather and compile information from student loan servicers to assemble data that assesses the total size of the student loan market in this state, the servicing of loans owed by borrowers at risk of default, the servicing of private student loans owed by borrowers experiencing financial distress, and the servicing of federal student loans for borrowers who seek to repay their loans under an Income Driven Repayment Plan as described in Section 1070 et seq. of Title 20 of the United States Code.

(2) The commissioner may, on a quarterly basis, develop and publicize metrics based on data collected pursuant to this subdivision, and those metrics may identify each student loan servicer and publish relevant metrics related to performance of student loan servicing by each person. In executing the function described in this subdivision, the commissioner may meet and confer with the Student Loan Ombudsman established pursuant to Chapter 4.

(e) Notwithstanding subdivision (l) of Section 1788.100, for purposes of this chapter, "student loan servicer" includes a state or nonprofit private institution or organization having an agreement with the United States Secretary of Education under the Higher Education Act of 1965 (20 U.S.C. Sec. 1078(b)) in connection with its responsibilities as a guaranty agency engaged in default aversion.

(f) This chapter shall become operative on July 1, 2021.

(g) The operation of this chapter is contingent upon the enactment of an appropriation in the annual Budget Act for its purposes. *(Added by Stats.2020, c. 154 (A.B.376), § 2, eff. July 1, 2021. Amended by Stats.2021, c. 124 (A.B.938), § 6, eff. Jan. 1, 2022.)*

Title 1.6C.15

PRIVATE STUDENT LOAN COLLECTIONS REFORM ACT

Section
1788.200. Short title.
1788.201. Definitions.
1788.202. Written statement to debtor for purpose of collection; information required to be obtained and provided to debtor.
1788.203. Settlement agreements; documentation in court or written agreement required; provision of statement to debtor following final payment.
1788.204. Initiation of legal proceedings prohibited following expiration of statute of limitations.
1788.205. Collection actions; requirements of complaint; disclosure of confidential information not required; exceptions.
1788.206. Entry of default judgment; documents required; exceptions.
1788.207. Motion to set aside default judgment.
1788.208. Violation of act; penalties; class actions; attorney's fees; exceptions; limitation of actions.
1788.209. Waiver.
1788.210. Severability.
1788.211. Operative date of title.

Operative Effect

For operative effect of Title 1.6C.15, see Civil Code § 1788.211.

§ 1788.200. Short title

This title shall be known and may be cited as the Private Student Loan Collections Reform Act. *(Added by Stats.2021, c. 559 (A.B.424), § 1, eff. Jan. 1, 2022, operative Jan. 1, 2022.)*

Operative Effect

For operative effect of Title 1.6C.15, see Civil Code § 1788.211.

§ 1788.201. Definitions

For purposes of this title, the following definitions apply:

(a) "Borrower" or "student loan borrower" means a person who has received or agreed to pay a private education loan.

(b) "Consumer report" and "consumer reporting agency" shall each have the same meaning that these terms have under the federal Fair Credit Reporting Act (15 U.S.C. Sec. 1681 et seq.).

(c)(1) "Cosigner" means any individual who is liable for the obligation of another without compensation, regardless of how the individual is designated in the contract or instrument with respect to that obligation, including an obligation under a private education loan extended to consolidate a borrower's preexisting private education loans, and shall include any person whose signature is requested as a condition to grant credit or to forbear on collection.

(2) "Cosigner" does not include a spouse of an individual described in paragraph (1), the signature of whom is needed to perfect the security interest in a loan.

(d) "Creditor" means any of the following:

(1) The original creditor, where ownership of a private education loan has not been sold, assigned, or transferred.

(2) The person or entity that owned the private education loan at the time the private education loan defaulted, even if that person or entity did not originate the private education loan, and where such a private education loan has not subsequently been sold, transferred, or assigned.

(3) A person or entity that purchased a defaulted private education loan, whether it collects the private education loan itself or hires a third party for collection, or hires an attorney for collection litigation.

(e) "Debtor" means a borrower, cosigner, or other person that owes or is alleged to owe an unpaid amount on a private education loan.

(f)(1) "Exempt entity" means an entity that meets both of the following requirements:

(A) It is a depository institution as defined in Section 1420 of the Financial Code.

(B) It, together with its affiliates, will be, in the aggregate, a plaintiff in 35 or fewer private student loan collection actions in the current calendar year. Private education loans assigned to a third party for the purposes of collection shall count towards the numerical limit set forth in this subparagraph.

(2) For purposes of this subdivision, an entity is an "affiliate" of another specified entity if it directly, or indirectly through one or more intermediaries, controls, is controlled by, or is under common control with, the other specified entity.

(g) "Original creditor" means the private education lender identified in a promissory note, loan agreement, or loan contract entered into with a student loan borrower or cosigner.

(h) "Private education lender" means either of the following:

§ 1788.201

(1) Any person or entity engaged in the business of securing, making, or extending private education loans.

(2) Any holder of a private education loan.

(i) "Private education loan" means an extension of credit that meets all of the following conditions:

(1) Is not made, insured, or guaranteed under Title IV of the Higher Education Act of 1965 (20 U.S.C. Sec. 1070 et seq.).

(2) Is extended to a consumer expressly, in whole or in part, for postsecondary educational expenses, regardless of whether the loan is provided by the educational institution that the student attends.

(3) Does not include open-end credit or any loan that is secured by real property or a dwelling.

(4) Does not include an extension of credit in which the covered educational institution is the original creditor if either:

(A) The term of the extension of credit is 90 days or less.

(B) An interest rate will not be applied to the credit balance and the term of the extension of credit is one year or less, even if the credit is payable in more than four installments.

(j) "Private education loan collection action" means any suit, arbitration, or other legal proceeding in which a claim is asserted to collect a private education loan.

(k) "Private education loan collector" means a person, other than a private education lender, collecting or attempting to collect on a defaulted private education loan. *(Added by Stats.2021, c. 559 (A.B.424), § 1, eff. Jan. 1, 2022, operative July 1, 2022.)*

Operative Effect

For operative effect of Title 1.6C.15, see Civil Code § 1788.211.

§ 1788.202. Written statement to debtor for purpose of collection; information required to be obtained and provided to debtor

(a) A private education lender or a private education loan collector shall not make any written statement to a debtor in an attempt to collect a private education loan unless the private education lender or private education loan collector possesses the following information:

(1) The name of the owner of the private education loan.

(2) The creditor's name at the time of default, if applicable.

(3) The creditor's account number used to identify the private education loan at the time of default, if the original creditor used an account number to identify the private education loan at the time of default.

(4) The amount due at default.

(5) An itemization of interest, if any, that has accrued on the private education loan.

(6) An itemization of fees, if any, claimed to be owed on the private education loan and whether those fees were imposed by the original creditor or any subsequent owners of the private education loan.

(7) The date that the private education loan was incurred.

(8) The date of the first partial payment or the first day that a payment was missed, whichever is earlier, that precipitated default.

(9) The date and amount of the last payment, if applicable.

(10) Any payments, settlement, or financial remuneration of any kind paid to the creditor by a guarantor, surety, or other party not obligated on the loan as compensation under a separate contract that provides coverage for financial losses incurred as a result of default, if applicable.

(11) The names of all persons or entities that owned the private education loan after the time of default, if applicable, and the date of each sale or transfer.

(12) A copy of the self-certification form and any other "needs analysis" conducted by the original creditor prior to origination of the loan.

(13) Documentation establishing that the creditor is the owner of the specific individual private education loan at issue. If the private education loan was assigned more than once, the creditor shall possess each assignment or other writing evidencing the transfer of ownership of the specific individual private education loan to establish an unbroken chain of ownership, beginning with the original creditor to the first subsequent creditor and each additional creditor. Each assignment or other writing evidencing transfer of ownership or the right to collect shall contain the original creditor's account number (redacted for security purposes to show only the last four digits) of the private education loan purchased or otherwise assigned, the date of purchase and assignment, and shall clearly show the borrower's correct name associated with the original account number. The assignment or other writing attached shall be that by which the creditor or other assignee acquired the private education loan, not a document prepared for litigation.

(14) A copy of all pages of the contract, application, or other documents evidencing the debtor's liability for the private education loan, stating all terms and conditions applicable to the private education loan.

(15) A list of all collection attempts made in the last 12 months, including date and time of all calls and written communications.

(16) A statement as to whether the creditor is willing to renegotiate the terms of the private student loan.

(17) Copies of all written settlement communications made in the last 12 months, or, in the alternative, a statement that the creditor has not attempted to settle or otherwise renegotiate the debt prior to suit.

(18) A statement as to whether the private education loan is eligible for an income-based repayment plan.

(b)(1) In addition to any other information required under applicable federal or state law, a private education lender or private education loan collector shall provide the information set forth in subdivision (a) in the first written collection communication with a debtor after the first of either of the following:

(A) Default and acceleration.

(B) A period of 12 consecutive months of default.

(2) A private education lender or private education loan collector shall provide the information set forth in subdivision (a) to the debtor upon the debtor's request if both of the following are true:

(A) An event described in subparagraph (A) or (B) of paragraph (1) has occurred.

(B) The debtor has not requested or received the information set forth in subdivision (a) within the previous 12 months. *(Added by Stats.2021, c. 559 (A.B.424), § 1, eff. Jan. 1, 2022, operative July 1, 2022.)*

Operative Effect

For operative effect of Title 1.6C.15, see Civil Code § 1788.211.

§ 1788.203. Settlement agreements; documentation in court or written agreement required; provision of statement to debtor following final payment

(a) All settlement agreements between a private education lender or private education loan collector and a debtor shall be documented in open court or otherwise reduced to writing. The private education lender or private education loan collector shall ensure that a copy of the written agreement is provided to the debtor.

(b) A private education lender or private education loan collector that accepts a payment as payment in full, or as a full and final compromise of a private education loan, shall provide, within 30 calendar days, a final statement that shall clearly and conspicuously show the amount and date paid, the name of the entity paid, the current account number, the name of the private education lender or private education loan collector, the account number issued by the private education lender or private education loan collector, the name of the owner of the private education loan, and that a zero balance is owing. The statement may be provided electronically if the parties agree. *(Added by Stats.2021, c. 559 (A.B.424), § 1, eff. Jan. 1, 2022, operative July 1, 2022.)*

Operative Effect

For operative effect of Title 1.6C.15, see Civil Code § 1788.211.

§ 1788.204. Initiation of legal proceedings prohibited following expiration of statute of limitations

A private education lender or private education loan collector shall not bring suit or initiate an arbitration or other legal proceeding to collect a private education loan if the applicable statute of limitations for the private education lender's or private education loan collector's claim has expired. *(Added by Stats.2021, c. 559 (A.B.424), § 1, eff. Jan. 1, 2022, operative July 1, 2022.)*

Operative Effect

For operative effect of Title 1.6C.15, see Civil Code § 1788.211.

§ 1788.205. Collection actions; requirements of complaint; disclosure of confidential information not required; exceptions

In an action brought by a private education lender or private education loan collector to collect a private education loan:

(a) The complaint shall allege all of the following:

(1) The information required by paragraphs (1) to (11), inclusive, of subdivision (a) of Section 1788.202.

(2) That the applicable statute of limitations has not expired.

(3) That the plaintiff has complied with Section 1788.202.

(b) Copies of the documents required by paragraphs (12) to (14), inclusive, of subdivision (a) of Section 1788.202 shall be attached to the complaint.

(c) The requirements of this title shall not be deemed to require the disclosure in public records of personal, financial, or medical information, the confidentiality of which is protected by any state or federal law.

(d) This section does not apply to a plaintiff that attaches to the complaint a declaration or affidavit pursuant to Section 2015.5 of the Code of Civil Procedure that is signed by a natural person and states all of the following:

(1) That the plaintiff is an exempt entity.

(2) The category in subdivision (a) of Section 1420 of the Financial Code under which the plaintiff falls.

(3) The name and title of the signer.

(4) That the signer has been authorized by the entity to make the affidavit or declaration. *(Added by Stats.2021, c. 559 (A.B.424), § 1, eff. Jan. 1, 2022, operative July 1, 2022.)*

Operative Effect

For operative effect of Title 1.6C.15, see Civil Code § 1788.211.

§ 1788.206. Entry of default judgment; documents required; exceptions

(a) In an action initiated by a private education lender or private education loan collector, no default or other judgment may be entered against a defendant unless documents are submitted by the plaintiff to the court to establish the facts required to be alleged by paragraphs (1) and (2) of subdivision (a) of Section 1788.205. The documents shall be properly authenticated and each shall be in a form that would be admissible as a business record under Section 1271 of the Evidence Code.

(b) In an action initiated by a private education lender or private education loan collector, no default or other judgment may be entered against a defendant unless copies of the documents described in subdivision (b) of Section 1788.205 have been submitted by the plaintiff to the court. These documents shall be properly authenticated and each shall be in a form that would be admissible as a business record under Section 1271 of the Evidence Code.

(c) In any action on a private education loan, if a plaintiff seeks a default judgment and has not complied with the requirements of this title, the court shall not enter a default judgment for the plaintiff and may, in its discretion, dismiss the action.

(d) Except as provided in this title, this section is not intended to modify or otherwise amend the procedures established in Section 585 of the Code of Civil Procedure.

§ 1788.206

(e) This section does not apply to a plaintiff that attaches to the complaint a declaration or affidavit pursuant to Section 2015.5 of the Code of Civil Procedure that is signed by a natural person and states all of the following:

(1) That the plaintiff is an exempt entity.

(2) The category in subdivision (a) of Section 1420 of the Financial Code under which the plaintiff falls.

(3) The name and title of the signer.

(4) That the signer has been authorized by the entity to make the affidavit or declaration. *(Added by Stats.2021, c. 559 (A.B.424), § 1, eff. Jan. 1, 2022, operative July 1, 2022.)*

Operative Effect

For operative effect of Title 1.6C.15, see Civil Code § 1788.211.

§ 1788.207. Motion to set aside default judgment

Notwithstanding Section 473.5 of the Code of Civil Procedure, if service of a summons has not resulted in actual notice to a person in time to defend an action brought by a private education lender or a private education loan collector and a default or default judgment has been entered against the person in the action, the person may serve and file a notice of motion and motion to set aside the default or default judgment and for leave to defend the action utilizing the procedures set forth in Section 1788.61. *(Added by Stats. 2021, c. 559 (A.B.424), § 1, eff. Jan. 1, 2022, operative July 1, 2022.)*

Operative Effect

For operative effect of Title 1.6C.15, see Civil Code § 1788.211.

§ 1788.208. Violation of act; penalties; class actions; attorney's fees; exceptions; limitation of actions

(a) A person may bring a cause of action against a creditor, private education lender, or private education loan collector for a violation of any provision of this title in order to recover or obtain any of the following:

(1) Damages in an amount equal to the sum of the following:

(A) Any actual damages sustained by that person as a result of the violation.

(B) Statutory damages in an amount as the court may allow, which shall not be less than five hundred dollars ($500) per violation.

(2) Damages pursuant to Section 3294.

(3) An order vacating any default judgment entered against that person.

(4) Restitution of all moneys taken from or paid by that person after a default judgment was entered in favor of the private education lender or private education loan collector.

(5) An order directing the private education lender or private education loan collector to do one or more of the following:

(A) Request that a consumer reporting agency correct a consumer report that it issues.

(B) Request that a consumer reporting agency remove derogatory information furnished to it after default.

(C) Furnish correct information to a consumer reporting agency.

(6) Any other relief that the court deems proper.

(b) In the case of a class action, a defendant that violates any provision of this title shall be liable for any statutory damages for each named plaintiff as provided in subparagraph (B) of paragraph (1) of subdivision (a). If the court finds that the defendant engaged in a pattern and practice of violating any provision of this title, the court may award additional damages to the class in an amount not to exceed the lesser of five hundred thousand dollars ($500,000) or 1 percent of the net worth of the defendant.

(c)(1) In the case of any successful cause of action under this section, the court shall award costs of the action, together with reasonable attorney's fees as determined by the court.

(2) Reasonable attorney's fees may be awarded to a prevailing defendant upon a finding by the court that the plaintiff's prosecution of the cause of action was not in good faith.

(d) A private education lender or private education loan collector shall have no civil liability for damages under this section if the private education lender or private education loan collector shows by a preponderance of evidence that the violation was not intentional and resulted from a bona fide error, and occurred notwithstanding the maintenance of procedures reasonably adopted to avoid any error.

(e) A cause of action to enforce any liability created by this title shall be brought within one year from the date of the discovery by the plaintiff of the last violation, or, in the event a default judgment is entered against the debtor, one year from the date the borrower first receives a writ, notice, or order under Division 1 (commencing with Section 680.010) or Division 2 (commencing with Section 695.010) of Title 9 of Part 2 of the Code of Civil Procedure, whichever is later. *(Added by Stats.2021, c. 559 (A.B.424), § 1, eff. Jan. 1, 2022, operative July 1, 2022.)*

Operative Effect

For operative effect of Title 1.6C.15, see Civil Code § 1788.211.

§ 1788.209. Waiver

Any waiver of the provisions of this title is contrary to public policy, and is void and unenforceable. *(Added by Stats.2021, c. 559 (A.B.424), § 1, eff. Jan. 1, 2022, operative July 1, 2022.)*

Operative Effect

For operative effect of Title 1.6C.15, see Civil Code § 1788.211.

§ 1788.210. Severability

The provisions of this title are severable. If any provision of this title or its application is held invalid, that invalidity shall not affect other provisions or applications that can be given effect without the invalid provision or application.

(Added by Stats.2021, c. 559 (A.B.424), § 1, eff. Jan. 1, 2022, operative July 1, 2022.)

Operative Effect

For operative effect of Title 1.6C.15, see Civil Code § 1788.211.

§ 1788.211. Operative date of title

This title shall become operative on July 1, 2022. *(Added by Stats.2021, c. 559 (A.B.424), § 1, eff. Jan. 1, 2022, operative July 1, 2022.)*

Title 1.6C.17

FAIR DEBT SETTLEMENT PRACTICES

Chapter	Section
1. General Provisions	1788.300
2. Application of the Fair Debt Settlement Practices Act	1788.303
3. Enforcement of the Fair Debt Settlement Practices Act	1788.305

CHAPTER 1. GENERAL PROVISIONS

Section
1788.300. Short title.
1788.301. Definitions.
1788.302. False, deceptive, or misleading acts or practices prohibited when providing debt settlement services; required disclosures; information required in contract; unfair, abusive, or deceptive acts or practices prohibited; termination of contract.

§ 1788.300. Short title

This title may be cited as the Fair Debt Settlement Practices Act. *(Added by Stats.2021, c. 454 (A.B.1405), § 1, eff. Jan. 1, 2022.)*

§ 1788.301. Definitions

For purposes of this title:

(a) "Debt settlement provider" means a person who, for compensation and on behalf of a consumer, provides debt settlement services.

(b) "Debt settlement services" means any of the following:

(1) Providing advice, or offering to act or acting as an intermediary, including, but not limited to, offering debt negotiation, debt reduction, or debt relief services between a consumer and one or more of the consumer's creditors, if the primary purpose of that advice or action is to obtain a settlement for less than the full amount of the debt.

(2) Advising, encouraging, or counseling a consumer to accumulate funds in an account for future payment of a reduced amount of debt to one or more of the consumer's creditors.

(c) "Settlement account" means a depository account established and used for the purpose of holding funds of a consumer to be distributed to a creditor in the event of a settlement of a consumer's debt with the creditor.

(d) "Consumer" means a person who is allegedly legally responsible for a debt.

(e) "Person" means a natural person or entity, whether a corporation, partnership, association, trust, limited liability company, cooperative, or other organization.

(f) "Creditor" means the person who originated the debt or is assigned, or has purchased for collection, a debt for which a consumer is allegedly legally responsible.

(g) "Debt" means money, whether in principal, interest, fees, or other charges, which is due or owing or alleged to be due or owing from a natural person to another person and incurred primarily for personal, family, or household purposes.

(h) "Payment processor" means a person who provides payment processing services.

(i) "Payment processing services" means accepting, maintaining, holding, or distributing funds, or facilitating the acceptance, maintenance, holding, or distribution of funds, on behalf of a consumer for the purpose of facilitating debt settlement services. *(Added by Stats.2021, c. 454 (A.B.1405), § 1, eff. Jan. 1, 2022.)*

§ 1788.302. False, deceptive, or misleading acts or practices prohibited when providing debt settlement services; required disclosures; information required in contract; unfair, abusive, or deceptive acts or practices prohibited; termination of contract

(a) A debt settlement provider shall not engage in false, deceptive, or misleading acts or practices when providing debt settlement services. Without limiting the general application of the foregoing, an act or practice is false, deceptive, or misleading, in connection with providing debt settlement services, if the act or practice consists of any of the following:

(1) Making or permitting another entity to publicly make on behalf of the debt settlement provider, a statement or representation that is false, deceptive, or misleading.

(2) Posting directly, or indirectly causing to be posted, an online review or ranking on an internet website if the debt settlement provider, or its agent, provided anything of value in exchange for favorable treatment in that review or ranking.

(3) Omitting any material information.

(b) A debt settlement provider shall provide to the consumer the following disclosures along with an unsigned copy of the written contract proposed to be entered into between the debt settlement provider and the consumer no less than three calendar days prior to the execution of that contract by the consumer. A fully executed copy of the contract shall be delivered to the consumer by the debt settlement provider immediately after the debt settlement provider receives the contract.

(1) The contract shall be preceded by a disclosure that contains all of the following information in conspicuous boldface type that is larger than the typeface provided in the contract typeface:

(A) There is no guarantee that any particular debt or all of the consumer's enrolled debts will be reduced, eliminated, or otherwise settled.

§ 1788.302

(B) The deposits made pursuant to the contract will not be distributed to the creditor until a settlement is obtained. This may take months to achieve.

(C) If the consumer stops paying any creditor, any of the following may occur:

(i) The creditors may still try to collect.

(ii) The creditors may sue.

(iii) If a creditor obtains a judgment against the consumer, the creditor may garnish the consumer's wages or levy the consumer's bank account or accounts, or both garnish the consumer's wages and levy the consumer's bank account or accounts.

(iv) The consumer's credit score or credit rating may be negatively impacted.

(D) Failing to pay debts on time may adversely affect the consumer's credit rating or credit scores.

(E) Specific results cannot be predicted or guaranteed, and the debt settlement provider cannot require a creditor to negotiate or settle a debt.

(F) A consumer may cancel the debt settlement contract at any time without any penalty.

(G) Debt settlement services may not be suitable for all individuals.

(H) Bankruptcy may provide an alternative to debt settlement.

(I) Canceled debt may be counted as income under federal tax law, and the consumer may have to pay income taxes on the amount of forgiven or reduced debt.

(J) Many sources of income may be protected from debt collection. Common sources of protected income include disability insurance benefits, life insurance benefits, military benefits, pension plans, retirement benefits, public assistance, social security benefits, supplemental security income (SSI), unemployment benefits, veterans benefits, workers compensation, and student aid. See form EJ–155 from the Judicial Council for a complete list.

(K) The number of months estimated to enter into settlement agreements that completely resolve all enrolled debts.

(L) All conditions that the consumer must satisfy before the debt settlement provider will make a settlement offer to a creditor.

(M) Whether the debt settlement provider pays or receives referral fees.

(2) Each contract between a consumer and debt settlement provider:

(A) Shall list each debt to be serviced, including, for each debt, the name of the creditor and the total amount of the debt. The total amount of the debt may be based on either a billing statement for the debt or information in the consumer's consumer report, as that term is defined under the federal Fair Credit Reporting Act (15 U.S.C. Sec. 1681 et seq.). The billing statement or consumer report must have been issued within 30 calendar days of the date of the contract.

(B) Shall provide the estimated period of time it will take the consumer to accumulate in a settlement account the amount of money estimated to be required to settle all debts.

(C) Shall provide the amount of time necessary to achieve the represented results.

(D) Shall provide, in terms easily understood by the least sophisticated consumer, the method that the debt settlement provider will use to calculate the charges and fees for debt settlement services.

(E) Shall provide the name and mailing address of the debt settlement provider and of the consumer.

(F) Shall provide a telephone number at which the consumer may speak, during normal business hours, with a live representative of the debt settlement provider during normal business hours who is able to access information about the consumer's account.

(G) Shall be provided to the consumer in English and in the language in which it was negotiated or in which the debt settlement services were offered, if that language is one of the languages set forth in Section 1632.

(H) Shall not require a compulsory agreement with any other party. A debt settlement provider may require that the consumer obtain a dedicated settlement account and provide a list of preferred vendors, however a payment processor who receives compensation from the consumer for payment processing services must supply its own contract to the consumer for engagement.

(I) Shall not be entered into by a consumer who is not already allegedly legally responsible for all the debt that will be enrolled in the debt settlement services. In the event multiple consumers engage in a single contract for debt settlement services, if any consumer is not proficient in English and speaks a language set forth in Section 1632, a translated copy of the disclosures and contract shall be provided to the consumer in that language and in a manner that complies with this subdivision.

(3) A debt settlement provider shall not communicate with any of a consumer's creditors until five calendar days after full execution of a contract for debt settlement services.

(c) A debt settlement provider and a payment processor shall not engage in unfair, abusive, or deceptive acts or practices when providing debt settlement services or payment processing services. Without limiting the general application of the foregoing, in connection with providing debt settlement services and payment processing services, an act or practice is unfair, abusive, or deceptive if the act or practice consists of any of the following:

(1) For a debt settlement provider and payment processor, offering to lend money or extend credit to the consumer, or purchase an enrolled debt.

(2) For a debt settlement provider requesting or receiving payment of any fee or consideration for debt settlement services, unless and until all of the following occur:

(A) The debt settlement provider has renegotiated, settled, reduced, or otherwise altered the terms of at least one debt pursuant to a settlement agreement approved and executed by the consumer.

(B) The consumer has made at least one payment pursuant to that settlement agreement between the consumer and the creditor.

(C) To the extent that debts enrolled in a debt settlement service are negotiated, settled, or modified individually, the fee or consideration must either:

(i) Bear the same proportional relationship to the total fee for renegotiating, settling, reducing, or altering the terms of the entire debt balance as the individual debt amount bears to the entire debt amount. The individual debt amount and the entire debt amount are those owed at the time the debt was enrolled in the service.

(ii) Represent a percentage of the amount saved as a result of the renegotiation, settlement, reduction, or alteration. The percentage charged cannot change from one individual debt to another. The amount saved is the difference between the amount owed at the time the debt was enrolled in the service and the amount agreed pursuant to the settlement agreement between the consumer and the creditor to satisfy the debt.

(3) Beginning July 1, 2022, for a payment processor, facilitating the distribution of payment of any fee or consideration for debt settlement services before the requirements set forth in paragraph (2) have been met.

(4) For a payment processor, failing to distribute a statement of accounting to a consumer at least once a month while the consumer is engaged with the payment processor, as well as on or before the fifth business day after a consumer requests a statement of accounting.

(A) When an accounting is available to the consumer online, the payment processor must make prominent and ongoing the ability for a consumer to opt in to a paper accounting to be mailed to the consumer under the terms of this section.

(B) The statement of accounting must contain the following information to the extent applicable:

(i) A list of deposits made into, and withdrawals from, the consumer's settlement account during the previous month.

(ii) The fees that the debt settlement provider has billed and collected in connection with each of the debts settled during the previous month.

(iii) The fees that the payment processor has billed and collected in connection with payment processing services during the previous month.

(iv) The amount of money that the consumer holds in the consumer's settlement account.

(C) Within five business days of a consumer's request, a payment processor shall provide a consolidated statement of accounting containing all of the following:

(i) A list of deposits made into, and withdrawals from, the consumer's settlement account starting from the outset of the contract.

(ii) A list of fees that the debt settlement provider has billed and collected in connection with each of the debts settled starting from the outset of the contract.

(iii) A list of fees that the payment processor has billed and collected in connection with payment processing services starting from the outset of the contract.

(iv) The amount of money that the consumer holds in the consumer's settlement account.

(5) For a debt settlement provider, failing to distribute a statement of accounting to a consumer at least once a month while the contract for debt settlement services is in effect, as well as on or before the fifth business day after a consumer requests a statement of accounting.

(A) When an accounting is available to the consumer online, the debt settlement provider must make prominent and ongoing the ability for a consumer to opt in to a paper accounting to be mailed to the consumer under the terms of this section.

(B) The statement of accounting must contain the following information to the extent applicable:

(i) The amounts, dates, and creditors associated with each settlement obtained by the debt settlement provider on behalf of the consumer.

(ii) The fees that the debt settlement provider has billed and collected in connection with each of the debts settled.

(iii) With respect to any debt settled by the debt settlement provider on behalf of the consumer, all of the following information:

(I) The total amount of money that the consumer paid or will pay to the creditor to settle the debt.

(II) The amount of the debt at the time the debt settlement provider and the consumer entered into the contract.

(III) The amount of the debt at the time the creditor agreed to settle the debt.

(IV) The amount of compensation that the debt settlement provider received, or may receive, to settle the debt.

(d)(1) A consumer may terminate a contract for debt settlement services at any time without a fee or penalty of any sort by notifying the debt settlement provider in writing, electronically, or orally.

(2) The notice described in paragraph (1) shall be deemed effective immediately upon being sent if made electronically, including via text message or orally. When the notice is sent via certified mail, notice shall be deemed effective upon receipt. When written notice is sent via noncertified mail, notice shall be deemed effective seven calendar days from the date of mailing.

(3) Upon effective notice of request for cancellation of the contract, the debt settlement provider shall do all of the following:

(A) Immediately cancel the contract.

(B) Immediately notify the payment processor that the consumer has canceled the debt settlement services and transmit to the payment processor the consumer's instruction to close the settlement account and deliver the balance in the settlement account to the consumer.

(C) Provide, within three business days, a detailed accounting of any amounts received or expected to be received by the debt settlement provider from the consumer's settlement account after the debt settlement provider received effective notice of request for cancellation. The detailed accounting shall include an explanation of how the amounts were calculated in accordance with the requirements of paragraph (2) of subdivision (c).

(D) Provide within three business days copies of all documents, notices, or other communications it has received from any creditor on behalf of the consumer.

(4) The items in subparagraphs (C) and (D) of paragraph (3) shall be sent by United States mail or by electronic means reasonably calculated to reach the consumer.

(5) Upon receipt of notice of cancellation of the contract from the consumer or debt settlement provider, the payment processor shall stop accumulating service fees, close the settlement account, and deliver to the consumer the balance in the settlement account within seven days. The payment processor shall provide, within 10 business days, a detailed accounting of the amount refunded and any amounts sent to the debt settlement provider after or upon the payment processor receiving notice of the cancellation of the contract.

(e) A debt settlement provider shall immediately forward the following notices to the consumer, either by United States mail or by electronic means reasonably calculated to reach the consumer:

(1) Any notice of a lawsuit on an enrolled debt from any person other than the consumer.

(2) Any settlement agreement that a debt settlement provider has negotiated on the consumer's behalf. *(Added by Stats.2021, c. 454 (A.B.1405), § 1, eff. Jan. 1, 2022.)*

CHAPTER 2. APPLICATION OF THE FAIR DEBT SETTLEMENT PRACTICES ACT

Section
1788.303. Application of title.
1788.304. Limits on application of title.

§ 1788.303. Application of title

This title applies to persons providing payment processing services, debt settlement services, and persons purporting to engage in debt settlement services. *(Added by Stats.2021, c. 454 (A.B.1405), § 1, eff. Jan. 1, 2022.)*

§ 1788.304. Limits on application of title

This title does not apply to any of the following:

(a) Any person, or the person's authorized agent, doing business under license and authority of the Commissioner of Financial Protection and Innovation under Divisions 1.1 (commencing with Section 1000), 2 (commencing with Section 5000), and 5 (commencing with Section 14000) of the Financial Code or under any law of this state or of the United States relating to banks or credit unions.

(b) Any nonprofit business organization that is certified as tax-exempt by the Internal Revenue Service and that does not receive compensation from the consumer for providing debt settlement services.

(c) Attorneys and law firms that meet all of the following criteria:

(1) The attorney or law firm does not charge for services regulated by this title.

(2) The fees and disbursements are not charges or costs shared, directly or indirectly, with a debt settlement provider.

(3) Any of the following is true:

(A) The attorney or law firm is retained by a consumer for the purpose of legal representation in consumer debt litigation.

(B) The attorney or law firm provides debt settlement services pursuant to representation by retainer for a debt collection matter that does not involve consumer debt.

(C) The attorney or law firm is retained by the consumer primarily for purposes other than the settlement of consumer debt.

(d) A merchant-owned credit or creditors association, or a member-owned, member-controlled, or member-directed association whose principal function is that of servicing the community as a reporting agency. *(Added by Stats.2021, c. 454 (A.B.1405), § 1, eff. Jan. 1, 2022.)*

CHAPTER 3. ENFORCEMENT OF THE FAIR DEBT SETTLEMENT PRACTICES ACT

Section
1788.305. Cause of action for violation of the provisions of title; damages and relief; unintentional violations; limitations period.
1788.306. Waiver.
1788.307. Severability.

§ 1788.305. Cause of action for violation of the provisions of title; damages and relief; unintentional violations; limitations period

(a) A debt settlement provider and a payment processor shall comply with this title.

(b) A consumer may bring a cause of action against a debt settlement provider and a payment processor for violation of any provision of this title in order to recover or obtain any of the following:

(1) Damages in an amount equal to the sum of the following:

(A) Statutory damages in an amount to be determined by the court of no less than one thousand dollars ($1,000) and no more than five thousand dollars ($5,000) per violation of this title.

(B) Any actual damages sustained by the consumer as a result of the violation.

(2) Injunctive relief.

(3) Any other relief that the court deems proper.

(c)(1) In the case of any successful cause of action under this section, the court shall award costs of the action, together with reasonable attorney's fees as determined by the court.

(2) Reasonable attorney's fees may be awarded to a prevailing debt settlement provider and a prevailing payment processor upon a finding by the court that the consumer's prosecution of the cause of action was not in good faith.

(d) A debt settlement provider or a prevailing payment processor shall have no civil liability for damages under this section if the debt settlement provider or a prevailing payment processor shows by a preponderance of evidence that the violation was not intentional and resulted from a bona fide error, and occurred notwithstanding the maintenance of procedures reasonably adopted to avoid any error.

(e) A cause of action brought under this section shall be brought within four years of the latter of the following dates:

(1) The last payment by or on behalf of the consumer.

(2) The date on which the consumer discovered or reasonably should have discovered the facts giving rise to the consumer's claim. *(Added by Stats.2021, c. 454 (A.B.1405), § 1, eff. Jan. 1, 2022.)*

§ 1788.306. Waiver

Any waiver of the provisions of this title is contrary to public policy, and is void and unenforceable. *(Added by Stats.2021, c. 454 (A.B.1405), § 1, eff. Jan. 1, 2022.)*

§ 1788.307. Severability

The provisions of this title are severable. If any provision of this title or its application is held invalid, that invalidity shall not affect other provisions or applications that can be given effect without the invalid provision or application. *(Added by Stats.2021, c. 454 (A.B.1405), § 1, eff. Jan. 1, 2022.)*

Title 1.6D

ELECTRONIC COMMERCE

Article	Section
1. General Provisions	1789

Application

For application of Title, see Civil Code §§ 1789.7, 1789.8.

ARTICLE 1. GENERAL PROVISIONS

Section
1789. Legislative findings and declarations.
1789.1. Short title.
1789.2. Definitions.
1789.3. Required information to consumers by providers of service.
1789.5. Violation; civil penalty; payment.
1789.6. Liability of provider for errors or omissions from operation of service.
1789.7. Application of title; federal law or regulation; credit cards; electronic fund transfer.
1789.8. Application of title; transactions on or after July 1, 1985.
1789.9. Public policy; waiver of rights.

§ 1789. Legislative findings and declarations

The Legislature hereby finds and declares that it is in the public interest that consumers have comprehensive knowledge of services available through electronic commerce and to that end hereby enacts the Electronic Commerce Act of 1984. *(Added by Stats.1984, c. 638, § 1.)*

Cross References

Consumer defined for purposes of this Title, see Civil Code § 1789.2.

§ 1789.1. Short title

This title may be cited as "The Electronic Commerce Act of 1984." *(Added by Stats.1984, c. 638, § 1.)*

§ 1789.2. Definitions

For the purposes of this title, the following terms have the meanings expressed in this section:

(a) "Electronic commercial service" or "service" means an electronic shopping system to conduct the purchase of goods and services via a telecommunications network, but does not mean conventional voice-only telephone service, one-way television or radio broadcasting, an electronic fund transfer system, or a service provided through an electronic terminal located at a place of business where the sale of goods or services sold through that service otherwise occurs.

(b) "Consumer" means a natural person who purchases goods or services using an electronic commercial service.

(c) "Provider of service" means a person who contracts with consumers to provide an electronic commercial service.

(d) "Goods or services" means tangible items or physical services provided to the consumer, or tickets or vouchers for such tangible items or physical services, but does not mean computerized data delivered to the consumer via a computer terminal or in printed form. *(Added by Stats.1984, c. 638, § 1. Amended by Stats.1987, c. 49, § 1, eff. June 17, 1987.)*

§ 1789.3. Required information to consumers by providers of service

The provider of an electronic commercial service shall provide to consumers with which it contracts to provide the service, at the time it contracts to provide the service and annually, on or before June 30 of each year thereafter, all of the following information:

(a) The name, address, and telephone number of the provider of service.

(b) Any charges to the consumer imposed by the provider for the use of the service.

(c) The procedures a consumer may follow in order to resolve a complaint regarding the service or to receive further information regarding use of the service, including the telephone number and address of the Complaint Assistance Unit of the Division of Consumer Services of the Department of Consumer Affairs. *(Added by Stats.1984, c. 638, § 1. Amended by Stats.1986, c. 508, § 1.)*

Cross References

Consumer defined for purposes of this Title, see Civil Code § 1789.2.
Electronic commercial service defined for purposes of this Title, see Civil Code § 1789.2.
Provider of service defined for purposes of this Title, see Civil Code § 1789.2.

§ 1789.5. Violation; civil penalty; payment

(a) Any provider who knowingly and willfully violates any provision of this title is liable for a civil penalty not to exceed five thousand dollars ($5,000) which may be assessed and recovered in a civil action brought in the name of the people of the State of California by the Attorney General, by any district attorney or city attorney, or by a city prosecutor in any city or city and county having a full-time city prosecutor, in any court of competent jurisdiction.

(b) If the action is brought by the Attorney General, one-half of the penalty collected shall be paid to the treasurer of the county in which the judgment was entered, and one-half

§ 1789.5 OBLIGATIONS

to the General Fund. If the action is brought by a district attorney, the penalty collected shall be paid to the treasurer of the county in which the judgment was entered. If the action is brought by a city attorney or city prosecutor, one-half of the penalty shall be paid to the treasurer of the city in which the judgment was entered, and one-half to the treasurer of the county in which the judgment was entered. *(Added by Stats.1984, c. 638, § 1.)*

Cross References

Attorney General, generally, see Government Code § 12500 et seq.

§ 1789.6. Liability of provider for errors or omissions from operation of service

Nothing in this title shall be construed to limit the liability of a provider of service to a consumer for errors or omissions arising from the operation of an electronic commercial service. *(Added by Stats.1984, c. 638, § 1.)*

Cross References

Consumer defined for purposes of this Title, see Civil Code § 1789.2.
Electronic commercial service defined for purposes of this Title, see Civil Code § 1789.2.
Provider of service defined for purposes of this Title, see Civil Code § 1789.2.

§ 1789.7. Application of title; federal law or regulation; credit cards; electronic fund transfer

(a) This title does not apply where it is inconsistent with, or infringes upon, federal law or regulation.

(b) This title does not apply to the rights and obligations of a cardholder and a card issuer with respect to the use of a credit card arising from the purchase of goods or services conducted through an electronic commercial service. For the purpose of this subdivision, "cardholder," "card issuer," and "credit card" have the same meaning as those terms are given in the federal Fair Credit Billing Act (15 U.S.C. Sec. 1601 et seq.) and regulations adopted thereunder, or, if applicable, the Song-Beverly Credit Card Act of 1971 (Title 1.3 (commencing with Section 1747)).

(c) This title does not apply to the rights and obligations of a consumer and a financial institution with respect to any electronic fund transfer arising from purchase of goods or services conducted through an electronic commercial service. For the purposes of this subdivision, "consumer," "financial institution," and "electronic fund transfer" have the same meaning as those terms are given in the Electronic Fund Transfer Act (15 U.S.C. Sec. 1601 et seq.) and regulations adopted thereunder. *(Added by Stats.1984, c. 638, § 1.)*

Cross References

Consumer defined for purposes of this Title, see Civil Code § 1789.2.
Consumers Legal Remedies Act, see Civil Code § 1750 et seq.
Electronic commercial service defined for purposes of this Title, see Civil Code § 1789.2.
Goods or services defined for purposes of this Title, see Civil Code § 1789.2.

§ 1789.8. Application of title; transactions on or after July 1, 1985

This title applies to transactions entered into on or after July 1, 1985. *(Added by Stats.1984, c. 638, § 1.)*

§ 1789.9. Public policy; waiver of rights

Any waiver of the provisions of this title is contrary to public policy, and is void and unenforceable. *(Added by Stats.2002, c. 815 (A.B.2331), § 13.)*

Title 1.6E

CREDIT SERVICES

Section
1789.10. Short title.
1789.11. Legislative findings and declarations; purposes; liberal construction.
1789.12. Definitions.
1789.13. Credit services organizations; prohibited activities.
1789.134. Communication with consumer represented by credit services organization.
1789.135. Redaction of consumer personal information.
1789.14. Information statement; necessity and time of delivery to consumer; acknowledgement of delivery; retention on file.
1789.15. Information statement; contents.
1789.16. Contracts; requirements; contents.
1789.17. Seller's breach of contract or obligation; violation of title.
1789.18. Surety bonds; compliance requirements; filing of copy.
1789.19. Waiver of rights by consumer; prohibition; attempt to obtain; violation of title; burden of proof on exemption or exception from definition.
1789.20. Violations; misdemeanor; injunction; prosecutor.
1789.21. Actions for recovery of damages or injunctive relief.
1789.22. Application of other laws; remedies as additional.
1789.23. Severability.
1789.24. Claims against deposits in lieu of bonds; establishment; approval; 240-day period; payment; approval of claims after 240-day period; deposits not subject to attachment, garnishment, or execution.
1789.25. Registration application; bond; fee; contents; investigation; notification of change in information; expiration of certificate of registration.
1789.26. Enforcement; filing fees.

Cross References

Areias Credit Card Full Disclosure Act, see Civil Code § 1748.10 et seq.
Areias-Robbins Charge Card Full Disclosure Act, see Civil Code § 1748.20 et seq.
Consumer Credit Reporting Agencies, see Civil Code § 1785.1 et seq.
Consumers Legal Remedies Act, see Civil Code § 1750 et seq.

§ 1789.10. Short title

This title shall be known and may be cited as the "Credit Services Act of 1984." *(Added by Stats.1984, c. 1177, § 1.)*

§ 1789.11. Legislative findings and declarations; purposes; liberal construction

The Legislature finds and declares that:

(a) The ability to obtain and use credit has become of great importance to consumers, who have a vital interest in establishing and maintaining their * * * creditworthiness and credit standing. As a result, consumers who have experienced credit problems may seek assistance from credit services organizations which offer to obtain credit or improve the credit standing of those consumers.

Certain advertising and business practices of some credit services organizations have worked a financial hardship upon the people of this state, often those who are of limited economic means and inexperienced in credit matters. Credit services organizations have significant impact upon the economy and well-being of this state and its people.

(b) The purposes of this title are to provide prospective consumers of services of credit services organizations with the information necessary to make an intelligent decision regarding the purchase of those services and to protect the public from unfair or deceptive advertising and business practices.

(c) This title shall be construed liberally to achieve these purposes. *(Added by Stats.1984, c. 1177, § 1. Amended by Stats.2022, c. 965 (A.B.2424), § 1, eff. Jan. 1, 2023.)*

Cross References

Buyer defined for purposes of this Title, see Civil Code § 1789.12.
Credit services organization defined for purposes of this Title, see Civil Code § 1789.12.

§ 1789.12. Definitions

As used in this title:

(a) "Communication" means the conveyance of any information regarding a debt, credit record, credit history, or credit rating, directly or indirectly, to any person by any means or through any medium.

(b) "Consumer" means any natural person who is solicited to purchase or who purchases the services of a credit services organization.

(c) "Consumer credit reporting agency" has the same meaning as in Section 1785.3.

(d) "Credit services organization" means a person who, with respect to the extension of credit by others, sells, provides, or performs, or represents that * * * the person can or will sell, provide, or perform, any of the following services, in return for the payment of money or other valuable consideration:

(1) Improving a consumer's credit record, history, or rating.

(2) Obtaining a loan or other extension of credit for a consumer.

(3) Providing advice or assistance to a consumer with regard to either paragraph (1) or (2).

(e) "Credit services organization" does not include any of the following:

(1) Any person holding a license to make loans or extensions of credit pursuant to the laws of this state or the United States who is subject to regulation and supervision with respect to the making of those loans or extensions of credit by an official or agency of this state or the United States and whose business is the making of those loans or extensions of credit.

(2) Any bank, as defined in Section 103 of the Financial Code, or any savings institution, as specified in subdivision (a) or (b) of Section 5102 of the Financial Code, whose deposits or accounts are eligible for insurance by the Federal Deposit Insurance Corporation.

(3) Any person licensed as a prorater by the Department of * * * Financial Protection and Innovation when the person is acting within the course and scope of that license.

(4) Any person licensed as a real estate broker performing an act for which a real estate license is required under the Real Estate Law (Part 1 (commencing with Section 10000) * * * of Division 4 * * * of the Business and Professions Code) and who is acting within the course and scope of that license.

(5) Any attorney licensed to practice law in this state, where the attorney renders services within the course and scope of the practice of law, unless the attorney is an employee of, or otherwise directly affiliated with, a credit services organization. This includes attorneys that regularly engage in litigation in furtherance of assisting consumers with credit issues.

(6) Any broker-dealer registered with the Securities and Exchange Commission or the Commodity Futures Trading Commission where the broker-dealer is acting within the course and scope of the regulation.

(7) Any nonprofit organization described in Section 501(c)(3) of the Internal Revenue Code [1] that, according to a final ruling or determination by the Internal Revenue Service, is both of the following:

(A) Exempt from taxation under Section 501(a) of the Internal Revenue Code.

(B) Not a private foundation as defined in Section 509 of the Internal Revenue Code.

An advance ruling or determination of tax-exempt or foundation status by the Internal Revenue Service does not meet the requirements of this paragraph.

* * *

(f) "Data furnisher" has the same meaning as the term "furnisher" is defined in Section 660.2 of Title 16 of the Code of Federal Regulations.

(g) "Extension of credit" means the right to defer payment of debt or to incur debt and defer its payment, offered or granted primarily for personal, family, or household purposes.

* * *

(h) "Person" includes an individual, corporation, partnership, joint venture, or any business entity. *(Added by Stats.1984, c. 1177, § 1. Amended by Stats.1992, c. 651 (A.B.2999), § 2; Stats.1994, c. 1010 (S.B.2053), § 38; Stats. 1994, c. 792 (A.B.1922), § 1; Stats.1996, c. 648 (A.B.2279), § 1; Stats.2015, c. 190 (A.B.1517), § 4, eff. Jan. 1, 2016; Stats.2022, c. 452 (S.B.1498), § 23, eff. Jan. 1, 2023; Stats. 2022, c. 965 (A.B.2424), § 2, eff. Jan. 1, 2023.)*

[1] Internal Revenue Code sections are in Title 26 of the U.S.C.A.

§ 1789.13. Credit services organizations; prohibited activities

A credit services organization and its salespersons, agents, representatives, and independent contractors who sell or attempt to sell the services of a credit services organization shall not do any of the following:

§ 1789.13 OBLIGATIONS

(a) Charge or receive any money or other valuable consideration prior to full and complete performance of the services the credit services organization has agreed to perform for or on behalf of the consumer.

(b) Fail to perform the agreed services within * * * 180 days following the date the consumer signs the contract for those services.

(c) Fail to provide a monthly statement to the consumer detailing the services performed.

(d) Charge or receive any money or other valuable consideration for referral of the consumer to a retail seller or other credit grantor who will or may extend credit to the consumer, if either of the following apply:

(1) The credit that is or will be extended to the consumer (A) is upon substantially the same terms as those available to the general public or (B) is upon substantially the same terms that would have been extended to the consumer without the assistance of the credit services organization.

(2) The money or consideration is paid by the credit grantor or is derived from the consumer's payments to the credit grantor for costs, fees, finance charges, or principal.

(e) Make, or counsel or advise a consumer to make, a statement that is untrue or misleading and that is known, or that by the exercise of reasonable care should be known, to be untrue or misleading, to a consumer credit reporting agency or to a person who has extended credit to a * * * consumer, to a data furnisher, or to any person with whom a consumer is applying for an extension of credit, such as statements concerning a consumer's identification, home address, creditworthiness, credit standing, or credit capacity.

(f) Remove, or assist or advise the consumer to remove, adverse information from the consumer's credit record that is accurate or not obsolete.

(g) Create, or assist or advise the consumer to create, a new credit record by using a different name, address, social security number, or employee identification number.

(h) Make or use untrue or misleading representations in the offer or sale of the services of a credit services organization, including either of the following:

(1) Guaranteeing or otherwise stating that the credit services organization is able to delete an adverse credit history, unless the representation clearly discloses, in a manner equally as conspicuous as the guarantee, that this can be done only if the credit history is inaccurate or obsolete and is not claimed to be accurate by the creditor who submitted the information.

(2) Guaranteeing or otherwise stating that the credit services organization is able to obtain an extension of credit, regardless of the consumer's previous credit problems or credit history, unless the representation clearly discloses, in a manner equally as conspicuous as the guarantee, the eligibility requirements for obtaining an extension of credit.

(i) Engage, directly or indirectly, in an act, practice, or course of business that operates or would operate as a fraud or deception upon a person in connection with the offer or sale of the services of a credit services organization.

(j) Advertise or cause to be advertised, in any manner, the services of the credit services organization, without being registered with the Department of Justice.

(k) Fail to maintain an agent for service of process in this state.

(*l*) Transfer or assign its certificate of registration.

(m) Call or submit any communication to a consumer credit reporting agency, creditor, debt collector, or debt buyer without the prior written authorization of the consumer. A relevant authorization in the agreement or contract between a consumer and a credit services organization is sufficient for the purpose of this subdivision.

(n) Submit a consumer's dispute to a consumer credit reporting agency * * *, creditor, debt collector, or debt buyer more than 180 days after the account subject to the dispute has been removed from the consumer's credit report.

(o) Use the online electronic portal, electronic mail system, or telephone system of a consumer credit reporting * * * agency, creditor, debt collector, or debt buyer * * * to submit a dispute of a consumer or * * * to request disclosure without the prior written authorization of the consumer. A relevant authorization in the agreement or contract between a consumer and a credit services organization is sufficient for the purpose of this subdivision.

(p) Directly or indirectly extend credit to a consumer.

(q) Refer a consumer to a credit grantor that is related to the credit services organization by a common ownership, management, or control, including a common owner, director, or officer.

(r) Refer a consumer to a credit grantor for which the credit services organization provides, or arranges for a third party to provide, services related to the extension of credit such as underwriting, billing, payment processing, or debt collection.

(s) Provide a credit grantor with an assurance that a portion of an extension of credit to a consumer referred by the credit services organization will be repaid, including providing a guaranty, letter of credit, or agreement to acquire a part of the credit grantor's financial interest in the extension of credit.

(t) Use a scheme, device, or contrivance to evade the prohibitions contained in this section.

(u) Fail to make a written communication sent on behalf of a consumer to any credit reporting agency, data furnisher, or legal counsel for either of the foregoing available to the consumer.

(v) Fail to provide along with its first written communication to a credit reporting agency or data furnisher any sufficient information to investigate an account.

(w) The seeking to obtain, or the obtaining of, a consumer's credit report and the performance of other services necessary to determine the needs of a consumer for the reinvestigation of any accounts shall not constitute services of a credit services organization for which a contract is required pursuant to subdivision (a) of Section 1789.16, if that activity is undertaken with the consumer's prior written, electronic, or recorded oral consent. (Added by Stats.1984, c. 1177, § 1. Amended by Stats.1992, c. 651 (A.B.2999), § 3; Stats.1994, c.

792 (A.B.1922), § 2; Stats.2007, c. 91 (S.B.500), § 1; Stats. 2008, c. 179 (S.B.1498), § 30; Stats.2022, c. 965 (A.B.2424), § 3, eff. Jan. 1, 2023.)

Cross References

Buyer defined for purposes of this Title, see Civil Code § 1789.12.
Consumer Credit Reporting Agencies, see Civil Code § 1785.1 et seq.
Consumer credit reporting agency defined for purposes of this Title, see Civil Code § 1789.12.
Credit services, grounds for denying certificate of registration, see Civil Code § 1789.25.
Credit services organization defined for purposes of this Title, see Civil Code § 1789.12.
Extension of credit defined for purposes of this Title, see Civil Code § 1789.12.
Person defined for purposes of this Title, see Civil Code § 1789.12.

§ 1789.134. Communication with consumer represented by credit services organization

(a) A consumer credit reporting agency, creditor, debt collector, or debt buyer that knows that a consumer is represented by a credit services organization, and that also has knowledge of, or can readily ascertain the credit services organization's name and address shall communicate with the credit services organization unless either of the following circumstances apply:

(1) The credit services organization fails to respond within 30 days to a communication from a consumer credit reporting agency, creditor, debt collector, or debt buyer.

(2) The consumer expressly directs the consumer credit reporting agency, creditor, debt collector, or debt buyer not to communicate with the credit services organization.

(b) Notwithstanding subdivision (a), a consumer credit reporting agency, creditor, or debt collector shall not be required to communicate with a credit services organization concerning an account that is subject to a dispute if any of the following apply:

(1) The account subject to the dispute has been paid, settled, or otherwise resolved and has been reported as paid, settled, or otherwise resolved on the consumer's credit report.

(2) The account subject to the dispute has been removed from the consumer's credit report.

(3) The debt collector has provided to the credit services organization or to the consumer the verification information or documentation described in Section 1692g(b) of Title 15 of the United States Code regarding the account subject to dispute.

(4) The debt buyer has provided to the credit services organization or to the consumer the information or documentation described in subdivisions (a) and (b) of Section 1788.52 regarding the account subject to the dispute.

(5) The consumer credit reporting agency, creditor, or debt collector reasonably determines that the dispute is frivolous or irrelevant pursuant to Section 1681i(a)(3) or Section 1681s–2(a)(1)(F) of Title 15 of the United States Code. (Added by Stats.2022, c. 965 (A.B.2424), § 4, eff. Jan. 1, 2023.)

§ 1789.135. Redaction of consumer personal information

To protect against fraud and identity theft, when a credit services organization sends a written communication by facsimile, electronic mail, United States mail, overnight courier, or other means that contains personal information of a consumer, the credit services organization shall redact the personal information to include only the last four digits of the social security number, taxpayer identification number, or state identification number, the last four digits of the financial account number, credit card number, or debit card number, or the month and year of the consumer's date of birth, unless the inclusion of the full number or date is otherwise required by law, or is legally permissible and required to achieve the desired objective. Redacting information pursuant to this subdivision shall not be considered a violation of subdivision (w) of Section 1789.13. (Added by Stats.2022, c. 965 (A.B.2424), § 5, eff. Jan. 1, 2023.)

§ 1789.14. Information statement; necessity and time of delivery to consumer; acknowledgement of delivery; retention on file

* * * <u>Before</u> the execution of a contract or agreement between the <u>consumer</u> and a credit services organization, the credit services organization shall provide the <u>consumer</u> a statement in writing * * * containing all the information required by Section 1789.15. The credit services organization shall maintain on file * * * for a period of <u>four</u> years <u>following the completion or termination of the credit services organization agreement with the consumer</u> an exact copy of the statement * * *. (Added by Stats.1984, c. 1177, § 1. Amended by Stats.1992, c. 651 (A.B.2999), § 4; Stats.2022, c. 965 (A.B.2424), § 6, eff. Jan. 1, 2023.)

Cross References

Buyer defined for purposes of this Title, see Civil Code § 1789.12.
Credit services organization defined for purposes of this Title, see Civil Code § 1789.12.

§ 1789.15. Information statement; contents

The information statement shall include all of the following:

(a) A complete and detailed description of the services to be performed by the credit services organization for or on behalf of the <u>consumer</u> and the total amount the <u>consumer</u> will have to pay, or become obligated to pay, for the services.

(b) The <u>consumer's</u> right to proceed against the bond under the circumstances and in the manner set forth in Section 1789.18.

(c) The name and address of the surety company which issued the bond.

(d) A complete and accurate statement of the availability of nonprofit credit counseling services.

(e) <u>The following notice: If you have a complaint about the services provided by this credit services organization or the fees charged by this credit services organization, you may</u>

§ 1789.15 OBLIGATIONS

submit that complaint to the Attorney General's office, California Department of Justice, Attn: ___, P.O. Box 944255, Sacramento, CA 94244–2550.

The information statement shall be printed in at least 10-point boldface type and shall include the following statement * * *:

"CONSUMER CREDIT FILE RIGHTS UNDER STATE AND FEDERAL LAW

You have a right to obtain a free copy of your credit report from a * * * credit reporting agency. You may * * * obtain this free copy of your credit report one time per year by visiting www.AnnualCreditReport.com. You will be able to view your credit report, dispute alleged inaccuracies, and obtain additional information at no fee. If requested, the consumer credit reporting agency must provide someone to help you interpret the information in your credit file.

You have a right to dispute inaccurate information by contacting the consumer credit reporting agency directly. However, neither you nor any credit repair company or credit services organization has the right to have accurate, current, and verifiable information removed from your credit report. Under the Federal Fair Credit Reporting Act, the consumer credit reporting agency must remove accurate, negative information from your report only if it is over seven years old. Bankruptcy information can be reported for 10 years.

If you have notified a credit reporting agency in writing that you dispute the accuracy of information in your credit file, the consumer credit reporting agency must then reinvestigate and modify or remove inaccurate information. The consumer credit reporting agency may not charge a fee for this service. Any pertinent information and copies of all documents you have concerning an error should be given to the consumer credit reporting agency.

If the reinvestigation does not resolve the dispute to your satisfaction, you may send a brief statement to the consumer credit reporting agency to keep in your file, explaining why you think the record is inaccurate. The consumer credit reporting agency must include your statement about disputed information in any report it issues about you.

You have a right to cancel the contract with the credit services organization for any reason * * * before midnight on the fifth working * * * day after you signed it. If for any reason you * * * cancel the contract during this time, you do not owe any money.

You have a right to sue a credit services organization if it misleads you." (Added by Stats.1984, c. 1177, § 1. Amended by Stats.1992, c. 651 (A.B.2999), § 5; Stats.2022, c. 965 (A.B.2424), § 7, eff. Jan. 1, 2023.)

Cross References

Buyer defined for purposes of this Title, see Civil Code § 1789.12.
Consumer credit reporting agency defined for purposes of this Title, see Civil Code § 1789.12.
Credit services organization defined for purposes of this Title, see Civil Code § 1789.12.

§ 1789.16. Contracts; requirements; contents

(a) A credit services organization shall not provide any service to a consumer except pursuant to a written contract that complies with this section. Every contract between the consumer and a credit services organization for the purchase of the services of the credit services organization shall identify the physical address, electronic mail address, and facsimile number if applicable, of the credit services organization, shall be in writing, shall be dated, shall be signed by the consumer, and shall include all of the following:

(1) A conspicuous statement in size equal to at least 10-point boldface type, in immediate proximity to the space reserved for the signature of the buyer, as follows:

"You, the consumer, may cancel this contract at any time * * * before midnight on the fifth working day after * * * you sign it. See the attached notice of cancellation form for an explanation of this right."

(2) The terms and conditions of payment, including the total of all payments to be made by the consumer, whether to the credit services organization or to some other person.

(3) A full and detailed description of the services to be performed by the credit services organization for the consumer, including a list of the information appearing on the consumer's credit report that the credit services organization will seek a reasonable reinvestigation of, as described in Title 15 of Section 1681i of the United States Code, all guarantees and all promises of full or partial refunds, and the estimated * * * length of time for performing the services, not to exceed * * * 180 days, or a shorter period consistent with the purposes of this title as may be prescribed by the Department of Justice.

(4) The credit services organization's principal business address and the name and address of its agent, other than the Secretary of State, in the State of California, authorized to receive service of process.

(b) The contract shall be accompanied by a completed form in duplicate, captioned "Notice of Cancellation," which shall be attached to the contract and easily detachable, and which shall contain in type of at least 10–point the following statement written in the same language as used in the contract:

"Notice of Cancellation"

"You may cancel this contract, without any penalty or obligation, * * * before midnight on the fifth working day after you sign it.

"If you cancel, any payment made by you under this contract must be returned within 15 days following receipt by the seller of your cancellation notice.

"To cancel this contract, mail or deliver a signed and dated copy of this cancellation notice, or any other written notice, to

_____ at

(name of seller)

_____   _____
(address of seller)   (place of business)
not later than midnight _____.
                         (date)
"I hereby cancel this transaction."

_____   _____
(date)   (purchaser's signature)

A copy of the fully completed contract and all other documents the credit services organization requires the buyer to sign shall be given to the consumer at the time they are signed. *(Added by Stats.1984, c. 1177, § 1. Amended by Stats.1992, c. 651 (A.B.2999), § 6; Stats.1993, c. 285 (A.B. 1340), § 10, eff. Aug. 2, 1993; Stats.1994, c. 792 (A.B.1922), § 3; Stats.2022, c. 965 (A.B.2424), § 8, eff. Jan. 1, 2023.)*

"_____ at
"(name of seller) "

Cross References

Buyer defined for purposes of this Title, see Civil Code § 1789.12.
Credit services organization defined for purposes of this Title, see Civil Code § 1789.12.
Person defined for purposes of this Title, see Civil Code § 1789.12.

§ 1789.17. Seller's breach of contract or obligation; violation of title

The seller's breach of a contract under this title or of any obligation arising therefrom shall constitute a violation of this title. *(Added by Stats.1984, c. 1177, § 1.)*

§ 1789.18. Surety bonds; compliance requirements; filing of copy

No credit services organization shall conduct business in this state unless the credit services organization has first obtained a surety bond in the principal amount of one hundred thousand dollars ($100,000) issued by an admitted surety and the bond complies with all of the following:

(a) The bond shall be in favor of the State of California for the benefit of any person who is damaged by any violation of this title. The bond shall also be in favor of any individual damaged by those practices.

(b) Any person claiming against the bond for a violation of this title may maintain an action at law against the credit services organization and against the surety. The surety shall be liable only for actual damages and not the punitive damages permitted under Section 1789.21. The aggregate liability of the surety to all persons damaged by a credit services organization's violation of this title shall in no event exceed the amount of the bond.

(c) The bond shall be maintained for two years following the date on which the credit services organization ceases to conduct business in this state.

A copy of the bond shall be filed with the Secretary of State. *(Added by Stats.1984, c. 1177, § 1. Amended by Stats.1992, c. 651 (A.B.2999), § 7.)*

Cross References

Claims against deposits in lieu of bonds, see Civil Code § 1789.24.
Credit services organization defined for purposes of this Title, see Civil Code § 1789.12.
Person defined for purposes of this Title, see Civil Code § 1789.12.

§ 1789.19. Waiver of rights by consumer; prohibition; attempt to obtain; violation of title; burden of proof on exemption or exception from definition

(a) Any waiver by a consumer of the provisions of this title shall be deemed contrary to public policy and shall be void and unenforceable. Any attempt by a credit services organization to have a consumer waive rights given by this title shall constitute a violation of this title.

(b) In any proceeding involving this title, the burden of proving an exemption or an exception from a definition is upon the person claiming it. *(Added by Stats.1984, c. 1177, § 1. Amended by Stats.2022, c. 965 (A.B.2424), § 9, eff. Jan. 1, 2023.)*

Cross References

Buyer defined for purposes of this Title, see Civil Code § 1789.12.
Credit services organization defined for purposes of this Title, see Civil Code § 1789.12.
Person defined for purposes of this Title, see Civil Code § 1789.12.

§ 1789.20. Violations; misdemeanor; injunction; prosecutor

(a) Any person who violates any provision of this title is guilty of a misdemeanor. Any superior court of this state shall have jurisdiction in equity to restrain and enjoin the violation of any provision of this title.

The duty to institute actions for violation of this title, including equity proceedings to restrain and enjoin such a violation, is hereby vested in the Attorney General, district attorneys, and city attorneys. The Attorney General, any district attorney, or any city attorney may prosecute misdemeanor actions or institute equity proceedings, or both.

This section shall not be deemed to prohibit the enforcement by any person of any right provided by this or any other law.

(b) The misdemeanor provision of this section does not apply to a seller's breach of a contract subject to this title. *(Added by Stats.1984, c. 1177, § 1.)*

§ 1789.20 OBLIGATIONS

Cross References

Attorney General, generally, see Government Code § 12500 et seq.

Misdemeanors, definition and penalties, see Penal Code §§ 17, 19, 19.2.

Person defined for purposes of this Title, see Civil Code § 1789.12.

§ 1789.21. Actions for recovery of damages or injunctive relief

(a) Any consumer injured by a violation of this title or by the credit services organization's breach of a contract subject to this title may bring any action for recovery of damages, or for injunctive relief, or both. Judgment shall be entered for actual damages, but in no case less than the amount paid by the consumer to the credit services organization, plus reasonable attorney's fees and costs. An award, if the trial court deems it proper, may be entered for punitive damages.

(b) Any person, including, but not limited to, a consumer credit reporting agency, as defined in subdivision (d) of Section 1785.3, and any consumer of, or user of, a consumer credit report under the Consumer Credit Reporting Agencies Act (Title 1.6 (commencing with Section 1785.1)), and any furnisher of credit information under the Consumer Credit Reporting Agencies Act, may bring an action for the recovery of damages or for injunctive relief, or both, for a violation of this title. Any person bringing such an action who prevails in the action shall be entitled to reasonable attorney's fees and costs. (Added by Stats.1984, c. 1177, § 1. Amended by Stats.1992, c. 651 (A.B.2999), § 8; Stats.1994, c. 792 (A.B. 1922), § 4; Stats.2004, c. 183 (A.B.3082), § 33; Stats.2022, c. 965 (A.B.2424), § 10, eff. Jan. 1, 2023.)

Cross References

Buyer defined for purposes of this Title, see Civil Code § 1789.12.

Consumer credit reporting agency defined for purposes of this Title, see Civil Code § 1789.12.

Credit services organization defined for purposes of this Title, see Civil Code § 1789.12.

Person defined for purposes of this Title, see Civil Code § 1789.12.

§ 1789.22. Application of other laws; remedies as additional

The provisions of this title are not exclusive and do not relieve the parties or the contracts subject thereto from compliance with any other applicable provision of law.

The remedies provided in this title for violation of any section of this title shall be in addition to any other procedures or remedies for any violation or conduct provided for in any other law. (Added by Stats.1984, c. 1177, § 1.)

§ 1789.23. Severability

If any provision of this title or if any application thereof to any person or circumstance is held invalid, the remainder of the title and the application of the provision to other persons and circumstances shall not be affected thereby. (Added by Stats.1984, c. 1177, § 1.)

Cross References

Person defined for purposes of this Title, see Civil Code § 1789.12.

§ 1789.24. Claims against deposits in lieu of bonds; establishment; approval; 240-day period; payment; approval of claims after 240-day period; deposits not subject to attachment, garnishment, or execution

(a) When a deposit has been made in lieu of a bond pursuant to Section 995.710 of the Code of Civil Procedure, the person asserting a claim against the deposit shall, in lieu of proceeding under Section 996.430 of the Code of Civil Procedure, establish the claim by furnishing evidence to the Secretary of State of a money judgment entered by a court, together with evidence that the claimant is a person described in subdivision (b) of Section 1789.18.

(b) When a person has established the claim with the Secretary of State, the Secretary of State shall review and approve the claim and enter the date of approval thereon. The claim shall be designated an "approved claim."

(c) When the first claim against a particular deposit has been approved, it shall not be paid until the expiration of a period of 240 days after the date of its approval by the Secretary of State. Subsequent claims that are approved by the Secretary of State within the same 240–day period shall similarly not be paid until the expiration of the 240–day period. Upon the expiration of the 240–day period, the Secretary of State shall pay all approved claims from that 240–day period in full unless the deposit is insufficient, in which case each approved claim shall be paid a pro rata share of the deposit.

(d) When the Secretary of State approves the first claim against a particular deposit after the expiration of a 240–day period, the date of approval of that claim shall begin a new 240–day period to which subdivision (c) shall apply with respect to any amount remaining in the deposit.

(e) After a deposit is exhausted, no further claims shall be paid by the Secretary of State. Claimants who have had their claims paid in full or in part pursuant to subdivision (c) or (d) shall not be required to return funds received from the deposit for the benefit of other claimants.

(f) When a deposit has been made in lieu of a bond, as specified in subdivision (a), the amount of the deposit shall not be subject to attachment, garnishment, or execution with respect to an action or judgment against the credit services organization, other than as to an amount as no longer needed or required for the purpose of this title which would otherwise be returned to the credit services organization by the Secretary of State.

(g) The Secretary of State shall retain a cash deposit for two years from the date the Secretary of State receives written notification from the assignor of the deposit that the assignor has ceased to engage in the business of a credit services organization or has filed a bond pursuant to Section 1789.18, provided that there are no outstanding claims against the deposit. The written notice shall include all of the following: (1) name, address, and telephone number of the assignor; (2) name, address, and telephone number of the bank at which the deposit is located; (3) account number of the deposit; and (4) a statement whether the assignor is ceasing to engage in the business of a credit services organization or has filed a bond with the Secretary of State. The Secretary of State shall forward an acknowledgment of receipt of the written notice to the assignor at the address indicated therein, specifying the date of receipt of the written notice and anticipated date of release of the deposit.

(h) This section shall apply to all deposits retained by the Secretary of State.

(i) A judge of a superior court may order the return of the deposit prior to the expiration of two years upon evidence satisfactory to the judge that there are no outstanding claims against the deposit or order the Secretary of State to retain the deposit for a sufficient period beyond the two years specified in subdivision (g) to resolve outstanding claims against the deposit account. *(Added by Stats.1985, c. 275, § 1. Amended by Stats.1996, c. 633 (S.B.1978), § 4; Stats. 1998, c. 829 (S.B.1652), § 6; Stats.2002, c. 784 (S.B.1316), § 13.)*

Cross References

Credit services organization defined for purposes of this Title, see Civil Code § 1789.12.

Person defined for purposes of this Title, see Civil Code § 1789.12.

§ 1789.25. Registration application; bond; fee; contents; investigation; notification of change in information; expiration of certificate of registration

(a) Every credit services organization shall file a registration application with, and receive a certificate of registration from, the Department of Justice before conducting business in this state. The Department of Justice shall not issue a certificate of registration until the bond required by Section 1789.18 has been filed with the Office of the Secretary of State and the department establishes that the organization seeking a certificate satisfies the requirements of subdivision (f). The application shall be accompanied by a registration fee of one hundred dollars ($100). The registration application shall contain all of the following information:

(1) The name and address where business is actually conducted of the credit services organization.

(2) The names, addresses, and driver's license numbers of any and all persons who directly or indirectly own or control 10 percent or more of the outstanding shares of stock in the credit services organization.

(3) Either of the following:

(A) A full and complete disclosure of any litigation commenced against the credit services organization or any resolved or unresolved complaint that relates to the operation of the credit services organization and that is filed with the Attorney General, or any other governmental authority of this state, any other state, or the federal government. With respect to each resolved complaint identified by the disclosure, the disclosure shall include a brief description of the resolution.

(B) An acknowledged declaration, under penalty of perjury, stating that no litigation has been commenced and no unresolved complaint relating to the operation of the organization has been filed with the Attorney General, or any other governmental authority of this state, any other state, or the federal government.

(4) Other information that the Department of Justice requires, either at the time of application or thereafter.

(b) The Department of Justice may conduct an investigation to verify the accuracy of the registration application. If the application involves investigation outside this state, the applicant credit services organization may be required by the Department of Justice to advance sufficient funds to pay the actual expenses of the investigation. Any nonresident applying for registration under this section shall designate and maintain a resident of this state as the applicant's agent for the purpose of receipt of service of process.

(c) Each credit services organization shall notify the Department of Justice in writing within 30 days after the date of a change in the information required by subdivision (a), except that 30 days' advance notice and approval by the Department of Justice shall be required before changing the corporate name or address, or persons owning more than 10 percent of the shares of stock in the organization. Each credit services organization registering under this section may use no more than one fictitious or trade name and shall maintain a copy of the registration application in its files. The organization shall allow a buyer to inspect the registration application upon request.

(d) A certificate of registration issued pursuant to this section shall expire * * * <u>one year after it was issued,</u> but may be renewed by filing a renewal application accompanied by a fee * * * <u>in an amount to be determined annually by the Department of * * * Justice as is reasonable and necessary to satisfy its costs * * * in complying with its duties under this title to regulate credit services organizations. The Department of Justice may, periodically, increase the fee, but the amount of the fee shall not exceed that which is reasonable and necessary to satisfy its costs in complying with its duties under this title to regulate credit services organizations.</u>

(e) The credit services organization shall attach to the registration statement a copy of the contract or contracts which the credit services organization intends to execute with its customers and a copy of the required bond.

(f) The Department of Justice shall not issue a certificate of registration under this title to any person who has engaged in, or proposes to engage in, any activity that is in violation of Section 1789.13, any law prohibiting the use of untrue or misleading statements, or any law related to the extension of credit to persons for personal, family, or household purposes.

(g) <u>The Department of Justice shall maintain on a publicly available internet website a list of the credit services organizations that are registered in this state.</u> *(Added by Stats.1992, c. 651 (A.B.2999), § 9. Amended by Stats.2007, c. 91 (S.B.500), § 2; Stats.2022, c. 965 (A.B.2424), § 11, eff. Jan. 1, 2023.)*

Cross References

Attorney General, generally, see Government Code § 12500 et seq.

Buyer defined for purposes of this Title, see Civil Code § 1789.12.

Credit services organization defined for purposes of this Title, see Civil Code § 1789.12.

Extension of credit defined for purposes of this Title, see Civil Code § 1789.12.

Person defined for purposes of this Title, see Civil Code § 1789.12.

§ 1789.26. Enforcement; filing fees

(a) The Secretary of State shall enforce the provisions of this title that govern the filing and maintenance of bonds and deposits in lieu of bonds.

(b) The Secretary of State shall charge and collect a filing fee not to exceed the cost of filing the bond or the deposit in lieu of a bond pursuant to Section 995.710 of the Code of Civil Procedure. *(Added by Stats.1996, c. 633 (S.B.1978), § 5.)*

Title 1.6F
CHECK CASHERS

Section
1789.30. Posting of schedule of fees and list of valid identification; return required for checks exceeding ten thousand dollars ($10,000).
1789.31. Check casher.
1789.32. Failure to post information or action contrary to posted information; unfair business practice.
1789.33. Repealed.
1789.35. Fees relating to check cashing services; identification and receipt requirements; violations and penalties; actions for relief.
1789.37. Permits; check cashing business; violations; penalties; deposit of forfeited bail and fines.
1789.38. Public policy; waiver of rights.
1789.39. Repealed.

Cross References

Credit card as condition of acceptance prohibited, see Civil Code § 1725.
Requirements for record keeping, see Penal Code § 14160.

§ 1789.30. Posting of schedule of fees and list of valid identification; return required for checks exceeding ten thousand dollars ($10,000)

(a)(1) Every check casher, as applicable to the services provided, shall post a complete, detailed, and unambiguous schedule of all fees for (A) cashing checks, drafts, money orders, or other commercial paper serving the same purpose, (B) the sale or issuance of money orders, and (C) the initial issuance of any identification card. Each check casher shall also post a list of valid identification which is acceptable in lieu of identification provided by the check casher. The information required by this section shall be clear, legible, and in letters not less than one-half inch in height. The information shall be posted in a conspicuous location in the unobstructed view of the public within the check casher's premises.

(2) A check casher may be required to file a return required by Section 18631.7 of the Revenue and Taxation Code.

(b)(1) Except as provided in paragraph (2), this section shall become operative December 31, 2004.

(2)(A) Except as provided in subparagraph (B), paragraph (2) of subdivision (a) shall apply to checks cashed on or after January 1, 2006.

(B) The amendments to this section made by the act[1] adding this subparagraph shall become operative on January 1, 2008. *(Added by Stats.2004, c. 17 (A.B.971), § 2, eff. Feb. 23, 2004, operative Dec. 31, 2004. Amended by Stats.2005, c. 74 (A.B.139), § 24, eff. July 19, 2005; Stats.2007, c. 341 (A.B.1747), § 1, operative Jan. 1, 2008.)*

[1] Stats.2007, c. 341 (A.B.1747).

Cross References

California deferred deposit transactions, enforcement of deferred deposits, see Financial Code § 23102.

§ 1789.31. Check casher

(a) As used in this title, a "check casher" means a person or entity that for compensation engages, in whole or in part, in the business of cashing checks, warrants, drafts, money orders, or other commercial paper serving the same purpose. "Check casher" does not include a state or federally chartered bank, savings association, credit union, or industrial loan company. "Check casher" also does not include a retail seller engaged primarily in the business of selling consumer goods, including consumables, to retail buyers that cashes checks or issues money orders for a fee not exceeding two dollars ($2) as a service to its customers that is incidental to its main purpose or business.

(b) This section shall become operative December 31, 2004. *(Added by Stats.2002, c. 777 (S.B.898), § 3, operative March 1, 2004. Amended by Stats.2004, c. 17 (A.B.971), § 4, eff. Feb. 23, 2004, operative Dec. 31, 2004.)*

Cross References

California deferred deposit transactions, enforcement of deferred deposits, see Financial Code § 23102.
Franchise and income tax laws, filing of returns, information returns by check cashiers, see Revenue and Taxation Code § 18631.7.

§ 1789.32. Failure to post information or action contrary to posted information; unfair business practice

Failure to post information as required by this title, or the imposition of fees or identification requirements contrary to the information posted, shall constitute an unfair business practice within the meaning of Section 17200 of the Business and Professions Code. *(Added by Stats.1990, c. 1391 (A.B. 3096), § 1.)*

Cross References

California deferred deposit transactions, enforcement of deferred deposits, see Financial Code § 23102.

§ 1789.33. Repealed by Stats.2004, c. 17 (A.B.971), § 5, operative Jan. 1, 2005

§ 1789.35. Fees relating to check cashing services; identification and receipt requirements; violations and penalties; actions for relief

(a) A check casher shall not charge a fee for cashing a payroll check or government check in excess of 3 percent if identification is provided by the customer, or 3.5 percent without the provision of identification, of the face amount of the check, or three dollars ($3), whichever is greater. Identification, for purposes of this section, is limited to a California driver's license, a California identification card, or a valid United States military identification card.

(b) A check casher may charge a fee of no more than ten dollars ($10) to set up an initial account and issue an optional identification card for providing check cashing services. A replacement optional identification card may be issued at a cost not to exceed five dollars ($5).

(c) A check casher shall provide a receipt to the customer for each transaction.

(d) A check casher may charge a fee for cashing a personal check, as posted pursuant to Section 1789.30, for immediate deposit in an amount not to exceed 12 percent of the face value of the check.

(e) Any person who violates any provision of this section shall be liable for a civil penalty not to exceed two thousand dollars ($2,000) for each violation, which shall be assessed and recovered in a civil action brought in the name of the people of the State of California by the Attorney General in any court of competent jurisdiction. Any action brought pursuant to this subdivision shall be commenced within four years of the date on which the act or transaction upon which the action is based occurred.

(f) A willful violation of this section is a misdemeanor.

(g) Any person who is injured by any violation of this section may bring an action for the recovery of damages, an equity proceeding to restrain and enjoin those violations, or both. The amount awarded may be up to three times the damages actually incurred, but in no event less than the amount paid by the aggrieved consumer to a person subject to this section. If the plaintiff prevails, the plaintiff shall be awarded reasonable attorney's fees and costs. If a court determines by clear and convincing evidence that a breach or violation was willful, the court, in its discretion, may award punitive damages in addition to the amounts set forth above.

(h) This section shall become operative December 31, 2004. *(Added by Stats.2002, c. 777 (S.B.898), § 6, operative March 1, 2004. Amended by Stats.2004, c. 17 (A.B.971), § 7, eff. Feb. 23, 2004, operative Dec. 31, 2004; Stats.2004, c. 28 (S.B.31), § 2, eff. April 1, 2004, operative Dec. 31, 2004.)*

Cross References

Attorney General, generally, see Government Code § 12500 et seq.
California deferred deposit transactions, enforcement of deferred deposits, see Financial Code § 23102.
Check cashiers cashing checks totalling more than ten thousand dollars, filing of informational return, violations and penalties, see Revenue and Taxation Code § 18631.7.
Franchise and income tax laws, filing of returns, information returns by check cashiers, see Revenue and Taxation Code § 18631.7.
Misdemeanors, definition and penalties, see Penal Code §§ 17, 19, 19.2.
Requirements for record keeping, see Penal Code § 14160.

§ 1789.37. Permits; check cashing business; violations; penalties; deposit of forfeited bail and fines

(a) Every owner of a check casher's business shall obtain a permit from the Department of Justice to conduct a check casher's business.

(b) All applications for a permit to conduct a check casher's business shall be filed with the department in writing, signed by the applicant, if an individual, or by a member or officer authorized to sign, if the applicant is a corporation or other entity, and shall state the name of the business, the type of business engaged in, and the business address. Each applicant shall be fingerprinted.

(c) Each applicant for a permit to conduct a check casher's business shall pay a fee not to exceed the cost of processing the application, fingerprinting the applicant, and checking or obtaining the criminal record of the applicant, at the time of filing the application.

(d) Each applicant shall annually, beginning one year from the date of issuance of a check casher's permit, file an application for renewal of the permit with the department, along with payment of a renewal fee not to exceed the cost of processing the application for renewal and checking or obtaining the criminal record of the applicant.

(e) The department shall deny an application for a permit to conduct a check casher's business, or for renewal of a permit, if the applicant has a felony conviction involving dishonesty, fraud, or deceit, if the crime is substantially related to the qualifications, functions, or duties of a person engaged in the business of check cashing.

(f) The department shall adopt regulations to implement this section and shall determine the amount of the application fees required by this section. The department shall prescribe forms for the applications and permit required by this section, which shall be uniform throughout the state.

(g) In any action brought by a city attorney or district attorney to enforce a violation of this section, an owner of a check casher's business who engages in the business of check cashing without holding a current and valid permit issued by the department pursuant to this section is subject to a civil penalty, as follows:

(1) For the first offense, not more than one thousand dollars ($1,000).

(2) For the second offense, not more than five thousand dollars ($5,000).

(h) Any person who has twice been found in violation of subdivision (g) and who, within 10 years of the date of the first offense, engages in the business of check cashing without holding a current and valid permit issued by the department pursuant to this section is guilty of a misdemeanor punishable by imprisonment in a county jail not exceeding six months, or by a fine not exceeding five thousand dollars ($5,000), or by both that fine and imprisonment.

(i) All civil penalties, forfeited bail, or fines received by any court pursuant to this section shall, as soon as practicable after the receipt thereof, be deposited with the county treasurer of the county in which the court is situated. Fines and forfeitures deposited shall be disbursed pursuant to the Penal Code. Civil penalties deposited shall be paid at least once a month as follows:

(1) Fifty percent to the Treasurer by warrant of the county auditor drawn upon the requisition of the clerk or judge of the court, to be deposited in the State Treasury on order of the Controller.

(2) Fifty percent to the city treasurer of the city, if the offense occurred in a city, otherwise to the treasurer of the county in which the prosecution is conducted. Any money deposited in the State Treasury under this section that is determined by the Controller to have been erroneously deposited shall be refunded out of any money in the State Treasury that is available by law for that purpose.

(j) This section shall become operative December 31, 2004. *(Added by Stats.2004, c. 17 (A.B.971), § 9, eff. Feb. 23, 2004, operative Dec. 31, 2004. Amended by Stats.2006, c. 538 (S.B.1852), § 47; Stats.2016, c. 31 (S.B.836), § 9, eff. June 27, 2016.)*

Cross References

California deferred deposit transactions,
 Enforcement, duties of check cashers, see Financial Code § 1789.37.
 Enforcement of deferred deposits, see Financial Code § 23102.

§ 1789.37 OBLIGATIONS

California Finance Lenders Law, application to check casher holding a valid permit issued pursuant to this section, see Financial Code § 22050.

California Victim Compensation and Government Claims Board (formerly State Control Board), see Government Code § 13900 et seq.

Duties of check cashers holding valid permits for making deferred deposits, see Financial Code § 23100.

Enforcement of deferred deposits, made pursuant to a permit issued under this section prior to December 31, 2004, see Financial Code § 23102.

Felonies, definition and penalties, see Penal Code §§ 17, 18.

Misdemeanors, definition and penalties, see Penal Code §§ 17, 19, 19.2.

State Controller, generally, see Government Code § 12402 et seq.

§ 1789.38. Public policy; waiver of rights

Any waiver of the provisions of this title is contrary to public policy, and is void and unenforceable. *(Added by Stats.2002, c. 815 (A.B.2331), § 14.)*

§ 1789.39. Repealed by Stats.2004, c. 17 (A.B.971), § 10, operative Jan. 1, 2005

Title 1.61

COMMERCIAL CREDIT REPORTS
[EDITORIAL NOTE]

For Title 1.61, "Commercial Credit Reports", added by Stats.1992, c. 101 (S.B.652), § 1, see Civil Code § 1785.41 et seq.

Title 1.7

CONSUMER WARRANTIES

Chapter	Section
1. Consumer Warranty Protection	1790
1.5. Motor Vehicle Warranty Adjustment Programs	1795.90
2. Standards for Warranty Work	1796
3. Mobilehome Warranties	1797
4. Grey Market Goods	1797.8
5. Home Roof Warranties	1797.90

Cross References

Emission standards, see Health and Safety Code § 43204 et seq.

Issuance of licenses and certificates to manufacturers, transporters, and dealers, suspension or revocation, violation of warranty responsibilities, see Vehicle Code § 11705.4.

Recreational vehicle transactions, complaints from the public seeking a refund, see Vehicle Code § 3078.

Sale of housecars, warranties, see Vehicle Code § 11930 et seq.

CHAPTER 1. CONSUMER WARRANTY PROTECTION

Article	Section
1. General Provisions	1790
2. Definitions	1791
3. Sale Warranties	1792

ARTICLE 1. GENERAL PROVISIONS

Section	
1790.	Short title.
1790.1.	Effect of waiver.
1790.2.	Severability.
1790.3.	Law governing; reference to Commercial Code.
1790.4.	Cumulative remedies; applicability of other remedies.

Cross References

Consumers Legal Remedies Act, see Civil Code § 1750 et seq.

§ 1790. Short title

This chapter may be cited as the "Song-Beverly Consumer Warranty Act." *(Added by Stats.1970, c. 1333, p. 2478, § 1.)*

Cross References

Consumer affairs, see Business and Professions Code § 300 et seq.

§ 1790.1. Effect of waiver

Any waiver by the buyer of consumer goods of the provisions of this chapter, except as expressly provided in this chapter, shall be deemed contrary to public policy and shall be unenforceable and void. *(Added by Stats.1970, c. 1333, p. 2478, § 1.)*

Cross References

Buyer or retail buyer defined for purposes of this Chapter, see Civil Code § 1791.

Consumer goods defined for purposes of this Chapter, see Civil Code § 1791.

Waiver of advantage, law established for public reason, see Civil Code § 3513.

Waiver of code provisions unless against public policy, see Civil Code § 3268.

§ 1790.2. Severability

If any provision of this chapter or the application thereof to any person or circumstance is held unconstitutional, such invalidity shall not affect other provisions or applications of this chapter which can be given effect without the invalid provision or application, and to this end the provisions of this chapter are severable. *(Added by Stats.1970, c. 1333, p. 2478, § 1.)*

§ 1790.3. Law governing; reference to Commercial Code

The provisions of this chapter shall not affect the rights and obligations of parties determined by reference to the Commercial Code except that, where the provisions of the Commercial Code conflict with the rights guaranteed to buyers of consumer goods under the provisions of this chapter, the provisions of this chapter shall prevail. *(Added by Stats.1970, c. 1333, p. 2478, § 1.)*

Cross References

Buyer or retail buyer defined for purposes of this Chapter, see Civil Code § 1791.

Consumer goods defined for purposes of this Chapter, see Civil Code § 1791.

Provisions of Commercial Code on warranties, see Commercial Code §§ 2312 et seq., 2607, 2714, 2715, 2725, 2801, 9206.

§ 1790.4. Cumulative remedies; applicability of other remedies

The remedies provided by this chapter are cumulative and shall not be construed as restricting any remedy that is otherwise available, and, in particular, shall not be construed to supplant the provisions of the Unfair Practices Act.[1] *(Added by Stats.1971, c. 1523, p. 3000, § 1, operative Jan. 1, 1972. Amended by Stats.1976, c. 416, p. 1068, § 1.)*

[1] Business and Professions Code § 17000 et seq.

ARTICLE 2. DEFINITIONS

Section
1791.   Definitions.
1791.1. Implied warranty; definition; duration; remedies of buyers.
1791.2. Express warranty; definition.
1791.3. Disclaimer of implied warranties; "as is" or "with all faults" sales.

§ 1791. Definitions

As used in this chapter:

(a) "Consumer goods" means any new product or part thereof that is used, bought, or leased for use primarily for personal, family, or household purposes, except for clothing and consumables. "Consumer goods" shall include new and used assistive devices sold at retail.

(b) "Buyer" or "retail buyer" means any individual who buys consumer goods from a person engaged in the business of manufacturing, distributing, or selling consumer goods at retail. As used in this subdivision, "person" means any individual, partnership, corporation, limited liability company, association, or other legal entity that engages in any of these businesses.

(c) "Clothing" means any wearing apparel, worn for any purpose, including under and outer garments, shoes, and accessories composed primarily of woven material, natural or synthetic yarn, fiber, or leather or similar fabric.

(d) "Consumables" means any product that is intended for consumption by individuals, or use by individuals for purposes of personal care or in the performance of services ordinarily rendered within the household, and that usually is consumed or expended in the course of consumption or use.

(e) "Distributor" means any individual, partnership, corporation, association, or other legal relationship that stands between the manufacturer and the retail seller in purchases, consignments, or contracts for sale of consumer goods.

(f) "Independent repair or service facility" or "independent service dealer" means any individual, partnership, corporation, association, or other legal entity, not an employee or subsidiary of a manufacturer or distributor, that engages in the business of servicing and repairing consumer goods.

(g) "Lease" means any contract for the lease or bailment for the use of consumer goods by an individual, for a term exceeding four months, primarily for personal, family, or household purposes, whether or not it is agreed that the lessee bears the risk of the consumer goods' depreciation.

(h) "Lessee" means an individual who leases consumer goods under a lease.

(i) "Lessor" means a person who regularly leases consumer goods under a lease.

(j) "Manufacturer" means any individual, partnership, corporation, association, or other legal relationship that manufactures, assembles, or produces consumer goods.

(k) "Place of business" means, for the purposes of any retail seller that sells consumer goods by catalog or mail order, the distribution point for consumer goods.

(*l*) "Retail seller," "seller," or "retailer" means any individual, partnership, corporation, association, or other legal relationship that engages in the business of selling or leasing consumer goods to retail buyers.

(m) "Return to the retail seller" means, for the purposes of any retail seller that sells consumer goods by catalog or mail order, the retail seller's place of business, as defined in subdivision (k).

(n) "Sale" means either of the following:

(1) The passing of title from the seller to the buyer for a price.

(2) A consignment for sale.

(*o*) "Service contract" means a contract in writing to perform, over a fixed period of time or for a specified duration, services relating to the maintenance or repair of a consumer product, except that this term does not include a policy of automobile insurance, as defined in Section 116 of the Insurance Code.

(p) "Assistive device" means any instrument, apparatus, or contrivance, including any component or part thereof or accessory thereto, that is used or intended to be used, to assist an individual with a disability in the mitigation or treatment of an injury or disease or to assist or affect or replace the structure or any function of the body of an individual with a disability, except that this term does not include prescriptive lenses and other ophthalmic goods unless they are sold or dispensed to a blind person, as defined in Section 19153 of the Welfare and Institutions Code and unless they are intended to assist the limited vision of the person so disabled.

(q) "Catalog or similar sale" means a sale in which neither the seller nor any employee or agent of the seller nor any person related to the seller nor any person with a financial interest in the sale participates in the diagnosis of the buyer's condition or in the selection or fitting of the device.

(r) "Home appliance" means any refrigerator, freezer, range, microwave oven, washer, dryer, dishwasher, garbage disposal, trash compactor, or room air-conditioner normally used or sold for personal, family, or household purposes.

(s) "Home electronic product" means any television, radio, antenna rotator, audio or video recorder or playback equipment, video camera, video game, video monitor, computer equipment, telephone, telecommunications equipment, electronic alarm system, electronic appliance control system, or other kind of electronic product, if it is normally used or sold for personal, family, or household purposes. The term includes any electronic accessory that is normally used or sold with a home electronic product for one of those purposes. The term excludes any single product with a wholesale price to the retail seller of less than fifty dollars ($50).

(t) "Member of the Armed Forces" means a person on full-time active duty in the Army, Navy, Marine Corps, Air Force, National Guard, Space Force, or Coast Guard. Full-time active duty shall also include active military service at a military service school designated by law or the Adjutant General of the Military Department concerned.

(u) "Clear and conspicuous" and "clearly and conspicuously" means a larger type than the surrounding text, or in a contrasting type, font, or color to the surrounding text of the same size, or set off from the surrounding text of the same size by symbols or other marks, in a manner that clearly calls attention to the language. For an audio disclosure, "clear and conspicuous" and "clearly and conspicuously" means in a volume and cadence sufficient to be readily audible and understandable. (Added by Stats.1993, c. 1265 (S.B.798), § 12.5, operative Jan. 1, 1998. Amended by Stats.1994, c. 1010 (S.B.2053), § 39.5, operative Jan. 1, 1998; Stats.1995, c. 461 (A.B.40), § 2, operative Jan. 1, 1998; Stats.1997, c. 401 (S.B.780), § 63, operative Jan. 1, 2003; Stats.2002, c. 405 (A.B.2973), § 62, operative Jan. 1, 2008; Stats.2007, c. 151 (S.B.234), § 1, operative Jan. 1, 2008; Stats.2021, c. 452 (A.B.1221), § 1, eff. Jan. 1, 2022; Stats.2022, c. 379 (A.B. 1715), § 2, eff. Jan. 1, 2023.)

Cross References

Mobilehome warranties, see Civil Code § 1797 et seq.
Used goods, application of this section, see Civil Code § 1795.5.

§ 1791.1. Implied warranty; definition; duration; remedies of buyers

As used in this chapter:

(a) "Implied warranty of merchantability" or "implied warranty that goods are merchantable" means that the consumer goods meet each of the following:

(1) Pass without objection in the trade under the contract description.

(2) Are fit for the ordinary purposes for which such goods are used.

(3) Are adequately contained, packaged, and labeled.

(4) Conform to the promises or affirmations of fact made on the container or label.

(b) "Implied warranty of fitness" means (1) that when the retailer, distributor, or manufacturer has reason to know any particular purpose for which the consumer goods are required, and further, that the buyer is relying on the skill and judgment of the seller to select and furnish suitable goods, then there is an implied warranty that the goods shall be fit for such purpose and (2) that when there is a sale of an assistive device sold at retail in this state, then there is an implied warranty by the retailer that the device is specifically fit for the particular needs of the buyer.

(c) The duration of the implied warranty of merchantability and where present the implied warranty of fitness shall be coextensive in duration with an express warranty which accompanies the consumer goods, provided the duration of the express warranty is reasonable; but in no event shall such implied warranty have a duration of less than 60 days nor more than one year following the sale of new consumer goods to a retail buyer. Where no duration for an express warranty is stated with respect to consumer goods, or parts thereof, the duration of the implied warranty shall be the maximum period prescribed above.

(d) Any buyer of consumer goods injured by a breach of the implied warranty of merchantability and where applicable by a breach of the implied warranty of fitness has the remedies provided in Chapter 6 (commencing with Section 2601) and Chapter 7 (commencing with Section 2701) of Division 2 of the Commercial Code, and, in any action brought under such provisions, Section 1794 of this chapter shall apply. (Added by Stats.1970, c. 1333, p. 2479, § 1. Amended by Stats.1971, c. 1523, p. 3002, § 3, operative Jan. 1, 1972; Stats.1978, c. 991, p. 3059, § 2; Stats.1979, c. 1023, p. 3494, § 1.5.)

Cross References

Assistive device defined for purposes of this Chapter, see Civil Code § 1791.
Buyer or retail buyer defined for purposes of this Chapter, see Civil Code § 1791.
Consumer goods defined for purposes of this Chapter, see Civil Code § 1791.
Distributor defined for purposes of this Chapter, see Civil Code § 1791.
Express warranty defined, see Civil Code § 1791.2.
Fair Practices of Equipment Manufacturers, Distributors, Wholesalers, and Dealers Act, termination or nonrenewal of contract, repurchase of inventory, see Business and Professions Code § 22905.
Implied warranties under Commercial Code, see Commercial Code §§ 2314, 2315.
Manufacturer defined for purposes of this Chapter, see Civil Code § 1791.
Retail seller, seller, or retailer defined for purposes of this Chapter, see Civil Code § 1791.
Sale defined for purposes of this Chapter, see Civil Code § 1791.

§ 1791.2. Express warranty; definition

(a) "Express warranty" means:

(1) A written statement arising out of a sale to the consumer of a consumer good pursuant to which the manufacturer, distributor, or retailer undertakes to preserve or maintain the utility or performance of the consumer good or provide compensation if there is a failure in utility or performance; or

(2) In the event of any sample or model, that the whole of the goods conforms to such sample or model.

(b) It is not necessary to the creation of an express warranty that formal words such as "warrant" or "guarantee" be used, but if such words are used then an express warranty is created. An affirmation merely of the value of the goods or a statement purporting to be merely an opinion or commendation of the goods does not create a warranty.

(c) Statements or representations such as expressions of general policy concerning customer satisfaction which are not subject to any limitation do not create an express warranty. (Added by Stats.1970, c. 1333, p. 2479, § 1. Amended by Stats.1978, c. 991, p. 3060, § 2.5.)

ARISING FROM PARTICULAR TRANSACTIONS

Cross References

Classes of insurance, express warranties, see Insurance Code § 116.6.

Distributor defined for purposes of this Chapter, see Civil Code § 1791.

Express warranties by affirmation, promise, description or sample, see Commercial Code § 2313.

Manufacturer defined for purposes of this Chapter, see Civil Code § 1791.

Retail seller, seller, or retailer defined for purposes of this Chapter, see Civil Code § 1791.

Sale defined for purposes of this Chapter, see Civil Code § 1791.

Vehicle protection products, express warranties, see Insurance Code § 116.6.

§ 1791.3. Disclaimer of implied warranties; "as is" or "with all faults" sales

As used in this chapter, a sale "as is" or "with all faults" means that the manufacturer, distributor, and retailer disclaim all implied warranties that would otherwise attach to the sale of consumer goods under the provisions of this chapter. *(Added by Stats.1970, c. 1333, p. 2479, § 1.)*

Cross References

Consumer goods defined for purposes of this Chapter, see Civil Code § 1791.

Distributor defined for purposes of this Chapter, see Civil Code § 1791.

Exclusion or modification of warranties, see Commercial Code § 2316.

Manufacturer defined for purposes of this Chapter, see Civil Code § 1791.

Retail seller, seller, or retailer defined for purposes of this Chapter, see Civil Code § 1791.

Sale defined for purposes of this Chapter, see Civil Code § 1791.

ARTICLE 3. SALE WARRANTIES

Section

1792. Implied warranty of merchantability; manufacturers and retail sellers; indemnity.

1792.1. Goods for particular purpose; implied warranty of fitness by manufacturer.

1792.2. Goods for particular purpose; assistive devices; implied warranty of fitness by retailer or distributor.

1792.3. Proscription against waiver of implied warranties; exception.

1792.4. Written notice to buyer; disclaimer of implied warranties on "as is" or "with all faults" sales.

1792.5. Sales on "as is" or "with all faults" basis; effect as to buyers.

1793. Right to make express warranties; limitation, modification or disclaimer of implied warranties.

1793.01. Express warranties that commence earlier than date of delivery.

1793.02. Assistive devices sold at retail; written warranty; warranty for hearing aids; remedies of buyer; exceptions; language not to constitute express warranty.

1793.025. Wheelchairs; express warranties.

1793.03. Electronic or appliance products; express warranty; service and repair facilities; time.

1793.05. Vehicle manufacturers; alteration of vehicles into housecars; assumption of original manufacturer's warranty.

1793.1. Language of express warranties; identification of warrantor; statement; warranty or product registration card or form; service and repair facilities.

1793.2. Consumer goods manufacturers; express warranties; service and repair facilities.

1793.22. Tanner Consumer Protection Act; presumption; third-party dispute resolution.

1793.23. Automotive Consumer Notification Act; legislative findings and declarations; reacquisition of vehicles; disclosure.

1793.24. Preparation of notice; contents of disclosure.

1793.25. Reimbursement of sales or use tax to manufacturer of vehicle making restitution to buyer or lessee; rules and regulations; application of sales and use tax to tangible personal property transactions; applicable laws; limitation on reimbursement amount.

1793.26. Reacquisition of motor vehicle; confidentiality or gag clause imposed upon dispossessed buyer or lessee; prohibitions.

1793.3. Return of nonconforming consumer goods; service, repair, replacement or refund; independent repair or service facilities; notice to buyers.

1793.35. Clothing; consumables; draperies; reimbursement or replacement; implied warranty of merchantability.

1793.4. Commencement of service and repair within reasonable time; tender of conforming goods within 30 days; extension of time.

1793.5. Liability of manufacturer to retailer.

1793.6. Liability of manufacturer to independent service and repair facility.

1794. Actions by buyers; measure of damages; civil penalties; costs and expenses; attorney's fees.

1794.1. Actions by retailer and independent serviceman.

1794.2. Repealed.

1794.3. Defect or nonconformity caused by unauthorized or unreasonable use; inapplicability of chapter.

1794.4. Service contract; contents; cancellation.

1794.41. Service contract provisions.

1794.45. Service contract; requirements while in effect; exclusions.

1794.5. Suggestions of methods of service and repair by manufacturer.

1795. Liability of warrantors other than manufacturers.

1795.1. Systems designed to heat, cool or condition air; equipment or component; application of chapter.

1795.4. Leases of new and used consumer goods; rules applicable.

1795.5. Used goods; obligation of distributor or retail seller; maintenance of service and repair facilities; duration of warranties.

1795.51. Buy-here-pay-here dealer; written warranty and receipt for sale or lease of vehicle; prohibited actions; notice of election to cancel; vehicle repairs.

1795.6. Tolling or expiration of warranty period during time of repairs or service; resumption of warranty period for hearing aids; warranty period deemed not expired; receipts.

1795.7. Liability of manufacturer; extension upon tolling of warranty period.

1795.8. Application of chapter to members of Armed Forces purchasing motor vehicle.

§ 1792. Implied warranty of merchantability; manufacturers and retail sellers; indemnity

Unless disclaimed in the manner prescribed by this chapter, every sale of consumer goods that are sold at retail in this state shall be accompanied by the manufacturer's and the retail seller's implied warranty that the goods are merchantable. The retail seller shall have a right of indemnity against the manufacturer in the amount of any liability under this section. (Added by Stats.1970, c. 1333, p. 2480, § 1. Amended by Stats.1971, c. 1523, p. 3003, § 4, operative Jan. 1, 1972; Stats.1978, c. 991, p. 3060, § 3.)

Cross References

Consumer goods defined for purposes of this Chapter, see Civil Code § 1791.
Implied warranty of merchantability, see Commercial Code § 2314.
Manufacturer defined for purposes of this Chapter, see Civil Code § 1791.
Retail seller, seller, or retailer defined for purposes of this Chapter, see Civil Code § 1791.
Sale defined for purposes of this Chapter, see Civil Code § 1791.

§ 1792.1. Goods for particular purpose; implied warranty of fitness by manufacturer

Every sale of consumer goods that are sold at retail in this state by a manufacturer who has reason to know at the time of the retail sale that the goods are required for a particular purpose and that the buyer is relying on the manufacturer's skill or judgment to select or furnish suitable goods shall be accompanied by such manufacturer's implied warranty of fitness. (Added by Stats.1970, c. 1333, p. 2480, § 1. Amended by Stats.1971, c. 1523, p. 3003, § 5, operative Jan. 1, 1972; Stats.1978, c. 991, p. 3060, § 4.)

Cross References

Buyer or retail buyer defined for purposes of this Chapter, see Civil Code § 1791.
Consumer goods defined for purposes of this Chapter, see Civil Code § 1791.
Implied warranty of fitness defined for purposes of this Chapter, see Civil Code § 1791.1.
Implied warranty of fitness for particular purpose, see Commercial Code § 2315.
Manufacturer defined for purposes of this Chapter, see Civil Code § 1791.
Sale defined for purposes of this Chapter, see Civil Code § 1791.

§ 1792.2. Goods for particular purpose; assistive devices; implied warranty of fitness by retailer or distributor

(a) Every sale of consumer goods that are sold at retail in this state by a retailer or distributor who has reason to know at the time of the retail sale that the goods are required for a particular purpose, and that the buyer is relying on the retailer's or distributor's skill or judgment to select or furnish suitable goods shall be accompanied by such retailer's or distributor's implied warranty that the goods are fit for that purpose.

(b) Every sale of an assistive device sold at retail in this state shall be accompanied by the retail seller's implied warranty that the device is specifically fit for the particular needs of the buyer. (Added by Stats.1970, c. 1333, p. 2480, § 1. Amended by Stats.1971, c. 1523, p. 3003, § 6, operative Jan. 1, 1972; Stats.1978, c. 991, p. 3060, § 5; Stats.1979, c. 1023, p. 3494, § 2.)

Cross References

Assistive device defined for purposes of this Chapter, see Civil Code § 1791.
Buyer or retail buyer defined for purposes of this Chapter, see Civil Code § 1791.
Consumer goods defined for purposes of this Chapter, see Civil Code § 1791.
Distributor defined for purposes of this Chapter, see Civil Code § 1791.
Implied warranty of fitness for particular purpose, see Commercial Code § 2315.
Retail seller, seller, or retailer defined for purposes of this Chapter, see Civil Code § 1791.
Sale defined for purposes of this Chapter, see Civil Code § 1791.

§ 1792.3. Proscription against waiver of implied warranties; exception

No implied warranty of merchantability and, where applicable, no implied warranty of fitness shall be waived, except in the case of a sale of consumer goods on an "as is" or "with all faults" basis where the provisions of this chapter affecting "as is" or "with all faults" sales are strictly complied with. (Added by Stats.1970, c. 1333, p. 2480, § 1.)

Cross References

As is or with all faults defined for purposes of this Chapter, see Civil Code § 1791.3.
Consumer goods defined for purposes of this Chapter, see Civil Code § 1791.
Implied warranty of fitness defined for purposes of this Chapter, see Civil Code § 1791.1.
Implied warranty of merchantability or implied warranty that goods are merchantable defined for purposes of this Chapter, see Civil Code § 1791.1.
Sale defined for purposes of this Chapter, see Civil Code § 1791.

§ 1792.4. Written notice to buyer; disclaimer of implied warranties on "as is" or "with all faults" sales

(a) No sale of goods, governed by the provisions of this chapter, on an "as is" or "with all faults" basis, shall be effective to disclaim the implied warranty of merchantability or, where applicable, the implied warranty of fitness, unless a conspicuous writing is attached to the goods which clearly informs the buyer, prior to the sale, in simple and concise language of each of the following:

(1) The goods are being sold on an "as is" or "with all faults" basis.

(2) The entire risk as to the quality and performance of the goods is with the buyer.

(3) Should the goods prove defective following their purchase, the buyer and not the manufacturer, distributor, or retailer assumes the entire cost of all necessary servicing or repair.

(b) In the event of sale of consumer goods by means of a mail order catalog, the catalog offering such goods shall contain the required writing as to each item so offered in lieu of the requirement of notification prior to the sale. (Added by Stats.1970, c. 1333, p. 2480, § 1. Amended by Stats.1971, c. 1523, p. 3003, § 6.5, operative Jan. 1, 1972.)

Cross References

As is or with all faults defined for purposes of this Chapter, see Civil Code § 1791.3.

Buyer or retail buyer defined for purposes of this Chapter, see Civil Code § 1791.

Consumer goods defined for purposes of this Chapter, see Civil Code § 1791.

Distributor defined for purposes of this Chapter, see Civil Code § 1791.

Exclusion or modification of warranties, see Commercial Code § 2316.

Implied warranty of fitness defined for purposes of this Chapter, see Civil Code § 1791.1.

Implied warranty of merchantability or implied warranty that goods are merchantable defined for purposes of this Chapter, see Civil Code § 1791.1.

Manufacturer defined for purposes of this Chapter, see Civil Code § 1791.

Retail seller, seller, or retailer defined for purposes of this Chapter, see Civil Code § 1791.

Sale defined for purposes of this Chapter, see Civil Code § 1791.

§ 1792.5. Sales on "as is" or "with all faults" basis; effect as to buyers

Every sale of goods that are governed by the provisions of this chapter, on an "as is" or "with all faults" basis, made in compliance with the provisions of this chapter, shall constitute a waiver by the buyer of the implied warranty of merchantability and, where applicable, of the implied warranty of fitness. *(Added by Stats.1970, c. 1333, p. 2480, § 1. Amended by Stats.1971, c. 1523, p. 3003, § 6.5, operative Jan. 1, 1972.)*

Cross References

As is or with all faults defined for purposes of this Chapter, see Civil Code § 1791.3.

Buyer or retail buyer defined for purposes of this Chapter, see Civil Code § 1791.

Exclusion or modification of warranties, see Commercial Code § 2316.

Implied warranty of fitness defined for purposes of this Chapter, see Civil Code § 1791.1.

Implied warranty of merchantability or implied warranty that goods are merchantable defined for purposes of this Chapter, see Civil Code § 1791.1.

Sale defined for purposes of this Chapter, see Civil Code § 1791.

§ 1793. Right to make express warranties; limitation, modification or disclaimer of implied warranties

Except as provided in * * * Sections 1793.01 and 1793.02, nothing in this chapter shall affect the right of the manufacturer, distributor, or retailer to make express warranties with respect to consumer goods. However, a manufacturer, distributor, or retailer, in transacting a sale in which express warranties are given, may not limit, modify, or disclaim the implied warranties guaranteed by this chapter to the sale of consumer goods. *(Added by Stats.1970, c. 1333, p. 2480, § 1. Amended by Stats.1971, c. 1523, p. 3004, § 7, operative Jan. 1, 1972; Stats.1978, c. 991, p. 3061, § 6; Stats.1979, c. 1023, p. 3494, § 3; Stats.2022, c. 464 (A.B.2912), § 1, eff. Jan. 1, 2023.)*

Cross References

Consumer goods defined for purposes of this Chapter, see Civil Code § 1791.

Distributor defined for purposes of this Chapter, see Civil Code § 1791.

Exclusion or modification of warranties, see Commercial Code § 2316.

Express warranty defined, see Civil Code § 1791.2.

Manufacturer defined for purposes of this Chapter, see Civil Code § 1791.

Retail seller, seller, or retailer defined for purposes of this Chapter, see Civil Code § 1791.

Sale defined for purposes of this Chapter, see Civil Code § 1791.

§ 1793.01. Express warranties that commence earlier than date of delivery

A manufacturer, distributor, or retail seller shall not make an express warranty with respect to a consumer good that commences earlier than the date of delivery of the good. This section does not limit an express warranty made before July 1, 2023. *(Added by Stats.2022, c. 464 (A.B.2912), § 2, eff. Jan. 1, 2023.)*

§ 1793.02. Assistive devices sold at retail; written warranty; warranty for hearing aids; remedies of buyer; exceptions; language not to constitute express warranty

(a)(1) Except as provided in paragraph (2), all new and used assistive devices sold at retail in this state shall be accompanied by the retail seller's written warranty which shall contain the following language: "This assistive device is warranted to be specifically fit for the particular needs of you, the buyer. If the device is not specifically fit for your particular needs, it may be returned to the seller within 30 days of the date of actual receipt by you or completion of fitting by the seller, whichever occurs later. If you return the device, the seller will either adjust or replace the device or promptly refund the total amount paid. This warranty does not affect the protections and remedies you have under other laws." In lieu of the words "30 days" the retail seller may specify any longer period.

(2)(A) All new and used hearing aids sold in this state shall be accompanied by the retail seller's written warranty and shall contain the following language: "This hearing aid is warranted to be specifically fit for the particular needs of you, the buyer. If the hearing aid is not initially fit for your particular needs, it may be returned to the seller within 45 days of the initial date of delivery to you. If you return the hearing aid, the seller will either adjust or replace the hearing aid or promptly refund the total amount paid. This warranty does not affect the protections and remedies you have under other laws."

(B) In lieu of the words "45 days" the retail seller may specify any longer period.

(C) On the initial date of delivery, the retail seller shall revise the written warranty to include the initial date of delivery to the buyer of the hearing aid and expiration date of the warranty.

(b) The language prescribed in subdivision (a) shall appear on the first page of the warranty in at least 10-point bold type. The warranty shall be delivered to the buyer at the time of the sale of the device.

(c) If the buyer returns the device within the period specified in the written warranty, the seller shall, without charge and within a reasonable time, adjust the device or, if appropriate, replace it with a device that is specifically fit for the particular needs of the buyer. If the seller does not adjust or replace the device so that it is specifically fit for the particular needs of the buyer, the seller shall promptly refund to the buyer the total amount paid, the transaction shall be deemed rescinded, and the seller shall promptly return to the buyer all payments and any assistive device or other consideration exchanged as part of the transaction and shall promptly cancel or cause to be canceled all contracts, instruments, and security agreements executed by the buyer in connection with the sale. When a sale is rescinded under this section, no charge, penalty, or other fee may be imposed in connection with the purchase, fitting, financing, or return of the device.

(d) With respect to the retail sale of an assistive device to an individual, organization, or agency known by the seller to be purchasing for the ultimate user of the device, this section and subdivision (b) of Section 1792.2 shall be construed to require that the device be specifically fit for the particular needs of the ultimate user.

(e) This section and subdivision (b) of Section 1792.2 shall not apply to any of the following sales of assistive devices:

(1) A catalog or similar sale, as defined in subdivision (q) of Section 1791, except a sale of a hearing aid.

(2) A sale which involves a retail sale price of less than fifteen dollars ($15).

(3) A surgical implant performed by a physician and surgeon, or a restoration or dental prosthesis provided by a dentist.

(f) The rights and remedies of the buyer under this section and subdivision (b) of Section 1792.2 are not subject to waiver under Section 1792.3. The rights and remedies of the buyer under this section and subdivision (b) of Section 1792.2 are cumulative, and shall not be construed to affect the obligations of the retail seller or any other party or to supplant the rights or remedies of the buyer under any other section of this chapter or under any other law or instrument.

(g) Section 1795.5 shall not apply to a sale of used assistive devices, and for the purposes of the Song–Beverly Consumer Warranty Act the buyer of a used assistive device shall have the same rights and remedies as the buyer of a new assistive device.

(h) The language in subdivision (a) shall not constitute an express warranty for purposes of Sections 1793.2 and 1793.3. (Added by Stats.1979, c. 1023, p. 3495, § 4. Amended by Stats.1982, c. 619, p. 2610, § 2; Stats.1991, c. 228 (A.B.1889), § 2; Stats.2014, c. 226 (S.B.1326), § 1, eff. Jan. 1, 2015.)

Cross References

Assistive device defined for purposes of this Chapter, see Civil Code § 1791.
Buyer or retail buyer defined for purposes of this Chapter, see Civil Code § 1791.
Catalog or similar sale defined for purposes of this Chapter, see Civil Code § 1791.
Express warranty defined, see Civil Code § 1791.2.
Retail seller, seller, or retailer defined for purposes of this Chapter, see Civil Code § 1791.
Sale defined for purposes of this Chapter, see Civil Code § 1791.
Speech-language pathologists and audiologists, unprofessional conduct based on violation of this section, see Business and Professions Code § 2533.

§ 1793.025. Wheelchairs; express warranties

(a) All new and used wheelchairs, including, but not limited to, wheelchairs that are motorized or have been otherwise customized to suit the needs of the user, shall be accompanied by the manufacturer's or lessor's written express warranty that the wheelchair is free of defects. The duration of the warranty shall be for a period of at least one year from the date of the first delivery of a new wheelchair to the consumer, or at least 60 days from the date of the first delivery of a used, refurbished, or reconditioned wheelchair to the consumer. If the written express warranty is not furnished to the consumer, the wheelchair nonetheless shall be deemed to be covered by the express warranty. This section shall not apply to wheelchairs manufactured specifically for athletic, competitive, or off-road use.

(b) The provisions of this chapter for express warranties govern the express warranty described in subdivision (a), whether or not those provisions only apply to the sale, and not the lease, of goods.

(c) A reasonable number of attempts have been made to conform a wheelchair to the express warranty if, within the warranty period or within one year of inception of the warranty, whichever occurs first, (1) the same nonconformity has been subject to repair four or more times by the manufacturer, lessor, or an agent thereof, and continues to exist, or (2) the wheelchair is out of service by reason of repair of nonconformities by the manufacturer, lessor, or an agent thereof, for a cumulative total of more than 30 calendar days since inception of the warranty.

(d) No wheelchair that has been returned to the manufacturer, lessor, or an agent thereof, by the consumer for failure to repair a nonconformity after a reasonable number of attempts, either in this state or in another state pursuant to a similar statute of that state, may be sold or leased again in this state unless the reasons for the return are fully disclosed to the prospective buyer or lessee.

(e) If the wheelchair is out of service for a period of at least 24 hours for the repair of a nonconformity by the manufacturer, lessor, or agent thereof, a temporary replacement wheelchair shall be made available to the consumer, if requested. The provider of the temporary replacement wheelchair may not charge the consumer more than the cost to the provider to make the wheelchair available to the consumer. Nothing in this subdivision is intended to prevent a consumer and a provider from negotiating an agreement in which the provider assumes the cost of providing a temporary replacement wheelchair to the consumer. (Added by Stats. 1993, c. 374 (A.B.1945), § 1. Amended by Stats.1995, c. 461 (A.B.40), § 3.)

Cross References

Buyer or retail buyer defined for purposes of this Chapter, see Civil Code § 1791.
Express warranty defined, see Civil Code § 1791.2.
Lease defined for purposes of this Chapter, see Civil Code § 1791.
Lessee defined for purposes of this Chapter, see Civil Code § 1791.
Lessor defined for purposes of this Chapter, see Civil Code § 1791.
Manufacturer defined for purposes of this Chapter, see Civil Code § 1791.

Sale defined for purposes of this Chapter, see Civil Code § 1791.

§ 1793.03. Electronic or appliance products; express warranty; service and repair facilities; time

(a) Every manufacturer making an express warranty with respect to an electronic or appliance product described in subdivision (h), (i), (j), or (k) of Section 9801 of the Business and Professions Code, with a wholesale price to the retailer of not less than fifty dollars ($50) and not more than ninety-nine dollars and ninety-nine cents ($99.99), shall make available to service and repair facilities sufficient service literature and functional parts to effect the repair of a product for at least three years after the date a product model or type was manufactured, regardless of whether the three-year period exceeds the warranty period for the product.

(b) Every manufacturer making an express warranty with respect to an electronic or appliance product described in subdivision (h), (i), (j), or (k) of Section 9801 of the Business and Professions Code, with a wholesale price to the retailer of one hundred dollars ($100) or more, shall make available to service and repair facilities sufficient service literature and functional parts to effect the repair of a product for at least seven years after the date a product model or type was manufactured, regardless of whether the seven-year period exceeds the warranty period for the product [1] *(Added by Stats.1986, c. 547, § 1.)*

[1] So in chaptered copy.

Cross References

Express warranty defined, see Civil Code § 1791.2.
Manufacturer defined for purposes of this Chapter, see Civil Code § 1791.
Retail seller, seller, or retailer defined for purposes of this Chapter, see Civil Code § 1791.

§ 1793.05. Vehicle manufacturers; alteration of vehicles into housecars; assumption of original manufacturer's warranty

Vehicle manufacturers who alter new vehicles into housecars shall, in addition to any new product warranty, assume any warranty responsibility of the original vehicle manufacturer for any and all components of the finished product which are, by virtue of any act of the alterer, no longer covered by the warranty issued by the original vehicle manufacturer. *(Added by Stats.1977, c. 873, p. 2634, § 1, operative July 1, 1978.)*

Cross References

House car, see Vehicle Code § 362.
Manufacturer defined for purposes of this Chapter, see Civil Code § 1791.
Vehicle manufacturer defined, see Vehicle Code § 672.

§ 1793.1. Language of express warranties; identification of warrantor; statement; warranty or product registration card or form; service and repair facilities

(a)(1) Every manufacturer, distributor, or retailer making express warranties with respect to consumer goods shall fully set forth those warranties in simple and readily understood language, which shall clearly identify the party making the express warranties, and which shall conform to the federal standards for disclosure of warranty terms and conditions set forth in the federal Magnuson-Moss Warranty-Federal Trade Commission Improvement Act (15 U.S.C. Sec. 2301 et seq.), and in the regulations of the Federal Trade Commission adopted pursuant to the provisions of that act. If the manufacturer, distributor, or retailer provides a warranty or product registration card or form, or an electronic online warranty or product registration form, to be completed and returned by the consumer, the card or form shall contain statements, each displayed in a clear and conspicuous manner, that do all of the following:

(A) Informs the consumer that the card or form is for product registration.

(B) Informs the consumer that failure to complete and return the card or form does not diminish his or her warranty rights.

(2) Every work order or repair invoice for warranty repairs or service shall clearly and conspicuously incorporate in 10-point boldface type the following statement either on the face of the work order or repair invoice, or on the reverse side, or on an attachment to the work order or repair invoice: "A buyer of this product in California has the right to have this product serviced or repaired during the warranty period. The warranty period will be extended for the number of whole days that the product has been out of the buyer's hands for warranty repairs. If a defect exists within the warranty period, the warranty will not expire until the defect has been fixed. The warranty period will also be extended if the warranty repairs have not been performed due to delays caused by circumstances beyond the control of the buyer, or if the warranty repairs did not remedy the defect and the buyer notifies the manufacturer or seller of the failure of the repairs within 60 days after they were completed. If, after a reasonable number of attempts, the defect has not been fixed, the buyer may return this product for a replacement or a refund subject, in either case, to deduction of a reasonable charge for usage. This time extension does not affect the protections or remedies the buyer has under other laws."

If the required notice is placed on the reverse side of the work order or repair invoice, the face of the work order or repair invoice shall include the following notice in 10-point boldface type: "Notice to Consumer: Please read important information on back."

A copy of the work order or repair invoice and any attachment shall be presented to the buyer at the time that warranty service or repairs are made.

(b) No warranty or product registration card or form, or an electronic online warranty or product registration form, may be labeled as a warranty registration or a warranty confirmation.

(c) The requirements imposed by this section on the distribution of any warranty or product registration card or form, or an electronic online warranty or product registration form, shall become effective on January 1, 2004.

(d) This section does not apply to any warranty or product registration card or form that was printed prior to January 1, 2004, and was shipped or included with a product that was placed in the stream of commerce prior to January 1, 2004.

(e) Every manufacturer, distributor, or retailer making express warranties and who elects to maintain service and

§ 1793.1

repair facilities within this state pursuant to this chapter shall perform one or more of the following:

(1) At the time of sale, provide the buyer with the name and address of each service and repair facility within this state.

(2) At the time of the sale, provide the buyer with the name and address and telephone number of a service and repair facility central directory within this state, or the toll-free telephone number of a service and repair facility central directory outside this state. It shall be the duty of the central directory to provide, upon inquiry, the name and address of the authorized service and repair facility nearest the buyer.

(3) Maintain at the premises of retail sellers of the warrantor's consumer goods a current listing of the warrantor's authorized service and repair facilities, or retail sellers to whom the consumer goods are to be returned for service and repair, whichever is applicable, within this state. It shall be the duty of every retail seller provided with that listing to provide, on inquiry, the name, address, and telephone number of the nearest authorized service and repair facility, or the retail seller to whom the consumer goods are to be returned for service and repair, whichever is applicable. (Added by Stats.1970, c. 1333, p. 2481, § 1. Amended by Stats.1971, c. 1523, p. 3004, § 8, operative Jan. 1, 1972; Stats.1972, c. 1293, p. 2584, § 1; Stats.1980, c. 394, p. 776, § 1; Stats.1981, c. 150, p. 953, § 1, eff. July 8, 1981; Stats.1982, c. 381, p. 1709, § 1; Stats.2002, c. 306 (S.B.1765), § 1.)

Cross References

Buyer or retail buyer defined for purposes of this Chapter, see Civil Code § 1791.

Consumer goods defined for purposes of this Chapter, see Civil Code § 1791.

Distributor defined for purposes of this Chapter, see Civil Code § 1791.

Enforceability of warranty without return of proof of purchase form, see Commercial Code § 2801.

Express warranties, see Commercial Code § 2313.

Express warranty defined, see Civil Code § 1791.2.

Manufacturer defined for purposes of this Chapter, see Civil Code § 1791.

Retail seller, seller, or retailer defined for purposes of this Chapter, see Civil Code § 1791.

Sale defined for purposes of this Chapter, see Civil Code § 1791.

§ 1793.2. Consumer goods manufacturers; express warranties; service and repair facilities

(a) Every manufacturer of consumer goods sold in this state and for which the manufacturer has made an express warranty shall:

(1)(A) Maintain in this state sufficient service and repair facilities reasonably close to all areas where its consumer goods are sold to carry out the terms of those warranties or designate and authorize in this state as service and repair facilities independent repair or service facilities reasonably close to all areas where its consumer goods are sold to carry out the terms of the warranties.

(B) As a means of complying with this paragraph, a manufacturer may enter into warranty service contracts with independent service and repair facilities. The warranty service contracts may provide for a fixed schedule of rates to be charged for warranty service or warranty repair work. However, the rates fixed by those contracts shall be in conformity with the requirements of subdivision (c) of Section 1793.3. The rates established pursuant to subdivision (c) of Section 1793.3, between the manufacturer and the independent service and repair facility, do not preclude a good faith discount that is reasonably related to reduced credit and general overhead cost factors arising from the manufacturer's payment of warranty charges direct to the independent service and repair facility. The warranty service contracts authorized by this paragraph may not be executed to cover a period of time in excess of one year, and may be renewed only by a separate, new contract or letter of agreement between the manufacturer and the independent service and repair facility.

(2) In the event of a failure to comply with paragraph (1) of this subdivision, be subject to Section 1793.5.

(3) Make available to authorized service and repair facilities sufficient service literature and replacement parts to effect repairs during the express warranty period.

(b) Where those service and repair facilities are maintained in this state and service or repair of the goods is necessary because they do not conform with the applicable express warranties, service and repair shall be commenced within a reasonable time by the manufacturer or its representative in this state. Unless the buyer agrees in writing to the contrary, the goods shall be serviced or repaired so as to conform to the applicable warranties within 30 days. Delay caused by conditions beyond the control of the manufacturer or its representatives shall serve to extend this 30–day requirement. Where delay arises, conforming goods shall be tendered as soon as possible following termination of the condition giving rise to the delay.

(c) The buyer shall deliver nonconforming goods to the manufacturer's service and repair facility within this state, unless, due to reasons of size and weight, or method of attachment, or method of installation, or nature of the nonconformity, delivery cannot reasonably be accomplished. If the buyer cannot return the nonconforming goods for any of these reasons, he or she shall notify the manufacturer or its nearest service and repair facility within the state. Written notice of nonconformity to the manufacturer or its service and repair facility shall constitute return of the goods for purposes of this section. Upon receipt of that notice of nonconformity, the manufacturer shall, at its option, service or repair the goods at the buyer's residence, or pick up the goods for service and repair, or arrange for transporting the goods to its service and repair facility. All reasonable costs of transporting the goods when a buyer cannot return them for any of the above reasons shall be at the manufacturer's expense. The reasonable costs of transporting nonconforming goods after delivery to the service and repair facility until return of the goods to the buyer shall be at the manufacturer's expense.

(d)(1) Except as provided in paragraph (2), if the manufacturer or its representative in this state does not service or repair the goods to conform to the applicable express warranties after a reasonable number of attempts, the manufacturer shall either replace the goods or reimburse the buyer in an amount equal to the purchase price paid by the buyer, less that amount directly attributable to use by the buyer prior to the discovery of the nonconformity.

(2) If the manufacturer or its representative in this state is unable to service or repair a new motor vehicle, as that term is defined in paragraph (2) of subdivision (e) of Section 1793.22, to conform to the applicable express warranties after a reasonable number of attempts, the manufacturer shall either promptly replace the new motor vehicle in accordance with subparagraph (A) or promptly make restitution to the buyer in accordance with subparagraph (B). However, the buyer shall be free to elect restitution in lieu of replacement, and in no event shall the buyer be required by the manufacturer to accept a replacement vehicle.

(A) In the case of replacement, the manufacturer shall replace the buyer's vehicle with a new motor vehicle substantially identical to the vehicle replaced. The replacement vehicle shall be accompanied by all express and implied warranties that normally accompany new motor vehicles of that specific kind. The manufacturer also shall pay for, or to, the buyer the amount of any sales or use tax, license fees, registration fees, and other official fees which the buyer is obligated to pay in connection with the replacement, plus any incidental damages to which the buyer is entitled under Section 1794, including, but not limited to, reasonable repair, towing, and rental car costs actually incurred by the buyer.

(B) In the case of restitution, the manufacturer shall make restitution in an amount equal to the actual price paid or payable by the buyer, including any charges for transportation and manufacturer-installed options, but excluding nonmanufacturer items installed by a dealer or the buyer, and including any collateral charges such as sales or use tax, license fees, registration fees, and other official fees, plus any incidental damages to which the buyer is entitled under Section 1794, including, but not limited to, reasonable repair, towing, and rental car costs actually incurred by the buyer.

(C) When the manufacturer replaces the new motor vehicle pursuant to subparagraph (A), the buyer shall only be liable to pay the manufacturer an amount directly attributable to use by the buyer of the replaced vehicle prior to the time the buyer first delivered the vehicle to the manufacturer or distributor, or its authorized service and repair facility for correction of the problem that gave rise to the nonconformity. When restitution is made pursuant to subparagraph (B), the amount to be paid by the manufacturer to the buyer may be reduced by the manufacturer by that amount directly attributable to use by the buyer prior to the time the buyer first delivered the vehicle to the manufacturer or distributor, or its authorized service and repair facility for correction of the problem that gave rise to the nonconformity. The amount directly attributable to use by the buyer shall be determined by multiplying the actual price of the new motor vehicle paid or payable by the buyer, including any charges for transportation and manufacturer-installed options, by a fraction having as its denominator 120,000 and having as its numerator the number of miles traveled by the new motor vehicle prior to the time the buyer first delivered the vehicle to the manufacturer or distributor, or its authorized service and repair facility for correction of the problem that gave rise to the nonconformity. Nothing in this paragraph shall in any way limit the rights or remedies available to the buyer under any other law.

(D) Pursuant to Section 1795.4, a buyer of a new motor vehicle shall also include a lessee of a new motor vehicle.

(e)(1) If the goods cannot practicably be serviced or repaired by the manufacturer or its representative to conform to the applicable express warranties because of the method of installation or because the goods have become so affixed to real property as to become a part thereof, the manufacturer shall either replace and install the goods or reimburse the buyer in an amount equal to the purchase price paid by the buyer, including installation costs, less that amount directly attributable to use by the buyer prior to the discovery of the nonconformity.

(2) With respect to claims arising out of deficiencies in the construction of a new residential dwelling, paragraph (1) shall not apply to either of the following:

(A) A product that is not a manufactured product, as defined in subdivision (g) of Section 896.

(B) A claim against a person or entity that is not the manufacturer that originally made the express warranty for that manufactured product. *(Added by Stats.1970, c. 1333, p. 2481, § 1. Amended by Stats.1971, c. 1523, p. 3004, § 9, operative Jan. 1, 1972; Stats.1976, c. 416, p. 1069, § 2; Stats.1978, c. 991, p. 3058, § 7; Stats.1982, c. 388, p. 1720, § 1; Stats.1986, c. 547, § 2; Stats.1987, c. 1280, § 2, operative Jan. 1, 1988; Stats.1988, c. 697, § 1; Stats.1989, c. 193, § 2; Stats.1991, c. 689 (A.B.211), § 10; Stats.1992, c. 1232 (S.B. 1762), § 6; Stats.2004, c. 331 (A.B.2723), § 1; Stats.2011, c. 727 (A.B.242), § 1.)*

Cross References

Buyer or retail buyer defined for purposes of this Chapter, see Civil Code § 1791.
Consumer goods defined for purposes of this Chapter, see Civil Code § 1791.
Distributor defined for purposes of this Chapter, see Civil Code § 1791.
Express warranty defined, see Civil Code § 1791.2.
Independent repair or service facility or independent service dealer defined for purposes of this Chapter, see Civil Code § 1791.
Manufacturer defined for purposes of this Chapter, see Civil Code § 1791.
Sale defined for purposes of this Chapter, see Civil Code § 1791.
Service contract defined for purposes of this Chapter, see Civil Code § 1791.

§ 1793.22. Tanner Consumer Protection Act; presumption; third-party dispute resolution

(a) This section shall be known and may be cited as the Tanner Consumer Protection Act.

(b) It shall be presumed that a reasonable number of attempts have been made to conform a new motor vehicle to the applicable express warranties if, within 18 months from delivery to the buyer or 18,000 miles on the odometer of the vehicle, whichever occurs first, one or more of the following occurs:

(1) The same nonconformity results in a condition that is likely to cause death or serious bodily injury if the vehicle is driven and the nonconformity has been subject to repair two or more times by the manufacturer or its agents, and the buyer or lessee has at least once directly notified the

manufacturer of the need for the repair of the nonconformity.

(2) The same nonconformity has been subject to repair four or more times by the manufacturer or its agents and the buyer has at least once directly notified the manufacturer of the need for the repair of the nonconformity.

(3) The vehicle is out of service by reason of repair of nonconformities by the manufacturer or its agents for a cumulative total of more than 30 calendar days since delivery of the vehicle to the buyer. The 30-day limit shall be extended only if repairs cannot be performed due to conditions beyond the control of the manufacturer or its agents. The buyer shall be required to directly notify the manufacturer pursuant to paragraphs (1) and (2) only if the manufacturer has clearly and conspicuously disclosed to the buyer, with the warranty or the owner's manual, the provisions of this section and that of subdivision (d) of Section 1793.2, including the requirement that the buyer must notify the manufacturer directly pursuant to paragraphs (1) and (2). The notification, if required, shall be sent to the address, if any, specified clearly and conspicuously by the manufacturer in the warranty or owner's manual. This presumption shall be a rebuttable presumption affecting the burden of proof, and it may be asserted by the buyer in any civil action, including an action in small claims court, or other formal or informal proceeding.

(c) If a qualified third-party dispute resolution process exists, and the buyer receives timely notification in writing of the availability of that qualified third-party dispute resolution process with a description of its operation and effect, the presumption in subdivision (b) may not be asserted by the buyer until after the buyer has initially resorted to the qualified third-party dispute resolution process as required in subdivision (d). Notification of the availability of the qualified third-party dispute resolution process is not timely if the buyer suffers any prejudice resulting from any delay in giving the notification. If a qualified third-party dispute resolution process does not exist, or if the buyer is dissatisfied with that third-party decision, or if the manufacturer or its agent neglects to promptly fulfill the terms of the qualified third-party dispute resolution process decision after the decision is accepted by the buyer, the buyer may assert the presumption provided in subdivision (b) in an action to enforce the buyer's rights under subdivision (d) of Section 1793.2. The findings and decision of a qualified third-party dispute resolution process shall be admissible in evidence in the action without further foundation. Any period of limitation of actions under any federal or California laws with respect to any person shall be extended for a period equal to the number of days between the date a complaint is filed with a third-party dispute resolution process and the date of its decision or the date before which the manufacturer or its agent is required by the decision to fulfill its terms if the decision is accepted by the buyer, whichever occurs later.

(d) A qualified third-party dispute resolution process shall be one that does all of the following:

(1) Complies with the minimum requirements of the Federal Trade Commission for informal dispute settlement procedures as set forth in Part 703 of Title 16 of the Code of Federal Regulations, as those regulations read on January 1, 1987.

(2) Renders decisions which are binding on the manufacturer if the buyer elects to accept the decision.

(3) Prescribes a reasonable time, not to exceed 30 days after the decision is accepted by the buyer, within which the manufacturer or its agent must fulfill the terms of its decisions.

(4) Provides arbitrators who are assigned to decide disputes with copies of, and instruction in, the provisions of the Federal Trade Commission's regulations in Part 703 of Title 16 of the Code of Federal Regulations as those regulations read on January 1, 1987, Division 2 (commencing with Section 2101) of the Commercial Code, and this chapter.

(5) Requires the manufacturer, when the process orders, under the terms of this chapter, either that the nonconforming motor vehicle be replaced if the buyer consents to this remedy or that restitution be made to the buyer, to replace the motor vehicle or make restitution in accordance with paragraph (2) of subdivision (d) of Section 1793.2.

(6) Provides, at the request of the arbitrator or a majority of the arbitration panel, for an inspection and written report on the condition of a nonconforming motor vehicle, at no cost to the buyer, by an automobile expert who is independent of the manufacturer.

(7) Takes into account, in rendering decisions, all legal and equitable factors, including, but not limited to, the written warranty, the rights and remedies conferred in regulations of the Federal Trade Commission contained in Part 703 of Title 16 of the Code of Federal Regulations as those regulations read on January 1, 1987, Division 2 (commencing with Section 2101) of the Commercial Code, this chapter, and any other equitable considerations appropriate in the circumstances. Nothing in this chapter requires that, to be certified as a qualified third-party dispute resolution process pursuant to this section, decisions of the process must consider or provide remedies in the form of awards of punitive damages or multiple damages, under subdivision (c) of Section 1794, or of attorneys' fees under subdivision (d) of Section 1794, or of consequential damages other than as provided in subdivisions (a) and (b) of Section 1794, including, but not limited to, reasonable repair, towing, and rental car costs actually incurred by the buyer.

(8) Requires that no arbitrator deciding a dispute may be a party to the dispute and that no other person, including an employee, agent, or dealer for the manufacturer, may be allowed to participate substantively in the merits of any dispute with the arbitrator unless the buyer is allowed to participate also. Nothing in this subdivision prohibits any member of an arbitration board from deciding a dispute.

(9) Obtains and maintains certification by the Department of Consumer Affairs pursuant to Chapter 9 (commencing with Section 472) of Division 1 of the Business and Professions Code.

(e) For the purposes of subdivision (d) of Section 1793.2 and this section, the following terms have the following meanings:

(1) "Nonconformity" means a nonconformity which substantially impairs the use, value, or safety of the new motor vehicle to the buyer or lessee.

(2) "New motor vehicle" means a new motor vehicle that is bought or used primarily for personal, family, or household purposes. "New motor vehicle" also means a new motor vehicle with a gross vehicle weight under 10,000 pounds that is bought or used primarily for business purposes by a person, including a partnership, limited liability company, corporation, association, or any other legal entity, to which not more than five motor vehicles are registered in this state. "New motor vehicle" includes the chassis, chassis cab, and that portion of a motor home devoted to its propulsion, but does not include any portion designed, used, or maintained primarily for human habitation, a dealer-owned vehicle and a "demonstrator" or other motor vehicle sold with a manufacturer's new car warranty but does not include a motorcycle or a motor vehicle which is not registered under the Vehicle Code because it is to be operated or used exclusively off the highways. A demonstrator is a vehicle assigned by a dealer for the purpose of demonstrating qualities and characteristics common to vehicles of the same or similar model and type.

(3) "Motor home" means a vehicular unit built on, or permanently attached to, a self-propelled motor vehicle chassis, chassis cab, or van, which becomes an integral part of the completed vehicle, designed for human habitation for recreational or emergency occupancy.

(f)(1) Except as provided in paragraph (2), no person shall sell, either at wholesale or retail, lease, or transfer a motor vehicle transferred by a buyer or lessee to a manufacturer pursuant to paragraph (2) of subdivision (d) of Section 1793.2 or a similar statute of any other state, unless the nature of the nonconformity experienced by the original buyer or lessee is clearly and conspicuously disclosed to the prospective buyer, lessee, or transferee, the nonconformity is corrected, and the manufacturer warrants to the new buyer, lessee, or transferee in writing for a period of one year that the motor vehicle is free of that nonconformity.

(2) Except for the requirement that the nature of the nonconformity be disclosed to the transferee, paragraph (1) does not apply to the transfer of a motor vehicle to an educational institution if the purpose of the transfer is to make the motor vehicle available for use in automotive repair courses. *(Added by Stats.1992, c. 1232 (S.B.1762), § 7. Amended by Stats.1998, c. 352 (A.B.1848), § 1; Stats.1999, c. 83 (S.B.966), § 21; Stats.1999, c. 448 (A.B.1290), § 1; Stats. 2000, c. 679 (S.B.1718), § 1.)*

Cross References

Burden of proof, generally, see Evidence Code § 500 et seq.
Buyer or retail buyer defined for purposes of this Chapter, see Civil Code § 1791.
Certification of third-party dispute resolution processes for new motor vehicles,
    Duties of Department of Consumer Affairs, see Business and Professions Code § 472.4.
    Establishment of program, see Business and Professions Code § 472.1.
    Manufacturer process for resolution of disputes, see Business and Professions Code § 472.2.
    Review of qualified process, notice of decertification, see Business and Professions Code § 472.3.

Express warranty defined, see Civil Code § 1791.2.
Lease defined for purposes of this Chapter, see Civil Code § 1791.
Lessee defined for purposes of this Chapter, see Civil Code § 1791.
Manufacturer defined for purposes of this Chapter, see Civil Code § 1791.
Members of Armed Forces purchasing motor vehicles, see Civil Code § 1795.8.

§ 1793.23. Automotive Consumer Notification Act; legislative findings and declarations; reacquisition of vehicles; disclosure

(a) The Legislature finds and declares all of the following:

(1) That the expansion of state warranty laws covering new and used cars has given important and valuable protection to consumers.

(2) That, in states without this valuable warranty protection, used and irrepairable motor vehicles are being resold in the marketplace without notice to the subsequent purchaser.

(3) That other states have addressed this problem by requiring notices on the title of these vehicles or other notice procedures to warn consumers that the motor vehicles were repurchased by a dealer or manufacturer because the vehicle could not be repaired in a reasonable length of time or a reasonable number of repair attempts or the dealer or manufacturer was not willing to repair the vehicle.

(4) That these notices serve the interests of consumers who have a right to information relevant to their buying decisions.

(5) That the disappearance of these notices upon the transfer of title from another state to this state encourages the transport of "lemons" to this state for sale to the drivers of this state.

(b) This section and Section 1793.24 shall be known, and may be cited as, the Automotive Consumer Notification Act.

(c) Any manufacturer who reacquires or assists a dealer or lienholder to reacquire a motor vehicle registered in this state, any other state, or a federally administered district shall, prior to any sale, lease, or transfer of the vehicle in this state, or prior to exporting the vehicle to another state for sale, lease, or transfer if the vehicle was registered in this state and reacquired pursuant to paragraph (2) of subdivision (d) of Section 1793.2, cause the vehicle to be retitled in the name of the manufacturer, request the Department of Motor Vehicles to inscribe the ownership certificate with the notation "Lemon Law Buyback," and affix a decal to the vehicle in accordance with Section 11713.12 of the Vehicle Code if the manufacturer knew or should have known that the vehicle is required by law to be replaced, accepted for restitution due to the failure of the manufacturer to conform the vehicle to applicable warranties pursuant to paragraph (2) of subdivision (d) of Section 1793.2, or accepted for restitution by the manufacturer due to the failure of the manufacturer to conform the vehicle to warranties required by any other applicable law of the state, any other state, or federal law.

(d) Any manufacturer who reacquires or assists a dealer or lienholder to reacquire a motor vehicle in response to a request by the buyer or lessee that the vehicle be either replaced or accepted for restitution because the vehicle did not conform to express warranties shall, prior to the sale, lease, or other transfer of the vehicle, execute and deliver to

§ 1793.23

the subsequent transferee a notice and obtain the transferee's written acknowledgment of a notice, as prescribed by Section 1793.24.

(e) Any person, including any dealer, who acquires a motor vehicle for resale and knows or should have known that the vehicle was reacquired by the vehicle's manufacturer in response to a request by the last retail owner or lessee of the vehicle that it be replaced or accepted for restitution because the vehicle did not conform to express warranties shall, prior to the sale, lease, or other transfer, execute and deliver to the subsequent transferee a notice and obtain the transferee's written acknowledgment of a notice, as prescribed by Section 1793.24.

(f) Any person, including any manufacturer or dealer, who sells, leases, or transfers ownership of a motor vehicle when the vehicle's ownership certificate is inscribed with the notation "Lemon Law Buyback" shall, prior to the sale, lease, or ownership transfer of the vehicle, provide the transferee with a disclosure statement signed by the transferee that states:

"THIS VEHICLE WAS REPURCHASED BY ITS MANUFACTURER DUE TO A DEFECT IN THE VEHICLE PURSUANT TO CONSUMER WARRANTY LAWS. THE TITLE TO THIS VEHICLE HAS BEEN PERMANENTLY BRANDED WITH THE NOTATION 'LEMON LAW BUYBACK'."

(g) The disclosure requirements in subdivisions (d), (e), and (f) are cumulative with all other consumer notice requirements and do not relieve any person, including any dealer or manufacturer, from complying with any other applicable law, including any requirement of subdivision (f) of Section 1793.22.

(h) For purposes of this section, "dealer" means any person engaged in the business of selling, offering for sale, or negotiating the retail sale of, a used motor vehicle or selling motor vehicles as a broker or agent for another, including the officers, agents, and employees of the person and any combination or association of dealers. *(Added by Stats.1995, c. 503 (A.B.1381), § 1. Amended by Stats.1998, c. 932 (A.B.1094), § 7.)*

Cross References

Affixation of Lemon Law Buyback decal, see Vehicle Code § 11713.12.
Buyer or retail buyer defined for purposes of this Chapter, see Civil Code § 1791.
Express warranty defined, see Civil Code § 1791.2.
Lease defined for purposes of this Chapter, see Civil Code § 1791.
Lessee defined for purposes of this Chapter, see Civil Code § 1791.
Manufacturer defined for purposes of this Chapter, see Civil Code § 1791.
Sale defined for purposes of this Chapter, see Civil Code § 1791.
Vehicle registration card, contents, see Vehicle Code § 4453.

§ 1793.24. Preparation of notice; contents of disclosure

(a) The notice required in subdivisions (d) and (e) of Section 1793.23 shall be prepared by the manufacturer of the reacquired vehicle and shall disclose all of the following:

(1) Year, make, model, and vehicle identification number of the vehicle.

(2) Whether the title to the vehicle has been inscribed with the notation "Lemon Law Buyback."

(3) The nature of each nonconformity reported by the original buyer or lessee of the vehicle.

(4) Repairs, if any, made to the vehicle in an attempt to correct each nonconformity reported by the original buyer or lessee.

(b) The notice shall be on a form 8½ x 11 inches in size and printed in no smaller than 10–point black type on a white background.

The form shall only contain the following information prior to it being filled out by the manufacturer:

WARRANTY BUYBACK NOTICE

(Check One)

☐ This vehicle was repurchased by the vehicle's manufacturer after the last retail owner or lessee requested its repurchase due to the problem(s) listed below.

☐ THIS VEHICLE WAS REPURCHASED BY ITS MANUFACTURER DUE TO A DEFECT IN THE VEHICLE PURSUANT TO CONSUMER WARRANTY LAWS. THE TITLE TO THIS VEHICLE HAS BEEN PERMANENTLY BRANDED WITH THE NOTATION "LEMON LAW BUYBACK." Under California law, the manufacturer must warrant to you, for a one year period, that the vehicle is free of the problem(s) listed below.

V.I.N.	Year Make Model
Problem(s) Reported by Original Owner	Repairs Made, if any, to Correct Reported Problem(s)
Signature of Manufacturer	Date
Signature of Dealer(s)	Date
Signature of Retail Buyer or Lessee	Date

(c) The manufacturer shall provide an executed copy of the notice to the manufacturer's transferee. Each transferee, including a dealer, to whom the motor vehicle is transferred prior to its sale to a retail buyer or lessee shall be provided an executed copy of the notice by the previous transferor. *(Added by Stats.1995, c. 503 (A.B.1381), § 2.)*

Cross References

Buyer or retail buyer defined for purposes of this Chapter, see Civil Code § 1791.
Lessee defined for purposes of this Chapter, see Civil Code § 1791.
Manufacturer defined for purposes of this Chapter, see Civil Code § 1791.

Sale defined for purposes of this Chapter, see Civil Code § 1791.

§ 1793.25. Reimbursement of sales or use tax to manufacturer of vehicle making restitution to buyer or lessee; rules and regulations; application of sales and use tax to tangible personal property transactions; applicable laws; limitation on reimbursement amount

(a) Notwithstanding Part 1 (commencing with Section 6001) of Division 2 of the Revenue and Taxation Code, the State Board of Equalization shall reimburse the manufacturer of a new motor vehicle for an amount equal to the sales tax or use tax which the manufacturer pays to or for the buyer or lessee when providing a replacement vehicle pursuant to subparagraph (A) of paragraph (2) of subdivision (d) of Section 1793.2 or includes in making restitution to the buyer or lessee pursuant to subparagraph (B) of paragraph (2) of subdivision (d) of Section 1793.2, when the manufacturer provides satisfactory proof that it has complied with subdivision (c) of Section 1793.23, and satisfactory proof is provided for one of the following:

(1) The retailer of the motor vehicle for which the manufacturer is making restitution has reported and paid the sales tax on the gross receipts from the sale of that motor vehicle.

(2) The buyer of the motor vehicle has paid the use tax on the sales price for the storage, use, or other consumption of that motor vehicle in this state.

(3) The lessee of the motor vehicle has paid the use tax on the rentals payable from the lease of that motor vehicle.

(b) The State Board of Equalization may adopt rules and regulations to carry out, facilitate compliance with, or prevent circumvention or evasion of, this section.

(c) This section shall not change the application of the sales and use tax to the gross receipts, the rentals payable, and the sales price from the sale, lease, and the storage, use, or other consumption, in this state of tangible personal property pursuant to Part 1 (commencing with Section 6001) of Division 2 of the Revenue and Taxation Code.

(d) The manufacturer's claim for reimbursement and the State Board of Equalization's approval or denial of the claim shall be subject to the provisions of Article 1 (commencing with Section 6901) of Chapter 7 of Part 1 of Division 2 of the Revenue and Taxation Code, except Sections 6907 and 6908, insofar as those provisions are not inconsistent with this section.

(e) For purposes of this section, the amount of use tax that the State Board of Equalization is required to reimburse the manufacturer shall be limited to the amount of use tax the manufacturer is required to pay to or for the lessee pursuant to Section 1793.2. *(Added by Stats.1987, c. 1280, § 3, operative Jan. 1, 1988. Amended by Stats.1995, c. 503 (A.B.1381), § 3; Stats.2011, c. 727 (A.B.242), § 2.)*

Cross References

Buyer or retail buyer defined for purposes of this Chapter, see Civil Code § 1791.
Manufacturer defined for purposes of this Chapter, see Civil Code § 1791.
Retail sales tax fund, withdrawal and transfer of funds, see Revenue and Taxation Code § 7102.

Retail seller, seller, or retailer defined for purposes of this Chapter, see Civil Code § 1791.
Sale defined for purposes of this Chapter, see Civil Code § 1791.

§ 1793.26. Reacquisition of motor vehicle; confidentiality or gag clause imposed upon dispossessed buyer or lessee; prohibitions

(a) Any automobile manufacturer, importer, distributor, dealer, or lienholder who reacquires, or who assists in reacquiring, a motor vehicle, whether by judgment, decree, arbitration award, settlement agreement, or voluntary agreement, is prohibited from doing either of the following:

(1) Requiring, as a condition of the reacquisition of the motor vehicle, that a buyer or lessee who is a resident of this state agree not to disclose the problems with the vehicle experienced by the buyer or lessee or the nonfinancial terms of the reacquisition.

(2) Including, in any release or other agreement, whether prepared by the manufacturer, importer, distributor, dealer, or lienholder, for signature by the buyer or lessee, a confidentiality clause, gag clause, or similar clause prohibiting the buyer or lessee from disclosing information to anyone about the problems with the vehicle, or the nonfinancial terms of the reacquisition of the vehicle by the manufacturer, importer, distributor, dealer, or lienholder.

(b) Any confidentiality clause, gag clause, or similar clause in such a release or other agreement in violation of this section shall be null and void as against the public policy of this state.

(c) Nothing in this section is intended to prevent any confidentiality clause, gag clause, or similar clause regarding the financial terms of the reacquisition of the vehicle. *(Added by Stats.1998, c. 1063 (A.B.2410), § 1. Amended by Stats.2000, c. 258 (A.B.2517), § 1.)*

Cross References

Buyer or retail buyer defined for purposes of this Chapter, see Civil Code § 1791.
Distributor defined for purposes of this Chapter, see Civil Code § 1791.
Lessee defined for purposes of this Chapter, see Civil Code § 1791.
Manufacturer defined for purposes of this Chapter, see Civil Code § 1791.

§ 1793.3. Return of nonconforming consumer goods; service, repair, replacement or refund; independent repair or service facilities; notice to buyers

If the manufacturer of consumer goods sold in this state for which the manufacturer has made an express warranty does not provide service and repair facilities within this state pursuant to subdivision (a) of Section 1793.2, or does not make available to authorized service and repair facilities service literature and replacement parts sufficient to effect repair during the express warranty period, the buyer of such manufacturer's nonconforming goods may follow the course of action prescribed in either subdivision (a), (b), or (c), below, as follows:

(a) Return the nonconforming consumer goods to the retail seller thereof. The retail seller shall do one of the following:

§ 1793.3

(1) Service or repair the nonconforming goods to conform to the applicable warranty.

(2) Direct the buyer to a reasonably close independent repair or service facility willing to accept service or repair under this section.

(3) Replace the nonconforming goods with goods that are identical or reasonably equivalent to the warranted goods.

(4) Refund to the buyer the original purchase price less that amount directly attributable to use by the buyer prior to the discovery of the nonconformity.

(b) Return the nonconforming consumer goods to any retail seller of like goods of the same manufacturer within this state who may do one of the following:

(1) Service or repair the nonconforming goods to conform to the applicable warranty.

(2) Direct the buyer to a reasonably close independent repair or service facility willing to accept service or repair under this section.

(3) Replace the nonconforming goods with goods that are identical or reasonably equivalent to the warranted goods.

(4) Refund to the buyer the original purchase price less that amount directly attributable to use by the buyer prior to the discovery of the nonconformity.

(c) Secure the services of an independent repair or service facility for the service or repair of the nonconforming consumer goods, when service or repair of the goods can be economically accomplished. In that event the manufacturer shall be liable to the buyer, or to the independent repair or service facility upon an assignment of the buyer's rights, for the actual and reasonable cost of service and repair, including any cost for parts and any reasonable cost of transporting the goods or parts, plus a reasonable profit. It shall be a rebuttable presumption affecting the burden of producing evidence that the reasonable cost of service or repair is an amount equal to that which is charged by the independent service dealer for like services or repairs rendered to service or repair customers who are not entitled to warranty protection. Any waiver of the liability of a manufacturer shall be void and unenforceable.

The course of action prescribed in this subdivision shall be available to the buyer only after the buyer has followed the course of action prescribed in either subdivision (a) or (b) and such course of action has not furnished the buyer with appropriate relief. In no event, shall the provisions of this subdivision be available to the buyer with regard to consumer goods with a wholesale price to the retailer of less than fifty dollars ($50). In no event shall the buyer be responsible or liable for service or repair costs charged by the independent repair or service facility which accepts service or repair of nonconforming consumer goods under this section. Such independent repair or service facility shall only be authorized to hold the manufacturer liable for such costs.

(d) A retail seller to which any nonconforming consumer good is returned pursuant to subdivision (a) or (b) shall have the option of providing service or repair itself or directing the buyer to a reasonably close independent repair or service facility willing to accept service or repair under this section. In the event the retail seller directs the buyer to an independent repair or service facility, the manufacturer shall be liable for the reasonable cost of repair services in the manner provided in subdivision (c).

(e) In the event a buyer is unable to return nonconforming goods to the retailer due to reasons of size and weight, or method of attachment, or method of installation, or nature of the nonconformity, the buyer shall give notice of the nonconformity to the retailer. Upon receipt of such notice of nonconformity the retailer shall, at its option, service or repair the goods at the buyer's residence, or pick up the goods for service or repair, or arrange for transporting the goods to its place of business. The reasonable costs of transporting the goods shall be at the retailer's expense. The retailer shall be entitled to recover all such reasonable costs of transportation from the manufacturer pursuant to Section 1793.5. The reasonable costs of transporting nonconforming goods after delivery to the retailer until return of the goods to the buyer, when incurred by a retailer, shall be recoverable from the manufacturer pursuant to Section 1793.5. Written notice of nonconformity to the retailer shall constitute return of the goods for the purposes of subdivisions (a) and (b).

(f) The manufacturer of consumer goods with a wholesale price to the retailer of fifty dollars ($50) or more for which the manufacturer has made express warranties shall provide written notice to the buyer of the courses of action available to him under subdivision (a), (b), or (c). *(Added by Stats.1970, c. 1333, p. 2481, § 1. Amended by Stats.1971, c. 1523, p. 3005, § 10, operative Jan. 1, 1972; Stats.1976, c. 416, p. 1070, § 3; Stats.1978, c. 991, p. 3062, § 8; Stats.1986, c. 547, § 3.)*

Cross References

Buyer or retail buyer defined for purposes of this Chapter, see Civil Code § 1791.

Buyer's damages for breach in regard to accepted goods, see Commercial Code § 2714.

Consumer goods defined for purposes of this Chapter, see Civil Code § 1791.

Express warranty defined, see Civil Code § 1791.2.

Independent repair or service facility or independent service dealer defined for purposes of this Chapter, see Civil Code § 1791.

Manufacturer defined for purposes of this Chapter, see Civil Code § 1791.

Place of business defined for purposes of this Chapter, see Civil Code § 1791.

Retail seller, seller, or retailer defined for purposes of this Chapter, see Civil Code § 1791.

§ 1793.35. Clothing; consumables; draperies; reimbursement or replacement; implied warranty of merchantability

(a) Where the retail sale of clothing or consumables is accompanied by an express warranty and such items do not conform with the terms of the express warranty, the buyer thereof may return the goods within 30 days of purchase or the period specified in the warranty, whichever is greater. The manufacturer may, in the express warranty, direct the purchaser to return nonconforming goods to a retail seller of like goods of the same manufacturer for replacement.

(b) When clothing or consumables are returned to a retail seller for the reason that they do not conform to an express warranty, the retailer shall replace the nonconforming goods where the manufacturer has directed replacement in the express warranty. In the event the manufacturer has not directed replacement in the express warranty, the retailer may replace the nonconforming goods or reimburse the buyer in an amount equal to the purchase price paid by the buyer for the goods, at the option of the retailer. Costs of reimbursement or replacement are recoverable by a retailer from the manufacturer in the manner provided in Section 1793.5.

(c) Where the retail sale of draperies is not accompanied by an express warranty and the sale of such draperies is accompanied by a conspicuous writing disclaiming the retailer's implied warranty of merchantability on the fabric, the retailer's implied warranty of merchantability shall not apply to the fabric. (Added by Stats.1971, c. 1523, p. 3006, § 10.5, operative Jan. 1, 1972. Amended by Stats.1978, c. 991, p. 3064, § 8.5.)

Cross References

Buyer or retail buyer defined for purposes of this Chapter, see Civil Code § 1791.
Clothing defined for purposes of this Chapter, see Civil Code § 1791.
Consumables defined for purposes of this Chapter, see Civil Code § 1791.
Express warranty defined, see Civil Code § 1791.2.
Implied warranty of merchantability or implied warranty that goods are merchantable defined for purposes of this Chapter, see Civil Code § 1791.1.
Manufacturer defined for purposes of this Chapter, see Civil Code § 1791.
Retail seller, seller, or retailer defined for purposes of this Chapter, see Civil Code § 1791.
Sale defined for purposes of this Chapter, see Civil Code § 1791.

§ 1793.4. Commencement of service and repair within reasonable time; tender of conforming goods within 30 days; extension of time

Where an option is exercised in favor of service and repair under Section 1793.3, such service and repair must be commenced within a reasonable time, and, unless the buyer agrees in writing to the contrary, goods conforming to the applicable express warranties shall be tendered within 30 days. Delay caused by conditions beyond the control of the retail seller or his representative shall serve to extend this 30-day requirement. Where such a delay arises, conforming goods shall be tendered as soon as possible following termination of the condition giving rise to the delay. (Added by Stats.1970, c. 1333, p. 2482, § 1. Amended by Stats.1971, c. 1523, p. 3006, § 11, operative Jan. 1, 1972; Stats.1978, c. 991, p. 3064, § 9.)

Cross References

Buyer or retail buyer defined for purposes of this Chapter, see Civil Code § 1791.
Express warranty defined, see Civil Code § 1791.2.
Retail seller, seller, or retailer defined for purposes of this Chapter, see Civil Code § 1791.

§ 1793.5. Liability of manufacturer to retailer

Every manufacturer making express warranties who does not provide service and repair facilities within this state pursuant to subdivision (a) of Section 1793.2 shall be liable as prescribed in this section to every retail seller of such manufacturer's goods who incurs obligations in giving effect to the express warranties that accompany such manufacturer's consumer goods. The amount of such liability shall be determined as follows:

(a) In the event of replacement, in an amount equal to the actual cost to the retail seller of the replaced goods, and cost of transporting the goods, if such costs are incurred plus a reasonable handling charge.

(b) In the event of service and repair, in an amount equal to that which would be received by the retail seller for like service rendered to retail consumers who are not entitled to warranty protection, including actual and reasonable costs of the service and repair and the cost of transporting the goods, if such costs are incurred, plus a reasonable profit.

(c) In the event of reimbursement under subdivision (a) of Section 1793.3, in an amount equal to that reimbursed to the buyer, plus a reasonable handling charge. (Added by Stats. 1970, c. 1333, p. 2482, § 1. Amended by Stats.1971, c. 1523, p. 3006, § 12, operative Jan. 1, 1972.)

Cross References

Buyer or retail buyer defined for purposes of this Chapter, see Civil Code § 1791.
Consumer goods defined for purposes of this Chapter, see Civil Code § 1791.
Express warranty defined, see Civil Code § 1791.2.
Manufacturer defined for purposes of this Chapter, see Civil Code § 1791.
Retail seller, seller, or retailer defined for purposes of this Chapter, see Civil Code § 1791.
Used goods, application of this section, see Civil Code § 1795.5.

§ 1793.6. Liability of manufacturer to independent service and repair facility

Except as otherwise provided in the terms of a warranty service contract, as specified in subdivision (a) of Section 1793.2, entered into between a manufacturer and an independent service and repair facility, every manufacturer making express warranties whose consumer goods are sold in this state shall be liable as prescribed in this section to every independent serviceman who performs services or incurs obligations in giving effect to the express warranties that accompany such manufacturer's consumer goods whether the independent serviceman is acting as an authorized service and repair facility designated by the manufacturer pursuant to paragraph (1) of subdivision (a) of Section 1793.2 or is acting as an independent serviceman pursuant to subdivisions (c) and (d) of Section 1793.3. The amount of such liability shall be an amount equal to the actual and reasonable costs of the service and repair, including any cost for parts and any reasonable cost of transporting the goods or parts, plus a reasonable profit. It shall be a rebuttable presumption affecting the burden of producing evidence that the reasonable cost of service or repair is an amount equal to that which is charged by the independent serviceman for like services or repairs rendered to service or repair customers who are not entitled to warranty protection. Any waiver of the liability of a manufacturer shall be void and unenforceable. (Added by Stats.1976, c. 416, p. 1072, § 4.)

§ 1793.6 OBLIGATIONS

Cross References

Consumer goods defined for purposes of this Chapter, see Civil Code § 1791.

Express warranty defined, see Civil Code § 1791.2.

Manufacturer defined for purposes of this Chapter, see Civil Code § 1791.

Service contract defined for purposes of this Chapter, see Civil Code § 1791.

§ 1794. Actions by buyers; measure of damages; civil penalties; costs and expenses; attorney's fees

(a) Any buyer of consumer goods who is damaged by a failure to comply with any obligation under this chapter or under an implied or express warranty or service contract may bring an action for the recovery of damages and other legal and equitable relief.

(b) The measure of the buyer's damages in an action under this section shall include the rights of replacement or reimbursement as set forth in subdivision (d) of Section 1793.2, and the following:

(1) Where the buyer has rightfully rejected or justifiably revoked acceptance of the goods or has exercised any right to cancel the sale, Sections 2711, 2712, and 2713 of the Commercial Code shall apply.

(2) Where the buyer has accepted the goods, Sections 2714 and 2715 of the Commercial Code shall apply, and the measure of damages shall include the cost of repairs necessary to make the goods conform.

(c) If the buyer establishes that the failure to comply was willful, the judgment may include, in addition to the amounts recovered under subdivision (a), a civil penalty which shall not exceed two times the amount of actual damages. This subdivision shall not apply in any class action under Section 382 of the Code of Civil Procedure or under Section 1781, or with respect to a claim based solely on a breach of an implied warranty.

(d) If the buyer prevails in an action under this section, the buyer shall be allowed by the court to recover as part of the judgment a sum equal to the aggregate amount of costs and expenses, including attorney's fees based on actual time expended, determined by the court to have been reasonably incurred by the buyer in connection with the commencement and prosecution of such action.

(e)(1) Except as otherwise provided in this subdivision, if the buyer establishes a violation of paragraph (2) of subdivision (d) of Section 1793.2, the buyer shall recover damages and reasonable attorney's fees and costs, and may recover a civil penalty of up to two times the amount of damages.

(2) If the manufacturer maintains a qualified third-party dispute resolution process which substantially complies with Section 1793.22, the manufacturer shall not be liable for any civil penalty pursuant to this subdivision.

(3) After the occurrence of the events giving rise to the presumption established in subdivision (b) of Section 1793.22, the buyer may serve upon the manufacturer a written notice requesting that the manufacturer comply with paragraph (2) of subdivision (d) of Section 1793.2. If the buyer fails to serve the notice, the manufacturer shall not be liable for a civil penalty pursuant to this subdivision.

(4) If the buyer serves the notice described in paragraph (3) and the manufacturer complies with paragraph (2) of subdivision (d) of Section 1793.2 within 30 days of the service of that notice, the manufacturer shall not be liable for a civil penalty pursuant to this subdivision.

(5) If the buyer recovers a civil penalty under subdivision (c), the buyer may not also recover a civil penalty under this subdivision for the same violation. (Added by Stats.1982, c. 385, p. 1716, § 2. Amended by Stats.1987, c. 1280, § 4, operative Jan. 1, 1988; Stats.1992, c. 1232 (S.B.1762), § 9.)

Cross References

Attorney's fees and costs, award, see Civil Code § 1717.

Automobile contract or purchase order, attorney's fees and costs, see Civil Code § 2983.4.

Buyer or retail buyer defined for purposes of this Chapter, see Civil Code § 1791.

Buyer's damages for breach in regard to accepted goods, see Commercial Code § 2714.

Consumer goods defined for purposes of this Chapter, see Civil Code § 1791.

Credit card holder, award of attorney's fees against issuer or retailer, see Civil Code § 1747.50 et seq.

Damages, generally, see Civil Code §§ 3274, 3281 et seq.

Express warranty defined, see Civil Code § 1791.2.

Manufacturer defined for purposes of this Chapter, see Civil Code § 1791.

Sale defined for purposes of this Chapter, see Civil Code § 1791.

Service contract defined for purposes of this Chapter, see Civil Code § 1791.

§ 1794.1. Actions by retailer and independent serviceman

(a) Any retail seller of consumer goods injured by the willful or repeated violation of the provisions of this chapter may bring an action for the recovery of damages. Judgment may be entered for three times the amount at which the actual damages are assessed plus reasonable attorney fees.

(b) Any independent serviceman of consumer goods injured by the willful or repeated violation of the provisions of this chapter may bring an action for the recovery of damages. Judgment may be entered for three times the amount at which the actual damages are assessed plus reasonable attorney fees. (Added by Stats.1970, c. 1333, p. 2482, § 1. Amended by Stats.1976, c. 416, p. 1072, § 5.)

Cross References

Attorney's fees and costs, award, see Civil Code § 1717.

Automobile conditional sales contract, attorney's fees, see Civil Code § 2983.4.

Consumer goods defined for purposes of this Chapter, see Civil Code § 1791.

Credit card holder, award of attorney's fees against issuer or retailer, see Civil Code §§ 1747.50, 1747.60, 1747.70.

Damages, generally, see Civil Code §§ 3274, 3281 et seq.

Retail seller, seller, or retailer defined for purposes of this Chapter, see Civil Code § 1791.

§ 1794.2. Repealed by Stats.1982, c. 385, p. 1716, § 3

§ 1794.3. Defect or nonconformity caused by unauthorized or unreasonable use; inapplicability of chapter

The provisions of this chapter shall not apply to any defect or nonconformity in consumer goods caused by the unauthorized or unreasonable use of the goods following sale.

(Added by Stats.1970, c. 1333, p. 2482, § 1. Amended by Stats.1971, c. 1523, p. 3007, § 15, operative Jan. 1, 1972.)

Cross References

Consumer goods defined for purposes of this Chapter, see Civil Code § 1791.

Sale defined for purposes of this Chapter, see Civil Code § 1791.

§ 1794.4. Service contract; contents; cancellation

(a) Nothing in this chapter shall be construed to prevent the sale of a service contract to the buyer in addition to or in lieu of an express warranty if that contract fully and conspicuously discloses in simple and readily understood language the terms, conditions, and exclusions of that contract, provided that nothing in this section shall apply to a home protection contract issued by a home protection company that is subject to Part 7 (commencing with Section 12740) of Division 2 of the Insurance Code.

(b) Except as otherwise expressly provided in the service contract, every service contract shall obligate the service contractor to provide to the buyer of the product all of the services and functional parts that may be necessary to maintain proper operation of the entire product under normal operation and service for the duration of the service contract and without additional charge.

(c) The service contract shall contain all of the following items of information:

(1) If the service contract covers a single product, a clear description and identification of the covered product. If the service contract covers a class of products, a description of the class of products covered by the service contract that is sufficiently clear so the buyer is able to discern the products covered.

(2) The point in time or event when the term of the service contract commences, and its duration measured by elapsed time or an objective measure of use.

(3)(A) A service contract may be offered on a month-to-month or other periodic basis and continue until canceled by the buyer or the service contractor in accordance with Section 1794.41 and, for electronic and appliance repair dealers, Section 9855.6 of the Business and Professions Code. If the service contract continues until canceled by the buyer or service contractor, the service contract shall do all of the following:

(i) Disclose to the buyer in a clear and conspicuous manner that the service contract shall continue until canceled by the buyer or service contractor and require the buyer's affirmative consent to this provision.

(ii) Disclose to the buyer all alternatives that the seller offering the service contract offers, including any fixed-term service contracts or other service contract basis that does not continue until it is canceled.

(iii) Provide, at a minimum, a toll-free number, email address, postal address, and, if one exists, internet website the buyer can use to cancel the service contract. Cancellation shall not require the use of more than one of these methods to be completed and shall be effective immediately upon receipt of the request for cancellation.

(iv) If the service contract was entered into online, allow the buyer the option to cancel the service contract exclusively online, without engaging in any unnecessary steps that obstruct or delay the buyer's ability to cancel the continuation of the service contract.

(v)(I) Provide for a refund to the buyer of any unearned amounts in accordance with Section 1794.41 and, for electronic and appliance repair dealers, Section 9855.6 of the Business and Professions Code.

(II) The amount of any refund, as well as any cancellation or administrative fees, under this paragraph shall be calculated based on the period, whether month to month or otherwise, for which payment is made and the amount of the payment for the period.

(III) A written notice of cancellation other than notice required by clauses (iii) and (iv) shall not be required to obtain a refund.

(B) This paragraph does not apply to vehicle service contracts.

(4) If the enforceability of the service contract is limited to the original buyer or is limited to persons other than every consumer owner of the covered product during the term of the service contract, a description of the limits on transfer or assignment of the service contract.

(5) A statement of the general obligation of the service contractor in the same language set forth in subdivision (b), with equally clear and conspicuous statements of the following:

(A) Any services, parts, characteristics, components, properties, defects, malfunctions, causes, conditions, repairs, or remedies that are excluded from the scope of the service contract.

(B) Any other limits on the application of the language in subdivision (b) such as a limit on the total number of service calls.

(C) Any additional services that the service contractor will provide.

(D) Whether the obligation of the service contractor includes preventive maintenance and, if so, the nature and frequency of the preventive maintenance that the service contractor will provide.

(E) Whether the buyer has an obligation to provide preventive maintenance or perform any other obligations and, if so, the nature and frequency of the preventive maintenance and of any other obligations, and the consequences of any noncompliance.

(6) A step-by-step explanation of the procedure that the buyer should follow in order to obtain performance of any obligation under the service contract including the following:

(A) The full legal and business name of the service contractor.

(B) The mailing address of the service contractor.

(C) The persons or class of persons that are authorized to perform service.

(D) The name or title and address of any agent, employee, or department of the service contractor that is responsible for the performance of any obligations.

(E) The method of giving notice to the service contractor of the need for service.

(F) Whether in-home service is provided or, if not, whether the costs of transporting the product for service or repairs will be paid by the service contractor.

(G) If the product must be transported to the service contractor, either the place where the product may be delivered for service or repairs or a toll-free telephone number that the buyer may call to obtain that information.

(H) All other steps that the buyer must take to obtain service.

(I) All fees, charges, and other costs that the buyer must pay to obtain service.

(7) An explanation of the steps that the service contractor will take to carry out its obligations under the service contract.

(8) A description of any right to cancel the contract if the buyer returns the product or the product is sold, lost, stolen, or destroyed, or, if there is no right to cancel or the right to cancel is limited, a statement of the fact.

(9) Information respecting the availability of any informal dispute settlement process.

(d) A service contractor may cancel a service contract offered on a month-to-month or other periodic basis only if any of the following occurs:

(1) The buyer fails to make timely payment.

(2) The buyer is otherwise in material breach of the service contract.

(3) The buyer has committed fraud in connection with the service contract.

(4)(A) The service contractor or its affiliate is the obligor under the service contract, and the service contractor or its affiliate is discontinuing this category of service contract no later than 30 days after the effective date of the cancellation.

(B) A cancellation or administrative fee shall not be charged to the buyer for a cancellation pursuant to this paragraph.

(5)(A) Neither the seller offering the service contract nor any of its affiliates is the obligor under the service contract, and the seller is discontinuing its offering of the service contract no later than 30 days after the effective date of the cancellation in favor of a service contract with a different obligor.

(B) A cancellation or administrative fee shall not be charged to the buyer for a cancellation pursuant to this paragraph.

(e) As used in this section:

(1) "Affiliate" means an entity that directly, or indirectly through one or more intermediaries, controls, is controlled by, or is under common control with another specified entity.

(2)(A) "Affirmative consent" means any freely given, specific, informed, and unambiguous indication of the consumer's wishes by which the consumer, or the consumer's legal guardian, a person who has power of attorney, or a person acting as a conservator for the consumer, including by a statement or by a clear affirmative action, signifies agreement to the continuous until canceled nature of the service contract.

(B) "Affirmative consent" does not mean any of the following:

(i) Acceptance of a general or broad terms of use, or similar document, that contains descriptions of the coverages under the service contract along with other, unrelated information.

(ii) Hovering over, muting, pausing, or closing a given piece of content.

(iii) Agreement obtained through the use of dark patterns.

(f) Subdivisions (b) and (c) are applicable to service contracts on new or used home appliances and home electronic products entered into on or after July 1, 1989. They are applicable to service contracts on all other new or used products entered into on and after July 1, 1991.

(g) The amendments to this section made by the act adding this subdivision are applicable only to a service contract entered into on or after January 1, 2022. *(Added by Stats.1993, c. 1265 (S.B.798), § 13.5, operative Jan. 1, 1998. Amended by Stats.1997, c. 401 (S.B.780), § 65, operative Jan. 1, 2003; Stats.2002, c. 405 (A.B.2973), § 64, operative Jan. 1, 2008; Stats.2021, c. 452 (A.B.1221), § 2, eff. Jan. 1, 2022.)*

Cross References

Buyer or retail buyer defined for purposes of this Chapter, see Civil Code § 1791.

Express warranty defined, see Civil Code § 1791.2.

Home appliance defined for purposes of this Chapter, see Civil Code § 1791.

Home electronic product defined for purposes of this Chapter, see Civil Code § 1791.

Sale defined for purposes of this Chapter, see Civil Code § 1791.

Service contract defined for purposes of this Chapter, see Civil Code § 1791.

Service contractors, compliance with the provisions of this section, see Business and Professions Code § 9855.5.

Vehicle service contract form offers, requirements, see Insurance Code § 12820.

Vehicle service contract forms, compliance with requirements of this section, see Insurance Code § 12820.

§ 1794.41. Service contract provisions

(a) No service contract covering any motor vehicle, home appliance, or home electronic product purchased for use in this state may be offered for sale or sold unless all of the following elements exist:

(1) The contract shall contain the disclosures specified in Section 1794.4 and shall disclose in the manner described in that section the buyer's cancellation and refund rights provided by this section.

(2) The contract shall be available for inspection by the buyer prior to purchase and either the contract, or a brochure which specifically describes the terms, conditions, and exclusions of the contract, and the provisions of this section relating to contract delivery, cancellation, and refund, shall be delivered to the buyer at or before the time of purchase of the contract. Within 60 days after the date of purchase, the contract itself shall be delivered to the buyer. If a service contract for a home appliance or a home electronic product is sold by means of a telephone solicitation, the seller may elect

to satisfy the requirements of this paragraph by mailing or delivering the contract to the buyer not later than 30 days after the date of the sale of the contract.

(3) The contract is applicable only to items, costs, and time periods not covered by the express warranty. However, a service contract may run concurrently with or overlap an express warranty if (A) the contract covers items or costs not covered by the express warranty or (B) the contract provides relief to the purchaser not available under the express warranty, such as automatic replacement of a product where the express warranty only provides for repair.

(4) The contract shall be cancelable by the purchaser under the following conditions:

(A) Unless the contract provides for a longer period, within the first 60 days after receipt of the contract, or with respect to a contract covering a used motor vehicle without manufacturer warranties, a home appliance, or a home electronic product, within the first 30 days after receipt of the contract, the full amount paid shall be refunded by the seller to the purchaser if the purchaser provides a written notice of cancellation to the person specified in the contract, and if no claims have been made against the contract. If a claim has been made against the contract either within the first 60 days after receipt of the contract, or with respect to a used motor vehicle without manufacturer warranties, home appliance, or home electronic product, within the first 30 days after receipt of the contract, a pro rata refund, based on either elapsed time or an objective measure of use, such as mileage or the retail value of any service performed, at the seller's option as indicated in the contract, or for a vehicle service contract at the obligor's option as determined at the time of cancellation, shall be made by the seller to the purchaser if the purchaser provides a written notice of cancellation to the person specified in the contract.

(B) Unless the contract provides for a longer period for obtaining a full refund, after the first 60 days after receipt of the contract, or with respect to a contract covering a used motor vehicle without manufacturer warranties, a home appliance, or a home electronic product, after the first 30 days after the receipt of the contract, a pro rata refund, based on either elapsed time or an objective measure of use, such as mileage or the retail value of any service performed, at the seller's option as indicated in the contract, or for a vehicle service contract at the obligor's option as determined at the time of cancellation, shall be made by the seller to the purchaser if the purchaser provides a written notice of cancellation to the person specified in the contract. In addition, the seller may assess a cancellation or administrative fee, not to exceed 10 percent of the price of the service contract or twenty-five dollars ($25), whichever is less.

(C) If the purchase of the service contract was financed, the seller may make the refund payable to the purchaser, the assignee, or lender of record, or both.

(b) Nothing in this section shall apply to a home protection plan that is issued by a home protection company which is subject to Part 7 (commencing with Section 12740) of Division 2 of the Insurance Code.

(c) If any provision of this section conflicts with any provision of Part 8 (commencing with Section 12800) of Division 2 of the Insurance Code, the provision of the Insurance Code shall apply instead of this section. (Added by Stats.1985, c. 1047, § 3. Amended by Stats.1988, c. 581, § 3; Stats.1990, c. 1183 (A.B.2226), § 1; Stats.2003, c. 439 (A.B. 984), § 1, operative July 1, 2004; Stats.2010, c. 543 (A.B.2111), § 7.)

Cross References

Buyer or retail buyer defined for purposes of this Chapter, see Civil Code § 1791.
Cancellation of service contracts, see Insurance Code § 12825.
Express warranty defined, see Civil Code § 1791.2.
Home appliance defined for purposes of this Chapter, see Civil Code § 1791.
Home electronic product defined for purposes of this Chapter, see Civil Code § 1791.
Insurance production agencies, licensing requirements, exemptions for certain employees of home protection companies, see Insurance Code § 1634.
Manufacturer defined for purposes of this Chapter, see Civil Code § 1791.
Retail seller, seller, or retailer defined for purposes of this Chapter, see Civil Code § 1791.
Sale defined for purposes of this Chapter, see Civil Code § 1791.
Service contract defined for purposes of this Chapter, see Civil Code § 1791.
Service contractors,
  Cancellation of service contract, time for refund or credit, see Business and Professions Code § 9855.6.
  Compliance with the provisions of this section, see Business and Professions Code § 9855.5.
Vehicle service contract form offers, requirements, see Insurance Code § 12820.
Vehicle service contract forms, compliance with requirements of this section, see Insurance Code § 12820.

§ 1794.45. Service contract; requirements while in effect; exclusions

(a) A retailer that sells a service contract pursuant to Section 1794.4 shall do either of the following during the period that the service contract is in effect:

(1) Maintain contract information that includes a description of the terms and conditions of the service contract, and provide that information to the purchaser of the service contract or other beneficiary upon request.

(2) Upon request from the purchaser of the service contract or other beneficiary, obtain a copy of the service contract, and provide that copy to the requester within 10 business days after receiving the request.

(b) This section shall not apply to a vehicle service contract, as defined in subdivision (c) of Section 12800 of the Insurance Code. (Added by Stats.2009, c. 74 (A.B.63), § 1.)

§ 1794.5. Suggestions of methods of service and repair by manufacturer

The provisions of this chapter shall not preclude a manufacturer making express warranties from suggesting methods of effecting service and repair, in accordance with the terms and conditions of the express warranties, other than those required by this chapter. (Added by Stats.1970, c. 1333, p. 2483, § 1.)

Cross References

Express warranty defined, see Civil Code § 1791.2.

Manufacturer defined for purposes of this Chapter, see Civil Code § 1791.

§ 1795. Liability of warrantors other than manufacturers

If express warranties are made by persons other than the manufacturer of the goods, the obligation of the person making such warranties shall be the same as that imposed on the manufacturer under this chapter. *(Added by Stats.1970, c. 1333, p. 2483, § 1.)*

Cross References

Express warranty defined, see Civil Code § 1791.2.
Manufacturer defined for purposes of this Chapter, see Civil Code § 1791.

§ 1795.1. Systems designed to heat, cool or condition air; equipment or component; application of chapter

This chapter shall apply to any equipment or mechanical, electrical, or thermal component of a system designed to heat, cool, or otherwise condition air, but, with that exception, shall not apply to the system as a whole where such a system becomes a fixed part of a structure. *(Added by Stats.1971, c. 1523, p. 3007, § 16.5, operative Jan. 1, 1972. Amended by Stats.1978, c. 991, p. 3065, § 11; Stats.1983, c. 728, § 1.)*

§ 1795.4. Leases of new and used consumer goods; rules applicable

For the purposes of this chapter only, the following rules apply to leases of both new and used consumer goods:

(a) If express warranties are regularly furnished to purchasers of substantially the same kind of goods, (1) those warranties will be deemed to apply to the leased goods and (2) the lessor and lessee shall each be deemed to be the first purchaser of the goods for the purpose of any warranty provision limiting warranty benefits to the original purchaser.

(b) The lessee of goods has the same rights under this chapter against the manufacturer and any person making express warranties that the lessee would have had under this chapter if the goods had been purchased by the lessee, and the manufacturer and any person making express warranties have the same duties and obligations under this chapter with respect to the goods that such manufacturer and other person would have had under this chapter if the goods had been sold to the lessee.

(c) If a lessor leases goods to a lessee from the lessor's inventory, the lessee has the same rights under this chapter against the lessor that the lessee would have had if the goods had been purchased by the lessee, and the lessor has the same duties and obligations under this chapter with respect to the goods that the lessor would have had under this chapter if the goods had been sold to the lessee. For purposes of this section, "inventory" shall include both goods in the lessor's possession prior to negotiation of the lease and goods ordered from another party in order to lease those goods to the lessee where the lessor is a dealer in goods of that type.

(d) If a lessor leases goods to a lessee which the lessor acquires other than from the lessor's inventory, the lessee has the same rights under this chapter against the seller of the goods to the lessor that the lessee would have had under this chapter if the goods had been purchased by the lessee from the seller, and the seller of the goods to the lessor has the same duties and obligations under this chapter with respect to the goods that the seller would have had under this chapter if the goods had been purchased by the lessee from the seller.

(e) A lessor who re-leases goods to a new lessee and does not retake possession of the goods prior to consummation of the re-lease may, notwithstanding the provisions of Section 1793, disclaim as to that lessee any and all warranties created by this chapter by conspicuously disclosing in the lease that these warranties are disclaimed.

(f) A lessor who has obligations to the lessee with relation to warranties in connection with a lease of goods and the seller of goods to a lessor have the same rights and remedies against the manufacturer and any person making express warranties that a seller of the goods would have had if the seller had sold the goods to the lessee. *(Added by Stats.1984, c. 1169, § 2.)*

Cross References

Consumer goods defined for purposes of this Chapter, see Civil Code § 1791.
Consumer goods manufacturers, express warranties, service and repair facilities, see Civil Code § 1793.2.
Express warranty defined, see Civil Code § 1791.2.
Lease defined for purposes of this Chapter, see Civil Code § 1791.
Lessee defined for purposes of this Chapter, see Civil Code § 1791.
Lessor defined for purposes of this Chapter, see Civil Code § 1791.
Manufacturer defined for purposes of this Chapter, see Civil Code § 1791.
Retail seller, seller, or retailer defined for purposes of this Chapter, see Civil Code § 1791.

§ 1795.5. Used goods; obligation of distributor or retail seller; maintenance of service and repair facilities; duration of warranties

Notwithstanding the provisions of subdivision (a) of Section 1791 defining consumer goods to mean "new" goods, the obligation of a distributor or retail seller of used consumer goods in a sale in which an express warranty is given shall be the same as that imposed on manufacturers under this chapter except:

(a) It shall be the obligation of the distributor or retail seller making express warranties with respect to used consumer goods (and not the original manufacturer, distributor, or retail seller making express warranties with respect to such goods when new) to maintain sufficient service and repair facilities within this state to carry out the terms of such express warranties.

(b) The provisions of Section 1793.5 shall not apply to the sale of used consumer goods sold in this state.

(c) The duration of the implied warranty of merchantability and where present the implied warranty of fitness with respect to used consumer goods sold in this state, where the sale is accompanied by an express warranty, shall be coextensive in duration with an express warranty which accompanies the consumer goods, provided the duration of the express warranty is reasonable, but in no event shall such implied warranties have a duration of less than 30 days nor more than three months following the sale of used consumer goods to a retail buyer. Where no duration for an express warranty is stated with respect to such goods, or parts thereof, the duration of the implied warranties shall be the maximum period prescribed above.

(d) The obligation of the distributor or retail seller who makes express warranties with respect to used goods that are sold in this state, shall extend to the sale of all such used goods, regardless of when such goods may have been manufactured. *(Added by Stats.1971, c. 1523, p. 3008, § 17, operative Jan. 1, 1972. Amended by Stats.1974, c. 169, p. 325, § 1; Stats.1978, c. 991, p. 3065, § 12; Stats.1983, c. 728, § 2.)*

Cross References

Buyer or retail buyer defined for purposes of this Chapter, see Civil Code § 1791.

Consumer goods defined for purposes of this Chapter, see Civil Code § 1791.

Distributor defined for purposes of this Chapter, see Civil Code § 1791.

Express warranty defined, see Civil Code § 1791.2.

Implied warranty of fitness defined for purposes of this Chapter, see Civil Code § 1791.1.

Implied warranty of merchantability or implied warranty that goods are merchantable defined for purposes of this Chapter, see Civil Code § 1791.1.

Manufacturer defined for purposes of this Chapter, see Civil Code § 1791.

Retail seller, seller, or retailer defined for purposes of this Chapter, see Civil Code § 1791.

Sale defined for purposes of this Chapter, see Civil Code § 1791.

Statute of limitations in contracts for sale, see Commercial Code § 2725.

Used assistive devises, inapplicability of this section, see Civil Code § 1793.02.

§ 1795.51. Buy-here-pay-here dealer; written warranty and receipt for sale or lease of vehicle; prohibited actions; notice of election to cancel; vehicle repairs

(a) No buy-here-pay-here dealer, as that term is defined in Section 241 of the Vehicle Code, shall sell or lease a used vehicle, as defined in Section 665 of the Vehicle Code, at retail price without giving the buyer or lessee a written warranty that shall have a minimum duration of at least 30 days from the date of delivery or when the odometer has registered 1,000 miles from what is shown on the contract, whichever occurs first.

(b) The written warranty shall provide that if the buyer or lessee notifies the buy-here-pay-here dealer that the vehicle does not conform to the written warranty, the buy-here-pay-here dealer shall either repair the vehicle to conform to the written warranty, reimburse the buyer or lessee for the reasonable cost of repairs, or cancel the sale or lease contract and provide the buyer or lessee with a full refund, less a reasonable amount for any damage sustained by the vehicle after the sale or lease, excepting damage caused by any nonconformity with the written warranty.

(c) The written warranty shall provide that the buy-here-pay-here dealer shall pay 100 percent of the cost of labor and parts for any repairs pursuant to the warranty, and may not charge the buyer or lessee for the cost of repairs or for inspecting the vehicle, tearing down the engine or transmission or other part, or for any deductible. Any person performing repairs pursuant to this subdivision shall comply with the requirements of an automotive repair dealer pursuant to Chapter 20.3 (commencing with Section 9880) of Division 3 of the Business and Professions Code.

(d) The buy-here-pay-here dealer or its agent may elect to refund the buyer or lessee a full refund, less a reasonable amount for any damage sustained by the vehicle after the sale or lease, excepting damage caused by any nonconformity with the written warranty, rather than performing a repair. In the event that the buy-here-pay-here dealer cancels the sale or lease, all of the following shall apply:

(1) The buy-here-pay-here dealer shall give written notice to the buyer or lessee of the election to cancel the sale or lease by personal delivery or first-class mail.

(2) The buyer or lessee shall return the vehicle in substantially the same condition as when it was delivered by the buy-here-pay-here dealer, reasonable wear and tear and any nonconformity with the written warranty excepted.

(3) The buy-here-pay-here dealer shall provide the buyer or lessee with a receipt stating all of the following:

(A) The date the vehicle was returned to the buy-here-pay-here dealer.

(B) The vehicle identification number.

(C) The make, year, and model of the vehicle.

(D) The odometer reading at the time that the vehicle was returned to the buy-here-pay-here dealer.

(E) A statement that the buy-here-pay-here dealer has canceled the sale or lease.

(F) The amount of the buyer's or lessee's refund.

(4) The buy-here-pay-here dealer shall not treat the return of the vehicle pursuant to the contract cancellation provisions of this subdivision as a repossession.

(5) The buyer or lessee shall execute the documents necessary to transfer any interest in the vehicle to the buy-here-pay-here dealer or to remove the buyer or lessee from any registration or title documents.

(6) The buy-here-pay-here dealer shall refund to the buyer or lessee, no later than the day after the day on which the buyer or lessee returns the vehicle and the notice of election to cancel is given to the buyer or lessee, all amounts paid under the sale or lease agreement, less a reasonable amount for property damage sustained by the vehicle after the sale or lease, excepting damage caused by any nonconformity with the warranty.

(e) The written warranty shall cover at least the following components:

(1) Engine, including all internally lubricated parts.

(2) Transmission and transaxle.

(3) Front and rear wheel drive components.

(4) Engine cooling system.

(5) Alternator, generator, starter, and ignition system, not including the battery.

(6) Braking system.

(7) Front and rear suspension systems.

(8) Steering system and components.

(9) Seatbelts.

§ 1795.51   OBLIGATIONS

(10) Inflatable restraint systems installed on the vehicle as originally manufactured.

(11) Catalytic converter and other emissions components necessary for the vehicle to pass a California emissions test.

(12) Heater.

(13) Seals and gaskets on components described in this subdivision.

(14) Electrical, electronic, and computer components, to the extent that those components substantially affect the functionality of other components described in this subdivision.

(f) Any Used Car Buyer's Guide displayed on a vehicle offered for sale or lease by a buy-here-pay-here dealer shall list each of the above systems and components and shall specify that the buy-here-pay-here dealer will pay 100 percent of the cost of parts and labor for repairs covered by the warranty.

(g) The buy-here-pay-here dealer shall make the repair or provide a refund notwithstanding the fact that the warranty period has expired if the buyer or lessee notified the buy-here-pay-here dealer of the failure of a covered system or part within the warranty period.

(h) This section shall not apply to any defect or nonconformity caused by the unauthorized or unreasonable use of the vehicle following the sale, or to any property damage not to the vehicle arising out of the failure of a covered part.

(i) In any proceeding in which the exclusion of coverage permitted by subdivision (h) or the deduction allowed by paragraph (6) of subdivision (d) is an issue, the buy-here-pay-here dealer shall have the burden of proof.

(j) A buy-here-pay-here dealer shall not sell or lease any vehicle unless the vehicle meets all of the equipment requirements of Division 12 (commencing with Section 24000) of the Vehicle Code.

(k) Any agreement between a buy-here-pay-here dealer and a buyer or lessee that disclaims, limits, or waives the rights set forth in this section shall be void as contrary to public policy.

(l) If a buy-here-pay-here dealer fails to give a buyer a written warranty pursuant to this section, the buy-here-pay-here dealer shall be deemed to have provided the warranty as a matter of law. (Added by Stats.2012, c. 740 (A.B.1447), § 2.)

Cross References

Buy-here-pay-here dealers, prohibited actions after sale, see Civil Code § 2983.37.

§ 1795.6. Tolling or expiration of warranty period during time of repairs or service; resumption of warranty period for hearing aids; warranty period deemed not expired; receipts

(a)(1) Except as provided in paragraph (2) warranty[1] period relating to an implied or express warranty accompanying a sale or consignment for sale of consumer goods selling for fifty dollars ($50) or more shall automatically be tolled for the period from the date upon which the buyer either (1) delivers nonconforming goods to the manufacturer or seller for warranty repairs or service or (2), pursuant to subdivision (c) of Section 1793.2 or Section 1793.22, notifies the manufacturer or seller of the nonconformity of the goods up to, and including, the date upon which (1) the repaired or serviced goods are delivered to the buyer, (2) the buyer is notified the goods are repaired or serviced and are available for the buyer's possession or (3) the buyer is notified that repairs or service is completed, if repairs or service is made at the buyer's residence.

(2) With respect to hearing aids, the warranty period shall resume on the date upon which (1) the repaired or serviced hearing aid is delivered to the buyer or (2) five days after the buyer is notified the hearing aid is repaired or serviced and is available for the buyer's possession, whichever is earlier.

(b) Notwithstanding the date or conditions set for the expiration of the warranty period, such warranty period shall not be deemed expired if either or both of the following situations occur: (1) after the buyer has satisfied the requirements of subdivision (a), the warranty repairs or service has not been performed due to delays caused by circumstances beyond the control of the buyer or (2) the warranty repairs or service performed upon the nonconforming goods did not remedy the nonconformity for which such repairs or service was performed and the buyer notified the manufacturer or seller of this failure within 60 days after the repairs or service was completed. When the warranty repairs or service has been performed so as to remedy the nonconformity, the warranty period shall expire in accordance with its terms, including any extension to the warranty period for warranty repairs or service.

(c) For purposes of this section only, "manufacturer" includes the manufacturer's service or repair facility.

(d)(1) Except as provided in paragraph (2), every manufacturer or seller of consumer goods selling for fifty dollars ($50) or more shall provide a receipt to the buyer showing the date of purchase. Every manufacturer or seller performing warranty repairs or service on the goods shall provide to the buyer a work order or receipt with the date of return and either the date the buyer was notified that the goods were repaired or serviced or, where applicable, the date the goods were shipped or delivered to the buyer.

(2) With respect to hearing aids, the seller, after receiving the hearing aid for warranty repairs or service, shall also provide at the time of delivery to the buyer a work order or receipt with the following: (1) the date the warranty period resumes and (2) the revised expiration date of the warranty, as adjusted to reflect the suspension of the warranty period provided under this section. (Added by Stats.1974, c. 844, p. 1809, § 1, operative July 1, 1975. Amended by Stats.1980, c. 394, p. 778, § 2; Stats.1983, c. 728, § 3; Stats.1992, c. 1232 (S.B.1762), § 10; Stats.2014, c. 226 (S.B.1326), § 2, eff. Jan. 1, 2015.)

[1] So in chaptered copy; probably should read "every warranty".

Cross References

Buyer or retail buyer defined for purposes of this Chapter, see Civil Code § 1791.

Consumer goods defined for purposes of this Chapter, see Civil Code § 1791.

Express warranty defined, see Civil Code § 1791.2.

Manufacturer defined for purposes of this Chapter, see Civil Code § 1791.

Retail seller, seller, or retailer defined for purposes of this Chapter, see Civil Code § 1791.
Sale defined for purposes of this Chapter, see Civil Code § 1791.

§ 1795.7. Liability of manufacturer; extension upon tolling of warranty period

Whenever a warranty, express or implied, is tolled pursuant to Section 1795.6 as a result of repairs or service performed by any retail seller, the warranty shall be extended with regard to the liability of the manufacturer to a retail seller pursuant to law. In such event, the manufacturer shall be liable in accordance with the provisions of Section 1793.5 for the period that an express warranty has been extended by virtue of Section 1795.6 to every retail seller who incurs obligations in giving effect to such express warranty. The manufacturer shall also be liable to every retail seller for the period that an implied warranty has been extended by virtue of Section 1795.6, in the same manner as he would be liable under Section 1793.5 for an express warranty. If a manufacturer provides for warranty repairs and service through its own service and repair facilities and through independent repair facilities in the state, its exclusive liability pursuant to this section shall be to such facilities. *(Added by Stats.1974, c. 844, p. 1809, § 2, operative July 1, 1975.)*

Cross References

Express warranty defined, see Civil Code § 1791.2.
Manufacturer defined for purposes of this Chapter, see Civil Code § 1791.
Retail seller, seller, or retailer defined for purposes of this Chapter, see Civil Code § 1791.

§ 1795.8. Application of chapter to members of Armed Forces purchasing motor vehicle

Notwithstanding any other provision of law, this chapter shall apply to a purchase in the United States of a motor vehicle, as defined in paragraph (2) of subdivision (e) of Section 1793.22, with a manufacturer's express warranty by a member of the Armed Forces regardless of in which state his or her motor vehicle is purchased or registered, if both of the following apply:

(a) The member of the Armed Forces purchases a motor vehicle, as defined in paragraph (2) of subdivision (e) of Section 1793.22, with a manufacturer's express warranty from a manufacturer who sells motor vehicles in this state or from an agent or representative of that manufacturer.

(b) The member of the Armed Forces was stationed in or a resident of this state at the time he or she purchased the motor vehicle or at the time he or she filed an action pursuant to this chapter. *(Added by Stats.2007, c. 151 (S.B.234), § 2.)*

Cross References

Express warrant defined, see Civil Code § 1791.2.
Manufacturer defined for purposes of this Chapter, see Civil Code § 1791.
Member of the Armed Forces defined for purposes of this Chapter, see Civil Code § 1791.

CHAPTER 1.5. MOTOR VEHICLE WARRANTY ADJUSTMENT PROGRAMS

Section
1795.90. Definitions.
1795.91. Dealers; duties.
1795.92. Manufacturers; duties.
1795.93. Consumer or lessee remedies; construction of chapter.

§ 1795.90. Definitions

For purposes of this chapter:

(a) "Consumer" means the purchaser, other than for purposes of resale, of a motor vehicle, a lessee of a motor vehicle, any person to whom the motor vehicle is transferred during the duration of an express warranty applicable to that motor vehicle, and any person entitled by the terms of the warranty to enforce the obligations of the warranty.

(b) "Manufacturer" means any person, firm, or corporation, whether resident or nonresident, that manufactures or assembles motor vehicles for sale or distribution in this state. In the case of motor vehicles not manufactured in the United States, the term "manufacturer" shall also include any person, firm, or corporation that is engaged in the business of importing motor vehicles.

(c) "Dealer" means any person, firm, or corporation selling or agreeing to sell in this state one or more new motor vehicles under a retail agreement with a manufacturer, manufacturer branch, distributor, distributor branch, or agent of any of them.

(d) "Adjustment program" means any program or policy that expands or extends the consumer's warranty beyond its stated limit or under which a manufacturer offers to pay for all or any part of the cost of repairing, or to reimburse consumers for all or any part of the cost of repairing, any condition that may substantially affect vehicle durability, reliability, or performance, other than service provided under a safety or emission-related recall campaign. "Adjustment program" does not include ad hoc adjustments made by a manufacturer on a case-by-case basis.

(e) "Motor vehicle" means a motor vehicle, excluding motorcycles, motor homes, and off-road vehicles, which is registered in this state.

(f) "Lessee" means any person who leases a motor vehicle pursuant to a written lease which provides that the lessee is responsible for repairs to the motor vehicle.

(g) "Service bulletin" means any notice issued by a manufacturer and filed with the National Highway Traffic Safety Administration relating to vehicle durability, reliability, or performance. *(Added by Stats.1993, c. 814 (S.B.486), § 1.)*

§ 1795.91. Dealers; duties

Dealers shall have the following duties:

(a) A dealer shall provide notice to prospective purchasers and lessees that provides information on how to get copies of service bulletins. This notice shall not be construed as an admission by the dealer or manufacturer of the existence or nonexistence of a vehicle defect.

The notice shall be deemed sufficient if posted in the showroom or other area conspicuous to motor vehicle purchasers and written in the following form:

§ 1795.91 OBLIGATIONS

FEDERAL LAW REQUIRES MANUFACTURERS TO FURNISH THE NATIONAL HIGHWAY TRAFFIC SAFETY ADMINISTRATION (NHTSA) WITH BULLETINS DESCRIBING ANY DEFECTS IN THEIR VEHICLES. THESE BULLETINS ARE NOT RECALLS.

YOU MAY OBTAIN COPIES OF THESE TECHNICAL SERVICE BULLETINS FROM THE NHTSA, THE MANUFACTURER (ASK YOUR DEALER FOR THE TOLL-FREE NUMBER), OR

CERTAIN CONSUMER PUBLICATIONS, WHICH PUBLISH THESE BULLETINS. SOME COMPANIES WILL SEND THEM TO YOU, FOR A FEE.

(b) A dealer shall disclose to a consumer seeking repairs for a particular condition at its repair shop, the principal terms and conditions of the manufacturer's adjustment program covering the condition if the dealer has received a service bulletin concerning the adjustment program. *(Added by Stats.1993, c. 814 (S.B.486), § 1. Amended by Stats.2019, c. 490 (A.B.596), § 1, eff. Jan. 1, 2020.)*

Cross References

Adjustment program defined for purposes of this Chapter, see Civil Code § 1795.90.
Consumer defined for purposes of this Chapter, see Civil Code § 1795.90.
Dealer defined for purposes of this Chapter, see Civil Code § 1795.90.
Lessee defined for purposes of this Chapter, see Civil Code § 1795.90.
Manufacturer defined for purposes of this Chapter, see Civil Code § 1795.90.
Motor vehicle defined for purposes of this Chapter, see Civil Code § 1795.90.
Service bulletin defined for purposes of this Chapter, see Civil Code § 1795.90.

§ 1795.92. Manufacturers; duties

Manufacturers shall have the following duties:

(a) A manufacturer shall, within 90 days of the adoption of an adjustment program, subject to priority for safety or emission-related recalls, notify by first-class mail all owners or lessees of motor vehicles eligible under the program of the condition giving rise to and the principal terms and conditions of the program.

(b) Copies of all notices mailed in accordance with subdivision (a) shall be sent to the New Motor Vehicle Board within the Department of Motor Vehicles and made available for public inquiries.

(c) A manufacturer shall, within 30 days of the adoption of any new adjustment program, notify its dealers, in writing, of all the terms and conditions thereof.

(d) A manufacturer who establishes an adjustment program shall implement procedures to assure reimbursement of each consumer eligible under an adjustment program who incurs expenses for repair of a condition subject to the program prior to acquiring knowledge of the program. The reimbursement shall be consistent with the terms and conditions of the particular program. The manufacturer shall notify the consumer within 21 business days of receiving a claim for reimbursement whether the claim will be allowed or denied. If the claim is denied, the specific reasons for the denial shall be stated in writing.

(e) Any consumer who, prior to acquiring knowledge of an adjustment program, incurs expenses for repair of a condition subject to the adjustment program may file a claim for reimbursement under subdivision (d). The claim shall be made in writing to the manufacturer within two years of the date of the consumer's payment for repair of the condition. *(Added by Stats.1993, c. 814 (S.B.486), § 1.)*

Cross References

Adjustment program defined for purposes of this Chapter, see Civil Code § 1795.90.
Consumer defined for purposes of this Chapter, see Civil Code § 1795.90.
Dealer defined for purposes of this Chapter, see Civil Code § 1795.90.
Department of Motor Vehicles, records, application of confidentiality of records law to specified entities, use of released address information, see Vehicle Code § 1808.23.
Lessee defined for purposes of this Chapter, see Civil Code § 1795.90.
Manufacturer defined for purposes of this Chapter, see Civil Code § 1795.90.
Motor vehicle defined for purposes of this Chapter, see Civil Code § 1795.90.

§ 1795.93. Consumer or lessee remedies; construction of chapter

Nothing in this chapter shall be construed to exclude, modify, or otherwise limit any other remedy provided by law to a consumer or lessee. *(Added by Stats.1993, c. 814 (S.B.486), § 1.)*

Cross References

Consumer defined for purposes of this Chapter, see Civil Code § 1795.90.
Lessee defined for purposes of this Chapter, see Civil Code § 1795.90.

CHAPTER 2. STANDARDS FOR WARRANTY WORK

Section
1796. Installation of consumer goods; duty owed to buyers.
1796.5. Service or repair to consumer goods; duty owed to purchasers.

§ 1796. Installation of consumer goods; duty owed to buyers

Any individual, partnership, corporation, association, or other legal relationship which engages in the business of installing new or used consumer goods, has a duty to the buyer to install them in a good and workmanlike manner. *(Added by Stats.1978, c. 991, p. 3065, § 13.)*

§ 1796.5. Service or repair to consumer goods; duty owed to purchasers

Any individual, partnership, corporation, association, or other legal relationship which engages in the business of providing service or repair to new or used consumer goods has a duty to the purchaser to perform those services in a good and workmanlike manner. *(Added by Stats.1978, c. 991, p. 3065, § 13.)*

CHAPTER 3. MOBILEHOME WARRANTIES

Section
1797. Necessity of warranty.
1797.1. Definitions.
1797.2. Application; warranty coverage; responsibility on sale to public agency.
1797.3. Written warranty; contents.
1797.4. Cumulative remedies; proscription against waiver.
1797.5. Copy of warranty provisions; display; posting.
1797.6. Records.
1797.7. Warranty service to be completed within specified time.

Cross References

Business practices of mobilehome licensees which are unlawful acts, see Health and Safety Code § 18060.5.
Manufactured Home Recovery Fund, grounds for claims for payment, see Health and Safety Code § 18070.3.
Sales involving foundation system installation, close of escrow, see Health and Safety Code § 18035.26.
Sales of new or used manufactured home or multiunit manufactured housing or used mobile home involving foundation system installation, warranty period, see Health and Safety Code § 18035.26.

§ 1797. Necessity of warranty

All new mobilehomes and manufactured homes sold to a buyer shall be covered by the warranty set forth in this chapter. *(Added by Stats.1971, c. 1492, p. 2944, § 1. Amended by Stats.1982, c. 730, p. 2904, § 1.)*

Cross References

Consumer affairs, see Business and Professions Code § 300 et seq.
Mobilehome and manufactured home defined for purposes of this Chapter, see Civil Code § 1797.1.
Sales involving foundation system installation, close of escrow, see Health and Safety Code § 18035.26.

§ 1797.1. Definitions

As used in this chapter:

(a) "Contractor" means any person who is a general building contractor within the meaning of Section 7057 of the Business and Professions Code.

(b) "Dealer" means any person who is a dealer within the meaning of Section 18002.6 of the Health and Safety Code.

(c) "Mobilehome" and "manufactured home" have the meanings, respectively, defined in Sections 18007 and 18008 of the Health and Safety Code.

(d) "Substantial defects in materials and workmanship" means defects objectively manifested by broken, ripped, cracked, stained, or missing parts or components, or workmanship resulting in improper function of materials, components, appliances, or systems as installed or manufactured by the contractor, dealer, or manufacturer. *(Added by Stats. 1971, c. 1492, p. 2944, § 1. Amended by Stats.1982, c. 730, p. 2904, § 2; Stats.1985, c. 763, § 1; Stats.1988, c. 793, § 1; Stats.1993, c. 458 (A.B.247), § 1.)*

Cross References

Mobilehome defined, see Health and Safety Code § 18211.

§ 1797.2. Application; warranty coverage; responsibility on sale to public agency

(a) The warranty provided for in this chapter shall apply to the manufacturer of the mobilehome or the manufactured home as well as to the contractor or dealer who sells the mobilehome or the manufactured home to the buyer. The warranty shall cover the electrical, plumbing, heating, cooling, fire safety, and structural systems, and all appliances of the mobilehome or manufactured home as installed or manufactured by the contractor, dealer, or manufacturer.

(b) Where a manufacturer sells a mobilehome or manufactured home directly to a city, city and county, or other public agency pursuant to the exception established in Section 18015.7, the manufacturer shall be responsible for providing the warranty required by this chapter. *(Added by Stats.1971, c. 1492, p. 2944, § 1. Amended by Stats.1982, c. 730, p. 2904, § 3; Stats.1985, c. 763, § 2; Stats.1993, c. 458 (A.B.247), § 2; Stats.1995, c. 185 (A.B.431), § 1.)*

Cross References

Contractor defined for purposes of this Chapter, see Civil Code § 1797.1.
Dealer defined for purposes of this Chapter, see Civil Code § 1797.1.
Mobilehome and manufactured home defined for purposes of this Chapter, see Civil Code § 1797.1.

§ 1797.3. Written warranty; contents

The mobilehome/manufactured home warranty from the contractor, manufacturer, or dealer to the buyer shall be set forth in a separate written document that reprints all of the provisions of this chapter and shall be delivered to the buyer by the contractor or dealer at the time the contract of sale is signed, and shall contain, but is not limited to, the following terms:

(a) That the mobilehome or manufactured home is free from any substantial defects in materials or workmanship.

(b) That the contractor, manufacturer, or dealer or any or all of them shall take appropriate corrective action at the site of the mobilehome or manufactured home in instances of substantial defects in materials or workmanship which become evident within one year from the date of delivery of the mobilehome or manufactured home to the buyer, provided the buyer or his or her transferee gives written notice of those defects to the contractor, manufacturer, or dealer at their business address not later than one year and 10 days after date of delivery.

(c) That the manufacturer and the contractor or dealer shall be jointly and severally liable to the buyer for the fulfillment of the terms of warranty, and that the buyer may notify either one or both of the need for appropriate corrective action in instances of substantial defects in materials or workmanship.

(d) That the address and the phone number of where to mail or deliver written notices of defects shall be set forth in the document.

(e) That the one-year warranty period applies to the plumbing, heating, electrical, cooling, fire safety, and struc-

§ 1797.3 OBLIGATIONS

tural systems and all appliances of the mobilehome or manufactured home.

(f) That, while the manufacturers of any or all appliances may also issue their own warranties, the primary responsibility for appropriate corrective action under the warranty rests with the contractor or dealer and the manufacturer, and the buyer should report all complaints to the contractor or dealer and the manufacturer initially.

(g) That, if corrective action taken by the manufacturer or the contractor or dealer fails to eliminate a substantial defect, then the material, system, appliance, or component shall be replaced in kind. As used in this subdivision, "replaced in kind" means (1) replacement with the identical material, system, appliance, or component, and, if not available (2) replacement with a comparable or better material, system, appliance, or component. (Added by Stats.1971, c. 1492, p. 2944, § 1. Amended by Stats.1973, c. 807, p. 1441, § 1; Stats.1982, c. 730, p. 2904, § 4; Stats.1985, c. 763, § 3; Stats.1990, c. 765 (A.B.4079), § 1; Stats.1993, c. 458 (A.B. 247), § 3.)

Cross References

Contractor defined for purposes of this Chapter, see Civil Code § 1797.1.
Dealer defined for purposes of this Chapter, see Civil Code § 1797.1.
Escrow accounts for new or used manufactured home or mobilehomes, see Health and Safety Code § 18035.
Manufactured housing, sales and escrows, contents of receipt for deposit, see Health and Safety Code § 18035.1.
Mobilehome accessory, equipment, see Health and Safety Code § 18008.5.
Mobilehome and manufactured home defined for purposes of this Chapter, see Civil Code § 1797.1.
Substantial defects in materials and workmanship defined for purposes of this Chapter, see Civil Code § 1797.1.

§ 1797.4. Cumulative remedies; proscription against waiver

The warranty under this chapter shall be in addition to, and not in derogation of, all other rights and privileges which the buyer may have under any other law or instrument. The contractor, manufacturer, or dealer shall not require the buyer to waive his or her rights under this chapter, and any waiver of these rights shall be deemed contrary to public policy and shall be unenforceable and void. (Added by Stats.1971, c. 1492, p. 2945, § 1. Amended by Stats.1993, c. 458 (A.B.247), § 4.)

Cross References

Contractor defined for purposes of this Chapter, see Civil Code § 1797.1.
Dealer defined for purposes of this Chapter, see Civil Code § 1797.1.
Waiver of advantage, law established for public reason, see Civil Code § 3513.
Waiver of code provisions unless against public policy, see Civil Code § 3268.
Warranties under sales contracts, see Civil Code § 1790 et seq.; Commercial Code § 2312 et seq.

§ 1797.5. Copy of warranty provisions; display; posting

Every contractor or dealer shall display a copy of all of the warranty provisions required by this chapter. The copy of the warranty provisions required by this chapter shall be posted in each area where purchase orders and conditional sales contracts are written. (Added by Stats.1974, c. 1286, p. 2792, § 1, operative July 1, 1975. Amended by Stats.1990, c. 765 (A.B.4079), § 2; Stats.1993, c. 458 (A.B.247), § 5.)

Cross References

Contractor defined for purposes of this Chapter, see Civil Code § 1797.1.
Dealer defined for purposes of this Chapter, see Civil Code § 1797.1.

§ 1797.6. Records

Manufacturers, contractors, and dealers shall keep records of all actions taken pursuant to this chapter, including all correspondence to or from the buyer for a period of three years from the date of delivery. (Added by Stats.1985, c. 763, § 4. Amended by Stats.1993, c. 458 (A.B.247), § 6.)

Cross References

Contractor defined for purposes of this Chapter, see Civil Code § 1797.1.
Dealer defined for purposes of this Chapter, see Civil Code § 1797.1.

§ 1797.7. Warranty service to be completed within specified time

The contractor, dealer, or manufacturer shall complete warranty service to correct all substantial defects within 90 days of receiving the buyer's written notice specified in subdivision (b) of Section 1797.3, unless there are circumstances which are beyond the control of the contractor, dealer, or manufacturer. (Added by Stats.1988, c. 793, § 2. Amended by Stats.1993, c. 458 (A.B.247), § 7.)

Cross References

Contractor defined for purposes of this Chapter, see Civil Code § 1797.1.
Dealer defined for purposes of this Chapter, see Civil Code § 1797.1.
Manufactured housing, citations and penalties for violation of specified sections, see Health and Safety Code § 18021.7.

CHAPTER 4. GREY MARKET GOODS

Section
1797.8. Definitions.
1797.81. Retail sellers; disclosures; signs; tickets, labels or tags.
1797.82. Retail dealers; disclosures in advertisements.
1797.83. Equivalent language.
1797.84. Construction with other laws.
1797.85. Retail sellers; violations; liability to buyer.
1797.86. Violations; unfair competition; grounds for rescission.

Cross References

Leases of new and used consumer goods, see Civil Code § 1795.4.
Reacquisition of vehicles, disclosure, see Civil Code § 1793.23.
Third-party dispute resolution, reasonable number of attempts, see Civil Code § 1793.22.

§ 1797.8. Definitions

(a) As used in this chapter, the term "grey market goods" means consumer goods bearing a trademark and normally accompanied by an express written warranty valid in the United States of America which are imported into the United States through channels other than the manufacturer's authorized United States distributor and which are not accompanied by the manufacturer's express written warranty valid in the United States.

(b) As used in this chapter, the term "sale" includes a lease of more than four months. *(Added by Stats.1986, c. 1497, § 2.)*

§ 1797.81. Retail sellers; disclosures; signs; tickets, labels or tags

(a) Every retail seller who offers grey market goods for sale shall post a conspicuous sign at the product's point of display and affix to the product or its package a conspicuous ticket, label, or tag disclosing any or all of the following, whichever is applicable:

(1) The item is not covered by a manufacturer's express written warranty valid in the United States (however, any implied warranty provided by law still exists).

(2) The item is not compatible with United States electrical currents.

(3) The item is not compatible with United States broadcast frequencies.

(4) Replacement parts are not available through the manufacturer's United States distributors.

(5) Compatible accessories are not available through the manufacturer's United States distributors.

(6) The item is not accompanied by instructions in English.

(7) The item is not eligible for a manufacturer's rebate.

(8) Any other incompatibility or nonconformity with relevant domestic standards known to the seller.

(b) The disclosure described in paragraph (1) of subdivision (a) shall not be required to be made by a retail seller with respect to grey market goods that are accompanied by an express written warranty provided by the retail seller, provided that each of the following conditions is satisfied:

(1) The protections and other benefits that are provided to the buyer by the express written warranty provided by the retail seller are equal to or better than the protections and other benefits that are provided to buyers in the United States of America by the manufacturer's express written warranty that normally accompanies the goods.

(2) The express written warranty conforms to the requirements of the Song-Beverly Consumer Warranty Act, (Chapter 1 (commencing with Section 1790)), including, but not limited to, the warranty disclosure standards specified in Section 1793.1, and the standards applicable to service and repair facilities specified in Section 1793.2.

(3) The retail seller has posted a conspicuous sign at the product's point of sale or display, or has affixed to the product or its package a conspicuous ticket, label, or tag that informs prospective buyers that copies of all of the warranties applicable to the products offered for sale by the retail seller are available to prospective buyers for inspection upon request.

(4) The retail seller has complied with the provisions on presale availability of written warranties set forth in the regulations of the Federal Trade Commission adopted pursuant to the federal Magnuson-Moss Warranty-Federal Trade Commission Improvement Act (see 15 U.S.C.A. Sec. 2302(b)(1)(A) and 16 C.F.R. 702.1 et seq.).

(c) Nothing in subdivision (b) shall affect the obligations of a retail seller to make the disclosures, if any, required by any other paragraph of subdivision (a). *(Added by Stats.1986, c. 1497, § 2.)*

Cross References

Grey market goods defined for purposes of this Chapter, see Civil Code § 1797.8.
Sale defined for purposes of this Chapter, see Civil Code § 1797.8.

§ 1797.82. Retail dealers; disclosures in advertisements

Every retail dealer who offers for sale grey market goods shall be required to disclose in any advertisement of those goods the disclosures required by Section 1797.81. The disclosure shall be made in a type of conspicuous size. *(Added by Stats.1986, c. 1497, § 2.)*

Cross References

Grey market goods defined for purposes of this Chapter, see Civil Code § 1797.8.
Sale defined for purposes of this Chapter, see Civil Code § 1797.8.

§ 1797.83. Equivalent language

In making the disclosures prescribed by this chapter, the retail seller may use reasonably equivalent language if necessary or appropriate to achieve a clearer, or more accurate, disclosure. *(Added by Stats.1986, c. 1497, § 2.)*

§ 1797.84. Construction with other laws

Nothing in this chapter shall be construed to authorize any sale of goods which is specifically prohibited by a federal or state statute or regulation or a local ordinance or regulation, or to relieve the seller of any responsibility for bringing the goods into compliance with any applicable federal or state statute or regulation or local ordinance or regulation. *(Added by Stats.1986, c. 1497, § 2.)*

Cross References

Sale defined for purposes of this Chapter, see Civil Code § 1797.8.

§ 1797.85. Retail sellers; violations; liability to buyer

Any retail seller who violates this chapter shall be liable to the buyer who returns the product for a refund, or credit on credit purchases, if the product purchased has not been used in a manner inconsistent with any printed instructions provided by the seller. *(Added by Stats.1986, c. 1497, § 2.)*

§ 1797.86. Violations; unfair competition; grounds for rescission

Any violation of this chapter constitutes unfair competition under Section 17200 of the Business and Professions Code, grounds for rescission under Section 1689 of this code, and an unfair method of competition or deceptive practice under Section 1770 of this code. *(Added by Stats.1986, c. 1497, § 2.)*

CHAPTER 5. HOME ROOF WARRANTIES

Section
1797.90. Application of chapter.

OBLIGATIONS

Section
1797.91. Contract for roofing materials or roof; warranty; writing requirement.
1797.92. Contracts on or after January 1, 1994; transferability of warranty.
1797.93. Lifetime warranty; disclosure of life to which it refers.
1797.94. Limit on transferability; form of provision.
1797.95. Roof warranties; standardization to meet requirements in other states.
1797.96. Newly constructed residential structure; provision of warranty disclosures prior to close of escrow.

Cross References

Leases of new and used consumer goods, see Civil Code § 1795.4.
Reacquisition of vehicles, disclosure, see Civil Code § 1793.23.
Third-party dispute resolution, reasonable number of attempts, see Civil Code § 1793.22.

§ 1797.90. Application of chapter

This chapter shall apply to all contracts and warranties for roofing materials used on a residential structure, including, but not limited to, a manufactured home or mobilehome, and to all contracts and warranties for the installation, repair, or replacement of all or any portion of the roof of a residential structure, including, but not limited to, a manufactured home or mobilehome. *(Added by Stats.1993, c. 835 (S.B.409), § 1.)*

§ 1797.91. Contract for roofing materials or roof; warranty; writing requirement

Any contract for roofing materials, or for the installation, repair, or replacement of all or any portion of the roof of a residential structure, including, but not limited to, a manufactured home or mobilehome, shall be in writing if the contract includes any warranty of the materials or workmanship that extends for any period of time beyond completion of the work. *(Added by Stats.1993, c. 835 (S.B.409), § 1.)*

§ 1797.92. Contracts on or after January 1, 1994; transferability of warranty

For any contract subject to this chapter that is entered into on or after January 1, 1994, the warranty obligations shall inure to the benefit of, and shall be directly enforceable by, all subsequent purchasers and transferees of the residential structure, without limitation, unless the contract contains a clear and conspicuous provision limiting transferability of the warranty. *(Added by Stats.1993, c. 835 (S.B.409), § 1.)*

§ 1797.93. Lifetime warranty; disclosure of life to which it refers

If any warranty subject to this chapter, uses the term "lifetime," "life," or a similar representation to describe the duration of the warranty, then the warranty shall disclose with such clarity and prominence as will be noticed and understood by prospective purchasers, the life to which the representation refers. *(Added by Stats.1993, c. 835 (S.B.409), § 1.)*

§ 1797.94. Limit on transferability; form of provision

Any warranty subject to this chapter, shall inure to the benefit of, and shall be directly enforceable by, all subsequent purchasers and transferees of the residential structure, without limitation, unless the warranty contains a provision limiting transferability of the warranty. A provision limiting transferability shall be set forth at the top of the first page of the warranty in 14-point boldface type, and shall be enclosed in a rectangular box in at least 4-point type.

(b)[1] Any disclosure required by Section 1797.93 shall also be set forth at the top of the first page of the warranty in 14-point boldface type, and shall be enclosed in a rectangular box in at least 4-point type. This disclosure may be included in a disclosure required under subdivision (a). *(Added by Stats.1993, c. 835 (S.B.409), § 1.)*

[1] Chaptered law did not contain a subdivision (a) designation.

§ 1797.95. Roof warranties; standardization to meet requirements in other states

A warrantor who provides roof warranties in multiple states may standardize the warranty to meet warranty requirements of other states. However, those standardized warranties shall meet requirements which are no less than those imposed by this chapter. *(Added by Stats.1993, c. 835 (S.B.409), § 1.)*

§ 1797.96. Newly constructed residential structure; provision of warranty disclosures prior to close of escrow

Where a warranty subject to this chapter is provided for the benefit of the purchaser of a newly constructed residential structure, the seller shall provide the warranty disclosures required by this chapter to the purchaser prior to the close of escrow. No transfer shall be invalidated for failure to comply with this section. *(Added by Stats.1993, c. 835 (S.B.409), § 1.)*

Title 1.8

PERSONAL DATA

Chapter	Section
1. Information Practices Act of 1977	1798

Cross References

Consumer fraud investigations, access to complaints and investigations by certain state agencies, see Government Code § 26509.
Disclosures of public records, by state or local agencies, waiver of exemptions, application of section, see Government Code § 6254.5.
Eligibility of disabled veteran business enterprise or small business enterprise, certification and determination, written declaration of applicant, transcripts of tax returns, see Government Code § 14840.
Office of Small Business and Disabled Veteran Business Enterprise Services, establishment, duties, see Government Code § 14839.
Public works, payroll records, rules and regulations, see Labor Code § 1776.
State agencies,
  Electronically collected personal information, distribution, see Government Code § 11015.5.
  Maintenance of permanent privacy policy, see Government Code § 11019.9.

CHAPTER 1. INFORMATION PRACTICES ACT OF 1977

Article	Section
1. General Provisions and Legislative Findings	1798

Article	Section
2. Definitions	1798.3
3. Office of Information Practices [Repealed]	
4. Notification Requirements [Repealed]	
5. Agency Requirements	1798.14
6. Conditions of Disclosure	1798.24
7. Accounting of Disclosures	1798.25
8. Access to Records and Administrative Remedies	1798.30
9. Civil Remedies	1798.45
10. Penalties	1798.55
11. Miscellaneous Provisions	1798.60
12. Construction with Other Laws	1798.70

Cross References

California Education Information System, see Education Code § 10601.

Childhood Lead Poisoning Prevention Act, legislative findings and declarations, posting of information, see Health and Safety Code § 124125.

Disclosure of tax return information to California Health Benefit Exchange, State Department of Health Care Services, Managed Risk Medical Insurance Board, and county departments and agencies, construction with these provisions, see Revenue and Taxation Code § 19548.5.

Duties of state agency heads relative to records and information collection practices, see Government Code § 12274.

Employees, wages, hours and working conditions, right to inspect records, see Labor Code § 1198.5.

Hazardous waste control,
  Facilities or transportable treatment units operating pursuant to permit-by-rule, notifications, see Health and Safety Code § 25205.13.
  Generators deemed to be operating under grants of conditional authorization, notification, see Health and Safety Code § 25200.3.

Health records, patient access, see Health and Safety Code § 123100 et seq.

Ken Maddy California Cancer Registry, confidentiality of information, see Health and Safety Code § 103885.

Medical information, inapplicability of this chapter to disclosure, see Civil Code § 56.29.

Office of Privacy Protection created, see Government Code § 11549.5.

Parkinson's Disease Registry, confidentiality of collected information, see Health and Safety Code § 103865.

Patient access to health records, see Health and Safety Code §§ 123135, 123140.

Privacy or confidentiality of information or material provided to Nationwide Multistate Licensing System and Registry, debt collector licensing, see Financial Code § 100016.

Privacy or confidentiality of information provided to Nationwide Mortgage Licensing System and Registry, see Financial Code § 50151.

Public Records Act, see Government Code § 6250 et seq.

Teacher credentialing, production of information, confidentiality, see Education Code § 44341.

Transfer of inmates, transmission of mental health records, confidentiality, see Penal Code § 5073.

Use of data identifying claimants owing past-due child support, compliance with privacy protection laws, see Insurance Code § 13552.

Vital records and health statistics, confidentiality of information, personal access to information, see Health and Safety Code § 103850.

ARTICLE 1. GENERAL PROVISIONS AND LEGISLATIVE FINDINGS

Section
1798. Citation of chapter.
1798.1. Legislative declaration and findings.
1798.2. Repealed.

Cross References

Investigative reporting agencies, remedies, disclosure of personal information obtained regarding consumer in lieu of using services of an investigative reporting agency, see Civil Code § 1786.53.

§ 1798. Citation of chapter

This chapter shall be known and may be cited as the Information Practices Act of 1977. *(Added by Stats.1977, c. 709, p. 2269, § 1, operative July 1, 1978.)*

Cross References

Drug Medi–Cal services, development of state plan amendment or waiver, criminal investigations, see Welfare and Institutions Code § 14124.24.

Office of Privacy Protection created, see Government Code § 11549.5.

Professional photocopiers, see Business and Professions Code § 22450 et seq.

§ 1798.1. Legislative declaration and findings

The Legislature declares that the right to privacy is a personal and fundamental right protected by Section 1 of Article I of the Constitution of California and by the United States Constitution and that all individuals have a right of privacy in information pertaining to them. The Legislature further makes the following findings:

(a) The right to privacy is being threatened by the indiscriminate collection, maintenance, and dissemination of personal information and the lack of effective laws and legal remedies.

(b) The increasing use of computers and other sophisticated information technology has greatly magnified the potential risk to individual privacy that can occur from the maintenance of personal information.

(c) In order to protect the privacy of individuals, it is necessary that the maintenance and dissemination of personal information be subject to strict limits. *(Added by Stats. 1977, c. 709, p. 2269, § 1, operative July 1, 1978.)*

Cross References

Individual defined for purposes of this Chapter, see Civil Code § 1798.3.

Personal information defined for purposes of this Chapter, see Civil Code § 1798.3.

§ 1798.2. Repealed by Stats.1985, c. 595, § 1

ARTICLE 2. DEFINITIONS

Section
1798.3. Definitions.

§ 1798.3. Definitions

As used in this chapter:

§ 1798.3

(a) The term "personal information" means any information that is maintained by an agency that identifies or describes an individual, including, but not limited to, the individual's name, social security number, physical description, home address, home telephone number, education, financial matters, and medical or employment history. It includes statements made by, or attributed to, the individual.

(b) The term "agency" means every state office, officer, department, division, bureau, board, commission, or other state agency, except that the term agency shall not include:

(1) The California Legislature.

(2) Any agency established under Article VI of the California Constitution.

(3) The State Compensation Insurance Fund, except as to any records that contain personal information about the employees of the State Compensation Insurance Fund.

(4) A local agency, as defined in Section 7920.510 of the Government Code.

(c) The term "disclose" means to disclose, release, transfer, disseminate, or otherwise communicate all or any part of any record orally, in writing, or by electronic or any other means to any person or entity.

(d) The term "individual" means a natural person.

(e) The term "maintain" includes maintain, acquire, use, or disclose.

(f) The term "person" means any natural person, corporation, partnership, limited liability company, firm, or association.

(g) The term "record" means any file or grouping of information about an individual that is maintained by an agency by reference to an identifying particular such as the individual's name, photograph, finger or voice print, or a number or symbol assigned to the individual.

(h) The term "system of records" means one or more records, which pertain to one or more individuals, which is maintained by any agency, from which information is retrieved by the name of an individual or by some identifying number, symbol, or other identifying particular assigned to the individual.

(i) The term "governmental entity," except as used in Section 1798.26, means any branch of the federal government or of the local government.

(j) The term "commercial purpose" means any purpose that has financial gain as a major objective. It does not include the gathering or dissemination of newsworthy facts by a publisher or broadcaster.

(k) The term "regulatory agency" means the Department of * * * Financial Protection and Innovation, the Department of Insurance, the Bureau of Real Estate, and agencies of the United States or of any other state responsible for regulating financial institutions. *(Added by Stats.1977, c. 709, p. 2269, § 1, operative July 1, 1978. Amended by Stats.1978, c. 874, p. 2741, § 1, eff. Sept. 19, 1978; Stats.1979, c. 143, p. 330, § 1, eff. June 22, 1979; Stats.1980, c. 174, p. 391, § 1; Stats.1982, c. 604, p. 2579, § 1; Stats.1985, c. 595, § 2; Stats.1987, c. 1453, § 1; Stats.1994, c. 1010 (S.B.2053), § 40; Stats.1996, c. 1064 (A.B.3351), § 4, operative July 1, 1997; Stats.2005, c. 677 (S.B.512), § 1, eff. Oct. 7, 2005; Stats.2013, c. 352 (A.B.1317), § 52, eff. Sept. 26, 2013, operative July 1, 2013; Stats.2021, c. 615 (A.B.474), § 43, eff. Jan. 1, 2022, operative Jan. 1, 2023; Stats.2022, c. 452 (S.B.1498), §§ 24, 25, eff. Jan. 1, 2023.)*

Cross References

Access to public records, disclosure of personal financial information not required, see Government Code § 7927.425.

Asilomar conference grounds, records, see Public Resources Code § 5080.25.

California Environmental Contaminant Biomonitoring Program, prohibition on sharing personal information, see Health and Safety Code § 105444.

Department of Corrections and Rehabilitation, prohibition on unauthorized removal from state prison of documents, computers, or computer accessible media containing personal information relating to Department of Corrections employees, see Penal Code § 5029.

Pacific Grove–Asilomar Operating Corporation, business and financial records, see Public Resources Code § 5080.24.

Subpoena duces tecum for records exempt from public disclosure under Public Records Act and maintained by state or local agency, see Code of Civil Procedure § 1985.4.

University of California, employee access to personal information in records, see Education Code § 92612.

ARTICLE 3. OFFICE OF INFORMATION PRACTICES [REPEALED]

§§ 1798.4 to 1798.8. Repealed by Stats.1991–1992, 1st Ex. Sess., c. 21 (A.B.66), § 33.1, eff. March 1, 1993

ARTICLE 4. NOTIFICATION REQUIREMENTS [REPEALED]

§§ 1798.9 to 1798.11. Repealed by Stats.1991–1992, 1st Ex.Sess., c. 21 (A.B.66), §§ 33.2 to 33.4, eff. March 1, 1993

ARTICLE 5. AGENCY REQUIREMENTS

Section
1798.14. Contents of records.
1798.15. Sources of information.
1798.16. Personal information; maintaining sources of information.
1798.17. Notice; periodic provision; contents.
1798.18. Maintenance of records; standards; transfers of records outside state government.
1798.19. Contracts for the operation or maintenance of records; requirements of chapter; employees of agency.
1798.20. Rules of conduct; instruction.
1798.21. Safeguards; administrative, technical and physical.
1798.22. Designation of employee responsible for agency compliance.
1798.23. Department of Justice; periodic review of personal information; exemption from access.

§ 1798.14. Contents of records

Each agency shall maintain in its records only personal information which is relevant and necessary to accomplish a purpose of the agency required or authorized by the California Constitution or statute or mandated by the federal government. *(Added by Stats.1977, c. 709, p. 2269, § 1, operative July 1, 1978. Amended by Stats.1985, c. 595, § 5.)*

Cross References

Agency defined for purposes of this Chapter, see Civil Code § 1798.3.
Maintain defined for purposes of this Chapter, see Civil Code § 1798.3.
Personal information defined for purposes of this Chapter, see Civil Code § 1798.3.
Record defined for purposes of this Chapter, see Civil Code § 1798.3.

§ 1798.15. Sources of information

Each agency shall collect personal information to the greatest extent practicable directly from the individual who is the subject of the information rather than from another source. *(Added by Stats.1977, c. 709, p. 2269, § 1, operative July 1, 1978. Amended by Stats.1985, c. 595, § 6.)*

Cross References

Agency defined for purposes of this Chapter, see Civil Code § 1798.3.
Individual defined for purposes of this Chapter, see Civil Code § 1798.3.
Personal information defined for purposes of this Chapter, see Civil Code § 1798.3.

§ 1798.16. Personal information; maintaining sources of information

(a) Whenever an agency collects personal information, the agency shall maintain the source or sources of the information, unless the source is the data subject or he or she has received a copy of the source document, including, but not limited to, the name of any source who is an individual acting in his or her own private or individual capacity. If the source is an agency, governmental entity or other organization, such as a corporation or association, this requirement can be met by maintaining the name of the agency, governmental entity, or organization, as long as the smallest reasonably identifiable unit of that agency, governmental entity, or organization is named.

(b) On or after July 1, 2001, unless otherwise authorized by the Department of Information Technology pursuant to Executive Order D–3–99, whenever an agency electronically collects personal information, as defined by Section 11015.5 of the Government Code, the agency shall retain the source or sources or any intermediate form of the information, if either are created or possessed by the agency, unless the source is the data subject that has requested that the information be discarded or the data subject has received a copy of the source document.

(c) The agency shall maintain the source or sources of the information in a readily accessible form so as to be able to provide it to the data subject when they inspect any record pursuant to Section 1798.34. This section shall not apply if the source or sources are exempt from disclosure under the provisions of this chapter. *(Added by Stats.1977, c. 709, p. 2269, § 1, operative July 1, 1978. Amended by Stats.1998, c. 429 (S.B.1386), § 1; Stats.1999, c. 784 (A.B.724), § 7, eff. Oct. 10, 1999.)*

Cross References

Agency defined for purposes of this Chapter, see Civil Code § 1798.3.
Governmental entity defined for purposes of this Chapter, see Civil Code § 1798.3.
Individual defined for purposes of this Chapter, see Civil Code § 1798.3.
Maintain defined for purposes of this Chapter, see Civil Code § 1798.3.
Personal information defined for purposes of this Chapter, see Civil Code § 1798.3.
Record defined for purposes of this Chapter, see Civil Code § 1798.3.

§ 1798.17. Notice; periodic provision; contents

Each agency shall provide on or with any form used to collect personal information from individuals the notice specified in this section. When contact with the individual is of a regularly recurring nature, an initial notice followed by a periodic notice of not more than one-year intervals shall satisfy this requirement. This requirement is also satisfied by notification to individuals of the availability of the notice in annual tax-related pamphlets or booklets provided for them. The notice shall include all of the following:

(a) The name of the agency and the division within the agency that is requesting the information.

(b) The title, business address, and telephone number of the agency official who is responsible for the system of records and who shall, upon request, inform an individual regarding the location of his or her records and the categories of any persons who use the information in those records.

(c) The authority, whether granted by statute, regulation, or executive order which authorizes the maintenance of the information.

(d) With respect to each item of information, whether submission of such information is mandatory or voluntary.

(e) The consequences, if any, of not providing all or any part of the requested information.

(f) The principal purpose or purposes within the agency for which the information is to be used.

(g) Any known or foreseeable disclosures which may be made of the information pursuant to subdivision (e) or (f) of Section 1798.24.

(h) The individual's right of access to records containing personal information which are maintained by the agency.

This section does not apply to any enforcement document issued by an employee of a law enforcement agency in the performance of his or her duties wherein the violator is provided an exact copy of the document, or to accident reports whereby the parties of interest may obtain a copy of the report pursuant to Section 20012 of the Vehicle Code.

The notice required by this section does not apply to agency requirements for an individual to provide his or her name, identifying number, photograph, address, or similar identifying information, if this information is used only for the purpose of identification and communication with the individual by the agency, except that requirements for an individual's social security number shall conform with the provisions of the Federal Privacy Act of 1974 (Public Law 93–579). *(Added by Stats.1977, c. 709, p. 2269, § 1, operative July*

1, 1978. Amended by Stats.1978, c. 874, p. 2744, § 3.5, eff. Sept. 19, 1978; Stats.1982, c. 604, p. 2582, § 2.5; Stats.1985, c. 595, § 7.)

Cross References

Agency defined for purposes of this Chapter, see Civil Code § 1798.3.
Escrow agents, employment applications, see Financial Code § 17419.
Individual defined for purposes of this Chapter, see Civil Code § 1798.3.
Person defined for purposes of this Chapter, see Civil Code § 1798.3.
Personal information defined for purposes of this Chapter, see Civil Code § 1798.3.
Record defined for purposes of this Chapter, see Civil Code § 1798.3.
State agencies, electronically collected personal information, distribution, see Government Code § 11015.5.
System of records defined for purposes of this Chapter, see Civil Code § 1798.3.

§ 1798.18. Maintenance of records; standards; transfers of records outside state government

Each agency shall maintain all records, to the maximum extent possible, with accuracy, relevance, timeliness, and completeness.

Such standard need not be met except when such records are used to make any determination about the individual. When an agency transfers a record outside of state government, it shall correct, update, withhold, or delete any portion of the record that it knows or has reason to believe is inaccurate or untimely. *(Added by Stats.1977, c. 709, p. 2269, § 1, operative July 1, 1978.)*

Cross References

Agency defined for purposes of this Chapter, see Civil Code § 1798.3.
Child Abuse and Neglect Reporting Act, index of reports, notice to child protection agencies or district attorneys, availability of information, see Penal Code § 11170.
Individual defined for purposes of this Chapter, see Civil Code § 1798.3.
Maintain defined for purposes of this Chapter, see Civil Code § 1798.3.
Record defined for purposes of this Chapter, see Civil Code § 1798.3.

§ 1798.19. Contracts for the operation or maintenance of records; requirements of chapter; employees of agency

Each agency when it provides by contract for the operation or maintenance of records containing personal information to accomplish an agency function, shall cause, consistent with its authority, the requirements of this chapter to be applied to those records. For purposes of Article 10 (commencing with Section 1798.55), any contractor and any employee of the contractor, if the contract is agreed to on or after July 1, 1978, shall be considered to be an employee of an agency. Local government functions mandated by the state are not deemed agency functions within the meaning of this section. *(Added by Stats.1977, c. 709, p. 2269, § 1, operative July 1, 1978. Amended by Stats.1978, c. 874, p. 2744, § 4, eff. Sept. 19, 1978; Stats.1985, c. 595, § 8.)*

Cross References

Agency defined for purposes of this Chapter, see Civil Code § 1798.3.
Personal information defined for purposes of this Chapter, see Civil Code § 1798.3.
Record defined for purposes of this Chapter, see Civil Code § 1798.3.

§ 1798.20. Rules of conduct; instruction

Each agency shall establish rules of conduct for persons involved in the design, development, operation, disclosure, or maintenance of records containing personal information and instruct each such person with respect to such rules and the requirements of this chapter, including any other rules and procedures adopted pursuant to this chapter and the remedies and penalties for noncompliance. *(Added by Stats.1977, c. 709, p. 2269, § 1, operative July 1, 1978. Amended by Stats.1985, c. 595, § 9.)*

Cross References

Agency defined for purposes of this Chapter, see Civil Code § 1798.3.
Person defined for purposes of this Chapter, see Civil Code § 1798.3.
Personal information defined for purposes of this Chapter, see Civil Code § 1798.3.
Record defined for purposes of this Chapter, see Civil Code § 1798.3.

§ 1798.21. Safeguards; administrative, technical and physical

Each agency shall establish appropriate and reasonable administrative, technical, and physical safeguards to ensure compliance with the provisions of this chapter, to ensure the security and confidentiality of records, and to protect against anticipated threats or hazards to their security or integrity which could result in any injury. *(Added by Stats.1977, c. 709, p. 2269, § 1, operative July 1, 1978.)*

Cross References

Agency defined for purposes of this Chapter, see Civil Code § 1798.3.
Record defined for purposes of this Chapter, see Civil Code § 1798.3.

§ 1798.22. Designation of employee responsible for agency compliance

Each agency shall designate an agency employee to be responsible for ensuring that the agency complies with all of the provisions of this chapter. *(Added by Stats.1977, c. 709, p. 2269, § 1, operative July 1, 1978.)*

Cross References

Agency defined for purposes of this Chapter, see Civil Code § 1798.3.
State agencies, electronically collected personal information, distribution, see Government Code § 11015.5.

§ 1798.23. Department of Justice; periodic review of personal information; exemption from access

The Department of Justice shall review all personal information in its possession every five years commencing July 1, 1978, to determine whether it should continue to be exempt from access pursuant to Section 1798.40. *(Added by*

Stats.1977, c. 709, p. 2269, § 1, operative July 1, 1978. Amended by Stats.1985, c. 595, § 10.)

Cross References

Personal information defined for purposes of this Chapter, see Civil Code § 1798.3.

ARTICLE 6. CONDITIONS OF DISCLOSURE

Section
1798.24. Personal information.
1798.24a. Exception; screening of prospective concessionaires.
1798.24b. Disclosure of information to protection and advocacy agency for rights of persons with disabilities.

§ 1798.24. Personal information

An agency shall not disclose any personal information in a manner that would link the information disclosed to the individual to whom it pertains unless the information is disclosed, as follows:

(a) To the individual to whom the information pertains.

(b) With the prior written voluntary consent of the individual to whom the information pertains, but only if that consent has been obtained not more than 30 days before the disclosure, or in the time limit agreed to by the individual in the written consent.

(c) To the duly appointed guardian or conservator of the individual or a person representing the individual if it can be proven with reasonable certainty through the possession of agency forms, documents, or correspondence that this person is the authorized representative of the individual to whom the information pertains.

(d) To those officers, employees, attorneys, agents, or volunteers of the agency that have custody of the information if the disclosure is relevant and necessary in the ordinary course of the performance of their official duties and is related to the purpose for which the information was acquired.

(e) To a person, or to another agency if the transfer is necessary for the transferee agency to perform its constitutional or statutory duties, and the use is compatible with a purpose for which the information was collected and the use or transfer is in accordance with Section 1798.25. With respect to information transferred from a law enforcement or regulatory agency, or information transferred to another law enforcement or regulatory agency, a use is compatible if the use of the information requested is needed in an investigation of unlawful activity under the jurisdiction of the requesting agency or for licensing, certification, or regulatory purposes by that agency.

(f) To a governmental entity if required by state or federal law.

(g) Pursuant to the California Public Records Act (* * * Division 10 (commencing with Section 7920.000) of * * * Title 1 of the Government Code).

(h) To a person who has provided the agency with advance, adequate written assurance that the information will be used solely for statistical research or reporting purposes, but only if the information to be disclosed is in a form that will not identify any individual.

(i) Pursuant to a determination by the agency that maintains information that compelling circumstances exist that affect the health or safety of an individual, if upon the disclosure notification is transmitted to the individual to whom the information pertains at the individual's last known address. Disclosure shall not be made if it is in conflict with other state or federal laws.

(j) To the State Archives as a record that has sufficient historical or other value to warrant its continued preservation by the California state government, or for evaluation by the Director of General Services or the director's designee to determine whether the record has further administrative, legal, or fiscal value.

(k) To any person pursuant to a subpoena, court order, or other compulsory legal process if, before the disclosure, the agency reasonably attempts to notify the individual to whom the record pertains, and if the notification is not prohibited by law.

(*l*) To any person pursuant to a search warrant.

(m) Pursuant to Article 3 (commencing with Section 1800) of Chapter 1 of Division 2 of the Vehicle Code.

(n) For the sole purpose of verifying and paying government health care service claims made pursuant to Division 9 (commencing with Section 10000) of the Welfare and Institutions Code.

(*o*) To a law enforcement or regulatory agency when required for an investigation of unlawful activity or for licensing, certification, or regulatory purposes, unless the disclosure is otherwise prohibited by law.

(p) To another person or governmental organization to the extent necessary to obtain information from the person or governmental organization for an investigation by the agency of a failure to comply with a specific state law that the agency is responsible for enforcing.

(q) To an adopted person and disclosure is limited to general background information pertaining to the adopted person's biological parents, if the information does not include or reveal the identity of the biological parents.

(r) To a child or a grandchild of an adopted person and disclosure is limited to medically necessary information pertaining to the adopted person's biological parents. However, the information, or the process for obtaining the information, shall not include or reveal the identity of the biological parents. The State Department of Social Services shall adopt regulations governing the release of information pursuant to this subdivision. The regulations shall require licensed adoption agencies to provide the same services provided by the department as established by this subdivision.

(s) To a committee of the Legislature or to a Member of the Legislature, or the member's staff if authorized in writing by the member, if the member has permission to obtain the information from the individual to whom it pertains or if the member provides reasonable assurance that the member is acting on behalf of the individual.

(t)(1) To the University of California, a nonprofit educational institution, an established nonprofit research institu-

§ 1798.24

tion performing health or social services research, the Cradle-to-Career Data System, for purposes consistent with the creation and execution of the Cradle-to-Career Data System Act pursuant to Article 2 (commencing with Section 10860) of Chapter 8.5 of Part 7 of Division 1 of Title 1 of the Education Code, or, in the case of education-related data, another nonprofit entity, conducting scientific research, if the request for information is approved by the Committee for the Protection of Human Subjects (CPHS) for the California Health and Human Services Agency (CHHSA) or an institutional review board, as authorized in paragraphs (5) and (6). The approval shall include a review and determination that all the following criteria have been satisfied:

(A) The researcher has provided a plan sufficient to protect personal information from improper use and disclosures, including sufficient administrative, physical, and technical safeguards to protect personal information from reasonable anticipated threats to the security or confidentiality of the information.

(B) The researcher has provided a sufficient plan to destroy or return all personal information as soon as it is no longer needed for the research project, unless the researcher has demonstrated an ongoing need for the personal information for the research project and has provided a long-term plan sufficient to protect the confidentiality of that information.

(C) The researcher has provided sufficient written assurances that the personal information will not be reused or disclosed to any other person or entity, or used in any manner, not approved in the research protocol, except as required by law or for authorized oversight of the research project.

(2) The CPHS shall enter into a written agreement with the Office of Cradle-to-Career Data, as defined in Section 10862 of the Education Code, to assist the managing entity of that office in its role as the institutional review board for the Cradle-to-Career Data System.

(3) The CPHS or institutional review board shall, at a minimum, accomplish all of the following as part of its review and approval of the research project for the purpose of protecting personal information held in agency databases:

(A) Determine whether the requested personal information is needed to conduct the research.

(B) Permit access to personal information only if it is needed for the research project.

(C) Permit access only to the minimum necessary personal information needed for the research project.

(D) Require the assignment of unique subject codes that are not derived from personal information in lieu of social security numbers if the research can still be conducted without social security numbers.

(E) If feasible, and if cost, time, and technical expertise permit, require the agency to conduct a portion of the data processing for the researcher to minimize the release of personal information.

(4) Reasonable costs to the agency associated with the agency's process of protecting personal information under the conditions of CPHS approval may be billed to the researcher, including, but not limited to, the agency's costs for conducting a portion of the data processing for the researcher, removing personal information, encrypting or otherwise securing personal information, or assigning subject codes.

(5) The CPHS may enter into written agreements to enable other institutional review boards to provide the data security approvals required by this subdivision, if the data security requirements set forth in this subdivision are satisfied.

(6) Pursuant to paragraph (5), the CPHS shall enter into a written agreement with the institutional review board established pursuant to former Section 49079.6 of the Education Code. The agreement shall authorize, commencing July 1, 2010, or the date upon which the written agreement is executed, whichever is later, that board to provide the data security approvals required by this subdivision, if the data security requirements set forth in this subdivision and the act specified in subdivision (a) of Section 49079.5 of the Education Code are satisfied.

(u) To an insurer if authorized by Chapter 5 (commencing with Section 10900) of Division 4 of the Vehicle Code.

(v) Pursuant to Section 450, 452, 8009, or 18396 of the Financial Code.

(w) For the sole purpose of participation in interstate data sharing of prescription drug monitoring program information pursuant to the California Uniform Controlled Substances Act (Division 10 (commencing with Section 11000) of the Health and Safety Code), if disclosure is limited to prescription drug monitoring program information.

This article does not require the disclosure of personal information to the individual to whom the information pertains if that information may otherwise be withheld as set forth in Section 1798.40. (Added by Stats.1977, c. 709, p. 2269, § 1, operative July 1, 1978. Amended by Stats.1978, c. 874, p. 2745, § 5, eff. Sept. 19, 1978; Stats.1979, c. 143, p. 332, § 2, eff. June 22, 1979; Stats.1982, c. 604, p. 2583, § 3; Stats.1982, c. 957, p. 3454, § 1; Stats.1984, c. 2, § 1; Stats.1984, c. 724, § 1; Stats.1985, c. 595, § 11; Stats.1987, c. 1453, § 2; Stats.1991–1992, 1st Ex.Sess., c. 21 (A.B.66), § 33.5; Stats.1995, c. 480 (A.B.1482), § 1.1, eff. Oct. 2, 1995, operative Oct. 2, 1995; Stats.2005, c. 241 (S.B.13), § 2; Stats.2006, c. 567 (A.B.2303), § 2.5; Stats.2008, c. 501 (A.B. 2749), § 1; Stats.2009–2010, 5th Ex.Sess., c. 1 (S.B.2), § 1, eff. April 12, 2010; Stats.2010, c. 725 (A.B.1612), § 1, eff. Oct. 19, 2010; Stats.2014, c. 64 (A.B.2742), § 2, eff. Jan. 1, 2015; Stats.2018, c. 478 (A.B.1751), § 1, eff. Jan. 1, 2019; Stats.2021, c. 615 (A.B.474), § 44, eff. Jan. 1, 2022, operative Jan. 1, 2023; Stats.2021, c. 144 (A.B.132), § 1, eff. July 27, 2021; Stats.2021, c. 696 (A.B.172), § 1, eff. Oct. 8, 2021; Stats.2022, c. 28 (S.B.1380), § 21, eff. Jan. 1, 2023.)

Cross References

Access to minimum amount of potentially identifiable data through research environment, violation of data use agreement, permissible access, limits on release of personal information, see Health and Safety Code § 127673.83.

Agency defined for purposes of this Chapter, see Civil Code § 1798.3.

Bond funds, application from prospective donor of property, signed authorization as consent to disclosure, see Public Resources Code § 37034.

Community Care Facilities Act, pre-license in-home interviews, prospective foster parents, licensing records, see Health and Safety Code § 1521.5.

Confidentiality of public social services records, see Welfare and Institutions Code § 10850.

Controlled Substance Utilization Review and Evaluation System (CURES), confidentiality, see Health and Safety Code § 11165.

Department of Motor Vehicles, records,
  Application of confidentiality of records law to specified entities, see Vehicle Code § 1808.23.
  Residence addresses, see Vehicle Code § 1808.21.

Disclose defined for purposes of this Chapter, see Civil Code § 1798.3.

Disclosure of medical information by authorization, see Civil Code § 56.20 et seq.

EMT–P employer reports relating to disciplinary action, disclosure of investigative files, see Health and Safety Code § 1799.112.

Establishment of procedures for providing materials to individuals for research related to firearm violence, identifying information, see Penal Code § 14240.

Exemptions from public disclosure of items in custody of State Archives, exemption not applicable to item 75 years after it was created, notice of public access, see Government Code § 12237.

Gambling Control Act, disclosure of information, see Business and Professions Code § 19821.

Governmental entity defined for purposes of this Chapter, see Civil Code § 1798.3.

Individual defined for purposes of this Chapter, see Civil Code § 1798.3.

Inspection of public records, other exemptions from disclosure, see Government Code § 6276.34.

Judges' Retirement Law, employment of retired judges, compensation reports, see Government Code § 75080.

Judges' Retirement System II, employment of retired judges, compensation reports, see Government Code § 75580.

Maintain defined for purposes of this Chapter, see Civil Code § 1798.3.

Person defined for purposes of this Chapter, see Civil Code § 1798.3.

Personal information defined for purposes of this Chapter, see Civil Code § 1798.3.

Record defined for purposes of this Chapter, see Civil Code § 1798.3.

Regulatory agency defined for purposes of this Chapter, see Civil Code § 1798.3.

Search warrants, see Penal Code § 1523 et seq.

Sharing of electronically collected personal information with California Community College district, user consent, proper use, see Government Code § 53087.9.

Standard form fire insurance policy, release of information to insurer in case of declaration of disaster, see Insurance Code § 2085.

State Civil Service Equal Employment Opportunity Program, departmental directors, responsibilities, see Government Code § 19794.

Teacher credentialing, nonpersonally identifiable teacher identification numbers, see Education Code § 44230.5.

§ 1798.24a. Exception; screening of prospective concessionaires

Notwithstanding Section 1798.24, information may be disclosed to any city, county, city and county, or district, or any officer or official thereof, if a written request is made to a local law enforcement agency and the information is needed to assist in the screening of a prospective concessionaire, and any affiliate or associate thereof, as these terms are defined in subdivision (k) of Section 432.7 of the Labor Code for purposes of consenting to, or approving of, the prospective concessionaire's application for, or acquisition of, any beneficial interest in a concession, lease, or other property interest. However, any summary criminal history information that may be disclosed pursuant to this section shall be limited to information pertaining to criminal convictions. *(Added by Stats.1992, c. 1026 (S.B.1769), § 2.)*

Cross References

Agency defined for purposes of this Chapter, see Civil Code § 1798.3.

§ 1798.24b. Disclosure of information to protection and advocacy agency for rights of persons with disabilities

(a) Notwithstanding Section 1798.24, except subdivision (v) thereof, information shall be disclosed to the protection and advocacy agency designated by the Governor in this state pursuant to federal law to protect and advocate for the rights of people with disabilities, as described in Division 4.7 (commencing with Section 4900) of the Welfare and Institutions Code.

(b) Information that shall be disclosed pursuant to this section includes all of the following information:

(1) Name.

(2) Address.

(3) Telephone number.

(4) Any other information necessary to identify that person whose consent is necessary for either of the following purposes:

(A) To enable the protection and advocacy agency to exercise its authority and investigate incidents of abuse or neglect of people with disabilities.

(B) To obtain access to records pursuant to Section 4903 of the Welfare and Institutions Code. *(Added by Stats.1991, c. 534 (S.B.1088), § 2. Amended by Stats.2003, c. 878 (S.B.577), § 2.)*

Cross References

Agency defined for purposes of this Chapter, see Civil Code § 1798.3.
Person defined for purposes of this Chapter, see Civil Code § 1798.3.
Record defined for purposes of this Chapter, see Civil Code § 1798.3.

ARTICLE 7. ACCOUNTING OF DISCLOSURES

Section
1798.25. Accounting for disclosure to law enforcement or regulatory agency; contents; routine disclosures.
1798.26. Motor vehicles; sale of registration information or information from drivers' licenses files; administrative procedures.
1798.27. Retention of accounting and original documents.
1798.28. Correction of errors; notation of disputes; notice.
1798.29. Agencies owning, licensing, or maintaining computerized data including personal information; disclosure of security breach; notice requirements.

§ 1798.25. Accounting for disclosure to law enforcement or regulatory agency; contents; routine disclosures

(a) Each agency shall keep an accurate accounting of the date, nature, and purpose of each disclosure of a record made pursuant to subdivision (i), (k), (*l*), (*o*), or (p) of Section

1798.24. This accounting shall also be required for disclosures made pursuant to subdivision (e) or (f) of Section 1798.24 unless notice of the type of disclosure has been provided pursuant to Sections 1798.9 and 1798.10. The accounting shall also include the name, title, and business address of the person or agency to whom the disclosure was made. For the purpose of an accounting of a disclosure made under subdivision (o) of Section 1798.24, it shall be sufficient for a law enforcement or regulatory agency to record the date of disclosure, the law enforcement or regulatory agency requesting the disclosure, and whether the purpose of the disclosure is for an investigation of unlawful activity under the jurisdiction of the requesting agency, or for licensing, certification, or regulatory purposes by that agency.

(b) Routine disclosures of information pertaining to crimes, offenders, and suspected offenders to law enforcement or regulatory agencies of federal, state, and local government shall be deemed to be disclosures pursuant to subdivision (e) of Section 1798.24 for the purpose of meeting this requirement. *(Added by Stats.1977, c. 709, p. 2269, § 1, operative July 1, 1978. Amended by Stats.1978, c. 874, p. 2747, § 6, eff. Sept. 19, 1978; Stats.1985, c. 595, § 12; Stats.1987, c. 1453, § 3; Stats.2018, c. 92 (S.B.1289), § 36, eff. Jan. 1, 2019.)*

Cross References

Agency defined for purposes of this Chapter, see Civil Code § 1798.3.
Person defined for purposes of this Chapter, see Civil Code § 1798.3.
Record defined for purposes of this Chapter, see Civil Code § 1798.3.
Regulatory agency defined for purposes of this Chapter, see Civil Code § 1798.3.

§ 1798.26. Motor vehicles; sale of registration information or information from drivers' licenses files; administrative procedures

With respect to the sale of information concerning the registration of any vehicle or the sale of information from the files of drivers' licenses, the Department of Motor Vehicles shall, by regulation, establish administrative procedures under which any person making a request for information shall be required to identify himself or herself and state the reason for making the request. These procedures shall provide for the verification of the name and address of the person making a request for the information and the department may require the person to produce the information as it determines is necessary in order to ensure that the name and address of the person are his or her true name and address. These procedures may provide for a 10-day delay in the release of the requested information. These procedures shall also provide for notification to the person to whom the information primarily relates, as to what information was provided and to whom it was provided. The department shall, by regulation, establish a reasonable period of time for which a record of all the foregoing shall be maintained.

The procedures required by this subdivision do not apply to any governmental entity, any person who has applied for and has been issued a requester code by the department, or any court of competent jurisdiction. *(Added by Stats.1977, c. 709, p. 2269, § 1, operative July 1, 1978. Amended by Stats.1987, c. 961, § 1; Stats.1989, c. 1213, § 2.)*

Cross References

Governmental entity defined for purposes of this Chapter, see Civil Code § 1798.3.
Person defined for purposes of this Chapter, see Civil Code § 1798.3.
Record defined for purposes of this Chapter, see Civil Code § 1798.3.

§ 1798.27. Retention of accounting and original documents

Each agency shall retain the accounting made pursuant to Section 1798.25 for at least three years after the disclosure for which the accounting is made, or until the record is destroyed, whichever is shorter.

Nothing in this section shall be construed to require retention of the original documents for a three-year period, providing that the agency can otherwise comply with the requirements of this section. *(Added by Stats.1977, c. 709, p. 2269, § 1, operative July 1, 1978.)*

Cross References

Agency defined for purposes of this Chapter, see Civil Code § 1798.3.
Record defined for purposes of this Chapter, see Civil Code § 1798.3.

§ 1798.28. Correction of errors; notation of disputes; notice

Each agency, after July 1, 1978, shall inform any person or agency to whom a record containing personal information has been disclosed during the preceding three years of any correction of an error or notation of dispute made pursuant to Sections 1798.35 and 1798.36 if (1) an accounting of the disclosure is required by Section 1798.25 or 1798.26, and the accounting has not been destroyed pursuant to Section 1798.27, or (2) the information provides the name of the person or agency to whom the disclosure was made, or (3) the person who is the subject of the disclosed record provides the name of the person or agency to whom the information was disclosed. *(Added by Stats.1977, c. 709, p. 2269, § 1, operative July 1, 1978. Amended by Stats.1985, c. 595, § 13.)*

Cross References

Agency defined for purposes of this Chapter, see Civil Code § 1798.3.
Person defined for purposes of this Chapter, see Civil Code § 1798.3.
Personal information defined for purposes of this Chapter, see Civil Code § 1798.3.
Record defined for purposes of this Chapter, see Civil Code § 1798.3.

§ 1798.29. Agencies owning, licensing, or maintaining computerized data including personal information; disclosure of security breach; notice requirements

(a) Any agency that owns or licenses computerized data that includes personal information shall disclose any breach of the security of the system following discovery or notification of the breach in the security of the data to any resident of California (1) whose unencrypted personal information was, or is reasonably believed to have been, acquired by an unauthorized person, or, (2) whose encrypted personal information was, or is reasonably believed to have been, acquired by an unauthorized person and the encryption key or security credential was, or is reasonably believed to have been, acquired by an unauthorized person and the agency that owns or licenses the encrypted information has a reasonable belief that the encryption key or security credential could render that personal information readable or usable. The disclosure shall be made in the most expedient time possible and without unreasonable delay, consistent with the legitimate needs of law enforcement, as provided in subdivision (c), or any measures necessary to determine the scope of the breach and restore the reasonable integrity of the data system.

(b) Any agency that maintains computerized data that includes personal information that the agency does not own shall notify the owner or licensee of the information of any breach of the security of the data immediately following discovery, if the personal information was, or is reasonably believed to have been, acquired by an unauthorized person.

(c) The notification required by this section may be delayed if a law enforcement agency determines that the notification will impede a criminal investigation. The notification required by this section shall be made after the law enforcement agency determines that it will not compromise the investigation.

(d) Any agency that is required to issue a security breach notification pursuant to this section shall meet all of the following requirements:

(1) The security breach notification shall be written in plain language, shall be titled "Notice of Data Breach," and shall present the information described in paragraph (2) under the following headings: "What Happened," "What Information Was Involved," "What We Are Doing," "What You Can Do," and "For More Information." Additional information may be provided as a supplement to the notice.

(A) The format of the notice shall be designed to call attention to the nature and significance of the information it contains.

(B) The title and headings in the notice shall be clearly and conspicuously displayed.

(C) The text of the notice and any other notice provided pursuant to this section shall be no smaller than 10–point type.

(D) For a written notice described in paragraph (1) of subdivision (i), use of the model security breach notification form prescribed below or use of the headings described in this paragraph with the information described in paragraph (2), written in plain language, shall be deemed to be in compliance with this subdivision.

[NAME OF INSTITUTION / LOGO]   Date: [insert date]

NOTICE OF DATA BREACH

What Happened?

What Information Was Involved?

What We Are Doing.

What You Can Do.

Other Important Information.
[insert other important information]

For More Information.   Call [telephone number] or go to [internet website]

(E) For an electronic notice described in paragraph (2) of subdivision (i), use of the headings described in this paragraph with the information described in paragraph (2), written in plain language, shall be deemed to be in compliance with this subdivision.

(2) The security breach notification described in paragraph (1) shall include, at a minimum, the following information:

(A) The name and contact information of the reporting agency subject to this section.

(B) A list of the types of personal information that were or are reasonably believed to have been the subject of a breach.

(C) If the information is possible to determine at the time the notice is provided, then any of the following: (i) the date of the breach, (ii) the estimated date of the breach, or (iii) the date range within which the breach occurred. The notification shall also include the date of the notice.

(D) Whether the notification was delayed as a result of a law enforcement investigation, if that information is possible to determine at the time the notice is provided.

(E) A general description of the breach incident, if that information is possible to determine at the time the notice is provided.

(F) The toll-free telephone numbers and addresses of the major credit reporting agencies, if the breach exposed a social security number or a driver's license or California identification card number.

§ 1798.29

(3) At the discretion of the agency, the security breach notification may also include any of the following:

(A) Information about what the agency has done to protect individuals whose information has been breached.

(B) Advice on steps that people whose information has been breached may take to protect themselves.

(e) Any agency that is required to issue a security breach notification pursuant to this section to more than 500 California residents as a result of a single breach of the security system shall electronically submit a single sample copy of that security breach notification, excluding any personally identifiable information, to the Attorney General. A single sample copy of a security breach notification shall not be deemed to be within * * * Article 1 (commencing with Section 7923.600) of Chapter 1 of Part 5 of Division 10 of Title 1 of the Government Code.

(f) For purposes of this section, "breach of the security of the system" means unauthorized acquisition of computerized data that compromises the security, confidentiality, or integrity of personal information maintained by the agency. Good faith acquisition of personal information by an employee or agent of the agency for the purposes of the agency is not a breach of the security of the system, provided that the personal information is not used or subject to further unauthorized disclosure.

(g) For purposes of this section, "personal information" means either of the following:

(1) An individual's first name or first initial and last name in combination with any one or more of the following data elements, when either the name or the data elements are not encrypted:

(A) Social security number.

(B) Driver's license number, California identification card number, tax identification number, passport number, military identification number, or other unique identification number issued on a government document commonly used to verify the identity of a specific individual.

(C) Account number or credit or debit card number, in combination with any required security code, access code, or password that would permit access to an individual's financial account.

(D) Medical information.

(E) Health insurance information.

(F) Unique biometric data generated from measurements or technical analysis of human body characteristics, such as a fingerprint, retina, or iris image, used to authenticate a specific individual. Unique biometric data does not include a physical or digital photograph, unless used or stored for facial recognition purposes.

(G) Information or data collected through the use or operation of an automated license plate recognition system, as defined in Section 1798.90.5.

(H) Genetic data.

(2) A username or email address, in combination with a password or security question and answer that would permit access to an online account.

OBLIGATIONS

(h)(1) For purposes of this section, "personal information" does not include publicly available information that is lawfully made available to the general public from federal, state, or local government records.

(2) For purposes of this section, "medical information" means any information regarding an individual's medical history, mental or physical condition, or medical treatment or diagnosis by a health care professional.

(3) For purposes of this section, "health insurance information" means an individual's health insurance policy number or subscriber identification number, any unique identifier used by a health insurer to identify the individual, or any information in an individual's application and claims history, including any appeals records.

(4) For purposes of this section, "encrypted" means rendered unusable, unreadable, or indecipherable to an unauthorized person through a security technology or methodology generally accepted in the field of information security.

(5) For purposes of this section, "genetic data" means any data, regardless of its format, that results from the analysis of a biological sample of an individual, or from another source enabling equivalent information to be obtained, and concerns genetic material. Genetic material includes, but is not limited to, deoxyribonucleic acids (DNA), ribonucleic acids (RNA), genes, chromosomes, alleles, genomes, alterations or modifications to DNA or RNA, single nucleotide polymorphisms (SNPs), uninterpreted data that results from analysis of the biological sample or other source, and any information extrapolated, derived, or inferred therefrom.

(i) For purposes of this section, "notice" may be provided by one of the following methods:

(1) Written notice.

(2) Electronic notice, if the notice provided is consistent with the provisions regarding electronic records and signatures set forth in Section 7001 of Title 15 of the United States Code.

(3) Substitute notice, if the agency demonstrates that the cost of providing notice would exceed two hundred fifty thousand dollars ($250,000), or that the affected class of subject persons to be notified exceeds 500,000, or the agency does not have sufficient contact information. Substitute notice shall consist of all of the following:

(A) Email notice when the agency has an email address for the subject persons.

(B) Conspicuous posting, for a minimum of 30 days, of the notice on the agency's internet website * * *, if the agency maintains one. For purposes of this subparagraph, conspicuous posting on the agency's internet website means providing a link to the notice on the home page or first significant page after entering the internet website that is in larger type than the surrounding text, or in contrasting type, font, or color to the surrounding text of the same size, or set off from the surrounding text of the same size by symbols or other marks that call attention to the link.

(C) Notification to major statewide media and the Office of Information Security within the Department of Technology.

(4) In the case of a breach of the security of the system involving personal information defined in paragraph (2) of subdivision (g) for an online account, and no other personal information defined in paragraph (1) of subdivision (g), the agency may comply with this section by providing the security breach notification in electronic or other form that directs the person whose personal information has been breached to promptly change the person's password and security question or answer, as applicable, or to take other steps appropriate to protect the online account with the agency and all other online accounts for which the person uses the same username or email address and password or security question or answer.

(5) In the case of a breach of the security of the system involving personal information defined in paragraph (2) of subdivision (g) for login credentials of an email account furnished by the agency, the agency shall not comply with this section by providing the security breach notification to that email address, but may, instead, comply with this section by providing notice by another method described in this subdivision or by clear and conspicuous notice delivered to the resident online when the resident is connected to the online account from an Internet Protocol address or online location from which the agency knows the resident customarily accesses the account.

(j) Notwithstanding subdivision (i), an agency that maintains its own notification procedures as part of an information security policy for the treatment of personal information and is otherwise consistent with the timing requirements of this part shall be deemed to be in compliance with the notification requirements of this section if it notifies subject persons in accordance with its policies in the event of a breach of security of the system.

(k) Notwithstanding the exception specified in paragraph (4) of subdivision (b) of Section 1798.3, for purposes of this section, "agency" includes a local agency, as defined in * * * Section 7920.510 of the Government Code.

(*l*) For purposes of this section, "encryption key" and "security credential" mean the confidential key or process designed to render the data usable, readable, and decipherable.

(m) Notwithstanding any other law, the State Bar of California shall comply with this section. This subdivision shall not be construed to apply other provisions of this chapter to the State Bar. (Added by Stats.2002, c. 1054 (A.B.700), § 2, operative July 1, 2003. Amended by Stats.2007, c. 699 (A.B.1298), § 4; Stats.2011, c. 197 (S.B.24), § 1; Stats.2013, c. 395 (A.B.1149), § 1; Stats.2013, c. 396 (S.B.46), § 1.5; Stats.2015, c. 522 (A.B.964), § 1, eff. Jan. 1, 2016; Stats.2015, c. 532 (S.B.34), § 1, eff. Jan. 1, 2016; Stats.2015, c. 543 (S.B.570), § 1.3, eff. Jan. 1, 2016; Stats.2016, c. 86 (S.B.1171), § 20, eff. Jan. 1, 2017; Stats.2016, c. 337 (A.B. 2828), § 1, eff. Jan. 1, 2017; Stats.2019, c. 750 (A.B.1130), § 1, eff. Jan. 1, 2020; Stats.2021, c. 615 (A.B.474), § 45, eff. Jan. 1, 2022, operative Jan. 1, 2023; Stats.2021, c. 527 (A.B.825), § 1, eff. Jan. 1, 2022; Stats.2022, c. 28 (S.B.1380), § 22, eff. Jan. 1, 2023; Stats.2022, c. 419 (A.B.2958), § 14, eff. Sept. 18, 2022.)

Cross References

Age verification when selling products that are illegal to sell to minor, reasonable steps, products requiring age verification, penalties, see Civil Code § 1798.99.1.

Agency defined for purposes of this Chapter, see Civil Code § 1798.3.

Disclose defined for purposes of this Chapter, see Civil Code § 1798.3.

Individual defined for purposes of this Chapter, see Civil Code § 1798.3.

Local educational agencies, reporting of cyberattacks, see Education Code § 35266.

Maintain defined for purposes of this Chapter, see Civil Code § 1798.3.

Person defined for purposes of this Chapter, see Civil Code § 1798.3.

Personal information defined for purposes of this Chapter, see Civil Code § 1798.3.

Record defined for purposes of this Chapter, see Civil Code § 1798.3.

Security breaches of computerized data including personal information, persons or businesses owning, licensing, or maintaining the data, disclosure and notice requirements, see Civil Code § 1798.82.

ARTICLE 8. ACCESS TO RECORDS AND ADMINISTRATIVE REMEDIES

Section
1798.30. Regulations or guidelines; procedure for implementation of article.
1798.31. Repealed.
1798.32. Maintenance of records; rights of inquiry and notice; contents of notice; rules and regulations.
1798.33. Copies of records; fees.
1798.34. Inspection of personal information in records and accounting; time; copies; form; availability.
1798.35. Amendment of records; procedure; notice.
1798.36. Refusal to amend records; review; final determination; time; statement of individual's disagreement.
1798.37. Disputed records; statements of individual's disagreement and rationale of agency for refusal of amendment; notation of disputed portions; copies.
1798.38. Promises or understandings concerning confidentiality of source; specified information in possession of agencies; protection of identity.
1798.39. Records evidencing property rights.
1798.40. Nondisclosure of personal information to individual to whom information pertains; criteria.
1798.41. Finding that requested information is exempt from access; written notice; review; ex parte orders authorizing responses of no maintenance.
1798.42. Disclosure of personal information relating to others; deletions.
1798.43. Disclosure of personal information to individual to whom information pertains; deletion of exempt information.
1798.44. Application of article.

§ 1798.30. Regulations or guidelines; procedure for implementation of article

Each agency shall either adopt regulations or publish guidelines specifying procedures to be followed in order fully to implement each of the rights of individuals set forth in this article. (Added by Stats.1977, c. 709, p. 2269, § 1, operative

July 1, 1978. Amended by Stats.1978, c. 874, p. 2747, § 7, eff. Sept. 19, 1978.)

Cross References

Agency defined for purposes of this Chapter, see Civil Code § 1798.3.
Individual defined for purposes of this Chapter, see Civil Code § 1798.3.

§ 1798.31. Repealed by Stats.1985, c. 595, § 14

§ 1798.32. Maintenance of records; rights of inquiry and notice; contents of notice; rules and regulations

Each individual shall have the right to inquire and be notified as to whether the agency maintains a record about himself or herself. Agencies shall take reasonable steps to assist individuals in making their requests sufficiently specific.

Any notice sent to an individual which in any way indicates that the agency maintains any record concerning that individual shall include the title and business address of the agency official responsible for maintaining the records, the procedures to be followed to gain access to the records, and the procedures to be followed for an individual to contest the contents of these records unless the individual has received this notice from the agency during the past year.

In implementing the right conferred by this section, an agency may specify in its rules or regulations reasonable times, places, and requirements for identifying an individual who requests access to a record, and for disclosing the contents of a record. (Added by Stats.1977, c. 709, p. 2269, § 1, operative July 1, 1978. Amended by Stats.1978, c. 874, p. 2747, § 8, eff. Sept. 19, 1978; Stats.1991–1992, 1st Ex.Sess., c. 21 (A.B.66), § 33.6, eff. March 1, 1993.)

Cross References

Agency defined for purposes of this Chapter, see Civil Code § 1798.3.
Individual defined for purposes of this Chapter, see Civil Code § 1798.3.
Maintain defined for purposes of this Chapter, see Civil Code § 1798.3.
Record defined for purposes of this Chapter, see Civil Code § 1798.3.

§ 1798.33. Copies of records; fees

Each agency may establish fees to be charged, if any, to an individual for making copies of a record. Such fees shall exclude the cost of any search for and review of the record, and shall not exceed ten cents ($0.10) per page, unless the agency fee for copying is established by statute. (Added by Stats.1977, c. 709, p. 2269, § 1, operative July 1, 1978. Amended by Stats.1978, c. 874, p. 2747, § 9, eff. Sept. 19, 1978.)

Cross References

Agency defined for purposes of this Chapter, see Civil Code § 1798.3.
Individual defined for purposes of this Chapter, see Civil Code § 1798.3.
Record defined for purposes of this Chapter, see Civil Code § 1798.3.

§ 1798.34. Inspection of personal information in records and accounting; time; copies; form; availability

(a) Except as otherwise provided in this chapter, each agency shall permit any individual upon request and proper identification to inspect all the personal information in any record containing personal information and maintained by reference to an identifying particular assigned to the individual within 30 days of the agency's receipt of the request for active records, and within 60 days of the agency's receipt of the request for records that are geographically dispersed or which are inactive and in central storage. Failure to respond within these time limits shall be deemed denial. In addition, the individual shall be permitted to inspect any personal information about himself or herself where it is maintained by reference to an identifying particular other than that of the individual, if the agency knows or should know that the information exists. The individual also shall be permitted to inspect the accounting made pursuant to Article 7 (commencing with Section 1798.25).

(b) The agency shall permit the individual, and, upon the individual's request, another person of the individual's own choosing to inspect all the personal information in the record and have an exact copy made of all or any portion thereof within 15 days of the inspection. It may require the individual to furnish a written statement authorizing disclosure of the individual's record to another person of the individual's choosing.

(c) The agency shall present the information in the record in a form reasonably comprehensible to the general public.

(d) Whenever an agency is unable to access a record by reference to name only, or when access by name only would impose an unreasonable administrative burden, it may require the individual to submit such other identifying information as will facilitate access to the record.

(e) When an individual is entitled under this chapter to gain access to the information in a record containing personal information, the information or a true copy thereof shall be made available to the individual at a location near the residence of the individual or by mail, whenever reasonable. (Added by Stats.1977, c. 709, p. 2269, § 1, operative July 1, 1978. Amended by Stats.1982, c. 604, p. 2584, § 4; Stats.1985, c. 595, § 15.)

Cross References

Access to records, extension of time limits, see Civil Code § 1798.66.
Agency defined for purposes of this Chapter, see Civil Code § 1798.3.
Individual defined for purposes of this Chapter, see Civil Code § 1798.3.
Person defined for purposes of this Chapter, see Civil Code § 1798.3.
Personal information defined for purposes of this Chapter, see Civil Code § 1798.3.
Record defined for purposes of this Chapter, see Civil Code § 1798.3.

§ 1798.35. Amendment of records; procedure; notice

Each agency shall permit an individual to request in writing an amendment of a record and, shall within 30 days of the date of receipt of such request:

(a) Make each correction in accordance with the individual's request of any portion of a record which the individual believes is not accurate, relevant, timely, or complete and inform the individual of the corrections made in accordance with their request; or

(b) Inform the individual of its refusal to amend the record in accordance with such individual's request, the reason for the refusal, the procedures established by the agency for the individual to request a review by the head of the agency or an official specifically designated by the head of the agency of the refusal to amend, and the name, title, and business address of the reviewing official. *(Added by Stats.1977, c. 709, p. 2269, § 1, operative July 1, 1978.)*

Cross References

Access to records, extension of time limits, see Civil Code § 1798.66.
Agency defined for purposes of this Chapter, see Civil Code § 1798.3.
Franchise and income tax laws, determinations of liability for tax, penalty, interest, fine, forfeiture, or other imposition or offense thereunder, application of specified provisions of Information Practices Act of 1977, see Revenue and Taxation Code § 19570.
Individual defined for purposes of this Chapter, see Civil Code § 1798.3.

§ 1798.36. Refusal to amend records; review; final determination; time; statement of individual's disagreement

Each agency shall permit any individual who disagrees with the refusal of the agency to amend a record to request a review of such refusal by the head of the agency or an official specifically designated by the head of such agency, and, not later than 30 days from the date on which the individual requests such review, complete such review and make a final determination unless, for good cause shown, the head of the agency extends such review period by 30 days. If, after such review, the reviewing official refuses to amend the record in accordance with the request, the agency shall permit the individual to file with the agency a statement of reasonable length setting forth the reasons for the individual's disagreement. *(Added by Stats.1977, c. 709, p. 2269, § 1, operative July 1, 1978.)*

Cross References

Access to records, extension of time limits, see Civil Code § 1798.66.
Agency defined for purposes of this Chapter, see Civil Code § 1798.3.
Franchise and income tax laws, determinations of liability for tax, penalty, interest, fine, forfeiture, or other imposition or offense thereunder, application of specified provisions of Information Practices Act of 1977, see Revenue and Taxation Code § 19570.
Individual defined for purposes of this Chapter, see Civil Code § 1798.3.
Record defined for purposes of this Chapter, see Civil Code § 1798.3.

§ 1798.37. Disputed records; statements of individual's disagreement and rationale of agency for refusal of amendment; notation of disputed portions; copies

The agency, with respect to any disclosure containing information about which the individual has filed a statement of disagreement, shall clearly note any portion of the record which is disputed and make available copies of such individual's statement and copies of a concise statement of the reasons of the agency for not making the amendment to any person or agency to whom the disputed record has been or is disclosed. *(Added by Stats.1977, c. 709, p. 2269, § 1, operative July 1, 1978.)*

Cross References

Agency defined for purposes of this Chapter, see Civil Code § 1798.3.
Franchise and income tax laws, determinations of liability for tax, penalty, interest, fine, forfeiture, or other imposition or offense thereunder, application of specified provisions of Information Practices Act of 1977, see Revenue and Taxation Code § 19570.
Individual defined for purposes of this Chapter, see Civil Code § 1798.3.

§ 1798.38. Promises or understandings concerning confidentiality of source; specified information in possession of agencies; protection of identity

If information, including letters of recommendation, compiled for the purpose of determining suitability, eligibility, or qualifications for employment, advancement, renewal of appointment or promotion, status as adoptive parents, or for the receipt of state contracts, or for licensing purposes, was received with the promise or, prior to July 1, 1978, with the understanding that the identity of the source of the information would be held in confidence and the source is not in a supervisory position with respect to the individual to whom the record pertains, the agency shall fully inform the individual of all personal information about that individual without identification of the source. This may be done by providing a copy of the text of the material with only such deletions as are necessary to protect the identity of the source or by providing a comprehensive summary of the substance of the material. Whichever method is used, the agency shall insure that full disclosure is made to the subject of any personal information that could reasonably in any way reflect or convey anything detrimental, disparaging, or threatening to an individual's reputation, rights, benefits, privileges, or qualifications, or be used by an agency to make a determination that would affect an individual's rights, benefits, privileges, or qualifications. In institutions of higher education, "supervisory positions" shall not be deemed to include chairpersons of academic departments. *(Added by Stats.1977, c. 709, p. 2269, § 1, operative July 1, 1978. Amended by Stats.1985, c. 595, § 16.)*

Cross References

Agency defined for purposes of this Chapter, see Civil Code § 1798.3.
Employee access to personal information in records, see Education Code § 92612.
Individual defined for purposes of this Chapter, see Civil Code § 1798.3.
Personal information defined for purposes of this Chapter, see Civil Code § 1798.3.

§ 1798.39. Records evidencing property rights

Sections 1798.35, 1798.36, and 1798.37 shall not apply to any record evidencing property rights. *(Added by Stats.1977, c. 709, p. 2269, § 1, operative July 1, 1978.)*

Cross References

Record defined for purposes of this Chapter, see Civil Code § 1798.3.

§ 1798.40. Nondisclosure of personal information to individual to whom information pertains; criteria

This chapter shall not be construed to require an agency to disclose personal information to the individual to whom the information pertains, if the information meets any of the following criteria:

(a) Is compiled for the purpose of identifying individual criminal offenders and alleged offenders and consists only of identifying data and notations of arrests, the nature and disposition of criminal charges, sentencing, confinement, release, and parole and probation status.

(b) Is compiled for the purpose of a criminal investigation of suspected criminal activities, including reports of informants and investigators, and associated with an identifiable individual.

(c) Is contained in any record which could identify an individual and which is compiled at any stage of the process of enforcement of the criminal laws, from the arrest or indictment stage through release from supervision and including the process of extradition or the exercise of executive clemency.

(d) Is maintained for the purpose of an investigation of an individual's fitness for licensure or public employment, or of a grievance or complaint, or a suspected civil offense, so long as the information is withheld only so as not to compromise the investigation, or a related investigation. The identities of individuals who provided information for the investigation may be withheld pursuant to Section 1798.38.

(e) Would compromise the objectivity or fairness of a competitive examination for appointment or promotion in public service, or to determine fitness for licensure, or to determine scholastic aptitude.

(f) Pertains to the physical or psychological condition of the individual, if the agency determines that disclosure would be detrimental to the individual. The information shall, upon the individual's written authorization, be disclosed to a licensed medical practitioner or psychologist designated by the individual.

(g) Relates to the settlement of claims for work related illnesses or injuries and is maintained exclusively by the State Compensation Insurance Fund.

(h) Is required by statute to be withheld from the individual to whom it pertains.

This section shall not be construed to deny an individual access to information relating to him or her if access is allowed by another statute or decisional law of this state. (Added by Stats.1985, c. 595, § 18.)

Cross References

Access to records, extension of time limits, see Civil Code § 1798.66.
Agency defined for purposes of this Chapter, see Civil Code § 1798.3.
Disclose defined for purposes of this Chapter, see Civil Code § 1798.3.
Individual defined for purposes of this Chapter, see Civil Code § 1798.3.
Personal information defined for purposes of this Chapter, see Civil Code § 1798.3.
Record defined for purposes of this Chapter, see Civil Code § 1798.3.
State Teachers' Retirement System, disclosure of confidential information, see Education Code § 22306.

§ 1798.41. Finding that requested information is exempt from access; written notice; review; ex parte orders authorizing responses of no maintenance

(a) Except as provided in subdivision (c), if the agency determines that information requested pursuant to Section 1798.34 is exempt from access, it shall inform the individual in writing of the agency's finding that disclosure is not required by law.

(b) Except as provided in subdivision (c), each agency shall conduct a review of its determination that particular information is exempt from access pursuant to Section 1798.40, within 30 days from the receipt of a request by an individual directly affected by the determination, and inform the individual in writing of the findings of the review. The review shall be conducted by the head of the agency or an official specifically designated by the head of the agency.

(c) If the agency believes that compliance with subdivision (a) would seriously interfere with attempts to apprehend persons who are wanted for committing a crime or attempts to prevent the commission of a crime or would endanger the life of an informant or other person submitting information contained in the record, it may petition the presiding judge of the superior court of the county in which the record is maintained to issue an ex parte order authorizing the agency to respond to the individual that no record is maintained. All proceedings before the court shall be in camera. If the presiding judge finds that there are reasonable grounds to believe that compliance with subdivision (a) will seriously interfere with attempts to apprehend persons who are wanted for committing a crime or attempts to prevent the commission of a crime or will endanger the life of an informant or other person submitting information contained in the record, the judge shall issue an order authorizing the agency to respond to the individual that no record is maintained by the agency. The order shall not be issued for longer than 30 days but can be renewed at 30-day intervals. If a request pursuant to this section is received after the expiration of the order, the agency must either respond pursuant to subdivision (a) or seek a new order pursuant to this subdivision. *(Formerly § 1798.40, added by Stats.1977, c. 709, p. 2269, § 1, operative July 1, 1978. Amended by Stats.1982, c. 604, p. 2585, § 5. Renumbered § 1798.41 and amended by Stats.1985, c. 595, § 17.)*

Cross References

Agency defined for purposes of this Chapter, see Civil Code § 1798.3.
Individual defined for purposes of this Chapter, see Civil Code § 1798.3.
Person defined for purposes of this Chapter, see Civil Code § 1798.3.
Record defined for purposes of this Chapter, see Civil Code § 1798.3.

§ 1798.42. Disclosure of personal information relating to others; deletions

In disclosing information contained in a record to an individual, an agency shall not disclose any personal information relating to another individual which may be contained in the record. To comply with this section, an agency shall, in disclosing information, delete from disclosure such information as may be necessary. This section shall not be construed to authorize withholding the identities of sources except as provided in Sections 1798.38 and 1798.40. *(Formerly § 1798.41, added by Stats.1977, c. 709, p. 2269, § 1, operative July 1, 1978. Amended by Stats.1982, c. 604, p. 2586, § 6. Renumbered § 1798.42 and amended by Stats.1985, c. 595, § 19.)*

Cross References

Agency defined for purposes of this Chapter, see Civil Code § 1798.3.
Disclose defined for purposes of this Chapter, see Civil Code § 1798.3.
Individual defined for purposes of this Chapter, see Civil Code § 1798.3.
Personal information defined for purposes of this Chapter, see Civil Code § 1798.3.
Record defined for purposes of this Chapter, see Civil Code § 1798.3.

§ 1798.43. Disclosure of personal information to individual to whom information pertains; deletion of exempt information

In disclosing information contained in a record to an individual, an agency need not disclose any information pertaining to that individual which is exempt under Section 1798.40. To comply with this section, an agency may, in disclosing personal information contained in a record, delete from the disclosure any exempt information. *(Formerly § 1798.42, added by Stats.1977, c. 709, p. 2269, § 1, operative July 1, 1978. Amended by Stats.1982, c. 604, p. 2586, § 7. Renumbered § 1798.43 and amended by Stats.1985, c. 595, § 20.)*

Cross References

Agency defined for purposes of this Chapter, see Civil Code § 1798.3.
Disclose defined for purposes of this Chapter, see Civil Code § 1798.3.
Individual defined for purposes of this Chapter, see Civil Code § 1798.3.
Personal information defined for purposes of this Chapter, see Civil Code § 1798.3.
Record defined for purposes of this Chapter, see Civil Code § 1798.3.

§ 1798.44. Application of article

This article applies to the rights of an individual to whom personal information pertains and not to the authority or right of any other person, agency, other state governmental entity, or governmental entity to obtain this information. *(Formerly § 1798.43, added by Stats.1978, c. 874, p. 2747, § 10, eff. Sept. 19, 1978. Renumbered § 1798.44 and amended by Stats.1985, c. 595, § 21.)*

Cross References

Agency defined for purposes of this Chapter, see Civil Code § 1798.3.
Governmental entity defined for purposes of this Chapter, see Civil Code § 1798.3.
Individual defined for purposes of this Chapter, see Civil Code § 1798.3.
Person defined for purposes of this Chapter, see Civil Code § 1798.3.
Personal information defined for purposes of this Chapter, see Civil Code § 1798.3.

ARTICLE 9. CIVIL REMEDIES

Section
1798.45. Civil actions against agencies; grounds.
1798.46. Actions for refusal to comply with requests for inspection; injunctions; proceedings de novo; in camera examination of records; attorney fees and costs.
1798.47. Injunctions; orders and judgments.
1798.48. Failure to maintain records properly; noncompliance with provisions of chapter and rules; actual damages; costs; attorney fees.
1798.49. Jurisdiction; limitation of actions; nonexclusive rights and remedies.
1798.50. Personnel actions; qualifications of individuals; subjective opinions; liability.
1798.51. Lapse of time; corrections to records.
1798.53. Invasion of privacy; intentional disclosure of personal information; state or federal records; exemplary damages; attorney fees and costs.

Cross References

Franchise and income tax laws, determinations of liability for tax, penalty, interest, fine, forfeiture, or other imposition or offense thereunder, application of specified provisions of Information Practices Act of 1977, see Revenue and Taxation Code § 19570.

§ 1798.45. Civil actions against agencies; grounds

An individual may bring a civil action against an agency whenever such agency does any of the following:

(a) Refuses to comply with an individual's lawful request to inspect pursuant to subdivision (a) of Section 1798.34.

(b) Fails to maintain any record concerning any individual with such accuracy, relevancy, timeliness, and completeness as is necessary to assure fairness in any determination relating to the qualifications, character, rights, opportunities of, or benefits to the individual that may be made on the basis of such record, if, as a proximate result of such failure, a determination is made which is adverse to the individual.

(c) Fails to comply with any other provision of this chapter, or any rule promulgated thereunder, in such a way as to have an adverse effect on an individual. *(Added by Stats.1977, c. 709, p. 2269, § 1, operative July 1, 1978.)*

Cross References

Agency defined for purposes of this Chapter, see Civil Code § 1798.3.
Individual defined for purposes of this Chapter, see Civil Code § 1798.3.
Maintain defined for purposes of this Chapter, see Civil Code § 1798.3.
Record defined for purposes of this Chapter, see Civil Code § 1798.3.

§ 1798.46. Actions for refusal to comply with requests for inspection; injunctions; proceedings de novo; in camera examination of records; attorney fees and costs

In any suit brought under the provisions of subdivision (a) of Section 1798.45:

§ 1798.46

(a) The court may enjoin the agency from withholding the records and order the production to the complainant of any agency records improperly withheld from the complainant. In such a suit the court shall determine the matter de novo, and may examine the contents of any agency records in camera to determine whether the records or any portion thereof may be withheld as being exempt from the individual's right of access and the burden is on the agency to sustain its action.

(b) The court shall assess against the agency reasonable attorney's fees and other litigation costs reasonably incurred in any suit under this section in which the complainant has prevailed. A party may be considered to have prevailed even though he or she does not prevail on all issues or against all parties. (Added by Stats.1977, c. 709, p. 2269, § 1, operative July 1, 1978. Amended by Stats.1985, c. 595, § 22.)

Cross References

Agency defined for purposes of this Chapter, see Civil Code § 1798.3.

Individual defined for purposes of this Chapter, see Civil Code § 1798.3.

Record defined for purposes of this Chapter, see Civil Code § 1798.3.

§ 1798.47. Injunctions; orders and judgments

Any agency that fails to comply with any provision of this chapter may be enjoined by any court of competent jurisdiction. The court may make any order or judgment as may be necessary to prevent the use or employment by an agency of any practices which violate this chapter.

Actions for injunction under this section may be prosecuted by the Attorney General, or any district attorney in this state, in the name of the people of the State of California whether upon his or her own complaint, or of a member of the general public, or by any individual acting in his or her own behalf. (Added by Stats.1977, c. 709, p. 2269, § 1, operative July 1, 1978. Amended by Stats.1991–1992, 1st Ex.Sess., c. 21 (A.B.66), § 33.7, eff. March 1, 1993.)

Cross References

Agency defined for purposes of this Chapter, see Civil Code § 1798.3.

Attorney General, generally, see Government Code § 12500 et seq.

Individual defined for purposes of this Chapter, see Civil Code § 1798.3.

§ 1798.48. Failure to maintain records properly; noncompliance with provisions of chapter and rules; actual damages; costs; attorney fees

In any suit brought under the provisions of subdivision (b) or (c) of Section 1798.45, the agency shall be liable to the individual in an amount equal to the sum of:

(a) Actual damages sustained by the individual, including damages for mental suffering.

(b) The costs of the action together with reasonable attorney's fees as determined by the court. (Added by Stats.1977, c. 709, p. 2269, § 1, operative July 1, 1978.)

Cross References

Agency defined for purposes of this Chapter, see Civil Code § 1798.3.

Individual defined for purposes of this Chapter, see Civil Code § 1798.3.

§ 1798.49. Jurisdiction; limitation of actions; nonexclusive rights and remedies

An action to enforce any liability created under Sections 1798.45 to 1798.48, inclusive, may be brought in any court of competent jurisdiction in the county in which the complainant resides, or has his principal place of business, or in which the defendant's records are situated, within two years from the date on which the cause of action arises, except that where a defendant has materially and willfully misrepresented any information required under this section to be disclosed to an individual who is the subject of the information and the information so misrepresented is material to the establishment of the defendant's liability to that individual under this section, the action may be brought at any time within two years after discovery by the complainant of the misrepresentation. Nothing in Sections 1798.45 to 1798.48, inclusive, shall be construed to authorize any civil action by reason of any injury sustained as the result of any information practice covered by this chapter prior to July 1, 1978.

The rights and remedies set forth in this chapter shall be deemed to be nonexclusive and are in addition to all those rights and remedies which are otherwise available under any other provision of law. (Added by Stats.1977, c. 709, p. 2269, § 1, operative July 1, 1978.)

Cross References

Individual defined for purposes of this Chapter, see Civil Code § 1798.3.

Record defined for purposes of this Chapter, see Civil Code § 1798.3.

§ 1798.50. Personnel actions; qualifications of individuals; subjective opinions; liability

A civil action shall not lie under this article based upon an allegation that an opinion which is subjective in nature, as distinguished from a factual assertion, about an individual's qualifications, in connection with a personnel action concerning such an individual, was not accurate, relevant, timely, or complete. (Added by Stats.1977, c. 709, p. 2269, § 1, operative July 1, 1978.)

Cross References

Individual defined for purposes of this Chapter, see Civil Code § 1798.3.

§ 1798.51. Lapse of time; corrections to records

Where a remedy other than those provided in Articles 8 and 9 is provided by law but is not available because of lapse of time an individual may obtain a correction to a record under this chapter but such correction shall not operate to revise or restore a right or remedy not provided by this chapter that has been barred because of lapse of time. (Added by Stats.1977, c. 709, p. 2269, § 1, operative July 1, 1978.)

Cross References

Individual defined for purposes of this Chapter, see Civil Code § 1798.3.

Record defined for purposes of this Chapter, see Civil Code § 1798.3.

§ 1798.53. Invasion of privacy; intentional disclosure of personal information; state or federal records; exemplary damages; attorney fees and costs

Any person, other than an employee of the state or of a local government agency acting solely in his or her official capacity, who intentionally discloses information, not otherwise public, which they know or should reasonably know was obtained from personal information maintained by a state agency or from "records" within a "system of records" (as these terms are defined in the Federal Privacy Act of 1974 (P.L. 93–579; 5 U.S.C. 552a)) maintained by a federal government agency, shall be subject to a civil action, for invasion of privacy, by the individual to whom the information pertains.

In any successful action brought under this section, the complainant, in addition to any special or general damages awarded, shall be awarded a minimum of two thousand five hundred dollars ($2,500) in exemplary damages as well as attorney's fees and other litigation costs reasonably incurred in the suit.

The right, remedy, and cause of action set forth in this section shall be nonexclusive and is in addition to all other rights, remedies, and causes of action for invasion of privacy, inherent in Section 1 of Article I of the California Constitution. (Added by Stats.1977, c. 709, p. 2269, § 1, operative July 1, 1978. Amended by Stats.1985, c. 595, § 23.)

Cross References

Agency defined for purposes of this Chapter, see Civil Code § 1798.3.
Disclose defined for purposes of this Chapter, see Civil Code § 1798.3.
Individual defined for purposes of this Chapter, see Civil Code § 1798.3.
Person defined for purposes of this Chapter, see Civil Code § 1798.3.
Personal information defined for purposes of this Chapter, see Civil Code § 1798.3.
Record defined for purposes of this Chapter, see Civil Code § 1798.3.
System of records defined for purposes of this Chapter, see Civil Code § 1798.3.

ARTICLE 10. PENALTIES

Section
1798.55. Intentional violations; agency officers and employees; discipline; termination of employment.
1798.56. False pretenses; requesting or obtaining records; misdemeanor.
1798.57. Wrongful disclosure of medical, psychiatric, or psychological information; economic loss or personal injury; misdemeanor.

§ 1798.55. Intentional violations; agency officers and employees; discipline; termination of employment

The intentional violation of any provision of this chapter or of any rules or regulations adopted thereunder, by an officer or employee of any agency shall constitute a cause for discipline, including termination of employment. (Added by Stats.1977, c. 709, p. 2269, § 1, operative July 1, 1978.)

Cross References

Agency defined for purposes of this Chapter, see Civil Code § 1798.3.

§ 1798.56. False pretenses; requesting or obtaining records; misdemeanor

Any person who willfully requests or obtains any record containing personal information from an agency under false pretenses shall be guilty of a misdemeanor and fined not more than five thousand dollars ($5,000), or imprisoned not more than one year, or both. (Added by Stats.1977, c. 709, p. 2269, § 1, operative July 1, 1978. Amended by Stats.1985, c. 595, § 24.)

Cross References

Access to minimum amount of potentially identifiable data through research environment, violation of data use agreement, permissible access, limits on release of personal information, see Health and Safety Code § 127673.83.
Agency defined for purposes of this Chapter, see Civil Code § 1798.3.
Misdemeanors, definition and penalties, see Penal Code §§ 17, 19, 19.2.
Person defined for purposes of this Chapter, see Civil Code § 1798.3.
Personal information defined for purposes of this Chapter, see Civil Code § 1798.3.
Record defined for purposes of this Chapter, see Civil Code § 1798.3.

§ 1798.57. Wrongful disclosure of medical, psychiatric, or psychological information; economic loss or personal injury; misdemeanor

Except for disclosures which are otherwise required or permitted by law, the intentional disclosure of medical, psychiatric, or psychological information in violation of the disclosure provisions of this chapter is punishable as a misdemeanor if the wrongful disclosure results in economic loss or personal injury to the individual to whom the information pertains. (Added by Stats.1986, c. 94, § 1, eff. May 13, 1986.)

Cross References

Individual defined for purposes of this Chapter, see Civil Code § 1798.3.
Misdemeanors, definition and penalties, see Penal Code §§ 17, 19, 19.2.

ARTICLE 11. MISCELLANEOUS PROVISIONS

Section
1798.60. Names and addresses; distribution for commercial purposes, sale or rental.
1798.61. Release of licensees' and applicants' names and addresses.
1798.62. Mailing lists; agencies; removal of names and addresses.
1798.63. Construction of chapter.
1798.64. Director of General Services; storage, processing and servicing of records; state archives; maintenance.
1798.65. Repealed.
1798.66. Access to records; time limitations; extension.
1798.67. Liens or encumbrances; state; disclosure of information relating to identity.

Section
1798.68. Disclosure of personal or confidential information to district attorney; petition to disclose.
1798.69. Release of names and addresses; State Board of Equalization.

§ 1798.60. Names and addresses; distribution for commercial purposes, sale or rental

An individual's name and address may not be distributed for commercial purposes, sold, or rented by an agency unless such action is specifically authorized by law. (Added by Stats.1977, c. 709, p. 2269, § 1, operative July 1, 1978.)

Cross References

Agency defined for purposes of this Chapter, see Civil Code § 1798.3.
Commercial purpose defined for purposes of this Chapter, see Civil Code § 1798.3.
Individual defined for purposes of this Chapter, see Civil Code § 1798.3.

§ 1798.61. Release of licensees' and applicants' names and addresses

(a) Nothing in this chapter shall prohibit the release of only names and addresses of persons possessing licenses to engage in professional occupations.

(b) Nothing in this chapter shall prohibit the release of only names and addresses of persons applying for licenses to engage in professional occupations for the sole purpose of providing those persons with informational materials relating to available professional educational materials or courses. (Added by Stats.1977, c. 709, p. 2269, § 1, operative July 1, 1978. Amended by Stats.1978, c. 874, p. 2747, § 11, eff. Sept. 19, 1978; Stats.1979, c. 143, p. 333, § 3, eff. June 22, 1979; Stats.1982, c. 1001, p. 3686, § 1; Stats.2000, c. 962 (A.B.1965), § 1.)

Cross References

Person defined for purposes of this Chapter, see Civil Code § 1798.3.

§ 1798.62. Mailing lists; agencies; removal of names and addresses

Upon written request of any individual, any agency which maintains a mailing list shall remove the individual's name and address from such list, except that such agency need not remove the individual's name if such name is exclusively used by the agency to directly contact the individual. (Added by Stats.1977, c. 709, p. 2269, § 1, operative July 1, 1978.)

Cross References

Agency defined for purposes of this Chapter, see Civil Code § 1798.3.
Individual defined for purposes of this Chapter, see Civil Code § 1798.3.
Maintain defined for purposes of this Chapter, see Civil Code § 1798.3.

§ 1798.63. Construction of chapter

The provisions of this chapter shall be liberally construed so as to protect the rights of privacy arising under this chapter or under the Federal or State Constitution. (Added by Stats.1977, c. 709, p. 2269, § 1, operative July 1, 1978.)

§ 1798.64. Director of General Services; storage, processing and servicing of records; state archives; maintenance

(a) Each agency record which is accepted by the Director of General Services for storage, processing, and servicing in accordance with provisions of the State Administrative Manual for the purposes of this chapter shall be considered to be maintained by the agency which deposited the record and shall continue to be subject to the provisions of this chapter. The Director of General Services shall not disclose the record except to the agency which maintains the record, or pursuant to rules established by such agency which are not inconsistent with the provisions of this chapter.

(b) Each agency record pertaining to an identifiable individual which was or is transferred to the State Archives as a record which has sufficient historical or other value to warrant its continued preservation by the California state government, prior to or after July 1, 1978, shall, for the purposes of this chapter, be considered to be maintained by the archives. (Added by Stats.1977, c. 709, p. 2269, § 1, operative July 1, 1978.)

Cross References

Agency defined for purposes of this Chapter, see Civil Code § 1798.3.
Disclose defined for purposes of this Chapter, see Civil Code § 1798.3.
Exemptions from public disclosure of items in custody of State Archives, exemption not applicable to item 75 years after it was created, notice of public access, see Government Code § 12237.
Individual defined for purposes of this Chapter, see Civil Code § 1798.3.
Maintain defined for purposes of this Chapter, see Civil Code § 1798.3.
Record defined for purposes of this Chapter, see Civil Code § 1798.3.

§ 1798.65. Repealed by Stats.1985, c. 595, § 25

§ 1798.66. Access to records; time limitations; extension

The time limits specified in Article 8 (commencing with Section 1798.30) may be extended to 60 days by the Franchise Tax Board if the following conditions exist:

(a) The request is made during the period January 1 through June 30; and

(b) The records requested are stored on magnetic tape. (Added by Stats.1977, c. 709, p. 2269, § 1, operative July 1, 1978.)

Cross References

Record defined for purposes of this Chapter, see Civil Code § 1798.3.

§ 1798.67. Liens or encumbrances; state; disclosure of information relating to identity

Where an agency has recorded a document creating a lien or encumbrance on real property in favor of the state, nothing herein shall prohibit any such agency from disclosing information relating to the identity of the person against whom such lien or encumbrance has been recorded for the purpose of distinguishing such person from another person bearing the same or a similar name. *(Added by Stats.1977, c. 709, p. 2269, § 1, operative July 1, 1978.)*

Cross References

Agency defined for purposes of this Chapter, see Civil Code § 1798.3.

Person defined for purposes of this Chapter, see Civil Code § 1798.3.

§ 1798.68. Disclosure of personal or confidential information to district attorney; petition to disclose

(a) Information which is permitted to be disclosed under the provisions of subdivision (e), (f), or (o), of Section 1798.24 shall be provided when requested by a district attorney.

A district attorney may petition a court of competent jurisdiction to require disclosure of information when an agency fails or refuses to provide the requested information within 10 working days of a request. The court may require the agency to permit inspection unless the public interest or good cause in withholding such records clearly outweighs the public interest in disclosure.

(b) Disclosure of information to a district attorney under the provisions of this chapter shall effect no change in the status of the records under any other provision of law. *(Added by Stats.1979, c. 601, p. 1873, § 1.)*

Cross References

Agency defined for purposes of this Chapter, see Civil Code § 1798.3.

Record defined for purposes of this Chapter, see Civil Code § 1798.3.

§ 1798.69. Release of names and addresses; State Board of Equalization

(a) Except as provided in subdivision (b), the State Board of Equalization may not release the names and addresses of individuals who are registered with, or are holding licenses or permits issued by, the State Board of Equalization except to the extent necessary to verify resale certificates or to administer the tax and fee provisions of the Revenue and Taxation Code.

(b) Nothing in this section shall prohibit the release by the State Board of Equalization to, or limit the use by, any federal or state agency, or local government, of any data collected by the board that is otherwise authorized by law. *(Added by Stats.2000, c. 962 (A.B.1965), § 2.)*

Cross References

Agency defined for purposes of this Chapter, see Civil Code § 1798.3.

Individual defined for purposes of this Chapter, see Civil Code § 1798.3.

ARTICLE 12. CONSTRUCTION WITH OTHER LAWS

Section
1798.70. Superseding other provisions of state law.
1798.71. Discovery; rights of litigants.
1798.72. Personal information; disclosure of records to other than the subject; violation of other law.
1798.73. Privacy; constitutional rights.
1798.74. Student records.
1798.75. Inspection of public records.

Section
1798.76. Law enforcement records; discovery in criminal or civil litigation.
1798.77. Modification, transfer, or destruction of records to avoid compliance with chapter prohibited; civil action; removal or destruction of requested information before access prohibited.
1798.78. Chapter deemed not to supersede Chapter 1299 of Statutes of 1976.

§ 1798.70. Superseding other provisions of state law

This chapter shall be construed to supersede any other provision of state law, including Article 2 (commencing with Section 7924.100) of Chapter 2 of Part 5 of Division 10 of Title 1 of the Government Code, or any exemption in Section 7922.000 of the Government Code or in any provision listed in Section 7920.505 of the Government Code, which authorizes any agency to withhold from an individual any record containing personal information that is otherwise accessible under the provisions of this chapter. *(Added by Stats.1977, c. 709, p. 2269, § 1, operative July 1, 1978. Amended by Stats.1978, c. 874, p. 2748, § 12, eff. Sept. 19, 1978; Stats.2021, c. 615 (A.B.474), § 46, eff. Jan. 1, 2022, operative Jan. 1, 2023.)*

Cross References

Agency defined for purposes of this Chapter, see Civil Code § 1798.3.

Individual defined for purposes of this Chapter, see Civil Code § 1798.3.

Inspection of public records, examination by proponents, see Government Code § 6253.5.

Personal information defined for purposes of this Chapter, see Civil Code § 1798.3.

Record defined for purposes of this Chapter, see Civil Code § 1798.3.

§ 1798.71. Discovery; rights of litigants

This chapter shall not be deemed to abridge or limit the rights of litigants, including parties to administrative proceedings, under the laws, or case law, of discovery of this state. *(Added by Stats.1977, c. 709, p. 2269, § 1, operative July 1, 1978.)*

§ 1798.72. Personal information; disclosure of records to other than the subject; violation of other law

Nothing in this chapter shall be construed to authorize the disclosure of any record containing personal information, other than to the subject of such records, in violation of any other law. *(Added by Stats.1977, c. 709, p. 2269, § 1, operative July 1, 1978.)*

Cross References

Personal information defined for purposes of this Chapter, see Civil Code § 1798.3.

Record defined for purposes of this Chapter, see Civil Code § 1798.3.

§ 1798.73. Privacy; constitutional rights

Nothing in this chapter shall be construed to deny or limit any right of privacy arising under Section 1 of Article I of the California Constitution. *(Added by Stats.1977, c. 709, p. 2269, § 1, operative July 1, 1978.)*

§ 1798.74. Student records

The provisions of Chapter 13 (commencing with Section 67110)[1] of Part 40 of the Education Code shall, with regard to student records, prevail over the provisions of this chapter. *(Added by Stats.1977, c. 709, p. 2269, § 1, operative July 1, 1978.)*

[1] So in chaptered copy. Repealed by Stats.1995, c. 758 (A.B.446), § 50.

Cross References

Record defined for purposes of this Chapter, see Civil Code § 1798.3.

§ 1798.75. Inspection of public records

This chapter shall not be deemed to supersede Division 10 (commencing with Section 7920.000) of Title 1 of the Government Code, except as to the provisions of Sections 1798.60, 1798.69, and 1798.70. *(Added by Stats.1977, c. 709, p. 2269, § 1, operative July 1, 1978. Amended by Stats.1979, c. 143, p. 334, § 4, eff. June 22, 1979; Stats.2000, c. 962 (A.B.1965), § 3; Stats.2021, c. 615 (A.B.474), § 47, eff. Jan. 1, 2022, operative Jan. 1, 2023.)*

Cross References

Inspection of public records, other exemptions from disclosure, see Government Code § 6276.34.

§ 1798.76. Law enforcement records; discovery in criminal or civil litigation

Nothing in this chapter shall be construed to revoke, modify, or alter in any manner any statutory provision or any judicial decision which (a) authorizes an individual to gain access to any law enforcement record, or (b) authorizes discovery in criminal or civil litigation. *(Added by Stats.1977, c. 709, p. 2269, § 1, operative July 1, 1978.)*

Cross References

Individual defined for purposes of this Chapter, see Civil Code § 1798.3.

Record defined for purposes of this Chapter, see Civil Code § 1798.3.

§ 1798.77. Modification, transfer, or destruction of records to avoid compliance with chapter prohibited; civil action; removal or destruction of requested information before access prohibited

Each agency shall ensure that no record containing personal information shall be modified, transferred, or destroyed to avoid compliance with any of the provisions of this chapter. In the event that an agency fails to comply with the provisions of this section, an individual may bring a civil action and seek the appropriate remedies and damages in accordance with the provisions of Article 9 (commencing with Section 1798.45).

An agency shall not remove or destroy personal information about an individual who has requested access to the information before allowing the individual access to the record containing the information. *(Added by Stats.1985, c. 595, § 26.)*

Cross References

Agency defined for purposes of this Chapter, see Civil Code § 1798.3.

Individual defined for purposes of this Chapter, see Civil Code § 1798.3.

Personal information defined for purposes of this Chapter, see Civil Code § 1798.3.

Record defined for purposes of this Chapter, see Civil Code § 1798.3.

§ 1798.78. Chapter deemed not to supersede Chapter 1299 of Statutes of 1976

This chapter shall not be deemed to supersede the provisions of Chapter 1299 of the Statutes of 1976.[1] *(Added by Stats.1985, c. 595, § 27.)*

[1] Stats.1976, c. 1299, added Education Code 1959, § 24317. See Education Code § 89546.

Title 1.80

IDENTIFICATION DOCUMENTS

Section
1798.79. Intentional reading or attempts to remotely read a person's identification document using radio frequency identification; disclosure of operational systems in a contactless identification system; penalties; application.
1798.795. Definitions.

§ 1798.79. Intentional reading or attempts to remotely read a person's identification document using radio frequency identification; disclosure of operational systems in a contactless identification system; penalties; application

(a) Except as provided in this section, a person or entity that intentionally remotely reads or attempts to remotely read a person's identification document using radio frequency identification (RFID), for the purpose of reading that person's identification document without that person's knowledge and prior consent, shall be punished by imprisonment in a county jail for up to one year, a fine of not more than one thousand five hundred dollars ($1,500), or both that fine and imprisonment.

(b) A person or entity that knowingly discloses, or causes to be disclosed, the operational system keys used in a contactless identification document system shall be punished by imprisonment in a county jail for up to one year, a fine of not more than one thousand five hundred dollars ($1,500), or both that fine and imprisonment.

(c) Subdivision (a) shall not apply to:

(1) The reading of a person's identification document for triage or medical care during a disaster and immediate hospitalization or immediate outpatient care directly related to a disaster, as defined by the local emergency medical services agency organized under Section 1797.200 of the Health and Safety Code.

(2) The reading of a person's identification document by a health care professional for reasons relating to the health or safety of that person or an identification document issued to a patient by emergency services.

(3) The reading of an identification document of a person who is incarcerated in the state prison or a county jail, detained in a juvenile facility operated by the Division of Juvenile Facilities in the Department of Corrections and Rehabilitation, or housed in a mental health facility, pursuant to a court order after having been charged with a crime, or to a person pursuant to a court-ordered electronic monitoring.

(4) Law enforcement or government personnel who need to read a lost identification document when the owner is unavailable for notice, knowledge, or consent, or those parties specifically authorized by law enforcement or government personnel for the limited purpose of reading a lost identification document when the owner is unavailable for notice, knowledge, or consent.

(5) Law enforcement personnel who need to read a person's identification document after an accident in which the person is unavailable for notice, knowledge, or consent.

(6) Law enforcement personnel who need to read a person's identification document pursuant to a search warrant.

(d) Subdivision (a) shall not apply to a person or entity that unintentionally remotely reads a person's identification document using RFID in the course of operating a contactless identification document system unless it knows it unintentionally read the document and thereafter intentionally does any of the following acts:

(1) Discloses what it read to a third party whose purpose is to read a person's identification document, or any information derived therefrom, without that person's knowledge and consent.

(2) Stores what it read for the purpose of reading a person's identification document, or any information derived therefrom, without that person's knowledge and prior consent.

(3) Uses what it read for the purpose of reading a person's identification document, or any information derived therefrom, without that person's knowledge and prior consent.

(e) Subdivisions (a) and (b) shall not apply to the reading, storage, use, or disclosure to a third party of a person's identification document, or information derived therefrom, in the course of an act of good faith security research, experimentation, or scientific inquiry, including, but not limited to, activities useful in identifying and analyzing security flaws and vulnerabilities.

(f) Nothing in this section shall affect the existing rights of law enforcement to access data stored electronically on driver's licenses.

(g) The penalties set forth in subdivisions (a) and (b) are independent of, and do not supersede, any other penalties provided by state law, and in the case of any conflict, the greater penalties shall apply. *(Added by Stats.2008, c. 746 (S.B.31), § 2. Amended by Stats.2009, c. 54 (S.B.544), § 5.)*

Cross References

Contactless identification document system defined for purposes of this Title, see Civil Code § 1798.795.
Data defined for purposes of this Title, see Civil Code § 1798.795.
Department of Corrections and Rehabilitation, generally, see Penal Code § 5000 et seq.
Identification document defined for purposes of this Title, see Civil Code § 1798.795.
Key defined for purposes of this Title, see Civil Code § 1798.795.
Radio frequency identification defined for purposes of this Title, see Civil Code § 1798.795.
Remotely defined for purposes of this Title, see Civil Code § 1798.795.
Search warrants, see Penal Code § 1523 et seq.

§ 1798.795. Definitions

For purposes of this title, the following definitions shall apply:

(a) "Contactless identification document system" means a group of identification documents issued and operated under a single authority that use RFID to transmit data remotely to readers intended to read that data. In a contactless identification document system, every reader must be able to read every identification document in the system.

(b) "Data" means any information stored or transmitted on an identification document in machine-readable form.

(c) "Identification document" means any document containing data that is issued to an individual and which that individual, and only that individual, uses alone or in conjunction with any other information for the primary purpose of establishing his or her identity. Identification documents specifically include, but are not limited to, the following:

(1) Driver's licenses or identification cards issued pursuant to Section 13000 of the Vehicle Code.

(2) Identification cards for employees or contractors.

(3) Identification cards issued by educational institutions.

(4) Health insurance or benefit cards.

(5) Benefit cards issued in conjunction with any government-supported aid program.

(6) Licenses, certificates, registration, or other means to engage in a business or profession regulated by the Business and Professions Code.

(7) Library cards issued by any public library.

(d) "Key" means a string of bits of information used as part of a cryptographic algorithm used in encryption.

(e) "Radio frequency identification" or "RFID" means the use of electromagnetic radiating waves or reactive field coupling in the radio frequency portion of the spectrum to communicate to or from an identification document through a variety of modulation and encoding schemes.

(f) "Reader" means a scanning device that is capable of using RFID to communicate with an identification document and read the data transmitted by that identification document.

(g) "Remotely" means that no physical contact between the identification document and a reader is necessary in order to transmit data using RFID. *(Added by Stats.2008, c. 746 (S.B.31), § 2.)*

Title 1.807

DOMESTIC VIOLENCE, SEXUAL ASSAULT, AND STALKING: PERSONAL INFORMATION

Section
1798.79.8. Definitions.

Section
1798.79.9. Prohibition on collection of personal identification information of clients from victim services providers receiving grants; statistical information excluded.
1798.79.95. Violations of title; injunctive relief; recovery of costs and attorney's fees; notice requirements.

§ 1798.79.8. Definitions

For purposes of this title:

(a) "Person or entity" means any individual, corporation, partnership, joint venture, or any business entity, or any state or local agency.

(b) "Personally identifying information" means:

(1) First and last name or last name only.

(2) Home or other physical address, including, but not limited to, a street name or ZIP Code, other than an address obtained pursuant to the California Safe At Home program or a business mailing address for the victim service provider.

(3) Electronic mail address or other online contact information, such as an instant messaging user identifier or a screen name that reveals an individual's electronic mail address.

(4) Telephone number, other than a business telephone number for the victim service provider.

(5) Social security number.

(6) Date of birth, with the exception of the year of birth.

(7) Internet protocol address or host name that identifies an individual.

(8) Any other information, including, but not limited to, the first and last names of children and relatives, racial or ethnic background, or religious affiliation, that, in combination with any other nonpersonally identifying information, would serve to identify any individual.

(c) "Victim service provider" means a nongovernmental organization or entity that provides shelter, programs, or services at low cost, no cost, or on a sliding scale to victims of domestic violence, dating violence, sexual assault, or stalking, or their children, either directly or through other contractual arrangements, including rape crisis centers, domestic violence shelters, domestic violence transitional housing programs, and other programs with the primary mission to provide services to victims of domestic violence, dating violence, sexual assault, or stalking, or their children, whether or not that program exists in an agency that provides additional services. *(Added by Stats.2006, c. 54 (S.B.1491), § 1.)*

Cross References

Award of reasonable expenses and attorney's fees in making a motion in an action arising from free speech rights on the Internet, see Code of Civil Procedure § 1987.2.
Subpoena, motion and order to quash, other orders, see Code of Civil Procedure § 1987.1.

§ 1798.79.9. Prohibition on collection of personal identification information of clients from victim services providers receiving grants; statistical information excluded

(a) In the course of awarding grants, including, but not limited to, requests for proposals, contracts, or billing procedures, implementing programs, or providing financial support or assistance for the purpose of providing shelter, programs, or services at low cost, no cost, or on a sliding scale to victims of domestic violence, dating violence, sexual assault, or stalking, or their children, to any victim service provider, it is unlawful for any person or entity to request or require that victim service provider to provide personally identifying information regarding any of the persons to whom it is providing services, it has provided services, or it has considered or is considering providing services.

(b) In the course of awarding grants, including, but not limited to, requests for proposals, contracts, or billing procedures, implementing programs, or providing financial support or assistance for the purpose of providing shelter, programs, or services at low cost, no cost, or on a sliding scale to victims of domestic violence, dating violence, sexual assault, or stalking, or their children, to any victim service provider, it is unlawful for any person or entity to request or require that victim service provider to use any computer software, computer program, computer protocol, or other computer system that requires the disclosure of personally identifying information regarding any of the persons to whom it is providing services, it has provided services, or it has considered or is considering providing services.

(c) Nothing in this section is intended to prevent the collection of information for statistical purposes that are necessary for the proper administration of the grant, program, or financial assistance, provided that collection does not require the disclosure of information that would serve to identify any specific individual. *(Added by Stats.2006, c. 54 (S.B.1491), § 1.)*

Cross References

Person or entity defined for purposes of this Title, see Civil Code § 1798.79.8.
Personally identifying information defined for purposes of this Title, see Civil Code § 1798.79.8.
Victim service provider defined for purposes of this Title, see Civil Code § 1798.79.8.

§ 1798.79.95. Violations of title; injunctive relief; recovery of costs and attorney's fees; notice requirements

Injunctive relief shall be available to any victim service provider aggrieved by a violation of this title. The prevailing plaintiff in any action commenced under this section shall be entitled to recover court costs and reasonable attorney's fees if the victim service provider has provided notice of this section and the asserted violation of this section to the defendant and the defendant has failed to cease the violation within five business days of receiving that notice. *(Added by Stats.2006, c. 54 (S.B.1491), § 1.)*

Cross References

Victim service provider defined for purposes of this Title, see Civil Code § 1798.79.8.

Title 1.81

CUSTOMER RECORDS

Section
1798.80. Definitions.
1798.81. Reasonable steps for disposal of customer records.

Section

1798.81.5. Security procedures and practices with respect to personal information about California residents.

1798.81.6. Computer system vulnerability; consumer credit agency; security procedures and practices with respect to personal information about California residents.

1798.82. Person or business who owns or licenses computerized data including personal information; breach of security of the system; disclosure requirements.

1798.83. Personal information; disclosure to direct marketers.

1798.83.5. Commercial online entertainment employment service providers; limits on publication of subscribers' age information.

1798.84. Waiver and violations of provisions of this title; civil actions and penalties; disposal of abandoned records containing personal information; attorney's fees and costs.

Cross References

California Consumer Privacy Act of 2018, intent, scope, and construction of title, see Civil Code § 1798.175.

Childhood Lead Poisoning Prevention Act, legislative findings and declarations, posting of information, see Health and Safety Code § 124125.

§ 1798.80. Definitions

The following definitions apply to this title:

(a) "Business" means a sole proprietorship, partnership, corporation, association, or other group, however organized and whether or not organized to operate at a profit, including a financial institution organized, chartered, or holding a license or authorization certificate under the law of this state, any other state, the United States, or of any other country, or the parent or the subsidiary of a financial institution. The term includes an entity that disposes of records.

(b) "Records" means any material, regardless of the physical form, on which information is recorded or preserved by any means, including in written or spoken words, graphically depicted, printed, or electromagnetically transmitted. "Records" does not include publicly available directories containing information an individual has voluntarily consented to have publicly disseminated or listed, such as name, address, or telephone number.

(c) "Customer" means an individual who provides personal information to a business for the purpose of purchasing or leasing a product or obtaining a service from the business.

(d) "Individual" means a natural person.

(e) "Personal information" means any information that identifies, relates to, describes, or is capable of being associated with, a particular individual, including, but not limited to, his or her name, signature, social security number, physical characteristics or description, address, telephone number, passport number, driver's license or state identification card number, insurance policy number, education, employment, employment history, bank account number, credit card number, debit card number, or any other financial information, medical information, or health insurance information. "Personal information" does not include publicly available information that is lawfully made available to the general public from federal, state, or local government records. *(Added by Stats.2000, c. 1039 (A.B.2246), § 1. Amended by Stats.2009, c. 134 (A.B.1094), § 1.)*

Cross References

California State University, personal information of alumni, disclosure, see Education Code § 89090.

Disclosure of personal information of alumni, see Education Code § 89090 et seq.

Restrictions on disclosure of personal information of book service users, personal information defined to include information specifically listed in this section, see Civil Code § 1798.90.

University of California, personal information of alumni, disclosure, see Education Code § 92630.

§ 1798.81. Reasonable steps for disposal of customer records

A business shall take all reasonable steps to dispose, or arrange for the disposal, of customer records within its custody or control containing personal information when the records are no longer to be retained by the business by (a) shredding, (b) erasing, or (c) otherwise modifying the personal information in those records to make it unreadable or undecipherable through any means. *(Added by Stats.2000, c. 1039 (A.B.2246), § 1. Amended by Stats.2009, c. 134 (A.B. 1094), § 2.)*

Cross References

Business defined for purposes of this Title, see Civil Code § 1798.80.

Customer defined for purposes of this Title, see Civil Code § 1798.80.

Motor vehicle records of residence or mailing address, destruction of records by contractor of insurance company, see Vehicle Code § 1808.22.

Parties to civil actions, protected persons, protection of identifying information, see Code of Civil Procedure § 367.3.

Personal information defined for purposes of this Title, see Civil Code § 1798.80.

Records defined for purposes of this Title, see Civil Code § 1798.80.

§ 1798.81.5. Security procedures and practices with respect to personal information about California residents

(a)(1) It is the intent of the Legislature to ensure that personal information about California residents is protected. To that end, the purpose of this section is to encourage businesses that own, license, or maintain personal information about Californians to provide reasonable security for that information.

(2) For the purpose of this section, the terms "own" and "license" include personal information that a business retains as part of the business' internal customer account or for the purpose of using that information in transactions with the person to whom the information relates. The term "maintain" includes personal information that a business maintains but does not own or license.

(b) A business that owns, licenses, or maintains personal information about a California resident shall implement and maintain reasonable security procedures and practices appropriate to the nature of the information, to protect the personal information from unauthorized access, destruction, use, modification, or disclosure.

(c) A business that discloses personal information about a California resident pursuant to a contract with a nonaffiliated third party that is not subject to subdivision (b) shall require

§ 1798.81.5

by contract that the third party implement and maintain reasonable security procedures and practices appropriate to the nature of the information, to protect the personal information from unauthorized access, destruction, use, modification, or disclosure.

(d) For purposes of this section, the following terms have the following meanings:

(1) "Personal information" means either of the following:

(A) An individual's first name or first initial and the individual's last name in combination with any one or more of the following data elements, when either the name or the data elements are not encrypted or redacted:

(i) Social security number.

(ii) Driver's license number, California identification card number, tax identification number, passport number, military identification number, or other unique identification number issued on a government document commonly used to verify the identity of a specific individual.

(iii) Account number or credit or debit card number, in combination with any required security code, access code, or password that would permit access to an individual's financial account.

(iv) Medical information.

(v) Health insurance information.

(vi) Unique biometric data generated from measurements or technical analysis of human body characteristics, such as a fingerprint, retina, or iris image, used to authenticate a specific individual. Unique biometric data does not include a physical or digital photograph, unless used or stored for facial recognition purposes.

(vii) Genetic data.

(B) A username or email address in combination with a password or security question and answer that would permit access to an online account.

(2) "Medical information" means any individually identifiable information, in electronic or physical form, regarding the individual's medical history or medical treatment or diagnosis by a health care professional.

(3) "Health insurance information" means an individual's insurance policy number or subscriber identification number, any unique identifier used by a health insurer to identify the individual, or any information in an individual's application and claims history, including any appeals records.

(4) "Personal information" does not include publicly available information that is lawfully made available to the general public from federal, state, or local government records.

(5) "Genetic data" means any data, regardless of its format, that results from the analysis of a biological sample of an individual, or from another source enabling equivalent information to be obtained, and concerns genetic material. Genetic material includes, but is not limited to, deoxyribonucleic acids (DNA), ribonucleic acids (RNA), genes, chromosomes, alleles, genomes, alterations or modifications to DNA or RNA, single nucleotide polymorphisms (SNPs), uninterpreted data that results from analysis of the biological sample or other source, and any information extrapolated, derived, or inferred therefrom.

(e) The provisions of this section do not apply to any of the following:

(1) A provider of health care, health care service plan, or contractor regulated by the Confidentiality of Medical Information Act (Part 2.6 (commencing with Section 56) of Division 1).

(2) A financial institution as defined in Section 4052 of the Financial Code and subject to the California Financial Information Privacy Act (Division 1.4 (commencing with Section 4050) of the Financial Code).

(3) A covered entity governed by the medical privacy and security rules issued by the federal Department of Health and Human Services, Parts 160 and 164 of Title 45 of the Code of Federal Regulations, established pursuant to the Health Insurance Portability and Availability Act of 1996 (HIPAA).

(4) An entity that obtains information under an agreement pursuant to Article 3 (commencing with Section 1800) of Chapter 1 of Division 2 of the Vehicle Code and is subject to the confidentiality requirements of the Vehicle Code.

(5) A business that is regulated by state or federal law providing greater protection to personal information than that provided by this section in regard to the subjects addressed by this section. Compliance with that state or federal law shall be deemed compliance with this section with regard to those subjects. This paragraph does not relieve a business from a duty to comply with any other requirements of other state and federal law regarding the protection and privacy of personal information. *(Added by Stats.2004, c. 877 (A.B.1950), § 1. Amended by Stats.2005, c. 22 (S.B.1108), § 15; Stats.2014, c. 855 (A.B.1710), § 1, eff. Jan. 1, 2015; Stats.2015, c. 96 (A.B.1541), § 1, eff. Jan. 1, 2016; Stats.2019, c. 750 (A.B.1130), § 2, eff. Jan. 1, 2020; Stats.2021, c. 527 (A.B.825), § 2, eff. Jan. 1, 2022.)*

Cross References

Age verification when selling products that are illegal to sell to minor, reasonable steps, products requiring age verification, penalties, see Civil Code § 1798.99.1.

Business defined for purposes of this Title, see Civil Code § 1798.80.

Cannabis, disclosure of consumer's personal information prohibited, exceptions, see Business and Professions Code § 26161.5.

Department of Health Care Services, generally, see Health and Safety Code § 100100 et seq.

Disclosure of a customer's personal information by business with an established business relationship within the preceding calendar year, customer's right to receive additional information relating to disclosure, see Civil Code § 1798.83.

Individual defined for purposes of this Title, see Civil Code § 1798.80.

Personal identification information upon credit card transaction form, prohibition upon collection of, civil penalties and injunctive relief, see Civil Code § 1747.08.

Personal information defined for purposes of this Title, see Civil Code § 1798.80.

Records defined for purposes of this Title, see Civil Code § 1798.80.

Specialty mental health services, see Welfare and Institutions Code § 14718.

§ 1798.81.6. Computer system vulnerability; consumer credit agency; security procedures and practices with respect to personal information about California residents

(a) A consumer credit reporting agency, as defined in 15 U.S.C. Sec. 1681a(p), that owns, licenses, or maintains personal information about a California resident, or a third party that maintains personal information about a California resident on behalf of a consumer credit reporting agency, that knows, or reasonably should know, that a computer system it owns, operates, or maintains, and for which it controls the security protocols, is subject to a security vulnerability that poses a significant risk, as defined in subdivision (c), to the security of computerized data that contains personal information, as defined in subdivision (h) of Section 1798.82, shall do all of the following:

(1) If a consumer credit reporting agency knows or reasonably should know that a software update is available to address the vulnerability as described in subdivision (a), the agency shall begin the necessary testing, planning, and assessment of its systems for implementation of that software update in the most expedient time possible and without unreasonable delay, in keeping with industry best practices, but in any case no later than three business days after becoming aware, or after the point at which it reasonably should have become aware, of the vulnerability and the available software update. The software update shall be completed in the most expedient time possible and without unreasonable delay, in keeping with industry best practices, but in any case no later than 90 days after becoming aware, or after the point at which it reasonably should have become aware, of the vulnerability and the available software update.

(2) Until the software update described in paragraph (1) is complete, the consumer credit reporting agency shall, in keeping with industry best practices, employ reasonable compensating controls to reduce the risk of a breach caused by computer system vulnerability as described in subdivision (a).

(b) Notwithstanding whether a software update is available, the consumer credit reporting agency, in keeping with industry best practices, shall do all of the following:

(1) Identify, prioritize, and address the highest risk security vulnerabilities most quickly in order to reduce the likelihood that the vulnerabilities that pose the greatest security risk will be exploited.

(2) Test and evaluate the impact of compensating controls and software updates and how they affect the vulnerability of the system to threats to the security of computerized data.

(3) Require, by contract, that the third party implement and maintain appropriate security measures for personal information. Contracting with a third party to maintain personal information about California residents shall not relieve the consumer credit agency of the requirements of this section.

(c) As used in this section, "significant risk" means a vulnerability score, calculated using a standard measurement system that is accepted as a best practice for the industry, to determine that the risk could reasonably result in a breach of the security of the system, as defined in subdivision (g) of Section 1798.82, of personal information, as defined in subdivision (h) of Section 1798.82.

(d) As used in this section, "compensating controls" means controls that the agency reasonably believes will prevent the computer system vulnerability as described in subdivision (a) from being exploited while the software update is being tested, assessed, and a plan for implementation is being developed, and have been adequately tested and confirmed to sufficiently offset the risk of breach caused by computer system vulnerability as described in subdivision (a).

(e) Nothing in this section shall reduce the responsibilities and obligations of a consumer credit reporting agency or third party under this title, including, but not limited to, Section 1798.81.5.

(f) The Attorney General has exclusive authority to enforce this section. *(Added by Stats.2018, c. 532 (A.B.1859), § 1, eff. Jan. 1, 2019.)*

§ 1798.82. Person or business who owns or licenses computerized data including personal information; breach of security of the system; disclosure requirements

(a) A person or business that conducts business in California, and that owns or licenses computerized data that includes personal information, shall disclose a breach of the security of the system following discovery or notification of the breach in the security of the data to a resident of California (1) whose unencrypted personal information was, or is reasonably believed to have been, acquired by an unauthorized person, or, (2) whose encrypted personal information was, or is reasonably believed to have been, acquired by an unauthorized person and the encryption key or security credential was, or is reasonably believed to have been, acquired by an unauthorized person and the person or business that owns or licenses the encrypted information has a reasonable belief that the encryption key or security credential could render that personal information readable or usable. The disclosure shall be made in the most expedient time possible and without unreasonable delay, consistent with the legitimate needs of law enforcement, as provided in subdivision (c), or any measures necessary to determine the scope of the breach and restore the reasonable integrity of the data system.

(b) A person or business that maintains computerized data that includes personal information that the person or business does not own shall notify the owner or licensee of the information of the breach of the security of the data immediately following discovery, if the personal information was, or is reasonably believed to have been, acquired by an unauthorized person.

(c) The notification required by this section may be delayed if a law enforcement agency determines that the notification will impede a criminal investigation. The notification required by this section shall be made promptly after the law enforcement agency determines that it will not compromise the investigation.

(d) A person or business that is required to issue a security breach notification pursuant to this section shall meet all of the following requirements:

(1) The security breach notification shall be written in plain language, shall be titled "Notice of Data Breach," and shall present the information described in paragraph (2) under the following headings: "What Happened," "What Information Was Involved," "What We Are Doing," "What

§ 1798.82 OBLIGATIONS

You Can Do," and "For More Information." Additional information may be provided as a supplement to the notice.

(A) The format of the notice shall be designed to call attention to the nature and significance of the information it contains.

(B) The title and headings in the notice shall be clearly and conspicuously displayed.

(C) The text of the notice and any other notice provided pursuant to this section shall be no smaller than 10-point type.

(D) For a written notice described in paragraph (1) of subdivision (j), use of the model security breach notification form prescribed below or use of the headings described in this paragraph with the information described in paragraph (2), written in plain language, shall be deemed to be in compliance with this subdivision.

[NAME OF INSTITUTION / LOGO]   Date: [insert date]

NOTICE OF DATA BREACH

What Happened?

What Information Was Involved?

What We Are Doing.

What You Can Do.

Other Important Information. [insert other important information]

For More Information.   Call [telephone number] or go to [internet website]

(E) For an electronic notice described in paragraph (2) of subdivision (j), use of the headings described in this paragraph with the information described in paragraph (2), written in plain language, shall be deemed to be in compliance with this subdivision.

(2) The security breach notification described in paragraph (1) shall include, at a minimum, the following information:

(A) The name and contact information of the reporting person or business subject to this section.

(B) A list of the types of personal information that were or are reasonably believed to have been the subject of a breach.

(C) If the information is possible to determine at the time the notice is provided, then any of the following: (i) the date of the breach, (ii) the estimated date of the breach, or (iii) the date range within which the breach occurred. The notification shall also include the date of the notice.

(D) Whether notification was delayed as a result of a law enforcement investigation, if that information is possible to determine at the time the notice is provided.

(E) A general description of the breach incident, if that information is possible to determine at the time the notice is provided.

(F) The toll-free telephone numbers and addresses of the major credit reporting agencies if the breach exposed a social security number or a driver's license or California identification card number.

(G) If the person or business providing the notification was the source of the breach, an offer to provide appropriate identity theft prevention and mitigation services, if any, shall be provided at no cost to the affected person for not less than 12 months along with all information necessary to take advantage of the offer to any person whose information was or may have been breached if the breach exposed or may have exposed personal information defined in subparagraphs (A) and (B) of paragraph (1) of subdivision (h).

(3) At the discretion of the person or business, the security breach notification may also include any of the following:

(A) Information about what the person or business has done to protect individuals whose information has been breached.

(B) Advice on steps that people whose information has been breached may take to protect themselves.

(C) In breaches involving biometric data, instructions on how to notify other entities that used the same type of biometric data as an authenticator to no longer rely on data for authentication purposes.

(e) A covered entity under the federal Health Insurance Portability and Accountability Act of 1996 (42 U.S.C. Sec. 1320d et seq.) will be deemed to have complied with the notice requirements in subdivision (d) if it has complied completely with Section 13402(f) of the federal Health Information Technology for Economic and Clinical Health Act (Public Law 111–5).[1] However, nothing in this subdivision shall be construed to exempt a covered entity from any other provision of this section.

(f) A person or business that is required to issue a security breach notification pursuant to this section to more than 500 California residents as a result of a single breach of the security system shall electronically submit a single sample copy of that security breach notification, excluding any personally identifiable information, to the Attorney General. A single sample copy of a security breach notification shall not be deemed to be within * * * <u>Article 1 (commencing with Section 7923.600) of Chapter 1 of Part 5 of Division 10 of Title 1 of the Government Code.</u>

(g) For purposes of this section, "breach of the security of the system" means unauthorized acquisition of computerized data that compromises the security, confidentiality, or integrity of personal information maintained by the person or business. Good faith acquisition of personal information by an employee or agent of the person or business for the purposes of the person or business is not a breach of the security of the system, provided that the personal information is not used or subject to further unauthorized disclosure.

(h) For purposes of this section, "personal information" means either of the following:

(1) An individual's first name or first initial and last name in combination with any one or more of the following data elements, when either the name or the data elements are not encrypted:

(A) Social security number.

(B) Driver's license number, California identification card number, tax identification number, passport number, military identification number, or other unique identification number issued on a government document commonly used to verify the identity of a specific individual.

(C) Account number or credit or debit card number, in combination with any required security code, access code, or password that would permit access to an individual's financial account.

(D) Medical information.

(E) Health insurance information.

(F) Unique biometric data generated from measurements or technical analysis of human body characteristics, such as a fingerprint, retina, or iris image, used to authenticate a specific individual. Unique biometric data does not include a physical or digital photograph, unless used or stored for facial recognition purposes.

(G) Information or data collected through the use or operation of an automated license plate recognition system, as defined in Section 1798.90.5.

(H) Genetic data.

(2) A username or email address, in combination with a password or security question and answer that would permit access to an online account.

(i)(1) For purposes of this section, "personal information" does not include publicly available information that is lawfully made available to the general public from federal, state, or local government records.

(2) For purposes of this section, "medical information" means any information regarding an individual's medical history, mental or physical condition, or medical treatment or diagnosis by a health care professional.

(3) For purposes of this section, "health insurance information" means an individual's health insurance policy number or subscriber identification number, any unique identifier used by a health insurer to identify the individual, or any information in an individual's application and claims history, including any appeals records.

(4) For purposes of this section, "encrypted" means rendered unusable, unreadable, or indecipherable to an unauthorized person through a security technology or methodology generally accepted in the field of information security.

(5) "Genetic data" means any data, regardless of its format, that results from the analysis of a biological sample of an individual, or from another source enabling equivalent information to be obtained, and concerns genetic material. Genetic material includes, but is not limited to, deoxyribonucleic acids (DNA), ribonucleic acids (RNA), genes, chromosomes, alleles, genomes, alterations or modifications to DNA or RNA, single nucleotide polymorphisms (SNPs), uninterpreted data that results from analysis of the biological sample or other source, and any information extrapolated, derived, or inferred therefrom.

(j) For purposes of this section, "notice" may be provided by one of the following methods:

(1) Written notice.

(2) Electronic notice, if the notice provided is consistent with the provisions regarding electronic records and signatures set forth in Section 7001 of Title 15 of the United States Code.

(3) Substitute notice, if the person or business demonstrates that the cost of providing notice would exceed two

§ 1798.82

hundred fifty thousand dollars ($250,000), or that the affected class of subject persons to be notified exceeds 500,000, or the person or business does not have sufficient contact information. Substitute notice shall consist of all of the following:

(A) Email notice when the person or business has an email address for the subject persons.

(B) Conspicuous posting, for a minimum of 30 days, of the notice on the internet website page of the person or business, if the person or business maintains one. For purposes of this subparagraph, conspicuous posting on the person's or business's internet website means providing a link to the notice on the home page or first significant page after entering the internet website that is in larger type than the surrounding text, or in contrasting type, font, or color to the surrounding text of the same size, or set off from the surrounding text of the same size by symbols or other marks that call attention to the link.

(C) Notification to major statewide media.

(4) In the case of a breach of the security of the system involving personal information defined in paragraph (2) of subdivision (h) for an online account, and no other personal information defined in paragraph (1) of subdivision (h), the person or business may comply with this section by providing the security breach notification in electronic or other form that directs the person whose personal information has been breached promptly to change the person's password and security question or answer, as applicable, or to take other steps appropriate to protect the online account with the person or business and all other online accounts for which the person whose personal information has been breached uses the same username or email address and password or security question or answer.

(5) In the case of a breach of the security of the system involving personal information defined in paragraph (2) of subdivision (h) for login credentials of an email account furnished by the person or business, the person or business shall not comply with this section by providing the security breach notification to that email address, but may, instead, comply with this section by providing notice by another method described in this subdivision or by clear and conspicuous notice delivered to the resident online when the resident is connected to the online account from an Internet Protocol address or online location from which the person or business knows the resident customarily accesses the account.

(k) For purposes of this section, "encryption key" and "security credential" mean the confidential key or process designed to render data usable, readable, and decipherable.

(l) Notwithstanding subdivision (j), a person or business that maintains its own notification procedures as part of an information security policy for the treatment of personal information and is otherwise consistent with the timing requirements of this part, shall be deemed to be in compliance with the notification requirements of this section if the person or business notifies subject persons in accordance with its policies in the event of a breach of security of the system.
(Added by Stats.2002, c. 1054 (A.B.700), § 4, operative July 1, 2003. Amended by Stats.2007, c. 699 (A.B.1298), § 6; Stats. 2011, c. 197 (S.B.24), § 2; Stats.2013, c. 396 (S.B.46), § 2; Stats.2014, c. 855 (A.B.1710), § 2, eff. Jan. 1, 2015; Stats.2015, c. 522 (A.B.964), § 2, eff. Jan. 1, 2016; Stats.2015, c. 532

OBLIGATIONS

(S.B.34), § 2, eff. Jan. 1, 2016; Stats.2015, c. 543 (S.B.570), § 2.3, eff. Jan. 1, 2016; Stats.2016, c. 86 (S.B.1171), § 21, eff. Jan. 1, 2017; Stats.2016, c. 337 (A.B.2828), § 2, eff. Jan. 1, 2017; Stats.2019, c. 750 (A.B.1130), § 3, eff. Jan. 1, 2020; Stats.2020, c. 370 (S.B.1371), § 29, eff. Jan. 1, 2021; Stats. 2021, c. 615 (A.B.474), § 48, eff. Jan. 1, 2022, operative Jan. 1, 2023; Stats.2021, c. 527 (A.B.825), § 3, eff. Jan. 1, 2022; Stats.2022, c. 28 (S.B.1380), § 23, eff. Jan. 1, 2023.)

[1] For public law sections classified to the U.S.C.A., see USCA–Tables.

Cross References

Age verification when selling products that are illegal to sell to minor, reasonable steps, products requiring age verification, penalties, see Civil Code § 1798.99.1.
Business defined for purposes of this Title, see Civil Code § 1798.80.
Identity theft actions, statute of limitations, see Civil Code § 1798.96.
Individual defined for purposes of this Title, see Civil Code § 1798.80.
Local educational agencies, reporting of cyberattacks, see Education Code § 35266.
Mental health digital service providers, information regarding how to find data breaches, see Civil Code § 56.251.
Personal information defined for purposes of this Title, see Civil Code § 1798.80.
Records defined for purposes of this Title, see Civil Code § 1798.80.
Security breaches of computerized data including personal information, agencies owning, licensing, or maintaining the data, disclosure and notice requirements, see Civil Code § 1798.29.

§ 1798.83. Personal information; disclosure to direct marketers

(a) Except as otherwise provided in subdivision (d), if a business has an established business relationship with a customer and has within the immediately preceding calendar year disclosed personal information that corresponds to any of the categories of personal information set forth in paragraph (6) of subdivision (e) to third parties, and if the business knows or reasonably should know that the third parties used the personal information for the third parties' direct marketing purposes, that business shall, after the receipt of a written or electronic mail request, or, if the business chooses to receive requests by toll-free telephone or facsimile numbers, a telephone or facsimile request from the customer, provide all of the following information to the customer free of charge:

(1) In writing or by electronic mail, a list of the categories set forth in paragraph (6) of subdivision (e) that correspond to the personal information disclosed by the business to third parties for the third parties' direct marketing purposes during the immediately preceding calendar year.

(2) In writing or by electronic mail, the names and addresses of all of the third parties that received personal information from the business for the third parties' direct marketing purposes during the preceding calendar year and, if the nature of the third parties' business cannot reasonably be determined from the third parties' name, examples of the products or services marketed, if known to the business, sufficient to give the customer a reasonable indication of the nature of the third parties' business.

(b)(1) A business required to comply with this section shall designate a mailing address, electronic mail address, or, if the business chooses to receive requests by telephone or facsimile, a toll-free telephone or facsimile number, to which customers may deliver requests pursuant to subdivision (a). A business required to comply with this section shall, at its election, do at least one of the following:

(A) Notify all agents and managers who directly supervise employees who regularly have contact with customers of the designated addresses or numbers or the means to obtain those addresses or numbers and instruct those employees that customers who inquire about the business's privacy practices or the business's compliance with this section shall be informed of the designated addresses or numbers or the means to obtain the addresses or numbers.

(B) Add to the home page of its Web site a link either to a page titled "Your Privacy Rights" or add the words "Your Privacy Rights" to the home page's link to the business's privacy policy. If the business elects to add the words "Your Privacy Rights" to the link to the business's privacy policy, the words "Your Privacy Rights" shall be in the same style and size as the link to the business's privacy policy. If the business does not display a link to its privacy policy on the home page of its Web site, or does not have a privacy policy, the words "Your Privacy Rights" shall be written in larger type than the surrounding text, or in contrasting type, font, or color to the surrounding text of the same size, or set off from the surrounding text of the same size by symbols or other marks that call attention to the language. The first page of the link shall describe a customer's rights pursuant to this section and shall provide the designated mailing address, e-mail address, as required, or toll-free telephone number or facsimile number, as appropriate. If the business elects to add the words "Your California Privacy Rights" to the home page's link to the business's privacy policy in a manner that complies with this subdivision, and the first page of the link describes a customer's rights pursuant to this section, and provides the designated mailing address, electronic mailing address, as required, or toll-free telephone or facsimile number, as appropriate, the business need not respond to requests that are not received at one of the designated addresses or numbers.

(C) Make the designated addresses or numbers, or means to obtain the designated addresses or numbers, readily available upon request of a customer at every place of business in California where the business or its agents regularly have contact with customers.

The response to a request pursuant to this section received at one of the designated addresses or numbers shall be provided within 30 days. Requests received by the business at other than one of the designated addresses or numbers shall be provided within a reasonable period, in light of the circumstances related to how the request was received, but not to exceed 150 days from the date received.

(2) A business that is required to comply with this section and Section 6803 of Title 15 of the United States Code may comply with this section by providing the customer the disclosure required by Section 6803 of Title 15 of the United States Code, but only if the disclosure also complies with this section.

(3) A business that is required to comply with this section is not obligated to provide information associated with specific individuals and may provide the information required by this section in standardized format.

(c)(1) A business that is required to comply with this section is not obligated to do so in response to a request from a customer more than once during the course of any calendar year. A business with fewer than 20 full-time or part-time employees is exempt from the requirements of this section.

(2) If a business that is required to comply with this section adopts and discloses to the public, in its privacy policy, a policy of not disclosing personal information of customers to third parties for the third parties' direct marketing purposes unless the customer first affirmatively agrees to that disclosure, or of not disclosing the personal information of customers to third parties for the third parties' direct marketing purposes if the customer has exercised an option that prevents that information from being disclosed to third parties for those purposes, as long as the business maintains and discloses the policies, the business may comply with subdivision (a) by notifying the customer of his or her right to prevent disclosure of personal information, and providing the customer with a cost-free means to exercise that right.

(d) The following are among the disclosures not deemed to be disclosures of personal information by a business for a third party's direct marketing purposes for purposes of this section:

(1) Disclosures between a business and a third party pursuant to contracts or arrangements pertaining to any of the following:

(A) The processing, storage, management, or organization of personal information, or the performance of services on behalf of the business during which personal information is disclosed, if the third party that processes, stores, manages, or organizes the personal information does not use the information for a third party's direct marketing purposes and does not disclose the information to additional third parties for their direct marketing purposes.

(B) Marketing products or services to customers with whom the business has an established business relationship where, as a part of the marketing, the business does not disclose personal information to third parties for the third parties' direct marketing purposes.

(C) Maintaining or servicing accounts, including credit accounts and disclosures pertaining to the denial of applications for credit or the status of applications for credit and processing bills or insurance claims for payment.

(D) Public record information relating to the right, title, or interest in real property or information relating to property characteristics, as defined in Section 408.3 of the Revenue and Taxation Code, obtained from a governmental agency or entity or from a multiple listing service, as defined in Section 1087, and not provided directly by the customer to a business in the course of an established business relationship.

(E) Jointly offering a product or service pursuant to a written agreement with the third party that receives the personal information, provided that all of the following requirements are met:

(i) The product or service offered is a product or service of, and is provided by, at least one of the businesses that is a party to the written agreement.

§ 1798.83

(ii) The product or service is jointly offered, endorsed, or sponsored by, and clearly and conspicuously identifies for the customer, the businesses that disclose and receive the disclosed personal information.

(iii) The written agreement provides that the third party that receives the personal information is required to maintain the confidentiality of the information and is prohibited from disclosing or using the information other than to carry out the joint offering or servicing of a product or service that is the subject of the written agreement.

(2) Disclosures to or from a consumer reporting agency of a customer's payment history or other information pertaining to transactions or experiences between the business and a customer if that information is to be reported in, or used to generate, a consumer report as defined in subdivision (d) of Section 1681a of Title 15 of the United States Code, and use of that information is limited by the federal Fair Credit Reporting Act (15 U.S.C. Sec. 1681 et seq.).

(3) Disclosures of personal information by a business to a third party financial institution solely for the purpose of the business obtaining payment for a transaction in which the customer paid the business for goods or services with a check, credit card, charge card, or debit card, if the customer seeks the information required by subdivision (a) from the business obtaining payment, whether or not the business obtaining payment knows or reasonably should know that the third party financial institution has used the personal information for its direct marketing purposes.

(4) Disclosures of personal information between a licensed agent and its principal, if the personal information disclosed is necessary to complete, effectuate, administer, or enforce transactions between the principal and the agent, whether or not the licensed agent or principal also uses the personal information for direct marketing purposes, if that personal information is used by each of them solely to market products and services directly to customers with whom both have established business relationships as a result of the principal and agent relationship.

(5) Disclosures of personal information between a financial institution and a business that has a private label credit card, affinity card, retail installment contract, or cobranded card program with the financial institution, if the personal information disclosed is necessary for the financial institution to maintain or service accounts on behalf of the business with which it has a private label credit card, affinity card, retail installment contract, or cobranded card program, or to complete, effectuate, administer, or enforce customer transactions or transactions between the institution and the business, whether or not the institution or the business also uses the personal information for direct marketing purposes, if that personal information is used solely to market products and services directly to customers with whom both the business and the financial institution have established business relationships as a result of the private label credit card, affinity card, retail installment contract, or cobranded card program.

(e) For purposes of this section, the following terms have the following meanings:

(1) "Customer" means an individual who is a resident of California who provides personal information to a business during the creation of, or throughout the duration of, an established business relationship if the business relationship is primarily for personal, family, or household purposes.

(2) "Direct marketing purposes" means the use of personal information to solicit or induce a purchase, rental, lease, or exchange of products, goods, property, or services directly to individuals by means of the mail, telephone, or electronic mail for their personal, family, or household purposes. The sale, rental, exchange, or lease of personal information for consideration to businesses is a direct marketing purpose of the business that sells, rents, exchanges, or obtains consideration for the personal information. "Direct marketing purposes" does not include the use of personal information (A) by bona fide tax exempt charitable or religious organizations to solicit charitable contributions, (B) to raise funds from and communicate with individuals regarding politics and government, (C) by a third party when the third party receives personal information solely as a consequence of having obtained for consideration permanent ownership of accounts that might contain personal information, or (D) by a third party when the third party receives personal information solely as a consequence of a single transaction where, as a part of the transaction, personal information had to be disclosed in order to effectuate the transaction.

(3) "Disclose" means to disclose, release, transfer, disseminate, or otherwise communicate orally, in writing, or by electronic or any other means to any third party.

(4) "Employees who regularly have contact with customers" means employees whose contact with customers is not incidental to their primary employment duties, and whose duties do not predominantly involve ensuring the safety or health of the business's customers. It includes, but is not limited to, employees whose primary employment duties are as cashier, clerk, customer service, sales, or promotion. It does not, by way of example, include employees whose primary employment duties consist of food or beverage preparation or service, maintenance and repair of the business's facilities or equipment, direct involvement in the operation of a motor vehicle, aircraft, watercraft, amusement ride, heavy machinery or similar equipment, security, or participation in a theatrical, literary, musical, artistic, or athletic performance or contest.

(5) "Established business relationship" means a relationship formed by a voluntary, two-way communication between a business and a customer, with or without an exchange of consideration, for the purpose of purchasing, renting, or leasing real or personal property, or any interest therein, or obtaining a product or service from the business, if the relationship is ongoing and has not been expressly terminated by the business or the customer, or if the relationship is not ongoing, but is solely established by the purchase, rental, or lease of real or personal property from a business, or the purchase of a product or service, and no more than 18 months have elapsed from the date of the purchase, rental, or lease.

(6)(A) The categories of personal information required to be disclosed pursuant to paragraph (1) of subdivision (a) are all of the following:

(i) Name and address.

(ii) Electronic mail address.

(iii) Age or date of birth.

(iv) Names of children.

(v) Electronic mail or other addresses of children.

(vi) Number of children.

(vii) The age or gender of children.

(viii) Height.

(ix) Weight.

(x) Race.

(xi) Religion.

(xii) Occupation.

(xiii) Telephone number.

(xiv) Education.

(xv) Political party affiliation.

(xvi) Medical condition.

(xvii) Drugs, therapies, or medical products or equipment used.

(xviii) The kind of product the customer purchased, leased, or rented.

(xix) Real property purchased, leased, or rented.

(xx) The kind of service provided.

(xxi) Social security number.

(xxii) Bank account number.

(xxiii) Credit card number.

(xxiv) Debit card number.

(xxv) Bank or investment account, debit card, or credit card balance.

(xxvi) Payment history.

(xxvii) Information pertaining to the customer's creditworthiness, assets, income, or liabilities.

(B) If a list, description, or grouping of customer names or addresses is derived using any of these categories, and is disclosed to a third party for direct marketing purposes in a manner that permits the third party to identify, determine, or extrapolate any other personal information from which the list was derived, and that personal information when it was disclosed identified, described, or was associated with an individual, the categories set forth in this subdivision that correspond to the personal information used to derive the list, description, or grouping shall be considered personal information for purposes of this section.

(7) "Personal information" as used in this section means any information that when it was disclosed identified, described, or was able to be associated with an individual and includes all of the following:

(A) An individual's name and address.

(B) Electronic mail address.

(C) Age or date of birth.

(D) Names of children.

(E) Electronic mail or other addresses of children.

(F) Number of children.

(G) The age or gender of children.

(H) Height.

(I) Weight.

(J) Race.

(K) Religion.

(L) Occupation.

(M) Telephone number.

(N) Education.

(O) Political party affiliation.

(P) Medical condition.

(Q) Drugs, therapies, or medical products or equipment used.

(R) The kind of product the customer purchased, leased, or rented.

(S) Real property purchased, leased, or rented.

(T) The kind of service provided.

(U) Social security number.

(V) Bank account number.

(W) Credit card number.

(X) Debit card number.

(Y) Bank or investment account, debit card, or credit card balance.

(Z) Payment history.

(AA) Information pertaining to creditworthiness, assets, income, or liabilities.

(8) "Third party" or "third parties" means one or more of the following:

(A) A business that is a separate legal entity from the business that has an established business relationship with a customer.

(B) A business that has access to a database that is shared among businesses, if the business is authorized to use the database for direct marketing purposes, unless the use of the database is exempt from being considered a disclosure for direct marketing purposes pursuant to subdivision (d).

(C) A business not affiliated by a common ownership or common corporate control with the business required to comply with subdivision (a).

(f)(1) Disclosures of personal information for direct marketing purposes between affiliated third parties that share the same brand name are exempt from the requirements of paragraph (1) of subdivision (a) unless the personal information disclosed corresponds to one of the following categories, in which case the customer shall be informed of those categories listed in this subdivision that correspond to the categories of personal information disclosed for direct marketing purposes and the third party recipients of personal information disclosed for direct marketing purposes pursuant to paragraph (2) of subdivision (a):

(A) Number of children.

(B) The age or gender of children.

(C) Electronic mail or other addresses of children.

(D) Height.

(E) Weight.

(F) Race.

§ 1798.83

(G) Religion.

(H) Telephone number.

(I) Medical condition.

(J) Drugs, therapies, or medical products or equipment used.

(K) Social security number.

(L) Bank account number.

(M) Credit card number.

(N) Debit card number.

(O) Bank or investment account, debit card, or credit card balance.

(2) If a list, description, or grouping of customer names or addresses is derived using any of these categories, and is disclosed to a third party or third parties sharing the same brand name for direct marketing purposes in a manner that permits the third party to identify, determine, or extrapolate the personal information from which the list was derived, and that personal information when it was disclosed identified, described, or was associated with an individual, any other personal information that corresponds to the categories set forth in this subdivision used to derive the list, description, or grouping shall be considered personal information for purposes of this section.

(3) If a business discloses personal information for direct marketing purposes to affiliated third parties that share the same brand name, the business that discloses personal information for direct marketing purposes between affiliated third parties that share the same brand name may comply with the requirements of paragraph (2) of subdivision (a) by providing the overall number of affiliated companies that share the same brand name.

(g) The provisions of this section are severable. If any provision of this section or its application is held invalid, that invalidity shall not affect other provisions or applications that can be given effect without the invalid provision or application.

(h) This section does not apply to a financial institution that is subject to the California Financial Information Privacy Act (Division 1.2 (commencing with Section 4050) of the Financial Code) if the financial institution is in compliance with Sections 4052, 4052.5, 4053, 4053.5, and 4054.6 of the Financial Code, as those sections read when they were chaptered on August 28, 2003, and as subsequently amended by the Legislature or by initiative.

(i) This section shall become operative on January 1, 2005. (Added by Stats.2003, c. 505 (S.B.27), § 3, operative Jan. 1, 2005. Amended by Stats.2004, c. 183 (A.B.3082), § 34, operative Jan. 1, 2005; Stats.2005, c. 22 (S.B.1108), § 16.)

Cross References

Business defined for purposes of this Title, see Civil Code § 1798.80.
Business solicitations, governmental term or symbol, use conditions, see Business and Professions Code § 17533.6.
Businesses that own or license personal identification information, duty to provide reasonable security to protect, see Civil Code § 1798.81.5.

Computer vendors, consent required from dealer to access, modify, or extract information from confidential dealer computer records or personally identifiable consumer data, see Vehicle Code § 11713.25.
Customer defined for purposes of this Title, see Civil Code § 1798.80.
Individual defined for purposes of this Title, see Civil Code § 1798.80.
Personal identification information upon credit card transaction form, prohibition upon collection of, civil penalties and injunctive relief, see Civil Code § 1747.08.
Personal information defined for purposes of this Title, see Civil Code § 1798.80.

§ 1798.83.5. Commercial online entertainment employment service providers; limits on publication of subscribers' age information

(a) The purpose of this section is to ensure that information obtained on an Internet Web site regarding an individual's age will not be used in furtherance of employment or age discrimination.

(b) A commercial online entertainment employment service provider that enters into a contractual agreement to provide employment services to an individual for a subscription payment shall not, upon request by the subscriber, do either of the following:

(1) Publish or make public the subscriber's date of birth or age information in an online profile of the subscriber.

(2) Share the subscriber's date of birth or age information with any Internet Web sites for the purpose of publication.

(c) A commercial online entertainment employment service provider subject to subdivision (b) shall, within five days, remove from public view in an online profile of the subscriber the subscriber's date of birth and age information on any companion Internet Web sites under its control upon specific request by the subscriber naming the Internet Web sites. A commercial online entertainment employment service provider that permits members of the public to upload or modify Internet content on its own Internet Web site or any Internet Web site under its control without prior review by that provider shall not be deemed in violation of this section unless first requested by the subscriber to remove age information.

(d) For purposes of this section, the following definitions apply:

(1) "Commercial online entertainment employment service provider" means a person or business that owns, licenses, or otherwise possesses computerized information, including, but not limited to, age and date of birth information, about individuals employed in the entertainment industry, including television, films, and video games, and that makes the information available to the public or potential employers.

(2) "Payment" means a fee in exchange for advertisements, or any other form of compensation or benefit.

(3) "Provide employment services" means post resumes, photographs, or other information about a subscriber when one of the purposes is to provide individually identifiable information about the subscriber to a prospective employer.

(4) "Subscriber" means a natural person who enters into a contractual agreement with a commercial online entertain-

ment employment service provider to receive employment services in return for a subscription payment. *(Added by Stats.2016, c. 555 (A.B.1687), § 1, eff. Jan. 1, 2017.)*

Validity

For validity of this section, see IMDb.com Inc. v. Becerra, C.A.9 (Cal.)2020, 962 F.3d 1111.

§ 1798.84. Waiver and violations of provisions of this title; civil actions and penalties; disposal of abandoned records containing personal information; attorney's fees and costs

(a) Any waiver of a provision of this title is contrary to public policy and is void and unenforceable.

(b) Any customer injured by a violation of this title may institute a civil action to recover damages.

(c) In addition, for a willful, intentional, or reckless violation of Section 1798.83, a customer may recover a civil penalty not to exceed three thousand dollars ($3,000) per violation; otherwise, the customer may recover a civil penalty of up to five hundred dollars ($500) per violation for a violation of Section 1798.83.

(d) Unless the violation is willful, intentional, or reckless, a business that is alleged to have not provided all the information required by subdivision (a) of Section 1798.83, to have provided inaccurate information, failed to provide any of the information required by subdivision (a) of Section 1798.83, or failed to provide information in the time period required by subdivision (b) of Section 1798.83, may assert as a complete defense in any action in law or equity that it thereafter provided regarding the information that was alleged to be untimely, all the information, or accurate information, to all customers who were provided incomplete or inaccurate information, respectively, within 90 days of the date the business knew that it had failed to provide the information, timely information, all the information, or the accurate information, respectively.

(e) Any business that violates, proposes to violate, or has violated this title may be enjoined.

(f)(1) A cause of action shall not lie against a business for disposing of abandoned records containing personal information by shredding, erasing, or otherwise modifying the personal information in the records to make it unreadable or undecipherable through any means.

(2) The Legislature finds and declares that when records containing personal information are abandoned by a business, they often end up in the possession of a storage company or commercial landlord. It is the intent of the Legislature in paragraph (1) to create a safe harbor for such a record custodian who properly disposes of the records in accordance with paragraph (1).

(g) A prevailing plaintiff in any action commenced under Section 1798.83 shall also be entitled to recover his or her reasonable attorney's fees and costs.

(h) The rights and remedies available under this section are cumulative to each other and to any other rights and remedies available under law. *(Formerly § 1798.82, added by Stats.2000, c. 1039 (A.B.2246), § 1. Renumbered § 1798.84 and amended by Stats.2002, c. 915 (S.B.1386), § 3, operative July 1, 2003; Stats.2002, c. 1054 (A.B.700), § 3, operative July 1, 2003. Amended by Stats.2003, c. 505 (S.B.27), § 4; Stats.2009, c. 134 (A.B.1094), § 3.)*

Cross References

Business defined for purposes of this Title, see Civil Code § 1798.80.
Customer defined for purposes of this Title, see Civil Code § 1798.80.
Identity theft actions, statute of limitations, see Civil Code § 1798.96.
Injunctions, provisional remedies and specific and preventive relief, generally, see Civil Code § 3420 et seq.; Code of Civil Procedure § 525 et seq.

Title 1.81.1

CONFIDENTIALITY OF SOCIAL SECURITY NUMBERS

Section
1798.85. Prohibited actions with respect to social security numbers; application and exceptions; operative dates with respect to specified entities.
1798.86. Public policy; waiver of rights.
1798.89. Recording or filing of documents; social security numbers; due diligence in using truncated social security numbers.

§ 1798.85. Prohibited actions with respect to social security numbers; application and exceptions; operative dates with respect to specified entities

(a) Except as provided in this section, a person or entity may not do any of the following:

(1) Publicly post or publicly display in any manner an individual's social security number. "Publicly post" or "publicly display" means to intentionally communicate or otherwise make available to the general public.

(2) Print an individual's social security number on any card required for the individual to access products or services provided by the person or entity.

(3) Require an individual to transmit the individual's social security number over the internet, unless the connection is secure or the social security number is encrypted.

(4) Require an individual to use the individual's social security number to access an internet website, unless a password or unique personal identification number or other authentication device is also required to access the internet website.

(5) Print an individual's social security number on any materials that are mailed to the individual, unless state or federal law requires the social security number to be on the document to be mailed. Notwithstanding this paragraph, social security numbers may be included in applications and forms sent by mail, including documents sent as part of an application or enrollment process, or to establish, amend, or terminate an account, contract, or policy, or to confirm the accuracy of the social security number. A social security number that is permitted to be mailed under this section may not be printed, in whole or in part, on a postcard or other

§ 1798.85

mailer not requiring an envelope, or visible on the envelope or without the envelope having been opened.

(6) Sell, advertise for sale, or offer to sell an individual's social security number. For purposes of this paragraph, the following apply:

(A) "Sell" shall not include the release of an individual's social security number if the release of the social security number is incidental to a larger transaction and is necessary to identify the individual in order to accomplish a legitimate business purpose. Release of an individual's social security number for marketing purposes is not permitted.

(B) "Sell" shall not include the release of an individual's social security number for a purpose specifically authorized or specifically allowed by federal or state law.

(b) This section does not prevent the collection, use, or release of a social security number as required by state or federal law or the use of a social security number for internal verification or administrative purposes.

(c) This section does not prevent an adult state correctional facility, an adult city jail, or an adult county jail from releasing an inmate's social security number, with the inmate's consent and upon request by the county veterans service officer or the United States Department of Veterans Affairs, for the purposes of determining the inmate's status as a military veteran and the inmate's eligibility for federal, state, or local veterans' benefits or services.

(d) This section does not apply to documents that are recorded or required to be open to the public pursuant to Chapter 14 (commencing with Section 7150) or Chapter 14.5 (commencing with Section 7220) of Division 7 of Title 1 of, Division 10 (commencing with Section 7920.000) of Title 1 of, Article 9 (commencing with Section 11120) of Chapter 1 of Part 1 of Division 3 of Title 2 of, or Chapter 9 (commencing with Section 54950) of Part 1 of Division 2 of Title 5 of, the Government Code. This section does not apply to records that are required by statute, case law, or California Rules of Court, to be made available to the public by entities provided for in Article VI of the California Constitution.

(e)(1) In the case of a health care service plan, a provider of health care, an insurer or a pharmacy benefits manager, a contractor as defined in Section 56.05, or the provision by any person or entity of administrative or other services relative to health care or insurance products or services, including third-party administration or administrative services only, this section shall become operative in the following manner:

(A) On or before January 1, 2003, the entities listed in paragraph (1) shall comply with paragraphs (1), (3), (4), and (5) of subdivision (a) as these requirements pertain to individual policyholders or individual contractholders.

(B) On or before January 1, 2004, the entities listed in paragraph (1) shall comply with paragraphs (1) to (5), inclusive, of subdivision (a) as these requirements pertain to new individual policyholders or new individual contractholders and new groups, including new groups administered or issued on or after January 1, 2004.

(C) On or before July 1, 2004, the entities listed in paragraph (1) shall comply with paragraphs (1) to (5), inclusive, of subdivision (a) for all individual policyholders and individual contractholders, for all groups, and for all enrollees of the Healthy Families and Medi-Cal programs, except that for individual policyholders, individual contractholders and groups in existence prior to January 1, 2004, the entities listed in paragraph (1) shall comply upon the renewal date of the policy, contract, or group on or after July 1, 2004, but no later than July 1, 2005.

(2) A health care service plan, a provider of health care, an insurer or a pharmacy benefits manager, a contractor, or another person or entity as described in paragraph (1) shall make reasonable efforts to cooperate, through systems testing and other means, to ensure that the requirements of this article are implemented on or before the dates specified in this section.

(3) Notwithstanding paragraph (2), the Director of the Department of Managed Health Care, pursuant to the authority granted under Section 1346 of the Health and Safety Code, or the Insurance Commissioner, pursuant to the authority granted under Section 12921 of the Insurance Code, and upon a determination of good cause, may grant extensions not to exceed six months for compliance by health care service plans and insurers with the requirements of this section when requested by the health care service plan or insurer. Any extension granted shall apply to the health care service plan or insurer's affected providers, pharmacy benefits manager, and contractors.

(f) If a federal law takes effect requiring the United States Department of Health and Human Services to establish a national unique patient health identifier program, a provider of health care, a health care service plan, a licensed health care professional, or a contractor, as those terms are defined in Section 56.05, that complies with the federal law shall be deemed in compliance with this section.

(g) A person or entity may not encode or embed a social security number in or on a card or document, including, but not limited to, using a barcode, chip, magnetic strip, or other technology, in place of removing the social security number, as required by this section.

(h) This section shall become operative, with respect to the University of California, in the following manner:

(1) On or before January 1, 2004, the University of California shall comply with paragraphs (1), (2), and (3) of subdivision (a).

(2) On or before January 1, 2005, the University of California shall comply with paragraphs (4) and (5) of subdivision (a).

(i) This section shall become operative with respect to the Franchise Tax Board on January 1, 2007.

(j) This section shall become operative with respect to the California community college districts on January 1, 2007.

(k) This section shall become operative with respect to the California State University system on July 1, 2005.

(*l*) This section shall become operative, with respect to the California Student Aid Commission and its auxiliary organization, in the following manner:

(1) On or before January 1, 2004, the commission and its auxiliary organization shall comply with paragraphs (1), (2), and (3) of subdivision (a).

(2) On or before January 1, 2005, the commission and its auxiliary organization shall comply with paragraphs (4) and (5) of subdivision (a). *(Added by Stats.2001, c. 720 (S.B.168), § 7. Amended by Stats.2002, c. 664 (A.B.3034), § 42; Stats.2002, c. 786 (S.B.1730), § 3; Stats.2003, c. 532 (A.B.763), § 1; Stats.2003, c. 907 (S.B.25), § 5.5; Stats.2004, c. 183 (A.B.3082), § 35; Stats.2004, c. 282 (A.B.3016), § 1, operative July 1, 2006; Stats.2013, c. 103 (A.B.555), § 1; Stats.2014, c. 855 (A.B.1710), § 3, eff. Jan. 1, 2015; Stats.2021, c. 615 (A.B.474), § 49, eff. Jan. 1, 2022, operative Jan. 1, 2023.)*

Operative Effect

For operative effect of this section, see its terms.

Cross References

Department of Health Care Services, generally, see Health and Safety Code § 100100 et seq.

Department of Managed Health Care, generally, see Health and Safety Code § 1341 et seq.

Investigative reporting agencies, remedies, permitting printing of social security numbers on account statements, see Civil Code § 1786.60.

§ 1798.86. Public policy; waiver of rights

Any waiver of the provisions of this title is contrary to public policy, and is void and unenforceable. *(Added by Stats.2002, c. 815 (A.B.2331), § 16.)*

§ 1798.89. Recording or filing of documents; social security numbers; due diligence in using truncated social security numbers

(a) Unless otherwise required to do so by state or federal law, no person, entity, or governmental agency shall present for recording or filing with a county recorder a document that is required by any provision of law to be open to the public if that record displays more than the last four digits of a social security number. Unless otherwise authorized by state or federal law, a document containing more than the last four digits of a social security number is not entitled for recording.

(b) A recorder shall be deemed to be in compliance with the requirements of this section if he or she uses due diligence to truncate social security numbers in documents recorded, as provided in Article 3.5 (commencing with Section 27300) of Chapter 6 of Part 3 of Division 2 of Title 3 of the Government Code.

(c) This section shall not apply to documents created prior to January 1, 2010. *(Added by Stats.2009, c. 552 (S.B.40), § 2.)*

Title 1.81.15

READER PRIVACY ACT

Section
1798.90. Short title; definitions; restrictions on disclosure of personal information of book service users; orders compelling disclosure; preservation of records and evidence; admissibility of evidence; penalties; defense; reports; actions by operators of certain commercial Web sites and online services.

Section
1798.90.05. Authority to obtain search warrants for personal information of book service users; provider compliance with proper search warrants.

§ 1798.90. Short title; definitions; restrictions on disclosure of personal information of book service users; orders compelling disclosure; preservation of records and evidence; admissibility of evidence; penalties; defense; reports; actions by operators of certain commercial Web sites and online services

(a) This title shall be known and may be cited as the Reader Privacy Act.

(b) For purposes of this section:

(1) "Book" means paginated or similarly organized content in printed, audio, electronic, or other format, including fiction, nonfiction, academic, or other works of the type normally published in a volume or finite number of volumes, excluding serial publications such as a magazine or newspaper.

(2) "Book service" means a service that, as its primary purpose, provides the rental, purchase, borrowing, browsing, or viewing of books. "Book service" does not include a store that sells a variety of consumer products when the book service sales do not exceed 2 percent of the store's total annual gross sales of consumer products sold in the United States.

(3) "Government entity" means any state or local agency, including, but not limited to, a law enforcement entity or any other investigative entity, agency, department, division, bureau, board, or commission, or any individual acting or purporting to act for or on behalf of a state or local agency.

(4) "Law enforcement entity" means a district attorney, a district attorney's office, a municipal police department, a sheriff's department, a county probation department, a county social services agency, the Department of Justice, the Department of Corrections and Rehabilitation, the Department of Corrections and Rehabilitation Division of Juvenile Facilities, the Department of the California Highway Patrol, the police department of a campus of a community college, the University of California, or the California State University, or any other department or agency of the state authorized to investigate or prosecute the commission of a crime.

(5) "Personal information" means all of the following:

(A) Any information that identifies, relates to, describes, or is associated with a particular user, including, but not limited to, the information specifically listed in Section 1798.80.

(B) A unique identifier or Internet Protocol address, when that identifier or address is used to identify, relate to, describe, or be associated with a particular user or book, in whole or in partial form.

(C) Any information that relates to, or is capable of being associated with, a particular user's access to or use of a book service or a book, in whole or in partial form.

(6) "Provider" means any commercial entity offering a book service to the public.

(7) "User" means any person or entity that uses a book service.

§ 1798.90

(c) A provider shall not knowingly disclose to any government entity, or be compelled to disclose to any person, private entity, or government entity, any personal information of a user, except under any of the following circumstances:

(1) A provider shall disclose personal information of a user to a law enforcement entity only pursuant to a court order issued by a duly authorized court with jurisdiction over an offense that is under investigation and only if all of the following conditions are met:

(A) The court issuing the order finds that probable cause exists to believe the personal information requested is relevant evidence to the investigation of an offense and any of the grounds in Section 1524 of the Penal Code is satisfied.

(B) The court issuing the order finds that the law enforcement entity seeking disclosure has a compelling interest in obtaining the personal information sought.

(C) The court issuing the order finds that the personal information sought cannot be obtained by the law enforcement entity seeking disclosure through less intrusive means.

(D) Prior to issuance of the court order, the law enforcement entity seeking disclosure provides, in a timely manner, the provider with reasonable notice of the proceeding to allow the provider the opportunity to appear and contest issuance of the order.

(E) The law enforcement entity seeking disclosure has informed the provider that it has given notice of the court order to the user contemporaneously with the execution of the order, unless there is a judicial determination of a strong showing of necessity to delay that notification for a reasonable period of time, not to exceed 90 days.

(2)(A) A provider shall disclose personal information of a user to any of the following only if all of the conditions listed in subparagraph (B) are satisfied:

(i) A government entity, other than a law enforcement entity, pursuant to a court order issued by a court having jurisdiction over an offense under investigation by that government entity.

(ii) A government entity, other than a law enforcement entity, or a person or private entity pursuant to a court order in a pending action brought by the government entity or by the person or private entity.

(B) A provider shall disclose personal information of a user pursuant to subparagraph (A) only if all of the following conditions are satisfied:

(i) The court issuing the order finds that the person or entity seeking disclosure has a compelling interest in obtaining the personal information sought.

(ii) The court issuing the order finds that the personal information sought cannot be obtained by the person or entity seeking disclosure through less intrusive means.

(iii) Prior to issuance of the court order, the person or entity seeking disclosure provides, in a timely manner, the provider with reasonable notice of the proceeding to allow the provider the opportunity to appear and contest the issuance of the court order.

(iv) The provider refrains from disclosing any personal information pursuant to the court order until it provides, in a timely manner, notice to the user about the issuance of the order and the ability to appear and quash the order, and the user has been given a minimum of 35 days prior to disclosure of the information within which to appear and quash the order.

(3) A provider shall disclose the personal information of a user to any person, private entity, or government entity if the user has given his or her informed, affirmative consent to the specific disclosure for a particular purpose.

(4) A provider may disclose personal information of a user to a government entity, if the government entity asserts, and the provider in good faith believes, that there is an imminent danger of death or serious physical injury requiring the immediate disclosure of the requested personal information and there is insufficient time to obtain a court order. The government entity seeking the disclosure shall provide the provider with a written statement setting forth the facts giving rise to the emergency upon request or no later than 48 hours after seeking disclosure.

(5) A provider may disclose personal information of a user to a government entity if the provider in good faith believes that the personal information is evidence directly related and relevant to a crime against the provider or that user.

(d)(1) Any court issuing a court order requiring the disclosure of personal information of a user shall impose appropriate safeguards against the unauthorized disclosure of personal information by the provider and by the person, private entity, or government entity seeking disclosure pursuant to the order.

(2) The court may, in its discretion, quash or modify a court order requiring the disclosure of the user's personal information upon a motion made by the user, provider, person, or entity seeking disclosure.

(e) A provider, upon the request of a law enforcement entity, shall take all necessary steps to preserve records and other evidence in its possession of a user's personal information related to the use of a book or part of a book, pending the issuance of a court order or a warrant pursuant to this section or Section 1798.90.05. The provider shall retain the records and evidence for a period of 90 days from the date of the request by the law enforcement entity, which shall be extended for an additional 90-day period upon a renewed request by the law enforcement entity.

(f) Except in an action for a violation of this section, no evidence obtained in violation of this section shall be admissible in any civil or administrative proceeding.

(g)(1) Violations of this section shall be subject to the following penalties:

(A) Any provider that knowingly provides personal information about a user to a government entity in violation of this section shall be subject to a civil penalty not to exceed five hundred dollars ($500) for each violation, which shall be paid to the user in a civil action brought by the user.

(B) Any provider that knowingly provides personal information about a user to a government entity in violation of this section shall, in addition to the penalty prescribed by subparagraph (A), be subject to a civil penalty not to exceed five hundred dollars ($500) for each violation, which may be assessed and recovered in a civil action brought by the Attorney General, by any district attorney or city attorney, or by a city prosecutor in any city having a full-time city prosecutor, in any court of competent jurisdiction.

(2) If an action is brought by the Attorney General, one-half of the penalty collected shall be paid to the treasurer of the county in which the judgment was entered, and one-half to the General Fund. If the action is brought by a district attorney, the penalty collected shall be paid to the treasurer of the county in which the judgment was entered. If the action is brought by a city attorney or city prosecutor, one-half of the penalty shall be paid to the treasurer of the city in which the judgment was entered, and one-half to the treasurer of the county in which the judgment was entered.

(3) The penalties provided by this section are not the exclusive remedy and do not affect any other relief or remedy provided by law.

(4) A civil action brought pursuant to this section shall be commenced within two years after the date upon which the claimant first discovered the violation.

(h) An objectively reasonable reliance by the provider on a warrant or court order for the disclosure of personal information of a user, or on any of the enumerated exceptions to the confidentiality of a user's personal information set forth in this section, is a complete defense to any civil action for the violation of this section.

(i)(1) Unless disclosure of information pertaining to a particular request or set of requests is specifically prohibited by law, a provider shall prepare a report including all of the following information, to the extent it can be reasonably determined:

(A) The number of federal and state warrants, federal and state grand jury subpoenas, federal and state civil and administrative subpoenas, federal and state civil and criminal court orders, and requests for information made with the informed consent of the user as described in paragraph (3) of subdivision (c), seeking disclosure of any personal information of a user related to the access or use of a book service or book, received by the provider from January 1 to December 31, inclusive, of the previous year.

(B) The number of disclosures made by the provider pursuant to paragraphs (4) and (5) of subdivision (c) from January 1 to December 31, inclusive, of the previous year.

(C) For each category of demand or disclosure, the provider shall include all of the following information:

(i) The number of times notice of a court order in a criminal, civil, or administrative action has been provided by the provider and the date the notice was provided.

(ii) The number of times personal information has been disclosed by the provider.

(iii) The number of times no personal information has been disclosed by the provider.

(iv) The number of times the provider contests the demand.

(v) The number of times the user contests the demand.

(vi) The number of users whose personal information was disclosed by the provider.

(vii) The type of personal information that was disclosed and the number of times that type of personal information was disclosed.

(2) Notwithstanding paragraph (1), a provider is not required to prepare a report pursuant to this subdivision unless it has disclosed personal information related to the access or use of a book service or book of more than 30 total users consisting of users located in this state or users whose location is unknown or of both types of users.

(3) The reporting requirements of this subdivision shall not apply to information disclosed to a government entity that is made by a provider serving a postsecondary educational institution when the provider is required to disclose the information in order to be reimbursed for the sale or rental of a book that was purchased or rented by a student using book vouchers or other financial aid subsidies for books.

(j) Reports prepared pursuant to subdivision (i) shall be made publicly available in an online, searchable format on or before March 1 of each year. If the provider does not have an Internet Web site, the provider shall post the reports prominently on its premises or send the reports to the Office of Privacy Protection on or before March 1 of each year.

(k) On or before March 1 of each year, a provider subject to Section 22575 of the Business and Professions Code shall complete one of the following actions:

(1) Create a prominent hyperlink to its latest report prepared pursuant to subdivision (i) in the disclosure section of its privacy policy applicable to its book service.

(2) Post the report prepared pursuant to subdivision (i) in the section of its Internet Web site explaining the way in which user information and privacy issues related to its book service are addressed.

(3) State on its Internet Web site in one of the areas described in paragraphs (1) and (2) that no report prepared pursuant to subdivision (i) is available because the provider is exempt from the reporting requirement pursuant to paragraph (2) of subdivision (i).

(*l*) Nothing in this section shall otherwise affect the rights of any person under the California Constitution or any other law or be construed as conflicting with the federal Privacy Protection Act of 1980 (42 U.S.C. 2000aa et seq.). *(Added by Stats.2011, c. 424 (S.B.602), § 1.)*

Cross References

Age verification when selling products that are illegal to sell to minor, reasonable steps, products requiring age verification, penalties, see Civil Code § 1798.99.1.

Production of or access to electronic communication information, circumstances allowing production or access, see Penal Code § 1546.1.

§ 1798.90.05. Authority to obtain search warrants for personal information of book service users; provider compliance with proper search warrants

Section 1798.90 does not make it unlawful for a law enforcement entity subject to Section 2000aa of Title 42 of the United States Code to obtain a search warrant for the personal information of a user pursuant to otherwise applicable law in connection with the investigation or prosecution of a criminal offense when probable cause exists to believe that

§ 1798.90.05

the person possessing the personal information has committed, or is committing, a criminal offense involving the production, possession, receipt, mailing, sale, distribution, shipment, or transportation of child pornography, the sexual exploitation of children, or the sale or purchase of children prohibited by Sections 2251, 2251A, 2252, and 2252A of Title 18 of the United States Code. Nothing in Section 1798.90 shall prevent a provider from complying with a proper search warrant issued by a duly authorized court in connection with the investigation or prosecution of any of those offenses. *(Added by Stats.2011, c. 424 (S.B.602), § 1.)*

Title 1.81.2

CONFIDENTIALITY OF DRIVER'S LICENSE INFORMATION

Section
1798.90.1. Information encoded on driver's license; authorization for use by businesses in electronic devices; violations; penalty.

Cross References

Unlawful use of personal identifying information by another, issuance of law enforcement investigation, determination of factual innocence of victim, see Penal Code § 530.6.

§ 1798.90.1. Information encoded on driver's license; authorization for use by businesses in electronic devices; violations; penalty

(a)(1) A business may scan or swipe a driver's license or identification card issued by the Department of Motor Vehicles in any electronic device for the following purposes:

(A) To verify age or the authenticity of the driver's license or identification card.

(B) To comply with a legal requirement to record, retain, or transmit that information.

(C) To transmit information to a check service company for the purpose of approving negotiable instruments, electronic funds transfers, or similar methods of payments, provided that only the name and identification number from the license or the card may be used or retained by the check service company.

(D) To collect or disclose personal information that is required for reporting, investigating, or preventing fraud, abuse, or material misrepresentation.

(2)(A) An organ procurement organization may scan or swipe a driver's license or identification card issued by the Department of Motor Vehicles in any electronic device to transmit information to the Donate Life California Organ and Tissue Donor Registry established pursuant to Section 7150.90 of the Health and Safety Code for the purposes of allowing an individual to identify himself or herself as a registered organ donor. Information gathered or transmitted pursuant to this paragraph shall comply with the Department of Motor Vehicles Information Security Agreement.

(B) Prior to scanning or swiping a driver's license or identification card issued by the Department of Motor Vehicles, an organ procurement organization shall provide clear and conspicuous notice to the applicant and shall follow the procedure prescribed in this subparagraph:

(i) Once the applicant's information is populated on the electronic form, the applicant shall verify that the information is accurate and shall click "submit" after reading a clear and conspicuous consent message, which shall not be combined with or contained within another message, acknowledging that the applicant's information will be used for the sole purpose of being added to the registry.

(ii) The applicant shall provide his or her signature to complete registration.

(iii) The organization or registry system shall provide a written confirmation to the applicant confirming that he or she is signed up as an organ and tissue donor.

(3) A business or organ procurement organization shall not retain or use any of the information obtained by that electronic means for any purpose other than as provided herein.

(b) As used in this section:

(1) "Business" means a proprietorship, partnership, corporation, or any other form of commercial enterprise.

(2) "Organ procurement organization" means a person designated by the Secretary of the federal Department of Health and Human Services as an organ procurement organization.

(c) A violation of this section constitutes a misdemeanor punishable by imprisonment in a county jail for no more than one year, or by a fine of no more than ten thousand dollars ($10,000), or by both. *(Added by Stats.2003, c. 533 (S.B.602), § 4. Amended by Stats.2014, c. 569 (A.B.2399), § 1, eff. Jan. 1, 2015; Stats.2018, c. 548 (A.B.2769), § 1, eff. Jan. 1, 2019.)*

Cross References

Age verification when selling products that are illegal to sell to minor, reasonable steps, products requiring age verification, penalties, see Civil Code § 1798.99.1.
Misdemeanor, definition, penalties, see Penal Code §§ 17, 19, 19.2.
Unlawful use of personal identifying information by another, issuance of law enforcement investigation, determination of factual innocence of victim, see Penal Code § 530.6.

Title 1.81.23

COLLECTION OF LICENSE PLATE INFORMATION

Section
1798.90.5. Definitions.
1798.90.51. Automated license plate recognition end-user "ALPR" operator duties; maintenance of reasonable security procedures; implementation of usage and privacy policy.
1798.90.52. Accessing or providing access to ALPR information by ALPR operator; maintenance of record of access; use of information for authorized purposes only.
1798.90.53. ALPR end-user duties; maintenance of reasonable security procedures and practices; implementation of usage and privacy policy.
1798.90.54. Civil action for harm caused by violation of title; award.

Section
1798.90.55. Public meeting requirement; selling, sharing, or transfer of ALPR information by public agency prohibited.

§ 1798.90.5. Definitions

The following definitions shall apply for purposes of this title:

(a) "Automated license plate recognition end-user" or "ALPR end-user" means a person that accesses or uses an ALPR system, but does not include any of the following:

(1) A transportation agency when subject to Section 31490 of the Streets and Highways Code.

(2) A person that is subject to Sections 6801 to 6809, inclusive, of Title 15 of the United States Code and state or federal statutes or regulations implementing those sections, if the person is subject to compliance oversight by a state or federal regulatory agency with respect to those sections.

(3) A person, other than a law enforcement agency, to whom information may be disclosed as a permissible use pursuant to Section 2721 of Title 18 of the United States Code.

(b) "Automated license plate recognition information," or "ALPR information" means information or data collected through the use of an ALPR system.

(c) "Automated license plate recognition operator" or "ALPR operator" means a person that operates an ALPR system, but does not include a transportation agency when subject to Section 31490 of the Streets and Highways Code.

(d) "Automated license plate recognition system" or "ALPR system" means a searchable computerized database resulting from the operation of one or more mobile or fixed cameras combined with computer algorithms to read and convert images of registration plates and the characters they contain into computer-readable data.

(e) "Person" means any natural person, public agency, partnership, firm, association, corporation, limited liability company, or other legal entity.

(f) "Public agency" means the state, any city, county, or city and county, or any agency or political subdivision of the state or a city, county, or city and county, including, but not limited to, a law enforcement agency. *(Added by Stats.2015, c. 532 (S.B.34), § 3, eff. Jan. 1, 2016.)*

§ 1798.90.51. Automated license plate recognition end-user "ALPR" operator duties; maintenance of reasonable security procedures; implementation of usage and privacy policy

An ALPR operator shall do all of the following:

(a) Maintain reasonable security procedures and practices, including operational, administrative, technical, and physical safeguards, to protect ALPR information from unauthorized access, destruction, use, modification, or disclosure.

(b)(1) Implement a usage and privacy policy in order to ensure that the collection, use, maintenance, sharing, and dissemination of ALPR information is consistent with respect for individuals' privacy and civil liberties. The usage and privacy policy shall be available to the public in writing, and, if the ALPR operator has an Internet Web site, the usage and privacy policy shall be posted conspicuously on that Internet Web site.

(2) The usage and privacy policy shall, at a minimum, include all of the following:

(A) The authorized purposes for using the ALPR system and collecting ALPR information.

(B) A description of the job title or other designation of the employees and independent contractors who are authorized to use or access the ALPR system, or to collect ALPR information. The policy shall identify the training requirements necessary for those authorized employees and independent contractors.

(C) A description of how the ALPR system will be monitored to ensure the security of the information and compliance with applicable privacy laws.

(D) The purposes of, process for, and restrictions on, the sale, sharing, or transfer of ALPR information to other persons.

(E) The title of the official custodian, or owner, of the ALPR system responsible for implementing this section.

(F) A description of the reasonable measures that will be used to ensure the accuracy of ALPR information and correct data errors.

(G) The length of time ALPR information will be retained, and the process the ALPR operator will utilize to determine if and when to destroy retained ALPR information. *(Added by Stats.2015, c. 532 (S.B.34), § 3, eff. Jan. 1, 2016.)*

§ 1798.90.52. Accessing or providing access to ALPR information by ALPR operator; maintenance of record of access; use of information for authorized purposes only

If an ALPR operator accesses or provides access to ALPR information, the ALPR operator shall do both of the following:

(a) Maintain a record of that access. At a minimum, the record shall include all of the following:

(1) The date and time the information is accessed.

(2) The license plate number or other data elements used to query the ALPR system.

(3) The username of the person who accesses the information, and, as applicable, the organization or entity with whom the person is affiliated.

(4) The purpose for accessing the information.

(b) Require that ALPR information only be used for the authorized purposes described in the usage and privacy policy required by subdivision (b) of Section 1798.90.51. *(Added by Stats.2015, c. 532 (S.B.34), § 3, eff. Jan. 1, 2016.)*

§ 1798.90.53. ALPR end-user duties; maintenance of reasonable security procedures and practices; implementation of usage and privacy policy

An ALPR end-user shall do all of the following:

(a) Maintain reasonable security procedures and practices, including operational, administrative, technical, and physical safeguards, to protect ALPR information from unauthorized access, destruction, use, modification, or disclosure.

§ 1798.90.53

(b)(1) Implement a usage and privacy policy in order to ensure that the access, use, sharing, and dissemination of ALPR information is consistent with respect for individuals' privacy and civil liberties. The usage and privacy policy shall be available to the public in writing, and, if the ALPR end-user has an Internet Web site, the usage and privacy policy shall be posted conspicuously on that Internet Web site.

(2) The usage and privacy policy shall, at a minimum, include all of the following:

(A) The authorized purposes for accessing and using ALPR information.

(B) A description of the job title or other designation of the employees and independent contractors who are authorized to access and use ALPR information. The policy shall identify the training requirements necessary for those authorized employees and independent contractors.

(C) A description of how the ALPR system will be monitored to ensure the security of the information accessed or used, and compliance with all applicable privacy laws and a process for periodic system audits.

(D) The purposes of, process for, and restrictions on, the sale, sharing, or transfer of ALPR information to other persons.

(E) The title of the official custodian, or owner, of the ALPR information responsible for implementing this section.

(F) A description of the reasonable measures that will be used to ensure the accuracy of ALPR information and correct data errors.

(G) The length of time ALPR information will be retained, and the process the ALPR end-user will utilize to determine if and when to destroy retained ALPR information. *(Added by Stats.2015, c. 532 (S.B.34), § 3, eff. Jan. 1, 2016.)*

§ 1798.90.54. Civil action for harm caused by violation of title; award

(a) In addition to any other sanctions, penalties, or remedies provided by law, an individual who has been harmed by a violation of this title, including, but not limited to, unauthorized access or use of ALPR information or a breach of security of an ALPR system, may bring a civil action in any court of competent jurisdiction against a person who knowingly caused the harm.

(b) The court may award a combination of any one or more of the following:

(1) Actual damages, but not less than liquidated damages in the amount of two thousand five hundred dollars ($2,500).

(2) Punitive damages upon proof of willful or reckless disregard of the law.

(3) Reasonable attorney's fees and other litigation costs reasonably incurred.

(4) Other preliminary and equitable relief as the court determines to be appropriate. *(Added by Stats.2015, c. 532 (S.B.34), § 3, eff. Jan. 1, 2016.)*

§ 1798.90.55. Public meeting requirement; selling, sharing, or transfer of ALPR information by public agency prohibited

Notwithstanding any other law or regulation:

(a) A public agency that operates or intends to operate an ALPR system shall provide an opportunity for public comment at a regularly scheduled public meeting of the governing body of the public agency before implementing the program.

(b) A public agency shall not sell, share, or transfer ALPR information, except to another public agency, and only as otherwise permitted by law. For purposes of this section, the provision of data hosting or towing services shall not be considered the sale, sharing, or transferring of ALPR information. *(Added by Stats.2015, c. 532 (S.B.34), § 3, eff. Jan. 1, 2016.)*

Title 1.81.25

CONSUMER PRIVACY PROTECTION

Section
1798.91. Definitions; oral and written requests by businesses for medical information; requirements; health care providers or contractors; insurance institutions, agents, or support organizations; telephone corporations.

§ 1798.91. Definitions; oral and written requests by businesses for medical information; requirements; health care providers or contractors; insurance institutions, agents, or support organizations; telephone corporations

(a) For purposes of this title, the following definitions shall apply:

(1) "Direct marketing purposes" means the use of personal information for marketing or advertising products, goods, or services directly to individuals. "Direct marketing purposes" does not include the use of personal information (A) by bona fide tax exempt charitable or religious organizations to solicit charitable contributions or (B) to raise funds from and communicate with individuals regarding politics and government.

(2) "Medical information" means any individually identifiable information, in electronic or physical form, regarding the individual's medical history, or medical treatment or diagnosis by a health care professional. "Individually identifiable" means that the medical information includes or contains any element of personal identifying information sufficient to allow identification of the individual, such as the individual's name, address, electronic mail address, telephone number, or social security number, or other information that, alone or in combination with other publicly available information, reveals the individual's identity. For purposes of this section, "medical information" does not mean a subscription to, purchase of, or request for a periodical, book, pamphlet, video, audio, or other multimedia product or nonprofit association information.

(3) "Clear and conspicuous" means in larger type than the surrounding text, or in contrasting type, font, or color to the surrounding text of the same size, or set off from the

surrounding text of the same size by symbols or other marks that call attention to the language.

(4) For purposes of this section, the collection of medical information online constitutes "in writing." For purposes of this section, "written consent" includes consent obtained online.

(b) A business may not orally request medical information directly from an individual regardless of whether the information pertains to the individual or not, and use, share, or otherwise disclose that information for direct marketing purposes, without doing both of the following prior to obtaining that information:

(1) Orally disclosing to the individual in the same conversation during which the business seeks to obtain the information, that it is obtaining the information to market or advertise products, goods, or services to the individual.

(2) Obtaining the consent of either the individual to whom the information pertains or a person legally authorized to consent for the individual, to permit his or her medical information to be used or shared to market or advertise products, goods, or services to the individual, and making and maintaining for two years after the date of the conversation, an audio recording of the entire conversation.

(c) A business may not request in writing medical information directly from an individual regardless of whether the information pertains to the individual or not, and use, share, or otherwise disclose that information for direct marketing purposes, without doing both of the following prior to obtaining that information:

(1) Disclosing in a clear and conspicuous manner that it is obtaining the information to market or advertise products, goods, or services to the individual.

(2) Obtaining the written consent of either the individual to whom the information pertains or a person legally authorized to consent for the individual, to permit his or her medical information to be used or shared to market or advertise products, goods, or services to the individual.

(d) This section does not apply to a provider of health care, health care service plan, or contractor, as defined in Section 56.05.

(e) This section shall not apply to an insurance institution, agent, or support organization, as defined in Section 791.02 of the Insurance Code, when engaged in an insurance transaction, as defined in Section 791.02 of the Insurance Code, pursuant to all the requirements of Article 6.6 (commencing with Section 791) of Chapter 1 of Part 2 of Division 1 of the Insurance Code, and the regulations promulgated thereunder.

(f) This section does not apply to a telephone corporation, as defined in Section 234 of the Public Utilities Code, when that corporation is engaged in providing telephone services and products pursuant to Sections 2881, 2881.1, and 2881.2 of the Public Utilities Code, if the corporation does not share or disclose medical information obtained as a consequence of complying with those sections of the Public Utilities Code, to third parties for direct marketing purposes. *(Added by Stats.2004, c. 861 (S.B.1633), § 1. Amended by Stats.2013, c. 444 (S.B.138), § 7.)*

Title 1.81.26

SECURITY OF CONNECTED DEVICES

Section
1798.91.04. Equipment of connected devices with security features; requirements.
1798.91.05. Definitions.
1798.91.06. Limits on application of title.

Operative Effect

For operative effect of Title 1.81.26, see Civil Code § 1798.91.06.

§ 1798.91.04. Equipment of connected devices with security features; requirements

(a) A manufacturer of a connected device shall equip the device with a reasonable security feature or features that are all of the following:

(1) Appropriate to the nature and function of the device.

(2) Appropriate to the information it may collect, contain, or transmit.

(3) Designed to protect the device and any information contained therein from unauthorized access, destruction, use, modification, or disclosure.

(b) Subject to all of the requirements of subdivision (a), if a connected device is equipped with a means for authentication outside a local area network, it shall be deemed a reasonable security feature under subdivision (a) if either of the following requirements are met:

(1) The preprogrammed password is unique to each device manufactured.

(2) The device contains a security feature that requires a user to generate a new means of authentication before access is granted to the device for the first time.

(c) A manufacturer of a connected device may elect to satisfy the requirements of subdivision (a) by ensuring the connected device does all of the following:

(1) Meets or exceeds the baseline product criteria of a NIST conforming labeling scheme.

(2) Satisfies a conformity assessment as described by a NIST conforming labeling scheme that includes a third-party test, inspection, or certification.

(3) Bears the binary label as described by a NIST conforming labeling scheme. *(Added by Stats.2018, c. 860 (A.B.1906), § 1, eff. Jan. 1, 2019, operative Jan. 1, 2020. Amended by Stats.2022, c. 785 (A.B.2392), § 2, eff. Jan. 1, 2023.)*

Operative Effect

For operative effect of Title 1.81.26, see Civil Code § 1798.91.06.

§ 1798.91.05. Definitions

For the purposes of this title, the following terms have the following meanings:

(a) "Authentication" means a method of verifying the authority of a user, process, or device to access resources in an information system.

§ 1798.91.05

(b) "Connected device" means any device, or other physical object that is capable of connecting to the <u>internet</u>, directly or indirectly, and that is assigned an * * * <u>internet protocol</u> address or Bluetooth address.

(c) "Manufacturer" means the person who manufactures, or contracts with another person to manufacture on the person's behalf, connected devices that are sold or offered for sale in California. For the purposes of this subdivision, a contract with another person to manufacture on the person's behalf does not include a contract only to purchase a connected device, or only to purchase and brand a connected device.

(d) <u>"NIST conforming labeling scheme" means a labeling scheme conforming to the Cybersecurity White Paper titled "Recommended Criteria for Cybersecurity Labeling for Consumer Internet of Things (IoT) Products" published by the National Institute of Standards and Technology (NIST) on February 4, 2022, including any revisions or successor publications.</u>

(e) "Security feature" means a feature of a device designed to provide security for that device.

(f) "Unauthorized access, destruction, use, modification, or disclosure" means access, destruction, use, modification, or disclosure that is not authorized by the consumer. *(Added by Stats.2018, c. 860 (A.B.1906), § 1, eff. Jan. 1, 2019, operative Jan. 1, 2020. Amended by Stats.2022, c. 785 (A.B.2392), § 3, eff. Jan. 1, 2023.)*

Operative Effect

For operative effect of Title 1.81.26, see Civil Code § 1798.91.06.

§ 1798.91.06. Limits on application of title

(a) This title shall not be construed to impose any duty upon the manufacturer of a connected device related to unaffiliated third-party software or applications that a user chooses to add to a connected device.

(b) This title shall not be construed to impose any duty upon a provider of an electronic store, gateway, marketplace, or other means of purchasing or downloading software or applications, to review or enforce compliance with this title.

(c) This title shall not be construed to impose any duty upon the manufacturer of a connected device to prevent a user from having full control over a connected device, including the ability to modify the software or firmware running on the device at the user's discretion.

(d) This title shall not apply to any connected device the functionality of which is subject to security requirements under federal law, regulations, or guidance promulgated by a federal agency pursuant to its regulatory enforcement authority.

(e) This title shall not be construed to provide a basis for a private right of action. The Attorney General, a city attorney, a county counsel, or a district attorney shall have the exclusive authority to enforce this title.

(f) The duties and obligations imposed by this title are cumulative with any other duties or obligations imposed under other law, and shall not be construed to relieve any party from any duties or obligations imposed under other law.

(g) This title shall not be construed to limit the authority of a law enforcement agency to obtain connected device information from a manufacturer as authorized by law or pursuant to an order of a court of competent jurisdiction.

(h) A covered entity, provider of health care, business associate, health care service plan, contractor, employer, or any other person subject to the federal Health Insurance Portability and Accountability Act of 1996 (HIPAA) (Public Law 104–191)[1] or the Confidentiality of Medical Information Act (Part 2.6 (commencing with Section 56) of Division 1) shall not be subject to this title with respect to any activity regulated by those acts.

(i) This title shall become operative on January 1, 2020. *(Added by Stats.2018, c. 860 (A.B.1906), § 1, eff. Jan. 1, 2019, operative Jan. 1, 2020.)*

[1] For public law sections classified to the U.S.C.A., see USCA–Tables.

Title 1.81.27

COMMERCIAL USE OF BOOKING PHOTOGRAPHS

Section
1798.91.1. Publication or dissemination of booking photographs; soliciting, requiring, or accepting fee to remove, correct, modify, or refrain from publishing or disseminating prohibited; damages.

§ 1798.91.1. Publication or dissemination of booking photographs; soliciting, requiring, or accepting fee to remove, correct, modify, or refrain from publishing or disseminating prohibited; damages

(a) For the purposes of this section, the following definitions shall apply:

(1) "Booking photograph" means a photograph of a subject individual taken pursuant to an arrest or other involvement in the criminal justice system.

(2) "Subject individual" means an individual who was arrested.

(3) "Person" means a natural person, partnership, joint venture, corporation, limited liability company, or other entity.

(4) "Public entity" means the state, county, city, special district, or other political subdivision therein.

(b) It shall be unlawful practice for any person engaged in publishing or otherwise disseminating a booking photograph through a print or electronic medium to solicit, require, or accept the payment of a fee or other consideration from a subject individual to remove, correct, modify, or to refrain from publishing or otherwise disseminating that booking photograph.

(c) Notwithstanding subdivision (b), a public entity may require and accept a reasonable administrative fee to correct a booking photograph.

(d) Each payment solicited or accepted in violation of these provisions constitutes a separate violation.

(e) In addition to any other sanctions, penalties, or remedies provided by law, a subject individual may bring a civil action in any court of competent jurisdiction against any person in violation of this section for damages in an amount equal to the greater of one thousand dollars ($1,000) per violation or the actual damages suffered by him or her as a result, along with costs, reasonable attorney's fees, and any other legal or equitable relief.

(f) The jurisdiction of a civil action brought pursuant to subdivision (e) shall also include the county in which the subject individual resides at the time of the violation of this section. *(Added by Stats.2014, c. 194 (S.B.1027), § 1, eff. Jan. 1, 2015.)*

Title 1.81.3

IDENTITY THEFT

Section
1798.92. Definitions.
1798.93. Actions and judgment for identity theft.
1798.94. Actions or cross-complaints joining other claimants as defendants in same action or cross-complaint; compliance with Code of Civil Procedure.
1798.95. Jurisdiction over action or cross-complaint filed pursuant to this title; joinder.
1798.96. Statute of limitations.
1798.97. Limits on application of identity theft actions; cumulative nature of title.

Cross References

Voter signatures or other information collected for initiative, referendum or recall petitions, prohibition on sending or making information available outside of United States, see Elections Code § 2188.5.

§ 1798.92. Definitions

For the purposes of this title:

(a) "Claimant" means a person who has or purports to have a claim for money or an interest in property in connection with a transaction procured through identity theft.

(b) "Identity theft" means the unauthorized use of another person's personal identifying information to obtain credit, goods, services, money, or property.

(c) "Personal identifying information" means a person's name, address, telephone number, driver's license number, social security number, place of employment, employee identification number, mother's maiden name, demand deposit account number, savings account number, or credit card number.

(d) "Victim of identity theft" means a person who had their personal identifying information used without authorization by another to obtain credit, goods, services, money, or property, and did not use or possess the credit, goods, services, money, or property obtained by the identity theft, and has submitted a Federal Trade Commission identity theft report. In the alternative, the person may have filed a police report in this regard pursuant to Section 530.5 of the Penal Code. *(Added by Stats.2001, c. 354 (A.B.655), § 21. Amended by Stats.2021, c. 265 (A.B.430), § 3, eff. Jan. 1, 2022.)*

Cross References

Consumer loans, instant loan checks and live checks, identity theft, see Financial Code § 22342.

Credit Reporting Agencies Act, obligation of agencies, consumer credit reports with credit approval, see Civil Code § 1785.20.3.
Deletion of inquiries for credit reports from consumer credit report with respect to identity theft, see Civil Code § 1785.16.1.
Sale of consumer debt by creditor where consumer is not obligated to pay debt because of identity theft, see Civil Code § 1785.16.2.
Use of consumer credit report in connection with credit transaction, reporting of consumer address error with respect to identity theft, see Civil Code § 1785.20.3.

§ 1798.93. Actions and judgment for identity theft

(a) A person may bring an action against a claimant to establish that the person is a victim of identity theft in connection with the claimant's claim against that person. If the claimant has brought an action to recover on its claim against the person, the person may file a cross-complaint to establish that the person is a victim of identity theft in connection with the claimant's claim.

(b) A person shall establish that they are a victim of identity theft by a preponderance of the evidence.

(c) A person who proves that they are a victim of identity theft, as defined in Section 530.5 of the Penal Code, as to a particular claim, shall be entitled to a judgment providing all of the following, as appropriate:

(1) A declaration that they are not obligated to the claimant on that claim.

(2) A declaration that any security interest or other interest the claimant had purportedly obtained in the victim's property in connection with that claim is void and unenforceable.

(3) An injunction restraining the claimant from collecting or attempting to collect from the victim on that claim, from enforcing or attempting to enforce any security interest or other interest in the victim's property in connection with that claim, or from enforcing or executing on any judgment against the victim on that claim.

(4) If the victim has filed a cross-complaint against the claimant, the dismissal of any cause of action in the complaint filed by the claimant based on a claim which arose as a result of the identity theft.

(5) Actual damages, attorney's fees, and costs, and any equitable relief that the court deems appropriate. In order to recover actual damages or attorney's fees in an action or cross-complaint filed by a person alleging that they are a victim of identity theft, the person shall show that they provided written notice to the claimant that a situation of identity theft might exist, including, upon written request of the claimant, a valid, signed Federal Trade Commission (FTC) identity theft report completed at least 30 days before filing the action, or within their cross-complaint pursuant to this section. In the alternative, the person may provide a valid copy of a police report or of a Department of Motor Vehicles (DMV) investigative report, filed pursuant to Section 530.5 of the Penal Code, at least 30 days before filing the action or within their cross-complaint pursuant to this section. For the purposes of this paragraph, if the person submits an FTC identity theft report, the claimant shall not also require a DMV or police report.

§ 1798.93

(6) A civil penalty, in addition to any other damages, of up to thirty thousand dollars ($30,000) if the victim establishes by clear and convincing evidence all of the following:

(A) That at least 30 days prior to filing an action or within the cross-complaint pursuant to this section, they provided written notice to the claimant at the address designated by the claimant for complaints related to credit reporting issues that a situation of identity theft might exist and explaining the basis for that belief.

(B) That the claimant failed to diligently investigate the victim's notification of a possible identity theft.

(C) That the claimant continued to pursue its claim against the victim after the claimant was presented with facts that were later held to entitle the victim to a judgment pursuant to this section. *(Added by Stats.2001, c. 354 (A.B.655), § 21. Amended by Stats.2021, c. 265 (A.B.430), § 4, eff. Jan. 1, 2022.)*

Cross References

Claimant defined for purposes of this Title, see Civil Code § 1798.92.
Collection of debt, theft of identity, debt collector duty to cease activities and conduct a review, see Civil Code § 1788.18.
Identity theft defined for purposes of this Title, see Civil Code § 1798.92.
Victim of identity theft defined for purposes of this Title, see Civil Code § 1798.92.

§ 1798.94. Actions or cross-complaints joining other claimants as defendants in same action or cross-complaint; compliance with Code of Civil Procedure

An action or cross-complaint brought under this title that joins other claimants as defendants in the same action or cross-complaint shall be deemed to comply with Section 379 of the Code of Civil Procedure. *(Added by Stats.2001, c. 354 (A.B.655), § 21.)*

Cross References

Claimant defined for purposes of this Title, see Civil Code § 1798.92.

§ 1798.95. Jurisdiction over action or cross-complaint filed pursuant to this title; joinder

A court shall have continuing jurisdiction over an action or cross-complaint filed pursuant to this title in order to provide for the joinder of related causes of action based on the theft of the same person's identity and the joinder of further defendants based upon the theft of the same person's identity, regardless of whether a final judgment has been entered as to any defendant. The court's continuing jurisdiction shall terminate 10 years after filing of the original action unless the court, prior to that date, finds good cause to extend jurisdiction over the matter. *(Added by Stats.2001, c. 354 (A.B.655), § 21.)*

§ 1798.96. Statute of limitations

Any action brought pursuant to this title or any joinder of a defendant pursuant to Section 1798.82 may be brought within four years of the date the person who alleges that he or she is a victim of identity theft knew or, in the exercise of reasonable diligence, should have known of the existence of facts which would give rise to the bringing of the action or joinder of the defendant. *(Added by Stats.2001, c. 354 (A.B.655), § 21.)*

Cross References

Identity theft defined for purposes of this Title, see Civil Code § 1798.92.
Victim of identity theft defined for purposes of this Title, see Civil Code § 1798.92.

§ 1798.97. Limits on application of identity theft actions; cumulative nature of title

(a) This title does not apply to a transaction subject to Section 1747.10.

(b) Nothing is this title shall be construed to affect a claimant's rights and remedies against a person who perpetrates identity theft or against any person who used or possessed the credit, goods, services, or property obtained by identity theft.

(c) This title is cumulative to the rights and remedies provided under other laws. *(Added by Stats.2001, c. 354 (A.B.655), § 21.)*

Cross References

Claimant defined for purposes of this Title, see Civil Code § 1798.92.
Identity theft defined for purposes of this Title, see Civil Code § 1798.92.

Title 1.81.35

COERCED DEBT

Section
1798.97.1. Definitions.
1798.97.2. Coerced debt; notification to claimant; credit reporting agency; intent to file action; possession of documents.
1798.97.3. Coerced debt; action to recover debt; relief; judgment; unnecessary delay; written findings; collection of debt; statute of limitations.
1798.97.4. Secured debts.
1798.97.5. Scope of title.
1798.97.6. Severability.

§ 1798.97.1. Definitions

For purposes of this title, the following definitions apply:

(a) "Adequate documentation" means documentation that identifies a particular debt, or portion thereof, as coerced debt, describes the circumstances under which the coerced debt was incurred, and takes the form of any of the following:

(1) A police report.

(2) A Federal Trade Commission identity theft report identifying a particular debt, or portion thereof, as coerced, but not as identity theft.

(3) A court order issued pursuant to Section 6340 of the Family Code relating to domestic violence, Section 213.5 of the Welfare and Institutions Code relating to a dependent or ward of the juvenile court, or Section 15657.03 of the Welfare and Institutions Code relating to elder or dependent adult abuse.

(4)(A) A sworn written certification from a qualified third-party professional based on information they received while acting in a professional capacity.

(B) The documentation described by subparagraph (A) shall be signed by a qualified third-party professional and display the letterhead, address, and telephone number of the office, institution, center, or organization, as appropriate, that engages or employs, whether financially compensated or not, the qualified third-party professional, or, if the qualified third-party professional is self-employed, the documentation shall display the letterhead, address, and telephone number of the qualified third-party professional.

(b) "Claim" means a right to payment, whether or not that right is reduced to judgment, liquidated, unliquidated, fixed, contingent, matured, unmatured, disputed, undisputed, legal, or equitable.

(c)(1) "Claimant" means a person or an entity who has or purports to have a claim against a debtor arising from coerced debt, or that person's or entity's successor or assignee. "Claimant" includes, but is not limited to, a debt collector or a debt buyer.

(2) Notwithstanding paragraph (1), "claimant" shall not include a person who caused the claim described in paragraph (1) to arise through duress, intimidation, threat of force, force, fraud, or undue influence perpetrated against the debtor.

(d) "Coerced debt" means a particular debt, or portion thereof, for personal, family, or household use in the name of a debtor who is a victim of domestic violence, or a victim of elder or dependent adult abuse, or a person who is a foster youth, incurred as a result of duress, intimidation, threat of force, force, fraud, or undue influence.

(1) For purposes of this subdivision, "domestic violence" has the same meaning as in Section 6211 of the Family Code.

(2) For the purposes of this subdivision, "foster youth" has the same meaning as in Section 42238.01 of the Education Code.

(3) For the purposes of this subdivision, "dependent adult" has the same meaning as in Section 15610.23 of the Welfare and Institutions Code.

(4) For the purposes of this subdivision, "elder" has the same meaning as in Section 15610.27 of the Welfare and Institutions Code.

(e) "Debtor" means a person who owes or is otherwise liable for coerced debt.

(f) "Fraud" means an initial fraudulent act that is perpetrated against the debtor.

(g) "Immediate family member" has the same meaning as defined in paragraph (3) of subdivision (h) of Section 1946.7.

(h) "Person" means a natural person.

(i) "Qualified third-party professional" means any of the following:

(1) A domestic violence counselor, as defined in Section 1037.1 of the Evidence Code.

(2) A sexual assault counselor, as defined in Section 1035.2 of the Evidence Code.

(3) A Court-Appointed Special Advocate, as defined in Section 101 of the Welfare and Institutions Code.

(4) A court-appointed attorney, as defined in subdivision (e) of Section 317 of the Welfare and Institutions Code.

(5) A board certified psychiatrist or psychologist.

(6) A licensed marriage and family therapist.

(7) A licensed professional clinical counselor.

(8) A licensed clinical social worker.

(9) A social worker or caseworker employed by an adult protective service agency for the purposes described in Chapter 13 (commencing with Section 15750) of Part 3 of Division 9 of the Welfare and Institutions Code.

(10) A social worker who has completed the child welfare training program described in Article 2 (commencing with Section 16205) of Chapter 3 of Part 4 of Division 9 of the Welfare and Institutions Code.

(j)(1) "Sworn written certification" means a document in which the author declares under penalty of perjury as true any material fact, and which is accompanied by the following, to the extent that an item listed below is relevant to the debtor's allegation that the debt is coerced debt:

(A) A copy of the debtor's driver's license or identification card, as issued by the state.

(B) Any other identification document that supports the statement that the particular debt, or portion thereof, is coerced debt.

(C) An express statement that the debtor did not willingly authorize the use of the debtor's name or personal information for incurring the coerced debt, and specific facts supporting the claim of coerced debt, if available, and, if not all of the debt was coerced, a statement identifying the portion thereof that was coerced.

(D) Any available correspondence disputing the coerced debt after transaction information has been provided to the debtor.

(E) Information, if known by the debtor, including, but not limited to, a credit card number or loan number, that can be used by the claimant to identify the account associated with the coerced debt and the person or persons in whose name the debt was incurred.

(F) The identity of the person or persons who coerced the debtor into incurring the debt and contact information for that person or persons, if known by the debtor, unless the debtor signs a sworn statement that disclosing this information is likely to result in abuse, as defined in Section 6203 of the Family Code, to the debtor or an immediate family member of the debtor.

(G) A telephone number for contacting the person signing the certification concerning any additional information or questions, or direction that further communications to the debtor be in writing only, with the mailing address specified in the statement.

(2) The certification required by this subdivision shall be sufficient if it is in substantially the following form:

"I declare under penalty of perjury that the representations made herein are true, correct, and contain no material omissions of fact.

(Date and Place)_____

(Signature)_____" *(Added by Stats.2022, c. 989 (S.B.975), § 2, eff. Jan. 1, 2023.)*

§ 1798.97.2. Coerced debt; notification to claimant; credit reporting agency; intent to file action; possession of documents

(a) A person shall not cause another person to incur a coerced debt. A person who causes another person to incur a coerced debt in violation of this subdivision shall be civilly liable to the claimant for the amount of the debt, or portion thereof, determined by a court to be coerced debt, plus the claimant's attorney's fees and costs.

(b) Upon receipt of both of the following, a claimant shall cease collection activities until completion of the review provided in subdivision (d):

(1) Adequate documentation.

(2) The debtor's sworn written certification that a particular debt, or portion thereof, being collected is coerced debt.

(c) If a debtor notifies a claimant orally that a particular debt, or portion thereof, being collected is coerced debt, the claimant shall notify the debtor, orally or in writing, that the debtor's notification must be in writing. If a debtor notifies a claimant in writing that a particular debt, or portion thereof, being collected is coerced debt, but omits information required by subdivision (b), and if the claimant does not cease collection activities, the claimant shall provide written notice to the debtor of the additional information that is required.

(d)(1) Within 10 business days of receiving the complete statement and information described in subdivision (b), the claimant shall, if the claimant furnished adverse information about the debtor to a consumer credit reporting agency, notify the consumer credit reporting agency that the account is disputed.

(2) The claimant shall initiate a review considering all of the information provided by the debtor and other information available to the claimant in its file.

(3) Within 10 business days of completing the review, the claimant shall notify the debtor in writing of the claimant's determination and the good faith basis for that determination.

(4) The claimant shall not recommence collection activities until the debtor has been notified in writing of the good faith determination that the information does not establish that the particular debt, or portion thereof, is coerced debt.

(e) No inference or presumption that the debt is valid or invalid, or that the debtor is liable or not liable for the particular debt, or portion thereof, shall arise if the claimant decides after the review described in subdivision (d) to cease or recommence collection activities. The exercise or nonexercise of rights under this section is not a waiver of any other right or defense of the debtor or claimant.

(f)(1) At least 30 days before filing an action pursuant to paragraph (2) of subdivision (a) of Section 1798.97.3 or other action against a claimant in connection with an allegedly coerced debt, a debtor shall submit notice of the debtor's intent to file an action against the claimant and documents that comply with subdivision (b) in writing to the claimant.

(2) The written notice described in paragraph (1) shall be sent by certified mail, overnight delivery, or other method that allows for confirmation of the delivery date.

(3) The written notice described in paragraph (1) shall be sent to an address made available to the debtor by the claimant for receipt of the notice, or, if an address has not been identified by the claimant, to the claimant's principal place of business as identified by the Secretary of State. If an address is unavailable through the Secretary of State's website, the debtor may use the correspondence address of the claimant, or in the case of a debt collector, the address on file with the Department of Financial Protection and Innovation for licensing purposes.

(4)(A) The debtor shall not commence an action described in subdivision (a) of Section 1798.97.3 or other action against a claimant in connection with an allegedly coerced debt if the claimant informs the debtor that it has ceased all efforts to collect on the particular debt, or portion thereof, identified in the written notice pursuant to paragraph (1) and the debtor receives written notice of this cessation before the expiration of the 30-day period.

(B) The debtor may commence an action described in subdivision (a) of Section 1798.97.3 or other action against a claimant in connection with an allegedly coerced debt if either of the following conditions is satisfied:

(i) The 30-day period described in paragraph (1) expires and the collection activities have not ceased or the debtor has not received written notice that collection activities have ceased.

(ii) The debtor receives written notice pursuant to paragraph (4) of subdivision (d) of the claimant's good faith determination that the information does not establish that the particular debt, or portion thereof, is coerced debt.

(5) For purposes of this subdivision, the 30-day period shall begin to run when the claimant receives the written notice.

(g) A claimant that ceases collection activities under this section and does not recommence those collection activities shall do both of the following:

(1) If the claimant has furnished adverse information to a consumer credit reporting agency regarding the debtor and a particular debt, or portion thereof, notify the agency to delete that information no later than 10 business days after making its determination.

(2) If the claimant is a debt collector, notify the creditor no later than 10 business days after making its determination that collection activities have been terminated based upon the debtor's assertion that a particular debt, or portion thereof, being collected is coerced debt.

(h) A claimant that has possession of documents that the debtor is entitled to request from a creditor pursuant to Section 530.8 of the Penal Code may provide those documents to the debtor. *(Added by Stats.2022, c. 989 (S.B.975), § 2, eff. Jan. 1, 2023.)*

§ 1798.97.3. Coerced debt; action to recover debt; relief; judgment; unnecessary delay; written findings; collection of debt; statute of limitations

(a)(1) A debtor may bring an action against a claimant to establish that a particular debt, or portion thereof, is coerced debt.

(2) In an action brought by a claimant to recover a particular debt against the debtor, the debtor may file a cross-complaint to establish that the particular debt, or portion thereof, is coerced debt. The notice described in subdivision (f) of Section 1798.97.2 shall not be required as a prerequisite to filing a cross-complaint.

(3) A debtor shall plead the allegations of coerced debt with particularity and shall do either of the following:

(A) Attach the documents provided to the claimant pursuant to subdivision (b) of Section 1798.97.2 to any complaint.

(B) Attach the documents identified in subdivision (b) of Section 1798.97.2 to any cross-complaint.

(b) If the debtor establishes by a preponderance of the evidence in an action described in subdivision (a) that the particular debt, or portion thereof, is coerced debt, the debtor shall be entitled to the following relief:

(1) A declaratory judgment that the debtor is not obligated to the claimant on the particular debt, or portion thereof, that is coerced debt.

(2) An injunction prohibiting the claimant from holding or attempting to hold the debtor personally liable on the particular debt, or portion thereof, that is coerced debt, and prohibiting the claimant from enforcing a judgment related to the particular debt, or portion thereof, that is coerced debt against the debtor.

(3) An order dismissing any cause of action brought by the claimant to enforce or collect on the particular debt from the debtor or, if only a portion of the debt is established as coerced debt, an order directing that the complaint and judgment, if any, in the action be amended to reflect only the portion of the particular debt that is not coerced debt.

(c)(1) If the debtor establishes by a preponderance of the evidence in an action described in subdivision (a) that the particular debt, or portion thereof, is coerced debt, the court shall issue a judgment in favor of the claimant against the person or persons who coerced the debtor into incurring the debt in the amount of the debt, or portion thereof, that is coerced debt, provided that the person or persons who coerced the debtor into incurring the debt or debts has been brought within the jurisdiction of the court and joined as a party to the action and the evidence supports such a judgment.

(2) The court presiding over the action shall take appropriate steps necessary to prevent abuse, as defined in Section 6203 of the Family Code, of the debtor or an immediate family member of the debtor, including, but not limited to, sealing court records, redacting personally identifiable information about the debtor and any immediate family member of the debtor, and directing that any deposition or evidentiary hearing be conducted remotely.

(d) A debtor who files knowingly false motions, pleadings, or other papers or engages in other tactics that are frivolous or intended to cause unnecessary delay against a claimant shall be liable for the claimant's attorney's fees and costs in defending the lawsuit.

(e) The claimant may move the court to make written findings regarding evidence related to the person who caused the coerced debt to be incurred.

(f) Where some or all of a claim is established as having arisen from coerced debt, a claimant shall have standing, and may use all rights and remedies, to collect by any lawful means that claim, or portion thereof, from the person or persons determined to have coerced the debt, or against a person who used or possessed money, goods, services, or property obtained through coerced debt.

(g) The statute of limitations for a claimant to bring an action to collect coerced debt from any person determined to have coerced the debt shall run from the date of the court's determination that the person caused the duress, intimidation, threat of force, force, fraud, or undue influence giving rise to the coerced debt at issue and shall be brought within five years of that determination. *(Added by Stats.2022, c. 989 (S.B.975), § 2, eff. Jan. 1, 2023.)*

§ 1798.97.4. Secured debts

(a) This title does not apply to secured debts.

(b) This title does not require a court to order a claimant to refund any moneys already paid on a debt that is determined to be coerced.

(c) This title does not diminish the rights of a claimant to recover payment for a coerced debt from the person or persons who coerced a debtor into incurring that debt.

(d) This title does not reduce or eliminate any other rights or defenses available to a debtor or claimant pursuant to any other law. *(Added by Stats.2022, c. 989 (S.B.975), § 2, eff. Jan. 1, 2023.)*

§ 1798.97.5. Scope of title

(a) Except as set forth in subdivision (b), this title applies only to debts incurred on or after July 1, 2023.

(b) Notwithstanding subdivision (a), a debtor may file a cross-complaint described by paragraph (2) of subdivision (a) of Section 1798.97.3 in an action filed by a claimant to collect a debt incurred prior to July 1, 2023, in which case, this title applies to that action, unless a final judgment has been entered in that action. *(Added by Stats.2022, c. 989 (S.B.975), § 2, eff. Jan. 1, 2023.)*

§ 1798.97.6. Severability

If any provision of this title or the application thereof to any person or circumstances is held invalid, such invalidity shall not affect other provisions or applications of this title that can be given effect without the invalid provision or application, and to this end the provisions of this title are severable. *(Added by Stats.2022, c. 989 (S.B.975), § 2, eff. Jan. 1, 2023.)*

Title 1.81.4

PRIVACY OF CUSTOMER ELECTRICAL OR NATURAL GAS USAGE DATA

Section
1798.98. Definitions; prohibition on sharing, disclosing, or making customer's data accessible to third parties without consent; required data security procedures and practices; incentives or discounts for

Section

        accessing data without prior consent prohibited; disposal of customer data; exemptions.

1798.99. Civil actions; limitation on damages; other rights, remedies, or penalties; enforcement authority of Attorney General.

§ 1798.98. Definitions; prohibition on sharing, disclosing, or making customer's data accessible to third parties without consent; required data security procedures and practices; incentives or discounts for accessing data without prior consent prohibited; disposal of customer data; exemptions

(a) For the purposes of this title, the following definitions shall apply:

(1) "Business" means a sole proprietorship, partnership, corporation, association, or other group, however organized and whether or not organized to operate at a profit, including a financial institution organized, chartered, or holding a license or authorization certificate under the law of this state, any other state, the United States, or of any other country, or the parent or the subsidiary of a financial institution.

(2) "Customer" means a customer of an electrical or gas corporation or a local publicly owned electric utility that permits a business to have access to data in association with purchasing or leasing a product or obtaining a service from the business.

(3) "Data" means a customer's electrical or natural gas usage that is made available to the business as part of an advanced metering infrastructure provided by an electrical corporation, a gas corporation, or a local publicly owned electric utility, and includes the name, account number, or physical address of the customer.

(4) "Electrical corporation" has the same meaning as in Section 218 of the Public Utilities Code.

(5) "Gas corporation" has the same meaning as in Section 222 of the Public Utilities Code.

(6) "Local publicly owned electric utility" has the same meaning as in Section 224.3 of the Public Utilities Code.

(b) Unless otherwise required or authorized by federal or state law, a business shall not share, disclose, or otherwise make accessible to any third party a customer's data without obtaining the express consent of the customer and conspicuously disclosing to whom the disclosure will be made and how the data will be used.

(c) A business that discloses data, with the express consent of the customer, pursuant to a contract with a nonaffiliated third party, shall require by contract that the third party implement and maintain reasonable security procedures and practices appropriate to the nature of the information, to protect the data from unauthorized access, destruction, use, modification, or disclosure.

(d) A business shall implement and maintain reasonable security procedures and practices appropriate to the nature of the information to protect the data from unauthorized access, destruction, use, modification, or disclosure.

(e) A business shall not provide an incentive or discount to the customer for accessing the data without the prior consent of the customer.

(f) A business shall take all reasonable steps to dispose, or arrange for the disposal, of customer data within its custody or control when the records are no longer to be retained by the business by (1) shredding, (2) erasing, or (3) otherwise modifying the data in those records to make it unreadable or undecipherable through any means.

(g) The provisions of this section do not apply to an electrical corporation, a gas corporation, or a local publicly owned electric utility or a business that secures the data as a result of a contract with an electrical or gas corporation or a local publicly owned electric utility under the provisions of subdivision (f) of Section 8380 or subdivision (f) of 8381 of the Public Utilities Code. *(Added by Stats.2013, c. 597 (A.B.1274), § 1. Amended by Stats.2020, c. 188 (A.B.2788), § 1, eff. Jan. 1, 2021.)*

§ 1798.99. Civil actions; limitation on damages; other rights, remedies, or penalties; enforcement authority of Attorney General

(a) A customer harmed by the release or unauthorized use of his or her customer data, in violation of Section 1798.98, may bring a civil action to recover actual damages in an amount not to exceed five hundred dollars ($500) for each willful violation.

(b) The rights, remedies, and penalties established by this title are in addition to the rights, remedies, or penalties established under any other law.

(c) Nothing in this title shall abrogate any authority of the Attorney General to enforce existing law. *(Added by Stats. 2013, c. 597 (A.B.1274), § 1.)*

Title 1.81.45

THE PARENT'S ACCOUNTABILITY AND CHILD PROTECTION ACT

Section

1798.99.1. Age verification when selling products that are illegal to sell to minor; reasonable steps; products requiring age verification; penalties; application of section.

§ 1798.99.1. Age verification when selling products that are illegal to sell to minor; reasonable steps; products requiring age verification; penalties; application of section

(a)(1) A person or business that conducts business in California, and that seeks to sell any product or service in or into California that is illegal under state law to sell to a minor, as described in subdivisions (b) and (c), shall, notwithstanding any general term or condition, take reasonable steps to ensure that the purchaser is of legal age at the time of purchase or delivery, including, but not limited to, verifying the age of the purchaser.

(2) Reasonable steps as used in paragraph (1) for the purchase of items described in subdivision (b) include, but are not limited to, any of the following:

(A) Requiring the purchaser or recipient to input, scan, provide, or display a government-issued identification, provided that the person or business complies with all laws governing the retention, use, and disclosure of personally identifiable information, including, but not limited to, subdivision (a) of Section 1749.65, paragraphs (3) to (7), inclusive, of subdivision (b) of, and subdivisions (c) to (f), inclusive, of, Section 1798.90, paragraph (1) of subdivision (a) of Section 1798.90.1, Sections 1798.29, 1798.81.5, and 1798.82, and Sections 22575 to 22579, inclusive, of the Business and Professions Code.

(B) Requiring the purchaser to use a nonprepaid credit card for an online purchase.

(C) Implementing a system that restricts individuals with accounts designated as minor accounts from purchasing the products listed in subdivision (b).

(D) Shipping the product or service to an individual who is of legal age.

(3) Reasonable steps as used in paragraph (1) for the purchase of items described in subdivision (c) include, but are not limited to, any of the following:

(A) Requiring the purchaser or recipient to input, scan, provide, or display a government-issued identification, provided that the person or business complies with all laws governing the retention, use, and disclosure of personally identifiable information, including, but not limited to, subdivision (a) of Section 1749.65, paragraphs (3) to (7), inclusive, of subdivision (b) of, and subdivisions (c) to (f), inclusive, of, Section 1798.90, paragraph (1) of subdivision (a) of Section 1798.90.1, Sections 1798.29, 1798.81.5, and 1798.82, and Sections 22575 to 22579, inclusive, of the Business and Professions Code.

(B) Shipping the product or service to an individual who is of legal age.

(4) Reasonable steps as used in paragraph (1) shall not include consent obtained through the minor.

(5) A seller's reasonable and good faith reliance on bona fide evidence of the purchaser or recipient's age shall constitute an affirmative defense to any action under this subdivision.

(6) A person or business required to comply with this section shall not retain, use, or disclose any information it receives from a purchaser or recipient in an effort to verify age pursuant to this section for any purpose other than as required to comply with, or as needed to demonstrate compliance with, this section, California law, or a state or federal court order.

(b) Products or services that are illegal to sell to a minor under state law that are subject to subdivision (a) include all of the following:

(1) An aerosol container of paint that is capable of defacing property, as referenced in Section 594.1 of the Penal Code.

(2) Etching cream that is capable of defacing property, as referenced in Section 594.1 of the Penal Code.

(3) Dangerous fireworks, as referenced in Sections 12505 and 12689 of the Health and Safety Code.

(4) Tanning in an ultraviolet tanning device, as referenced in Sections 22702 and 22706 of the Business and Professions Code.

(5) Dietary supplement products containing ephedrine group alkaloids, as referenced in Section 110423.2 of the Health and Safety Code.

(6) Body branding, as referenced in Sections 119301 and 119302 of the Health and Safety Code.

(c) Products or services that are illegal to sell to a minor under state law that are subject to subdivision (a) include all of the following:

(1) Firearms or handguns, as referenced in Sections 16520, 16640, and 27505 of the Penal Code.

(2) A BB device, as referenced in Sections 16250 and 19910 of the Penal Code.

(3) Ammunition or reloaded ammunition, as referenced in Sections 16150 and 30300 of the Penal Code.

(4) Any tobacco, cigarette, cigarette papers, blunt wraps, any other preparation of tobacco, any other instrument or paraphernalia that is designed for the smoking or ingestion of tobacco, products prepared from tobacco, or any controlled substance, as referenced in Division 8.5 (commencing with Section 22950) of the Business and Professions Code, and Sections 308, 308.1, 308.2, and 308.3 of the Penal Code.

(5) Electronic cigarettes, as referenced in Section 119406 of the Health and Safety Code.

(6) A less lethal weapon, as referenced in Sections 16780 and 19405 of the Penal Code.

(d) In an action brought by a public prosecutor, a business or person that violates this section shall be subject to a civil penalty not exceeding seven thousand five hundred dollars ($7,500) for each violation.

(e) The provisions of this section do not apply to a business that is regulated by state or federal law providing greater protection to personal information or requiring greater age verification than provided by this section in regard to the subjects addressed by this section. Compliance with state or federal law shall be deemed compliance with this section with regard to those subjects. This subdivision does not relieve a business from a duty to comply with any other requirements of other state and federal law regarding the protection and privacy of personal information or age verification.

(f) For purposes of this section, a government-issued identification means any of the following:

(1) A document issued by a federal, state, county, or municipal government, or subdivision or agency thereof, including, but not limited to, an identification card or a valid motor vehicle operator's license, including licenses or identification cards issued pursuant to Section 12801.9 of the Vehicle Code, that contains the name, date of birth, description, and picture of the person.

(2) A valid passport issued by the United States or by a foreign government.

(3) A valid identification card issued to a member of the United States Armed Forces that includes the date of birth and picture of the person.

(4) A valid consular identification document.

(5) An identification card issued by a federally recognized tribal government.

(g) This section shall become operative on January 1, 2020. *(Added by Stats.2018, c. 872 (A.B.2511), § 1, eff. Jan. 1, 2019, operative Jan. 1, 2020. Amended by Stats.2022, c. 482 (A.B.1766), § 1, eff. Jan. 1, 2023.)*

Title 1.81.46

ONLINE VIOLENCE PREVENTION ACT

Section
1798.99.20. Definitions.
1798.99.21. Social media platforms; mechanism for reporting violent posts.
1798.99.22. Person who is target of violent post; request for order requiring removal of post and related violent posts; costs and attorney's fees.
1798.99.23. Application of title.

§ 1798.99.20. Definitions

For purposes of this section:[1]

(a)(1) "Content" means statements or comments made by users and media that are created, posted, shared, or otherwise interacted with by users on an internet-based service or application.

(2) "Content" does not include media put on a service or application exclusively for the purpose of cloud storage, transmitting files, or file collaboration.

(b) "Social media platform" means a public or semipublic internet-based service or application that has users in California and that meets both of the following criteria:

(1)(A) A substantial function of the service or application is to connect users in order to allow users to interact socially with each other within the service or application.

(B) A service or application that provides email or direct messaging services shall not be considered to meet this criterion on the basis of that function alone.

(2) The service or application allows users to do all of the following:

(A) Construct a public or semipublic profile for purposes of signing into and using the service or application.

(B) Populate a list of other users with whom an individual shares a social connection within the system.

(C) Create or post content viewable by other users, including, but not limited to, on message boards, in chat rooms, or through a landing page or main feed that presents the user with content generated by other users.

(c) "Public or semipublic internet-based service or application" does not include a service or application used to facilitate communication with a business or enterprise among employees or affiliates of the business or enterprise, provided that access to the service or application is restricted to employees or affiliates of the business or enterprise using the service or application.

(d) "User" means a person with an account on a social media platform.

(e) "Violent post" means content on a social media platform that contains a true threat against a specific person that is not protected by the First Amendment to the United States Constitution. *(Added by Stats.2022, c. 881 (S.B.1056), § 1, eff. Jan. 1, 2023.)*

[1] So in enrolled bill; probably should be "title".

§ 1798.99.21. Social media platforms; mechanism for reporting violent posts

(a) A social media platform shall clearly and conspicuously state whether it has a mechanism for reporting violent posts that is available to users and nonusers of the platform.

(b) If the social media platform has a reporting mechanism, the statement required by this subdivision shall include a link to the reporting mechanism. *(Added by Stats.2022, c. 881 (S.B.1056), § 1, eff. Jan. 1, 2023.)*

§ 1798.99.22. Person who is target of violent post; request for order requiring removal of post and related violent posts; costs and attorney's fees

(a)(1)(A) A person who is the target of a violent post, or reasonably believes the person is the target of a violent post, may seek an order requiring the social media platform to remove the violent post and any related violent post the court determines shall be removed in the interests of justice.

(B)(i) A person may bring an action pursuant to this paragraph before 48 hours have passed since providing notice to a social media platform pursuant to paragraph (2), but the court shall not rule on the request for an order until 48 hours have passed from the provision of notice.

(ii) The court may dismiss an action described by clause (i) if the social media platform deletes the post before 48 hours have passed from the provision of notice.

(C) Except as provided in subparagraph (D), a person may bring an action pursuant to this paragraph at any time, and the court may rule on the request at any time, if the social media platform does not have a reporting mechanism described in Section 1798.99.21.

(D) A person shall not bring an action pursuant to this paragraph, nor shall a court issue an order requiring a social medial platform to remove a violent post or any related violent post, based upon content containing a true threat against a specific person if the date and time when the true threat that was threatened to occur has passed.

(2) If the social media platform has a reporting mechanism described in Section 1798.99.21, a person shall not bring an action pursuant to paragraph (1) until the person has notified the social media platform of the violent post and requested that it be removed through the reporting mechanism.

(b)(1) A court shall award court costs and reasonable attorney's fees to a prevailing plaintiff in an action brought pursuant to this section.

(2) Reasonable attorney's fees may be awarded to a prevailing defendant upon a finding by the court that the plaintiff's prosecution of the action was not in good faith. *(Added by Stats.2022, c. 881 (S.B.1056), § 1, eff. Jan. 1, 2023.)*

§ 1798.99.23. Application of title

This title does not apply to a social media platform with fewer than 1,000,000 discrete monthly users. *(Added by Stats.2022, c. 881 (S.B.1056), § 1, eff. Jan. 1, 2023.)*

Title 1.81.47

THE CALIFORNIA AGE–APPROPRIATE DESIGN CODE ACT

Section
1798.99.28. Short title.
1798.99.29. Legislative findings and declarations.
1798.99.30. Definitions.
1798.99.31. Business that provides an online service, product, or feature likely to be accessed by children; required actions; prohibited actions.
1798.99.32. California Children's Data Protection Working Group.
1798.99.33. Completion of Data Protection Impact Assessment; exception.
1798.99.35. Violations and penalties; business in substantial compliance.
1798.99.40. Application of title.

§ 1798.99.28. Short title

This title shall be known, and may be cited, as the California Age-Appropriate Design Code Act. *(Added by Stats.2022, c. 320 (A.B.2273), § 2, eff. Jan. 1, 2023.)*

§ 1798.99.29. Legislative findings and declarations

The Legislature declares that children should be afforded protections not only by online products and services specifically directed at them but by all online products and services they are likely to access and makes the following findings:

(a) Businesses that develop and provide online services, products, or features that children are likely to access should consider the best interests of children when designing, developing, and providing that online service, product, or feature.

(b) If a conflict arises between commercial interests and the best interests of children, companies should prioritize the privacy, safety, and well-being of children over commercial interests. *(Added by Stats.2022, c. 320 (A.B.2273), § 2, eff. Jan. 1, 2023.)*

§ 1798.99.30. Definitions

(a) For purposes of this title, the definitions in Section 1798.140 shall apply unless otherwise specified in this title.

(b) For the purposes of this title:

(1) "Child" or "children," unless otherwise specified, means a consumer or consumers who are under 18 years of age.

(2) "Data Protection Impact Assessment" means a systematic survey to assess and mitigate risks that arise from the data management practices of the business to children who are reasonably likely to access the online service, product, or feature at issue that arises from the provision of that online service, product, or feature.

(3) "Default" means a preselected option adopted by the business for the online service, product, or feature.

(4) "Likely to be accessed by children" means it is reasonable to expect, based on the following indicators, that the online service, product, or feature would be accessed by children:

(A) The online service, product, or feature is directed to children as defined by the Children's Online Privacy Protection Act (15 U.S.C. Sec. 6501 et seq.).

(B) The online service, product, or feature is determined, based on competent and reliable evidence regarding audience composition, to be routinely accessed by a significant number of children.

(C) An online service, product, or feature with advertisements marketed to children.

(D) An online service, product, or feature that is substantially similar or the same as an online service, product, or feature subject to subparagraph (B).

(E) An online service, product, or feature that has design elements that are known to be of interest to children, including, but not limited to, games, cartoons, music, and celebrities who appeal to children.

(F) A significant amount of the audience of the online service, product, or feature is determined, based on internal company research, to be children.

(5) "Online service, product, or feature" does not mean any of the following:

(A) A broadband internet access service, as defined in Section 3100.

(B) A telecommunications service, as defined in Section 153 of Title 47 of the United States Code.

(C) The delivery or use of a physical product.

(6) "Profiling" means any form of automated processing of personal information that uses personal information to evaluate certain aspects relating to a natural person, including analyzing or predicting aspects concerning a natural person's performance at work, economic situation, health, personal preferences, interests, reliability, behavior, location, or movements. *(Added by Stats.2022, c. 320 (A.B.2273), § 2, eff. Jan. 1, 2023.)*

§ 1798.99.31. Business that provides an online service, product, or feature likely to be accessed by children; required actions; prohibited actions

Section operative July 1, 2024.

(a) A business that provides an online service, product, or feature likely to be accessed by children shall take all of the following actions:

(1)(A) Before any new online services, products, or features are offered to the public, complete a Data Protection Impact Assessment for any online service, product, or feature likely to be accessed by children and maintain documentation of this assessment as long as the online service, product, or feature is likely to be accessed by children. A business shall biennially review all Data Protection Impact Assessments.

(B) The Data Protection Impact Assessment required by this paragraph shall identify the purpose of the online service, product, or feature, how it uses children's personal information, and the risks of material detriment to children that arise from the data management practices of the business. The Data Protection Impact Assessment shall address, to the extent applicable, all of the following:

§ 1798.99.31

(i) Whether the design of the online product, service, or feature could harm children, including by exposing children to harmful, or potentially harmful, content on the online product, service, or feature.

(ii) Whether the design of the online product, service, or feature could lead to children experiencing or being targeted by harmful, or potentially harmful, contacts on the online product, service, or feature.

(iii) Whether the design of the online product, service, or feature could permit children to witness, participate in, or be subject to harmful, or potentially harmful, conduct on the online product, service, or feature.

(iv) Whether the design of the online product, service, or feature could allow children to be party to or exploited by a harmful, or potentially harmful, contact on the online product, service, or feature.

(v) Whether algorithms used by the online product, service, or feature could harm children.

(vi) Whether targeted advertising systems used by the online product, service, or feature could harm children.

(vii) Whether and how the online product, service, or feature uses system design features to increase, sustain, or extend use of the online product, service, or feature by children, including the automatic playing of media, rewards for time spent, and notifications.

(viii) Whether, how, and for what purpose the online product, service, or feature collects or processes sensitive personal information of children.

(2) Document any risk of material detriment to children that arises from the data management practices of the business identified in the Data Protection Impact Assessment required by paragraph (1) and create a timed plan to mitigate or eliminate the risk before the online service, product, or feature is accessed by children.

(3) Within three business days of a written request by the Attorney General, provide to the Attorney General a list of all Data Protection Impact Assessments the business has completed.

(4)(A) For any Data Protection Impact Assessment completed pursuant to paragraph (1), make the Data Protection Impact Assessment available, within five business days, to the Attorney General pursuant to a written request.

(B) Notwithstanding any other law, a Data Protection Impact Assessment is protected as confidential and shall be exempt from public disclosure, including under the California Public Records Act (Chapter 3.5 (commencing with Section 6250) of Division 7 of Title 1 of the Government Code).

(C) To the extent any information contained in a Data Protection Impact Assessment disclosed to the Attorney General includes information subject to attorney-client privilege or work product protection, disclosure pursuant to this paragraph shall not constitute a waiver of that privilege or protection.

(5) Estimate the age of child users with a reasonable level of certainty appropriate to the risks that arise from the data management practices of the business or apply the privacy and data protections afforded to children to all consumers.

(6) Configure all default privacy settings provided to children by the online service, product, or feature to settings that offer a high level of privacy, unless the business can demonstrate a compelling reason that a different setting is in the best interests of children.

(7) Provide any privacy information, terms of service, policies, and community standards concisely, prominently, and using clear language suited to the age of children likely to access that online service, product, or feature.

(8) If the online service, product, or feature allows the child's parent, guardian, or any other consumer to monitor the child's online activity or track the child's location, provide an obvious signal to the child when the child is being monitored or tracked.

(9) Enforce published terms, policies, and community standards established by the business, including, but not limited to, privacy policies and those concerning children.

(10) Provide prominent, accessible, and responsive tools to help children, or if applicable their parents or guardians, exercise their privacy rights and report concerns.

(b) A business that provides an online service, product, or feature likely to be accessed by children shall not take any of the following actions:

(1) Use the personal information of any child in a way that the business knows, or has reason to know, is materially detrimental to the physical health, mental health, or well-being of a child.

(2) Profile a child by default unless both of the following criteria are met:

(A) The business can demonstrate it has appropriate safeguards in place to protect children.

(B) Either of the following is true:

(i) Profiling is necessary to provide the online service, product, or feature requested and only with respect to the aspects of the online service, product, or feature with which the child is actively and knowingly engaged.

(ii) The business can demonstrate a compelling reason that profiling is in the best interests of children.

(3) Collect, sell, share, or retain any personal information that is not necessary to provide an online service, product, or feature with which a child is actively and knowingly engaged, or as described in paragraphs (1) to (4), inclusive, of subdivision (a) of Section 1798.145, unless the business can demonstrate a compelling reason that the collecting, selling, sharing, or retaining of the personal information is in the best interests of children likely to access the online service, product, or feature.

(4) If the end user is a child, use personal information for any reason other than a reason for which that personal information was collected, unless the business can demonstrate a compelling reason that use of the personal information is in the best interests of children.

(5) Collect, sell, or share any precise geolocation information of children by default unless the collection of that precise geolocation information is strictly necessary for the business to provide the service, product, or feature requested and then only for the limited time that the collection of precise

geolocation information is necessary to provide the service, product, or feature.

(6) Collect any precise geolocation information of a child without providing an obvious sign to the child for the duration of that collection that precise geolocation information is being collected.

(7) Use dark patterns to lead or encourage children to provide personal information beyond what is reasonably expected to provide that online service, product, or feature to forego privacy protections, or to take any action that the business knows, or has reason to know, is materially detrimental to the child's physical health, mental health, or well-being.

(8) Use any personal information collected to estimate age or age range for any other purpose or retain that personal information longer than necessary to estimate age. Age assurance shall be proportionate to the risks and data practice of an online service, product, or feature.

(c)(1) A Data Protection Impact Assessment conducted by a business for the purpose of compliance with any other law complies with this section if the Data Protection Impact Assessment meets the requirements of this title.

(2) A single data protection impact assessment may contain multiple similar processing operations that present similar risks only if each relevant online service, product, or feature is addressed.

(d) This section shall become operative on July 1, 2024. *(Added by Stats.2022, c. 320 (A.B.2273), § 2, eff. Jan. 1, 2023, operative July 1, 2024.)*

§ 1798.99.32. California Children's Data Protection Working Group

(a) The California Children's Data Protection Working Group is hereby created to deliver a report to the Legislature, pursuant to subdivision (e), regarding best practices for the implementation of this title.

(b) Working Group members shall consist of Californians with expertise in at least two of the following areas:

(1) Children's data privacy.

(2) Physical health.

(3) Mental health and well-being.

(4) Computer science.

(5) Children's rights.

(c) The working group shall select a chair and a vice chair from among its members and shall consist of the following 10 members:

(1) Two appointees by the Governor.

(2) Two appointees by the President Pro Tempore of the Senate.

(3) Two appointees by the Speaker of the Assembly.

(4) Two appointees by the Attorney General.

(5) Two appointees by the California Privacy Protection Agency.

(d) The working group shall take input from a broad range of stakeholders, including from academia, consumer advocacy groups, and small, medium, and large businesses affected by data privacy policies and shall make recommendations to the Legislature on best practices regarding, at minimum, all of the following:

(1) Identifying online services, products, or features likely to be accessed by children.

(2) Evaluating and prioritizing the best interests of children with respect to their privacy, physical health, and mental health and well-being and evaluating how those interests may be furthered by the design, development, and implementation of an online service, product, or feature.

(3) Ensuring that age assurance methods used by businesses that provide online services, products, or features likely to be accessed by children are proportionate to the risks that arise from the data management practices of the business, privacy protective, and minimally invasive.

(4) Assessing and mitigating risks to children that arise from the use of an online service, product, or feature.

(5) Publishing privacy information, policies, and standards in concise, clear language suited for the age of children likely to access an online service, product, or feature.

(6) How the working group and the Department of Justice may leverage the substantial and growing expertise of the California Privacy Protection Agency in the long-term development of data privacy policies that affect the privacy, rights, and safety of children online.

(e) On or before January 1, 2024, and every two years thereafter, the working group shall submit, pursuant to Section 9795 of the Government Code, a report to the Legislature regarding the recommendations described in subdivision (d).

(f) The members of the working group shall serve without compensation but shall be reimbursed for all necessary expenses actually incurred in the performance of their duties.

(g) This section shall remain in effect until January 1, 2030, and as of that date is repealed. *(Added by Stats.2022, c. 320 (A.B.2273), § 2, eff. Jan. 1, 2023.)*

Repeal

For repeal of this section, see its terms.

§ 1798.99.33. Completion of Data Protection Impact Assessment; exception

(a) A business shall complete a Data Protection Impact Assessment on or before July 1, 2024, for any online service, product, or feature likely to be accessed by children offered to the public before July 1, 2024.

(b) This section does not apply to an online service, product, or feature that is not offered to the public on or after July 1, 2024. *(Added by Stats.2022, c. 320 (A.B.2273), § 2, eff. Jan. 1, 2023.)*

§ 1798.99.35. Violations and penalties; business in substantial compliance

(a) Any business that violates this title shall be subject to an injunction and liable for a civil penalty of not more than two thousand five hundred dollars ($2,500) per affected child for each negligent violation or not more than seven thousand five hundred dollars ($7,500) per affected child for each

§ 1798.99.35

intentional violation, which shall be assessed and recovered only in a civil action brought in the name of the people of the State of California by the Attorney General.

(b) Any penalties, fees, and expenses recovered in an action brought under this title shall be deposited in the Consumer Privacy Fund, created within the General Fund pursuant to subdivision (a) of Section 1798.160, with the intent that they be used to fully offset costs incurred by the Attorney General in connection with this title.

(c)(1) If a business is in substantial compliance with the requirements of paragraphs (1) through (4), inclusive, of subdivision (a) of Section 1798.99.31, the Attorney General shall provide written notice to the business, before initiating an action under this title, identifying the specific provisions of this title that the Attorney General alleges have been or are being violated.

(2) If, within 90 days of the notice required by this subdivision, the business cures any noticed violation and provides the Attorney General a written statement that the alleged violations have been cured, and sufficient measures have been taken to prevent future violations, the business shall not be liable for a civil penalty for any violation cured pursuant to this subdivision.

(d) Nothing in this title shall be interpreted to serve as the basis for a private right of action under this title or any other law.

(e) The Attorney General may solicit broad public participation and adopt regulations to clarify the requirements of this title. (Added by Stats.2022, c. 320 (A.B.2273), § 2, eff. Jan. 1, 2023.)

§ 1798.99.40. Application of title

This title does not apply to the information or entities described in subdivision (c) of Section 1798.145. (Added by Stats.2022, c. 320 (A.B.2273), § 2, eff. Jan. 1, 2023.)

Title 1.81.48

DATA BROKER REGISTRATION

Section
1798.99.80. Definitions.
1798.99.81. Data Brokers' Registry Fund.
1798.99.82. Registration; deadline; fee; information required; penalties.
1798.99.84. Posting on internet website.
1798.99.88. Construction of title.

§ 1798.99.80. Definitions

For purposes of this title:

(a) "Business" has the meaning provided in subdivision (d) of Section 1798.140.

(b) "Collects" and "collection" have the meaning provided in subdivision (f) of Section 1798.140.

(c) "Consumer" has the meaning provided in subdivision (i) of Section 1798.140.

(d) "Data broker" means a business that knowingly collects and sells to third parties the personal information of a consumer with whom the business does not have a direct relationship. "Data broker" does not include any of the following:

(1) A consumer reporting agency to the extent that it is covered by the federal Fair Credit Reporting Act (15 U.S.C. Sec. 1681 et seq.).

(2) A financial institution to the extent that it is covered by the Gramm-Leach-Bliley Act (Public Law 106–102)[1] and implementing regulations.

(3) An entity to the extent that it is covered by the Insurance Information and Privacy Protection Act (Article 6.6 (commencing with Section 791) of Chapter 1 of Part 2 of Division 1 of the Insurance Code).

(e) "Personal information" has the meaning provided in subdivision (v) of Section 1798.140.

(f) "Sell" * * * has the meaning provided in subdivision (ad) of Section 1798.140.

(g) "Third party" has the meaning provided in subdivision (ai) of Section 1798.140. (Added by Stats.2019, c. 753 (A.B.1202), § 2, eff. Jan. 1, 2020. Amended by Stats.2022, c. 420 (A.B.2960), § 10, eff. Jan. 1, 2023.)

[1] For public law sections classified to the U.S.C.A., see USCA–Tables.

§ 1798.99.81. Data Brokers' Registry Fund

A fund to be known as the "Data Brokers' Registry Fund" is hereby created within the State Treasury. All registration fees received pursuant to paragraph (1) of subdivision (b) of Section 1798.99.82 shall be deposited into the Data Brokers' Registry Fund, to be available for expenditure by the Department of Justice, upon appropriation by the Legislature, to offset costs of establishing and maintaining the informational internet website described in Section 1798.99.84. (Added by Stats.2020, c. 14 (A.B.82), § 3, eff. June 29, 2020.)

§ 1798.99.82. Registration; deadline; fee; information required; penalties

(a) On or before January 31 following each year in which a business meets the definition of data broker as provided in this title, the business shall register with the Attorney General pursuant to the requirements of this section.

(b) In registering with the Attorney General, as described in subdivision (a), a data broker shall do all of the following:

(1) Pay a registration fee in an amount determined by the Attorney General, not to exceed the reasonable costs of establishing and maintaining the informational internet website described in Section 1798.99.84. Registration fees shall be deposited in the Data Brokers' Registry Fund, created within the State Treasury pursuant to Section 1798.99.81, and used for the purposes outlined in this paragraph.

(2) Provide the following information:

(A) The name of the data broker and its primary physical, email, and internet website addresses.

(B) Any additional information or explanation the data broker chooses to provide concerning its data collection practices.

(c) A data broker that fails to register as required by this section is subject to injunction and is liable for civil penalties, fees, and costs in an action brought in the name of the people of the State of California by the Attorney General as follows:

(1) A civil penalty of one hundred dollars ($100) for each day the data broker fails to register as required by this section.

(2) An amount equal to the fees that were due during the period it failed to register.

(3) Expenses incurred by the Attorney General in the investigation and prosecution of the action as the court deems appropriate.

(d) Any penalties, fees, and expenses recovered in an action prosecuted under subdivision (c) shall be deposited in the Consumer Privacy Fund, created within the General Fund pursuant to subdivision (a) of Section 1798.160, with the intent that they be used to fully offset costs incurred by the state courts and the Attorney General in connection with this title. *(Added by Stats.2019, c. 753 (A.B.1202), § 2, eff. Jan. 1, 2020. Amended by Stats.2020, c. 14 (A.B.82), § 4, eff. June 29, 2020.)*

§ 1798.99.84. Posting on internet website

The Attorney General shall create a page on its internet website where the information provided by data brokers under this title shall be accessible to the public. *(Added by Stats.2019, c. 753 (A.B.1202), § 2, eff. Jan. 1, 2020.)*

§ 1798.99.88. Construction of title

Nothing in this title shall be construed to supersede or interfere with the operation of the California Consumer Privacy Act of 2018 (Title 1.81.5 (commencing with Section 1798.100)). *(Added by Stats.2019, c. 753 (A.B.1202), § 2, eff. Jan. 1, 2020.)*

Title 1.81.5

CALIFORNIA CONSUMER PRIVACY ACT OF 2018

Section	
1798.100.	General Duties of Businesses that Collect Personal Information.
1798.105.	Consumers' Right to Delete Personal Information.
1798.106.	Consumers' Right to Correct Inaccurate Personal Information.
1798.110.	Consumers' Right to Know What Personal Information is Being Collected. Right to Access Personal Information.
1798.115.	Consumers' Right to Know What Personal Information is Sold or Shared and to Whom.
1798.120.	Consumers' Right to Opt Out of Sale or Sharing of Personal Information.
1798.121.	Consumers' Right to Limit Use and Disclosure of Sensitive Personal Information.
1798.125.	Consumers' Right of No Retaliation Following Opt Out or Exercise of Other Rights.
1798.130.	Notice, Disclosure, Correction, and Deletion Requirements.
1798.135.	Methods of Limiting Sale, Sharing, and Use of Personal Information and Use of Sensitive Personal Information.
1798.140.	Definitions.
1798.145.	Exemptions.
1798.146.	Collection of confidential medical information; protected health information; covered entity or business governed by federal law.
1798.148.	Reidentification of confidential medical information; exceptions.
1798.150.	Personal Information Security Breaches.
1798.155.	Administrative Enforcement.
1798.160.	Consumer Privacy Fund.
1798.175.	Conflicting Provisions.
1798.180.	Preemption.
1798.185.	Regulations.
1798.190.	Anti–Avoidance.
1798.192.	Waiver.
1798.194.	Liberal construction of title.
1798.196.	Construction with federal law, United States Constitution, and California Constitution.
1798.198.	Operative date of title.
1798.199.	Operative date of Section 1798.180.
1798.199.10.	California Privacy Protection Agency; establishment; appointments.
1798.199.15.	Members of the board; qualifications; conduct.
1798.199.20.	Duration of service.
1798.199.25.	Compensation.
1798.199.30.	Executive director; officers, counsel, and employees.
1798.199.35.	Delegation of authority.
1798.199.40.	Functions of agency.
1798.199.45.	Investigation of possible violations; considerations.
1798.199.50.	Consideration of probable cause; notice to alleged violator.
1798.199.55.	Determination of probable cause; notice and hearing; issuance of order; joint and several liability.
1798.199.60.	Rejection of decision of administrative law judge; written statement of reasons.
1798.199.65.	Subpoenas; oaths and affirmations; evidence.
1798.199.70.	Time for bringing action.
1798.199.75.	Civil action for collection of unpaid administrative fines.
1798.199.80.	Application for judgment to collect administrative fines imposed by order or decision.
1798.199.85.	Agency decisions subject to judicial review.
1798.199.90.	Penalties for violations; Attorney General enforcement.
1798.199.95.	Appropriations.
1798.199.100.	Consideration of good faith cooperation.

Operative Effect

For operative effect of Title 1.81.5, see Civil Code § 1798.198.

Cross References

Data broker registration, construction with this Title, see Civil Code § 1798.99.88.

Program to issue alternative devices for license plates, stickers, tabs, and registration cards, see Vehicle Code § 4854.

§ 1798.100. General Duties of Businesses that Collect Personal Information [1]

(a) A business that controls the collection of a consumer's personal information shall, at or before the point of collection, inform consumers of the following:

§ 1798.100

(1) The categories of personal information to be collected and the purposes for which the categories of personal information are collected or used and whether that information is sold or shared. A business shall not collect additional categories of personal information or use personal information collected for additional purposes that are incompatible with the disclosed purpose for which the personal information was collected without providing the consumer with notice consistent with this section.

(2) If the business collects sensitive personal information, the categories of sensitive personal information to be collected and the purposes for which the categories of sensitive personal information are collected or used, and whether that information is sold or shared. A business shall not collect additional categories of sensitive personal information or use sensitive personal information collected for additional purposes that are incompatible with the disclosed purpose for which the sensitive personal information was collected without providing the consumer with notice consistent with this section.

(3) The length of time the business intends to retain each category of personal information, including sensitive personal information, or if that is not possible, the criteria used to determine that period provided that a business shall not retain a consumer's personal information or sensitive personal information for each disclosed purpose for which the personal information was collected for longer than is reasonably necessary for that disclosed purpose.

(b) A business that, acting as a third party, controls the collection of personal information about a consumer may satisfy its obligation under subdivision (a) by providing the required information prominently and conspicuously on the homepage of its internet website. In addition, if a business acting as a third party controls the collection of personal information about a consumer on its premises, including in a vehicle, then the business shall, at or before the point of collection, inform consumers as to the categories of personal information to be collected and the purposes for which the categories of personal information are used, and whether that personal information is sold, in a clear and conspicuous manner at the location.

(c) A business' collection, use, retention, and sharing of a consumer's personal information shall be reasonably necessary and proportionate to achieve the purposes for which the personal information was collected or processed, or for another disclosed purpose that is compatible with the context in which the personal information was collected, and not further processed in a manner that is incompatible with those purposes.

(d) A business that collects a consumer's personal information and that sells that personal information to, or shares it with, a third party or that discloses it to a service provider or contractor for a business purpose shall enter into an agreement with the third party, service provider, or contractor, that:

(1) Specifies that the personal information is sold or disclosed by the business only for limited and specified purposes.

(2) Obligates the third party, service provider, or contractor to comply with applicable obligations under this title and obligate those persons to provide the same level of privacy protection as is required by this title.

(3) Grants the business rights to take reasonable and appropriate steps to help ensure that the third party, service provider, or contractor uses the personal information transferred in a manner consistent with the business' obligations under this title.

(4) Requires the third party, service provider, or contractor to notify the business if it makes a determination that it can no longer meet its obligations under this title.

(5) Grants the business the right, upon notice, including under paragraph (4), to take reasonable and appropriate steps to stop and remediate unauthorized use of personal information.

(e) A business that collects a consumer's personal information shall implement reasonable security procedures and practices appropriate to the nature of the personal information to protect the personal information from unauthorized or illegal access, destruction, use, modification, or disclosure in accordance with Section 1798.81.5.

(f) Nothing in this section shall require a business to disclose trade secrets, as specified in regulations adopted pursuant to paragraph (3) of subdivision (a) of Section 1798.185. *(Added by Stats.2018, c. 55 (A.B.375), § 3, eff. Jan. 1, 2019, operative Jan. 1, 2020. Amended by Stats.2018, c. 735 (S.B.1121), § 1, eff. Sept. 23, 2018, operative Jan. 1, 2020; Stats.2019, c. 757 (A.B.1355), § 1, eff. Jan. 1, 2020; Initiative Measure (Prop. 24, § 4, approved Nov. 3, 2020, eff. Dec. 16, 2020, operative Jan. 1, 2023).)*

[1] Section caption supplied by Prop. 24.

Operative Effect

For effective and operative dates of Initiative Measure (Prop. 24), see § 31 of the Measure.

For operative effect of Title 1.81.5, see Civil Code § 1798.198.

§ 1798.105. Consumers' Right to Delete Personal Information[1]

(a) A consumer shall have the right to request that a business delete any personal information about the consumer which the business has collected from the consumer.

(b) A business that collects personal information about consumers shall disclose, pursuant to Section 1798.130, the consumer's rights to request the deletion of the consumer's personal information.

(c)(1) A business that receives a verifiable consumer request from a consumer to delete the consumer's personal information pursuant to subdivision (a) of this section shall delete the consumer's personal information from its records, notify any service providers or contractors to delete the consumer's personal information from their records, and notify all third parties to whom the business has sold or shared the personal information to delete the consumer's personal information unless this proves impossible or involves disproportionate effort.

(2) The business may maintain a confidential record of deletion requests solely for the purpose of preventing the personal information of a consumer who has submitted a deletion request from being sold, for compliance with laws or for other purposes, solely to the extent permissible under this title.

(3) A service provider or contractor shall cooperate with the business in responding to a verifiable consumer request, and at the direction of the business, shall delete, or enable the business to delete and shall notify any of its own service providers or contractors to delete personal information about the consumer collected, used, processed, or retained by the service provider or the contractor. The service provider or contractor shall notify any service providers, contractors, or third parties who may have accessed personal information from or through the service provider or contractor, unless the information was accessed at the direction of the business, to delete the consumer's personal information unless this proves impossible or involves disproportionate effort. A service provider or contractor shall not be required to comply with a deletion request submitted by the consumer directly to the service provider or contractor to the extent that the service provider or contractor has collected, used, processed, or retained the consumer's personal information in its role as a service provider or contractor to the business.

(d) A business, or a service provider or contractor acting pursuant to its contract with the business, another service provider, or another contractor, shall not be required to comply with a consumer's request to delete the consumer's personal information if it is reasonably necessary for the business, service provider, or contractor to maintain the consumer's personal information in order to:

(1) Complete the transaction for which the personal information was collected, fulfill the terms of a written warranty or product recall conducted in accordance with federal law, provide a good or service requested by the consumer, or reasonably anticipated by the consumer within the context of a business' ongoing business relationship with the consumer, or otherwise perform a contract between the business and the consumer.

(2) Help to ensure security and integrity to the extent the use of the consumer's personal information is reasonably necessary and proportionate for those purposes.

(3) Debug to identify and repair errors that impair existing intended functionality.

(4) Exercise free speech, ensure the right of another consumer to exercise that consumer's right of free speech, or exercise another right provided for by law.

(5) Comply with the California Electronic Communications Privacy Act pursuant to Chapter 3.6 (commencing with Section 1546) of Title 12 of Part 2 of the Penal Code.

(6) Engage in public or peer-reviewed scientific, historical, or statistical research that conforms or adheres to all other applicable ethics and privacy laws, when the business' deletion of the information is likely to render impossible or seriously impair the ability to complete such research, if the consumer has provided informed consent.

(7) To enable solely internal uses that are reasonably aligned with the expectations of the consumer based on the consumer's relationship with the business and compatible with the context in which the consumer provided the information.

(8) Comply with a legal obligation. *(Added by Stats.2018, c. 55 (A.B.375), § 3, eff. Jan. 1, 2019, operative Jan. 1, 2020. Amended by Stats.2018, c. 735 (S.B.1121), § 2, eff. Sept. 23, 2018, operative Jan. 1, 2020; Stats.2019, c. 751 (A.B.1146), § 1, eff. Jan. 1, 2020; Initiative Measure (Prop. 24, § 5, approved Nov. 3, 2020, eff. Dec. 16, 2020, operative Jan. 1, 2023).)*

[1] Section caption supplied by Prop. 24.

Operative Effect

For effective and operative dates of Initiative Measure (Prop. 24), see § 31 of the Measure.

For operative effect of Title 1.81.5, see Civil Code § 1798.198.

§ 1798.106. Consumers' Right to Correct Inaccurate Personal Information [1]

(a) A consumer shall have the right to request a business that maintains inaccurate personal information about the consumer to correct that inaccurate personal information, taking into account the nature of the personal information and the purposes of the processing of the personal information.

(b) A business that collects personal information about consumers shall disclose, pursuant to Section 1798.130, the consumer's right to request correction of inaccurate personal information.

(c) A business that receives a verifiable consumer request to correct inaccurate personal information shall use commercially reasonable efforts to correct the inaccurate personal information as directed by the consumer, pursuant to Section 1798.130 and regulations adopted pursuant to paragraph (8) of subdivision (a) of Section 1798.185. *(Added by Initiative Measure (Prop. 24, § 6, approved Nov. 3, 2020, eff. Dec. 16, 2020, operative Jan. 1, 2023).)*

[1] Section caption supplied by Prop. 24.

Operative Effect

For effective and operative dates of Initiative Measure (Prop. 24), see § 31 of the Measure.

For operative effect of Title 1.81.5, see Civil Code § 1798.198.

§ 1798.110. Consumers' Right to Know What Personal Information is Being Collected. Right to Access Personal Information [1]

(a) A consumer shall have the right to request that a business that collects personal information about the consumer disclose to the consumer the following:

(1) The categories of personal information it has collected about that consumer.

(2) The categories of sources from which the personal information is collected.

§ 1798.110

(3) The business or commercial purpose for collecting, selling, or sharing personal information.

(4) The categories of third parties to whom the business discloses personal information.

(5) The specific pieces of personal information it has collected about that consumer.

(b) A business that collects personal information about a consumer shall disclose to the consumer, pursuant to subparagraph (B) of paragraph (3) of subdivision (a) of Section 1798.130, the information specified in subdivision (a) upon receipt of a verifiable consumer request from the consumer, provided that a business shall be deemed to be in compliance with paragraphs (1) to (4), inclusive, of subdivision (a) to the extent that the categories of information and the business or commercial purpose for collecting, selling, or sharing personal information it would be required to disclose to the consumer pursuant to paragraphs (1) to (4), inclusive, of subdivision (a) is the same as the information it has disclosed pursuant to paragraphs (1) to (4), inclusive, of subdivision (c).

(c) A business that collects personal information about consumers shall disclose, pursuant to subparagraph (B) of paragraph (5) of subdivision (a) of Section 1798.130:

(1) The categories of personal information it has collected about consumers.

(2) The categories of sources from which the personal information is collected.

(3) The business or commercial purpose for collecting, selling, or sharing personal information.

(4) The categories of third parties to whom the business discloses personal information.

(5) That a consumer has the right to request the specific pieces of personal information the business has collected about that consumer. *(Added by Stats.2018, c. 55 (A.B.375), § 3, eff. Jan. 1, 2019, operative Jan. 1, 2020. Amended by Stats.2018, c. 735 (S.B.1121), § 3, eff. Sept. 23, 2018, operative Jan. 1, 2020; Stats.2019, c. 757 (A.B.1355), § 2, eff. Jan. 1, 2020; Initiative Measure (Prop. 24, § 7, approved Nov. 3, 2020, eff. Dec. 16, 2020, operative Jan. 1, 2023).)*

[1] Section caption supplied by Prop. 24.

Operative Effect

For effective and operative dates of Initiative Measure (Prop. 24), see § 31 of the Measure.

For operative effect of Title 1.81.5, see Civil Code § 1798.198.

§ 1798.115. Consumers' Right to Know What Personal Information is Sold or Shared and to Whom [1]

(a) A consumer shall have the right to request that a business that sells or shares the consumer's personal information, or that discloses it for a business purpose, disclose to that consumer:

(1) The categories of personal information that the business collected about the consumer.

(2) The categories of personal information that the business sold or shared about the consumer and the categories of third parties to whom the personal information was sold or shared, by category or categories of personal information for each category of third parties to whom the personal information was sold or shared.

(3) The categories of personal information that the business disclosed about the consumer for a business purpose and the categories of persons to whom it was disclosed for a business purpose.

(b) A business that sells or shares personal information about a consumer, or that discloses a consumer's personal information for a business purpose, shall disclose, pursuant to paragraph (4) of subdivision (a) of Section 1798.130, the information specified in subdivision (a) to the consumer upon receipt of a verifiable consumer request from the consumer.

(c) A business that sells or shares consumers' personal information, or that discloses consumers' personal information for a business purpose, shall disclose, pursuant to subparagraph (C) of paragraph (5) of subdivision (a) of Section 1798.130:

(1) The category or categories of consumers' personal information it has sold or shared, or if the business has not sold or shared consumers' personal information, it shall disclose that fact.

(2) The category or categories of consumers' personal information it has disclosed for a business purpose, or if the business has not disclosed consumers' personal information for a business purpose, it shall disclose that fact.

(d) A third party shall not sell or share personal information about a consumer that has been sold to, or shared with, the third party by a business unless the consumer has received explicit notice and is provided an opportunity to exercise the right to opt-out pursuant to Section 1798.120. *(Added by Stats.2018, c. 55 (A.B.375), § 3, eff. Jan. 1, 2019, operative Jan. 1, 2020. Amended by Stats.2018, c. 735 (S.B.1121), § 4, eff. Sept. 23, 2018, operative Jan. 1, 2020; Stats.2019, c. 757 (A.B.1355), § 3, eff. Jan. 1, 2020; Initiative Measure (Prop. 24, § 8, approved Nov. 3, 2020, eff. Dec. 16, 2020, operative Jan. 1, 2023).)*

[1] Section caption supplied by Prop. 24.

Operative Effect

For effective and operative dates of Initiative Measure (Prop. 24), see § 31 of the Measure.

For operative effect of Title 1.81.5, see Civil Code § 1798.198.

§ 1798.120. Consumers' Right to Opt Out of Sale or Sharing of Personal Information [1]

(a) A consumer shall have the right, at any time, to direct a business that sells or shares personal information about the consumer to third parties not to sell or share the consumer's personal information. This right may be referred to as the right to opt-out of sale or sharing.

(b) A business that sells consumers' personal information to, or shares it with, third parties shall provide notice to consumers, pursuant to subdivision (a) of Section 1798.135, that this information may be sold or shared and that consumers have the "right to opt-out" of the sale or sharing of their personal information.

(c) Notwithstanding subdivision (a), a business shall not sell or share the personal information of consumers if the business has actual knowledge that the consumer is less than 16 years of age, unless the consumer, in the case of consumers at least 13 years of age and less than 16 years of age, or the consumer's parent or guardian, in the case of consumers who are less than 13 years of age, has affirmatively authorized the sale or sharing of the consumer's personal information. A business that willfully disregards the consumer's age shall be deemed to have had actual knowledge of the consumer's age.

(d) A business that has received direction from a consumer not to sell or share the consumer's personal information or, in the case of a minor consumer's personal information has not received consent to sell or share the minor consumer's personal information, shall be prohibited, pursuant to paragraph (4) of subdivision (c) of Section 1798.135, from selling or sharing the consumer's personal information after its receipt of the consumer's direction, unless the consumer subsequently provides consent, for the sale or sharing of the consumer's personal information. *(Added by Stats.2018, c. 55 (A.B.375), § 3, eff. Jan. 1, 2019, operative Jan. 1, 2020. Amended by Stats.2018, c. 735 (S.B.1121), § 5, eff. Sept. 23, 2018, operative Jan. 1, 2020; Stats.2019, c. 757 (A.B.1355), § 4, eff. Jan. 1, 2020; Initiative Measure (Prop. 24, § 9, approved Nov. 3, 2020, eff. Dec. 16, 2020, operative Jan. 1, 2023).)*

[1] Section caption supplied by Prop. 24.

Operative Effect

For effective and operative dates of Initiative Measure (Prop. 24), see § 31 of the Measure.

For operative effect of Title 1.81.5, see Civil Code § 1798.198.

§ 1798.121. Consumers' Right to Limit Use and Disclosure of Sensitive Personal Information [1]

(a) A consumer shall have the right, at any time, to direct a business that collects sensitive personal information about the consumer to limit its use of the consumer's sensitive personal information to that use which is necessary to perform the services or provide the goods reasonably expected by an average consumer who requests those goods or services, to perform the services set forth in paragraphs (2), (4), (5), and (8) of subdivision (e) of Section 1798.140, and as authorized by regulations adopted pursuant to subparagraph (C) of paragraph (19) of subdivision (a) of Section 1798.185. A business that uses or discloses a consumer's sensitive personal information for purposes other than those specified in this subdivision shall provide notice to consumers, pursuant to subdivision (a) of Section 1798.135, that this information may be used, or disclosed to a service provider or contractor, for additional, specified purposes and that consumers have the right to limit the use or disclosure of their sensitive personal information.

(b) A business that has received direction from a consumer not to use or disclose the consumer's sensitive personal information, except as authorized by subdivision (a), shall be prohibited, pursuant to paragraph (4) of subdivision (c) of Section 1798.135, from using or disclosing the consumer's sensitive personal information for any other purpose after its receipt of the consumer's direction unless the consumer subsequently provides consent for the use or disclosure of the consumer's sensitive personal information for additional purposes.

(c) A service provider or contractor that assists a business in performing the purposes authorized by subdivision (a) may not use the sensitive personal information after it has received instructions from the business and to the extent it has actual knowledge that the personal information is sensitive personal information for any other purpose. A service provider or contractor is only required to limit its use of sensitive personal information received pursuant to a written contract with the business in response to instructions from the business and only with respect to its relationship with that business.

(d) Sensitive personal information that is collected or processed without the purpose of inferring characteristics about a consumer is not subject to this section, as further defined in regulations adopted pursuant to subparagraph (C) of paragraph (19) of subdivision (a) of Section 1798.185, and shall be treated as personal information for purposes of all other sections of this act, including Section 1798.100. *(Added by Initiative Measure (Prop. 24, § 10, approved Nov. 3, 2020, eff. Dec. 16, 2020, operative Jan. 1, 2023).)*

[1] Section caption supplied by Prop. 24.

Operative Effect

For effective and operative dates of Initiative Measure (Prop. 24), see § 31 of the Measure.

For operative effect of Title 1.81.5, see Civil Code § 1798.198.

§ 1798.125. Consumers' Right of No Retaliation Following Opt Out or Exercise of Other Rights [1]

(a)(1) A business shall not discriminate against a consumer because the consumer exercised any of the consumer's rights under this title, including, but not limited to, by:

(A) Denying goods or services to the consumer.

(B) Charging different prices or rates for goods or services, including through the use of discounts or other benefits or imposing penalties.

(C) Providing a different level or quality of goods or services to the consumer.

(D) Suggesting that the consumer will receive a different price or rate for goods or services or a different level or quality of goods or services.

(E) Retaliating against an employee, applicant for employment, or independent contractor, as defined in subparagraph (A) of paragraph (2) of subdivision (m) of Section 1798.145, for exercising their rights under this title.

(2) Nothing in this subdivision prohibits a business, pursuant to subdivision (b), from charging a consumer a different price or rate, or from providing a different level or quality of goods or services to the consumer, if that difference is

§ 1798.125

reasonably related to the value provided to the business by the consumer's data.

(3) This subdivision does not prohibit a business from offering loyalty, rewards, premium features, discounts, or club card programs consistent with this title.

(b)(1) A business may offer financial incentives, including payments to consumers as compensation, for the collection of personal information, the sale or sharing of personal information, or the retention of personal information. A business may also offer a different price, rate, level, or quality of goods or services to the consumer if that price or difference is reasonably related to the value provided to the business by the consumer's data.

(2) A business that offers any financial incentives pursuant to this subdivision, shall notify consumers of the financial incentives pursuant to Section 1798.130.

(3) A business may enter a consumer into a financial incentive program only if the consumer gives the business prior opt-in consent pursuant to Section 1798.130 that clearly describes the material terms of the financial incentive program, and which may be revoked by the consumer at any time. If a consumer refuses to provide opt-in consent, then the business shall wait for at least 12 months before next requesting that the consumer provide opt-in consent, or as prescribed by regulations adopted pursuant to Section 1798.185.

(4) A business shall not use financial incentive practices that are unjust, unreasonable, coercive, or usurious in nature. *(Added by Stats.2018, c. 55 (A.B.375), § 3, eff. Jan. 1, 2019, operative Jan. 1, 2020. Amended by Stats.2018, c. 735 (S.B.1121), § 6, eff. Sept. 23, 2018, operative Jan. 1, 2020; Stats.2019, c. 757 (A.B.1355), § 5, eff. Jan. 1, 2020; Initiative Measure (Prop. 24, § 11, approved Nov. 3, 2020, eff. Dec. 16, 2020, operative Jan. 1, 2023).)*

[1] Section caption supplied by Prop. 24.

Operative Effect

For effective and operative dates of Initiative Measure (Prop. 24), see § 31 of the Measure.

For operative effect of Title 1.81.5, see Civil Code § 1798.198.

§ 1798.130. Notice, Disclosure, Correction, and Deletion Requirements [1]

(a) In order to comply with Sections 1798.100, 1798.105, 1798.106, 1798.110, 1798.115, and 1798.125, a business shall, in a form that is reasonably accessible to consumers:

(1)(A) Make available to consumers two or more designated methods for submitting requests for information required to be disclosed pursuant to Sections 1798.110 and 1798.115, or requests for deletion or correction pursuant to Sections 1798.105 and 1798.106, respectively, including, at a minimum, a toll-free telephone number. A business that operates exclusively online and has a direct relationship with a consumer from whom it collects personal information shall only be required to provide an email address for submitting requests for information required to be disclosed pursuant to Sections 1798.110 and 1798.115, or for requests for deletion or correction pursuant to Sections 1798.105 and 1798.106, respectively.

(B) If the business maintains an internet website, make the internet website available to consumers to submit requests for information required to be disclosed pursuant to Sections 1798.110 and 1798.115, or requests for deletion or correction pursuant to Sections 1798.105 and 1798.106, respectively.

(2)(A) Disclose and deliver the required information to a consumer free of charge, correct inaccurate personal information, or delete a consumer's personal information, based on the consumer's request, within 45 days of receiving a verifiable consumer request from the consumer. The business shall promptly take steps to determine whether the request is a verifiable consumer request, but this shall not extend the business's duty to disclose and deliver the information, to correct inaccurate personal information, or to delete personal information within 45 days of receipt of the consumer's request. The time period to provide the required information, to correct inaccurate personal information, or to delete personal information may be extended once by an additional 45 days when reasonably necessary, provided the consumer is provided notice of the extension within the first 45–day period. The disclosure of the required information shall be made in writing and delivered through the consumer's account with the business, if the consumer maintains an account with the business, or by mail or electronically at the consumer's option if the consumer does not maintain an account with the business, in a readily useable format that allows the consumer to transmit this information from one entity to another entity without hindrance. The business may require authentication of the consumer that is reasonable in light of the nature of the personal information requested, but shall not require the consumer to create an account with the business in order to make a verifiable consumer request provided that if the consumer, has an account with the business, the business may require the consumer to use that account to submit a verifiable consumer request.

(B) The disclosure of the required information shall cover the 12–month period preceding the business' receipt of the verifiable consumer request provided that, upon the adoption of a regulation pursuant to paragraph (9) of subdivision (a) of Section 1798.185, a consumer may request that the business disclose the required information beyond the 12–month period, and the business shall be required to provide that information unless doing so proves impossible or would involve a disproportionate effort. A consumer's right to request required information beyond the 12–month period, and a business's obligation to provide that information, shall only apply to personal information collected on or after January 1, 2022. Nothing in this subparagraph shall require a business to keep personal information for any length of time.

(3)(A) A business that receives a verifiable consumer request pursuant to Section 1798.110 or 1798.115 shall disclose any personal information it has collected about a consumer, directly or indirectly, including through or by a service provider or contractor, to the consumer. A service provider or contractor shall not be required to comply with a verifiable consumer request received directly from a consumer or a consumer's authorized agent, pursuant to Section 1798.110 or 1798.115, to the extent that the service provider or contractor has collected personal information about the consumer in its role as a service provider or contractor. A service provider or contractor shall provide assistance to a business with which it has a contractual relationship with respect to the business' response to a verifiable consumer request, including, but not limited to, by providing to the business the consumer's personal information in the service provider or contractor's possession, which the service provider or contractor obtained as a result of providing services to the business, and by correcting inaccurate information or by enabling the business to do the same. A service provider or contractor that collects personal information pursuant to a written contract with a business shall be required to assist the business through appropriate technical and organizational measures in complying with the requirements of subdivisions (d) to (f), inclusive, of Section 1798.100, taking into account the nature of the processing.

(B) For purposes of subdivision (b) of Section 1798.110:

(i) To identify the consumer, associate the information provided by the consumer in the verifiable consumer request to any personal information previously collected by the business about the consumer.

(ii) Identify by category or categories the personal information collected about the consumer for the applicable period of time by reference to the enumerated category or categories in subdivision (c) that most closely describes the personal information collected; the categories of sources from which the consumer's personal information was collected; the business or commercial purpose for collecting, selling, or sharing the consumer's personal information; and the categories of third parties to whom the business discloses the consumer's personal information.

(iii) Provide the specific pieces of personal information obtained from the consumer in a format that is easily understandable to the average consumer, and to the extent technically feasible, in a structured, commonly used, machine-readable format that may also be transmitted to another entity at the consumer's request without hindrance. "Specific pieces of information" do not include data generated to help ensure security and integrity or as prescribed by regulation. Personal information is not considered to have been disclosed by a business when a consumer instructs a business to transfer the consumer's personal information from one business to another in the context of switching services.

(4) For purposes of subdivision (b) of Section 1798.115:

(A) Identify the consumer and associate the information provided by the consumer in the verifiable consumer request to any personal information previously collected by the business about the consumer.

(B) Identify by category or categories the personal information of the consumer that the business sold or shared during the applicable period of time by reference to the enumerated category in subdivision (c) that most closely describes the personal information, and provide the categories of third parties to whom the consumer's personal information was sold or shared during the applicable period of time by reference to the enumerated category or categories in subdivision (c) that most closely describes the personal information sold or shared. The business shall disclose the information in a list that is separate from a list generated for the purposes of subparagraph (C).

(C) Identify by category or categories the personal information of the consumer that the business disclosed for a business purpose during the applicable period of time by reference to the enumerated category or categories in subdivision (c) that most closely describes the personal information, and provide the categories of persons to whom the consumer's personal information was disclosed for a business purpose during the applicable period of time by reference to the enumerated category or categories in subdivision (c) that most closely describes the personal information disclosed. The business shall disclose the information in a list that is separate from a list generated for the purposes of subparagraph (B).

(5) Disclose the following information in its online privacy policy or policies if the business has an online privacy policy or policies and in any California-specific description of consumers' privacy rights, or if the business does not maintain those policies, on its internet website, and update that information at least once every 12 months:

(A) A description of a consumer's rights pursuant to Sections 1798.100, 1798.105, 1798.106, 1798.110, 1798.115, and 1798.125 and two or more designated methods for submitting requests, except as provided in subparagraph (A) of paragraph (1) of subdivision (a).

(B) For purposes of subdivision (c) of Section 1798.110:

(i) A list of the categories of personal information it has collected about consumers in the preceding 12 months by reference to the enumerated category or categories in subdivision (c) that most closely describe the personal information collected.

(ii) The categories of sources from which consumers' personal information is collected.

(iii) The business or commercial purpose for collecting, selling, or sharing consumers' personal information.

(iv) The categories of third parties to whom the business discloses consumers' personal information.

(C) For purposes of paragraphs (1) and (2) of subdivision (c) of Section 1798.115, two separate lists:

(i) A list of the categories of personal information it has sold or shared about consumers in the preceding 12 months by reference to the enumerated category or categories in subdivision (c) that most closely describe the personal information sold or shared, or if the business has not sold or shared consumers' personal information in the preceding 12 months, the business shall prominently disclose that fact in its privacy policy.

(ii) A list of the categories of personal information it has disclosed about consumers for a business purpose in the preceding 12 months by reference to the enumerated category in subdivision (c) that most closely describes the personal information disclosed, or if the business has not disclosed consumers' personal information for a business purpose in the preceding 12 months, the business shall disclose that fact.

(6) Ensure that all individuals responsible for handling consumer inquiries about the business' privacy practices or the business' compliance with this title are informed of all

§ 1798.130

requirements in Sections 1798.100, 1798.105, 1798.106, 1798.110, 1798.115, 1798.125, and this section, and how to direct consumers to exercise their rights under those sections.

(7) Use any personal information collected from the consumer in connection with the business' verification of the consumer's request solely for the purposes of verification and shall not further disclose the personal information, retain it longer than necessary for purposes of verification, or use it for unrelated purposes.

(b) A business is not obligated to provide the information required by Sections 1798.110 and 1798.115 to the same consumer more than twice in a 12–month period.

(c) The categories of personal information required to be disclosed pursuant to Sections 1798.100, 1798.110, and 1798.115 shall follow the definitions of personal information and sensitive personal information in Section 1798.140 by describing the categories of personal information using the specific terms set forth in subparagraphs (A) to (K), inclusive, of paragraph (1) of subdivision (v) of Section 1798.140 and by describing the categories of sensitive personal information using the specific terms set forth in paragraphs (1) to (9), inclusive, of subdivision (ae) of Section 1798.140. (Added by Stats.2018, c. 55 (A.B.375), § 3, eff. Jan. 1, 2019, operative Jan. 1, 2020. Amended by Stats.2018, c. 735 (S.B.1121), § 7, eff. Sept. 23, 2018, operative Jan. 1, 2020; Stats.2019, c. 757 (A.B.1355), § 6, eff. Jan. 1, 2020; Stats.2019, c. 759 (A.B. 1564), § 1, eff. Jan. 1, 2020; Stats.2019, c. 763 (A.B.25), § 1.3, eff. Jan. 1, 2020; Initiative Measure (Prop. 24, § 12, approved Nov. 3, 2020, eff. Dec. 16, 2020, operative Jan. 1, 2023).)

[1] Section caption supplied by Prop. 24.

Operative Effect

For effective and operative dates of Initiative Measure (Prop. 24), see § 31 of the Measure.

For operative effect of Title 1.81.5, see Civil Code § 1798.198.

§ 1798.135. Methods of Limiting Sale, Sharing, and Use of Personal Information and Use of Sensitive Personal Information [1]

(a) A business that sells or shares consumers' personal information or uses or discloses consumers' sensitive personal information for purposes other than those authorized by subdivision (a) of Section 1798.121 shall, in a form that is reasonably accessible to consumers:

(1) Provide a clear and conspicuous link on the business's internet homepages, titled "Do Not Sell or Share My Personal Information," to an internet web page that enables a consumer, or a person authorized by the consumer, to opt-out of the sale or sharing of the consumer's personal information.

(2) Provide a clear and conspicuous link on the business' internet homepages, titled "Limit the Use of My Sensitive Personal Information," that enables a consumer, or a person authorized by the consumer, to limit the use or disclosure of the consumer's sensitive personal information to those uses authorized by subdivision (a) of Section 1798.121.

(3) At the business' discretion, utilize a single, clearly labeled link on the business' internet homepages, in lieu of complying with paragraphs (1) and (2), if that link easily allows a consumer to opt out of the sale or sharing of the consumer's personal information and to limit the use or disclosure of the consumer's sensitive personal information.

(4) In the event that a business responds to opt-out requests received pursuant to paragraph (1), (2), or (3) by informing the consumer of a charge for the use of any product or service, present the terms of any financial incentive offered pursuant to subdivision (b) of Section 1798.125 for the retention, use, sale, or sharing of the consumer's personal information.

(b)(1) A business shall not be required to comply with subdivision (a) if the business allows consumers to opt out of the sale or sharing of their personal information and to limit the use of their sensitive personal information through an opt-out preference signal sent with the consumer's consent by a platform, technology, or mechanism, based on technical specifications set forth in regulations adopted pursuant to paragraph (20) of subdivision (a) of Section 1798.185, to the business indicating the consumer's intent to opt out of the business' sale or sharing of the consumer's personal information or to limit the use or disclosure of the consumer's sensitive personal information, or both.

(2) A business that allows consumers to opt out of the sale or sharing of their personal information and to limit the use of their sensitive personal information pursuant to paragraph (1) may provide a link to a web page that enables the consumer to consent to the business ignoring the opt-out preference signal with respect to that business' sale or sharing of the consumer's personal information or the use of the consumer's sensitive personal information for additional purposes provided that:

(A) The consent web page also allows the consumer or a person authorized by the consumer to revoke the consent as easily as it is affirmatively provided.

(B) The link to the web page does not degrade the consumer's experience on the web page the consumer intends to visit and has a similar look, feel, and size relative to other links on the same web page.

(C) The consent web page complies with technical specifications set forth in regulations adopted pursuant to paragraph (20) of subdivision (a) of Section 1798.185.

(3) A business that complies with subdivision (a) is not required to comply with subdivision (b). For the purposes of clarity, a business may elect whether to comply with subdivision (a) or subdivision (b).

(c) A business that is subject to this section shall:

(1) Not require a consumer to create an account or provide additional information beyond what is necessary in order to direct the business not to sell or share the consumer's personal information or to limit use or disclosure of the consumer's sensitive personal information.

(2) Include a description of a consumer's rights pursuant to Sections 1798.120 and 1798.121, along with a separate link to the "Do Not Sell or Share My Personal Information" internet web page and a separate link to the "Limit the Use of My Sensitive Personal Information" internet web page, if

applicable, or a single link to both choices, or a statement that the business responds to and abides by opt-out preference signals sent by a platform, technology, or mechanism in accordance with subdivision (b), in:

(A) Its online privacy policy or policies if the business has an online privacy policy or policies.

(B) Any California-specific description of consumers' privacy rights.

(3) Ensure that all individuals responsible for handling consumer inquiries about the business's privacy practices or the business's compliance with this title are informed of all requirements in Sections 1798.120, 1798.121, and this section and how to direct consumers to exercise their rights under those sections.

(4) For consumers who exercise their right to opt-out of the sale or sharing of their personal information or limit the use or disclosure of their sensitive personal information, refrain from selling or sharing the consumer's personal information or using or disclosing the consumer's sensitive personal information and wait for at least 12 months before requesting that the consumer authorize the sale or sharing of the consumer's personal information or the use and disclosure of the consumer's sensitive personal information for additional purposes, or as authorized by regulations.

(5) For consumers under 16 years of age who do not consent to the sale or sharing of their personal information, refrain from selling or sharing the personal information of the consumer under 16 years of age and wait for at least 12 months before requesting the consumer's consent again, or as authorized by regulations or until the consumer attains 16 years of age.

(6) Use any personal information collected from the consumer in connection with the submission of the consumer's opt-out request solely for the purposes of complying with the opt-out request.

(d) Nothing in this title shall be construed to require a business to comply with the title by including the required links and text on the homepage that the business makes available to the public generally, if the business maintains a separate and additional homepage that is dedicated to California consumers and that includes the required links and text, and the business takes reasonable steps to ensure that California consumers are directed to the homepage for California consumers and not the homepage made available to the public generally.

(e) A consumer may authorize another person to opt-out of the sale or sharing of the consumer's personal information and to limit the use of the consumer's sensitive personal information on the consumer's behalf, including through an opt-out preference signal, as defined in paragraph (1) of subdivision (b), indicating the consumer's intent to opt out, and a business shall comply with an opt-out request received from a person authorized by the consumer to act on the consumer's behalf, pursuant to regulations adopted by the Attorney General regardless of whether the business has elected to comply with subdivision (a) or (b). For purposes of clarity, a business that elects to comply with subdivision (a) may respond to the consumer's opt-out consistent with Section 1798.125.

(f) If a business communicates a consumer's opt-out request to any person authorized by the business to collect personal information, the person shall thereafter only use that consumer's personal information for a business purpose specified by the business, or as otherwise permitted by this title, and shall be prohibited from:

(1) Selling or sharing the personal information.

(2) Retaining, using, or disclosing that consumer's personal information.

(A) For any purpose other than for the specific purpose of performing the services offered to the business.

(B) Outside of the direct business relationship between the person and the business.

(C) For a commercial purpose other than providing the services to the business.

(g) A business that communicates a consumer's opt-out request to a person pursuant to subdivision (f) shall not be liable under this title if the person receiving the opt-out request violates the restrictions set forth in the title provided that, at the time of communicating the opt-out request, the business does not have actual knowledge, or reason to believe, that the person intends to commit such a violation. Any provision of a contract or agreement of any kind that purports to waive or limit in any way this subdivision shall be void and unenforceable. *(Added by Stats.2018, c. 55 (A.B. 375), § 3, eff. Jan. 1, 2019, operative Jan. 1, 2020. Amended by Stats.2018, c. 735 (S.B.1121), § 8, eff. Sept. 23, 2018, operative Jan. 1, 2020; Initiative Measure (Prop. 24, § 13, approved Nov. 3, 2020, eff. Dec. 16, 2020, operative Jan. 1, 2023).)*

[1] Section caption supplied by Prop. 24.

Operative Effect

For effective and operative dates of Initiative Measure (Prop. 24), see § 31 of the Measure.

For operative effect of Title 1.81.5, see Civil Code § 1798.198.

§ 1798.140. Definitions [1]

For purposes of this title:

(a) "Advertising and marketing" means a communication by a business or a person acting on the business' behalf in any medium intended to induce a consumer to obtain goods, services, or employment.

(b) "Aggregate consumer information" means information that relates to a group or category of consumers, from which individual consumer identities have been removed, that is not linked or reasonably linkable to any consumer or household, including via a device. "Aggregate consumer information" does not mean one or more individual consumer records that have been deidentified.

(c) "Biometric information" means an individual's physiological, biological, or behavioral characteristics, including information pertaining to an individual's deoxyribonucleic acid (DNA), that is used or is intended to be used singly or in combination with each other or with other identifying data, to establish individual identity. Biometric information includes,

§ 1798.140

but is not limited to, imagery of the iris, retina, fingerprint, face, hand, palm, vein patterns, and voice recordings, from which an identifier template, such as a faceprint, a minutiae template, or a voiceprint, can be extracted, and keystroke patterns or rhythms, gait patterns or rhythms, and sleep, health, or exercise data that contain identifying information.

(d) "Business" means:

(1) A sole proprietorship, partnership, limited liability company, corporation, association, or other legal entity that is organized or operated for the profit or financial benefit of its shareholders or other owners, that collects consumers' personal information, or on the behalf of which such information is collected and that alone, or jointly with others, determines the purposes and means of the processing of consumers' personal information, that does business in the State of California, and that satisfies one or more of the following thresholds:

(A) As of January 1 of the calendar year, had annual gross revenues in excess of twenty-five million dollars ($25,000,000) in the preceding calendar year, as adjusted pursuant to paragraph (5) of subdivision (a) of Section 1798.185.

(B) Alone or in combination, annually buys, sells, or shares the personal information of 100,000 or more consumers or households.

(C) Derives 50 percent or more of its annual revenues from selling or sharing consumers' personal information.

(2) Any entity that controls or is controlled by a business, as defined in paragraph (1), and that shares common branding with the business and with whom the business shares consumers' personal information. "Control" or "controlled" means ownership of, or the power to vote, more than 50 percent of the outstanding shares of any class of voting security of a business; control in any manner over the election of a majority of the directors, or of individuals exercising similar functions; or the power to exercise a controlling influence over the management of a company. "Common branding" means a shared name, servicemark, or trademark that the average consumer would understand that two or more entities are commonly owned.

(3) A joint venture or partnership composed of businesses in which each business has at least a 40 percent interest. For purposes of this title, the joint venture or partnership and each business that composes the joint venture or partnership shall separately be considered a single business, except that personal information in the possession of each business and disclosed to the joint venture or partnership shall not be shared with the other business.

(4) A person that does business in California, that is not covered by paragraph (1), (2), or (3), and that voluntarily certifies to the California Privacy Protection Agency that it is in compliance with, and agrees to be bound by, this title.

(e) "Business purpose" means the use of personal information for the business' operational purposes, or other notified purposes, or for the service provider or contractor's operational purposes, as defined by regulations adopted pursuant to paragraph (11) of subdivision (a) of Section 1798.185, provided that the use of personal information shall be reasonably necessary and proportionate to achieve the purpose for which the personal information was collected or processed or for another purpose that is compatible with the context in which the personal information was collected. Business purposes are:

(1) Auditing related to counting ad impressions to unique visitors, verifying positioning and quality of ad impressions, and auditing compliance with this specification and other standards.

(2) Helping to ensure security and integrity to the extent the use of the consumer's personal information is reasonably necessary and proportionate for these purposes.

(3) Debugging to identify and repair errors that impair existing intended functionality.

(4) Short-term, transient use, including, but not limited to, nonpersonalized advertising shown as part of a consumer's current interaction with the business, provided that the consumer's personal information is not disclosed to another third party and is not used to build a profile about the consumer or otherwise alter the consumer's experience outside the current interaction with the business.

(5) Performing services on behalf of the business, including maintaining or servicing accounts, providing customer service, processing or fulfilling orders and transactions, verifying customer information, processing payments, providing financing, providing analytic services, providing storage, or providing similar services on behalf of the business.

(6) Providing advertising and marketing services, except for cross-context behavioral advertising, to the consumer provided that, for the purpose of advertising and marketing, a service provider or contractor shall not combine the personal information of opted-out consumers that the service provider or contractor receives from, or on behalf of, the business with personal information that the service provider or contractor receives from, or on behalf of, another person or persons or collects from its own interaction with consumers.

(7) Undertaking internal research for technological development and demonstration.

(8) Undertaking activities to verify or maintain the quality or safety of a service or device that is owned, manufactured, manufactured for, or controlled by the business, and to improve, upgrade, or enhance the service or device that is owned, manufactured, manufactured for, or controlled by the business.

(f) "Collects," "collected," or "collection" means buying, renting, gathering, obtaining, receiving, or accessing any personal information pertaining to a consumer by any means. This includes receiving information from the consumer, either actively or passively, or by observing the consumer's behavior.

(g) "Commercial purposes" means to advance a person's commercial or economic interests, such as by inducing another person to buy, rent, lease, join, subscribe to, provide, or exchange products, goods, property, information, or services, or enabling or effecting, directly or indirectly, a commercial transaction.

(h) "Consent" means any freely given, specific, informed, and unambiguous indication of the consumer's wishes by which the consumer, or the consumer's legal guardian, a person who has power of attorney, or a person acting as a conservator for the consumer, including by a statement or by a clear affirmative action, signifies agreement to the processing of personal information relating to the consumer for a narrowly defined particular purpose. Acceptance of a general or broad terms of use, or similar document, that contains descriptions of personal information processing along with other, unrelated information, does not constitute consent. Hovering over, muting, pausing, or closing a given piece of content does not constitute consent. Likewise, agreement obtained through use of dark patterns does not constitute consent.

(i) "Consumer" means a natural person who is a California resident, as defined in Section 17014 of Title 18 of the California Code of Regulations, as that section read on September 1, 2017, however identified, including by any unique identifier.

(j)(1) "Contractor" means a person to whom the business makes available a consumer's personal information for a business purpose, pursuant to a written contract with the business, provided that the contract:

(A) Prohibits the contractor from:

(i) Selling or sharing the personal information.

(ii) Retaining, using, or disclosing the personal information for any purpose other than for the business purposes specified in the contract, including retaining, using, or disclosing the personal information for a commercial purpose other than the business purposes specified in the contract, or as otherwise permitted by this title.

(iii) Retaining, using, or disclosing the information outside of the direct business relationship between the contractor and the business.

(iv) Combining the personal information that the contractor receives pursuant to a written contract with the business with personal information that it receives from or on behalf of another person or persons, or collects from its own interaction with the consumer, provided that the contractor may combine personal information to perform any business purpose as defined in regulations adopted pursuant to paragraph (10) of subdivision (a) of Section 1798.185, except as provided for in paragraph (6) of subdivision (e) and in regulations adopted by the California Privacy Protection Agency.

(B) Includes a certification made by the contractor that the contractor understands the restrictions in subparagraph (A) and will comply with them.

(C) Permits, subject to agreement with the contractor, the business to monitor the contractor's compliance with the contract through measures, including, but not limited to, ongoing manual reviews and automated scans and regular assessments, audits, or other technical and operational testing at least once every 12 months.

(2) If a contractor engages any other person to assist it in processing personal information for a business purpose on behalf of the business, or if any other person engaged by the contractor engages another person to assist in processing personal information for that business purpose, it shall notify the business of that engagement, and the engagement shall be pursuant to a written contract binding the other person to observe all the requirements set forth in paragraph (1).

(k) "Cross-context behavioral advertising" means the targeting of advertising to a consumer based on the consumer's personal information obtained from the consumer's activity across businesses, distinctly-branded websites, applications, or services, other than the business, distinctly-branded website, application, or service with which the consumer intentionally interacts.

(*l*) "Dark pattern" means a user interface designed or manipulated with the substantial effect of subverting or impairing user autonomy, decisionmaking, or choice, as further defined by regulation.

(m) "Deidentified" means information that cannot reasonably be used to infer information about, or otherwise be linked to, a particular consumer provided that the business that possesses the information:

(1) Takes reasonable measures to ensure that the information cannot be associated with a consumer or household.

(2) Publicly commits to maintain and use the information in deidentified form and not to attempt to reidentify the information, except that the business may attempt to reidentify the information solely for the purpose of determining whether its deidentification processes satisfy the requirements of this subdivision.

(3) Contractually obligates any recipients of the information to comply with all provisions of this subdivision.

(n) "Designated methods for submitting requests" means a mailing address, email address, internet web page, internet web portal, toll-free telephone number, or other applicable contact information, whereby consumers may submit a request or direction under this title, and any new, consumer-friendly means of contacting a business, as approved by the Attorney General pursuant to Section 1798.185.

(*o*) "Device" means any physical object that is capable of connecting to the Internet, directly or indirectly, or to another device.

(p) "Homepage" means the introductory page of an internet website and any internet web page where personal information is collected. In the case of an online service, such as a mobile application, homepage means the application's platform page or download page, a link within the application, such as from the application configuration, "About," "Information," or settings page, and any other location that allows consumers to review the notices required by this title, including, but not limited to, before downloading the application.

(q) "Household" means a group, however identified, of consumers who cohabitate with one another at the same residential address and share use of common devices or services.

(r) "Infer" or "inference" means the derivation of information, data, assumptions, or conclusions from facts, evidence, or another source of information or data.

(s) "Intentionally interacts" means when the consumer intends to interact with a person, or disclose personal information to a person, via one or more deliberate interactions, including visiting the person's website or purchasing a good or service from the person. Hovering over, muting,

§ 1798.140

pausing, or closing a given piece of content does not constitute a consumer's intent to interact with a person.

(t) "Nonpersonalized advertising" means advertising and marketing that is based solely on a consumer's personal information derived from the consumer's current interaction with the business with the exception of the consumer's precise geolocation.

(u) "Person" means an individual, proprietorship, firm, partnership, joint venture, syndicate, business trust, company, corporation, limited liability company, association, committee, and any other organization or group of persons acting in concert.

(v)(1) "Personal information" means information that identifies, relates to, describes, is reasonably capable of being associated with, or could reasonably be linked, directly or indirectly, with a particular consumer or household. Personal information includes, but is not limited to, the following if it identifies, relates to, describes, is reasonably capable of being associated with, or could be reasonably linked, directly or indirectly, with a particular consumer or household:

(A) Identifiers such as a real name, alias, postal address, unique personal identifier, online identifier, Internet Protocol address, email address, account name, social security number, driver's license number, passport number, or other similar identifiers.

(B) Any personal information described in subdivision (e) of Section 1798.80.

(C) Characteristics of protected classifications under California or federal law.

(D) Commercial information, including records of personal property, products or services purchased, obtained, or considered, or other purchasing or consuming histories or tendencies.

(E) Biometric information.

(F) Internet or other electronic network activity information, including, but not limited to, browsing history, search history, and information regarding a consumer's interaction with an internet website application, or advertisement.

(G) Geolocation data.

(H) Audio, electronic, visual, thermal, olfactory, or similar information.

(I) Professional or employment-related information.

(J) Education information, defined as information that is not publicly available personally identifiable information as defined in the Family Educational Rights and Privacy Act (20 U.S.C. Sec. 1232g; 34 C.F.R. Part 99).

(K) Inferences drawn from any of the information identified in this subdivision to create a profile about a consumer reflecting the consumer's preferences, characteristics, psychological trends, predispositions, behavior, attitudes, intelligence, abilities, and aptitudes.

(L) Sensitive personal information.

(2) "Personal information" does not include publicly available information or lawfully obtained, truthful information that is a matter of public concern. For purposes of this paragraph, "publicly available" means: information that is lawfully made available from federal, state, or local government records, or information that a business has a reasonable basis to believe is lawfully made available to the general public by the consumer or from widely distributed media; or information made available by a person to whom the consumer has disclosed the information if the consumer has not restricted the information to a specific audience. "Publicly available" does not mean biometric information collected by a business about a consumer without the consumer's knowledge.

(3) "Personal information" does not include consumer information that is deidentified or aggregate consumer information.

(w) "Precise geolocation" means any data that is derived from a device and that is used or intended to be used to locate a consumer within a geographic area that is equal to or less than the area of a circle with a radius of 1,850 feet, except as prescribed by regulations.

(x) "Probabilistic identifier" means the identification of a consumer or a consumer's device to a degree of certainty of more probable than not based on any categories of personal information included in, or similar to, the categories enumerated in the definition of personal information.

(y) "Processing" means any operation or set of operations that are performed on personal information or on sets of personal information, whether or not by automated means.

(z) "Profiling" means any form of automated processing of personal information, as further defined by regulations pursuant to paragraph (16) of subdivision (a) of Section 1798.185, to evaluate certain personal aspects relating to a natural person and in particular to analyze or predict aspects concerning that natural person's performance at work, economic situation, health, personal preferences, interests, reliability, behavior, location, or movements.

(aa) "Pseudonymize" or "Pseudonymization" means the processing of personal information in a manner that renders the personal information no longer attributable to a specific consumer without the use of additional information, provided that the additional information is kept separately and is subject to technical and organizational measures to ensure that the personal information is not attributed to an identified or identifiable consumer.

(ab) "Research" means scientific analysis, systematic study, and observation, including basic research or applied research that is designed to develop or contribute to public or scientific knowledge and that adheres or otherwise conforms to all other applicable ethics and privacy laws, including, but not limited to, studies conducted in the public interest in the area of public health. Research with personal information that may have been collected from a consumer in the course of the consumer's interactions with a business' service or device for other purposes shall be:

(1) Compatible with the business purpose for which the personal information was collected.

(2) Subsequently pseudonymized and deidentified, or deidentified and in the aggregate, such that the information cannot reasonably identify, relate to, describe, be capable of being associated with, or be linked, directly or indirectly, to a particular consumer, by a business.

(3) Made subject to technical safeguards that prohibit reidentification of the consumer to whom the information may pertain, other than as needed to support the research.

(4) Subject to business processes that specifically prohibit reidentification of the information, other than as needed to support the research.

(5) Made subject to business processes to prevent inadvertent release of deidentified information.

(6) Protected from any reidentification attempts.

(7) Used solely for research purposes that are compatible with the context in which the personal information was collected.

(8) Subjected by the business conducting the research to additional security controls that limit access to the research data to only those individuals as are necessary to carry out the research purpose.

(ac) "Security and integrity" means the ability of:

(1) Networks or information systems to detect security incidents that compromise the availability, authenticity, integrity, and confidentiality of stored or transmitted personal information.

(2) Businesses to detect security incidents, resist malicious, deceptive, fraudulent, or illegal actions and to help prosecute those responsible for those actions.

(3) Businesses to ensure the physical safety of natural persons.

(ad)(1) "Sell," "selling," "sale," or "sold," means selling, renting, releasing, disclosing, disseminating, making available, transferring, or otherwise communicating orally, in writing, or by electronic or other means, a consumer's personal information by the business to a third party for monetary or other valuable consideration.

(2) For purposes of this title, a business does not sell personal information when:

(A) A consumer uses or directs the business to intentionally:

(i) Disclose personal information.

(ii) Interact with one or more third parties.

(B) The business uses or shares an identifier for a consumer who has opted out of the sale of the consumer's personal information or limited the use of the consumer's sensitive personal information for the purposes of alerting persons that the consumer has opted out of the sale of the consumer's personal information or limited the use of the consumer's sensitive personal information.

(C) The business transfers to a third party the personal information of a consumer as an asset that is part of a merger, acquisition, bankruptcy, or other transaction in which the third party assumes control of all or part of the business, provided that information is used or shared consistently with this title. If a third party materially alters how it uses or shares the personal information of a consumer in a manner that is materially inconsistent with the promises made at the time of collection, it shall provide prior notice of the new or changed practice to the consumer. The notice shall be sufficiently prominent and robust to ensure that existing consumers can easily exercise their choices consistently with this title. This subparagraph does not authorize a business to make material, retroactive privacy policy changes or make other changes in their privacy policy in a manner that would violate the Unfair and Deceptive Practices Act (Chapter 5 (commencing with Section 17200) of Part 2 of Division 7 of the Business and Professions Code).

(ae) "Sensitive personal information" means:

(1) Personal information that reveals:

(A) A consumer's social security, driver's license, state identification card, or passport number.

(B) A consumer's account log-in, financial account, debit card, or credit card number in combination with any required security or access code, password, or credentials allowing access to an account.

(C) A consumer's precise geolocation.

(D) A consumer's racial or ethnic origin, religious or philosophical beliefs, or union membership.

(E) The contents of a consumer's mail, email, and text messages unless the business is the intended recipient of the communication.

(F) A consumer's genetic data.

(2)(A) The processing of biometric information for the purpose of uniquely identifying a consumer.

(B) Personal information collected and analyzed concerning a consumer's health.

(C) Personal information collected and analyzed concerning a consumer's sex life or sexual orientation.

(3) Sensitive personal information that is "publicly available" pursuant to paragraph (2) of subdivision (v) shall not be considered sensitive personal information or personal information.

(af) "Service" or "services" means work, labor, and services, including services furnished in connection with the sale or repair of goods.

(ag)(1) "Service provider" means a person that processes personal information on behalf of a business and that receives from or on behalf of the business consumer's personal information for a business purpose pursuant to a written contract, provided that the contract prohibits the person from:

(A) Selling or sharing the personal information.

(B) Retaining, using, or disclosing the personal information for any purpose other than for the business purposes specified in the contract for the business, including retaining, using, or disclosing the personal information for a commercial purpose other than the business purposes specified in the contract with the business, or as otherwise permitted by this title.

(C) Retaining, using, or disclosing the information outside of the direct business relationship between the service provider and the business.

(D) Combining the personal information that the service provider receives from, or on behalf of, the business with personal information that it receives from, or on behalf of, another person or persons, or collects from its own interaction with the consumer, provided that the service provider may combine personal information to perform any business purpose as defined in regulations adopted pursuant to paragraph (10) of subdivision (a) of Section 1798.185, except as provided for in paragraph (6) of subdivision (e) of this section and in regulations adopted by the California Privacy Protection Agency. The contract may, subject to agreement with the service provider, permit the business to monitor the service provider's compliance with the contract through measures, including, but not limited to, ongoing manual reviews and automated scans and regular assessments, audits, or other technical and operational testing at least once every 12 months.

(2) If a service provider engages any other person to assist it in processing personal information for a business purpose on behalf of the business, or if any other person engaged by the service provider engages another person to assist in processing personal information for that business purpose, it shall notify the business of that engagement, and the engagement shall be pursuant to a written contract binding the other person to observe all the requirements set forth in paragraph (1).

(ah)(1) "Share," "shared," or "sharing" means sharing, renting, releasing, disclosing, disseminating, making available, transferring, or otherwise communicating orally, in writing, or by electronic or other means, a consumer's personal information by the business to a third party for cross-context behavioral advertising, whether or not for monetary or other valuable consideration, including transactions between a business and a third party for cross-context behavioral advertising for the benefit of a business in which no money is exchanged.

(2) For purposes of this title, a business does not share personal information when:

(A) A consumer uses or directs the business to intentionally disclose personal information or intentionally interact with one or more third parties.

(B) The business uses or shares an identifier for a consumer who has opted out of the sharing of the consumer's personal information or limited the use of the consumer's sensitive personal information for the purposes of alerting persons that the consumer has opted out of the sharing of the consumer's personal information or limited the use of the consumer's sensitive personal information.

(C) The business transfers to a third party the personal information of a consumer as an asset that is part of a merger, acquisition, bankruptcy, or other transaction in which the third party assumes control of all or part of the business, provided that information is used or shared consistently with this title. If a third party materially alters how it uses or shares the personal information of a consumer in a manner that is materially inconsistent with the promises made at the time of collection, it shall provide prior notice of the new or changed practice to the consumer. The notice shall be sufficiently prominent and robust to ensure that existing consumers can easily exercise their choices consistently with this title. This subparagraph does not authorize a business to make material, retroactive privacy policy changes or make other changes in their privacy policy in a manner that would violate the Unfair and Deceptive Practices Act (Chapter 5 (commencing with Section 17200) of Part 2 of Division 7 of the Business and Professions Code).

(ai) "Third party" means a person who is not any of the following:

(1) The business with whom the consumer intentionally interacts and that collects personal information from the consumer as part of the consumer's current interaction with the business under this title.

(2) A service provider to the business.

(3) A contractor.

(aj) "Unique identifier" or "unique personal identifier" means a persistent identifier that can be used to recognize a consumer, a family, or a device that is linked to a consumer or family, over time and across different services, including, but not limited to, a device identifier; an Internet Protocol address; cookies, beacons, pixel tags, mobile ad identifiers, or similar technology; customer number, unique pseudonym, or user alias; telephone numbers, or other forms of persistent or probabilistic identifiers that can be used to identify a particular consumer or device that is linked to a consumer or family. For purposes of this subdivision, "family" means a custodial parent or guardian and any children under 18 years of age over which the parent or guardian has custody.

(ak) "Verifiable consumer request" means a request that is made by a consumer, by a consumer on behalf of the consumer's minor child, by a natural person or a person registered with the Secretary of State, authorized by the consumer to act on the consumer's behalf, or by a person who has power of attorney or is acting as a conservator for the consumer, and that the business can verify, using commercially reasonable methods, pursuant to regulations adopted by the Attorney General pursuant to paragraph (7) of subdivision (a) of Section 1798.185 to be the consumer about whom the business has collected personal information. A business is not obligated to provide information to the consumer pursuant to Sections 1798.110 and 1798.115, to delete personal information pursuant to Section 1798.105, or to correct inaccurate personal information pursuant to Section 1798.106, if the business cannot verify, pursuant to this subdivision and regulations adopted by the Attorney General pursuant to paragraph (7) of subdivision (a) of Section 1798.185, that the consumer making the request is the consumer about whom the business has collected information or is a person authorized by the consumer to act on such consumer's behalf. *(Added by Stats.2018, c. 55 (A.B.375), § 3, eff. Jan. 1, 2019, operative Jan. 1, 2020. Amended by Stats.2018, c. 735 (S.B.1121), § 9, eff. Sept. 23, 2018, operative Jan. 1, 2020; Stats.2019, c. 748 (A.B.874), § 1, eff. Jan. 1, 2020; Stats.2019, c. 757 (A.B.1355), § 7.5, eff. Jan. 1, 2020; Initiative Measure (Prop. 24, § 14, approved Nov. 3, 2020, eff. Dec. 16, 2020, operative Jan. 1, 2023); Stats.2021, c. 525 (A.B.694), § 3, eff. Jan. 1, 2022, operative Jan. 1, 2023.)*

[1] Section caption supplied by Prop. 24.

Operative Effect

For effective and operative dates of Initiative Measure (Prop. 24), see § 31 of the Measure.

For operative effect of Title 1.81.5, see Civil Code § 1798.198.

Cross References

Business providing proctoring services, personal information, scope of section, see Business and Professions Code § 22588.

§ 1798.145. Exemptions [1]

(a) The obligations imposed on businesses by this title shall not restrict a business' ability to:

(1) Comply with federal, state, or local laws or comply with a court order or subpoena to provide information.

(2) Comply with a civil, criminal, or regulatory inquiry, investigation, subpoena, or summons by federal, state, or local authorities. Law enforcement agencies, including police and sheriff's departments, may direct a business pursuant to a law enforcement agency-approved investigation with an active case number not to delete a consumer's personal information, and, upon receipt of that direction, a business shall not delete the personal information for 90 days in order to allow the law enforcement agency to obtain a court-issued subpoena, order, or warrant to obtain a consumer's personal information. For good cause and only to the extent necessary for investigatory purposes, a law enforcement agency may direct a business not to delete the consumer's personal information for additional 90–day periods. A business that has received direction from a law enforcement agency not to delete the personal information of a consumer who has requested deletion of the consumer's personal information shall not use the consumer's personal information for any purpose other than retaining it to produce to law enforcement in response to a court-issued subpoena, order, or warrant unless the consumer's deletion request is subject to an exemption from deletion under this title.

(3) Cooperate with law enforcement agencies concerning conduct or activity that the business, service provider, or third party reasonably and in good faith believes may violate federal, state, or local law.

(4) Cooperate with a government agency request for emergency access to a consumer's personal information if a natural person is at risk or danger of death or serious physical injury provided that:

(A) The request is approved by a high-ranking agency officer for emergency access to a consumer's personal information.

(B) The request is based on the agency's good faith determination that it has a lawful basis to access the information on a nonemergency basis.

(C) The agency agrees to petition a court for an appropriate order within three days and to destroy the information if that order is not granted.

(5) Exercise or defend legal claims.

(6) Collect, use, retain, sell, share, or disclose consumers' personal information that is deidentified or aggregate consumer information.

(7) Collect, sell, or share a consumer's personal information if every aspect of that commercial conduct takes place wholly outside of California. For purposes of this title, commercial conduct takes place wholly outside of California if the business collected that information while the consumer was outside of California, no part of the sale of the consumer's personal information occurred in California, and no personal information collected while the consumer was in California is sold. This paragraph shall not prohibit a business from storing, including on a device, personal information about a consumer when the consumer is in California and then collecting that personal information when the consumer and stored personal information is outside of California.

(b) The obligations imposed on businesses by Sections 1798.110, 1798.115, 1798.120, 1798.121, 1798.130, and 1798.135 shall not apply where compliance by the business with the title would violate an evidentiary privilege under California law and shall not prevent a business from providing the personal information of a consumer to a person covered by an evidentiary privilege under California law as part of a privileged communication.

(c)(1) This title shall not apply to any of the following:

(A) Medical information governed by the Confidentiality of Medical Information Act (Part 2.6 (commencing with Section 56) of Division 1) or protected health information that is collected by a covered entity or business associate governed by the privacy, security, and breach notification rules issued by the United States Department of Health and Human Services, Parts 160 and 164 of Title 45 of the Code of Federal Regulations, established pursuant to the Health Insurance Portability and Accountability Act of 1996 (Public Law 104–191)[2] and the Health Information Technology for Economic and Clinical Health Act (Public Law 111–5).

(B) A provider of health care governed by the Confidentiality of Medical Information Act (Part 2.6 (commencing with Section 56) of Division 1) or a covered entity governed by the privacy, security, and breach notification rules issued by the United States Department of Health and Human Services, Parts 160 and 164 of Title 45 of the Code of Federal Regulations, established pursuant to the Health Insurance Portability and Accountability Act of 1996 (Public Law 104–191), to the extent the provider or covered entity maintains patient information in the same manner as medical information or protected health information as described in subparagraph (A) of this section.

(C) Personal information collected as part of a clinical trial or other biomedical research study subject to, or conducted in accordance with, the Federal Policy for the Protection of Human Subjects, also known as the Common Rule, pursuant to good clinical practice guidelines issued by the International Council for Harmonisation or pursuant to human subject protection requirements of the United States Food and Drug Administration, provided that the information is not sold or shared in a manner not permitted by this subparagraph, and, if it is inconsistent, that participants be informed of that use and provide consent.

(2) For purposes of this subdivision, the definitions of "medical information" and "provider of health care" in Section 56.05 shall apply and the definitions of "business associate," "covered entity," and "protected health information" in Section 160.103 of Title 45 of the Code of Federal Regulations shall apply.

§ 1798.145

(d)(1) This title shall not apply to an activity involving the collection, maintenance, disclosure, sale, communication, or use of any personal information bearing on a consumer's creditworthiness, credit standing, credit capacity, character, general reputation, personal characteristics, or mode of living by a consumer reporting agency, as defined in subdivision (f) of Section 1681a of Title 15 of the United States Code, by a furnisher of information, as set forth in Section 1681s–2 of Title 15 of the United States Code, who provides information for use in a consumer report, as defined in subdivision (d) of Section 1681a of Title 15 of the United States Code, and by a user of a consumer report as set forth in Section 1681b of Title 15 of the United States Code.

(2) Paragraph (1) shall apply only to the extent that such activity involving the collection, maintenance, disclosure, sale, communication, or use of such information by that agency, furnisher, or user is subject to regulation under the Fair Credit Reporting Act, Section 1681 et seq., Title 15 of the United States Code and the information is not collected, maintained, used, communicated, disclosed, or sold except as authorized by the Fair Credit Reporting Act.

(3) This subdivision shall not apply to Section 1798.150.

(e) This title shall not apply to personal information collected, processed, sold, or disclosed subject to the federal Gramm-Leach-Bliley Act (Public Law 106–102), and implementing regulations, or the California Financial Information Privacy Act (Division 1.4 (commencing with Section 4050) of the Financial Code), or the federal Farm Credit Act of 1971 (as amended in 12 U.S.C. 2001–2279cc and implementing regulations, 12 C.F.R. 600, et seq.). This subdivision shall not apply to Section 1798.150.

(f) This title shall not apply to personal information collected, processed, sold, or disclosed pursuant to the Driver's Privacy Protection Act of 1994 (18 U.S.C. Sec. 2721 et seq.). This subdivision shall not apply to Section 1798.150.

(g)(1) Section 1798.120 shall not apply to vehicle information or ownership information retained or shared between a new motor vehicle dealer, as defined in Section 426 of the Vehicle Code, and the vehicle's manufacturer, as defined in Section 672 of the Vehicle Code, if the vehicle information or ownership information is shared for the purpose of effectuating, or in anticipation of effectuating, a vehicle repair covered by a vehicle warranty or a recall conducted pursuant to Sections 30118 to 30120, inclusive, of Title 49 of the United States Code, provided that the new motor vehicle dealer or vehicle manufacturer with which that vehicle information or ownership information is shared does not sell, share, or use that information for any other purpose.

(2) Section 1798.120 shall not apply to vessel information or ownership information retained or shared between a vessel dealer and the vessel's manufacturer, as defined in Section 651 of the Harbors and Navigation Code, if the vessel information or ownership information is shared for the purpose of effectuating, or in anticipation of effectuating, a vessel repair covered by a vessel warranty or a recall conducted pursuant to Section 4310 of Title 46 of the United States Code, provided that the vessel dealer or vessel manufacturer with which that vessel information or ownership information is shared does not sell, share, or use that information for any other purpose.

(3) For purposes of this subdivision:

(A) "Ownership information" means the name or names of the registered owner or owners and the contact information for the owner or owners.

(B) "Vehicle information" means the vehicle information number, make, model, year, and odometer reading.

(C) "Vessel dealer" means a person who is engaged, wholly or in part, in the business of selling or offering for sale, buying or taking in trade for the purpose of resale, or exchanging, any vessel or vessels, as defined in Section 651 of the Harbors and Navigation Code, and receives or expects to receive money, profit, or any other thing of value.

(D) "Vessel information" means the hull identification number, model, year, month and year of production, and information describing any of the following equipment as shipped, transferred, or sold from the place of manufacture, including all attached parts and accessories:

(i) An inboard engine.

(ii) An outboard engine.

(iii) A stern drive unit.

(iv) An inflatable personal floatation device approved under Section 160.076 of Title 46 of the Code of Federal Regulations.

(h) Notwithstanding a business' obligations to respond to and honor consumer rights requests pursuant to this title:

(1) A time period for a business to respond to a consumer for any verifiable consumer request may be extended by up to a total of 90 days where necessary, taking into account the complexity and number of the requests. The business shall inform the consumer of any such extension within 45 days of receipt of the request, together with the reasons for the delay.

(2) If the business does not take action on the request of the consumer, the business shall inform the consumer, without delay and at the latest within the time period permitted of response by this section, of the reasons for not taking action and any rights the consumer may have to appeal the decision to the business.

(3) If requests from a consumer are manifestly unfounded or excessive, in particular because of their repetitive character, a business may either charge a reasonable fee, taking into account the administrative costs of providing the information or communication or taking the action requested, or refuse to act on the request and notify the consumer of the reason for refusing the request. The business shall bear the burden of demonstrating that any verifiable consumer request is manifestly unfounded or excessive.

(i)(1) A business that discloses personal information to a service provider or contractor in compliance with this title shall not be liable under this title if the service provider or contractor receiving the personal information uses it in violation of the restrictions set forth in the title, provided that, at the time of disclosing the personal information, the business does not have actual knowledge, or reason to believe, that the service provider or contractor intends to commit such a violation. A service provider or contractor shall likewise not be liable under this title for the obligations of a business for which it provides services as set forth in this title provided that the service provider or contractor shall be liable for its own violations of this title.

(2) A business that discloses personal information of a consumer, with the exception of consumers who have exercised their right to opt out of the sale or sharing of their personal information, consumers who have limited the use or disclosure of their sensitive personal information, and minor consumers who have not opted in to the collection or sale of their personal information, to a third party pursuant to a written contract that requires the third party to provide the same level of protection of the consumer's rights under this title as provided by the business shall not be liable under this title if the third party receiving the personal information uses it in violation of the restrictions set forth in this title provided that, at the time of disclosing the personal information, the business does not have actual knowledge, or reason to believe, that the third party intends to commit such a violation.

(j) This title shall not be construed to require a business, service provider, or contractor to:

(1) Reidentify or otherwise link information that, in the ordinary course of business, is not maintained in a manner that would be considered personal information.

(2) Retain any personal information about a consumer if, in the ordinary course of business, that information about the consumer would not be retained.

(3) Maintain information in identifiable, linkable, or associable form, or collect, obtain, retain, or access any data or technology, in order to be capable of linking or associating a verifiable consumer request with personal information.

(k) The rights afforded to consumers and the obligations imposed on the business in this title shall not adversely affect the rights and freedoms of other natural persons. A verifiable consumer request for specific pieces of personal information pursuant to Section 1798.110, to delete a consumer's personal information pursuant to Section 1798.105, or to correct inaccurate personal information pursuant to Section 1798.106, shall not extend to personal information about the consumer that belongs to, or the business maintains on behalf of, another natural person. A business may rely on representations made in a verifiable consumer request as to rights with respect to personal information and is under no legal requirement to seek out other persons that may have or claim to have rights to personal information, and a business is under no legal obligation under this title or any other provision of law to take any action under this title in the event of a dispute between or among persons claiming rights to personal information in the business' possession.

(*l*) The rights afforded to consumers and the obligations imposed on any business under this title shall not apply to the extent that they infringe on the noncommercial activities of a person or entity described in subdivision (b) of Section 2 of Article I of the California Constitution.

(m)(1) This title shall not apply to any of the following:

(A) Personal information that is collected by a business about a natural person in the course of the natural person acting as a job applicant to, an employee of, owner of, director of, officer of, medical staff member of, or independent contractor of, that business to the extent that the natural person's personal information is collected and used by the business solely within the context of the natural person's role or former role as a job applicant to, an employee of, owner of, director of, officer of, medical staff member of, or an independent contractor of, that business.

(B) Personal information that is collected by a business that is emergency contact information of the natural person acting as a job applicant to, an employee of, owner of, director of, officer of, medical staff member of, or independent contractor of, that business to the extent that the personal information is collected and used solely within the context of having an emergency contact on file.

(C) Personal information that is necessary for the business to retain to administer benefits for another natural person relating to the natural person acting as a job applicant to, an employee of, owner of, director of, officer of, medical staff member of, or independent contractor of, that business to the extent that the personal information is collected and used solely within the context of administering those benefits.

(2) For purposes of this subdivision:

(A) "Independent contractor" means a natural person who provides any service to a business pursuant to a written contract.

(B) "Director" means a natural person designated in the articles of incorporation as director, or elected by the incorporators and natural persons designated, elected, or appointed by any other name or title to act as directors, and their successors.

(C) "Medical staff member" means a licensed physician and surgeon, dentist, or podiatrist, licensed pursuant to Division 2 (commencing with Section 500) of the Business and Professions Code and a clinical psychologist as defined in Section 1316.5 of the Health and Safety Code.

(D) "Officer" means a natural person elected or appointed by the board of directors to manage the daily operations of a corporation, including a chief executive officer, president, secretary, or treasurer.

(E) "Owner" means a natural person who meets one of the following criteria:

(i) Has ownership of, or the power to vote, more than 50 percent of the outstanding shares of any class of voting security of a business.

(ii) Has control in any manner over the election of a majority of the directors or of individuals exercising similar functions.

(iii) Has the power to exercise a controlling influence over the management of a company.

(3) This subdivision shall not apply to subdivision (a) of Section 1798.100 or Section 1798.150.

(4) This subdivision shall become inoperative on January 1, 2023.

(n)(1) The obligations imposed on businesses by Sections 1798.100, 1798.105, 1798.106, 1798.110, 1798.115, 1798.121, 1798.130, and 1798.135 shall not apply to personal information reflecting a written or verbal communication or a transaction between the business and the consumer, where the consumer is a natural person who acted or is acting as an employee, owner, director, officer, or independent contractor

§ 1798.145 OBLIGATIONS

of a company, partnership, sole proprietorship, nonprofit, or government agency and whose communications or transaction with the business occur solely within the context of the business conducting due diligence regarding, or providing or receiving a product or service to or from such company, partnership, sole proprietorship, nonprofit, or government agency.

(2) For purposes of this subdivision:

(A) "Independent contractor" means a natural person who provides any service to a business pursuant to a written contract.

(B) "Director" means a natural person designated in the articles of incorporation as such or elected by the incorporators and natural persons designated, elected, or appointed by any other name or title to act as directors, and their successors.

(C) "Officer" means a natural person elected or appointed by the board of directors to manage the daily operations of a corporation, such as a chief executive officer, president, secretary, or treasurer.

(D) "Owner" means a natural person who meets one of the following:

(i) Has ownership of, or the power to vote, more than 50 percent of the outstanding shares of any class of voting security of a business.

(ii) Has control in any manner over the election of a majority of the directors or of individuals exercising similar functions.

(iii) Has the power to exercise a controlling influence over the management of a company.

(3) This subdivision shall become inoperative on January 1, 2023.

(o)(1) Sections 1798.105 and 1798.120 shall not apply to a commercial credit reporting agency's collection, processing, sale, or disclosure of business controller information to the extent the commercial credit reporting agency uses the business controller information solely to identify the relationship of a consumer to a business that the consumer owns or contact the consumer only in the consumer's role as the owner, director, officer, or management employee of the business.

(2) For the purposes of this subdivision:

(A) "Business controller information" means the name or names of the owner or owners, director, officer, or management employee of a business and the contact information, including a business title, for the owner or owners, director, officer, or management employee.

(B) "Commercial credit reporting agency" has the meaning set forth in subdivision (b) of Section 1785.42.

(C) "Owner" means a natural person that meets one of the following:

(i) Has ownership of, or the power to vote, more than 50 percent of the outstanding shares of any class of voting security of a business.

(ii) Has control in any manner over the election of a majority of the directors or of individuals exercising similar functions.

(iii) Has the power to exercise a controlling influence over the management of a company.

(D) "Director" means a natural person designated in the articles of incorporation of a business as director, or elected by the incorporators and natural persons designated, elected, or appointed by any other name or title to act as directors, and their successors.

(E) "Officer" means a natural person elected or appointed by the board of directors of a business to manage the daily operations of a corporation, including a chief executive officer, president, secretary, or treasurer.

(F) "Management employee" means a natural person whose name and contact information is reported to or collected by a commercial credit reporting agency as the primary manager of a business and used solely within the context of the natural person's role as the primary manager of the business.

(p) The obligations imposed on businesses in Sections 1798.105, 1798.106, 1798.110, and 1798.115 shall not apply to household data.

(q)(1) This title does not require a business to comply with a verifiable consumer request to delete a consumer's personal information under Section 1798.105 to the extent the verifiable consumer request applies to a student's grades, educational scores, or educational test results that the business holds on behalf of a local educational agency, as defined in subdivision (d) of Section 49073.1 of the Education Code, at which the student is currently enrolled. If a business does not comply with a request pursuant to this section, it shall notify the consumer that it is acting pursuant to this exception.

(2) This title does not require, in response to a request pursuant to Section 1798.110, that a business disclose on educational standardized assessment or educational assessment or a consumer's specific responses to the educational standardized assessment or educational assessment if consumer access, possession, or control would jeopardize the validity and reliability of that educational standardized assessment or educational assessment. If a business does not comply with a request pursuant to this section, it shall notify the consumer that it is acting pursuant to this exception.

(3) For purposes of this subdivision:

(A) "Educational standardized assessment or educational assessment" means a standardized or nonstandardized quiz, test, or other assessment used to evaluate students in or for entry to kindergarten and grades 1 to 12, inclusive, schools, postsecondary institutions, vocational programs, and postgraduate programs that are accredited by an accrediting agency or organization recognized by the State of California or the United States Department of Education, as well as certification and licensure examinations used to determine competency and eligibility to receive certification or licensure from a government agency or government certification body.

(B) "Jeopardize the validity and reliability of that educational standardized assessment or educational assessment" means releasing information that would provide an advantage to the consumer who has submitted a verifiable consumer request or to another natural person.

(r) Sections 1798.105 and 1798.120 shall not apply to a business' use, disclosure, or sale of particular pieces of a consumer's personal information if the consumer has consented to the business' use, disclosure, or sale of that information to produce a physical item, including a school yearbook containing the consumer's photograph if:

(1) The business has incurred significant expense in reliance on the consumer's consent.

(2) Compliance with the consumer's request to opt out of the sale of the consumer's personal information or to delete the consumer's personal information would not be commercially reasonable.

(3) The business complies with the consumer's request as soon as it is commercially reasonable to do so. *(Added by Stats.2018, c. 55 (A.B.375), § 3, eff. Jan. 1, 2019, operative Jan. 1, 2020. Amended by Stats.2018, c. 735 (S.B.1121), § 10, eff. Sept. 23, 2018, operative Jan. 1, 2020; Stats.2019, c. 751 (A.B.1146), § 2, eff. Jan. 1, 2020; Stats.2019, c. 757 (A.B. 1355), § 8, eff. Jan. 1, 2020; Stats.2019, c. 763 (A.B.25), § 2.3, eff. Jan. 1, 2020; Initiative Measure (Prop. 24, § 15, approved Nov. 3, 2020, eff. Dec. 16, 2020); Initiative Measure (Prop. 24, § 15, approved Nov. 3, 2020, eff. Dec. 16, 2020, operative Jan. 1, 2023); Stats.2021, c. 525 (A.B.694), § 4, eff. Jan. 1, 2022, operative Jan. 1, 2023; Stats.2021, c. 700 (A.B.335), § 2.5, eff. Jan. 1, 2022, operative Jan. 1, 2023.)*

[1] Section caption supplied by Prop. 24.

[2] For public law sections classified to U.S.C.A., see U.S.C.A. Tables.

Operative Effect

For effective and operative dates of Initiative Measure (Prop. 24), see § 31 of the Measure.

For operative effect of Title 1.81.5, see Civil Code § 1798.198.

Cross References

Business that provides an online service, product, or feature likely to be accessed by children, prohibited actions, see Civil Code § 1798.99.31.

California Age-Appropriate Design Code Act, application of title, see Civil Code § 1798.99.40.

§ 1798.146. Collection of confidential medical information; protected health information; covered entity or business governed by federal law

(a) This title shall not apply to any of the following:

(1) Medical information governed by the Confidentiality of Medical Information Act (Part 2.6 (commencing with Section 56) of Division 1) or protected health information that is collected by a covered entity or business associate governed by the privacy, security, and breach notification rules issued by the United States Department of Health and Human Services, Parts 160 and 164 of Title 45 of the Code of Federal Regulations, established pursuant to the federal Health Insurance Portability and Accountability Act of 1996 (Public Law 104–191)[1] and the federal Health Information Technology for Economic and Clinical Health Act, Title XIII of the federal American Recovery and Reinvestment Act of 2009 (Public Law 111–5).

(2) A provider of health care governed by the Confidentiality of Medical Information Act (Part 2.6 (commencing with Section 56) of Division 1) or a covered entity governed by the privacy, security, and breach notification rules issued by the United States Department of Health and Human Services, Parts 160 and 164 of Title 45 of the Code of Federal Regulations, established pursuant to the federal Health Insurance Portability and Accountability Act of 1996 (Public Law 104–191), to the extent the provider or covered entity maintains, uses, and discloses patient information in the same manner as medical information or protected health information as described in paragraph (1).

(3) A business associate of a covered entity governed by the privacy, security, and data breach notification rules issued by the United States Department of Health and Human Services, Parts 160 and 164 of Title 45 of the Code of Federal Regulations, established pursuant to the federal Health Insurance Portability and Accountability Act of 1996 (Public Law 104–191) and the federal Health Information Technology for Economic and Clinical Health Act, Title XIII of the federal American Recovery and Reinvestment Act of 2009 (Public Law 111–5), to the extent that the business associate maintains, uses, and discloses patient information in the same manner as medical information or protected health information as described in paragraph (1).

(4)(A) Information that meets both of the following conditions:

(i) It is deidentified in accordance with the requirements for deidentification set forth in Section 164.514 of Part 164 of Title 45 of the Code of Federal Regulations.

(ii) It is derived from patient information that was originally collected, created, transmitted, or maintained by an entity regulated by the Health Insurance Portability and Accountability Act, the Confidentiality Of Medical Information Act, or the Federal Policy for the Protection of Human Subjects, also known as the Common Rule.

(B) Information that met the requirements of subparagraph (A) but is subsequently reidentified shall no longer be eligible for the exemption in this paragraph, and shall be subject to applicable federal and state data privacy and security laws, including, but not limited to, the Health Insurance Portability and Accountability Act, the Confidentiality Of Medical Information Act, and this title.

(5) Information that is collected, used, or disclosed in research, as defined in Section 164.501 of Title 45 of the Code of Federal Regulations, including, but not limited to, a clinical trial, and that is conducted in accordance with applicable ethics, confidentiality, privacy, and security rules of Part 164 of Title 45 of the Code of Federal Regulations, the Federal Policy for the Protection of Human Subjects, also known as the Common Rule, good clinical practice guidelines issued by the International Council for Harmonisation, or human subject protection requirements of the United States Food and Drug Administration.

(b) For purposes of this section, all of the following shall apply:

(1) "Business associate" has the same meaning as defined in Section 160.103 of Title 45 of the Code of Federal Regulations.

§ 1798.146

(2) "Covered entity" has the same meaning as defined in Section 160.103 of Title 45 of the Code of Federal Regulations.

(3) "Identifiable private information" has the same meaning as defined in Section 46.102 of Title 45 of the Code of Federal Regulations.

(4) "Individually identifiable health information" has the same meaning as defined in Section 160.103 of Title 45 of the Code of Federal Regulations.

(5) "Medical information" has the same meaning as defined in Section 56.05.

(6) "Patient information" shall mean identifiable private information, protected health information, individually identifiable health information, or medical information.

(7) "Protected health information" has the same meaning as defined in Section 160.103 of Title 45 of the Code of Federal Regulations.

(8) "Provider of health care" has the same meaning as defined in Section 56.05. (Added by Stats.2020, c. 172 (A.B.713), § 2, eff. Sept. 25, 2020.)

[1] For public law sections classified to the U.S.C.A., see USCA–Tables.

Operative Effect

For operative effect of Title 1.81.5, see Civil Code § 1798.198.

§ 1798.148. Reidentification of confidential medical information; exceptions

(a) A business or other person shall not reidentify, or attempt to reidentify, information that has met the requirements of paragraph (4) of subdivision (a) of Section 1798.146, except for one or more of the following purposes:

(1) Treatment, payment, or health care operations conducted by a covered entity or business associate acting on behalf of, and at the written direction of, the covered entity. For purposes of this paragraph, "treatment," "payment," "health care operations," "covered entity," and "business associate" have the same meaning as defined in Section 164.501 of Title 45 of the Code of Federal Regulations.

(2) Public health activities or purposes as described in Section 164.512 of Title 45 of the Code of Federal Regulations.

(3) Research, as defined in Section 164.501 of Title 45 of the Code of Federal Regulations, that is conducted in accordance with Part 46 of Title 45 of the Code of Federal Regulations, the Federal Policy for the Protection of Human Subjects, also known as the Common Rule.

(4) Pursuant to a contract where the lawful holder of the deidentified information that met the requirements of paragraph (4) of subdivision (a) of Section 1798.146 expressly engages a person or entity to attempt to reidentify the deidentified information in order to conduct testing, analysis, or validation of deidentification, or related statistical techniques, if the contract bans any other use or disclosure of the reidentified information and requires the return or destruction of the information that was reidentified upon completion of the contract.

(5) If otherwise required by law.

(b) In accordance with paragraph (4) of subdivision (a) of Section 1798.146, information reidentified pursuant this section shall be subject to applicable federal and state data privacy and security laws including, but not limited to, the Health Insurance Portability and Accountability Act, the Confidentiality of Medical Information Act, and this title.

(c) Beginning January 1, 2021, any contract for the sale or license of deidentified information that has met the requirements of paragraph (4) of subdivision (a) of Section 1798.146, where one of the parties is a person residing or doing business in the state, shall include the following, or substantially similar, provisions:

(1) A statement that the deidentified information being sold or licensed includes deidentified patient information.

(2) A statement that reidentification, and attempted reidentification, of the deidentified information by the purchaser or licensee of the information is prohibited pursuant to this section.

(3) A requirement that, unless otherwise required by law, the purchaser or licensee of the deidentified information may not further disclose the deidentified information to any third party unless the third party is contractually bound by the same or stricter restrictions and conditions.

(d) For purposes of this section, "reidentify" means the process of reversal of deidentification techniques, including, but not limited to, the addition of specific pieces of information or data elements that can, individually or in combination, be used to uniquely identify an individual or usage of any statistical method, contrivance, computer software, or other means that have the effect of associating deidentified information with a specific identifiable individual. (Added by Stats.2020, c. 172 (A.B.713), § 3, eff. Sept. 25, 2020.)

Operative Effect

For operative effect of Title 1.81.5, see Civil Code § 1798.198.

§ 1798.150. Personal Information Security Breaches [1]

(a)(1) Any consumer whose nonencrypted and nonredacted personal information, as defined in subparagraph (A) of paragraph (1) of subdivision (d) of Section 1798.81.5, or whose email address in combination with a password or security question and answer that would permit access to the account is subject to an unauthorized access and exfiltration, theft, or disclosure as a result of the business's violation of the duty to implement and maintain reasonable security procedures and practices appropriate to the nature of the information to protect the personal information may institute a civil action for any of the following:

(A) To recover damages in an amount not less than one hundred dollars ($100) and not greater than seven hundred and fifty ($750) per consumer per incident or actual damages, whichever is greater.

(B) Injunctive or declaratory relief.

(C) Any other relief the court deems proper.

(2) In assessing the amount of statutory damages, the court shall consider any one or more of the relevant

circumstances presented by any of the parties to the case, including, but not limited to, the nature and seriousness of the misconduct, the number of violations, the persistence of the misconduct, the length of time over which the misconduct occurred, the willfulness of the defendant's misconduct, and the defendant's assets, liabilities, and net worth.

(b) Actions pursuant to this section may be brought by a consumer if, prior to initiating any action against a business for statutory damages on an individual or class-wide basis, a consumer provides a business 30 days' written notice identifying the specific provisions of this title the consumer alleges have been or are being violated. In the event a cure is possible, if within the 30 days the business actually cures the noticed violation and provides the consumer an express written statement that the violations have been cured and that no further violations shall occur, no action for individual statutory damages or class-wide statutory damages may be initiated against the business. The implementation and maintenance of reasonable security procedures and practices pursuant to Section 1798.81.5 following a breach does not constitute a cure with respect to that breach. No notice shall be required prior to an individual consumer initiating an action solely for actual pecuniary damages suffered as a result of the alleged violations of this title. If a business continues to violate this title in breach of the express written statement provided to the consumer under this section, the consumer may initiate an action against the business to enforce the written statement and may pursue statutory damages for each breach of the express written statement, as well as any other violation of the title that postdates the written statement.

(c) The cause of action established by this section shall apply only to violations as defined in subdivision (a) and shall not be based on violations of any other section of this title. Nothing in this title shall be interpreted to serve as the basis for a private right of action under any other law. This shall not be construed to relieve any party from any duties or obligations imposed under other law or the United States or California Constitution. *(Added by Stats.2018, c. 55 (A.B. 375), § 3, eff. Jan. 1, 2019, operative Jan. 1, 2020. Amended by Stats.2018, c. 735 (S.B.1121), § 11, eff. Sept. 23, 2018, operative Jan. 1, 2020; Stats.2019, c. 757 (A.B.1355), § 9, eff. Jan. 1, 2020; Initiative Measure (Prop. 24, § 16, approved Nov. 3, 2020, eff. Dec. 16, 2020, operative Jan. 1, 2023).)*

[1] Section caption supplied by Prop. 24.

Operative Effect

For effective and operative dates of Initiative Measure (Prop. 24), see § 31 of the Measure.

For operative effect of Title 1.81.5, see Civil Code § 1798.198.

§ 1798.155. Administrative Enforcement [1]

(a) Any business, service provider, contractor, or other person that violates this title shall be liable for an administrative fine of not more than two thousand five hundred dollars ($2,500) for each violation or seven thousand five hundred dollars ($7,500) for each intentional violation or violations involving the personal information of consumers whom the business, service provider, contractor, or other person has actual knowledge are under 16 years of age, as adjusted pursuant to paragraph (5) of subdivision (a) of Section 1798.185, in an administrative enforcement action brought by the California Privacy Protection Agency.

(b) Any administrative fine assessed for a violation of this title, and the proceeds of any settlement of an action brought pursuant to subdivision (a), shall be deposited in the Consumer Privacy Fund, created within the General Fund pursuant to subdivision (a) of Section 1798.160 with the intent to fully offset any costs incurred by the state courts, the Attorney General, and the California Privacy Protection Agency in connection with this title. *(Added by Stats.2018, c. 55 (A.B.375), § 3, eff. Jan. 1, 2019, operative Jan. 1, 2020. Amended by Stats.2018, c. 735 (S.B.1121), § 12, eff. Sept. 23, 2018, operative Jan. 1, 2020; Initiative Measure (Prop. 24, § 17, approved Nov. 3, 2020, eff. Dec. 16, 2020, operative Jan. 1, 2023).)*

[1] Section caption supplied by Prop. 24.

Operative Effect

For effective and operative dates of Initiative Measure (Prop. 24), see § 31 of the Measure.

For operative effect of Title 1.81.5, see Civil Code § 1798.198.

§ 1798.160. Consumer Privacy Fund [1]

(a) A special fund to be known as the "Consumer Privacy Fund" is hereby created within the General Fund in the State Treasury, and is available upon appropriation by the Legislature first to offset any costs incurred by the state courts in connection with actions brought to enforce this title, the costs incurred by the Attorney General in carrying out the Attorney General's duties under this title, and then for the purposes of establishing an investment fund in the State Treasury, with any earnings or interest from the fund to be deposited in the General Fund, and making grants to promote and protect consumer privacy, educate children in the area of online privacy, and fund cooperative programs with international law enforcement organizations to combat fraudulent activities with respect to consumer data breaches.

(b) Funds transferred to the Consumer Privacy Fund shall be used exclusively as follows:

(1) To offset any costs incurred by the state courts and the Attorney General in connection with this title.

(2) After satisfying the obligations under paragraph (1), the remaining funds shall be allocated each fiscal year as follows:

(A) Ninety–one percent shall be invested by the Treasurer in financial assets with the goal of maximizing long term yields consistent with a prudent level of risk. The principal shall not be subject to transfer or appropriation, provided that any interest and earnings shall be transferred on an annual basis to the General Fund for appropriation by the Legislature for General Fund purposes.

(B) Nine percent shall be made available to the California Privacy Protection Agency for the purposes of making grants in California, with 3 percent allocated to each of the following grant recipients:

(i) Nonprofit organizations to promote and protect consumer privacy.

§ 1798.160

(ii) Nonprofit organizations and public agencies, including school districts, to educate children in the area of online privacy.

(iii) State and local law enforcement agencies to fund cooperative programs with international law enforcement organizations to combat fraudulent activities with respect to consumer data breaches.

(c) Funds in the Consumer Privacy Fund shall not be subject to appropriation or transfer by the Legislature for any other purpose. *(Added by Stats.2018, c. 55 (A.B.375), § 3, eff. Jan. 1, 2019, operative Jan. 1, 2020. Amended by Initiative Measure (Prop. 24, § 18, approved Nov. 3, 2020, eff. Dec. 16, 2020).)*

[1] Section caption supplied by Prop. 24.

Operative Effect

For effective and operative dates of Initiative Measure (Prop. 24), see § 31 of the Measure.

For operative effect of Title 1.81.5, see Civil Code § 1798.198.

Cross References

Data broker registration, penalties for failure to register, see Civil Code § 1798.99.82.

§ 1798.175. Conflicting Provisions [1]

This title is intended to further the constitutional right of privacy and to supplement existing laws relating to consumers' personal information, including, but not limited to, Chapter 22 (commencing with Section 22575) of Division 8 of the Business and Professions Code and Title 1.81 (commencing with Section 1798.80). The provisions of this title are not limited to information collected electronically or over the Internet, but apply to the collection and sale of all personal information collected by a business from consumers. Wherever possible, law relating to consumers' personal information should be construed to harmonize with the provisions of this title, but in the event of a conflict between other laws and the provisions of this title, the provisions of the law that afford the greatest protection for the right of privacy for consumers shall control. *(Added by Stats.2018, c. 55 (A.B. 375), § 3, eff. Jan. 1, 2019, operative Jan. 1, 2020. Amended by Initiative Measure (Prop. 24, § 19, approved Nov. 3, 2020, eff. Dec. 16, 2020, operative Jan. 1, 2023).)*

[1] Section caption supplied by Prop. 24.

Operative Effect

For effective and operative dates of Initiative Measure (Prop. 24), see § 31 of the Measure.

For operative effect of Title 1.81.5, see Civil Code § 1798.198.

§ 1798.180. Preemption [1]

This title is a matter of statewide concern and supersedes and preempts all rules, regulations, codes, ordinances, and other laws adopted by a city, county, city and county, municipality, or local agency regarding the collection and sale of consumers' personal information by a business. *(Added by Stats.2018, c. 55 (A.B.375), § 3, eff. Jan. 1, 2019, operative Sept. 23, 2018. Amended by Initiative Measure (Prop. 24, § 20, approved Nov. 3, 2020, eff. Dec. 16, 2020, operative Jan. 1, 2023).)*

[1] Section caption supplied by Prop. 24.

Operative Effect

For effective and operative dates of Initiative Measure (Prop. 24), see § 31 of the Measure.

For operative effect of Title 1.81.5, see Civil Code § 1798.198.

§ 1798.185. Regulations [1]

(a) On or before July 1, 2020, the Attorney General shall solicit broad public participation and adopt regulations to further the purposes of this title, including, but not limited to, the following areas:

(1) Updating or adding categories of personal information to those enumerated in subdivision (c) of Section 1798.130 and subdivision (v) of Section 1798.140, and updating or adding categories of sensitive personal information to those enumerated in subdivision (ae) of Section 1798.140 in order to address changes in technology, data collection practices, obstacles to implementation, and privacy concerns.

(2) Updating as needed the definitions of "deidentified" and "unique identifier" to address changes in technology, data collection, obstacles to implementation, and privacy concerns, and adding, modifying, or deleting categories to the definition of designated methods for submitting requests to facilitate a consumer's ability to obtain information from a business pursuant to Section 1798.130. The authority to update the definition of "deidentified" shall not apply to deidentification standards set forth in Section 164.514 of Title 45 of the Code of Federal Regulations, where such information previously was "protected health information" as defined in Section 160.103 of Title 45 of the Code of Federal Regulations.

(3) Establishing any exceptions necessary to comply with state or federal law, including, but not limited to, those relating to trade secrets and intellectual property rights, within one year of passage of this title and as needed thereafter, with the intention that trade secrets should not be disclosed in response to a verifiable consumer request.

(4) Establishing rules and procedures for the following:

(A) To facilitate and govern the submission of a request by a consumer to opt-out of the sale or sharing of personal information pursuant to Section 1798.120 and to limit the use of a consumer's sensitive personal information pursuant to Section 1798.121 to ensure that consumers have the ability to exercise their choices without undue burden and to prevent business from engaging in deceptive or harassing conduct, including in retaliation against consumers for exercising their rights, while allowing businesses to inform consumers of the consequences of their decision to opt out of the sale or sharing of their personal information or to limit the use of their sensitive personal information.

(B) To govern business compliance with a consumer's opt-out request.

(C) For the development and use of a recognizable and uniform opt-out logo or button by all businesses to promote consumer awareness of the opportunity to opt-out of the sale of personal information.

(5) Adjusting the monetary thresholds, in January of every odd-numbered year to reflect any increase in the Consumer Price Index, in: subparagraph (A) of paragraph (1) of subdivision (d) of Section 1798.140; subparagraph (A) of paragraph (1) of subdivision (a) of Section 1798.150; subdivision (a) of Section 1798.155; Section 1798.199.25; and subdivision (a) of Section 1798.199.90.

(6) Establishing rules, procedures, and any exceptions necessary to ensure that the notices and information that businesses are required to provide pursuant to this title are provided in a manner that may be easily understood by the average consumer, are accessible to consumers with disabilities, and are available in the language primarily used to interact with the consumer, including establishing rules and guidelines regarding financial incentives within one year of passage of this title and as needed thereafter.

(7) Establishing rules and procedures to further the purposes of Sections 1798.105, 1798.106, 1798.110, and 1798.115 and to facilitate a consumer's or the consumer's authorized agent's ability to delete personal information, correct inaccurate personal information pursuant to Section 1798.106, or obtain information pursuant to Section 1798.130, with the goal of minimizing the administrative burden on consumers, taking into account available technology, security concerns, and the burden on the business, to govern a business's determination that a request for information received from a consumer is a verifiable consumer request, including treating a request submitted through a password-protected account maintained by the consumer with the business while the consumer is logged into the account as a verifiable consumer request and providing a mechanism for a consumer who does not maintain an account with the business to request information through the business's authentication of the consumer's identity, within one year of passage of this title and as needed thereafter.

(8) Establishing how often, and under what circumstances, a consumer may request a correction pursuant to Section 1798.106, including standards governing the following:

(A) How a business responds to a request for correction, including exceptions for requests to which a response is impossible or would involve disproportionate effort, and requests for correction of accurate information.

(B) How concerns regarding the accuracy of the information may be resolved.

(C) The steps a business may take to prevent fraud.

(D) If a business rejects a request to correct personal information collected and analyzed concerning a consumer's health, the right of a consumer to provide a written addendum to the business with respect to any item or statement regarding any such personal information that the consumer believes to be incomplete or incorrect. The addendum shall be limited to 250 words per alleged incomplete or incorrect item and shall clearly indicate in writing that the consumer requests the addendum to be made a part of the consumer's record.

(9) Establishing the standard to govern a business' determination, pursuant to subparagraph (B) of paragraph (2) of subdivision (a) of Section 1798.130, that providing information beyond the 12–month period in a response to a verifiable consumer request is impossible or would involve a disproportionate effort.

(10) Issuing regulations further defining and adding to the business purposes, including other notified purposes, for which businesses, service providers, and contractors may use consumers' personal information consistent with consumers' expectations, and further defining the business purposes for which service providers and contractors may combine consumers' personal information obtained from different sources, except as provided for in paragraph (6) of subdivision (e) of Section 1798.140.

(11) Issuing regulations identifying those business purposes, including other notified purposes, for which service providers and contractors may use consumers' personal information received pursuant to a written contract with a business, for the service provider or contractor's own business purposes, with the goal of maximizing consumer privacy.

(12) Issuing regulations to further define "intentionally interacts," with the goal of maximizing consumer privacy.

(13) Issuing regulations to further define "precise geolocation," including if the size defined is not sufficient to protect consumer privacy in sparsely populated areas or when the personal information is used for normal operational purposes, including billing.

(14) Issuing regulations to define the term "specific pieces of information obtained from the consumer" with the goal of maximizing a consumer's right to access relevant personal information while minimizing the delivery of information to a consumer that would not be useful to the consumer, including system log information and other technical data. For delivery of the most sensitive personal information, the regulations may require a higher standard of authentication provided that the agency shall monitor the impact of the higher standard on the right of consumers to obtain their personal information to ensure that the requirements of verification do not result in the unreasonable denial of verifiable consumer requests.

(15) Issuing regulations requiring businesses whose processing of consumers' personal information presents significant risk to consumers' privacy or security, to:

(A) Perform a cybersecurity audit on an annual basis, including defining the scope of the audit and establishing a process to ensure that audits are thorough and independent. The factors to be considered in determining when processing may result in significant risk to the security of personal information shall include the size and complexity of the business and the nature and scope of processing activities.

(B) Submit to the California Privacy Protection Agency on a regular basis a risk assessment with respect to their processing of personal information, including whether the processing involves sensitive personal information, and identifying and weighing the benefits resulting from the processing to the business, the consumer, other stakeholders, and the public, against the potential risks to the rights of the consumer associated with that processing, with the goal of

§ 1798.185

restricting or prohibiting the processing if the risks to privacy of the consumer outweigh the benefits resulting from processing to the consumer, the business, other stakeholders, and the public. Nothing in this section shall require a business to divulge trade secrets.

(16) Issuing regulations governing access and opt-out rights with respect to businesses' use of automated decisionmaking technology, including profiling and requiring businesses' response to access requests to include meaningful information about the logic involved in those decisionmaking processes, as well as a description of the likely outcome of the process with respect to the consumer.

(17) Issuing regulations to further define a "law enforcement agency-approved investigation" for purposes of the exception in paragraph (2) of subdivision (a) of Section 1798.145.

(18) Issuing regulations to define the scope and process for the exercise of the agency's audit authority, to establish criteria for selection of persons to audit, and to protect consumers' personal information from disclosure to an auditor in the absence of a court order, warrant, or subpoena.

(19)(A) Issuing regulations to define the requirements and technical specifications for an opt-out preference signal sent by a platform, technology, or mechanism, to indicate a consumer's intent to opt out of the sale or sharing of the consumer's personal information and to limit the use or disclosure of the consumer's sensitive personal information. The requirements and specifications for the opt-out preference signal should be updated from time to time to reflect the means by which consumers interact with businesses, and should:

(i) Ensure that the manufacturer of a platform or browser or device that sends the opt-out preference signal cannot unfairly disadvantage another business.

(ii) Ensure that the opt-out preference signal is consumer-friendly, clearly described, and easy to use by an average consumer and does not require that the consumer provide additional information beyond what is necessary.

(iii) Clearly represent a consumer's intent and be free of defaults constraining or presupposing that intent.

(iv) Ensure that the opt-out preference signal does not conflict with other commonly used privacy settings or tools that consumers may employ.

(v) Provide a mechanism for the consumer to selectively consent to a business' sale of the consumer's personal information, or the use or disclosure of the consumer's sensitive personal information, without affecting the consumer's preferences with respect to other businesses or disabling the opt-out preference signal globally.

(vi) State that in the case of a page or setting view that the consumer accesses to set the opt-out preference signal, the consumer should see up to three choices, including:

(I) Global opt out from sale and sharing of personal information, including a direction to limit the use of sensitive personal information.

(II) Choice to "Limit the Use of My Sensitive Personal Information."

(III) Choice titled "Do Not Sell/Do Not Share My Personal Information for Cross–Context Behavioral Advertising."

(B) Issuing regulations to establish technical specifications for an opt-out preference signal that allows the consumer, or the consumer's parent or guardian, to specify that the consumer is less than 13 years of age or at least 13 years of age and less than 16 years of age.

(C) Issuing regulations, with the goal of strengthening consumer privacy while considering the legitimate operational interests of businesses, to govern the use or disclosure of a consumer's sensitive personal information, notwithstanding the consumer's direction to limit the use or disclosure of the consumer's sensitive personal information, including:

(i) Determining any additional purposes for which a business may use or disclose a consumer's sensitive personal information.

(ii) Determining the scope of activities permitted under paragraph (8) of subdivision (e) of Section 1798.140, as authorized by subdivision (a) of Section 1798.121, to ensure that the activities do not involve health-related research.

(iii) Ensuring the functionality of the business' operations.

(iv) Ensuring that the exemption in subdivision (d) of Section 1798.121 for sensitive personal information applies to information that is collected or processed incidentally, or without the purpose of inferring characteristics about a consumer, while ensuring that businesses do not use the exemption for the purpose of evading consumers' rights to limit the use and disclosure of their sensitive personal information under Section 1798.121.

(20) Issuing regulations to govern how a business that has elected to comply with subdivision (b) of Section 1798.135 responds to the opt-out preference signal and provides consumers with the opportunity subsequently to consent to the sale or sharing of their personal information or the use and disclosure of their sensitive personal information for purposes in addition to those authorized by subdivision (a) of Section 1798.121. The regulations should:

(A) Strive to promote competition and consumer choice and be technology neutral.

(B) Ensure that the business does not respond to an opt-out preference signal by:

(i) Intentionally degrading the functionality of the consumer experience.

(ii) Charging the consumer a fee in response to the consumer's opt-out preferences.

(iii) Making any products or services not function properly or fully for the consumer, as compared to consumers who do not use the opt-out preference signal.

(iv) Attempting to coerce the consumer to opt in to the sale or sharing of the consumer's personal information, or the use or disclosure of the consumer's sensitive personal information, by stating or implying that the use of the opt-out preference signal will adversely affect the consumer as compared to consumers who do not use the opt-out preference signal, including stating or implying that the consumer will not be able to use the business' products or services or that those products or services may not function properly or fully.

(v) Displaying any notification or pop-up in response to the consumer's opt-out preference signal.

(C) Ensure that any link to a web page or its supporting content that allows the consumer to consent to opt in:

(i) Is not part of a popup, notice, banner, or other intrusive design that obscures any part of the web page the consumer intended to visit from full view or that interferes with or impedes in any way the consumer's experience visiting or browsing the web page or website the consumer intended to visit.

(ii) Does not require or imply that the consumer must click the link to receive full functionality of any products or services, including the website.

(iii) Does not make use of any dark patterns.

(iv) Applies only to the business with which the consumer intends to interact.

(D) Strive to curb coercive or deceptive practices in response to an opt-out preference signal but should not unduly restrict businesses that are trying in good faith to comply with Section 1798.135.

(21) Review existing Insurance Code provisions and regulations relating to consumer privacy, except those relating to insurance rates or pricing, to determine whether any provisions of the Insurance Code provide greater protection to consumers than the provisions of this title. Upon completing its review, the agency shall adopt a regulation that applies only the more protective provisions of this title to insurance companies. For the purpose of clarity, the Insurance Commissioner shall have jurisdiction over insurance rates and pricing.

(22) Harmonizing the regulations governing opt-out mechanisms, notices to consumers, and other operational mechanisms in this title to promote clarity and the functionality of this title for consumers.

(b) The Attorney General may adopt additional regulations as necessary to further the purposes of this title.

(c) The Attorney General shall not bring an enforcement action under this title until six months after the publication of the final regulations issued pursuant to this section or July 1, 2020, whichever is sooner.

(d) Notwithstanding subdivision (a), the timeline for adopting final regulations required by the act adding this subdivision shall be July 1, 2022. Beginning the later of July 1, 2021, or six months after the agency provides notice to the Attorney General that it is prepared to begin rulemaking under this title, the authority assigned to the Attorney General to adopt regulations under this section shall be exercised by the California Privacy Protection Agency. Notwithstanding any other law, civil and administrative enforcement of the provisions of law added or amended by this act shall not commence until July 1, 2023, and shall only apply to violations occurring on or after that date. Enforcement of provisions of law contained in the California Consumer Privacy Act of 2018 amended by this act shall remain in effect and shall be enforceable until the same provisions of this act become enforceable. *(Added by Stats.2018, c. 55 (A.B.375), § 3, eff. Jan. 1, 2019, operative Jan. 1, 2020. Amended by Stats.2018, c. 735 (S.B.1121), § 13, eff. Sept. 23, 2018,* operative Jan. 1, 2020; Stats.2019, c. 757 (A.B.1355), § 10, eff. Jan. 1, 2020; Initiative Measure (Prop. 24, § 21, approved Nov. 3, 2020, eff. Dec. 16, 2020).)

[1] Section caption supplied by Prop. 24.

Operative Effect

For effective and operative dates of Initiative Measure (Prop. 24), see § 31 of the Measure.

For operative effect of Title 1.81.5, see Civil Code § 1798.198.

§ 1798.190. Anti–Avoidance [1]

A court or the agency shall disregard the intermediate steps or transactions for purposes of effectuating the purposes of this title:

(a) If a series of steps or transactions were component parts of a single transaction intended from the beginning to be taken with the intention of avoiding the reach of this title, including the disclosure of information by a business to a third party in order to avoid the definition of sell or share.

(b) If steps or transactions were taken to purposely avoid the definition of sell or share by eliminating any monetary or other valuable consideration, including by entering into contracts that do not include an exchange for monetary or other valuable consideration, but where a party is obtaining something of value or use. *(Added by Stats.2018, c. 55 (A.B.375), § 3, eff. Jan. 1, 2019, operative Jan. 1, 2020. Amended by Initiative Measure (Prop. 24, § 22, approved Nov. 3, 2020, eff. Dec. 16, 2020, operative Jan. 1, 2023).)*

[1] Section caption supplied by Prop. 24.

Operative Effect

For effective and operative dates of Initiative Measure (Prop. 24), see § 31 of the Measure.

For operative effect of Title 1.81.5, see Civil Code § 1798.198.

§ 1798.192. Waiver [1]

Any provision of a contract or agreement of any kind, including a representative action waiver, that purports to waive or limit in any way rights under this title, including, but not limited to, any right to a remedy or means of enforcement, shall be deemed contrary to public policy and shall be void and unenforceable. This section shall not prevent a consumer from declining to request information from a business, declining to opt out of a business's sale of the consumer's personal information, or authorizing a business to sell or share the consumer's personal information after previously opting out. *(Added by Stats.2018, c. 55 (A.B.375), § 3, eff. Jan. 1, 2019, operative Jan. 1, 2020. Amended by Stats.2018, c. 735 (S.B.1121), § 14, eff. Sept. 23, 2018, operative Jan. 1, 2020; Initiative Measure (Prop. 24, § 23, approved Nov. 3, 2020, eff. Dec. 16, 2020, operative Jan. 1, 2023).)*

[1] Section caption supplied by Prop. 24.

Operative Effect

For effective and operative dates of Initiative Measure (Prop. 24), see § 31 of the Measure.

For operative effect of Title 1.81.5, see Civil Code § 1798.198.

§ 1798.194. Liberal construction of title

This title shall be liberally construed to effectuate its purposes. *(Added by Stats.2018, c. 55 (A.B.375), § 3, eff. Jan. 1, 2019, operative Jan. 1, 2020.)*

Operative Effect

For operative effect of Title 1.81.5, see Civil Code § 1798.198.

§ 1798.196. Construction with federal law, United States Constitution, and California Constitution

This title is intended to supplement federal and state law, if permissible, but shall not apply if such application is preempted by, or in conflict with, federal law or the United States or California Constitution. *(Added by Stats.2018, c. 55 (A.B. 375), § 3, eff. Jan. 1, 2019, operative Jan. 1, 2020. Amended by Stats.2018, c. 735 (S.B.1121), § 15, eff. Sept. 23, 2018, operative Jan. 1, 2020.)*

Operative Effect

For operative effect of Title 1.81.5, see Civil Code § 1798.198.

§ 1798.198. Operative date of title

(a) Subject to limitation provided in subdivision (b), and in Section 1798.199, this title shall be operative January 1, 2020.

(b) This title shall become operative only if initiative measure No. 17–0039, The Consumer Right to Privacy Act of 2018, is withdrawn from the ballot pursuant to Section 9604 of the Elections Code.[1] *(Added by Stats.2018, c. 55 (A.B. 375), § 3, eff. Jan. 1, 2019, operative Jan. 1, 2020. Amended by Stats.2018, c. 735 (S.B.1121), § 16, eff. Sept. 23, 2018, operative Jan. 1, 2020.)*

[1] Initiative measure No. 17–0039 was withdrawn from the ballot June 28, 2018.

§ 1798.199. Operative date of Section 1798.180

Notwithstanding Section 1798.198, Section 1798.180 shall be operative on the effective date of the act[1] adding this section. *(Added by Stats.2018, c. 735 (S.B.1121), § 17, eff. Sept. 23, 2018, operative Jan. 1, 2020.)*

[1] Stats.2018, c. 735 (S.B.1121), eff. Sept. 23, 2018.

Operative Effect

For operative effect of Title 1.81.5, see Civil Code § 1798.198.

§ 1798.199.10. California Privacy Protection Agency; establishment; appointments

(a) There is hereby established in state government the California Privacy Protection Agency, which is vested with full administrative power, authority, and jurisdiction to implement and enforce the California Consumer Privacy Act of 2018. The agency shall be governed by a five-member board, including the chairperson. The chairperson and one member of the board shall be appointed by the Governor. The Attorney General, Senate Rules Committee, and Speaker of the Assembly shall each appoint one member. These appointments should be made from among Californians with expertise in the areas of privacy, technology, and consumer rights.

(b) The initial appointments to the agency shall be made within 90 days of the effective date of the act adding this section. *(Added by Initiative Measure (Prop. 24, § 24.1, approved Nov. 3, 2020, eff. Dec. 16, 2020).)*

Operative Effect

For effective and operative dates of Initiative Measure (Prop. 24), see § 31 of the Measure.

For operative effect of Title 1.81.5, see Civil Code § 1798.198.

§ 1798.199.15. Members of the board; qualifications; conduct

Members of the agency board shall:

(a) Have qualifications, experience, and skills, in particular in the areas of privacy and technology, required to perform the duties of the agency and exercise its powers.

(b) Maintain the confidentiality of information which has come to their knowledge in the course of the performance of their tasks or exercise of their powers, except to the extent that disclosure is required by the Public Records Act.

(c) Remain free from external influence, whether direct or indirect, and shall neither seek nor take instructions from another.

(d) Refrain from any action incompatible with their duties and engaging in any incompatible occupation, whether gainful or not, during their term.

(e) Have the right of access to all information made available by the agency to the chairperson.

(f) Be precluded, for a period of one year after leaving office, from accepting employment with a business that was subject to an enforcement action or civil action under this title during the member's tenure or during the five-year period preceding the member's appointment.

(g) Be precluded for a period of two years after leaving office from acting, for compensation, as an agent or attorney for, or otherwise representing, any other person in a matter pending before the agency if the purpose is to influence an action of the agency. *(Added by Initiative Measure (Prop. 24, § 24.2, approved Nov. 3, 2020, eff. Dec. 16, 2020).)*

Operative Effect

For effective and operative dates of Initiative Measure (Prop. 24), see § 31 of the Measure.

For operative effect of Title 1.81.5, see Civil Code § 1798.198.

§ 1798.199.20. Duration of service

Members of the agency board, including the chairperson, shall serve at the pleasure of their appointing authority but shall serve for no longer than eight consecutive years. *(Added by Initiative Measure (Prop. 24, § 24.3, approved Nov. 3, 2020, eff. Dec. 16, 2020).)*

Operative Effect

For effective and operative dates of Initiative Measure (Prop. 24), see § 31 of the Measure.

For operative effect of Title 1.81.5, see Civil Code § 1798.198.

§ 1798.199.25. Compensation

For each day on which they engage in official duties, members of the agency board shall be compensated at the rate of one hundred dollars ($100), adjusted biennially to reflect changes in the cost of living, and shall be reimbursed for expenses incurred in performance of their official duties. *(Added by Initiative Measure (Prop. 24, § 24.4, approved Nov. 3, 2020, eff. Dec. 16, 2020).)*

Operative Effect

For effective and operative dates of Initiative Measure (Prop. 24), see § 31 of the Measure.

For operative effect of Title 1.81.5, see Civil Code § 1798.198.

§ 1798.199.30. Executive director; officers, counsel, and employees

The agency board shall appoint an executive director who shall act in accordance with agency policies and regulations and with applicable law. The agency shall appoint and discharge officers, counsel, and employees, consistent with applicable civil service laws, and shall fix the compensation of employees and prescribe their duties. The agency may contract for services that cannot be provided by its employees. *(Added by Initiative Measure (Prop. 24, § 24.5, approved Nov. 3, 2020, eff. Dec. 16, 2020).)*

Operative Effect

For effective and operative dates of Initiative Measure (Prop. 24), see § 31 of the Measure.

For operative effect of Title 1.81.5, see Civil Code § 1798.198.

§ 1798.199.35. Delegation of authority

The agency board may delegate authority to the chairperson or the executive director to act in the name of the agency between meetings of the agency, except with respect to resolution of enforcement actions and rulemaking authority. *(Added by Initiative Measure (Prop. 24, § 24.6, approved Nov. 3, 2020, eff. Dec. 16, 2020).)*

Operative Effect

For effective and operative dates of Initiative Measure (Prop. 24), see § 31 of the Measure.

For operative effect of Title 1.81.5, see Civil Code § 1798.198.

§ 1798.199.40. Functions of agency

The agency shall perform the following functions:

(a) Administer, implement, and enforce through administrative actions this title.

(b) On and after the later of July 1, 2021, or within six months of the agency providing the Attorney General with notice that it is prepared to assume rulemaking responsibilities under this title, adopt, amend, and rescind regulations pursuant to Section 1798.185 to carry out the purposes and provisions of the California Consumer Privacy Act of 2018, including regulations specifying recordkeeping requirements for businesses to ensure compliance with this title.

(c) Through the implementation of this title, protect the fundamental privacy rights of natural persons with respect to the use of their personal information.

(d) Promote public awareness and understanding of the risks, rules, responsibilities, safeguards, and rights in relation to the collection, use, sale, and disclosure of personal information, including the rights of minors with respect to their own information, and provide a public report summarizing the risk assessments filed with the agency pursuant to paragraph (15) of subdivision (a) of Section 1798.185 while ensuring that data security is not compromised.

(e) Provide guidance to consumers regarding their rights under this title.

(f) Provide guidance to businesses regarding their duties and responsibilities under this title and appoint a Chief Privacy Auditor to conduct audits of businesses to ensure compliance with this title pursuant to regulations adopted pursuant to paragraph (18) of subdivision (a) of Section 1798.185.

(g) Provide technical assistance and advice to the Legislature, upon request, with respect to privacy-related legislation.

(h) Monitor relevant developments relating to the protection of personal information and, in particular, the development of information and communication technologies and commercial practices.

(i) Cooperate with other agencies with jurisdiction over privacy laws and with data processing authorities in California, other states, territories, and countries to ensure consistent application of privacy protections.

(j) Establish a mechanism pursuant to which persons doing business in California that do not meet the definition of business set forth in paragraph (1), (2), or (3) of subdivision (d) of Section 1798.140 may voluntarily certify that they are in compliance with this title, as set forth in paragraph (4) of subdivision (d) of Section 1798.140, and make a list of those entities available to the public.

(k) Solicit, review, and approve applications for grants to the extent funds are available pursuant to paragraph (2) of subdivision (b) of Section 1798.160.

(*l*) Perform all other acts necessary or appropriate in the exercise of its power, authority, and jurisdiction and seek to balance the goals of strengthening consumer privacy while giving attention to the impact on businesses. *(Added by Initiative Measure (Prop. 24, § 24.7, approved Nov. 3, 2020, eff. Dec. 16, 2020). Amended by Stats.2021, c. 525 (A.B.694), § 5, eff. Jan. 1, 2022.)*

Operative Effect

For effective and operative dates of Initiative Measure (Prop. 24), see § 31 of the Measure.

For operative effect of Title 1.81.5, see Civil Code § 1798.198.

§ 1798.199.45. Investigation of possible violations; considerations

(a) Upon the sworn complaint of any person or on its own initiative, the agency may investigate possible violations of this title relating to any business, service provider, contractor, or person. The agency may decide not to investigate a complaint or decide to provide a business with a time period to cure the alleged violation. In making a decision not to investigate or provide more time to cure, the agency may consider the following:

(1) Lack of intent to violate this title.

(2) Voluntary efforts undertaken by the business, service provider, contractor, or person to cure the alleged violation prior to being notified by the agency of the complaint.

(b) The agency shall notify in writing the person who made the complaint of the action, if any, the agency has taken or plans to take on the complaint, together with the reasons for that action or nonaction. (Added by Initiative Measure (Prop. 24, § 24.8, approved Nov. 3, 2020, eff. Dec. 16, 2020, operative Jan. 1, 2023).)

Operative Effect

For effective and operative dates of Initiative Measure (Prop. 24), see § 31 of the Measure.

For operative effect of Title 1.81.5, see Civil Code § 1798.198.

§ 1798.199.50. Consideration of probable cause; notice to alleged violator

No finding of probable cause to believe this title has been violated shall be made by the agency unless, at least 30 days prior to the agency's consideration of the alleged violation, the business, service provider, contractor, or person alleged to have violated this title is notified of the violation by service of process or registered mail with return receipt requested, provided with a summary of the evidence, and informed of their right to be present in person and represented by counsel at any proceeding of the agency held for the purpose of considering whether probable cause exists for believing the person violated this title. Notice to the alleged violator shall be deemed made on the date of service, the date the registered mail receipt is signed, or if the registered mail receipt is not signed, the date returned by the post office. A proceeding held for the purpose of considering probable cause shall be private unless the alleged violator files with the agency a written request that the proceeding be public. (Added by Initiative Measure (Prop. 24, § 24.9, approved Nov. 3, 2020, eff. Dec. 16, 2020, operative Jan. 1, 2023).)

Operative Effect

For effective and operative dates of Initiative Measure (Prop. 24), see § 31 of the Measure.

For operative effect of Title 1.81.5, see Civil Code § 1798.198.

§ 1798.199.55. Determination of probable cause; notice and hearing; issuance of order; joint and several liability

(a) When the agency determines there is probable cause for believing this title has been violated, it shall hold a hearing to determine if a violation has or violations have occurred. Notice shall be given and the hearing conducted in accordance with the Administrative Procedure Act (Chapter 5 (commencing with Section 11500), Part 1, Division 3, Title 2, Government Code). The agency shall have all the powers granted by that chapter. If the agency determines on the basis of the hearing conducted pursuant to this subdivision that a violation or violations have occurred, it shall issue an order that may require the violator to do all or any of the following:

(1) Cease and desist violation of this title.

(2) Subject to Section 1798.155, pay an administrative fine of up to two thousand five hundred dollars ($2,500) for each violation, or up to seven thousand five hundred dollars ($7,500) for each intentional violation and each violation involving the personal information of minor consumers to the Consumer Privacy Fund within the General Fund of the state. When the agency determines that no violation has occurred, it shall publish a declaration so stating.

(b) If two or more persons are responsible for any violation or violations, they shall be jointly and severally liable. (Added by Initiative Measure (Prop. 24, § 24.10, approved Nov. 3, 2020, eff. Dec. 16, 2020, operative Jan. 1, 2023).)

Operative Effect

For effective and operative dates of Initiative Measure (Prop. 24), see § 31 of the Measure.

For operative effect of Title 1.81.5, see Civil Code § 1798.198.

§ 1798.199.60. Rejection of decision of administrative law judge; written statement of reasons

Whenever the agency rejects the decision of an administrative law judge made pursuant to Section 11517 of the Government Code, the agency shall state the reasons in writing for rejecting the decision. (Added by Initiative Measure (Prop. 24, § 24.11, approved Nov. 3, 2020, eff. Dec. 16, 2020, operative Jan. 1, 2023).)

Operative Effect

For effective and operative dates of Initiative Measure (Prop. 24), see § 31 of the Measure.

For operative effect of Title 1.81.5, see Civil Code § 1798.198.

§ 1798.199.65. Subpoenas; oaths and affirmations; evidence

The agency may subpoena witnesses, compel their attendance and testimony, administer oaths and affirmations, take evidence and require by subpoena the production of any books, papers, records, or other items material to the performance of the agency's duties or exercise of its powers, including, but not limited to, its power to audit a business' compliance with this title. (Added by Initiative Measure (Prop. 24, § 24.12, approved Nov. 3, 2020, eff. Dec. 16, 2020, operative Jan. 1, 2023).)

Operative Effect

For effective and operative dates of Initiative Measure (Prop. 24), see § 31 of the Measure.

For operative effect of Title 1.81.5, see Civil Code § 1798.198.

§ 1798.199.70. Time for bringing action

No administrative action brought pursuant to this title alleging a violation of any of the provisions of this title shall be commenced more than five years after the date on which the violation occurred.

(a) The service of the probable cause hearing notice, as required by Section 1798.199.50, upon the person alleged to have violated this title shall constitute the commencement of the administrative action.

(b) If the person alleged to have violated this title engages in the fraudulent concealment of the person's acts or identity, the five-year period shall be tolled for the period of the concealment. For purposes of this subdivision, "fraudulent concealment" means the person knows of material facts related to the person's duties under this title and knowingly conceals them in performing or omitting to perform those duties for the purpose of defrauding the public of information to which it is entitled under this title.

(c) If, upon being ordered by a superior court to produce any documents sought by a subpoena in any administrative proceeding under this title, the person alleged to have violated this title fails to produce documents in response to the order by the date ordered to comply therewith, the five-year period shall be tolled for the period of the delay from the date of filing of the motion to compel until the date the documents are produced. *(Added by Initiative Measure (Prop. 24, § 24.13, approved Nov. 3, 2020, eff. Dec. 16, 2020, operative Jan. 1, 2023).)*

Operative Effect

For effective and operative dates of Initiative Measure (Prop. 24), see § 31 of the Measure.

For operative effect of Title 1.81.5, see Civil Code § 1798.198.

§ 1798.199.75. Civil action for collection of unpaid administrative fines

(a) In addition to any other available remedies, the agency may bring a civil action and obtain a judgment in superior court for the purpose of collecting any unpaid administrative fines imposed pursuant to this title after exhaustion of judicial review of the agency's action. The action may be filed as a small claims, limited civil, or unlimited civil case depending on the jurisdictional amount. The venue for this action shall be in the county where the administrative fines were imposed by the agency. In order to obtain a judgment in a proceeding under this section, the agency shall show, following the procedures and rules of evidence as applied in ordinary civil actions, all of the following:

(1) That the administrative fines were imposed following the procedures set forth in this title and implementing regulations.

(2) That the defendant or defendants in the action were notified, by actual or constructive notice, of the imposition of the administrative fines.

(3) That a demand for payment has been made by the agency and full payment has not been received.

(b) A civil action brought pursuant to subdivision (a) shall be commenced within four years after the date on which the administrative fines were imposed. *(Added by Initiative Measure (Prop. 24, § 24.14, approved Nov. 3, 2020, eff. Dec. 16, 2020, operative Jan. 1, 2023).)*

Operative Effect

For effective and operative dates of Initiative Measure (Prop. 24), see § 31 of the Measure.

For operative effect of Title 1.81.5, see Civil Code § 1798.198.

§ 1798.199.80. Application for judgment to collect administrative fines imposed by order or decision

(a) If the time for judicial review of a final agency order or decision has lapsed, or if all means of judicial review of the order or decision have been exhausted, the agency may apply to the clerk of the court for a judgment to collect the administrative fines imposed by the order or decision, or the order as modified in accordance with a decision on judicial review.

(b) The application, which shall include a certified copy of the order or decision, or the order as modified in accordance with a decision on judicial review, and proof of service of the order or decision, constitutes a sufficient showing to warrant issuance of the judgment to collect the administrative fines. The clerk of the court shall enter the judgment immediately in conformity with the application.

(c) An application made pursuant to this section shall be made to the clerk of the superior court in the county where the administrative fines were imposed by the agency.

(d) A judgment entered in accordance with this section has the same force and effect as, and is subject to all the provisions of law relating to, a judgment in a civil action and may be enforced in the same manner as any other judgment of the court in which it is entered.

(e) The agency may bring an application pursuant to this section only within four years after the date on which all means of judicial review of the order or decision have been exhausted.

(f) The remedy available under this section is in addition to those available under any other law. *(Added by Initiative Measure (Prop. 24, § 24.15, approved Nov. 3, 2020, eff. Dec. 16, 2020, operative Jan. 1, 2023).)*

Operative Effect

For effective and operative dates of Initiative Measure (Prop. 24), see § 31 of the Measure.

For operative effect of Title 1.81.5, see Civil Code § 1798.198.

§ 1798.199.85. Agency decisions subject to judicial review

Any decision of the agency with respect to a complaint or administrative fine shall be subject to judicial review in an action brought by an interested party to the complaint or administrative fine and shall be subject to an abuse of discretion standard. *(Added by Initiative Measure (Prop. 24, § 24.16, approved Nov. 3, 2020, eff. Dec. 16, 2020, operative Jan. 1, 2023).)*

Operative Effect

For effective and operative dates of Initiative Measure (Prop. 24), see § 31 of the Measure.

For operative effect of Title 1.81.5, see Civil Code § 1798.198.

§ 1798.199.90. Penalties for violations; Attorney General enforcement

(a) Any business, service provider, contractor, or other person that violates this title shall be subject to an injunction and liable for a civil penalty of not more than two thousand five hundred dollars ($2,500) for each violation or seven thousand five hundred dollars ($7,500) for each intentional violation and each violation involving the personal information of minor consumers, as adjusted pursuant to paragraph (5) of subdivision (a) of Section 1798.185, which shall be assessed and recovered in a civil action brought in the name of the people of the State of California by the Attorney General. The court may consider the good faith cooperation of the business, service provider, contractor, or other person in determining the amount of the civil penalty.

(b) Any civil penalty recovered by an action brought by the Attorney General for a violation of this title, and the proceeds of any settlement of any said action, shall be deposited in the Consumer Privacy Fund.

(c) The agency shall, upon request by the Attorney General, stay an administrative action or investigation under this title to permit the Attorney General to proceed with an investigation or civil action and shall not pursue an administrative action or investigation, unless the Attorney General subsequently determines not to pursue an investigation or civil action. The agency may not limit the authority of the Attorney General to enforce this title.

(d) No civil action may be filed by the Attorney General under this section for any violation of this title after the agency has issued a decision pursuant to Section 1798.199.85 or an order pursuant to Section 1798.199.55 against that person for the same violation.

(e) This section shall not affect the private right of action provided for in Section 1798.150. *(Added by Initiative Measure (Prop. 24, § 24.17, approved Nov. 3, 2020, eff. Dec. 16, 2020, operative Jan. 1, 2023).)*

Operative Effect

For effective and operative dates of Initiative Measure (Prop. 24), see § 31 of the Measure.

For operative effect of Title 1.81.5, see Civil Code § 1798.198.

§ 1798.199.95. Appropriations

(a) There is hereby appropriated from the General Fund of the state to the agency the sum of five million dollars ($5,000,000) during the fiscal year 2020–2021, and the sum of ten million dollars ($10,000,000) adjusted for cost-of-living changes, during each fiscal year thereafter, for expenditure to support the operations of the agency pursuant to this title. The expenditure of funds under this appropriation shall be subject to the normal administrative review given to other state appropriations. The Legislature shall appropriate those additional amounts to the commission and other agencies as may be necessary to carry out the provisions of this title.

(b) The Department of Finance, in preparing the state budget and the Budget Act bill submitted to the Legislature, shall include an item for the support of this title that shall indicate all of the following:

(1) The amounts to be appropriated to other agencies to carry out their duties under this title, which amounts shall be in augmentation of the support items of those agencies.

(2) The additional amounts required to be appropriated by the Legislature to the agency to carry out the purposes of this title, as provided for in this section.

(3) In parentheses, for informational purposes, the continuing appropriation during each fiscal year of ten million dollars ($10,000,000), adjusted for cost-of-living changes made pursuant to this section.

(c) The Attorney General shall provide staff support to the agency until the agency has hired its own staff. The Attorney General shall be reimbursed by the agency for these services. *(Added by Initiative Measure (Prop. 24, § 24.18, approved Nov. 3, 2020, eff. Dec. 16, 2020).)*

Operative Effect

For effective and operative dates of Initiative Measure (Prop. 24), see § 31 of the Measure.

For operative effect of Title 1.81.5, see Civil Code § 1798.198.

§ 1798.199.100. Consideration of good faith cooperation

The agency and any court, as applicable, shall consider the good faith cooperation of the business, service provider, contractor, or other person in determining the amount of any administrative fine or civil penalty for a violation of this title. A business shall not be required by the agency, a court, or otherwise to pay both an administrative fine and a civil penalty for the same violation. *(Added by Initiative Measure (Prop. 24, § 24.19, approved Nov. 3, 2020, eff. Dec. 16, 2020, operative Jan. 1, 2023).)*

Operative Effect

For effective and operative dates of Initiative Measure (Prop. 24), see § 31 of the Measure.

For operative effect of Title 1.81.5, see Civil Code § 1798.198.

Title 1.81.6

IDENTITY THEFT IN BUSINESS ENTITY FILINGS

Section
1798.200. Definitions.

Section
1798.201. Petition filed in superior court; order for alleged perpetrator to appear and show cause for information in personal identifying business entity filing.

1798.202. Petition heard and determination made part of record of court; procedures if petition is meritorious; vacation of determination for cause; form for order of determination; filing with Secretary of State.

§ 1798.200. Definitions

For purposes of this title, the following terms are defined as follows:

(a) "Business entity filing" means a document required by law to be filed with the Secretary of State pursuant to the Corporations Code, the Financial Code, or the Insurance Code.

(b) "Personal identifying information" has the same meaning as defined in subdivision (b) of Section 530.55 of the Penal Code.

(c) "Person" means a natural person, firm, association, organization, partnership, business trust, company, corporation, limited liability company, or public entity. (Added by Stats.2018, c. 696 (S.B.1196), § 1, eff. Jan. 1, 2019.)

§ 1798.201. Petition filed in superior court; order for alleged perpetrator to appear and show cause for information in personal identifying business entity filing

A person who has learned or reasonably suspects that his or her personal identifying information has been used unlawfully, as described in subdivision (a) of Section 530.5 of the Penal Code, in a business entity filing, and has initiated a law enforcement investigation in accordance with subdivision (a) of Section 530.6 of the Penal Code, may petition the superior court in the county in which the person resides for an order, which may be granted ex parte, directing the alleged perpetrator of the act described in paragraph (1) of subdivision (c) of Section 530.5 of the Penal Code, if known, and the person using the personal identifying information in the business entity filing to appear at a hearing before the court and show cause for both of the following:

(a) Why the personal identifying information should not be labeled to show the information is impersonated and does not reflect the person's identity.

(b) Why the personal identifying information should be associated with the business entity. (Added by Stats.2018, c. 696 (S.B.1196), § 1, eff. Jan. 1, 2019.)

§ 1798.202. Petition heard and determination made part of record of court; procedures if petition is meritorious; vacation of determination for cause; form for order of determination; filing with Secretary of State

(a) A petition filed pursuant to Section 1798.201 shall be heard and determined based on declarations, affidavits, police reports, or other material, relevant, and reliable information submitted by the parties or ordered to be made part of the record by the court.

(b) If the court determines the petition is meritorious and there is no reasonable cause to believe that the victim's personal identifying information has been used lawfully in the business entity filing, the court shall make a finding that the victim's personal identifying information has been used unlawfully in the business entity filing and shall issue an order certifying this determination.

(c) Upon making a determination pursuant to subdivision (b), the court shall do the following:

(1) Order the name and associated personal identifying information in the business entity filing to be redacted or labeled to show that the data is impersonated and does not reflect the victim's identity.

(2) Order the data to be removed from publicly accessible electronic indexes and databases.

(d) A determination made pursuant to subdivision (b) may be vacated at any time if the petition or any information submitted in support of the petition is found to contain any material misrepresentation or was obtained by fraud.

(e) The Judicial Council shall develop a form for issuing an order of determination pursuant to this section.

(f) An order issued pursuant to subdivision (c) shall be filed with the Secretary of State. (Added by Stats.2018, c. 696 (S.B.1196), § 1, eff. Jan. 1, 2019.)

Title 1.82

BUSINESS RECORDS

Chapter	Section
1. Definitions	1799
2. Disclosures	1799.1
3. Civil Remedies	1799.2

CHAPTER 1. DEFINITIONS

Section
1799. Bookkeeping services; business entity; individual; person; record.

§ 1799. Bookkeeping services; business entity; individual; person; record

As used in this title:

(a) The term "bookkeeping services" means keeping books, making trial balances, preparing statements, making audits, or preparing reports, all as a part of bookkeeping operations, provided that such trial balances, statements, or reports are not issued over the name of such person as having been prepared or examined by a certified public accountant or public accountant.

(b) The term "business entity" means a sole proprietorship, partnership, corporation, association or other group, however organized and whether or not organized to operate at a profit, but does not mean a financial institution organized, chartered, or holding a license or authorization certificate under a law of this state or the United States to make loans or extend credit and subject to supervision by an official or agency of this state or the United States, nor the parent of any such financial institution, nor any subsidiary of any such financial institution or parent.

(c) The term "individual" means a natural person.

(d) The term "person" means any natural person, corporation, partnership, limited liability company, firm, association, or governmental entity.

(e) The term "record" means any item, collection, or grouping of information about an individual or business entity. *(Added by Stats.1977, c. 221, p. 1017, § 1. Amended by Stats.1994, c. 1010 (S.B.2053), § 41.)*

CHAPTER 2. DISCLOSURES

Section
1799.1. Prohibition against disclosure except upon written consent; application of section.
1799.1a. Income tax returns.
1799.1b. Credit card holders and telephone accountholders; change of address requests; requirements and restrictions for credit card issuers and business entities providing telephone accounts; change of address notifications.

§ 1799.1. Prohibition against disclosure except upon written consent; application of section

(a) No business entity which performs bookkeeping services shall disclose in whole or in part the contents of any record, including the disclosure of information in the record in any composite of information, which is prepared or maintained by such business entity to any person, other than the individual or business entity which is the subject of the record, without the express written consent of such individual or business entity.

(b) This section shall not apply to the following:

(1) To a disclosure to any person pursuant to a subpoena or court order.

(2) To a disclosure which is discoverable.

(3) To a disclosure to any person acting pursuant to a lawful search warrant.

(4) To a disclosure to a law enforcement agency when required for investigations of criminal activity, unless such disclosure is prohibited by law.

(5) To a disclosure to a taxing agency for purposes of tax administration. *(Added by Stats.1977, c. 221, p. 1017, § 1.)*

Cross References

Bookkeeping services defined for purposes of this Title, see Civil Code § 1799.
Business entity defined for purposes of this Title, see Civil Code § 1799.
Individual defined for purposes of this Title, see Civil Code § 1799.
Person defined for purposes of this Title, see Civil Code § 1799.
Record defined for purposes of this Title, see Civil Code § 1799.
Search warrants, see Penal Code § 1523 et seq.

§ 1799.1a. Income tax returns

(a) No person, including an individual, firm, corporation, association, partnership, or joint venture, or any employee or agent thereof, shall disclose information obtained from a federal or state income tax return or any information obtained from a tax schedule submitted with the return by a consumer in connection with a financial or other business-related transaction unless the disclosure is within any of the following:

(1) Consented to in writing by the consumer in a separate document that states to whom the disclosure will be made and how the information will be used. If the consumer agrees, this separate consent document may be in the form of an electronic record, executed by an electronic signature as provided by Title 2.5 (commencing with Section 1633.1) of Part 2 of Division 3 of the Civil Code.

(2) Authorized or required by state or federal law.

(3) Necessary to complete or service the financial or business-related transaction or to effect, administer, or enforce a financial or business-related transaction requested by the consumer.

(4) Pursuant to court order.

(5) Required to complete any of the transactions described in subparagraphs (A) to (D), inclusive, by a person, including an individual, firm, corporation, association, partnership or joint venture, if the disclosure is made solely for that purpose. The provisions of this section apply to any person, including an individual, firm, corporation, association, partnership, or joint venture, and any employee or agent thereof, receiving information as a result of a disclosure authorized by this paragraph.

(A) A proposed or actual sale, merger, transfer, or exchange of all or a portion of a business or operating unit.

(B) A proposed or actual securitization or secondary market sale, including the sale of servicing rights.

(C) To provide information to insurance rate advisory organizations, guaranty funds or agencies, rating agencies, and other persons assessing compliance with industry standards.

(D) To protect against or to prevent actual or potential fraud and unauthorized transactions and claims and for institutional risk control activities.

(b) No unrelated use shall be made of a federal or state tax return or any information obtained therefrom or any information submitted with the return by a consumer in connection with a financial or other business-related transaction. "Unrelated use" means any use that is not necessary to effect, administer, or enforce the financial or other business-related transaction with the consumer or that is beyond the scope of the stated purpose to which the consumer consented for the use of the return or any other information he or she submitted.

(c)(1) For purposes of this section, the following definitions shall apply:

(A) "Affiliate" means any entity that, directly or indirectly, through one or more intermediaries, controls, is controlled by, or is under common control with, another entity.

(B) "Consumer" means an individual who requests or obtains financial or other business-related services.

(C) "Tax return" means a return, declaration, statement, refund claim, or other document required to be made or to be filed in connection with state or federal income taxes or state bank and corporation franchise taxes.

(2) A disclosure prohibited by this section includes a disclosure made internally within the entity or by that entity to any of its subsidiaries or affiliates.

(3) The information described in subdivision (a) includes that information obtained through an electronic medium.

(d) No person, including an individual, firm, corporation, association, partnership, or joint venture, or any employee or agent thereof, shall dispose of any of the information described in subdivision (a) in a manner in which the identity of the consumer may be determined from the disposed information alone or in combination with other publicly available information. This subdivision shall not become operative if Assembly Bill 2246 of the 1999–2000 Regular Session is enacted and becomes effective on or before January 1, 2001.

(e) The civil remedies in Chapter 3 (commencing with Section 1799.2) shall be applicable to a violation of this section. Each violation of this section shall constitute a separate cause of action for which damages are recoverable.

(f) The treatment of tax returns by tax preparers, as defined in Section 22251 of the Business and Professions Code, shall be governed by Section 17530.5 of the Business and Professions Code. *(Added by Stats.2000, c. 1084 (S.B. 1724), § 5.)*

Cross References

Individual defined for purposes of this Title, see Civil Code § 1799.
Person defined for purposes of this Title, see Civil Code § 1799.
Tax preparers, disclosure of confidential information concerning client or prospective client, written permission required, legislative intent, see Business and Professions Code § 22252.1.

§ 1799.1b. Credit card holders and telephone accountholders; change of address requests; requirements and restrictions for credit card issuers and business entities providing telephone accounts; change of address notifications

(a) Any credit card issuer that receives a change of address request, other than for a correction of a typographical error, from a cardholder who orders a replacement credit card within 60 days before or after that request is received shall send to that cardholder a change of address notification that is addressed to the cardholder at the cardholder's previous address of record. If the replacement credit card is requested prior to the effective date of the change of address, the notification shall be sent within 30 days of the change of address request. If the replacement credit card is requested after the effective date of the change of address, the notification shall be sent within 30 days of the request for the replacement credit card.

(b) Any business entity that provides telephone accounts that receives a change of address request, other than for a correction of a typographical error, from an accountholder who orders new service, shall send to that accountholder a change of address notification that is addressed to the accountholder at the accountholder's previous address of record. The notification shall be sent within 30 days of the request for new service.

(c) The notice required pursuant to subdivision (a) or (b) may be given by telephone or e-mail communication if the credit card issuer or business entity that provides telephone accounts reasonably believes that it has the current telephone number or e-mail address for the accountholder or cardholder who has requested a change of address. If the notification is in writing it may not contain the consumer's account number, social security number, or other personal identifying information, but may contain the consumer's name, previous address, and new address of record. For business entities described in subdivision (b), the notification may also contain the accountholder's telephone number.

(d) A credit card issuer or a business entity that provides telephone accounts is not required to send a change of address notification when a change of address request is made in person by a consumer who has presented valid identification, or is made by telephone and the requester has provided a unique alpha-numeric password.

(e) The following definitions shall apply to this section:

(1) "Credit account" has the same meaning as "credit card," as defined in subdivision (a) of Section 1747.02.

(2) "Telephone account" means an account with a telephone corporation, as defined in Section 234 of the Public Utilities Code. *(Added by Stats.2003, c. 533 (S.B.602), § 5. Amended by Stats.2004, c. 183 (A.B.3082), § 36.)*

Cross References

Business entity defined for purposes of this Title, see Civil Code § 1799.
Person defined for purposes of this Title, see Civil Code § 1799.
Record defined for purposes of this Title, see Civil Code § 1799.
Telephone corporations, customer right of privacy, restrictions on availability of information, see Public Utilities Code § 2891.
Unlawful use of personal identifying information by another, issuance of law enforcement investigation, determination of factual innocence of victim, see Penal Code § 530.6.

CHAPTER 3. CIVIL REMEDIES

Section
1799.2. Initiation of civil action; liability for damages; limitation.
1799.3. Prohibition of disclosure by persons providing video recording sales or rentals without written consent; exceptions; violations; penalties.

§ 1799.2. Initiation of civil action; liability for damages; limitation

(a) A person may initiate a civil action against a business entity in accordance with state law whenever a business entity violates the provisions of Section 1799.1.

(b) In any suit brought pursuant to the provisions of subdivision (a) a business entity which has violated Section 1799.1 shall be liable to the person in an amount equal to the actual damages sustained by the person as a result of such violation, but in no case less than five hundred dollars ($500), and the attendant court costs and reasonable attorneys' fees.

(c) An action to enforce any liability created under this section may be brought in any court of competent jurisdiction within two years from the date on which the cause of action arose. *(Added by Stats.1977, c. 221, p. 1017, § 1.)*

Cross References

Business entity defined for purposes of this Title, see Civil Code § 1799.

§ 1799.2

Person defined for purposes of this Title, see Civil Code § 1799.

§ 1799.3. Prohibition of disclosure by persons providing video recording sales or rentals without written consent; exceptions; violations; penalties

(a) No person providing video recording sales or rental services shall disclose any personal information or the contents of any record, including sales or rental information, which is prepared or maintained by that person, to any person, other than the individual who is the subject of the record, without the written consent of that individual.

(b) This section does not apply to any of the following:

(1) To a disclosure to any person pursuant to a subpoena or court order.

(2) To a disclosure that is in response to the proper use of discovery in a pending civil action.

(3) To a disclosure to any person acting pursuant to a lawful search warrant.

(4) To a disclosure to a law enforcement agency when required for investigations of criminal activity, unless that disclosure is prohibited by law.

(5) To a disclosure to a taxing agency for purposes of tax administration.

(6) To a disclosure of names and addresses only for commercial purposes.

(c) Any willful violation of this section shall be subject to a civil penalty not to exceed five hundred dollars ($500) for each violation, which may be recovered in a civil action brought by the person who is the subject of the records.

(d)(1) Any person who willfully violates this section on three or more occasions in any six-month period shall, in addition, be subject to a civil penalty not to exceed five hundred dollars ($500) for each violation, which may be assessed and recovered in a civil action brought in the name of the people of the State of California by the Attorney General, by any district attorney or city attorney, or by a city prosecutor in any city or city and county having a full-time city prosecutor, in any court of competent jurisdiction.

(2) If the action is brought by the Attorney General, one-half of the penalty collected shall be paid to the treasurer of the county in which the judgment was entered, and one-half to the General Fund. If the action is brought by a district attorney, the penalty collected shall be paid to the treasurer of the county in which the judgment was entered. If the action is brought by a city attorney or city prosecutor, one-half of the penalty shall be paid to the treasurer of the city in which the judgment was entered, and one-half to the treasurer of the county in which the judgment was entered.

(e) The penalty provided by this section is not an exclusive remedy, and does not affect any other relief or remedy provided by law. *(Added by Stats.1988, c. 1050, § 1. Amended by Stats.2009, c. 88 (A.B.176), § 14.)*

Cross References

Attorney General, generally, see Government Code § 12500 et seq.
Individual defined for purposes of this Title, see Civil Code § 1799.
Person defined for purposes of this Title, see Civil Code § 1799.
Record defined for purposes of this Title, see Civil Code § 1799.

Search warrants, see Penal Code § 1523 et seq.

Title 1.83

PRECOMPUTED INTEREST

Section
1799.5. Definition; limitation of duration of loan for personal, family or household purposes; written statement of intended purpose; signature; date of application.
1799.6. Public policy; waiver of rights.

§ 1799.5. Definition; limitation of duration of loan for personal, family or household purposes; written statement of intended purpose; signature; date of application

(a) "Precomputed interest" means interest, as that term is contemplated by the Truth in Lending Act, 15 United States Code 1605(a)(1), which is (1) computed by multiplying the original balance of the loan by a rate and multiplying that product by the number of payment periods elapsing between the date of the loan and the date of the last scheduled payment and (2) either added to the original principal balance of the loan in advance or subtracted from the loan proceeds.

(b) No loan which is made to a natural person primarily for personal, family, or household purposes shall provide for the payment of precomputed interest if the date on which the final installment is due, according to the original terms of the loan, is more than 62 months after the date of the loan.

(c) For purposes of determining whether a loan is covered by this title, the lender may conclusively rely on any written statement of intended purpose signed by the borrower. Such written statement may be a separate statement signed by the borrower or may be contained in a loan application or other document signed by the borrower.

(d) For purposes of this title, the term "loan" does not include the forbearance of a debt arising from a sale or lease of property and does not include any loan arising under an open end credit plan.

(e) This title shall apply only to loans made on or after January 1, 1983. *(Added by Stats.1979, c. 805, p. 2769, § 1. Amended by Stats.1980, c. 1380, p. 5005, § 2, eff. Oct. 1, 1980.)*

§ 1799.6. Public policy; waiver of rights

Any waiver of the provisions of this title is contrary to public policy, and is void and unenforceable. *(Added by Stats.2002, c. 815 (A.B.2331), § 17.)*

Title 1.84

PRECOMPUTED FINANCE CHARGE CONTRACT

Section
1799.8. Definitions; limitation of duration of contract for personal, family or household purposes; written statement of purpose; signature; date of application.
1799.85. Public policy; waiver of rights.

§ 1799.8. Definitions; limitation of duration of contract for personal, family or household purposes; written statement of purpose; signature; date of application

(a) "Precomputed finance charge" means a finance charge which is (1) computed by multiplying the original contract balance by a rate and multiplying that product by the number of payment periods elapsing between the date of the contract and the date of the last scheduled payment and (2) either added to the original contract balance in advance or subtracted from the contract balance.

(b) "Contract" means any agreement (1) providing for the construction, sale, or construction and sale of an entire residence, with or without a parcel of real property or an interest therein, or for the sale of a lot or parcel of real property, including any site preparation incidental to such sale, and (2) where the purchaser is a natural person who enters into such agreement primarily for personal, family, or household purposes.

(c) No contract as defined in subdivision (b) shall provide for the payment of a precomputed finance charge if the date on which the final installment is due, according to the original terms of the contract, is more than 62 months after the date of the contract.

(d) For purposes of determining whether a contract is covered by this title, the seller may conclusively rely on any written statement of intended purpose signed by the purchaser. Such written statement may be a separate statement signed by the purchaser or may be contained in a credit application or other document signed by the purchaser.

(e) This title shall apply only to contracts entered into on or after January 1, 1983. *(Added by Stats.1979, c. 805, p. 2770, § 2.)*

§ 1799.85. Public policy; waiver of rights

Any waiver of the provisions of this title is contrary to public policy, and is void and unenforceable. *(Added by Stats.2002, c. 815 (A.B.2331), § 18.)*

Title 1.85

CONSUMER CREDIT CONTRACTS

Section
1799.90. Definitions.
1799.91. Multiple signatures on consumer credit contracts; delivery of notice of liability to each signatory who does not receive any of the subject matter of the contract.
1799.92. Notice; method of inclusion in contract.
1799.93. Obtaining signatures on consumer credit contract containing blank spaces prohibited; notice; documents given to persons receiving notice.
1799.94. Rights and obligations of parties; nonapplication of statement.
1799.95. Action or enforcement by creditor or assignee against any person not in receipt of subject matter of contract without compliance with title; prohibition.
1799.96. Notice required by federal law; substitution.
1799.97. Security interests in religious books, artifacts or materials.

Section
1799.98. Application of provisions of title; evidentiary effect of delivery of notice to contract signatory.
1799.99. Transactions other than consumer credit contracts; action or enforcement against persons not receiving notice in manner prescribed; prohibition.
1799.100. Taking of security interest in household goods with consumer credit contract; statement of description; enforcement; civil action.
1799.101. Cosigners; delinquency; adverse information provided by creditor to consumer reporting agency; notice to cosigner; curing delinquency; operative date.
1799.102. Action by cosigner; amount; attorney fees; notification; resolution; operative date.
1799.103. Security interests in investment property pledged as collateral; conditions for provision in consumer credit contract or guarantee thereof.
1799.104. Public policy; waiver of rights.

Cross References

Fair debt collection practices, see Civil Code § 1788 et seq.

§ 1799.90. Definitions

As used in this title:

(a) "Consumer credit contract" means any of the following obligations to pay money on a deferred payment basis, where the money, property, services or other consideration which is the subject matter of the contract is primarily for personal, family or household purposes:

(1) Retail installment contracts, as defined in Section 1802.6.

(2) Retail installment accounts, as defined in Section 1802.7.

(3) Conditional sales contracts, as defined in Section 2981.

(4) Loans or extensions of credit secured by other than real property, or unsecured, for use primarily for personal, family or household purposes.

(5) Loans or extensions of credit for use primarily for personal, family or household purposes where such loans or extensions of credit are subject to the provisions of Article 7 (commencing with Section 10240) of Chapter 3 of Part I of Division 4 of the Business and Professions Code, Division 7 (commencing with Section 18000), Division 9 (commencing with Section 22000), or Division 10 (commencing with Section 24000) of the Financial Code, whether secured by real property or otherwise.

(6) Lease contracts, as defined in Section 2985.7.

(b) "Creditor" means an individual, partnership, corporation, association or other entity, however designated, who enters into or arranges for consumer credit contracts in the ordinary course of business. *(Added by Stats.1975, c. 847, p. 1912, § 1, operative April 1, 1976. Amended by Stats.1984, c. 890, § 1; Stats.1997, c. 800 (S.B.1291), § 1.)*

§ 1799.91. Multiple signatures on consumer credit contracts; delivery of notice of liability to each signatory who does not receive any of the subject matter of the contract

(a) * * * <u>Each</u> creditor who obtains the signature of more than one person on a consumer credit contract shall deliver

§ 1799.91 OBLIGATIONS

to each person who does not in fact receive any of the money, property, or services which are the subject matter of the consumer credit contract, prior to that person's becoming obligated on the consumer credit contract, a notice in English and * * * the languages set forth in subdivision (b) of Section 1632 in a clear and conspicuous manner in at least 10–point Arial equivalent type as follows:

NOTICE TO COSIGNER * * *

You are being asked to guarantee this debt. Think carefully before you do. If the borrower doesn't pay the debt, you will have to. Be sure you can afford to pay if you have to, and that you want to accept this responsibility.

You may have to pay up to the full amount of the debt if the borrower does not pay. You may also have to pay late fees or collection costs, which increase this amount.

The creditor can collect this debt from you without first trying to collect from the borrower. The creditor can use the same collection methods against you that can be used against the borrower, such as suing you, garnishing your wages, etc. If this debt is ever in default, that fact may become a part of *your* credit record.

This notice is not the contract that makes you liable for the debt.

* * *

(b) Whenever notice is required to be given under subdivision (a) or (d) and the consumer credit contract is written in a language other than English or * * * a language set forth in subdivision (b) of Section 1632, the creditor shall deliver the notice as required in subdivision (a) or (d) in English and * * * in the language in which the consumer contract is written.

(c) The requirements of subdivisions (a) and (b) do not apply to a creditor offering or extending open-end credit, as defined in Regulation Z, to joint applicants if all of the following conditions are satisfied:

(1) The application or agreement signed by each applicant clearly and conspicuously discloses that after credit approval each applicant shall have the right to use the open-end credit plan to the extent of any limit set by the creditor and may be liable for all amounts extended under the plan to any joint applicant.

(2) After credit approval, the creditor issues for the use of each applicant any credit device such as a credit card which may be used to obtain credit under the open-end credit plan and sends the credit device to the address specified in the application or otherwise delivers the credit device in a manner specified in the application or agreement signed by each applicant.

This paragraph does not apply to a creditor who does not issue a credit card or other credit device in order to obtain credit under the creditor's open-end credit plan.

(d) * * * A lessor under a lease shall deliver to each person who does not in fact receive the vehicle which is the subject of the lease contract, prior to that person becoming liable on the lease contract, the following notice in English and * * * the languages set forth in subdivision (b) of Section 1632 in a clear and conspicuous manner in at least 10–point Arial equivalent type in lieu of the notice required by subdivision (a):

NOTICE TO COSIGNER * * *

You are being asked to guarantee this lease. Think carefully before you do. If the lessee doesn't pay, you will have to. Be sure you can afford to pay if you have to, and that you want to accept this responsibility.

You may have to pay up to the full amount owed on the lease if the lessee does not pay. You may also have to pay late fees or other collection costs, which increase this amount.

The lessor can collect on the lease from you without first trying to collect from the lessee. The lessor can use the same collection methods against you that can be used against the lessee, such as suing you, garnishing your wages, etc. If this lease is ever in default, that fact may become part of *your* credit record.

This notice is not the contract that makes you liable for the lease obligation.

* * *

(e) "Regulation Z" has the meaning set forth in Section 1802.18.

(f) The word "your" in the last sentence of the third paragraph of the notice in English set forth in subdivisions (a) and (d) shall be italicized.

(g)(1) On or before January 1, 2023, the Department of Financial Protection and Innovation shall make available for download on its internet website translations of the notices set forth in subdivisions (a) and (d), which may be used to satisfy the requirements of this section.

(2) If additional languages are added to Section 1632 by subsequent amendment, the department shall make available for download on its internet website translations of the notices set forth in subdivisions (a) and (d) in the new language. (Added by Stats.1975, c. 847, p. 1912, § 1, operative April 1, 1976. Amended by Stats.1985, c. 987, § 1; Stats.1986, c. 280, § 1; Stats.1987, c. 295, § 1, eff. July 30, 1987; Stats.1997, c. 800 (S.B.1291), § 2; Stats.2022, c. 149 (S.B.633), § 1, eff. Jan. 1, 2023.)

Cross References

Consumer credit contract defined for purposes of this Title, see Civil Code § 1799.90.
Creditor defined for purposes of this Title, see Civil Code § 1799.90.

§ 1799.92. Notice; method of inclusion in contract

(a) * * * The notice required by Section 1799.91 * * * shall be provided on a separate sheet that meets the following requirements:

(1) It shall not contain any other text except as is necessary to identify the creditor and consumer credit contract or lessor and lease to which the statement refers * * *.

(2) It shall provide for the date and the person's acknowledgment of receipt.

(3) It shall be attached to and precede the consumer credit contract or lease.

(b) The creditor or lessor may develop the separate sheet described in subdivision (a) so long as it conforms to the requirements of this title. *(Added by Stats.1975, c. 847, p. 1914, § 1, operative April 1, 1976. Amended by Stats.1985, c. 987, § 2; Stats.2022, c. 149 (S.B.633), § 2, eff. Jan. 1, 2023.)*

Cross References

Consumer credit contract defined for purposes of this Title, see Civil Code § 1799.90.

Creditor defined for purposes of this Title, see Civil Code § 1799.90.

§ 1799.93. Obtaining signatures on consumer credit contract containing blank spaces prohibited; notice; documents given to persons receiving notice

(a) The creditor shall not obtain the signature of any person entitled to notice under Section 1799.91 if the consumer credit contract contains blank spaces to be filled in after the person's signature has been obtained.

(b) The creditor shall give each person entitled to notice under Section 1799.91 a copy of the debt instrument and security agreement or deed of trust, if any, evidencing the consumer credit contract and, if separate therefrom, a copy of the notice required by Section 1799.91 and a copy of the document evidencing that person's obligations. *(Added by Stats.1975, c. 847, p. 1914, § 1, operative April 1, 1976. Amended by Stats.1985, c. 987, § 3.)*

Cross References

Consumer credit contract defined for purposes of this Title, see Civil Code § 1799.90.

Creditor defined for purposes of this Title, see Civil Code § 1799.90.

§ 1799.94. Rights and obligations of parties; nonapplication of statement

The text of the statement required by Section 1799.91 of this title shall not be construed to alter or affect the rights and obligations of the parties to any consumer credit contract. *(Added by Stats.1975, c. 847, p. 1914, § 1, operative April 1, 1976.)*

Cross References

Consumer credit contract defined for purposes of this Title, see Civil Code § 1799.90.

§ 1799.95. Action or enforcement by creditor or assignee against any person not in receipt of subject matter of contract without compliance with title; prohibition

No action shall be brought, nor shall any security interest be enforced, by any creditor or any assignee of a creditor on any consumer credit contract which fails to comply with this title against any person, however designated, who is entitled to notice under Section 1799.91 and who does not in fact receive any of the money, property or services which are the subject matter of the consumer credit contract.

Nothing herein shall affect the rights of any bona fide purchaser for value of property sold pursuant to the enforcement of a security interest if the purchase was made without notice of any facts constituting a violation of this title. *(Added by Stats.1975, c. 847, p. 1914, § 1, operative April 1, 1976. Amended by Stats.1985, c. 987, § 4.)*

Cross References

Consumer credit contract defined for purposes of this Title, see Civil Code § 1799.90.

Creditor defined for purposes of this Title, see Civil Code § 1799.90.

§ 1799.96. Notice required by federal law; substitution

If federal law or regulations require or permit the use of a notice substantially similar to that required by Section 1799.91, the use of such federally sanctioned notice and an accurate * * * translation thereof into the languages set forth in subdivision (b) of Section 1632 shall constitute compliance with Section 1799.91. However, the other provisions of this title shall remain unaffected. *(Added by Stats.1975, c. 847, p. 1914, § 1, operative April 1, 1976. Amended by Stats.2022, c. 149 (S.B.633), § 3, eff. Jan. 1, 2023.)*

§ 1799.97. Security interests in religious books, artifacts or materials

(a) No consumer credit contract shall provide for a security interest in any religious books, religious artifacts, or religious materials, valued at less than five hundred dollars ($500), unless the religious books, artifacts, or materials are specifically pledged as collateral.

(b) Any provision in any contract which provides for a security interest in violation of subdivision (a) shall be void and unenforceable. *(Added by Stats.1984, c. 732, § 1.)*

Cross References

Consumer credit contract defined for purposes of this Title, see Civil Code § 1799.90.

§ 1799.98. Application of provisions of title; evidentiary effect of delivery of notice to contract signatory

(a) Nothing in this title shall be construed to make applicable or affect or operate as a waiver of any of the provisions of any of the following:

(1) Title 13 (commencing with Section 2787) of Part 4 of Division 3 of this code.

(2) Parts 1 (commencing with Section 700), 2 (commencing with Section 760), 3 (commencing with Section 900), and 4 (commencing with Section 1100) of Division 4 of the Family Code.

(3) Sections 4301 and 4302 of the Family Code.

(b) The delivery of notice pursuant to Section 1799.91 is not evidence that the person to whom the notice was delivered entered or did not enter the transaction in the capacity of a surety. *(Added by Stats.1985, c. 987, § 5. Amended by Stats.1992, c. 163 (A.B.2641), § 10, operative Jan. 1, 1994; Stats.1993, c. 219 (A.B.1500), § 28.5.)*

§ 1799.99. Transactions other than consumer credit contracts; action or enforcement against persons not receiving notice in manner prescribed; prohibition

(a) This section applies to transactions, other than consumer credit contracts as defined in Section 1799.90, which are subject to 16 C.F.R. 444.3, 12 C.F.R. 227.14, or 12 C.F.R. 535.3, whichever is applicable to the creditor.

(b) Unless the persons who are obligated under the transaction are married to each other, no action shall be brought, nor shall any security interest be enforced, against any person entitled to receive notice under 16 C.F.R. 444.3, 12 C.F.R. 227.14, or 12 C.F.R. 535.3, whichever is applicable to the creditor, if that person did not receive the notice in the manner prescribed by the applicable regulation and an accurate Spanish translation of the notice. *(Added by Stats.1985, c. 987, § 6. Amended by Stats.1988, c. 160, § 15.)*

Cross References

Consumer credit contract defined for purposes of this Title, see Civil Code § 1799.90.

Creditor defined for purposes of this Title, see Civil Code § 1799.90.

§ 1799.100. Taking of security interest in household goods with consumer credit contract; statement of description; enforcement; civil action

(a) It is unlawful for any person to take a security interest in any household goods, as defined in subdivision (g), in connection with a consumer credit contract or other credit obligation incurred primarily for personal, family, or household purposes unless (1) the person takes possession of the household goods or (2) the purchase price of the household goods was financed through the consumer credit contract or credit obligation.

(b) An agreement or other document creating a nonpossessory security interest in personal property as defined in subdivision (d) in connection with a consumer credit contract or other credit obligation incurred primarily for personal, family, or household purposes shall contain a statement of description reviewed and signed by the consumer indicating each specific item of the personal property in which the security interest is taken. A consumer credit contract or other credit obligation subject to the Unruh Act (Chapter 1 (commencing with Section 1801) of Title 2) that complies with the provisions of subdivision (a) of Section 1803.3, or of subdivision (f) of Section 1810.1, shall be deemed to comply with this subdivision.

(c) Notwithstanding any other provision of law, a person who has a nonpossessory security interest in personal property, described in subdivision (d), taken in connection with a consumer credit contract or other credit obligation incurred primarily for personal, family, or household purposes shall only enforce the security interest by judicial action unless the property is abandoned or freely and voluntarily surrendered by the consumer.

(d) The provisions of subdivisions (b) and (c) apply only to the following types of personal property:

(1) Any goods, as defined in paragraph (44) of subdivision (a) of Section 9102 of the Commercial Code, except for vessels, vehicles, and aircraft, that are used or bought for use primarily for personal, family, or household purposes and that has a fair market value of less than one thousand dollars ($1,000) per individual item at the time the security interest is created.

(2) The property described in Section 704.050 and subdivision (a) of Section 704.060 of the Code of Civil Procedure, except for vessels, vehicles, and aircraft.

(e) Any security interest taken in violation of either subdivision (a) or (b) is void and unenforceable.

(f) Any person injured by a violation of this section may bring a civil action for the recovery of damages, equitable relief, and attorney's fees and costs.

(g) For the purpose of this section:

(1) "Household goods" means and includes clothing, furniture, appliances, one radio, one television, linens, china, crockery, kitchenware, personal effects, and wedding rings. "Household goods" does not include works of art, electronic entertainment equipment (except one radio and one television), items acquired as antiques, and jewelry (except wedding rings).

(2) "Antique" means any item over one hundred years of age, including such items that have been repaired or renovated without changing their original form or character. *(Added by Stats.1989, c. 525, § 1. Amended by Stats.1990, c. 31 (A.B.1259), § 1, eff. March 26, 1990; Stats.1999, c. 991 (S.B.45), § 3.5, operative July 1, 2001.)*

Cross References

Consumer credit contract defined for purposes of this Title, see Civil Code § 1799.90.

Secured transactions, sufficiency of description, see Commercial Code § 9108.

§ 1799.101. Cosigners; delinquency; adverse information provided by creditor to consumer reporting agency; notice to cosigner; curing delinquency; operative date

(a) For the purposes of this section, the following terms are defined as follows:

(1) "Adverse information" means information directly or indirectly indicating that a delinquency has occurred, because a cosigner has not complied with the contractual provisions of a consumer credit contract.

(2) "Collection action" means requesting a cosigner to pay all or part of the obligation on a consumer credit contract.

(3) "Cosigner" means a natural person, other than the primary obligor or the spouse of the primary obligor, who renders himself or herself liable for the obligation on a consumer credit contract without compensation. The term includes a person whose signature is requested by a creditor as a condition to granting credit to another person. A person who does not receive goods, services, or money in return for executing a consumer credit contract does not receive compensation within the meaning of this section. "Cosigner" does not include a joint applicant for open-end credit pursuant to subdivision (c) of Section 1799.91. A person is a cosigner within the meaning of this section whether or not he or she is designated as such on a consumer credit contract or other document creating the consumer credit contract obligation for the cosigner.

(4) "Delinquency" means a failure to make timely payment to the creditor of all or a portion of any installment under a consumer credit contract.

(5) "Notice" means a writing which describes, recites, or otherwise refers to a delinquency.

(6) "Obligation" means an indebtedness incurred by an individual for personal, family, or household purposes.

(7) "Person" means an individual, firm, partnership, association, limited liability company, or corporation.

(8) "Primary obligor" means one or more persons, other than a cosigner, who sign a consumer credit contract and assume an obligation as debtor under that contract.

(b) Except as provided in subdivisions (d) and (e), no creditor shall provide any adverse information with respect to any cosigner, to a consumer credit reporting agency regarding a delinquency on a consumer credit contract entered into on or after July 1, 1992, unless, at or before the time the information is provided to the consumer credit reporting agency, written notice of the delinquency is provided to the cosigner.

(c) No creditor shall provide any information regarding the cosigner's obligation on a consumer credit contract to a debt collector, as defined in subdivision (c) of Section 1788.2, until notice has been provided to the cosigner under subdivision (b).

(d) The notice requirements of subdivisions (b) and (c) do not apply to any cosigner whose address, as shown in the creditor's records respecting the consumer credit contract, is the same as the primary obligor.

(e) The notice requirements of subdivisions (b) and (c) shall be satisfied by mailing a copy of the required notice to the cosigner at the cosigner's address, as shown in the creditor's records respecting the consumer credit contract. However, if more than one cosigner reside at the same address, as shown in the creditor's records respecting the consumer credit contract, a notice addressed to any cosigner at that address shall be deemed notice to all the cosigners residing at that address.

(f) Nothing in this section shall require any particular form or language with respect to a notice of delinquency sent to either a primary obligor or cosigner.

(g) Within a reasonable time after a creditor has reported to a credit reporting agency that a delinquency or delinquencies that have been reported to the consumer credit reporting agency and included in the cosigner's file maintained by the consumer credit reporting agency have been cured, the consumer credit reporting agency shall indicate in the file that the payment was made.

(h) Nothing in this section shall be construed to require notice of a delinquency to be provided to a cosigner in any instance not expressly specified in this section, or to provide notice to persons other than cosigners.

(i) This section shall become operative on July 1, 1992. (Added by Stats.1990, c. 1549 (A.B.2729), § 1, operative July 1, 1992. Amended by Stats.1991, c. 131 (A.B.956), § 1, operative July 1, 1992; Stats.1994, c. 1010 (S.B.2053), § 42.)

Cross References

Consumer credit contract defined for purposes of this Title, see Civil Code § 1799.90.
Creditor defined for purposes of this Title, see Civil Code § 1799.90.

§ 1799.102. Action by cosigner; amount; attorney fees; notification; resolution; operative date

(a) A cosigner who suffers a loss as a result of a violation of Section 1799.101 may bring an action to recover actual damages or two hundred fifty dollars ($250), whichever is greater, and reasonable attorney fees.

(b) The cosigner shall, not less than 30 days prior to bringing an action pursuant to subdivision (a), notify the person alleged to have violated Section 1799.101 of the cosigner's intention to bring an action. The notice shall include a statement of the specific evidence that proves the loss suffered by the cosigner. If within 25 days after the date of receiving the notice, the person alleged to have violated Section 1799.101 tenders to the cosigner an amount equal to the loss, or otherwise resolves the matter to the cosigner's satisfaction, the cosigner shall be barred from further recovery of that loss, including reasonable attorney fees.

(c) This section shall become operative on July 1, 1992. (Added by Stats.1990, c. 1549 (A.B.2729), § 2, operative July 1, 1992.)

§ 1799.103. Security interests in investment property pledged as collateral; conditions for provision in consumer credit contract or guarantee thereof

No consumer credit contract or guarantee of a consumer credit contract shall provide for a security interest in any investment property, as defined in paragraph (49) of subdivision (a) of Section 9102 of the Commercial Code, that is pledged as collateral, unless (a) the contract either specifically identifies the investment property as collateral or (b) the secured party is a securities intermediary, as defined in paragraph (14) of subdivision (a) of Section 8102 of the Commercial Code, or commodity intermediary, as defined in paragraph (17) of subdivision (a) of Section 9102 of the Commercial Code, with respect to the investment property. The identification of an account shall include the name of the holder, account number, and name of the institute holding the investment property. In the event that a consumer credit contract or guarantee does not comply with this section, the security interest in the investment property is void. (Added by Stats.1996, c. 497 (S.B.1591), § 1, operative Jan. 1, 1997. Amended by Stats.1999, c. 991 (S.B.45), § 4, operative July 1, 2001.)

Cross References

Consumer credit contract defined for purposes of this Title, see Civil Code § 1799.90.
Secured transactions, sufficiency of description, see Commercial Code § 9108.

§ 1799.104. Public policy; waiver of rights

Any waiver of the provisions of this title is contrary to public policy, and is void and unenforceable. (Added by Stats.2002, c. 815 (A.B.2331), § 19.)

Title 1.86

CONSUMER CONTRACT AWARENESS ACT OF 1990

Section
1799.200. Short title.
1799.201. Definitions.
1799.202. Contract; mailing or delivery; copies.
1799.203. Compliance with and application of § 1799.202.
1799.204. Contract signed by more than one consumer; mailing or delivery.
1799.205. Failure to comply; liability; remedies; basis for rescission.
1799.206. Delivery of copy to guarantor; failure to comply with section; liability; basis for rescission.
1799.207. Public policy; waiver of rights.
1800. Repealed.

Cross References

Insurance, arranging premium financing, requirements, see Insurance Code § 778.4.

§ 1799.200. Short title

This title shall be known and may be cited as the Consumer Contract Awareness Act of 1990. *(Added by Stats.1990, c. 1079 (S.B.1107), § 1, operative July 1, 1991.)*

§ 1799.201. Definitions

As used in this title:

(a) "Consumer" means a natural person who has entered into a consumer contract with a seller.

(b) "Consumer contract" means a writing prepared by a seller and, except as provided in subdivision (c) of Section 1799.202, signed, or to be signed, by a consumer, which provides (1) for the sale or lease of goods or services that are purchased or leased primarily for personal, family, or household purposes, or (2) for extension of credit, the proceeds of which are used primarily for personal, family, or household purposes. Without affecting the enforceability of any incidental provision contained therein, an application for credit shall not be considered to be a consumer contract for purposes of this section even if it contains incidental provisions, such as the consumer's consent to a credit review, a certification of the accuracy of the information furnished, or the consumer's agreement to the terms that will be furnished to the consumer pursuant to this title.

(c) "Consumer contract guaranty" means a writing prepared by a seller and signed, or to be signed, by a guarantor which guarantees the obligation of a consumer under a consumer contract.

(d) "Copy" means a reproduction, facsimile, or duplicate.

(e) "Days" means calendar days.

(f) "Goods" means tangible and intangible personal property.

(g) "Guarantor" means a person who guarantees the obligation of a consumer under a consumer contract by signing a consumer contract guaranty.

(h) "Seller" means a person who has entered into a consumer contract with a consumer.

(i) "Services" means work, labor, and services, including depository services and other banking services.

(j) "Financial institution" means any commercial bank, trust company, savings and loan association, credit union, industrial loan company, insurance company, or person engaged in the business of lending money. *(Added by Stats.1990, c. 1079 (S.B.1107), § 1, operative July 1, 1991. Amended by Stats.1991, c. 1129 (S.B.108), § 1; Stats.1992, c. 879 (A.B.3468), § 1.)*

§ 1799.202. Contract; mailing or delivery; copies

(a) Except as otherwise provided in this title, a seller shall deliver a copy of a consumer contract to the consumer at the time it is signed by the consumer if the consumer contract is signed at a place of business of the seller. If the consumer contract is not signed by the consumer at a place of business of the seller, and the seller has not provided a copy of the consumer contract for the consumer which the consumer is instructed to keep, the seller shall mail or deliver a copy of it to the consumer within 10 calendar days after the seller receives the signed consumer contract. In any case, the copy of the contract provided to the consumer shall not contain any blank spaces to be completed after the consumer signs the contract, shall contain the signature of the seller if it provides for that signature, and may also contain the signature of the consumer.

(b) A seller that is a financial institution need not deliver to the consumer, pursuant to subdivision (a), any writing which the consumer contract incorporates by reference if either of the following conditions apply:

(1) The writing was previously delivered or mailed to the consumer.

(2) The writing was not prepared by the seller.

(c) If the consumer contract (1) is wholly or partly contained on a card or other writing which is used to identify the consumer in connection with a deposit account, safe deposit box, safekeeping agreement, or other service offered by a financial institution, and (2) contains information particular to the consumer's account, box, or other arrangement that, if known by a third party, could be used by the third party to cause loss to the consumer or financial institution, the copy of the contract furnished to the consumer need not contain the consumer's signature or any of the identifying information particular to the consumer's account, box, or other arrangement.

For purposes of this subdivision, a document which includes the same terms as those contained in the consumer contract shall be deemed a copy.

(d) Within a reasonable time after receipt of a written request from a consumer, a seller or financial institution shall mail a copy of the consumer's completed consumer credit application, which may, but need not, contain any information completed or added by the seller or financial institution, to the consumer at the address indicated on the request. By making a written request, the consumer shall conclusively be deemed to have waived any action against the seller or financial institution, as well as its employees or agents, on any theory, at law or in equity, arising directly or indirectly out of the mailing or other delivery of the copy, including any information added to the application by the seller or financial institution and included in the copy. The seller or financial institution may specify the address to which such a request may be sent, may charge the consumer a reasonable copying fee, and shall not be obligated to provide the copy until the fee is paid. *(Added by Stats.1990, c. 1079 (S.B.1107), § 1, operative July 1, 1991. Amended by Stats.1991, c. 1129 (S.B.108), § 2; Stats.1992, c. 879 (A.B.3468), § 2.)*

§ 1799.203. Compliance with and application of § 1799.202

(a) It shall be deemed compliance with Section 1799.202 if a copy of any consumer contract which is subject to Article 10 (commencing with Section 1810.1) of Chapter 1 of Title 2, or which is an open-end consumer credit plan subject to Section 127 of the federal Truth in Lending Act (15 U.S.C. 1637), is delivered or mailed to the consumer before the consumer enters into a transaction covered and permitted by the consumer contract.

(b) Section 1799.202 does not apply to any of the following:

(1) A consumer contract for the purchase of goods by mail if the seller permits the consumer to examine the goods for seven calendar days and cancel the consumer contract and receive a full refund within 30 calendar days for returned unused and undamaged goods.

(2) A written contract created by, and consisting of, an exchange of letters by mail.

(3) Any consumer contract which is required to be mailed or delivered at a time prescribed by another law of this state or the United States. *(Added by Stats.1990, c. 1079 (S.B. 1107), § 1, operative July 1, 1991. Amended by Stats.1991, c. 1129 (S.B.108), § 3.)*

§ 1799.204. Contract signed by more than one consumer; mailing or delivery

If more than one consumer has signed a consumer contact,[1] the seller may comply with Section 1799.202 by mailing or delivering the copy to any one of the consumers who reside at the same address. A copy shall also be mailed or delivered to any other consumer who has signed the consumer contract and who does not reside at the same address. *(Added by Stats.1990, c. 1079 (S.B.1107), § 1, operative July 1, 1991.)*

[1] So in enrolled bill. Probably should be "contract".

§ 1799.205. Failure to comply; liability; remedies; basis for rescission

(a) A seller who fails to comply with Section 1799.202 is liable to the consumer for any actual damages suffered by the consumer as the result of that failure. The remedy provided by this subdivision is nonexclusive and is in addition to any other remedies or penalties available under other laws of this state.

(b) Failure to comply with Section 1799.202 does not create an independent basis for the rescission, but is admissible to establish a basis for the rescission of the contract otherwise authorized by law. *(Added by Stats.1990, c. 1079 (S.B.1107), § 1, operative July 1, 1991. Amended by Stats. 1991, c. 1129 (S.B.108), § 4.)*

§ 1799.206. Delivery of copy to guarantor; failure to comply with section; liability; basis for rescission

(a) Except as otherwise provided in this section, a seller shall deliver a copy of the consumer contract guaranty to the guarantor at the time the consumer contract guaranty is signed by the guarantor if the consumer contract guaranty is signed by the guarantor at a place of business of the seller. If the consumer contract guaranty is not signed by the guarantor at a place of business of the seller, and the seller has not provided a copy of the consumer contract guaranty for the guarantor which the guarantor is able to keep, the seller shall mail or deliver a copy of the consumer contract guaranty to the guarantor within 10 calendar days after the seller receives the signed consumer contract guaranty. In any case, the copy of the consumer contract guaranty provided to the guarantor shall not contain any blank spaces to be completed after the guarantor signs the guaranty, shall contain the signature of the seller if it provides for that signature, and may also contain the signature of the guarantor.

(b) If more than one guarantor has signed the consumer contract guaranty, the seller may comply with subdivision (a) by mailing or delivering the copy to any one of the guarantors who reside at the same address. A copy shall also be mailed or delivered to any guarantor who has signed the consumer contract guaranty and who does not reside at the same address.

(c) A seller that fails to comply with this section is liable to the guarantor for any actual damages suffered by the guarantor as the result of that failure. The remedy provided by this subdivision is nonexclusive and in addition to any other remedies or penalties available under other laws of this state.

(d) Failure to comply with this section does not create a new basis for rescission, but is admissible to establish a basis for rescission of the consumer contract guaranty otherwise authorized by law. *(Added by Stats.1990, c. 1079 (S.B.1107), § 1, operative July 1, 1991. Amended by Stats.1991, c. 1129 (S.B.108), § 5; Stats.1992, c. 879 (A.B.3468), § 3.)*

§ 1799.207. Public policy; waiver of rights

Any waiver of the provisions of this title is contrary to public policy, and is void and unenforceable. *(Added by Stats.2002, c. 815 (A.B.2331), § 20.)*

§ 1800. Repealed by Stats.1963, c. 819, p. 1997, § 2, eff. Jan. 1, 1965

Title 2

CREDIT SALES

Chapter	Section
1. Retail Installment Sales	1801
2. Credit Transactions Regarding Women	1812.30
3. Retail Credit Advisory Committee [Repealed]	

Cross References

Savings association, issuance of credit cards, application of this Title, see Financial Code § 7454.

Spanish language translation of contracts or agreements, necessity, exceptions, see Civil Code § 1632.

CHAPTER 1. RETAIL INSTALLMENT SALES

Article	Section
1. General Provisions	1801
2. Definitions	1802
3. Provisions of Retail Installment Contracts	1803.1
4. Restrictions on Retail Installment Contracts	1804.1
5. Finance Charge Limitation	1805.1
6. Payments	1806.1
7. Refinancing and Consolidation	1807.1
8. Add-On Sales	1808.1
9. Terms of Purchase by Financing Agency	1809.1
10. Retail Installment Accounts	1810
10.5. Retail Installment Account Credit Card Periodic Rate Disclosures	1810.20
11. Attorney's Fees and Court Costs	1811.1

OBLIGATIONS

Article		Section
12.	Attachment [Repealed]	
12.1.	Repossession and Resale	1812.2
12.2.	Penalties	1812.6
12.3.	Actions	1812.10
12.4.	Financing Retail Purchases	1812.20

Cross References

Refinancing of loan subject to this chapter, required conditions, see Financial Code § 22341.

Secured transactions, action in which deficiency or surplus is in issue, see Commercial Code § 9626.

ARTICLE 1. GENERAL PROVISIONS

Section
1801. Citation.
1801.1. Waiver of provisions.
1801.2. Partial invalidity.
1801.3. Repealed.
1801.4. Application of chapter.
1801.5. Regulation Z; disclosures.
1801.6. Legislative finding and purpose; application of chapter; loans by supervised financial organization.
1801.7. Application of chapter; premium finance agreements entered into by industrial loan company.

Cross References

Consumer credit contracts, notice to multiple signatories, see Civil Code § 1799.90 et seq.

Finance charges, prejudgment interest, see Civil Code § 3289.5.

Finance lenders law, loan conditions to refinance retail installment contracts, see Financial Code § 22341.

Membership camping contracts, application of this act, see Civil Code § 1812.301.

§ 1801. Citation

This chapter may be cited as the "Unruh Act." *(Added by Stats.1959, c. 201, p. 2092, § 1, operative Jan. 1, 1960.)*

Cross References

Automobile Sales Finance Act, see Civil Code § 2981 et seq.

Conflicts between Retail Installment Sales Act and Division 9 of the Commercial Code, see Commercial Code § 9203.

Extinction of contracts, see Civil Code § 1682 et seq.

Sales, see Commercial Code § 2101 et seq.

Secured transactions, see Commercial Code § 9101 et seq.

Unlawful contracts, see Civil Code § 1667 et seq.

§ 1801.1. Waiver of provisions

Any waiver by the buyer of the provisions of this chapter shall be deemed contrary to public policy and shall be unenforceable and void. *(Added by Stats.1959, c. 201, p. 2092, § 1. Amended by Stats.1963, c. 1603, p. 3181, § 1.)*

Cross References

Civil actions, place of trial, consent to retention of case, see Code of Civil Procedure § 396a.

Retail buyer or buyer defined for purposes of this Chapter, see Civil Code § 1802.4.

Waiver of advantage, law established for public reason, see Civil Code § 3513.

Waiver of code provisions, generally, see Civil Code § 3268.

§ 1801.2. Partial invalidity

If any provision of this chapter or the application thereof to any person or circumstances is held unconstitutional, the remainder of the chapter and the application of such provision to other persons or circumstances shall not be affected thereby. *(Added by Stats.1959, c. 201, p. 2092, § 1, operative Jan. 1, 1960.)*

Cross References

Person defined for purposes of this Chapter, see Civil Code § 1802.15.

§ 1801.3. Repealed by Stats.1963, c. 1603, p. 3181, § 2

§ 1801.4. Application of chapter

The provisions of this chapter shall not apply to any contract or series of contracts providing for: (a) the construction, sale, or construction and sale of an entire residence, including a mobilehome, or all or part of a structure designed for commerical[1] or industrial occupancy, with or without a parcel of real property or an interest therein, (b) for the sale of a lot or parcel of real property, including any site preparation incidental to such sale, (c) the sale of any aircraft required to be registered under the Federal Aviation Act of 1958, or (d) the sale of any vessel as defined in subdivision (a) of Section 9840 of the Vehicle Code if the cash price of such vessel, including accessories and equipment sold in conjunction therewith, exceeds twenty-five thousand dollars ($25,000). *(Added by Stats.1969, c. 554, p. 1180, § 1. Amended by Stats.1980, c. 437, p. 922, § 1; Stats.1980, c. 1149, p. 3722, § 6.)*

[1] So in chaptered copy. Probably should be "commercial".

Cross References

Cash price defined for purposes of this Chapter, see Civil Code § 1802.8.

Retail installment contract or contract defined for purposes of this Chapter, see Civil Code § 1802.6.

Retail installment sale or sale defined for purposes of this Chapter, see Civil Code § 1802.5.

§ 1801.5. Regulation Z; disclosures

Notwithstanding any other provision of this chapter to the contrary, any information required to be disclosed in a retail installment contract or other document under this chapter may be disclosed in any manner, method, or terminology required or permitted under Regulation Z, as in effect at the time such disclosure is made, except that permitted by paragraph (2) of subdivision (c) of Section 226.18 of Regulation Z, provided that all of the requirements and limitations set forth in subdivision (b) of Section 1803.3 are satisfied. Nothing contained in this chapter shall be deemed to prohibit the disclosure in such contract or other document of additional information required or permitted under Regulation Z, as in effect at the time such disclosure is made. *(Added by Stats.1970, c. 546, p. 1041, § 1. Amended by Stats.1979, c. 805, p. 2770, § 3; Stats.1981, c. 1075, p. 4114, § 1, operative Oct. 1, 1982.)*

Cross References

Regulation Z, see Civil Code § 1802.18.

Retail installment contract or contract defined for purposes of this Chapter, see Civil Code § 1802.6.

§ 1801.6. Legislative finding and purpose; application of chapter; loans by supervised financial organization

(a) The Legislature finds that the decisional law of this state regarding the characterization of credit transactions as either loans or credit sales has been made unclear by the holding in King v. Central Bank, 18 Cal.3d 840. It is the purpose of subdivision (b) to clarify such law by establishing standards for determining whether a transaction is subject to the Unruh Act. However, subdivision (b) is not intended to abrogate the judicial principle that the substance of a transaction rather than its form is determinative of its characterization as a loan or credit sale as exemplified by such decisions as Verbeck v. Clymer, 202 Cal. 557, Milana v. Credit Discount Co., 27 Cal.2d 335, and Boerner v. Colwell Co., 21 Cal.3d 37. Subdivision (b) also is not intended to abrogate the decision in Morgan v. Reasor Corp., 69 Cal.2d 881, to the extent such decision has not been modified by Chapter 554 of the Statutes of 1969 or other legislative amendments to the Unruh Act.

(b) The provisions of this chapter shall not apply to any transaction in the form of a loan made by a supervised financial organization to a buyer of goods or services where all or a portion of the loan proceeds are used to purchase such goods or services, whether or not the seller of such goods or services arranges the loan or participates in the preparation of the loan documents, unless the supervised financial organization and the seller:

(1) Are related by common ownership and control and the relationship was a material factor in the loan transaction; or

(2) Share in the profits and losses of either or both the sale and the loan.

(c) For purposes of this section:

(1) The term "supervised financial organization" means a person organized, chartered, or holding a license or authorization certificate to make loans pursuant to the laws of this state or the United States who is subject to supervision by an official or agency of this state or the United States.

(2) Receipt of a loan commission, brokerage or referral fee by a seller from a supervised financial organization shall not constitute a sharing of profits of the supervised financial organization, provided that such payment (i) is reasonable under the circumstances existing at the time the loan is consummated, and (ii) is not refundable or is wholly or partly refundable only if the loan is voluntarily paid in full prior to its scheduled maturity. For purposes of this paragraph, a loan commission, brokerage or referral fee not exceeding the greater of 1 percent of the amount financed (as that term is defined by Regulation Z with respect to loans), or twenty dollars ($20), is reasonable under the circumstances existing at the time the loan is consummated.

(3) Payment of money by a seller to a supervised financial organization pursuant to an actual or alleged contractual or statutory obligation to indemnify a supervised financial organization for losses incurred as a result of the assertion by a buyer of claims or defenses with respect to goods or services purchased with loan proceeds shall not constitute participation in or sharing of loan losses by the seller. (Added by Stats.1979, c. 1151, p. 4221, § 1. Amended by Stats.1980, c. 438, p. 922, § 1.)

Cross References

Amount financed defined for purposes of this Chapter, see Civil Code § 1802.11.
Goods defined for purposes of this Chapter, see Civil Code § 1802.1.
Person defined for purposes of this Chapter, see Civil Code § 1802.15.
Prohibition against requiring purchaser to obtain financing from particular source, see Civil Code § 1812.20.
Regulation Z defined for purposes of this Chapter, see Civil Code § 1802.18.
Retail buyer or buyer defined for purposes of this Chapter, see Civil Code § 1802.4.
Retail installment sale or sale defined for purposes of this Chapter, see Civil Code § 1802.5.
Retail seller or seller defined for purposes of this Chapter, see Civil Code § 1802.3.
Services defined for purposes of this Chapter, see Civil Code § 1802.2.

§ 1801.7. Application of chapter; premium finance agreements entered into by industrial loan company

The provisions of this chapter shall not apply to any premium finance agreement entered into by an industrial loan company pursuant to Chapter 8 (commencing with Section 18560) of Division 7 of the Financial Code. (Added by Stats.1979, c. 1151, p. 4221, § 2.)

ARTICLE 2. DEFINITIONS

Section
Section	
1802.	Construction of chapter.
1802.1.	Goods.
1802.2.	Services.
1802.3.	Retail seller; seller.
1802.4.	Retail buyer; buyer.
1802.5.	Retail installment sale; sale.
1802.6.	Retail installment contract; contract.
1802.7.	Retail installment account; installment account; revolving account.
1802.8.	Cash price.
1802.9.	Total sale price.
1802.10.	Finance charge.
1802.11.	Amount financed; unpaid balance.
1802.12.	Total of payments.
1802.13.	Holder.
1802.14.	Official fees.
1802.15.	Person.
1802.16.	Financing agency.
1802.17.	Billing cycle.
1802.18.	Regulation Z.
1802.19.	Contracts and accounts; offer or agreement to sell or buy in this state; application of chapter.
1802.20.	Simple-interest basis.
1802.21.	Precomputed basis.

§ 1802. Construction of chapter

Unless the context or subject matter otherwise requires, the definitions given in this article govern the construction of this chapter. (Added by Stats.1959, c. 201, p. 2092, § 1, operative Jan. 1, 1960.)

§ 1802

Cross References

Words and phrases, construction, see Civil Code § 13.

§ 1802.1. Goods

"Goods" means tangible chattels bought for use primarily for personal, family or household purposes, including certificates or coupons exchangeable for such goods, and including goods which, at the time of the sale or subsequently are to be so affixed to real property as to become a part of such real property whether or not severable therefrom, but does not include any vehicle required to be registered under the Vehicle Code, nor any goods sold or leased with such a vehicle if sold under a contract governed by Section 2982 or leased under a contract governed by Section 2985.7. "Goods" also includes a trailer which is sold in conjunction with a vessel, as defined in subdivision (a) of Section 9840 of the Vehicle Code, unless the sales transaction is exempted under Section 1801.4. As used in this section, "trailer" means a vehicle designed solely for carrying vessels. *(Added by Stats.1959, c. 201, p. 2092, § 1, operative Jan. 1, 1960. Amended by Stats.1984, c. 1114, § 1; Stats.1985, c. 1186, § 1.)*

Cross References

Goods defined,
   Consumers Legal Remedies Act, see Civil Code § 1761.
   Sales Act, see Commercial Code § 2105.
Retail installment contract or contract defined for purposes of this Chapter, see Civil Code § 1802.6.
Retail installment sale or sale defined for purposes of this Chapter, see Civil Code § 1802.5.
Vehicles subject to registration, see Vehicle Code § 4000 et seq.

§ 1802.2. Services

"Services" means work, labor and services, for other than a commercial or business use, including services furnished in connection with the sale or repair of goods as defined in Section 1802.1 or furnished in connection with the repair of motor vehicles (except for service contracts as defined by subdivision (p) of Section 2981 which are sold in conjunction with the sale or lease of a vehicle required to be registered under the Vehicle Code) or in connection with the improvement of real property or the providing of insurance, but does not include the services of physicians or dentists, nor services for which the tariffs, rates, charges, costs or expenses, including in each instance the deferred payment price, are required by law to be filed with and approved by the federal government or any official, department, division, commission or agency of the United States. *(Added by Stats.1959, c. 201, p. 2092, § 1, operative Jan. 1, 1960. Amended by Stats.1968, c. 48, p. 188, § 1; Stats.1970, c. 546, p. 1041, § 2; Stats.1980, c. 1380, p. 5005, § 3, eff. Oct. 1, 1980; Stats.1981, c. 1075, p. 4114, § 1.5, operative Oct. 1, 1982; Stats.1984, c. 1114, § 2.)*

Cross References

Retail installment contract or contract defined for purposes of this Chapter, see Civil Code § 1802.6.
Retail installment sale or sale defined for purposes of this Chapter, see Civil Code § 1802.5.

§ 1802.3. Retail seller; seller

"Retail seller" or "seller" means a person engaged in the business of selling goods or furnishing services to retail buyers. *(Added by Stats.1959, c. 201, p. 2093, § 1, operative Jan. 1, 1960.)*

Cross References

Goods defined for purposes of this Chapter, see Civil Code § 1802.1.
Person defined for purposes of this Chapter, see Civil Code § 1802.15.
Retail buyer or buyer defined for purposes of this Chapter, see Civil Code § 1802.4.
Seller defined, see Commercial Code § 2103.
Services defined for purposes of this Chapter, see Civil Code § 1802.2.

§ 1802.4. Retail buyer; buyer

"Retail buyer" or "buyer" means a person who buys goods or obtains services from a retail seller in a retail installment sale and not principally for the purpose of resale. *(Added by Stats.1959, c. 201, p. 2093, § 1, operative Jan. 1, 1960.)*

Cross References

Buyer defined, see Commercial Code § 2103.
Goods defined for purposes of this Chapter, see Civil Code § 1802.1.
Person defined for purposes of this Chapter, see Civil Code § 1802.15.
Retail installment sale or sale defined for purposes of this Chapter, see Civil Code § 1802.5.
Retail seller or seller defined for purposes of this Chapter, see Civil Code § 1802.3.
Services defined for purposes of this Chapter, see Civil Code § 1802.2.

§ 1802.5. Retail installment sale; sale

"Retail installment sale" or "sale" means the sale of goods or the furnishing of services by a retail seller to a retail buyer for a deferred payment price payable in installments. *(Added by Stats.1959, c. 201, p. 2093, § 1, operative Jan. 1, 1960. Amended by Stats.1970, c. 546, p. 1041, § 3.)*

Cross References

Goods defined for purposes of this Chapter, see Civil Code § 1802.1.
Retail buyer or buyer defined for purposes of this Chapter, see Civil Code § 1802.4.
Retail seller or seller defined for purposes of this Chapter, see Civil Code § 1802.3.
Sale defined, see Commercial Code § 2106.
Services defined for purposes of this Chapter, see Civil Code § 1802.2.

§ 1802.6. Retail installment contract; contract

"Retail installment contract" or "contract" means any contract for a retail installment sale between a buyer and seller, entered into or performed in this state, which provides for (a) repayment in installments, whether or not such contract contains a title retention provision, and in which the buyer agrees to pay a finance charge, or in which the buyer does not agree to pay a finance charge but the goods or services are available at a lesser price if paid for by either cash or credit card, or in which the buyer would have received any additional goods or services or any higher quality goods or services at no added cost over the total amount payable in installments if the sale had been for cash, or (b) which provides for payment in more than four installments. When taken or given in connection with a retail installment sale, the term includes but is not limited to a security agreement and a contract for the bailment or leasing of goods by which the bailee or lessee contracts to pay as compensation for their use a sum substantially equivalent to or in excess of their value and by which it is agreed that the bailee or lessee will become, or for no other or for a nominal consideration has the option of becoming, the owner of the goods upon full compliance with the terms of the contract. *(Added by Stats.1959, c. 201, p. 2093, § 1. Amended by Stats.1961, c. 1214, p. 2948, § 1; Stats.1963, c. 819, p. 1998, § 6, eff. Jan. 1, 1965; Stats.1969, c. 1192, p. 2322, § 1; Stats.1970, c. 546, p. 1041, § 4; Stats.1979, c. 805, p. 2771, § 4.)*

Cross References

Contract defined, see Civil Code § 1549.
Finance charge defined for purposes of this Chapter, see Civil Code § 1802.10.
Goods defined for purposes of this Chapter, see Civil Code § 1802.1.
Installment contract defined, breach, see Commercial Code § 2612.
Iraq–Kuwait military reservists, see Military and Veterans Code § 800.
Military Families Financial Relief Act, see Military and Veterans Code § 800 et seq.
Retail buyer or buyer defined for purposes of this Chapter, see Civil Code § 1802.4.
Retail installment sale or sale defined for purposes of this Chapter, see Civil Code § 1802.5.
Retail seller or seller defined for purposes of this Chapter, see Civil Code § 1802.3.
Secured transactions, see Commercial Code § 9101 et seq.
Security agreement defined, see Commercial Code § 9105.
Services defined for purposes of this Chapter, see Civil Code § 1802.2.

§ 1802.7. Retail installment account; installment account; revolving account

"Retail installment account" or "installment account" or "revolving account" means an account established by an agreement entered into in this state, pursuant to which the buyer promises to pay, in installments, to a retail seller, his outstanding balance incurred in retail installment sales, whether or not a security interest in the goods sold is retained by the seller, and which provides for a finance charge which is expressed as a percent of the periodic balances to accrue thereafter providing such charge is not capitalized or stated as a dollar amount in such agreement. *(Added by Stats.1959, c. 201, p. 2093, § 1, operative Jan. 1, 1960. Amended by Stats.1970, c. 546, p. 1042, § 5.)*

Cross References

Finance charge defined for purposes of this Chapter, see Civil Code § 1802.10.
Goods defined for purposes of this Chapter, see Civil Code § 1802.1.
Iraq–Kuwait military reservists, see Military and Veterans Code § 800.
Military Families Financial Relief Act, see Military and Veterans Code § 800 et seq.
Penalty for failure of obligee to give timely response to inquiry concerning debit or credit, see Civil Code § 1720.
Retail buyer or buyer defined for purposes of this Chapter, see Civil Code § 1802.4.
Retail installment accounts, see Civil Code § 1810.1 et seq.
Retail installment sale or sale defined for purposes of this Chapter, see Civil Code § 1802.5.
Retail seller or seller defined for purposes of this Chapter, see Civil Code § 1802.3.

§ 1802.8. Cash price

"Cash price" means the cash price stated in a retail installment contract for which the seller would sell or furnish to the buyer and the buyer would buy or obtain from the seller the goods or services which are the subject matter of a retail installment contract if the sale were a sale for cash instead of a retail installment sale. The cash price shall include any taxes and cash prices for accessories and services, if any, included in a retail installment sale. *(Added by Stats.1959, c. 201, p. 2093, § 1, operative Jan. 1, 1960. Amended by Stats.1969, c. 625, p. 1264, § 1; Stats.1981, c. 1075, p. 4115, § 2, operative Oct. 1, 1982.)*

Cross References

Goods defined for purposes of this Chapter, see Civil Code § 1802.1.
Retail buyer or buyer defined for purposes of this Chapter, see Civil Code § 1802.4.
Retail installment contract or contract defined for purposes of this Chapter, see Civil Code § 1802.6.
Retail installment sale or sale defined for purposes of this Chapter, see Civil Code § 1802.5.
Retail seller or seller defined for purposes of this Chapter, see Civil Code § 1802.3.
Services defined for purposes of this Chapter, see Civil Code § 1802.2.

§ 1802.9. Total sale price

"Total sale price" means the total of the cash price of the goods or services, the amounts, if any, included for insurance, official fees, and the finance charge. *(Added by Stats.1959, c. 201, p. 2094, § 1, operative Jan. 1, 1960. Amended by Stats.1969, c. 625, p. 1264, § 2; Stats.1970, c. 546, p. 1042, § 6; Stats.1981, c. 1075, p. 4115, § 3, operative Oct. 1, 1982.)*

Cross References

Cash price defined for purposes of this Chapter, see Civil Code § 1802.8.
Finance charge defined for purposes of this Chapter, see Civil Code § 1802.10.
Goods defined for purposes of this Chapter, see Civil Code § 1802.1.
Official fees defined for purposes of this Chapter, see Civil Code § 1802.14.
Retail installment sale or sale defined for purposes of this Chapter, see Civil Code § 1802.5.
Services defined for purposes of this Chapter, see Civil Code § 1802.2.

§ 1802.10. Finance charge

"Finance charge" means the amount however denominated or expressed which the retail buyer contracts to pay or pays for the privilege of purchasing goods or services to be paid for by the buyer in installments. "Finance charge" does not include the amounts, if any, charged for insurance premiums, including premiums of the kind and to the extent described in paragraph (2) of subsection (e) of Section 226.4 of Regulation Z, delinquency charges, attorney's fees, court costs, collection expenses, official fees, extension or deferral agreement charges as provided by Section 1807.1, or amounts for insurance, repairs to or preservation of the goods, or preservation of the holder's security interest therein advanced by the holder subsequent to the execution of a contract.

(Added by Stats.1959, c. 201, p. 2094, § 1, operative Jan. 1, 1960. Amended by Stats.1969, c. 625, p. 1265, § 3; Stats.1970, c. 546, p. 1042, § 7; Stats.1980, c. 1380, p. 5005, § 4, eff. Oct. 1, 1980; Stats.1984, c. 199, § 1.)

Cross References

Determination of finance charge, see Civil Code § 1808.5.
Finance charge, authorization, see Civil Code § 1810.2.
Finance charge limitation, see Civil Code § 1805.1 et seq.
Goods defined for purposes of this Chapter, see Civil Code § 1802.1.
Holder defined for purposes of this Chapter, see Civil Code § 1802.13.
Official fees defined for purposes of this Chapter, see Civil Code § 1802.14.
Regulation Z defined for purposes of this Chapter, see Civil Code § 1802.18.
Retail buyer or buyer defined for purposes of this Chapter, see Civil Code § 1802.4.
Retail installment contract or contract defined for purposes of this Chapter, see Civil Code § 1802.6.
Services defined for purposes of this Chapter, see Civil Code § 1802.2.
Willful violation of law affecting recovery of charges, see Civil Code § 1812.9.

§ 1802.11. Amount financed; unpaid balance

(a) "Amount financed" means the amount required to be disclosed pursuant to paragraph (7) of subdivision (c) of Section 1803.3.

(b) "Unpaid balance" means the cash price of the goods or services which are the subject matter of the retail installment sale, plus the amounts, if any, included in a retail installment sale for insurance and official fees, minus the amount of the buyer's downpayment in money or goods. *(Added by Stats. 1959, c. 201, p. 2094, § 1, operative Jan. 1, 1960. Amended by Stats.1969, c. 625, p. 1265, § 4; Stats.1970, c. 546, p. 1042, § 8; Stats.1980, c. 1380, p. 5006, § 5, eff. Oct. 1, 1980; Stats.1981, c. 1075, p. 4115, § 4, operative Oct. 1, 1982.)*

Cross References

Cash price defined for purposes of this Chapter, see Civil Code § 1802.8.
Goods defined for purposes of this Chapter, see Civil Code § 1802.1.
Official fees defined for purposes of this Chapter, see Civil Code § 1802.14.
Payments, see Civil Code § 1806.1 et seq.
Retail buyer or buyer defined for purposes of this Chapter, see Civil Code § 1802.4.
Retail installment sale or sale defined for purposes of this Chapter, see Civil Code § 1802.5.
Services defined for purposes of this Chapter, see Civil Code § 1802.2.
Statement of unpaid balance, see Civil Code § 1806.2.

§ 1802.12. Total of payments

"Total of payments" means the amount required to be disclosed pursuant to subdivision (h) of Section 226.18 of Regulation Z. The term includes any portion of the downpayment deferred until not later than the second otherwise scheduled payment and which is not subject to a finance charge. *(Added by Stats.1959, c. 201, p. 2094, § 1, operative Jan. 1, 1960. Amended by Stats.1970, c. 546, p. 1042, § 9; Stats.1981, c. 1075, p. 4115, § 5, operative Oct. 1, 1982.)*

Cross References

Finance charge, see Civil Code § 1802.10.
Regulation Z defined for purposes of this Chapter, see Civil Code § 1802.18.

§ 1802.13. Holder

"Holder" means the retail seller who acquires a retail installment contract or installment account executed, incurred or entered into by a retail buyer, or if the contract or installment account is purchased by a financing agency or other assignee, the financing agency or other assignee. The term does not include the pledgee of or the holder of a security interest in an aggregate number of such contracts or installment accounts to secure a bona fide loan thereon. *(Added by Stats.1959, c. 201, p. 2094, § 1, operative Jan. 1, 1960.)*

Cross References

Financing agency defined for purposes of this Chapter, see Civil Code § 1802.16.
Holder, see Commercial Code § 1201.
Retail buyer or buyer defined for purposes of this Chapter, see Civil Code § 1802.4.
Retail installment account or installment account defined for purposes of this Chapter, see Civil Code § 1802.7.
Retail installment contract or contract defined for purposes of this Chapter, see Civil Code § 1802.6.
Retail seller or seller defined for purposes of this Chapter, see Civil Code § 1802.3.

§ 1802.14. Official fees

"Official fees" means the fees required by law and actually to be paid to the appropriate public officer to perfect a lien or other security interest, on or in goods, retained or taken by a seller under a retail installment contract or installment account, and license, certificate of title, and registration fees imposed by law. *(Added by Stats.1959, c. 201, p. 2094, § 1, operative Jan. 1, 1960. Amended by Stats.1970, c. 546, p. 1043, § 10.)*

Cross References

Goods defined for purposes of this Chapter, see Civil Code § 1802.1.
Retail installment account or installment account defined for purposes of this Chapter, see Civil Code § 1802.7.
Retail installment contract or contract defined for purposes of this Chapter, see Civil Code § 1802.6.
Retail seller or seller defined for purposes of this Chapter, see Civil Code § 1802.3.

§ 1802.15. Person

"Person" means an individual, partnership, corporation, limited liability company, association or other group, however organized. *(Added by Stats.1959, c. 201, p. 2094, § 1, operative Jan. 1, 1960. Amended by Stats.1994, c. 1010 (S.B.2053), § 43.)*

Cross References

Person defined, see Civil Code § 14.

§ 1802.16. Financing agency

"Financing agency" means a person engaged in this State in whole or in part in the business of purchasing retail installment contracts, or installment accounts from one or more retail sellers. The term includes but is not limited to a bank, trust company, private banker, or investment company, if so engaged. *(Added by Stats.1959, c. 201, p. 2094, § 1, operative Jan. 1, 1960.)*

Cross References

Person defined for purposes of this Chapter, see Civil Code § 1802.15.
Retail installment account or installment account defined for purposes of this Chapter, see Civil Code § 1802.7.
Retail installment contract or contract defined for purposes of this Chapter, see Civil Code § 1802.6.
Retail seller or seller defined for purposes of this Chapter, see Civil Code § 1802.3.

§ 1802.17. Billing cycle

"Billing cycle" means the time interval between regular monthly billing statement dates. *(Added by Stats.1970, c. 546, p. 1043, § 12.)*

§ 1802.18. Regulation Z

"Regulation Z" means any rule, regulation, or interpretation promulgated by the Board of Governors of the Federal Reserve System ("Board") under the Federal Truth in Lending Act, as amended (15 U.S.C. 1601, et seq.), and any interpretation or approval issued by an official or employee of the Federal Reserve System duly authorized by the board under the Truth in Lending Act, as amended, to issue such interpretations or approvals. *(Added by Stats.1970, c. 546, p. 1043, § 13. Amended by Stats.1979, c. 805, p. 2771, § 5.)*

§ 1802.19. Contracts and accounts; offer or agreement to sell or buy in this state; application of chapter

(a) For the purposes of this chapter, a retail installment contract, contract, retail installment account, installment account, or revolving account shall be deemed to have been made in this state and, therefore, subject to the provisions of this chapter, if either the seller offers or agrees in this state to sell to a buyer who is a resident of this state or if such buyer accepts or makes the offer in this state to buy, regardless of the situs of the contract as specified therein.

(b) Any solicitation or communication to sell, oral or written, originating outside of this state, but forwarded to, and received in this state by, a buyer who is a resident of this state, shall be deemed to be an offer or agreement to sell in this state.

(c) Any solicitation or communication to buy, oral or written, originating within this state, from a buyer who is a resident of this state, but forwarded to, and received by, a retail seller outside of this state, shall be deemed to be an acceptance or offer to buy in this state. *(Added by Stats.1976, c. 508, p. 1258, § 1.)*

Cross References

Retail buyer or buyer defined for purposes of this Chapter, see Civil Code § 1802.4.
Retail installment account or installment account defined for purposes of this Chapter, see Civil Code § 1802.7.
Retail installment contract or contract defined for purposes of this Chapter, see Civil Code § 1802.6.
Retail seller or seller defined for purposes of this Chapter, see Civil Code § 1802.3.

§ 1802.20. Simple-interest basis

"Simple-interest basis" means the determination of a finance charge, other than an administrative finance charge, by applying a constant rate to the unpaid balance as it changes from time to time, either:

(a) Calculated on the basis of a 365-day year and actual days elapsed (although the seller may, but need not, adjust its calculations to account for leap years); reference in this chapter to the "365-day basis" shall mean this method of determining the finance charge, or

(b) For contracts entered into prior to January 1, 1988, calculated on the basis of a 360-day year consisting of 12 months of 30 days each and on the assumption that all payments will be received by the seller on their respective due dates; reference in this chapter to the "360-day basis" shall mean this method of determining the finance charge. *(Added by Stats.1979, c. 805, p. 2771, § 6.)*

Cross References

Finance charge defined for purposes of this Chapter, see Civil Code § 1802.10.
Retail installment contract or contract defined for purposes of this Chapter, see Civil Code § 1802.6.
Retail seller or seller defined for purposes of this Chapter, see Civil Code § 1802.3.
Unpaid balance defined for purposes of this Chapter, see Civil Code § 1802.11.

§ 1802.21. Precomputed basis

"Precomputed basis" means the determination of a finance charge by multiplying the original unpaid balance of the contract by a rate and multiplying that product by the number of payment periods elapsing between the date on which the finance charge begins to be assessed and the date of the last scheduled payment. *(Added by Stats.1979, c. 805, p. 2771, § 7.)*

Cross References

Finance charge defined for purposes of this Chapter, see Civil Code § 1802.10.
Retail installment contract or contract defined for purposes of this Chapter, see Civil Code § 1802.6.
Unpaid balance defined for purposes of this Chapter, see Civil Code § 1802.11.

ARTICLE 3. PROVISIONS OF RETAIL INSTALLMENT CONTRACTS

Section
1803.1. Date; writing; size of type.
1803.2. Single document; contents.
1803.3. Contract; contents.
1803.4. Obtaining signature of buyer to contract containing blank spaces.
1803.5. Cost of insurance included in contract and separate charge made to buyer.
1803.6. Delinquency charges; costs of collection.
1803.7. Delivery of copy of completed contract or other document to buyer; penalties; acknowledgment of delivery; rebuttable presumption.
1803.8. Negotiation of sales by mail or telephone.

Section	
1803.9.	Contract contingent on loan to be obtained by buyer; rescission upon failure; time; return of consideration.
1803.10.	Rebates, discounts, commissions, or other consideration.
1803.11.	Advertisements; solicitation to enter into contract without intent to sell contract to financing agency or assignee; requirements.
1804.	Repealed.

Cross References

Add-on sales, see Civil Code § 1808.1 et seq.
Retail installment accounts, see Civil Code § 1810.1 et seq.

§ 1803.1. Date; writing; size of type

A retail installment contract shall be dated and in writing; the printed portion thereof shall be in at least eight-point type. (Added by Stats.1959, c. 201, p. 2094, § 1, operative Jan. 1, 1960.)

Cross References

Invalidity of prohibited provisions, effect on contract, see Civil Code § 1804.4.
Retail installment contract, see Civil Code § 1802.6.

§ 1803.2. Single document; contents

Except as provided in Section 1808.3, every retail installment contract shall be contained in a single document that shall contain:

(a) The entire agreement of the parties with respect to the cost and terms of payment for the goods and services, including any promissory notes or any other evidences of indebtedness between the parties relating to the transaction.

(b)(1) At the top of the contract the words "Security Agreement" shall appear in at least 12–point bold type where a security interest in the goods is retained or a security interest on other goods or realty is obtained by the seller as security for the goods or services purchased.

(2) At the top of the contract the words "Retail Installment Contract" shall appear in at least 12–point bold type where a security interest is not retained or obtained by the seller as security for the goods or services purchased.

(3) Any contract for goods or services that provides for a security interest in real property shall also provide the following notice, written in the same language, e.g., Spanish, as used in the contract: "WARNING TO BUYER: IF YOU SIGN THIS CONTRACT, YOU WILL BE PUTTING UP YOUR HOME AS SECURITY. THIS MEANS THAT YOUR HOME COULD BE SOLD WITHOUT YOUR PERMISSION AND WITHOUT ANY COURT ACTION IF YOU MISS ANY PAYMENT AS REQUIRED BY THIS CONTRACT." This notice shall be printed in at least 14–point boldface type, shall be set apart from the rest of the contract by a border, and shall appear directly above the space reserved for the signature of the buyer. A security interest created in any contract described in this paragraph that does not provide the notice as required by this paragraph shall be void and unenforceable.

As used in this subdivision, the term "security interest" refers to a contractual interest in property and not to a mechanic's lien or other interest in property arising by operation of law.

(c) Where the contract includes a finance charge that is determined on the precomputed basis and provides that the unearned portion of the finance charge to be refunded upon full prepayment of the contract is to be determined by a method other than actuarial, a notice in at least 10–point bold type if the contract is printed reading as follows: "Notice to buyer: (1) Do not sign this agreement before you read it or if it contains any blank spaces to be filled in. (2) You are entitled to a completely filled-in copy of this agreement. (3) You can prepay the full amount due under this agreement at any time and obtain a partial refund of the finance charge if it is $1 or more. Because of the way the amount of this refund will be figured, the time when you prepay could increase the ultimate cost of credit under this agreement. (4) If you desire to pay off in advance the full amount due, the amount of the refund you are entitled to, if any, will be furnished upon request."

(d) Where the contract includes a finance charge that is determined on the precomputed basis and provides for the actuarial method for computing the unearned portion of the finance charge upon prepayment in full, a notice in at least 10–point bold type if the contract is printed reading as follows: "Notice to buyer: (1) Do not sign this agreement before you read it or if it contains any blank spaces to be filled in. (2) You are entitled to a completely filled-in copy of this agreement. (3) You can prepay the full amount due under this agreement at any time and obtain a partial refund of the finance charge if it is $1 or more. (4) If you desire to pay off in advance the full amount due, the amount of the refund you are entitled to, if any, will be furnished upon request."

(e) Where the contract includes a finance charge that is determined on the simple-interest basis, a notice in at least 10–point bold type if the contract is printed reading as follows: "Notice to buyer: (1) Do not sign this agreement before you read it or if it contains any blank spaces to be filled in. (2) You are entitled to a completely filled-in copy of this agreement. (3) You can prepay the full amount due under this agreement at any time. (4) If you desire to pay off in advance the full amount due, the amount which is outstanding will be furnished upon request."

(f) This section shall become operative on October 1, 1995.

(g) The form specified in this section may be used before October 1, 1995, to comply with the provisions of this section as amended and repealed by Section 2 of Chapter 888 of the Statutes of 1994. (Added by Stats.1994, c. 888 (A.B.3269), § 3, operative Oct. 1, 1995. Amended by Stats.1995, c. 91 (S.B.975), § 17, operative Oct. 1, 1995; Stats.1995, c. 153 (A.B.1635), § 1, eff. July 24, 1995, operative Oct. 1, 1995.)

Cross References

Buyer, see Civil Code § 1802.4; Commercial Code § 2103.
Finance charge,
   Generally, see Civil Code § 1802.10.
   Authorization, see Civil Code § 1810.2.
Goods defined for purposes of this Chapter, see Civil Code § 1802.1.
Lien defined, see Civil Code § 2872; Code of Civil Procedure § 1180.

Obtaining signature of buyer to contract containing blank spaces, see Civil Code § 1803.4.
Precomputed basis defined for purposes of this Chapter, see Civil Code § 1802.21.
Prohibited provisions, see Civil Code § 1804.1.
Retail installment contract, see Civil Code § 1802.6.
Retail seller or seller defined for purposes of this Chapter, see Civil Code § 1802.3.
Security interest defined, see Commercial Code § 1201.
Services defined for purposes of this Chapter, see Civil Code § 1802.2.
Simple-interest basis defined for purposes of this Chapter, see Civil Code § 1802.20.

§ 1803.3. Contract; contents

Except as provided in Article 8 (commencing with Section 1808.1) of this chapter, a contract shall contain the following:

(a) The names of the seller and the buyer, the place of business of the seller, the residence or place of business of the buyer as specified by the buyer and a description of the goods or services sufficient to identify them. Services or multiple items of goods may be described in general terms and may be described in detail sufficient to identify them in a separate writing.

(b) Every contract subject to this chapter shall contain the disclosures required by Regulation Z whether or not Regulation Z applies to the transaction. In addition, to the extent applicable, the contract shall contain the other disclosures and notices required by, and shall satisfy the requirements and limitations of, this section. The disclosures required by subdivision (c) may be itemized or subtotaled to a greater extent than as required by that subdivision and shall be made together and in the sequence set forth in that subdivision. No particular terminology is required to disclose the items set forth in subdivision (c) except as therein expressly provided. Except as otherwise provided by this subdivision (b), these disclosures and notices may appear in the contract in any location or sequence and may be combined or interspersed with other provisions of the contract.

(c) The contract shall contain the following disclosures, as applicable, which shall be labeled "itemization of the amount financed":

(1)(A) The cash price, exclusive of taxes imposed on the sale.

(B) Taxes imposed on the sale.

(C) The total of the above.

(2) An itemization of the amount to be paid to any public officer for official fees.

(3) The aggregate amount of premiums agreed, upon execution of the contract, to be paid for policies of insurance included in the contract, excluding the amount of any insurance premium included in the finance charge.

(4) A subtotal representing the sum of the foregoing items.

(5) The amount of the buyer's downpayment, which downpayment shall not include any administrative finance charge charged, received, or collected by the seller pursuant to subdivision (c) of Section 1805.1 and as shown as item (6), itemized to show the following:

(A) The net agreed value of the property being traded in.

(B) The amount of any portion of downpayment to be deferred until not later than the due date of the second regularly scheduled installment under the contract and which is not subject to a finance charge.

(C) The amount of any manufacturer's rebate applied or to be applied to the downpayment.

(D) The remaining amount paid or to be paid by the buyer as a downpayment.

(6) The amount of any administrative finance charge, labeled "prepaid finance charge."

(7) The difference between item (4) and the sum of items (5) and (6), labeled "amount financed."

(d) If the payment of all or a portion of the downpayment is to be deferred, the deferred payment shall be reflected in the payment schedule disclosed pursuant to Regulation Z.

(e) If the downpayment includes property being traded in, the contract shall contain a brief description of that property.

(f)(1) Where the contract includes a finance charge determined on the precomputed basis, the contract shall identify the method of computing the unearned portion of the finance charge in the event of prepayment in full of the buyer's obligation and contain a statement of the amount or method of computation of any charge that may be deducted from the amount of any such unearned finance charge in computing the amount that will be credited to the obligation or refunded to the buyer. Reference to the Rule of 78's, the sum of the digits, the sum of the periodic time balances or the actuarial method shall constitute a sufficient identification of the method of computing the unearned portion of the finance charge.

(2) Where the contract includes a finance charge which is determined on the simple-interest basis but provides for a minimum finance charge in the event of prepayment in full, the contract shall contain a statement of that fact and the amount of the minimum finance charge or its method of calculation.

(g) The contract shall contain an itemization of any insurance included as part of the amount financed disclosed pursuant to paragraph (3) of subdivision (c) and of any insurance included as part of the finance charge. The itemization shall identify the type of insurance coverage and the premium charged therefor, and, if the insurance expires before the date of the last scheduled installment included in the repayment schedule, the term of the insurance shall be stated. (Added by Stats.1959, c. 201, p. 2095, § 1, operative Jan. 1, 1960. Amended by Stats.1969, c. 625, p. 1266, § 6; Stats.1970, c. 546, p. 1044, § 15; Stats.1979, c. 805, p. 2774, § 8; Stats.1980, c. 1380, p. 5009, § 8, eff. Oct. 1, 1980; Stats.1981, c. 1075, p. 4115, § 6, operative Oct. 1, 1982.)

Cross References

Add-on sales,
   Generally, see Civil Code § 1808.1 et seq.
   Contents of memorandum, see Civil Code § 1808.2.
Amount financed defined for purposes of this Chapter, see Civil Code § 1802.11.
Attorney's fees and court costs, see Civil Code §§ 1810.4, 1811.1.
Buyer, see Civil Code § 1802.4; Commercial Code § 2103.
Cash price defined for purposes of this Chapter, see Civil Code § 1802.8.

§ 1803.3

Contract, see Civil Code §§ 1549, 1802.6.
Effect of prohibited provisions in contract, see Civil Code § 1804.4.
Finance charge,
   Generally, see Civil Code § 1802.10.
   As inclusive, see Civil Code §§ 1805.4, 1810.4.
   Authorization, see Civil Code § 1810.2.
   Determination, see Civil Code § 1808.5.
   Limitation, see Civil Code § 1805.1 et seq.
Goods defined for purposes of this Chapter, see Civil Code § 1802.1.
Insurance cost, see Civil Code § 1810.5.
Official fees defined for purposes of this Chapter, see Civil Code § 1802.14.
Precomputed basis defined for purposes of this Chapter, see Civil Code § 1802.21.
Prohibited provisions, see Civil Code §§ 1804.1, 1804.3.
Refund credit on prepayment, see Civil Code § 1806.3.
Regulation Z, disclosures, see Civil Code § 1801.5.
Regulation Z defined for purposes of this Chapter, see Civil Code § 1802.18.
Retail installment sale or sale defined for purposes of this Chapter, see Civil Code § 1802.5.
Retail seller or seller defined for purposes of this Chapter, see Civil Code § 1802.3.
Services defined for purposes of this Chapter, see Civil Code § 1802.2.
Simple-interest basis defined for purposes of this Chapter, see Civil Code § 1802.20.
Total sale price defined for purposes of this Chapter, see Civil Code § 1802.9.

§ 1803.4. Obtaining signature of buyer to contract containing blank spaces

The seller shall not obtain the signature of the buyer to a contract when it contains blank spaces to be filled in after it has been signed. *(Added by Stats.1959, c. 201, p. 2096, § 1, operative Jan. 1, 1960.)*

Cross References

Buyer, see Civil Code § 1802.4; Commercial Code § 2103.
Contract, see Civil Code §§ 1549, 1802.6.
Presumption of compliance, see Civil Code § 1803.7.
Retail seller or seller defined for purposes of this Chapter, see Civil Code § 1802.3.

§ 1803.5. Cost of insurance included in contract and separate charge made to buyer

If the cost of any insurance is included in the contract and a separate charge is made to the buyer for such insurance:

(a) The contract shall state whether the insurance is to be procured by the buyer or the seller.

(b) The amount, included for such insurance, shall not exceed the premiums chargeable in accordance with rate fixed for such insurance by the insurer.

(c) If the insurance is to be procured by the seller or holder, he shall, within 45 days after delivery of the goods or furnishing of the services under the contract, deliver, mail or cause to be mailed to the buyer, at his address as specified in the contract, a notice thereof or a copy of the policy or policies of insurance or a certificate or certificates of the insurance so procured.

(d) The provisions of Insurance Code Section 1668 shall apply to any violation of this section. *(Added by Stats.1959, c. 201, p. 2096, § 1, operative Jan. 1, 1960.)*

Cross References

Application of this section when insurance procured by seller or holder, see Civil Code § 1810.5.
Buyer, see Civil Code § 1802.4; Commercial Code § 2103.
Contract, see Civil Code §§ 1549, 1802.6.
Cost of insurance separately charged to buyer, agreement, see Civil Code § 1810.5.
Denial of application for license, grounds, see Insurance Code § 1668.
Extension of due date or deferment of payment, see Civil Code § 1807.1.
Goods defined for purposes of this Chapter, see Civil Code § 1802.1.
Holder, see Civil Code § 1802.13; Commercial Code § 1201.
Refinancing, insurance cost, see Civil Code § 1807.2.
Retail seller or seller defined for purposes of this Chapter, see Civil Code § 1802.3.
Services defined for purposes of this Chapter, see Civil Code § 1802.2.

§ 1803.6. Delinquency charges; costs of collection

(a) A contract may provide that for each installment in default the buyer shall pay a delinquency charge not in excess of one of the following amounts:

(1) For a period in default of not less than 10 days, an amount not in excess of ten dollars ($10).

(2) For a period in default of not less than 15 days, an amount not in excess of fifteen dollars ($15).

(b) Only one delinquency charge may be collected on any installment regardless of the period during which it remains in default. Payments timely received by the seller under a written extension or deferral agreement shall not be subject to any delinquency charge. The contract may also provide for payment of any actual and reasonable costs of collection occasioned by removal of the goods from the state without written permission of the holder, or by the failure of the buyer to notify the holder of any change of residence, or by the failure of the buyer to communicate with the holder for a period of 45 days after any default in making payments due under the contract. *(Added by Stats.1959, c. 201, p. 2096, § 1, operative Jan. 1, 1960. Amended by Stats.1980, c. 1380, p. 5011, § 9, eff. Oct. 1, 1980; Stats.1994, c. 168 (S.B.1583), § 1; Stats.1996, c. 301 (S.B.2050), § 1.)*

Cross References

Buyer, see Civil Code § 1802.4; Commercial Code § 2103.
Contract, see Civil Code §§ 1549, 1802.6.
Default on balloon payment, right to new payment schedule, see Civil Code § 1807.3.
Delinquent payment charges on mortgages of real property, see Civil Code § 2954.5.
Extension of due date or deferment of payment, see Civil Code § 1807.1.
Goods defined for purposes of this Chapter, see Civil Code § 1802.1.
Holder defined for purposes of this Chapter, see Civil Code § 1802.13.
Refinancing and consolidation, charges, see Civil Code § 1807.1 et seq.
Retail seller or seller defined for purposes of this Chapter, see Civil Code § 1802.3.

§ 1803.7. Delivery of copy of completed contract or other document to buyer; penalties; acknowledgment of delivery; rebuttable presumption

The seller shall deliver to the buyer at the time of the buyer's signature a legible copy of the contract or of any other document which the seller has required or requested the buyer to sign, and which he has signed, during the contract negotiation. In addition to the penalties provided under Article 12.2 (commencing with Section 1812.6) of this chapter, until the seller delivers such documents, the buyer shall be obligated to pay only the cash price. Any acknowledgment by the buyer of delivery of a copy of such documents shall be printed or written in a size equal to at least 10-point bold type and, if contained in the contract shall also appear directly above the space reserved for the buyer's signature. The buyer's written acknowledgment, conforming to the requirements of this section of delivery of a copy of such documents shall be a rebuttable presumption of such delivery and of compliance with this section and Section 1803.4, in any action or proceeding by or against an assignee of the contract without knowledge to the contrary when he purchases the contract. If the holder furnishes the buyer a copy of such documents, or a notice containing the items required by Section 1803.3 and stating that the buyer should notify the holder in writing within 30 days if he was not furnished a copy of the contract or of any other document which the seller had required or requested the buyer to sign, and which he did sign, during the contract negotiation, and no such notification is given, it shall be conclusively presumed in favor of the third party that copies of such documents were furnished as required by Sections 1803.4 and 1803.7. *(Added by Stats. 1959, c. 201, p. 2096, § 1. Amended by Stats.1961, c. 1214, p. 2950, § 3; Stats.1969, c. 353, p. 730, § 1; Stats.1970, c. 546, p. 1044, § 16.)*

Cross References

Add-on sale memorandum, nondelivery, obligation restricted to cash price, see Civil Code § 1808.4.
Buyer, see Civil Code § 1802.4; Commercial Code § 2103.
Cash price, see Civil Code § 1802.8.
Contract, see Civil Code §§ 1549, 1802.6.
Holder, see Civil Code § 1802.13; Commercial Code § 1201.
Presumptions, see Evidence Code § 601 et seq.
Retail installment account statement nondelivery, obligation restricted to cash price, see Civil Code § 1810.1.
Retail seller or seller defined for purposes of this Chapter, see Civil Code § 1802.3.

§ 1803.8. Negotiation of sales by mail or telephone

Retail installment sales negotiated and entered into by mail or telephone without personal solicitation by a salesman or other representative of the seller, where the seller's cash and deferred payment prices and other terms are clearly set forth in a catalog or other printed solicitation of business which is generally available to the public, may be made as hereinafter provided. All of the provisions of this chapter shall apply to such sales except that the seller shall not be required to deliver a copy of the contract to the buyer as provided in Section 1803.7, and if, when the proposed retail installment sale contract is received by the seller from the buyer, there are blank spaces to be filled in, the seller may insert in the appropriate blank spaces the amounts of money and other terms which are set forth in the seller's catalog which is then in effect. In lieu of the copy of the contract provided for in Section 1803.7 the seller shall, within 15 days from the date of shipment of goods, furnish to the buyer a written statement of the items inserted in such blank spaces. *(Added by Stats. 1959, c. 201, p. 2097, § 1, operative Jan. 1, 1960.)*

Cross References

Buyer, see Civil Code § 1802.4; Commercial Code § 2103.
Cash price, see Civil Code § 1802.8.
Goods, see Civil Code § 1802.1.
Retail installment contract, see Civil Code § 1802.6.
Retail installment sale, see Civil Code § 1802.5.
Retail seller or seller defined for purposes of this Chapter, see Civil Code § 1802.3.
Total sale price, see Civil Code § 1802.9.

§ 1803.9. Contract contingent on loan to be obtained by buyer; rescission upon failure; time; return of consideration

If it is explicitly understood between the seller and the buyer that all or any part of the cash price will be paid from the proceeds of a loan to be obtained by the buyer from a third party, the contract of sale or purchase order may be rescinded at the election of the buyer, and all considerations thereupon shall be returned by the respective parties without further demand, if the buyer is unable to obtain such third-party financing upon reasonable terms after having made a reasonable effort to obtain it, and buyer notifies the seller of the rescission within three business days. *(Added by Stats. 1979, c. 1151, p. 4222, § 3.)*

Cross References

Cash price defined for purposes of this Chapter, see Civil Code § 1802.8.
Retail buyer or buyer defined for purposes of this Chapter, see Civil Code § 1802.4.
Retail installment contract or contract defined for purposes of this Chapter, see Civil Code § 1802.6.
Retail installment sale or sale defined for purposes of this Chapter, see Civil Code § 1802.5.
Retail seller or seller defined for purposes of this Chapter, see Civil Code § 1802.3.

§ 1803.10. Rebates, discounts, commissions, or other consideration

It shall be unlawful for any seller to induce or attempt to induce any person to enter into a contract subject to this act by offering a rebate, discount, commission, or other consideration, contingent upon the happening of a future event, on the condition that the buyer either sells, or gives information or assistance for the purpose of leading to a sale by the seller of, the same or related goods. *(Added by Stats.1968, c. 452, p. 1074, § 2.)*

Cross References

Buyer, see Civil Code § 1802.4; Commercial Code § 2103.
Goods defined for purposes of this Chapter, see Civil Code § 1802.1.
Person, see Civil Code §§ 14, 1802.15.
Retail installment contract or contract defined for purposes of this Chapter, see Civil Code § 1802.6.
Retail installment sale or sale defined for purposes of this Chapter, see Civil Code § 1802.5.
Retail seller or seller defined for purposes of this Chapter, see Civil Code § 1802.3.

§ 1803.11. Advertisements; solicitation to enter into contract without intent to sell contract to financing agency or assignee; requirements

It shall be unlawful for any seller to solicit buyers, in any advertisement, to enter into a retail installment contract with it if the seller does not intend to sell that retail installment contract to a financing agency or other assignee, unless the advertisement clearly states the periodic rate or range of periodic rates, expressed as an annual percentage rate or a range of annual percentage rates that will be used to determine the finance charge imposed on the retail installment contract. *(Added by Stats.1991, c. 819 (S.B.1105), § 1.)*

Cross References

Finance charge defined for purposes of this Chapter, see Civil Code § 1802.10.
Financing agency defined for purposes of this Chapter, see Civil Code § 1802.16.
Retail buyer or buyer defined for purposes of this Chapter, see Civil Code § 1802.4.
Retail installment contract or contract defined for purposes of this Chapter, see Civil Code § 1802.6.
Retail seller or seller defined for purposes of this Chapter, see Civil Code § 1802.3.

§ 1804. Repealed by Stats.1931, c. 1070, p. 2234, § 1

ARTICLE 4. RESTRICTIONS ON RETAIL INSTALLMENT CONTRACTS

Section
1804.1. Prohibited provisions.
1804.2. Assignment of seller's rights; recourse.
1804.3. Security interest in goods paid for or not sold; security interest in real property for sale of unattached goods.
1804.4. Invalidity of prohibited provisions; effect upon contract.
1805. Repealed.

Cross References

Provisions of retail installment contracts, see Civil Code § 1803.1 et seq.

§ 1804.1. Prohibited provisions

No contract or obligation shall contain any provision by which:

(a) The buyer agrees not to assert against a seller a claim or defense arising out of the sale or agrees not to assert against an assignee such a claim or defense other than as provided in Section 1804.2.

(b) In the absence of the buyer's default in the performance of any of his or her obligations, the holder may accelerate the maturity of any part or all of the amount owing thereunder.

(c) A power of attorney is given to confess judgment in this state, or an assignment of wages is given; provided, that nothing herein contained shall prohibit the giving of an assignment of wages contained in a separate instrument, executed pursuant to Section 300 of the Labor Code.

(d) The seller or holder of the contract or other person acting on his or her behalf is given authority to enter upon the buyer's premises unlawfully or to commit any breach of the peace in the repossession of goods.

(e) The buyer waives any right of action against the seller or holder of the contract or other person acting on his or her behalf, for any illegal act committed in the collection of payments under the contract or in the repossession of goods.

(f) The buyer executes a power of attorney appointing the seller or holder of the contract, or other person acting on his or her behalf, as the buyer's agent in collection of payments under the contract or in the repossession of goods.

(g) The buyer relieves the seller from liability for any legal remedies which the buyer may have against the seller under the contract or any separate instrument executed in connection therewith.

(h) The buyer agrees to the payment of any charge by reason of the exercise of his or her right to rescind or void the contract.

(i) The seller or holder of the contract is given the right to commence an action on a contract under the provisions of this chapter in a county other than the county in which the contract was in fact signed by the buyer, the county in which the buyer resides at the commencement of the action, the county in which the buyer resided at the time that the contract was entered into, or in the county in which the goods purchased pursuant to the contract have been so affixed to real property as to become a part of such real property.

(j) The seller takes a security interest, other than a mechanics' lien, in the buyer's real property which is the buyer's primary residence where the buyer is a person who is 65 years of age or older and the contract is for a home improvement, as defined in Section 7151.2 of the Business and Professions Code. *(Added by Stats.1959, c. 201, p. 2097, § 1. Amended by Stats.1961, c. 1214, p. 2950, § 4; Stats.1963, c. 1310, p. 2833, § 1; Stats.1965, c. 776, p. 2361, § 1; Stats.1999, c. 512 (S.B.187), § 2.)*

Cross References

Confession of judgment without action, see Code of Civil Procedure § 1132 et seq.
Contract, see Civil Code §§ 1549, 1802.6.
Goods defined for purposes of this Chapter, see Civil Code § 1802.1.
Holder, see Civil Code § 1802.13; Commercial Code § 1201.
Liquidated damages, see Civil Code § 1671.
Person defined for purposes of this Chapter, see Civil Code § 1802.15.
Retail buyer or buyer defined for purposes of this Chapter, see Civil Code § 1802.4.
Retail seller or seller defined for purposes of this Chapter, see Civil Code § 1802.3.
Sale, see Civil Code § 1802.5; Commercial Code § 2106.

§ 1804.2. Assignment of seller's rights; recourse

(a) An assignee of the seller's rights is subject to all equities and defenses of the buyer against the seller arising out of the sale, notwithstanding an agreement to the contrary, but the assignee's liability may not exceed the amount of the debt owing to the assignee at the time of the assignment.

(b) The assignee shall have recourse against the seller to the extent of any liability incurred by the assignee pursuant to this section regardless of whether the assignment was with or without recourse. *(Added by Stats.1967, c. 1294, p. 3099, § 2. Amended by Stats.1971, c. 999, p. 1917, § 1; Stats.1975, c. 66, p. 128, § 1.)*

Cross References

Retail buyer or buyer defined for purposes of this Chapter, see Civil Code § 1802.4.

Retail installment sale or sale defined for purposes of this Chapter, see Civil Code § 1802.5.

Retail seller or seller defined for purposes of this Chapter, see Civil Code § 1802.3.

§ 1804.3. Security interest in goods paid for or not sold; security interest in real property for sale of unattached goods

(a) No contract other than one for services shall provide for a security interest in any goods theretofore fully paid for or which have not been sold by the seller.

(b) Any contract for goods which provides for a security interest in real property where the primary goods sold are not to be attached to the real property shall be a violation of this chapter and subject to the penalties set forth in Article 12.2 (commencing with Section 1812.6).

(c) This section shall become operative October 1, 1982. *(Added by Stats.1980, c. 1380, p. 5012, § 11, eff. Oct. 1, 1980. Amended by Stats.1981, c. 107, p. 817, § 4, eff. June 29, 1981, operative April 1, 1982; Stats.1982, c. 129, p. 403, § 4, eff. March 25, 1982, operative Oct. 1, 1982.)*

Cross References

Consumer loans, retail installment contracts held by licensee, refinancing loans, required conditions, see Financial Code § 22341.
Contract, see Civil Code §§ 1549, 1802.6.
Goods, see Civil Code § 1802.1.
Lien defined, see Civil Code § 2872; Code of Civil Procedure § 1180.
Retail seller or seller defined for purposes of this Chapter, see Civil Code § 1802.3.
Sale, see Civil Code § 1802.5; Commercial Code § 2106.
Services defined for purposes of this Chapter, see Civil Code § 1802.2.

§ 1804.4. Invalidity of prohibited provisions; effect upon contract

Any provision in a contract which is prohibited by this chapter shall be void but shall not otherwise affect the validity of the contract. *(Added by Stats.1959, c. 201, p. 2098, § 1, operative Jan. 1, 1960.)*

Cross References

Contract, see Civil Code §§ 1549, 1802.6.
Penalties, see Civil Code § 1812.6 et seq.
Unlawful contracts, see Civil Code § 1667 et seq.

§ 1805. Repealed by Stats.1931, c. 1070, p. 2234, § 1

ARTICLE 5. FINANCE CHARGE LIMITATION

Section
1805.1. Rates; prohibition of annual fee or charge in retail installment contract.
1805.1a. Repealed.
1805.2. Installment payments.
1805.3. Repealed.
1805.4. Inclusive charge; additional fee for return of dishonored check, negotiable order of withdrawal or share draft.
1805.5. Repealed.

Section
1805.6. Undelivered goods.
1805.7. Finance charge; calculation after January 1, 1983.
1805.8. Amounts advanced subsequent to execution of contract; maximum rate of finance charge.
1805.9. Determination of finance charge on precomputed and simple-interest bases; exception.
1806. Repealed.

Cross References

Legal rate of interest, see Cal. Const. Art. 15, § 1; Civil Code § 1916–1 et seq.
Unlawful contracts, see Civil Code § 1667 et seq.

§ 1805.1. Rates; prohibition of annual fee or charge in retail installment contract

The holder of the contract shall not charge, collect, or receive a finance charge which exceeds the dollar amount shown pursuant to subdivision (b) of Section 1803.3, except to the extent (a) caused by the holder's receipt of one or more payments under a contract which provides for determination of the finance charge or a portion thereof on the 365-day basis at a time or times other than as originally scheduled, whether or not the parties enter into an agreement pursuant to Section 1807.1, (b) permitted by paragraph (2), (3), or (4) of subdivision (c) of Section 226.17 of Regulation Z, or (3) permitted by Section 1805.8.

No annual fee or charge shall be made in any retail installment contract. *(Added by Stats.1982, c. 129, p. 405, § 10, eff. March 25, 1982, operative Oct. 1, 1982. Amended by Stats.1982, c. 1611, p. 6443, § 2, eff. Sept. 30, 1982, operative Jan. 1, 1984; Stats.1983, c. 1157, § 2, operative Jan. 1, 1986; Stats.1985, c. 227, § 2, operative Jan. 1, 1988; Stats.1988, c. 479, § 1; Stats.1991, c. 819 (S.B.1105), § 2.)*

Cross References

Amount financed, see Civil Code § 1802.11.
Application to add-on transactions, see Civil Code § 1808.5.
Contract, see Civil Code §§ 1549, 1802.6.
Finance charge,
   Generally, see Civil Code § 1802.10.
   Authorization, see Civil Code § 1810.2.
   Determination, see Civil Code § 1808.5.
Holder, see Civil Code § 1802.13; Commercial Code § 1201.
Regulation Z defined for purposes of this Chapter, see Civil Code § 1802.18.
Retail installment contract, see Civil Code § 1802.6.
Retail seller, see Civil Code § 1802.3.

§ 1805.1a. Repealed by Stats.1991, c. 819 (S.B.1105), § 4

§ 1805.2. Installment payments

Contracts may be payable in successive monthly, semi-monthly or weekly installments. *(Added by Stats.1959, c. 201, p. 2098, § 1, operative Jan. 1, 1960.)*

Cross References

Contract, see Civil Code §§ 1549, 1802.6.
Installment contract, see Commercial Code § 2612.
Payments, see Civil Code § 1806.1 et seq.

§ 1805.3. Repealed by Stats.1991, c. 819 (S.B.1105), § 5

§ 1805.4. Inclusive charge; additional fee for return of dishonored check, negotiable order of withdrawal or share draft

The finance charge shall be inclusive of all charges incident to investigating and making the contract and for the extension of the credit provided for in the contract, and no fee, expense or other charge whatsoever shall be taken, received, reserved or contracted for except as otherwise provided in this chapter.

The seller or holder of a retail installment contract may charge and collect a fee not to exceed fifteen dollars ($15) for the return by a depository institution of a dishonored check, negotiable order of withdrawal, or share draft issued in connection with the retail installment contract. The fee is not included in charges as defined in this chapter or in determining the applicable charges which may be made under this chapter. (Added by Stats.1959, c. 201, p. 2098, § 1, operative Jan. 1, 1960. Amended by Stats.1970, c. 546, p. 1046, § 20; Stats.1982, c. 512, p. 2289, § 1; Stats.1993, c. 101 (S.B.329), § 1.)

Cross References

Attorney's fees and court costs, see Civil Code § 1811.1.
Contract, see Civil Code §§ 1549, 1802.6.
Finance charge,
    Generally, see Civil Code § 1802.10.
    Authorization, see Civil Code § 1810.2.
    Determination, see Civil Code § 1808.5.
Holder defined for purposes of this Chapter, see Civil Code § 1802.13.
Retail seller or seller defined for purposes of this Chapter, see Civil Code § 1802.3.

§ 1805.5. Repealed by Stats.1991, c. 819 (S.B.1105), § 6

§ 1805.6. Undelivered goods

(a) Notwithstanding the provisions of any contract to the contrary, except as provided in subdivision (b) or (c), no retail seller shall assess any finance charge for goods purchased under a retail installment contract until the goods are in the buyer's possession.

(b) A finance charge may be assessed for such undelivered goods, as follows:

(1) From the date when such goods are available for pickup by the buyer and the buyer is notified of their availability, or

(2) From the date of purchase, when such goods are delivered or available for pickup by the buyer within 10 days of the date of purchase.

(c) In the case of a home improvement contract as defined in Section 7151.2 of the Business and Professions Code, a finance charge may be assessed from the approximate date of commencement of the work as set forth in the home improvement contract. (Added by Stats.1975, c. 1041, p. 2455, § 1. Amended by Stats.1976, c. 1271, p. 5625, § 3, eff. Sept. 28, 1976, operative Jan. 1, 1978; Stats.1977, c. 868, p. 2622, § 3; Stats.1979, c. 1000, p. 3400, § 4; Stats.1980, c. 1380, p. 5015, § 15, eff. Oct. 1, 1980; Stats.1981, c. 1075, p. 4120, § 8, operative Oct. 1, 1982.)

Cross References

Finance charge defined for purposes of this Chapter, see Civil Code § 1802.10.
Goods defined for purposes of this Chapter, see Civil Code § 1802.1.
Retail buyer or buyer defined for purposes of this Chapter, see Civil Code § 1802.4.
Retail installment contract or contract defined for purposes of this Chapter, see Civil Code § 1802.6.
Retail seller or seller defined for purposes of this Chapter, see Civil Code § 1802.3.

§ 1805.7. Finance charge; calculation after January 1, 1983

All contracts entered into between a buyer and a seller on or after January 1, 1983, shall provide for the calculation of the finance charge contemplated by item (1) of subdivision (a) of Section 1805.1 on the simple-interest basis if the date on which the final installment is due, according to the original terms of the contract, is more than 62 months after the date of the contract. (Added by Stats.1979, c. 805, p. 2776, § 11.)

Cross References

Finance charge defined for purposes of this Chapter, see Civil Code § 1802.10.
Retail buyer or buyer defined for purposes of this Chapter, see Civil Code § 1802.4.
Retail installment contract or contract defined for purposes of this Chapter, see Civil Code § 1802.6.
Retail seller or seller defined for purposes of this Chapter, see Civil Code § 1802.3.
Simple-interest basis defined for purposes of this Chapter, see Civil Code § 1802.20.

§ 1805.8. Amounts advanced subsequent to execution of contract; maximum rate of finance charge

The maximum rate of finance charge which may be imposed on amounts advanced by the holder subsequent to the execution of the contract for insurance, repairs to or preservation of the goods, or preservation of the holder's security interest therein, shall not exceed the annual percentage rate disclosed pursuant to item (b) of Section 1803.3. (Added by Stats.1979, c. 805, p. 2776, § 11.5. Amended by Stats.1981, c. 1075, p. 4120, § 9, operative Oct. 1, 1982.)

Cross References

Finance charge defined for purposes of this Chapter, see Civil Code § 1802.10.
Goods defined for purposes of this Chapter, see Civil Code § 1802.1.
Holder defined for purposes of this Chapter, see Civil Code § 1802.13.
Retail installment contract or contract defined for purposes of this Chapter, see Civil Code § 1802.6.

§ 1805.9. Determination of finance charge on precomputed and simple-interest bases; exception

No contract shall provide for a finance charge which is determined in part by the precomputed basis and in part by the simple-interest basis, except for any finance charge permitted by Section 1805.8. (Added by Stats.1979, c. 805, p. 2776, § 11.7.)

Cross References

Finance charge defined for purposes of this Chapter, see Civil Code § 1802.10.

Precomputed basis defined for purposes of this Chapter, see Civil Code § 1802.21.

Retail installment contract or contract defined for purposes of this Chapter, see Civil Code § 1802.6.

Simple-interest basis defined for purposes of this Chapter, see Civil Code § 1802.20.

§ 1806. Repealed by Stats.1931, c. 1070, p. 2234, § 1

ARTICLE 6. PAYMENTS

Section
1806.1. Payment to last known holder of contract or installment account; discharge of obligation.
1806.2. Statement of unpaid balance.
1806.3. Payment or satisfaction before maturity; refund credit.
1806.4. Acknowledgment of payments; release of security.
1807. Repealed.

Cross References

Extinction of contracts, see Civil Code § 1682 et seq.
Extinction of obligations, see Civil Code § 1473 et seq.

§ 1806.1. Payment to last known holder of contract or installment account; discharge of obligation

Unless the buyer has notice of actual or intended assignment of a contract or installment account, payment thereunder made by the buyer to the last known holder of such contract or installment account, shall to the extent of the payment, discharge the buyer's obligation. *(Added by Stats. 1959, c. 201, p. 2099, § 1, operative Jan. 1, 1960.)*

Cross References

Application of section to retail installment accounts, see Civil Code § 1810.8.
Holder, see Civil Code § 1802.13.
Retail buyer or buyer defined for purposes of this Chapter, see Civil Code § 1802.4.
Retail installment account, see Civil Code § 1802.7.
Retail installment contract or contract defined for purposes of this Chapter, see Civil Code § 1802.6.

§ 1806.2. Statement of unpaid balance

At any time after its execution, but not later than one year after the last payment thereunder, the holder of a contract shall, upon written request of the buyer made in good faith, promptly give or forward to the buyer a detailed written statement which will state with accuracy the total amount, if any, unpaid thereunder. Such a statement shall be supplied by the holder once each year without charge; if any additional statement is requested by the buyer, the holder shall supply such statement to the buyer at a charge not exceeding one dollar ($1) for each additional statement supplied to the buyer. The provisions of this section shall apply only to those transactions wherein, instead of periodic statements of account, the buyer is provided with a passbook or payment book in which all payments, credits, charges and the unpaid balance is entered. *(Added by Stats.1959, c. 201, p. 2099, § 1, operative Jan. 1, 1960. Amended by Stats.1969, c. 625, p. 1266, § 7.)*

Cross References

Add-on sales, contents of memorandum, see Civil Code § 1808.2.

Holder defined for purposes of this Chapter, see Civil Code § 1802.13.
Retail buyer or buyer defined for purposes of this Chapter, see Civil Code § 1802.4.
Retail installment contract or contract defined for purposes of this Chapter, see Civil Code § 1802.6.
Unpaid balance defined for purposes of this Chapter, see Civil Code § 1802.11.

§ 1806.3. Payment or satisfaction before maturity; refund credit

(a) Notwithstanding any provision of a contract to the contrary, the buyer may pay at any time before maturity the entire indebtedness evidenced by the contract without penalty. In the event of prepayment in full:

(1) If the finance charge was determined on the precomputed basis, the amount required to repay the contract shall be the outstanding contract balance as of that date, provided, however, that the buyer shall be entitled to a refund credit in the amount of the unearned portion of the finance charge. The amount of the unearned portion of the finance charge shall be at least as great a proportion of the finance charge, or if the contract has been extended, deferred, or refinanced, of the additional charge therefor, as the sum of the periodic monthly time balances payable more than 15 days after the date of prepayment bears to the sum of all the periodic monthly time balances under the schedule of installments in the contract or, if the contract has been extended, deferred or refinanced, as so extended, deferred or refinanced. Where the amount of the refund credit is less than one dollar ($1), no refund credit need be made by the holder. Any refund credit in the amount of one dollar ($1) or more may be made in cash or credited to the outstanding obligations of the buyer under the contract.

(2) If the finance charge or a portion thereof was determined on the simple-interest basis, the amount required to prepay the contract shall be the outstanding contract balance as of that date, including any earned finance charges which are unpaid as of that date, and provided further that in cases where the finance charge or a portion thereof is determined on the 360-day basis, the payments theretofore received will be assumed to have been received on their respective due dates regardless of the actual dates on which those payments were received.

(b) Notwithstanding any provision of a contract to the contrary, whenever the indebtedness created by any retail installment contract is satisfied prior to its maturity through surrender of the collateral, repossession of the collateral, redemption of the collateral after repossession, or any judgment, the outstanding obligation of the buyer shall be determined as provided in subdivision (a); provided further that the buyer's outstanding obligation shall be computed by the holder as of the date the holder recovers the value of the collateral through disposition thereof or judgment is entered or, if the holder elects to keep the collateral in satisfaction of the buyer's indebtedness, as of the date the holder takes possession of the collateral.

(c) This section does not preclude the collection or retention by the holder of any delinquency charge made pursuant to Section 1803.6. *(Added by Stats.1959, c. 201, p. 2099, § 1, operative Jan. 1, 1960. Amended by Stats.1970, c.*

§ 1806.3

546, p. 1046, § 22; Stats.1973, c. 793, p. 1409, § 1; Stats.1979, c. 805, p. 2777, § 12; Stats.1980, c. 1380, p. 5015, § 16, eff. Oct. 1, 1980; Stats.1988, c. 479, § 5; Stats.1991, c. 819 (S.B.1105), § 7.)

Cross References

Application of refund credit in computing refinancing charges, see Civil Code § 1807.2.
Buyer defined, see Civil Code § 1802.4.
Finance charge,
   Generally, see Civil Code § 1802.10.
   Determination, see Civil Code § 1808.5.
   Limitation, see Civil Code § 1805.1 et seq.
Holder defined for purposes of this Chapter, see Civil Code § 1802.13.
Precomputed basis defined for purposes of this Chapter, see Civil Code § 1802.21.
Retail installment contract or contract defined for purposes of this Chapter, see Civil Code § 1802.6.
Simple-interest basis defined for purposes of this Chapter, see Civil Code § 1802.20.
Total of payments, see Civil Code § 1802.12.

§ 1806.4. Acknowledgment of payments; release of security

After the payment of all sums for which the buyer is obligated under a contract and upon demand made by the buyer, the holder shall deliver, or mail to the buyer at his last known address, such one or more good and sufficient instruments as may be necessary to acknowledge payment in full and to release all security in the goods under such contract. (Added by Stats.1959, c. 201, p. 2099, § 1, operative Jan. 1, 1960.)

Cross References

Application of section to retail installment accounts, see Civil Code § 1810.8.
Downpayment, allocation in the case of add-on sales, see Civil Code § 1808.2.
Goods defined for purposes of this Chapter, see Civil Code § 1802.1.
Holder defined for purposes of this Chapter, see Civil Code § 1802.13.
Retail buyer or buyer defined for purposes of this Chapter, see Civil Code § 1802.4.
Retail installment contract or contract defined for purposes of this Chapter, see Civil Code § 1802.6.

§ 1807. Repealed by Stats.1931, c. 1070, p. 2234, § 1

ARTICLE 7. REFINANCING AND CONSOLIDATION

Section
1807.1. Extension of due date or deferment of payment; agreement; charge.
1807.2. Refinancing; agreement; charge; provisions applicable to consolidation of contracts.
1807.3. Installment more than double amount of regularly scheduled equal payment; balloon payment; right to new payment schedule; necessary provision.

§ 1807.1. Extension of due date or deferment of payment; agreement; charge

(a) The holder of a retail installment contract may, upon agreement with the buyer, extend the scheduled due date or defer the scheduled payment of all or of any part of any installment or installments payable thereunder. No charge shall be made for any such extension or deferment unless the agreement for such extension or deferment is in writing and signed by the parties thereto.

(b) Where the contract includes a finance charge determined on the precomputed basis, the holder may charge and contract for the payment of an extension or deferral agreement charge by the buyer and collect and receive the same, but such charge may not exceed an amount equal to 1 percent per month simple interest on the amount of the installment or installments, or part thereof, extended or deferred for the period of extension or deferral. Such period shall not exceed the period from the date when such extended or deferred installment or installments, or part thereof, would have been payable in the absence of such extension or deferral, to the date when such installment or installments, or part thereof, are made payable under the agreement of extension or deferment; except that a minimum charge of one dollar ($1) for the period of extension or deferral may be made in any case where the extension or deferral agreement charge, when computed at such rate, amounts to less than one dollar ($1).

(c) Where the contract includes a finance charge determined on the simple-interest basis, the holder may charge and contract for the payment of an extension or deferral agreement charge by the buyer and collect and receive the same, but the charge for the extension or deferral agreement may not exceed the lesser of twenty-five dollars ($25) or 10 percent of the then unpaid balance of the contract. Such charge shall be in addition to any finance charges which accrue because such extended or deferred payments are received at a time other than as originally scheduled.

(d) An extension or deferral agreement may also provide for the payment by the buyer of the additional cost to the holder of the contract of premiums for continuing in force, until the end of such period of extension or deferral, any insurance coverages provided for in the contract, subject to the provisions of Section 1803.5. (Added by Stats.1959, c. 201, p. 2100, § 1, operative Jan. 1, 1960. Amended by Stats.1980, c. 1380, p. 5016, § 17, eff. Oct. 1, 1980.)

Cross References

Cost of insurance, see Civil Code § 1803.5.
Delinquency charge, see Civil Code § 1803.6.
Finance charge defined for purposes of this Chapter, see Civil Code § 1802.10.
Holder defined for purposes of this Chapter, see Civil Code § 1802.13.
Precomputed basis defined for purposes of this Chapter, see Civil Code § 1802.21.
Retail buyer or buyer defined for purposes of this Chapter, see Civil Code § 1802.4.
Retail installment contract or contract defined for purposes of this Chapter, see Civil Code § 1802.6.
Simple-interest basis defined for purposes of this Chapter, see Civil Code § 1802.20.
Unpaid balance defined for purposes of this Chapter, see Civil Code § 1802.11.

§ 1807.2. Refinancing; agreement; charge; provisions applicable to consolidation of contracts

The holder of a retail installment contract or contracts may, upon agreement in writing with the buyer, refinance the remaining amount owing on the contract or contracts by providing for a new schedule of installment payments. The holder may charge and contract for the payment of a refinance charge by the buyer and collect and receive the same, but such refinance charge shall be based upon the amount refinanced, plus any additional cost of insurance and of official fees incident to the refinancing, after the deduction of a refund credit in an amount equal to that to which the buyer would have been entitled under Section 1806.3 if he or she had prepaid in full his or her obligations under the contract or contracts. The agreement for refinancing may also provide for the payment by the buyer of the additional cost to the holder of the contract or contracts of premiums for continuing in force, until the maturity of the contract or contracts as refinanced, any insurance coverages provided for therein, subject to Section 1803.5. The refinancing agreement shall set forth:

(a) The amount of the existing outstanding balance to be refinanced, which consists of the remaining amount owing to be refinanced.

(b) The amount of any refund credit.

(c) The difference between subdivisions (a) and (b), which is the net outstanding balance to be refinanced.

(d) Any additional cost of insurance and of official fees to the buyer.

(e) The sum of subdivisions (c) and (d), which is the amount financed.

(f) The finance charge (1) as expressed as the annual percentage rate as defined in Regulation Z and (2) expressed in dollars.

(g) The number amount, and due dates or periods of payments scheduled to repay the indebtedness and the sum of those payments.

The items need not be stated in the sequence or order set forth above; additional items may be included to explain the computations made in determining the amount to be paid by the buyer. Where there is a consolidation of two or more contracts then Sections 1808.1 and 1808.2 shall apply. If the finance charge or any portion thereof is calculated on the 365-day basis, the amount of the finance charge shown pursuant to subdivision (f) shall be that amount which will be incurred by the buyer if all payments are received by the seller on their respective due dates. *(Added by Stats.1959, c. 201, p. 2100, § 1, operative Jan. 1, 1960. Amended by Stats.1970, c. 546, p. 1046, § 23; Stats.1979, c. 805, p. 2777, § 13; Stats.1981, c. 1075, p. 4120, § 10, operative Oct. 1, 1982; Stats.1988, c. 479, § 6; Stats.1991, c. 819 (S.B.1105), § 9.)*

Cross References

Amount financed defined for purposes of this Chapter, see Civil Code § 1802.11.
Contract, see Civil Code §§ 1549, 1802.6.
Finance charge,
  Generally, see Civil Code § 1802.10.
  Determination, see Civil Code § 1808.5.
  Limitation, see Civil Code § 1805.1 et seq.
Holder defined for purposes of this Chapter, see Civil Code § 1802.13.
Official fees defined for purposes of this Chapter, see Civil Code § 1802.14.
Prohibited provisions, effect, see Civil Code § 1804.4.
Regulation Z defined for purposes of this Chapter, see Civil Code § 1802.18.
Retail buyer or buyer defined for purposes of this Chapter, see Civil Code § 1802.4.
Retail seller or seller defined for purposes of this Chapter, see Civil Code § 1802.3.
Unpaid balance defined for purposes of this Chapter, see Civil Code § 1802.11.

§ 1807.3. Installment more than double amount of regularly scheduled equal payment; balloon payment; right to new payment schedule; necessary provision

(a) If any payment, other than a deferred downpayment, under a contract or refinancing agreement is more than twice the amount of an otherwise regularly scheduled equal payment, the contract or refinancing agreement shall contain the following provision:

> "The payment schedule contained in this contract requires that you make a balloon payment of $_____ which is a pay-
>   *(Amount of balloon payment)*
> ment more than double the amount of the regular payments. You have an absolute right to obtain a new payment schedule if you default in the payment of any balloon payment."

(b) If the buyer defaults in the payment of any balloon payment, he or she shall be given an absolute right to obtain a new payment schedule. Unless agreed to by the buyer, the periodic payments under the new schedule shall not be substantially greater than the average of the preceding installments. *(Added by Stats.1959, c. 201, p. 2101, § 1, operative Jan. 1, 1960. Amended by Stats.1969, c. 625, p. 1267, § 8; Stats.1970, c. 546, p. 1047, § 23.5; Stats.1981, c. 1075, p. 4121, § 11, operative Oct. 1, 1982.)*

Cross References

Contract, contents, see Civil Code § 1803.3.
Provision in contract for balloon payment, see Civil Code §§ 1808.2, 1808.3.
Retail buyer or buyer defined for purposes of this Chapter, see Civil Code § 1802.4.
Retail installment contract or contract defined for purposes of this Chapter, see Civil Code § 1802.6.
Right of prepayment, see Civil Code § 1806.3.

ARTICLE 8. ADD–ON SALES

Section
1808.1. Contract provisions.
1808.2. Subsequent purchase; memorandum; contents; delivery to buyer.
1808.3. Series of transactions; memorandum; contents; delivery to buyer.
1808.4. Obligation of buyer prior to delivery of memorandum.
1808.5. Finance charge; determination.
1808.6. Repealed.

§ 1808.1. Contract provisions

A retail installment contract, which otherwise conforms to the requirements of this chapter, may contain the provision that the seller may at his option add subsequent purchases made by the buyer to the contract, and that the total price of

§ 1808.1

the goods or services covered by the contract shall be increased by the price of such additional goods or services, and that all finance charges and installment payments may at the seller's option be increased proportionately, and that all terms and conditions of the contract shall apply equally to such additional goods or services. The contract may also provide that the goods purchased under the previous contract or contracts shall be security for the goods purchased under the subsequent contract but only until such time as the total of payments under the previous contract or contracts is fully paid. *(Added by Stats.1959, c. 201, p. 2101, § 1, operative Jan. 1, 1960. Amended by Stats.1969, c. 625, p. 1267, § 9; Stats.1970, c. 546, p. 1047, § 24.)*

Cross References

Contents of contract, see Civil Code § 1803.3.
Contract, see Civil Code §§ 1549, 1802.6.
Finance charge defined for purposes of this Chapter, see Civil Code § 1802.10.
Goods defined for purposes of this Chapter, see Civil Code § 1802.1.
Installment contract, see Commercial Code § 2612.
Payments, see Civil Code § 1806.1 et seq.
Price, see Commercial Code § 2304 et seq.
Provisions of retail installment contracts, see Civil Code § 1803.1 et seq.
Restrictions on retail installment contracts, see Civil Code § 1804.1 et seq.
Retail buyer or buyer defined for purposes of this Chapter, see Civil Code § 1802.4.
Retail installment contract or contract defined for purposes of this Chapter, see Civil Code § 1802.6.
Retail seller or seller defined for purposes of this Chapter, see Civil Code § 1802.3.
Services defined for purposes of this Chapter, see Civil Code § 1802.2.
Total of payments defined for purposes of this Chapter, see Civil Code § 1802.12.
Total sale price defined for purposes of this Chapter, see Civil Code § 1802.9.

§ 1808.2. Subsequent purchase; memorandum; contents; delivery to buyer

When a subsequent purchase is made, the entire amount of all payments made previous thereto shall be deemed to have been applied toward the payment of the previous deferred payment price or deferred payment prices. Each payment thereafter received shall be deemed to be allocated to all of the various deferred payment prices in the same proportion or ratio as the original cash sale prices of the various purchases bear to one another; where the amount of each installment payment is increased in connection with the subsequent purchase, the subsequent payments (at the seller's election) may be deemed to be allocated as follows: an amount equal to the original payment to the previous deferred payment price, and an amount equal to the increase, to the subsequent deferred payment price. However, the amount of any initial or downpayment on the subsequent purchase shall be deemed to be allocated in its entirety to such purchase.

When a subsequent purchase under this section is made the seller shall deliver to the buyer, prior to the due date of the first installment, a memorandum which shall set forth the following:

(a) The names of the seller and the buyer, the place of business of the seller, the residence or place of business of the buyer as specified by the buyer and a description of the goods and services sufficient to identify them. Services or multiple items of goods may be described in general terms and may be described in detail in a separate writing.

(b) The cash price of the goods, services and accessories which are the subject matter of the new retail installment sale.

(c) The amount of the buyer's downpayment, itemizing the amounts paid in money and in goods and containing a brief description of the goods, if any, traded in.

(d) The difference between item (b) and item (c) which is the unpaid balance of cash price.

(e) The amount of the existing outstanding balance to be consolidated, which consists of the unpaid time balance or balances of the prior contract or contracts to be consolidated.

(f) The amount of any unearned finance charge, determined by deducting from the amount of item (e) any then unearned finance charge in an amount not less than the refund credit provided for in Article 6 (commencing with Section 1806.1) of this chapter (computed, however, without the allowance of any minimum earned finance charge).

(g) The difference between items (e) and (f), which is the net outstanding balance to be consolidated.

(h) The amount, if any, included for insurance, specifying the coverages.

(i) The amount, if any, of official fees.

(j) The unpaid balance, which is the sum of items (d), (g), (h) and (i).

(k) The finance charge (1) expressed as the annual percentage rate as defined in Regulation Z and (2) expressed in dollars, and computed in conformity with Section 1808.5.

(*l*) The number, amount, and due dates or periods of payment scheduled to repay the indebtedness and the sum of such payments.

(m) Any "balloon payments" as described in Section 1807.3.

The items need not be stated in the sequence or order set forth above; additional items may be included to explain the computations made in determining the amount to be paid by the buyer. If the finance charge or any portion thereof is calculated on the 365-day basis, the amount of the finance charge shown pursuant to item (k) shall be that amount which will be incurred by the buyer if all payments are received by the seller on their respective due dates. *(Added by Stats. 1959, c. 201, p. 2101, § 1, operative Jan. 1, 1960. Amended by Stats.1969, c. 625, p. 1267, § 10; Stats.1970, c. 546, p. 1048, § 25; Stats.1979, c. 805, p. 2778, § 14.)*

Cross References

Cash price defined for purposes of this Chapter, see Civil Code § 1802.8.
Contents of contract, see Civil Code § 1803.3.
Contract, see Civil Code §§ 1549, 1802.6.
Finance charge defined for purposes of this Chapter, see Civil Code § 1802.10.
Goods defined for purposes of this Chapter, see Civil Code § 1802.1.

Official fees defined for purposes of this Chapter, see Civil Code § 1802.14.

Regulation Z defined for purposes of this Chapter, see Civil Code § 1802.18.

Retail buyer or buyer defined for purposes of this Chapter, see Civil Code § 1802.4.

Retail installment sale or sale defined for purposes of this Chapter, see Civil Code § 1802.5.

Retail seller or seller defined for purposes of this Chapter, see Civil Code § 1802.3.

Retention by seller of security interest in goods, allocation of payments, see Civil Code § 1810.6.

Services defined for purposes of this Chapter, see Civil Code § 1802.2.

Total sale price defined for purposes of this Chapter, see Civil Code § 1802.9.

Unpaid balance defined for purposes of this Chapter, see Civil Code § 1802.11.

§ 1808.3. Series of transactions; memorandum; contents; delivery to buyer

If a credit sale is one of a series of transactions made pursuant to an agreement providing for the addition of the amount financed plus the finance charge for the current sale to an existing outstanding balance, and the disclosures required under this article for the initial sale and each subsequent sale are delayed until some date prior to the date the first payment for that particular sale is due; and

(1) The customer has approved in writing both the annual percentage rate or rates and the method of treating any unearned finance charge on an existing outstanding balance in computing the finance charge or charges; and

(2) The seller retains no security interest in any property as to which he has received payments aggregating the amount of the sale price including any finance charges attributable thereto; then, for the purposes of this section, in the case of items purchased on different dates, the first purchased shall be deemed first paid for, and in the case of items purchased on the same date the lowest priced shall be deemed first paid for.

When a credit sale under this section is made, the seller shall deliver to the buyer, prior to the due date of the first installment, a memorandum which shall set forth the following:

(a) The names of the seller and the buyer, the place of business of the seller, the residence or place of business of the buyer as specified by the buyer and a description of the goods and services sufficient to identify them. Services or multiple items of goods may be described in general terms and may be described in detail in a separate writing.

(b) The cash price of the goods, services and accessories which are the subject matter of the new retail installment sale.

(c) The amount of the buyer's downpayment, itemizing the amounts paid in money and in goods and containing a brief description of the goods, if any, traded in.

(d) The difference between item (b) and item (c), which is the unpaid balance of cash price.

(e) The amount, if any, included for insurance, specifying the coverages.

(f) The amount, if any, of official fees.

(g) The amount financed, which is the sum of items (d), (e) and (f).

(h) The amount of the finance charge (1) expressed as the annual percentage rate as defined in Regulation Z and (2) expressed in dollars, which is to be computed in accordance with this chapter.

(i) The deferred payment price, which is the sum of the amounts determined under items (b), (e), (f) and (h).

(j) The previous balance, which is the amount owing on prior purchases.

(k) The number, amount, and due dates or periods of payments scheduled to repay the indebtedness and the sum of such payments.

(*l*) Any "balloon payments," as described in Section 1807.3.

The items need not be stated in the sequence or order set forth above; additional items may be included to explain the computations made in determining the amount to be paid by the buyer. If the finance charge or any portion thereof is calculated on the 365-day basis, the amount of the finance charge shown pursuant to item (h) shall be that amount which will be incurred by the buyer if all payments are received by the seller on their respective due dates. (Added by Stats.1959, c. 201, p. 2102, § 1, operative Jan. 1, 1960. Amended by Stats.1969, c. 625, p. 1268, § 11; Stats.1970, c. 546, p. 1049, § 26; Stats.1979, c. 805, p. 2779, § 15.)

Cross References

Amount financed defined for purposes of this Chapter, see Civil Code § 1802.11.

Buyer defined for purposes of this Chapter, see Civil Code § 1802.4.

Cash price defined for purposes of this Chapter, see Civil Code § 1802.8.

Contents of contract, see Civil Code § 1803.3.

Contract, see Civil Code §§ 1549, 1802.6.

Finance charge defined for purposes of this Chapter, see Civil Code § 1802.10.

Goods defined for purposes of this Chapter, see Civil Code § 1802.1.

Official fees defined for purposes of this Chapter, see Civil Code § 1802.14.

Regulation Z defined for purposes of this Chapter, see Civil Code § 1802.18.

Retail seller or seller defined for purposes of this Chapter, see Civil Code § 1802.3.

Sale, see Civil Code § 1802.5; Commercial Code § 2106.

Security interest defined, see Commercial Code § 1201.

Services defined for purposes of this Chapter, see Civil Code § 1802.2.

Unpaid balance defined for purposes of this Chapter, see Civil Code § 1802.11.

§ 1808.4. Obligation of buyer prior to delivery of memorandum

Until the seller delivers to the buyer the memorandum as provided in Sections 1808.2 and 1808.3, the buyer shall be obligated to pay only the cash price of the subsequent purchase. (Added by Stats.1959, c. 201, p. 2102, § 1, operative Jan. 1, 1960. Amended by Stats.1970, c. 546, p. 1050, § 27.)

Cross References

Cash price defined for purposes of this Chapter, see Civil Code § 1802.8.

§ 1808.4

Retail buyer or buyer defined for purposes of this Chapter, see Civil Code § 1802.4.

Retail installment account statement nondelivery, obligation restricted to cash price, see Civil Code § 1810.1.

Retail installment contract, nondelivery of documents, obligation restricted to cash price, see Civil Code § 1803.7.

Retail seller or seller defined for purposes of this Chapter, see Civil Code § 1802.3.

§ 1808.5. Finance charge; determination

Subject to the other provisions of Article 5 (commencing with Section 1805.1), the finance charge to be included in a consolidated total of payments under subdivision (*l*) of Section 1808.2 shall be determined by applying the finance charge at the applicable rate to the unpaid balance under subdivision (j) of Section 1808.2, for the period from the date of the consolidation to and including the date when the final installment of the consolidated total is payable. *(Added by Stats.1959, c. 201, p. 2102, § 1, operative Jan. 1, 1960. Amended by Stats.1970, c. 546, p. 1050, § 28; Stats.1979, c. 805, p. 2781, § 16; Stats.1988, c. 479, § 7; Stats.1991, c. 819 (S.B.1105), § 11.)*

Cross References

Finance charge defined for purposes of this Chapter, see Civil Code § 1802.10.

Total of payments defined for purposes of this Chapter, see Civil Code § 1802.12.

Unpaid balance defined for purposes of this Chapter, see Civil Code § 1802.11.

§ 1808.6. Repealed by Stats.1991, c. 819 (S.B.1105), § 13

ARTICLE 9. TERMS OF PURCHASE BY FINANCING AGENCY

Section
1809.1. Authority to purchase; terms; conditions and price.

§ 1809.1. Authority to purchase; terms; conditions and price

Notwithstanding any contrary provision of this title a financing agency may purchase a retail installment contract or installment account from a seller on such terms and conditions and for such price as may be mutually agreed upon. No filing of notice or of the assignment, no notice to the buyer of the assignment, and no requirement that the seller be deprived of dominion over payments upon the contract or installment account or over the goods if repossessed by the seller, shall be necessary to the validity of a written assignment of a contract or installment account as against creditors, subsequent purchasers, pledgees, mortgagees or encumbrancers of the seller, except as may otherwise be required by law. *(Added by Stats.1959, c. 201, p. 2103, § 1, operative Jan. 1, 1960.)*

Cross References

Alienability of debtor's rights in collateral, see Commercial Code § 9311.

Application of Commercial Code, see Commercial Code § 9104.

Assignment of security interest, duties of filing officer, see Commercial Code § 9406.

Defenses against assignee, see Commercial Code § 9318.

OBLIGATIONS

Filing to protect security interests, exceptions, see Commercial Code § 9302.

Financing agency defined for purposes of this Chapter, see Civil Code § 1802.16.

Goods defined for purposes of this Chapter, see Civil Code § 1802.1.

Price, see Commercial Code § 2304 et seq.

Retail buyer or buyer defined for purposes of this Chapter, see Civil Code § 1802.4.

Retail installment account or installment account defined for purposes of this Chapter, see Civil Code § 1802.7.

Retail installment contract or contract defined for purposes of this Chapter, see Civil Code § 1802.6.

Retail seller or seller defined for purposes of this Chapter, see Civil Code § 1802.3.

ARTICLE 10. RETAIL INSTALLMENT ACCOUNTS

Section
1810. Agreements; acceptance by buyer; disclosures; notices of change.
1810.1. Written statement by creditor; contents.
1810.2. Finance charge.
1810.3. Periodic statement; contents; disclosure of change in terms; credit balances; notice; disposition.
1810.4. Finance charge as inclusive of all incidental charges; agreement for payment of attorney's fees and costs; annual fee for credit cards; fee for dishonored checks.
1810.5. Cost of insurance separately charged to buyer; agreement.
1810.6. Retention by seller of security interest in goods; allocation of payments.
1810.7. Execution of notes or series of notes.
1810.8. Applicability of provisions relating to payments.
1810.9. Repealed.
1810.10. Finance charge on undelivered goods.
1810.11. Statement of finance charges; request; form; time.
1810.12. Delinquency charge for default in payment of installment; agreement with and copy to buyer; collection cost.

§ 1810. Agreements; acceptance by buyer; disclosures; notices of change

For the purposes of this article, a retail installment account agreement shall be deemed to be accepted by the buyer if (1) the buyer signs the agreement, including signing an application containing the terms of the agreement, or (2) the account is used by the buyer or a person who has been authorized by the buyer to use the account, and the buyer has been notified in writing that the use of the credit card will mean that the agreement has been accepted by the buyer. The agreement shall not become effective unless and until the buyer has been given or provided with the disclosures required pursuant to Section 1810.1, and has accepted the agreement as provided in this section. A subsequent change in any term of the agreement shall not become effective until the seller has given notice of the change and complies with the provisions of subdivision (d) of Section 1810.3. *(Added by Stats.1995, c. 566 (S.B.538), § 1.)*

Cross References

Person defined for purposes of this Chapter, see Civil Code § 1802.15.

Retail buyer or buyer defined for purposes of this Chapter, see Civil Code § 1802.4.

Retail installment account or installment account defined for purposes of this Chapter, see Civil Code § 1802.7.

Retail seller or seller defined for purposes of this Chapter, see Civil Code § 1802.3.

§ 1810.1. Written statement by creditor; contents

Notwithstanding any other provisions of this article to the contrary, before the first transaction is made on any retail installment account, the seller shall disclose to the buyer in a single written statement, which the buyer may retain, in terminology consistent with the requirements of Section 1810.3, each of the following items, to the extent applicable:

(a) The conditions under which a finance charge may be imposed, including an explanation of the time period, if any, within which any credit extended may be paid without incurring a finance charge.

(b) The method of determining the balance upon which a finance charge may be imposed.

(c) The method of determining the amount of the finance charge, including the method of determining any minimum, charge which may be imposed as a finance charge.

(d) Where one or more periodic rates may be used to compute the finance charge, each such rate, the range of balances to which it is applicable, and the corresponding annual percentage rate determined by multiplying the periodic rate by the number of periods in a year.

(e) The conditions under which any other charges may be imposed, and the method by which they will be determined.

(f) The conditions under which the creditor may retain or acquire any security interest in any property to secure the payment of any credit extended on the account, and a description or identification of the type of the interest or interests which may be so retained, or acquired.

(g) The minimum periodic payment required.

In addition to the penalties provided under Article 12.2 (commencing with Section 1812.6) of this chapter, until the seller delivers the written statement required by this section, the buyer shall be obligated to pay only the cash price of the goods or services. *(Added by Stats.1969, c. 625, p. 1269, § 13. Amended by Stats.1970, c. 304, p. 698, § 1, operative Jan. 1, 1971; Stats.1970, c. 546, p. 1051, § 29.5, operative Jan. 1, 1971.)*

Cross References

Add-on sale memorandum, nondelivery, obligation restricted to cash price, see Civil Code § 1808.4.

Cash price defined for purposes of this Chapter, see Civil Code § 1802.8.

Finance charge, see Civil Code § 1802.10.

Goods defined for purposes of this Chapter, see Civil Code § 1802.1.

Retail buyer or buyer defined for purposes of this Chapter, see Civil Code § 1802.4.

Retail installment account, see Civil Code § 1802.7.

Retail installment contract, nondelivery of documents, obligation restricted to cash price, see Civil Code § 1803.7.

Retail seller or seller defined for purposes of this Chapter, see Civil Code § 1802.3.

Services defined for purposes of this Chapter, see Civil Code § 1802.2.

§ 1810.2. Finance charge

Subject to the other provisions of this article, the seller or holder of a retail installment account may charge, receive and collect a finance charge as disclosed to the buyer pursuant to Section 1810.3. *(Added by Stats.1980, c. 1381, p. 5047, § 6, operative April 1, 1982. Amended by Stats.1981, c. 26, p. 61, § 2, eff. April 30, 1981, operative Oct. 1, 1982; Stats.1982, c. 1611, p. 6445, § 4, eff. Sept. 30, 1982, operative Jan. 1, 1984; Stats.1983, c. 1157, § 4, operative Jan. 1, 1986; Stats.1985, c. 227, § 4, operative Jan. 1, 1988; Stats.1988, c. 479, § 9; Stats.1991, c. 819 (S.B.1105), § 14.)*

Cross References

Finance charge,
  Generally, see Civil Code § 1802.10.
  Determination, see Civil Code § 1808.5.
  Limitation, see Civil Code § 1805.1 et seq.
  Statement of amount and method of computation in contract, see Civil Code § 1803.3.

Holder defined for purposes of this Chapter, see Civil Code § 1802.13.

Retail buyer or buyer defined for purposes of this Chapter, see Civil Code § 1802.4.

Retail installment account or installment account defined for purposes of this Chapter, see Civil Code § 1802.7.

Retail seller or seller defined for purposes of this Chapter, see Civil Code § 1802.3.

§ 1810.3. Periodic statement; contents; disclosure of change in terms; credit balances; notice; disposition

(a) Except in the case of an account which the seller deems to be uncollectible or with respect to which delinquency collection procedures have been instituted, the seller of any retail installment account shall mail or deliver to the buyer for each billing cycle at the end of which there is an outstanding debit balance in excess of one dollar ($1) in that account or with respect to which a finance charge is imposed, a statement or statements which the buyer may retain, setting forth in accordance with subdivision (c) each of the following items to the extent applicable:

(1) The outstanding balance in the account at the beginning of the billing cycle, using the term "previous balance."

(2) The amount and date of each extension of credit or the date the extension of credit is debited to the account during the billing cycle and, unless previously furnished, a brief identification of any goods or services purchased or other extension of credit.

(3) The total amounts credited to the account during the billing cycle for payments, using the term "payment," and for other credits, including returns, rebates of finance charges, and adjustments, using the term "credits," and unless previously furnished, a brief identification of each of the items included in the other credits.

(4) The amount of any finance charge, using the term "finance charge," debited to the account during the billing cycle, itemized and identified to show the amounts, if any, due to the application of periodic rates and the amount of any other charge included in the finance charge, such as a minimum charge, using appropriate descriptive terminology.

(5) Each periodic rate, using the term "periodic rate" (or "rates"), that may be used to compute the finance charge (whether or not applied during the billing cycle), and the range of balances to which it is applicable.

(6) The balance on which the finance charge was computed, and a statement of how that balance was determined. If any balance is determined without first deducting all credits during the billing cycle, that fact and the amount of the credits shall also be disclosed.

(7) The closing date of the billing cycle and the outstanding balance in the account on that date, using the term "new balance," accompanied by the statement of the date by which, or the period, if any, within which, payment must be made to avoid additional finance charges.

(b) The seller shall mail or deliver the statements required by subdivision (a) at least 14 days prior to any date or the end of any time period required to be disclosed under paragraph (7) of subdivision (a) in order for the consumer to avoid an additional finance or other charge. A seller that fails to meet this requirement shall not collect any finance or other charges imposed as a result of the failure.

(c) The disclosures required by subdivision (a) may be made on the face of the periodic statement or on its reverse side. In addition, the disclosures required by subdivision (a) may be made on the periodic statement supplemented by separate statement forms if they are enclosed together and delivered to the customer at the same time and if all of the following conditions are met:

(1) The disclosures required by paragraph (1) of subdivision (a) shall appear on the face of the periodic statement. If the amounts and dates of the charges and credits required to be disclosed under paragraphs (2) and (3) of subdivision (a) are not itemized on the face or reverse side of the periodic statement, they shall be disclosed on a separate statement or separate slips which shall accompany the periodic statement and identify each charge and credit and show the date and amount thereof. Identification of goods or services purchased may be made on an accompanying slip or by symbol relating to an identification list printed on the statement. If the disclosures required under paragraph (4) of subdivision (a) are not itemized on the face or reverse side of the periodic statement, they shall be disclosed on a separate statement which shall accompany the periodic statement.

(2) The disclosures required by paragraph (5) of subdivision (a) and a reference to the amounts required to be disclosed under paragraphs (4) and (6) of subdivision (a), if not disclosed together on the face or the reverse side of the periodic statement, shall appear together on the face of a single supplemental statement which shall accompany the periodic statement.

(3) The face of the periodic statement shall contain one of the following notices, as applicable: "NOTICE: See reverse side for important information" or "NOTICE: See accompanying statement(s) for important information" or "NOTICE: See reverse side and accompanying statement(s) for important information."

(4) The disclosures shall not be separated so as to confuse or mislead the customer, or to obscure or detract attention from the information required to be disclosed.

(d) If any change is to be made in terms of a retail installment account previously disclosed to the buyer, the seller shall mail or deliver to the buyer written disclosure of the proposed change not less than 30 days prior to the effective date of the change or 30 days prior to the beginning of the billing cycle within which the change will become effective, whichever is the earlier date. When the change involves a reduction of any component of a finance charge or other charge, the notice shall be sufficient if it appears on or accompanies the periodic statements mailed or delivered to buyers receiving periodic statements in the ordinary course of business. When the change involves an increase in any component of a finance charge, as defined in Section 1802.10, or involves a change in a charge permitted by Section 1810.4 or a change in the attorney's fee provision in the agreement pursuant to Section 1810.4, the change shall be effective only with respect to purchases made on or after the effective date of the change.

(e)(1) If any outstanding credit balance in excess of one dollar ($1) exists in a retail installment account, the seller shall mail or deliver to the buyer at the end of the billing cycle in which the credit balance is created either of the following:

(A) A cash refund in the amount of the outstanding credit.

(B) A statement setting forth the credit balance, and thereafter shall mail or deliver to the buyer a statement setting forth the credit balance no fewer than two additional times during the six-month period following creation of the credit balance.

(2) If the credit balance exists for a period of 90 days, the seller shall, at his or her option, do either of the following:

(A) Notify the buyer of his or her right to request and receive a cash refund in the amount of the outstanding credit balance in two successive statements covering, respectively, each of the two successive billing cycles immediately following the 90-day period. The notice is to be accomplished by a clear and conspicuous disclosure on or enclosed with each of the two successive statements, each of which shall be accompanied by a self-addressed return envelope. The disclosure shall contain the following information and may be in the following form:

"We owe you ____. Your credit balance will be refunded on request. If you don't request a refund, six months from the first appearance of a "credit balance" on your bill, your credit balance will be refunded automatically.

"If your credit balance is $1.00 or less, it will not be refunded unless requested, and after 6 months, it will not be credited against future purchases.

"You may obtain a refund of your credit balance by mail by presenting your statement at our store or by returning the top half of your statement in the enclosed envelope."

If between the sending of the first notice and the sending of the second notice required by this subparagraph, the outstanding credit balance is refunded to the buyer or otherwise disposed of, the sending of the second notice shall not be required.

(B) Refund to the buyer the outstanding credit balance at any time after the credit balance is created in the buyer's account and prior to the date by which the first notice of the outstanding balance would have been sent had the seller elected to proceed under subparagraph (A).

(f)(1) If a retail installment account with an outstanding credit balance in excess of one dollar ($1) which has been determined to be correct by the seller is dormant for a period of 180 days after the credit balance is created in the buyer's account, the seller shall mail or deliver a refund in the amount of the outstanding credit balance to the buyer at the buyer's last known address.

(2) If any refund is returned to the seller with a notification to the effect that the addressee is not located at the address to which it was sent, the seller shall make one remailing of the refund with an address correction request, and shall mail the refund to the corrected address, if it is obtained.

(3) If the refund reflecting an outstanding credit balance in excess of twenty-five dollars ($25) is again returned, the seller shall reinstate the full amount of the outstanding credit balance on the buyer's account to be retained and credited against future purchases for one year from the date on which the remailed refund was returned. The seller may continue to attempt to obtain a current mailing address for the buyer by whatever means the seller deems appropriate. Except as provided in subdivision (g), the seller shall not be required to take any further action with respect to sending any statement of the credit balance or otherwise with respect to the credit balance, unless the buyer of the account thereafter requests a refund of the credit balance, in which event the seller shall either make the refund or provide a written explanation as provided in paragraph (5) of this subdivision.

(4) If a remailed refund reflecting an outstanding credit balance of twenty-five dollars ($25) or less is again returned, the seller, except as provided in subdivision (g), shall not be required to take any further action with respect to sending any statement of the credit balance to the buyer or otherwise with respect to the credit balance, unless the buyer of the account thereafter requests a refund of the credit balance, in which event the seller shall either make the refund or provide a written explanation as provided in paragraph (5) of this subdivision.

(5) If a buyer requests, in person or by mail, a refund of a credit balance in any amount which has been reflected at any time on the buyer's account, the seller shall, within 30 days of receipt of the request, either refund the amount requested, or furnish the customer with a written explanation, with supporting documentation when available, of the reasons for refusing to refund the amount requested.

(6) If a buyer, in writing, requests a seller to retain an outstanding credit balance on his or her account, the seller shall not be required to give notification as otherwise required by subdivisions (e) and (f).

(g) If an outstanding credit balance remains unrefundable for three years from the date it was created in the buyer's account, then the amount of the buyer's outstanding credit balance shall escheat to the state as property included within Section 1520 of the Code of Civil Procedure. Those funds shall be paid or delivered to the Controller, and may thereafter be claimed, as specified in Chapter 7 (commencing with Section 1500) of Title 10 of Part 4 of the Code of Civil Procedure.

(h) For the purposes of this section, an outstanding credit balance is created at the end of the billing cycle in which the credit balance is first recorded on a buyer's account and is created anew at the end of the billing cycle in which the recorded amount of an existing credit balance is changed because of the buyer's use of his or her account. *(Formerly § 1810.5, added by Stats.1959, c. 201, p. 2104, § 1, operative Jan. 1, 1960. Renumbered § 1810.3 and amended by Stats. 1969, c. 625, p. 1270, § 17. Amended by Stats.1970, c. 546, p. 1052, § 31; Stats.1975, c. 947, p. 2117, § 1; Stats.1981, c. 452, p. 1700, § 1; Stats.1988, c. 1402, § 1; Stats.1995, c. 566 (S.B.538), § 2; Stats.1996, c. 762 (S.B.2014), § 1.)*

Cross References

Billing cycle defined for purposes of this Chapter, see Civil Code § 1802.17.
Goods defined for purposes of this Chapter, see Civil Code § 1802.1.
Payments, see Civil Code § 1806.1 et seq.
Person defined for purposes of this Chapter, see Civil Code § 1802.15.
Retail buyer or buyer defined for purposes of this Chapter, see Civil Code § 1802.4.
Retail installment account or installment account defined for purposes of this Chapter, see Civil Code § 1802.7.
Retail seller or seller defined for purposes of this Chapter, see Civil Code § 1802.3.
Services defined for purposes of this Chapter, see Civil Code § 1802.2.
State Controller, generally, see Government Code § 12402 et seq.
Unpaid balance, see Civil Code § 1802.11.

§ 1810.4. Finance charge as inclusive of all incidental charges; agreement for payment of attorney's fees and costs; annual fee for credit cards; fee for dishonored checks

The finance charge shall include all charges incident to investigating and making the retail installment account. No fee, expense, delinquency, collection, or other charge whatsoever shall be taken, received, reserved, or contracted by the seller or holder of a retail installment account except as provided in this section. A seller may, however, in an agreement which is accepted by the buyer and of which a copy is given or furnished to the buyer provide for the payment of attorney's fees and costs in conformity with Article 11 (commencing with Section 1811.1). Any subsequent change in any term of the agreement shall not become effective until the seller has given notice of the change and complies with the provisions of subdivision (d) of Section 1810.3. When credit cards are issued in connection with a retail installment account, the seller, either in the agreement or after giving the notice required by subdivision (d) of Section 1810.3, may require the payment of an annual fee of not more than fifteen dollars ($15) for membership in the credit card plan, which fee shall not be deemed a finance charge or interest for any purpose of the law.

The seller or holder of a retail installment account may charge and collect a fee not to exceed fifteen dollars ($15) for the return by a depository institution of a dishonored check, negotiable order of withdrawal, or share draft issued in connection with the retail installment account. The fee is not included in charges as defined in this chapter or in determining the applicable charges which may be made under this chapter. *(Formerly § 1810.6, added by Stats.1959, c. 201, p.*

§ 1810.4

2105, § 1, operative Jan. 1, 1960. Renumbered § 1810.4 and amended by Stats.1969, c. 625, p. 1272, § 18. Amended by Stats.1970, c. 546, p. 1054, § 32; Stats.1982, c. 371, p. 1690, § 1; Stats.1982, c. 512, p. 2290, § 3; Stats.1993, c. 101 (S.B.329), § 2; Stats.1995, c. 566 (S.B.538), § 3.)

Cross References

Action on contract, award of attorney's fees and costs, see Civil Code § 1717.
Attorney's fees, payment from proceeds of resale, see Civil Code § 1812.4.
Attorney's fees and costs, see Civil Code §§ 1717, 1811.1.
Automobile conditional sales contract, attorney's fees, see Civil Code § 2983.4.
Breach of warranty, award of attorney's fees, see Civil Code §§ 1794, 1794.1.
Commercial paper, provision for attorney's fees and collection costs, see Commercial Code § 3106.
Credit card holder, award of attorney's fees against issuer or retailer, see Civil Code § 1747.50 et seq.
Finance charge,
  Generally, see Civil Code § 1802.10.
  Determination, see Civil Code § 1808.5.
  Limitation, see Civil Code § 1805.1 et seq.
Holder defined for purposes of this Chapter, see Civil Code § 1802.13.
Prohibited provision, effect, see Civil Code § 1804.4.
Retail buyer or buyer defined for purposes of this Chapter, see Civil Code § 1802.4.
Retail installment account or installment account defined for purposes of this Chapter, see Civil Code § 1802.7.
Retail seller or seller defined for purposes of this Chapter, see Civil Code § 1802.3.
Swimming pool construction contracts, award of attorney's fees, see Business and Professions Code § 7168.

§ 1810.5. Cost of insurance separately charged to buyer; agreement

If the cost of any insurance is to be separately charged to the buyer, there shall be an agreement to this effect, signed by both the buyer and the seller, a copy of which shall be given or furnished to the buyer. Such agreement shall state whether the insurance is to be procured by the buyer or the seller or holder. If the insurance is to be procured by the seller or holder, the seller or holder shall comply with the provisions of Section 1803.5. (Formerly § 1810.7, added by Stats.1959, c. 201, p. 2105, § 1, operative Jan. 1, 1960. Renumbered § 1810.5 and amended by Stats.1969, c. 625, p. 1272, § 19.)

Cross References

Holder defined for purposes of this Chapter, see Civil Code § 1802.13.
Insurance cost, see Civil Code § 1803.5.
Retail buyer or buyer defined for purposes of this Chapter, see Civil Code § 1802.4.
Retail seller or seller defined for purposes of this Chapter, see Civil Code § 1802.3.

§ 1810.6. Retention by seller of security interest in goods; allocation of payments

Nothing in this article prohibits the execution of an agreement between a buyer and seller whereby the seller retains a security interest in goods sold to the buyer until full payment therefor has been made. For purposes of release of the security interests, in the case of goods or services purchased on different dates, the first purchased shall be deemed first paid for, and in the case of goods or services purchased on the same date, the lowest priced shall be deemed first paid for, and all amounts allocated to payment of these goods or services shall be applied to accomplish that result. However, any downpayment on a specific purchase shall be deemed to be allocated in its entirety to such purchase. (Formerly § 1810.8, added by Stats.1959, c. 201, p. 2105, § 1, operative Jan. 1, 1960. Renumbered § 1810.6 and amended by Stats.1969, c. 625, p. 1272, § 20. Amended by Stats.1974, c. 563, p. 1382, § 1; Stats.1981, c. 26, p. 61, § 3, eff. April 30, 1981.)

Cross References

Goods defined for purposes of this Chapter, see Civil Code § 1802.1.
Retail buyer or buyer defined for purposes of this Chapter, see Civil Code § 1802.4.
Retail seller or seller defined for purposes of this Chapter, see Civil Code § 1802.3.
Secured transactions, see Commercial Code § 9101 et seq.
Services defined for purposes of this Chapter, see Civil Code § 1802.2.

§ 1810.7. Execution of notes or series of notes

No retail installment account shall require or entail the execution of any note or series of notes by the buyer which when separately negotiated will cut off as to third parties any right of action or defense which the buyer may have against the seller. (Formerly § 1810.9, added by Stats.1959, c. 201, p. 2105, § 1, operative Jan. 1, 1960. Renumbered § 1810.7 and amended by Stats.1969, c. 625, p. 1272, § 21.)

Cross References

Invalidity of prohibited provisions, effect on contract, see Civil Code § 1804.4.
Retail buyer or buyer defined for purposes of this Chapter, see Civil Code § 1802.4.
Retail installment account or installment account defined for purposes of this Chapter, see Civil Code § 1802.7.
Retail seller or seller defined for purposes of this Chapter, see Civil Code § 1802.3.

§ 1810.8. Applicability of provisions relating to payments

The provisions of Sections 1806.1 and 1806.4 shall be applicable to retail installment accounts. (Formerly § 1810.10, added by Stats.1959, c. 201, p. 2105, § 1, operative Jan. 1, 1960. Renumbered § 1810.8 and amended by Stats. 1969, c. 625, p. 1272, § 22.)

Cross References

Retail installment account or installment account defined for purposes of this Chapter, see Civil Code § 1802.7.

§ 1810.9. Repealed by Stats.1988, c. 1402, § 2

§ 1810.10. Finance charge on undelivered goods

(a) Notwithstanding the provision of any contract to the contrary, except as provided in subdivision (b) or (c), no retail seller shall assess any finance charge against the outstanding balance for goods purchased under a retail installment account until the goods are in the buyer's possession.

(b) A finance charge may be assessed against the outstanding balance for such undelivered goods, as follows:

(1) From the date when such goods are available for pickup by the buyer and the buyer is notified of their availability, or

(2) From the date of purchase, when such goods are delivered or available for pickup by the buyer within 10 days of the date of purchase.

(c) In the case of a home improvement contract as defined in Section 7151.2 of the Business and Professions Code, a finance charge may be assessed against the amount financed from the approximate date of commencement of the work as set forth in the home improvement contract. (Added by Stats.1975, c. 1041, p. 2455, § 2. Amended by Stats.1976, c. 1271, p. 5626, § 5, eff. Sept. 28, 1976, operative Jan. 1, 1978; Stats.1977, c. 868, p. 2622, § 5; Stats.1979, c. 1000, p. 3400, § 6.)

Cross References

Amount financed defined for purposes of this Chapter, see Civil Code § 1802.11.
Finance charge defined for purposes of this Chapter, see Civil Code § 1802.10.
Goods defined for purposes of this Chapter, see Civil Code § 1802.1.
Retail buyer or buyer defined for purposes of this Chapter, see Civil Code § 1802.4.
Retail installment account or installment account defined for purposes of this Chapter, see Civil Code § 1802.7.
Retail installment contract or contract defined for purposes of this Chapter, see Civil Code § 1802.6.
Retail seller or seller defined for purposes of this Chapter, see Civil Code § 1802.3.

§ 1810.11. Statement of finance charges; request; form; time

The buyer may request, not more frequently than once a year, that the seller inform the buyer of the total amount of finance charges assessed on the account during the preceding calendar year and the seller shall provide that information to the buyer within 30 days of receiving the request, without charge.

If the buyer's request for the information is made in writing, the seller shall provide the information in writing, provided, however, that if the seller is required to furnish the buyer with a periodic billing or periodic statement of account or furnishes the billing or statement of account, the requested statement of finance charges may be furnished along with the periodic billing or periodic statement of account.

"Seller," for the purposes of this section, means a person engaged in the business of selling goods or furnishing services to retail buyers whose annual sales pursuant to retail installment accounts in California have exceeded one hundred fifty million dollars ($150,000,000) in the seller's last two consecutive years. (Added by Stats.1995, c. 693 (S.B.539), § 2.)

Cross References

Finance charge defined for purposes of this Chapter, see Civil Code § 1802.10.
Goods defined for purposes of this Chapter, see Civil Code § 1802.1.
Person defined for purposes of this Chapter, see Civil Code § 1802.15.
Retail buyer or buyer defined for purposes of this Chapter, see Civil Code § 1802.4.
Retail installment account or installment account defined for purposes of this Chapter, see Civil Code § 1802.7.
Retail installment sale or sale defined for purposes of this Chapter, see Civil Code § 1802.5.
Retail seller or seller defined for purposes of this Chapter, see Civil Code § 1802.3.
Services defined for purposes of this Chapter, see Civil Code § 1802.2.

§ 1810.12. Delinquency charge for default in payment of installment; agreement with and copy to buyer; collection cost

(a) Notwithstanding Section 1810.4, a seller or holder of a retail installment account may, subject to subdivision (d) of Section 1810.3, provide that for each installment in default the buyer shall pay a delinquency charge not in excess of one of the following amounts:

(1) For a period in default of not less than 10 days, an amount not in excess of ten dollars ($10).

(2) For a period in default of not less than 15 days, an amount not in excess of fifteen dollars ($15).

(b) Only one delinquency charge may be collected on any installment regardless of the period during which it remains in default. No delinquency charge shall be imposed for any default of payment on any payment due prior to the mailing or delivery to the buyer of the written disclosure concerning the delinquency charge provided by the seller or holder of a retail installment account pursuant to subdivision (d) of Section 1810.3. Payments timely received by the seller under a written extension or deferral agreement shall not be subject to any delinquency charge. The agreement may also provide for payment of any actual and reasonable costs of collection occasioned by removal of the goods from the state without written permission of the holder, or by the failure of the buyer to notify the holder of any change of residence, or by the failure of the buyer to communicate with the holder for a period of 45 days after any default in making payments due under the agreement.

(c) Notwithstanding subdivision (b) of Section 1810.3, the seller or holder of a retail installment account shall provide a minimum of 20 days between the monthly billing date and the date upon which the minimum payment is due, exclusive of the applicable grace period provided in subdivision (a). (Added by Stats.1983, c. 763, § 1. Amended by Stats.1988, c. 1402, § 3; Stats.1994, c. 168 (S.B.1583), § 2; Stats.1996, c. 301 (S.B.2050), § 2.)

Cross References

Goods defined for purposes of this Chapter, see Civil Code § 1802.1.
Holder defined for purposes of this Chapter, see Civil Code § 1802.13.
Retail buyer or buyer defined for purposes of this Chapter, see Civil Code § 1802.4.
Retail installment account or installment account defined for purposes of this Chapter, see Civil Code § 1802.7.
Retail seller or seller defined for purposes of this Chapter, see Civil Code § 1802.3.

ARTICLE 10.5. RETAIL INSTALLMENT ACCOUNT CREDIT CARD PERIODIC RATE DISCLOSURES

Section
1810.20. Short title.

Section
1810.21. Disclosures to accompany application form; manner of disclosure; "Regulation Z"; additional terms, etc.; federal disclosure requirement; statement offering disclosures; application of article.

§ 1810.20. Short title

This article shall be known and may be cited as the "Areias Retail Installment Account Full Disclosure Act of 1986." *(Added by Stats.1986, c. 1397, § 4. Amended by Stats.2000, c. 375 (A.B.1331), § 6.)*

Cross References

Retail installment account or installment account defined for purposes of this Chapter, see Civil Code § 1802.7.

§ 1810.21. Disclosures to accompany application form; manner of disclosure; "Regulation Z"; additional terms, etc.; federal disclosure requirement; statement offering disclosures; application of article

(a) Any application form or preapproved written solicitation for a credit card issued in connection with a retail installment account that is mailed on or after October 1, 1987, to a retail buyer residing in this state by or on behalf of a retail seller, whether or not the retail seller is located in this state, other than an application form or solicitation included in a magazine, newspaper, or other publication distributed by someone other than the retail seller, shall contain or be accompanied by either of the following disclosures:

(1) A disclosure of each of the following, if applicable:

(A) Any periodic rate or rates that will be used to determine the finance charge imposed on the balance due under the terms of a retail installment account, expressed as an annual percentage rate or rates.

(B) Any membership or participation fee that will be imposed for availability of a retail installment account in connection with which a credit card is issued expressed as an annualized amount.

(C) If the retail seller provides a period during which the retail buyer may repay the full balance reflected on a billing statement that is attributable to purchases of goods or services from the retail seller without the imposition of additional finance charges, the retail seller shall either disclose the minimum number of days of that period, calculated from the closing date of the prior billing cycle to the date designated in the billing statement sent to the retail buyer as the date by which that payment must be received to avoid additional finance charges, or describe the manner in which the period is calculated. For purposes of this section, the period shall be referred to as the "free period" or "free-ride period." If the retail seller does not provide this period for purchases, the disclosure shall so indicate.

(2) A disclosure that satisfies the initial disclosure statement requirements of Regulation Z (12 C.F.R. 226.6).

(b) In the event that an unsolicited application form is mailed or otherwise delivered to retail buyers in more than one state, the requirements of subdivision (a) shall be satisfied if on the application form or the soliciting material there is a notice that credit terms may vary from state to state and that provides either the disclosures required by subdivision (a) or an address or phone number for the customer to use to obtain the disclosure. The notice shall be in boldface type no smaller than the largest type used in the narrative portion, excluding headlines, of the material soliciting the application. Any person responding to the notice shall be given the disclosures required by subdivision (a).

(c) A retail seller need not present the disclosures required by paragraph (1) of subdivision (a) in chart form or use any specific terminology, except as expressly provided in this section. The following chart shall not be construed in any way as a standard by which to determine whether a retail seller who elects not to use the chart has provided the required disclosures in a manner which satisfies paragraph (1) of subdivision (a). However, disclosures shall be conclusively presumed to satisfy the requirements of paragraph (1) of subdivision (a) if a chart with captions substantially as follows is completed with the applicable terms offered by the retail seller, or if the retail seller presents the applicable terms in tabular, list, or narrative format using terminology substantially similar to the captions included in the following chart:

THE FOLLOWING INFORMATION IS PROVIDED PURSUANT TO THE AREIAS RETAIL INSTALLMENT ACCOUNT FULL DISCLOSURE ACT OF 1986:

CREDIT CARD TERMS VARY AMONG RETAIL SELLERS—SELECTED TERMS FOR PURCHASES UNDER THIS RETAIL INSTALLMENT ACCOUNT ARE SET OUT BELOW

PERIODIC RATES (as APRs)	ANNUAL FEES	FREE–RIDE PERIOD

(d) For purposes of this section, "Regulation Z" has the meaning attributed to it under Section 1802.18, and all of the terms used in this section have the same meaning as attributed to them in federal Regulation Z (12 C.F.R. 226.1 et seq.).

(e) Nothing in this section shall be deemed or construed to prohibit a retail seller from disclosing additional terms, conditions, or information, whether or not relating to the disclosures required under this section, in conjunction with the disclosures required by this section. Notwithstanding subdivision (g) of Section 1748.11, a retail seller that complies with the requirements of Section 1748.11 shall be deemed to have complied with the requirements of this section.

(f) If a retail seller is required under federal law to make any disclosure of the terms applicable to a retail installment account in connection with application forms or solicitations, the retail seller shall be deemed to have complied with the requirements of paragraph (1) of subdivision (a) with respect to those application forms or solicitations if the retail seller complies with the federal disclosure requirement.

(g) If the disclosure required by this section does not otherwise appear on an application form or an accompanying retail installment agreement distributed in this state on or after October 1, 1987, other than by mail, the application form shall include a statement in substantially the following form:

"If you wish to receive disclosure of the terms of this retail installment account, pursuant to the Areias Retail Installment Account Full Disclosure Act of 1986, check here and return to the address on this form."

A box shall be printed in or next to this statement for placing such a checkmark.

(h) This article does not apply to (1) any application form or preapproved written solicitation for a retail installment account credit card where the credit to be extended will be secured by a lien on real or personal property, or both real and personal property, (2) any application form or written solicitation that invites a person or persons to apply for a retail installment account credit card and which is included as part of a catalog which is sent to one or more persons by a creditor in order to facilitate a credit sale of goods offered in the catalog, (3) any advertisement which does not invite, directly or indirectly, an application for a retail installment account credit card, and (4) any application form or written advertisement included in a magazine, newspaper, or other publication distributed in more than one state by someone other than the creditor. *(Added by Stats.1986, c. 1397, § 4. Amended by Stats.2000, c. 375 (A.B.1331), § 7; Stats.2001, c. 159 (S.B.662), § 34.)*

Cross References

Billing cycle defined for purposes of this Chapter, see Civil Code § 1802.17.
Disclosures, see Civil Code §§ 1748.11, 1748.22.
Finance charge defined for purposes of this Chapter, see Civil Code § 1802.10.
Goods defined for purposes of this Chapter, see Civil Code § 1802.1.
Person defined for purposes of this Chapter, see Civil Code § 1802.15.
Retail buyer or buyer defined for purposes of this Chapter, see Civil Code § 1802.4.
Retail installment account or installment account defined for purposes of this Chapter, see Civil Code § 1802.7.
Retail installment sale or sale defined for purposes of this Chapter, see Civil Code § 1802.5.
Retail seller or seller defined for purposes of this Chapter, see Civil Code § 1802.3.
Services defined for purposes of this Chapter, see Civil Code § 1802.2.

ARTICLE 11. ATTORNEY'S FEES AND COURT COSTS

Section
1811.1. Award to prevailing party.

§ 1811.1. Award to prevailing party

Reasonable attorney's fees and costs shall be awarded to the prevailing party in any action on a contract or installment account subject to the provisions of this chapter regardless of whether such action is instituted by the seller, holder or buyer. Where the defendant alleges in his answer that he tendered to the plaintiff the full amount to which he was entitled, and thereupon deposits in court, for the plaintiff, the amount so tendered, and the allegation is found to be true, then the defendant is deemed to be a prevailing party within the meaning of this article. *(Added by Stats.1959, c. 201, p. 2105, § 1. Amended by Stats.1961, c. 1214, p. 2951, § 6.)*

Cross References

Action on contract, award of attorney's fees and costs, see Civil Code § 1717.
Automobile conditional sales contract, attorney's fees, see Civil Code § 2983.4.
Breach of warranty, award of attorney's fees, see Civil Code §§ 1794, 1794.1.
Contract, see Civil Code §§ 1549, 1802.6.
Contractual provision for attorney's fees and costs, see Civil Code § 1717.
Credit card holder, award of attorney's fees against issuer or retailer, see Civil Code § 1747.50 et seq.
Holder defined for purposes of this Chapter, see Civil Code § 1802.13.
Retail buyer or buyer defined for purposes of this Chapter, see Civil Code § 1802.4.
Retail installment account or installment account defined for purposes of this Chapter, see Civil Code § 1802.7.
Retail installment accounts, provision for attorney's fees, see Civil Code § 1810.4.
Retail seller or seller defined for purposes of this Chapter, see Civil Code § 1802.3.
Swimming pool construction contracts, award of attorney's fees, see Business and Professions Code § 7168.

ARTICLE 12. ATTACHMENT [REPEALED]

§ 1812. Repealed by Stats.1974, c. 1516, p. 3335, § 2; Stats.1975, c. 200, p. 574, § 2, operative Jan. 1, 1977

§ 1812.1. Repealed by Stats.1970, c. 1523, p. 3058, § 1

ARTICLE 12.1. REPOSSESSION AND RESALE

Section
1812.2. Default by buyer; rights of holder; notice of sale or retention of goods; redemption; statement of sum due.
1812.3. Notice; contents; service.
1812.4. Application of proceeds of resale.
1812.5. Recovery of deficiency prohibited.

§ 1812.2. Default by buyer; rights of holder; notice of sale or retention of goods; redemption; statement of sum due

In the event of any default by the buyer in the performance of his obligations under a contract or installment account, the holder, pursuant to any rights granted therein, may proceed to recover judgment for the balance due without retaking the goods, or he may retake the goods and proceed as hereinafter provided. If he retakes the goods, he shall, within 10 days, give notice to the buyer of his intention to sell the goods at public sale or give notice to the buyer of his intention to retain the goods in satisfaction of the balance due. The notice must state the amount of the overdue payments, that

§ 1812.2 OBLIGATIONS

the buyer must pay, if he pays within 10 days of the notice, in order to redeem the goods. In either case the buyer shall have an absolute right to redeem the goods within 10 days after the notice is given by paying or tendering the amount owing under the contract. If the holder gives notice of election to sell the goods the buyer shall also have the absolute right to redeem the goods at any time before sale by paying or tendering the amounts specified above and also any expense reasonably incurred by the seller or holder in good faith in repairing, reconditioning the goods or preparing them for sale. If the holder gives notice of his intention to retain the goods in satisfaction of the indebtedness he shall be deemed to have done so at the end of the 10-day period if the goods are not redeemed; at the time the notice is given, the holder shall furnish the buyer a written statement of the sum due under the contract and the expenses provided for in this section. For failure to render such a statement the holder shall forfeit to the buyer ten dollars ($10) and also be liable to him for all damages suffered because of such failure. *(Added by Stats.1959, c. 201, p. 2106, § 1. Amended by Stats.1961, c. 1214, p. 2951, § 7; Stats.1963, c. 1952, p. 4017, § 1.)*

Cross References

Buyer, see Civil Code § 1802.4; Commercial Code § 2103.
Default in secured transaction, remedies and procedure, see Commercial Code § 9501 et seq.
Goods defined for purposes of this Chapter, see Civil Code § 1802.1.
Holder, see Civil Code § 1802.13; Commercial Code § 1201.
Remedies of seller, see Commercial Code § 2702 et seq.
Resale of goods as remedy of seller, see Commercial Code § 2706.
Retail installment account or installment account defined for purposes of this Chapter, see Civil Code § 1802.7.
Retail installment contract or contract defined for purposes of this Chapter, see Civil Code § 1802.6.
Retail installment sale or sale defined for purposes of this Chapter, see Civil Code § 1802.5.
Retail seller or seller defined for purposes of this Chapter, see Civil Code § 1802.3.

§ 1812.3. Notice; contents; service

The notice provided for in Section 1812.2 shall be given to the buyer and any other person liable by causing it to be delivered personally or to be deposited in the United States mail addressed to the buyer or to such other person at his last known address and shall advise the buyer or such other person of his right to redeem as provided for in Section 1812.2. If the holder determines to sell the goods at public sale he shall give notice of the time and place of sale at least 10 days before the date of sale by delivering a copy of the notice personally to the buyer or other person liable or depositing the same in the United States mail addressed to the buyer or such other person at his last known address. *(Added by Stats.1959, c. 201, p. 2106, § 1. Amended by Stats.1961, c. 1214, p. 2952, § 8.)*

Cross References

Goods defined for purposes of this Chapter, see Civil Code § 1802.1.
Holder defined for purposes of this Chapter, see Civil Code § 1802.13.
Person defined for purposes of this Chapter, see Civil Code § 1802.15.
Retail buyer or buyer defined for purposes of this Chapter, see Civil Code § 1802.4.
Retail installment sale or sale defined for purposes of this Chapter, see Civil Code § 1802.5.

§ 1812.4. Application of proceeds of resale

The proceeds of a resale shall be applied (1) to the payment of the expenses thereof, (2) to the payment of any expenses of retaking, including reasonable attorney's fees actually incurred, and of any expenses of keeping, storing, repairing, reconditioning or preparing the goods for sale to which the holder may be entitled, (3) to the satisfaction of the balance due under the contract. Any sum remaining after the satisfaction of such claims shall be paid to the buyer. *(Added by Stats.1959, c. 201, p. 2107, § 1, operative Jan. 1, 1960.)*

Cross References

Attorney's fees and costs, see Civil Code §§ 1717, 1811.1.
Goods defined for purposes of this Chapter, see Civil Code § 1802.1.
Holder defined for purposes of this Chapter, see Civil Code § 1802.13.
Retail buyer or buyer defined for purposes of this Chapter, see Civil Code § 1802.4.
Retail installment accounts, provision for attorney's fees, see Civil Code § 1810.4.
Retail installment contract or contract defined for purposes of this Chapter, see Civil Code § 1802.6.
Retail installment sale or sale defined for purposes of this Chapter, see Civil Code § 1802.5.
Surplus and deficiency in secured transaction, see Commercial Code § 9504.

§ 1812.5. Recovery of deficiency prohibited

If the proceeds of the sale are not sufficient to cover items (1), (2) and (3) of Section 1812.4, the holder may not recover the deficiency from the buyer or from anyone who has succeeded to the obligations of the buyer. *(Added by Stats.1959, c. 201, p. 2107, § 1. Amended by Stats.1963, c. 1952, p. 4018, § 2.)*

Cross References

Holder defined for purposes of this Chapter, see Civil Code § 1802.13.
Retail buyer or buyer defined for purposes of this Chapter, see Civil Code § 1802.4.
Retail installment sale or sale defined for purposes of this Chapter, see Civil Code § 1802.5.
Secured transactions, action in which deficiency or surplus is in issue, see Commercial Code § 9626.
Surplus and deficiency in secured transaction, see Commercial Code § 9504.

ARTICLE 12.2. PENALTIES

Section
1812.6. Violation; misdemeanor.
1812.7. Noncompliance with provisions as barring right of recovery; remedy of buyer.
1812.8. Correction of failure to comply with provisions.
1812.9. Willful violation; triple damages.

Cross References

Add-on sale memorandum, nondelivery, obligation restricted to cash price, see Civil Code § 1808.4.

Nondelivery of copy of contract to buyer, application of penalties, see Civil Code § 1803.7.

§ 1812.6. Violation; misdemeanor

Any person who shall willfully violate any provision of this chapter shall be guilty of a misdemeanor. (Added by Stats.1959, c. 201, p. 2107, § 1, operative Jan. 1, 1960.)

Cross References

Misdemeanor,
  Defined, see Penal Code § 17.
  Punishment, see Penal Code §§ 19, 19.2.
Person defined for purposes of this Chapter, see Civil Code § 1802.15.
Prohibited provisions in contract, effect, see Civil Code § 1804.4.

§ 1812.7. Noncompliance with provisions as barring right of recovery; remedy of buyer

In case of failure by any person to comply with the provisions of this chapter, such person or any person who acquires a contract or installment account with knowledge of such noncompliance is barred from recovery of any finance charge or of any delinquency, collection, extension, deferral or refinance charge imposed in connection with such contract or installment account and the buyer shall have the right to recover from such person an amount equal to any of such charges paid by the buyer. (Added by Stats.1959, c. 201, p. 2107, § 1, operative Jan. 1, 1960. Amended by Stats.1970, c. 546, p. 1054, § 33.)

Cross References

Delinquency charge, see Civil Code § 1803.6.
Finance charge defined for purposes of this Chapter, see Civil Code § 1802.10.
Invalidity of prohibited provisions, effect on contract, see Civil Code § 1804.4.
Person defined for purposes of this Chapter, see Civil Code § 1802.15.
Retail buyer or buyer defined for purposes of this Chapter, see Civil Code § 1802.4.
Retail installment account or installment account defined for purposes of this Chapter, see Civil Code § 1802.7.
Retail installment contract or contract defined for purposes of this Chapter, see Civil Code § 1802.6.

§ 1812.8. Correction of failure to comply with provisions

Notwithstanding the provisions of this article, any failure to comply with any provision of this chapter may be corrected by the holder in accordance with the provisions of this section, provided that a willful violation may not be corrected, and a correction which will increase the amount owed by the buyer or the amount of any payment shall not be effective unless the buyer concurs in writing to the correction. If a violation is corrected by the holder in accordance with the provisions of this section, neither the seller nor the holder shall be subject to any penalty under this article. The correction shall be made by delivery to the buyer of a corrected copy of the contract within 30 days of the execution of the original contract by the buyer. Any amount improperly collected from the buyer shall be credited against the indebtedness evidenced by the contract. (Added by Stats.1959, c. 201, p. 2107, § 1. Amended by Stats.1961, c. 1214, p. 2952, § 9.)

Cross References

Holder defined for purposes of this Chapter, see Civil Code § 1802.13.
Invalidity of prohibited provisions, effect on contract, see Civil Code § 1804.4.
Retail buyer or buyer defined for purposes of this Chapter, see Civil Code § 1802.4.
Retail installment contract or contract defined for purposes of this Chapter, see Civil Code § 1802.6.
Retail seller or seller defined for purposes of this Chapter, see Civil Code § 1802.3.

§ 1812.9. Willful violation; triple damages

In any case in which a person willfully violates any provision of this chapter in connection with the imposition, computation or disclosures of or relating to a finance charge on a consolidated total of two or more contracts under the provisions of Article 8 (commencing with Section 1808.1) of this chapter, the buyer may recover from such person an amount equal to three times the total of the finance charges and any delinquency, collection, extension, deferral or refinance charges imposed, contracted for or received on all contracts included in the consolidated total and the seller shall be barred from the recovery of any such charges. (Added by Stats.1959, c. 201, p. 2108, § 1. Amended by Stats.1961, c. 1214, p. 2953, § 10; Stats.1970, c. 546, p. 1054, § 34.)

Cross References

Finance charge defined for purposes of this Chapter, see Civil Code § 1802.10.
Person defined for purposes of this Chapter, see Civil Code § 1802.15.
Retail buyer or buyer defined for purposes of this Chapter, see Civil Code § 1802.4.
Retail installment contract or contract defined for purposes of this Chapter, see Civil Code § 1802.6.
Retail seller or seller defined for purposes of this Chapter, see Civil Code § 1802.3.

ARTICLE 12.3. ACTIONS

Section
1812.10. Venue; jurisdiction.

§ 1812.10. Venue; jurisdiction

(a) An action on a contract or installment account under this chapter shall be tried in the superior court in the county where the contract was in fact signed by the buyer, where the buyer resided at the time the contract was entered into, where the buyer resides at the commencement of the action, or where the goods purchased pursuant to the contract have been so affixed to real property as to become a part of that real property.

(b) In the superior court designated as the proper court in subdivision (a), the proper court location for trial of an action under this chapter is the location where the court tries that type of action that is nearest or most accessible to where the contract was in fact signed by the buyer, where the buyer resided at the time the contract was entered into, where the buyer resides at the commencement of the action, or where the goods purchased pursuant to the contract have been so affixed to real property as to become a part of that real

§ 1812.10

property. Otherwise, any location of the superior court designated as the proper court in subdivision (a) is the proper court location for the trial of the action. The court may specify by local rule the nearest or most accessible court location where the court tries that type of case.

(c) In any action subject to this section, concurrently with the filing of the complaint, the plaintiff shall file an affidavit stating facts showing that the action has been commenced in a superior court and court location described in this section as a proper place for the trial of the action. Those facts may be stated in a verified complaint and shall not be stated on information or belief. When that affidavit is filed with the complaint, a copy thereof shall be served with the summons. If a plaintiff fails to file the affidavit or state facts in a verified complaint required by this section, no further proceedings may occur, but the court shall, upon its own motion or upon motion of any party, dismiss the action without prejudice. The court may, on terms that are just, permit the affidavit to be filed subsequent to the filing of the complaint and a copy of the affidavit shall be served on the defendant. The time to answer or otherwise plead shall date from that service. *(Added by Stats.1965, c. 792, p. 2382, § 1. Amended by Stats.1968, c. 743, p. 1446, § 1; Stats.1969, c. 186, p. 466, § 1; Stats.1970, c. 725, p. 1352, § 1; Stats.1971, c. 1529, p. 3020, § 1; Stats.1998, c. 931 (S.B.2139), § 16, eff. Sept. 28, 1998; Stats.2002, c. 806 (A.B.3027), § 1.)*

Cross References

Actions in which attachment is authorized, see Code of Civil Procedure § 483.010 et seq.
Affidavit accompanying application to enter default, see Code of Civil Procedure § 585.5.
Civil actions,
    Affidavit accompanying application to enter default, motion to set aside default and for leave to defend, procedure, see Code of Civil Procedure § 585.5.
    Cases subject to this section, statement of jurisdictional facts, transfers, consent to retention of case, see Code of Civil Procedure § 396a.
Goods defined for purposes of this Chapter, see Civil Code § 1802.1.
Justice courts, original jurisdiction, see Code of Civil Procedure § 86.
Place of trial, see Code of Civil Procedure § 392 et seq.
Retail buyer or buyer defined for purposes of this Chapter, see Civil Code § 1802.4.
Retail installment account or installment account defined for purposes of this Chapter, see Civil Code § 1802.7.
Retail installment contract or contract defined for purposes of this Chapter, see Civil Code § 1802.6.

ARTICLE 12.4. FINANCING RETAIL PURCHASES

Section
1812.20. Requirement that purchaser obtain financing from particular source; prohibition; penalty.

§ 1812.20. Requirement that purchaser obtain financing from particular source; prohibition; penalty

Notwithstanding Section 1801.6, no person shall require a purchaser of goods or services to obtain financing from any particular source. Any person who violates this section shall be subject to the penalty provided in Section 1812.6. *(Added by Stats.1979, c. 1151, p. 4222, § 4.)*

Cross References

Goods defined for purposes of this Chapter, see Civil Code § 1802.1.
Person defined for purposes of this Chapter, see Civil Code § 1802.15.
Services defined for purposes of this Chapter, see Civil Code § 1802.2.

CHAPTER 2. CREDIT TRANSACTIONS REGARDING WOMEN

Section
1812.30. Denial of credit to person regardless of marital status; prohibition; conditions; reporting agency.
1812.31. Right of action; damages; individual and class suits.
1812.32. Injunction.
1812.33. Civil penalties; precedence of action; distribution of proceeds.
1812.34. Costs and attorney fees.
1812.35. Commencement of action; limitations.

§ 1812.30. Denial of credit to person regardless of marital status; prohibition; conditions; reporting agency

(a) No person, regardless of marital status, shall be denied credit in his or her own name if the earnings and other property over which he or she has management and control are such that a person of the opposite sex managing and controlling the same amount of earnings and other property would receive credit.

(b) No person, regardless of marital status, managing and controlling earnings and other property shall be offered credit on terms less favorable than those offered to a person of the opposite sex seeking the same type of credit and managing and controlling the same amount of earnings and other property.

(c) No unmarried person shall be denied credit if his or her earnings and other property are such that a married person managing and controlling the same amount of earnings and other property would receive credit.

(d) No unmarried person shall be offered credit on terms less favorable than those offered to a married person managing and controlling the same amount of earnings and other property.

(e) For accounts established after January 1, 1977 or for accounts in existence on January 1, 1977 where information on that account is received after January 1, 1977, a credit reporting agency which in its normal course of business receives information on joint credit accounts identifying the persons responsible for such accounts, or receives information which reflects the participation of both spouses, shall: (1) at the time such information is received file such information separately under the names of each person or spouse, or file such information in another manner which would enable either person or spouse to automatically gain access to the credit history without having in any way to list or refer to the name of the other person, and (2) provide access to all information about the account in the name of each person or spouse.

(f) For all accounts established prior to January 1, 1977, a credit reporting agency shall at any time upon the written or personal request of a person who is or has been married, verify the contractual liability, liability by operation of law, or authorized use by such person, of joint credit accounts appearing in the file of the person's spouse or former spouse, and, if applicable, shall file such information separately and thereafter continue to do so under the names of each person responsible for the joint account or in another manner which would enable either person responsible for the joint account to automatically gain access to the credit history without having in any way to list or refer to the name of the other person.

(g) For the purposes of this chapter "credit" means obtainment of money, property, labor, or services on a deferred-payment basis.

(h) For the purposes of this chapter, earnings shall include, but not be limited to, spousal, family, and child support payments, pensions, social security, disability or survivorship benefits. Spousal, family, and child support payments shall be considered in the same manner as earnings from salary, wages, or other sources where the payments are received pursuant to a written agreement or court decree to the extent that the reliability of such payments is established. The factors which a creditor may consider in evaluating the reliability of such payments are the length of time payments have been received; the regularity of receipt; and whether full or partial payments have been made.

(i) Nothing in this chapter shall be construed to prohibit a person from: (1) utilizing an evaluation of the reliability of earnings provided that such an evaluation is applied to persons without regard to their sex or marital status; or (2) inquiring into and utilizing an evaluation of the obligations for which community property is liable pursuant to the Family Code for the sole purpose of determining the creditor's rights and remedies with respect to the particular extension of credit, provided that such is done with respect to all applicants without regard to their sex; or (3) utilizing any other relevant factors or methods in determining whether to extend credit to an applicant provided that such factors or methods are applicable to all applicants without regard to their sex or marital status. For the purpose of this subdivision, the fact that an applicant is of childbearing age is not a relevant factor.

(j) Credit applications for the obtainment of money, goods, labor, or services shall clearly specify that the applicant, if married, may apply for a separate account. *(Added by Stats.1973, c. 999, p. 1987, § 1. Amended by Stats.1975, c. 332, p. 778, § 1; Stats.1976, c. 1361, p. 6203, § 1; Stats.1992, c. 163 (A.B.2641), § 11, operative Jan. 1, 1994.)*

§ 1812.31. Right of action; damages; individual and class suits

(a) Whoever violates Section 1812.30 shall be liable to the aggrieved person in an amount equal to the sum of any actual damages sustained by such person acting either in an individual capacity or as a representative of a class.

(b) Whoever violates Section 1812.30 shall be liable to the aggrieved person for punitive damages in an amount not greater than ten thousand dollars ($10,000), as determined by the court, in addition to any actual damages provided in subdivision (a); provided, however, that in pursuing the recovery allowed under this subdivision, the aggrieved person may proceed only in an individual capacity and not as a representative of a class.

(c) Notwithstanding subdivision (b), whoever violates Section 1812.30 may be liable for punitive damages in the case of a class action in such amount as the court may allow, except that as to each member of the class no minimum recovery shall be applicable, and the total recovery in such action shall not exceed the lesser of one hundred thousand dollars ($100,000) or one percent (1%) of the net worth of the creditor. In determining the amount of the award in any class action, the court shall consider, among other relevant factors, the amount of any actual damages awarded, the frequency and persistence of violations, the resources of the creditor, the number of persons adversely affected, and the extent to which the creditor's violation was intentional. *(Added by Stats.1973, c. 999, p. 1987, § 1. Amended by Stats.1975, c. 332, p. 779, § 2.)*

§ 1812.32. Injunction

Any person, corporation, firm, partnership, joint stock company, or any other association or organization which violates or proposes to violate this chapter may be enjoined by any court of competent jurisdiction. Actions for injunction under this section may be prosecuted by the Attorney General or any district attorney, county counsel, city attorney, or city prosecutor in this state in the name of the people of the State of California or by any person denied credit or offered credit in violation of Section 1812.30. *(Added by Stats.1975, c. 332, p. 780, § 3.)*

Cross References

Attorney General, generally, see Government Code § 12500 et seq.

§ 1812.33. Civil penalties; precedence of action; distribution of proceeds

(a) Any person who intentionally violates any injunction issued pursuant to this chapter shall be liable for a civil penalty not to exceed two thousand five hundred dollars ($2,500) for each day that such person violates the injunction.

(b) The civil penalty prescribed by this section shall be assessed and recovered in a civil action brought in the name of the people of the State of California by the Attorney General or by any district attorney, county counsel, or city attorney in any court of competent jurisdiction. An action brought pursuant to this section to recover such civil penalties shall take special precedence over all civil matters on the calendar of the court except those matters to which equal precedence on the calendar is granted by law.

(c) If such an action is brought by the Attorney General, one-half of the penalty collected pursuant to this section shall be paid to the treasurer of the county in which the judgment was entered, and one-half to the State Treasurer. If brought by a district attorney or county counsel, the entire amount of the penalty collected shall be paid to the treasurer of the county in which the judgment was entered. If brought by a city attorney or city prosecutor, one-half of the penalty shall be paid to the treasurer of the county in which the judgment was entered and one-half to the city. *(Added by Stats.1975, c. 332, p. 780, § 4.)*

§ 1812.33

Cross References

Attorney General, generally, see Government Code § 12500 et seq.
State Treasurer, generally, see Government Code § 12302 et seq.

§ 1812.34. Costs and attorney fees

Any person denied credit or offered credit in violation of Section 1812.30 who brings an action pursuant to Section 1812.31 or 1812.32 of this code may petition the court for award of costs and reasonable attorney's fees which the court shall award if the action is successful. *(Added by Stats.1975, c. 332, p. 781, § 5.)*

§ 1812.35. Commencement of action; limitations

Any action commenced pursuant to Section 1812.31 shall be commenced within two years from the date on which the person is denied credit or is offered credit in violation of Section 1812.30. *(Added by Stats.1975, c. 332, p. 781, § 6.)*

CHAPTER 3. RETAIL CREDIT ADVISORY COMMITTEE [REPEALED]

§§ 1812.40, 1812.41. Repealed by Stats.2004, c. 193 (S.B. 111), § 10

Title 2.4

CONTRACTS FOR DANCE STUDIO LESSONS AND OTHER SERVICES

Section	
1812.50.	Legislative findings and declarations; purpose.
1812.51.	Contract for dance studio lessons and other services; exceptions from application of title.
1812.51a.	Repealed.
1812.52.	Written contract required.
1812.53.	Limitation on payment period; prohibition against life contract; permissible service period; single contract.
1812.54.	Performance of contract; cancellation and refund; statement of hourly rate and on bond of studio.
1812.55.	Prohibition of notes cutting off, as to third parties, buyer's right of action or defense against seller.
1812.56.	Prohibition against assignment of contract cutting off buyer's right of action or defense against seller; conditions.
1812.57.	Relief from payment upon death or disability.
1812.58.	Provisions not exclusive.
1812.59.	Noncomplying contracts void.
1812.60.	Fraud rendering contract void.
1812.61.	Waiver of provisions.
1812.62.	Recovery of triple damages and attorney fee; correction of contract; "holder" defined.
1812.63.	Violation of provisions; offense; injunction; duty to institute actions.
1812.64.	Bond; amount; filing.
1812.65.	Bond; persons protected.
1812.66.	Repealed.
1812.67.	Exclusions from application of certain sections.
1812.68.	Severability clause.
1812.69.	Enforcement; filing fees.

Cross References

Contracts for health studio services, see Civil Code § 1812.80 et seq.

§ 1812.50. Legislative findings and declarations; purpose

(a) The Legislature finds that there exists in connection with a substantial number of contracts for dance studio lessons and other services, sales practices, and business and financing methods which have worked a fraud, deceit, imposition, and financial hardship upon the people of this state; that existing legal remedies are inadequate to correct these abuses; that the dance studio industry has a significant impact upon the economy and well-being of this state and its local communities; and that the provisions of this title relating to these contracts are necessary for the public welfare.

(b) The Legislature declares that the purpose of this title is to safeguard the public against fraud, deceit, imposition, and financial hardship, and to foster and encourage competition, fair dealing, and prosperity in the field of dance studio lessons and other services by prohibiting or restricting false or misleading advertising, onerous contract terms, harmful financial practices, and other unfair, dishonest, deceptive, destructive, unscrupulous, fraudulent, and discriminatory practices by which the public has been injured in connection with contracts for dance studio lessons and other services. *(Added by Stats.1969, c. 1571, p. 3190, § 1. Amended by Stats.1987, c. 449, § 2; Stats.1988, c. 1043, § 2.)*

§ 1812.51. Contract for dance studio lessons and other services; exceptions from application of title

As used in this title, "contract for dance studio lessons and other services" means a contract for instruction in ballroom or other types of dancing, and includes lessons and other services, whether given to students individually or in groups. This title does not include contracts for professional services rendered or furnished by a person licensed under Division 2 (commencing with Section 500) of the Business and Professions Code, or contracts for instruction at schools operating pursuant to the Education Code. *(Added by Stats.1969, c. 1571, p. 3190, § 1. Amended by Stats.1987, c. 449, § 3; Stats.1988, c. 1043, § 3.)*

Cross References

Contract defined, see Civil Code §§ 1549, 1802.6.

§ 1812.51a. Repealed by Stats.1988, c. 1043, § 4

§ 1812.52. Written contract required

Every contract for dance studio lessons and other services shall be in writing and shall be subject to this title. A copy of the written contract shall be given to the customer at the time he or she signs the contract. *(Added by Stats.1969, c. 1571, p. 3190, § 1. Amended by Stats.1987, c. 449, § 5; Stats.1988, c. 1043, § 5.)*

Cross References

Statute of frauds, see Civil Code § 1624.

§ 1812.53. Limitation on payment period; prohibition against life contract; permissible service period; single contract

(a) No contract for dance studio lessons and other services shall require payments or financing by the buyer over a period in excess of one year from the date the contract is entered into, nor shall the term of any contract be measured by the life of the buyer. However, the lessons and other services to be rendered to the buyer under the contract may extend over a period not to exceed seven years from the date the contract is entered into.

(b) All contracts for dance studio lessons and other services that may be in effect between the same seller and the same buyer, the terms of which overlap for any period, shall be considered as one contract for the purposes of this title. (Added by Stats.1969, c. 1571, p. 3190, § 1. Amended by Stats.1983, c. 259, § 1; Stats.1987, c. 449, § 6; Stats.1988, c. 1043, § 6; Stats.1999, c. 1024 (A.B.648), § 1.)

§ 1812.54. Performance of contract; cancellation and refund; statement of hourly rate and on bond of studio

(a) Every contract for dance studio lessons and other services shall provide that performance of the agreed-upon lessons will begin within six months from the date the contract is entered into.

(b) A contract for dance studio lessons and other services may be canceled by the student at any time provided he or she gives written notice to the dance studio at the address specified in the contract. When a contract for dance studio lessons and other services is canceled the dance studio shall calculate the refund on the contract, if any, on a pro rata basis. The dance studio shall refund any moneys owed to the student within 10 days of receiving the cancellation notice, unless the student owes the dance studio money for studio lessons or other services received prior to the cancellation, in which case any moneys owed the dance studio shall be deducted by the dance studio from the refund owed to the student and the balance, if any, shall be refunded as specified above. A dance studio shall not charge a cancellation fee, or other fee, for cancellation of the contract by the student.

(c) Every contract for dance studio lessons and other services shall contain a written statement of the hourly rate charged for each type of lesson for which the student has contracted. If the contract includes dance studio lessons that are sold at different per-hour rates, the contract shall contain separate hourly rates for each different type of lesson sold. All other services for which the student has contracted that are not capable of a per-hour charge shall be set forth in writing in specific terms. The statement shall be contained in the dance studio contract before the contract is signed by the buyer.

(d) Every dance studio subject to Sections 1812.64 and 1812.65 shall include in every contract for dance studio lessons or other services a statement that the studio is bonded and that information concerning the bond may be obtained by writing to the office of the Secretary of State. (Added by Stats.1969, c. 1571, p. 3191, § 1. Amended by Stats.1976, c. 1200, p. 5474, § 1; Stats.1982, c. 517, p. 2321, § 58; Stats. 1983, c. 259, § 2; Stats.1987, c. 449, § 7; Stats.1988, c. 1043, § 7; Stats.1997, c. 112 (S.B.338), § 1; Stats.1998, c. 829 (S.B.1652), § 7; Stats.1999, c. 1024 (A.B.648), § 2.)

Cross References

Deposits in lieu of bond, see Code of Civil Procedure § 995.710 et seq.

§ 1812.55. Prohibition of notes cutting off, as to third parties, buyer's right of action or defense against seller

No contract for dance studio lessons and other services shall require or entail the execution of any note or series of notes by the buyer which, when separately negotiated, will cut off as to third parties any right of action or defense which the buyer may have against the seller. (Added by Stats.1969, c. 1571, p. 3191, § 1. Amended by Stats.1987, c. 449, § 8; Stats.1988, c. 1043, § 8.)

§ 1812.56. Prohibition against assignment of contract cutting off buyer's right of action or defense against seller; conditions

No right of action or defense arising out of a contract for dance studio lessons and other services which the buyer has against the seller, and which would be cut off by assignment, shall be cut off by assignment of the contract to any third party whether or not he or she acquires the contract in good faith and for value unless the assignee gives notice of the assignment to the buyer as provided in this section and, within 30 days of the mailing of notice, receives no written notice of the facts giving rise to the claim or defense of the buyer. A notice of assignment shall be in writing addressed to the buyer at the address shown on the contract and shall identify the contract and inform the buyer that he or she shall, within 30 days of the date of mailing of the notice, notify the assignee in writing of any facts giving rise to a claim or defense which he or she may have. The notice of assignment shall state the name of the seller and buyer, a description of the lessons and other services, the contract balance, and the number and amount of the installments. (Added by Stats.1969, c. 1571, p. 3191, § 1. Amended by Stats.1987, c. 449, § 9; Stats.1988, c. 1043, § 9.)

Cross References

Rights of holder in due course and of non-holder in due course, see Commercial Code §§ 3305, 3306.

§ 1812.57. Relief from payment upon death or disability

(a) Every contract for dance studio lessons and other services shall contain a clause providing that if, by reason of death or disability, the person agreeing to receive lessons and other services is unable to receive all lessons and other services for which he or she has contracted, the person and his or her estate shall be relieved from the obligation of making payment for lessons and other services other than those received prior to death or the onset of disability, and that if the buyer has prepaid any sum for lessons and other services so much of that sum as is allocable to lessons and other services he or she has not taken shall be promptly refunded to the buyer or his or her representative.

(b) Notwithstanding the provisions of any contract to the contrary, whenever the contract price is payable in installments and the buyer is relieved from making further payments or entitled to a refund under this section, the buyer shall be entitled to receive a refund or refund credit of so much of the cash price as is allocable to the lessons or other services not actually received by the buyer. The refund of the finance charge shall be computed according to the "sum of the balances method," also known as the "Rule of 78". (Added by Stats.1969, c. 1571, p. 3192, § 1. Amended by Stats.1976, c. 1200, p. 5475, § 2; Stats.1987, c. 449, § 10; Stats.1988, c. 1043, § 10.)

§ 1812.58. Provisions not exclusive

The provisions of this title are not exclusive and do not relieve the parties or the contracts subject thereto from compliance with all other applicable provisions of law. (Added by Stats.1969, c. 1571, p. 3192, § 1.)

§ 1812.59. Noncomplying contracts void

Any contract for dance studio lessons and other services which does not comply with the applicable provisions of this title shall be void and unenforceable as contrary to public policy. (Added by Stats.1969, c. 1571, p. 3192, § 1. Amended by Stats.1987, c. 449, § 11; Stats.1988, c. 1043, § 11.)

§ 1812.60. Fraud rendering contract void

Any contract for dance studio lessons and other services entered into in reliance upon any willful and false, fraudulent, or misleading information, representation, notice, or advertisement of the seller shall be void and unenforceable. (Added by Stats.1969, c. 1571, p. 3192, § 1. Amended by Stats.1987, c. 449, § 12; Stats.1988, c. 1043, § 12.)

Cross References

Actual fraud, see Civil Code § 1572.
Disregard of provisions of written contract which fail to express real intention of parties due to fraud, mistake or accident, see Civil Code § 1640.

§ 1812.61. Waiver of provisions

Any waiver of the buyer of the provisions of this title shall be deemed contrary to public policy and shall be void and unenforceable. (Added by Stats.1969, c. 1571, p. 3192, § 1.)

Cross References

Waiver of advantage, law established for public reason, see Civil Code § 3513.
Waiver of code provisions, generally, see Civil Code § 3268.

§ 1812.62. Recovery of triple damages and attorney fee; correction of contract; "holder" defined

(a) Any buyer injured by a violation of this title may bring an action for the recovery of damages. Judgment may be entered for three times the amount at which the actual damages are assessed plus reasonable attorney fees.

(b) Notwithstanding the provisions of this title, any failure to comply with any provision of this title may be corrected within 30 days after the execution of the contract by the buyer, and, if so corrected, neither the seller nor the holder shall be subject to any penalty under this title, provided that any correction which increases any monthly payment, the number of payments, or the total amount due, must be concurred in, in writing, by the buyer. "Holder" includes the seller who acquires the contract, or, if the contract is purchased by a financing agency or other assignee, the financing agency or other assignee. (Added by Stats.1969, c. 1571, p. 3193, § 1.)

Cross References

Action on contract, award of attorney's fees and costs, see Civil Code § 1717.
Attorney's fees and costs, see Civil Code §§ 1717, 1811.1.
Damages, generally, see Civil Code §§ 3274, 3281 et seq.
Holder, see Civil Code § 1802.13; Commercial Code § 1201.

§ 1812.63. Violation of provisions; offense; injunction; duty to institute actions

Any person who violates any provision of this title relating to dance studio contracts is guilty of a misdemeanor. Any superior court of this state has jurisdiction in equity to restrain and enjoin the violation of any of the provisions of this title relating to dance studio contracts.

The duty to institute actions for violation of those provisions of this title, including equity proceedings to restrain and enjoin violations, is hereby vested in the Attorney General, district attorneys, and city attorneys. The Attorney General, any district attorney, or any city attorney may prosecute misdemeanor actions or institute equity proceedings, or both.

This section shall not be deemed to prohibit the enforcement by any person of any right provided by this or any other law. (Added by Stats.1969, c. 1571, p. 3193, § 1. Amended by Stats.1987, c. 449, § 13; Stats.1988, c. 1043, § 13.)

Cross References

Attorney general, see Government Code § 12500 et seq.
District attorney, see Government Code § 26500 et seq.
Injunction, see Civil Code § 3420 et seq.; Code of Civil Procedure § 525 et seq.
Misdemeanor,
  Defined, see Penal Code § 17.
  Punishment, see Penal Code §§ 19, 19.2.

§ 1812.64. Bond; amount; filing

Every dance studio shall maintain a bond issued by a surety company admitted to do business in this state. The principal sum of the bond shall be 25 percent of the dance studio's gross income from the studio business in this state during the studio's last fiscal year, except that the principal sum of the bond shall not be less than twenty-five thousand dollars ($25,000) in the first or any subsequent year of operation.

A copy of the bond shall be filed with the Secretary of State, together with a declaration under penalty of perjury signed by the owner of the studio stating the dance studio's gross income from the dance studio business in this state during the last fiscal year. The information contained in the declaration shall not be subject to public inspection. If the person in whose name the bond is issued severs his or her relationship with the bonded dance studio, the new owner shall, as a condition of doing business, notify the Secretary of State of the change of ownership and of proof of compliance with Sections 1812.64 and 1812.65. (Added by Stats.1969, c. 1571, p. 3193, § 1. Amended by Stats.1976, c. 1200, p. 5476, § 3; Stats.1987, c. 449, § 14; Stats.1988, c. 1043, § 14; Stats.1999, c. 1024 (A.B.648), § 3.)

§ 1812.65. Bond; persons protected

The bond required by Section 1812.64 shall be in favor of the State of California for the benefit of any person who, after entering into a contract for dance studio lessons and other services with the dance studio, is damaged by fraud or dishonesty or failure to provide the services of the studio in performance of the contract. (Added by Stats.1969, c. 1571, p. 3193, § 1. Amended by Stats.1982, c. 517, p. 2322, § 59; Stats.1987, c. 449, § 15; Stats.1988, c. 1043, § 15.)

Cross References

Bond and Undertaking Law, see Code of Civil Procedure § 995.010 et seq.

§ 1812.66. Repealed by Stats.1999, c. 1024 (A.B.648), § 4

§ 1812.67. Exclusions from application of certain sections

(a) Sections 1812.64 and 1812.65 do not apply to any dance studio which requires or receives less than fifty dollars ($50) in advance payments from or on behalf of each student for dance studio lessons or other services which are to be rendered by the studio in the future and such advance payments are not required or received by the studio from each student more frequently than once every 30 days.

(b) Sections 1812.53, 1812.54, 1812.64, and 1812.65 do not apply to a dance studio which only offers instruction in ballet, modern, jazz, tap dance, or any combination thereof, to persons under 21 years of age pursuant to a contract for dance studio lessons that provides all of the following: (1) a total payment of less than five hundred dollars ($500), (2) that all agreed-upon lessons will be offered within four months from the date the contract is entered, and (3) that the contract may be canceled and all money paid for instruction not yet received will be refunded within 10 days of cancellation, if the dance student cancels within three days after receiving the first lesson, or if the dance student cancels at any time after moving his or her residence to a location more than 15 miles from the location of the dance studio.

(c) Sections 1812.53, 1812.54, 1812.64, and 1812.65 do not apply to any organization that has qualified for a tax exemption under Section 501(c)(3) of the Internal Revenue Code and which receives a direct grant of funds from the California Arts Council. *(Added by Stats.1969, c. 1571, p. 3190, § 1. Amended by Stats.1971, c. 903, p. 1752, § 2; Stats.1976, c. 1200, p. 5476, § 4; Stats.1982, c. 517, p. 2322, § 61; Stats.1987, c. 449, § 16; Stats.1988, c. 1043, § 16.)*

§ 1812.68. Severability clause

If any provision of this title or the application thereof to any person or circumstances is held unconstitutional, the remainder of the title and the application of such provision to other persons and circumstances shall not be affected thereby. *(Added by Stats.1969, c. 1571, p. 3194, § 1.)*

§ 1812.69. Enforcement; filing fees

(a) The Secretary of State shall enforce the provisions of this title that govern the filing and maintenance of bonds.

(b) The Secretary of State shall charge a filing fee not to exceed the cost of filing the bond. *(Added by Stats.1996, c. 633 (S.B.1978), § 7. Amended by Stats.1999, c. 1024 (A.B. 648), § 5.)*

Title 2.5

CONTRACTS FOR HEALTH STUDIO SERVICES

Section
1812.80. Purpose.
1812.81. "Contract for health studio services" defined.
1812.82. Written contract required; copy to customer.
1812.83. Overlapping contracts; consideration as one.

Section
1812.84. Payment period and contract term limitations; statement disclosing length of term; cancellations.
1812.85. Time for beginning performance of services; grounds for cancellation and refunds; statement and notice of cancellation; consumer liability.
1812.86. Limitation on amount of payment.
1812.87. Prohibition of notes cutting off, as to third parties, buyer's right of action or defense against seller.
1812.88. Prohibition against assignment of contract cutting off buyer's right of action or defense against seller; conditions.
1812.89. Relief from payment upon death, disability or movement; refund of prepayments; predetermined fee.
1812.90. Provisions not exclusive.
1812.91. Noncomplying contracts void.
1812.92. Fraud rendering contract void.
1812.93. Waiver of provisions.
1812.94. Recovery of triple damages and attorney fee; correction of contract; holder defined.
1812.95. Severability clause.
1812.96. Money to be held in trust until business opens; use of funds; cancellation rights.
1812.98. Month-to-month contracts; declaration of existing law.

Cross References

Contracts for dance studio lessons and other services, see Civil Code § 1812.50 et seq.

Installation or maintenance of two-way mirrors in restrooms, toilets, hotel rooms, etc., see Penal Code § 653n.

§ 1812.80. Purpose

(a) The Legislature finds that the health studio industry has a significant impact upon the economy and well-being of this state and its local communities; and that the provisions of this title relating to contracts for health studio services are necessary for the public welfare.

(b) The Legislature declares that the purpose of this title is to safeguard the public against fraud, deceit, imposition and financial hardship, and to foster and encourage competition, fair dealing, and prosperity in the field of health studio services by prohibiting or restricting false or misleading advertising, onerous contract terms, harmful financial practices, and other unfair, dishonest, deceptive, destructive, unscrupulous, fraudulent, and discriminatory practices by which the public has been injured in connection with contracts for health studio services. *(Added by Stats.1961, c. 1675, p. 3641, § 1. Amended by Stats.1969, c. 1571, p. 3194, § 3; Stats.2005, c. 439 (S.B.581), § 1.)*

Cross References

Contract for health studio services defined for purposes of this Title, see Civil Code § 1812.81.

§ 1812.81. "Contract for health studio services" defined

As used in this title, "contract for health studio services" means a contract for instruction, training or assistance in physical culture, body building, exercising, reducing, figure development, or any other such physical skill, or for the use by an individual patron of the facilities of a health studio, gymnasium or other facility used for any of the above purposes, or for membership in any group, club, association or organization formed for any of the above purposes; but does not include (a) contracts for professional services rendered or furnished by a person licensed under the provisions of Division 2 (commencing with Section 500) of the Business and Professions Code, (b) contracts for instruction at schools operating pursuant to the provisions of the Education Code, or (c) contracts for instruction, training, or assistance relating to diet or control of eating habits not involving physical culture, body building, exercising, figure development, or any other such physical skill. (Added by Stats.1961, c. 1675, p. 3642, § 1. Amended by Stats.1969, c. 1571, p. 3195, § 4; Stats.1980, c. 690, p. 2081, § 1.)

Cross References

Contract defined, see Civil Code § 1549.

§ 1812.82. Written contract required; copy to customer

Every contract for health studio services shall be in writing and shall be subject to the provisions of this title. A copy of the written contract shall be physically given to or delivered by email to the customer at the time he or she signs the contract. (Added by Stats.1961, c. 1675, p. 3642, § 1. Amended by Stats.1969, c. 611, p. 1251, § 1; Stats.1969, c. 1571, p. 3195, § 5; Stats.2016, c. 189 (A.B.2810), § 1, eff. Jan. 1, 2017.)

Cross References

Contract for health studio services defined for purposes of this Title, see Civil Code § 1812.81.
Statute of frauds, see Civil Code § 1624.

§ 1812.83. Overlapping contracts; consideration as one

All contracts for health studio services, which may be in effect between the same seller and the same buyer, the terms of which overlap for any period, shall be considered as one contract for the purposes of this title. (Added by Stats.1961, c. 1675, p. 3642, § 1. Amended by Stats.1969, c. 1571, p. 3195, § 6.)

Cross References

Contract for health studio services defined for purposes of this Title, see Civil Code § 1812.81.

§ 1812.84. Payment period and contract term limitations; statement disclosing length of term; cancellations

(a) A contract for health studio services may not require payments or financing by the buyer to exceed the term of the contract, nor may the term of the contract exceed three years. This subdivision does not apply to a member's obligation to pay valid, outstanding moneys due under the contract, including moneys to be paid pursuant to a termination notice period in the contract in which the termination notice period does not exceed 30 days.

(b) A contract for health studio services shall include a statement printed in a size at least 14–point type or presented in an equally legible electronic format that discloses the initial or minimum length of the term of the contract. This statement shall be placed above the space reserved for the signature of the buyer.

(c) At any time a cancellation is authorized by this title, a contract for health studio services may be canceled by the buyer in person, via email from an email address on file with the health studio, or via first-class mail. (Added by Stats.

1961, c. 1675, p. 3642, § 1. Amended by Stats.1969, c. 1571, p. 3195, § 7; Stats.1980, c. 651, p. 1825, § 1; Stats.1993, c. 339 (A.B.626), § 1; Stats.2001, c. 233 (S.B.85), § 1; Stats.2005, c. 439 (S.B.581), § 2; Stats.2006, c. 219 (A.B.2664), § 1; Stats.2016, c. 189 (A.B.2810), § 2, eff. Jan. 1, 2017.)

Cross References

Contract for health studio services defined for purposes of this Title, see Civil Code § 1812.81.

§ 1812.85. Time for beginning performance of services; grounds for cancellation and refunds; statement and notice of cancellation; consumer liability

(a) Every contract for health studio services shall provide that performance of the agreed-upon services will begin within six months after the date the contract is entered into. The consumer may cancel the contract and receive a pro rata refund if the health studio fails to provide the specific facilities advertised or offered in writing by the time indicated. If no time is indicated in the contract, the consumer may cancel the contract within six months after the execution of the contract and shall receive a pro rata refund. If a health studio fails to meet a timeline set forth in this section, the consumer may cancel the contract at any time after the expiration of the timeline. However, if following the expiration of the timeline, the health studio provides the advertised or agreed-upon services, the consumer may cancel the contract up to 10 days after those services are provided.

(b)(1) Every contract for health studio services shall, in addition, contain on its face, and in close proximity to the space reserved for the signature of the buyer, a conspicuous statement in a size equal to at least 10–point boldface type, as follows:

"You, the buyer, may choose to cancel this agreement at any time prior to midnight of the fifth business day of the health studio after the date of this agreement, excluding Sundays and holidays. To cancel this agreement, mail, email, or deliver a signed and dated notice that states that you, the buyer, are canceling this agreement, or words of similar effect. The notice shall be sent via first-class mail, via email from an email address on file with the health studio, or delivered in person to

_____
(Name of health studio operator)
at _____
(Address and email address of health studio operator)."

(2) The contract for health studio services shall contain on the first page, in a type size no smaller than that generally used in the body of the document, the following: (A) the name and mailing address of the health studio operator to which the notice of cancellation is to be mailed, (B) the email address of the health studio operator to which a notice of cancellation email is to be sent, and (C) the date the buyer signed the contract.

(3) The contract shall provide a description of the services, facilities, and hours of access to which the consumer is entitled or state where that information is available on the health studio operator's Internet Web site. Any services, facilities, and hours of access that are not described in the contract or on the health studio operator's Internet Web site

shall be considered optional services, and these optional services shall be considered as separate contracts for the purposes of this title and Section 1812.83.

(4) Until the health studio operator has complied with this section, the buyer may cancel the contract for health studio services.

(5) All moneys paid pursuant to a contract for health studio services shall be refunded within 10 days after receipt of the notice of cancellation, except that payment shall be made for any health studio services received prior to cancellation.

(c) If at any time during the term of the contract, including a transfer of the contractual obligation, the health studio eliminates or substantially reduces the scope of the facilities, such as swimming pools or tennis courts, that were described in the contract, in an advertisement relating to the specific location, or in a written offer, and available to the consumer upon execution of the contract, the consumer may cancel the contract and receive a pro rata refund. The consumer may not cancel the contract pursuant to this subdivision if the health studio, after giving reasonable notice to its members, temporarily takes facilities out of operation for reasonable repairs, modifications, substitutions, or improvements. This subdivision shall not be interpreted to give the consumer the right to cancel a contract because of changes to the type or quantity of classes or equipment offered, provided the consumer is informed in the contract that the health studio reserves the right to make changes to the type or quantity of classes or equipment offered and the changes to the type or quantity of classes or equipment offered are reasonable under the circumstances.

(d)(1) If a contract for health studio services requires payment of one thousand five hundred dollars ($1,500) to two thousand dollars ($2,000), inclusive, including initiation fees or initial membership fees, by the person receiving the services or the use of the facility, the person shall have the right to cancel the contract within 20 days after the contract is executed.

(2) If a contract for health studio services requires payment of two thousand one dollars ($2,001) to two thousand five hundred dollars ($2,500), inclusive, including initiation fees or initial membership fees, by the person receiving the services or the use of the facility, the person shall have the right to cancel the contract within 30 days after the contract is executed.

(3) If a contract for health studio services requires payment of two thousand five hundred one dollars ($2,501) or more, including initiation fees or initial membership fees, by the person receiving the services or the use of the facility, the person shall have the right to cancel the contract within 45 days after the contract is executed.

(4) The right of cancellation provided in this subdivision shall be set out in the membership contract.

(5) The rights and remedies under this paragraph are cumulative to any rights and remedies under other law.

(6) A health studio entering into a contract for health studio services that requires a payment of less than one thousand five hundred dollars ($1,500), including initiation or initial membership fees and exclusive of interest or finance charges, by the person receiving the services or the use of the facilities, is not required to comply with paragraph (1), (2), or (3).

(e) Upon cancellation, the consumer shall be liable only for that portion of the total contract payment, including initiation fees and other charges however denominated, that has been available for use by the consumer, based upon a pro rata calculation over the term of the contract. The remaining portion of the contract payment shall be returned to the consumer by the health studio. (Added by Stats.1961, c. 1675, p. 3642, § 1. Amended by Stats.1967, c. 1613, p. 3854, § 1; Stats.1969, c. 611, p. 1251, § 2; Stats.1969, c. 1571, p. 3195, § 8; Stats.1980, c. 651, p. 1825, § 2; Stats.2005, c. 439 (S.B.581), § 3; Stats.2006, c. 538 (S.B.1852), § 48; Stats. 2006, c. 219 (A.B.2664), § 2; Stats.2016, c. 189 (A.B.2810), § 3, eff. Jan. 1, 2017.)

Cross References

Contract for health studio services defined for purposes of this Title, see Civil Code § 1812.81.

§ 1812.86. Limitation on amount of payment

(a) No contract for health studio services shall require payment by the person receiving the services or the use of the facilities of a total amount in excess of the amount specified in subdivision (b) or (c).

(b) The limit specified in subdivision (a) shall, on and after January 1, 2006, be three thousand dollars ($3,000), inclusive of initiation or initial membership fees and exclusive of interest or finance charges.

(c) The limit in subdivision (a) shall, on and after January 1, 2010, be four thousand four hundred dollars ($4,400), inclusive of initiation or initial membership fees and exclusive of interest or finance charges. (Added by Stats.1961, c. 1675, p. 3642, § 1. Amended by Stats.1967, c. 1613, p. 3855, § 2; Stats.1969, c. 1571, p. 3195, § 9; Stats.1980, c. 651, p. 1825, § 3; Stats.2005, c. 439 (S.B.581), § 4.)

Cross References

Contract for health studio services defined for purposes of this Title, see Civil Code § 1812.81.

§ 1812.87. Prohibition of notes cutting off, as to third parties, buyer's right of action or defense against seller

No contract for health studio services shall require or entail the execution of any note or series of notes by the buyer which when separately negotiated will cut off as to third parties any right of action or defense which the buyer may have against the seller. (Added by Stats.1961, c. 1675, p. 3642, § 1. Amended by Stats.1969, c. 1571, p. 3195, § 10.)

Cross References

Contract for health studio services defined for purposes of this Title, see Civil Code § 1812.81.

§ 1812.88. Prohibition against assignment of contract cutting off buyer's right of action or defense against seller; conditions

No right of action or defense arising out of a contract for health studio services which the buyer has against the seller, and which would be cut off by assignment, shall be cut off by

§ 1812.88   OBLIGATIONS

assignment of the contract to any third party whether or not he acquires the contract in good faith and for value unless the assignee gives notice of the assignment to the buyer as provided in this section and within 30 days of the mailing of notice receives no written notice of the facts giving rise to the claim or defense of the buyer. A notice of assignment shall be in writing addressed to the buyer at the address shown on the contract and shall identify the contract and inform the buyer that he must, within 30 days of the date of mailing of the notice, notify the assignee in writing of any facts giving rise to a claim or defense which he may have. The notice of assignment shall state the name of the seller and buyer, a description of the services, the contract balance and the number and amount of the installments. *(Added by Stats. 1961, c. 1675, p. 3643, § 1. Amended by Stats.1969, c. 1571, p. 3196, § 11.)*

Cross References

Contract for health studio services defined for purposes of this Title, see Civil Code § 1812.81.

Rights of holder in due course and of non-holder in due course, see Commercial Code §§ 3305, 3306.

§ 1812.89. Relief from payment upon death, disability or movement; refund of prepayments; predetermined fee

(a)(1) Every contract for health studio services shall contain a clause providing that if, by reason of death or disability, the person agreeing to receive services is unable to receive all services for which he has contracted, he and his estate shall be relieved from the obligation of making payment for services other than those received prior to death or the onset of disability, and that if he has prepaid any sum for services, so much of such sum as is allocable to services he has not taken shall be promptly refunded to him or his representative.

(2) In every case in which a person has prepaid a sum for services under a contract for health studio services, and by reason of death or disability, is unable to receive all such services, the party agreeing to furnish such services shall, on request, immediately refund to such person or his personal representative such amount of the sum prepaid as is proportionate to the amount of services not received.

(3) For the purposes of this section, "disability" means a condition which precludes the buyer from physically using the facilities and the condition is verified by a physician.

(4) Notwithstanding the provisions of any contract to the contrary, whenever the contract price is payable in installments and the buyer is relieved from making further payments or entitled to a refund under this section, the amount of the contract price allocable to services not received shall represent at least as great a proportion of the total contract price as the sum of the periodic monthly balances not yet due bears to the sum of all the periodic monthly balances under the schedule of installments in the contract.

(b)(1) Except as provided in paragraph (2), every contract for health studio services shall contain a clause providing that if the person agreeing to receive health studio services moves further than 25 miles from the health studio and is unable to transfer the contract to a comparable facility, such person shall be relieved from the obligation of making payment for services other than those received prior to the move, and if such person has prepaid any sum for health studio services, so much of such sum as is allocable to services he or she has not taken shall be promptly refunded.

(2) Notwithstanding paragraph (1), a contract for health studio services may contain a clause providing that if the person agreeing to receive health studio services moves further than 25 miles from the health studio and is unable to transfer the contract to a comparable facility, such person may be charged a predetermined fee not exceeding one hundred dollars ($100), or, if more than half the life of the contract has expired, such person may be charged a predetermined fee not exceeding fifty dollars ($50). *(Added by Stats.1961, c. 1675, p. 3643, § 1. Amended by Stats.1969, c. 1571, p. 3196, § 12; Stats.1980, c. 651, p. 1826, § 4.)*

Cross References

Contract for health studio services defined for purposes of this Title, see Civil Code § 1812.81.

§ 1812.90. Provisions not exclusive

The provisions of this title are not exclusive and do not relieve the parties or the contracts subject thereto from compliance with all other applicable provisions of law. *(Added by Stats.1961, c. 1675, p. 3643, § 1.)*

§ 1812.91. Noncomplying contracts void

Any contract for health studio services which does not comply with the applicable provisions of this title shall be void and unenforceable as contrary to public policy. *(Added by Stats.1961, c. 1675, p. 3643, § 1. Amended by Stats.1969, c. 1571, p. 3197, § 13.)*

Cross References

Contract for health studio services defined for purposes of this Title, see Civil Code § 1812.81.

§ 1812.92. Fraud rendering contract void

Any contract for health studio services entered into in reliance upon any willful and false, fraudulent, or misleading information, representation, notice or advertisement of the seller shall be void and unenforceable. *(Added by Stats.1961, c. 1675, p. 3644, § 1. Amended by Stats.1969, c. 1571, p. 3197, § 14.)*

Cross References

Actual fraud, see Civil Code § 1572.

Contract for health studio services defined for purposes of this Title, see Civil Code § 1812.81.

Disregard of provisions of written contract which fail to express real intention of parties due to fraud, mistake or accident, see Civil Code § 1640.

§ 1812.93. Waiver of provisions

Any waiver of the buyer of the provisions of this title shall be deemed contrary to public policy and shall be void and unenforceable. *(Added by Stats.1961, c. 1675, p. 3644, § 1.)*

Cross References

Waiver of advantage, law established for public reason, see Civil Code § 3513.

Waiver of code provisions, generally, see Civil Code § 3268.

§ 1812.94. Recovery of triple damages and attorney fee; correction of contract; holder defined

(a) Any buyer injured by a violation of this title may bring an action for the recovery of damages. Judgment may be entered for three times the amount at which the actual damages are assessed plus reasonable attorney fees.

(b) Notwithstanding the provisions of this title, any failure to comply with any provision of this title may be corrected within 30 days after the execution of the contract by the buyer, and, if so corrected, neither the seller nor the holder shall be subject to any penalty under this title, provided that any correction which increases any monthly payment, the number of payments, or the total amount due, must be concurred in, in writing, by the buyer. "Holder" includes the seller who acquires the contract or, if the contract is purchased by a financing agency or other assignee, the financing agency or other assignee. (Added by Stats.1961, c. 1675, p. 3644, § 1. Amended by Stats.1963, c. 299, p. 1072, § 1.)

Cross References

Action on contract, award of attorney's fees and costs, see Civil Code § 1717.

§ 1812.95. Severability clause

If any provision of this title or the application thereof to any person or circumstances is held unconstitutional, the remainder of the title and the application of such provision to other persons and circumstances shall not be affected thereby. (Added by Stats.1961, c. 1675, p. 3644, § 1.)

§ 1812.96. Money to be held in trust until business opens; use of funds; cancellation rights

(a) Except as provided in subdivision (c) or (d), all money received by the seller of health studio services from a consumer for a health studio facility that has not yet opened for business shall be held in trust and shall be deposited in a trust account established in a state or federally chartered bank or savings association. The seller shall not draw, transfer, or encumber any of the money held in trust until five business days after the health studio facility has opened and the seller has fully paid refunds to consumers who canceled their contracts as provided in subdivision (b) or in Section 1812.85.

(b) In addition to any other cancellation rights, a consumer who pays any money under a contract for health studio services for a health studio facility that has not yet opened for business has the right to cancel the contract and receive a full refund at any time prior to midnight of the fifth business day after the date the health studio opens for business. The cancellation right shall be set forth in the contract. The refund shall be paid within 10 days of receipt of notice of cancellation.

(c) Notwithstanding subdivision (a), a seller of health studio services may draw on money held in trust to pay refunds or may draw, transfer, or encumber funds to the extent that the amount is offset by a bond of equal or greater amount that satisfies this subdivision. The bond shall be issued by a surety insurer admitted to do business in this state and shall be filed with the Secretary of State. The bond shall be in favor of the State of California for the benefit of consumers harmed by a violation of this title.

(d) Subdivision (a) does not apply to a seller of health studio services that is, at the time money is received from the consumer, operating at least five health studio facilities in this state that have been in operation for a period of at least five years, and that has an excess of current assets over current liabilities of at least one million dollars ($1,000,000). (Added by Stats.2005, c. 439 (S.B.581), § 5.)

Cross References

Contract for health studio services defined for purposes of this Title, see Civil Code § 1812.81.

§ 1812.97. Editorial Note

For a section of this number as added by Stats.1986, c. 565, § 1, see Civil Code § 1812.97 under Title 2.55.

§ 1812.98. Month-to-month contracts; declaration of existing law

Nothing in this title is intended to prohibit month-to-month contracts. This section is declaratory of existing law. (Formerly § 1812.97, added by Stats.2005, c. 439 (S.B.581), § 6. Renumbered § 1812.98 and amended by Stats.2006, c. 538 (S.B.1852), § 49.)

Title 2.55

CONTRACTS FOR THE LEASE OR RENTAL OF ATHLETIC FACILITIES

Section
1812.97. Warning statement; posting; athletic facilities; anabolic steroids.
1812.99. Repealed.
1812.995. Repealed.

§ 1812.97. Warning statement; posting; athletic facilities; anabolic steroids

(a) Every contract which has as its purpose the lease or rental of athletic facilities for instruction, training, or assistance in physical culture, body building, exercising, reducing, figure development, or any other related physical skill, or for baseball, football, tennis, basketball, gymnastics, track and field, hockey, ice skating, weightlifting, wrestling, or bicycling shall contain the following warning statement in 10-point bold type:

Warning: Use of steroids to increase strength or growth can cause serious health problems. Steroids can keep teenagers from growing to their full height; they can also cause heart disease, stroke, and damaged liver function. Men and women using steriods[1] may develop fertility problems, personality changes, and acne. Men can also experience premature balding and development of breast tissue. These health hazards are in addition to the civil and criminal penalties for unauthorized sale, use, or exchange of anabolic steroids.

(b) Commencing June 1, 1990, the warning statement required pursuant to subdivision (a) shall be conspicuously posted in all athletic facilities in this state which have locker

§ 1812.97

rooms. At least one warning statement shall be posted in every locker room of the athletic facility.

(c) As used in this section, "athletic facilities" includes a health studio regulated pursuant to Title 2.5 (commencing with Section 1812.80), a professional boxers' training gymnasium, as defined in Section 18685 of the Business and Professions Code, any privately owned sports facility or stadium in this state which is open to the general public, and any publicly owned sports facility or stadium in this state, including facilities in institutions of higher learning and schools that include any or all grades 7 to 12, inclusive.

(d) As used in this section, "anabolic steroids" include, but are not limited to, the following:

(1) Dianabol (methandrostenelone).

(2) Winstrol (stabozalol).

(3) Maxibolin (ethyl estrenol).

(4) Durabolin (nandrolone phenpropionate).

(5) Deca-Durabolin (nandrolone decanote).

(6) Testosterone propionate.

(7) Pregnyl (chorionic gonadotropin).

(8) Anavar (toxandroprione).

(e) When an athletic facility seeks to renew an operating license, if it can be demonstrated by a preponderance of the evidence that an athletic facility has not posted the sign required pursuant to this section, the licensing agency may impose a fine in the amount of fifty dollars ($50) per day for each day that the violation occurred, as a condition of obtaining the license renewal. (Added by Stats.1986, c. 565, § 1. Amended by Stats.1989, c. 807, § 2, operative June 1, 1990.)

[1] So in chaptered copy. Probably should be "steroids".

§ 1812.98. Editorial Note

For a section of this number as added by Stats.2005, c. 439 (S.B.581), § 6, see Civil Code § 1812.98 under Title 2.5.

§ 1812.99. Repealed by Stats.1969, c. 1571, § 18.

§ 1812.995. Repealed by Stats.1969, c. 1571, p. 3197, § 19

Title 2.6

CONTRACTS FOR DISCOUNT BUYING SERVICES

Section	
1812.100.	Legislative findings; purpose.
1812.101.	Definitions.
1812.103.	Bond; amount; copy.
1812.104.	Bond; beneficiaries; liability.
1812.105.	Deposit in lieu of bond; claim against deposit; review and approval; payment; attachment, garnishment, or execution.
1812.106.	Disclosures by buying organization; nature of services; listing of items; warranties or guarantees; charges; criminal or civil actions.
1812.107.	Written contract; contents.
1812.108.	Overlapping contracts; consideration as one.
1812.109.	Payment or financing period; limitation.
1812.110.	Availability of services; time.
1812.113.	Prohibition of notes cutting off, as to third parties, buyer's right of action or defense against seller.
1812.114.	Prohibition against assignment or transfer of contract cutting off buyer's right of action or defense against organization.
1812.116.	Receipt of payment or funds; delivery or availability of goods; time; refund; trust account; deposits and withdrawals.
1812.117.	Trust account withdrawal provisions; conditions for compliance with alternate trust account provisions; bond requirements: letter of credit; enforcement.
1812.118.	Cancellation of contract; time.
1812.119.	Voidable contracts; reference to compliance with title.
1812.120.	Misrepresentation; contract void and unenforceable.
1812.121.	Rescission and pro rata refund; removal of place of business; discontinuance of goods or services.
1812.122.	Transfer to another entity of duty or obligation to provide services; defense in action for enforcement or collection on contract.
1812.123.	Action for damages and restitution of moneys paid; treble damages and attorney fees and costs; correction of contract; transferee defined.
1812.125.	Violations; punishment; misdemeanor.
1812.126.	Provisions not exclusive.
1812.127.	Waiver.
1812.128.	Severability.
1812.129.	Enforcement; filing fees.

Cross References

Real estate, regulation of vacation ownership and time-share transactions, exemption from contracts for discount buying services provisions, see Business and Professions Code § 11211.7.

Seller of travel discount program, see Business and Professions Code § 17550.27.

Travel business discount program, see Business and Professions Code § 17550.26.

§ 1812.100. Legislative findings; purpose

(a) The Legislature finds that there exist in connection with a substantial number of contracts for discount buying services, sales practices and business and financing practices which result in fraud, deceit, and financial hardships being perpetrated on the people of the state; that existing legal remedies are inadequate to correct these abuses; that the discount buying industry has a significant impact upon the economy and well-being of the state and its local communities; and that the provisions of this title relating to such contracts are necessary for the public welfare.

(b) The purpose of this title is to safeguard the public against fraud, deceit, and financial hardship, and to foster and encourage competition, fair dealing, and prosperity in the field of discount buying services by prohibiting or restricting false or misleading advertising, unfair contract terms, harmful financial practices, and other unfair, deceptive, destructive, unscrupulous, fraudulent and discriminatory practices by which the public has been endangered and by which the public may in the future be harmed in connection with contracts for discount buying services. This title shall be construed liberally in order to achieve the foregoing purposes. (Added by Stats.1976, c. 237, p. 447, § 1.)

Cross References

Contract for discount buying services defined for purposes of this Title, see Civil Code § 1812.101.

§ 1812.101. Definitions

For the purpose of this title, the following definitions shall be used:

(a) "Discount buying organization" means any person or persons, corporation, unincorporated association, or other organization which, for a consideration, provides or purports to provide its clients or the clients or members of any other discount buying organization with the ability to purchase goods or services at discount prices, except that a discount buying organization does not include any of the following:

(1) Any discount buying organization in which the total consideration paid by each client or member in any manner whatsoever for the purchase of discount buying services from the organization that either:

(A) Does not exceed a one-time fee of fifty dollars ($50) or an annual fee of twenty-five dollars ($25) to be paid on a yearly basis.

(B) Does not exceed a one-time or annual fee of fifty dollars ($50) and the organization provides a majority of the goods and services through purchases by members who walk in to a fixed location operated by the organization.

(2) Any discount buying organization in which the total consideration paid by each client or member in any manner whatsoever for the purchase of discount buying services from the organization does not exceed a one-time or annual fee of one hundred dollars ($100) and the organization does all of the following in subparagraphs (A) to (F), inclusive, and subject to subparagraph (G):

(A) Offers buying services to clients or members through toll-free telephone access, computer access, or video shopping terminals.

(B)(i) During the first year of membership of each member, upon the request of the member, provides a full refund of membership fees, exclusive of any fees, however designated, not exceeding ten dollars ($10) in the aggregate, without conditions other than the surrender or destruction of materials which allow the member to access or use the service.

(ii)(I) The organization shall establish an escrow account of fifty thousand dollars ($50,000) for the purpose of providing refunds to members, pursuant to clause (i). If the fifty thousand dollars ($50,000) deposited in escrow is depleted during the first year of the existence of the escrow account, the organization shall within three business days of depletion replenish the account in the amount of fifty thousand dollars ($50,000). For each calendar year thereafter, the organization shall deposit in the account an amount equal to refunds made from the account in the prior calendar year, but not less than fifty thousand dollars ($50,000). At any time the balance in the escrow account decreases to 50 percent of the amount funded that year, the organization shall within three business days replenish the account back to the balance required at the beginning of that calendar year. The organization shall provide proof of the establishment of the escrow account to the Secretary of State and shall maintain records of all member requests for refunds and refunds made pursuant to this clause. The records shall be made available for review upon request by the Attorney General, any district attorney, or the Department of Justice.

(II) The escrow account shall be established and maintained at a federally insured bank or federally insured financial institution independent of the organization with escrow instructions making the bank or financial institution or an officer or employee thereof the escrow trustee.

(III) Refunds shall be made from the escrow account to any member who provides proof of membership while a California resident and requests, in writing, a membership refund, and has not previously been refunded his or her membership fee. The escrow trustee shall issue the refund within 10 days of the date the written request is received by the escrow trustee. In addition, requests for refunds may be made directly to and paid directly by the organization.

(IV) Proof of creation of the escrow account, and membership refund information, shall be provided to the members in the following form:

"The _____ (organization) has established an escrow account for the refund of membership fees at _____ (financial institution). Refunds from the escrow account may, in addition to other remedies and sources available to you, be obtained by mailing a written request along with proof of membership to _____ (escrow trustee). This refund request shall not affect or limit any other remedy at law available to you."

(C) Provides at least 15 toll-free service lines to California consumers devoted exclusively to customer service questions and complaints.

(D) Maintains a bond which meets the requirements of Sections 1812.103 and 1812.104, except that the principal sum of the bond need only be twenty thousand dollars ($20,000).

(E)(i) Possesses an unrevoked acknowledgment from the Attorney General that the organization has provided to the Attorney General, to the Attorney General's reasonable satisfaction, marketing procedures and documents that clearly explain membership fee cancellation and refund terms which include:

(I) The amount of the initial membership fee and how and when it will be collected.

(II) If applicable, that a member must be advised, before any charges are applied, that they need not provide billing information in order to be charged a membership fee, in circumstances in which the telemarketing firm has prior access to the member's billing information.

(III) In the case of trial membership offers, the duration of the trial period and that if the member does not cancel within the trial period he or she will automatically be charged the membership fee.

(IV) Specifically how the member may cancel membership.

(V) The written disclosure, printed in capital letters with a minimum 14–point boldface type, indicating who to contact, both directly through the company and through the escrow account, for a refund.

§ 1812.101 OBLIGATIONS

(VI) The written disclosure made at the time of solicitation and at the time an enrollment package is sent to consumers.

(ii) When an organization provides documentation that clearly explains membership fee cancellation and refund terms to the Attorney General's reasonable satisfaction, which includes the information required by subclauses (I) to (VI), inclusive, of clause (i) of subparagraph (E), the Attorney General shall issue a revocable acknowledgment to the organization for it to obtain this exception. The acknowledgment issued by the Attorney General is not evidence of the adequacy or accuracy of the organization's actual disclosures and representations provided to consumers. No organization in any marketing to consumers may make any reference to an acknowledgment issued by the Attorney General under this clause.

(F) Provides the disclosures listed in subclauses (I) to (VI), inclusive, of clause (i) of subparagraph (E) to every prospective member.

(G) The exemption is null and void if the organization fails to comply with the conditions set forth in this section or if the Attorney General's office revokes the exemption due to a organization not being in full compliance with all of the provisions of this section.

(3) Any discount buying organization in which persons receive discount buying services incidentally as part of a package of services provided to or available to the individual on account of his or her membership in the organization, which is not organized for the profit of any person or organization, and which does not have as one of its primary purposes or businesses, the provision of discount buying services.

(4) Any person, corporation, unincorporated association, or other organization, which, for a consideration collected from another entity, provides or purports to provide the clients of the other entity with the ability to purchase goods or services at discount prices, if the clients of the other entity do not order from, or pay any money to, that person, corporation, unincorporated association, or other organization; however, the entity, from which the customer purchases the right to obtain goods or services at discount prices, shall comply with the requirements of this title.

(b) "Contract for discount buying services" means a contract between one party (hereinafter referred to as the "buyer") who is purchasing the service for personal or family use, and a discount buying organization, whereby the buyer for a consideration receives the right to obtain goods or services from the discount buying organization, or to utilize the discount buying organization services in obtaining goods and services, at discount prices.

(c) "Discount prices" means prices which are represented to be lower on most or all offered goods or services than those generally charged for the items in the locality in which the representation is made.

This definition is not intended to affect the degree of savings which must be offered on an item or selection of items in order to truthfully and without misleading consumers represent an item, selection of items, or entire store as being "discount" or "discounted." *(Added by Stats.1976, c. 237, p. 447, § 1. Amended by Stats.1985, c. 558, § 1; Stats.1986, c. 345, § 1, eff. July 15, 1986; Stats.1992, c. 304 (A.B.2859), § 1; Stats.2001, c. 178 (S.B.916), § 1.)*

Cross References

Attorney General, generally, see Government Code § 12500 et seq.

§ 1812.103. Bond; amount; copy

Every discount buying organization shall maintain a bond issued by a surety company admitted to do business in this state. The principal sum of the bond shall be twenty thousand dollars ($20,000). A copy of such bond shall be filed with the Secretary of State. *(Added by Stats.1976, c. 237, p. 447, § 1. Amended by Stats.1996, c. 633 (S.B.1978), § 8.)*

Cross References

Discount buying organization defined for purposes of this Title, see Civil Code § 1812.101.

§ 1812.104. Bond; beneficiaries; liability

The bond required by Section 1812.103 shall be in favor of the State of California for the benefit of any person who is damaged by any violation of this title or by fraud or dishonesty or failure to provide the services of the discount buying organization in performance of the contract. The surety shall be liable only for the actual damages plus restitution and not the treble damages permitted under subdivision (a) of Section 1812.123. *(Added by Stats.1976, c. 237, p. 447, § 1. Amended by Stats.1982, c. 517, p. 2322, § 62.)*

Cross References

Bond and Undertaking Law, see Code of Civil Procedure § 995.010 et seq.
Discount buying organization defined for purposes of this Title, see Civil Code § 1812.101.

§ 1812.105. Deposit in lieu of bond; claim against deposit; review and approval; payment; attachment, garnishment, or execution

(a) When a deposit has been made in lieu of a bond pursuant to Section 995.710 of the Code of Civil Procedure, the person asserting a claim against the deposit shall, in lieu of Section 996.430 of the Code of Civil Procedure, establish the claim by furnishing evidence to the Secretary of State of a money judgment entered by a court together with evidence that the claimant is a person described in Section 1812.104.

(b) When a person has established the claim with the Secretary of State, the Secretary of State shall review and approve the claim and enter the date of approval on the claim. The claim shall be designated an "approved claim."

(c) When the first claim against a particular deposit has been approved, it shall not be paid until the expiration of a period of 240 days after the date of its approval by the Secretary of State. Subsequent claims that are approved by the Secretary of State within the same 240–day period shall similarly not be paid until the expiration of the 240–day period. Upon the expiration of the 240–day period, the Secretary of State shall pay all approved claims from that 240–day period in full unless the deposit is insufficient, in which case each approved claim shall be paid a pro rata share of the deposit.

(d) When the Secretary of State approves the first claim against a particular deposit after the expiration of a 240-day period, the date of approval of that claim shall begin a new 240-day period to which subdivision (c) shall apply with respect to the amount remaining in the deposit.

(e) After a deposit is exhausted, no further claims shall be paid by the Secretary of State. Claimants who have had their claims paid in full or in part pursuant to subdivisions (c) and (d) shall not be required to return funds received from the deposit for the benefit of other claimants.

(f) When a deposit has been made in lieu of a bond, the amount of the deposit shall not be subject to attachment, garnishment, or execution with respect to an action or judgment against the discount buying organization, other than as to an amount as no longer needed or required for the purpose of this title that would otherwise be returned to the discount buying organization by the Secretary of State.

(g) The Secretary of State shall retain a cash deposit for two years from the date the Secretary of State receives written notification from the assignor of the deposit that the assignor has ceased to engage in the business of a discount buying organization or has filed a bond pursuant to Section 1812.103, provided that there are no outstanding claims against the deposit. This written notice shall include all of the following: (1) name, address, and telephone number of the assignor; (2) name, address, and telephone number of the bank at which the deposit is located; (3) account number of the deposit; and (4) a statement whether the assignor is ceasing to engage in the business of a discount buying organization or has filed a bond with the Secretary of State. The Secretary of State shall forward an acknowledgment of receipt of the written notice to the assignor at the address indicated therein, specifying the date of receipt of the written notice and anticipated date of release of the deposit, provided there are no outstanding claims against the deposit.

(h) A judge of a superior court may order the return of the deposit prior to the expiration of two years upon evidence satisfactory to the judge that there are no outstanding claims against the deposit or order the Secretary of State to retain the deposit for a sufficient period beyond the two years specified in subdivision (g) to resolve outstanding claims against the deposit. (Added by Stats.1984, c. 545, § 3. Amended by Stats.1996, c. 633 (S.B.1978), § 9; Stats.1998, c. 829 (S.B.1652), § 9; Stats.2002, c. 784 (S.B.1316), § 14.)

Cross References

Auctioneers and auction companies, deposits in lieu of surety bond, procedures, approval and payment of claims, see Civil Code § 1812.600.
Discount buying organization defined for purposes of this Title, see Civil Code § 1812.101.

§ 1812.106. Disclosures by buying organization; nature of services; listing of items; warranties or guarantees; charges; criminal or civil actions

Every discount buying organization, before obtaining the signature of a potential buyer on any application or contract for discount buying services, shall provide to the buyer, and shall allow the buyer to retain, the following written disclosures:

(a) The exact nature of the services it provides, specifying the general categories of goods that are available at the discount buying organization's place of business or warehouse, those categories of goods, if any, that must be ordered or obtained through stores to which the discount buying organization will refer the customer, and those categories of goods, if any, that must be ordered or obtained through the mail.

(b) A list, current within the previous 60 days, of at least 100 items that are sold by or through the organization or available to those who contract with the organization, identified by brand name, model, and total price including a reasonable estimate of freight charges, if any are to be imposed; a reasonable estimate of delivery charges, if any are to be imposed; a reasonable estimate of setup charges, if any are to be imposed; the discount buying organization's price markup; and a reasonable estimate of any other charges the discount buying organization imposes. These items shall be reasonably representative as to the type of goods available. In lieu of providing this list, the discount buying organization shall provide and allow the buyer to retain a list of at least 100 items that were purchased by its members through the discount buying organization during the preceding 60 days. This list shall identify the items by brand name, model, and total selling price including freight charges, if any; delivery charges, if any; setup charges, if any; the discount buying organization's price markup; and any other charges imposed by the discount buying organization, and shall be representative as to the type of goods sold and the prices charged for the listed goods sold during that period. If the maximum number of items available through a discount buying organization is fewer than 100 in number, it may comply with this section by furnishing a list of the total items available, identified as described above with a statement that those are the only goods presently available. Any list required by this subdivision shall state the date on which it was prepared.

(c) A statement of the discount buying organization's policy with respect to warranties or guarantees on goods ordered, and the policy with respect to the return of ordered goods, cancellation of orders by the buyer, and refunds for cancellation or return.

(d) A description of any charges, such as freight charges, delivery charges, setup charges, seller's markup, and any other charges that are incidental to the purchase of goods through the discount buying organization and are to be paid by the buyer. A disclosure of these costs in specific monetary amounts shall also be made on each order placed through the discount buying organization.

(e) If any stockholder, director, officer, or general or limited partner of the discount buying organization, as the case may be:

(1) Has been convicted of a felony or misdemeanor or pleaded nolo contendere to a felony or misdemeanor charge, if the felony or misdemeanor involved fraud, embezzlement, fraudulent conversion, misappropriation of property, or a violation of this title.

(2) Has been held liable in a civil action by final judgment or consented to the entry of a stipulated judgment if the civil action alleged fraud, embezzlement, fraudulent conversion, or misappropriation of property, a violation of this title, the

§ 1812.106

use of untrue or misleading representations in an attempt to sell or dispose of real or personal property, or the use of unfair, unlawful, or deceptive business practices.

(3) Is subject to any currently effective injunction or restrictive order relating to business activity as the result of an action brought by a public agency or department, including, but not limited to, an action affecting any vocational license, a statement so stating, and including the name of the court, the date of the conviction, judgment, order, or injunction and, if applicable, the name of the governmental agency that filed the action resulting in the conviction, judgment, order, or injunction. *(Added by Stats.1976, c. 237, p. 447, § 1. Amended by Stats.1980, c. 1001, p. 3190, § 1, eff. Sept. 21, 1980; Stats.2006, c. 538 (S.B.1852), § 50.)*

Cross References

Contract for discount buying services defined for purposes of this Title, see Civil Code § 1812.101.
Discount buying organization defined for purposes of this Title, see Civil Code § 1812.101.
Felonies, definition and penalties, see Penal Code §§ 17, 18.
Misdemeanors, definition and penalties, see Penal Code §§ 17, 19, 19.2.

§ 1812.107. Written contract; contents

Every contract for discount buying services shall be in writing and shall be subject to the provisions of this title. The address of the seller's discount buying facility and the residence address of the buyer shall be clearly indicated on the face of the contract. A copy of the written contract shall be given to the buyer at the time he signs the contract. All blank spaces in the contract shall be filled in before the contract is signed by the buyer. Provisions or terms written by hand on the buyer's copy shall be legible. The contract shall disclose that a bond has been obtained by the discount buying organization and that a copy of such bond is on file with the Secretary of State. The contract shall be specific as to the period of time for which the discount buying services will be available to the buyer. This time period shall not be measured by the life of the buyer. *(Added by Stats.1976, c. 237, p. 447, § 1.)*

Cross References

Contract for discount buying services defined for purposes of this Title, see Civil Code § 1812.101.
Discount buying organization defined for purposes of this Title, see Civil Code § 1812.101.

§ 1812.108. Overlapping contracts; consideration as one

All contracts for discount buying services, which may be in effect between a seller or related sellers and a buyer, the terms of which overlap for any period of time, shall be considered as one contract for the purpose of this title. *(Added by Stats.1976, c. 237, p. 447, § 1.)*

Cross References

Contract for discount buying services defined for purposes of this Title, see Civil Code § 1812.101.

§ 1812.109. Payment or financing period; limitation

No contract for discount buying services shall require payments or financing by the buyer over a period in excess of two years from the date the contract was entered into. *(Added by Stats.1976, c. 237, p. 447, § 1.)*

Cross References

Contract for discount buying services defined for purposes of this Title, see Civil Code § 1812.101.

§ 1812.110. Availability of services; time

Every contract for discount buying services shall provide that the buying services shall become available to the buyer within seven days from the date the contract was entered into. *(Added by Stats.1976, c. 237, p. 447, § 1.)*

Cross References

Contract for discount buying services defined for purposes of this Title, see Civil Code § 1812.101.

§ 1812.113. Prohibition of notes cutting off, as to third parties, buyer's right of action or defense against seller

No contract for discount buying services shall require or entail the execution of any note or series of notes by the buyer which, when separately negotiated, will cut off as to any third party any right of action or defense which the buyer may have against the seller. *(Added by Stats.1976, c. 237, p. 447, § 1.)*

Cross References

Contract for discount buying services defined for purposes of this Title, see Civil Code § 1812.101.

§ 1812.114. Prohibition against assignment or transfer of contract cutting off buyer's right of action or defense against organization

No right of action or defense arising out of a contract for discount buying services which the buyer has against the discount buying organization shall be cut off by assignment or transfer of the contract to any third party. *(Added by Stats.1976, c. 237, p. 447, § 1.)*

Cross References

Contract for discount buying services defined for purposes of this Title, see Civil Code § 1812.101.
Discount buying organization defined for purposes of this Title, see Civil Code § 1812.101.

§ 1812.116. Receipt of payment or funds; delivery or availability of goods; time; refund; trust account; deposits and withdrawals

(a) Every contract for discount buying services shall provide that if any goods ordered by the buyer from the seller are not delivered to the buyer or available for pickup by the buyer at a location within his county of residence within six weeks from the date the buyer placed an order for such goods, then any moneys paid by the buyer for such goods in advance of delivery shall, upon the buyer's request, be fully refunded unless a predetermined delivery date has been furnished to the buyer in writing at the time he ordered such goods and the goods are delivered to the buyer or are available for pickup by that date.

(b) Prior to receiving from a buyer any payments pursuant to the terms of a contract for discount buying services, the discount buying organization shall establish a trust account at a federally insured bank or savings and loan association for the deposit, except for the first fifty dollars ($50) of a downpayment, of the contract payments as they are received.

If the discount buying organization sells or assigns the contract for discount buying services to a third party and such third party pays the discount buying organization as consideration an amount which is commercially reasonable for the sale or assignment of the contract, the discount buying organization shall deposit all funds received from the third party into the trust account.

If the discount buying organization in any manner transfers the contract for discount buying services to a third party which is to act as the recipient of contract payments from the buyer and such third party does not pay the discount buying organization as consideration for such transfer an amount which is commercially reasonable, then all sums received by the third party from the buyer shall be deposited in the discount buying organization's trust account for contract payments.

As to each buyer, during the first one-fourth or first six months of the buyer's membership period, whichever is shorter, funds representing no more than one-fourth of the contract price may be withdrawn from the trust account. During each subsequent one-fourth or six-month period, whichever is shorter, funds representing an additional one-fourth of the contract price may be withdrawn from the trust account.

(c)(1) Prior to receiving funds for an order of goods or services from any buyer, the discount buying organization shall establish a trust account at a federally insured bank or savings and loan association for the deposit of the funds. The discount buying organization shall deposit into the account all funds received from buyers for orders of goods or services regardless of how the funds are styled, including but not limited to, down payment, partial payment, payment in full, freight charge, or any other terms. If the total cost of goods or services ordered by a buyer on any one day does not exceed fifty dollars ($50), including taxes, freight charges, delivery charges, markup and all other charges collected by the discount buying organization, then the funds received from the buyer need not be deposited in the trust account.

(2) The trust account required by this section shall be created and maintained for the benefit of buyers who order goods or services from or through the discount buying organization. The discount buying organization shall not in any manner encumber the corpus of the account and shall not withdraw money deposited therein on behalf of a buyer except: (i) in partial or full payment to the discount buying organization's source for the goods or services ordered by the buyer, or (ii) to make a refund to the buyer. After the withdrawal of money from a buyer's deposit pursuant to (i) or (ii) above, only that portion of the remainder of the deposit which represents compensation to the discount buying organization may be withdrawn. *(Added by Stats.1976, c. 237, p. 447, § 1. Amended by Stats.1980, c. 1001, p. 3191, § 2, eff. Sept. 21, 1980.)*

Cross References

Contract for discount buying services defined for purposes of this Title, see Civil Code § 1812.101.

Discount buying organization defined for purposes of this Title, see Civil Code § 1812.101.

§ 1812.117. Trust account withdrawal provisions; conditions for compliance with alternate trust account provisions; bond requirements: letter of credit; enforcement

(a) An affiliate discount buying organization may, at its option, and with the express written consent of its parent, comply with the trust account withdrawal provisions set forth in subdivision (b), in lieu of those contained in subdivision (b) of Section 1812.116.

(b) The affiliate shall comply with the trust account provisions of subdivision (b) of Section 1812.116, except that:

(1) As to each buyer, during the first one-fourth or first six months of the buyer's membership period, whichever is shorter, funds representing no more than one-half of the contract price may be withdrawn from the trust account.

(2) During the subsequent one-fourth or six-month period of the buyer's membership period, whichever is shorter, the remaining balance of the contract price may be withdrawn from the trust account.

(c) To qualify for the provisions set forth in subdivision (b), (1) the affiliate shall maintain a surety bond of two hundred fifty thousand dollars ($250,000), and (2) the parent shall maintain an aggregate surety bond of two million five hundred thousand dollars ($2,500,000) and a letter of credit, as set forth in subdivision (d), for all of its affiliates that qualify for the withdrawal provisions of subdivision (b). The bonds shall be issued by a surety company admitted to do business in this state. A copy of each bond shall be filed with the Secretary of State, with a copy provided to the Attorney General. The affiliate's bond shall be in lieu of the bond required by subdivision (a) of Section 1812.103. The surety bonds shall comply with the requirements of this section and shall be in favor of the State of California for the benefit of consumers harmed by any violation of this title by the affiliate, the failure of the affiliate to comply with the terms of its membership contracts with consumers, and the failure of the affiliate to comply with the terms of any agreement with consumers for the purchase of goods or services, provided the bonds shall cover only pecuniary loss and not exemplary damages or treble damages permitted under subdivision (a) of Section 1812.123, and provided further the parent's bond shall not be drawn on until the affiliate's bond is exhausted.

(d) The parent shall continuously maintain and provide to the Attorney General as beneficiary an irrevocable letter of credit issued by a California state chartered bank or a national bank with its principal place of business in the State of California, in the amount of one million dollars ($1,000,000), in a form satisfactory to the Attorney General. After the bonds described in subdivision (c) have been exhausted, only the Attorney General, by and through the Attorney General's deputy or assistant, may draw on the letter of credit for the satisfaction of any final judgments based on any violation of this title by the affiliate, the failure of the affiliate to comply with the terms of its membership contracts with consumers, or the failure of an affiliate to comply with the terms of any agreement with consumers for the purchase of goods or services, provided the liability is established by final

§ 1812.117

judgment of a court of competent jurisdiction and the time for appeal has expired or, if an appeal is taken, the appeal is finally determined and the judgment is affirmed, and provided further the letter of credit shall cover only pecuniary loss and not exemplary damages or treble damages permitted under subdivision (a) of Section 1812.123. The letter of credit shall provide that payment shall be made to the Attorney General upon presentation to the issuer of a sight draft stating only the amount drawn and signed by the Attorney General or by an Assistant or Deputy Attorney General. Any amount received by the Attorney General under the letter of credit shall be used exclusively to satisfy final judgments as described in this subdivision. The Attorney General may apply to the court for orders as desired or needed to carry out the provisions of this subdivision.

(e) In addition to other lawful means for the enforcement of the surety's liability on the bonds required by this section, the surety's liability may be enforced by motion after a final judgment has been obtained against an affiliate based on any violation of this title by the affiliate, the failure of the affiliate to comply with the terms of its membership contracts with consumers, or the failure of the affiliate to comply with the terms of any agreement with consumers for the purchase of goods or services. The bond of the parent shall not be drawn on until the bond of the affiliate has been exhausted, as provided in subdivisions (c) and (d). The motion may be filed by the Attorney General, a public prosecutor, or any person who obtained the judgment without first attempting to enforce the judgment against any party liable under the judgment. The notice of motion, motion, and a copy of the judgment shall be served on the surety as provided in Chapter 5 (commencing with Section 1010) of Title 14 of Part 2 of the Code of Civil Procedure. The notice shall set forth the amount of the claim, a brief statement indicating that the claim is covered by the bond, and, if the motion is to enforce liability under the bond provided by the parent, a statement that the bond provided by the affiliate has been exhausted or will be exhausted if the motion is granted. Service shall also be made on the Attorney General directed to the Consumer Law section. The court shall grant the motion unless the surety establishes that the claim is not covered by the bond or unless the court sustains an objection made by the Attorney General that the grant of the motion might impair the rights of actual or potential claimants or is not in the public interest. The court may, in the interest of justice, order a pro rata or other equitable distribution of the bond proceeds.

(f)(1) The bond required by subdivision (c) for an affiliate shall be continuously maintained by the affiliate until the date the affiliate ceases to make the election under subdivision (a) or ceases to engage in the business of a discount buying organization. The bond required by subdivision (c) for the parent shall be continuously maintained by the parent until the date all affiliates cease to make the election under subdivision (a) or all affiliates cease to engage in the business of a discount buying organization.

(2) Notwithstanding the expiration or termination of any bond required under this section, the bond remains in full force and effect for all liabilities incurred before, and for acts, omissions, and causes existing or which arose before, the expiration or termination of the bond. Legal proceedings may be had therefor in all respects as though the bond were in effect.

(3) The letter of credit required under subdivisions (c) and (d) shall be continuously maintained for a period of four years after all affiliates cease to make the election under subdivision (a) or cease to engage in the business of a discount buying organization, provided the period shall be extended until there is a final judgment, as described in subdivision (d), entered in each action seeking relief that may be covered by the letter of credit if the action was filed before the expiration of the four-year period.

(g) Subdivision (a) of Section 1812.121 does not apply to a discount buying organization that offers substantially equivalent alternative at-home ordering service through other generally available channels of communications, such as the Internet, for the same categories of goods and services, provided the ordered goods are shipped either to the home or to a freight receiver within 20 miles of the buyer's residence at the time the buyer entered into the contract for discount buying services.

(h) For purposes of this section, the following terms apply:

(1) "Affiliate" or "affiliate discount buying organization" means a discount buying organization that is a subsidiary of a parent, as defined in paragraph (4), or operates under a franchise, as defined in paragraph (3), granted by a parent.

(2) "Consumer" or "buyer" means and includes a client or member of an affiliate discount buying organization.

(3) "Franchise" has the same meaning as in Section 31005 of the Corporations Code.

(4) "Parent" means a business entity that directly or indirectly has franchised or operated 25 or more discount buying organizations for 10 years or more. *(Added by Stats.2004, c. 451 (A.B.2613), § 1.)*

Cross References

Attorney General, generally, see Government Code § 12500 et seq.
Bond and Undertaking Law, bonds or undertakings given as security, see Code of Civil Procedure § 995.010 et seq.
Contract for discount buying services defined for purposes of this Title, see Civil Code § 1812.101.
Discount buying organization defined for purposes of this Title, see Civil Code § 1812.101.
Legislative intent, construction of statutes, see Code of Civil Procedure § 1859.
Suretyship, see Civil Code § 2787 et seq.

§ 1812.118. Cancellation of contract; time

Every contract for discount buying services shall further provide that such contract may be canceled at any time within three days after the date of receipt by the buyer of a copy of the contract by written notice to the seller at the address specified in the contract. If such cancellation is made, all moneys paid pursuant to the contract shall be refunded. Every contract for discount buying services shall be subject to the cancellation privileges and comply with the requirements of Sections 1689.6 and 1689.7 of this code. *(Added by Stats.1976, c. 237, p. 447, § 1.)*

Cross References

Contract for discount buying services defined for purposes of this Title, see Civil Code § 1812.101.

§ 1812.119. Voidable contracts; reference to compliance with title

(a) Any contract for discount buying services which does not comply with the applicable provisions of this title shall be voidable by the buyer.

(b) No discount buying organization shall make or authorize the making of any reference to its compliance with this title. *(Added by Stats.1976, c. 237, p. 447, § 1. Amended by Stats.1980, c. 1001, p. 3193, § 3, eff. Sept. 21, 1980.)*

Cross References

Contract for discount buying services defined for purposes of this Title, see Civil Code § 1812.101.

Discount buying organization defined for purposes of this Title, see Civil Code § 1812.101.

§ 1812.120. Misrepresentation; contract void and unenforceable

Any untrue or misleading information, representation, notice or advertisement of the seller which has been received by or made to the buyer prior to his signing a contract for discount buying services shall render the contract for discount buying services void and unenforceable by the seller. No seller shall make or disseminate such information, representations, notices or advertisements. The phrase "untrue or misleading information, representation, notice, or advertisement" shall include any acts which constitute violations of Chapter 1 (commencing with Section 17500) of Part 3 of Division 7 of the Business and Professions Code. However, neither this section nor any other section of this title shall operate to exempt discount buying services from any other provisions of law, including the penalty provisions of Section 17536 of the Business and Professions Code and Section 3370.1 of this code. *(Added by Stats.1976, c. 237, p. 447, § 1.)*

Cross References

Contract for discount buying services defined for purposes of this Title, see Civil Code § 1812.101.

§ 1812.121. Rescission and pro rata refund; removal of place of business; discontinuance of goods or services

(a) If a discount buying organization removes its place of business or, if it conducts business at more than one location, that place of business which is geographically closest to the buyer's residence indicated on the face of the contract, more than 20 miles farther from the buyer's residence than it was at the time the contract for discount buying services was entered into, the organization shall offer rescission and a pro rata refund to each buyer affected, based upon the amount of time for which the buyer has been a member of the organization.

(b) If a discount buying organization discontinues providing any category of goods or services disclosed in compliance with Section 1812.106 or otherwise represented to the buyer to be available at or before the buyer's signing of the contract for discount buying services, the organization shall offer rescission and a pro rata refund based upon the amount of time for which the buyer has been a member of the organization, to each buyer who was informed of the availability of the category of goods or services to be discontinued and signed a contract for discount buying services within the six months immediately preceding the discontinuance of said category of goods or services. *(Added by Stats.1976, c. 237, p. 447, § 1.)*

Cross References

Contract for discount buying services defined for purposes of this Title, see Civil Code § 1812.101.

Discount buying organization defined for purposes of this Title, see Civil Code § 1812.101.

§ 1812.122. Transfer to another entity of duty or obligation to provide services; defense in action for enforcement or collection on contract

Any transfer by a discount buying organization of its duty or obligation to provide services to buyers under its contracts for discount buying services to another individual, corporation, or other business entity, as a result of which a buyer shall have available substantially fewer goods and services, shall constitute a complete defense to an action for further enforcement of or collection on such a contract for discount buying services which may be asserted by any buyer who did not consent in writing, after a full and fair disclosure of the categories of goods and services to be provided by the new discount buying organization, to such transfer of the duty or obligation of performance, and shall entitle such a nonconsenting individual to rescind the contract and obtain a pro rata refund from the transferor. *(Added by Stats.1976, c. 237, p. 447, § 1.)*

Cross References

Contract for discount buying services defined for purposes of this Title, see Civil Code § 1812.101.

Discount buying organization defined for purposes of this Title, see Civil Code § 1812.101.

§ 1812.123. Action for damages and restitution of moneys paid; treble damages and attorney fees and costs; correction of contract; transferee defined

(a) Any buyer injured by a violation of this title may bring an action for the recovery of damages and return of all moneys paid by the buyer to the seller. Judgment shall be entered for three times the amount at which the actual damages, plus such restitution, are assessed plus reasonable attorney's fees and costs. In the event that the court finds a violation of Section 1812.120 relating to untrue or misleading statements, judgment shall be entered for one thousand dollars ($1,000) plus reasonable attorney's fees or three times the amount of actual damages plus restitution plus reasonable attorney's fees, whichever is greater.

(b) Notwithstanding any other provision of this title, any failure to comply with any provision of this title except Section 1812.120 may be corrected within 30 days after the execution of the contract by the buyer, and if so corrected, neither the seller nor his transferee shall be subject to any liability under this title except that of a suit for actual damages plus reasonable attorney's fees and costs, provided that any correction must be concurred in, in writing, by the buyer, or the contract shall be void and unenforceable by the seller, who shall forthwith tender to the buyer a full refund.

"Transferee" includes holders and assignees. *(Added by Stats.1976, c. 237, p. 447, § 1.)*

Cross References

Action on contract, award of attorney's fees and costs, see Civil Code § 1717.

§ 1812.125. Violations; punishment; misdemeanor

(a) Any person who violates subdivision (b) or (c) of Section 1812.116 shall, upon conviction, be fined not more than ten thousand dollars ($10,000) for each violation, or imprisoned pursuant to subdivision (h) of Section 1170 of the Penal Code, or imprisoned in a county jail for not more than one year, or be punished by both that fine and imprisonment.

(b) Any person who violates any other provision of this title shall be guilty of a misdemeanor. *(Added by Stats.1976, c. 237, p. 447, § 1. Amended by Stats.1980, c. 1001, p. 3193, § 4, eff. Sept. 21, 1980; Stats.2011, c. 15 (A.B.109), § 33, eff. April 4, 2011, operative Oct. 1, 2011.)*

Cross References

Misdemeanors, definition and penalties, see Penal Code §§ 17, 19, 19.2.

§ 1812.126. Provisions not exclusive

The prohibitions [1] of this title are not exclusive and do not relieve the parties or the contracts subject thereto from compliance with any other applicable provision of law. *(Added by Stats.1976, c. 237, p. 447, § 1.)*

[1] So in chaptered copy. Probably should read "provisions".

§ 1812.127. Waiver

Any waiver by the buyer of the provisions of this title shall be deemed contrary to public policy and shall be void and unenforceable. *(Added by Stats.1976, c. 237, p. 447, § 1.)*

§ 1812.128. Severability

If any provision of this title or the application thereof to any person or circumstances is held invalid, such invalidity shall not affect other provisions or applications of the title which can be given effect without the invalid provision or application, and to this end the provisions of this title are severable. *(Added by Stats.1976, c. 237, p. 447, § 1.)*

§ 1812.129. Enforcement; filing fees

(a) The Secretary of State shall enforce the provisions of this title that govern the filing and maintenance of bonds and deposits in lieu of bonds.

(b) The Secretary of State shall charge a filing fee not to exceed the cost of filing the bond or the deposit in lieu of a bond pursuant to Section 995.710 of the Code of Civil Procedure. *(Added by Stats.1996, c. 633 (S.B.1978), § 10. Amended by Stats.1998, c. 829 (S.B.1652), § 10.)*

Title 2.7

CONTRACTS FOR SELLER ASSISTED MARKETING PLANS

Section
1812.200. Legislative findings, declarations, and intent.

Section
1812.201. Definitions.
1812.202. Offer in state.
1812.203. Filing disclosure statements and lists of salespersons; notice of intent to issue stop orders; refutation.
1812.204. Prohibited representations and activities.
1812.205. Disclosure statement.
1812.206. Information sheet.
1812.207. Written contracts; delivery of copies.
1812.208. Right to cancel; time; notice.
1812.209. Mandatory contract provisions.
1812.210. Notes; downpayment restrictions; escrow.
1812.211. Rights of purchaser against seller's assignee.
1812.212. Reference to compliance.
1812.213. Books, records and accounts; preservation of documents.
1812.214. Attorney to receive process; service of process; bond or trust accounts; escrow account procedures.
1812.215. Purchaser's right to void contract.
1812.216. Waiver of rights by purchaser; burden of proving exemption or exception from definitions.
1812.217. Violations; punishment.
1812.218. Damages.
1812.219. Additional remedies.
1812.220. Partial invalidity.
1812.221. Deposit in lieu of bond; claim against deposit; review and approval; payment; attachment, garnishment, or execution.

Cross References

Telephonic sellers, exclusions from definition, see Business and Professions Code § 17511.1.

§ 1812.200. Legislative findings, declarations, and intent

(a) The Legislature finds and declares that the widespread sale of seller assisted marketing plans, often connected with the sale of vending machines, racks or work-at-home paraphernalia, has created numerous problems in California for purchasers which are inimical to good business practice. Often purchasers of seller assisted marketing plans are individuals inexperienced in business matters who use their life savings to purchase the seller assisted marketing plan in the hope that they will earn enough money in addition to retirement income or salary to become or remain self-sufficient. Many purchasers are the elderly who are seeking a way to supplement their fixed incomes. The initial payment is usually in the form of a purchase of overpriced equipment or products. California purchasers have suffered substantial losses when they have failed to receive full and complete information regarding the seller assisted marketing plan, the amount of money they can reasonably expect to earn, and the previous experience of the seller assisted marketing plan seller. Seller assisted marketing plan sellers have a significant impact upon the economy and well-being of this state and its local communities. The provisions of this title relating to seller assisted marketing plans are necessary for the public welfare.

(b) It is the intent of this title to provide each prospective seller assisted marketing plan purchaser with the information necessary to make an intelligent decision regarding seller assisted marketing plans being offered; to safeguard the public against deceit and financial hardship; to insure, foster and encourage competition and fair dealing in the sale of seller assisted marketing plans by requiring adequate disclosure; to prohibit representations that tend to mislead; and to prohibit or restrict unfair contract terms. This title shall be construed liberally in order to achieve the foregoing purposes. *(Added by Stats.1978, c. 876, p. 2749, § 1.)*

Cross References

Equipment defined for purposes of this Title, see Civil Code § 1812.201.
Initial payment defined for purposes of this Title, see Civil Code § 1812.201.
Product defined for purposes of this Title, see Civil Code § 1812.201.
Purchaser defined for purposes of this Title, see Civil Code § 1812.201.
Seller assisted marketing plan contract or contract defined for purposes of this Title, see Civil Code § 1812.201.
Seller assisted marketing plan defined for purposes of this Title, see Civil Code § 1812.201.
Seller defined for purposes of this Title, see Civil Code § 1812.201.

§ 1812.201. Definitions

For the purposes of this title, the following definitions shall apply:

(a) "Seller assisted marketing plan" means any sale or lease or offer to sell or lease any product, equipment, supplies, or services that requires a total initial payment exceeding five hundred dollars ($500), but requires an initial cash payment of less than fifty thousand dollars ($50,000), that will aid a purchaser or will be used by or on behalf of the purchaser in connection with or incidental to beginning, maintaining, or operating a business when the seller assisted marketing plan seller has advertised or in any other manner solicited the purchase or lease of the seller assisted marketing plan and done any of the following acts:

(1) Represented that the purchaser will earn, is likely to earn, or can earn an amount in excess of the initial payment paid by the purchaser for participation in the seller assisted marketing plan.

(2) Represented that there is a market for the product, equipment, supplies, or services, or any product marketed by the user of the product, equipment, supplies, or services sold or leased or offered for sale or lease to the purchaser by the seller, or anything, be it tangible or intangible, made, produced, fabricated, grown, bred, modified, or developed by the purchaser using, in whole or in part, the product, supplies, equipment, or services that were sold or leased or offered for sale or lease to the purchaser by the seller assisted marketing plan seller.

(3) Represented that the seller will buy back or is likely to buy back any product made, produced, fabricated, grown, or bred by the purchaser using, in whole or in part, the product, supplies, equipment, or services that were initially sold or leased or offered for sale or lease to the purchaser by the seller assisted marketing plan seller.

(b) A "seller assisted marketing plan" shall not include:

(1) A security, as defined in the Corporate Securities Law of 1968 (Division 1 (commencing with Section 25000) of Title 4 of the Corporations Code), that has been qualified for sale by the Department of * * * <u>Financial Protection and Innovation</u>, or is exempt under Chapter 1 (commencing with Section 25100) of Part 2 of Division 1 of Title 4 of the Corporations Code from the necessity to qualify.

(2) A franchise defined by the Franchise Investment Law (Division 5 (commencing with Section 31000) of Title 4 of the Corporations Code) that is registered with the Department of * * * <u>Financial Protection and Innovation</u> or is exempt under Chapter 1 (commencing with Section 31100) of Part 2 of Division 5 of Title 4 of the Corporations Code from the necessity of registering.

(3) Any transaction in which either the seller or purchaser or the lessor or lessee is licensed pursuant to and the transaction is governed by the Real Estate Law, Division 4 (commencing with Section 10000) of the Business and Professions Code.

(4) A license granted by a general merchandise retailer that allows the licensee to sell goods, equipment, supplies, products, or services to the general public under the retailer's trademark, trade name, or service mark if all of the following criteria are satisfied:

(A) The general merchandise retailer has been doing business in this state continually for five years prior to the granting of the license.

(B) The general merchandise retailer sells diverse kinds of goods, equipment, supplies, products, or services.

(C) The general merchandise retailer also sells the same goods, equipment, supplies, products, or services directly to the general public.

(D) During the previous 12 months the general merchandise retailer's direct sales of the same goods, equipment, supplies, products, or services to the public account for at least 50 percent of its yearly sales of these goods, equipment, supplies, products, or services made under the retailer's trademark, trade name, or service mark.

(5) A newspaper distribution system distributing newspapers as defined in Section 6362 of the Revenue and Taxation Code.

(6) A sale or lease to an existing or beginning business enterprise that also sells or leases equipment, products, supplies, or performs services that are not supplied by the seller and that the purchaser does not utilize with the equipment, products, supplies, or services of the seller, if the equipment, products, supplies, or services not supplied by the seller account for more than 25 percent of the purchaser's gross sales.

(7) The sale in the entirety of an "ongoing business." For purposes of this paragraph, an "ongoing business" means a business that for at least six months previous to the sale has been operated from a particular specific location, has been open for business to the general public, and has had all equipment and supplies necessary for operating the business located at that location. The sale shall be of the entire "ongoing business" and not merely a portion of the ongoing business.

(8) A sale or lease or offer to sell or lease to a purchaser (A) who has for a period of at least six months previously bought products, supplies, services, or equipment that were sold under the same trademark or trade name or that were produced by the seller and, (B) who has received on resale of

§ 1812.201   OBLIGATIONS

the product, supplies, services, or equipment an amount that is at least equal to the amount of the initial payment.

(9) The renewal or extension of an existing seller assisted marketing plan contract.

(10) A product distributorship that meets each of the following requirements:

(A) The seller sells products to the purchaser for resale by the purchaser, and it is reasonably contemplated that substantially all of the purchaser's sales of the product will be at wholesale.

(B) The agreement between the parties does not require that the purchaser pay the seller, or any person associated with the seller, a fee or any other payment for the right to enter into the agreement, and does not require the purchaser to buy a minimum or specified quantity of the products, or to buy products for a minimum or specified period of time. For purposes of this paragraph, a "person associated with the seller" means a person, including an individual or a business entity, controlling, controlled by, or under the same control as the seller.

(C) The seller is a corporation, partnership, limited liability company, joint venture, or any other business entity.

(D) The seller has a net worth of at least ten million dollars ($10,000,000) according to audited financial statements of the seller done during the 18 months preceding the date of the initial sale of products to the purchaser. Net worth may be determined on a consolidated basis if the seller is a subsidiary of another business entity that is permitted by generally accepted accounting standards to prepare financial statements on a consolidated basis and that business entity absolutely and irrevocably agrees in writing to guarantee the seller's obligations to the purchaser. The seller's net worth shall be verified by a certification to the Attorney General from an independent certified public accountant that the audited financial statement reflects a net worth of at least ten million dollars ($10,000,000). This certification shall be provided within 30 days following receipt of a written request from the Attorney General.

(E) The seller grants the purchaser a license to use a trademark that is registered under federal law.

(F) It is not an agreement or arrangement encouraging a distributor to recruit others to participate in the program and compensating the distributor for recruiting others into the program or for sales made by others recruited into the program.

(c) "Person" includes an individual, corporation, partnership, limited liability company, joint venture, or any business entity.

(d) "Seller" means a person who sells or leases or offers to sell or lease a seller assisted marketing plan and who meets either of the following conditions:

(1) Has sold or leased or represents or implies that the seller has sold or leased, whether in California or elsewhere, at least five seller assisted marketing plans within 24 months prior to a solicitation.

(2) Intends or represents or implies that the seller intends to sell or lease, whether in California or elsewhere, at least five seller assisted marketing plans within 12 months following a solicitation.

For purposes of this title, the seller is the person to whom the purchaser becomes contractually obligated. A "seller" does not include a licensed real estate broker or salesman who engages in the sale or lease of a "business opportunity" as that term is used in Sections 10000 to 10030, inclusive, of the Business and Professions Code, or elsewhere in Chapter 1 (commencing with Section 10000), Chapter 2 (commencing with Section 10050), or Chapter 6 (commencing with Section 10450) of Part 1 of Division 4 of the Business and Professions Code.

(e) "Purchaser" means a person who is solicited to become obligated or does become obligated on a seller assisted marketing plan contract.

(f) "Equipment" includes machines, all electrical devices, video or audio devices, molds, display racks, vending machines, coin operated game machines, machines that dispense products, and display units of all kinds.

(g) "Supplies" includes any and all materials used to produce, grow, breed, fabricate, modify, develop, or make any product or item.

(h) "Product" includes any tangible chattel, including food or living animals, that the purchaser intends to:

(1) Sell or lease.

(2) Use to perform a service.

(3) Resell or attempt to resell to the seller assisted marketing plan seller.

(4) Provide or attempt to provide to the seller assisted marketing plan seller or to any other person whom the seller suggests the purchaser contact so that the seller assisted marketing plan seller or that other person may assist, either directly or indirectly, the purchaser in distributing, selling, leasing, or otherwise disposing of the product.

(i) "Services" includes any assistance, guidance, direction, work, labor, or services provided by the seller to initiate or maintain or assist in the initiation or maintenance of a business.

(j) "Seller assisted marketing plan contract" or "contract" means any contract or agreement that obligates a purchaser to a seller.

(k) "Initial payment" means the total amount a purchaser is obligated to pay to the seller under the terms of the seller assisted marketing plan contract prior to or at the time of delivery of the equipment, supplies, products, or services or within six months of the purchaser commencing operation of the seller assisted marketing plan. If the contract sets forth a specific total sale price for purchase of the seller assisted marketing plan which total price is to be paid partially as a downpayment and then in specific monthly payments, the "initial payment" means the entire total sale price.

(*l*) "Initial cash payment" or "downpayment" means that portion of the initial payment that the purchaser is obligated to pay to the seller prior to or at the time of delivery of equipment, supplies, products, or services. It does not include any amount financed by or for which financing is to be obtained by the seller, or financing that the seller assists in obtaining.

(m) "Buy-back" or "secured investment" means any representation that implies in any manner that the purchaser's initial payment is protected from loss. These terms include a representation or implication of any of the following:

(1) That the seller may repurchase either all or part of what it sold to the purchaser.

(2) That the seller may at some future time pay the purchaser the difference between what has been earned and the initial payment.

(3) That the seller may in the ordinary course buy from the purchaser items made, produced, fabricated, grown, bred, modified, or developed by the purchaser using, in whole or in part, the product, supplies, equipment, or services that were initially sold or leased to the purchaser by the seller.

(4) That the seller or a person to whom the seller will refer the purchaser may in the ordinary course sell, lease, or distribute the items the purchaser has for sale or lease. *(Added by Stats.1978, c. 876, p. 2749, § 1. Amended by Stats.1980, c. 567, p. 1554, § 1; Stats.1981, c. 258, p. 1324, § 1; Stats.1989, c. 1021, § 1; Stats.1990, c. 216 (S.B.2510), § 6; Stats.1994, c. 1010 (S.B.2053), § 44; Stats.2000, c. 413 (A.B.2699), § 1; Stats.2015, c. 190 (A.B.1517), § 5, eff. Jan. 1, 2016; Stats.2022, c. 452 (S.B.1498), § 26, eff. Jan. 1, 2023.)*

Cross References
Attorney General, generally, see Government Code § 12500 et seq.

§ 1812.202. Offer in state

(a) An offer to sell or offer to lease a seller assisted marketing plan shall occur in this state whenever:

(1) The offer to sell or offer to lease is made in this state;

(2) The purchaser resides in this state at the time of the offer; or

(3) The offer to sell or offer to lease either originates from this state or is directed by the seller or lessor to this state and received at the place to which it is directed.

(b) A sale or lease of a seller assisted marketing plan shall occur in this state whenever:

(1) The offer to sell or offer to lease is accepted in this state;

(2) The purchaser resides in this state at the time of the sale; or

(3) The acceptance is communicated to a seller situated in this state. *(Added by Stats.1978, c. 876, p. 2749, § 1.)*

Cross References
Purchaser defined for purposes of this Title, see Civil Code § 1812.201.

Seller assisted marketing plan defined for purposes of this Title, see Civil Code § 1812.201.

Seller defined for purposes of this Title, see Civil Code § 1812.201.

§ 1812.203. Filing disclosure statements and lists of salespersons; notice of intent to issue stop orders; refutation

(a) The seller of any seller assisted marketing plan shall pay an annual fee in the amount of one hundred dollars ($100) and annually file with the Attorney General a copy of the disclosure statements required under Sections 1812.205 and 1812.206, as well as a list of the names and resident addresses of those individuals who sell the seller assisted marketing plan on behalf of the seller. The first filing shall be made at least 30 days prior to placing any advertisement or making any other representations to prospective purchasers. The first filing shall not be deemed to be effective until a notice of filing has been issued by the Attorney General. The seller may not make any advertisement or other representation to prospective purchasers until a notice of filing has been issued by the Attorney General. The disclosure statements on file shall be updated through a new filing and payment of a fee in the amount of thirty dollars ($30), whenever material changes occur during the year following the annual filing and the updated filing shall include all disclosure statements required by Sections 1812.205 and 1812.206 and a list of the names and resident addresses of all current salespersons and all salespersons who have acted on behalf of the seller since the previous filing, whether the annual filing or an updated filing, indicating which salespersons are still active and which no longer act on behalf of the seller. Each seller of a seller assisted marketing plan shall file the annual renewal filing, whether or not any update filings have been made, at least 10 days before one year has elapsed from the date of the notice of filing issued by the Attorney General, and at least 10 days before the same date every year thereafter. The annual renewal filing shall include all disclosure statements required by Sections 1812.205 and 1812.206 and a list of the names and addresses of the residences of all current salespersons and all salespersons who have acted on behalf of the seller since the previous filing (whether the annual filing or an updated filing), indicating which salespersons are still active and which no longer act on behalf of the seller. The annual renewal filing fee shall be one hundred dollars ($100). If an annual renewal filing is not filed as required, the previous filing shall be deemed to have lapsed and the seller shall be prohibited from placing any seller assisted marketing plan advertisements or making any other representations to prospective purchasers of seller assisted marketing plan until a new annual filing is made and a new notice of filing has been issued by the Attorney General.

(b) The Attorney General may send by certified mail to the address set forth in the seller assisted marketing plan filing an intent to issue a stop order denying the effectiveness of or suspending or revoking the effectiveness of any filing if he or she finds the following:

(1) That there has been a failure to comply with any of the provisions of this title.

(2) That the offer or sale of the seller assisted marketing plan would constitute a misrepresentation to, or deceit of, or fraud on, the purchaser.

(3) That any person identified in the filing has been convicted of an offense under paragraph (1) of subdivision (b) of Section 1812.206, or is subject to an order or has had a civil judgment entered against him or her as described in paragraphs (2) and (3) of subdivision (b) of Section 1812.206, and the involvement of that person in the sale or management of the seller assisted marketing plan creates an unreasonable risk to prospective purchasers.

(c) The notice referred to shall include facts supporting a suspension or revocation. If the seller assisted marketing

§ 1812.203

plan does not submit to the Attorney General, under penalties of perjury signed by an owner or officer of the seller assisted marketing plan, within 10 days of receipt of the intent to issue a stop order, a refutation of each and every supporting fact set forth in the notice, and each fact not refuted shall be deemed, for purposes of issuance of the order, an admission that the fact is true. If, in the opinion of the Attorney General, and based upon supporting facts not refuted by the seller assisted marketing plan, the plan is offered to the public without compliance with this title, the Attorney General may order the seller to desist and refrain from the further sale or attempted sale of the seller assisted marketing plan unless and until a notice of filing has been issued pursuant to this section. Until that time, the registration shall be void. The order shall be in effect until and unless the seller assisted marketing plan files a proceeding in superior court pursuant to Section 1085 or 1094.5 of the Code of Civil Procedure or seeks other judicial relief and serves a copy of the proceeding upon the Attorney General. *(Added by Stats.1978, c. 876, p. 2749, § 1. Amended by Stats.1989, c. 1021, § 2; Stats.1990, c. 1491, (A.B.3765), § 2; Stats.1998, c. 595 (A.B.1830), § 1.)*

Cross References

Attorney General, generally, see Government Code § 12500 et seq.
Person defined for purposes of this Title, see Civil Code § 1812.201.
Purchaser defined for purposes of this Title, see Civil Code § 1812.201.
Seller assisted marketing plan defined for purposes of this Title, see Civil Code § 1812.201.
Seller defined for purposes of this Title, see Civil Code § 1812.201.
Telephonic sellers, exclusions from definition, see Business and Professions Code § 17511.1.

§ 1812.204. Prohibited representations and activities

In selling, leasing, or offering to sell or lease a seller assisted marketing plan in this state, sellers shall not:

(a) Use the phrase "buy-back" or "secured investment" or similar phrase orally or in writing when soliciting, offering, leasing, or selling a seller assisted marketing plan if the "security" is the value of the equipment, supplies, products or services supplied by the seller to the purchaser.

(b) Use the phrase "buy-back" or "secured investment" or similar phrase orally or in writing when soliciting, offering, leasing, or selling a seller assisted marketing plan unless there are no restrictions or qualifications whatsoever preventing or limiting a purchaser from being able to invoke the "buy-back" or "secured" portion of the seller assisted marketing plan contract at any time the purchaser desires during the one-year period following the contract date. Upon invocation of the "buy-back" or "security" provision, the minimum amount a purchaser shall be entitled to have returned to him is the full amount of his initial payment, less the amount actually received by him from the operation of the seller assisted marketing plan. The "amount actually received" means either the amount the purchaser actually obtained from the seller for any product resold to the seller or the amount of money the purchaser received for use of the purchaser's product, equipment, supplies or services, less any amount: (1) the purchaser has paid the owner or manager of the location at which the purchaser's products, equipment, supplies or services are placed; and (2) the purchaser has paid to obtain other items needed in order to sell, make, produce, fabricate, grow, breed, modify, or develop the item which the seller assisted marketing plan purchaser intends to sell, lease, distribute, or otherwise dispose of.

(c) Represent that a purchaser's initial payment is "secured" in any manner or to any degree or that the seller provides a "buy-back" arrangement unless the seller has, in conformity with subdivision (b) of Section 1812.214, either obtained a surety bond issued by a surety company admitted to do business in this state or established a trust account at a federally insured bank or savings and loan association located in this state.

(d) Represent that the seller assisted marketing plan provides income or earning potential of any kind unless the seller has data to substantiate the claims of income or earning potential and discloses this data to the purchaser at the time the claim is made, if made in person, or if made through written or telephonic communication, at the first in-person communication thereafter and, when disclosed, the data is left with the purchaser. A mathematical computation of the number of sales multiplied by the amount of profit per sale to reach a projected income figure is not sufficient data to substantiate an income or earning potential claim. Income or earning potential claims cannot be made or implied at all unless they are based on the experience of at least 10 purchasers from the seller assisted marketing plan being offered. The data left by the seller must, at a minimum, disclose:

(1) The length of time the seller has been selling the particular seller assisted marketing plan being offered;

(2) The number of purchasers from the seller known to the seller to have made at least the same sales, income or profits as those represented; and

(3) The percentage the number represents of the total number of purchasers from the seller.

(e) Use the trademark, service mark, trade name, logotype, advertising or other commercial symbol of any business which does not either control the ownership interest in the seller or accept responsibility for all representations made by the seller in regard to the seller assisted marketing plan, unless the nature of the seller's relationship to such other business entity is set forth immediately adjacent to and in type size equal to or larger than that used to depict the commercial symbol of such other business. If a member of a trade association, the seller may use the logo or registration mark of the trade association in advertisements and materials without regard to this subdivision.

(f) Place or cause to be placed any advertisement for a seller assisted marketing plan which does not include the actual business name of the seller, and if it differs, the name under which the seller assisted marketing plan is operated and the street address of the principal place of business of the seller. *(Added by Stats.1978, c. 876, p. 2749, § 1. Amended by Stats.1981, c. 258, p. 1327, § 2.)*

Cross References

Buy-back or secured investment defined for purposes of this Title, see Civil Code § 1812.201.
Equipment defined for purposes of this Title, see Civil Code § 1812.201.

Initial payment defined for purposes of this Title, see Civil Code § 1812.201.
Person defined for purposes of this Title, see Civil Code § 1812.201.
Product defined for purposes of this Title, see Civil Code § 1812.201.
Purchaser defined for purposes of this Title, see Civil Code § 1812.201.
Seller assisted marketing plan contract or contract defined for purposes of this Title, see Civil Code § 1812.201.
Seller assisted marketing plan defined for purposes of this Title, see Civil Code § 1812.201.
Seller defined for purposes of this Title, see Civil Code § 1812.201.
Services defined for purposes of this Title, see Civil Code § 1812.201.
Supplies defined for purposes of this Title, see Civil Code § 1812.201.

§ 1812.205. Disclosure statement

At the first in-person communication with a potential purchaser or in the first written response to an inquiry by a potential purchaser, whichever occurs first, wherein the seller assisted marketing plan is described, the seller or his or her representative shall provide the prospective purchaser a written document, the cover sheet of which is entitled in at least 16-point boldface capital letters "DISCLOSURE REQUIRED BY CALIFORNIA LAW." Under the title shall appear in boldface of at least 10-point type, the statement: "The State of California has not reviewed and does not approve, recommend, endorse or sponsor any seller assisted marketing plan. The information contained in this disclosure has not been checked by the state. If you have any questions about this purchase, see an attorney or other financial adviser before you sign a contract or agreement." Nothing shall appear on the cover sheet except the title and the statement required above. The disclosure document shall contain the following information:

(a) The name of the seller, the name under which the seller is doing or intends to do business and the name of any parent or affiliated company that will engage in business transactions with purchasers or accept responsibility for statements made by the seller.

(b) A statement of the initial payment to be paid by the purchaser to the seller, or when not known, a statement of the approximate initial payment charged, the amount of the initial payment to be paid to a person inducing, directly or indirectly, a purchaser to contract for the seller assisted marketing plan.

(c) A full and detailed description of the actual services the seller will undertake to perform for the purchaser.

(d) When the seller makes any statement concerning earnings or range of earnings that may be made through the seller assisted marketing plan, he must comply with subdivision (d) of Section 1812.204 and set forth in complete form in this disclosure statement the following:

"No guarantee of earnings or ranges of earnings can be made. The number of purchasers who have earned through this business an amount in excess of the amount of their initial payment is at least _____, which represents _____ percent of the total number of purchasers of this seller assisted marketing plan."

(e) If training of any type is promised by the seller, a complete description of the training and the length of the training.

(f) If the seller promises services to be performed in connection with the placement of the equipment, product or supplies at a location from which they will be sold or used, the full nature of those services as well as the nature of the agreements to be made with the owner or manager of the location at which the purchaser's equipment, product or supplies will be placed, must be set forth.

(g) If the seller represents orally or in writing when soliciting or offering for sale or lease or selling or leasing a seller assisted marketing plan that there is a "buy-back" arrangement or that the initial payment is in some manner protected from loss or "secured," the entire and precise nature of the "buy-back", "protection" or "security" arrangement shall be completely and clearly disclosed. (Added by Stats.1978, c. 876, p. 2749, § 1. Amended by Stats.1981, c. 258, p. 1329, § 3.)

Cross References

Buy-back or secured investment defined for purposes of this Title, see Civil Code § 1812.201.
Equipment defined for purposes of this Title, see Civil Code § 1812.201.
Initial payment defined for purposes of this Title, see Civil Code § 1812.201.
Person defined for purposes of this Title, see Civil Code § 1812.201.
Product defined for purposes of this Title, see Civil Code § 1812.201.
Purchaser defined for purposes of this Title, see Civil Code § 1812.201.
Seller assisted marketing plan contract or contract defined for purposes of this Title, see Civil Code § 1812.201.
Seller assisted marketing plan defined for purposes of this Title, see Civil Code § 1812.201.
Seller defined for purposes of this Title, see Civil Code § 1812.201.
Services defined for purposes of this Title, see Civil Code § 1812.201.
Supplies defined for purposes of this Title, see Civil Code § 1812.201.

§ 1812.206. Information sheet

At least 48 hours prior to the execution of a seller assisted marketing plan contract or agreement or at least 48 hours prior to the receipt of any consideration, whichever occurs first, the seller or his or her representative shall provide to the prospective purchaser in writing a document entitled "SELLER ASSISTED MARKETING PLAN INFORMATION SHEET." The seller may combine the information required under this section with the information required under Section 1812.205 and, if done, shall utilize the single title "DISCLOSURES REQUIRED BY CALIFORNIA LAW," and the title page required by Section 1812.205. If a combined document is used, it shall be given at the time required by Section 1812.205, provided that this time meets the 48-hour test of this section. The information sheet required by this section shall contain the following:

(a) The name of and the office held by the seller's owners, officers, directors, trustees and general or limited partners, as the case may be, and the names of those individuals who have management responsibilities in connection with the seller's business activities.

(b) A statement whether the seller, any person identified in subdivision (a), and any other company managed by a person identified in subdivision (a):

(1) Has been convicted of a felony or misdemeanor or pleaded nolo contendere to a felony or misdemeanor charge if the felony or misdemeanor involved an alleged violation of this title, fraud, embezzlement, fraudulent conversion or misappropriation of property.

(2) Has been held liable in a civil action by final judgment or consented to the entry of a stipulated judgment if the civil action alleged a violation of this title, fraud, embezzlement, fraudulent conversion or misappropriation of property or the use of untrue or misleading representations in an attempt to sell or dispose of real or personal property or the use of unfair, unlawful or deceptive business practices.

(3) Is subject to any currently effective agreement, injunction, or restrictive order, including, but not limited to, a "cease and desist" order, an "assurance of discontinuance," or other comparable agreement or order, relating to business activity as the result of an action or investigation brought by a public agency or department, including, but not limited to, an action affecting any vocational license.

The statements required by paragraphs (1), (2) and (3) of this subdivision shall set forth the terms of the agreement, or the court, the docket number of the matter, the date of the conviction or of the judgment and, when involved, the name of the governmental agency that initiated the investigation or brought the action resulting in the conviction or judgment.

(4) Has at any time during the previous seven fiscal years been the subject of an order for relief in bankruptcy, been reorganized due to insolvency, or been a principal, director, officer, trustee, general or limited partner, or had management responsibilities of any other person, as defined in subdivision (b) of Section 1812.201, that has so filed or was so reorganized, during or within one year after the period that the individual held that position. If so, the name and location of the person having so filed, or having been so reorganized, the date thereof, the court which exercised jurisdiction, and the docket number of the matter shall be set forth.

(c) The length of time the seller:

(1) Has sold seller assisted marketing plans.

(2) Has sold the specific seller assisted marketing plan being offered to the purchaser.

(d) If the seller is required to secure a bond or establish a trust account pursuant to the requirements of Section 1812.204, the information sheet shall state either:

(1) "Seller has secured a bond issued by

———————————————————————
(name and address of surety company)

a surety company admitted to do business in this state. Before signing a contract to purchase this seller assisted marketing plan, you should check with the surety company to determine the bond's current status," or

(2) "Seller has deposited with the office of the Attorney General information regarding its trust account. Before signing a contract to purchase this seller assisted marketing plan, you should check with the Attorney General to determine the current status of the trust account."

(e) A copy of a recent, not more than 12 months old, financial statement of the seller, together with a statement of any material changes in the financial condition of the seller from the date thereof. That financial statement shall either be audited or be under penalty of perjury signed by one of the seller's officers, directors, trustees or general or limited partners. The declaration under penalty of perjury shall indicate that to the best of the signatory's knowledge and belief the information in the financial statement is true and accurate; the date of signature and the location where signed shall also be indicated. Provided, however, that where a seller is a subsidiary of another corporation which is permitted by generally accepted accounting standards to prepare financial statements on a consolidated basis, the above information may be submitted in the same manner for the parent if the corresponding financial statement of the seller is also provided and the parent absolutely and irrevocably has agreed to guarantee all obligations of the seller.

(f) An unexecuted copy of the entire seller assisted marketing plan contract.

(g) For purposes of this section, "seller's owners" means any individual who holds an equity interest of at least 10 percent in the seller. *(Added by Stats.1978, c. 876, p. 2749, § 1. Amended by Stats.1981, c. 258, p. 1330, § 4; Stats.1989, c. 1021, § 3; Stats.1997, c. 377 (A.B.1548), § 1; Stats.1998, c. 595 (A.B.1830), § 2; Stats.2009, c. 500 (A.B.1059), § 13.)*

Cross References

Attorney General, generally, see Government Code § 12500 et seq.
Buy-back or secured investment defined for purposes of this Title, see Civil Code § 1812.201.
Felonies, definition and penalties, see Penal Code §§ 17, 18.
Misdemeanors, definition and penalties, see Penal Code §§ 17, 19, 19.2.
Person defined for purposes of this Title, see Civil Code § 1812.201.
Purchaser defined for purposes of this Title, see Civil Code § 1812.201.
Seller assisted marketing plan contract or contract defined for purposes of this Title, see Civil Code § 1812.201.
Seller assisted marketing plan defined for purposes of this Title, see Civil Code § 1812.201.
Seller defined for purposes of this Title, see Civil Code § 1812.201.

§ 1812.207. Written contracts; delivery of copies

Every contract for sale or lease of a seller assisted marketing plan in this state shall be in writing and shall be subject to the provisions of this title. A copy of the fully completed contract and all other documents the seller requires the purchaser to sign shall be given to the purchaser at the time they are signed. *(Added by Stats.1978, c. 876, p. 2749, § 1.)*

Cross References

Purchaser defined for purposes of this Title, see Civil Code § 1812.201.
Seller assisted marketing plan contract or contract defined for purposes of this Title, see Civil Code § 1812.201.
Seller assisted marketing plan defined for purposes of this Title, see Civil Code § 1812.201.

Seller defined for purposes of this Title, see Civil Code § 1812.201.

§ 1812.208. Right to cancel; time; notice

The purchaser shall have the right to cancel a seller assisted marketing plan contract for any reason at any time within three business days of the date the purchaser and the seller sign the contract. The notice of the right to cancel and the procedures to be followed when a contract is canceled shall comply with Section 1812.209. (Added by Stats.1978, c. 876, p. 2749, § 1.)

Cross References

Purchaser defined for purposes of this Title, see Civil Code § 1812.201.
Seller assisted marketing plan contract or contract defined for purposes of this Title, see Civil Code § 1812.201.
Seller assisted marketing plan defined for purposes of this Title, see Civil Code § 1812.201.
Seller defined for purposes of this Title, see Civil Code § 1812.201.

§ 1812.209. Mandatory contract provisions

Every seller assisted marketing plan contract shall set forth in at least 10-point type or equivalent size if handwritten, all of the following:

(a) The terms and conditions of payment including the initial payment, additional payments, and downpayment required. If the contract provides for the seller to receive more than 20 percent of the initial payment before delivery to the purchaser of the equipment, supplies or products or services to be furnished under the terms of the contract, the contract shall clearly set forth for the escrow account established pursuant to subdivision (b) of Section 1812.210 and the name and address of the escrow account holder, as well as the institution, branch, and account number of the escrow account. If the contract provides for payment of any amount in excess of 20 percent of the initial payment prior to delivery of the equipment, supplies or products or services to be furnished under the terms of the contract, the contract shall set forth that payment of the amount in excess of 20 percent shall be by separate instrument made payable to the escrow account.

(b) Immediately above the place at which the purchaser signs the contract the following notification, in boldface type, of the purchaser's right to cancel the contract:

"You have three business days in which you may cancel this contract for any reason by mailing or delivering written notice to the seller assisted marketing plan seller. The three business days shall expire on

_____
(last date to mail or deliver notice)
and notice of cancellation should be mailed or delivered to _____
_____
(seller assisted marketing plan seller's
name and business street address)

If you choose to mail your notice, it must be placed in the United States mail properly addressed, first-class postage prepaid, and postmarked before midnight of the above date. If you choose to deliver your notice to the seller directly, it must be delivered to him by the end of his normal business day on the above date. Within five business days of receipt of the notice of cancellation, the seller shall return to the purchaser all sums paid by the purchaser to the seller pursuant to this contract. Within five business days after receipt of all such sums, the purchaser shall make available at his address or at the place at which they were caused to be located, all equipment, products and supplies provided to the purchaser pursuant to this contract. Upon demand of the seller, such equipment, products and supplies shall be made available at the time the purchaser receives full repayment by cash, money order or certified check."

(c) A full and detailed description of the acts or services the seller will undertake to perform for the purchaser.

(d) The seller's principal business address and the name and the address of its agent, other than the Secretary of State, in the State of California authorized to receive service of process.

(e) The business form of the seller, whether corporate, partnership or otherwise.

(f) The delivery date or, when the contract provides for a staggered delivery of items to the purchaser, the approximate delivery date of those products, equipment or supplies the seller is to deliver to the purchaser to enable the purchaser to begin or maintain his business and whether the products, equipment or supplies are to be delivered to the purchaser's home or business address or are to be placed or caused to be placed by the seller at locations owned or managed by persons other than the purchaser.

(g) A complete description of the nature of the "buy-back", "protection", or "security" arrangement, if the seller has represented orally or in writing when selling or leasing, soliciting or offering a seller assisted marketing plan that there is a "buy-back" or that the initial payment or any part of it is "protected" or "secured."

(h) A statement which accurately sets forth a purchaser's right to void the contract under the circumstances and in the manner set forth in subdivisions (a) and (b) of Section 1812.215.

(i) The name of the supplier and the address of such supplier of the products, equipment, or supplies the seller is to deliver to the purchaser to enable the purchaser to begin or maintain his business. (Added by Stats.1978, c. 876, p. 2749, § 1. Amended by Stats.1981, c. 258, p. 1332, § 5; Stats.1989, c. 1021, § 4.)

Cross References

Buy-back or secured investment defined for purposes of this Title, see Civil Code § 1812.201.
Equipment defined for purposes of this Title, see Civil Code § 1812.201.
Initial cash payment or downpayment defined for purposes of this Title, see Civil Code § 1812.201.
Initial payment defined for purposes of this Title, see Civil Code § 1812.201.
Person defined for purposes of this Title, see Civil Code § 1812.201.
Product defined for purposes of this Title, see Civil Code § 1812.201.
Purchaser defined for purposes of this Title, see Civil Code § 1812.201.
Seller assisted marketing plan contract or contract defined for purposes of this Title, see Civil Code § 1812.201.

§ 1812.209

OBLIGATIONS

Seller assisted marketing plan defined for purposes of this Title, see Civil Code § 1812.201.
Seller defined for purposes of this Title, see Civil Code § 1812.201.
Services defined for purposes of this Title, see Civil Code § 1812.201.
Supplies defined for purposes of this Title, see Civil Code § 1812.201.

§ 1812.210. Notes; downpayment restrictions; escrow

(a) No seller assisted marketing plan contract shall require or entail the execution of any note or series of notes by the purchaser which, when separately negotiated, will cut off as to third parties any right of action or defense which the purchaser may have against the seller.

(b) If the contract referred to in Section 1812.209 provides for a downpayment to be paid to the seller, the downpayment shall not exceed 20 percent of the initial payment amount. In no event shall the contract payment schedule provide for the seller to receive more than 20 percent of the initial payment before delivery to the purchaser, or to the place at which they are to be located, the equipment, supplies or products, unless all sums in excess of 20 percent are placed in an escrow account as provided for in subdivision (c) of Section 1812.214. Funds placed in an escrow account shall not be released until the purchaser notifies the escrow holder in writing of the delivery of such equipment, supplies or products within the time limits set forth in the seller assisted marketing plan contract. Notification of delivery by the purchaser to the escrow holder shall not be unreasonably withheld. *(Added by Stats.1978, c. 876, p. 2749, § 1. Amended by Stats.1981, c. 258, p. 1333, § 6; Stats.1989, c. 1021, § 5.)*

Cross References

Equipment defined for purposes of this Title, see Civil Code § 1812.201.
Initial cash payment or downpayment defined for purposes of this Title, see Civil Code § 1812.201.
Initial payment defined for purposes of this Title, see Civil Code § 1812.201.
Product defined for purposes of this Title, see Civil Code § 1812.201.
Purchaser defined for purposes of this Title, see Civil Code § 1812.201.
Seller assisted marketing plan contract or contract defined for purposes of this Title, see Civil Code § 1812.201.
Seller assisted marketing plan defined for purposes of this Title, see Civil Code § 1812.201.
Seller defined for purposes of this Title, see Civil Code § 1812.201.
Supplies defined for purposes of this Title, see Civil Code § 1812.201.

§ 1812.211. Rights of purchaser against seller's assignee

Any assignee of the seller assisted marketing plan contract or the seller's rights is subject to all equities, rights and defenses of the purchaser against the seller. *(Added by Stats.1978, c. 876, p. 2749, § 1.)*

Cross References

Purchaser defined for purposes of this Title, see Civil Code § 1812.201.
Seller assisted marketing plan contract or contract defined for purposes of this Title, see Civil Code § 1812.201.
Seller assisted marketing plan defined for purposes of this Title, see Civil Code § 1812.201.
Seller defined for purposes of this Title, see Civil Code § 1812.201.

§ 1812.212. Reference to compliance

No seller shall make or authorize the making of any reference to its compliance with this title. *(Added by Stats.1978, c. 876, p. 2749, § 1.)*

Cross References

Seller defined for purposes of this Title, see Civil Code § 1812.201.

§ 1812.213. Books, records and accounts; preservation of documents

Every seller shall at all times keep and maintain a complete set of books, records and accounts of seller assisted marketing plan sales made by the seller. All documents relating to each specific seller assisted marketing plan sold or leased shall be maintained for four years after the date of the seller assisted marketing plan contract. *(Added by Stats.1978, c. 876, p. 2749, § 1.)*

Cross References

Seller assisted marketing plan contract or contract defined for purposes of this Title, see Civil Code § 1812.201.
Seller assisted marketing plan defined for purposes of this Title, see Civil Code § 1812.201.
Seller defined for purposes of this Title, see Civil Code § 1812.201.

§ 1812.214. Attorney to receive process; service of process; bond or trust accounts; escrow account procedures

(a) Every seller of seller-assisted marketing plans other than a California corporation shall file with the Attorney General an irrevocable consent appointing the Secretary of State or successor in office to act as the seller's attorney to receive service or any lawful process in any noncriminal suit, action or proceeding against the seller or the seller's successor, executor or administrator, which may arise under this title. When service is made upon the Secretary of State, it shall have the same force and validity as if served personally on the seller. Service may be made by leaving a copy of the process in the office of the Secretary of State, but it shall not be effective unless:

(1) The plaintiff forthwith sends by first-class mail a notice of the service upon the Secretary of State and a copy of the process to the defendant or respondent at the last address on file with the Attorney General; and

(2) The plaintiff's affidavit of compliance with this section is filed in the case on or before the return date of the process, if any, or within such further time as the court allows.

(b) If, pursuant to subdivision (c) of Section 1812.204, a seller must obtain a surety bond or establish a trust account, the following procedures apply:

(1) If a bond is obtained, a copy of it shall be filed with the Attorney General; if a trust account is established, notification of the depository, the trustee and the account number shall be filed with the Attorney General.

(2) The bond or trust account required shall be in favor of the State of California for the benefit of any person who is damaged by any violation of this title or by the seller's breach of a contract subject to this title or of any obligation arising therefrom. The trust account shall also be in favor of any person damaged by these practices.

(3) Any person claiming against the trust account for a violation of this title may maintain an action at law against the seller and the trustee. The surety or trustee shall be liable only for actual damages and not the punitive damages permitted under Section 1812.218. The aggregate liability of the trustee to all persons damaged by a seller's violation of this title shall in no event exceed the amount of the trust account.

(4) The bond or the trust account shall be in an amount equal to the total amount of the "initial payment" section of all seller-assisted marketing plan contracts the seller has entered into during the previous year or three hundred thousand dollars ($300,000), whichever is less, but in no case shall the amount be less than fifty thousand dollars ($50,000). The amount required shall be adjusted twice a year, no later than the tenth day of the first month of the seller's fiscal year and no later than the tenth day of the seventh month of the seller's fiscal year. A seller need only establish a bond or trust account in the amount of fifty thousand dollars ($50,-000) at the commencement of business and during the first six months the seller is in business. By the tenth day of the seller's seventh month in business, the amount of the bond or trust account shall be established as provided for herein as if the seller had been in business for a year.

(c) If, pursuant to subdivision (b) of Section 1812.210, a seller utilizes an escrow account to receive those portions of the downpayment in excess of 20 percent of the initial payment before delivery to the purchaser of the equipment, supplies or products or services to be furnished under the terms of the contract, the following procedures shall apply:

(1) The holder of the escrow account shall be independent of the seller, and the seller shall not have any authority to direct disbursements from the escrow account by the holder except upon written notification by the purchaser to the holder of the escrow account of the delivery of the equipment, supplies, or products as required by and within the time limits set forth in the seller assisted marketing plan contract.

(2) The name and address of the escrow account holder, the name of the institution, the branch and account number of the escrow account shall be reported to the Attorney General by the seller.

(3) Any person claiming against the escrow account for a violation of this title may maintain an action at law against the seller and the escrow account holder. The escrow account holder shall be liable only for actual damages and not the punitive damages permitted under Section 1812.218. The aggregate liability of the escrow account holder to all persons damaged by a seller's violation of this title shall in no event exceed the amount of the escrow account. (Added by Stats.1978, c. 876, p. 2749, § 1. Amended by Stats.1981, c. 258, p. 1333, § 7; Stats.1982, c. 517, p. 2322, § 64; Stats.1989, c. 1021, § 6; Stats.1990, c. 1491 (A.B.3765), § 3.)

Cross References

Attorney General, generally, see Government Code § 12500 et seq.
Bond and Undertaking Law, see Code of Civil Procedure § 995.010 et seq.
Equipment defined for purposes of this Title, see Civil Code § 1812.201.
Initial cash payment or downpayment defined for purposes of this Title, see Civil Code § 1812.201.
Initial payment defined for purposes of this Title, see Civil Code § 1812.201.
Person defined for purposes of this Title, see Civil Code § 1812.201.
Product defined for purposes of this Title, see Civil Code § 1812.201.
Purchaser defined for purposes of this Title, see Civil Code § 1812.201.
Seller assisted marketing plan contract or contract defined for purposes of this Title, see Civil Code § 1812.201.
Seller assisted marketing plan defined for purposes of this Title, see Civil Code § 1812.201.
Seller defined for purposes of this Title, see Civil Code § 1812.201.
Services defined for purposes of this Title, see Civil Code § 1812.201.
Supplies defined for purposes of this Title, see Civil Code § 1812.201.

§ 1812.215. Purchaser's right to void contract

(a) If a seller uses any untrue or misleading statements to sell or lease a seller assisted marketing plan, or fails to comply with Section 1812.203, or fails to give the disclosure documents or disclose any of the information required by Sections 1812.205 and 1812.206, or the contract does not comply with the requirements of this title, then within one year of the date of the contract at the election of the purchaser upon written notice to the seller, the contract shall be voidable by the purchaser and unenforceable by the seller or his assignee as contrary to public policy and the purchaser shall be entitled to receive from the seller all sums paid to the seller when the purchaser is able to return all equipment, supplies or products delivered by the seller; when such complete return cannot be made, the purchaser shall be entitled to receive from the seller all sums paid to the seller less the fair market value at the time of delivery of the equipment, supplies or products not returned by the purchaser, but delivered by the seller. Upon the receipt of such sums, the purchaser shall make available to the seller at the purchaser's address or at the places at which they are located at the time the purchaser gives notice pursuant to this section, the products, equipment or supplies received by the purchaser from the seller. Provided, however, if the seller inadvertently has failed to make any of the disclosures required by Section 1812.205 or 1812.206 or the contract inadvertently fails to comply with the requirements of this title, the seller may cure such inadvertent defect by providing the purchaser with the correct disclosure statements or contract if at the time of providing such correct disclosures or contract the seller also informs the purchaser in writing that because of the seller's error, the purchaser has an additional 15-day period after receipt of the correct disclosures or contract within which to cancel the contract and receive a full return of all moneys paid in exchange for return of whatever equipment, supplies or products the purchaser has. If the purchaser does not cancel the contract within 15 days after receipt of the correct disclosures or contract, he may not in the future exercise his right to void the contract under this section due to such noncompliance with the disclosure or contract requirements of this title.

(b) If a seller fails to deliver the equipment, supplies or product within 30 days of the delivery date stated in the contract, unless such delivery delay is beyond the control of the seller, then at any time prior to delivery or within 30 days after delivery, at the election of the purchaser upon written notice to the seller, the contract shall be voidable by the

§ 1812.215

purchaser and unenforceable by the seller or his assignee as contrary to public policy.

The rights of the purchaser set forth in this section shall be cumulative to all other rights under this title or otherwise. (Added by Stats.1978, c. 876, p. 2749, § 1. Amended by Stats.1981, c. 258, p. 1334, § 8.)

Cross References

Equipment defined for purposes of this Title, see Civil Code § 1812.201.
Product defined for purposes of this Title, see Civil Code § 1812.201.
Purchaser defined for purposes of this Title, see Civil Code § 1812.201.
Seller assisted marketing plan contract or contract defined for purposes of this Title, see Civil Code § 1812.201.
Seller assisted marketing plan defined for purposes of this Title, see Civil Code § 1812.201.
Seller defined for purposes of this Title, see Civil Code § 1812.201.
Supplies defined for purposes of this Title, see Civil Code § 1812.201.

§ 1812.216. Waiver of rights by purchaser; burden of proving exemption or exception from definitions

(a) Any waiver by a purchaser of the provisions of this title shall be deemed contrary to public policy and shall be void and unenforceable. Any attempt by a seller to have a purchaser waive rights given by this title shall be a violation of this title.

(b) In any proceeding involving this title, the burden of proving an exemption or an exception from a definition is upon the person claiming it. (Added by Stats.1978, c. 876, p. 2749, § 1. Amended by Stats.1981, c. 258, p. 1335, § 9.)

Cross References

Person defined for purposes of this Title, see Civil Code § 1812.201.
Purchaser defined for purposes of this Title, see Civil Code § 1812.201.
Seller defined for purposes of this Title, see Civil Code § 1812.201.

§ 1812.217. Violations; punishment

Any person, including, but not limited to, the seller, a salesman, agent or representative of the seller or an independent contractor who attempts to sell or lease or sells or leases a seller assisted marketing plan, who willfully violates any provision of this title or employs, directly or indirectly, any device, scheme or artifice to deceive in connection with the offer or sale of any seller assisted marketing plan, or willfully engages, directly or indirectly, in any act, practice or course of business which operates or would operate as a fraud or deceit upon any person in connection with the offer, purchase, lease or sale of any seller assisted marketing plan shall, upon conviction, be fined not more than ten thousand dollars ($10,000) for each unlawful transaction, or imprisoned pursuant to subdivision (h) of Section 1170 of the Penal Code, or imprisoned in a county jail for not more than one year, or be punished by both that fine and imprisonment. (Added by Stats.1978, c. 876, p. 2749, § 1. Amended by Stats.2011, c. 15 (A.B.109), § 34, eff. April 4, 2011, operative Oct. 1, 2011.)

Cross References

Classification of offenses, see Penal Code § 17.
Person defined for purposes of this Title, see Civil Code § 1812.201.

Seller assisted marketing plan defined for purposes of this Title, see Civil Code § 1812.201.
Seller defined for purposes of this Title, see Civil Code § 1812.201.

§ 1812.218. Damages

Any purchaser injured by a violation of this title or by the seller's breach of a contract subject to this title or of any obligation arising from the sale or lease of the seller assisted marketing plan may bring any action for recovery of damages. Judgment shall be entered for actual damages, plus reasonable attorney's fees and costs, but in no case shall the award of damages be less than the amount of the initial payment provided the purchaser is able to return all the equipment, supplies or products delivered by the seller; when such complete return cannot be made, the minimum award shall be no less than the amount of the initial payment less the fair market value at the time of delivery of the equipment, supplies or products that cannot be returned but were actually delivered by the seller. An award, if the trial court deems it proper, may be entered for punitive damages. (Added by Stats.1978, c. 876, p. 2749, § 1.)

Cross References

Equipment defined for purposes of this Title, see Civil Code § 1812.201.
Initial payment defined for purposes of this Title, see Civil Code § 1812.201.
Product defined for purposes of this Title, see Civil Code § 1812.201.
Purchaser defined for purposes of this Title, see Civil Code § 1812.201.
Seller assisted marketing plan contract or contract defined for purposes of this Title, see Civil Code § 1812.201.
Seller assisted marketing plan defined for purposes of this Title, see Civil Code § 1812.201.
Seller defined for purposes of this Title, see Civil Code § 1812.201.
Supplies defined for purposes of this Title, see Civil Code § 1812.201.

§ 1812.219. Additional remedies

The provisions of this title are not exclusive. The remedies provided herein for violation of any section of this title or for conduct proscribed by any section of this title shall be in addition to any other procedures or remedies for any violation or conduct provided for in any other law.

Nothing in this title shall limit any other statutory or any common law rights of the Attorney General, any district attorney or city attorney, or any other person. If any act or practice proscribed under this title also constitutes a cause of action in common law or a violation of another statute, the purchaser may assert such common law or statutory cause of action under the procedures and with the remedies provided for in such other law. (Added by Stats.1978, c. 876, p. 2749, § 1.)

Cross References

Attorney General, generally, see Government Code § 12500 et seq.
Person defined for purposes of this Title, see Civil Code § 1812.201.
Purchaser defined for purposes of this Title, see Civil Code § 1812.201.

§ 1812.220. Partial invalidity

If any provision of this act or if any application thereof to any person or circumstance is held unconstitutional, the remainder of the title and the application of such provision to other persons and circumstances shall not be affected thereby. *(Added by Stats.1978, c. 876, p. 2749, § 1.)*

Cross References

Person defined for purposes of this Title, see Civil Code § 1812.201.

§ 1812.221. Deposit in lieu of bond; claim against deposit; review and approval; payment; attachment, garnishment, or execution

(a) When a deposit has been made in lieu of bond pursuant to paragraph (1) of subdivision (b) of Section 1812.214 and Section 995.710 of the Code of Civil Procedure, the person asserting a claim against the deposit shall, in lieu of the provisions of Section 996.430 of the Code of Civil Procedure, establish the claim by furnishing evidence to the Attorney General of a money judgment entered by a court together with evidence that the claimant is a person described in paragraph (2) of subdivision (b) of Section 1812.214.

(b) When a person has completely established the claim with the Attorney General, the Attorney General shall forthwith review and approve the claim and enter the date of approval thereon. The claim shall be designated an "approved claim."

(c) When the first claim against a particular deposit account has been approved, it shall not be paid until the expiration of a period of 240 days after the date of its approval by the Attorney General. Subsequent claims which are approved by the Attorney General within the same 240-day period shall similarly not be paid until the expiration of the 240-day period. Forthwith upon the expiration of the 240-day period, the Attorney General shall pay all approved claims from that 240-day period in full unless there are insufficient funds in the deposit account in which case each approved claim shall be paid a proportionate amount to exhaust the deposit account.

(d) When the Attorney General approves the first claim against a particular deposit account after the expiration of a 240-day period, the date of approval of that claim shall begin a new 240-day period to which subdivision (c) shall apply with respect to the amount remaining in the deposit account.

(e) After a deposit account is exhausted, no further claims shall be paid by the Attorney General. Claimants who have had their claims paid in full or in part pursuant to subdivisions (c) and (d) shall not be required to make a contribution back to the deposit account for the benefit of other claimants.

(f) When a deposit has been made in lieu of bond, the amount of the deposit shall not be subject to attachment, garnishment, or execution with respect to an action or judgment against the seller, other than as to an amount as no longer needed or required for the purpose of this title which would otherwise be returned to the seller by the Attorney General. *(Added by Stats.1984, c. 545, § 4. Amended by Stats.1989, c. 1021, § 7.)*

Cross References

Attorney General, generally, see Government Code § 12500 et seq.
Person defined for purposes of this Title, see Civil Code § 1812.201.

Seller defined for purposes of this Title, see Civil Code § 1812.201.

Title 2.8

MEMBERSHIP CAMPING CONTRACTS

Section
1812.300. Definitions.
1812.301. Unruh Act; application to contracts and persons covered by the title.
1812.302. Written disclosures by operator to purchaser.
1812.303. Language of contract; date and signature; notice of cancellation; refunds after cancellation.
1812.304. Notice of cancellation rights to purchaser failing to inspect campgrounds; return of payment and negotiable instruments upon cancellation.
1812.305. Exempt transactions.
1812.306. Remedy of purchaser for errors or omissions; attorney's fees; corrections.
1812.307. Withdrawal of campgrounds; conditions.
1812.308. Sale, lease, assignment or transfer of campground.
1812.309. Availability of campgrounds for use; conditions.
1812.314. Membership camping contract brokers; fees; escrows; disclosures to new purchaser; notice of cancellation to purchaser.
1812.315. Severability.
1812.316. Public policy; waiver of rights.

Cross References

Employment agency deemed not the employer of domestic workers, withholding tax on wages, see Unemployment Insurance Code § 13005.7.

§ 1812.300. Definitions

For the purposes of this title:

(a) "Membership camping operator" means any enterprise, other than one that is tax exempt under Section 501(c)(3) of the Internal Revenue Code of 1954, as amended, that has as one of its purposes the ownership or operation of campgrounds which include or may include use of camping sites, that solicits membership paid for by a fee or periodic payments, such as annual dues, and the contractual members are the primary intended users. "Membership camping operator" does not include camping or recreational trailer parks, as defined in Section 18215 of the Health and Safety Code, which are open to the general public and which contain camping sites rented for a per use fee, or a "mobilehome park," as defined in either Section 798.4 of the Civil Code or Section 18214 of the Health and Safety Code.

As used in this title, "seller" means membership camping operator.

(b) "Membership camping contract" means an agreement offered or sold within the State of California by a membership camping operator or membership camping broker evidencing a purchaser's right or license to use for more than 14 days in a year, the campgrounds of a membership camping operator and includes a membership which provides for this use.

(c) "Camping site" means a space designed and promoted for the purpose of locating a trailer, tent, tent trailer, pickup camper, or other similar device used for camping.

(d) "Offer" means any solicitation reasonably designed to result in entering into a membership camping contract.

§ 1812.300

(e) "Person" means any individual, corporation, partnership, limited liability company, trust, association, or other organization other than a government or a subdivision thereof.

(f) "Purchaser" means a person who enters into a membership camping contract and thereby obtains the right to use the campgrounds of a membership camping operator.

(g) "Sale" or "sell" means entering into, or other disposition, of a membership camping contract for value. The term "value" does not include a reasonable fee to offset the administrative costs of transfer of a membership camping contract.

(h) "Campground" means real property within this state owned or operated by a membership camping operator and designated in whole or in part by the membership camping operator as available for camping or outdoor recreation by purchasers of membership camping contracts.

(i) "Blanket encumbrance" means any mortgage, deed of trust, option to purchase, vendor's lien or interest under a contract or agreement of sale, or other financing lien or encumbrance granted by the membership camping operator or affiliate which secures or evidences the obligation to pay money or to sell or convey any campgrounds made available to purchasers by the membership camping operator or any portion thereof, and which authorizes, permits, or requires the foreclosure or other disposition of the campground.

(j) "Nondisturbance agreement" means an instrument in recordable form by which the holder of a blanket encumbrance agrees to all of the following:

(1) The holder's rights in any campground made available to purchasers, prior or subsequent to the agreement, by the membership camping operator shall be subordinate to the rights of purchasers from and after the recordation of the nondisturbance agreement.

(2) The holder and all successors and assignees of the holder, and any person who acquires the campground through foreclosure or by deed in lieu of foreclosure of the blanket encumbrance shall take the campground subject to the rights of purchasers.

(3) The holder or any successor acquiring the campground through the blanket encumbrance shall not use or cause the campground to be used in a manner which would materially prevent purchasers from using or occupying the campground in a manner contemplated by the purchasers' membership camping contracts. However, the holder shall have no obligation to, and no liability for failure to assume the responsibilities or obligations of, the membership camping operator under the membership camping contracts.

(k) "Membership camping contract broker" means a person who, for compensation, resells or offers to resell a membership camping contract to a new purchaser on behalf of a prior purchaser. Membership camping contract broker does not include a membership camping operator or its employees or agents. *(Added by Stats.1983, c. 847, § 1. Amended by Stats.1990, c. 1529 (S.B.2203), § 4; Stats.1994, c. 1010 (S.B.2053), § 45.)*

§ 1812.301. Unruh Act; application to contracts and persons covered by the title

The membership camping contracts and persons covered by this title shall be subject to Chapter 5 (commencing with Section 17200) of Part 2 of Division 7 and Article 1 (commencing with Section 17500) of Chapter 1 of Part 3 of Division 7 of the Business and Professions Code and the Unruh Act (Chapter 1 (commencing with Section 1801) of Title 2 of Part 4 of Division 3). *(Added by Stats.1983, c. 847, § 1. Amended by Stats.1990, c. 1529 (S.B.2203), § 5.)*

Cross References

Membership camping contract defined for purposes of this Title, see Civil Code § 1812.300.

Person defined for purposes of this Title, see Civil Code § 1812.300.

§ 1812.302. Written disclosures by operator to purchaser

A membership camping operator shall provide to a purchaser the following written disclosures in any format which clearly communicates the following reasonably current information before the purchaser signs a membership camping contract, or gives any money or thing of value for the purchase of a membership camping contract. The written disclosures shall be included in or attached to the contract before the time the contract is signed. The following information shall be updated once a year.

(a) The name and address of the membership camping operator and any material affiliate membership camping operator.

(b) A brief description of the membership camping operator's experience in the membership camping business, including the number of years the operator has been in the membership camping business; a brief description of the past five years' business experience of the chairman, the president and chief executive officer, and if other than the foregoing, the person in charge of marketing of the membership camping operator, or persons in comparable positions in noncorporate operators, including the number of other membership camping operators with which the executive has been associated and the length of time with each.

(c) A brief description of the nature of the purchaser's right or license to use the membership camping operator's property or facilities.

(d) The location of each of the membership camping operator's campgrounds and a brief description for each campground of the significant facilities then available for use by purchasers and those which are represented to purchasers as being planned, together with a brief description of any significant facilities that are or will be available to nonpurchasers or nonmembers.

"Significant facilities" shall include, but are not limited to, each of the following: the number of campsites, in each campground; the number of campsites in each campground with full or partial hookups; swimming pools; tennis courts; recreation buildings; restrooms and showers; laundry rooms; trading posts; or grocery stores. "Partial hookups" mean those hookups with at least one of the following connections: electricity, water, or sewer connections.

Following such description there shall appear in 10-point bold type the following disclosure:

NOTICE: PURCHASE A MEMBERSHIP CAMPING CONTRACT ONLY ON THE BASIS OF EXISTING FACILITIES. CONSTRUCTION OF PLANNED FACILITIES IS SOMETIMES DEFERRED OR REVISED FOR A VARIETY OF REASONS. SHOULD THE SALESPERSON DESCRIBE A SIGNIFICANT FACILITY WHICH IS NEITHER LISTED AS EXISTING NOR PLANNED, TELEPHONE COLLECT OR TOLL FREE DURING WEEKDAY BUSINESS HOURS TO [insert headquarter's telephone number] TO VERIFY THE OPERATOR'S PLAN FOR SUCH A FACILITY.

(e) A brief description of the membership camping operator's ownership of, or other right to use, the campgrounds represented to be available for use by purchasers, together with the duration and expiration date of any lease, license, franchise, or reciprocal agreement entitling the membership camping operator to use the campgrounds, and any material provisions of any agreements, land use permits, or operating licenses which could materially restrict a purchaser's use of the campgrounds under the terms of the purchaser's camping contract.

(f) A summary or copy of the rules, restrictions, or covenants regulating the purchaser's use of the membership camping operator's properties, including a statement of whether and how the rules, restrictions, or covenants may be changed.

(g) A brief description of all payments of a purchaser under a membership camping contract, including initial fees and any further fees, charges, or assessments, together with any provisions for changing the payments.

(h) A description of any restraints on the transfer of the membership camping contract.

(i) A brief description of the policies relating to the availability of camping sites and whether reservations are required.

(j) A brief description of any grounds for forfeiture of a purchaser's membership camping contract.

(k) A copy of the membership camping contract form. (Added by Stats.1983, c. 847, § 1. Amended by Stats.1990, c. 1529 (S.B.2203), § 6.)

Cross References

Campground defined for purposes of this Title, see Civil Code § 1812.300.
Camping site defined for purposes of this Title, see Civil Code § 1812.300.
Membership camping contract defined for purposes of this Title, see Civil Code § 1812.300.
Membership camping operator defined for purposes of this Title, see Civil Code § 1812.300.
Person defined for purposes of this Title, see Civil Code § 1812.300.
Purchaser defined for purposes of this Title, see Civil Code § 1812.300.

§ 1812.303. Language of contract; date and signature; notice of cancellation; refunds after cancellation

(a) A membership camping contract shall be written in the same language as that principally used in any oral sales presentation (e.g., Spanish). A membership camping contract shall be dated, signed by the purchaser, and contain, in immediate proximity to the space reserved for the signature of the purchaser, a conspicuous statement in a size equal to at least 10-point bold type, as follows: "You, the purchaser, may cancel this contract at any time prior to midnight of the third business day after the date of the transaction. See an explanation of this right as set forth in this contract or on the attached notice of cancellation form." In the alternative the notice of cancellation as set forth in subdivision (b) may be placed in immediate proximity to the signature line of the contract in lieu of the foregoing statement.

(b) The contract shall be accompanied by a completed form in duplicate, captioned "Notice of Cancellation", which shall be attached to the contract and easily detachable. In the alternative, the seller may include all of the cancellation information on the contract and provide the consumer with a carbon copy which may be retained after cancellation. Both shall contain, in type of at least 10-point, the following statement written in the same language as used in the contract:

"Notice of Cancellation"

"You may cancel this contract, without any penalty or obligation, within three business days from the date the contract is executed.

"To cancel this contract, mail or deliver a signed and dated copy of this cancellation notice or a copy of this contract if it contains the cancellation instructions, or any other written notice, or send a telegram to

_____, at
(Name of seller)

_____
(Address of seller's place of business)
not later than midnight of _____.
(Date)
I hereby cancel this transaction _____.
(Date)

_____
(Purchaser's signature)

"With the notice of cancellation, or separately if a telegram is sent, you must return the original membership camping contract, membership card and all other evidence of membership to the seller. You should promptly return these documents with the notice of cancellation, or separately if a telegram is sent. Failure to send the documents promptly could delay your refund. You should retain for your records one copy of the cancellation notice, or a carbon of the contract when it provides the cancellation information, or other writing showing intent to cancel. Mailing by ordinary mail is adequate but certified mail return receipt requested is recommended."

(c) On the date of purchase the membership camping operator shall provide the purchaser with a copy of the contract and duplicate of the notice of cancellation. The membership camping operator shall inform the purchaser orally of the right to cancel at the time the contract is executed.

(d) Within 20 days after the membership camping operator receives a notice of cancellation, the membership camping contract, the membership card and all other evidence of purchase or membership, the membership camping operator

§ 1812.303

shall refund to the purchaser any sums paid as a deposit, downpayment or other payment therefor. If the purchaser does not promptly return the evidence of membership, the 20-day period shall be extended until such evidence of membership is returned.

(e) Until the membership camping operator has complied with this section, the purchaser shall have the right to cancel the contract.

(f) "Business day" means any calendar day except Sunday, or the following business holidays: New Year's Day, Washington's Birthday, Memorial Day, Independence Day, Labor Day, Columbus Day, Veteran's Day, Thanksgiving Day, and Christmas Day. *(Added by Stats.1983, c. 847, § 1. Amended by Stats.1990, c. 1529 (S.B.2203), § 7.)*

Cross References

Membership camping contract defined for purposes of this Title, see Civil Code § 1812.300.
Membership camping operator defined for purposes of this Title, see Civil Code § 1812.300.
Purchaser defined for purposes of this Title, see Civil Code § 1812.300.
Sale or sell defined for purposes of this Title, see Civil Code § 1812.300.
Seller defined for purposes of this Title, see Civil Code § 1812.300.

§ 1812.304. Notice of cancellation rights to purchaser failing to inspect campgrounds; return of payment and negotiable instruments upon cancellation

(a) If the purchaser has not inspected at least one of the membership camping operator's campgrounds prior to purchase of a membership camping contract, the notice shall contain the following additional language:

"If you sign this contract without having first inspected one of the membership camping operator's campgrounds, you may also cancel this contract at any time prior to midnight of the 10th business day after date of purchase by mailing or delivering the signed and dated attached written notice of cancellation or a copy of the contract when that contains the cancellation instructions together with the original camping club contract, membership card and any other evidence of membership."

(b) The seller shall return any payment made by the purchaser under the contract or offer to purchase, and any negotiable instrument executed by the purchaser, within 10 days of the return of evidence of membership and cancellation of the contract by the purchaser. If the purchaser does not promptly return the evidence of membership, the 10-day period shall be extended until the evidence of membership is returned. *(Added by Stats.1983, c. 847, § 1. Amended by Stats.1990, c. 1529 (S.B.2203), § 8.)*

Cross References

Campground defined for purposes of this Title, see Civil Code § 1812.300.
Membership camping contract defined for purposes of this Title, see Civil Code § 1812.300.
Membership camping operator defined for purposes of this Title, see Civil Code § 1812.300.
Offer defined for purposes of this Title, see Civil Code § 1812.300.
Purchaser defined for purposes of this Title, see Civil Code § 1812.300.
Seller defined for purposes of this Title, see Civil Code § 1812.300.

§ 1812.305. Exempt transactions

The following transactions are exempt from the provisions of this title.

(a) An offer, sale or transfer by any one person of not more than one membership camping contract for any given membership camping operator in any 12-month period.

(b) An offer or sale by a government or governmental agency.

(c) A bona fide pledge of a membership camping contract. *(Added by Stats.1983, c. 847, § 1.)*

Cross References

Membership camping contract defined for purposes of this Title, see Civil Code § 1812.300.
Membership camping operator defined for purposes of this Title, see Civil Code § 1812.300.
Offer defined for purposes of this Title, see Civil Code § 1812.300.
Person defined for purposes of this Title, see Civil Code § 1812.300.
Sale or sell defined for purposes of this Title, see Civil Code § 1812.300.

§ 1812.306. Remedy of purchaser for errors or omissions; attorney's fees; corrections

(a) A purchaser's remedy for errors in or omissions from the membership camping contract of any of the disclosures or requirements of Sections 1812.302 to 1812.304, inclusive, shall be limited to a right of rescission and refund. Reasonable attorney's fees shall be awarded to the prevailing party in any action under this title. This limitation does not apply to errors or omissions from the contract, or disclosures or other requirements of this title, which are a part of a scheme to willfully misstate or omit the information required, or other requirements imposed by this title.

(b) Any failure, except a willful or material failure, to comply with any provision of Sections 1812.302 to 1812.304, inclusive, may be corrected within 30 days after receipt of written notice to the membership camping operator from the purchaser, and, if so corrected, there shall be no right of rescission. The membership camping operator or the holder shall not be subject to any penalty under this title. However, there can be no correction that increases any monthly payment, the number of payments, or the total amount due, unless concurred to, in writing, by the purchaser. "Holder" includes the seller who acquires the contract, or if the contract is purchased, a financing agency or other assignee who purchases the contract. *(Added by Stats.1983, c. 847, § 1. Amended by Stats.2006, c. 538 (S.B.1852), § 51.)*

Cross References

Action on contract, award of attorney's fees and costs, see Civil Code § 1717.
Membership camping contract defined for purposes of this Title, see Civil Code § 1812.300.
Membership camping operator defined for purposes of this Title, see Civil Code § 1812.300.
Purchaser defined for purposes of this Title, see Civil Code § 1812.300.

Seller defined for purposes of this Title, see Civil Code § 1812.300.

§ 1812.307. Withdrawal of campgrounds; conditions

No membership camping operator shall withdraw from the use by purchasers of membership camping contracts any campground unless one of the following conditions is satisfied:

(a) Adequate provision is made to provide within a reasonable time, a substitute campground in the same general area that is as desirable for the purpose of camping and outdoor recreation.

(b) The campground is withdrawn from use because, despite good faith efforts by the membership camping operator, a person not affiliated with the membership camping operator has exercised a superior right to possession (such as the right of a lessor to take possession following expiration of a lease of the property) and the terms and date of the withdrawal were disclosed in writing to all purchasers at or prior to the time of any sale of a membership camping contract after the membership camping operator represented to purchasers that the campground would be available for camping or recreation purposes.

(c) The rights of all purchasers of membership camping contracts who are entitled to use the campground have expired or have been lawfully terminated. *(Added by Stats. 1990, c. 1529 (S.B.2203), § 10.)*

Cross References

Campground defined for purposes of this Title, see Civil Code § 1812.300.
Membership camping contract defined for purposes of this Title, see Civil Code § 1812.300.
Membership camping operator defined for purposes of this Title, see Civil Code § 1812.300.
Person defined for purposes of this Title, see Civil Code § 1812.300.
Purchaser defined for purposes of this Title, see Civil Code § 1812.300.
Sale or sell defined for purposes of this Title, see Civil Code § 1812.300.

§ 1812.308. Sale, lease, assignment or transfer of campground

(a) Except in the case of a membership camping operator substituting a campground in accordance with Section 1812.307, no membership camping operator or owner of the underlying fee shall sell, lease, assign, or otherwise transfer his or her interest in a campground except by an instrument evidencing the transfer recorded in the office of the county recorder for the county in which the campground is located. The instrument shall be in recordable form and be executed by both the transferor and transferee and shall state each of the following:

(1) That the instrument is intended to protect the rights of all purchasers of membership camping contracts.

(2) That its terms may be enforced by any prior or subsequent purchaser so long as that purchaser is not in default on his or her obligations under the membership camping contract.

(3) That the transferee shall fully honor the rights of the purchasers to occupy and use the campground as provided in the purchaser's original membership camping contracts.

(4) That the transferee shall fully honor all rights of purchasers to cancel their contracts and receive appropriate refunds.

(5) That the obligations of the transferee under the instrument will continue to exist despite any cancellation or rejection of the contracts between the membership camping operator and purchaser arising out of bankruptcy proceedings.

(b) If any transfer of the interest of the membership camping operator or owner of the underlying fee occurs in a manner which is not in compliance with this section, the terms set forth in this section shall be presumed to be a part of the transfer and shall be deemed to be included in the instrument of transfer. Notice of the transfer shall be mailed to each purchaser within 30 days of the transfer. Persons who hold blanket encumbrances on a campground shall not be considered transferees for the purposes of this section. *(Added by Stats.1990, c. 1529 (S.B.2203), § 12.)*

Cross References

Blanket encumbrance defined for purposes of this Title, see Civil Code § 1812.300.
Campground defined for purposes of this Title, see Civil Code § 1812.300.
Membership camping contract defined for purposes of this Title, see Civil Code § 1812.300.
Membership camping operator defined for purposes of this Title, see Civil Code § 1812.300.
Person defined for purposes of this Title, see Civil Code § 1812.300.
Purchaser defined for purposes of this Title, see Civil Code § 1812.300.
Sale or sell defined for purposes of this Title, see Civil Code § 1812.300.

§ 1812.309. Availability of campgrounds for use; conditions

(a) Campgrounds subject to this section include any campground which is offered or made available by an operator for the first time after January 1, 1991, or any campground which becomes subject to a new or refinanced blanket encumbrance after January 1, 1991. A membership camping operator shall not offer or represent that any campground subject to this section is available for use by the purchasers of its camping contracts unless one of the following conditions has been satisfied:

(1) The membership camping operator obtains and records a nondisturbance agreement from each holder of a blanket encumbrance. The nondisturbance agreement is executed by the membership camping operator and each holder of the blanket encumbrance and includes the provisions set forth in subdivision (j) of Section 1812.300 and each of the following:

(A) The instrument may be enforced by purchasers of membership camping contracts. If the membership camping operator is not in default under its obligations to the holder of the blanket encumbrance, the agreement may be enforced by both the membership camping operator and the purchasers.

(B) The nondisturbance agreement is effective as between each purchaser and the holder of the blanket encumbrance despite any rejection or cancellation of the purchaser's contract during any bankruptcy proceedings of the membership camping operator.

(C) The agreement is binding upon the successors in the interest of both the membership camping operator and the holder of the blanket encumbrance.

(D) A holder of the blanket encumbrance who obtains title or possession, or who causes a change in title or possession in a campground by foreclosure or otherwise, and who does not continue to operate the campground upon conditions no less favorable to members than existed prior to the change of title or possession shall either:

(i) Offer the title or possession of the campground to an association of members to operate the campground.

(ii) Obtain a commitment from another entity which obtains title or possession to undertake the responsibility of operating the campground.

(2) The membership camping operator posts a surety bond or irrevocable letter of credit with a trustee in favor of purchasers and which guarantees that the payments on the blanket encumbrance are made as they become due. A trustee shall be either a corporate trustee or an attorney licensed to practice law in this state.

(3) The membership camping operator delivers to a trustee an encumbrance trust agreement which contains each of the following provisions:

(A) The membership camping operator shall collaterally assign to the trustee all of its membership camping contracts receivable or other receivables of the membership camping operator in an amount calculated in accordance with subparagraph (B). The membership camping operator shall provide the trustee with a security interest in the receivables and all proceeds therefrom. For purposes of this section, the membership camping operator shall be credited with 100 percent of the outstanding principal balance of each receivable assigned to the trustee. All proceeds of the receivables shall be held in a trust account by the trustee subject to this section for the use and benefit of the purchasers to make the payments of principal and interest due under the blanket encumbrance. However, if the proceeds of the receivables during any calendar year exceed the amount due under the blanket encumbrance in the following calendar quarter, these excess funds shall be returned by the trustee to the membership camping operator.

(B) The amount of membership camping contracts receivable or other receivables to be collaterally assigned as described in subparagraph (A) shall be calculated based upon the maximum number of contracts per camping site to be offered on or after January 1, 1991, in connection with the campground in question, which number of contracts per camping site shall not exceed 15 multiplied by the total number of camping sites available at the campground thereby yielding the anticipated total number of contracts to be sold in connection with the campground. The outstanding balance due under the blanket encumbrance shall then be divided by the anticipated total number of contracts to arrive at the amount per contract sold to be paid over to the trustee in the form of collaterally assigned receivables as described in subparagraph (A). The membership camping operator shall make the required collateral assignments to the trustee on a quarterly basis based upon the actual sales of contracts at the campground in question during the previous calendar quarter. However, the membership camping operator's obligation to collaterally assign receivables to the trustee shall cease when the membership camping operator has collaterally assigned to the trustee an aggregate principal amount of receivables equal to 100 percent of the aggregate principal indebtedness remaining due under the blanket encumbrance.

(C) If the outstanding balance due under the blanket encumbrance at the time of execution of the encumbrance trust agreement exceeds the anticipated gross revenue based upon the membership camping operator's price list to be generated by the sale of the anticipated total number of contracts as calculated in subparagraph (B), the membership camping operator shall meet the conditions specified in paragraph (1), (2), or (4) of this subdivision as to the full amount of the excess.

(D) It may be terminated by the membership camping operator if the membership camping operator has satisfied the obligation secured by the blanket encumbrance in full or has complied with paragraph (1), (2), or (4) of this subdivision. Upon termination of the agreement, all receivables and proceeds thereof held by the trustee shall be immediately assigned and delivered to the membership camping operator. All costs of administering this trust, filing, and perfecting the security interest, and foreclosing the lien shall be borne by the membership camping operator.

(4) Any financial institution which has made a hypothecation loan to the membership camping operator (a "hypothecation lender") shall have a lien on, or security interest in, the membership camping operator's interest in the campground, and the hypothecation lender shall have executed and recorded a nondisturbance agreement at the county recorder's office for the county in which the campground is located. Each person holding an interest in a blanket encumbrance superior to the interest held by the hypothecation lender shall execute and record at the county recorder's office, an instrument stating that the person shall give the hypothecation lender notice of, and at least 30 days to cure, any default under the blanket encumbrance before the person commences any foreclosure action affecting the campground. For the purposes of this paragraph, a "hypothecation loan to a membership camping operator" means a loan or line of credit secured by membership camping contracts receivable arising from the sale of membership camping contracts by the membership camping operator, which exceeds in the aggregate all outstanding indebtedness secured by blanket encumbrances superior to the interest held by the hypothecation lender.

A hypothecation lender who obtains title or possession, or who causes a change in title or possession, in a campground, by foreclosure or otherwise, and who does not continue to operate the campground upon conditions no less favorable to purchasers than existed prior to the change of title or possession shall either:

(A) Offer the title or possession to an association of members to operate the campground.

(B) Obtain a commitment from another entity which obtains title to, or possession of, the campground to undertake the responsibility of operating the campground.

(b) Any membership camping operator which does not comply at all times with subdivision (a) with regard to any blanket encumbrance in connection with any campground subject to that subdivision is prohibited from offering any membership camping contracts for sale during the period of noncompliance. (Added by Stats.1990, c. 1529 (S.B.2203), § 13.)

Cross References

Blanket encumbrance defined for purposes of this Title, see Civil Code § 1812.300.
Campground defined for purposes of this Title, see Civil Code § 1812.300.
Camping site defined for purposes of this Title, see Civil Code § 1812.300.
Membership camping contract defined for purposes of this Title, see Civil Code § 1812.300.
Membership camping operator defined for purposes of this Title, see Civil Code § 1812.300.
Nondisturbance agreement defined for purposes of this Title, see Civil Code § 1812.300.
Offer defined for purposes of this Title, see Civil Code § 1812.300.
Person defined for purposes of this Title, see Civil Code § 1812.300.
Purchaser defined for purposes of this Title, see Civil Code § 1812.300.
Sale or sell defined for purposes of this Title, see Civil Code § 1812.300.

§ 1812.314. Membership camping contract brokers; fees; escrows; disclosures to new purchaser; notice of cancellation to purchaser

(a) All money received from the owner of a membership camping contract or the prospective purchaser thereof, by a membership camping contract broker in advance of the completion of any membership camping contract resale, including, but not limited to, listing fees, and fees for services, shall be deposited into an escrow account. The money shall not be disbursed until the transaction is complete, or until the escrow agent has received written instructions to disburse the funds signed by the owner of the membership camping contract or the prospective purchaser and the broker. For purposes of this section, a transaction is complete when ownership of the membership camping contract has been transferred from the prior purchaser to the new purchaser in the manner required by the terms of the membership camping contract, all documents necessary to complete the transfer have been fully executed, and the new purchaser has not exercised the right to cancel provided in paragraph (2) of subdivision (c).

(b) The broker shall inform the new purchaser in writing of the following:

(1) The risks of purchasing a membership camping contract without visiting at least one of the membership camping operator's campgrounds.

(2) That the membership camping operator may have a valid reason for not transferring the contract to the new purchaser such as a default in payment on contract or annual dues, or that the new purchaser does not meet the same credit standards applied to other new purchasers.

(3) That there may have been changes in the rules or regulations concerning the rights and obligations of the membership camping operator or its members including changes with respect to annual dues, fees, assessments, use restrictions or that some campgrounds may have been withdrawn.

(4) Any material changes or risks to the purchaser known to the broker.

(c)(1) Every broker shall provide in writing the following notice of cancellation to the new purchaser:

"You may cancel your contract of purchase, without any penalty or obligation, within 10 business days from the above date of purchase by mailing notice of cancellation together with the membership camping contract, if any, any contract for transfer, membership card or other evidence of membership to

_____,
(Name and address of broker)
the membership camping operator
_____
(Name and address of membership camping operator)
and the escrow company
_____,
(Name and address of escrow company)
if any, not later than midnight of _____.
(Date)

I hereby cancel this transaction _____
(Purchaser's signature)
_____
(Date)

Notice by ordinary mail is adequate but certified mail return receipt requested is recommended."

(2) Any escrow company which receives a notice of cancellation from a purchaser shall, within 72 hours of receipt of the notice, notify the membership camping operator of the cancellation and shall refund any sums paid by the purchaser of the contract within 10 days of receipt of the notice of the cancellation and other documents. The escrow company shall incur no liability to the seller, purchaser, or broker as a result of its compliance with this section. (Formerly § 1812.307, added by Stats.1983, c. 847, § 1. Renumbered § 1812.314 and amended by Stats.1990, c. 1529 (S.B.2203), § 9.)

Cross References

Campground defined for purposes of this Title, see Civil Code § 1812.300.
Membership camping contract broker defined for purposes of this Title, see Civil Code § 1812.300.
Membership camping contract defined for purposes of this Title, see Civil Code § 1812.300.
Membership camping operator defined for purposes of this Title, see Civil Code § 1812.300.
Purchaser defined for purposes of this Title, see Civil Code § 1812.300.
Seller defined for purposes of this Title, see Civil Code § 1812.300.

§ 1812.315. Severability

If any provision of this title or the application thereof to any person or circumstances is held invalid, the invalidity shall not affect other provisions or applications of this title which can be given effect without the invalid provision or application, and to this end the provisions of this title are

§ 1812.315

severable. *(Formerly § 1812.308, added by Stats.1983, c. 847, § 1. Renumbered § 1812.315 and amended by Stats.1990, c. 1529 (S.B.2203), § 11.)*

Cross References

Person defined for purposes of this Title, see Civil Code § 1812.300.

§ 1812.316. Public policy; waiver of rights

Any waiver of the provisions of this title is contrary to public policy, and is void and unenforceable. *(Added by Stats.2002, c. 815 (A.B.2331), § 21.)*

Title 2.9

CREDITOR REMEDIES: DISABILITY INSURANCE

Section

1812.400.	Legislative findings and declarations.
1812.401.	Definitions.
1812.402.	Prohibition of invocation of creditor's remedies because of nonpayment of sum due during any credit insurance disability claim period; prior indebtedness; foreclosure of lien; payments; disclosure; cumulative rights and remedies.
1812.403.	Invocation of creditor's remedies; cessation of payment of claim because of debtor's failure to timely submit forms to credit insurer.
1812.404.	Application of title; creditors arranging or participating in sale or receiving commission or compensation for sale of credit disability insurance to debtor.
1812.405.	Invocation of creditor's remedies; nonpayment of amount due under open-end credit plan.
1812.406.	Application of title; credit insurance covering key person; certain loans or transactions secured by mortgage or deed of trust.
1812.407.	Application of title; nonpayment of sums due after April 1, 1984.
1812.408.	Waiver by debtor; invalidity.
1812.409.	Effect of title; after-acquired property interest by bona fide purchaser or encumbrancer.
1812.410.	Severability.

§ 1812.400. Legislative findings and declarations

The Legislature finds and declares that it is unfair for a creditor who has directly participated in, arranged, or received a commission or other compensation for the sale of credit disability insurance to the debtor, or that creditor's successor in interest, to invoke a creditor's remedy because of a debtor's nonpayment of any sum which has become due during a period of disability until a reasonable time has passed for the disability insurance claim to be filed, verified and processed. *(Added by Stats.1983, c. 973, § 1.)*

Cross References

Credit disability insurance defined for purposes of this Title, see Civil Code § 1812.401.

Creditor defined for purposes of this Title, see Civil Code § 1812.401.

Creditor's remedy defined for purposes of this Title, see Civil Code § 1812.401.

Debtor defined for purposes of this Title, see Civil Code § 1812.401.

§ 1812.401. Definitions

For the purposes of this title:

(a) "Credit disability insurance" means insurance of a debtor to provide indemnity for payments becoming due on a specific loan or other credit transaction while the debtor is disabled as defined in the policy.

(b) "Creditor" means the lender of money or vendor or lessor of goods, services, property, rights, or privileges, for which payment is arranged through a credit transaction, who has directly participated in, arranged, or received a commission or other compensation for the sale of credit disability insurance to the debtor, or any successor to the right, title, or interest of any such lender, vendor, or lessor, and an affiliate, associate, or subsidiary of any of them or any director, officer, or employee of any of them, or any other person in any way associated with any of them.

(c) "Debtor" means a borrower of money or a purchaser or lessee of goods, services, property, rights, or privileges for which payment is arranged through a credit transaction.

(d) "Creditor's remedy" means and includes the imposition of any late charge or penalty, the acceleration of the maturity of all or any part of the indebtedness, the collection or assignment for the collection of all or any part of the indebtedness, the commencement of any action or special proceeding, or the enforcement of any security interest in any manner, including, but not limited to, repossession, foreclosure, or the exercise of a power of sale contained in a deed of trust or mortgage.

(e) "Disability claim period" or "claim period" means the period beginning on the due date of the first payment not paid by the debtor for which the debtor claims disability coverage arising from a then current disability and continuing until three calendar months thereafter or until the insurer pays or rejects the claim, whichever occurs sooner.

(f) "Notice" to a creditor means written notice deposited in the United States mail, postage prepaid, addressed to the creditor at the location where payments on the loan or credit transaction are normally required to be sent by the debtor. A creditor may elect to require that written notice, otherwise complying with the requirements of this subdivision, be sent to a different location or may elect to accept telephonic notice to a telephone number specified by the creditor, in either case in lieu of notice being sent to the location where payments are regularly required to be sent, if that location or telephone number is clearly and conspicuously disclosed as the proper place to direct any notice to the creditor relating to any claim of disability on each monthly billing, or on or in each payment coupon book (by adhesive attachment, republication, or otherwise), as the case may be, or (if payments are automatically deducted from an account of the debtor) on the annual statement of loan activity. In any particular instance a creditor may waive the requirement that notice be in writing and accept oral notice. *(Added by Stats.1983, c. 973, § 1. Amended by Stats.1984, c. 1200, § 1, eff. Sept. 17, 1984.)*

§ 1812.402. Prohibition of invocation of creditor's remedies because of nonpayment of sum due during any credit insurance disability claim period; prior indebtedness; foreclosure of lien; payments; disclosure; cumulative rights and remedies

(a) No creditor, as defined in Section 1812.401, shall invoke any creditor's remedy against a debtor because of the debtor's nonpayment of any sum which becomes due during any disability claim period and for which credit disability insurance coverage, subject to this title, is provided.

(b) Upon initially receiving notice, as defined in subdivision (f) of Section 1812.401, of the debtor's claim of disability, the creditor shall inform the debtor in writing of the name, address, and telephone number of the insurer or its designated representative from whom the debtor may obtain claim forms. Upon receiving notice of the disability claim, the insurer or its designated representative shall send necessary claim forms to the debtor. The debtor shall submit the claim to the insurer or its designated representative and shall notify the creditor, as specified in subdivision (f) of Section 1812.401, that a claim has been submitted.

This subdivision shall apply to the original creditor who sold the disability insurance and shall not apply to that creditor's successor in interest if the successor in interest (1) is not related by common ownership or control to that creditor and (2) has no information regarding the name, address, and telephone number of the insurer or its designated representative.

(c) Nothing in this section prohibits a creditor from invoking any creditor's remedy during or after the claim period for the debtor's nonpayment of any sum due prior to the claim period, whether or not the nonpayment is related to the claimed disability, or for the debtor's nonpayment of any interest, finance charge, or late charge accruing during the claim period of any sum due prior to the period.

(d) Nothing in this section prohibits a creditor from foreclosing a lien on any property to protect that creditor's security interest if a senior lienholder on that property (1) has initiated the foreclosure of its lien, (2) is not prohibited from continuing the foreclosure by any law or order of court, or (3) will not otherwise suspend or delay its foreclosure proceeding until after the disability claim period.

(e) If the insurer pays the claim within the disability claim period, the creditor shall treat each payment made by the insurer as though it were timely made by the debtor. If the insurer rejects the claim within the disability claim period or accepts the claim within the claim period as a partial disability which results in a payment of less than the full benefit which would be paid for the total disability, the debtor shall have the opportunity to pay the entire amount which became due during the claim period or the difference between the amount which became due during the claim period and the amount paid by the insurer for the partial disability without being subject to any creditor's remedy, except the imposition of late charges, for 35 days following the date on which the insurer sends notice of the rejection of the claim or acceptance of the claim as a partial disability. In the event the debtor does not pay the entire amount which became due during the claim period plus any accrued late charges within 35 days from that date, the creditor may then invoke any creditor's remedy.

(f) The obligations of the creditor and debtor pursuant to this section shall be disclosed in writing in at least 10-point type by the creditor to the debtor at the time the creditor sells the insurance, in the manner provided in paragraph (1), and by the insurer to the debtor at the time the insurer sends claim forms pursuant to subdivision (b), in the manner provided in paragraph (2).

(1) The disclosure required by the creditor shall be substantially in the following form:

CLAIM PROCEDURE

If you become disabled, tell us (your creditor) right away. (We advise you to send this information to the same address to which you are normally required to send your payments, unless a different address or telephone number is given to you in writing by us as the location where we would like to be notified.) We will tell you where to get claim forms. Send in the completed form to the insurance company as soon as possible and tell us as soon as you do.

If your disability insurance covers all of your missed payment, WE CANNOT TRY TO COLLECT WHAT YOU OWE OR FORECLOSE UPON OR REPOSSESS ANY COLLATERAL UNTIL THREE CALENDAR MONTHS AFTER your first missed payment is due or until the insurance company pays or rejects your claim, whichever comes first. We can, however, try to collect, foreclose, or repossess if you have money due and owing us or are otherwise in default when your disability claim is made or if a senior mortgage or lien holder is foreclosing.

If the insurance company pays the claim within the three calendar months, we must accept the money as though you paid on time. If the insurance company rejects the claim within the three calendar months or accepts the claim within the three calendar months as a partial disability and pays less than for a total disability, you will have 35 days from the date that the rejection or the acceptance of the partial disability claim is sent to pay past due payments, or the difference between past due payments and what the insurance company pays for the partial disability, plus late charges. You can contact us, and we will tell you how much you owe. After that time, we can take action to collect or foreclose or repossess any collateral you may have given.

If the insurance company accepts your claim but requires that you send in additional forms to remain eligible for continued payments, you should send in these completed additional forms no later than required. If you do not send in these forms on time, the insurance company may stop paying, and we will then be able to take action to collect or foreclose or repossess any collateral you may have given.

(2) The disclosure required by the insurer shall be substantially in the following form:

CLAIM PROCEDURE

Send in the completed form to the insurance company as soon as possible and tell your creditor as soon as you do. (Your creditor has already advised you of the address or telephone number to use to confirm that you have submitted your completed form to the insurance company.)

§ 1812.402 OBLIGATIONS

If your disability insurance covers all of your missed payments, YOUR CREDITOR CANNOT TRY TO COLLECT WHAT YOU OWE OR FORECLOSE UPON OR REPOSSESS ANY COLLATERAL UNTIL THREE CALENDAR MONTHS AFTER your first missed payment is due or until the insurance company pays or rejects your claim, whichever comes first. Your creditor can, however, try to collect, foreclose, or repossess if you have money due and owing or are otherwise in default when your disability claim is made or if a senior mortgage or lienholder is foreclosing.

If the insurance company pays the claim within the three calendar months, your creditor must accept the money as though you paid on time. If the insurance company rejects the claim within the three calendar months or accepts the claim within the three calendar months as a partial disability and pays less than for a total disability, you will have 35 days from the date that the rejection or the acceptance of the partial disability claim was sent to pay past due payments, or the difference between past due payments and what the insurance company pays for the partial disability, plus late charges. You can contact your creditor who will tell you how much you owe. After that time, your creditor can take action to collect or foreclose or repossess any collateral you may have given.

If the insurance company accepts your claim, but requires that you send in additional forms to remain eligible for continued payments, you should send in these completed additional forms no later than required. If you do not send in these forms on time, the insurance company may stop paying, and your creditor will then be able to take action to collect or foreclose or repossess any collateral you have given.

(g) If a debtor does not make a payment for which the debtor claims disability coverage arising from a then current disability and if the creditor, after sending the debtor notice of the debtor's delinquency, invokes any creditor's remedy because of the nonpayment without knowledge of the debtor's claim of disability coverage, subject to this title, the following provisions apply:

(1) Upon receiving notice of the debtor's claim, the creditor shall not invoke any further creditor's remedy during the remainder of the claim period and the period provided in subdivision (e).

(2) Upon receiving notice, as specified in subdivision (f) of Section 1812.401, of the debtor's claim, the creditor shall rescind every creditor's remedy that has been invoked relating to the delinquency for which coverage is claimed, except that the creditor shall not be obligated to restore property which has been sold in a bona fide lawful sale to any person not related by common ownership or control to the creditor.

(3) The debtor shall be liable for costs and expenses actually incurred in connection with the invocation or rescission of any creditor's remedy.

(4) The creditor shall not be in violation of this title and shall not be liable under subdivision (i) provided the creditor complies with paragraphs (1) and (2) of this subdivision.

(h) The rights and remedies afforded debtors by this title shall be cumulative to each other and to all other rights and remedies which the debtors may have under other laws.

(i) The debtor may bring an action for damages, equitable relief, or other relief for any violation of this title. *(Added by Stats.1983, c. 973, § 1. Amended by Stats.1984, c. 1200, § 2, eff. Sept. 17, 1984.)*

Cross References

Credit disability insurance defined for purposes of this Title, see Civil Code § 1812.401.
Creditor defined for purposes of this Title, see Civil Code § 1812.401.
Creditor's remedy defined for purposes of this Title, see Civil Code § 1812.401.
Debtor defined for purposes of this Title, see Civil Code § 1812.401.
Disability claim period or claim period defined for purposes of this Title, see Civil Code § 1812.401.

§ 1812.403. Invocation of creditor's remedies; cessation of payment of claim because of debtor's failure to timely submit forms to credit insurer

A creditor may invoke any creditor's remedy 15 days after receiving notice that the insurer has ceased making payments on a credit disability insurance claim because of the debtor's failure to timely submit any forms required by the insurer for recertification of a temporary disability. *(Added by Stats. 1983, c. 973, § 1.)*

Cross References

Credit disability insurance defined for purposes of this Title, see Civil Code § 1812.401.
Creditor defined for purposes of this Title, see Civil Code § 1812.401.
Creditor's remedy defined for purposes of this Title, see Civil Code § 1812.401.
Debtor defined for purposes of this Title, see Civil Code § 1812.401.
Notice defined for purposes of this Title, see Civil Code § 1812.401.

§ 1812.404. Application of title; creditors arranging or participating in sale or receiving commission or compensation for sale of credit disability insurance to debtor

This title shall apply to a creditor only if the creditor, the predecessor to the right, title, or interest of the creditor, or the representative of either of them directly arranges or participates in the sale or receives a commission or other compensation for the sale of credit disability insurance to the debtor. *(Added by Stats.1983, c. 973, § 1.)*

Cross References

Credit disability insurance defined for purposes of this Title, see Civil Code § 1812.401.
Creditor defined for purposes of this Title, see Civil Code § 1812.401.
Debtor defined for purposes of this Title, see Civil Code § 1812.401.

§ 1812.405. Invocation of creditor's remedies; nonpayment of amount due under open-end credit plan

This title shall not prohibit a creditor from invoking any creditor's remedy as a result of a debtor's nonpayment when due of any amount obtained under an open-end credit plan, as hereafter defined, after the debtor has given notice of a disability claim unless the nonpayment is related to a covered disability then affecting the debtor other than the disability previously claimed. The creditor's termination of the open-end credit plan because the debtor does not meet the creditor's customary credit standards at the time the debtor notifies the creditor of the disability claim is not a creditor's remedy.

An "open-end credit plan" means credit extended by a creditor under a plan in which the creditor reasonably contemplates repeated transactions, the creditor may impose a finance charge from time to time on an outstanding unpaid balance, and the amount of credit that may be extended to the debtor during the term of the plan (up to any limit set by the creditor) is generally made available to the extent that any outstanding balance is repaid. *(Added by Stats.1983, c. 973, § 1.)*

Cross References

Creditor defined for purposes of this Title, see Civil Code § 1812.401.
Creditor's remedy defined for purposes of this Title, see Civil Code § 1812.401.
Debtor defined for purposes of this Title, see Civil Code § 1812.401.
Notice defined for purposes of this Title, see Civil Code § 1812.401.

§ 1812.406. Application of title; credit insurance covering key person; certain loans or transactions secured by mortgage or deed of trust

(a) This title does not apply to credit disability insurance covering a key person, as hereinafter defined, which a creditor requires as a condition to making a loan of at least twenty-five thousand dollars ($25,000) to be used in the operation of a business in which the key person is employed or has an ownership interest.

For the purposes of this subdivision, a "key person" is a person who the creditor and the debtor or debtors mutually agree must be involved in the operation of the business to assure its success.

(b) This title does not apply to a loan or other credit transaction (including an open line of credit) of more than 10 years' duration which is secured by a mortgage or deed of trust unless (1) the principal purpose of the loan or credit transaction is for the construction (other than initial construction), rehabilitation, or improvement (including "home improvement" as defined in Section 7151 of the Business and Professions Code) of real property consisting of four or fewer residential units, and (2) any document incident to the loan or credit transaction at the time the loan or extension of credit is made, or any course of dealing between the creditor and a contractor or material supplier assisting the borrower in obtaining the loan or extension of credit, would indicate that purpose.

(c) Subdivision (b) shall not apply to debtors who were entitled to receive notice from the creditor pursuant to subdivision (f) of Section 1812.402 on or after January 1, 1984, and prior to the effective date of the act which added this subdivision, unless the debtor receives written notice that the remedies provided in this title are revoked, the debtor is given an opportunity to cancel the coverage, and no claim has been made or notice provided as specified in Section 1812.401. If the debtor fails to cancel the insurance following receipt of the notice required under this subdivision, subdivision (b) shall apply to that policy upon payment by the debtor of the next installment of premium, whether to the insurer or to a creditor pursuant to a premium finance agreement. *(Added by Stats.1983, c. 973, § 1. Amended by Stats.1984, c. 1200, § 3, eff. Sept. 17, 1984.)*

Cross References

Credit disability insurance defined for purposes of this Title, see Civil Code § 1812.401.
Creditor defined for purposes of this Title, see Civil Code § 1812.401.
Debtor defined for purposes of this Title, see Civil Code § 1812.401.

§ 1812.407. Application of title; nonpayment of sums due after April 1, 1984

The provisions of this title shall apply to the nonpayment of any sum which becomes due on or after April 1, 1984, and for which the debtor claims disability coverage. *(Added by Stats.1983, c. 973, § 1.)*

Cross References

Debtor defined for purposes of this Title, see Civil Code § 1812.401.

§ 1812.408. Waiver by debtor; invalidity

Any waiver by the debtor of the provisions of this title shall be void and unenforceable. *(Added by Stats.1983, c. 973, § 1.)*

Cross References

Debtor defined for purposes of this Title, see Civil Code § 1812.401.

§ 1812.409. Effect of title; after-acquired property interest by bona fide purchaser or encumbrancer

This title shall not affect or defeat an interest in the debtor's property, acquired after the creditor invokes a creditor's remedy in violation of this title, by a bona fide purchaser or encumbrancer for value and without notice of facts that constitute a violation of this title. *(Added by Stats.1984, c. 1200, § 4, eff. Sept. 17, 1984.)*

Cross References

Creditor defined for purposes of this Title, see Civil Code § 1812.401.
Creditor's remedy defined for purposes of this Title, see Civil Code § 1812.401.
Debtor defined for purposes of this Title, see Civil Code § 1812.401.
Notice defined for purposes of this Title, see Civil Code § 1812.401.

§ 1812.410. Severability

If any provision of this title or the application thereof to any person or circumstance is held to be unconstitutional, the remainder of the title and the application of the provision to other persons and circumstances shall not be affected thereby. *(Formerly § 1812.409, added by Stats.1983, c. 973, § 1. Renumbered § 1812.410 and amended by Stats.1984, c. 1200, § 5, eff. Sept. 17, 1984.)*

Title 2.91

EMPLOYMENT AGENCY, EMPLOYMENT COUNSELING, AND JOB LISTING SERVICES ACT

Chapter	Section
1. General Provisions	1812.500
2. Employment Agencies	1812.503

Chapter	Section
3. Employment Counseling Services	1812.510
4. Job Listing Services	1812.515
5. Records	1812.522
6. Remedies and Enforcement	1812.523
7. Nurses' Registries	1812.524
8. Long–Term Care Facilities	1812.540

CHAPTER 1. GENERAL PROVISIONS

Section
1812.500. Short title.
1812.501. Definitions.
1812.502. Application of title; person charging employer exclusively; nonprofit corporation; labor organization; nursing, business, or vocational school; job listing service.

§ 1812.500. Short title

This title shall be known and cited as the Employment Agency, Employment Counseling, and Job Listing Services Act. *(Added by Stats.1989, c. 704, § 2.)*

Cross References

Employment agency or agency defined, see Civil Code § 1812.501.
Job listing service defined, see Civil Code § 1812.501.

§ 1812.501. Definitions

(a)(1) "Employment agency" or "agency" means:

(A) Any person who, for a fee or other valuable consideration to be paid, directly or indirectly by a jobseeker, performs, offers to perform, or represents it can or will perform any of the following services:

(i) Procures, offers, promises, or attempts to procure employment or engagements for others or employees for employers.

(ii) Registers persons seeking to procure or retain employment or engagement.

(iii) Gives information as to where and from whom this help, employment, or engagement may be procured.

(iv) Provides employment or engagements.

(B) Any person who offers, as one of its main objects or purposes, to procure employment for any person who will pay for its services, or that collects dues, tuition, or membership or registration fees of any sort, if the main object of the person paying those fees is to secure employment.

(C) Any person who, for a fee or other valuable consideration, procures, offers, promises, provides, or attempts to procure babysitting or domestic employment for others or domestics or babysitters for others.

(2) "Employment agency" or "agency" shall not include any employment counseling service or any job listing service.

(b)(1) "Employment counseling service" means any person who offers, advertises, or represents it can or will provide any of the following services for a fee: career counseling, vocational guidance, aptitude testing, executive consulting, personnel consulting, career management, evaluation, or planning, or the development of résumés and other promotional materials relating to the preparation for employment. "Employment counseling service" shall not include persons who provide services strictly on an hourly basis with no financial obligation required of the consumer beyond the hourly fee for services rendered. An "employment counseling service" does not include the functions of an "employment agency" as defined in subdivision (a).

(2) "Employment counseling service" does not include:

(A) Businesses that are retained by, act solely on behalf of, and are compensated solely by prior or current employers that do not require any "customer" to sign a contract and do not in any way hold any "customer" liable for fees.

(B)(i) Any provider of vocational rehabilitation in which the counseling services are paid for by insurance benefits, if the counseling is provided as a result of marital dissolution or separation proceedings to prepare one of the spouses for reentry into the job market and if the fees are paid by some party other than the person receiving the counseling services.

(ii) The exemption provided in this subparagraph does not apply to any vocational rehabilitation counselor who receives any payments directly from the individual customer receiving the counseling.

(C) Any person who engages solely in the preparation of résumés and cover letters, provided that the résumé writing service does not advertise or hold itself out as offering other job seeking or placement services and does not charge more than three hundred dollars ($300) for any résumé, cover letter, or combination of both to any single customer in any individual transaction.

(D) Any public educational institution.

(E) Any private educational institution established solely for educational purposes that, as a part of its curriculum, offers employment counseling to its student body and conforms to the requirements of Article 3.5 (commencing with Section 94760) of Chapter 7 of Part 59 of the Education Code.

(F) A psychologist or psychological corporation licensed pursuant to Chapter 6.6 (commencing with Section 2900) of Division 2 of the Business and Professions Code, providing psychological assessment, career or occupational counseling, or consultation and related professional services within his, her, or its scope of practice.

(G) An educational psychologist licensed pursuant to Article 5 (commencing with Section 4986) of Chapter 13 of Division 2 of the Business and Professions Code, providing counseling services within his or her scope of practice.

(c) "Job listing service" means any person who provides, offers, or represents it can or will provide any of the following services, for a fee or other valuable consideration to be paid, directly or indirectly, by the jobseeker in advance of, or contemporaneously with, performance of these services: matches jobseekers with employment opportunities, providing or offering to provide jobseekers lists of employers or lists of job openings or like publications, or preparing résumés or lists of jobseekers for distribution to potential employers.

(d) A "nurses' registry" as defined in subdivision (b) of Section 1812.524 is an employment agency. However, unless otherwise provided for in this title, a nurses' registry shall not be required to comply with Chapter 2 (commencing with Section 1812.503) regulating employment agencies but, instead, shall be required to comply with Chapter 7 (commencing with Section 1812.524).

(e) "Jobseeker" means a person seeking employment.

(f) "Employer" means any individual, company, partnership, association, corporation, agent, employee, or representative for whom or for which an employment agency or job listing service attempts to obtain an employee or to place a jobseeker.

(g) "Job order" means any written or oral instruction, direction, or permission granted by an employer or its agent to an employment agency or job listing service to refer jobseekers for a specified job.

(h) "Domestic agency" means any agency that provides, or attempts to provide, employment by placement of domestic help in private homes.

(i) "Deposit" means any money or valuable consideration received by an employment agency or job listing service from a jobseeker for referring the jobseeker to a position of employment prior to the jobseeker's acceptance of a position.

(j) "Fee" means:

(1) Any money or other valuable consideration paid, or promised to be paid, for services rendered or to be rendered by any person conducting an employment agency, employment counseling service, or job listing service under this title.

(2) Any money received by any person in excess of that which has been paid out by him or her for transportation, transfer of baggage, or board and lodging for any applicant for employment.

(k) "Registration fee" means any charge made, or attempted to be made, by an employment agency for registering or listing an applicant for employment, for letter writing, or any charge of a like nature made, or attempted to be made without having a bona fide order for the placement of the applicant in a position.

(*l*) "Person" means any individual, corporation, partnership, limited liability company, trust, association, or other organization.

(m) This section shall become operative on January 1, 1997. *(Added by Stats.1995, c. 758 (A.B.446), § 8.5, operative Jan. 1, 1997. Amended by Stats.2006, c. 538 (S.B.1852), § 52.)*

Cross References

Domestic workers, withholding tax on wages, see Unemployment Insurance Code § 13005.7.
Employment agencies, domestic workers, see Unemployment Insurance Code § 687.2.

§ 1812.502. Application of title; person charging employer exclusively; nonprofit corporation; labor organization; nursing, business, or vocational school; job listing service

(a) This title does not apply to any person who provides any of the services described in subdivision (a) of Section 1812.501 and who charges fees exclusively to employers for those services. The exemption from regulation provided by this subdivision does not apply to any person who provides babysitting or domestic employment for others. This subdivision does not apply to an employment counseling service as defined in subdivision (b) of Section 1812.501.

(b) This title shall not apply to any nonprofit corporation, organized for the purpose of economic adjustment, civic betterment, and the giving of vocational guidance and placement to its members, or others, including employment counseling services, when all of the following conditions exist:

(1) None of the directors, officers, or employees thereof receive any profit other than a nominal salary for services performed for the organization or corporation.

(2) No fee is charged for those services, though a voluntary contribution may be requested.

(3) Membership dues or fees charged are used solely for maintenance of the organization or corporation.

(c) Nothing in this title shall apply to a nonprofit corporation which has been formed in good faith for the promotion and advancement of the general professional interests of its members and which maintains a placement service principally engaged in securing employment for such members with the state or any county, city, district or other public agency under contracts providing employment for one year or longer, or any nonprofit corporation exempted by subdivision (b).

(d) This title shall not apply to a labor organization as defined in Section 1117 of the Labor Code, a newspaper of general circulation, bona fide newsletter, magazine, trade or professional journal, or other publication of general circulation, the main purpose of which is dissemination of news, reports, trade or professional information, or information not intended to assist in locating, securing, or procuring employment or assignments for others.

(e) As used in this title, "employment agency" or "agency" does not include a nursing school, business school, or vocational school, except that if such a school charges a fee for placement, the school shall be an employment agency within the meaning of this title.

(f)(1) A job listing service which meets the requirements specified in paragraph (2) or (3) shall not be subject to any of the following: Sections 1812.515, 1812.516, 1812.517, and 1812.518; subdivisions (a) and (b), and paragraph (3) of subdivision (c), and subdivision (d) of Section 1812.519; paragraph (2) of subdivision (b), and subdivisions (c), (d), (e), and (f) of Section 1812.520; and Section 1812.521.

(2) A job listing service shall be exempt pursuant to paragraph (1) if it complies with all of the following:

(A) Does not provide, offer, or imply the offer of, services related to employment.

(B) Does not offer or sell lists of employers or job openings to jobseekers on an in-person basis.

(C) Maintains records of all its advertisements, identified by date and publication, and the sources of information used for the preparation of lists of employers and job openings, from which can be determined the accuracy of any statistics regarding success rate or similar statistics used in its advertising, promotional materials, or oral or written statements to jobseekers.

(D) Identifies, on each list of employers and job openings, its general source of information for jobs included on that list when the source of information is a publication or other public record.

(E) Provides, at or before the time of delivery of the list, a prominent written statement to the jobseeker granting the jobseeker a right to return the list for an immediate refund of the purchase price during a stated period of time which expires not less than 10 days from the date of delivery of the list. The list shall be deemed returned upon delivery to the address from which it was obtained or upon deposit in the mail properly addressed to that address, with postage prepaid.

(3) A job listing service shall be exempt pursuant to paragraph (1) if it complies with all of the following:

(A) A majority interest in the job listing service is owned by one or more colleges or universities, or alumni associations affiliated therewith, and each college or university is accredited by both (i) an accrediting agency recognized as such by the United States Department of Education and (ii) a member organization of the Council of Postsecondary Accreditation.

(B) The job listing service provides services related to employment exclusively for jobseekers who are the alumni of colleges or universities specified in subparagraph (A).

(C) The job listing service does not require, as a condition to receiving employment services, that the applicant have completed courses or examinations beyond the requirements for graduation from the college or university specified in subparagraph (A).

(D) More than 50 percent of the annual revenues received by the job listing service are derived from paid subscriptions of prospective employers. *(Added by Stats.1989, c. 704, § 2. Amended by Stats.1990, c. 1256 (A.B.2649), § 4.)*

Cross References
Employment agency or agency defined, see Civil Code § 1812.501.

CHAPTER 2. EMPLOYMENT AGENCIES

Section
1812.503. Bond; deposit in lieu of bond.
1812.504. Contract.
1812.505. Fees; schedule; payment terms; notice; change; confession of judgment, note, or wage assignment as payment; deposit; termination of employment; interagency disputes; splitting; employer interest in agency.
1812.506. Fees; deposit; return; delay; notice; permanent employment; termination of employment; refusal to refund.
1812.507. Job order; referring jobseeker.
1812.508. False or misleading representations; advertisements; name, address, and telephone number; designation in name; fee; records.
1812.509. Employment of minors; notification required to be given to jobseekers; necessity of personal interview.
1812.5093. Child care provider referral; disclosure.
1812.5095. Domestic worker; relationship with employment agency; agency referral authority and duties.

§ 1812.503. Bond; deposit in lieu of bond

(a) Every employment agency subject to this title shall maintain a bond issued by a surety company admitted to do business in this state. The principal sum of the bond shall be three thousand dollars ($3,000). A copy of the bond shall be filed with the Secretary of State.

(b) The bond required by this section shall be in favor of, and payable to, the people of the State of California and shall be conditioned that the person obtaining the bond will comply with this title and will pay all sums due any individual or group of individuals when the person or his or her representative, agent, or employee has received those sums. The bond shall be for the benefit of any person or persons damaged by any violation of this title or by fraud, dishonesty, misstatement, misrepresentation, deceit, unlawful acts or omissions, or failure to provide the services of the employment agency in performance of the contract with the jobseeker, by the employment agency or its agents, representatives, or employees while acting within the scope of their employment.

(c)(1) No employment agency shall conduct any business without having a current surety bond in the amount prescribed by this title and filing a copy of the bond with the Secretary of State.

(2) Thirty days prior to the cancellation or termination of any surety bond required by this section, the surety shall send a written notice of that cancellation or termination to both the employment agency and the Secretary of State, identifying the bond and the date of cancellation or termination.

(3) If any employment agency fails to obtain a new bond and file a copy of that bond with the Secretary of State by the effective date of the cancellation or termination of the former bond, the employment agency shall cease to conduct any business unless and until a new surety bond is obtained and a copy of that bond is filed with the Secretary of State.

(d) When a deposit has been made in lieu of the bond pursuant to Section 995.710 of the Code of Civil Procedure, the person asserting a claim against the deposit shall, in lieu of Section 996.430 of the Code of Civil Procedure, establish the claim by furnishing evidence to the Secretary of State of a money judgment entered by a court together with evidence that the claimant is a person described in subdivision (b).

(e) When a claimant has established the claim with the Secretary of State, the Secretary of State shall review and approve the claim and enter the date of approval thereon. The claim shall be designated an "approved claim."

(f) When the first claim against a particular deposit has been approved, it shall not be paid until the expiration of a period of 240 days after the date of its approval by the Secretary of State. Subsequent claims that are approved by the Secretary of State within the same 240–day period shall similarly not be paid until the expiration of the 240–day period. Upon the expiration of the 240–day period, the Secretary of State shall pay all approved claims from that 240–day period in full unless the deposit is insufficient, in which case each approved claim shall be paid a pro rata share of the deposit.

(g) When the Secretary of State approves the first claim against a particular deposit after the expiration of a 240–day period, the date of approval of that claim shall begin a new 240–day period to which subdivision (f) shall apply with respect to any amount remaining in the deposit.

(h) After a deposit is exhausted, no further claims shall be paid by the Secretary of State. Claimants who have had their claims paid in full or in part pursuant to subdivision (f) or (g) shall not be required to return funds received from the deposit for the benefit of other claimants.

(i) When a deposit has been made in lieu of a bond, the amount of the deposit shall not be subject to attachment, garnishment, or execution with respect to an action or judgment against the employment agency, other than as to an amount as no longer needed or required for the purpose of this title that would otherwise be returned to the employment agency by the Secretary of State.

(j) The Secretary of State shall retain a cash deposit for two years from the date the Secretary of State receives written notification from the assignor of the deposit that the assignor has ceased to engage in the business of an employment agency or has filed a bond pursuant to subdivision (a), provided that there are no outstanding claims against the deposit. This written notice shall include all of the following: (1) name, address, and telephone number of the assignor; (2) name, address, and telephone number of the bank at which the deposit is located; (3) account number of the deposit; and (4) a statement whether the assignor is ceasing to engage in the business of an employment agency or has filed a bond with the Secretary of State. The Secretary of State shall forward an acknowledgment of receipt of the written notice to the assignor at the address indicated therein, specifying the date of receipt of the written notice and anticipated date of release of the deposit, provided there are no outstanding claims against the deposit.

(k) A judge of a superior court may order the return of the deposit prior to the expiration of two years upon evidence satisfactory to the judge that there are no outstanding claims against the deposit or order the Secretary of State to retain the deposit for a sufficient period beyond the two years pursuant to subdivision (j) to resolve outstanding claims against the deposit account.

(l) The Secretary of State shall charge a filing fee not to exceed the cost of filing the bond or deposit filed in lieu of a bond as set forth in Section 995.710 of the Code of Civil Procedure.

(m) The Secretary of State shall enforce the provisions of this chapter that govern the filing and maintenance of bonds and deposits in lieu of bonds. *(Added by Stats.1989, c. 704, § 2. Amended by Stats.1996, c. 633 (S.B.1978), § 11; Stats. 1998, c. 829 (S.B.1652), § 11; Stats.2002, c. 784 (S.B.1316), § 15.)*

Cross References

Deposit defined, see Civil Code § 1812.501.
Employment agency or agency defined, see Civil Code § 1812.501.
Fee defined, see Civil Code § 1812.501.
Jobseeker defined, see Civil Code § 1812.501.
Person defined, see Civil Code § 1812.501.

§ 1812.504. Contract

(a) Every employment agency shall give a written contract to every jobseeker from whom a fee or deposit is to be received, whether directly or indirectly. The original of the contract shall be given to the jobseeker at the time the jobseeker signs the contract and before the employment agency accepts any fee or deposit or the jobseeker becomes obligated to pay any such fee or deposit. The contract shall contain all of the following:

(1) The name, address, and telephone number of the employment agency, and, if the employment agency has more than one office or location, the address and telephone number of the principal office or location providing services to the jobseeker.

(2) The name and address of the person giving the order for help, the date and consecutive number of the receipt of the order by the agency, and its manner of transmission.

(3) The name of the jobseeker, the name and address of the person to whom the jobseeker is sent for employment, and the address where the jobseeker is to report for employment.

(4) The date and consecutive number of the contract.

(5) The amount of the fee to be charged and to be collected from the jobseeker, including a statement that if the employment is terminated, the fee may not exceed gross earnings of the jobseeker in that employment, and the amount of the fee paid or advanced by the prospective employer and by whom paid or advanced.

(6) The kind of work or employment.

(7) The daily hours of work; the wages or salary, including any consideration or privilege; the benefits; and any other conditions of employment.

(8) If any labor trouble exists at the place of employment, that fact shall be stated in the contract.

(9) A contract expiration date which shall not be later than 180 days from the date of the referral or signing of the contract, whichever occurs first; however, a domestic agency operating as a registry may enter into a continuing contract subject to termination by written notice by either the domestic worker or the agency.

(10) Any other term, condition, or understanding agreed upon between the agency and the jobseeker.

(11) The following statement, with the caption in type no smaller than 10-point boldfaced type and the remainder in a size no smaller than that generally used throughout the contract, and in full capitals, boldface, or italics:

RIGHT TO REFUND

"If you pay all or any portion of a fee and fail to accept employment, the employment agency shall, upon your request, return the amount paid to you within 48 hours after your request for a refund.

"If you leave employment for just cause or are discharged for reasons other than misconduct connected with your work within 90 days from the starting date of employment, the agency shall reduce your fee to that payable for temporary employment and shall refund any excess paid within 10 days of your request for a refund.

"No fee larger than that for temporary employment may be charged to you for employment lasting 90 days or less unless the agency's fee schedules, contracts, and agreements provide for a further charge if you leave employment without just cause or are discharged for misconduct in connection with your work.

"If any refund due is not made within the time limits set forth above, the employment agency shall pay you an additional sum equal to the amount of the refund."

(b) All contracts shall be dated and shall be made and numbered consecutively, both copies to be signed by the jobseeker and the person acting for the employment agency. The original shall be given to the jobseeker and one copy shall be kept on file at the employment agency.

(c) The full agreement between the parties shall be contained in a single document containing those elements set forth in this section.

(d) When a referral is made by telephone the agency shall execute the contract or receipt in triplicate and shall mail the original and duplicate to the jobseeker on the day the referral is made, with instructions that they be signed by the jobseeker and the duplicate returned to the agency. The date of mailing the contract or receipt to the jobseeker shall be entered thereon by the agency. The same contract or receipt shall not be used for more than one referral.

(e) For purposes of this section, a "domestic agency operating as a registry" means a domestic agency that engages in the business of obtaining and filling commitments for domestic help. (Added by Stats.1989, c. 704, § 2. Amended by Stats.1996, c. 102 (S.B.2030), § 1.)

Cross References
Civil actions and proceedings, false or misleading representation voiding contract, see Civil Code § 1812.523.
Deposit defined, see Civil Code § 1812.501.
Domestic agency defined, see Civil Code § 1812.501.
Employer defined, see Civil Code § 1812.501.
Employment agency or agency defined, see Civil Code § 1812.501.
Fee defined, see Civil Code § 1812.501.
Jobseeker defined, see Civil Code § 1812.501.
Person defined, see Civil Code § 1812.501.

§ 1812.505. Fees; schedule; payment terms; notice; change; confession of judgment, note, or wage assignment as payment; deposit; termination of employment; interagency disputes; splitting; employer interest in agency

(a)(1) An employment agency shall provide a copy of the agency's jobseeker fee schedule and payment terms to any jobseeker from whom a fee or deposit is to be received, prior to the jobseeker being interviewed by a counselor. The jobseeker fee schedule shall indicate the percentage of both the projected annual and first month's total gross earnings represented by those fees.

(2) In the schedule, the various employments or salary ranges by which the fee is to be computed or determined shall be classified, and in each class the maximum fee shall be fixed and shall include the charges of every kind rendered by the agency in each case or transaction on behalf of the prospective employee. Changes in the schedule may be made, but no change shall become effective until posted for not less than seven days in a conspicuous place in the agency.

(3) A copy of the schedule in effect shall be kept posted in the employment agency in a conspicuous place, and the posted schedule and the changes therein shall be in lettering or printing of not less than standard pica capitals. The date of the taking effect of the schedule and of each change therein shall appear on the posted copies.

(4) A copy of all fee schedules, and of all changes therein, shall be kept on file at the employment agency, retrospectively, for a period of one year.

(b) No fee charged or collected shall be in excess of the fee as scheduled.

(c) No employment agency shall accept, directly or indirectly, a registration fee of any kind.

(d) No employment agency may take from a jobseeker a confession of judgment, a promissory note or notes, or an assignment of wages to cover its fees.

(e) The employment agency shall give a receipt to every jobseeker from whom a deposit is received. No other deposit or prepayment of any kind may be required by an agency. If the jobseeker accepts employment, the deposit shall be applied to the fee to be paid by the jobseeker.

(f)(1) If a jobseeker leaves employment for just cause or is discharged for reasons other than misconduct connected with the jobseeker's work within 90 days from the starting date of employment, the agency shall reduce the fee payable by the jobseeker to that payable for temporary employment under subdivision (g) and shall refund any fee paid in excess of that amount.

(2) No charge may be made to or obligation to pay incurred by any jobseeker beyond that authorized by subdivision (g) for employment lasting 90 days or less, unless the agency's fee schedules, contracts, and agreements specifically provide for a further charge if the jobseeker leaves employment without just cause or is discharged for misconduct in connection with his or her work, and then only if lack of just cause or misconduct exists. Otherwise, the agency shall retain or charge only the fee for temporary employment for any employment lasting 90 days or less from the starting date of employment.

(3) Notwithstanding subdivision (a) and this subdivision, in no instance in which the employment accepted is subsequently terminated shall the fee charged or obligation to pay incurred by a jobseeker be greater than the total gross earnings of the jobseeker in that employment. This provision shall be stated in all agency contracts issued pursuant to Section 1812.504.

(g) The fee payable by the jobseeker for temporary employment shall not exceed $1/90$ of the fee for permanent employment for each consecutive calendar day during the period that the jobseeker is employed or compensated as though employed.

(h)(1) If a jobseeker accepts employment in which the jobseeker is to be paid on the basis of straight commissions, or a drawing account against commissions, or either a drawing account or salary plus commissions, the fee payable by the jobseeker may be predicated upon the projected total gross earnings during the first year of employment as estimated by the employer.

(2) Upon the conclusion of a jobseeker's first 12 months of employment, a computation of his or her actual total gross earnings may be provided by the jobseeker to the agency, and, predicated upon appropriate proof of earnings, an

adjustment in the fee shall be made in which either the agency shall refund to the jobseeker any excess fee paid by him or her or the jobseeker shall pay to the agency any deficiency thereon.

(3) If the jobseeker's employment is terminated prior to the conclusion of the first 12 months of employment, the actual total gross earnings of the jobseeker for the period of employment shall be projected to 12 months on a pro rata basis as though the jobseeker had been employed for the entire period of 12 months, and a computation shall be made thereon. The fee paid or payable by the jobseeker shall be predicated upon that computation as though the jobseeker had been so employed.

(i) If an employment agency sends a jobseeker for employment and the jobseeker accepts employment other than that position specified in the bona fide order for employment to which the jobseeker was sent, but with the same employer, then the agency shall be entitled to a fee for the employment of the jobseeker, payable by the jobseeker, computed under the terms of the fee schedule in effect in the agency at the time of referral, provided that the jobseeker accepts employment within 180 days of the date of referral. The expiration date of the referral shall be stated in the contract.

In interagency disputes concerning the earning of a fee for placement of a jobseeker, the fee shall be earned by the agency responsible for the jobseeker being placed. A reasonable effort shall be made by the billing agency that it is entitled to the fee. The jobseeker shall be responsible for only one full fee for any single placement, and that fact shall be so stated in the contract.

(j)(1) No employment agency shall divide fees with an employer, an agent, or other employee of an employer or person to whom help is furnished.

(2) No employment agency shall charge any jobseeker a fee for accepting employment with such employment agency or any subsidiary of that agency.

(3) No employment agency shall charge any jobseeker a fee when help is furnished to an employer, an agent, any employee of an employer, a member, or person who has a financial interest in the employment agency. *(Added by Stats.1989, c. 704, § 2.)*

Cross References

Deposit defined, see Civil Code § 1812.501.
Employer defined, see Civil Code § 1812.501.
Employment agency or agency defined, see Civil Code § 1812.501.
Farm labor contractors, see Labor Code § 1698.8.
Fee defined, see Civil Code § 1812.501.
Jobseeker defined, see Civil Code § 1812.501.
Person defined, see Civil Code § 1812.501.
Registration fee defined, see Civil Code § 1812.501.

§ 1812.506. Fees; deposit; return; delay; notice; permanent employment; termination of employment; refusal to refund

(a) If a jobseeker paying or becoming obligated to pay a fee, or making a deposit on a fee for placement fails to accept employment, the employment agency shall, upon request by the jobseeker, repay the amount of the deposit or fee to the jobseeker. Unless the deposit is returned within 48 hours after request, the employment agency shall pay to the jobseeker an additional sum equal to the amount of the deposit. A notice to this effect shall be inserted in all contracts between the agency and the jobseeker, and in all receipts given to the jobseeker for cash payment in advance of employment, and in the schedule of fees posted in the office of the agency.

(b)(1) All employment provided by any employment agency to any jobseeker from whom a fee is to be received shall be considered permanent only if it lasts longer than 90 days. If a jobseeker leaves the job or is discharged within the first 90 days of employment, the agency shall make a refund or reduction of the fee to the temporary fee amount unless the agency's fee schedules, contracts, and agreements specifically provide for a further charge if the jobseeker leaves employment without just cause or is discharged for misconduct in connection with his or her work.

(2) "Just cause" or "discharge for reasons other than misconduct" includes, but is not limited to, the following:

(A) Wages or salary less than that agreed upon between the jobseeker and the employer.

(B) Receiving a payroll check which is not honored by the bank upon which it was drawn.

(C) Working hours, working days, or working shifts significantly different than those agreed upon between the jobseeker and the employer.

(D) Receiving a work assignment, subsequent to accepting the job, which is substantially different from that agreed upon between the jobseeker and the employer.

(E) Being assigned to a job location different from that which was agreed upon between the jobseeker and the employer.

(F) The jobseeker's lack of physical ability to perform duties connected with the position agreed upon between the jobseeker and the employer unless the provisions of subparagraph (E) of paragraph (3) apply.

(G) A lockout or strike causing loss of pay.

(H) The jobseeker's lack of physical ability to perform duties connected with the position unless the provisions of subparagraph (E) of paragraph (3) apply.

(J)[1] The jobseeker's entry into active service in the armed forces.

(K) Physical or economic destruction of the business.

(L) The death of the jobseeker (any refund in that case shall be paid to the estate of the jobseeker).

(3) "Lack of just cause" or a discharge for "misconduct" includes, but is not limited, to:

(A) Abandonment of the job by the jobseeker.

(B) Conviction of the jobseeker, subsequent to employment, of a crime when conviction temporarily or permanently prevents the jobseeker from fulfilling the terms of employment.

(C) Willful violation of lawful company policies or rules by the jobseeker.

(D) Willful failure to perform lawful duties appropriate to employment by the jobseeker.

(E) Acts of the jobseeker constituting misrepresentation or withholding of information directly related to education, work experience, responsibility, physical ability, or training, that would have caused the employer to refuse employment.

(c)(1) Except as otherwise provided in subdivision (a), a refund when due shall be made within 10 working days after request therefor from the jobseeker.

(2) Alternatively, if the decision of the agency is not to make a refund, the agency shall notify the jobseeker in writing, within the 10-day working period specified in paragraph (1), as to the specific reasons why the refund is not being made.

(3) If the agency fails to properly notify the jobseeker pursuant to paragraph (2) or fails to tender a refund within the time allowed, the agency shall be liable to the jobseeker in the amount of an additional sum equal to the amount of the refund. *(Added by Stats.1989, c. 704, § 2.)*

[1] No (I) in enrolled copy.

Cross References

Deposit defined, see Civil Code § 1812.501.
Employer defined, see Civil Code § 1812.501.
Employment agency or agency defined, see Civil Code § 1812.501.
Fee defined, see Civil Code § 1812.501.
Jobseeker defined, see Civil Code § 1812.501.

§ 1812.507. Job order; referring jobseeker

(a) No employment agency shall accept a fee from any jobseeker, or send any jobseeker for employment, without having obtained, orally or in writing, a bona fide job order for employment.

(b) An agency shall identify itself as an employment agency to the employer in all instances in which it contacts an employer for the purpose of soliciting a job order. All job orders shall be recorded in writing. A job order for employment shall be considered to have been given by an employer to an employment agency under the following conditions:

(1) The employer, or his or her agent, orally or in writing, registers a request or gives permission that the agency recruit or refer jobseekers who meet the employer's stated job specifications and the employer furnishes such information as required by subdivision (a) of Section 1812.504. A job order is valid for the referral of any qualified jobseeker until it is filled or canceled by the employer, and may serve as the basis for agency advertising. The agency is required to recontact the employer within 30 days to ensure that the position is still vacant prior to any additional advertising or referral of jobseekers.

(2) When an agency has brought the qualifications of a specific jobseeker to the attention of an employer and the employer has expressed interest in that jobseeker either by agreeing to interview the jobseeker, or by requesting that the agency furnish him or her with the jobseeker's resumé or other written history or data, or by initiating direct contact with the jobseeker as a result of information furnished by the agency, that action by the employer shall constitute a job order only for the jobseeker discussed and is not valid for advertisement, unless the contact by the agency resulted in a job order for a specific position sufficient under paragraph (1). If the employer has no position open but merely wishes to explore the possible employment of the jobseeker and the jobseeker is to be responsible for the placement fee, that fact shall be indicated on the jobseeker's referral contract.

(c) No employment agency shall refer a jobseeker to a job knowing or having reason to know that:

(1) The job does not exist or the jobseeker is not qualified for the job.

(2) The job has been described or advertised by or on behalf of the agency in a false, misleading, or deceptive manner.

(3) The agency has not obtained written or oral permission to list the job from the employer or an authorized agent of the employer. *(Added by Stats.1989, c. 704, § 2.)*

Cross References

Employer defined, see Civil Code § 1812.501.
Employment agency or agency defined, see Civil Code § 1812.501.
Fee defined, see Civil Code § 1812.501.
Job order defined, see Civil Code § 1812.501.
Jobseeker defined, see Civil Code § 1812.501.

§ 1812.508. False or misleading representations; advertisements; name, address, and telephone number; designation in name; fee; records

(a) No employment agency shall make, or cause to be made, any false, misleading, or deceptive advertisements or representations concerning the services that the agency will provide to jobseekers.

(b)(1) No employment agency shall publish or cause to be published any false, fraudulent, or misleading information, representation, notice, or advertisements.

(2) All advertisements of an employment agency shall contain the correct name of the employment agency and one of the following:

(A) The street address of the agency's place of business.

(B) The correct telephone number of the agency at its place of business.

(3) Every employment agency, except a nurses' registry shall use, as part of its name, either the designation "agency" or "personnel service."

(4) No employment agency shall give any false information or make any false promises or representations concerning an engagement or employment to any jobseeker who registers or applies for an engagement or employment or help.

(5) No employment agency shall, by its name, advertisement, or any other representation, represent itself to be a home health agency, as defined by subdivision (a) of Section 1727 of the Health and Safety Code, or to perform the services of a home health agency. An employment agency shall provide a written disclosure to each individual receiving nursing services in his or her place of residence stating that it does not perform the services of a home health agency and clearly describing that it is an employment agency only and that any complaints against personnel providing nursing services who are neither licensed nor certified shall be submitted to the local district attorney, complaints against certified nursing assistants and certified home health aides providing nursing services shall be submitted to the local

district attorney and the State Department of Health Services, and complaints against licensed personnel providing nursing services shall be submitted to the local district attorney and the Department of Consumer Affairs. The address and telephone number of each agency and board to which complaints are required to be submitted shall be provided by the employment agency to all patients prior to the time they are under the care of any nursing services personnel.

(6) Any person may refer complaints concerning employment agencies to the proper law enforcement agency for action.

(c)(1) Where an employment agency job advertisement includes a description of the placement fee associated with the advertised job, the employment agency shall describe the placement fee in a manner which either clearly indicates whether or not a jobseeker shall be responsible for the placement fee or in accordance with the following terms and provisions:

(A) "FEE" means the jobseeker pays the entire placement fee.

(B) "NO FEE" means the jobseeker pays no portion of the placement fee.

(2) Where "NO FEE" jobs are advertised and the agency also administers placement for "FEE" jobs, the advertisement shall state "ALSO FEE JOBS" in type of equal size, prominence, and boldness as "NO FEE" notations.

(3) A group job advertisement which includes a description of the placement fee shall describe the placement fee either separately for each job, or by use of the proper term as a heading under which all applicable jobs shall be listed. All those headings shall be in type and of the same size, prominence, and boldness.

(d) Special requirements not usually associated with a job shall be specified in any advertisement. When the location of the position advertised is more than 50 miles from the employment agency office responsible for the advertisement, it shall state either the location or that the job is "nonlocal." Special benefits of the job, if advertised, shall be specifically described and substitute terms or symbols such as "extras" or "+" shall not be sufficient.

(e) An advertised salary shall be based upon the starting salary contained in the job order. An advertised range of starting salaries shall be specified by preceding the minimum salary and maximum salary by the terms "from" and "to" respectively. When the job order contains only the maximum amount of a salary range, that advertised salary shall be preceded by the word "to." If a maximum salary is dependent upon the jobseeker's experience, the advertised salary may be described by listing the minimum salary and the term "up Depending on Experience" or "up D.O.E." The words "open" and "negotiable" or words or symbols of like import shall not be used as a substitute for the salary. If an advertised salary is based in whole or in part on commissions, that fact shall be indicated in the advertisement.

(f) All employment agencies shall maintain a record of all advertised jobs, correlated to show the date and the publication in which the advertisement appeared and the job order number of each job advertised, retrospectively for a period of one year. *(Added by Stats.1989, c. 704, § 2. Amended by Stats.1990, c. 761 (A.B.3924), § 1.)*

Cross References

Department of Health Care Services, generally, see Health and Safety Code § 100100 et seq.
Employment agency or agency defined, see Civil Code § 1812.501.
Fee defined, see Civil Code § 1812.501.
Job order defined, see Civil Code § 1812.501.
Jobseeker defined, see Civil Code § 1812.501.
Nurses' registry as employment agency, required compliance, see Civil Code § 1812.501.
Person defined, see Civil Code § 1812.501.
Requirements of record keeping, separation from records of other business, see Civil Code § 1812.522.

§ 1812.509. Employment of minors; notification required to be given to jobseekers; necessity of personal interview

(a) No employment agency shall, when employment would be in violation of Chapter 1 (commencing with Section 1171) of Part 4 of Division 2 of the Labor Code or Part 27 (commencing with Section 48000) of the Education Code, accept any application for employment made by, or on behalf of, any minor, or place or assist in placing any minor in that employment.

(b) Every employment agency shall notify each jobseeker before sending the jobseeker in response to a request for employment whether a labor contract is in existence at the establishment to which the jobseeker is being sent, and whether union membership is required.

(c) No employment agency shall send a jobseeker to any place where a strike, lockout, or other labor trouble exists without notifying the jobseeker of that fact and shall in addition thereto enter a statement of those conditions upon the contract or receipt given to the jobseeker.

(d) No babysitting, domestic, or other employment agency which procures babysitting or domestic employment for employers shall refer babysitters or domestics for any employment without first conducting a personal interview of the jobseeker and making a reasonable effort to verify the experience or training of the jobseeker.

(e) No employment agency that procures temporary employment for long-term health care employers shall refer certified nurse assistants or licensed nursing staff as defined in Section 1812.540, for any employment without first conducting a personal interview of the individual, verifying the experience, training, and references of the individual, and verifying that the individual is in good standing with the appropriate licensing or certification board, including verification that the individual has successfully secured a criminal record clearance. *(Added by Stats.1989, c. 704, § 2. Amended by Stats.1990, c. 1256 (A.B.2649), § 5; Stats.2001, c. 326 (A.B.1643), § 1.)*

Cross References

Employer defined, see Civil Code § 1812.501.
Employment agency or agency defined, see Civil Code § 1812.501.
Jobseeker defined, see Civil Code § 1812.501.

§ 1812.5093. Child care provider referral; disclosure

(a) Every employment agency that refers a child care provider to an employer who is not required to be a licensed

§ 1812.5093

child day care facility pursuant to Section 1596.792 of the Health and Safety Code shall provide the employer with all the following:

(1) A description of the child care provider trustline registry established pursuant to Chapter 3.35 (commencing with Section 1596.60) of Division 2 of the Health and Safety Code that provides criminal history checks on child care providers.

(2) An explanation of how an employer may obtain more information about the child care provider trustline registry.

(3) A statement that an employment agency is prohibited by law from placing a child care provider unless the provider is a trustline applicant or a registered child care provider.

(4) An explanation of how the employer may verify the prospective child care provider's trustline registry registration.

(b) Receipt of the information required to be provided pursuant to subdivision (a) shall be verified in writing by the employer. *(Added by Stats.1998, c. 287 (A.B.2001), § 1.)*

Cross References

Child care provider to parents who are not required to be a licensed facility shall not make placement of a child care provider who is not a trustline applicant or a registered child care provider, see Health and Safety Code § 1596.65.
Employer defined, see Civil Code § 1812.501.
Employment agency or agency defined, see Civil Code § 1812.501.

§ 1812.5095. Domestic worker; relationship with employment agency; agency referral authority and duties

(a) For purposes of this section, the term "employment agency" means an employment agency, as defined in paragraph (3) of subdivision (a) of Section 1812.501, or a domestic agency, as defined in subdivision (h) of Section 1812.501.

(b) An employment agency is not the employer of a domestic worker for whom it procures, offers, refers, provides, or attempts to provide work, if all of the following factors characterize the nature of the relationship between the employment agency and the domestic worker for whom the agency procures, offers, refers, provides, or attempts to provide domestic work:

(1) There is a signed contract or agreement between the employment agency and the domestic worker that contains, at a minimum, provisions that specify all of the following:

(A) That the employment agency shall assist the domestic worker in securing work.

(B) How the employment agency's referral fee shall be paid.

(C) That the domestic worker is free to sign an agreement with other employment agencies and to perform domestic work for persons not referred by the employment agency.

(2) The domestic worker informs the employment agency of any restrictions on hours, location, conditions, or type of work he or she will accept and the domestic worker is free to select or reject any work opportunity procured, offered, referred, or provided by the employment agency.

(3) The domestic worker is free to renegotiate with the person hiring him or her the amount proposed to be paid for the work.

(4) The domestic worker does not receive any training from the employment agency with respect to the performance of domestic work. However, an employment agency may provide a voluntary orientation session in which the relationship between the employment agency and the domestic worker, including the employment agency's administrative and operating procedures, and the provisions of the contract or agreement between the employment agency and the domestic worker are explained.

(5) The domestic worker performs domestic work without any direction, control, or supervision exercised by the employment agency with respect to the manner and means of performing the domestic work. An employment agency shall not be deemed to be exercising direction, control, or supervision when it takes any of the following actions:

(A) Informs the domestic worker about the services to be provided and the conditions of work specified by the person seeking to hire a domestic worker.

(B) Contacts the person who has hired the domestic worker to determine whether that person is satisfied with the agency's referral service.

(C) Informs the domestic worker of the time during which new referrals are available.

(D) Requests the domestic worker to inform the employment agency if the domestic worker is unable to perform the work accepted.

(6) The employment agency does not provide tools, supplies, or equipment necessary to perform the domestic work.

(7) The domestic worker is not obligated to pay the employment agency's referral fee, and the employment agency is not obligated to pay the domestic worker if the person for whom the services were performed fails or refuses to pay for the domestic work.

(8) Payments for domestic services are made directly to either the domestic worker or to the employment agency. Payments made directly to the employment agency shall be deposited into a trust account until payment can be made to the domestic worker.

(9) The relationship between a domestic worker and the person for whom the domestic worker performs services may only be terminated by either of those parties and not by the employment agency that referred the domestic worker. However, an employment agency may decline to make additional referrals to a particular domestic worker, and the domestic worker may decline to accept a particular referral.

(c) The fee charged by an employment agency for its services shall be reasonable, negotiable, and based on a fixed percentage of the job cost.

(d) An employment agency referring a domestic worker to a job shall inform that domestic worker, in writing, on or before the signing of the contract pursuant to paragraph (1) of subdivision (b), that the domestic worker may be obligated to obtain business permits or licenses, where required by any state or local law, ordinance, or regulation, and that he or she is not eligible for unemployment insurance, state disability insurance, social security, or workers' compensation benefits through an employment agency complying with subdivision (b). The employment agency referring a domestic worker shall also inform that domestic worker, if the domestic worker is self-employed, that he or she is required to pay self-employment tax, state tax, and federal income taxes.

(e) An employment agency referring a domestic worker to a job shall verify the worker's legal status or authorization to work prior to providing referral services in accordance with procedures established under federal law.

(f) An employment agency referring a domestic worker to a job shall orally communicate to the person seeking domestic services the disclosure set forth below prior to the referral of the domestic worker the following disclosure statement:

"(Name of agency) is not the employer of the domestic worker it referred to you. Depending on your arrangement with the domestic worker, you may have employer responsibilities."

Within three business days after the employment agency refers a domestic worker to the person seeking domestic services, the following statement printed in not less than 10-point type shall be mailed to the person seeking domestic services:

"(Name of agency) is not the employer of the domestic worker it referred to you. The domestic worker may be your employee or an independent contractor depending on the relationship you have with him or her. If you direct and control the manner and means by which the domestic worker performs his or her work you may have employer responsibilities, including employment taxes and workers' compensation, under state and federal law. For additional information contact your local Employment Development Department and the Internal Revenue Service."

(g) An employment agency referring a domestic worker to a job shall not specify that a worker is self-employed or an independent contractor in any notice, advertisement, or brochure provided to either the worker or the customer.

(h) Every employment agency referring a domestic worker to a job and who is not the employer of the domestic worker being referred, shall in any paid telephone directory advertisement or any other promotional literature or advertising distributed or placed by such an employment agency, on or after January 1, 1995, insert the following statement, in no less than 6-point type which shall be in print which contrasts with the background of the advertisement so as to be easily legible:

"(Name of agency) is a referral agency."

(i) An employment agency may not refer, in its advertising, soliciting, or other presentments to the public, to any bond required to be filed pursuant to this chapter.

(j) An employment agency may not refer, in its advertising, soliciting, or other presentments to the public, to any licensure acquired by the agency.

(k) Any violation of this section with the intent to directly or indirectly mislead the public on the nature of services provided by an employment agency shall constitute unfair competition which includes any unlawful, unfair, or fraudulent business acts or practices and unfair, deceptive, untrue, or misleading advertising. Any person or entity that engages in unfair competition shall be liable for a civil penalty not to exceed two thousand five hundred dollars ($2,500) for each violation. *(Added by Stats.1993, c. 1275 (A.B.1370), § 1. Amended by Stats.1994, c. 1081 (S.B.1418), § 1.)*

Cross References

Employment agency or agency defined, see Civil Code § 1812.501.
Workers' compensation, see Labor Code § 3200 et seq.

CHAPTER 3. EMPLOYMENT COUNSELING SERVICES

Section
1812.510. Bond; deposit in lieu of bond.
1812.511. Contract; cancellation.
1812.512. Fees; schedule; payment terms; notice; change; confession of judgment, note, or wage assignment as payment.
1812.513. False or misleading representations; advertisements; name, address, and telephone number; guarantee; records.

§ 1812.510. Bond; deposit in lieu of bond

(a) Every employment counseling service subject to this title shall maintain a bond issued by a surety company admitted to do business in this state. The principal sum of the bond shall be ten thousand dollars ($10,000). A copy of the bond shall be filed with the Secretary of State.

(b) The bond required by this section shall be in favor of, and payable to, the people of the State of California, and shall be conditioned that the person obtaining the bond will comply with this title and will pay all sums due any individual or group of individuals when the person or his or her representative, agent, or employee has received those sums. The bond shall be for the benefit of any person or persons damaged by any violation of this title or by fraud, dishonesty, misstatement, misrepresentation, deceit, unlawful acts or omissions, or failure to provide the services of the employment counseling service in performance of the contract with the customer by the employment counseling service or its agents, representatives, or employees while acting within the scope of their employment.

(c)(1) No employment counseling service shall conduct any business without having a current surety bond in the amount prescribed by this title and filing a copy of the bond with the Secretary of State.

(2) Thirty days prior to the cancellation or termination of any surety bond required by this section, the surety shall send a written notice of that cancellation or termination to both the employment counseling service and the Secretary of State, identifying the bond and the date of cancellation or termination.

(3) If any employment counseling service fails to obtain a new bond and file a copy of that bond with the Secretary of State by the effective date of the cancellation or termination of the former bond, the employment counseling service shall cease to conduct any business unless and until a new surety bond is obtained and a copy of that bond is filed with the Secretary of State.

§ 1812.510

(d) When a deposit has been made in lieu of the bond pursuant to Section 995.710 of the Code of Civil Procedure, the person asserting a claim against the deposit shall, in lieu of Section 996.430 of the Code of Civil Procedure, establish the claim by furnishing evidence to the Secretary of State of a money judgment entered by a court together with evidence that the claimant is a person described in subdivision (b).

(e) When a person has established the claim with the Secretary of State, the Secretary of State shall immediately review and approve the claim and enter the date of approval on the claim. The claim shall be designated an "approved claim."

(f) When the first claim against a particular deposit has been approved, it shall not be paid until the expiration of a period of 240 days after the date of its approval by the Secretary of State. Subsequent claims that are approved by the Secretary of State within the same 240-day period shall similarly not be paid until the expiration of the 240-day period. Upon the expiration of the 240-day period, the Secretary of State shall pay all approved claims from that 240-day period in full unless the deposit is insufficient, in which case each approved claim shall be paid a pro rata share of the deposit.

(g) When the Secretary of State approves the first claim against a particular deposit account after the expiration of the 240-day period, the date of approval of that claim shall begin a new 240-day period to which subdivision (f) shall apply with respect to the amount remaining in the deposit account.

(h) After a deposit account is exhausted, no further claims shall be paid by the Secretary of State. Claimants who have had their claims paid in full or in part pursuant to subdivisions (f) and (g) shall not be required to return funds received from the deposit for the benefit of other claimants.

(i) When a deposit has been made in lieu of a bond, the amount of the deposit shall not be subject to attachment, garnishment, or execution with respect to an action or judgment against the employment counseling service, other than as to an amount as no longer needed or required for the purpose of this title that would otherwise be returned to the employment counseling service by the Secretary of State.

(j) The Secretary of State shall retain a cash deposit for two years from the date the Secretary of State receives written notification from the assignor of the deposit that the assignor has ceased to engage in the business of a counseling service or has filed a bond pursuant to subdivision (a), provided that there are no outstanding claims against the deposit. Written notification to the Secretary of State shall include all of the following: (1) name, address, and telephone number of the assignor; (2) name, address, and telephone number of the bank at which the deposit is located; (3) account number of the deposit; and (4) a statement whether the assignor is ceasing to engage in the business of a counseling service or has filed a bond with the Secretary of State. The Secretary of State shall forward an acknowledgment of receipt of the written notice to the assignor at the address indicated in the notice, specifying the date of receipt of the written notice and anticipated date of release of the deposit, provided there are no outstanding claims against the deposit account.

(k) A judge of a superior court may order the return of the deposit prior to the expiration of two years upon evidence satisfactory to the judge that there are no outstanding claims against the deposit or order the Secretary of State to retain the deposit for a sufficient period beyond the two years pursuant to subdivision (j) to resolve outstanding claims against the deposit account.

(*l*) The Secretary of State shall charge a filing fee not to exceed the cost of filing the bond or the deposit filed in lieu of a bond pursuant to Section 995.710 of the Code of Civil Procedure.

(m) The Secretary of State shall enforce the provisions of this chapter that govern the filing and maintenance of bonds and deposits in lieu of bonds. *(Added by Stats.1989, c. 704, § 2. Amended by Stats.1996, c. 633 (S.B.1978), § 12; Stats. 1998, c. 829 (S.B.1652), § 12; Stats.2002, c. 784 (S.B.1316), § 16.)*

Cross References

Deposit defined, see Civil Code § 1812.501.
Employment counseling service defined, see Civil Code § 1812.501.
Fee defined, see Civil Code § 1812.501.
Person defined, see Civil Code § 1812.501.

§ 1812.511. Contract; cancellation

(a) Every contract for employment counseling services shall be in writing. An original and one copy of the contract shall be given to the customer at the time the customer signs the contract and before the employment counseling service accepts any fee or deposit or the customer becomes obligated to pay any such fee or deposit. The contract shall contain all of the following:

(1) The name, address, and telephone number of the employment counseling service.

(2) The name and address of the person signing the contract and the person to whom the employment counseling services are to be provided.

(3) A description of the services to be provided; a statement when those services are to be provided; the duration of the contract; and refund provisions as appropriate, to be applicable if the described services are not provided according to the contract.

(4) The amount of the fee to be charged to or collected from the person receiving the services or any other person, and the date or dates when that fee is required to be paid.

(5) The following statement, in type no smaller than 10-point boldfaced type:

"No verbal or written promise or guarantee of any job or employment is made or implied under the terms of this contract."

(6) The following statement, in immediate proximity to the space reserved for the customer's signature, in type no smaller than 10-point boldfaced type:

YOUR RIGHT TO CANCEL

/enter date of transaction/

"You may cancel this contract for employment counseling services, without any penalty or obligation, if notice of cancellation is given, in writing, within three business days from the above date.

"To cancel this contract, just mail or deliver a signed and dated copy of the following cancellation notice or any other written notice of cancellation, or send a telegram containing a notice of cancellation, to (name of employment counseling service) at (address of its place of business), NOT LATER THAN MIDNIGHT OF /date/."

CANCELLATION NOTICE

I hereby cancel this contract.

Dated: _____

_____ Customer's Signature"

Until the employment counseling service has complied with this section the customer may cancel the employment counseling services contract.

(b) All contracts shall be dated and shall be made and numbered consecutively in triplicate, the original and each copy to be signed by the customer and the person acting for the employment counseling service. The original and one copy shall be given to the customer and the other copy shall be kept on file at the employment counseling service.

(c) The full agreement between the parties shall be contained in a single document containing those elements set forth in this section. *(Added by Stats.1989, c. 704, § 2.)*

Cross References

Deposit defined, see Civil Code § 1812.501.
Employment counseling service defined, see Civil Code § 1812.501.
Fee defined, see Civil Code § 1812.501.
Person defined, see Civil Code § 1812.501.

§ 1812.512. Fees; schedule; payment terms; notice; change; confession of judgment, note, or wage assignment as payment

(a)(1) An employment counseling service shall provide a copy of its fee schedule and payment terms to any customer from whom a fee or deposit is to be received, prior to the customer being interviewed by a counselor, agent, or employee.

(2) In the schedule, the maximum fee shall be fixed and shall include the charges of every kind rendered by the employment counseling service in each case or transaction on behalf of the prospective employee. Changes in the fee schedule may be made, but no change shall become effective until posted for not less than seven days in a conspicuous place in the employment counseling service.

(3) A copy of the schedule in effect shall be kept posted in the employment counseling service in a conspicuous place, and the posted schedule and the changes therein shall be in lettering or printing of not less than standard pica capitals. The date of the taking effect of the schedule and of each change therein shall appear on the posted copies.

(4) A copy of all fee schedules, and of all changes therein, shall be kept on file at the employment counseling service, retrospectively for a period of one year.

(b) No fee charged or collected shall be in excess of the fee as scheduled.

(c) No employment counseling service shall accept, directly or indirectly, a registration fee of any kind.

(d) No employment counseling service may take from a customer a confession of judgment, a promissory note or notes, or an assignment of wages to cover its fees. *(Added by Stats.1989, c. 704, § 2.)*

Cross References

Deposit defined, see Civil Code § 1812.501.
Employment counseling service defined, see Civil Code § 1812.501.
Fee defined, see Civil Code § 1812.501.

§ 1812.513. False or misleading representations; advertisements; name, address, and telephone number; guarantee; records

(a) No employment counseling service shall make or cause to be made any false, misleading, or deceptive advertisements or representations concerning the services that the employment counseling service will provide to customers.

(b)(1) No employment counseling service shall publish or cause to be published any false, fraudulent, or misleading information, representation, notice, or advertisements.

(2) All advertisements of an employment counseling service shall contain the correct name of the employment counseling service and one of the following:

(A) The street address of the employment counseling service's place of business.

(B) The correct telephone number of the employment counseling service at its place of business.

(c) No employment counseling service shall give any false information or make any false promises or representations concerning engagement or employment to any customer, or make any verbal or written promise or guarantee of any job or employment.

(d) An employment counseling service shall maintain a record of all advertisements for the service, correlated to show the date and the publication in which the advertisement appeared, retrospectively, for a period of one year.

(e) No employment counseling service shall, by its choice of name or by advertisement or representation, represent itself to be an employment agency or to perform the job placement services of an employment agency. *(Added by Stats.1989, c. 704, § 2.)*

Cross References

Employment agency or agency defined, see Civil Code § 1812.501.
Employment counseling service defined, see Civil Code § 1812.501.

CHAPTER 4. JOB LISTING SERVICES

Section
1812.515. Bond; deposit in lieu of bond.
1812.516. Contracts; cancellation.
1812.517. Fees; schedule; payment terms; notice; change; confession of judgment, note, or wage assignment as payment; splitting.
1812.518. Refunds; failure to meet contract specifications; job not obtained or lasting less than 90 days; penalty.

Section

1812.519. Job order; prerequisite to fee acceptance; conditions; referrals; exchange with employment agency.

1812.520. False or misleading representations; advertisements; contents; records.

1812.521. Illegal employment; minors; labor contract; union membership; labor trouble; notice.

§ 1812.515. Bond; deposit in lieu of bond

(a) Every job listing service subject to this title shall maintain a bond issued by a surety company admitted to do business in this state. The principal sum of the bond shall be ten thousand dollars ($10,000) for each location. A copy of the bond shall be filed with the Secretary of State.

(b) The bond required by this section shall be in favor of, and payable to, the people of the State of California, and shall be conditioned that the person obtaining the bond will comply with this title and will pay all sums due any individual or group of individuals when the person or his or her representative, agent, or employee has received those sums. The bond shall be for the benefit of any person or persons damaged by any violation of misrepresentation, deceit, unlawful acts of omissions, or failure to provide the services of the job listing service in performance of the contract with the jobseeker, by the job listing service or its agent, representatives, or employees while acting within the scope of their employment.

(c)(1) No job listing service shall conduct any business without having a current surety bond in the amount prescribed by this chapter and filing a copy of the bond with the Secretary of State, identifying the bond and the date of cancellation or termination.

(2) Thirty days prior to the cancellation or termination of any surety bond required by this section, the surety shall send a written notice of that cancellation or termination to both the job listing service and the Secretary of State, identifying the bond and the date of cancellation or termination.

(3) If any job listing service fails to obtain a new bond and file a copy of that bond with the Secretary of State by the effective date of the cancellation or termination of the former bond, the job listing service shall cease to conduct any business unless and until a new surety bond is obtained and a copy of that bond is filed with the Secretary of State.

(d) When a deposit has been made in lieu of a bond pursuant to Section 995.710 of the Code of Civil Procedure, the person asserting a claim against the deposit shall, in lieu of Section 996.430 of the Code of Civil Procedure, establish the claim by furnishing evidence to the Secretary of State of a money judgment entered by a court together with evidence that the claimant is a person described in subdivision (b).

(e) When a person has established the claim with the Secretary of State, the Secretary of State shall review and approve the claim and enter the date of approval on the claim. The claim shall be designated an "approved claim."

(f) When the first claim against a particular deposit has been approved, it shall not be paid until the expiration of a period of 240 days after the date of its approval by the Secretary of State. Subsequent claims that are approved by the Secretary of State within the same 240-day period shall similarly not be paid until the expiration of the 240-day period. Upon the expiration of the 240-day period, the Secretary of State shall pay all approved claims from that 240-day period in full unless the deposit is insufficient, in which case each approved claim shall be paid in a pro rata share of the deposit.

(g) When the Secretary of State approves the first claim against a particular deposit after the expiration of the 240-day period, the date of approval of that claim shall begin a new 240-day period to which subdivision (f) shall apply with respect to the amount remaining in the deposit.

(h) After a deposit is exhausted, no further claims shall be paid by the Secretary of State. Claimants who have had their claims paid in full or in part pursuant to subdivisions (f) and (g) shall not be required to return funds received from the deposit for the benefit of other claimants.

(i) When a deposit has been made in lieu of a bond, the amount of the deposit shall not be subject to attachment, garnishment, or execution with respect to an action or judgment against the job listing service, other than as to an amount as no longer needed or required for the purpose of this title that would otherwise be returned to the job listing service by the Secretary of State.

(j) The Secretary of State shall retain a cash deposit for two years from the date the Secretary of State receives written notification from the assignor of the deposit that the assignor has ceased to engage in the business of a job listing service or has filed a bond pursuant to subdivision (a), provided that there are no outstanding claims against the deposit. Written notification to the Secretary of State shall include all of the following: (1) name, address, and telephone number of the assignor; (2) name, address, and telephone number of the bank at which the deposit is located; (3) account number of the deposit; and (4) a statement whether the assignor is ceasing to engage in the business of a job listing service or has filed a bond with the Secretary of State. The Secretary of State shall forward an acknowledgment of receipt of the written notice to the assignor at the address indicated therein, specifying the date of receipt of the written notice and anticipated date of release of the deposit, provided there are no outstanding claims against the deposit.

(k) A judge of a superior court may order the return of the deposit prior to the expiration of two years upon evidence satisfactory to the judge that there are no outstanding claims against the deposit or order the Secretary of State to retain the deposit for a specified period beyond the two years pursuant to subdivision (j) to resolve outstanding claims against the deposit account.

(*l*) The Secretary of State shall charge a filing fee not to exceed the cost of filing the bond or deposit filed in lieu of a bond pursuant to Section 995.710 of the Code of Civil Procedure.

(m) The Secretary of State shall enforce the provisions of this chapter that govern the filing and maintenance of bonds and deposits in lieu of bonds. *(Added by Stats.1989, c. 704, § 2. Amended by Stats.1996, c. 633 (S.B.1978), § 13; Stats. 1998, c. 829 (S.B.1652), § 13; Stats.2002, c. 784 (S.B.1316), § 17.)*

Cross References

Deposit defined, see Civil Code § 1812.501.
Fee defined, see Civil Code § 1812.501.
Job listing service defined, see Civil Code § 1812.501.
Jobseeker defined, see Civil Code § 1812.501.
Person defined, see Civil Code § 1812.501.

§ 1812.516. Contracts; cancellation

(a) Every job listing service shall give a written contract to every jobseeker from whom a fee or deposit is to be received, whether directly or indirectly. The original and one copy of the contract shall be given to the jobseeker at the time the jobseeker signs the contract and before the job listing service accepts any fee or deposit or the jobseeker becomes obligated to pay any such fee or deposit. The contract shall contain all of the following:

(1) The name of the job listing service and the addresses and telephone numbers of the principal office of the job listing service and the location providing the listing services to the jobseeker.

(2) The amount of the fee to be charged and to be collected from the jobseeker.

(3) A description of the service to be performed by the job listing service, including significant conditions, restrictions, and limitations where applicable.

(4) A description of the jobseeker's specifications for the employment opportunity in clear language understandable to the jobseeker, including, but not limited to, the following:

(A) Kind of work or employment.

(B) Interests of jobseeker.

(C) Qualifications of jobseeker.

(D) Daily hours of work, the wages or salary, benefits, and other conditions of employment.

(E) Location of job.

(5) The contract expiration date, which shall not be later than 90 days from the date of execution of the contract.

(6) The following statement, in immediate proximity to the space reserved for the jobseeker's signature, in type no smaller than 10-point boldfaced type:

YOUR RIGHT TO CANCEL

/enter date of transaction/

"You may cancel this contract for job listing services without any penalty or obligation, if notice of cancellation is given, in writing, within three business days from the above date.

"To cancel this contract, just mail or deliver a signed and dated copy of the following cancellation notice or any other written notice of cancellation, to (name of job listing service) at (address of its place of business), NOT LATER THAN MIDNIGHT OF /date/."

CANCELLATION NOTICE

I hereby cancel this contract.

Dated: _____

_____ Customer's Signature"

Until the job listing service has complied with this section the jobseeker may cancel the job listing service's contract.

(7) The following statement, with the caption in type no smaller than 10-point boldfaced type and the remainder in a size no smaller than that generally used throughout the contract, and in full capitals, boldface, or italics:

"RIGHT TO REFUND"

"If, within seven business days after payment of a fee or deposit, the job listing service has not supplied you with at least three available employment opportunities meeting the specifications of the contract as to type of job; interests of jobseeker; qualifications of jobseeker; hours, salary, benefits, and other conditions of employment; location of job; and any other specifications expressly set forth in the contract, the full amount of the fee or deposit paid shall be refunded to you upon your request.

"If you do not obtain a job through the services of the job listing service, or if you obtain employment which lasts less than 90 days, any amount paid in fees or deposits in excess of a twenty-five dollar ($25) service charge shall be refunded to you, upon your request after expiration of the contract.

"Any refund due must be made to you within 10 days of your request. If the refund is not made in that time, the job listing service must pay to you an additional sum equal to the amount of your fee or deposit."

(8) If any labor trouble exists at the place of employment, that fact shall be stated in the listing of that employment provided to the jobseeker.

(b) All contracts shall be dated and shall be made and numbered consecutively in triplicate, the original and each copy to be signed by the jobseeker and the person acting for the job listing service. The original and one copy shall be given to the jobseeker and the other copy shall be kept on file at the job listing service.

(c) The full agreement between the parties shall be contained in a single document containing those elements set forth in this section. (Added by Stats.1989, c. 704, § 2. Amended by Stats.1990, c. 1256 (A.B.2649), § 6.)

Cross References

Deposit defined, see Civil Code § 1812.501.
Fee defined, see Civil Code § 1812.501.
Job listing service defined, see Civil Code § 1812.501.
Jobseeker defined, see Civil Code § 1812.501.
Person defined, see Civil Code § 1812.501.

§ 1812.517. Fees; schedule; payment terms; notice; change; confession of judgment, note, or wage assignment as payment; splitting

(a)(1) A job listing service shall provide a copy of the service's fee schedule and payment terms to any jobseeker from whom a fee or deposit is to be received, prior to the jobseeker being interviewed by a counselor or other agent or employee.

(2) In the schedule, the maximum fee shall be fixed and shall include the charges of every kind rendered by the job listing service in each case or transaction on behalf of the prospective employee. Changes in the fee schedule may be made, but no change shall become effective until posted for

§ 1812.517

not less than seven days in a conspicuous place in the job listing service.

(3) A copy of the schedule in effect shall be kept posted in the job listing service in a conspicuous place, and the posted schedule and the changes therein shall be in lettering or printing of not less than standard pica capitals. The date of the taking effect of the schedule and of each change therein shall appear on the posted copies.

(4) A copy of all fee schedules, and of all changes therein, shall be kept on file at the job listing service, retrospectively, for a period of one year.

(b) No fee charged or collected shall be in excess of the fee as scheduled.

(c) No job listing service may take from a jobseeker a confession of judgment, a promissory note or notes, or an assignment of wages to cover its fees.

(d) The fee charged shall not be based on a portion or percentage of the salary or wages earned or to be earned in the employment obtained through use of the job listing service.

(e)(1) No job listing service shall divide fees with an employer, an agent, or other employee of any employer or person to whom help is furnished.

(2) No job listing service shall charge any jobseeker a fee for accepting employment with that job listing service or any subsidiary of that service.

(3) No job listing service shall charge any jobseeker a fee when help is furnished to an employer, an agent, any employee of any employer, a member, or person who has a financial interest in the job listing service. (Added by Stats.1989, c. 704, § 2.)

Cross References

Deposit defined, see Civil Code § 1812.501.
Employer defined, see Civil Code § 1812.501.
Fee defined, see Civil Code § 1812.501.
Job listing service defined, see Civil Code § 1812.501.
Jobseeker defined, see Civil Code § 1812.501.
Person defined, see Civil Code § 1812.501.

§ 1812.518. Refunds; failure to meet contract specifications; job not obtained or lasting less than 90 days; penalty

(a)(1) A job listing service shall refund in full any advance fee paid and cancel any other obligation incurred by the jobseeker if the job listing service does not, within seven business days after execution of the contract, supply at least three employment opportunities then available to the jobseeker and meeting the specifications of the contract.

(2) A job listing service will be deemed to have supplied information meeting the specifications of the jobseeker if the information supplied meets the contract specifications with reference to: type of job; interests of jobseeker; qualifications of jobseeker; hours, salary, benefits, and other conditions of employment; location of job; and any other specifications expressly set forth in the contract.

(b) A job listing service shall refund any amount over and above a twenty-five dollar ($25) service charge and cancel any other obligation incurred by the jobseeker if the jobseeker

OBLIGATIONS

does not obtain a job, or if employment, once obtained, lasts less than 90 days.

(c) A job listing service shall make all refunds required under this section within 10 days after the jobseeker requests such refund. Unless the refund is made within that time, the job listing service shall pay the jobseeker an additional sum equal to the amount of the deposit. (Added by Stats.1989, c. 704, § 2.)

Cross References

Deposit defined, see Civil Code § 1812.501.
Fee defined, see Civil Code § 1812.501.
Job listing service defined, see Civil Code § 1812.501.
Jobseeker defined, see Civil Code § 1812.501.

§ 1812.519. Job order; prerequisite to fee acceptance; conditions; referrals; exchange with employment agency

(a) No job listing service shall accept a fee from any jobseeker, or send any jobseeker for employment, without having obtained, in writing, a bona fide job order for employment.

(b) A job listing service shall identify itself as a job listing service to the employer in all instances in which it contacts an employer for the purposes of soliciting a job order. All job orders shall be recorded in writing. A job order for employment shall be considered to have been given by an employer to a job listing service under the following conditions:

(1) The employer, or his or her agent, in writing, registers a request or gives permission that the job listing service recruit or refer jobseekers who meet the employer's stated job specifications and the employer furnishes such information as required by subdivision (a) of Section 1812.516.

(2) A job order is valid for the referral of any qualified jobseeker until it is filled or canceled by the employer, and may serve as the basis for job listing service advertising. The job listing service is required to recontact the employer within the four-day period immediately preceding dissemination of the job listing information to ensure that the position is still vacant prior to any additional advertising or referral of jobseekers.

(c) No job listing service shall refer a jobseeker to a job knowing or having reason to know that:

(1) The job does not exist or the jobseeker is not qualified for the job.

(2) The job has been described or advertised by or on behalf of the job listing service in a false, misleading, or deceptive manner.

(3) The job listing service has not obtained written permission to list the job from the employer or an authorized agent of the employer.

(d) No job listing service shall exchange job orders with an employment agency which charges a placement fee. (Added by Stats.1989, c. 704, § 2. Amended by Stats.1991, c. 654 (A.B.1893), § 51.)

Cross References

Employer defined, see Civil Code § 1812.501.
Employment agency or agency defined, see Civil Code § 1812.501.

Fee defined, see Civil Code § 1812.501.
Job listing service defined, see Civil Code § 1812.501.
Job order defined, see Civil Code § 1812.501.
Jobseeker defined, see Civil Code § 1812.501.

§ 1812.520. False or misleading representations; advertisements; contents; records

(a) No job listing service shall make or cause to be made any false, misleading or deceptive advertisements or representations concerning the services that the job listing service will provide to jobseekers.

(b)(1) No job listing service shall publish or cause to be published any false, fraudulent, or misleading information, representation, notice, or advertisements.

(2) All advertisements of a job listing service shall contain the correct name of the job listing service and one of the following:

(A) The street address of the job listing service's place of business.

(B) The correct telephone number of the job listing service at its place of business.

(3) No job listing service shall give any false information or make any false promises or representations concerning an engagement or employment to any jobseeker.

(4) No job listing service shall, by its choice of name or by advertisement or representation, represent itself to be an employment agency or to perform the services of an employment agency.

(c) Special requirements not usually associated with a job shall be specified in any advertisement. When the location of the position advertised is more than 50 miles from the job listing service office responsible for the advertisement, it shall state either the location or that the job is "nonlocal." Special benefits of the job, if advertised, shall be specifically described and substitute terms or symbols such as "extras" or "+" shall not be sufficient.

(d) An advertised salary shall be based upon the starting salary contained in the job order. An advertised range of starting salaries shall be specified by preceding the minimum salary and maximum salary by terms "from" and "to" respectively. When the job order contains only the maximum amount of a salary range, that advertised salary shall be preceded by the word "to." If a maximum salary is dependent upon the jobseeker's experience, the advertised salary may be described by listing the minimum salary and the term "up Depending on Experience" or "up D.O.E." The words "open" and "negotiable" or words or symbols of like import shall not be used as a substitute for the salary. If an advertised salary is based in whole or in part on commissions, that fact shall be indicated in the advertisement.

(e) All job listing services shall maintain a record of all advertised jobs, correlated to show the date and the publication in which the advertisement appeared and the job order number of each job advertised, retrospectively for a period of one year. *(Added by Stats.1989, c. 704, § 2. Amended by Stats.1990, c. 1256 (A.B.2649), § 7.)*

Cross References

Employment agency or agency defined, see Civil Code § 1812.501.
Job listing service defined, see Civil Code § 1812.501.
Job order defined, see Civil Code § 1812.501.
Jobseeker defined, see Civil Code § 1812.501.

§ 1812.521. Illegal employment; minors; labor contract; union membership; labor trouble; notice

(a) No job listing service shall, when employment would be in violation of Chapter 1 (commencing with Section 1171) of Part 4 of Division 2 of the Labor Code or Part 27 (commencing with Section 48000) of the Education Code, accept any application for employment made by, or on behalf of, any minor, or place or assist in placing any minor in that employment.

(b) Every job listing service shall notify each jobseeker before sending the jobseeker in response to a request for employment whether a labor contract is in existence at the establishment to which the jobseeker is being sent, and whether union membership is required.

(c) No job listing service shall send a jobseeker to any place where a strike, lockout, or other labor trouble exists without notifying the jobseeker of that fact and shall in addition thereto enter a statement of those conditions upon the contract or receipt given to the jobseeker. *(Added by Stats.1989, c. 704, § 2. Amended by Stats.1990, c. 1256 (A.B.2649), § 8.)*

Cross References

Job listing service defined, see Civil Code § 1812.501.
Jobseeker defined, see Civil Code § 1812.501.

CHAPTER 5. RECORDS

Section
1812.522. Inspection; reports; separation from records of other business.

§ 1812.522. Inspection; reports; separation from records of other business

(a) All books, records, files, the schedules, and other papers required by this title to be kept by any employment agency, employment counseling service, or job listing service shall be open at all reasonable hours to the inspection of the representative of the Attorney General, any district attorney, or any city attorney. Every employment agency, employment counseling service, and job listing service shall furnish to the representative of the Attorney General, any district attorney, or any city attorney upon request a true copy of those books, records, files, the schedules, and papers or any portion thereof, and shall make such reports as the Attorney General prescribes.

(b) If any employment agency, employment counseling service, or job listing service also engages in any other business which is not subject to this title, the records of the agency or service pertaining to matters under the jurisdictions of this title shall be kept separate and apart from the records of that other business. *(Added by Stats.1989, c. 704, § 2.)*

Cross References

Attorney General, generally, see Government Code § 12500 et seq.
Employment agency or agency defined, see Civil Code § 1812.501.
Employment counseling service defined, see Civil Code § 1812.501.

§ 1812.522

Job listing service defined, see Civil Code § 1812.501.

CHAPTER 6. REMEDIES AND ENFORCEMENT

Section
1812.523. Misdemeanors; civil actions and proceedings; false or misleading representation voiding contract; refund; damages; attorney fees; costs; other laws; waiver of provisions; severability.

§ 1812.523. Misdemeanors; civil actions and proceedings; false or misleading representation voiding contract; refund; damages; attorney fees; costs; other laws; waiver of provisions; severability

(a) Any person who violates any provision of this title is guilty of a misdemeanor. The Attorney General, any district attorney, or any city attorney may prosecute misdemeanor actions.

(b) Actions for violation of this title, including, but not limited to, equity proceedings to restrain and enjoin such a violation, may be instituted by the Attorney General, any district attorney, or any city attorney. This section shall not be deemed to prohibit the enforcement by any person of any right provided by this or any other law.

(c) If any person uses any untrue or misleading statement, information, or advertisement to sell its services or fails to comply with the applicable provisions of this title, or the contract does not comply with the applicable provisions of this title, then the contract shall be void and unenforceable as contrary to public policy and the jobseeker, customer, or nurse shall be entitled to the return of all sums paid.

(d) Any person who is injured by any violation of this title or by the breach of a contract subject to this title may bring an action for the recovery of damages, an equity proceeding to restrain and enjoin those violations, or both. The amount awarded may be up to three times the damages actually incurred, but in no event less than the amount paid by the jobseeker, customer, or nurse to the person subject to this title. If the person subject to this title refuses or is unwilling to pay the damages awarded, the amount awarded may be satisfied out of the security required by this title. If the plaintiff prevails, the plaintiff shall be awarded a reasonable attorney's fee and costs. If the court determines that the breach or violation was willful, by clear and convincing evidence, the court, in its discretion, may award punitive damages in addition to the amounts set forth above.

(e) The provisions of this title are not exclusive and do not relieve the parties subject to this title from the duty to comply with all other applicable laws.

(f) The remedies provided in this title are not exclusive and shall be in addition to any other remedies or procedures provided in any other law.

(g) Any waiver by the consumer, jobseeker, or nurse of the provisions of this title shall be deemed contrary to public policy and shall be void and unenforceable. Any attempt by a person subject to this title to have a jobseeker, customer, or nurse waive rights given by this title shall constitute a violation of this title.

(h) If any provisions of this title or the application thereof to any person or circumstances is held unconstitutional, the remainder of the title and the application of that provision to other persons and circumstances shall not be affected thereby. *(Added by Stats.1989, c. 704, § 2.)*

Cross References

Attorney General, generally, see Government Code § 12500 et seq.
Fee defined, see Civil Code § 1812.501.
Jobseeker defined, see Civil Code § 1812.501.
Misdemeanor, see Penal Code §§ 16, 17, 19, 19.2.
Person defined, see Civil Code § 1812.501.

CHAPTER 7. NURSES' REGISTRIES

Section
1812.524. Definitions.
1812.525. Bond; deposit in lieu of bond.
1812.526. Continuing contract; contents.
1812.527. Fees; schedule; payment terms; notice; change.
1812.528. Experience, training, license; verification.
1812.529. Records.
1812.530. Registration fee; confession of judgment, note, or wage assignment as fee payment.
1812.531. Splitting fees.
1812.532. Failure to obtain or be paid for assignment; refund; delay; penalty.
1812.533. False or misleading representations; advertisements; contents.

§ 1812.524. Definitions

(a) "Nursing service" means the assignment of a nurse, as a private duty, self-employed, licensed registered nurse, licensed vocational nurse, or practical nurse to render service to a patient under the direction or supervision of a physician or surgeon registered to practice in this state.

(b) "Nurses' registry" means a person who engages in the business of obtaining and filling commitments for nursing service. A nurses' registry which makes or plans to make referrals for nurses' employment other than private duty nursing shall comply with Chapters 1 (commencing with Section 1812.500) and 2 (commencing with Section 1812.503) of this title with respect to those referrals.

(c) "Private duty nurse" means a self-employed nurse rendering service in the care of either a physically or mentally ill patient under the direction of a physician or surgeon, but who is paid by either the patient or the designated agent of the patient and who accepts the responsibilities of a self-employed private contractor. *(Added by Stats.1989, c. 704, § 2. Amended by Stats.1990, c. 1256 (A.B.2649), § 9.)*

Cross References

Nurses' registry as employment agency, required compliance, see Civil Code § 1812.501.
Person defined, see Civil Code § 1812.501.

§ 1812.525. Bond; deposit in lieu of bond

(a) Every nurses' registry subject to this title shall maintain a bond issued by a surety company admitted to do business in this state. The principal sum of the bond shall be three thousand dollars ($3,000). A copy of the bond shall be filed with the Secretary of State.

(b) The bond required by this section shall be in favor of, and payable to, the people of the State of California, and shall be conditioned that the person obtaining the bond will comply with this title and will pay all sums due any individual or group of individuals when the person or his or her representative, agent, or employee has received those sums. The bond shall be for the benefit of any person or persons damaged by any violation of this title or by fraud, dishonesty, misstatement, misrepresentation, deceit, unlawful acts or omissions, or failure to provide the services of the nurses' registry in performance of the contract with the nurse by the nurses' registry or its agents, representatives, or employees while acting within the scope of their employment.

(c)(1) No nurses' registry shall conduct any business without having a current surety bond in the amount prescribed by this title and filing a copy of the bond with the Secretary of State.

(2) Thirty days prior to the cancellation or termination of any surety bond required by this section, the surety shall send a written notice of that cancellation or termination to both the nurses' registry and the Secretary of State, identifying the bond and the date of cancellation or termination.

(3) If any nurses' registry fails to obtain a new bond and file a copy of that bond with the Secretary of State by the effective date of the cancellation or termination of the former bond, the nurses' registry shall cease to conduct any business unless and until a new surety bond is obtained and a copy of that bond is filed with the Secretary of State.

(d) When a deposit has been made in lieu of a bond pursuant to Section 995.710 of the Code of Civil Procedure, the person asserting a claim against the deposit shall, in lieu of Section 996.430 of the Code of Civil Procedure, establish the claim by furnishing evidence to the Secretary of State of a money judgment entered by a court together with evidence that the claimant is a person described in subdivision (b).

(e) When a person has established the claim with the Secretary of State, the Secretary of State shall review and approve the claim and enter the date of approval on the claim. The claim shall be designated an "approved claim."

(f) When the first claim against a particular deposit has been approved, it shall not be paid until the expiration of a period of 240 days after the date of its approval by the Secretary of State. Subsequent claims that are approved by the Secretary of State within the same 240–day period shall similarly not be paid until the expiration of the 240–day period. Upon the expiration of the 240–day period, the Secretary of State shall pay all approved claims from that 240–day period in full unless the deposit is insufficient, in which case each approved claim shall be paid a pro rata share of the deposit.

(g) When the Secretary of State approves the first claim against a particular deposit after the expiration of a 240–day period, the date of approval of that claim shall begin a new 240–day period to which subdivision (f) shall apply with respect to the amount remaining in the deposit.

(h) After a deposit is exhausted, no further claims shall be paid by the Secretary of State. Claimants who have had their claims paid in full or in part pursuant to subdivisions (f) and (g) shall not be required to return funds received from the deposit for the benefit of other claimants.

(i) When a deposit has been made in lieu of a bond, the amount of the deposit shall not be subject to attachment, garnishment, or execution with respect to an action or judgment against the nurses' registry, other than as to an amount as no longer needed or required for the purpose of this title that would otherwise be returned to the nurses' registry by the Secretary of State.

(j) The Secretary of State shall retain a cash deposit for two years from the date the Secretary of State receives written notification from the assignor of the deposit that the assignor has ceased to engage in the business of a nurses' registry or has filed a bond pursuant to subdivision (a), provided that there are no outstanding claims against the deposit. The written notice to the Secretary of State shall include all of the following: (1) name, address, and telephone number of the assignor; (2) name, address, and telephone number of the bank at which the deposit is located; (3) account number of the deposit; and (4) a statement whether the assignor is ceasing to engage in the business of a nurses' registry or has filed a bond with the Secretary of State. The Secretary of State shall forward an acknowledgment of receipt of the written notice to the assignor at the address indicated therein, specifying the date of receipt of the written notice and anticipated date of release of the deposit, provided there are no outstanding claims against the deposit.

(k) A judge of a superior court may order the return of the deposit prior to the expiration of two years upon evidence satisfactory to the judge that there are no outstanding claims against the deposit or order the Secretary of State to retain the deposit for a specified period beyond the two years pursuant to subdivision (j) to resolve outstanding claims against the deposit.

(*l*) The Secretary of State shall charge a filing fee not to exceed the cost of filing the bond or deposit filed in lieu of a bond pursuant to Section 995.710 of the Code of Civil Procedure.

(m) The Secretary of State shall enforce the provisions of this chapter that govern the filing and maintenance of bonds and deposits in lieu of bonds. *(Added by Stats.1989, c. 704, § 2. Amended by Stats.1996, c. 633 (S.B.1978), § 14; Stats. 1998, c. 829 (S.B.1652), § 14; Stats.2002, c. 784 (S.B.1316), § 18.)*

Cross References

Deposit defined, see Civil Code § 1812.501.
Fee defined, see Civil Code § 1812.501.
Nurses' registry as employment agency, required compliance, see Civil Code § 1812.501.
Nurses' registry defined, see Civil Code § 1812.524.
Person defined, see Civil Code § 1812.501.

§ 1812.526. Continuing contract; contents

Nurses' registries may enter into a continuing contract with private duty nurses covering the assignment of those nurses by the nurses' registries. The continuing contract shall state:

(a) The name, address, and telephone number of the nurses' registry.

(b) The name, address, and telephone number of the nurse.

(c) The current fee schedule of the nurses' registry.

(d) The date of its execution by the nurses' registry and the nurse.

§ 1812.526

(e) The contract shall specify that the provisions thereof are to govern only the assignment of private duty nurses and shall do all of the following:

(1) Designate the nurses' registry as the continuous agent of the nurse for purposes of assignment.

(2) Provide that the contract in effect may be terminated at any time by written notice given by one to the other for any future assignment.

(3) Provide for delivery to the nurse at the time of the execution of the contract a written schedule of the rates of nurses' charges currently agreed to between the nurses' registry and the nurse for the nurse's services to the patient.

(4) State that the nurses' registry will immediately notify the nurse in writing of all subsequent changes in the rates to be charged the patient for services, and that the nurse shall agree to abide by these rates.

(5) Contain express undertakings by the nurses' registry that it shall continuously maintain true and correct records of orders and assignments as provided in this title.

(6) Provide that the nurses' registry shall periodically and at least once each month render to the nurse a written statement of all fees claimed to be due the nurses' registry, and further that the statement shall adequately identify each assignment as to the inception date and period of service covered by the claim, including the name of the patient and the amount of service fee claimed.

(7) Contain appropriate wording advising the nurse of his or her right to dispute the correctness of any service fee claimed by the nurses' registry in the written statement referred to above, and that in the absence of objections within a reasonable time, any such service fee may be presumed to be correctly charged.

(8) Include any other term, condition, or understanding agreed upon between the nurses' registry and the nurse.

(f) Each contract shall be numbered consecutively in original and duplicate, both to be signed by the nurse and the nurses' registry. The original shall be given to the nurse and the duplicate shall be kept on file at the nurses' registry within the nurse's records.

(g) The full agreement between the parties shall be contained in a single document containing those elements set forth in this section. (Added by Stats.1989, c. 704, § 2. Amended by Stats.1990, c. 1256 (A.B.2649), § 10.)

Cross References

Fee defined, see Civil Code § 1812.501.
Nurses' registry as employment agency, required compliance, see Civil Code § 1812.501.
Nurses' registry defined, see Civil Code § 1812.524.
Private duty nurse defined, see Civil Code § 1812.524.

§ 1812.527. Fees; schedule; payment terms; notice; change

(a)(1)[1] A nurses' registry shall provide a copy of the registry's fee schedule and payment terms to any nurse from whom a fee or deposit is to be received, prior to the nurse being interviewed by the registry.

(2) In the schedule, the maximum fee shall be fixed and shall include the charges of every kind rendered by the nurses' registry in each case or transaction on behalf of the nurse. Changes in the fee schedule may be made, but no change shall become effective until posted for not less than seven days in a conspicuous place in the nurses' registry.

(3) A copy of the schedule in effect shall be kept posted in the nurses' registry in a conspicuous place, and the posted schedule and the changes therein shall be in lettering or printing of not less than standard pica capitals. The date of the taking effect of the schedule and of each change therein shall appear on the posted copies.

(4) A copy of all fee schedules, and of all changes therein, shall be kept on file at the nurses' registry, retrospectively for a period of one year. (Added by Stats.1989, c. 704, § 2.)

[1] No subd. (b) in enrolled bill.

Cross References

Deposit defined, see Civil Code § 1812.501.
Fee defined, see Civil Code § 1812.501.
Nurses' registry as employment agency, required compliance, see Civil Code § 1812.501.
Nurses' registry defined, see Civil Code § 1812.524.

§ 1812.528. Experience, training, license; verification

It shall be the duty of the nurses' registry to verify in writing the claims as to the experience or training listed on the application and to keep a file of those records in the nurse's folder within the nurses' registry. It shall also be the duty of the person interviewing the jobseeker to require the jobseeker to exhibit his or her license as issued by the Board of Registered Nursing or the Board of Vocational Nurse and Psychiatric Technician Examiners, with a notation to be made on the application by the interviewer that the license has been inspected and the date of expiration of the license. (Added by Stats.1989, c. 704, § 2.)

Cross References

Jobseeker defined, see Civil Code § 1812.501.
Nurses' registry as employment agency, required compliance, see Civil Code § 1812.501.
Nurses' registry defined, see Civil Code § 1812.524.
Person defined, see Civil Code § 1812.501.

§ 1812.529. Records

Each nurses' registry shall continuously maintain in its offices true and correct permanent log sheets and other records which shall disclose, in addition to the other information required, the date and hour of the receipt by the nurses' registry of each order for a private duty nurse, and the date and hour of the making or giving of each assignment to the nurse by the nurses' registry, the name of the nurse assigned, the name of the patient and the address where the nurse is assigned, the name of the attending physician, the date the assignment is to start, the period of actual service for each assignment, and the amount of the fee charged for each assignment. No nurses' registry, his or her agent or employees, shall make any false entry in those records. The nurses' registry shall maintain the log sheets and records required by this section respectively for a period of one year. (Added by Stats.1989. c. 704, § 2.)

Cross References

Fee defined, see Civil Code § 1812.501.

Nurses' registry as employment agency, required compliance, see Civil Code § 1812.501.
Nurses' registry defined, see Civil Code § 1812.524.
Private duty nurse defined, see Civil Code § 1812.524.

§ 1812.530. Registration fee; confession of judgment, note, or wage assignment as fee payment

(a) No nurses' registry shall accept, directly or indirectly, a registration fee of any kind.

(b) No nurses' registry may take from a nurse a confession of judgment, or promissory note, or an assignment of wages to cover its fees. (Added by Stats.1989, c. 704, § 2.)

Cross References

Fee defined, see Civil Code § 1812.501.
Nurses' registry as employment agency, required compliance, see Civil Code § 1812.501.
Nurses' registry defined, see Civil Code § 1812.524.
Registration fee defined, see Civil Code § 1812.501.

§ 1812.531. Splitting fees

No nurses' registry shall divide fees with any physician and surgeon, nurse, hospital, patient, or any agent or employee of any of these. (Added by Stats.1989, c. 704, § 2.)

Cross References

Fee defined, see Civil Code § 1812.501.
Nurses' registry as employment agency, required compliance, see Civil Code § 1812.501.
Nurses' registry defined, see Civil Code § 1812.524.

§ 1812.532. Failure to obtain or be paid for assignment; refund; delay; penalty

In the event that a nurses' registry collects from a nurse a fee or expenses for an assignment, and the nurse fails to obtain the assignment, or the nurse fails to be paid for the assignment, the nurses' registry shall upon demand therefor, repay to the nurse the fee and expenses so collected. Unless repayment is made within 48 hours after demand, the nurses' registry shall pay to the nurse an additional sum equal to the amount of the fee. (Added by Stats.1989, c. 704, § 2.)

Cross References

Fee defined, see Civil Code § 1812.501.
Nurses' registry as employment agency, required compliance, see Civil Code § 1812.501.
Nurses' registry defined, see Civil Code § 1812.524.

§ 1812.533. False or misleading representations; advertisements; contents

(a) No nurses' registry shall make, or cause to be made, any false, misleading, or deceptive advertisements or representations concerning the services that registry will provide to nurses.

(b)(1) No nurses' registry shall publish or cause to be published any false, fraudulent, or misleading information, representation, notice, or advertisements.

(2) All advertisements of a nurses' registry shall contain the correct name of the nurses' registry and one of the following:

(A) The street address of the registry's place of business.

(B) The correct telephone number of the registry at its place of business.

(3) No nurses' registry shall give any false information or make any false promises or representations concerning an assignment or employment to any nurse who registers or applies for an assignment or employment.

(4) No nurses' registry shall, by its name, advertisement, or any other representation, represent itself to be a home health agency, as defined by subdivision (a) of Section 1727 of the Health and Safety Code, or to perform the services of a home health agency. A nurses' registry shall provide a written disclosure to each individual receiving nursing services, as defined in subdivision (a) of Section 1812.524, in his or her place of residence stating that it does not perform the services of a home health agency and clearly describing that it is a nurses' registry only and that any complaints against licensed personnel providing a nursing service shall be brought to the local district attorney and the Department of Consumer Affairs. The address and telephone number of each agency and board to which complaints are required to be submitted shall be provided to all patients prior to the time they are under the care of any nursing services personnel.

(5) Any person may refer complaints concerning nurses' registries to the proper law enforcement agency for action.

(c) Every nurses' registry shall maintain a record of all advertisements, correlated to show the date and the publication in which the advertisement appeared, retrospectively for a period of one year. (Added by Stats.1989, c. 704, § 2. Amended by Stats.1990, c. 761, (A.B.3924), § 2.)

Cross References

Employment agency or agency defined, see Civil Code § 1812.501.
Nurses' registry as employment agency, required compliance, see Civil Code § 1812.501.
Person defined, see Civil Code § 1812.501.

CHAPTER 8. LONG–TERM CARE FACILITIES

Section
1812.540. Definitions.
1812.541. Information or material to be provided to long-term health care facility with respect to the referral of a temporary certified nurse assistant.
1812.542. Information or material to be provided to long-term health care facility with respect to the referral of a temporary licensed nursing staff.
1812.543. Adoption of policies and procedures by employment agency regarding prevention of resident or patient abuse by temporary staff.
1812.544. Maintaining records of all advertisements by employment agencies making referrals of licensed nursing staff or certified nurse assistants for temporary employment in a long-term health care facility.

§ 1812.540. Definitions

For purposes of this chapter, the following definitions shall apply:

(a) "Direct care service" means the temporary assignment of certified nurse assistants to render basic care services directed at the safety, comfort, personal hygiene, or protec-

§ 1812.540

tion of a patient who is a resident of a long-term health care facility.

(b) "Nursing service" means the temporary assignment of a licensed registered nurse, licensed vocational nurse, or psychiatric technician to render nursing and basic care services to a patient who is a resident of a long-term health care facility.

(c) "Licensed nursing staff" means a licensed registered nurse, licensed vocational nurse, or psychiatric technician.

(d) "Long-term health care facility" means a licensed facility, as defined in Section 1418 of the Health and Safety Code. *(Added by Stats.2001, c. 326 (A.B.1643), § 2.)*

§ 1812.541. Information or material to be provided to long-term health care facility with respect to the referral of a temporary certified nurse assistant

Every employment agency that refers temporary certified nurse assistants to an employer that is a long-term health care facility shall provide the employer with all of the following:

(a) Written verification that the employment agency has verified that any certified nurse assistant referred by the agency is registered on the state registry of certified nurse assistants and is in good standing. The employment agency shall provide to the employer the certified nurse assistant's professional certification number and date of expiration.

(b) A statement that the certified nurse assistant has at least six months of experience working in a long-term health care facility.

(c) A statement that the certified nurse assistant has had a health examination within 90 days prior to employment with the employment agency or seven days after employment with the employment agency and at least annually thereafter by a person lawfully authorized to perform that procedure. Each examination shall include a medical history and physical evaluation. The employment agency shall also provide verification that the individual has had tuberculosis screening within 90 days prior to employment and annually thereafter.

(d) A statement that the certified nurse assistant will participate in the facility's orientation program and any in-service training programs at the request of the long-term health care employer.

(e) A statement that a certified nurse assistant is in compliance with the in-service training requirements of paragraph (1) of subdivision (a) of Section 1337.6 of the Health and Safety Code. *(Added by Stats.2001, c. 326 (A.B.1643), § 2.)*

Cross References

Employer defined, see Civil Code § 1812.501.
Employment agency or agency defined, see Civil Code § 1812.501.
Long-term health care facility defined for purposes of this Chapter, see Civil Code § 1812.540.
Person defined, see Civil Code § 1812.501.

§ 1812.542. Information or material to be provided to long-term health care facility with respect to the referral of a temporary licensed nursing staff

Every employment agency that refers temporary licensed nursing staff to an employer who is a licensed long-term health care facility shall provide the employer with all of the following:

(a) Written verification that the individual is in good standing with the Board of Registered Nursing or the Board of Vocational Nursing and Psychiatric Technicians, as applicable, and has successfully secured a criminal record clearance. The employment agency shall provide to the employer the individual's professional license and registration number and date of expiration.

(b) A statement that the licensed nursing staff person has had a health examination within 90 days prior to employment with the employment agency or seven days after employment with the employment agency and at least annually thereafter by a person lawfully authorized to perform that procedure. Each examination shall include a medical history and physical evaluation. The employment agency shall also provide verification that the individual has had tuberculosis screening within 90 days prior to employment and annually thereafter. *(Added by Stats.2001, c. 326 (A.B.1643), § 2.)*

Cross References

Employer defined, see Civil Code § 1812.501.
Employment agency or agency defined, see Civil Code § 1812.501.
Licensed nursing staff defined for purposes of this Chapter, see Civil Code § 1812.540.
Long-term health care facility defined for purposes of this Chapter, see Civil Code § 1812.540.
Person defined, see Civil Code § 1812.501.

§ 1812.543. Adoption of policies and procedures by employment agency regarding prevention of resident or patient abuse by temporary staff

(a) An employment agency that makes referrals of licensed nursing staff or certified nurse assistants for temporary employment in a long-term health care facility shall adopt policies and procedures regarding prevention of resident or patient abuse by temporary staff.

(b) The employment agency shall provide written verification to the long-term health care facility that any certified nurse assistants or licensed nursing staff referred by the agency do not have any unresolved allegations against them involving the mistreatment, neglect, or abuse of a patient, including injuries of unknown source and misappropriation of resident property.

(c) No temporary staff person referred by an employment agency may be solely responsible for a unit unless that person has received a full orientation to the facility and the applicable unit for which he or she is assigned.

(d) Upon the request of the State Department of Health Services, an employment agency shall provide a list of temporary employees who have been referred to a specified facility during the period in which the facility is involved in a labor action.

(e) An employment agency shall require that any employee referred to a long-term care facility be identified as a temporary staff person in the facility's daily staffing levels required to be posted in accordance with the standards set forth in Section 941 of Appendix F of Public Law 106–554 (42 U.S.C. Sec. 1395i–3(b)(8) and 42 U.S.C. Sec. 1395r(b)(8)). *(Added by Stats.2001, c. 326 (A.B.1643), § 2.)*

Cross References

Department of Health Care Services, generally, see Health and Safety Code § 100100 et seq.

Employment agency or agency defined, see Civil Code § 1812.501.

Licensed nursing staff defined for purposes of this Chapter, see Civil Code § 1812.540.

Long-term health care facility defined for purposes of this Chapter, see Civil Code § 1812.540.

Person defined, see Civil Code § 1812.501.

§ 1812.544. Maintaining records of all advertisements by employment agencies making referrals of licensed nursing staff or certified nurse assistants for temporary employment in a long-term health care facility

(a) Every employment agency that makes referrals of licensed nursing staff or certified nurse assistants for temporary employment in a long-term health care facility shall maintain a record of all advertisements, showing the date of publication and the publication in which the advertisement appeared, for a period of one year from the date of the advertisement.

(b) No employment agency that makes referrals for employment to a long-term health care facility shall, by its name, advertisement, or any other representation, represent itself to be a home health agency, as defined by subdivision (a) of Section 1727 of the Health and Safety Code, or to perform the services of a home health agency. The employment agency shall provide a written disclosure to each employer stating that it does not perform the services of a home health agency and clearly describing that it is an employment agency only.

(c) Any facility or individual may refer complaints concerning employment agencies which place licensed nursing staff or certified nurse assistants in long-term health care facilities to the appropriate licensing, certification, ombudsman, adult protective services, or proper law enforcement agency for action. *(Added by Stats.2001, c. 326 (A.B.1643), § 2.)*

Cross References

Employer defined, see Civil Code § 1812.501.

Employment agency or agency defined, see Civil Code § 1812.501.

Licensed nursing staff defined for purposes of this Chapter, see Civil Code § 1812.540.

Long-term health care facility defined for purposes of this Chapter, see Civil Code § 1812.540.

Title 2.95

AUCTIONEER AND AUCTION COMPANIES

Section
1812.600. Necessity of surety bond; amount; cancellation; deposits in lieu of bonds; enforcement; civil penalties; attorney fees.
1812.601. Definitions.
1812.602. Restraining order; injunction.
1812.603. Restitution order; reimbursement for expenses; additional remedies.
1812.604. Violations; misdemeanor; punishment.
1812.605. Business of auctioneering; requirements.
1812.606. Auctioneer or auction company; liability.

Section
1812.607. Requirements of auctioneer or auction company; punishment.
1812.608. Additional violations; punishment.
1812.609. Public policy; waiver of rights.
1812.610. Auctioneers stating increased bids when no person has made an increased bid; online auctions of real property; notice.

Cross References

Dealers, auction of vehicles to the public, prohibitions, see Vehicle Code § 11713.11.

Estate management, contracts with auctioneers, terms and liability of estate or personal representative, see Probate Code § 10151.

Mock auctions, obtaining money or property from another by means of any false or fraudulent sale of property, see Penal Code § 535.

Real estate auctioneer license fee, see Business and Professions Code § 16002.1.

Unlawfully acting as auctioneer, see Penal Code § 436.

§ 1812.600. Necessity of surety bond; amount; cancellation; deposits in lieu of bonds; enforcement; civil penalties; attorney fees

(a) Every auctioneer and auction company shall maintain a bond issued by a surety company admitted to do business in this state. The principal sum of the bond shall be twenty thousand dollars ($20,000). A copy of the bond shall be filed with the Secretary of State.

(b) The bond required by this section shall be in favor of, and payable to, the people of the State of California and shall be for the benefit of any person or persons damaged by any fraud, dishonesty, misstatement, misrepresentation, deceit, unlawful acts or omissions, or failure to provide the services of the auctioneer or auction company in performance of the auction by the auctioneer or auction company or its agents, representatives, or employees while acting within the scope of their employment.

(c)(1) No auctioneer or auction company shall conduct any business without having a current surety bond in the amount prescribed by this section and without filing a copy of the bond with the Secretary of State.

(2) Thirty days prior to the cancellation or termination of any surety bond required by this section, the surety shall send a written notice of that cancellation or termination to both the auctioneer or auction company and the Secretary of State, identifying the bond and the date of cancellation or termination.

(3) If any auctioneer or auction company fails to obtain a new bond and file a copy of that bond with the Secretary of State by the effective date of the cancellation or termination of the former bond, the auctioneer or auction company shall cease to conduct any business unless and until that time as a new surety bond is obtained and a copy of that bond is filed with the Secretary of State.

(d) A deposit may be made in lieu of a bond as set forth in Section 995.710 of the Code of Civil Procedure. When a deposit is made in lieu of the bond, the person asserting the claim against the deposit shall establish the claim by furnishing evidence to the Secretary of State of a money judgment entered by a court together with evidence that the claimant is a person described in subdivision (b).

§ 1812.600 OBLIGATIONS

(e) When a claimant has established the claim with the Secretary of State, the Secretary of State shall review and approve the claim and enter the date of approval on the claim. The claim shall be designated an "approved claim."

(f) When the first claim against a particular deposit has been approved, it shall not be paid until the expiration of a period of 240 days after the date of its approval by the Secretary of State. Subsequent claims that are approved by the Secretary of State within the same 240–day period shall similarly not be paid until the expiration of the 240–day period. Upon expiration of the 240–day period, the Secretary of State shall pay all approved claims from that 240–day period in full unless the deposit is insufficient, in which case each approved claim shall be paid a pro rata share of the deposit.

(g) When the Secretary of State approves the first claim against a particular deposit after the expiration of a 240–day period, the date of approval of that claim shall begin a new 240–day period to which subdivision (f) shall apply with respect to any amount remaining in the deposit.

(h) After a deposit is exhausted, no further claims shall be paid by the Secretary of State. Claimants who have had their claims paid in full or in part pursuant to subdivision (f) or (g) shall not be required to return funds received from the deposit for the benefit of other claimants.

(i) When a deposit has been made in lieu of a bond, the amount of the deposit shall not be subject to attachment, garnishment, or execution with respect to an action or judgment against the auctioneer or auction company, other than as to that amount that is no longer needed or required for the purpose of this section that otherwise would be returned to the auctioneer or auction company by the Secretary of State.

(j) The Secretary of State shall retain a cash deposit for two years from the date the Secretary of State receives written notification from the assignor of the deposit that the assignor has ceased to engage in the business of an auctioneer or auction company or has filed a bond pursuant to subdivision (a), provided that there are no outstanding claims against the deposit. Written notification to the Secretary of State shall include all of the following: (1) name, address, and telephone number of the assignor; (2) name, address, and telephone number of the bank at which the deposit is located; (3) account number of the deposit; and (4) a statement whether the assignor is ceasing to engage in the business of an auctioneer or auction company or has filed a bond with the Secretary of State. The Secretary of State shall forward an acknowledgment of receipt of the written notice to the assignor at the address indicated in the notice, specifying the date of receipt of the written notice and anticipated date of release of the deposit, provided there are no outstanding claims against the deposit.

(k) A judge of a superior court may order the return of the deposit prior to the expiration of two years upon evidence satisfactory to the judge that there are no outstanding claims against the deposit or order the Secretary of State to retain the deposit for a specified period beyond the two years pursuant to subdivision (j) to resolve outstanding claims against the deposit.

(*l*) If an auctioneer or auction company fails to perform any of the duties specifically imposed upon him or her pursuant to this title, any person may maintain an action for enforcement of those duties or to recover a civil penalty in the amount of one thousand dollars ($1,000), or for both enforcement and recovery.

(m) In any action to enforce these duties or to recover civil penalties, or for both enforcement and recovery, the prevailing plaintiff shall be entitled to reasonable attorney's fees and costs, in addition to the civil penalties provided under subdivision (*l*).

(n) Notwithstanding the repeal of Chapter 3.7 (commencing with Section 5700) of Division 3 of the Business and Professions Code by the act adding this chapter, any cash security in lieu of the surety bond formerly required and authorized by former Chapter 3.7 (commencing with Section 5700) of Division 3 of the Business and Professions Code, shall be transferred to, and maintained by, the Secretary of State.

(o) The Secretary of State shall charge and collect a filing fee not to exceed the cost of filing the bond or deposit filed in lieu of a bond as set forth in Section 995.710 of the Code of Civil Procedure.

(p) The Secretary of State shall enforce the provisions of this chapter that govern the filing and maintenance of bonds and deposits in lieu of bonds. *(Added by Stats.1993, c. 1170 (A.B.259), § 2, eff. Oct. 11, 1993. Amended by Stats.1996, c. 633 (S.B.1978), § 15; Stats.1998, c. 829 (S.B.1652), § 15; Stats.2002, c. 784 (S.B.1316), § 19.)*

Cross References

Auction company defined, see Civil Code § 1812.601.
Auction defined, see Civil Code § 1812.601.
Auctioneer defined, see Civil Code § 1812.601.
Employee defined, see Civil Code § 1812.601.
Person defined, see Civil Code § 1812.601.

§ 1812.601. Definitions

(a) "Advertisement" means any of the following:

(1) Any written or printed communication for the purpose of soliciting, describing, or offering to act as an auctioneer or provide auction company services, including any brochure, pamphlet, newspaper, periodical, or publication.

(2) A telephone or other directory listing caused or permitted by an auctioneer or auction company to be published that indicates the offer to practice auctioneering or auction company services.

(3) A radio, television, or similar airwave transmission that solicits or offers the practice of auctioneering or auction company services.

(b) "Auction" means a sale transaction conducted by means of oral or written exchanges, which include exchanges made in person or through electronic media, between an auctioneer and the members of his or her audience, which exchanges consist of a series of invitations for offers for the purchase of goods made by the auctioneer and offers to purchase made by members of the audience and culminate in the acceptance by the auctioneer of the highest or most favorable offer made by a member of the participating audience. However, auction does not include either of the following:

(1) A wholesale motor vehicle auction subject to regulation by the Department of Motor Vehicles.

(2) A sale of real estate or a sale in any sequence of real estate with personal property or fixtures or both in a unified sale pursuant to subparagraph (B) of paragraph (1) of subdivision (a) of Section 9604 of the Commercial Code.

(c) "Auction company" means any person who arranges, manages, sponsors, advertises, accounts for the proceeds of, or carries out auction sales at locations, including, but not limited to, any fixed location, including an auction barn, gallery place of business, sale barn, sale yard, sale pavilion, and the contiguous surroundings of each.

(d) "Auctioneer" means any individual who is engaged in, or who by advertising or otherwise holds himself or herself out as being available to engage in, the calling for, the recognition of, and the acceptance of, offers for the purchase of goods at an auction.

(e) "Employee" means an individual who works for an employer, is listed on the employer's payroll records, and is under the employer's control.

(f) "Employer" means a person who employs an individual for wages or salary, lists the individual on the person's payroll records, and withholds legally required deductions and contributions.

(g) "Goods" means any goods, wares, chattels, merchandise, or other personal property, including domestic animals and farm products.

(h) "Person" means an individual, corporation, partnership, trust, including a business trust, firm, association, organization, or any other form of business enterprise. *(Added by Stats.1993, c. 1170 (A.B.259), § 2, eff. Oct. 11, 1993. Amended by Stats.1994, c. 1010 (S.B.2053), § 46.1; Stats.1994, c. 180 (A.B.375), § 2, eff. July 11, 1994; Stats.1999, c. 991 (S.B.45), § 5, operative July 1, 2001; Stats.2004, c. 194 (S.B.1832), § 1.)*

Cross References

Action for specific recovery of fine art against museum, gallery, auctioneer, or dealer, statute of limitations, auctioneer defined, see Code of Civil Procedure § 338.

§ 1812.602. Restraining order; injunction

The superior court for the county in which any person has engaged or is about to engage in any act that constitutes a violation of this title may, upon a petition filed by any person, issue an injunction or other appropriate order restraining the violative conduct. Proceedings under this section shall be governed by Chapter 3 (commencing with Section 525) of Title 7 of Part 2 of the Code of Civil Procedure, except that no undertaking shall be required. *(Added by Stats.1993, c. 1170 (A.B.259), § 2, eff. Oct. 11, 1993.)*

Cross References

Person defined, see Civil Code § 1812.601.

§ 1812.603. Restitution order; reimbursement for expenses; additional remedies

(a) The superior court for the county in which any person has engaged in any act that constitutes a violation of this title may, upon a petition filed by any person, order the person who committed the violation to make restitution to any person injured as a result of the violation.

(b) The court may order any person against whom an injunction or restraining order pursuant to subdivision (a), or an order requiring restitution pursuant to subdivision (b), is directed, to reimburse the petitioner for expenses incurred in the investigation related to its petition.

(c) The remedies set forth in this section are in addition to, and not a limitation on, the authority provided for in any other section of this code. *(Added by Stats.1993, c. 1170 (A.B.259), § 2, eff. Oct. 11, 1993.)*

Cross References

Person defined, see Civil Code § 1812.601.

§ 1812.604. Violations; misdemeanor; punishment

Except as otherwise provided in this title, any person who violates any provision of this title is guilty of a misdemeanor, which offense is punishable by a fine not exceeding one thousand dollars ($1,000), or by imprisonment in a county jail for not more than one year, or by both that fine and imprisonment. In addition, upon a conviction of any violation of this chapter, or of any crime related to the conduct of an auctioneer, the court may issue an injunction and prohibit the convicted person from acting as an auctioneer or an auction company in this state, in which case the court shall inform the Secretary of State of that action. *(Added by Stats.1993, c. 1170 (A.B.259), § 2, eff. Oct. 11, 1993.)*

Cross References

Auction company defined, see Civil Code § 1812.601.
Auction defined, see Civil Code § 1812.601.
Auctioneer defined, see Civil Code § 1812.601.
Misdemeanors, definition and penalties, see Penal Code §§ 17, 19, 19.2.
Person defined, see Civil Code § 1812.601.

§ 1812.605. Business of auctioneering; requirements

In conducting the business of auctioneering, each auctioneer and auction company, and the company's owners, partners, officers, agents, and employees, shall do all of the following:

(a) Follow all lawful requests of the owner or consignor of the goods being sold at auction with regard to the sale of those goods.

(b) Perform his or her duties so that the highest or most favorable offer made by a member of his or her audience is accepted, except to the extent that any item or sale is offered with reserve or subject to confirmation.

(c) Truthfully represent the goods to be auctioned.

(d) Otherwise perform his or her duties in accordance with the laws of this state. *(Added by Stats.1993, c. 1170 (A.B. 259), § 2, eff. Oct. 11, 1993.)*

Cross References

Auction company defined, see Civil Code § 1812.601.
Auction defined, see Civil Code § 1812.601.
Auctioneer defined, see Civil Code § 1812.601.
Employee defined, see Civil Code § 1812.601.

§ 1812.605

Goods defined, see Civil Code § 1812.601.

§ 1812.606. Auctioneer or auction company; liability

Every auctioneer who operates his or her own auction company as a sole proprietor, and every auction company, together with its owners, partners, and officers, that employs an auctioneer, shall be responsible for all violations committed by the auctioneer or by any company employee in the conduct of auction business. An auctioneer who is employed by an auctioneer or auction company shall be responsible for all violations committed by him or her in the conduct of auction business.

It is a violation of this title for any auctioneer or auction company, or the company's owners, partners, and officers, to direct or knowingly permit any violation of this title by any auctioneer employed by or under contract with that auctioneer or auction company, or by any owner, partner, officer, agent, or employee of the auction company. (Added by Stats.1993, c. 1170 (A.B.259), § 2, eff. Oct. 11, 1993.)

Cross References

Auction company defined, see Civil Code § 1812.601.
Auction defined, see Civil Code § 1812.601.
Auctioneer defined, see Civil Code § 1812.601.
Employee defined, see Civil Code § 1812.601.

§ 1812.607. Requirements of auctioneer or auction company; punishment

Every auction company and auctioneer shall do all of the following:

(a) Disclose his or her name, trade or business name, telephone number, and bond number in all advertising of auctions. A first violation of this subdivision is an infraction subject to a fine of fifty dollars ($50); a second violation is subject to a fine of seventy-five dollars ($75); and a third or subsequent violation is subject to a fine of one hundred dollars ($100). This section shall not apply to business cards, business stationery, or to any advertisement that does not specify an auction date.

(b) Post a sign, the dimensions of which shall be at least 18 inches by 24 inches, at the main entrance to each auction, stating that the auction is being conducted in compliance with Section 2328 of the Commercial Code, Section 535 of the Penal Code, and the provisions of the California Civil Code. A first violation of this subdivision is an infraction subject to a fine of fifty dollars ($50); a second violation is subject to a fine of seventy-five dollars ($75); and a third or subsequent violation is subject to a fine of one hundred dollars ($100).

(c) Post or distribute to the audience the terms, conditions, restrictions, and procedures whereby goods will be sold at the auction, and announce any changes to those terms, conditions, restrictions, and procedures prior to the beginning of the auction sale. A first violation of this subdivision is an infraction subject to a fine of fifty dollars ($50); a second violation is subject to a fine of one hundred dollars ($100); and a third or subsequent violation is subject to a fine of two hundred fifty dollars ($250).

(d) Notify the Secretary of State of any change in address of record within 30 days of the change. A violation of this subdivision is an infraction subject to a fine of fifty dollars ($50).

(e) Notify the Secretary of State of any change in the officers of a corporate license within 30 days of the change. A violation of this subdivision is an infraction subject to a fine of fifty dollars ($50).

(f) Notify the Secretary of State of any change in the business or trade name of the auctioneer or auction company within 30 days of the change. A violation of this subdivision is an infraction subject to a fine of fifty dollars ($50).

(g) Keep and maintain, at the auctioneer's or auction company's address of record, complete and correct records and accounts pertaining to the auctioneer's or auction company's activity for a period of not less than two years. The records shall include the name and address of the owner or consignor and of any buyer of goods at any auction sale engaged in or conducted by the auctioneer or auction company, a description of the goods, the terms and conditions of the acceptance and sale of the goods, all written contracts with owners and consignors, and accounts of all moneys received and paid out, whether on the auctioneer's or auction company's own behalf or as agent, as a result of those activities. A first violation of this subdivision is a misdemeanor subject to a fine of five hundred dollars ($500); and a second or subsequent violation is subject to a fine of one thousand dollars ($1,000).

(h) Within 30 working days after the sale transaction, provide, or cause to be provided, an account to the owner or consignor of all goods that are the subject of an auction engaged in or conducted by the auctioneer or auction company. A first violation of this subdivision is a misdemeanor subject to a fine of five hundred dollars ($500); and a second or subsequent violation is subject to a fine of one thousand dollars ($1,000).

(i) Within 30 working days after a sale transaction of goods, pay or cause to be paid all moneys and proceeds due to the owner or the consignor of all goods that were the subject of an auction engaged in or conducted by the auctioneer or auction company, unless delay is compelled by legal proceedings or the inability of the auctioneer or auction company, through no fault of his or her own, to transfer title to the goods or to comply with any provision of this chapter, the Commercial Code, or the Code of Civil Procedure, or with any other applicable provision of law. A first violation of this subdivision is a misdemeanor subject to a fine of one thousand dollars ($1,000); a second violation is subject to a fine of one thousand five hundred dollars ($1,500); and a third or subsequent violation is subject to a fine of two thousand dollars ($2,000).

(j) Maintain the funds of all owners, consignors, buyers, and other clients and customers separate from his or her personal funds and accounts. A violation of this subdivision is an infraction subject to a fine of two hundred fifty dollars ($250).

(k) Immediately prior to offering any item for sale, disclose to the audience the existence and amount of any liens or other encumbrances on the item, unless the item is sold as free and clear. For the purposes of this subdivision, an item is "free and clear" if all liens and encumbrances on the item are to be paid prior to the transfer of title. A violation of this subdivision is an infraction subject to a fine of two hundred fifty dollars ($250) in addition to the requirement that the buyer be refunded, upon demand, the amount paid for any item that is the subject of the violation.

(*l*) Within two working days after an auction sale, return the blank check or deposit of each buyer who purchased no goods at the sale. A first violation of this subdivision is an infraction subject to a fine of one hundred dollars ($100); and a second or subsequent violation is subject to a fine of two hundred fifty dollars ($250).

(m) Within 30 working days of any auction sale, refund that portion of the deposit of each buyer that exceeds the cost of the goods purchased, unless delay is compelled by legal proceedings or the inability of the auctioneer or auction company, through no fault of his or her own, to transfer title to the goods or to comply with any provision of this chapter, the Commercial Code, or the Code of Civil Procedure, or with other applicable provisions of law, or unless the buyer violated the terms of a written agreement that he or she take possession of purchased goods within a specified period of time. A first violation of this subdivision is an infraction subject to a fine of one hundred dollars ($100); and a second or subsequent violation is subject to a fine of two hundred fifty dollars ($250). *(Formerly § 1861.607, added by Stats. 1993, c. 1170 (A.B.259), § 2, eff. Oct. 11, 1993. Renumbered § 1812.607 and amended by Stats.1997, c. 17 (S.B.947), § 16.)*

Cross References

Advertisement defined, see Civil Code § 1812.601.
Auction company defined, see Civil Code § 1812.601.
Auction defined, see Civil Code § 1812.601.
Auctioneer defined, see Civil Code § 1812.601.
Goods defined, see Civil Code § 1812.601.
Misdemeanors, definition and penalties, see Penal Code §§ 17, 19, 19.2.

§ 1812.608. Additional violations; punishment

In addition to other requirements and prohibitions of this title, it is a violation of this title for any person to do any of the following:

(a) Fail to comply with any provision of this code, or with any provision of the Vehicle Code, the Commercial Code, any regulation of the Secretary of State, the Code of Civil Procedure, the Penal Code, or any law administered by the State Board of Equalization, relating to the auctioneering business, including, but not limited to, sales and the transfer of title of goods.

(b) Aid or abet the activity of any other person that violates any provision of this title. A violation of this subdivision is a misdemeanor subject to a fine of one thousand dollars ($1,000).

(c) Place or use any misleading or untruthful advertising or statements or make any substantial misrepresentation in conducting auctioneering business. A first violation of this subdivision is a misdemeanor subject to a fine of five hundred dollars ($500); and a second or subsequent violation is subject to a fine of one thousand dollars ($1,000).

(d) Sell goods at auction before the auctioneer or auction company involved has first entered into a written contract with the owner or consignor of the goods, which contract sets forth the terms and conditions upon which the auctioneer or auction company accepts the goods for sale. The written contract shall include all of the following:

(1) The auctioneer's or auction company's name, trade or business name, business address, and business telephone number.

(2) An inventory of the item or items to be sold at auction.

(3) A description of the services to be provided and the agreed consideration for the services, which description shall explicitly state which party shall be responsible for advertising and other expenses.

(4) The approximate date or dates when the item or items will be sold at auction.

(5) A statement as to which party shall be responsible for insuring the item or items against loss by theft, fire, or other means.

(6) A disclosure that the auctioneer or auction company has a bond on file with the Secretary of State. A first violation of this subdivision is an infraction subject to a fine of two hundred fifty dollars ($250); a second violation is subject to a fine of five hundred dollars ($500); and a third or subsequent violation is subject to a fine of one thousand dollars ($1,000).

(e) Sell goods at auction before the auctioneer or auction company involved has first entered into a written contract with the auctioneer who is to conduct the auction. A first violation of this subdivision is an infraction subject to a fine of one hundred dollars ($100); and a second or subsequent violation is subject to a fine of two hundred fifty dollars ($250).

(f) Fail to reduce to writing all amendments or addenda to any written contract with an owner or consignor or an auctioneer. A first violation of this subdivision is an infraction subject to a fine of one hundred dollars ($100); and a second or subsequent violation is subject to a fine of two hundred fifty dollars ($250).

(g) Fail to abide by the terms of any written contract required by this section. A first violation of this subdivision is an infraction subject to a fine of one hundred dollars ($100); and a second or subsequent violation is subject to a fine of two hundred fifty dollars ($250).

(h) Cause or allow any person to bid at a sale for the sole purpose of increasing the bid on any item or items being sold by the auctioneer, except as authorized by Section 2328 of the Commercial Code or by this title. A violation of this subdivision includes, but is not limited to, either of the following:

(1) Stating any increased bid greater than that offered by the last highest bidder when, in fact, no person has made such a bid.

(2) Allowing the owner, consignor, or agent thereof, of any item or items to bid on the item or items, without disclosing to the audience that the owner, consignor, or agent thereof has reserved the right to so bid.

A violation of this subdivision is an infraction subject to a fine of one hundred dollars ($100).

(i) Knowingly misrepresent the nature of any item or items to be sold at auction, including, but not limited to, age, authenticity, value, condition, or origin. A violation of this subdivision is an infraction subject to a fine of two hundred fifty dollars ($250). In addition, it shall be required that the

§ 1812.608 OBLIGATIONS

buyer of the misrepresented item be refunded the purchase price of the item or items within 24 hours of return to the auctioneer or auction company of the item by the buyer, provided that the item is returned within five days after the date of the auction sale.

(j) Misrepresent the terms, conditions, restrictions, or procedures under which goods will be sold at auction. A violation of this subdivision is an infraction subject to a fine of seventy-five dollars ($75).

(k) Sell any item subject to sales tax without possessing a valid and unrevoked seller's permit from the State Board of Equalization. A violation of this subdivision is an infraction subject to a fine of five hundred dollars ($500). *(Formerly § 1861.608, added by Stats.1993, c. 1170 (A.B.259), § 2, eff. Oct. 11, 1993. Renumbered § 1812.608 and amended by Stats.1997, c. 17 (S.B.947), § 17.)*

Cross References

Auction company defined, see Civil Code § 1812.601.
Auction defined, see Civil Code § 1812.601.
Auctioneer defined, see Civil Code § 1812.601.
Goods defined, see Civil Code § 1812.601.
Misdemeanors, definition and penalties, see Penal Code §§ 17, 19, 19.2.
Person defined, see Civil Code § 1812.601.

§ 1812.609. Public policy; waiver of rights

Any waiver of the provisions of this title is contrary to public policy, and is void and unenforceable. *(Added by Stats.2002, c. 815 (A.B.2331), § 22.)*

§ 1812.610. Auctioneers stating increased bids when no person has made an increased bid; online auctions of real property; notice

(a) Notwithstanding Section 1812.601, for purposes of this section, an auction includes the sale of real property and an "auctioneer" means any individual who is engaged in, or who by advertising or otherwise holds himself or herself out as being available to engage in, the calling for, the recognition of, and the acceptance of, offers for the purchase of real property at an auction.

(b) An auctioneer shall not state at an auction that an increased bid greater than that offered by the last highest bidder has been made when, in fact, no person has made an increased bid. Notwithstanding the foregoing, an auctioneer or another authorized person may place a bid on the seller's behalf during an auction of real property that would not result in a sale of the real property, if both of the following are true:

(1) Notice is given to all auction participants, including all other bidders, that liberty for that type of bidding is reserved and that type of bid will not result in the sale of the real property.

(2) The person placing that type of bid contemporaneously discloses to all auction participants, including all other bidders, that the particular bid has been placed on behalf of the seller.

(c) For the purpose of the conduct of online auctions of real property, "notice" means a statement of the information required to be given under paragraph (1) of subdivision (b) within the end user license agreement, terms of service, or equivalent policy posted on, or provided by, the operator of an Internet Web site, online service, online application, or mobile application, and by conspicuously posting the information required to be given under paragraph (1) of subdivision (b) in any of the following ways:

(1) Upon the Internet Web page or its equivalent through which a user directly interacts with the site, service, or application during the online auction.

(2) With an icon that hyperlinks to an Internet Web page or its equivalent upon which the required information is posted, if the icon is located on the Internet Web page or its equivalent through which a user directly interacts with the site, service, or application during the online auction. The icon shall use a color that contrasts with the background color of the Internet Web page or is otherwise readily distinguishable.

(3) With a text link that hyperlinks to an Internet Web page or its equivalent upon which the required information is posted, if the text link is located on the Internet Web page or its equivalent through which a user directly interacts with the site, service, or application during the online auction. The text link shall be written in capital letters that are in larger type than the surrounding text, or shall be written in contrasting type, font, or color to the surrounding text of the same size, or shall be set off from the surrounding text of the same size by symbols or other marks that call attention to the language.

(4) With any other functional hyperlink or its equivalent that is displayed on the site, service, or application through which a user directly interacts with the site, service, or application during the online auction so that a reasonable person would notice it and understand it to hyperlink to the required information. *(Added by Stats.2014, c. 893 (A.B. 2039), § 1, eff. Jan. 1, 2015, operative July 1, 2015. Amended by Stats.2015, c. 354 (S.B.474), § 1, eff. Sept. 28, 2015.)*

Title 2.96

CALIFORNIA RENTAL–PURCHASE ACT

Section	
1812.620.	Short title.
1812.621.	Legislative findings, declarations and intent.
1812.622.	Definitions.
1812.623.	Rental-purchase agreement; form; contents.
1812.624.	Prohibited provisions; effect.
1812.625.	Security deposits; amount; purpose; return.
1812.626.	Late payment fee; conditions; limit.
1812.627.	Consumer's liability for loss or damage to the property; limit.
1812.628.	Right of cancellation.
1812.629.	Information and documents to be provided to consumer; execution of rental-purchase agreement; receipts.
1812.630.	Advertisements.
1812.631.	Default; reinstatement.
1812.632.	Acquisition of ownership; reduction of periodic rental payment.
1812.633.	Lessor's duty to maintain the property.
1812.634.	Transfer of warranties.
1812.635.	Service contracts.
1812.636.	Violations; damages; fees and costs; equitable relief.

Section	
1812.637.	Bona fide errors.
1812.638.	Unfair, unlawful or deceptive conduct; collection or repossession; communications to locate consumer or rental property; communications with consumer; harassment.
1812.639.	Unfair, unlawful or deceptive conduct; untrue or misleading statements; rental-purchase agreement.
1812.640.	Report of late payment, default or repossession to consumer credit reporting agency or investigative consumer reporting agency.
1812.641.	Solicitation or promotional material to consumer reference to verify consumer's income, assets, credit history or residence.
1812.642.	Discrimination against prospective consumers.
1812.643.	Notice to joint signers of rental-purchase agreement.
1812.644.	Records of lessor's cost; maximum cash price; maximum total of payments.
1812.645.	Action on rental-purchase agreement; venue.
1812.646.	Waiver or modification of provisions of title.
1812.647.	Violation; punishment.
1812.648.	Cumulative remedies.
1812.649.	Severability.
1812.650.	Geophysical location tracking; use by lessor; clear and prominent notice and consent.

§ 1812.620. Short title

This title shall be known and may be cited as the Karnette Rental-Purchase Act. *(Added by Stats.1994, c. 1026 (A.B. 722), § 1.)*

§ 1812.621. Legislative findings, declarations and intent

The Legislature hereby finds and declares that consumers enter into rental-purchase contracts that do not adequately disclose the actual terms and cost of the transaction or the consumer's liability for certain breaches of the contract, and that contain unfair provisions, including unfair terms related to fees and charges, the exercise or the termination of purchase option rights, property loss and damage, and the repair or replacement of improperly functioning rental property.

It is, therefore, the intent of the Legislature in enacting this title to ensure that consumers are protected from misrepresentations and unfair dealings by ensuring that consumers are adequately informed of all relevant terms, including the cash price, periodic payments, total purchase price, and other applicable charges or fees, before they enter into rental-purchase contracts.

It is further the intent of the Legislature to (a) prohibit unfair or unconscionable conduct toward consumers in connection with rental-purchase transactions, (b) prohibit unfair contract terms, including unreasonable charges, (c) prevent the forfeiture of contract rights by consumers, (d) provide a right of reinstatement and a reasonable formula for the exercise of purchase option rights under a rental-purchase contract, (e) provide reasonable requirements for the servicing, repair, and replacement of improperly functioning rental property, and (f) cover rental-purchase transactions under existing laws, including laws governing debt collection, cosigners, home solicitation contracts, and warranties. This title shall be liberally construed to achieve its remedial objectives. *(Added by Stats.1994, c. 1026 (A.B.722), § 1.)*

Cross References

Cash price defined for purposes of this Title, see Civil Code § 1812.622.

Consumer defined for purposes of this Title, see Civil Code § 1812.622.

Fee defined for purposes of this Title, see Civil Code § 1812.622.

§ 1812.622. Definitions

As used in this title:

(a) "Advertisement" means a commercial message in any medium that directly or indirectly solicits or promotes one or more specific rental-purchase transactions, excluding instore [1] merchandising aids. This definition does not limit or alter the application of other laws, including Chapter 5 (commencing with Section 17200) of Part 2 and Chapter 1 (commencing with Section 17500) of Part 3, of Division 7 of the Business and Professions Code, to rental-purchase transactions.

(b) "Consumer" means a natural person or persons who rent or lease personal property from a lessor pursuant to a rental-purchase agreement or to whom a lessor offers personal property for use pursuant to a rental-purchase agreement.

(c) "Lessor" means any person or entity that provides or offers to provide personal property for use by consumers pursuant to a rental-purchase agreement.

(d) "Rental–purchase agreement," except as otherwise provided in this subdivision, means an agreement between a lessor and a consumer pursuant to which the lessor rents or leases, for valuable consideration, personal property for use by a consumer for personal, family, or household purposes for an initial term not exceeding four months that may be renewed or otherwise extended, if under the terms of the agreement the consumer acquires an option or other legally enforceable right to become owner of the property. A rental-purchase agreement is a lease subject to Title 1.5 (commencing with Section 1750) and Title 1.7 (commencing with Section 1790).

"Rental-purchase agreement" shall not be construed to be, nor be governed by, and shall not apply to, any of the following:

(1) A retail installment sale, as defined in Section 1802.5.

(2) A retail installment contract, as defined in Section 1802.6.

(3) A retail installment account, as defined in Section 1802.7.

(4) A lease or agreement that constitutes a security interest, as defined in Section 1201 of the Commercial Code.

(5) A consumer credit contract, as defined in Section 1799.90.

(e) "Cash price" means the price of the personal property described in the rental-purchase agreement that the consumer may pay in cash to the lessor at the inception of the rental-purchase agreement to acquire ownership of that personal property.

(f) "Cost of rental" means the difference between the total of all periodic payments necessary to acquire ownership under the rental-purchase agreement and the cash price of the rental property that is subject to the rental-purchase agreement.

§ 1812.622

(g) "Fee" means any payment, charge, fee, cost, or expense, however denominated, other than a rental payment.

(h) "Appliance" means and includes any refrigerator, freezer, range including any cooktop or oven, microwave oven, washer, dryer, dishwasher, or room air-conditioner or air purifier.

(i) "Electronic set" means and includes any television, radio, camera, video game, or any type of device for the recording, storage, copying, printing, transmission, display, or playback of any sound or image, but does not include any item that is part of a computer system.

(j) "Computer system" means a computer processor and a video monitor, printer, and peripheral items primarily designed for use with a computer. Audio and video devices, which are commonly used for entertainment and into which data may be downloaded from a computer, are not part of a computer system.

(k) "Lessor's cost" means the documented actual cost, including actual freight charges, of the rental property to the lessor from a wholesaler, distributor, supplier, or manufacturer and net of any discounts, rebates, and incentives.

(l) "Total of payments" means the total amount of periodic payments necessary to acquire ownership of the property that is the subject of the rental-purchase agreement if the consumer makes all regularly scheduled payments.

(m) "Electronic device" means a desktop or laptop computer, handheld device, tablet, smartphone, or other electronic product or device that has a platform on which to download, install, or run any software program, code, script, or other content.

(n) "Geophysical location tracking technology" means hardware, software, or an application that collects and reports data or information that identifies the precise geophysical location of an item, including technologies that report the GPS coordinates of an electronic device, the WiFi signals available to or actually used by an electronic device to access the Internet, the telecommunication towers or connections available to or actually used by an electronic device, the processing of any reported data or information through geolocation lookup services, or any information derived from any combination of the foregoing.

(o) "Monitoring technology" means any hardware, software, or application utilized in conjunction with an electronic device that can cause the electronic device to capture, monitor, record, or report information about user activities with or without the user's knowledge.

(p) "Remote technical assistance" means collaborative access by the user and technician to connect to an electronic device for the purpose of providing technical support to the user.

(q) "Express consent" means the affirmative agreement to any use or installation of geophysical location tracking technology or remote technical assistance. Express consent does not include consent given when either option is highlighted or preselected as a default setting. (Added by Stats.1994, c. 1026 (A.B.722), § 1. Amended by Stats.2006, c. 254 (S.B.1481), § 2; Stats.2006, c. 410 (A.B.594), § 1; Stats. 2014, c. 426 (A.B.2667), § 1, eff. Jan. 1, 2015.)

[1] So in chaptered copy; probably should be "in-store".

§ 1812.623. Rental-purchase agreement; form; contents

(a) Every rental-purchase agreement shall be contained in a single document which shall set forth all of the agreements of the lessor and the consumer with respect to the rights and obligations of each party. Every rental-purchase agreement shall be written in at least 10–point type in the same language as principally used in any oral sales presentation or negotiations leading to the execution of the agreement, and shall clearly and conspicuously disclose all of the following:

(1) The names of the lessor and the consumer, the lessor's business address and telephone number, the consumer's address, the date on which the agreement is executed, and a description of the property sufficient to identify it.

(2) Whether the property subject to the rental-purchase agreement is new or used. If the property is new, the lessor shall disclose the model year or, if the model year is not known by the lessor, the date of the lessor's acquisition of the property. If the property is used, the age or model year shall be disclosed if known by the lessor.

(3) The minimum period for which the consumer is obligated under the rental-purchase agreement; the duration of the rental-purchase agreement if all regularly scheduled periodic payments are made, designated as the "rental period"; and the amount of each periodic payment.

(4) The total of payments and the total number of periodic payments necessary to acquire ownership of the property if the renter makes all regularly scheduled periodic payments.

(5) The cash price of the property subject to the rental purchase agreement.

(6) The cost of rental.

(7) The amount and purpose of any other payment or fee permitted by this title in addition to those specified pursuant to paragraphs (3) and (4), including any late payment fee.

(8) A statement that the total number and dollar amount of payments necessary to acquire ownership of the rental property disclosed under paragraph (4) does not include other fees permitted by this title, such as late payment fees, and that the consumer should read the rental-purchase agreement for an explanation of any applicable additional fees.

(9) Whether the consumer is liable for loss or damage to the rental property and, if so, the maximum amount for which the consumer may be liable as provided in subdivision (a) of Section 1812.627.

(10) The following notice:

NOTICE

You are renting this property. You will not own it until you make all of the regularly scheduled payments or you use the early purchase option.

You do not have the right to keep the property if you do not make required payments or do not use the early purchase option. If you miss a payment, the lessor can repossess the property, but, you may have the right to the return of the same or similar property.

See the contract for an explanation of your rights.

(11) A description of the consumer's right to acquire ownership of the property before the end of the rental period as provided in subdivisions (a) and (b) of Section 1812.632.

(12) A description of the consumer's reinstatement rights as provided in Section 1812.631.

(13) If warranty coverage is transferable to a consumer who acquires ownership of the property, a statement that the unexpired portion of all warranties provided by the manufacturer, distributor, or seller of the property that is the subject of the rental-purchase agreement will be transferred by the lessor to the consumer at the time the consumer acquires ownership of the property from the lessor.

(14) A description of the lessor's obligation to maintain the rental property and to repair or replace rental property that is not operating properly, as provided in Section 1812.633.

(b)(1) The disclosures required by paragraphs (3), (4), (5), and (6) of subdivision (a) shall be printed in at least 10–point boldface type or capital letters if typed and shall be grouped together in a box formed by a heavy line in the following form:

TOTAL OF PAYMENTS	COST OF RENTAL	CASH PRICE	
$	$ Amount over cash price you will pay if you make all regular payments.	$ Property available at this price for cash from the lessor. See about your early purchase option rights.	
You must pay this amount to own the property if you make all the regular payments. You can buy the property for less under the early purchase option.	AMOUNT OF EACH PAYMENT $ per _____ (insert period)	NUMBER OF PAYMENTS	RENTAL PERIOD

(2) The box described in paragraph (1) shall appear immediately above the space reserved for the buyer's signature.

(c) The disclosures required by paragraphs (3), (4), (5), and (6) of subdivision (a) shall be grouped together in a box formed by a heavy line in the form prescribed in subdivision (b) and shall be clearly and conspicuously placed on a tag or sticker affixed to the property available for rental-purchase. If the property available for rental-purchase is not displayed at the lessor's place of business but appears in a photograph or catalog shown to consumers, a tag or sticker shall be affixed to the photograph of the property or catalog shown to consumers or shall be given to consumers. The disclosure required by paragraph (2) of subdivision (a) also shall be clearly and conspicuously placed on the tag or sticker.

(d) All disclosures required by this section shall be printed or typed in a color or shade that clearly contrasts with the background. *(Added by Stats.1994, c. 1026 (A.B.722), § 1. Amended by Stats.1997, c. 112 (S.B.338), § 2; Stats.2006, c. 410 (A.B.594), § 2.)*

Cross References

Cash price defined for purposes of this Title, see Civil Code § 1812.622.
Consumer defined for purposes of this Title, see Civil Code § 1812.622.
Cost of rental defined for purposes of this Title, see Civil Code § 1812.622.
Fee defined for purposes of this Title, see Civil Code § 1812.622.
Lessor defined for purposes of this Title, see Civil Code § 1812.622.
Rental-purchase agreement defined for purposes of this Title, see Civil Code § 1812.622.
Total of payments defined for purposes of this Title, see Civil Code § 1812.622.

§ 1812.624. Prohibited provisions; effect

(a) No rental-purchase agreement or any document that the lessor requests the consumer to sign shall contain any provision by which:

(1) A power of attorney is given to confess judgment in this state or to appoint the lessor, its agents, or its successors in interest as the consumer's agent in the collection of payments or the repossession of the rental property.

(2) The consumer authorizes the lessor or its agent to commit any breach of the peace in repossessing the rental property or to enter the consumer's dwelling or other premises without obtaining the consumer's consent at the time of entry.

(3) The consumer agrees to purchase from the lessor insurance or a liability waiver against loss or damage to the rental property.

(4) The consumer waives or agrees to waive any defense, counterclaim, or right the consumer may have against the lessor, its agent, or its successor in interest.

§ 1812.624

(5) The consumer is required to pay any fee in connection with reinstatement except as provided in Section 1812.631.

(6) The consumer is required to pay a fee in connection with the pickup of the property or the termination or rescission of the rental-purchase agreement.

(7) The consumer is required to pay any fee permitted by the rental-purchase agreement and this title that is not reasonable and actually incurred by the lessor. The lessor has the burden of proof to establish that a fee was reasonable and was an actual cost incurred by the lessor.

(8) The consumer is required to pay a downpayment, more than one advance periodic rental payment, or any other payment except a security deposit permitted under Section 1812.625.

(9) Except to the extent permitted by subdivision (b) of Section 1812.627, the consumer waives any rights under Sections 1928 or 1929.

(10) The consumer grants a security interest in any property.

(11) The consumer's liability for loss or damage to the property which is the subject of the rental-purchase agreement may exceed the maximum described in subdivision (a) of Section 1812.627.

(12) Except under the circumstances authorized by subdivision (a) or (b) of Section 1812.632, the consumer is obligated to make any balloon payment. A "balloon payment" is any payment for the purchase or use of the rental property which is more than the regularly scheduled periodic payment amount.

(13) The consumer is required to pay a late payment fee that is not permitted under Section 1812.626.

(14) The consumer is required to pay both a late payment fee and a fee for the lessor's collection of a past due payment at the consumer's home or other location.

(15) The consumer waives or offers to waive any right or remedy against the lessor, its agents, or its successors in interest for any violation of this title or any other illegal act. This subdivision does not apply to a document executed in connection with the bona fide settlement, compromise, or release of a specific disputed claim.

(16) The lessor, its agents, or its successors in interest may commence any judicial action against the consumer in a county other than the county in which (A) the rental-purchase agreement was signed or (B) the consumer resides at the time the action is commenced.

(17) The amount stated as the cash price for any item of personal property exceeds the cash price permitted under Section 1812.644.

(18) The total of payments exceeds the amount permitted under Section 1812.644.

(b) Any provision in a rental-purchase agreement that is prohibited by this title shall be void and unenforceable and a violation of this title. A rental-purchase agreement which contains any provision that is prohibited by this title is voidable by the consumer. *(Added by Stats.1994, c. 1026 (A.B.722), § 1. Amended by Stats.2006, c. 410 (A.B.594), § 3.)*

Cross References

Burden of proof, generally, see Evidence Code § 500 et seq.
Cash price defined for purposes of this Title, see Civil Code § 1812.622.
Consumer defined for purposes of this Title, see Civil Code § 1812.622.
Fee defined for purposes of this Title, see Civil Code § 1812.622.
Lessor defined for purposes of this Title, see Civil Code § 1812.622.
Rental-purchase agreement defined for purposes of this Title, see Civil Code § 1812.622.
Total of payments defined for purposes of this Title, see Civil Code § 1812.622.

§ 1812.625. Security deposits; amount; purpose; return

(a) The lessor may require the consumer to pay a security deposit, however denominated, in an amount not to exceed the equivalent of one month's rental only for the purpose of satisfying any lawful claim by the lessor, up to the maximum described in subdivision (a) of Section 1812.627, for those amounts reasonably necessary to pay for the loss of the property or the repair of damage, exclusive of reasonable wear and tear.

(b) Within two weeks after the lessor has taken possession of the property from the consumer, the lessor shall deliver to the consumer the amount of the security deposit less the amount, if any, deducted for loss or repair as permitted by this title. If any amount is deducted, the lessor shall also deliver to the consumer at that time a copy of an itemized statement indicating the amount of the security deposit, the amount deducted for loss or repair, and a detailed statement of the basis for the deduction. Delivery may be made by personal delivery or by first-class mail, postage prepaid. *(Added by Stats.1994, c. 1026 (A.B.722), § 1.)*

Cross References

Consumer defined for purposes of this Title, see Civil Code § 1812.622.
Lessor defined for purposes of this Title, see Civil Code § 1812.622.

§ 1812.626. Late payment fee; conditions; limit

(a) The lessor may assess a late payment fee if the late payment fee is specified in the rental-purchase agreement and is permitted by this section.

(b) No fee shall be assessed for a payment which is less than three days late if the rental-purchase agreement specifies weekly periodic payments.

(c) No fee shall be assessed for a payment which is less than 7 days late if the rental-purchase agreement specifies longer than weekly periodic payments.

(d) The lessor may assess more than one late fee for a particular late payment if the total of all fees assessed for that late payment does not exceed the maximum provided in subdivision (e). If the maximum total late payment fee has been imposed for a particular payment, no additional late payment fee may be imposed for that payment.

(e) The total of all fees for a late payment shall not exceed the lesser of 5 percent of the payment or five dollars ($5), except that a minimum total fee of two dollars ($2) may be required. *(Added by Stats.1994, c. 1026 (A.B.722), § 1.)*

Cross References

Fee defined for purposes of this Title, see Civil Code § 1812.622.
Lessor defined for purposes of this Title, see Civil Code § 1812.622.
Rental-purchase agreement defined for purposes of this Title, see Civil Code § 1812.622.

§ 1812.627. Consumer's liability for loss or damage to the property; limit

(a) The consumer's liability for loss or damage to the property which is the subject of the rental-purchase agreement shall in no event exceed the lesser of (1) the fair market value at the time of the loss or damage or (2) the amount that would be necessary for the renter to exercise the purchase option provided in subdivision (a) of Section 1812.632.

(b) A lessor and a consumer may agree that the consumer may be liable for loss only up to the maximum amount described in subdivision (a) and only for one of the following:

(1) Loss caused by the consumer's negligent, reckless, or intentional acts.

(2) Loss caused by the theft of the property subject to the rental-purchase agreement unless one of the following is applicable:

(A) There is evidence of a burglary of the premises in which the property is located, such as physical evidence or an official report filed by the consumer with the police or other law enforcement agency.

(B) The consumer establishes by the preponderance of the evidence that the consumer has not committed or aided or abetted in the commission of the theft of the property. *(Added by Stats.1994, c. 1026 (A.B.722), § 1.)*

Cross References

Consumer defined for purposes of this Title, see Civil Code § 1812.622.
Lessor defined for purposes of this Title, see Civil Code § 1812.622.
Rental-purchase agreement defined for purposes of this Title, see Civil Code § 1812.622.

§ 1812.628. Right of cancellation

(a) In addition to the circumstances described in subdivision (a) of Section 1689.5, a rental-purchase agreement regardless of the amount involved shall be deemed a home solicitation contract or offer if the rental-purchase agreement has an initial term that exceeds one week and was made at other than appropriate trade premises, as defined in subdivision (b) of Section 1689.5.

(b) In addition to any other right of cancellation, a consumer has the right to cancel a rental-purchase agreement, without penalty or obligation if the consumer has not taken possession of the property. *(Added by Stats.1994, c. 1026 (A.B.722), § 1.)*

Cross References

Consumer defined for purposes of this Title, see Civil Code § 1812.622.
Rental-purchase agreement defined for purposes of this Title, see Civil Code § 1812.622.

§ 1812.629. Information and documents to be provided to consumer; execution of rental-purchase agreement; receipts

(a) Upon the request of the consumer, the lessor shall provide the information as required by subdivision (b) of Section 1812.623 in an exemplar of the rental-purchase agreement covering the property specified by the consumer and shall provide the consumer with a copy of the proposed rental-purchase agreement prior to its execution. The consumer may take this copy from the lessor's premises.

(b) The lessor shall not obtain the consumer's signature to a rental-purchase agreement if it contains blank spaces to be filled in after it has been signed.

(c) A copy of the fully completed rental-purchase agreement and all other documents which the lessor requests the consumer to sign shall be given to the consumer at the time they are signed. The rental-purchase agreement shall not be enforceable against the consumer until the consumer has received a signed copy.

(d) The lessor shall deliver to the consumer a written receipt for each payment made by the consumer. *(Added by Stats.1994, c. 1026 (A.B.722), § 1.)*

Cross References

Consumer defined for purposes of this Title, see Civil Code § 1812.622.
Lessor defined for purposes of this Title, see Civil Code § 1812.622.
Rental-purchase agreement defined for purposes of this Title, see Civil Code § 1812.622.

§ 1812.630. Advertisements

(a)(1) Any advertisement of a rental-purchase agreement that states the amount of any payment shall clearly and conspicuously disclose all of the following in the same language used in the advertisement:

(A) That the agreement advertised is a rental-purchase agreement.

(B) That the property is used if that is the case.

(C) That ownership is not acquired until all of the payments necessary to acquire ownership have been made.

(D) The total amount and number of periodic payments necessary to acquire ownership.

(2) If more than one item is advertised in one print advertisement, the lessor may comply with paragraph (1) by clearly and conspicuously including in the advertisement a table or schedule sufficient in detail to permit determination of the total amount and number of periodic payments necessary to acquire ownership of the items advertised having the highest and lowest total amount of periodic payments necessary to acquire ownership.

(b) A lessor who advertises "no credit check" or otherwise states or implies that no inquiry will be made of a consumer's credit history or creditworthiness shall not (1) make any inquiry or request a consumer to complete any document concerning the consumer's assets or credit history, (2) obtain a consumer credit report as defined in subdivision (c) of Section 1785.3, or (3) obtain an investigative consumer report as defined in subdivision (c) of Section 1786.2. *(Added by Stats.1994, c. 1026 (A.B.722), § 1.)*

Cross References

Advertisement defined for purposes of this Title, see Civil Code § 1812.622.
Consumer defined for purposes of this Title, see Civil Code § 1812.622.

§ 1812.630

Lessor defined for purposes of this Title, see Civil Code § 1812.622.
Rental-purchase agreement defined for purposes of this Title, see Civil Code § 1812.622.

§ 1812.631. Default; reinstatement

(a) A consumer may be deemed in default under the rental-purchase agreement if either of the following applies:

(1) The rental-purchase agreement requires weekly periodic rental payments and the consumer has not made a payment by the end of the seventh day after its due date.

(2) The rental-purchase agreement requires rental payments in periodic intervals longer than one week and the consumer has not made a payment by the end of the 10th day after its due date.

(b) A consumer who is in default under a rental-purchase agreement requiring weekly periodic rental payments may reinstate the rental-purchase agreement, without losing any rights or options under that agreement, by paying all past due payments, including late payment fees, by the end of the seventh day after the due date of the payment in default if the consumer retains possession of the property and within one year after the due date of the payment in default if the consumer returns or tenders the property to the lessor, unless the lessor permits the consumer to retain the property during this period.

(c) A consumer who is in default under a rental-purchase agreement requiring rental payments in periodic intervals longer than one week may reinstate the rental-purchase agreement, without losing any rights or options under that agreement, by paying all past due payments, including late payment fees, by the end of the 10th day after the due date of the payment in default if the consumer retains possession of the property and within one year after the due date of the payment in default if the consumer returns or tenders the property to the lessor, unless the lessor permits the consumer to retain the property during this period.

(d) Upon reinstatement, the lessor shall provide the consumer with the same rental property, if available, or substitute property of the same brand, if available, and comparable quality, age, condition, and warranty coverage. If substitute property is provided, the lessor shall provide the lessee with the disclosures required in paragraph (2) of subdivision (a) of Section 1812.623.

(e)(1) Except as provided in paragraph (2), a lessor shall not deny a consumer the right of reinstatement provided in this section.

(2) This section does not apply to a consumer who has (A) stolen or unlawfully disposed of the property, (B) damaged the property as the result of the consumer's intentional, willful, wanton, or reckless conduct, or (C) defaulted in making payments as described in subdivision (a) on three consecutive occasions.

(3) If the lessor denies a consumer the right to reinstate pursuant to paragraph (2), the lessor has the burden of proof to establish that the denial was in good faith and was permitted under paragraph (2).

(f) Nothing in this subdivision prohibits the lessor from contacting the consumer provided that the lessor does not violate Section 1812.638. *(Added by Stats.1994, c. 1026 (A.B.722), § 1.)*

Cross References

Consumer defined for purposes of this Title, see Civil Code § 1812.622.
Fee defined for purposes of this Title, see Civil Code § 1812.622.
Lessor defined for purposes of this Title, see Civil Code § 1812.622.
Rental-purchase agreement defined for purposes of this Title, see Civil Code § 1812.622.

§ 1812.632. Acquisition of ownership; reduction of periodic rental payment

(a)(1) The consumer has the right to acquire ownership of the property within three months of the date on which the consumer executed the rental-purchase agreement by tendering to the lessor an amount equal to the cash price and any past due fees less all periodic payments that the consumer has paid.

(2) Within 10 days after the consumer executes the rental purchase agreement, the lessor shall personally deliver or send by first-class mail to the consumer a notice informing the consumer of the right described in paragraph (1), including the amount the consumer must pay to acquire ownership and the date by which payment must be made. The statement shall not be accompanied by any other written information including solicitations for other rental-purchase agreements.

(b) After the expiration of the three-month period following the execution of the rental-purchase agreement, the consumer has the right to acquire ownership of the property at any time by tendering to the lessor all past due payments and fees and an amount equal to the cash price stated in the rental-purchase agreement multiplied by a fraction that has as its numerator the number of periodic payments remaining under the agreement and that has as its denominator the total number of periodic payments.

(c)(1) The lessor shall, in connection with a consumer's rights under subdivision (b), provide the consumer with a written statement in the manner set forth in paragraph (2) below that clearly states (A) the total amount the consumer would have to pay to acquire ownership of the rental property if the consumer makes all regularly scheduled payments remaining under the rental-purchase agreement and (B) the total amount the consumer would have to pay to acquire ownership of that property pursuant to subdivision (a).

(2) The statement required by paragraph (1) shall be personally delivered or sent by first-class mail to the consumer within seven days after (A) the date the consumer requests information about the amount required to purchase the rental property and (B) the date the consumer has made one-half of the total number of periodic payments required to acquire ownership of the rental property. The statement shall not be accompanied by any other written information including solicitations for other rental-purchase agreements.

(d)(1) Subject to paragraph (2), if any consumer who has signed the rental-purchase agreement has experienced an interruption or reduction of 25 percent or more of income due to involuntary job loss, involuntary reduced employment, illness, pregnancy, or disability after one-half or more of the total amount of the periodic payments necessary to acquire ownership under the agreement has been paid, the lessor shall reduce the amount of each periodic rental payment by (A) the percentage of the reduction in the consumer's income or (B) 50 percent, whichever is less, for the period during which the consumer's income is interrupted or reduced. If payments are reduced, the total dollar amount of payments necessary to acquire ownership shall not be increased, and the rights and duties of the lessor and the consumer shall not otherwise be affected. When the consumer's income is restored, the lessor may increase the amount of rental payments, but in no event shall rental payments exceed the originally scheduled amount of rental payments.

(2) Paragraph (1) applies only after the consumer provides to the lessor some evidence of the amount and cause of the interruption or reduction of income. *(Added by Stats.1994, c. 1026 (A.B.722), § 1. Amended by Stats.2006, c. 410 (A.B. 594), § 4.)*

Cross References

Cash price defined for purposes of this Title, see Civil Code § 1812.622.
Consumer defined for purposes of this Title, see Civil Code § 1812.622.
Fee defined for purposes of this Title, see Civil Code § 1812.622.
Lessor defined for purposes of this Title, see Civil Code § 1812.622.
Rental-purchase agreement defined for purposes of this Title, see Civil Code § 1812.622.

§ 1812.633. Lessor's duty to maintain the property

(a) The lessor shall maintain the property subject to the rental-purchase agreement in good working order while the agreement is in effect without charging any fee to the consumer in addition to the regularly scheduled rental payments set forth in the rental-purchase agreement.

(b) By the end of the second business day following the day on which the lessor received notice from the consumer that the property is not operating properly, the lessor shall repair or replace the property without any fee to the consumer in addition to the regularly scheduled rental payments set forth in the rental-purchase agreement.

(c) If a repair or replacement cannot be immediately effected, the lessor shall temporarily substitute property of comparable quality and condition while repairs are being effected. If repairs cannot be completed to the reasonable satisfaction of the consumer within 30 days after the lessor receives notice from the consumer or within a longer period voluntarily agreed to by the consumer, the lessor shall permanently replace the property.

(d) All replacement property shall be the same brand, if available, and comparable in quality, age, condition, and warranty coverage to the replaced property. If the same brand is not available, the brand of the replacement property shall be agreeable to the consumer.

(e) All of the consumer's and lessor's rights and obligations under the rental-purchase agreement and this title that applied to the property originally subject to the rental-purchase agreement shall apply to any replacement property.

(f) The consumer shall not be charged, or held liable for, any rental fee for any period of time during which the property that is the subject of the rental-purchase agreement or any property substituted for it pursuant to this section is not in good working order.

(g) This section does not apply to the repair of damage resulting from the consumer's intentional, willful, wanton, reckless, or negligent conduct. If the lessor does not comply with this section because of this subdivision, the lessor has the burden of proof to establish that noncompliance was justified and in good faith.

(h) A lessor shall not deliver to a consumer any property which the lessor knows or has reason to know is defective. *(Added by Stats.1994, c. 1026 (A.B.722), § 1.)*

Cross References

Burden of proof, generally, see Evidence Code § 500 et seq.
Consumer defined for purposes of this Title, see Civil Code § 1812.622.
Fee defined for purposes of this Title, see Civil Code § 1812.622.
Lessor defined for purposes of this Title, see Civil Code § 1812.622.
Rental-purchase agreement defined for purposes of this Title, see Civil Code § 1812.622.

§ 1812.634. Transfer of warranties

When the lessor transfers ownership of the rental property, the lessor shall also transfer to the consumer the unexpired portion of any transferable warranties provided by the manufacturer, distributor, or seller of the rental property, and these warranties shall apply as if the consumer were the original purchaser of the goods. *(Added by Stats.1994, c. 1026 (A.B.722), § 1.)*

Cross References

Consumer defined for purposes of this Title, see Civil Code § 1812.622.
Lessor defined for purposes of this Title, see Civil Code § 1812.622.

§ 1812.635. Service contracts

(a) A lessor shall not sell, or offer for sale, a service contract for the rental property if that service contract provides any coverage while the rental-purchase agreement is in effect.

(b) A lessor may sell, or offer for sale, a service contract providing coverage for the rental property after the consumer acquires ownership of that property, if both of the following conditions are satisfied:

(1) The lessor does not sell, or offer to sell, the service contract before (A) the consumer pays at least one-half of the total number of periodic payments necessary to acquire ownership of the property or (B) the consumer acquires ownership of the property, as provided in Section 1812.632, whichever occurs first.

(2) The lessor clearly and conspicuously indicates to the consumer in writing before the consumer's purchase of the service contract that the purchase is optional.

(c) If the consumer chooses to purchase a service contract before the expiration of the rental-purchase agreement and defaults or otherwise does not make all payments necessary to acquire ownership within the rental period specified in the agreement, the lessor shall refund all consideration paid for the service contract to the consumer within two weeks after the lessor has received the consumer's last rental payment. This subdivision does not limit or alter any of the consumer's

§ 1812.635

cancellation or refund rights under the service contract or under other provisions of law.

(d) "Service contract" has the meaning set forth in subdivision (o) of Section 1791. (Added by Stats.1994, c. 1026 (A.B.722), § 1.)

Cross References

Consumer defined for purposes of this Title, see Civil Code § 1812.622.
Lessor defined for purposes of this Title, see Civil Code § 1812.622.
Rental-purchase agreement defined for purposes of this Title, see Civil Code § 1812.622.

§ 1812.636. Violations; damages; fees and costs; equitable relief

(a) A consumer damaged by a violation of this title by a lessor is entitled to recover all of the following:

(1) Actual damages.

(2) Twenty-five percent of an amount equal to the total amount of payments required to obtain ownership if all payments were made under the rental-purchase agreement, but not less than one hundred dollars ($100) nor more than one thousand dollars ($1,000).

(3) The consumer's reasonable attorney's fees and court costs.

(4) Exemplary damages, in the amount the court deems proper, for intentional or willful violations of this title.

(5) Equitable relief as the court deems proper.

(b) Where more than one consumer is a party to a rental-purchase agreement, the limitations of subdivision (a) shall apply to all those consumers in the aggregate, and no more than one recovery shall be permitted for each violation. (Added by Stats.1994, c. 1026 (A.B.722), § 1.)

Cross References

Consumer defined for purposes of this Title, see Civil Code § 1812.622.
Fee defined for purposes of this Title, see Civil Code § 1812.622.
Lessor defined for purposes of this Title, see Civil Code § 1812.622.
Rental-purchase agreement defined for purposes of this Title, see Civil Code § 1812.622.

§ 1812.637. Bona fide errors

(a) A lessor is not liable for a violation of this title if, before the 30th calendar day after the date the lessor discovers a bona fide error and before an action under this title is filed or written notice of the error is received by the lessor from the consumer, the lessor gives the consumer written notice of the error. "Bona fide error," as used in this section, means a violation that was not intentional and resulted from a bona fide error notwithstanding the maintenance of procedures reasonably adapted to avoid that error. Examples of a bona fide error include clerical errors, calculation errors, errors due to unintentionally improper computer programming or data entry, and printing errors, but does not include an error of legal judgment with respect to a lessor's obligations under this title.

(b) Notwithstanding subdivision (a), if the lessor notifies the consumer of a bona fide error the correction of which would increase the amount of any payment, the lessor may not collect the amount of the increase, and the consumer may enforce the rental-purchase agreement as initially written.

(c) Notwithstanding subdivision (a), if the lessor notifies the consumer of a bona fide error the correction of which would lower the amount of any payment, the lessor shall immediately refund to the consumer the difference between what the consumer paid and what the consumer should have paid if the agreement were correct at the inception of the transaction. (Added by Stats.1994, c. 1026 (A.B.722), § 1.)

Cross References

Consumer defined for purposes of this Title, see Civil Code § 1812.622.
Lessor defined for purposes of this Title, see Civil Code § 1812.622.
Rental-purchase agreement defined for purposes of this Title, see Civil Code § 1812.622.

§ 1812.638. Unfair, unlawful or deceptive conduct; collection or repossession; communications to locate consumer or rental property; communications with consumer; harassment

(a) A lessor shall not engage in any unfair, unlawful, or deceptive conduct, or make any untrue or misleading statement in connection with the collection of any payment owed by a consumer or the repossession of any property or attempt to collect or collect any payment in a manner that would be unlawful to collect a debt pursuant to Title 1.6C (commencing with Section 1788).

(b) All of the following apply to any communication by a lessor with any person other than the consumer for the purpose of acquiring information about the location of a consumer or of any rental property:

(1) The lessor shall identify itself and state that the lessor is confirming or correcting location information concerning the consumer.

(2) The lessor shall not communicate with any person more than once unless requested to do so by the person or unless the lessor reasonably believes that the earlier response is erroneous or incomplete and that the person now has correct or complete location information.

(3) The lessor shall not communicate by postcard.

(4) The lessor shall not use any language or symbol on any envelope or in the contents of any communication that indicates that the communication relates to the collection of any payment or the recovery or repossession of rental property.

(5) The lessor shall not communicate with any person other than the consumer's attorney, after the lessor knows the consumer is represented by an attorney with regard to the rental-purchase agreement and has knowledge of, or can readily ascertain, the attorney's name and address, unless the attorney fails to respond within a reasonable period of time to communication from the lessor or unless the attorney consents to direct communication with the consumer.

(c) Without the prior consent of the consumer given directly to the lessor or the express permission of a court of competent jurisdiction, a lessor shall not communicate with a consumer in connection with the collection of any payment or the recovery or repossession of rental property at any of the following:

(1) The consumer's place of employment.

(2) Any unusual time or place or a time or place known or that should be known to be inconvenient to the consumer. In the absence of knowledge of circumstances to the contrary, a lessor shall assume that the convenient time for communicating with a consumer is after 8 a.m. and before 9 p.m., local time at the consumer's location.

(d) A lessor shall not communicate, in connection with the rental-purchase agreement, with any person other than the consumer, the consumer's attorney, or the lessor's attorney, except to the extent the communication is any of the following:

(1) Reasonably necessary to acquire location information concerning the consumer or the rental property, as provided in subdivision (b).

(2) Upon the prior consent of the consumer given directly to the lessor.

(3) Upon the express permission of a court of competent jurisdiction.

(4) Reasonably necessary to effectuate a postjudgment judicial remedy.

(e) If a consumer notifies the lessor in writing that the consumer wishes the lessor to cease further communication with the consumer, the lessor shall not communicate further with the consumer with respect to the rental-purchase agreement, except for any of the following:

(1) To advise the consumer that the lessor's further efforts are being terminated.

(2) To notify the consumer that the lessor may invoke specified remedies allowable by law which are ordinarily invoked by the lessor.

(3) Where necessary to effectuate any postjudgment remedy.

(f) A lessor shall not harass, oppress, or abuse any person in connection with a rental-purchase agreement, including engaging in any of the following conduct:

(1) Using or threatening the use of violence or any criminal means to harm the physical person, reputation, or property of any person.

(2) Using obscene, profane, or abusive language.

(3) Causing a telephone to ring, or engaging any person in telephone conversation repeatedly or continuously with intent to annoy, abuse, or harass any person.

(4) Placing telephone calls without disclosure of the caller's identity. *(Added by Stats.1994, c. 1026 (A.B.722), § 1.)*

Cross References

Consumer defined for purposes of this Title, see Civil Code § 1812.622.
Lessor defined for purposes of this Title, see Civil Code § 1812.622.
Rental-purchase agreement defined for purposes of this Title, see Civil Code § 1812.622.

§ 1812.639. Unfair, unlawful or deceptive conduct; untrue or misleading statements; rental-purchase agreement

A lessor shall not engage in any unfair, unlawful, or deceptive conduct or make any untrue or misleading statement in connection with a rental-purchase agreement, including any violation of this title. *(Added by Stats.1994, c. 1026 (A.B.722), § 1.)*

Cross References

Lessor defined for purposes of this Title, see Civil Code § 1812.622.
Rental-purchase agreement defined for purposes of this Title, see Civil Code § 1812.622.

§ 1812.640. Report of late payment, default or repossession to consumer credit reporting agency or investigative consumer reporting agency

A lessor shall not report any late payment, default, or repossession to a consumer credit reporting agency, as defined in subdivision (d) of Section 1785.3, or to an investigative consumer reporting agency, as defined in subdivision (d) of Section 1786.2 if the lessor (a) advertises "no credit check" or otherwise states or implies that no inquiry will be made of a consumer's credit history or creditworthiness or (b) does not obtain a consumer credit report or investigative consumer report on a consumer before entering into a rental-purchase agreement with that consumer. *(Added by Stats.1994, c. 1026 (A.B.722), § 1.)*

Cross References

Consumer defined for purposes of this Title, see Civil Code § 1812.622.
Lessor defined for purposes of this Title, see Civil Code § 1812.622.
Rental-purchase agreement defined for purposes of this Title, see Civil Code § 1812.622.

§ 1812.641. Solicitation or promotional material to consumer reference to verify consumer's income, assets, credit history or residence

(a) A lessor shall not send any solicitation or other promotional material to a person identified by the consumer as a reference to verify the consumer's income, assets, credit history, or residence unless all of the following occur:

(1) The lessor clearly discloses in the rental-purchase agreement or application that (A) the lessor may send solicitations or other promotional material to references provided by the consumer unless the consumer objects and (B) the consumer has the right to object without incurring any additional rental charge or fee or any loss of contractual rights.

(2) A space on the rental-purchase agreement or application adjacent to the disclosure described in paragraph (1) is provided for the consumer to indicate the consumer's approval or disapproval of the lessor's sending solicitations or other promotional material.

(3) The consumer affirmatively indicates approval.

(4) The lessor does not vary any term required to be disclosed pursuant to Section 1812.623 depending on whether the consumer approves or disapproves of the lessor's sending of solicitations or other promotional material to references.

(b) The first solicitation or other promotional material directed to a person whom the consumer has identified as a reference shall clearly offer the reference the opportunity, without cost, to instruct the lessor to refrain from sending further solicitations or other promotional material to the reference. If so instructed, the lessor shall not send any further solicitations or other promotional material to the

§ 1812.641 OBLIGATIONS

reference and shall remove the reference's name and address from the lessor's mailing list.

(c) This section shall not apply to solicitations or other promotional material sent generally to people solely on the basis of demographic, geographic, or postal zip code criteria and without regard to whether the people have been identified as references by consumers. *(Added by Stats.1994, c. 1026 (A.B.722), § 1.)*

Cross References

Consumer defined for purposes of this Title, see Civil Code § 1812.622.
Fee defined for purposes of this Title, see Civil Code § 1812.622.
Lessor defined for purposes of this Title, see Civil Code § 1812.622.
Rental-purchase agreement defined for purposes of this Title, see Civil Code § 1812.622.

§ 1812.642. Discrimination against prospective consumers

A lessor shall not discriminate against a prospective consumer on any ground that would be a prohibited basis for a creditor to discriminate against an applicant for credit as provided in the Equal Credit Opportunity Act (15 U.S.C. Sec. 1691 et seq.) and Regulation B (12 C.F.R. Part 202) as if they applied to a rental-purchase agreement. Nothing in this section shall be construed in any manner to mean that a rental-purchase agreement is a credit transaction. *(Added by Stats.1994, c. 1026 (A.B.722), § 1.)*

Cross References

Consumer defined for purposes of this Title, see Civil Code § 1812.622.
Lessor defined for purposes of this Title, see Civil Code § 1812.622.
Rental-purchase agreement defined for purposes of this Title, see Civil Code § 1812.622.

§ 1812.643. Notice to joint signers of rental-purchase agreement

(a) Except as provided in subdivision (b), a lessor who obtains the signature of more than one person on a rental-purchase agreement shall deliver the notice set forth in subdivision (c) to each person before that person signs the agreement.

(b) This section does not apply if the persons signing the agreement are married to each other or in fact receive possession of the property described in the agreement.

(c) The notice required by this section is as follows:

"NOTICE TO COSIGNER

If you sign this contract, you will have the same responsibility for the property and the same obligation to make payments that every renter has.

If any renter does not pay, you may have to pay the full amount owed, including late fees, and you may have to pay for certain loss or damage to the property.

The lessor may collect from you without first trying to collect from any other renter. The lessor can use the same collection methods against you that can be used against any renter, such as suing you or garnishing your wages.

This notice is not the contract that makes you responsible.

Before you sign, be sure you can afford to pay if you have to, and that you want to accept this responsibility."

(d) The notice required by subdivision (c) shall be printed in at least 10-point boldface type in English and Spanish. If the rental-purchase agreement is required to be written in a language other than English or Spanish, the notice shall be written in English and, in addition or in lieu of Spanish, in that other language.

(e) If the notice set forth in subdivision (c) is included with the text of the rental-purchase agreement, the notice shall appear immediately above or adjacent to the disclosures required by subdivision (b) of Section 1812.623. If the notice is not included with the text of the agreement, the notice shall be on a separate sheet which shall not contain any other text except as is necessary to identify the lessor and agreement to which the notice refers and to provide for the date and the person's acknowledgment of receipt.

(f) The lessor shall give each person entitled to notice under this section a copy of the completed rental-purchase agreement before obtaining that person's signature.

(g) If a person entitled to receive notice and a copy of the rental-purchase agreement under this section does not receive the notice or agreement in the manner required, that person has no liability in connection with the rental-purchase transaction. *(Added by Stats.1994, c. 1026 (A.B.722), § 1.)*

Cross References

Fee defined for purposes of this Title, see Civil Code § 1812.622.
Lessor defined for purposes of this Title, see Civil Code § 1812.622.
Rental-purchase agreement defined for purposes of this Title, see Civil Code § 1812.622.

§ 1812.644. Records of lessor's cost; maximum cash price; maximum total of payments

(a) A lessor shall maintain records that establish the lessor's cost, as defined in subdivision (k) of Section 1812.622, for each item of personal property that is the subject of the rental-purchase agreement. A copy of each rental-purchase agreement and of the records required by this subdivision shall be maintained for two years following the termination of the agreement.

(b) The maximum cash price for the lessor's first rental of the property that is the subject of the rental-purchase agreement may not exceed 1.65 times the lessor's cost for computer systems and appliances, 1.7 times the lessor's cost for electronic sets, 1.9 times the lessor's cost for automotive accessories, furniture, jewelry, and musical instruments, and 1.65 times the lessor's cost for all other items.

(c) The maximum total of payments may not exceed 2.25 times the maximum cash price that could have been charged for the first rental of the property under subdivision (b).

(d) The maximum total of payments for the lessor's second and subsequent rental of the property that is the subject of the rental-purchase agreement may not exceed the maximum total of payments permitted under subdivision (c) for the first rental of that property less (1) for appliances and electronic sets, one-third the amount of all rental payments paid to the lessor by consumers who previously rented that property or (2) for furniture, computer systems, and all other items, one-half the amount of all rental payments paid to the lessor by consumers who previously rented that property.

(e) The maximum cash price for property on its second or subsequent rental may not exceed the maximum total of payments for that property as permitted under subdivision (d) divided by 2.25.

(f) Upon the written request of the Attorney General, any district attorney or city attorney, or the Director of the Department of Consumer Affairs, a lessor shall provide copies of the records described in this section.

(g) If a lessor willfully discloses a cash price or a total of payments that exceeds the amount permitted by this section, the rental-purchase agreement is void, the consumer shall retain the property without any obligation, and the lessor shall refund to the consumer all amounts paid. *(Added by Stats.1994, c. 1026 (A.B.722), § 1. Amended by Stats.2006, c. 410 (A.B.594), § 5.)*

Cross References

Attorney General, generally, see Government Code § 12500 et seq.
California Rental-Purchase Act, rental-purchase agreements, prohibited provisions, see Civil Code § 1812.624.

§ 1812.645. Action on rental-purchase agreement; venue

An action on a rental-purchase agreement shall be tried in the county in which the rental-purchase agreement was signed or the consumer resides at the time the action is commenced. *(Added by Stats.1994, c. 1026 (A.B.722), § 1.)*

Cross References

Consumer defined for purposes of this Title, see Civil Code § 1812.622.
Rental-purchase agreement defined for purposes of this Title, see Civil Code § 1812.622.

§ 1812.646. Waiver or modification of provisions of title

Any waiver or modification of the provisions of this title by the consumer or lessor shall be void and unenforceable as contrary to public policy. *(Added by Stats.1994, c. 1026 (A.B.722), § 1.)*

Cross References

Consumer defined for purposes of this Title, see Civil Code § 1812.622.
Lessor defined for purposes of this Title, see Civil Code § 1812.622.

§ 1812.647. Violation; punishment

Any person who willfully violates any provision of this title is guilty of a misdemeanor. *(Added by Stats.1994, c. 1026 (A.B.722), § 1.)*

Cross References

Misdemeanors, definition and penalties, see Penal Code §§ 17, 19, 19.2.

§ 1812.648. Cumulative remedies

The rights, remedies, and penalties established by this title are cumulative to the rights, remedies, or penalties established under other laws. *(Added by Stats.1994, c. 1026 (A.B.722), § 1.)*

§ 1812.649. Severability

If any provision of this title or the application thereof to any person or circumstances is held invalid, that invalidity shall not affect other provisions or applications of the title that can be given effect without the invalid provision or application, and to this end the provisions of this title are severable. *(Added by Stats.1994, c. 1026 (A.B.722), § 1.)*

§ 1812.650. Geophysical location tracking; use by lessor; clear and prominent notice and consent

(a) A lessor shall provide clear and prominent notice to a consumer and obtain express consent from the consumer at the time the lessor and the consumer enter into a rental-purchase agreement for an electronic device if that device has geophysical location tracking technology installed by the lessor, and at any time the geophysical location tracking technology is activated or used by the lessor.

(b) For purposes of this section, "clear and prominent notice" means notice presented in an understandable language and syntax, in the predominantly used language for that communication, and that:

(1) In textual communications, the required disclosures are separate and apart from a privacy policy, data use policy, terms of service, end-user license agreement, lease agreement, or other similar document, and of a type, size, and location sufficiently noticeable for an ordinary consumer to read and comprehend in print that contrasts highly with the background on which they appear.

(2) In communications disseminated orally or through audible means, the required disclosures are unavoidable and delivered in a volume and cadence sufficient for an ordinary consumer to hear and comprehend.

(3) In communications disseminated through video means, the required disclosures are in writing in a form consistent with paragraph (1) and appear on the screen for a duration sufficient for an ordinary consumer to read and comprehend them.

(4) In communications made through interactive media, including the Internet, online services, and software, the required disclosures are unavoidable and presented in a form consistent with paragraph (1), in addition to any audio or video presentation.

(c) A lessor shall not use, sell, or share geophysical location tracking technology on an electronic device for any purpose other than the repossession of the electronic device when there is a violation of the rental-purchase agreement, pursuant to law, or when requested by the consumer.

(d) Clear and prominent notification shall be displayed on an electronic device if geophysical location tracking technology is activated or used by the lessor. This notification requirement shall be suspended if the consumer or lessor reports that the electronic device has been stolen and has filed a police report stating that the electronic device has been stolen. For purposes of this subdivision, "filing a police report" means the filing of a consumer's or lessor's complaint with the police department in any form recognized by that jurisdiction.

(e) A lessor shall provide that any geophysical location tracking technology that has been installed by the lessor on an

§ 1812.650

electronic device, or can be activated by the lessor, expires upon the first instance the electronic device connects to the Internet after completion of the purchase of the electronic device.

(f) A lessor shall not use or install monitoring technology on an electronic device for any purpose other than to provide remote technical assistance when requested by the consumer.

(g) A lessor shall provide clear and prominent notice to a consumer and obtain express consent from the consumer for the installation or use of any software that allows the lessor to provide remote technical assistance and upon the activation and deactivation of any remote technical assistance when requested by the consumer.

(h) A lessor shall not acquire any data when providing remote technical assistance beyond what is necessary to provide assistance to the user and beyond what the user has consented to. Any data acquired during the period of consumer consented technical assistance shall not be retained, used, or sold for any purpose.

(i) This section shall not be interpreted to require a lessor to enter into a rental-purchase agreement with any consumer who does not provide express consent to the above-described provisions of the rental-purchase agreement. *(Added by Stats.2014, c. 426 (A.B.2667), § 2, eff. Jan. 1, 2015.)*

Title 2.97

CONSUMER COLLECTION NOTICE

Section
1812.700. Notice to be provided to debtors by third-party collectors subject to federal Fair Debt Collection Practices Act.
1812.701. Change in notice; type-sized used.
1812.702. Violations.

§ 1812.700. Notice to be provided to debtors by third-party collectors subject to federal Fair Debt Collection Practices Act

(a) In addition to the requirements imposed by Article 2 (commencing with Section 1788.10) of Title 1.6C, third-party debt collectors subject to the federal Fair Debt Collection Practices Act (15 U.S.C. Sec. 1692 et seq.) shall provide a notice to debtors that shall include the following description of debtor rights:

"The state Rosenthal Fair Debt Collection Practices Act and the federal Fair Debt Collection Practices Act require that, except under unusual circumstances, collectors may not contact you before 8 a.m. or after 9 p.m. They may not harass you by using threats of violence or arrest or by using obscene language. Collectors may not use false or misleading statements or call you at work if they know or have reason to know that you may not receive personal calls at work. For the most part, collectors may not tell another person, other than your attorney or spouse, about your debt. Collectors may contact another person to confirm your location or enforce a judgment. For more information about debt collection activities, you may contact the Federal Trade Commission at 1–877–FTC–HELP or www.ftc.gov."

(b) The notice shall be included with the first written notice initially addressed to a California address of a debtor in connection with collecting the debt by the third-party debt collector.

(c) If a language other than English is principally used by the third-party debt collector in the initial oral contact with the debtor, a notice shall be provided to the debtor in that language within five working days. *(Added by Stats.2003, c. 259 (S.B.1022), § 1, operative July 1, 2004.)*

§ 1812.701. Change in notice; type-sized used

(a) The notice required in this title may be changed only as necessary to reflect changes under the federal Fair Debt Collection Practices Act (15 U.S.C. Sec. 1692 et seq.) that would otherwise make the disclosure inaccurate.

(b) The type-size used in the disclosure shall be at least the same type-size as that used to inform the debtor of his or her specific debt, but is not required to be larger than 12–point type. *(Added by Stats.2003, c. 259 (S.B.1022), § 1, operative July 1, 2004. Amended by Stats.2004, c. 183 (A.B.3082), § 37.)*

§ 1812.702. Violations

Any violation of this act shall be considered a violation of the Rosenthal Fair Debt Collection Practices Act (Title 1.6C (commencing with Section 1788)). *(Added by Stats.2003, c. 259 (S.B.1022), § 1, operative July 1, 2004.)*

Title 3

DEPOSIT

Chapter	Section
1. Deposit in General	1813
2. Deposit for Keeping	1833
3. Deposit for Exchange	1878
4. Private Bulk Storage of Grain	1880

CHAPTER 1. DEPOSIT IN GENERAL

Article	Section
1. Nature and Creation of Deposit	1813
2. Obligations of the Depositary	1822

ARTICLE 1. NATURE AND CREATION OF DEPOSIT

Section
1813. Kinds of deposit.
1814. Voluntary deposit; depositor and depositary defined.
1815. Involuntary deposit.
1816. Involuntary deposit; animal control notification; duty of depositary.
1817. Deposit for keeping defined.
1818. Deposit for exchange defined.
1821.23. Renumbered.

Cross References

Common carriers, see Civil Code § 2085 et seq.
Deposit for exchange, see Civil Code § 1878.
Deposit for keeping, see Civil Code § 1833 et seq.
Gratuitous deposit, see Civil Code § 1844 et seq.

Hiring, see Civil Code § 1925 et seq.
Innkeepers, see Civil Code § 1859 et seq.
Loan for exchange, see Civil Code § 1902 et seq.
Loan for use, see Civil Code § 1884 et seq.
Loan of money, see Civil Code § 1912 et seq.
Storage, deposit for hire, see Civil Code § 1851 et seq.

§ 1813. Kinds of deposit

A deposit may be voluntary or involuntary; and for safe keeping or for exchange. *(Enacted in 1872.)*

§ 1814. Voluntary deposit; depositor and depositary defined

A voluntary deposit is made by one giving to another, with his consent, the possession of personal property to keep for the benefit of the former, or of a third party. The person giving is called the depositor, and the person receiving the depositary. *(Enacted in 1872.)*

Cross References
Involuntary deposits, see Civil Code §§ 1815, 1816.
Obligations of depositary, see Civil Code § 1822 et seq.

§ 1815. Involuntary deposit

An involuntary deposit is made:

(a) By the accidental leaving or placing of personal property in the possession of any person, without negligence on the part of its owner.

(b) In cases of fire, shipwreck, inundation, insurrection, riot, or like extraordinary emergencies, by the owner of personal property committing it, out of necessity, to the care of any person.

(c) By the delivery to, or picking up by, and the holding of, a stray live animal by any person or public or private entity.

(d) By the abandonment or leaving of a live animal, as proscribed by Section 597.1 of the Penal Code, in or about any premises or real property that has been vacated upon, or immediately preceding, the termination of a lease or other rental agreement or foreclosure of the property. *(Enacted in 1872. Amended by Stats.1998, c. 752 (S.B.1785), § 2; Stats. 1999, c. 83 (S.B.966), § 22; Stats.2008, c. 265 (A.B.2949), § 1.)*

Cross References
Degree of care required, see Civil Code § 1846.
Involuntary deposit, duty of depositary, see Civil Code § 1816.
Involuntary gratuitous deposit, see Civil Code § 1845.
Termination of duties of depositary, see Civil Code § 1847.

§ 1816. Involuntary deposit; animal control notification; duty of depositary

(a) The person or private entity with whom a thing is deposited in the manner described in Section 1815 is bound to take charge of it, if able to do so.

(b) Any person or private entity with whom a live animal is deposited in the manner described in subdivision (d) of Section 1815 shall immediately notify animal control officials for the purpose of retrieving the animal pursuant to Section 597.1 of the Penal Code. Animal control officers who respond shall be entitled to exercise the right afforded them pursuant to that section to secure a lien for the purpose of recovering the costs of attempting to rescue the animal. Nothing in this subdivision shall impose any new or additional civil or criminal liability upon a depositary who complies with this subdivision.

(c) A public agency or shelter with whom an abandoned animal is deposited in the manner described in Section 1815 is bound to take charge of it, as provided in Section 597.1 of the Penal Code.

(d) The person in possession of the abandoned animal is subject to all local ordinances and state laws that govern the proper care and treatment of those animals.

(e) For purposes of this section, the person or private entity that notifies animal control officials to retrieve the animal or the successor property owner shall not be considered the keeper of the animal or the agent of the animal's owner as those terms are used in Section 597.1 of the Penal Code. *(Enacted in 1872. Amended by Stats.1998, c. 752 (S.B.1785), § 3; Stats.2008, c. 265 (A.B.2949), § 2.)*

Cross References
Depositary defined, see Civil Code § 1814.
Involuntary deposit, see Civil Code § 1815.

§ 1817. Deposit for keeping defined

A deposit for keeping is one in which the depositary is bound to return the identical thing deposited. *(Enacted in 1872.)*

Cross References
Deposit for exchange defined, see Civil Code § 1818.
Deposit for keeping, general provisions, see Civil Code § 1833 et seq.
Depositary defined, see Civil Code § 1814.
Transfer of title, relationship between parties, see Civil Code § 1878.

§ 1818. Deposit for exchange defined

A deposit for exchange is one in which the depositary is only bound to return a thing corresponding in kind to that which is deposited. *(Enacted in 1872.)*

Cross References
Deposit for keeping, general provisions, see Civil Code § 1833 et seq.
Deposit for keeping defined, see Civil Code § 1817.
Depositary defined, see Civil Code § 1814.
Loan for exchange, see Civil Code § 1902 et seq.
Transfer of title, relationship between parties, see Civil Code § 1878.

§ 1821.23. Renumbered § 1861.23 and amended by Stats. 1981, c. 714, p. 2591, § 53

ARTICLE 2.   OBLIGATIONS OF THE DEPOSITARY

Section
1822. Delivery on demand.
1823. Necessity of demand.
1824. Place of delivery.
1825. Adverse claims; notice to beneficiary of deposit.
1826. Notice of deposit to true owner.
1827. Delivery to co-owners.
1828. Joint tenancy deposits; delivery.

Cross References
Banks, deposits, see Civil Code § 850 et seq.
Deposit for keeping, general provisions, see Civil Code § 1833 et seq.

Private bulk storage of grain, see Civil Code § 1880 et seq.
Transfer of title, relationship between parties, see Civil Code § 1878.

§ 1822. Delivery on demand

A depositary must deliver the thing to the person for whose benefit it was deposited, on demand, whether the deposit was made for a specified time or not, unless he has a lien upon the thing deposited, or has been forbidden or prevented from doing so by the real owner thereof, or by the act of the law, and has given the notice required by Section 1825. *(Enacted in 1872.)*

Cross References

Adverse claims, notice to beneficiary of deposit, see Civil Code § 1825.
Degree of care required to storage of deposits, see Civil Code § 1852.
Delivery, necessity of demand, see Civil Code § 1823.
Delivery to co-owners, see Civil Code § 1827.
Depositary defined, see Civil Code § 1814.
Innkeeper's lien, see Civil Code § 1861.
Possessory liens for services, repairs, etc., see Civil Code § 3051.

§ 1823. Necessity of demand

A depositary is not bound to deliver a thing deposited without demand, even where the deposit is made for a specified time. *(Enacted in 1872.)*

Cross References

Demand, duty to deliver on, see Civil Code § 1822.
Depositary defined, see Civil Code § 1814.

§ 1824. Place of delivery

A depositary must deliver the thing deposited at his residence or place of business, as may be most convenient for him. *(Enacted in 1872.)*

Cross References

Delivery of joint tenancy deposits, see Civil Code § 1828.
Delivery of jointly owned items to co-owners, see Civil Code § 1827.
Depositary defined, see Civil Code § 1814.

§ 1825. Adverse claims; notice to beneficiary of deposit

A depositary must give prompt notice to the person for whose benefit the deposit was made, of any proceedings taken adversely to his interest in the thing deposited, which may tend to excuse the depositary from delivering the thing to him. *(Enacted in 1872.)*

Cross References

Adverse claim to bank deposit, see Financial Code § 1450.
Depositary defined, see Civil Code § 1814.
Inability to deliver, see Civil Code § 1822.
Notice of deposit to true owner, see Civil Code § 1826.

§ 1826. Notice of deposit to true owner

A depositary, who believes that a thing deposited with him is wrongfully detained from its true owner, may give him notice of the deposit; and if within a reasonable time afterwards he does not claim it, and sufficiently establish his right thereto, and indemnify the depositary against the claim of the depositor, the depositary is exonerated from liability to the person to whom he gave the notice, upon returning the thing to the depositor, or assuming, in good faith, a new obligation changing his position in respect to the thing, to his prejudice. *(Enacted in 1872.)*

Cross References

Adverse claims, notice to beneficiary of deposit, see Civil Code § 1825.
Depositary defined, see Civil Code § 1814.
Depositor defined, see Civil Code § 1814.

§ 1827. Delivery to co-owners

If a thing deposited is owned jointly or in common by persons who cannot agree upon the manner of its delivery, the depositary may deliver to each his proper share thereof, if it can be done without injury to the thing. *(Enacted in 1872.)*

Cross References

Depositary defined, see Civil Code § 1814.
Place of delivery, see Civil Code § 1824.

§ 1828. Joint tenancy deposits; delivery

When a deposit is made in the name of two or more persons, deliverable or payable to either or to their survivor or survivors, such deposit or any part thereof, or increase thereof, may be delivered or paid to either of said persons or to the survivor or survivors in due course of business. *(Added by Stats.1907, c. 75, p. 92, § 1.)*

Cross References

Delivery of jointly owned items to co-owners, see Civil Code § 1827.
Joint tenancy, definition and method of creation, see Civil Code § 683.
Multiple party accounts, see Financial Code § 1402.
Performance to any joint obligee, see Civil Code § 1475.
Place of delivery, see Civil Code § 1824.

CHAPTER 2. DEPOSIT FOR KEEPING

Article		Section
1.	General Provisions	1833
2.	Gratuitous Deposit	1844
3.	Storage	1851
3.5.	Deposits for Repair, Alteration or Sale	1858
3A.	Warehousemen [Repealed]	
3B.	Warehouse Receipts Act [Repealed]	
3C.	Warehouse Receipts for Goods Out-of-State [Repealed]	
4.	Innkeepers	1859
5.	Finding [Repealed]	

Cross References

Banks, deposits, see Civil Code § 850 et seq.
Deposit for keeping defined, see Civil Code § 1817.
Private bulk storage of grain, see Civil Code § 1880 et seq.
Transfer of title, relationship between parties, see Civil Code § 1878.

ARTICLE 1. GENERAL PROVISIONS

Section	
1833.	Indemnification of depositary.
1834.	Depositary of animals; duties.
1834.4.	Euthanasia.
1834.5.	Abandoned animals; disposition; notice.
1834.6.	Repealed.

Section

1834.7. Use of animals turned over to animal shelter entity for biological supply or research facility; sign on animal shelter entity.
1834.8. Public auctions or sales of equines; notice of sale for slaughter; minimum bids; posting of slaughter prices.
1834.9. Alternative animal test methods; required use by manufacturers and contract testing facilities.
1834.9.3. Prohibition of canine or feline toxicological experiments; exceptions; penalties.
1834.9.5. Prohibition on cosmetics developed or manufactured using animal testing; applicability of section.
1835. Use of thing deposited; opening fastened thing.
1836. Wrongful use; damages.
1837. Sale of thing in danger of perishing.
1838. Loss of or injury to thing deposited.
1839. Services by depositary.
1840. Negligence; limitation of liability.

Cross References

Deposits for repair, alteration or sale, see Civil Code § 1858 et seq.
Gratuitous deposit, see Civil Code § 1844 et seq.
Innkeepers, see Civil Code § 1859 et seq.
Storage, see Civil Code § 1851 et seq.

§ 1833. Indemnification of depositary

A depositor must indemnify the depositary:

1. For all damage caused to him by the defects or vices of the thing deposited; and,

2. For all expenses necessarily incurred by him about the thing, other than such as are involved in the nature of the undertaking. *(Enacted in 1872.)*

Cross References

Defects concealed from borrower, lender's liability, see Civil Code § 1893.
Depositary defined, see Civil Code § 1814.
Depositary of animals, see Civil Code § 1834 et seq.
Depositor defined, see Civil Code § 1814.
Liability for damage arising from wrongful use, see Civil Code §§ 1836, 1840.
Loss of or injury of thing deposited, see Civil Code § 1838.
Sale of thing in danger of perishing, see Civil Code § 1837.
Use of thing deposited, see Civil Code § 1835.

§ 1834. Depositary of animals; duties

A depositary of living animals shall provide the animals with necessary and prompt veterinary care, nutrition, and shelter, and treat them kindly. Any depositary that fails to perform these duties may be liable for civil damages as provided by law. *(Enacted in 1872. Amended by Stats.1998, c. 752 (S.B.1785), § 4.)*

Cross References

Abandoned animals, see Civil Code § 1834.5.
Crimes involving cruelty to animals, see Penal Code § 597 et seq.
Depositary defined, see Civil Code § 1814.
Identification and payment of costs mandated by the state, legislative findings and declarations, see Government Code § 17572.
Indemnification of depositary, see Civil Code § 1833.
Liability for damage arising from wrongful use, see Civil Code §§ 1836, 1840.
Liens, animals, keeping and services, see Civil Code §§ 3051, 3062 et seq.
Use of abandoned animals for scientific or other experimentation prohibited, see Civil Code § 1834.5.
Use of animals turned over to pound or animal regulation department for biological supply or research facility, see Civil Code § 1834.7.
Use of thing deposited, see Civil Code § 1835.

§ 1834.4. Euthanasia

(a) It is the policy of the state that no adoptable animal should be euthanized if it can be adopted into a suitable home. Adoptable animals include only those animals eight weeks of age or older that, at or subsequent to the time the animal is impounded or otherwise taken into possession, have manifested no sign of a behavioral or temperamental defect that could pose a health or safety risk or otherwise make the animal unsuitable for placement as a pet, and have manifested no sign of disease, injury, or congenital or hereditary condition that adversely affects the health of the animal or that is likely to adversely affect the animal's health in the future.

(b) It is the policy of the state that no treatable animal should be euthanized. A treatable animal shall include any animal that is not adoptable but that could become adoptable with reasonable efforts. This subdivision, by itself, shall not be the basis of liability for damages regarding euthanasia. *(Added by Stats.1998, c. 752 (S.B.1785), § 5.)*

§ 1834.5. Abandoned animals; disposition; notice

(a) Notwithstanding any other provision of law, whenever an animal is delivered to a veterinarian, dog kennel, cat kennel, pet-grooming parlor, animal hospital, or any other animal care facility pursuant to a written or oral agreement entered into after the effective date of this section, and the owner of the animal does not pick up the animal within 14 calendar days after the day the animal was initially due to be picked up, the animal shall be deemed to be abandoned. The person into whose custody the animal was placed for care shall first try for a period of not less than 10 days to find a new owner for the animal or turn the animal over to a public animal control agency or shelter, society for the prevention of cruelty to animals shelter, humane society shelter, or nonprofit animal rescue group, provided that the shelter or rescue group has been contacted and has agreed to take the animal. If unable to place the animal with a new owner, shelter, or rescue group, the animal care facility may have the abandoned animal euthanized.

(b) If an animal so abandoned was left with a veterinarian or with a facility that has a veterinarian, and a new owner cannot be found pursuant to this section, the veterinarian may euthanize the animal.

(c) Nothing in this section shall be construed to require an animal care facility or a veterinarian to euthanize an abandoned animal upon the expiration of the 10-day period described in subdivision (a).

(d) There shall be a notice posted in a conspicuous place, or in conspicuous type in a written receipt given, to warn a person depositing an animal at an animal care facility of the provisions of this section.

(e) An abandoned animal shall not be used for scientific or any other type of experimentation. *(Added by Stats.1969, c. 1138, p. 2205, § 1. Amended by Stats.1970, c. 1166, p. 2071, § 1; Stats.1971, c. 477, p. 962, § 1; Stats.2014, c. 86 (A.B.1810), § 1, eff. Jan. 1, 2015.)*

Cross References

Abandonment of animals, misdemeanor, see Penal Code § 597s.
Indemnification of depositary, see Civil Code § 1833.

§ 1834.6. Repealed by Stats.2014, c. 86 (A.B.1810), § 2, eff. Jan. 1, 2015

§ 1834.7. Use of animals turned over to animal shelter entity for biological supply or research facility; sign on animal shelter entity

(a) For purposes of this section:

(1) "Animal dealer" means a person who, in commerce, for compensation or profit, delivers for transportation, or transports, except as a carrier, or who buys, sells, or negotiates the purchase or sale of any animal, whether alive or dead, for research, teaching, exhibition, or biological supply.

(2) "Animal shelter entity" includes, but is not limited to, an animal regulation agency, humane society, society for the prevention of cruelty to animals, or other private or public animal shelter.

(3) "Person" means an individual, partnership, firm, limited liability company, joint-stock company, corporation, association, trust, estate, governmental agency, or other legal entity.

(4) "Research facility" means a research facility as defined by Section 2132 of Title 7 of the United States Code, effective February 7, 2014.

(b)(1) An animal shelter entity where dead animals are turned over to a biological supply facility or a research facility for research purposes or to supply blood, tissue, or other biological products shall post a sign as described by this paragraph in a place where it will be clearly visible to a majority of persons when turning animals over to the shelter. The sign shall measure a minimum of 28x21 cm— 11x8 ½ inches —with lettering of a minimum of 3.2 cm high and 1.2 cm wide— 1 ¼ x ½ inch —(91 point) and shall state:

"Animals Euthanized at This Shelter May Be Used for Research Purposes or to Supply Blood, Tissue, or Other Biological Products"

(2) The statement in paragraph (1) shall also be included on owner surrender forms.

(3) An animal shelter or other person shall not euthanize an animal for the purpose of transferring the carcass to a research facility or animal dealer.

(c)(1) An animal shelter entity or other person that accepts animals from the public or takes in stray or unwanted animals shall not sell, give, or otherwise transfer a living animal to a research facility, an animal dealer, or other person for the purpose of research, experimentation, or testing.

(2) A research facility, animal dealer, or other person shall not procure, purchase, receive, accept, or use a living animal for the purpose of research, experimentation, or testing if that animal is transferred from, or received from, an animal shelter entity or other person that accepts animals from the public or takes in stray or unwanted animals.

(d) Nothing in this section shall prohibit a research facility from working in collaboration with an animal shelter to investigate problems and provide services to shelter animals.

(e) A violation of this section is subject to a civil penalty of one thousand dollars ($1,000) in an action to be brought by the district attorney or city attorney of the county or city where the violation occurred. When collected, the civil penalty shall be payable to the general fund of the governmental entity that brought the action to assess the penalty. *(Added by Stats.2016, c. 568 (A.B.2269), § 2, eff. Jan. 1, 2017.)*

Cross References

Abandoned animals, see Civil Code § 1834.5.
Use of abandoned animals for scientific or other experimentation prohibited, see Civil Code § 1834.5.

§ 1834.8. Public auctions or sales of equines; notice of sale for slaughter; minimum bids; posting of slaughter prices

(a) At any public auction or sale where equines are sold, the management of the auction or sale shall post a sign (measuring a minimum of 15 x 9 inches with lettering of a minimum of 1 ¼ x ½ (91 point)) or shall insert into its consignment agreement with the seller in boldface type the notice stated in subdivision (b). If a sign is posted, it shall be posted in a conspicuous place so that it will be clearly visible to a majority of persons attending the sale. If the notice is inserted into the consignment agreement, space shall be provided adjacent to the notice for the seller to initial their acknowledgment of the notice.

(b) The notice required by subdivision (a) shall read as follows:

"WARNING

The sale of horses in California for slaughter for human consumption is a felony."

(c) For the purposes of this section, the management of the auction or sale shall post current slaughter prices or make them available to sellers upon request. *(Added by Stats.1995, c. 99 (S.B.1219), § 1. Amended by Stats.2006, c. 538 (S.B. 1852), § 53; Stats.2019, c. 765 (A.B.128), § 2, eff. Jan. 1, 2020.)*

§ 1834.9. Alternative animal test methods; required use by manufacturers and contract testing facilities

(a) Manufacturers and contract testing facilities shall not use traditional animal test methods within this state for which an appropriate alternative test method has been scientifically validated and recommended by the Inter-Agency Coordinating Committee for the Validation of Alternative Methods (ICCVAM) and adopted by the relevant federal agency or agencies or program within an agency responsible for regulating the specific product or activity for which the test is being conducted.

(b) Nothing in this section shall prohibit the use of any alternative nonanimal test method for the testing of any product, product formulation, chemical, or ingredient that is not recommended by ICCVAM.

(c) Nothing in this section shall prohibit the use of animal tests to comply with requirements of state agencies. Nothing in this section shall prohibit the use of animal tests to comply with requirements of federal agencies when the federal agency has approved an alternative nonanimal test pursuant to subdivision (a) and the federal agency staff concludes that the alternative nonanimal test does not assure the health or safety of consumers.

(d) Notwithstanding any other provision of law, the exclusive remedy for enforcing this section shall be a civil action for injunctive relief brought by the Attorney General, the district attorney of the county in which the violation is alleged to have occurred, or a city attorney of a city or a city and county having a population in excess of 750,000 and in which the violation is alleged to have occurred. If the court determines that the Attorney General or district attorney is the prevailing party in the enforcement action, the official may also recover costs, attorney fees, and a civil penalty not to exceed five thousand dollars ($5,000) in that action.

(e) This section shall not apply to any animal test performed for the purpose of medical research.

(f) For the purposes of this section, these terms have the following meanings:

(1) "Animal" means vertebrate nonhuman animal.

(2) "Manufacturer" means any partnership, corporation, association, or other legal relationship that produces chemicals, ingredients, product formulations, or products in this state.

(3) "Contract testing facility" means any partnership, corporation, association, or other legal relationship that tests chemicals, ingredients, product formulations, or products in this state.

(4) "ICCVAM" means the Inter-Agency Coordinating Committee for the Validation of Alternative Methods, a federal committee comprised of representatives from 14 federal regulatory or research agencies, including the Food and Drug Administration, Environmental Protection Agency, and Consumer Products Safety Commission, that reviews the validity of alternative test methods. The committee is the federal mechanism for recommending appropriate, valid test methods to relevant federal agencies.

(5) "Medical research" means research related to the causes, diagnosis, treatment, control, or prevention of physical or mental diseases and impairments of humans and animals or related to the development of biomedical products, devices, or drugs as defined in Section 321(g)(1) of Title 21 of the United States Code. Medical research does not include the testing of an ingredient that was formerly used in a drug, tested for the drug use with traditional animal methods to characterize the ingredient and to substantiate its safety for human use, and is now proposed for use in a product other than a biomedical product, medical device, or drug.

(6) "Traditional animal test method" means a process or procedure using animals to obtain information on the characteristics of a chemical or agent. Toxicological test methods generate information regarding the ability of a chemical or agent to produce a specific biological effect under specified conditions.

(7) "Validated alternative test method" means a test method that does not use animals, or in some cases reduces or refines the current use of animals, for which the reliability and relevance for a specific purpose has been established in validation studies as specified in the ICCVAM report provided to the relevant federal agencies.

(8) "Person" means an individual with managerial control, or a partnership, corporation, association, or other legal relationship.

(9) "Adopted by a federal agency" means a final action taken by an agency, published in the Federal Register, for public notice. *(Formerly § 1834.8, added by Stats.2000, c. 476 (S.B.2082), § 1. Renumbered § 1834.9 and amended by Stats.2001, c. 159 (S.B.662), § 34.5.)*

Cross References

Attorney General, generally, see Government Code § 12500 et seq.

§ 1834.9.3. Prohibition of canine or feline toxicological experiments; exceptions; penalties

(a) For purposes of this section, the following definitions apply:

(1) "Alternative test method" means a test method that does not use animals, or in some cases reduces or refines the use of animals, for which the reliability and relevance for a specific purpose has been established by validation bodies, including, but not limited to, the Interagency Coordinating Committee for the Validation of Alternative Methods and the Organization for Economic Co-operation and Development. Alternative test methods include, but are not limited to, high-throughput screening methods, testing of categories of chemical substances, tiered testing methods, in vitro studies, and systems biology.

(2) "Canine or feline toxicological experiment" means any test or study of any duration that seeks to determine the effect, if any, of the application or exposure, whether internal or external, of any amount of a chemical substance on a dog or cat. "Application or exposure" includes, but is not limited to, oral ingestion, skin or eye contact, or inhalation.

(3) "Cat" means any member of the species Felis catus.

(4) "Chemical substance" shall have the same meaning as that term is defined under subsection (2) of Section 2602 of Title 15 of the United States Code, except that for purposes of this section, such term shall include any pesticide, as defined under subsection (u) of Section 136 of Title 7 of the United States Code, and any food additive, as defined under subsection (s) of Section 321 of Title 21 of the United States Code.

(5) "Dog" means any member of the species Canis familiaris.

(6) "Food additive" shall have the same meaning as that term is defined in subsection (s) of Section 321 of Title 21 of the United States Code.

(7) "Medical research" means research related to the causes, diagnosis, treatment, control, or prevention of physical or mental diseases and impairments of humans and animals or related to the development of biomedical drugs or

§ 1834.9.3

devices as those terms are defined in subsections (g) and (h), inclusive, of Section 321 of Title 21 of the United States Code. Medical research does not include experimentation or testing of a chemical substance or ingredient proposed for use in a product other than a biomedical drug or device as those terms are defined in the Federal Food, Drug, and Cosmetic Act (21 U.S.C. Sec. 321).

(8) "Pesticide" shall have the same meaning as that term is defined in subsection (u) of Section 136 of Title 7 of the United States Code.

(9) "Testing facility" means any partnership, corporation, association, school, institution, organization, or other legal relationship, whether privately or government owned, leased, or operated, that tests chemicals, ingredients, product formulations, or products in this state.

(b) Notwithstanding any other law, and in addition to the prohibitions set forth in Sections 1834.9 and 1834.9.5, a testing facility shall not conduct a canine or feline toxicological experiment in this state to achieve discovery, approval, maintenance of approval, notification, registration, or maintenance of a pesticide or chemical substance, unless the experiment is conducted pursuant to any of the following:

(1) To satisfy an express requirement imposed by the United States Environmental Protection Agency (EPA) under the authority of the Federal Insecticide, Fungicide, and Rodenticide Act (7 U.S.C. Sec. 136 et seq.) and the Toxic Substances Control Act (15 U.S.C. Sec. 2601 et seq.), including any EPA rule, regulation, or order.

(2) To support an application to the EPA for a waiver from the requirements in paragraph (1), provided that testing is conducted solely to reduce the total number of animals needed for experiments to achieve discovery, approval, maintenance of approval, notification, registration, or maintenance of a pesticide or chemical substance.

(3) To satisfy an express requirement imposed by the Food and Drug Administration (FDA) per the Federal Food, Drug, and Cosmetic Act (21 U.S.C. Sec. 301 et seq.) or any binding agency regulation promulgated upon notice and comment thereunder.

(c)(1) Notwithstanding any other law, the Attorney General, the district attorney of the county in which the violation is alleged to have occurred, or a city attorney of a city or city and county having a population in excess of 750,000 and in which the violation is alleged to have occurred, may bring a civil action for injunctive relief pursuant to this paragraph. If the court determines that the Attorney General, district attorney, or city attorney is the prevailing party in the enforcement action, the official may also recover costs, attorney fees, and a civil penalty not to exceed five thousand dollars ($5,000) for each day that each dog or each cat is used in a canine or feline toxicological experiment in violation of this section.

(2) The procedure set forth in paragraph (1) is the exclusive remedy for enforcing this section.

(d) The prohibition in subdivision (b) shall not apply to either of the following:

(1) Medical research.

(2) Testing or experimentation conducted for the purpose of developing, manufacturing, or marketing any product intended for beneficial use in dogs or cats. *(Added by Stats.2022, c. 551 (S.B.879), § 2, eff. Jan. 1, 2023.)*

§ 1834.9.5. Prohibition on cosmetics developed or manufactured using animal testing; applicability of section

(a) Notwithstanding any other law, it is unlawful for a manufacturer to import for profit, sell, or offer for sale in this state, any cosmetic, if the cosmetic was developed or manufactured using an animal test that was conducted or contracted by the manufacturer, or any supplier of the manufacturer, on or after January 1, 2020.

(b) For purposes of this section, the following terms apply:

(1) "Animal test" means the internal or external application of a cosmetic, either in its final form or any ingredient thereof, to the skin, eyes, or other body part of a live, nonhuman vertebrate.

(2) "Cosmetic" means any article intended to be rubbed, poured, sprinkled, or sprayed on, introduced into, or otherwise applied to the human body or any part thereof for cleansing, beautifying, promoting attractiveness, or altering the appearance, including, but not limited to, personal hygiene products such as deodorant, shampoo, or conditioner.

(3) "Ingredient" means any component of a cosmetic as defined by Section 700.3 of Title 21 of the Code of Federal Regulations.

(4) "Manufacturer" means any person whose name appears on the label of a cosmetic product pursuant to the requirements of Section 701.12 of Title 21 of the Code of Federal Regulations.

(5) "Supplier" means any entity that supplies, directly or through a third party, any ingredient used in the formulation of a manufacturer's cosmetic.

(c) The prohibitions in subdivision (a) do not apply to the following:

(1) An animal test of any cosmetic that is required by a federal or state regulatory authority if all of the following apply:

(A) The ingredient is in wide use and cannot be replaced by another ingredient capable of performing a similar function.

(B) A specific human health problem is substantiated and the need to conduct animal tests is justified and is supported by a detailed research protocol proposed as the basis for the evaluation.

(C) There is not a nonanimal alternative method accepted for the relevant endpoint by the relevant federal or state regulatory authority.

(2) An animal test that was conducted to comply with a requirement of a foreign regulatory authority, if no evidence derived from the test was relied upon to substantiate the safety of the cosmetic sold in California by the manufacturer.

(3) An animal test that was conducted on any product or ingredient subject to the requirements of Chapter V of the Federal Food, Drug, and Cosmetic Act (21 U.S.C. 351 et seq.).

(4) An animal test that was conducted for noncosmetic purposes in response to a requirement of a federal, state, or foreign regulatory authority, if no evidence derived from the test was relied upon to substantiate the safety of the cosmetic sold in California by the manufacturer. A manufacturer is not prohibited from reviewing, assessing, or retaining evidence from an animal test conducted pursuant to this paragraph.

(d) A violation of this section shall be punishable by a fine of five thousand dollars ($5,000) and an additional one thousand dollars ($1,000) for each day the violation continues.

(e) A violation of this section may be enforced by the district attorney of the county in which the violation occurred, or by the city attorney of the city in which the violation occurred. The civil fine shall be paid to the entity that is authorized to bring the action.

(f) A district attorney or city attorney may, upon a determination that there is a reasonable likelihood of a violation of this section, review the testing data upon which a cosmetic manufacturer has relied in the development or manufacturing of the relevant cosmetic product sold in the state. Information provided under this section shall be protected as a trade secret as defined in subdivision (d) of Section 3426.1. Consistent with the procedures described in Section 3426.5, a district attorney or city attorney shall enter a protective order with a manufacturer before receipt of information from a manufacturer pursuant to this section, and shall take other appropriate measures necessary to preserve the confidentiality of information provided pursuant to this section.

(g) This section shall not apply to either of the following:

(1) A cosmetic, if the cosmetic, in its final form, was sold in California or tested on animals prior to January 1, 2020, even if the cosmetic is manufactured after that date.

(2) An ingredient, if the ingredient was sold in California or tested on animals prior to January 1, 2020, even if the ingredient is manufactured after that date.

(h) Notwithstanding any other provision of this section, cosmetic inventory found to be in violation of this section may be sold for a period of 180 days.

(i) No county or political subdivision of the state may establish or continue any prohibition on or relating to animal tests, as defined in this section, that is not identical to the prohibitions set forth in this section and that does not include the exemptions contained in subdivision (c).

(j) This section shall become operative on January 1, 2020. *(Added by Stats.2018, c. 899 (S.B.1249), § 1, eff. Jan. 1, 2019, operative Jan. 1, 2020.)*

§ 1835. Use of thing deposited; opening fastened thing

A depositary may not use the thing deposited, or permit it to be used, for any purpose, without the consent of the depositor. He may not, if it is purposely fastened by the depositor, open it without the consent of the latter, except in case of necessity. *(Enacted in 1872.)*

Cross References

Depositary defined, see Civil Code § 1814.
Depositary of animals, see Civil Code § 1834 et seq.
Depositor defined, see Civil Code § 1814.
Hiring, see Civil Code § 1925 et seq.
Indemnification of depositary, see Civil Code § 1833.
Liability for damage arising from wrongful use, see Civil Code §§ 1836, 1840.
Loss of or injury of thing deposited, see Civil Code § 1838.
Sale of thing in danger of perishing, see Civil Code § 1837.

§ 1836. Wrongful use; damages

A depositary is liable for any damage happening to the thing deposited, during his wrongful use thereof, unless such damage must inevitably have happened though the property had not been thus used. *(Enacted in 1872.)*

Cross References

Depositary defined, see Civil Code § 1814.
Depositary of animals, see Civil Code § 1834 et seq.
Indemnification of depositary, see Civil Code § 1833.
Liability of depositary for negligence, see Civil Code §§ 1840, 1852.
Loss of or injury of thing deposited, see Civil Code § 1838.
Sale of thing in danger of perishing, see Civil Code § 1837.
Use of thing deposited, see Civil Code § 1835.

§ 1837. Sale of thing in danger of perishing

If a thing deposited is in actual danger of perishing before instructions can be obtained from the depositor, the depositary may sell it for the best price obtainable, and retain the proceeds as a deposit, giving immediate notice of his proceedings to the depositor. *(Enacted in 1872.)*

Cross References

Depositary defined, see Civil Code § 1814.
Depositary of animals, see Civil Code § 1834 et seq.
Depositor defined, see Civil Code § 1814.
Indemnification of depositary, see Civil Code § 1833.
Liability for damage arising from wrongful use, see Civil Code §§ 1836, 1840.
Loss of or injury of thing deposited, see Civil Code § 1838.
Storage, sale of perishables, see Civil Code § 1857.
Use of thing deposited, see Civil Code § 1835.

§ 1838. Loss of or injury to thing deposited

If a thing is lost or injured during its deposit, and the depositary refuses to inform the depositor of the circumstances under which the loss or injury occurred, so far as he has information concerning them, or willfully misrepresents the circumstances to him, the depositary is presumed to have willfully, or by gross negligence, permitted the loss or injury to occur. *(Enacted in 1872.)*

Cross References

Depositary defined, see Civil Code § 1814.
Depositary of animals, see Civil Code § 1834 et seq.
Depositor defined, see Civil Code § 1814.
Indemnification of depositary, see Civil Code § 1833.
Liability for damage arising from wrongful use, see Civil Code §§ 1836, 1840.
Sale to satisfy depositary's lien for storage, see Civil Code § 1857.
Use of thing deposited, see Civil Code § 1835.

§ 1839. Services by depositary

So far as any service is rendered by a depositary, or required from him, his duties and liabilities are prescribed by the Title on Employment and Service. *(Enacted in 1872.)*

Cross References

Agency, see Civil Code § 2295 et seq.
Depositary defined, see Civil Code § 1814.
Depositary of animals, see Civil Code § 1834 et seq.
Employer and employee, see Labor Code § 2800 et seq.
Indemnification of depositary, see Civil Code § 1833.
Liability for damage arising from wrongful use, see Civil Code §§ 1836, 1840.
Loss of or injury of thing deposited, see Civil Code § 1838.
Use of thing deposited, see Civil Code § 1835.

§ 1840. Negligence; limitation of liability

The liability of a depositary for negligence cannot exceed the amount which he is informed by the depositor, or has reason to suppose, the thing deposited to be worth. *(Enacted in 1872. Amended by Code Am.1873–74, c. 612, p. 244, § 200.)*

Cross References

Depositary defined, see Civil Code § 1814.
Depositor defined, see Civil Code § 1814.
Indemnification of depositary, see Civil Code § 1833.
Services of depositary, see Civil Code § 1839.

ARTICLE 2. GRATUITOUS DEPOSIT

Section
1844. Gratuitous deposit defined.
1845. Involuntary deposit.
1846. Degree of care required.
1847. Termination of duties of depositary.

Cross References

Deposits for keeping, see Civil Code § 1833 et seq.
Deposits for repair, alteration or sale, see Civil Code § 1858 et seq.
Storage, see Civil Code § 1851 et seq.

§ 1844. Gratuitous deposit defined

Gratuitous deposit is a deposit for which the depositary receives no consideration beyond the mere possession of the thing deposited. *(Enacted in 1872.)*

Cross References

Degree of care required, see Civil Code § 1846.
Depositary defined, see Civil Code § 1814.
Involuntary deposits gratuitous, see Civil Code § 1845.

§ 1845. Involuntary deposit

An involuntary deposit is gratuitous, the depositary being entitled to no reward. However, an involuntary depositary of any live animal may accept advertised rewards or rewards freely offered by the owner of the animal. *(Enacted in 1872. Amended by Stats.1998, c. 752 (S.B.1785), § 6.)*

Cross References

Depositary defined, see Civil Code § 1814.
Involuntary deposit, how made, see Civil Code § 1815.

§ 1846. Degree of care required

(a) A gratuitous depositary must use, at least, slight care for the preservation of the thing deposited.

(b) A gratuitous depositary of a living animal shall provide the animal with necessary and prompt veterinary care, adequate nutrition and water, and shelter, and shall treat it humanely and, if the animal has any identification, make reasonable attempts to notify the owner of the animal's location. Any gratuitous depositary that does not have sufficient resources or desire to provide that care shall promptly turn the animal over to an appropriate care facility.

(c) If the gratuitous depositary of a living animal is a public animal shelter, shelter operated by a society for the prevention of cruelty to animals, or humane shelter, the depositary shall comply with all other requirements of the Food and Agricultural Code regarding the impounding of live animals. *(Enacted in 1872. Amended by Stats.1998, c. 752 (S.B.1785), § 7; Stats.2019, c. 7 (A.B.1553), § 2, eff. Jan. 1, 2020.)*

Cross References

Depositary defined, see Civil Code § 1814.
Gratuitous deposit defined, see Civil Code § 1844.
Identification and payment of costs mandated by the state, legislative findings and declarations, see Government Code § 17572.
Termination of duties of depositary, see Civil Code § 1847.

§ 1847. Termination of duties of depositary

The duties of a gratuitous depositary cease:

(a) Upon restoration by the depositary of the thing deposited to its owner.

(b) Upon reasonable notice given by the depositary to the owner to remove it, and the owner failing to do so within a reasonable time. But an involuntary depositary, under subdivision (b) of Section 1815, may not give notice until the emergency that gave rise to the deposit is past. This subdivision shall not apply to a public animal shelter, a shelter operated by a society for the prevention of cruelty to animals, or a humane shelter. The duty to provide care, as required by Section 1846, continues until the public or private animal shelter is lawfully relieved of responsibility for the animal. *(Enacted in 1872. Amended by Stats.1998, c. 752 (S.B.1785), § 8; Stats.2019, c. 7 (A.B.1553), § 3, eff. Jan. 1, 2020.)*

Cross References

Degree of care required by depositary, see Civil Code § 1846.
Depositary defined, see Civil Code § 1814.
Gratuitous deposit defined, see Civil Code § 1844.

ARTICLE 3. STORAGE

Section
1851. Storage; deposit for hire.
1852. Degree of care required.
1853. Hire for fraction of week or month.
1854. Termination of deposit.
1855. Termination of deposit; agreement respecting time.
1856. Depositary's lien.
1857. Depositary's lien; sale.

Cross References

Deposit for keeping, see Civil Code § 1833 et seq.
Deposits for repair, alteration or sale, see Civil Code § 1858 et seq.
Gratuitous deposit, see Civil Code § 1844 et seq.

§ 1851. Storage; deposit for hire

A deposit not gratuitous is called storage. The depositary in such case is called a depositary for hire. *(Enacted in 1872.)*

Cross References

Depositary defined, see Civil Code § 1814.
Gratuitous deposit, see Civil Code § 1844 et seq.
Hiring in general, see Civil Code § 1925 et seq.

§ 1852. Degree of care required

A depositary for hire must use at least ordinary care for the preservation of the thing deposited. *(Enacted in 1872.)*

Cross References

Care required of carriers, see Civil Code §§ 2096, 2114, 2194.
Consignee's failure to accept and remove freight, see Civil Code § 2121.
Degree of care, hirer, see Civil Code § 1928 et seq.
Deposit for hire, see Civil Code § 1851.
Depositary defined, see Civil Code § 1814.
Innkeepers, liability, see Civil Code § 1859.
Notice to consignee of arrival, see Civil Code § 2120.

§ 1853. Hire for fraction of week or month

In the absence of a different agreement or usage, a depositary for hire is entitled to one week's hire for the sustenance and shelter of living animals during any fraction of a week, and to half a month's hire for the storage of any other property during any fraction of a half month. *(Enacted in 1872.)*

Cross References

Advances, effect upon sale of unclaimed property, see Civil Code § 2081.5.
Deposit for hire, see Civil Code § 1851.
Depositary defined, see Civil Code § 1814.

§ 1854. Termination of deposit

In the absence of an agreement as to the length of time during which a deposit is to continue, it may be terminated by the depositor at any time, and by the depositary upon reasonable notice. *(Enacted in 1872.)*

Cross References

Depositary defined, see Civil Code § 1814.
Depositor defined, see Civil Code § 1814.

§ 1855. Termination of deposit; agreement respecting time

Notwithstanding an agreement respecting the length of time during which a deposit is to continue, it may be terminated by the depositor on paying all that would become due to the depositary in case of the deposit so continuing. *(Enacted in 1872.)*

Cross References

Depositary defined, see Civil Code § 1814.
Depositor defined, see Civil Code § 1814.

§ 1856. Depositary's lien

A depositary for hire has a lien for storage charges and for advances and insurance incurred at the request of the bailor, and for money necessarily expended in and about the care, preservation and keeping of the property stored, and he also has a lien for money advanced at the request of the bailor, to discharge a prior lien, and for the expenses of a sale where default has been made in satisfying a valid lien. The rights of the depositary for hire to such lien are regulated by the title on liens. *(Added by Stats.1891, c. 249, p. 470, § 1. Amended by Stats.1909, c. 664, p. 1001, § 1.)*

Cross References

Depositary defined, see Civil Code § 1814.
Liens, see Civil Code § 2872 et seq.
Storage until payment of freight and charges, see Civil Code § 2081.
Termination of bailee's responsibility, see Civil Code § 2081.4.

§ 1857. Depositary's lien; sale

If from any cause other than want of ordinary care and diligence on his part, a depositary for hire is unable to deliver perishable property, baggage, or luggage received by him for storage, or to collect his charges for storage due thereon, he may cause such property to be sold, in open market, to satisfy his lien for storage; *provided*, that no property except perishable property shall be sold, under the provisions of this section, upon which storage charges shall not be due and unpaid for one year at the time of such sale.

All Acts and parts of Acts in conflict with the provisions of this Act are hereby repealed.

This Act shall take effect from and after its passage. *(Added by Stats.1891, c. 249, p. 470, § 2.)*

Cross References

Advances, effect upon sale of unclaimed property, see Civil Code § 2081.5.
Depositary defined, see Civil Code § 1814.
Liens, extinction by sale, etc., see Civil Code § 2910.
Perishables, sale, see Civil Code § 1837.
Sale by lienholder at auction, see Civil Code § 3052.
Unclaimed property, sale, proceeds, see Civil Code § 2081.1 et seq.

ARTICLE 3.5. DEPOSITS FOR REPAIR, ALTERATION OR SALE

Section
1858. Definitions.
1858.1. Customer's receipt; contents.
1858.2. Failure to furnish receipt; strict liability.
1858.3. Insurance protection.

Cross References

Deposit for keeping, see Civil Code § 1833 et seq.
Gratuitous deposit, see Civil Code § 1844 et seq.
Storage, see Civil Code § 1851 et seq.

§ 1858. Definitions

As used in this article:

(a) "Customer" means a natural person who deals with a depositary.

(b) "Depositary" means a person who in the ordinary course of business regularly receives property from customers for the purpose of repair or alteration.

(c) "Property" means personal property used for or intended for personal, family, or household purposes, but does not include any motor vehicle within the meaning of Section 415 of the Vehicle Code. *(Added by Stats.1970, c. 1185, p. 2093, § 1. Amended by Stats.1971, c. 180, p. 247, § 1, eff. June 25, 1971.)*

§ 1858

Cross References

Depositary defined, see Civil Code § 1814.

§ 1858.1. Customer's receipt; contents

Every depositary shall, upon accepting property from a customer, present the customer with written receipt which shall include a statement, if such is the case, that such deposited property is not insured or protected to the amount of the actual cash value thereof by the depositary against loss occasioned by theft, fire, and vandalism while such property remains with the depositary. (Added by Stats.1970, c. 1185, p. 2093, § 1.)

Cross References

Customer defined for purposes of this Article, see Civil Code § 1858.
Depositary defined, see Civil Code § 1814.
Depositary defined for purposes of this Article, see Civil Code § 1858.
Property defined for purposes of this Article, see Civil Code § 1858.

§ 1858.2. Failure to furnish receipt; strict liability

Every depositary who fails to furnish the receipt, or a statement thereon as required by Section 1858.1, or who makes any misrepresentation in such receipt, shall be strictly liable to the customer for any loss occasioned by theft, fire, or vandalism while such property remains with the depositary and shall forfeit any lien or other right to hold the property arising from services rendered in holding, repairing, altering, or selling the property. When liability is imposed upon a depositary under this section it shall be deemed as having been imposed for the commission of a willful act for the purposes of Section 533 of the Insurance Code. (Added by Stats.1970, c. 1185, p. 2093, § 1.)

Cross References

Customer defined for purposes of this Article, see Civil Code § 1858.
Depositary defined, see Civil Code § 1814.
Depositary defined for purposes of this Article, see Civil Code § 1858.
Property defined for purposes of this Article, see Civil Code § 1858.

§ 1858.3. Insurance protection

If the depositary by insurance or by self-insurance does protect property deposited by customers for loss or damage occasioned by theft, fire or vandalism while such property remains with the depositary, such depositary need not make or deliver to customer any notice thereof. (Added by Stats.1970, c. 1185, p. 2093, § 1.)

Cross References

Customer defined for purposes of this Article, see Civil Code § 1858.
Depositary defined, see Civil Code § 1814.
Depositary defined for purposes of this Article, see Civil Code § 1858.
Property defined for purposes of this Article, see Civil Code § 1858.

ARTICLE 3A. WAREHOUSEMEN [REPEALED]

§§ 1858a to 1858f. Repealed by Stats.1963, c. 819, p. 1997, § 2, eff. Jan. 1, 1965

ARTICLE 3B. WAREHOUSE RECEIPTS ACT [REPEALED]

§§ 1858.01 to 1858.35. Repealed by Stats.1963, c. 819, p. 1997, § 2, eff. Jan. 1, 1965

§§ 1858.50 to 1858.85. Repealed by Stats.1963, c. 819, p. 1997, § 2, eff. Jan. 1, 1965

ARTICLE 3C. WAREHOUSE RECEIPTS FOR GOODS OUT–OF–STATE [REPEALED]

§§ 1858.90 to 1858.93. Repealed by Stats.1963, c. 819, p. 1997, § 2, eff. Jan. 1, 1965

ARTICLE 4. INNKEEPERS

Section
1859. Innkeepers, etc., liability as depositaries for hire; limit of liability; special contracts.
1860. Fireproof safe; notice of nonliability; limit of liability.
1861. Innkeeper's lien; enforcement; writ of possession; third party claims; exemptions.
1861.1. Definitions.
1861.5. Application for writ of possession.
1861.6. Writ of possession; hearing; issuance; probable cause; conditions; papers served with writ; motion to quash; damages.
1861.7. Documents to be served.
1861.8. Notice of Application and Hearing.
1861.9. Affidavits; points and authorities; basis for determination; continuance; additional evidence.
1861.10. Issuance of writ of possession; required findings.
1861.12. Writ of possession; requirements.
1861.13. Effect of failure to defend.
1861.14. Effect of determinations.
1861.15. Failure to recover judgment; redelivery of property; liability for damages.
1861.16. Temporary restraining order; preliminary injunction.
1861.17. Scope of temporary restraining order.
1861.18. Service by levying officer.
1861.19. Duties of levying officer; undertaking for redelivery; objection; perishables.
1861.20. Return of writ of possession; time.
1861.21. Plaintiff's undertaking.
1861.22. Defendant's undertaking.
1861.23. Objections to undertakings; time; notice; determination of sufficiency; order of court.
1861.24. Nonpayment of judgment; sale of baggage or property; procedure; distribution of proceeds.
1861.25. Application of rules and proceedings applicable to third-party claims.
1861.27. Affidavits; particularity; qualifications of affiant; verified complaint.
1861.28. Subordinate judicial duties.
1861.607. Renumbered.
1861.608. Renumbered.
1861a. Keepers of apartment houses, etc.; lien; enforcement procedure; disposition of proceeds; exemptions.
1862. Repealed.
1862.5. Unclaimed property in hospital; sale; notice; expenses; surplus.
1863. Rates of charges; posting.

Section
1864. Solicitation or acceptance of reservations or money for transient occupancies in certain dwelling units; duties.
1865. Eviction of guest by innkeeper; possession of guests' property; responsibility for minors.
1866. Special occupancy parks; eviction; possession and removal of property; rights of minors.
1867. Special occupancy parks; movement of guest if imminent danger.

Cross References

Deposit for keeping, see Civil Code § 1833 et seq.
Gratuitous deposit, see Civil Code § 1844 et seq.
Storage, see Civil Code § 1851 et seq.

§ 1859. Innkeepers, etc., liability as depositaries for hire; limit of liability; special contracts

The liability of an innkeeper, hotelkeeper, operator of a licensed hospital, rest home or sanitarium, furnished apartment house keeper, furnished bungalow court keeper, boardinghouse or lodginghouse keeper, for losses of or injuries to personal property, is that of a depositary for hire; provided, however, that in no case shall such liability exceed the sum of one thousand dollars ($1,000) in the aggregate. In no case shall liability exceed, for each item of described property, the respective sums of five hundred dollars ($500) for each trunk and its contents, two hundred fifty dollars ($250) for each valise or traveling bag and its contents, two hundred fifty dollars ($250) for each box, bundle or package and its contents, and two hundred fifty dollars ($250) for all other personal property of any kind, unless he shall have consented in writing with the owner thereof to assume a greater liability. (Enacted in 1872. Amended by Stats.1895, c. 47, p. 49, § 1; Stats.1921, c. 151, p. 149, § 1; Stats.1927, c. 593, p. 1028, § 1; Stats.1931, c. 1190, p. 2501, § 1; Stats.1943, c. 363, p. 1599, § 1; Stats.1957, c. 1251, p. 2557, § 1; Stats.1979, c. 705, p. 2183, § 1.)

Cross References

Action for recovery of personal property, baggage, etc., left at hotel, hospital, etc., limitation, see Code of Civil Procedure § 341a.
Depositary defined, see Civil Code § 1814.
Depositary for hire, care required, see Civil Code § 1852.
Innkeepers, limit of liability, see Civil Code § 1860.
Innkeeper's lien, see Civil Code § 1861.
Innkeeper's refusal to receive and entertain guest, misdemeanor, see Penal Code § 365.

§ 1860. Fireproof safe; notice of nonliability; limit of liability

If an innkeeper, hotelkeeper, operator of a licensed hospital, rest home or sanitarium, boardinghouse or lodginghouse keeper, keeps a fireproof safe and gives notice to a guest, patient, boarder or lodger, either personally or by putting up a printed notice in a prominent place in the office or the room occupied by the guest, patient, boarder, or lodger, that he keeps such a safe and will not be liable for money, jewelry, documents, furs, fur coats and fur garments, or other articles of unusual value and small compass, unless placed therein, he is not liable, except so far as his own acts shall contribute thereto, for any loss of or injury to such articles, if not deposited with him to be placed therein, nor in any case for more than the sum of five hundred dollars ($500) for any or all such property of any individual guest, patient, boarder, or lodger, unless he shall have given a receipt in writing therefor to such guest, patient, boarder or lodger. (Enacted in 1872. Amended by Stats.1895, c. 47, p. 50, § 2; Stats.1921, c. 150, p. 149, § 1; Stats.1943, c. 363, p. 1600, § 2; Stats.1957, c. 1251, p. 2557, § 2; Stats.1979, c. 705, p. 2183, § 2.)

Cross References

Contracts explained by circumstances, see Civil Code § 1647.
Innkeepers, liability as depositaries for hire, see Civil Code § 1859.
Innkeeper's lien, see Civil Code § 1861.

§ 1861. Innkeeper's lien; enforcement; writ of possession; third party claims; exemptions

Hotel, motel, inn, boardinghouse, and lodginghouse keepers shall have a lien upon the baggage and other property belonging to or legally under the control of their guests, boarders, tenants, or lodgers which may be in such hotel, motel, inn, or boarding or lodging house for the proper charges due from such guests, boarders, tenants, or lodgers, for their accommodation, board and lodging and room rent, and such extras as are furnished at their request, and for all money paid for or advanced to such guests, boarders, tenants, or lodgers, and for the costs of enforcing such lien. The lien may be enforced only after final judgment in an action brought to recover such charges or moneys. During the pendency of the proceeding, the plaintiff may take possession of the baggage and property pursuant to a writ of possession as provided by Sections 1861.1 to 1861.27, inclusive. However, if any baggage or property becoming subject to the lien herein provided for does not belong to the guest, lodger, tenant, or boarder who incurred the charges or indebtedness secured thereby, at the time when such charges or indebtedness was incurred, and if the hotel, motel, inn, boarding or lodging house keeper entitled to such lien receives notice of such fact at any time before the sale of such baggage or property hereunder, then, and in that event, such baggage and property which is subject to said lien and did not belong to said guest, boarder, tenant, or lodger at the time when such charges or indebtedness was incurred shall not be subject to this lien.

Any property which is exempt from enforcement of a money judgment is not subject to the lien provided for in this section. (Added by Code Am.1875–76, c. 486, p. 78, § 1. Amended by Stats.1915, c. 650, p. 1285, § 1; Stats.1939, c. 483, p. 1829, § 1; Stats.1953, c. 261, p. 1417, § 1; Stats.1957, c. 42, p. 600, § 1; Stats.1957, c. 591, p. 1686, § 1; Stats.1965, c. 1540, p. 3632, § 1; Stats.1967, c. 1387, p. 3246, § 1; Stats. 1968, c. 1182, p. 2240, § 1; Stats.1970, c. 1247, p. 2237, § 1; Stats.1974, c. 546, p. 1357, § 13; Stats.1979, c. 964, p. 3309, § 1.5; Stats.1982, c. 497, p. 2137, § 9, operative July 1, 1983.)

Cross References

Boardinghouse defined for purposes of Civil Code §§ 1861 to 1861.27, see Civil Code § 1861.1.
Defrauding innkeepers, etc., see Penal Code § 537.
Hotel defined for purposes of Civil Code §§ 1861 to 1861.27, see Civil Code § 1861.1.
Inn defined for purposes of Civil Code §§ 1861 to 1861.27, see Civil Code § 1861.1.
Innkeepers, liability as depositaries for hire, see Civil Code § 1859.
Innkeepers, limit of liability, see Civil Code § 1860.

§ 1861

Keepers of apartment houses, lien, see Civil Code § 1861a.
Lodginghouse defined for purposes of Civil Code §§ 1861 to 1861.27, see Civil Code § 1861.1.
Motel defined for purposes of Civil Code §§ 1861 to 1861.27, see Civil Code § 1861.1.
Plaintiff defined for purposes of Civil Code §§ 1861 to 1861.27, see Civil Code § 1861.1.
Recreational vehicle parks, removal of vehicles, lien on vehicle and contents, see Civil Code §§ 799.55 et seq., 799.75.
Unclaimed property, see Civil Code § 2081 et seq.

§ 1861.1. Definitions

Definitions for purposes of Sections 1861 through 1861.27 include the following:

(a) "Hotel", "motel", "inn", "boardinghouse", and "lodginghouse keeper" means any person, corporation, partnership, unincorporated association, public entity, or agent of any of the aforementioned, who offers and accepts payment for rooms, sleeping accommodations, or board and lodging and retains the right of access to, and control of, the dwelling unit.

(b) "Levying officer" means the sheriff or marshal who is directed to execute a writ of possession issued pursuant to this article.

(c) "Plaintiff" means any party filing a complaint or cross complaint.

(d) "Probable validity" means that the plaintiff, more likely than not, will obtain a judgment against the defendant on the plaintiff's claim. *(Added by Stats.1979, c. 964, p. 3310, § 2. Amended by Stats.1996, c. 872 (A.B.3472), § 23.)*

Cross References

Application for writ, time and contents, see Code of Civil Procedure § 512.010.

§ 1861.5. Application for writ of possession

(a) Upon the filing of a complaint, or at any time thereafter, the plaintiff may apply, pursuant to this article, for a writ of possession by filing an application for the writ with the court in which the action was filed.

(b) The application shall be executed under oath and shall include all of the following:

(1) A showing of the basis of the plaintiff's claim, including a showing that the plaintiff is entitled to possession of the property claimed pursuant to an innkeepers' lien.

(2) A general description of the property and a statement of its value.

(3) A statement of the amount of money claimed to be owed by the guest, lodger, tenant, or boarder.

(c) The requirements of subdivision (b) may be satisfied by one or more affidavits filed with the application. *(Added by Stats.1979, c. 964, p. 3310, § 3.)*

Cross References

Innkeeper's,
  Documents to be served, see Civil Code § 1861.7.
  Liability as depositaries for hire, see Civil Code § 1859.
  Lien, see Civil Code § 1861.
  Limit of liability, see Civil Code § 1860.
  Notice of application and hearing, see Civil Code § 1861.8.
  Requirements of writ of possession, see Civil Code § 1861.12.
Temporary restraining order, see Civil Code § 1861.17.
Writ of possession issued, see Civil Code §§ 1861.6, 1861.10.
Plaintiff defined for purposes of Civil Code §§ 1861 to 1861.27, see Civil Code § 1861.1.
Small claims court,
  Generally, see Code of Civil Procedure § 116.110 et seq.
  Jurisdiction over writs authorized by this section, see Code of Civil Procedure § 116.220.

§ 1861.6. Writ of possession; hearing; issuance; probable cause; conditions; papers served with writ; motion to quash; damages

(a) Except as otherwise provided in this section, no writ shall be issued under this article except after a hearing on a noticed motion.

(b) A writ of possession may be issued ex parte pursuant to this subdivision, if probable cause appears that the following conditions exist:

(1) The property is not necessary for the support of the defendant or his family;

(2) There is an immediate danger that the property will become unavailable to levy, by reason of being transferred, concealed, or removed from the state, or the premises of the motel, hotel, inn, boardinghouse, or lodginghouse, or will become substantially impaired in value by acts of destruction or by failure to take care of the property in a reasonable manner; and

(3) The ex parte issuance of a writ of possession is necessary to protect the property.

(4) The plaintiff establishes the probable validity of the plaintiff's claim.

The plaintiff's application for the writ shall satisfy the requirements of Section 1861.5 and, in addition, shall include a showing that the conditions required by this subdivision exist. A writ of possession may issue if the court finds that the conditions required by this subdivision exist, and the requirements of Section 1861.5 are met. Where a writ of possession has been issued pursuant to this subdivision, a copy of the summons and complaint, a copy of the application and any affidavit in support thereof, and a notice which satisfies the requirements of subdivisions (b) and (c) of Section 1861.8 and informs the defendant of his rights under this subdivision shall be served upon the defendant, and any other person required by Section 1861.8 to be served with a writ of possession. Any defendant whose property has been taken pursuant to a writ of possession issued under this subdivision may apply for an order that the writ be quashed, and any property levied on pursuant to the writ be released. Such application shall be made by noticed motion, and the provisions of Section 1861.9 shall apply. Pending the hearing of the defendant's application, the court may order that delivery pursuant to Section 1861.19 of any property previously levied upon be stayed. If the court determines that the plaintiff is not entitled to a writ of possession, the court shall quash the writ of possession and order the release and redelivery of any property previously levied upon, and shall award the defendant any damages sustained by the defendant which were proximately caused by the levy of the writ of possession and the loss of possession of the property pursuant to such levy. *(Added by Stats.1979, c. 964, p. 3310, § 4.)*

Cross References

Boardinghouse defined for purposes for Civil Code §§ 1861 to 1861.27, see Civil Code § 1861.1.
Hotel defined for purposes of Civil Code §§ 1861 to 1861.27, see Civil Code § 1861.1.
Inn defined for purposes of Civil Code §§ 1861 to 1861.27, see Civil Code § 1861.1.
Issuance of writ after hearing or ex parte, see Code of Civil Procedure § 512.020.
Motel defined for purposes of Civil Code §§ 1861 to 1861.27, see Civil Code § 1861.1.
Plaintiff defined for purposes of Civil Code §§ 1861 to 1861.27, see Civil Code § 1861.1.
Plaintiff's undertaking, see Civil Code § 1861.21.
Probable validity defined for purposes of Civil Code §§ 1861 to 1861.27, see Civil Code § 1861.1.
Seizure of property at place not specified in writ, see Code of Civil Procedure § 512.090.

§ 1861.7. Documents to be served

Prior to the hearing required by subdivision (a) of Section 1861.6, the defendant shall be served with all of the following:

(a) A copy of the summons and complaint.

(b) Notice of application and hearing.

(c) A copy of the application and any affidavit filed in support thereof. *(Added by Stats.1979, c. 964, p. 3311, § 5.)*

Cross References

Service of documents on defendant prior to hearing, see Code of Civil Procedure § 512.030.

§ 1861.8. Notice of Application and Hearing

The "Notice of Application and Hearing" shall inform the defendant of all of the following:

(a) The hearing will be held at a place and at a time, to be specified in the notice, on plaintiff's application for writ of possession.

(b) The writ shall be issued if the court finds that the plaintiff's claim has probable validity and the other requirements for issuing the writ are established. The hearing is not for the purpose of determining whether the claim is actually valid; such determination shall be made in subsequent proceedings in the action.

(c) If the defendant desires to oppose the issuance of the writ, he shall file with the court either an affidavit providing evidence sufficient to defeat the plaintiff's right to issuance of the writ, or an undertaking to stay the delivery of the property in accordance with Section 1861.22.

(d) The notice shall contain the following statement in 10-point bold type:

"If you believe the plaintiff may not be entitled to possession of the property claimed, you may wish to seek the advice of an attorney. Such attorney should be consulted promptly so that he may assist you before the time set for the hearing." *(Added by Stats.1979, c. 964, p. 3311, § 6.)*

Cross References

Notice of application and hearing on writ, contents, see Code of Civil Procedure § 512.040.
Plaintiff defined for purposes of Civil Code §§ 1861 to 1861.27, see Civil Code § 1861.1.
Probable validity defined for purposes of Civil Code §§ 1861 to 1861.27, see Civil Code § 1861.1.

§ 1861.9. Affidavits; points and authorities; basis for determination; continuance; additional evidence

Each party shall file with the court and serve upon the other party within the time prescribed by rule, any affidavits and points and authorities intended to be relied upon at the hearing. At the hearing, the court shall make its determination upon the basis of the pleadings and other papers in the record; but, upon good cause shown, the court may receive and consider additional evidence and authority produced at the hearing, or may continue the hearing for the production of additional evidence, oral or documentary, and the filing of other affidavits or points and authorities. *(Added by Stats. 1979, c. 964, p. 3312, § 7.)*

Cross References

Filing of affidavits and briefs with court, see Code of Civil Procedure § 512.050.

§ 1861.10. Issuance of writ of possession; required findings

(a) At the hearing a writ of possession shall issue if all of the following are found:

(1) The plaintiff has established the probable validity of his claim to possession of the property of the tenant, boarder, or lodger.

(2) That the property which is described within the application for the writ is located on the premises of the motel, hotel, boardinghouse or lodginghouse.

(3) The plaintiff has provided an undertaking as required by Section 1861.21.

(b) No writ directing the levying officer to enter any premises to take possession of any property shall be issued unless the plaintiff has established that there is probable cause to believe that such property is located there. *(Added by Stats.1979, c. 964, p. 3312, § 8.)*

Cross References

Boardinghouse defined for purposes for Civil Code §§ 1861 to 1861.27, see Civil Code § 1861.1.
Hotel defined for purposes of Civil Code §§ 1861 to 1861.27, see Civil Code § 1861.1.
Issuance of writ, requirements, see Code of Civil Procedure § 512.060.
Levying officer defined for purposes of Civil Code §§ 1861 to 1861.27, see Civil Code § 1861.1.
Motel defined for purposes of Civil Code §§ 1861 to 1861.27, see Civil Code § 1861.1.
Plaintiff defined for purposes of Civil Code §§ 1861 to 1861.27, see Civil Code § 1861.1.
Probable validity defined for purposes of Civil Code §§ 1861 to 1861.27, see Civil Code § 1861.1.

§ 1861.12. Writ of possession; requirements

The writ of possession shall meet all of the following requirements:

(a) Be directed to the levying officer within whose jurisdiction the property is located.

(b) Generally describe the property to be seized.

§ 1861.12

(c) Specify the apartment, motel, or other boarding premises that may be entered to take possession of the property, or some part of it.

(d) Direct the levying officer to levy on the property pursuant to Section 1861.18 if found on the described premises, and to retain custody of it until released or sold pursuant to Section 1861.19.

(e) Inform the defendant of the right to object to the plaintiff's undertaking, a copy of which shall be attached to the writ, or to obtain the delivery of the property by filing an undertaking as prescribed by Section 1861.22. (Added by Stats.1979, c. 964, p. 3312, § 9. Amended by Stats.1982, c. 517, p. 2323, § 65.)

Cross References

Bond and Undertaking Law, see Code of Civil Procedure § 995.010 et seq.
Levying officer defined for purposes of Civil Code §§ 1861 to 1861.27, see Civil Code § 1861.1.
Motel defined for purposes of Civil Code §§ 1861 to 1861.27, see Civil Code § 1861.1.
Plaintiff defined for purposes of Civil Code §§ 1861 to 1861.27, see Civil Code § 1861.1.
Writ of possession, requirements, see Code of Civil Procedure § 512.080.

§ 1861.13. Effect of failure to defend

Neither the failure of the defendant to oppose the issuance of a writ of possession under this article, nor his failure to rebut any evidence produced by the plaintiff in connection with proceedings under this article, shall constitute a waiver of any defense to the plaintiff's claim in the action, or any other action, or have any effect on the right of the defendant to produce or exclude evidence at the trial of any such action. (Added by Stats.1979, c. 964, p. 3313, § 10.)

Cross References

Failure of defendant to oppose issuance of writ or to rebut evidence, see Code of Civil Procedure § 512.100.
Plaintiff defined for purposes of Civil Code §§ 1861 to 1861.27, see Civil Code § 1861.1.

§ 1861.14. Effect of determinations

The determinations of the court under this article shall have no effect on the determination of any issues in the action, other than the issues relevant to proceedings under this article, nor shall they affect the rights of any party in any other action arising out of the same claim. The determinations of the court under this article shall not be given in evidence, or referred to in the trial. (Added by Stats.1979, c. 964, p. 3313, § 11.)

Cross References

Effect of court determinations, see Code of Civil Procedure § 512.110.

§ 1861.15. Failure to recover judgment; redelivery of property; liability for damages

If the plaintiff fails to recover judgment in the action, he shall redeliver the property to the defendant, and be liable for all damages sustained by the defendant, which are proximately caused by operation of the temporary restraining order and preliminary injunction, if any, the levy of the writ of possession, and the loss of possession of the property pursuant to the levy of the writ of possession. (Added by Stats.1979, c. 964, p. 3313, § 12.)

Cross References

Failure of plaintiff to recover judgment, see Code of Civil Procedure § 512.120.
Plaintiff defined for purposes of Civil Code §§ 1861 to 1861.27, see Civil Code § 1861.1.

§ 1861.16. Temporary restraining order; preliminary injunction

(a) At or after the time he files an application for a writ of possession, the plaintiff may apply for a temporary restraining order by setting forth in the application a statement of grounds justifying the issuance of such order.

(b) A temporary restraining order may issue ex parte if all the following are found:

(1) The plaintiff has established the probable validity of his claim and entitlement to possession of the property, pursuant to an innkeepers' lien.

(2) The plaintiff has provided an undertaking as required by Section 1861.21.

(3) The plaintiff has established the probable validity that there is an immediate danger that the property claimed may become unavailable to levy by reason of being transferred, concealed, or removed, or may become substantially impaired in value.

(c) If at the hearing on the issuance of the writ of possession the court determines that the plaintiff is not entitled to a writ of possession, the court shall dissolve any temporary restraining order; otherwise, the court may issue a preliminary injunction to remain in effect until the property claimed is seized pursuant to the writ of possession. (Added by Stats.1979, c. 964, p. 3313, § 13.)

Cross References

Application for temporary restraining order, see Code of Civil Procedure § 513.010.
Plaintiff defined for purposes of Civil Code §§ 1861 to 1861.27, see Civil Code § 1861.1.
Probable validity defined for purposes of Civil Code §§ 1861 to 1861.27, see Civil Code § 1861.1.

§ 1861.17. Scope of temporary restraining order

In the discretion of the court, the temporary restraining order may prohibit the defendant from doing any or all of the following:

(a) Transferring any interest in the property by sale, pledge, or grant of security interest, or otherwise disposing of, or encumbering, the property.

(b) Concealing or otherwise removing the property in such a manner as to make it less available to seizure by the levying officer.

(c) Impairing the value of the property either by acts of destruction or by failure to care for the property in a reasonable manner. (Added by Stats.1979, c. 964, p. 3314, § 14.)

Cross References

Levying officer defined for purposes of Civil Code §§ 1861 to 1861.27, see Civil Code § 1861.1.

Prohibition of certain acts by defendant, see Code of Civil Procedure § 513.020.

§ 1861.18. Service by levying officer

(a) At the time of levy, the levying officer shall deliver to the person in possession of the property a copy of the writ of possession, with a copy of the plaintiff's undertaking attached.

(b) If no one is in possession of the property at the time of levy, the levying officer shall subsequently serve the writ and attached undertaking on the defendant. If the defendant has appeared in the action, service shall be accomplished in the manner provided by Chapter 5 (commencing with Section 1010) of Title 14 of Part 2. If the defendant has not appeared in the action, service shall be accomplished in the manner provided for the service of summons and complaint by Article 3 (commencing with Section 415.10) of Chapter 4 of Title 5 of Part 2. (Added by Stats.1979, c. 964, p. 3314, § 15.)

Cross References

Delivery of copy of writ and undertaking, see Code of Civil Procedure § 514.020.

Levying officer defined for purposes of Civil Code §§ 1861 to 1861.27, see Civil Code § 1861.1.

Plaintiff defined for purposes of Civil Code §§ 1861 to 1861.27, see Civil Code § 1861.1.

Undertakings, see Civil Code § 1861.21 et seq.

§ 1861.19. Duties of levying officer; undertaking for redelivery; objection; perishables

(a) After the levying officer takes possession pursuant to the writ of possession, the levying officer shall keep the property in a secure place. Except as otherwise provided in Section 1861.6:

(1) If notice of the filing of an undertaking for redelivery or notice of objection to the undertaking is not received by the levying officer within 10 days after levy of the writ of possession, the levying officer shall deliver the property to plaintiff, upon receiving the fees for taking, and necessary expenses for keeping, the property.

(2) If notice of the filing of an undertaking for redelivery is received by the levying officer within 10 days after levy of the writ of possession, and no objection is made to the defendant's undertaking, the levying officer shall redeliver the property to defendant upon expiration of the time to object, upon receiving the fees for taking and necessary expenses for keeping the property not already paid or advanced by the plaintiff.

(3) If notice of objection to the plaintiff's undertaking or notice of the filing of an undertaking for redelivery is received within 10 days after levy of the writ of possession, and objection is made to the defendant's undertaking, the levying officer shall not deliver or redeliver the property until the time provided in Section 1861.23.

(b) Notwithstanding subdivision (a), when not otherwise provided by contract, and where an undertaking for redelivery has not been filed, upon a showing that the property is perishable, or will greatly deteriorate or depreciate in value, or for some other reason that the interest of the parties will be best served thereby, the court may order that the property be sold and the proceeds deposited in the court to abide the judgment in the action. (Added by Stats.1979, c. 964, p. 3314, § 16. Amended by Stats.1982, c. 517, p. 2323, § 66.)

Cross References

Custody, delivery or redelivery of property, see Code of Civil Procedure § 514.030.

Levying officer defined for purposes of Civil Code §§ 1861 to 1861.27, see Civil Code § 1861.1.

Objections to bonds, see Code of Civil Procedure § 995.910 et seq.

Plaintiff defined for purposes of Civil Code §§ 1861 to 1861.27, see Civil Code § 1861.1.

§ 1861.20. Return of writ of possession; time

The levying officer shall return the writ of possession, with his proceedings thereon, to the court in which the action is pending, within 30 days after a levy, but in no event more than 60 days after the writ is issued. (Added by Stats.1979, c. 964, p. 3315, § 17.)

Cross References

Levying officer defined for purposes of Civil Code §§ 1861 to 1861.27, see Civil Code § 1861.1.

Return by levying officer, see Code of Civil Procedure § 514.040.

§ 1861.21. Plaintiff's undertaking

The court shall not issue a temporary restraining order or a writ of possession until the plaintiff has filed with the court an undertaking. The undertaking shall provide that the sureties are bound to the defendant in the amount of the undertaking for the return of the property to the defendant, if the return thereof be ordered, and for the payment to the defendant of any sum recovered against plaintiff. The undertaking shall be in an amount not less than twice the value of the property. (Added by Stats.1979, c. 964, p. 3315, § 18. Amended by Stats.1982, c. 517, p. 2324, § 67.)

Cross References

Defendant's undertaking, see Civil Code § 1861.22.

Objections to undertakings, see Civil Code § 1861.23.

Plaintiff defined for purposes of Civil Code §§ 1861 to 1861.27, see Civil Code § 1861.1.

Undertaking by plaintiff, see Code of Civil Procedure § 515.010.

§ 1861.22. Defendant's undertaking

(a) The defendant may prevent the plaintiff from taking possession of property, pursuant to a writ of possession, or regain possession of property so taken, by filing with the court in which the action was brought an undertaking in an amount equal to the amount of the plaintiff's undertaking required by Section 1861.21. The undertaking shall state that, if the plaintiff recovers judgment on the action, the defendant shall pay all costs awarded to the plaintiff and all damages that the plaintiff may sustain by reason of the loss of possession of the property, not exceeding the amount of the undertaking.

(b) The defendant's undertaking may be filed at any time before or after the levy of the writ of possession. The defendant shall mail a copy of the undertaking to the levying officer.

§ 1861.22 OBLIGATIONS

(c) If an undertaking for redelivery is filed, and no objection is made to the undertaking, the levying officer shall deliver the property to the defendant, or, if the plaintiff has previously been given possession of the property, the plaintiff shall deliver the property to the defendant. If an undertaking for redelivery is filed and an objection to the undertaking is made, the provisions of Section 1861.23 apply. (Added by Stats.1979, c. 964, p. 3315, § 19. Amended by Stats.1982, c. 517, p. 2324, § 68.)

Cross References

Bond and Undertaking Law, see Code of Civil Procedure § 995.010 et seq.
Levying officer defined for purposes of Civil Code §§ 1861 to 1861.27, see Civil Code § 1861.1.
Plaintiff defined for purposes of Civil Code §§ 1861 to 1861.27, see Civil Code § 1861.1.
Undertaking by defendant, see Code of Civil Procedure § 515.020.
Undertakings, see Civil Code § 1861.21 et seq.

§ 1861.23. Objections to undertakings; time; notice; determination of sufficiency; order of court

(a) The defendant may object to the plaintiff's undertaking not later than 10 days after levy of the writ of possession. The defendant shall mail notice of objection to the levying officer.

(b) The plaintiff may object to the defendant's undertaking not later than 10 days after the defendant's undertaking is filed. The plaintiff shall mail notice of objection to the levying officer.

(c) If the court determines that the plaintiff's undertaking is not sufficient and a sufficient undertaking is not given within the time provided by statute, the court shall vacate the temporary restraining order or preliminary injunction, if any, and the writ of possession and, if levy has occurred, order the levying officer or the plaintiff to return the property to the defendant. If the court determines that the plaintiff's undertaking is sufficient, the court shall order the levying officer to deliver the property to the plaintiff.

(d) If the court determines that the defendant's undertaking is not sufficient and a sufficient undertaking is not given within the time required by statute, the court shall order the levying officer to deliver the property to the plaintiff, or, if the plaintiff has previously been given possession of the property, the plaintiff shall retain possession. If the court determines the defendant's undertaking is sufficient, the court shall order the levying officer or the plaintiff to deliver the property to the defendant. (Formerly § 1821.23, added by Stats.1979, c. 964, p. 3316, § 20. Renumbered § 1861.23 and amended by Stats.1981, c. 714, p. 2591, § 53. Amended by Stats.1982, c. 517, p. 2325, § 69.)

Cross References

Defendant's undertaking, see Civil Code § 1861.22.
Levying officer defined for purposes of Civil Code §§ 1861 to 1861.27, see Civil Code § 1861.1.
Objection to defendant's undertaking, see Code of Civil Procedure § 515.030.
Objections to bonds, see Code of Civil Procedure § 995.910 et seq.
Plaintiff defined for purposes of Civil Code §§ 1861 to 1861.27, see Civil Code § 1861.1.

Plaintiff's undertaking, see Civil Code § 1861.21.

§ 1861.24. Nonpayment of judgment; sale of baggage or property; procedure; distribution of proceeds

Unless the judgment is paid within 30 days from the date it becomes final, the plaintiff may sell the baggage and property at public auction to the highest bidder, after giving notice of the sale by publication. The notice shall contain the name of the debtor, the amount due, a brief description of the property to be sold, and the time and place of sale, in the manner required by Section 6061 of the Government Code in the county in which the premises are situated. A copy of the notice shall be mailed, at least 15 days prior to the date of sale, to the tenant or guest at his or her residence or other known address, and if not known, to the tenant or guest at the place where the premises are situated. After satisfying the lien out of the proceeds of the sale, together with any reasonable costs that may have been incurred in enforcing the lien, the balance of the proceeds of the sale, if any, which have not been claimed by the tenant or guest shall, within 30 days from the date of the sale, be paid into the treasury of the county in which the sale took place. If that balance is not claimed by the owner thereof, or his legal representative, within one year thereafter, by making application to the treasurer or other official designated by the county, it shall be paid into the general fund of the county. Any sale conducted pursuant to this section shall be a bar to any action against the plaintiff for the recovery of the baggage or property, or of the value thereof, or for any damages arising out of the failure of the tenant or guest to receive the baggage or property. (Added by Stats.1979, c. 964, p. 3316, § 21.)

Cross References

Plaintiff defined for purposes of Civil Code §§ 1861 to 1861.27, see Civil Code § 1861.1.

§ 1861.25. Application of rules and proceedings applicable to third-party claims

Where the property taken is claimed by a third person, the rules and proceedings applicable in cases of third-party claims under Division 4 (commencing with Section 720.010) of Title 9 of Part 2 of the Code of Civil Procedure apply. (Added by Stats.1982, c. 497, p. 2139, § 10.5, operative July 1, 1983.)

§ 1861.27. Affidavits; particularity; qualifications of affiant; verified complaint

The facts stated in each affidavit filed pursuant to this article shall be set forth with particularity. Except where matters are specifically permitted by this article to be shown by information and belief, each affidavit shall show affirmatively that the affiant, if sworn as a witness, can testify competently to the facts stated therein. The affiant may be any person, whether or not a party to this action, who has knowledge of the facts. A verified complaint that satisfies the requirements of this section may be used in lieu of, or in addition to, an ordinary affidavit. (Added by Stats.1979, c. 964, p. 3317, § 22.)

Cross References

Affidavits, see Code of Civil Procedure § 516.030.

§ 1861.28. Subordinate judicial duties

The judicial duties to be performed under this article are "subordinate judicial duties" within the meaning of Section

22 of Article VI of the California Constitution, and may be performed by appointed officers such as court commissioners. *(Added by Stats.1979, c. 964, p. 3317, § 23.)*

Cross References

Subordinate judicial duties, see Code of Civil Procedure § 516.040.

§ 1861.607. Renumbered Civil Code § 1812.607 and amended by Stats.1997, c. 17 (S.B.947), § 16

§ 1861.608. Renumbered Civil Code § 1812.608 and amended by Stats.1997, c. 17 (S.B.947), § 17

§ 1861a. Keepers of apartment houses, etc.; lien; enforcement procedure; disposition of proceeds; exemptions

Keepers of furnished and unfurnished apartment houses, apartments, cottages, or bungalow courts shall have a lien upon the baggage and other property of value belonging to their tenants or guests, and upon all the right, title and interest of their tenants or guests in and to all property in the possession of such tenants or guests which may be in such apartment house, apartment, cottage, or bungalow court, for the proper charges due from such tenants or guests, for their accommodation, rent, services, meals, and such extras as are furnished at their request, and for all moneys expended for them, at their request, and for the costs of enforcing such lien.

Such lien may be enforced only after final judgment in an action brought to recover such charges or moneys. During the pendency of the proceeding, the plaintiff may take possession of such baggage and property upon an order issued by the court, where it appears to the satisfaction of the court from an affidavit filed by or on behalf of the plaintiff that the baggage or property is about to be destroyed, substantially devalued, or removed from the premises. Ten days written notice of the hearing on the motion for such order shall be served on the defendant and shall inform the defendant that the defendant may file affidavits on the defendant's behalf and present testimony in the defendant's behalf and that if the defendant fails to appear the plaintiff will apply to the court for such order. The plaintiff shall file an undertaking with good and sufficient sureties, to be approved by the court, in such sum as may be fixed by the court.

Upon such order, the plaintiff shall have the right to enter peaceably the unfurnished apartment house, apartment, cottage, or bungalow court used by the guest or tenant without liability to the guest or tenant, including any possible claim of liability for conversion, trespass, or forcible entry. The plaintiff shall have the same duties and liabilities as a depository for hire as to property which the plaintiff takes into possession. An entry shall be considered peaceable when accomplished with a key or passkey or through an unlocked door during the hours between sunrise and sunset. Unless the judgment shall be paid within 30 days from the date when it becomes final, the plaintiff may sell the baggage and property, at public auction to the highest bidder, after giving notice of such sale by publication of a notice containing the name of the debtor, the amount due, a brief description of the property to be sold, and the time and place of such sale, pursuant to Section 6064 of the Government Code in the county in which said apartment house, apartment, cottage, or bungalow court is situated, and after by mailing, at least 15 days prior to the date of sale, a copy of such notice addressed to such tenant or guest at the residence or other known address of the tenant or guest, and if not known, such notice shall be addressed to the tenant or guest at the place where such apartment house, apartment, cottage, or bungalow court is situated; and, after satisfying such lien out of the proceeds of such sale, together with any reasonable costs, that may have been incurred in enforcing said lien, the residue of said proceeds of sale, if any, shall, upon demand made within six months after such sale, be paid to such tenant or guest; and if not demanded within six months from the date of such sale, said residue, if any, shall be paid into the treasury of the county in which such sale took place; and if the same be not claimed by the owner thereof, or the owner's legal representative within one year thereafter, it shall be paid into the general fund of the county; and such sale shall be a perpetual bar to any action against said keeper for the recovery of such baggage or property, or of the value thereof, or for any damages, growing out of the failure of such tenant or guest to receive such baggage or property.

When the baggage and property are not in the possession of the keeper as provided herein, such lien shall be enforced only in the manner provided for enforcement of a money judgment.

Any property which is exempt from enforcement of a money judgment is not subject to the lien provided for in this section. *(Added by Stats.1917, c. 794, p. 1662, § 1. Amended by Stats.1933, c. 900, p. 2341, § 1; Stats.1939, c. 483, p. 1831, § 2; Stats.1941, c. 515, p. 1825, § 1; Stats.1953, c. 250, p. 1385, § 1; Stats.1953, c. 1453, p. 3051, § 1; Stats.1957, c. 454, p. 1306, § 1; Stats.1961, c. 2041, p. 4258, § 1; Stats.1965, c. 1540, p. 3634, § 1.5; Stats.1967, c. 1387, p. 3247, § 2; Stats.1968, c. 1182, p. 2242, § 2; Stats.1970, c. 1247, p. 2238, § 2; Stats.1982, c. 517, p. 2325, § 70; Stats.1982, c. 497, p. 2139, § 10, operative July 1, 1983.)*

Cross References

Bond and Undertaking Law, see Code of Civil Procedure § 995.010 et seq.
Innkeeper's lien, see Civil Code § 1861.
Recreational vehicle park, lien of owner or manager, see Civil Code § 799.75.
Unclaimed property, auction, see Civil Code § 2081.1.
Unclaimed property, effect of advances upon sale of unclaimed property, see Civil Code § 2081.5.
Unclaimed property, surplus, see Civil Code §§ 2081.2, 2081.3.

§ 1862. Repealed by Stats.1974, c. 331, p. 653, § 1

§ 1862.5. Unclaimed property in hospital; sale; notice; expenses; surplus

Whenever any personal property has heretofore been found in or deposited with, or is hereafter found in or deposited with any licensed hospital and has remained or shall remain unclaimed for a period of 180 days following the departure of the owner from the hospital, such hospital may proceed to sell the same at public auction, and out of the proceeds of such sale may retain the charges for storage, if any, the reasonable expenses of sale thereof and all sums due the hospital from the last known owner. No such sale shall

§ 1862.5 OBLIGATIONS

be made until the expiration of four weeks from the time written notice of such sale is given to the last known owner. Said notice shall contain a description of each item of personal property to be sold, the name of the last owner, the name of the hospital and the time and place of sale and may be sent by regular mail, postage prepaid, to the last known owner at his last known address. In case there should be any balance from such sale after the deductions herein provided for, and such balance shall not be claimed by the rightful owner or his legal representative within one week of said sale, the same shall be paid into the treasury of the county wherein said hospital is located; and if the same be not claimed by the owner thereof, or his legal representative within one year thereafter, the same shall be paid into the general fund of said county. Proceedings in substantial compliance with this section shall exonerate the hospital from any liability for property so sold. This section shall not be construed as limiting or in any way amending any other provision of law limiting the liabilities of any licensed hospital. *(Added by Stats.1963, c. 810, p. 1840, § 1.)*

Cross References

Optional procedure for disposition of property remaining on premises after commercial tenancy is terminated, see Civil Code § 1993.02.

§ 1863. Rates of charges; posting

(a) Every keeper of a hotel, inn, boardinghouse or lodginghouse, shall post in a conspicuous place in the office or public room, and in every bedroom of said hotel, boardinghouse, inn, or lodginghouse, a printed copy of this section, and a statement of rate or range of rates by the day for lodging.

(b) No charge or sum shall be collected or received for any greater sum than is specified in subdivision (a). For any violation of this subdivision, the offender shall forfeit to the injured party one hundred dollars ($100) or three times the amount of the sum charged in excess of what he is entitled to, whichever is greater. There shall be no forfeiture under this subdivision unless notice be given of the overcharge to such keeper within 30 days after payment of such charges and such keeper shall fail or refuse to make proper adjustment of such overcharge. *(Added by Code Am.1875–76, c. 486, p. 79, § 1. Amended by Stats.1969, c. 826, p. 1655, § 1.)*

§ 1864. Solicitation or acceptance of reservations or money for transient occupancies in certain dwelling units; duties

Any person or entity, including a person employed by a real estate broker, who, on behalf of another or others, solicits or arranges, or accepts reservations or money, or both, for transient occupancies described in paragraphs (1) and (2) of subdivision (b) of Section 1940, in a dwelling unit in a common interest development, as defined in Section 4100, in a dwelling unit in an apartment building or complex, or in a single-family home, shall do each of the following:

(a) Prepare and maintain, in accordance with a written agreement with the owner, complete and accurate records and books of account, kept in accordance with generally accepted accounting principles, of all reservations made and money received and spent with respect to each dwelling unit. All money received shall be kept in a trust account maintained for the benefit of owners of the dwelling units.

(b) Render, monthly, to each owner of the dwelling unit, or to that owner's designee, an accounting for each month in which there are any deposits or disbursements on behalf of that owner, however, in no event shall this accounting be rendered any less frequently than quarterly.

(c) Make all records and books of account with respect to a dwelling unit available, upon reasonable advance notice, for inspection and copying by the dwelling unit's owner. The records shall be maintained for a period of at least three years.

(d) Comply fully with all collection, payment, and record-keeping requirements of a transient occupancy tax ordinance, if any, applicable to the occupancy.

(e) In no event shall any activities described in this section subject the person or entity performing those activities in any manner to Part 1 (commencing with Section 10000) of Division 4 of the Business and Professions Code. However, a real estate licensee subject to this section may satisfy the requirements of this section by compliance with the Real Estate Law. *(Added by Stats.1992, c. 134 (A.B.814), § 2. Amended by Stats.2012, c. 181 (A.B.806), § 37, operative Jan. 1, 2014.)*

Cross References

Exceptions to definition of real estate broker, see Business and Professions Code § 10131.01.

§ 1865. Eviction of guest by innkeeper; possession of guests' property; responsibility for minors

(a) For purposes of this section, "hotel" means any hotel, motel, bed and breakfast inn, or other similar transient lodging establishment, but it shall not include any residential hotel as defined in Section 50519 of the Health and Safety Code. "Innkeeper" means the owner or operator of a hotel, or the duly authorized agent or employee of the owner or operator.

(b) For purposes of this section, "guest" means, and is specifically limited to, an occupant of a hotel whose occupancy is exempt, pursuant to subdivision (b) of Section 1940, from Chapter 2 (commencing with Section 1940) of Title 5 of Part 4 of Division 3.

(c) In addition to, and not in derogation of, any other provision of law, every innkeeper shall have the right to evict a guest in the manner specified in this subdivision if the guest refuses or otherwise fails to fully depart the guest room at or before the innkeeper's posted checkout time on the date agreed to by the guest, but only if both of the following conditions are met:

(1) If the guest is provided written notice, at the time that he or she was received and provided accommodations by the innkeeper, that the innkeeper needs that guest's room to accommodate an arriving person with a contractual right thereto, and that if the guest fails to fully depart at the time agreed to the innkeeper may enter the guest's guest room, take possession of the guest's property, re-key the door to the guest room, and make the guest room available to a new guest. The written notice shall be signed by the guest.

(2) At the time that the innkeeper actually undertakes to evict the guest as specified in this subdivision, the innkeeper in fact has a contractual obligation to provide the guest room to an arriving person.

In the above cases, the innkeeper may enter the guest's guest room, take possession of the guest's property, re-key the door to the guest room, and make the guest room available to a new guest. The evicted guest shall be entitled to immediate possession of his or her property upon request therefor, subject to the rights of the innkeeper pursuant to Sections 1861 to 1861.28, inclusive.

(d) As pertains to a minor, the rights of an innkeeper include, but are not limited to, the following:

(1) Where a minor unaccompanied by an adult seeks accommodations, the innkeeper may require a parent or guardian of the minor, or another responsible adult, to assume, in writing, full liability for any and all proper charges and other obligations incurred by the minor for accommodations, food and beverages, and other services provided by or through the innkeeper, as well as for any and all injuries or damage caused by the minor to any person or property.

(2) Where a minor is accompanied by an adult, the innkeeper may require the adult to agree, in writing, not to leave any minor 12 years of age or younger unattended on the innkeeper's premises at any time during their stay, and to control the minor's behavior during their stay so as to preserve the peace and quiet of the innkeeper's other guests and to prevent any injury to any person and damage to any property. *(Added by Stats.1999, c. 354 (S.B.1171), § 2. Amended by Stats.2004, c. 183 (A.B.3082), § 38.)*

Cross References

Innkeepers or common carriers refusing to receive guests and passengers, see Penal Code § 365.

§ 1866. Special occupancy parks; eviction; possession and removal of property; rights of minors

(a) For purposes of this section, the following definitions apply:

(1) "Camping cabin" has the same meaning as in Section 18862.5 of the Health and Safety Code.

(2) "Campsite" has the same meaning as in Section 18862.9 of the Health and Safety Code.

(3) "Guest" is interchangeable with "occupant" and has the same meaning as used in Chapter 2.6 (commencing with Section 799.20) of Title 2 of Part 2 of Division 1.

(4) "Lot" has the same meaning as in Section 18862.23 of the Health and Safety Code.

(5) "Motor vehicle" has the same meaning as in Section 415 of the Vehicle Code.

(6) "Occupant" is interchangeable with "guest" and has the same meaning as used in Chapter 2.6 (commencing with Section 799.20) of Title 2 of Part 2 of Division 1.

(7) "Park trailer" has the same meaning as in Section 18009.3 of the Health and Safety Code.

(8) "Recreational vehicle" has the same meaning as in Section 18010 of the Health and Safety Code.

(9) "Site" means the campsite, camping cabin, lot, or rental unit.

(10) "Special occupancy park" has the same meaning as in Section 18862.43 of the Health and Safety Code.

(11) "Tent" has the same meaning as in Section 18862.49 of the Health and Safety Code.

(b)(1) Notwithstanding any other provision of law, the park management of a special occupancy park shall have the right to evict a guest if the guest refuses or otherwise fails to fully depart from the campsite, camping cabin, lot, or other rental unit at the park management's posted checkout time on the date agreed to by the guest, but only if the following conditions are met:

(A) The guest is provided with written notice, at the time that he or she was provided accommodations by the park management, that the park management needs that guest's campsite, camping cabin, lot, or rental unit to accommodate an arriving person with a contractual right thereto, and that if the guest fails to fully depart at the time agreed to, the park management may take possession of the guest's property left in the site, subject to the limits of paragraph (2), including any tent, park trailer, or recreational vehicle, and make the campsite, camping cabin, lot, or rental unit available to new guests. The written notice shall be signed by the guest.

(B)(i) At the time that the park management actually undertakes to evict the guest as specified in this subdivision, the park management has a contractual obligation to provide the guest's campsite, camping cabin, lot, or rental unit to an arriving person and there are no other substantially similar campsites, camping cabins, lots, or rental units available for the arriving person.

(ii) Subject to the same requirements described in subparagraph (i), a guest may be provided with the notice described in subparagraph (A) subsequent to the time he or she was provided accommodations by park management, if the notice is provided at least 24 hours prior to the guest's scheduled checkout time. If park management provides a notice under this subparagraph in bad faith or with the knowledge that the contractual obligation is not a bona fide obligation, it shall be liable to the evicted guest for actual damages, plus a civil penalty of two hundred fifty dollars ($250).

(C) At the time that the park management actually undertakes to evict the guest as specified in this subdivision, the park management offers another campsite, camping cabin, lot, or rental unit to the guest, if one is available.

(2) In addition to the requirements of paragraph (1), in order for management to remove a recreational vehicle or motor vehicle, the park management shall do all of the following:

(A) Management shall have an oral, face-to-face communication with the registered guest after the guest has held over that does all of the following:

(i) Alerts the guest that he or she is in violation of the terms of the reservation because he or she has failed to depart the site at the agreed-upon time.

(ii) Reminds the guest that failure to remove a recreational vehicle, motor vehicle, or any other property from the space within two hours may result in the park management removing the recreational vehicle, motor vehicle, or any other property.

(iii) Discloses that the cost of towing a recreational vehicle or motor vehicle is substantial and that these costs will be incurred by the guest.

(iv) Identifies another location in the park to which the guest may temporarily move his or her recreational vehicle or motor vehicle.

(B) The park management gives the guest two hours after the park management has communicated with the guest, pursuant to subparagraph (A), to remove the guest's recreational vehicle, motor vehicle, or other property from the site.

(c) Except as provided in subdivision (f), if the conditions specified in subdivision (b) are met, the park management may take possession of the guest's property left at the site and have the guest's recreational vehicle or motor vehicle towed from the special occupancy park and make the guest's campsite, camping cabin, lot, or rental unit available to a new guest. Park management may enter a campsite, camping cabin, park trailer, lot, or rental unit owned by the park management to take possession of the guest's possessions. The evicted guest shall be entitled to immediate possession of his or her property upon request, subject to the enforcement rights of the park management, which are the same as those accorded to a hotel, motel, inn, boarding house, or lodging housekeeper, pursuant to Sections 1861 to 1861.28, inclusive. If a guest's recreational vehicle or motor vehicle has been towed from the premises, the guest shall be entitled to immediate possession of his or her vehicle upon request, subject to the conditions of the towing company.

(d) When the park management moves or causes the removal of a guest's recreational vehicle, motor vehicle, or other property, the management and the individual or entity that removes the recreational vehicle, motor vehicle, or other property shall exercise reasonable and ordinary care in removing the recreational vehicle, motor vehicle, or other property.

(e) This section does not apply to a manufactured home, as defined in Section 18007 of the Health and Safety Code, or a mobilehome, as defined in Section 18008 of the Health and Safety Code.

(f) In the event that a guest is incapable of removing his or her recreational vehicle or motor vehicle from the lot because of: (1) a physical incapacity, (2) the recreational vehicle or motor vehicle is not motorized and cannot be moved by the guest's vehicle, or (3) the recreational vehicle or motor vehicle is inoperable due to mechanical difficulties, the guest shall be provided with 72 hours in which to remove the vehicle. If the guest has not removed the vehicle within 72 hours, park management may remove the vehicle without further notice.

(g) As pertains to a minor, the rights of guests include, but are not limited to, the following:

(1) If a minor who is unaccompanied by an adult seeks accommodations, the park management may require a parent or guardian of the minor, or another responsible adult, to assume, in writing, full liability for any and all proper charges and other obligations incurred by the minor for accommodations, food and beverages, and other services provided by or through the park management, as well as for any and all injuries or damage caused by the minor to any person or property.

(2) If a minor is accompanied by an adult, the park management may require the adult to agree, in writing, not to leave any minor 12 years of age or younger unattended on the park management's premises at any time during their stay, and to control the minor's behavior during their stay so as to preserve the peace and quiet of the other guests and to prevent any injury to any person and damage to any property. *(Added by Stats.2004, c. 530 (A.B.1964), § 4.)*

Cross References

Removal of recreational vehicle, display of warning signs, see Civil Code § 799.46.

§ 1867. Special occupancy parks; movement of guest if imminent danger

(a) The park management of a special occupancy park may require a guest to move from a space in the special occupancy park to a different space in the special occupancy park if an imminent danger is present, as determined by the park management. If possible, the park management shall offer to return the guest to his or her original space once the park management has determined that the imminent danger is removed or resolved.

(b) For purposes of this section, the following definitions apply:

(1) "Imminent danger" means a danger that poses an immediate and likely risk to the health or safety of a guest or guests in the special occupancy park.

(2) "Space" means any of the following:

(A) "Camping cabin," as defined in Section 18862.5 of the Health and Safety Code.

(B) "Campsite," as defined in Section 18862.9 of the Health and Safety Code.

(C) "Lot," as defined in Section 18862.23 of the Health and Safety Code, or other rental unit.

(3) "Special occupancy park" has the same meaning as in Section 18862.43 of the Health and Safety Code. *(Added by Stats.2004, c. 530 (A.B.1964), § 5.)*

ARTICLE 5. FINDING [REPEALED]

§§ 1868 to 1874. Repealed by Stats.1967, c. 1512, p. 3601, § 1

§ 1875. Repealed by Stats.1968, c. 48, § 3

CHAPTER 3. DEPOSIT FOR EXCHANGE

Section
1878. Transfer of title; relationship between parties.

§ 1878. Transfer of title; relationship between parties

A deposit for exchange transfers to the depositary the title to the thing deposited, and creates between him and the depositor the relation of debtor and creditor merely. *(Enacted in 1872.)*

Cross References

Banks, deposits, see Financial Code § 1400 et seq.
Deposit for exchange defined, see Civil Code § 1818.
Deposit for keeping, see Civil Code § 1833 et seq.
Depositary defined, see Civil Code § 1814.
Depositor defined, see Civil Code § 1814.
Loan for exchange, see Civil Code § 1902 et seq.
Private bulk storage of grain, see Civil Code § 1880 et seq.

CHAPTER 4. PRIVATE BULK STORAGE OF GRAIN

Section
1880. Short title.
1880.1. Definitions.
1880.2. Storage facilities; marking.
1880.3. Sale by bill of sale without delivery.
1880.4. Bill of sale; contents.
1880.5. Bill of sale; optional contracts.
1880.6. Bill of sale; title passing by delivery and endorsement.
1880.7. Notice of sale; posting; form.
1880.8. Delivery; necessity of presenting bill of sale; endorsement of amount delivered.
1880.9. Bill of sale; presumptive evidence of right to delivery.
1881. Storage after delivery date.
1881.1. Offense and punishment; irregularity of notice or posting, effect on sale.
1881.2. Depositary; legal status.
1881.3. Repealed.

Cross References

Banks, deposits, see Financial Code § 1400 et seq.
Deposit for keeping, see Civil Code § 1833 et seq.
Transfer of title, relationship between parties, see Civil Code § 1878.

§ 1880. Short title

This chapter may be cited as the Private Bulk Grain Storage Law. *(Added by Stats.1944, 4th Ex.Sess., c. 54, p. 211, § 1.)*

Cross References

Grain defined for purposes of this Chapter, see Civil Code § 1880.1.

§ 1880.1. Definitions

As used in this chapter:

(a) "Grain" includes barley, corn, flax, hay, grain sorghums, oats, rice, rye, and wheat.

(b) "Seller" means a producer of grain who continues to store grain after sale thereof by him in storage facilities owned, operated, or controlled by him.

(c) "Storage facilities" means any bin, building, elevator, protected enclosure, or other structure owned, operated, or controlled by the seller of the grain stored therein.

(d) "Private bulk storage" means the storage of grain in storage facilities after sale of such grain by a seller.

(e) "Buyer" means a purchaser of grain which is thereafter stored in private bulk storage, and includes the assigns and successors in interest of such buyer.

(f) "Bill of sale" means a written instrument, conforming to the requirements of this chapter, which evidences a transfer of grain. *(Added by Stats.1944, 4th Ex.Sess., c. 54, p. 211, § 1.)*

§ 1880.2. Storage facilities; marking

The seller shall conspicuously mark on all storage facilities "Private bulk storage only" and with a designating number on each such facility and such markings shall be maintained at all times during which grain remains in private bulk storage therein. *(Added by Stats.1944, 4th Ex.Sess., c. 54, p. 212, § 1.)*

Cross References

Failure to comply with notice and posting requirements for private bulk storage facilities, see Civil Code § 1881.1.
Grain defined for purposes of this Chapter, see Civil Code § 1880.1.
Private bulk storage defined for purposes of this Chapter, see Civil Code § 1880.1.
Seller defined for purposes of this Chapter, see Civil Code § 1880.1.
Storage facilities defined for purposes of this Chapter, see Civil Code § 1880.1.

§ 1880.3. Sale by bill of sale without delivery

Grain in private bulk storage facilities may be sold in conformity with this chapter by bill of sale without delivery and no provision of Section 3440 of this code or of any other law requiring delivery or actual and continued change of possession shall be applicable to grain so sold. *(Added by Stats.1944, 4th Ex.Sess., c. 54, p. 212, § 1.)*

Cross References

Bill of sale defined for purposes of this Chapter, see Civil Code § 1880.1.
Grain defined for purposes of this Chapter, see Civil Code § 1880.1.
Private bulk storage defined for purposes of this Chapter, see Civil Code § 1880.1.
Storage facilities defined for purposes of this Chapter, see Civil Code § 1880.1.

§ 1880.4. Bill of sale; contents

Upon sale of grain which is to remain in private bulk storage the seller shall execute and deliver to the buyer a bill of sale which shall contain all of the following:

(a) The date and place where made.

(b) The names of the seller and the buyer.

(c) A statement of the estimated quantity and kind of grain.

(d) A statement of the location and designating numbers of the storage facilities in which the grain is stored.

(e) A statement of the price per unit and a statement of the amount received by the seller. *(Added by Stats.1944, 4th Ex.Sess., c. 54, p. 212, § 1.)*

Cross References

Bill of sale defined for purposes of this Chapter, see Civil Code § 1880.1.
Buyer defined for purposes of this Chapter, see Civil Code § 1880.1.
Grain defined for purposes of this Chapter, see Civil Code § 1880.1.
Private bulk storage defined for purposes of this Chapter, see Civil Code § 1880.1.
Seller defined for purposes of this Chapter, see Civil Code § 1880.1.
Storage facilities defined for purposes of this Chapter, see Civil Code § 1880.1.

§ 1880.5. Bill of sale; optional contracts

The bill of sale may contain other provisions, including reference to or provision for any one or more of the following:

§ 1880.5 OBLIGATIONS

(a) Provision that the total price is based upon the estimated weight and that the total price may be adjusted in accordance with the outturn weight.

(b) A statement that the buyer may have free use of the designated storage facilities until a specified date and that any extension beyond the specified date granted by seller must be endorsed under the signature of seller on the bill of sale.

(c) A statement that seller has the legal right to extend to buyer the use of designated storage facilities.

(d) A statement that actual possession of the grain by the buyer is to be taken on board trucks at the storage facility, or on railroad cars, or in the storage facility, or as may be agreed upon.

(e) A statement that if actual possession be not taken within the time specified, due to any cause not chargeable to seller, the seller may consign the same at buyer's risk and expense to a specified destination. *(Added by Stats.1944, 4th Ex.Sess., c. 54, p. 212, § 1.)*

Cross References

Bill of sale defined for purposes of this Chapter, see Civil Code § 1880.1.
Buyer defined for purposes of this Chapter, see Civil Code § 1880.1.
Grain defined for purposes of this Chapter, see Civil Code § 1880.1.
Seller defined for purposes of this Chapter, see Civil Code § 1880.1.
Storage facilities defined for purposes of this Chapter, see Civil Code § 1880.1.

§ 1880.6. Bill of sale; title passing by delivery and endorsement

Execution and delivery by a seller of a bill of sale shall pass seller's title to the grain covered thereby to the buyer and such title passes to the assignees of the buyer upon further endorsement and delivery of the bill of sale. *(Added by Stats.1944, 4th Ex.Sess., c. 54, p. 212, § 1.)*

Cross References

Bill of sale defined for purposes of this Chapter, see Civil Code § 1880.1.
Buyer defined for purposes of this Chapter, see Civil Code § 1880.1.
Grain defined for purposes of this Chapter, see Civil Code § 1880.1.
Notice of sale, see Civil Code § 1880.7.
Seller defined for purposes of this Chapter, see Civil Code § 1880.1.

§ 1880.7. Notice of sale; posting; form

Upon the issuance of any such bill of sale, the seller shall immediately post upon the storage facilities containing the grain a notice in substantially the following form:

"Notice of Sale

On this _____ day of _____, 19__, grain in this storage facility numbered _____, estimated to be _____ bushels of _____ (designating the kind of grain) was transferred and sold as follows:

Name of Seller _____   Name of original Buyer __
Address of Seller _____   Address of Buyer _____

Grain to be removed by buyer on or before _____, 19___.
(If date extended such fact and the date to which extended must appear on the notice)."

Such notice shall be maintained by seller in a conspicuous place upon the storage facility at all times during which the grain involved continues to be stored therein. *(Added by Stats.1944, 4th Ex.Sess., c. 54, p. 212, § 1.)*

Cross References

Bill of sale defined for purposes of this Chapter, see Civil Code § 1880.1.
Buyer defined for purposes of this Chapter, see Civil Code § 1880.1.
Failure to comply with notice and posting requirements for private bulk storage facilities, see Civil Code § 1881.1.
Grain defined for purposes of this Chapter, see Civil Code § 1880.1.
Seller defined for purposes of this Chapter, see Civil Code § 1880.1.
Storage facilities defined for purposes of this Chapter, see Civil Code § 1880.1.

§ 1880.8. Delivery; necessity of presenting bill of sale; endorsement of amount delivered

No delivery shall be made of any portion of the grain so privately stored unless the bill of sale therefor is presented to the seller, or other person in charge of the storage facility, and the amount of grain so delivered plainly endorsed upon the bill of sale; but this provision shall not apply to any consignment of the grain by the seller to the buyer upon the expiration of the time for delivery specified in the bill of sale. *(Added by Stats.1944, 4th Ex.Sess., c. 54, p. 213, § 1.)*

Cross References

Bill of sale defined for purposes of this Chapter, see Civil Code § 1880.1.
Buyer defined for purposes of this Chapter, see Civil Code § 1880.1.
Grain defined for purposes of this Chapter, see Civil Code § 1880.1.
Seller defined for purposes of this Chapter, see Civil Code § 1880.1.

§ 1880.9. Bill of sale; presumptive evidence of right to delivery

The presentment of the bill of sale by the holder to seller shall be presumptive evidence that the person presenting it is entitled to delivery of the grain described therein unless the seller has knowledge of facts or circumstances sufficient to place him on notice that the possession of the instrument by such person is unlawful. *(Added by Stats.1944, 4th Ex.Sess., c. 54, p. 213, § 1.)*

Cross References

Bill of sale defined for purposes of this Chapter, see Civil Code § 1880.1.
Grain defined for purposes of this Chapter, see Civil Code § 1880.1.
Seller defined for purposes of this Chapter, see Civil Code § 1880.1.

§ 1881. Storage after delivery date

If any grain in private bulk storage is not removed or delivered on or before the original date of delivery specified in the bill of sale and in the notice of sale, it shall be lawful for the seller to continue to store such grain to the order of the buyer upon such terms as may be agreed upon. *(Added by Stats.1944, 4th Ex.Sess., c. 54, p. 213, § 1.)*

Cross References

Bill of sale defined for purposes of this Chapter, see Civil Code § 1880.1.
Buyer defined for purposes of this Chapter, see Civil Code § 1880.1.
Grain defined for purposes of this Chapter, see Civil Code § 1880.1.

Private bulk storage defined for purposes of this Chapter, see Civil Code § 1880.1.

Seller defined for purposes of this Chapter, see Civil Code § 1880.1.

§ 1881.1. Offense and punishment; irregularity of notice or posting, effect on sale

A seller who shall willfully fail to comply with the requirements of notice and posting as provided for in Section 1880.2 or in Section 1880.7 shall be guilty of a misdemeanor and punishable by imprisonment in the county jail not exceeding six months, or by fine not exceeding one thousand dollars ($1,000), or by both. No sale of grain shall be invalidated by reason of any lack or irregularity in connection with such notice or posting. *(Added by Stats.1944, 4th Ex.Sess., c. 54, p. 213, § 1. Amended by Stats.1983, c. 1092, § 66, eff. Sept. 27, 1983, operative Jan. 1, 1984.)*

Cross References

Grain defined for purposes of this Chapter, see Civil Code § 1880.1.
Misdemeanors, definition and penalties, see Penal Code §§ 17, 19, 19.2.
Seller defined for purposes of this Chapter, see Civil Code § 1880.1.

§ 1881.2. Depositary; legal status

The storage of grain pursuant to this chapter shall not constitute the depositary a warehouseman or storer of goods for hire and no storage facility shall be deemed to constitute a warehouse or public place of storage. *(Added by Stats.1944, 4th Ex.Sess., c. 54, p. 213, § 1.)*

Cross References

Depositary defined, see Civil Code § 1814.
Grain defined for purposes of this Chapter, see Civil Code § 1880.1.

§ 1881.3. Repealed by Stats.1953, c. 867, p. 2212, § 1

Title 3.5

UTILITY SERVICES

Section
1882. Definitions.
1882.1. Civil actions for diversion, unauthorized connections, tampering with meter, etc.
1882.2. Treble damages; costs; attorney fees.
1882.3. Presumptions; certain apparatus or altered meter found on premises.
1882.4. Action to enjoin or restrain unauthorized use permitted; damages recoverable in same action.
1882.5. Action to enjoin or restrain unauthorized use; monetary damages or threat thereof not a prerequisite.
1882.6. Damages exceeding actual loss; consideration in establishing utility rates.

Cross References

Crimes involving telegraph, telephone, cable television or electric lines, see Penal Code §§ 591, 593b.
Crimes involving water works, facilities, or pipes, see Penal Code § 624.
Injury to public utility property, see Public Utilities Code § 7951 et seq.
Public utilities, collection of tariff charges, see Public Utilities Code § 737.
Public utilities, termination of residential service for nonpayment of delinquent account, see Public Utilities Code § 779.
Public utilities, termination of services on weekends, legal holidays or time when business office is not open, see Public Utilities Code § 780.
Public Utilities Act, liability for damage or injury caused by a violation, see Public Utilities Code § 2106.

§ 1882. Definitions

Unless the context requires otherwise, the following definitions govern the construction of this title:

(a) "Customer" means the person in whose name a utility service is provided.

(b) "Divert" means to change the intended course or path of electricity, gas, or water without the authorization or consent of the utility.

(c) "Person" means any individual, a partnership, firm, association, limited liability company, or corporation.

(d) "Reconnection" means the commencement of utility service to a customer or other person after service has been lawfully discontinued by the utility.

(e) "Tamper" means to rearrange, injure, alter, interfere with, or otherwise to prevent from performing normal or customary function.

(f) "Utility" means any electrical, gas, or water corporation as those terms are defined in the Public Utilities Code and includes any electrical, gas, or water system operated by any public agency.

(g) "Utility service" means the provision of electricity, gas, water, or any other service or commodity furnished by the utility for compensation. *(Added by Stats.1981, c. 981, p. 3807, § 1. Amended by Stats.1994, c. 1010 (S.B.2053), § 47.)*

§ 1882.1. Civil actions for diversion, unauthorized connections, tampering with meter, etc.

A utility may bring a civil action for damages against any person who commits, authorizes, solicits, aids, abets, or attempts any of the following acts:

(a) Diverts, or causes to be diverted, utility services by any means whatsoever.

(b) Makes, or causes to be made, any connection or reconnection with property owned or used by the utility to provide utility service without the authorization or consent of the utility.

(c) Prevents any utility meter, or other device used in determining the charge for utility services, from accurately performing its measuring function by tampering or by any other means.

(d) Tampers with any property owned or used by the utility to provide utility services.

(e) Uses or receives the direct benefit of all, or a portion, of the utility service with knowledge of, or reason to believe that, the diversion, tampering, or unauthorized connection existed at the time of the use, or that the use or receipt, was without the authorization or consent of the utility. *(Added by Stats.1981, c. 981, p. 3807, § 1.)*

Cross References

Divert defined for purposes of this Title, see Civil Code § 1882.
Person defined for purposes of this Title, see Civil Code § 1882.

§ 1882.1

Reconnection defined for purposes of this Title, see Civil Code § 1882.
Tamper defined for purposes of this Title, see Civil Code § 1882.
Utility defined for purposes of this Title, see Civil Code § 1882.
Utility service defined for purposes of this Title, see Civil Code § 1882.

§ 1882.2. Treble damages; costs; attorney fees

In any civil action brought pursuant to Section 1882.1, the utility may recover as damages three times the amount of actual damages, if any, plus the cost of the suit and reasonable attorney's fees. *(Added by Stats.1981, c. 981, p. 3807, § 1.)*

Cross References

Action by a utility to enjoin or restrain unauthorized use permitted, see Civil Code § 1882.4.
Damages recovered by utility exceeding actual loss taken into consideration in establishing utility rates, see Civil Code § 1882.6.
Utility defined for purposes of this Title, see Civil Code § 1882.
Utility services, presumptions when a certain apparatus or altered meter is found on the premises, see Civil Code § 1882.3.

§ 1882.3. Presumptions; certain apparatus or altered meter found on premises

There is a rebuttable presumption that there is a violation of Section 1882.1 if, on premises controlled by the customer or by the person using or receiving the direct benefit of utility service, there is either, or both, of the following:

(a) Any instrument, apparatus, or device primarily designed to be used to obtain utility service without paying the full lawful charge therefor.

(b) Any meter that has been altered, tampered with, or bypassed so as to cause no measurement or inaccurate measurement of utility services. *(Added by Stats.1981, c. 981, p. 3807, § 1.)*

Cross References

Customer defined for purposes of this Title, see Civil Code § 1882.
Person defined for purposes of this Title, see Civil Code § 1882.
Utility service defined for purposes of this Title, see Civil Code § 1882.

§ 1882.4. Action to enjoin or restrain unauthorized use permitted; damages recoverable in same action

A utility may, in accordance with Chapter 3 (commencing with Section 525) of Title 7 of Part 2 of the Code of Civil Procedure, bring an action to enjoin and restrain any of the acts specified in Section 1882.1.

The utility may, in the same action, seek damages for any of the acts specified in Section 1882.1. *(Added by Stats.1981, c. 981, p. 3807, § 1.)*

Cross References

Utility service defined for purposes of this Title, see Civil Code § 1882.
Utility services, presumptions when a certain apparatus or altered meter is found on the premises, see Civil Code § 1882.3.
Utility services, treble damages, see Civil Code § 1882.2.

§ 1882.5. Action to enjoin or restrain unauthorized use; monetary damages or threat thereof not a prerequisite

It is not a necessary prerequisite to an action pursuant to Section 1882.4 that the utility have suffered, or be threatened with, monetary damages. *(Added by Stats.1981, c. 981, p. 3807, § 1.)*

Cross References

Action by a utility to enjoin or restrain unauthorized use permitted, see Civil Code § 1882.4.
Civil actions by utility for diversion, unauthorized connections, tampering with meter, etc., see Civil Code § 1882.1.
Utility service defined for purposes of this Title, see Civil Code § 1882.
Utility services, presumptions when a certain apparatus or altered meter is found on the premises, see Civil Code § 1882.3.
Utility services, treble damages, see Civil Code § 1882.2.

§ 1882.6. Damages exceeding actual loss; consideration in establishing utility rates

Any damages recovered pursuant to this title in excess of the actual damages sustained by the utility may be taken into account by the Public Utilities Commission or other applicable ratemaking agency in establishing utility rates. *(Added by Stats.1981, c. 981, p. 3807, § 1.)*

Cross References

Civil actions by utility for diversion, unauthorized connections, tampering with meter, etc., see Civil Code § 1882.1.
Utility service defined for purposes of this Title, see Civil Code § 1882.
Utility services, treble damages, see Civil Code § 1882.2.

Title 4

LOAN

Chapter		Section
1.	Loan for Use	1884
1.5.	Loans to Museums for Indefinite or Long Terms	1899
2.	Loan for Exchange	1902
3.	Loan of Money	1912
3.5.	Shared Appreciation Loans	1917
4.	Shared Appreciation Loans of E.R.I.S.A. Pension Funds [Inoperative]	1917.010
5.	Shared Appreciation Loans [Inoperative]	1917.110
6.	Loans of E.R.I.S.A. Pension Funds	1917.210
7.	Shared Appreciation Loans for Seniors	1917.320
7.5.	Mortgage Loans	1918
8.	Reverse Mortgages	1923

CHAPTER 1. LOAN FOR USE

Section
1884. Loan for use defined.
1885. Title and increase of thing lent.
1886. Borrower; degree of care.
1887. Borrower; treatment of animals.
1888. Borrower; degree of skill.
1889. Repairs.
1890. Use of thing; purposes.
1891. Relending.

Section
1892. Expenses of thing lent.
1893. Concealed defects; lender's liability.
1894. Return of thing; time; indemnification for loss.
1895. Return of thing; demand.
1896. Return of thing; place.

Cross References

Bribery to procure a loan, see Penal Code §§ 639, 639a.
County museums, and historical records and property, see Public Resources Code § 5120 et seq.
Deposit in general, see Civil Code § 1813 et seq.
Establishment of museums, see Government Code §§ 37541, 37542.
Hiring in general, see Civil Code § 1925 et seq.
Home Equity Loan Disclosure Act, see Civil Code § 2970 et seq.
Insurance in connection with sales and loans, see Insurance Code § 770 et seq.
Insurance loans and investments, see Insurance Code § 1100 et seq.
Interest, see Civil Code § 1914 et seq.
Liability of lender financing design, manufacture, construction, repair, modification or improvement of real or personal property, see Civil Code § 3434.
Loan for exchange, see Civil Code § 1902 et seq.
Loan for use, see Civil Code § 1884 et seq.
Loan of money, see Civil Code § 1912 et seq.
Loans of E.R.I.S.A. pension funds, see Civil Code § 1917.210 et seq.
Mortgage loans, see Civil Code § 1918.5 et seq.
National Housing Act loans, see Financial Code § 27000 et seq.
Shared appreciation loans, see Civil Code § 1917 et seq.
Shared appreciation loans for seniors, see Civil Code § 1917.320 et seq.
Translation of contracts negotiated in language other than English, see Civil Code § 1632.

§ 1884. Loan for use defined

A loan for use is a contract by which one gives to another the temporary possession and use of personal property, and the latter agrees to return the same thing to him at a future time, without reward for its use. *(Enacted in 1872.)*

Cross References

Degree of care required of borrower, see Civil Code § 1886.
Gratuitous deposit defined, see Civil Code § 1844.
Lender's liability for concealed defects, see Civil Code § 1893.
Personal property defined, see Civil Code §§ 14, 663.
Title and increase of property lent, see Civil Code § 1885.

§ 1885. Title and increase of thing lent

A loan for use does not transfer the title to the thing; and all its increase during the period of the loan belongs to the lender. *(Enacted in 1872.)*

Cross References

Degree of care required of borrower, see Civil Code § 1886.
Lender's liability for concealed defects, see Civil Code § 1893.
Loan for use defined, see Civil Code § 1884.
Rights of owners, see Civil Code §§ 732, 733.
Title, expense and increase of property lent, see Civil Code § 1904.

§ 1886. Borrower; degree of care

A borrower for use must use great care for the preservation in safety and in good condition of the thing lent. *(Enacted in 1872.)*

Cross References

Degree of skill required by borrower, see Civil Code § 1888.
Lender's liability for concealed defects, see Civil Code § 1893.
Malicious injury to property in a library, gallery, museum, etc., see Education Code § 19910.
Title and increase of property lent, see Civil Code § 1885.
Treatment of borrowed animals, see Civil Code § 1887.
Trustee, care required of, see Probate Code § 16041.
Vandalism, see Penal Code § 594 et seq.

§ 1887. Borrower; treatment of animals

One who borrows a living animal for use, must treat it with great kindness, and provide everything necessary and suitable for it. *(Enacted in 1872.)*

Cross References

Cruelty to animals, see Penal Code § 596 et seq.
Degree of care required of borrower, see Civil Code § 1886.
Degree of skill required by borrower, see Civil Code § 1888.
Depositary of animals, see Civil Code § 1834.
Lender's liability for concealed defects, see Civil Code § 1893.
Title and increase of property lent, see Civil Code § 1885.

§ 1888. Borrower; degree of skill

A borrower for use is bound to have and to exercise such skill in the care of the thing lent as he causes the lender to believe him to possess. *(Enacted in 1872.)*

Cross References

Degree of care required of borrower, see Civil Code § 1886.
Degree of skill required by borrower, see Civil Code § 1888.
Lender's liability for concealed defects, see Civil Code § 1893.
Malicious mischief, see Penal Code § 594 et seq.
Title and increase of property lent, see Civil Code § 1885.
Treatment of borrowed animals, see Civil Code § 1887.
Service at own request, performance required, see Labor Code § 2851.

§ 1889. Repairs

A borrower for use must repair all deteriorations or injuries to the thing lent, which are occasioned by his negligence, however slight. *(Enacted in 1872.)*

Cross References

Degree of care required of borrower, see Civil Code § 1886.
Degree of skill required by borrower, see Civil Code § 1888.
Expenses of item lent, see Civil Code § 1892.
Gratuitous depositary, degree of care required of, see Civil Code § 1846.
Lender's liability for concealed defects, see Civil Code § 1893.
Malicious mischief, see Penal Code § 594 et seq.
Negligence defined, see Penal Code § 7.
Title and increase of property lent, see Civil Code § 1885.
Treatment of borrowed animals, see Civil Code § 1887.
Trustee, care required of, see Probate Code § 16041.

§ 1890. Use of thing; purposes

The borrower of a thing for use may use it for such purposes only as the lender might reasonably anticipate at the time of lending. *(Enacted in 1872.)*

Cross References

Degree of care required of borrower, see Civil Code § 1886.
Degree of skill required by borrower, see Civil Code § 1888.
Malicious mischief, see Penal Code § 594 et seq.
Relending forbidden, see Civil Code § 1891.
Title and increase of property lent, see Civil Code § 1885.

Treatment of borrowed animals, see Civil Code § 1887.

§ 1891. Relending

The borrower of a thing for use must not part with it to a third person, without the consent of the lender. *(Enacted in 1872.)*

Cross References

Degree of care required of borrower, see Civil Code § 1886.
Degree of skill required by borrower, see Civil Code § 1888.
Title and increase of property lent, see Civil Code § 1885.
Treatment of borrowed animals, see Civil Code § 1887.

§ 1892. Expenses of thing lent

The borrower of a thing for use must bear all its expenses during the loan, except such as are necessarily incurred by him to preserve it from unexpected and unusual injury. For such expenses he is entitled to compensation from the lender, who may, however, exonerate himself by surrendering the thing to the borrower. *(Enacted in 1872.)*

Cross References

Degree of care required of borrower, see Civil Code § 1886.
Degree of skill required by borrower, see Civil Code § 1888.
Lender's liability for concealed defects, see Civil Code § 1893.
Repairs borrower required to make, see Civil Code § 1889.
Title, expense and increase of property lent, see Civil Code § 1904.
Title and increase of property lent, see Civil Code § 1885.
Treatment of borrowed animals, see Civil Code § 1887.

§ 1893. Concealed defects; lender's liability

The lender of a thing for use must indemnify the borrower for damage caused by defects or vices in it, which he knew at the time of lending, and concealed from the borrower. *(Enacted in 1872.)*

Cross References

Application of this section to loan for exchange, see Civil Code § 1906.
Damages generally, see Civil Code § 3281 et seq.
Degree of care required of borrower, see Civil Code § 1886.
Indemnification of depositary, see Civil Code § 1833.
Lender's liability for concealed defects, see Civil Code § 1893.
Title and increase of property lent, see Civil Code § 1885.
Treatment of borrowed animals, see Civil Code § 1887.

§ 1894. Return of thing; time; indemnification for loss

The lender of a thing for use may at any time require its return, even though he lent it for a specified time or purpose. But if, on the faith of such an agreement, the borrower has made such arrangements that a return of the thing before the period agreed upon would cause him loss, exceeding the benefit derived by him from the loan, the lender must indemnify him for such loss, if he compels such return, the borrower not having in any manner violated his duty. *(Enacted in 1872.)*

Cross References

Degree of care required of borrower, see Civil Code § 1886.
Indemnity,
  Defined, see Civil Code § 2772.
  Depositor's duty, see Civil Code § 1833.
Lender's liability for concealed defects, see Civil Code § 1893.
Place for return of item, see Civil Code § 1896.
Return of item without demand, see Civil Code § 1895.
Title and increase of property lent, see Civil Code § 1885.
Treatment of borrowed animals, see Civil Code § 1887.

§ 1895. Return of thing; demand

If a thing is lent for use for a specified time or purpose, it must be returned to the lender without demand, as soon as the time has expired, or the purpose has been accomplished. In other cases it need not be returned until demanded. *(Enacted in 1872.)*

Cross References

Application of this section to loan for exchange, see Civil Code § 1906.
Degree of care required of borrower, see Civil Code § 1886.
Lender may require return of item lent, see Civil Code § 1894.
Lender's liability for concealed defects, see Civil Code § 1893.
Place for return of item, see Civil Code § 1896.
Title and increase of property lent, see Civil Code § 1885.
Treatment of borrowed animals, see Civil Code § 1887.

§ 1896. Return of thing; place

The borrower of a thing for use must return it to the lender, at the place contemplated by the parties at the time of lending; or if no particular place was so contemplated by them, then at the place where it was at that time. *(Enacted in 1872.)*

Cross References

Application of this section to loan for exchange, see Civil Code § 1906.
Degree of care required of borrower, see Civil Code § 1886.
Lender may require return of item lent, see Civil Code § 1894.
Lender's liability for concealed defects, see Civil Code § 1893.
Return of item without demand, see Civil Code § 1895.
Title and increase of property lent, see Civil Code § 1885.
Treatment of borrowed animals, see Civil Code § 1887.

CHAPTER 1.5. LOANS TO MUSEUMS FOR INDEFINITE OR LONG TERMS

Section	
1899.	Legislative findings and declarations.
1899.1.	Definitions.
1899.2.	Notice to lender; manner; contents; location of museum.
1899.3.	Notice of provisions of chapter; retention of claimant notices; receipts for notices of intent to preserve interest; notice of injury or loss.
1899.4.	Property owners' notices; change of address or ownership; intent to preserve an interest in property; effect.
1899.5.	Notice of intent to preserve an interest in property; requirements; retention by museum; form; disclosure.
1899.6.	Conservation or disposal of loaned property without permission; conditions; lien; liability of museum.
1899.7.	Publication of statement in lieu of notice of injury or loss; informing claimant; time limit.
1899.8.	Limitations of actions.
1899.9.	Intent to terminate loan; form; transformation of specified term to indefinite term.
1899.10.	Action to recover property; limitations; donation presumed; title of purchaser.
1899.11.	Construction with Unclaimed Property Law; notice of intent to report property to controller.

§ 1899. Legislative findings and declarations

The Legislature finds and declares as follows:

(a) Many museums have benefited greatly from having property loaned to them for study or display. Problems have arisen, however, in connection with loans for indefinite or long terms, when museums and lenders have failed to maintain contact. Many of these problems could be avoided by a clarification and regularization of the rights and obligations of the parties to loans for indefinite or long terms.

(b) An existing law, the Unclaimed Property Law (commencing with Section 1500 of the Code of Civil Procedure), is technically applicable to property on loan to a museum which has been left unclaimed by its owner for at least seven years.

(c) While the Unclaimed Property Law addresses problems similar to those which arise in the museum context when the parties to loans fail to maintain contact, there is need for an alternative method of dealing with unclaimed property in the hands of museums, one tailored to the unique circumstances of unclaimed loans to museums. These circumstances include the likelihood that the unclaimed property has significant scientific, historical, aesthetic, or cultural value but does not have great monetary value; that the public's interest in the intangible values of unclaimed property loaned to museums can best be realized if title is transferred to the museums holding the property; that often lenders intend eventually to donate property but place it on indefinite or long term loan initially for tax and other reasons; and that many museums have incurred unreimbursed expenses in caring for and storing unclaimed loaned property.

(d) There is an inherent tendency for the condition of tangible property to change over time. Loaned property often requires conservation work and conservation measures may be expensive or potentially detrimental to the property. Organic materials and specimens may serve as breeding grounds for insects, fungi, or diseases which threaten other more valuable property.

(e) Museums cannot reasonably be expected to make decisions regarding conservation or disposition of loaned property at their own risk and expense. Over time, however, lenders die or move, and museums and lenders lose contact. If a lender has failed to maintain contact with a museum, it is often impossible to locate the lender so that the lender can make decisions regarding conservation or disposition of loaned property.

(f) Since museums rarely relocate, it is easier for lenders, and those who claim through them, to notify museums of address or ownership changes so that museums can readily contact lenders when decisions must be made regarding conservation or disposition of loaned property.

(g) The best evidence of ownership of property on loan to a museum is generally the original loan receipt. The longer property remains on loan, the less likely it is that the original lender will claim it, and the more likely it is that any claim which is made will be made by someone who does not have the original loan receipt or other clear evidence of ownership. The state has a substantial interest in cutting off stale and uncertain claims to tangible personal property loaned to nonprofit and public museums.

(h) Most of the tangible personal property which escheats to the state under the Unclaimed Property Law is found in safe deposit boxes. Although 40–50 percent of the intangible property which escheats to the state is subsequently claimed, less than 1 percent of escheated tangible personal property is claimed. Of the few claims which are presented to the Controller for tangible personal property, most are presented within two years of the date the Controller gives notice of the escheat.

(i) The public interest is served by requiring lenders to notify museums of changes in address or ownership of loaned property, by establishing a uniform procedure for lenders to preserve their interests in property loaned to museums for indefinite or long terms, and by vesting title to unclaimed property on loan to museums in the museums which have custody of the property. *(Added by Stats.1983, c. 61, § 1.)*

Cross References

Interest defined, see Civil Code § 1915.
Loan, loaned, and on loan defined for purposes of this Chapter, see Civil Code § 1899.1.
Museum defined for purposes of this Chapter, see Civil Code § 1899.1.
Property defined for purposes of this Chapter, see Civil Code § 1899.1.
State Controller, generally, see Government Code § 12402 et seq.

§ 1899.1. Definitions

For the purposes of this chapter:

(a) A "museum" is an institution located in California and operated by a nonprofit corporation or public agency, primarily educational, scientific, or aesthetic in purpose, which owns, borrows, or cares for, and studies, archives, or exhibits property.

(b) A "lender's address" is the most recent address as shown on the museum's records pertaining to the property on loan from the lender.

(c) The terms "loan," "loaned," and "on loan" include all deposits of property with a museum which are not accompanied by a transfer of title to the property.

(d) "Property" includes all tangible objects, animate and inanimate, under a museum's care which have intrinsic value to science, history, art, or culture, except that it does not include botanical or zoological specimens loaned to a museum for scientific research purposes. *(Added by Stats.1983, c. 61, § 1.)*

§ 1899.2. Notice to lender; manner; contents; location of museum

(a) When a museum is required to give a lender notice pursuant to the provisions of this chapter, the museum shall be deemed to have given a lender notice if the museum mails the notice to the lender at the lender's address and proof of receipt is received by the museum within 30 days from the date the notice was mailed. If the museum does not have an address for the lender, or if proof of receipt is not received by the museum, notice shall be deemed given if the museum publishes notice at least once a week for three successive weeks in a newspaper of general circulation in both the county in which the museum is located and the county of the lender's address, if any.

§ 1899.2 OBLIGATIONS

(b) In addition to any other information prescribed in this chapter, notices given pursuant to it shall contain the lender's name, the lender's address, if known, the date of the loan and, if the notice is being given by the museum, the name, address, and telephone number of the appropriate office or official to be contacted at the museum for information regarding the loan.

(c) For the purposes of this section, a museum is "located" in the county of a branch of the museum to which a loan is made. In all other instances, a museum is located in the county in which it has its principal place of business. *(Added by Stats.1983, c. 61, § 1.)*

Cross References

Conservation or disposal of loaned property without permission, see Civil Code § 1899.6.
Duties of museums that accept loans of property for indefinite terms, see Civil Code § 1899.3.
Lender's address defined for purposes of this Chapter, see Civil Code § 1899.1.
Loan defined for purposes of this Chapter, see Civil Code § 1899.1.
Museum defined for purposes of this Chapter, see Civil Code § 1899.1.
Notice of intent to preserve an interest in property, see Civil Code § 1899.5.
Publication of statement in lieu of notice of injury or loss, see Civil Code § 1899.7.
Responsibilities of owners of property on loan to museums, see Civil Code § 1899.4.

§ 1899.3. Notice of provisions of chapter; retention of claimant notices; receipts for notices of intent to preserve interest; notice of injury or loss

(a) If, on or after January 1, 1984, a museum accepts a loan of property for an indefinite term, or for a term in excess of seven years, the museum shall inform the lender in writing at the time of the loan of the provisions of this chapter. A copy of the form notice prescribed in Section 1899.5, or a citation to this chapter, is adequate for this purpose.

(b) Unless the loaned property is returned to the claimant, the museum shall retain for a period of not less than 25 years the original or an accurate copy of each notice filed by a claimant pursuant to Section 1899.4.

(c) The museum shall furnish anyone who files a notice of intent to preserve an interest in property on loan proof of receipt of the notice by mailing an original receipt or a copy of the receipt portion of the form notice prescribed in Section 1899.5 to the lender or other claimant at the address given on the notice within 30 days of receiving the notice.

(d) A museum shall give a lender prompt notice of any known injury to or loss of property on loan. *(Added by Stats.1983, c. 61, § 1.)*

Cross References

Conservation or disposal of loaned property without permission, see Civil Code § 1899.6.
Interest defined, see Civil Code § 1915.
Loan, loaned, and on loan defined for purposes of this Chapter, see Civil Code § 1899.1.
Museum defined for purposes of this Chapter, see Civil Code § 1899.1.
Notice of intent to preserve an interest in property, see Civil Code § 1899.5.
Notice of lender, see Civil Code § 1899.2.
Property defined for purposes of this Chapter, see Civil Code § 1899.1.
Publication of statement in lieu of notice of injury or loss, see Civil Code § 1899.7.
Responsibilities of owners of property on loan to museums, see Civil Code § 1899.4.

§ 1899.4. Property owners' notices; change of address or ownership; intent to preserve an interest in property; effect

(a) It is the responsibility of the owner of property on loan to a museum to notify the museum promptly in writing of any change of address or change in ownership of the property. Failure to notify the museum of these changes may result in the owner's loss of rights in the property.

(b) The owner of property on loan to a museum may file with the museum a notice of intent to preserve an interest in the property as provided for in Section 1899.5. The filing of a notice of intent to preserve an interest in property on loan to a museum does not validate or make enforceable any claim which would be extinguished under the terms of a written loan agreement, or which would otherwise be invalid or unenforceable. *(Added by Stats.1983, c. 61, § 1.)*

Cross References

Conservation or disposal of loaned property without permission, see Civil Code § 1899.6.
Duties of museums that accept loans of property for indefinite terms, see Civil Code § 1899.3.
Interest defined, see Civil Code § 1915.
Loan and on loan defined for purposes of this Chapter, see Civil Code § 1899.1.
Museum defined for purposes of this Chapter, see Civil Code § 1899.1.
Notice of lender, see Civil Code § 1899.2.
Property defined for purposes of this Chapter, see Civil Code § 1899.1.
Publication of statement in lieu of notice of injury or loss, see Civil Code § 1899.7.

§ 1899.5. Notice of intent to preserve an interest in property; requirements; retention by museum; form; disclosure

(a) A notice of intent to preserve an interest in property on loan to a museum filed pursuant to this chapter shall be in writing, shall contain a description of the property adequate to enable the museum to identify the property, shall be accompanied by documentation sufficient to establish the claimant as owner of the property, and shall be signed under penalty of perjury by the claimant or by a person authorized to act on behalf of the claimant.

(b) The museum need not retain a notice that does not meet the requirements set forth in subdivision (a). If, however, the museum does not intend to retain a notice for this reason, the museum shall promptly notify the claimant at the address given on the notice that it believes the notice is ineffective to preserve an interest, and the reasons therefor. The fact that the museum retains a notice shall not be construed to mean that the museum accepts the sufficiency or accuracy of the notice or that the notice is effective to preserve an interest in property on loan to the museum.

(c) A notice of intent to preserve an interest in property on loan to a museum which is in substantially the following form, and contains the information and attachments described, satisfies the requirements of subdivision (a):

NOTICE OF INTENT TO PRESERVE AN INTEREST IN PROPERTY ON LOAN TO A MUSEUM

TO THE LENDER: Section 1899.4 of the California Civil Code requires that you notify the museum promptly in writing of any change of address or ownership of the property. If the museum is unable to contact you regarding your loan, you may lose rights in the loaned property. If you choose to file this form with the museum to preserve your interest in the property, the museum is required to maintain it, or a copy of it, for 25 years. For full details, see Section 1899, et seq. of the California Civil Code.

TO THE MUSEUM: You are hereby notified that the undersigned claims an interest in the property described herein.

Claimant
   Name: _____
   Address: _____
            _____
            _____
   Telephone: _____
   Social Security Number (optional): _____
Museum Name: _____
Date Property Loaned: _____
Interest in Property:

If you are not the original lender, describe the origin of your interest in the property and attach a copy of any document creating your interest:
      _____
      _____
      _____
      _____

Description of Property:

Unless an accurate, legible copy of the original loan receipt is attached, give a detailed description of the claimed property, including its nature and general characteristics and the museum registration number assigned to the property, if known, and attach any documentary evidence you have establishing the loan:
   Registration # _____
   Description: _____
            _____
            _____
            _____
            _____

(Attach additional sheets if necessary.)

I understand that I must promptly notify the museum in writing of any change of address or change in ownership of the loaned property.

I declare under penalty of perjury that to the best of my knowledge the information contained in this notice is true.

   Signed: _____ Date: _____
           (claimant)

OR

I declare under penalty of perjury that I am authorized to act on behalf of the claimant and am informed and believe that the information contained in this notice is true.

   Signed: _____ Date: _____
     (claimant's representative)

RECEIPT FOR NOTICE OF INTENT
TO PRESERVE AN INTEREST IN PROPERTY

(For use by the museum.)

Notice received by: _____
Date of receipt: _____
Copy of receipt returned to claimant:
   By _____
   Date: _____

(d) Notices of intent to preserve an interest in property on loan to a museum filed pursuant to this chapter are exempt from the disclosure requirements of the California Public Records Act (Division 10 (commencing with Section 7920.000) of the Government Code). *(Added by Stats.1983, c. 61, § 1. Amended by Stats.2021, c. 615 (A.B.474), § 50, eff. Jan. 1, 2022, operative Jan. 1, 2023.)*

Cross References

Duties of museums that accept loans of property for indefinite terms, see Civil Code § 1899.3.
Interest defined, see Civil Code § 1915.
Limitations of actions, see Civil Code § 1899.8.
Loan, loaned, and on loan defined for purposes of this Chapter, see Civil Code § 1899.1.
Museum defined for purposes of this Chapter, see Civil Code § 1899.1.
Notice of lender, see Civil Code § 1899.2.
Property defined for purposes of this Chapter, see Civil Code § 1899.1.

§ 1899.6. Conservation or disposal of loaned property without permission; conditions; lien; liability of museum

(a) Unless there is a written loan agreement to the contrary, a museum may apply conservation measures to or dispose of property on loan to the museum without a lender's permission if:

(1) Immediate action is required to protect the property on loan or to protect other property in the custody of the museum, or because the property on loan has become a hazard to the health and safety of the public or of the museum's staff, and:

§ 1899.6 OBLIGATIONS

(A) The museum is unable to reach the lender at the lender's last address of record so that the museum and the lender can promptly agree upon a solution; or

(B) The lender will not agree to the protective measures the museum recommends, yet is unwilling or unable to terminate the loan and retrieve the property.

(2) In the case of a lender who cannot be contacted in person, the museum publishes a notice containing the information described in subdivision (a) of Section 1899.7 and there is no response for 120 days.

(b) If a museum applies conservation measures to or disposes of property pursuant to subdivision (a):

(1) The museum shall have a lien on the property and on the proceeds from any disposition thereof for the costs incurred by the museum; and

(2) The museum shall not be liable for injury to or loss of the property:

(A) If the museum had a reasonable belief at the time the action was taken that the action was necessary to protect the property on loan or other property in the custody of the museum, or that the property on loan constituted a hazard to the health and safety of the public or the museum's staff; and

(B) If the museum applied conservation measures, the museum exercised reasonable care in the choice and application of the conservation measures. *(Added by Stats.1983, c. 61, § 1.)*

Cross References

Duties of museums that accept loans of property for indefinite terms, see Civil Code § 1899.3.
Limitations of actions, see Civil Code § 1899.8.
Loan and on loan defined for purposes of this Chapter, see Civil Code § 1899.1.
Museum defined for purposes of this Chapter, see Civil Code § 1899.1.
Notice of lender, see Civil Code § 1899.2.
Property defined for purposes of this Chapter, see Civil Code § 1899.1.

§ 1899.7. Publication of statement in lieu of notice of injury or loss; informing claimant; time limit

(a) Except as provided in subdivision (b), if a museum is unable to give the lender the notice required by subdivision (d) of Section 1899.3 of injury to or loss of property on loan by mail, the museum shall be deemed to have given the lender notice of any injury or loss if in addition to the information required by subdivision (b) of Section 1899.2 the published notice includes a statement containing substantially the following information:

"The records of _____
(name of museum)
indicate that you have property on loan to it. Your failure to notify it in writing of a change of address or ownership of property on loan or to contact it in writing regarding the loan may result in the loss of rights in the loaned property. See California Civil Code Sections 1899, et seq."

(b) If, within three years of giving notice of injury to or loss of loaned property by publishing the notice set forth in subdivision (a), the museum receives a notice from a claimant pursuant to Section 1899.4, the museum shall promptly advise the claimant in writing of the nature of the injury to or the fact of the loss of property on loan and the approximate date thereof. For the purposes of the limitation period in Section 1899.8, if the museum mails the information to the claimant within 30 days of the date the museum receives the notice from the claimant, the museum shall be deemed to have given the claimant notice of the injury to or loss of property on loan on the date notice by publication pursuant to subdivision (a) was completed. *(Added by Stats.1983, c. 61, § 1.)*

Cross References

Duties of museums that accept loans of property for indefinite terms, see Civil Code § 1899.3.
Loan, loaned, and on loan defined for purposes of this Chapter, see Civil Code § 1899.1.
Museum defined for purposes of this Chapter, see Civil Code § 1899.1.
Notice of lender, see Civil Code § 1899.2.
Property defined for purposes of this Chapter, see Civil Code § 1899.1.

§ 1899.8. Limitations of actions

Effective January 1, 1985, no action shall be brought against a museum for damages because of injury to or loss of property loaned to the museum more than (1) three years from the date the museum gives the lender notice of the injury or loss, or (2) ten years from the date of the injury or loss, whichever occurs earlier. *(Added by Stats.1983, c. 61, § 1.)*

Cross References

Duties of museums that accept loans of property for indefinite terms, see Civil Code § 1899.3.
Loaned defined for purposes of this Chapter, see Civil Code § 1899.1.
Museum defined for purposes of this Chapter, see Civil Code § 1899.1.
Notice of lender, see Civil Code § 1899.2.
Property defined for purposes of this Chapter, see Civil Code § 1899.1.

§ 1899.9. Intent to terminate loan; form; transformation of specified term to indefinite term

(a) A museum may give the lender notice of the museum's intent to terminate a loan which was made for an indefinite term, or which was made on or after January 1, 1984, for a term in excess of seven years.

A notice of intent to terminate a loan given pursuant to this section shall include a statement containing substantially the following information:

"The records of _____
(name of museum)
indicate that you have property on loan to it. The institution wishes to terminate the loan. You must contact the institution, establish your ownership of the property, and make arrangements to collect the property. If you fail to do so promptly, you will be deemed to have donated the property to the institution. See California Civil Code Sections 1899, et seq."

(b) For the purposes of this chapter, a loan for a specified term becomes a loan for an indefinite term if the property remains in the custody of the museum when the specified term expires. *(Added by Stats.1983, c. 61, § 1.)*

Cross References

Construction with Unclaimed Property Law, notice of intent to report property to controller, see Civil Code § 1899.11.

Loan and on loan defined for purposes of this Chapter, see Civil Code § 1899.1.

Museum defined for purposes of this Chapter, see Civil Code § 1899.1.

Property defined for purposes of this Chapter, see Civil Code § 1899.1.

§ 1899.10. Action to recover property; limitations; donation presumed; title of purchaser

(a) The three-year limitation on actions to recover personal property prescribed in Code of Civil Procedure Section 338.3 shall run from the date the museum gives the lender notice of its intent to terminate the loan pursuant to Section 1899.9.

(b) Except as provided in subdivision (e), effective January 1, 1985, no action shall be brought against a museum to recover property on loan when more than 25 years have passed from the date of the last written contact between the lender and the museum, as evidenced in the museum's records.

(c) A lender shall be deemed to have donated loaned property to a museum if the lender fails to file an action to recover the property on loan to the museum within the periods specified in subdivisions (a) and (b).

(d) One who purchases property from a museum acquires good title to the property if the museum represents that it has acquired title to the property pursuant to subdivision (c).

(e) Notwithstanding subdivisions (b) and (c), a lender who was not given notice that the museum intended to terminate a loan and who proves that the museum received a notice of intent to preserve an interest in loaned property within the 25 years immediately preceding the date on which the lender's right to recover the property otherwise expired under subdivision (b) may recover the property or, if the property has been disposed of, the reasonable value of the property at the time the property was disposed of with interest at the rate on judgments set by the Legislature pursuant to Section 1 of Article XV of the California Constitution. *(Added by Stats.1983, c. 61, § 1. Amended by Stats.1984, c. 541, § 1, eff. July 17, 1984.)*

Cross References

Interest defined, see Civil Code § 1915.

Loan, loaned, and on loan defined for purposes of this Chapter, see Civil Code § 1899.1.

Museum defined for purposes of this Chapter, see Civil Code § 1899.1.

Property defined for purposes of this Chapter, see Civil Code § 1899.1.

§ 1899.11. Construction with Unclaimed Property Law; notice of intent to report property to controller

(a) The provisions of this chapter supersede the provisions of the Unclaimed Property Law (commencing with Section 1500 of the Code of Civil Procedure) except that at its option, a museum may report property which has been on loan unclaimed by its owner for more than seven years to the Controller pursuant to Section 1530 of the Code of Civil Procedure for disposition in accordance with the provisions of the Unclaimed Property Law.

(b) Not less than six months or more than 12 months before reporting any loaned property to the Controller, a museum shall mail to the lender at the lender's address, if known, a notice of intent to report the property to the Controller. The notice shall include a statement containing substantially the following information:

"The records of _____
(name of museum)
indicate that you have property on loan to the institution. The institution wishes to terminate the loan. You must contact the institution, establish your ownership of the property and make arrangements to collect the property before _____
(fill in date)
or the property will be disposed of in accordance with the provisions of the Unclaimed Property Law (commencing with Section 1500 of the Code of Civil Procedure)."

(Added by Stats.1983, c. 61, § 1.)

Cross References

Lender's address defined for purposes of this Chapter, see Civil Code § 1899.1.

Loan, loaned, and on loan defined for purposes of this Chapter, see Civil Code § 1899.1.

Museum defined for purposes of this Chapter, see Civil Code § 1899.1.

Property defined for purposes of this Chapter, see Civil Code § 1899.1.

State Controller, generally, see Government Code § 12402 et seq.

CHAPTER 2. LOAN FOR EXCHANGE

Section
1902. Loan for exchange defined.
1903. Optional loan; application of chapter.
1904. Title, expense and increase of thing lent.
1905. Modification of contract.
1906. Applicability of other sections.

Cross References

Loan for use defined, see Civil Code § 1884.
Loan of money, see Civil Code § 1912 et seq.
Loans to museums for indefinite or long terms, see Civil Code § 1899 et seq.

§ 1902. Loan for exchange defined

A loan for exchange is a contract by which one delivers personal property to another, and the latter agrees to return to the lender a similar thing at a future time, without reward for its use. *(Enacted in 1872.)*

Cross References

Deposit for exchange defined, see Civil Code § 1818.
Personal property defined, see Civil Code §§ 14, 663.

§ 1902 OBLIGATIONS

Trusts defined, see Probate Code § 82 et seq.

§ 1903. Optional loan; application of chapter

A loan, which the borrower is allowed by the lender to treat as a loan for use, or for exchange, at his option, is subject to all the provisions of this Chapter. *(Enacted in 1872.)*

Cross References

Loan for use defined, see Civil Code § 1884.

§ 1904. Title, expense and increase of thing lent

By a loan for exchange the title to the thing lent is transferred to the borrower, and he must bear all its expenses, and is entitled to all its increase. *(Enacted in 1872.)*

Cross References

Acquisition of property, see Civil Code § 1000.
Expenses of property lent, see Civil Code § 1892.
Loan for exchange defined, see Civil Code § 1902.
Products and accessions of property, see Civil Code § 732.
Title and increase of property lent, see Civil Code § 1885.

§ 1905. Modification of contract

A lender for exchange cannot require the borrower to fulfill his obligations at a time, or in a manner, different from that which was originally agreed upon. *(Enacted in 1872.)*

§ 1906. Applicability of other sections

Sections 1893, 1895, and 1896, apply to a loan for exchange. *(Enacted in 1872.)*

Cross References

Lender may require return of item lent, see Civil Code § 1894.
Lender's liability for concealed defects, see Civil Code § 1893.
Loan for exchange defined, see Civil Code § 1902.
Return of item without demand, see Civil Code § 1895.

CHAPTER 3. LOAN OF MONEY

Section	
1912.	"Loan of money" defined.
1913.	Payment in current money.
1914.	Interest; presumption.
1915.	Interest defined.
1916.	Interest; annual rate.
1916.1.	Constitutional restrictions; application to loans secured by real property; licensed real estate brokers; arrangement of loan or forbearance.
1916.2.	Constitutional restrictions; application to loans by out-of-state public retirement or pension systems; exemption.
1916.5.	Variable interest; requirements.
1916.6.	Variable interest; change; five year period.
1916.7.	Adjustable-payment, adjustable-rate loan secured by owner occupied real property; exemption from other laws; disclosure notice.
1916.8.	Renegotiable rate mortgage loans; interest rate changes at renewal; costs or fees; notice to borrower; disclosure to applicant.
1916.9.	Offer of fixed rate mortgage loan as alternative to renegotiable rate mortgage loan.
1916.10.	Repealed.
1916.11.	Lien of mortgage or deed of trust; validity.
1916.12.	Legislative findings; purpose; mortgage parity between state and federal institutions; rules and regulations.
1916–1.	Legal rate of interest; contract rate.
1916–2.	Maximum rate of interest; compound interest; effect of contract provisions for excessive interest.
1916–3.	Civil and criminal liability for violations.
1916–4.	Repeals.
1916–5.	Usury Law, citation.

The Usury Law, an initiative measure approved by the electors Nov. 5, 1918, while not included in the Civil Code by the Legislature, is set out herein as §§ 1916–1 to 1916–5, for convenient reference by the Bench and Bar. This disposition is in accordance with the recommendation made by the California Code Commission in its final report, dated Sept. 1, 1953, on page 8, reading as follows:

"j. Initiative acts. These acts cannot be codified by the Legislature because of the constitutional limitations on the powers of the Legislature with reference to them. The commission recommends to the publishers of the codes that the initiative act be published as an appendix to the appropriate code, rather than as a separate volume."

Cross References

Home Equity Loan Disclosure Act, see Civil Code § 2970 et seq.
Insurance in connection with sales and loans, see Insurance Code § 770 et seq.
Liability of lender financing design, manufacture, construction, repair, modification or improvement of real or personal property, see Civil Code § 3434.
Loan for exchange, see Civil Code § 1902 et seq.
Loan of money, interest, see Civil Code § 1914 et seq.
Loans of E.R.I.S.A. pension funds, see Civil Code § 1917.210 et seq.
Loans to museums for indefinite or long terms, see Civil Code § 1899 et seq.
Mortgage loans, see Civil Code § 1918.5 et seq.
National Housing Act loans, see Financial Code § 27000 et seq.
Precomputed interest, see Civil Code § 1799.5.
Shared appreciation loans, see Civil Code § 1917 et seq.
Shared appreciation loans for seniors, see Civil Code § 1917.320 et seq.
Translation of contracts negotiated in language other than English, see Civil Code § 1632.

§ 1912. "Loan of money" defined

A loan of money is a contract by which one delivers a sum of money to another, and the latter agrees to return at a future time a sum equivalent to that which he borrowed. A loan for mere use is governed by the Chapter on Loan for Use. *(Enacted in 1872.)*

Cross References

Loan for use defined, see Civil Code § 1884 et seq.
Loan of money, interest, see Civil Code § 1914 et seq.
Trusts, definitions of, see Probate Code § 82 et seq.

§ 1913. Payment in current money

A borrower of money, unless there is an express contract to the contrary, must pay the amount due in such money as is current at the time when the loan becomes due, whether such money is worth more or less than the actual money lent. *(Enacted in 1872.)*

Cross References

Loan of money, interest, see Civil Code § 1914 et seq.

§ 1914. Interest; presumption

Whenever a loan of money is made, it is presumed to be made upon interest, unless it is otherwise expressly stipulated at the time in writing. *(Enacted in 1872. Amended by Code Am.1873–74, c. 612, p. 244, § 201.)*

Cross References

Effect of offer on interest and incidents of obligation, see Civil Code § 1504.
Interest defined, see Civil Code § 1915.
Loan of money defined, see Civil Code § 1912.
Presumption defined, see Evidence Code § 600.
Usury law, see Civil Code § 1916–1 et seq.

§ 1915. Interest defined

Interest is the compensation allowed by law or fixed by the parties for the use, or forbearance, or detention of money. *(Enacted in 1872. Amended by Code Am.1873–74, c. 612, p. 245, § 202.)*

Cross References

Administration of estates of decedents, interest on debt, see Probate Code § 11423.
Conversion, right to interest for, see Civil Code § 3336.
Eminent domain law, interest on damages, see Code of Civil Procedure § 1268.310 et seq.
Interest and costs, see Code of Civil Procedure § 685.010 et seq.
Interest and income accruing during administration of estates of decedents, see Probate Code § 12000 et seq.
Interest on damages, see Civil Code § 3287 et seq.
Interest on damages for noncontractual obligations, see Civil Code § 3288.
Interest on demand deposits, see Financial Code § 1403.
Interest on time warrants not paid due to lack of funds, see Water Code § 53047.
Orders authorizing borrowing or giving security interests, see Probate Code § 9804.
Petition for escheated property, see Code of Civil Procedure § 1355.
Profit or loss from increase or decrease of estate, see Probate Code § 9657.
Reclamation districts, interest rate on demand warrants, see Water Code § 53022.
Usury law, see Civil Code § 1916–1 et seq.
Waiver of interest, see Civil Code § 3290.

§ 1916. Interest; annual rate

When a rate of interest is prescribed by a law or contract, without specifying the period of time by which such rate is to be calculated, it is to be deemed an annual rate. *(Enacted in 1872.)*

Cross References

Interest and costs, see Code of Civil Procedure § 685.010 et seq.
Interest defined, see Civil Code § 1915.
Interest on damages, see Civil Code § 3287 et seq.
Pawnbrokers, maximum compensation and violations, see Financial Code §§ 21200, 21209.
Rate of interest chargeable after breach of contract, see Civil Code § 3289.

Usury, interest rates, see Cal. Const. Art. 15, § 1.
Usury law, see Civil Code § 1916–1 et seq.

§ 1916.1. Constitutional restrictions; application to loans secured by real property; licensed real estate brokers; arrangement of loan or forbearance

The restrictions upon rates of interest contained in Section 1 of Article XV of the California Constitution shall not apply to any loan or forbearance made or arranged by any person licensed as a real estate broker by the State of California, and secured, directly or collaterally, in whole or in part by liens on real property. For purposes of this section, a loan or forbearance is arranged by a person licensed as a real estate broker when the broker (1) acts for compensation or in expectation of compensation for soliciting, negotiating, or arranging the loan for another, (2) acts for compensation or in expectation of compensation for selling, buying, leasing, exchanging, or negotiating the sale, purchase, lease, or exchange of real property or a business for another and (A) arranges a loan to pay all or any portion of the purchase price of, or of an improvement to, that property or business or (B) arranges a forbearance, extension, or refinancing of any loan in connection with that sale, purchase, lease, exchange of, or an improvement to, real property or a business, or (3) arranges or negotiates for another a forbearance, extension, or refinancing of any loan secured by real property in connection with a past transaction in which the broker had acted for compensation or in expectation of compensation for selling, buying, leasing, exchanging, or negotiating the sale, purchase, lease, or exchange of real property or a business. The term "made or arranged" includes any loan made by a person licensed as a real estate broker as a principal or as an agent for others, and whether or not the person is acting within the course and scope of such license. *(Added by Stats.1983, c. 307, § 1. Amended by Stats.1985, c. 489, § 1.)*

Cross References

Annual rate of interest, see Civil Code § 1916.
Interest defined, see Civil Code § 1915.

§ 1916.2. Constitutional restrictions; application to loans by out-of-state public retirement or pension systems; exemption

The restrictions upon rates of interest contained in Section 1 of Article XV of the California Constitution do not apply to any loans made by, or forbearances of, a public retirement or pension system that is created, authorized, and regulated by the laws of a state other than California, or the laws of a local agency of a state other than California.

This section establishes as an exempt class of persons pursuant to Section 1 of Article XV of the California Constitution, any public retirement or pension system that is created, authorized, and regulated by the laws of a state other than California, or the laws of a local agency of a state other than California. *(Added by Stats.1987, c. 764, § 5.)*

Cross References

Annual rate of interest, see Civil Code § 1916.
Constitutional restrictions on rates of interest, see Civil Code § 1916.1.
Interest defined, see Civil Code § 1915.

Usury, interest rates, see Cal. Const. Art. 15, § 1.

§ 1916.5. Variable interest; requirements

(a) No increase in interest provided for in any provision for a variable interest rate contained in a security document, or evidence of debt issued in connection therewith, by a lender other than a supervised financial organization is valid unless that provision is set forth in the security document, and in any evidence of debt issued in connection therewith, and the document or documents contain the following provisions:

(1) A requirement that when an increase in the interest rate is required or permitted by a movement in a particular direction of a prescribed standard an identical decrease is required in the interest rate by a movement in the opposite direction of the prescribed standard.

(2) The rate of interest shall not change more often than once during any semiannual period, and at least six months shall elapse between any two changes.

(3) The change in the interest rate shall not exceed one-fourth of 1 percent in any semiannual period, and shall not result in a rate more than 2.5 percentage points greater than the rate for the first loan payment due after the closing of the loan.

(4) The rate of interest shall not change during the first semiannual period.

(5) The borrower is permitted to prepay the loan in whole or in part without a prepayment charge within 90 days of notification of any increase in the rate of interest.

(6) A statement attached to the security document and to any evidence of debt issued in connection therewith printed or written in a size equal to at least 10–point boldface type, consisting of the following language:

NOTICE TO BORROWER: THIS DOCUMENT CONTAINS PROVISIONS FOR A VARIABLE INTEREST RATE.

(b)(1) This section shall be applicable only to a mortgage contract, deed of trust, real estate sales contract, or any note or negotiable instrument issued in connection therewith, when its purpose is to finance the purchase or construction of real property containing four or fewer residential units or on which four or fewer residential units are to be constructed.

(2) This section does not apply to unamortized construction loans with an original term of two years or less or to loans made for the purpose of the purchase or construction of improvements to existing residential dwellings.

(c) Regulations setting forth the prescribed standard upon which variations in the interest rate shall be based may be adopted by the Commissioner of * * * Financial Protection and Innovation with respect to savings associations and by the Insurance Commissioner with respect to insurers. Regulations adopted by the Commissioner of * * * Financial Protection and Innovation shall apply to all loans made by savings associations pursuant to this section before January 1, 1990.

(d) As used in this section:

(1) "Supervised financial organization" means a state or federally regulated bank, savings association, savings bank, or credit union, or state regulated industrial loan company, a licensed finance lender under the California Financing Law,[1] a licensed residential mortgage lender under the California Residential Mortgage Lending Act,[2] or holding company, affiliate, or subsidiary thereof, or institution of the Farm Credit System, as specified in Section 2002 of Title 12 of the United States Code.

(2) "Insurer" includes, but is not limited to, a nonadmitted insurance company.

(3) "Semiannual period" means each of the successive periods of six calendar months commencing with the first day of the calendar month in which the instrument creating the obligation is dated.

(4) "Security document" means a mortgage contract, deed of trust, or real estate sales contract.

(5) "Evidence of debt" means a note or negotiable instrument.

(e) This section is applicable only to instruments executed on and after the effective date of this section.

(f) This section does not apply to nonprofit public corporations.

(g) This section is not intended to apply to a loan made where the rate of interest provided for is less than the then current market rate for a similar loan in order to accommodate the borrower because of a special relationship, including, but not limited to, an employment or business relationship, of the borrower with the lender or with a customer of the lender and the sole increase in interest provided for with respect to the loan will result only by reason of the termination of that relationship or upon the sale, deed, or transfer of the property securing the loan to a person not having that relationship. (Added by Stats.1970, c. 1584, p. 3300, § 1. Amended by Stats.1971, c. 1265, p. 2482, § 1; Stats.1975, c. 338, p. 787, § 1; Stats.1980, c. 1139, p. 3681, § 1; Stats.1982, c. 1307, p. 4816, § 1; Stats.1984, c. 975, § 1; Stats.1989, c. 188, § 1; Stats.1990, c. 157 (A.B.2728), § 1; Stats.1996, c. 1064 (A.B.3351), § 5, operative July 1, 1997; Stats.2004, c. 939 (A.B.1979), § 1; Stats.2004, c. 940 (A.B.2693), § 3; Stats. 2019, c. 143 (S.B.251), § 15, eff. Jan. 1, 2020; Stats.2022, c. 452 (S.B.1498), § 27, eff. Jan. 1, 2023.)

[1] Financial Code § 22000 et seq.
[2] Financial Code § 50000 et seq.

Cross References

Adjustable-payment, adjustable-rate loan secured by owner occupied real property, see Civil Code § 1916.7.
Assumption of mortgages, housing and infrastructure finance agency, see Health and Safety Code § 51068.
Cooperative housing corporations, loans secured by stock or membership certificates, see Financial Code § 1494.
Exemption from this section of loans by state institutions under regulations to establish parity with federal institutions, see Civil Code § 1916.12.
Fees, charges and interest rates for financing residential rehabilitation, see Health and Safety Code § 37917.
Housing purchase or rehabilitation loans by state or local public entity, denial of or change in mortgage on assumption, see Civil Code § 711.5.
Interest defined, see Civil Code § 1915.
Offer of fixed rate mortgage loan as alternative to renegotiable rate mortgage loan, see Civil Code § 1916.9.
Renegotiable rate mortgage loans, see Civil Code § 1916.8.

Variable interest rate, see Civil Code § 1916.6.

§ 1916.6. Variable interest; change; five year period

A security document, or evidence of debt issued in connection therewith, executed pursuant to Section 1916.5 may provide that the rate of interest shall not change until five years after execution of such document or documents, and not more frequently than every five years thereafter. In every security document, or evidence of debt issued in connection therewith, executed pursuant to this section all the provisions of Section 1916.5 shall be applicable, except those provisions specifying the frequency of interest rate changes and limiting rate changes to one-fourth of 1 percent in any semiannual period. For the purposes of this section "five years" means each of the successive periods of five years commencing with the first day of the calendar month in which the instrument creating the obligation is dated. (Added by Stats.1977, c. 575, p. 1821, § 1.)

Cross References

Adjustable-payment, adjustable-rate loan secured by owner occupied real property, see Civil Code § 1916.7.
Exemption from this section of loans by state institutions under regulations to establish parity with federal institutions, see Civil Code § 1916.12.
Interest defined, see Civil Code § 1915.
Offer of fixed rate mortgage loan as alternative to renegotiable rate mortgage loan, see Civil Code § 1916.9.
Renegotiable rate mortgage loans, see Civil Code § 1916.8.

§ 1916.7. Adjustable-payment, adjustable-rate loan secured by owner occupied real property; exemption from other laws; disclosure notice

(a) Sections 1916.5, 1916.6, 1916.8, and 1916.9 of the Civil Code, and any other provision of law restricting or setting forth requirements for changes in the rate of interest on loans, shall not be applicable to loans made pursuant to this section.

(b) A mortgage loan made pursuant to the provisions of this section is an adjustable-payment, adjustable-rate loan, on the security of real property occupied or intended to be occupied by the borrower containing four or fewer residential units and incorporating terms substantially as follows:

(1) The term of the loan shall be not less than 29 years, repayable in monthly installments amortized over a period of not less than 30 years.

(2) Monthly payments may be adjusted to reflect changes in the variable interest rate of the loan. Changes in interest and monthly payment shall not occur more often than twice during any annual period and at least six months shall elapse between any two changes. The rate of interest and monthly payments shall not change during the first semiannual period. The amount of any increase in monthly payment shall not exceed 7.5 percent annually.

(3) Monthly payments may also be established on a graduated basis within the parameters of a loan originated pursuant to the provisions of this section. A graduated payment adjustable mortgage loan shall meet all the requirements of this section and shall set forth in the note, at the time of origination, limitations on the rate of increase in the scheduled payments due both to graduation and to changes in the interest rate.

(4) Whenever any monthly installment is less than the amount of interest accrued during the month with respect to which the installment is payable, the borrower shall have the option to select one, or any combination of, the following:

(A) Notwithstanding paragraph (2) of subdivision (b), increase the monthly installment in an amount which at least covers the increase in interest.

(B) Have the difference added to the principal of the loan as of the due date of the installment and thereafter shall bear interest as part of the principal. In no instance shall the difference which is added to the principal be an amount which causes the resulting loan-to-value ratio to exceed the loan-to-value ratio at the time of loan origination.

(C) Extend the term of the loan up to, but not exceeding, 40 years.

(5) Changes in the rate of interest on the loan shall reflect the movement, in reference to the date of the original loan, of a periodically published index selected by the lender which may be either of the following:

(A) The contract interest rate on the purchase of previously occupied homes in the most recent monthly national average mortgage rate index for all major lenders published periodically by the Federal Home Loan Bank Board.

(B) The weighted average cost of funds for California Associations of the Eleventh District Savings and Loan Associations as published periodically by the Federal Home Loan Bank of San Francisco.

(6) Any change in the interest rate shall not exceed the limit, specified by the lender in the loan contract, for rate increases in any semiannual period and shall not exceed the limit, specified by the lender in the loan contract, for rate increases greater than the base index rate.

(7) Notwithstanding any change in the interest rate indicated by a movement of the index, increases in the interest rate shall be optional with the lender, while decreases are mandatory. Such decreases, upon the option of the borrower, shall be used (1) to pay off any negative amortization accrued when the interest rate was increased, or (2) to decrease the monthly payment as reflected in the decrease in the interest rate.

(8) The borrower is permitted to prepay the loan in whole or in part without a prepayment charge at any time, and no fee or other charge may be required by the lender of the borrower as a result of any change in the interest rate or the exercise of any option or election extended to the borrower pursuant to this section.

(9) The borrower, after initiation of the loan, shall not be subsequently required to demonstrate his or her qualification for the loan, except that this paragraph shall not limit any remedy available to the lender by law for default or other breach of contract.

(10) In the event the remaining principal due on a loan made pursuant to this section will not be paid off during the current term, within 90 days of expiration of the term a borrower may elect in writing to repay the remaining balance in full or in substantially equal installments of principal and interest over an additional period not to exceed 10 years, during which period the interest rate shall remain fixed.

§ 1916.7   OBLIGATIONS

(c) An applicant for a loan originated pursuant to the provisions of this section must be given, at the time he or she requests an application, a disclosure notice in the following form:

NOTICE TO BORROWER

IMPORTANT INFORMATION ABOUT THE ADJUSTABLE–PAYMENT, ADJUSTABLE–RATE LOAN

PLEASE READ CAREFULLY

(at least 10-point bold type)

You have received an application form for an adjustable-payment, adjustable-rate mortgage loan. This loan may differ from other mortgages with which you are familiar.

I. GENERAL DESCRIPTION OF ADJUSTABLE–PAYMENT, ADJUSTABLE–RATE LOAN

The adjustable-payment, adjustable-rate mortgage loan is a flexible loan instrument. This means that the interest, monthly payment and/or the length of the loan may be changed during the course of the loan contract.

The first flexible feature of this loan is the interest rate. The interest rate on the loan may be changed by the lender every six months. Changes in the interest rate must reflect the movement of an index that is selected by the lender. Changes in the interest rate may result in increases or decreases in your monthly payment, in the outstanding principal loan balance, in the loan term, or in all three.

The lender is required by law to limit the amount that the interest can change at any one time or over the life of the loan. The law does not specify what these limits are. That is a matter you should negotiate with the lender.

You may also want to make inquiries concerning the lending terms offered by other lenders on adjustable-payment, adjustable-rate mortgage loans to compare the terms and conditions.

Another flexible feature of the adjustable-payment, adjustable-rate mortgage loan is the monthly payment. The amount of the monthly payment may be increased or decreased by the lender every six months to reflect the changes in the interest rate. State law prohibits the lender from increasing your monthly payment by more than 7.5 percent per year. There may be circumstances, however, in which you, the borrower, may want to increase the amount of your monthly payment beyond the 7.5 percent limit. This option would be available to you whenever changes in the interest rate threaten to increase the outstanding principal loan balance on the loan.

A third flexible feature of the adjustable-payment, adjustable-rate mortgage loan is that the outstanding principal loan balance (the total amount you owe) may be increased from time to time. This situation, called "negative amortization," can occur when rising interest rates make the monthly payment too small to cover the interest due on the loan. The difference between the monthly payment and the actual amount due in interest is added to the outstanding loan balance.

Under the terms of this mortgage, you as a borrower would always have the option of either incurring additions to the amount you owe on the loan or voluntarily increasing your monthly payments beyond the 7.5 percent annual limit to an amount needed to pay off the rising interest costs.

Continual increases in the outstanding loan balance may cause a situation in which the loan balance is not entirely paid off at the end of the 30-year loan term. If this occurs, you may elect in writing to repay the outstanding principal all at once, or with a series of fixed payments at a fixed rate of interest for up to 10 years.

The final flexible feature of the adjustable-payment, adjustable-rate mortgage loan is that you may lengthen the loan term from 30 to up to 40 years. Extending the loan term will lower your monthly payment slightly less than they would have been had the loan term not been extended.

II. INDEX

Adjustments to the interest rate of an adjustable-payment, adjustable-rate mortgage loan must correspond directly to the movement of an index which is selected, but not controlled, by the lender. Any adjustments to the interest rate are subject to limitations provided in the loan contract.

If the index moves down, the lender must reduce the interest rate by at least the decrease in the index. If the index moves up, the lender has the right to increase the interest rate by that amount. Although making such an increase is optional by the lender, you should be aware that the lender has this right and may be contractually obligated to exercise it.

The index used is [Name and description of index to be used for applicant's loan, initial index value (if known) and date of initial index value, a source or sources where the index may be readily obtained by the borrower, and the high and low index rates during the previous calendar year].

III. KEY PROVISIONS OF [Name of Institution] ADJUSTABLE–PAYMENT, ADJUSTABLE–RATE MORTGAGE LOAN

The following information is a summary of the basic terms on the mortgage loan being offered to you. This summary is intended for reference purposes only. Important information relating specifically to your loan will be contained in the loan agreement.

[Provide a summary of basic terms of the loan, including the loan term, the frequency of rate changes, the frequency of payment changes, the maximum rate change at any one time, the maximum rate change over the life of the loan, the maximum annual payment change, and whether additions to the principal loan balance are possible, in the following format:]

LOAN TERM

FREQUENCY OF RATE CHANGES

FREQUENCY OF PAYMENT CHANGES

IV. HOW YOUR ADJUSTABLE–PAYMENT, ADJUSTABLE–RATE MORTGAGE LOAN WOULD WORK

A. INITIAL INTEREST RATE

The initial interest rate offered by [Name of Institution] on your adjustable-payment, adjustable-rate mortgage loan will be established and disclosed to you on [commitment date, etc.] based on market conditions at that time.

[Insert a short description of each of the key provisions of the loan to be offered to the borrower, using headings where appropriate.]

B. NOTICE OF PAYMENT ADJUSTMENTS

[Name of Institution] will send you notice of an adjustment to the payment amount at least 60 days before it becomes effective. [Describe what information the notice will contain.]

C. PREPAYMENT PENALTY

You may prepay your adjustable-payment, adjustable-rate mortgage in whole or in part without penalty at any time during the term of the loan.

D. FEES

You will be charged fees by [Name of Institution] and by other persons in connection with the origination of your loan. The association will give you an estimate of these fees after receiving your loan application. However, you will not be charged any costs of fees in connection with any regularly scheduled adjustment to the interest rate, the payment, the outstanding principal loan balance, or the loan term.

V. EXAMPLE OF OPERATION OF YOUR ADJUSTABLE–PAYMENT, ADJUSTABLE–RATE MORTGAGE LOAN

[Set out an example of the operation of the mortgage loan, including the use of a table. In at least one of the examples, create a situation showing how negative amortization could occur.]

(d) At least 60 days prior to the due date of a monthly installment to be revised due to a change in the interest rate, notice shall be mailed to the borrower of the following:

(1) The base index.

(2) The most recently published index at the date of the change in the rate.

(3) The interest rate in effect as a result of the change.

(4) The amount of the unpaid principal balance.

(5) If the interest scheduled to be paid on the due date exceeds the amount of the installment, a statement to that effect, including the amount of excess and extent of borrower options as described in paragraph (4) of subdivision (b).

(6) The amount of the revised monthly installment.

(7) The borrower's right to prepayment under paragraph (8) of subdivision (b).

(8) The address and telephone number of the office of the lender to which inquiries may be made.

(e) As used in this section:

(1) "Base index" means the last published index at the date of the note.

(2) "Base index rate" means the interest rate initially applicable to the loan as specified in the note.

(3) "Graduated Payment Adjustable Mortgage Loan" means a loan on which the monthly payments begin at a level lower than that necessary to pay off the remaining principal balance over an amortization period of not less than 30 years. During a period the length of which is fixed at loan origination (the "graduation period"), the scheduled payments gradually rise to a level sufficient to pay off the remaining principal balance over the stipulated amortization period. Limitations on the rate of increase in the scheduled payments due both to graduation and to changes in the interest rate are also fixed at loan origination.

(4) "Note" means the note or other loan contract evidencing an adjustable-payment, adjustable-rate mortgage loan.
(Added by Stats.1981, c. 1079, p. 4152, § 1.)

Cross References

Exemption from this section of loans by state institutions under regulations to establish parity with federal institutions, see Civil Code § 1916.12.
Interest defined, see Civil Code § 1915.

§ 1916.8. Renegotiable rate mortgage loans; interest rate changes at renewal; costs or fees; notice to borrower; disclosure to applicant

Any lender may make, purchase or participate in a renegotiable rate mortgage loan under this section if the loan complies with the provisions of this section pertaining to one- to four-family home loans.

(a) For purposes of this section, a renegotiable rate mortgage loan is a loan issued for a term of three, four or five years, secured by a long-term mortgage or deed of trust of up to 30 years, and automatically renewable at equal intervals except as provided in paragraph (1) of subdivision (b). The loan must be repayable in equal monthly installments of principal and interest during the loan term, in an amount at least sufficient to amortize a loan with the same principal and at the same interest rate over the remaining term of the mortgage or deed of trust. Only one of the indices described in paragraph (1) of subdivision (b) shall be used and no other index shall be used during the term of the mortgage or deed of trust securing the loan. At renewal, no change other than in the interest rate may be made in the terms or conditions of the initial loan. Prepayment in full or in part of the loan balance secured by the mortgage or deed of trust may be made without penalty at any time after the beginning of the minimum notice period for the first renewal, or at any earlier time specified in the loan contract.

(b) Interest rate changes at renewal shall be determined as follows:

(1) Subject to the provisions of subdivision (a) the interest rate offered at renewal shall reflect the movement, in reference to the date of the original loan, of an index, which may be either (i) the contract interest rate on the purchase of previously occupied homes in the most recent monthly national average mortgage rate index for all major lenders published by the Federal Home Loan Bank Board, or (ii) the

§ 1916.8 OBLIGATIONS

weighted average cost of funds for the 11th District Savings and Loan Associations as computed by the Federal Home Loan Bank of San Francisco; provided that a lender may extend the initial terms of loans for a period less than six months so that they may mature on the same date three, four or five years after the end of such period of extension, in which case the interest rate offered at renewal shall reflect the movement of the index from the end of such period so that loans may be grouped as though all loans of such group had originated at the end of the extension period.

(2) The maximum rate increase or decrease shall be ½ of 1 percentage point per year multiplied by the number of years in the loan term, with a maximum increase or decrease of 5 percentage points over the life of the mortgage or deed of trust. The lender may offer a borrower a renegotiable rate mortgage loan with maximum annual and total interest rate decreases smaller than the maximum set out in this paragraph, except that in such a case the maximum annual and total interest rate increases offered shall not exceed the maximum annual and total decreases set out in the loan contract.

(3) Interest rate decreases from the previous loan term shall be mandatory. Interest rate increases are optional with the lender, but the lender may obligate itself to a third party to take the maximum increase permitted by this paragraph.

(c) The borrower may not be charged any costs or fees in connection with the renewal of such loan.

(d) At least 90 days before the due date of the loan, the lender shall send written notification in the following form to the borrower:

NOTICE

Your loan with [name of lender], secured by a [mortgage/deed of trust] on property located at [address], is due and payable on [90 days from the date of notice].

If you do not pay by that date, your loan will be renewed automatically for _____ years, upon the same terms and conditions as the current loan, except that the interest rate will be _____%. (See accompanying Truth-In-Lending statement for further credit information.)

Your monthly payment, based on that rate, will be $_____, beginning with the payment due on _____, 19___.

You may pay off the entire loan or a part of it without penalty at any time.

If you have questions about this notice, please contact [title and telephone number of lender's employee].

(e) An applicant for a renegotiable rate mortgage loan must be given, at the time he or she requests an application, a disclosure notice in the following form:

INFORMATION ABOUT THE RENEGOTIABLE–RATE MORTGAGE

You have received an application form for a renegotiable-rate mortgage ("RRM"). The RRM differs from the fixed-rate mortgage with which you may be familiar. In the fixed-rate mortgage the length of the loan and the length of the underlying mortgage are the same, but in the RRM the loan is short-term (3–5 years) and is automatically renewable for a period equal to the mortgage (up to 30 years). Therefore, instead of having an interest rate that is set at the beginning of the mortgage and remains the same, the RRM has an interest rate that may increase or decrease at each renewal of the short-term loan. This means that the amount of your monthly payment may also increase or decrease.

The term of the RRM loan is _____ years, and the length of the underlying mortgage is _____ years. The initial loan term may be up to six months longer than later terms.

The lender must offer to renew the loan, and the only loan provision that may be changed at renewal is the interest rate. The interest rate offered at renewal is based on changes in an index rate. The index used is (either of the following statements shall be given): [computed monthly by the Federal Home Loan Bank Board, an agency of the federal government. The index is based on the national average contract rate for all major lenders for the purchase of previously occupied, single-family homes.] [the weighted average cost of savings, borrowings and Federal Home Loan Bank advances to California members of the Federal Home Loan Bank Board of San Francisco as computed from statistics tabulated by the Federal Home Loan Bank of San Francisco. The index used is computed by the Federal Home Loan Bank of San Francisco.]

At renewal, if the index has moved higher than it was at the beginning of the mortgage, the lender has the right to offer a renewal of the loan at an interest rate equaling the original interest rate plus the increase in the index rate. This is the maximum increase permitted to the lender. Although taking such an increase is optional with the lender, you should be aware that the lender has this right and may become contractually obligated to exercise it.

If the index has moved down, the lender must at renewal reduce the original interest rate by the decrease in the index rate. No matter how much the index rate increases or decreases, THE LENDER, AT RENEWAL, MAY NOT INCREASE OR DECREASE THE INTEREST RATE ON YOUR RRM LOAN BY AN AMOUNT GREATER THAN _____ OF ONE PERCENTAGE POINT PER YEAR OF THE LOAN, AND THE TOTAL INCREASE OR DECREASE OVER THE LIFE OF THE MORTGAGE MAY NOT BE MORE THAN _____ PERCENTAGE POINTS.

As the borrower, you have the right to decline the lender's offer of renewal. If you decide not to renew, you will have to pay off the remaining balance of the mortgage. Even if you decide to renew, you have the right to prepay the loan in part or in full without penalty at any time after the beginning of the minimum notice period for the first renewal. To give you enough time to make this decision, the lender, 90 days before renewal, will send a notice stating the due date of the loan, the new interest rate and the monthly payment amount. If you do not respond to the notice, the loan will be automatically renewed at the new rate. You will not have to pay any fees or charges at renewal time.

The maximum interest rate increase at the first renewal is _____ percentage points. On a $50,000 mortgage with a loan term of _____ years and an original interest rate of [lender's current commitment rate] percent, this rate change would increase the monthly payment (principal and interest) from $_____ to $_____. Using the same example, the highest rate you might have to pay over the life of the mortgage would be _____ percent, and the lowest would be _____ percent. *(Added by Stats.1980, c. 1139, p. 3681, § 2.)*

Cross References

Exemption from this section of loans by state institutions under regulations to establish parity with federal institutions, see Civil Code § 1916.12.

Interest defined, see Civil Code § 1915.

Offer to fixed rate mortgage loan as alternative to renegotiable rate mortgage loan, see Civil Code § 1916.9.

Variable interest rates, see Civil Code § 1916.5 et seq.

§ 1916.9. Offer of fixed rate mortgage loan as alternative to renegotiable rate mortgage loan

(a) Every lender who offers a renegotiable rate mortgage loan pursuant to Section 1916.8 to a borrower who occupies or intends to occupy the property which is security for the loan shall also offer to such borrower a fixed rate mortgage loan in the same amount with a term of at least 29 years.

(b) Nothing in this section shall require that the terms of such alternative loans, including the rates of interest thereon, must be the same as those terms offered with regard to the fixed-payment adjustable-rate loan or the renegotiable rate mortgage loan also offered.

(c) This section does not apply to any lender who makes less than 10 loans per year. *(Added by Stats.1980, c. 1139, p. 3685, § 3.)*

Cross References

Exemption from this section of loans by state institutions under regulations to establish parity with federal institutions, see Civil Code § 1916.12.

Interest defined, see Civil Code § 1915.

Variable interest rates, see Civil Code § 1916.5 et seq.

§ 1916.10. Repealed by Stats.1981, c. 1079, p. 4151, § 2, operative Dec. 31, 1983

§ 1916.11. Lien of mortgage or deed of trust; validity

Notwithstanding any other remedy a borrower may have based on an alleged failure to comply with Sections 1916.5 through 1916.9, the lien of the mortgage or deed of trust shall be valid. *(Added by Stats.1981, c. 274, p. 1370, § 2, eff. Aug. 27, 1981.)*

§ 1916.12. Legislative findings; purpose; mortgage parity between state and federal institutions; rules and regulations

(a) The Legislature finds that the economic environment of financial institutions has become increasingly volatile as a result of regulatory revisions enacted by the United States Congress and federal agencies including, but not necessarily limited to, the Comptroller of the Currency, the Federal Home Loan Bank Board, Federal Reserve Board, and the Depository Institutions Deregulation Committee. The Legislature further finds that deposit rate ceilings are being phased out while the cost of and competition for funds have escalated. It is the purpose of this section to maintain the quality of competition between state-licensed and federally regulated financial institutions in the field of mortgage lending, as well as promote the convenience, advantage and best interests of California residents in their pursuit of adequate and available housing. In order to remain competitive and provide the optimum housing environment for the citizens of California, state institutions require the ability to respond in a timely manner to changes in mortgage lending parameters initiated at the federal level. Local regulatory guidelines must promote continued parity between the state and federal levels in order to avoid creation of discriminatory burdens upon state institutions and to protect interests held by California citizens. It is the intent of the Legislature to eliminate past and prevent future inequities between state and federal financial institutions doing business in the State of California by creating a sensitive and responsive mortgage parity procedure.

(b) The Secretary of the Business, Consumer Services, and Housing Agency, or the secretary's designee as defined by subdivision (c) of Section 1918.5 of the Civil Code, shall have the authority to prescribe rules and regulations extending to lenders who make loans upon the security of residential real property any right, power, privilege or duty relating to mortgage instruments that is equivalent to authority extended to federally regulated financial institutions by federal statute or regulation.

(c) In order to grant equivalent mortgage lending authority to state financial institutions to that which has been extended to federal financial institutions, the secretary or the secretary's designee shall adopt such regulations within 60 days of the effective date of the statute or regulation extending the comparable right, power, privilege, or duty to federally regulated financial institutions.

(d) The provisions of Sections 1916.5, 1916.6, 1916.7, 1916.8, and 1916.9, and any other provisions of law relating to the requirements for changes in the rate of interest on loans, shall not be applicable to loans made pursuant to the provisions of this section and regulations promulgated thereunder.

(e) Any regulations adopted pursuant to this section shall expire on January 1 of the second succeeding year following the end of the calendar year in which the regulation was promulgated. Subsequent amendments to these regulations cannot extend this expiration date.

(f) This section shall become operative on December 31, 1983. *(Added by Stats.1981, c. 1079, p. 4151, § 3, operative Dec. 31, 1983. Amended by Stats.2013, c. 353 (S.B.820), § 10, eff. Sept. 26, 2013, operative July 1, 2013.)*

Cross References

Interest defined, see Civil Code § 1915.

§ 1916–1. Legal rate of interest; contract rate

The rate of interest upon the loan or forbearance of any money, goods or things in action or on accounts after demand or judgments rendered in any court of this state, shall be seven dollars upon the one hundred dollars for one year and at that rate for a greater or less sum or for a longer or a shorter time; but it shall be competent for parties to contract

§ 1916–1

for the payment and receipt of a rate of interest not exceeding twelve dollars on the one hundred dollars for one year and not exceeding that rate for a greater or less sum or for a longer or shorter time, in which case such rate exceeding seven dollars on one hundred dollars shall be clearly expressed in writing. *(Initiative Measure, Stats.1919, p. lxxxiii, § 1.)*

Cross References

Commercial loans, see Financial Code § 22500 et seq.
Finance lenders law, see Financial Code § 22000 et seq.
Interest defined, see Civil Code § 1915.

§ 1916–2. Maximum rate of interest; compound interest; effect of contract provisions for excessive interest

No person, company, association or corporation shall directly or indirectly take or receive in money, goods or things in action, or in any other manner whatsoever, any greater sum or any greater value for the loan or forbearance of money, goods or things in action than at the rate of twelve dollars upon one hundred dollars for one year; and in the computation of interest upon any bond, note, or other instrument or agreement, interest shall not be compounded, nor shall the interest thereon be construed to bear interest unless an agreement to that effect is clearly expressed in writing and signed by the party to be charged therewith. Any agreement or contract of any nature in conflict with the provisions of this section shall be null and void as to any agreement or stipulation therein contained to pay interest and no action at law to recover interest in any sum shall be maintained and the debt can not be declared due until the full period of time it was contracted for has elapsed. *(Initiative Measure, Stats. 1919, p. lxxxiii, § 2.)*

Cross References

Interest defined, see Civil Code § 1915.
Maximum interest rate prescribed by constitutional provision adopted in 1976, see Cal. Const. Art. 15, § 1.

§ 1916–3. Civil and criminal liability for violations

(a) Every person, company, association or corporation, who for any loan or forbearance of money, goods or things in action shall have paid or delivered any greater sum or value than is allowed to be received under the preceding sections, one and two, may either in person or his or its personal representative, recover in an action at law against the person, company, association or corporation who shall have taken or received the same, or his or its personal representative, treble the amount of the money so paid or value delivered in violation of said sections, providing such action shall be brought within one year after such payment or delivery.

(b) Any person who willfully makes or negotiates, for himself or another, a loan of money, credit, goods, or things in action, and who directly or indirectly charges, contracts for, or receives with respect to any such loan any interest or charge of any nature, the value of which is in excess of that allowed by law, is guilty of loan-sharking, a felony, and is punishable by imprisonment in the state prison for not more than five years or in the county jail for not more than one year. This subdivision shall not apply to any person licensed to make or negotiate, for himself or another, loans of money, credit, goods, or things in action, or expressly exempted from compliance by the laws of this state with respect to such licensure or interest or other charge, or to any agent or employee of such person when acting within the scope of his agency or employment. *(Initiative Measure, Stats.1919, p. lxxxiii, § 3. Amended by Stats.1970, c. 784, p. 1497, § 1.)*

Cross References

Commercial loans, see Financial Code § 22500 et seq.
Felonies, definition and penalties, see Penal Code §§ 17, 18.
Finance lenders law, see Financial Code § 22000 et seq.
Interest defined, see Civil Code § 1915.
Loan of money defined, see Civil Code § 1912.
Maximum interest rate prescribed by constitutional provision adopted in 1976, see Cal. Const. Art. 15, § 1.

§ 1916–4. Repeals

Sections one thousand nine hundred seventeen, one thousand nine hundred eighteen, one thousand nine hundred nineteen and one thousand nine hundred twenty of the Civil Code and all acts and parts of acts in conflict with this act are hereby repealed. *(Initiative Measure, Stats.1919, p. lxxxiv, § 4.)*

§ 1916–5. Usury Law, citation

This act whenever cited, referred to, or amended may be designated simply as the "usury law." *(Initiative Measure, Stats.1919, p. lxxxiv, § 5.)*

CHAPTER 3.5. SHARED APPRECIATION LOANS

Section
1917. Definitions; contingent deferred interest; shared appreciation loan.
1917.001. Relationship of borrower and lender.
1917.002. Statutes governing variable, adjustable, or renegotiable interest rate instruments; application.
1917.003. Liens of deeds of trust; included amounts.
1917.004. Lien of deed of trust securing loan; attachment; priority; indication of type of loan on document.
1917.005. Usury exemption.
1917.006. Definitions; shared appreciation loan; local public entity; owner-occupied residence.

Cross References

Bribery to procure a loan, see Penal Code §§ 639, 639a.
Home Equity Loan Disclosure Act, see Civil Code § 2970 et seq.
Insurance in connection with sales and loans, see Insurance Code § 770 et seq.
Insurance loans and investments, see Insurance Code § 1100 et seq.
Interest, see Civil Code § 1914 et seq.
Liability of lender financing design, manufacture, construction, repair, modification or improvement of real or personal property, see Civil Code § 3434.
Loan for exchange, see Civil Code § 1902 et seq.
Loans of E.R.I.S.A. pension funds, see Civil Code § 1917.210 et seq.
Mortgage loans, see Civil Code § 1920 et seq.
National Housing Act loans, see Financial Code § 27000 et seq.
Precomputed interest, see Civil Code § 1799.5.
Shared appreciation loans for seniors, see Civil Code § 1917.320 et seq.
Translation of contracts negotiated in language other than English, see Civil Code § 1632.

§ 1917. Definitions; contingent deferred interest; shared appreciation loan

For purposes of this chapter:

(a) "Contingent deferred interest" means the sum a borrower is obligated to pay to a lender pursuant to the documentation of a shared appreciation loan as a share of (1) the appreciation in the value of the security property (2) rents and profits attributable to the subject property, or (3) both.

(b) A "shared appreciation loan" means any loan made upon the security of an interest in real property which additionally obligates the borrower to pay to the lender contingent deferred interest pursuant to the loan documentation. "Shared appreciation loan" does not include any loan made upon the security of an interest in real property containing one to four residential units at least one of which at the time the loan is made is or is to be occupied by the borrower. *(Added by Stats.1987, c. 652, § 1.)*

Cross References

Interest defined, see Civil Code § 1915.
Local public entity defined for purposes of this Chapter, see Civil Code § 1917.006.
Owner occupied residence defined for purposes of this Chapter, see Civil Code § 1917.006.
Shared appreciation loan defined for purposes of this Chapter, see Civil Code § 1917.006.

§ 1917.001. Relationship of borrower and lender

The relationship of the borrower and the lender in a shared appreciation loan transaction is that of debtor and creditor and shall not be, or be construed to be, a joint venture, equity venture, partnership, or other relationship. *(Added by Stats. 1987, c. 652, § 1.)*

Cross References

Relationship of borrower and lender, see Civil Code § 1917.610.
Shared appreciation loan defined for purposes of this Chapter, see Civil Code §§ 1917, 1917.006.

§ 1917.002. Statutes governing variable, adjustable, or renegotiable interest rate instruments; application

A shared appreciation loan shall not be subject to any provisions of this code or the Financial Code which limits the interest rate or change of interest rate of variable, adjustable, or renegotiable interest instruments, or which requires particular language or provisions in security instruments securing variable, adjustable, or renegotiable rate obligations or in evidences of such debts except for those specifically imposed by Chapter 4 (commencing with Section 1917.010) or Chapter 7 (commencing with Section 1917.320) for loans subject to those chapters. This section is declaratory of existing law. *(Added by Stats.1987, c. 652, § 1.)*

Cross References

Interest defined, see Civil Code § 1915.
Shared appreciation loan defined for purposes of this Chapter, see Civil Code §§ 1917, 1917.006.
Usury exemption, see Civil Code § 1917.005.

§ 1917.003. Liens of deeds of trust; included amounts

The lien or liens of a deed or deeds of trust securing a shared appreciation loan shall include and secure the principal amount of the shared appreciation loan, and all interest, whether accrued or to be accrued, including all amounts of contingent deferred interest. *(Added by Stats.1987, c. 652, § 1. Amended by Stats.1989, c. 1416, § 5.)*

Cross References

Contingent deferred interest defined for purposes of this Chapter, see Civil Code § 1917.
Interest defined, see Civil Code § 1915.
Lien of deed of trust securing loan, see Civil Code §§ 1917.004, 1917.614.
Shared appreciation loan defined for purposes of this Chapter, see Civil Code §§ 1917, 1917.006.

§ 1917.004. Lien of deed of trust securing loan; attachment; priority; indication of type of loan on document

(a) The lien of a shared appreciation loan, including the principle[1] amount and all interest, whether accrued or to be accrued, and all amounts of contingent deferred interest, shall attach from the time of the recordation of the deed of trust securing the loan, and the lien, including the lien of the interest accrued, or to be accrued, and of the contingent deferred interest, shall have priority over any other lien or encumbrance affecting the property encumbered by the shared appreciation deed of trust which is recorded after the time of recordation of the shared appreciation deed of trust. Nothing in this section shall preclude a junior or subordinate lien to the deed of trust securing the shared appreciation loan.

(b) Any deed of trust that acts as security for a shared appreciation loan shall indicate on the document that the deed of trust secures a shared appreciation loan. *(Added by Stats.1987, c. 652, § 1.)*

[1] So in chaptered copy. Probably should read "principal".

Cross References

Attachment priority of lien, see Civil Code § 1917.615.
Contingent deferred interest defined for purposes of this Chapter, see Civil Code § 1917.
Interest defined, see Civil Code § 1915.
Liens of deed of trust, see Civil Code § 1917.003.
Shared appreciation loan defined for purposes of this Chapter, see Civil Code §§ 1917, 1917.006.

§ 1917.005. Usury exemption

Lenders shall be exempt from the usury provisions of Article XV of the California Constitution with respect to shared appreciation loan transactions. This section is declaratory of existing law. *(Added by Stats.1987, c. 652, § 1.)*

Cross References

Shared appreciation loan defined for purposes of this Chapter, see Civil Code §§ 1917, 1917.006.

§ 1917.006. Definitions; shared appreciation loan; local public entity; owner-occupied residence

For purposes of this chapter:

(a) "Shared appreciation loan" means, in addition to the meaning defined in Section 1917, a loan that obligates the borrower to pay to the lender contingent deferred interest pursuant to the loan documentation and that is made upon the security of an interest in real property that is an owner-occupied residence in compliance with all of the following conditions:

(1) The loan is made by, and all contingent deferred interest paid with respect to the loan is used by, a local public entity to provide financial assistance in the acquisition of

§ 1917.006

housing that is affordable to persons and families of low or moderate income, as defined in Section 50093 of the Health and Safety Code.

(2) The loan is made or acquired with assets of the local public entity other than the proceeds of a bond meeting the requirements of Section 143 of the United States Internal Revenue Code of 1986.

(3) The loan documentation assures that the obligation to pay contingent deferred interest is subject to a superior right of the borrower, upon termination of the loan, to receive repayment of money paid by the borrower for purchase of the security property (including downpayment, installment payments of mortgage principal, escrow fees, transfer taxes, recording fees, brokerage commissions and similar costs of acquisition actually paid by the borrower) and money paid by the borrower for capital improvements to the security property, plus not less than the legal rate of interest on those cash payments.

(4) The loan documentation assures that the amount of contingent deferred interest shall not exceed that percentage of the appreciation in appraised fair market value of the security property that equals the local public entity's proportionate share of the total initial equity in the security property. The amount of the total initial equity and of the local public entity's share of the initial equity shall be agreed upon by the borrower and the local public entity at the time of executing the shared appreciation loan and shall include the local public entity's cash investment, the difference between the price of land provided by the local public entity and the fair market value of the land, the amount of fees waived by the local public entity, and the value of in-kind contributions made by or on behalf of the local public entity. Funds borrowed by the borrower, the repayment of which are secured by the security property, shall not be included in the calculation of total initial equity of the borrower.

(5) At least 30 days in advance of executing the loan documentation, the borrower receives full disclosure of the terms and conditions of the loan, including the economic consequences to the borrower of the obligation to pay contingent deferred interest.

(b) "Local public entity" means a city and county, or a housing authority or redevelopment agency of a city and county.

(c) "Owner-occupied residence" means real property containing one to four residential units at least one of which at the time the loan is made is, or is to be, occupied by the borrower. (Added by Stats.1990, c. 1606 (S.B.2716), § 1.)

Cross References

Contingent deferred interest defined for purposes of this Chapter, see Civil Code § 1917.
Interest defined, see Civil Code § 1915.
Shared appreciation loan defined for purposes of this Chapter, see Civil Code § 1917.

CHAPTER 4. SHARED APPRECIATION LOANS OF E.R.I.S.A. PENSION FUNDS [INOPERATIVE]

Article	Section
1. Legislative Findings and Declarations [Inoperative]	1917.010
2. Definitions [Inoperative]	1917.020
3. Terms and Conditions [Inoperative]	1917.030
4. Annual Appraisals [Inoperative]	1917.040
5. Improvements [Inoperative]	1917.050
6. General Provisions [Inoperative]	1917.060
7. Notices and Disclosures [Inoperative]	1917.070

Chapter 4, added as "Shared Appreciation Loans of E.R.I.S.A. Pension Funds" by Stats.1982, c. 466, p. 1975, § 11, consisting of §§ 1917.010 to 1917.075, became inoperative January 1, 1990 pursuant to Stats.1982, c. 466, § 11.5. For continuing application of Chapter 4, see Historical and Statutory Notes under Civil Code § 1917.010.

ARTICLE 1. LEGISLATIVE FINDINGS AND DECLARATIONS [INOPERATIVE]

Section
1917.010. Legislative findings and declarations.

Article 1 was added by Stats.1982, c. 466, p. 1975, § 11.

Operative Effect

Chapter 4 became inoperative January 1, 1990 pursuant to Stats.1982, c. 466, § 11.5. For continuing application of Chapter 4, see Historical and Statutory Notes under Civil Code § 1917.010.

§ 1917.010. Legislative findings and declarations

The Legislature hereby finds and declares that:

(a) It is necessary and essential that the state provide and promote alternative means of supplying affordable housing to the citizens of the state.

(b) High interest rates have caused payment schedules for new long-term, fixed-rate and adjustable-rate mortgages to exceed affordable levels for the vast majority of the state's households.

(c) Because of current economic conditions, including high and volatile interest rates, alternative mortgage instruments must be developed to supplement the standard long-term, fixed-rate mortgage.

(d) Because the interest to which the lender is entitled under a shared appreciation mortgage includes a share of the appreciated value of the property securing the loan, the periodic payments under a shared appreciation mortgage are lower and, therefore, more affordable to borrowers than under a mortgage in which the lender's interest does not include a share of the appreciated value of the property. State authorization of the shared appreciation loan for pension fund lenders will serve the need to develop alternative and more affordable means of financing the construction of new housing and the subsequent marketing of new homes, and to create vitally needed jobs in the construction industry.

(e) Pension funds may find shared appreciation loans suited to their investment needs since yields are keyed to appreciation in property values, which may serve as a hedge against inflation. (Added by Stats.1982, c. 466, p. 1975, § 11.)

Operative Effect

Chapter 4 became inoperative January 1, 1990 pursuant to Stats.1982, c. 466, § 11.5. For continuing application of Chapter 4, see Historical and Statutory Notes under this section.

Cross References

Interest defined, see Civil Code § 1915.
Lender defined for purposes of this Chapter, see Civil Code § 1917.320.
Shared appreciation loan defined for purposes of this Chapter, see Civil Code § 1917.020.

ARTICLE 2. DEFINITIONS [INOPERATIVE]

Section
1917.020. Definitions.

Article 2 was added by Stats.1982, c. 466, p. 1975, § 11.

Operative Effect

Chapter 4 became inoperative January 1, 1990 pursuant to Stats.1982, c. 466, § 11.5. For continuing application of Chapter 4, see Historical and Statutory Notes under Civil Code § 1917.010.

§ 1917.020. Definitions

For purposes of this chapter:

(a) "Adjusted fair market value" means all of the following:

(1) The net sale price, in the case of a bona fide sale made in good faith prior to the maturity date of the shared appreciation loan, but excluding any sale upon a foreclosure or trustee's sale pursuant to Section 726 of the Code of Civil Procedure or Section 2924.

(2) In all other cases, the amount of value of the property specified in the most recent annual appraisal performed pursuant to Section 1917.040 or 1917.042.

(b) "Borrower's cost of the property" means the total cost to the borrower incident to the purchase of the property, including documentary transfer taxes, escrow and recording fees, and title insurance premiums.

(c) "Contingent deferred interest" means the sum resulting upon multiplying the net appreciated value by one-third.

(d) "Cost of capital improvements" means the amount of the credit, if any, determined pursuant to Article 5 (commencing with Section 1917.050).

(e) "Lender" means any person who makes a shared appreciation loan on behalf of a pension fund specified in Section 1917.030. Subsequent to an assignment of a shared appreciation loan to a pension fund pursuant to Section 1917.030, "lender" shall mean the pension fund assignee (or any subsequent assignee) and its agents designated to service the shared appreciation loan.

(f) "Net appreciated value" means the adjusted fair market value less the sum of the borrower's cost of the property and the cost of capital improvements.

(g) "Net sale price" means the gross sale price less expenses of sale actually paid by the borrower, including real estate commissions, advertising, documentary transfer taxes, legal, escrow and recording fees, and title insurance premiums.

(h) "Prevailing rate" means the weighted average yield accepted by the Federal National Mortgage Association in its most recent free market system auction for four-month conventional mortgage commitments or, if the Federal National Mortgage Association alters its free market system auction, then the system which is adopted by the Federal National Mortgage Association which substantially replaces or supersedes the present free market system auction for four-month commitments, or if no auction or equivalent thereof has been conducted within the six months immediately preceding the date the application for a shared appreciation mortgage loan is executed, the weighted average cost of funds for the 11th District Savings and Loan Associations as computed by the Federal Home Loan Bank of San Francisco.

(i) "Shared appreciation loan" means any loan made pursuant to this chapter upon the security of owner-occupied real property of a type specified in Section 1917.030, and in connection with which the lender has a right to receive a share of the appreciation in the value of the security property. "Shared appreciation loan" includes a deed of trust and any evidence of debt issued in connection with the loan. (Added by Stats.1982, c. 466, p. 1975, § 11. Amended by Stats.1984, c. 1267, § 1.)

Operative Effect

Chapter 4 became inoperative January 1, 1990 pursuant to Stats.1982, c. 466, § 11.5. For continuing application of Chapter 4, see Historical and Statutory Notes under Civil Code § 1917.010.

Cross References

Interest defined, see Civil Code § 1915.
Value of property determination of adjusted fair market value, see Civil Code § 1917.043.

ARTICLE 3. TERMS AND CONDITIONS [INOPERATIVE]

Section
1917.030. Authority to make loans on owner-occupied property; pension funds.
1917.031. General terms and conditions.
1917.032. Right to prepay; prepayment charge.
1917.033. Refinancing.
1917.034. Alternative refinancing.

Article 3 was added by Stats.1982, c. 466, p. 1975, § 11.

Operative Effect

Chapter 4 became inoperative January 1, 1990 pursuant to Stats.1982, c. 466, § 11.5. For continuing application of Chapter 4, see Historical and Statutory Notes under Civil Code § 1917.010.

§ 1917.030. Authority to make loans on owner-occupied property; pension funds

Lenders may make shared appreciation loans pursuant to this chapter for the purchase of real property improved with one- to four-family dwelling units, including structures ancil-

§ 1917.030

lary to such dwelling units and including attached single-family dwelling units, single-family mobilehome units placed upon permanent foundations, residential condominium units and dwelling units within a planned unit development. Shared appreciation loans shall be made to finance only owner-occupied dwelling units, but in the case of two- to four-unit dwellings financed under this chapter only one of the units need be owner-occupied. The original recipient of a shared appreciation loan shall certify in writing to the lender that he or she will occupy the security property as his or her principal residence, provided that failure to so occupy the security property shall not void a shared appreciation loan, but at the option of the lender the loan may be accelerated in accordance with the terms and conditions provided in the shared appreciation loan. All shared appreciation loans shall be originated by the lender on behalf of a pension fund which is subject to the Employee Retirement Income Security Act of 1974 (P.L. 93–406, 88 Stat. 829),[1] pursuant to a prior written commitment to purchase the loan. *(Added by Stats.1982, c. 466, p. 1975, § 11.)*

[1] 29 U.S.C.A. § 1001 et seq.

Operative Effect

Chapter 4 became inoperative January 1, 1990 pursuant to Stats.1982, c. 466, § 11.5. For continuing application of Chapter 4, see Historical and Statutory Notes under Civil Code § 1917.010.

Cross References

Lender defined for purposes of this Chapter, see Civil Code § 1917.320.
Shared appreciation loan defined for purposes of this Chapter, see Civil Code § 1917.020.

§ 1917.031. General terms and conditions

A shared appreciation loan shall include the following terms and conditions:

(a) The term of the loan, excluding refinancing under Section 1917.033, shall be at least seven years, but not more than 30 years.

(b) The repayment schedule for the loan, excluding refinancing under Section 1917.033, shall be cast so that full amortization of the principal amount of the loan would occur in 30 years, regardless of the actual term of the loan. Any principal balance remaining at maturity shall be due and payable at that time, unless refinanced as provided in Section 1917.033. Monthly installment payments shall be equal in amount and in addition to amortization of principal, shall include fixed interest pursuant to subdivision (d).

(c) The loan shall be secured by a deed of trust or mortgage on the real property financed.

(d) The loan shall bear interest at a fixed rate, which shall be one-third below the prevailing rate in effect 90 days prior to the loan closing, or at another date between that date and the loan closing if mutually agreed by the lender and borrower.

(e) The borrower shall additionally be obligated to pay contingent deferred interest in the amount of one-third of the net appreciated value of the real property which secures the loan, at the time the property is sold (including a sale pursuant to a land sale contract), when title is transferred, other than a transfer specified in Section 2924.6, when a lease with an option to purchase is entered into, when a partnership is formed which in effect transfers the beneficial ownership to another person, when a trust is created which affects title to the property, upon a judicial or nonjudicial foreclosure sale, at the time the loan is prepaid in full, or upon the maturity of the loan, whichever first occurs. *(Added by Stats.1982, c. 466, p. 1975, § 11.)*

Operative Effect

Chapter 4 became inoperative January 1, 1990 pursuant to Stats.1982, c. 466, § 11.5. For continuing application of Chapter 4, see Historical and Statutory Notes under Civil Code § 1917.010.

Cross References

Contingent deferred interest defined for purposes of this Chapter, see Civil Code § 1917.020.
Interest defined, see Civil Code § 1915.
Lender defined for purposes of this Chapter, see Civil Code § 1917.320.
Net appreciated value defined for purposes of this Chapter, see Civil Code § 1917.020.
Prevailing rate defined for purposes of this Chapter, see Civil Code § 1917.020.
Shared appreciation loan, validity of "due-on-sale" clause, see Civil Code § 1917.062.
Shared appreciation loan defined for purposes of this Chapter, see Civil Code § 1917.020.

§ 1917.032. Right to prepay; prepayment charge

(a) The borrower shall have the right to prepay, at any time, in full or in part, the principal loan balance of the shared appreciation loan, together with accrued interest, including deferred contingent interest.

(b) Nothing in this chapter shall prevent a borrower from obligating himself or herself, by an agreement in writing, to pay a prepayment charge, as authorized by this section, upon prepayment of the loan, in full or in part, within five years of the date of execution of the shared appreciation loan.

(c) Any prepayment charge imposed upon the prepayment of a shared appreciation loan shall not exceed the amount authorized and specified in subdivision (b) of Section 2954.9.

(d) No prepayment charge shall be imposed as to any portion of the contingent deferred interest. *(Added by Stats.1982, c. 466, p. 1975, § 11.)*

Operative Effect

Chapter 4 became inoperative January 1, 1990 pursuant to Stats.1982, c. 466, § 11.5. For continuing application of Chapter 4, see Historical and Statutory Notes under Civil Code § 1917.010.

Cross References

Contingent deferred interest defined for purposes of this Chapter, see Civil Code § 1917.020.
Interest defined, see Civil Code § 1915.
Shared appreciation loan defined for purposes of this Chapter, see Civil Code § 1917.020.

§ 1917.033. Refinancing

(a) If the shared appreciation loan is not prepaid in full or the real property securing the loan is not sold or transferred prior to maturity of the loan, the lender shall offer to the original borrower refinancing of the unpaid balance of the loan and all contingent deferred interest.

(b) The term of the refinancing loan shall be at least 30 years from the date of the refinancing, provided that if the interest rate of the refinancing loan is not adjustable or variable during the term of such loan, the loan may contain a call provision giving the lender an option to accelerate the principal loan balance making it, together with accrued interest, payable in full at a date specified in the shared appreciation loan, which shall be no earlier than seven years following the date of refinancing under this section. If such a call provision is included in the refinancing loan, a concise description thereof shall be included in upper case print in the disclosures on refinancing required by Section 1917.071.

(c) The interest rate for the refinancing loan shall not exceed the prevailing rate existing at maturity of the shared appreciation loan.

(d) The lender may require as a condition of the refinancing loan that it be secured by a deed of trust or mortgage of first priority on the property financed.

(e) The terms and conditions of refinancing pursuant to this section shall be specified in the shared appreciation loan, shall be a part of the shared appreciation loan contract, and shall be subject to the applicable laws in effect on the date of execution of the shared appreciation loan. The refinancing shall be fully amortizing and the interest rate may be either fixed or adjustable as permitted by law for home financing offered by banks or savings and loan associations doing business in this state to the public for financing housing similar to the borrower's property, provided that nothing in this section shall preclude such other lawful refinancing terms as may be mutually acceptable to the borrower and lender. If the lender offers more than one form of refinancing, the borrower may select from among the types of refinancing offered by the lender. (Added by Stats.1982, c. 466, p. 1975, § 11.)

Operative Effect

Chapter 4 became inoperative January 1, 1990 pursuant to Stats.1982, c. 466, § 11.5. For continuing application of Chapter 4, see Historical and Statutory Notes under Civil Code § 1917.010.

Cross References

Contingent deferred interest defined for purposes of this Chapter, see Civil Code § 1917.020.
Interest defined, see Civil Code § 1915.
Lender defined for purposes of this Chapter, see Civil Code § 1917.320.
Prevailing rate defined for purposes of this Chapter, see Civil Code § 1917.020.
Shared appreciation loan defined for purposes of this Chapter, see Civil Code § 1917.020.

§ 1917.034. Alternative refinancing

Nothing in this chapter shall preclude the borrower from obtaining any other financing, in lieu of the refinancing provided for in Section 1917.033, including refinancing on other terms that are mutually agreeable to the borrower and lender. (Added by Stats.1982, c. 466, p. 1975, § 11.)

Operative Effect

Chapter 4 became inoperative January 1, 1990 pursuant to Stats.1982, c. 466, § 11.5. For continuing application of Chapter 4, see Historical and Statutory Notes under Civil Code § 1917.010.

Cross References

Lender defined for purposes of this Chapter, see Civil Code § 1917.320.

ARTICLE 4. ANNUAL APPRAISALS [INOPERATIVE]

Section
1917.040. Appraisal for lender; time; copy for borrower; notice; payment of cost.
1917.041. Appraisal for borrower; time; copy to lender.
1917.042. Differing appraisals; determination of amount.
1917.043. Value of property; determination of adjusted fair market value.
1917.044. Qualifications of appraisers; specification by loan terms.

Article 4 was added by Stats.1982, c. 466, p. 1975, § 11.

Operative Effect

Chapter 4 became inoperative January 1, 1990 pursuant to Stats.1982, c. 466, § 11.5. For continuing application of Chapter 4, see Historical and Statutory Notes under Civil Code § 1917.010.

§ 1917.040. Appraisal for lender; time; copy for borrower; notice; payment of cost

The fair market value of the real property securing a shared appreciation loan shall be determined annually as provided in this article. The lender shall select an independent appraiser annually to perform an appraisal of the property subject to a shared appreciation loan. The appraisal shall be performed within 30 days preceding the anniversary date of the loan and a copy of the current appraisal shall be sent by first-class mail to the borrower no later than five days following the anniversary date of the loan, together with a notice informing the borrower that the appraisal will constitute a final and conclusive determination of the value of the property for certain purposes and that if the borrower disputes the amount of the appraisal, the borrower may procure an independent appraisal as provided in Section 1917.041. The lender may require the borrower to pay for the cost of the appraisal. (Added by Stats.1982, c. 466, p. 1975, § 11.)

Operative Effect

Chapter 4 became inoperative January 1, 1990 pursuant to Stats.1982, c. 466, § 11.5. For continuing application of Chapter 4, see Historical and Statutory Notes under Civil Code § 1917.010.

Cross References

Lender defined for purposes of this Chapter, see Civil Code § 1917.320.

§ 1917.040 OBLIGATIONS

Shared appreciation loan defined for purposes of this Chapter, see Civil Code § 1917.020.

§ 1917.041. Appraisal for borrower; time; copy to lender

If the borrower disputes the amount of the appraisal, the borrower, within 30 days of the anniversary date of the loan, may procure an appraisal of the property at the borrower's expense by a qualified independent appraiser, and a copy of the appraisal shall be sent by first-class mail to the lender within the 30-day period. (Added by Stats.1982, c. 466, p. 1975, § 11.)

Operative Effect

Chapter 4 became inoperative January 1, 1990 pursuant to Stats.1982, c. 466, § 11.5. For continuing application of Chapter 4, see Historical and Statutory Notes under Civil Code § 1917.010.

Cross References

Lender defined for purposes of this Chapter, see Civil Code § 1917.320.

§ 1917.042. Differing appraisals; determination of amount

If the appraisal by the appraiser selected by the borrower is lower in amount than the appraisal by the appraiser selected by the lender, the amount to be used to calculate the annual adjustment shall be one-half of the sum of the two appraisals. (Added by Stats.1982, c. 466, p. 1975, § 11.)

Operative Effect

Chapter 4 became inoperative January 1, 1990 pursuant to Stats.1982, c. 466, § 11.5. For continuing application of Chapter 4, see Historical and Statutory Notes under Civil Code § 1917.010.

Cross References

Lender defined for purposes of this Chapter, see Civil Code § 1917.320.

§ 1917.043. Value of property; determination of adjusted fair market value

The appraisal amount, as determined pursuant to Section 1917.040 if the borrower does not dispute the appraisal amount, or 1917.042 if the borrower disputes the appraisal amount, shall constitute the value of the property from and after the anniversary date of the loan for the purpose of determining the property's adjusted fair market value under Section 1917.020. (Added by Stats.1982, c. 466, p. 1975, § 11.)

Operative Effect

Chapter 4 became inoperative January 1, 1990 pursuant to Stats.1982, c. 466, § 11.5. For continuing application of Chapter 4, see Historical and Statutory Notes under Civil Code § 1917.010.

Cross References

Adjusted fair market value defined for purposes of this Chapter, see Civil Code § 1917.020.

§ 1917.044. Qualifications of appraisers; specification by loan terms

The qualifications of the appraisers may be specified by the terms of the shared appreciation loan for purposes of this article and Article 5 (commencing with Section 1917.050). (Added by Stats.1982, c. 466, p. 1975, § 11.)

Operative Effect

Chapter 4 became inoperative January 1, 1990 pursuant to Stats.1982, c. 466, § 11.5. For continuing application of Chapter 4, see Historical and Statutory Notes under Civil Code § 1917.010.

Cross References

Shared appreciation loan defined for purposes of this Chapter, see Civil Code § 1917.020.

ARTICLE 5. IMPROVEMENTS [INOPERATIVE]

Section
1917.050. Addition of cost of improvements to borrower's cost in determining contingent deferred interest; procedure.

Article 5 was added by Stats.1982, c. 466, p. 1975, § 11.

Operative Effect

Chapter 4 became inoperative January 1, 1990 pursuant to Stats.1982, c. 466, § 11.5. For continuing application of Chapter 4, see Historical and Statutory Notes under Civil Code § 1917.010.

§ 1917.050. Addition of cost of improvements to borrower's cost in determining contingent deferred interest; procedure

The borrower may have the cost of capital improvements to the security property completed within any 12-month period, and with an appraised value in excess of two thousand five hundred dollars ($2,500), added to the borrower's cost of the property, for purposes of determining the contingent deferred interest, but only if the procedures set forth in this article are followed.

(a) Within 60 days following the completion of the improvements, the borrower shall send by first-class mail a notice of the completion of the improvements to the lender and shall submit proof of cost of the improvements.

(b) Within 90 days following the completion of the improvements, the lender shall select an appraiser to perform an appraisal to determine the increase in value of the property, if any, by reason of the improvements. A copy of the appraisal shall be sent by first-class mail to the borrower, together with a notice informing the borrower that the appraisal will constitute a final and conclusive determination of the increase in the value of the property by reason of the improvement for purposes of computing the net appreciated value of the property, and that if the borrower disputes the amount of the appraisal, the borrower may procure an independent appraisal as provided in subdivision (c). The lender may require the borrower to pay for the cost of the appraisal.

(c) If the borrower disputes the amount of the appraisal, the borrower, within 120 days of the completion of the improvements, may secure at borrower's expense, a qualified, independent appraiser to perform an appraisal to determine the increase in value of the property, if any, by reason of the improvements, and a copy of the appraisal shall be sent by first-class mail to the lender within that period of time.

(d) If the appraisal of the appraiser selected by the borrower is greater in amount than the appraisal by the appraiser selected by the lender, the amount of the appraisal, for the purposes of this section, shall be one-half of the sum of the two appraisals.

(e) The lesser of the borrower's actual cost or the appraised increase in the value of the property by reason of the improvements shall be available as a credit to the buyer for purposes of determining net appreciated value, except as provided in subdivision (f).

(f) If 50 percent or more of the value of the labor or other work on the improvements was performed by the borrower, then the appraised increase in the value of the property by reason of the improvements shall be the cost of capital improvements for purposes of establishing the credit under this section. *(Added by Stats.1982, c. 466, p. 1975, § 11.)*

Operative Effect

Chapter 4 became inoperative January 1, 1990 pursuant to Stats.1982, c. 466, § 11.5. For continuing application of Chapter 4, see Historical and Statutory Notes under Civil Code § 1917.010.

Cross References

Borrower's cost of the property defined for purposes of this Chapter, see Civil Code § 1917.020.
Contingent deferred interest defined for purposes of this Chapter, see Civil Code § 1917.020.
Cost of capital improvements defined for purposes of this Chapter, see Civil Code § 1917.020.
Interest defined, see Civil Code § 1915.
Lender defined for purposes of this Chapter, see Civil Code § 1917.320.
Net appreciated value defined for purposes of this Chapter, see Civil Code § 1917.020.
Qualifications of appraisers, see Civil Code § 1917.044.

ARTICLE 6. GENERAL PROVISIONS [INOPERATIVE]

Section
1917.060. Relationship of borrower and lender.
1917.061. Waiver of borrower's rights; prohibition.
1917.062. Acceleration of maturity upon sale or transfer.
1917.063. Conformity of loan terms and conditions to chapter; application.
1917.064. Exemption of loans under this chapter from laws applicable to other loans.
1917.065. Scope of lien.
1917.066. Lien; time of attachment; priority; junior lien.
1917.067. Usury exemption.
1917.068. Exemption from qualification requirements for corporate securities.
1917.069. Fees and charges.

Article 6 was added by Stats.1982, c. 466, p. 1975, § 11.

Operative Effect

Chapter 4 became inoperative January 1, 1990 pursuant to Stats.1982, c. 466, § 11.5. For continuing application of Chapter 4, see Historical and Statutory Notes under Civil Code § 1917.010.

§ 1917.060. Relationship of borrower and lender

The relationship of the borrower and the lender, as to a shared appreciation loan, is that of debtor and creditor and shall not be, or be construed to be, a joint venture, equity venture, partnership, or other relationship. *(Added by Stats.1982, c. 466, p. 1975, § 11.)*

Operative Effect

Chapter 4 became inoperative January 1, 1990 pursuant to Stats.1982, c. 466, § 11.5. For continuing application of Chapter 4, see Historical and Statutory Notes under Civil Code § 1917.010.

Cross References

Lender defined for purposes of this Chapter, see Civil Code § 1917.320.
Shared appreciation loan defined for purposes of this Chapter, see Civil Code § 1917.020.

§ 1917.061. Waiver of borrower's rights; prohibition

Any waiver of any right of a borrower under the provisions of this chapter shall be void and unenforceable. *(Added by Stats.1982, c. 466, p. 1975, § 11.)*

Operative Effect

Chapter 4 became inoperative January 1, 1990 pursuant to Stats.1982, c. 466, § 11.5. For continuing application of Chapter 4, see Historical and Statutory Notes under Civil Code § 1917.010.

§ 1917.062. Acceleration of maturity upon sale or transfer

(a) Notwithstanding Section 711, a provision in a shared appreciation loan (not including the refinancing obligation) permitting the lender to accelerate the maturity date of the principal and accrued interest on the loan upon a sale or other transfer of the property, as specified in subdivision (e) of Section 1917.031, shall be valid and enforceable against the borrower, except as may be precluded by Section 2924.6.

(b) The Legislature finds and declares that potential exposure to liability for enforcement of a "due-on-sale" clause consistent with Section 711, as interpreted by the courts, makes use of such a provision impractical. Moreover, the additional risks to the lender inherent in shared appreciation financing are greater with longer loan terms (which are more desirable from the standpoint of housing affordability), but this risk is reduced with an enforceable "due-on-sale" clause. Therefore, in order to facilitate shared appreciation financing, it is necessary to establish the exception specified in subdivision (a). *(Added by Stats.1982, c. 466, p. 1975, § 11.)*

Operative Effect

Chapter 4 became inoperative January 1, 1990 pursuant to Stats.1982, c. 466, § 11.5. For continuing application of Chapter 4, see Historical and Statutory Notes under Civil Code § 1917.010.

Cross References

Interest defined, see Civil Code § 1915.

§ 1917.062

Lender defined for purposes of this Chapter, see Civil Code § 1917.320.

Shared appreciation loan defined for purposes of this Chapter, see Civil Code § 1917.020.

§ 1917.063. Conformity of loan terms and conditions to chapter; application

This chapter facilitates the making of shared appreciation financing in this state which conforms to the provisions of this chapter. The terms and conditions of any shared appreciation loan made pursuant to this chapter shall be consistent with this chapter. This chapter does not, however, apply to or limit shared appreciation financing of real property of a type specified in Section 1917.030 that is made pursuant to other provisions of law, or which is not otherwise unlawful. Nothing in this chapter shall be construed to in any way affect shared appreciation financing of commercial property or residential property not meeting the criteria specified in Section 1917.030.

Nothing in this chapter precludes a pension fund specified in Section 1917.030 from providing shared appreciation financing pursuant to Chapter 5 (commencing with Section 1917.110) or any other provision of law, or which is not otherwise unlawful. *(Added by Stats.1982, c. 1346, p. 5032, § 5.)*

Operative Effect

Chapter 4 became inoperative January 1, 1990 pursuant to Stats.1982, c. 466, § 11.5. For continuing application of Chapter 4, see Historical and Statutory Notes under Civil Code § 1917.010.

Cross References

Shared appreciation loan defined for purposes of this Chapter, see Civil Code § 1917.020.

§ 1917.064. Exemption of loans under this chapter from laws applicable to other loans

A shared appreciation loan shall not be subject to any provision of this code or the Financial Code which limits the interest rate or change of interest rate of variable, adjustable, or renegotiable interest instruments, or which requires particular language or provisions in security instruments securing variable, adjustable, or renegotiable rate obligations or in evidences of such debts.

This section is declaratory of existing law. *(Added by Stats.1982, c. 466, p. 1981, § 11.)*

Operative Effect

Chapter 4 became inoperative January 1, 1990 pursuant to Stats.1982, c. 466, § 11.5. For continuing application of Chapter 4, see Historical and Statutory Notes under Civil Code § 1917.010.

Cross References

Interest defined, see Civil Code § 1915.

Shared appreciation loan defined for purposes of this Chapter, see Civil Code § 1917.020.

§ 1917.065. Scope of lien

The lien of a deed of trust securing a shared appreciation loan shall include and secure the principal amount of the shared appreciation loan, and all interest, whether accrued or to be accrued, including all amounts of contingent deferred interest. *(Added by Stats.1982, c. 466, p. 1982, § 11.)*

Operative Effect

Chapter 4 became inoperative January 1, 1990 pursuant to Stats.1982, c. 466, § 11.5. For continuing application of Chapter 4, see Historical and Statutory Notes under Civil Code § 1917.010.

Cross References

Contingent deferred interest defined for purposes of this Chapter, see Civil Code § 1917.020.

Interest defined, see Civil Code § 1915.

Shared appreciation loan defined for purposes of this Chapter, see Civil Code § 1917.020.

§ 1917.066. Lien; time of attachment; priority; junior lien

The lien of a shared appreciation loan, including the principal amount and all interest, whether accrued or to be accrued, and all amounts of contingent deferred interest, shall attach from the time of the recordation of the deed of trust securing the loan, and the lien, including the lien of the interest accrued or to be accrued and of the contingent deferred interest, shall have priority over any other lien or encumbrance affecting the property secured by the shared appreciation instrument which is recorded after the time of recordation of the shared appreciation instrument. However, nothing in this section or Section 1917.165 shall preclude a junior lien or encumbrance subordinate to the obligation of the shared appreciation loan. *(Added by Stats.1982, c. 466, p. 1982, § 11.)*

Operative Effect

Chapter 4 became inoperative January 1, 1990 pursuant to Stats.1982, c. 466, § 11.5. For continuing application of Chapter 4, see Historical and Statutory Notes under Civil Code § 1917.010.

Cross References

Contingent deferred interest defined for purposes of this Chapter, see Civil Code § 1917.020.

Interest defined, see Civil Code § 1915.

Shared appreciation loan defined for purposes of this Chapter, see Civil Code § 1917.020.

§ 1917.067. Usury exemption

Lenders shall be exempt from the usury provisions of Article XV of the California Constitution with respect to shared appreciation loans made pursuant to this chapter.

This section is declaratory of existing law. *(Added by Stats.1982, c. 466, p. 1982, § 11. Amended by Stats.1983, c. 557, § 1.)*

Operative Effect

Chapter 4 became inoperative January 1, 1990 pursuant to Stats.1982, c. 466, § 11.5. For continuing application of Chapter 4, see Historical and Statutory Notes under Civil Code § 1917.010.

Cross References

Lender defined for purposes of this Chapter, see Civil Code § 1917.320.

Shared appreciation loan defined for purposes of this Chapter, see Civil Code § 1917.020.

§ 1917.068. Exemption from qualification requirements for corporate securities

The qualification requirements of Sections 25110, 25120, and 25130 of the Corporations Code shall not apply to a shared appreciation loan, provided (1) the loan obligation is evidenced by one promissory note secured by a deed of trust which is not one of a series of notes secured by interests in the same real property and (2) the loan obligation is not evidenced by fractional undivided interests in one promissory note secured by interests in the same real property. *(Added by Stats.1982, c. 466, p. 1982, § 11.)*

Operative Effect

Chapter 4 became inoperative January 1, 1990 pursuant to Stats.1982, c. 466, § 11.5. For continuing application of Chapter 4, see Historical and Statutory Notes under Civil Code § 1917.010.

Cross References

Interest defined, see Civil Code § 1915.
Shared appreciation loan defined for purposes of this Chapter, see Civil Code § 1917.020.

§ 1917.069. Fees and charges

The aggregate amount of any fee charged to the borrower for processing an application and preparing any necessary documents in connection with originating a shared appreciation loan shall not exceed the reasonable cost of providing the service. No prepaid interest shall be charged to the borrower, but nothing in this chapter shall preclude a lender from requiring a fee for providing commitments for shared appreciation loans to builders or others who will not be the ultimate borrower. *(Added by Stats.1982, c. 466, p. 1982, § 11.)*

Operative Effect

Chapter 4 became inoperative January 1, 1990 pursuant to Stats.1982, c. 466, § 11.5. For continuing application of Chapter 4, see Historical and Statutory Notes under Civil Code § 1917.010.

Cross References

Interest defined, see Civil Code § 1915.
Lender defined for purposes of this Chapter, see Civil Code § 1917.320.
Shared appreciation loan defined for purposes of this Chapter, see Civil Code § 1917.020.

ARTICLE 7. NOTICES AND DISCLOSURES [INOPERATIVE]

Section
1917.070. Exemption from disclosures required by other laws; exceptions; use of equivalent language.
1917.071. Initial disclosure; time; form.
1917.072. Disclosures required by federal regulations.
1917.073. Statement to be given prospective borrower.
1917.074. Statement in deed of trust and evidence of debt.
1917.075. Interest disclosure.

Article 7 was added by Stats.1982, c. 466, p. 1982, § 11.

Operative Effect

Chapter 4 became inoperative January 1, 1990 pursuant to Stats.1982, c. 466, § 11.5. For continuing application of Chapter 4, see Historical and Statutory Notes under Civil Code § 1917.010.

§ 1917.070. Exemption from disclosures required by other laws; exceptions; use of equivalent language

(a) The disclosures made pursuant to this chapter, as required, shall be the only disclosures required to be made pursuant to state law for shared appreciation loans, notwithstanding any contrary provisions applicable to loans not made under this chapter, except those, if any, that may be required by reason of the application of Division 1 (commencing with Section 25000) of the Corporations Code, or Chapter 1 (commencing with Section 11000) of Part 2 of Division 4 of the Business and Professions Code. A lender may, but shall not be required to, supplement the disclosures required by this article with additional disclosures that are not inconsistent with the disclosures required by this article.

(b) When very specific language is prescribed by this chapter, substantially the same language shall be utilized if possible, but reasonably equivalent language may be used to the extent necessary or appropriate to achieve a clearer or more accurate disclosure. *(Added by Stats.1982, c. 466, p. 1982, § 11.)*

Operative Effect

Chapter 4 became inoperative January 1, 1990 pursuant to Stats.1982, c. 466, § 11.5. For continuing application of Chapter 4, see Historical and Statutory Notes under Civil Code § 1917.010.

Cross References

Lender defined for purposes of this Chapter, see Civil Code § 1917.320.
Shared appreciation loan defined for purposes of this Chapter, see Civil Code § 1917.020.

§ 1917.071. Initial disclosure; time; form

(a) Each lender offering shared appreciation loans shall furnish to a prospective borrower, on the earlier of the date on which the lender first provides written information concerning shared appreciation loans from such lender or provides a loan application form to the prospective borrower, a written disclosure as provided in this section.

(b) The disclosure shall be entitled "INFORMATION ABOUT THE (Name of Lender) SHARED APPRECIATION LOAN," and shall describe the operation and effect of the shared appreciation loan including a brief summary of its terms and conditions, together with a statement consisting of substantially the following language, to the extent applicable to such loan:

INFORMATION ABOUT THE [Name of Lender]
SHARED APPRECIATION LOAN

(Name of Lender) is pleased to offer you the opportunity to finance your home through a shared appreciation loan.

§ 1917.071

Because the shared appreciation loan differs from the usual mortgage loan, the law requires that you should read and understand before you sign the loan documents.

The loan will bear a stated rate of interest which will be one-third below the prevailing market interest rate. In exchange for a stated interest rate which is below the prevailing rate, you will be obligated to pay us additional interest later. This additional interest is called "contingent deferred interest."

Contingent Deferred Interest

This loan provides that you, as borrower, must pay to us, as lender, as contingent deferred interest, one-third of the net appreciated value of the real property which secures the loan. This contingent interest is due and payable when the property is sold or transferred, when the loan is paid in full, upon any acceleration of the loan upon default, or at the end of the term of the loan, whichever first occurs. The dollar amount of contingent interest which you will be required to pay cannot be determined at this time. If the property does not appreciate, you will owe us nothing.

Your obligation to pay contingent interest will reduce the amount of the appreciation, if any, that you will realize on the property. This appreciation will not produce a real gain in your equity in the property, unless the appreciation rate exceeds the general inflation rate, but you will be required to pay a portion of the appreciation as contingent interest without regard to whether the appreciation has resulted in a real gain.

When you sell or refinance your home, you normally will receive enough cash to pay the shared appreciation loan balance, accrued interest, prepayment penalty (if applicable), the contingent interest, and expenses of sale. However, if you sell with only a small downpayment, you may possibly not receive enough cash to pay the contingent interest, and, in that event, it will be necessary for you to provide cash from other funds.

If you do not sell the property before the end of the term of this loan, you will need to refinance this loan at that time. The term of this loan is (duration) years. We will offer to refinance the outstanding obligation, including any contingent interest, at that time. If you refinance this loan, your monthly payments may increase substantially if the property appreciates significantly or if the interest rate on the refinancing loan is much higher than today's prevailing rates. In general, the more your property appreciated, the larger will be the amount of the contingent interest that you will have an obligation to pay or refinance.

The contingent interest will not become due if title to the property is transferred on your death to a spouse, or where a transfer results from a decree of dissolution of a marriage and a spouse becomes the sole owner.

Calculating the Contingent Interest

Contingent interest will be calculated as follows:

FAIR MARKET VALUE OF THE PROPERTY
(Sale price or amount of value determined by appraisal.)

− (less) BORROWER'S COST OF THE PROPERTY
(This amount includes certain costs paid by you incident to the purchase.)

− (less) COST OF CAPITAL IMPROVEMENTS MADE BY YOU IN ANY 12-MONTH PERIOD
(Must exceed $2,500 in value. The actual amount may be the lesser of actual cost or appraised value.)

= (equals) NET APPRECIATED VALUE
× (times) ONE-THIRD PERCENTAGE OWED TO LENDER
= (equals) TOTAL CONTINGENT INTEREST

Determining Net Appreciated Value

We are entitled to receive one-third of the net appreciated value of the property as contingent interest. As explained above, net appreciated value equals (1) the fair market value of the property at the time of the sale or appraisal, less (2) your cost of the property, less (3) the value of any capital improvements for which you are entitled to credit.

Determining Fair Market Value

Fair market value is the sale price of the property in the case of a bona fide sale of the property made before the maturity of the shared appreciation loan, excluding certain foreclosure related sales. In all other cases, fair market value is determined by our most recent annual appraisal of the property. If you desire to contest the amount of our annual appraisal, you may obtain another appraisal by a qualified independent appraiser within 30 days after the anniversary date of the loan and send a copy of the appraisal to us by first-class mail within that 30-day period. If your appraiser's appraisal is lower than our appraisal, the annual appraisal shall equal one-half the sum of the two appraisals.

Determining Value of Capital Improvements

The cost or value of certain capital improvements (but no maintenance or repair costs) may be added to your cost of the property for the purpose of determining the net appreciated value, but only if the procedures set forth in the shared appreciation loan documents are followed. It is important to note that capital improvements completed and for which a credit is claimed in any 12-month period must cost or be appraised at more than two thousand five hundred dollars ($2,500). The lesser of the cost or appraised value will control. However, if you have performed at least half the value of the labor or other work involved, then the appraised value of the improvements will control. The appraised value of the improvements shall be considered to be the increase in the value of the property resulting from the improvements. You will receive no credit for improvements that are not appraised at more than two thousand five hundred dollars ($2,500).

Cost of Appraisals

The terms of this loan call for annual appraisals of the property, and for additional appraisals to value improvements or in the event of a dispute regarding the value of the property or improvements. The cost of the appraisals will be paid as follows:

Your Right to Refinance This Loan

If the property is not sold or transferred prior to the maturity of the loan, we will offer to refinance the outstanding obligation on the loan, including any contingent interest. We will offer refinancing at the then prevailing interest rate either directly or through another mortgage lender.

The terms of the refinancing loan will be like home loans offered at that time by banks or savings and loan associations, but you are assured that at least one of the options will be a fully amortizing 30-year loan. The interest rate on the refinancing loan may be either fixed or adjustable, as provided in your shared appreciation loan.

We will not be permitted to look to the forecast of your income in offering to refinance. The interest rate and monthly payment upon refinancing cannot be determined at this time. They may be either more or less burdensome to you than the currently prevailing rates and terms.

Tax Consequences

Use of the shared appreciation loan will have income tax or estate planning consequences which will depend upon your own financial and tax situation. FOR FURTHER INFORMATION, YOU ARE URGED TO CONSULT YOUR OWN ACCOUNTANT, ATTORNEY OR OTHER FINANCIAL ADVISER. THE QUESTIONS YOU SHOULD DISCUSS INCLUDE THE TAX DEDUCTIBILITY OF THE CONTINGENT INTEREST PAYMENT, YOUR RIGHT TO UTILIZE THAT DEDUCTION IN YEARS OTHER THAN THE YEAR IT IS PAID, AND THE EFFECT OF THE LOSS OF TAX BENEFITS BEFORE THAT TIME.

Other Important Information

(Here insert additional description, if necessary, of the operation and effect of the shared appreciation loan.)

The foregoing describes our shared appreciation loan, includes a summary of all of its important provisions, and informs you of some of the risks of a shared appreciation loan.

If your loan application is accepted by us, we will provide you with more information about your particular shared appreciation loan, which will include a comparison with conventional mortgages, an illustration of the possible increase in your monthly payments upon refinancing, and other important information.

Before you enter into a shared appreciation loan with us, we recommend that you and your attorney or tax accountant review the loan documents for the full text of all of the terms and conditions which will govern the loan. *(Added by Stats.1982, c. 466, p. 1983, § 11.)*

Operative Effect

Chapter 4 became inoperative January 1, 1990 pursuant to Stats.1982, c. 466, § 11.5. For continuing application of Chapter 4, see Historical and Statutory Notes under Civil Code § 1917.010.

Cross References

Borrower's cost of the property defined for purposes of this Chapter, see Civil Code § 1917.020.

Call provision, inclusion in disclosures, see Civil Code § 1917.033.
Contingent deferred interest defined for purposes of this Chapter, see Civil Code § 1917.020.
Cost of capital improvements defined for purposes of this Chapter, see Civil Code § 1917.020.
Interest defined, see Civil Code § 1915.
Lender defined for purposes of this Chapter, see Civil Code § 1917.320.
Net appreciated value defined for purposes of this Chapter, see Civil Code § 1917.020.
Prevailing rate defined for purposes of this Chapter, see Civil Code § 1917.020.
Shared appreciation loan defined for purposes of this Chapter, see Civil Code § 1917.020.

§ 1917.072. Disclosures required by federal regulations

(a) Each lender making a shared appreciation loan shall also furnish to the prospective borrower, prior to the consummation of the loan, the disclosures required by Subpart C of Federal Reserve Board Regulation Z (12 CFR Part 226), including 12 CFR Section 226.18(f), to the extent applicable to the transaction.

(b) The disclosure made pursuant to paragraph (a) and Regulation Z shall be based on the fixed interest rate of the shared appreciation loan, and shall include a description of the shared appreciation feature, including (1) the conditions for its imposition, the time at which it would be collected, and the limitations on the lender's share, as required by the Federal Reserve Board in the information published by the Board at 46 Federal Register 20877 and 20878 (April 7, 1981), and (2) the lender's share of the net appreciated value and the prevailing interest rate as defined in Section 1917.120(h).

(c) The disclosure made pursuant to paragraph (a) and Regulation Z shall be accompanied by (1) one or more transaction-specific examples of the operation and effect the shared appreciation loan, and (2) the following charts, comparing the shared appreciation loan and a conventional loan made at the prevailing interest rate, and illustrating the possible increase in the monthly payments, and the possible annual percentage rate of finance charge, on the assumptions therein stated:

Chart 1

CONVENTIONAL MORTGAGE AT __%
If the same loan balance were financed under a conventional, 30-year, fixed-rate, level-payment mortgage, your monthly payments would be:
Years 1–30
$_____/mo.

Chart 2

IF YOU REFINANCE THIS TRANSACTION at __%
If your property appreciates at 10% per year, and if your loan balance (including contingent deferred interest due) at the end of ___ years is refinanced at __% (the prevailing market interest rate now), your monthly payments will be:

Years 1-____	Refinancing loan
$_____/mo.	$_____/mo.*

§ 1917.072   OBLIGATIONS

* Refinancing loan, assuming a conventional, 30-year, fixed-rate level-payment mortgage. Other mortgage instruments, e.g., graduated-payment or shared appreciation, if available, may result in lower payments.

Chart 3

APR IF PROPERTY APPRECIATES AT 10%

If your property appreciates at 10% per year, the total finance charge on your shared appreciation loan (including contingent interest) will equal $_____, and the annual percentage rate of the total finance charge (including contingent interest) will equal _____%.

(d) The disclosures required by paragraph (c) shall be separated from the disclosures required by Regulation Z, and may be presented in the document containing the disclosures required by Regulation Z or in one or more separate documents.

(e) Except to the extent that this section requires disclosure of additional information not required by Regulation Z, compliance with the applicable credit disclosure requirements of Regulation Z shall constitute compliance with the requirements of this section.

(f) The disclosures prescribed in Section 1917.171 shall be physically attached to the disclosures required by this section and Regulation Z at the time such disclosures are furnished to the borrower.

(g) In the event federal law is amended so that this section is inconsistent therewith, the federal law shall prevail as to the disclosures required by this section. *(Added by Stats. 1982, c. 466, p. 1986, § 11.)*

Operative Effect

Chapter 4 became inoperative January 1, 1990 pursuant to Stats.1982, c. 466, § 11.5. For continuing application of Chapter 4, see Historical and Statutory Notes under Civil Code § 1917.010.

Cross References

Contingent deferred interest defined for purposes of this Chapter, see Civil Code § 1917.020.
Interest defined, see Civil Code § 1915.
Lender defined for purposes of this Chapter, see Civil Code § 1917.320.
Net appreciated value defined for purposes of this Chapter, see Civil Code § 1917.020.
Shared appreciation loan defined for purposes of this Chapter, see Civil Code § 1917.020.

§ 1917.073. Statement to be given prospective borrower

Each lender making a shared appreciation loan shall additionally furnish to the prospective borrower, prior to the consummation of the loan, a statement containing the following information:

IMPORTANT INFORMATION ABOUT YOUR
SHARED APPRECIATION LOAN

You are being offered a shared appreciation loan. Before you decide to accept this loan read this statement, which is designed to provide important information that you should consider.

1. Prevailing interest rate: ____%.
2. Fixed interest rate on this loan: ____%.
3. Lender's share of net appreciated value: one-third.
4. Amount of this loan: $____.
5. Amount of the monthly payments: $____.
6. Term of this loan: ____ years.
7. Amortization period on which payments are calculated: 30 years.
8. Prepayment penalty (if any) ____. *(Added by Stats. 1982, c. 466, p. 1988, § 11.)*

Operative Effect

Chapter 4 became inoperative January 1, 1990 pursuant to Stats.1982, c. 466, § 11.5. For continuing application of Chapter 4, see Historical and Statutory Notes under Civil Code § 1917.010.

Cross References

Interest defined, see Civil Code § 1915.
Lender defined for purposes of this Chapter, see Civil Code § 1917.320.
Net appreciated value defined for purposes of this Chapter, see Civil Code § 1917.020.
Shared appreciation loan defined for purposes of this Chapter, see Civil Code § 1917.020.

§ 1917.074. Statement in deed of trust and evidence of debt

Each deed of trust and evidence of debt executed in connection with a shared appreciation loan shall contain a statement, printed or written in a size equal to at least 12-point bold type, consisting of substantially the following language: "THIS IS A [DURATION] SHARED APPRECIATION LOAN. THE LENDER'S INTEREST INCLUDES ONE–THIRD OF THE NET APPRECIATED VALUE OF THE PROPERTY. FOR FURTHER INFORMATION, READ THE FLYER 'INFORMATION ABOUT THE [NAME OF LENDER] SHARED APPRECIATION LOAN.'" The notice required by this section shall be completed to state the term of the shared appreciation loan. *(Added by Stats.1982, c. 466, p. 1989, § 11.)*

Operative Effect

Chapter 4 became inoperative January 1, 1990 pursuant to Stats.1982, c. 466, § 11.5. For continuing application of Chapter 4, see Historical and Statutory Notes under Civil Code § 1917.010.

Cross References

Interest defined, see Civil Code § 1915.
Lender defined for purposes of this Chapter, see Civil Code § 1917.320.
Net appreciated value defined for purposes of this Chapter, see Civil Code § 1917.020.
Shared appreciation loan defined for purposes of this Chapter, see Civil Code § 1917.020.

§ 1917.075. Interest disclosure

Where, pursuant to any provision of law, the lender is required to disclose the amount of interest due or to be due under a shared appreciation loan and the amount of contingent deferred interest due or to be due is not known, the lender may disclose that fact and specify in the disclosure the method for calculating contingent deferred interest. *(Added by Stats.1982, c. 466, p. 1989, § 11.)*

Operative Effect

Chapter 4 became inoperative January 1, 1990 pursuant to Stats.1982, c. 466, § 11.5. For continuing application of Chapter 4, see Historical and Statutory Notes under Civil Code § 1917.010.

Cross References

Contingent deferred interest defined for purposes of this Chapter, see Civil Code § 1917.020.
Interest defined, see Civil Code § 1915.
Lender defined for purposes of this Chapter, see Civil Code § 1917.320.
Shared appreciation loan defined for purposes of this Chapter, see Civil Code § 1917.020.

CHAPTER 5. SHARED APPRECIATION LOANS [INOPERATIVE]

Article	Section
1. Legislative Findings and Declarations [Inoperative]	1917.110
2. Definitions [Inoperative]	1917.120
3. Terms and Conditions [Inoperative]	1917.130
4. Determination of Fair Market Value [Inoperative]	1917.140
5. Improvements [Inoperative]	1917.150
6. General Provisions [Inoperative]	1917.160
7. Notices and Disclosures [Inoperative]	1917.170

Chapter 5, added as "Shared Appreciation Loans" by Stats.1982, c. 466, p. 1989, § 12, consisting of §§ 1917.110 to 1917.175, became inoperative January 1, 1987, pursuant to Stats.1982, c. 466, § 12.5. For continuing application of Chapter 5, see Historical and Statutory Notes under Civil Code § 1917.110.

ARTICLE 1. LEGISLATIVE FINDINGS AND DECLARATIONS [INOPERATIVE]

Section
1917.110. Legislative findings and declarations.

Article 1 was added by Stats.1982, c. 466, p. 1989, § 12.

Operative Effect

Chapter 5 became inoperative January 1, 1987 pursuant to Stats.1982, c. 466, § 12.5. For continuing application of Chapter 5, see Historical and Statutory Notes under Civil Code § 1917.110.

§ 1917.110. Legislative findings and declarations

The Legislature hereby finds and declares that:

(a) It is necessary and essential that the state provide and promote alternative means of supplying affordable housing to the citizens of the state.

(b) Because of current economic conditions, including the unprecedented fluctuation in interest rates, alternative mortgage instruments must be developed to supplement the standard long-term, fixed-rate mortgage.

(c) State facilitation of the shared appreciation loan will serve the need to develop alternative means of financing housing, particularly new homes, and will help to create vitally needed jobs in the construction industry. *(Added by Stats.1982, c. 466, p. 1989, § 12.)*

Operative Effect

Chapter 5 became inoperative January 1, 1987 pursuant to Stats.1982, c. 466, § 12.5. For continuing application of Chapter 5, see Historical and Statutory Notes under this section.

Cross References

Interest defined, see Civil Code § 1915.
Shared appreciation loan defined for purposes of this Chapter, see Civil Code § 1917.120.

ARTICLE 2. DEFINITIONS [INOPERATIVE]

Section
1917.120. Definitions.

Article 2 was added by Stats.1982, c. 466, p. 1989, § 12.

Operative Effect

Chapter 5 became inoperative January 1, 1987 pursuant to Stats.1982, c. 466, § 12.5. For continuing application of Chapter 5, see Historical and Statutory Notes under Civil Code § 1917.110.

§ 1917.120. Definitions

For purposes of this chapter:

(a) "Borrower" means the recipient or recipients of a shared appreciation loan and includes any successor in interest to the borrower under a shared appreciation loan, to the extent such succession is permitted by law or by the terms of the shared appreciation loan.

(b) "Borrower's cost of the property" means the price paid by the borrower for the purchase of the property to be financed with a shared appreciation loan and also includes documentary transfer taxes, escrow and recording fees, title insurance premiums, and any other fees directly paid by the borrower as a necessary or customary cost of consummating acquisition of the property. However, if the purchase price to be paid for the property does not reasonably reflect the true value of the property, the borrower may request that, in lieu of the actual price paid, the "borrower's cost of the property" be established at an amount mutually agreed by the lender and borrower or be established by averaging two appraisals in the same manner as specified in Section 1917.142 for determination of fair market value. Nothing in this subdivision shall be construed to require a lender to make shared appreciation loans with the borrower's cost of the property established on the basis of appraisals.

(c) "Contingent deferred interest" means the lender's share of net appreciated value, calculated as the sum resulting upon multiplying the net appreciated value by a percentage agreed by the lender and borrower, not to exceed 50 percent.

(d) "Fair market value" means the highest price on the date of valuation that would be agreed to by a seller, being

§ 1917.120 OBLIGATIONS

willing to sell but under no particular or urgent necessity for so doing, nor obliged to sell, and a buyer, being ready, willing, and able to buy but under no particular necessity for so doing, each dealing with the other with full knowledge of all the uses and purposes for which the property is reasonably adaptable and available.

Fair market value shall be determined pursuant to Article 4 (commencing with Section 1917.140).

(e) "Lender" means any person who makes a shared appreciation loan or the successor in interest to any such person.

(f) "Net appreciated value" means the fair market value less the sum of the borrower's cost of the property and the value of capital improvements. Nothing in this chapter shall, however, preclude a shared appreciation loan from additionally including a provision requiring deduction of any or all of the borrower's costs of selling the property from fair market value in determining, "net appreciated value," and if such a provision is included, the disclosures required by Section 1917.171 shall be modified accordingly.

(g) "Prevailing rate" means the weighted average yield accepted by the Federal National Mortgage Association in its most recent free market system auction for four-month conventional mortgage commitments. In the event that the Federal National Mortgage Association discontinues or substantially alters its free market system auction for conventional mortgages then the "prevailing rate" shall be the average yield established at the most recent immediate delivery auction of the Federal Home Loan Mortgage Corporation, or if the auction has been discontinued, then the "prevailing rate" shall be specified in the shared appreciation loan as either (1) the most recently published Federal Home Loan Bank Board mortgage contract rate or (2) the average single-family home mortgage rate for the 10 largest savings and loan associations with principal offices in this state.

(h) "Property" means the property financed by the shared appreciation loan.

(i) "Sale" means any transfer of title to the property and additionally includes the execution of an installment sale contract giving the purchaser a right to possess the property before transfer of title, refinancing, judicial sale on execution or other legal process of foreclosure or trustee's sale (regardless of whether initiated by the lender), but "sale" does not include a transfer specified in Section 2924.6.

(j) "Shared appreciation loan" means any loan made pursuant to this chapter upon the security of owner-occupied real property of a type specified in Section 1917.130, and in connection with which the lender has a right to receive a share of the appreciation in the value of the security property. "Shared appreciation loan" includes a deed of trust and any evidence of debt issued in connection with the loan.

(k) "Value of capital improvements" means the amount of the credit or credits for capital improvements, if any, determined pursuant to Article 5 (commencing with Section 1917.150). *(Added by Stats.1982, c. 466, p. 1989, § 12.)*

Operative Effect

Chapter 5 became inoperative January 1, 1987 pursuant to Stats.1982, c. 466, § 12.5. For continuing application of Chapter 5, see Historical and Statutory Notes under Civil Code § 1917.110.

Cross References

Disclosure of prevailing rate, see Civil Code § 1917.172.
Interest defined, see Civil Code § 1915.

ARTICLE 3. TERMS AND CONDITIONS [INOPERATIVE]

Section
1917.130. Authority to make loans on owner-occupied property.
1917.131. General terms and conditions.
1917.132. Right to prepay; prepayment charge.
1917.133. Refinancing.
1917.134. Laws applicable to refinancing.
1917.135. Alternative refinancing.

Article 3 was added by Stats.1982, c. 466, p. 1991, § 12.

Operative Effect

Chapter 5 became inoperative January 1, 1987 pursuant to Stats.1982, c. 466, § 12.5. For continuing application of Chapter 5, see Historical and Statutory Notes under Civil Code § 1917.110.

§ 1917.130. Authority to make loans on owner-occupied property

Lenders may make shared appreciation loans pursuant to this chapter for the purchase of real property improved with one- to four-dwelling units, including structures ancillary to such dwelling units and including attached single-family dwelling units, single-family mobilehome units placed upon permanent foundations, residential condominium units, and dwelling units within a planned unit development. Shared appreciation loans shall be made to finance only owner-occupied dwelling units, but in the case of two- to four-unit dwellings financed under this chapter only one of the units need be owner-occupied. A dwelling unit shall be conclusively deemed to be owner-occupied for purposes of this chapter if an original recipient of the shared appreciation loan certifies in writing to the lender at the time the loan is made that he or she will occupy the property. *(Added by Stats.1982, c. 466, p. 1991, § 12.)*

Operative Effect

Chapter 5 became inoperative January 1, 1987 pursuant to Stats.1982, c. 466, § 12.5. For continuing application of Chapter 5, see Historical and Statutory Notes under Civil Code § 1917.110.

Cross References

Lender defined for purposes of this Chapter, see Civil Code § 1917.120.
Property defined for purposes of this Chapter, see Civil Code § 1917.120.
Shared appreciation financing under other laws, see Civil Code § 1917.163.

Shared appreciation loan defined for purposes of this Chapter, see Civil Code § 1917.120.

§ 1917.131. General terms and conditions

A shared appreciation loan shall include the following terms and conditions:

(a) The term of the loan, excluding any refinancing under Section 1917.133, shall be at least seven years, but not more than 30 years.

(b) The repayment schedule for the loan, excluding any refinancing under Section 1917.133, shall be cast so that full amortization of the principal amount of the loan would occur in not less than 30 nor more than 40 years, regardless of the actual term of the loan. Any principal balance remaining at maturity shall be due and payable at that time, unless refinanced as provided in Section 1917.133. Monthly installment payments shall be equal in amount, except for the final payment when a principal balance is remaining at maturity, and in addition to amortization of principal shall include fixed interest pursuant to subdivision (d).

(c) The loan shall be secured by a deed of trust on the real property financed.

(d) The loan shall bear interest at a fixed rate, which shall be established in relation to the prevailing rate (1) in effect 90 days prior to the loan closing, (2) in effect at another date between that date and the loan closing if and as mutually agreed by the lender and borrower, or (3) in effect at the time of the lender's loan commitment given to the borrower or to the person from whom the borrower purchases the property. The percentage by which the fixed interest rate is reduced below the applicable prevailing rate shall be at least one-half the lender's percentage share of net appreciated value which is contingent deferred interest, except that if the shared appreciation loan is for less than 80 percent of the borrower's purchase price of the property, the percentage by which the fixed interest rate is reduced below the applicable prevailing rate shall be at least two-thirds the lender's percentage share of net appreciated value which is contingent deferred interest.

(e) The borrower shall additionally be obligated to pay to the lender contingent deferred interest (1) at the time of sale of the property if the lender accelerates the principal balance of the loan in accordance with a provision in the shared appreciation loan authorized by Section 1917.162, (2) at the time the loan is prepaid in full, upon acceleration of the loan upon default, or (3) upon the maturity of the loan, whichever first occurs.

(f) The aggregate amount of any fee charged to the borrower by the lender for processing an application, preparing any necessary documents, obtaining a credit report, or any other costs incurred by the lender in connection with originating a shared appreciation loan shall not exceed two percent of the principal amount of the loan or five hundred dollars ($500), whichever is greater. No prepaid interest shall be charged to the borrower, but nothing in this chapter shall preclude a lender from requiring a fee for providing commitments for shared appreciation loans to builders or others who purchase such commitments and who will not be the ultimate borrower. *(Added by Stats.1982, c. 466, p. 1991, § 12.)*

Operative Effect

Chapter 5 became inoperative January 1, 1987 pursuant to Stats.1982, c. 466, § 12.5. For continuing application of Chapter 5, see Historical and Statutory Notes under Civil Code § 1917.110.

Cross References

Borrower defined for purposes of this Chapter, see Civil Code § 1917.120.

Contingent deferred interest defined for purposes of this Chapter, see Civil Code § 1917.120.

Interest defined, see Civil Code § 1915.

Lender defined for purposes of this Chapter, see Civil Code § 1917.120.

Net appreciated value defined for purposes of this Chapter, see Civil Code § 1917.120.

Prevailing rate defined for purposes of this Chapter, see Civil Code § 1917.120.

Property defined for purposes of this Chapter, see Civil Code § 1917.120.

Sale defined for purposes of this Chapter, see Civil Code § 1917.120.

Shared appreciation loan defined for purposes of this Chapter, see Civil Code § 1917.120.

§ 1917.132. Right to prepay; prepayment charge

(a) The borrower shall have the right to prepay, at any time, in full or in part, the principal loan balance of the shared appreciation loan, together with accrued interest, including contingent deferred interest.

(b) Nothing in this chapter shall prevent a borrower from obligating himself or herself, by an agreement in writing, to pay a prepayment charge upon prepayment of the loan, in full or in part, made within five years of the date of execution of the shared appreciation loan.

(c) Any prepayment charge imposed upon the prepayment of a shared appreciation loan shall not exceed the amount authorized and specified in subdivision (b) of Section 2954.9.

(d) No prepayment charge shall be imposed as to any portion of the contingent deferred interest. *(Added by Stats.1982, c. 466, p. 1992, § 12.)*

Operative Effect

Chapter 5 became inoperative January 1, 1987 pursuant to Stats.1982, c. 466, § 12.5. For continuing application of Chapter 5, see Historical and Statutory Notes under Civil Code § 1917.110.

Cross References

Borrower defined for purposes of this Chapter, see Civil Code § 1917.120.

Contingent deferred interest defined for purposes of this Chapter, see Civil Code § 1917.120.

Interest defined, see Civil Code § 1915.

Shared appreciation loan defined for purposes of this Chapter, see Civil Code § 1917.120.

§ 1917.133. Refinancing

(a) If a shared appreciation loan with an original term of less than 10 years is not prepaid in full or the property is not sold or transferred prior to maturity of the loan, and provided the borrower is not then in default, the lender shall offer or arrange for refinancing of the unpaid balance of the loan upon maturity and all contingent deferred interest. The refinancing may be provided directly by the lender or another mortgage lender, or the lender may arrange at the time of making the shared appreciation loan for the refinancing to be provided by a federally or state chartered bank or savings and loan association doing business in this state or by a qualified mortgage banker. As used in this section "qualified mortgage banker" means a lender (1) meeting the criteria established by the Government National Mortgage Association for lenders selling over ten million dollars ($10,000,000) in mortgage loans to that organization annually and (2) which either has conducted an ongoing business of mortgage lending in this state for not less than five years immediately preceding the making of the shared appreciation loans, or made over fifty million dollars ($50,000,000) in mortgage loans in this state during the 12 months immediately preceding the making of the shared appreciation loan. If a refinancing commitment is arranged by the lender upon origination of the shared appreciation loan, this fact shall be fully and fairly disclosed to the borrower, a copy of the lender's contract with the bank, savings and loan association or qualified mortgage banker making the commitment shall be supplied to the borrower at such time, and the contract shall be fully enforceable by the borrower as a third-party beneficiary thereto, but the lender shall not be a guarantor of the obligation of the bank, savings and loan association, or qualified mortgage banker to provide refinancing.

If the original lender is a bank or savings and loan association doing business in this state or a qualified mortgage banker, it may provide the refinancing commitment to the borrower required by this section and assignees or successors in interest of the original lender shall not be guarantors of the refinancing obligation, provided the shared appreciation loan contains this limitation, which is fully and fairly disclosed to the borrower, and the original lender's refinancing commitment is fully enforceable by the borrower.

(b) The term of the loan for refinancing shall be established so that the borrower's repayment schedule provides for the final installment payment not less than 30 years from the date of origination of the shared appreciation loan. However, if loans at that duration are not available, within the meaning of subdivision (d), the lender or other obligor shall give the borrower a choice of any form of loan and maturity for that type of loan which is available at the time of refinancing, within the meaning of subdivision (d). The lender or other obligor shall inform the borrower of the types of loans (and maturities) available for refinancing under this section not less than 60 days prior to maturity of the shared appreciation loan.

(c) The interest rate for the refinancing loan shall not exceed rates generally available in the market for the type of loan instrument provided under subdivision (d) at the time of maturity of the shared appreciation loan. No loan origination fees shall be required of the borrower, either as prepaid interest or for processing services, as a condition of obtaining a refinancing loan pursuant to this section, but the borrower may be required to pay the costs of obtaining a policy of title insurance in accordance with the lender's requirements. The refinancing loan need not be a fixed interest rate loan, subject to the limitations of subdivision (d).

(d) The refinancing loan may be any form of loan which, at the time of refinancing, is generally offered to and utilized by the public for financing housing like the borrower's property by banks or savings and loan associations doing business in this state.

(e) The lender may require as a condition of the refinancing loan that it be secured by a deed of trust having a lien of first priority. (Added by Stats.1982, c. 466, p. 1993, § 12.)

Operative Effect

Chapter 5 became inoperative January 1, 1987 pursuant to Stats.1982, c. 466, § 12.5. For continuing application of Chapter 5, see Historical and Statutory Notes under Civil Code § 1917.110.

Cross References

Borrower defined for purposes of this Chapter, see Civil Code § 1917.120.
Contingent deferred interest defined for purposes of this Chapter, see Civil Code § 1917.120.
Interest defined, see Civil Code § 1915.
Lender defined for purposes of this Chapter, see Civil Code § 1917.120.
Property defined for purposes of this Chapter, see Civil Code § 1917.120.
Shared appreciation loan defined for purposes of this Chapter, see Civil Code § 1917.120.

§ 1917.134. Laws applicable to refinancing

Except as provided in this article, the terms and conditions of the refinancing loan shall be subject to all laws applicable to loans in effect on the date of refinancing. (Added by Stats.1982, c. 466, p. 1994, § 12.)

Operative Effect

Chapter 5 became inoperative January 1, 1987 pursuant to Stats.1982, c. 466, § 12.5. For continuing application of Chapter 5, see Historical and Statutory Notes under Civil Code § 1917.110.

§ 1917.135. Alternative refinancing

Nothing in this chapter shall preclude the borrower from obtaining any other financing, in lieu of the refinancing provided for in Section 1917.133, including refinancing on other terms mutually agreeable to the borrower and lender. (Added by Stats.1982, c. 466, p. 1994, § 12.)

Operative Effect

Chapter 5 became inoperative January 1, 1987 pursuant to Stats.1982, c. 466, § 12.5. For continuing application of Chapter 5, see Historical and Statutory Notes under Civil Code § 1917.110.

Cross References

Borrower defined for purposes of this Chapter, see Civil Code § 1917.120.
Lender defined for purposes of this Chapter, see Civil Code § 1917.120.

ARTICLE 4. DETERMINATION OF FAIR MARKET VALUE [INOPERATIVE]

Section
1917.140. Lender's estimate; good faith.
1917.141. Cash sale; challenge to reasonableness of price.
1917.142. Average of two appraisals; selection and qualifications of appraisers; costs.

Article 4 was added by Stats.1982, c. 466, p. 1994, § 12.

Operative Effect

Chapter 5 became inoperative January 1, 1987 pursuant to Stats.1982, c. 466, § 12.5. For continuing application of Chapter 5, see Historical and Statutory Notes under Civil Code § 1917.110.

Cross References

Fair market value, see Civil Code § 1917.120.

§ 1917.140. Lender's estimate; good faith

The borrower may, at any time for the purpose of facilitating a sale of the property, request the lender to stipulate the minimum amount which the lender considers to be the fair market value of the property for the purposes of this chapter. The lender shall advise the borrower within 10 working days of the receipt of such request of the lender's estimate of the minimum fair market value. The estimate shall remain effective for purposes of this section for 90 days. For the purposes of this section and Section 1917.141, a sale of the property shall be deemed to have occurred within the 90-day period if there is a valid contract entered by an offer and acceptance within the 90-day period for the sale of the property. The lender's stipulation shall remain effective for an additional 60 days following execution of the sale contract to permit completion of the sale and close of escrow.

The lender shall not be liable to the borrower or any other party on account of damages alleged as a result of providing the stipulation or estimate required by this section if such stipulation or estimate is made in good faith. Evidence of lack of good faith shall include, but not be limited to, a showing that the lender has willfully or repeatedly overrepresented the fair market value of other properties in similar situations, applying equitable principles to those determinations. The lender shall be conclusively presumed to have acted in good faith and no action may be brought or maintained against a lender which arises out of the provision by the lender of such stipulation or estimate, if the lender relied upon an appraisal of an independent appraiser approved by the Federal National Mortgage Association. *(Added by Stats.1982, c. 466, p. 1994, § 12.)*

Operative Effect

Chapter 5 became inoperative January 1, 1987 pursuant to Stats.1982, c. 466, § 12.5. For continuing application of Chapter 5, see Historical and Statutory Notes under Civil Code § 1917.110.

Cross References

Borrower defined for purposes of this Chapter, see Civil Code § 1917.120.
Fair market value defined for purposes of this Chapter, see Civil Code § 1917.120.
Lender defined for purposes of this Chapter, see Civil Code § 1917.120.
Property defined for purposes of this Chapter, see Civil Code § 1917.120.

Sale defined for purposes of this Chapter, see Civil Code § 1917.120.

§ 1917.141. Cash sale; challenge to reasonableness of price

(a) In the case of a sale for cash within 90 days after the lender stipulates, under the provisions of Section 1917.140, a minimum amount which the lender considers to be the fair market value of the property, the fair market value shall be the gross sale price, unless the gross sales price is below the minimum amount stipulated by the lender and the lender contests in writing the reasonableness of the gross sale price in relation to the fair market value within 10 working days of the lender's receipt of notice of the gross sale price from borrower, in which case fair market value shall be the greater of gross sale price or the amount determined under Section 1917.142.

(b) In the case of a sale for cash where the borrower has not requested the lender under the provisions of Section 1917.140 to stipulate to the minimum amount which the lender considers to be the fair market value of the property or where the stipulated minimum amount was provided by the lender more than 90 days prior to the date of sale, fair market value shall be the gross sale price, unless lender contests in writing the reasonableness of the gross sale price in relation to the fair market value within 10 working days of the lender's receipt of notice of the gross sale price from borrower, in which case fair market value shall be the greater of gross sale price or the amount determined under Section 1917.142.

(c) In the case of a sale which includes consideration to the seller other than cash, fair market value shall be as determined under Section 1917.142.

(d) In the case the shared appreciation loan is prepaid in full, or upon acceleration of the shared appreciation loan upon default, or upon maturity of the shared appreciation loan, fair market value shall be as determined under Section 1917.142. *(Added by Stats.1982, c. 466, p. 1995, § 12.)*

Operative Effect

Chapter 5 became inoperative January 1, 1987 pursuant to Stats.1982, c. 466, § 12.5. For continuing application of Chapter 5, see Historical and Statutory Notes under Civil Code § 1917.110.

Cross References

Borrower defined for purposes of this Chapter, see Civil Code § 1917.120.
Fair market value defined for purposes of this Chapter, see Civil Code § 1917.120.
Lender defined for purposes of this Chapter, see Civil Code § 1917.120.
Property defined for purposes of this Chapter, see Civil Code § 1917.120.
Sale defined for purposes of this Chapter, see Civil Code § 1917.120.
Shared appreciation loan defined for purposes of this Chapter, see Civil Code § 1917.120.

§ 1917.142. Average of two appraisals; selection and qualifications of appraisers; costs

When Section 1917.141 requires the application of this section, the fair market value shall be determined as the average of two appraisals of the property performed as described in this section. If possible, the appraisals shall be based on the sale prices of comparable properties in the

§ 1917.142

market area sold within the preceding three-month period. The appraisals shall be made upon request of the lender by two independent residential appraisers, one to be selected by the lender and one by the borrower. Each appraiser shall be approved by the Federal National Mortgage Association. The cost of the appraiser selected by the lender shall be borne by the lender, and the cost of the appraiser selected by the borrower shall be borne by the borrower, unless the average of the two appraisals equals or is less than the gross sale price of the property, in which case the lender shall also pay the fee of the borrower's appraiser up to two hundred dollars ($200). If either of the appraisers determines that the gross sale price does not reasonably reflect the fair market value of the property, or, in the case of a sale for which appraisal is required by this section, then the fair market value of the property shall be determined as the average of the two appraisals. If the borrower fails to select a qualified appraiser within 15 days after the lender has notified the borrower in writing of the lender's request for an appraisal of the property, the reasons therefor, and the borrower's option to select an independent appraiser within 15 days after the lender's request is submitted to the borrower, the lender may designate the second appraiser, provided the lender's request informs the borrower of this time limitation, and that the lender will select an appraiser on behalf of the borrower in the event the borrower fails to designate an appraiser, with consequent cost to the borrower. If pursuant to this section the lender designates the second appraiser, the cost of both appraisals shall be borne equally by the borrower and lender. If in any case the property has been damaged (other than normal wear and tear) and the damage has not been fully repaired, the determination of fair market value shall be based on the condition of the property not including the damage.

Nothing in this section shall preclude the borrower and lender from establishing the fair market value of the property by mutual agreement in lieu of appraisals pursuant to this section. (Added by Stats.1982, c. 466, p. 1995, § 12.)

Operative Effect

Chapter 5 became inoperative January 1, 1987 pursuant to Stats.1982, c. 466, § 12.5. For continuing application of Chapter 5, see Historical and Statutory Notes under Civil Code § 1917.110.

Cross References

Appraisal of improvements, selection of appraisers, see Civil Code § 1917.150.
Borrower defined for purposes of this Chapter, see Civil Code § 1917.120.
Fair market value defined for purposes of this Chapter, see Civil Code § 1917.120.
Lender defined for purposes of this Chapter, see Civil Code § 1917.120.
Property defined for purposes of this Chapter, see Civil Code § 1917.120.
Sale defined for purposes of this Chapter, see Civil Code § 1917.120.

ARTICLE 5. IMPROVEMENTS [INOPERATIVE]

Section
1917.150. Addition of value of improvements to borrower's cost; appraisal.
1917.151. Additional credit.

Article 5 was added by Stats.1982, c. 466, p. 1996, § 12.

Operative Effect

Chapter 5 became inoperative January 1, 1987 pursuant to Stats.1982, c. 466, § 12.5. For continuing application of Chapter 5, see Historical and Statutory Notes under Civil Code § 1917.110.

Cross References

Value of capital improvements defined for purposes of this Chapter, see Civil Code § 1917.120.

§ 1917.150. Addition of value of improvements to borrower's cost; appraisal

The borrower may have the value of capital improvements added to the borrower's cost of the property, for purposes of determining net appreciated value and the amount of contingent deferred interest, but only if the procedures set forth in this article are followed.

(a) Within 60 days following the completion of capital improvements during any 12-month period with a cost in excess of two thousand five hundred dollars ($2,500), the borrower shall send by first-class mail a notice of the completion of the improvements to the lender and shall submit proof of cost and an estimate of the increase in value of the property by reason of the improvements.

(b) If, within 30 days of receipt of the notice, the lender questions the claimed increase in value of the property by reason of the improvements, the lender and the borrower may, by mutual agreement, establish the value of the capital improvements or the lender may require appraisal of the property. An appraisal shall be made to determine the increase in value of the property, if any, by reason of the improvements, by two appraisers selected in the same manner specified in Section 1917.142. If appraisals are performed, the increase in value resulting from the improvements for the purposes of this section, shall be one-half of the sum of the two appraisals. The cost of the appraiser selected by the borrower shall be borne by the borrower, and the cost of the appraiser selected by the lender shall be borne by the lender.

(c) A credit for the value of capital improvements shall be provided if the increase in value of the property resulting therefrom is determined pursuant to subdivision (b) to exceed two thousand five hundred dollars ($2,500).

(d) If 50 percent or more of the value of the labor or other work on the improvements was performed by the borrower, then the actual cost of the improvements need not exceed two thousand five hundred dollars ($2,500) for purposes of making application under subdivision (a). (Added by Stats. 1982, c. 466, p. 1996, § 12.)

Operative Effect

Chapter 5 became inoperative January 1, 1987 pursuant to Stats.1982, c. 466, § 12.5. For continuing application of Chapter 5, see Historical and Statutory Notes under Civil Code § 1917.110.

Cross References

Borrower defined for purposes of this Chapter, see Civil Code § 1917.120.

Borrower's cost of the property defined for purposes of this Chapter, see Civil Code § 1917.120.

Contingent deferred interest defined for purposes of this Chapter, see Civil Code § 1917.120.

Interest defined, see Civil Code § 1915.

Lender defined for purposes of this Chapter, see Civil Code § 1917.120.

Net appreciated value defined for purposes of this Chapter, see Civil Code § 1917.120.

Property defined for purposes of this Chapter, see Civil Code § 1917.120.

Value of capital improvements defined for purposes of this Chapter, see Civil Code § 1917.120.

§ 1917.151. Additional credit

Nothing in this article shall preclude a shared appreciation loan from providing the borrower with a greater credit for improvements than specified in this article, provided the relevant disclosures required by Article 7 (commencing with Section 1917.170) are appropriately modified to accurately disclose the terms of the credit. *(Added by Stats.1982, c. 466, p. 1997, § 12.)*

Operative Effect

Chapter 5 became inoperative January 1, 1987 pursuant to Stats.1982, c. 466, § 12.5. For continuing application of Chapter 5, see Historical and Statutory Notes under Civil Code § 1917.110.

Cross References

Borrower defined for purposes of this Chapter, see Civil Code § 1917.120.

Shared appreciation loan defined for purposes of this Chapter, see Civil Code § 1917.120.

ARTICLE 6. GENERAL PROVISIONS [INOPERATIVE]

Section
1917.160. Relationship of borrower and lender.
1917.161. Waiver of borrower's rights; prohibition.
1917.162. Acceleration of maturity upon sale or transfer.
1917.163. Conformity of loan terms and conditions to chapter; application of chapter.
1917.164. Exemption of loans under this chapter from interest laws applicable to other loans.
1917.165. Scope of lien.
1917.166. Lien; time of attachment; priority; junior lien.
1917.167. Usury exemption.
1917.168. Exemption from qualification requirements for corporate securities.

Article 6 was added by Stats.1982, c. 466, p. 1989, § 12.

Operative Effect

Chapter 5 became inoperative January 1, 1987 pursuant to Stats.1982, c. 466, § 12.5. For continuing application of Chapter 5, see Historical and Statutory Notes under Civil Code § 1917.110.

§ 1917.160. Relationship of borrower and lender

The relationship of the borrower and the lender, as to a shared appreciation loan, is that of debtor and creditor and shall not be, or be construed to be, a joint venture, equity venture, partnership, or other relationship. *(Added by Stats.1982, c. 466, p. 1997, § 12.)*

Operative Effect

Chapter 5 became inoperative January 1, 1987 pursuant to Stats.1982, c. 466, § 12.5. For continuing application of Chapter 5, see Historical and Statutory Notes under Civil Code § 1917.110.

Cross References

Borrower defined for purposes of this Chapter, see Civil Code § 1917.120.

Lender defined for purposes of this Chapter, see Civil Code § 1917.120.

Shared appreciation loan defined for purposes of this Chapter, see Civil Code § 1917.120.

§ 1917.161. Waiver of borrower's rights; prohibition

Any waiver of any right of a borrower under the provisions of this chapter shall be void and unenforceable. *(Added by Stats.1982, c. 466, p. 1997, § 12.)*

Operative Effect

Chapter 5 became inoperative January 1, 1987 pursuant to Stats.1982, c. 466, § 12.5. For continuing application of Chapter 5, see Historical and Statutory Notes under Civil Code § 1917.110.

Cross References

Borrower defined for purposes of this Chapter, see Civil Code § 1917.120.

§ 1917.162. Acceleration of maturity upon sale or transfer

(a) Notwithstanding Section 711, a provision in a shared appreciation loan made pursuant to this chapter permitting the lender to accelerate the maturity date of the principal and accrued interest on the loan upon sale of the property shall be valid and enforceable against the borrower, except as may be precluded by Section 2924.6.

(b) The Legislature finds and declares that potential exposure to liability for enforcement of a "due-on-sale" clause consistent with Section 711, as interpreted by the courts, makes use of such a provision impractical. Moreover, the additional risks to the lender inherent in shared appreciation financing are greater with longer loan terms (which are more desirable from the standpoint of housing affordability), but this risk is reduced with an enforceable "due-on-sale" clause. Therefore, in order to facilitate shared appreciation financing, it is necessary to establish the exception specified in subdivision (a). *(Added by Stats.1982, c. 466, p. 1997, § 12.)*

Operative Effect

Chapter 5 became inoperative January 1, 1987 pursuant to Stats.1982, c. 466, § 12.5. For continuing application of Chapter 5, see Historical and Statutory Notes under Civil Code § 1917.110.

Cross References

Borrower defined for purposes of this Chapter, see Civil Code § 1917.120.

Interest defined, see Civil Code § 1915.

Lender defined for purposes of this Chapter, see Civil Code § 1917.120.

§ 1917.162

Obligation to pay contingent deferred interest upon acceleration of loan, see Civil Code § 1917.131.
Property defined for purposes of this Chapter, see Civil Code § 1917.120.
Sale defined for purposes of this Chapter, see Civil Code § 1917.120.
Shared appreciation loan defined for purposes of this Chapter, see Civil Code § 1917.120.

§ 1917.163. Conformity of loan terms and conditions to chapter; application of chapter

This chapter facilitates the making of shared appreciation financing in this state which conforms to the provisions of this chapter. The terms and conditions of any shared appreciation loan made pursuant to this chapter shall be consistent with this chapter. This chapter does not, however, apply to or limit shared appreciation financing of real property of a type specified in Section 1917.130 that is made pursuant to other provisions of law, or which is not otherwise unlawful. Nothing in this chapter shall be construed to in any way affect shared appreciation financing of commercial property or residential property not meeting the criteria specified in Section 1917.130. *(Added by Stats.1982, c. 466, p. 1997, § 12.)*

Operative Effect

Chapter 5 became inoperative January 1, 1987 pursuant to Stats.1982, c. 466, § 12.5. For continuing application of Chapter 5, see Historical and Statutory Notes under Civil Code § 1917.110.

Cross References

Property defined for purposes of this Chapter, see Civil Code § 1917.120.
Shared appreciation loan defined for purposes of this Chapter, see Civil Code § 1917.120.

§ 1917.164. Exemption of loans under this chapter from interest laws applicable to other loans

A shared appreciation loan shall not be subject to any provision of this code or the Financial Code which limits the interest rate or change of interest rate of variable interest rate or renegotiable interest instruments, or which requires particular language or provisions in security instruments securing variable or renegotiable rate obligations or in evidences of those debts.

This section is declaratory of existing law. *(Added by Stats.1982, c. 466, p. 1998, § 12.)*

Operative Effect

Chapter 5 became inoperative January 1, 1987 pursuant to Stats.1982, c. 466, § 12.5. For continuing application of Chapter 5, see Historical and Statutory Notes under Civil Code § 1917.110.

Cross References

Interest defined, see Civil Code § 1915.
Shared appreciation loan defined for purposes of this Chapter, see Civil Code § 1917.120.

§ 1917.165. Scope of lien

The lien of a deed of trust securing a shared appreciation loan shall include and secure the principal amount of the shared appreciation loan, and all interest, whether accrued or to be accrued, including all amounts of contingent deferred interest. *(Added by Stats.1982, c. 466, p. 1998, § 12.)*

Operative Effect

Chapter 5 became inoperative January 1, 1987 pursuant to Stats.1982, c. 466, § 12.5. For continuing application of Chapter 5, see Historical and Statutory Notes under Civil Code § 1917.110.

Cross References

Contingent deferred interest defined for purposes of this Chapter, see Civil Code § 1917.120.
Interest defined, see Civil Code § 1915.
Shared appreciation loan, junior lien, see Civil Code § 1917.066.
Shared appreciation loan defined for purposes of this Chapter, see Civil Code § 1917.120.

§ 1917.166. Lien; time of attachment; priority; junior lien

The lien of a shared appreciation loan, including the principal amount and all interest, whether accrued or to be accrued, and all amounts of contingent deferred interest, shall attach from the time of the recordation of the deed of trust securing the loan, and the lien, including the lien of the interest accrued or to be accrued and of the contingent deferred interest, shall have priority over any other lien or encumbrance affecting the property secured by the shared appreciation instrument, recorded after the time of recordation of the shared appreciation instrument. However, nothing in this section or Section 1917.165 shall preclude a junior lien or encumbrance subordinate to the obligation of the shared appreciation loan. In no case may a junior lien achieve priority over the lien securing the obligation of the shared appreciation loan, provided that nothing in this section shall be construed to supersede Section 8450. *(Added by Stats.1982, c. 466, p. 1998, § 12. Amended by Stats. 2010, c. 697 (S.B.189), § 11, operative July 1, 2012.)*

Operative Effect

Chapter 5 became inoperative January 1, 1987 pursuant to Stats.1982, c. 466, § 12.5. For continuing application of Chapter 5, see Historical and Statutory Notes under Civil Code § 1917.110.

Cross References

Contingent deferred interest defined for purposes of this Chapter, see Civil Code § 1917.120.
Interest defined, see Civil Code § 1915.
Property defined for purposes of this Chapter, see Civil Code § 1917.120.
Shared appreciation loan defined for purposes of this Chapter, see Civil Code § 1917.120.

§ 1917.167. Usury exemption

A shared appreciation loan which at origination bears a fixed interest rate complying with the usury provisions of Article XV of the California Constitution shall not be deemed to become usurious by reason of the payment of contingent deferred interest pursuant to this chapter. *(Added by Stats.1982, c. 466, p. 1998, § 12.)*

Operative Effect

Chapter 5 became inoperative January 1, 1987 pursuant to Stats.1982, c. 466, § 12.5. For continu-

ing application of Chapter 5, see Historical and Statutory Notes under Civil Code § 1917.110.

Cross References

Contingent deferred interest defined for purposes of this Chapter, see Civil Code § 1917.120.
Interest defined, see Civil Code § 1915.
Shared appreciation loan defined for purposes of this Chapter, see Civil Code § 1917.120.

§ 1917.168. Exemption from qualification requirements for corporate securities

The qualification requirements of Sections 25110, 25120, and 25130 of the Corporations Code do not apply to a shared appreciation loan to the extent the exemption afforded by subdivision (p) of Section 25100 of that code is applicable. (Added by Stats.1982, c. 466, p. 1998, § 12.)

Operative Effect

Chapter 5 became inoperative January 1, 1987 pursuant to Stats.1982, c. 466, § 12.5. For continuing application of Chapter 5, see Historical and Statutory Notes under Civil Code § 1917.110.

Cross References

Shared appreciation loan defined for purposes of this Chapter, see Civil Code § 1917.120.

ARTICLE 7. NOTICES AND DISCLOSURES [INOPERATIVE]

Section
1917.170. Exemption from disclosures required by other laws; exceptions; use of equivalent language.
1917.171. Initial disclosure; time; form.
1917.172. Disclosures required by federal regulation.
1917.173. Statement to be given prospective borrower.
1917.174. Statement in deed of trust and evidence of debt.
1917.175. Interest disclosure.

Article 7 was added by Stats.1982, c. 466, p. 1998, § 12.

Operative Effect

Chapter 5 became inoperative January 1, 1987 pursuant to Stats.1982, c. 466, § 12.5. For continuing application of Chapter 5, see Historical and Statutory Notes under Civil Code § 1917.110.

Cross References

Additional credit for improvements, modification of disclosures, see Civil Code § 1917.151.

§ 1917.170. Exemption from disclosures required by other laws; exceptions; use of equivalent language

(a) The disclosures made pursuant to this chapter, as required, shall be the only disclosures required to be made pursuant to state law for shared appreciation loans, notwithstanding any contrary provision applicable to loans not made under this chapter, except those, if any, that may be required by reason of the application of Division 1 (commencing with Section 25000) of the Corporations Code, or Chapter 1 (commencing with Section 11000) of Part 2 of Division 4 of the Business and Professions Code. However, a lender shall not be precluded from supplementing the disclosures required by this chapter with additional disclosures that are not inconsistent with the disclosures required by this chapter.

(b) Whenever specific language is prescribed by this chapter, substantially the same language shall be utilized if possible, but reasonably equivalent language may be used to the extent necessary or appropriate to achieve a clearer or more accurate disclosure. (Added by Stats.1982, c. 466, p. 1998, § 12.)

Operative Effect

Chapter 5 became inoperative January 1, 1987 pursuant to Stats.1982, c. 466, § 12.5. For continuing application of Chapter 5, see Historical and Statutory Notes under Civil Code § 1917.110.

Cross References

Lender defined for purposes of this Chapter, see Civil Code § 1917.120.
Shared appreciation loan defined for purposes of this Chapter, see Civil Code § 1917.120.

§ 1917.171. Initial disclosure; time; form

(a) Each lender offering shared appreciation loans shall furnish to a prospective borrower, on the earlier of the dates on which the lender first provides written information concerning shared appreciation loans from the lender or provides a loan application form to the prospective borrower, a written disclosure as provided in this section.

(b) The disclosure shall be entitled "INFORMATION ABOUT THE (Name of Lender) SHARED APPRECIATION LOAN," and shall describe the operation and effect of the shared appreciation loan including a brief summary of its terms and conditions, together with a statement consisting of substantially the following language, to the extent applicable to such loan:

INFORMATION ABOUT THE (Name of Lender)
SHARED
APPRECIATION LOAN

(Name of Lender) is pleased to offer you the opportunity to finance your home through a shared appreciation loan.

Because the shared appreciation loan differs from the usual mortgage loan, the law requires that you have a detailed explanation of the special features of the loan before you apply. Before you sign your particular shared appreciation loan documents, you will receive more information about your particular shared appreciation loan, which you should read and understand before you sign the loan documents.

The loan will bear a stated rate of interest which will be (percent) below the prevailing market interest rate. In exchange for a stated interest rate which is below the prevailing rate, you will be obligated to pay us additional interest later. This additional interest is called "contingent interest."

The loan will require a balloon payment at the end of the _____ year. Thus, if you do not sell the property before that time, you will need to refinance the loan at that time.

§ 1917.171

Contingent Interest

This loan provides that you, as borrower, must pay to us, as lender, as contingent interest, (percent) of the net appreciated value of the real property which secures the loan. This contingent interest is due and payable when the property is sold or transferred, when the loan is paid in full, upon any acceleration of the loan upon default, or at the end of the term of the loan, whichever first occurs. The dollar amount of contingent interest, if any, which you will be required to pay cannot be determined at this time. If the property does not appreciate, you will owe us nothing. The contingent interest will not become due if title to the property is transferred on your death to a spouse, or where a transfer results from a decree of dissolution of a marriage and a spouse becomes the sole owner.

Your obligation to pay contingent interest will reduce the amount of the appreciation, if any, that you will realize on the property. This appreciation will not produce a real gain in your equity in the property, unless the appreciation rate exceeds the general inflation rate, but you will be required to pay a portion of the appreciation as contingent interest without regard to whether the appreciation has resulted in a real gain.

When you sell or refinance your home, you normally will receive enough cash to pay the shared appreciation loan balance, accrued interest, prepayment charge (if applicable), contingent interest, and expenses of sale. However, if you sell with only a small downpayment, you may possibly not receive enough cash to pay the contingent interest, and, in that event, it will be necessary for you to provide cash from other funds.

Calculating the Contingent Interest

Contingent interest will be calculated as follows:

		FAIR MARKET VALUE OF THE PROPERTY (Sale price or appraised value.)
−	(less)	BORROWER'S COST OF THE PROPERTY (This amount includes certain costs paid by you incident to the purchase.)
−	(less)	VALUE OF CAPITAL IMPROVEMENTS MADE BY YOU (Must exceed $2,500 in value. Must also exceed $2,500 in cost unless you perform more than 50% of the value of the labor or work on the improvement.)
=	(equals)	NET APPRECIATED VALUE
×	(times)	_____ PERCENT OWED TO LENDER
=	(equals)	TOTAL CONTINGENT INTEREST

Determining Fair Market Value

If you sell your property for cash before maturity of your shared appreciation loan, the gross sale price will be the fair market value of the property, unless appraisals are requested by us and the appraisals average more than the gross sale price. However, at your request, we also will tell you what we consider to be the fair market value of the property. If you sell for cash for a gross sale price that equals or exceeds that amount, the gross sale price will control and appraisals will not be needed.

Fair market value is determined by appraisals in the event of sales involving a consideration other than cash, prepayment of the loan in full, or maturity of the loan.

When appraisals are required, fair market value is determined by averaging two independent appraisals of the property. You may select one of the two appraisers from a list approved by the Federal National Mortgage Association. If appraisals are requested by us, we will provide you with full information on how to select an appraiser.

In lieu of appraisals, we may establish fair market value at an agreed amount if an agreement can be reached between you and us.

Determining Value of Capital Improvements

Capital improvements with a value exceeding $2,500 (but no maintenance or repair costs) may be added to your cost of the property for the purpose of determining the net appreciated value, but only if the procedures set forth in the shared appreciation loan documents are followed. It is important to note that capital improvements completed and claimed in any 12-month period must add more than $2,500 in value to the property and must generally also cost more than $2,500. However, if you have performed at least half the value of the labor or other work involved, then the cost of the improvements will not be considered. The appraised value of the improvements will be the increase in the value of the property resulting from the improvements. You will receive no credit for minor or major repairs or for improvements that are not appraised at more than $2,500, but the lender will acquire a share of any resulting appreciation in the value of the property.

Determining Net Appreciated Value

We are entitled to receive _____ percent of the net appreciated value of the property as contingent interest. As shown in the chart above, net appreciated value equals (1) the fair market value of the property at the time of the sale or appraisal, less (2) your cost of the property, less (3) the value of any capital improvements for which you are entitled to credit.

Balloon Payment of Principal

If you do not sell the property before the end of the term of this loan, you will need to refinance this loan at that time. The term of this loan is (duration) years. We [are not obligated to refinance either the unpaid balance of the loan or the contingent interest at that time; you alone will be responsible for obtaining refinancing] [will offer or arrange with another lender to refinance the outstanding obligation, including any contingent interest, at that time]. If you refinance this loan, your monthly payments may increase substantially if the property appreciates significantly or if the interest rate on the refinancing loan is much higher than today's prevailing rates. In general, the more your property appreciates, the larger will be the amount of the contingent interest that you will have an obligation to pay or refinance.

Your Right to Refinance This Loan

(For loans with a refinancing obligation)

If the property is not sold or transferred prior to the maturity of the loan, we will offer or arrange with another lender to refinance the outstanding obligation of the loan, including any contingent interest. The refinancing will be at the then prevailing interest rate.

The terms of the refinancing loan will be like those of home loans offered at that time by banks or savings and loan associations. If at the time of refinancing, banks or savings and loan associations in this state offer loans of sufficient duration, you are assured that the combined length of your shared appreciation loan and refinancing loan will be at least 30 years. However, if loans of sufficient duration are not then offered by banks or savings and loan associations, you may elect any type and maturity of loan then offered by banks or savings and loan associations.

We will not be permitted to look to the forecast of your income in offering or arranging for your refinancing loan. The interest rate and specific terms of any refinancing loan will be subject to then-prevailing market conditions. The interest rate and monthly payment upon refinancing cannot be determined at this time. They may be either more or less burdensome to you than the currently prevailing rates and terms.

Tax Consequences

(For all loans)

USE OF THE SHARED APPRECIATION LOAN WILL HAVE INCOME TAX OR ESTATE PLANNING CONSEQUENCES WHICH WILL DEPEND UPON YOUR OWN FINANCIAL AND TAX SITUATION. FOR FURTHER INFORMATION, YOU ARE URGED TO CONSULT YOUR OWN ACCOUNTANT, ATTORNEY, OR OTHER FINANCIAL ADVISOR.

THE QUESTIONS YOU SHOULD DISCUSS INCLUDE THE TAX DEDUCTIBILITY OF THE CONTINGENT INTEREST PAYMENT, YOUR RIGHT TO UTILIZE THAT DEDUCTION IN YEARS OTHER THAN THE YEAR IT IS PAID, AND THE EFFECT OF THE LOSS OF TAX BENEFITS BEFORE THAT TIME.

Other Important Information

(Here insert additional description, if necessary, of the operation and effect of the shared appreciation loan.)

The foregoing describes our shared appreciation loan, includes a summary of all of its important provisions, and informs you of some of the risks of a shared appreciation loan.

If your loan application is accepted by us, we will provide you with more information about your particular shared appreciation loan, which will include a comparison with conventional mortgages, an illustration of the possible increase in your monthly payments upon refinancing, and other important information.

Before you enter into a shared appreciation loan with us, we recommend that you and your attorney or tax accountant review the loan documents for the full text of all of the terms and conditions which will govern the loan. *(Added by Stats.1982, c. 466, p. 1999, § 12.)*

Operative Effect

Chapter 5 became inoperative January 1, 1987 pursuant to Stats.1982, c. 466, § 12.5. For continuing application of Chapter 5, see Historical and Statutory Notes under Civil Code § 1917.110.

Cross References

Borrower defined for purposes of this Chapter, see Civil Code § 1917.120.
Borrower's cost of the property defined for purposes of this Chapter, see Civil Code § 1917.120.
Fair market value defined for purposes of this Chapter, see Civil Code § 1917.120.
Interest defined, see Civil Code § 1915.
Lender defined for purposes of this Chapter, see Civil Code § 1917.120.
Loan for use defined, see Civil Code § 1884.
Modification of disclosures when deduction of borrowers costs of selling allowed, see Civil Code § 1917.120.
Net appreciated value defined for purposes of this Chapter, see Civil Code § 1917.120.
Prevailing rate defined for purposes of this Chapter, see Civil Code § 1917.120.
Property defined for purposes of this Chapter, see Civil Code § 1917.120.
Sale defined for purposes of this Chapter, see Civil Code § 1917.120.
Shared appreciation loan defined for purposes of this Chapter, see Civil Code § 1917.120.
Shared appreciation loans of E.R.I.S.A. pension funds, notices and disclosures, see Civil Code § 1917.072.
Value of capital improvements defined for purposes of this Chapter, see Civil Code § 1917.120.

§ 1917.172. Disclosures required by federal regulation

(a) Each lender making a shared appreciation loan shall also furnish to the prospective borrower, prior to the consummation of the loan, the disclosures required by Subpart C of Federal Reserve Board Regulation Z (12 CFR Part 226), including 12 CFR Section 226.18(f), to the extent applicable to the transaction.

(b) The disclosure made pursuant to subdivision (a) and Regulation Z shall be based on the fixed interest rate of the shared appreciation loan, and shall include a description of the shared appreciation feature, including (1) the conditions for its imposition, the time at which it would be collected, and the limitations on the lender's share, as required by the Federal Reserve Board in the information published by the board in 46 Federal Register 20877–78 (April 7, 1981), and (2) the lender's share of the net appreciated value and the prevailing interest rate as defined in Section 1917.120 of the Civil Code.

(c) The disclosure made pursuant to subdivision (a) and Regulation Z shall be accompanied by (1) one or more transaction-specific examples of the operation and effect of the shared appreciation loan and (2) the following charts comparing the shared appreciation loan and a conventional loan made at the prevailing interest rate, and illustrating the possible increase in the monthly payments, and the possible annual percentage rate of finance charge, on the assumptions therein stated:

§ 1917.172   OBLIGATIONS

Chart 1

CONVENTIONAL MORTGAGE AT __%

If the same loan balance were financed under a conventional, 30-year, fixed-rate, level-payment mortgage, your monthly payments would be:

Years 1-30

$_____/mo.

Chart 2

IF YOU REFINANCE THIS TRANSACTION at __%

If your property appreciates at 10% per year, and if your loan balance (including contingent interest due) at the end of ____ years is refinanced at __% (the prevailing market interest rate now), your monthly payments will be:

Years 1-__	Refinancing loan
$_____/mo.	$_____/mo.*

* Refinancing loan, assuming a conventional 30-year fixed-rate, level-payment mortgage. Other mortgage instruments, e.g., graduated-payment or shared-appreciation, if available, may result in lower payments.

Chart 3

APR IF PROPERTY APPRECIATES AT 10%

If your property appreciates at 10% per year, and if your loan balance on your shared appreciation loan (including contingent interest) will equal $_____, and the annual percentage rate of the total finance charge (including contingent interest) will equal _____%.

(d) The disclosures required by subdivision (c) shall be separate from the disclosures required by Regulation Z, and may be presented in the document containing the disclosures required by Regulation Z or in one or more separate documents.

(e) Except to the extent that this section requires disclosure of additional information not required by Regulation Z, compliance with the applicable credit disclosure requirements of Regulation Z shall constitute compliance with the requirements of this section.

(f) The disclosure prescribed in Section 1917.171 shall be physically attached to the disclosures required by this section and Regulation Z at the time the Regulation Z disclosures are furnished to the borrower.

(g) In the event federal law is amended so that this section is inconsistent therewith, the federal law shall prevail as to the disclosures required by this section. (Added by Stats. 1982, c. 466, p. 2003, § 12.)

Operative Effect

Chapter 5 became inoperative January 1, 1987 pursuant to Stats.1982, c. 466, § 12.5. For continuing application of Chapter 5, see Historical and Statutory Notes under Civil Code § 1917.110.

Cross References

Borrower defined for purposes of this Chapter, see Civil Code § 1917.120.
Interest defined, see Civil Code § 1915.
Lender defined for purposes of this Chapter, see Civil Code § 1917.120.
Net appreciated value defined for purposes of this Chapter, see Civil Code § 1917.120.
Property defined for purposes of this Chapter, see Civil Code § 1917.120.
Shared appreciation loan defined for purposes of this Chapter, see Civil Code § 1917.120.

§ 1917.173. Statement to be given prospective borrower

Each lender making a shared appreciation loan shall additionally furnish to the prospective borrower, prior to consummation of the loan, a statement containing the following information:

IMPORTANT INFORMATION ABOUT YOUR SHARED APPRECIATION LOAN

You are being offered a shared appreciation loan. Before you decide to accept this loan, read this statement, which is designed to provide important information you should consider.

1. Prevailing interest rate: ____%.
2. Interest rate on this loan: ____%.
3. Lender's share of net appreciated value: ____%.
4. Amount of this loan: $____.
5. Amount of the monthly payments: $____.
6. Term of this loan: ____ years.
7. Amortization period on which payments are calculated: ____ years.
8. Prepayment charge (if any): ____. *(Added by Stats. 1982, c. 466, p. 2005, § 12.)*

Operative Effect

Chapter 5 became inoperative January 1, 1987 pursuant to Stats.1982, c. 466, § 12.5. For continuing application of Chapter 5, see Historical and Statutory Notes under Civil Code § 1917.110.

Cross References

Borrower defined for purposes of this Chapter, see Civil Code § 1917.120.
Interest defined, see Civil Code § 1915.
Lender defined for purposes of this Chapter, see Civil Code § 1917.120.
Net appreciated value defined for purposes of this Chapter, see Civil Code § 1917.120.
Shared appreciation loan defined for purposes of this Chapter, see Civil Code § 1917.120.

§ 1917.174. Statement in deed of trust and evidence of debt

Each deed of trust and evidence of debt executed in connection with a shared appreciation loan shall contain a statement, printed or written in a size equal to at least 12-point bold type, consisting of substantially the following language: "THIS IS A [DURATION] SHARED APPRECIATION LOAN. THE LENDER'S INTEREST INCLUDES [PERCENT] OF THE NET APPRECIATED VALUE OF THE PROPERTY. A BALLOON PAYMENT OF PRINCIPAL WILL BE REQUIRED. FOR FURTHER INFORMATION, READ THE FLYER ENTITLED 'INFORMA-

TION ABOUT THE [NAME OF LENDER] SHARED APPRECIATION LOAN.'" The notice required by this section shall be completed to state the terms of the shared appreciation loan and the lender's share of the net appreciated value. *(Added by Stats.1982, c. 466, p. 2005, § 12.)*

Operative Effect

Chapter 5 became inoperative January 1, 1987 pursuant to Stats.1982, c. 466, § 12.5. For continuing application of Chapter 5, see Historical and Statutory Notes under Civil Code § 1917.110.

Cross References

Interest defined, see Civil Code § 1915.
Lender defined for purposes of this Chapter, see Civil Code § 1917.120.
Net appreciated value defined for purposes of this Chapter, see Civil Code § 1917.120.
Property defined for purposes of this Chapter, see Civil Code § 1917.120.
Shared appreciation loan defined for purposes of this Chapter, see Civil Code § 1917.120.

§ 1917.175. Interest disclosure

Where, pursuant to any provision of law, the lender is required to disclose the amount of interest due or to be due under a shared appreciation loan and the amount of contingent deferred interest due or to be due is not known, the lender may disclose that fact and specify in the disclosure the method for calculating contingent deferred interest. *(Added by Stats.1982, c. 466, p. 2005, § 12.)*

Operative Effect

Chapter 5 became inoperative January 1, 1987 pursuant to Stats.1982, c. 466, § 12.5. For continuing application of Chapter 5, see Historical and Statutory Notes under Civil Code § 1917.110.

Cross References

Contingent deferred interest defined for purposes of this Chapter, see Civil Code § 1917.120.
Interest defined, see Civil Code § 1915.
Lender defined for purposes of this Chapter, see Civil Code § 1917.120.
Shared appreciation loan defined for purposes of this Chapter, see Civil Code § 1917.120.

CHAPTER 6. LOANS OF E.R.I.S.A. PENSION FUNDS

Section
1917.210. License or certificate; exemption.
1917.220. Usury exemption.

Cross References

Bribery to procure a loan, see Penal Code §§ 639, 639a.
Home Equity Loan Disclosure Act, see Civil Code § 2970 et seq.
Insurance in connection with sales and loans, see Insurance Code § 770 et seq.
Insurance loans and investments, see Insurance Code § 1100 et seq.
Interest, see Civil Code § 1914 et seq.
Liability of lender financing design, manufacture, construction, repair, modification or improvement of real or personal property, see Civil Code § 3434.
Loan for exchange, see Civil Code § 1902 et seq.
Loans of E.R.I.S.A. pension funds, see Civil Code § 1917.210 et seq.
Mortgage loans, see Civil Code § 1920 et seq.
National Housing Act loans, see Financial Code § 27000 et seq.
Precomputed interest, see Civil Code § 1799.5.
Shared appreciation loans, see Civil Code § 1917 et seq.
Shared appreciation loans for seniors, see Civil Code § 1917.320 et seq.
Translation of contracts negotiated in language other than English, see Civil Code § 1632.

§ 1917.210. License or certificate; exemption

Each pension fund or retirement system which is subject to the Employee Retirement Income Security Act of 1974 (P.L. 93–406),[1] shall not be required to obtain any license or certificate in order to provide funds for any type of loan transaction permitted by law. *(Added by Stats.1983, c. 557, § 2.)*

[1] 29 U.S.C.A. § 1001 et seq.

§ 1917.220. Usury exemption

Pursuant to the authority contained in Section 1 of Article XV of the California Constitution, the restrictions upon rates of interest contained in Section 1 of Article XV of the California Constitution shall not apply to any obligation of, loan made by, or forbearance of, any pension fund or retirement system which is subject to the Employee Retirement Income Security Act of 1974 (P.L. 93–406).[1]

This section creates and authorizes pension funds or retirement systems subject to the Employee Retirement Income Security Act of 1974 (P.L. 93–406) as an exempt class of persons pursuant to Section 1 of Article XV of the Constitution. *(Added by Stats.1983, c. 557, § 2.)*

[1] 29 U.S.C.A. § 1001 et seq.

Cross References

Interest defined, see Civil Code § 1915.

CHAPTER 7. SHARED APPRECIATION LOANS FOR SENIORS

Article	Section
1. Definitions	1917.320
2. Terms and Conditions	1917.330
3. Determination of Fair Market Value	1917.410
4. Improvements	1917.510
5. General Provisions	1917.610
6. Notices and Disclosures	1917.710

Cross References

Bribery to procure a loan, see Penal Code §§ 639, 639a.
Home Equity Loan Disclosure Act, see Civil Code § 2970 et seq.
Insurance in connection with sales and loans, see Insurance Code § 770 et seq.
Insurance loans and investments, see Insurance Code § 1100 et seq.
Interest, see Civil Code § 1914 et seq.
Liability of lender financing design, manufacture, construction, repair, modification or improvement of real or personal property, see Civil Code § 3434.
Loan for exchange, see Civil Code § 1902 et seq.
Loans of E.R.I.S.A. pension funds, see Civil Code § 1917.210 et seq.
Mortgage loans, see Civil Code § 1920 et seq.
National Housing Act loans, see Financial Code § 27000 et seq.
Precomputed interest, see Civil Code § 1799.5.
Shared appreciation loans, see Civil Code § 1917 et seq.

Translation of contracts negotiated in language other than English, see Civil Code § 1632.

ARTICLE 1. DEFINITIONS

Section
1917.320. Definitions.

§ 1917.320. Definitions

For the purposes of this chapter:

(a) "Actual contingent interest" means the lender's appreciation share of the net appreciated amount. In no event, however, shall the rate of appreciation upon which actual contingent interest is calculated at the end of the loan term exceed 2 ½ times the rate at which projected contingent interest had been calculated.

(b) "Actual life expectancy" shall be calculated based upon actuarial tables for women only, regardless of the sex of the borrower, and acceptable to both the state and the insurance industry.

(c) "Annuity base amount" means the projected loan amount less (1) the initial advance and (2) the projected contingent interest based on the reasonable appreciation rate used in calculating the projected loan amount.

(d) "Borrower" means the recipient or recipients of a shared appreciation loan for seniors who is obligated by execution of a promissory note and who is at least 65 years of age.

(e) "Borrower's life expectancy" means the actual life expectancy of the borrower plus no more than five years. In the case of a loan executed by two borrowers, the actual life expectancy shall be based upon the youngest of the two.

(f) "Cessation of occupancy" means the rental to a third party of the right of exclusive occupancy of the subject property, or the abandonment by all coborrowers of the property as his or her residence.

(g) "Lender" means any corporation organized as a public benefit corporation pursuant to the Nonprofit Corporation Law (Part 2 (commencing with Section 5110), Div. 2, Title 1, Corp. C.).

(h) "Lender's appreciation share" means a proportion not to exceed 25 percent of the appreciation of the property securing the loan calculated in accordance with this chapter.

(i) "Shared appreciation loan for seniors" means any loan made pursuant to this chapter upon the security of owner-occupied real property of a type specified in Section 1917.330, and in connection with which the lender has a right to receive a share of the appreciation in the value of the security property. "Shared appreciation loan" includes a deed of trust and any evidence of debt issued in connection with the loan.

(j) "Maturity event" means the earliest of any of the following:

(1) The death of the borrower. In the case of a married couple who are coborrowers, the death of the surviving spouse.

(2) The date of sale.

(3) The date a loan made pursuant to this chapter is refinanced or repaid in full.

(4) Cessation of occupancy.

(k) "Monthly annuity" means an amount paid in equal monthly installments to the borrower which, together with interest calculated at the stated rate, shall exhaust the annuity base amount during the borrower's life expectancy.

In the event that the calculated monthly annuity exceeds the cap or ceiling determined in accordance with this subdivision, the lender may limit the actual monthly annuity payment to an amount not lower than the cap. If the cap is imposed, the lender's appreciation share shall be limited to 25 percent times the ratio between the actual capped monthly payment and the monthly payment calculated in accordance with the first sentence of this subdivision. For example, if the monthly payment calculated in the first sentence is five thousand dollars ($5,000), but the lender applies a two thousand five hundred dollar ($2,500) ceiling, the lender's share of the home's appreciation shall be likewise reduced by 50 percent.

The minimum cap shall be two thousand five hundred dollars ($2,500) for loans made during the calendar year 1989. In subsequent calendar years, the minimum cap shall be two thousand five hundred dollars ($2,500) increased to reflect the proportional increase in the Consumer Price Index for the State of California, as determined by the United States Bureau of Labor Statistics, for the period from January 1, 1989, until the November monthly index figure for the year prior to the year in which the loan agreement is entered into.

(*l*) "Net advance" means any lump-sum advance of funds by the lender to the borrower made at the time of the loan closing. Net advance shall not exceed 15 percent of the projected loan amount.

(m) "Net appreciated value" means the difference between the fair market value of the property securing the loan at the time the loan is made and the fair market value of the property securing the loan at the time of the maturity event, less any credit for approved improvements made during the term of the loan.

(n) "Prevailing rate" means the yield of a 30–year mortgage commitment for delivery within 30 days for a standard conventional fixed rate mortgage of the Federal Home Loan Mortgage Corporation.

(o) "Projected contingent interest" means the lender's appreciation share of the projected appreciation of the property securing the loan from the date of the loan until the end of the borrower's life expectancy, using the same reasonable projection of annual appreciation used in determining the projected loan amount.

(p) "Projected loan amount" means not less than 75 percent of the estimated fair market value of the borrower's home at the end of the borrower's life expectancy, calculated by applying to the fair market value a reasonable projection of appreciation over the borrower's life expectancy based on a reasonable projected annual appreciation rate of the fair market value of the home.

(q) "Sale" means any transfer of title to the property and includes the execution of an installment sale contract giving the purchaser a right to possess the property before transfer of title, refinancing, judicial sale on execution, or other legal process of foreclosure or trustee's sale, but "sale" does not include a transfer specified in Section 2924.6 if any spouse to whom the property is transferred is also a coborrower.

(r) "Stated interest rate" means a total interest rate of not more than four-fifths of the prevailing rate.

(s) "Total loan obligation" means the net original loan and the sum total of all monthly annuity payments received by the borrower, with interest on all outstanding amounts calculated no more often than monthly at the stated interest rate, and actual contingent interest plus interest at the prevailing rate as disclosed to the borrower at the time the loan was entered into on all of the above amounts from the date of any maturity event until the outstanding loan obligation is repaid in full. In no event shall the total loan obligation exceed the actual fair market value of the home on the date of the maturity event. *(Added by Stats.1984, c. 1701, § 1. Amended by Stats.1988, c. 1406, § 1.)*

Cross References

Interest defined, see Civil Code § 1915.
Similar provisions, see Civil Code § 1917.120.

ARTICLE 2. TERMS AND CONDITIONS

Section
1917.330. Refinancing real property improved with one- to four-dwelling units; owner-occupied dwelling units.
1917.331. Terms and conditions; security; fee.
1917.332. Discontinuation or termination of monthly annuity.
1917.333. Right to prepay.
1917.334. Laws applicable.

Cross References

Definitions for purposes of this Chapter, see Civil Code § 1917.320.

§ 1917.330. Refinancing real property improved with one- to four-dwelling units; owner-occupied dwelling units

Lenders may make shared appreciation loans for seniors pursuant to this chapter for the refinancing of real property improved with one- to four-dwelling units, including structures ancillary to such dwelling units and including attached single-family dwelling units, single-family mobilehome units, residential condominium units, and dwelling units within a planned unit development. Shared appreciation loans shall be made to refinance only owner-occupied dwelling units, but in the case of two- to four-unit dwellings financed under this chapter, only one of the units need be owner-occupied. A dwelling unit shall be conclusively deemed to be owner-occupied for purposes of this chapter with respect to initial qualification for participation in the loan program if a borrower certifies in writing to the lender at the time the loan is made that he or she will occupy the property.

Nothing contained herein shall be deemed or interpreted to restrict a lender from providing a shared appreciation loan based solely upon the value of the real property upon which the borrower's dwelling is situated, secured only by that real property and not by the improvements thereon. In that case, the lender's actual contingent interest, and any other necessary calculations, shall be based upon the land value alone, not taking into account any improvements thereon. This paragraph is declaratory of existing law. *(Added by Stats. 1984, c. 1701, § 1. Amended by Stats.1988, c. 1406, § 2.)*

Cross References

Actual contingent interest defined for purposes of this Chapter, see Civil Code § 1917.320.
Authority, general terms and conditions, shared appreciation loans, see Civil Code § 1917.130 et seq.
Borrower defined for purposes of this Chapter, see Civil Code § 1917.320.
Interest defined, see Civil Code § 1915.
Lender defined for purposes of this Chapter, see Civil Code § 1917.320.
Shared appreciation loan for seniors defined for purposes of this Chapter, see Civil Code § 1917.320.
Specified type of property, loan security, see Civil Code § 1917.320.

§ 1917.331. Terms and conditions; security; fee

(a) A shared appreciation loan for seniors shall include all of the following:

(1) The term of the loan shall be for an open-ended term, terminating upon the occurrence of a maturity event, or the failure of the borrower to meet the terms of a deed of trust granted by the borrower to the lender which are normally and customarily used by mortgage lenders in this state for loans secured by residential real property. However, if the maturity event is either cessation of occupancy of the property by the borrower or death of the borrower, the term shall be extended until the earlier of the sale or refinancing of the property or 12 months after the occurrence of the maturity event.

(2) An initial advance, if desired by the borrower.

(3) Monthly annuity payments which shall continue until the occurrence of a maturity event, or earlier termination in accordance with paragraph (1).

(4) Interest on (2) and (3), calculated no more often than monthly at the stated interest rate.

(5) Actual contingent interest.

(6) Interest on paragraphs (2) to (5), inclusive, compounded no more often than monthly, from the date of a maturity event until the loan is repaid in full.

(b) The loan shall be secured by a deed of trust on the real property financed.

(c) The aggregate amount of any fee charged to the borrower by the lender for processing an application, preparing any necessary documents, obtaining a credit report, or any other costs incurred by the lender in connection with originating a shared appreciation loan for seniors shall not exceed five hundred dollars ($500). No prepaid interest shall be charged to the borrower. *(Added by Stats.1984, c. 1701, § 1. Amended by Stats.1988, c. 1406, § 3.)*

Cross References

Actual contingent interest defined for purposes of this Chapter, see Civil Code § 1917.320.
Borrower defined for purposes of this Chapter, see Civil Code § 1917.320.
Cessation of occupancy defined for purposes of this Chapter, see Civil Code § 1917.320.
Interest defined, see Civil Code § 1915.

§ 1917.331

Lender defined for purposes of this Chapter, see Civil Code § 1917.320.
Maturity event defined for purposes of this Chapter, see Civil Code § 1917.320.
Monthly annuity defined for purposes of this Chapter, see Civil Code § 1917.320.
Sale defined for purposes of this Chapter, see Civil Code § 1917.320.
Shared appreciation loan for seniors defined for purposes of this Chapter, see Civil Code § 1917.320.
Stated interest rate defined for purposes of this Chapter, see Civil Code § 1917.320.

§ 1917.332. Discontinuation or termination of monthly annuity

Any provision in any loan made pursuant to this chapter for the discontinuation or termination of a monthly annuity other than upon the occurrence of a maturity event is void and unenforceable. *(Added by Stats.1984, c. 1701, § 1.)*

Cross References

Maturity event defined for purposes of this Chapter, see Civil Code § 1917.320.
Monthly annuity defined for purposes of this Chapter, see Civil Code § 1917.320.

§ 1917.333. Right to prepay

(a)[1] The borrower shall have the right to prepay, at any time, in full or in part, the total loan obligation. *(Added by Stats.1984, c. 1701, § 1.)*

[1] No subd. (b) in enrolled bill.

Cross References

Borrower defined for purposes of this Chapter, see Civil Code § 1917.320.
Similar provisions, see Civil Code § 1917.132.
Total loan obligation defined for purposes of this Chapter, see Civil Code § 1917.320.

§ 1917.334. Laws applicable

Except as provided in this article, the terms and conditions of the shared appreciation loan for seniors shall be subject to all laws applicable to loans in effect on the date the loan is made. *(Added by Stats.1984, c. 1701, § 1.)*

Cross References

Refinancing, laws applicable, see Civil Code § 1917.133 et seq.
Shared appreciation loan for seniors defined for purposes of this Chapter, see Civil Code § 1917.320.

ARTICLE 3. DETERMINATION OF FAIR MARKET VALUE

Section
1917.410. Lender's estimate of minimum fair market value.
1917.411. Sales for cash; sale including consideration other than cash; prepaid in full or upon occurrence of maturity event.
1917.412. Appraisals; mutual agreement.

Cross References

Definitions for purposes of this Chapter, see Civil Code § 1917.320.

Improvements, see Civil Code § 1917.510 et seq.

§ 1917.410. Lender's estimate of minimum fair market value

The borrower, at any time for the purpose of facilitating a sale of the property or prepaying or refinancing the loan, may request the lender to stipulate the minimum amount which the lender considers to be the fair market value of the property for the purposes of this chapter. The lender shall advise the borrower within 10 working days of the receipt of such request of the lender's estimate of the minimum fair market value. The estimate shall remain effective for purposes of this section for 90 days. For the purposes of this section and Section 1917.411, a sale of the property shall be deemed to have occurred within the 90-day period if there is a valid contract entered by an offer and acceptance within the 90-day period for the sale of the property. The lender's stipulation shall remain effective for an additional 60 days following execution of the sale contract to permit completion of the sale and close of escrow.

The lender shall not be liable to the borrower or any other party on account of damages alleged as a result of providing the stipulation or estimate required by this section if such stipulation or estimate is made in good faith. Evidence of lack of good faith shall include, but not be limited to, a showing that the lender has willfully or repeatedly overrepresented the fair market value of other properties in similar situations, applying equitable principles to those determinations. The lender shall be conclusively presumed to have acted in good faith and no action may be brought or maintained against a lender which arises out of the provision by the lender of such stipulation or estimate, if the lender relied upon an appraisal of an independent appraiser approved by the Federal National Mortgage Association. *(Added by Stats.1984, c. 1701, § 1.)*

Cross References

Borrower defined for purposes of this Chapter, see Civil Code § 1917.320.
Lender defined for purposes of this Chapter, see Civil Code § 1917.320.
Sale defined for purposes of this Chapter, see Civil Code § 1917.320.
Similar provisions, see Civil Code § 1917.140.

§ 1917.411. Sales for cash; sale including consideration other than cash; prepaid in full or upon occurrence of maturity event

(a) In the case of a sale for cash within 90 days after the lender stipulates, under the provisions of Section 1917.410, a minimum amount which the lender considers to be the fair market value of the property, the fair market value shall be the gross sale price, unless the gross sale price is below the minimum amount stipulated by the lender and the lender contests in writing the reasonableness of the gross sale price in relation to the fair market value within 10 working days of the lender's receipt of notice of the gross sale price from the borrower, in which case fair market value shall be the greater of gross sale price or the amount determined under Section 1917.412.

(b) In the case of a sale for cash where the borrower has not requested the lender under the provisions of Section 1917.410 to stipulate to the minimum amount which the lender considers to be the fair market value of the property or where the stipulated minimum amount was provided by the lender more than 90 days prior to the date of sale, fair market value shall be the gross sale price, unless the lender contests in writing the reasonableness of the gross sale price in relation to the fair market value within 10 working days of the lender's receipt of notice of the gross sale price from borrower, in which case fair market value shall be the greater of the gross sale price or the amount determined under Section 1917.412.

(c) In the case of a sale which includes consideration to the seller other than cash, fair market value shall be as determined under Section 1917.412.

(d) If the shared appreciation loan is prepaid in full, or upon the occurrence of a maturity event, fair market value shall be as determined under Section 1917.412. *(Added by Stats.1984, c. 1701, § 1.)*

Cross References

Borrower defined for purposes of this Chapter, see Civil Code § 1917.320.
Lender defined for purposes of this Chapter, see Civil Code § 1917.320.
Maturity event defined for purposes of this Chapter, see Civil Code § 1917.320.
Sale defined for purposes of this Chapter, see Civil Code § 1917.320.
Similar provisions, see Civil Code § 1917.141.

§ 1917.412. Appraisals; mutual agreement

When Section 1917.411 requires the application of this section, the fair market value shall be determined by averaging two appraisals of the property performed as described in this section. If possible, the appraisals shall be based on the sale prices of comparable properties in the market area sold within the preceding three-month period. The appraisals shall be made upon request of the lender by two independent residential appraisers, one to be selected by the lender and one by the borrower. Each appraiser shall be approved by the Federal National Mortgage Association. The cost of the appraiser selected by the lender shall be borne by the lender, and the cost of the appraiser selected by the borrower shall be borne by the borrower, unless the average of the two appraisals equals or is less than the gross sale price of the property, in which case the lender shall also pay the fee of the borrower's appraiser up to two hundred dollars ($200). If either of the appraisers determines that the gross sale price does not reasonably reflect the fair market value of the property, or, in the case of a sale for which appraisal is required by this section, then the fair market value of the property shall be determined as the average of the two appraisals. If the borrower fails to select a qualified appraiser within 15 days after the lender has notified the borrower in writing of the lender's request for an appraisal of the property, the reasons therefor, and the borrower's option to select an independent appraiser within 15 days after the lender's request is submitted to the borrower, the lender may designate the second appraiser, provided the lender's request informs the borrower of this time limitation, and that the lender will select an appraiser on behalf of the borrower in the event the borrower fails to designate an appraiser, with consequent cost to the borrower. If pursuant to this section the lender designates the second appraiser, the cost of both appraisals shall be borne equally by the borrower and lender. If in any case the property has been damaged (other than normal wear and tear) and the damage has not been fully repaired, the determination of fair market value shall be based on the condition of the property not including the damage.

Nothing in this section shall preclude the borrower and lender from establishing the fair market value of the property by mutual agreement in lieu of appraisals pursuant to this section. *(Added by Stats.1984, c. 1701, § 1.)*

Cross References

Appraisal of improvements, selection of appraisers, see Civil Code § 1917.510.
Borrower defined for purposes of this Chapter, see Civil Code § 1917.320.
Lender defined for purposes of this Chapter, see Civil Code § 1917.320.
Sale defined for purposes of this Chapter, see Civil Code § 1917.320.
Similar provisions, see Civil Code § 1917.142.

ARTICLE 4. IMPROVEMENTS

Section
1917.510. Procedures for adding value of capital improvements to fair market value.
1917.511. Greater credit for improvements than specified in article.

Cross References

Definitions for purposes of this Chapter, see Civil Code § 1917.320.
Determination of fair market value, see Civil Code § 1917.410 et seq.

§ 1917.510. Procedures for adding value of capital improvements to fair market value

The borrower may have the value of capital improvements added to the fair market value of the borrower's property, for purposes of determining the total loan obligation, but only if the procedures set forth in this article are followed.

(a) Within 60 days following the completion of capital improvements during any 12-month period with a cost in excess of one thousand dollars ($1,000), the borrower shall send by first-class mail a notice of the completion of the improvements to the lender and shall submit proof of cost and an estimate of the increase in value of the property by reason of the improvements.

(b) If, within 30 days of receipt of the notice, the lender questions the claimed increase in value of the property by reason of the improvements, the lender and the borrower may, by mutual agreement, establish the value of the capital improvements or the lender may require appraisal of the property. An appraisal shall be made to determine the increase in value of the property, if any, by reason of the improvements, by two appraisers selected in the same manner specified in Section 1917.412. If appraisals are performed, the increase in value resulting from the improvements for the purposes of this section, shall be one-half of the sum of the two appraisals. The cost of the appraiser selected by the borrower shall be borne by the borrower, and the cost of the appraiser selected by the lender shall be borne by the lender.

(c) A credit for the value of capital improvements shall be provided if the increase in value of the property resulting

§ 1917.510

therefrom is determined pursuant to subdivision (b) to exceed one thousand dollars ($1,000).

(d) If 50 percent or more of the value of the labor or other work on the improvements was performed by the borrower, then the actual cost of the improvements need not exceed one thousand dollars ($1,000) for purposes of making application under subdivision (a). *(Added by Stats.1984, c. 1701, § 1.)*

Cross References

Borrower defined for purposes of this Chapter, see Civil Code § 1917.320.
Lender defined for purposes of this Chapter, see Civil Code § 1917.320.
Similar provisions, see Civil Code § 1917.150.
Total loan obligation defined for purposes of this Chapter, see Civil Code § 1917.320.

§ 1917.511. Greater credit for improvements than specified in article

Nothing in this article shall preclude a shared appreciation loan for seniors from providing the borrower with a greater credit for improvements than specified in this article, provided the relevant disclosures required by Article 7 (commencing with Section 1917.710) are appropriately modified to accurately disclose the terms of the credit. *(Added by Stats.1984, c. 1701, § 1.)*

Cross References

Borrower defined for purposes of this Chapter, see Civil Code § 1917.320.
Shared appreciation loan for seniors defined for purposes of this Chapter, see Civil Code § 1917.320.
Similar provisions, see Civil Code § 1917.151.

ARTICLE 5. GENERAL PROVISIONS

Section
1917.610. Relationship of borrower and lender; debtor and creditor.
1917.611. Waiver of borrower's rights; void and unenforceable.
1917.612. Terms and conditions of loans made pursuant to chapter to be consistent with chapter; other shared appreciation financing, application and effect of chapter.
1917.613. Application of interest rate provisions.
1917.614. Lien of deed of trust securing loan.
1917.615. Lien; attachment, priority.
1917.616. Contingent interest; usury.
1917.617. Application of qualification requirements of Corporations Code §§ 25110, 25120, and 25130.
1917.618. Loans subject to Code of Civil Procedure § 580b.
1917.619. Nonapplication of interest rate restrictions contained in Const. Art. XV, § 1.

Cross References

Definitions for purposes of this Chapter, see Civil Code § 1917.320.
Determination of fair market value, see Civil Code § 1917.410 et seq.
Improvements, see Civil Code § 1917.510 et seq.
Notices and disclosures, see Civil Code § 1917.710 et seq.

§ 1917.610. Relationship of borrower and lender; debtor and creditor

The relationship of the borrower and the lender of a shared appreciation loan for seniors is that of debtor and creditor and shall not be, or be construed to be, a joint venture, an equity venture, a partnership, or other relationship. *(Added by Stats.1984, c. 1701, § 1.)*

Cross References

Borrower defined for purposes of this Chapter, see Civil Code § 1917.320.
Lender defined for purposes of this Chapter, see Civil Code § 1917.320.
Relationship of borrower and lender, see Civil Code § 1917.001.
Shared appreciation loan for seniors defined for purposes of this Chapter, see Civil Code § 1917.320.
Similar provisions, see Civil Code § 1917.160.

§ 1917.611. Waiver of borrower's rights; void and unenforceable

Any waiver of any right of a borrower under the provisions of this chapter shall be void and unenforceable. *(Added by Stats.1984, c. 1701, § 1.)*

Cross References

Borrower defined for purposes of this Chapter, see Civil Code § 1917.320.
Similar provisions, see Civil Code § 1917.161.

§ 1917.612. Terms and conditions of loans made pursuant to chapter to be consistent with chapter; other shared appreciation financing, application and effect of chapter

This chapter facilitates one method of making shared appreciation loans to senior citizens in this state. The terms and conditions of any shared appreciation loan for seniors made pursuant to this chapter shall be consistent with this chapter. This chapter does not, however, apply to or limit shared appreciation financing of real property of a type made pursuant to other provisions of law, or which is not otherwise unlawful. Nothing in this chapter shall be construed in any way to affect shared appreciation financing of residential property of senior citizens not meeting the criteria specified in this chapter. *(Added by Stats.1984, c. 1701, § 1.)*

Cross References

Shared appreciation loan for seniors defined for purposes of this Chapter, see Civil Code § 1917.320.
Similar provisions, see Civil Code § 1917.163.

§ 1917.613. Application of interest rate provisions

A shared appreciation loan for seniors shall not be subject to any provision of this code or the Financial Code which limits the interest rate or change of interest rate of variable interest rate or renegotiable interest instruments, or which requires particular language or provisions in security instruments securing variable or renegotiable rate obligations or in evidences of those debts.

This section is declaratory of existing law. *(Added by Stats.1984, c. 1701, § 1.)*

Cross References

Interest defined, see Civil Code § 1915.
Shared appreciation loan for seniors defined for purposes of this Chapter, see Civil Code § 1917.320.
Similar provisions, see Civil Code § 1917.164.

§ 1917.614. Lien of deed of trust securing loan

The lien of a deed of trust securing a shared appreciation loan for seniors shall include and secure the total loan obligation of the shared appreciation loan for seniors. *(Added by Stats.1984, c. 1701, § 1.)*

Cross References

Attachment priority of lien, see Civil Code § 1917.615.
Liens of deed of trust, see Civil Code § 1917.003.
Shared appreciation loan for seniors defined for purposes of this Chapter, see Civil Code § 1917.320.
Similar provisions, see Civil Code § 1917.165.
Total loan obligation defined for purposes of this Chapter, see Civil Code § 1917.320.

§ 1917.615. Lien; attachment, priority

The lien of a shared appreciation loan for seniors, including the total loan obligation, shall attach from the time of the recordation of the deed of trust securing the loan, and the lien, including the lien of the total loan obligation accrued or to be accrued, shall have priority over any other lien or encumbrance affecting the property secured by the shared appreciation instrument and recorded after the time of recordation of the shared appreciation instrument. However, nothing in this section or Section 1917.614 shall preclude a junior lien or encumbrance subordinate to the total loan obligation of the shared appreciation loan for seniors. In no case may a junior lien achieve priority over the lien securing the total loan obligation of the shared appreciation loan, provided that nothing in this section shall be construed to supersede Section 8450. *(Added by Stats.1984, c. 1701, § 1. Amended by Stats.2010, c. 697 (S.B.189), § 12, operative July 1, 2012.)*

Cross References

Lien of deed of trust securing loan, see Civil Code § 1917.004.
Shared appreciation loan for seniors defined for purposes of this Chapter, see Civil Code § 1917.320.
Similar provisions, see Civil Code § 1917.166.
Total loan obligation defined for purposes of this Chapter, see Civil Code § 1917.320.

§ 1917.616. Contingent interest; usury

A shared appreciation loan for seniors which bears a fixed interest rate complying with the usury provisions of Article XV of the California Constitution shall not be deemed to become usurious by reason of the payment of actual contingent interest pursuant to this chapter; provided, however, that in no event may the amount of actual contingent interest received by the lender, plus the stated interest received by the lender, result in an annual percentage rate in excess of 1.5 times the applicable usury rate calculated pursuant to Article XV of the California Constitution, when all of such interest is applied over the actual term of the loan. *(Added by Stats.1984, c. 1701, § 1.)*

Cross References

Actual contingent interest defined for purposes of this Chapter, see Civil Code § 1917.320.
Interest defined, see Civil Code § 1915.
Lender defined for purposes of this Chapter, see Civil Code § 1917.320.
Shared appreciation loan for seniors defined for purposes of this Chapter, see Civil Code § 1917.320.
Similar provisions, see Civil Code § 1917.167.

§ 1917.617. Application of qualification requirements of Corporations Code §§ 25110, 25120, and 25130

The qualification requirements of Sections 25110, 25120, and 25130 of the Corporations Code do not apply to a shared appreciation loan for seniors to the extent the exemption afforded by subdivision (p) of Section 25100 of that code is applicable. *(Added by Stats.1984, c. 1701, § 1.)*

Cross References

Shared appreciation loan for seniors defined for purposes of this Chapter, see Civil Code § 1917.320.
Similar provisions, see Civil Code § 1917.168.

§ 1917.618. Loans subject to Code of Civil Procedure § 580b

Any loan made pursuant to this chapter shall be subject to Section 580b of the Code of Civil Procedure. *(Added by Stats.1984, c. 1701, § 1.)*

§ 1917.619. Nonapplication of interest rate restrictions contained in Const. Art. XV, § 1

Pursuant to the authority contained in Section 1 of Article XV of the California Constitution, the restrictions upon rates of interest contained in Section 1 of Article XV of the California Constitution shall not apply to any obligation of any loan made by any lender pursuant to this chapter.

This section creates and authorizes lenders under this chapter as an exempt class of persons pursuant to Section 1 of Article XV of the Constitution. *(Added by Stats.1984, c. 1701, § 1.)*

Cross References

Interest defined, see Civil Code § 1915.
Lender defined for purposes of this Chapter, see Civil Code § 1917.320.

ARTICLE 6. NOTICES AND DISCLOSURES

Section
1917.710. Required disclosures; additional disclosures; language.
1917.711. Written disclosure to prospective borrower; "Information About the Shared Appreciation Loans For Seniors".
1917.712. Disclosures required by Subpart C of Federal Reserve Board Regulation Z.
1917.713. Statement furnished to prospective borrower prior to consummation of loan.
1917.714. Statement in deed of trust and evidence of debt; notice stating terms and lender's share of net appreciated value.

Cross References

Determination of fair market value, see Civil Code § 1917.410 et seq.

Improvements, see Civil Code § 1917.510 et seq.
Shared appreciation loans for seniors, see Civil Code § 1917.320 et seq.

§ 1917.710. Required disclosures; additional disclosures; language

(a) The disclosures made pursuant to this chapter, as required, shall be the only disclosures required to be made pursuant to state law for shared appreciation loans for seniors, notwithstanding any contrary provision applicable to loans not made under this chapter, except those, if any, that may be required by reason of the application of Division 1 (commencing with Section 25000) of the Corporations Code, or Chapter 1 (commencing with Section 11000) of Part 2 of Division 4 of the Business and Professions Code. However, a lender shall not be precluded from supplementing the disclosures required by this chapter with additional disclosures that are not inconsistent with the disclosures required by this chapter.

(b) Whenever specific language is prescribed by this chapter, substantially the same language shall be utilized if possible, but reasonably equivalent language may be used to the extent necessary or appropriate to achieve a clearer or more accurate disclosure. *(Added by Stats.1984, c. 1701, § 1.)*

Cross References

Greater credit for improvements, modification of disclosures, see Civil Code § 1917.511.
Lender defined for purposes of this Chapter, see Civil Code § 1917.320.
Shared appreciation loan for seniors defined for purposes of this Chapter, see Civil Code § 1917.320.
Similar provisions, see Civil Code § 1917.170.

§ 1917.711. Written disclosure to prospective borrower; "Information About the Shared Appreciation Loans For Seniors"

(a) Each lender offering shared appreciation loans for seniors shall furnish to a prospective borrower, on the earlier of the dates on which the lender first provides written information concerning shared appreciation loans for seniors by the lender or provides a loan application form to the prospective borrower, a written disclosure as provided in this section, in type of not less than 10 point.

(b) The disclosure shall be entitled "INFORMATION ABOUT THE (Name of Lender) SHARED APPRECIATION LOAN FOR SENIORS," and shall describe the operation and effect of the shared appreciation loan for seniors, including a brief summary of its terms and conditions, together with a statement consisting of substantially the following language, to the extent applicable to such loan:

INFORMATION ABOUT THE SHARED APPRECIATION LOANS FOR SENIORS

Your lender is pleased to offer you the opportunity to borrow against the equity in your home through a Shared Appreciation Loan for Seniors.

Because the Shared Appreciation Loan for Seniors differs from the usual mortgage loan, the law requires that you have a detailed explanation of the special features of the loan before you apply. Before you sign your particular Shared Appreciation Loan for Seniors documents, you will receive more information about your particular Shared Appreciation Loan for Seniors, which you should read and understand before you sign the loan documents.

Receipt of shared appreciation loan proceeds could be considered income, thereby reducing payments received under government benefit programs, such as Supplemental Security Income (SSI). If this income is accumulated, the payments will be considered a resource, and could terminate your eligibility for SSI or Medi–Cal. See your legal adviser for more information.

I

GENERAL TERMS

A Shared Appreciation Loan for Seniors will provide you with funds to pay off any existing indebtedness on your home and to pay the closing costs for the loan, and will then advance funds to you each month (monthly annuity) (1) for so long as you or your spouse who is a coborrower live; or (2) until you sell the house; or (3) until you decide to refinance the property and pay off your Shared Appreciation Loan for Seniors; or (4) until you cease to occupy the property as your residence, meaning either that the property has been rented out for exclusive use by a nonborrower, or the abandonment by all coborrowers of the property as their residence. Any of these four events are considered "maturity events," and will constitute the end of the obligation to advance funds to you. The maturity events are described more fully in the promissory note. Your monthly annuity is calculated according to the method described in Section II, below. You will also be required to fulfill any customary terms or conditions included in the deed of trust encumbering your property.

Each advance of funds you receive, including both initial advances (net original loan) and each monthly annuity, will be considered outstanding principal on your loan and will bear a stated interest rate which will be not more than 80 percent of the prevailing rate of interest in the locality in which you live. No payments on your total loan obligation need be made by you until the occurrence of one of the four maturity events described above.

In exchange for a stated interest rate which is below the prevailing rate, you will be obligated to pay us additional interest later, in the form of a share of the appreciation of your home between the time you execute the promissory note and the occurrence of a maturity event. This additional interest is called "actual contingent interest" and is described more fully below at Section III. Once a maturity event has occurred, interest at the prevailing rate compounded not more often than monthly shall accrue on the entire outstanding loan balance, including the actual contingent interest, until repayment in full of the loan.

Balloon Payment of Principal. If you do not sell the property before the occurrence of a maturity event, you or your successors will need to refinance or pay this loan at that time. The term of this loan is until occurrence of a maturity event. However, if the maturity event is cessation of occupancy or death of the borrowers, the term shall be extended until the earlier of the sale or refinancing of the property, or 12 months after occurrence of the maturity event. We will not refinance either the unpaid balance of the loan or the contingent interest at that time; you or your successors alone will be responsible for obtaining refinancing. If you refinance this loan, your monthly payments may increase substantially if the property has appreciated significantly or if the interest rate on the refinancing loan is much higher than today's prevailing rates. In general, the more your property appreciates, the larger will be the amount of the actual contingent interest that you will have an obligation to pay or refinance.

Tax and Estate Consequences. USE OF THE SHARED APPRECIATION LOAN FOR SENIORS WILL HAVE INCOME TAX OR ESTATE PLANNING CONSEQUENCES WHICH WILL DEPEND UPON YOUR OWN FINANCIAL AND TAX SITUATION. FOR FURTHER INFORMATION, YOU ARE URGED TO CONSULT YOUR OWN ACCOUNTANT, ATTORNEY, OR OTHER FINANCIAL ADVISER.

THE QUESTIONS YOU SHOULD DISCUSS INCLUDE THE TAX DEDUCTIBILITY OF THE CONTINGENT INTEREST PAYMENT, YOUR RIGHT TO UTILIZE THAT DEDUCTION IN YEARS OTHER THAN THE YEAR IT IS PAID, AND THE EFFECT OF THE LOSS OF TAX BENEFITS BEFORE THAT TIME. BECAUSE YOU WILL BE BORROWING A SIGNIFICANT AMOUNT OF THE EQUITY IN YOUR HOME, WHEN A MATURITY EVENT OCCURS AND YOUR LOAN IS REPAID, LITTLE OR NO EQUITY MAY REMAIN FOR YOU OR YOUR HEIRS.

Determining Fair Market Value. If you sell your property, the gross sale price will be the fair market value of the property, unless appraisals are requested by us and the appraisals average more than the gross sale price. However, at your request, we also will tell you what we consider to be the fair market value of the property. If you sell for cash for a gross sale price that equals or exceeds that amount, the gross sale price will control and appraisals will not be needed.

Fair market value is determined by appraisals in the event of sales involving a consideration other than cash, prepayment of the loan in full, or any other maturity event.

When appraisals are required, fair market value is determined by averaging two independent appraisals of the property. You may select one of the two appraisers from a list approved by the Federal National Mortgage Association. If appraisals are requested by us, we will provide you with full information on how to select an appraiser.

In lieu of appraisals, we may establish fair market value at an agreed amount if an agreement can be reached between you and us.

Determining Value of Capital Improvements. Capital improvements with a value exceeding one thousand dollars ($1,000) (but no maintenance or repair costs) may be added to the value of the property for the purpose of determining the net appreciated value, but only if the procedures set forth in the shared appreciation loan documents are followed. It is important to note that capital improvements completed and claimed in any 12-month period must add more than one thousand dollars ($1,000) in value to the property and must generally also cost more than one thousand dollars ($1,000). However, if you have performed at least one-half the value of the labor or other work involved, then the cost of the improvements will not be considered. The appraised value of the improvements will be the increase in the value of the property resulting from the improvements. You will receive no credit for minor or major repairs or for improvements that are not appraised at more than one thousand dollars ($1,000), but the lender will acquire a share of any resulting appreciation in the value of the property.

II

CALCULATION OF MONTHLY ANNUITY

Your Shared Appreciation Loan for Seniors consists of two components: first, an initial advance to cover the cost of paying off any existing liens which you wish to pay off, and to cover closing costs; and second, a monthly annuity.

Your Shared Appreciation Loan for Seniors is designed to provide a monthly stream of funds for the remainder of the lives of the borrowers, with no payments on the loan due at any time during the lives of the borrowers unless the property is sold or the loan is refinanced or repaid in full or until you cease to occupy the property. In determining the amount that it is able to lend, the lender estimates what at least 75 percent of the value of the borrower's home is likely to be at the end of the borrower's life expectancy, based on a reasonable projected appreciation rate per year. Borrowers' estimated life spans are predicted on the basis of "actuarial tables" prepared by the government and the insurance industry; and are based only upon estimated female life span, plus up to five years, to avoid any discriminatory effect between the sexes in determining loan amounts and for conservative lending practices. Once the maximum amount which may be loaned has been determined, the amount necessary to pay off existing liens and for closing costs, plus interest at the stated interest rate on that amount for the borrower's life expectancy, is subtracted. The "projected contingent interest" that is predicted to have been earned at the end of the estimated life span is also subtracted. A monthly annuity is then calculated on the remaining amount, based on the stated interest and the borrower's life expectancy.

This complex calculation is illustrated by the following example:

Mr. and Mrs. Smith, who are 73 and 71 years of age, respectively, live in a home with a current value of one hundred fifty thousand dollars ($150,000), and apply for a Shared Appreciation Loan for Seniors. According to acceptable actuarial tables, Mrs. Smith, the younger of the two, has a remaining actuarial life span of 18 years. At the end of the 18 years, at a 4 percent per year projected appreciation rate, the house would be worth three hundred thousand dollars ($300,000), 80 percent of which equals two hundred forty thousand dollars ($240,000) (the lender could have based the calculation on as little as 75 percent of the three hundred thousand dollar ($300,000) projected value). The house currently has a fifteen thousand dollar ($15,000) first mortgage, and closing costs will be approximately two thousand dollars ($2,000), and the Smiths' wish to receive an initial advance to pay off the mortgage and to cover closing costs.

At the time the Smiths apply, the average of the 30–year fixed interest rate for home mortgages of the Federal Home Loan Mortgage Corporation is 13 percent, which is the "prevailing rate." The "stated interest rate" on the Smiths' loan will be 75 percent of the "prevailing rate," or 9 ¾ percent (the lender could have charged up to 80 percent of the prevailing rate).

The Smiths' payments will be calculated so that at the end of the projected loan term of 18 years, the total of all payments owed to the lender will be two hundred forty thousand dollars ($240,000), 80 percent of the estimated value of the Smiths' home after 18 years.

Two items must be subtracted from the two hundred forty thousand dollar ($240,000) future value before the Smiths' payment can be calculated:

(a) Since the Smiths' are requesting an advance of seventeen thousand dollars ($17,000) to pay off their existing mortgage and for closing costs, seventeen thousand dollars ($17,000), plus interest on seventeen thousand dollars ($17,000) at 9 ¾ percent for 18 years, for a total of ninety-six thousand fifty-seven dollars ($96,057), must be subtracted from the two hundred forty thousand dollars ($240,000) available for lending. This leaves one hundred forty-three thousand nine hundred forty-three dollars ($143,943).

(b) The lender's share of appreciation of the value of the home is also subtracted before calculating the monthly payment. Since the home is projected to increase in value by one hundred fifty thousand dollars ($150,000), the lender's share, 25 percent, equals thirty-seven thousand five hundred dollars ($37,500). When subtracted from one hundred forty-three thousand nine hundred forty-three dollars ($143,943), this leaves one hundred six thousand four hundred forty-three dollars ($106,443) for monthly payments.

The monthly payment is calculated on the basis of one hundred six thousand four hundred forty-three dollars ($106,443), over an 18–year term with interest at 9 ¾ percent. This equals one hundred eighty-four dollars ($184) per month. The Smiths' will receive one hundred eighty-four dollars ($184) per month until a maturity event occurs.

At the time of occurrence of a maturity event, the Smiths, or their successors, if they are both deceased, will owe the seventeen thousand dollars ($17,000) advanced initially, plus the sum of all the monthly payments of one hundred eighty-four dollars ($184) received by them until the occurrence of the maturity event, plus interest at 9 ¾ percent on all of the above from the time the funds were advanced until occurrence of the maturity event, plus actual contingent interest calculated as described in Section III below. Interest, compounded no more often than monthly, on all of the above shall accrue at the prevailing rate from the date of any maturity event until the loan is paid in full.

Because interest accumulates rapidly, when a large initial advance is received, or the projected loan term is relatively long, the monthly payment is significantly lower. For instance, if the Smiths' were 80 years old, and received no lump-sum advance, their monthly payment would be seven hundred forty-nine dollars ($749) per month.

The longer the loan has been in effect, of course, the greater the amount that will be owed, as monthly payments and interest accumulate, and as the home appreciates in value. Unless the borrowers choose to sell the home or refinance the loan, monthly payments will continue until both are deceased, no matter how long they live so long as they continue to occupy the property. Thus, the total loan obligation is not limited to the projected life span of the borrowers, nor to any set dollar amount, regardless of the projected maximum. Regardless of how much principal has been advanced by Shared Appreciation Loans for Seniors, and regardless of how much stated interest and actual contingent interest have accumulated or been earned, payments will continue. If the borrower lives substantially longer than the actuarial prediction, it is possible that the total of principal and acquired stated interest plus actual contingent interest, may exceed the value of the home. IN NO EVENT, HOWEVER, WILL A BORROWER OR A BORROWER'S ESTATE BE LIABLE ON THE SHARED APPRECIATION LOAN FOR SENIORS IN AN AMOUNT GREATER THAN THE VALUE OF THE HOME.

The Smith example can be illustrated as follows:

A. $150,000 = Value of home at time of loan.
B. $300,000 = Estimated value of home at end of life expectancy (18 years, 4% annual appreciation).
C. $240,000 = Loan (80% of B).
D. $150,000 = Total appreciation (B less A).
E. $ 37,500 = Lender's share of appreciation (25% × D).
F. $ 96,057 = Payoff of preexisting mortgage, plus interest.
G. $106,443 = Amount from which monthly payment is calculated (C less E less F).
H. $ 184 = Monthly payment (based on G) to the Smiths. At death or other maturity event, the sum of all monthly payments, plus interest, plus the lender's share of appreciation, plus the amount owing from payoff of the old mortgage, must be paid to the lender.

III

ACTUAL CONTINGENT INTEREST

This Shared Appreciation Loan for Seniors provides that you, as borrower, must pay to the lender, as actual contingent interest, a share of up to 25 percent of the net appreciated value of the real property which secures the loan. This actual contingent interest is due and payable whenever a maturity event occurs. The dollar amount of actual contingent interest, if any, which you will be required to pay cannot be determined at this time. If the property does not appreciate, you will owe us nothing as actual contingent interest, and will only have to repay principal and stated interest. Actual contingent interest will not become due if title to the property is transferred on your death to a spouse who is a coborrower, or where a transfer results from a decree of dissolution of a marriage and a spouse who is a coborrower becomes the sole owner.

Your obligation to pay actual contingent interest and stated interest will reduce the amount of the appreciation, if any, that you will realize on the property over and above its value today. Appreciation will not produce a real gain in your equity in the property unless the appreciation rate exceeds the general inflation rate, but you will be required to pay a portion of the appreciation as actual contingent interest without regard to whether the appreciation has resulted in a real gain.

When your home is sold or refinanced, you normally will receive enough cash to pay the total loan obligation. However, if you sell and provide financing to the buyer, you may possibly not receive enough cash to pay the actual contingent interest, and, in that event, it will be necessary for you to provide cash from other funds. In no event, however, will your total loan obligation exceed the value of your home at the time of occurrence of a maturity event, unless you have willfully caused damage to the property.

Calculating the actual contingent interest. Actual contingent interest will be calculated as follows:

    FAIR MARKET VALUE OF THE PROPERTY ON DATE OF MATURITY EVENT
    (Sale Price or Appraised Value)

− (less) CURRENT VALUE OF THE PROPERTY

− (less) VALUE OF CAPITAL IMPROVEMENTS MADE BY YOU
    (Must exceed $1,000 in cost.)

× (times) LENDER'S APPRECIATION SHARE (up to 25%)

= (equals) ACTUAL CONTINGENT INTEREST

Below are answers to two frequently asked questions about the Shared Appreciation Loans for Seniors program. If you have any further questions, feel free to call the lender at _____, or write to the lender at _____.

Question. What if I marry, or my spouse is not a coborrower?

Answer. Your Shared Appreciation Loan for Seniors will be due upon the death of the last surviving coborrower. Your lender will be happy to include a new or present spouse as a coborrower, provided the new spouse is over age _____ at the time he or she becomes a coborrower. Because the monthly payment annuity is based upon the projected life span of the youngest coborrower, the annuity will be readjusted if a new, younger coborrower is added. The annuity will be adjusted to reflect the annuity that would have existed had the new coborrower been a coborrower from the beginning of the loan period. Since the monthly annuity is based on a fixed "lendable amount" derived from projected appreciation of the home (see Section II, above), a longer projected loan period, because of the younger age of the new coborrower, will result in a decrease in the size of the monthly annuity.

Question. Can I obtain an additional advance for home improvements?

Answer. Yes, provided your lender approves of the improvement. Your lender will act reasonably in reviewing your request. At the time the advance is made, your lender will calculate the amount of interest at the stated interest rate that will accrue through the projected life of the loan, as it was determined at the time the loan was made. This amount will be deducted from the original lendable amount, and a new annuity calculated, based upon the calculations described in Section II. The effect is the same as if the advance had been made at the outset of the loan, except, of course, you will not be responsible for any interest until the funds are actually advanced. Your annuity will, however, be smaller. (Added by Stats.1984, c. 1701, § 1. Amended by Stats.1988, c. 1406, § 4.)

Cross References

Actual contingent interest defined for purposes of this Chapter, see Civil Code § 1917.320.
Borrower defined for purposes of this Chapter, see Civil Code § 1917.320.
Borrower's life expectancy defined for purposes of this Chapter, see Civil Code § 1917.320.
Cessation of occupancy defined for purposes of this Chapter, see Civil Code § 1917.320.
Interest defined, see Civil Code § 1915.
Lender defined for purposes of this Chapter, see Civil Code § 1917.320.
Lender's appreciation share defined for purposes of this Chapter, see Civil Code § 1917.320.
Maturity event defined for purposes of this Chapter, see Civil Code § 1917.320.
Monthly annuity defined for purposes of this Chapter, see Civil Code § 1917.320.
Net appreciated value defined for purposes of this Chapter, see Civil Code § 1917.320.
Prevailing rate defined for purposes of this Chapter, see Civil Code § 1917.320.
Projected contingent interest defined for purposes of this Chapter, see Civil Code § 1917.320.
Sale defined for purposes of this Chapter, see Civil Code § 1917.320.
Shared appreciation loan for seniors defined for purposes of this Chapter, see Civil Code § 1917.320.
Similar provisions, see Civil Code § 1917.171.
Stated interest rate defined for purposes of this Chapter, see Civil Code § 1917.320.
Total loan obligation defined for purposes of this Chapter, see Civil Code § 1917.320.

§ 1917.712. Disclosures required by Subpart C of Federal Reserve Board Regulation Z

(a) Each lender making a shared appreciation loan for seniors shall also furnish to the prospective borrower, prior to the consummation of the loan, the disclosures required by Subpart C of Federal Reserve Board Regulation Z (12 C.F.R. Part 226), including 12 C.F.R. Section 226.18(f), to the extent applicable to the transaction.

(b) The disclosure made pursuant to subdivision (a) and Regulation Z shall be based on the fixed interest rate of the shared appreciation loan for seniors, and shall include a description of the shared appreciation feature, including (1) the conditions for its imposition, the time at which it would be collected, and the limitations on the lender's share, as required by the Federal Reserve Board in the information published by the board in 46 Federal Register 20877–78 (April 7, 1981), and (2) the lender's share of the appreciated value and the prevailing interest rate as defined in Section 1917.320.

(c) The disclosure made pursuant to subdivision (a) and Regulation Z shall be accompanied by (1) several transaction-specific examples of the operation and effect of the shared appreciation loan and (2) the following charts com-

§ 1917.712

paring the shared appreciation loan and a conventional loan made at the prevailing interest rate, and illustrating the possible increase in the monthly payments, and the possible annual percentage rate of finance charge, on the assumptions therein stated:

Chart 1

CONVENTIONAL MORTGAGE AT __%

If the same loan balance were financed under a conventional, 30-year, fixed-rate, level-payment mortgage, your monthly payments would be:

Years 1–30

$_____ /mo.

Chart 2

IF YOU REFINANCE THIS TRANSACTION AT __%

If your property appreciates at 10% per year, and if your total loan obligation (including actual contingent interest due) at the end of ___ years is refinanced at __% (the prevailing market interest rate now), your monthly payments will be:

Years 1–___   Refinancing loan
$_____ /mo. $_____ /mo.*

* Refinancing loan, assuming a conventional 30-year, fixed-rate, level-payment mortgage. Other mortgage instruments, e.g., graduated-payment or shared-appreciation, if available, may result in lower payments.

Chart 3

APR IF PROPERTY APPRECIATES AT 10%

If your property appreciates at 10% per year, the total finance charge on your shared appreciation loan for seniors (including actual contingent interest) will equal $_____, and the annual percentage rate of the total finance charge (including actual contingent interest) will equal _____%.

(d) The disclosures required by subdivision (c) shall be separate from the disclosures required by Regulation Z, and may be presented in the document containing the disclosures required by Regulation Z or in one or more separate documents.

(e) Except to the extent that this section requires disclosure of additional information not required by Regulation Z, compliance with the applicable credit disclosure requirements of Regulation Z shall constitute compliance with the requirements of this section.

(f) The disclosure prescribed in Section 1917.711 shall be physically attached to the disclosures required by this section and Regulation Z at the time the Regulation Z disclosures are furnished to the borrower.

(g) In the event federal law is amended so that this section is inconsistent therewith, the federal law shall prevail as to the disclosures required by this section. *(Added by Stats. 1984, c. 1701, § 1.)*

Cross References

Borrower defined for purposes of this Chapter, see Civil Code § 1917.320.
Interest defined, see Civil Code § 1915.
Lender defined for purposes of this Chapter, see Civil Code § 1917.320.
Shared appreciation loan for seniors defined for purposes of this Chapter, see Civil Code § 1917.320.
Similar provisions, see Civil Code § 1917.172.

§ 1917.713. Statement furnished to prospective borrower prior to consummation of loan

Each lender making a shared appreciation loan for seniors shall additionally furnish to the prospective borrower, prior to consummation of the loan, a statement containing the following information:

IMPORTANT INFORMATION ABOUT YOUR SHARED APPRECIATION LOAN FOR SENIORS

You are being offered a shared appreciation loan. Before you decide to accept this loan, read this statement, which is designed to provide important information you should consider.

1. Prevailing interest rate: ____%.
2. Stated interest rate on this loan: ____%.
3. Projected contingent interest: ____%.
4. Initial amount of this loan: $____.
5. Amount of the monthly annuity payments you will receive: $____.
6. Projected term of this loan: ____ years.
7. Projected total loan obligation you will have to pay, assuming the loan continues to the end of the "borrower's" life expectancy: $____.

(Added by Stats.1984, c. 1701, § 1.)

Cross References

Borrower defined for purposes of this Chapter, see Civil Code § 1917.320.
Borrower's life expectancy defined for purposes of this Chapter, see Civil Code § 1917.320.
Interest defined, see Civil Code § 1915.
Lender defined for purposes of this Chapter, see Civil Code § 1917.320.
Monthly annuity defined for purposes of this Chapter, see Civil Code § 1917.320.
Projected contingent interest defined for purposes of this Chapter, see Civil Code § 1917.320.
Shared appreciation loan for seniors defined for purposes of this Chapter, see Civil Code § 1917.320.
Similar provisions, see Civil Code § 1917.173.
Stated interest rate defined for purposes of this Chapter, see Civil Code § 1917.320.
Total loan obligation defined for purposes of this Chapter, see Civil Code § 1917.320.

§ 1917.714. Statement in deed of trust and evidence of debt; notice stating terms and lender's share of net appreciated value

Each deed of trust and evidence of debt executed in connection with a shared appreciation loan for seniors shall contain a statement, printed or written in a size equal to at

least 12-point bold type, consisting of substantially the following language: "THIS IS A [DURATION] SHARED APPRECIATION LOAN FOR SENIORS. THE LENDER'S INTEREST INCLUDES [PERCENT] OF THE NET APPRECIATED VALUE OF THE PROPERTY. A BALLOON PAYMENT OF PRINCIPAL WILL BE REQUIRED. FOR FURTHER INFORMATION, READ THE FLYER ENTITLED 'INFORMATION ABOUT THE [NAME OF LENDER] SHARED APPRECIATION LOAN FOR SENIORS.' " The notice required by this section shall be completed to state the terms of the shared appreciation loan and the lender's share of the net appreciated value.
(Added by Stats.1984, c. 1701, § 1.)

Cross References

Interest defined, see Civil Code § 1915.
Lender defined for purposes of this Chapter, see Civil Code § 1917.320.
Net appreciated value defined for purposes of this Chapter, see Civil Code § 1917.320.
Shared appreciation loan for seniors defined for purposes of this Chapter, see Civil Code § 1917.320.
Similar provisions, see Civil Code § 1917.174.

CHAPTER 7.5. MORTGAGE LOANS

Section
1918. Repealed.
1918.5. Definitions.
1919. Repealed.
1920. Requirements of mortgage instrument.
1921. Definitions; providing prospective borrowers with publications on adjustable-rate mortgages; failure of lender to comply; liability for damages.
1922 to 1922.11. Repealed.
1922.12. Repealed.
1922.13, 1922.14. Repealed.

Cross References

Exemption from this chapter of loans by state institutions under regulations to establish parity with federal institutions, see Civil Code § 1916.12.

§ 1918. Repealed by Stats.1997, c. 232 (A.B.447), § 22

§ 1918.5. Definitions

As used in this chapter:

(a) "Evidence of debt" means a note or negotiable instrument.

(b) "Secretary" means the Secretary of the Business, Consumer Services, and Housing.

(c) "Secretary's designee" means the director of a department within the agency that licenses or regulates the institutions, organizations, or persons engaged in a business related to or affecting compliance with this chapter.

(d) "Security document" means a mortgage contract, deed of trust, real estate sales contract, or any note or negotiable instrument issued in connection therewith, when its purpose is to finance the purchase or construction of real property occupied or intended to be occupied by the borrower, containing four or fewer residential units or on which four or fewer residential units are to be constructed. *(Added by Stats.1981, c. 1079, p. 4159, § 4, operative Jan. 1, 1983.*

Amended by Stats.2013, c. 353 (S.B.820), § 11, eff. Sept. 26, 2013, operative July 1, 2013.)

Cross References

Authority of secretary's designee, see Civil Code § 1916.12.

§ 1919. Repealed by Stats.1997, c. 232 (A.B.447), § 23

§ 1920. Requirements of mortgage instrument

Any mortgage instrument that is made pursuant to the provisions of this chapter shall meet the following requirements:

(a) Standards for the adjustment of interest rates or monthly payments shall consider factors which can reasonably be deemed to affect the ability of borrowers to meet their mortgage obligations.

(b) No change in interest provided for in any provision for a variable interest rate contained in a security document, or evidence of debt issued in connection therewith, shall be valid unless the provision is set forth in the security document, and in any evidence of debt issued in connection therewith, and the document or documents contain the following provisions:

(1) A statement attached to the security document and to any evidence of debt issued in connection therewith printed or written in a size equal to at least 10-point bold type, consisting of language authorized by the secretary or the secretary's designee notifying the borrower that the mortgage may provide for changes in interest, principal loan balance, payment, or the loan term.

(2) Before the due date of the first monthly installment following each change in the interest rate, notice shall be mailed to the borrower of the following:

(A) The base index.

(B) The most recently published index at the date of the change in the rate.

(C) The interest rate in effect as a result of the change.

(D) Any change in the monthly installment.

(E) The amount of the unpaid principal balance.

(F) If the interest scheduled to be paid on the due date exceeds the amount of the installment, a statement to that effect and the amount of the excess, and the address and telephone number of the office of the lender to which inquiries may be made.

(c) The borrower is permitted to prepay the loan in whole or in part without a prepayment charge at any time, and no fee or other charge may be required by the lender of the borrower as a result of any change in the interest rate, the payment, the outstanding principal loan balance, or the loan term.

(d) Changes in the rate of interest on the loan shall reflect the movement of an index, which shall be authorized by the secretary or the secretary's designee.

(e) To the extent that any monthly installment is less than the amount of interest accrued during the month with respect to which the installment is payable, the borrower shall be notified of such instance in a form and manner prescribed by the secretary or the secretary's designee. Such notice shall include, but not be limited to, the amount of interest exceeding the monthly installment, and any borrower options under these circumstances.

(f) The lender shall provide to the borrower, prior to the execution by the borrower of any mortgage payment instrument authorized pursuant to this chapter, full and complete disclosure, as specified by the secretary or the secretary's designee, of the nature and effect of the mortgage payment instrument, and all costs or savings attributed to the mortgage instrument. *(Added by Stats.1981, c. 1079, p. 4159, § 4, operative Jan. 1, 1983. Amended by Stats.1997, c. 232 (A.B.447), § 24.)*

Cross References

Evidence of debt defined for purposes of this Chapter, see Civil Code § 1918.5.
Interest defined, see Civil Code § 1915.
Secretary defined for purposes of this Chapter, see Civil Code § 1918.5.
Secretary's designee defined for purposes of this Chapter, see Civil Code § 1918.5.
Security document defined for purposes of this Chapter, see Civil Code § 1918.5.

§ 1921. Definitions; providing prospective borrowers with publications on adjustable-rate mortgages; failure of lender to comply; liability for damages

(a) As used in this section:

(1) "Adjustable-rate residential mortgage loan" means any loan or credit sale which is primarily for personal, family, or household purposes which bears interest at a rate subject to change during the term of the loan, whether predetermined or otherwise, and which is made upon the security of real property containing not less than one nor more than four dwelling units.

(2) "Lender" means any person, association, corporation, partnership, limited partnership, or other business entity making, in any 12–month period, more than 10 loans or credit sales upon the security of residential real property containing not less than one nor more than four dwelling units.

(b) Any lender offering adjustable-rate residential mortgage loans shall provide to prospective borrowers a copy of the most recent available publication of the Federal Reserve Board that is designed to provide the public with descriptive information concerning adjustable-rate mortgages (currently entitled "Consumer Handbook on Adjustable Rate Mortgages"), either upon the prospective borrower's request or at the same time the lender first provides written information, other than direct-mail advertising, concerning any adjustable-rate residential mortgage loan or credit sale to the prospective borrower, whichever is earlier. Any lender who fails to comply with the requirements of this section may be enjoined by any court of competent jurisdiction and shall be liable for actual damages, the costs of the action, and reasonable attorney's fees as determined by the court. The court may make those orders as may be necessary to prevent future violations of this section.

(c) A lender that makes adjustable-rate mortgage loan disclosures pursuant to either Part 29 of Chapter I of, or Part 563 of Chapter V of, Title 12 of the Code of Federal Regulations, may comply with this section by providing the descriptive information required by subdivision (b) at the same time and under the same circumstances that it makes disclosures in accordance with those federal regulations. Such a lender shall also display and make the descriptive information available to the public in an area of the lender's office that is open to the public. *(Added by Stats.1985, c. 1284, § 1. Amended by Stats.1987, c. 56, § 19.)*

Cross References

Interest defined, see Civil Code § 1915.

§§ 1922 to 1922.11. Repealed by Stats.1990, c. 491 (A.B. 527), § 2

§ 1922.12. Repealed by Stats.1987, c. 699, § 1

§§ 1922.13, 1922.14. Repealed by Stats.1990, c. 491 (A.B. 527), § 2

CHAPTER 8. REVERSE MORTGAGES

Section
1923. Reverse mortgage; defining criteria.
1923.2. Reverse mortgage loans; requirements.
1923.3. Reverse mortgages constituting lien against subject property.
1923.4. Property deemed to be owner-occupied; occupant as trust beneficiary.
1923.5. Reverse mortgage loan application; plain language statement.
1923.6. Disclosure statement.
1923.7. Failure of lender to comply with requirements; effect on liens.
1923.9. Reverse mortgage loan payments; treatment for means-tested programs of aid to individuals.
1923.10. Application of chapter.

Cross References

Manner of creating contracts, translation of contracts negotiated in language other than English, see Civil Code § 1632.

§ 1923. Reverse mortgage; defining criteria

For purposes of this chapter, "reverse mortgage" means a nonrecourse loan secured by real property that meets all of the following criteria:

(a) The loan provides cash advances to a borrower based on the equity or the value in a borrower's owner-occupied principal residence.

(b) The loan requires no payment of principal or interest until the entire loan becomes due and payable.

(c) The loan is made by a lender licensed or chartered pursuant to the laws of this state or the United States. *(Added by Stats.1997, c. 797 (A.B.456), § 1.)*

Cross References

Interest defined, see Civil Code § 1915.

§ 1923.2. Reverse mortgage loans; requirements

A reverse mortgage loan shall comply with all of the following requirements:

(a) Prepayment, in whole or in part, shall be permitted without penalty at any time during the term of the reverse mortgage loan. For the purposes of this section, penalty does not include any fees, payments, or other charges that would have otherwise been due upon the reverse mortgage being due and payable.

(b) A reverse mortgage loan may provide for a fixed or adjustable interest rate or combination thereof, including compound interest, and may also provide for interest that is contingent on the value of the property upon execution of the loan or at maturity, or on changes in value between closing and maturity.

(c) A reverse mortgage may include costs and fees that are charged by the lender, or the lender's designee, originator, or servicer, including costs and fees charged upon execution of the loan, on a periodic basis, or upon maturity.

(d) If a reverse mortgage loan provides for periodic advances to a borrower, these advances shall not be reduced in amount or number based on any adjustment in the interest rate.

(e) A lender who fails to make loan advances as required in the loan documents, and fails to cure an actual default after notice as specified in the loan documents, shall forfeit to the borrower treble the amount wrongfully withheld plus interest at the legal rate.

(f) The reverse mortgage loan may become due and payable upon the occurrence of any one of the following events:

(1) The home securing the loan is sold or title to the home is otherwise transferred.

(2) All borrowers cease occupying the home as a principal residence, except as provided in subdivision (g).

(3) Any fixed maturity date agreed to by the lender and the borrower occurs.

(4) An event occurs which is specified in the loan documents and which jeopardizes the lender's security.

(g) Repayment of the reverse mortgage loan shall be subject to the following additional conditions:

(1) Temporary absences from the home not exceeding 60 consecutive days shall not cause the mortgage to become due and payable.

(2) Extended absences from the home exceeding 60 consecutive days, but less than one year, shall not cause the mortgage to become due and payable if the borrower has taken prior action which secures and protects the home in a manner satisfactory to the lender, as specified in the loan documents.

(3) The lender's right to collect reverse mortgage loan proceeds shall be subject to the applicable statute of limitations for written loan contracts. Notwithstanding any other provision of law, the statute of limitations shall commence on the date that the reverse mortgage loan becomes due and payable as provided in the loan agreement.

(4) The lender shall prominently disclose in the loan agreement any interest rate or other fees to be charged during the period that commences on the date that the reverse mortgage loan becomes due and payable, and that ends when repayment in full is made.

(h) The first page of any deed of trust securing a reverse mortgage loan shall contain the following statement in 10-point boldface type: "This deed of trust secures a reverse mortgage loan."

(i) A lender or any other person that participates in the origination of the mortgage shall not require an applicant for a reverse mortgage to purchase an annuity as a condition of obtaining a reverse mortgage loan.

(1) The lender or any other person that participates in the origination of the mortgage shall not do either of the following:

(A) Participate in, be associated with, or employ any party that participates in or is associated with any other financial or insurance activity, unless the lender maintains procedural safeguards designed to ensure that individuals participating in the origination of the mortgage shall have no involvement with, or incentive to provide the prospective borrower with, any other financial or insurance product.

(B) Refer the borrower to anyone for the purchase of an annuity or other financial or insurance product prior to the closing of the reverse mortgage or before the expiration of the right of the borrower to rescind the reverse mortgage agreement.

(2) This subdivision does not prevent a lender from offering or referring borrowers for title insurance, hazard, flood, or other peril insurance, or other similar products that are customary and normal under a reverse mortgage loan.

(3) A lender or any other person who participates in the origination of a reverse mortgage loan to which this subdivision would apply, and who complies with paragraph (1) of subsection (n), and with subsection (o), of Section 1715z–20 of Title 12 of the United States Code, and any regulations and guidance promulgated under that section, as amended from time to time, in offering the loan, regardless of whether the loan is originated pursuant to the program authorized under Section 1715z–20 of Title 12 of the United States Code, and any regulations and guidance promulgated under that section, shall be deemed to have complied with this subdivision.

(j) Prior to accepting a final and complete application for a reverse mortgage the lender shall provide the borrower with a list of not fewer than 10 counseling agencies that are approved by the United States Department of Housing and Urban Development to engage in reverse mortgage counseling as provided in Subpart B of Part 214 of Title 24 of the Code of Federal Regulation. The counseling agency shall not receive any compensation, either directly or indirectly, from the lender or from any other person or entity involved in originating or servicing the mortgage or the sale of annuities, investments, long-term care insurance, or any other type of financial or insurance product. This subdivision does not prevent a counseling agency from receiving financial assistance that is unrelated to the offering or selling of a reverse mortgage loan and that is provided by the lender as part of charitable or philanthropic activities.

(k) A lender shall not accept a final and complete application for a reverse mortgage loan from a prospective applicant or assess any fees upon a prospective applicant until the lapse of seven days from the date of counseling, as evidenced by the counseling certification, and without first receiving certification from the applicant or the applicant's

§ 1923.2

authorized representative that the applicant has received counseling from an agency as described in subdivision (j) and that the counseling was conducted in person, unless the certification specifies that the applicant elected to receive the counseling in a manner other than in person. The certification shall be signed by the borrower and the agency counselor, and shall include the date of the counseling and the name, address, and telephone number of both the counselor and the applicant. Electronic facsimile copy of the housing counseling certification satisfies the requirements of this subdivision. The lender shall maintain the certification in an accurate, reproducible, and accessible format for the term of the reverse mortgage.

(*l*) A lender shall not make a reverse mortgage loan without first complying with, or in the case of brokered loans ensuring compliance with, the requirements of Section 1632, if applicable. (Added by Stats.1997, c. 797 (A.B.456), § 1. Amended by Stats.2006, c. 202 (S.B.1609), § 2; Stats.2009, c. 236 (A.B.329), § 3; Stats.2012, c. 641 (A.B.2010), § 1; Stats.2014, c. 854 (A.B.1700), § 2, eff. Jan. 1, 2015.)

Cross References

Interest defined, see Civil Code § 1915.
Reverse mortgage defined for purposes of this Chapter, see Civil Code § 1923.

§ 1923.3. Reverse mortgages constituting lien against subject property

A reverse mortgage shall constitute a lien against the subject property to the extent of all advances made pursuant to the reverse mortgage and all interest accrued on these advances, and that lien shall have priority over any lien filed or recorded after recordation of a reverse mortgage loan. (Added by Stats.1997, c. 797 (A.B.456), § 1.)

Cross References

Interest defined, see Civil Code § 1915.
Reverse mortgage defined for purposes of this Chapter, see Civil Code § 1923.

§ 1923.4. Property deemed to be owner-occupied; occupant as trust beneficiary

For the purposes of this chapter, a property shall be deemed to be owner-occupied, notwithstanding that the legal title to the property is held in the name of a trust, provided that the occupant of the property is a beneficiary of that trust. (Added by Stats.1997, c. 797 (A.B.456), § 1.)

§ 1923.5. Reverse mortgage loan application; plain language statement

(a) No reverse mortgage loan application shall be taken by a lender unless the loan applicant, prior to receiving counseling, has received from the lender the following plain language statement in conspicuous 16–point type or larger, advising the prospective borrower about counseling prior to obtaining the reverse mortgage loan:

IMPORTANT NOTICE TO REVERSE MORTGAGE LOAN APPLICANT

A REVERSE MORTGAGE IS A COMPLEX FINANCIAL TRANSACTION. IF YOU DECIDE TO OBTAIN A REVERSE MORTGAGE LOAN, YOU WILL SIGN BINDING LEGAL DOCUMENTS THAT WILL HAVE IMPORTANT LEGAL AND FINANCIAL IMPLICATIONS FOR YOU AND YOUR ESTATE. IT IS THEREFORE IMPORTANT TO UNDERSTAND THE TERMS OF THE REVERSE MORTGAGE AND ITS EFFECT ON YOUR FUTURE NEEDS. BEFORE ENTERING INTO THIS TRANSACTION, YOU ARE REQUIRED TO CONSULT WITH AN INDEPENDENT REVERSE MORTGAGE LOAN COUNSELOR TO DISCUSS WHETHER OR NOT A REVERSE MORTGAGE IS RIGHT FOR YOU. A LIST OF APPROVED COUNSELORS WILL BE PROVIDED TO YOU BY THE LENDER.

SENIOR CITIZEN ADVOCACY GROUPS ADVISE AGAINST USING THE PROCEEDS OF A REVERSE MORTGAGE TO PURCHASE AN ANNUITY OR RELATED FINANCIAL PRODUCTS. IF YOU ARE CONSIDERING USING YOUR PROCEEDS FOR THIS PURPOSE, YOU SHOULD DISCUSS THE FINANCIAL IMPLICATIONS OF DOING SO WITH YOUR COUNSELOR AND FAMILY MEMBERS.

(b)(1) In addition to the plain language notice described in subdivision (a), no reverse mortgage loan application shall be taken by a lender unless the lender provides the prospective borrower, prior to his or her meeting with a counseling agency on reverse mortgages, with a reverse mortgage worksheet guide, or in the event that the prospective borrower seeks counseling prior to requesting a reverse mortgage loan application from the reverse mortgage lender, the counseling agency shall provide the prospective borrower with the following plain language reverse mortgage worksheet guide in 14–point type or larger:

Reverse Mortgage Worksheet Guide–Is a Reverse Mortgage Right for Me?

To decide if a recommended purchase of a reverse mortgage is right for you, consider all of your goals, needs, and available options. This self-evaluation worksheet has five essential questions for you to consider when deciding if a reverse mortgage is right for you.

Directions: The State of California advises you to carefully read and complete this worksheet, and bring it with you to your counseling session. You may make notes on a separate piece of paper with questions you may have about whether a reverse mortgage is right for you. During the counseling session, you can speak openly and confidentially with a professional reverse mortgage counselor, independent of the lender, who can help you understand what it means for you to become involved with this particular loan.

1. What happens to others in your home after you die or move out?

Rule: When the borrower dies, moves, or is absent from the home for 12 consecutive months, the loan may become due.

Considerations: Having a reverse mortgage affects the future of all those living with you. If the loan cannot be paid off, then the home will have to be sold in order to satisfy the lender. To determine if this is an issue for you, ask yourself:

(A) Who is currently living in the home with you?

(B) What will they do when you die or permanently move from the home?

(C) Have you discussed this with all those living with you or any family members?

(D) Who will pay off the loan, and have you discussed this with them?

(E) If your heirs do not have enough money to pay off the loan, the home will pass into foreclosure.

Do you need to discuss this with your counselor? Yes or No

2. Do you know that you can default on a reverse mortgage?

Rule: There are three continuous financial obligations. If you fail to keep up with your insurance, property taxes, and home maintenance, you will go into default. Uncured defaults lead to foreclosures.

Considerations: Will you have adequate resources and income to support your financial needs and obligations once you have removed all of your available equity with a reverse mortgage? To determine if this is an issue for you, ask yourself:

(A) Are you contemplating a lump-sum withdrawal?

(B) What other resources will you have once you have reached your equity withdrawal limit?

(C) Will you have funds to pay for unexpected medical expenses?

(D) Will you have the ability to finance alternative living accommodations, such as independent living, assisted living, or a long-term care nursing home?

(E) Will you have the ability to finance routine or catastrophic home repairs, especially if maintenance is a factor that may determine when the mortgage becomes payable?

Do you need to discuss this with your counselor? Yes or No

3. Have you fully explored other options?

Rule: Less costly options may exist.

Consideration: Reverse mortgages are compounding-interest loans, and the debt to the lender increases as time goes on. You may want to consider using less expensive alternatives or other assets you may have before you commit to a reverse mortgage. To determine if this is an issue for you, consider:

(A) Alternative financial options for seniors may include, but not be limited to, less costly home equity lines of credit, property tax deferral programs, or governmental aid programs.

(B) Other types of lending arrangements may be available and less costly. You may be able to use your home equity to secure loans from family members, friends, or would-be heirs.

Do you need to discuss this with your counselor? Yes or No

4. Are you intending to use the reverse mortgage to purchase a financial product?

Rule: Reverse mortgages are interest-accruing loans.

Considerations: Due to the high cost and increasing debt incurred by reverse mortgage borrowers, using home equity to finance investments is not suitable in most instances. To determine if this is an issue for you, consider:

(A) The cost of the reverse mortgage loan may exceed any financial gain from any product purchased.

(B) Will the financial product you are considering freeze or otherwise tie up your money?

(C) There may be high surrender fees, service charges, or undisclosed costs on the financial products purchased with the proceeds of a reverse mortgage.

(D) Has the sales agent offering the financial product discussed suitability with you?

Do you need to discuss this with your counselor? Yes or No

5. Do you know that a reverse mortgage may impact your eligibility for government assistance programs?

Rule: Income received from investments will count against individuals seeking government assistance.

Considerations: Converting your home equity into investments may create nonexempt asset statuses. To determine if this is an issue for you, consider:

(A) There are state and federal taxes on the income investments financed through home equity.

(B) If you go into a nursing home for an extended period of time, the reverse mortgage loan will become due, the home may be sold, and any proceeds from the sale of the home may make you ineligible for government benefits.

(C) If the homeowner is a Medi–Cal beneficiary, a reverse mortgage may make it difficult to transfer ownership of the home, thus resulting in Medi–Cal recovery.

Do you need to discuss this with your counselor? Yes or No

(2) The reverse mortgage worksheet guide required in paragraph (1) shall be signed by the agency counselor, if the counseling is done in person, and by the prospective borrower and returned to the lender along with the certification of counseling required under subdivision (k) of Section 1923.2, and the loan application shall not be approved until the signed reverse mortgage worksheet guide is provided to the lender. A copy of the reverse mortgage worksheet guide shall be provided to the borrower. (Added by Stats.1997, c. 797 (A.B.456), § 1. Amended by Stats.2006, c. 202 (S.B. 1609), § 3; Stats.2009, c. 236 (A.B.329), § 4; Stats.2014, c. 854 (A.B.1700), § 3, eff. Jan. 1, 2015.)

Cross References

Reverse mortgage defined for purposes of this Chapter, see Civil Code § 1923.

§ 1923.6. Disclosure statement

The lender shall be presumed to have satisfied any disclosure duty imposed by this chapter if the lender provides a disclosure statement in the same form as provided in this chapter. (Added by Stats.1997, c. 797 (A.B.456), § 1.)

§ 1923.7. Failure of lender to comply with requirements; effect on liens

No arrangement, transfer, or lien subject to this chapter shall be invalidated solely because of the failure of a lender to comply with any provision of this chapter. However, nothing in this section shall preclude the application of any other existing civil remedies provided by law. *(Added by Stats.1997, c. 797 (A.B.456), § 1.)*

§ 1923.9. Reverse mortgage loan payments; treatment for means-tested programs of aid to individuals

(a) To the extent that implementation of this section does not conflict with federal law resulting in the loss of federal funding, reverse mortgage loan payments made to a borrower shall be treated as proceeds from a loan and not as income for the purpose of determining eligibility and benefits under means-tested programs of aid to individuals.

(b) Undisbursed reverse mortgage funds shall be treated as equity in the borrower's home and not as proceeds from a loan, resources, or assets for the purpose of determining eligibility and benefits under means-tested programs of aid to individuals.

(c) This section applies to any law or program relating to payments, allowances, benefits, or services provided on a means-tested basis, by this state, including, but not limited to, optional state supplements to the federal supplemental security income program, low-income energy assistance, property tax relief, general assistance, and medical assistance only to the extent this section does not conflict with Title 19 of the federal Social Security Act.

(d) For the purposes of this section, "means-tested programs and aid to individuals" includes, but is not limited to, programs set forth in Chapter 2 (commencing with Section 11200) of Part 3 of Division 9, and Part 5 (commencing with Section 17000) of Division 9, of the Welfare and Institutions Code. *(Added by Stats.1997, c. 797 (A.B.456), § 1.)*

Cross References

Reverse mortgage defined for purposes of this Chapter, see Civil Code § 1923.

§ 1923.10. Application of chapter

This chapter shall only apply to those reverse mortgage loans executed on or after January 1, 1998. *(Added by Stats.1997, c. 797 (A.B.456), § 1.)*

Cross References

Reverse mortgage defined for purposes of this Chapter, see Civil Code § 1923.

Title 4.5

APPRAISALS OF REAL PROPERTY [REPEALED]

Title 5

HIRING

Chapter		Section
1.	Hiring in General	1925
1.5.	Rental Passenger Vehicle Transactions	1939.01
2.	Hiring of Real Property	1940
2.4.	Occupancy in Interim Homelessness Programs	1954.08
2.5.	Transitional Housing Participant Misconduct	1954.10
2.5.	Water Service	1954.201
2.6.	Commercial Rental Control	1954.25
2.7.	Residential Rent Control	1954.50
2.8.	Bed Bug Infestations	1954.600
3.	Hiring of Personal Property	1955
4.	Identification of Property Owners	1961
4.5.	Disposition of Personal Property Upon Request of Tenant	1965
5.	Disposition of Personal Property Remaining on Premises at Termination of Tenancy	1980
5.5.	Disposition of Property Remaining on Premises at Termination of Commercial Tenancy	1993
6.	Assignment and Sublease	1995.010
7.	Use Restrictions	1997.010

CHAPTER 1. HIRING IN GENERAL

Section	
1925.	Hiring defined.
1926.	Title to products of thing hired.
1927.	Quiet possession of hire.
1928.	Degree of care.
1929.	Repairs.
1930.	Use of thing lent for particular purpose; damages.
1931.	Termination of hiring by letter.
1932.	Termination of hiring by hirer.
1933.	Termination of hiring.
1934.	Death or incapacity of party; effect.
1934.5.	Accommodations from month to month in nursing or convalescent home; termination on death of patient.
1935.	Termination of hiring; apportionment of hire.
1936.	Repealed.
1936.01.	Repealed.
1936.015.	Repealed.
1936.05.	Repealed.
1936.1.	Repealed.
1936.5.	Repealed.
1938.	Commercial property lease form or rental agreement; statement regarding Certified Access Specialist (CASp) inspection; copy of CASp report and inspection certificate; presumption regarding responsibility to correct violations; notice of right to obtain CASp inspection.

Cross References

Provisions of this Title, in respect to rights and obligations of parties to contract, as subordinate to intention of parties and waiver of benefit thereof, see Civil Code § 3268.

§ 1925. Hiring defined

Hiring is a contract by which one gives to another the temporary possession and use of property, other than money, for reward, and the latter agrees to return the same to the former at a future time. *(Enacted in 1872.)*

Cross References

Hiring of personal property, see Civil Code § 1955 et seq.

Hiring of real property, see Civil Code § 1941 et seq.

§ 1926. Title to products of thing hired

The products of a thing hired, during the hiring, belong to the hirer. *(Enacted in 1872.)*

Cross References

Hiring defined, see Civil Code § 1925.

§ 1927. Quiet possession of hire

An agreement to let upon hire binds the letter to secure to the hirer the quiet possession of the thing hired during the term of the hiring, against all persons lawfully claiming the same. *(Enacted in 1872.)*

Cross References

Covenant for quiet enjoyment running with the land, see Civil Code § 1463.
Damages for breach of covenant of quiet enjoyment, see Civil Code § 3304.
Hiring defined, see Civil Code § 1925.
Hiring of real property, unlawful actions by landlord to influence tenant to vacate, civil penalties, see Civil Code § 1940.2.
Obligations of lessor of personal property, see Civil Code § 1955.

§ 1928. Degree of care

The hirer of a thing must use ordinary care for its preservation in safety and in good condition. *(Enacted in 1872.)*

Cross References

Degree of care required of depositary for hire, see Civil Code § 1852.

§ 1929. Repairs

The hirer of a thing must repair all deteriorations or injuries thereto occasioned by his want of ordinary care. *(Enacted in 1872. Amended by Stats.1905, c. 454, p. 614, § 1.)*

Cross References

Buildings for human occupancy, see Civil Code § 1941.
Personal property, see Civil Code § 1955.
Vessels, responsibility for repairs and supplies, see Harbors and Navigation Code § 404.

§ 1930. Use of thing lent for particular purpose; damages

When a thing is let for a particular purpose the hirer must not use it for any other purpose; and if he does, he is liable to the letter for all damages resulting from such use, or the letter may treat the contract as thereby rescinded. *(Enacted in 1872. Amended by Stats.1905, c. 454, p. 614, § 2.)*

Cross References

Grounds for rescission of contract, see Civil Code § 1689.

§ 1931. Termination of hiring by letter

The letter of a thing may terminate the hiring and reclaim the thing before the end of the term agreed upon:

1. When the hirer uses or permits a use of the thing hired in a manner contrary to the agreement of the parties; or,

2. When the hirer does not, within a reasonable time after request, make such repairs as he is bound to make. *(Enacted in 1872.)*

Cross References

Hiring defined, see Civil Code § 1925.

§ 1932. Termination of hiring by hirer

The hirer of a thing may terminate the hiring before the end of the term agreed upon:

1. When the letter does not, within a reasonable time after request, fulfill his obligations, if any, as to placing and securing the hirer in the quiet possession of the thing hired, or putting it into good condition, or repairing; or,

2. When the greater part of the thing hired, or that part which was and which the letter had at the time of the hiring reason to believe was the material inducement to the hirer to enter into the contract, perishes from any other cause than the want of ordinary care of the hirer. *(Enacted in 1872. Amended by Stats.1905, c. 454, p. 614, § 3.)*

Cross References

Hiring defined, see Civil Code § 1925.
Personal property, see Civil Code § 1955.

§ 1933. Termination of hiring

The hiring of a thing terminates:

1. At the end of the term agreed upon;

2. By the mutual consent of the parties;

3. By the hirer acquiring a title to the thing hired superior to that of the letter; or,

4. By the destruction of the thing hired. *(Enacted in 1872.)*

Cross References

Hiring defined, see Civil Code § 1925.
Termination of lease, remedy of lessor, see Civil Code § 1951.2.

§ 1934. Death or incapacity of party; effect

If the hiring of a thing is terminable at the pleasure of one of the parties, it is terminated by notice to the other of his death or incapacity to contract. In other cases it is not terminated thereby. *(Enacted in 1872.)*

Cross References

Hiring defined, see Civil Code § 1925.

§ 1934.5. Accommodations from month to month in nursing or convalescent home; termination on death of patient

Notwithstanding the provisions of Section 1934, the hiring of accommodations from month to month in a nursing or convalescent home shall be terminated by the death of the patient by or for whom the hiring was made. The hirer or his heir, legatee, or personal representative shall not be liable for any rent due for such accommodations under the hiring agreement beyond that rent due for the date on which such patient died. No advance payment of rent made by the hirer shall be subject to the claim of, or retention by, the nursing or convalescent home and shall be returned to the heir, legatee, or personal representative no later than two weeks after such patient has died. Any provision in the hiring agreement by which the hirer agrees to modify or waive any of his rights under this section shall be void as contrary to public policy.

§ 1934.5

The provisions of this section shall be applicable to all hiring agreements executed on or after January 1, 1979. *(Added by Stats.1978, c. 628, p. 2081, § 1.)*

Cross References

Hiring defined, see Civil Code § 1925.

§ 1935. Termination of hiring; apportionment of hire

When the hiring of a thing is terminated before the time originally agreed upon, the hirer must pay the due proportion of the hire for such use as he has actually made of the thing, unless such use is merely nominal, and of no benefit to him. *(Enacted in 1872.)*

Cross References

Hiring defined, see Civil Code § 1925.
Rate of compensation for fraction of week, termination of deposit, see Civil Code §§ 1853, 1854, 1855.

§ 1936. Repealed by Stats.2016, c. 183 (A.B.2051), § 1, eff. Jan. 1, 2017

§ 1936.01. Repealed by Stats.2015, c. 333 (A.B.675), § 3, eff. Jan. 1, 2016

§ 1936.015. Repealed by Stats.2015, c. 333 (A.B.675), § 4, eff. Jan. 1, 2016

§ 1936.05. Repealed by Stats.2016, c. 183 (A.B.2051), § 2, eff. Jan. 1, 2017

§ 1936.1. Repealed by Stats.2016, c. 183 (A.B.2051), § 3, eff. Jan. 1, 2017

§ 1936.5. Repealed by Stats.2016, c. 183 (A.B.2051), § 4, eff. Jan. 1, 2017

§ 1938. Commercial property lease form or rental agreement; statement regarding Certified Access Specialist (CASp) inspection; copy of CASp report and inspection certificate; presumption regarding responsibility to correct violations; notice of right to obtain CASp inspection

(a) A commercial property owner or lessor shall state on every lease form or rental agreement executed on or after January 1, 2017, whether or not the subject premises have undergone inspection by a Certified Access Specialist (CASp).

(b) If the subject premises have undergone inspection by a CASp and, to the best of the commercial property owner's or lessor's knowledge, there have been no modifications or alterations completed or commenced between the date of the inspection and the date of the lease or rental agreement that have impacted the subject premises' compliance with construction-related accessibility standards, the commercial property owner or lessor shall provide, prior to execution of the lease or rental agreement, a copy of any report prepared by the CASp with an agreement from the prospective lessee or tenant that information in the report shall remain confidential, except as necessary for the tenant to complete repairs and corrections of violations of construction-related accessibility standards that the lessee or tenant agrees to make.

(c) Making any repairs or modifications necessary to correct violations of construction-related accessibility standards that are noted in a CASp report is presumed to be the responsibility of the commercial property owner or lessor, unless otherwise mutually agreed upon by the commercial property owner or lessor and the lessee or tenant. The prospective lessee or tenant shall have the opportunity to review any CASp report prior to execution of the lease or rental agreement. If the report is not provided to the prospective lessee or tenant at least 48 hours prior to execution of the lease or rental agreement, the prospective lessee or tenant shall have the right to rescind the lease or rental agreement, based upon the information contained in the report, for 72 hours after execution of the agreement.

(d) If the subject premises have been issued an inspection report by a CASp, as described in paragraph (1) of subdivision (a) of Section 55.53, indicating that it meets applicable standards, as defined in paragraph (4) of subdivision (a) of Section 55.52, the commercial property owner or lessor shall provide a copy of the current disability access inspection certificate and any inspection report to the lessee or tenant not already provided pursuant to subdivision (b) within seven days of the date of the execution of the lease form or rental agreement.

(e) If the subject premises have not been issued a disability access inspection certificate, as described in subdivision (e) of Section 55.53, the commercial property owner or lessor shall state the following on the lease form or rental agreement:

"A Certified Access Specialist (CASp) can inspect the subject premises and determine whether the subject premises comply with all of the applicable construction-related accessibility standards under state law. Although state law does not require a CASp inspection of the subject premises, the commercial property owner or lessor may not prohibit the lessee or tenant from obtaining a CASp inspection of the subject premises for the occupancy or potential occupancy of the lessee or tenant, if requested by the lessee or tenant. The parties shall mutually agree on the arrangements for the time and manner of the CASp inspection, the payment of the fee for the CASp inspection, and the cost of making any repairs necessary to correct violations of construction-related accessibility standards within the premises."

(f) As used in this section, "commercial property" means property that is offered for rent or lease to persons operating, or intending to operate, a place of public accommodation as defined in Section 202 of Chapter 2 of Part 2 of Title 24 of the California Code of Regulations, or a facility to which the general public is invited, at those premises. *(Added by Stats.2012, c. 383 (S.B.1186), § 12, eff. Sept. 19, 2012. Amended by Stats.2016, c. 379 (A.B.2093), § 1, eff. Sept. 16, 2016; Stats.2017, c. 87 (A.B.1148), § 1, eff. July 21, 2017; Stats.2018, c. 92 (S.B.1289), § 37, eff. Jan. 1, 2019.)*

CHAPTER 1.5. RENTAL PASSENGER VEHICLE TRANSACTIONS

Section
1939.01. Definitions.

Section	
1939.03.	Agreement for renter responsibility.
1939.05.	Limit on total amount of renter's liability.
1939.07.	Claim against renter; reasonable and rational relationship to loss; submission of insurance claims; recovery from other sources.
1939.09.	Damage waiver; contents; rate limitations.
1939.13.	Purchase of damage waiver, optional insurance, or another optional good or service; prohibited rental company practices.
1939.15.	Recovery on claim; express permission required to process credit card charge; other prohibited tactics.
1939.17.	Customer facility charges.
1939.19.	Providing quote or imposing charges for rental; disclosure of additional mandatory charges.
1939.21.	Qualified business rentals; definitions; additional charges.
1939.22.	Rental or lease agreement; electronic communication; denial of rental or lease agreement prohibited.
1939.23.	Use of electronic surveillance technology prohibited; exceptions.
1939.25.	Action against rental company for violation of chapter; attorney's fees and costs.
1939.27.	Action against renter for loss due to theft of vehicle; jurisdiction.
1939.29.	Waiver of provisions void and unenforceable.
1939.31.	Renters enrolled in membership program; disclosure requirements.
1939.33.	Foreign renters; service of process.
1939.35.	15–passenger vans; renter documentation.
1939.37.	Rental company not subject to specified vehicle rental requirements; conditions.

Cross References

Annual device registration fee to recover costs of inspecting or testing weighing and measuring devices, see Business and Professions Code § 12240.

§ 1939.01. Definitions

For the purpose of this chapter, the following definitions shall apply:

(a) "Rental company" means a person or entity in the business of renting passenger vehicles to the public.

(b) "Renter" means any person in a manner obligated under a contract for the lease or hire of a passenger vehicle from a rental company for a period of less than 30 days.

(c) "Additional mandatory charges" means any separately stated charges that the rental company requires the renter to pay to hire or lease the vehicle for the period of time to which the rental rate applies, which are imposed by a governmental entity and specifically relate to the operation of a rental vehicle business, including, but not limited to, a customer facility charge, airport concession fee, tourism commission assessment, vehicle license recovery fee, or other government-imposed taxes or fees.

(d) "Airport concession fee" means a charge collected by a rental company from a renter that is the renter's proportionate share of the amount paid by the rental company to the owner or operator of an airport for the right or privilege of conducting a vehicle rental business on the airport's premises.

(e) "Authorized driver" means all of the following:

(1) The renter.

(2) The renter's spouse, if that person is a licensed driver and satisfies the rental company's minimum age requirement.

(3) The renter's employer or coworker, if he or she is engaged in business activity with the renter, is a licensed driver, and satisfies the rental company's minimum age requirement.

(4) A person expressly listed by the rental company on that renter's contract as an authorized driver.

(f) "Customer facility charge" means any fee, including an alternative fee, required by an airport to be collected by a rental company from a renter pursuant to Section 50474.21 of the Government Code.

(g) "Damage waiver" means a rental company's agreement not to hold a renter liable for all or any portion of any damage or loss related to the rented vehicle, any loss of use of the rented vehicle, or any storage, impound, towing, or administrative charges.

(h) "Electronic surveillance technology" means a technological method or system used to observe, monitor, or collect information, including telematics, Global Positioning System (GPS), wireless technology, or location-based technologies. "Electronic surveillance technology" does not include event data recorders (EDR), sensing and diagnostic modules (SDM), or other systems that are used either:

(1) For the purpose of identifying, diagnosing, or monitoring functions related to the potential need to repair, service, or perform maintenance on the rental vehicle.

(2) As part of the vehicle's airbag sensing and diagnostic system in order to capture safety systems-related data for retrieval after a crash has occurred or in the event that the collision sensors are activated to prepare the decisionmaking computer to make the determination to deploy or not to deploy the airbag.

(i) "Estimated time for replacement" means the number of hours of labor, or fraction thereof, needed to replace damaged vehicle parts as set forth in collision damage estimating guides generally used in the vehicle repair business and commonly known as "crash books."

(j) "Estimated time for repair" means a good faith estimate of the reasonable number of hours of labor, or fraction thereof, needed to repair damaged vehicle parts.

(k) "Membership program" means a service offered by a rental company that permits customers to bypass the rental counter and go directly to the vehicle previously reserved or select an alternate vehicle. A membership program shall meet all of the following requirements:

(1) The renter initiates enrollment by completing an application on which the renter can specify a preference for type of vehicle and acceptance or declination of optional services.

(2) The rental company fully discloses, prior to the enrollee's first rental as a participant in the program, all terms and conditions of the rental agreement as well as all required disclosures.

(3) The renter may terminate enrollment at any time.

(4) The rental company fully explains to the renter that designated preferences, as well as acceptance or declination

of optional services, may be changed by the renter at any time for the next and future rentals.

(5) An employee is available at the lot where the renter takes possession of the vehicle, to receive any change in the rental agreement from the renter.

(*l*) "Passenger vehicle" or "vehicle" means a "passenger vehicle" as defined in Section 465 of the Vehicle Code.

(m) "Quote" means an estimated cost of rental provided by a rental company or a third party to a potential customer that is based on information provided by the potential customer and used to generate an estimated cost of rental, including, but not limited to, potential dates of rental, locations, or classes of vehicle.

(n) "Tourism commission assessment" means the charge collected by a rental company from a renter that has been established by the California Travel and Tourism Commission pursuant to Section 13995.65 of the Government Code.

(*o*) "Vehicle license fee" means the tax imposed pursuant to the Vehicle License Fee Law (Part 5 (commencing with Section 10701) of Division 2 of the Revenue and Taxation Code).

(p) "Vehicle registration fee" means any fee imposed pursuant to any provision of Chapter 6 (commencing with Section 9101) of Division 3 of the Vehicle Code or any other law that imposes a fee upon the registration of vehicles in this state.

(q) "Vehicle license recovery fee" means a charge that seeks to recover the amount of any vehicle license fee and vehicle registration fee paid by a rental company for the particular class of vehicle being rented. If imposed, the vehicle license recovery fee shall be separately stated as a single charge in the quote and rental contract. *(Added by Stats.2016, c. 183 (A.B.2051), § 5, eff. Jan. 1, 2017.)*

§ 1939.03. Agreement for renter responsibility

Except as limited by Section 1939.05, a rental company and a renter may agree that the renter will be responsible for no more than all of the following:

(a) Physical or mechanical damage to the rented vehicle up to its fair market value, as determined in the customary market for the sale of that vehicle, resulting from collision regardless of the cause of the damage.

(b) Loss due to theft of the rented vehicle up to its fair market value, as determined in the customary market for the sale of that vehicle, provided that the rental company establishes by clear and convincing evidence that the renter or the authorized driver failed to exercise ordinary care while in possession of the vehicle. In addition, the renter shall be presumed to have no liability for any loss due to theft if (1) an authorized driver has possession of the ignition key furnished by the rental company or an authorized driver establishes that the ignition key furnished by the rental company was not in the vehicle at the time of the theft, and (2) an authorized driver files an official report of the theft with the police or other law enforcement agency within 24 hours of learning of the theft and reasonably cooperates with the rental company and the police or other law enforcement agency in providing information concerning the theft. The presumption set forth in this subdivision is a presumption affecting the burden of proof which the rental company may rebut by establishing that an authorized driver committed, or aided and abetted the commission of, the theft.

(c) Physical damage to the rented vehicle up to its fair market value, as determined in the customary market for the sale of that vehicle, resulting from vandalism occurring after, or in connection with, the theft of the rented vehicle. However, the renter shall have no liability for any damage due to vandalism if the renter would have no liability for theft pursuant to subdivision (b).

(d) Physical damage to the rented vehicle up to a total of five hundred dollars ($500) resulting from vandalism unrelated to the theft of the rented vehicle.

(e) Actual charges for towing, storage, and impound fees paid by the rental company if the renter is liable for damage or loss.

(f) An administrative charge, which shall include the cost of appraisal and all other costs and expenses incident to the damage, loss, repair, or replacement of the rented vehicle. *(Added by Stats.2016, c. 183 (A.B.2051), § 5, eff. Jan. 1, 2017.)*

§ 1939.05. Limit on total amount of renter's liability

(a) The total amount of the renter's liability to the rental company resulting from damage to the rented vehicle shall not exceed the sum of the following:

(1) The estimated cost of parts which the rental company would have to pay to replace damaged vehicle parts.

(2) The estimated cost of labor to replace damaged vehicle parts, which shall not exceed the product of (A) the rate for labor usually paid by the rental company to replace vehicle parts of the type that were damaged and (B) the estimated time for replacement.

(3) The estimated cost of labor to repair damaged vehicle parts, which shall not exceed the lesser of the following:

(A) The product of the rate for labor usually paid by the rental company to repair vehicle parts of the type that were damaged and the estimated time for repair.

(B) The sum of the estimated labor and parts costs determined under paragraphs (1) and (2) to replace the same vehicle parts.

(4) Actual charges for towing, storage, and impound fees paid by the rental company.

(b) For purposes of subdivision (a), all discounts and price reductions or adjustments that are or will be received by the rental company shall be subtracted from the estimate to the extent not already incorporated in the estimate, or otherwise promptly credited or refunded to the renter.

(c) For the purpose of converting the estimated time for repair into the same units of time in which the rental rate is expressed, a day shall be deemed to consist of eight hours.

(d) The administrative charge described in subdivision (f) of Section 1939.03 shall not exceed (1) fifty dollars ($50) if the total estimated cost for parts and labor is more than one hundred dollars ($100) up to and including five hundred dollars ($500), (2) one hundred dollars ($100) if the total estimated cost for parts and labor exceeds five hundred dollars ($500) up to and including one thousand five hundred dollars ($1,500), or (3) one hundred fifty dollars ($150) if the total estimated cost for parts and labor exceeds one thousand five hundred dollars ($1,500). An administrative charge shall not be imposed if the total estimated cost of parts and labor is one hundred dollars ($100) or less.

(e) The total amount of an authorized driver's liability to the rental company, if any, for damage occurring during the authorized driver's operation of the rented vehicle shall not exceed the amount of the renter's liability under this section.

(f) A rental company shall not recover from an authorized driver an amount exceeding the renter's liability under this section. *(Added by Stats.2016, c. 183 (A.B.2051), § 5, eff. Jan. 1, 2017.)*

§ 1939.07. Claim against renter; reasonable and rational relationship to loss; submission of insurance claims; recovery from other sources

(a) A claim against a renter resulting from damage or loss, excluding loss of use, to a rental vehicle shall be reasonably and rationally related to the actual loss incurred. A rental company shall mitigate damages where possible and shall not assert or collect a claim for physical damage which exceeds the actual costs of the repairs performed or the estimated cost of repairs, if the rental company chooses not to repair the vehicle, including all discounts and price reductions. However, if the vehicle is a total loss vehicle, the claim shall not exceed the total loss vehicle value established in accordance with procedures that are customarily used by insurance companies when paying claims on total loss vehicles, less the proceeds from salvaging the vehicle, if those proceeds are retained by the rental company.

(b) If insurance coverage exists under the renter's applicable personal or business insurance policy and the coverage is confirmed during regular business hours, the renter may require that the rental company submit any claims to the renter's applicable personal or business insurance carrier. The rental company shall not make any written or oral representations that it will not present claims or negotiate with the renter's insurance carrier. For purposes of this subdivision, confirmation of coverage includes telephone confirmation from insurance company representatives during regular business hours. Upon request of the renter and after confirmation of coverage, the amount of claim shall be resolved between the insurance carrier and the rental company. The renter shall remain responsible for payment to the rental company for any loss sustained that the renter's applicable personal or business insurance policy does not cover.

(c) A rental company shall not recover from an authorized driver for an item described in Section 1939.03 to the extent the rental company obtains recovery from another person.

(d) This chapter applies only to the maximum liability of an authorized driver to the rental company resulting from damage to the rented vehicle and not to the liability of another person. *(Added by Stats.2016, c. 183 (A.B.2051), § 5, eff. Jan. 1, 2017.)*

§ 1939.09. Damage waiver; contents; rate limitations

(a)(1) Except as provided in subdivision (b), a damage waiver shall provide or, if not expressly stated in writing, shall be deemed to provide that the renter has no liability for damage, loss, loss of use, or a cost or expense incident thereto.

(2) Except as provided in subdivision (b), every limitation, exception, or exclusion to a damage waiver is void and unenforceable.

(b) A rental company may provide in the rental contract that a damage waiver does not apply under any of the following circumstances:

(1) Damage or loss results from an authorized driver's (A) intentional, willful, wanton, or reckless conduct, (B) operation of the vehicle under the influence of drugs or alcohol in violation of Section 23152 of the Vehicle Code, (C) towing or pushing anything, or (D) operation of the vehicle on an unpaved road if the damage or loss is a direct result of the road or driving conditions.

(2) Damage or loss occurs while the vehicle is (A) used for commercial hire, (B) used in connection with conduct that could be properly charged as a felony, (C) involved in a speed test or contest or in driver training activity, (D) operated by a person other than an authorized driver, or (E) operated outside the United States.

(3) An authorized driver who has (A) provided fraudulent information to the rental company, or (B) provided false information and the rental company would not have rented the vehicle if it had instead received true information.

(c)(1) A rental company that offers or provides a damage waiver for any consideration in addition to the rental rate shall clearly and conspicuously disclose the following information in the rental contract or holder in which the contract is placed and, also, in signs posted at the location where the renter signs the rental contract, and, for renters who are enrolled in the rental company's membership program, in a sign that shall be posted in a location clearly visible to those renters as they enter the location where their reserved rental vehicles are parked or near the exit of the bus or other conveyance that transports the enrollee to a reserved vehicle: (A) the nature of the renter's liability, such as liability for all collision damage regardless of cause, (B) the extent of the renter's liability, such as liability for damage or loss up to a specified amount, (C) the renter's personal insurance policy or the credit card used to pay for the vehicle rental transaction may provide coverage for all or a portion of the renter's potential liability, (D) the renter should consult with their insurer to determine the scope of insurance coverage, including the amount of the deductible, if any, for which the renter is obligated, (E) the renter may purchase an optional damage waiver to cover all liability, subject to whatever exceptions the rental company expressly lists that are permitted under subdivision (b), and (F) the range of charges for the damage waiver.

(2) In addition to the requirements of paragraph (1), a rental company that offers or provides a damage waiver shall orally disclose to all renters, except those who are participants in the rental company's membership program, that the damage waiver may be duplicative of coverage that the customer maintains under their own policy of motor vehicle insurance. The renter shall acknowledge receipt of the oral disclosure near that part of the contract where the renter indicates, by the renter's own initials, their acceptance or declination of the damage waiver. Adjacent to that same

§ 1939.09   OBLIGATIONS

part, the contract also shall state that the damage waiver is optional. Further, the contract for these renters shall include a clear and conspicuous written disclosure that the damage waiver may be duplicative of coverage that the customer maintains under their own policy of motor vehicle insurance.

(3)(A) The following is an example, for purposes of illustration and not limitation, of a notice fulfilling the requirements of paragraph (1) for a rental company that imposes liability on the renter for collision damage to the full value of the vehicle:

"NOTICE ABOUT YOUR FINANCIAL RESPONSIBILITY AND OPTIONAL DAMAGE WAIVER

You are responsible for all collision damage to the rented vehicle even if someone else caused it or the cause is unknown. You are responsible for the cost of repair up to the value of the vehicle, and towing, storage, and impound fees.

Your own insurance, or the issuer of the credit card you use to pay for the vehicle rental transaction, may cover all or part of your financial responsibility for the rented vehicle. You should check with your insurance company, or credit card issuer, to find out about your coverage and the amount of the deductible, if any, for which you may be liable.

Further, if you use a credit card that provides coverage for your potential liability, you should check with the issuer to determine if you must first exhaust the coverage limits of your own insurance before the credit card coverage applies.

The rental company will not hold you responsible if you buy a damage waiver. But a damage waiver will not protect you if (list exceptions)."

(B) When the notice in subparagraph (A) is printed in the rental contract or holder in which the contract is placed, the following shall be printed immediately following the notice:

"The cost of an optional damage waiver is $____ for every (day or week)."

(C) When the notice in subparagraph (A) appears on a sign, the following shall appear immediately adjacent to the notice:

"The cost of an optional damage waiver is $____ to $____ for every (day or week), depending upon the vehicle rented."

(d) Notwithstanding any other law, a rental company may sell a damage waiver for each full or partial 24-hour rental day for the damage waiver, subject to the following rate limitations:

(1) For rental vehicles that the rental company designates as an "economy car," "compact car," "intermediate car," "standard car," "full-size car," or another term having similar meaning to the five smallest body-size categories of vehicles established by the Association of Car Rental Industry Systems Standards for North America when offered for rental, the rate shall not exceed twenty-five dollars ($25).

(2) Starting January 1, 2023, and each January thereafter, the rate cap shall be increased based on the increase in the Consumer Price Index for All Urban Consumers (CPI–U) over the previous year as reported by the United States Bureau of Labor Statistics. *(Added by Stats.2016, c. 183 (A.B.2051), § 5, eff. Jan. 1, 2017. Amended by Stats.2021, c. 415 (A.B.901), § 1, eff. Jan. 1, 2022.)*

§ 1939.13. Purchase of damage waiver, optional insurance, or another optional good or service; prohibited rental company practices

(a) A rental company shall not require the purchase of a damage waiver, optional insurance, or another optional good or service.

(b) A rental company shall not engage in any unfair, deceptive, or coercive conduct to induce a renter to purchase the damage waiver, optional insurance, or another optional good or service, including conduct such as, but not limited to, refusing to honor the renter's reservation, limiting the availability of vehicles, requiring a deposit, or debiting or blocking the renter's credit card account for a sum equivalent to a deposit if the renter declines to purchase the damage waiver, optional insurance, or another optional good or service. *(Added by Stats.2016, c. 183 (A.B.2051), § 5, eff. Jan. 1, 2017.)*

§ 1939.15. Recovery on claim; express permission required to process credit card charge; other prohibited tactics

(a) In the absence of express permission granted by the renter subsequent to damage to, or loss of, the rented vehicle, a rental company shall not seek to recover any portion of a claim arising out of damage to, or loss of, the vehicle by processing a credit card charge or causing a debit or block to be placed on the renter's credit card account.

(b) A rental company shall not engage in any unfair, deceptive, or coercive tactics in attempting to recover or in recovering on any claim arising out of damage to, or loss of, the rented vehicle. *(Added by Stats.2016, c. 183 (A.B.2051), § 5, eff. Jan. 1, 2017.)*

§ 1939.17. Customer facility charges

A customer facility charge or alternative customer facility charge may be collected by a rental company pursuant to Section 50474.3 of the Government Code. *(Added by Stats.2016, c. 183 (A.B.2051), § 5, eff. Jan. 1, 2017.)*

§ 1939.19. Providing quote or imposing charges for rental; disclosure of additional mandatory charges

(a) When providing a quote, or imposing charges for a rental, the rental company may separately state the rental rate, additional mandatory charges, if any, and a mileage charge, if any, that a renter must pay to hire or lease the vehicle for the period of time to which the rental rate applies. A rental company shall not charge in addition to the rental rate, additional mandatory charges, or a mileage charge, as those may be applicable, any other fee that is required to be paid by the renter as a condition of hiring or leasing the vehicle.

(b) If additional mandatory charges are imposed, the rental company shall do each of the following:

(1) At the time the quote is given, provide the person receiving the quote with a good faith estimate of the rental rate and all additional mandatory charges, as well as the total charges for the entire rental. The total charges, if provided on an internet website page, shall be displayed in a typeface at least as large as any rental rate disclosed on that page and shall be provided on a page that the person receiving the quote may reach by following a link directly from the page on

which the rental rate is first provided. The good faith estimate may exclude mileage charges and charges for optional items that cannot be determined prior to completing the reservation based upon the information provided by the person.

(2) At the time and place the rental commences, clearly and conspicuously disclose in the rental contract, or that portion of the contract that is provided to the renter, the total of the rental rate and additional mandatory charges, for the entire rental, exclusive of charges that cannot be determined at the time the rental commences. Charges imposed pursuant to this paragraph shall be no more than the amount of the quote provided in a confirmed reservation, unless the person changes the terms of the rental contract subsequent to making the reservation.

(3) Provide each person, other than those persons within the rental company, offering quotes to actual or prospective customers access to information about additional mandatory charges, as well as access to information about when those charges apply. Any person providing quotes to actual or prospective customers for the hire or lease of a vehicle from a rental company shall provide the quotes in the manner described in paragraph (1).

(c) In addition to the rental rate, taxes, additional mandatory charges, if any, and mileage charges, if any, a rental company may charge for an item or service provided in connection with a particular rental transaction if the renter could have avoided incurring the charge by choosing not to obtain or utilize the optional item or service. Items and services for which the rental company may impose an additional charge include, but are not limited to, optional insurance and accessories requested by the renter, service charges incident to the renter's optional return of the vehicle to a location other than the location where the vehicle was hired or leased, and charges for refueling the vehicle at the conclusion of the rental transaction in the event the renter did not return the vehicle with as much fuel as was in the fuel tank at the beginning of the rental. A rental company also may impose an additional charge based on reasonable age criteria established by the rental company.

(d) A rental company may charge a fee for an authorized driver, in addition to the rental charge for an individual renter, unless the authorized driver is either of the following:

(1) The renter's spouse, as described in paragraph (2) of subdivision (e) of Section 1939.01, the renter's child or person for whom the renter is a legal guardian, the renter's sibling, or the renter's parent or grandparent.

(2) The renter's employer or coworker, as described in paragraph (3) of subdivision (e) of Section 1939.01.

(e) In the event that a rental company learns that an additional driver who was not previously authorized in the rental agreement has driven the rental car, the rental company may charge up to twice the authorized driver fee.

(f) If a rental company states a rental rate in print advertisement or in a quotation, the rental company shall disclose clearly in that advertisement or quotation the terms of mileage conditions relating to the advertised or quoted rental rate, including, but not limited to, to the extent applicable, the amount of mileage and gas charges, the number of miles for which no charges will be imposed, and a description of geographic driving limitations within the United States and Canada.

(g) All rate advertisements shall include a disclaimer, which shall be prominently displayed, providing that additional mandatory charges may be imposed, including, but not limited to, airport fees, tourism fees, vehicle license recovery fees, or other government imposed taxes or fees, and indicating that this information, including an estimate of the total rental cost, is displayed on the rental company's internet website. All rate advertisements shall also include a statement that additional charges may apply if an optional good or service, such as a damage waiver, is purchased.

(h) If any person or entity other than a rental company, including a passenger carrier or a seller of travel services, advertises a rental rate for a vehicle rental that includes additional mandatory charges, that person or entity shall clearly disclose the existence and amount of the charges. If a rental company provides the person or entity with rental rate and additional mandatory charges information, the rental car company is not responsible for the failure of that person or entity to comply with this subdivision.

(i) If a rental company delivers a vehicle to a renter at a location other than the location where the rental company normally carries on its business, the rental company shall not charge the renter an amount for the rental for the period before the delivery of the vehicle. If a rental company picks up a rented vehicle from a renter at a location other than the location where the rental company normally carries on its business, the rental company shall not charge the renter an amount for the rental for the period after the renter notifies the rental company to pick up the vehicle.

(j) Except as otherwise permitted pursuant to the customer facility charge, a rental company shall not separately charge, in addition to the rental rate, a fee for transporting the renter to a location where the rented vehicle will be delivered to the renter. (Added by Stats.2016, c. 183 (A.B. 2051), § 5, eff. Jan. 1, 2017. Amended by Stats.2021, c. 415 (A.B.901), § 2, eff. Jan. 1, 2022.)

§ 1939.21. Qualified business rentals; definitions; additional charges

(a) For purposes of this section:

(1) "Additional charges" means charges other than a per period base rental rate established by the business program.

(2) "Business program" means either of the following:

(A) A contract between a rental company and a business program sponsor that has established the per period base rental rate, and any other material terms relating to additional charges, on which the rental company will rent passenger vehicles to persons authorized by the sponsor.

(B) A plan, program, or other arrangement established by a rental company at the request of, or with the consent of, a business program sponsor under which the rental company offers to rent passenger vehicles to persons authorized by the sponsor at per period base rental rates, and any other material terms relating to additional charges, that are not the same as those generally offered by the rental company to the public.

§ 1939.21

(3) "Business program sponsor" means a legal entity, other than a natural person, that is a corporation, limited liability company, or partnership.

(4) "Business renter" means, for any business program sponsor, a person who is authorized by the sponsor, through the use of an identifying number or program name or code, to enter into a rental contract under the sponsor's business program. In no case shall the term "business renter" include a person renting as any of the following:

(A) A nonemployee member of a not-for-profit organization.

(B) The purchaser of a voucher or other prepaid rental arrangement from a person, including a tour operator, engaged in the business of reselling those vouchers or prepaid rental arrangements to the general public.

(C) An individual whose vehicle rental is eligible for reimbursement in whole or in part as a result of the person being insured or provided coverage under a policy of insurance issued by an insurance company.

(D) An individual whose vehicle rental is eligible for reimbursement in whole or in part as a result of the person purchasing passenger vehicle repair services from a person licensed to perform such services.

(5) "Qualified business rental" under a business program established for a business program sponsor by a rental company means the rental of a passenger vehicle under the business program if either: (A) in the 12–month period ending on the date of the rental or in the calendar year immediately preceding the year in which the rental occurs, the rentals under all business programs established by the rental company for the business program sponsor and its affiliates produced gross rental revenues in excess of twenty-five thousand dollars ($25,000) or (B) the rental company in good faith estimates that rentals under all the business programs established by the rental company for the business program sponsor and its affiliates will produce gross rental revenues in excess of twenty-five thousand dollars ($25,000) in the 12–month period commencing with the date of the rental or in the calendar year in which the rental occurs. The rental company has the burden of establishing by objectively verifiable evidence that the rental was a qualified business rental.

(6) "Quote" means telephonic, in-person, and computer-transmitted quotations.

(b) Notwithstanding any provision to the contrary contained in Section 1939.19 or 1939.23, a rental company may, in connection with the qualified business rental of a passenger vehicle to a business renter of a business program sponsor under the sponsor's business program, do both of the following:

(1) Separately quote additional charges for the rental if, at the time the quote is provided, the person receiving the quote is also provided a good faith estimate of the total of all the charges for the entire rental. The estimate may exclude mileage charges and charges for optional items and services that cannot be determined prior to completing the reservation based upon the information provided by the renter.

(2) Separately impose additional charges for the rental, if the rental contract, or another document provided to the business renter at the time and place the rental commences, clearly and conspicuously discloses the total of all the charges for the entire rental, exclusive of charges that cannot be determined at the time the rental commences.

(c) A renter may bring an action against a rental company for the recovery of damages and appropriate equitable relief for a violation of this section. The prevailing party shall be entitled to recover reasonable attorney's fees and costs.

(d) Any waiver of any of the provisions of this section shall be void and unenforceable as contrary to public policy.

(e) This section shall not be interpreted to mean that a rental company is not required to comply with the requirements of subdivisions (c) to (h), inclusive, of Section 1939.19. *(Added by Stats.2016, c. 183 (A.B.2051), § 5, eff. Jan. 1, 2017.)*

§ 1939.22. Rental or lease agreement; electronic communication; denial of rental or lease agreement prohibited

A rental company shall send communications to a renter electronically if the renter agrees to that communication in the rental or lease agreement. A rental company shall not deny a rental or lease agreement if the renter chooses not to receive communications electronically. For purposes of this section, "electronically" does not include a cellular telephone. *(Added by Stats.2018, c. 344 (A.B.2620), § 1, eff. Jan. 1, 2019.)*

§ 1939.23. Use of electronic surveillance technology prohibited; exceptions

(a) A rental company shall not use, access, or obtain any information relating to the renter's use of the rental vehicle that was obtained using electronic surveillance technology, except in the following circumstances:

(1)(A) When the equipment is used by the rental company only for the purpose of locating a stolen, abandoned, or missing rental vehicle after one of the following:

(i) The renter or law enforcement has informed the rental company that the vehicle is missing or has been stolen or abandoned.

(ii) Until January 1, 2024, and for purposes of this clause, if the rental vehicle has not been returned following 72 hours after the contracted return date or by 72 hours following the end of an extension of that return date, the rental company may activate electronic surveillance technology. The rental company shall provide notice of activation of the electronic surveillance technology 24 hours prior to activation, by telephone and electronically pursuant to Section 1939.22, unless the renter has not provided a telephone number or the renter has not agreed to electronic communication pursuant to Section 1939.22. The rental or lease agreement shall advise the renter that electronic surveillance technology may be activated if the rental vehicle has not been returned within 72 hours after the contracted return date or extension of the return date. The renter shall acknowledge this advisement in the rental or lease agreement by initials. The advisement shall also be made orally to the renter at the time of executing the rental or lease agreement. The advisements are not required to be made to members of the rental company's membership program executing a rental or lease agreement; however, a renter shall be given those advisements upon enrolling in the rental company's membership program.

(iii) Notwithstanding clause (ii), if the rental vehicle has not been returned following one week after the contracted return date or by one week following the end of an extension of that return date.

(iv) The rental company discovers the rental vehicle has been stolen or abandoned, and, if stolen, the rental company shall report the vehicle stolen to law enforcement by filing a stolen vehicle report, unless law enforcement has already informed the rental company that the vehicle is missing or has been stolen or abandoned.

(v) The rental vehicle is the subject of an AMBER Alert issued pursuant to Section 8594 of the Government Code. If the rental company uses the equipment in connection with this provision relating to an AMBER Alert, the rental company shall notify law enforcement that one of the rental company's vehicles is the subject of an AMBER Alert upon becoming aware of the situation, unless law enforcement has already informed the rental company that the vehicle was the subject of an AMBER Alert.

(B) If electronic surveillance technology is activated pursuant to subparagraph (A), a rental company shall maintain a record, in either electronic or written form, of information relevant to the activation of that technology. That information shall include the rental agreement, including the return date, and the date and time the electronic surveillance technology was activated. The record shall also include, if relevant, a record of written or other communication with the renter, including communications regarding extensions of the rental, police reports, or other written communication with law enforcement officials. The record shall be maintained for a period of at least 12 months from the time the record is created and shall be made available upon the renter's request. The rental company shall maintain and furnish explanatory codes necessary to read the record. A rental company shall not be required to maintain a record if electronic surveillance technology is activated to recover a rental vehicle that is stolen or missing at a time other than during a rental period.

(2) In response to a specific request from law enforcement pursuant to a subpoena or search warrant.

(b) Subdivision (a) does not prohibit a rental company from equipping rental vehicles with any of the following:

(1) GPS–based technology that provides navigation assistance to the occupants of the rental vehicle, if the rental company does not use, access, or obtain information relating to the renter's use of the rental vehicle that was obtained using that technology, except for the purposes of discovering or repairing a defect in the technology and the information may then be used only for that purpose.

(2) Electronic surveillance technology that allows for the remote locking or unlocking of the vehicle at the request of the renter, if the rental company does not use, access, or obtain information relating to the renter's use of the rental vehicle that was obtained using that technology, except as necessary to lock or unlock the vehicle.

(3) Electronic surveillance technology that allows the company to provide roadside assistance, such as towing, flat tire, or fuel services, at the request of the renter, if the rental company does not use, access, or obtain information relating to the renter's use of the rental vehicle that was obtained using that technology except as necessary to provide the requested roadside assistance.

(c) Subdivision (a) does not prohibit a rental company from obtaining, accessing, or using information from electronic surveillance technology for the sole purpose of determining the date and time the vehicle departs from and is returned to the rental company, and the total mileage driven and the vehicle fuel level of the returned vehicle. The information obtained or accessed from this electronic surveillance technology shall only be used for the purpose described in this subdivision.

(d) A rental company shall not use electronic surveillance technology to track a renter in order to impose fines or surcharges relating to the renter's use of the rental vehicle. *(Added by Stats.2016, c. 183 (A.B.2051), § 5, eff. Jan. 1, 2017. Amended by Stats.2017, c. 163 (S.B.466), § 1, eff. Jan. 1, 2018; Stats.2018, c. 344 (A.B.2620), § 2, eff. Jan. 1, 2019.)*

§ 1939.25. Action against rental company for violation of chapter; attorney's fees and costs

A renter may bring an action against a rental company for the recovery of damages and appropriate equitable relief for a violation of this chapter, except for Sections 1939.21, 1939.35, and 1939.37. The prevailing party shall be entitled to recover reasonable attorney's fees and costs. *(Added by Stats.2016, c. 183 (A.B.2051), § 5, eff. Jan. 1, 2017.)*

§ 1939.27. Action against renter for loss due to theft of vehicle; jurisdiction

A rental company that brings an action against a renter for loss due to theft of the vehicle shall bring the action in the county in which the renter resides or, if the renter is not a resident of this state, in the jurisdiction in which the renter resides. *(Added by Stats.2016, c. 183 (A.B.2051), § 5, eff. Jan. 1, 2017.)*

§ 1939.29. Waiver of provisions void and unenforceable

A waiver of any of the provisions of this chapter, except for Sections 1939.21, 1939.35, and 1939.37, shall be void and unenforceable as contrary to public policy. *(Added by Stats.2016, c. 183 (A.B.2051), § 5, eff. Jan. 1, 2017.)*

§ 1939.31. Renters enrolled in membership program; disclosure requirements

(a) A rental company's disclosure requirements shall be satisfied for renters who are enrolled in the rental company's membership program if all of the following conditions are met:

(1) Prior to the enrollee's first rental as a participant in the program, the renter receives, in writing, the following:

(A) All of the disclosures required by paragraph (1) of subdivision (c) of Section 1939.09, including the terms and conditions of the rental agreement then in effect.

(B) An internet website address, as well as a contact number or address, where the enrollee can learn of changes to the rental agreement or to the laws of this state governing rental agreements since the effective date of the rental company's most recent restatement of the rental agreement and distribution of that restatement to its members.

(2) At the commencement of each rental period, the renter is provided, on the rental record or the folder in which it is inserted, with a printed notice stating that the renter had either previously selected or declined an optional damage waiver and that the renter has the right to change preferences.

(b) This section does not relieve the rental company from the disclosures required to be made within the text of a contract or holder in which the contract is placed; in or on an advertisement containing a rental rate; or in a telephonic, in-person, or computer-transmitted quotation or reservation. *(Added by Stats.2016, c. 183 (A.B.2051), § 5, eff. Jan. 1, 2017. Amended by Stats.2021, c. 415 (A.B.901), § 3, eff. Jan. 1, 2022.)*

§ 1939.33. Foreign renters; service of process

(a) When a rental company enters into a rental agreement in the state for the rental of a vehicle to any renter who is not a resident of this country and, as part of, or associated with, the rental agreement, the renter purchases liability insurance, as defined in subdivision (b) of Section 1758.85 of the Insurance Code, from the rental company in its capacity as a rental vehicle agent for an authorized insurer, the rental company shall be authorized to accept, and, if served as set forth in this section, shall accept, service of a summons and complaint and any other required documents against the foreign renter for any accident or collision resulting from the operation of the rental vehicle within the state during the rental period. If the rental company has a registered agent for service of process on file with the Secretary of State, process shall be served on the rental company's registered agent, either by first-class mail, return receipt requested, or by personal service.

(b) Within 30 days of acceptance of service of process, the rental company shall provide a copy of the summons and complaint and any other required documents served in accordance with this section to the foreign renter by first-class mail, return receipt requested.

(c) Any plaintiff, or his or her representative, who elects to serve the foreign renter by delivering a copy of the summons and complaint and any other required documents to the rental company pursuant to subdivision (a) shall agree to limit his or her recovery against the foreign renter and the rental company to the limits of the protection extended by the liability insurance.

(d) Notwithstanding the requirements of Sections 17450 to 17456, inclusive, of the Vehicle Code, service of process in compliance with subdivision (a) shall be deemed a valid and effective service.

(e) Notwithstanding any other law, the requirement that the rental company accept service of process pursuant to subdivision (a) shall not create any duty, obligation, or agency relationship other than that provided in subdivision (a). *(Added by Stats.2016, c. 183 (A.B.2051), § 5, eff. Jan. 1, 2017.)*

§ 1939.35. 15–passenger vans; renter documentation

(a)(1) A rental company shall provide a renter of a 15–passenger van with a copy of the United States Department of Transportation, National Highway Traffic Safety Administration's consumer advisory for 15-passenger vans titled "Reducing the Risk of Rollover Crashes" or, if that advisory is updated, a copy of the updated advisory. The renter shall acknowledge receipt of that copy by signing an acknowledgment of receipt on the rental agreement or on an attached form.

(2) If the rental of that 15–passenger van is for a business purpose or use, the rental company shall also provide on the document described in paragraph (1) that only an employee with the proper licensing may drive that vehicle. The renter shall acknowledge the receipt thereof in the same manner as described in paragraph (1).

(b)(1) Except as provided in paragraph (2), for purposes of this section, a "15–passenger van" means any van manufactured to accommodate 15 passengers, including the driver, regardless of whether that van has been altered to accommodate fewer than 15 passengers.

(2) For purposes of this section, a "15–passenger van" does not mean a 15–passenger van with dual rear wheels that has a gross weight rating equal to, or greater than, 11,500 pounds. *(Added by Stats.2016, c. 183 (A.B.2051), § 5, eff. Jan. 1, 2017.)*

§ 1939.37. Rental company not subject to specified vehicle rental requirements; conditions

A rental company is not subject to the requirements of Section 14608 of the Vehicle Code if the rental is subject to the terms of a membership agreement that allows the renter to gain physical access to a vehicle without a key through use of a code, key card, or by other means that allow the vehicle to be accessed at a remote location, or at a business location of the rental company outside of that location's regular hours of operation. *(Added by Stats.2016, c. 183 (A.B.2051), § 5, eff. Jan. 1, 2017.)*

CHAPTER 2. HIRING OF REAL PROPERTY

Section	
1940.	Application of chapter; "persons who hire" and "dwelling unit".
1940.05.	"Immigration or citizenship status" defined.
1940.1.	Occupants of residential hotels; moving or checking out and reregistering.
1940.2.	Unlawful actions by landlord to influence tenant to vacate; civil penalties; oral or written notice of violations of lease.
1940.3.	Immigration or citizenship status; public entity legislation prohibited; unlawful actions by landlord.
1940.35.	Immigration or citizenship status; disclosure by landlord prohibited; exception for compliance with legal obligation; remedies.
1940.4.	Posting or displaying political signs by tenant; landlord not to prohibit; exceptions; location; time limit; notice and enforcement of changes in terms of tenancy.
1940.45.	Posting or displaying religious items; landlord not to prohibit; exceptions; location; size.
1940.5.	Refusal to rent to otherwise qualified tenant on basis of possession of waterbed prohibited; requirements and conditions.
1940.6.	Demolition of residential dwelling unit; notice to prospective tenants; contents; remedies and civil penalties for noncompliance; attorney's fees.

ARISING FROM PARTICULAR TRANSACTIONS

Section
1940.7. Disclosure of former federal or state ordnance locations.
1940.7.5. Repealed.
1940.8. Pest control company notices.
1940.8.5. Written notice of pesticide application; contents.
1940.9. Gas and electric meters; notice to tenant when meter serves area outside tenant's dwelling unit; cost of services; remedies.
1940.10. Personal agriculture; tenant's authority to maintain portable containers under certain conditions; use of pesticides or other synthetic chemical products; landlord inspections.
1940.20. Tenant use of clothesline or drying rack; conditions.
1941. Buildings for human occupancy; fitness; repairs.
1941.1. Untenantable dwellings; program assistance for heating or hot water system repairs or replacement.
1941.2. Tenant's affirmative obligations.
1941.3. Buildings intended for human habitation; landlord's duties; tenants' duties; violations; exempt buildings.
1941.4. Residential buildings; lessors' responsibilities; inside telephone wiring.
1941.5. Tenant protected by restraining order against nontenant; change of locks on dwelling unit; definitions.
1941.6. Tenant protected by restraining order against another tenant; change of locks on dwelling unit; liability regarding person excluded; definitions.
1941.7. Obligation of lessor to repair dilapidation relating to presence of mold; notice; authority to enter dwelling unit for repair.
1942. Repairs by tenant; rent deduction or vacation of premises; presumption; limit; nonavailability of remedy; additional remedy.
1942.1. Waiver of rights; public policy; arbitration of untenantability.
1942.2. Payment to utility or district; deduction from rent.
1942.3. Unlawful detainer; burden of proof; rebuttable presumption landlord breached habitability requirements; conditions.
1942.4. Demand, collection or increase of rent under certain enumerated conditions; landlord liability; attorney's fees; abatement and repair; additional remedies.
1942.5. Retaliation; prohibited acts; violations; remedies; penalties.
1942.6. Entry on property for purposes of tenants' rights.
1942.7. Conditions on occupancy based on declawing or devocalizing animals allowed on the premises; restrictions on persons or corporations occupying, owning, managing, or providing services in connection with real property; declaratory or injunctive relief; civil penalties.
1942.8. Temporarily permitting the occupancy of dwelling unit by person at risk of homelessness; rights and obligations of landlord, tenant, and person at risk of homelessness.
1942.9. Tenant having COVID–19 rental debt who has submitted declaration of COVID–19–related financial distress; prohibited landlord actions; service or amenity reductions as a result of compliance with public health orders or guidelines.
1943. Term of hiring; presumption.
1944. Term of hiring; presumption; lodgings or dwelling house.

Section
1945. Renewal by continued possession and acceptance of rent.
1945.5. Automatic renewal or extension; recitals in contract; size of type, etc.
1946. Renewable hiring; notice of termination.
1946.1. Renewal and termination with respect to hiring of residential real property for a term not specified by the parties; notice.
1946.2. Termination of tenancy after continuous and lawful occupation of residential real property for 12 months; just cause required; notice; additional tenants; opportunity to cure violation; relocation assistance or rent waiver; application of section.
1946.5. Room by single lodger on periodic basis within dwelling unit occupied by owner; termination; written notice; removal from premises.
1946.7. Victims of domestic violence, sexual assault, stalking, human trafficking, or abuse of elder or dependent adult; written notice to terminate tenancy; requirements of notice; landlord disclosure to third party; violations and remedies.
1946.8. Summoning law enforcement assistance or emergency assistance; lease or rental agreement provisions prohibiting or limiting right void; penalties prohibited; establishing belief; waiver void and unenforceable; affirmative defense; remedies.
1947. Rent; time of payment.
1947.3. Cash or electronic funds transfer as exclusive form of payment of rent or security deposit; conditions; payment of rent by third party; right to terminate tenancy; form; mutual agreement; waiver.
1947.5. Prohibition by residential dwelling unit landlord of smoking cigarettes or other tobacco products; lease or rental agreement provisions.
1947.6. Installation of electric vehicle charging station upon request by lessee; leases executed, extended or renewed on and after July 1, 2015; exceptions; requirements.
1947.7. Local rent stabilization and rent control programs; enforcement; confidential information.
1947.8. Local rent controls; establishment and certification of permissible rent levels; appeal; fee; public record.
1947.9. San Francisco rent stabilization ordinance; limitations on compensation for temporary displacement; interpretation of section.
1947.10. Evictions based on fraudulent intent to occupy; treble damages.
1947.11. Rent charged in excess of certified lawful rent ceiling; refunds.
1947.12. Limitation of rent increase; subleases; application of section; notice; report to Legislature; legislative findings, declarations, and intent.
1947.13. Assisted housing developments; rental rates and increases.
1947.15. Rent control; calculation of fair return to owner; reasonable expenses, fees and costs for professional services.
1948. Attornment to a stranger.
1949. Tenant's obligation to deliver certain notices to landlord; damages.
1950. Letting parts of rooms; double letting of rooms.
1950.1. Reusable tenant screening report; required information; currency; fees; definitions; construction with state and local laws; landlord discretion to accept reusable tenant screening reports.

OBLIGATIONS

Section

1950.5. Security for rental agreement for residential property used as dwelling of tenant; amount and disposition; damages.

1950.6. Rental application screening fees; amount; receipt; copies of credit reports; construction of section with housing assistance programs.

1950.7. Payment or deposit of money to secure performance of rental agreement for other than residential property; status of and claims against deposit; duty of landlord on termination of interest.

1950.8. Payment of money, including but not limited to key money, or the lessor's attorney's fees incurred in preparation of lease or rental agreement, as a condition of initiating, continuing, or renewing a lease or rental agreement; statement of payment amount in agreement; penalties.

1951. "Rent" and "lease" defined.

1951.2. Termination of lease; remedy of lessor.

1951.3. Abandonment of real property other than commercial real property; notice by lessor; form; defenses of lessee.

1951.35. Abandonment of commercial property by lessee; notice by lessor; form; defenses of lessee.

1951.4. Remedy provided by lease; provisions.

1951.5. Liquidated damages.

1951.7. "Advance payment" defined; notice of reletting.

1951.8. Equitable relief.

1952. Actions for unlawful detainer, forcible entry, and forcible detainer; effect.

1952.2. Inapplicability of Sections 1951 to 1952, inclusive, to certain leases.

1952.3. Unlawful detainer; possession not in issue; conversion to action for damages.

1952.4. Agreement for exploration for or removal of natural resources not lease of real property.

1952.6. Applicability to leases between public entities and nonprofit corporations; substitution of remedies for breach.

1952.7. Enforceability of lease terms prohibiting or unreasonably restricting installation of electric vehicle charging station; exceptions; charging station requirements.

1952.8. Gasoline service stations; leases; vapor control system; requirements.

1953. Waiver or modification of lessee's rights; void as contrary to public policy; exception; applicability of section.

1954. Entry of dwelling by landlord; conditions; oral agreement between tenant and landlord.

1954.05. Assignment for the benefit of creditors; right of assignee to occupy business premises; payment of rent; time.

1954.06. Assisted housing development; election to have rental payment information reported to credit agency; fee; evaluation of impact of rental payment reporting.

Cross References

Employee housing, termination or modification of tenancy or retaliatory employment actions, enforcement of tenants' rights, see Health and Safety Code §§ 17031.5, 17031.7.

Immigration or citizenship status irrelevant to issues of liability or remedy in specified proceedings, discovery, see Civil Code § 3339.10.

§ 1940. Application of chapter; "persons who hire" and "dwelling unit"

(a) Except as provided in subdivision (b), this chapter shall apply to all persons who hire dwelling units located within this state including tenants, lessees, boarders, lodgers, and others, however denominated.

(b) The term "persons who hire" shall not include a person who maintains either of the following:

(1) Transient occupancy in a hotel, motel, residence club, or other facility when the transient occupancy is or would be subject to tax under Section 7280 of the Revenue and Taxation Code. The term "persons who hire" shall not include a person to whom this paragraph pertains if the person has not made valid payment for all room and other related charges owing as of the last day on which his or her occupancy is or would be subject to tax under Section 7280 of the Revenue and Taxation Code.

(2) Occupancy at a hotel or motel where the innkeeper retains a right of access to and control of the dwelling unit and the hotel or motel provides or offers all of the following services to all of the residents:

(A) Facilities for the safeguarding of personal property pursuant to Section 1860.

(B) Central telephone service subject to tariffs covering the same filed with the California Public Utilities Commission.

(C) Maid, mail, and room services.

(D) Occupancy for periods of less than seven days.

(E) Food service provided by a food establishment, as defined in Section 113780 of the Health and Safety Code, located on or adjacent to the premises of the hotel or motel and owned or operated by the innkeeper or owned or operated by a person or entity pursuant to a lease or similar relationship with the innkeeper or person or entity affiliated with the innkeeper.

(c) "Dwelling unit" means a structure or the part of a structure that is used as a home, residence, or sleeping place by one person who maintains a household or by two or more persons who maintain a common household.

(d) Nothing in this section shall be construed to limit the application of any provision of this chapter to tenancy in a dwelling unit unless the provision is so limited by its specific terms. (Added by Stats.1976, c. 712, p. 1727, § 1. Amended by Stats.1994, c. 680 (S.B.2088), § 1; Stats.1996, c. 1023 (S.B.1497), § 28, eff. Sept. 29, 1996.)

Cross References

Real estate brokers, solicitation for transient occupancies, Definition exemption, see Business and Professions Code § 10131.01.

Records and account books, maintenance, see Civil Code § 1864.

§ 1940.05. "Immigration or citizenship status" defined

For purposes of this chapter, "immigration or citizenship status" includes a perception that the person has a particular immigration status or citizenship status, or that the person is associated with a person who has, or is perceived to have, a particular immigration status or citizenship status. (Added by Stats.2017, c. 489 (A.B.291), § 2, eff. Jan. 1, 2018.)

§ 1940.1. Occupants of residential hotels; moving or checking out and reregistering

(a) No person may require an occupant of a residential hotel, as defined in Section 50519 of the Health and Safety Code, to move, or to check out and reregister, before the expiration of 30 days occupancy if a purpose is to have that occupant maintain transient occupancy status pursuant to paragraph (1) of subdivision (b) of Section 1940. Evidence that an occupant was required to check out and reregister shall create a rebuttable presumption, which shall affect solely the burden of producing evidence, of the purpose referred to in this subdivision.

(b) In addition to any remedies provided by local ordinance, any violation of subdivision (a) is punishable by a civil penalty of five hundred dollars ($500). In any action brought pursuant to this section, the prevailing party shall be entitled to reasonable attorney's fees.

(c) Nothing in this section shall prevent a local governing body from establishing inspection authority or reporting or recordkeeping requirements to ensure compliance with this section. (Added by Stats.1990, c. 1235 (A.B.3926), § 1. Amended by Stats.1991, c. 245 (A.B.537), § 1, eff. July 29, 1991; Stats.2004, c. 950 (A.B.2867), § 1.)

Cross References

Levy on privilege of occupying rooms or living space in a hotel, see Revenue and Taxation Code § 7280.

§ 1940.2. Unlawful actions by landlord to influence tenant to vacate; civil penalties; oral or written notice of violations of lease

(a) It is unlawful for a landlord to do any of the following for the purpose of influencing a tenant to vacate a dwelling:

(1) Engage in conduct that violates subdivision (a) of Section 484 of the Penal Code.

(2) Engage in conduct that violates Section 518 of the Penal Code.

(3) Use, or threaten to use, force, willful threats, or menacing conduct constituting a course of conduct that interferes with the tenant's quiet enjoyment of the premises in violation of Section 1927 that would create an apprehension of harm in a reasonable person. Nothing in this paragraph requires a tenant to be actually or constructively evicted in order to obtain relief.

(4) Commit a significant and intentional violation of Section 1954.

(5) Threaten to disclose information regarding or relating to the immigration or citizenship status of a tenant, occupant, or other person known to the landlord to be associated with a tenant or occupant. This paragraph does not require a tenant to be actually or constructively evicted in order to obtain relief.

(b) A tenant who prevails in a civil action, including an action in small claims court, to enforce his or her rights under this section is entitled to a civil penalty in an amount not to exceed two thousand dollars ($2,000) for each violation.

(c) An oral or written warning notice, given in good faith, regarding conduct by a tenant, occupant, or guest that violates, may violate, or violated the applicable rental agreement, rules, regulations, lease, or laws, is not a violation of this section. An oral or written explanation of the rental agreement, rules, regulations, lease, or laws given in the normal course of business is not a violation of this section.

(d) This section does not enlarge or diminish a landlord's right to terminate a tenancy pursuant to existing state or local law; nor does this section enlarge or diminish any ability of local government to regulate or enforce a prohibition against a landlord's harassment of a tenant. (Added by Stats.2003, c. 542 (A.B.1059), § 1. Amended by Stats.2017, c. 489 (A.B. 291), § 3, eff. Jan. 1, 2018.)

§ 1940.3. Immigration or citizenship status; public entity legislation prohibited; unlawful actions by landlord

(a) A public entity shall not, by ordinance, regulation, policy, or administrative action implementing any ordinance, regulation, policy, or administrative action, compel a landlord or any agent of the landlord to make any inquiry, compile, disclose, report, or provide any information, prohibit offering or continuing to offer, accommodations in the property for rent or lease, or otherwise take any action regarding or based on the immigration or citizenship status of a tenant, prospective tenant, occupant, or prospective occupant of residential rental property.

(b) A landlord, or any agent of the landlord, shall not do any of the following:

(1) Make any inquiry regarding or based on the immigration or citizenship status of a tenant, prospective tenant, occupant, or prospective occupant of residential rental property.

(2) Require that any tenant, prospective tenant, occupant, or prospective occupant of the rental property disclose or make any statement, representation, or certification concerning his or her immigration or citizenship status.

(3) Disclose to any person or entity information regarding or relating to the immigration or citizenship status of any tenant, prospective tenant, occupant, or prospective occupant of the rental property for the purpose of, or with the intent of, harassing or intimidating a tenant, prospective tenant, occupant, or prospective occupant, retaliating against a tenant or occupant for the exercise of his or her rights, influencing a tenant or occupant to vacate a dwelling, or recovering possession of the dwelling.

(c) This section does not prohibit a landlord from doing any of the following:

(1) Complying with any legal obligation under federal law, including, but not limited to, any legal obligation under any federal government program that provides for rent limitations or rental assistance to a qualified tenant, or a subpoena, warrant, or other order issued by a court.

(2) Requesting information or documentation necessary to determine or verify the financial qualifications of a prospective tenant, or to determine or verify the identity of a prospective tenant or prospective occupant.

(d) For purposes of this section, both of the following shall apply:

(1) "Public entity" includes the state, a city, county, city and county, district, public authority, public agency, and any other political subdivision or public corporation in the state.

(2) "State" includes any state office, department, division, bureau, board, or commission and the Trustees of the California State University and the California State University. *(Added by Stats.2007, c. 403 (A.B.976), § 1. Amended by Stats.2017, c. 489 (A.B.291), § 4, eff. Jan. 1, 2018; Stats.2017, c. 490 (A.B.299), § 1.5, eff. Jan. 1, 2018.)*

Cross References

Immigration or citizenship status, prohibited landlord actions, rebuttable presumptions, see Code of Civil Procedure § 1161.4.

§ 1940.35. Immigration or citizenship status; disclosure by landlord prohibited; exception for compliance with legal obligation; remedies

(a) It is unlawful for a landlord to disclose to any immigration authority, law enforcement agency, or local, state, or federal agency information regarding or relating to the immigration or citizenship status of any tenant, occupant, or other person known to the landlord to be associated with a tenant or occupant, for the purpose of, or with the intent of, harassing or intimidating a tenant or occupant, retaliating against a tenant or occupant for the exercise of his or her rights, influencing a tenant or occupant to vacate a dwelling, or recovering possession of the dwelling, irrespective of whether the tenant or occupant currently resides in the dwelling.

(b) If a court of applicable jurisdiction finds a violation of this section in a proceeding initiated by a party or upon a motion of the court, the court shall do all of the following:

(1) For each person whose status was so disclosed, order the landlord to pay statutory damages in an amount to be determined in the court's discretion that is between 6 and 12 times the monthly rent charged for the dwelling in which the tenant or occupant resides or resided.

(2) Issue injunctive relief to prevent the landlord from engaging in similar conduct with respect to other tenants, occupants, and persons known to the landlord to be associated with the tenants or occupants.

(3) Notify the district attorney of the county in which the real property for hire is located of a potential violation of Section 519 of the Penal Code.

(c) A landlord is not in violation of this section if he or she is complying with any legal obligation under federal law, or subpoena, warrant, or order issued by a court.

(d) In making findings in a proceeding under this section, a court may take judicial notice under subdivision (d) of Section 452 of the Evidence Code of the proceedings and records of any federal removal, inadmissibility, or deportation proceeding.

(e) A court shall award to the prevailing party in an action under this section attorney's fees and costs.

(f) The remedies provided by this section shall be in addition to any other remedies provided by statutory or decisional law.

(g) Any waiver of a right under this section by a tenant, occupant, or person known to the landlord to be associated with a tenant or occupant shall be void as a matter of public policy.

(h) An action for injunctive relief pursuant to this section may be brought by a nonprofit organization exempt from federal income taxation under Section 501(c)(3) of the Internal Revenue Code,[1] as amended. That organization shall be considered a party for purposes of this section. *(Added by Stats.2017, c. 489 (A.B.291), § 5, eff. Jan. 1, 2018.)*

[1] Internal Revenue Code sections are in Title 26 of the U.S.C.A.

§ 1940.4. Posting or displaying political signs by tenant; landlord not to prohibit; exceptions; location; time limit; notice and enforcement of changes in terms of tenancy

(a) Except as provided in subdivision (c), a landlord shall not prohibit a tenant from posting or displaying political signs relating to any of the following:

(1) An election or legislative vote, including an election of a candidate to public office.

(2) The initiative, referendum, or recall process.

(3) Issues that are before a public commission, public board, or elected local body for a vote.

(b) Political signs may be posted or displayed in the window or on the door of the premises leased by the tenant in a multifamily dwelling, or from the yard, window, door, balcony, or outside wall of the premises leased by a tenant of a single-family dwelling.

(c) A landlord may prohibit a tenant from posting or displaying political signs in the following circumstances:

(1) The political sign is more than six square feet in size.

(2) The posting or displaying would violate a local, state, or federal law.

(3) The posting or displaying would violate a lawful provision in a common interest development governing a document that satisfies the criteria of Section 1353.6.

(d) A tenant shall post and remove political signs in compliance with the time limits set by the ordinance for the jurisdiction where the premises are located. A tenant shall be solely responsible for any violation of a local ordinance. If no local ordinance exists or if the local ordinance does not include a time limit for posting and removing political signs on private property, the landlord may establish a reasonable time period for the posting and removal of political signs. A reasonable time period for this purpose shall begin at least 90 days prior to the date of the election or vote to which the sign relates and end at least 15 days following the date of the election or vote.

(e) Notwithstanding any other provision of law, any changes in the terms of a tenancy that are made to implement the provisions of this section and are noticed pursuant to Section 827 shall not be deemed to cause a diminution in housing services, and may be enforced in accordance with Section 1161 of the Code of Civil Procedure. *(Added by Stats.2011, c. 383 (S.B.337), § 1.)*

§ 1940.45. Posting or displaying religious items; landlord not to prohibit; exceptions; location; size

(a) Except as otherwise provided by this section, a property owner shall not enforce or adopt a restrictive covenant or any other restriction that prohibits one or more religious items from being displayed or affixed on any entry door or entry door frame of a dwelling.

(b) To the extent permitted by Article 1, Section 4, of the California Constitution and the First Amendment to the United States Constitution, this section does not prohibit the enforcement or adoption of a restrictive covenant or other restriction prohibiting the display or affixing of a religious item on any entry door or entry door frame to a dwelling that:

(1) Threatens the public health or safety.

(2) Hinders the opening or closing of any entry door.

(3) Violates any federal, state, or local law.

(4) Contains graphics, language or any display that is obscene or otherwise illegal.

(5) Individually or in combination with any other religious item displayed or affixed on any entry door or door frame that has a total size greater than 36 by 12 square inches, provided it does not exceed the size of the door.

(c) As used in this section, the following terms have the following meanings:

(1) "Property owner" means all of the following:

(A) An association, as that term is defined in Section 4080.

(B) A board, as that term is defined in Section 4085.

(C) A member, as that term is defined in Section 4160.

(D) A landlord, as that term is defined in Section 1940.8.5.

(E) A sublessor.

(2) "Religious item" means an item displayed because of sincerely held religious beliefs.   *(Added by Stats.2019, c. 154 (S.B.652), § 1, eff. Jan. 1, 2020.)*

§ 1940.5. Refusal to rent to otherwise qualified tenant on basis of possession of waterbed prohibited; requirements and conditions

An owner or an owner's agent shall not refuse to rent a dwelling unit in a structure which received its valid certificate of occupancy after January 1, 1973, to an otherwise qualified prospective tenant or refuse to continue to rent to an existing tenant solely on the basis of that tenant's possession of a waterbed or other bedding with liquid filling material where all of the following requirements and conditions are met:

(a) A tenant or prospective tenant furnishes to the owner, prior to installation, a valid waterbed insurance policy or certificate of insurance for property damage. The policy shall be issued by a company licensed to do business in California and possessing a Best's Insurance Report rating of "B" or higher. The insurance policy shall be maintained in full force and effect until the bedding is permanently removed from the rental premises. The policy shall be written for no less than one hundred thousand dollars ($100,000) of coverage. The policy shall cover, up to the limits of the policy, replacement value of all property damage, including loss of use, incurred by the rental property owner or other caused by or arising out of the ownership, maintenance, use, or removal of the waterbed on the rental premises only, except for any damage caused intentionally or at the direction of the insured, or for any damage caused by or resulting from fire. The owner may require the tenant to produce evidence of insurance at any time. The carrier shall give the owner notice of cancellation or nonrenewal 10 days prior to this action. Every application for a policy shall contain the information as provided in subdivisions (a), (b), and (c) of Section 1962 and Section 1962.5.

(b) The bedding shall conform to the pounds-per-square foot weight limitation and placement as dictated by the floor load capacity of the residential structure. The weight shall be distributed on a pedestal or frame which is substantially the dimensions of the mattress itself.

(c) The tenant or prospective tenant shall install, maintain and remove the bedding, including, but not limited to, the mattress and frame, according to standard methods of installation, maintenance, and removal as prescribed by the manufacturer, retailer, or state law, whichever provides the higher degree of safety. The tenant shall notify the owner or owner's agent in writing of the intent to install, remove, or move the waterbed. The notice shall be delivered 24 hours prior to the installation, removal, or movement. The owner or the owner's agent may be present at the time of installation, removal, or movement at the owner's or the owner's agent's option. If the bedding is installed or moved by any person other than the tenant or prospective tenant, the tenant or prospective tenant shall deliver to the owner or to the owner's agent a written installation receipt stating the installer's name, address, and business affiliation where appropriate.

(d) Any new bedding installation shall conform to the owner's or the owner's agent's reasonable structural specifications for placement within the rental property and shall be consistent with floor capacity of the rental dwelling unit.

(e) The tenant or prospective tenant shall comply with the minimum component specification list prescribed by the manufacturer, retailer, or state law, whichever provides the higher degree of safety.

(f) Subject to the notice requirements of Section 1954, the owner, or the owner's agent, shall have the right to inspect the bedding installation upon completion, and periodically thereafter, to insure its conformity with this section. If installation or maintenance is not in conformity with this section, the owner may serve the tenant with a written notice of breach of the rental agreement. The owner may give the tenant three days either to bring the installation into conformity with those standards or to remove the bedding, unless there is an immediate danger to the structure, in which case there shall be immediate corrective action. If the bedding is installed by any person other than the tenant or prospective tenant, the tenant or prospective tenant shall deliver to the owner or to the owner's agent a written installation receipt stating the installer's name and business affiliation where appropriate.

(g) Notwithstanding Section 1950.5, an owner or owner's agent is entitled to increase the security deposit on the dwelling unit in an amount equal to one-half of one months' rent. The owner or owner's agent may charge a tenant, lessee, or sublessee a reasonable fee to cover administration costs. In no event does this section authorize the payment of a rebate of premium in violation of Article 5 (commencing with Section 750) of Chapter 1 of Part 2 of Division 1 of the Insurance Code.

§ 1940.5

(h) Failure of the owner, or owner's agent, to exercise any of his or her rights pursuant to this section does not constitute grounds for denial of an insurance claim.

(i) As used in this section, "tenant" includes any lessee, and "rental" means any rental or lease. *(Added by Stats. 1987, c. 1503, § 1. Amended by Stats.1996, c. 1137 (S.B. 1077), § 52.)*

§ 1940.6. Demolition of residential dwelling unit; notice to prospective tenants; contents; remedies and civil penalties for noncompliance; attorney's fees

(a) The owner of a residential dwelling unit or the owner's agent who applies to any public agency for a permit to demolish that residential dwelling unit shall give written notice of that fact to:

(1) A prospective tenant prior to the occurrence of any of the following actions by the owner or the owner's agent:

(A) Entering into a rental agreement with a prospective tenant.

(B) Requiring or accepting payment from the prospective tenant for an application screening fee, as provided in Section 1950.6.

(C) Requiring or accepting any other fees from a prospective tenant.

(D) Requiring or accepting any writings that would initiate a tenancy.

(2) A current tenant, including a tenant who has entered into a rental agreement but has not yet taken possession of the dwelling unit, prior to applying to the public agency for the permit to demolish that residential dwelling unit.

(b) The notice shall include the earliest possible approximate date on which the owner expects the demolition to occur and the approximate date on which the owner will terminate the tenancy. However, in no case may the demolition for which the owner or the owner's agent has applied occur prior to the earliest possible approximate date noticed.

(c) If a landlord fails to comply with subdivision (a) or (b), a tenant may bring an action in a court of competent jurisdiction. The remedies the court may order shall include, but are not limited to, the following:

(1) In the case of a prospective tenant who moved into a residential dwelling unit and was not informed as required by subdivision (a) or (b), the actual damages suffered, moving expenses, and a civil penalty not to exceed two thousand five hundred dollars ($2,500) to be paid by the landlord to the tenant.

(2) In the case of a current tenant who was not informed as required by subdivision (a) or (b), the actual damages suffered, and a civil penalty not to exceed two thousand five hundred dollars ($2,500) to be paid by the landlord to the tenant.

(3) In any action brought pursuant to this section, the prevailing party shall be entitled to reasonable attorney's fees.

(d) The remedies available under this section are cumulative to other remedies available under law.

(e) This section shall not be construed to preempt other laws regarding landlord obligations or disclosures, including, but not limited to, those arising pursuant to Chapter 12.75 (commencing with Section 7060) of Division 7 of Title 1 of the Government Code.

(f) For purposes of this section:

(1) "Residential dwelling unit" has the same meaning as that contained in Section 1940.

(2) "Public agency" has the same meaning as that contained in Section 21063 of the Public Resources Code. *(Added by Stats.2002, c. 285 (S.B.1576), § 1.)*

§ 1940.7. Disclosure of former federal or state ordnance locations

(a) The Legislature finds and declares that the December 10, 1983, tragedy in Tierra Santa, in which lives were lost as a result of a live munition exploding in a residential area that was formerly a military ordnance location, has demonstrated (1) the unique and heretofore unknown risk that there are other live munitions in former ordnance locations in California, (2) that these former ordnance locations need to be identified by the federal, state, or local authorities, and (3) that the people living in the neighborhood of these former ordnance locations should be notified of their existence. Therefore, it is the intent of the Legislature that the disclosure required by this section is solely warranted and limited by (1) the fact that these former ordnance locations cannot be readily observed or discovered by landlords and tenants, and (2) the ability of a landlord who has actual knowledge of a former ordnance location within the neighborhood of his or her rental property to disclose this information for the safety of the tenant.

(b) The landlord of a residential dwelling unit who has actual knowledge of any former federal or state ordnance locations in the neighborhood area shall give written notice to a prospective tenant of that knowledege [1] prior to the execution of a rental agreement. In cases of tenancies in existence on January 1, 1990, this written notice shall be given to tenants as soon as practicable thereafter.

(c) For purposes of this section:

(1) "Former federal or state ordnance location" means an area identified by an agency or instrumentality of the federal or state government as an area once used for military training purposes and which may contain potentially explosive munitions.

(2) "Neighborhood area" means within one mile of the residential dwelling. *(Added by Stats.1989, c. 294, § 2.)*

[1] So in chaptered copy. Probably should be "knowledge".

Cross References

Disclosure of former federal or state ordnance locations by seller of residential real property, see Civil Code § 1102.15.

§ 1940.7.5. Repealed by Stats.2003, c. 422 (A.B.24), § 2, operative Jan. 1, 2006

§ 1940.8. Pest control company notices

A landlord of a residential dwelling unit shall provide each new tenant that occupies the unit with a copy of the notice provided by a registered structural pest control company pursuant to Section 8538 of the Business and Professions

Code, if a contract for periodic pest control service has been executed. *(Added by Stats.2000, c. 234 (S.B.2143), § 2.)*

§ 1940.8.5. Written notice of pesticide application; contents

(a) For purposes of this section, the following terms have the following meanings:

(1) "Adjacent dwelling unit" means a dwelling unit that is directly beside, above, or below a particular dwelling unit.

(2) "Authorized agent" means an individual, organization, or other entity that has entered into an agreement with a landlord to act on the landlord's behalf in relation to the management of a residential rental property.

(3) "Broadcast application" means spreading pesticide over an area greater than two square feet.

(4) "Electronic delivery" means delivery of a document by electronic means to the electronic address at or through which a tenant, landlord, or authorized agent has authorized electronic delivery.

(5) "Landlord" means an owner of residential rental property.

(6) "Pest" means a living organism that causes damage to property or economic loss, or transmits or produces diseases.

(7) "Pesticide" means any substance, or mixture of substances, that is intended to be used for controlling, destroying, repelling, or mitigating any pest or organism, excluding antimicrobial pesticides as defined by the Federal Insecticide, Fungicide, and Rodenticide Act (7 U.S.C. Sec. 136(mm)).

(8) "Licensed pest control operator" means anyone licensed by the state to apply pesticides.

(b)(1) A landlord or authorized agent that applies any pesticide to a dwelling unit without a licensed pest control operator shall provide a tenant of that dwelling unit and, if making broadcast applications, or using total release foggers or aerosol sprays, any tenant in an adjacent dwelling unit that could reasonably be impacted by the pesticide use with written notice that contains the following statements and information using words with common and everyday meaning:

(A) The pest or pests to be controlled.

(B) The name and brand of the pesticide product proposed to be used.

(C) "State law requires that you be given the following information:

CAUTION—PESTICIDES ARE TOXIC CHEMICALS. The California Department of Pesticide Regulation and the United States Environmental Protection Agency allow the unlicensed use of certain pesticides based on existing scientific evidence that there are no appreciable risks if proper use conditions are followed or that the risks are outweighed by the benefits. The degree of risk depends upon the degree of exposure, so exposure should be minimized.

If within 24 hours following application of a pesticide, a person experiences symptoms similar to common seasonal illness comparable to influenza, the person should contact a physician, appropriate licensed health care provider, or the California Poison Control System (1–800–222–1222).

For further information, contact any of the following: for Health Questions—the County Health Department (telephone number) and for Regulatory Information—the Department of Pesticide Regulation (916–324–4100)."

(D) The approximate date, time, and frequency with which the pesticide will be applied.

(E) The following notification:

"The approximate date, time, and frequency of this pesticide application is subject to change."

(2) At least 24 hours prior to application of the pesticide to the dwelling unit, the landlord or authorized agent shall provide the notice to the tenant of the dwelling unit, as well as any tenants in adjacent units that are required to be notified pursuant to paragraph (1), in at least one of the following ways:

(A) First–class mail.

(B) Personal delivery to the tenant, someone of suitable age and discretion at the premises, or under the usual entry door of the premises.

(C) Electronic delivery, if an electronic mailing address has been provided by the tenant.

(D) Posting a written notice in a conspicuous place at the unit entry in a manner in which a reasonable person would discover the notice.

(3)(A) Upon receipt of written notification, the tenant may agree in writing, or if notification was electronically delivered, the tenant may agree through electronic delivery, to allow the landlord or authorized agent to apply a pesticide immediately or at an agreed upon time.

(B)(i) Prior to receipt of written notification, the tenant and the landlord or authorized agent may agree orally to an immediate pesticide application if a tenant requests that the pesticide be applied before 24–hour advance notice can be given. The oral agreement shall include the name and brand of the pesticide product proposed to be used.

(ii) With respect to a tenant entering into an oral agreement for immediate pesticide application, the landlord or authorized agent, no later than the time of pesticide application, shall leave the written notice specified in paragraph (1) in a conspicuous place in the dwelling unit, or at the entrance of the unit in a manner in which a reasonable person would discover the notice.

(iii) If any tenants in adjacent dwelling units are also required to be notified pursuant to this subdivision, the landlord or authorized agent shall provide those tenants with this notice as soon as practicable after the oral agreement is made authorizing immediate pesticide application, but in no case later than commencement of application of the pesticide.

(4)(A) This subdivision shall not be construed to require an association, as defined in Section 4080, to provide notice of pesticide use in a separate interest, as defined in Section 4185, within a common interest development, as defined in Section 4100.

§ 1940.8.5 OBLIGATIONS

(B) Notwithstanding subparagraph (A), an association, as defined in Section 4080, that has taken title to a separate interest, as defined in Section 4185, shall provide notification to tenants as specified in this subdivision.

(c)(1) A landlord or authorized agent that applies any pesticide to a common area without a licensed pest control operator, excluding routine pesticide applications described in subdivision (d), shall post written notice in a conspicuous place in the common area in which a pesticide is to be applied that contains the following statements and information using words with common and everyday meaning:

(A) The pest or pests to be controlled.

(B) The name and brand of the pesticide product proposed to be used.

(C) "State law requires that you be given the following information:

CAUTION—PESTICIDES ARE TOXIC CHEMICALS. The California Department of Pesticide Regulation and the United States Environmental Protection Agency allow the unlicensed use of certain pesticides based on existing scientific evidence that there are no appreciable risks if proper use conditions are followed or that the risks are outweighed by the benefits. The degree of risk depends upon the degree of exposure, so exposure should be minimized.

If within 24 hours following application of a pesticide, a person experiences symptoms similar to common seasonal illness comparable to influenza, the person should contact a physician, appropriate licensed health care provider, or the California Poison Control System (1–800–222–1222).

For further information, contact any of the following: for Health Questions—the County Health Department (telephone number) and for Regulatory Information—the Department of Pesticide Regulation (916–324–4100)."

(D) The approximate date, time, and frequency with which the pesticide will be applied.

(2)(A) The notice shall be posted before a pesticide application in a common area and shall remain posted for at least 24 hours after the pesticide is applied.

(B) Landlords and their authorized agents are not liable for any notice removed from a common area without the knowledge or consent of the landlord or authorized agent.

(C) If the pest poses an immediate threat to health and safety, thereby making compliance with notification prior to the pesticide application required in subparagraph (A) unreasonable, a landlord or authorized agent shall post the notification as soon as practicable, but not later than one hour after the pesticide is applied.

(3) If a common area lacks a suitable place to post a notice, then the landlord shall provide the notice to each dwelling unit in at least one of the following ways:

(A) First–class mail.

(B) Personal delivery to the tenant, someone of suitable age and discretion at the premises, or under the usual entry door of the premises.

(C) Electronic delivery, if an electronic mailing address has been provided by the tenant.

(D) Posting a written notice in a conspicuous place at the unit entry in a manner in which a reasonable person would discover the notice.

(4) This subdivision shall not be construed to require any landlord or authorized agent, or an association, as defined in Section 4080, to provide notice of pesticide use in common areas within a common interest development, as defined in Section 4100.

(d)(1) A landlord or authorized agent that routinely applies pesticide in a common area on a set schedule without a licensed pest control operator shall provide a tenant in each dwelling unit with written notice that contains the following statements and information using words with common and everyday meaning:

(A) The pest or pests to be controlled.

(B) The name and brand of the pesticide product proposed to be used.

(C) "State law requires that you be given the following information:

CAUTION—PESTICIDES ARE TOXIC CHEMICALS. The California Department of Pesticide Regulation and the United States Environmental Protection Agency allow the unlicensed use of certain pesticides based on existing scientific evidence that there are no appreciable risks if proper use conditions are followed or that the risks are outweighed by the benefits. The degree of risk depends upon the degree of exposure, so exposure should be minimized.

If within 24 hours following application of a pesticide, a person experiences symptoms similar to common seasonal illness comparable to influenza, the person should contact a physician, appropriate licensed health care provider, or the California Poison Control System (1–800–222–1222).

For further information, contact any of the following: for Health Questions—the County Health Department (telephone number) and for Regulatory Information—the Department of Pesticide Regulation (916–324–4100)."

(D) The schedule pursuant to which the pesticide will be routinely applied.

(2)(A) The landlord or authorized agent shall provide the notice to both of the following:

(i) Existing tenants prior to the initial pesticide application.

(ii) Each new tenant prior to entering into a lease agreement.

(B) The landlord or authorized agent shall provide the notice to the tenant in at least one of the following ways:

(i) First–class mail.

(ii) Personal delivery to the tenant, someone of suitable age and discretion at the premises, or under the usual entry door of the premises.

(iii) Electronic delivery, if an electronic mailing address has been provided by the tenant.

(iv) Posting a written notice in a conspicuous place at the unit entry in a manner in which a reasonable person would discover the notice.

(C) If the pesticide to be used is changed, a landlord or authorized agent shall provide a new notice pursuant to paragraph (1).

(D) This subdivision shall not be construed to require any landlord or authorized agent, or an association, as defined in Section 4080, to provide notice of pesticide use in common areas within a common interest development, as defined in Section 4100.

(e) Nothing in this section abrogates the responsibility of a registered structural pest control company to abide by the notification requirements of Section 8538 of the Business and Professions Code.

(f) Nothing in this section authorizes a landlord or authorized agent to enter a tenant's dwelling unit in violation of Section 1954.

(g) If a tenant is provided notice in compliance with this section, a landlord or authorized agent is not required to provide additional information, and the information shall be deemed adequate to inform the tenant regarding the application of pesticides. *(Added by Stats.2015, c. 278 (S.B.328), § 2, eff. Jan. 1, 2016.)*

Cross References

Common interest developments, written notice of pesticide application, contents, see Civil Code § 4777.

§ 1940.9. Gas and electric meters; notice to tenant when meter serves area outside tenant's dwelling unit; cost of services; remedies

(a) If the landlord does not provide separate gas and electric meters for each tenant's dwelling unit so that each tenant's meter measures only the electric or gas service to that tenant's dwelling unit and the landlord or his or her agent has knowledge that gas or electric service provided through a tenant's meter serves an area outside the tenant's dwelling unit, the landlord, prior to the inception of the tenancy or upon discovery, shall explicitly disclose that condition to the tenant and shall do either of the following:

(1) Execute a mutual written agreement with the tenant for payment by the tenant of the cost of the gas or electric service provided through the tenant's meter to serve areas outside the tenant's dwelling unit.

(2) Make other arrangements, as are mutually agreed in writing, for payment for the gas or electric service provided through the tenant's meter to serve areas outside the tenant's dwelling unit. These arrangements may include, but are not limited to, the landlord becoming the customer of record for the tenant's meter, or the landlord separately metering and becoming the customer of record for the area outside the tenant's dwelling unit.

(b) If a landlord fails to comply with subdivision (a), the aggrieved tenant may bring an action in a court of competent jurisdiction. The remedies the court may order shall include, but are not limited to, the following:

(1) Requiring the landlord to be made the customer of record with the utility for the tenant's meter.

(2) Ordering the landlord to reimburse the tenant for payments made by the tenant to the utility for service to areas outside of the tenant's dwelling unit. Payments to be reimbursed pursuant to this paragraph shall commence from the date the obligation to disclose arose under subdivision (a).

(c) Nothing in this section limits any remedies available to a landlord or tenant under other provisions of this chapter, the rental agreement, or applicable statutory or common law. *(Added by Stats.1989, c. 861, § 1.)*

§ 1940.10. Personal agriculture; tenant's authority to maintain portable containers under certain conditions; use of pesticides or other synthetic chemical products; landlord inspections

(a) For the purposes of this section, the following definitions shall apply:

(1) "Private area" means an outdoor backyard area that is on the ground level of the rental unit.

(2) "Personal agriculture" means a use of land where an individual cultivates edible plant crops for personal use or donation.

(3) "Plant crop" means any crop in its raw or natural state, which comes from a plant that will bear edible fruits or vegetables. It shall not include marijuana or any unlawful crops or substances.

(b) A landlord shall permit a tenant to participate in personal agriculture in portable containers approved by the landlord in the tenant's private area if the following conditions are met:

(1) The tenant regularly removes any dead plant material and weeds, with the exception of straw, mulch, compost, and any other organic materials intended to encourage vegetation and retention of moisture in soil, unless the landlord and tenant have a preexisting or separate agreement regarding garden maintenance where the tenant is not responsible for removing or maintaining plant crop and weeds.

(2) The plant crop will not interfere with the maintenance of the rental property.

(3) The placement of the portable containers does not interfere with any tenant's parking spot.

(4) The placement and location of the portable containers may be determined by the landlord. The portable containers may not create a health and safety hazard, block doorways, or interfere with walkways or utility services or equipment.

(c) The cultivation of plant crops on the rental property other than that which is contained in portable containers shall be subject to approval from the landlord.

(d) A landlord may prohibit the use of synthetic chemical herbicides, pesticides, fungicides, rodenticides, insecticides, or any other synthetic chemical product commonly used in the growing of plant crops.

(e) A landlord may require the tenant to enter into a written agreement regarding the payment of any excess water and waste collection bills arising from the tenant's personal agriculture activities.

(f) Subject to the notice required by Section 1954, a landlord has a right to periodically inspect any area where the

§ 1940.10

tenant is engaging in personal agriculture to ensure compliance with this section.

(g) This section shall only apply to residential real property that is improved with, or consisting of, a building containing not more than two units that are intended for human habitation. *(Added by Stats.2014, c. 584 (A.B.2561), § 2, eff. Jan. 1, 2015.)*

§ 1940.20. Tenant use of clothesline or drying rack; conditions

(a) For purposes of this section, the following definitions shall apply:

(1) "Clothesline" includes a cord, rope, or wire from which laundered items may be hung to dry or air. A balcony, railing, awning, or other part of a structure or building shall not qualify as a clothesline.

(2) "Drying rack" means an apparatus from which laundered items may be hung to dry or air. A balcony, railing, awning, or other part of a structure or building shall not qualify as a drying rack.

(3) "Private area" means an outdoor area or an area in the tenant's premises enclosed by a wall or fence with access from a door of the premises.

(b) A tenant may utilize a clothesline or drying rack in the tenant's private area if all of the following conditions are met:

(1) The clothesline or drying rack will not interfere with the maintenance of the rental property.

(2) The clothesline or drying rack will not create a health or safety hazard, block doorways, or interfere with walkways or utility service equipment.

(3) The tenant seeks the landlord's consent before affixing a clothesline to a building.

(4) Use of the clothesline or drying rack does not violate reasonable time or location restrictions imposed by the landlord.

(5) The tenant has received approval of the clothesline or drying rack, or the type of clothesline or drying rack, from the landlord. *(Added by Stats.2015, c. 602 (A.B.1448), § 1, eff. Jan. 1, 2016.)*

§ 1941. Buildings for human occupancy; fitness; repairs

The lessor of a building intended for the occupation of human beings must, in the absence of an agreement to the contrary, put it into a condition fit for such occupation, and repair all subsequent dilapidations thereof, which render it untenantable, except such as are mentioned in section nineteen hundred and twenty-nine. *(Enacted in 1872. Amended by Code Am.1873–74, c. 612, p. 245, § 205.)*

Cross References

Conversion of residential real property into condominium, community apartment project, or stock cooperative project, rights and obligations of parties under this section, see Government Code § 66427.1.

Repairs by hirer, see Civil Code § 1929.

Shelter crisis, emergency housing, homeless shelters, see Government Code § 8698.4.

§ 1941.1. Untenantable dwellings; program assistance for heating or hot water system repairs or replacement

(a) A dwelling shall be deemed untenantable for purposes of Section 1941 if it substantially lacks any of the following affirmative standard characteristics or is a residential unit described in Section 17920.3 or 17920.10 of the Health and Safety Code:

(1) Effective waterproofing and weather protection of roof and exterior walls, including unbroken windows and doors.

(2) Plumbing or gas facilities that conformed to applicable law in effect at the time of installation, maintained in good working order.

(3) A water supply approved under applicable law that is under the control of the tenant, capable of producing hot and cold running water, or a system that is under the control of the landlord, that produces hot and cold running water, furnished to appropriate fixtures, and connected to a sewage disposal system approved under applicable law.

(4) Heating facilities that conformed with applicable law at the time of installation, maintained in good working order.

(5) Electrical lighting, with wiring and electrical equipment that conformed with applicable law at the time of installation, maintained in good working order.

(6) Building, grounds, and appurtenances at the time of the commencement of the lease or rental agreement, and all areas under control of the landlord, kept in every part clean, sanitary, and free from all accumulations of debris, filth, rubbish, garbage, rodents, and vermin.

(7) An adequate number of appropriate receptacles for garbage and rubbish, in clean condition and good repair at the time of the commencement of the lease or rental agreement, with the landlord providing appropriate serviceable receptacles thereafter and being responsible for the clean condition and good repair of the receptacles under his or her control.

(8) Floors, stairways, and railings maintained in good repair.

(9) A locking mail receptacle for each residential unit in a residential hotel, as required by Section 17958.3 of the Health and Safety Code. This subdivision shall become operative on July 1, 2008.

(b) Nothing in this section shall be interpreted to prohibit a tenant or owner of rental properties from qualifying for a utility energy savings assistance program, or any other program assistance, for heating or hot water system repairs or replacement, or a combination of heating and hot water system repairs or replacements, that would achieve energy savings. *(Added by Stats.1970, c. 1280, p. 2314, § 1. Amended by Stats.1979, c. 307, p. 1125, § 1; Stats.2002, c. 931 (S.B.460), § 1; Stats.2007, c. 599 (A.B.607), § 1; Stats.2012, c. 600 (A.B.1124), § 1.)*

Cross References

Conversion of residential real property into condominium, community apartment project, or stock cooperative project, rights and obligations of parties under this section, see Government Code § 66427.1.

Notices and orders to building owners, public records, see Government Code § 7924.700.

Public nuisances, abatement, lead paint, see Civil Code § 3494.5.

Records of notices and orders concerning violations of standards provided in this section, inspection of public records, see Government Code § 6254.7.

Shelter crisis, emergency housing, homeless shelters, see Government Code § 8698.4.

Tenants who may be found guilty of unlawful detainer, assistance for tenant in relocating, see Code of Civil Procedure § 1179.03.5.

§ 1941.2. Tenant's affirmative obligations

(a) No duty on the part of the landlord to repair a dilapidation shall arise under Section 1941 or 1942 if the tenant is in substantial violation of any of the following affirmative obligations, provided the tenant's violation contributes substantially to the existence of the dilapidation or interferes substantially with the landlord's obligation under Section 1941 to effect the necessary repairs:

(1) To keep that part of the premises which he occupies and uses clean and sanitary as the condition of the premises permits.

(2) To dispose from his dwelling unit of all rubbish, garbage and other waste, in a clean and sanitary manner.

(3) To properly use and operate all electrical, gas and plumbing fixtures and keep them as clean and sanitary as their condition permits.

(4) Not to permit any person on the premises, with his permission, to willfully or wantonly destroy, deface, damage, impair or remove any part of the structure or dwelling unit or the facilities, equipment, or appurtenances thereto, nor himself do any such thing.

(5) To occupy the premises as his abode, utilizing portions thereof for living, sleeping, cooking or dining purposes only which were respectively designed or intended to be used for such occupancies.

(b) Paragraphs (1) and (2) of subdivision (a) shall not apply if the landlord has expressly agreed in writing to perform the act or acts mentioned therein. *(Added by Stats.1970, c. 1280, p. 2315, § 2. Amended by Stats.1979, c. 307, p. 1125, § 2.)*

Cross References

Conversion of residential real property into condominium, community apartment project, or stock cooperative project, rights and obligations of parties under this section, see Government Code § 66427.1.

Shelter crisis, emergency housing, homeless shelters, see Government Code § 8698.4.

§ 1941.3. Buildings intended for human habitation; landlord's duties; tenants' duties; violations; exempt buildings

(a) On and after July 1, 1998, the landlord, or his or her agent, of a building intended for human habitation shall do all of the following:

(1) Install and maintain an operable dead bolt lock on each main swinging entry door of a dwelling unit. The dead bolt lock shall be installed in conformance with the manufacturer's specifications and shall comply with applicable state and local codes including, but not limited to, those provisions relating to fire and life safety and accessibility for the disabled. When in the locked position, the bolt shall extend a minimum of $13/16$ of an inch in length beyond the strike edge of the door and protrude into the doorjamb.

This section shall not apply to horizontal sliding doors. Existing dead bolts of at least one-half inch in length shall satisfy the requirements of this section. Existing locks with a thumb-turn deadlock that have a strike plate attached to the doorjamb and a latch bolt that is held in a vertical position by a guard bolt, a plunger, or an auxiliary mechanism shall also satisfy the requirements of this section. These locks, however, shall be replaced with a dead bolt at least $13/16$ of an inch in length the first time after July 1, 1998, that the lock requires repair or replacement.

Existing doors which cannot be equipped with dead bolt locks shall satisfy the requirements of this section if the door is equipped with a metal strap affixed horizontally across the midsection of the door with a dead bolt which extends $13/16$ of an inch in length beyond the strike edge of the door and protrudes into the doorjamb. Locks and security devices other than those described herein which are inspected and approved by an appropriate state or local government agency as providing adequate security shall satisfy the requirements of this section.

(2) Install and maintain operable window security or locking devices for windows that are designed to be opened. Louvered windows, casement windows, and all windows more than 12 feet vertically or six feet horizontally from the ground, a roof, or any other platform are excluded from this subdivision.

(3) Install locking mechanisms that comply with applicable fire and safety codes on the exterior doors that provide ingress or egress to common areas with access to dwelling units in multifamily developments. This paragraph does not require the installation of a door or gate where none exists on January 1, 1998.

(b) The tenant shall be responsible for notifying the owner or his or her authorized agent when the tenant becomes aware of an inoperable dead bolt lock or window security or locking device in the dwelling unit. The landlord, or his or her authorized agent, shall not be liable for a violation of subdivision (a) unless he or she fails to correct the violation within a reasonable time after he or she either has actual notice of a deficiency or receives notice of a deficiency.

(c) On and after July 1, 1998, the rights and remedies of tenant for a violation of this section by the landlord shall include those available pursuant to Sections 1942, 1942.4, and 1942.5, an action for breach of contract, and an action for injunctive relief pursuant to Section 526 of the Code of Civil Procedure. Additionally, in an unlawful detainer action, after a default in the payment of rent, a tenant may raise the violation of this section as an affirmative defense and shall have a right to the remedies provided by Section 1174.2 of the Code of Civil Procedure.

§ 1941.3

(d) A violation of this section shall not broaden, limit, or otherwise affect the duty of care owed by a landlord pursuant to existing law, including any duty that may exist pursuant to Section 1714. The delayed applicability of the requirements of subdivision (a) shall not affect a landlord's duty to maintain the premises in safe condition.

(e) Nothing in this section shall be construed to affect any authority of any public entity that may otherwise exist to impose any additional security requirements upon a landlord.

(f) This section shall not apply to any building which has been designated as historically significant by an appropriate local, state, or federal governmental jurisdiction.

(g) Subdivisions (a) and (b) shall not apply to any building intended for human habitation which is managed, directly or indirectly, and controlled by the Department of Transportation. This exemption shall not be construed to affect the duty of the Department of Transportation to maintain the premises of these buildings in a safe condition or abrogate any express or implied statement or promise of the Department of Transportation to provide secure premises. Additionally, this exemption shall not apply to residential dwellings acquired prior to July 1, 1997, by the Department of Transportation to complete construction of state highway routes 710 and 238 and related interchanges. *(Added by Stats.1997, c. 537 (S.B.548), § 1.)*

Cross References

Shelter crisis, emergency housing, homeless shelters, see Government Code § 8698.4.

§ 1941.4. Residential buildings; lessors' responsibilities; inside telephone wiring

The lessor of a building intended for the residential occupation of human beings shall be responsible for installing at least one usable telephone jack and for placing and maintaining the inside telephone wiring in good working order, shall ensure that the inside telephone wiring meets the applicable standards of the most recent California Electrical Code, and shall make any required repairs. The lessor shall not restrict or interfere with access by the telephone utility to its telephone network facilities up to the demarcation point separating the inside wiring.

"Inside telephone wiring" for purposes of this section, means that portion of the telephone wire that connects the telephone equipment at the customer's premises to the telephone network at a demarcation point determined by the telephone corporation in accordance with orders of the Public Utilities Commission. *(Added by Stats.1991, c. 1001 (S.B.841), § 2. Amended by Stats.2013, c. 183 (S.B.745), § 5.)*

Cross References

Shelter crisis, emergency housing, homeless shelters, see Government Code § 8698.4.

§ 1941.5. Tenant protected by restraining order against non-tenant; change of locks on dwelling unit; definitions

(a) This section shall apply if a person who is restrained from contact with the protected tenant under a court order or is named in a police report is not a tenant of the same dwelling unit as the protected tenant.

(b) A landlord shall change the locks of a protected tenant's dwelling unit upon written request of the protected tenant not later than 24 hours after the protected tenant gives the landlord a copy of a court order or police report, and shall give the protected tenant a key to the new locks.

(c)(1) If a landlord fails to change the locks within 24 hours, the protected tenant may change the locks without the landlord's permission, notwithstanding any provision in the lease to the contrary.

(2) If the protected tenant changes the locks pursuant to this subdivision, the protected tenant shall do all of the following:

(A) Change the locks in a workmanlike manner with locks of similar or better quality than the original lock.

(B) Notify the landlord within 24 hours that the locks have been changed.

(C) Provide the landlord with a key by any reasonable method agreed upon by the landlord and protected tenant.

(3) This subdivision shall apply to leases executed on or after the date the act that added this section takes effect.

(d) For the purposes of this section, the following definitions shall apply:

(1) "Court order" means a court order lawfully issued within the last 180 days pursuant to Section 527.6 of the Code of Civil Procedure, Part 3 (commencing with Section 6240), Part 4 (commencing with Section 6300), or Part 5 (commencing with Section 6400) of Division 10 of the Family Code, Section 136.2 of the Penal Code, or Section 213.5 of the Welfare and Institutions Code.

(2) "Locks" means any exterior lock that provides access to the dwelling.

(3) "Police report" means a written report, written within the last 180 days, by a peace officer employed by a state or local law enforcement agency acting in his or her official capacity, stating that the protected tenant or a household member has filed a report alleging that the protected tenant or the household member is a victim of domestic violence, sexual assault, or stalking.

(4) "Protected tenant" means a tenant who has obtained a court order or has a copy of a police report.

(5) "Tenant" means tenant, subtenant, lessee, or sublessee. *(Added by Stats.2010, c. 626 (S.B.782), § 2.)*

Cross References

Shelter crisis, emergency housing, homeless shelters, see Government Code § 8698.4.

§ 1941.6. Tenant protected by restraining order against another tenant; change of locks on dwelling unit; liability regarding person excluded; definitions

(a) This section shall apply if a person who is restrained from contact with a protected tenant under a court order is a tenant of the same dwelling unit as the protected tenant.

(b) A landlord shall change the locks of a protected tenant's dwelling unit upon written request of the protected tenant not later than 24 hours after the protected tenant gives the landlord a copy of a court order that excludes from the dwelling unit the restrained person referred to in subdivision (a). The landlord shall give the protected tenant a key to the new locks.

(c)(1) If a landlord fails to change the locks within 24 hours, the protected tenant may change the locks without the landlord's permission, notwithstanding any provision in the lease to the contrary.

(2) If the protected tenant changes the locks pursuant to this subdivision, the protected tenant shall do all of the following:

(A) Change the locks in a workmanlike manner with locks of similar or better quality than the original lock.

(B) Notify the landlord within 24 hours that the locks have been changed.

(C) Provide the landlord with a key by any reasonable method agreed upon by the landlord and protected tenant.

(3) This subdivision shall apply to leases executed on or after the date the act that added this section takes effect.

(d) Notwithstanding Section 789.3, if the locks are changed pursuant to this section, the landlord is not liable to a person excluded from the dwelling unit pursuant to this section.

(e) A person who has been excluded from a dwelling unit under this section remains liable under the lease with all other tenants of the dwelling unit for rent as provided in the lease.

(f) For the purposes of this section, the following definitions shall apply:

(1) "Court order" means a court order lawfully issued within the last 180 days pursuant to Section 527.6 of the Code of Civil Procedure, Part 3 (commencing with Section 6240), Part 4 (commencing with Section 6300), or Part 5 (commencing with Section 6400) of Division 10 of the Family Code, Section 136.2 of the Penal Code, or Section 213.5 of the Welfare and Institutions Code.

(2) "Locks" means any exterior lock that provides access to the dwelling.

(3) "Protected tenant" means a tenant who has obtained a court order.

(4) "Tenant" means tenant, subtenant, lessee, or sublessee. *(Added by Stats.2010, c. 626 (S.B.782), § 3.)*

Cross References

Shelter crisis, emergency housing, homeless shelters, see Government Code § 8698.4.

§ 1941.7. Obligation of lessor to repair dilapidation relating to presence of mold; notice; authority to enter dwelling unit for repair

(a) An obligation shall not arise under Section 1941 or 1942 to repair a dilapidation relating to the presence of mold pursuant to paragraph (13) of subdivision (a) of Section 17920.3 of the Health and Safety Code until the lessor has notice of the dilapidation or if the tenant is in violation of Section 1941.2.

(b) A landlord may enter a dwelling unit to repair a dilapidation relating to the presence of mold pursuant to paragraph (13) of subdivision (a) of Section 17920.3 of the Health and Safety Code provided the landlord complies with the provisions of Section 1954. *(Added by Stats.2015, c. 720 (S.B.655), § 1, eff. Jan. 1, 2016.)*

Cross References

Shelter crisis, emergency housing, homeless shelters, see Government Code § 8698.4.

§ 1942. Repairs by tenant; rent deduction or vacation of premises; presumption; limit; nonavailability of remedy; additional remedy

(a) If within a reasonable time after written or oral notice to the landlord or his agent, as defined in subdivision (a) of Section 1962, of dilapidations rendering the premises untenantable which the landlord ought to repair, the landlord neglects to do so, the tenant may repair the same himself where the cost of such repairs does not require an expenditure more than one month's rent of the premises and deduct the expenses of such repairs from the rent when due, or the tenant may vacate the premises, in which case the tenant shall be discharged from further payment of rent, or performance of other conditions as of the date of vacating the premises. This remedy shall not be available to the tenant more than twice in any 12-month period.

(b) For the purposes of this section, if a tenant acts to repair and deduct after the 30th day following notice, he is presumed to have acted after a reasonable time. The presumption established by this subdivision is a rebuttable presumption affecting the burden of producing evidence and shall not be construed to prevent a tenant from repairing and deducting after a shorter notice if all the circumstances require shorter notice.

(c) The tenant's remedy under subdivision (a) shall not be available if the condition was caused by the violation of Section 1929 or 1941.2.

(d) The remedy provided by this section is in addition to any other remedy provided by this chapter, the rental agreement, or other applicable statutory or common law. *(Enacted in 1872. Amended by Code Am.1873–74, c. 612, p. 246, § 206; Stats.1970, c. 1280, p. 2315, § 3; Stats.1979, c. 307, p. 1126, § 3.)*

Cross References

Expenses of lessee in making good lessor's default, see Civil Code § 1957.
Operation and management of housing projects, waiver of rights under this section prohibited, see Health and Safety Code § 34331.
Shelter crisis, emergency housing, homeless shelters, see Government Code § 8698.4.

§ 1942.1. Waiver of rights; public policy; arbitration of untenantability

Any agreement by a lessee of a dwelling waiving or modifying his rights under Section 1941 or 1942 shall be void as contrary to public policy with respect to any condition which renders the premises untenantable, except that the lessor and the lessee may agree that the lessee shall undertake to improve, repair or maintain all or stipulated portions of the dwelling as part of the consideration for rental.

§ 1942.1

The lessor and lessee may, if an agreement is in writing, set forth the provisions of Sections 1941 to 1942.1, inclusive, and provide that any controversy relating to a condition of the premises claimed to make them untenantable may by application of either party be submitted to arbitration, pursuant to the provisions of Title 9 (commencing with Section 1280), Part 3 of the Code of Civil Procedure, and that the costs of such arbitration shall be apportioned by the arbitrator between the parties. *(Added by Stats.1970, c. 1280, p. 2316, § 4.)*

Cross References

Shelter crisis, emergency housing, homeless shelters, see Government Code § 8698.4.

§ 1942.2. Payment to utility or district; deduction from rent

A tenant who has made a payment to a utility pursuant to Section 777, 777.1, 10009, 10009.1, 12822, 12822.1, 16481, or 16481.1 of the Public Utilities Code, or to a district pursuant to Section 60371 of the Government Code, may deduct the payment from the rent as provided in that section. *(Added by Stats.2009, c. 560 (S.B.120), § 1. Amended by Stats.2014, c. 913 (A.B.2747), § 6, eff. Jan. 1, 2015.)*

Cross References

Shelter crisis, emergency housing, homeless shelters, see Government Code § 8698.4.

§ 1942.3. Unlawful detainer; burden of proof; rebuttable presumption landlord breached habitability requirements; conditions

(a) In any unlawful detainer action by the landlord to recover possession from a tenant, a rebuttable presumption affecting the burden of producing evidence that the landlord has breached the habitability requirements in Section 1941 is created if all of the following conditions exist:

(1) The dwelling substantially lacks any of the affirmative standard characteristics listed in Section 1941.1, is deemed and declared substandard pursuant to Section 17920.3 of the Health and Safety Code, or contains lead hazards as defined in Section 17920.10 of the Health and Safety Code.

(2) A public officer or employee who is responsible for the enforcement of any housing law has notified the landlord, or an agent of the landlord, in a written notice issued after inspection of the premises which informs the landlord of his or her obligation to abate the nuisance or repair the substandard or unsafe conditions identified under the authority described in paragraph (1).

(3) The conditions have existed and have not been abated 60 days beyond the date of issuance of the notice specified in paragraph (2) and the delay is without good cause.

(4) The conditions were not caused by an act or omission of the tenant or lessee in violation of Section 1929 or 1941.2.

(b) The presumption specified in subdivision (a) does not arise unless all of the conditions set forth therein are proven, but failure to so establish the presumption shall not otherwise affect the right of the tenant to raise and pursue any defense based on the landlord's breach of the implied warranty of habitability.

(c) The presumption provided in this section shall apply only to rental agreements or leases entered into or renewed on or after January 1, 1986. *(Added by Stats.1985, c. 1279, § 1. Amended by Stats.2005, c. 595 (S.B.253), § 2.)*

Cross References

Shelter crisis, emergency housing, homeless shelters, see Government Code § 8698.4.

§ 1942.4. Demand, collection or increase of rent under certain enumerated conditions; landlord liability; attorney's fees; abatement and repair; additional remedies

(a) A landlord of a dwelling may not demand rent, collect rent, issue a notice of a rent increase, or issue a three-day notice to pay rent or quit pursuant to subdivision (2) of Section 1161 of the Code of Civil Procedure, if all of the following conditions exist prior to the landlord's demand or notice:

(1) The dwelling substantially lacks any of the affirmative standard characteristics listed in Section 1941.1 or violates Section 17920.10 of the Health and Safety Code, or is deemed and declared substandard as set forth in Section 17920.3 of the Health and Safety Code because conditions listed in that section exist to an extent that endangers the life, limb, health, property, safety, or welfare of the public or the occupants of the dwelling.

(2) A public officer or employee who is responsible for the enforcement of any housing law, after inspecting the premises, has notified the landlord or the landlord's agent in writing of his or her obligations to abate the nuisance or repair the substandard conditions.

(3) The conditions have existed and have not been abated 35 days beyond the date of service of the notice specified in paragraph (2) and the delay is without good cause. For purposes of this subdivision, service shall be complete at the time of deposit in the United States mail.

(4) The conditions were not caused by an act or omission of the tenant or lessee in violation of Section 1929 or 1941.2.

(b)(1) A landlord who violates this section is liable to the tenant or lessee for the actual damages sustained by the tenant or lessee and special damages of not less than one hundred dollars ($100) and not more than five thousand dollars ($5,000).

(2) The prevailing party shall be entitled to recovery of reasonable attorney's fees and costs of the suit in an amount fixed by the court.

(c) Any court that awards damages under this section may also order the landlord to abate any nuisance at the rental dwelling and to repair any substandard conditions of the rental dwelling, as defined in Section 1941.1, which significantly or materially affect the health or safety of the occupants of the rental dwelling and are uncorrected. If the court orders repairs or corrections, or both, the court's jurisdiction continues over the matter for the purpose of ensuring compliance.

(d) The tenant or lessee shall be under no obligation to undertake any other remedy prior to exercising his or her rights under this section.

(e) Any action under this section may be maintained in small claims court if the claim does not exceed the jurisdictional limit of that court.

(f) The remedy provided by this section may be utilized in addition to any other remedy provided by this chapter, the rental agreement, lease, or other applicable statutory or common law. Nothing in this section shall require any landlord to comply with this section if he or she pursues his or her rights pursuant to Chapter 12.75 (commencing with Section 7060) of Division 7 of Title 1 of the Government Code. *(Added by Stats.1985, c. 1279, § 2. Amended by Stats.1990, c. 1305 (S.B.2627), § 1; Stats.1992, c. 488 (A.B. 2574), § 1; Stats.1993, c. 589 (A.B.2211), § 23; Stats.2003, c. 109 (A.B.647), § 1.)*

Cross References

Shelter crisis, emergency housing, homeless shelters, see Government Code § 8698.4.

Unlawful detainer proceedings, award of attorneys' fees and costs, landlord liability, see Code of Civil Procedure § 1174.21.

§ 1942.5. Retaliation; prohibited acts; violations; remedies; penalties

(a) If the lessor retaliates against the lessee because of the exercise by the lessee of the lessee's rights under this chapter or because of the lessee's complaint to an appropriate agency as to tenantability of a dwelling, and if the lessee of a dwelling is not in default as to the payment of rent, the lessor may not recover possession of a dwelling in any action or proceeding, cause the lessee to quit involuntarily, increase the rent, or decrease any services within 180 days of any of the following:

(1) After the date upon which the lessee, in good faith, has given notice pursuant to Section 1942, has provided notice of a suspected bed bug infestation, or has made an oral complaint to the lessor regarding tenantability.

(2) After the date upon which the lessee, in good faith, has filed a written complaint, or an oral complaint which is registered or otherwise recorded in writing, with an appropriate agency, of which the lessor has notice, for the purpose of obtaining correction of a condition relating to tenantability.

(3) After the date of an inspection or issuance of a citation, resulting from a complaint described in paragraph (2) of which the lessor did not have notice.

(4) After the filing of appropriate documents commencing a judicial or arbitration proceeding involving the issue of tenantability.

(5) After entry of judgment or the signing of an arbitration award, if any, when in the judicial proceeding or arbitration the issue of tenantability is determined adversely to the lessor.

In each instance, the 180-day period shall run from the latest applicable date referred to in paragraphs (1) to (5), inclusive.

(b) A lessee may not invoke subdivision (a) more than once in any 12-month period.

(c) To report, or to threaten to report, the lessee or individuals known to the landlord to be associated with the lessee to immigration authorities is a form of retaliatory conduct prohibited under subdivision (a). This subdivision shall in no way limit the definition of retaliatory conduct prohibited under this section.

(d) Notwithstanding subdivision (a), it is unlawful for a lessor to increase rent, decrease services, cause a lessee to quit involuntarily, bring an action to recover possession, or threaten to do any of those acts, for the purpose of retaliating against the lessee because the lessee has lawfully organized or participated in a lessees' association or an organization advocating lessees' rights or has lawfully and peaceably exercised any rights under the law. In an action brought by or against the lessee pursuant to this subdivision, the lessee shall bear the burden of producing evidence that the lessor's conduct was, in fact, retaliatory.

(e) To report, or to threaten to report, the lessee or individuals known to the landlord to be associated with the lessee to immigration authorities is a form of retaliatory conduct prohibited under subdivision (d). This subdivision shall in no way limit the definition of retaliatory conduct prohibited under this section.

(f) This section does not limit in any way the exercise by the lessor of the lessor's rights under any lease or agreement or any law pertaining to the hiring of property or the lessor's right to do any of the acts described in subdivision (a) or (d) for any lawful cause. Any waiver by a lessee of the lessee's rights under this section is void as contrary to public policy.

(g) Notwithstanding subdivisions (a) to (f), inclusive, a lessor may recover possession of a dwelling and do any of the other acts described in subdivision (a) within the period or periods prescribed therein, or within subdivision (d), if the notice of termination, rent increase, or other act, and any pleading or statement of issues in an arbitration, if any, states the ground upon which the lessor, in good faith, seeks to recover possession, increase rent, or do any of the other acts described in subdivision (a) or (d). If the statement is controverted, the lessor shall establish its truth at the trial or other hearing.

(h) Any lessor or agent of a lessor who violates this section shall be liable to the lessee in a civil action for all of the following:

(1) The actual damages sustained by the lessee.

(2) Punitive damages in an amount of not less than one hundred dollars ($100) nor more than two thousand dollars ($2,000) for each retaliatory act where the lessor or agent has been guilty of fraud, oppression, or malice with respect to that act.

(i) In any action brought for damages for retaliatory eviction, the court shall award reasonable attorney's fees to the prevailing party if either party requests attorney's fees upon the initiation of the action.

(j) The remedies provided by this section shall be in addition to any other remedies provided by statutory or decisional law.

(k) A lessor does not violate subdivision (c) or (e) by complying with any legal obligation under any federal government program that provides for rent limitations or rental assistance to a qualified tenant.

(*l*) This section shall become operative on October 1, 2021. *(Added by Stats.2020, c. 37 (A.B.3088), § 7, eff. Aug. 31, 2020,*

§ 1942.5

operative Feb. 1, 2021. Amended by Stats.2021, c. 2 (S.B.91), § 6, eff. Jan. 29, 2021, operative July 1, 2021; Stats.2021, c. 27 (A.B.832), § 5, eff. June 28, 2021, operative Oct. 1, 2021.)

Cross References

Employee community housing, application of this section to retaliatory employment actions against tenants, see Health and Safety Code § 17031.7.

Employee housing, enforcement of tenants' rights, see Health and Safety Code § 17031.5.

Employee housing eviction proceedings, defense of protected activity under this section, see Health and Safety Code § 17031.6.

Hiring defined, see Civil Code § 1925.

Shelter crisis, emergency housing, homeless shelters, see Government Code § 8698.4.

§ 1942.6. Entry on property for purposes of tenants' rights

Any person entering onto residential real property, upon the invitation of an occupant, during reasonable hours or because of emergency circumstances, for the purpose of providing information regarding tenants' rights or to participate in a lessees' association or association of tenants or an association that advocates tenants' rights shall not be liable in any criminal or civil action for trespass.

The Legislature finds and declares that this section is declaratory of existing law. Nothing in this section shall be construed to enlarge or diminish the rights of any person under existing law. *(Added by Stats.1999, c. 590 (S.B.1098), § 1.)*

§ 1942.7. Conditions on occupancy based on declawing or devocalizing animals allowed on the premises; restrictions on persons or corporations occupying, owning, managing, or providing services in connection with real property; declaratory or injunctive relief; civil penalties

(a) A person or corporation that occupies, owns, manages, or provides services in connection with any real property, including the individual's or corporation's agents or successors in interest, and that allows an animal on the premises, shall not do any of the following:

(1) Advertise, through any means, the availability of real property for occupancy in a manner designed to discourage application for occupancy of that real property because an applicant's animal has not been declawed or devocalized.

(2) Refuse to allow the occupancy of any real property, refuse to negotiate the occupancy of any real property, or otherwise make unavailable or deny to any other person the occupancy of any real property because of that person's refusal to declaw or devocalize any animal.

(3) Require any tenant or occupant of real property to declaw or devocalize any animal allowed on the premises.

(b) For purposes of this section, the following definitions apply:

(1) "Animal" means any mammal, bird, reptile, or amphibian.

(2) "Application for occupancy" means all phases of the process of applying for the right to occupy real property, including, but not limited to, filling out applications, interviewing, and submitting references.

(3) "Claw" means a hardened keratinized modification of the epidermis, or a hardened keratinized growth, that extends from the end of the digits of certain mammals, birds, reptiles, and amphibians, often commonly referred to as a "claw," "talon," or "nail."

(4) "Declawing" means performing, procuring, or arranging for any procedure, such as an onychectomy, tendonectomy, or phalangectomy, to remove or to prevent the normal function of an animal's claw or claws.

(5) "Devocalizing" means performing, procuring, or arranging for any surgical procedure such as a vocal cordectomy, to remove an animal's vocal cords or to prevent the normal function of an animal's vocal cords.

(6) "Owner" means any person who has any right, title, or interest in real property.

(c)(1) A city attorney, district attorney, or other law enforcement prosecutorial entity has standing to enforce this section and may sue for declaratory relief or injunctive relief for a violation of this section, and to enforce the civil penalties provided in paragraphs (2) and (3).

(2) In addition to any other penalty allowed by law, a violation of paragraph (1) of subdivision (a) shall result in a civil penalty of not more than one thousand dollars ($1,000) per advertisement, to be paid to the entity that is authorized to bring the action under this section.

(3) In addition to any other penalty allowed by law, a violation of paragraph (2) or (3) of subdivision (a) shall result in a civil penalty of not more than one thousand dollars ($1,000) per animal, to be paid to the entity that is authorized to bring the action under this section. *(Added by Stats.2012, c. 596 (S.B.1229), § 2.)*

§ 1942.8. Temporarily permitting the occupancy of dwelling unit by person at risk of homelessness; rights and obligations of landlord, tenant, and person at risk of homelessness

(a) It is the intent of the Legislature in enacting this section to assist those at risk of homelessness and to encourage landlords and tenants to permit those persons to temporarily reside on their property.

(b) Notwithstanding any other law, and regardless of the terms of the lease or rental agreement, a tenant may, with the written approval of the owner or landlord of the property, temporarily permit the occupancy of their dwelling unit by a person who is at risk of homelessness.

(c)(1) An owner or landlord may adjust the rent payable under the lease or rental agreement during the time the person who is at risk of homelessness is occupying the tenant's dwelling unit, as compensation for the occupancy of that person. The terms regarding the rent payable shall be agreed to in writing by the owner or landlord and the tenant, and shall be consistent with any applicable rent stabilization law or regulation.

(2) If the person who is at risk of homelessness moves out during the term of the lease or rental agreement to which the tenant was already subject, the landlord shall adjust the rent back to the amount that was due from the tenant before the time the person at risk of homelessness occupied the unit plus

any lawful intervening rent increases that were not based on the occupancy of the person at risk of homelessness.

(3) The tenant shall be liable for the timely and total payment of the rent, pursuant to the lease or property agreement, in its entirety.

(d) The person at risk of homelessness shall have all of the rights and obligations of a lodger under California law, except that termination of the right of occupancy of the person at risk of homelessness shall be governed exclusively by subdivision (g).

(e) For purposes of this section, the tenant shall have the same rights and obligations toward the person at risk of homelessness as an owner has to a lodger under California law, except that termination of the right of occupancy of the person at risk of homelessness shall be governed exclusively by subdivision (g).

(f) Unless otherwise agreed upon by all parties, all of the following apply:

(1) The tenant shall be liable for the actions of the person at risk of homelessness to the extent those actions are bound by the terms of the lease or property agreement to which the tenant was already subject, and the tenant shall inform the person at risk of homelessness of all rules and regulations applicable to the premises, and occupants thereof.

(2) The tenant and the landlord shall enter into a written agreement, signed by both parties, indicating that the tenant is liable for the actions of the person at risk of homelessness as provided in paragraph (1). The agreement shall include a provision that states that failure by the tenant to terminate the occupancy of the person at risk of homelessness upon that person's violation of the rules and regulations pursuant to the lease or property agreement of the tenant could result in termination of the lease or property agreement of the tenant.

(3) The tenant shall provide the person at risk of homelessness with a copy of the lease or property agreement with the landlord to which the tenant was already subject.

(4) The tenant and the person at risk of homelessness shall enter into a written agreement, signed by both parties, acknowledging that the person at risk of homelessness shall abide by the rules and regulations prescribed under the lease or property agreement to which the tenant was already subject.

(5) The tenant shall provide the person at risk of homelessness and the landlord with a copy of the signed written agreement described in paragraph (4).

(g)(1) The person at risk of homelessness' right to occupy the premises shall terminate on the earlier of any of the following:

(A) The date agreed to by the landlord.

(B) The termination of the tenant's tenancy for any reason.

(C) The tenant vacating the premises.

(D) At least seven days after the tenant provides notice that specifies the date and time by which the person at risk of homelessness must vacate the premises, unless either of the following apply:

(i) If the landlord has served the tenant with a three-day notice to cure or quit the property pursuant to paragraph (3) of Section 1161 of the Code of Civil Procedure, then the person at risk of homelessness' right to occupy shall terminate 24 hours after the tenant provides notice in writing to the person at risk of homelessness that specifies the date and time by which the person at risk of homelessness must vacate the premises.

(ii) The person at risk of homelessness' right to occupy the premises may be terminated immediately, without notice, if that person has engaged in criminal conduct on the premises.

(2) Upon termination of the person at risk of homelessness' right to remain in the dwelling unit, the person at risk of homelessness may be removed from the premises pursuant to Section 602.3 of the Penal Code, as though the person at risk of homelessness were a lodger.

(h) Prior to terminating the tenant's lease or property agreement based on a violation of the rules and regulations by the person at risk of homelessness, the landlord shall provide the tenant with notice and an opportunity to cure the violation pursuant to paragraph (3) of Section 1161 of the Code of Civil Procedure. Termination of the occupancy of the person at risk of homelessness shall constitute cure of the violation.

(i) Nothing in this section shall be construed to compel a landlord or property owner to agree to permit the occupancy of the person at risk of homelessness in the unit.

(j) Notwithstanding subdivision (b), occupancy by a person who is at risk of homelessness pursuant to this section is not permissible if the addition of another person in the dwelling unit would violate the building's occupancy limits or other applicable building standards.

(k) For the purposes of this section, "person who is at risk of homelessness" has the same meaning as defined in Section 578.3 of Title 24 of the Code of Federal Regulations, except that the criterion provided in subdivision (ii) of subsection (1) of that definition shall not apply.

(*l*) This section does not apply to federal Section 8 housing (42 U.S.C. Sec. 1437 et seq.) or to any other federally funded or assisted low-income housing.

(m) This section is not intended to supersede any other applicable law or regulation governing the ability of tenants to add additional members to their household with or without prior approval from the landlord.

(n) This section shall remain in effect only until January 1, 2024, and as of that date is repealed. *(Added by Stats.2019, c. 339 (A.B.1188), § 1, eff. Jan. 1, 2020.)*

Repeal

For repeal of this section, see its terms.

§ 1942.9. Tenant having COVID–19 rental debt who has submitted declaration of COVID–19–related financial distress; prohibited landlord actions; service or amenity reductions as a result of compliance with public health orders or guidelines

(a) Notwithstanding any other law, a landlord shall not, with respect to a tenant who has COVID–19 rental debt, as that term is defined in Section 1179.02 of the Code of Civil

Procedure, and who has submitted a declaration of COVID–19–related financial distress, as defined in Section 1179.02 of the Code of Civil Procedure, do either of the following:

(1) Charge a tenant, or attempt to collect from a tenant, fees assessed for the late payment of that COVID–19 rental debt.

(2) Increase fees charged to the tenant or charge the tenant fees for services previously provided by the landlord without charge.

(b) Notwithstanding any other law, a landlord who temporarily reduces or makes unavailable a service or amenity as the result of compliance with federal, state, or local public health orders or guidelines shall not be considered to have violated the rental or lease agreement, nor to have provided different terms or conditions of tenancy or reduced services for purposes of any law, ordinance, rule, regulation, or initiative measure adopted by a local governmental entity that establishes a maximum amount that a landlord may charge a tenant for rent. (Added by Stats.2021, c. 2 (S.B.91), § 7, eff. Jan. 29, 2021. Amended by Stats.2021, c. 5 (A.B.81), § 6, eff. Feb. 23, 2021.)

§ 1943. Term of hiring; presumption

A hiring of real property, other than lodgings and dwelling-houses, in places where there is no custom or usage on the subject, is presumed to be a month to month tenancy unless otherwise designated in writing; except that, in the case of real property used for agricultural or grazing purposes a hiring is presumed to be for one year from its commencement unless otherwise expressed in the hiring. (Enacted in 1872. Amended by Stats.1953, c. 1541, p. 3212, § 1.)

Cross References

Hiring defined, see Civil Code § 1925.
Statute of frauds, see Civil Code § 1624.

§ 1944. Term of hiring; presumption; lodgings or dwelling house

A hiring of lodgings or a dwelling house for an unspecified term is presumed to have been made for such length of time as the parties adopt for the estimation of the rent. Thus a hiring at a monthly rate of rent is presumed to be for one month. In the absence of any agreement respecting the length of time or the rent, the hiring is presumed to be monthly. (Enacted in 1872.)

Cross References

Estates in real property, see Civil Code § 761.
Hiring defined, see Civil Code § 1925.

§ 1945. Renewal by continued possession and acceptance of rent

If a lessee of real property remains in possession thereof after the expiration of the hiring, and the lessor accepts rent from him, the parties are presumed to have renewed the hiring on the same terms and for the same time, not exceeding one month when the rent is payable monthly, nor in any case one year. (Enacted in 1872.)

Cross References

Hiring defined, see Civil Code § 1925.

§ 1945.5. Automatic renewal or extension; recitals in contract; size of type, etc.

Notwithstanding any other provision of law, any term of a lease executed after the effective date of this section for the hiring of residential real property which provides for the automatic renewal or extension of the lease for all or part of the full term of the lease if the lessee remains in possession after the expiration of the lease or fails to give notice of his intent not to renew or extend before the expiration of the lease shall be voidable by the party who did not prepare the lease unless such renewal or extension provision appears in at least eight-point boldface type, if the contract is printed, in the body of the lease agreement and a recital of the fact that such provision is contained in the body of the agreement appears in at least eight-point boldface type, if the contract is printed, immediately prior to the place where the lessee executes the agreement. In such case, the presumption in Section 1945 of this code shall apply.

Any waiver of the provisions of this section is void as against public policy. (Added by Stats.1965, c. 1664, p. 3779, § 1, operative June 30, 1966. Amended by Stats.1976, c. 1107, p. 4991, § 1.)

Cross References

Hiring defined, see Civil Code § 1925.

§ 1946. Renewable hiring; notice of termination

A hiring of real property, for a term not specified by the parties, is deemed to be renewed as stated in Section 1945, at the end of the term implied by law unless one of the parties gives written notice to the other of that party's intention to terminate the same, at least as long before the expiration thereof as the term of the hiring itself, not exceeding 30 days; provided, however, that as to tenancies from month to month either of the parties may terminate the same by giving at least 30 days' written notice thereof at any time and the rent shall be due and payable to and including the date of termination. It shall be competent for the parties to provide by an agreement at the time the tenancy is created that a notice of the intention to terminate the same may be given at any time not less than seven days before the expiration of the term thereof. The notice herein required shall be given in the manner prescribed in Section 1162 of the Code of Civil Procedure or by sending a copy by certified or registered mail addressed to the other party. In addition, the lessee may give the notice by sending a copy by certified or registered mail addressed to the agent of the lessor to whom the lessee has paid the rent for the month prior to the date of the notice or by delivering a copy to the agent personally. The notice given by the lessor shall also contain, in substantially the same form, the following:

"State law permits former tenants to reclaim abandoned personal property left at the former address of the tenant, subject to certain conditions. You may or may not be able to reclaim property without incurring additional costs, depending on the cost of storing the property and the length of time before it is reclaimed. In general, these costs will be lower the sooner you contact your former landlord after being notified that property belonging to you was left behind after you moved out." *(Enacted in 1872. Amended by Stats.1931, c. 643, p. 1385, § 1; Stats.1937, c. 354, p. 773, § 1; Stats.1941, c. 784, p. 2325, § 1; Stats.1947, c. 676, p. 1709, § 2; Stats.1969, c. 442, p. 993, § 1; Stats.1973, c. 167, p. 468, § 10; Stats.2012, c. 560 (A.B.2521), § 1; Stats.2018, c. 104 (A.B. 2847), § 1, eff. Jan. 1, 2019.)*

Cross References

Determination of tenancy or other estate at will, see Civil Code § 789.

Eviction of tenant of housing development or residential structure financed by California Housing Finance Agency, required notice and hearing, see Health and Safety Code § 51066.

Hiring defined, see Civil Code § 1925.

Notice of change in terms of lease before expiration of term, see Civil Code § 827.

Possession after expiration of term as unlawful detainer, see Code of Civil Procedure § 1161.

Rent increases, tenants of housing developments financed under California Housing and Infrastructure Finance Agency supervision, notice of meetings to review increase and notice of right to receive specified information, see Health and Safety Code § 51200.

Service of notice in forcible entry and detainer proceedings, see Code of Civil Procedure § 1162.

§ 1946.1. Renewal and termination with respect to hiring of residential real property for a term not specified by the parties; notice

(a) Notwithstanding Section 1946, a hiring of residential real property for a term not specified by the parties, is deemed to be renewed as stated in Section 1945, at the end of the term implied by law unless one of the parties gives written notice to the other of his or her intention to terminate the tenancy, as provided in this section.

(b) An owner of a residential dwelling giving notice pursuant to this section shall give notice at least 60 days prior to the proposed date of termination. A tenant giving notice pursuant to this section shall give notice for a period at least as long as the term of the periodic tenancy prior to the proposed date of termination.

(c) Notwithstanding subdivision (b), an owner of a residential dwelling giving notice pursuant to this section shall give notice at least 30 days prior to the proposed date of termination if any tenant or resident has resided in the dwelling for less than one year.

(d) Notwithstanding subdivision (b), an owner of a residential dwelling giving notice pursuant to this section shall give notice at least 30 days prior to the proposed date of termination if all of the following apply:

(1) The dwelling or unit is alienable separate from the title to any other dwelling unit.

(2) The owner has contracted to sell the dwelling or unit to a bona fide purchaser for value, and has established an escrow with a title insurer or an underwritten title company, as defined in Sections 12340.4 and 12340.5 of the Insurance Code, respectively, a licensed escrow agent, as defined in Sections 17004 and 17200 of the Financial Code, or a licensed real estate broker, as defined in Section 10131 of the Business and Professions Code.

(3) The purchaser is a natural person or persons.

(4) The notice is given no more than 120 days after the escrow has been established.

(5) Notice was not previously given to the tenant pursuant to this section.

(6) The purchaser in good faith intends to reside in the property for at least one full year after the termination of the tenancy.

(e) After an owner has given notice of his or her intention to terminate the tenancy pursuant to this section, a tenant may also give notice of his or her intention to terminate the tenancy pursuant to this section, provided that the tenant's notice is for a period at least as long as the term of the periodic tenancy and the proposed date of termination occurs before the owner's proposed date of termination.

(f) The notices required by this section shall be given in the manner prescribed in Section 1162 of the Code of Civil Procedure or by sending a copy by certified or registered mail.

(g) This section may not be construed to affect the authority of a public entity that otherwise exists to regulate or monitor the basis for eviction.

(h) Any notice given by an owner pursuant to this section shall contain, in substantially the same form, the following:

"State law permits former tenants to reclaim abandoned personal property left at the former address of the tenant, subject to certain conditions. You may or may not be able to reclaim property without incurring additional costs, depending on the cost of storing the property and the length of time before it is reclaimed. In general, these costs will be lower the sooner you contact your former landlord after being notified that property belonging to you was left behind after you moved out." *(Added by Stats.2006, c. 842 (A.B.1169), § 1. Amended by Stats.2009, c. 347 (S.B.290), § 1; Stats. 2012, c. 560 (A.B.2521), § 2; Stats.2012, c. 786 (A.B.2303), § 2.5.)*

Cross References

Hiring defined, see Civil Code § 1925.

§ 1946.2. Termination of tenancy after continuous and lawful occupation of residential real property for 12 months; just cause required; notice; additional tenants; opportunity to cure violation; relocation assistance or rent waiver; application of section

(a) Notwithstanding any other law, after a tenant has continuously and lawfully occupied a residential real property for 12 months, the owner of the residential real property shall not terminate the tenancy without just cause, which shall be stated in the written notice to terminate tenancy. If any additional adult tenants are added to the lease before an existing tenant has continuously and lawfully occupied the residential real property for 24 months, then this subdivision shall only apply if either of the following are satisfied:

(1) All of the tenants have continuously and lawfully occupied the residential real property for 12 months or more.

(2) One or more tenants have continuously and lawfully occupied the residential real property for 24 months or more.

(b) For purposes of this section, "just cause" includes either of the following:

(1) At-fault just cause, which is any of the following:

(A) Default in the payment of rent.

(B) A breach of a material term of the lease, as described in paragraph (3) of Section 1161 of the Code of Civil Procedure, including, but not limited to, violation of a provision of the lease after being issued a written notice to correct the violation.

(C) Maintaining, committing, or permitting the maintenance or commission of a nuisance as described in paragraph (4) of Section 1161 of the Code of Civil Procedure.

(D) Committing waste as described in paragraph (4) of Section 1161 of the Code of Civil Procedure.

(E) The tenant had a written lease that terminated on or after January 1, 2020, or January 1, 2022, if the lease is for a tenancy in a mobilehome, and after a written request or demand from the owner, the tenant has refused to execute a written extension or renewal of the lease for an additional term of similar duration with similar provisions, provided that those terms do not violate this section or any other provision of law.

(F) Criminal activity by the tenant on the residential real property, including any common areas, or any criminal activity or criminal threat, as defined in subdivision (a) of Section 422 of the Penal Code, on or off the residential real property, that is directed at any owner or agent of the owner of the residential real property.

(G) Assigning or subletting the premises in violation of the tenant's lease, as described in paragraph (4) of Section 1161 of the Code of Civil Procedure.

(H) The tenant's refusal to allow the owner to enter the residential real property as authorized by Sections 1101.5 and 1954 of this code, and Sections 13113.7 and 17926.1 of the Health and Safety Code.

(I) Using the premises for an unlawful purpose as described in paragraph (4) of Section 1161 of the Code of Civil Procedure.

(J) The employee, agent, or licensee's failure to vacate after their termination as an employee, agent, or a licensee as described in paragraph (1) of Section 1161 of the Code of Civil Procedure.

(K) When the tenant fails to deliver possession of the residential real property after providing the owner written notice as provided in Section 1946 of the tenant's intention to terminate the hiring of the real property, or makes a written offer to surrender that is accepted in writing by the landlord, but fails to deliver possession at the time specified in that written notice as described in paragraph (5) of Section 1161 of the Code of Civil Procedure.

(2) No-fault just cause, which includes any of the following:

(A)(i) Intent to occupy the residential real property by the owner or their spouse, domestic partner, children, grandchildren, parents, or grandparents.

(ii) For leases entered into on or after July 1, 2020, or July 1, 2022, if the lease is for a tenancy in a mobilehome, clause (i) shall apply only if the tenant agrees, in writing, to the termination, or if a provision of the lease allows the owner to terminate the lease if the owner, or their spouse, domestic partner, children, grandchildren, parents, or grandparents, unilaterally decides to occupy the residential real property. Addition of a provision allowing the owner to terminate the lease as described in this clause to a new or renewed rental agreement or fixed-term lease constitutes a similar provision for the purposes of subparagraph (E) of paragraph (1).

(B) Withdrawal of the residential real property from the rental market.

(C)(i) The owner complying with any of the following:

(I) An order issued by a government agency or court relating to habitability that necessitates vacating the residential real property.

(II) An order issued by a government agency or court to vacate the residential real property.

(III) A local ordinance that necessitates vacating the residential real property.

(ii) If it is determined by any government agency or court that the tenant is at fault for the condition or conditions triggering the order or need to vacate under clause (i), the tenant shall not be entitled to relocation assistance as outlined in paragraph (3) of subdivision (d).

(D)(i) Intent to demolish or to substantially remodel the residential real property.

(ii) For purposes of this subparagraph, "substantially remodel" means the replacement or substantial modification of any structural, electrical, plumbing, or mechanical system that requires a permit from a governmental agency, or the abatement of hazardous materials, including lead-based paint, mold, or asbestos, in accordance with applicable federal, state, and local laws, that cannot be reasonably accomplished in a safe manner with the tenant in place and that requires the tenant to vacate the residential real property for at least 30 days. Cosmetic improvements alone, including painting, decorating, and minor repairs, or other work that can be performed safely without having the residential real property vacated, do not qualify as substantial rehabilitation.

(c) Before an owner of residential real property issues a notice to terminate a tenancy for just cause that is a curable lease violation, the owner shall first give notice of the violation to the tenant with an opportunity to cure the violation pursuant to paragraph (3) of Section 1161 of the Code of Civil Procedure. If the violation is not cured within the time period set forth in the notice, a three-day notice to quit without an opportunity to cure may thereafter be served to terminate the tenancy.

(d)(1) For a tenancy for which just cause is required to terminate the tenancy under subdivision (a), if an owner of residential real property issues a termination notice based on a no-fault just cause described in paragraph (2) of subdivision (b), the owner shall, regardless of the tenant's income, at the owner's option, do one of the following:

(A) Assist the tenant to relocate by providing a direct payment to the tenant as described in paragraph (3).

(B) Waive in writing the payment of rent for the final month of the tenancy, prior to the rent becoming due.

(2) If an owner issues a notice to terminate a tenancy for no-fault just cause, the owner shall notify the tenant of the tenant's right to relocation assistance or rent waiver pursuant to this section. If the owner elects to waive the rent for the final month of the tenancy as provided in subparagraph (B) of paragraph (1), the notice shall state the amount of rent waived and that no rent is due for the final month of the tenancy.

(3)(A) The amount of relocation assistance or rent waiver shall be equal to one month of the tenant's rent that was in effect when the owner issued the notice to terminate the tenancy. Any relocation assistance shall be provided within 15 calendar days of service of the notice.

(B) If a tenant fails to vacate after the expiration of the notice to terminate the tenancy, the actual amount of any relocation assistance or rent waiver provided pursuant to this subdivision shall be recoverable as damages in an action to recover possession.

(C) The relocation assistance or rent waiver required by this subdivision shall be credited against any other relocation assistance required by any other law.

(4) An owner's failure to strictly comply with this subdivision shall render the notice of termination void.

(e) This section shall not apply to the following types of residential real properties or residential circumstances:

(1) Transient and tourist hotel occupancy as defined in subdivision (b) of Section 1940.

(2) Housing accommodations in a nonprofit hospital, religious facility, extended care facility, licensed residential care facility for the elderly, as defined in Section 1569.2 of the Health and Safety Code, or an adult residential facility, as defined in Chapter 6 of Division 6 of Title 22 of the Manual of Policies and Procedures published by the State Department of Social Services.

(3) Dormitories owned and operated by an institution of higher education or a kindergarten and grades 1 to 12, inclusive, school.

(4) Housing accommodations in which the tenant shares bathroom or kitchen facilities with the owner who maintains their principal residence at the residential real property.

(5) Single–family owner-occupied residences, including both of the following:

(A) A residence in which the owner-occupant rents or leases no more than two units or bedrooms, including, but not limited to, an accessory dwelling unit or a junior accessory dwelling unit.

(B) A mobilehome.

(6) A property containing two separate dwelling units within a single structure in which the owner occupied one of the units as the owner's principal place of residence at the beginning of the tenancy, so long as the owner continues in occupancy, and neither unit is an accessory dwelling unit or a junior accessory dwelling unit.

(7) Housing that has been issued a certificate of occupancy within the previous 15 years, unless the housing is a mobilehome.

(8) Residential real property, including a mobilehome, that is alienable separate from the title to any other dwelling unit, provided that both of the following apply:

(A) The owner is not any of the following:

(i) A real estate investment trust, as defined in Section 856 of the Internal Revenue Code.[1]

(ii) A corporation.

(iii) A limited liability company in which at least one member is a corporation.

(iv.) Management of a mobilehome park, as defined in Section 798.2.

(B)(i) The tenants have been provided written notice that the residential property is exempt from this section using the following statement:

"This property is not subject to the rent limits imposed by Section 1947.12 of the Civil Code and is not subject to the just cause requirements of Section 1946.2 of the Civil Code. This property meets the requirements of Sections 1947.12 (d)(5) and 1946.2 (e)(8) of the Civil Code and the owner is not any of the following: (1) a real estate investment trust, as defined by Section 856 of the Internal Revenue Code; (2) a corporation; or (3) a limited liability company in which at least one member is a corporation."

(ii)(I) Except as provided in subclause (II), for a tenancy existing before July 1, 2020, the notice required under clause (i) may, but is not required to, be provided in the rental agreement.

(II) For a tenancy in a mobilehome existing before July 1, 2022, the notice required under clause (i) may, but is not required to, be provided in the rental agreement.

(iii)(I) Except as provided in subclause (II), for any tenancy commenced or renewed on or after July 1, 2020, the notice required under clause (i) must be provided in the rental agreement.

(II) For any tenancy in a mobilehome commenced or renewed on or after July 1, 2022, the notice required under clause (i) shall be provided in the rental agreement.

(iv) Addition of a provision containing the notice required under clause (i) to any new or renewed rental agreement or fixed-term lease constitutes a similar provision for the purposes of subparagraph (E) of paragraph (1) of subdivision (b).

(9) Housing restricted by deed, regulatory restriction contained in an agreement with a government agency, or other recorded document as affordable housing for persons and families of very low, low, or moderate income, as defined in Section 50093 of the Health and Safety Code, or subject to an agreement that provides housing subsidies for affordable housing for persons and families of very low, low, or moderate income, as defined in Section 50093 of the Health and Safety Code or comparable federal statutes.

(f) An owner of residential real property subject to this section shall provide notice to the tenant as follows:

(1)(A) Except as provided in subparagraph (B), for any tenancy commenced or renewed on or after July 1, 2020, as an addendum to the lease or rental agreement, or as a written notice signed by the tenant, with a copy provided to the tenant.

(B) For a tenancy in a mobilehome commenced or renewed on or after July 1, 2022, as an addendum to the lease or rental agreement, or as a written notice signed by the tenant, with a copy provided to the tenant.

(2)(A) Except as provided in subparagraph (B), for a tenancy existing prior to July 1, 2020, by written notice to the tenant no later than August 1, 2020, or as an addendum to the lease or rental agreement.

(B) For a tenancy in a mobilehome existing prior to July 1, 2022, by written notice to the tenant no later than August 1, 2022, or as an addendum to the lease or rental agreement.

(3) The notification or lease provision shall be in no less than 12–point type, and shall include the following:

"California law limits the amount your rent can be increased. See Section 1947.12 of the Civil Code for more information. California law also provides that after all of the tenants have continuously and lawfully occupied the property for 12 months or more or at least one of the tenants has continuously and lawfully occupied the property for 24 months or more, a landlord must provide a statement of cause in any notice to terminate a tenancy. See Section 1946.2 of the Civil Code for more information."

The provision of the notice shall be subject to Section 1632.

(g)(1) This section does not apply to the following residential real property:

(A) Residential real property subject to a local ordinance requiring just cause for termination of a residential tenancy adopted on or before September 1, 2019, in which case the local ordinance shall apply.

(B) Residential real property subject to a local ordinance requiring just cause for termination of a residential tenancy adopted or amended after September 1, 2019, that is more protective than this section, in which case the local ordinance shall apply. For purposes of this subparagraph, an ordinance is "more protective" if it meets all of the following criteria:

(i) The just cause for termination of a residential tenancy under the local ordinance is consistent with this section.

(ii) The ordinance further limits the reasons for termination of a residential tenancy, provides for higher relocation assistance amounts, or provides additional tenant protections that are not prohibited by any other provision of law.

(iii) The local government has made a binding finding within their local ordinance that the ordinance is more protective than the provisions of this section.

(2) A residential real property shall not be subject to both a local ordinance requiring just cause for termination of a residential tenancy and this section.

(3) A local ordinance adopted after September 1, 2019, that is less protective than this section shall not be enforced unless this section is repealed.

(h) Any waiver of the rights under this section shall be void as contrary to public policy.

(i) For the purposes of this section, the following definitions shall apply:

(1) "Owner" includes any person, acting as principal or through an agent, having the right to offer residential real property for rent, and includes a predecessor in interest to the owner.

(2) "Residential real property" means any dwelling or unit that is intended for human habitation, including any dwelling or unit in a mobilehome park.

(3) "Tenancy" means the lawful occupation of residential real property and includes a lease or sublease.

(j) This section shall not apply to a homeowner of a mobilehome, as defined in Section 798.9.

(k) This section shall remain in effect only until January 1, 2030, and as of that date is repealed. *(Added by Stats.2019, c. 597 (A.B.1482), § 2, eff. Jan. 1, 2020. Amended by Stats.2020, c. 370 (S.B.1371), § 32, eff. Jan. 1, 2021; Stats.2020, c. 37 (A.B.3088), § 8, eff. Aug. 31, 2020; Stats.2021, c. 125 (A.B. 978), § 3, eff. Jan. 1, 2022.)*

[1] Internal Revenue Code sections are in Title 26 of the U.S.C.A.

Repeal

For repeal of this section, see its terms.

Cross References

City and county ordinances, resolutions, regulations, or administrative actions adopted in response to the COVID–19 pandemic, requirements, one-year limitation, legislative intent, see Code of Civil Procedure § 1179.05.

Tenants who may be found guilty of unlawful detainer, assistance for tenant in relocating, see Code of Civil Procedure § 1179.03.5.

§ 1946.5. Room by single lodger on periodic basis within dwelling unit occupied by owner; termination; written notice; removal from premises

(a) The hiring of a room by a lodger on a periodic basis within a dwelling unit occupied by the owner may be terminated by either party giving written notice to the other of his or her intention to terminate the hiring, at least as long before the expiration of the term of the hiring as specified in Section 1946. The notice shall be given in a manner prescribed in Section 1162 of the Code of Civil Procedure or by certified or registered mail, restricted delivery, to the other party, with a return receipt requested.

(b) Upon expiration of the notice period provided in the notice of termination given pursuant to subdivision (a), any right of the lodger to remain in the dwelling unit or any part thereof is terminated by operation of law. The lodger's removal from the premises may thereafter be effected pursuant to the provisions of Section 602.3 of the Penal Code or other applicable provisions of law.

(c) As used in this section, "lodger" means a person contracting with the owner of a dwelling unit for a room or room and board within the dwelling unit personally occupied by the owner, where the owner retains a right of access to all areas of the dwelling unit occupied by the lodger and has overall control of the dwelling unit.

(d) This section applies only to owner-occupied dwellings where a single lodger resides. Nothing in this section shall be construed to determine or affect in any way the rights of persons residing as lodgers in an owner-occupied dwelling where more than one lodger resides. *(Added by Stats.1986, c. 1010, § 1.)*

Cross References

Hiring defined, see Civil Code § 1925.

§ 1946.7. Victims of domestic violence, sexual assault, stalking, human trafficking, or abuse of elder or dependent adult; written notice to terminate tenancy; requirements of notice; landlord disclosure to third party; violations and remedies

(a) A tenant may notify the landlord that the tenant intends to terminate the tenancy if the tenant, a household member, or an immediate family member was the victim of an act that constitutes any of the following:

(1) Domestic violence as defined in Section 6211 of the Family Code.

(2) Sexual assault as defined in Section 261, 261.5, 286, 287, or 289 of the Penal Code.

(3) Stalking as defined in Section 1708.7.

(4) Human trafficking as defined in Section 236.1 of the Penal Code.

(5) Abuse of an elder or a dependent adult as defined in Section 15610.07 of the Welfare and Institutions Code.

(6) A crime that caused bodily injury or death.

(7) A crime that included the exhibition, drawing, brandishing, or use of a firearm or other deadly weapon or instrument.

(8) A crime that included the use of force against the victim or a threat of force against the victim.

(b) A notice to terminate a tenancy under this section shall be in writing, with one of the following attached to the notice:

(1) A copy of a temporary restraining order, emergency protective order, or protective order lawfully issued pursuant to Part 3 (commencing with Section 6240) or Part 4 (commencing with Section 6300) of Division 10 of the Family Code, Section 136.2 of the Penal Code, Section 527.6 of the Code of Civil Procedure, or Section 213.5 or 15657.03 of the Welfare and Institutions Code that protects the tenant, household member, or immediate family member from further domestic violence, sexual assault, stalking, human trafficking, abuse of an elder or a dependent adult, or any act or crime listed in subdivision (a).

(2) A copy of a written report by a peace officer employed by a state or local law enforcement agency acting in the peace officer's official capacity stating that the tenant, household member, or immediate family member has filed a report alleging that the tenant, the household member, or the immediate family member is a victim of an act or crime listed in subdivision (a).

(3)(A) Documentation from a qualified third party based on information received by that third party while acting in the third party's professional capacity to indicate that the tenant, household member, or immediate family member is seeking assistance for physical or mental injuries or abuse resulting from an act or crime listed in subdivision (a).

(B) The documentation shall contain, in substantially the same form, the following:

Tenant Statement and Qualified Third Party Statement under Civil Code Section 1946.7

Part I. Statement By Tenant

I, [insert name of tenant], state as follows:

I, or a member of my household or immediate family, have been a victim of:

[insert one or more of the following: domestic violence, sexual assault, stalking, human trafficking, elder abuse, dependent adult abuse, or a crime that caused bodily injury or death, a crime that included the exhibition, drawing, brandishing, or use of a firearm or other deadly weapon or instrument, or a crime that included the use of force against the victim or a threat of force against the victim.]

The most recent incident(s) happened on or about:

[insert date or dates.]

The incident(s) was/were committed by the following person(s), with these physical description(s), if known and safe to provide:

[if known and safe to provide, insert name(s) and physical description(s).]

_____   _____
(signature of tenant)   (date)

Part II. Qualified Third Party Statement

I, [insert name of qualified third party], state as follows:

My business address and phone number are:

[insert business address and phone number.]

Check and complete one of the following:

_____I meet the requirements for a sexual assault counselor provided in Section 1035.2 of the Evidence Code and I am either engaged in an office, hospital, institution, or center commonly known as a rape crisis center described in that section or employed by an organization providing the programs specified in Section 13835.2 of the Penal Code.

_____I meet the requirements for a domestic violence counselor provided in Section 1037.1 of the Evidence Code and I am employed, whether financially compensated or not, by a domestic violence victim service organization, as defined in that section.

_____I meet the requirements for a human trafficking caseworker provided in Section 1038.2 of the Evidence Code and I am employed, whether financially compensated or not, by an organization that provides programs specified in Section 18294 of the Welfare and Institutions Code or in Section 13835.2 of the Penal Code.

_____I meet the definition of "victim of violent crime advocate" provided in Section 1947.6 of the Civil Code and I am employed, whether financially compensated or not, by * * * an agency or organization that has a documented record of providing services to victims of violent crime or provides those services under the auspices or supervision of a court or a law enforcement or prosecution agency.

_____I am licensed by the State of California as a:
[insert one of the following: physician and surgeon, osteopathic physician and surgeon, registered nurse, psychiatrist, psychologist, licensed clinical social worker, licensed marriage and family therapist, or licensed professional clinical counselor.] and I am licensed by, and my license number is:
[insert name of state licensing entity and license number.]

The person who signed the Statement By Tenant above stated to me that the person, or a member of the person's household or immediate family, is a victim of:
[insert one or more of the following: domestic violence, sexual assault, stalking, human trafficking, elder abuse, dependent adult abuse, or a crime that caused physical injury, emotional injury and the threat of physical injury, or death.]

The person further stated to me the incident(s) occurred on or about the date(s) stated above.

I understand that the person who made the Statement By Tenant may use this document as a basis for terminating a lease with the person's landlord.

_____   _____
(signature of qualified third party)   (date)

(C) The documentation may be signed by a person who meets the requirements for a sexual assault counselor, domestic violence counselor, a human trafficking caseworker, or a victim of violent crime advocate only if the documentation displays the letterhead of the office, hospital, institution, center, or organization, as appropriate, that engages or employs, whether financially compensated or not, this counselor, caseworker, or advocate.

(4) Any other form of documentation that reasonably verifies that the crime or act listed in subdivision (a) occurred.

(c) If the tenant is terminating tenancy pursuant to subdivision (a) because an immediate family member is a victim of an eligible act or crime listed in subdivision (a) and that tenant did not live in the same household as the immediate family member at the time of the act or crime, and no part of the act or crime occurred within the dwelling unit or within 1,000 feet of the dwelling unit of the tenant, the tenant shall attach to the notice and other documentation required by subdivision (b) a written statement stating all of the following:

(1) The tenant's immediate family member was a victim of an act or crime listed in subdivision (a).

(2) The tenant intends to relocate as a result of the tenant's immediate family member being a victim of an act or crime listed in subdivision (a).

(3) The tenant is relocating to increase the safety, physical well-being, emotional well-being, psychological well-being, or financial security of the tenant or of the tenant's immediate family member as a result of the act or crime.

(d) The notice to terminate the tenancy shall be given within 180 days of the date that any order described in paragraph (1) of subdivision (b) was issued, within 180 days of the date that any written report described in paragraph (2) of subdivision (b) was made, within 180 days of the date that an act or a crime described in * * * subdivision (a) occurred, or within the time period described in Section 1946.

(e) If notice to terminate the tenancy is provided to the landlord under this section, the tenant shall be responsible for payment of rent for no more than 14 calendar days following the giving of the notice, or for any shorter appropriate period as described in Section 1946 or the lease or rental agreement. The tenant shall be released without penalty from any further rent or other payment obligation to the landlord under the lease or rental agreement * * *. If the premises are relet to another party prior to the end of the obligation to pay rent, the rent owed under this subdivision shall be prorated.

(f) Notwithstanding any law, a landlord shall not, due to the termination, require a tenant who terminates a lease or rental agreement pursuant to this section to forfeit any security deposit money or advance rent paid * * *. A tenant who terminates a rental agreement pursuant to this section shall not be considered for any purpose, by reason of the termination, to have breached the lease or rental agreement. * * * In all other respects, the law governing the security deposit shall apply.

(g) This section does not relieve a tenant, other than the tenant who is, or who has a household member or immediate family member who is, a victim of an act or crime listed in subdivision (a) and members of that tenant's household, from their obligations under the lease or rental agreement.

(h) For purposes of this section, the following definitions apply:

(1) "Household member" means a member of the tenant's family who lives in the same * * * residential unit as the tenant.

(2) "Health practitioner" means a physician and surgeon, osteopathic physician and surgeon, psychiatrist, psychologist, registered nurse, licensed clinical social worker, licensed marriage and family therapist, * * * licensed professional clinical counselor, or a victim of violent crime advocate.

(3) "Immediate family member" means the parent, stepparent, spouse, child, child-in-law, stepchild, or sibling of the tenant, or any person living in the tenant's household at the time the crime or act listed in subdivision (a) occurred who has a relationship with the tenant that is substantially similar to that of a family member.

(4) "Qualified third party" means a health practitioner, domestic violence counselor, as defined in Section 1037.1 of

the Evidence Code, a sexual assault counselor, as defined in Section 1035.2 of the Evidence Code, or a human trafficking caseworker, as defined in Section 1038.2 of the Evidence Code.

(5) "Victim of violent crime advocate" means a person who is employed, whether financially compensated or not, for the purpose of rendering advice or assistance to victims of violent crimes for * * * an agency or organization that has a documented record of providing services to victims of violent crime or provides those services under the auspices or supervision of a court or a law enforcement or prosecution agency.

(i)(1) A landlord shall not disclose any information provided by a tenant under this section to a third party unless the disclosure satisfies * * * one or more of the following:

(A) The tenant consents in writing to the disclosure.

(B) The disclosure is required by law or order of the court.

(2) A landlord's communication to a qualified third party who provides documentation under paragraph (3) of subdivision (b) to verify the contents of that documentation is not disclosure for purposes of this subdivision.

(j) An owner or an owner's agent shall not refuse to rent a dwelling unit to an otherwise qualified prospective tenant or refuse to continue to rent to an existing tenant solely on the basis that the tenant has previously exercised the tenant's rights under this section or has previously terminated a tenancy because of the circumstances described in subdivision (a).

(k) A landlord or agent of a landlord who violates this section shall be liable to the tenant in a civil action for both of the following:

(1) The actual damages sustained by the tenant.

(2)(A) Statutory damages of not less than one hundred dollars ($100) and not more than five thousand dollars ($5,000).

(B) Notwithstanding subparagraph (A), a landlord or agent of a landlord who violates this section shall not be liable for statutory damages if the tenant provided documentation of the crime or act to the landlord or the agent of the landlord pursuant to paragraph (4) of subdivision (b) only.

(*l*) The remedies provided by this section shall be in addition to any other remedy provided by law. (Added by Stats.2008, c. 440 (A.B.2052), § 1, eff. Sept. 27, 2008. Amended by Stats.2011, c. 76 (A.B.588), § 1; Stats.2012, c. 516 (S.B.1403), § 1; Stats.2013, c. 130 (S.B.612), § 1; Stats.2015, c. 70 (A.B.418), § 1, eff. Jan. 1, 2016; Stats.2018, c. 423 (S.B.1494), § 6, eff. Jan. 1, 2019; Stats.2019, c. 497 (A.B.991), § 26, eff. Jan. 1, 2020; Stats.2020, c. 205 (S.B.1190), § 1, eff. Jan. 1, 2021; Stats.2021, c. 626 (A.B.1171), § 5, eff. Jan. 1, 2022; Stats.2022, c. 28 (S.B.1380), § 24, eff. Jan. 1, 2023; Stats.2022, c. 558 (S.B.1017), § 1, eff. Jan. 1, 2023.)

Cross References

Informing crime victims of their rights, Victim Protections and Resources card, see Penal Code § 679.027.

§ 1946.8. Summoning law enforcement assistance or emergency assistance; lease or rental agreement provisions prohibiting or limiting right void; penalties prohibited; establishing belief; waiver void and unenforceable; affirmative defense; remedies

(a) For purposes of this section:

(1) "Individual in an emergency" means a person who believes that immediate action is required to prevent or mitigate the loss or impairment of life, health, or property.

(2) "Occupant" means a person residing in a dwelling unit with the tenant. "Occupant" includes lodgers as defined in Section 1946.5.

(3) "Penalties" means the following:

(A) The actual or threatened assessment of fees, fines, or penalties.

(B) The actual or threatened termination of a tenancy or the actual or threatened failure to renew a tenancy.

(C) Subjecting a tenant to inferior terms, privileges, and conditions of tenancy in comparison to tenants who have not sought law enforcement assistance or emergency assistance.

(4) "Resident" means a member of the tenant's household or any other occupant living in the dwelling unit with the consent of the tenant.

(5) "Victim of abuse" includes:

(A) A victim of domestic violence as defined in Section 6211 of the Family Code.

(B) A victim of elder or dependent adult abuse as defined in Section 15610.07 of the Welfare and Institutions Code.

(C) A victim of human trafficking as described in Section 236.1 of the Penal Code.

(D) A victim of sexual assault, meaning a victim of any act made punishable by Section 261, 264.1, 285, 286, 288, 288a, or 289 of the Penal Code.

(E) A victim of stalking as described in Section 1708.7 of this code or Section 646.9 of the Penal Code.

(6) "Victim of crime" means any victim of a misdemeanor or felony.

(b) Any provision in a rental or lease agreement for a dwelling unit that prohibits or limits, or threatens to prohibit or limit, a tenant's, resident's, or other person's right to summon law enforcement assistance or emergency assistance as, or on behalf of, a victim of abuse, a victim of crime, or an individual in an emergency, if the tenant, resident, or other person believes that the law enforcement assistance or emergency assistance is necessary to prevent or address the perpetration, escalation, or exacerbation of the abuse, crime, or emergency, shall be void as contrary to public policy.

(c) A landlord shall not impose, or threaten to impose, penalties on a tenant or resident who exercises the tenant's or resident's right to summon law enforcement assistance or emergency assistance as, or on behalf of, a victim of abuse, a victim of crime, or an individual in an emergency, based on the person's belief that the assistance is necessary, as described in subdivision (b). A landlord shall not impose, or threaten to impose, penalties on a tenant or resident as a consequence of a person who is not a resident or tenant summoning law enforcement assistance or emergency assistance on the tenant's, resident's, or other person's behalf, based on the person's belief that the assistance is necessary.

(d) Documentation is not required to establish belief for purposes of subdivision (b) or (c), but belief may be established by documents such as those described in Section 1161.3 of the Code of Civil Procedure.

(e) Any waiver of the provisions of this section is contrary to public policy and is void and unenforceable.

(f)(1) In an action for unlawful detainer, a tenant, resident, or occupant may raise, as an affirmative defense, that the landlord or owner violated this section.

(2) There is a rebuttable presumption that a tenant, resident, or occupant has established an affirmative defense under this subdivision if the landlord or owner files a complaint for unlawful detainer within 30 days of a resident, tenant, or other person summoning law enforcement assistance or emergency assistance and the complaint is based upon a notice that alleges that the act of summoning law enforcement assistance or emergency assistance as, or on behalf of, a victim of abuse, a victim of crime, or an individual in an emergency constitutes a rental agreement violation, lease violation, or a nuisance. A reference to a person summoning law enforcement in a notice that is the basis for a complaint for unlawful detainer that is necessary to describe conduct that is alleged to constitute a violation of a rental agreement or lease is not, in itself, an allegation for purposes of this paragraph.

(3) A landlord or owner may rebut the presumption described in paragraph (2) by demonstrating that a reason other than the summoning of law enforcement or emergency assistance as, or on behalf of, a victim of abuse, a victim of crime, or an individual in an emergency was a substantial motivating factor for filing the complaint.

(g) In addition to other remedies provided by law, a violation of this section entitles a tenant, a resident, or other aggrieved person to seek injunctive relief prohibiting the landlord from creating or enforcing policies in violation of this section, or from imposing or threatening to impose penalties against the tenant, resident, or other aggrieved person based on summoning law enforcement or emergency assistance as, or on behalf of, a victim of abuse, a victim of crime, or an individual in an emergency.

(h) This section does not permit an injunction to be entered that would prohibit the filing of an unlawful detainer action.

(i) This section does not limit a landlord's exercise of the landlord's other rights under a lease or rental agreement, or under other law pertaining to the hiring of property, with regard to matters that are not addressed by this section. *(Added by Stats.2018, c. 190 (A.B.2413), § 1, eff. Jan. 1, 2019. Amended by Stats.2021, c. 626 (A.B.1171), § 6, eff. Jan. 1, 2022.)*

§ 1947. Rent; time of payment

When there is no usage or contract to the contrary, rents are payable at the termination of the holding, when it does not exceed one year. If the holding is by the day, week, month, quarter, or year, rent is payable at the termination of the respective periods, as it successively becomes due. *(Enacted in 1872.)*

§ 1947.3. Cash or electronic funds transfer as exclusive form of payment of rent or security deposit; conditions; payment of rent by third party; right to terminate tenancy; form; mutual agreement; waiver

(a)(1) Except as provided in paragraph (2), a landlord or a landlord's agent shall allow a tenant to pay rent and deposit of security by at least one form of payment that is neither cash nor electronic funds transfer.

(2) A landlord or a landlord's agent may demand or require cash as the exclusive form of payment of rent or deposit of security if the tenant has previously attempted to pay the landlord or landlord's agent with a check drawn on insufficient funds or the tenant has instructed the drawee to stop payment on a check, draft, or order for the payment of money. The landlord may demand or require cash as the exclusive form of payment only for a period not exceeding three months following an attempt to pay with a check on insufficient funds or following a tenant's instruction to stop payment. If the landlord chooses to demand or require cash payment under these circumstances, the landlord shall give the tenant a written notice stating that the payment instrument was dishonored and informing the tenant that the tenant shall pay in cash for a period determined by the landlord, not to exceed three months, and attach a copy of the dishonored instrument to the notice. The notice shall comply with Section 827 if demanding or requiring payment in cash constitutes a change in the terms of the lease.

(3) Subject to the limitations below, a landlord or a landlord's agent shall allow a tenant to pay rent through a third party.

(A) A landlord or landlord's agent is not required to accept the rent payment tendered by a third party unless the third party has provided to the landlord or landlord's agent a signed acknowledgment stating that they are not currently a tenant of the premises for which the rent payment is being made and that acceptance of the rent payment does not create a new tenancy with the third party.

(B) Failure by a third party to provide the signed acknowledgment to the landlord or landlord's agent shall void the obligation of a landlord or landlord's agent to accept a tenant's rent tendered by a third party.

(C) The landlord or landlord's agent may, but is not required to, provide a form acknowledgment to be used by third parties, as provided for in subparagraph (A), provided however that a landlord shall accept as sufficient for compliance with subparagraph (A) an acknowledgment in substantially the following form:

I, [insert name of third party], state as follows:

I am not currently a tenant of the premises located at [insert address of premises].

I acknowledge that acceptance of the rent payment I am offering for the premises does not create a new tenancy.

_____ _____
(signature of third party)   (date)

(D) A landlord or landlord's agent may require a signed acknowledgment for each rent payment made by the third party. A landlord or landlord's agent and the third party may agree that one acknowledgment shall be sufficient for when the third party makes more than one rent payment during a period of time.

(E) Nothing in this paragraph shall be construed to require a landlord or landlord's agent to enter into a contract in connection with a federal, state, or local housing assistance program, including, but not limited to, the federal housing assistance voucher programs under Section 8 of the United States Housing Act of 1937 (42 U.S.C. Sec. 1437f).

(4) Paragraphs (2) and (3) do not enlarge or diminish a landlord's or landlord's agent's legal right to terminate a tenancy. Nothing in paragraph (3) is intended to extend the due date for any rent payment or require a landlord or landlord's agent to accept tender of rent beyond the expiration of the period stated in paragraph (2) of Section 1161 of the Code of Civil Procedure.

(b) For the purposes of this section, the issuance of a money order or a cashier's check is direct evidence only that the instrument was issued.

(c) For purposes of this section, "electronic funds transfer" means any transfer of funds, other than a transaction originated by check, draft, or similar paper instrument, that is initiated through an electronic terminal, telephonic instrument, computer, or magnetic tape so as to order, instruct, or authorize a financial institution to debit or credit an account. "Electronic funds transfer" includes, but is not limited to, point-of-sale transfers, direct deposits or withdrawals of funds, transfers initiated by telephone, transfers via an automated clearinghouse, transfers initiated electronically that deliver a paper instrument, and transfers authorized in advance to recur at substantially regular intervals.

(d) Nothing in this section shall be construed to prohibit the tenant and landlord or agent to mutually agree that rent payments may be made in cash or by electronic funds transfer, so long as another form of payment is also authorized, subject to the requirements of subdivision (a).

(e) A waiver of the provisions of this section is contrary to public policy, and is void and unenforceable. *(Added by Stats.2004, c. 76 (S.B.115), § 1. Amended by Stats.2012, c. 268 (S.B.1055), § 1; Stats.2018, c. 233 (A.B.2219), § 1, eff. Jan. 1, 2019.)*

Cross References

Actions to recover COVID–19 rental debt, attorneys' fees, see Code of Civil Procedure § 871.11.
Actions to recover COVID–19 rental debt, documentation of good faith effort regarding governmental rental assistance for tenant, reduction of damages for landlord refusal to obtain rental assistance, exceptions, see Code of Civil Procedure § 871.10.
Legislative findings and declarations, small claims court jurisdictions for COVID–19 rental debt, see Code of Civil Procedure § 116.223.

§ 1947.5. Prohibition by residential dwelling unit landlord of smoking cigarettes or other tobacco products; lease or rental agreement provisions

(a) A landlord of a residential dwelling unit, as defined in Section 1940, or his or her agent, may prohibit the smoking of a cigarette, as defined in Section 104556 of the Health and Safety Code, or other tobacco product on the property or in any building or portion of the building, including any dwelling unit, other interior or exterior area, or the premises on which it is located, in accordance with this article.

(b)(1) Every lease or rental agreement entered into on or after January 1, 2012, for a residential dwelling unit on property on any portion of which the landlord has prohibited the smoking of cigarettes or other tobacco products pursuant to this article shall include a provision that specifies the areas on the property where smoking is prohibited, if the lessee has not previously occupied the dwelling unit.

(2) For a lease or rental agreement entered into before January 1, 2012, a prohibition against the smoking of cigarettes or other tobacco products in any portion of the property in which smoking was previously permitted shall constitute a change of the terms of tenancy, requiring adequate notice in writing, to be provided in the manner prescribed in Section 827.

(c) A landlord who exercises the authority provided in subdivision (a) to prohibit smoking shall be subject to federal, state, and local requirements governing changes to the terms of a lease or rental agreement for tenants with leases or rental agreements that are in existence at the time that the policy limiting or prohibiting smoking is adopted.

(d) This section shall not be construed to preempt any local ordinance in effect on or before January 1, 2012, or any provision of a local ordinance in effect on or after January 1, 2012, that restricts the smoking of cigarettes or other tobacco products.

(e) A limitation or prohibition of the use of any tobacco product shall not affect any other term or condition of the tenancy, nor shall this section be construed to require statutory authority to establish or enforce any other lawful term or condition of the tenancy.

(f) For purposes of this section, "smoking" has the same meaning as in subdivision (c) of Section 22950.5 of the Business and Professions Code.

(g) For purposes of this section, "tobacco product" means a product or device as defined in subdivision (d) of Section 22950.5 of the Business and Professions Code. *(Added by Stats.2011, c. 264 (S.B.332), § 2. Amended by Stats.2015–2016, 2nd Ex.Sess., c. 7 (S.B.5), § 8, eff. June 9, 2016.)*

§ 1947.6. Installation of electric vehicle charging station upon request by lessee; leases executed, extended or renewed on and after July 1, 2015; exceptions; requirements

(a) For any lease executed, extended, or renewed on and after July 1, 2015, a lessor of a dwelling shall approve a written request of a lessee to install an electric vehicle charging station at a parking space allotted for the lessee that meets the requirements of this section and complies with the lessor's procedural approval process for modification to the property.

(b) This section does not apply to residential rental properties where:

(1) Electric vehicle charging stations already exist for lessees in a ratio that is equal to or greater than 10 percent of the designated parking spaces.

(2) Parking is not provided as part of the lease agreement.

(3) There are fewer than five parking spaces.

(4) The dwelling is subject to a residential rent control ordinance. This paragraph shall not apply to a lease executed, extended, or renewed on and after January 1, 2019.

(5) The dwelling is subject to both a residential rent control ordinance and an ordinance, adopted on or before January 1, 2018, that requires the lessor to approve a lessee's written request to install an electric vehicle charging station at a parking space allotted to the lessee.

(c) For purposes of this section, "electric vehicle charging station" or "charging station" means any level of electric vehicle supply equipment station that is designed and built in compliance with Article 625 of the California Electrical Code, as it reads on the effective date of this section, and delivers electricity from a source outside an electric vehicle into a plug-in electric vehicle.

(d) A lessor shall not be obligated to provide an additional parking space to a lessee in order to accommodate an electric vehicle charging station.

(e) If the electric vehicle charging station has the effect of providing the lessee with a reserved parking space, the lessor may charge a monthly rental amount for that parking space.

(f) An electric vehicle charging station and all modifications and improvements to the property shall comply with federal, state, and local law, and all applicable zoning requirements, land use requirements, and covenants, conditions, and restrictions.

(g) A lessee's written request to make a modification to the property in order to install and use an electric vehicle charging station shall include, but is not limited to, the lessee's consent to enter into a written agreement that includes, but is not limited to, the following:

(1) Compliance with the lessor's requirements for the installation, use, maintenance, and removal of the charging station and installation, use, and maintenance of the infrastructure for the charging station.

(2) Compliance with the lessor's requirements for the lessee to provide a complete financial analysis and scope of work regarding the installation of the charging station and its infrastructure.

(3) A written description of how, when, and where the modifications and improvements to the property are proposed to be made consistent with those items specified in the "Permitting Checklist" of the "Zero-Emission Vehicles in California: Community Readiness Guidebook" published by the Office of Planning and Research.

(4) Obligation of the lessee to pay the lessor all costs associated with the lessor's installation of the charging station and its infrastructure prior to any modification or improvement being made to the leased property. The costs associated with modifications and improvements shall include, but are not limited to, the cost of permits, supervision, construction, and, solely if required by the contractor, consistent with its past performance of work for the lessor, performance bonds.

(5) Obligation of the lessee to pay as part of rent for the costs associated with the electrical usage of the charging station, and cost for damage, maintenance, repair, removal, and replacement of the charging station, and modifications or improvements made to the property associated with the charging station.

(h) The lessee and each successor lessee shall obtain personal liability coverage, as described in Section 108 of the Insurance Code, in an amount not to exceed 10 times the annual rent changed for the dwelling, covering property damage and personal injury proximately caused by the installation or operation of the electric vehicle charging station. The policy shall be maintained in full force and effect from the time of installation of the electric vehicle charging station until the electric vehicle charging station is removed or the lessee forfeits possession of the dwelling to the lessor.

(i) Notwithstanding subdivision (h), no insurance shall be required of a lessee installing an electric vehicle charging station if both of the following are satisfied:

(1) The electric vehicle charging station has been certified by a Nationally Recognized Testing Laboratory that is approved by the Occupational Safety and Health Administration of the United States Department of Labor.

(2) The electric vehicle charging station and any associated alterations to the dwelling's electrical system are performed by a licensed electrician. (Added by Stats.2014, c. 529 (A.B.2565), § 1, eff. Jan. 1, 2015. Amended by Stats.2018, c. 163 (A.B.1796), § 1, eff. Jan. 1, 2019; Stats.2019, c. 855 (S.B.638), § 1, eff. Jan. 1, 2020.)

§ 1947.7. Local rent stabilization and rent control programs; enforcement; confidential information

(a) The Legislature finds and declares that the operation of local rent stabilization programs can be complex and that disputes often arise with regard to standards of compliance with the regulatory processes of those programs. Therefore, it is the intent of the Legislature to limit the imposition of penalties and sanctions against an owner of residential rental units where that person has attempted in good faith to fully comply with the regulatory processes.

(b) An owner of a residential rental unit who is in substantial compliance with an ordinance or charter that controls or establishes a system of controls on the price at which residential rental units may be offered for rent or lease and which requires the registration of rents, or any regulation adopted pursuant thereto, shall not be assessed a penalty or any other sanction for noncompliance with the ordinance, charter, or regulation.

Restitution to the tenant or recovery of the registration or filing fees due to the local agency shall be the exclusive remedies which may be imposed against an owner of a residential rental unit who is in substantial compliance with the ordinance, charter, or regulation.

"Substantial compliance," as used in this subdivision, means that the owner of a residential rental unit has made a good faith attempt to comply with the ordinance, charter, or regulation sufficient to reasonably carry out the intent and purpose of the ordinance, charter, or regulation, but is not in full compliance, and has, after receiving notice of a deficiency from the local agency, cured the defect in a timely manner, as reasonably determined by the local agency.

"Local agency," as used in this subdivision, means the public entity responsible for the implementation of the ordinance, charter, or regulation.

(c) For any residential unit which has been registered and for which a base rent has been listed or for any residential unit which an owner can show, by a preponderance of the evidence, a good faith attempt to comply with the registration requirements or who was exempt from registration requirements in a previous version of the ordinance or charter and for which the owner of that residential unit has subsequently found not to have been in compliance with the ordinance, charter, or regulation, all annual rent adjustments which may have been denied during the period of the owner's noncompliance shall be restored prospectively once the owner is in compliance with the ordinance, charter, or regulation.

(d) In those jurisdictions where, prior to January 1, 1990, the local ordinance did not allow the restoration of annual rent adjustment, once the owner is in compliance with this section the local agency may phase in any increase in rent caused by the restoration of the annual rent adjustments that is in excess of 20 percent over the rent previously paid by the tenant, in equal installments over three years, if the tenant demonstrates undue financial hardship due to the restoration of the full annual rent adjustments. This subdivision shall remain operative only until January 1, 1993, unless a later enacted statute which is chaptered by January 1, 1993, deletes or extends that date.

(e) For purposes of this subdivision, an owner shall be deemed in compliance with the ordinance, charter, or regulation if he or she is in substantial compliance with the applicable local rental registration requirements and applicable local and state housing code provisions, has paid all fees and penalties owed to the local agency which have not otherwise been barred by the applicable statute of limitations, and has satisfied all claims for refunds of rental overcharges brought by tenants or by the local rent control board on behalf of tenants of the affected unit.

(f) Nothing in this section shall be construed to grant to any public entity any power which it does not possess independent of this section to control or establish a system of control on the price at which accommodations may be offered for rent or lease, or to diminish any power to do so which that public entity may possess, except as specifically provided in this section.

(g) In those jurisdictions where an ordinance or charter controls, or establishes a system of controls on, the price at which residential rental units may be offered for rent or lease and requires the periodic registration of rents, and where, for purposes of compliance with subdivision (e) of Section 1954.53, the local agency requires an owner to provide the name of a present or former tenant, the tenant's name and any additional information provided concerning the tenant, is confidential and shall be treated as confidential information within the meaning of the Information Practices Act of 1977 (Chapter 1 (commencing with Section 1798) of Title 1.8 of this part). A local agency shall, to the extent required by this subdivision, be considered an "agency" as defined in subdivision (b) of Section 1798.3. For purposes of compliance with subdivision (e) of Section 1954.53, a local agency subject to this subdivision may request, but shall not compel, an owner to provide any information regarding a tenant other than the tenant's name. *(Added by Stats.1986, c. 1199, § 1. Amended by Stats.1989, c. 987, § 1; Stats.1996, c. 566 (S.B.1632), § 1.)*

§ 1947.8. Local rent controls; establishment and certification of permissible rent levels; appeal; fee; public record

(a) If an ordinance or charter controls or establishes a system of controls on the price at which residential rental units may be offered for rent or lease and requires the registration of rents, the ordinance or charter, or any regulation adopted pursuant thereto, shall provide for the establishment and certification of permissible rent levels for the registered rental units, and any changes thereafter to those rent levels, by the local agency as provided in this section.

(b) If the ordinance, charter, or regulation is in effect on January 1, 1987, the ordinance, charter, or regulation shall provide for the establishment and certification of permissible rent levels on or before January 1, 1988, including completion of all appeals and administrative proceedings connected therewith. After July 1, 1990, no local agency may maintain any action to recover excess rent against any property owner who has registered the unit with the local agency within the time limits set forth in this section if the initial certification of permissible rent levels affecting that particular property has not been completed, unless the delay is willfully and intentionally caused by the property owner or is a result of court proceedings or further administrative proceedings ordered by a court. If the ordinance, charter, or regulation is adopted on or after January 1, 1987, the ordinance, charter, or regulation shall provide for the establishment and certification of permissible rent levels within one year after it is adopted, including completion of all appeals and administrative proceedings connected therewith. Upon the request of the landlord or the tenant, the local agency shall provide the landlord and the tenant with a certificate or other documentation reflecting the permissible rent levels of the rental unit. A landlord may request a certificate of permissible rent levels for rental units that have a base rent established, but are vacant and not exempt from registration under this section. The landlord or the tenant may appeal the determination of the permissible rent levels reflected in the certificate. The permissible rent levels reflected in the certificate or other documentation shall, in the absence of intentional misrepresentation or fraud, be binding and conclusive upon the local agency unless the determination of the permissible rent levels is being appealed.

(c) After the establishment and certification of permissible rent levels under subdivision (b), the local agency shall, upon the request of the landlord or the tenant, provide the landlord and the tenant with a certificate of the permissible rent levels of the rental unit. The certificate shall be issued within five business days from the date of request by the landlord or the tenant. The permissible rent levels reflected in the certificate shall, in the absence of intentional misrepresentation or fraud, be binding and conclusive upon the local agency unless the determination of the permissible rent levels is being appealed. The landlord or the tenant may appeal the determination of the permissible rent levels reflected in the certificate. Any appeal of a determination of permissible rent levels as reflected in the certificate, other than an appeal

§ 1947.8

made pursuant to subdivision (b), shall be filed with the local agency within 15 days from issuance of the certificate. The local agency shall notify, in writing, the landlord and the tenant of its decision within 60 days following the filing of the appeal.

(d) The local agency may charge the person to whom a certificate is issued a fee in the amount necessary to cover the reasonable costs incurred by the local agency in issuing the certificate.

(e) The absence of a certification of permissible rent levels shall not impair, restrict, abridge, or otherwise interfere with either of the following:

(1) A judicial or administrative hearing.

(2) Any matter in connection with a conveyance of an interest in property.

(f) The record of permissible rent levels is a public record for purposes of the California Public Records Act (Division 10 (commencing with Section 7920.000) of Title 1 of the Government Code).

(g) Any notice specifying the rents applicable to residential rental units that is given by an owner to a public entity or tenant in order to comply with Chapter 12.75 (commencing with Section 7060) of Division 7 of Title 1 of the Government Code shall not be considered a registration of rents for purposes of this section.

(h) "Local agency," as used in this section, means the public entity responsible for the implementation of the ordinance, charter, or regulation.

(i) Nothing in this section shall be construed:

(1) To grant to any public entity any power that it does not possess independent of this section to control or establish a system of control on the price at which accommodations may be offered for rent or lease, or to diminish any power of this type that the public entity may possess, except as specifically provided in this section.

(2) On and after January 1, 2016, to apply to tenancies commencing on or after January 1, 1999, for which the owner of residential property may establish the initial rent under Chapter 2.7 (commencing with Section 1954.50). However, for a tenancy that commenced on or after January 1, 1999, if a property owner has provided the local agency with the tenancy's initial rent in compliance with that agency's registration requirements in a writing signed under penalty of perjury, there shall be a rebuttable presumption that the statement of the initial rent is correct. *(Added by Stats.1986, c. 1199, § 2. Amended by Stats.1989, c. 987, § 2; Stats.2016, c. 83 (S.B.775), § 1, eff. Jan. 1, 2017; Stats.2021, c. 615 (A.B.474), § 51, eff. Jan. 1, 2022, operative Jan. 1, 2023.)*

§ 1947.9. San Francisco rent stabilization ordinance; limitations on compensation for temporary displacement; interpretation of section

(a)(1) Notwithstanding any local law to the contrary, for those units governed by the local rent stabilization ordinance in the City and County of San Francisco, levels of compensation for the temporary displacement of a tenant household for less than 20 days shall be limited to both of the following:

(A) Temporary housing and living expenses, of two hundred seventy-five dollars ($275) per day per tenant household. This limit may be adjusted annually by the city and county in an amount equal to the Consumer Price Index, beginning on January 1, 2014.

(B) Actual moving expenses if it is necessary to move the possessions of the tenant household.

(2) The landlord shall have the option to provide a comparable dwelling unit and pay any actual moving expenses, in lieu of the compensation specified in subparagraph (A) of paragraph (1). The rental housing shall be comparable to the tenant household's existing housing in location, size, number of bedrooms, accessibility, type, and quality of construction, and proximity to services and institutions upon which the displaced tenant household depends.

(b) This section shall not be construed to do any of the following:

(1) To terminate, interrupt, or amend, in any way, a tenancy subject to the lease provisions, or the rights and obligations of either party, including, but not limited to, the payment of rent.

(2) To create or affect any grounds for displacement or requirements of a landlord seeking temporary displacement, except the payment of relocation fees pursuant to subdivision (a) for displacement not exceeding 20 days.

(3) To affect the authority of a public entity that may regulate or monitor the basis for eviction.

(c) If a federal or state law regarding relocation compensation is also applicable to the temporary displacement, the tenant may elect to be compensated under those other provisions, and subdivision (a) shall be inapplicable.

(d) This section shall affect only levels of compensation for a temporary displacement of less than 20 days, and does not affect any other local procedures governing temporary relocation. *(Added by Stats.2012, c. 243 (A.B.1925), § 1.)*

§ 1947.10. Evictions based on fraudulent intent to occupy; treble damages

(a) After July 1, 1990, in any city, county, or city and county which administers a system of controls on the price at which residential rental units may be offered for rent or lease and which requires the registration of rents, any owner who evicts a tenant based upon the owner's or the owner's immediate relative's intention to occupy the tenant's unit, shall be required to maintain residence in the unit for at least six continuous months. If a court determines that the eviction was based upon fraud by the owner or the owner's immediate relative to not fulfill this six-month requirement, a court may order the owner to pay treble the cost of relocating the tenant from his or her existing unit back into the previous unit and may order the owner to pay treble the amount of any increase in rent which the tenant has paid. If the tenant decides not to relocate back into the previous unit, the court may order the owner to pay treble the amount of one month's rent paid by the tenant for the unit from which he or she was evicted and treble the amount of any costs incurred in relocating to a different unit. The prevailing party shall be awarded attorney's fees and court costs.

(b) The remedy provided by this section shall not be construed to prohibit any other remedies available to a any party affected by this section. *(Added by Stats.1989, c. 987, § 3.)*

§ 1947.11. Rent charged in excess of certified lawful rent ceiling; refunds

(a) In any city, county, or city and county which administers a system of controls on the price at which residential rental units may be offered for rent or lease and which requires the registration of rents, upon the establishment of a certified rent level, any owner who charges rent to a tenant in excess of the certified lawful rent ceiling shall refund the excess rent to the tenant upon demand. If the owner refuses to refund the excess rent and if a court determines that the owner willfully or intentionally charged the tenant rent in excess of the certified lawful rent ceiling, the court shall award the tenant a judgment for the excess amount of rent and may treble that amount. The prevailing party shall be awarded attorney's fees and court costs.

(b) The remedy provided by this section shall not be construed to prohibit any other remedies available to any party affected by this section.

(c) This section shall not be construed to extend the time within which actions are required to be brought beyond the otherwise applicable limitation set forth in the Code of Civil Procedure. *(Added by Stats.1989, c. 987, § 4. Amended by Stats.1990, c. 216 (S.B.2510), § 7.)*

§ 1947.12. Limitation of rent increase; subleases; application of section; notice; report to Legislature; legislative findings, declarations, and intent

(a)(1) Subject to subdivision (b), an owner of residential real property shall not, over the course of any 12–month period, increase the gross rental rate for a dwelling or a unit more than 5 percent plus the percentage change in the cost of living, or 10 percent, whichever is lower, of the lowest gross rental rate charged for that dwelling or unit at any time during the 12 months prior to the effective date of the increase. In determining the lowest gross rental amount pursuant to this section, any rent discounts, incentives, concessions, or credits offered by the owner of such unit of residential real property and accepted by the tenant shall be excluded. The gross per-month rental rate and any owner-offered discounts, incentives, concessions, or credits shall be separately listed and identified in the lease or rental agreement or any amendments to an existing lease or rental agreement.

(2) If the same tenant remains in occupancy of a unit of residential real property over any 12–month period, the gross rental rate for the unit of residential real property shall not be increased in more than two increments over that 12–month period, subject to the other restrictions of this subdivision governing gross rental rate increase.

(b) For a new tenancy in which no tenant from the prior tenancy remains in lawful possession of the residential real property, the owner may establish the initial rental rate not subject to subdivision (a). Subdivision (a) is only applicable to subsequent increases after that initial rental rate has been established.

(c) A tenant of residential real property subject to this section shall not enter into a sublease that results in a total rent for the premises that exceeds the allowable rental rate authorized by subdivision (a). Nothing in this subdivision authorizes a tenant to sublet or assign the tenant's interest where otherwise prohibited.

(d) This section shall not apply to the following residential real properties:

(1) Housing restricted by deed, regulatory restriction contained in an agreement with a government agency, or other recorded document as affordable housing for persons and families of very low, low, or moderate income, as defined in Section 50093 of the Health and Safety Code, or subject to an agreement that provides housing subsidies for affordable housing for persons and families of very low, low, or moderate income, as defined in Section 50093 of the Health and Safety Code or comparable federal statutes.

(2) Dormitories owned and operated by an institution of higher education or a kindergarten and grades 1 to 12, inclusive, school.

(3) Housing subject to rent or price control through a public entity's valid exercise of its police power consistent with Chapter 2.7 (commencing with Section 1954.50) that restricts annual increases in the rental rate to an amount less than that provided in subdivision (a).

(4) Housing that has been issued a certificate of occupancy within the previous 15 years, unless the housing is a mobilehome.

(5) Residential real property that is alienable separate from the title to any other dwelling unit, including a mobilehome, provided that both of the following apply:

(A) The owner is not any of the following:

(i) A real estate investment trust, as defined in Section 856 of the Internal Revenue Code.[1]

(ii) A corporation.

(iii) A limited liability company in which at least one member is a corporation.

(iv) Management of a mobilehome park, as defined in Section 798.2.

(B)(i) The tenants have been provided written notice that the residential real property is exempt from this section using the following statement:

"This property is not subject to the rent limits imposed by Section 1947.12 of the Civil Code and is not subject to the just cause requirements of Section 1946.2 of the Civil Code. This property meets the requirements of Sections 1947.12 (d)(5) and 1946.2 (e)(8) of the Civil Code and the owner is not any of the following: (1) a real estate investment trust, as defined by Section 856 of the Internal Revenue Code; (2) a corporation; or (3) a limited liability company in which at least one member is a corporation."

(ii) For a tenancy existing before July 1, 2020, or July 1, 2022, if the lease is for a tenancy in a mobilehome, the notice required under clause (i) may, but is not required to, be provided in the rental agreement.

§ 1947.12

(iii) For a tenancy commenced or renewed on or after July 1, 2020, or July 1, 2022, if the lease is for a tenancy in a mobilehome, the notice required under clause (i) must be provided in the rental agreement.

(iv) Addition of a provision containing the notice required under clause (i) to any new or renewed rental agreement or fixed-term lease constitutes a similar provision for the purposes of subparagraph (E) of paragraph (1) of subdivision (b) of Section 1946.2.

(6) A property containing two separate dwelling units within a single structure in which the owner occupied one of the units as the owner's principal place of residence at the beginning of the tenancy, so long as the owner continues in occupancy, and neither unit is an accessory dwelling unit or a junior accessory dwelling unit.

(e) An owner shall provide notice of any increase in the rental rate, pursuant to subdivision (a), to each tenant in accordance with Section 827.

(f)(1) On or before January 1, 2030, the Legislative Analyst's Office shall report to the Legislature regarding the effectiveness of this section and Section 1947.13. The report shall include, but not be limited to, the impact of the rental rate cap pursuant to subdivision (a) on the housing market within the state.

(2) The report required by paragraph (1) shall be submitted in compliance with Section 9795 of the Government Code.

(g) For the purposes of this section, the following definitions shall apply:

(1) "Consumer Price Index for All Urban Consumers for All Items" means the following:

(A) The Consumer Price Index for All Urban Consumers for All Items (CPI–U) for the metropolitan area in which the property is located, as published by the United States Bureau of Labor Statistics, which are as follows:

(i) The CPI–U for the Los Angeles–Long Beach–Anaheim metropolitan area covering the Counties of Los Angeles and Orange.

(ii) The CPI–U for the Riverside–San Bernardo–Ontario metropolitan area covering the Counties of Riverside and San Bernardino.

(iii) The CPI–U for the San Diego–Carlsbad metropolitan area covering the County of San Diego.

(iv) The CPI–U for the San Francisco–Oakland–Hayward metropolitan area covering the Counties of Alameda, Contra Costa, Marin, San Francisco, and San Mateo.

(v) Any successor metropolitan area index to any of the indexes listed in clauses (i) to (iv), inclusive.

(B) If the United States Bureau of Labor Statistics does not publish a CPI–U for the metropolitan area in which the property is located, the California Consumer Price Index for All Urban Consumers for All Items as published by the Department of Industrial Relations.

(C) On or after January 1, 2021, if the United States Bureau of Labor Statistics publishes a CPI–U index for one or more metropolitan areas not listed in subparagraph (A), that CPI–U index shall apply in those areas with respect to

rent increases that take effect on or after August 1 of the calendar year in which the 12–month change in that CPI–U, as described in subparagraph (B) of paragraph (3), is first published.

(2) "Owner" includes any person, acting as principal or through an agent, having the right to offer residential real property for rent, and includes a predecessor in interest to the owner.

(3)(A) "Percentage change in the cost of living" means the percentage change, computed pursuant to subparagraph (B), in the applicable, as determined pursuant to paragraph (1), Consumer Price Index for All Urban Consumers for All Items.

(B)(i) For rent increases that take effect before August 1 of any calendar year, the following shall apply:

(I) The percentage change shall be the percentage change in the amount published for April of the immediately preceding calendar year and April of the year before that.

(II) If there is not an amount published in April for the applicable geographic area, the percentage change shall be the percentage change in the amount published for March of the immediately preceding calendar year and March of the year before that.

(ii) For rent increases that take effect on or after August 1 of any calendar year, the following shall apply:

(I) The percentage change shall be the percentage change in the amount published for April of that calendar year and April of the immediately preceding calendar year.

(II) If there is not an amount published in April for the applicable geographic area, the percentage change shall be the percentage change in the amount published for March of that calendar year and March of the immediately preceding calendar year.

(iii) The percentage change shall be rounded to the nearest one-tenth of 1 percent.

(4) "Residential real property" means any dwelling or unit that is intended for human habitation, including any dwelling or unit in a mobilehome park.

(5) "Tenancy" means the lawful occupation of residential real property and includes a lease or sublease.

(h)(1) This section shall apply to all rent increases subject to subdivision (a) occurring on or after March 15, 2019, except as provided in subdivision (i).

(2) In the event that an owner has increased the rent by more than the amount permissible under subdivision (a) between March 15, 2019, and January 1, 2020, both of the following shall apply:

(A) The applicable rent on January 1, 2020, shall be the rent as of March 15, 2019, plus the maximum permissible increase under subdivision (a).

(B) An owner shall not be liable to the tenant for any corresponding rent overpayment.

(3) An owner of residential real property subject to subdivision (a) who increased the rental rate on that residential real property on or after March 15, 2019, but prior to January 1, 2020, by an amount less than the rental rate increase permitted by subdivision (a) shall be allowed to

increase the rental rate twice, as provided in paragraph (2) of subdivision (a), within 12 months of March 15, 2019, but in no event shall that rental rate increase exceed the maximum rental rate increase permitted by subdivision (a).

(i)(1) Notwithstanding subdivision (h), this section shall apply only to rent increases for a tenancy in a mobilehome subject to subdivision (a) occurring on or after February 18, 2021.

(2) In the event that an owner has increased the rent for a tenancy in a mobilehome by more than the amount permissible under subdivision (a) between February 18, 2021, and January 1, 2022, both of the following shall apply:

(A) The applicable rent on January 1, 2022, shall be the rent as of February 18, 2021, plus the maximum permissible increase under subdivision (a).

(B) An owner shall not be liable to the tenant for any corresponding rent overpayment.

(3) An owner of residential real property subject to subdivision (a) who increased the rental rate on that residential real property on or after February 18, 2021, but prior to January 1, 2022, by an amount less than the rental rate increase permitted by subdivision (a) shall be allowed to increase the rental rate twice, as provided in paragraph (2) of subdivision (a), within 12 months of February 18, 2021, but in no event shall that rental rate increase exceed the maximum rental rate increase permitted by subdivision (a).

(j) This section shall not apply to a homeowner of a mobilehome, as defined in Section 798.9.

(k) Any waiver of the rights under this section shall be void as contrary to public policy.

(*l*) This section shall remain in effect until January 1, 2030, and as of that date is repealed.

(m)(1) The Legislature finds and declares that the unique circumstances of the current housing crisis require a statewide response to address rent gouging by establishing statewide limitations on gross rental rate increases.

(2) It is the intent of the Legislature that this section should apply only for the limited time needed to address the current statewide housing crisis, as described in paragraph (1). This section is not intended to expand or limit the authority of local governments to establish local policies regulating rents consistent with Chapter 2.7 (commencing with Section 1954.50), nor is it a statement regarding the appropriate, allowable rental rate increase when a local government adopts a policy regulating rent that is otherwise consistent with Chapter 2.7 (commencing with Section 1954.50).

(3) Nothing in this section authorizes a local government to establish limitations on any rental rate increases not otherwise permissible under Chapter 2.7 (commencing with Section 1954.50), or affects the existing authority of a local government to adopt or maintain rent controls or price controls consistent with that chapter. *(Added by Stats.2019, c. 597 (A.B.1482), § 3, eff. Jan. 1, 2020. Amended by Stats.2020, c. 37 (A.B.3088), § 9, eff. Aug. 31, 2020; Stats. 2021, c. 125 (A.B.978), § 4, eff. Jan. 1, 2022.)*

[1] Internal Revenue Code sections are in Title 26 of the U.S.C.A.

Repeal

For repeal of this section, see its terms.

§ 1947.13. Assisted housing developments; rental rates and increases

(a) Notwithstanding subdivision (a) of Section 1947.12, upon the expiration of rental restrictions, the following shall apply:

(1) The owner of an assisted housing development who demonstrates, under penalty of perjury, compliance with all applicable provisions of Sections 65863.10, 65863.11, and 65863.13 of the Government Code and any other applicable federal, state, or local law or regulation may establish the initial unassisted rental rate for units in the applicable housing development. Any subsequent rent increase in the development shall be subject to Section 1947.12.

(2) The owner of a deed-restricted affordable housing unit or an affordable housing unit subject to a regulatory restriction contained in an agreement with a government agency limiting rental rates that is not within an assisted housing development may, subject to any applicable federal, state, or local law or regulation, establish the initial rental rate for the unit upon the expiration of the restriction. Any subsequent rent increase for the unit shall be subject to Section 1947.12.

(b) For purposes of this section:

(1) "Assisted housing development" has the same meaning as defined in paragraph (3) of subdivision (a) of Section 65863.10 of the Government Code.

(2) "Expiration of rental restrictions" has the same meaning as defined in paragraph (5) of subdivision (a) of Section 65863.10 of the Government Code.

(c) This section shall remain in effect until January 1, 2030, and as of that date is repealed.

(d) Any waiver of the rights under this section shall be void as contrary to public policy.

(e) This section shall not be construed to preempt any local law. *(Added by Stats.2019, c. 597 (A.B.1482), § 4, eff. Jan. 1, 2020. Amended by Stats.2020, c. 37 (A.B.3088), § 10, eff. Aug. 31, 2020.)*

Repeal

For repeal of this section, see its terms.

§ 1947.15. Rent control; calculation of fair return to owner; reasonable expenses, fees and costs for professional services

(a) The Legislature declares the purpose of this section is to:

(1) Ensure that owners of residential rental units that are subject to a system of controls on the price at which the units may be offered for rent or lease, or controls on the adjustment of the rent level, are not precluded or discouraged from obtaining a fair return on their properties as guaranteed by the United States Constitution and California Constitution because the professional expenses reasonably required in the course of the administrative proceedings, in order to obtain the rent increases necessary to provide a fair return, are not treated as a legitimate business expense.

§ 1947.15

(2) Encourage agencies which administer a system of controls on the price at which residential rental units may be offered for rent or lease, or controls the adjustment of the rent level, to enact streamlined administrative procedures governing rent adjustment petitions which minimize, to the extent possible, the cost and expense of these administrative proceedings.

(3) Ensure that the cost of professional services reasonably incurred and required by owners of residential rental units subject to a system of controls in the price at which the units may be offered for rent or lease, or controls on the adjustments of the rent level in the course of defending rights related to the rent control system, be treated as a legitimate business expense.

(b) Any city, county, or city and county, including a charter city, which administers an ordinance, charter provision, rule, or regulation that controls or establishes a system of controls on the price at which all or any portion of the residential rental units located within the city, county, or city and county, may be offered for rent or lease, or controls the adjustment of the rent level, and which does not include a system of vacancy decontrol, as defined in subdivision (i), shall permit reasonable expenses, fees, and other costs for professional services, including, but not limited to, legal, accounting, appraisal, bookkeeping, consulting, property management, or architectural services, reasonably incurred in the course of successfully pursuing rights under or in relationship to, that ordinance, charter provision, rule, or regulation, or the right to a fair return on an owner's property as protected by the United States Constitution or California Constitution, to be included in any calculation of net operating income and operating expenses used to determine a fair return to the owner of the property. All expenses, fees, and other costs reasonably incurred by an owner of property in relation to administrative proceedings for purposes specified in this subdivision shall be included in the calculation specified in this subdivision.

(c) Reasonable fees that are incurred by the owner in successfully obtaining a judicial reversal of an adverse administrative decision regarding a petition for upward adjustment of rents shall be assessed against the respondent public agency which issued the adverse administrative decision, and shall not be included in the calculations specified in subdivisions (b) and (d).

(d)(1) Notwithstanding subdivision (b), the city, county, or city and county, on the basis of substantial evidence in the record that the expenses reasonably incurred in the underlying proceeding will not reoccur annually, may amortize the expenses for a period not to exceed five years, except that in extraordinary circumstances, the amortization period may be extended to a period of eight years. The extended amortization period shall not apply to vacant units and shall end if the unit becomes vacant during the period that the expense is being amortized. An amortization schedule shall include a reasonable rate of interest.

(2) Any determination of the reasonableness of the expenses claimed, of an appropriate amortization period, or of the award of an upward adjustment of rents to compensate the owner for expenses and costs incurred shall be made as part of, or immediately following, the decision in the underlying administrative proceeding.

(e) Any and all of the following factors shall be considered in the determination of the reasonableness of the expenses, fees, or other costs authorized by this section:

(1) The rate charged for those professional services in the relevant geographic area.

(2) The complexity of the matter.

(3) The degree of administrative burden or judicial burden, or both, imposed upon the property owner.

(4) The amount of adjustment sought or the significance of the rights defended and the results obtained.

(5) The relationship of the result obtained to the expenses, fees, and other costs incurred (that is, whether professional assistance was reasonably related to the result achieved).

(f) This section shall not be applicable to any ordinance, rule, regulation, or charter provision of any city, county, or city and county, including a charter city, to the extent that the ordinance, rule, or regulation, or charter provision places a limit on the amount of rent that an owner may charge a tenant of a mobilehome park.

(g) For purposes of this section, the rights of a property owner shall be deemed to be successfully pursued or defended if the owner obtains an upward adjustment in rents, successfully defends his or her rights in an administrative proceeding brought by the tenant or the local rent board, or prevails in a proceeding, brought pursuant to Section 1947.8 concerning certification of maximum lawful rents.

(h)(1) If it is determined that a landlord petition assisted by attorneys or consultants is wholly without merit, the tenant shall be awarded a reduction in rent to compensate for the reasonable costs of attorneys or consultants retained by the tenant to defend the petition brought by the landlord. The reasonableness of the costs of the tenant's defense of the action brought by the landlord shall be determined pursuant to the same provisions established by this section for determining the reasonableness of the landlord's costs for the professional services. The determination of the reasonableness of the expenses claimed, an appropriate amortization period, and the award of a reduction in rents to compensate the tenant for costs incurred shall be made immediately following the decision in the underlying administrative proceeding.

(2) If it is determined that a landlord's appeal of an adverse administrative decision is frivolous or solely intended to cause unnecessary delay, the public agency which defended the action shall be awarded its reasonably incurred expenses, including attorney's fees, in defending the action. As used in this paragraph, "frivolous" means either (A) totally and completely without merit; or (B) for the sole purpose of harassing an opposing party.

(i) For purposes of this section, the following terms shall have the following meanings:

(1) "Vacancy decontrol" means a system of controls on the price at which residential rental units may be offered for rent or lease which permits the rent to be increased to its market level, without restriction, each time a vacancy occurs. "Vacancy decontrol" includes systems which reimpose controls on the price at which residential rental units may be offered for rent or lease upon rerental of the unit.

(2) "Vacancy decontrol" includes circumstances where the tenant vacates the unit of his or her own volition, or where the local jurisdiction permits the rent to be raised to market rate after an eviction for cause, as specified in the ordinance, charter provision, rule, or regulation.

(j) This section shall not be construed to affect in any way the ability of a local agency to set its own fair return standards or to limit other actions under its local rent control program other than those expressly set forth in this section.

(k) This section is not operative unless the Costa-Hawkins Rental Housing Act (Chapter 2.7 (commencing with Section 1954.50) of Title 5 of Part 4 of Division 3) is repealed. *(Added by Stats.1993, c. 843 (A.B.264), § 1. Amended by Stats.1996, c. 566 (S.B.1632), § 2; Stats.2002, c. 301 (S.B. 1403), § 2.)*

Operative Effect

By its own terms, this section is not operative unless the Costa-Hawkins Rental Housing Act (Chapter 2.7 (commencing with Section 1954.50) of Title 5 of Part 4 of Division 3) is repealed. See Civil Code § 1954.50 et seq.

Cross References

Costa-Hawkins Rental Housing Act, see Civil Code § 1954.50 et seq.

§ 1948. Attornment to a stranger

The attornment of a tenant to a stranger is void, unless it is made with the consent of the landlord, or in consequence of a judgment of a Court of competent jurisdiction. *(Enacted in 1872.)*

Cross References

Estoppel of tenant to deny title of landlord, see Evidence Code § 624.
Grants of rents, reversions, and remainders good without attornments of the tenants, see Civil Code § 1111.
Rights of owners, see Civil Code § 821 et seq.

§ 1949. Tenant's obligation to deliver certain notices to landlord; damages

Every tenant who receives notice of any proceeding to recover the real property occupied by him or her, or the possession of the real property, shall immediately inform his or her landlord of the proceeding, and also deliver to the landlord the notice, if in writing, and is responsible to the landlord for all damages which he or she may sustain by reason of any omission to inform the landlord of the notice, or to deliver it to him or her if in writing. *(Enacted in 1872. Amended by Code Am.1873–74, c. 612, p. 246, § 207; Stats. 1989, c. 1360, § 11.)*

§ 1950. Letting parts of rooms; double letting of rooms

One who hires part of a room for a dwelling is entitled to the whole of the room, notwithstanding any agreement to the contrary; and if a landlord lets a room as a dwelling for more than one family, the person to whom he first lets any part of it is entitled to the possession of the whole room for the term agreed upon, and every tenant in the building, under the same landlord, is relieved from all obligation to pay rent to him while such double letting of any room continues. *(Enacted in 1872.)*

§ 1950.1. Reusable tenant screening report; required information; currency; fees; definitions; construction with state and local laws; landlord discretion to accept reusable tenant screening reports

(a) A reusable tenant screening report shall include all of the following information regarding an applicant:

(1) Name.

(2) Contact information.

(3) Verification of employment.

(4) Last known address.

(5) Results of an eviction history check in a manner and for a period of time consistent with applicable law related to the consideration of eviction history in housing.

(b) A reusable tenant screening report shall prominently state the date through which the information contained in the report is current.

(c) A landlord may elect to accept reusable tenant screening reports and may require an applicant to state that there has not been a material change to the information in the reusable tenant screening report.

(d) Notwithstanding Section 1950.6, if an applicant provides a reusable tenant screening report to a landlord that accepts reusable tenant screening reports, the landlord shall not charge the applicant either of the following:

(1) A fee for the landlord to access the report.

(2) An application screening fee.

(e) As used in this section:

(1) "Applicant" has the same meaning as defined in Section 1950.6.

(2) "Application screening fee" has the same meaning as defined in Section 1950.6.

(3) "Consumer report" has the same meaning as defined in Section 1681a of Title 15 of the United States Code.

(4) "Consumer reporting agency" means a person which, for monetary fees, dues, or on a cooperative nonprofit basis, regularly engages in whole or in part in the practice of assembling or evaluating consumer credit information or other information on consumers for the purpose of furnishing consumer reports to third parties and that uses any means or facility of interstate commerce for the purpose of preparing or furnishing consumer reports.

(5) "Landlord" means an owner of residential rental property or the owner's agent.

(6) "Reusable tenant screening report" means a consumer report that meets all of the following criteria:

(A) Was prepared within the previous 30 days by a consumer reporting agency at the request and expense of an applicant.

(B) Is made directly available to a landlord for use in the rental application process or is provided through a third-party website that regularly engages in the business of providing a reusable tenant screening report and complies with all state and federal laws pertaining to use and disclosure of information contained in a consumer report by a consumer reporting agency.

§ 1950.1

(C) Is available to the landlord at no cost to access or use.

(f) This section does not affect any other applicable law related to the consideration of criminal history information in housing, including, but not limited to, Article 24 (commencing with Section 12264) of Subchapter 7 of Chapter 5 of Division 4.1 of Title 2 of the California Code of Regulations and local ordinances governing the information that landlords may review and consider when determining to whom they will rent.

(g) If an ordinance, resolution, regulation, administrative action, initiative, or other policy adopted by a city, county, or city and county conflicts with this section, the policy that provides greater protections to applicants shall apply.

(h) This section does not require a landlord to accept reusable tenant screening reports. *(Added by Stats.2022, c. 288 (A.B.2559), § 1, eff. Jan. 1, 2023.)*

§ 1950.5. Security for rental agreement for residential property used as dwelling of tenant; amount and disposition; damages

(a) This section applies to security for a rental agreement for residential property that is used as the dwelling of the tenant.

(b) As used in this section, "security" means any payment, fee, deposit, or charge, including, but not limited to, any payment, fee, deposit, or charge, except as provided in Section 1950.6, that is imposed at the beginning of the tenancy to be used to reimburse the landlord for costs associated with processing a new tenant or that is imposed as an advance payment of rent, used or to be used for any purpose, including, but not limited to, any of the following:

(1) The compensation of a landlord for a tenant's default in the payment of rent.

(2) The repair of damages to the premises, exclusive of ordinary wear and tear, caused by the tenant or by a guest or licensee of the tenant.

(3) The cleaning of the premises upon termination of the tenancy necessary to return the unit to the same level of cleanliness it was in at the inception of the tenancy. The amendments to this paragraph enacted by the act adding this sentence shall apply only to tenancies for which the tenant's right to occupy begins after January 1, 2003.

(4) To remedy future defaults by the tenant in any obligation under the rental agreement to restore, replace, or return personal property or appurtenances, exclusive of ordinary wear and tear, if the security deposit is authorized to be applied thereto by the rental agreement.

(c)(1) Except as provided in paragraph (2), (3), or (4), a landlord may not demand or receive security, however denominated, in an amount or value in excess of an amount equal to two months' rent, in the case of unfurnished residential property, and an amount equal to three months' rent, in the case of furnished residential property, in addition to any rent for the first month paid on or before initial occupancy.

(2) Notwithstanding paragraph (1), and except as provided in subparagraphs (A) and (B), a landlord shall not demand or receive security, however denominated, from a service member who rents residential property in which the service member will reside in an amount or value in excess of an amount equal to one months' rent, in the case of unfurnished residential property, or in excess of an amount equal to two months' rent, in the case of furnished residential property, in addition to any rent for the first month paid on or before initial occupancy. A landlord shall not refuse to enter into a rental agreement for residential property with a prospective tenant who is a service member because this paragraph prohibits the landlord from demanding or receiving a greater amount of security than that which is established in paragraph (1). For purposes of this paragraph, "service member" has the same meaning as in Section 400 of the Military and Veterans Code.

(A) A landlord may demand or receive security from a service member who rents residential property in which the service member will reside as provided in paragraph (1), if the tenant has a history of poor credit or of causing damage to the rental property or its furnishings.

(B) This paragraph does not apply to a situation in which the property is rented to a group of individuals, one or more of whom is not the service member's spouse, parent, domestic partner, or dependent.

(C) For purposes of this paragraph "resides" means that the service member will be listed as a tenant on the residential property lease agreement.

(3) This subdivision does not prohibit an advance payment of not less than six months' rent if the term of the lease is six months or longer.

(4) This subdivision does not preclude a landlord and a tenant from entering into a mutual agreement for the landlord, at the request of the tenant and for a specified fee or charge, to make structural, decorative, furnishing, or other similar alterations, if the alterations are other than cleaning or repairing for which the landlord may charge the previous tenant as provided by subdivision (e).

(d) Any security shall be held by the landlord for the tenant who is party to the lease or agreement. The claim of a tenant to the security shall be prior to the claim of any creditor of the landlord.

(e) The landlord may claim of the security only those amounts as are reasonably necessary for the purposes specified in subdivision (b). The landlord may not assert a claim against the tenant or the security for damages to the premises or any defective conditions that preexisted the tenancy, for ordinary wear and tear or the effects thereof, whether the wear and tear preexisted the tenancy or occurred during the tenancy, or for the cumulative effects of ordinary wear and tear occurring during any one or more tenancies.

(f)(1) Within a reasonable time after notification of either party's intention to terminate the tenancy, or before the end of the lease term, the landlord shall notify the tenant in writing of the tenant's option to request an initial inspection and of the tenant's right to be present at the inspection. The requirements of this subdivision do not apply when the tenancy is terminated pursuant to subdivision (2), (3), or (4) of Section 1161 of the Code of Civil Procedure. At a reasonable time, but no earlier than two weeks before the termination or the end of lease date, the landlord, or an agent of the landlord, shall, upon the request of the tenant, make an initial inspection of the premises prior to any final inspection the landlord makes after the tenant has vacated the premises. The purpose of the initial inspection shall be to allow the tenant an opportunity to remedy identified deficiencies, in a manner consistent with the rights and obligations of the parties under the rental agreement, in order to avoid deductions from the security. If a tenant chooses not to request an initial inspection, the duties of the landlord under this subdivision are discharged. If an inspection is requested, the parties shall attempt to schedule the inspection at a mutually acceptable date and time. The landlord shall give at least 48 hours' prior written notice of the date and time of the inspection if either a mutual time is agreed upon, or if a mutually agreed time cannot be scheduled but the tenant still wishes an inspection. The tenant and landlord may agree to forgo the 48-hour prior written notice by both signing a written waiver. The landlord shall proceed with the inspection whether the tenant is present or not, unless the tenant previously withdrew their request for the inspection. Written notice by the landlord shall contain, in substantially the same form, the following:

"State law permits former tenants to reclaim abandoned personal property left at the former address of the tenant, subject to certain conditions. You may or may not be able to reclaim property without incurring additional costs, depending on the cost of storing the property and the length of time before it is reclaimed. In general, these costs will be lower the sooner you contact your former landlord after being notified that property belonging to you was left behind after you moved out."

(2) Based on the inspection, the landlord shall give the tenant an itemized statement specifying repairs or cleanings that are proposed to be the basis of any deductions from the security the landlord intends to make pursuant to paragraphs (1) to (4), inclusive, of subdivision (b). This statement shall also include the texts of paragraphs (1) to (4), inclusive, of subdivision (b). The statement shall be given to the tenant, if the tenant is present for the inspection, or shall be left inside the premises.

(3) The tenant shall have the opportunity during the period following the initial inspection until termination of the tenancy to remedy identified deficiencies, in a manner consistent with the rights and obligations of the parties under the rental agreement, in order to avoid deductions from the security.

(4) Nothing in this subdivision shall prevent a landlord from using the security for deductions itemized in the statement provided for in paragraph (2) that were not cured by the tenant so long as the deductions are for damages authorized by this section.

(5) Nothing in this subdivision shall prevent a landlord from using the security for any purpose specified in paragraphs (1) to (4), inclusive, of subdivision (b) that occurs between completion of the initial inspection and termination of the tenancy or was not identified during the initial inspection due to the presence of a tenant's possessions.

(g)(1) No later than 21 calendar days after the tenant has vacated the premises, but not earlier than the time that either the landlord or the tenant provides a notice to terminate the tenancy under Section 1946 or 1946.1, Section 1161 of the Code of Civil Procedure, or not earlier than 60 calendar days prior to the expiration of a fixed-term lease, the landlord shall furnish the tenant, by personal delivery or by first-class mail, postage prepaid, a copy of an itemized statement indicating the basis for, and the amount of, any security received and the disposition of the security, and shall return any remaining portion of the security to the tenant. After either the landlord or the tenant provides notice to terminate the tenancy, the landlord and tenant may mutually agree to have the landlord deposit any remaining portion of the security deposit electronically to a bank account or other financial institution designated by the tenant. After either the landlord or the tenant provides notice to terminate the tenancy, the landlord and the tenant may also agree to have the landlord provide a copy of the itemized statement along with the copies required by paragraph (2) to an email account provided by the tenant.

(2) Along with the itemized statement, the landlord shall also include copies of documents showing charges incurred and deducted by the landlord to repair or clean the premises, as follows:

(A) If the landlord or landlord's employee did the work, the itemized statement shall reasonably describe the work performed. The itemized statement shall include the time spent and the reasonable hourly rate charged.

(B) If the landlord or landlord's employee did not do the work, the landlord shall provide the tenant a copy of the bill, invoice, or receipt supplied by the person or entity performing the work. The itemized statement shall provide the tenant with the name, address, and telephone number of the person or entity, if the bill, invoice, or receipt does not include that information.

(C) If a deduction is made for materials or supplies, the landlord shall provide a copy of the bill, invoice, or receipt. If a particular material or supply item is purchased by the landlord on an ongoing basis, the landlord may document the cost of the item by providing a copy of a bill, invoice, receipt, vendor price list, or other vendor document that reasonably documents the cost of the item used in the repair or cleaning of the unit.

(3) If a repair to be done by the landlord or the landlord's employee cannot reasonably be completed within 21 calendar days after the tenant has vacated the premises, or if the documents from a person or entity providing services, materials, or supplies are not in the landlord's possession within 21 calendar days after the tenant has vacated the premises, the landlord may deduct the amount of a good faith estimate of the charges that will be incurred and provide that estimate with the itemized statement. If the reason for the estimate is because the documents from a person or entity providing services, materials, or supplies are not in the landlord's possession, the itemized statement shall include the name, address, and telephone number of the person or entity. Within 14 calendar days of completing the repair or receiving the documentation, the landlord shall complete the requirements in paragraphs (1) and (2) in the manner specified.

(4) The landlord need not comply with paragraph (2) or (3) if either of the following applies:

(A) The deductions for repairs and cleaning together do not exceed one hundred twenty-five dollars ($125).

(B) The tenant waived the rights specified in paragraphs (2) and (3). The waiver shall only be effective if it is signed by the tenant at the same time or after a notice to terminate a tenancy under Section 1946 or 1946.1 has been given, a notice under Section 1161 of the Code of Civil Procedure has been given, or no earlier than 60 calendar days prior to the expiration of a fixed-term lease. The waiver shall substantially include the text of paragraph (2).

(5) Notwithstanding paragraph (4), the landlord shall comply with paragraphs (2) and (3) when a tenant makes a request for documentation within 14 calendar days after receiving the itemized statement specified in paragraph (1). The landlord shall comply within 14 calendar days after receiving the request from the tenant.

(6) Any mailings to the tenant pursuant to this subdivision shall be sent to the address provided by the tenant. If the tenant does not provide an address, mailings pursuant to this subdivision shall be sent to the unit that has been vacated.

(h) Upon termination of the landlord's interest in the premises, whether by sale, assignment, death, appointment of receiver, or otherwise, the landlord or the landlord's agent shall, within a reasonable time, do one of the following acts, either of which shall relieve the landlord of further liability with respect to the security held:

(1) Transfer the portion of the security remaining after any lawful deductions made under subdivision (e) to the landlord's successor in interest. The landlord shall thereafter notify the tenant by personal delivery or by first-class mail, postage prepaid, of the transfer, of any claims made against the security, of the amount of the security deposited, and of the names of the successors in interest, their addresses, and their telephone numbers. If the notice to the tenant is made by personal delivery, the tenant shall acknowledge receipt of the notice and sign their name on the landlord's copy of the notice.

(2) Return the portion of the security remaining after any lawful deductions made under subdivision (e) to the tenant, together with an accounting as provided in subdivision (g).

(i) Prior to the voluntary transfer of a landlord's interest in the premises, the landlord shall deliver to the landlord's successor in interest a written statement indicating the following:

(1) The security remaining after any lawful deductions are made.

(2) An itemization of any lawful deductions from any security received.

(3) Their election under paragraph (1) or (2) of subdivision (h).

This subdivision does not affect the validity of title to the real property transferred in violation of this subdivision.

(j)(1) In the event of noncompliance with subdivision (h), the landlord's successors in interest shall be jointly and severally liable with the landlord for repayment of the security, or that portion thereof to which the tenant is entitled, when and as provided in subdivisions (e) and (g). A successor in interest of a landlord may not require the tenant to post any security to replace that amount not transferred to the tenant or successors in interest as provided in subdivision (h), unless and until the successor in interest first makes restitution of the initial security as provided in paragraph (2) of subdivision (h) or provides the tenant with an accounting as provided in subdivision (g).

(2) This subdivision does not preclude a successor in interest from recovering from the tenant compensatory damages that are in excess of the security received from the landlord previously paid by the tenant to the landlord.

(3) Notwithstanding this subdivision, if, upon inquiry and reasonable investigation, a landlord's successor in interest has a good faith belief that the lawfully remaining security deposit is transferred to the successor in interest or returned to the tenant pursuant to subdivision (h), the successor in interest is not liable for damages as provided in subdivision (*l*), or any security not transferred pursuant to subdivision (h).

(k) Upon receipt of any portion of the security under paragraph (1) of subdivision (h), the landlord's successors in interest shall have all of the rights and obligations of a landlord holding the security with respect to the security.

(*l*) The bad faith claim or retention by a landlord or the landlord's successors in interest of the security or any portion thereof in violation of this section, or the bad faith demand of replacement security in violation of subdivision (j), may subject the landlord or the landlord's successors in interest to statutory damages of up to twice the amount of the security, in addition to actual damages. The court may award damages for bad faith whenever the facts warrant that award, regardless of whether the injured party has specifically requested relief. In an action under this section, the landlord or the landlord's successors in interest shall have the burden of proof as to the reasonableness of the amounts claimed or the authority pursuant to this section to demand additional security deposits.

(m) No lease or rental agreement may contain a provision characterizing any security as "nonrefundable."

(n) An action under this section may be maintained in small claims court if the damages claimed, whether actual, statutory, or both, are within the jurisdictional amount allowed by Section 116.220 or 116.221 of the Code of Civil Procedure.

(o) Proof of the existence of and the amount of a security deposit may be established by any credible evidence, including, but not limited to, a canceled check, a receipt, a lease indicating the requirement of a deposit as well as the amount, prior consistent statements or actions of the landlord or tenant, or a statement under penalty of perjury that satisfies the credibility requirements set forth in Section 780 of the Evidence Code.

(p) The amendments to this section made during the 1985 portion of the 1985–86 Regular Session of the Legislature that are set forth in subdivision (e) are declaratory of existing law.

(q) The amendments to this section made during the 2003 portion of the 2003–04 Regular Session of the Legislature that are set forth in paragraph (1) of subdivision (f) are declaratory of existing law. *(Added by Stats.1977, c. 971, p. 2939, § 2. Amended by Stats.1985, c. 1291, § 1; Stats.1985, c. 1555, § 2; Stats.1986, c. 564, § 1; Stats.1993, c. 755 (S.B. 444), § 1; Stats.1994, c. 146 (A.B.3601), § 13; Stats.2002, c. 1061 (A.B.2330), § 1; Stats.2003, c. 335 (S.B.90), § 1; Stats. 2003, c. 576 (A.B.1384), § 1.5; Stats.2004, c. 568 (S.B.1145), § 3; Stats.2006, c. 167 (A.B.2618), § 3; Stats.2012, c. 557 (A.B.1679), § 1; Stats.2012, c. 560 (A.B.2521), § 3.5; Stats. 2013, c. 76 (A.B.383), § 12; Stats.2019, c. 602 (S.B.644), § 2, eff. Jan. 1, 2020.)*

Cross References

Burden of proof, generally, see Evidence Code § 500 et seq.
Pet Friendly Housing Act of 2017, see Health and Safety Code § 50466.

§ 1950.6. Rental application screening fees; amount; receipt; copies of credit reports; construction of section with housing assistance programs

(a) Notwithstanding Section 1950.5, when a landlord or his or her agent receives a request to rent a residential property from an applicant, the landlord or his or her agent may charge that applicant an application screening fee to cover the costs of obtaining information about the applicant. The information requested and obtained by the landlord or his or her agent may include, but is not limited to, personal reference checks and consumer credit reports produced by consumer credit reporting agencies as defined in Section 1785.3. A landlord or his or her agent may, but is not required to, accept and rely upon a consumer credit report presented by an applicant.

(b) The amount of the application screening fee shall not be greater than the actual out-of-pocket costs of gathering information concerning the applicant, including, but not limited to, the cost of using a tenant screening service or a consumer credit reporting service, and the reasonable value of time spent by the landlord or his or her agent in obtaining information on the applicant. In no case shall the amount of the application screening fee charged by the landlord or his or her agent be greater than thirty dollars ($30) per applicant. The thirty dollar ($30) application screening fee may be adjusted annually by the landlord or his or her agent commensurate with an increase in the Consumer Price Index, beginning on January 1, 1998.

(c) Unless the applicant agrees in writing, a landlord or his or her agent may not charge an applicant an application screening fee when he or she knows or should have known that no rental unit is available at that time or will be available within a reasonable period of time.

(d) The landlord or his or her agent shall provide, personally, or by mail, the applicant with a receipt for the fee paid by the applicant, which receipt shall itemize the out-of-pocket expenses and time spent by the landlord or his or her agent to obtain and process the information about the applicant.

(e) If the landlord or his or her agent does not perform a personal reference check or does not obtain a consumer credit report, the landlord or his or her agent shall return any amount of the screening fee that is not used for the purposes authorized by this section to the applicant.

(f) If an application screening fee has been paid by the applicant and if requested by the applicant, the landlord or his or her agent shall provide a copy of the consumer credit report to the applicant who is the subject of that report.

(g) As used in this section, "landlord" means an owner of residential rental property.

(h) As used in this section, "application screening fee" means any nonrefundable payment of money charged by a landlord or his or her agent to an applicant, the purpose of which is to purchase a consumer credit report and to validate, review, or otherwise process an application for the rent or lease of residential rental property.

(i) As used in this section, "applicant" means any entity or individual who makes a request to a landlord or his or her agent to rent a residential housing unit, or an entity or individual who agrees to act as a guarantor or cosignor on a rental agreement.

(j) The application screening fee shall not be considered an "advance fee" as that term is used in Section 10026 of the Business and Professions Code, and shall not be considered "security" as that term is used in Section 1950.5.

(k) This section is not intended to preempt any provisions or regulations that govern the collection of deposits and fees under federal or state housing assistance programs. *(Added by Stats.1996, c. 525 (A.B.2263), § 1.)*

§ 1950.7. Payment or deposit of money to secure performance of rental agreement for other than residential property; status of and claims against deposit; duty of landlord on termination of interest

(a) Any payment or deposit of money the primary function of which is to secure the performance of a rental agreement for other than residential property or any part of the agreement, other than a payment or deposit, including an advance payment of rent, made to secure the execution of a rental agreement, shall be governed by the provisions of this section. With respect to residential property, the provisions of Section 1950.5 shall prevail.

(b) The payment or deposit of money shall be held by the landlord for the tenant who is party to the agreement. The claim of a tenant to the payment or deposit shall be prior to the claim of any creditor of the landlord, except a trustee in bankruptcy.

(c) The landlord may claim of the payment or deposit only those amounts as are reasonably necessary to remedy tenant defaults in the payment of rent, to repair damages to the premises caused by the tenant, or to clean the premises upon termination of the tenancy, if the payment or deposit is made for any or all of those specific purposes.

(1) If the claim of the landlord upon the payment or deposit is only for defaults in the payment of rent and the security deposit equals no more than one month's rent plus a deposit amount clearly described as the payment of the last month's rent, then any remaining portion of the payment or deposit shall be returned to the tenant at a time as may be mutually agreed upon by landlord and tenant, but in no event later than 30 days from the date the landlord receives possession of the premises.

(2) If the claim of the landlord upon the payment or deposit is only for defaults in the payment of rent and the security deposit exceeds the amount of one month's rent plus a deposit amount clearly described as the payment of the last month's rent, then any remaining portion of the payment or deposit in excess of an amount equal to one month's rent shall be returned to the tenant no later than two weeks after the date the landlord receives possession of the premises, with the remainder to be returned or accounted for within 30 days from the date the landlord receives possession of the premises.

(3) If the claim of the landlord upon the payment or deposit includes amounts reasonably necessary to repair damages to the premises caused by the tenant or to clean the premises, then any remaining portion of the payment or deposit shall be returned to the tenant at a time as may be mutually agreed upon by landlord and tenant, but in no event later than 30 days from the date the landlord receives possession of the premises.

(d) Upon termination of the landlord's interest in the unit in question, whether by sale, assignment, death, appointment of receiver or otherwise, the landlord or the landlord's agent shall, within a reasonable time, do one of the following acts, either of which shall relieve the landlord of further liability with respect to the payment or deposit:

(1) Transfer the portion of the payment or deposit remaining after any lawful deductions made under subdivision (c) to the landlord's successor in interest, and thereafter notify the tenant by personal delivery or certified mail of the transfer, of any claims made against the payment or deposit, and of the transferee's name and address. If the notice to the tenant is made by personal delivery, the tenant shall acknowledge receipt of the notice and sign his or her name on the landlord's copy of the notice.

(2) Return the portion of the payment or deposit remaining after any lawful deductions made under subdivision (c) to the tenant.

(e) Upon receipt of any portion of the payment or deposit under paragraph (1) of subdivision (d), the transferee shall have all of the rights and obligations of a landlord holding the payment or deposit with respect to the payment or deposit.

(f) The bad faith retention by a landlord or transferee of a payment or deposit or any portion thereof, in violation of this section, may subject the landlord or the transferee to damages not to exceed two hundred dollars ($200), in addition to any actual damages.

(g) This section is declarative of existing law and therefore operative as to all tenancies, leases, or rental agreements for other than residential property created or renewed on or after January 1, 1971. *(Added by Stats.1977, c. 971, p. 2941, § 3. Amended by Stats.1981, c. 259, p. 1336, § 1; Stats.2003, c. 89 (A.B.1361), § 1.)*

§ 1950.8. Payment of money, including but not limited to key money, or the lessor's attorney's fees incurred in preparation of lease or rental agreement, as a condition of initiating, continuing, or renewing a lease or rental agreement; statement of payment amount in agreement; penalties

(a) This section applies only to commercial leases and nonresidential tenancies of real property.

(b) It shall be unlawful for any person to require, demand, or cause to make payable any payment of money, including, but not limited to, "key money," however denominated, or the lessor's attorney's fees reasonably incurred in preparing the lease or rental agreement, as a condition of initiating, continuing, or renewing a lease or rental agreement, unless the amount of payment is stated in the written lease or rental agreement.

(c) Any person who requires, demands, or causes to make payable any payment in violation of subdivision (a), shall be subject to civil penalty of three times the amount of actual damages proximately suffered by the person seeking to obtain the lease or rental of real property, and the person so damaged shall be entitled to an award of costs, including reasonable attorney's fees, reasonable incurred in connection with obtaining the civil penalty.

(d) Nothing in this section shall prohibit the advance payment of rent, if the amount and character of the payment are clearly stated in a written lease or rental agreement.

(e) Nothing in this section shall prohibit any person from charging a reasonable amount for the purpose of conducting reasonable business activity in connection with initiating, continuing, or renewing a lease or rental agreement for nonresidential real property, including, but not limited to, verifying creditworthiness or qualifications of any person seeking to initiate, continue, or renew a lease or rental agreement for any use other than residential use, or cleaning fees, reasonably incurred in connection with the hiring of the real property.

(f) Nothing in this section shall prohibit a person from increasing a tenant's rent for nonresidential real property in order to recover building operating costs incurred on behalf of the tenant, if the right to the rent, the method of calculating the increase, and the period of time covered by the increase is stated in the lease or rental agreement. *(Added by Stats.2001, c. 368 (A.B.533), § 1.)*

Cross References

Hiring defined, see Civil Code § 1925.

§ 1951. "Rent" and "lease" defined

As used in Sections 1951.2 to 1952.6, inclusive:

(a) "Rent" includes charges equivalent to rent.

(b) "Lease" includes a sublease. *(Added by Stats.1970, c. 89, p. 104, § 1, operative July 1, 1971.)*

§ 1951.2. Termination of lease; remedy of lessor

(a) Except as otherwise provided in Section 1951.4, if a lessee of real property breaches the lease and abandons the property before the end of the term or if his right to possession is terminated by the lessor because of a breach of the lease, the lease terminates. Upon such termination, the lessor may recover from the lessee:

(1) The worth at the time of award of the unpaid rent which had been earned at the time of termination;

(2) The worth at the time of award of the amount by which the unpaid rent which would have been earned after termination until the time of award exceeds the amount of such

rental loss that the lessee proves could have been reasonably avoided;

(3) Subject to subdivision (c), the worth at the time of award of the amount by which the unpaid rent for the balance of the term after the time of award exceeds the amount of such rental loss that the lessee proves could be reasonably avoided; and

(4) Any other amount necessary to compensate the lessor for all the detriment proximately caused by the lessee's failure to perform his obligations under the lease or which in the ordinary course of things would be likely to result therefrom.

(b) The "worth at the time of award" of the amounts referred to in paragraphs (1) and (2) of subdivision (a) is computed by allowing interest at such lawful rate as may be specified in the lease or, if no such rate is specified in the lease, at the legal rate. The worth at the time of award of the amount referred to in paragraph (3) of subdivision (a) is computed by discounting such amount at the discount rate of the Federal Reserve Bank of San Francisco at the time of award plus 1 percent.

(c) The lessor may recover damages under paragraph (3) of subdivision (a) only if:

(1) The lease provides that the damages he may recover include the worth at the time of award of the amount by which the unpaid rent for the balance of the term after the time of award, or for any shorter period of time specified in the lease, exceeds the amount of such rental loss for the same period that the lessee proves could be reasonably avoided; or

(2) The lessor relet the property prior to the time of award and proves that in reletting the property he acted reasonably and in a good-faith effort to mitigate the damages, but the recovery of damages under this paragraph is subject to any limitations specified in the lease.

(d) Efforts by the lessor to mitigate the damages caused by the lessee's breach of the lease do not waive the lessor's right to recover damages under this section.

(e) Nothing in this section affects the right of the lessor under a lease of real property to indemnification for liability arising prior to the termination of the lease for personal injuries or property damage where the lease provides for such indemnification. *(Added by Stats.1970, c. 89, p. 104, § 2, operative July 1, 1971.)*

Cross References

Lease defined for purposes of Civil Code §§ 1951.2 to 1952.6, see Civil Code § 1951.
Liability of lessee pursuant to this section despite judgment declaring forfeiture of lease or agreement, see Code of Civil Procedure § 1174.5.
Limitation of actions, see Code of Civil Procedure §§ 337.2, 339.5.
Rent defined for purposes of Civil Code §§ 1951.2 to 1952.6, see Civil Code § 1951.
Termination of hiring, generally, see Civil Code § 1931 et seq.

§ 1951.3. Abandonment of real property other than commercial real property; notice by lessor; form; defenses of lessee

(a) This section applies to real property other than commercial real property, as defined in subdivision (d) of Section 1954.26.

(b) Real property shall be deemed abandoned by the lessee, within the meaning of Section 1951.2, and the lease shall terminate if the lessor gives written notice of belief of abandonment as provided in this section and the lessee fails to give the lessor written notice, prior to the date of termination specified in the lessor's notice, stating that the lessee does not intend to abandon the real property and stating an address at which the lessee may be served by certified mail in any action for unlawful detainer of the real property.

(c) The lessor may give a notice of belief of abandonment to the lessee pursuant to this section only where the rent on the property has been due and unpaid for at least 14 consecutive days and the lessor reasonably believes that the lessee has abandoned the property. The date of termination of the lease shall be specified in the lessor's notice and shall be not less than 15 days after the notice is served personally or, if mailed, not less than 18 days after the notice is deposited in the mail.

(d) The lessor's notice of belief of abandonment shall be personally delivered to the lessee or sent by first-class mail, postage prepaid, to the lessee at the lessee's last known address and, if there is reason to believe that the notice sent to that address will not be received by the lessee, also to any other address known to the lessor where the lessee may reasonably be expected to receive the notice.

(e) The notice of belief of abandonment shall be in substantially the following form:

Notice of Belief of Abandonment

To: _____
(Name of lessee/tenant)

_____
(Address of lessee/tenant)

This notice is given pursuant to Section 1951.3 of the Civil Code concerning the real property leased by you at _____ (state location of the property by address or other sufficient description). The rent on this property has been due and unpaid for 14 consecutive days and the lessor/landlord believes that you have abandoned the property.

The real property will be deemed abandoned within the meaning of Section 1951.2 of the Civil Code and your lease will terminate on _____ (here insert a date not less than 15 days after this notice is served personally or, if mailed, not less than 18 days after this notice is deposited in the mail) unless before that date the lessor/landlord receives at the address indicated below a written notice from you stating both of the following:

(1) Your intent not to abandon the real property.

(2) An address at which you may be served by certified mail in any action for unlawful detainer of the real property.

You are required to pay the rent due and unpaid on this real property as required by the lease, and your failure to do so can lead to a court proceeding against you.

Dated: _____

_____
(Signature of lessor/landlord)

_____
(Type or print name of lessor/landlord)

_____
(Address to which lessee/tenant is to send notice)

§ 1951.3   OBLIGATIONS

(f) The real property shall not be deemed to be abandoned pursuant to this section if the lessee proves any of the following:

(1) At the time the notice of belief of abandonment was given, the rent was not due and unpaid for 14 consecutive days.

(2) At the time the notice of belief of abandonment was given, it was not reasonable for the lessor to believe that the lessee had abandoned the real property. The fact that the lessor knew that the lessee left personal property on the real property does not, of itself, justify a finding that the lessor did not reasonably believe that the lessee had abandoned the real property.

(3) Before the date specified in the lessor's notice, the lessee gave written notice to the lessor stating the lessee's intent not to abandon the real property and stating an address at which the lessee may be served by certified mail in any action for unlawful detainer of the real property.

(4) During the period beginning 14 days before the time the notice of belief of abandonment was given and ending on the date the lease would have terminated pursuant to the notice, the lessee paid to the lessor all or a portion of the rent due and unpaid on the real property.

(g) Nothing in this section precludes the lessor or the lessee from otherwise proving that the real property has been abandoned by the lessee within the meaning of Section 1951.2.

(h) Nothing in this section precludes the lessor from serving a notice requiring the lessee to pay rent or quit as provided in Sections 1161 and 1162 of the Code of Civil Procedure at any time permitted by those sections, or affects the time and manner of giving any other notice required or permitted by law. The giving of the notice provided by this section does not satisfy the requirements of Sections 1161 and 1162 of the Code of Civil Procedure. *(Added by Stats.1974, c. 332, p. 661, § 1. Amended by Stats.2018, c. 104 (A.B.2847), § 2, eff. Jan. 1, 2019.)*

Cross References

Lease defined for purposes of Civil Code §§ 1951.2 to 1952.6, see Civil Code § 1951.
Notice of belief of abandonment, see Civil Code § 1993.09.
Notice of belief of abandonment combined with notice to former tenant given pursuant to § 1983, see Civil Code § 1991.
Rent defined for purposes of Civil Code §§ 1951.2 to 1952.6, see Civil Code § 1951.

§ 1951.35. Abandonment of commercial property by lessee; notice by lessor; form; defenses of lessee

(a) This section applies only to commercial real property, as defined in subdivision (d) of Section 1954.26.

(b) Commercial real property shall be deemed abandoned by the lessee within the meaning of Section 1951.2 and the lease shall terminate if the lessor gives written notice of belief of abandonment pursuant to subdivision (c) and, prior to the date of termination specified in the lessor's notice of belief of abandonment, the lessee fails to give the lessor written notice stating that the lessee does not intend to abandon the commercial real property and provides an address at which the lessee may be served by certified mail in an action for unlawful detainer of real property.

(c) The lessor may give notice of belief of abandonment pursuant to this section only if the rent on the property has been due and unpaid for at least the number of days required for the lessor to declare a rent default under the terms of the lease, but in no case less than three days, and the lessor reasonably believes that the lessee has abandoned the property. The date of termination of the lease shall be specified in the notice and shall be not less than 15 days after the notice is served personally, sent to the lessee by an overnight courier service, or deposited in the mail.

(d) The lessor's notice of belief of abandonment shall be personally delivered to the lessee, sent by a recognized overnight carrier, or sent by first-class mail, postage prepaid, to the lessee at the lessee's last known address, and, if there is reason to believe that the notice sent to that address will not be received by the lessee, also to any other address known to the lessor where the lessee may reasonably be expected to receive the notice.

(e) The notice of belief of abandonment shall be in substantially the following form:

Notice of Belief of Abandonment

To: _____
(Name of lessee/tenant)

_____
(Address of lessee/tenant)

This notice is given pursuant to Section 1951.35 of the Civil Code concerning the real property leased by you at _____ (state location of the property by address or other sufficient description). The rent on this property has been due and unpaid for the number of days necessary to declare a rent default under your lease and the lessor/landlord believes that you have abandoned the property.

The real property will be deemed abandoned within the meaning of Section 1951.2 of the Civil Code and your lease will terminate on _____ (here insert a date not less than 15 days after this notice is served personally, sent by overnight courier service, or deposited in the mail) unless before that date the lessor/landlord receives at the address below a written notice from you stating both of the following:

(1) Your intent not to abandon the real property.

(2) An address at which you may be served by certified mail in any action for unlawful detainer of the real property.

You are required to pay the rent due and unpaid on this real property as required by the lease, and your failure to do so can lead to a court proceeding against you.

Dated: _____   _____
(Signature of lessor/landlord)

_____
(Type or print name of lessor/landlord)

_____
(Address to which lessee/tenant is to send notice)

(f) The real property shall not be deemed to be abandoned pursuant to this section if the lessee provides any of the following:

(1) At the time the notice of belief of abandonment was given, the rent was not due and unpaid for the time period necessary to declare a rent default under the lessee's lease.

(2) At the time the notice of belief of abandonment was given, it was not reasonable for the lessor to believe that the lessee had abandoned the real property. The fact that the lessor knew that the lessee left personal property on the real property does not, by itself, justify a finding that the lessor did not believe that the lessee had abandoned the real property.

(3) Before the date specified in the lessor's notice, the lessee gave written notice to the lessor stating the lessee's intent not to abandon the real property and provided an address at which the lessee may be served by certified mail in an action for unlawful detainer of real property.

(4) During the period beginning at the start of the applicable rent default period and ending on the date the lease would have terminated pursuant to the notice, the lessee paid to the lessor all or a portion of the rent due and unpaid on the real property.

(g) Nothing in this section precludes the lessor or the lessee from otherwise proving that the real property has been abandoned by the lessee within the meaning of Section 1951.2.

(h) Nothing in this section precludes the lessor from serving a notice requiring the lessee to pay rent or quit as provided in Section 1161 or 1162 of the Code of Civil Procedure at any time permitted by those sections, or affects the time and manner of giving any other notice required or permitted by law. Giving notice pursuant to this section does not satisfy the requirements of Section 1161 or 1162 of the Code of Civil Procedure. *(Added by Stats.2018, c. 104 (A.B.2847), § 3, eff. Jan. 1, 2019.)*

§ 1951.4. Remedy provided by lease; provisions

(a) The remedy described in this section is available only if the lease provides for this remedy. In addition to any other type of provision used in a lease to provide for the remedy described in this section, a provision in the lease in substantially the following form satisfies this subdivision:

"The lessor has the remedy described in California Civil Code Section 1951.4 (lessor may continue lease in effect after lessee's breach and abandonment and recover rent as it becomes due, if lessee has right to sublet or assign, subject only to reasonable limitations)."

(b) Even though a lessee of real property has breached the lease and abandoned the property, the lease continues in effect for so long as the lessor does not terminate the lessee's right to possession, and the lessor may enforce all the lessor's rights and remedies under the lease, including the right to recover the rent as it becomes due under the lease, if any of the following conditions is satisfied:

(1) The lease permits the lessee, or does not prohibit or otherwise restrict the right of the lessee, to sublet the property, assign the lessee's interest in the lease, or both.

(2) The lease permits the lessee to sublet the property, assign the lessee's interest in the lease, or both, subject to express standards or conditions, provided the standards and conditions are reasonable at the time the lease is executed and the lessor does not require compliance with any standard or condition that has become unreasonable at the time the lessee seeks to sublet or assign. For purposes of this paragraph, an express standard or condition is presumed to be reasonable; this presumption is a presumption affecting the burden of proof.

(3) The lease permits the lessee to sublet the property, assign the lessee's interest in the lease, or both, with the consent of the lessor, and the lease provides that the consent shall not be unreasonably withheld or the lease includes a standard implied by law that consent shall not be unreasonably withheld.

(c) For the purposes of subdivision (b), the following do not constitute a termination of the lessee's right to possession:

(1) Acts of maintenance or preservation or efforts to relet the property.

(2) The appointment of a receiver upon initiative of the lessor to protect the lessor's interest under the lease.

(3) Withholding consent to a subletting or assignment, or terminating a subletting or assignment, if the withholding or termination does not violate the rights of the lessee specified in subdivision (b). *(Added by Stats.1970, c. 89, p. 105, § 3, operative July 1, 1971. Amended by Stats.1989, c. 982, § 1; Stats.1991, c. 67 (S.B.256), § 1.)*

Cross References

Burden of proof, generally, see Evidence Code § 500 et seq.
Computation of rental loss if lease contains restrictions, see Civil Code § 1997.040.
Landlord's right to terminate lease, see Civil Code § 1995.330.
Lease defined for purposes of Civil Code §§ 1951.2 to 1952.6, see Civil Code § 1951.
Rent defined for purposes of Civil Code §§ 1951.2 to 1952.6, see Civil Code § 1951.
Restrictions on transfers of tenant's interest in lease, see Civil Code § 1995.230.

§ 1951.5. Liquidated damages

Section 1671, relating to liquidated damages, applies to a lease of real property. *(Added by Stats.1970, c. 89, p. 105, § 4, operative July 1, 1971. Amended by Stats.1977, c. 198, p. 720, § 8, operative July 1, 1978.)*

Cross References

Lease defined for purposes of Civil Code §§ 1951.2 to 1952.6, see Civil Code § 1951.
Rent defined for purposes of Civil Code §§ 1951.2 to 1952.6, see Civil Code § 1951.

§ 1951.7. "Advance payment" defined; notice of reletting

(a) As used in this section, "advance payment" means moneys paid to the lessor of real property as prepayment of rent, or as a deposit to secure faithful performance of the terms of the lease, or another payment that is the substantial equivalent of either of these. A payment that is not in excess of the amount of one month's rent is not an advance payment for purposes of this section.

§ 1951.7

(b) The notice provided by subdivision (c) is required to be given only if all of the following apply:

(1) The lessee has made an advance payment.

(2) The lease is terminated pursuant to Section 1951.2.

(3) The lessee has made a request, in writing, to the lessor that he or she be given notice under subdivision (c).

(c) Upon the initial reletting of the property, the lessor shall send a written notice to the lessee stating that the property has been relet, the name and address of the new lessee, and the length of the new lease and the amount of the rent. The notice shall be delivered to the lessee personally, or be sent by regular mail to the lessee at the address shown on the request, not later than 30 days after the new lessee takes possession of the property. Notice is not required if the amount of the rent due and unpaid at the time of termination exceeds the amount of the advance payment. *(Added by Stats.1970, c. 89, p. 105, § 5, operative July 1, 1971. Amended by Stats.2008, c. 179 (S.B.1498), § 32.)*

Cross References

Lease defined for purposes of Civil Code §§ 1951.2 to 1952.6, see Civil Code § 1951.

Rent defined for purposes of Civil Code §§ 1951.2 to 1952.6, see Civil Code § 1951.

§ 1951.8. Equitable relief

Nothing in Section 1951.2 or 1951.4 affects the right of the lessor under a lease of real property to equitable relief where such relief is appropriate. *(Added by Stats.1970, c. 89, p. 106, § 6, operative July 1, 1971.)*

Cross References

Lease defined for purposes of Civil Code §§ 1951.2 to 1952.6, see Civil Code § 1951.

Rent defined for purposes of Civil Code §§ 1951.2 to 1952.6, see Civil Code § 1951.

§ 1952. Actions for unlawful detainer, forcible entry, and forcible detainer; effect

(a) Except as provided in subdivision (c), nothing in Sections 1951 to 1951.8, inclusive, affects the provisions of Chapter 4 (commencing with Section 1159) of Title 3 of Part 3 of the Code of Civil Procedure, relating to actions for unlawful detainer, forcible entry, and forcible detainer.

(b) Unless the lessor amends the complaint as provided in paragraph (1) of subdivision (a) of Section 1952.3 to state a claim for damages not recoverable in the unlawful detainer proceeding, the bringing of an action under the provisions of Chapter 4 (commencing with Section 1159) of Title 3 of Part 3 of the Code of Civil Procedure does not affect the lessor's right to bring a separate action for relief under Sections 1951.2, 1951.5, and 1951.8, but no damages shall be recovered in the subsequent action for any detriment for which a claim for damages was made and determined on the merits in the previous action.

(c) After the lessor obtains possession of the property under a judgment pursuant to Section 1174 of the Code of Civil Procedure, he is no longer entitled to the remedy provided under Section 1951.4 unless the lessee obtains relief under Section 1179 of the Code of Civil Procedure. *(Added by Stats.1970, c. 89, p. 106, § 7, operative July 1, 1971. Amended by Stats.1977, c. 49, p. 426, § 1.)*

Cross References

Lease defined for purposes of Civil Code §§ 1951.2 to 1952.6, see Civil Code § 1951.

Rent defined for purposes of Civil Code §§ 1951.2 to 1952.6, see Civil Code § 1951.

§ 1952.2. Inapplicability of Sections 1951 to 1952, inclusive, to certain leases

Sections 1951 to 1952, inclusive, do not apply to:

(a) Any lease executed before July 1, 1971.

(b) Any lease executed on or after July 1, 1971, if the terms of the lease were fixed by a lease, option, or other agreement executed before July 1, 1971. *(Added by Stats.1970, c. 89, p. 106, § 8, operative July 1, 1971.)*

Cross References

Lease defined for purposes of Civil Code §§ 1951.2 to 1952.6, see Civil Code § 1951.

Rent defined for purposes of Civil Code §§ 1951.2 to 1952.6, see Civil Code § 1951.

§ 1952.3. Unlawful detainer; possession not in issue; conversion to action for damages

(a) Except as provided in subdivisions (b) and (c), if the lessor brings an unlawful detainer proceeding and possession of the property is no longer in issue because possession of the property has been delivered to the lessor before trial or, if there is no trial, before judgment is entered, the case becomes an ordinary civil action in which:

(1) The lessor may obtain any relief to which he is entitled, including, where applicable, relief authorized by Section 1951.2; but, if the lessor seeks to recover damages described in paragraph (3) of subdivision (a) of Section 1951.2 or any other damages not recoverable in the unlawful detainer proceeding, the lessor shall first amend the complaint pursuant to Section 472 or 473 of the Code of Civil Procedure so that possession of the property is no longer in issue and to state a claim for such damages and shall serve a copy of the amended complaint on the defendant in the same manner as a copy of a summons and original complaint is served.

(2) The defendant may, by appropriate pleadings or amendments to pleadings, seek any affirmative relief, and assert all defenses, to which he is entitled, whether or not the lessor has amended the complaint; but subdivision (a) of Section 426.30 of the Code of Civil Procedure does not apply unless, after delivering possession of the property to the lessor, the defendant (i) files a cross-complaint or (ii) files an answer or an amended answer in response to an amended complaint filed pursuant to paragraph (1).

(b) The defendant's time to respond to a complaint for unlawful detainer is not affected by the delivery of possession of the property to the lessor; but, if the complaint is amended as provided in paragraph (1) of subdivision (a), the defendant has the same time to respond to the amended complaint as in an ordinary civil action.

(c) The case shall proceed as an unlawful detainer proceeding if the defendant's default (1) has been entered on the unlawful detainer complaint and (2) has not been opened by an amendment of the complaint or otherwise set aside.

(d) Nothing in this section affects the pleadings that may be filed, relief that may be sought, or defenses that may be asserted in an unlawful detainer proceeding that has not become an ordinary civil action as provided in subdivision (a). *(Added by Stats.1977, c. 49, p. 427, § 2.)*

Cross References

Lease defined for purposes of Civil Code §§ 1951.2 to 1952.6, see Civil Code § 1951.

Rent defined for purposes of Civil Code §§ 1951.2 to 1952.6, see Civil Code § 1951.

§ 1952.4. Agreement for exploration for or removal of natural resources not lease of real property

An agreement for the exploration for or the removal of natural resources is not a lease of real property within the meaning of Sections 1951 to 1952.2, inclusive. *(Added by Stats.1970, c. 89, p. 106, § 9, operative July 1, 1971.)*

Cross References

Lease defined for purposes of Civil Code §§ 1951.2 to 1952.6, see Civil Code § 1951.

Rent defined for purposes of Civil Code §§ 1951.2 to 1952.6, see Civil Code § 1951.

§ 1952.6. Applicability to leases between public entities and nonprofit corporations; substitution of remedies for breach

(a) Sections 1951 to 1952.2, inclusive, shall not apply to any lease or agreement for a lease of real property between any public entity and any nonprofit corporation whose title or interest in the property is subject to reversion to or vesting in a public entity and which issues bonds or other evidences of indebtedness, the interest on which is exempt from federal income taxes for the purpose of acquiring, constructing, or improving the property or a building or other facility thereon, or between any public entity and any other public entity, unless the lease or the agreement shall specifically provide that Sections 1951 to 1952.2, inclusive, or any portions thereof, are applicable to the lease or the agreement.

(b) Except as provided in subdivision (a), a public entity lessee in a contract for a capital lease of real property involving the payment of rents of one million dollars ($1,000,000) or more may elect to waive any of the remedies for a breach of the lease provided in Sections 1951 to 1952.2, inclusive, and contract instead for any other remedy permitted by law. As used in this subdivision, "capital lease" refers to a lease entered into for the purpose of acquiring, constructing, or improving the property or a building or other facility thereon.

(c) As used in this section, "public entity" includes the state, a county, city and county, city, district, public authority, public agency, or any other political subdivision or public corporation. *(Added by Stats.1970, c. 89, p. 106, § 10, operative July 1, 1971. Amended by Stats.1971, c. 732, p. 1457, § 1, eff. Aug. 24, 1971; Stats.1989, c. 613, § 1.)*

Cross References

Lease defined for purposes of Civil Code §§ 1951.2 to 1952.6, see Civil Code § 1951.

Rent defined for purposes of Civil Code §§ 1951.2 to 1952.6, see Civil Code § 1951.

§ 1952.7. Enforceability of lease terms prohibiting or unreasonably restricting installation of electric vehicle charging station; exceptions; charging station requirements

(a)(1) Any term in a lease that is executed, renewed, or extended on or after January 1, 2015, that conveys any possessory interest in commercial property that either prohibits or unreasonably restricts the installation or use of an electric vehicle charging station in a parking space associated with the commercial property, or that is otherwise in conflict with the provisions of this section, is void and unenforceable.

(2) This subdivision does not apply to provisions that impose reasonable restrictions on the installation of electric vehicle charging stations. However, it is the policy of the state to promote, encourage, and remove obstacles to the use of electric vehicle charging stations.

(3) This subdivision shall not grant the holder of a possessory interest under the lease described in paragraph (1) the right to install electric vehicle charging stations in more parking spaces than are allotted to the leaseholder in his or her lease, or, if no parking spaces are allotted, a number of parking spaces determined by multiplying the total number of parking spaces located at the commercial property by a fraction, the denominator of which is the total rentable square feet at the property, and the numerator of which is the number of total square feet rented by the leaseholder.

(4) If the installation of an electric vehicle charging station has the effect of granting the leaseholder a reserved parking space and a reserved parking space is not allotted to the leaseholder in the lease, the owner of the commercial property may charge a reasonable monthly rental amount for the parking space.

(b) This section shall not apply to any of the following:

(1) A commercial property where charging stations already exist for use by tenants in a ratio that is equal to or greater than 2 available parking spaces for every 100 parking spaces at the commercial property.

(2) A commercial property where there are less than 50 parking spaces.

(c) For purposes of this section:

(1) "Electric vehicle charging station" or "charging station" means a station that is designed in compliance with Article 625 of the California Electrical Code, as it reads on the effective date of this section, and delivers electricity from a source outside an electric vehicle into one or more electric vehicles.

(2) "Reasonable costs" includes, but is not limited to, costs associated with those items specified in the "Permitting Checklist" of the "Zero-Emission Vehicles in California: Community Readiness Guidebook" published by the Office of Planning and Research.

(3) "Reasonable restrictions" or "reasonable standards" are restrictions or standards that do not significantly increase the cost of the electric vehicle charging station or its installation or significantly decrease the charging station's efficiency or specified performance.

(d) An electric vehicle charging station shall meet applicable health and safety standards and requirements imposed by state and local authorities as well as all other applicable zoning, land use, or other ordinances, or land use permit requirements.

(e) If lessor approval is required for the installation or use of an electric vehicle charging station, the application for approval shall not be willfully avoided or delayed. The approval or denial of an application shall be in writing.

(f) An electric vehicle charging station installed by a lessee shall satisfy the following provisions:

(1) If lessor approval is required, the lessee first shall obtain approval from the lessor to install the electric vehicle charging station and the lessor shall approve the installation if the lessee complies with the applicable provisions of the lease consistent with the provisions of this section and agrees in writing to do all of the following:

(A) Comply with the lessor's reasonable standards for the installation of the charging station.

(B) Engage a licensed contractor to install the charging station.

(C) Within 14 days of approval, provide a certificate of insurance that names the lessor as an additional insured under the lessee's insurance policy in the amount set forth in paragraph (3).

(2) The lessee shall be responsible for all of the following:

(A) Costs for damage to property and the charging station resulting from the installation, maintenance, repair, removal, or replacement of the charging station.

(B) Costs for the maintenance, repair, and replacement of the charging station.

(C) The cost of electricity associated with the charging station.

(3) The lessee at all times, shall maintain a lessee liability coverage policy in the amount of one million dollars ($1,000,000), and shall name the lessor as a named additional insured under the policy with a right to notice of cancellation and property insurance covering any damage or destruction caused by the charging station, naming the lessor as its interests may appear.

(g) A lessor may, in its sole discretion, create a new parking space where one did not previously exist to facilitate the installation of an electric vehicle charging station, in compliance with all applicable laws.

(h) Any installation by a lessor or a lessee of an electric vehicle charging station in a common interest development is also subject to all of the requirements of subdivision (f) of Section 4745. *(Added by Stats.2014, c. 529 (A.B.2565), § 2, eff. Jan. 1, 2015. Amended by Stats.2016, c. 714 (S.B.944), § 4, eff. Jan. 1, 2017.)*

§ 1952.8. Gasoline service stations; leases; vapor control system; requirements

On and after the effective date of this section, no owner of a gasoline service station shall enter into a lease with any person for the leasing of the station for the purpose of operating a gasoline service station, unless (a) the station is equipped with a vapor control system for the control of gasoline vapor emissions during gasoline marketing operations, including storage, transport, and transfer operations, if such vapor control system is required by law or by any rule or regulation of the State Air Resources Board or of the air pollution control district in which the station is located or (b) no vapor control system has been certified by the board prior to the date of the lease.

A lease entered into in violation of this section shall be voidable at the option of the lessee. *(Added by Stats.1976, c. 1030, p. 4619, § 1, eff. Sept. 20, 1976.)*

Cross References

Gasoline vapor control, see Health and Safety Code § 41950 et seq.

§ 1953. Waiver or modification of lessee's rights; void as contrary to public policy; exception; applicability of section

(a) Any provision of a lease or rental agreement of a dwelling by which the lessee agrees to modify or waive any of the following rights shall be void as contrary to public policy:

(1) His rights or remedies under Section 1950.5 or 1954.

(2) His right to assert a cause of action against the lessor which may arise in the future.

(3) His right to a notice or hearing required by law.

(4) His procedural rights in litigation in any action involving his rights and obligations as a tenant.

(5) His right to have the landlord exercise a duty of care to prevent personal injury or personal property damage where that duty is imposed by law.

(b) Any provision of a lease or rental agreement of a dwelling by which the lessee agrees to modify or waive a statutory right, where the modification or waiver is not void under subdivision (a) or under Section 1942.1, 1942.5, or 1954, shall be void as contrary to public policy unless the lease or rental agreement is presented to the lessee before he takes actual possession of the premises. This subdivision does not apply to any provisions modifying or waiving a statutory right in agreements renewing leases or rental agreements where the same provision was also contained in the lease or rental agreement which is being renewed.

(c) This section shall apply only to leases and rental agreements executed on or after January 1, 1976. *(Added by Stats.1975, c. 302, p. 749, § 1.)*

Cross References

Freedom from violence or intimidation, waiver of civil rights by contract, provisions of this section not abrogated, see Civil Code § 51.7.

§ 1954. Entry of dwelling by landlord; conditions; oral agreement between tenant and landlord

(a) A landlord may enter the dwelling unit only in the following cases:

(1) In case of emergency.

(2) To make necessary or agreed repairs, decorations, alterations or improvements, supply necessary or agreed services, or exhibit the dwelling unit to prospective or actual purchasers, mortgagees, tenants, workers, or contractors or to

make an inspection pursuant to subdivision (f) of Section 1950.5.

(3) When the tenant has abandoned or surrendered the premises.

(4) Pursuant to court order.

(5) For the purposes set forth in Chapter 2.5 (commencing with Section 1954.201).

(6) To comply with the provisions of Article 2.2 (commencing with Section 17973) of Chapter 5 of Part 1.5 of Division 13 of the Health and Safety Code.

(b) Except in cases of emergency or when the tenant has abandoned or surrendered the premises, entry may not be made during other than normal business hours unless the tenant consents to an entry during other than normal business hours at the time of entry.

(c) The landlord may not abuse the right of access or use it to harass the tenant.

(d)(1) Except as provided in subdivision (e), or as provided in paragraph (2) or (3), the landlord shall give the tenant reasonable notice in writing of his or her intent to enter and enter only during normal business hours. The notice shall include the date, approximate time, and purpose of the entry. The notice may be personally delivered to the tenant, left with someone of a suitable age and discretion at the premises, or, left on, near, or under the usual entry door of the premises in a manner in which a reasonable person would discover the notice. Twenty–four hours shall be presumed to be reasonable notice in absence of evidence to the contrary. The notice may be mailed to the tenant. Mailing of the notice at least six days prior to an intended entry is presumed reasonable notice in the absence of evidence to the contrary.

(2) If the purpose of the entry is to exhibit the dwelling unit to prospective or actual purchasers, the notice may be given orally, in person or by telephone, if the landlord or his or her agent has notified the tenant in writing within 120 days of the oral notice that the property is for sale and that the landlord or agent may contact the tenant orally for the purpose described above. Twenty–four hours is presumed reasonable notice in the absence of evidence to the contrary. The notice shall include the date, approximate time, and purpose of the entry. At the time of entry, the landlord or agent shall leave written evidence of the entry inside the unit.

(3) The tenant and the landlord may agree orally to an entry to make agreed repairs or supply agreed services. The agreement shall include the date and approximate time of the entry, which shall be within one week of the agreement. In this case, the landlord is not required to provide the tenant a written notice.

(e) No notice of entry is required under this section:

(1) To respond to an emergency.

(2) If the tenant is present and consents to the entry at the time of entry.

(3) After the tenant has abandoned or surrendered the unit. *(Added by Stats.1975, c. 302, p. 750, § 2. Amended by Stats.2002, c. 301 (S.B.1403), § 3; Stats.2002, c. 1061 (A.B. 2330), § 2.5; Stats.2003, c. 62 (S.B.600), § 18; Stats.2003, c. 787 (S.B.345), § 1; Stats.2016, c. 623 (S.B.7), § 1, eff. Jan. 1, 2017; Stats.2018, c. 445 (S.B.721), § 1, eff. Jan. 1, 2019.)*

Cross References

Hiring of real property, unlawful actions by landlord to influence tenant to vacate, civil penalties, see Civil Code § 1940.2.
Multifamily residential real property and commercial real property, installation and maintenance of water-conserving plumbing fixtures, see Civil Code § 1101.5.
Refusal to rent to qualified tenant on basis of possession of waterbed prohibited, see Civil Code § 1940.5.
Rental housing developments, entry or inspection by local public entity, see Health and Safety Code § 50760.

§ 1954.05. Assignment for the benefit of creditors; right of assignee to occupy business premises; payment of rent; time

In any general assignment for the benefit of creditors, as defined in Section 493.010 of the Code of Civil Procedure, the assignee shall have the right to occupy, for a period of up to 90 days after the date of the assignment, any business premises held under a lease by the assignor upon payment when due of the monthly rental reserved in the lease for the period of such occupancy, notwithstanding any provision in the lease, whether heretofore or hereafter entered into, for the termination thereof upon the making of the assignment or the insolvency of the lessee or other condition relating to the financial condition of the lessee. This section shall be construed as establishing the reasonable rental value of the premises recoverable by a landlord upon a holding-over by the tenant upon the termination of a lease under the circumstances specified herein. *(Formerly § 1954.1, added by Stats.1982, c. 35, p. 63, § 1, eff. Feb. 17, 1982. Renumbered § 1954.05 and amended by Stats.2016, c. 599 (A.B.551), § 2, eff. Jan. 1, 2017.)*

§ 1954.06. Assisted housing development; election to have rental payment information reported to credit agency; fee; evaluation of impact of rental payment reporting

(a) As specified in subdivision (b), and except as provided in subdivision (j), beginning July 1, 2021, any landlord of an assisted housing development shall offer the tenant or tenants obligated on the lease of each unit in that housing development the option of having the tenant's rental payment information reported to at least one nationwide consumer reporting agency that meets the definition in Section 603(p) of the federal Fair Credit Reporting Act (15 U.S.C. Section 1681a(p)) or any other consumer reporting agency that meets the definition in Section 603(f) of the federal Fair Credit Reporting Act (15 U.S.C. Section 1681a(f)) so long as the consumer reporting agency resells or otherwise furnishes rental payment information to a nationwide consumer reporting agency that meets the definition in Section 603(p) of the federal Fair Credit Reporting Act (15 U.S.C. Section 1681a(p)). A tenant's election to have rent reported under this subdivision shall be in writing, as described in subdivision (c).

(b) For leases entered into on and after July 1, 2021, the offer of rent reporting shall be made at the time of the lease agreement and at least once annually thereafter. For leases outstanding as of July 1, 2021, the offer of rent reporting shall be made no later than October 1, 2021, and at least once annually thereafter.

(c) The offer of rent reporting shall include a written election of rent reporting that contains all of the following:

§ 1954.06

(1) A statement that reporting of the tenant's rental payment information is optional.

(2) Identification of each consumer reporting agency to which rental payment information will be reported.

(3) A statement that all of the tenant's rental payments will be reported, regardless of whether the payments are timely, late, or missed.

(4) The amount of any fee charged pursuant to subdivision (f).

(5) Instructions on how to submit the written election of rent reporting to the landlord by mail.

(6) A statement that the tenant may opt into rent reporting at any time following the initial offer by the landlord.

(7) A statement that the tenant may elect to stop rent reporting at any time, but that they will not be able to resume rent reporting for at least six months after their election to opt out.

(8) Instructions on how to opt out of reporting rental payment information.

(9) A signature block that the tenant shall date and sign in order to accept the offer of rent reporting.

(d) When the offer of rent reporting is made, the landlord shall provide the tenant with a self-addressed, stamped envelope to return the written election of rent reporting.

(e) The written election to begin rent reporting shall not be accepted from the tenant at the time of the offer. A tenant may submit their completed written election of rent reporting at any time after they receive the offer of rent reporting from the landlord. A tenant may request and shall obtain additional copies of the written election of rent reporting form from the landlord at any time.

(f) If a tenant elects to have that tenant's rental payments reported to a consumer reporting agency under subdivision (a), the landlord may require that tenant to pay a fee not to exceed the lesser of the actual cost to the landlord to provide the service or ten dollars ($10) per month. The payment or nonpayment of this fee by the tenant shall not be reported to a consumer reporting agency.

(g) If a tenant fails to pay any fee required by the landlord pursuant to subdivision (f), all of the following shall apply:

(1) The failure to pay the fee shall not be cause for termination of the tenancy, whether pursuant to Section 1161 of the Code of Civil Procedure or otherwise.

(2) The landlord shall not deduct the unpaid fee from the tenant's security deposit.

(3) If the fee remains unpaid for 30 days or more, the landlord may stop reporting the tenant's rental payments and the tenant shall be unable to elect rent reporting again for a period of six months from the date on which the fee first became due.

(h) A tenant who elects to have rent reported as described in subdivision (a) may subsequently file a written request with their landlord to stop that reporting with which the landlord shall comply. A tenant who elects to stop reporting shall not be allowed to elect rent reporting again for a period of at least six months from the date of the tenant's written request to stop reporting.

(i) A tenant who elects to have rent reported does not forfeit any rights under Sections 1941 to 1942, inclusive. If a tenant makes deductions from rent or otherwise withholds rent as authorized by those sections, the deductions or withholding of rent shall not constitute a late rental payment. A tenant invoking the right to repair and deduct or withhold rent under those sections shall notify their landlord of the deduction or withholding prior to the date rent is due. This subdivision shall not be construed to relieve a housing provider of the obligation to maintain habitable premises.

(j) This section shall not apply to any landlord of an assisted housing development that contains 15 or fewer dwelling units, unless both of the following apply:

(1) The landlord owns more than one assisted housing development, regardless of the number of units in each assisted housing development.

(2) The landlord is one of the following:

(A) A real estate investment trust, as defined in Section 856 of Title 26 of the United States Code.

(B) A corporation.

(C) A limited liability company in which at least one member is a corporation.

(k) For purposes of this section, the following definitions shall apply:

(1) "Assisted housing development" has the same meaning as defined in Section 65863.10 of the Government Code.

(2) "Landlord" means an owner of residential real property containing five or more dwelling units.

(*l*) An independent evaluator, upon appropriation by the Legislature for this purpose, shall be selected by the Department of Financial Protection and Innovation and shall be responsible for conducting an evaluation of the impact of rental payment reporting in this state pursuant to this section.

(1) The evaluator shall be selected through a competitive process to be completed on or before March 1, 2024.

(2) The evaluator shall conduct the evaluation of the impact of rental payment reporting in this state pursuant to this section from July 1, 2021, through June 30, 2024, or a later date chosen by the evaluator with the approval of the Department of Financial Protection and Innovation.

(3) Based on the evaluation described in paragraph (2), the evaluator shall create a report that includes, but is not limited to, information about all of the following:

(A) The estimated percentage of assisted housing developments in compliance with this section.

(B) Any significant barriers to compliance with this section experienced by assisted housing developments.

(C) The estimated number of participating tenants.

(D) Any significant barriers to participation experienced by tenants.

(E) The estimated impact of participation on the credit scores of participating tenants living in assisted housing developments.

(F) Recommendations, if any, for changes to the rental payment reporting process established by this section that could positively impact tenants of assisted housing developments.

(4) In complying with this subdivision, the Department of Financial Protection and Innovation and the evaluator may employ statistical probability methods and other sampling methods to provide estimates.

(5) If the information required in paragraph (3) cannot be obtained due to an absence of data or other methodological constraints, the Department of Financial Protection and Innovation shall notify the Legislature by January 1, 2024. This notification shall describe in detail the actions taken to attempt to obtain the information, why the required information was unable to be obtained, and recommendations for statutory changes that could produce data to satisfy the requirements enumerated in paragraph (3).

(6) On or before January 1, 2025, the annual report required pursuant to paragraph (3) shall be posted on the internet website of the Department of Financial Protection and Innovation and distributed to the appropriate policy committees of the Legislature for review.

(m) This section shall remain in effect only until July 1, 2025, and as of that date is repealed, unless a later enacted statute that is enacted before July 1, 2025, deletes or extends that date. *(Added by Stats.2020, c. 204 (S.B.1157), § 1, eff. Jan. 1, 2021. Amended by Stats.2022, c. 670 (S.B.1396), § 1, eff. Jan. 1, 2023.)*

Repeal

For repeal of this section, see its terms.

CHAPTER 2.4. OCCUPANCY IN INTERIM HOMELESSNESS PROGRAMS

Section
1954.08. Definitions.
1954.09. Shelter program participant continued occupancy does not constitute new tenancy, and not considered person who hires; shelter program requirements; responsibilities of shelter program administrator; property being converted to permanent housing site.
1954.091. Duration of occupancy; tenant rights.
1954.092. Motel or hotel may not be designated as nontransient motel or nontransient hotel solely as result of shelter program participant's length of occupancy; prohibited hotel or motel policies.
1954.093. Duration of chapter.
1954.1. Renumbered.

Repeal

For repeal of Chapter 2.4, see Civil Code § 1954.093.

§ 1954.08. Definitions

For the purposes of this chapter, the following definitions apply:

(a) "Harm-reduction" means a set of strategies, policies, and practices aimed at mitigating the negative social and physical consequences associated with various human behaviors, including, but not limited to, substance use, and that do not rely on punitive measures to gain program compliance.

(b) "Motel or hotel" means a dwelling unit, as defined by subdivision (c) of Section 1940, that an innkeeper retains a right of access to and control of, and that provides or offers all of the following services to all of the residents:

(1) Facilities for the safeguarding of personal property pursuant to Section 1860.

(2) Central telephone service subject to tariffs covering the same filed with the California Public Utilities Commission.

(3) Maid, mail, and room services.

(c) "Shelter program" means a city-, county-, continuum of care-, state-, or federally funded shelter, interim housing, motel voucher, or emergency shelter program in which the city, county, continuum of care, state, or federal governmental entity retains an oversight and accountability role in ensuring compliance with program regulations and proper program administration.

(d) "Shelter program administrator" means a city, county, or continuum of care entity that retains an oversight role in ensuring compliance with program regulations and proper program administration.

(e) "Shelter program operator" means a service provider agency that is contracting with a shelter program administrator to carry out the operations of the shelter program. A "shelter program operator" may include community-based service providers as well as public government agencies carrying out program operations.

(f) "Shelter program participant" means an occupant of a motel, hotel, or other shelter site whose occupancy is solely due to their participation in a shelter program.

(g) "Trauma-informed" means a set of practices that promote safety, empowerment, and healing in recognition that program participants may have experienced trauma that informs their experiences and responses. *(Added by Stats. 2022, c. 645 (A.B.1991), § 1, eff. Jan. 1, 2023.)*

Repeal

For repeal of Chapter 2.4, see Civil Code § 1954.093.

§ 1954.09. Shelter program participant continued occupancy does not constitute new tenancy, and not considered person who hires; shelter program requirements; responsibilities of shelter program administrator; property being converted to permanent housing site

(a) Notwithstanding paragraph (1) of subdivision (b) of Section 1954.091, shelter program participants shall not have their continued occupancy in a motel, hotel, or shelter program constitute a new tenancy and shall not be considered persons who hire pursuant to Section 1940 for the purposes of Section 1161 of the Code of Civil Procedure, if the shelter program meets all of the following requirements:

(1) The shelter program adheres to the core components of Housing First, pursuant to subdivision (b) of Section 8255 of the Welfare and Institutions Code.

(2) The shelter program establishes, adopts, and clearly documents rules governing how and for what reasons a shelter program participant's enrollment may be terminated and the shelter program operator discloses the termination

policy to program participants in writing, in plain language, at the commencement of their occupancy.

(A) Permissible reasons for termination shall include sexual assault, verbally or physically threatening behaviors, which rise to the level of a "direct threat" to persons or property, as defined in paragraph (3) of subdivision (b) of Section 12179 of Title 2 of the Code of California Regulations, physical violence to staff or other program participants, direct observation of participant engaging in illegal activity onsite, or time limits established by the shelter program.

(B) Terminations for reasons not stated in subparagraph (A) and any operational policies negotiated prior to the commencement of the shelter program shall be approved by the shelter program administrator and shared with their shelter program participants in a clearly labeled document.

(C) The shelter program administrator shall endeavor to ensure terminations are performed by the shelter program operator in a trauma-informed manner utilizing a harm-reduction approach, and shall ensure that the termination policies and procedures of the hotel, motel, and shelter program, including the required grievance procedure, comply with all applicable disability laws, including requirements for reasonable accommodation.

(3) The shelter program administrator establishes procedures regarding how a shelter program participant will be provided a written termination notice if a termination occurs and the shelter program operator discloses those procedures to shelter program participants in writing at the commencement of their occupancy.

(A) The shelter program operator shall provide the termination notice to the participant at least 30 days prior to the proposed termination or, if the underlying cause for a proposed termination constitutes a "direct threat," as defined in paragraph (3) of subdivision (b) of Section 12179 of Title 2 of the Code of California Regulations, the shelter program operator may remove the participant from the premises immediately, provided that the operator advises the participant of their right to utilize the grievance process described in paragraph (5).

(B) The termination notice shall contain a clear, plain-language statement of the reason for the termination, shall notify the participant of their right to request a reasonable accommodation if they are a qualified person with a disability, and shall notify the participant of their right to utilize the grievance process described in subparagraph (E).

(C) The established procedures developed regarding participant guideline violations shall include an escalation continuum that incorporates documented warnings and documented shelter program operator staff and participant problem solving methods prior to instituting terminations from the shelter program.

(4) The shelter program operator shall provide an exit plan upon termination of a shelter program participant that includes referrals to any available local shelter service for which the participant is eligible and the shelter program operator shall make a good faith, reasonable effort to facilitate an intake for that participant in an available bed or unit.

(A) The shelter program operator shall document good faith, reasonable efforts and shall make that documentation available upon request.

(B) The shelter program administrator, in cases where the grievance process is utilized, shall determine whether the shelter program operator's efforts constitute a good faith effort to facilitate a participant into an alternative available shelter site or program.

(C)(i) The shelter program administrator shall make good faith efforts to provide reasonable transportation accommodations upon termination of a shelter program participant from a program or upon transfer of a shelter program participant to an alternative available bed or unit.

(ii) In exigent circumstances that necessitate the presence of first responders, police, or fire department and render it infeasible to provide a termination letter at that time or coordinate a postexit plan, the shelter program operator shall create a termination letter that satisfies the above-described requirements and make that documentation available to participants within 24 hours of their request.

(5) The shelter program administrator shall establish a grievance process that complies with due process and the shelter program operator shall disclose the grievance process to occupants in writing, in plain language, at the commencement of their occupancy.

(A) The grievance process shall give shelter program participants a right to due process appeal through the shelter program administrator if the shelter program participant believes they were or are being wrongfully terminated from the program, and shall inform shelter program participants on how to access and initiate the grievance process.

(B)(i) Program participants shall be provided the opportunity to initiate the grievance process 30 days prior to their proposed termination date or at any point thereafter.

(ii) In cases where participants are subject to immediate removal based on circumstances that present a "direct threat," as defined in paragraph (3) of subdivision (b) of Section 12179 of Title 2 of the Code of California Regulations, participants shall be provided the opportunity to initiate the grievance process at the time of removal or at any point thereafter.

(C) If, following the grievance process, the proposed termination is not carried out, any participant already removed shall be granted the right to resume their participation in the program. If the shelter program operator is unable to place the individual in the original site, the shelter program operator shall facilitate a placement for the individual in an alternative available motel, hotel, or shelter site.

(b) Where a shelter program administrator is also the shelter program operator, the shelter program administrator is responsible for all of the duties described in subdivision (a).

(c) For properties that are being converted from use as a motel or hotel, or from use as a shelter, interim housing, emergency shelter, or other interim facility to a permanent housing site, paragraph (2) shall not apply to occupants of the site from the date that the site receives a certificate of occupancy as a permanent housing site. *(Added by Stats. 2022, c. 645 (A.B.1991), § 1, eff. Jan. 1, 2023.)*

Repeal

For repeal of Chapter 2.4, see Civil Code § 1954.093.

§ 1954.091. Duration of occupancy; tenant rights

(a) Section 310.3 of Chapter 3 (commencing with Section 301.1) of Part 2 of Title 24 (the California Building Standards Code) of the California Code of Regulations shall not be interpreted to restrict the duration of occupancy for shelter program participants.

(b)(1) This chapter shall not be interpreted to either confer or deny any tenant rights or protections for persons who hire pursuant to Section 1940, or any rights that the tenant may otherwise be entitled to under any applicable federal, state, or local law.

(2) Notwithstanding paragraph (1), a shelter program participant of a shelter program that complies with the requirements described in Section 1954.09 shall be entitled to all of the following:

(A) A shelter program participant's continued occupancy in a motel or hotel does not constitute a new tenancy.

(B) A shelter program participant shall not be considered a person who hires pursuant to Section 1940 for the purposes of Section 1161 of the Code of Civil Procedure.

(C) Receipt of a written termination policy.

(D) Disclosure of a termination notice procedure.

(E) Thirty days' notice prior to termination, except as described in Section 1954.09.

(F) Right to appeal termination pursuant to the grievance policy required by Section 1954.09. *(Added by Stats.2022, c. 645 (A.B.1991), § 1, eff. Jan. 1, 2023.)*

Repeal

For repeal of Chapter 2.4, see Civil Code § 1954.093.

§ 1954.092. Motel or hotel may not be designated as nontransient motel or nontransient hotel solely as result of shelter program participant's length of occupancy; prohibited hotel or motel policies

(a) A motel or hotel shall not be designated as a nontransient motel or a nontransient hotel pursuant to Section 310.4 of Chapter 3 (commencing with Section 301.1) of Part 2 of Title 24 (the California Building Standards Code) of the California Code of Regulations solely as a result of a shelter program participant's occupancy in the motel or hotel beyond a 30–day period.

(b) A hotel or motel shall not do either of the following:

(1)(A) Adopt termination policies specifically for motel or hotel occupants who are shelter program participants that do not apply to other motel or hotel occupants who are not participating in a shelter program, impose restrictions on the ability of program participants to freely enter or exit the property or access certain areas or amenities of the property that do not apply to other motel or hotel occupants, or levy charges and fees, including fees for room card replacements, that do not apply to other motel or hotel occupants.

(B) This paragraph sets minimum standards for shelter program terminations and shall not be construed to restrict shelter program operating standards that confer greater rights to participants with regard to shelter program terminations.

(2) Require shelter program participants to check out and reregister, move out of rooms or between rooms, or from the hotel or motel while actively enrolled in the shelter program for the purposes of preventing an occupant from establishing rights of tenancy. *(Added by Stats.2022, c. 645 (A.B.1991), § 1, eff. Jan. 1, 2023.)*

Repeal

For repeal of Chapter 2.4, see Civil Code § 1954.093.

§ 1954.093. Duration of chapter

This chapter shall remain in effect only until January 1, 2025, and as of that date is repealed. *(Added by Stats.2022, c. 645 (A.B.1991), § 1, eff. Jan. 1, 2023.)*

§ 1954.1. Renumbered § 1954.05 and amended by Stats. 2016, c. 599 (A.B.551), § 2, eff. Jan. 1, 2017

CHAPTER 2.5. TRANSITIONAL HOUSING PARTICIPANT MISCONDUCT

Article	Section
1. General Provisions and Definitions	1954.10
2. Temporary Restraining Order and Injunction	1954.13
3. Recovery of Dwelling	1954.17

Explanatory Note

For another Chapter 2.5, "Water Service", added by Stats.2016, c. 623 (S.B.7), § 2, eff. Jan. 1, 2017, operative Jan. 1, 2018, see Civil Code § 1954.201 et seq.

ARTICLE 1. GENERAL PROVISIONS AND DEFINITIONS

Section
1954.10. Short title.
1954.11. Legislative intent.
1954.12. Definitions.

§ 1954.10. Short title

This chapter shall be known and may be cited as the Transitional Housing Participant Misconduct Act. *(Added by Stats.2016, c. 714 (S.B.944), § 5, eff. Jan. 1, 2017.)*

§ 1954.11. Legislative intent

In enacting this chapter, it is the intent of the Legislature to prevent the recurrence of acts of substantial disruption or violence by participants in transitional housing programs against other such participants, program staff, or immediate neighbors of the participants. *(Added by Stats.2016, c. 714 (S.B.944), § 5, eff. Jan. 1, 2017.)*

§ 1954.12. Definitions

The following definitions shall govern the construction of this chapter:

(a) "Abuse" means intentionally or recklessly causing or attempting to cause bodily injury, or sexual assault or placing

§ 1954.12 OBLIGATIONS

another person in reasonable apprehension of imminent serious bodily injury to himself, herself, or another, where the injured person is another participant, program operator's staff, or a person residing within 100 feet of the program site.

(b) "Homeless person" means an individual or family who, prior to participation in a transitional housing program, either lacked a fixed, regular, and adequate nighttime residence or had a primary nighttime residence, that was one of the following:

(1) A supervised publicly or privately operated shelter designed to provide temporary living accommodations, including, but not limited to, welfare hotels, congregate shelters, and transitional housing for the mentally ill.

(2) An institution that provides a temporary residence for individuals intended to be institutionalized.

(3) A public or private place not designed for, or ordinarily used as, a regular sleeping accommodation for human beings.

(c) "Participant" means a homeless person under contract with a program operator to participate in a transitional housing program and to use a dwelling unit in the program site. For the purposes of naming a defendant under this part, or a person to be protected under this part, "participant" shall include a person living with a participant at the program site. The contract shall specifically include the transitional housing program rules and regulations, a statement of the program operator's right of control over and access to the program unit occupied by the participant, and a restatement of the requirements and procedures of this chapter.

(d) "Program misconduct" means any intentional violation of the transitional housing program rules and regulations which (1) substantially interferes with the orderly operation of the transitional housing program, and (2) relates to drunkenness on the program site, unlawful use or sale of controlled substances, theft, arson, or destruction of the property of the program operator, persons living within 100 feet of the program site, program employees, or other participants, or (3) relates to violence or threats of violence, and harassment of persons living within 100 feet of the program site, program employees, or of other participants.

(e) "Program operator" means a governmental agency, or private nonprofit corporation receiving any portion of its transitional housing program funds from a governmental agency, which is operating a transitional housing program. "Program operator" also includes any other manager or operator hired by a governmental agency or nonprofit corporation to operate its transitional housing program.

(f) "Program site" means the real property containing a dwelling unit, the use of which is granted to a participant, and other locations where program activities or services are carried out or provided, subject to the participant's compliance with the transitional housing program rules and regulations.

(g) "Transitional housing program" means any program which is designed to assist homeless persons in obtaining skills necessary for independent living in permanent housing and which has all of the following components:

(1) Comprehensive social service programs which include regular individualized case management services and which may include alcohol and drug abuse counseling, self-improvement education, employment and training assistance services, and independent living skills development.

(2) Use of a program unit as a temporary housing unit in a structured living environment which use is conditioned upon compliance with the transitional housing program rules and regulations.

(3) A rule or regulation which specifies an occupancy period of not less than 30 days, but not more than 24 months. *(Added by Stats.2016, c. 714 (S.B.944), § 5, eff. Jan. 1, 2017.)*

ARTICLE 2. TEMPORARY RESTRAINING ORDER AND INJUNCTION

Section
1954.13. Temporary restraining order and injunction; procedures.
1954.14. Transmission of copy to law enforcement agency having jurisdiction over program site; willful disobedience; contempt.
1954.15. Violation of order; breach of agreement; subsequent performance prohibited.
1954.16. Forms and instructions.

§ 1954.13. Temporary restraining order and injunction; procedures

(a) The program operator may seek, on its own behalf or on behalf of other participants, project employees, or persons residing within 100 feet of the program site, a temporary restraining order and an injunction prohibiting abuse or program misconduct as provided in this chapter. A program operator may not seek a temporary restraining order, pursuant to this section, against a participant after the participant has been under contract with the program operator for at least six months or longer, except when an action is pending against the participant or a temporary restraining order is in effect and subject to further orders. Nothing in this section shall be construed to authorize a person residing within 100 feet of the program site to seek a temporary restraining order or injunction under this chapter.

(b) Upon filing a petition for an injunction under this chapter, the program operator may obtain a temporary restraining order in accordance with the provisions of this section. No temporary restraining order shall be issued without notice to the opposite party, unless it shall appear from the facts shown by the affidavit that great or irreparable harm would result to the program operator, a program participant, or an individual residing within 100 feet of the program site before the matter can be heard on notice. The program operator or the program operator's attorney shall state in an affidavit to the court (1) that within a reasonable time prior to the application for a temporary restraining order he or she informed the opposing party or his or her attorney at what time and where the application would be made, (2) that he or she in good faith attempted to so inform the opposing party and his or her attorney but was unable to so inform the opposing attorney or his or her party, specifying the efforts made to contact them, or (3) that for reasons specified he or she should not be required to inform the opposing party or his or her attorney.

A temporary restraining order may be granted upon an affidavit which, to the satisfaction of the court, shows reasonable proof of program misconduct or abuse by the participant, and that great or irreparable harm would result. A temporary restraining order granted under this section shall remain in effect, at the court's discretion, for a period not to exceed five days, unless otherwise modified, extended, or terminated by the court.

(c) The matter shall be made returnable on an order requiring cause to be shown why the injunction should not be granted, not later than five days from the date of the order. When the matter comes up for hearing, the party who obtained the temporary restraining order shall be ready to proceed and shall have personally served upon the opposite party at least two days prior to the hearing, a copy of the petition, a copy of the temporary restraining order, if any, the notice of hearing, copies of all affidavits to be used in the application, and a copy of any points and authorities in support of the petition. If the party who obtained the temporary restraining order is not ready, or if he or she fails to serve a copy of his or her petition, affidavits, and points and authorities, as herein required, the court shall dissolve the temporary restraining order. The court may, upon the filing of an affidavit by the program operator or his or her attorney, that the participant could not be served on time, reissue any temporary restraining order previously issued pursuant to this section and dissolved by the court for failure to serve the participant. An order reissued under this section shall state on its face the new date of expiration of the order. No fees shall be charged for the reissuance of any order under this section. The participant shall be entitled to a continuance, provided that the request is made on or before the hearing date and the hearing shall be set for a date within 15 days of the application, unless the participant requests a later date. The court may extend, or modify and extend, any temporary restraining order until the date and time upon which the hearing is held. The participant may file a response which explains, excuses, justifies, or denies the alleged conduct. No fee shall be charged for the filing of a response. At the hearing, the judge shall receive any testimony or evidence that is relevant, and may make an independent inquiry. If the judge finds by clear and convincing evidence that program misconduct or abuse exists, an injunction shall issue prohibiting that conduct. An injunction issued pursuant to this section shall have a duration of not more than one year. At any time within the three months before the expiration of the injunction, the program operator may apply for renewal of the injunction by filing a new petition for an injunction under this section.

(d) In addition to orders restraining abuse, the court may, upon clear and convincing evidence of abuse, issue an order excluding the participant from the program site, or restraining the participant from coming within 200 feet of the program site, upon an affidavit which, to the satisfaction of the court, shows clear and convincing evidence of abuse of a project employee, another participant, or a person who resides within 100 feet of the program site, by the participant and that great or irreparable injury would result to one of these individuals if the order is not issued. An order excluding the participant from the program site may be included in the temporary restraining order only in an emergency where it is necessary to protect another participant, a project employee, or an individual who lives within 100 feet of the project site from imminent serious bodily injury.

(e) Nothing in this chapter shall preclude either party from representation by private counsel or from appearing on his or her own behalf.

(f) The notice of hearing specified in subdivision (c) shall contain on its face the name and phone number of an office funded by the federal Legal Services Corporation which provides legal services to low-income persons in the county in which the action is filed. The notice shall indicate that this number may be called for legal advice concerning the filing of a response to the petition.

(g) Nothing in this chapter shall preclude the program operator's right to utilize other existing civil remedies. An order issued under this section shall not affect the rights of anyone not named in the order. *(Added by Stats.2016, c. 714 (S.B.944), § 5, eff. Jan. 1, 2017.)*

§ 1954.14. Transmission of copy to law enforcement agency having jurisdiction over program site; willful disobedience; contempt

(a) The clerk shall transmit a copy of each temporary restraining order or injunction or modification or termination thereof, granted under this chapter, by the close of the business day on which the order was granted, to the law enforcement agencies having jurisdiction over the program site. Each law enforcement agency may make available information as to the existence and current status of these orders to law enforcement officers responding to the scene of reported abuse or program misconduct.

(b) Any willful disobedience of any temporary restraining order or injunction granted under this section shall be a misdemeanor pursuant to Section 166 of the Penal Code.

(c) If a participant is found in contempt of a court order issued pursuant to this section, the court may, in addition to any other punishment, modify the order to exclude the participant from the program site. *(Added by Stats.2016, c. 714 (S.B.944), § 5, eff. Jan. 1, 2017.)*

§ 1954.15. Violation of order; breach of agreement; subsequent performance prohibited

If a participant has violated an order issued under Section 1954.13, the participant shall be considered to have failed to perform the conditions of the agreement under which the property is held as provided in subsection 3 of Section 1161 of the Code of Civil Procedure, which conditions cannot afterward be performed. *(Added by Stats.2016, c. 714 (S.B.944), § 5, eff. Jan. 1, 2017.)*

§ 1954.16. Forms and instructions

The Judicial Council shall promulgate forms and related instructions to implement the procedures required by this chapter. The petition and response forms shall be simple and concise. *(Added by Stats.2016, c. 714 (S.B.944), § 5, eff. Jan. 1, 2017.)*

ARTICLE 3. RECOVERY OF DWELLING

Section
1954.17. Recovery of possession of dwelling unit without further notice; abandonment deemed to affect only named individuals.
1954.18. Participant's property; opportunity for removal from unit; remaining property deemed abandoned.

§ 1954.17. Recovery of possession of dwelling unit without further notice; abandonment deemed to affect only named individuals

If, after hearing pursuant to this chapter, an order excluding the participant from the program site is issued, the program operator may, without further notice, take possession of the participant's dwelling unit on the program site. The program operator shall have the same rights to the dwelling unit as if it had been recovered after abandonment in accordance with Section 1951.3 and without objection of the participant. If other participants, including the defendant participant's family members, reside in the dwelling unit, the abandonment shall be deemed only to affect the rights of the individual or individuals against whom the order was issued. *(Added by Stats.2016, c. 714 (S.B.944), § 5, eff. Jan. 1, 2017.)*

§ 1954.18. Participant's property; opportunity for removal from unit; remaining property deemed abandoned

If the program operator takes possession of the property, pursuant to this article, the program operator shall give the subject participant a reasonable opportunity to remove the participant's property from his or her dwelling unit on the program site, and, thereafter, the program operator may consider the remaining subject participant's property to be abandoned property pursuant to Chapter 5 (commencing with Section 1980). *(Added by Stats.2016, c. 714 (S.B.944), § 5, eff. Jan. 1, 2017.)*

CHAPTER 2.5. WATER SERVICE

Section
1954.201. Legislative intent.
1954.202. Definitions.
1954.203. Requirements for submeters; responsibilities of water purveyors.
1954.204. Landlord intending to charge for water service separate from rent in property with submeters; required disclosures.
1954.205. Bill for water service; calculation; inclusion of other lawful charges.
1954.206. Time for reading submeter; due date for payments; information to be included in bill; past due amounts.
1954.207. Beginning and ending of tenancy; submeter readings; deduction of unpaid water service bill from security deposit.
1954.208. Penalty for wasting of water; tenant liability.
1954.209. Information to be maintained and made available at tenant's request.
1954.210. Leak, drip, etc. causing constant or abnormally high water usage; landlord to investigate and rectify condition; tenant may not remove water fixtures or water-saving devices installed by landlord; delays in rectifying condition; tenant failure to provide access; notice from local water purveyor.
1954.211. Landlord entry for purposes relating to submeters.
1954.212. Monthly submeter readings unavailable; charges.
1954.213. Late fees; termination of tenancy; water service may not be shut off.
1954.214. Effect of chapter on ordinances and regulations.
1954.215. Rights or obligations may not be waived.
1954.216. Application of chapter.
1954.217. Submetering systems measuring only portion of water usage put in service before January 1, 2018; exemption.
1954.218. Operative date of chapter.
1954.219. Multiunit structures required to install individual submeters; billing pursuant to this chapter required.

Operative Effect

For operative effect of Chapter 2.5, see Civil Code § 1954.218.

Explanatory Note

For another Chapter 2.5, "Transitional Housing Participant Misconduct", added by Stats.2016, c. 714 (S.B.944), § 5, eff. Jan. 1, 2017, see Civil Code § 1954.10 et seq.

§ 1954.201. Legislative intent

It is the intent of the Legislature in enacting this chapter to do both of the following:

(a) To encourage the conservation of water in multifamily residential rental buildings through means either within the landlord's or the tenant's control.

(b) To establish that the practices involving the submetering of dwelling units for water service are just and reasonable, and include appropriate safeguards for both tenants and landlords. *(Added by Stats.2016, c. 623 (S.B.7), § 2, eff. Jan. 1, 2017, operative Jan. 1, 2018.)*

Operative Effect

For operative effect of Chapter 2.5, see Civil Code § 1954.218.

§ 1954.202. Definitions

For the purposes of this chapter:

(a) "Billing agent" means a person or entity who contracts to provide submetering services to a landlord, including billing.

(b) "Landlord" means an owner of residential rental property. "Landlord" does not include a tenant who rents all or a portion of a dwelling unit to subtenants. "Landlord" does not include a common interest development, as defined in Section 4100 of the Civil Code.

(c) "Property" means real property containing two or more dwelling units that is served by a single master meter.

(d) "Ratio utility billing system" means the allocation of water and sewer costs to tenants based on the square footage, occupancy, or other physical factors of a dwelling unit.

(e) "Rental agreement" includes a fixed-term lease.

(f) "Renting" includes leasing, whether on a periodic or fixed-term basis.

(g) "Submeter" means a device that measures water consumption of an individual rental unit within a multiunit residential structure or mixed-use residential and commercial structure, and that is owned and operated by the landlord of the structure or the landlord's agent. As used in this section, "multiunit residential structure" and "mixed-use residential and commercial structure" mean real property containing two or more dwelling units.

(h) "Water service" includes any charges, whether presented for payment on local water purveyor bills, tax bills, or bills from other entities, related to water treatment, distribution, or usage, including, but not limited to, water, sewer, stormwater, and flood control.

(i) "Water purveyor" means a water purveyor as defined in Section 512 of the Water Code. *(Added by Stats.2016, c. 623 (S.B.7), § 2, eff. Jan. 1, 2017, operative Jan. 1, 2018.)*

Operative Effect

For operative effect of Chapter 2.5, see Civil Code § 1954.218.

§ 1954.203. Requirements for submeters; responsibilities of water purveyors

(a) Submeters used to separately bill tenants for water service shall satisfy each of the following requirements:

(1) The submeter shall be inspected, tested, and verified for commercial purposes pursuant to law, including, but not limited to, Section 12500.5 of the Business and Professions Code.

(2) The submeter shall conform to all laws regarding installation, maintenance, repair, and use, including, but not limited to, regulations established pursuant to Section 12107 of the Business and Professions Code.

(3) The submeter shall measure only water that is supplied for the exclusive use of the particular dwelling unit, and only to an area within the exclusive possession and control of the tenant of the dwelling unit.

(4) The submeter shall be capable of being accessed and read by the tenant of the dwelling unit and read by the landlord without entering the dwelling unit. A submeter installed before January 1, 2018, may be read by the landlord after entry into the unit, in accordance with this chapter and Section 1954.

(5) The submeter shall be reinspected and recalibrated within the time limits specified in law or regulation.

(b) This section does not require a water purveyor to assume responsibility for ensuring compliance with any law or regulation governing installation, certification, maintenance, and testing of submeters and associated onsite plumbing. *(Added by Stats.2016, c. 623 (S.B.7), § 2, eff. Jan. 1, 2017, operative Jan. 1, 2018.)*

Operative Effect

For operative effect of Chapter 2.5, see Civil Code § 1954.218.

§ 1954.204. Landlord intending to charge for water service separate from rent in property with submeters; required disclosures

Before executing a rental agreement, a landlord who intends to charge a tenant separately from rent for water service in a property with submeters shall clearly disclose the following information to the tenant, in writing, in at least 10–point type, which may be incorporated into the rental agreement:

(a) That the tenant will be billed for water service separately from the rent.

(b) An estimate of the monthly bill for water service for dwelling units at the property based on either of the following:

(1) The average or median bill for water service for comparative dwelling units at the property over any three of the past six months.

(2) The amount of the bill based upon average indoor water use of a family of four of approximately 200 gallons per day, and including all other monthly charges that will be assessed. Estimates for other gallons per day may also be included. The estimate shall include a statement that the average family of four uses about 200 gallons of water each day.

(c) The due dates and payment procedures for bills for water service.

(d) A mailing address, an email address, and a toll-free telephone number or a local telephone number for the tenant to contact the landlord or billing agent with questions regarding the water service billing and the days and hours for regular telephone service at either number.

(e) That the monthly bill for water service may only include the following charges:

(1) Payment due for the amount of usage as measured by the submeter and charged at allowable rates in accordance with subdivision (a) of Section 1954.205.

(2) Payment of a portion of the fixed fee charged by the water purveyors for water service.

(3) A fee for the landlord's or billing agent's costs in accordance with paragraph (3) of subdivision (a) of Section 1954.205.

(4) Any late fee, with the amounts and times assessed, in compliance with Section 1954.213.

(f) A statement that the tenant shall notify the landlord of any leaks, drips, water fixtures that do not shut off properly, including, but not limited to, a toilet, or other problems with the water system, including, but not limited to, problems with water-saving devices, and that the landlord is required to investigate, and, if necessary, repair these problems within 21 days, otherwise, the water bill will be adjusted pursuant to law.

(g) A mailing address, an email address, and a toll-free telephone number or a local telephone number for the tenant to use to contact the landlord, or an agent of the landlord, to report any leaks, drips, water fixtures that do not shut off properly, including, but not limited to, a toilet, or other problems with the water system, including, but not limited to, problems with water-saving devices.

§ 1954.204

(h) A statement that the landlord shall provide any of the following information if asked by the tenant:

(1) The location of the submeter.

(2) The calculations used to determine a monthly bill.

(3) The date the submeter was last certified for use, and the date it is next scheduled for certification, if known.

(i) A statement that if the tenant believes that the submeter reading is inaccurate or the submeter is malfunctioning, the tenant shall first notify the landlord in writing and request an investigation. A tenant shall be provided with notice that if an alleged submeter malfunction is not resolved by the landlord, a tenant may contact the local county sealer and request that the submeter be tested. Contact information for the county sealer shall be included in the disclosure to the tenant.

(j) A statement that this disclosure is only a general overview of the laws regarding submeters and that the laws can be found at Chapter 2.5 (commencing with Section 1954.201) of Title 5 of Part 4 of Division 3 of the Civil Code, available online or at most libraries. *(Added by Stats.2016, c. 623 (S.B.7), § 2, eff. Jan. 1, 2017, operative Jan. 1, 2018.)*

Operative Effect

For operative effect of Chapter 2.5, see Civil Code § 1954.218.

§ 1954.205. Bill for water service; calculation; inclusion of other lawful charges

(a) As part of the regular bill for water service, a landlord shall only bill a tenant for the following water service:

(1) A charge for volumetric usage, which may be calculated in any the following ways:

(A) The amount shall be calculated by first determining the proportion of the tenant's usage, as shown by the submeter, to the total usage as shown by the water purveyor's billing. The dollar amount billed to the tenant for usage shall be in that same proportion to the dollar amount for usage shown by the water purveyor's billing.

(B) If the water purveyor charges for volumetric usage based on a tiered rate schedule, the landlord may calculate the charge for a tenant's volumetric usage as described in subparagraph (A) or the landlord may instead divide each tier's volume evenly among the number of dwelling units, and the rate applicable to each block shall be applied to the consumption recorded for each dwelling unit.

(C) If the water purveyor charges the property rates on a per-dwelling unit basis, the tenants may be charged at those exact per unit rates.

(2) Any recurring fixed charge for water service billed to the property by the water purveyors that, at the landlord's discretion, shall be calculated by either of the following:

(A) The tenant's proportion of the total fixed charges charged to the property. The tenant's proportion shall be based on the percentage of the tenant's volumetric water use in relation to the total volumetric water use of the entire property, as shown on the property's water bill during that period.

(B) Dividing the total fixed charges charged to the property equally among the total number of residential units and nonresidential units at the property.

(3) A billing, administrative, or other fee for the landlord's and billing agent's costs, which shall be the lesser of an amount not to exceed four dollars and seventy-five cents ($4.75), as adjusted pursuant to this paragraph or 25 percent of the amount billed pursuant to paragraph (1). Beginning January 1, 2018, the maximum fee authorized by this paragraph may be adjusted each calendar year by the landlord, no higher than a commensurate increase in the Consumer Price Index based on a California fiscal year average for the previous fiscal year, for all urban consumers, as determined by the Department of Finance.

(4) A late charge as assessed pursuant to Section 1954.213.

(b) If a submeter reading for the beginning or end of a billing period is, in good faith, not available, the landlord shall bill the tenant according to Section 1954.212.

(c) This section does not prohibit a landlord or the landlord's billing agent from including any other lawful charges, including, but not limited to, rent, on the same bill. *(Added by Stats.2016, c. 623 (S.B.7), § 2, eff. Jan. 1, 2017, operative Jan. 1, 2018.)*

Operative Effect

For operative effect of Chapter 2.5, see Civil Code § 1954.218.

§ 1954.206. Time for reading submeter; due date for payments; information to be included in bill; past due amounts

(a) Submeters shall be read within three days of the same point in each billing cycle.

(b) Payments shall be due at the same point in each billing cycle. A tenant may agree in writing to receive a bill electronically. A tenant may rescind authorization for electronic delivery of bills at any time. The landlord shall have 30 days to comply with any change in how a tenant requests to receive a bill. A tenant shall not be required to pay a bill electronically.

(c) A bill shall include and separately set forth the following information:

(1) The submeter reading for the beginning date and ending date of the billing cycle, the dates read, and the indicated consumption as determined by subtracting the amount of the beginning date submeter reading from the amount of the ending date submeter reading. If the unit of measure is in something other than gallons, the indicated consumption shall be expressed in gallons.

(2) The amounts charged pursuant to subdivision (a) of Section 1954.205.

(3) The rate or rates charged for the volumetric charge per unit of measure.

(4) The amount, if any, due from the previous month's bill.

(5) The amount, if any, due from bills prior to the previous month's bill.

(6) The late fee, if any, imposed on amounts specified in paragraph (4) or (5).

(7) The total amount due for the billing period.

(8) The due date for the payment.

(9) If a late fee is charged by the landlord, a statement of when the late fees would apply.

(10) The procedure to contact the landlord or billing agent with questions or concerns regarding the bill. Upon request of the tenant, the landlord or billing agent shall respond in writing to any questions or disputes from the tenant. If a billing agent is used, the name of the billing agent shall be disclosed. The tenant shall be provided a mailing address, email address, and telephone number, which shall be either a toll-free or a local number, and the time of regular telephone hours for contact regarding billing inquiries.

(11) A statement that the landlord or billing agent is not the water purveyor that includes the name of the local water purveyor providing the water service to the master meter.

(12) A mailing address, an email address, and a toll-free telephone number or a local telephone number for the tenant to use to contact the landlord, or an agent of the landlord, to report any leaks, drips, water fixtures that do not shut off properly, including, but not limited to, a toilet, or other problems with the water system, including, but not limited to, problems with water-saving devices.

(d) Notwithstanding paragraphs (4) and (5) of subdivision (c), a separate bill may be provided for past due amounts if past due amounts are not included on the current month's bill. *(Added by Stats.2016, c. 623 (S.B.7), § 2, eff. Jan. 1, 2017, operative Jan. 1, 2018.)*

Operative Effect

For operative effect of Chapter 2.5, see Civil Code § 1954.218.

§ 1954.207. Beginning and ending of tenancy; submeter readings; deduction of unpaid water service bill from security deposit

(a) At the beginning of a tenancy, a submeter shall be read after the tenant takes possession. If the regular reading occurs less than five days prior to the tenant taking possession, that reading may be substituted to establish usage. If the submeter is manually read, the first bill may be estimated based on the rate established in subdivision (b) of Section 1954.212.

(b) For a water-service bill at the end of a tenancy, the submeter shall be read within five days, if possible. If the submeter cannot be read within five days at the end of a tenancy, the bill amount for the final month shall be based on the bill amount for the previous month.

(c) The landlord may, at his or her discretion, deduct an unpaid water service bill from the security deposit during or upon termination of a tenancy, if the last water service bill showing the amount due is attached to the documentation required by Section 1950.5. *(Added by Stats.2016, c. 623 (S.B.7), § 2, eff. Jan. 1, 2017, operative Jan. 1, 2018.)*

Operative Effect

For operative effect of Chapter 2.5, see Civil Code § 1954.218.

§ 1954.208. Penalty for wasting of water; tenant liability

Unless it can be documented that a penalty is primarily the result of a tenant's or tenants' failure to comply with state or local water use regulations or restrictions, or both, regarding wasting of water, a landlord shall not charge, recover, or allow to be charged or recovered, fees incurred by the landlord from the water purveyors, billing agent, or any other person for any deposit, disconnection, reconnection, late payment by the landlord, or any other penalty assessed against the landlord. This section shall not prevent a landlord from charging a tenant for the tenant's late payment of any bill. *(Added by Stats.2016, c. 623 (S.B.7), § 2, eff. Jan. 1, 2017, operative Jan. 1, 2018.)*

Operative Effect

For operative effect of Chapter 2.5, see Civil Code § 1954.218.

§ 1954.209. Information to be maintained and made available at tenant's request

The landlord shall maintain and make available in writing, at the tenant's written or electronic request, within seven days after the request, the following:

(a) The date the submeter was last inspected, tested, and verified, and the date by which it shall be reinspected, tested, and verified under law, if available. If this information is not available, the landlord shall disclose that the information is not available.

(b) The data used to calculate the tenant's bill, as follows:

(1) The most recent water bill for the property's master water meter showing the recurring fixed charge for water service billed to the property by the water purveyor, and the usage charges for the property, including any tiered amounts.

(2) Any other bills for water service, as defined in subdivision (h) of Section 1954.202, for the property.

(3) The number of dwelling units in the property used in the last billing period to calculate the tenant's water service charges.

(4) If not shown on the bill for the property, the per unit charges for volumetric water usage, including any tiered amounts.

(5) The formula used to calculate the charge for the tenant's volumetric water usage.

(c) The location of the submeter. *(Added by Stats.2016, c. 623 (S.B.7), § 2, eff. Jan. 1, 2017, operative Jan. 1, 2018.)*

Operative Effect

For operative effect of Chapter 2.5, see Civil Code § 1954.218.

§ 1954.210. Leak, drip, etc. causing constant or abnormally high water usage; landlord to investigate and rectify condition; tenant may not remove water fixtures or water-saving devices installed by landlord; delays in rectifying condition; tenant failure to provide access; notice from local water purveyor

(a) If a tenant notifies the landlord of, or the landlord otherwise becomes aware of, a leak, a drip, a water fixture

§ 1954.210 OBLIGATIONS

that does not shut off property,[1] including, but not limited to, a toilet, a problem with a water-saving device, or other problem with the water system that causes constant or abnormally high water usage, or a submeter reading indicates constant or abnormal high water usage, the landlord shall have the condition investigated, and, if warranted, rectify the condition.

(b) A tenant shall not remove any water fixtures or water-saving devices that have been installed by the landlord.

(c) If the condition is rectified more than 21 days after the tenant provides notice to the landlord or the landlord otherwise becomes aware of a leak, a drip, a water fixture that does not shut off properly, including, but not limited to, a toilet, a problem with a water-saving device, or other problem with the water system that causes constant or abnormally high water usage, or a submeter reading indicates constant or abnormally high water usage, pursuant to subdivision (a), the tenant's volumetric usage for any month or months that include the period between 21 days after the initial investigation and the repair shall be deemed to be fifteen dollars ($15) or actual usage, whichever is less. At the landlord's option, if submeter readings are available to determine the usage at a point prior to investigation and a point following repair, usage shall be deemed to be fifty cents ($0.50) per day for those days between the two submeter readings or actual usage, whichever is less.

(d) If the condition remains unrectified for 180 days after investigation, no further volumetric usage charges may be imposed until the condition is repaired.

(e) If, in order to comply with subdivision (a), the landlord has provided notice pursuant to Section 1954, and the tenant has failed to provide access to the dwelling unit, then the charges shall not be determined pursuant to subdivisions (c) and (d).

(f) If the local water purveyor notifies the landlord of constant or abnormally high water usage at the property, the landlord shall investigate and, if possible, rectify the cause of the high water usage. *(Added by Stats.2016, c. 623 (S.B.7), § 2, eff. Jan. 1, 2017, operative Jan. 1, 2018.)*

[1] So in enrolled bill. Probably should be "properly".

Operative Effect

For operative effect of Chapter 2.5, see Civil Code § 1954.218.

§ 1954.211. Landlord entry for purposes relating to submeters

The landlord may enter a dwelling unit as follows:

(a) For the purpose of installing, repairing, or replacing a submeter, or for the purpose of investigating or rectifying a condition causing constant or abnormally high water usage, as required by subdivision (a) of Section 1954.210, if the requirements of Section 1954 are met.

(b) To read a submeter, if the requirements of this chapter and Section 1954 are met. Notwithstanding paragraph (3) of subdivision (d) of Section 1954, notice shall be given only in writing. *(Added by Stats.2016, c. 623 (S.B.7), § 2, eff. Jan. 1, 2017, operative Jan. 1, 2018.)*

Operative Effect

For operative effect of Chapter 2.5, see Civil Code § 1954.218.

§ 1954.212. Monthly submeter readings unavailable; charges

(a) If a monthly submeter reading necessary to measure volumetric usage is unavailable, and the tenant has provided access to the submeter, the tenant may be charged 75 percent of the average amount billed for volumetric usage for the last three months for which complete billing information is available. The adjustment shall be disclosed on the bill.

(b) If no complete billing information is available for the prior three months, the volumetric usage charge shall be deemed to be fifty cents ($0.50) per day that the data is not available.

(c) If monthly submeter readings remain unavailable for more than six months, the volumetric usage charge shall be deemed to be zero for any subsequent month that the data is not available. *(Added by Stats.2016, c. 623 (S.B.7), § 2, eff. Jan. 1, 2017, operative Jan. 1, 2018.)*

Operative Effect

For operative effect of Chapter 2.5, see Civil Code § 1954.218.

§ 1954.213. Late fees; termination of tenancy; water service may not be shut off

(a) A tenant may be charged a late fee for any water service bill not paid 25 days after mailing or other transmittal of the bill. If the 25th day falls on a Saturday, Sunday, or holiday, the late fee shall not be imposed until the day after the first business day following the 25th day.

(b)(1) A late fee of up to seven dollars ($7) may be imposed if any amount of a water service bill remains unpaid after the time described in subdivision (a). A late fee of up to ten dollars ($10) may be imposed in each subsequent bill if any amount remains unpaid.

(2) The total late fee imposed in any 12–month period upon the amount of a bill that remains unpaid shall not exceed 10 percent of the unpaid amount, exclusive of the administrative fee imposed pursuant to paragraph (3) of subdivision (a) of Section 1954.205 and the late fee imposed pursuant to paragraph (1).

(3) If any partial payments are made, they shall be credited against the bill that has been outstanding the longest.

(c) Notwithstanding subdivision (c) of Section 1954.207, if the water bill remains unpaid for 180 days after the date upon which it is due or the amount of the unpaid water bill equals or exceeds two hundred dollars ($200), the landlord may terminate the tenancy in accordance with Section 1161 of the Code of Civil Procedure with the service of a three-day notice to perform the conditions or covenants or quit upon the tenant.

(d) Water service charges under this chapter shall not constitute rent.

(e) The water service to a dwelling unit shall not be shut off or otherwise interfered with by the landlord for any reason, including nonpayment of a bill. Notwithstanding the foregoing, a landlord or its agent may shut off water service to a dwelling unit or the property, in order to make repairs, replacements of equipment, or perform other maintenance at the property. (Added by Stats.2016, c. 623 (S.B.7), § 2, eff. Jan. 1, 2017, operative Jan. 1, 2018.)

Operative Effect

For operative effect of Chapter 2.5, see Civil Code § 1954.218.

§ 1954.214. Effect of chapter on ordinances and regulations

This chapter does not preclude or preempt an ordinance or regulation adopted prior to January 1, 2013, that regulates the approval of submeter types or the installation, maintenance, reading, billing, or testing of submeters and associated onsite plumbing. (Added by Stats.2016, c. 623 (S.B.7), § 2, eff. Jan. 1, 2017, operative Jan. 1, 2018.)

Operative Effect

For operative effect of Chapter 2.5, see Civil Code § 1954.218.

§ 1954.215. Rights or obligations may not be waived

The rights or obligations established under this chapter shall not be waived. Any purported waiver is void. (Added by Stats.2016, c. 623 (S.B.7), § 2, eff. Jan. 1, 2017, operative Jan. 1, 2018.)

Operative Effect

For operative effect of Chapter 2.5, see Civil Code § 1954.218.

§ 1954.216. Application of chapter

(a) This chapter applies to the following:

(1) All dwelling units offered for rent or rented in a building where submeters were required to be installed pursuant to a building standard adopted in accordance with Section 17922.14 of the Health and Safety Code.

(2) All dwelling units where submeters are used to charge a tenant separately for water service.

(b) Nothing in this chapter shall be construed to apply to any dwelling units other than those described in subdivision (a).

(c) Nothing in this chapter shall be construed to apply or create a public policy or requirement that favors or disfavors the use of a ratio utility billing system. (Added by Stats.2016, c. 623 (S.B.7), § 2, eff. Jan. 1, 2017, operative Jan. 1, 2018.)

Operative Effect

For operative effect of Chapter 2.5, see Civil Code § 1954.218.

§ 1954.217. Submetering systems measuring only portion of water usage put in service before January 1, 2018; exemption

A submetering system that measures only a portion of a dwelling unit's water usage, including, but not limited to, a system that measures only hot water usage, shall not be subject to this chapter if the system was first put in service before January 1, 2018. (Added by Stats.2016, c. 623 (S.B.7), § 2, eff. Jan. 1, 2017, operative Jan. 1, 2018.)

Operative Effect

For operative effect of Chapter 2.5, see Civil Code § 1954.218.

§ 1954.218. Operative date of chapter

This chapter shall become operative on January 1, 2018. (Added by Stats.2016, c. 623 (S.B.7), § 2, eff. Jan. 1, 2017, operative Jan. 1, 2018.)

§ 1954.219. Multiunit structures required to install individual submeters; billing pursuant to this chapter required

Any property that is required to install individual submeters pursuant to Article 5 (commencing with Section 537) of Chapter 8 of Division 1 of the Water Code shall at all times be required to bill residents for water service pursuant to this chapter. (Added by Stats.2016, c. 623 (S.B.7), § 2, eff. Jan. 1, 2017, operative Jan. 1, 2018.)

Operative Effect

For operative effect of Chapter 2.5, see Civil Code § 1954.218.

CHAPTER 2.6. COMMERCIAL RENTAL CONTROL

Section
1954.25. Legislative findings.
1954.26. Definitions.
1954.27. Rental control enactment or enforcement by public entity; limitations on construction of chapter.
1954.28. Permissible regulation by or agreements with public entities.
1954.29. Zoning and planning and business licenses; effect of chapter on public entity powers.
1954.30. Effect of chapter on powers of public entity.
1954.31. Public entity enactment relating to lease termination upon expiration of its term; contents; construction; application.

§ 1954.25. Legislative findings

The Legislature finds that the price charged for commercial real property is a matter of statewide concern. Price controls on commercial rents discourage expansion of commercial development and entrepreneurial enterprise. These controls also discourage competition in the open market by giving artificial price benefits to one enterprise to the disadvantage of another. Because the impact of these controls goes beyond the local boundaries within which the controls are imposed, the adverse economic consquences [1] become statewide.

In order to prevent this statewide economic drain from occurring, the Legislature hereby enacts a uniform system with respect to commercial rents, which shall apply to every local jurisdiction in the state. This legislative action is needed to prevent the imposition of artificial barriers on commercial rents, as well as to define those areas not included within the definition of commercial real property.

In making these findings and in enacting this chapter, the Legislature expressly declares its intent that this chapter shall not apply or be interpreted to apply to local rental controls on residential real property. *(Added by Stats.1987, c. 824, § 2.)*

[1] So in chaptered copy. Probably should be "consequences".

Cross References

Commercial real property defined for purposes of this Chapter, see Civil Code § 1954.26.
Rent defined for purposes of this Chapter, see Civil Code § 1954.26.

§ 1954.26. Definitions

As used in this chapter, the following terms have the following meanings:

(a) "Owner" includes any person, acting as principal or through an agent, having the right to offer commercial real property for rent, and includes any predecessor in interest to the owner.

(b) "Price" includes any charge or fee, however denominated, for the hiring of commercial real property and includes any security or deposit subject to Section 1950.7.

(c) "Public entity" has the same meaning as defined in Section 811.2 of the Government Code.

(d) "Commercial real property" includes any part, portion, or unit thereof, and any related facilities, space, or services, except the following:

(1) Any dwelling or dwelling unit subject to the provisions of Section 1940.

(2) Any accommodation in any residential hotel, as defined in Section 50519 of the Health and Safety Code, or comparable accommodations which are specifically regulated by a public entity in structures where 20 percent or more of the accommodations are occupied by persons as their primary residence.

(3) Any hotel unit not otherwise specified in paragraph (1) or (2) that is located in a structure with 20 or more units or in which 20 percent or more of the accommodations were occupied as of August 5, 1987, by persons as their primary residence, if, in either circumstance, the unit was subject to rental controls on August 5, 1987, provided that any control exercised thereafter is in accordance with the system of controls in effect on August 5, 1987.

(4) Any space or dwelling unit in any mobilehome park, as defined in Section 18214 of the Health and Safety Code.

(e) "Rent" means to hire real property and includes a lease or sublease.

(f) "Commercial rental control" includes any action of a public entity taken by statute, charter, ordinance, resolution, administrative regulation, or any other governmental enactment to establish, continue, implement, or enforce any control or system of controls, on the price at which, or the term for which, commercial real property may be offered for rent, or control or system of controls which would select, mandate, dictate, or otherwise designate a specific tenant or specific person or entity with whom the owner must negotiate on the formation, extension, or renewal of a tenancy; or any other enactment which has such a purpose.

(g) "Tenant" includes a lessee, subtenant, and sublessee.

(h) "Term" means the period of time for which real property is rented or offered for rent, and includes any provision for a termination or extension of such a period or renewal thereof, except that nothing in this chapter supersedes the specific provisions of this code or of the Code of Civil Procedure which of themselves establish, prescribe, limit, or define the term for which real property may be rented.

(i) "Impasse notice" means a written notice which states either of the following:

(1) That the owner has not received from the tenant an offer of any terms for an extension or renewal of the lease which are acceptable to the owner, or an acceptance by the tenant of any offer of terms by the owner, and that an impasse with respect to any agreement on a lease extension or renewal has been reached.

(2) That the owner is not willing to extend or renew the lease.

(j) "Negotiation notice" means a written notice by a tenant in privity of estate, and in privity of contract with the owner, stating either of the following:

(1) That the tenant offers to extend or renew the lease on terms set forth in the notice.

(2) That the tenant solicits an offer for the extension or renewal of the lease from the owner.

(k) "Deliver" means to deliver by personal service or by placing a copy of the notice in the mail, postage prepaid, by certified mail, return receipt requested, addressed to the party at the address for the receipt of notices under the lease.

(*l*) "Developer" means any person who enters into an agreement with a redevelopment agency for the purpose of developing specific commercial real property within a redevelopment project area with the intention of acquiring ownership of that property, even if that person does not own that property when the agreement is executed. *(Added by Stats.1987, c. 824, § 2.)*

Cross References

Abandonment of commercial property by lessee, notice by lessor, form, defenses of lessee, see Civil Code § 1951.35.
Disposition of personal property remaining on premises at termination of tenancy, application to commercial real property, see Civil Code § 1980.5.
Hiring defined, see Civil Code § 1925.

§ 1954.27. Rental control enactment or enforcement by public entity; limitations on construction of chapter

(a) No public entity shall enact any measure constituting commercial rental control, nor shall any public entity enforce any commercial rental control, whether enacted prior to or on or after January 1, 1988.

(b) However, nothing in this chapter shall be construed to do any of the following:

(1) Relieve any party to a commercial lease or rental agreement of the duty to perform any obligation thereunder.

(2) Preclude express establishment in a commercial lease or rental agreement of the price at which real property may be offered to a subtenant or sublessee.

(3) Impair any obligation of any contract entered into prior to January 1, 1988.

(4) Affect any provision of, or requirement for mitigation of damages under, Sections 1951 to 1952.6, inclusive.

(5) Limit any adjustment of price required or permitted by law due to constructive eviction.

(6) Enlarge or diminish in any way any power which a public entity may have with respect to regulation of rental rates or the ownership, conveyance, or use of any property specified in paragraph (1), (2), or (3) of subdivision (d) of Section 1954.26.

(7) Relieve any party of any requirement or mandate to arbitrate, or deprive any party of any right to arbitrate or compel arbitration, which mandate or right exists pursuant to Title 9 (commencing with Section 1280) of Part 3 of the Code of Civil Procedure, titled "Arbitration," Chapter 2.5 (commencing with Section 1141.10) of Title 3 of Part 3 of the Code of Civil Procedure, titled "Judicial Arbitration," Title 1 (commencing with Section 1823) of Part 3 of the Code of Civil Procedure, titled "Pilot Projects," or any other provision of state law.

(8) Affect in any way, or preclude the inclusion of, any provision in a lease creating any lawful option, right of first refusal, or any covenant to renew or extend the lease or sell the real property or any interest therein.

(9) Relieve any person of any duty or deprive any person of any right or cause of action which may exist pursuant to Section 51, 53, or 782. *(Added by Stats.1987, c. 824, § 2.)*

Cross References

Commercial rental control defined for purposes of this Chapter, see Civil Code § 1954.26.
Price defined for purposes of this Chapter, see Civil Code § 1954.26.
Public entity defined for purposes of this Chapter, see Civil Code § 1954.26.

§ 1954.28. Permissible regulation by or agreements with public entities

Nothing in this chapter limits or affects public entities with respect to any of the following:

(a) The Eminent Domain Law, Title 7 (commencing with Section 1230.10) of Part 3 of the Code of Civil Procedure.

(b) Abatement of nuisances. However, except as to conditions expressly defined as nuisances by statute, authority to abate or bring actions to abate nuisances shall not be used to circumvent the limitations of this chapter with respect to conditions not manifesting the quantum and character of unreasonableness and injuriousness to constitute a nuisance under law.

(c) The Airport Approaches Zoning Law, Article 6.5 (commencing with Section 50485) of Chapter 2 of Part 1 of Division 1 of Title 5 of the Government Code.

(d) Any contract or agreement by which an owner agrees with a public entity to offer any real property for rent at a stipulated or maximum price or under a specified formula for ascertaining a stipulated or maximum price, in consideration for a direct financial contribution; any written contract between a redevelopment agency and an owner or developer of commercial real property within a redevelopment project area; or any written development agreement entered into pursuant to Article 2.5 (commencing with Section 65864) of Chapter 4 of Division 1 of Title 7 of the Government Code. Any contract or agreement specified in this subdivision is not enforceable against an owner who became an owner (1) without actual knowledge of the contract or agreement, and (2) more than 30 days prior to the recording with the county recorder of a written memorandum of the contract or agreement specifically describing its terms and identifying the real property and the owner. The county recorder shall index these memorandums in the grantor-grantee index.

(e) Article 2 (commencing with Section 5020) of Chapter 1 of Division 5 of the Public Resources Code, relating to historical resources.

(f) The Subdivision Map Act, Division 2 (commencing with Section 66410) of Title 7 of the Government Code.

(g) Any contract or agreement entered into by a public entity relating to the transfer, lease, or license of commercial real property owned or leased by that public entity, except any requirement enacted pursuant to Section 1954.31. *(Added by Stats.1987, c. 824, § 2.)*

Cross References

Commercial real property defined for purposes of this Chapter, see Civil Code § 1954.26.
Developer defined for purposes of this Chapter, see Civil Code § 1954.26.
Owner defined for purposes of this Chapter, see Civil Code § 1954.26.
Price defined for purposes of this Chapter, see Civil Code § 1954.26.
Public entity defined for purposes of this Chapter, see Civil Code § 1954.26.
Rent defined for purposes of this Chapter, see Civil Code § 1954.26.
Term defined for purposes of this Chapter, see Civil Code § 1954.26.

§ 1954.29. Zoning and planning and business licenses; effect of chapter on public entity powers

Nothing in this chapter shall, with respect to a public entity:

(a) Grant, enlarge, or diminish any power (1) which it may possess under the provisions of, and for the purposes of, Division 1 (commencing with Section 65000) of Title 7 of the Government Code, (2) with respect to charter cities, planning, or zoning powers granted under Section 5 of Article XI of the California Constitution, or (3) any power which it may possess to mitigate the impact caused by the construction, reconstruction, demolition, or alteration of the size of any commercial real property. However, this subdivision does not apply to any actions taken for the clear or systematic purpose of circumventing this chapter.

(b) Grant, repeal, enlarge, or diminish any authority to require a business license, whether for regulation or revenue. *(Added by Stats.1987, c. 824, § 2.)*

Cross References

Commercial real property defined for purposes of this Chapter, see Civil Code § 1954.26.
Public entity defined for purposes of this Chapter, see Civil Code § 1954.26.

§ 1954.30. Effect of chapter on powers of public entity

Nothing in this chapter grants or augments any authority of a public entity which it does not possess independent of this

§ 1954.30

chapter, nor diminish any power of a public entity except as expressly provided in this chapter. *(Added by Stats.1987, c. 824, § 2.)*

Cross References

Public entity defined for purposes of this Chapter, see Civil Code § 1954.26.

§ 1954.31. Public entity enactment relating to lease termination upon expiration of its term; contents; construction; application

A public entity may by enactment of a statute, charter or charter amendment, or ordinance, establish a requirement for notice relating to the termination of a lease of commercial real property due to the expiration of its term.

(a) The enactment shall contain provisions dealing with any or all of the following:

(1) The delivery of a negotiation notice by a tenant.

(2) A requirement for an owner to deliver an impasse notice at any time after delivery of the negotiation notice, except that:

(A) The requirement shall be inapplicable unless the tenant has been required to deliver a negotiation notice not less than 270 days before the expiration of the lease, and has done so.

(B) The mandate for delivery of an impasse notice shall not occur earlier than 180 days before expiration of the lease.

(C) No impasse notice shall be required if the parties have executed a renewal or extension of the lease.

(D) Provision shall be made that the notice will include, in a form of type which will distinguish it from the body of the text of the balance of the notice, a disclosure reading, either:

(i) The giving of this notice does not necessarily preclude further dialogue or negotiation on an extension or renewal of the lease if the parties choose to negotiate, but the delivery of this notice discharges all obligations of _____ (the owner) under provisions of _____ (the enactment) and Section 1954.31 of the Civil Code; or

(ii) By giving this notice _____ (the owner) declares that he or she does not intend to negotiate further on any extension or renewal of the lease.

(3) Establish that a bad faith failure to comply with the enactment is subject to a remedy for actual damages.

(4) Any remedy under the enactment or Section 1954.31 shall be available only by an action brought by the owner or the tenant.

(b) The enactment shall contain (or shall be deemed to contain), a provision that:

(1) A tenant may not exercise any right pursuant to the enactment or this chapter, unless the tenant has performed the terms of the lease in such manner as would entitle the tenant to exercise any option he or she might possess under the lease.

(2) No right or cause of action accruing to a tenant pursuant to the enactment or this chapter, may be assigned other than to a person who is a lawful assignee of the lease, is in lawful possession of the premises under the lease, and is in compliance with paragraph (1).

(3) Nothing in the enactment or this chapter creates or imposes, nor shall be construed to create or impose, a duty to extend or renew, or to negotiate on an extension or renewal, of any lease; nor shall the delivery or receipt of any notice provided for by the enactment or by this chapter, constitute a waiver of any rights to continued performance under the covenants under the lease or to actions for possession.

(4) The delivery of any notice pursuant to the enactment or this chapter shall create a rebuttable presumption affecting the burden of proof, that the notice has been properly given.

(c) No enactment shall provide, or be deemed to provide:

(1) For any extension of the term of any lease without the mutual, written consent of the owner and the tenant.

(2) For any requirement on either party to offer to extend or renew or to negotiate an extension or renewal of the lease.

(3) Bar any action brought to recover possession whether by ejectment, unlawful detainer, or other lawful means.

(4) Any remedy under the enactment or this chapter, other than that which may be provided pursuant to paragraph (3) of subdivision (a).

(d) The provisions of any enactment adopted pursuant to this section shall not apply to:

(1) Any lease or rental agreement which is not in writing, which constitutes a tenancy at will, which is for a term of less than one year or for an unspecified term, which is a month-to-month tenancy or a tenancy at sufferance.

(2) Any lease, the term of which expires within 270 days after the effective date of the enactment. *(Added by Stats.1987, c. 824, § 2.)*

Cross References

Burden of proof, generally, see Evidence Code § 500 et seq.
Commercial real property defined for purposes of this Chapter, see Civil Code § 1954.26.
Deliver defined for purposes of this Chapter, see Civil Code § 1954.26.
Impasse notice defined for purposes of this Chapter, see Civil Code § 1954.26.
Negotiation notice defined for purposes of this Chapter, see Civil Code § 1954.26.
Owner defined for purposes of this Chapter, see Civil Code § 1954.26.
Public entity defined for purposes of this Chapter, see Civil Code § 1954.26.
Tenant defined for purposes of this Chapter, see Civil Code § 1954.26.
Term defined for purposes of this Chapter, see Civil Code § 1954.26.

CHAPTER 2.7. RESIDENTIAL RENT CONTROL

Section
1954.50. Short title.
1954.51. Definitions.
1954.52. Rental rates; establishment by owner; conditions.
1954.53. Initial rental rate; establishment by owner; conditions; exceptions.
1954.535. Written notice of termination by owner.
1954.54. Rejected,.

Cross References

Hiring of real property, rent control, application to initial rent established under this chapter, see Civil Code § 1947.8.

Real property, limitation of rent increase, subleases, notice, see Civil Code § 1947.12.

Rent control, calculation of fair return to owner, operation of provisions dependent upon repeal of this chapter, see Civil Code § 1947.15.

§ 1954.50. Short title

This chapter shall be known and may be cited as the Costa–Hawkins Rental Housing Act. *(Added by Stats.1995, c. 331 (A.B.1164), § 1.)*

§ 1954.51. Definitions

As used in this chapter, the following terms have the following meanings:

(a) "Comparable units" means rental units that have approximately the same living space, have the same number of bedrooms, are located in the same or similar neighborhoods, and feature the same, similar, or equal amenities and housing services.

(b) "Owner" includes any person, acting as principal or through an agent, having the right to offer residential real property for rent, and includes a predecessor in interest to the owner, except that this term does not include the owner or operator of a mobilehome park, or the owner of a mobilehome or his or her agent.

(c) "Prevailing market rent" means the rental rate that would be authorized pursuant to 42 U.S.C.A. 1437(f), as calculated by the United States Department of Housing and Urban Development pursuant to Part 888 of Title 24 of the Code of Federal Regulations.

(d) "Public entity" has the same meaning as set forth in Section 811.2 of the Government Code.

(e) "Residential real property" includes any dwelling or unit that is intended for human habitation.

(f) "Tenancy" includes the lawful occupation of property and includes a lease or sublease. *(Added by Stats.1995, c. 331 (A.B.1164), § 1.)*

§ 1954.52. Rental rates; establishment by owner; conditions

(a) Notwithstanding any other provision of law, an owner of residential real property may establish the initial and all subsequent rental rates for a dwelling or a unit about which any of the following is true:

(1) It has a certificate of occupancy issued after February 1, 1995.

(2) It has already been exempt from the residential rent control ordinance of a public entity on or before February 1, 1995, pursuant to a local exemption for newly constructed units.

(3)(A) It is alienable separate from the title to any other dwelling unit or is a subdivided interest in a subdivision, as specified in subdivision (b), (d), or (f) of Section 11004.5 of the Business and Professions Code.

(B) This paragraph does not apply to either of the following:

(i) A dwelling or unit where the preceding tenancy has been terminated by the owner by notice pursuant to Section 1946.1 or has been terminated upon a change in the terms of the tenancy noticed pursuant to Section 827.

(ii) A condominium dwelling or unit that has not been sold separately by the subdivider to a bona fide purchaser for value. The initial rent amount of the unit for purposes of this chapter shall be the lawful rent in effect on May 7, 2001, unless the rent amount is governed by a different provision of this chapter. However, if a condominium dwelling or unit meets the criteria of paragraph (1) or (2) of subdivision (a), or if all the dwellings or units except one have been sold separately by the subdivider to bona fide purchasers for value, and the subdivider has occupied that remaining unsold condominium dwelling or unit as his or her principal residence for at least one year after the subdivision occurred, then subparagraph (A) of paragraph (3) shall apply to that unsold condominium dwelling or unit.

(C) Where a dwelling or unit in which the initial or subsequent rental rates are controlled by an ordinance or charter provision in effect on January 1, 1995, the following shall apply:

(i) An owner of real property as described in this paragraph may establish the initial and all subsequent rental rates for all existing and new tenancies in effect on or after January 1, 1999, if the tenancy in effect on or after January 1, 1999, was created between January 1, 1996, and December 31, 1998.

(ii) Commencing on January 1, 1999, an owner of real property as described in this paragraph may establish the initial and all subsequent rental rates for all new tenancies if the previous tenancy was in effect on December 31, 1995.

(iii) The initial rental rate for a dwelling or unit as described in this paragraph in which the initial rental rate is controlled by an ordinance or charter provision in effect on January 1, 1995, may not, until January 1, 1999, exceed the amount calculated pursuant to subdivision (c) of Section 1954.53. An owner of residential real property as described in this paragraph may, until January 1, 1999, establish the initial rental rate for a dwelling or unit only where the tenant has voluntarily vacated, abandoned, or been evicted pursuant to paragraph (2) of Section 1161 of the Code of Civil Procedure.

(b) Subdivision (a) does not apply where the owner has otherwise agreed by contract with a public entity in consideration for a direct financial contribution or any other forms of assistance specified in Chapter 4.3 (commencing with Section 65915) of Division 1 of Title 7 of the Government Code.

(c) Nothing in this section shall be construed to affect the authority of a public entity that may otherwise exist to regulate or monitor the basis for eviction.

(d) This section does not apply to any dwelling or unit that contains serious health, safety, fire, or building code violations, excluding those caused by disasters for which a citation has been issued by the appropriate governmental agency and which has remained unabated for six months or longer preceding the vacancy. *(Added by Stats.1995, c. 331 (A.B. 1164), § 1. Amended by Stats.2001, c. 729 (S.B.985), § 2; Stats.2004, c. 568 (S.B.1145), § 4.)*

§ 1954.53. Initial rental rate; establishment by owner; conditions; exceptions

(a) Notwithstanding any other provision of law, an owner of residential real property may establish the initial rental rate for a dwelling or unit, except where any of the following applies:

(1) The previous tenancy has been terminated by the owner by notice pursuant to Section 1946.1 or has been terminated upon a change in the terms of the tenancy noticed pursuant to Section 827, except a change permitted by law in the amount of rent or fees. For the purpose of this paragraph, the owner's termination or nonrenewal of a contract or recorded agreement with a governmental agency that provides for a rent limitation to a qualified tenant, shall be construed as a change in the terms of the tenancy pursuant to Section 827.

(A) In a jurisdiction that controls by ordinance or charter provision the rental rate for a dwelling or unit, an owner who terminates or fails to renew a contract or recorded agreement with a governmental agency that provides for a rent limitation to a qualified tenant may not set an initial rent for three years following the date of the termination or nonrenewal of the contract or agreement. For any new tenancy established during the three-year period, the rental rate for a new tenancy established in that vacated dwelling or unit shall be at the same rate as the rent under the terminated or nonrenewed contract or recorded agreement with a governmental agency that provided for a rent limitation to a qualified tenant, plus any increases authorized after the termination or cancellation of the contract or recorded agreement.

(B) Subparagraph (A) does not apply to any new tenancy of 12 months or more duration established after January 1, 2000, pursuant to the owner's contract or recorded agreement with a governmental agency that provides for a rent limitation to a qualified tenant, unless the prior vacancy in that dwelling or unit was pursuant to a nonrenewed or canceled contract or recorded agreement with a governmental agency that provides for a rent limitation to a qualified tenant as set forth in that subparagraph.

(2) The owner has otherwise agreed by contract with a public entity in consideration for a direct financial contribution or any other forms of assistance specified in Chapter 4.3 (commencing with Section 65915) of Division 1 of Title 7 of the Government Code.

(3) The initial rental rate for a dwelling or unit whose initial rental rate is controlled by an ordinance or charter provision in effect on January 1, 1995, may not until January 1, 1999, exceed the amount calculated pursuant to subdivision (c).

(b) Subdivision (a) applies to, and includes, renewal of the initial hiring by the same tenant, lessee, authorized subtenant, or authorized sublessee for the entire period of his or her occupancy at the rental rate established for the initial hiring.

(c) The rental rate of a dwelling or unit whose initial rental rate is controlled by ordinance or charter provision in effect on January 1, 1995, shall, until January 1, 1999, be established in accordance with this subdivision. Where the previous tenant has voluntarily vacated, abandoned, or been evicted pursuant to paragraph (2) of Section 1161 of Code of Civil Procedure, an owner of residential real property may, no more than twice, establish the initial rental rate for a dwelling or unit in an amount that is no greater than 15 percent more than the rental rate in effect for the immediately preceding tenancy or in an amount that is 70 percent of the prevailing market rent for comparable units, whichever amount is greater.

The initial rental rate established pursuant to this subdivision may not substitute for or replace increases in rental rates otherwise authorized pursuant to law.

(d)(1) Nothing in this section or any other provision of law shall be construed to preclude express establishment in a lease or rental agreement of the rental rates to be applicable in the event the rental unit subject thereto is sublet. Nothing in this section shall be construed to impair the obligations of contracts entered into prior to January 1, 1996.

(2) If the original occupant or occupants who took possession of the dwelling or unit pursuant to the rental agreement with the owner no longer permanently reside there, an owner may increase the rent by any amount allowed by this section to a lawful sublessee or assignee who did not reside at the dwelling or unit prior to January 1, 1996.

(3) This subdivision does not apply to partial changes in occupancy of a dwelling or unit where one or more of the occupants of the premises, pursuant to the agreement with the owner provided for above, remains an occupant in lawful possession of the dwelling or unit, or where a lawful sublessee or assignee who resided at the dwelling or unit prior to January 1, 1996, remains in possession of the dwelling or unit. Nothing contained in this section shall be construed to enlarge or diminish an owner's right to withhold consent to a sublease or assignment.

(4) Acceptance of rent by the owner does not operate as a waiver or otherwise prevent enforcement of a covenant prohibiting sublease or assignment or as a waiver of an owner's rights to establish the initial rental rate, unless the owner has received written notice from the tenant that is party to the agreement and thereafter accepted rent.

(e) Nothing in this section shall be construed to affect any authority of a public entity that may otherwise exist to regulate or monitor the grounds for eviction.

(f) This section does not apply to any dwelling or unit if all the following conditions are met:

(1) The dwelling or unit has been cited in an inspection report by the appropriate governmental agency as containing serious health, safety, fire, or building code violations, as defined by Section 17920.3 of the Health and Safety Code, excluding any violation caused by a disaster.

(2) The citation was issued at least 60 days prior to the date of the vacancy.

(3) The cited violation had not been abated when the prior tenant vacated and had remained unabated for 60 days or for a longer period of time. However, the 60-day time period may be extended by the appropriate governmental agency that issued the citation. *(Added by Stats.1995, c. 331 (A.B.1164), § 1. Amended by Stats.1996, c. 1031 (A.B.3244), § 1; Stats.1999, c. 590 (S.B.1098), § 2; Stats.2004, c. 568 (S.B.1145), § 5.)*

Cross References

Hiring defined, see Civil Code § 1925.

§ 1954.535. Written notice of termination by owner

Where an owner terminates or fails to renew a contract or recorded agreement with a governmental agency that provides for rent limitations to a qualified tenant, the tenant or tenants who were the beneficiaries of the contract or recorded agreement shall be given at least 90 days' written notice of the effective date of the termination and shall not be obligated to pay more than the tenant's portion of the rent, as calculated under the contract or recorded agreement to be terminated, for 90 days following receipt of the notice of termination of nonrenewal of the contract. *(Added by Stats.1999, c. 590 (S.B.1098), § 3.)*

§ 1954.54. Rejected, eff. Nov. 6, 2018

CHAPTER 2.8. BED BUG INFESTATIONS

Section
1954.600. Legislative findings and declarations.
1954.601. "Pest control operator" defined.
1954.602. No showing, renting, or leasing unit during bed bug infestation; duty to inspect.
1954.603. Written notice to be provided to tenants; contents.
1954.604. Entry into dwelling for inspection; cooperation by tenants.
1954.605. Notification of pest control findings; requirements.

§ 1954.600. Legislative findings and declarations

The Legislature finds and declares:

(a) Controlling bed bugs is uniquely challenging, as bed bug resistance to existing insecticidal control measures is significant. Cooperation among landlords, tenants, and pest control operators is required for successful control. With cooperation among landlords, tenants, and pest control operators, most bed bug infestations can be successfully controlled.

(b) Effective control is more likely to occur when landlords and tenants are informed of the best practices for bed bug control.

(c) Early detection and reporting of bed bugs is an important component required for preventing bed bug infestations. Tenants should not face retaliation for reporting a problem.

(d) Lack of cooperation by landlords and tenants can undermine pest control operator efforts to identify the presence of bed bugs and control an infestation. Depending on the treatment strategy, it is often critical that tenants cooperate with pest control operators by reducing clutter, washing clothes, or performing other activities. Likewise, inadequate or untimely response or planning by landlords may exacerbate an infestation.

(e) Pest control operators with knowledge and education in current best practices for bed bug management, such as those created by the National Pest Management Association (NPMA), are best equipped to help property owners and tenants eradicate bed bugs from their home.

(f) The Structural Pest Control Board should incorporate training in bed bug management based on the National Pest Management Association (NPMA) best practices for the issuance or renewal of a Branch 2 operator, field representative, or applicator license. *(Added by Stats.2016, c. 599 (A.B.551), § 3, eff. Jan. 1, 2017.)*

§ 1954.601. "Pest control operator" defined

For purposes of this chapter, the term "pest control operator" means an individual holding a Branch 2 operator, field representative, or applicator license from the Structural Pest Control Board. *(Added by Stats.2016, c. 599 (A.B.551), § 3, eff. Jan. 1, 2017.)*

§ 1954.602. No showing, renting, or leasing unit during bed bug infestation; duty to inspect

(a) A landlord shall not show, rent, or lease to a prospective tenant any vacant dwelling unit that the landlord knows has a current bed bug infestation.

(b) This section does not impose a duty on a landlord to inspect a dwelling unit or the common areas of the premises for bed bugs if the landlord has no notice of a suspected or actual bed bug infestation. If a bed bug infestation is evident on visual inspection, the landlord shall be considered to have notice pursuant to this section. *(Added by Stats.2016, c. 599 (A.B.551), § 3, eff. Jan. 1, 2017.)*

§ 1954.603. Written notice to be provided to tenants; contents

On and after July 1, 2017, prior to creating a new tenancy for a dwelling unit, a landlord shall provide a written notice to the prospective tenant as provided in this section. This notice shall be provided to all other tenants by January 1, 2018. The notice shall be in at least 10–point type and shall include, but is not limited to, the following:

(a) General information about bed bug identification, behavior and biology, the importance of cooperation for prevention and treatment, and the importance of and for prompt written reporting of suspected infestations to the landlord. The information shall be in substantially the following form:

Information about Bed Bugs

Bed bug Appearance: Bed bugs have six legs. Adult bed bugs have flat bodies about ¼ of an inch in length. Their color can vary from red and brown to copper colored. Young bed bugs are very small. Their bodies are about 1/16 of an inch in length. They have almost no color. When a bed bug feeds, its body swells, may lengthen, and becomes bright red, sometimes making it appear to be a different insect. Bed bugs do not fly. They can either crawl or be carried from place to place on objects, people, or animals. Bed bugs can be hard to find and identify because they are tiny and try to stay hidden.

Life Cycle and Reproduction: An average bed bug lives for about 10 months. Female bed bugs lay one to five eggs per day. Bed bugs grow to full adulthood in about 21 days.

Bed bugs can survive for months without feeding.

Bed bug Bites: Because bed bugs usually feed at night, most people are bitten in their sleep and do not realize they were bitten. A person's reaction to insect bites is an immune

§ 1954.603

response and so varies from person to person. Sometimes the red welts caused by the bites will not be noticed until many days after a person was bitten, if at all.

Common signs and symptoms of a possible bed bug infestation:

- Small red to reddish brown fecal spots on mattresses, box springs, bed frames, mattresses, linens, upholstery, or walls.
- Molted bed bug skins, white, sticky eggs, or empty eggshells.
- Very heavily infested areas may have a characteristically sweet odor.
- Red, itchy bite marks, especially on the legs, arms, and other body parts exposed while sleeping. However, some people do not show bed bug lesions on their bodies even though bed bugs may have fed on them.

For more information, see the Internet Web sites of the United States Environmental Protection Agency and the National Pest Management Association.

(b) The procedure to report suspected infestations to the landlord. *(Added by Stats.2016, c. 599 (A.B.551), § 3, eff. Jan. 1, 2017.)*

§ 1954.604. Entry into dwelling for inspection; cooperation by tenants

Entry to inspect a tenant's dwelling unit shall comply with Section 1954. Entry to inspect any unit selected by the pest control operator and to conduct followup inspections of surrounding units until bed bugs are eliminated is a necessary service for the purpose of Section 1954. Tenants shall cooperate with the inspection to facilitate the detection and treatment of bed bugs, including providing requested information that is necessary to facilitate the detection and treatment of bed bugs to the pest control operator. *(Added by Stats.2016, c. 599 (A.B.551), § 3, eff. Jan. 1, 2017.)*

§ 1954.605. Notification of pest control findings; requirements

The landlord shall notify the tenants of those units inspected by the pest control operator pursuant to Section 1954.604 of the pest control operator's findings. The notification shall be in writing and made within two business days of receipt of the pest control operator's findings. For confirmed infestations in common areas, all tenants shall be provided notice of the pest control operator's findings. *(Added by Stats.2016, c. 599 (A.B.551), § 3, eff. Jan. 1, 2017.)*

CHAPTER 3. HIRING OF PERSONAL PROPERTY

Section
1955. Obligations of lessor.
1956. Expenses.
1957. Expenses of lessee in making good lessor's default.
1958. Return; time and place.
1959. Charter party defined.

§ 1955. Obligations of lessor

Except as otherwise agreed by the lessor and the lessee in lease agreements for a term of more than 20 days, one who leases personal property must deliver it to the lessee, secure his or her quiet enjoyment thereof against all lawful claimants, put it into a condition fit for the purpose for which he or she leases it, and repair all deteriorations thereof not occasioned by the fault of the lessee and not the natural result of its use. *(Enacted in 1872. Amended by Stats.1982, c. 561, p. 2507, § 1.)*

Cross References

Expenses of lessee in making good lessor's default, see Civil Code § 1957.
Quiet possession of hire, see Civil Code § 1927.
Responsibility for willful acts and negligence, see Civil Code § 1714.

§ 1956. Expenses

Except as otherwise agreed by the lessor and lessee, a lessee of personal property must bear all such expenses concerning it as might naturally be foreseen to attend it during its use by him or her, and all other expenses must be borne by the lessor. *(Enacted in 1872. Amended by Stats. 1982, c. 561, p. 2507, § 2.)*

§ 1957. Expenses of lessee in making good lessor's default

If a lessor fails to fulfill his or her obligations, as prescribed by Section 1955, the lessee, after giving him or her notice to do so, if the notice can conveniently be given, may expend any reasonable amount necessary to make good the lessor's default, and may recover such amount from him or her. *(Enacted in 1872. Amended by Stats.1982, c. 561, p. 2507, § 3.)*

Cross References

Obligations of lessor, see Civil Code § 1955.
Repairs by tenant after notice to repair, see Civil Code § 1942.

§ 1958. Return; time and place

At the expiration of the term for which personal property is leased, the lessee must return it to the lessor at the place contemplated by the parties at the time of leasing; or, if no particular place was so contemplated by them, at the place at which it was at that time. *(Enacted in 1872. Amended by Stats.1982, c. 561, p. 2507, § 4.)*

§ 1959. Charter party defined

The contract by which a ship is let is termed a charter party. By it the owner may either let the capacity or burden of the ship, continuing the employment of the owner's master, crew, and equipments, or may surrender the entire ship to the charterer, who then provides them himself. The master or a part owner may be a charterer. *(Enacted in 1872.)*

Cross References

Contract of carriage, see Civil Code § 2085 et seq.
Manager's authority to contract, see Harbors and Navigation Code § 833.
Manager's power to enter into charter parties, see Harbors and Navigation Code § 833.
Responsibility for repairs and supplies, see Harbors and Navigation Code § 404.

CHAPTER 4. IDENTIFICATION OF PROPERTY OWNERS

Section
1961. Application of chapter.

Section
1962. Disclosures by owner or rental agent to tenant; agent failing to make disclosure as agent of owner.
1962.5. Optional methods of disclosure.
1962.7. Failure to comply; service of process; mailing to address at which rent is paid.

§ 1961. Application of chapter

This chapter shall apply to every dwelling structure containing one or more units offered to the public for rent or for lease for residential purposes. *(Added by Stats.1972, c. 941, p. 1698, § 1, operative July 1, 1973. Amended by Stats.1987, c. 769, § 1.)*

§ 1962. Disclosures by owner or rental agent to tenant; agent failing to make disclosure as agent of owner

(a) Any owner of a dwelling structure specified in Section 1961 or a party signing a rental agreement or lease on behalf of the owner shall do all of the following:

(1) Disclose therein the name, telephone number, and usual street address at which personal service may be effected of each person who is:

(A) Authorized to manage the premises.

(B) An owner of the premises or a person who is authorized to act for and on behalf of the owner for the purpose of service of process and for the purpose of receiving and receipting for all notices and demands.

(2) Disclose therein the name, telephone number, and address of the person or entity to whom rent payments shall be made.

(A) If rent payments may be made personally, the usual days and hours that the person will be available to receive the payments shall also be disclosed.

(B) At the owner's option, the rental agreement or lease shall instead disclose the number of either:

(i) The account in a financial institution into which rent payments may be made, and the name and street address of the institution; provided that the institution is located within five miles of the rental property.

(ii) The information necessary to establish an electronic funds transfer procedure for paying the rent.

(3) Disclose therein the form or forms in which rent payments are to be made.

(4) Provide a copy of the rental agreement or lease to the tenant within 15 days of its execution by the tenant. Once each calendar year thereafter, upon request by the tenant, the owner or owner's agent shall provide an additional copy to the tenant within 15 days. If the owner or owner's agent does not possess the rental agreement or lease or a copy of it, the owner or owner's agent shall instead furnish the tenant with a written statement stating that fact and containing the information required by paragraphs (1), (2), and (3).

(b) In the case of an oral rental agreement, the owner, or a person acting on behalf of the owner for the receipt of rent or otherwise, shall furnish the tenant, within 15 days of the agreement, with a written statement containing the information required by paragraphs (1), (2), and (3) of subdivision (a). Once each calendar year thereafter, upon request by the tenant, the owner or owner's agent shall provide an additional copy of the statement to the tenant within 15 days.

(c) The information required by this section shall be kept current and this section shall extend to and be enforceable against any successor owner or manager, who shall comply with this section within 15 days of succeeding the previous owner or manager. A successor owner or manager shall not serve a notice pursuant to paragraph (2) of Section 1161 of the Code of Civil Procedure or otherwise evict a tenant for nonpayment of rent that accrued during the period of noncompliance by a successor owner or manager with this subdivision. Nothing in this subdivision shall relieve the tenant of any liability for unpaid rent.

(d) A party who enters into a rental agreement on behalf of the owner who fails to comply with this section is deemed an agent of each person who is an owner:

(1) For the purpose of service of process and receiving and receipting for notices and demands.

(2) For the purpose of performing the obligations of the owner under law and under the rental agreement.

(3) For the purpose of receiving rental payments, which may be made in cash, by check, by money order, or in any form previously accepted by the owner or owner's agent, unless the form of payment has been specified in the oral or written agreement, or the tenant has been notified by the owner in writing that a particular form of payment is unacceptable.

(e) Nothing in this section limits or excludes the liability of any undisclosed owner.

(f) If the address provided by the owner does not allow for personal delivery, then it shall be conclusively presumed that upon the mailing of any rent or notice to the owner by the tenant to the name and address provided, the notice or rent is deemed receivable by the owner on the date posted, if the tenant can show proof of mailing to the name and address provided by the owner. *(Added by Stats.1972, c. 941, p. 1998, § 1, operative July 1, 1973. Amended by Stats.1987, c. 769, § 2; Stats.2001, c. 729 (S.B.985), § 3; Stats.2012, c. 695 (A.B.1953), § 1.)*

§ 1962.5. Optional methods of disclosure

(a) Notwithstanding subdivisions (a) and (b) of Section 1962, the information required by paragraph (1) of subdivision (a) of Section 1962 to be disclosed to a tenant may, instead of being disclosed in the manner described in subdivisions (a) and (b) of Section 1962, be disclosed by the following method:

(1) In each dwelling structure containing an elevator a printed or typewritten notice containing the information required by paragraph (1) of subdivision (a) of Section 1962 shall be placed in every elevator and in one other conspicuous place.

(2) In each structure not containing an elevator, a printed or typewritten notice containing the information required by paragraph (1) of subdivision (a) of Section 1962 shall be placed in at least two conspicuous places.

(3) In the case of a single unit dwelling structure, the information to be disclosed under this section may be disclosed by complying with either paragraph (1) or (2).

§ 1962.5

(b) Except as provided in subdivision (a), all the provisions of Section 1962 shall be applicable. *(Added by Stats.1972, c. 941, p. 1699, § 1, operative July 1, 1973. Amended by Stats.1987, c. 769, § 3; Stats.2001, c. 729 (S.B.985), § 4.)*

§ 1962.7. Failure to comply; service of process; mailing to address at which rent is paid

In the event an owner, successor owner, manager, or agent specified in Section 1961 fails to comply with the requirements of this chapter, service of process by a tenant with respect to a dispute arising out of the tenancy may be made by registered or certified mail sent to the address at which rent is paid, in which case the provisions of Section 1013 of the Code of Civil Procedure shall apply. *(Added by Stats. 1987, c. 769, § 4. Amended by Stats.2001, c. 729 (S.B.985), § 5.)*

CHAPTER 4.5. DISPOSITION OF PERSONAL PROPERTY UPON REQUEST OF TENANT

Section
1965. Surrender of personal property to tenant or representative; costs; exemptions; landlord liability; actions.
1969 to 1979. Repealed.

§ 1965. Surrender of personal property to tenant or representative; costs; exemptions; landlord liability; actions

(a) A residential landlord shall not refuse to surrender, to a residential tenant or to a residential tenant's duly authorized representative, any personal property not owned by the landlord which has been left on the premises after the tenant has vacated the residential premises and the return of which has been requested by the tenant or by the authorized representative of the tenant if all of the following occur:

(1) The tenant requests, in writing, within 18 days of vacating the premises, the surrender of the personal property and the request includes a description of the personal property held by the landlord and specifies the mailing address of the tenant.

(2) The landlord or the landlord's agent has control or possession of the tenant's personal property at the time the request is received.

(3) The tenant, prior to the surrender of the personal property by the landlord and upon written demand by the landlord, tenders payment of all reasonable costs associated with the landlord's removal and storage of the personal property. The landlord's demand for payment of reasonable costs associated with the removal and storage of personal property shall be in writing and shall either be mailed to the tenant at the address provided by the tenant pursuant to paragraph (1) or shall be personally presented to the tenant or to the tenant's authorized representative, within five days after the actual receipt of the tenant's request for surrender of the personal property, unless the property is returned first. The demand shall itemize all charges, specifying the nature and amount of each item of cost.

(4) The tenant agrees to claim and remove the personal property at a reasonable time mutually agreed upon by the landlord and tenant but not later than 72 hours after the tender provided for under paragraph (3).

(b) For the purposes of this chapter, "reasonable costs associated with the landlord's removal and storage of the personal property" shall include, but not be limited to, each of the following:

(1) Reasonable costs actually incurred, or the reasonable value of labor actually provided, or both, in removing the personal property from its original location to the place of storage, including disassembly and transportation.

(2) Reasonable storage costs actually incurred, which shall not exceed the fair rental value of the space reasonably required for the storage of the personal property.

(c) This chapter shall not apply when disposition of the personal property has been initiated or completed pursuant to the procedure set forth in Chapter 5 (commencing with Section 1980) or the occupancy is one defined by subdivision (b) of Section 1940.

(d) A landlord who complies with this chapter shall not be liable to any person with respect to that person's personal property that is given to another person. In the event of conflicting demands, the first timely request for surrender of personal property received by the landlord shall prevail.

(e) Any landlord who retains personal property in violation of this chapter shall be liable to the tenant in a civil action for all the following:

(1) Actual damages not to exceed the value of the personal property, if the personal property is not surrendered by the later of either of the following: (A) within a reasonable time after the tenant's request for surrender of the personal property, or (B) if the landlord has demanded payment of reasonable costs associated with removal and storage and the tenant has complied with the requirements set forth in paragraphs (3) and (4) of subdivision (a), whichever is later. Three days is presumed to be a reasonable time in the absence of evidence to the contrary.

(2) An amount not to exceed two hundred fifty dollars ($250) for each bad faith violation of this section. In determining the amount of the award, the court shall consider proof of matters as justice may require.

(3) The court may award reasonable attorney's fees and cost to the prevailing party.

(f) The remedy provided by this chapter is not exclusive and shall not preclude either the landlord or the tenant from pursuing any other remedy provided by law. *(Added by Stats.1988, c. 797, § 2.)*

Cross References

Proceedings to get possession of real property, see Code of Civil Procedure § 1159 et seq.

§§ 1969 to 1979. Repealed by Stats.1937, c. 90, p. 326, § 8100

CHAPTER 5. DISPOSITION OF PERSONAL PROPERTY REMAINING ON PREMISES AT TERMINATION OF TENANCY

Section
1980. Definitions.
1980.5. Commercial real property; application of chapter.

Section	
1981.	Optional procedure; construction of chapter.
1982.	Lost property; disposition.
1983.	Notice to former tenant and owner of property; description; delivery.
1984.	Notice to former tenant; form; contents.
1985.	Notice to owner; form.
1986.	Storage of property; place; reasonable care.
1987.	Release of property; payment of storage and expenses.
1988.	Sale of property; notice; publication; proceeds.
1989.	Liability of landlord.
1990.	Costs of storage; assessment.
1991.	Notice of belief of abandonment to lessee; notice to former tenant; combined notices.
1992.	Repealed.

Cross References

Shelter crisis, emergency housing, homeless shelters, see Government Code § 8698.4.

§ 1980. Definitions

As used in this chapter:

(a) "Landlord" means any operator, keeper, lessor, or sublessor of any furnished or unfurnished premises for hire, or his or her agent or successor in interest.

(b) "Owner" means any person other than the landlord who has any right, title, or interest in personal property.

(c) "Premises" includes any common areas associated therewith.

(d) "Reasonable belief" means the actual knowledge or belief a prudent person would have without making an investigation (including any investigation of public records) except that, where the landlord has specific information indicating that such an investigation would more probably than not reveal pertinent information and the cost of such an investigation would be reasonable in relation to the probable value of the personal property involved, "reasonable belief" includes the actual knowledge or belief a prudent person would have if such an investigation were made.

(e) "Records" means any material, regardless of the physical form, on which information is recorded or preserved by any means, including in written or spoken words, graphically depicted, printed, or electromagnetically transmitted. "Records" does not include publicly available directories containing information an individual has voluntarily consented to have publicly disseminated or listed, such as name, address, or telephone number.

(f) "Tenant" includes any paying guest, lessee, or sublessee of any premises for hire. *(Added by Stats.1974, c. 331, p. 653, § 2. Amended by Stats.2009, c. 134 (A.B.1094), § 4.)*

Cross References

Judgment for possession of premises, see Code of Civil Procedure § 1174.
Recreational vehicle parks, removed vehicles, disposition of abandoned possessions, see Civil Code §§ 799.55 et seq., 799.75.

§ 1980.5. Commercial real property; application of chapter

Except as provided in Section 1993.01, the provisions of this chapter shall not apply to commercial real property, as defined in subdivision (d) of Section 1954.26. For purposes of this section, commercial real property shall not include self-storage units. *(Added by Stats.2008, c. 161 (A.B.2025), § 1.)*

Cross References

Requirements for property remaining on premises at termination of tenancy, see Civil Code § 1993.01.

§ 1981. Optional procedure; construction of chapter

(a) This chapter provides an optional procedure for the disposition of personal property that remains on the premises after a tenancy has terminated and the premises have been vacated by the tenant.

(b) This chapter does not apply whenever Section 1862.5, 2080.8, 2080.9, or 2081 to 2081.6, inclusive, applies. This chapter does not apply to property that exists for the purpose of providing utility services and is owned by a public utility, whether or not that property is actually in operation to provide those utility services.

(c) This chapter does not apply to any manufactured home as defined in Section 18007 of the Health and Safety Code, any mobilehome as defined in Section 18008 of the Health and Safety Code, or to any commercial coach as defined in Section 18001.8 of the Health and Safety Code, including attachments thereto or contents thereof, whether or not the manufactured home, mobilehome, or commercial coach is subject to registration under the Health and Safety Code.

(d) This chapter does not apply to the disposition of an animal to which subdivision (d) of Section 1815 or Chapter 7 (commencing with Section 17001) of Part 1 of Division 9 of the Food and Agricultural Code applies, and those animals shall be disposed of in accordance with those provisions.

(e) If the requirements of this chapter are not satisfied, nothing in this chapter affects the rights and liabilities of the landlord, former tenant, or any other person. *(Added by Stats.1974, c. 331, p. 654, § 2. Amended by Stats.1983, c. 1124, § 5, operative Jan. 1, 1984; Stats.1996, c. 653 (A.B. 2605), § 1; Stats.2008, c. 265 (A.B.2949), § 3.)*

Cross References

Landlord defined for purposes of this Chapter, see Civil Code § 1980.
Premises defined for purposes of this Chapter, see Civil Code § 1980.
Tenant defined for purposes of this Chapter, see Civil Code § 1980.

§ 1982. Lost property; disposition

(a) Personal property which the landlord reasonably believes to have been lost shall be disposed of pursuant to Article 1 (commencing with Section 2080) of Chapter 4 of Title 6. The landlord is not liable to the owner of the property if he complies with this subdivision.

(b) If the appropriate police or sheriff's department refuses to accept property pursuant to subdivision (a), the landlord may dispose of the property pursuant to this chapter. *(Added by Stats.1974, c. 331, p. 654, § 2.)*

Cross References

Landlord defined for purposes of this Chapter, see Civil Code § 1980.

§ 1982

Owner defined for purposes of this Chapter, see Civil Code § 1980.
Requirements for property remaining on premises at termination of tenancy, see Civil Code § 1993.01.

§ 1983. Notice to former tenant and owner of property; description; delivery

(a) Where personal property remains on the premises after a tenancy has terminated and the premises have been vacated by the tenant, the landlord shall give written notice to the tenant and to any other person the landlord reasonably believes to be the owner of the property. If the property consists of records, the tenant shall be presumed to be the owner of the records for the purposes of this chapter.

(b) The notice shall describe the property in a manner reasonably adequate to permit the owner of the property to identify it. The notice may describe all or a portion of the property, but the limitation of liability provided by Section 1989 does not protect the landlord from any liability arising from the disposition of property not described in the notice except that a trunk, valise, box, or other container which is locked, fastened, or tied in a manner which deters immediate access to its contents may be described as such without describing its contents. The notice shall advise the person to be notified that reasonable costs of storage may be charged before the property is returned, where the property may be claimed, and the date before which the claim must be made. The date specified in the notice shall be a date not less than 15 days after the notice is personally delivered or, if mailed, not less than 18 days after the notice is deposited in the mail.

(c) The notice shall be personally delivered to the person to be notified or sent by first-class mail, postage prepaid, to the person to be notified at his or her last known address and, if there is reason to believe that the notice sent to that address will not be received by that person, also to any other address known to the landlord where the person may reasonably be expected to receive the notice. If the notice is sent by mail to the former tenant, one copy shall be sent to the premises vacated by the tenant. If the former tenant provided the landlord with the tenant's email address, the landlord may also send the notice by email. *(Added by Stats.1974, c. 331, p. 654, § 2. Amended by Stats.2009, c. 134 (A.B.1094), § 5; Stats.2012, c. 560 (A.B.2521), § 4.)*

Cross References

Judgment for possession of premises, notice to owners of personal property on the premises, see Code of Civil Procedure § 1174.
Landlord defined for purposes of this Chapter, see Civil Code § 1980.
Owner defined for purposes of this Chapter, see Civil Code § 1980.
Premises defined for purposes of this Chapter, see Civil Code § 1980.
Records defined for purposes of this Chapter, see Civil Code § 1980.
Tenant defined for purposes of this Chapter, see Civil Code § 1980.

§ 1984. Notice to former tenant; form; contents

(a) A notice given to the former tenant which is in substantially the following form satisfies the requirements of Section 1983:

Notice of Right to Reclaim Abandoned Property

To: _____
(Name of former tenant)

_____
(Address of former tenant)

When you vacated the premises at _____
(Address of premises, including room or apartment number, if any)
the following personal property remained:

_____
(Insert description of the personal property)

You may claim this property at _____

_____
(Address where property may be claimed).

If you claim this property by _____ (insert date not less than 2 days after the former tenant vacated the premises), you may minimize the costs of storage. If you fail to claim this property by _____ (insert date not less than 2 days after the former tenant vacated the premises), unless you pay the landlord's reasonable cost of storage for all the above-described property, and take possession of the property which you claim, not later than _____ (insert date not less than 15 days after notice is personally delivered or, if mailed, not less than 18 days after notice is deposited in the mail) this property may be disposed of pursuant to Civil Code Section 1988.

(Insert here the statement required by subdivision (b) of this section)
Dated: _____

_____
(Signature of landlord)

_____
(Type or print name of landlord)

_____
(Telephone number)

_____
(Address)

(b) The notice set forth in subdivision (a) shall also contain one of the following statements:

(1) "If you fail to reclaim the property, it will be sold at a public sale after notice of the sale has been given by publication. You have the right to bid on the property at this sale. After the property is sold and the cost of storage, advertising, and sale is deducted, the remaining money will be paid over to the county. You may claim the remaining money at any time within one year after the county receives the money."

(2) "Because this property is believed to be worth less than $700, it may be kept, sold, or destroyed without further notice if you fail to reclaim it within the time indicated above." *(Added by Stats.1974, c. 331, p. 654, § 2. Amended by Stats.1984, c. 1249, § 1; Stats.2012, c. 560 (A.B.2521), § 5.)*

Cross References

Landlord defined for purposes of this Chapter, see Civil Code § 1980.
Premises defined for purposes of this Chapter, see Civil Code § 1980.
Tenant defined for purposes of this Chapter, see Civil Code § 1980.

§ 1985. Notice to owner; form

A notice which is in substantially the following form given to a person (other than the former tenant) the landlord reasonably believes to be the owner of personal property satisfies the requirements of Section 1983:

Notice of Right to Reclaim Abandoned Property

To: _____
(Name)

_____
(Address)

When _____ vacated the premises at
    (name of former tenant)
_____,
(address of premises, including room or apartment number, if any) the following personal property remained:
_____
        (insert description of the personal property)
If you own any of this property, you may claim it at
_____
(address where property may be claimed).
If you claim this property by ____ (insert date not less than 2 days after the former tenant vacated the premises), you may minimize the costs of storage. If you fail to claim this property by ____ (insert date not less than 2 days after the former tenant vacated the premises), unless you pay the landlord's reasonable cost of storage and take possession of the property to which you are entitled not later than _____ (insert date not less than 15 days after notice is personally delivered or, if mailed, not less than 18 days after notice is deposited in the mail) this property may be disposed of pursuant to Civil Code Section 1988.

Dated: _____

_____
                    (Signature of landlord)
_____
                (Type or print name of landlord)
_____
                    (Telephone number)
_____
                         (Address)

(Added by Stats.1974, c. 331, p. 655, § 2. Amended by Stats.2012, c. 560 (A.B.2521), § 6.)

Cross References

Landlord defined for purposes of this Chapter, see Civil Code § 1980.
Owner defined for purposes of this Chapter, see Civil Code § 1980.
Premises defined for purposes of this Chapter, see Civil Code § 1980.
Subpoenas for dependent child hearings, see Welfare and Institutions Code § 341.
Tenant defined for purposes of this Chapter, see Civil Code § 1980.

§ 1986. Storage of property; place; reasonable care

The personal property described in the notice shall either be left on the vacated premises or be stored by the landlord in a place of safekeeping until the landlord either releases the property pursuant to Section 1987 or disposes of the property pursuant to Section 1988. The landlord shall exercise reasonable care in storing the property, but he is not liable to the tenant or any other owner for any loss not caused by his deliberate or negligent act. (Added by Stats.1974, c. 331, p. 656, § 2.)

Cross References

Landlord defined for purposes of this Chapter, see Civil Code § 1980.
Owner defined for purposes of this Chapter, see Civil Code § 1980.
Premises defined for purposes of this Chapter, see Civil Code § 1980.
Tenant defined for purposes of this Chapter, see Civil Code § 1980.

§ 1987. Release of property; payment of storage and expenses

(a) The personal property described in the notice shall be released by the landlord to the former tenant or, at the landlord's option, to any person reasonably believed by the landlord to be its owner if that tenant or other person pays the reasonable cost of storage and takes possession of the property not later than the date specified in the notice for taking possession.

(b) Where personal property is not released pursuant to subdivision (a) and the notice stated that the personal property would be sold at a public sale, the landlord shall release the personal property to the former tenant if he or she claims it prior to the time it is sold and pays the reasonable cost of storage, advertising, and sale incurred prior to the time the property is withdrawn from sale.

(c) Notwithstanding subdivision (a), the landlord shall release the personal property described in the notice to the former tenant and shall not require the former tenant to pay the cost of storage if the property remained in the dwelling and the former tenant or other person reasonably believed by the landlord to be its owner reclaims the property within two days of vacating the dwelling. (Added by Stats.1974, c. 331, p. 656, § 2. Amended by Stats.2012, c. 560 (A.B.2521), § 7.)

Cross References

Landlord defined for purposes of this Chapter, see Civil Code § 1980.
Owner defined for purposes of this Chapter, see Civil Code § 1980.
Requirements for property remaining on premises at termination of tenancy, see Civil Code § 1993.01.
Tenant defined for purposes of this Chapter, see Civil Code § 1980.

§ 1988. Sale of property; notice; publication; proceeds

(a) If the personal property described in the notice is not released pursuant to Section 1987, it shall be sold at public sale by competitive bidding. However, if the landlord reasonably believes that the total resale value of the property not released is less than seven hundred dollars ($700), the landlord may retain the property for his or her own use or dispose of it in any manner. Nothing in this section shall be construed to preclude the landlord or tenant from bidding on the property at the public sale.

(b) Notice of the time and place of the public sale shall be given by publication pursuant to Section 6066 of the Government Code in a newspaper of general circulation published in the county where the sale is to be held. The last publication shall be not less than five days before the sale is to be held. The notice of the sale shall not be published before the last of the dates specified for taking possession of the property in any notice given pursuant to Section 1983. The notice of the sale shall describe the property to be sold in a manner reasonably adequate to permit the owner of the property to identify it. The notice may describe all or a portion of the property, but the limitation of liability provided by Section 1989 does not protect the landlord from any liability arising from the disposition of property not described in the notice, except that a trunk, valise, box, or other container which is locked, fastened, or tied in a manner which deters immediate access to its contents may be described as such without describing its contents.

(c) After deduction of the costs of storage, advertising, and sale, any balance of the proceeds of the sale which is not claimed by the former tenant or an owner other than such tenant shall be paid into the treasury of the county in which the sale took place not later than 30 days after the date of sale. The former tenant or other owner may claim the balance within one year from the date of payment to the county by making application to the county treasurer or other official designated by the county. If the county pays the balance or any part thereof to a claimant, neither the county nor any officer or employee thereof is liable to any other claimant as to the amount paid. (Added by Stats.1974, c. 331, p. 657, § 2. Amended by Stats.1982, c. 811, p. 3099, § 1; Stats.2012, c. 560 (A.B.2521), § 8.)

Cross References

Judgment for possession of premises, disposition of personal property not released, see Code of Civil Procedure § 1174.
Landlord defined for purposes of this Chapter, see Civil Code § 1980.
Owner defined for purposes of this Chapter, see Civil Code § 1980.
Tenant defined for purposes of this Chapter, see Civil Code § 1980.

§ 1989. Liability of landlord

(a) Notwithstanding subdivision (c) of Section 1981, where the landlord releases to the former tenant property which remains on the premises after a tenancy is terminated, the landlord is not liable with respect to that property to any person.

(b) Where the landlord releases property pursuant to Section 1987 to a person (other than the former tenant) reasonably believed by the landlord to be the owner of the property, the landlord is not liable with respect to that property to:

(1) Any person to whom notice was given pursuant to Section 1983; or

(2) Any person to whom notice was not given pursuant to Section 1983 unless such person proves that, prior to releasing the property, the landlord believed or reasonably should have believed that such person had an interest in the property and also that the landlord knew or should have known upon reasonable investigation the address of such person.

(c) Where property is disposed of pursuant to Section 1988, the landlord is not liable with respect to that property to:

(1) Any person to whom notice was given pursuant to Section 1983; or

(2) Any person to whom notice was not given pursuant to Section 1983 unless such person proves that, prior to disposing of the property pursuant to Section 1988, the landlord believed or reasonably should have believed that such person had an interest in the property and also that the landlord knew or should have known upon reasonable investigation the address of such person. (Added by Stats. 1974, c. 331, p. 657, § 2.)

Cross References

Landlord defined for purposes of this Chapter, see Civil Code § 1980.
Owner defined for purposes of this Chapter, see Civil Code § 1980.
Premises defined for purposes of this Chapter, see Civil Code § 1980.
Tenant defined for purposes of this Chapter, see Civil Code § 1980.

§ 1990. Costs of storage; assessment

(a) Costs of storage which may be required to be paid under this chapter shall be assessed in the following manner:

(1) Where a former tenant claims property pursuant to Section 1987, he or she may be required to pay the reasonable costs of storage for all the personal property remaining on the premises at the termination of the tenancy which are unpaid at the time the claim is made.

(2) Where an owner other than the former tenant claims property pursuant to Section 1987, he or she may be required to pay the reasonable costs of storage for only the property in which he or she claims an interest.

(b) In determining the costs to be assessed under subdivision (a), the landlord shall not charge more than one person for the same costs.

(c) If the landlord stores the personal property on the premises, the cost of storage shall be the fair rental value of the space reasonably required for that storage for the term of the storage. Costs shall not be assessed if the former tenant reclaims property stored on the premises within two days of having vacated the premises. (Added by Stats.1974, c. 331, p. 658, § 2. Amended by Stats.2012, c. 560 (A.B.2521), § 9.)

Cross References

Judgment for possession of premises, cost for storage of personal property remaining on premises, see Code of Civil Procedure § 1174.
Landlord defined for purposes of this Chapter, see Civil Code § 1980.
Owner defined for purposes of this Chapter, see Civil Code § 1980.
Premises defined for purposes of this Chapter, see Civil Code § 1980.
Requirements for property remaining on premises at termination of tenancy, see Civil Code § 1993.01.
Tenant defined for purposes of this Chapter, see Civil Code § 1980.

§ 1991. Notice of belief of abandonment to lessee; notice to former tenant; combined notices

Where a notice of belief of abandonment is given to a lessee pursuant to Section 1951.3, the notice to the former tenant given pursuant to Section 1983 may, but need not, be given at the same time as the notice of belief of abandonment even though the tenancy is not terminated until the end of the period specified in the notice of belief of abandonment. If the notices are so given, the notices may, but need not, be combined in one notice that contains all the information required by the sections under which the notices are given. (Added by Stats.1974, c. 331, p. 658, § 2.)

Cross References

Tenant defined for purposes of this Chapter, see Civil Code § 1980.

§ 1992. Repealed by Stats.1937, c. 90, § 8100

CHAPTER 5.5. DISPOSITION OF PROPERTY REMAINING ON PREMISES AT TERMINATION OF COMMERCIAL TENANCY

Section
1993.   Definitions.

Section
1993.01. Requirements applicable to this chapter.
1993.02. Optional procedure for disposition of property; application of chapter.
1993.03. Written notice provided; contents; delivery.
1993.04. Written notice to former tenant by landlord; requirements.
1993.05. Written notice given owner of personal property; form.
1993.06. Storage of property; place of safekeeping; reasonable care.
1993.07. Property in notice not released; public sale; publication of time and place; proceeds.
1993.08. Release of property to former tenant; landlord liability; notice.
1993.09. Notice of belief of abandonment.

§ 1993. Definitions

This chapter shall only apply to commercial real property. As used in this chapter:

(a) "Commercial real property" has the meaning specified in subdivision (d) of Section 1954.26. For purposes of this chapter, commercial real property shall not include self-storage units.

(b) "Landlord" means any operator, keeper, lessor, or sublessor of any furnished or unfurnished premises for hire, or his or her agent or successor in interest.

(c) "Owner" means any person other than the landlord who has any right, title, or interest in property.

(d) "Premises" includes any common areas associated therewith.

(e) "Reasonable belief" means the actual knowledge or belief a prudent person would have without making an investigation, including any investigation of public records, except that, if the landlord has specific information indicating that an investigation would more probably than not reveal pertinent information and the cost of an investigation would be reasonable in relation to the probable value of the property involved, "reasonable belief" includes the actual knowledge or belief a prudent person would have if an investigation were made.

(f) "Records" means any material, regardless of the physical form, on which information is recorded or preserved by any means, including in written or spoken words, graphically depicted, printed, or electromagnetically transmitted. "Records" does not include publicly available directories containing information an individual has voluntarily consented to have publicly disseminated or listed, such as name, address, or telephone number.

(g) "Tenant" includes any lessee or sublessee of any commercial real property and its premises for hire. (Added by Stats.2008, c. 161 (A.B.2025), § 2. Amended by Stats.2009, c. 140 (A.B.1164), § 29; Stats.2009, c. 134 (A.B.1094), § 6.)

§ 1993.01. Requirements applicable to this chapter

Notwithstanding Section 1980.5, the requirements of Sections 1982, 1987, and 1990 shall apply to property that is subject to this chapter. (Added by Stats.2008, c. 161 (A.B. 2025), § 2.)

Cross References

Inclusion of self-storage units for purposes of this section, see Civil Code § 1980.5.

§ 1993.02. Optional procedure for disposition of property; application of chapter

(a) This chapter provides an optional procedure for the disposition of property that remains on the premises after a tenancy of commercial real property has terminated and the premises have been vacated by the tenant.

(b) This chapter does not apply if Section 1862.5, 2080.8, or 2080.9, or Article 2 (commencing with Section 2081) of Chapter 4 of Title 6, apply. This chapter does not apply to property that exists for the purpose of providing utility services and is owned by a public utility, whether or not that property is actually in operation to provide those utility services.

(c) This chapter does not apply to a manufactured home, as defined in Section 18007 of the Health and Safety Code, a mobilehome, as defined in Section 18008 of the Health and Safety Code, or a commercial coach, as defined in Section 18001.8 of the Health and Safety Code, including any attachments or contents, whether or not the manufactured home, mobilehome, or commercial coach is subject to registration under the Health and Safety Code.

(d) This chapter does not apply to the disposition of animals subject to Chapter 7 (commencing with Section 17001) of Part 1 of Division 9 of the Food and Agricultural Code.

(e) This chapter does not apply to residential property or self-storage units.

(f) If the requirements of this chapter are not satisfied, nothing in this chapter affects the rights and liabilities of the landlord, former tenant, or any other person. (Added by Stats.2008, c. 161 (A.B.2025), § 2. Amended by Stats.2009, c. 140 (A.B.1164), § 30.)

§ 1993.03. Written notice provided; contents; delivery

(a) If property remains on the premises after a tenancy has terminated and the premises have been vacated by the tenant, the landlord shall give written notice to the tenant and to any other person the landlord reasonably believes to be the owner of the property. If the property consists of records, the tenant shall be presumed to be the owner of the records for the purposes of this chapter.

(b) The notice shall describe the property in a manner reasonably adequate to permit the owner of the property to identify it. The notice may describe all or a portion of the property, but the limitation of liability provided by Section 1993.08 does not protect the landlord from any liability arising from the disposition of property not described in the notice, except that a trunk, valise, box, safe, vault, or other container that is locked, fastened, or tied in a manner that deters immediate access to its contents may be described as such without describing its contents. The notice shall advise the person to be notified that reasonable costs of storage may be charged before the property is returned, where the property may be claimed, and the date before which the claim must be made. The date specified in the notice shall be a date not less than 15 days after the notice is personally

§ 1993.03

delivered or, if mailed, not less than 18 days after the notice is deposited in the mail.

(c) The notice shall be personally delivered to the person to be notified or sent by first-class mail, postage prepaid, to the person to be notified at his or her last known address and, if there is reason to believe that the notice sent to that address will not be received by that person, also to any other address known to the landlord where the person may reasonably be expected to receive the notice. If the notice is sent by mail to the former tenant, one copy shall be sent to the premises vacated by the tenant. *(Added by Stats.2008, c. 161 (A.B.2025), § 2. Amended by Stats.2009, c. 140 (A.B.1164), § 31; Stats.2009, c. 134 (A.B.1094), § 7.)*

§ 1993.04. Written notice to former tenant by landlord; requirements

(a) A notice given to the former tenant that is in substantially the following form satisfies the requirements of Section 1993.03:

Notice of Right to Reclaim Abandoned Property

To: _____
(Name of former tenant)

_____
(Address of former tenant)

When you vacated the premises at _____
(Address of premises, including room, if any)
the following personal property remained:

_____
(Insert description of the personal property)

You may claim this property at _____
(Address where property may be claimed)

Unless you pay the reasonable cost of storage for all of the above-described property, and take possession of the property which you claim, not later than _____ (insert date not less than 15 days after notice is personally delivered or, if mailed, not less than 18 days after notice is deposited in the mail) this property may be disposed of pursuant to Section 1993.07 of the Civil Code.

(Insert here the statement required by subdivision (b) of this section)

Dated: _____

_____
(Signature of landlord)

_____
(Type or print name of landlord)

_____
(Telephone number of landlord)

_____
(Address of landlord)

(b) The notice set forth in subdivision (a) shall also contain one of the following statements:

(1) "If you fail to reclaim the property, it will be sold at a public sale after notice of the sale has been given by publication. You have the right to bid on the property at this sale. After the property is sold and the cost of storage, advertising, and sale is deducted, the remaining money will be paid over to the county. You may claim the remaining money at any time within one year after the county receives the money."

(2) "Because you were a commercial tenant and this property is believed to be worth less than either two thousand five hundred dollars ($2,500) or an amount equal to one month's rent for the premises you occupied, whichever is greater, it may be kept, sold, or destroyed without further notice if you fail to reclaim it within the time indicated above." *(Added by Stats.2008, c. 161 (A.B.2025), § 2. Amended by Stats.2009, c. 140 (A.B.1164), § 32; Stats.2018, c. 74 (A.B.2173), § 2, eff. Jan. 1, 2019.)*

§ 1993.05. Written notice given owner of personal property; form

A notice in substantially the following form given to a person (other than the former tenant) the landlord reasonably believes to be the owner of personal property satisfies the requirements of Section 1993.03:

Notice of Right to Reclaim Abandoned Property

To: _____
(Name of owner)

_____
(Address of owner)

When _____ vacated the premises at
(Name of former tenant)

_____
(Address of premises, including room, if any)
the following personal property remained:

_____
(Insert description of the personal property)

You may claim this property at _____
(Address where property may be claimed)

Unless you pay the reasonable cost of storage for all of the above-described property, and take possession of the property that you claim, not later than _____ (insert date not less than 15 days after notice is personally delivered or, if mailed, not less than 18 days after notice is deposited in the mail) this property may be disposed of pursuant to Section 1993.07 of the Civil Code.

(Insert here the statement required by subdivision (b) of this section)

Dated: _____

_____
(Signature of landlord)

_____
(Type or print name of landlord)

_____
(Telephone number of landlord)

_____
(Address of landlord)

(Added by Stats.2008, c. 161 (A.B.2025), § 2. Amended by Stats.2009, c. 140 (A.B.1164), § 33.)

§ 1993.06. Storage of property; place of safekeeping; reasonable care

The personal property described in the notice shall either be left on the vacated premises or be stored by the landlord in a place of safekeeping until the landlord either releases the property pursuant to Section 1987 or disposes of the property pursuant to Section 1993.07. The landlord shall exercise reasonable care in storing the property, but he or she is not liable to the tenant or any other owner for any loss not caused by his or her deliberate or negligent act. *(Added by Stats.2008, c. 161 (A.B.2025), § 2.)*

§ 1993.07. Property in notice not released; public sale; publication of time and place; proceeds

(a)(1) The property described in the notice that is not released pursuant to Section 1987 shall be sold at public sale by competitive bidding except that, if the landlord reasonably believes that the total resale value of the property is less than the threshold amount, the landlord may retain the property for his or her own use or dispose of it in any manner.

(2) For the purposes of this section, "threshold amount" means either two thousand five hundred dollars ($2,500) or an amount equal to one month's rent for the premises occupied by the tenant, whichever is greater.

(b)(1) Notice of the time and place of the public sale shall be given by publication pursuant to Section 6066 of the Government Code in a newspaper of general circulation published in the county where the sale is to be held.

(2) The last publication shall be not less than five days before the sale is to be held.

(3) The notice of the sale shall not be published before the last of the dates specified for taking possession of the property in any notice given pursuant to Section 1993.03.

(4) The notice of the sale shall describe the property to be sold in a manner reasonably adequate to permit the owner of the property to identify it.

(5) The notice may describe all or a portion of the property, but the limitation of liability provided by Section 1993.08 does not protect the landlord from any liability arising from the disposition of property not described in the notice, except that a trunk, valise, box, safe, vault, or other container that is locked, fastened, or tied in a manner that deters immediate access to its contents may be described as such without describing its contents.

(c)(1) After deduction of the costs of storage, advertising, and sale, any balance of the proceeds of the sale that is not claimed by the former tenant or an owner other than the tenant shall be paid into the treasury of the county in which the sale took place not later than 30 days after the date of sale.

(2) The former tenant or other owner may claim the balance within one year from the date of payment to the county by making application to the county treasurer or other official designated by the county.

(3) If the county pays the balance or any part thereof to a claimant, neither the county nor any officer or employee thereof shall be liable to any other claimant as to the amount paid.

(d) Nothing in this section precludes a landlord or tenant from bidding on the property at the public sale. *(Added by Stats.2008, c. 161 (A.B.2025), § 2. Amended by Stats.2009, c. 140 (A.B.1164), § 34; Stats.2018, c. 74 (A.B.2173), § 3, eff. Jan. 1, 2019.)*

§ 1993.08. Release of property to former tenant; landlord liability; notice

(a) Notwithstanding subdivision (c) of Section 1993.02, if the landlord releases to the former tenant property that remains on the premises after a tenancy is terminated, the landlord shall not be liable with respect to that property to any person.

(b) If the landlord releases property pursuant to Section 1987 to a person, other than the former tenant, who is reasonably believed by the landlord to be the owner of the property, the landlord shall not be liable with respect to that property to any of the following persons:

(1) A person to whom notice was given pursuant to Section 1993.03.

(2) A person to whom notice was not given pursuant to Section 1993.03, unless the person proves that, prior to releasing the property, the landlord believed or reasonably should have believed that the person had an interest in the property and also that the landlord knew or should have known upon reasonable investigation the address of the person.

(c) If property is disposed of pursuant to Section 1993.07, the landlord shall not be liable with respect to that property to any of the following persons:

(1) A person to whom notice was given pursuant to Section 1993.03.

(2) A person to whom notice was not given pursuant to Section 1993.03, unless the person proves that, prior to disposing of the property pursuant to Section 1993.07, the landlord believed or reasonably should have believed that the person had an interest in the property and also that the landlord knew or should have known upon reasonable investigation the address of the person. *(Added by Stats. 2008, c. 161 (A.B.2025), § 2. Amended by Stats.2009, c. 140 (A.B.1164), § 35.)*

§ 1993.09. Notice of belief of abandonment

If a notice of belief of abandonment is given to a lessee pursuant to Section 1951.3, the notice to the former tenant given pursuant to Section 1993.03 may be given at the same time as the notice of belief of abandonment, even though the tenancy is not terminated until the end of the period specified in the notice of belief of abandonment. The notices may be combined in one notice that contains all the information required by the sections under which the notices are given. *(Added by Stats.2008, c. 161 (A.B.2025), § 2. Amended by Stats.2009, c. 140 (A.B.1164), § 36.)*

CHAPTER 6. ASSIGNMENT AND SUBLEASE

Article	Section
1. General Provisions	1995.010
2. Restrictions on Transfer	1995.210
3. Breach and Remedies	1995.300

ARTICLE 1. GENERAL PROVISIONS

Section
1995.010. Application of chapter.
1995.020. Definitions.
1995.030. Further application of chapter.

§ 1995.010. Application of chapter

This chapter applies to transfer of a tenant's interest in a lease of real property for other than residential purposes. *(Added by Stats.1989, c. 982, § 2.)*

Cross References

Tenant defined for purposes of this Chapter, see Civil Code § 1995.020.
Transfer defined for purposes of this Chapter, see Civil Code § 1995.020.

§ 1995.020. Definitions

As used in this chapter:

(a) "Landlord" includes a tenant who is a sublandlord under a sublease.

(b) "Lease" means a lease or sublease of real property for other than residential purposes, and includes modifications and other agreements affecting a lease.

(c) "Restriction on transfer" means a provision in a lease that restricts the right of transfer of the tenant's interest in the lease.

(d) "Tenant" includes a subtenant or assignee.

(e) "Transfer" of a tenant's interest in a lease means an assignment, sublease, or other voluntary or involuntary transfer or encumbrance of all or part of a tenant's interest in the lease. *(Added by Stats.1989, c. 982, § 2.)*

§ 1995.030. Further application of chapter

Except as provided in Section 1995.270, this chapter applies to a lease executed before, on, or after January 1, 1990. *(Added by Stats.1989, c. 982, § 2.)*

ARTICLE 2. RESTRICTIONS ON TRANSFER

Section
1995.210. Restrictions on transfer of tenant's interest.
1995.220. Construction in favor of transferability.
1995.230. Prohibition of transfer.
1995.240. Express standards or conditions of transfer.
1995.250. Consent of landlord; requirements.
1995.260. Unreasonably withheld consent; burden of proof.
1995.270. Legislative findings and declarations.

§ 1995.210. Restrictions on transfer of tenant's interest

(a) Subject to the limitations in this chapter, a lease may include a restriction on transfer of the tenant's interest in the lease.

(b) Unless a lease includes a restriction on transfer, a tenant's rights under the lease include unrestricted transfer of the tenant's interest in the lease. *(Added by Stats.1989, c. 982, § 2.)*

Cross References

Restriction on transfer defined for purposes of this Chapter, see Civil Code § 1995.020.
Tenant defined for purposes of this Chapter, see Civil Code § 1995.020.
Transfer defined for purposes of this Chapter, see Civil Code § 1995.020.

§ 1995.220. Construction in favor of transferability

An ambiguity in a restriction on transfer of a tenant's interest in a lease shall be construed in favor of transferability. *(Added by Stats.1989, c. 982, § 2.)*

Cross References

Restriction on transfer defined for purposes of this Chapter, see Civil Code § 1995.020.
Tenant defined for purposes of this Chapter, see Civil Code § 1995.020.
Transfer defined for purposes of this Chapter, see Civil Code § 1995.020.

§ 1995.230. Prohibition of transfer

A restriction on transfer of a tenant's interest in a lease may absolutely prohibit transfer. *(Added by Stats.1989, c. 982, § 2.)*

Cross References

Restriction on transfer defined for purposes of this Chapter, see Civil Code § 1995.020.
Tenant defined for purposes of this Chapter, see Civil Code § 1995.020.
Transfer defined for purposes of this Chapter, see Civil Code § 1995.020.

§ 1995.240. Express standards or conditions of transfer

A restriction on transfer of a tenant's interest in a lease may provide that the transfer is subject to any express standard or condition, including, but not limited to, a provision that the landlord is entitled to some or all of any consideration the tenant receives from a transferee in excess of the rent under the lease. *(Added by Stats.1989, c. 982, § 2.)*

Cross References

Landlord defined for purposes of this Chapter, see Civil Code § 1995.020.
Restriction on transfer defined for purposes of this Chapter, see Civil Code § 1995.020.
Tenant defined for purposes of this Chapter, see Civil Code § 1995.020.
Transfer defined for purposes of this Chapter, see Civil Code § 1995.020.

§ 1995.250. Consent of landlord; requirements

A restriction on transfer of a tenant's interest in a lease may require the landlord's consent for transfer subject to any express standard or condition for giving or withholding consent, including, but not limited to, either of the following:

(a) The landlord's consent may not be unreasonably withheld.

(b) The landlord's consent may be withheld subject to express standards or conditions. *(Added by Stats.1989, c. 982, § 2.)*

Cross References

Landlord defined for purposes of this Chapter, see Civil Code § 1995.020.
Restriction on transfer defined for purposes of this Chapter, see Civil Code § 1995.020.

Tenant defined for purposes of this Chapter, see Civil Code § 1995.020.

Transfer defined for purposes of this Chapter, see Civil Code § 1995.020.

§ 1995.260. Unreasonably withheld consent; burden of proof

If a restriction on transfer of the tenant's interest in a lease requires the landlord's consent for transfer but provides no standard for giving or withholding consent, the restriction on transfer shall be construed to include an implied standard that the landlord's consent may not be unreasonably withheld. Whether the landlord's consent has been unreasonably withheld in a particular case is a question of fact on which the tenant has the burden of proof. The tenant may satisfy the burden of proof by showing that, in response to the tenant's written request for a statement of reasons for withholding consent, the landlord has failed, within a reasonable time, to state in writing a reasonable objection to the transfer. *(Added by Stats.1989, c. 982, § 2.)*

Cross References

Burden of proof, generally, see Evidence Code § 500 et seq.

Landlord defined for purposes of this Chapter, see Civil Code § 1995.020.

Restriction on transfer defined for purposes of this Chapter, see Civil Code § 1995.020.

Tenant defined for purposes of this Chapter, see Civil Code § 1995.020.

Transfer defined for purposes of this Chapter, see Civil Code § 1995.020.

§ 1995.270. Legislative findings and declarations

(a) The Legislature finds and declares:

(1) It is the public policy of the state and fundamental to the commerce and economic development of the state to enable and facilitate freedom of contract by the parties to commercial real property leases.

(2) The parties to commercial real property leases must be able to negotiate and conduct their affairs in reasonable reliance on the rights and protections given them under the laws of the state.

(3) Until the case of Kendall v. Ernest Pestana, Inc., 40 Cal.3d 488 (1985), and its predecessor, Cohen v. Ratinoff, 147 Cal.App.3d 321 (1983), the parties to commercial real property leases could reasonably rely on the law of the state to provide that if a lease restriction requires the landlord's consent for transfer of the tenant's interest in the lease but provides no standard for giving or withholding consent, the landlord's consent may be unreasonably withheld.

(4) The Kendall and Cohen decisions reversed the law on which parties to commercial real property leases executed before September 23, 1983, the date of the Cohen decision, could reasonably rely, thereby frustrating the expectations of the parties, with the result of impairing commerce and economic development.

(b) Section 1995.260 applies to a restriction on transfer executed on or after September 23, 1983. If a restriction on transfer executed before September 23, 1983, requires the landlord's consent for the tenant's transfer but provides no standard for giving or withholding consent, the landlord's consent may be unreasonably withheld. For purposes of this subdivision, if the terms of a restriction on transfer are fixed by an option or other agreement, the restriction on transfer is deemed to be executed on the date of execution of the option or other agreement. *(Added by Stats.1989, c. 982, § 2.)*

Cross References

Landlord defined for purposes of this Chapter, see Civil Code § 1995.020.

Restriction on transfer defined for purposes of this Chapter, see Civil Code § 1995.020.

Tenant defined for purposes of this Chapter, see Civil Code § 1995.020.

Transfer defined for purposes of this Chapter, see Civil Code § 1995.020.

ARTICLE 3. BREACH AND REMEDIES

Section
1995.300. Restrictions on remedies.
1995.310. Consent of landlord to transfer; unreasonable withholding of consent.
1995.320. Transfer by tenant of interest in violation of lease.
1995.330. Transfers to assignees; joint and several liability for transfers in violation; termination by landlord.
1995.340. Subsequent transfers; effect of landlord's consent to or waiver of restrictions for prior transfers.
1996, 1997. Repealed.

§ 1995.300. Restrictions on remedies

A remedy provided by law for violation of the rights of the tenant or of the landlord concerning transfer of a tenant's interest in a lease, including a remedy provided in this article, is (a) subject to an express provision in the lease that affects the remedy and (b) subject to any applicable defense, whether legal or equitable, including, but not limited to, waiver and estoppel. *(Added by Stats.1991, c. 67 (S.B.256), § 2.)*

Cross References

Landlord defined for purposes of this Chapter, see Civil Code § 1995.020.

Tenant defined for purposes of this Chapter, see Civil Code § 1995.020.

Transfer defined for purposes of this Chapter, see Civil Code § 1995.020.

§ 1995.310. Consent of landlord to transfer; unreasonable withholding of consent

If a restriction on transfer of a tenant's interest in a lease requires the landlord's consent for transfer subject to an express or implied standard that the landlord's consent may not be unreasonably withheld, and the landlord unreasonably withholds consent to a transfer in violation of the tenant's rights under the lease, in addition to any other remedies provided by law for breach of a lease, the tenant has all the remedies provided for breach of contract, including, but not limited to, either or both of the following:

(a) The right to contract damages caused by the landlord's breach.

(b) The right to terminate the lease. *(Added by Stats.1991, c. 67 (S.B.256), § 2.)*

§ 1995.310 OBLIGATIONS

Cross References

Landlord defined for purposes of this Chapter, see Civil Code § 1995.020.
Restriction on transfer defined for purposes of this Chapter, see Civil Code § 1995.020.
Tenant defined for purposes of this Chapter, see Civil Code § 1995.020.
Transfer defined for purposes of this Chapter, see Civil Code § 1995.020.

§ 1995.320. Transfer by tenant of interest in violation of lease

If a tenant transfers the tenant's interest in a lease in violation of a restriction on transfer of the tenant's interest in the lease, in addition to any other remedies provided by law for breach of a lease, the landlord has all the remedies provided for breach of contract, including, but not limited to, either or both of the following:

(a) The right to contract damages caused by the tenant's breach.

(b) The right to terminate the lease. *(Added by Stats.1991, c. 67 (S.B.256), § 2.)*

Cross References

Landlord defined for purposes of this Chapter, see Civil Code § 1995.020.
Restriction on transfer defined for purposes of this Chapter, see Civil Code § 1995.020.
Tenant defined for purposes of this Chapter, see Civil Code § 1995.020.
Transfer defined for purposes of this Chapter, see Civil Code § 1995.020.

§ 1995.330. Transfers to assignees; joint and several liability for transfers in violation; termination by landlord

(a) An assignee who receives or makes a transfer in violation of a restriction on transfer of a tenant's interest in a lease is jointly and severally liable with the tenant for contract damages under Section 1995.320. For this purpose, the provisions of Section 1951.2 applicable to a lessee apply to an assignee.

(b) The landlord's right to terminate a lease under Section 1995.320 includes the right to terminate a transfer without terminating the lease. If the landlord terminates a transfer without terminating the lease, the assignee or subtenant in possession is guilty of unlawful detainer and the landlord may obtain possession from the assignee or subtenant without terminating the right to possession of the tenant. For this purpose, the landlord may use the procedure provided in Chapter 4 (commencing with Section 1159) of Title 3 of Part 3 of the Code of Civil Procedure, with the changes necessary to make the procedure applicable to this subdivision. *(Added by Stats.1991, c. 67 (S.B.256), § 2.)*

Cross References

Landlord defined for purposes of this Chapter, see Civil Code § 1995.020.
Remedy provided by lease, see Civil Code § 1951.4.
Restriction on transfer defined for purposes of this Chapter, see Civil Code § 1995.020.
Tenant defined for purposes of this Chapter, see Civil Code § 1995.020.
Transfer defined for purposes of this Chapter, see Civil Code § 1995.020.

§ 1995.340. Subsequent transfers; effect of landlord's consent to or waiver of restrictions for prior transfers

(a) Subject to subdivision (b), a restriction on transfer of a tenant's interest in a lease applies to a subsequent transfer by a tenant, an assignee, or a subtenant notwithstanding the landlord's consent to a prior transfer or the landlord's waiver of a standard or condition for a prior transfer.

(b) Subdivision (a) does not apply if either of the following conditions is satisfied:

(1) The lease provides expressly that the restriction on transfer is limited to the original tenant.

(2) The landlord states expressly in writing that the consent or waiver applies to a subsequent transfer. *(Added by Stats.1991, c. 67 (S.B.256), § 2.)*

Cross References

Landlord defined for purposes of this Chapter, see Civil Code § 1995.020.
Restriction on transfer defined for purposes of this Chapter, see Civil Code § 1995.020.
Tenant defined for purposes of this Chapter, see Civil Code § 1995.020.
Transfer defined for purposes of this Chapter, see Civil Code § 1995.020.

§§ 1996, 1997. Repealed by Stats.1937, c. 90, § 8100

CHAPTER 7. USE RESTRICTIONS

Article	Section
1. General Provisions	1997.010
2. Use Restrictions	1997.210

ARTICLE 1. GENERAL PROVISIONS

Section
1997.010. Application of chapter.
1997.020. Definitions.
1997.030. Restrictions otherwise prohibited by law.
1997.040. Computation of rental loss; availability of remedy provided by lease.
1997.050. Retrospective and prospective application of chapter to leases.

§ 1997.010. Application of chapter

This chapter applies to a restriction on use of leased property by a tenant under a lease of real property for other than residential purposes. *(Added by Stats.1991, c. 67 (S.B.256), § 3.)*

Cross References

Lease defined for purposes of this Chapter, see Civil Code § 1997.020.
Restriction on use defined for purposes of this Chapter, see Civil Code § 1997.020.
Tenant defined for purposes of this Chapter, see Civil Code § 1997.020.

§ 1997.020. Definitions

As used in this chapter:

(a) "Landlord" includes a tenant who is a sublandlord under a sublease.

(b) "Lease" means a lease or sublease of real property for other than residential purposes, and includes modifications and other agreements affecting a lease.

(c) "Restriction on use" means a provision in a lease that restricts the use of leased property by a tenant, whether by limiting use to a specified purpose, mandating use for a specified purpose, prohibiting use for a specified purpose, limiting or prohibiting a change in use, or otherwise.

(d) "Tenant" includes a subtenant or assignee. *(Added by Stats.1991, c. 67 (S.B.256), § 3.)*

§ 1997.030. Restrictions otherwise prohibited by law

Nothing in this chapter authorizes a restriction on use that is otherwise prohibited by law. *(Added by Stats.1991, c. 67 (S.B.256), § 3.)*

Cross References

Restriction on use defined for purposes of this Chapter, see Civil Code § 1997.020.

§ 1997.040. Computation of rental loss; availability of remedy provided by lease

(a) For the purpose of subdivision (a) of Section 1951.2 (damages on termination for breach), the amount of rental loss that could be or could have been reasonably avoided is computed by taking into account any reasonable use of the leased property. However, if the lease contains a restriction on use that is enforceable under this chapter, the computation shall take into account the restricted use of the property except to the extent the tenant proves that under all the circumstances enforcement of the restriction would be unreasonable. The circumstances include, but are not limited to, those involving both the leased property and any building or complex in which it is located.

(b) The remedy described in Section 1951.4 (continuation of lease after breach and abandonment) is available notwithstanding the presence in the lease of a restriction on use of the leased property. The restriction on use applies under Section 1951.4 if it is enforceable under this chapter except to the extent the tenant proves that under all the circumstances enforcement of the restriction would be unreasonable. The circumstances include, but are not limited to, those involving both the leased property and any building or complex in which it is located. *(Added by Stats.1991, c. 67 (S.B.256), § 3.)*

Cross References

Lease defined for purposes of this Chapter, see Civil Code § 1997.020.
Restriction on use defined for purposes of this Chapter, see Civil Code § 1997.020.
Tenant defined for purposes of this Chapter, see Civil Code § 1997.020.

§ 1997.050. Retrospective and prospective application of chapter to leases

Except as provided in Section 1997.270, this chapter applies to a lease executed before, on, or after January 1, 1992. *(Added by Stats.1991, c. 67 (S.B.256), § 3.)*

Cross References

Lease defined for purposes of this Chapter, see Civil Code § 1997.020.

ARTICLE 2. USE RESTRICTIONS

Section
1997.210. Restrictions included in lease.
1997.220. Ambiguities in use restrictions; construction.
1997.230. Prohibitions on change in use.
1997.240. Change in use subject to express standards or conditions.
1997.250. Consent of landlord; standards or conditions for giving or withholding consent.
1997.260. Consent of landlord; absence of standards for giving or withholding consent.
1997.270. Application of § 1997.260; restrictions on use executed prior to Jan. 1, 1992; discretion to give or withhold consent.

§ 1997.210. Restrictions included in lease

(a) Subject to the limitations in this chapter, a lease may include a restriction on use of leased property by a tenant.

(b) Unless the lease includes a restriction on use, a tenant's rights under a lease include any reasonable use of leased property. *(Added by Stats.1991, c. 67 (S.B.256), § 3.)*

Cross References

Lease defined for purposes of this Chapter, see Civil Code § 1997.020.
Restriction on use defined for purposes of this Chapter, see Civil Code § 1997.020.
Tenant defined for purposes of this Chapter, see Civil Code § 1997.020.

§ 1997.220. Ambiguities in use restrictions; construction

An ambiguity in a restriction on use of leased property by a tenant shall be construed in favor of unrestricted use. *(Added by Stats.1991, c. 67 (S.B.256), § 3.)*

Cross References

Restriction on use defined for purposes of this Chapter, see Civil Code § 1997.020.
Tenant defined for purposes of this Chapter, see Civil Code § 1997.020.

§ 1997.230. Prohibitions on change in use

A restriction on use of leased property by a tenant may absolutely prohibit a change in use. *(Added by Stats.1991, c. 67 (S.B.256), § 3.)*

Cross References

Restriction on use defined for purposes of this Chapter, see Civil Code § 1997.020.
Tenant defined for purposes of this Chapter, see Civil Code § 1997.020.

§ 1997.240. Change in use subject to express standards or conditions

A restriction on use of leased property by a tenant may provide that a change in use is subject to any express standard or condition. *(Added by Stats.1991, c. 67 (S.B.256), § 3.)*

§ 1997.240

Cross References

Restriction on use defined for purposes of this Chapter, see Civil Code § 1997.020.

Tenant defined for purposes of this Chapter, see Civil Code § 1997.020.

§ 1997.250. Consent of landlord; standards or conditions for giving or withholding consent

A restriction on use of leased property by a tenant may require the landlord's consent for a change in use subject to any express standard or condition for giving or withholding consent, including, but not limited to, either of the following:

(a) The landlord's consent may not be unreasonably withheld.

(b) The landlord's consent may be withheld subject to express standards or conditions. *(Added by Stats.1991, c. 67 (S.B.256), § 3.)*

Cross References

Landlord defined for purposes of this Chapter, see Civil Code § 1997.020.

Restriction on use defined for purposes of this Chapter, see Civil Code § 1997.020.

Tenant defined for purposes of this Chapter, see Civil Code § 1997.020.

§ 1997.260. Consent of landlord; absence of standards for giving or withholding consent

If a restriction on use of leased property by a tenant requires the landlord's consent for a change in use but provides no standard for giving or withholding consent, the restriction shall be construed to include an implied standard that the landlord's consent may not be unreasonably withheld. Whether the landlord's consent has been unreasonably withheld in a particular case is a question of fact on which the tenant has the burden of proof. The tenant may satisfy the burden of proof by showing that, in response to the tenant's written request for a statement of reasons for withholding consent, the landlord has failed, within a reasonable time, to state in writing a reasonable objection to the change in use. *(Added by Stats.1991, c. 67 (S.B.256), § 3.)*

Cross References

Burden of proof, generally, see Evidence Code § 500 et seq.

Landlord defined for purposes of this Chapter, see Civil Code § 1997.020.

Restriction on use defined for purposes of this Chapter, see Civil Code § 1997.020.

Tenant defined for purposes of this Chapter, see Civil Code § 1997.020.

§ 1997.270. Application of § 1997.260; restrictions on use executed prior to Jan. 1, 1992; discretion to give or withhold consent

(a) Section 1997.260 applies to a restriction on use executed on or after January 1, 1992. If a restriction on use executed before January 1, 1992, requires the landlord's consent for a change in use of leased premises by a tenant, but provides no standard for giving or withholding consent, the landlord has sole and absolute discretion to give or withhold consent.

(b) For purposes of this section, if the terms of a restriction on change in use are fixed by an option or other agreement, the restriction on change in use is deemed to be executed on the date of execution of the option or other agreement. *(Added by Stats.1991, c. 67 (S.B.256), § 3.)*

Cross References

Landlord defined for purposes of this Chapter, see Civil Code § 1997.020.

Restriction on use defined for purposes of this Chapter, see Civil Code § 1997.020.

Tenant defined for purposes of this Chapter, see Civil Code § 1997.020.

Title 6

SERVICE

Chapter	Section
1. Service With Employment [Repealed]	
2. Particular Employments	2009
3. Service Without Employment	2078
4. Lost and Unclaimed Property	2080

CHAPTER 1. SERVICE WITH EMPLOYMENT [REPEALED]

§§ 1998 to 2004. Repealed by Stats.1937, c. 90, p. 326, § 8100

CHAPTER 2. PARTICULAR EMPLOYMENTS

Article	Section
1. Master and Servant [Repealed]	
2. Agents	2019
3. Factors	2026
4. Shipmasters [Repealed]	
5. Mates and Seamen [Repealed]	
6. Ships' Managers [Repealed]	

ARTICLE 1. MASTER AND SERVANT [REPEALED]

§§ 2009 to 2012. Repealed by Stats.1937, c. 90, p. 328, § 8100

§ 2013. Repealed by Stats.1921, c. 99, p. 95, § 1

§§ 2014, 2015. Repealed by Stats.1937, c. 90, p. 328, § 8100

ARTICLE 2. AGENTS

Section	
2019.	Conformity to limits of authority.
2020.	Duty to keep principal informed.
2021.	Duties of collecting agent.
2022.	Responsibility of agent of agent.

Cross References

Provisions of this Title, in respect to rights and obligations of parties to contract, as subordinate to intention of parties and waiver of benefit thereof, see Civil Code § 3268.

§ 2019. Conformity to limits of authority

An agent must not exceed the limits of his actual authority, as defined by the Title on Agency. *(Enacted in 1872.)*

Cross References

Agency, see Civil Code § 2295 et seq.
Authority of agents, see Civil Code § 2304 et seq.

§ 2020. Duty to keep principal informed

An agent must use ordinary diligence to keep his principal informed of his acts in the course of the agency. *(Enacted in 1872.)*

Cross References

Employee's duty to account to employer, see Labor Code § 2861.

§ 2021. Duties of collecting agent

An agent employed to collect a negotiable instrument must collect it promptly, and take all measures necessary to charge the parties thereto, in case of its dishonor; and, if it is a bill of exchange, must present it for acceptance with reasonable diligence. *(Enacted in 1872.)*

Cross References

Bank deposits and collections, see Commercial Code § 4101 et seq.

§ 2022. Responsibility of agent of agent

A mere agent of an agent is not responsible as such to the principal of the latter. *(Enacted in 1872.)*

Cross References

Authorized sub-agent, see Civil Code § 2351.
Unauthorized sub-agent, see Civil Code § 2350.

ARTICLE 3. FACTORS

Section
2026. "Factor" defined.
2027. Obedience to instructions; exception.
2028. Credit sales.
2029. Guaranty commission; liability to pay price.
2030. Relief from responsibility to guarantee sales or remittance.

§ 2026. "Factor" defined

A factor is an agent who, in the pursuit of an independent calling, is employed by another to sell property for him, and is vested by the latter with the possession or control of the property, or authorized to receive payment therefor from the purchaser. *(Enacted in 1872.)*

Cross References

Actual authority of factor, see Civil Code § 2368.
Authority of agents, generally, see Civil Code § 2304 et seq.
Factor defined, see Civil Code § 2367.
Ostensible authority of factor, see Civil Code § 2369.

§ 2027. Obedience to instructions; exception

A factor must obey the instructions of his principal to the same extent as any other employé,[1] notwithstanding any advances he may have made to his principal upon the property consigned to him, except that if the principal forbids him to sell at the market price, he may, nevertheless, sell for his reimbursement, after giving to his principal reasonable notice of his intention to do so, and of the time and place of sale, and proceeding in all respects as a pledgee. *(Enacted in 1872.)*

[1] So in chaptered copy.

Cross References

Actual authority of factor, see Civil Code § 2368.
Factor defined, see Civil Code § 2026.
Factor's lien, see Civil Code § 3053.
Ostensible authority of factor, see Civil Code § 2369.
Waiver of suretyship rights and defenses, see Labor Code § 2856.

§ 2028. Credit sales

A factor may sell property consigned to him on such credit as is usual; but, having once agreed with the purchaser upon the term of credit, may not extend it. *(Enacted in 1872.)*

Cross References

Factor authorized to sell on credit, see Civil Code § 2368.
Factor defined, see Civil Code § 2026.

§ 2029. Guaranty commission; liability to pay price

A factor who charges his principal with a guaranty commission upon a sale, thereby assumes absolutely to pay the price when it falls due, as if it were a debt of his own, and not as a mere guarantor for the purchaser; but he does not thereby assume any additional responsibility for the safety of his remittance of the proceeds. *(Enacted in 1872.)*

Cross References

Factor defined, see Civil Code § 2026.

§ 2030. Relief from responsibility to guarantee sales or remittance

A factor who receives property for sale, under a general agreement or usage to guarantee the sales or the remittance of the proceeds, cannot relieve himself from responsibility therefor without the consent of his principal. *(Enacted in 1872.)*

Cross References

Factor defined, see Civil Code § 2026.

ARTICLE 4. SHIPMASTERS [REPEALED]

§§ 2034 to 2044. Repealed by Stats.1937, c. 368, p. 1002, § 10001

ARTICLE 5. MATES AND SEAMEN [REPEALED]

§§ 2048 to 2064. Repealed by Stats.1937, c. 368, p. 1002, § 10001

§ 2065. Repealed by Code Am.1873–74, c. 612, p. 247, § 211

§ 2066. Repealed by Stats.1937, c. 368, p. 1002, § 10001

OBLIGATIONS

ARTICLE 6. SHIPS' MANAGERS [REPEALED]

§§ 2070 to 2072. Repealed by Stats.1937, c. 368, p. 1002, § 10001

CHAPTER 3. SERVICE WITHOUT EMPLOYMENT

Article	Section
1. Voluntary Interference with Property	2078
2. Duty to Prospective Purchaser of Real Property	2079

ARTICLE 1. VOLUNTARY INTERFERENCE WITH PROPERTY

Section	
2078.	Voluntary interference with property.

§ 2078. Voluntary interference with property

One who officiously, and without the consent of the real or apparent owner of a thing, takes it into his possession for the purpose of rendering a service about it, must complete such service, and use ordinary care, diligence, and reasonable skill about the same. He is not entitled to any compensation for his service or expenses, except that he may deduct actual and necessary expenses incurred by him about such service from any profits which his service has caused the thing to acquire for its owner, and must account to the owner for the residue. *(Enacted in 1872.)*

Cross References

Obligations of employee, gratuitous service, see Labor Code § 2850 et seq.

ARTICLE 2. DUTY TO PROSPECTIVE PURCHASER OF REAL PROPERTY

Section	
2079.	Real estate brokers and salespersons; inspections and disclosures; standards of professional conduct.
2079.1.	Application of article; leases with options; ground leases; real property sales contracts.
2079.2.	Real estate brokers; standard of care.
2079.3.	Scope of inspection.
2079.4.	Breach of duty; limitation of actions.
2079.5.	Buyers or prospective buyers; duty of reasonable care.
2079.6.	Subdivision sales subject to certain reporting requirements.
2079.7.	Environmental hazards; duty to disclose.
2079.7.	Environmental hazards; duty to disclose.
2079.8.	Delivery of Homeowner's Guide to Earthquake Safety to buyer of real property; effect on duty of sellers or brokers to disclose existence of known hazards.
2079.9.	Delivery of Commercial Property Owner's Guide to Earthquake Safety to buyer of real property; effect on duty of sellers and brokers to disclose existence of known hazards.
2079.10.	Home energy rating program; information booklet.
2079.10.5.	Contracts for sale; required notice; gas and hazardous liquid transmission pipelines.
2079.10a.	Specified residential real property transactions; contents of notice.
2079.11.	Consumer information publications; earthquake guide; costs.
2079.12.	Duty of care for real estate licensees; legislative findings and declarations.
2079.13.	Definitions.
2079.14.	Disclosure form; furnishing to buyer and seller; exceptions.
2079.15.	Acknowledgment of receipt; refusal to sign.
2079.16.	Disclosure form.
2079.17.	Agency relationship; disclosure and confirmation.
2079.18.	Repealed.
2079.19.	Payment of compensation; effect on determination of agency relationship.
2079.20.	Form of agency relationship; selection; condition of employment.
2079.21.	Dual agents; disclosures prohibited.
2079.22.	Seller's agent may also be buyer's agent.
2079.23.	Agency contract; modification or alteration; indemnification of lender or auction company by homeowner or listing agent prohibited as condition of lender's approval.
2079.24.	Disclosure and fiduciary duties; effect of article.
2079.25.	Application of Section 1102.1(d).

Cross References

Professional liability insurance, real estate licensees, exclusions, see Insurance Code § 11589.5.

§ 2079. Real estate brokers and salespersons; inspections and disclosures; standards of professional conduct

(a) It is the duty of a real estate broker or salesperson, licensed under Division 4 (commencing with Section 10000) of the Business and Professions Code, to a prospective buyer of residential real property improved with one to four dwelling units or a manufactured home as defined in Section 18007 of the Health and Safety Code, to conduct a reasonably competent and diligent visual inspection of the property offered for sale and to disclose to that prospective buyer all facts materially affecting the value or desirability of the property that an investigation would reveal, if that broker has a written contract with the seller to find or obtain a buyer or is a broker who acts in cooperation with that broker to find and obtain a buyer.

(b) It is the duty of a real estate broker or salesperson, licensed under Division 4 (commencing with Section 10000) of the Business and Professions Code, to comply with this section and any regulations imposing standards of professional conduct adopted pursuant to Section 10080 of the Business and Professions Code with reference to Sections 10176 and 10177 of the Business and Professions Code. *(Added by Stats.1985, c. 223, § 2. Amended by Stats.1994, c. 339 (S.B.1509), § 1; Stats.1996, c. 812 (A.B.2221), § 2; Stats. 2018, c. 907 (A.B.1289), § 30, eff. Jan. 1, 2019; Stats.2019, c. 310 (A.B.892), § 8, eff. Jan. 1, 2020.)*

Cross References

Contracts for sale, required notice, gas and hazardous liquid transmission pipelines, see Civil Code § 2079.10.5.

Toxic Mold Protection Act of 2001, see Health and Safety Code § 26100 et seq.

§ 2079.1. Application of article; leases with options; ground leases; real property sales contracts

The provisions of this article relating sale transactions of residential real property comprising one to four dwelling units apply with equal force to leases of that property that include an option to purchase, ground leases of land on which one to four dwelling units have been constructed, or real property sales contracts, as defined in Section 2985, for that property. *(Added by Stats.1985, c. 223, § 2.)*

§ 2079.2. Real estate brokers; standard of care

The standard of care owed by a broker under this article is the degree of care that a reasonably prudent real estate licensee would exercise and is measured by the degree of knowledge through education, experience, and examination, required to obtain a license under Division 4 (commencing with Section 10000) of the Business and Professions Code. *(Added by Stats.1985, c. 223, § 2.)*

§ 2079.3. Scope of inspection

The inspection to be performed pursuant to this article does not include or involve an inspection of areas that are reasonably and normally inaccessible to this type of an inspection, nor an affirmative inspection of areas off the site of the subject property or public records or permits concerning the title or use of the property, and, if the property comprises a unit in a planned development as defined in Section 11003 of the Business and Professions Code, a condominium as defined in Section 783, or a stock cooperative as defined in Section 11003.2 of the Business and Professions Code, does not include an inspection of more than the unit offered for sale, if the seller or the broker complies with the provisions of Sections 4525 to 4580, inclusive. *(Added by Stats.1985, c. 223, § 2. Amended by Stats.1994, c. 339 (S.B.1509), § 2; Stats.2012, c. 181 (A.B. 806), § 38, operative Jan. 1, 2014.)*

§ 2079.4. Breach of duty; limitation of actions

In no event shall the time for commencement of legal action for breach of duty imposed by this article exceed two years from the date of possession, which means the date of recordation, the date of close of escrow, or the date of occupancy, whichever occurs first. *(Added by Stats.1985, c. 223, § 2.)*

§ 2079.5. Buyers or prospective buyers; duty of reasonable care

Nothing in this article relieves a buyer or prospective buyer of the duty to exercise reasonable care to protect himself or herself, including those facts which are known to or within the diligent attention and observation of the buyer or prospective buyer. *(Added by Stats.1985, c. 223, § 2.)*

§ 2079.6. Subdivision sales subject to certain reporting requirements

This article does not apply to sales which are required to be preceded by the furnishing, to a prospective buyer, of a copy of a public report pursuant to Section 11018.1 or Section 11234 of the Business and Professions Code and sales that can be made without a public report pursuant to Section 11010.4 of the Business and Professions Code, unless the property has been previously occupied. *(Added by Stats.1988, c. 274, § 1. Amended by Stats.2015, c. 88 (A.B.905), § 3, eff. Jan. 1, 2016; Stats.2018, c. 907 (A.B.1289), § 31, eff. Jan. 1, 2019.)*

§ 2079.7. Environmental hazards; duty to disclose

Section operative until Jan. 1, 2024. See, also, § 2079.7 operative Jan. 1, 2024.

(a) If a consumer information booklet described in Section 10084.1 of the Business and Professions Code is delivered to a buyer in connection with the sale of real property, including property specified in Section 1102 of the Civil Code, or manufactured housing, as defined in Section 18007 of the Health and Safety Code, a seller or broker is not required to provide additional information concerning, and the information shall be deemed to be adequate to inform the buyer regarding, common environmental hazards, as described in the booklet, that can affect real property.

(b) Notwithstanding subdivision (a), nothing in this section either increases or decreases the duties, if any, of sellers or brokers, including, but not limited to, the duties of a seller or broker under this article, Article 1.5 (commencing with Section 1102) of Chapter 2 of Title 4 of Part 4 of Division 2, or Section 25359.7 of the Health and Safety Code, or alters the duty of a seller or broker to disclose the existence of known environmental hazards on or affecting the real property. *(Added by Stats.1989, c. 969, § 2. Amended by Stats.2018, c. 907 (A.B.1289), § 32, eff. Jan. 1, 2019.)*

§ 2079.7. Environmental hazards; duty to disclose

Section operative Jan. 1, 2024. See, also, § 2079.7 operative until Jan. 1, 2024.

(a) If a consumer information booklet described in Section 10084.1 of the Business and Professions Code is delivered to a buyer in connection with the sale of real property, including property specified in Section 1102 of the Civil Code, or manufactured housing, as defined in Section 18007 of the Health and Safety Code, a seller or broker is not required to provide additional information concerning, and the information shall be deemed to be adequate to inform the buyer regarding, common environmental hazards, as described in the booklet, that can affect real property.

(b) Notwithstanding subdivision (a), nothing in this section either increases or decreases the duties, if any, of sellers or brokers, including, but not limited to, the duties of a seller or broker under this article, Article 1.5 (commencing with Section 1102) of Chapter 2 of Title 4 of Part 4 of Division 2, or Section 78700 of the Health and Safety Code, or alters the duty of a seller or broker to disclose the existence of known environmental hazards on or affecting the real property. *(Added by Stats.1989, c. 969, § 2. Amended by Stats.2018, c. 907 (A.B.1289), § 32, eff. Jan. 1, 2019; Stats.2022, c. 258 (A.B.2327), § 5, eff. Jan. 1, 2023, operative Jan. 1, 2024.)*

§ 2079.8. Delivery of Homeowner's Guide to Earthquake Safety to buyer of real property; effect on duty of sellers or brokers to disclose existence of known hazards

(a) If a Homeowner's Guide to Earthquake Safety described in Section 10149 of the Business and Professions

§ 2079.8

Code is delivered to a buyer in connection with the sale of real property, including property specified in Section 1102 or under Chapter 7.5 (commencing with Section 2621) of Division 2 of the Public Resources Code, a seller or broker is not required to provide additional information concerning, and the information shall be deemed to be adequate to inform the buyer regarding, geologic and seismic hazards, in general, as described in the guide, that may affect real property and mitigating measures that the buyer or seller might consider.

(b) Notwithstanding subdivision (a), nothing in this section increases or decreases the duties, if any, of sellers or brokers, including, but not limited to, the duties of a seller or broker under this article, Article 1.5 (commencing with Section 1102) of Chapter 2 of Title 4 of Part 4 of Division 2, or under Chapter 7.5 (commencing with Section 2621) of Division 2 of the Public Resources Code, or alters the duty of a seller or broker to disclose the existence of known hazards on or affecting the real property. *(Added by Stats.1990, c. 1499 (A.B.2959), § 2. Amended by Stats.1991, c. 550 (A.B.29), § 2; Stats.2018, c. 907 (A.B.1289), § 33, eff. Jan. 1, 2019.)*

§ 2079.9. Delivery of Commercial Property Owner's Guide to Earthquake Safety to buyer of real property; effect on duty of sellers and brokers to disclose existence of known hazards

(a) If a Commercial Property Owner's Guide to Earthquake Safety described in Section 10147 of the Business and Professions Code is delivered to a buyer in connection with the sale of real property, including property specified in Section 1102 or under Chapter 7.5 (commencing with Section 2621) of Division 2 of the Public Resources Code, a seller or broker is not required to provide additional information concerning, and the information shall be deemed to be adequate to inform the buyer regarding, geologic and seismic hazards, in general, as described in the guide, that may affect real property and mitigating measures that the buyer or seller might consider.

(b) Notwithstanding subdivision (a), nothing in this section increases or decreases the duties, if any, of sellers, their real estate brokers or agents under this article or under Chapter 7.5 (commencing with Section 2621) or Chapter 7.8 (commencing with Section 2690) of Division 2 of the Public Resources Code, or alters the duty of a seller, agent, or broker to disclose the existence of known hazards on or affecting the real property. *(Added by Stats.1991, c. 859 (A.B.1968), § 2. Amended by Stats.2018, c. 907 (A.B.1289), § 34, eff. Jan. 1, 2019.)*

Cross References

Application of article, waiver of requirements, see Civil Code § 1102.

§ 2079.10. Home energy rating program; information booklet

(a) If the informational booklet published pursuant to Section 25402.9 of the Public Resources Code, concerning the statewide home energy rating program adopted pursuant to Section 25942 of the Public Resources Code, is delivered to a buyer in connection with the sale of real property, including, but not limited to, property specified in Section 1102, manufactured homes as defined in Section 18007 of the Health and Safety Code, and property subject to Chapter 7.5 (commencing with Section 2621) of Division 2 of the Public Resources Code, the seller or broker is not required to provide information additional to that contained in the booklet concerning home energy ratings, and the information in the booklet shall be deemed to be adequate to inform the buyer about the existence of a statewide home energy rating program.

(b) Notwithstanding subdivision (a), nothing in this section alters any existing duty of the seller or broker under any other law including, but not limited to, the duties of a seller or broker under this article, Article 1.5 (commencing with Section 1102) of Chapter 2 of Title 4 of Part 4 of Division 2 of the Civil Code, or Chapter 7.5 (commencing with Section 2621) of Division 2 of the Public Resources Code, to disclose information concerning the existence of a home energy rating program affecting the real property.

(c) If the informational booklet or materials described in Section 375.5 of the Water Code concerning water conservation and water conservation programs are delivered to a buyer in connection with the sale of real property, including property described in subdivision (a), the seller or broker is not required to provide information concerning water conservation and water conservation programs that is additional to that contained in the booklet or materials, and the information in the booklet or materials shall be deemed to be adequate to inform the buyer about water conservation and water conservation programs. *(Added by Stats.1992, c. 769 (S.B.1207), § 2. Amended by Stats.2004, c. 111 (A.B.2470), § 1; Stats.2018, c. 907 (A.B.1289), § 35, eff. Jan. 1, 2019.)*

Cross References

Public entities, water supplies, information booklets and materials, see Water Code § 375.5.

§ 2079.10.5. Contracts for sale; required notice; gas and hazardous liquid transmission pipelines

(a) Every contract for the sale of single-family residential real property entered into on or after July 1, 2013, shall contain, in not less than 8–point type, a notice as specified below:

NOTICE REGARDING GAS AND HAZARDOUS LIQUID TRANSMISSION PIPELINES

This notice is being provided simply to inform you that information about the general location of gas and hazardous liquid transmission pipelines is available to the public via the National Pipeline Mapping System (NPMS) Internet Web site maintained by the United States Department of Transportation at http://www.npms.phmsa.dot.gov/. To seek further information about possible transmission pipelines near the property, you may contact your local gas utility or other pipeline operators in the area. Contact information for pipeline operators is searchable by ZIP Code and county on the NPMS Internet Web site.

(b) Upon delivery of the notice to the buyer of the real property, the seller or broker is not required to provide information in addition to that contained in the notice regarding gas and hazardous liquid transmission pipelines in subdivision (a). The information in the notice shall be deemed to be adequate to inform the buyer about the existence of a statewide database of the locations of gas and hazardous liquid transmission pipelines and information from the database regarding those locations.

(c) Nothing in this section shall alter any existing duty under any other statute or decisional law imposed upon the seller or broker, including, but not limited to, the duties of a seller or broker under this article, or the duties of a seller or broker under Article 1.5 (commencing with Section 1102) of Chapter 2 of Title 4 of Part 4 of Division 2. *(Added by Stats.2012, c. 91 (A.B.1511), § 1. Amended by Stats.2018, c. 907 (A.B.1289), § 36, eff. Jan. 1, 2019.)*

§ 2079.10a. Specified residential real property transactions; contents of notice

(a) Every lease or rental agreement for single-family residential real property entered into on or after July 1, 1999, any leasehold interest in real property consisting of multiunit residential property with more than four dwelling units entered into after that date, and every contract for the sale of residential real property comprised of one to four dwelling units entered into on or after that date, shall contain, in not less than 8–point type, a notice as specified in paragraph (1), (2), or (3).

(1) A contract entered into by the parties on or after July 1, 1999, and before September 1, 2005, shall contain the following notice:

Notice: The California Department of Justice, sheriff's departments, police departments serving jurisdictions of 200,000 or more, and many other local law enforcement authorities maintain for public access a database of the locations of persons required to register pursuant to subdivision (a) of Section 290.4 of the Penal Code. The database is updated on a quarterly basis and is a source of information about the presence of these individuals in any neighborhood. The Department of Justice also maintains a Sex Offender Identification Line through which inquiries about individuals may be made. This is a "900" telephone service. Callers shall have specific information about individuals they are checking. Information regarding neighborhoods is not available through the "900" telephone service.

(2) A contract entered into by the parties on or after September 1, 2005, and before April 1, 2006, shall contain either the notice specified in paragraph (1) or the notice specified in paragraph (3).

(3) A contract entered into by the parties on or after April 1, 2006, shall contain the following notice:

Notice: Pursuant to Section 290.46 of the Penal Code, information about specified registered sex offenders is made available to the public via an Internet Web site maintained by the Department of Justice at www.meganslaw.ca.gov. Depending on an offender's criminal history, this information will include either the address at which the offender resides or the community of residence and ZIP Code in which the offender resides.

(b) Subject to subdivision (c), upon delivery of the notice to the lessee or buyer of the real property, the lessor, seller, or broker is not required to provide information in addition to that contained in the notice regarding the proximity of registered sex offenders. The information in the notice shall be deemed to be adequate to inform the lessee or buyer about the existence of a statewide database of the locations of registered sex offenders and information from the database regarding those locations. The information in the notice shall not give rise to any cause of action against the disclosing party by a registered sex offender.

(c) Notwithstanding subdivisions (a) and (b), nothing in this section shall alter any existing duty of the lessor, seller, or broker under any other statute or decisional law including, but not limited to, the duties of a lessor, seller, or broker under this article, or the duties of a seller or broker under Article 1.5 (commencing with Section 1102) of Chapter 2 of Title 4 of Part 4 of Division 2. *(Added by Stats.1998, c. 645 (S.B.1989), § 1. Amended by Stats.1999, c. 876 (A.B.248), § 4; Stats.2005, c. 722 (A.B.1323), § 1, eff. Oct. 7, 2005; Stats.2018, c. 907 (A.B.1289), § 37, eff. Jan. 1, 2019.)*

§ 2079.11. Consumer information publications; earthquake guide; costs

(a) Except as provided in subdivision (b), to the extent permitted by law, the consumer information publications referred to in this article, including, but not limited to, the information booklets described in Section 10084.1 of the Business and Professions Code and Section 25402.9 of the Public Resources Code, shall be in the public domain and freely available.

(b) Notwithstanding subdivision (a), the Seismic Safety Commission's Homeowner's Guide to Earthquake Safety, published pursuant to Section 10149 of the Business and Professions Code, shall be made available to the public at cost and for reproduction at no cost to any vendor who wishes to publish the guide, provided the vendor agrees to submit the guide to the commission prior to publication for content approval. *(Added by Stats.1994, c. 66 (S.B.1229), § 1. Amended by Stats.1998, c. 65 (A.B.1195), § 4, eff. June 9, 1998, operative June 1, 1998.)*

§ 2079.12. Duty of care for real estate licensees; legislative findings and declarations

(a) The Legislature hereby finds and declares all of the following:

(1) That the imprecision of terms in the opinion rendered in Easton v. Strassburger, 152 Cal.App.3d 90, and the absence of a comprehensive declaration of duties, standards, and exceptions, has caused insurers to modify professional liability coverage of real estate licensees and has caused confusion among real estate licensees as to the manner of performing the duty ascribed to them by the court.

(2) That it is necessary to resolve and make precise these issues in an expeditious manner.

(3) That it is desirable to facilitate the issuance of professional liability insurance as a resource for aggrieved members of the public.

(4) That Sections 2079 to 2079.6, inclusive, of this article should be construed as a definition of the duty of care found to exist by the holding of Easton v. Strassburger, 152 Cal.App.3d 90, and the manner of its discharge, and is declarative of the common law regarding this duty. Howev-

§ 2079.12

er, nothing in this section is intended to affect the court's ability to interpret Sections 2079 to 2079.6, inclusive.

(b) It is the intent of the Legislature to codify and make precise the holding of Easton v. Strassburger, 152 Cal.App.3d 90. It is not the intent of the Legislature to modify or restrict existing duties owed by real estate licensees. *(Added by Stats.1995, c. 428 (S.B.467), § 1. Amended by Stats.1996, c. 124 (A.B.3470), § 7; Stats.1996, c. 476 (A.B.2935), § 1.)*

§ 2079.13. Definitions

As used in this section and Sections 2079.7 and 2079.14 to 2079.24, inclusive, the following terms have the following meanings:

(a) "Agent" means a person acting under provisions of Title 9 (commencing with Section 2295) in a real property transaction, and includes a person who is licensed as a real estate broker under Chapter 3 (commencing with Section 10130) of Part 1 of Division 4 of the Business and Professions Code, and under whose license a listing is executed or an offer to purchase is obtained.

The agent in the real property transaction bears responsibility for that agent's salespersons or broker associates who perform as agents of the agent. When a salesperson or broker associate owes a duty to any principal, or to any buyer or seller who is not a principal, in a real property transaction, that duty is equivalent to the duty owed to that party by the broker for whom the salesperson or broker associate functions.

(b) "Buyer" means a transferee in a real property transaction, and includes a person who executes an offer to purchase real property from a seller through an agent, or who seeks the services of an agent in more than a casual, transitory, or preliminary manner, with the object of entering into a real property transaction. "Buyer" includes a vendee or lessee of real property.

(c) "Commercial real property" means all real property in the state, except (1) single-family residential real property, (2) dwelling units made subject to Chapter 2 (commencing with Section 1940) of Title 5, (3) a mobilehome, as defined in Section 798.3, (4) vacant land, or (5) a recreational vehicle, as defined in Section 799.29.

(d) "Dual agent" means an agent acting, either directly or through a salesperson or broker associate, as agent for both the seller and the buyer in a real property transaction.

(e) "Listing agreement" means a written contract between a seller of real property and an agent, by which the agent has been authorized to sell the real property or to find or obtain a buyer, including rendering other services for which a real estate license is required to the seller pursuant to the terms of the agreement.

(f) "Seller's agent" means a person who has obtained a listing of real property to act as an agent for compensation.

(g) "Listing price" is the amount expressed in dollars specified in the listing for which the seller is willing to sell the real property through the seller's agent.

(h) "Offering price" is the amount expressed in dollars specified in an offer to purchase for which the buyer is willing to buy the real property.

(i) "Offer to purchase" means a written contract executed by a buyer acting through a buyer's agent that becomes the contract for the sale of the real property upon acceptance by the seller.

(j) "Real property" means any estate specified by subdivision (1) or (2) of Section 761 in property, and includes (1) single-family residential property, (2) multiunit residential property with more than four dwelling units, (3) commercial real property, (4) vacant land, (5) a ground lease coupled with improvements, or (6) a manufactured home as defined in Section 18007 of the Health and Safety Code, or a mobilehome as defined in Section 18008 of the Health and Safety Code, when offered for sale or sold through an agent pursuant to the authority contained in Section 10131.6 of the Business and Professions Code.

(k) "Real property transaction" means a transaction for the sale of real property in which an agent is retained by a buyer, seller, or both a buyer and seller to act in that transaction, and includes a listing or an offer to purchase.

(*l*) "Single–family residential property" or "single-family residential real property" means any of the following:

(1) Real property improved with one to four dwelling units, including a leasehold exceeding one year's duration.

(2) A unit in a residential stock cooperative, condominium, or planned unit development.

(3) A mobilehome or manufactured home when offered for sale or sold through a real estate broker pursuant to Section 10131.6 of the Business and Professions Code.

(m) "Sell," "sale," or "sold" refers to a transaction for the transfer of real property from the seller to the buyer and includes exchanges of real property between the seller and buyer, transactions for the creation of a real property sales contract within the meaning of Section 2985, and transactions for the creation of a leasehold exceeding one year's duration.

(n) "Seller" means the transferor in a real property transaction and includes an owner who lists real property with an agent, whether or not a transfer results, or who receives an offer to purchase real property of which they are the owner from an agent on behalf of another. "Seller" includes both a vendor and a lessor of real property.

(o) "Buyer's agent" means an agent who represents a buyer in a real property transaction. *(Added by Stats.1995, c. 428 (S.B.467), § 2. Amended by Stats.2014, c. 200 (S.B.1171), § 2, eff. Jan. 1, 2015; Stats.2016, c. 125 (A.B.1750), § 1, eff. Jan. 1, 2017; Stats.2017, c. 561 (A.B.1516), § 18, eff. Jan. 1, 2018; Stats.2018, c. 907 (A.B.1289), § 38, eff. Jan. 1, 2019; Stats.2019, c. 310 (A.B.892), § 9, eff. Jan. 1, 2020.)*

§ 2079.14. Disclosure form; furnishing to buyer and seller; exceptions

(a) A copy of the disclosure form specified in Section 2079.16 shall be provided in a real property transaction as follows:

(1) The seller's agent, if any, shall provide the disclosure form to the seller before entering into the listing agreement.

(2) The buyer's agent shall provide the disclosure form to the buyer as soon as practicable before execution of the buyer's offer to purchase. If the offer to purchase is not

prepared by the buyer's agent, the buyer's agent shall present the disclosure form to the buyer not later than the next business day after receiving the offer to purchase from the buyer.

(b) The agent providing the disclosure form specified in Section 2079.16 shall obtain a signed acknowledgment of receipt from the buyer or seller except as provided in Section 2079.15. *(Added by Stats.1995, c. 428 (S.B.467), § 3. Amended by Stats.2018, c. 907 (A.B.1289), § 39, eff. Jan. 1, 2019; Stats.2019, c. 310 (A.B.892), § 10, eff. Jan. 1, 2020.)*

Cross References

Agent defined for purposes of Civil Code §§ 2079.14 to 2079.24, see Civil Code § 2079.13.

Buyer defined for purposes of Civil Code §§ 2079.14 to 2079.24, see Civil Code § 2079.13.

Listing agreement defined for purposes of Civil Code §§ 2079.14 to 2079.24, see Civil Code § 2079.13.

Offer to purchase defined for purposes of Civil Code §§ 2079.14 to 2079.24, see Civil Code § 2079.13.

Real property defined for purposes of Civil Code §§ 2079.14 to 2079.24, see Civil Code § 2079.13.

Real property transaction defined for purposes of Civil Code §§ 2079.14 to 2079.24, see Civil Code § 2079.13.

Seller defined for purposes of Civil Code §§ 2079.14 to 2079.24, see Civil Code § 2079.13.

Selling agents defined for purposes of Civil Code §§ 2079.14 to 2079.24, see Civil Code § 2079.13.

§ 2079.15. Acknowledgment of receipt; refusal to sign

In any circumstance in which the seller or buyer refuses to sign an acknowledgment of receipt pursuant to Section 2079.14, the agent shall set forth, sign, and date a written declaration of the facts of the refusal. *(Added by Stats.1995, c. 428 (S.B.467), § 4. Amended by Stats.2018, c. 907 (A.B. 1289), § 40, eff. Jan. 1, 2019.)*

Cross References

Agent defined for purposes of Civil Code §§ 2079.14 to 2079.24, see Civil Code § 2079.13.

Associate licensee defined for purposes of Civil Code §§ 2079.14 to 2079.24, see Civil Code § 2079.13.

Buyer defined for purposes of Civil Code §§ 2079.14 to 2079.24, see Civil Code § 2079.13.

Seller defined for purposes of Civil Code §§ 2079.14 to 2079.24, see Civil Code § 2079.13.

§ 2079.16. Disclosure form

The disclosure form required by Section 2079.14 shall have Sections 2079.13 to 2079.24, inclusive, excluding this section, printed on the back, and on the front of the disclosure form the following shall appear:

DISCLOSURE REGARDING REAL ESTATE AGENCY RELATIONSHIP
(As required by the Civil Code)

When you enter into a discussion with a real estate agent regarding a real estate transaction, you should from the outset understand what type of agency relationship or representation you wish to have with the agent in the transaction.

SELLER'S AGENT

A Seller's agent under a listing agreement with the Seller acts as the agent for the Seller only. A Seller's agent or a subagent of that agent has the following affirmative obligations:

To the Seller:

A fiduciary duty of utmost care, integrity, honesty, and loyalty in dealings with the Seller.

To the Buyer and the Seller:

(a) Diligent exercise of reasonable skill and care in performance of the agent's duties.

(b) A duty of honest and fair dealing and good faith.

(c) A duty to disclose all facts known to the agent materially affecting the value or desirability of the property that are not known to, or within the diligent attention and observation of, the parties.

An agent is not obligated to reveal to either party any confidential information obtained from the other party that does not involve the affirmative duties set forth above.

BUYER'S AGENT

A Buyer's agent can, with a Buyer's consent, agree to act as agent for the Buyer only. In these situations, the agent is not the Seller's agent, even if by agreement the agent may receive compensation for services rendered, either in full or in part from the Seller. An agent acting only for a Buyer has the following affirmative obligations:

To the Buyer:

A fiduciary duty of utmost care, integrity, honesty, and loyalty in dealings with the Buyer.

To the Buyer and the Seller:

(a) Diligent exercise of reasonable skill and care in performance of the agent's duties.

(b) A duty of honest and fair dealing and good faith.

(c) A duty to disclose all facts known to the agent materially affecting the value or desirability of the property that are not known to, or within the diligent attention and observation of, the parties. An agent is not obligated to reveal to either party any confidential information obtained from the other party that does not involve the affirmative duties set forth above.

AGENT REPRESENTING BOTH SELLER AND BUYER

A real estate agent, either acting directly or through one or more salespersons and broker associates, can legally be the agent of both the Seller and the Buyer in a transaction, but only with the knowledge and consent of both the Seller and the Buyer.

In a dual agency situation, the agent has the following affirmative obligations to both the Seller and the Buyer:

(a) A fiduciary duty of utmost care, integrity, honesty, and loyalty in the dealings with either the Seller or the Buyer.

(b) Other duties to the Seller and the Buyer as stated above in their respective sections.

§ 2079.16 OBLIGATIONS

In representing both Seller and Buyer, a dual agent may not, without the express permission of the respective party, disclose to the other party confidential information, including, but not limited to, facts relating to either the Buyer's or Seller's financial position, motivations, bargaining position, or other personal information that may impact price, including the Seller's willingness to accept a price less than the listing price or the Buyer's willingness to pay a price greater than the price offered.

SELLER AND BUYER RESPONSIBILITIES

Either the purchase agreement or a separate document will contain a confirmation of which agent is representing you and whether that agent is representing you exclusively in the transaction or acting as a dual agent. Please pay attention to that confirmation to make sure it accurately reflects your understanding of your agent's role.

The above duties of the agent in a real estate transaction do not relieve a Seller or Buyer from the responsibility to protect his or her own interests. You should carefully read all agreements to assure that they adequately express your understanding of the transaction. A real estate agent is a person qualified to advise about real estate. If legal or tax advice is desired, consult a competent professional.

If you are a Buyer, you have the duty to exercise reasonable care to protect yourself, including as to those facts about the property which are known to you or within your diligent attention and observation.

Both Sellers and Buyers should strongly consider obtaining tax advice from a competent professional because the federal and state tax consequences of a transaction can be complex and subject to change.

Throughout your real property transaction you may receive more than one disclosure form, depending upon the number of agents assisting in the transaction. The law requires each agent with whom you have more than a casual relationship to present you with this disclosure form. You should read its contents each time it is presented to you, considering the relationship between you and the real estate agent in your specific transaction.

This disclosure form includes the provisions of Sections 2079.13 to 2079.24, inclusive, of the Civil Code set forth on the reverse hereof. Read it carefully.

_____   _____
Agent   (date)   Buyer/Seller
                                 (date)
                                 (Signature)

_____   _____
Salesperson or Broker Associate, if   Buyer/Seller
any   (date)   (date)
(Signature)   (Signature)

(Added by Stats.1995, c. 428 (S.B.467), § 5. Amended by Stats.1996, c. 240 (A.B.2383), § 4; Stats.2018, c. 907 (A.B. 1289), § 41, eff. Jan. 1, 2019.)

Cross References

Agent defined for purposes of Civil Code §§ 2079.14 to 2079.24, see Civil Code § 2079.13.

Associate licensee defined for purposes of Civil Code §§ 2079.14 to 2079.24, see Civil Code § 2079.13.

Buyer defined for purposes of Civil Code §§ 2079.14 to 2079.24, see Civil Code § 2079.13.

Listing agreement defined for purposes of Civil Code §§ 2079.14 to 2079.24, see Civil Code § 2079.13.

Listing price defined for purposes of Civil Code §§ 2079.14 to 2079.24, see Civil Code § 2079.13.

Real property defined for purposes of Civil Code §§ 2079.14 to 2079.24, see Civil Code § 2079.13.

Real property transaction defined for purposes of Civil Code §§ 2079.14 to 2079.24, see Civil Code § 2079.13.

Seller defined for purposes of Civil Code §§ 2079.14 to 2079.24, see Civil Code § 2079.13.

Selling agents defined for purposes of Civil Code §§ 2079.14 to 2079.24, see Civil Code § 2079.13.

Subagent defined for purposes of Civil Code §§ 2079.14 to 2079.24, see Civil Code § 2079.13.

§ 2079.17. Agency relationship; disclosure and confirmation

(a) As soon as practicable, the buyer's agent shall disclose to the buyer and seller whether the agent is acting in the real property transaction as the buyer's agent, or as a dual agent representing both the buyer and the seller. This relationship shall be confirmed in the contract to purchase and sell real property or in a separate writing executed or acknowledged by the seller, the buyer, and the buyer's agent prior to or coincident with execution of that contract by the buyer and the seller, respectively.

(b) As soon as practicable, the seller's agent shall disclose to the seller whether the seller's agent is acting in the real property transaction as the seller's agent, or as a dual agent representing both the buyer and seller. This relationship shall be confirmed in the contract to purchase and sell real property or in a separate writing executed or acknowledged by the seller and the seller's agent prior to or coincident with the execution of that contract by the seller.

(c) The confirmation required by subdivisions (a) and (b) shall be in the following form:

_____
(Name of Seller's Agent, Brokerage firm and license number)
is the broker of (check one):
[ ]   the seller; or
[ ]   both the buyer and seller. (dual agent)

_____
(Name of Seller's Agent and license number)
is (check one):
[ ]   is the Seller's Agent. (salesperson or broker associate)
[ ]   is both the Buyer's and Seller's Agent. (dual agent)

_____
(Name of Buyer's Agent, Brokerage firm and license number)
is the broker of (check one):
[ ]   the buyer; or
[ ]   both the buyer and seller. (dual agent)

_____
(Name of Buyer's Agent and license number)
is (check one):
[ ]   the Buyer's Agent. (salesperson or broker associate)
[ ]   both the Buyer's and Seller's Agent. (dual agent)

(d) The disclosures and confirmation required by this section shall be in addition to the disclosure required by

Section 2079.14. An agent's duty to provide disclosure and confirmation of representation in this section may be performed by a real estate salesperson or broker associate affiliated with that broker. *(Added by Stats.1995, c. 428 (S.B.467), § 6. Amended by Stats.2018, c. 907 (A.B.1289), § 42, eff. Jan. 1, 2019.)*

Cross References

Agent defined for purposes of Civil Code §§ 2079.14 to 2079.24, see Civil Code § 2079.13.
Buyer defined for purposes of Civil Code §§ 2079.14 to 2079.24, see Civil Code § 2079.13.
Dual agent defined for purposes of Civil Code §§ 2079.14 to 2079.24, see Civil Code § 2079.13.
Listing agent defined for purposes of Civil Code §§ 2079.14 to 2079.24, see Civil Code § 2079.13.
Real property defined for purposes of Civil Code §§ 2079.14 to 2079.24, see Civil Code § 2079.13.
Real property transaction defined for purposes of Civil Code §§ 2079.14 to 2079.24, see Civil Code § 2079.13.
Sell defined for purposes of Civil Code §§ 2079.14 to 2079.24, see Civil Code § 2079.13.
Seller defined for purposes of Civil Code §§ 2079.14 to 2079.24, see Civil Code § 2079.13.
Selling agents defined for purposes of Civil Code §§ 2079.14 to 2079.24, see Civil Code § 2079.13.

§ 2079.18. Repealed by Stats.2018, c. 907 (A.B.1289), § 43, eff. Jan. 1, 2019

§ 2079.19. Payment of compensation; effect on determination of agency relationship

The payment of compensation or the obligation to pay compensation to an agent by the seller or buyer is not necessarily determinative of a particular agency relationship between an agent and the seller or buyer. A listing agent and a selling agent may agree to share any compensation or commission paid, or any right to any compensation or commission for which an obligation arises as the result of a real estate transaction, and the terms of any such agreement shall not necessarily be determinative of a particular relationship. *(Added by Stats.1995, c. 428 (S.B.467), § 8.)*

Cross References

Agent defined for purposes of Civil Code §§ 2079.14 to 2079.24, see Civil Code § 2079.13.
Buyer defined for purposes of Civil Code §§ 2079.14 to 2079.24, see Civil Code § 2079.13.
Listing agent defined for purposes of Civil Code §§ 2079.14 to 2079.24, see Civil Code § 2079.13.
Seller defined for purposes of Civil Code §§ 2079.14 to 2079.24, see Civil Code § 2079.13.
Selling agents defined for purposes of Civil Code §§ 2079.14 to 2079.24, see Civil Code § 2079.13.

§ 2079.20. Form of agency relationship; selection; condition of employment

Nothing in this article prevents an agent from selecting, as a condition of the agent's employment, a specific form of agency relationship not specifically prohibited by this article if the requirements of Section 2079.14 and Section 2079.17 are complied with. *(Added by Stats.1995, c. 428 (S.B.467), § 9.)*

Cross References

Agent defined for purposes of Civil Code §§ 2079.14 to 2079.24, see Civil Code § 2079.13.

§ 2079.21. Dual agents; disclosures prohibited

(a) A dual agent may not, without the express permission of the seller, disclose to the buyer any confidential information obtained from the seller.

(b) A dual agent may not, without the express permission of the buyer, disclose to the seller any confidential information obtained from the buyer.

(c) "Confidential information" means facts relating to the client's financial position, motivations, bargaining position, or other personal information that may impact price, such as the seller is willing to accept a price less than the listing price or the buyer is willing to pay a price greater than the price offered.

(d) This section does not alter in any way the duty or responsibility of a dual agent to any principal with respect to confidential information other than price. *(Added by Stats. 1995, c. 428 (S.B.467), § 10. Amended by Stats.2018, c. 907 (A.B.1289), § 44, eff. Jan. 1, 2019.)*

Cross References

Agent defined for purposes of Civil Code §§ 2079.14 to 2079.24, see Civil Code § 2079.13.
Buyer defined for purposes of Civil Code §§ 2079.14 to 2079.24, see Civil Code § 2079.13.
Dual agent defined for purposes of Civil Code §§ 2079.14 to 2079.24, see Civil Code § 2079.13.
Listing price defined for purposes of Civil Code §§ 2079.14 to 2079.24, see Civil Code § 2079.13.
Offering price defined for purposes of Civil Code §§ 2079.14 to 2079.24, see Civil Code § 2079.13.
Sell defined for purposes of Civil Code §§ 2079.14 to 2079.24, see Civil Code § 2079.13.
Seller defined for purposes of Civil Code §§ 2079.14 to 2079.24, see Civil Code § 2079.13.

§ 2079.22. Seller's agent may also be buyer's agent

Nothing in this article precludes a seller's agent from also being a buyer's agent. If a seller or buyer in a transaction chooses to not be represented by an agent, that does not, of itself, make that agent a dual agent. *(Added by Stats.1995, c. 428 (S.B.467), § 11. Amended by Stats.2018, c. 907 (A.B. 1289), § 45, eff. Jan. 1, 2019.)*

Cross References

Agent defined for purposes of Civil Code §§ 2079.14 to 2079.24, see Civil Code § 2079.13.
Dual agent defined for purposes of Civil Code §§ 2079.14 to 2079.24, see Civil Code § 2079.13.
Listing agent defined for purposes of Civil Code §§ 2079.14 to 2079.24, see Civil Code § 2079.13.
Selling agents defined for purposes of Civil Code §§ 2079.14 to 2079.24, see Civil Code § 2079.13.

§ 2079.23. Agency contract; modification or alteration; indemnification of lender or auction company by homeowner or listing agent prohibited as condition of lender's approval

(a) A contract between the principal and agent may be modified or altered to change the agency relationship at any

§ 2079.23

time before the performance of the act which is the object of the agency with the written consent of the parties to the agency relationship.

(b) A lender or an auction company retained by a lender to control aspects of a transaction of real property subject to this part, including validating the sales price, shall not require, as a condition of receiving the lender's approval of the transaction, the homeowner or listing agent to defend or indemnify the lender or auction company from any liability alleged to result from the actions of the lender or auction company. Any clause, provision, covenant, or agreement purporting to impose an obligation to defend or indemnify a lender or an auction company in violation of this subdivision is against public policy, void, and unenforceable. (Added by Stats.1995, c. 428 (S.B.467), § 12. Amended by Stats.2014, c. 893 (A.B.2039), § 2, eff. Jan. 1, 2015.)

Cross References

Agent defined for purposes of Civil Code §§ 2079.14 to 2079.24, see Civil Code § 2079.13.

§ 2079.24. Disclosure and fiduciary duties; effect of article

Nothing in this article shall be construed to either diminish the duty of disclosure owed buyers and sellers by agents and their associate licensees, subagents, and employees or to relieve agents and their associate licensees, subagents, and employees from liability for their conduct in connection with acts governed by this article or for any breach of a fiduciary duty or a duty of disclosure. (Added by Stats.1995, c. 428 (S.B.467), § 13.)

Cross References

Associate licensee defined for purposes of Civil Code §§ 2079.14 to 2079.24, see Civil Code § 2079.13.
Buyer defined for purposes of Civil Code §§ 2079.14 to 2079.24, see Civil Code § 2079.13.
Seller defined for purposes of Civil Code §§ 2079.14 to 2079.24, see Civil Code § 2079.13.
Subagent defined for purposes of Civil Code §§ 2079.14 to 2079.24, see Civil Code § 2079.13.

§ 2079.25. Application of Section 1102.1(d)

The provisions of subdivision (d) of Section 1102.1 shall apply to this article. (Added by Stats.2018, c. 907 (A.B.1289), § 46, eff. Jan. 1, 2019.)

CHAPTER 4. LOST AND UNCLAIMED PROPERTY

Article	Section
1. Lost Money and Goods	2080
2. Unclaimed Property	2081
3. Fees of Officers	2082

Cross References

Retrieval of lost or abandoned commercial crab traps, regulations, retrieval permit program, see Fish and Game Code § 9002.5.
San Diego County Regional Airport Authority, authority to act in municipal role for purposes of this Chapter, see Public Utilities Code § 170036.

ARTICLE 1. LOST MONEY AND GOODS

Section	
2080.	Duties of finder.
2080.1.	Delivery to police or sheriff; affidavit; charges.
2080.2.	Restoration to owner.
2080.3.	Advertisement; payment of cost; vesting of title in finder.
2080.4.	Local regulations.
2080.5.	Authority to sell.
2080.6.	Public agency; adoption of regulations.
2080.7.	Abandoned property.
2080.8.	Property in possession of Regents of University of California, University of California Police Department, or any state university.
2080.9.	Repealed.
2080.10.	Public agency temporarily receiving personalty for safekeeping; duties.

Cross References

Delivery or transportation of firearm to law enforcement agency, application of Penal Code § 26350, see Penal Code § 26392.
Transportation and delivery of firearm to law enforcement agency, application of Penal Code § 26400, see Penal Code § 26406.

§ 2080. Duties of finder

Any person who finds a thing lost is not bound to take charge of it, unless the person is otherwise required to do so by contract or law, but when the person does take charge of it he or she is thenceforward a depositary for the owner, with the rights and obligations of a depositary for hire. Any person or any public or private entity that finds and takes possession of any money, goods, things in action, or other personal property, or saves any domestic animal from harm, neglect, drowning, or starvation, shall, within a reasonable time, inform the owner, if known, and make restitution without compensation, except a reasonable charge for saving and taking care of the property. Any person who takes possession of a live domestic animal shall provide for humane treatment of the animal. (Added by Stats.1967, c. 1512, p. 3601, § 3. Amended by Stats.1998, c. 752 (S.B.1785), § 9.)

Cross References

Affidavit when owner unknown, see Civil Code § 2080.1.
Appropriation of lost property with knowledge as to true owner, see Penal Code § 485.
Depositary for hire, see Civil Code § 1851 et seq.

§ 2080.1. Delivery to police or sheriff; affidavit; charges

(a) If the owner is unknown or has not claimed the property, the person saving or finding the property shall, if the property is of the value of one hundred dollars ($100) or more, within a reasonable time turn the property over to the police department of the city or city and county, if found therein, or to the sheriff's department of the county if found outside of city limits, and shall make an affidavit, stating when and where he or she found or saved the property, particularly describing it. If the property was saved, the affidavit shall state:

(1) From what and how it was saved.

(2) Whether the owner of the property is known to the affiant.

(3) That the affiant has not secreted, withheld, or disposed of any part of the property.

(b) The police department or the sheriff's department shall notify the owner, if his or her identity is reasonably ascertainable, that it possesses the property and where it may be claimed. The police department or sheriff's department may require payment by the owner of a reasonable charge to defray costs of storage and care of the property. *(Added by Stats.1967, c. 1512, p. 3601, § 3. Amended by Stats.1992, c. 138 (A.B.2457), § 1.)*

§ 2080.2. Restoration to owner

If the owner appears within 90 days, after receipt of the property by the police department or sheriff's department, proves his ownership of the property, and pays all reasonable charges, the police department or sheriff's department shall restore the property to him. *(Added by Stats.1967, c. 1512, p. 3601, § 3.)*

§ 2080.3. Advertisement; payment of cost; vesting of title in finder

(a) If the reported value of the property is two hundred fifty dollars ($250) or more and no owner appears and proves his or her ownership of the property within 90 days, the police department or sheriff's department shall cause notice of the property to be published at least once in a newspaper of general circulation. If, after seven days following the first publication of the notice, no owner appears and proves his or her ownership of the property and the person who found or saved the property pays the cost of the publication, the title shall vest in the person who found or saved the property unless the property was found in the course of employment by an employee of any public agency, in which case the property shall be sold at public auction. Title to the property shall not vest in the person who found or saved the property or in the successful bidder at the public auction unless the cost of publication is first paid to the city, county, or city and county whose police or sheriff's department caused the notice to be published.

(b) If the reported value of the property is less than two hundred fifty dollars ($250) and no owner appears and proves his or her ownership of the property within 90 days, the title shall vest in the person who found or saved the property, unless the property was found in the course of employment by an employee of any public agency, in which case the property shall be sold at public auction. *(Added by Stats. 1967, c. 1512, p. 3601, § 3. Amended by Stats.1970, c. 260, p. 524, § 1; Stats.1971, c. 1254, p. 2465, § 1; Stats.1977, c. 250, p. 1136, § 1; Stats.1992, c. 138 (A.B.2457), § 2.)*

§ 2080.4. Local regulations

Notwithstanding the provisions of Section 2080.3 or Section 2080.6, the legislative body of any city, city and county, or county may provide by ordinance for the care, restitution, sale or destruction of unclaimed property in the possession of the police department of such city or city and county or of the sheriff of such county. Any city, city and county, or county adopting such an ordinance shall provide therein (1) that such unclaimed property shall be held by the police department or sheriff for a period of at least three months, and (2) that thereafter such property will be sold at public auction to the highest bidder, with notice of such sale being given by the chief of police or sheriff at least five days before the time fixed therefor by publication once in a newspaper of general circulation published in the county, or that thereafter such property will be transferred to the local government purchasing and stores agency or other similar agency for sale to the public at public auction. If such property is transferred to a county purchasing agent it may be sold in the manner provided by Article 7 (commencing with Section 25500) of Chapter 5 of Part 2 of Division 2 of Title 3 of the Government Code for the sale of surplus personal property. If property is transferred to the local government purchasing and stores agency or other similar agency pursuant to this section, such property shall not be redeemable by the owner or other person entitled to possession. If the local government purchasing and stores agency or other similar agency determines that any such property transferred to it for sale is needed for a public use, such property may be retained by the agency and need not be sold. *(Added by Stats.1967, c. 1512, p. 3601, § 3. Amended by Stats.1969, c. 857, p. 1689, § 1; Stats.1983, c. 878, § 1.)*

§ 2080.5. Authority to sell

The police department or sheriff's department may sell such property by public auction, in the manner and upon the notice of sale of personal property under execution, if it is a thing which is commonly the subject of sale, when the owner cannot, with reasonable diligence, be found, or, being found, refuses upon demand to pay the lawful charges provided by Sections 2080 and 2080.1, in the following cases:

(1) When the thing is in danger of perishing, or of losing the greater part of its value; or,

(2) When the lawful charges provided by Sections 2080 and 2080.1 amount to two-thirds of its value. *(Added by Stats.1967, c. 1512, p. 3601, § 3.)*

Cross References

Unclaimed personal property for use in programs to prevent delinquency, see Welfare and Institutions Code § 217.

§ 2080.6. Public agency; adoption of regulations

(a) Any public agency may elect to be governed by the provisions of this article with respect to disposition of personal property found or saved on property subject to its jurisdiction, or may adopt reasonable regulations for the care, restitution, sale or destruction of unclaimed property in its possession. Any public agency adopting such regulations shall provide therein (1) that such unclaimed property shall be held by such agency for a period of at least three months, (2) that thereafter such property will be sold at public auction to the highest bidder, and (3) that notice of such sale shall be given by the chief administrative officer of such agency at least five days before the time fixed therefor by publication once in a newspaper of general circulation published in the county in which such property was found. Any property remaining unsold after being offered at such public auction may be destroyed or otherwise disposed of by the public agency. In a county having a purchasing agent, the purchasing agent may conduct such sale, in which case the provisions of subdivisions (2) and (3) of this section shall not be applicable. Such sale shall be made by the county purchasing agent in the manner provided by Article 7 (commencing with Section 25500) of Chapter 5 of Part 2 of Division 2 of Title 3

§ 2080.6 OBLIGATIONS

of the Government Code for the sale of surplus personal property. If the public agency determines that any such property transferred to it for sale is needed for a public use, such property may be retained by the agency and need not be sold.

(b) "Public agency" as used in this section means any state agency, including the Department of General Services and the Department of Parks and Recreation, any city, county, city and county, special district, or other political subdivision. *(Added by Stats.1967, c. 1512, p. 3601, § 3. Amended by Stats.1969, c. 857, p. 1690, § 2; Stats.1988, c. 1282, § 1.)*

Cross References

Department of General Services, generally, see Government Code § 14600 et seq.

§ 2080.7. Abandoned property

The provisions of this article have no application to things which have been intentionally abandoned by their owner. *(Added by Stats.1967, c. 1512, p. 3601, § 3.)*

§ 2080.8. Property in possession of Regents of University of California, University of California Police Department, or any state university

(a) The Regents of the University of California and the Trustees of the California State University, as applicable, may provide by resolution or regulation for the care, restitution, sale, or destruction of unclaimed, lost, or abandoned property in the possession of the Regents of the University of California, the University of California Police Department, or any state university.

(b) Any resolution or regulation adopted pursuant to this section shall provide therein (1) that unclaimed, lost, or abandoned property valued at or above three hundred dollars ($300) shall be held by the Regents of the University of California, the University of California Police Department, or the particular state university for a period of at least three months, (2) that thereafter the property will be sold at public auction to the highest bidder, and (3) that notice of that sale shall be given by the Regents of the University of California, the University of California Police Department, or the Trustees of the California State University at least five days before the time therefor by publication once in a newspaper of general circulation published in the county in which the property is held.

(c) The Regents of the University of California or the Trustees of the California State University may dispose of any of that property upon which no bid is made at any sale. *(Added by Stats.1967, c. 1512, p. 3601, § 3. Amended by Stats.1969, c. 857, p. 1690, § 3; Stats.2010, c. 199 (A.B.1890), § 1.)*

Cross References

Optional procedure for disposition of property remaining on premises after commercial tenancy is terminated, see Civil Code § 1993.02.

§ 2080.9. Repealed by Stats.2010, c. 199 (A.B.1890), § 2

§ 2080.10. Public agency temporarily receiving personalty for safekeeping; duties

(a) When a public agency obtains possession of personal property from a person for temporary safekeeping, the public agency shall do all of the following:

(1) Take responsibility for the storage, documentation, and disposition of the property.

(2) Provide the person from whom the property was taken with a receipt and instructions for the retrieval of the property. The receipt and instructions shall either be given to the person from whom the property was taken at the time the public agency obtains the property or immediately mailed, by first-class mail, to the person from whom the property was taken.

(3) If the public agency has knowledge that the person from whom the property was taken is not the owner, the agency shall make reasonable efforts to identify the owner. If the owner is identified, the public agency shall mail, by first-class mail, a receipt and instructions for the retrieval of the property.

(b) The receipt and instructions shall notify the person from whom the property was taken that the property must be claimed within 60 days after the public agency obtains possession or the property will be disposed of in accordance with the disposal provisions of this article. Within 60 days, the person may do one of the following:

(1) Retrieve the property.

(2) Authorize in writing another person to retrieve the property.

(3) Notify the public agency in writing that he or she is unable to retrieve the property, because he or she is in custody, and request the public agency to hold the property. If a person notifies the public agency that he or she is unable to retrieve the property within 60 days, or have an authorized person retrieve the property, the public agency shall hold the property for not longer than 10 additional months.

(c) The public agency shall not be liable for damages caused by any official action performed with due care regarding the disposition of personal property pursuant to this section and the disposal provisions of this article.

(d) As used in this section, "public agency" means any state agency, any city, county, city and county, special district, or other political subdivision. *(Added by Stats.1998, c. 540 (S.B.1707), § 1.)*

ARTICLE 2. UNCLAIMED PROPERTY

Section
2081.	Storage by bailee until freight and charges paid.
2081.1.	Auction; notice.
2081.2.	Surplus; disposition.
2081.3.	Surplus; failure of owner to demand; payment to county treasury.
2081.4.	Termination of bailee's responsibility; liability of warehousemen.
2081.5.	Advances; effect upon sale of unclaimed property.
2081.6.	Applicable law.

ARISING FROM PARTICULAR TRANSACTIONS

Cross References

Property in federal custody, see Code of Civil Procedure § 1600 et seq.
Unclaimed property, see Code of Civil Procedure § 1300.
Unclaimed Property Law, see Code of Civil Procedure § 1500 et seq.

§ 2081. Storage by bailee until freight and charges paid

When any goods, merchandise, or other property has been received by any railroad or express company, other common carrier, commission merchant, innkeeper, or warehouseman, for transportation or safekeeping, and is not delivered to the owner, consignee, or other authorized person, the carrier, commission merchant, innkeeper, or warehouseman may hold or store the property with some responsible person until the freight and all just and reasonable charges are paid. (Added by Stats.1951, c. 656, p. 1867, § 2.)

Cross References

Optional procedure for disposition of property remaining on premises after commercial tenancy is terminated, see Civil Code § 1993.02.

§ 2081.1. Auction; notice

If within 60 days after its receipt no person calls for the property and pays the freight and charges upon it, the carrier, commission merchant, innkeeper, or warehouseman may sell the property, or so much of it as will pay freight and charges, to the highest bidder at public auction, after first causing such notice of sale to be given as is customary in sales of goods by auction at the place where the goods are held or stored. (Added by Stats.1951, c. 656, p. 1866, § 2.)

Cross References

Optional procedure for disposition of property remaining on premises after commercial tenancy is terminated, see Civil Code § 1993.02.

§ 2081.2. Surplus; disposition

If any surplus remains after paying the freight, storage, expenses of sale, and other reasonable charges, the sum remaining shall be paid over to the owner of the property, upon his demand at any time within 60 days after the sale. (Added by Stats.1951, c. 656, p. 1867, § 2.)

Cross References

Optional procedure for disposition of property remaining on premises after commercial tenancy is terminated, see Civil Code § 1993.02.

§ 2081.3. Surplus; failure of owner to demand; payment to county treasury

If the owner or his agent fails to demand the surplus within 60 days after the sale, it shall be paid into the county treasury, subject to the order of the owner. (Added by Stats.1951, c. 656, p. 1867, § 2.)

Cross References

Disposition of unclaimed property, see Code of Civil Procedure § 1440 et seq.
Optional procedure for disposition of property remaining on premises after commercial tenancy is terminated, see Civil Code § 1993.02.

§ 2081.4. Termination of bailee's responsibility; liability of warehousemen

After the storage of the property the responsibility of the carrier, commission merchant, innkeeper, or warehouseman ceases. The person with whom the property is stored is not liable for loss or damage on its account unless the loss or damage results from his negligence or want of proper care. (Added by Stats.1951, c. 656, p. 1868, § 2.)

Cross References

Optional procedure for disposition of property remaining on premises after commercial tenancy is terminated, see Civil Code § 1993.02.

§ 2081.5. Advances; effect upon sale of unclaimed property

When any commission merchant or warehouseman receives produce, merchandise, or other property on consignment and makes advances upon it, either to the owner or for freight and charges, if the advances are not paid to him within 60 days from the date made, he may cause the produce, merchandise, or property on which the advances were made, to be advertised and sold pursuant to this article. (Added by Stats.1951, c. 656, p. 1868, § 2.)

Cross References

Optional procedure for disposition of property remaining on premises after commercial tenancy is terminated, see Civil Code § 1993.02.

§ 2081.6. Applicable law

All proceedings pursuant to this article are governed entirely by its provisions and are not controlled or affected by Article 2, Chapter 3, Title 7, Part 4, Division 3 of this code.[1] (Added by Stats.1951, c. 656, p. 1868, § 2.)

[1] Civil Code § 2114 et seq.

Cross References

Optional procedure for disposition of property remaining on premises after commercial tenancy is terminated, see Civil Code § 1993.02.

ARTICLE 3. FEES OF OFFICERS

Section
2082. Amount of fees; payment.

§ 2082. Amount of fees; payment

The fees of officers under this chapter are the same allowed by law for similar services, and shall be paid by the taker up or finder and recovered from the owner. (Added by Stats.1951, c. 656, p. 1868, § 2.)

Title 7

CARRIAGE

Chapter	Section
1. Carriage in General	2085
2. Carriage of Persons	2096
3. Carriage of Property	2110
4. Carriage of Messages	2161
5. Common Carriers	2168

OBLIGATIONS

CHAPTER 1. CARRIAGE IN GENERAL

Section
2085. Contract of carriage defined.
2086. Kinds of carriage.
2087. Marine and inland carriers defined.
2088. Marine carriers governed by federal law.
2089. Gratuitous carriers; obligations.
2090. Gratuitous carriers; obligations after commencing to carry.

Cross References

Provisions of this Title, in respect to rights and obligations of parties to contract, as subordinate to intention of parties and waiver of benefit thereof, see Civil Code § 3268.

§ 2085. Contract of carriage defined

The contract of carriage is a contract for the conveyance of property, persons, or messages, from one place to another. *(Enacted in 1872.)*

Cross References

Bills of lading, special provisions, see Commercial Code § 7301 et seq.
Carriage of,
  Messages, see Civil Code §§ 2161, 2162.
  Persons, see Civil Code § 2096.
  Property, see Civil Code § 2110.
Charter party, see Harbors and Navigation Code § 833.
Damages for breach of carriage contract, see Civil Code § 3315 et seq.

§ 2086. Kinds of carriage

Carriage is either:

1. Inland; or,
2. Marine. *(Enacted in 1872.)*

§ 2087. Marine and inland carriers defined

Carriers upon the ocean and upon arms of the sea are marine carriers. All others are inland carriers. *(Enacted in 1872.)*

Cross References

Inland carriers, liability for loss, see Civil Code §§ 2194, 2195.
Liability of marine carrier, generally, see Harbors and Navigation Code § 420 et seq.

§ 2088. Marine carriers governed by federal law

Rights and duties peculiar to carriers by sea are defined by Acts of Congress. *(Enacted in 1872.)*

Cross References

Inland carrier's liability for loss, see Civil Code § 2194.
Liability of marine carriers, see Harbors and Navigation Code §§ 420, 421.

§ 2089. Gratuitous carriers; obligations

Carriers without reward are subject to the same rules as employé's [1] without reward, except so far as is otherwise provided by this Title. *(Enacted in 1872.)*

[1] So in chaptered copy.

Cross References

Care and diligence required of carriers without reward, see Civil Code §§ 2096, 2114.
Gratuitous employment, see Labor Code § 2850 et seq.
Service without employment, see Civil Code § 2078.

§ 2090. Gratuitous carriers; obligations after commencing to carry

A carrier without reward, who has begun to perform his undertaking, must complete it in like manner as if he had received a reward, unless he restores the person or thing carried to as favorable a position as before he commenced the carriage. *(Enacted in 1872.)*

Cross References

Care and diligence required of carriers without reward, see Civil Code §§ 2096, 2114.
Gratuitous employment, see Labor Code § 2850 et seq.

CHAPTER 2. CARRIAGE OF PERSONS

Article	Section
1. Gratuitous Carriage of Persons	2096
2. Carriage for Reward	2100

ARTICLE 1. GRATUITOUS CARRIAGE OF PERSONS

Section
2096. Degree of care.

§ 2096. Degree of care

A carrier of persons without reward must use ordinary care and diligence for their safe carriage. *(Enacted in 1872.)*

Cross References

Care and diligence required of carriers without reward, see Civil Code § 2114.
Common carriers of persons, see Civil Code § 2180 et seq.
Gratuitous employment, see Labor Code § 2850 et seq.
Responsibility for willful acts and negligence, see Civil Code § 1714.

ARTICLE 2. CARRIAGE FOR REWARD

Section
2100. Care, skill and equipment.
2101. Provision of safe vehicles.
2102. Overcrowding or overloading.
2103. Passengers' accommodations, treatment and attention.
2104. Speed; delays; deviations from route.

§ 2100. Care, skill and equipment

A carrier of persons for reward must use the utmost care and diligence for their safe carriage, must provide everything necessary for that purpose, and must exercise to that end a reasonable degree of skill. *(Enacted in 1872.)*

Cross References

Contractual limitation on liability of carrier, see Civil Code § 2174 et seq.
Malicious mischief, see Penal Code § 594 et seq.

Responsibility for willful acts and negligence, see Civil Code § 1714.

§ 2101. Provision of safe vehicles

A carrier of persons for reward is bound to provide vehicles safe and fit for the purposes to which they are put, and is not excused for default in this respect by any degree of care. *(Enacted in 1872.)*

Cross References

Number of vehicles, see Civil Code § 2184.
Safety and fitness of street railroads, see Public Utilities Code § 7810.

§ 2102. Overcrowding or overloading

A carrier of persons for reward must not overcrowd or overload his vehicle. *(Enacted in 1872.)*

Cross References

Duty of railroad to furnish sufficient room and accommodations, see Public Utilities Code § 7653.
Similar provision, see Civil Code § 2185.

§ 2103. Passengers' accommodations, treatment and attention

A carrier of persons for reward must give to passengers all such accommodations as are usual and reasonable, and must treat them with civility, and give them a reasonable degree of attention. *(Enacted in 1872.)*

Cross References

Accommodations for passengers, see Civil Code § 2184; Public Utilities Code § 7653.

§ 2104. Speed; delays; deviations from route

A carrier of persons for reward must travel at a reasonable rate of speed, and without any unreasonable delay, or deviation from his proper route. *(Enacted in 1872.)*

Cross References

Liability for delay, see Civil Code § 2196.

CHAPTER 3. CARRIAGE OF PROPERTY

Article	Section
1. General Definitions	2110
2. Obligations of the Carrier	2114
3. Bills of Lading [Repealed]	
4. Freightage	2136
5. General Average [Repealed]	

ARTICLE 1. GENERAL DEFINITIONS

Section
2110. Freight, freightage, consignor, and consignee defined.

§ 2110. Freight, freightage, consignor, and consignee defined

Property carried is called freight; the reward, if any, to be paid for its carriage is called freightage; the person who delivers the freight to the carrier is called the consignor; and the person to whom it is to be delivered is called the consignee. *(Enacted in 1872.)*

Cross References

Definition of freightage in marine insurance, see Insurance Code § 1882.
Freightage, see Civil Code § 2136 et seq.

ARTICLE 2. OBLIGATIONS OF THE CARRIER

Section
2114. Degree of care and diligence required.
2115. Obedience to directions.
2116. Repealed.
2117. Repealed.
2118. Place and manner of delivery.
2119. Place of delivery.
2120. Notice to consignee of arrival.
2121. Consignee's failure to accept and remove freight, storage.
2122. Repealed.

§ 2114. Degree of care and diligence required

A carrier of property for reward must use at least ordinary care and diligence in the performance of all his duties. A carrier without reward must use at least slight care and diligence. *(Enacted in 1872.)*

Cross References

Common carriers of persons, liability for luggage, see Civil Code § 2182.
Contractual limitation on liability, see Civil Code § 2174 et seq.
Gratuitous carriers, see Civil Code § 2089 et seq.
Inland carrier's liability for loss, see Civil Code § 2194.
Marine carrier's liability for loss, see Harbors and Navigation Code § 420.
Unclaimed property, proceedings excluded from coverage of this Article, see Civil Code § 2081.6.

§ 2115. Obedience to directions

Subject to Section 7303 of the Uniform Commercial Code, a carrier must comply with the directions of the consignor or consignee to the same extent that an employee is bound to comply with those of his employer. *(Enacted in 1872. Amended by Stats.1963, c. 819, p. 1999, § 8, eff. Jan. 1, 1965.)*

Cross References

Consignee defined, see Civil Code § 2110.
Consignor defined, see Civil Code § 2110.
Employee's duty to obey employer, see Labor Code § 2856.

§ 2116. Repealed by Stats.1963, c. 819, p. 1999, § 9, eff. Jan. 1, 1965

§ 2117. Repealed by Stats.1937, c. 368, p. 1002, § 10001

§ 2118. Place and manner of delivery

Subject to Section 7303 of the Uniform Commercial Code, a carrier of property must deliver it to the consignee, at the place to which it is addressed, in the manner usual at that place. *(Enacted in 1872. Amended by Stats.1963, c. 819, p. 1999, § 10, eff. Jan. 1, 1965.)*

Cross References

Carrier's delay in delivery, see Civil Code § 3317.
Compensation, see Civil Code § 2173.
Compliance with this section as relieving inland carrier from liability for loss, see Civil Code § 2194.

§ 2118 OBLIGATIONS

Consignee defined, see Civil Code § 2110.
Damages for breach of carrier's obligation to deliver, see Civil Code § 3316.
Freightage, see Civil Code § 2136 et seq.
Limitation of obligations, see Civil Code § 2174.
Obligation to accept freight, see Civil Code § 2169.

§ 2119. Place of delivery

If there is no usage to the contrary at the place of delivery, freight must be delivered as follows:

1. If carried upon a railway owned or managed by the carrier, it may be delivered at the station nearest to the place to which it is addressed;

2. If carried by sea from a foreign country, it may be delivered at the wharf where the ship moors, within a reasonable distance from the place of address; or, if there is no wharf, on board a lighter alongside the ship; or,

3. Subject to Section 7303 of the Uniform Commercial Code, in other cases, it must be delivered to the consignee or his agent, personally, if either can, with reasonable diligence, be found. *(Enacted in 1872. Amended by Stats.1963, c. 819, p. 1999, § 11, eff. Jan. 1, 1965.)*

Cross References

Compliance with this section as relieving inland carrier from liability for loss, see Civil Code § 2194.
Consignee defined, see Civil Code § 2110.
Delivery to connecting carrier, see Commercial Code § 7302.
Freight defined, see Civil Code § 2110.

§ 2120. Notice to consignee of arrival

If, for any reason, a carrier does not deliver freight to the consignee or his agent personally, he must give notice to the consignee of its arrival, and keep the same in safety, upon his responsibility as a warehouseman, until the consignee has had a reasonable time to remove it. If the place of residence or business of the consignee be unknown to the carrier, he may give the notice by letter dropped in the nearest Post Office. *(Enacted in 1872. Amended by Code Am.1873–74, c. 612, p. 247, § 213.)*

Cross References

Compliance with this section as relieving inland carrier from liability for loss, see Civil Code § 2194.
Consignee defined, see Civil Code § 2110.
Freight defined, see Civil Code § 2110.
Warehouse receipts, see Commercial Code § 7201 et seq.

§ 2121. Consignee's failure to accept and remove freight, storage

If a consignee does not accept and remove freight within a reasonable time after the carrier has fulfilled his obligation to deliver, or duly offered to fulfill the same, the carrier may exonerate himself from further liability by placing the freight in a suitable warehouse, on storage, on account of the consignee, and giving notice thereof to him. *(Enacted in 1872. Amended by Code Am.1873–74, c. 612, p. 248, § 214.)*

Cross References

Compliance with this section as relieving inland carrier from liability for loss, see Civil Code § 2194.
Consignee defined, see Civil Code § 2110.
Freight defined, see Civil Code § 2110.

§ 2122. Repealed by Code Am.1873–74, c. 612, p. 248, § 215

ARTICLE 3. BILLS OF LADING [REPEALED]

§§ 2126 to 2126i. Repealed by Stats.1963, c. 819, p. 1997, § 2, eff. Jan. 1, 1965

§§ 2127 to 2128k. Repealed by Stats.1963, c. 819, p. 1997, § 2, eff. Jan. 1, 1965

§§ 2129 to 2130g. Repealed by Stats.1963, c. 819, p. 1997, § 2, eff. Jan. 1, 1965

§§ 2131 to 2131f. Repealed by Stats.1963, c. 819, p. 1997, § 2, eff. Jan. 1, 1965

§§ 2132 to 2132c. Repealed by Stats.1963, c. 819, p. 1997, § 2, eff. Jan. 1, 1965

ARTICLE 4. FREIGHTAGE

Section
2136. Time for payment.
2137. Liability of consignor.
2138. Liability of consignee.
2139. Natural increase of freight.
2140. Apportionment by bill of lading or other contract.
2141. Apportionment; part of freight not delivered.
2142. Apportionment according to distance.
2143. Freight carried further or more expeditiously than agreed upon; compensation; delivery.
2144. Carrier's lien.

§ 2136. Time for payment

A carrier may require his freightage to be paid upon his receiving the freight; but if he does not demand it then, he cannot until he is ready to deliver the freight to the consignee. *(Enacted in 1872.)*

Cross References

Compensation of common carrier, see Civil Code § 2173.
Consignee defined, see Civil Code § 2110.
Freight defined, see Civil Code § 2110.
Freightage defined, see Civil Code § 2110.
Reasonable charges, see Public Utilities Code §§ 451, 728, 730.
Tariff schedules, see Public Utilities Code § 486 et seq.
Unclaimed property by carriers, see Civil Code § 2081 et seq.

§ 2137. Liability of consignor

The consignor of freight is presumed to be liable for the freightage, but if the contract between him and the carrier provides that the consignee shall pay it, and the carrier allows the consignee to take the freight, he cannot afterwards recover the freightage from the consignor. *(Enacted in 1872.)*

Cross References

Consignee defined, see Civil Code § 2110.
Consignor defined, see Civil Code § 2110.
Freight defined, see Civil Code § 2110.

Freightage defined, see Civil Code § 2110.

§ 2138. Liability of consignee

The consignee of freight is liable for the freightage, if he accepts the freight with notice of the intention of the consignor that he should pay it. *(Enacted in 1872.)*

Cross References

Consignee defined, see Civil Code § 2110.
Consignor defined, see Civil Code § 2110.
Freight defined, see Civil Code § 2110.
Freightage defined, see Civil Code § 2110.

§ 2139. Natural increase of freight

No freightage can be charged upon the natural increase of freight. *(Enacted in 1872.)*

Cross References

Freight defined, see Civil Code § 2110.
Freightage defined, see Civil Code § 2110.

§ 2140. Apportionment by bill of lading or other contract

If freightage is apportioned by a bill of lading or other contract made between a consignor and carrier, the carrier is entitled to payment, according to the apportionment, for so much as he delivers. *(Enacted in 1872.)*

Cross References

Consignor defined, see Civil Code § 2110.
Freightage defined, see Civil Code § 2110.

§ 2141. Apportionment; part of freight not delivered

If a part of the freight is accepted by a consignee, without a specific objection that the rest is not delivered, the freightage must be apportioned and paid as to that part, though not apportioned in the original contract. *(Enacted in 1872.)*

Cross References

Consignee defined, see Civil Code § 2110.
Freight defined, see Civil Code § 2110.
Freightage defined, see Civil Code § 2110.

§ 2142. Apportionment according to distance

If a consignee voluntarily receives freight at a place short of the one appointed for delivery, the carrier is entitled to a just proportion of the freightage, according to distance. If the carrier, being ready and willing, offers to complete the transit, he is entitled to the full freightage. If he does not thus offer completion, and the consignee receives the freight only from necessity, the carrier is not entitled to any freightage. *(Enacted in 1872.)*

Cross References

Consignee defined, see Civil Code § 2110.
Freight defined, see Civil Code § 2110.
Freightage defined, see Civil Code § 2110.

§ 2143. Freight carried further or more expeditiously than agreed upon; compensation; delivery

If freight is carried further, or more expeditiously, than was agreed upon by the parties, the carrier is not entitled to additional compensation, and cannot refuse to deliver it, on the demand of the consignee, at the place and time of its arrival. *(Enacted in 1872.)*

Cross References

Consignee defined, see Civil Code § 2110.
Freight defined, see Civil Code § 2110.

§ 2144. Carrier's lien

A carrier has a lien for (a) freightage and for services rendered at request of shipper or consignee in and about the transportation of the property, (b) care and preservation of the property, (c) money advanced at request of shipper or consignee to discharge a prior lien, and (d), subject to the limitations specified in Section 3051.6, any fines, penalties, costs, expenses, and interest arising from the provision of false or erroneous certifications of gross cargo weight as required by Section 508 of Title 49 of the United States Code. The carrier's rights to this lien are regulated by the title on liens. *(Enacted in 1872. Amended by Stats.1909, c. 663, p. 1000, § 1; Stats.1993, c. 757 (S.B.619), § 1.)*

Cross References

Consignee defined, see Civil Code § 2110.
Freightage defined, see Civil Code § 2110.
Liens,
   Generally, see Civil Code § 2872 et seq.
   Freight, see Civil Code § 2204.
   Passenger's luggage, see Civil Code § 2191.

ARTICLE 5. GENERAL AVERAGE [REPEALED]

§§ 2148 to 2155. Repealed by Stats.1937, c. 368, p. 1002, § 10001

CHAPTER 4. CARRIAGE OF MESSAGES

Section
2161. Carrier of messages; delivery; toll or ferriage; compensation for messenger.
2162. Care and diligence in transmission and delivery.

§ 2161. Carrier of messages; delivery; toll or ferriage; compensation for messenger

A carrier of messages for reward, other than by telegraph or telephone, must deliver them at the place to which they are addressed, or to the person for whom they are intended. Such carrier, by telegraph or telephone, must deliver them at such place and to such person, *provided* the place of address, or the person for whom they are intended, is within a distance of two miles from the main office of the carrier in the city or town to which the messages are transmitted, and the carrier is not required, in making the delivery, to pay on his route toll or ferriage; but for any distance beyond one mile from such office, compensation may be charged for a messenger employed by the carrier. *(Enacted in 1872. Amended by Code Am.1873–74, c. 612, p. 248, § 216; Stats.1905, c. 469, p. 627, § 1.)*

Cross References

Bribery of telephone or telegraph employee to disclose message, see Penal Code § 641.
Common carriers of messages, see Civil Code § 2207 et seq.
Refusal to accept messages, see Civil Code § 3315.

§ 2161

Rights and obligations of public utilities, see Public Utilities Code § 451 et seq.

Telephone or telegraph corporations, see Public Utilities Code § 7901 et seq.

§ 2162. Care and diligence in transmission and delivery

A carrier of messages for reward, must use great care and diligence in the transmission and delivery of messages. *(Enacted in 1872. Amended by Code Am.1873–74, c. 612, p. 249, § 217.)*

Cross References

Common carriers of messages, see Civil Code § 2207 et seq.

CHAPTER 5. COMMON CARRIERS

Article	Section
1. Common Carriers in General	2168
2. Common Carriers of Persons	2180
3. Common Carriers of Property	2194
4. Common Carriers of Messages	2207
5. Space Flight Liability and Immunity	2210

ARTICLE 1. COMMON CARRIERS IN GENERAL

Section	
2168.	Common carrier defined.
2169.	Obligation to accept freight.
2170.	Preferences prohibited; schedules of starting times; penalty.
2171.	Preferences to State and United States.
2172.	Starting on time; permissible delays.
2173.	Compensation.
2174.	Limitation of obligations.
2175.	Invalid agreements of exoneration.
2176.	Limitation of liability by contract.
2177.	Valuable letters; nonliability for loss unless informed of value.
2178.	Baggage; limitation of railroad's liability.

Cross References

Exemption from local sales and use taxes, see Revenue and Taxation Code §§ 7202, 7203.

§ 2168. Common carrier defined

Every one who offers to the public to carry persons, property, or messages, excepting only telegraphic messages, is a common carrier of whatever he thus offers to carry. *(Enacted in 1872. Amended by Code Am.1873–74, c. 612, p. 249, § 218.)*

Cross References

Additional definition, see Public Utilities Code § 211.
Common carriers,
  Generally, see Civil Code § 2085 et seq.
  Messages, see Civil Code § 2207 et seq.
  Persons, see Civil Code § 2180 et seq.
  Property, see Civil Code § 2194 et seq.
Railroads, powers and duties, see Public Utilities Code § 7526 et seq.
Regulation of public utilities, see Public Utilities Code § 701 et seq.

§ 2169. Obligation to accept freight

A common carrier must, if able to do so, accept and carry whatever is offered to him, at a reasonable time and place, of a kind that he undertakes or is accustomed to carry. *(Enacted in 1872.)*

Cross References

Common carrier defined, see Civil Code § 2168.
Damages for failure to accept freight, see Civil Code § 3315.
Freight defined, see Civil Code § 2110.
Obligation to provide seats on carriers, see Civil Code § 2185.

§ 2170. Preferences prohibited; schedules of starting times; penalty

A common carrier must not give preference in time, price, or otherwise, to one person over another. Every common carrier of passengers by railroad, or by vessel plying upon waters lying wholly within this State, shall establish a schedule time for the starting of trains or vessel from their respective stations or wharves, of which public notice shall be given, and shall, weather permitting, except in case of accident or detention caused by connecting lines, start their said trains or vessel at or within ten minutes after the schedule time so established and notice given, under a penalty of two hundred and fifty dollars for each neglect so to do, to be recovered by action before any Court of competent jurisdiction, upon complaint filed by the District Attorney of the county in the name of the people, and paid into the Common School Fund of the said county. *(Enacted in 1872. Amended by Code Am.1880, c. 37, p. 1, § 1.)*

Cross References

Common carrier defined, see Civil Code § 2168.
Similar provision, see Public Utilities Code § 453.

§ 2171. Preferences to State and United States

A common carrier must always give a preference in time, and may give a preference in price, to the United States and to this State. *(Enacted in 1872.)*

Cross References

Common carrier defined, see Civil Code § 2168.

§ 2172. Starting on time; permissible delays

A common carrier must start at such time and place as he announces to the public, unless detained by accident or the elements, or in order to connect with carriers on other lines of travel. *(Enacted in 1872. Amended by Code Am.1873–74, c. 612, p. 249, § 219.)*

Cross References

Common carrier defined, see Civil Code § 2168.
Liability for delay, see Civil Code § 2196.
Rights and obligations of public utilities, see Public Utilities Code § 451 et seq.

§ 2173. Compensation

A common carrier is entitled to a reasonable compensation and no more, which he may require to be paid in advance. If payment thereof is refused, he may refuse to carry. *(Enacted in 1872.)*

Cross References

Carrier's lien, see Civil Code § 2144.
Common carrier defined, see Civil Code § 2168.
Passenger fare, time for payment, see Civil Code § 2187.

Payment of freightage, see Civil Code § 2136.
Reasonable charges, see Public Utilities Code §§ 451, 728, 730.
Tariff schedules, see Public Utilities Code § 486 et seq.

§ 2174. Limitation of obligations

The obligations of a common carrier cannot be limited by general notice on his part, but may be limited by special contract. *(Enacted in 1872. Amended by Code Am.1873–74, c. 612, p. 249, § 220.)*

Cross References

Common carrier defined, see Civil Code § 2168.

§ 2175. Invalid agreements of exoneration

A common carrier cannot be exonerated, by any agreement made in anticipation thereof, from liability for the gross negligence, fraud, or willful wrong of himself or his servants. *(Enacted in 1872.)*

Cross References

Common carrier defined, see Civil Code § 2168.
Contractual exemptions on fraud or wilful injury as unlawful, see Civil Code § 1668.
Fraud, see Civil Code § 1571 et seq.

§ 2176. Limitation of liability by contract

A passenger, consignor, or consignee, by accepting a ticket, bill of lading, or written contract for carriage, with a knowledge of its terms, assents to the rate of hire, the time, place, and manner of delivery therein stated; and also to the limitation stated therein upon the amount of the carrier's liability in case property carried in packages, trunks, or boxes, is lost or injured, when the value of such property is not named; and also to the limitation stated therein to the carrier's liability for loss or injury to live animals carried. But his assent to any other modification of the carrier's obligations contained in such instrument can be manifested only by his signature to the same. *(Enacted in 1872. Amended by Code Am.1873–74, c. 612, p. 249, § 221.)*

Cross References

Consignee defined, see Civil Code § 2110.
Consignor defined, see Civil Code § 2110.
Contract of carriage defined, see Civil Code § 2085.

§ 2177. Valuable letters; nonliability for loss unless informed of value

A common carrier is not responsible for loss or miscarriage of a letter, or package having the form of a letter, containing money or notes, bills of exchange, or other papers of value, unless he be informed at the time of its receipt of the value of its contents. *(Added by Code Am.1873–74, c. 612, p. 250, § 222.)*

Cross References

Common carrier defined, see Civil Code § 2168.
Liability of common carrier for negotiable paper or valuable writings when value not declared, see Civil Code § 2200.

§ 2178. Baggage; limitation of railroad's liability

A common carrier of property by steam or electric railroad which accepts for transportation, storage, handling or safekeeping, as a part of or in connection with passenger transportation, property carried in trunks, valises, suit cases, traveling bags, boxes, bundles or packages, shall not be liable, in the event of loss of or injury to the same, for more than one hundred dollars for each trunk and contents, nor more than fifty dollars for each valise and contents, or suit case and contents, or traveling bag and contents, nor more than ten dollars for each box, bundle or package and contents, unless the carrier shall have consented in writing to assume a greater liability. The term "common carrier" as used in this section shall include sleeping car companies. *(Added by Stats.1931, c. 614, p. 1323, § 1.)*

Cross References

Common carrier defined, see Civil Code § 2168.
Limitation of liability of stages for baggage, see Civil Code § 2205.

ARTICLE 2. COMMON CARRIERS OF PERSONS

Section
2180. Baggage; obligation to carry; charges.
2181. Luggage defined; bicycles.
2182. Liability for luggage.
2183. Luggage; delivery; checking; risk.
2184. Obligation to provide vehicles; exceptions.
2185. Obligation to provide seats; exceptions.
2186. Rules for conduct of business.
2187. Payment of fare.
2188. Ejection of passengers; method; place.
2189. Repealed.
2190. Fare not payable after ejection.
2191. Lien on luggage.

Cross References

Exemption from local sales and use taxes, see Revenue and Taxation Code §§ 7202, 7203.

§ 2180. Baggage; obligation to carry; charges

A common carrier of persons, unless his vehicle is fitted for the reception of persons exclusively, must receive and carry a reasonable amount of baggage for each passenger without charge, except for an excess of weight over one hundred pounds to a passenger; if such carrier is a proprietor of a stage line, he need not receive and carry for each passenger by such stage line, without charge, more than sixty pounds of baggage. *(Enacted in 1872. Amended by Code Am.1877–78, c. 159, p. 87, § 1; Stats.1905, c. 455, p. 615, § 1.)*

Cross References

Baggage checks, see Public Utilities Code § 7655.
Common carrier defined, see Civil Code § 2168.
Gratuitous carriage of persons, see Civil Code § 2096.

§ 2181. Luggage defined; bicycles

Luggage may consist of whatever the passenger takes with him for his personal use and convenience, according to the habits or wants of the particular class to which he belongs, either with reference to the important necessities or to the ultimate purposes of his journey. Luggage within the meaning of this section shall include the samples, case, wares, appliances and catalogs of commercial travelers or their employers, used by them for the purpose of transacting their business and carried with them solely for that purpose, when securely packed and locked in substantial trunks or sample cases of convenient shape and weight for handling. No crate cover or other protection shall be required for any bicycle carried as luggage, but no passenger shall be entitled to carry as luggage more than one bicycle. *(Enacted in 1872. Amended by Code Am.1897, c. 4, p. 4, § 1; Stats.1911, c. 363, p. 638, § 1.)*

§ 2182. Liability for luggage

The liability of a carrier for luggage received by him with a passenger is the same as that of a common carrier of property. *(Enacted in 1872.)*

Cross References

Carriage of property, degree of care and diligence required, see Civil Code § 2114.
Common carrier defined, see Civil Code § 2168.
Inland carrier's liability for loss, see Civil Code § 2194.
Liability of stage lines for baggage, see Civil Code § 2205.
Luggage defined, see Civil Code § 2181.
Railroad baggage liability limited, see Civil Code § 2178.

§ 2183. Luggage; delivery; checking; risk

A common carrier must deliver every passenger's luggage, whether within the prescribed weight or not, immediately upon the arrival of the passenger at his destination; and, unless the vehicle would be overcrowded or overloaded thereby, must carry it on the same vehicle by which he carries the passenger to whom it belonged, except that where luggage is transported by rail, it must be checked and carried in a regular baggage car; and whenever passengers neglect or refuse to have their luggage so checked and transported, it is carried at their risk. *(Enacted in 1872. Amended by Code Am.1873–74, c. 612, p. 250, § 223.)*

Cross References

Baggage checks, see Public Utilities Code § 7655.
Common carrier defined, see Civil Code § 2168.
Luggage defined, see Civil Code § 2181.

§ 2184. Obligation to provide vehicles; exceptions

A common carrier of persons must provide a sufficient number of vehicles to accommodate all the passengers who can be reasonably expected to require carriage at any one time. This section shall not apply, however, to any passenger stage corporation or street railroad corporation, as defined in Sections 226 and 232, respectively, of the Public Utilities Code, which is subject to the jurisdiction of the Public Utilities Commission. *(Enacted in 1872. Amended by Stats. 1957, c. 511, p. 1548, § 1.)*

Cross References

Carrier not to overload vehicle, see Civil Code § 2102.
Common carrier defined, see Civil Code § 2168.
Duty of railroad to furnish sufficient room and accommodations, see Public Utilities Code § 7653.
Passengers' accommodations, treatment and attention, see Civil Code § 2103.

§ 2185. Obligation to provide seats; exceptions

A common carrier of persons must provide every passenger with a seat. He must not overload his vehicle by receiving and carrying more passengers than its rated capacity allows. This section shall not apply, however, to any city, county, city and county that operates a transportation system, or to any passenger stage corporation or street railroad corporation, as defined in Sections 226 and 232, respectively, of the Public Utilities Code, which is subject to the jurisdiction of the Public Utilities Commission. *(Enacted in 1872. Amended by Stats.1957, c. 511, p. 1549, § 2; Stats.1963, c. 1409, p. 2947, § 1.)*

Cross References

Carrier not to overload vehicle, see Civil Code § 2102.
Common carrier defined, see Civil Code § 2168.
Duty of railroad to furnish sufficient room and accommodations, see Public Utilities Code § 7653.
Passengers' accommodations, treatment and attention, see Civil Code § 2103.

§ 2186. Rules for conduct of business

A common carrier of persons may make rules for the conduct of his business, and may require passengers to conform to them, if they are lawful, public, uniform in their application, and reasonable. *(Enacted in 1872.)*

Cross References

Common carrier defined, see Civil Code § 2168.
Posting of rules and regulations, see Public Utilities Code § 7654.
Power of railroad to establish rules and regulations, see Public Utilities Code § 7527.

§ 2187. Payment of fare

A common carrier may demand the fare of passengers, either at starting or at any subsequent time. *(Enacted in 1872.)*

Cross References

Common carrier defined, see Civil Code § 2168.
Compensation of common carrier, see Civil Code § 2173.
Tariff schedules, see Public Utilities Code § 486 et seq.

§ 2188. Ejection of passengers; method; place

A passenger who refuses to pay his fare or to conform to any lawful regulation of the carrier, may be ejected from the vehicle by the carrier. But this must be done with as little violence as possible, and at any usual stopping place or near some dwelling house. *(Enacted in 1872.)*

Cross References

Railroad passengers, ejection, see Public Utilities Code § 7656.

§ 2189. Repealed by Stats.1951, c. 764, p. 2258, § 25003

§ 2190. Fare not payable after ejection

After having ejected a passenger, a carrier has no right to require the payment of any part of his fare. *(Enacted in 1872.)*

§ 2191. Lien on luggage

A common carrier has a lien upon the luggage of a passenger for the payment of such fare as he is entitled to from him. This lien is regulated by the Title on Liens. *(Enacted in 1872.)*

Cross References

Carrier's lien, see Civil Code § 2144.
Common carrier defined, see Civil Code § 2168.
Liens, generally, see Civil Code § 2872 et seq.

Luggage defined, see Civil Code § 2181.

ARTICLE 3. COMMON CARRIERS OF PROPERTY

Section
2194. Inland carrier's liability for loss; exceptions.
2195. Inland carrier's liability for negligence.
2196. Liability for delay.
2197. Liability for storage or equipment rental charges of consignor and consignee causing delay.
2197.5. Liability of consignee on prepaid shipments for delay caused by consignor or consignee.
2198, 2199. Repealed.
2200. Valuables; limitation of liability; notice of nature of freight; declaration of value.
2201, 2202. Repealed.
2203. Services other than carriage and delivery.
2204. Perishable property; sale for freightage.
2205. Stagelines, etc.; limitation on liability for damage to baggage.

Cross References

Exemption from local sales and use taxes, see Revenue and Taxation Code §§ 7202, 7203.

§ 2194. Inland carrier's liability for loss; exceptions

Unless the consignor accompanies the freight and retains exclusive control thereof, an inland common carrier of property is liable, from the time that he accepts until he relieves himself from liability pursuant to Sections 2118 to 2122, for the loss or injury thereof from any cause whatever, except:

1. An inherent defect, vice, or weakness, or a spontaneous action, of the property itself;

2. The act of a public enemy of the United States, or of this State;

3. The act of the law; or,

4. Any irresistible superhuman cause. *(Enacted in 1872.)*

Cross References

Carrier's responsibility as warehouseman, see Civil Code § 2120.
Common carrier defined, see Civil Code § 2168.
Consignor defined, see Civil Code § 2110.
Contractual limitation of liability, see Civil Code § 2174 et seq.
Degree of care and diligence required, see Civil Code § 2114.
Freight defined, see Civil Code § 2110.
Marine and inland carrier defined, see Civil Code § 2087.
Marine carrier's liability for loss, see Harbors and Navigation Code § 420.

§ 2195. Inland carrier's liability for negligence

A common carrier is liable, even in the cases excepted by the last section, if his want of ordinary care exposes the property to the cause of the loss. *(Enacted in 1872. Amended by Stats.1905, c. 455, p. 615, § 2.)*

Cross References

Common carrier defined, see Civil Code § 2168.

Contractual limitations on liability, see Civil Code § 2174 et seq.

§ 2196. Liability for delay

A common carrier is liable for delay only when it is caused by his want of ordinary care and diligence. *(Enacted in 1872. Amended by Code Am.1873–74, c. 612, p. 251, § 224.)*

Cross References

Common carrier defined, see Civil Code § 2168.
Damages for delay, see Civil Code § 3317.
Delay by carrier of persons, see Civil Code § 2104.

§ 2197. Liability for storage or equipment rental charges of consignor and consignee causing delay

(a) Liability for storage or equipment rental charges assessed against a motor carrier by a railroad or steamship company shall be as follows if the charges arise out of a delay caused by the consignor or consignee of the freight:

(1) The consignor is liable to the motor carrier for the charges if the consignor caused the delay.

(2) The consignee is liable to the motor carrier for the charges if the consignee caused the delay.

(b) Nothing in this section shall affect the rights, duties, and obligations between a railroad or steamship company and a motor carrier. *(Added by Stats.1988, c. 937, § 1.)*

Cross References

Consignee defined, see Civil Code § 2110.
Consignor defined, see Civil Code § 2110.
Freight defined, see Civil Code § 2110.

§ 2197.5. Liability of consignee on prepaid shipments for delay caused by consignor or consignee

(a) In addition to the liability established by Section 2197, the consignee is liable to the motor carrier for the charges if the freight is shipped prepaid and the delay was caused by either the consignor or the consignee.

(b) Nothing in this section shall affect the rights, duties, and obligations between a railroad or steamship company and a motor carrier. *(Added by Stats.1988, c. 937, § 2. Amended by Stats.1992, c. 466 (A.B.2387), § 1.)*

Cross References

Consignee defined, see Civil Code § 2110.
Consignor defined, see Civil Code § 2110.
Freight defined, see Civil Code § 2110.

§§ 2198, 2199. Repealed by Stats.1937, c. 368, p. 1002, § 10001

§ 2200. Valuables; limitation of liability; notice of nature of freight; declaration of value

A common carrier of gold, silver, platina, or precious stones, or of imitations thereof, in a manufactured or unmanufactured state; of timepieces of any description; of negotiable paper or other valuable writings; of pictures, glass, or chinaware; of statuary, silk, or laces; or of plated ware of any kind, is not liable for more than fifty dollars upon the loss or injury of any one package of such articles, unless he has notice, upon his receipt thereof, by mark upon the package or otherwise, of the nature of the freight; nor is such carrier liable upon any package carried for more than the value of the articles named in the receipt or the bill of lading. *(Enacted in 1872. Amended by Code Am.1873–74, c. 612, p. 251, § 225.)*

Cross References

Common carrier defined, see Civil Code § 2168.
Freight defined, see Civil Code § 2110.
Liability for,
  Loss of packages containing valuable letters or currency, see Civil Code § 2177.
  Property carried in packages when the value is not declared, see Civil Code § 2176.

§§ 2201, 2202. Repealed by Stats.1963, c. 819, p. 1999, §§ 12, 13, eff. Jan. 1, 1965

§ 2203. Services other than carriage and delivery

In respect to any service rendered by a common carrier about freight, other than its carriage and delivery, his rights and obligations are defined by the Titles on Deposit and Service. *(Enacted in 1872.)*

Cross References

Common carrier defined, see Civil Code § 2168.
Compensation of common carrier, see Civil Code § 2173.
Deposit, see Civil Code § 1813 et seq.
Freight defined, see Civil Code § 2110.

§ 2204. Perishable property; sale for freightage

If, from any cause other than want of ordinary care and diligence on his part, a common carrier is unable to deliver perishable property transported by him, and collect his charges thereon, he may cause the property to be sold in open market to satisfy his lien for freightage. *(Added by Code Am.1873–74, c. 612, p. 251, § 226.)*

Cross References

Common carrier defined, see Civil Code § 2168.
Freightage defined, see Civil Code § 2110.
Lien for freight, see Civil Code § 2144.
Unclaimed property, see Civil Code § 2081 et seq.

§ 2205. Stagelines, etc.; limitation on liability for damage to baggage

The liability of any stageline, transfer company, or other common carriers operating over the public highways for the loss of or for damage to any baggage shall not exceed the sum of five hundred dollars ($500) for each trunk and its contents; two hundred fifty dollars ($250) for each valise, suitcase or traveling bag and its contents; or two hundred fifty dollars ($250) for each box, bundle, or package and its contents, unless a higher valuation is declared at the time of delivery of such baggage to the carrier and assented thereto in writing by such carrier.

All baggage presented to the carrier for checking shall be appropriately tagged by the owner with his name and address. *(Added Stats.1925, c. 146, p. 299, § 1. Amended by Stats. 1965, c. 104, p. 1045, § 1; Stats.1969, c. 982, p. 1950, § 1; Stats.1971, c. 1653, p. 3558, § 1.)*

Cross References

Carrier's lien on luggage for fare, see Civil Code § 2191.
Common carrier defined, see Civil Code § 2168.

Liability of common carrier for luggage, see Civil Code § 2182.
Limitation of liability for railroad baggage, see Civil Code § 2178.

ARTICLE 4. COMMON CARRIERS OF MESSAGES

Section
2207. Telegraphic messages; order of transmission.
2208. Messages other than telegraphic; order of transmission.
2209. Damages for refusing or postponing messages.

Cross References

Exemption from local sales and use taxes, see Revenue and Taxation Code §§ 7202, 7203.

§ 2207. Telegraphic messages; order of transmission

A carrier of messages by telegraph must, if it is practicable, transmit every such message immediately upon its receipt. But if this is not practicable, and several messages accumulate upon his hands, he must transmit them in the following order:

1. Messages from public agents of the United States or of this State, on public business;

2. Messages intended in good faith for immediate publication in newspapers, and not for any secret use;

3. Messages giving information relating to the sickness or death of any person;

4. Other messages in the order in which they were received. *(Enacted in 1872.)*

Cross References

Damages,
  For breach of obligation to accept messages, see Civil Code § 3315.
  When message is refused or postponed, see Civil Code § 2209.
Obligations and duties of carriers of messages, see Civil Code §§ 2161, 2162.
Penalty for refusal or neglect to transmit or deliver message, see Public Utilities Code § 7904.

§ 2208. Messages other than telegraphic; order of transmission

A common carrier of messages, otherwise than by telegraph, must transmit messages in the order in which he receives them, except messages from agents of the United States or of this State, on public business, to which he must always give priority. But he may fix upon certain times for the simultaneous transmission of messages previously received. *(Enacted in 1872.)*

Cross References

Common carrier defined, see Civil Code § 2168.

§ 2209. Damages for refusing or postponing messages

Every person whose message is refused or postponed, contrary to the provisions of this Chapter, is entitled to recover from the carrier his actual damages, and fifty dollars in addition thereto. *(Enacted in 1872.)*

Cross References

Damages for breach of obligation to accept messages, see Civil Code § 3315.
Obligations and duties of carriers of messages, see Civil Code §§ 2161, 2162.

Penalty for refusal or neglect to transmit or deliver message, see Public Utilities Code § 7904.

ARTICLE 5. SPACE FLIGHT LIABILITY AND IMMUNITY

Section
2210. Definitions.
2211. Warning statement; immunity.
2212. Limitation of liability for injuries arising out of space flight activities; conditions.

§ 2210. Definitions

For purposes of this article:

(a) "Participant" means a space flight participant as defined in Section 50902 of Title 51 of the United States Code.

(b) "Participant injury" means a bodily injury, including death, emotional injury, or property damage, sustained by the participant.

(c) "Space flight activities" means launch services or reentry services as defined in Section 50902 of Title 51 of the United States Code.

(d) "Space flight entity" means any public or private entity that holds, either directly or through a corporate subsidiary or parent, a license, permit, or other authorization issued by the United States Federal Aviation Administration pursuant to the federal Commercial Space Launch Amendments Act of 2004 (51 U.S.C. Sec. 50905 et seq.), including, but not limited to, a safety approval and a payload determination. *(Added by Stats.2012, c. 416 (A.B.2243), § 2.)*

§ 2211. Warning statement; immunity

(a) A space flight entity providing space flight activities to a participant shall have each participant sign a warning statement that shall contain, at a minimum, and in addition to any language required by federal law, the following notice:

"WARNING AND ACKNOWLEDGMENT: I understand and acknowledge that, under California law, there is limited civil liability for bodily injury, including death, emotional injury, or property damage, sustained by a participant as a result of the inherent risks associated with space flight activities provided by a space flight entity. I have given my informed consent to participate in space flight activities after receiving a description of the inherent risks associated with space flight activities, as required by federal law pursuant to Section 50905 of Title 51 of the United States Code and Section 460.45 of Title 14 of the Code of Federal Regulations. The consent that I have given acknowledges that the inherent risks associated with space flight activities include, but are not limited to, risk of bodily injury, including death, emotional injury, and property damage. I understand and acknowledge that I am participating in space flight activities at my own risk. I have been given the opportunity to consult with an attorney before signing this statement."

(b) Failure to comply with the requirements provided in this section shall prevent a space flight entity from invoking the privileges of immunity provided by Section 2212.

(c) Nothing in this section shall be construed to be contrary to the public policy of this state. *(Added by Stats.2012, c. 416 (A.B.2243), § 2. Amended by Stats.2014, c. 48 (S.B.415), § 1, eff. Jan. 1, 2015.)*

§ 2212. Limitation of liability for injuries arising out of space flight activities; conditions

(a) Except as provided in subdivision (c), a space flight entity shall not be liable for participant injury arising out of space flight activities if both of the following apply:

(1) The participant has been informed of the risks associated with space flight activities as required by federal law and Section 2211.

(2) The participant has given his or her informed consent that he or she is voluntarily participating in space flight activities after having been informed of the risks associated with those activities, as required by federal law and Section 2211.

(b) If informed consent is given pursuant to subdivision (a), a participant, his or her representative, including the heirs, administrators, executors, assignees, next of kin, and estate of the participant, or any person who attempts to bring a claim on behalf of the participant for a participant injury, shall not be authorized to maintain an action against, or recover from, a space flight entity for a participant injury that resulted from the risks associated with space flight activities, except as provided in subdivision (c).

(c) Nothing in this section shall prevent or limit the liability of a space flight entity that does any of the following:

(1) Commits an act or omission that constitutes gross negligence or willful or wanton disregard for the safety of the participant, and that act or omission proximately causes a participant injury.

(2) Intentionally causes a participant injury.

(3) Has actual knowledge or reasonably should have known of a dangerous condition on the land or in the facilities or equipment used in space flight activities and the dangerous condition proximately causes injury, damage, or death to the participant.

(d) Any limitation on legal liability afforded by this section to a space flight entity is in addition to any other limitations of legal liability otherwise provided by law.

(e) Nothing in this section shall be construed to limit the liability of a manufacturer of a part or component used in space flight activities if a defective part or component proximately causes an injury to the participant. *(Added by Stats.2012, c. 416 (A.B.2243), § 2.)*

Title 8

INVOLUNTARY TRUSTS

Section
2215 to 2222. Repealed.
2223. Involuntary trustee.
2224. Wrongful act.
2224.1. Repealed.
2224.5. Limitation of action by Attorney General.

Section
2225. Definitions; proceeds from sale of story of felony; involuntary trust; action to recover proceeds; transfer to Controller; allocation to Restitution Fund; violations; remedies cumulative; limitation of actions.
2228 to 2290.9. Repealed.
2290.10. Repealed.
2290.11, 2290.12. Repealed.

Cross References

Administration of trusts, see Probate Code § 16000 et seq.
Guardian and ward relationship as subject to provisions of law relating to trusts, see Probate Code § 2101.
Provisions of this Title, in respect to rights and obligations of parties to contract, as subordinate to intention of parties and waiver of benefit thereof, see Civil Code § 3268.
Trusts, see Probate Code § 15002 et seq.
Uniform Principal and Income Act, see Probate Code § 16320 et seq.

§§ 2215 to 2222. Repealed by Stats.1986, c. 820, § 7, operative July 1, 1987

§ 2223. Involuntary trustee

One who wrongfully detains a thing is an involuntary trustee thereof, for the benefit of the owner. *(Added by Stats.1986, c. 820, § 8, eff. Sept. 15, 1986, operative July 1, 1987.)*

Cross References

Charitable trusts, civil actions by Attorney General, time for commencement, see Government Code § 12596.
Third persons as involuntary trustees, see Probate Code § 18100.

§ 2224. Wrongful act

One who gains a thing by fraud, accident, mistake, undue influence, the violation of a trust, or other wrongful act, is, unless he or she has some other and better right thereto, an involuntary trustee of the thing gained, for the benefit of the person who would otherwise have had it. *(Added by Stats. 1986, c. 820, § 8, eff. Sept. 15, 1986, operative July 1, 1987.)*

Cross References

Actual and constructive fraud defined under contract law, see Civil Code §§ 1572, 1573.
Charitable trusts, civil actions by Attorney General, time for commencement, see Government Code § 12596.
Influence to obtain advantage from beneficiary, see Probate Code § 16004.

§ 2224.1. Repealed by Stats.1986, c. 820, § 7, operative July 1, 1987

§ 2224.5. Limitation of action by Attorney General

An action brought by the Attorney General pursuant to Section 2223 or 2224 may be brought at any time within 10 years after the cause of action accrued. *(Added by Stats.2015, c. 299 (A.B.556), § 2, eff. Jan. 1, 2016.)*

§ 2225. Definitions; proceeds from sale of story of felony; involuntary trust; action to recover proceeds; transfer to Controller; allocation to Restitution Fund; violations; remedies cumulative; limitation of actions

(a) As used in this section:

(1) "Convicted felon" means any person convicted of a felony, or found not guilty by reason of insanity of a felony committed in California, either by a court or jury trial or by entry of a plea in court.

(2) "Felony" means a felony defined by any California or United States statute.

(3)(A) "Representative of the felon" means any person or entity receiving proceeds or profits by designation of that felon, on behalf of that felon, or in the stead of that felon, whether by the felon's designation or by operation of law.

(B) "Profiteer of the felony" means any person who sells or transfers for profit any memorabilia or other property or thing of the felon, the value of which is enhanced by the notoriety gained from the commission of the felony for which the felon was convicted. This subparagraph shall not apply to any media entity reporting on the felon's story or on the sale of the materials, memorabilia, or other property or thing of the felon. Nor shall it apply to the sale of the materials, as the term is defined in paragraph (6), where the seller is exercising his or her first amendment rights. This subparagraph also shall not apply to the sale or transfer by a profiteer of any other expressive work protected by the First Amendment unless the sale or transfer is primarily for a commercial or speculative purpose.

(4)(A) "Beneficiary" means a person who, under applicable law, other than the provisions of this section, has or had a right to recover damages from the convicted felon for physical, mental, or emotional injury, or pecuniary loss proximately caused by the convicted felon as a result of the crime for which the felon was convicted.

(B) If a beneficiary described in subparagraph (A) has died, "beneficiary" also includes a person or estate entitled to recover damages pursuant to Chapter 4 (commencing with Section 377.10) of Title 3 of Part 2 of the Code of Civil Procedure.

(C) If a person has died and the death was proximately caused by the convicted felon as a result of the crime for which the felon was convicted, "beneficiary" also includes a person described in Section 377.60 of the Code of Civil Procedure and any beneficiary of a will of the decedent who had a right under that will to receive more than 25 percent of the value of the estate of the decedent.

(5) "Beneficiary's interest" means that portion of the proceeds or profits necessary to pay the following:

(A) In the case of a beneficiary described in subparagraph (A) or (B) of paragraph (4), those damages that, under applicable law, other than the provisions of this section, the beneficiary has or had a right to recover from the convicted felon for injuries proximately caused by the convicted felon as a result of the crime for which the felon was convicted.

(B) In the case of a beneficiary described in subparagraph (C) of paragraph (4), those damages that, under all the circumstances of the case, may be just.

(C) A beneficiary's interest shall be reduced by the following amount:

(i) Money paid to the beneficiary from the Restitution Fund because of the crime for which the felon was convicted.

(ii) Money paid to the beneficiary by the convicted felon because of a requirement of restitution imposed by a court in connection with the crime for which the felon was convicted.

(iii) Money paid to the beneficiary because of a judgment against the convicted felon based upon the crime for which the felon was convicted.

(D) In the case of an unsatisfied existing judgment or order of restitution against the convicted felon and in favor of a beneficiary, any money paid to the beneficiary pursuant to this section shall be applied to reduce the amount of the unsatisfied judgment or order.

(6) "Materials" means books, magazine or newspaper articles, movies, films, videotapes, sound recordings, interviews or appearances on television and radio stations, and live presentations of any kind.

(7) "Story" means a depiction, portrayal, or reenactment of a felony and shall not be taken to mean a passing mention of the felony, as in a footnote or bibliography.

(8) "Sale" includes lease, license, or any other transfer or alienation taking place in California or elsewhere.

(9) "Proceeds" means all fees, royalties, real property, or other consideration of any and every kind or nature received by or owing to a felon or his or her representatives for the preparation for the purpose of sale of materials, for the sale of the rights to materials, or the sale or distribution by the convicted felon of materials whether earned, accrued, or paid before or after the conviction. It includes any interest, earnings, or accretions upon proceeds, and any property received in exchange for proceeds.

(10) "Profits" means all income from anything sold or transferred by the felon, a representative of the felon, or a profiteer of the felony, including any right, the value of which thing or right is enhanced by the notoriety gained from the commission of a felony for which a convicted felon was convicted. This income may have been accrued, earned, or paid before or after the conviction. However, voluntary donations or contributions to a defendant to assist in the defense of criminal charges shall not be deemed to be "profits," provided the donation or contribution to that defense is not given in exchange for some material of value.

(b)(1) All proceeds from the preparation for the purpose of sale, the sale of the rights to, or the sale of materials that include or are based on the story of a felony for which a convicted felon was convicted, shall be subject to an involuntary trust for the benefit of the beneficiaries set forth in this section. That trust shall continue until five years after the time of payment of the proceeds to the felon or five years after the date of conviction, whichever is later. If an action is filed by a beneficiary to recover his or her interest in a trust within those time limitations, the trust character of the property shall continue until the conclusion of the action. At the end of the five-year trust period, any proceeds that remain in trust that have not been claimed by a beneficiary shall be transferred to the Controller, to be allocated to the Restitution Fund for the payment of claims pursuant to Section 13969 of the Government Code.

(2) All profits shall be subject to an involuntary trust for the benefit of the beneficiaries set forth in this section. That trust shall continue until five years after the time of payment of the profits to the felon or five years after the date of conviction, whichever is later. If an action is filed by a beneficiary to recover his or her interest in a trust within those time limitations, the trust character of the property shall continue until the conclusion of the action. At the end of the five-year trust period, any profits that remain in trust that have not been claimed by a beneficiary shall be transferred to the Controller, to be allocated to the Restitution Fund for the payment of claims pursuant to Section 13969 of the Government Code.

(3) Notwithstanding paragraph (2), in the case of a sale or transfer by a profiteer of the felony, the court in an action under subdivision (c) shall, upon an adequate showing by the profiteer of the felony, exclude from the involuntary trust that portion of the profits that represents the inherent value of the memorabilia, property, or thing sold or transferred and exclusive of the amount of the enhancement to the value due to the notoriety of the convicted felon.

(c)(1) Any beneficiary may bring an action against a convicted felon, representative of the felon, or a profiteer of a felony to recover his or her interest in the trust established by this section.

(2) That action may be brought in the superior court of the county in which the beneficiary resides, or of the county in which the convicted felon resides, or of the county in which proceeds or profits are located.

(3) If the court determines that a beneficiary is entitled to proceeds or profits pursuant to this section, the court shall order the payment from proceeds or profits that have been received, and, if that is insufficient, from proceeds or profits that may be received in the future.

(d) If there are two or more beneficiaries and if the available proceeds or profits are insufficient to pay all beneficiaries, the proceeds or profits shall be equitably apportioned among the beneficiaries taking into account the impact of the crime upon them.

Prior to any distribution of any proceeds to a beneficiary, the court shall determine whether the convicted felon has failed to pay any portion of a restitution fine or penalty fine imposed by a court, or any restitution imposed as a condition of probation. The court shall also determine whether the felon is obligated to reimburse a governmental entity for the costs of his or her defense and whether a portion of the proceeds is needed to cover his or her reasonable attorney's fees incurred in the criminal proceeding related to the felony, or any appeal or other related proceeding, or in the defense of the action brought under this section. The court shall order payment of these obligations prior to any payment to a beneficiary, except that 60 percent of the proceeds or profits shall be reserved for payment to the beneficiaries.

(e)(1) The Attorney General may bring an action to require proceeds or profits received by a convicted felon to be held in an express trust in a bank authorized to act as a trustee.

(2) An action may be brought under this subdivision within one year after the receipt of proceeds or profits by a convicted felon or one year after the date of conviction, whichever is later.

That action may be brought in the superior court of any county in which the Attorney General has an office.

(3) If the Attorney General proves that the proceeds or profits are proceeds or profits from the sale of a story or thing of value that are subject to an involuntary trust pursuant to this section, and that it is more probable than not that there are beneficiaries within the meaning of this section, the court shall order that all proceeds or profits be deposited in a bank and held by the bank as trustee of the trust until an order of disposition is made by a court pursuant to subdivision (d), or until the expiration of the period specified in subdivision (b).

(4) If the Attorney General prevails in an action under this subdivision, the court shall order the payment from the proceeds or profits to the Attorney General of reasonable costs and attorney's fees.

(f)(1) In any action brought pursuant to this section, upon motion of a party the court shall grant a preliminary injunction to prevent any waste of proceeds or profits if it appears that the proceeds or profits are subject to the provisions of this section, and that they may be subject to waste.

(2) Upon motion of the Attorney General or any potential beneficiary, the court shall grant a preliminary injunction against a person against whom an indictment or information for a felony has been filed in superior court to prevent any waste of proceeds or profits if there is probable cause to believe that the proceeds or profits would be subject to an involuntary trust pursuant to this section upon conviction of this person, and that they may be subject to waste.

(g) Any violation of an order of a court made pursuant to this section shall be punishable as contempt.

(h) The remedies provided by this section are in addition to other remedies provided by law.

No period of limitations, except those provided by this section, shall limit the right of recovery under this section. (Added by Stats.1986, c. 820, § 8, eff. Sept. 15, 1986, operative July 1, 1987. Amended by Stats.1992, c. 178 (S.B.1496), § 2; Stats.1994, c. 556 (S.B.1330), § 1, eff. Sept. 13, 1994; Stats. 1995, c. 262 (S.B.287), § 1; Stats.2000, c. 261 (S.B.1565), § 2.)

Validity

This section was held unconstitutional as a content-based restriction on speech in the case of Keenan v. Superior Court of Los Angeles County (2002) 117 Cal.Rptr.2d 1, 27 Cal.4th 413, 40 P.3d 718, certiorari denied 123 S.Ct. 94, 537 U.S. 818, 154 L.Ed.2d 25.

§§ 2228 to 2290.9. Repealed by Stats.1986, c. 820, § 7, operative July 1, 1987

§ 2290.10. Repealed by Stats.1978, c. 806, p. 2581, § 3, operative Jan. 1, 1983

§§ 2290.11, 2290.12. Repealed by Stats.1986, c. 820, § 7, operative July 1, 1987

Title 9

AGENCY

Chapter	Section
1. Agency in General	2295
2. Particular Agencies	2362
3. Statutory Short Form Power of Attorney [Repealed]	
3.5. Uniform Statutory Form Power of Attorney Act [Repealed]	
4. Statutory Form Durable Power of Attorney for Health Care [Repealed]	
5. Miscellaneous Provisions Relating to Powers of Attorney [Repealed]	

CHAPTER 1. AGENCY IN GENERAL

Article	Section
1. Definition of Agency	2295
2. Authority of Agents	2304
3. Mutual Obligations of Principals and Third Persons	2330
4. Obligations of Agents to Third Persons	2342
5. Delegation of Agency	2349
6. Termination of Agency	2355

ARTICLE 1. DEFINITION OF AGENCY

Section
2295. "Agent" defined.
2296. Capacity to appoint agent; capacity to be agent.
2297. Special agents; general agents.
2298. Actual or ostensible agency.
2299. "Actual agency" defined.
2300. "Ostensible agency" defined.

Cross References

Partner as agent of partnership, see Corporations Code § 16301.
Provisions of this Title as subordinate to intention of parties and waiver of benefit thereof, see Civil Code § 3268.

§ 2295. "Agent" defined

An agent is one who represents another, called the principal, in dealings with third persons. Such representation is called agency. *(Enacted in 1872.)*

Cross References

Agency defined, see Government Code § 11500.
Agent defined, gratuities, see Labor Code § 350.
Agents, see Civil Code § 2019 et seq.
Factors, see Civil Code §§ 2026 et seq., 2367 et seq.
Waiver of code provisions, see Civil Code § 3268.

§ 2296. Capacity to appoint agent; capacity to be agent

Any person having capacity to contract may appoint an agent, and any person may be an agent. *(Enacted in 1872.)*

Cross References

Minors as parties to contracts, see Family Code § 6700.

Persons with unsound mind as parties to contracts, see Civil Code §§ 38 et seq., 1556, 1557.

§ 2297. Special agents; general agents

An agent for a particular act or transaction is called a special agent. All others are general agents. *(Enacted in 1872.)*

§ 2298. Actual or ostensible agency

An agency is either actual or ostensible. *(Enacted in 1872.)*

Cross References

Actual authority, see Civil Code § 2316.
Ostensible authority, see Civil Code §§ 2317, 2334.

§ 2299. "Actual agency" defined

An agency is actual when the agent is really employed by the principal. *(Enacted in 1872.)*

Cross References

Actual authority, see Civil Code § 2316.

§ 2300. "Ostensible agency" defined

An agency is ostensible when the principal intentionally, or by want of ordinary care, causes a third person to believe another to be his agent who is not really employed by him. *(Enacted in 1872.)*

Cross References

Liability for acts under ostensible authority, see Civil Code § 2334.
Ostensible authority, see Civil Code § 2317.

ARTICLE 2. AUTHORITY OF AGENTS

Section
2304. Authority conferrable; scope.
2305. Performance of acts required of principal by code.
2306. Defrauding principal; absence of authority.
2307. Creation of agency; manner.
2307.1. Repealed.
2308. Consideration unnecessary.
2309. Oral and written authorizations.
2310. Ratification; manner.
2311. Ratification; part of indivisible transaction.
2312. Ratification; invalidity unless principal had power to confer authority.
2313. Ratification; rights of third persons.
2314. Ratification; rescission.
2315. Measure of authority.
2316. Actual authority.
2317. Ostensible authority.
2318. Authority as to persons having notice of restrictions.
2319. Necessary authority.
2320. Power to disobey instructions.
2321. Authority partly in general and partly in specific terms; construction.
2322. Authority of agent.
2323. Sale of personal property; included authority.
2324. Sale of real estate; included authority.
2325. General agent; authority to receive price.
2326. Special agent; authority to receive price.

§ 2304. Authority conferrable; scope

An agent may be authorized to do any acts which his principal might do, except those to which the latter is bound to give his personal attention. *(Enacted in 1872.)*

Cross References

Conformity to authority, see Civil Code § 2019.
Employment of subagents, see Civil Code § 2349 et seq.

§ 2305. Performance of acts required of principal by code

Every act which, according to this Code, may be done by or to any person, may be done by or to the agent of such person for that purpose, unless a contrary intention clearly appears. *(Enacted in 1872.)*

Cross References

Conformity to authority, see Civil Code § 2019.

§ 2306. Defrauding principal; absence of authority

An agent can never have authority, either actual or ostensible, to do an act which is, and is known or suspected by the person with whom he deals, to be a fraud upon the principal. *(Enacted in 1872.)*

Cross References

Actual authority, see Civil Code § 2316.
Ostensible authority, see Civil Code § 2317.

§ 2307. Creation of agency; manner

An agency may be created, and an authority may be conferred, by a precedent authorization or a subsequent ratification. *(Enacted in 1872.)*

§ 2307.1. Repealed by Stats.1981, c. 511, p. 1866, § 1

§ 2308. Consideration unnecessary

A consideration is not necessary to make an authority, whether precedent or subsequent, binding upon the principal. *(Enacted in 1872.)*

§ 2309. Oral and written authorizations

An oral authorization is sufficient for any purpose, except that an authority to enter into a contract required by law to be in writing can only be given by an instrument in writing. *(Enacted in 1872.)*

Cross References

Conformity to authority, see Civil Code § 2019.
Contracts required to be in writing, see Civil Code § 1624; Commercial Code §§ 1206, 2201, 8113.
Enforceability of oral contract required to be in writing, see Civil Code § 1623.
Execution of writing, see Code of Civil Procedure § 1933.
Power of attorney to execute a mortgage, see Civil Code § 2933.

§ 2310. Ratification; manner

A ratification can be made only in the manner that would have been necessary to confer an original authority for the act ratified, or where an oral authorization would suffice, by accepting or retaining the benefit of the act, with notice thereof. *(Enacted in 1872.)*

§ 2311. Ratification; part of indivisible transaction

Ratification of part of an indivisible transaction is a ratification of the whole. *(Enacted in 1872.)*

Cross References

Ratification of voidable contract, see Civil Code § 1588.

§ 2312. Ratification; invalidity unless principal had power to confer authority

A ratification is not valid unless, at the time of ratifying the act done, the principal has power to confer authority for such an act. *(Enacted in 1872.)*

§ 2313. Ratification; rights of third persons

No unauthorized act can be made valid, retroactively, to the prejudice of third persons, without their consent. *(Enacted in 1872.)*

§ 2314. Ratification; rescission

A ratification may be rescinded when made without such consent as is required in a contract, or with an imperfect knowledge of the material facts of the transaction ratified, but not otherwise. *(Enacted in 1872.)*

Cross References

Consent, see Civil Code § 1565 et seq.

§ 2315. Measure of authority

An agent has such authority as the principal, actually or ostensibly, confers upon him. *(Enacted in 1872.)*

Cross References

Actual agency, see Civil Code § 2299.
Effect of agent's authorized acts upon principal, see Civil Code § 2330.
Ostensible agency, see Civil Code § 2300.

§ 2316. Actual authority

Actual authority is such as a principal intentionally confers upon the agent, or intentionally, or by want of ordinary care, allows the agent to believe himself to possess. *(Enacted in 1872.)*

Cross References

Actual agency, see Civil Code § 2299.

§ 2317. Ostensible authority

Ostensible authority is such as a principal, intentionally or by want of ordinary care, causes or allows a third person to believe the agent to possess. *(Enacted in 1872.)*

Cross References

Ostensible agency, see Civil Code § 2300.

§ 2318. Authority as to persons having notice of restrictions

Every agent has actually such authority as is defined by this Title, unless specially deprived thereof by his principal, and has even then such authority ostensibly, except as to persons who have actual or constructive notice of the restriction upon his authority. *(Enacted in 1872.)*

Cross References

Notice, see Civil Code §§ 18, 19.

§ 2319. Necessary authority

An agent has authority:

1. To do everything necessary or proper and usual, in the ordinary course of business, for effecting the purpose of his agency; and,

2. To make a representation respecting any matter of fact, not including the terms of his authority, but upon which his right to use his authority depends, and the truth of which cannot be determined by the use of reasonable diligence on the part of the person to whom the representation is made. *(Enacted in 1872.)*

Cross References

Effect of agent's acts upon principal, see Civil Code § 2330.

§ 2320. Power to disobey instructions

An agent has power to disobey instructions in dealing with the subject of the agency, in cases where it is clearly for the interest of his principal that he should do so, and there is not time to communicate with the principal. *(Enacted in 1872.)*

Cross References

Effect of agent's acts upon principal, see Civil Code § 2330.

§ 2321. Authority partly in general and partly in specific terms; construction

When an authority is given partly in general and partly in specific terms, the general authority gives no higher powers than those specifically mentioned. *(Enacted in 1872.)*

§ 2322. Authority of agent

An authority expressed in general terms, however broad, does not authorize an agent to do any of the following:

(a) Act in the agent's own name, unless it is the usual course of business to do so.

(b) Define the scope of the agency.

(c) Violate a duty to which a trustee is subject under Section 16002, 16004, 16005, or 16009 of the Probate Code. *(Enacted in 1872. Amended by Stats.1986, c. 820, § 9, eff. Sept. 15, 1986, operative July 1, 1987; Stats.1988, c. 113, § 5, eff. May 25, 1988.)*

Cross References

Set off against principal where agent acts for himself, see Civil Code § 2336.

§ 2323. Sale of personal property; included authority

An authority to sell personal property includes authority to warrant the title of the principal, and the quality and quantity of the property. *(Enacted in 1872.)*

Cross References

Warrant by auctioneer, see Civil Code § 2362.

§ 2324. Sale of real estate; included authority

An authority to sell and convey real property includes authority to give the usual covenants of warranty. *(Enacted in 1872.)*

Cross References

Breach of covenant of warranty, damages, see Civil Code § 3304.
Covenants of warranty, running with the land, see Civil Code § 1463.
Implied covenants, see Civil Code § 1113.

§ 2325. General agent; authority to receive price

A general agent to sell, who is intrusted by the principal with the possession of the thing sold, has authority to receive the price. *(Enacted in 1872.)*

Cross References

Collection of negotiable instrument, see Civil Code § 2021.
General agent defined, see Civil Code § 2297.

§ 2326. Special agent; authority to receive price

A special agent to sell has authority to receive the price on delivery of the thing sold, but not afterwards. *(Enacted in 1872.)*

Cross References

Special agent defined, see Civil Code § 2297.

ARTICLE 3. MUTUAL OBLIGATIONS OF PRINCIPALS AND THIRD PERSONS

Section
2330. Principal's rights and liabilities from acts of agent within scope of authority.
2331. Incomplete execution of authority.
2332. Notice to principal or agent as notice to the other.
2333. Principal's obligation where authority exceeded.
2334. Principal bound by acts under ostensible authority.
2335. Exclusive credit to agent; exoneration of principal.
2336. Rights of person dealing with agent without knowledge of agency.
2337. Instrument within scope of agency intended to bind principal.
2338. Responsibility for agent's negligence or omission.
2339. Responsibility for agent's other wrongs.

Cross References

Authority of agents, see Civil Code § 2304 et seq.
Definition of agency, see Civil Code § 2295 et seq.
Delegation of agency, see Civil Code § 2349 et seq.
Obligations of agents to third parties, see Civil Code § 2342 et seq.
Termination of agency, see Civil Code § 2355.

§ 2330. Principal's rights and liabilities from acts of agent within scope of authority

An agent represents his principal for all purposes within the scope of his actual or ostensible authority, and all the rights and liabilities which would accrue to the agent from transactions within such limit, if they had been entered into on his own account, accrue to the principal. *(Enacted in 1872.)*

Cross References

Actual agency defined, see Civil Code § 2299.
Actual authority defined, see Civil Code § 2316.
Ostensible agency defined, see Civil Code § 2300.
Ostensible authority defined, see Civil Code § 2317.

§ 2331. Incomplete execution of authority

A principal is bound by an incomplete execution of an authority, when it is consistent with the whole purpose and scope thereof, but not otherwise. *(Enacted in 1872.)*

§ 2332. Notice to principal or agent as notice to the other

As against a principal, both principal and agent are deemed to have notice of whatever either has notice of, and ought, in good faith and the exercise of ordinary care and diligence, to communicate to the other. *(Enacted in 1872.)*

§ 2333. Principal's obligation where authority exceeded

When an agent exceeds his authority, his principal is bound by his authorized acts so far only as they can be plainly separated from those which are unauthorized. *(Enacted in 1872.)*

Cross References

Ratification of agent's acts, see Civil Code § 2310 et seq.

§ 2334. Principal bound by acts under ostensible authority

A principal is bound by acts of his agent, under a merely ostensible authority, to those persons only who have in good faith, and without want of ordinary care, incurred a liability or parted with value, upon the faith thereof. *(Enacted in 1872. Amended by Stats.1905, c. 457, p. 616, § 1.)*

Cross References

Ostensible agency defined, see Civil Code § 2300.
Ostensible authority defined, see Civil Code § 2317.

§ 2335. Exclusive credit to agent; exoneration of principal

If exclusive credit is given to an agent by the person dealing with him, his principal is exonerated by payment or other satisfaction made by him to his agent in good faith, before receiving notice of the creditor's election to hold him responsible. *(Enacted in 1872).*

Cross References

Liability of agent for personally extended credit, see Civil Code § 2343.

§ 2336. Rights of person dealing with agent without knowledge of agency

One who deals with an agent without knowing or having reason to believe that the agent acts as such in the transaction, may set off against any claim of the principal arising out of the same, all claims which he might have set off against the agent before notice of the agency. *(Enacted in 1872.)*

§ 2337. Instrument within scope of agency intended to bind principal

An instrument within the scope of his authority by which an agent intends to bind his principal, does bind him if such intent is plainly inferable from the instrument itself. *(Enacted in 1872.)*

§ 2338. Responsibility for agent's negligence or omission

Unless required by or under the authority of law to employ that particular agent, a principal is responsible to third

§ 2338

persons for the negligence of his agent in the transaction of the business of the agency, including wrongful acts committed by such agent in and as a part of the transaction of such business, and for his willful omission to fulfill the obligations of the principal. *(Enacted in 1872.)*

Cross References

Damages for torts, see Civil Code § 3333.
Negligence, see Civil Code § 1714.
Negligence of pilot and persons employed in navigation, see Harbors and Navigation Code § 820.

§ 2339. Responsibility for agent's other wrongs

A principal is responsible for no other wrongs committed by his agent than those mentioned in the last section, unless he has authorized or ratified them, even though they are committed while the agent is engaged in his service. *(Enacted in 1872.)*

Cross References

Ratification, see Civil Code § 2310 et seq.

ARTICLE 4. OBLIGATIONS OF AGENTS TO THIRD PERSONS

Section
2342. Warranty of authority.
2343. Responsibility to third persons.
2344. Surrender of property to third persons.
2345. Applicability of law of persons.

Cross References

Authority of agents, see Civil Code § 2304 et seq.
Breach of warranty of agent's authority, damages, see Civil Code § 3318.
Definition of agency, see Civil Code § 2295 et seq.
Delegation of agency, see Civil Code § 2349 et seq.
Mutual obligations of principals and third persons, see Civil Code § 2330 et seq.
Termination of agency, see Civil Code § 2355.

§ 2342. Warranty of authority

One who assumes to act as an agent thereby warrants, to all who deal with him in that capacity, that he has the authority which he assumes. *(Enacted in 1872.)*

§ 2343. Responsibility to third persons

One who assumes to act as an agent is responsible to third persons as a principal for his acts in the course of his agency, in any of the following cases, and in no others:

1. When, with his consent, credit is given to him personally in a transaction;

2. When he enters into a written contract in the name of his principal, without believing, in good faith, that he has authority to do so; or,

3. When his acts are wrongful in their nature. *(Enacted in 1872.)*

Cross References

Personal liability of master of vessel on contracts, see Harbors and Navigation Code § 819.

§ 2344. Surrender of property to third persons

If an agent receives anything for the benefit of his principal, to the possession of which another person is entitled, he must, on demand, surrender it to such person, or so much of it as he has under his control at the time of demand, on being indemnified for any advance which he has made to his principal, in good faith, on account of the same; and is responsible therefor, if, after notice from the owner, he delivers it to his principal. *(Enacted in 1872.)*

Cross References

Depositary, delivery on demand, see Civil Code § 1822 et seq.

§ 2345. Applicability of law of persons

The provisions of this Article are subject to the provisions of Part 1, Division First, of this Code. *(Enacted in 1872.)*

ARTICLE 5. DELEGATION OF AGENCY

Section
2349. Authority to delegate powers.
2350. Unauthorized sub-agent; relationship of parties.
2351. Authorized sub-agent; relationship of parties.

§ 2349. Authority to delegate powers

An agent, unless specially forbidden by his principal to do so, can delegate his powers to another person in any of the following cases, and in no others:

1. When the act to be done is purely mechanical;

2. When it is such as the agent cannot himself, and the sub-agent can lawfully perform;

3. When it is the usage of the place to delegate such powers; or,

4. When such delegation is specially authorized by the principal. *(Enacted in 1872.)*

§ 2350. Unauthorized sub-agent; relationship of parties

If an agent employs a sub-agent without authority, the former is a principal and the latter his agent, and the principal of the former has no connection with the latter. *(Enacted in 1872.)*

Cross References

Responsibility of agent of agent, see Civil Code § 2022.

§ 2351. Authorized sub-agent; relationship of parties

A sub-agent, lawfully appointed, represents the principal in like manner with the original agent; and the original agent is not responsible to third persons for the acts of the sub-agent. *(Enacted in 1872.)*

ARTICLE 6. TERMINATION OF AGENCY

Section
2355. Means of termination.

Section
2356. Agency not coupled with an interest; bona fide transaction; proxies.
2357. Absentee principal; knowledge.

§ 2355. Means of termination

An agency is terminated, as to every person having notice thereof, by any of the following:

(a) The expiration of its term.

(b) The extinction of its subject.

(c) The death of the agent.

(d) The agent's renunciation of the agency.

(e) The incapacity of the agent to act as such. *(Enacted in 1872. Amended by Stats.1972, c. 988, p. 1799, § 1, eff. Aug. 16, 1972; Stats.1980, c. 246, p. 491, § 1; Stats.1983, c. 99, § 5; Stats.1994, c. 307 (S.B.1907), § 1.)*

§ 2356. Agency not coupled with an interest; bona fide transaction; proxies

(a) Unless the power of an agent is coupled with an interest in the subject of the agency, it is terminated by any of the following:

(1) Its revocation by the principal.

(2) The death of the principal.

(3) The incapacity of the principal to contract.

(b) Notwithstanding subdivision (a), any bona fide transaction entered into with an agent by any person acting without actual knowledge of the revocation, death, or incapacity shall be binding upon the principal, his or her heirs, devisees, legatees, and other successors in interest.

(c) Nothing in this section shall affect the provisions of Section 1216.

(d) With respect to a proxy given by a person to another person relating to the exercise of voting rights, to the extent the provisions of this section conflict with or contravene any other provisions of the statutes of California pertaining to the proxy, the latter provisions shall prevail. *(Enacted in 1872. Amended by Stats.1943, c. 413, p. 1951, § 1; Stats.1972, c. 988, p. 1799, § 2, eff. Aug. 16, 1972; Stats.1979, c. 234, p. 488, § 2; Stats.1980, c. 246, p. 491, § 2; Stats.1981, c. 511, p. 1867, § 2; Stats.1983, c. 1204, § 1; Stats.1994, c. 307 (S.B.1907), § 2.)*

Cross References

Proxies, form, etc., see Corporations Code §§ 604, 705.

§ 2357. Absentee principal; knowledge

For the purposes of subdivision (b) of Section 2356, in the case of a principal who is an absentee as defined in Section 1403 of the Probate Code, a person shall be deemed to be without actual knowledge of:

(a) The principal's death or incapacity while the absentee continues in missing status and until the person receives notice of the determination of the death of the absentee by the secretary concerned or the head of the department or agency concerned or the delegate of the secretary or head.

(b) Revocation by the principal during the period described in subdivision (a). *(Added by Stats.1981, c. 511, p. 1867, § 3. Amended by Stats.1994, c. 307 (S.B.1907), § 3.)*

CHAPTER 2. PARTICULAR AGENCIES

Article	Section
1. Auctioneers	2362
2. Factors	2367
2.5 Agency Relationships in Residential Real Property Transactions [Repealed]	
3. Powers of Attorney Under Probate Code	2400
4. Court Enforcement of Duties of Attorney in Fact [Repealed]	
5. Durable Power of Attorney for Health Care [Repealed]	

ARTICLE 1. AUCTIONEERS

Section
2362. Authority from seller.
2363. Authority from bidder.

Cross References

Bulk sales, auction, notice, see Commercial Code § 6105 et seq.
Obtaining money, property or signature by mock auction, punishment, see Penal Code § 535.
Sale by auction, see Commercial Code § 2328.
Unlawfully acting as auctioneer, misdemeanor, see Penal Code § 436.

§ 2362. Authority from seller

An auctioneer, in the absence of special authorization or usage to the contrary, has authority from the seller, only as follows:

1. To sell by public auction to the highest bidder;

2. To sell for cash only, except such articles as are usually sold on credit at auction;

3. To warrant, in like manner with other agents to sell, according to Section 2323;

4. To prescribe reasonable rules and terms of sale;

5. To deliver the thing sold, upon payment of the price;

6. To collect the price; and,

7. To do whatever else is necessary, or proper and usual, in the ordinary course of business, for effecting these purposes. *(Enacted in 1872.)*

Cross References

Proxies, see Corporations Code §§ 604, 705.

§ 2363. Authority from bidder

An auctioneer has authority from a bidder at the auction, as well as from the seller, to bind both by a memorandum of the contract, as prescribed in the Title on Sale. *(Enacted in 1872.)*

ARTICLE 2. FACTORS

Section
2367. "Factor" defined.
2368. Actual authority of factor.
2369. Ostensible authority of factor.

Cross References

Factors,
Generally, see Civil Code § 2026.

False statements to principal, see Penal Code §§ 536, 536a.
Guaranty commission, see Civil Code § 2029.
Lien, see Civil Code § 3053.
Obedience to instructions, see Civil Code § 2027.
Relief from responsibility to guarantee sales or remittance, see Civil Code § 2030.
Sales on credit, see Civil Code § 2028.

§ 2367. "Factor" defined

A factor is an agent, as defined by Section 2026. *(Enacted in 1872.)*

Cross References

Credit sales by factor, see Civil Code § 2028.
Factor's lien, see Civil Code § 3053.
Guarantee sales, general agreement or usage, liability of factor, see Civil Code § 2030.
Obedience of factor to instructions of principal, see Civil Code § 2027.
Statement of sales by factor, see Penal Code §§ 536, 536a.

§ 2368. Actual authority of factor

In addition to the authority of agents in general, a factor has actual authority from his principal, unless specially restricted:

1. To insure property consigned to him uninsured;
2. To sell, on credit, anything intrusted to him for sale, except such things as it is contrary to usage to sell on credit; but not to pledge, mortgage, or barter the same; and,
3. To delegate his authority to his partner or servant, but not to any person in an independent employment. *(Enacted in 1872.)*

Cross References

Credit sales, extension of credit term, see Civil Code § 2028.

§ 2369. Ostensible authority of factor

A factor has ostensible authority to deal with the property of his principal as his own, in transactions with persons not having notice of the actual ownership. *(Enacted in 1872.)*

Cross References

Ostensible agency defined, see Civil Code § 2300.

ARTICLE 2.5. AGENCY RELATIONSHIPS IN RESIDENTIAL REAL PROPERTY TRANSACTIONS [REPEALED]

§§ 2373 to 2382. Repealed by Stats.1995, c. 428 (S.B.467), § 2

§§ 2383 to 2385. Repealed by Stats.1937, c. 368, p. 1002, § 10001

§§ 2388, 2389. Repealed by Stats.1937, c. 368, p. 1002, § 10001

ARTICLE 3. POWERS OF ATTORNEY UNDER PROBATE CODE

Section
2395 to 2399. Repealed.

Section
2400. Powers of attorney; applicable law.
2400.5 to 2407. Repealed.
2408, 2409. Repealed.

§§ 2395 to 2399. Repealed by Stats.1949, c. 383, § 2

§ 2400. Powers of attorney; applicable law

Powers of attorney are governed by the Power of Attorney Law (Division 4.5 (commencing with Section 4000) of the Probate Code) to the extent provided in that law. *(Added by Stats.1994, c. 307 (S.B.1907), § 5.)*

§§ 2400.5 to 2407. Repealed by Stats.1994, c. 307 (S.B. 1907), § 4

§§ 2408, 2409. Repealed by Stats.1949, c. 383, p. 697, § 2

ARTICLE 4. COURT ENFORCEMENT OF DUTIES OF ATTORNEY IN FACT [REPEALED]

§§ 2410 to 2423. Repealed by Stats.1994, c. 307 (S.B.1907), § 6

§§ 2424 to 2429. Repealed by Stats.1949, c. 383, § 2

ARTICLE 5. DURABLE POWER OF ATTORNEY FOR HEALTH CARE [REPEALED]

§§ 2430 to 2445. Repealed by Stats.1994, c. 307 (S.B.1907), § 7

§ 2446. Inoperative

§ 2449. Repealed by Stats.1929, c. 864, § 1

CHAPTER 3. STATUTORY SHORT FORM POWER OF ATTORNEY [REPEALED]

§ 2450. Repealed by Stats.1994, c. 307 (S.B.1907), § 8

§§ 2451 to 2457. Repealed by Stats.1990, c. 986 (S.B.1777), § 1

§§ 2458, 2459. Repealed by Stats.1929, c. 864, p. 1896, § 1

§§ 2460 to 2469. Repealed by Stats.1990, c. 986 (S.B.1777), § 1

§§ 2469.1 to 2469.3. Repealed by Stats.1970, c. 618, p. 1229, § 5, operative July 1, 1971

§§ 2470 to 2473. Repealed by Stats.1990, c. 986 (S.B.1777), § 1

CHAPTER 3.5. UNIFORM STATUTORY FORM POWER OF ATTORNEY ACT [REPEALED]

CHAPTER 4. STATUTORY FORM DURABLE POWER OF ATTORNEY FOR HEALTH CARE [REPEALED]

CHAPTER 5. MISCELLANEOUS PROVISIONS RELATING TO POWERS OF ATTORNEY [REPEALED]

Title 10
RECORDING ARTIST CONTRACTS

Section
2500. Definitions.
2501. Audit of books and records of royalty reporting party; conditions.
2502 to 2504. Repealed.

§ 2500. Definitions

As used in this title:

(a) "Royalty recipient" means a party to a contract for the furnishing of services in the production of sound recordings, as defined in Section 101 of Title 17 of the United States Code, who has the right to receive royalties under that contract.

(b) A "royalty reporting party" is the party obligated to pay royalties to the royalty recipient under the contract described in subdivision (a). *(Added by Stats.2004, c. 150 (S.B.1034), § 2.)*

§ 2501. Audit of books and records of royalty reporting party; conditions

Notwithstanding any provision of a contract described in Section 2500:

(a) A royalty recipient may audit the books and records of the royalty reporting party to determine if the royalty recipient earned all of the royalties due the royalty recipient pursuant to the contract, subject to the following:

(1) A royalty recipient may conduct an audit not more than once per year.

(2) A royalty recipient shall request an audit within three years after the end of a royalty earnings period under the contract.

(3) A royalty recipient may not audit a particular royalty earnings period more than once.

(b) The royalty recipient shall retain a qualified royalty auditor of the royalty recipient's choice to conduct an audit described in this section.

(c) The royalty recipient may enter into a contingency fee agreement with the auditor described in subdivision (b).

(d) A qualified royalty auditor may conduct individual audits of the books and records of a royalty reporting party on behalf of different royalty recipients simultaneously.

(e) Except as required by law, a qualified royalty auditor shall not disclose any confidential information obtained solely during an audit without the express consent of the party or parties to whom that information is confidential. This subdivision shall not prohibit the auditor from disclosing to the royalty recipient, or an agent of the recipient, on behalf of whom the auditor is conducting the audit information directly pertaining to that royalty recipient's contract, as described in Section 2500.

(f) The provisions of subdivisions (a), (b), (c), (d), and (e) are in addition to any other rights provided by a contract, as described in Section 2500, between a royalty recipient and a royalty reporting party.

(g) Nothing in subdivision (a), (b), (c), (d), or (e) shall be deemed to extend any limitations period applicable to royalty accounting or payments not specifically addressed in this section.

(h) Nothing in subdivision (a), (b), (c), (d), or (e) shall be deemed to limit any rights provided by collective bargaining agreement or by applicable state or federal law. *(Added by Stats.2004, c. 150 (S.B.1034), § 2.)*

§§ 2502 to 2504. Repealed by Stats.1994, c. 307 (S.B.1907), § 10

Title 10.1
SHARED MOBILITY DEVICES

Section
2505. Requirement of agreement or permit for shared mobility service provider; insurance coverage; pedestrian liability coverage; adoption of rules regarding shared mobility devices.
2505.5. Department of Insurance study and report.
2506. Braille affixed to each shared mobility device; identification; information.
2507, 2508. Repealed.
2509. Repealed.
2510 to 2514. Repealed.
2515 to 2520. Repealed.

§ 2505. Requirement of agreement or permit for shared mobility service provider; insurance coverage; pedestrian liability coverage; adoption of rules regarding shared mobility devices

(a) For purposes of this title:

(1) "Assistive technology device" has the same meaning as in Section 7002 of Title 9 of the California Code of Regulations.

(2) "Shared mobility device" means an electrically motorized board as defined in Section 313.5 of the Vehicle Code, motorized scooter as defined in Section 407.5 of the Vehicle Code, electric bicycle as defined in Section 312.5 of the Vehicle Code, bicycle as defined in Section 231 of the Vehicle Code, or other similar personal transportation device, except as provided in subdivision (b) of Section 415 of the Vehicle Code, that is made available to the public by a shared mobility service provider for shared use and transportation in exchange for financial compensation via a digital application or other electronic or digital platform.

(3) "Shared mobility service provider" or "provider" means a person or entity that offers, makes available, or provides a shared mobility device in exchange for financial

§ 2505   OBLIGATIONS

compensation or membership via a digital application or other electronic or digital platform.

(b)(1) Before distribution of a shared mobility device, a shared mobility service provider shall enter into an agreement with, or obtain a permit from, the city or county with jurisdiction over the area of use. The agreement or permit shall, at a minimum, require that the shared mobility service provider maintain commercial general liability insurance coverage with an admitted insurer, or a * * * nonadmitted insurer that is eligible to insure a home state insured under Chapter 6 (commencing with Section 1760) of Part 2 of Division 1 of the Insurance Code, with limits not less than one million dollars ($1,000,000) for each occurrence for bodily injury or property damage, including contractual liability, personal injury, and product liability and completed operations, and not less than five million dollars ($5,000,000) aggregate for all occurrences during the policy period. The insurance shall not exclude coverage for injuries or damages caused by the shared mobility service provider to the shared mobility device user.

(2)(A)(i) Notwithstanding any other law, effective July 1, 2023, the agreement or permit required pursuant to paragraph (1) shall require, in addition to the coverage required by paragraph (1), a shared mobility service provider to offer or make available, or to confirm the user of a shared mobility device maintains, insurance coverage for bodily injury or death suffered by a pedestrian when the injury or death involves, in whole or in part, the negligent conduct of the shared mobility device user, of ten thousand dollars ($10,000) for each occurrence of bodily injury to, or death of, one pedestrian in any one accident, and for property damage to an assistive technology device, of one thousand dollars ($1,000), for each occurrence.

(ii) Notwithstanding clause (i) or any other law, a shared mobility service provider or user of a shared mobility device is not required to maintain insurance coverage, as described in clause (i), for injuries of, or death to, a pedestrian or property damage involving the following devices:

(I) A bicycle propelled exclusively by human power, as described in Section 231 of the Vehicle Code. For purposes of this paragraph, "bicycle" shall not include an electric bicycle.

(II) A class 1 electric bicycle as defined in paragraph (1) of subdivision (a) of Section 312.5 of the Vehicle Code.

(III) A class 2 electric bicycle as defined in paragraph (2) of subdivision (a) of Section 312.5 of the Vehicle Code.

(iii) The Legislature finds and declares that bicycles may be recognized as safer than motorized devices when in use, and recognizes there may remain a propensity for pedestrian injuries or death resulting from shared mobility bicycles and shared mobility electric bicycles being left negligently abandoned on pedestrian walkways.

(B) A shared mobility service provider may partner with an insurer to provide an option to its users via its digital application or other electronic platform where the user may purchase insurance coverage that meets or exceeds the requirements of subparagraph (A). The shared mobility service provider shall disclose via its digital application or other electronic platform the name, contact information, and location to make a claim with the insurer they chose to partner with. The shared mobility service provider may fund the cost of providing this coverage itself and pass the cost on in its standard fee to users, or through a separate charge to users. If a user of a shared mobility device does not maintain their own insurance policy, then that coverage shall be offered or made available by the shared mobility service provider. A shared mobility service provider shall not allow a user or individual to operate or utilize a shared mobility device without the coverage identified in subparagraph (A). If a user or individual gains access to a shared mobility device without obtaining coverage through the options outlined in this subparagraph or subparagraph (C), and uses or operates it uninsured, the shared mobility service provider shall be required to provide the insurance coverage identified in subparagraph (A).

(C)(i) A shared mobility service provider may enter into separate individual agreements with users maintaining their own liability insurance coverage that meets or exceeds the requirements of subparagraph (A), to exclude the user from the provider's insurance coverage required in subparagraph (A) when, in consideration for such an agreement, the user shall not pay a separate charge for the coverage or shall be refunded the portion of the provider's fee that pays for the provider's coverage. The agreement shall be null and void upon lapse, cancellation, or expiration of the user's policy. If a shared mobility device user entering into an agreement under this subparagraph misrepresents their maintenance of a policy or through an error or act of omission does not provide coverage, the shared mobility service provider shall be required to maintain the insurance to cover any claims resulting in injury, death, or property damage described in subparagraph (A).

(ii) It is the intent of the Legislature that, in enacting this subparagraph, shared mobility service providers have the flexibility to offer or make available insurance options to their users, while also ensuring the shared mobility service providers' insurance serves as the backstop to cover any pedestrian injuries or death, or property damage, should there be any unintended gaps in coverage as a result of users misrepresenting or not maintaining the insurance.

(D) A shared mobility service provider shall keep an up-to-date list of its users that maintain their own liability insurance coverage that meets or exceeds the requirements of subparagraph (A). The provider shall annually transmit information on the percentage of its total users in the state that maintain their own insurance coverage, in the same manner as proscribed in subdivision (b) of Section 2505.5 of the Civil Code, to the Department of Insurance.

(3) Effective July 1, 2023, nothing in this section shall prohibit a provider from requiring a user to enter into an indemnity contract whereby the user will indemnify the provider for the user's proportionate share of liability. The indemnity contract shall not require the user to defend or indemnify the provider for the provider's negligence or willful misconduct. This section shall not be waived or modified by contractual agreement, act, or omission of the parties.

(c)(1) A city or county that authorizes a provider to operate within its jurisdiction on or after January 1, 2021, shall adopt rules for the operation, parking, and maintenance of shared mobility devices before a provider may offer any shared mobility device for rent or use in the city or county by any of the following:

(A) Ordinance.

(B) Agreement.

(C) Permit terms.

(2) A city or county that authorized a provider to operate within its jurisdiction before January 1, 2021, and continues to provide that authorization shall adopt rules for the operation, parking, and maintenance of shared mobility devices by January 1, 2022, by any of the following:

(A) Ordinance.

(B) Agreement.

(C) Permit terms.

(3) A provider shall comply with all applicable rules, agreements, and permit terms established pursuant to this subdivision.

(d) Nothing in this section shall prohibit a city or county from adopting any ordinance or regulation that is not inconsistent with this title.

(e) On or before July 1, 2023, a shared mobility service provider shall disclose to its customers that the customer's existing homeowner's, renter's, or automobile insurance policies might not provide coverage for liability resulting from the use of shared mobility devices and that the customer should contact their insurance company or insurance agent to determine if coverage is provided, prior to allowing a user to initiate their first use of a device.

(1) The disclosure shall be made to, and acknowledged by, the customer via the provider's digital application or electronic platform and posted on the provider's internet website.

(2) The disclosure shall include the following language in capital letters:

"YOUR HOMEOWNER'S, RENTER'S, OR AUTOMOBILE INSURANCE POLICIES MIGHT NOT PROVIDE COVERAGE FOR ACCIDENTS INVOLVING THE USE OF THIS DEVICE. TO DETERMINE IF COVERAGE IS PROVIDED YOU SHOULD CONTACT YOUR INSURANCE COMPANY OR AGENT." (Added by Stats.2020, c. 91 (A.B.1286), § 1, eff. Jan. 1, 2021. Amended by Stats.2022, c. 740 (A.B.371), § 1, eff. Jan. 1, 2023.)

§ 2505.5. Department of Insurance study and report

(a) The Department of Insurance shall conduct a study and report the findings to the Legislature and the insurance committees of both houses no later than December 31, 2026, that does all of the following:

(1) In collaboration with a city or county with jurisdiction over areas of shared mobility device use and shared mobility device insurers and operators, assesses whether coverage requirements for shared mobility devices are appropriate to the risk of shared mobility device services and provide recommendations to update coverage requirements, if found to be necessary. The Department of Insurance may specify by bulletin the time periods and elements of data to be provided by admitted and nonadmitted insurers writing coverage pursuant to subdivision (b) of Section 2505.

(2) With input from shared mobility device providers, analyzes the process by which providers give users an option to purchase their own insurance coverage, and make recommendations, if necessary, on how to strengthen the market for individual mobility device liability coverage, including on ensuring agreements between a provider and user to remove the user from the provider's policy do not result in circumstances where there is a gap in coverage providing recovery for injured pedestrians.

(3)(A) In collaboration with a city or county with jurisdiction over areas of shared mobility device use and shared mobility device insurers and operators, assesses whether there is a need for insurance coverage for injuries to, or death of, a pedestrian or property damage to assistive technology devices when the injury, death, or property damage involves, in whole or in part, the following devices:

(i) A bicycle propelled exclusively by human power, as described in Section 231 of the Vehicle Code. For purposes of this paragraph, "bicycle" shall not include an electric bicycle.

(ii) A class 1 electric bicycle as defined in paragraph (1) of subdivision (a) of Section 312.5 of the Vehicle Code.

(iii) A class 2 electric bicycle as defined in paragraph (2) of subdivision (a) of Section 312.5 of the Vehicle Code.

(B) It is the intent of the Legislature that the assessment in subparagraph (A) of this section will provide data on the prevalence of injuries, death, or property damage resulting from the devices described in clauses (i), (ii), and (iii) of subparagraph (A), including, but not limited to, resulting from such devices being negligently abandoned on pedestrian walkways, and determine whether additional insurance coverage is necessary to account for such pedestrian injuries or death and property damage.

(b) Data collected by the Department of Insurance pursuant to this section shall not include information that identifies or describes an individual, including, but not limited to, an individual's name, social security number, home address, home telephone number, education, financial matters, medical or employment history, geolocation, or statements made by, or attributed to, the individual, or that may otherwise compromise the privacy of the individual under existing law.

(c)(1) A report to be submitted pursuant to this section shall be submitted in compliance with Section 9795 of the Government Code.

(2) Pursuant to Section 10231.5 of the Government Code, this section is repealed on January 1, 2027. (Added by Stats.2022, c. 740 (A.B.371), § 2, eff. Jan. 1, 2023.)

Repeal

For repeal of this section, see its terms.

§ 2506. Braille affixed to each shared mobility device; identification; information

A shared mobility service provider shall affix to each shared mobility device a readily accessible, single, and clearly displayed tactile sign containing raised characters and accompanying Braille, complying with Section 11B–703 of the

Building Code, to identify the device for the purpose of reporting illegal or negligent activity. The sign shall minimally consist of the company name, phone number, and email address of the service provider that is visible a minimum of five feet and not obfuscated by branding or other markings. (Added by Stats.2022, c. 740 (A.B.371), § 3, eff. Jan. 1, 2023.)

§§ 2507, 2508. Repealed by Stats.1994, c. 307 (S.B.1907), § 10

§ 2509. Repealed by Stats.1929, c. 865, § 1

§§ 2510 to 2514. Repealed by Stats.1994, c. 307 (S.B.1907), § 11

§§ 2515 to 2520. Repealed by Stats.1939, c. 93, § 1002

Title 10A

UNINCORPORATED NONPROFIT ASSOCIATIONS AND THEIR MEMBERS [REPEALED]

§§ 2523, 2524. Repealed by Stats.1947, c. 1038, p. 2441, § 10003

Title 10.5

DEATH WITH DIGNITY ACT [REJECTED]

§§ 2525 to 2525.24. Rejected, eff. Nov. 3, 1992

Title 11

PHARMACEUTICAL SERVICES

Section
2527. Prescription drug claims processors; requirements; fee studies.
2528. Violations; civil remedy; damages; attorney's fees and costs; standing; notice.
2531 to 2709. Repealed.
2710. Repealed.
2711 to 2746. Repealed.
2752. Repealed.
2753 to 2769. Repealed.

§ 2527. Prescription drug claims processors; requirements; fee studies

(a) On or after January 1, 1984, no prescription drug claims processor, as defined in subdivision (b), shall enter into or perform any provision of any new contract, or perform any provision of any existing contract, with a licensed California pharmacy, or process or assist in the processing of any prescription drug claim submitted by or otherwise involving a service of a licensed California pharmacy unless the processor is in compliance with subdivisions (c) and (d).

(b) A "prescription drug claims processor," as used in this part, means any nongovernmental entity which has a contractual relationship with purchasers of prepaid or insured prescription drug benefits, and which processes, consults, advises on, or otherwise assists in the processing of prepaid or insured prescription drug benefit claims submitted by a licensed California pharmacy or patron thereof. A "prescription drug claims processor" shall not include insurers (as defined in Section 23 of the Insurance Code), health care service plans (as defined in subdivision (f) of Section 1345 of the Health and Safety Code), nonprofit hospital service plans (pursuant to Chapter 11A, (commencing with Section 11491) of Part 2 of Division 2 of the Insurance Code), pharmacy permitholders (pursuant to Section 4080 of the Business and Professions Code), employers, trusts, and other entities which assume the risks of pharmaceutical services for designated beneficiaries. Also, a "prescription drug claims processor" shall not include insurers, health care service plans, and nonprofit hospital service plans which process claims on a nonrisk basis for self-insured clients.

(c) On or before January 1, 1984, every prescription drug claims processor shall have conducted or obtained the results of a study or studies which identifies the fees, separate from ingredient costs, of all, or of a statistically significant sample, of California pharmacies, for pharmaceutical dispensing services to private consumers. The study or studies shall meet reasonable professional standards of the statistical profession. The determination of the pharmacy's fee made for purposes of the study or studies shall be computed by reviewing a sample of the pharmacy's usual charges for a random or other representative sample of commonly prescribed drug products, subtracting the average wholesale price of drug ingredients, and averaging the resulting fees by dividing the aggregate of the fees by the number of prescriptions reviewed. A study report shall include a preface, an explanatory summary of the results and findings including a comparison of the fees of California pharmacies by setting forth the mean fee and standard deviation, the range of fees and fee percentiles (10th, 20th, 30th, 40th, 50th, 60th, 70th, 80th, 90th). This study or these studies shall be conducted or obtained no less often than every 24 months.

(d) The study report or reports obtained pursuant to subdivision (c) shall be transmitted by certified mail by each prescription drug claims processor to the chief executive officer or designee, of each client for whom it performs claims processing services. Consistent with subdivision (c), the processor shall transmit the study or studies to clients no less often than every 24 months.

Nothing in this section shall be construed to require a prescription drug claims processor to transmit to its clients more than two studies meeting the requirements of subdivision (c) during any such 24-month period.

Effective January 1, 1986, a claims processor may comply with subdivision (c) and this subdivision, in the event that no new study or studies meeting the criteria of subdivision (c) have been conducted or obtained subsequent to January 1, 1984, by transmitting the same study or studies previously transmitted, with notice of cost-of-living changes as measured by the Consumer Price Index (CPI) of the United States Department of Labor. (Added by Stats.1982, c. 296, p. 937, § 1.)

Validity

This statute was held unconstitutional as a restriction on freedom of speech, in the decision of ARP Pharmacy Services, Inc. v. Gallagher Bassett Services, Inc. (App. 2 Dist. 2006) 42 Cal.Rptr.3d 256, 138 Cal.App.4th 1307.

§ 2528. Violations; civil remedy; damages; attorney's fees and costs; standing; notice

A violation of Section 2527 may result only in imposition of a civil remedy, which includes, but is not limited to, imposition of statutory damages of not less than one thousand dollars ($1,000) or more than ten thousand dollars ($10,000) depending on the severity or gravity of the violation, plus reasonable attorney's fees and costs, declaratory and injunctive relief, and any other relief which the court deems proper. Any owner of a licensed California pharmacy shall have standing to bring an action seeking a civil remedy pursuant to this section so long as his or her pharmacy has a contractual relationship with, or renders pharmaceutical services to, a beneficiary of a client of the prescription drug claims processor, against whom the action is brought provided that no such action may be commenced by the owner unless he or she has notified the processor in writing as to the nature of the alleged violation and the processor fails to remedy the violation within 30 days from the receipt of the notice or fails to undertake steps to remedy the violation within that period and complete the steps promptly thereafter. *(Added by Stats.1982, c. 296, p. 938, § 1.)*

Validity

This statute was held unconstitutional in the decision of ARP Pharmacy Services, Inc. v. Gallagher Bassett Services, Inc. (App. 2 Dist. 2006) 42 Cal. Rptr.3d 256, 138 Cal.App.4th 1307.

§§ 2531 to 2709. Repealed by Stats.1935, c. 145, p. 778, § 13001

§ 2710. Repealed by Code Am.1873–74, c. 612, p. 258, § 248

§§ 2711 to 2746. Repealed by Stats.1935, c. 145, p. 778, § 13001

§ 2752. Repealed by Code Am.1873–74, c. 612, p. 259, § 252

§§ 2753 to 2769. Repealed by Stats.1935, c. 145, p. 778, § 13001

Title 12

INDEMNITY

Section
2772. Definitions.
2773. Future wrongful act; invalidity.
2774. Past wrongful act; validity.
2775. Extension to acts of agents.
2776. Agreement to indemnify several persons; application.
2777. Joint or separate liability.
2778. Rules of interpretation.
2779. Reimbursement of person indemnifying; manner.
2780, 2781. Repealed.
2782. Construction contracts; void and unenforceable indemnification provisions; agreements between subcontractors, builders, or general contractors.
2782.05. Construction contracts; void and unenforceable indemnification provisions; agreements between general contractors, construction managers, or subcontractors.
2782.1. Agreement to enter adjacent property; indemnification.
2782.2. Agreement to indemnify professional engineers or agents or employees of engineers; liability for negligence in providing inspection services; requirements.
2782.5. Agreements as to allocation or limitation of liability for design defects or of promisee to promisor.
2782.6. Professional engineers or geologists; agreements indemnifying work with hazardous materials; criteria; gross negligence or willful misconduct excepted.
2782.6. Professional engineers or geologists; agreements indemnifying work with hazardous materials; criteria; gross negligence or willful misconduct excepted.
2782.8. Contracts for design professional services; indemnification provisions.
2782.9. Residential construction projects; unenforceable indemnity agreements.
2782.95. Residential improvements; wrap-up insurance policies or other consolidated insurance programs; disclosures.
2782.96. Public works; wrap-up insurance policy or other consolidated insurance programs; disclosures.
2783. "Construction contract" defined.
2784. "Design defect" defined.
2784.5. Hauling, trucking, or cartage contracts; provisions indemnifying against liability for negligence void; exception.

Cross References

Bovine animals, indemnity for slaughter, see Food and Agricultural Code § 10405 et seq.
Bovine tuberculosis, indemnity for slaughter, see Food and Agricultural Code § 10061 et seq.
Central Valley project, indemnity bonds, see Water Code § 11850 et seq.
Contract rights and obligations, provisions of title subordinate to intentions of the parties, see Civil Code § 3268.
Covenant of indemnity, effect of judgment upon, see Code of Civil Procedure § 1055.
Crimes, indemnification of private citizens, see Government Code § 13959 et seq.
Expenses and losses of employees, indemnification, see Labor Code § 2802.
Fire insurance contract, measure of indemnity, see Insurance Code § 2050 et seq.
Indemnification of partners, see Corporations Code § 16401.
Joint tortfeasors, releases and contribution, see Code of Civil Procedure § 875 et seq.
Letters of credit, indemnitees, see Commercial Code § 5113.
Life and disability insurance, indemnity defined, see Insurance Code § 10272.
Lost or destroyed documents, indemnity bond, see Civil Code § 3415.

Mutilated or defaced bonds of local agencies, duplicates, indemnity bond, see Government Code § 53435.
Patent infringement, indemnity, see Public Contract Code § 10318.
Persons erroneously convicted and pardoned, indemnity, see Penal Code § 4900 et seq.
Position of sureties, see Civil Code § 2832 et seq.
Securities law, indemnity, see Corporations Code § 25505.

§ 2772. Definitions

Indemnity is a contract by which one engages to save another from a legal consequence of the conduct of one of the parties, or of some other person. *(Enacted in 1872.)*

Cross References

Suretyship, see Civil Code § 2787 et seq.

§ 2773. Future wrongful act; invalidity

An agreement to indemnify a person against an act thereafter to be done, is void, if the act be known by such person at the time of doing it to be unlawful. *(Enacted in 1872. Amended by Code Am. 1873–74, c. 612, p. 259, § 253.)*

§ 2774. Past wrongful act; validity

An agreement to indemnify a person against an act already done, is valid, even though the act was known to be wrongful, unless it was a felony. *(Enacted in 1872.)*

§ 2775. Extension to acts of agents

An agreement to indemnify against the acts of a certain person, applies not only to his acts and their consequences, but also to those of his agents. *(Enacted in 1872.)*

§ 2776. Agreement to indemnify several persons; application

An agreement to indemnify several persons applies to each, unless a contrary intention appears. *(Enacted in 1872.)*

§ 2777. Joint or separate liability

One who indemnifies another against an act to be done by the latter, is liable jointly with the person indemnified, and separately, to every person injured by such act. *(Enacted in 1872.)*

§ 2778. Rules of interpretation

In the interpretation of a contract of indemnity, the following rules are to be applied, unless a contrary intention appears:

1. Upon an indemnity against liability, expressly, or in other equivalent terms, the person indemnified is entitled to recover upon becoming liable;

2. Upon an indemnity against claims, or demands, or damages, or costs, expressly, or in other equivalent terms, the person indemnified is not entitled to recover without payment thereof;

3. An indemnity against claims, or demands, or liability expressly, or in other equivalent terms, embraces the costs of defense against such claims, demands, or liability incurred in good faith, and in the exercise of a reasonable discretion;

4. The person indemnifying is bound, on request of the person indemnified, to defend actions or proceedings brought against the latter in respect to the matters embraced by the indemnity, but the person indemnified has the right to conduct such defenses, if he chooses to do so;

5. If, after request, the person indemnifying neglects to defend the person indemnified, a recovery against the latter suffered by him in good faith, is conclusive in his favor against the former;

6. If the person indemnifying, whether he is a principal or a surety in the agreement, has not reasonable notice of the action or proceeding against the person indemnified, or is not allowed to control its defense, judgment against the latter is only presumptive evidence against the former;

7. A stipulation that a judgment against the person indemnified shall be conclusive upon the person indemnifying, is inapplicable if he had a good defense upon the merits, which by want of ordinary care he failed to establish in the action. *(Enacted in 1872.)*

Cross References

Rule for interpretation of surety contracts, see Civil Code § 2837.

§ 2779. Reimbursement of person indemnifying; manner

Where one, at the request of another, engages to answer in damages, whether liquidated or unliquidated, for any violation of duty on the part of the latter, he is entitled to be reimbursed in the same manner as a surety, for whatever he may pay. *(Enacted in 1872.)*

Cross References

Duty of principal to reimburse surety, see Civil Code § 2847.
Position of sureties, see Civil Code § 2832 et seq.

§§ 2780, 2781. Repealed by Stats.1982, c. 517, p. 2327, §§ 71, 72

§ 2782. Construction contracts; void and unenforceable indemnification provisions; agreements between subcontractors, builders, or general contractors

(a) Except as provided in Sections 2782.1, 2782.2, 2782.5, and 2782.6, provisions, clauses, covenants, or agreements contained in, collateral to, or affecting any construction contract and that purport to indemnify the promisee against liability for damages for death or bodily injury to persons, injury to property, or any other loss, damage or expense arising from the sole negligence or willful misconduct of the promisee or the promisee's agents, servants, or independent contractors who are directly responsible to the promisee, or for defects in design furnished by those persons, are against public policy and are void and unenforceable; provided, however, that this section shall not affect the validity of any insurance contract, workers' compensation, or agreement issued by an admitted insurer as defined by the Insurance Code.

(b)(1) Except as provided in Sections 2782.1, 2782.2, and 2782.5, provisions, clauses, covenants, or agreements contained in, collateral to, or affecting any construction contract with a public agency entered into before January 1, 2013, that purport to impose on the contractor, or relieve the public agency from, liability for the active negligence of the public agency are void and unenforceable.

(2) Except as provided in Sections 2782.1, 2782.2, and 2782.5, provisions, clauses, covenants, or agreements con-

tained in, collateral to, or affecting any construction contract with a public agency entered into on or after January 1, 2013, that purport to impose on any contractor, subcontractor, or supplier of goods or services, or relieve the public agency from, liability for the active negligence of the public agency are void and unenforceable.

(c)(1) Except as provided in subdivision (d) and Sections 2782.1, 2782.2, and 2782.5, provisions, clauses, covenants, or agreements contained in, collateral to, or affecting any construction contract entered into on or after January 1, 2013, with the owner of privately owned real property to be improved and as to which the owner is not acting as a contractor or supplier of materials or equipment to the work, that purport to impose on any contractor, subcontractor, or supplier of goods or services, or relieve the owner from, liability are unenforceable to the extent of the active negligence of the owner, including that of its employees.

(2) For purposes of this subdivision, an owner of privately owned real property to be improved includes the owner of any interest therein, other than a mortgage or other interest that is held solely as security for performance of an obligation.

(3) This subdivision shall not apply to a homeowner performing a home improvement project on his or her own single family dwelling.

(d) For all construction contracts, and amendments thereto, entered into after January 1, 2009, for residential construction, as used in Title 7 (commencing with Section 895) of Part 2 of Division 2, all provisions, clauses, covenants, and agreements contained in, collateral to, or affecting any construction contract, and amendments thereto, that purport to insure or indemnify, including the cost to defend, the builder, as defined in Section 911, or the general contractor or contractor not affiliated with the builder, as described in subdivision (b) of Section 911, by a subcontractor against liability for claims of construction defects are unenforceable to the extent the claims arise out of, pertain to, or relate to the negligence of the builder or contractor or the builder's or contractor's other agents, other servants, or other independent contractors who are directly responsible to the builder, or for defects in design furnished by those persons, or to the extent the claims do not arise out of, pertain to, or relate to the scope of work in the written agreement between the parties. This section shall not be waived or modified by contractual agreement, act, or omission of the parties. Contractual provisions, clauses, covenants, or agreements not expressly prohibited herein are reserved to the agreement of the parties. Nothing in this subdivision shall prevent any party from exercising its rights under subdivision (a) of Section 910. This subdivision shall not affect the obligations of an insurance carrier under the holding of Presley Homes, Inc. v. American States Insurance Company (2001) 90 Cal.App.4th 571. Nor shall this subdivision affect the obligations of a builder or subcontractor pursuant to Title 7 (commencing with Section 895) of Part 2 of Division 2.

(e) Subdivision (d) does not prohibit a subcontractor and builder or general contractor from mutually agreeing to the timing or immediacy of the defense and provisions for reimbursement of defense fees and costs, so long as that agreement does not waive or modify the provisions of subdivision (d) subject, however, to paragraphs (1) and (2). A subcontractor shall owe no defense or indemnity obligation to a builder or general contractor for a construction defect claim unless and until the builder or general contractor provides a written tender of the claim, or portion thereof, to the subcontractor which includes all of the information provided to the builder or general contractor by the claimant or claimants, including, but not limited to, information provided pursuant to subdivision (a) of Section 910, relating to claims caused by that subcontractor's scope of work. This written tender shall have the same force and effect as a notice of commencement of a legal proceeding. If a builder or general contractor tenders a claim for construction defects, or a portion thereof, to a subcontractor in the manner specified by this provision, the subcontractor shall elect to perform either of the following, the performance of which shall be deemed to satisfy the subcontractor's defense obligation to the builder or general contractor:

(1) Defend the claim with counsel of its choice, and the subcontractor shall maintain control of the defense for any claim or portion of claim to which the defense obligation applies. If a subcontractor elects to defend under this paragraph, the subcontractor shall provide written notice of the election to the builder or general contractor within a reasonable time period following receipt of the written tender, and in no event later than 90 days following that receipt. Consistent with subdivision (d), the defense by the subcontractor shall be a complete defense of the builder or general contractor of all claims or portions thereof to the extent alleged to be caused by the subcontractor, including any vicarious liability claims against the builder or general contractor resulting from the subcontractor's scope of work, but not including claims resulting from the scope of work, actions, or omissions of the builder, general contractor, or any other party. Any vicarious liability imposed upon a builder or general contractor for claims caused by the subcontractor electing to defend under this paragraph shall be directly enforceable against the subcontractor by the builder, general contractor, or claimant.

(2) Pay, within 30 days of receipt of an invoice from the builder or general contractor, no more than a reasonable allocated share of the builder's or general contractor's defense fees and costs, on an ongoing basis during the pendency of the claim, subject to reallocation consistent with subdivision (d), and including any amounts reallocated upon final resolution of the claim, either by settlement or judgment. The builder or general contractor shall allocate a share to itself to the extent a claim or claims are alleged to be caused by its work, actions, or omissions, and a share to each subcontractor to the extent a claim or claims are alleged to be caused by the subcontractor's work, actions, or omissions, regardless of whether the builder or general contractor actually tenders the claim to any particular subcontractor, and regardless of whether that subcontractor is participating in the defense. Any amounts not collected from any particular subcontractor may not be collected from any other subcontractor.

(f) Notwithstanding any other provision of law, if a subcontractor fails to timely and adequately perform its obligations under paragraph (1) of subdivision (e), the builder or general contractor shall have the right to pursue a claim against the subcontractor for any resulting compensatory damages, consequential damages, and reasonable attorney's fees. If a subcontractor fails to timely perform its obligations under paragraph (2) of subdivision (e), the builder or general contractor shall have the right to pursue a claim against the subcontractor for any resulting compensatory and consequential damages, as well as for interest on defense and indemnity costs, from the date incurred, at the rate set forth in subdivision (g) of Section 3260, and for the builder's or general contractor's reasonable attorney's fees incurred to recover these amounts. The builder or general contractor shall bear the burden of proof to establish both the subcontractor's failure to perform under either paragraph (1) or (2) of subdivision (e) and any resulting damages. If, upon request by a subcontractor, a builder or general contractor does not reallocate defense fees to subcontractors within 30 days following final resolution of the claim as described above, the subcontractor shall have the right to pursue a claim against the builder or general contractor for any resulting compensatory and consequential damages, as well as for interest on the fees, from the date of final resolution of the claim, at the rate set forth in subdivision (g) of Section 3260, and the subcontractor's reasonable attorney's fees incurred in connection therewith. The subcontractor shall bear the burden of proof to establish both the failure to reallocate the fees and any resulting damages. Nothing in this section shall prohibit the parties from mutually agreeing to reasonable contractual provisions for damages if any party fails to elect for or perform its obligations as stated in this section.

(g) A builder, general contractor, or subcontractor shall have the right to seek equitable indemnity for any claim governed by this section.

(h) Nothing in this section limits, restricts, or prohibits the right of a builder, general contractor, or subcontractor to seek equitable indemnity against any supplier, design professional, or product manufacturer.

(i) As used in this section, "construction defect" means a violation of the standards set forth in Sections 896 and 897. *(Added by Stats.1967, c. 1327, p. 3158, § 1. Amended by Stats.1980, c. 211, p. 442, § 1; Stats.1982, c. 386, p. 1717, § 1; Stats.1985, c. 567, § 1; Stats.1990, c. 814 (S.B.1922), § 1; Stats.2005, c. 394 (A.B.758), § 1; Stats.2007, c. 32 (S.B.138), § 1; Stats.2008, c. 467 (A.B.2738), § 1; Stats.2011, c. 707 (S.B.474), § 2.)*

Cross References

Construction manager at-risk contracts, county construction projects, contracts between county and construction manager at-risk entity subject to provisions of this section, see Public Contract Code § 20146.

§ 2782.05. Construction contracts; void and unenforceable indemnification provisions; agreements between general contractors, construction managers, or subcontractors

(a) Except as provided in subdivision (b), provisions, clauses, covenants, and agreements contained in, collateral to, or affecting any construction contract and amendments thereto entered into on or after January 1, 2013, that purport to insure or indemnify, including the cost to defend, a general contractor, construction manager, or other subcontractor, by a subcontractor against liability for claims of death or bodily injury to persons, injury to property, or any other loss, damage, or expense are void and unenforceable to the extent the claims arise out of, pertain to, or relate to the active negligence or willful misconduct of that general contractor, construction manager, or other subcontractor, or their other agents, other servants, or other independent contractors who are responsible to the general contractor, construction manager, or other subcontractor, or for defects in design furnished by those persons, or to the extent the claims do not arise out of the scope of work of the subcontractor pursuant to the construction contract. This section shall not be waived or modified by contractual agreement, act, or omission of the parties. Contractual provisions, clauses, covenants, or agreements not expressly prohibited herein are reserved to the agreement of the parties. This section shall not affect the obligations of an insurance carrier under the holding of Presley Homes, Inc. v. American States Insurance Company (2001) 90 Cal.App.4th 571, nor the rights of an insurance carrier under the holding of Buss v. Superior Court (1997) 16 Cal.4th 35.

(b) This section does not apply to:

(1) Contracts for residential construction that are subject to any part of Title 7 (commencing with Section 895) of Part 2 of Division 2.

(2) Direct contracts with a public agency that are governed by subdivision (b) of Section 2782.

(3) Direct contracts with the owner of privately owned real property to be improved that are governed by subdivision (c) of Section 2782.

(4) Any wrap-up insurance policy or program.

(5) A cause of action for breach of contract or warranty that exists independently of an indemnity obligation.

(6) A provision in a construction contract that requires the promisor to purchase or maintain insurance covering the acts or omissions of the promisor, including additional insurance endorsements covering the acts or omissions of the promisor during ongoing and completed operations.

(7) Indemnity provisions contained in loan and financing documents, other than construction contracts to which the contractor and a contracting project owner's lender are parties.

(8) General agreements of indemnity required by sureties as a condition of execution of bonds for construction contracts.

(9) The benefits and protections provided by the workers' compensation laws.

(10) The benefits or protections provided by the governmental immunity laws.

(11) Provisions that require the purchase of any of the following:

(A) Owners and contractors protective liability insurance.

(B) Railroad protective liability insurance.

(C) Contractors all-risk insurance.

(D) Builders all-risk or named perils property insurance.

(12) Contracts with design professionals.

(13) Any agreement between a promisor and an admitted surety insurer regarding the promisor's obligations as a principal or indemnitor on a bond.

(c) Notwithstanding any choice-of-law rules that would apply the laws of another jurisdiction, the law of California shall apply to every contract to which this section applies.

(d) Any waiver of the provisions of this section is contrary to public policy and is void and unenforceable.

(e) Subdivision (a) does not prohibit a subcontractor and a general contractor or construction manager from mutually agreeing to the timing or immediacy of the defense and provisions for reimbursement of defense fees and costs, so long as that agreement does not waive or modify the provisions of subdivision (a) subject, however, to paragraphs (1) and (2). A subcontractor shall owe no defense or indemnity obligation to a general contractor or construction manager for a claim unless and until the general contractor or construction manager provides a written tender of the claim, or portion thereof, to the subcontractor that includes the information provided by the claimant or claimants relating to claims caused by that subcontractor's scope of work. In addition, the general contractor or construction manager shall provide a written statement regarding how the reasonable allocated share of fees and costs was determined. The written tender shall have the same force and effect as a notice of commencement of a legal proceeding. If a general contractor or construction manager tenders a claim, or portion thereof, to a subcontractor in the manner specified by this subdivision, the subcontractor shall elect to perform either of the following, the performance of which shall be deemed to satisfy the subcontractor's defense obligation to the general contractor or construction manager:

(1) Defend the claim with counsel of its choice, and the subcontractor shall maintain control of the defense for any claim or portion of claim to which the defense obligation applies. If a subcontractor elects to defend under this paragraph, the subcontractor shall provide written notice of the election to the general contractor or construction manager within a reasonable time period following receipt of the written tender, and in no event later than 30 days following that receipt. Consistent with subdivision (a), the defense by the subcontractor shall be a complete defense of the general contractor or construction manager of all claims or portions thereof to the extent alleged to be caused by the subcontractor, including any vicarious liability claims against the general contractor or construction manager resulting from the subcontractor's scope of work, but not including claims resulting from the scope of work, actions, or omissions of the general contractor or construction manager, or any other party. Any vicarious liability imposed upon a general contractor or construction manager for claims caused by the subcontractor electing to defend under this paragraph shall be directly enforceable against the subcontractor by the general contractor, construction manager, or claimant. All information, documentation, or evidence, if any, relating to a subcontractor's assertion that another party is responsible for the claim shall be provided by that subcontractor to the general contractor or construction manager that tendered the claim.

(2) Pay, within 30 days of receipt of an invoice from the general contractor or construction manager, no more than a reasonable allocated share of the general contractor's or construction manager's defense fees and costs, on an ongoing basis during the pendency of the claim, subject to reallocation consistent with subdivision (a), and including any amounts reallocated upon final resolution of the claim, either by settlement or judgment. The general contractor or construction manager shall allocate a share to itself to the extent a claim or claims are alleged to be caused by its work, actions, or omissions, and a share to each subcontractor to the extent a claim or claims are alleged to be caused by the subcontractor's work, actions, or omissions, regardless of whether the general contractor or construction manager actually tenders the claim to any particular subcontractor, and regardless of whether that subcontractor is participating in the defense. Any amounts not collected from any particular subcontractor may not be collected from any other subcontractor.

(f) Notwithstanding any other provision of law, if a subcontractor fails to timely and adequately perform its obligations under paragraph (1) of subdivision (e), the general contractor or construction manager shall have the right to pursue a claim against the subcontractor for any resulting compensatory damages, consequential damages, and reasonable attorney's fees. If a subcontractor fails to timely perform its obligations under paragraph (2) of subdivision (e), the general contractor or construction manager shall have the right to pursue a claim against the subcontractor for any resulting compensatory damages, interest on defense and indemnity costs, from the date incurred, at the rate set forth in subdivision (g) of Section 3260, consequential damages, and reasonable attorney's fees incurred to recover these amounts. The general contractor or construction manager shall bear the burden of proof to establish both the subcontractor's failure to perform under either paragraph (1) or (2) of subdivision (e) and any resulting damages. If, upon request by a subcontractor, a general contractor or construction manager does not reallocate defense fees to subcontractors within 30 days following final resolution of the claim, the subcontractor shall have the right to pursue a claim against the general contractor or construction manager for any resulting compensatory damages with interest, from the date of final resolution of the claim, at the rate set forth in subdivision (g) of Section 3260. The subcontractor shall bear the burden of proof to establish both the failure to reallocate the fees and any resulting damages. Nothing in this section shall prohibit the parties from mutually agreeing to reasonable contractual provisions for damages if any party fails to elect for or perform its obligations as stated in this section.

(g) For purposes of this section, "construction manager" means a person or entity, other than a public agency or owner of privately owned real property to be improved, who is contracted by a public agency or the owner of privately owned real property to be improved to direct, schedule, or coordinate the work of contractors for a work of improvement, but does not itself perform the work.

(h) For purposes of this section, "general contractor," in relation to a given subcontractor, means a person who has entered into a construction contract and who has entered into a subcontract with that subcontractor under which the subcontractor agrees to perform a portion of that scope of work. Where a subcontractor has itself subcontracted a portion of its work, that subcontractor, along with its general

§ 2782.05

contractor, shall be considered a general contractor as to its subcontractors.

(i) For purposes of this section, "subcontractor" means a person who has entered into a construction contract either with a contractor to perform a portion of that contractor's work under a construction contract or with any person to perform a construction contract subject to the direction or control of a general contractor or construction manager.

(j) A general contractor, construction manager, or subcontractor shall have the right to seek equitable indemnity for any claim governed by this section.

(k) Nothing in this section limits, restricts, or prohibits the right of a general contractor, construction manager, or subcontractor to seek equitable indemnity against any supplier, design professional, product manufacturer, or other independent contractor or subcontractor.

(*l*) This section shall not affect the validity of any existing insurance contract or agreement, including, but not limited to, a contract or agreement for workers' compensation or an agreement issued on or before January 1, 2012, by an admitted insurer, as defined in the Insurance Code.

(m) Nothing in this section shall be construed to affect the obligation, if any, of either a contractor or construction manager to indemnify, including defending or paying the costs to defend, a public agency against any claim arising from the alleged active negligence of the public agency under subdivision (b) of Section 2782 or to indemnify, including defending or paying the costs to defend, an owner of privately owned real property to be improved against any claim arising from the alleged active negligence of the owner under subdivision (c) of Section 2782.

(n) Nothing in this section shall be construed to affect the obligation, if any, of either a contractor or construction manager to provide or maintain insurance covering the acts or omissions of the promisor, including additional insurance endorsements covering the acts or omissions of the promisor during ongoing and completed operations pursuant to a construction contract with a public agency under subdivision (b) of Section 2782 or an owner of privately owned real property to be improved under subdivision (c) of Section 2782. *(Added by Stats.2011, c. 707 (S.B.474), § 3.)*

Cross References

Construction manager at-risk contracts, county construction projects, contracts between construction manager at-risk entity and contractor or subcontractors subject to provisions of this section, see Public Contract Code § 20146.

§ 2782.1. Agreement to enter adjacent property; indemnification

Nothing contained in Section 2782 shall prevent a contractor responsible for the performance of a construction contract, as defined in Section 2783, from indemnifying fully a person, firm, corporation, state or other agency for whose account the construction contract is not being performed but who, as an accommodation, enters into an agreement with the contractor permitting such contractor to enter upon or adjacent to its property for the purpose of performing such construction contract for others. *(Added by Stats.1968, c. 466, p. 1097, § 1.)*

§ 2782.2. Agreement to indemnify professional engineers or agents or employees of engineers; liability for negligence in providing inspection services; requirements

(a) Nothing contained in subdivision (a) of Section 2782 prevents an agreement to indemnify a professional engineer against liability for the negligence of the engineer, or the engineer's agents or employees, in providing inspection services to plants or other facilities if all the following criteria are satisfied:

(1) The promisor is the owner of the plants or facilities inspected.

(2) The promisor is audited annually by an independent certified public accountant, public accountant, or accounting licentiate of another state authorized by the laws of that state to perform the audit.

(3) The net worth of the promisor exceeds ten million dollars ($10,000,000), as determined by the promisor's most recent annual independent audit. The requirement of this paragraph shall be satisfied at the time the contract for indemnification is entered, and a subsequent reduction of the promisor's net worth shall not void the obligation to indemnify.

(4) The promisor is self-insured with respect to liability arising from ownership of the plant or facility.

(5) The indemnification shall not be applicable to the first two hundred fifty thousand dollars ($250,000) of liability.

(b) Subdivision (a) does not authorize contracts for indemnification of liability arising from willful misconduct. *(Added by Stats.1985, c. 567, § 2.)*

§ 2782.5. Agreements as to allocation or limitation of liability for design defects or of promisee to promisor

Nothing contained in Section 2782 shall prevent a party to a construction contract and the owner or other party for whose account the construction contract is being performed from negotiating and expressly agreeing with respect to the allocation, release, liquidation, exclusion, or limitation as between the parties of any liability (a) for design defects, or (b) of the promisee to the promisor arising out of or relating to the construction contract. *(Added by Stats.1967, c. 1327, p. 3159, § 2. Amended by Stats.1980, c. 211, p. 442, § 2.)*

§ 2782.6. Professional engineers or geologists; agreements indemnifying work with hazardous materials; criteria; gross negligence or willful misconduct excepted

Section operative until Jan. 1, 2024. See, also, § 2782.6 operative Jan. 1, 2024.

(a) Nothing in subdivision (a) of Section 2782 prevents an agreement to indemnify a professional engineer or geologist or the agents, servants, independent contractors, subsidiaries, or employees of that engineer or geologist from liability as described in Section 2782 in providing hazardous materials identification, evaluation, preliminary assessment, design, remediation services, or other services of the types described in Sections 25322 and 25323 of the Health and Safety Code or the federal National Oil and Hazardous Substances Pollution Contingency Plan (40 C.F.R. Sec. 300.1 et seq.), if all of the following criteria are satisfied:

(1) The services in whole or in part address subterranean contamination or other concealed conditions caused by the hazardous materials.

(2) The promisor is responsible, or potentially responsible, for all or part of the contamination.

(b) The indemnification described in this section is valid only for damages arising from, or related to, subterranean contamination or concealed conditions, and is not applicable to the first two hundred fifty thousand dollars ($250,000) of liability or a greater amount as is agreed to by the parties.

(c) This section does not authorize contracts for indemnification, by promisors specified in paragraph (2) of subdivision (a), of any liability of a promisee arising from the gross negligence or willful misconduct of the promisee.

(d) "Hazardous materials," as used in this section, means any hazardous or toxic substance, material, or waste that is or becomes subject to regulation by any agency of the state, any municipality or political subdivision of the state, or the United States. "Hazardous materials" includes, but is not limited to, any material or substance that is any of the following:

(1) A hazardous substance, as defined in Section 25316 of the Health and Safety Code.

(2) Hazardous material, as defined in subdivision (n) of Section 25501 of the Health and Safety Code.

(3) A regulated substance, as defined in subdivision (i) of Section 25532 of the Health and Safety Code.

(4) Hazardous waste, as defined in Section 25117 of the Health and Safety Code.

(5) Extremely hazardous waste, as defined in Section 25115 of the Health and Safety Code.

(6) Petroleum.

(7) Asbestos.

(8) Designated as a hazardous substance for purposes of Section 311 of the Federal Water Pollution Control Act, as amended (33 U.S.C. Sec. 1321).

(9) Hazardous waste, as defined by subsection (5) of Section 1004 of the federal Resource Conservation and Recovery Act of 1976, as amended (42 U.S.C. Sec. 6903).

(10) A hazardous substance, as defined by subsection (14) of Section 101 of the federal Comprehensive Environmental Response, Compensation, and Liability Act of 1980, as amended (42 U.S.C. Sec. 9601).

(11) A regulated substance, as defined by subsection (7) of Section 9001 of the federal Solid Waste Disposal Act, as amended (42 U.S.C. Sec. 6991).

(e) Nothing in this section shall be construed to alter, modify, or otherwise affect the liability of the promisor or promisee, under an indemnity agreement meeting the criteria of this section, to third parties for damages for death or bodily injury to persons, injury to property, or any other loss, damage, or expense.

(f) This section does not apply to public entities, as defined by Section 811.2 of the Government Code. (Added by Stats.1990, c. 814 (S.B.1922), § 2. Amended by Stats.2018, c. 59 (S.B.1502), § 1, eff. Jan. 1, 2019; Stats.2021, c. 115 (A.B.148), § 1, eff. July 22, 2021.)

§ 2782.6. Professional engineers or geologists; agreements indemnifying work with hazardous materials; criteria; gross negligence or willful misconduct excepted

Section operative Jan. 1, 2024. See, also, § 2782.6 operative until Jan. 1, 2024.

(a) Nothing in subdivision (a) of Section 2782 prevents an agreement to indemnify a professional engineer or geologist or the agents, servants, independent contractors, subsidiaries, or employees of that engineer or geologist from liability as described in Section 2782 in providing hazardous materials identification, evaluation, preliminary assessment, design, remediation services, or other services of the types described in Sections 78125 and 78135 of the Health and Safety Code or the federal National Oil and Hazardous Substances Pollution Contingency Plan (40 C.F.R. Sec. 300.1 et seq.), if all of the following criteria are satisfied:

(1) The services in whole or in part address subterranean contamination or other concealed conditions caused by the hazardous materials.

(2) The promisor is responsible, or potentially responsible, for all or part of the contamination.

(b) The indemnification described in this section is valid only for damages arising from, or related to, subterranean contamination or concealed conditions, and is not applicable to the first two hundred fifty thousand dollars ($250,000) of liability or a greater amount as is agreed to by the parties.

(c) This section does not authorize contracts for indemnification, by promisors specified in paragraph (2) of subdivision (a), of any liability of a promisee arising from the gross negligence or willful misconduct of the promisee.

(d) "Hazardous materials," as used in this section, means any hazardous or toxic substance, material, or waste that is or becomes subject to regulation by any agency of the state, any municipality or political subdivision of the state, or the United States. "Hazardous materials" includes, but is not limited to, any material or substance that is any of the following:

(1) A hazardous substance, as defined in subdivision (a) of Section 78075 of the Health and Safety Code.

(2) Hazardous material, as defined in subdivision (n) of Section 25501 of the Health and Safety Code.

(3) A regulated substance, as defined in subdivision (i) of Section 25532 of the Health and Safety Code.

(4) Hazardous waste, as defined in Section 25117 of the Health and Safety Code.

(5) Extremely hazardous waste, as defined in Section 25115 of the Health and Safety Code.

(6) Petroleum.

(7) Asbestos.

(8) Designated as a hazardous substance for purposes of Section 311 of the Federal Water Pollution Control Act, as amended (33 U.S.C. Sec. 1321).

(9) Hazardous waste, as defined by subsection (5) of Section 1004 of the federal Resource Conservation and Recovery Act of 1976, as amended (42 U.S.C. Sec. 6903).

(10) A hazardous substance, as defined by subsection (14) of Section 101 of the federal Comprehensive Environmental

§ 2782.6 OBLIGATIONS

Response, Compensation, and Liability Act of 1980, as amended (42 U.S.C. Sec. 9601).

(11) A regulated substance, as defined by subsection (7) of Section 9001 of the federal Solid Waste Disposal Act, as amended (42 U.S.C. Sec. 6991).

(e) Nothing in this section shall be construed to alter, modify, or otherwise affect the liability of the promisor or promisee, under an indemnity agreement meeting the criteria of this section, to third parties for damages for death or bodily injury to persons, injury to property, or any other loss, damage, or expense.

(f) This section does not apply to public entities, as defined by Section 811.2 of the Government Code. *(Added by Stats.1990, c. 814 (S.B.1922), § 2. Amended by Stats.2018, c. 59 (S.B.1502), § 1, eff. Jan. 1, 2019; Stats.2021, c. 115 (A.B.148), § 1, eff. July 22, 2021; Stats.2022, c. 258 (A.B. 2327), § 6, eff. Jan. 1, 2023, operative Jan. 1, 2024.)*

§ 2782.8. Contracts for design professional services; indemnification provisions

(a) For all contracts, and amendments thereto, entered into on or after January 1, 2018, for design professional services, all provisions, clauses, covenants, and agreements contained in, collateral to, or affecting any such contract, and amendments thereto, that purport to indemnify, including the duty and the cost to defend, the indemnitee by a design professional against liability for claims against the indemnitee, are unenforceable, except to the extent that the claims against the indemnitee arise out of, pertain to, or relate to the negligence, recklessness, or willful misconduct of the design professional. In no event shall the cost to defend charged to the design professional exceed the design professional's proportionate percentage of fault. However, notwithstanding the previous sentence, in the event one or more defendants is unable to pay its share of defense costs due to bankruptcy or dissolution of the business, the design professional shall meet and confer with other parties regarding unpaid defense costs. The duty to indemnify, including the duty and the cost to defend, is limited as provided in this section. This section shall not be waived or modified by contractual agreement, act, or omission of the parties. Contractual provisions, clauses, covenants, or agreements not expressly prohibited herein are reserved to the agreement of the parties.

(b) All contracts and all solicitation documents, including requests for proposal, invitations for bid, and other solicitation documents for design professional services are deemed to incorporate by reference the provisions of this section.

(c) For purposes of this section, "design professional" includes all of the following:

(1) An individual licensed as an architect pursuant to Chapter 3 (commencing with Section 5500) of Division 3 of the Business and Professions Code, and a business entity offering architectural services in accordance with that chapter.

(2) An individual licensed as a landscape architect pursuant to Chapter 3.5 (commencing with Section 5615) of Division 3 of the Business and Professions Code, and a business entity offering landscape architectural services in accordance with that chapter.

(3) An individual registered as a professional engineer pursuant to Chapter 7 (commencing with Section 6700) of Division 3 of the Business and Professions Code, and a business entity offering professional engineering services in accordance with that chapter.

(4) An individual licensed as a professional land surveyor pursuant to Chapter 15 (commencing with Section 8700) of Division 3 of the Business and Professions Code, and a business entity offering professional land surveying services in accordance with that chapter.

(d) This section shall apply only to a professional service contract, or any amendment thereto, entered into on or after January 1, 2018.

(e) The provisions of this section pertaining to the duty and cost to defend shall not apply to either of the following:

(1) Any contract for design professional services, or amendments thereto, where a project-specific general liability policy insures all project participants for general liability exposures on a primary basis and also covers all design professionals for their legal liability arising out of their professional services on a primary basis.

(2) A design professional who is a party to a written design-build joint venture agreement.

(f) Nothing in this section shall abrogate the provisions of Section 1104 of the Public Contract Code.

(g) Indemnitee, for purposes of this section, does not include any agency of the state. *(Added by Stats.2006, c. 455 (A.B.573), § 1. Amended by Stats.2010, c. 510 (S.B.972), § 1; Stats.2017, c. 8 (S.B.496), § 1, eff. Jan. 1, 2018.)*

§ 2782.9. Residential construction projects; unenforceable indemnity agreements

(a) All contracts, provisions, clauses, amendments, or agreements contained therein entered into after January 1, 2009, for a residential construction project on which a wrap-up insurance policy, as defined in subdivision (b) of Section 11751.82 of the Insurance Code, or other consolidated insurance program, is applicable, that require an enrolled and participating subcontractor or other participant to indemnify, hold harmless, or defend another for any claim or action covered by that program, arising out of that project are unenforceable.

(b) To the extent any contractual provision is deemed unenforceable pursuant to this section, any party may pursue an equitable indemnity claim against another party for a claim or action unless there is coverage for the claim or action under the wrap-up policy or policies. Nothing in this section shall prohibit a builder or general contractor from requiring a reasonably allocated contribution from a subcontractor or other participant to the self-insured retention or deductible required under the wrap-up policy or other consolidated insurance program, if the maximum amount and method of collection of the participant's contribution is disclosed in the contract with the participant and the contribution is reasonably limited so that each participant may have some financial obligation in the event of a claim alleged to be caused by that participant's scope of work. The contribution shall only be collected when and as any such self-insured retention or deductible is incurred by the builder or general contractor and in an amount that bears a reasonable and proportionate relationship to the alleged liability arising from the claim or claims alleged to be caused by the participant's scope of work, when viewed in the context of the entirety of the alleged claim or claims. Any contribution shall only be collected from a participant after written notice to the participant of the amount of and basis for the contribution. In no event shall the total amount of contributions collected from participants exceed the amount of any self-insured retention or deductible due and payable by the builder or general contractor for the claim or claims. However, this requirement does not prohibit any legally permissible recovery of costs and legal fees to collect a participant's contribution if the contribution satisfies the requirements of this subdivision and is not paid by the participant when due.

(c) This section shall not be waived or modified by contractual agreement, act, or omission of the parties. *(Added by Stats.2008, c. 467 (A.B.2738), § 2.)*

§ 2782.95. Residential improvements; wrap-up insurance policies or other consolidated insurance programs; disclosures

For any wrap-up insurance policy or other consolidated insurance program that insures a private residential (as that term is used in Title 7 (commencing with Section 895) of Part 2 of Division 2) work of improvement that first commences construction after January 1, 2009, the following shall apply:

(a) The owner, builder, or general contractor obtaining the wrap-up insurance policy or other consolidated insurance program shall disclose the total amount or method of calculation of any credit or compensation for premium required from a subcontractor or other participant for that wrap-up policy in the contract documents.

(b) The contract documents shall disclose, if and to the extent known:

(1) The policy limits.

(2) The scope of policy coverage.

(3) The policy term.

(4) The basis upon which the deductible or occurrence is triggered by the insurance carrier.

(5) If the policy covers more than one work of improvement, the number of units, if any, indicated on the application for the insurance policy.

(6) A good faith estimate of the amount of available limits remaining under the policy as of a date indicated in the disclosure obtained from the insurer.

(7) Disclosures made pursuant to paragraphs (5) and (6) are recognized to be based upon information at a given moment in time and may not accurately reflect the actual number of units covered by the policy nor the amount of insurance available, if any, when a later claim is made. These disclosures are presumptively made in good faith if the disclosure pursuant to paragraph (5) is the same as that contained in the application to the wrap-up insurer and the disclosure pursuant to paragraph (6) was obtained from the wrap-up insurer or broker. The presumptions stated above shall be overcome only by a showing that the insurer, broker, builder, or general contractor intentionally misrepresented the facts identified in paragraphs (5) or (6).

(c) Upon the written request of any participant, a copy of the insurance policy shall be provided, if available, that shows the coverage terms and items in paragraphs (1) to (4), inclusive, of subdivision (b) above. If the policy is not available at the time of the request, a copy of the insurance binder or declaration of coverage may be provided in lieu of the actual policy. Paragraphs (1) to (4), inclusive, of subdivision (b) may be satisfied by providing the participant with a copy of the binder or declaration. Any party receiving a copy of the policy, binder, or declaration shall not disclose it to third parties other than the participant's insurance broker or attorney unless required to do so by law. The participant's insurance broker or attorney may not disclose the policy, binder, or declaration to any third party unless required to do so by law.

(d) If the owner, builder, or general contractor obtaining the wrap-up insurance policy or other consolidated insurance program does not disclose the total amount or method of calculation of the premium credit or compensation to be charged to the participant prior to the time the participant submits its bid, the participant shall not be legally bound by the bid unless that participant has the right to increase the bid up to the amount equal to the difference between the amount the participant included, if any, for insurance in the original bid and the amount of the actual bid credit required by the owner, builder, or general contractor obtaining the wrap-up insurance policy or other consolidated insurance program. This subdivision shall not apply if the owner, builder, or general contractor obtaining the wrap-up insurance policy or other consolidated insurance program did not require the subcontractor to offset the original bid amount with a deduction for the wrap-up insurance policy or program. *(Added by Stats.2008, c. 467 (A.B.2738), § 3.)*

§ 2782.96. Public works; wrap-up insurance policy or other consolidated insurance programs; disclosures

If an owner, builder, or general contractor obtains a wrap-up insurance policy or other consolidated insurance program for a public work as defined in Section 1720 of the Labor Code or any other project other than residential construction, as that term is used in Title 7 (commencing with Section 895) of Part 2 of Division 2, that is put out for bid after January 1, 2009, the following shall apply:

(a) The total amount or method of calculation of any credit or compensation for premium required from a subcontractor or other participant for that policy shall be clearly delineated in the bid documents.

(b) The named insured, to the extent known, shall disclose to the subcontractor or other participant in the contract documents the policy limits, known exclusions, and the length of time the policy is intended to remain in effect. In addition, upon written request, once available, the named insured shall provide copies of insurance policies to all those who are covered by the policy. Until such time as the policies are available, the named insured may also satisfy the disclosure requirements of this subdivision by providing the subcontractor or other participant with a copy of the insurance binder or declaration of coverage. Any party receiving a copy of the policy, binder, or declaration shall not disclose it

§ 2782.96

to third parties other than the participant's insurance broker or attorney unless required to do so by law. The participant's insurance broker or attorney may not disclose the policy, binder, or declaration to any third party unless required to do so by law.

(c) The disclosure requirements in subdivisions (a) and (b) do not apply to an insurance policy purchased by an owner, builder, or general contractor that provides additional coverage beyond what was contained in the original wrap-up policy or other consolidated insurance program if no credit or compensation for premium is required of the subcontractor for the additional insurance policy. (Added by Stats.2008, c. 467 (A.B.2738), § 4. Amended by Stats.2009, c. 140 (A.B. 1164), § 37.)

§ 2783. "Construction contract" defined

As used in Sections 2782 and 2782.5, "construction contract" is defined as any agreement or understanding, written or oral, respecting the construction, surveying, design, specifications, alteration, repair, improvement, renovation, maintenance, removal of or demolition of any building, highway, road, parking facility, bridge, water line, sewer line, oil line, gas line, electric utility transmission or distribution line, railroad, airport, pier or dock, excavation or other structure, appurtenance, development or other improvement to real or personal property, or an agreement to perform any portion thereof or any act collateral thereto, or to perform any service reasonably related thereto, including, but not limited to, the erection of all structures or performance of work in connection therewith, electrical power line clearing, tree trimming, vegetation maintenance, the rental of all equipment, all incidental transportation, moving, lifting, crane and rigging service and other goods and services furnished in connection therewith. (Added by Stats.1967, c. 1327, p. 3159, § 3. Amended by Stats.2011, c. 707 (S.B.474), § 4.)

§ 2784. "Design defect" defined

As used in Sections 2782 and 2782.5, a "design defect" is defined as a condition arising out of its design which renders a structure, item of equipment or machinery or any other similar object, movable or immovable, when constructed substantially in accordance with its design, inherently unfit, either wholly or in part, for its intended use or which impairs or renders the use of such structure, equipment, machinery or property dangerous. (Added by Stats.1967, c. 1327, p. 3159, § 4.)

§ 2784.5. Hauling, trucking, or cartage contracts; provisions indemnifying against liability for negligence void; exception

Any provision, promise, agreement, clause, or covenant contained in, collateral to, or affecting any hauling, trucking, or cartage contract or agreement is against public policy, void and unenforceable if it purports to indemnify the promisee against liability for any of the following damages which are caused by the sole negligence or willful misconduct of the promisee, agents, servants, or the independent contractors directly responsible to the promisee, except when such agents, servants, or independent contractors are under the direct supervision and control of the promisor:

(a) Damages arising out of bodily injury or death to persons.

(b) Damage to property.

(c) Any other damage or expense arising under either (a) or (b).

This section shall not affect the validity of any insurance contract, workmen's compensation insurance contract, or agreement issued by an admitted insurer as defined by Sections 23 and 24 of the Insurance Code or insurance effected by surplus line brokers under Sections 1760 through 1780 of the Insurance Code. (Added by Stats.1967, c. 1314, p. 3138, § 1.)

Title 13

SURETYSHIP

Article	Section
1. Definition of Suretyship	2787
2. Creation of Suretyship	2792
3. Interpretation of Suretyship	2799
4. Liability of Sureties	2806
5. Continuing Guaranty	2814
6. Exoneration of Sureties	2819
7. Position of Sureties	2831
8. Letter of Credit [Repealed]	

Cross References

Contractual rights and obligations, subordination to intent of parties, waiver, see Civil Code § 3268.
Surety insurance, see Insurance Code § 105.
Waiver of suretyship rights or defenses available to guarantors, see Civil Code § 2856.

ARTICLE 1. DEFINITION OF SURETYSHIP

Section
2787. Sureties and guarantors; distinction abolished; definitions; letters of credit.
2788. Surety without knowledge or consent of principal.

§ 2787. Sureties and guarantors; distinction abolished; definitions; letters of credit

The distinction between sureties and guarantors is hereby abolished. The terms and their derivatives, wherever used in this code or in any other statute or law of this state now in force or hereafter enacted, shall have the same meaning as defined in this section. A surety or guarantor is one who promises to answer for the debt, default, or miscarriage of another, or hypothecates property as security therefor. Guaranties of collection and continuing guaranties are forms of suretyship obligations, and except in so far as necessary in order to give effect to provisions specially relating thereto, shall be subject to all provisions of law relating to suretyships in general. A letter of credit is not a form of suretyship obligation. For purposes of this section, the term "letter of credit" means a "letter of credit" as defined in paragraph (10) of subdivision (a) of Section 5102 of the Commercial Code whether or not the engagement is governed by Division 5 (commencing with Section 5101) of the Commercial Code. (Enacted in 1872. Amended by Stats.1939, c. 453, p. 1796,

§ 10; Stats.1994, c. 611 (S.B.1612), § 1, eff. Sept. 16, 1994; Stats.1996, c. 176 (S.B.1599), § 1.)

Cross References

Continuing guaranty, see Civil Code §§ 2814, 2815.
Guaranty of collection, see Civil Code § 2800 et seq.
Indemnity, see Civil Code § 2772 et seq.
Surety insurance, see Insurance Code § 105.

§ 2788. Surety without knowledge or consent of principal

A person may become surety even without the knowledge or consent of the principal. *(Enacted in 1872. Amended by Stats.1939, c. 453, p. 1797, § 11.)*

Cross References

Apparent principal as surety, see Civil Code § 2832.

ARTICLE 2. CREATION OF SURETYSHIP

Section
2792. Consideration.
2793. Writing; signature.
2794. Original obligations not requiring a writing.
2795. Acceptance of offer; notice.

§ 2792. Consideration

Where a suretyship obligation is entered into at the same time with the original obligation, or with the acceptance of the latter by the creditor, and forms with that obligation a part of the consideration to him, no other consideration need exist. In all other cases there must be a consideration distinct from that of the original obligation. *(Enacted in 1872. Amended by Stats.1939, c. 453, p. 1797, § 12.)*

Cross References

Consideration, generally, see Civil Code § 1605 et seq.
Necessity of writing, see Commercial Code § 2201.

§ 2793. Writing; signature

Except as prescribed by the next section, a suretyship obligation must be in writing, and signed by the surety; but the writing need not express a consideration. *(Enacted in 1872. Amended by Stats.1939, c. 453, p. 1797, § 13.)*

Cross References

Statute of frauds, generally, see Civil Code § 1624.

§ 2794. Original obligations not requiring a writing

A promise to answer for the obligation of another, in any of the following cases, is deemed an original obligation of the promisor, and need not be in writing:

(1) Where the promise is made by one who has received property of another upon an undertaking to apply it pursuant to such promise; or by one who has received a discharge from an obligation in whole or in part, in consideration of such promise;

(2) Where the creditor parts with value, or enters into an obligation, in consideration of the obligation in respect to which the promise is made, in terms or under circumstances such as to render the party making the promise the principal debtor and the person in whose behalf it is made, his surety;

(3) Where the promise, being for an antecedent obligation of another, is made upon the consideration that the party receiving it cancels the antecedent obligation, accepting the new promise as a substitute therefor; or upon the consideration that the party receiving it releases the property of another from a levy, or his person from imprisonment under an execution on a judgment obtained upon the antecedent obligation;

(4) Where the promise is upon a consideration beneficial to the promisor, whether moving from either party to the antecedent obligation, or from another person;

(5) Where a factor undertakes, for a commission, to sell merchandise and act as surety in connection with the sale;

(6) Where the holder of an instrument for the payment of money, upon which a third person is or may become liable to him, transfers it in payment of a precedent debt of his own, or for a new consideration, and in connection with such transfer enters into a promise respecting such instrument. *(Enacted in 1872. Amended by Stats.1939, c. 453, p. 1797, § 14.)*

Cross References

Positions of surety for consideration and gratuitous surety, see Civil Code § 2837.
Real estate transfers, required writing, see Code of Civil Procedure §§ 1971, 1972.
Statute of frauds, see Civil Code § 1624.

§ 2795. Acceptance of offer; notice

Unless notice of acceptance is expressly required, an offer to become a surety may be accepted by acting upon it, or by acceptance upon other consideration. An absolute suretyship obligation is binding upon the surety without notice of acceptance. *(Enacted in 1872. Amended by Stats.1939, c. 453, p. 1798, § 15.)*

Cross References

Acceptance by creditor of ostensible principal as a surety, see Civil Code § 2832.
Unconditional suretyship, see Civil Code § 2806.

ARTICLE 3. INTERPRETATION OF SURETYSHIP

Section
2799. Incomplete contract; implied terms.
2800. Guaranty that obligation is good or collectible.
2801. Guaranty that obligation is good or collectible; recovery.
2802. Guaranty that obligation is good or collectible; surety's liability.

§ 2799. Incomplete contract; implied terms

In an assumption of liability as surety in connection with a contract, the terms of which are not then settled, it is implied that its terms shall be such as will not expose the surety to greater risks than he would incur under those terms which are most common in similar contracts at the place where the principal contract is to be performed. *(Enacted in 1872. Amended by Stats.1939, c. 453, p. 1798, § 16.)*

§ 2800. Guaranty that obligation is good or collectible

A guaranty to the effect that an obligation is good, or is collectible, imports that the debtor is solvent, and that the demand is collectible by the usual legal proceedings, if taken with reasonable diligence. *(Enacted in 1872.)*

Cross References

Guaranty of collection as suretyship, see Civil Code § 2787.

§ 2801. Guaranty that obligation is good or collectible; recovery

A guaranty, such as is mentioned in the last section, is not discharged by an omission to take proceedings upon the principal debt, or upon any collateral security for its payment, if no part of the debt could have been collected thereby. *(Enacted in 1872.)*

§ 2802. Guaranty that obligation is good or collectible; surety's liability

In the cases mentioned in Section 2800, the removal of the principal from the state, leaving no property therein from which the obligation might be satisfied, is equivalent to the insolvency of the principal in its effect upon the rights and obligations of the guarantor. *(Enacted in 1872.)*

ARTICLE 4. LIABILITY OF SURETIES

Section
2806. Conditional and unconditional obligations.
2807. Surety for payment or performance; liability without demand or notice.
2808. Surety upon conditional obligation; notice of default.
2809. Surety's obligation commensurate with principal obligation.
2810. Surety's obligation; principal's personal disability.
2811. Bonded principal; agreement with surety, deposit of money and assets, withdrawals.

§ 2806. Conditional and unconditional obligations

A suretyship obligation is to be deemed unconditional unless its terms import some condition precedent to the liability of the surety. *(Enacted in 1872. Amended by Stats.1939, c. 453, p. 1798, § 17.)*

Cross References

Absolute suretyship binding without notice of acceptance, see Civil Code § 2795.
Measure of liability, see Civil Code § 2809.
Situations not releasing sureties, see Civil Code § 8152.

§ 2807. Surety for payment or performance; liability without demand or notice

A surety who has assumed liability for payment or performance is liable to the creditor immediately upon the default of the principal, and without demand or notice. *(Enacted in 1872. Amended by Stats.1939, c. 453, p. 1798, § 18.)*

Cross References

Exoneration of sureties, see Civil Code § 2819 et seq.
Measure of liability, see Civil Code § 2809.

§ 2808. Surety upon conditional obligation; notice of default

Where one assumes liability as surety upon a conditional obligation, his liability is commensurate with that of the principal, and he is not entitled to notice of the default of the principal, unless he is unable, by the exercise of reasonable diligence, to acquire information of such default, and the creditor has actual notice thereof. *(Enacted in 1872. Amended by Stats.1939, c. 453, p. 1798, § 19.)*

§ 2809. Surety's obligation commensurate with principal obligation

The obligation of a surety must be neither larger in amount nor in other respects more burdensome than that of the principal; and if in its terms it exceeds it, it is reducible in proportion to the principal obligation. *(Enacted in 1872. Amended by Stats.1939, c. 453, p. 1798, § 20.)*

Cross References

Exoneration, see Civil Code § 2819 et seq.

§ 2810. Surety's obligation; principal's personal disability

A surety is liable, notwithstanding any mere personal disability of the principal, though the disability be such as to make the contract void against the principal; but he is not liable if for any other reason there is no liability upon the part of the principal at the time of the execution of the contract, or the liability of the principal thereafter ceases, unless the surety has assumed liability with knowledge of the existence of the defense. Where the principal is not liable because of mere personal disability, recovery back by the creditor of any res which formed all or part of the consideration for the contract shall have the effect upon the liability of the surety which is attributed to the recovery back of such a res under the law of sales generally. *(Enacted in 1872. Amended by Stats.1939, c. 453, p. 1798, § 21.)*

§ 2811. Bonded principal; agreement with surety, deposit of money and assets, withdrawals

Any party required to give a bond undertaking or other obligation may agree with his surety for the deposit of any money and assets for which the surety is responsible with a bank, savings bank, safe deposit, or trust company authorized by law to do business as such, or other depository approved by the court or a judge thereof, if such deposit is otherwise proper, for the safekeeping of such money and assets and in such manner as to prevent the withdrawal of any or all such money and assets without the written consent of the surety, or an order of court or a judge thereof, made on such notice to the surety as the court or judge may direct. Such agreement shall not in any manner release, or change the liability of, the principal or surety as established by the terms of the bond. *(Added by Stats.1953, c. 37, p. 675, § 4.)*

ARTICLE 5. CONTINUING GUARANTY

Section
2814. Definition.
2815. Revocation.

§ 2814. Definition

A guaranty relating to a future liability of the principal, under successive transactions, which either continue his liability or from time to time renew it after it has been satisfied, is called a continuing guaranty. *(Enacted in 1872.)*

ARISING FROM PARTICULAR TRANSACTIONS

Cross References

Continuing guaranty as form of suretyship, see Civil Code § 2787.
Letter of credit, time and effect of establishment of credit, see Commercial Code § 5106.

§ 2815. Revocation

A continuing guaranty may be revoked at any time by the guarantor, in respect to future transactions, unless there is a continuing consideration as to such transactions which he does not renounce. *(Enacted in 1872.)*

ARTICLE 6. EXONERATION OF SURETIES

Section
2819. Alteration of original obligation; suspension or impairment of remedies or rights against principal.
2820. Suspension or impairment of remedy; creditor's void promise.
2821. Rescission of agreement altering obligation or impairing remedy.
2822. Partial satisfaction of obligation; effect on obligation of surety.
2823. Delay in proceeding by creditor.
2824. Indemnified surety; liability notwithstanding modification or release.
2825. Discharge of principal.

§ 2819. Alteration of original obligation; suspension or impairment of remedies or rights against principal

A surety is exonerated, except so far as he or she may be indemnified by the principal, if by any act of the creditor, without the consent of the surety the original obligation of the principal is altered in any respect, or the remedies or rights of the creditor against the principal, in respect thereto, in any way impaired or suspended. However, nothing in this section shall be construed to supersede subdivision (b) of Section 2822. *(Enacted in 1872. Amended by Stats.1939, c. 453, p. 1799, § 22; Stats.1993, c. 149 (A.B.1402), § 1, eff. July 19, 1993.)*

Cross References

Creditor entitled to benefit of securities held by surety, see Civil Code § 2854.
Exoneration of surety,
  Negligence of creditor, see Civil Code § 2845.
  Performance of principal obligation, see Civil Code § 2839.
Release of surety, see Civil Code § 8152.

§ 2820. Suspension or impairment of remedy; creditor's void promise

That a promise by a creditor is for any cause void, or voidable by him at his option, shall not prevent it from altering the obligation or suspending or impairing the remedy within the meaning of the last section. *(Enacted in 1872. Amended by Stats.1939, c. 453, p. 1795, § 34.)*

§ 2821. Rescission of agreement altering obligation or impairing remedy

The rescission of an agreement altering the original obligation of a debtor, or impairing the remedy of a creditor, does not restore the liability of a surety who has been exonerated by such agreement. *(Enacted in 1872. Amended by Stats.1939, c. 453, p. 1799, § 23.)*

Cross References

Rescission of contracts, see Civil Code § 1688 et seq.

§ 2822. Partial satisfaction of obligation; effect on obligation of surety

(a) The acceptance, by a creditor, of anything in partial satisfaction of an obligation, reduces the obligation of a surety thereof, in the same measure as that of the principal, but does not otherwise affect it. However, if the surety is liable upon only a portion of an obligation and the principal provides partial satisfaction of the obligation, the principal may designate the portion of the obligation that is to be satisfied.

(b) For purposes of this section and Section 2819, an agreement by a creditor to accept from the principal debtor a sum less than the balance owed on the original obligation, without the prior consent of the surety and without any other change to the underlying agreement between the creditor and principal debtor, shall not exonerate the surety for the lesser sum agreed upon by the creditor and principal debtor. *(Enacted in 1872. Amended by Stats.1939, c. 453, p. 1799, § 24; Stats.1993, c. 149 (A.B.1402), § 2, eff. July 19, 1993.)*

Cross References

Part performance, satisfaction, see Civil Code § 1524.
Partial performance, extinction of obligations, see Civil Code § 1477.
Satisfaction defined, see Civil Code § 1523.

§ 2823. Delay in proceeding by creditor

Mere delay on the part of a creditor to proceed against the principal, or to enforce any other remedy, does not exonerate a surety. *(Enacted in 1872. Amended by Stats.1939, c. 453, p. 1799, § 25.)*

Cross References

Effect of creditor's neglect to proceed against principal, see Civil Code § 2845.

§ 2824. Indemnified surety; liability notwithstanding modification or release

A surety, who has been indemnified by the principal, is liable to the creditor to the extent of the indemnity, notwithstanding that the creditor, without the assent of the surety, may have modified the contract or released the principal. *(Enacted in 1872. Amended by Stats.1939, c. 453, p. 1799, § 26.)*

Cross References

Creditor entitled to benefit of securities held by surety, see Civil Code § 2854.

§ 2825. Discharge of principal

A surety is not exonerated by the discharge of his principal by operation of law, without the intervention or omission of the creditor. *(Enacted in 1872. Amended by Stats.1939, c. 453, p. 1799, § 27.)*

ARTICLE 7. POSITION OF SURETIES

Section
2831. Repealed.
2832. Ostensible principal may show suretyship.

Section
2836. Repealed.
2837. Rules of interpretation.
2838. Judgment against surety; effect on relationship of parties.
2839. Exoneration by performance or offer of performance.
2840. Repealed.
2844. Repealed.
2845. Requiring creditor to pursue certain remedies; exoneration of surety by creditor's neglect to proceed.
2846. Compelling principal to perform.
2847. Reimbursement of surety by principal.
2848. Enforcement of creditor's remedies against principal; contribution by co-sureties.
2849. Surety entitled to benefits of securities for performance.
2850. Property of principal first applied to discharge of obligation.
2851, 2852. Repealed.
2854. Creditor entitled to benefits of securities for performance held by surety.
2855. Arbitration award against principal alone; effect on surety.
2856. Waiver of suretyship rights and defenses; contract language; effectiveness; applicability; validity of waivers executed prior to January 1, 1997.

§ 2831. Repealed by Stats.1939, c. 453, p. 1800, § 31

§ 2832. Ostensible principal may show suretyship

One who appears to be a principal, whether by the terms of a written instrument or otherwise, may show that he is in fact a surety, except as against persons who have acted on the faith of his apparent character of principal. It is not necessary for him to show that the creditor accepted him as surety. *(Enacted in 1872. Amended by Stats.1939, c. 453, p. 1799, § 28.)*

Cross References

Acceptance of suretyship, see Civil Code § 2795.
Creation of suretyship not dependent on knowledge or consent of principal, see Civil Code § 2788.
Release of sureties, see Civil Code § 8152.

§ 2836. Repealed by Stats.1939, c. 453, p. 1800, § 31

§ 2837. Rules of interpretation

In interpreting the terms of a contract of suretyship, the same rules are to be observed as in the case of other contracts. Except as provided in section 2794, the position of a surety to whom consideration moves is the same as that of one who is gratuitous. *(Enacted in 1872. Amended by Stats.1939, c. 453, p. 1799, § 29.)*

Cross References

Interpretation of contracts, see Civil Code § 1635 et seq.
Rules for interpretation of indemnity contracts, see Civil Code § 2778.

§ 2838. Judgment against surety; effect on relationship of parties

Notwithstanding the recovery of judgment by a creditor against a surety, the latter still occupies the relation of surety. *(Enacted in 1872.)*

Cross References

Conclusiveness of judgment against surety, see Code of Civil Procedure § 1055.

§ 2839. Exoneration by performance or offer of performance

Performance of the principal obligation, or an offer of such performance, duly made as provided in this code, exonerates a surety. *(Enacted in 1872. Amended by Code Am.1873–74, c. 612, p. 260, § 254.)*

Cross References

Exoneration, generally, see Civil Code § 2819 et seq.
Offer of performance, see Civil Code § 1485 et seq.

§ 2840. Repealed by Stats.1939, c. 453, p. 1800, § 31

§ 2844. Repealed by Stats.1939, c. 453, p. 1800, § 31

§ 2845. Requiring creditor to pursue certain remedies; exoneration of surety by creditor's neglect to proceed

A surety may require the creditor, subject to Section 996.440 of the Code of Civil Procedure, to proceed against the principal, or to pursue any other remedy in the creditor's power which the surety cannot pursue, and which would lighten the surety's burden; and if the creditor neglects to do so, the surety is exonerated to the extent to which the surety is thereby prejudiced. *(Enacted in 1872. Amended by Stats.1939, c. 453, p. 1800, § 30; Stats.1972, c. 391, p. 714, § 1; Stats.1982, c. 517, p. 2300, § 73.)*

Cross References

Delay in proceeding against principal, see Civil Code § 2823.
Exoneration, generally, see Civil Code § 2819 et seq.

§ 2846. Compelling principal to perform

A surety may compel his principal to perform the obligation when due. *(Enacted in 1872.)*

Cross References

Right of action to compel principal to satisfy the debt, see Code of Civil Procedure § 1050.

§ 2847. Reimbursement of surety by principal

If a surety satisfies the principal obligation, or any part thereof, whether with or without legal proceedings, the principal is bound to reimburse what he has disbursed, including necessary costs and expenses; but the surety has no claim for reimbursement against other persons, though they may have been benefited by his act, except as prescribed by the next section. *(Enacted in 1872.)*

Cross References

Reimbursement when person indemnifying is a surety, see Civil Code § 2779.

§ 2848. Enforcement of creditor's remedies against principal; contribution by co-sureties

A surety, upon satisfying the obligation of the principal, is entitled to enforce every remedy which the creditor then has against the principal to the extent of reimbursing what he has expended, and also to require all his co-sureties to contribute thereto, without regard to the order of time in which they became such. *(Enacted in 1872.)*

Cross References

Contribution, see Code of Civil Procedure §§ 882, 883.

§ 2849. Surety entitled to benefits of securities for performance

A surety is entitled to the benefit of every security for the performance of the principal obligation held by the creditor, or by a co-surety at the time of entering into the contract of suretyship, or acquired by him afterwards, whether the surety was aware of the security or not. *(Enacted in 1872.)*

§ 2850. Property of principal first applied to discharge of obligation

Whenever property of a surety is hypothecated with property of the principal, the surety is entitled to have the property of the principal first applied to the discharge of the obligation. *(Enacted in 1872.)*

Cross References

Surety may require creditor to proceed against the principal, see Civil Code § 2845.

§§ 2851, 2852. Repealed by Stats.1982, c. 517, p. 2327, §§ 74, 75

§ 2854. Creditor entitled to benefits of securities for performance held by surety

A creditor is entitled to the benefit of everything which a surety has received from the debtor by way of security for the performance of the obligation, and may, upon the maturity of the obligation, compel the application of such security to its satisfaction. *(Enacted in 1872.)*

§ 2855. Arbitration award against principal alone; effect on surety

An arbitration award rendered against a principal alone shall not be, be deemed to be, or be utilized as, an award against his surety.

The intent of this legislation is to apply existing law to arbitration awards. *(Added by Stats.1979, c. 346, p. 1211, § 1.)*

§ 2856. Waiver of suretyship rights and defenses; contract language; effectiveness; applicability; validity of waivers executed prior to January 1, 1997

(a) Any guarantor or other surety, including a guarantor of a note or other obligation secured by real property or an estate for years, may waive any or all of the following:

(1) The guarantor or other surety's rights of subrogation, reimbursement, indemnification, and contribution and any other rights and defenses that are or may become available to the guarantor or other surety by reason of Sections 2787 to 2855, inclusive.

(2) Any rights or defenses the guarantor or other surety may have in respect of his or her obligations as a guarantor or other surety by reason of any election of remedies by the creditor.

(3) Any rights or defenses the guarantor or other surety may have because the principal's note or other obligation is secured by real property or an estate for years. These rights or defenses include, but are not limited to, any rights or defenses that are based upon, directly or indirectly, the application of Section 580a, 580b, 580d, or 726 of the Code of Civil Procedure to the principal's note or other obligation.

(b) A contractual provision that expresses an intent to waive any or all of the rights and defenses described in subdivision (a) shall be effective to waive these rights and defenses without regard to the inclusion of any particular language or phrases in the contract to waive any rights and defenses or any references to statutory provisions or judicial decisions.

(c) Without limiting any rights of the creditor or any guarantor or other surety to use any other language to express an intent to waive any or all of the rights and defenses described in paragraphs (2) and (3) of subdivision (a), the following provisions in a contract shall effectively waive all rights and defenses described in paragraphs (2) and (3) of subdivision (a):

The guarantor waives all rights and defenses that the guarantor may have because the debtor's debt is secured by real property. This means, among other things:

(1) The creditor may collect from the guarantor without first foreclosing on any real or personal property collateral pledged by the debtor.

(2) If the creditor forecloses on any real property collateral pledged by the debtor:

(A) The amount of the debt may be reduced only by the price for which that collateral is sold at the foreclosure sale, even if the collateral is worth more than the sale price.

(B) The creditor may collect from the guarantor even if the creditor, by foreclosing on the real property collateral, has destroyed any right the guarantor may have to collect from the debtor.

This is an unconditional and irrevocable waiver of any rights and defenses the guarantor may have because the debtor's debt is secured by real property. These rights and defenses include, but are not limited to, any rights or defenses based upon Section 580a, 580b, 580d, or 726 of the Code of Civil Procedure.

(d) Without limiting any rights of the creditor or any guarantor or other surety to use any other language to express an intent to waive all rights and defenses of the surety by reason of any election of remedies by the creditor, the following provision shall be effective to waive all rights and defenses the guarantor or other surety may have in respect of his or her obligations as a surety by reason of an election of remedies by the creditor:

The guarantor waives all rights and defenses arising out of an election of remedies by the creditor, even though that election of remedies, such as a nonjudicial foreclosure with respect to security for a guaranteed obligation, has destroyed the guarantor's rights of subrogation and reimbursement against the principal by the operation of Section 580d of the Code of Civil Procedure or otherwise.

(e) Subdivisions (b), (c), and (d) shall not apply to a guaranty or other type of suretyship obligation made in respect of a loan secured by a deed of trust or mortgage on a dwelling for not more than four families when the dwelling is occupied, entirely or in part, by the borrower and that loan was in fact used to pay all or part of the purchase price of that dwelling.

(f) The validity of a waiver executed before January 1, 1997, shall be determined by the application of the law that existed on the date that the waiver was executed. *(Added by Stats.1996, c. 1013 (A.B.2585), § 2.)*

ARTICLE 8. LETTER OF CREDIT [REPEALED]

§§ 2858, 2859. Repealed by Stats.1963, c. 819, p. 1997, § 2, eff. Jan. 1, 1965

Title 13.5

OBLIGATION TO DEFEND ACTION

Section
2860. Conflict of interest; duty to provide independent counsel; waiver; qualifications of independent counsel; fees; disclosure of information.
2861 to 2866. Repealed.

§ 2860. Conflict of interest; duty to provide independent counsel; waiver; qualifications of independent counsel; fees; disclosure of information

(a) If the provisions of a policy of insurance impose a duty to defend upon an insurer and a conflict of interest arises which creates a duty on the part of the insurer to provide independent counsel to the insured, the insurer shall provide independent counsel to represent the insured unless, at the time the insured is informed that a possible conflict may arise or does exist, the insured expressly waives, in writing, the right to independent counsel. An insurance contract may contain a provision which sets forth the method of selecting that counsel consistent with this section.

(b) For purposes of this section, a conflict of interest does not exist as to allegations or facts in the litigation for which the insurer denies coverage; however, when an insurer reserves its rights on a given issue and the outcome of that coverage issue can be controlled by counsel first retained by the insurer for the defense of the claim, a conflict of interest may exist. No conflict of interest shall be deemed to exist as to allegations of punitive damages or be deemed to exist solely because an insured is sued for an amount in excess of the insurance policy limits.

(c) When the insured has selected independent counsel to represent him or her, the insurer may exercise its right to require that the counsel selected by the insured possess certain minimum qualifications which may include that the selected counsel have (1) at least five years of civil litigation practice which includes substantial defense experience in the subject at issue in the litigation, and (2) errors and omissions coverage. The insurer's obligation to pay fees to the independent counsel selected by the insured is limited to the rates which are actually paid by the insurer to attorneys retained by it in the ordinary course of business in the defense of similar actions in the community where the claim arose or is being defended. This subdivision does not invalidate other different or additional policy provisions pertaining to attorney's fees or providing for methods of settlement of disputes concerning those fees. Any dispute concerning attorney's fees not resolved by these methods shall be resolved by final and binding arbitration by a single neutral arbitrator selected by the parties to the dispute.

(d) When independent counsel has been selected by the insured, it shall be the duty of that counsel and the insured to disclose to the insurer all information concerning the action except privileged materials relevant to coverage disputes, and timely to inform and consult with the insurer on all matters relating to the action. Any claim of privilege asserted is subject to in camera review in the appropriate law and motion department of the superior court. Any information disclosed by the insured or by independent counsel is not a waiver of the privilege as to any other party.

(e) The insured may waive its right to select independent counsel by signing the following statement: "I have been advised and informed of my right to select independent counsel to represent me in this lawsuit. I have considered this matter fully and freely waive my right to select independent counsel at this time. I authorize my insurer to select a defense attorney to represent me in this lawsuit."

(f) Where the insured selects independent counsel pursuant to the provisions of this section, both the counsel provided by the insurer and independent counsel selected by the insured shall be allowed to participate in all aspects of the litigation. Counsel shall cooperate fully in the exchange of information that is consistent with each counsel's ethical and legal obligation to the insured. Nothing in this section shall relieve the insured of his or her duty to cooperate with the insurer under the terms of the insurance contract. *(Added by Stats.1987, c. 1498, § 4. Amended by Stats.1988, c. 1114, § 1.)*

§§ 2861 to 2866. Repealed by Stats.1963, c. 819, § 2, eff. Jan. 1, 1965

Title 13.7

OBLIGATION TO SETTLE INSURANCE CLAIMS FAIRLY [REJECTED]

§§ 2870, 2871. Rejected, eff. March 7, 2000

Title 14

LIEN

Chapter		Section
1.	Liens in General	2872
2.	Mortgage	2920
2a.	Home Equity Loan Disclosure Act	2970
2b.	Automobile Sales Finance Act	2981
2c.	Real Property Sales Contracts	2985
2d.	Vehicle Leasing Act	2985.7
2e.	Controlled Escrows	2995
3.	Pledge [Repealed]	
3a.	Trust Receipts [Repealed]	

Chapter		Section
3b.	Assignments of Accounts Receivable [Repealed]	
3c.	Inventory Liens [Repealed]	
3.5.	Health Care Liens	3040
4.	Hospital Liens	3045.1
5.	Respondentia [Repealed]	
6.	Other Liens	3046
6.5.	Liens on Vehicles	3067
6.7.	Livestock Service Lien	3080
7.	Stoppage in Transit	3081
8.	Design Professionals' Liens [Repealed]	

CHAPTER 1. LIENS IN GENERAL

Article		Section
1.	Definition of Liens	2872
2.	Creation of Liens	2881
3.	Effect of Liens	2888
4.	Priority of Liens	2897
5.	Redemption from Liens	2903
6.	Extinction of Lien	2909

ARTICLE 1. DEFINITION OF LIENS

Section
2872. Definition.
2873. Classification of liens.
2874. "General lien" defined.
2875. "Special lien" defined.
2876. Prior lien satisfied by holder of special lien.
2877. Contracts governed by chapter.

Cross References

Provisions of this Title, in respect to rights and obligations of parties to contract, as subordinate to intention of parties and waiver of benefit thereof, see Civil Code § 3268.

§ 2872. Definition

A lien is a charge imposed in some mode other than by a transfer in trust upon specific property by which it is made security for the performance of an act. *(Enacted in 1872. Amended by Code Am.1877–78, c. 74, p. 88, § 1.)*

Cross References

Aircraft repair, special liens, see Business and Professions Code § 9798.1.
Attachment lien, see Code of Civil Procedure §§ 488.500, 488.510.
Enforcement of liens, see Code of Civil Procedure § 1180 et seq.
Lien defined, see Code of Civil Procedure § 1180.
Mechanics liens, see Civil Code § 8400 et seq.; Cal. Const. Art. 14, § 3.
Tax liens,
  Generation skipping transfer tax, see Revenue and Taxation Code § 16810.
  Personal income tax, see Revenue and Taxation Code § 19203 et seq.
  State tax lien, see Revenue and Taxation Code § 13610.

§ 2873. Classification of liens

Liens are either general or special. *(Enacted in 1872.)*

§ 2874. "General lien" defined

A general lien is one which the holder thereof is entitled to enforce as a security for the performance of all the obligations, or all of a particular class of obligations, which exist in his favor against the owner of the property. *(Enacted in 1872.)*

Cross References

Banker's lien, see Civil Code § 3054.
Factor's lien, see Civil Code § 3053.
Master's lien, see Harbors and Navigation Code § 492.
Seamen's lien, see Harbors and Navigation Code § 493.
Services lien, see Civil Code § 3051.
Vendor's lien, see Civil Code § 3046 et seq.

§ 2875. "Special lien" defined

A special lien is one which the holder thereof can enforce only as security for the performance of a particular act or obligation, and of such obligations as may be incidental thereto. *(Enacted in 1872.)*

Cross References

Aircraft repair, special liens, see Business and Professions Code § 9798.1.
Mortgage as special lien, see Civil Code § 2923.
Officer's lien by levy of attachment or execution, see Code of Civil Procedure §§ 488.100, 687.050.
Possessory lien for services, repairs, etc., see Civil Code § 3051.
Purchaser's lien, see Civil Code § 3050.

§ 2876. Prior lien satisfied by holder of special lien

Where the holder of a special lien is compelled to satisfy a prior lien for his own protection, he may enforce payment of the amount so paid by him, as a part of the claim for which his own lien exists. *(Enacted in 1872.)*

Cross References

Contracts in restraint of the right of redemption, validity, see Civil Code § 2889.
Enforcement of liens, see Code of Civil Procedure § 1180.
Mechanics liens, priorities, see Civil Code § 8450.
Satisfaction of prior liens, redemption and subrogation, see Civil Code §§ 2903, 2904.

§ 2877. Contracts governed by chapter

Contracts of mortgage, pledge, bottomry, or respondentia are subject to all of the provisions of this chapter. *(Enacted in 1872. Amended by Stats.2013, c. 76 (A.B.383), § 13.)*

Cross References

Bottomry, see Harbors and Navigation Code § 450 et seq.
Mortgages defined, see Civil Code § 2920.
Respondentia, see Harbors and Navigation Code § 470 et seq.

ARTICLE 2. CREATION OF LIENS

Section
2881. Creation.
2882. Claim not due; no lien by operation of law.
2883. Agreement to create a lien; property not yet acquired; undistributed real property of an estate.
2884. Obligations not in existence at time of creating lien.
2885. Recordation of state tax liens; notice to tax debtor.

§ 2881. Creation

A lien is created:

1. By contract of the parties; or,
2. By operation of law. *(Enacted in 1872.)*

§ 2882. Claim not due; no lien by operation of law

No lien arises by mere operation of law until the time at which the act to be secured thereby ought to be performed. *(Enacted in 1872.)*

§ 2883. Agreement to create a lien; property not yet acquired; undistributed real property of an estate

(a) An agreement may be made to create a lien upon property not yet acquired by the party agreeing to give the lien, or not yet in existence. In that case the lien agreed for attaches from the time when the party agreeing to give it acquires an interest in the thing, to the extent of such interest.

(b) For purposes of subdivision (a), an agreement by a beneficiary of an estate that is subject to administration, as provided in Division 7 (commencing with Section 7000) of the Probate Code, to create a lien upon real property in the estate that is undistributed at the time the agreement is entered into, shall create no lien upon the real property unless and until the real property is distributed to that beneficiary. Upon recordation of an order confirming the sale of the real property pursuant to Section 10313 of the Probate Code and the recording of a duly executed deed in accordance therewith, any expectancy of a lien in the real property under the agreement shall be extinguished. *(Enacted in 1872. Amended by Stats.1993, c. 382 (S.B.848), § 1; Stats.1993, c. 527 (A.B.908), § 1.)*

Cross References

Future interests, see Civil Code § 690.

§ 2884. Obligations not in existence at time of creating lien

A lien may be created by contract, to take immediate effect, as security for the performance of obligations not then in existence. *(Enacted in 1872.)*

Cross References

Aircraft repair, special liens, see Business and Professions Code § 9798.1.
Secured transactions, after-acquired property, see Commercial Code § 9204.

§ 2885. Recordation of state tax liens; notice to tax debtor

Any state agency, upon recording a state tax lien against real property, shall mail written notice of the recordation to the tax debtor, unless previous correspondence mailed to the address of record was returned undelivered with no forwarding address. Failure to notify the tax debtor shall not affect the constructive notice otherwise imparted by recordation, nor shall it affect the force, effect, or priority otherwise accorded such tax lien. *(Added by Stats.1980, c. 1281, p. 4326, § 1. Amended by Stats.1983, c. 643, § 1, eff. Sept. 1, 1983.)*

ARTICLE 3. EFFECT OF LIENS

Section
2888. Title not transferred.
2889. Forfeitures and restraints upon redemption; validity.
2890. Personal obligation not implied.
2891. Security of other obligations.
2892. Compensation of lien holder.

§ 2888. Title not transferred

Notwithstanding an agreement to the contrary, a lien, or a contract for a lien, transfers no title to the property subject to the lien. *(Enacted in 1872.)*

Cross References

Mortgage not deemed a conveyance, see Code of Civil Procedure § 744.
Possession of mortgaged property, see Civil Code § 2927.
Title subsequently acquired by mortgagor, see Civil Code § 2930.
Title to thing offered in performance of an obligation, see Civil Code § 1502.
Transfer of interest in property, see Civil Code § 2924.

§ 2889. Forfeitures and restraints upon redemption; validity

All contracts for the forfeiture of property subject to a lien, in satisfaction of the obligation secured thereby, and all contracts in restraint of the right of redemption from a lien, are void. *(Enacted in 1872.)*

Cross References

Redemption and subrogation, right of, see Civil Code § 2903 et seq.
Works of improvement, waiver and release, see Civil Code § 8122 et seq.

§ 2890. Personal obligation not implied

The creation of a lien does not of itself imply that any person is bound to perform the act for which the lien is a security. *(Enacted in 1872.)*

Cross References

Mortgage not a personal obligation, see Civil Code § 2928.

§ 2891. Security of other obligations

The existence of a lien upon property does not of itself entitle the person in whose favor it exists to a lien upon the same property for the performance of any other obligation than that which the lien originally secured. *(Enacted in 1872.)*

§ 2892. Compensation of lien holder

One who holds property by virtue of a lien thereon, is not entitled to compensation from the owner thereof for any trouble or expense which he incurs respecting it, except to the same extent as a borrower, under sections 1892 and 1893. *(Enacted in 1872.)*

§ 2893. Inoperative

ARTICLE 4. PRIORITY OF LIENS

Section
2897. Time of creation; exception.
2898. Mortgages or deeds of trust.
2899. Marshaling liens.

§ 2897. Time of creation; exception

Other things being equal, different liens upon the same property have priority according to the time of their creation, except in cases of bottomry and respondentia. *(Enacted in 1872.)*

Cross References

Filing to perfect security interest, see Commercial Code §§ 9401, 9402.
First lien on realty, determination, see Financial Code § 1496.
Instruments subordinating or waiving priority, see Civil Code § 2934.
Mechanics liens, priority over lands, deeds of trust, mortgages, see Civil Code § 8450 et seq.
Oil and gas liens, preferences, see Code of Civil Procedure §§ 1203.56, 1203.57.
Personal income tax, priority of, see Revenue and Taxation Code §§ 19222, 19253.
Property taxation, priority of liens, see Revenue and Taxation Code § 2192.1.
Repair of aircraft, priority of liens, see Business and Professions Code § 9798.4.
Sales tax, priority of, see Revenue and Taxation Code § 6756.
State tax liens, priority, see Government Code § 7170.5.

§ 2898. Mortgages or deeds of trust

(a) A mortgage or deed of trust given for the price of real property, at the time of its conveyance, has priority over all other liens created against the purchaser, subject to the operation of the recording laws.

(b) The priority of the lien of a mortgage or deed of trust on an estate for years in real property shall be determined in the same manner as for determining the priority of a lien of a mortgage or deed of trust on real property. *(Enacted in 1872. Amended by Stats.1939, c. 520, p. 1905, § 1; Stats.1989, c. 698, § 3.)*

Cross References

Recording of deeds of trust, see Civil Code § 2934.
Recording of mortgages, see Civil Code § 2952.
Vendor's lien, priority, see Civil Code § 3046 et seq.

§ 2899. Marshaling liens

Where one has a lien upon several things, and other persons have subordinate liens upon, or interests in, some but not all of the same things, the person having the prior lien, if he can do so without risk of loss to himself, or of injustice to other persons, must resort to the property in the following order, on the demand of any party interested:

1. To the things upon which he has an exclusive lien;

2. To the things which are subject to the fewest subordinate liens;

3. In like manner inversely to the number of subordinate liens upon the same thing; and,

4. When several things are within one of the foregoing classes, and subject to the same number of liens, resort must be had—

(1.) To the things which have not been transferred since the prior lien was created;

(2.) To the things which have been so transferred without a valuable consideration; and,

(3.) To the things which have been so transferred for a valuable consideration in the inverse order of the transfer. *(Enacted in 1872.)*

Cross References

Marshaling assets, relative rights of different creditors, see Civil Code § 3433.

ARTICLE 5. REDEMPTION FROM LIEN

Section
2903. Right of redemption; subrogation.
2904. Rights of inferior lien holder.
2905. Redemption; procedure.
2906. Secured party; option to acquire interest in real property collateral; priority; validity.

§ 2903. Right of redemption; subrogation

Every person, having an interest in property subject to a lien, has a right to redeem it from the lien, at any time after the claim is due, and before his right of redemption is foreclosed, and, by such redemption, becomes subrogated to all the benefits of the lien, as against all owners of other interests in the property, except in so far as he was bound to make such redemption for their benefit. *(Enacted in 1872. Amended by Stats.1905, c. 459, p. 617, § 1.)*

Cross References

Prior lien satisfied by holder of special lien, see Civil Code § 2876.
Redemption,
  Contracts in restraint, see Civil Code § 2889.
  Foreclosure of right, generally, see Civil Code § 2931.
  Mortgages, see Code of Civil Procedure §§ 726, 729.010 et seq.
  Time, see Code of Civil Procedure § 729.030.
Secured transactions, debtor's right to redeem collateral, see Commercial Code § 9506.

§ 2904. Rights of inferior lien holder

One who has a lien inferior to another, upon the same property, has a right:

1. To redeem the property in the same manner as its owner might, from the superior lien; and,

2. To be subrogated to all the benefits of the superior lien, when necessary for the protection of his interests, upon satisfying the claim secured thereby. *(Enacted in 1872.)*

Cross References

Prior lien satisfied by holder of special lien, see Civil Code § 2876.
Redemption,
  Contracts in restraint, see Civil Code § 2889.
  Foreclosure of right, generally, see Civil Code § 2931.
  Time, see Code of Civil Procedure § 729.030.
Rights of holder of subordinate assessment or bond, see Streets and Highways Code § 5373.

§ 2905. Redemption; procedure

Redemption from a lien is made by performing, or offering to perform, the act for the performance of which it is a security, and paying, or offering to pay, the damages, if any, to which the holder of the lien is entitled for delay. *(Enacted in 1872.)*

Cross References

Extinguishment of debt, see Civil Code § 1500.

§ 2906. Secured party; option to acquire interest in real property collateral; priority; validity

An option granted to a secured party by a debtor to acquire an interest in real property collateral takes priority as of its recording and is effective according to its terms if the right to exercise the option is not dependent upon the occurrence of a default with respect to the security agreement and, where the real property which is the subject of the option is other than residential real property containing four or fewer units, shall not be deemed invalid or ineffective on the basis that the secured party has impaired the debtor's equity of redemption in violation of common law or Section 2889. This section shall not be construed to make valid or effective an otherwise unlawful option nor shall any inference be drawn from this section as to the validity or application of common law with respect to residential real property containing four or fewer units. *(Added by Stats.1984, c. 565, § 1.)*

ARTICLE 6. EXTINCTION OF LIENS

Section
2909. Extinction as accessory obligation.
2910. Sale or conversion.
2911. Lapse of time; presumption as to public improvement liens.
2912. Partial performance.
2913. Lien dependent upon possession; restoration of property.
2914. Transactions and security interests governed by Commercial Code.

§ 2909. Extinction as accessory obligation

A lien is to be deemed accessory to the act for the performance of which it is a security, whether any person is bound for such performance or not, and is extinguishable in like manner with any other accessory obligation. *(Enacted in 1872.)*

Cross References

Enforcement of mechanics lien, see Civil Code § 8460 et seq.
Extinction of debt by loss of possession, see Civil Code § 2913.
Extinguishment of debt, see Civil Code § 1500.
Insurance tax lien, see Revenue and Taxation Code § 12494.

§ 2910. Sale or conversion

The sale of any property on which there is a lien, in satisfaction of the claim secured thereby, or in case of personal property, its wrongful conversion by the person holding the lien, extinguishes the lien thereon. *(Enacted in 1872.)*

Cross References

Conversion of personal property, see Civil Code § 3336 et seq.
Limitation of actions for conversion, see Code of Civil Procedure § 338.
Sale by lienholder at auction, see Civil Code § 3052.

§ 2911. Lapse of time; presumption as to public improvement liens

A lien is extinguished by the lapse of time within which, under the provisions of the Code of Civil Procedure, either:

1. An action can be brought upon the principal obligation, or

2. A treasurer, street superintendent or other public official may sell any real property to satisfy a public improvement assessment or any bond issued to represent such assessment and which assessment is secured by a lien upon said real property; whichever is later.

Anything to the contrary notwithstanding, any lien heretofore existing or which may hereafter exist upon real property to secure the payment of a public improvement assessment shall be presumed to have been extinguished at the expiration of four years after the due date of such assessment or the last installment thereof, or four years after the date the lien attaches, or on January 1, 1947, whichever is later, or in the event bonds were or shall be issued to represent such assessment, the lien shall then be presumed to have been extinguished at the expiration of four years after the due date of said bonds or of the last installment thereof or of the last principal coupon attached thereto, or on January 1, 1947, whichever is later. The presumptions mentioned in this paragraph shall be conclusive in favor of a bona fide purchaser for value of said property after such dates. *(Enacted in 1872. Amended by Stats.1945, c. 361, p. 821, § 1.)*

Cross References

Action to determine adverse interests where lien is presumptively extinguished under this section, see Code of Civil Procedure § 801.1.
Constructive presumption of payment, see Code of Civil Procedure § 329.
Periods of limitation, see Code of Civil Procedure § 335 et seq.
Sale of lands under public improvement assessment liens, see Code of Civil Procedure § 330.

§ 2912. Partial performance

The partial performance of an act secured by a lien does not extinguish the lien upon any part of the property subject thereto, even if it is divisible. *(Enacted in 1872.)*

Cross References

Partial performance, effect of, see Civil Code §§ 1477, 1486, 1524.

§ 2913. Lien dependent upon possession; restoration of property

The voluntary restoration of property to its owner by the holder of a lien thereon dependent upon possession extinguishes the lien as to such property, unless otherwise agreed by the parties, and extinguishes it, notwithstanding any such agreement, as to creditors of the owner and persons, subsequently acquiring a title to the property, or a lien thereon, in good faith, and for value. *(Enacted in 1872. Amended by Code Am.1873–74, c. 612, p. 260, § 255; Stats.1905, c. 459, p. 617, § 2.)*

Cross References

Liens on vehicles, see Civil Code § 3067 et seq.
Presumption of ownership from possession, see Evidence Code § 637.

§ 2914. Transactions and security interests governed by Commercial Code

None of the provisions of this chapter apply to any transaction or security interest governed by the Uniform Commercial Code. *(Added by Stats.1963, c. 819, p. 1999, § 14, eff. Jan. 1, 1965.)*

ARISING FROM PARTICULAR TRANSACTIONS

Cross References

Secured transactions, see Commercial Code § 9101 et seq.

CHAPTER 2. MORTGAGE

Article		Section
1.	Mortgages in General	2920
1.5.	Mortgage Foreclosure Consultants	2945
2.	Mortgage of Real Property	2947
3.	Disclosures on Purchase Money Liens on Residential Property	2956

Cross References

Real estate regulations, grounds for disciplinary action, see Business and Professions Code § 10177.

ARTICLE 1. MORTGAGES IN GENERAL

Section
- 2920. "Mortgage" defined.
- 2920.5. Definitions.
- 2920.7. Repealed.
- 2921. Property adversely held.
- 2922. Writing; formalities.
- 2923. Special lien independent of possession.
- 2923.1. Fiduciary of borrower; violation; duty.
- 2923.3. Notice of default; summary of key information; delivery requirements; translations.
- 2923.4. Purpose of act; availability of loss mitigation options in nonjudicial foreclosure process.
- 2923.5. Notice of default; recording; contact of borrower by mortgage servicer.
- 2923.52. Repealed.
- 2923.53. Repealed.
- 2923.54. Repealed.
- 2923.55. Notice of default; recording; sending of written information to borrower by mortgage servicer.
- 2923.6. Legislative findings and declarations; pooling and servicing agreements; loan modification or workout plan; application for a first lien loan modification; contents of written notice of denial; time allowed to file appeal; application of section.
- 2923.7. Receipt of borrower request for foreclosure prevention alternative; establishment of single point of contact; application.
- 2924. Transfer as security deemed mortgage or pledge; power of sale; requirements prior to sale; trustee liability; evidence of compliance; privileged communications; rebuttable presumption.
- 2924.1. Transfers of property in common interest developments; recording; validity of sale not affected by failure.
- 2924.3. Persons undertaking loan collections; notice of default and sale; exemptions.
- 2924.5. Acceleration clause in deed of trust or mortgage on property containing four or fewer residential units.
- 2924.6. Acceleration clauses; inapplicability to certain transfers; prohibition of waiver; date of application.
- 2924.7. Acceleration clause for nonpayment of taxes, rents, assessments, insurance premiums, advances; provision for payment of hazard insurance proceeds to beneficiary, trustee, mortgagee or agent; enforcement of clauses despite impairment of security interest.
- 2924.8. Required notice for residents of property subject to foreclosure sale.
- 2924.85. Repealed.

Section
- 2924.9. Mortgage service providers offering one or more foreclosure prevention alternatives; sending of written communication to borrower.
- 2924.10. Submission of first lien modification application document; written acknowledgment of receipt.
- 2924.11. Approval of foreclosure prevention alternative in writing; circumstances prohibiting recordation of notice of default, recording of notice of sale, or conducting trustee's sale; copy of agreement; recording of rescission of notice of default or cancellation of pending trustee's sale; fees; transfer of loan.
- 2924.12. Material violations of specified foreclosure provisions; action for injunctive relief by borrower prior to recording of trustee's deed upon sale; liability to borrower after recording of trustee's deed upon sale; effect of violation on validity of sale; third-party encumbrancer; attorney's fees and costs.
- 2924.15. Application of specified provisions only to first lien mortgages or deeds of trust secured by owner-occupied residential real property containing no more than four dwelling units.
- 2924.15. Application of specified provisions only to first lien mortgages or deeds of trust secured by residential real property containing no more than four dwelling units and meeting specified conditions.
- 2924.17. Requirement that specified declarations or affidavits be accurate and complete and supported by competent and reliable evidence; review by mortgage servicer; liability for multiple and repeated uncorrected recording or filing violations.
- 2924.18. Submission of complete first lien loan modification application; prohibition on recording notice of default, notice of sale, or conducting trustee's sale while application is pending; approval of foreclosure prevention alternative in writing; circumstances prohibiting recordation of notice of default, recording of notice of sale, or conducting trustee's sale; application to specified entities meeting foreclosure threshold; notification to primary regulator when threshold is excee
- 2924.19. Material violations of specified foreclosure provisions; action for injunctive relief by borrower prior to recording of trustee's deed upon sale; liability to borrower after recording of trustee's deed upon sale; effect of violation on validity of sale; third-party encumbrancer; attorney's fees and costs; application to entities described in subdivision (b) of Section 2924.18.
- 2924.20. Regulations; adoption by Department of Financial Protection and Innovation and the Bureau of Real Estate; enforcement.
- 2924.25. Repealed.
- 2924.26. Licensed title company or underwritten title company; violation of Section 2923.5 or 2924.11; exemption.
- 2924a. Attorney's and authorized agent's authority to conduct trustee's sale.
- 2924b. Notices of default and of sale; mailing upon request for copies and to certain interested persons.
- 2924c. Cure of default; payment of arrearages, costs and fees; effect on acceleration; notice of default; trustee's or attorney's fees; reinstatement period.
- 2924d. Costs and expenses of enforcement; trustee's or attorney's fees; rebates and kickbacks.
- 2924d. Costs and expenses of enforcement; trustee's or attorney's fees; rebates and kickbacks.
- 2924e. Junior lienholder requests for written notice of delinquencies; duration; liability for failure to give

OBLIGATIONS

Section	
	notice; satisfaction of obligations secured by junior liens.
2924f.	Sale or resale of property where there is a default on the obligation secured by the property; notice; contents; posting and publication.
2924f.	Sale or resale of property where there is a default on the obligation secured by the property; notice; contents; posting and publication.
2924g.	Conduct of sale; time; place; interested parties; postponement; order of sale.
2924g.	Conduct of sale; time; place; interested parties; postponement; order of sale.
2924h.	Bidders at sale; bid as irrevocable offer; security deposit; finality of sale; rescission for failure of consideration; delivery of payment; restraint of bidding; remedies.
2924h.	Bidders at sale; bid as irrevocable offer; security deposit; finality of sale; rescission for failure of consideration; delivery of payment; restraint of bidding; remedies.
2924i.	Balloon payment loans; final payment due date; notice; effect; validity of documents; date of application.
2924j.	Execution of trustee's deed resulting from surplus proceeds of trustee's sale; notice; priority of claims; due diligence; declaration of unresolved claims; deposit of funds.
2924k.	Distribution of proceeds of trustee's sale; priority.
2924l.	Declaration of nonmonetary status; trustee named in action or proceeding in trustee capacity; objections.
2924m.	Sale of property containing one to four residential units; finality of sale; notice of sale by trustee.
2924n.	Compliance with law regarding eviction or displacement of tenants.
2924o.	Eligible bidder; affordable housing cost or rent; tenants; enforcement.
2924p.	Sale of real property containing one to four residential dwelling units acquired through foreclosure under a mortgage or deed of trust by an institution or that is acquired at a foreclosure sale by an institution.
2924½.	Repealed.
2925.	Transfer subject to defeasance on a condition; proof.
2926.	Scope of mortgage lien.
2927.	Possession of mortgaged property.
2928.	Personal obligation.
2929.	Waste.
2929.3.	Maintenance of vacant residential property purchased at foreclosure sale; violation; fines and penalties; notice of violation.
2929.4.	Failure to maintain vacant property subject to notice of default, purchased at foreclosure sale, or acquired through foreclosure; notice of violation prior to imposition of fine or penalty; opportunity to correct; exception for public health or safety.
2929.45.	Limit upon nuisance abatement costs recoverable against property subject to notice of default, purchased at foreclosure sale, or acquired through foreclosure; costs adopted by elected officials.
2929.5.	Hazardous substances; inspection by secured lender.
2930.	Title subsequently acquired by mortgagor.
2931.	Foreclosure.
2931a.	Actions relating to real property; tax lien; state agency as party; jurisdiction; contents of complaint or petition; service of process; duties of Attorney General.
2931b.	Tax sale; purchase by state.

Section	
2931c.	Action by Attorney General to enforce lien to secure payment of taxes or other obligations to state.
2932.	Power of sale.
2932.5.	Power of sale; vesting in assignee.
2932.6.	Financial institution repair of property acquired through foreclosure.
2933.	Power of attorney; formalities.
2934.	Assignments; instruments subordinating or waiving priority; recording; effect.
2934a.	Substitution of trustee; mailing; recording; contents of substitution; substitution after notice of default; authorization of trustee to act; resignation of trustee; new notice of sale.
2934b.	Application of probate provisions.
2935.	Record of assignment not notice to debtor; validity of payments.
2936.	Assignment of debt carries security.
2937.	Notices to borrower of transfer of service by existing and new servicing agent of mortgage or deed of trust on single family residential real property.
2937.7.	Service of process on trustee under deed of trust or mortgage; effect on trustor.
2938.	Assignment of rents; recordation; enforcement; demand; cash proceeds; application of section.
2938.1.	Repealed.
2939.	Discharge; recording certificate of payment, satisfaction, or discharge.
2939½.	Renumbered.
2939.5.	Satisfaction; foreign executors, administrators and guardians.
2940.	Certificate of discharge; recording.
2941.	Satisfaction; obligation to issue discharge certificate or reconvey; failure to execute or record reconveyance; damages; fee; reproduced "original" instruments.
2941.1.	Charging a reconveyance fee where no payoff demand statement is issued.
2941.5.	Obligation to execute certificate of discharge, satisfaction, or request for reconveyance; penalty.
2941.7.	Satisfaction of mortgage or deed of trust; release of lien when mortgagee or beneficiary cannot be found or refuses to issue certificate of discharge or to reconvey.
2941.9.	Trust deed beneficiaries; agreements to be governed by beneficiaries holding more than 50 percent of the record beneficial interest.
2942.	Bottomry and respondentia excluded from chapter.
2943.	Definitions; copy of note and modifications; payoff demand statement; reliance by entitled person on beneficiary statement or payoff demand statement.
2943.1.	Borrower's Instruction to Suspend and Close Equity Line of Credit; delivery information included in payoff demand statement; form; duties of beneficiary upon receipt of instruction and payment; reliance.
2944.	Transactions and security interests governed by Commercial Code.
2944.5.	Insurance policies; acceptance; lender, mortgagee, or third party with interest in real or personal property.
2944.6.	Person who negotiates or offers to perform mortgage loan modifications for fee; violations.
2944.7.	Person negotiating or offering to perform mortgage loan modification for compensation paid by borrower; unlawful acts; penalties; allowable acts.
2944.8.	Person negotiating or offering to perform mortgage loan modification for compensation paid by bor-

Section
rower; additional penalties where victim is senior citizen or disabled person.
2944.10. Person negotiating or offering to perform mortgage loan modification for compensation paid by borrower; limitation of actions.

Cross References

Home equity sales contracts,
  Equity purchaser defined to exclude purchaser who acquires deed from trustee at foreclosure sale conducted pursuant to this article, see Civil Code § 1695.1.
  Residence in foreclosure defined to include residence which was the subject of a default notice recorded pursuant to this article, see Civil Code § 1695.1.
Mobilehome affixed to real property, notice of default and sale governed by this chapter, see Health and Safety Code § 18039.1.
Mortgage foreclosure consultants, residence in foreclosure defined to include residence subject to foreclosure notice recorded pursuant to this Article, see Civil Code § 2945.1.
Trustee holding power of sale under deed of trust or mortgage, authority to sue to exercise powers and duties pursuant to this chapter, see Code of Civil Procedure § 369.

§ 2920. "Mortgage" defined

(a) A mortgage is a contract by which specific property, including an estate for years in real property, is hypothecated for the performance of an act, without the necessity of a change of possession.

(b) For purposes of Sections 2924 to 2924h, inclusive, "mortgage" also means any security device or instrument, other than a deed of trust, that confers a power of sale affecting real property or an estate for years therein, to be exercised after breach of the obligation so secured, including a real property sales contract, as defined in Section 2985, which contains such a provision. *(Enacted in 1872. Amended by Stats.1986, c. 1385, § 1; Stats.1989, c. 698, § 4.)*

Cross References

Consideration, see Civil Code § 1605.
Definition of lien, see Civil Code § 2872.
Form of mortgage,
  Personal property, see Civil Code § 2956.
  Real property, see Civil Code §§ 2922, 2948.
Iraq-Kuwait military reservists, see Military and Veterans Code § 800.
Mortgage not a conveyance, see Code of Civil Procedure § 744.
Possession of mortgaged property, see Civil Code § 2927.
Record of mortgage, see Civil Code § 1213.
Title not transferred by lien or contract for lien, see Civil Code § 2888.
Transfer as security, mortgage or pledge, see Civil Code § 2924.
Transfer subject to defeasance on condition, see Civil Code § 2925.

§ 2920.5. Definitions

For purposes of this article, the following definitions apply:

(a) "Mortgage servicer" means a person or entity who directly services a loan, or who is responsible for interacting with the borrower, managing the loan account on a daily basis including collecting and crediting periodic loan payments, managing any escrow account, or enforcing the note and security instrument, either as the current owner of the promissory note or as the current owner's authorized agent. "Mortgage servicer" also means a subservicing agent to a master servicer by contract. "Mortgage servicer" shall not include a trustee, or a trustee's authorized agent, acting under a power of sale pursuant to a deed of trust.

(b) "Foreclosure prevention alternative" means a first lien loan modification or another available loss mitigation option.

(c)(1) Unless otherwise provided and for purposes of Sections 2923.4, 2923.5, 2923.55, 2923.6, 2923.7, 2924.9, 2924.10, 2924.11, 2924.18, and 2924.19, "borrower" means any natural person who is a mortgagor or trustor and who is potentially eligible for any federal, state, or proprietary foreclosure prevention alternative program offered by, or through, his or her mortgage servicer.

(2) For purposes of the sections listed in paragraph (1), "borrower" shall not include any of the following:

(A) An individual who has surrendered the secured property as evidenced by either a letter confirming the surrender or delivery of the keys to the property to the mortgagee, trustee, beneficiary, or authorized agent.

(B) An individual who has contracted with an organization, person, or entity whose primary business is advising people who have decided to leave their homes on how to extend the foreclosure process and avoid their contractual obligations to mortgagees or beneficiaries.

(C) An individual who has filed a case under Chapter 7, 11, 12, or 13 of Title 11 of the United States Code and the bankruptcy court has not entered an order closing or dismissing the bankruptcy case, or granting relief from a stay of foreclosure.

(d) "First lien" means the most senior mortgage or deed of trust on the property that is the subject of the notice of default or notice of sale. *(Added by Stats.2012, c. 87 (S.B.900), § 2.)*

§ 2920.7. Repealed by Stats.2019, c. 497 (A.B.991), § 27, operative Jan. 1, 2020

§ 2921. Property adversely held

A mortgage may be created upon property held adversely to the mortgagor. *(Enacted in 1872.)*

§ 2922. Writing; formalities

A mortgage can be created, renewed, or extended, only by writing, executed with the formalities required in the case of a grant of real property. *(Enacted in 1872.)*

Cross References

Form of mortgage, see Civil Code § 2948.
Mode of transfer of real property generally, see Civil Code § 1091 et seq.
Written power of attorney to execute mortgage, see Civil Code § 2933.

§ 2923. Special lien independent of possession

The lien of a mortgage is special, unless otherwise expressly agreed, and is independent of possession. *(Enacted in 1872.)*

Cross References

Special lien defined, see Civil Code § 2875.

§ 2923.1. Fiduciary of borrower; violation; duty

(a) A mortgage broker providing mortgage brokerage services to a borrower is the fiduciary of the borrower, and any violation of the broker's fiduciary duties shall be a violation of the mortgage broker's license law. This fiduciary duty includes a requirement that the mortgage broker place the economic interest of the borrower ahead of his or her own economic interest. A mortgage broker who provides mortgage brokerage services to the borrower owes this fiduciary duty to the borrower regardless of whether the mortgage broker is acting as an agent for any other party in connection with the residential mortgage loan transaction.

(b) For purposes of this section, the following definitions apply:

(1) "Licensed person" means a real estate broker licensed under the Real Estate Law (Part 1 (commencing with Section 10000) of Division 4 of the Business and Professions Code), a finance lender or broker licensed under the California Finance Lenders Law (Division 9 (commencing with Section 22000) of the Financial Code), a residential mortgage lender licensed under the California Residential Mortgage Lending Act (Division 20 (commencing with Section 50000) of the Financial Code), a commercial or industrial bank organized under the Banking Law (Division 1 (commencing with Section 99) of the Financial Code), a savings association organized under the Savings Association Law (Division 2 (commencing with Section 5000) of the Financial Code), and a credit union organized under the California Credit Union Law (Division 5 (commencing with Section 14000) of the Financial Code).

(2) "Mortgage broker" means a licensed person who provides mortgage brokerage services. For purposes of this section, a licensed person who makes a residential mortgage loan is a "mortgage broker," and subject to the requirements of this section applicable to mortgage brokers, only with respect to transactions in which the licensed person provides mortgage brokerage services.

(3) "Mortgage brokerage services" means arranging or attempting to arrange, as exclusive agent for the borrower or as dual agent for the borrower and lender, for compensation or in expectation of compensation, paid directly or indirectly, a residential mortgage loan made by an unaffiliated third party.

(4) "Residential mortgage loan" means a consumer credit transaction that is secured by residential real property that is improved by four or fewer residential units.

(c) The duties set forth in this section shall not be construed to limit or narrow any other fiduciary duty of a mortgage broker. *(Added by Stats.2009, c. 629 (A.B.260), § 2.)*

Cross References

Higher-priced mortgage loans, violations and enforcement, see Financial Code § 4995.3.

§ 2923.3. Notice of default; summary of key information; delivery requirements; translations

(a) With respect to residential real property containing no more than four dwelling units, a mortgagee, trustee, beneficiary, or authorized agent shall provide to the mortgagor or trustor a copy of the recorded notice of default with an attached separate summary document of the notice of default in English and the languages described in Section 1632, as set forth in subdivision (c), and a copy of the recorded notice of sale with an attached separate summary document of the information required to be contained in the notice of sale in English and the languages described in Section 1632, as set forth in subdivision (d). These summaries are not required to be recorded or published. This subdivision shall become operative on April 1, 2013, or 90 days following the issuance of the translations by the Department of * * * <u>Financial Protection and Innovation</u> pursuant to subdivision (b), whichever is later.

(b)(1) The Department of * * * <u>Financial Protection and Innovation</u> shall provide a standard translation of the statement in paragraph (1) of subdivision (c), and of the summary of the notice of default, as set forth in paragraph (2) of subdivision (c) in the languages described in Section 1632.

(2) The Department of * * * <u>Financial Protection and Innovation</u> shall provide a standard translation of the statement in paragraph (1) of subdivision (d), and of the summary of the notice of sale, as set forth in paragraph (2) of subdivision (d).

(3) The department shall make the translations described in paragraphs (1) and (2) available without charge on its * * * <u>internet website</u>. Any mortgagee, trustee, beneficiary, or authorized agent who provides the department's translations in the manner prescribed by this section shall be in compliance with this section.

(c)(1) The following statement shall appear in the languages described in Section 1632 at the beginning of the notice of default:

NOTE: THERE IS A SUMMARY OF THE INFORMATION IN THIS DOCUMENT ATTACHED.

(2) The following summary of key information shall be attached to the copy of the notice of default provided to the mortgagor or trustor:

SUMMARY OF KEY INFORMATION

The attached notice of default was sent to [name of the trustor], in relation to [description of the property that secures the mortgage or deed of trust in default]. This property may be sold to satisfy your obligation and any other obligation secured by the deed of trust or mortgage that is in default. [Trustor] has, as described in the notice of default, breached the mortgage or deed of trust on the property described above.

IMPORTANT NOTICE: IF YOUR PROPERTY IS IN FORECLOSURE BECAUSE YOU ARE BEHIND IN YOUR PAYMENTS, IT MAY BE SOLD WITHOUT ANY COURT ACTION, and you may have the legal right to bring your account in good standing by paying all of your past due payments plus permitted costs and expenses within the time permitted by law for reinstatement of your account, which is normally five business days prior to the date set for the sale of your property. No sale date may be set until approximately 90 days from the date the attached notice of default may be recorded (which date of recordation appears on the notice).

This amount is _____ as of ___(date)_____ and will increase until your account becomes current.

While your property is in foreclosure, you still must pay other obligations (such as insurance and taxes) required by your note and deed of trust or mortgage. If you fail to make future payments on the loan, pay taxes on the property, provide insurance on the property, or pay other obligations as required in the note and deed of trust or mortgage, the beneficiary or mortgagee may insist that you do so in order to reinstate your account in good standing. In addition, the beneficiary or mortgagee may require as a condition to reinstatement that you provide reliable written evidence that you paid all senior liens, property taxes, and hazard insurance premiums.

Upon your written request, the beneficiary or mortgagee will give you a written itemization of the entire amount you must pay. You may not have to pay the entire unpaid portion of your account, even though full payment was demanded, but you must pay all amounts in default at the time payment is made. However, you and your beneficiary or mortgagee may mutually agree in writing prior to the time the notice of sale is posted (which may not be earlier than three months after this notice of default is recorded) to, among other things, (1) provide additional time in which to cure the default by transfer of the property or otherwise; or (2) establish a schedule of payments in order to cure your default; or both (1) and (2).

Following the expiration of the time period referred to in the first paragraph of this notice, unless the obligation being foreclosed upon or a separate written agreement between you and your creditor permits a longer period, you have only the legal right to stop the sale of your property by paying the entire amount demanded by your creditor.

To find out the amount you must pay, or to arrange for payment to stop the foreclosure, or if your property is in foreclosure for any other reason, contact:

_____
(Name of beneficiary or mortgagee)

_____
(Mailing address)

_____
(Telephone)

If you have any questions, you should contact a lawyer or the governmental agency which may have insured your loan.

Notwithstanding the fact that your property is in foreclosure, you may offer your property for sale, provided the sale is concluded prior to the conclusion of the foreclosure.

Remember, YOU MAY LOSE LEGAL RIGHTS IF YOU DO NOT TAKE PROMPT ACTION.

If you would like additional copies of this summary, you may obtain them by calling [insert telephone number].

(d)(1) The following statement shall appear in the languages described in Section 1632 at the beginning of the notice of sale:

NOTE: THERE IS A SUMMARY OF THE INFORMATION IN THIS DOCUMENT ATTACHED.

(2) The following summary of key information shall be attached to the copy of the notice of sale provided to the mortgagor or trustor:

SUMMARY OF KEY INFORMATION

The attached notice of sale was sent to [trustor], in relation to [description of the property that secures the mortgage or deed of trust in default].

YOU ARE IN DEFAULT UNDER A (Deed of trust or mortgage) DATED ___. UNLESS YOU TAKE ACTION TO PROTECT YOUR PROPERTY, IT MAY BE SOLD AT A PUBLIC SALE.

IF YOU NEED AN EXPLANATION OF THE NATURE OF THE PROCEEDING AGAINST YOU, YOU SHOULD CONTACT A LAWYER.

The total amount due in the notice of sale is ___.

Your property is scheduled to be sold on [insert date and time of sale] at [insert location of sale].

However, the sale date shown on the attached notice of sale may be postponed one or more times by the mortgagee, beneficiary, trustee, or a court, pursuant to Section 2924g of the California Civil Code. The law requires that information about trustee sale postponements be made available to you and to the public, as a courtesy to those not present at the sale. If you wish to learn whether your sale date has been postponed, and, if applicable, the rescheduled time and date for the sale of this property, you may call [telephone number for information regarding the trustee's sale] or visit this * * * internet website [* * * internet website address for information regarding the sale of this property], using the file number assigned to this case [case file number]. Information about postponements that are very short in duration or that occur close in time to the scheduled sale may not immediately be reflected in the telephone information or on the * * * internet website. The best way to verify postponement information is to attend the scheduled sale.

If you would like additional copies of this summary, you may obtain them by calling [insert telephone number].

(e) Failure to provide these summaries to the mortgagor or trustor shall have the same effect as if the notice of default or notice of sale were incomplete or not provided.

(f) This section sets forth a requirement for translation in languages other than English, and a document complying with the provisions of this section may be recorded pursuant to subdivision (b) of Section 27293 of the Government Code. A document that complies with this section shall not be rejected for recordation on the ground that some part of the document is in a language other than English. *(Added by Stats.2012, c. 556 (A.B.1599), § 1. Amended by Stats.2015, c. 190 (A.B.1517), § 6, eff. Jan. 1, 2016; Stats.2022, c. 452 (S.B.1498), § 28, eff. Jan. 1, 2023.)*

§ 2923.4. Purpose of act; availability of loss mitigation options in nonjudicial foreclosure process

The purpose of the act that added this section is to ensure that, as part of the nonjudicial foreclosure process, borrowers are considered for, and have a meaningful opportunity to obtain, available loss mitigation options, if any, offered by or through the borrower's mortgage servicer, such as loan modifications or other alternatives to foreclosure. Nothing in the act that added this section, however, shall be interpreted to require a particular result of that process. (Added by Stats.2012, c. 87 (S.B.900), § 3. Amended by Stats.2018, c. 404 (S.B.818), § 2, eff. Jan. 1, 2019.)

§ 2923.5. Notice of default; recording; contact of borrower by mortgage servicer

(a)(1) A mortgage servicer, mortgagee, trustee, beneficiary, or authorized agent shall not record a notice of default pursuant to Section 2924 until both of the following:

(A) Either 30 days after initial contact is made as required by paragraph (2) or 30 days after satisfying the due diligence requirements as described in subdivision (e).

(B) The mortgage servicer complies with paragraph (1) of subdivision (a) of Section 2924.18, if the borrower has provided a complete application as defined in subdivision (d) of Section 2924.18.

(2) A mortgage servicer shall contact the borrower in person or by telephone in order to assess the borrower's financial situation and explore options for the borrower to avoid foreclosure. During the initial contact, the mortgage servicer shall advise the borrower that he or she has the right to request a subsequent meeting and, if requested, the mortgage servicer shall schedule the meeting to occur within 14 days. The assessment of the borrower's financial situation and discussion of options may occur during the first contact, or at the subsequent meeting scheduled for that purpose. In either case, the borrower shall be provided the toll-free telephone number made available by the United States Department of Housing and Urban Development (HUD) to find a HUD-certified housing counseling agency. Any meeting may occur telephonically.

(b) A notice of default recorded pursuant to Section 2924 shall include a declaration that the mortgage servicer has contacted the borrower, has tried with due diligence to contact the borrower as required by this section, or that no contact was required because the individual did not meet the definition of "borrower" pursuant to subdivision (c) of Section 2920.5.

(c) A mortgage servicer's loss mitigation personnel may participate by telephone during any contact required by this section.

(d) A borrower may designate, with consent given in writing, a HUD-certified housing counseling agency, attorney, or other advisor to discuss with the mortgage servicer, on the borrower's behalf, the borrower's financial situation and options for the borrower to avoid foreclosure. That contact made at the direction of the borrower shall satisfy the contact requirements of paragraph (2) of subdivision (a). Any loan modification or workout plan offered at the meeting by the mortgage servicer is subject to approval by the borrower.

(e) A notice of default may be recorded pursuant to Section 2924 when a mortgage servicer has not contacted a borrower as required by paragraph (2) of subdivision (a) provided that the failure to contact the borrower occurred despite the due diligence of the mortgage servicer. For purposes of this section, "due diligence" shall require and mean all of the following:

(1) A mortgage servicer shall first attempt to contact a borrower by sending a first-class letter that includes the toll-free telephone number made available by HUD to find a HUD-certified housing counseling agency.

(2)(A) After the letter has been sent, the mortgage servicer shall attempt to contact the borrower by telephone at least three times at different hours and on different days. Telephone calls shall be made to the primary telephone number on file.

(B) A mortgage servicer may attempt to contact a borrower using an automated system to dial borrowers, provided that, if the telephone call is answered, the call is connected to a live representative of the mortgage servicer.

(C) A mortgage servicer satisfies the telephone contact requirements of this paragraph:

(i) If it determines, after attempting contact pursuant to this paragraph, that the borrower's primary telephone number and secondary telephone number or numbers on file, if any, have been disconnected.

(ii) If the borrower or his or her authorized agent notifies the mortgage servicer in writing to cease further communication with the borrower. The cease communication notification shall explicitly pertain to the mortgage loan account to be effective. The cease communication notification shall be effective until the borrower or his or her authorized agent rescinds it in writing.

(3) If the borrower does not respond within two weeks after the telephone call requirements of paragraph (2) have been satisfied, the mortgage servicer shall then send a certified letter, with return receipt requested.

(4) The mortgage servicer shall provide a means for the borrower to contact it in a timely manner, including a toll-free telephone number that will provide access to a live representative during business hours.

(5) The mortgage servicer has posted a prominent link on the homepage of its Internet Web site, if any, to the following information:

(A) Options that may be available to borrowers who are unable to afford their mortgage payments and who wish to avoid foreclosure, and instructions to borrowers advising them on steps to take to explore those options.

(B) A list of financial documents borrowers should collect and be prepared to present to the mortgage servicer when discussing options for avoiding foreclosure.

(C) A toll-free telephone number for borrowers who wish to discuss options for avoiding foreclosure with their mortgage servicer.

(D) The toll-free telephone number made available by HUD to find a HUD-certified housing counseling agency.

(f) This section shall apply only to mortgages or deeds of trust described in Section 2924.15.

(g) This section shall apply only to entities described in subdivision (b) of Section 2924.18. *(Added by Stats.2012, c. 87 (S.B.900), § 5, operative Jan. 1, 2018. Amended by Stats.2018, c. 404 (S.B.818), § 4, eff. Jan. 1, 2019.)*

Cross References

Material violations of specified foreclosure provisions, action for injunctive relief by borrower prior to recording of trustee's deed upon sale, liability to borrower after recording of trustee's deed upon sale, effect of violation on validity of sale, third-party encumbrancer, attorney's fees and costs, see Civil Code § 2924.12.

Material violations of specified foreclosure provisions, action for injunctive relief by borrower prior to recording of trustee's deed upon sale, liability to borrower after recording of trustee's deed upon sale, effect of violation on validity of sale, third-party encumbrancer, attorney's fees and costs, application to entities described in subdivision (b) of Section 2924.18, see Civil Code § 2924.19.

Requirement that specified declarations or affidavits be accurate and complete and supported by competent and reliable evidence, review by mortgage servicer, liability for multiple and repeated uncorrected recording or filing violations, see Civil Code § 2924.17.

Written notice of forbearance request denial, identification of defects in request, see Civil Code § 3273.10.

§ 2923.52. Repealed by Stats.2009–2010, 2nd Ex.Sess., c. 5 (A.B.7), § 3, operative Jan. 1, 2011

§ 2923.53. Repealed by Stats.2009–2010, 2nd Ex.Sess., c. 5 (A.B.7), § 4, operative Jan. 1, 2011

§ 2923.54. Repealed by Stats.2009–2010, 2nd Ex.Sess., c. 5 (A.B.7), § 5, operative Jan. 1, 2011

§ 2923.55. Notice of default; recording; sending of written information to borrower by mortgage servicer

(a) A mortgage servicer, mortgagee, trustee, beneficiary, or authorized agent shall not record a notice of default pursuant to Section 2924 until all of the following:

(1) The mortgage servicer has satisfied the requirements of paragraph (1) of subdivision (b).

(2) Either 30 days after initial contact is made as required by paragraph (2) of subdivision (b) or 30 days after satisfying the due diligence requirements as described in subdivision (f).

(3) The mortgage servicer complies with subdivision (c) of Section 2923.6, if the borrower has provided a complete application as defined in subdivision (h) of Section 2923.6.

(b)(1) As specified in subdivision (a), a mortgage servicer shall send the following information in writing to the borrower:

(A) A statement that if the borrower is a servicemember or a dependent of a servicemember, he or she may be entitled to certain protections under the federal Servicemembers Civil Relief Act (50 U.S.C. Sec. 3901 et seq.) regarding the servicemember's interest rate and the risk of foreclosure, and counseling for covered servicemembers that is available at agencies such as Military OneSource and Armed Forces Legal Assistance.

(B) A statement that the borrower may request the following:

(i) A copy of the borrower's promissory note or other evidence of indebtedness.

(ii) A copy of the borrower's deed of trust or mortgage.

(iii) A copy of any assignment, if applicable, of the borrower's mortgage or deed of trust required to demonstrate the right of the mortgage servicer to foreclose.

(iv) A copy of the borrower's payment history since the borrower was last less than 60 days past due.

(2) A mortgage servicer shall contact the borrower in person or by telephone in order to assess the borrower's financial situation and explore options for the borrower to avoid foreclosure. During the initial contact, the mortgage servicer shall advise the borrower that he or she has the right to request a subsequent meeting and, if requested, the mortgage servicer shall schedule the meeting to occur within 14 days. The assessment of the borrower's financial situation and discussion of options may occur during the first contact, or at the subsequent meeting scheduled for that purpose. In either case, the borrower shall be provided the toll-free telephone number made available by the United States Department of Housing and Urban Development (HUD) to find a HUD-certified housing counseling agency. Any meeting may occur telephonically.

(c) A notice of default recorded pursuant to Section 2924 shall include a declaration that the mortgage servicer has contacted the borrower, has tried with due diligence to contact the borrower as required by this section, or that no contact was required because the individual did not meet the definition of "borrower" pursuant to subdivision (c) of Section 2920.5.

(d) A mortgage servicer's loss mitigation personnel may participate by telephone during any contact required by this section.

(e) A borrower may designate, with consent given in writing, a HUD-certified housing counseling agency, attorney, or other adviser to discuss with the mortgage servicer, on the borrower's behalf, the borrower's financial situation and options for the borrower to avoid foreclosure. That contact made at the direction of the borrower shall satisfy the contact requirements of paragraph (2) of subdivision (b). Any foreclosure prevention alternative offered at the meeting by the mortgage servicer is subject to approval by the borrower.

(f) A notice of default may be recorded pursuant to Section 2924 when a mortgage servicer has not contacted a borrower as required by paragraph (2) of subdivision (b), provided that the failure to contact the borrower occurred despite the due diligence of the mortgage servicer. For purposes of this section, "due diligence" shall require and mean all of the following:

(1) A mortgage servicer shall first attempt to contact a borrower by sending a first-class letter that includes the toll-free telephone number made available by HUD to find a HUD-certified housing counseling agency.

(2)(A) After the letter has been sent, the mortgage servicer shall attempt to contact the borrower by telephone at least three times at different hours and on different days.

Telephone calls shall be made to the primary telephone number on file.

(B) A mortgage servicer may attempt to contact a borrower using an automated system to dial borrowers, provided that, if the telephone call is answered, the call is connected to a live representative of the mortgage servicer.

(C) A mortgage servicer satisfies the telephone contact requirements of this paragraph:

(i) If it determines, after attempting contact pursuant to this paragraph, that the borrower's primary telephone number and secondary telephone number or numbers on file, if any, have been disconnected.

(ii) If the borrower or his or her authorized agent notifies the mortgage servicer in writing to cease further communication with the borrower. The cease communication notification shall explicitly pertain to the mortgage loan account to be effective. The cease communication notification shall be effective until the borrower or his or her authorized agent rescinds it in writing.

(3) If the borrower does not respond within two weeks after the telephone call requirements of paragraph (2) have been satisfied, the mortgage servicer shall then send a certified letter, with return receipt requested, that includes the toll-free telephone number made available by HUD to find a HUD-certified housing counseling agency.

(4) The mortgage servicer shall provide a means for the borrower to contact it in a timely manner, including a toll-free telephone number that will provide access to a live representative during business hours.

(5) The mortgage servicer has posted a prominent link on the homepage of its Internet Web site, if any, to the following information:

(A) Options that may be available to borrowers who are unable to afford their mortgage payments and who wish to avoid foreclosure, and instructions to borrowers advising them on steps to take to explore those options.

(B) A list of financial documents borrowers should collect and be prepared to present to the mortgage servicer when discussing options for avoiding foreclosure.

(C) A toll-free telephone number for borrowers who wish to discuss options for avoiding foreclosure with their mortgage servicer.

(D) The toll-free telephone number made available by HUD to find a HUD-certified housing counseling agency.

(g) This section shall not apply to entities described in subdivision (b) of Section 2924.18.

(h) This section shall apply only to mortgages or deeds of trust described in Section 2924.15. (Added by Stats.2018, c. 404 (S.B.818), § 6, eff. Jan. 1, 2019.)

§ 2923.6. **Legislative findings and declarations; pooling and servicing agreements; loan modification or workout plan; application for a first lien loan modification; contents of written notice of denial; time allowed to file appeal; application of section**

(a) The Legislature finds and declares that any duty mortgage servicers may have to maximize net present value under their pooling and servicing agreements is owed to all parties in a loan pool, or to all investors under a pooling and servicing agreement, not to any particular party in the loan pool or investor under a pooling and servicing agreement, and that a mortgage servicer acts in the best interests of all parties to the loan pool or investors in the pooling and servicing agreement if it agrees to or implements a loan modification or workout plan for which both of the following apply:

(1) The loan is in payment default, or payment default is reasonably foreseeable.

(2) Anticipated recovery under the loan modification or workout plan exceeds the anticipated recovery through foreclosure on a net present value basis.

(b) It is the intent of the Legislature that the mortgage servicer offer the borrower a loan modification or workout plan if such a modification or plan is consistent with its contractual or other authority.

(c) If a borrower submits a complete application for a first lien loan modification offered by, or through, the borrower's mortgage servicer at least five business days before a scheduled foreclosure sale, a mortgage servicer, mortgagee, trustee, beneficiary, or authorized agent shall not record a notice of default or notice of sale, or conduct a trustee's sale, while the complete first lien loan modification application is pending. A mortgage servicer, mortgagee, trustee, beneficiary, or authorized agent shall not record a notice of default or notice of sale or conduct a trustee's sale until any of the following occurs:

(1) The mortgage servicer makes a written determination that the borrower is not eligible for a first lien loan modification, and any appeal period pursuant to subdivision (d) has expired.

(2) The borrower does not accept an offered first lien loan modification within 14 days of the offer.

(3) The borrower accepts a written first lien loan modification, but defaults on, or otherwise breaches the borrower's obligations under, the first lien loan modification.

(d) If the borrower's application for a first lien loan modification is denied, the borrower shall have at least 30 days from the date of the written denial to appeal the denial and to provide evidence that the mortgage servicer's determination was in error.

(e) If the borrower's application for a first lien loan modification is denied, the mortgage servicer, mortgagee, trustee, beneficiary, or authorized agent shall not record a notice of default or, if a notice of default has already been recorded, record a notice of sale or conduct a trustee's sale until the later of:

(1) Thirty-one days after the borrower is notified in writing of the denial.

(2) If the borrower appeals the denial pursuant to subdivision (d), the later of 15 days after the denial of the appeal or 14 days after a first lien loan modification is offered after appeal but declined by the borrower, or, if a first lien loan modification is offered and accepted after appeal, the date on which the borrower fails to timely submit the first payment or otherwise breaches the terms of the offer.

(f) Following the denial of a first lien loan modification application, the mortgage servicer shall send a written notice to the borrower identifying the reasons for denial, including the following:

(1) The amount of time from the date of the denial letter in which the borrower may request an appeal of the denial of the first lien loan modification and instructions regarding how to appeal the denial.

(2) If the denial was based on investor disallowance, the specific reasons for the investor disallowance.

(3) If the denial is the result of a net present value calculation, the monthly gross income and property value used to calculate the net present value and a statement that the borrower may obtain all of the inputs used in the net present value calculation upon written request to the mortgage servicer.

(4) If applicable, a finding that the borrower was previously offered a first lien loan modification and failed to successfully make payments under the terms of the modified loan.

(5) If applicable, a description of other foreclosure prevention alternatives for which the borrower may be eligible, and a list of the steps the borrower must take in order to be considered for those options. If the mortgage servicer has already approved the borrower for another foreclosure prevention alternative, information necessary to complete the foreclosure prevention alternative.

(g) In order to minimize the risk of borrowers submitting multiple applications for first lien loan modifications for the purpose of delay, the mortgage servicer shall not be obligated to evaluate applications from borrowers who have been evaluated or afforded a fair opportunity to be evaluated consistent with the requirements of this section, unless there has been a material change in the borrower's financial circumstances since the date of the borrower's previous application and that change is documented by the borrower and submitted to the mortgage servicer.

(h) For purposes of this section, an application shall be deemed "complete" when a borrower has supplied the mortgage servicer with all documents required by the mortgage servicer within the reasonable timeframes specified by the mortgage servicer.

(i) Subdivisions (c) to (h), inclusive, shall not apply to entities described in subdivision (b) of Section 2924.18.

(j) This section shall apply only to mortgages or deeds of trust described in Section 2924.15. *(Added by Stats.2012, c. 87 (S.B.900), § 8, operative Jan. 1, 2018. Amended by Stats.2018, c. 404 (S.B.818), § 7, eff. Jan. 1, 2019.)*

Cross References

Material violations of specified foreclosure provisions, action for injunctive relief by borrower prior to recording of trustee's deed upon sale, liability to borrower after recording of trustee's deed upon sale, effect of violation on validity of sale, third-party encumbrancer, signatory to specified consent judgment, attorney's fees and costs, see Civil Code § 2924.12.

Mortgage service providers offering one or more foreclosure prevention alternatives, sending of written communication to borrower, see Civil Code § 2924.9.

§ 2923.7. Receipt of borrower request for foreclosure prevention alternative; establishment of single point of contact; application

(a) When a borrower requests a foreclosure prevention alternative, the mortgage servicer shall promptly establish a single point of contact and provide to the borrower one or more direct means of communication with the single point of contact.

(b) The single point of contact shall be responsible for doing all of the following:

(1) Communicating the process by which a borrower may apply for an available foreclosure prevention alternative and the deadline for any required submissions to be considered for these options.

(2) Coordinating receipt of all documents associated with available foreclosure prevention alternatives and notifying the borrower of any missing documents necessary to complete the application.

(3) Having access to current information and personnel sufficient to timely, accurately, and adequately inform the borrower of the current status of the foreclosure prevention alternative.

(4) Ensuring that a borrower is considered for all foreclosure prevention alternatives offered by, or through, the mortgage servicer, if any.

(5) Having access to individuals with the ability and authority to stop foreclosure proceedings when necessary.

(c) The single point of contact shall remain assigned to the borrower's account until the mortgage servicer determines that all loss mitigation options offered by, or through, the mortgage servicer have been exhausted or the borrower's account becomes current.

(d) The mortgage servicer shall ensure that a single point of contact refers and transfers a borrower to an appropriate supervisor upon request of the borrower, if the single point of contact has a supervisor.

(e) For purposes of this section, "single point of contact" means an individual or team of personnel each of whom has the ability and authority to perform the responsibilities described in subdivisions (b) to (d), inclusive. The mortgage servicer shall ensure that each member of the team is knowledgeable about the borrower's situation and current status in the alternatives to foreclosure process.

(f) This section shall apply only to mortgages or deeds of trust described in Section 2924.15.

(g)(1) This section shall not apply to a depository institution chartered under state or federal law, a person licensed pursuant to Division 9 (commencing with Section 22000) or Division 20 (commencing with Section 50000) of the Financial Code, or a person licensed pursuant to Part 1 (commencing with Section 10000) of Division 4 of the Business and Professions Code, that, during its immediately preceding annual reporting period, as established with its primary regulator, foreclosed on 175 or fewer residential real properties, containing no more than four dwelling units, that are located in California.

(2) Within three months after the close of any calendar year or annual reporting period as established with its

§ 2923.7

primary regulator during which an entity or person described in paragraph (1) exceeds the threshold of 175 specified in paragraph (1), that entity shall notify its primary regulator, in a manner acceptable to its primary regulator, and any mortgagor or trustor who is delinquent on a residential mortgage loan serviced by that entity of the date on which that entity will be subject to this section, which date shall be the first day of the first month that is six months after the close of the calendar year or annual reporting period during which that entity exceeded the threshold. *(Added by Stats. 2012, c. 87 (S.B.900), § 9. Amended by Stats.2018, c. 404 (S.B.818), § 9, eff. Jan. 1, 2019.)*

Cross References

Material violations of specified foreclosure provisions, action for injunctive relief by borrower prior to recording of trustee's deed upon sale, liability to borrower after recording of trustee's deed upon sale, effect of violation on validity of sale, third-party encumbrancer, signatory to specified consent judgment, attorney's fees and costs, see Civil Code § 2924.12.

Submission of complete first lien loan modification application, prohibition on recording notice default, notice of sale, or conducting trustee's sale while application is pending, approval of foreclosure prevention alternative in writing, circumstances prohibiting recordation of notice of default, recording of notice of sale, or conducting trustee's sale, application to specified entities meeting foreclosure threshold, notification to primary regulator when threshold is exceeded, transfer of loan, see Civil Code § 2924.18.

§ 2924. Transfer as security deemed mortgage or pledge; power of sale; requirements prior to sale; trustee liability; evidence of compliance; privileged communications; rebuttable presumption

(a) Every transfer of an interest in property, other than in trust, made only as a security for the performance of another act, is to be deemed a mortgage, except when in the case of personal property it is accompanied by actual change of possession, in which case it is to be deemed a pledge. If, by a mortgage created after July 27, 1917, of any estate in real property, other than an estate at will or for years, less than two, or in any transfer in trust made after July 27, 1917, of a like estate to secure the performance of an obligation, a power of sale is conferred upon the mortgagee, trustee, or any other person, to be exercised after a breach of the obligation for which that mortgage or transfer is a security, the power shall not be exercised except where the mortgage or transfer is made pursuant to an order, judgment, or decree of a court of record, or to secure the payment of bonds or other evidences of indebtedness authorized or permitted to be issued by the Commissioner of * * * <u>Financial Protection and Innovation</u>, or is made by a public utility subject to the provisions of the Public Utilities Act, until all of the following apply:

(1) The trustee, mortgagee, or beneficiary, or any of their authorized agents shall first file for record, in the office of the recorder of each county wherein the mortgaged or trust property or some part or parcel thereof is situated, a notice of default. That notice of default shall include all of the following:

(A) A statement identifying the mortgage or deed of trust by stating the name or names of the trustor or trustors and giving the book and page, or instrument number, if applicable, where the mortgage or deed of trust is recorded or a description of the mortgaged or trust property.

(B) A statement that a breach of the obligation for which the mortgage or transfer in trust is security has occurred.

(C) A statement setting forth the nature of each breach actually known to the beneficiary and of the beneficiary's election to sell or cause to be sold the property to satisfy that obligation and any other obligation secured by the deed of trust or mortgage that is in default.

(D) If the default is curable pursuant to Section 2924c, the statement specified in paragraph (1) of subdivision (b) of Section 2924c.

(2) Not less than three months shall elapse from the filing of the notice of default.

(3) Except as provided in paragraph (4), after the lapse of the three months described in paragraph (2), the mortgagee, trustee, or other person authorized to take the sale shall give notice of sale, stating the time and place thereof, in the manner and for a time not less than that set forth in Section 2924f.

(4) Notwithstanding paragraph (3), the mortgagee, trustee, or other person authorized to take sale may record a notice of sale pursuant to Section 2924f up to five days before the lapse of the three-month period described in paragraph (2), provided that the date of sale is no earlier than three months and 20 days after the recording of the notice of default.

(5) Whenever a sale is postponed for a period of at least 10 business days pursuant to Section 2924g, a mortgagee, beneficiary, or authorized agent shall provide written notice to a borrower regarding the new sale date and time, within five business days following the postponement. Information provided pursuant to this paragraph shall not constitute the public declaration required by subdivision (d) of Section 2924g. Failure to comply with this paragraph shall not invalidate any sale that would otherwise be valid under Section 2924f.

(6) An entity shall not record or cause a notice of default to be recorded or otherwise initiate the foreclosure process unless it is the holder of the beneficial interest under the mortgage or deed of trust, the original trustee or the substituted trustee under the deed of trust, or the designated agent of the holder of the beneficial interest. An agent of the holder of the beneficial interest under the mortgage or deed of trust, original trustee or substituted trustee under the deed of trust shall not record a notice of default or otherwise commence the foreclosure process except when acting within the scope of authority designated by the holder of the beneficial interest.

(b) In performing acts required by this article, the trustee shall incur no liability for any good faith error resulting from reliance on information provided in good faith by the beneficiary regarding the nature and the amount of the default under the secured obligation, deed of trust, or mortgage. In performing the acts required by this article, a trustee shall not be subject to Title 1.6c (commencing with Section 1788) of Part 4.

(c) A recital in the deed executed pursuant to the power of sale of compliance with all requirements of law regarding the mailing of copies of notices or the publication of a copy of the notice of default or the personal delivery of the copy of the notice of default or the posting of copies of the notice of sale or the publication of a copy thereof shall constitute prima facie evidence of compliance with these requirements and conclusive evidence thereof in favor of bona fide purchasers and encumbrancers for value and without notice.

(d) All of the following shall constitute privileged communications pursuant to Section 47:

(1) The mailing, publication, and delivery of notices as required by this section.

(2) Performance of the procedures set forth in this article.

(3) Performance of the functions and procedures set forth in this article if those functions and procedures are necessary to carry out the duties described in Sections 729.040, 729.050, and 729.080 of the Code of Civil Procedure.

(e) There is a rebuttable presumption that the beneficiary actually knew of all unpaid loan payments on the obligation owed to the beneficiary and secured by the deed of trust or mortgage subject to the notice of default. However, the failure to include an actually known default shall not invalidate the notice of sale and the beneficiary shall not be precluded from asserting a claim to this omitted default or defaults in a separate notice of default.

(f) With respect to residential real property containing no more than four dwelling units, a separate document containing a summary of the notice of default information in English and the languages described in Section 1632 shall be attached to the notice of default provided to the mortgagor or trustor pursuant to Section 2923.3. *(Added by Stats.2009–2010, 2nd Ex.Sess., c. 4 (S.B.7), § 8, eff. May 21, 2009, operative Jan. 1, 2011. Amended by Stats.2010, c. 180 (S.B.1221), § 1; Stats. 2012, c. 86 (A.B.278), § 10; Stats.2012, c. 87 (S.B.900), § 10; Stats.2012, c. 556 (A.B.1599), § 2.5; Stats.2018, c. 404 (S.B. 818), § 11, eff. Jan. 1, 2019; Stats.2019, c. 143 (S.B.251), § 16, eff. Jan. 1, 2020; Stats.2022, c. 452 (S.B.1498), § 29, eff. Jan. 1, 2023.)*

Cross References

Actions for foreclosure of trust deeds and mortgages, see Code of Civil Procedure § 725a et seq.
Adjusted fair market value, shared appreciation loans, exclusion of trustee's sale, see Civil Code § 1917.020.
Application of specified provisions only to first lien mortgages or deeds of trust secured by owner-occupied residential real property containing no more than four dwelling units, see Civil Code § 2924.15.
Bids at sales, see Civil Code § 2924h.
Commercial and industrial common interest developments, monetary charge for repair of damage to common area and facilities, monetary penalties, see Civil Code § 6824.
Commercial and industrial common interest developments, trustee sale, procedure, see Civil Code § 6822.
Conduct of sale, see Civil Code § 2924g.
Consideration, see Civil Code § 1605.
Definition of mortgage, see Civil Code § 2920.
Forfeitures and restraints upon redemption invalid, see Civil Code § 2889.
Invalidity of waiver of rights or privileges conferred by this section upon borrower, see Civil Code § 2953.
Mortgage foreclosure actions, see Code of Civil Procedure § 726 et seq.
Mortgage not personal obligation, see Civil Code § 2928.
Mortgage service providers offering one or more foreclosure prevention alternatives, sending of written communication to borrower, see Civil Code § 2924.9.
Notice of default, recording, sending of written information to borrower by mortgage servicer, see Civil Code § 2923.55.
Notice of sale of interest in real property, see Code of Civil Procedure § 701.540.
Power of sale in mortgage, see Civil Code § 2932.
Priority of mechanics liens to mortgages, see Civil Code § 8450.
Record of conveyances, see Civil Code § 1213.
Redemption from lien, see Civil Code § 2903 et seq.
Removal of occupant after sale of property under this section, see Code of Civil Procedure § 1161a.
Request for copy of notice of default and sale, see Civil Code § 2924b.
Requirement that specified declarations or affidavits be accurate and complete and supported by competent and reliable evidence, review by mortgage servicer, liability for multiple and repeated uncorrected recording or filing violations, see Civil Code § 2924.17.
Sale of encumbered property by judgment in foreclosure action, see Code of Civil Procedure § 726.
Sale of property, posting and publication of notice, see Civil Code § 2924f.
Time and manner of sale under execution of real property, see Code of Civil Procedure §§ 701.570, 701.580.
Transfer or encumbrance of utility property, see Public Utilities Code § 851 et seq.
Transfer subject to defeasance on condition, see Civil Code § 2925.
Transfers without delivery, see Civil Code § 3440.

§ 2924.1. Transfers of property in common interest developments; recording; validity of sale not affected by failure

(a) Notwithstanding any other law, the transfer, following the sale, of property in a common interest development, as defined by Section 1351, executed under the power of sale contained in any deed of trust or mortgage, shall be recorded within 30 days after the date of sale in the office of the county recorder where the property or a portion of the property is located.

(b) Any failure to comply with the provisions of this section shall not affect the validity of a trustee's sale or a sale in favor of a bona fide purchaser. *(Added by Stats.2012, c. 255 (A.B.2273), § 1.)*

§ 2924.3. Persons undertaking loan collections; notice of default and sale; exemptions

(a) Except as provided in subdivisions (b) and (c), a person who has undertaken as an agent of a mortgagee, beneficiary, or owner of a promissory note secured directly or collaterally by a mortgage or deed of trust on real property or an estate for years therein, to make collections of payments from an obligor under the note, shall mail the following notices, postage prepaid, to each mortgagee, beneficiary or owner for whom the agent has agreed to make collections from the obligor under the note:

(1) A copy of the notice of default filed in the office of the county recorder pursuant to Section 2924 on account of a breach of obligation under the promissory note on which the agent has agreed to make collections of payments, within 15 days after recordation.

(2) Notice that a notice of default has been recorded pursuant to Section 2924 on account of a breach of an

§ 2924.3

obligation secured by a mortgage or deed of trust against the same property or estate for years therein having priority over the mortgage or deed of trust securing the obligation described in paragraph (1), within 15 days after recordation or within three business days after the agent receives the information, whichever is later.

(3) Notice of the time and place scheduled for the sale of the real property or estate for years therein pursuant to Section 2924f under a power of sale in a mortgage or deed of trust securing an obligation described in paragraphs (1) or (2), not less than 15 days before the scheduled date of the sale or not later than the next business day after the agent receives the information, whichever is later.

(b) An agent who has undertaken to make collections on behalf of mortgagees, beneficiaries or owners of promissory notes secured by mortgages or deeds of trust on real property or an estate for years therein shall not be required to comply with the provisions of subdivision (a) with respect to a mortgagee, beneficiary or owner who is entitled to receive notice pursuant to subdivision (c) of Section 2924b or for whom a request for notice has been recorded pursuant to subdivision (b) of Section 2924b if the agent reasonably believes that the address of the mortgagee, beneficiary, or owner described in Section 2924b is the current business or residence address of that person.

(c) An agent who has undertaken to make collections on behalf of mortgagees, beneficiaries or owners of promissory notes secured by mortgages or deeds of trust on real property or an estate for years therein shall not be required to comply with the provisions of paragraph (1) or (2) of subdivision (a) if the agent knows or reasonably believes that the default has already been cured by or on behalf of the obligor.

(d) Any failure to comply with the provisions of this section shall not affect the validity of a sale in favor of a bona fide purchaser or the rights of an encumbrancer for value and without notice. (Added by Stats.1982, c. 711, p. 2874, § 4. Amended by Stats.1989, c. 698, § 7; Stats.1998, c. 932 (A.B.1094), § 10.)

§ 2924.5. Acceleration clause in deed of trust or mortgage on property containing four or fewer residential units

No clause in any deed of trust or mortgage on property containing four or fewer residential units or on which four or fewer residential units are to be constructed or in any obligation secured by any deed of trust or mortgage on property containing four or fewer residential units or on which four or fewer residential units are to be constructed that provides for the acceleration of the due date of the obligation upon the sale, conveyance, alienation, lease, succession, assignment or other transfer of the property subject to the deed of trust or mortgage shall be valid unless the clause is set forth, in its entirety in both the body of the deed of trust or mortgage and the promissory note or other document evidencing the secured obligation. This section shall apply to all such deeds of trust, mortgages, and obligations secured thereby executed on or after July 1, 1972. (Added by Stats.1971, c. 429, p. 830, § 1. Amended by Stats.1972, c. 216, p. 451, § 1, eff. June 30, 1972.)

OBLIGATIONS

Cross References
Addition of junior encumbrance by owner of single-family, owner-occupied dwelling, effect on acceleration of maturity, see Civil Code § 2949.

§ 2924.6. Acceleration clauses; inapplicability to certain transfers; prohibition of waiver; date of application

(a) An obligee may not accelerate the maturity date of the principal and accrued interest on any loan secured by a mortgage or deed of trust on residential real property solely by reason of any one or more of the following transfers in the title to the real property:

(1) A transfer resulting from the death of an obligor where the transfer is to the spouse who is also an obligor.

(2) A transfer by an obligor where the spouse becomes a coowner of the property.

(3) A transfer resulting from a decree of dissolution of the marriage or legal separation or from a property settlement agreement incidental to such a decree which requires the obligor to continue to make the loan payments by which a spouse who is an obligor becomes the sole owner of the property.

(4) A transfer by an obligor or obligors into an inter vivos trust in which the obligor or obligors are beneficiaries.

(5) Such real property or any portion thereof is made subject to a junior encumbrance or lien.

(b) Any waiver of the provisions of this section by an obligor is void and unenforceable and is contrary to public policy.

(c) For the purposes of this section, "residential real property" means any real property which contains at least one but not more than four housing units.

(d) This act applies only to loans executed or refinanced on or after January 1, 1976. (Added by Stats.1975, c. 850, p. 1916, § 1.)

Cross References
Shared appreciation loan, exclusion of transfer under this section from "sale", see Civil Code § 1917.120.
Shared appreciation loan, transfers requiring payment of contingent deferred interest, exclusion of transfers under this section, see Civil Code § 1917.031.
Shared appreciation loan, validity of "due-on-sale" clause, see Civil Code § 1917.062.

§ 2924.7. Acceleration clause for nonpayment of taxes, rents, assessments, insurance premiums, advances; provision for payment of hazard insurance proceeds to beneficiary, trustee, mortgagee or agent; enforcement of clauses despite impairment of security interest

(a) The provisions of any deed of trust or mortgage on real property which authorize any beneficiary, trustee, mortgagee, or his or her agent or successor in interest, to accelerate the maturity date of the principal and interest on any loan secured thereby or to exercise any power of sale or other remedy contained therein upon the failure of the trustor or mortgagor to pay, at the times provided for under the terms of the deed of trust or mortgage, any taxes, rents, assessments, or insurance premiums with respect to the property or the loan, or any advances made by the beneficiary, mortgagee, or his or her agent or successor in interest shall be enforceable whether or not impairment of the security interest in the property has resulted from the failure of the trustor or mortgagor to pay the taxes, rents, assessments, insurance premiums, or advances.

(b) The provisions of any deed of trust or mortgage on real property which authorize any beneficiary, trustee, mortgagee, or his or her agent or successor in interest, to receive and control the disbursement of the proceeds of any policy of fire, flood, or other hazard insurance respecting the property shall be enforceable whether or not impairment of the security interest in the property has resulted from the event that caused the proceeds of the insurance policy to become payable. *(Added by Stats.1988, c. 179, § 2.)*

§ 2924.8. Required notice for residents of property subject to foreclosure sale

(a) Upon posting a notice of sale pursuant to Section 2924f, a trustee or authorized agent shall also post the following notice, in the manner required for posting the notice of sale on the property to be sold, and a mortgagee, trustee, beneficiary, or authorized agent, concurrently with the mailing of the notice of sale pursuant to Section 2924b, shall send by first-class mail in an envelope addressed to the "Resident of property subject to foreclosure sale" the following notice in English and the languages described in Section 1632:

Foreclosure process has begun on this property, which may affect your right to continue to live in this property. Twenty days or more after the date of this notice, this property may be sold at foreclosure. If you are renting this property, the new property owner may either give you a new lease or rental agreement or provide you with a 90–day eviction notice. You may have a right to stay in your home for longer than 90 days. If you have a fixed-term lease, the new owner must honor the lease unless the new owner will occupy the property as a primary residence or in other limited circumstances. Also, in some cases and in some cities with a "just cause for eviction" law, you may not have to move at all. All rights and obligations under your lease or tenancy, including your obligation to pay rent, will continue after the foreclosure sale. You may wish to contact a lawyer or your local legal aid office or housing counseling agency to discuss any rights you may have.

(b) It is an infraction to tear down the notice described in subdivision (a) within 72 hours of posting. Violators shall be subject to a fine of one hundred dollars ($100).

(c) The Department of * * * <u>Financial Protection and Innovation</u> and the Department of Real Estate shall make available translations of the notice described in subdivision (a) which may be used by a mortgagee, trustee, beneficiary, or authorized agent to satisfy the requirements of this section.

(d) This section shall only apply to loans secured by residential real property, and if the billing address for the mortgage note is different than the property address.

(e) This section shall become operative on March 1, 2021. *(Added by Stats.2020, c. 36 (A.B.3364), § 14, eff. Jan. 1, 2021, operative March 1, 2021. Amended by Stats.2022, c. 452 (S.B.1498), § 30, eff. Jan. 1, 2023.)*

§ 2924.85. Repealed by Stats.2012, c. 566 (S.B.1191), § 1, operative Jan. 1, 2018

§ 2924.9. Mortgage service providers offering one or more foreclosure prevention alternatives; sending of written communication to borrower

(a) Unless a borrower has previously exhausted the first lien loan modification process offered by, or through, his or her mortgage servicer described in Section 2923.6, within five business days after recording a notice of default pursuant to Section 2924, a mortgage servicer that offers one or more foreclosure prevention alternatives shall send a written communication to the borrower that includes all of the following information:

(1) That the borrower may be evaluated for a foreclosure prevention alternative or, if applicable, foreclosure prevention alternatives.

(2) Whether an application is required to be submitted by the borrower in order to be considered for a foreclosure prevention alternative.

(3) The means and process by which a borrower may obtain an application for a foreclosure prevention alternative.

(b) This section shall not apply to entities described in subdivision (b) of Section 2924.18.

(c) This section shall apply only to mortgages or deeds of trust described in Section 2924.15. *(Added by Stats.2018, c. 404 (S.B.818), § 12, eff. Jan. 1, 2019.)*

§ 2924.10. Submission of first lien modification application document; written acknowledgment of receipt

(a) When a borrower submits a complete first lien modification application or any document in connection with a first lien modification application, the mortgage servicer shall provide written acknowledgment of the receipt of the documentation within five business days of receipt. In its initial acknowledgment of receipt of the loan modification application, the mortgage servicer shall include the following information:

(1) A description of the loan modification process, including an estimate of when a decision on the loan modification will be made after a complete application has been submitted by the borrower and the length of time the borrower will have to consider an offer of a loan modification or other foreclosure prevention alternative.

(2) Any deadlines, including deadlines to submit missing documentation, that would affect the processing of a first lien loan modification application.

(3) Any expiration dates for submitted documents.

(4) Any deficiency in the borrower's first lien loan modification application.

(b) For purposes of this section, a borrower's first lien loan modification application shall be deemed to be "complete" when a borrower has supplied the mortgage servicer with all documents required by the mortgage servicer within the reasonable timeframes specified by the mortgage servicer.

(c) This section shall not apply to entities described in subdivision (b) of Section 2924.18.

§ 2924.10

(d) This section shall apply only to mortgages or deeds of trust described in Section 2924.15. *(Added by Stats.2018, c. 404 (S.B.818), § 13, eff. Jan. 1, 2019.)*

§ 2924.11. Approval of foreclosure prevention alternative in writing; circumstances prohibiting recordation of notice of default, recording of notice of sale, or conducting trustee's sale; copy of agreement; recording of rescission of notice of default or cancellation of pending trustee's sale; fees; transfer of loan

(a) If a foreclosure prevention alternative is approved in writing prior to the recordation of a notice of default, a mortgage servicer, mortgagee, trustee, beneficiary, or authorized agent shall not record a notice of default under either of the following circumstances:

(1) The borrower is in compliance with the terms of a written trial or permanent loan modification, forbearance, or repayment plan.

(2) A foreclosure prevention alternative has been approved in writing by all parties, including, for example, the first lien investor, junior lienholder, and mortgage insurer, as applicable, and proof of funds or financing has been provided to the servicer.

(b) If a foreclosure prevention alternative is approved in writing after the recordation of a notice of default, a mortgage servicer, mortgagee, trustee, beneficiary, or authorized agent shall not record a notice of sale or conduct a trustee's sale under either of the following circumstances:

(1) The borrower is in compliance with the terms of a written trial or permanent loan modification, forbearance, or repayment plan.

(2) A foreclosure prevention alternative has been approved in writing by all parties, including, for example, the first lien investor, junior lienholder, and mortgage insurer, as applicable, and proof of funds or financing has been provided to the servicer.

(c) When a borrower accepts an offered first lien loan modification or other foreclosure prevention alternative, the mortgage servicer shall provide the borrower with a copy of the fully executed loan modification agreement or agreement evidencing the foreclosure prevention alternative following receipt of the executed copy from the borrower.

(d) A mortgagee, beneficiary, or authorized agent shall record a rescission of a notice of default or cancel a pending trustee's sale, if applicable, upon the borrower executing a permanent foreclosure prevention alternative. In the case of a short sale, the cancellation of the pending trustee's sale shall occur when the short sale has been approved by all parties and proof of funds or financing has been provided to the mortgagee, beneficiary, or authorized agent.

(e) The mortgage servicer shall not charge any application, processing, or other fee for a first lien loan modification or other foreclosure prevention alternative.

(f) The mortgage servicer shall not collect any late fees for periods during which a complete first lien loan modification application is under consideration or a denial is being appealed, the borrower is making timely modification payments, or a foreclosure prevention alternative is being evaluated or exercised.

(g) If a borrower has been approved in writing for a first lien loan modification or other foreclosure prevention alternative, and the servicing of that borrower's loan is transferred or sold to another mortgage servicer, the subsequent mortgage servicer shall continue to honor any previously approved first lien loan modification or other foreclosure prevention alternative, in accordance with the provisions of the act that added this section.

(h) This section shall apply only to mortgages or deeds of trust described in Section 2924.15.

(i) This section shall not apply to entities described in subdivision (b) of Section 2924.18. *(Added by Stats.2018, c. 404 (S.B.818), § 16, eff. Jan. 1, 2019.)*

Cross References

Material violations of specified foreclosure provisions, action for injunctive relief by borrower prior to recording of trustee's deed upon sale, liability to borrower after recording of trustee's deed upon sale, effect of violation on validity of sale, third-party encumbrancer, signatory to specified consent judgment, attorney's fees and costs, see Civil Code § 2924.12.

§ 2924.12. Material violations of specified foreclosure provisions; action for injunctive relief by borrower prior to recording of trustee's deed upon sale; liability to borrower after recording of trustee's deed upon sale; effect of violation on validity of sale; third-party encumbrancer; attorney's fees and costs

(a)(1) If a trustee's deed upon sale has not been recorded, a borrower may bring an action for injunctive relief to enjoin a material violation of Section 2923.55, 2923.6, 2923.7, 2924.9, 2924.10, 2924.11, or 2924.17.

(2) Any injunction shall remain in place and any trustee's sale shall be enjoined until the court determines that the mortgage servicer, mortgagee, trustee, beneficiary, or authorized agent has corrected and remedied the violation or violations giving rise to the action for injunctive relief. An enjoined entity may move to dissolve an injunction based on a showing that the material violation has been corrected and remedied.

(b) After a trustee's deed upon sale has been recorded, a mortgage servicer, mortgagee, trustee, beneficiary, or authorized agent shall be liable to a borrower for actual economic damages pursuant to Section 3281, resulting from a material violation of Section 2923.55, 2923.6, 2923.7, 2924.9, 2924.10, 2924.11, or 2924.17 by that mortgage servicer, mortgagee, trustee, beneficiary, or authorized agent where the violation was not corrected and remedied prior to the recordation of the trustee's deed upon sale. If the court finds that the material violation was intentional or reckless, or resulted from willful misconduct by a mortgage servicer, mortgagee, trustee, beneficiary, or authorized agent, the court may award the borrower the greater of treble actual damages or statutory damages of fifty thousand dollars ($50,000).

(c) A mortgage servicer, mortgagee, trustee, beneficiary, or authorized agent shall not be liable for any violation that it has corrected and remedied prior to the recordation of the trustee's deed upon sale, or that has been corrected and remedied by third parties working on its behalf prior to the recordation of the trustee's deed upon sale.

(d) A violation of Section 2923.55, 2923.6, 2923.7, 2924.9, 2924.10, 2924.11, or 2924.17 by a person licensed by the Department of * * * Financial Protection and Innovation or the Department of Real Estate shall be deemed to be a violation of that person's licensing law.

(e) No violation of this article shall affect the validity of a sale in favor of a bona fide purchaser and any of its encumbrancers for value without notice.

(f) A third-party encumbrancer shall not be relieved of liability resulting from violations of Section 2923.55, 2923.6, 2923.7, 2924.9, 2924.10, 2924.11, or 2924.17 committed by that third-party encumbrancer, that occurred prior to the sale of the subject property to the bona fide purchaser.

(g) The rights, remedies, and procedures provided by this section are in addition to and independent of any other rights, remedies, or procedures under any other law. Nothing in this section shall be construed to alter, limit, or negate any other rights, remedies, or procedures provided by law.

(h) A court may award a prevailing borrower reasonable attorney's fees and costs in an action brought pursuant to this section. A borrower shall be deemed to have prevailed for purposes of this subdivision if the borrower obtained injunctive relief or was awarded damages pursuant to this section.

(i) This section shall not apply to entities described in subdivision (b) of Section 2924.18. *(Added by Stats.2012, c. 87 (S.B.900), § 17, operative Jan. 1, 2018. Amended by Stats.2014, c. 401 (A.B.2763), § 7, eff. Jan. 1, 2015, operative Jan. 1, 2018; Stats.2018, c. 404 (S.B.818), § 17, eff. Jan. 1, 2019; Stats.2022, c. 452 (S.B.1498), § 31, eff. Jan. 1, 2023.)*

Cross References

Material violations of specified foreclosure provisions, action for injunctive relief by borrower prior to recording of trustee's deed upon sale, liability to borrower after recording of trustee's deed upon sale, effect of violation on validity of sale, third-party encumbrancer, signatory to specified consent judgment, attorney's fees and costs, see Civil Code § 2924.12.

§ 2924.15. Application of specified provisions only to first lien mortgages or deeds of trust secured by residential real property containing no more than four dwelling units and meeting specified conditions

(a) Unless otherwise provided, paragraph (5) of subdivision (a) of Section 2924 and Sections 2923.5, 2923.55, 2923.6, 2923.7, 2924.9, 2924.10, 2924.11, and 2924.18 shall apply only to a first lien mortgage or deed of trust that meets either of the following conditions:

(1)(A) The first lien mortgage or deed of trust is secured by owner-occupied residential real property containing no more than four dwelling units.

(B) For purposes of this paragraph, "owner-occupied" means that the property is the principal residence of the borrower and is security for a loan made for personal, family, or household purposes.

(2) The first lien mortgage or deed of trust is secured by residential real property that is occupied by a tenant and that contains no more than four dwelling units and meets all of the conditions described in subparagraph (B) and one of the conditions described in subparagraph (C).

(A) For purposes of this paragraph:

(i) "Applicable lease" means a lease entered pursuant to an arm's length transaction before, and in effect on, March 4, 2020.

(ii) "Arm's length transaction" means a lease entered into in good faith and for valuable consideration that reflects the fair market value in the open market between informed and willing parties.

(iii) "Occupied by a tenant" means that the property is the principal residence of a tenant.

(B) To meet the conditions of this paragraph, a first lien mortgage or deed of trust shall have all of the following characteristics:

(i) The property is owned by an individual who owns no more than three residential real properties, each of which contains no more than four dwelling units.

(ii) The property shall have been occupied by a tenant pursuant to an applicable lease.

(iii) A tenant occupying the property shall have been unable to pay rent due to a reduction in income resulting from COVID–19.

(C) For a first lien mortgage or deed of trust to meet the conditions of this paragraph, the borrower shall satisfy either of the following characteristics:

(i) The borrower has been approved in writing for a first lien loan modification or other foreclosure prevention alternative before January 1, 2023.

(ii) The borrower submits a completed application for a first lien loan modification before January 1, 2023, and, as of January 1, 2023, either the mortgage servicer has not yet determined whether the applicant is eligible for a first lien loan modification, or the appeal period for the mortgage servicer's denial of the application has not yet expired.

(D) Relief shall be available pursuant to subdivision (a) of Section 2924 and Sections 2923.5, 2923.55, 2923.6, 2923.7, 2924.9, 2924.10, 2924.11, and 2924.18 for so long as the property remains occupied by a tenant pursuant to a lease entered into an arm's length transaction.

(b) This section shall become operative on January 1, 2023. *(Added by Stats.2020, c. 37 (A.B.3088), § 12, effective Aug. 31, 2020, operative Jan. 1, 2023. Amended by Stats.2021, c. 360 (A.B.1584), § 5, eff. Jan. 1, 2022, operative Jan. 1, 2023.)*

§ 2924.17. Requirement that specified declarations or affidavits be accurate and complete and supported by competent and reliable evidence; review by mortgage servicer; liability for multiple and repeated uncorrected recording or filing violations

(a) A declaration recorded pursuant to Section 2923.5 or pursuant to Section 2923.55, a notice of default, notice of sale, assignment of a deed of trust, or substitution of trustee recorded by or on behalf of a mortgage servicer in connection with a foreclosure subject to the requirements of Section 2924, or a declaration or affidavit filed in any court relative to a foreclosure proceeding shall be accurate and complete and supported by competent and reliable evidence.

(b) Before recording or filing any of the documents described in subdivision (a), a mortgage servicer shall ensure that it has reviewed competent and reliable evidence to substantiate the borrower's default and the right to foreclose, including the borrower's loan status and loan information.

(c) Any mortgage servicer that engages in multiple and repeated uncorrected violations of subdivision (b) in recording documents or filing documents in any court relative to a foreclosure proceeding shall be liable for a civil penalty of up to seven thousand five hundred dollars ($7,500) per mortgage or deed of trust in an action brought by a government entity identified in Section 17204 of the Business and Professions Code, or in an administrative proceeding brought by the Department of * * * Financial Protection and Innovation or the Department of Real Estate against a respective licensee, in addition to any other remedies available to these entities. *(Added by Stats.2012, c. 87 (S.B.900), § 20. Amended by Stats.2014, c. 401 (A.B.2763), § 9, eff. Jan. 1, 2015; Stats.2018, c. 404 (S.B.818), § 21, eff. Jan. 1, 2019; Stats.2022, c. 452 (S.B.1498), § 32, eff. Jan. 1, 2023.)*

Cross References

Material violations of specified foreclosure provisions, action for injunctive relief by borrower prior to recording of trustee's deed upon sale, liability to borrower after recording of trustee's deed upon sale, effect of violation on validity of sale, third-party encumbrancer, attorney's fees and costs, application to entities described in subdivision (b) of Section 2924.18, see Civil Code § 2924.19.

Material violations of specified foreclosure provisions, action for injunctive relief by borrower prior to recording of trustee's deed upon sale, liability to borrower after recording of trustee's deed upon sale, effect of violation on validity of sale, third-party encumbrancer, signatory to specified consent judgment, attorney's fees and costs, see Civil Code § 2924.12.

§ 2924.18. Submission of complete first lien loan modification application; prohibition on recording notice of default, notice of sale, or conducting trustee's sale while application is pending; approval of foreclosure prevention alternative in writing; circumstances prohibiting recordation of notice of default, recording of notice of sale, or conducting trustee's sale; application to specified entities meeting foreclosure threshold; notification to primary regulator when threshold is exceeded; transfer of loan

(a)(1) If a borrower submits a complete application for a first lien loan modification offered by, or through, the borrower's mortgage servicer at least five business days before a scheduled foreclosure sale, a mortgage servicer, trustee, mortgagee, beneficiary, or authorized agent shall not record a notice of default, notice of sale, or conduct a trustee's sale while the complete first lien loan modification application is pending, and until the borrower has been provided with a written determination by the mortgage servicer regarding that borrower's eligibility for the requested loan modification.

(2) If a foreclosure prevention alternative has been approved in writing prior to the recordation of a notice of

default, a mortgage servicer, mortgagee, trustee, beneficiary, or authorized agent shall not record a notice of default under either of the following circumstances:

(A) The borrower is in compliance with the terms of a written trial or permanent loan modification, forbearance, or repayment plan.

(B) A foreclosure prevention alternative has been approved in writing by all parties, including, for example, the first lien investor, junior lienholder, and mortgage insurer, as applicable, and proof of funds or financing has been provided to the servicer.

(3) If a foreclosure prevention alternative is approved in writing after the recordation of a notice of default, a mortgage servicer, mortgagee, trustee, beneficiary, or authorized agent shall not record a notice of sale or conduct a trustee's sale under either of the following circumstances:

(A) The borrower is in compliance with the terms of a written trial or permanent loan modification, forbearance, or repayment plan.

(B) A foreclosure prevention alternative has been approved in writing by all parties, including, for example, the first lien investor, junior lienholder, and mortgage insurer, as applicable, and proof of funds or financing has been provided to the servicer.

(b) This section shall apply only to a depository institution chartered under state or federal law, a person licensed pursuant to Division 9 (commencing with Section 22000) or Division 20 (commencing with Section 50000) of the Financial Code, or a person licensed pursuant to Part 1 (commencing with Section 10000) of Division 4 of the Business and Professions Code, that, during its immediately preceding annual reporting period, as established with its primary regulator, foreclosed on 175 or fewer residential real properties, containing no more than four dwelling units, that are located in California.

(c) Within three months after the close of any calendar year or annual reporting period as established with its primary regulator during which an entity or person described in subdivision (b) exceeds the threshold of 175 specified in subdivision (b), that entity shall notify its primary regulator, in a manner acceptable to its primary regulator, and any mortgagor or trustor who is delinquent on a residential mortgage loan serviced by that entity of the date on which that entity will be subject to Sections 2923.55, 2923.6, 2923.7, 2924.9, 2924.10, 2924.11, and 2924.12, which date shall be the first day of the first month that is six months after the close of the calendar year or annual reporting period during which that entity exceeded the threshold.

(d) For purposes of this section, an application shall be deemed "complete" when a borrower has supplied the mortgage servicer with all documents required by the mortgage servicer within the reasonable timeframes specified by the mortgage servicer.

(e) If a borrower has been approved in writing for a first lien loan modification or other foreclosure prevention alternative, and the servicing of the borrower's loan is transferred or sold to another mortgage servicer, the subsequent mortgage servicer shall continue to honor any previously approved first lien loan modification or other foreclosure prevention alternative, in accordance with the provisions of the act that added this section.

(f) This section shall apply only to mortgages or deeds of trust described in Section 2924.15. *(Added by Stats.2018, c. 404 (S.B.818), § 23, eff. Jan. 1, 2019.)*

§ 2924.19. Material violations of specified foreclosure provisions; action for injunctive relief by borrower prior to recording of trustee's deed upon sale; liability to borrower after recording of trustee's deed upon sale; effect of violation on validity of sale; third-party encumbrancer; attorney's fees and costs; application to entities described in subdivision (b) of Section 2924.18

(a)(1) If a trustee's deed upon sale has not been recorded, a borrower may bring an action for injunctive relief to enjoin a material violation of Section 2923.5, 2924.17, or 2924.18.

(2) An injunction shall remain in place and any trustee's sale shall be enjoined until the court determines that the mortgage servicer, mortgagee, beneficiary, or authorized agent has corrected and remedied the violation or violations giving rise to the action for injunctive relief. An enjoined entity may move to dissolve an injunction based on a showing that the material violation has been corrected and remedied.

(b) After a trustee's deed upon sale has been recorded, a mortgage servicer, mortgagee, beneficiary, or authorized agent shall be liable to a borrower for actual economic damages pursuant to Section 3281, resulting from a material violation of Section 2923.5, 2924.17, or 2924.18 by that mortgage servicer, mortgagee, beneficiary, or authorized agent where the violation was not corrected and remedied prior to the recordation of the trustee's deed upon sale. If the court finds that the material violation was intentional or reckless, or resulted from willful misconduct by a mortgage servicer, mortgagee, beneficiary, or authorized agent, the court may award the borrower the greater of treble actual damages or statutory damages of fifty thousand dollars ($50,000).

(c) A mortgage servicer, mortgagee, beneficiary, or authorized agent shall not be liable for any violation that it has corrected and remedied prior to the recordation of the trustee's deed upon sale, or that has been corrected and remedied by third parties working on its behalf prior to the recordation of the trustee's deed upon sale.

(d) A violation of Section 2923.5, 2924.17, or 2924.18 by a person licensed by the Department of * * * <u>Financial Protection and Innovation</u> or the Department of Real Estate shall be deemed to be a violation of that person's licensing law.

(e) A violation of this article shall not affect the validity of a sale in favor of a bona fide purchaser and any of its encumbrancers for value without notice.

(f) A third-party encumbrancer shall not be relieved of liability resulting from violations of Section 2923.5, 2924.17, or 2924.18, committed by that third-party encumbrancer, that occurred prior to the sale of the subject property to the bona fide purchaser.

(g) The rights, remedies, and procedures provided by this section are in addition to and independent of any other rights, remedies, or procedures under any other law. Noth-

§ 2924.19

ing in this section shall be construed to alter, limit, or negate any other rights, remedies, or procedures provided by law.

(h) A court may award a prevailing borrower reasonable attorney's fees and costs in an action brought pursuant to this section. A borrower shall be deemed to have prevailed for purposes of this subdivision if the borrower obtained injunctive relief or damages pursuant to this section.

(i) This section shall apply only to entities described in subdivision (b) of Section 2924.18. *(Added by Stats.2018, c. 404 (S.B.818), § 24, eff. Jan. 1, 2019. Amended by Stats.2022, c. 452 (S.B.1498), § 33, eff. Jan. 1, 2023.)*

§ 2924.20. Regulations; adoption by Department of Financial Protection and Innovation and the Bureau of Real Estate; enforcement

Consistent with their general regulatory authority, and notwithstanding subdivisions (b) and (c) of Section 2924.18, the Department of * * * <u>Financial Protection and Innovation</u> and the Bureau of Real Estate may adopt regulations applicable to any entity or person under their respective jurisdictions that are necessary to carry out the purposes of the act that added this section. A violation of the regulations adopted pursuant to this section shall only be enforceable by the regulatory agency. *(Added by Stats.2012, c. 87 (S.B.900), § 23. Amended by Stats.2014, c. 401 (A.B.2763), § 13, eff. Jan. 1, 2015; Stats.2022, c. 452 (S.B.1498), § 34, eff. Jan. 1, 2023.)*

§ 2924.25. Repealed by Stats.2013, c. 251 (S.B.310), § 1, operative Jan. 1, 2018

§ 2924.26. Licensed title company or underwritten title company; violation of Section 2923.5 or 2924.11; exemption

(a) Unless acting in the capacity of a trustee, a licensed title company or underwritten title company shall not be liable for a violation of Section 2923.5 or 2924.11 if it records or causes to record a notice of default or notice of sale at the request of a trustee, substitute trustee, or beneficiary, in good faith and in the normal course of its business activities.

(b) This section shall become operative on January 1, 2018. *(Added by Stats.2013, c. 251 (S.B.310), § 2, operative Jan. 1, 2018.)*

§ 2924a. Attorney's and authorized agent's authority to conduct trustee's sale

If, by the terms of any trust or deed of trust a power of sale is conferred upon the trustee, the attorney for the trustee, or any duly authorized agent, may conduct the sale and act in the sale as the auctioneer for the trustee. *(Added by Stats.1929, c. 610, p. 1019, § 1. Amended by Stats.2006, c. 575 (A.B.2624), § 5.)*

Cross References

Mortgage foreclosure actions, see Code of Civil Procedure § 726 et seq.

§ 2924b. Notices of default and of sale; mailing upon request for copies and to certain interested persons

(a) Any person desiring a copy of any notice of default and of any notice of sale under any deed of trust or mortgage with power of sale upon real property or an estate for years therein, as to which deed of trust or mortgage the power of sale cannot be exercised until these notices are given for the time and in the manner provided in Section 2924 may, at any time subsequent to recordation of the deed of trust or mortgage and prior to recordation of notice of default thereunder, cause to be filed for record in the office of the recorder of any county in which any part or parcel of the real property is situated, a duly acknowledged request for a copy of the notice of default and of sale. This request shall be signed and acknowledged by the person making the request, specifying the name and address of the person to whom the notice is to be mailed, shall identify the deed of trust or mortgage by stating the names of the parties thereto, the date of recordation thereof, and the book and page where the deed of trust or mortgage is recorded or the recorder's number, and shall be in substantially the following form:

"In accordance with Section 2924b, Civil Code, request is hereby made that a copy of any notice of default and a copy of any notice of sale under the deed of trust (or mortgage) recorded _____, _____, in Book _____ page _____ records of _____ County, (or filed for record with recorder's serial number _____, _____ County) California, executed by _____ as trustor (or mortgagor) in which _____ is named as beneficiary (or mortgagee) and _____ as trustee be mailed to

_____ at _____.
       Name   Address

NOTICE: A copy of any notice of default and of any notice of sale will be sent only to the address contained in this recorded request. If your address changes, a new request must be recorded.

Signature _____"

Upon the filing for record of the request, the recorder shall index in the general index of grantors the names of the trustors (or mortgagors) recited therein and the names of persons requesting copies.

(b) The mortgagee, trustee, or other person authorized to record the notice of default or the notice of sale shall do each of the following:

(1) Within 10 business days following recordation of the notice of default, deposit or cause to be deposited in the United States mail an envelope, sent by registered or certified mail with postage prepaid, containing a copy of the notice with the recording date shown thereon, addressed to each person whose name and address are set forth in a duly recorded request therefor, directed to the address designated in the request and to each trustor or mortgagor at his or her last known address if different than the address specified in the deed of trust or mortgage with power of sale.

(2) At least 20 days before the date of sale, deposit or cause to be deposited in the United States mail an envelope, sent by registered or certified mail with postage prepaid, containing a copy of the notice of the time and place of sale, addressed to each person whose name and address are set forth in a duly recorded request therefor, directed to the address designated in the request and to each trustor or mortgagor at his or her last known address if different than the address specified in the deed of trust or mortgage with power of sale.

(3) As used in paragraphs (1) and (2), the "last known address" of each trustor or mortgagor means the last business or residence physical address actually known by the mortgagee, beneficiary, trustee, or other person authorized to record the notice of default. For the purposes of this subdivision, an address is "actually known" if it is contained in the original deed of trust or mortgage, or in any subsequent written notification of a change of physical address from the trustor or mortgagor pursuant to the deed of trust or mortgage. For the purposes of this subdivision, "physical address" does not include an email or any form of electronic address for a trustor or mortgagor. The beneficiary shall inform the trustee of the trustor's last address actually known by the beneficiary. However, the trustee shall incur no liability for failing to send any notice to the last address unless the trustee has actual knowledge of it.

(4) A "person authorized to record the notice of default or the notice of sale" shall include an agent for the mortgagee or beneficiary, an agent of the named trustee, any person designated in an executed substitution of trustee, or an agent of that substituted trustee.

(c) The mortgagee, trustee, or other person authorized to record the notice of default or the notice of sale shall do the following:

(1) Within one month following recordation of the notice of default, deposit or cause to be deposited in the United States mail an envelope, sent by registered or certified mail with postage prepaid, containing a copy of the notice with the recording date shown thereon, addressed to each person set forth in paragraph (2), provided that the estate or interest of any person entitled to receive notice under this subdivision is acquired by an instrument sufficient to impart constructive notice of the estate or interest in the land or portion thereof that is subject to the deed of trust or mortgage being foreclosed, and provided the instrument is recorded in the office of the county recorder so as to impart that constructive notice prior to the recording date of the notice of default and provided the instrument as so recorded sets forth a mailing address that the county recorder shall use, as instructed within the instrument, for the return of the instrument after recording, and which address shall be the address used for the purposes of mailing notices herein.

(2) The persons to whom notice shall be mailed under this subdivision are:

(A) The successor in interest, as of the recording date of the notice of default, of the estate or interest or any portion thereof of the trustor or mortgagor of the deed of trust or mortgage being foreclosed.

(B) The beneficiary or mortgagee of any deed of trust or mortgage recorded subsequent to the deed of trust or mortgage being foreclosed, or recorded prior to or concurrently with the deed of trust or mortgage being foreclosed but subject to a recorded agreement or a recorded statement of subordination to the deed of trust or mortgage being foreclosed.

(C) The assignee of any interest of the beneficiary or mortgagee described in subparagraph (B), as of the recording date of the notice of default.

(D) The vendee of any contract of sale, or the lessee of any lease, of the estate or interest being foreclosed that is recorded subsequent to the deed of trust or mortgage being foreclosed, or recorded prior to or concurrently with the deed of trust or mortgage being foreclosed but subject to a recorded agreement or statement of subordination to the deed of trust or mortgage being foreclosed.

(E) The successor in interest to the vendee or lessee described in subparagraph (D), as of the recording date of the notice of default.

(F) The office of the Controller, Sacramento, California, where, as of the recording date of the notice of default, a "Notice of Lien for Postponed Property Taxes" has been recorded against the real property to which the notice of default applies.

(3) At least 20 days before the date of sale, deposit or cause to be deposited in the United States mail an envelope, sent by registered or certified mail with postage prepaid, containing a copy of the notice of the time and place of sale addressed to each person to whom a copy of the notice of default is to be mailed as provided in paragraphs (1) and (2), and addressed to the office of any state taxing agency, Sacramento, California, that has recorded, subsequent to the deed of trust or mortgage being foreclosed, a notice of tax lien prior to the recording date of the notice of default against the real property to which the notice of default applies.

(4) Provide a copy of the notice of sale to the Internal Revenue Service, in accordance with Section 7425 of the Internal Revenue Code [1] and any applicable federal regulation, if a "Notice of Federal Tax Lien under Internal Revenue Laws" has been recorded, subsequent to the deed of trust or mortgage being foreclosed, against the real property to which the notice of sale applies. The failure to provide the Internal Revenue Service with a copy of the notice of sale pursuant to this paragraph shall be sufficient cause to rescind the trustee's sale and invalidate the trustee's deed, at the option of either the successful bidder at the trustee's sale or the trustee, and in either case with the consent of the beneficiary. Any option to rescind the trustee's sale pursuant to this paragraph shall be exercised prior to any transfer of the property by the successful bidder to a bona fide purchaser for value. A rescission of the trustee's sale pursuant to this paragraph may be recorded in a notice of rescission pursuant to Section 1058.5.

(5) The mailing of notices in the manner set forth in paragraph (1) shall not impose upon any licensed attorney, agent, or employee of any person entitled to receive notices as herein set forth any duty to communicate the notice to the entitled person from the fact that the mailing address used by the county recorder is the address of the attorney, agent, or employee.

(d) Any deed of trust or mortgage with power of sale hereafter executed upon real property or an estate for years therein may contain a request that a copy of any notice of default and a copy of any notice of sale thereunder shall be mailed to any person or party thereto at the address of the person given therein, and a copy of any notice of default and of any notice of sale shall be mailed to each of these at the same time and in the same manner required as though a separate request therefor had been filed by each of these persons as herein authorized. If any deed of trust or mortgage with power of sale executed after September 19, 1939, except a deed of trust or mortgage of any of the classes excepted from the provisions of Section 2924, does not contain a mailing address of the trustor or mortgagor therein named, and if no request for special notice by the trustor or mortgagor in substantially the form set forth in this section has subsequently been recorded, a copy of the notice of default shall be published once a week for at least four weeks in a newspaper of general circulation in the county in which the property is situated, the publication to commence within 10 business days after the filing of the notice of default. In lieu of publication, a copy of the notice of default may be delivered personally to the trustor or mortgagor within the 10 business days or at any time before publication is completed, or by posting the notice of default in a conspicuous place on the property and mailing the notice to the last known address of the trustor or mortgagor.

(e) Any person required to mail a copy of a notice of default or notice of sale to each trustor or mortgagor pursuant to subdivision (b) or (c) by registered or certified mail shall simultaneously cause to be deposited in the United States mail, with postage prepaid and mailed by first-class mail, an envelope containing an additional copy of the required notice addressed to each trustor or mortgagor at the same address to which the notice is sent by registered or certified mail pursuant to subdivision (b) or (c). The person shall execute and retain an affidavit identifying the notice mailed, showing the name and residence or business address of that person, that he or she is over 18 years of age, the date of deposit in the mail, the name and address of the trustor or mortgagor to whom sent, and that the envelope was sealed and deposited in the mail with postage fully prepaid. In the absence of fraud, the affidavit required by this subdivision shall establish a conclusive presumption of mailing.

(f)(1) Notwithstanding subdivision (a), with respect to separate interests governed by an association, as defined in Section 4080 or 6528, the association may cause to be filed in the office of the recorder in the county in which the separate interests are situated a request that a mortgagee, trustee, or other person authorized to record a notice of default regarding any of those separate interests mail to the association a copy of any trustee's deed upon sale concerning a separate interest. The request shall include a legal description or the assessor's parcel number of all the separate interests. A request recorded pursuant to this subdivision shall include the name and address of the association and a statement that it is an association as defined in Section 4080 or 6528. Subsequent requests of an association shall supersede prior requests. A request pursuant to this subdivision shall be recorded before the filing of a notice of default. The mortgagee, trustee, or other authorized person shall mail the requested information to the association within 15 business days following the date of the trustee's sale. Failure to mail the request, pursuant to this subdivision, shall not affect the title to real property.

(2) A request filed pursuant to paragraph (1) does not, for purposes of Section 27288.1 of the Government Code, constitute a document that either effects or evidences a transfer or encumbrance of an interest in real property or that releases or terminates any interest, right, or encumbrance of an interest in real property.

(g) No request for a copy of any notice filed for record pursuant to this section, no statement or allegation in the request, and no record thereof shall affect the title to real property or be deemed notice to any person that any person requesting copies of notice has or claims any right, title, or interest in, or lien or charge upon the property described in the deed of trust or mortgage referred to therein.

(h) "Business day," as used in this section, has the meaning specified in Section 9. *(Added by Stats.1933, c. 642, p. 1670, § 2. Re-enacted by Stats.1935, c. 650, p. 1803, § 2. Amended by Stats.1939, c. 983, p. 2737, § 2; Stats.1951, c. 417, p. 1392, § 2; Stats.1957, c. 1865, p. 3269, § 11; Stats.1959, c. 425, p. 2362, § 1; Stats.1959, c. 1890, p. 4456, § 2; Stats.1961, c. 2218, p. 4567, § 1; Stats.1976, c. 1149, p. 5206, § 1, operative July 1, 1977; Stats.1977, c. 1242, p. 4187, § 2, eff. Oct. 1, 1977; Stats.1978, c. 43, p. 127, § 1, eff. March 16, 1978; Stats.1979, c. 1015, p. 3464, § 1; Stats.1980, c. 925, p. 2933, § 1, eff. Aug. 18, 1980; Stats.1985, c. 154, § 1; Stats.1985, c. 1206, § 1; Stats.1986, c. 1361, § 3; Stats.1986, c. 1385, § 2.5; Stats.1989, c. 698, § 5; Stats.1992, c. 351 (A.B.2981), § 1; Stats.1993, c. 686 (A.B.1219), § 3; Stats.2001, c. 438 (S.B. 958), § 2, eff. Oct. 2, 2001; Stats.2002, c. 809 (S.B.1504), § 1; Stats.2004, c. 177 (S.B.1277), § 1; Stats.2005, c. 224 (A.B. 885), § 1; Stats.2008, c. 527 (S.B.1511), § 1; Stats.2010, c. 133 (A.B.2016), § 1; Stats.2012, c. 181 (A.B.806), § 39, operative Jan. 1, 2014; Stats.2012, c. 255 (A.B.2273), § 2; Stats.2013, c. 183 (S.B.745), § 6; Stats.2013, c. 605 (S.B.752), § 17.)*

[1] Internal Revenue Code sections are in Title 26 of the U.S.C.A.

Cross References

Address of trustor or mortgagor of deed of trust or mortgage with power of sale upon real property, as requirement for recordation, see Government Code § 27321.5.

Commercial and industrial common interest developments, monetary charge for repair of damage to common area and facilities, monetary penalties, see Civil Code § 6824.

Commercial and industrial common interest developments, trustee sale, procedure, see Civil Code § 6822.

Common interest developments, monetary charge for repair of damage to common area and facilities, monetary penalties, see Civil Code § 5725.

Common interest developments, trustee sale, procedure, see Civil Code § 5710.

Liens and mortgages, substitution of trustee, mailing and recording, see Civil Code § 2934a.

Mortgage foreclosure actions, see Code of Civil Procedure § 726 et seq.

Property taxation, sale to private parties after deed to state, power to sell and sale of part of parcel, see Revenue and Taxation Code § 3691.

Waiver of rights or privileges conferred by this section upon borrower, validity, see Civil Code § 2953.

§ 2924c. Cure of default; payment of arrearages, costs and fees; effect on acceleration; notice of default; trustee's or attorney's fees; reinstatement period

(a)(1) Whenever all or a portion of the principal sum of any obligation secured by deed of trust or mortgage on real property or an estate for years therein hereafter executed has, prior to the maturity date fixed in that obligation, become due or been declared due by reason of default in payment of interest or of any installment of principal, or by reason of failure of trustor or mortgagor to pay, in accordance with the terms of that obligation or of the deed of trust or mortgage, taxes, assessments, premiums for insurance, or advances made by beneficiary or mortgagee in accordance with the terms of that obligation or of the deed of trust or mortgage, the trustor or mortgagor or * * * their successor in interest in the mortgaged or trust property or any part thereof, or any beneficiary under a subordinate deed of trust or any other person having a subordinate lien or encumbrance of record thereon, at any time within the period specified in subdivision (e), if the power of sale therein is to be exercised, or, otherwise at any time prior to entry of the decree of foreclosure, may pay to the beneficiary or the mortgagee or their successors in interest, respectively, the entire amount due, at the time payment is tendered, with respect to (A) all amounts of principal, interest, taxes, assessments, insurance premiums, or advances actually known by the beneficiary to be, and that are, in default and shown in the notice of default, under the terms of the deed of trust or mortgage and the obligation secured thereby, (B) all amounts in default on recurring obligations not shown in the notice of default, and (C) all reasonable costs and expenses, subject to subdivision (c), that are actually incurred in enforcing the terms of the obligation, deed of trust, or mortgage, and trustee's or attorney's fees, subject to subdivision (d), other than the portion of principal as would not then be due had no default occurred, and thereby cure the default theretofore existing, and thereupon, all proceedings theretofore had or instituted shall be dismissed or discontinued and the obligation and deed of trust or mortgage shall be reinstated and shall be and remain in force and effect, the same as if the acceleration had not occurred. This section does not apply to bonds or other evidences of indebtedness authorized or permitted to be issued by the Department of * * * Financial Protection and Innovation or made by a public utility subject to the Public Utilities Code. For the purposes of this subdivision, the term "recurring obligation" means all amounts of principal and interest on the loan, or rents, subject to the deed of trust or mortgage in default due after the notice of default is recorded; all amounts of principal and interest or rents advanced on senior liens or leaseholds that are advanced after the recordation of the notice of default; and payments of taxes, assessments, and hazard insurance advanced after recordation of the notice of default. If the beneficiary or mortgagee has made no advances on defaults that would constitute recurring obligations, the beneficiary or mortgagee may require the trustor or mortgagor to provide reliable written evidence that the amounts have been paid prior to reinstatement.

(2) If the trustor, mortgagor, or other person authorized to cure the default pursuant to this subdivision does cure the default, the beneficiary or mortgagee or the agent for the beneficiary or mortgagee shall, within 21 days following the reinstatement, execute and deliver to the trustee a notice of rescission that rescinds the declaration of default and demand for sale and advises the trustee of the date of reinstatement. The trustee shall cause the notice of rescission to be recorded within 30 days of receipt of the notice of rescission and of all allowable fees and costs.

No charge, except for the recording fee, shall be made against the trustor or mortgagor for the execution and recordation of the notice which rescinds the declaration of default and demand for sale.

(b)(1) The notice, of any default described in this section, recorded pursuant to Section 2924, and mailed to any person pursuant to Section 2924b, shall begin with the following statement, printed or typed thereon:

"IMPORTANT NOTICE [14–point boldface type if printed or in capital letters if typed]

IF YOUR PROPERTY IS IN FORECLOSURE BECAUSE YOU ARE BEHIND IN YOUR PAYMENTS, IT MAY BE SOLD WITHOUT ANY COURT ACTION, [14–point boldface type if printed or in capital letters if typed] and you may have the legal right to bring your account in good standing by paying all of your past due payments plus permitted costs and expenses within the time permitted by law for reinstatement of your account, which is normally five business days prior to the date set for the sale of your property. No sale date may be set until approximately 90 days from the date this notice of default may be recorded (which date of recordation appears on this notice).

This amount is _____ as of _____
(Date)

and will increase until your account becomes current.

While your property is in foreclosure, you still must pay other obligations (such as insurance and taxes) required by your note and deed of trust or mortgage. If you fail to make future payments on the loan, pay taxes on the property, provide insurance on the property, or pay other obligations as required in the note and deed of trust or mortgage, the beneficiary or mortgagee may insist that you do so in order to reinstate your account in good standing. In addition, the beneficiary or mortgagee may require as a condition to reinstatement that you provide reliable written evidence that you paid all senior liens, property taxes, and hazard insurance premiums.

Upon your written request, the beneficiary or mortgagee will give you a written itemization of the entire amount you must pay. You may not have to pay the entire unpaid portion of your account, even though full payment was demanded, but you must pay all amounts in default at the time payment is made. However, you and your beneficiary or mortgagee may mutually agree in writing prior to the time the notice of sale is posted (which may not be earlier than three months after this notice of default is recorded) to, among other things, (1) provide additional time in which to cure the default by transfer of the property or otherwise; or (2) establish a schedule of payments in order to cure your default; or both (1) and (2).

Following the expiration of the time period referred to in the first paragraph of this notice, unless the obligation being foreclosed upon or a separate written agreement between you and your creditor permits a longer period, you have only the legal right to stop the sale of your property by paying the entire amount demanded by your creditor.

To find out the amount you must pay, or to arrange for payment to stop the foreclosure, or if your property is in foreclosure for any other reason, contact:

_____
(Name of beneficiary or mortgagee)

_____
(Mailing address)

_____
(Telephone)

If you have any questions, you should contact a lawyer or the governmental agency that may have insured your loan.

Notwithstanding the fact that your property is in foreclosure, you may offer your property for sale, provided the sale is concluded prior to the conclusion of the foreclosure.

Remember, YOU MAY LOSE LEGAL RIGHTS IF YOU DO NOT TAKE PROMPT ACTION. [14–point boldface type if printed or in capital letters if typed]"

Unless otherwise specified, the notice, if printed, shall appear in at least 12–point boldface type.

If the obligation secured by the deed of trust or mortgage is a contract or agreement described in paragraph (1) or (4) of subdivision (a) of Section 1632, the notice required herein shall be in Spanish if the trustor requested a Spanish language translation of the contract or agreement pursuant to Section 1632. If the obligation secured by the deed of trust or mortgage is contained in a home improvement contract, as defined in Sections 7151.2 and 7159 of the Business and Professions Code, which is subject to Title 2 (commencing with Section 1801), the seller shall specify on the contract whether or not the contract was principally negotiated in Spanish and if the contract was principally negotiated in Spanish, the notice required herein shall be in Spanish. No assignee of the contract or person authorized to record the notice of default shall incur any obligation or liability for failing to mail a notice in Spanish unless Spanish is specified in the contract or the assignee or person has actual knowledge that the secured obligation was principally negotiated in Spanish. Unless specified in writing to the contrary, a copy of the notice required by subdivision (c) of Section 2924b shall be in English.

(2) Any failure to comply with the provisions of this subdivision shall not affect the validity of a sale in favor of a bona fide purchaser or the rights of an encumbrancer for value and without notice.

(c) Costs and expenses that may be charged pursuant to Sections 2924 to 2924i, inclusive, shall be limited to the costs incurred for recording, mailing, including certified and express mail charges, publishing, and posting notices required by Sections 2924 to 2924i, inclusive, postponement pursuant to Section 2924g not to exceed fifty dollars ($50) per postponement and a fee for a trustee's sale guarantee or, in the event of judicial foreclosure, a litigation guarantee. For purposes of this subdivision, a trustee or beneficiary may purchase a trustee's sale guarantee at a rate meeting the standards contained in Sections 12401.1 and 12401.3 of the Insurance Code.

(d)(1) Trustee's or attorney's fees that may be charged pursuant to subdivision (a), or until the notice of sale is deposited in the mail to the trustor as provided in Section 2924b, if the sale is by power of sale contained in the deed of trust or mortgage, or, otherwise at any time prior to the decree of foreclosure, are hereby authorized to be in an amount as follows:

(A) If the unpaid principal sum secured is fifty thousand dollars ($50,000) or less, then in a base amount that does not exceed three hundred fifty dollars ($350).

(B) If the unpaid principal sum secured is greater than fifty thousand dollars ($50,000) but does not exceed one hundred fifty thousand dollars ($150,000), then in a base amount that does not exceed three hundred fifty dollars ($350) plus one-half of 1 percent of the unpaid principal sum secured exceeding fifty thousand dollars ($50,000).

(C) If the unpaid principal sum secured is greater than one hundred fifty thousand dollars ($150,000) but does not exceed five hundred thousand dollars ($500,000), then in a base amount that does not exceed three hundred dollars ($300) plus one-half of 1 percent of the unpaid principal sum secured exceeding fifty thousand dollars ($50,000) up to and including one hundred fifty thousand dollars ($150,000) plus one-quarter of 1 percent of any portion of the unpaid principal sum secured exceeding one hundred fifty thousand dollars ($150,000).

(D) If the unpaid principal sum secured is greater than five hundred thousand dollars ($500,000), then in a base amount that does not exceed three hundred dollars ($300) plus one-half of 1 percent of the unpaid principal sum secured exceeding fifty thousand dollars ($50,000) up to and including one hundred fifty thousand dollars ($150,000) plus one-quarter of 1 percent of any portion of the unpaid principal sum secured exceeding one hundred fifty thousand dollars ($150,000) up to and including five hundred thousand dollars ($500,000) plus one-eighth of 1 percent of any portion of the unpaid principal sum secured exceeding five hundred thousand dollars ($500,000).

(2) Any charge for trustee's or attorney's fees authorized by this subdivision shall be conclusively presumed to be lawful and valid where the charge does not exceed the amounts authorized in this subdivision. For purposes of this subdivision, the unpaid principal sum secured shall be determined as of the date the notice of default is recorded.

(e) Reinstatement of a monetary default under the terms of an obligation secured by a deed of trust, or mortgage may be made at any time within the period commencing with the date of recordation of the notice of default until five business days prior to the date of sale set forth in the initial recorded notice of sale.

In the event the sale does not take place on the date set forth in the initial recorded notice of sale or a subsequent recorded notice of sale is required to be given, the right of reinstatement shall be revived as of the date of recordation of the subsequent notice of sale, and shall continue from that date until five business days prior to the date of sale set forth in the subsequently recorded notice of sale.

In the event the date of sale is postponed on the date of sale set forth in either an initial or any subsequent notice of sale, or is postponed on the date declared for sale at an immediately preceding postponement of sale, and, the postponement is for a period that exceeds five business days from the date set forth in the notice of sale, or declared at the time of postponement, then the right of reinstatement is revived as of the date of postponement and shall continue from that date until five business days prior to the date of sale declared at the time of the postponement.

Nothing contained herein shall give rise to a right of reinstatement during the period of five business days prior to the date of sale, whether the date of sale is noticed in a notice of sale or declared at a postponement of sale.

Pursuant to the terms of this subdivision, no beneficiary, trustee, mortgagee, or their agents or successors shall be liable in any manner to a trustor, mortgagor, their agents or successors or any beneficiary under a subordinate deed of trust or mortgage or any other person having a subordinate lien or encumbrance of record thereon for the failure to allow a reinstatement of the obligation secured by a deed of trust or mortgage during the period of five business days prior to the sale of the security property, and no such right of reinstatement during this period is created by this section. Any right of reinstatement created by this section is terminated five business days prior to the date of sale set forth in the initial date of sale, and is revived only as prescribed herein and only as of the date set forth herein.

As used in this subdivision, the term "business day" has the same meaning as specified in Section 9. *(Added by Stats. 1933, c. 642, p. 1671, § 3. Re-enacted by Stats.1935, c. 650, p. 1807, § 3. Amended by Stats.1949, c. 1437, p. 2501, § 1; Stats.1951, c. 417, p. 1392, § 1; Stats.1957, c. 40, p. 599, § 1; Stats.1957, c. 362, p. 1176, § 1; Stats.1973, c. 817, § 2, operative July 1, 1974; Stats.1974, c. 308, § 1, eff. May 31, 1974, operative July 1, 1974; Stats.1979, c. 655, p. 2019, § 4, eff. Sept. 14, 1979, operative Jan. 1, 1980; Stats.1979, c. 1015, p. 3468, § 2; Stats.1980, c. 423, p. 839, § 12, eff. July 11, 1980; Stats.1980, c. 1380, p. 5017, § 18.5, eff. Oct. 1, 1980, operative Jan. 1, 1981; Stats.1981, c. 427, p. 1657, § 2; Stats.1983, c. 112, § 1; Stats.1983, c. 1217, § 1; Stats.1984, c. 919, § 1, operative July 1, 1985; Stats.1984, c. 1730, § 1; Stats.1984, c. 1730, § 1.5, operative July 1, 1985; Stats.1985, c. 1206, § 2; Stats.1986, c. 1385, § 3; Stats.1989, c. 698, § 6; Stats.1990, c. 657 (S.B.2339), § 2; Stats.1992, c. 351 (A.B.2981), § 2; Stats.1993, c. 686 (A.B.1219), § 4; Stats.1996, c. 483 (S.B. 1488), § 2; Stats.1997, c. 74 (S.B.665), § 2; Stats.1998, c. 485 (A.B.2803), § 39; Stats.1998, c. 932 (A.B.1094), § 8; Stats. 1999, c. 974 (A.B.431), § 9; Stats.2000, c. 135 (A.B.2539), § 13; Stats.2001, c. 438 (S.B.958), § 3, eff. Oct. 2, 2001, operative Jan. 1, 2002; Stats.2010, c. 180 (S.B.1221), § 3; Stats.2016, c. 170 (S.B.983), § 3, eff. Jan. 1, 2017; Stats.2017, c. 217 (S.B.479), § 1, eff. Jan. 1, 2018; Stats.2022, c. 452 (S.B.1498), § 35, eff. Jan. 1, 2023.)*

Cross References

Commercial and industrial common interest developments, monetary charge for repair of damage to common area and facilities, monetary penalties, see Civil Code § 6824.

Commercial and industrial common interest developments, trustee sale, procedure, see Civil Code § 6822.

Common interest developments, monetary charge for repair of damage to common area and facilities, monetary penalties, see Civil Code § 5725.

Common interest developments, sale to satisfy assessment, application of this section, see Civil Code § 5740.

Common interest developments, trustee sale, procedure, see Civil Code § 5710.

Mortgage foreclosure actions, see Code of Civil Procedure § 726 et seq.

Reinstatement, assistance of mortgage foreclosure consultant, see Civil Code § 2945.1.

Waiver of rights or privileges conferred by this section upon borrower, validity, see Civil Code § 2953.

§ 2924d. Costs and expenses of enforcement; trustee's or attorney's fees; rebates and kickbacks

Section operative until Jan. 1, 2031. See, also, § 2924d operative Jan. 1, 2031.

(a)(1) Commencing with the date that the notice of sale is deposited in the mail, as provided in Section 2924b, and until the property is sold pursuant to the power of sale contained in the mortgage or deed of trust, a beneficiary, trustee, mortgagee, or * * * their agent or successor in interest may demand and receive from a trustor, mortgagor, or * * * their agent or successor in interest or any beneficiary under a subordinate deed of trust, or any other person having a subordinate lien or encumbrance of record those reasonable costs and expenses, to the extent allowed by subdivision (c) of Section 2924c, that are actually incurred in enforcing the terms of the obligation and trustee's or attorney's fees that are hereby authorized to be in an amount as follows:

(A) If the unpaid principal sum secured is fifty thousand dollars ($50,000) or less, then in a base amount that does not exceed four hundred seventy-five dollars ($475).

(B) If the unpaid principal sum secured is greater than fifty thousand dollars ($50,000) but does not exceed one hundred fifty thousand dollars ($150,000), then in a base amount that does not exceed four hundred seventy-five dollars ($475) plus 1 percent of the unpaid principal sum secured exceeding fifty thousand dollars ($50,000).

(C) If the unpaid principal sum secured is greater than one hundred fifty thousand dollars ($150,000) but does not exceed five hundred thousand dollars ($500,000), then in a base amount that does not exceed four hundred ten dollars ($410) plus 1 percent of the unpaid principal sum secured exceeding fifty thousand dollars ($50,000) up to and including one hundred fifty thousand dollars ($150,000), plus one-half of 1 percent of any portion of the unpaid principal sum secured exceeding one hundred fifty thousand dollars ($150,000).

(D) If the unpaid principal sum secured exceeds five hundred thousand dollars ($500,000), then in a base amount that does not exceed four hundred ten dollars ($410) plus 1 percent of the unpaid principal sum secured exceeding fifty thousand dollars ($50,000) up to and including one hundred fifty thousand dollars ($150,000), plus one-half of 1 percent of any portion of the unpaid principal sum secured exceeding one hundred fifty thousand dollars ($150,000) up to and including five hundred thousand dollars ($500,000), plus one-quarter of 1 percent of any portion of the unpaid principal sum secured exceeding five hundred thousand dollars ($500,000).

(2) For purposes of this subdivision, the unpaid principal sum secured shall be determined as of the date the notice of

§ 2924d OBLIGATIONS

default is recorded. Any charge for trustee's or attorney's fees authorized by this subdivision shall be conclusively presumed to be lawful and valid where that charge does not exceed the amounts authorized in this subdivision. Any charge for trustee's or attorney's fees made pursuant to this subdivision shall be in lieu of and not in addition to those charges authorized by subdivision (d) of Section 2924c.

(b)<u>(1)</u> Upon the sale of property pursuant to a power of sale, a trustee, or * * * <u>their</u> agent or successor in interest, may demand and receive from a beneficiary, or * * * <u>their</u> agent or successor in interest, or may deduct from the proceeds of the sale, those reasonable costs and expenses, to the extent allowed by subdivision (c) of Section 2924c, that are actually incurred in enforcing the terms of the obligation and trustee's or attorney's fees that are hereby authorized to be in an amount which does not exceed four hundred seventy-five dollars ($475) or 1 percent of the unpaid principal sum secured, whichever is greater. For purposes of this subdivision, the unpaid principal sum secured shall be determined as of the date the notice of default is recorded.

<u>(2) In addition to the amounts authorized under paragraph (1), if at least one eligible tenant buyer or eligible bidder submits to the trustee either a bid or a nonbinding written notice of intent to place a bid pursuant to paragraph (2) of subdivision (c) of Section 2924m, the trustee may deduct from the proceeds of the sale trustee's or attorney's fees for providing services pursuant to Section 2924m that are hereby authorized to be in an amount which does not exceed two hundred dollars ($200) or one-sixth of 1 percent of the unpaid principal sum secured, whichever is greater.</u>

(3) Any charge for trustee's or attorney's fees authorized by this subdivision shall be conclusively presumed to be lawful and valid where that charge does not exceed the amount authorized herein. Any charges for trustee's or attorney's fees made pursuant to this subdivision shall be in lieu of and not in addition to those charges authorized by subdivision (a) of this section and subdivision (d) of Section 2924c.

(c)(1) No person shall pay or offer to pay or collect any rebate or kickback for the referral of business involving the performance of any act required by this article.

(2) Any person who violates this subdivision shall be liable to the trustor for three times the amount of any rebate or kickback, plus reasonable attorney's fees and costs, in addition to any other remedies provided by law.

(3) No violation of this subdivision shall affect the validity of a sale in favor of a bona fide purchaser or the rights of an encumbrancer for value without notice.

(d) It shall not be unlawful for a trustee to pay or offer to pay a fee to an agent or subagent of the trustee for work performed by the agent or subagent in discharging the trustee's obligations under the terms of the deed of trust. Any payment of a fee by a trustee to an agent or subagent of the trustee for work performed by the agent or subagent in discharging the trustee's obligations under the terms of the deed of trust shall be conclusively presumed to be lawful and valid if the fee, when combined with other fees of the trustee, does not exceed in the aggregate the trustee's fee authorized by subdivision (d) of Section 2924c or subdivision (a) or (b) of this section.

(e) When a court issues a decree of foreclosure, it shall have discretion to award attorney's fees, costs, and expenses as are reasonable, if provided for in the note, deed of trust, or mortgage, pursuant to Section 580c of the Code of Civil Procedure.

<u>(f) This section shall remain in effect only until January 1, 2031, and as of that date is repealed.</u> (Added by Stats.1983, c. 1217, § 2. Amended by Stats.1984, c. 1730, § 2; Stats.1985, c. 560, § 1; Stats.1985, c. 1206, § 4; Stats.1993, c. 686 (A.B. 1219), § 5; Stats.1997, c. 74 (S.B.665), § 3; Stats.2001, c. 438 (S.B.958), § 4, eff. Oct. 2, 2001, operative Jan. 1, 2002; Stats.2016, c. 170 (S.B.983), § 4, eff. Jan. 1, 2017; Stats.2017, c. 217 (S.B.479), § 2, eff. Jan. 1, 2018; Stats.2022, c. 642 (A.B.1837), § 1, eff. Jan. 1, 2023.)

Repeal

For repeal of this section, see its terms.

Cross References

Commercial and industrial common interest developments, trustee sale, trustee fees, see Civil Code § 6822.
Common interest developments, trustee sale, procedure, see Civil Code § 5710.
Mortgage foreclosure actions, see Code of Civil Procedure § 726 et seq.

§ 2924d. Costs and expenses of enforcement; trustee's or attorney's fees; rebates and kickbacks

Section operative Jan. 1, 2031. See, also, § 2924d operative until Jan. 1, 2031.

(a)(1) Commencing with the date that the notice of sale is deposited in the mail, as provided in Section 2924b, and until the property is sold pursuant to the power of sale contained in the mortgage or deed of trust, a beneficiary, trustee, mortgagee, or their agent or successor in interest may demand and receive from a trustor, mortgagor, or their agent or successor in interest or any beneficiary under a subordinate deed of trust, or any other person having a subordinate lien or encumbrance of record those reasonable costs and expenses, to the extent allowed by subdivision (c) of Section 2924c, that are actually incurred in enforcing the terms of the obligation and trustee's or attorney's fees that are hereby authorized to be in an amount as follows:

(A) If the unpaid principal sum secured is fifty thousand dollars ($50,000) or less, then in a base amount that does not exceed four hundred seventy-five dollars ($475).

(B) If the unpaid principal sum secured is greater than fifty thousand dollars ($50,000) but does not exceed one hundred fifty thousand dollars ($150,000), then in a base amount that does not exceed four hundred seventy-five dollars ($475) plus 1 percent of the unpaid principal sum secured exceeding fifty thousand dollars ($50,000).

(C) If the unpaid principal sum secured is greater than one hundred fifty thousand dollars ($150,000) but does not exceed five hundred thousand dollars ($500,000), then in a base amount that does not exceed four hundred ten dollars ($410) plus 1 percent of the unpaid principal sum secured exceeding fifty thousand dollars ($50,000) up to and including one hundred fifty thousand dollars ($150,000), plus one-half of 1 percent of any portion of the unpaid principal sum secured exceeding one hundred fifty thousand dollars ($150,000).

(D) If the unpaid principal sum secured exceeds five hundred thousand dollars ($500,000), then in a base amount that does not exceed four hundred ten dollars ($410) plus 1 percent of the unpaid principal sum secured exceeding fifty thousand dollars ($50,000) up to and including one hundred fifty thousand dollars ($150,000), plus one-half of 1 percent of any portion of the unpaid principal sum secured exceeding one hundred fifty thousand dollars ($150,000) up to and including five hundred thousand dollars ($500,000), plus one-quarter of 1 percent of any portion of the unpaid principal sum secured exceeding five hundred thousand dollars ($500,000).

(2) For purposes of this subdivision, the unpaid principal sum secured shall be determined as of the date the notice of default is recorded. Any charge for trustee's or attorney's fees authorized by this subdivision shall be conclusively presumed to be lawful and valid where that charge does not exceed the amounts authorized in this subdivision. Any charge for trustee's or attorney's fees made pursuant to this subdivision shall be in lieu of and not in addition to those charges authorized by subdivision (d) of Section 2924c.

(b) Upon the sale of property pursuant to a power of sale, a trustee, or their agent or successor in interest, may demand and receive from a beneficiary, or their agent or successor in interest, or may deduct from the proceeds of the sale, those reasonable costs and expenses, to the extent allowed by subdivision (c) of Section 2924c, that are actually incurred in enforcing the terms of the obligation and trustee's or attorney's fees that are hereby authorized to be in an amount which does not exceed four hundred seventy-five dollars ($475) or 1 percent of the unpaid principal sum secured, whichever is greater. For purposes of this subdivision, the unpaid principal sum secured shall be determined as of the date the notice of default is recorded. Any charge for trustee's or attorney's fees authorized by this subdivision shall be conclusively presumed to be lawful and valid where that charge does not exceed the amount authorized herein. Any charges for trustee's or attorney's fees made pursuant to this subdivision shall be in lieu of and not in addition to those charges authorized by subdivision (a) of this section and subdivision (d) of Section 2924c.

(c)(1) No person shall pay or offer to pay or collect any rebate or kickback for the referral of business involving the performance of any act required by this article.

(2) Any person who violates this subdivision shall be liable to the trustor for three times the amount of any rebate or kickback, plus reasonable attorney's fees and costs, in addition to any other remedies provided by law.

(3) No violation of this subdivision shall affect the validity of a sale in favor of a bona fide purchaser or the rights of an encumbrancer for value without notice.

(d) It shall not be unlawful for a trustee to pay or offer to pay a fee to an agent or subagent of the trustee for work performed by the agent or subagent in discharging the trustee's obligations under the terms of the deed of trust. Any payment of a fee by a trustee to an agent or subagent of the trustee for work performed by the agent or subagent in discharging the trustee's obligations under the terms of the deed of trust shall be conclusively presumed to be lawful and valid if the fee, when combined with other fees of the trustee, does not exceed in the aggregate the trustee's fee authorized by subdivision (d) of Section 2924c or subdivision (a) or (b) of this section.

(e) When a court issues a decree of foreclosure, it shall have discretion to award attorney's fees, costs, and expenses as are reasonable, if provided for in the note, deed of trust, or mortgage, pursuant to Section 580c of the Code of Civil Procedure.

(f) This section shall be operative January 1, 2031. *(Added by Stats.2022, c. 642 (A.B.1837), § 2, eff. Jan. 1, 2023, operative Jan. 1, 2031.)*

Cross References

Commercial and industrial common interest developments, trustee sale, trustee fees, see Civil Code § 6822.
Common interest developments, trustee sale, procedure, see Civil Code § 5710.
Mortgage foreclosure actions, see Code of Civil Procedure § 726 et seq.

§ 2924e. Junior lienholder requests for written notice of delinquencies; duration; liability for failure to give notice; satisfaction of obligations secured by junior liens

(a) The beneficiary or mortgagee of any deed of trust or mortgage on real property either containing one to four residential units or given to secure an original obligation not to exceed three hundred thousand dollars ($300,000) may, with the written consent of the trustor or mortgagor that is either effected through a signed and dated agreement which shall be separate from other loan and security documents or disclosed to the trustor or mortgagor in at least 10-point type, submit a written request by certified mail to the beneficiary or mortgagee of any lien which is senior to the lien of the requester, for written notice of any or all delinquencies of four months or more, in payments of principal or interest on any obligation secured by that senior lien notwithstanding that the loan secured by the lien of the requester is not then in default as to payments of principal or interest.

The request shall be sent to the beneficiary or mortgagee, or agent which it might designate for the purpose of receiving loan payments, at the address specified for the receipt of these payments, if known, or, if not known, at the address shown on the recorded deed of trust or mortgage.

(b) The request for notice shall identify the ownership or security interest of the requester, the date on which the interest of the requester will terminate as evidenced by the maturity date of the note of the trustor or mortgagor in favor of the requester, the name of the trustor or mortgagor and the name of the current owner of the security property if different from the trustor or mortgagor, the street address or other description of the security property, the loan number (if available to the requester) of the loan secured by the senior lien, the name and address to which notice is to be sent, and shall include or be accompanied by the signed written consent of the trustor or mortgagor, and a fee of forty dollars ($40). For obligations secured by residential properties, the request shall remain valid until withdrawn in writing and shall be applicable to all delinquencies as provided in this section, which occur prior to the date on which the interest of the requester will terminate as specified in the request or the expiration date, as appropriate. For obligations secured by nonresidential properties, the request shall remain valid until withdrawn in writing and shall be applicable to all delinquencies as provided in this section, which occur prior to the date on which the interest of the requester will terminate as specified in the request or the expiration date, as appropriate. The beneficiary or mortgagee of obligations secured by nonresidential properties that have sent five or more notices prior to the expiration of the effective period of the request may charge a fee up to fifteen dollars ($15) for each subsequent notice. A request for notice shall be effective for five years from the mailing of the request or the recording of that request, whichever occurs later, and may be renewed within six months prior to its expiration date by sending the beneficiary or mortgagee, or agent, as the case may be, at the address to which original requests for notice are to be sent, a copy of the earlier request for notice together with a signed statement that the request is renewed and a renewal fee of fifteen dollars ($15). Upon timely submittal of a renewal request for notice, the effectiveness of the original request is continued for five years from the time when it would otherwise have lapsed. Succeeding renewal requests may be submitted in the same manner. The request for notice and renewals thereof shall be recorded in the office of the county recorder of the county in which the security real property is situated. The rights and obligations specified in this section shall inure to the benefit of, or pass to, as the case may be, successors in interest of parties specified in this section. Any successor in interest of a party entitled to notice under this section shall file a request for that notice with any beneficiary or mortgagee of the senior lien and shall pay a processing fee of fifteen dollars ($15). No new written consent shall be required from the trustor or mortgagor.

(c) Unless the delinquency has been cured, within 15 days following the end of four months from any delinquency in payments of principal or interest on any obligation secured by the senior lien which delinquency exists or occurs on or after 10 days from the mailing of the request for notice or the recording of that request, whichever occurs later, the beneficiary or mortgagee shall give written notice to the requester of the fact of any delinquency and the amount thereof.

The notice shall be given by personal service, or by deposit in the mail, first-class postage paid. Following the recording of any notice of default pursuant to Section 2924 with respect to the same delinquency, no notice or further notice shall be required pursuant to this section.

(d) If the beneficiary or mortgagee of any such senior lien fails to give notice to the requester as required in subdivision (c), and a subsequent foreclosure or trustee's sale of the security property occurs, the beneficiary or mortgagee shall be liable to the requester for any monetary damage due to the failure to provide notice within the time period specified in subdivision (c) which the requester has sustained from the date on which notice should have been given to the earlier of the date on which the notice is given or the date of the recording of the notice of default under Section 2924, and shall also forfeit to the requester the sum of three hundred dollars ($300). A showing by the beneficiary or mortgagee by a preponderance of the evidence that the failure to provide timely notice as required by subdivision (c) resulted from a bona fide error notwithstanding the maintenance of procedures reasonably adapted to avoid any such error shall be a defense to any liability for that failure.

(e) If any beneficiary or mortgagee, or agent which it had designated for the purpose of receiving loan payments, has been succeeded in interest by any other person, any request for notice received pursuant to this section shall be transmitted promptly to that person.

(f) Any failure to comply with the provisions of this section shall not affect the validity of a sale in favor of a bona fide purchaser or the rights of an encumbrancer for value and without notice.

(g) Upon satisfaction of an obligation secured by a junior lien with respect to which a notice request was made pursuant to this section, the beneficiary or mortgagee that made the request shall communicate that fact in writing to the senior lienholder to whom the request was made. The communication shall specify that provision of notice pursuant to the prior request under this section is no longer required. *(Added by Stats.1984, c. 1331, § 1, operative July 1, 1985. Amended by Stats.1986, c. 618, § 1; Stats.1988, c. 510, § 1; Stats.1990, c. 788 (S.B.2042), § 1.)*

Cross References

Mortgage foreclosure actions, see Code of Civil Procedure § 726 et seq.

§ 2924f. Sale or resale of property where there is a default on the obligation secured by the property; notice; contents; posting and publication

Section operative until Jan. 1, 2031. See, also, § 2924f operative Jan. 1, 2031.

(a) As used in this section and Sections 2924g and 2924h, "property" means real property or a leasehold estate therein, and "calendar week" means Monday through Saturday, inclusive.

(b)(1) Except as provided in subdivision (c), before any sale of property can be made under the power of sale contained in any deed of trust or mortgage, or any resale resulting from a rescission for a failure of consideration pursuant to subdivision (c) of Section 2924h, notice of the sale thereof shall be given by posting a written notice of the time of sale and of the street address and the specific place at the street address where the sale will be held, and describing the property to be sold, at least 20 days before the date of sale in one public place in the city where the property is to be sold, if the property is to be sold in a city, or, if not, then in one public place in the county seat of the county where the property is to be sold, and publishing a copy once a week for three consecutive calendar weeks.

(2) The first publication to be at least 20 days before the date of sale, in a newspaper of general circulation published in the public notice district in which the property or some part thereof is situated, or in case no newspaper of general circulation is published in the public notice district, in a newspaper of general circulation published in the county in which the property or some part thereof is situated, or in case no newspaper of general circulation is published in the public notice district or county, as the case may be, in a newspaper

of general circulation published in the county in this state that is contiguous to the county in which the property or some part thereof is situated and has, by comparison with all similarly contiguous counties, the highest population based upon total county population as determined by the most recent federal decennial census published by the Bureau of the Census. For the purposes of this section, publication of notice in a public notice district is governed by Chapter 1.1 (commencing with Section 6080) of Division 7 of Title 1 of the Government Code.

(3) A copy of the notice of sale shall also be posted in a conspicuous place on the property to be sold at least 20 days before the date of sale, where possible and where not restricted for any reason. If the property is a single-family residence the posting shall be on a door of the residence, but, if not possible or restricted, then the notice shall be posted in a conspicuous place on the property; however, if access is denied because a common entrance to the property is restricted by a guard gate or similar impediment, the property may be posted at that guard gate or similar impediment to any development community.

(4) The notice of sale shall conform to the minimum requirements of Section 6043 of the Government Code and be recorded with the county recorder of the county in which the property or some part thereof is situated at least 20 days prior to the date of sale.

(5) The notice of sale shall contain the name, street address in this state, which may reflect an agent of the trustee, and either a toll-free telephone number or telephone number in this state of the trustee, and the name of the original trustor, and also shall contain the statement required by paragraph (3) of subdivision (c). In addition to any other description of the property, the notice shall describe the property by giving its street address, if any, or other common designation, if any, and a county assessor's parcel number; but if the property has no street address or other common designation, the notice shall contain a legal description of the property, the name and address of the beneficiary at whose request the sale is to be conducted, and a statement that directions may be obtained pursuant to a written request submitted to the beneficiary within 10 days from the first publication of the notice. Directions shall be deemed reasonably sufficient to locate the property if information as to the location of the property is given by reference to the direction and approximate distance from the nearest crossroads, frontage road, or access road. If a legal description or a county assessor's parcel number and either a street address or another common designation of the property is given, the validity of the notice and the validity of the sale shall not be affected by the fact that the street address, other common designation, name and address of the beneficiary, or the directions obtained therefrom are erroneous or that the street address, other common designation, name and address of the beneficiary, or directions obtained therefrom are omitted.

(6) The term "newspaper of general circulation," as used in this section, has the same meaning as defined in Article 1 (commencing with Section 6000) of Chapter 1 of Division 7 of Title 1 of the Government Code.

(7) The notice of sale shall contain a statement of the total amount of the unpaid balance of the obligation secured by the property to be sold and reasonably estimated costs, expenses, advances at the time of the initial publication of the notice of sale, and, if republished pursuant to a cancellation of a cash equivalent pursuant to subdivision (d) of Section 2924h, a reference of that fact; provided, that the trustee shall incur no liability for any good faith error in stating the proper amount, including any amount provided in good faith by or on behalf of the beneficiary. An inaccurate statement of this amount shall not affect the validity of any sale to a bona fide purchaser for value, nor shall the failure to post the notice of sale on a door as provided by this subdivision affect the validity of any sale to a bona fide purchaser for value.

(8)(A) On and after April 1, 2012, if the deed of trust or mortgage containing a power of sale is secured by real property containing from one to four single-family residences, the notice of sale shall contain substantially the following language, in addition to the language required pursuant to paragraphs (1) to (7), inclusive:

NOTICE TO POTENTIAL BIDDERS: If you are considering bidding on this property lien, you should understand that there are risks involved in bidding at a trustee auction. You will be bidding on a lien, not on the property itself. Placing the highest bid at a trustee auction does not automatically entitle you to free and clear ownership of the property. You should also be aware that the lien being auctioned off may be a junior lien. If you are the highest bidder at the auction, you are or may be responsible for paying off all liens senior to the lien being auctioned off, before you can receive clear title to the property. You are encouraged to investigate the existence, priority, and size of outstanding liens that may exist on this property by contacting the county recorder's office or a title insurance company, either of which may charge you a fee for this information. If you consult either of these resources, you should be aware that the same lender may hold more than one mortgage or deed of trust on the property.

NOTICE TO PROPERTY OWNER: The sale date shown on this notice of sale may be postponed one or more times by the mortgagee, beneficiary, trustee, or a court, pursuant to Section 2924g of the California Civil Code. The law requires that information about trustee sale postponements be made available to you and to the public, as a courtesy to those not present at the sale. If you wish to learn whether your sale date has been postponed, and, if applicable, the rescheduled time and date for the sale of this property, you may call [telephone number for information regarding the trustee's sale] or visit this internet website [internet website address for information regarding the sale of this property], using the file number assigned to this case [case file number]. Information about postponements that are very short in duration or that occur close in time to the scheduled sale may not immediately be reflected in the telephone information or on the internet website. The best way to verify postponement information is to attend the scheduled sale.

§ 2924f OBLIGATIONS

NOTICE TO TENANT: You may have a right to purchase this property after the trustee auction pursuant to Section 2924m of the California Civil Code. If you are an "eligible tenant buyer," you can purchase the property if you match the last and highest bid placed at the trustee auction. If you are an "eligible bidder," you may be able to purchase the property if you exceed the last and highest bid placed at the trustee auction. There are three steps to exercising this right of purchase. First, 48 hours after the date of the trustee sale, you can call [telephone number for information regarding the trustee's sale], or visit this internet website [internet website address for information regarding the sale of this property], using the file number assigned to this case [case file number] to find the date on which the trustee's sale was held, the amount of the last and highest bid, and the address of the trustee. Second, you must send a written notice of intent to place a bid so that the trustee receives it no more than 15 days after the trustee's sale. Third, you must submit a bid so that the trustee receives it no more than 45 days after the trustee's sale. If you think you may qualify as an "eligible tenant buyer" or "eligible bidder," you should consider contacting an attorney or appropriate real estate professional immediately for advice regarding this potential right to purchase.

(B) A mortgagee, beneficiary, trustee, or authorized agent shall make a good faith effort to provide up-to-date information regarding sale dates and postponements to persons who wish this information. This information shall be made available free of charge. It may be made available via an internet website, a telephone recording that is accessible 24 hours a day, seven days a week, or through any other means that allows 24 hours a day, seven days a week, no-cost access to updated information. A disruption of any of these methods of providing sale date and postponement information to allow for reasonable maintenance or due to a service outage shall not be deemed to be a violation of the good faith standard.

(C) Except as provided in subparagraph (B), nothing in the wording of the notices required by subparagraph (A) is intended to modify or create any substantive rights or obligations for any person providing, or specified in, either of the required notices. Failure to comply with subparagraph (A) or (B) shall not invalidate any sale that would otherwise be valid under Section 2924f.

(D) Information provided pursuant to subparagraph (A) does not constitute the public declaration required by subdivision (d) of Section 2924g.

(E) For purposes of a property subject to this paragraph and of satisfying the requirements of Section 2924m, a trustee or an authorized agent shall maintain an internet website and a telephone number to provide information on applicable properties to persons who wish the information. In addition to any other information required by subparagraph (B), a trustee or an authorized agent shall provide information regarding the sale date, amount of the last and highest bid, and the trustee's address, to be accessible using the file number assigned to the case and listed on the NOTICE TO TENANT required by subparagraph (A). This information shall be made available free of charge and shall be available 24 hours a day, seven days a week.

(9) If the sale of the property is to be a unified sale as provided in subparagraph (B) of paragraph (1) of subdivision (a) of Section 9604 of the Commercial Code, the notice of sale shall also contain a description of the personal property or fixtures to be sold. In the case where it is contemplated that all of the personal property or fixtures are to be sold, the description in the notice of the personal property or fixtures shall be sufficient if it is the same as the description of the personal property or fixtures contained in the agreement creating the security interest in or encumbrance on the personal property or fixtures or the filed financing statement relating to the personal property or fixtures. In all other cases, the description in the notice shall be sufficient if it would be a sufficient description of the personal property or fixtures under Section 9108 of the Commercial Code. Inclusion of a reference to or a description of personal property or fixtures in a notice of sale hereunder shall not constitute an election by the secured party to conduct a unified sale pursuant to subparagraph (B) of paragraph (1) of subdivision (a) of Section 9604 of the Commercial Code, shall not obligate the secured party to conduct a unified sale pursuant to subparagraph (B) of paragraph (1) of subdivision (a) of Section 9604 of the Commercial Code, and in no way shall render defective or noncomplying either that notice or a sale pursuant to that notice by reason of the fact that the sale includes none or less than all of the personal property or fixtures referred to or described in the notice. This paragraph shall not otherwise affect the obligations or duties of a secured party under the Commercial Code.

(c)(1) This subdivision applies only to deeds of trust or mortgages which contain a power of sale and which are secured by real property containing a single-family, owner-occupied residence, where the obligation secured by the deed of trust or mortgage is contained in a contract for goods or services subject to the provisions of the Unruh Act (Chapter 1 (commencing with Section 1801) of Title 2 of Part 4 of Division 3).

(2) Except as otherwise expressly set forth in this subdivision, all other provisions of law relating to the exercise of a power of sale shall govern the exercise of a power of sale contained in a deed of trust or mortgage described in paragraph (1).

(3) If any default of the obligation secured by a deed of trust or mortgage described in paragraph (1) has not been cured within 30 days after the recordation of the notice of default, the trustee or mortgagee shall mail to the trustor or mortgagor, at their last known address, a copy of the following statement:

YOU ARE IN DEFAULT UNDER A
_____
,
(Deed of trust or mortgage)
DATED ____. UNLESS YOU TAKE ACTION TO PROTECT YOUR PROPERTY, IT MAY BE SOLD AT A PUBLIC SALE. IF YOU NEED AN EXPLANATION OF THE NATURE OF THE PROCEEDING AGAINST YOU, YOU SHOULD CONTACT A LAWYER.

(4) All sales of real property pursuant to a power of sale contained in any deed of trust or mortgage described in paragraph (1) shall be held in the county where the residence is located and shall be made to the person making the highest offer. The trustee may receive offers during the 10-day period immediately prior to the date of sale and if any offer is accepted in writing by both the trustor or mortgagor and the beneficiary or mortgagee prior to the time set for sale, the sale shall be postponed to a date certain and prior to which the property may be conveyed by the trustor to the person making the offer according to its terms. The offer is revocable until accepted. The performance of the offer, following acceptance, according to its terms, by a conveyance of the property to the offeror, shall operate to terminate any further proceeding under the notice of sale and it shall be deemed revoked.

(5) In addition to the trustee fee pursuant to Section 2924c, the trustee or mortgagee pursuant to a deed of trust or mortgage subject to this subdivision shall be entitled to charge an additional fee of fifty dollars ($50).

(6) This subdivision applies only to property on which notices of default were filed on or after the effective date of this subdivision.

(d) With respect to residential real property containing no more than four dwelling units, a separate document containing a summary of the notice of sale information in English and the languages described in Section 1632 shall be attached to the notice of sale provided to the mortgagor or trustor pursuant to Section 2923.3.

(e) This section shall remain in effect only until January 1, 2031, and as of that date is repealed, unless a later enacted statute that is enacted before January 1, 2031, deletes or extends that date. (Added by Stats.2010, c. 597 (A.B.2347), § 2, operative Jan. 1, 2013. Amended by Stats.2011, c. 229 (S.B.4), § 2, operative Jan. 1, 2013; Stats.2012, c. 556 (A.B. 1599), § 4; Stats.2016, c. 703 (A.B.2881), § 3, eff. Jan. 1, 2017; Stats.2020, c. 202 (S.B.1079), § 1, eff. Jan. 1, 2021; Stats.2020, c. 203 (S.B.1148), § 1.3, eff. Jan. 1, 2021; Stats. 2022, c. 642 (A.B.1837), § 3, eff. Jan. 1, 2023.)

Repeal

For repeal of this section, see its terms.

Cross References

Common interest developments, debts for assessments that arise on and after Jan. 1, 2006, nonjudicial foreclosure, see Civil Code § 5715.

Mortgage foreclosure actions, see Code of Civil Procedure § 726 et seq.

Transfer as security deemed mortgage or pledge, power of sale, requirements prior to sale, see Civil Code § 2924.

§ 2924f. Sale or resale of property where there is a default on the obligation secured by the property; notice; contents; posting and publication

Section operative Jan. 1, 2031. See, also, § 2924f operative until Jan. 1, 2031.

(a) As used in this section and Sections 2924g and 2924h, "property" means real property or a leasehold estate therein, and "calendar week" means Monday through Saturday, inclusive.

(b)(1) Except as provided in subdivision (c), before any sale of property can be made under the power of sale contained in any deed of trust or mortgage, or any resale resulting from a rescission for a failure of consideration pursuant to subdivision (c) of Section 2924h, notice of the sale thereof shall be given by posting a written notice of the time of sale and of the street address and the specific place at the street address where the sale will be held, and describing the property to be sold, at least 20 days before the date of sale in one public place in the city where the property is to be sold, if the property is to be sold in a city, or, if not, then in one public place in the county seat of the county where the property is to be sold, and publishing a copy once a week for three consecutive calendar weeks.

(2) The first publication to be at least 20 days before the date of sale, in a newspaper of general circulation published in the public notice district in which the property or some part thereof is situated, or in case no newspaper of general circulation is published in the public notice district, in a newspaper of general circulation published in the county in which the property or some part thereof is situated, or in case no newspaper of general circulation is published in the public notice district or county, as the case may be, in a newspaper of general circulation published in the county in this state that is contiguous to the county in which the property or some part thereof is situated and has, by comparison with all similarly contiguous counties, the highest population based upon total county population as determined by the most recent federal decennial census published by the Bureau of the Census. For the purposes of this section, publication of notice in a public notice district is governed by Chapter 1.1 (commencing with Section 6080) of Division 7 of Title 1 of the Government Code.

(3) A copy of the notice of sale shall also be posted in a conspicuous place on the property to be sold at least 20 days before the date of sale, where possible and where not restricted for any reason. If the property is a single-family residence the posting shall be on a door of the residence, but, if not possible or restricted, then the notice shall be posted in

§ 2924f OBLIGATIONS

a conspicuous place on the property; however, if access is denied because a common entrance to the property is restricted by a guard gate or similar impediment, the property may be posted at that guard gate or similar impediment to any development community.

(4) The notice of sale shall conform to the minimum requirements of Section 6043 of the Government Code and be recorded with the county recorder of the county in which the property or some part thereof is situated at least 20 days prior to the date of sale.

(5) The notice of sale shall contain the name, street address in this state, which may reflect an agent of the trustee, and either a toll-free telephone number or telephone number in this state of the trustee, and the name of the original trustor, and also shall contain the statement required by paragraph (3) of subdivision (c). In addition to any other description of the property, the notice shall describe the property by giving its street address, if any, or other common designation, if any, and a county assessor's parcel number; but if the property has no street address or other common designation, the notice shall contain a legal description of the property, the name and address of the beneficiary at whose request the sale is to be conducted, and a statement that directions may be obtained pursuant to a written request submitted to the beneficiary within 10 days from the first publication of the notice. Directions shall be deemed reasonably sufficient to locate the property if information as to the location of the property is given by reference to the direction and approximate distance from the nearest crossroads, frontage road, or access road. If a legal description or a county assessor's parcel number and either a street address or another common designation of the property is given, the validity of the notice and the validity of the sale shall not be affected by the fact that the street address, other common designation, name and address of the beneficiary, or the directions obtained therefrom are erroneous or that the street address, other common designation, name and address of the beneficiary, or directions obtained therefrom are omitted.

(6) The term "newspaper of general circulation," as used in this section, has the same meaning as defined in Article 1 (commencing with Section 6000) of Chapter 1 of Division 7 of Title 1 of the Government Code.

(7) The notice of sale shall contain a statement of the total amount of the unpaid balance of the obligation secured by the property to be sold and reasonably estimated costs, expenses, advances at the time of the initial publication of the notice of sale, and, if republished pursuant to a cancellation of a cash equivalent pursuant to subdivision (d) of Section 2924h, a reference of that fact; provided, that the trustee shall incur no liability for any good faith error in stating the proper amount, including any amount provided in good faith by or on behalf of the beneficiary. An inaccurate statement of this amount shall not affect the validity of any sale to a bona fide purchaser for value, nor shall the failure to post the notice of sale on a door as provided by this subdivision affect the validity of any sale to a bona fide purchaser for value.

(8)(A) On and after April 1, 2012, if the deed of trust or mortgage containing a power of sale is secured by real property containing from one to four single-family residences, the notice of sale shall contain substantially the following language, in addition to the language required pursuant to paragraphs (1) to (7), inclusive:

NOTICE TO POTENTIAL BIDDERS: If you are considering bidding on this property lien, you should understand that there are risks involved in bidding at a trustee auction. You will be bidding on a lien, not on the property itself. Placing the highest bid at a trustee auction does not automatically entitle you to free and clear ownership of the property. You should also be aware that the lien being auctioned off may be a junior lien. If you are the highest bidder at the auction, you are or may be responsible for paying off all liens senior to the lien being auctioned off, before you can receive clear title to the property. You are encouraged to investigate the existence, priority, and size of outstanding liens that may exist on this property by contacting the county recorder's office or a title insurance company, either of which may charge you a fee for this information. If you consult either of these resources, you should be aware that the same lender may hold more than one mortgage or deed of trust on the property.

NOTICE TO PROPERTY OWNER: The sale date shown on this notice of sale may be postponed one or more times by the mortgagee, beneficiary, trustee, or a court, pursuant to Section 2924g of the California Civil Code. The law requires that information about trustee sale postponements be made available to you and to the public, as a courtesy to those not present at the sale. If you wish to learn whether your sale date has been postponed, and, if applicable, the rescheduled time and date for the sale of this property, you may call [telephone number for information regarding the trustee's sale] or visit this internet website [internet website address for information regarding the sale of this property], using the file number assigned to this case [case file number]. Information about postponements that are very short in duration or that occur close in time to the scheduled sale may not immediately be reflected in the telephone information or on the internet website. The best way to verify postponement information is to attend the scheduled sale.

(B) A mortgagee, beneficiary, trustee, or authorized agent shall make a good faith effort to provide up-to-date information regarding sale dates and postponements to persons who wish this information. This information shall be made available free of charge. It may be made available via an internet website, a telephone recording that is accessible 24 hours a day, seven days a week, or through any other means that allows 24 hours a day, seven days a week, no-cost access to updated information. A disruption of any of these methods of providing sale date and postponement information to allow for reasonable maintenance or due to a service outage shall not be deemed to be a violation of the good faith standard.

(C) Except as provided in subparagraph (B), nothing in the wording of the notices required by subparagraph (A) is intended to modify or create any substantive rights or obligations for any person providing, or specified in, either of the required notices. Failure to comply with subparagraph (A) or (B) shall not invalidate any sale that would otherwise be valid under Section 2924f.

(D) Information provided pursuant to subparagraph (A) does not constitute the public declaration required by subdivision (d) of Section 2924g.

(9) If the sale of the property is to be a unified sale as provided in subparagraph (B) of paragraph (1) of subdivision (a) of Section 9604 of the Commercial Code, the notice of sale shall also contain a description of the personal property or fixtures to be sold. In the case where it is contemplated that all of the personal property or fixtures are to be sold, the description in the notice of the personal property or fixtures shall be sufficient if it is the same as the description of the personal property or fixtures contained in the agreement creating the security interest in or encumbrance on the personal property or fixtures or the filed financing statement relating to the personal property or fixtures. In all other cases, the description in the notice shall be sufficient if it would be a sufficient description of the personal property or fixtures under Section 9108 of the Commercial Code. Inclusion of a reference to or a description of personal property or fixtures in a notice of sale hereunder shall not constitute an election by the secured party to conduct a unified sale pursuant to subparagraph (B) of paragraph (1) of subdivision (a) of Section 9604 of the Commercial Code, shall not obligate the secured party to conduct a unified sale pursuant to subparagraph (B) of paragraph (1) of subdivision (a) of Section 9604 of the Commercial Code, and in no way shall render defective or noncomplying either that notice or a sale pursuant to that notice by reason of the fact that the sale includes none or less than all of the personal property or fixtures referred to or described in the notice. This paragraph shall not otherwise affect the obligations or duties of a secured party under the Commercial Code.

(c)(1) This subdivision applies only to deeds of trust or mortgages which contain a power of sale and which are secured by real property containing a single-family, owner-occupied residence, where the obligation secured by the deed of trust or mortgage is contained in a contract for goods or services subject to the provisions of the Unruh Act (Chapter 1 (commencing with Section 1801) of Title 2 of Part 4 of Division 3).

(2) Except as otherwise expressly set forth in this subdivision, all other provisions of law relating to the exercise of a power of sale shall govern the exercise of a power of sale contained in a deed of trust or mortgage described in paragraph (1).

(3) If any default of the obligation secured by a deed of trust or mortgage described in paragraph (1) has not been cured within 30 days after the recordation of the notice of default, the trustee or mortgagee shall mail to the trustor or mortgagor, at their last known address, a copy of the following statement:

YOU ARE IN DEFAULT UNDER A

_____,

(Deed of trust or mortgage)

DATED ____. UNLESS YOU TAKE ACTION TO PROTECT

YOUR PROPERTY, IT MAY BE SOLD AT A PUBLIC SALE.

IF YOU NEED AN EXPLANATION OF THE NATURE OF THE

PROCEEDING AGAINST YOU, YOU SHOULD CONTACT

A

LAWYER.[1]

(4) All sales of real property pursuant to a power of sale contained in any deed of trust or mortgage described in paragraph (1) shall be held in the county where the residence is located and shall be made to the person making the highest offer. The trustee may receive offers during the 10–day period immediately prior to the date of sale and if any offer is accepted in writing by both the trustor or mortgagor and the beneficiary or mortgagee prior to the time set for sale, the sale shall be postponed to a date certain and prior to which the property may be conveyed by the trustor to the person making the offer according to its terms. The offer is revocable until accepted. The performance of the offer, following acceptance, according to its terms, by a conveyance of the property to the offeror, shall operate to terminate any further proceeding under the notice of sale and it shall be deemed revoked.

(5) In addition to the trustee fee pursuant to Section 2924c, the trustee or mortgagee pursuant to a deed of trust or mortgage subject to this subdivision shall be entitled to charge an additional fee of fifty dollars ($50).

(6) This subdivision applies only to property on which notices of default were filed on or after the effective date of this subdivision.

(d) With respect to residential real property containing no more than four dwelling units, a separate document containing a summary of the notice of sale information in English and the languages described in Section 1632 shall be attached to the notice of sale provided to the mortgagor or trustor pursuant to Section 2923.3.

(e) This section shall be operative January 1, 2031. *(Added by Stats.2020, c. 203 (S.B.1148), § 1.5, eff. Jan. 1, 2021, operative Jan. 1, 2026. Amended by Stats.2022, c. 642 (A.B.1837), § 4, eff. Jan. 1, 2023, operative Jan. 1, 2031.)*

[1] So in enrolled bill.

Cross References

Common interest developments, debts for assessments that arise on and after Jan. 1, 2006, nonjudicial foreclosure, see Civil Code § 5715.

Mortgage foreclosure actions, see Code of Civil Procedure § 726 et seq.

Transfer as security deemed mortgage or pledge, power of sale, requirements prior to sale, see Civil Code § 2924.

§ 2924g. Conduct of sale; time; place; interested parties; postponement; order of sale

Section operative until Jan. 1, 2031. See, also, § 2924g operative Jan. 1, 2031.

(a)(1) All sales of property under the power of sale contained in any deed of trust or mortgage shall be held in the county where the property or some part thereof is situated, and shall be made at auction, to the highest bidder, between the hours of 9 a.m. and 5 p.m. on any business day, Monday through Friday.

(2) The sale shall commence at the time and location specified in the notice of sale. Any postponement shall be announced at the time and location specified in the notice of sale for commencement of the sale or pursuant to paragraph (1) of subdivision (c).

(3) If the sale of more than one parcel of real property has been scheduled for the same time and location by the same trustee, (A) any postponement of any of the sales shall be announced at the time published in the notice of sale, (B) the first sale shall commence at the time published in the notice of sale or immediately after the announcement of any postponement, and (C) each subsequent sale shall take place as soon as possible after the preceding sale has been completed.

(4) Notwithstanding any other law, a sale of property under the power of sale contained in any deed of trust or mortgage shall be subject to the following restriction: a trustee shall not bundle properties for the purpose of sale and each property shall be bid on separately, unless the deed of trust or mortgage requires otherwise.

(b) When the property consists of several known lots or parcels, they shall be sold separately unless the deed of trust or mortgage provides otherwise. When a portion of the property is claimed by a third person, who requires it to be sold separately, the portion subject to the claim may be thus sold. The trustor, if present at the sale, may also, unless the deed of trust or mortgage otherwise provides, direct the order in which property shall be sold, when the property consists of several known lots or parcels which may be sold to advantage separately, and the trustee shall follow that direction. After sufficient property has been sold to satisfy the indebtedness, no more can be sold.

If the property under power of sale is in two or more counties, the public auction sale of all of the property under the power of sale may take place in any one of the counties where the property or a portion thereof is located.

(c)(1) There may be a postponement or postponements of the sale proceedings, including a postponement upon instruction by the beneficiary to the trustee that the sale proceedings be postponed, at any time prior to the completion of the sale for any period of time not to exceed a total of 365 days from the date set forth in the notice of sale. The trustee shall postpone the sale in accordance with any of the following:

(A) Upon the order of any court of competent jurisdiction.

(B) If stayed by operation of law.

(C) By mutual agreement, whether oral or in writing, of any trustor and any beneficiary or any mortgagor and any mortgagee.

(D) At the discretion of the trustee.

(2) In the event that the sale proceedings are postponed for a period or periods totaling more than 365 days, the scheduling of any further sale proceedings shall be preceded by giving a new notice of sale in the manner prescribed in Section 2924f. New fees incurred for the new notice of sale shall not exceed the amounts specified in Sections 2924c and 2924d, and shall not exceed reasonable costs that are necessary to comply with this paragraph.

(d) The notice of each postponement and the reason therefor shall be given by public declaration by the trustee at the time and place last appointed for sale. A public declaration of postponement shall also set forth the new date, time, and place of sale and the place of sale shall be the same place as originally fixed by the trustee for the sale. No other notice of postponement need be given. However, the sale shall be conducted no sooner than on the seventh day after the earlier of (1) dismissal of the action or (2) expiration or termination of the injunction, restraining order, or stay that required postponement of the sale, whether by entry of an order by a court of competent jurisdiction, operation of law, or otherwise, unless the injunction, restraining order, or subsequent order expressly directs the conduct of the sale within that seven-day period. For purposes of this subdivision, the seven-day period shall not include the day on which the action is dismissed, or the day on which the injunction, restraining order, or stay expires or is terminated. If the sale had been scheduled to occur, but this subdivision precludes its conduct during that seven-day period, a new notice of postponement shall be given if the sale had been scheduled to occur during that seven-day period. The trustee shall maintain records of each postponement and the reason therefor.

(e) Notwithstanding the time periods established under subdivision (d), if postponement of a sale is based on a stay imposed by Title 11 of the United States Code (bankruptcy), the sale shall be conducted no sooner than the expiration of the stay imposed by that title and the seven-day provision of subdivision (d) shall not apply.

(f) This section shall remain in effect only until January 1, 2031, and as of that date is repealed, unless a later enacted statute that is enacted before January 1, 2031, deletes or extends that date. *(Added by Stats.1972, c. 1056, p. 1943, § 4. Amended by Stats.1979, c. 1015, p. 3474, § 4; Stats.1980, c. 423, p. 844, § 14, eff. July 11, 1980; Stats.1984, c. 1730, § 4; Stats.1985, c. 1206, § 5; Stats.1986, c. 1385, § 4; Stats.1992, c. 351 (A.B.2981), § 4; Stats.1993, c. 686 (A.B.1219), § 7; Stats.1994, c. 587 (A.B.3600), § 1.2; Stats.1997, c. 74 (S.B. 665), § 5; Stats.2000, c. 636 (A.B.2284), § 7; Stats.2001, c. 438 (S.B.958), § 5, eff. Oct. 2, 2001, operative Jan. 1, 2002; Stats.2005, c. 224 (A.B.885), § 2; Stats.2020, c. 202 (S.B. 1079), § 3, eff. Jan. 1, 2021; Stats.2022, c. 642 (A.B.1837), § 5, eff. Jan. 1, 2023.)*

Repeal

For repeal of this section, see its terms.

Cross References

Mortgage foreclosure actions, see Code of Civil Procedure § 726 et seq.

Transfer as security deemed mortgage or pledge, power of sale, requirements prior to sale, see Civil Code § 2924.

§ 2924g. Conduct of sale; time; place; interested parties; postponement; order of sale

Section operative Jan. 1, 2031. See, also, § 2924g operative until Jan. 1, 2031.

(a) All sales of property under the power of sale contained in any deed of trust or mortgage shall be held in the county where the property or some part thereof is situated, and shall be made at auction, to the highest bidder, between the hours of 9 a.m. and 5 p.m. on any business day, Monday through Friday.

The sale shall commence at the time and location specified in the notice of sale. Any postponement shall be announced at the time and location specified in the notice of sale for commencement of the sale or pursuant to paragraph (1) of subdivision (c).

If the sale of more than one parcel of real property has been scheduled for the same time and location by the same trustee, (1) any postponement of any of the sales shall be announced at the time published in the notice of sale, (2) the first sale shall commence at the time published in the notice of sale or immediately after the announcement of any postponement, and (3) each subsequent sale shall take place as soon as possible after the preceding sale has been completed.

(b) When the property consists of several known lots or parcels, they shall be sold separately unless the deed of trust or mortgage provides otherwise. When a portion of the property is claimed by a third person, who requires it to be sold separately, the portion subject to the claim may be thus sold. The trustor, if present at the sale, may also, unless the deed of trust or mortgage otherwise provides, direct the order in which property shall be sold, when the property consists of several known lots or parcels which may be sold to advantage separately, and the trustee shall follow that direction. After sufficient property has been sold to satisfy the indebtedness, no more can be sold.

If the property under power of sale is in two or more counties, the public auction sale of all of the property under the power of sale may take place in any one of the counties where the property or a portion thereof is located.

(c)(1) There may be a postponement or postponements of the sale proceedings, including a postponement upon instruction by the beneficiary to the trustee that the sale proceedings be postponed, at any time prior to the completion of the sale for any period of time not to exceed a total of 365 days from the date set forth in the notice of sale. The trustee shall postpone the sale in accordance with any of the following:

(A) Upon the order of any court of competent jurisdiction.

(B) If stayed by operation of law.

(C) By mutual agreement, whether oral or in writing, of any trustor and any beneficiary or any mortgagor and any mortgagee.

(D) At the discretion of the trustee.

(2) In the event that the sale proceedings are postponed for a period or periods totaling more than 365 days, the scheduling of any further sale proceedings shall be preceded by giving a new notice of sale in the manner prescribed in Section 2924f. New fees incurred for the new notice of sale shall not exceed the amounts specified in Sections 2924c and 2924d, and shall not exceed reasonable costs that are necessary to comply with this paragraph.

(d) The notice of each postponement and the reason therefor shall be given by public declaration by the trustee at the time and place last appointed for sale. A public declaration of postponement shall also set forth the new date, time, and place of sale and the place of sale shall be the same place as originally fixed by the trustee for the sale. No other notice of postponement need be given. However, the sale shall be conducted no sooner than on the seventh day after the earlier of (1) dismissal of the action or (2) expiration or termination of the injunction, restraining order, or stay that required postponement of the sale, whether by entry of an order by a court of competent jurisdiction, operation of law, or otherwise, unless the injunction, restraining order, or subsequent order expressly directs the conduct of the sale within that seven-day period. For purposes of this subdivision, the seven-day period shall not include the day on which the action is dismissed, or the day on which the injunction, restraining order, or stay expires or is terminated. If the sale had been scheduled to occur, but this subdivision precludes its conduct during that seven-day period, a new notice of postponement shall be given if the sale had been scheduled to occur during that seven-day period. The trustee shall maintain records of each postponement and the reason therefor.

(e) Notwithstanding the time periods established under subdivision (d), if postponement of a sale is based on a stay imposed by Title 11 of the United States Code (bankruptcy), the sale shall be conducted no sooner than the expiration of the stay imposed by that title and the seven-day provision of subdivision (d) shall not apply.

(f) This section shall be operative January 1, 2031. *(Added by Stats.2020, c. 202 (S.B.1079), § 4, eff. Jan. 1, 2021, operative Jan. 1, 2026. Amended by Stats.2022, c. 642 (A.B.1837), § 6, eff. Jan. 1, 2023, operative Jan. 1, 2031.)*

Cross References

Mortgage foreclosure actions, see Code of Civil Procedure § 726 et seq.
Transfer as security deemed mortgage or pledge, power of sale, requirements prior to sale, see Civil Code § 2924.

§ 2924h. Bidders at sale; bid as irrevocable offer; security deposit; finality of sale; rescission for failure of consideration; delivery of payment; restraint of bidding; remedies

Section operative until Jan. 1, 2031. See, also, § 2924h operative Jan. 1, 2031.

(a) Each and every bid made by a bidder at a trustee's sale under a power of sale contained in a deed of trust or mortgage shall be deemed to be an irrevocable offer by that bidder to purchase the property being sold by the trustee under the power of sale for the amount of the bid. Any second or subsequent bid by the same bidder or any other bidder for a higher amount shall be a cancellation of the prior bid.

(b) At the trustee's sale the trustee shall have the right (1) to require every bidder to show evidence of the bidder's ability to deposit with the trustee the full amount of their final bid in cash, a cashier's check drawn on a state or national bank, a check drawn by a state or federal credit union, or a check drawn by a state or federal savings and loan

§ 2924h

association, savings association, or savings bank specified in Section 5102 of the Financial Code and authorized to do business in this state, or a cash equivalent which has been designated in the notice of sale as acceptable to the trustee prior to, and as a condition to, the recognizing of the bid, and to conditionally accept and hold these amounts for the duration of the sale, and (2) to require the last and highest bidder to deposit, if not deposited previously, the full amount of the bidder's final bid in cash, a cashier's check drawn on a state or national bank, a check drawn by a state or federal credit union, or a check drawn by a state or federal savings and loan association, savings association, or savings bank specified in Section 5102 of the Financial Code and authorized to do business in this state, or a cash equivalent which has been designated in the notice of sale as acceptable to the trustee, immediately prior to the completion of the sale, the completion of the sale being so announced by the fall of the hammer or in another customary manner. The present beneficiary of the deed of trust under foreclosure shall have the right to offset their bid or bids only to the extent of the total amount due the beneficiary including the trustee's fees and expenses.

(c) In the event the trustee accepts a check drawn by a credit union or a savings and loan association pursuant to this subdivision or a cash equivalent designated in the notice of sale, the trustee may withhold the issuance of the trustee's deed to the successful bidder submitting the check drawn by a state or federal credit union or savings and loan association or the cash equivalent until funds become available to the payee or endorsee as a matter of right.

For the purposes of this subdivision, the trustee's sale shall be deemed final upon the acceptance of the last and highest bid, and shall be deemed perfected as of 8 a.m. on the actual date of sale if the trustee's deed is recorded within 21 calendar days after the sale, or the next business day following the 21st day if the county recorder in which the property is located is closed on the 21st day. If an eligible bidder submits a written notice of intent to bid pursuant to paragraph (3) of subdivision (c) of Section 2924m, the trustee's sale shall be deemed perfected as of 8 a.m. on the actual date of sale if the trustee's deed is recorded within 60 calendar days after the sale or the next business day following the 60th day if the county recorder in which the property is located is closed on the 60th day. However, the sale is subject to an automatic rescission for a failure of consideration in the event the funds are not "available for withdrawal" as defined in Section 12413.1 of the Insurance Code. The trustee shall send a notice of rescission for a failure of consideration to the last and highest bidder submitting the check or alternative instrument, if the address of the last and highest bidder is known to the trustee.

If a sale results in an automatic right of rescission for failure of consideration pursuant to this subdivision, the interest of any lienholder shall be reinstated in the same priority as if the previous sale had not occurred.

(d) If the trustee has not required the last and highest bidder to deposit the cash, a cashier's check drawn on a state or national bank, a check drawn by a state or federal credit union, or a check drawn by a state or federal savings and loan association, savings association, or savings bank specified in Section 5102 of the Financial Code and authorized to do business in this state, or a cash equivalent which has been designated in the notice of sale as acceptable to the trustee in the manner set forth in paragraph (2) of subdivision (b), the trustee shall complete the sale. If the last and highest bidder then fails to deliver to the trustee, when demanded, the amount of their final bid in cash, a cashier's check drawn on a state or national bank, a check drawn by a state or federal credit union, or a check drawn by a state or federal savings and loan association, savings association, or savings bank specified in Section 5102 of the Financial Code and authorized to do business in this state, or a cash equivalent which has been designated in the notice of sale as acceptable to the trustee, that bidder shall be liable to the trustee for all damages which the trustee may sustain by the refusal to deliver to the trustee the amount of the final bid, including any court costs and reasonable attorneys' fees.

If the last and highest bidder willfully fails to deliver to the trustee the amount of their final bid in cash, a cashier's check drawn on a state or national bank, a check drawn by a state or federal credit union, or a check drawn by a state or federal savings and loan association, savings association, or savings bank specified in Section 5102 of the Financial Code and authorized to do business in this state, or a cash equivalent which has been designated in the notice of sale as acceptable to the trustee, or if the last and highest bidder cancels a cashiers check drawn on a state or national bank, a check drawn by a state or federal credit union, or a check drawn by a state or federal savings and loan association, savings association, or savings bank specified in Section 5102 of the Financial Code and authorized to do business in this state, or a cash equivalent that has been designated in the notice of sale as acceptable to the trustee, that bidder shall be guilty of a misdemeanor punishable by a fine of not more than two thousand five hundred dollars ($2,500).

In the event the last and highest bidder cancels an instrument submitted to the trustee as a cash equivalent, the trustee shall provide a new notice of sale in the manner set forth in Section 2924f and shall be entitled to recover the costs of the new notice of sale as provided in Section 2924c.

(e) Any postponement or discontinuance of the sale proceedings shall be a cancellation of the last bid.

(f) Except as specifically provided in Section 2924m, in the event that this section conflicts with any other statute, then this section shall prevail.

(g) It shall be unlawful for any person, acting alone or in concert with others, (1) to offer to accept or accept from another, any consideration of any type not to bid, or (2) to fix or restrain bidding in any manner, at a sale of property conducted pursuant to a power of sale in a deed of trust or mortgage. However, it shall not be unlawful for any person, including a trustee, to state that a property subject to a recorded notice of default or subject to a sale conducted pursuant to this chapter is being sold in an "as-is" condition.

In addition to any other remedies, any person committing any act declared unlawful by this subdivision or any act which would operate as a fraud or deceit upon any beneficiary, trustor, or junior lienor shall, upon conviction, be fined not more than ten thousand dollars ($10,000) or imprisoned in the county jail for not more than one year, or be punished by both that fine and imprisonment.

(h) This section shall remain in effect only until January 1, 2031, and as of that date is repealed, unless a later enacted statute that is enacted before January 1, 2031, deletes or extends that date.

(i) The amendments made to this section by the bill adding this subdivision [1] shall become operative on January 1, 2022. (Added by Stats.1972, c. 1056, p. 1943, § 5. Amended by Stats.1979, c. 1015, p. 3476, § 5; Stats.1981, c. 427, p. 1660, § 3; Stats.1986, c. 1385, § 6; Stats.1987, c. 725, § 2; Stats. 1992, c. 351 (A.B.2981), § 5; Stats.1993, c. 724 (A.B.1196), § 3; Stats.1995, c. 752 (A.B.1695), § 3; Stats.2004, c. 177 (S.B.1277), § 2; Stats.2020, c. 202 (S.B.1079), § 5, eff. Jan. 1, 2021; Stats.2021, c. 255 (A.B.175), § 1, eff. Sept. 23, 2021, operative Jan. 1, 2022; Stats.2022, c. 642 (A.B.1837), § 7, eff. Jan. 1, 2023.)

[1] Stats.2021, c. 255 (A.B.175).

Repeal

For repeal of this section, see its terms.

Cross References

Mortgage foreclosure actions, see Code of Civil Procedure § 726 et seq.

§ 2924h. Bidders at sale; bid as irrevocable offer; security deposit; finality of sale; rescission for failure of consideration; delivery of payment; restraint of bidding; remedies

Section operative Jan. 1, 2031. See, also, § 2924h operative until Jan. 1, 2031.

(a) Each and every bid made by a bidder at a trustee's sale under a power of sale contained in a deed of trust or mortgage shall be deemed to be an irrevocable offer by that bidder to purchase the property being sold by the trustee under the power of sale for the amount of the bid. Any second or subsequent bid by the same bidder or any other bidder for a higher amount shall be a cancellation of the prior bid.

(b) At the trustee's sale the trustee shall have the right (1) to require every bidder to show evidence of the bidder's ability to deposit with the trustee the full amount of their final bid in cash, a cashier's check drawn on a state or national bank, a check drawn by a state or federal credit union, or a check drawn by a state or federal savings and loan association, savings association, or savings bank specified in Section 5102 of the Financial Code and authorized to do business in this state, or a cash equivalent which has been designated in the notice of sale as acceptable to the trustee prior to, and as a condition to, the recognizing of the bid, and to conditionally accept and hold these amounts for the duration of the sale, and (2) to require the last and highest bidder to deposit, if not deposited previously, the full amount of the bidder's final bid in cash, a cashier's check drawn on a state or national bank, a check drawn by a state or federal credit union, or a check drawn by a state or federal savings and loan association, savings association, or savings bank specified in Section 5102 of the Financial Code and authorized to do business in this state, or a cash equivalent which has been designated in the notice of sale as acceptable to the trustee, immediately prior to the completion of the sale, the completion of the sale being so announced by the fall of the hammer or in another customary manner. The present beneficiary of the deed of trust under foreclosure shall have the right to offset their bid or bids only to the extent of the total amount due the beneficiary including the trustee's fees and expenses.

(c) In the event the trustee accepts a check drawn by a credit union or a savings and loan association pursuant to this subdivision or a cash equivalent designated in the notice of sale, the trustee may withhold the issuance of the trustee's deed to the successful bidder submitting the check drawn by a state or federal credit union or savings and loan association or the cash equivalent until funds become available to the payee or endorsee as a matter of right.

For the purposes of this subdivision, the trustee's sale shall be deemed final upon the acceptance of the last and highest bid, and shall be deemed perfected as of 8 a.m. on the actual date of sale if the trustee's deed is recorded within 15 calendar days after the sale, or the next business day following the 15th day if the county recorder in which the property is located is closed on the 15th day. However, the sale is subject to an automatic rescission for a failure of consideration in the event the funds are not "available for withdrawal" as defined in Section 12413.1 of the Insurance Code. The trustee shall send a notice of rescission for a failure of consideration to the last and highest bidder submitting the check or alternative instrument, if the address of the last and highest bidder is known to the trustee.

If a sale results in an automatic right of rescission for failure of consideration pursuant to this subdivision, the interest of any lienholder shall be reinstated in the same priority as if the previous sale had not occurred.

(d) If the trustee has not required the last and highest bidder to deposit the cash, a cashier's check drawn on a state or national bank, a check drawn by a state or federal credit union, or a check drawn by a state or federal savings and loan association, savings association, or savings bank specified in Section 5102 of the Financial Code and authorized to do business in this state, or a cash equivalent which has been designated in the notice of sale as acceptable to the trustee in the manner set forth in paragraph (2) of subdivision (b), the trustee shall complete the sale. If the last and highest bidder then fails to deliver to the trustee, when demanded, the amount of their final bid in cash, a cashier's check drawn on a state or national bank, a check drawn by a state or federal credit union, or a check drawn by a state or federal savings and loan association, savings association, or savings bank specified in Section 5102 of the Financial Code and authorized to do business in this state, or a cash equivalent which has been designated in the notice of sale as acceptable to the trustee, that bidder shall be liable to the trustee for all damages which the trustee may sustain by the refusal to deliver to the trustee the amount of the final bid, including any court costs and reasonable attorneys' fees.

If the last and highest bidder willfully fails to deliver to the trustee the amount of their final bid in cash, a cashier's check drawn on a state or national bank, a check drawn by a state or federal credit union, or a check drawn by a state or federal savings and loan association, savings association, or savings bank specified in Section 5102 of the Financial Code and authorized to do business in this state, or a cash equivalent

§ 2924h OBLIGATIONS

which has been designated in the notice of sale as acceptable to the trustee, or if the last and highest bidder cancels a cashiers check drawn on a state or national bank, a check drawn by a state or federal credit union, or a check drawn by a state or federal savings and loan association, savings association, or savings bank specified in Section 5102 of the Financial Code and authorized to do business in this state, or a cash equivalent that has been designated in the notice of sale as acceptable to the trustee, that bidder shall be guilty of a misdemeanor punishable by a fine of not more than two thousand five hundred dollars ($2,500).

In the event the last and highest bidder cancels an instrument submitted to the trustee as a cash equivalent, the trustee shall provide a new notice of sale in the manner set forth in Section 2924f and shall be entitled to recover the costs of the new notice of sale as provided in Section 2924c.

(e) Any postponement or discontinuance of the sale proceedings shall be a cancellation of the last bid.

(f) In the event that this section conflicts with any other statute, then this section shall prevail.

(g) It shall be unlawful for any person, acting alone or in concert with others, (1) to offer to accept or accept from another, any consideration of any type not to bid, or (2) to fix or restrain bidding in any manner, at a sale of property conducted pursuant to a power of sale in a deed of trust or mortgage. However, it shall not be unlawful for any person, including a trustee, to state that a property subject to a recorded notice of default or subject to a sale conducted pursuant to this chapter is being sold in an "as-is" condition.

In addition to any other remedies, any person committing any act declared unlawful by this subdivision or any act which would operate as a fraud or deceit upon any beneficiary, trustor, or junior lienor shall, upon conviction, be fined not more than ten thousand dollars ($10,000) or imprisoned in the county jail for not more than one year, or be punished by both that fine and imprisonment.

(h) This section shall be operative January 1, 2031. *(Added by Stats.2020, c. 202 (S.B.1079), § 6, eff. Jan. 1, 2021, operative Jan. 1, 2026. Amended by Stats.2022, c. 642 (A.B.1837), § 8, eff. Jan. 1, 2023, operative Jan. 1, 2031.)*

Cross References

Mortgage foreclosure actions, see Code of Civil Procedure § 726 et seq.

§ 2924i. Balloon payment loans; final payment due date; notice; effect; validity of documents; date of application

(a) This section applies to loans secured by a deed of trust or mortgage on real property containing one to four residential units at least one of which at the time the loan is made is or is to be occupied by the borrower if the loan is for a period in excess of one year and is a balloon payment loan.

(b) This section shall not apply to (1) open end credit as defined in Regulation Z, whether or not the transaction is otherwise subject to Regulation Z, (2) transactions subject to Section 2956, or (3) loans made for the principal purpose of financing the construction of one or more residential units.

(c) At least 90 days but not more than 150 days prior to the due date of the final payment on a loan that is subject to this section, the holder of the loan shall deliver or mail by first-class mail, with a certificate of mailing obtained from the United States Postal Service, to the trustor, or his or her successor in interest, at the last known address of that person, a written notice which shall include all of the following:

(1) A statement of the name and address of the person to whom the final payment is required to be paid.

(2) The date on or before which the final payment is required to be paid.

(3) The amount of the final payment, or if the exact amount is unknown, a good faith estimate of the amount thereof, including unpaid principal, interest and any other charges, such amount to be determined assuming timely payment in full of all scheduled installments coming due between the date the notice is prepared and the date when the final payment is due.

(4) If the borrower has a contractual right to refinance the final payment, a statement to that effect.

If the due date of the final payment of a loan subject to this section is extended prior to the time notice is otherwise required under this subdivision, this notice requirement shall apply only to the due date as extended (or as subsequently extended).

(d) For purposes of this section:

(1) A "balloon payment loan" is a loan which provides for a final payment as originally scheduled which is more than twice the amount of any of the immediately preceding six regularly scheduled payments or which contains a call provision; provided, however, that if the call provision is not exercised by the holder of the loan, the existence of the unexercised call provision shall not cause the loan to be deemed to be a balloon payment loan.

(2) "Call provision" means a loan contract term that provides the holder of the loan with the right to call the loan due and payable either after a specified period has elapsed following closing or after a specified date.

(3) "Regulation Z" means any rule, regulation, or interpretation promulgated by the Board of Governors of the Federal Reserve System under the Federal Truth in Lending Act, as amended (15 U.S.C. Sec. 1601 et seq.), and any interpretation or approval thereof issued by an official or employee of the Federal Reserve System duly authorized by the board under the Truth in Lending Act, as amended, to issue such interpretations or approvals.

(e) Failure to provide notice as required by subdivision (a) does not extinguish any obligation of payment by the borrower, except that the due date for any balloon payment shall be the date specified in the balloon payment note, or 90 days from the date of delivery or mailing of the notice required by subdivision (a), or the due date specified in the notice required by subdivision (a), whichever date is later. If the operation of this section acts to extend the term of any note, interest shall continue to accrue for the extended term at the contract rate and payments shall continue to be due at any periodic interval and on any payment schedule specified in the note and shall be credited to principal or interest under the terms of the note. Default in any extended periodic payment shall be considered a default under terms of the note or security instrument.

(f)(1) The validity of any credit document or of any security document subject to the provisions of this section shall not be invalidated solely because of the failure of any person to comply with this section. However, any person who willfully violates any provision of this section shall be liable in the amount of actual damages suffered by the debtor as the proximate result of the violation, and, if the debtor prevails in any suit to recover that amount, for reasonable attorney's fees.

(2) No person may be held liable in any action under this section if it is shown by a preponderance of the evidence that the violation was not intentional and resulted from a bona fide error notwithstanding the maintenance of procedures reasonably adopted to avoid any such error.

(g) The provisions of this section shall apply to any note executed on or after January 1, 1984. *(Added by Stats.1983, c. 1094, § 1. Amended by Stats.1986, c. 1360, § 1.)*

§ 2924j. Execution of trustee's deed resulting from surplus proceeds of trustee's sale; notice; priority of claims; due diligence; declaration of unresolved claims; deposit of funds

(a) Unless an interpleader action has been filed, within 30 days of the execution of the trustee's deed resulting from a sale in which there are proceeds remaining after payment of the amounts required by paragraphs (1) and (2) of subdivision (a) of Section 2924k, the trustee shall send written notice to all persons with recorded interests in the real property as of the date immediately prior to the trustee's sale who would be entitled to notice pursuant to subdivisions (b) and (c) of Section 2924b. The notice shall be sent by first-class mail in the manner provided in paragraph (1) of subdivision (c) of Section 2924b and inform each entitled person of each of the following:

(1) That there has been a trustee's sale of the described real property.

(2) That the noticed person may have a claim to all or a portion of the sale proceeds remaining after payment of the amounts required by paragraphs (1) and (2) of subdivision (a) of Section 2924k.

(3) The noticed person may contact the trustee at the address provided in the notice to pursue any potential claim.

(4) That before the trustee can act, the noticed person may be required to present proof that the person holds the beneficial interest in the obligation and the security interest therefor. In the case of a promissory note secured by a deed of trust, proof that the person holds the beneficial interest may include the original promissory note and assignment of beneficial interests related thereto. The noticed person shall also submit a written claim to the trustee, executed under penalty of perjury, stating the following:

(A) The amount of the claim to the date of trustee's sale.

(B) An itemized statement of the principal, interest, and other charges.

(C) That claims must be received by the trustee at the address stated in the notice no later than 30 days after the date the trustee sends notice to the potential claimant.

(b) The trustee shall exercise due diligence to determine the priority of the written claims received by the trustee to the trustee's sale surplus proceeds from those persons to whom notice was sent pursuant to subdivision (a). In the event there is no dispute as to the priority of the written claims submitted to the trustee, proceeds shall be paid within 30 days after the conclusion of the notice period. If the trustee has failed to determine the priority of written claims within 90 days following the 30-day notice period, then within 10 days thereafter the trustee shall deposit the funds with the clerk of the court pursuant to subdivision (c) or file an interpleader action pursuant to subdivision (e). Nothing in this section shall preclude any person from pursuing other remedies or claims as to surplus proceeds.

(c) If, after due diligence, the trustee is unable to determine the priority of the written claims received by the trustee to the trustee's sale surplus of multiple persons or if the trustee determines there is a conflict between potential claimants, the trustee may file a declaration of the unresolved claims and deposit with the clerk of the superior court of the county in which the sale occurred, that portion of the sales proceeds that cannot be distributed, less any fees charged by the clerk pursuant to this subdivision. The declaration shall specify the date of the trustee's sale, a description of the property, the names and addresses of all persons sent notice pursuant to subdivision (a), a statement that the trustee exercised due diligence pursuant to subdivision (b), that the trustee provided written notice as required by subdivisions (a) and (d) and the amount of the sales proceeds deposited by the trustee with the court. Further, the trustee shall submit a copy of the trustee's sales guarantee and any information relevant to the identity, location, and priority of the potential claimants with the court and shall file proof of service of the notice required by subdivision (d) on all persons described in subdivision (a).

The clerk shall deposit the amount with the county treasurer or, if a bank account has been established for moneys held in trust under paragraph (2) of subdivision (a) of Section 77009 of the Government Code, in that account, subject to order of the court upon the application of any interested party. The clerk may charge a reasonable fee for the performance of activities pursuant to this subdivision equal to the fee for filing an interpleader action pursuant to Chapter 5.8 (commencing with Section 70600) of Title 8 of the Government Code. Upon deposit of that portion of the sale proceeds that cannot be distributed by due diligence, the trustee shall be discharged of further responsibility for the disbursement of sale proceeds. A deposit with the clerk of the court pursuant to this subdivision may be either for the total proceeds of the trustee's sale, less any fees charged by the clerk, if a conflict or conflicts exist with respect to the total proceeds, or that portion that cannot be distributed after due diligence, less any fees charged by the clerk.

(d) Before the trustee deposits the funds with the clerk of the court pursuant to subdivision (c), the trustee shall send written notice by first-class mail, postage prepaid, to all persons described in subdivision (a) informing them that the trustee intends to deposit the funds with the clerk of the court and that a claim for the funds must be filed with the court within 30 days from the date of the notice, providing the address of the court in which the funds were deposited, and a telephone number for obtaining further information.

§ 2924j

Within 90 days after deposit with the clerk, the court shall consider all claims filed at least 15 days before the date on which the hearing is scheduled by the court, the clerk shall serve written notice of the hearing by first-class mail on all claimants identified in the trustee's declaration at the addresses specified therein. Where the amount of the deposit is twenty-five thousand dollars ($25,000) or less, a proceeding pursuant to this section is a limited civil case. The court shall distribute the deposited funds to any and all claimants entitled thereto.

(e) Nothing in this section restricts the ability of a trustee to file an interpleader action in order to resolve a dispute about the proceeds of a trustee's sale. Once an interpleader action has been filed, thereafter the provisions of this section do not apply.

(f) "Due diligence," for the purposes of this section means that the trustee researched the written claims submitted or other evidence of conflicts and determined that a conflict of priorities exists between two or more claimants which the trustee is unable to resolve.

(g) To the extent required by the Unclaimed Property Law, a trustee in possession of surplus proceeds not required to be deposited with the court pursuant to subdivision (b) shall comply with the Unclaimed Property Law (Chapter 7 (commencing with Section 1500) of Title 10 of Part 3 of the Code of Civil Procedure).

(h) The trustee, beneficiary, or counsel to the trustee or beneficiary, is not liable for providing to any person who is entitled to notice pursuant to this section, information set forth in, or a copy of, subdivision (h) of Section 2945.3. *(Added by Stats.1989, c. 849, § 1. Amended by Stats.1990, c. 287 (A.B.3078), § 1; Stats.1992, c. 351 (A.B.2981), § 6; Stats.1998, c. 932 (A.B.1094), § 9; Stats.1999, c. 974 (A.B. 431), § 11; Stats.2002, c. 784 (S.B.1316), § 20; Stats.2003, c. 62 (S.B.600), § 19; Stats.2004, c. 177 (S.B.1277), § 3; Stats. 2005, c. 75 (A.B.145), § 15, eff. July 19, 2005, operative Jan. 1, 2006.)*

Cross References

Liens and mortgages, legislative findings and declarations regarding reliance of vulnerable homeowners upon foreclosure consultants, see Civil Code § 2945.

§ 2924k. Distribution of proceeds of trustee's sale; priority

(a) The trustee, or the clerk of the court upon order to the clerk pursuant to subdivision (d) of Section 2924j, shall distribute the proceeds, or a portion of the proceeds, as the case may be, of the trustee's sale conducted pursuant to Section 2924h in the following order of priority:

(1) To the costs and expenses of exercising the power of sale and of sale, including the payment of the trustee's fees and attorney's fees permitted pursuant to subdivision (b) of Section 2924d and subdivision (b) of this section.

(2) To the payment of the obligations secured by the deed of trust or mortgage which is the subject of the trustee's sale.

(3) To satisfy the outstanding balance of obligations secured by any junior liens or encumbrances in the order of their priority.

(4) To the trustor or the trustor's successor in interest. In the event the property is sold or transferred to another, to the vested owner of record at the time of the trustee's sale.

(b) A trustee may charge costs and expenses incurred for such items as mailing and a reasonable fee for services rendered in connection with the distribution of the proceeds from a trustee's sale, including, but not limited to, the investigation of priority and validity of claims and the disbursement of funds. If the fee charged for services rendered pursuant to this subdivision does not exceed one hundred dollars ($100), or one hundred twenty-five dollars ($125) where there are obligations specified in paragraph (3) of subdivision (a), the fee is conclusively presumed to be reasonable. *(Added by Stats.1990, c. 287 (A.B.3078), § 2. Amended by Stats.1999, c. 974 (A.B.431), § 12.)*

§ 2924l. Declaration of nonmonetary status; trustee named in action or proceeding in trustee capacity; objections

(a) In the event that a trustee under a deed of trust is named in an action or proceeding in which that deed of trust is the subject, and in the event that the trustee maintains a reasonable belief that it has been named in the action or proceeding solely in its capacity as trustee, and not arising out of any wrongful acts or omissions on its part in the performance of its duties as trustee, then, at any time, the trustee may file a declaration of nonmonetary status. The declaration shall be served on the parties in the manner set forth in Chapter 5 (commencing with Section 1010) of Title 14 of the Code of Civil Procedure.

(b) The declaration of nonmonetary status shall set forth the status of the trustee as trustee under the deed of trust that is the subject of the action or proceeding, that the trustee knows or maintains a reasonable belief that it has been named as a defendant in the proceeding solely in its capacity as a trustee under the deed of trust, its reasonable belief that it has not been named as a defendant due to any acts or omissions on its part in the performance of its duties as trustee, the basis for that knowledge or reasonable belief, and that it agrees to be bound by whatever order or judgment is issued by the court regarding the subject deed of trust.

(c) The parties who have appeared in the action or proceeding shall have 15 days from the service of the declaration by the trustee in which to object to the nonmonetary judgment status of the trustee. Any objection shall set forth the factual basis on which the objection is based and shall be served on the trustee.

(d) In the event that no objection is served within the 15-day objection period, the trustee shall not be required to participate any further in the action or proceeding, shall not be subject to any monetary awards as and for damages, attorneys' fees or costs, shall be required to respond to any discovery requests as a nonparty, and shall be bound by any court order relating to the subject deed of trust that is the subject of the action or proceeding.

(e) In the event of a timely objection to the declaration of nonmonetary status, the trustee shall thereafter be required to participate in the action or proceeding.

Additionally, in the event that the parties elect not to, or fail to, timely object to the declaration of nonmonetary status, but later through discovery, or otherwise, determine that the trustee should participate in the action because of the performance of its duties as a trustee, the parties may file and serve on all parties and the trustee a motion pursuant to Section 473 of the Code of Civil Procedure that specifies the factual basis for the demand. Upon the court's granting of the motion, the trustee shall thereafter be required to participate in the action or proceeding, and the court shall provide sufficient time prior to trial for the trustee to be able to respond to the complaint, to conduct discovery, and to bring other pretrial motions in accordance with the Code of Civil Procedure.

(f) Upon the filing of the declaration of nonmonetary status, the time within which the trustee is required to file an answer or other responsive pleading shall be tolled for the period of time within which the opposing parties may respond to the declaration. Upon the timely service of an objection to the declaration on nonmonetary status, the trustee shall have 30 days from the date of service within which to file an answer or other responsive pleading to the complaint or cross-complaint.

(g) For purposes of this section, "trustee" includes any agent or employee of the trustee who performs some or all of the duties of a trustee under this article, and includes substituted trustees and agents of the beneficiary or trustee.

(h) A fee shall not be charged for the filing of a declaration of nonmonetary status pursuant to this section. (Added by Stats.1995, c. 752 (A.B.1695), § 4. Amended by Stats.1997, c. 74 (S.B.665), § 6; Stats.1999, c. 974 (A.B.431), § 13; Stats.2004, c. 177 (S.B.1277), § 4; Stats.2020, c. 203 (S.B.1148), § 2, eff. Jan. 1, 2021.)

§ 2924m. Sale of property containing one to four residential units; finality of sale; notice of sale by trustee

(a) For purposes of this section:

(1) "Prospective owner-occupant" means a natural person who presents to the trustee an affidavit or declaration, pursuant to Section 2015.5 of the Code of Civil Procedure, that:

(A) They will occupy the property as their primary residence within 60 days of the trustee's deed being recorded.

(B) They will maintain their occupancy for at least one year.

(C) They are not any of the following:

(i) The mortgagor or trustor.

(ii) The child, spouse, or parent of the mortgagor or trustor.

(iii) The grantor of a living trust that was named in the title to the property when the notice of default was recorded.

(iv) An employee, officer, or member of the mortgagor or trustor.

(v) A person with an ownership interest in the mortgagor, unless the mortgagor is a publicly traded company.

(D) They are not acting as the agent of any other person or entity in purchasing the real property.

(2) "Eligible tenant buyer" means a natural person who at the time of the trustee's sale:

(A) Is occupying the real property as their primary residence.

(B) Is occupying the real property under a rental or lease agreement entered into as the result of an arm's length transaction with the mortgagor or trustor, or with the mortgagor or trustor's predecessor in interest, on a date prior to the recording of the notice of default against the property, and who attaches evidence demonstrating the existence of the tenancy to the affidavit or declaration required pursuant to subparagraph (B) of paragraph (2) of subdivision (c).

(C) Is not the mortgagor or trustor, or the child, spouse, or parent of the mortgagor or trustor.

(D) Is not acting as the agent of any other person or entity in purchasing the real property. Submission of a bid pursuant to paragraph (3) of subdivision (c) does not violate this subparagraph.

(E) Has not filed a petition under Chapter 7, 11, 12, or 13 of Title 11 of the United States Code at any time during the period from the date of the trustee's sale of the property to the 45th day after the trustee's sale, or the next business day following the 45th day if the 45th day is a weekend or holiday.

(3) "Eligible bidder" means any of the following:

(A) An eligible tenant buyer.

(B) A prospective owner-occupant.

(C) A nonprofit association, nonprofit corporation, or cooperative corporation in which an eligible tenant buyer * * * is a voting member or director.

(D) An eligible nonprofit corporation * * * with all of the following attributes:

(i) It has a determination letter from the Internal Revenue Service affirming its tax-exempt status pursuant to Section 501(c)(3) of the Internal Revenue Code [1] and is not a private foundation as that term is defined in Section 509 of the Internal Revenue Code.

(ii) It has its principal place of business in California.

(iii) The primary residences of all board members are located in California.

(iv) One of its primary activities is the development and preservation of affordable rental or homeownership housing in California.

* * *

(v) It is registered and in good standing with the Attorney General's Registry of Charitable Trusts, pursuant to the Supervision of Trustees and Fundraisers for Charitable Purposes Act (Article 7 (commencing with Section 12580) of Chapter 6 of Part 2 of Division 3 of Title 2 of the Government Code).

(E) A limited liability company * * * wholly owned by one or more eligible nonprofit * * * corporations as described in subparagraph (C) or (D).

(F) A community land trust, as defined in clause (ii) of subparagraph (C) of paragraph (11) of subdivision (a) of Section 402.1 of the Revenue and Taxation Code.

(G) A limited-equity housing cooperative as defined in Section 817.

(H) The state, the Regents of the University of California, a county, city, district, public authority, or public agency, and any other political subdivision or public corporation in the state.

(4) "Evidence demonstrating the existence of the tenancy" means a copy of the dated and signed rental or lease agreement or, if a copy of the dated and signed rental or lease agreement is not available, then one of the following:

(A) Evidence of rent payments made for the property by the person asserting that they are an eligible tenant buyer for the six months prior to the recording of the notice of default.

(B) Copies of utility bills for the property payable by the person asserting that they are an eligible tenant buyer for the six months prior to the recording of the notice of default.

(b) Nothing in this section shall prevent an eligible tenant buyer who meets the conditions set forth in paragraph (1) of subdivision (a) from being deemed a prospective owner-occupant.

(c) A trustee's sale of property under a power of sale contained in a deed of trust or mortgage on real property containing one to four residential units pursuant to Section 2924g shall not be deemed final until the earliest of the following:

(1) If a prospective owner-occupant is the last and highest bidder at the trustee's sale, the date upon which the conditions set forth in Section 2924h for the sale to become final are met. The * * * prospective owner-occupant shall submit to the trustee the affidavit or declaration described in paragraph (1) of subdivision (a) at the trustee's sale or to the trustee by 5 p.m. on the next business day following the trustee's sale. * * *

(2) Fifteen days after the trustee's sale unless at least one eligible tenant buyer or eligible bidder submits to the trustee either a bid pursuant to paragraph (3) or (4) or a nonbinding written notice of intent to place such a bid. The bid or written notice of intent to place a bid shall:

(A) Be sent to the trustee by certified mail, overnight delivery, or other method that allows for confirmation of the delivery date.

(B) Be accompanied by an affidavit or declaration, pursuant to Section 2015.5 of the Code of Civil Procedure, identifying the category set forth in paragraph (3) of subdivision (a) to which the person or entity submitting the bid or nonbinding written notice of intent belongs and stating that the person meets the criteria for that category. * * * If the winning bid is placed by an eligible bidder described in subparagraphs (C) to (G), inclusive, of paragraph (3) of subdivision (a), the affidavit or declaration shall affirm the bidder's duty to comply with subdivision (a) of Section 2924o for the benefit of tenants occupying the property.

(C) Be received by the trustee no later than 5 p.m. on the 15th day after the trustee's sale, or the next business day following the 15th day if the 15th day is a weekend or holiday.

(D) Contain a current telephone number and return mailing address for the person submitting the bid or nonbinding written notice of intent.

(3)(A) The date upon which a representative of all of the eligible tenant buyers submits to the trustee a bid in an amount equal to the full amount of the last and highest bid at the trustee's sale, in the form of cash, a cashier's check drawn on a state or national bank, a cashier's check drawn by a state or federal credit union, or a cashier's check drawn by a state or federal savings and loan association, savings association, or savings bank specified in Section 5102 of the Financial Code and authorized to do business in this state. This bid shall:

(i) Be sent to the trustee by certified mail, overnight delivery, or other method that allows for confirmation of the delivery date and shall

(ii) Be accompanied by an affidavit or declaration, pursuant to Section 2015.5 of the Code of Civil Procedure, stating that the persons represented meet the criteria set forth in paragraph (2) of subdivision (a), and that the persons represented are all of the eligible tenant buyers. * * *

(iii) Meet either of the following criteria:

(I) Be received by the trustee no later than 5 p.m. on the 15th day after the trustee's sale, the next business day following the 15th day if the 15th day is a weekend or holiday.

(II) Be received by the trustee no later than 5 p.m. on the 45th day after the trustee's sale, or the next business day following the 45th day if the 45th day is a weekend or holiday, if at least one of the eligible tenant buyers submitted a nonbinding written notice of intent to place a bid pursuant to paragraph (2).

(iv) Contain a current telephone number and return mailing address for the person submitting the bid.

(v) Be limited to a single bid amount and not contain instructions for successive bid amounts.

(B) If the conditions in this paragraph are satisfied, the eligible tenant buyers shall be deemed the last and highest bidder pursuant to the power of sale.

(4)(A) Forty-five days after the trustee's sale, except that during the 45-day period, an eligible bidder may submit to the trustee a bid in an amount that exceeds the last and highest bid at the trustee's sale, in the form of cash, a cashier's check drawn on a state or national bank, a cashier's check drawn by a state or federal credit union, or a cashier's check drawn by a state or federal savings and loan association, savings association, or savings bank specified in Section 5102 of the Financial Code and authorized to do business in this state. The bid shall:

(i) Be sent to the trustee by certified mail, overnight delivery, or other method that allows for confirmation of the delivery date.

(ii) Be accompanied by an affidavit or declaration, pursuant to Section 2015.5 of the Code of Civil Procedure, identifying the category set forth in paragraph (3) of subdivision (a) to which the eligible bidder belongs and stating that the eligible bidder meets the criteria for that category. * * *

(iii) Be received by the trustee no later than 5 p.m. on the 45th day after the trustee's sale, or the next business day following the 45th day if the 45th day is a weekend or holiday, if the eligible bidder submitted a nonbinding written notice of intent to bid pursuant to paragraph (2). Notwithstanding clause (i), on the last day that bids are eligible to be received by the trustee under this clause, the trustee shall not receive any bid that is not sent by certified mail or overnight mail.

(iv) Contain a current telephone number and return mailing address for the person submitting the bid.

(B) As of 5 p.m. on the 45th day after the trustee's sale, if one or more eligible bidders has submitted a bid that meets the conditions in this paragraph, the eligible bidder that submitted the highest bid shall be deemed the last and highest bidder pursuant to the power of sale. The trustee shall return any losing bid to the eligible bidder that submitted it.

(d) The trustee may reasonably rely on affidavits and declarations regarding bidder eligibility received under this section. The affidavit or declaration of the winning bidder shall be attached as an exhibit to the trustee's deed and recorded.

(e) If the conditions set forth in paragraph (1) of subdivision (c) for a sale to be deemed final are not met, then:

(1) Not later than 48 hours after the trustee's sale of property under Section 2924g, the trustee or an authorized agent shall post on the internet website set forth on the notice of sale, as required under paragraph (8) of subdivision (b) of Section 2924f, the following information:

(A) The date on which the trustee's sale took place.

(B) The amount of the last and highest bid at the trustee's sale.

(C) An address at which the trustee can receive documents sent by United States mail and by a method of delivery providing for overnight delivery.

(2) The information required to be posted on the internet website under paragraph (1) shall also be made available not later than 48 hours after the trustee's sale of property under Section 2924g by calling the telephone number set forth on the notice of sale as required under paragraph (8) of subdivision (b) of Section 2924f.

(3) The information required to be provided under paragraphs (1) and (2) shall be made available using the file number assigned to the case that is set forth on the notice of sale as required under paragraph (8) of subdivision (b) of Section 2924f.

(4) The information required to be provided under paragraphs (1) and (2) shall be made available for a period of not less than 45 days after the sale of property under Section 2924g.

(5) A disruption of any of these methods of providing the information required under paragraphs (1) and (2) to allow for reasonable maintenance or due to a service outage shall not be deemed to be a violation of this subdivision.

(6) The information to be provided by the trustee to eligible bidders or to persons considering whether to submit a bid or notice of intent to bid pursuant to this section is limited to the information set forth in paragraph (1).

(f) Title to the property shall remain with the mortgagor or trustor until the property sale is deemed final as provided in this section.

(g) A prospective owner-occupant shall not be in violation of this section if a legal owner's compliance with the requirements of Section 2924n renders them unable to occupy the property as their primary residence within 60 days of the trustee's deed being recorded.

(h) This section shall prevail over any conflicting provision of Section 2924h.

(i) For trustee's sales where the winning bidder is an eligible bidder under this section, the trustee or an authorized agent shall electronically send the following information to the office of the Attorney General within 15 days of the sale being deemed final:

(1) The dates when the trustee's sale took place and when it was deemed final.

(2) The name of the winning bidder.

(3) The street address and assessor's parcel number of the subject property.

(4) A copy of the trustee's deed, as recorded, including the attached affidavit or declaration of the winning bidder.

(5) The category set forth in paragraph (3) of subdivision (a) to which the eligible bidder belongs.

(j) The Attorney General, a county counsel, a city attorney, or a district attorney may bring an action for specific performance or any other remedy at equity or at law to enforce this section.

(k) The Department of Justice shall include a summary of information contained in the reports received pursuant to subdivision (i) in a searchable repository on its official internet website.

(*l*) The pendency of a determination of finality under subdivision (c) shall not cause termination of any hazard insurance coverage in effect at the time of the trustee's sale.

(m) This section shall remain in effect only until January 1, 2031, and as of that date is repealed, unless a later enacted statute that is enacted before January 1, 2031, deletes or extends that date.

(n) The amendments made to this section by the bill adding this subdivision [2] shall become operative on January 1, 2022.

(*o*) The amendments made to this section by the bill adding this subdivision shall become operative on January 1, 2023. *(Added by Stats.2020, c. 202 (S.B.1079), § 7, eff. Jan. 1, 2021. Amended by Stats.2021, c. 255 (A.B.175), § 2, eff. Sept. 23, 2021, operative Jan. 1, 2022; Stats.2022, c. 642 (A.B.1837), § 9, eff. Jan. 1, 2023.)*

[1] Internal Revenue Code sections are in Title 26 of the U.S.C.A.
[2] Stats.2021, c. 255 (A.B.175).

Repeal

For repeal of this section, see its terms.

§ 2924n. Compliance with law regarding eviction or displacement of tenants

Nothing in this article shall relieve a person deemed the legal owner of real property when the trustee's deed is recorded from complying with applicable law regarding the eviction or displacement of tenants, including, but not limited to, notice requirements, requirements for the provision of temporary or permanent relocation assistance, the right to return, and just cause eviction requirements. *(Added by Stats.2020, c. 202 (S.B.1079), § 8, eff. Jan. 1, 2021.)*

§ 2924o. Eligible bidder; affordable housing cost or rent; tenants; enforcement

(a) On and after January 1, 2023, in the case of any real property purchased pursuant to Section 2924m by an eligible bidder described in subparagraphs (C) to (G), inclusive, of paragraph (3) of subdivision (a) of that section, the property shall be subject to a recorded covenant that ensures the property shall be sold at an affordable housing cost, as defined in Section 50052.5 of the Health and Safety Code, or rented at an affordable rent, as defined in Section 50053 of the Health and Safety Code, for lower income households for 30 years from the date the trustee's deed is issued, or a greater period of time if any of the following apply:

(1) The terms of a federal, state, or local grant, tax credit, or other source of project financing funding the purchase or maintenance of the property by an eligible bidder require a longer term.

(2) The property becomes subject to a contract as described in paragraph (11) of subdivision (a) of Section 402.1 of the Revenue and Taxation Code.

(b) Tenants, if any, of a property purchased pursuant to Section 2924m by an eligible bidder described in subparagraphs (C) to (G), inclusive, of paragraph (3) of subdivision (a) of that section may exercise any rights available at equity or in law, including, without limitation, to defend an unlawful detainer or institute an action to enforce this section.

(c) For purposes of this section, "lower income households" has the same meaning as described in Section 50079.5 of the Health and Safety Code.

(d) This section shall remain in effect only until January 1, 2031, and as of that date is repealed, unless a later enacted statute that is enacted before January 1, 2031, deletes or extends that date. *(Added by Stats.2022, c. 642 (A.B.1837), § 10, eff. Jan. 1, 2023.)*

Repeal

For repeal of this section, see its terms.

§ 2924p. Sale of real property containing one to four residential dwelling units acquired through foreclosure under a mortgage or deed of trust by an institution or that is acquired at a foreclosure sale by an institution

(a) For purposes of this section, it is the intent of the Legislature to do all of the following:

(1) Allow for prospective owner-occupants and eligible bidders to have the first opportunity to purchase properties that have been acquired through the foreclosure process by an entity that annually forecloses on 175 or more residential real properties in California.

(2) Promote owner occupancy by enacting legislation consistent with the provisions of the federal First Look program that provides owner-occupants and affordable housing providers an opportunity for their offers to be considered on foreclosed properties prior to other offers.

(3) Ensure that the requirements of this section are consistent with the original stated goals of the federal First Look program, which were to expand home ownership opportunities, strengthen neighborhoods and communities, while also providing that sellers are required to respond to offers received during the first look period before accepting or considering investor offers to purchase single-family homes.

(b) For purpose of this section:

(1) "Bundled sale" means the sale of two or more parcels of real property containing one to four residential dwelling units, inclusive, at least two of which have been acquired through foreclosure under a mortgage or deed of trust.

(2) "Eligible bidder" means any of the following:

(A) A prospective owner-occupant.

(B) A nonprofit corporation that meets all of the following requirements:

(i) The nonprofit corporation has a determination letter from the Internal Revenue Service affirming its tax-exempt status pursuant to Section 501(c)(3) of the Internal Revenue Code [1] and is not a private foundation as that term is defined in Section 509 of the Internal Revenue Code.

(ii) The nonprofit corporation is based in California.

(iii) All of the board members of the nonprofit corporation have their primary residence in California.

(iv) The primary activity of the nonprofit corporation is the development and preservation of affordable rental or home ownership housing in California.

(C) A community land trust based in California, as defined in clause (ii) of subparagraph (C) of paragraph (11) of subdivision (a) of Section 402.1 of the Revenue and Taxation Code.

(D) A limited-equity housing cooperative, as defined in Section 817, that is based in California.

(E) The state, the Regents of the University of California, a county, city, district, public authority, or public agency, and any other political subdivision or public corporation in the state.

(3) "Institution" means any of the following, if that person or entity, during its immediately preceding annual reporting period, as established with its primary regulator, foreclosed on 175 or more residential real properties, containing no more than 4 dwelling units:

(A) A depository institution chartered under state or federal law.

(B) A person licensed pursuant to Division 9 (commencing with Section 22000) or Division 20 (commencing with Section 50000) of the Financial Code.

(C) A person licensed pursuant to Part 1 (commencing with Section 10000) of Division 4 of the Business and Professions Code.

(4) "Prospective owner-occupant" means a natural person whose affidavit or declaration under paragraph (2) of subdivision (c) states all of the following:

(A) They will occupy the property as their primary residence within 60 days of the trustee's deed being recorded.

(B) They will maintain their occupancy for at least one year.

(C) They are not any of the following:

(i) The mortgagor or trustor.

(ii) The child, spouse, or parent of the mortgagor or trustor.

(iii) The grantor of a living trust that was named in the title to the property when the notice of default was recorded.

(iv) An employee, officer, or member of the mortgagor or trustor.

(v) A person with an ownership interest in the mortgagor, unless the mortgagor is a publicly traded company.

(D) They are not acting as the agent of any other person or entity in purchasing the real property.

(c) All of the following shall apply to sales of real property containing one to four residential dwelling units, inclusive, that is acquired through foreclosure under a mortgage or deed of trust by an institution or that is acquired at a foreclosure sale by an institution:

(1) During the first 30 days after the property is listed for sale, the institution shall only accept offers from eligible bidders.

(2) An eligible bidder shall submit with their offer to the institution an affidavit or declaration, pursuant to Section 2015.5 of the Code of Civil Procedure, that states they are either of the following:

(A) An eligible bidder pursuant to subparagraphs (B) through (E) of paragraph (2) of subdivision (b).

(B) A prospective owner-occupant purchasing the property as a primary residence pursuant to this subdivision.

(3) Any fraudulent statements may be subject to criminal or civil liability.

(4) The institution shall respond, in writing, to all offers received from eligible bidders during the first 30 days after the property is listed for sale before considering any other offers.

(5) Notwithstanding any other law, an institution shall not conduct a bundled sale.

(d) The provisions of this section are severable. If any provision of this section or its application is held invalid, that invalidity shall not affect other provisions or applications that can be given effect without the invalid provision or application. *(Added by Stats.2022, c. 865 (A.B.2170), § 1, eff. Jan. 1, 2023.)*

[1] Internal Revenue Code sections are in Title 26 of the U.S.C.A.

§ 2924½. Repealed by Stats.1959, c. 593, p. 2564, § 3

§ 2925. Transfer subject to defeasance on a condition; proof

The fact that a transfer was made subject to defeasance on a condition, may, for the purpose of showing such transfer to be a mortgage, be proved (except as against a subsequent purchaser or incumbrancer for value and without notice), though the fact does not appear by the terms of the instrument. *(Enacted in 1872.)*

Cross References

Instrument of defeasance affecting absolute grant to be recorded, see Civil Code § 2950.

Title not transferred by lien or contract for lien, see Civil Code § 2888.

§ 2926. Scope of mortgage lien

A mortgage is a lien upon everything that would pass by a grant of the property. *(Enacted in 1872.)*

Cross References

Effect of,
   Liens generally, see Civil Code § 2888 et seq.
   Transfer of real property generally, see Civil Code § 1104 et seq.
Extinction of liens generally, see Civil Code § 2909 et seq.
Fixtures defined, see Civil Code § 660.
Priority of,
   Liens generally, see Civil Code § 2897 et seq.
   Mechanics liens over mortgages, see Civil Code § 8450 et seq.
Real property defined, see Civil Code § 658.
Real property mortgageable, see Civil Code § 2947.

§ 2927. Possession of mortgaged property

A mortgage does not entitle the mortgagee to the possession of the property, unless authorized by the express terms of the mortgage; but after the execution of the mortgage the mortgagor may agree to such change of possession without a new consideration. *(Enacted in 1872.)*

Cross References

Definition of mortgage, see Civil Code § 2920.
Independence of lien of a mortgage from possession, see Civil Code § 2923.
Mortgage not deemed conveyance, see Code of Civil Procedure § 744.
Mortgage on property held adversely to mortgagor, see Civil Code § 2921.
Title not transferred by lien or contract for lien, see Civil Code § 2888.

§ 2928. Personal obligation

A mortgage does not bind the mortgagor personally to perform the act for the performance of which it is a security, unless there is an express covenant therein to that effect. *(Enacted in 1872.)*

Cross References

Deficiency judgment, foreclosure under power of sale, see Code of Civil Procedure § 580d.
Discharge of mortgage, see Civil Code § 2939 et seq.
Personal liability of defendant in foreclosure proceedings, see Code of Civil Procedure § 726.
Personal obligation not implied by creation of lien, see Civil Code § 2890.

§ 2929. Waste

No person whose interest is subject to the lien of a mortgage may do any act which will substantially impair the mortgagee's security. *(Enacted in 1872.)*

Cross References

Actions for waste, see Code of Civil Procedure § 732.
Damages for wrongs, see Civil Code § 3333 et seq.
Injunction against injury to real property,
   During foreclosure, see Code of Civil Procedure § 745.
   During litigation, see Code of Civil Procedure § 526.

§ 2929.3. Maintenance of vacant residential property purchased at foreclosure sale; violation; fines and penalties; notice of violation

(a)(1) A legal owner shall maintain vacant residential property purchased by that owner at a foreclosure sale once that sale is deemed final, or acquired by that owner through foreclosure under a mortgage or deed of trust. A governmental entity may impose a civil fine upon the legal owner of the property for a violation as set forth in this section. The governmental entity is not required to impose a civil fine if the violation is not remedied.

(2) If the governmental entity chooses to impose a fine pursuant to this section, it shall give the legal owner, prior to the imposition of the fine, a notice containing the following information:

(A) Notice of the alleged violation, including a detailed description of the conditions that gave rise to the allegation.

(B) Notice of the entity's intent to assess a civil fine if the legal owner does not do both of the following:

(i) Within a period determined by the entity, consisting of not less than 14 business days following the date of the notice, commence action to remedy the violation and notify the entity of that action. This time period shall be extended by an additional 10 business days if requested by the legal owner in order to clarify with the entity the actions necessary to remedy the violation.

(ii) Complete the action described in clause (i) within a period of no less than 16 business days following the end of the period set forth in clause (i).

(C) The notice required under this paragraph shall be mailed to the address provided in the deed or other instrument as specified in subdivision (a) of Section 27321.5 of the Government Code, or, if none, to the return address provided on the deed or other instrument.

(3) The governmental entity shall provide a period of not less than the time set forth in clauses (i) and (ii) of subparagraph (B) of paragraph (2) to remedy the violation prior to imposing a civil fine and shall allow for a hearing and opportunity to contest any fine imposed. In determining the amount of the fine, the governmental entity shall take into consideration any timely and good faith efforts by the legal owner to remedy the violation. The maximum civil fine authorized by this section for each day that the owner fails to maintain the property, commencing on the day following the expiration of the period to remedy the violation established by the governmental entity, is as follows:

(A) Up to a maximum of two thousand dollars ($2,000) per day for the first 30 days.

(B) Up to a maximum of five thousand dollars ($5,000) per day thereafter.

(4) Subject to the provisions of this section, a governmental entity may establish different compliance periods for different conditions on the same property in the notice of alleged violation mailed to the legal owner.

(b) For purposes of this section, "failure to maintain" means failure to care for the exterior of the property, including, but not limited to, permitting excessive foliage growth that diminishes the value of surrounding properties, failing to take action to prevent trespassers or squatters from remaining on the property, or failing to take action to prevent mosquito larvae from growing in standing water or other conditions that create a public nuisance.

(c) Notwithstanding subdivisions (a) and (b), a governmental entity may provide less than 30 days' notice to remedy a condition before imposing a civil fine if the entity determines that a specific condition of the property threatens public health or safety and provided that notice of that determination and time for compliance is given.

(d) Fines and penalties collected pursuant to this section shall be directed to local nuisance abatement programs, including, but not limited to, legal abatement proceedings.

(e) A governmental entity may not impose fines on a legal owner under both this section and a local ordinance.

(f) These provisions shall not preempt any local ordinance.

(g) This section shall only apply to residential real property.

(h) The rights and remedies provided in this section are cumulative and in addition to any other rights and remedies provided by law. *(Added by Stats.2008, c. 69 (S.B.1137), § 5, eff. July 8, 2008. Amended by Stats.2012, c. 201 (A.B.2314), § 1; Stats.2020, c. 202 (S.B.1079), § 9, eff. Jan. 1, 2021.)*

§ 2929.4. Failure to maintain vacant property subject to notice of default, purchased at foreclosure sale, or acquired through foreclosure; notice of violation prior to imposition of fine or penalty; opportunity to correct; exception for public health or safety

(a) Prior to imposing a fine or penalty for failure to maintain a vacant property that is subject to a notice of default, that is purchased at a foreclosure sale, or that is acquired through foreclosure under a mortgage or deed of trust, a governmental entity shall provide the owner of that property with a notice of the violation and an opportunity to correct that violation.

(b) This section shall not apply if the governmental entity determines that a specific condition of the property threatens public health or safety. *(Added by Stats.2010, c. 527 (S.B. 1427), § 1.)*

§ 2929.45. Limit upon nuisance abatement costs recoverable against property subject to notice of default, purchased at foreclosure sale, or acquired through foreclosure; costs adopted by elected officials

(a) An assessment or lien to recover the costs of nuisance abatement measures taken by a governmental entity with regard to property that is subject to a notice of default, that is purchased at a foreclosure sale, or that is acquired through foreclosure under a mortgage or deed of trust, shall not exceed the actual and reasonable costs of nuisance abatement.

(b) A governmental entity shall not impose an assessment or lien unless the costs that constitute the assessment or lien have been adopted by the elected officials of that governmental entity at a public hearing. *(Added by Stats.2010, c. 527 (S.B.1427), § 2.)*

§ 2929.5. Hazardous substances; inspection by secured lender

(a) A secured lender may enter and inspect the real property security for the purpose of determining the existence, location, nature, and magnitude of any past or present release or threatened release of any hazardous substance into, onto, beneath, or from the real property security on either of the following:

(1) Upon reasonable belief of the existence of a past or present release or threatened release of any hazardous substance into, onto, beneath, or from the real property security not previously disclosed in writing to the secured lender in conjunction with the making, renewal, or modification of a loan, extension of credit, guaranty, or other obligation involving the borrower.

(2) After the commencement of nonjudicial or judicial foreclosure proceedings against the real property security.

(b) The secured lender shall not abuse the right of entry and inspection or use it to harass the borrower or tenant of the property. Except in case of an emergency, when the borrower or tenant of the property has abandoned the premises, or if it is impracticable to do so, the secured lender shall give the borrower or tenant of the property reasonable notice of the secured lender's intent to enter, and enter only during the borrower's or tenant's normal business hours. Twenty-four hours' notice shall be presumed to be reasonable notice in the absence of evidence to the contrary.

(c) The secured lender shall reimburse the borrower for the cost of repair of any physical injury to the real property security caused by the entry and inspection.

(d) If a secured lender is refused the right of entry and inspection by the borrower or tenant of the property, or is otherwise unable to enter and inspect the property without a breach of the peace, the secured lender may, upon petition, obtain an order from a court of competent jurisdiction to exercise the secured lender's rights under subdivision (a), and that action shall not constitute an action within the meaning of subdivision (a) of Section 726 of the Code of Civil Procedure.

(e) For purposes of this section:

(1) "Borrower" means the trustor under a deed of trust, or a mortgagor under a mortgage, where the deed of trust or mortgage encumbers real property security and secures the performance of the trustor or mortgagor under a loan, extension of credit, guaranty, or other obligation. The term includes any successor-in-interest of the trustor or mortgagor to the real property security before the deed of trust or mortgage has been discharged, reconveyed, or foreclosed upon.

(2) "Hazardous substance" includes all of the following:

(A) Any "hazardous substance" as defined in subdivision (h) of Section 25281 of the Health and Safety Code.

(B) Any "waste" as defined in subdivision (d) of Section 13050 of the Water Code.

(C) Petroleum, including crude oil or any fraction thereof, natural gas, natural gas liquids, liquefied natural gas, or synthetic gas usable for fuel, or any mixture thereof.

(3) "Real property security" means any real property and improvements, other than a separate interest and any related interest in the common area of a residential common interest development, as the terms "separate interest," "common area," and "common interest development" are defined in Sections 4095, 4100, and 4185, or real property consisting of one acre or less which contains 1 to 15 dwelling units.

(4) "Release" means any spilling, leaking, pumping, pouring, emitting, emptying, discharging, injecting, escaping, leaching, dumping, or disposing into the environment, including continuing migration, of hazardous substances into, onto, or through soil, surface water, or groundwater.

(5) "Secured lender" means the beneficiary under a deed of trust against the real property security, or the mortgagee under a mortgage against the real property security, and any successor-in-interest of the beneficiary or mortgagee to the deed of trust or mortgage. *(Added by Stats.1991, c. 1167 (A.B.1735), § 1. Amended by Stats.1992, c. 167 (A.B.2750), § 1; Stats.2002, c. 999 (A.B.2481), § 2; Stats.2012, c. 181 (A.B.806), § 40, operative Jan. 1, 2014.)*

Cross References

Jurisdictional classification of proceeding to distribute excess sale proceeds,
    Limited civil cases, see Code of Civil Procedure § 85.
    Unlimited civil cases, see Code of Civil Procedure § 88.

§ 2930. Title subsequently acquired by mortgagor

Title acquired by the mortgagor subsequent to the execution of the mortgage, inures to the mortgagee as security for the debt in like manner as if acquired before the execution. *(Enacted in 1872. Amended by Code Am. 1873–74, c. 612, p. 260, § 257.)*

Cross References

Subsequently acquired title, passage by operation of law, see Civil Code § 1106.
Title not transferred by lien or contract for lien, see Civil Code § 2888.

§ 2931. Foreclosure

A mortgagee may foreclose the right of redemption of the mortgagor in the manner prescribed by the Code of Civil Procedure. *(Enacted in 1872.)*

Cross References

Action to redeem mortgages, see Code of Civil Procedure §§ 346, 347.
Actions for foreclosure of trust deeds and mortgages, see Code of Civil Procedure § 725a et seq.
Receiver, appointment in mortgage foreclosure proceeding, see Code of Civil Procedure § 564.
Redemption from lien generally, see Civil Code § 2903 et seq.

§ 2931a. Actions relating to real property; tax lien; state agency as party; jurisdiction; contents of complaint or petition; service of process; duties of Attorney General

In any action brought to determine conflicting claims to real property, or for partition of real property or an estate for years therein, or to foreclose a deed of trust, mortgage, or other lien upon real property, or in all eminent domain proceedings under Section 1250.110 et seq., of the Code of Civil Procedure against real property upon which exists a lien to secure the payment of taxes or other obligations to an agency of the State of California, other than ad valorem taxes upon the real property, the state agency charged with the collection of the tax obligation may be made a party. In such an action, the court shall have jurisdiction to determine the priority and effect of the liens described in the complaint in or upon the real property or estate for years therein, but the jurisdiction of the court in the action shall not include a determination of the validity of the tax giving rise to the lien or claim of lien. The complaint or petition in the action shall contain a description of the lien sufficient to enable the tax or other obligation, payment of which it secures, to be identified with certainty, and shall include the name and address of the person owing the tax or other obligation, the name of the state agency that recorded the lien, and the date and place where the lien was recorded. Services of process in the action shall be made upon the agency, officer, board, commission, department, division, or other body charged with the collection of the tax or obligation. It shall be the duty of the Attorney General to represent the state agency in the action. (Added by Stats.1935, c. 464, p. 1521, § 1. Amended by Stats.1941, c. 1193, p. 2966, § 1; Stats.1980, c. 44, p. 108, § 2; Stats.1986, c. 81, § 1; Stats.1989, c. 698, § 8.)

Cross References

Actions for partition of real and personal property, see Code of Civil Procedure § 872.010 et seq.

§ 2931b. Tax sale; purchase by state

In all actions in which the State of California is named a party pursuant to the provisions of Section 2931a and in which real property or an estate for years therein is sought to be sold, the Attorney General may, with the consent of the Department of Finance, bid upon and purchase that real property or estate for years. (Added by Stats.1953, c. 1675, p. 3408, § 1. Amended by Stats.1989, c. 698, § 9.)

§ 2931c. Action by Attorney General to enforce lien to secure payment of taxes or other obligations to state

The Attorney General may bring an action in the courts of this or any other state or of the United States to enforce any lien to secure the payment of taxes or other obligations to the State of California under the Unemployment Insurance Code, the Revenue and Taxation Code, or Chapter 6 (commencing with Section 16180) of Part 1 of Division 4 of Title 2 of the Government Code or to subject to payment of the liability giving rise to the lien any property in which the debtor has any right, title, or interest. In any action brought under this section the court shall have jurisdiction to determine the priority and effect of the lien in or upon the property, but the jurisdiction of the court in such action shall not extend to a determination of the validity of the liability giving rise to the lien. (Added by Stats.1963, c. 1308, p. 2832, § 1. Amended by Stats.1977, c. 1242, p. 4190, § 3, eff. Oct. 1, 1977.)

§ 2932. Power of sale

A power of sale may be conferred by a mortgage upon the mortgagee or any other person, to be exercised after a breach of the obligation for which the mortgage is a security. (Enacted in 1872.)

Cross References

Attorney's authority to conduct trustee's sale, see Civil Code § 2924a.
Conduct of sale, see Civil Code §§ 2924g, 2924h.
Forfeitures and restraints upon redemption, invalid, see Civil Code § 2889.
Notice of sale of property,
  Execution, see Code of Civil Procedure § 699.070.
  Power of sale in mortgage or deed of trust, see Civil Code § 2924f.
Power of sale in mortgage after breach of obligation, see Civil Code § 2924.
Sale of encumbered property by judgment in foreclosure action, see Code of Civil Procedure § 726.

§ 2932.5. Power of sale; vesting in assignee

Where a power to sell real property is given to a mortgagee, or other encumbrancer, in an instrument intended to secure the payment of money, the power is part of the security and vests in any person who by assignment becomes entitled to payment of the money secured by the instrument. The power of sale may be exercised by the assignee if the assignment is duly acknowledged and recorded. (Added by Stats.1986, c. 820, § 11, operative July 1, 1987.)

§ 2932.6. Financial institution repair of property acquired through foreclosure

(a) Notwithstanding any other provision of law, a financial institution may undertake to repair any property acquired through foreclosure under a mortgage or deed of trust.

(b) As used in this section, the term "financial institution" includes, but is not limited to, banks, savings associations, credit unions, and industrial loan companies.

(c) The rights granted to a financial institution by this section are in addition to, and not in derogation of, the rights of a financial institution which otherwise exist. (Added by Stats.1987, c. 187, § 1. Amended by Stats.1988, c. 125, § 1.)

§ 2933. Power of attorney; formalities

A power of attorney to execute a mortgage must be in writing, subscribed, acknowledged, or proved, certified, and recorded in like manner as powers of attorney for grants of real property. (Enacted in 1872.)

Cross References

Attorney in fact, execution of written instruments transferring estate in real property, see Civil Code § 1095.
Index of powers of attorney, see Government Code § 27238.
Mode of transfer of real property generally, see Civil Code § 1091 et seq.
Oral and written authorizations of agents, see Civil Code § 2309.
Power of attorney, revocation, see Civil Code § 1216.
Proof and acknowledgment of instruments, see Civil Code § 1180 et seq.
Recording instruments or judgments affecting real property, see Government Code § 27280 et seq.
Recording of mortgage on real property, see Civil Code § 2952.

§ 2934. Assignments; instruments subordinating or waiving priority; recording; effect

Any assignment of a mortgage and any assignment of the beneficial interest under a deed of trust may be recorded, and from the time the same is filed for record operates as constructive notice of the contents thereof to all persons; and any instrument by which any mortgage or deed of trust of, lien upon or interest in real property, (or by which any mortgage of, lien upon or interest in personal property a document evidencing or creating which is required or permitted by law to be recorded), is subordinated or waived as to priority may be recorded, and from the time the same is filed for record operates as constructive notice of the contents thereof, to all persons. *(Enacted in 1872. Amended by Code Am.1873–74, c. 612, p. 261, § 258; Stats.1931, c. 80, p. 101, § 1; Stats.1935, c. 818, p. 2229, § 1.)*

Cross References

Lien, mortgage, satisfaction, see Civil Code § 2941.
Prior recording of subsequent mortgages, see Civil Code § 1214.
Purchaser's lien on real property, see Civil Code § 3050.
Recordation of assignments of trust deed by real estate licensees, see Business and Professions Code § 10234.
Recording instruments or judgments affecting real property, see Government Code § 27280 et seq.
Recording of mortgage on real property, see Civil Code § 2952.

§ 2934a. Substitution of trustee; mailing; recording; contents of substitution; substitution after notice of default; authorization of trustee to act; resignation of trustee; new notice of sale

(a)(1) The trustee under a trust deed upon real property or an estate for years given to secure an obligation to pay money and conferring no other duties upon the trustee than those which are incidental to the exercise of the power of sale therein conferred, may be substituted by the recording in the county in which the property is located of a substitution executed and acknowledged by either of the following:

(A) All of the beneficiaries under the trust deed, or their successors in interest, and the substitution shall be effective notwithstanding any contrary provision in any trust deed executed on or after January 1, 1968.

(B) The holders of more than 50 percent of the record beneficial interest of a series of notes secured by the same real property or of undivided interests in a note secured by real property equivalent to a series transaction, exclusive of any notes or interests of a licensed real estate broker that is the issuer or servicer of the notes or interests or of any affiliate of that licensed real estate broker.

(2) A substitution executed pursuant to subparagraph (B) of paragraph (1) is not effective unless all the parties signing the substitution sign, under penalty of perjury, a separate written document stating the following:

(A) The substitution has been signed pursuant to subparagraph (B) of paragraph (1).

(B) None of the undersigned is a licensed real estate broker or an affiliate of the broker that is the issuer or servicer of the obligation secured by the deed of trust.

(C) The undersigned together hold more than 50 percent of the record beneficial interest of a series of notes secured by the same real property or of undivided interests in a note secured by real property equivalent to a series transaction.

(D) Notice of the substitution was sent by certified mail, postage prepaid, with return receipt requested to each holder of an interest in the obligation secured by the deed of trust who has not joined in the execution of the substitution or the separate document.

The separate document shall be attached to the substitution and recorded in the office of the county recorder of each county in which the real property described in the deed of trust is located. Once the document is recorded, it shall constitute conclusive evidence of compliance with the requirements of this paragraph in favor of substituted trustees acting pursuant to this section, subsequent assignees of the obligation secured by the deed of trust and subsequent bona fide purchasers or encumbrancers for value of the real property described therein.

(3) For purposes of this section, "affiliate of the licensed real estate broker" includes any person as defined in Section 25013 of the Corporations Code that is controlled by, or is under common control with, or who controls, a licensed real estate broker. "Control" means the possession, direct or indirect, of the power to direct or cause the direction of management and policies.

(4) The substitution shall contain the date of recordation of the trust deed, the name of the trustor, the book and page or instrument number where the trust deed is recorded, and the name of the new trustee. From the time the substitution is filed for record, the new trustee shall succeed to all the powers, duties, authority, and title granted and delegated to the trustee named in the deed of trust. A substitution may be accomplished, with respect to multiple deeds of trust that are recorded in the same county in which the substitution is being recorded and that all have the same trustee and beneficiary or beneficiaries, by recording a single document, complying with the requirements of this section, substituting trustees for all those deeds of trust.

(b) If the substitution is executed, but not recorded, prior to or concurrently with the recording of the notice of default, the beneficiary or beneficiaries or their authorized agents shall mail notice of the substitution before or concurrently with the recording thereof, in the manner provided in Section 2924b, to all persons to whom a copy of the notice of default would be required to be mailed by Section 2924b. An affidavit shall be attached to the substitution that notice has been given to those persons, as required by this subdivision.

(c) If the substitution is effected after a notice of default has been recorded but prior to the recording of the notice of sale, the beneficiary or beneficiaries or their authorized agents shall mail a copy of the substitution, before, or concurrently with, the recording thereof, as provided in Section 2924b, to the trustee then of record and to all persons to whom a copy of the notice of default would be required to be mailed by Section 2924b. An affidavit shall be attached to the substitution that notice has been given to those persons, as required by this subdivision.

(d)(1) A trustee named in a recorded substitution of trustee shall be deemed to be authorized to act as the trustee under the mortgage or deed of trust for all purposes from the date the substitution is executed by the mortgagee, beneficiaries, or by their authorized agents. A trustee under a recorded substitution is not required to accept the substitution, and may either resign or refuse to accept appointment as trustee pursuant to this subdivision.

(2)(A) A trustee named in a recorded substitution of trustee may resign or refuse to accept appointment as trustee at that trustee's own election without the consent of the beneficiary or beneficiaries or their authorized agents. The trustee shall give prompt written notice of that resignation or refusal to accept appointment as trustee to the beneficiary or beneficiaries or their authorized agents by doing both of the following:

(i) Depositing or causing to be deposited in the United States mail an envelope containing a notice of resignation of trustee, sent by registered or certified mail with postage prepaid, to all beneficiaries or their authorized agents at the address shown on the last-recorded substitution of trustee for that real property or estate for years in that county.

(ii) Recording the notice of resignation of trustee, mailed in the manner described in clause (i), in each county in which the substitution of trustee under which the trustee was appointed is recorded. An affidavit stating that notice has been mailed to all beneficiaries and their authorized agents in the manner provided in clause (i) shall be attached to the recorded notice of resignation of trustee.

(B) The resignation of the trustee or refusal to accept appointment as trustee pursuant to this subdivision shall become effective upon the recording of the notice of resignation of trustee in each county in which the substitution of trustee under which the trustee was appointed is recorded.

(C) The resignation of the trustee or refusal to accept appointment as trustee pursuant to this subdivision does not affect the validity of the mortgage or deed of trust, except that no action required to be performed by the trustee under this chapter or under the mortgage or deed of trust may be taken until a substituted trustee is appointed pursuant to this section. If a trustee is not designated in the deed of trust, or upon the resignation, incapacity, disability, absence or death of the trustee, or the election of the beneficiary or beneficiaries to replace the trustee, the beneficiary or beneficiaries or their authorized agents shall appoint a trustee or a successor trustee.

(D) A notice of resignation of trustee mailed and recorded pursuant to this paragraph shall set forth the intention of the trustee to resign or refuse appointment as trustee and the recording date and instrument number of the recorded substitution of trustee under which the trustee was appointed.

(E) A notice of resignation of trustee mailed and recorded pursuant to this paragraph shall contain an address at which the trustee and any successor in interest will be available for service of process for at least five years after the date that the notice of resignation is recorded.

(F) For at least five years after a notice of resignation of trustee is mailed and recorded pursuant to this paragraph, the trustee and any successor in interest to that trustee shall retain and preserve every writing, as that term is defined in Section 250 of the Evidence Code, relating to the trust deed or estate for years under which the trustee was appointed.

(3) For purposes of this section, paragraph (2) sets forth the exclusive procedure for a trustee to either resign or refuse to accept appointment as trustee.

(4) Once recorded, the substitution shall constitute conclusive evidence of the authority of the substituted trustee or their authorized agents to act pursuant to this section, unless prompt written notice of resignation of trustee has been given in accordance with the procedures set forth in paragraph (2).

(e) Notwithstanding any provision of this section or any provision in any deed of trust, unless a new notice of sale containing the name, street address, and telephone number of the substituted trustee is given pursuant to Section 2924f after execution of the substitution, any sale conducted by the substituted trustee shall be void. *(Added by Stats.1993, c. 754 (S.B.313), § 2.5, eff. Oct. 4, 1993, operative Jan. 1, 1998. Amended by Stats.1996, c. 839 (S.B.1638), § 2, operative Jan. 1, 1998; Stats.1999, c. 974 (A.B.431), § 14; Stats.2004, c. 177 (S.B.1277), § 5; Stats.2019, c. 474 (S.B.306), § 1, eff. Jan. 1, 2020.)*

Cross References

Appointment of new trustees by court, see Probate Code § 15660.

Commercial and industrial common interest developments, enforcement of lien, sale by trustee substituted pursuant to this section, see Civil Code § 6820.

Common interest developments, assessment collection, enforcement of lien, see Civil Code § 5700.

Lien, mortgage, satisfaction, see Civil Code § 2941.

Notice of default, see Civil Code § 2924b.

Power of sale in deed of trust or mortgage, see Civil Code §§ 2924, 2932.

Recording deeds of trust, see Civil Code § 2952.

Recording instruments or judgments affecting real property, see Government Code § 27280 et seq.

§ 2934b. Application of probate provisions

Sections 15643 and 18102 of the Probate Code apply to trustees under deeds of trust given to secure obligations. *(Added by Stats.1986, c. 820, § 12, operative July 1, 1987.)*

§ 2935. Record of assignment not notice to debtor; validity of payments

When a mortgage or deed of trust is executed as security for money due or to become due, on a promissory note, bond, or other instrument, designated in the mortgage or deed of trust, the record of the assignment of the mortgage or of the assignment of the beneficial interest under the deed of trust, is not of itself notice to the debtor, his heirs, or personal representatives, so as to invalidate any payment made by them, or any of them, to the person holding such note, bond, or other instrument. *(Enacted in 1872. Amended by Code Am.1873–74, c. 612, p. 261, § 259; Stats.1931, c. 80, p. 101, § 2.)*

§ 2936. Assignment of debt carries security

The assignment of a debt secured by mortgage carries with it the security. *(Enacted in 1872.)*

Cross References

Power of sale instrument to secure payment, see Civil Code § 2932.5.

§ 2937. Notices to borrower of transfer of service by existing and new servicing agent of mortgage or deed of trust on single family residential real property

(a) The Legislature hereby finds and declares that borrowers or subsequent obligors have the right to know when a person holding a promissory note, bond, or other instrument transfers servicing of the indebtedness secured by a mortgage or deed of trust on real property containing one to four residential units located in this state. The Legislature also finds that notification to the borrower or subsequent obligor of the transfer may protect the borrower or subsequent obligor from fraudulent business practices and may ensure timely payments.

It is the intent of the Legislature in enacting this section to mandate that a borrower or subsequent obligor be given written notice when a person transfers the servicing of the indebtedness on notes, bonds, or other instruments secured by a mortgage or deed of trust on real property containing one to four residential units and located in this state.

(b) Any person transferring the servicing of indebtedness as provided in subdivision (a) to a different servicing agent and any person assuming from another responsibility for servicing the instrument evidencing indebtedness, shall give written notice to the borrower or subsequent obligor before the borrower or subsequent obligor becomes obligated to make payments to a new servicing agent.

(c) In the event a notice of default has been recorded or a judicial foreclosure proceeding has been commenced, the person transferring the servicing of the indebtedness and the person assuming from another the duty of servicing the indebtedness shall give written notice to the trustee or attorney named in the notice of default or judicial foreclosure of the transfer. A notice of default, notice of sale, or judicial foreclosure shall not be invalidated solely because the servicing agent is changed during the foreclosure process.

(d) Any person transferring the servicing of indebtedness as provided in subdivision (a) to a different servicing agent shall provide to the new servicing agent all existing insurance policy information that the person is responsible for maintaining, including, but not limited to, flood and hazard insurance policy information.

(e) The notices required by subdivision (b) shall be sent by first- class mail, postage prepaid, to the borrower's or subsequent obligor's address designated for loan payment billings, or if escrow is pending, as provided in the escrow, and shall contain each of the following:

(1) The name and address of the person to which the transfer of the servicing of the indebtedness is made.

(2) The date the transfer was or will be completed.

(3) The address where all payments pursuant to the transfer are to be made.

(f) Any person assuming from another responsibility for servicing the instrument evidencing indebtedness shall include in the notice required by subdivision (b) a statement of the due date of the next payment.

(g) The borrower or subsequent obligor shall not be liable to the holder of the note, bond, or other instrument or to any servicing agent for payments made to the previous servicing agent or for late charges if these payments were made prior to the borrower or subsequent obligor receiving written notice of the transfer as provided by subdivision (e) and the payments were otherwise on time.

(h) For purposes of this section, the term servicing agent shall not include a trustee exercising a power of sale pursuant to a deed of trust. *(Added by Stats.1988, c. 1190, § 1.*

Amended by Stats.1989, c. 96, § 1, eff. July 7, 1989; Stats.2002, c. 70 (S.B.1370), § 1.)

§ 2937.7. Service of process on trustee under deed of trust or mortgage; effect on trustor

In any action affecting the interest of any trustor or beneficiary under a deed of trust or mortgage, service of process to the trustee does not constitute service to the trustor or beneficiary and does not impose any obligation on the trustee to notify the trustor or beneficiary of the action. *(Added by Stats.1988, c. 530, § 1.)*

§ 2938. Assignment of rents; recordation; enforcement; demand; cash proceeds; application of section

(a) A written assignment of an interest in leases, rents, issues, or profits of real property made in connection with an obligation secured by real property, irrespective of whether the assignment is denoted as absolute, absolute conditioned upon default, additional security for an obligation, or otherwise, shall, upon execution and delivery by the assignor, be effective to create a present security interest in existing and future leases, rents, issues, or profits of that real property. As used in this section, "leases, rents, issues, and profits of real property" includes the cash proceeds thereof. "Cash proceeds" means cash, checks, deposit accounts, and the like.

(b) An assignment of an interest in leases, rents, issues, or profits of real property may be recorded in the records of the county recorder in the county in which the underlying real property is located in the same manner as any other conveyance of an interest in real property, whether the assignment is in a separate document or part of a mortgage or deed of trust, and when so duly recorded in accordance with the methods, procedures, and requirements for recordation of conveyances of other interests in real property, (1) the assignment shall be deemed to give constructive notice of the content of the assignment with the same force and effect as any other duly recorded conveyance of an interest in real property and (2) the interest granted by the assignment shall be deemed fully perfected as of the time of recordation with the same force and effect as any other duly recorded conveyance of an interest in real property, notwithstanding a provision of the assignment or a provision of law that would otherwise preclude or defer enforcement of the rights granted the assignee under the assignment until the occurrence of a subsequent event, including, but not limited to, a subsequent default of the assignor, or the assignee's obtaining possession of the real property or the appointment of a receiver.

(c) Upon default of the assignor under the obligation secured by the assignment of leases, rents, issues, and profits, the assignee shall be entitled to enforce the assignment in accordance with this section. On and after the date the assignee takes one or more of the enforcement steps described in this subdivision, the assignee shall be entitled to collect and receive all rents, issues, and profits that have accrued but remain unpaid and uncollected by the assignor or its agent or for the assignor's benefit on that date, and all rents, issues, and profits that accrue on or after the date. The assignment shall be enforced by one or more of the following:

(1) The appointment of a receiver.

(2) Obtaining possession of the rents, issues, or profits.

(3) Delivery to any one or more of the tenants of a written demand for turnover of rents, issues, and profits in the form specified in subdivision (k), a copy of which demand shall also be delivered to the assignor; and a copy of which shall be mailed to all other assignees of record of the leases, rents, issues, and profits of the real property at the address for notices provided in the assignment or, if none, to the address to which the recorded assignment was to be mailed after recording.

(4) Delivery to the assignor of a written demand for the rents, issues, or profits, a copy of which shall be mailed to all other assignees of record of the leases, rents, issues, and profits of the real property at the address for notices provided in the assignment or, if none, to the address to which the recorded assignment was to be mailed after recording.

Moneys received by the assignee pursuant to this subdivision, net of amounts paid pursuant to subdivision (g), if any, shall be applied by the assignee to the debt or otherwise in accordance with the assignment or the promissory note, deed of trust, or other instrument evidencing the obligation, provided, however, that neither the application nor the failure to so apply the rents, issues, or profits shall result in a loss of any lien or security interest that the assignee may have in the underlying real property or any other collateral, render the obligation unenforceable, constitute a violation of Section 726 of the Code of Civil Procedure, or otherwise limit a right available to the assignee with respect to its security.

(d) If an assignee elects to take the action provided for under paragraph (3) of subdivision (c), the demand provided for therein shall be signed under penalty of perjury by the assignee or an authorized agent of the assignee and shall be effective as against the tenant when actually received by the tenant at the address for notices provided under the lease or other contractual agreement under which the tenant occupies the property or, if no address for notices is so provided, at the property. Upon receipt of this demand, the tenant shall be obligated to pay to the assignee all rents, issues, and profits that are past due and payable on the date of receipt of the demand, and all rents, issues, and profits coming due under the lease following the date of receipt of the demand, unless either of the following occurs:

(1) The tenant has previously received a demand that is valid on its face from another assignee of the leases, issues, rents, and profits sent by the other assignee in accordance with this subdivision and subdivision (c).

(2) The tenant, in good faith and in a manner that is not inconsistent with the lease, has previously paid, or within 10 days following receipt of the demand notice pays, the rent to the assignor.

Payment of rent to an assignee following a demand under an assignment of leases, rents, issues, and profits shall satisfy the tenant's obligation to pay the amounts under the lease. If a tenant pays rent to the assignor after receipt of a demand other than under the circumstances described in this subdivision, the tenant shall not be discharged of the obligation to pay rent to the assignee, unless the tenant occupies the property for residential purposes. The obligation of a tenant to pay rent pursuant to this subdivision and subdivision (c) shall continue until receipt by the tenant of a written notice from a court directing the tenant to pay the rent in a different manner or receipt by the tenant of a written notice from the assignee from whom the demand was received canceling the demand, whichever occurs first. This subdivision does not affect the entitlement to rents, issues, or profits as between assignees as set forth in subdivision (h).

(e) An enforcement action of the type authorized by subdivision (c), and a collection, distribution, or application of rents, issues, or profits by the assignee following an enforcement action of the type authorized by subdivision (c), shall not do any of the following:

(1) Make the assignee a mortgagee in possession of the property, except if the assignee obtains actual possession of the real property, or an agent of the assignor.

(2) Constitute an action, render the obligation unenforceable, violate Section 726 of the Code of Civil Procedure, or, other than with respect to marshaling requirements, otherwise limit any rights available to the assignee with respect to its security.

(3) Be deemed to create a bar to a deficiency judgment pursuant to a provision of law governing or relating to deficiency judgments following the enforcement of any encumbrance, lien, or security interest, notwithstanding that the action, collection, distribution, or application may reduce the indebtedness secured by the assignment or by a deed of trust or other security instrument.

The application of rents, issues, or profits to the secured obligation shall satisfy the secured obligation to the extent of those rents, issues, or profits, and, notwithstanding any provisions of the assignment or other loan documents to the contrary, shall be credited against any amounts necessary to cure any monetary default for purposes of reinstatement under Section 2924c.

(f) If cash proceeds of rents, issues, or profits to which the assignee is entitled following enforcement as set forth in subdivision (c) are received by the assignor or its agent for collection or by another person who has collected such rents, issues, or profits for the assignor's benefit, or for the benefit of a subsequent assignee under the circumstances described in subdivision (h), following the taking by the assignee of either of the enforcement actions authorized in paragraph (3) or (4) of subdivision (c), and the assignee has not authorized the assignor's disposition of the cash proceeds in a writing signed by the assignee, the rights to the cash proceeds and to the recovery of the cash proceeds shall be determined by the following:

(1) The assignee shall be entitled to an immediate turnover of the cash proceeds received by the assignor or its agent for collection or any other person who has collected the rents, issues, or profits for the assignor's benefit, or for the benefit of a subsequent assignee under the circumstances described in subdivision (h), and the assignor or other described party in possession of those cash proceeds shall turn over the full amount of cash proceeds to the assignee, less any amount representing payment of expenses authorized by the assignee in writing. The assignee shall have a right to bring an action for recovery of the cash proceeds, and to recover the cash proceeds, without the necessity of bringing an action to foreclose a security interest that it may have in the real property. This action shall not violate Section 726 of the

Code of Civil Procedure or otherwise limit a right available to the assignee with respect to its security.

(2) As between an assignee with an interest in cash proceeds perfected in the manner set forth in subdivision (b) and enforced in accordance with paragraph (3) or (4) of subdivision (c) and another person claiming an interest in the cash proceeds, other than the assignor or its agent for collection or one collecting rents, issues, and profits for the benefit of the assignor, and subject to subdivision (h), the assignee shall have a continuously perfected security interest in the cash proceeds to the extent that the cash proceeds are identifiable. For purposes hereof, cash proceeds are identifiable if they are either (A) segregated or (B) if commingled with other funds of the assignor or its agent or one acting on its behalf, can be traced using the lowest intermediate balance principle, unless the assignor or other party claiming an interest in proceeds shows that some other method of tracing would better serve the interests of justice and equity under the circumstances of the case. The provisions of this paragraph are subject to any generally applicable law with respect to payments made in the operation of the assignor's business.

(g)(1) If the assignee enforces the assignment under subdivision (c) by means other than the appointment of a receiver and receives rents, issues, or profits pursuant to this enforcement, the assignor or another assignee of the affected real property may make written demand upon the assignee to pay the reasonable costs of protecting and preserving the property, including payment of taxes and insurance and compliance with building and housing codes, if any.

(2) On and after the date of receipt of the demand, the assignee shall pay for the reasonable costs of protecting and preserving the real property to the extent of any rents, issues, or profits actually received by the assignee, provided, however, that no such acts by the assignee shall cause the assignee to become a mortgagee in possession and the assignee's duties under this subdivision, upon receipt of a demand from the assignor or any other assignee of the leases, rents, issues, and profits pursuant to paragraph (1), shall not be construed to require the assignee to operate or manage the property, which obligation shall remain that of the assignor.

(3) The obligation of the assignee hereunder shall continue until the earlier of (A) the date on which the assignee obtains the appointment of a receiver for the real property pursuant to application to a court of competent jurisdiction, or (B) the date on which the assignee ceases to enforce the assignment.

(4) This subdivision does not supersede or diminish the right of the assignee to the appointment of a receiver.

(h) The lien priorities, rights, and interests among creditors concerning rents, issues, or profits collected before the enforcement by the assignee shall be governed by subdivisions (a) and (b). Without limiting the generality of the foregoing, if an assignee who has recorded its interest in leases, rents, issues, and profits prior to the recordation of that interest by a subsequent assignee seeks to enforce its interest in those rents, issues, or profits in accordance with this section after any enforcement action has been taken by a subsequent assignee, the prior assignee shall be entitled only to the rents, issues, and profits that are accrued and unpaid as of the date of its enforcement action and unpaid rents, issues, and profits accruing thereafter. The prior assignee shall have no right to rents, issues, or profits paid prior to the date of the enforcement action, whether in the hands of the assignor or any subsequent assignee. Upon receipt of notice that the prior assignee has enforced its interest in the rents, issues, and profits, the subsequent assignee shall immediately send a notice to any tenant to whom it has given notice under subdivision (c). The notice shall inform the tenant that the subsequent assignee cancels its demand that the tenant pay rent to the subsequent assignee.

(i)(1) This section shall apply to contracts entered into on or after January 1, 1997.

(2) Sections 2938 and 2938.1, as these sections were in effect prior to January 1, 1997, shall govern contracts entered into prior to January 1, 1997, and shall govern actions and proceedings initiated on the basis of these contracts.

(j) "Real property," as used in this section, means real property or any estate or interest therein.

(k) The demand required by paragraph (3) of subdivision (c) shall be in the following form:

DEMAND TO PAY RENT TO

PARTY OTHER THAN LANDLORD

(SECTION 2938 OF THE CIVIL CODE)

Tenant: [Name of Tenant]

Property Occupied by Tenant: [Address]

Landlord: [Name of Landlord]

Secured Party: [Name of Secured Party]

Address: [Address for Payment of Rent to Secured Party and for Further Information]:

The secured party named above is the assignee of leases, rents, issues, and profits under [name of document] dated ___, and recorded at [recording information] in the official records of ___ County, California. You may request a copy of the assignment from the secured party at ___ (address).

THIS NOTICE AFFECTS YOUR LEASE OR RENTAL AGREEMENT RIGHTS AND OBLIGATIONS. YOU ARE THEREFORE ADVISED TO CONSULT AN ATTORNEY CONCERNING THOSE RIGHTS AND OBLIGATIONS IF YOU HAVE ANY QUESTIONS REGARDING YOUR RIGHTS AND OBLIGATIONS UNDER THIS NOTICE.

IN ACCORDANCE WITH SUBDIVISION (C) OF SECTION 2938 OF THE CIVIL CODE, YOU ARE HEREBY

DIRECTED TO PAY TO THE SECURED PARTY, ___ (NAME OF SECURED PARTY) AT ___ (ADDRESS), ALL RENTS UNDER YOUR LEASE OR OTHER RENTAL AGREEMENT WITH THE LANDLORD OR PREDECESSOR IN INTEREST OF LANDLORD, FOR THE OCCUPANCY OF THE PROPERTY AT ___ (ADDRESS OF RENTAL PREMISES) WHICH ARE PAST DUE AND PAYABLE ON THE DATE YOU RECEIVE THIS DEMAND, AND ALL RENTS COMING DUE UNDER THE LEASE OR OTHER RENTAL AGREEMENT FOLLOWING THE DATE YOU RECEIVE THIS DEMAND UNLESS YOU HAVE ALREADY PAID THIS RENT TO THE LANDLORD IN GOOD FAITH AND IN A MANNER NOT INCONSISTENT WITH THE AGREEMENT BETWEEN YOU AND THE LANDLORD. IN THIS CASE, THIS DEMAND NOTICE SHALL REQUIRE YOU TO PAY TO THE SECURED PARTY, ___ (NAME OF THE SECURED PARTY), ALL RENTS THAT COME DUE FOLLOWING THE DATE OF THE PAYMENT TO THE LANDLORD.

IF YOU PAY THE RENT TO THE UNDERSIGNED SECURED PARTY, ___ (NAME OF SECURED PARTY), IN ACCORDANCE WITH THIS NOTICE, YOU DO NOT HAVE TO PAY THE RENT TO THE LANDLORD. YOU WILL NOT BE SUBJECT TO DAMAGES OR OBLIGATED TO PAY RENT TO THE SECURED PARTY IF YOU HAVE PREVIOUSLY RECEIVED A DEMAND OF THIS TYPE FROM A DIFFERENT SECURED PARTY.

[For other than residential tenants] IF YOU PAY RENT TO THE LANDLORD THAT BY THE TERMS OF THIS DEMAND YOU ARE REQUIRED TO PAY TO THE SECURED PARTY, YOU MAY BE SUBJECT TO DAMAGES INCURRED BY THE SECURED PARTY BY REASON OF YOUR FAILURE TO COMPLY WITH THIS DEMAND, AND YOU MAY NOT BE DISCHARGED FROM YOUR OBLIGATION TO PAY THAT RENT TO THE SECURED PARTY. YOU WILL NOT BE SUBJECT TO THOSE DAMAGES OR OBLIGATED TO PAY THAT RENT TO THE SECURED PARTY IF YOU HAVE PREVIOUSLY RECEIVED A DEMAND OF THIS TYPE FROM A DIFFERENT ASSIGNEE.

Your obligation to pay rent under this demand shall continue until you receive either (1) a written notice from a court directing you to pay the rent in a manner provided therein, or (2) a written notice from the secured party named above canceling this demand.

The undersigned hereby certifies, under penalty of perjury, that the undersigned is an authorized officer or agent of the secured party and that the secured party is the assignee, or the current successor to the assignee, under an assignment of leases, rents, issues, or profits executed by the landlord, or a predecessor in interest, that is being enforced pursuant to and in accordance with Section 2938 of the Civil Code.

Executed at _____, California, this ___ day of _____, ___.

[Secured Party]
Name: _____

Title: _____

(Added by Stats.1996, c. 49 (S.B.947), § 2. Amended by Stats.1997, c. 8 (S.B.23), § 1, eff. April 15, 1997; Stats.2008, c. 179 (S.B.1498), § 33.)

§ 2938.1. Repealed by Stats.1996, c. 49 (S.B.947), § 3

§ 2939. Discharge; recording certificate of payment, satisfaction, or discharge

A recorded mortgage must be discharged by a certificate signed by the mortgagee, his personal representatives or assigns, acknowledged or proved and certified as prescribed by the chapter on "recording transfers," stating that the mortgage has been paid, satisfied, or discharged. Reference shall be made in said certificate to the book and page where the mortgage is recorded. (Enacted in 1872. Amended by Stats.1945, c. 1074, p. 2073, § 1; Stats.1957, c. 297, p. 939, § 1; Stats.1957, c. 1865, p. 3271, § 12.)

Cross References

Recording instruments or judgments affecting title, see Government Code § 27280 et seq.

§ 2939½. Renumbered § 2939.5 and amended by Stats. 1979, c. 730, p. 2469, § 10, operative Jan. 1, 1981

§ 2939.5. Satisfaction; foreign executors, administrators and guardians

Foreign executors, administrators and guardians may satisfy mortgages upon the records of any county in this state, upon producing and recording in the office of the county recorder of the county in which such mortgage is recorded, a duly certified and authenticated copy of their letters testamentary, or of administration or of guardianship, and which certificate or authentication shall also recite that said letters have not been revoked. For the purposes of this section, "guardian" includes a foreign conservator, committee, or comparable fiduciary. (Formerly § 2939½, added by Stats. 1895, c. 22, p. 29, § 1. Amended by Stats.1913, c. 128, p. 216, § 1. Renumbered § 2939.5 and amended by Stats.1979, c. 730, p. 2469, § 10, operative Jan. 1, 1981.)

§ 2940. Certificate of discharge; recording

A certificate of the discharge of a mortgage, and the proof or acknowledgment thereof, must be recorded in the office of the county recorder in which the mortgage is recorded. (Enacted in 1872. Amended by Stats.1945, c. 1074, p. 2073, § 2; Stats.1957, c. 1865, p. 3271, § 13.)

§ 2941. Satisfaction; obligation to issue discharge certificate or reconvey; failure to execute or record reconveyance; damages; fee; reproduced "original" instruments

(a) Within 30 days after any mortgage has been satisfied, the mortgagee or the assignee of the mortgagee shall execute a certificate of the discharge thereof, as provided in Section 2939, and shall record or cause to be recorded in the office of the county recorder in which the mortgage is recorded. The mortgagee shall then deliver, upon the written request of the mortgagor or the mortgagor's heirs, successors, or assignees, as the case may be, the original note and mortgage to the person making the request.

(b)(1) Within 30 calendar days after the obligation secured by any deed of trust has been satisfied, the beneficiary or the assignee of the beneficiary shall execute and deliver to the trustee the original note, deed of trust, request for a full reconveyance, and other documents as may be necessary to reconvey, or cause to be reconveyed, the deed of trust.

(A) The trustee shall execute the full reconveyance and shall record or cause it to be recorded in the office of the county recorder in which the deed of trust is recorded within 21 calendar days after receipt by the trustee of the original note, deed of trust, request for a full reconveyance, the fee that may be charged pursuant to subdivision (e), recorder's fees, and other documents as may be necessary to reconvey, or cause to be reconveyed, the deed of trust.

(B) The trustee shall deliver a copy of the reconveyance to the beneficiary, its successor in interest, or its servicing agent, if known. The reconveyance instrument shall specify one of the following options for delivery of the instrument, the addresses of which the recorder has no duty to validate:

(i) The trustor or successor in interest, and that person's last known address, as the person to whom the recorder will deliver the recorded instrument pursuant to Section 27321 of the Government Code.

(ii) That the recorder shall deliver the recorded instrument to the trustee's address. If the trustee's address is specified for delivery, the trustee shall mail the recorded instrument to the trustor or the successor in interest to the last known address for that party.

(C) Following execution and recordation of the full reconveyance, upon receipt of a written request by the trustor or the trustor's heirs, successors, or assignees, the trustee shall then deliver, or caused to be delivered, the original note and deed of trust to the person making that request.

(D) If the note or deed of trust, or any copy of the note or deed of trust, is electronic, upon satisfaction of an obligation secured by a deed of trust, any electronic original, or electronic copy which has not been previously marked solely for use as a copy, of the note and deed of trust, shall be altered to indicate that the obligation is paid in full.

(2) If the trustee has failed to execute and record, or cause to be recorded, the full reconveyance within 60 calendar days of satisfaction of the obligation, the beneficiary, upon receipt of a written request by the trustor or trustor's heirs, successor in interest, agent, or assignee, shall execute and acknowledge a document pursuant to Section 2934a substituting itself or another as trustee and issue a full reconveyance.

(3) If a full reconveyance has not been executed and recorded pursuant to either paragraph (1) or paragraph (2) within 75 calendar days of satisfaction of the obligation, then a title insurance company may prepare and record a release of the obligation. However, at least 10 days prior to the issuance and recording of a full release pursuant to this paragraph, the title insurance company shall mail by first-class mail with postage prepaid, the intention to release the obligation to the trustee, trustor, and beneficiary of record, or their successor in interest of record, at the last known address.

(A) The release shall set forth:

(i) The name of the beneficiary.

(ii) The name of the trustor.

(iii) The recording reference to the deed of trust.

(iv) A recital that the obligation secured by the deed of trust has been paid in full.

(v) The date and amount of payment.

(B) The release issued pursuant to this subdivision shall be entitled to recordation and, when recorded, shall be deemed to be the equivalent of a reconveyance of a deed of trust.

(4) Where an obligation secured by a deed of trust was paid in full prior to July 1, 1989, and no reconveyance has been issued and recorded by October 1, 1989, then a release of obligation as provided for in paragraph (3) may be issued.

(5) Paragraphs (2) and (3) do not excuse the beneficiary or the trustee from compliance with paragraph (1). Paragraph (3) does not excuse the beneficiary from compliance with paragraph (2).

(6) In addition to any other remedy provided by law, a title insurance company preparing or recording the release of the obligation shall be liable to any party for damages, including attorney's fees, which any person may sustain by reason of the issuance and recording of the release, pursuant to paragraphs (3) and (4).

(7) A beneficiary may, at its discretion, in accordance with the requirements and procedures of Section 2934a, substitute the title company conducting the escrow through which the obligation is satisfied for the trustee of record, in which case the title company assumes the obligation of a trustee under this subdivision, and may collect the fee authorized by subdivision (e).

(8) In lieu of delivering the original note and deed of trust to the trustee within 30 days of loan satisfaction, as required by paragraph (1) of subdivision (b), a beneficiary who executes and delivers to the trustee a request for a full reconveyance within 30 days of loan satisfaction may, within 120 days of loan satisfaction, deliver the original note and deed of trust to either the trustee or trustor. If the note and deed of trust are delivered as provided in this paragraph, upon satisfaction of the note and deed of trust, the note and deed of trust shall be altered to indicate that the obligation is paid in full. Nothing in this paragraph alters the requirements and obligations set forth in paragraphs (2) and (3).

(c) For the purposes of this section, the phrases "cause to be recorded" and "cause it to be recorded" include, but are not limited to, sending by certified mail with the United States Postal Service or by an independent courier service using its tracking service that provides documentation of receipt and delivery, including the signature of the recipient, the full reconveyance or certificate of discharge in a recordable form, together with payment for all required fees, in an envelope addressed to the county recorder's office of the county in which the deed of trust or mortgage is recorded. Within two business days from the day of receipt, if received in recordable form together with all required fees, the county recorder shall stamp and record the full reconveyance or certificate of discharge. Compliance with this subdivision shall entitle the trustee to the benefit of the presumption found in Section 641 of the Evidence Code.

(d) The violation of this section shall make the violator liable to the person affected by the violation for all damages which that person may sustain by reason of the violation, and shall require that the violator forfeit to that person the sum of five hundred dollars ($500).

(e)(1) The trustee, beneficiary, or mortgagee may charge a reasonable fee to the trustor or mortgagor, or the owner of the land, as the case may be, for all services involved in the preparation, execution, and recordation of the full reconveyance, including, but not limited to, document preparation and forwarding services rendered to effect the full reconveyance, and, in addition, may collect official fees. This fee may be made payable no earlier than the opening of a bona fide escrow or no more than 60 days prior to the full satisfaction of the obligation secured by the deed of trust or mortgage.

(2) If the fee charged pursuant to this subdivision does not exceed forty-five dollars ($45), the fee is conclusively presumed to be reasonable.

(3) The fee described in paragraph (1) may not be charged unless demand for the fee was included in the payoff demand statement described in Section 2943.

(f) For purposes of this section, "original" may include an optically imaged reproduction when the following requirements are met:

(1) The trustee receiving the request for reconveyance and executing the reconveyance as provided in subdivision (b) is an affiliate or subsidiary of the beneficiary or an affiliate or subsidiary of the assignee of the beneficiary, respectively.

(2) The optical image storage media used to store the document shall be nonerasable write once, read many (WORM) optical image media that does not allow changes to the stored document.

(3) The optical image reproduction shall be made consistent with the minimum standards of quality approved by either the National Institute of Standards and Technology or the Association for Information and Image Management.

(4) Written authentication identifying the optical image reproduction as an unaltered copy of the note, deed of trust, or mortgage shall be stamped or printed on the optical image reproduction.

(g) No fee or charge may be imposed on the trustor in connection with, or relating to, any act described in this section except as expressly authorized by this section.

(h) The amendments to this section enacted at the 1999–2000 Regular Session shall apply only to a mortgage or an obligation secured by a deed of trust that is satisfied on or after January 1, 2001.

(i)(1) In any action filed before January 1, 2002, that is dismissed as a result of the amendments to this section enacted at the 2001–02 Regular Session, the plaintiff shall not be required to pay the defendant's costs.

(2) Any claimant, including a claimant in a class action lawsuit, whose claim is dismissed or barred as a result of the amendments to this section enacted at the 2001–02 Regular Session, may, within 6 months of the dismissal or barring of the action or claim, file or refile a claim for actual damages occurring before January 1, 2002, that were proximately caused by a time lapse between loan satisfaction and the completion of the beneficiary's obligations as required under paragraph (1) of subdivision (b). In any action brought under this section, the defendant may be found liable for actual damages, but may not be found liable for any civil penalty authorized by Section 2941.

(j) Notwithstanding any other penalties, if a beneficiary collects a fee for reconveyance and thereafter has knowledge, or should have knowledge, that no reconveyance has been recorded, the beneficiary shall cause to be recorded the reconveyance, or in the event a release of obligation is earlier and timely recorded, the beneficiary shall refund to the trustor the fee charged to perform the reconveyance. Evidence of knowledge includes, but is not limited to, notice of a release of obligation pursuant to paragraph (3) of subdivision (b). *(Enacted in 1872. Amended by Code Am.1873–74, c. 612, p. 261, § 261; Code Am.1880, c. 81, p. 10, § 1; Stats.1946, 1st Ex.Sess., c. 58, p. 82, § 1, eff. Feb. 25, 1946; Stats.1947, c. 1411, p. 2972, § 1; Stats.1974, c. 267, § 1; Stats.1978, c. 509, p. 1657, § 1; Stats.1988, c. 1006, § 1, operative July 1, 1989; Stats.1991, c. 1155 (A.B.2146), § 2; Stats.1993, c. 754 (S.B.313), § 3, eff. Oct. 4, 1993; Stats.1994, c. 374 (A.B.3397), § 1; Stats.1996, c. 230 (A.B.372), § 1; Stats.1997, c. 74 (S.B.665), § 7; Stats.2000, c. 1013 (A.B.996), § 1; Stats.2001, c. 560 (A.B.1090), § 1; Stats.2002, c. 809 (S.B.1504), § 2; Stats.2003, c. 62 (S.B.600), § 20.)*

§ 2941.1. Charging a reconveyance fee where no payoff demand statement is issued

Notwithstanding any other provision of law, if no payoff demand statement is issued pursuant to Section 2943, nothing in Section 2941 shall be construed to prohibit the charging of a reconveyance fee. *(Added by Stats.2001, c. 438 (S.B.958), § 6, eff. Oct. 2, 2001, operative Jan. 1, 2002.)*

§ 2941.5. Obligation to execute certificate of discharge, satisfaction, or request for reconveyance; penalty

Every person who willfully violates Section 2941 is guilty of a misdemeanor punishable by fine of not less than fifty dollars ($50) nor more than four hundred dollars ($400), or by imprisonment in the county jail for not to exceed six months, or by both such fine and imprisonment.

For purposes of this section, "willfully" means simply a purpose or willingness to commit the act, or make the omission referred to. It does not require an intent to violate the law, to injure another, or to acquire any advantage. *(Added by Stats.1946, 1st Ex.Sess., c. 58, p. 82, § 2, eff. Feb. 25, 1946. Amended by Stats.1983, c. 1092, § 67, eff. Sept. 27, 1983, operative Jan. 1, 1984; Stats.1988, c. 1006, § 2, operative July 1, 1989.)*

§ 2941.7. Satisfaction of mortgage or deed of trust; release of lien when mortgagee or beneficiary cannot be found or refuses to issue certificate of discharge or to reconvey

Whenever the obligation secured by a mortgage or deed of trust has been fully satisfied and the present mortgagee or beneficiary of record cannot be located after diligent search, or refuses to execute and deliver a proper certificate of discharge or request for reconveyance, or whenever a specified balance, including principal and interest, remains due and the mortgagor or trustor or the mortgagor's or trustor's successor in interest cannot, after diligent search, locate the then mortgagee or beneficiary of record, the lien of any mortgage or deed of trust shall be released when the mortgagor or trustor or the mortgagor's or trustor's successor in interest records or causes to be recorded, in the office of the county recorder of the county in which the encumbered property is located, a corporate bond accompanied by a declaration, as specified in subdivision (b), and with respect to a deed of trust, a reconveyance as hereinafter provided.

(a) The bond shall be acceptable to the trustee and shall be issued by a corporation lawfully authorized to issue surety bonds in the State of California in a sum equal to the greater of either (1) two times the amount of the original obligation secured by the mortgage or deed of trust and any additional principal amounts, including advances, shown in any recorded amendment thereto, or (2) one-half of the total amount computed pursuant to (1) and any accrued interest on such amount, and shall be conditioned for payment of any sum which the mortgagee or beneficiary may recover in an action on the obligation secured by the mortgage or deed of trust, with costs of suit and reasonable attorneys' fees. The obligees under the bond shall be the mortgagee or mortgagee's successor in interest or the trustee who executes a reconveyance under this section and the beneficiary or beneficiary's successor in interest.

The bond recorded by the mortgagor or trustor or mortgagor's or trustor's successor in interest shall contain the following information describing the mortgage or deed of trust:

(1) Recording date and instrument number or book and page number of the recorded instrument.

(2) Names of original mortgagor and mortgagee or trustor and beneficiary.

(3) Amount shown as original principal sum secured thereby.

(4) The recording information and new principal amount shown in any recorded amendment thereto.

(b) The declaration accompanying the corporate bond recorded by the mortgagor or trustor or the mortgagor's or trustor's successor in interest shall state:

(1) That it is recorded pursuant to this section.

(2) The name of the original mortgagor or trustor and mortgagee or beneficiary.

(3) The name and address of the person making the declaration.

(4) That either the obligation secured by the mortgage or deed of trust has been fully satisfied and the present mortgagee or beneficiary of record cannot be located after diligent search, or refuses to execute and deliver a proper certificate of discharge or request for reconveyance as required under Section 2941; or that a specified balance, including principal and interest, remains due and the mortgagor or trustor or mortgagor's or trustor's successor in interest cannot, after diligent search, locate the then mortgagee or beneficiary.

(5) That the declarant has mailed by certified mail, return receipt requested, to the last address of the person to whom payments under the mortgage or deed of trust were made and to the last mortgagee or beneficiary of record at the address for such mortgagee or beneficiary shown on the instrument creating, assigning, or conveying the interest, a notice of recording a declaration and bond under this section and informing the recipient of the name and address of the mortgagor or trustee, if any, and of the right to record a written objection with respect to the release of the lien of the mortgage or, with respect to a deed of trust, notify the trustee in writing of any objection to the reconveyance of the deed of trust. The declaration shall state the date any notices were mailed pursuant to this section and the names and addresses of all persons to whom mailed.

The declaration provided for in this section shall be signed by the mortgagor or trustor under penalty of perjury.

(c) With respect to a deed of trust, after the expiration of 30 days following the recording of the corporate bond and accompanying declaration provided in subdivisions (a) and (b), and delivery to the trustee of the usual reconveyance fees plus costs and a demand for reconveyance under this section, the trustee shall execute and record, or otherwise deliver as provided in Section 2941, a reconveyance in the same form as if the beneficiary had delivered to the trustee a proper request for reconveyance, provided that the trustee has not received a written objection to the reconveyance from the beneficiary of record. No trustee shall have any liability to any person by reason of its execution of a reconveyance in reliance upon a trustor's or trustor's successor's in interest substantial compliance with this section. The sole remedy of any person damaged by reason of the reconveyance shall be against the trustor, the affiant, or the bond. With respect to a mortgage, a mortgage shall be satisfied of record when 30 days have expired following recordation of the corporate bond and accompanying declaration, provided no objection to satisfaction has been recorded by the mortgagee within that period. A bona fide purchaser or encumbrancer for value shall take the interest conveyed free of such mortgage, provided there has been compliance with subdivisions (a) and (b) and the deed to the purchaser recites that no objections by the mortgagee have been recorded.

Upon recording of a reconveyance under this section, or, in the case of a mortgage the expiration of 30 days following recordation of the corporate bond and accompanying declaration without objection thereto having been recorded, interest shall no longer accrue as to any balance remaining due to the extent the balance due has been alleged in the declaration recorded under subdivision (b).

The sum of any specified balance, including principal and interest, which remains due and which is remitted to any issuer of a corporate bond in conjunction with the issuance of a bond pursuant to this section shall, if unclaimed, escheat to the state after three years pursuant to the Unclaimed Property Law. From the date of escheat the issuer of the bond shall be relieved of any liability to pay to the beneficiary or his or her heirs or other successors in interest the escheated funds and the sole remedy shall be a claim for property paid or delivered to the Controller pursuant to the Unclaimed Property Law.

§ 2941.7

(d) The term "diligent search," as used in this section, shall mean all of the following:

(1) The mailing of notices as provided in paragraph (5) of subdivision (b), and to any other address that the declarant has used to correspond with or contact the mortgagee or beneficiary.

(2) A check of the telephone directory in the city where the mortgagee or beneficiary maintained the mortgagee's or beneficiary's last known address or place of business.

(3) In the event the mortgagee or beneficiary or the mortgagee's or beneficiary's successor in interest is a corporation, a check of the records of the California Secretary of State and the secretary of state in the state of incorporation, if known.

(4) In the event the mortgagee or beneficiary is a state or national bank or a state or federal savings and loan association, an inquiry of the regulatory authority of such bank or savings and loan association.

(e) This section shall not be deemed to create an exclusive procedure for the issuance of reconveyances and the issuance of bonds and declarations to release the lien of a mortgage and shall not affect any other procedures, whether or not such procedures are set forth in statute, for the issuance of reconveyances and the issuance of bonds and declarations to release the lien of a mortgage.

(f) For purposes of this section, the trustor or trustor's successor in interest may substitute the present trustee of record without conferring any duties upon the trustee other than those that are incidental to the execution of a reconveyance pursuant to this section if all of the following requirements are met:

(1) The present trustee of record and the present mortgagee or beneficiary of record cannot be located after diligent search.

(2) The declaration filed pursuant to subdivision (b) shall state in addition that it is filed pursuant to this subdivision, and shall, in lieu of the provisions of paragraph (4) of subdivision (b), state that the obligation secured by the mortgage or deed of trust has been fully satisfied and the present trustee of record and present mortgagee or beneficiary of record cannot be located after diligent search.

(3) The substitute trustee is a title insurance company that agrees to accept the substitution. This subdivision shall not impose a duty upon a title insurance company to accept the substitution.

(4) The corporate bond required in subdivision (a) is for a period of five or more years. *(Added by Stats.1980, c. 529, p. 1470, § 1. Amended by Stats.1995, c. 244 (S.B.784), § 1; Stats.1996, c. 762 (S.B.2014), § 2.)*

§ 2941.9. Trust deed beneficiaries; agreements to be governed by beneficiaries holding more than 50 percent of the record beneficial interest

(a) The purpose of this section is to establish a process through which all of the beneficiaries under a trust deed may agree to be governed by beneficiaries holding more than 50 percent of the record beneficial interest of a series of notes secured by the same real property or of undivided interests in a note secured by real property equivalent to a series transaction, exclusive of any notes or interests of a licensed real estate broker that is the issuer or servicer of the notes or interests or any affiliate of that licensed real estate broker.

(b) All holders of notes secured by the same real property or a series of undivided interests in notes secured by real property equivalent to a series transaction may agree in writing to be governed by the desires of the holders of more than 50 percent of the record beneficial interest of those notes or interests, exclusive of any notes or interests of a licensed real estate broker that is the issuer or servicer of the notes or interests of any affiliate of the licensed real estate broker, with respect to actions to be taken on behalf of all holders in the event of default or foreclosure for matters that require direction or approval of the holders, including designation of the broker, servicing agent, or other person acting on their behalf, and the sale, encumbrance, or lease of real property owned by the holders resulting from foreclosure or receipt of a deed in lieu of foreclosure.

(c) A description of the agreement authorized in subdivision (b) of this section shall be disclosed pursuant to Section 10232.5 of the Business and Professions Code and shall be included in a recorded document such as the deed of trust or the assignment of interests.

(d) Any action taken pursuant to the authority granted in this section is not effective unless all the parties agreeing to the action sign, under penalty of perjury, a separate written document entitled "Majority Action Affidavit" stating the following:

(1) The action has been authorized pursuant to this section.

(2) None of the undersigned is a licensed real estate broker or an affiliate of the broker that is the issuer or servicer of the obligation secured by the deed of trust.

(3) The undersigned together hold more than 50 percent of the record beneficial interest of a series of notes secured by the same real property or of undivided interests in a note secured by real property equivalent to a series transaction.

(4) Notice of the action was sent by certified mail, postage prepaid, with return receipt requested, to each holder of an interest in the obligation secured by the deed of trust who has not joined in the execution of the substitution or this document.

This document shall be recorded in the office of the county recorder of each county in which the real property described in the deed of trust is located. Once the document in this subdivision is recorded, it shall constitute conclusive evidence of compliance with the requirements of this subdivision in favor of trustees acting pursuant to this section, substituted trustees acting pursuant to Section 2934a, subsequent assignees of the obligation secured by the deed of trust, and subsequent bona fide purchasers or encumbrancers for value of the real property described therein.

(e) For purposes of this section, "affiliate of the licensed real estate broker" includes any person as defined in Section 25013 of the Corporations Code who is controlled by, or is under common control with, or who controls, a licensed real estate broker. "Control" means the possession, direct or indirect, of the power to direct or cause the direction of management and policies. *(Added by Stats.1996, c. 839 (S.B.1638), § 3.)*

§ 2942. Bottomry and respondentia excluded from chapter

Contracts of bottomry or respondentia, although in the nature of mortgages, are not affected by any of the provisions of this Chapter. *(Enacted in 1872.)*

Cross References

Bottomry, see Harbors and Navigation Code § 450 et seq.
Respondentia, see Harbors and Navigation Code § 470 et seq.

§ 2943. Definitions; copy of note and modifications; payoff demand statement; reliance by entitled person on beneficiary statement or payoff demand statement

(a) As used in this section:

(1) "Beneficiary" means a mortgagee or beneficiary of a mortgage or deed of trust, or his or her assignees.

(2) "Beneficiary statement" means a written statement showing:

(A) The amount of the unpaid balance of the obligation secured by the mortgage or deed of trust and the interest rate, together with the total amounts, if any, of all overdue installments of either principal or interest, or both.

(B) The amounts of periodic payments, if any.

(C) The date on which the obligation is due in whole or in part.

(D) The date to which real estate taxes and special assessments have been paid to the extent the information is known to the beneficiary.

(E) The amount of hazard insurance in effect and the term and premium of that insurance to the extent the information is known to the beneficiary.

(F) The amount in an account, if any, maintained for the accumulation of funds with which to pay taxes and insurance premiums.

(G) The nature and, if known, the amount of any additional charges, costs, or expenses paid or incurred by the beneficiary which have become a lien on the real property involved.

(H) Whether the obligation secured by the mortgage or deed of trust can or may be transferred to a new borrower.

(3) "Delivery" means depositing or causing to be deposited in the United States mail an envelope with postage prepaid, containing a copy of the document to be delivered, addressed to the person whose name and address is set forth in the demand therefor. The document may also be transmitted by facsimile machine to the person whose name and address is set forth in the demand therefor.

(4) "Entitled person" means the trustor or mortgagor of, or his or her successor in interest in, the mortgaged or trust property or any part thereof, any beneficiary under a deed of trust, any person having a subordinate lien or encumbrance of record thereon, the escrowholder licensed as an agent pursuant to Division 6 (commencing with Section 17000) of the Financial Code, or the party exempt by virtue of Section 17006 of the Financial Code who is acting as the escrowholder.

(5) "Payoff demand statement" means a written statement, prepared in response to a written demand made by an entitled person or authorized agent, setting forth the amounts required as of the date of preparation by the beneficiary, to fully satisfy all obligations secured by the loan that is the subject of the payoff demand statement. The written statement shall include information reasonably necessary to calculate the payoff amount on a per diem basis for the period of time, not to exceed 30 days, during which the per diem amount is not changed by the terms of the note.

(b)(1) A beneficiary, or his or her authorized agent, shall, within 21 days of the receipt of a written demand by an entitled person or his or her authorized agent, prepare and deliver to the person demanding it a true, correct, and complete copy of the note or other evidence of indebtedness with any modification thereto, and a beneficiary statement.

(2) A request pursuant to this subdivision may be made by an entitled person or his or her authorized agent at any time before, or within two months after, the recording of a notice of default under a mortgage or deed of trust, or may otherwise be made more than 30 days prior to the entry of the decree of foreclosure.

(c) A beneficiary, or his or her authorized agent, shall, on the written demand of an entitled person, or his or her authorized agent, prepare and deliver a payoff demand statement to the person demanding it within 21 days of the receipt of the demand. However, if the loan is subject to a recorded notice of default or a filed complaint commencing a judicial foreclosure, the beneficiary shall have no obligation to prepare and deliver this statement as prescribed unless the written demand is received prior to the first publication of a notice of sale or the notice of the first date of sale established by a court.

(d)(1) A beneficiary statement or payoff demand statement may be relied upon by the entitled person or his or her authorized agent in accordance with its terms, including with respect to the payoff demand statement reliance for the purpose of establishing the amount necessary to pay the obligation in full. If the beneficiary notifies the entitled person or his or her authorized agent of any amendment to the statement, then the amended statement may be relied upon by the entitled person or his or her authorized agent as provided in this subdivision.

(2) If notification of any amendment to the statement is not given in writing, then a written amendment to the statement shall be delivered to the entitled person or his or her authorized agent no later than the next business day after notification.

(3) Upon the dates specified in subparagraphs (A) and (B) any sums that were due and for any reason not included in the statement or amended statement shall continue to be recoverable by the beneficiary as an unsecured obligation of the obligor pursuant to the terms of the note and existing provisions of law.

(A) If the transaction is voluntary, the entitled party or his or her authorized agent may rely upon the statement or amended statement upon the earlier of (i) the close of escrow, (ii) transfer of title, or (iii) recordation of a lien.

(B) If the loan is subject to a recorded notice of default or a filed complaint commencing a judicial foreclosure, the entitled party or his or her authorized agent may rely upon the statement or amended statement upon the acceptance of the last and highest bid at a trustee's sale or a court supervised sale.

(e) The following provisions apply to a demand for either a beneficiary statement or a payoff demand statement:

(1) If an entitled person or his or her authorized agent requests a statement pursuant to this section and does not specify a beneficiary statement or a payoff demand statement the beneficiary shall treat the request as a request for a payoff demand statement.

(2) If the entitled person or the entitled person's authorized agent includes in the written demand a specific request for a copy of the deed of trust or mortgage, it shall be furnished with the written statement at no additional charge.

(3) The beneficiary may, before delivering a statement, require reasonable proof that the person making the demand is, in fact, an entitled person or an authorized agent of an entitled person, in which event the beneficiary shall not be subject to the penalties of this section until 21 days after receipt of the proof herein provided for. A statement in writing signed by the entitled person appointing an authorized agent when delivered personally to the beneficiary or delivered by registered return receipt mail shall constitute reasonable proof as to the identity of an agent. Similar delivery of a policy of title insurance, preliminary report issued by a title company, original or photographic copy of a grant deed or certified copy of letters testamentary, guardianship, or conservatorship shall constitute reasonable proof as to the identity of a successor in interest, provided the person demanding a statement is named as successor in interest in the document.

(4) If a beneficiary for a period of 21 days after receipt of the written demand willfully fails to prepare and deliver the statement, he or she is liable to the entitled person for all damages which he or she may sustain by reason of the refusal and, whether or not actual damages are sustained, he or she shall forfeit to the entitled person the sum of three hundred dollars ($300). Each failure to prepare and deliver the statement, occurring at a time when, pursuant to this section, the beneficiary is required to prepare and deliver the statement, creates a separate cause of action, but a judgment awarding an entitled person a forfeiture, or damages and forfeiture, for any failure to prepare and deliver a statement bars recovery of damages and forfeiture for any other failure to prepare and deliver a statement, with respect to the same obligation, in compliance with a demand therefor made within six months before or after the demand as to which the award was made. For the purposes of this subdivision, "willfully" means an intentional failure to comply with the requirements of this section without just cause or excuse.

(5) If the beneficiary has more than one branch, office, or other place of business, then the demand shall be made to the branch or office address set forth in the payment billing notice or payment book, and the statement, unless it specifies otherwise, shall be deemed to apply only to the unpaid balance of the single obligation named in the request and secured by the mortgage or deed of trust which is payable at the branch or office whose address appears on the aforesaid billing notice or payment book.

(6) The beneficiary may make a charge not to exceed thirty dollars ($30) for furnishing each required statement. The provisions of this paragraph shall not apply to mortgages or deeds of trust insured by the Federal Housing Administrator or guaranteed by the Administrator of Veterans Affairs.

(f) The preparation and delivery of a beneficiary statement or a payoff demand statement pursuant to this section shall not change a date of sale established pursuant to Section 2924g.

(g) This section shall become operative on January 1, 2014. *(Added by Stats.2009, c. 43 (S.B.306), § 6, operative Jan. 1, 2014.)*

§ 2943.1. Borrower's Instruction to Suspend and Close Equity Line of Credit; delivery information included in payoff demand statement; form; duties of beneficiary upon receipt of instruction and payment; reliance

(a) For purposes of this section, the following definitions apply:

(1) "Beneficiary" has the same meaning as defined in Section 2943.

(2) "Borrower's Instruction to Suspend and Close Equity Line of Credit" means the instruction described in subdivision (c), signed by the borrower or borrowers under an equity line of credit.

(3) "Entitled person" has the same meaning as defined in Section 2943.

(4) "Equity line of credit" means a revolving line of credit used for consumer purposes, which is secured by a mortgage or deed of trust encumbering residential real property consisting of one to four dwelling units, at least one of which is occupied by the borrower.

(5) "Payoff demand statement" has the same meaning as defined in Section 2943.

(6) "Suspend" means to prohibit the borrower from drawing on, increasing, or incurring any additional principal debt on the equity line of credit.

(b) Notwithstanding paragraph (5) of subdivision (a) of Section 2943, a payoff demand statement issued by a beneficiary in connection with an equity line of credit shall include an email address, fax number, or mailing address designated by the beneficiary for delivery of the Borrower's Instruction to Suspend and Close Equity Line of Credit by the entitled person.

(c) Upon receipt from an entitled person of a Borrower's Instruction to Suspend and Close Equity Line of Credit, that has been prepared and presented to the borrower by the entitled person and signed by a borrower, a beneficiary shall suspend the equity line of credit for a minimum of 30 days. A Borrower's Instruction to Suspend and Close Equity Line of Credit shall be effective if made substantially in the following form and signed by the borrower:

"Borrower's Instruction to Suspend and Close
Equity Line of Credit

Lender: [Name of Lender]

Borrower(s): [Name of Borrower(s)]

Account Number of the Equity Line of Credit: [Account Number]

Encumbered Property Address: [Property Address]

Escrow or Settlement Agent: [Name of Agent]:

In connection with a sale or refinance of the above-referenced property, my Escrow or Settlement Agent has requested a payoff demand statement for the above-described equity line of credit. I understand my ability to use this equity line of credit has been suspended for at least 30 days to accommodate this pending transaction. I understand that I cannot use any credit cards, debit cards, or checks associated with this equity line of credit while it is suspended and all amounts will be due and payable upon close of escrow. I also understand that when payment is made in accordance with the payoff demand statement, my equity line of credit will be closed. If any amounts remain due after the payment is made, I understand I will remain personally liable for those amounts even if the equity line of credit has been closed and the property released.

This is my written authorization and instruction that you are to close my equity line of credit and cause the secured lien against this property to be released when you are in receipt of both this instruction and payment in accordance with your payoff demand statement.

_____   _____
(Date)   (Signature of Each Borrower)"

(d) When a beneficiary is in receipt of both a Borrower's Instruction to Suspend and Close Equity Line of Credit and payment in accordance with the payoff demand statement as set forth in Section 2943, the beneficiary shall do all of the following:

(1) Close the equity line of credit.

(2) Release or reconvey the property securing the equity line of credit, as provided by this chapter.

(e) The beneficiary may conclusively rely on the Borrower's Instruction to Suspend and Close Equity Line of Credit provided by the entitled person as coming from the borrower.

(f) This section shall become operative on July 1, 2015. *(Added by Stats.2014, c. 206 (A.B.1770), § 1, eff. Jan. 1, 2015, operative July 1, 2015. Amended by Stats.2018, c. 90 (S.B. 1139), § 1, eff. Jan. 1, 2019.)*

§ 2944. Transactions and security interests governed by Commercial Code

None of the provisions of this chapter applies to any transaction or security interest governed by the Commercial Code, except to the extent made applicable by reason of an election made by the secured party pursuant to subparagraph (B) of paragraph (1) of subdivision (a) of Section 9604 of the Commercial Code. *(Added by Stats.1963, c. 819, p. 2000, § 15, eff. Jan. 1, 1965. Amended by Stats.1992, c. 1095 (A.B.2734), § 3; Stats.1999, c. 991 (S.B.45), § 7, operative July 1, 2001.)*

§ 2944.5. Insurance policies; acceptance; lender, mortgagee, or third party with interest in real or personal property

No lender, mortgagee, or any third party having an interest in real or personal property shall refuse to accept a policy issued by an admitted insurer solely because the policy is issued for a continuous period without a fixed expiration date even though the policy premium is due and payable every six months, provided the lender, mortgagee, or third party is entitled to receive (a) notice of renewal from the insurer within 15 days of receipt of payment on the policy by the insured or (b) notice of cancellation or nonrenewal under the terms and conditions set forth in Sections 678 and 2074.8 of the Insurance Code, whichever is applicable. *(Added by Stats.1993, c. 522 (A.B.421), § 1.)*

§ 2944.6. Person who negotiates or offers to perform mortgage loan modifications for fee; violations

(a) Notwithstanding any other provision of law, any person who negotiates, attempts to negotiate, arranges, attempts to arrange, or otherwise offers to perform a mortgage loan modification or other form of mortgage loan forbearance for a fee or other compensation paid by the borrower, shall provide the following to the borrower, as a separate statement, in not less than 14–point bold type, prior to entering into any fee agreement with the borrower:

It is not necessary to pay a third party to arrange for a loan modification or other form of forbearance from your mortgage lender or servicer. You may call your lender directly to ask for a change in your loan terms. Nonprofit housing counseling agencies also offer these and other forms of borrower assistance free of charge. A list of nonprofit housing counseling agencies approved by the United States Department of Housing and Urban Development (HUD) is available from your local HUD office or by visiting www.hud.gov.

(b) If loan modification or other mortgage loan forbearance services are offered or negotiated in one of the languages set forth in Section 1632, a translated copy of the statement in subdivision (a) shall be provided to the borrower in that foreign language.

(c) A violation of this section by a natural person is a public offense punishable by a fine not exceeding ten thousand dollars ($10,000), by imprisonment in the county jail for a term not to exceed one year, or by both that fine and imprisonment, or if by a business entity, the violation is punishable by a fine not exceeding fifty thousand dollars ($50,000). These penalties are cumulative to any other remedies or penalties provided by law.

(d) This section does not apply to a person, or an agent acting on that person's behalf, offering loan modification or other loan forbearance services for a loan owned or serviced by that person.

(e) This section shall apply only to mortgages and deeds of trust secured by residential real property containing four or fewer dwelling units. *(Added by Stats.2009, c. 630 (S.B.94), § 9, eff. Oct. 11, 2009.)*

§ 2944.6

Cross References

Imposition of discipline of attorney, violation, see Business and Professions Code § 6106.3.

§ 2944.7. Person negotiating or offering to perform mortgage loan modification for compensation paid by borrower; unlawful acts; penalties; allowable acts

(a) Notwithstanding any other law, it shall be unlawful for any person who negotiates, attempts to negotiate, arranges, attempts to arrange, or otherwise offers to perform a mortgage loan modification or other form of mortgage loan forbearance for a fee or other compensation paid by the borrower, to do any of the following:

(1) Claim, demand, charge, collect, or receive any compensation until after the person has fully performed each and every service the person contracted to perform or represented that he or she would perform.

(2) Take any wage assignment, any lien of any type on real or personal property, or other security to secure the payment of compensation.

(3) Take any power of attorney from the borrower for any purpose.

(b) A violation of this section by a natural person is punishable by a fine not exceeding ten thousand dollars ($10,000), by imprisonment in the county jail for a term not to exceed one year, or by both that fine and imprisonment, or if by a business entity, the violation is punishable by a fine not exceeding fifty thousand dollars ($50,000). These penalties are cumulative to any other remedies or penalties provided by law.

(c) In addition to the penalties and remedies provided by Chapter 5 (commencing with Section 17200) of Part 2 of Division 7 of the Business and Professions Code, a person who violates this section shall be liable for a civil penalty not to exceed twenty thousand dollars ($20,000) for each violation, which shall be assessed and recovered in a civil action brought in the name of the people of the State of California by the Attorney General, by any district attorney, by any county counsel authorized by agreement with the district attorney in actions involving a violation of a county ordinance, by any city attorney of a city having a population in excess of 750,000, by any city attorney of any city and county, or, with the consent of the district attorney, by a city prosecutor in any city having a full-time city prosecutor, in any court of competent jurisdiction pursuant to Chapter 5 (commencing with Section 17200) of Part 2 of Division 7 of the Business and Professions Code.

(d) Nothing in this section precludes a person, or an agent acting on that person's behalf, who offers loan modification or other loan forbearance services for a loan owned or serviced by that person, from doing any of the following:

(1) Collecting principal, interest, or other charges under the terms of a loan, before the loan is modified, including charges to establish a new payment schedule for a nondelinquent loan, after the borrower reduces the unpaid principal balance of that loan for the express purpose of lowering the monthly payment due under the terms of the loan.

(2) Collecting principal, interest, or other charges under the terms of a loan, after the loan is modified.

(3) Accepting payment from a federal agency in connection with the federal Making Home Affordable Plan or other federal plan intended to help borrowers refinance or modify their loans or otherwise avoid foreclosures.

(e) This section shall apply only to mortgages and deeds of trust secured by residential real property containing four or fewer dwelling units. *(Added by Stats.2009, c. 630 (S.B.94), § 10, eff. Oct. 11, 2009. Amended by Stats.2012, c. 563 (S.B.980), § 4; Stats.2012, c. 569 (A.B.1950), § 3; Stats.2014, c. 457 (A.B.1730), § 1, eff. Jan. 1, 2015.)*

Cross References

Imposition of discipline of attorney, violation, see Business and Professions Code § 6106.3.

§ 2944.8. Person negotiating or offering to perform mortgage loan modification for compensation paid by borrower; additional penalties where victim is senior citizen or disabled person

(a) In addition to any liability for a civil penalty pursuant to Section 2944.7, if a person violates Section 2944.7 with respect to a victim who is a senior citizen or a disabled person, the violator may be liable for a civil penalty not to exceed two thousand five hundred dollars ($2,500) for each violation, which may be assessed and recovered in a civil action.

(b) As used in this section, the following terms have the following meanings:

(1) "Disabled person" means a person who has a physical or mental disability, as defined in Sections 12926 and 12926.1 of the Government Code.

(2) "Senior citizen" means a person who is 65 years of age or older.

(c) In determining whether to impose a civil penalty pursuant to subdivision (a) and the amount thereof, the court shall consider, in addition to any other appropriate factors, the extent to which one or more of the following factors are present:

(1) Whether the defendant knew or should have known that his or her conduct was directed to one or more senior citizens or disabled persons.

(2) Whether the defendant's conduct caused one or more senior citizens or disabled persons to suffer any of the following: loss or encumbrance of a primary residence, principal employment, or source of income, substantial loss of property set aside for retirement, or for personal or family care and maintenance, or substantial loss of payments received under a pension or retirement plan or a government benefits program, or assets essential to the health or welfare of the senior citizen or disabled person.

(3) Whether one or more senior citizens or disabled persons are substantially more vulnerable than other members of the public to the defendant's conduct because of age, poor health or infirmity, impaired understanding, restricted mobility, or disability, and actually suffered substantial physical, emotional, or economic damage resulting from the defendant's conduct.

(d) A court of competent jurisdiction hearing an action pursuant to this section may make orders and judgments as necessary to restore to a senior citizen or disabled person money or property, real or personal, that may have been acquired by means of a violation of Section 2944.7. *(Added by Stats.2014, c. 457 (A.B.1730), § 2, eff. Jan. 1, 2015.)*

§ 2944.10. Person negotiating or offering to perform mortgage loan modification for compensation paid by borrower; limitation of actions

Any action to enforce any cause of action pursuant to Section 2944.7 or 2944.8 shall be commenced within four years after the cause of action accrued. No cause of action barred under existing law on the effective date of this section shall be revived by its enactment. *(Added by Stats.2014, c. 457 (A.B.1730), § 3, eff. Jan. 1, 2015.)*

ARTICLE 1.5. MORTGAGE FORECLOSURE CONSULTANTS

Section
2945. Legislative findings and declarations.
2945.1. Definitions.
2945.2. Owner's right to cancel contract with consultant; time and manner of cancellation.
2945.3. Written contract; contents; language, date, and signature; notice of cancellation; form.
2945.4. Prohibited practices.
2945.45. Foreclosure consultants; registration and certification; requirements; Foreclosure Consultant Regulation Fund; refusal or revocation of registration; fines and penalties for violation.
2945.5. Waiver.
2945.6. Action against consultant; judgment; cumulative remedies; limitation of actions.
2945.7. Violations; punishment; cumulative remedies.
2945.8. Severability.
2945.9. Liability of consultant for statements or acts committed by representative.
2945.10. Limitation of liability under section 2945.9; voiding provision or contract; arbitration.
2945.11. Representative of consultant; statements to be provided to owner; remedies.

§ 2945. Legislative findings and declarations

(a) The Legislature finds and declares that homeowners whose residences are in foreclosure are subject to fraud, deception, harassment, and unfair dealing by foreclosure consultants from the time a Notice of Default is recorded pursuant to Section 2924 until the time surplus funds from any foreclosure sale are distributed to the homeowner or his or her successor. Foreclosure consultants represent that they can assist homeowners who have defaulted on obligations secured by their residences. These foreclosure consultants, however, often charge high fees, the payment of which is often secured by a deed of trust on the residence to be saved, and perform no service or essentially a worthless service. Homeowners, relying on the foreclosure consultants' promises of help, take no other action, are diverted from lawful businesses which could render beneficial services, and often lose their homes, sometimes to the foreclosure consultants who purchase homes at a fraction of their value before the sale. Vulnerable homeowners are increasingly relying on the services of foreclosure consultants who advise the homeowner that the foreclosure consultant can obtain the remaining funds from the foreclosure sale if the homeowner executes an assignment of the surplus, a deed, or a power of attorney in favor of the foreclosure consultant. This results in the homeowner paying an exorbitant fee for a service when the homeowner could have obtained the remaining funds from the trustee's sale from the trustee directly for minimal cost if the homeowner had consulted legal counsel or had sufficient time to receive notices from the trustee pursuant to Section 2924j regarding how and where to make a claim for excess proceeds.

(b) The Legislature further finds and declares that foreclosure consultants have a significant impact on the economy of this state and on the welfare of its citizens.

(c) The intent and purposes of this article are the following:

(1) To require that foreclosure consultant service agreements be expressed in writing; to safeguard the public against deceit and financial hardship; to permit rescission of foreclosure consultation contracts; to prohibit representations that tend to mislead; and to encourage fair dealing in the rendition of foreclosure services.

(2) The provisions of this article shall be liberally construed to effectuate this intent and to achieve these purposes. *(Added by Stats.1979, c. 1029, p. 3541, § 2. Amended by Stats.1980, c. 676, p. 1896, § 51; Stats.2004, c. 177 (S.B.1277), § 6.)*

§ 2945.1. Definitions

The following definitions apply to this chapter:

(a) "Foreclosure consultant" means any person who makes any solicitation, representation, or offer to any owner to perform for compensation or who, for compensation, performs any service which the person in any manner represents will in any manner do any of the following:

(1) Stop or postpone the foreclosure sale.

(2) Obtain any forbearance from any beneficiary or mortgagee.

(3) Assist the owner to exercise the right of reinstatement provided in Section 2924c.

(4) Obtain any extension of the period within which the owner may reinstate his or her obligation.

(5) Obtain any waiver of an acceleration clause contained in any promissory note or contract secured by a deed of trust or mortgage on a residence in foreclosure or contained that deed of trust or mortgage.

(6) Assist the owner to obtain a loan or advance of funds.

(7) Avoid or ameliorate the impairment of the owner's credit resulting from the recording of a notice of default or the conduct of a foreclosure sale.

(8) Save the owner's residence from foreclosure.

(9) Assist the owner in obtaining from the beneficiary, mortgagee, trustee under a power of sale, or counsel for the beneficiary, mortgagee, or trustee, the remaining proceeds from the foreclosure sale of the owner's residence.

(b) A foreclosure consultant does not include any of the following:

(1) A person licensed to practice law in this state when the person renders service in the course of his or her practice as an attorney at law.

(2) A person licensed under Division 3 (commencing with Section 12000) of the Financial Code when the person is acting as a prorater as defined therein.

(3) A person licensed under Part 1 (commencing with Section 10000) of Division 4 of the Business and Professions Code when the person is acting under the authority of that license, as described in Section 10131 or 10131.1 of the Business and Professions Code.

(4) A person licensed under Chapter 1 (commencing with Section 5000) of Division 3 of the Business and Professions Code when the person is acting in any capacity for which the person is licensed under those provisions.

(5) A person or his or her authorized agent acting under the express authority or written approval of the Department of Housing and Urban Development or other department or agency of the United States or this state to provide services.

(6) A person who holds or is owed an obligation secured by a lien on any residence in foreclosure when the person performs services in connection with this obligation or lien.

(7) Any person licensed to make loans pursuant to Division 9 (commencing with Section 22000) of the Financial Code when the person is acting under the authority of that license.

(8) Any person or entity doing business under any law of this state, or of the United States relating to banks, trust companies, savings and loan associations, industrial loan companies, pension trusts, credit unions, insurance companies, or any person or entity authorized under the laws of this state to conduct a title or escrow business, or a mortgagee which is a United States Department of Housing and Urban Development approved mortgagee and any subsidiary or affiliate of the above, and any agent or employee of the above while engaged in the business of these persons or entities.

(9) A person licensed as a residential mortgage lender or servicer pursuant to Division 20 (commencing with Section 50000) of the Financial Code, when acting under the authority of that license.

(c) Notwithstanding subdivision (b), any person who provides services pursuant to paragraph (9) of subdivision (a) is a foreclosure consultant unless he or she is the owner's attorney.

(d) "Person" means any individual, partnership, corporation, limited liability company, association or other group, however organized.

(e) "Service" means and includes, but is not limited to, any of the following:

(1) Debt, budget, or financial counseling of any type.

(2) Receiving money for the purpose of distributing it to creditors in payment or partial payment of any obligation secured by a lien on a residence in foreclosure.

(3) Contacting creditors on behalf of an owner of a residence in foreclosure.

(4) Arranging or attempting to arrange for an extension of the period within which the owner of a residence in foreclosure may cure his or her default and reinstate his or her obligation pursuant to Section 2924c.

(5) Arranging or attempting to arrange for any delay or postponement of the time of sale of the residence in foreclosure.

(6) Advising the filing of any document or assisting in any manner in the preparation of any document for filing with any bankruptcy court.

(7) Giving any advice, explanation, or instruction to an owner of a residence in foreclosure which in any manner relates to the cure of a default in or the reinstatement of an obligation secured by a lien on the residence in foreclosure, the full satisfaction of that obligation, or the postponement or avoidance of a sale of a residence in foreclosure pursuant to a power of sale contained in any deed of trust.

(8) Arranging or attempting to arrange for the payment by the beneficiary, mortgagee, trustee under a power of sale, or counsel for the beneficiary, mortgagee, or trustee, of the remaining proceeds to which the owner is entitled from a foreclosure sale of the owner's residence in foreclosure. Arranging or attempting to arrange for the payment shall include any arrangement where the owner transfers or assigns the right to the remaining proceeds of a foreclosure sale to the foreclosure consultant or any person designated by the foreclosure consultant, whether that transfer is effected by agreement, assignment, deed, power of attorney, or assignment of claim.

(9) Arranging or attempting to arrange an audit of any obligation secured by a lien on a residence in foreclosure.

(f) "Residence in foreclosure" means a residence in foreclosure as defined in Section 1695.1.

(g) "Owner" means a property owner as defined in Section 1695.1.

(h) "Contract" means any agreement, or any term thereof, between a foreclosure consultant and an owner for the rendition of any service as defined in subdivision (e). (Added by Stats.1979, c. 1029, p. 3541, § 2. Amended by Stats.1980, c. 108, p. 252, § 3, eff. May 20, 1980; Stats.1980, c. 423, p. 845, § 15, eff. July 11, 1980; Stats.1980, c. 676, p. 1897, § 52; Stats.1980, c. 706, p. 2115, § 2; Stats.1981, c. 724, p. 2835, § 4; Stats.1982, c. 1082, p. 3920, § 3; Stats.1986, c. 248, § 17; Stats.1994, c. 1010 (S.B.2053), § 49; Stats.1995, c. 564 (S.B.946), § 4; Stats.2004, c. 177 (S.B.1277), § 7; Stats.2009, c. 630 (S.B.94), § 11, eff. Oct. 11, 2009; Stats.2010, c. 596 (A.B.2325), § 1.)

§ 2945.2. Owner's right to cancel contract with consultant; time and manner of cancellation

(a) In addition to any other right under law to rescind a contract, an owner has the right to cancel such a contract until midnight of the fifth business day, as defined in subdivision (e) of Section 1689.5, after the day on which the owner signs a contract that complies with Section 2945.3.

(b) Cancellation occurs when the owner gives written notice of cancellation to the foreclosure consultant by mail at the address specified in the contract, or by facsimile or electronic mail at the number or address identified in the contract.

(c) Notice of cancellation, if given by mail, is effective when deposited in the mail properly addressed with postage prepaid. If given by facsimile or electronic mail, notice of cancellation is effective when successfully transmitted.

(d) Notice of cancellation given by the owner need not take the particular form as provided with the contract and, however expressed, is effective if it indicates the intention of the owner not to be bound by the contract. *(Added by Stats.1979, c. 1029, p. 3541, § 2. Amended by Stats.2008, c. 278 (A.B.180), § 2, operative July 1, 2009.)*

Cross References

Inducement or attempted inducement of owner to enter contract which does not comply with this section a prohibited practice, see Civil Code § 2945.4.

§ 2945.3. Written contract; contents; language, date, and signature; notice of cancellation; form

(a) Every contract shall be in writing and shall fully disclose the exact nature of the foreclosure consultant's services and the total amount and terms of compensation.

(b) The following notice, printed in at least 14–point boldface type and completed with the name of the foreclosure consultant, shall be printed immediately above the statement required by subdivision (d):

"NOTICE REQUIRED BY CALIFORNIA LAW

_____ or anyone working
(Name)

for him or her CANNOT:

(1) Take any money from you or ask you for money

until _____ has
(Name)
completely finished doing everything he or she said he or she would do; and

(2) Ask you to sign or have you sign any lien, deed of trust, or deed."

(c) The contract shall be written in the same language as principally used by the foreclosure consultant to describe his or her services or to negotiate the contract. In addition, the foreclosure consultant shall provide the owner, before the owner signs the contract, with a copy of a completed contract written in any other language used in any communication between the foreclosure consultant and the owner and in any language described in subdivision (b) of Section 1632 and requested by the owner. If English is the language principally used by the foreclosure consultant to describe the foreclosure consultant's services or to negotiate the contract, the foreclosure consultant shall notify the owner orally and in writing before the owner signs the contract that the owner has the right to ask for a completed copy of the contract in a language described in subdivision (b) of Section 1632.

(d) The contract shall be dated and signed by the owner and shall contain in immediate proximity to the space reserved for the owner's signature a conspicuous statement in a size equal to at least 10–point boldface type, as follows: "You, the owner, may cancel this transaction at any time prior to midnight of the fifth business day after the date of this transaction. See the attached notice of cancellation form for an explanation of this right."

(e) The contract shall contain on the first page, in a type size no smaller than that generally used in the body of the document, each of the following:

(1) The name, mailing address, electronic mail address, and facsimile number of the foreclosure consultant to which the notice of cancellation is to be mailed.

(2) The date the owner signed the contract.

(f) The contract shall be accompanied by a completed form in duplicate, captioned "notice of cancellation," which shall be attached to the contract, shall be easily detachable, and shall contain in type of at least 10–point the following statement written in the same language as used in the contract:

"NOTICE OF CANCELLATION

_____
(Enter date of transaction)   (Date)

You may cancel this transaction, without any penalty or obligation, within five business days from the above date.

To cancel this transaction, mail or deliver a signed and dated copy of this cancellation notice, or any other written notice, or send a telegram,

to _____
(Name of foreclosure consultant)

at _____
(Address of foreclosure consultant's place of business)

You may also cancel by sending a facsimile (fax) of signed and dated copy of this cancellation notice, or any other written notice, to the following number:

_____
(Facsimile telephone number of foreclosure consultant's place of business)

You may also cancel by sending an e-mail canceling this transaction to the following e-mail address:

_____
(E-mail address of foreclosure consultant's business)

I hereby cancel this transaction

_____
(Date)

_____"
(Owner's signature)

(g) The foreclosure consultant shall provide the owner with a copy of the contract and the attached notice of cancellation.

(h) Until the foreclosure consultant has complied with this section, the owner may cancel the contract. *(Added by Stats.1979, c. 1029, p. 3541, § 2. Amended by Stats.1980, c. 423, p. 850, § 16, eff. July 11, 1980; Stats.1997, c. 50 (A.B.669), § 4; Stats.2004, c. 183 (A.B.3082), § 39; Stats. 2004, c. 177 (S.B.1277), § 8; Stats.2006, c. 538 (S.B.1852), § 54; Stats.2008, c. 278 (A.B.180), § 3, operative July 1, 2009.)*

§ 2945.3

Cross References

Liens, mortgages, execution of trustee's deed resulting from surplus proceeds of trustee's sale, see Civil Code § 2924j.

§ 2945.4. Prohibited practices

It shall be a violation for a foreclosure consultant to:

(a) Claim, demand, charge, collect, or receive any compensation until after the foreclosure consultant has fully performed each and every service the foreclosure consultant contracted to perform or represented that he or she would perform.

(b) Claim, demand, charge, collect, or receive any fee, interest, or any other compensation for any reason which exceeds 10 percent per annum of the amount of any loan which the foreclosure consultant may make to the owner.

(c) Take any wage assignment, any lien of any type on real or personal property, or other security to secure the payment of compensation. That security shall be void and unenforceable.

(d) Receive any consideration from any third party in connection with services rendered to an owner unless that consideration is fully disclosed to the owner.

(e) Acquire any interest in a residence in foreclosure from an owner with whom the foreclosure consultant has contracted. Any interest acquired in violation of this subdivision shall be voidable, provided that nothing herein shall affect or defeat the title of a bona fide purchaser or encumbrancer for value and without notice of a violation of this article. Knowledge that the property was "residential real property in foreclosure," does not constitute notice of a violation of this article. This subdivision may not be deemed to abrogate any duty of inquiry which exists as to rights or interests of persons in possession of residential real property in foreclosure.

(f) Take any power of attorney from an owner for any purpose.

(g) Induce or attempt to induce any owner to enter into a contract which does not comply in all respects with Sections 2945.2 and 2945.3.

(h) Enter into an agreement at any time to assist the owner in arranging, or arrange for the owner, the release of surplus funds after the trustee's sale is conducted, whether the agreement involves direct payment, assignment, deed, power of attorney, assignment of claim from an owner to the foreclosure consultant or any person designated by the foreclosure consultant, or any other compensation. (Added by Stats.1979, c. 1029, p. 3541, § 2. Amended by Stats.1980, c. 423, p. 851, § 17, eff. July 11, 1980; Stats.2004, c. 177 (S.B.1277), § 9; Stats.2008, c. 278 (A.B.180), § 4, operative July 1, 2009.)

Cross References

Treble damages for violating certain provisions of this section, see Civil Code § 2945.6.

§ 2945.45. Foreclosure consultants; registration and certification; requirements; Foreclosure Consultant Regulation Fund; refusal or revocation of registration; fines and penalties for violation

(a) Except as provided in subdivision (b) of Section 2945.1, a person shall not take any action specified in subdivision (a) of Section 2945.1 unless the person satisfies the following requirements:

(1) The person registers with, and is issued and maintains a certificate of registration from, the Department of Justice in accordance with the following requirements:

(A) The person shall submit a completed registration form, along with applicable fees, to the department. The registration form shall include the name, address, and telephone number of the foreclosure consultant, all of the names, addresses, telephone numbers, Internet Web sites, and e-mail addresses used or proposed to be used in connection with acting as a foreclosure consultant, a statement that the person has not been convicted of, or pled nolo contendere to, any crime involving fraud, misrepresentation, dishonesty, or a violation of this article, a statement that the person has not been liable under any civil judgment for fraud, misrepresentation, or violations of this article or of Section 17200 or 17500 of the Business and Professions Code, and any additional information required by the department.

(B) The registration form shall be accompanied by a copy of all print or electronic advertising and other promotional material, and scripts of all telephonic or broadcast advertising and other statements used or proposed to be used in connection with acting as a foreclosure consultant.

(C) The registration form shall be accompanied by a copy of the bond required pursuant to paragraph (2).

(D) The person shall file an update of any material change in the information required by subparagraphs (A) and (B) with the department.

(E) The person shall pay any fee set by the department to defray reasonable costs incurred in connection with the department's responsibilities under this article.

(2) The person obtains and maintains in force a surety bond in the amount of one hundred thousand dollars ($100,000). The bond shall be executed by a corporate surety admitted to do business in this state. The bond shall be made in favor of the State of California for the benefit of homeowners for damages caused by the foreclosure consultant's violation of this article or any other provision of law. A copy of the bond shall be filed with the Secretary of State, with a copy provided to the department pursuant to subparagraph (C) of paragraph (1).

(b) The Foreclosure Consultant Regulation Fund is hereby created in the State Treasury for the deposit of fees submitted to the Department of Justice pursuant to subparagraph (A) of paragraph (1) of subdivision (a) for registration as a foreclosure consultant. Moneys in the fund shall be available, upon appropriation by the Legislature, for the costs of the department incurred in connection with the administration of the registration program.

(c) The Department of Justice may refuse to issue, or may revoke, a certificate of registration because of any misstatement in the registration form, because the foreclosure consultant has been held liable for the violation of any law described in subparagraph (A) of paragraph (1) of subdivision (a), because the foreclosure consultant has failed to maintain the bond required under paragraph (2) of subdivision (a), or because of any violation of this chapter.

(d) A person who violates subdivision (a) shall be punished, for each violation, by a fine of not less than one thousand dollars ($1,000) and not more than twenty-five thousand dollars ($25,000), by imprisonment in the county jail for not more than one year, or by both that fine and imprisonment. The imposition of a penalty pursuant to this subdivision shall not be affected by the availability of any other relief, remedy, or penalty provided by law, and shall not affect the availability of any such relief, remedy, or penalty. (Added by Stats.2008, c. 278 (A.B.180), § 5, operative July 1, 2009.)

§ 2945.5. Waiver

Any waiver by an owner of the provisions of this article shall be deemed void and unenforceable as contrary to public policy. Any attempt by a foreclosure consultant to induce an owner to waive his rights shall be deemed a violation of this article. (Added by Stats.1979, c. 1029, p. 3541, § 2. Amended by Stats.1980, c. 676, p. 1899, § 53.)

§ 2945.6. Action against consultant; judgment; cumulative remedies; limitation of actions

(a) An owner may bring an action against a foreclosure consultant for any violation of this chapter. Judgment shall be entered for actual damages, reasonable attorneys' fees and costs, and appropriate equitable relief. The court also may, in its discretion, award exemplary damages and shall award exemplary damages equivalent to at least three times the compensation received by the foreclosure consultant in violation of subdivision (a), (b), or (d) of Section 2945.4, and three times the owner's actual damages for any violation of subdivision (c), (e), or (g) of Section 2945.4, in addition to any other award of actual or exemplary damages.

(b) The rights and remedies provided in subdivision (a) are cumulative to, and not a limitation of, any other rights and remedies provided by law. Any action brought pursuant to this section shall be commenced within four years from the date of the alleged violation. (Added by Stats.1979, c. 1029, p. 3541, § 2. Amended by Stats.1980, c. 676, p. 1899, § 54; Stats.1980, c. 423, p. 852, § 18, eff. July 11, 1980; Stats.1997, c. 50 (A.B.669), § 5.)

§ 2945.7. Violations; punishment; cumulative remedies

Any person who commits any violation described in Section 2945.4 shall be punished by a fine of not more than ten thousand dollars ($10,000), by imprisonment in the county jail for not more than one year, or pursuant to subdivision (h) of Section 1170 of the Penal Code, or by both that fine and imprisonment for each violation. These penalties are cumulative to any other remedies or penalties provided by law. (Added by Stats.1979, c. 1029, p. 3541, § 2. Amended by Stats.1980, c. 423, p. 852, § 19, eff. July 11, 1980; Stats.1985, c. 270, § 2; Stats.2011, c. 15 (A.B.109), § 35, eff. April 4, 2011, operative Oct. 1, 2011.)

Cross References

Misdemeanor, see Penal Code §§ 16, 17, 19, 19.2.

§ 2945.8. Severability

If any provision of this article or the application thereof to any person or circumstance is held to be unconstitutional, the remainder of the article and the application of such provision to other persons and circumstances shall not be affected thereby. (Added by Stats.1979, c. 1029, p. 3541, § 2.)

§ 2945.9. Liability of consultant for statements or acts committed by representative

(a) A foreclosure consultant is liable for all damages resulting from any statement made or act committed by the foreclosure consultant's representative in any manner connected with the foreclosure consultant's (1) performance, offer to perform, or contract to perform any of the services described in subdivision (a) of Section 2945.1, (2) receipt of any consideration or property from or on behalf of an owner, or (3) performance of any act prohibited by this article.

(b) "Representative" for the purposes of this section means a person who in any manner solicits, induces, or causes (1) any owner to contract with a foreclosure consultant, (2) any owner to pay any consideration or transfer title to the residence in foreclosure to the foreclosure consultant, or (3) any member of the owner's family or household to induce or cause any owner to pay any consideration or transfer title to the residence in foreclosure to the foreclosure consultant. (Added by Stats.1990, c. 1537 (S.B.2641), § 4. Amended by Stats.2006, c. 538 (S.B.1852), § 55.)

§ 2945.10. Limitation of liability under section 2945.9; voiding provision or contract; arbitration

(a) Any provision in a contract which attempts or purports to limit the liability of the foreclosure consultant under Section 2945.9 shall be void and shall at the option of the owner render the contract void. The foreclosure consultant shall be liable to the owner for all damages proximately caused by that provision. Any provision in a contract which attempts or purports to require arbitration of any dispute arising under this chapter shall be void at the option of the owner only upon grounds as exist for the revocation of any contract.

(b) This section shall apply to any contract entered into on or after January 1, 1991. (Added by Stats.1990, c. 1537 (S.B.2641), § 5.)

§ 2945.11. Representative of consultant; statements to be provided to owner; remedies

(a) Any representative, as defined in subdivision (b) of Section 2945.9, deemed to be the agent or employee or both the agent and the employee of the foreclosure consultant shall be required to provide both of the following:

(1) Written proof to the owner that the representative has a valid current California Real Estate Sales License and that the representative is bonded by an admitted surety insurer in an amount equal to at least twice the fair market value of the real property that is the subject of the contract.

(2) A statement in writing, under penalty of perjury, that the representative has a valid current California Real Estate Sales License, that the representative is bonded by an admitted surety insurer in an amount equal to at least twice the value of the real property that is the subject of the contract and has complied with paragraph (1). The written statement required by this paragraph shall be provided to all parties to the contract prior to the transfer of any interest in the real property that is the subject of the contract.

§ 2945.11

(b) The failure to comply with subdivision (a) shall, at the option of the owner, render the contract void and the foreclosure consultant shall be liable to the owner for all damages proximately caused by the failure to comply. *(Added by Stats.1990, c. 1537 (S.B.2641), § 6. Amended by Stats.1996, c. 124 (A.B.3470), § 8.)*

ARTICLE 2. MORTGAGE OF REAL PROPERTY

Section
- 2947. Property subject to mortgage.
- 2948. Form.
- 2948.5. Interest on principal obligation under promissory note secured by mortgage or deed of trust on real property improved with residential dwelling units; conditions; accrual of interest; conditions; applicability.
- 2949. Single-family, owner-occupied dwelling; addition of junior encumbrance by owner; no default or acceleration of maturity.
- 2950. Instrument of defeasance affecting grant in absolute form; necessity of recording.
- 2951. Repealed.
- 2952. Recording and acknowledgment; fictitious mortgages and deeds of trust; indexing; incorporation of terms by reference; constructive notice; designation of items not to be recorded.
- 2953. Waiver by borrower of statutory rights; validity; exceptions.
- 2953.1. Real property security instrument; subordination clause; subordination agreement.
- 2953.2. Real property security instrument containing subordination clause; contents.
- 2953.3. Subordination agreements; contents.
- 2953.4. Voidability of subordination clause or agreement; election; waiver.
- 2953.5. Application of §§ 2953.1 through 2953.4 to specified loans.
- 2954. Impound, trust, or other account for payment of taxes, insurance, or other purposes; conditions; accounting.
- 2954.1. Impound, trust, or other accounts maintained for property-related payments; restrictions.
- 2954.2. One- to four-family residences; written statement by mortgagee; moneys received and disbursed; additional accountings; charges; operative effect.
- 2954.4. Single-family, owner occupied dwellings late payment charge; maximum; tender; inapplicable loans.
- 2954.5. Delinquent payment charge; prerequisites to imposition.
- 2954.6. Private mortgage insurance or mortgage guaranty insurance; cancellation rights; notification.
- 2954.65. Refund of unused premiums.
- 2954.7. Termination of mortgage insurance payments; conditions; exclusion of specified instruments.
- 2954.8. Impound accounts; payment of interest; restrictions; exceptions; application.
- 2954.9. Loans for residential property of four units or less; right to prepayment.
- 2954.10. Acceleration of maturity date; penalty for prepayment.
- 2954.11. Installment loans; definitions; right to prepay and prepayment charges; disclosure; application of section.
- 2954.12. Private mortgage insurance or mortgage guaranty insurance; collection of future payments.

Section
- 2955. Impound account funds; investments; deposits; injunction for violations.
- 2955.1. Condominium loans; underwriting requirements for earthquake insurance or fees; disclosures.
- 2955.5. Hazard insurance; lender requiring amount exceeding replacement value; disclosure; relief.

§ 2947. Property subject to mortgage

Any interest in real property which is capable of being transferred may be mortgaged. *(Enacted in 1872.)*

Cross References

Accession to real property, see Civil Code § 1013 et seq.
Appurtenances to land defined, see Civil Code § 662.
Estates in real property, see Civil Code § 761 et seq.
Fixtures,
   Defined, see Civil Code § 660.
   Inclusion in lien of mortgage, see Civil Code § 2926.
Mortgage on property held adversely to mortgagor, see Civil Code § 2921.
Possibility, transferability, see Civil Code § 1045.
Real property defined, see Civil Code §§ 14, 658; Code of Civil Procedure § 17.

§ 2948. Form

A mortgage of real property may be made in substantially the following form:

This mortgage, made the _____ day of _____, in the year _____, by A. B., of _____, mortgagor, to C. D., of _____, mortgagee, witnesseth:

That the mortgagor mortgages to the mortgagee [here describe the property], as security for the payment to him of _____ dollars, on [or before] the _____ day of _____, in the year _____, with interest thereon [or as security for the payment of an obligation, describing it, etc.] A.B. *(Enacted in 1872.)*

Cross References

Mortgage as security, see Civil Code § 2920.
Necessity of writing to create a mortgage, see Civil Code § 2922.
Real property descriptions, construction, see Code of Civil Procedure § 2077.
Transfer as security for performance of another act as mortgage, see Civil Code § 2924.
Transfer subject to defeasance as mortgage, see Civil Code §§ 2925, 2950.

§ 2948.5. Interest on principal obligation under promissory note secured by mortgage or deed of trust on real property improved with residential dwelling units; conditions; accrual of interest; conditions; applicability

(a) A borrower shall not be required to pay interest on a principal obligation under a promissory note secured by a mortgage or deed of trust on real property improved with between one to four residential dwelling units for any period that meets any of the following requirements:

(1) Is more than one day prior to the date that the loan proceeds are disbursed from escrow.

(2) In the event of no escrow, if a request for recording is made in connection with the disbursement, is more than one day prior to the date the loan proceeds are disbursed to the

borrower, to a third party on behalf of the borrower, or to the lender to satisfy an existing obligation of the borrower.

(3) In all other circumstances where there is no escrow and no request for recording, is prior to the date funds are disbursed to the borrower, to a third party on behalf of the borrower, or to the lender to satisfy an existing obligation of the borrower.

(b) Interest may commence to accrue on the business day immediately preceding the day of disbursement, for obligations described in paragraphs (1) and (2) of subdivision (a) if both of the following occur:

(1) The borrower affirmatively requests, and the lender agrees, that the disbursement will occur on Monday, or a day immediately following a bank holiday.

(2) The following information is disclosed to the borrower in writing: (A) the amount of additional per diem interest charged to facilitate disbursement on Monday or the day following a holiday, as the case may be, and (B) that it may be possible to avoid the additional per diem interest charge by disbursing the loan proceeds on a day immediately following a business day. This disclosure shall be provided to the borrower and acknowledged by the borrower by signing a copy of the disclosure document prior to placing funds in escrow.

(c) This section does not apply to a loan that is subject to subdivision (c) of Section 10242 of the Business and Professions Code. *(Added by Stats.1985, c. 1393, § 1. Amended by Stats.1990, c. 872 (A.B.4267), § 1; Stats.2001, c. 302 (S.B. 364), § 1; Stats.2003, c. 554 (A.B.313), § 1.)*

Cross References

Licensed residential mortgage lenders, prohibited acts, see Financial Code § 50204.

§ 2949. Single-family, owner-occupied dwelling; addition of junior encumbrance by owner; no default or acceleration of maturity

(a) No mortgage or deed of trust on real property containing only a single-family, owner-occupied dwelling may be declared in default, nor may the maturity date of the indebtedness secured thereby be accelerated, solely by reason of the owner further encumbering the real property or any portion thereof, with a junior mortgage or junior deed of trust.

(b) As used in this section, "single-family, owner-occupied dwelling" means a dwelling which will be owned and occupied by a signatory to the mortgage or deed of trust secured by such dwelling within 90 days of the execution of such mortgage or deed of trust. *(Added by Stats.1972, c. 698, p. 1278, § 1.)*

§ 2950. Instrument of defeasance affecting grant in absolute form; necessity of recording

When a grant of real property purports to be an absolute conveyance, but is intended to be defeasible on the performance of certain conditions, such grant is not defeated or affected as against any person other than the grantee or his or her heirs or devisees, or persons having actual notice, unless an instrument of defeasance, duly executed and acknowledged, shall have been recorded in the office of the county recorder of the county where the property is situated. *(Enacted in 1872. Amended by Stats.2013, c. 76 (A.B.383), § 19.)*

Cross References

Proof that transfer made subject to defeasance is actually a mortgage, see Civil Code § 2925.
Validity of an unrecorded instrument as between parties, see Civil Code § 1217.

§ 2951. Repealed by Code Am.1873–74, c. 612, p. 262, § 262

§ 2952. Recording and acknowledgment; fictitious mortgages and deeds of trust; indexing; incorporation of terms by reference; constructive notice; designation of items not to be recorded

Mortgages and deeds of trust of real property may be acknowledged or proved, certified and recorded, in like manner and with like effect, as grants thereof; provided, however, that a mortgage or deed of trust of real property may be recorded and constructive notice of the same and the contents thereof given in the following manner:

Any person may record in the office of the county recorder of any county fictitious mortgages and deeds of trust of real property. Those fictitious mortgages and deeds of trust need not be acknowledged, or proved or certified to be recorded or entitled to record. Those mortgages and deeds of trust shall have noted upon the face thereof that they are fictitious. The county recorder shall index and record fictitious mortgages and deeds of trust in the same manner as other mortgages and deeds of trust are recorded, and shall note on all indices and records of the same that they are fictitious. Thereafter, any of the provisions of any recorded fictitious mortgage or deed of trust may be included for any and all purposes in any mortgage or deed of trust by reference therein to any of those provisions, without setting the same forth in full; provided, the fictitious mortgage or deed of trust is of record in the county in which the mortgage or deed of trust adopting or including by reference any of the provisions thereof is recorded. The reference shall contain a statement, as to each county in which the mortgage or deed of trust containing such a reference is recorded, of the date the fictitious mortgage or deed of trust was recorded, the county recorder's office wherein it is recorded, and the book or volume and the first page of the records in the recorder's office wherein and at which the fictitious mortgage or deed of trust was recorded, and a statement by paragraph numbers or any other method that will definitely identify the same, of the specific provisions of the fictitious mortgage or deed of trust that are being so adopted and included therein. The recording of any mortgage or deed of trust which has included therein any of those provisions by reference as aforesaid shall operate as constructive notice of the whole thereof including the terms, as a part of the written contents of the mortgage or deed of trust, of those provisions so included by reference as though the same were written in full therein. The parties bound or to be bound by provisions so adopted and included by reference shall be bound thereby in the same manner and with like effect for all purposes as though those provisions had been and were set forth in full in any mortgage or deed of trust.

§ 2952

The amendment to this section enacted by the 1957 Regular Session of the Legislature does not constitute a change in, but is declaratory of, the preexisting law. *(Enacted in 1872. Amended by Code Am.1873–74, c. 612, p. 262, § 263; Stats.1947, c. 1497, p. 3098, § 5; Stats.1949, c. 443, p. 788, § 1; Stats.1957, c. 1220, p. 2503, § 1; Stats.1969, c. 287, p. 638, § 1, operative July 1, 1970; Stats.2000, c. 924 (A.B.2935), § 1.)*

Cross References

Effect of recording, see Civil Code § 1213 et seq.
Mode of recording, see Civil Code § 1169 et seq.

§ 2953. Waiver by borrower of statutory rights; validity; exceptions

Any express agreement made or entered into by a borrower at the time of or in connection with the making of or renewing of any loan secured by a deed of trust, mortgage or other instrument creating a lien on real property, whereby the borrower agrees to waive the rights, or privileges conferred upon the borrower by Sections 2924, 2924b, or 2924c of the Civil Code or by Sections 580a or 726 of the Code of Civil Procedure, shall be void and of no effect. The provisions of this section shall not apply to any deed of trust, mortgage, or other liens given to secure the payment of bonds or other evidences of indebtedness authorized or permitted to be issued by the Commissioner of * * * Financial Protection and Innovation, or made by a public utility subject to the provisions of the Public Utilities Act. *(Added by Stats.1937, c. 564, p. 1605, § 1. Amended by Stats.1939, c. 585, p. 1991, § 1; Stats.1941, c. 599, p. 1983, § 1; Stats.2019, c. 143 (S.B.251), § 17, eff. Jan. 1, 2020; Stats.2022, c. 452 (S.B. 1498), § 36, eff. Jan. 1, 2023.)*

§ 2953.1. Real property security instrument; subordination clause; subordination agreement

As used in this section:

(a) "Real property security instrument" shall include any mortgage or trust deed or land contract in or on real property.

(b) "Subordination clause" shall mean a clause in a real property security instrument whereby the holder of the security interest under such instrument agrees that upon the occurrence of conditions or circumstances specified therein his security interest will become subordinate to or he will execute an agreement subordinating his interest to the lien of another real property security instrument which would otherwise be of lower priority than his lien or security interest.

(c) "Subordination agreement" shall mean a separate agreement or instrument whereby the holder of the security interest under a real property security instrument agrees that (1) his existing security interest is subordinate to, or (2) upon the occurrence of conditions or circumstances specified in such separate agreement his security interest will become subordinate to, or (3) he will execute an agreement subordinating his interest to, the lien of another real property security instrument which would otherwise be of lower priority than his lien or security interest. *(Added by Stats. 1963, c. 1861, p. 3841, § 1, operative Jan. 2, 1964.)*

§ 2953.2. Real property security instrument containing subordination clause; contents

Every real property security instrument which contains or has attached a subordination clause shall contain:

(a) At the top of the real property security instrument there shall appear in at least 10-point bold type, or, if typewritten, in capital letters and underlined, the word "Subordinated" followed by a description of the type of security instrument.

(b) A notice in at least eight-point bold type, or, if typewritten, in capital letters, shall appear immediately below the legend required by subdivision (a) of this section reading as follows: "Notice: This (insert description of real property security instrument) contains a subordination clause which may result in your security interest in the property becoming subject to and of lower priority than the lien of some other or later security instrument."

(c) If the terms of the subordination clause allow the obligor on the debt secured by the real property security instrument to obtain a loan, secured by another real property security instrument covering all or any part of the same parcel of real property, the proceeds of which may be used for any purpose or purposes other than defraying the costs for improvement of the land covered by the real property security instrument containing the subordination clause, a notice in at least eight-point bold type, or, if typewritten, in capital letters shall appear directly above the space reserved for the signature of the person whose security interest is to be subordinated, reading as follows: "Notice: This (insert description of real property security instrument) contains a subordination clause which allows the person obligated on your real property security instrument to obtain a loan a portion of which may be expended for other purposes than improvement of the land." *(Added by Stats.1963, c. 1861, p. 3842, § 2, operative Jan. 2, 1964.)*

§ 2953.3. Subordination agreements; contents

Every subordination agreement shall contain:

(a) At the top of the subordination agreement there shall appear in at least 10-point bold type, or, if typewritten, in capital letters and underlined, the words "Subordination Agreement."

(b) A notice in at least eight-point bold type, or, if typewritten, in capital letters, shall appear immediately below the legend required by subdivision (a) of this section reading as follows:

"Notice: This subordination agreement ("may result" or "results" as appropriate) in your security interest in the property becoming subject to and of lower priority than the lien of some other or later security instrument."

(c) If the terms of the subordination agreement provide that the obligor on the debt secured by the real property security instrument may either obtain a loan, or obtain an agreement from the holder of the real property security which will allow him to obtain a loan, the proceeds of which may be used for any purpose or purposes other than defraying the actual contract costs for improvement of the land, covered by the real property security instrument which is, or is to become subordinated, a notice in at least eight-point bold type or, if typewritten, in capital letters, shall appear directly above the space reserved for the signature of the person whose security interest is to be subordinated, reading as follows: "NOTICE: This subordination agreement contains a provision which ("allows" or "may allow" as appropriate) the person obligated on your real property security to obtain a loan a portion of which may be expended for other purposes than improvement of the land." (Added by Stats.1963, c. 1861, p. 3842, § 3, operative Jan. 2, 1964.)

§ 2953.4. Voidability of subordination clause or agreement; election; waiver

(a) Any subordination clause and any subordination agreement which is executed after the effective date of this act and which does not substantially comply with the provisions of Section 2953.2 or Section 2953.3 shall be voidable upon the election of the person whose security interest is to be subordinated or his successor-in-interest exercised within two years of the date on which the instrument to which his security interest is subordinated is executed; provided that such power of avoidance shall not be exercisable by any person having actual knowledge of the existence and terms of the subordination clause or agreement.

(b) The person whose security interest was to be subordinated or his successor-in-interest shall exercise his election to void the subordination clause or subordination agreement provided by subdivision (a) of this section by recording a notice stating that the provisions of Civil Code Section 2953.2 or Civil Code Section 2953.3 have not been complied with, and that he is the holder of the security instrument which is or was to become subordinated and that he elects to avoid the effect of the subordination clause or subordination agreement.

(c) The provisions of this section may be waived by the subsequent execution and recordation by the holder of the security interest which is or may become subordinated, of a statement that he knows of the existence of the subordination clause or agreement and of its terms and that he waives the provisions of this section and the requirements of Sections 2953.1, 2953.2, and 2953.3. (Added by Stats.1963, c. 1861, p. 3843, § 4, operative Jan. 2, 1964.)

§ 2953.5. Application of §§ 2953.1 through 2953.4 to specified loans

(a) Sections 2953.1 through 2953.4 shall not apply to any subordination clause or subordination agreement which expressly states that the subordinating loan shall exceed twenty-five thousand dollars ($25,000).

(b) Sections 2953.1 through 2953.4 shall not apply to any subordination clause or subordination agreement which is executed in connection with a loan which exceeds twenty-five thousand dollars ($25,000). (Added by Stats.1963, c. 1861, p. 3843, § 5, operative Jan. 2, 1964.)

§ 2954. Impound, trust, or other account for payment of taxes, insurance, or other purposes; conditions; accounting

(a)(1) No impound, trust, or other type of account for payment of taxes on the property, insurance premiums, or other purposes relating to the property shall be required as a condition of a real property sale contract or a loan secured by a deed of trust or mortgage on real property containing only a single-family, owner-occupied dwelling, except: (A) where required by a state or federal regulatory authority, (B) where a loan is made, guaranteed, or insured by a state or federal governmental lending or insuring agency, (C) upon a failure of the purchaser or borrower to pay two consecutive tax installments on the property prior to the delinquency date for such payments, (D) where the original principal amount of such a loan is (i) 90 percent or more of the sale price, if the property involved is sold, or is (ii) 90 percent or more of the appraised value of the property securing the loan, (E) whenever the combined principal amount of all loans secured by the real property exceeds 80 percent of the appraised value of the property securing the loans, (F) where a loan is made in compliance with the requirements for higher priced mortgage loans established in Regulation Z, whether or not the loan is a higher priced mortgage loan, or (G) where a loan is refinanced or modified in connection with a lender's homeownership preservation program or a lender's participation in such a program sponsored by a federal, state, or local government authority or a nonprofit organization. Nothing contained in this section shall preclude establishment of such an account on terms mutually agreeable to the parties to the loan, if, prior to the execution of the loan or sale agreement, the seller or lender has furnished to the purchaser or borrower a statement in writing, which may be set forth in the loan application, to the effect that the establishment of such an account shall not be required as a condition to the execution of the loan or sale agreement, and further, stating whether or not interest will be paid on the funds in such an account.

An impound, trust, or other type of account for the payment of taxes, insurance premiums, or other purposes relating to property established in violation of this subdivision is voidable, at the option of the purchaser or borrower, at any time, but shall not otherwise affect the validity of the loan or sale.

(2) For the purposes of this subdivision, "Regulation Z" means any rule, regulation, or interpretation promulgated by the Board of Governors of the Federal Reserve System and any interpretation or approval issued by an official or employee duly authorized by the board to issue interpretations or approvals dealing with, respectively, consumer leasing or consumer lending, pursuant to the federal Truth in Lending Act, as amended (15 U.S.C. Sec. 1601 et seq.).

(b) Every mortgagee of real property, beneficiary under a deed of trust on real property, or vendor on a real property sale contract upon the written request of the mortgagor, trustor, or vendee shall furnish to the mortgagor, trustor, or vendee for each calendar year within 60 days after the end of the year an itemized accounting of moneys received for interest and principal repayment and received and held in or disbursed from an impound or trust account, if any, for payment of taxes on the property, insurance premiums, or other purposes relating to the property subject to the mortgage, deed of trust, or real property sale contract. The mortgagor, trustor, or vendee shall be entitled to receive one such accounting for each calendar year without charge and shall be entitled to additional similar accountings for one or more months upon written request and on payment in advance of fees as follows:

§ 2954

(1) Fifty cents ($0.50) per statement when requested in advance on a monthly basis for one or more years.

(2) One dollar ($1) per statement when requested for only one month.

(3) Five dollars ($5) if requested for a single cumulative statement giving all the information described above back to the last statement rendered.

If the mortgagee, beneficiary, or vendor transmits to the mortgagor, trustor, or vendee a monthly statement or passbook showing moneys received for interest and principal repayment and received and held in and disbursed from an impound or trust account, if any, the mortgagee, beneficiary, or vendor shall be deemed to have complied with this section.

No increase in the monthly rate of payment of a mortgagor, trustor, or vendee on a real property sale contract for impound or trust accounts shall be effective until after the mortgagee, beneficiary, or vendor has furnished the mortgagor, trustor, or vendee with an itemized accounting of the moneys presently held by it in the accounts, and a statement of the new monthly rate of payment, and an explanation of the factors necessitating the increase.

The provisions of this section shall be in addition to the obligations of the parties as stated by Section 2943.

Every person who willfully or repeatedly violates this subdivision shall be subject to punishment by a fine of not less than fifty dollars ($50) nor more than two hundred dollars ($200).

(c) As used in this section, "single-family, owner-occupied dwelling" means a dwelling that will be owned and occupied by a signatory to the mortgage or deed of trust secured by that dwelling within 90 days of the execution of the mortgage or deed of trust. (Added by Stats.1961, c. 1452, p. 3298, § 1. Amended by Stats.1963, c. 1543, p. 3125, § 1; Stats.1971, c. 117, p. 151, § 1; Stats.1973, c. 975, § 1; Stats.1974, c. 389, § 1; Stats.1982, c. 1196, p. 4265, § 1; Stats.1983, c. 1092, § 68, eff. Sept. 27, 1983, operative Jan. 1. 1984; Stats.2009, c. 57 (S.B.633), § 1; Stats.2010, c. 328 (S.B.1330), § 30.)

Cross References

County deferred property tax program for senior citizens and disabled citizens, effect of deferral on obligation with respect to impound account, trust, or other accounts maintained for property-related payments, see Revenue and Taxation Code § 20823.

Effect of postponement of property taxes, see Revenue and Taxation Code § 20605.

§ 2954.1. Impound, trust, or other accounts maintained for property-related payments; restrictions

No lender or person who purchases obligations secured by real property, or any agent of such lender or person, who maintains an impound, trust, or other type of account for the payment of taxes and assessments on real property, insurance premiums, or other purposes relating to such property shall do any of the following:

(a) Require the borrower or vendee to deposit in such account in any month an amount in excess of that which would be permitted in connection with a federally related mortgage loan pursuant to Section 10 of the Real Estate Settlement Procedures Act of 1974 (12 U.S.C. 2609), as amended.

(b) Require the sums maintained in such account to exceed at any time the amount or amounts reasonably necessary to pay such obligations as they become due. Any sum held in excess of the reasonable amount shall be refunded within 30 days unless the parties mutually agree to the contrary. Such an agreement may be rescinded at any time by any party.

(c) Make payments from the account in a manner so as to cause any policy of insurance to be canceled or so as to cause property taxes or other similar payments to become delinquent.

Nothing contained herein shall prohibit requiring additional amounts to be paid into an impound account in order to recover any deficiency which may exist in the account.

Any person harmed by a violation of this section shall be entitled to sue to recover his or her damages or for injunctive relief; but such violation shall not otherwise affect the validity of the loan or sale.

This section applies to all such accounts maintained after the effective date of this act. (Added by Stats.1979, c. 257, p. 574, § 1, eff. July 11, 1979. Amended by Stats.1983, c. 74, § 1.)

§ 2954.2. One- to four-family residences; written statement by mortgagee; moneys received and disbursed; additional accountings; charges; operative effect

(a) Every mortgagee of record of real property containing only a one- to four-family residence, when the mortgage is given to secure payment of the balance of the purchase price of the property or to refinance such a mortgage, shall furnish to the mortgagor within 60 days after the end of each calendar year a written statement showing the amount of moneys received for interest and principal repayment, late charges, moneys received and held in or disbursed from an impound account, if any, for the payment of taxes on the property, insurance premiums, bond assessments, or other purposes relating to the property, and interest credited to the account, if any. The written statement required to be furnished by this section shall be deemed furnished if the mortgagee of record transmits to the mortgagor of record cumulative statements or receipts which, for each calendar year, provide in one of the statements or receipts the information required by this section. The mortgagor, trustor or vendee shall be entitled to receive one such statement for each calendar year without charge and without request. Such statement shall include a notification in 10-point type that additional accountings can be requested by the mortgagor, trustor, or vendee, pursuant to Section 2954.

(b) For the purposes of this section:

(1) "Mortgagee" includes a beneficiary under a deed of trust, a vendor under a real property sale contract, and an organization which services a mortgage or deed of trust by receiving and disbursing payments for the mortgagee or beneficiary.

(2) "Mortgage" includes a first or second mortgage, a first or second deed of trust, and a real property sale contract.

(3) "Impound account" includes a trust or other type of account established for the purposes described in subdivision (a).

(c) The requirements of this section shall be in addition to the requirements of Section 2954.

(d) This section shall become operative on December 31, 1978, and apply to moneys received by a mortgagee on and after January 1, 1978. *(Added by Stats.1976, c. 774, p. 1815, § 1, operative Dec. 31, 1978.)*

§ 2954.4. Single-family, owner occupied dwellings late payment charge; maximum; tender; inapplicable loans

(a) A charge that may be imposed for late payment of an installment due on a loan secured by a mortgage or a deed of trust on real property containing only a single-family, owner-occupied dwelling, shall not exceed either (1) the equivalent of 6 percent of the installment due that is applicable to payment of principal and interest on the loan, or (2) five dollars ($5), whichever is greater. A charge may not be imposed more than once for the late payment of the same installment. However, the imposition of a late charge on any late payment does not eliminate or supersede late charges imposed on prior late payments. A payment is not a "late payment" for the purposes of this section until at least 10 days following the due date of the installment.

(b) A late charge may not be imposed on any installment which is paid or tendered in full on or before its due date, or within 10 days thereafter, even though an earlier installment or installments, or any late charge thereon, may not have been paid in full when due. For the purposes of determining whether late charges may be imposed, any payment tendered by the borrower shall be applied by the lender to the most recent installment due.

(c) A late payment charge described in subdivision (a) is valid if it satisfies the requirements of this section and Section 2954.5.

(d) Nothing in this section shall be construed to alter in any way the duty of the borrower to pay any installment then due or to alter the rights of the lender to enforce the payment of the installments.

(e) This section is not applicable to loans made by a credit union subject to Division 5 (commencing with Section 14000) of the Financial Code, by an industrial loan company subject to Division 7 (commencing with Section 18000) of the Financial Code, or by a finance lender subject to Division 9 (commencing with Section 22000) of the Financial Code, and is not applicable to loans made or negotiated by a real estate broker subject to Article 7 (commencing with Section 10240) of Chapter 3 of Part 1 of Division 4 of the Business and Professions Code.

(f) As used in this section, "single-family, owner-occupied dwelling" means a dwelling that will be owned and occupied by a signatory to the mortgage or deed of trust secured by the dwelling within 90 days of the execution of the mortgage or deed of trust.

(g) This section applies to loans executed on and after January 1, 1976. *(Added by Stats.1975, c. 736, p. 1729, § 1. Amended by Stats.1984, c. 890, § 2; Stats.2001, c. 159 (S.B.662), § 35.)*

§ 2954.5. Delinquent payment charge; prerequisites to imposition

(a) Before the first default, delinquency, or late payment charge may be assessed by any lender on a delinquent payment of a loan, other than a loan made pursuant to Division 9 (commencing with Section 22000) of the Financial Code, secured by real property, and before the borrower becomes obligated to pay this charge, the borrower shall either (1) be notified in writing and given at least 10 days from mailing of the notice in which to cure the delinquency, or (2) be informed, by a billing or notice sent for each payment due on the loan, of the date after which this charge will be assessed.

The notice provided in either paragraph (1) or (2) shall contain the amount of the charge or the method by which it is calculated.

(b) If a subsequent payment becomes delinquent the borrower shall be notified in writing, before the late charge is to be imposed, that the charge will be imposed if payment is not received, or the borrower shall be notified at least semiannually of the total amount of late charges imposed during the period covered by the notice.

(c) Notice provided by this section shall be sent to the address specified by the borrower, or, if no address is specified, to the borrower's address as shown in the lender's records.

(d) In case of multiple borrowers obligated on the same loan, a notice mailed to one shall be deemed to comply with this section.

(e) The failure of the lender to comply with the requirements of this section does not excuse or defer the borrower's performance of any obligation incurred in the loan transaction, other than his or her obligation to pay a late payment charge, nor does it impair or defer the right of the lender to enforce any other obligation including the costs and expenses incurred in any enforcement authorized by law.

(f) The provisions of this section as added by Chapter 1430 of the Statutes of 1970 shall only affect loans made on and after January 1, 1971.

The amendments to this section made at the 1975–76 Regular Session of the Legislature shall only apply to loans executed on and after January 1, 1976. *(Added by Stats.1970, c. 1430, p. 2773, § 1. Amended by Stats.1971, c. 813, p. 1571, § 1, eff. Sept. 29, 1971; Stats.1975, c. 736, p. 1730, § 2; Stats.1984, c. 890, § 3; Stats.2001, c. 159 (S.B.662), § 36.)*

§ 2954.6. Private mortgage insurance or mortgage guaranty insurance; cancellation rights; notification

(a) If private mortgage insurance or mortgage guaranty insurance, as defined in subdivision (a) of Section 12640.02 of the Insurance Code, is required as a condition of a loan secured by a deed of trust or mortgage on real property, the lender or person making or arranging the loan shall notify the borrower whether or not the borrower has the right to cancel the insurance. If the borrower has the right to cancel, then the lender or person making or arranging the loan shall notify the borrower in writing of the following:

§ 2954.6

(1) Any identifying loan or insurance information necessary to permit the borrower to communicate with the insurer or the lender concerning the insurance.

(2) The conditions that are required to be satisfied before the private mortgage insurance or mortgage guaranty insurance may be subject to cancellation, which shall include, but is not limited to, both of the following:

(A) If the condition is a minimum ratio between the remaining principal balance of the loan and the original or current value of the property, that ratio shall be stated.

(B) Information concerning whether or not an appraisal may be necessary.

(3) The procedure the borrower is required to follow to cancel the private mortgage insurance or mortgage guaranty insurance.

(b) The notice required in subdivision (a) shall be given to the borrower no later than 30 days after the close of escrow. The notice shall be set forth in at least 10–point bold type.

(c) With respect to any loan specified in subdivision (a) for which private mortgage insurance or mortgage guaranty insurance is still maintained, the lender or person making, arranging, or servicing the loan shall provide the borrower with a notice containing the same information as specified in subdivision (a) or a clear and conspicuous written statement indicating that (1) the borrower may be able to cancel the private mortgage insurance or mortgage guaranty insurance based upon various factors, including appreciation of the value of the property derived from a current appraisal performed by an appraiser selected by the lender or servicer, and paid for by the borrower, and (2) the borrower may contact the lender or person making, arranging, or servicing the loan at a designated address and telephone number to determine whether the borrower has a right of cancellation and, if so, the conditions and procedure to effect cancellation. The notice or statement required by this subdivision shall be provided in or with each written statement required by Section 2954.2.

(d) The notice required under this section shall be provided without cost to the borrower.

(e) Any person harmed by a violation of this section may obtain injunctive relief and may recover treble damages and reasonable attorney's fees and costs.

(f) This section shall not apply to any mortgage funded with bond proceeds issued under an indenture requiring mortgage insurance for the life of the loan nor to any insurance issued pursuant to Part 4 (commencing with Section 51600) of Division 31 of the Health and Safety Code, or loans insured by the Federal Housing Administration or Veterans Administration. (Added by Stats.1988, c. 569, § 1. Amended by Stats.1990, c. 1099 (A.B.3746), § 1; Stats.2001, c. 137 (S.B.270), § 1, operative July 1, 2002.)

§ 2954.65. Refund of unused premiums

Within 30 days after notice of cancellation from the insured, a private mortgage insurer or mortgage guaranty insurer shall, if the policy is cancellable, refund the remaining portion of the unused premium to the person or persons designated by the insured. (Added by Stats.1990, c. 1099 (A.B.3746), § 2.)

§ 2954.7. Termination of mortgage insurance payments; conditions; exclusion of specified instruments

Except when a statute, regulation, rule, or written guideline promulgated by an institutional third party applicable to notes or evidence of indebtedness secured by a deed of trust or mortgage purchased in whole or in part by an institutional third party specifically prohibits cancellation during the term of the indebtedness, if a borrower so requests and the conditions established by paragraphs (1) to (5), inclusive, of subdivision (a) are met, a borrower may terminate future payments for private mortgage insurance, or mortgage guaranty insurance as defined in subdivision (a) of Section 12640.02 of the Insurance Code, issued as a condition to the extension of credit in the form of a loan evidenced by a note or other evidence of indebtedness that is secured by a deed of trust or mortgage on the subject real property.

(a) The following conditions shall be satisfied in order for a borrower to be entitled to terminate payments for private mortgage insurance or mortgage guaranty insurance:

(1) The request to terminate future payments for private mortgage insurance or mortgage guaranty insurance shall be in writing.

(2) The origination date of the note or evidence of indebtedness shall be at least two years prior to the date of the request.

(3) The note or evidence of indebtedness shall be for personal, family, household, or purchase money purposes, secured by a deed of trust or mortgage on owner-occupied, one- to four-unit, residential real property.

(4) The unpaid principal balance owed on the secured obligation that is the subject of the private mortgage insurance or mortgage guaranty insurance shall not be more than 75 percent, unless the borrower and lender or servicer of the loan agree in writing upon a higher loan-to-value ratio, of either of the following:

(A) The sale price of the property at the origination date of the note or evidence of indebtedness, provided that the current fair market value of the property is equal to or greater than the original appraised value used at the origination date.

(B) The current fair market value of the property as determined by an appraisal, the cost of which shall be paid for by the borrower. The appraisal shall be ordered and the appraiser shall be selected by the lender or servicer of the loan.

(5) The borrower's monthly installments of principal, interest, and escrow obligations on the encumbrance or encumbrances secured by the real property shall be current at the time the request is made and those installments shall not have been more than 30 days past due over the 24–month period immediately preceding the request, provided further, that no notice of default has been recorded against the security real property pursuant to Section 2924, as a result of a nonmonetary default by the borrower (trustor) during the 24–month period immediately preceding the request.

(b) This section does not apply to any of the following:

(1) A note or evidence of indebtedness secured by a deed of trust or mortgage, or mortgage insurance, executed under

the authority of Part 3 (commencing with Section 50900) or Part 4 (commencing with Section 51600) of Division 31 of the Health and Safety Code.

(2) Any note or evidence of indebtedness secured by a deed of trust or mortgage that is funded in whole or in part pursuant to authority granted by statute, regulation, or rule that, as a condition of that funding, prohibits or limits termination of payments for private mortgage insurance or mortgage guaranty insurance during the term of the indebtedness.

(3) Notes or evidence of indebtedness that require private mortgage insurance and were executed prior to January 1, 1991.

(c) If the note secured by the deed of trust or mortgage will be or has been sold in whole or in part to an institutional third party, adherence to the institutional third party's standards for termination of future payments for private mortgage insurance or mortgage guaranty insurance shall be deemed in compliance with the requirements of this section.

(d) For the purposes of this section, "institutional third party" means the Federal National Mortgage Association, the Federal Home Loan Mortgage Corporation, the Government National Mortgage Association, and other substantially similar institutions, whether public or private, provided the institutions establish and adhere to rules applicable to the right of cancellation of private mortgage insurance or mortgage guaranty insurance, which are the same or substantially the same as those utilized by the above-named institutions. *(Added by Stats.1990, c. 1098 (A.B.3610), § 1. Amended by Stats.1994, c. 356 (A.B.2481), § 1; Stats.2006, c. 538 (S.B. 1852), § 56.)*

§ 2954.8. Impound accounts; payment of interest; restrictions; exceptions; application

(a) Every financial institution that makes loans upon the security of real property containing only a one- to four-family residence and located in this state or purchases obligations secured by such property and that receives money in advance for payment of taxes and assessments on the property, for insurance, or for other purposes relating to the property, shall pay interest on the amount so held to the borrower. The interest on such amounts shall be at the rate of at least 2 percent simple interest per annum. Such interest shall be credited to the borrower's account annually or upon termination of such account, whichever is earlier.

(b) No financial institution subject to the provisions of this section shall impose any fee or charge in connection with the maintenance or disbursement of money received in advance for the payment of taxes and assessments on real property securing loans made by such financial institution, or for the payment of insurance, or for other purposes relating to such real property, that will result in an interest rate of less than 2 percent per annum being paid on the moneys so received.

(c) For the purposes of this section, "financial institution" means a bank, savings and loan association or credit union chartered under the laws of this state or the United States, or any other person or organization making loans upon the security of real property containing only a one- to four-family residence.

(d) The provisions of this section do not apply to any of the following:

(1) Loans executed prior to the effective date of this section.

(2) Moneys which are required by a state or federal regulatory authority to be placed by a financial institution other than a bank in a non-interest-bearing demand trust fund account of a bank.

The amendment of this section made by the 1979–80 Regular Session of the Legislature shall only apply to loans executed on or after January 1, 1980. *(Added by Stats.1976, c. 25, p. 40, § 1. Amended by Stats.1979, c. 803, p. 2765, § 1.)*

Validity

For validity of this section, see McShannock v. JP Morgan Chase Bank NA, C.A.9 (Cal.)2020, 976 F.3d 881.

§ 2954.9. Loans for residential property of four units or less; right to prepayment

(a) (1) Except as otherwise provided by statute, where the original principal obligation is a loan for residential property of four units or less, the borrower under any note or evidence of indebtedness secured by a deed of trust or mortgage or any other lien on real property shall be entitled to prepay the whole or any part of the balance due, together with accrued interest, at any time.

(2) Nothing in this subdivision shall prevent a borrower from obligating himself, by an agreement in writing, to pay a prepayment charge.

(3) This subdivision does not apply during any calendar year to a bona fide loan secured by a deed of trust or mortgage given back during such calendar year to the seller by the purchaser on account of the purchase price if the seller does not take back four or more such deeds of trust or mortgages during such calendar year. Nothing in this subdivision shall be construed to prohibit a borrower from making a prepayment by an agreement in writing with the lender.

(b) Except as otherwise provided in Section 10242.6 of the Business and Professions Code, the principal and accrued interest on any loan secured by a mortgage or deed of trust on owner-occupied residential real property containing only four units or less may be prepaid in whole or in part at any time but only a prepayment made within five years of the date of execution of such mortgage or deed of trust may be subject to a prepayment charge and then solely as herein set forth. An amount not exceeding 20 percent of the original principal amount may be prepaid in any 12-month period without penalty. A prepayment charge may be imposed on any amount prepaid in any 12-month period in excess of 20 percent of the original principal amount of the loan which charge shall not exceed an amount equal to the payment of six months' advance interest on the amount prepaid in excess of 20 percent of the original principal amount.

(c) Notwithstanding subdivisions (a) and (b), there shall be no prepayment penalty charged to a borrower under a loan subject to this section if the residential structure securing the loan has been damaged to such an extent by a natural disaster for which a state of emergency is declared by the Governor, pursuant to Chapter 7 (commencing with Section 8550) of Division 1 of Title 2 of the Government Code, that the residential structure cannot be occupied and the prepayment is causally related thereto. *(Added by Stats.1974, c. 1059, p. 2280, § 1. Amended by Stats.1975, c. 763, p. 1775, § 2; Stats.1977, c. 579, p. 1825, § 32; Stats.1979, c. 391, p. 1458, § 1; Stats.1990, c. 663 (A.B.3660), § 2.)*

§ 2954.10. Acceleration of maturity date; penalty for prepayment

An obligee which accelerates the maturity date of the principal and accrued interest, pursuant to contract, on any loan secured by a mortgage or deed of trust on real property or an estate for years therein, upon the conveyance of any right, title, or interest in that property, may not claim, exact, or collect any charge, fee, or penalty for any prepayment resulting from that acceleration.

The provisions of this section shall not apply to a loan other than a loan secured by residential real property or any interest therein containing four units or less, in which the obligor has expressly waived, in writing, the right to repay in whole or part without penalty, or has expressly agreed, in writing, to the payment of a penalty for prepayment upon acceleration. For any loan executed on or after January 1, 1984, this waiver or agreement shall be separately signed or initialed by the obligor and its enforcement shall be supported by evidence of a course of conduct by the obligee of individual weight to the consideration in that transaction for the waiver or agreement. *(Added by Stats.1983, c. 1115, § 1, eff. Sept. 28, 1983. Amended by Stats.1989, c. 698, § 11.)*

§ 2954.11. Installment loans; definitions; right to prepay and prepayment charges; disclosure; application of section

(a) As used in this section:

(1) "Open-end credit plan" has the meaning set forth in Regulation Z of the Federal Reserve System (12 C.F.R. 226.2(a)(20)).

(2) "Installment loan" means any loan specified in subdivision (h) extended under an installment loan feature.

(3) "Installment loan feature" means a feature of an open-end credit plan which provides for a separate subaccount of the open-end credit plan pursuant to which the principal of, and interest on, the loan associated with that subaccount are to be repaid in substantially equal installments over a specified period without regard to the amount outstanding under any other feature of the open-end credit plan or the payment schedule with respect to the other feature.

(b)(1) Except as otherwise provided by statute, the borrower under any installment loan shall be entitled to prepay the whole or any part of the installment loan, together with any accrued interest, at any time.

(2) With respect to any installment loan, nothing in this section shall preclude a borrower from becoming obligated, by an agreement in writing, to pay a prepayment charge; but only a prepayment made within five years of the date the installment loan is made may be subject to a prepayment charge and then solely as herein set forth. An amount not exceeding 20 percent of the original principal amount of the installment loan may be prepaid in any one 12-month period without incurring a prepayment charge. A prepayment charge may be imposed on any amount prepaid in any 12-month period in excess of 20 percent of the original principal amount of the installment loan, which charge shall not exceed an amount equal to the payment of six months' advance interest on the amount prepaid in excess of 20 percent of the original principal amount of the installment loan.

(c) For purposes of subdivision (b):

(1) If the deed of trust or mortgage secures repayment of more than one installment loan, each of the installment loans shall be deemed to have been separately made on the date that the proceeds of the installment loan are advanced.

(2) If the outstanding balance of a loan advanced pursuant to an open-end credit plan thereafter becomes subject to an installment loan feature of the credit plan, the loan shall be deemed to have been made when the loan becomes subject to the installment loan feature, whether the feature was available at the borrower's option under original terms of the open-end credit plan or the feature thereafter became available upon modification of the original terms of the open-end credit plan.

(d) Notwithstanding subdivision (b), no prepayment charge may be imposed with respect to an installment loan subject to this section if any of the following apply:

(1) The residential structure securing the installment loan has been damaged to such an extent by a natural disaster for which a state of emergency is declared by the Governor, pursuant to Chapter 7 (commencing with Section 8550) of Division 1 of Title 2 of the Government Code, that the residential structure cannot be occupied and the prepayment is causally related thereto.

(2) The prepayment is made in conjunction with a bona fide sale of the real property securing the installment loan.

(3) The lender does not comply with subdivision (e).

(4) The term of the installment loan is for not more than five years and the original principal amount of the installment loan is less than five thousand dollars ($5,000).

(e)(1) The lender receiving a borrower's obligation to pay a prepayment charge authorized by subdivision (b) shall furnish the borrower with a written disclosure describing the existence of the prepayment charge obligation, the conditions under which the prepayment charge shall be payable, and the method by which the amount of the prepayment charge shall be determined. If subdivision (f) provides the borrower with a right to rescind the installment loan and the related obligation to pay a prepayment charge, the disclosure required by this subdivision shall also inform the borrower of this right to rescind, how and when to exercise the right, and where to mail or deliver a notice of rescission.

(2) The amount of, or the method for determining the amount of, the prepayment charge for an installment loan shall be set forth in the agreement governing the open-end credit plan.

(f)(1) The disclosure required by paragraph (1) of subdivision (e) shall be furnished when or up to 30 days before the borrower signs the agreement or other documents required by the lender for the installment loan, or no earlier than 30 days before nor later than 10 days following the making of the installment loan, if made without the borrower having to sign an agreement or other documentation, such as may be the case if the installment loan may be made on the basis of telephone or other discussions between the lender and the borrower not taking place in person. If the installment loan is made before the borrower has been furnished with the disclosure required by paragraph (1) of subdivision (e), the borrower shall have the right to rescind the installment loan and the related obligation to pay a prepayment charge by personally delivering or mailing notice to that effect to the lender, by first-class mail with postage prepaid, at the lender's location stated in its disclosure concerning the right to rescind within 10 days following the furnishing of the disclosure.

(2) If the disclosure required by paragraph (1) of subdivision (e) is included in the agreement or other document signed by the borrower for the installment loan, the disclosure shall be deemed given at that time. In other cases, the disclosure shall be deemed furnished when personally delivered to the borrower or three days after it is mailed to the borrower, first-class mail with postage prepaid, at the address to which billing statements for the open-end credit plan are being sent.

(3) The disclosure required by paragraph (1) of subdivision (e) may be separately furnished or may be included in the agreement or other document for the installment loan, provided that a copy of the disclosure that the borrower may retain is furnished to the borrower.

(4) If there is more than one borrower with respect to the open-end credit plan, a disclosure to any one of them pursuant to subdivision (e) shall satisfy the requirements of that subdivision with respect to all of them.

(g) If after an installment loan is made the lender receives the borrower's timely notice of the rescission of the installment loan in accordance with subdivision (f), the balance of the installment loan shall be transferred to the open-end subaccount of the open-end credit plan and the borrower shall be obligated to repay the amount under the same terms and conditions, and subject to the same fees and other charges, as would be applicable had the loan initially been extended pursuant to the open-end credit plan or had the installment loan never been made.

(h) This section applies to any installment loan secured by a deed of trust or mortgage or any other lien on residential property of four units or less and Section 2954.9 does not apply to such installment loans. This section shall not apply to any loan that is subject to Section 10242.6 of the Business and Professions Code. (Added by Stats.1996, c. 32 (S.B. 1106), § 1.)

§ 2954.12. Private mortgage insurance or mortgage guaranty insurance; collection of future payments

(a) Notwithstanding Section 2954.7, and except when a statute, regulation, rule, or written guideline promulgated by an institutional third party applicable to notes or evidence of indebtedness secured by a deed of trust or mortgage purchased in whole or in part by an institutional third party specifically prohibits cancellation during the term of the indebtedness, the lender or servicer of a loan evidenced by a note or other evidence of indebtedness that is secured by a deed of trust or mortgage on the subject property may not charge or collect future payments from a borrower for private mortgage insurance or mortgage guaranty insurance as defined in subdivision (a) of Section 12640.02 of the Insurance Code, if all of the following conditions are satisfied:

(1) The loan is for personal, family, household, or purchase money purposes, the subject property is owner-occupied, one-to-four unit residential real property, and the outstanding principal balance of the note or evidence of indebtedness secured by the senior deed of trust or mortgage on the subject property is equal to or less than 75 percent of the lesser of (A) if the loan was made for purchase of the property, the sales price of the property under such purchase; or (B) the appraised value of the property, as determined by the appraisal conducted in connection with the making of the loan.

(2) The borrower's scheduled payment of monthly installments of principal, interest, and escrow obligations is current at the time the right to cancellation of mortgage insurance accrues.

(3) During the 12 months prior to the date upon which the right to cancellation accrues, the borrower has not been assessed more than one late penalty for any scheduled payment and has not made any scheduled payment more than 30 days late.

(4) The loan evidenced by a note or evidence of indebtedness was made or executed on or after January 1, 1998.

(5) No notice of default has been recorded against the real property pursuant to Section 2924, as a result of a nonmonetary default on the extension of credit by the borrower during the last 12 months prior to the accrual of the borrower's right to cancellation.

(b) This section does not apply to any of the following:

(1) A note or evidence of indebtedness secured by a deed of trust or mortgage, or mortgage insurance, executed under the authority of Part 3 (commencing with Section 50900) or Part 4 (commencing with Section 51600) of Division 31 of the Health and Safety Code.

(2) Any note or evidence of indebtedness secured by a deed of trust or mortgage that is funded in whole or in part pursuant to authority granted by statute, regulation, or rule that, as a condition of that funding, prohibits or limits termination of payments for private mortgage insurance or mortgage guaranty insurance during the term of the indebtedness.

(c) If the note secured by the deed of trust or mortgage will be or has been sold in whole or in part to an institutional third party, adherence to the institutional third party's standards for termination of future payments for private mortgage insurance or mortgage guaranty insurance shall be deemed in compliance with the requirements of this section.

(d) For the purposes of this section, "institutional third party" means the Federal National Mortgage Association, the Federal Home Loan Mortgage Corporation, the Government National Mortgage Association and other substantially similar institutions, whether public or private, provided the institutions establish and adhere to rules applicable to the right of cancellation of private mortgage insurance or mortgage guaranty insurance, which are the same or substantially the same as those utilized by the above-named institutions. *(Added by Stats.1997, c. 62 (A.B.1160), § 1.)*

§ 2955. Impound account funds; investments; deposits; injunction for violations

(a) Money held by a mortgagee or a beneficiary of a deed of trust on real property in this state, or held by a vendor on a contract of sale of real property in this state, in an impound account for the payment of taxes and assessments or insurance premiums or other purposes on or relating to the property, shall be retained in this state and, if invested, shall be invested only with residents of this state in the case of individuals, or with partnerships, corporations, or other persons, or the branches or subsidiaries thereof, which are engaged in business within this state.

(b) Notwithstanding subdivision (a), a mortgagee or beneficiary of a deed of trust, secured by a first lien on real property, may deposit money held for the payment of taxes and assessments or insurance premiums or other purposes in an impound account in an out-of-state depository institution insured by the Federal Deposit Insurance Corporation if the mortgagee or beneficiary is any one of the following:

(1) The Federal National Mortgage Association, the Government National Mortgage Association, the Federal Home Loan Mortgage Corporation, the Federal Housing Administration, or the Veteran's Administration.

(2) A bank or subsidiary thereof, bank holding company or subsidiary thereof, trust company, savings bank or savings and loan association or subsidiary thereof, savings bank or savings association holding company or subsidiary thereof, credit union, industrial bank or industrial loan company, commercial finance lender, personal property broker, consumer finance lender, or insurer doing business under the authority of and in accordance with the laws of this state, any other state, or of the United States relating to banks, trust companies, savings banks or savings associations, credit unions, industrial banks or industrial loan companies, commercial finance lenders, personal property brokers, consumer finance lenders, or insurers, as evidenced by a license, certificate, or charter issued by the United States or a state, district, territory, or commonwealth of the United States.

(3) Trustees of a pension, profit-sharing, or welfare fund, if the pension, profit-sharing, or welfare fund has a net worth of not less than fifteen million dollars ($15,000,000).

(4) A corporation with outstanding securities registered under Section 12 of the Securities Exchange Act of 1934,[1] or a wholly owned subsidiary of that corporation.

(5) A syndication or other combination of any of the entities specified in paragraphs (1) to (4), inclusive, that is organized to purchase the promissory note.

(6) The California Housing Finance Agency or a local housing finance agency organized under the Health and Safety Code.

(7) A licensed real estate broker selling all or part of the loan, note, or contract to a lender or purchaser described in paragraphs (1) to (6), inclusive, of this subdivision.

(8) A licensed residential mortgage lender or servicer when acting under the authority of that license.

(c) A mortgagee or beneficiary of a deed of trust who deposits funds held in trust in an out-of-state depository institution in accordance with subdivision (b) shall make available, in this state, the books, records, and files pertaining to those trust accounts to the appropriate state regulatory department or agency, or pay the reasonable expenses for travel and lodging incurred by the regulatory department or agency in order to conduct an examination at an out-of-state location.

(d) The Attorney General may bring an action on behalf of the people of California to enjoin a violation of subdivision (a) or subdivision (b). *(Added by Stats.1970, c. 1212, p. 2130, § 1. Amended by Stats.1992, c. 1055 (A.B.3342), § 3; Stats. 1995, c. 564 (S.B.946), § 5.)*

[1] 15 U.S.C.A. § 78l.

§ 2955.1. Condominium loans; underwriting requirements for earthquake insurance or fees; disclosures

(a) Any lender originating a loan secured by the borrower's separate interest in a condominium project, as defined in Section 4125 or 6542, which requires earthquake insurance or imposes a fee or any other condition in lieu thereof pursuant to an underwriting requirement imposed by an institutional third-party purchaser shall disclose all of the following to the potential borrower:

(1) That the lender or the institutional third party in question requires earthquake insurance or imposes a fee or any other condition in lieu thereof pursuant to an underwriting requirement imposed by an institutional third-party purchaser.

(2) That not all lenders or institutional third parties require earthquake insurance or impose a fee or any other condition in lieu thereof pursuant to an underwriting requirement imposed by an institutional third-party purchaser.

(3) Earthquake insurance may be required on the entire condominium project.

(4) That lenders or institutional third parties may also require that a condominium project maintain, or demonstrate an ability to maintain, financial reserves in the amount of the earthquake insurance deductible.

(b) For the purposes of this section, "institutional third party" means the Federal Home Loan Mortgage Corporation, the Federal National Mortgage Association, the Government National Mortgage Association, and other substantially similar institutions, whether public or private.

(c) The disclosure required by this section shall be made in writing by the lender as soon as reasonably practicable. *(Added by Stats.1995, c. 925 (S.B.1326), § 1, eff. Oct. 16, 1995. Amended by Stats.2012, c. 181 (A.B.806), § 41, operative Jan. 1, 2014; Stats.2013, c. 605 (S.B.752), § 18.)*

§ 2955.5. Hazard insurance; lender requiring amount exceeding replacement value; disclosure; relief

(a) No lender shall require a borrower, as a condition of receiving or maintaining a loan secured by real property, to provide hazard insurance coverage against risks to the improvements on that real property in an amount exceeding the replacement value of the improvements on the property.

(b) A lender shall disclose to a borrower, in writing, the contents of subdivision (a), as soon as practicable, but before execution of any note or security documents.

(c) Any person harmed by a violation of this section shall be entitled to obtain injunctive relief and may recover damages and reasonable attorney's fees and costs.

(d) A violation of this section does not affect the validity of the loan, note secured by a deed of trust, mortgage, or deed of trust.

(e) For purposes of this section:

(1) "Hazard insurance coverage" means insurance against losses caused by perils which are commonly covered in policies described as a "Homeowner's Policy," "General Property Form," "Guaranteed Replacement Cost Insurance," "Special Building Form," "Standard Fire," "Standard Fire with Extended Coverage," "Standard Fire with Special Form Endorsement," or comparable insurance coverage to protect the real property against loss or damage from fire and other perils covered within the scope of a standard extended coverage endorsement.

(2) "Improvements" means buildings or structures attached to the real property. *(Added by Stats.1987, c. 715, § 1. Amended by Stats.1988, c. 276, § 1, eff. July 6, 1988; Stats. 1999, c. 412 (A.B.1454), § 1, operative July 1, 2000.)*

ARTICLE 3. DISCLOSURES ON PURCHASE MONEY LIENS ON RESIDENTIAL PROPERTY

Section
2956. Form and contents of disclosure; multiple arrangers.
2957. Definitions.
2958. Transactions exempt from disclosure requirements.
2958a. Repealed.
2959. Timeliness and effect of disclosures; disclosure statement; receipt; signature; copies.
2959a. Repealed.
2960. Information disclosed, subsequently rendered inaccurate; approximations.
2961. Good faith; definition; requirement.
2962. Amendment of disclosure.
2963. Disclosures required.
2964. Disclosure obligations arising outside this article.
2965. Noncompliance with this article; effect on credit or security documents; damages; bona fide errors.
2966. Balloon payment note containing term exceeding one year.
2967. Limitation of actions.
2968. Repealed.
2969. Repealed.

§ 2956. Form and contents of disclosure; multiple arrangers

In a transaction for the purchase of a dwelling for not more than four families in which there is an arranger of credit, which purchase includes an extension of credit by the vendor, a written disclosure with respect to that credit transaction shall be made, as required by this article:

(a) To the purchaser, by the arranger of credit and the vendor (with respect to information within the knowledge of the vendor).

(b) To the vendor, by the arranger of credit and the purchaser (with respect to information within the knowledge of the purchaser).

If there is more than one arranger of credit and one of those arrangers has obtained the offer by the purchaser to purchase the property, that arranger shall make the disclosure, unless the parties designate another person in writing. *(Added by Stats.1982, c. 968, p. 3475, § 1, operative July 1, 1983.)*

§ 2957. Definitions

The following definitions shall apply for the purposes of this article:

(a) "Arranger of credit" means:

(1) A person, other than a party to the credit transaction (except as provided in paragraph (2)), who is involved in developing or negotiating credit terms, participates in the completion of the credit documents, and directly or indirectly receives compensation for arrangement of the credit or from any transaction or transfer of the real property which is facilitated by that extension of credit. As used in this paragraph, "arranger of credit" does not apply to an attorney who is representing one of the parties to the credit transaction.

(2) A party to the transaction who is either a real estate licensee, licensed under provisions of Part 1 (commencing with Section 10000) of Division 4 of the Business and Professions Code, or is an attorney licensed under Chapter 4 (commencing with Section 6000) of Division 3 of the Business and Professions Code if neither party to the transaction is represented by an agent who is a real estate licensee. In any transaction in which disclosure is required solely by the provisions of this paragraph, the obligations of this article shall apply only to a real estate licensee or attorney who is a party to the transaction, and not to any other party.

(3) An arranger of credit does not include a person acting in the capacity as an escrow in the transaction.

(4) Persons described in paragraph (2) who are acting in the capacity as an escrowholder in the transaction shall nevertheless be deemed arrangers of credit where such persons act on behalf of a party to the transaction or an agent of such party in the development or negotiation of credit terms. Neither the completion of credit documents in accordance with instructions of a party or his or her agent nor the furnishing of information regarding credit terms to a party or his or her agent shall be considered to be the development or negotiation of credit terms.

(b) "Balloon payment note" means a note which provides for a final payment as originally scheduled which is more than twice the amount of any of the immediately preceding six regularly scheduled payments or which contains a call provision; provided, however, that if the call provision is not exercised by the holder of the note, the existence of the unexercised call provision shall not cause the note to be deemed to be a balloon payment note.

(c) "Call provision" means a note contract term that provides the holder of the note with the right to call the note due and payable either after a specified period has elapsed following closing or after a specified date.

(d) "Credit" means the right granted by a vendor to a purchaser to purchase property and to defer payment therefore.

The credit involved must be subject to a finance charge or payable by written agreement in more than four installments, whether providing for payment of principal and interest, or interest only, not including a downpayment.

(e) "Credit documents" are those documents which contain the binding credit terms, and include a note or a contract of sale if the contract spells out terms upon which a vendor agrees to provide financing for a purchaser.

(f) "Purchase" includes acquisition of equitable title by a real property sales contract as defined in Section 2985, or lease with an option to purchase, where the facts demonstrate intent to transfer equitable title.

(g) "Security documents" include a mortgage, deed of trust, real property sales contract as defined in Section 2985, or lease with an option to purchase, where the facts demonstrate an intent to transfer equitable title.

(h) "All inclusive trust deed" is an instrument which secures indebtedness owed by the trustor to the beneficiary, which indebtedness includes a debt or debts owed by that beneficiary to the beneficiary of another security document secured by the same property which is senior in priority. *(Added by Stats.1982, c. 968, p. 3475, § 1, operative July 1, 1983. Amended by Stats.1983, c. 1217, § 3; Stats.1986, c. 1360, § 2.)*

§ 2958. Transactions exempt from disclosure requirements

A disclosure is not required under this article, to a purchaser when that purchaser is entitled to receive, a disclosure pursuant to the Federal Truth-In-Lending Act (15 U.S. Code 1604, as amended), the Real Estate Settlement Procedures Act (12 U.S. Code 2601, as amended), or Section 10240 of the Business and Professions Code; or to a vendor if the vendor is entitled to receive, a disclosure pursuant to Sections 10232.4 and 10232.5 of the Business and Professions Code, or disclosure pursuant to a qualification under Section 25110 of the Corporations Code or disclosure pursuant to regulations of the Department of Corporations granting an exemption from Section 25110 of the Corporations Code. *(Added by Stats.1982, c. 968, p. 3476, § 1, operative July 1, 1983.)*

§ 2958a. Repealed by Stats.1963, c. 819, § 2, eff. Jan. 1, 1965

§ 2959. Timeliness and effect of disclosures; disclosure statement; receipt; signature; copies

The disclosures required by this article shall be made as soon as practicable, but before execution of any note or security documents. If any disclosure is made after the execution of credit documents by the purchaser, such documents shall be contingent on the purchaser's approval of the disclosures prior to execution of the security documents. The disclosure statement shall be receipted for by the purchaser and the vendor. The disclosure shall be signed by the arranger of credit and a copy shall be delivered respectively to the purchaser and the vendor and the arranger shall retain a true copy of the executed statements for three years.

The provisions of this section do not apply to the disclosures required by Section 2966. *(Added by Stats.1982, c. 968, p. 3476, § 1, operative July 1, 1983.)*

§ 2959a. Repealed by Stats.1963, c. 819, § 2, eff. Jan. 1, 1965

§ 2960. Information disclosed, subsequently rendered inaccurate; approximations

If information disclosed in accordance with this article is subsequently rendered inaccurate as a result of any act, occurrence, or agreement between the parties to the transaction subsequent to the delivery of the required disclosures, the inaccuracy resulting therefrom shall not constitute a violation of this article. If, at the time disclosure is to be made, an item of information required to be disclosed is unknown or not available to the vendor, purchaser, or arranger of credit, and the arranger of credit has made a reasonable effort to ascertain it, the disclosure may employ an approximation of the information, provided the approximation is clearly identified as such, is reasonable, is based on the best information available to the arranger, and is not used for the purpose of circumventing or evading the provisions of this article. *(Added by Stats.1982, c. 968, p. 3477, § 1, operative July 1, 1983.)*

§ 2961. Good faith; definition; requirement

Every disclosure required by this article and every act which is to be performed in making that disclosure shall be made in good faith. For the purposes of this article, "good faith" means honesty in fact in the conduct of the transaction. *(Added by Stats.1982, c. 968, p. 3477, § 1, operative July 1, 1983.)*

§ 2962. Amendment of disclosure

Any disclosure made pursuant to this article may be amended in writing by the person making the disclosure, provided that any amendment shall be subject to the provisions of Section 2959. *(Added by Stats.1982, c. 968, p. 3477, § 1, operative July 1, 1983.)*

§ 2963. Disclosures required

The disclosures required to both purchaser and vendor by this article are:

(a) An identification of the note or other credit documents or security documents and of the property which is the security for the transaction.

(b) A description of the terms of the promissory note or other credit documents or a copy of the note or other credit documents.

(c) Insofar as available, the principal terms and conditions of each recorded encumbrance which constitutes a lien upon the property which is or will be senior to the financing being arranged, including the original balance, the current balance, the periodic payment, any balloon payment, the interest rate (and any provisions with respect to variations in the interest rate), the maturity date, and whether or not there is any current default in payment on that encumbrance.

(d) A warning that, if refinancing would be required as a result of lack of full amortization under the terms of any existing or proposed loans, such refinancing might be difficult or impossible in the conventional mortgage marketplace.

(e) If negative amortization is possible as a result of any variable or adjustable rate financing being arranged, a clear disclosure of this fact and an explanation of its potential effect.

(f) In the event that the financing involves an all inclusive trust deed, the disclosure shall indicate whether the credit or security documents specify who is liable for payment or responsible for defense in the case of an attempted acceleration by a lender or other obligee under a prior encumbrance, and whether or not the credit or security documents specify the responsibilities and rights of the parties in the event of a loan prepayment respecting a prior encumbrance which may result in a requirement for refinancing, a prepayment penalty, or a prepayment discount and, if such specification occurs, a recital of the provisions which apply.

(g) If the financing being arranged or any of the financing represented by a prior encumbrance could result in a balloon payment, or in a right in the lender or other obligee under such financing to require a prepayment of the principal balance at or after a stipulated date, or upon the occurrence of a stipulated event, a disclosure of the date and amount of any balloon payment or the amount which would be due upon the exercise of such right by the lender or obligee, and a statement that there is no assurance that new financing or loan extension will be available at the time of such occurrence.

(h) If the financing being arranged involves an all inclusive trust deed or real property sales contract, a disclosure of the party to whom payments will be made and who will be responsible for remitting these funds to payees under prior encumbrances and vendors under this transaction and a warning that, if that person is not a neutral third party, the parties may wish to agree to have a neutral third party designated for these purposes.

(i) A disclosure on the identity, occupation, employment, income, and credit data about the prospective purchaser, as represented to the arranger by the prospective purchaser; or, specifically, that no representation as to the credit-worthiness of the specific prospective purchaser is made by the arranger. A warning should also be expressed that Section 580b of the Code of Civil Procedure may limit any recovery by the vendor to the net proceeds of the sale of the security property in the event of foreclosure.

(j) A statement that loss payee clauses have been added to property insurance protecting the vendor, or that instructions have been or will be directed to the escrowholder, if any, in the transaction or the appropriate insurance carriers for addition of such loss payee clauses, or a statement that, if such provisions have not been made, that the vendor should consider protecting himself or herself by securing such clauses.

(k) A statement that a request for notice of default under Section 2924b has been recorded, or that, if it has not been recorded, the vendor should consider recording a request for notice of default.

(*l*) That a policy of title insurance has been obtained or will be obtained and be furnished to the vendor and purchaser, insuring the respective interests of the vendor and purchaser, or that the vendor and purchaser individually should consider obtaining a policy of title insurance.

(m) That a tax service has been arranged to report to the vendor whether property taxes have been paid on the property, and who will be responsible for the continued retention and compensation of tax service; or that the vendor should otherwise assure for himself or herself that the taxes on the property have been paid.

(n) A disclosure whether the security documents on the financing being arranged have been or will be recorded pursuant to Section 27280 of the Government Code, or a statement that the security of the vendor may be subject to intervening liens or judgments which may occur after the note is executed and before any resort to security occurs if the security documents are not recorded.

(*o*) If the purchaser is to receive any cash from the proceeds of the transaction, a statement of that fact, the amount, the source of the funds, and the purpose of the disbursement as represented by the purchaser.

(p) A statement that a request for notice of delinquency under Section 2924e has been made, or that, if it has not been made, the vendor should consider making a request for a notice of delinquency. (*Added by Stats.1982, c. 968, p. 3477, § 1, operative July 1, 1983. Amended by Stats.1983, c. 1217, § 4; Stats.1984, c. 1331, § 4, operative July 1, 1985; Stats. 1990, c. 788 (S.B.2042), § 2.*)

§ 2964. Disclosure obligations arising outside this article

The specification of items for disclosure in this article does not limit or abridge any obligation for disclosure created by any other provision of law or which may exist in order to avoid fraud, misrepresentation, or deceit in the transaction. (*Added by Stats.1982, c. 968, p. 3479, § 1, operative July 1, 1983.*)

§ 2965. Noncompliance with this article; effect on credit or security documents; damages; bona fide errors

The validity of any credit document or of any security document subject to the provisions of this article shall not be invalidated solely because of the failure of any person to comply with this article. However, any person who willfully violates any provision of this article shall be liable in the amount of actual damages suffered by the vendor or purchaser as the proximate result of the violation.

No person may be held liable in any action under this article if it is shown by a preponderance of the evidence that the violation was not intentional and resulted from a bona fide error notwithstanding the maintenance of procedures reasonably adopted to avoid any such error. (*Added by Stats.1982, c. 968, p. 3479, § 1, operative July 1, 1983.*)

§ 2966. Balloon payment note containing term exceeding one year

(a) In a transaction regulated by this article, which includes a balloon payment note when the term for repayment is for a period in excess of one year, the holder of the note shall, not less than 90 nor more than 150 days before the balloon payment is due, deliver or mail by first-class mail, with a certificate of mailing obtained from the United States

Postal Service, to the trustor, or his or her successor in interest, at the last known address of such person a written notice, to include:

(1) A statement of the name and address of the person to whom the balloon payment is required to be paid.

(2) The date on or before which the balloon payment was or is required to be paid.

(3) The amount of the balloon payment, or if its exact amount is unknown a good faith estimate of the amount thereof, including unpaid principal, interest, and any other charges (assuming payment in full of all scheduled installments coming due between the date of the notice and the date when the balloon payment is due).

(4) A description of the trustor's right, if any, to refinance the balloon payment, including a summary of the actual terms of the refinancing or an estimate or approximation thereof, to the extent known.

If the due date of the balloon payment of a note subject to this subdivision is extended prior to the time notice is otherwise required under this subdivision, this notice requirement shall apply only to the due date as extended (or as subsequently extended).

(b) Failure to provide notice as required by subdivision (a) does not extinguish any obligation of payment by the trustor, except that the due date for any balloon payment shall be the date specified in the note, or 90 days from the date the delivery or mailing of the notice, or the date specified in the notice, whichever date is later. If the operation of this section acts to extend the term of any such note, interest shall continue to accrue for the extended term at the contract rate and payments shall continue to be due at any periodic interval and on any scheduled payment schedule specified in the note and shall be credited to principal or interest under terms of the note. Default in any extended periodic payment shall be considered a default under terms of the note or security instrument.

(c) Any failure to comply with the provisions of this section shall not affect the validity of a sale in favor of a bona fide purchaser or the rights of an encumbrancer for value and without notice.

(d) Every note subject to the provisions of this section shall include the following statement:

"This note is subject to Section 2966 of the Civil Code, which provides that the holder of this note shall give written notice to the trustor, or his successor in interest, of prescribed information at least 90 and not more than 150 days before any balloon payment is due."

Failure to include this notice shall not invalidate the note.

(e) The provisions of this section shall apply to any note executed on or after July 1, 1983. (Added by Stats.1982, c. 968, p. 3479, § 1, operative July 1, 1983. Amended by Stats.1986, c. 1360, § 3.)

§ 2967. Limitation of actions

Any action arising under this article may be brought within two years from the date on which the liability arises, except that where any material disclosure under this article has been materially and willfully misrepresented, the action may be brought within two years of discovery of the misrepresentation. (Added by Stats.1982, c. 968, p. 3480, § 1, operative July 1, 1983.)

§ 2968. Repealed by Stats.1963, c. 819, § 2, eff. Jan. 1, 1965

§ 2969. Repealed by Stats.1947, c. 723, § 1

CHAPTER 2A. HOME EQUITY LOAN DISCLOSURE ACT

Section
2970. "Home equity loan" defined.
2971. Disclosure to customer by creditor at time of initial application.
2972, 2973. Repealed.
2974. Repealed.
2975 to 2978. Repealed.
2980. Repealed.
2980.5. Repealed.

§ 2970. "Home equity loan" defined

For purposes of this chapter "home equity loan" means any open end consumer credit plan in which a consensual security interest is created or retained against the consumer's dwelling. (Added by Stats.1988, c. 1315, § 1.)

§ 2971. Disclosure to customer by creditor at time of initial application

(a) At the time that a customer makes an initial application to a creditor for a home equity loan in person, or within three business days if the customer applies by mail or telephone, the creditor shall provide the applicant with a disclosure in either of the following forms:

(1) The statement: "This home equity loan that you are applying for will be secured by your home and your failure to repay the loan for any reason could cause you to lose your home!"

(2) A statement to the effect that a home equity loan is secured by a lien against the home of the consumer and in the event of any default the consumer risks the loss of the home.

(b) The disclosure required in subdivision (a) shall be made by either of the following means:

(1) A separate and specific document attached to or accompanying the application.

(2) A clear and conspicuous statement on the application.

(c) If a creditor is required by federal statute or regulation to make a substantially similar disclosure to that required by subdivision (a), and the creditor complies with that federal statute or regulation, the creditor shall be deemed to have complied with the requirements of this chapter. (Added by Stats.1988, c. 1315, § 1.)

§§ 2972, 2973. Repealed by Stats.1963, c. 819, § 2, eff. Jan. 1, 1965

§ 2974. Repealed by Stats.1959, c. 528, § 1

§§ 2975 to 2978. Repealed by Stats.1963, c. 819, § 2, eff. Jan. 1, 1965

§ 2980. Repealed by Stats.1963, c. 819, p. 2000, § 16, eff. Jan. 1, 1965

§ 2980.5. Repealed by Stats.1984, c. 859, § 1

CHAPTER 2B. AUTOMOBILE SALES FINANCE ACT

Section
2981. Definitions.
2981.5. Bailments or leases not considered conditional sale contracts.
2981.7. Finance charge; calculation on or after January 1, 1983.
2981.8. Finance charge; determination on precomputed basis and simple interest basis; exception.
2981.9. Requirements of conditional sale contracts.
2982. Formalities of conditional sale contracts.
2982.05. Repealed.
2982.1. Rebates, discounts, commissions, etc.
2982.2. Disclosures required for conditional sale contracts.
2982.3. Extension of due date; deferment of payment; charges.
2982.5. Exemptions from chapter; conditions; proceeds of loan.
2982.7. Refund of down payment; breach after leaving motor vehicle as down payment; recovery by buyer.
2982.8. Amounts advanced by holder to procure insurance; repayment options for buyer; security; notice to buyer.
2982.9. Inability of buyer to obtain financing through third party; rescission of contract.
2982.10. Consideration for assignment of conditional sale contract.
2982.11. Conditional sale contract including charge for electric vehicle charging station; written disclosure.
2982.12. Guaranteed asset protection waiver; termination.
2983. Enforceability of contract; violation of specified provisions by seller; correction; recovery by buyer; disclosure violations relating to payment of state fees.
2983.1. Enforceability of contract; violation of provisions relating to guaranteed asset protection waiver; violation of provisions relating to prepayment, refinancing, or refund of finance charge by seller or holder; recovery by buyer; election to enforce or rescind; disclosure violations relating to payment of state fees.
2983.2. Disposition after repossession or surrender; notice of intent; service prerequisite to liability for delinquency; contents; accounting of disposition to person liable on contract; surplus; disposition; application of section.
2983.3. Default; prerequisite to acceleration of maturity; repossession or surrender; right of reinstatement by person liable on contract; exceptions; methods; right to deficiency; abrogation; application of section.
2983.35. Cosigners; notice of delinquency; service; application of section.
2983.37. Buy-here-pay-here dealer; prohibited actions after sale of vehicle; violations.
2983.4. Prevailing party's right to attorney's fees and costs.
2983.5. Assignment of sellers rights; recourse.
2983.6. Violations; offense.
2983.7. Prohibition of certain provisions.
2983.8. Deficiency judgment on conditional sale contract for mobilehome or motor vehicle.

Section
2984. Correction of contract to comply with chapter.
2984.1. Contract provision regarding insurance coverage.
2984.2. Provision for title to or lien upon other property prohibited; exceptions.
2984.3. Buyer's acknowledgment of delivery of copy of contract; presumptions.
2984.4. Actions on contract or purchase order; venue.
2984.5. Conditional sales contracts; maintenance of documents by seller.
2984.6. Repossession of vehicle connected with incident of violence notice; notice to subsequent assignee.

Cross References

Automobile Dealers Anti-Coercion Act, see Business and Professions Code § 18400 et seq.
Automobile Leasing Act, see Civil Code § 2985.7 et seq.
Business practices of mobilehome licensees which are unlawful acts, see Health and Safety Code § 18060.5.
Buy-here-pay-here dealer defined, see Vehicle Code §§ 241, 241.1.
Consumer credit contracts, notice to multiple signatories, see Civil Code § 1799.90 et seq.
Military Families Financial Relief Act, see Military and Veterans Code § 800 et seq.
Retail installment sales, exclusion of motor vehicles, see Civil Code § 1802.1.
Spanish language translation of contracts or agreements, necessity, exceptions, see Civil Code § 1632.
Vehicle manufacturers, transporters and dealers, license suspension or revocation for violation of this chapter, see Vehicle Code § 11705.

§ 2981. Definitions

As used in this chapter, unless the context otherwise requires:

(a) "Conditional sale contract" means:

(1) A contract for the sale of a motor vehicle between a buyer and a seller, with or without accessories, under which possession is delivered to the buyer and either of the following:

(A) The title vests in the buyer thereafter only upon the payment of all or a part of the price, or the performance of any other condition.

(B) A lien on the property is to vest in the seller as security for the payment of part or all of the price, or for the performance of any other condition.

(2) A contract for the bailment of a motor vehicle between a buyer and a seller, with or without accessories, by which the bailee or lessee agrees to pay as compensation for use a sum substantially equivalent to or in excess of the aggregate value of the vehicle and its accessories, if any, at the time the contract is executed, and by which it is agreed that the bailee or lessee will become, or for no other or for a nominal consideration has the option of becoming, the owner of the vehicle upon full compliance with the terms of the contract.

(b) "Seller" means a person engaged in the business of selling or leasing motor vehicles under conditional sale contracts.

(c) "Buyer" means the person who buys or hires a motor vehicle under a conditional sale contract.

(d) "Person" includes an individual, company, firm, association, partnership, trust, corporation, limited liability company, or other legal entity.

(e) "Holder" means the person entitled to enforce the conditional sale contract against the buyer at the time.

(f) "Cash price" means the amount for which the seller would sell and transfer to the buyer unqualified title to the motor vehicle described in the conditional sale contract, if the property were sold for cash at the seller's place of business on the date the contract is executed, and shall include taxes to the extent imposed on the cash sale and the cash price of accessories or services related to the sale, including, but not limited to, delivery, installation, alterations, modifications, improvements, document preparation fees, a service contract, a vehicle contract cancellation option agreement, and payment of a prior credit or lease balance remaining on property being traded in.

(g) "Downpayment" means a payment that the buyer pays or agrees to pay to the seller in cash or property value or money's worth at or prior to delivery by the seller to the buyer of the motor vehicle described in the conditional sale contract. The term shall also include the amount of any portion of the downpayment the payment of which is deferred until not later than the due date of the second otherwise scheduled payment, if the amount of the deferred downpayment is not subject to a finance charge. The term does not include any administrative finance charge charged, received, or collected by the seller as provided in this chapter.

(h) "Amount financed" means the amount required to be disclosed pursuant to paragraph (8) of subdivision (a) of Section 2982.

(i) "Unpaid balance" means the difference between * * * subdivisions (f) and (g), plus all insurance premiums (except for credit life or disability insurance when the amount thereof is included in the finance charge), which are included in the contract balance, and the total amount paid or to be paid as follows:

(1) To a public officer in connection with the transaction.

(2) For license, certificate of title, and registration fees imposed by law, and the amount of the state fee for issuance of a certificate of compliance or certificate of waiver pursuant to Section 9889.56 of the Business and Professions Code.

(j) "Finance charge" has the meaning set forth for that term in Section 226.4 of Regulation Z. The term shall not include delinquency charges or collection costs and fees as provided by subdivision (k) of Section 2982, extension or deferral agreement charges as provided by Section 2982.3, or amounts for insurance, repairs to or preservation of the motor vehicle, or preservation of the security interest therein advanced by the holder under the terms of the contract.

(k) "Total of payments" means the amount required to be disclosed pursuant to subdivision (h) of Section 226.18 of Regulation Z. The term includes any portion of the downpayment that is deferred until not later than the second otherwise scheduled payment and that is not subject to a finance charge. The term shall not include amounts for which the buyer may later become obligated under the terms of the contract in connection with insurance, repairs to or preservation of the motor vehicle, preservation of the security interest therein, or otherwise.

(l) "Motor vehicle" means a vehicle required to be registered under the Vehicle Code that is bought for use primarily for personal or family purposes, and does not mean any vehicle that is bought for use primarily for business or commercial purposes or a mobilehome, as defined in Section 18008 of the Health and Safety Code that is sold on or after July 1, 1981. "Motor vehicle" does not include any trailer that is sold in conjunction with a vessel and that comes within the definition of "goods" under Section 1802.1.

(m) "Purchase order" means a sales order, car reservation, statement of transaction, or any other such instrument used in the conditional sale of a motor vehicle pending execution of a conditional sale contract. The purchase order shall conform to the disclosure requirements of subdivision (a) of Section 2982 and Section 2984.1, and subdivision (m) of Section 2982 shall apply.

(n) "Regulation Z" means a rule, regulation, or interpretation promulgated by the Board of Governors of the Federal Reserve System ("Board") under the federal Truth in Lending Act, as amended (15 U.S.C. Sec. 1601, et seq.), and an interpretation or approval issued by an official or employee of the Federal Reserve System duly authorized by the board under the Truth in Lending Act, as amended, to issue the interpretations or approvals.

(o) "Simple-interest basis" means the determination of a finance charge, other than an administrative finance charge, by applying a constant rate to the unpaid balance as it changes from time to time either:

(1) Calculated on the basis of a 365-day year and actual days elapsed (although the seller may, but need not, adjust its calculations to account for leap years); reference in this chapter to the "365-day basis" shall mean this method of determining the finance charge, or

(2) For contracts entered into prior to January 1, 1988, calculated on the basis of a 360-day year consisting of 12 months of 30 days each and on the assumption that all payments will be received by the seller on their respective due dates; reference in this chapter to the "360-day basis" shall mean this method of determining the finance charge.

(p) "Precomputed basis" means the determination of a finance charge by multiplying the original unpaid balance of the contract by a rate and multiplying that product by the number of payment periods elapsing between the date of the contract and the date of the last scheduled payment.

(q) "Service contract" means "vehicle service contract" as defined in subdivision (c) of Section 12800 of the Insurance Code.

(r) "Surface protection product" means the following products installed by the seller after the motor vehicle is sold:

(1) Undercoating.

(2) Rustproofing.

(3) Chemical or film paint sealant or protectant.

(4) Chemical sealant or stain inhibitor for carpet and fabric.

(s) "Theft deterrent device" means the following devices installed by the seller after the motor vehicle is sold:

(1) A vehicle alarm system.

(2) A window etch product.

(3) A body part marking product.

(4) A steering lock.

(5) A pedal or ignition lock.

(6) A fuel or ignition kill switch.

(t) "Guaranteed asset protection waiver" means an optional contractual obligation under which a seller agrees, for additional consideration, to cancel or waive all or part of amounts due on the buyer's conditional sale contract subject to this chapter in the event of a total loss or unrecovered theft of the motor vehicle specified in the conditional sale contract. *(Added by Stats.1961, c. 1626, p. 3534, § 4, eff. Jan. 1, 1962. Amended by Stats.1968, c. 1338, p. 2556, § 1; Stats.1970, c. 1003, p. 1800, § 1; Stats.1973, c. 696, § 1; Stats.1976, c. 1285, p. 5722, § 1; Stats.1979, c. 805, p. 2781, § 18; Stats.1980, c. 1149, p. 3722, § 7; Stats.1980, c. 1380, p. 5019, § 19, eff. Oct. 1, 1980; Stats.1981, c. 134, p. 892, § 1, eff. July 1, 1981, operative July 1, 1981; Stats.1981, c. 1075, p. 4122, § 12, operative Oct. 1, 1982; Stats.1985, c. 1186, § 2; Stats.1994, c. 1010 (S.B.2053), § 50; Stats.1999, c. 212 (S.B.1092), § 1; Stats.2005, c. 128 (A.B.68), § 2, operative July 1, 2006; Stats.2022, c. 283 (A.B.2311), § 1, eff. Jan. 1, 2023.)*

Cross References

Bailments, see Civil Code § 1955 et seq.
Buy-here-pay-here dealer defined, see Vehicle Code §§ 241, 241.1.
Sales, see Commercial Code § 2101 et seq.

§ 2981.5. Bailments or leases not considered conditional sale contracts

A contract for the bailment or leasing of a motor vehicle, with or without accessories, which establishes the maximum for which a bailee or lessee could be held liable at the end of the lease or bailment period, or upon an earlier termination, by reference to the value of the vehicle at such time, is not a contract by which the bailee or lessee will become or for no other or for a nominal consideration has the option of becoming the owner of the vehicle, for the purposes of paragraph (2) of subdivision (a) of Section 2981 or any other provision of this chapter. *(Added by Stats.1973, c. 696, § 2.)*

§ 2981.7. Finance charge; calculation on or after January 1, 1983

All contracts entered into between a buyer and a seller on or after January 1, 1983, shall provide for the calculation of the finance charge contemplated by item (A) of paragraph (1) of subdivision (j) of Section 2982 on the simple-interest basis, if the date on which the final installment is due, according to the original terms of the contract, is more than 62 months after the date of the contract. *(Added by Stats.1979, c. 805, p. 2783, § 19. Amended by Stats.1983, c. 142, § 3.)*

§ 2981.8. Finance charge; determination on precomputed basis and simple interest basis; exception

No contract shall provide for a finance charge which is determined in part by the precomputed basis and in part by the simple-interest basis except for any finance charge permitted by subdivisions (a) and (c) of Section 2982.8.

(Added by Stats.1979, c. 805, p. 2783, § 19.5. Amended by Stats.1980, c. 1380, p. 5021, § 20, eff. Oct. 1, 1980.)

§ 2981.9. Requirements of conditional sale contracts

Every conditional sale contract subject to this chapter shall be in writing and, if printed, shall be printed in type no smaller than 6-point, and shall contain in a single document all of the agreements of the buyer and seller with respect to the total cost and the terms of payment for the motor vehicle, including any promissory notes or any other evidences of indebtedness. The conditional sale contract or a purchase order shall be signed by the buyer or his or her authorized representative and by the seller or its authorized representative. An exact copy of the contract or purchase order shall be furnished to the buyer by the seller at the time the buyer and the seller have signed it. No motor vehicle shall be delivered pursuant to a contract subject to this chapter until the seller delivers to the buyer a fully executed copy of the conditional sale contract or purchase order and any vehicle purchase proposal and any credit statement which the seller has required or requested the buyer to sign and which he or she has signed during the contract negotiations. The seller shall not obtain the signature of the buyer to a contract when it contains blank spaces to be filled in after it has been signed. *(Added by Stats.1981, c. 1075, p. 4124, § 13, operative Oct. 1, 1982.)*

Cross References

Contract cancellation option agreement required, exceptions, purchase price, form, and cancellation procedures, see Vehicle Code § 11713.21.

§ 2982. Formalities of conditional sale contracts

A conditional sale contract subject to this chapter shall contain the disclosures required by Regulation Z, whether or not Regulation Z applies to the transaction. In addition, to the extent applicable, the contract shall contain the other disclosures and notices required by, and shall satisfy the requirements and limitations of, this section. The disclosures required by subdivision (a) may be itemized or subtotaled to a greater extent than as required by that subdivision and shall be made together and in the sequence set forth in that subdivision. All other disclosures and notices may appear in the contract in any location or sequence and may be combined or interspersed with other provisions of the contract.

(a) The contract shall contain the following disclosures, as applicable, which shall be labeled "itemization of the amount financed":

(1)(A) The cash price, exclusive of document processing charges, charges to electronically register or transfer the vehicle, taxes imposed on the sale, pollution control certification fees, prior credit or lease balance on property being traded in, the amount charged for a service contract, the amount charged for a theft deterrent system, the amount charged for a surface protection product, the amount charged for an optional debt cancellation agreement or guaranteed asset protection waiver, and the amount charged for a contract cancellation option agreement.

(B) The charge to be retained by the seller for document processing authorized pursuant to Section 4456.5 of the Vehicle Code.

(C) The fee charged by the seller for certifying that the motor vehicle complies with applicable pollution control requirements.

(D) A charge for a theft deterrent device.

(E) A charge for a surface protection product.

(F) The total amount charged by the seller for an electric vehicle charging station, which may include only the charges for the electric vehicle charging station device, any materials and wiring, and any installation services. The total amount shall be labeled "EV Charging Station."

(G) Taxes imposed on the sale.

(H) The charge to electronically register or transfer the vehicle authorized pursuant to Section 4456.5 of the Vehicle Code.

(I) The amount charged for a service contract.

(J) The prior credit or lease balance remaining on property being traded in, as required by paragraph (6). The disclosure required by this subparagraph shall be labeled "prior credit or lease balance (see downpayment and trade-in calculation)."

(K) Any charge for an optional debt cancellation agreement or guaranteed asset protection waiver.

(L) Any charge for a used vehicle contract cancellation option agreement.

(M) The total cash price, which is the sum of subparagraphs (A) to (L), inclusive.

(N) The disclosures described in subparagraphs (D), (E), and (L) are not required on contracts involving the sale of a motorcycle, as defined in Section 400 of the Vehicle Code, or on contracts involving the sale of an off-highway motor vehicle that is subject to identification under Section 38010 of the Vehicle Code, and the amounts of those charges, if any, are not required to be reflected in the total price under subparagraph (M).

(2) Amounts paid to public officials for the following:

(A) Vehicle license fees.

(B) Registration, transfer, and titling fees.

(C) California tire fees imposed pursuant to Section 42885 of the Public Resources Code.

(3) The aggregate amount of premiums agreed, upon execution of the contract, to be paid for policies of insurance included in the contract, excluding the amount of any insurance premium included in the finance charge.

(4) The amount of the state fee for issuance of a certificate of compliance, noncompliance, exemption, or waiver pursuant to any applicable pollution control statute.

(5) A subtotal representing the sum of the amounts described in paragraphs (1) to (4), inclusive.

(6) The amount of the buyer's downpayment itemized to show the following:

(A) The agreed value of the property being traded in.

(B) The prior credit or lease balance, if any, owing on the property being traded in.

(C) The net agreed value of the property being traded in, which is the difference between the amounts disclosed in subparagraphs (A) and (B). If the prior credit or lease balance of the property being traded in exceeds the agreed value of the property, a negative number shall be stated.

(D) The amount of any portion of the downpayment to be deferred until not later than the due date of the second regularly scheduled installment under the contract and that is not subject to a finance charge.

(E) The amount of any manufacturer's rebate applied or to be applied to the downpayment.

(F) The remaining amount paid or to be paid by the buyer as a downpayment.

(G) The total downpayment. If the sum of subparagraphs (C) to (F), inclusive, is zero or more, that sum shall be stated as the total downpayment, and no amount shall be stated as the prior credit or lease balance under subparagraph (I) of paragraph (1). If the sum of subparagraphs (C) to (F), inclusive, is less than zero, then that sum, expressed as a positive number, shall be stated as the prior credit or lease balance under subparagraph (I) of paragraph (1), and zero shall be stated as the total downpayment. The disclosure required by this subparagraph shall be labeled "total downpayment" and shall contain a descriptor indicating that if the total downpayment is a negative number, a zero shall be disclosed as the total downpayment and a reference made that the remainder shall be included in the disclosure required pursuant to subparagraph (I) of paragraph (1).

(7) The amount of any administrative finance charge, labeled "prepaid finance charge."

(8) The difference between the amount described in paragraph (5) and the sum of the amounts described in paragraphs (6) and (7), labeled "amount financed."

(b) No particular terminology is required to disclose the items set forth in subdivision (a) except as expressly provided in that subdivision.

(c) If payment of all or a portion of the downpayment is to be deferred, the deferred payment shall be reflected in the payment schedule disclosed pursuant to Regulation Z.

(d) If the downpayment includes property being traded in, the contract shall contain a brief description of that property.

(e) The contract shall contain the names and addresses of all persons to whom the notice required pursuant to Section 2983.2 and permitted pursuant to Sections 2983.5 and 2984 is to be sent.

(f)(1) If the contract includes a finance charge determined on the precomputed basis, the contract shall identify the method of computing the unearned portion of the finance charge in the event of prepayment in full of the buyer's obligation and contain a statement of the amount or method of computation of any charge that may be deducted from the amount of any unearned finance charge in computing the amount that will be credited to the obligation or refunded to the buyer. The method of computing the unearned portion of the finance charge shall be sufficiently identified with a reference to the actuarial method if the computation will be under that method. The method of computing the unearned portion of the finance charge shall be sufficiently identified with a reference to the Rule of 78's, the sum of the digits, or the sum of the periodic time balances method in all other cases, and those references shall be deemed to be equivalent for disclosure purposes.

(2) If the contract includes a finance charge that is determined on the simple-interest basis but provides for a minimum finance charge in the event of prepayment in full, the contract shall contain a statement of that fact and the amount of the minimum finance charge or its method of calculation.

(g)(1) If the contract includes a finance charge that is determined on the precomputed basis and provides that the unearned portion of the finance charge to be refunded upon full prepayment of the contract is to be determined by a method other than actuarial, the contract shall contain a notice, in at least 10–point boldface type if the contract is printed, reading as follows: "Notice to buyer: (1) Do not sign this agreement before you read it or if it contains any blank spaces to be filled in. (2) You are entitled to a completely filled-in copy of this agreement. (3) You can prepay the full amount due under this agreement at any time and obtain a partial refund of the finance charge if it is $1 or more. Because of the way the amount of this refund will be figured, the time when you prepay could increase the ultimate cost of credit under this agreement. (4) If you default in the performance of your obligations under this agreement, the vehicle may be repossessed and you may be subject to suit and liability for the unpaid indebtedness evidenced by this agreement."

(2) If the contract includes a finance charge that is determined on the precomputed basis and provides for the actuarial method for computing the unearned portion of the finance charge upon prepayment in full, the contract shall contain a notice, in at least 10–point boldface type if the contract is printed, reading as follows: "Notice to buyer: (1) Do not sign this agreement before you read it or if it contains any blank spaces to be filled in. (2) You are entitled to a completely filled-in copy of this agreement. (3) You can prepay the full amount due under this agreement at any time and obtain a partial refund of the finance charge if it is $1 or more. (4) If you default in the performance of your obligations under this agreement, the vehicle may be repossessed and you may be subject to suit and liability for the unpaid indebtedness evidenced by this agreement."

(3) If the contract includes a finance charge that is determined on the simple-interest basis, the contract shall contain a notice, in at least 10–point boldface type if the contract is printed, reading as follows: "Notice to buyer: (1) Do not sign this agreement before you read it or if it contains any blank spaces to be filled in. (2) You are entitled to a completely filled-in copy of this agreement. (3) You can prepay the full amount due under this agreement at any time. (4) If you default in the performance of your obligations under this agreement, the vehicle may be repossessed and you may be subject to suit and liability for the unpaid indebtedness evidenced by this agreement."

(h) The contract shall contain a notice in at least 8–point boldface type, acknowledged by the buyer, that reads as follows:

"If you have a complaint concerning this sale, you should try to resolve it with the seller.

Complaints concerning unfair or deceptive practices or methods by the seller may be referred to the city attorney, the district attorney, or an investigator for the Department of Motor Vehicles, or any combination thereof.

After this contract is signed, the seller may not change the financing or payment terms unless you agree in writing to the change. You do not have to agree to any change, and it is an unfair or deceptive practice for the seller to make a unilateral change.

Buyer's
Signa-
ture"

(i)(1) The contract shall contain an itemization of any insurance included as part of the amount financed disclosed pursuant to paragraph (3) of subdivision (a) and of any insurance included as part of the finance charge. The itemization shall identify the type of insurance coverage and the premium charged therefor, and, if the insurance expires before the date of the last scheduled installment included in the repayment schedule, the term of the insurance shall be stated.

(2) If any charge for insurance, other than for credit life or disability, is included in the contract balance and disbursement of any part thereof is to be made more than one year after the date of the conditional sale contract, any finance charge on the amount to be disbursed after one year shall be computed from the month the disbursement is to be made to the due date of the last installment under the conditional sale contract.

(j)(1) Except for contracts in which the finance charge or a portion of the finance charge is determined by the simple-interest basis and the amount financed disclosed pursuant to paragraph (8) of subdivision (a) is more than two thousand five hundred dollars ($2,500), the dollar amount of the disclosed finance charge may not exceed the greater of:

(A)(i) One and one-half percent on so much of the unpaid balance as does not exceed two hundred twenty-five dollars ($225), 1⅙ percent on so much of the unpaid balance in excess of two hundred twenty-five dollars ($225) as does not exceed nine hundred dollars ($900) and five-sixths of 1 percent on so much of the unpaid balance in excess of nine hundred dollars ($900) as does not exceed two thousand five hundred dollars ($2,500).

(ii) One percent of the entire unpaid balance; multiplied in either case by the number of months (computed on the basis of a full month for any fractional month period in excess of 15 days) elapsing between the date of the contract and the due date of the last installment.

(B) If the finance charge is determined by the precomputed basis, twenty-five dollars ($25).

(C) If the finance charge or a portion thereof is determined by the simple-interest basis:

(i) Twenty-five dollars ($25) if the unpaid balance does not exceed one thousand dollars ($1,000).

(ii) Fifty dollars ($50) if the unpaid balance exceeds one thousand dollars ($1,000) but does not exceed two thousand dollars ($2,000).

(iii) Seventy-five dollars ($75) if the unpaid balance exceeds two thousand dollars ($2,000).

(2) The holder of the contract shall not charge, collect, or receive a finance charge that exceeds the disclosed finance charge, except to the extent (A) caused by the holder's receipt of one or more payments under a contract that provides for determination of the finance charge or a portion thereof on the 365-day basis at a time or times other than as originally scheduled whether or not the parties enter into an agreement pursuant to Section 2982.3, (B) permitted by paragraph (2), (3), or (4) of subdivision (c) of Section 226.17 of Regulation Z, or (C) permitted by subdivisions (a) and (c) of Section 2982.8.

(3) If the finance charge or a portion thereof is determined by the simple-interest basis and the amount of the unpaid balance exceeds five thousand dollars ($5,000), the holder of the contract may, in lieu of its right to a minimum finance charge under subparagraph (C) of paragraph (1), charge, receive, or collect on the date of the contract an administrative finance charge not to exceed seventy-five dollars ($75), provided that the sum of the administrative finance charge and the portion of the finance charge determined by the simple-interest basis shall not exceed the maximum total finance charge permitted by subparagraph (A) of paragraph (1). Any administrative finance charge that is charged, received, or collected by a holder shall be deemed a finance charge earned on the date of the contract.

(4) If a contract provides for unequal or irregular payments, or payments on other than a monthly basis, the maximum finance charge shall be at the effective rate provided for in paragraph (1), having due regard for the schedule of installments.

(k) The contract may provide that for each installment in default for a period of not less than 10 days the buyer shall pay a delinquency charge in an amount not to exceed in the aggregate 5 percent of the delinquent installment, which amount may be collected only once on any installment regardless of the period during which it remains in default. Payments timely received by the seller under an extension or deferral agreement may not be subject to a delinquency charge unless the charge is permitted by Section 2982.3. The contract may provide for reasonable collection costs and fees in the event of delinquency.

(*l*) Notwithstanding any provision of a contract to the contrary, the buyer may pay at any time before maturity the entire indebtedness evidenced by the contract without penalty. In the event of prepayment in full:

(1) If the finance charge was determined on the precomputed basis, the amount required to prepay the contract shall be the outstanding contract balance as of that date, provided, however, that the buyer shall be entitled to a refund credit in the amount of the unearned portion of the finance charge, except as provided in paragraphs (3) and (4). The amount of the unearned portion of the finance charge shall be at least as great a proportion of the finance charge, including any additional finance charge imposed pursuant to Section 2982.8 or other additional charge imposed because the contract has been extended, deferred, or refinanced, as the sum of the periodic monthly time balances payable more than 15 days after the date of prepayment bears to the sum of all the periodic monthly time balances under the schedule of installments in the contract or, if the contract has been extended, deferred, or refinanced, as so extended, deferred, or refinanced. If the amount of the refund credit is less than one dollar ($1), no refund credit need be made by the holder. Any refund credit may be made in cash or credited to the outstanding obligations of the buyer under the contract.

(2) If the finance charge or a portion of the finance charge was determined on the simple-interest basis, the amount required to prepay the contract shall be the outstanding contract balance as of that date, including any earned finance charges that are unpaid as of that date and, if applicable, the amount provided in paragraph (3), and provided further that in cases where a finance charge is determined on the 360-day basis, the payments received under the contract shall be assumed to have been received on their respective due dates regardless of the actual dates on which the payments were received.

(3) If the minimum finance charge provided by subparagraph (B) or subparagraph (C) of paragraph (1) of subdivision (j), if either is applicable, is greater than the earned finance charge as of the date of prepayment, the holder shall be additionally entitled to the difference.

(4) This subdivision shall not impair the right of the seller or the seller's assignee to receive delinquency charges on delinquent installments and reasonable costs and fees as provided in subdivision (k) or extension or deferral agreement charges as provided in Section 2982.3.

(5) Notwithstanding any provision of a contract to the contrary, if the indebtedness created by any contract is satisfied prior to its maturity through surrender of the motor vehicle, repossession of the motor vehicle, redemption of the motor vehicle after repossession, or any judgment, the outstanding obligation of the buyer shall be determined as provided in paragraph (1) or (2). Notwithstanding, the buyer's outstanding obligation shall be computed by the holder as of the date the holder recovers the value of the motor vehicle through disposition thereof or judgment is entered or, if the holder elects to keep the motor vehicle in satisfaction of the buyer's indebtedness, as of the date the holder takes possession of the motor vehicle.

(m) Notwithstanding any other provision of this chapter to the contrary, any information required to be disclosed in a conditional sale contract under this chapter may be disclosed in any manner, method, or terminology required or permitted under Regulation Z, as in effect at the time that disclosure is made, except that permitted by paragraph (2) of subdivision (c) of Section 226.18 of Regulation Z, if all of the requirements and limitations set forth in subdivision (a) are satisfied. This chapter does not prohibit the disclosure in that contract of additional information required or permitted under Regulation Z, as in effect at the time that disclosure is made.

(n) If the seller imposes a charge for document processing or to electronically register or transfer the vehicle, the contract shall contain a disclosure that the charge is not a governmental fee.

(o) A seller shall not impose an application fee for a transaction governed by this chapter.

(p) The seller or holder may charge and collect a fee not to exceed fifteen dollars ($15) for the return by a depository institution of a dishonored check, negotiated order of withdrawal, or share draft issued in connection with the contract if the contract so provides or if the contract contains a generalized statement that the buyer may be liable for collection costs incurred in connection with the contract.

(q) The contract shall disclose on its face, by printing the word "new" or "used" within a box outlined in red, that is not smaller than one-half inch high and one-half inch wide, whether the vehicle is sold as a new vehicle, as defined in Section 430 of the Vehicle Code, or as a used vehicle, as defined in Section 665 of the Vehicle Code.

(r) The contract shall contain a notice with a heading in at least 12–point bold type and the text in at least 10–point bold type, circumscribed by a line, immediately above the contract signature line, that reads as follows:

THERE IS NO COOLING–OFF PERIOD UNLESS YOU OBTAIN A CONTRACT CANCELLATION OPTION

California law does not provide for a "cooling-off" or other cancellation period for vehicle sales. Therefore, you cannot later cancel this contract simply because you change your mind, decide the vehicle costs too much, or wish you had acquired a different vehicle. After you sign below, you may only cancel this contract with the agreement of the seller or for legal cause, such as fraud.

However, California law does require a seller to offer a two-day contract cancellation option on used vehicles with a purchase price of less than forty thousand dollars ($40,000), subject to certain statutory conditions. This contract cancellation option requirement does not apply to the sale of a recreational vehicle, a motorcycle, or an off-highway motor vehicle subject to identification under California law. See the vehicle contract cancellation option agreement for details.

(s) This section shall become operative on July 1, 2013. *(Added by Stats.2012, c. 675 (A.B.2502), § 2, eff. Sept. 27, 2012, operative July 1, 2013. Amended by Stats.2022, c. 283 (A.B.2311), § 2, eff. Jan. 1, 2023.)*

Cross References

Automobile dealers, insurance assignment, see Business and Professions Code §§ 18450, 18451.

Contract cancellation option agreement required, exceptions, purchase price, form, and cancellation procedures, see Vehicle Code § 11713.21.

§ 2982.05. Repealed by Stats.1990, c. 189 (A.B.2618), § 2, eff. June 29, 1990

§ 2982.1. Rebates, discounts, commissions, etc.

It shall be unlawful for any seller to induce or attempt to induce any person to enter into a contract subject to this chapter by offering a rebate, discount, commission, or other consideration, contingent upon the happening of a future event, on the condition that the buyer either sells, or gives information or assistance for the purpose of leading to a sale by the seller of, the same or related goods. *(Added by Stats.1968, c. 452, p. 1075, § 3.)*

§ 2982.2. Disclosures required for conditional sale contracts

(a) Prior to the execution of a conditional sale contract, the seller shall provide to a buyer, and obtain the buyer's signature on, a written disclosure that sets forth the following information:

(1)(A) A description and the price of each item sold if the contract includes a charge for the item.

(B) Subparagraph (A) applies to each item in the following categories:

(i) A service contract.

(ii) An insurance product.

(iii) A debt cancellation agreement or guaranteed asset protection waiver agreement.

(iv) A theft deterrent device.

(v) A surface protection product.

(vi) A vehicle contract cancellation option agreement.

(2) The sum of all of the charges disclosed under subdivision (a), labeled "total."

(3) The amount that would be calculated under the contract as the regular installment payment if charges for the items disclosed pursuant to subdivision (a) are not included in the contract. The amount disclosed pursuant to this subdivision shall be labeled "Installment Payment EXCLUDING Listed Items."

(4) The amount that would be calculated under the contract as the regular installment payment if charges for the items disclosed under subdivision (a) are included in the contract. The amount disclosed pursuant to this subdivision shall be labeled "Installment Payment INCLUDING Listed Items."

(b) The disclosures required under this section shall be in at least 10–point type and shall be contained in a document that is separate from the conditional sale contract and a purchase order.

(c) This section does not apply to the sale of a motorcycle, as defined in Section 400 of the Vehicle Code, or an off-highway vehicle subject to identification under Section 38010 of the Vehicle Code. *(Added by Stats.2005, c. 128 (A.B.68), § 4, operative July 1, 2006. Amended by Stats.2006, c. 567 (A.B.2303), § 3.5; Stats.2022, c. 283 (A.B.2311), § 3, eff. Jan. 1, 2023.)*

§ 2982.3. Extension of due date; deferment of payment; charges

(a) The holder of a conditional sale contract may, upon agreement with the buyer, extend the scheduled due date or defer the scheduled payment of all or of any part of any installment or installments payable thereunder. No charge shall be made for any such extension or deferment unless the agreement for such extension or deferment is in writing and signed by the parties thereto. However, the seller or holder may, as an adjunct to or to assist in efforts to collect one or more delinquent installments on the contract, advise one or more obligors on the contract, either in writing or orally, that the due date for one or more installments under the contract shall be extended, with no charge being made for such extension other than any applicable late charge provided for in the contract.

(b) Where the contract includes a finance charge determined on the precomputed basis, the holder may charge and contract for the payment of an extension or deferral agreement charge by the buyer and collect and receive the same, but such charge may not exceed an amount equal to 1 percent per month simple interest on the amount of the installment or installments, or part thereof, extended or deferred for the period of extension or deferral. Such period shall not exceed the period from the date when such extended or deferred installment or installments, or part thereof, would have been payable in the absence of such extension or deferral to the date when such installment or installments, or part thereof, are made payable under the agreement of extension or deferment; except that a minimum charge of one dollar ($1) for the period of extension or deferral may be made in any case where the extension or deferral agreement charge, when computed at such rate, amounts to less than one dollar ($1).

(c) Where the contract includes a finance charge determined on the simple-interest basis, the holder may charge and contract for the payment of an extension or deferral agreement charge by the buyer and collect and receive the same, but the charge for the extension or deferral agreement may not exceed the lesser of twenty-five dollars ($25) or 10 percent of the then outstanding principal balance of the contract. Such charge shall be in addition to any finance charges which accrue because such extended or deferred payments are received at a time other than as originally scheduled. (Added by Stats.1980, c. 1380, p. 5039, § 23, eff. Oct. 1, 1980. Amended by Stats.1981, c. 1075, p. 4130, § 15, operative Oct. 1, 1982; Stats.1987, c. 448, § 2.)

§ 2982.5. Exemptions from chapter; conditions; proceeds of loan

(a) This chapter may not be deemed to affect a loan, or the security therefor, between a purchaser of a motor vehicle and a supervised financial organization, other than the seller of the motor vehicle, all or a portion of which loan is used in connection with the purchase of a motor vehicle. As used in this chapter, "supervised financial organization" means a person organized, chartered, or holding a license or authorization certificate under a law of this state or the United States to make loans and subject to supervision by an official or agency of this state or the United States.

(b) This chapter may not be deemed to prohibit the seller's assisting the buyer in obtaining a loan upon any security from any third party to be used as a part or all of the downpayment or any other payment on a conditional sale contract or purchase order; provided that the conditional sale contract sets forth on its face the amount of the loan, the finance charge, the total thereof, the number of installments scheduled to repay the loan and the amount of each installment, that the buyer may be required to pledge security for the loan, which security shall be mutually agreed to by the buyer and the lender and notice to the buyer in at least 8-point type that he or she is obligated for the installment payments on both the conditional sale contract and the loan. The seller may not provide any security or other guarantee of payment on the loan, nor shall the seller receive any commission or other remuneration for assisting the buyer to obtain the loan. If the buyer obligates himself or herself to purchase, or receives possession of, the motor vehicle prior to securing the loan, and if the buyer upon appropriate application for the loan is unable to secure the loan, on the conditions stated in the conditional sale contract, the conditional sale contract or purchase order shall be deemed rescinded and all consideration thereupon shall be returned by the respective parties without demand.

(c) The proceeds of any loan payable to the seller after the date of the contract but prior to the due date of the second payment otherwise scheduled thereunder may not be subject to a finance charge and the amount thereof shall be disclosed pursuant to subparagraph (D) of paragraph (6) of subdivision (a) of Section 2982.

(d) This chapter may not be deemed to prohibit the seller's assisting the buyer in obtaining a loan from any third party to be used to pay for the full purchase price, or any part thereof, of a motor vehicle, if each of the following provisions applies:

(1) The loan may be upon any security, but except as provided in paragraph (2), the loan may not be secured in whole or in part by a lien on real property. Any lien on real property taken in violation of this section shall be void and unenforceable.

(2) A lien on real property may be taken to secure a loan of seven thousand five hundred dollars ($7,500) or more used to pay the full purchase price, or any part thereof, of a recreational vehicle, as defined in Section 18010 of the Health and Safety Code, which is not less than 20 feet in length.

(3) The provisions of Sections 2983.2, 2983.3, and 2984.4 shall apply to the loan, but may not authorize the lender or the lender's successor in interest to charge for any costs, fees, or expenses or to obtain any other benefit which the lender is prohibited from charging or obtaining under any regulatory law applicable to the lender. Notwithstanding this paragraph, the provisions of Sections 2983.2 and 2983.3 may not apply to a loan made by a lender licensed under Division 9 (commencing with Section 22000) or Division 10 (commencing with Section 24000) of the Financial Code.

(4) The lender or the lender's successor in interest shall be subject to all claims and defenses which the buyer could assert against the seller, but liability may not exceed the amount of the loan.

(5) If the buyer becomes obligated to purchase, or receives possession of, the motor vehicle prior to obtaining the loan, the agreement between the buyer and the seller shall set forth

on its face the amount of the loan, the finance charge, the total thereof, the number of installments scheduled to repay the loan and the amount of each installment, that the buyer may be required to pledge security for the loan, which security must be mutually agreed to by the buyer and the lender, and notice to the buyer in at least 8-point type that the buyer is obligated for the installment payments on the loan and for any payments which may be due on the agreement between the buyer and the seller. The seller may not provide any security or other guarantee of payment on the loan, and the seller may not receive any commission or other remuneration for assisting the buyer to obtain the loan. If the buyer upon proper application for the loan is unable to obtain the loan, on the condition stated in the agreement between the buyer and the seller, the agreement shall be deemed rescinded and all consideration thereupon shall be returned by the respective parties without demand.

(6) Any waiver by the buyer of the provisions of this section shall be void and unenforceable.

This subdivision does not apply to state or federally chartered banks and savings and loan associations and may not be construed to affect existing law regarding a seller's assisting a buyer to obtain a loan from a bank or savings and loan association or any loan obtained by the buyer from those lenders. (Added by Stats.1968, c. 979, p. 1866, § 1. Amended by Stats.1970, c. 1003, p. 1804, § 3; Stats.1979, c. 805, p. 2793, § 21; Stats.1981, c. 1075, p. 4131, § 16, operative Oct. 1, 1982; Stats.1983, c. 405, § 1; Stats.1985, c. 226, § 1; Stats.2003, c. 37 (A.B.964), § 2.)

§ 2982.7. Refund of down payment; breach after leaving motor vehicle as down payment; recovery by buyer

(a) Any payment made by a buyer to a seller pending execution of a conditional sale contract shall be refunded to the buyer in the event the conditional sale contract is not executed.

(b) In the event of breach by the seller of a conditional sale contract or purchase order where the buyer leaves his motor vehicle with the seller as downpayment and such motor vehicle is not returned by the seller to the buyer for whatever reason, the buyer may recover from the seller either the fair market value of the motor vehicle left as a downpayment or its value as stated in the contract or purchase order, whichever is greater. The recovery shall be tendered to the buyer within five business days after the breach.

(c) The remedies of the buyer provided for in subdivision (b) are nonexclusive and cumulative and shall not preclude the buyer from pursuing any other remedy which he may have under any other provision of law. (Added by Stats.1968, c. 1338, p. 2558, § 2. Amended by Stats.1970, c. 1003, p. 1805, § 4; Stats.1976, c. 1285, p. 5735, § 4.)

§ 2982.8. Amounts advanced by holder to procure insurance; repayment options for buyer; security; notice to buyer

(a) If a buyer is obligated under the terms of the conditional sale contract to maintain insurance on the vehicle and subsequent to the execution of the contract the buyer either fails to maintain or requests the holder to procure the insurance, any amounts advanced by the holder to procure the insurance may be the subject of finance charges from the date of advance as provided in subdivision (e).

(b) These amounts shall be secured as provided in the contract and permitted by Section 2984.2 if the holder notifies the buyer in writing of his or her option to repay those amounts in any one of the following ways:

(1) Full payment within 10 days from the date of giving or mailing the notice.

(2) Full amortization during the term of the insurance.

(3) If offered by the holder, full amortization after the term of the conditional sale contract, to be payable in installments which do not exceed the average payment allocable to a monthly period under the contract.

(4) If offered by the holder, a combination of the methods described in paragraphs (2) and (3), so that there is some amortization during the term of the insurance, with the remainder of the amortization being accomplished after the term of the conditional sale contract, to be payable in installments which do not exceed the average payment allocable to a monthly period under the original terms of the contract.

(5) If offered by the holder, any other amortization plan.

If the buyer neither pays in full the amounts advanced nor notifies the holder in writing of his or her choice regarding amortization options before the expiration of 10 days from the date of giving or mailing the notice by the holder, the holder may amortize the amounts advanced on a secured basis pursuant to paragraph (2) or, if offered by the holder as an option to the buyer, paragraph (3) or (4).

(c) The written notification described in subdivision (b) shall also set forth the amounts advanced by the holder and, with respect to each amortization plan the amount of the additional finance charge, the sum of the amounts advanced and the additional finance charge, the number of installments required, the amount of each installment and the date for payment of the installments.

In addition, the notice shall contain a statement in contrasting red print in at least 8-point bold type, which reads as follows:

"WARNING—IT IS YOUR RESPONSIBILITY UNDER CALIFORNIA LAW TO OBTAIN LIABILITY INSURANCE OR BE SUBJECT TO PENALTIES FOR VIOLATING SECTION 16020 OF THE VEHICLE CODE, WHICH MAY INCLUDE LOSS OF LICENSE OR A FINE. THE INSURANCE ACQUIRED BY THE LIENHOLDER DOES NOT PROVIDE LIABILITY COVERAGE AND DOES NOT SATISFY YOUR RESPONSIBILITY UNDER CALIFORNIA LAW."

(d) If subsequent to the execution of the contract the holder advances amounts for repairs to or preservation of the motor vehicle or preservation of the holder's security interest therein and such advances are occasioned by the buyer's default under the contract, such advances may be the subject of finance charges from the date of advance as provided in subdivision (e) and shall be secured as provided in the contract and permitted by Section 2984.2.

(e) The maximum rate of finance charge which may be imposed on amounts advanced by the holder subsequent to the execution of the contract for insurance, repairs to or preservation of the motor vehicle, or preservation of the holder's security interest therein, shall not exceed the annual percentage rate disclosed pursuant to Section 2982. (Added by Stats.1976, c. 1265, p. 5601, § 2. Amended by Stats.1977, c. 777, p. 2411, § 1, eff. Sept. 13, 1977; Stats.1978, c. 1057, p. 3264, § 1; Stats.1979, c. 805, p. 2793, § 22; Stats.1980, c. 1149, p. 3736, § 9; Stats.1980, c. 1380, p. 5040, § 24, eff. Oct. 1, 1980; Stats.1981, c. 134, p. 911, § 5, eff. July 1, 1981; Stats.1981, c. 1075, p. 4131, § 17, operative Oct. 1, 1982; Stats.1983, c. 33, § 1; Stats.1985, c. 1292, § 1; Stats.1986, c. 412, § 1; Stats.1987, c. 448, § 3; Stats.1988, c. 1092, § 2.)

§ 2982.9. Inability of buyer to obtain financing through third party; rescission of contract

In the event a buyer obligates himself to purchase, or receive possession of, a motor vehicle pursuant to a contract or purchase order, and the seller knows that the buyer intends to obtain financing from a third party without the assistance of the seller, and the buyer is unable to obtain such financing, the contract or purchase order shall be deemed rescinded and all consideration thereupon shall be returned by the respective parties without demand. (Added by Stats. 1976, c. 1285, p. 5736, § 4.5.)

§ 2982.10. Consideration for assignment of conditional sale contract

(a) In consideration of the assignment of a conditional sale contract, the seller shall not receive or accept from the assignee any payment or credit based upon any amount collected or received, or to be collected or received, under the contract as a finance charge except to the extent the payment or credit does not exceed the amount that would be calculated in accordance with Regulation Z, whether or not Regulation Z applies to the contract, as the contract's finance charge using, for the purposes of the calculation, an annual percentage rate equal to 2.5 percent for a contract having an original scheduled term of 60 monthly payments or less or 2 percent for a contract having an original scheduled term of more than 60 monthly payments.

(b) Subdivision (a) does not apply in the following circumstances:

(1) An assignment that is with full recourse or under other terms requiring the seller to bear the entire risk of financial performance of the buyer.

(2) An assignment that is more than six months following the date of the conditional sale contract.

(3) Isolated instances resulting from bona fide errors that would otherwise constitute a violation of subdivision (a) if the seller maintains reasonable procedures to guard against any errors and promptly, upon notice of the error, remits to the assignee any consideration received in excess of that permitted by subdivision (a).

(4) The assignment of a conditional sale contract involving the sale of a motorcycle, as defined in Section 400 of the Vehicle Code.

(5) The assignment of a conditional sale contract involving the sale of an off-highway motor vehicle that is subject to identification under Section 38010 of the Vehicle Code.

(Added by Stats.2005, c. 128 (A.B.68), § 5, operative July 1, 2006.)

§ 2982.11. Conditional sale contract including charge for electric vehicle charging station; written disclosure

(a) Prior to the execution of a conditional sale contract that includes a charge for an electric vehicle charging station, the seller shall provide the buyer with, and obtain the buyer's signature on, a written disclosure that includes a description and price of each of the following:

(1) The electric vehicle charging station device.

(2) Any materials and wiring.

(3) Any installation services included in the total charge.

(b) The disclosures required under this section shall be in at least 12–point type and shall be contained in a document that is separate from the conditional sale contract or purchase order.

(c) This section shall become operative July 1, 2013. (Added by Stats.2012, c. 675 (A.B.2502), § 3, eff. Sept. 27, 2012, operative July 1, 2013.)

§ 2982.12. Guaranteed asset protection waiver; termination

(a)(1) A guaranteed asset protection waiver may be offered, sold, or provided to a buyer, or administered, in connection with a conditional sale contract subject to this chapter only in compliance with this chapter and paragraph (2) of subdivision (h) of Section 1758.992 of the Insurance Code.

(2) A guaranteed asset protection waiver, which may be titled as an addendum, forms part of the conditional sale contract and remains a part of the conditional sale contract upon the assignment, sale, or transfer of that conditional sale contract.

(3) Neither the extension of credit, the term of credit, nor the terms of a conditional sale contract may be conditioned upon the purchase of a guaranteed asset protection waiver.

(4)(A) The terms and conditions of the guaranteed asset protection waiver, including those terms required by subdivision (b), shall appear on a document separate from the conditional sale contract and a buyer or potential buyer shall separately sign the document setting forth the guaranteed asset protection waiver's terms and conditions in addition to the conditional sale contract.

(B) The separate document displaying the guaranteed asset protection waiver's terms and conditions shall do the following:

(i) Conspicuously state that the guaranteed asset protection waiver is an optional addition to the conditional sale contract, and that the holder of the conditional sale contract is the contracting party to the guaranteed asset protection waiver, and state the name and mailing address of the seller. If the conditional sale contract is assigned, written notice of the assignment of both the conditional sale contract and guaranteed asset protection waiver, and the assignee's name and mailing address, shall be provided to the buyer in person or by mail, or by a means of notice that the buyer previously agreed to with the seller or holder in connection with the conditional sale contract within 30 days of the assignment.

(ii) Conspicuously disclose the name and mailing address of any administrator known as of the date of the sale. In this section, "administrator" means any person, other than an insurer, that performs administrative or operational functions in connection with the guaranteed asset protection waiver. An administrator is deemed to be an agent of the contemporaneous holder with respect to performance of the holder's obligations under the guaranteed asset protection waiver and this section.

(iii) Contain a notice with a heading in at least 12–point bold type and the text in at least 10–point bold type, circumscribed by a line, immediately above the contract signature line, that reads as follows:

STOP AND READ:
YOU CANNOT BE REQUIRED TO BUY A GAP WAIVER OR ANY OTHER OPTIONAL ADD–ON PRODUCTS OR SERVICES. IT IS OPTIONAL.

NO ONE CAN MAKE YOU BUY A GAP WAIVER OR ANY OTHER OPTIONAL ADD–ON PRODUCTS OR SERVICES TO GET FINANCING, TO GET CERTAIN FINANCING TERMS, OR TO GET CERTAIN TERMS FOR THE SALE OF A VEHICLE.

IT IS UNLAWFUL TO REQUIRE OR ATTEMPT TO REQUIRE THE PURCHASE OF THIS GAP WAIVER OR ANY OTHER OPTIONAL ADD–ON PRODUCTS OR SERVICES.

(5) A person that sells a guaranteed asset protection waiver subject to this chapter shall not do either of the following:

(A) Charge more for the guaranteed asset protection waiver than 4 percent of the amount the buyer finances under a conditional sale contract.

(B) Sell a guaranteed asset protection waiver if one of the following applies:

(i) The amount financed through the conditional sale contract exceeds a maximum dollar amount covered by the guaranteed asset protection waiver.

(ii) The conditional sale contract's loan-to-value ratio at the contracting date exceeds the maximum loan-to-value ratio covered by the guaranteed asset protection waiver, unless the terms of the guaranteed asset protection waiver conspicuously disclose the maximum loan-to-value ratio limitation, including the method by which the limitation is applied, and the buyer is informed in a writing, acknowledged by the buyer, that the amount financed in the buyer's conditional sale contract exceeds the waiver's maximum loan-to-value limitation and therefore the waiver will not cover the total amount owed on the conditional sale contract. As used in this subclause, "loan-to-value ratio" means the total amount financed through a conditional sale contract as a percentage of the manufacturer suggested retail price for a new motor vehicle or the average retail value for a used motor vehicle, as determined by a nationally recognized pricing guide, as defined in paragraph (2) of subdivision (c) of Section 11950 of the Vehicle Code.

(iii) The amount financed through a conditional sale contract is less than 70 percent of the manufacturer suggested retail price for a new motor vehicle or the average retail value for a used motor vehicle, as determined by a nationally recognized pricing guide, as defined in paragraph (2) of subdivision (c) of Section 11950 of the Vehicle Code.

(6) Notwithstanding any provision in any conditional sale contract for the sale of a motor vehicle to the contrary, when communicating in writing an itemized contract balance to the buyer, including a payoff letter, payoff quote, or any written notice required under subdivision (a) of Section 2983.2 of this code or subdivision (b) of Section 22328 of the Financial Code, the holder of a conditional sale contract that includes a guaranteed asset protection waiver shall do either of the following:

(A) Individually identify as a credit or refund available to the buyer the unearned portion of all guaranteed asset protection waiver charges paid by the buyer as of the date of the communication on a pro rata basis.

(B) Conspicuously state that a buyer who purchased a guaranteed asset protection waiver is generally entitled to a refund of the unearned portion of the guaranteed asset protection waiver charges on a pro rata basis upon early termination of their conditional sale contract or cancellation of the guaranteed asset protection waiver, and that the buyer should contact the administrator identified in the buyer's guaranteed asset protection waiver, or any other appropriate person designated by the holder, for identification of the amount of such a refund available to the buyer at that time.

(b)(1) A guaranteed asset protection waiver terminates no later than the earliest of the following events:

(A) Cancellation of the guaranteed asset protection waiver by the buyer, as provided by paragraph (4).

(B) Payment in full by the buyer of the conditional sale contract.

(C) Expiration of any redemption and reinstatement periods after a repossession or surrender of the motor vehicle specified in the conditional sale contract pursuant to subdivision (a) of Section 2983.2.

(D) Upon total loss or unrecovered theft of the motor vehicle specified in the conditional sale contract, after the holder has applied all applicable benefits required under the guaranteed asset protection waiver.

(E) Upon any other event that occurs earlier than the events listed in subparagraphs (A) to (D), inclusive, as specified in the guaranteed asset protection waiver.

(2) Subject to paragraph (3), upon termination of a guaranteed asset protection waiver, the buyer is entitled to a refund as follows:

(A) If the termination occurs within 30 days after the date the buyer purchased the guaranteed asset protection waiver, the buyer is entitled to a full refund of the guaranteed asset protection waiver charges plus all finance charges attributable to the guaranteed asset protection waiver.

(B) If the termination occurs later than 30 days after the date the buyer purchased the guaranteed asset protection waiver, the buyer is entitled to a refund of the unearned guaranteed asset protection waiver charges, which shall be

§ 2982.12   OBLIGATIONS

calculated on a pro rata basis. For the purposes of this section, "calculating a refund on a pro rata basis" shall require multiplying the total dollar amount of guaranteed asset protection waiver charges by the quotient of the number of calendar days from the termination date to the conditional sale contract's original full term date, including the termination date as a full calendar day, divided by the total number of calendar days in the conditional sale contract's original term.

(C) No refund is required upon termination if there has been a total loss or unrecovered theft of the motor vehicle specified in the conditional sale contract and the buyer has or will receive the benefit of the guaranteed asset protection waiver.

(3) Within 60 business days from the termination of a guaranteed asset protection waiver, the holder shall tender the refund required under paragraph (2) or shall cause to be made the refund under paragraph (2) by instructing in writing the administrator or any other appropriate party to make the refund.

(A) A refund owed under this section may be applied by the holder as a reduction of the amount owed under the conditional sale contract unless the conditional sale contract has been paid in full.

(B) Refunds owed under this section are not exclusive and shall be in addition to any other refunds provided for in this chapter.

(4) A guaranteed asset protection waiver may be canceled by the buyer at any time without penalty.

(5) A cancellation fee, termination fee, or similar fee shall not be assessed in connection with the termination of a guaranteed asset protection waiver.

(6) In addition to the requirements of Section 2984.5, the holder shall maintain records identifying any refund made and tendered under paragraphs (2) and (3) of this subdivision, including those refunds the holder instructed the administrator or other appropriate party to make, and provide electronic access to those records, in response to any subpoena or other administratively or judicially enforceable request, until four years after the date the refund was tendered. *(Added by Stats.2022, c. 283 (A.B.2311), § 4, eff. Jan. 1, 2023.)*

§ 2983. Enforceability of contract; violation of specified provisions by seller; correction; recovery by buyer; disclosure violations relating to payment of state fees

(a) Except as provided in subdivision (b), if the seller, except as the result of an accidental or bona fide error in computation, violates any provision of Section 2981.9, or of subdivision (a), (j), or (k) of Section 2982, the conditional sale contract shall not be enforceable, except by a bona fide purchaser, assignee, or pledgee for value, or until after the violation is corrected as provided in Section 2984, and, if the violation is not corrected, the buyer may recover from the seller the total amount paid, pursuant to the terms of the contract, by the buyer to the seller or his or her assignee. The amount recoverable for property traded in as all or part of the downpayment shall be equal to the agreed cash value of the property as the value appears on the conditional sale contract or the fair market value of the property as of the time the contract is made, whichever is greater.

(b) A conditional sale contract executed or entered into on or after January 1, 2012, shall not be made unenforceable solely because of a violation by the seller of paragraph (2) or (5) of subdivision (a) of Section 2982. In addition to any other remedies that may be available, the buyer is entitled to any actual damages sustained as a result of a violation of those provisions. Nothing in this subdivision affects any legal rights, claims, or remedies otherwise available under law. *(Added by Stats.1961, c. 1626, p. 3537, § 4, eff. Jan. 1, 1962. Amended by Stats.1967, c. 815, p. 2239, § 1; Stats.1979, c. 805, p. 2794, § 23; Stats.1981, c. 1075, p. 4132, § 18, operative Oct. 1, 1982; Stats.2011, c. 526 (A.B.238), § 2, eff. Oct. 7, 2011; Stats.2012, c. 162 (S.B.1171), § 11.)*

§ 2983.1. Enforceability of contract; violation of provisions relating to guaranteed asset protection waiver; violation of provisions relating to prepayment, refinancing, or refund of finance charge by seller or holder; recovery by buyer; election to enforce or rescind; disclosure violations relating to payment of state fees

(a) If the seller or holder of a conditional sale contract, except as the result of an accidental or bona fide error of computation, violates any provision of subdivision (*l*) of Section 2982, the buyer may recover from the person three times the amount of any finance charge paid to that person.

(b) If a holder of a conditional sale contract that includes a guaranteed asset protection waiver, except as the result of an accidental or bona fide error of computation, violates any provision of subdivision (b) of Section 2982.12, the buyer may recover from the holder three times the amount of any guaranteed asset protection charges paid.

(c) Except as provided in subdivision (f), if a holder acquires a conditional sale contract without actual knowledge of the violation by the seller of Section 2981.9, or of subdivision (a), (j), or (k) of Section 2982, the contract shall be valid and enforceable by the holder except the buyer is excused from payment of the unpaid finance charge, unless the violation is corrected as provided in Section 2984.

(d) Except as provided in subdivision (f), if a holder acquires a conditional sale contract with knowledge of a violation of Section 2981.9, or of subdivision (a), (j), or (k) of Section 2982, the conditional sale contract shall not be enforceable except by a bona fide purchaser, assignee, or pledgee for value, or unless the violation is corrected as provided in Section 2984, and, if the violation is not corrected, the buyer may recover the amounts specified in Section 2983 from the person to whom payment was made.

(e) When a conditional sale contract is not enforceable under Section 2983 or this section, the buyer may elect to retain the motor vehicle and continue the contract in force, or may, with reasonable diligence, elect to rescind the contract and return the motor vehicle. The value of the motor vehicle returned shall be credited as restitution by the buyer without any decrease that results from the passage of time in the cash price of the motor vehicle as the price appears on the conditional sale contract.

(f) A conditional sale contract executed or entered into on or after January 1, 2012, shall not be made unenforceable, and the buyer shall not be excused from payment of any finance charge, solely because of a violation by the seller of paragraph (2) or (5) of subdivision (a) of Section 2982. In addition to any other remedies that may be available, the buyer is entitled to any actual damages sustained as a result of a violation of those provisions. Nothing in this subdivision affects any legal rights, claims, or remedies otherwise available under law. *(Added by Stats.1961, c. 1626, p. 3538, § 4, eff. Jan. 1, 1962. Amended by Stats.1979, c. 805, p. 2794, § 24; Stats.1981, c. 1075, p. 4133, § 19, operative Oct. 1, 1982; Stats.2011, c. 526 (A.B.238), § 3, eff. Oct. 7, 2011; Stats.2022, c. 283 (A.B.2311), § 5, eff. Jan. 1, 2023.)*

§ 2983.2. Disposition after repossession or surrender; notice of intent; service prerequisite to liability for delinquency; contents; accounting of disposition to person liable on contract; surplus; disposition; application of section

(a) Except where the motor vehicle has been seized as described in paragraph (6) of subdivision (b) of Section 2983.3, any provision in any conditional sale contract for the sale of a motor vehicle to the contrary notwithstanding, at least 15 days' written notice of intent to dispose of a repossessed or surrendered motor vehicle shall be given to all persons liable on the contract. The notice shall be personally served or shall be sent by certified mail, return receipt requested, or first-class mail, postage prepaid, directed to the last known address of the persons liable on the contract. If those persons are married to each other, and, according to the most recent records of the seller or holder of the contract, reside at the same address, one notice addressed to both persons at that address is sufficient. Except as otherwise provided in Section 2983.8, those persons shall be liable for any deficiency after disposition of the repossessed or surrendered motor vehicle only if the notice prescribed by this section is given within 60 days of repossession or surrender and does all of the following:

(1) Sets forth that those persons shall have a right to redeem the motor vehicle by paying in full the indebtedness evidenced by the contract until the expiration of 15 days from the date of giving or mailing the notice and provides an itemization of the contract balance and of any delinquency, collection or repossession costs and fees and sets forth the computation or estimate of the amount of any credit for unearned finance charges or canceled insurance as of the date of the notice.

(2) States either that there is a conditional right to reinstate the contract until the expiration of 15 days from the date of giving or mailing the notice and all the conditions precedent thereto or that there is no right of reinstatement and provides a statement of reasons therefor.

(3) States that, upon written request, the seller or holder shall extend for an additional 10 days the redemption period or, if entitled to the conditional right of reinstatement, both the redemption and reinstatement periods. The seller or holder shall provide the proper form for applying for the extensions with the substance of the form being limited to the extension request, spaces for the requesting party to sign and date the form, and instructions that it must be personally served or sent by certified or registered mail, return receipt requested, to a person or office and address designated by the seller or holder and received before the expiration of the initial redemption and reinstatement periods.

(4) Discloses the place at which the motor vehicle will be returned to those persons upon redemption or reinstatement.

(5) Designates the name and address of the person or office to whom payment shall be made.

(6) States the seller's or holder's intent to dispose of the motor vehicle upon the expiration of 15 days from the date of giving or mailing the notice, or if by mail and either the place of deposit in the mail or the place of address is outside of this state, the period shall be 20 days instead of 15 days, and further, that upon written request to extend the redemption period and any applicable reinstatement period for 10 days, the seller or holder shall without further notice extend the period accordingly.

(7) Informs those persons that upon written request, the seller or holder will furnish a written accounting regarding the disposition of the motor vehicle as provided for in subdivision (b). The seller or holder shall advise them that this request must be personally served or sent first-class mail, postage prepaid, or certified mail, return receipt requested, to a person or office and address designated by the seller or holder.

(8) Includes notice, in at least 10–point bold type if the notice is printed, reading as follows: "NOTICE. YOU MAY BE SUBJECT TO SUIT AND LIABILITY IF THE AMOUNT OBTAINED UPON DISPOSITION OF THE VEHICLE IS INSUFFICIENT TO PAY THE CONTRACT BALANCE AND ANY OTHER AMOUNTS DUE."

(9) Informs those persons that upon the disposition of the motor vehicle, they will be liable for the deficiency balance plus interest at the contract rate, or at the legal rate of interest pursuant to Section 3289 if there is no contract rate of interest, from the date of disposition of the motor vehicle to the date of entry of judgment.

The notice prescribed by this section shall not affect the discretion of the court to strike out an unconscionable interest rate in the contract for which the notice is required, nor affect the court in its determination of whether the rate is unconscionable.

(b) Unless automatically provided to the buyer within 45 days after the disposition of the motor vehicle, the seller or holder shall provide to any person liable on the contract within 45 days after their written request, if the request is made within one year after the disposition, a written accounting regarding the disposition. The accounting shall itemize:

(1) The gross proceeds of the disposition.

(2) The reasonable and necessary expenses incurred for retaking, holding, preparing for and conducting the sale and to the extent provided for in the agreement and not prohibited by law, reasonable attorney fees and legal expenses incurred by the seller or holder in retaking the motor vehicle from any person not a party to the contract.

(3) The satisfaction of indebtedness secured by any subordinate lien or encumbrance on the motor vehicle if written notification of demand therefor is received before distribution of the proceeds is completed. If requested by the seller or holder, the holder of a subordinate lien or encumbrance

must seasonably furnish reasonable proof of its interest, and unless it does so, the seller or holder need not comply with its demand.

(c) In all sales which result in a surplus, the seller or holder shall furnish an accounting as provided in subdivision (b) whether or not requested by the buyer. Any surplus shall be returned to the buyer within 45 days after the sale is conducted.

(d) This section does not apply to a loan made by a lender licensed under Division 9 (commencing with Section 22000) of the Financial Code. *(Added by Stats.1977, c. 777, p. 2413, § 3, eff. Sept. 13, 1977, operative Jan. 1, 1978. Amended by Stats.1985, c. 226, § 2; Stats.1987, c. 448, § 4; Stats.1988, c. 1092, § 3; Stats.1996, c. 124 (A.B.3470), § 9; Stats.1996, c. 313 (S.B.1639), § 1; Stats.2019, c. 497 (A.B.991), § 28, eff. Jan. 1, 2020.)*

Cross References

Notification of repossession to police department, see Vehicle Code § 28.

§ 2983.3. Default; prerequisite to acceleration of maturity; repossession or surrender; right of reinstatement by person liable on contract; exceptions; methods; right to deficiency; abrogation; application of section

(a)(1) In the absence of default in the performance of any of the buyer's obligations under the contract, the seller or holder may not accelerate the maturity of any part or all of the amount due thereunder or repossess the motor vehicle.

(2) Neither the act of filing a petition commencing a case for bankruptcy under Title 11 of the United States Code by the buyer or other individual liable on the contract nor the status of either of those persons as a debtor in bankruptcy constitutes a default in the performance of any of the buyer's obligations under the contract, and neither may be used as a basis for accelerating the maturity of any part or all of the amount due under the contract or for repossessing the motor vehicle. A provision of a contract that states that the act of filing a petition commencing a case for bankruptcy under Title 11 of the United States Code by the buyer or other individual liable on the contract or the status of either of those persons as a debtor in bankruptcy is a default is void and unenforceable.

(b) If after default by the buyer, the seller or holder repossesses or voluntarily accepts surrender of the motor vehicle, any person liable on the contract shall have a right to reinstate the contract and the seller or holder shall not accelerate the maturity of any part or all of the contract prior to expiration of the right to reinstate, unless the seller or holder reasonably and in good faith determines that any of the following has occurred:

(1) The buyer or any other person liable on the contract by omission or commission intentionally provided false or misleading information of material importance on the buyer's or other person's credit application.

(2) The buyer, any other person liable on the contract, or any permissive user in possession of the motor vehicle, in order to avoid repossession has concealed the motor vehicle or removed it from the state.

(3) The buyer, any other person liable on the contract, or any permissive user in possession of the motor vehicle, has committed or threatens to commit acts of destruction, or has failed to take care of the motor vehicle in a reasonable manner, so that the motor vehicle has become substantially impaired in value, or the buyer, any other person liable on the contract, or any nonoccasional permissive user in possession of the motor vehicle has failed to take care of the motor vehicle in a reasonable manner, so that the motor vehicle may become substantially impaired in value.

(4) The buyer or any other person liable on the contract has committed, attempted to commit, or threatened to commit criminal acts of violence or bodily harm against an agent, employee, or officer of the seller or holder in connection with the seller's or holder's repossession of or attempt to repossess the motor vehicle.

(5) The buyer has knowingly used the motor vehicle, or has knowingly permitted it to be used, in connection with the commission of a criminal offense, other than an infraction, as a consequence of which the motor vehicle has been seized by a federal, state, or local agency or authority pursuant to federal, state, or local law.

(6) The motor vehicle has been seized by a federal, state, or local public agency or authority pursuant to (A) Section 1324 of Title 8 of the United States Code or Part 274 of Title 8 of the Code of Federal Regulations, (B) Section 881 of Title 21 of the United States Code or Part 9 of Title 28 of the Code of Federal Regulations, or (C) other federal, state, or local law, including regulations, and, pursuant to that other law, the seizing authority, as a precondition to the return of the motor vehicle to the seller or holder, prohibits the return of the motor vehicle to the buyer or other person liable on the contract or any third person claiming the motor vehicle by or through them or otherwise effects or requires the termination of the property rights in the motor vehicle of the buyer or other person liable on the contract or claimants by or through them.

(c) Exercise of the right to reinstate the contract shall be limited to once in any 12–month period and twice during the term of the contract.

(d) The provisions of this subdivision cover the method by which a contract shall be reinstated with respect to curing events of default which were a ground for repossession or occurred subsequent to repossession:

(1) When the default is the result of the buyer's failure to make any payment due under the contract, the buyer or any other person liable on the contract shall make the defaulted payments and pay any applicable delinquency charges.

(2) When the default is the result of the buyer's failure to keep and maintain the motor vehicle free from all encumbrances and liens of every kind, the buyer or any other person liable on the contract shall either satisfy all encumbrances and liens or, in the event the seller or holder satisfies the encumbrances and liens, the buyer or any other person liable on the contract shall reimburse the seller or holder for all reasonable costs and expenses incurred therefor.

(3) When the default is the result of the buyer's failure to keep and maintain insurance on the motor vehicle, the buyer or any other person liable on the contract shall either obtain

the insurance or, in the event the seller or holder has obtained the insurance, the buyer or any other person liable on the contract shall reimburse the seller or holder for premiums paid and all reasonable costs and expenses, including, but not limited to, any finance charge in connection with the premiums permitted by Section 2982.8, incurred therefor.

(4) When the default is the result of the buyer's failure to perform any other obligation under the contract, unless the seller or holder has made a good faith determination that the default is so substantial as to be incurable, the buyer or any other person liable on the contract shall either cure the default or, if the seller or holder has performed the obligation, reimburse the seller or holder for all reasonable costs and expenses incurred in connection therewith.

(5) Additionally, the buyer or any other person liable on the contract shall, in all cases, reimburse the seller or holder for all reasonable and necessary collection and repossession costs and fees actually paid by the seller or holder, including attorney's fees and legal expenses expended in retaking and holding the vehicle.

(e) If the seller or holder denies the right to reinstatement under subdivision (b) or paragraph (4) of subdivision (d), the seller or holder shall have the burden of proof that the denial was justified in that it was reasonable and made in good faith. If the seller or holder fails to sustain the burden of proof, the seller or holder shall not be entitled to a deficiency, but it shall not be presumed that the buyer is entitled to damages by reason of the failure of the seller or holder to sustain the burden of proof.

(f) This section does not apply to a loan made by a lender licensed under Division 9 (commencing with Section 22000) of the Financial Code. *(Added by Stats.1961, c. 1626, p. 3539, § 4, eff. Jan. 1, 1962. Amended by Stats.1976, c. 1265, p. 5603, § 4; Stats.1985, c. 226, § 3; Stats.1986, c. 1236, § 1; Stats. 1987, c. 448, § 5; Stats.2019, c. 497 (A.B.991), § 29, eff. Jan. 1, 2020; Stats.2021, c. 401 (A.B.1578), § 2, eff. Jan. 1, 2022; Stats.2022, c. 716 (S.B.1099), § 1, eff. Jan. 1, 2023.)*

§ 2983.35. Cosigners; notice of delinquency; service; application of section

(a) If a creditor has requested a cosigner as a condition of granting credit to any person for the purpose of acquisition of a motor vehicle, the creditor or holder shall give the cosigner a written notice of delinquency prior to the repossession of the motor vehicle if the motor vehicle is to be repossessed pursuant to the motor vehicle credit agreement. The written notice of delinquency shall be personally served or shall be sent by certified mail, return receipt requested, or first-class mail, postage prepaid, directed to the last known address of the cosigner. If the last known address of the buyer and the cosigner are the same, a single written notice of delinquency given to both the borrower and cosigner prior to repossession satisfies the cosigner notice requirement of this section.

(b) A creditor or holder who fails to comply with this section may not recover any costs associated with the repossession of the vehicle from the cosigner.

(c) This section applies to any motor vehicle credit agreement, notwithstanding Section 2982.5.

(d) The following definitions govern the construction of this section.

(1) "Cosigner" means a buyer who executes a motor vehicle credit agreement but does not in fact receive possession of the motor vehicle that is the subject of the agreement.

(2) "Creditor" means a seller or lender described in paragraph (4).

(3) "Holder" means any other person who is entitled to enforce the motor vehicle credit agreement.

(4) "Motor vehicle credit agreement" means any conditional sales contract as defined in Section 2981 and any contract or agreement in which a lender gives value to enable a purchaser to acquire a motor vehicle and in which the lender obtains a security interest in the motor vehicle. *(Added by Stats.1996, c. 313 (S.B.1639), § 2.)*

§ 2983.37. Buy-here-pay-here dealer; prohibited actions after sale of vehicle; violations

(a) After a sale of a vehicle under this chapter, a buy-here-pay-here dealer, as defined in Section 241 of the Vehicle Code, shall not do any of the following:

(1) Utilize electronic tracking technology to obtain or record the location of the vehicle, unless the buyer is expressly made aware of the existence and use of the tracking technology by the buy-here-pay-here dealer, the buyer's written consent is obtained, and either subparagraph (A) or (B), or both, apply:

(A) The electronic tracking technology is used solely to verify and maintain the operational status of the tracking technology, to repossess the vehicle, or to locate the vehicle to service the loan or keep the loan current.

(B) The electronic tracking technology is used solely for any optional service to the buyer and both of the following conditions are met:

(i) The agreement to utilize electronic tracking technology for the optional service is separate from the purchase and sale agreement, is not a condition of the purchase or sale agreement for the vehicle, and is executed after the completion of the purchase or sale agreement for the vehicle.

(ii) The buyer is permitted to cancel the optional service at any point in the future without affecting the sale of the vehicle, and is informed of his or her ability to do so.

(2) Disable the vehicle by using starter interrupt technology, unless the buy-here-pay-here dealer complies with all of the following provisions:

(A) Notifies the buyer in writing at the time of the sale that the vehicle is equipped with starter interrupt technology, which the buy-here-pay-here dealer can use to shut down the vehicle remotely.

(B) The written disclosure provided to the buyer at the time of sale informs the buyer that a warning will be provided five days before the use of the starter interrupt technology for all weekly payment term contracts and 10 days before the use of starter interrupt technology on all other contracts, and a final warning will be provided no less than 48 hours before the use of the starter interrupt technology to shut down the vehicle remotely and discloses the manner and method in which that warning will occur. The dealer shall offer the buyer a choice of warning methods, including warning from the device, telephone call, email, or text message, if available, provided that the warning method does not violate applicable state or federal law.

(C) The written disclosure provided to the buyer at the time of sale informs the buyer that in the event of an emergency, the buyer will be provided with the ability to start a dealer-disabled vehicle for no less than 24 hours after the vehicle's initial disablement.

(b) A buy-here-pay-here dealer shall not require the buyer to make payments to the seller in person. For purposes of this subdivision, "payments" does not include the downpayment. If the buyer tenders timely payment of a deferred downpayment, the dealer shall not repossess the vehicle or impose any other charge or penalty on the grounds that the payment was not made in person.

(c) Each violation of this section is a misdemeanor punishable by a fine not exceeding two thousand dollars ($2,000). (Added by Stats.2012, c. 740 (A.B.1447), § 3. Amended by Stats.2015, c. 179 (A.B.265), § 1, eff. Jan. 1, 2016.)

Cross References
Buy-here-pay-here dealers, warranties and receipts for sales or leases, prohibited actions, notice of election to cancel, repairs, see Civil Code § 1795.51.

§ 2983.4. Prevailing party's right to attorney's fees and costs

Reasonable attorney's fees and costs shall be awarded to the prevailing party in any action on a contract or purchase order subject to the provisions of this chapter regardless of whether the action is instituted by the seller, holder or buyer. Where the defendant alleges in his answer that he tendered to the plaintiff the full amount to which he was entitled, and thereupon deposits in court, for the plaintiff, the amount so tendered, and the allegation is found to be true, then the defendant is deemed to be a prevailing party within the meaning of this section. (Added by Stats.1961, c. 1626, p. 3539, § 4, eff. Jan. 1, 1962. Amended by Stats.1976, c. 1285, p. 5736, § 5.)

Cross References
Attorney's fees and costs, see Civil Code §§ 1717, 1811.1.
Retail installment, award of attorney's fees, see Civil Code § 1811.1.

§ 2983.5. Assignment of sellers rights; recourse

(a) An assignee of the seller's right is subject to all equities and defenses of the buyer against the seller, notwithstanding an agreement to the contrary, but the assignee's liability may not exceed the amount of the debt owing to the assignee at the time of the assignment.

(b) The assignee shall have recourse against the seller to the extent of any liability incurred by the assignee pursuant to this section regardless of whether the assignment was with or without recourse. (Added by Stats.1961, c. 1626, p. 3539, § 4, eff. Jan. 1, 1962. Amended by Stats.1965, c. 327, p. 1436, § 1; Stats.1971, c. 999, p. 1917, § 2; Stats.1975, c. 66, p. 129, § 2.)

§ 2983.6. Violations; offense

Any person who shall willfully violate any provision of this chapter shall be guilty of a misdemeanor. (Added by Stats.1968, c. 1338, p. 2558, § 3.)

Cross References
Correction of contract to comply with chapter, see Civil Code § 2984.
Misdemeanor,
    Defined, see Penal Code § 17.
    Punishment, see Penal Code §§ 19, 19.2.

§ 2983.7. Prohibition of certain provisions

No conditional sale contract shall contain any provision by which:

(a) The buyer agrees not to assert against the seller a claim or defense arising out of the sale or agrees not to assert against an assignee such a claim or defense.

(b) A power of attorney is given to confess judgment in this state, or an assignment of wages is given; provided, that nothing herein contained shall prohibit the giving of an assignment of wages contained in a separate instrument pursuant to Section 300 of the Labor Code.

(c) The buyer waives any right of action against the seller or holder of the contract or other person acting on his behalf, for any illegal act committed in the collection of payments under the contract or in the repossession of the motor vehicle.

(d) The buyer executes a power of attorney appointing the seller or holder of the contract, or other person acting on his behalf, as the buyer's agent in the collection of payments under the contract or in the repossession of the motor vehicle.

(e) The buyer relieves the seller from liability for any legal remedies which the buyer may have against the seller under the contract or any separate instrument executed in connection therewith.

(f) The seller or holder of the contract is given the right to commence action on a contract under the provisions of this chapter in a county other than the county in which the contract was in fact signed by the buyer, the county in which the buyer resides at the commencement of the action, the county in which the buyer resided at the time the contract was entered into, or in the county in which the motor vehicle purchased pursuant to such contract is permanently garaged. (Added by Stats.1968, c. 1288, p. 2428, § 1.)

§ 2983.8. Deficiency judgment on conditional sale contract for mobilehome or motor vehicle

Notwithstanding Section 2983.2 or any other provision of law, no deficiency judgment shall lie in any event in any of the following instances:

(a) After any sale of any mobilehome for which a permit is required pursuant to Section 35780 or 35790 of the Vehicle Code for failure of the purchaser to complete his or her conditional sale contract given to the seller to secure payment of the balance of the purchase price of such mobilehome. The provisions of this subdivision shall not apply in the event there is substantial damage to the mobilehome other than wear and tear from normal usage. This subdivision shall apply only to contracts entered into on or after the effective date of the act that enacted this subdivision and before July 1, 1981.

(b) After any sale or other disposition of a motor vehicle unless the court has determined that the sale or other disposition was in conformity with the provisions of this chapter and the relevant provisions of Division 9 (commencing with Section 9101) of the Commercial Code, including Sections 9610, 9611, 9612, 9613, 9614, 9615, and 9626. The determination may be made upon an affidavit unless the court requires a hearing in the particular case. *(Added by Stats.1972, c. 1001, p. 1829, § 3. Amended by Stats.1980, c. 1149, p. 3738, § 10; Stats.1984, c. 1376, § 1; Stats.1999, c. 991 (S.B.45), § 8, operative July 1, 2001.)*

§ 2984. Correction of contract to comply with chapter

Any failure to comply with any provision of this chapter (commencing with Section 2981) may be corrected by the holder, provided, however, that a willful violation may not be corrected unless it is a violation appearing on the face of the contract and is corrected within 30 days of the execution of the contract or within 20 days of its sale, assignment or pledge, whichever is later, provided that the 20-day period shall commence with the initial sale, assignment or pledge of the contract, and provided that any other violation appearing on the face of the contract may be corrected only within such time periods. A correction which will increase the amount of the contract balance or the amount of any installment as such amounts appear on the conditional sale contract shall not be effective unless the buyer concurs in writing to the correction. If notified in writing by the buyer of such a failure to comply with any provision of this chapter, the correction shall be made within 10 days of notice. Where any provision of a conditional sale contract fails to comply with any provision of this chapter, the correction shall be made by mailing or delivering a corrected copy of the contract to the buyer. Any amount improperly collected by the holder from the buyer shall be credited against the indebtedness evidenced by the contract or returned to the buyer. A violation corrected as provided in this section shall not be the basis of any recovery by the buyer or affect the enforceability of the contract by the holder and shall not be deemed to be a substantive change in the agreement of the parties. *(Added by Stats.1961, c. 1626, p. 3539, § 4, eff. Jan. 1, 1962. Amended by Stats.1963, c. 838, p. 2037, § 1.)*

§ 2984.1. Contract provision regarding insurance coverage

Every conditional sale contract shall contain a statement in contrasting red print in at least 8–point bold type which shall satisfy the requirements of Section 5604 of the Vehicle Code and be signed or initialed by the buyer, as follows:

THE MINIMUM PUBLIC LIABILITY INSURANCE LIMITS PROVIDED IN LAW MUST BE MET BY EVERY PERSON WHO PURCHASES A VEHICLE. IF YOU ARE UNSURE WHETHER OR NOT YOUR CURRENT INSURANCE POLICY WILL COVER YOUR NEWLY ACQUIRED VEHICLE IN THE EVENT OF AN ACCIDENT, YOU SHOULD CONTACT YOUR INSURANCE AGENT.
WARNING:
YOUR PRESENT POLICY MAY NOT COVER COLLISION DAMAGE OR MAY NOT PROVIDE FOR FULL REPLACEMENT COSTS FOR THE VEHICLE BEING PURCHASED. IF YOU DO NOT HAVE FULL COVERAGE, SUPPLEMENTAL COVERAGE FOR COLLISION DAMAGE MAY BE AVAILABLE TO YOU THROUGH YOUR INSURANCE AGENT OR THROUGH THE SELLING DEALER. HOWEVER, UNLESS OTHERWISE SPECIFIED, THE COVERAGE YOU OBTAIN THROUGH THE DEALER PROTECTS ONLY THE DEALER, USUALLY UP TO THE AMOUNT OF THE UNPAID BALANCE REMAINING AFTER THE VEHICLE HAS BEEN REPOSSESSED AND SOLD.
FOR ADVICE ON FULL COVERAGE THAT WILL PROTECT YOU IN THE EVENT OF LOSS OR DAMAGE TO YOUR VEHICLE, YOU SHOULD CONTACT YOUR INSURANCE AGENT.
THE BUYER SHALL SIGN TO ACKNOWLEDGE THAT HE/SHE UNDERSTANDS THESE PUBLIC LIABILITY TERMS AND CONDITIONS.
S/S _____.

No person shall print for use as a sales contract form, any form which does not comply with this section. *(Added by Stats.1961, c. 1626, p. 3540, § 4, eff. Jan. 1, 1962. Amended by Stats.1965, c. 666, p. 2042, § 1; Stats.1974, c. 577, p. 1396, § 1; Stats.1988, c. 177, § 1.)*

§ 2984.2. Provision for title to or lien upon other property prohibited; exceptions

(a) No conditional sale contract, and no agreement between a seller and a buyer made in connection with a conditional sale contract, may provide for the inclusion of title to or a lien upon any property other than the following:

(1) The motor vehicle which is the subject matter of the sale, including any replacement of that motor vehicle, or accessories, accessions, or replacement of those accessories or accessions, or proceeds thereof.

(2) The proceeds of any insurance policies covering the motor vehicle which are required by the seller or the returned premiums of any such policies if the premiums for such policies are included in the amount financed.

(3) The proceeds of any credit insurance policies which the buyer purchases in connection with the motor vehicle conditional sale contract or the returned premiums of any such policies if the premiums for such policies are included in the amount financed.

(4) The proceeds and returned price of any service contract if the cost of such contract is included in the amount financed.

(b) Subdivision (a) shall not apply to any agreement which meets the requirements of subdivision (b) of Section 2982.5 and otherwise complies with this chapter, nor, with respect to a mobilehome sold prior to July 1, 1981, to any agreement whereby a security interest is taken in real property on which the mobilehome is installed on a foundation system pursuant to Section 18551 of the Health and Safety Code.

(c) A provision in violation of this section shall be void. *(Added by Stats.1980, c. 1380, p. 5040, § 26, eff. Oct. 1, 1980. Amended by Stats.1981, c. 134, p. 912, § 6, eff. July 1, 1981, operative July 1, 1981; Stats.1981, c. 1075, p. 4133, § 20, operative Oct. 1, 1982; Stats.1987, c. 1043, § 1.)*

§ 2984.3. Buyer's acknowledgment of delivery of copy of contract; presumptions

Cross References

Similar provision applicable to leases of motor vehicles, see Civil Code § 2986.6.

§ 2984.3. Buyer's acknowledgment of delivery of copy of contract; presumptions

Any acknowledgment by the buyer of delivery of a copy of a conditional sale contract or purchase order and any vehicle purchase proposal and any credit statement that the seller has required or requested the buyer to sign, and that he or she has signed, during the contract negotiations, shall be printed or written in size equal to at least 10-point boldface type and, if contained in the contract, shall appear directly above the space reserved for the buyer's signature or adjacent to any other notices required by law to be placed immediately above the signature space. The buyer's written acknowledgment, conforming to the requirements of this section, of delivery of a completely filled-in copy of the contract, and a copy of the other documents shall be a rebuttable presumption of delivery in any action or proceeding by or against a third party without knowledge to the contrary when he or she acquired his or her interest in the contract. If the third party furnishes the buyer a copy of the documents, or a notice containing the disclosures identified in subdivision (a) of Section 2982, and stating that the buyer shall notify the third party in writing within 30 days if a copy of the documents was not furnished, and that notification is not given, it shall be conclusively presumed in favor of the third party that copies of the documents were furnished as required by this chapter. *(Added by Stats.1961, c. 1626, p. 3540, § 4, eff. Jan. 1, 1962. Amended by Stats.1970, c. 1003, p. 1805, § 5; Stats.1979, c. 805, p. 2795, § 25; Stats.1980, c. 1149, p. 3739, § 12; Stats.1993, c. 1092 (A.B.431), § 3, operative July 1, 1994; Stats.1994, c. 146 (A.B.3601), § 15.)*

Cross References

Conclusive presumptions, see Evidence Code § 620 et seq.
Rebuttable presumptions, see Evidence Code § 601 et seq.

§ 2984.4. Actions on contract or purchase order; venue

(a) An action on a contract or purchase order under this chapter shall be tried in the superior court in the county where the contract or purchase order was in fact signed by the buyer, where the buyer resided at the time the contract or purchase order was entered into, where the buyer resides at the commencement of the action, or where the motor vehicle purchased pursuant to the contract or purchase order is permanently garaged.

In any action involving multiple claims, or causes of action, venue shall lie in those courts if there is at least one claim or cause of action arising from a contract subject to this chapter.

(b) In the superior court designated as the proper court in subdivision (a), the proper court location for trial of an action under this chapter is the location where the court tries that type of action that is nearest or most accessible to where the contract, conditional sale contract, or purchase order was in fact signed by the buyer, where the buyer resided at the time the contract, conditional sale contract, or purchase order was entered into, where the buyer resides at the commencement of the action, or where the motor vehicle purchased pursuant to the contract is permanently garaged. Otherwise, any location of the superior court designated as the proper superior court in subdivision (a) is the proper court location for the trial of the action. The court may specify by local rule the nearest or most accessible court location where the court tries that type of case.

(c) In any action subject to this section, concurrently with the filing of the complaint, the plaintiff shall file an affidavit stating facts showing that the action has been commenced in a superior court and court location described in this section as a proper place for the trial of the action. Those facts may be stated in a verified complaint and shall not be stated on information or belief. When that affidavit is filed with the complaint, a copy shall be served with the summons. If a plaintiff fails to file the affidavit or state facts in a verified complaint required by this section, no further proceedings may occur, but the court shall, upon its own motion or upon motion of any party, dismiss the action without prejudice. The court may, on terms that are just, permit the affidavit to be filed subsequent to the filing of the complaint and a copy of the affidavit shall be served on the defendant. The time to answer or otherwise plead shall date from that service. *(Added by Stats.1969, c. 724, p. 1455, § 1. Amended by Stats.1970, c. 725, p. 1325, § 2; Stats.1971, c. 1529, p. 3021, § 2; Stats.1974, c. 1516, p. 3335, § 3, operative Jan. 1, 1977; Stats.1976, c. 1285, p. 5736, § 6; Stats.1998, c. 931 (S.B.2139), § 17, eff. Sept. 28, 1998; Stats.2002, c. 806 (A.B.3027), § 2.)*

§ 2984.5. Conditional sales contracts; maintenance of documents by seller

(a) A seller shall maintain the following documents for at least seven years or the length of the conditional sales contract, whichever is longer:

(1) A copy of each buyer's conditional sales contract.

(2) Any documents relied upon by the seller to determine a buyer's creditworthiness, including, but not limited to, any consumer credit report, as defined in Section 1785.3, or any other document containing a buyer's credit score, as defined in Section 1785.15.1.

(3) If the conditional sales contract is sold, assigned, or otherwise transferred, a copy of the terms of that sale, assignment, or transfer.

(b) A seller that unlawfully fails to comply with a court order to produce the documents described in subdivision (a) shall be liable in an action brought by the Attorney General for a civil penalty of five thousand dollars ($5,000) per violation. The penalties provided by this section are in addition to all rights and remedies that are otherwise available under law. *(Added by Stats.2003, c. 59 (S.B.508), § 1.)*

§ 2984.6. Repossession of vehicle connected with incident of violence notice; notice to subsequent assignee

A holder of a conditional sales contract, purchase order, or security interest, or the agent of a holder, who has received a notice pursuant to Section 7507.6 of the Business and Professions Code, shall not make a subsequent assignment to skip trace, locate, or repossess the vehicle without simultaneously, and in the same manner by which the assignment is given, advising the assignee of the assignment of the information contained in the notice. As used in this section, "assignment" has the same meaning set forth in Section 7500.1 of the Business and Professions Code. *(Added by Stats.2007, c. 192 (S.B.659), § 4, eff. Sept. 7, 2007.)*

CHAPTER 2C. REAL PROPERTY SALES CONTRACTS

Section
2985. Definition.
2985.1. Transferability.
2985.2. Encumbering realty sold under unrecorded sales contract in amount exceeding amount due under contract without consent; misdemeanor.
2985.3. Appropriation by seller of payment by buyer when payment by seller on obligation secured by encumbrance on realty due; misdemeanor.
2985.4. Holding pro rata payments for insurance and taxes in trust; applicability of section.
2985.5. Required contents of sales contracts; number of years required to complete payments; basis for tax estimate.
2985.51. Divisions of real property; statement of compliance with Subdivision Map Act; violations; remedies of vendee; misdemeanor.
2985.6. Prepayment of balance due on real property sales contracts; effect of waiver of provisions.

Cross References

Equipment, conditions of contract, see Vehicle Code § 24010.
Notification of insurance coverage by dealer or lending agency, see Vehicle Code § 5604.

§ 2985. Definition

(a) A real property sales contract is an agreement in which one party agrees to convey title to real property to another party upon the satisfaction of specified conditions set forth in the contract and that does not require conveyance of title within one year from the date of formation of the contract.

(b) For purposes of this chapter only, a real property sales contract does not include a contract for purchase of an attached residential condominium unit entered into pursuant to a conditional public report issued by the Bureau of Real Estate pursuant to Section 11018.12 of the Business and Professions Code. *(Added by Stats.1961, c. 886, p. 2343, § 30. Amended by Stats.1963, c. 560, p. 1442, § 6; Stats.2006, c. 51 (S.B.504), § 1, eff. June 30, 2006; Stats.2013, c. 352 (A.B. 1317), § 53, eff. Sept. 26, 2013, operative July 1, 2013.)*

Cross References

Common interest developments, sale or title transfer, provision of specified items to prospective purchasers, see Civil Code § 4525.
Duty to prospective purchasers, see Civil Code § 2079.1.
Real property sales contract defined, see Business and Professions Code § 10029.

§ 2985.1. Transferability

A real property sales contract may not be transferred by the fee owner of the real property unless accompanied by a transfer of the real property which is the subject of the contract, and real property may not be transferred by the fee owner thereof unless accompanied by an assignment of the contract.

Nothing herein shall be deemed to prohibit the assignment or pledge of a real property sales contract, as security or for the purpose of effecting collection thereon, to the holder of a first lien on the real property which is the subject of the contract without a transfer of the real property or the transfer of a fee title in trust without the concurrent assignment of the sales contract. *(Added by Stats.1961, c. 886, p. 2344, § 30, eff. June 28, 1961. Amended by Stats.1963, c. 71, p. 699, § 1.)*

Cross References

Transfer of real property, see Civil Code § 1091 et seq.

§ 2985.2. Encumbering realty sold under unrecorded sales contract in amount exceeding amount due under contract without consent; misdemeanor

Any person, or the assignee of such person, who sells a parcel of land under a sales contract which is not recorded and who thereafter causes an encumbrance or encumbrances not consented to in writing by the parties upon such property in an amount which, together with existing encumbrances thereon exceeds the amount then due under the contract, or under which the aggregate amount of any periodic payments exceeds the periodic payments due on the contract, excluding any pro rata amount for insurance and taxes, shall be guilty of a public offense punishable by a fine not exceeding ten thousand dollars ($10,000), or by imprisonment pursuant to subdivision (h) of Section 1170 of the Penal Code, or in a county jail not exceeding one year, or by both that fine and imprisonment. *(Added by Stats.1963, c. 560, p. 1441, § 3. Amended by Stats.1976, c. 1139, p. 5064, § 7, operative July 1, 1977; Stats.1983, c. 1092, § 69, eff. Sept. 27, 1983, operative Jan. 1, 1984; Stats.2011, c. 15 (A.B.109), § 36, eff. April 4, 2011, operative Oct. 1, 2011.)*

§ 2985.3. Appropriation by seller of payment by buyer when payment by seller on obligation secured by encumbrance on realty due; misdemeanor

Every seller of improved or unimproved real property under a real property sales contract, or his assignee, who knowingly receives an installment payment from the buyer under a real property sales contract at a time when there is then due any payment by the seller, or his assignee, on an obligation secured by an encumbrance on the property subject to the real property sales contract, and who appropriates such payment received from the buyer to a use other than payment of the amount then due on the seller's or assignee's obligation, except to the extent the payment received from the buyer exceeds the amount due from the seller or assignee, is guilty of a public offense punishable by a fine not exceeding ten thousand dollars ($10,000), or by imprisonment pursuant to subdivision (h) of Section 1170 of the Penal Code, or in a county jail not exceeding one year, or by both that fine and imprisonment. *(Added by Stats.1963, c. 560, p. 1442, § 4. Amended by Stats.1976, c. 1139, p. 5064, § 8, operative July 1, 1977; Stats.1983, c. 1092, § 70, eff. Sept. 27, 1983, operative Jan. 1, 1984; Stats.2011, c. 15 (A.B.109), § 37, eff. April 4, 2011, operative Oct. 1, 2011.)*

Cross References

Penalty for violation of this section, see Penal Code § 506b.

§ 2985.4. Holding pro rata payments for insurance and taxes in trust; applicability of section

Every seller of improved or unimproved real property under a real property sales contract who receives pro rata

§ 2985.4

payments for insurance and taxes shall hold these amounts in trust for the purpose designated. These amounts shall not be disbursed for any other purpose without the consent of the payor and any person or corporation holding an encumbrance on the property.

This section shall not apply to a state- or federal-supervised assignee of a seller who as agent for the seller receives and disburses payments. *(Added by Stats.1963, c. 560, p. 1442, § 5.)*

Cross References

Penalty for violation of this section, see Penal Code § 506b.

§ 2985.5. Required contents of sales contracts; number of years required to complete payments; basis for tax estimate

Every real property sales contract entered into after January 1, 1966, shall contain a statement of:

(a) The number of years required to complete payment in accordance with the terms of the contract.

(b) The basis upon which the tax estimate is made. *(Added by Stats.1965, c. 1214, p. 3034, § 1.)*

§ 2985.51. Divisions of real property; statement of compliance with Subdivision Map Act; violations; remedies of vendee; misdemeanor

(a) Every real property sales contract entered into on and after January 1, 1978, where the real property that is the subject of such contract resulted from a division of real property occurring on or after January 1, 1978, shall contain or have attached thereto a statement indicating the fact that the division creating the parcel or parcels to be conveyed:

(1) Was made in compliance with the provisions of the Subdivision Map Act, Division 2 (commencing with Section 66410) of Title 7 of the Government Code and local ordinances adopted pursuant thereto, and in such event the statement shall expressly refer to the location, in the records of the county recorder for the county in which the real property is located, of a previously recorded certificate of compliance or conditional certificate of compliance issued pursuant to Section 66499.35 of the Government Code with respect to the real property being sold, or the statement shall describe the real property to be conveyed as an entire lot or parcel by referencing the recorded final or parcel map creating the parcel or parcels to be conveyed and such description shall constitute a certificate of compliance as set forth in subdivision (d) of Section 66499.35 of the Government Code. Provided, however, where reference is made to a recorded parcel map and the approval of such map was conditioned upon the construction of specified offsite and onsite improvements as a precondition to the issuance of a permit or grant of approval for the development of such parcel and the construction of the improvements has not been completed as of the date of execution of the real property sales contract, then the statement shall expressly set forth all such required offsite and onsite improvements; or

(2) Was exempt from the provisions of the Subdivision Map Act and local ordinances adopted pursuant thereto, and in such event the statement shall expressly set forth the basis for such exemption; or

(3) Was the subject of a waiver of the provisions of the Subdivision Map Act and local ordinances adopted pursuant thereto, and in such event the contract shall have attached thereto a copy of the document issued by the local agency granting the waiver. Provided, however, where the granting of the waiver was conditioned upon the construction of specified offsite and onsite improvements as a precondition to the issuance of a permit or grant of approval for the development of the parcel and the construction of the improvements has not been completed as of the date of execution of the real property sales contract, then such statement shall expressly set forth all such required offsite and onsite improvements; or

(4) Was not subject to the provisions of the Subdivision Map Act and local ordinances adopted pursuant thereto, and in such event the statement shall expressly set forth the basis for the nonapplicability of the Subdivision Map Act to the division.

(b) Every real property sales contract entered into after January 1, 1978, where the real property that is the subject of such contract resulted from a division of real property occurring prior to January 1, 1978, shall:

(1) Contain or have attached thereto a signed statement by the vendor that the parcel or parcels which are the subject of the contract have been created in compliance with, or a waiver has been granted with respect to, the provisions of the Subdivision Map Act, Division 2 (commencing with Section 66410) of Title 7 of the Government Code and local ordinances adopted pursuant thereto, or any prior law regulating the division of land, or, were exempt from or not otherwise subject to any such law at the time of their creation. Provided, however, where the division creating the parcel or parcels being conveyed was by means of a parcel map, or in the event that a waiver of the provisions of the Subdivision Map Act has been granted, and the approval of the parcel map or the granting of the waiver was conditioned upon the construction of specified offsite and onsite improvements as a precondition to the issuance of a permit or grant of approval for the development of such parcel and the construction of the improvements has not been completed as of the date of execution of the real property sales contract, then such contract shall expressly set forth all such required offsite and onsite improvements.

(2) In lieu of the above, the vendor may include in the real property sales contract a description of the real property being conveyed as an entire lot or parcel by referencing the recorded final or parcel map creating the parcel or parcels being conveyed and such description shall constitute a certificate of compliance as set forth in subdivision (d) of Section 66499.35 of the Government Code. Provided, however, where reference is made to a recorded parcel map, or in the event that a waiver of the provisions of the Subdivision Map Act has been granted, and the approval of the parcel map or the granting of the waiver was conditioned upon the construction of specified offsite and onsite improvements as a precondition to the issuance of a permit or grant of approval for the development of such parcel and the construction of the improvements has not been completed as of the date of execution of the real property sales contract, then such contract shall expressly set forth all such required offsite and onsite improvements.

(3) Notwithstanding paragraphs (1) and (2), in the event that the parcel or parcels which are the subject of the real property sales contract were not created in compliance with the provisions of the Subdivision Map Act, Division 2 (commencing with Section 66410) of Title 7 of the Government Code and local ordinances adopted pursuant thereto, or any other prior law regulating the division of land, and were not exempt from, or were otherwise subject to any such law at the time of their creation, the real property sales contract shall contain a statement signed by the vendor and vendee acknowledging such fact. In addition, the vendor shall attach to the real property sales contract a conditional certificate of compliance issued pursuant to Section 66499.35 of the Government Code.

(c) In the event that the parcel or parcels which are the subject of the real property sales contract are found not to have been created in compliance with, or a waiver has not been granted with respect to, the provisions of the Subdivision Map Act, Division 2 (commencing with Section 66410) of Title 7 of the Government Code, or any other prior law regulating the division of land nor to be exempt from, or otherwise subject to such laws and the vendee has reasonably relied upon the statement of such compliance or exemption made by the vendor, or in the event that the vendor has failed to provide the conditional certificate of compliance as required by paragraph (3) of subdivision (b), and the vendor knew or should have known of the fact of such noncompliance, or lack of exemption, or the failure to provide the conditional certificate of compliance, the vendee, or his successor in interest, shall be entitled to: (1) recover from the vendor or his assigns the amount of all costs incurred by the vendee or his successor in interest in complying with all conditions imposed pursuant to Section 66499.35 of the Government Code; or, (2) the real property sales contract, at the sole option of the vendee, or his successor in interest, shall be voidable and in such event the vendee or his successor in interest shall be entitled to damages from the vendor or his assigns. For purposes of this section, damages shall mean all amounts paid under the real estate sales contract with interest thereon at the rate of 9 percent per annum, and in addition thereto a civil penalty in the amount of five hundred dollars ($500) plus attorney's fees and costs. Any action to enforce the rights of a vendee or his successor in interest shall be commenced within one year of the date of discovery of the failure to comply with the provisions of this section.

(d) Any vendor who willfully violates the provisions of subdivision (a) of this section by knowingly providing a vendee with a false statement of compliance with, exemption from, waiver of, or nonapplicability of, the provisions of the Subdivision Map Act, with respect to the real property that is the subject of the real property sales contract, shall be guilty of a misdemeanor punishable by a fine of not to exceed one thousand dollars ($1,000), or imprisonment for not to exceed six months, or both such fine and imprisonment.

(e) For purposes of this section a real property sales contract is an agreement wherein one party agrees to convey title to unimproved real property to another party upon the satisfaction of specified conditions set forth in the contract and which does not require conveyance of title within one year from the date of formation of the contract. Unimproved real property means real property upon which no permanent structure intended for human occupancy or commercial use is located.

(f) The provisions of this section shall not apply to a real property sales contract which, by its terms, requires either a good faith downpayment and a single payment of the balance of the purchase price or a single payment of the purchase price upon completion of the contract, and the provisions of such contract do not require periodic payment of principal or interest. *(Added by Stats.1977, c. 1228, p. 4125, § 1.)*

§ 2985.6. Prepayment of balance due on real property sales contracts; effect of waiver of provisions

(a) A buyer shall be entitled to prepay all or any part of the balance due on any real property sales contract with respect to the sale of land which has been subdivided into a residential lot or lots which contain a dwelling for not more than four families entered into on or after January 1, 1969; provided, however, that the seller, by an agreement in writing with the buyer, may prohibit prepayment for up to a 12-month period following the sale.

(b) Any waiver by the buyer of the provisions of this section shall be deemed contrary to public policy and shall be unenforceable and void; provided, however, that any such waiver shall in no way affect the validity of the remainder of the contract. *(Added by Stats.1968, c. 437, p. 1041, § 1. Amended by Stats.1969, c. 399, p. 930, § 1; Stats.1978, c. 565, p. 1739, § 1.)*

CHAPTER 2D. VEHICLE LEASING ACT

Section
2985.7.	Definitions.
2985.71.	Solicitation including statement concerning payments; contents; restriction; violation; liability.
2985.8.	Lease contract; requirements; contents.
2985.81.	Repealed.
2985.9.	Documents and agreements not required in a lease contract.
2985.91 to 2985.93.	Repealed.
2986.	Repealed.
2986.2.	Repealed.
2986.3.	Prohibited provisions.
2986.4.	Delivery of copy of lease contract, purchase order, lease proposal and credit statement; acknowledgment; effect; failure to notify third party of nondelivery.
2986.5.	Used motor vehicle; requirements for lease; excess charges for licensing or transfer of title; return to lessee.
2986.6.	Agreement for inclusion of other property as security; unenforceability.
2986.10.	Assignee of lessor; rights and liabilities.
2986.12.	Rebate, discount, etc. for information or assistance in lease or sale of motor vehicle; prohibition.
2986.13.	Payment pending execution of lease contract; refund upon nonexecution; exceptions; remedies.
2987.	Lessee's right to early termination of lease contract; conditions; notice.
2988.	Legislative findings; liability of lessee on expiration of lease based on estimated residual value; reasonableness; rebuttable presumption.
2988.5.	Failure to comply with requirements of §§ 2985.8, 2988; liability; failure to disclose information

Section	
	required by chapter; multiple offenses; limitation of actions.
2988.7.	Failure to comply with § 2985.8; rescission of contract.
2988.9.	Award of reasonable attorney's fees and costs.
2989.	Preemption of civil action; federal civil action on same facts.
2989.2.	Fair market value at expiration of lease; depreciation; method of establishment; notice of intent to sell motor vehicle; service on lessee; exception; contents.
2989.4.	Lessor; prohibited acts; nonliability for violations.
2989.5.	Records; availability to Department of Motor Vehicles; affidavit; court order; financial institution; report to supervising agency; report of action taken.
2989.6.	Rules and regulations.
2989.8.	Violations; misdemeanor.
2990.	Inapplicability of chapter to transaction regulated by Automobile Sales Finance Act.
2991.	Forms; Spanish language translations.
2992.	Preprinted lease contract; design requirements and contents.
2993.	Repossession of vehicle connected with incident of violence notice; notice to subsequent assignee.
2994.	Repealed.

Cross References

Automobile Sales Finance Act, see Civil Code § 2981 et seq.
Buy-here-pay-here dealer defined, see Vehicle Code §§ 241, 241.1.
Records of rental, see Vehicle Code § 14609.
Spanish language translation of contracts or agreements, necessity, exceptions, see Civil Code § 1632.
Unlawful subleasing of motor vehicles, see Penal Code § 570 et seq.

§ 2985.7. Definitions

(a) "Motor vehicle" means any vehicle required to be registered under the Vehicle Code. Motor vehicle does not include any trailer which is sold in conjunction with a vessel.

(b) "Lessor" includes "bailor" and is a person who is engaged in the business of leasing, offering to lease or arranging the lease of a motor vehicle under a lease contract.

For the purpose of this subdivision, "person" means an individual, partnership, corporation, limited liability company, estate, trust, cooperative, association or any other legal entity.

(c) "Lessee" includes "bailee" and is a natural person who leases, offers to lease or is offered the lease of a motor vehicle under a lease contract.

(d) "Lease contract" means any contract for or in contemplation of the lease or bailment for the use of a motor vehicle, and the purchase of services incidental thereto, by a natural person for a term exceeding four months, primarily for personal, family or household purposes, whether or not it is agreed that the lessee bear the risk of the motor vehicle's depreciation. Lease contract does not include a lease for agricultural, business or commercial purposes, or to a government or governmental agency or instrumentality.

(e) "Regulation M" means any rule, regulation, or interpretation promulgated by the Board of Governors of the Federal Reserve System under the federal Consumer Leasing Act (15 U.S.C. Secs. 1667–1667e), and any interpretation or approval issued by an official or employee of the Federal Reserve System duly authorized by the board to issue such interpretations or approvals.

(f) "Constant yield method" means the following:

(1) In the case of a periodic payment lease, the method of determining the rent charge portion of each base payment in which the rent charge for each computational period is earned in advance by multiplying the constant rate implicit in the lease contract times the balance subject to rent charge as it declines during the scheduled lease term. At any time during the scheduled term of a periodic payment lease, the balance subject to rent charge is the difference between the adjusted capitalized cost and the sum of (A) all depreciation and other amortized amounts accrued during the preceding computational periods and (B) the first base periodic payment.

(2) In the case of a single payment lease, the method of determining the periodic earning of rent charges in which the rent charge for each computational period is earned in advance by multiplying the constant rate implicit in the lease contract times the balance subject to rent charge as it increases during the scheduled lease term. At any time during the scheduled term of a single payment lease, the balance subject to rent charge is determined by subtracting from the residual value the total rent charge scheduled to be earned over the term of the lease contract and adding to the difference all rent charges accrued during the preceding computational periods.

(3) Periodic rent charge calculations are based on the assumption that the lessor will receive the lease payments on their exact due dates and that the lease does not end before its scheduled termination date. *(Added by Stats.1976, c. 1284, p. 5700, § 2, operative March 23, 1977. Amended by Stats. 1984, c. 1114, § 4; Stats.1994, c. 1010 (S.B.2053), § 51; Stats.1997, c. 800 (S.B.1291), § 3.)*

Cross References

Buy-here-pay-here dealer defined, see Vehicle Code §§ 241, 241.1.

§ 2985.71. Solicitation including statement concerning payments; contents; restriction; violation; liability

(a) Any solicitation to enter into a lease contract that includes any of the following items shall contain the disclosures described in subdivision (b):

(1) The amount of any payment.

(2) A statement of any capitalized cost reduction or other payment required prior to or at consummation or by delivery, if delivery occurs after consummation.

(3) A statement that no capitalized cost reduction or other payment is required prior to or at consummation or by delivery, if delivery occurs after consummation.

(b) A solicitation to enter into a lease contract that includes any item listed in subdivision (a) shall also clearly and conspicuously state all of the following items:

(1) All of the disclosures prescribed by Regulation M set forth in the manner required or permitted by Regulation M, whether or not Regulation M applies to the transaction.

(2) The mileage limit after which mileage charges may accrue and the charge per mile for mileage in excess of the stated mileage limit.

(3) The statement "Plus tax and license" or a substantially similar statement, if amounts due for use tax, license fees, and registration fees are not included in the payments.

(c) No solicitation to aid, promote, or assist directly or indirectly any lease contract may state that a specific lease of any motor vehicle at specific amounts or terms is available unless the lessor usually and customarily leases or will lease that motor vehicle at those amounts or terms.

(d) A failure to comply with the provisions of this section shall not affect the validity of the leasing contract. No owner or employee of any entity, other than the lessor, that serves as a medium in which a lease solicitation appears or through which a lease solicitation is disseminated, shall be liable under this section. *(Added by Stats.1997, c. 800 (S.B.1291), § 5.)*

§ 2985.8. Lease contract; requirements; contents

(a) A lease contract shall be in writing, and the print portion of the contract shall be printed in at least 8–point type and shall contain in a single document all of the agreements of the lessor and lessee with respect to the obligations of each party.

(b) At the top of the lease contract, a title that contains the words "LEASE CONTRACT" or "LEASE AGREEMENT" shall appear in at least 12–point boldface type.

(c) A lease contract shall disclose all of the following:

(1) All of the information prescribed by Regulation M set forth in the manner required or permitted by Regulation M, whether or not Regulation M applies to the transaction.

(2) A separate statement labeled "Itemization of Gross Capitalized Cost" that shall appear immediately following or directly adjacent to the disclosures required to be segregated by Regulation M. The Itemization of Gross Capitalized Cost shall include all of the following and shall be circumscribed by a line:

(A) The agreed-upon value of the vehicle as equipped at the time of signing the lease.

(B) The agreed-upon value and a description of each accessory and item of optional equipment the lessor agrees to add to the vehicle after signing the lease.

(C) The premium for each policy of insurance.

(D) The amount charged for each service contract.

(E) Any charge for an optional debt cancellation agreement.

(F) Any outstanding prior credit or lease balance.

(G) An itemization by type and agreed-upon value of each good or service included in the gross capitalized cost other than those items included in the disclosures required in subparagraphs (A) to (F), inclusive.

(3) The vehicle identification number of the leased vehicle.

(4) A brief description of each vehicle or other property being traded in and the agreed-upon value of the vehicle or property if the amount due at the time of signing the lease or upon delivery is paid in whole or in part with a net trade-in allowance or the "Itemization of Gross Capitalized Cost" includes any portion of the outstanding prior credit or lease balance from the trade-in property.

(5) The charge, if any, to be retained by the lessor for document processing authorized pursuant to Section 4456.5 of the Vehicle Code, which may not be represented as a governmental fee.

(6) The charge, if any, to electronically register or transfer the vehicle authorized pursuant to Section 4456.5 of the Vehicle Code, which shall not be represented as a governmental fee.

(d) A lease contract shall contain, in at least 8–point boldface type, above the space provided for the lessee's signature and circumscribed by a line, the following notice: "(1) Do not sign this lease before you read it or if it contains any blank spaces to be filled in; (2) You are entitled to a completely filled in copy of this lease; (3) Warning—Unless a charge is included in this lease for public liability or property damage insurance, payment for that coverage is not provided by this lease."

(e) A lease contract shall contain, in at least 8–point boldface type, on the first page of the contract and circumscribed by a line, the following notice:

"THERE IS NO COOLING OFF PERIOD

California law does not provide for a "cooling off" or other cancellation period for vehicle leases. Therefore, you cannot later cancel this lease simply because you change your mind, decided the vehicle costs too much, or wish you had acquired a different vehicle. You may cancel this lease only with the agreement of the lessor or for legal cause, such as fraud."

(f) A lease contract shall contain, in at least 8–point boldface type, the following notice: "You have the right to return the vehicle, and receive a refund of any payments made if the credit application is not approved, unless nonapproval results from an incomplete application or from incorrect information provided by you."

(g) The lease contract shall be signed by the lessor and lessee, or their authorized representatives, and an exact copy of the fully executed lease contract shall be provided to the lessee at the time of signing.

(h) A motor vehicle shall not be delivered under a lease contract subject to this chapter until the lessor provides to the lessee a fully executed copy of the lease contract.

(i) The lessor shall not obtain the signature of the lessee to a contract when it contains blank spaces to be filled in after it has been signed.

(j) If the lease contract contains a provision that holds the lessee liable for the difference between (1) the adjusted capitalized cost disclosed in the lease contract reduced by the amounts described in subparagraph (A) of paragraph (5) of subdivision (b) of Section 2987 and (2) the settlement proceeds of the lessee's required insurance and deductible in the event of theft or damage to the vehicle that results in a total loss, the lease contract shall contain the following notice in at least 8–point boldface type on the first page of the contract:

§ 2985.8

"GAP LIABILITY NOTICE

In the event of theft or damage to the vehicle that results in a total loss, there may be a GAP between the amount due upon early termination and the proceeds of your insurance settlement and deductible. THIS LEASE PROVIDES THAT YOU ARE LIABLE FOR THE GAP AMOUNT. Optional coverage for the GAP amount may be offered for an additional price."

(k) This section shall become operative on July 1, 2012. *(Added by Stats.2011, c. 329 (A.B.1215), § 6, operative July 1, 2012.)*

§ 2985.81. Repealed by Stats.1976, c. 1284, p. 5700, § 1, operative March 23, 1977

§ 2985.9. Documents and agreements not required in a lease contract

The following documents and agreements are not required to be contained in a lease contract:

(a) An "express warranty," as that term is defined in paragraph (1) of subdivision (a) of Section 1791.2, whether it relates to the sale or lease of a consumer good.

(b) Titling and transfer documents utilized to register, title, or transfer ownership of vehicles described in the lease contract with government registration authorities.

(c) Insurance policies, service contracts, and optional debt cancellation agreements.

(d) Documents that memorialize the sale or lease of goods or services, relating to the leased vehicle, between the provider of those goods or services and lessee that are included in the gross capitalized cost of the lease and separately itemized in the "Itemization of Gross Capitalized Cost." *(Added by Stats.2001, c. 287 (S.B.281), § 3.)*

Operative Effect

For operative effect of Stats.2001, c. 287 (S.B.281), see § 5 of that Act.

§§ 2985.91 to 2985.93. Repealed by Stats.1976, c. 1284, p. 5700, § 1, operative March 23, 1977

§ 2986. Repealed by Stats.1963, c. 819, § 2, eff. Jan. 1, 1965

§ 2986.2. Repealed by Stats.1997, c. 800 (S.B.1291), § 8

§ 2986.3. Prohibited provisions

No lease contract shall contain any provision by which:

(a) A power of attorney is given to confess judgment in this state, or an assignment of wages is given; provided that nothing herein contained shall prohibit the giving of an assignment of wages contained in a separate instrument pursuant to Section 300 of the Labor Code.

(b) The lessee waives any right of action against the lessor or holder of the contract or other person acting on his or her behalf for any illegal act committed in the collection of payments under the contract or in the repossession of the motor vehicle.

(c) The lessee relieves the lessor from liability for any legal remedies which the lessee may have against the lessor under the contract or any separate instruments executed in connection therewith.

(d) The lessor or holder of the contract is given the right to commence action on a contract under the provisions of this chapter in a county other than the county in which the contract was in fact signed by the lessee, the county in which the lessee resides at the commencement of the action, the county in which the lessee resided at the time the contract was entered into or in the county in which the motor vehicle leased pursuant to such contract is permanently garaged. *(Added by Stats.1976, c. 1284, p. 5700, § 2, operative March 23, 1977. Amended by Stats.1997, c. 800 (S.B.1291), § 9.)*

§ 2986.4. Delivery of copy of lease contract, purchase order, lease proposal and credit statement; acknowledgment; effect; failure to notify third party of nondelivery

Any acknowledgment by the lessee of delivery of a copy of a lease contract or purchase order and any vehicle lease proposal and any credit statement which the lessor has required or requested the lessee to sign, and which the lessee has signed, during the contract negotiations, shall be printed or written in size equal to at least 10–point bold type and, if contained in the contract, shall appear directly above the space reserved for the lessee's signature. The lessee's written acknowledgment, conforming to the requirements of this section, of delivery of a completely filled in copy of the contract, and a copy of such other documents shall be a rebuttable presumption of delivery in any action or proceeding by or against a third party without knowledge to the contrary when he or she acquired his or her interest in the contract. If such third party furnishes the lessee a copy of such documents, or a notice containing items set forth in subdivision (c) of Section 2985.8, and stating that the lessee shall notify such third party in writing within 30 days if he or she was not furnished a copy of such documents, and no such notification is given, it shall be conclusively presumed in favor of such a third party that copies of the documents were furnished as required by this chapter. *(Added by Stats.1976, c. 1284, p. 5700, § 2, operative March 23, 1977. Amended by Stats.1997, c. 800 (S.B.1291), § 10.)*

§ 2986.5. Used motor vehicle; requirements for lease; excess charges for licensing or transfer of title; return to lessee

(a) No person shall lease a used motor vehicle for operation on California highways if such vehicle does not meet all of the equipment requirements of Division 12 (commencing with Section 24000) of the Vehicle Code. This subdivision does not apply to an extension or a subsequent lease of the same motor vehicle to the same lessee.

(b) If a lessee of a vehicle pays to the lessor an amount for the licensing or transfer of title of the vehicle which amount is in excess of the actual fees due for such licensing or transfer, or which amount is in excess of the amount which has been paid, prior to the sale, by the lessor to the state in order to avoid penalties that would have accrued because of late payment of such fees, the lessor shall return such excess amount to the lessee, whether or not such lessee requests the return of the excess amount. *(Added by Stats.1976, c. 1284, p. 5700, § 2, operative March 23, 1977.)*

§ 2986.6. Agreement for inclusion of other property as security; unenforceability

No agreement in connection with a lease contract which provides for the inclusion of title to or a lien upon any personal or real property, other than the motor vehicle which is the subject matter of the lease contract, or accessories therefor, or special and auxiliary equipment used in connection therewith, as security for the payment of the contract obligations, shall be enforceable. This section does not apply to a security deposit, advance payment of rent or other cash prepayment. *(Added by Stats.1976, c. 1284, p. 5700, § 2, operative March 23, 1977.)*

Cross References

Similar provision on conditional sales of motor vehicles, see Civil Code § 2984.2.

§ 2986.10. Assignee of lessor; rights and liabilities

(a) An assignee of the lessor's rights is subject to all equities and defenses of the lessee against the lessor, notwithstanding an agreement to the contrary, but the assignee's liability may not exceed the amount of the obligation owing to the assignee at the time of the assignment.

(b) The assignee shall have recourse against the lessor to the extent of any liability incurred by the assignee pursuant to this section regardless of whether the assignment was with or without recourse. *(Added by Stats.1976, c. 1284, p. 5700, § 2, operative March 23, 1977.)*

§ 2986.12. Rebate, discount, etc. for information or assistance in lease or sale of motor vehicle; prohibition

It shall be unlawful for any lessor to induce or attempt to induce any person to enter into a contract subject to this chapter by offering a rebate, discount, commission or other consideration, on the condition that the lessee gives information or assistance for the purpose of enabling a lessor to either lease or sell a motor vehicle to another. *(Added by Stats.1976, c. 1284, p. 5700, § 2, operative March 23, 1977.)*

§ 2986.13. Payment pending execution of lease contract; refund upon nonexecution; exceptions; remedies

(a) Any payment made by a lessee to a lessor pending the execution of a lease contract shall be refunded to the lessee in the event the lease contract is not executed.

(b) In the event of breach by the lessor of a lease contract where the lessee leaves his or her motor vehicle with the lessor as a trade-in downpayment and the motor vehicle is not returned by the lessor to the lessee for whatever reason, the lessee may recover from the lessor either the fair market value of the motor vehicle left as a downpayment or its value as stated in the lease contract, whichever is greater. The recovery shall be tendered to the lessee within five business days after the breach.

(c) The remedies of the buyer provided for in subdivision (b) are nonexclusive and cumulative and shall not preclude the lessee from pursuing any other remedy which he or she may have under any other provision of law. *(Added by Stats.1976, c. 1284, p. 5700, § 2, operative March 23, 1977. Amended by Stats.1997, c. 800 (S.B.1291), § 11.)*

§ 2987. Lessee's right to early termination of lease contract; conditions; notice

(a) A lessee has the right to terminate a lease contract at any time prior to the scheduled expiration date specified in the lease contract. Except as provided in subdivision (f), all of the following subdivisions of this section apply in the event of an early termination.

(b) The lessee's liability shall not exceed the sum of the following:

(1) All unpaid periodic lease payments that have accrued up to the date of termination.

(2) All other amounts due and unpaid by the lessee under the lease contract, other than excess wear and mileage charges and unpaid periodic lease payments.

(3) Any charges, however denominated, that the lessor or holder of the lease contract may assess in connection with termination not to exceed in the aggregate the amount of a reasonable disposition fee, if any, disclosed in the lease contract and assessed upon termination of the lease contract.

(4) In the event of the lessee's default, reasonable fees paid by the lessor or holder for reconditioning of the leased vehicle and reasonable and necessary fees paid by the lessor or holder, if any, in connection with the repossession and storage of the leased vehicle.

(5) The difference, if any, between the adjusted capitalized cost disclosed in the lease contract and the sum of (A) all depreciation and other amortized amounts accrued through the date of early termination, calculated in accordance with the constant yield or other generally accepted actuarial method, and (B) the realized value of the vehicle as provided in subdivision (c).

(c) Subject to subdivision (d), the realized value of the vehicle used to calculate the lessee's liability under paragraph (5) of subdivision (b) shall be (1) if the lessee maintains insurance on the leased vehicle as required in the lease contract and the vehicle is a total loss as a result of theft or damage, the amount of any applicable insurance deductible owed by the lessee and the proceeds of the settlement of the insurance claim, unless a higher amount is agreed to by the holder of the lease contract, (2) if the lessee elects to have an appraisal conducted as provided in Regulation M, the value determined on appraisal, (3) if the holder of the lease contract or lessor elects to retain ownership of the vehicle for use or to lease to a subsequent lessee, the wholesale value of the vehicle as specified in the current edition of a recognized used vehicle value guide customarily used by California motor vehicle dealers to value vehicles in this state, including, but not limited to, the Kelley Blue Book Auto Market Report and the N.A.D.A. Official Used Car Guide, or (4) under all other circumstances, the higher of (A) the price paid for the vehicle upon disposition, or (B) any other amount established by the lessor or the lease contract.

(d)(1) The lessor or holder of the lease contract shall act in good faith and in a commercially reasonable manner in connection with the disposition of the vehicle.

§ 2987

(2) In addition to the requirements of paragraph (1), any disposition of the vehicle shall be preceded by a notice complying with both of the following:

(A) The notice shall be in writing and given by the holder of the contract to each lessee and guarantor at least 10 days in advance of any disposition or the date by which the value of the vehicle will be determined pursuant to paragraph (3) of subdivision (c). The notice shall be personally served or shall be sent by certified mail, return receipt requested, or first-class mail, postage prepaid, directed to the last known address of each lessee and guarantor. One notice is sufficient if those persons are married to each other and the most recent records of the holder of the lease contract indicate that they reside at the same address. The last known address of each lessee and guarantor shall be presumed to be the address stated in the lease contract or guaranty for each lessee and guarantor unless the lessee or guarantor notifies the holder of the lease contract of a change of address.

(B) The notice shall set forth (i) the time and place of any public sale, the time on or after which a private sale or other intended disposition is to be made, or the date by which the value of the vehicle will be determined pursuant to paragraph (3) of subdivision (c), (ii) an itemization of all amounts claimed under paragraphs (1) to (4), inclusive, of subdivision (b), (iii) the amount of the difference between the adjusted capitalized cost and the sum of all depreciation and other amortized amounts paid through the date of early termination as provided in paragraph (5) of subdivision (b), (iv) the total of these amounts identified as the "Gross Early Termination Amount," and (v) one of the following statements, whichever is applicable:

[To be inserted when the realized value will be determined pursuant to paragraph (3) of subdivision (c)]

"The amount you owe for early termination will be no more than the difference between the Gross Early Termination Amount stated above and (1) the appraised value of the vehicle or (2) if there is no appraisal, the wholesale value specified in a recognized used vehicle value guide.

You have the right to get a professional appraisal to establish the value of the vehicle for the purpose of figuring how much you owe on the lease. If you want an appraisal, you will have to arrange for it to be completed at least three days before the scheduled valuation date. The appraiser has to be an independent person acceptable to the holder of the lease. You will have to pay for the appraiser. The appraised value will be considered final and binding on you and the holder of the lease."

[To be inserted in all other circumstances]

"The amount you owe for early termination will be no more than the difference between the Gross Early Termination Amount stated above and (1) the appraised value of the vehicle or (2) if there is no appraisal, either the price received for the vehicle upon disposition or a greater amount established by the lessor or the lease contract.

You have the right to get a professional appraisal to establish the value of the vehicle for the purpose of figuring how much you owe on the lease. If you want an appraisal, you will have to arrange for it to be completed at least three days before the scheduled sale date of the vehicle. The appraiser has to be an independent person acceptable to the holder of the lease. You will have to pay for the appraiser. The appraised value will be considered final and binding on you and the holder of the lease."

(3) The lessee shall have no liability under subdivision (b) if the lessor or holder of the lease contract does not comply with this subdivision. This paragraph does not apply under all the following conditions:

(A) Noncompliance was the result of a bona fide error in stating an amount required to be disclosed pursuant to clause (ii), (iii), or (iv) of subparagraph (B) of paragraph (2).

(B) The holder of the lease gives the lessee written notice of the error within 30 days after discovering the error and before (i) an action is filed to recover the amount claimed to be owed or (ii) written notice of the error is received by the holder of the lease from the lessee.

(C) The lessee is liable for the lesser of the originally claimed amount or the correct amount.

(D) The holder of the lease refunds any amount collected in excess of the amount described in subparagraph (C) within 10 days after notice of the error is given. "Bona fide error," as used in this paragraph, means an error that was not intentional and occurred notwithstanding the maintenance of procedures reasonably adapted to avoid that error. Examples of a bona fide error include clerical errors, calculation errors, errors due to unintentionally improper computer programming or data entry, and printing errors, but does not include an error of legal judgment with respect to a lessor's or lease contractholder's obligations under this section.

(4) This subdivision does not apply when the lessee maintains insurance on the leased vehicle as required in the lease contract and the vehicle is declared a total loss by the insurer as a result of theft or damage.

(e) The lessor or holder of the lease contract shall credit any security deposit or advance rental payment held by the lessor or holder of the lease contract against the lessee's liability under the lease contract as limited by this section. The portion of a security deposit or advance rental payment, if any, remaining after the lessee's liability under the lease contract as limited by this section has been satisfied shall be returned to the lessee within 30 days of the satisfaction of the obligation.

(f) Subdivisions (b) to (d), inclusive, do not apply if, prior to the scheduled expiration date specified in the lease contract, the lessee terminates the lease and purchases the vehicle or trades in the vehicle in connection with the purchase or lease of another vehicle. In such an event, the selling price of the leased vehicle, exclusive of taxes and other charges incidental to the sale, shall not exceed the sum of the following and shall relieve the lessee of any further liability under the lease contract:

(1) All unpaid periodic lease payments that have accrued up to the date of termination.

(2) All other amounts due and unpaid by the lessee under the lease contract, other than excess wear and mileage charges and unpaid periodic lease payments.

(3) Any charges, however denominated, that the lessor or holder of the lease contract may assess in connection with

termination of the lease contract and the acquisition of the vehicle, not to exceed in the aggregate the amount of a reasonable purchase option fee, if any, disclosed in the lease contract and assessed upon the scheduled termination of the lease contract.

(4) The adjusted capitalized cost disclosed in the lease contract less all depreciation and other amortized amounts accrued through the date of early termination, calculated in accordance with the constant yield or other generally accepted actuarial method.

(g) If the lessee terminates a lease contract, voluntarily returns possession of the vehicle to the lessor, and timely pays all sums required under the lease contract as limited by this section, the lessor or holder shall not provide any adverse information concerning the early termination to any consumer credit reporting agency.

(h) The Rule of 78 shall not be used to calculate accrued rent charges.

(i) This section shall only apply to lease contracts entered into on and after January 1, 1998. *(Added by Stats.1997, c. 800 (S.B.1291), § 12.)*

§ 2988. Legislative findings; liability of lessee on expiration of lease based on estimated residual value; reasonableness; rebuttable presumption

(a) The Legislature finds that it is necessary to provide some protection for consumers who enter into lease contracts in which the lessee will bear the risk of the motor vehicle's depreciation. This section is intended to provide relief to the consumer when an ostensibly inexpensive lease contract establishes an excessively low level of periodic payment which results, conversely, in an excessively high liability being imposed on the lessee at the expiration of the lease term because the lessor has failed to act in good faith in either estimating a residual value of the motor vehicle or establishing a level of periodic payment which bears no reasonable relation to the motor vehicle's reasonably expected depreciation during the lease term. Therefore, the lessor will have the obligation to act in good faith and to come forward with competent evidence showing that the estimated residual value was so determined given the circumstances existing at the inception of the lease contract.

(b) Where the lessee is to bear the risk of the motor vehicle's depreciation and the lessee's liability on expiration of a consumer lease is based on the estimated residual value of the motor vehicle such estimated residual value shall be a reasonable approximation of the anticipated actual fair market value of the motor vehicle on lease expiration. There shall be a rebuttable presumption that the estimated residual value is unreasonable to the extent that the estimated residual value exceeds the actual residual value by more than three times the average payment allocable to a monthly period under the lease. The presumption stated in the preceding sentence shall not apply to the extent the excess of estimated over actual residual value is due to physical damage to the motor vehicle beyond reasonable wear and use, or to excessive use, and the lease may set standards for such wear and use if such standards are not unreasonable.

(c) For the purposes of this chapter, "fair market value" means the value the motor vehicle would have when sold in a commercially reasonable manner in the customary market for such motor vehicle. *(Added by Stats.1976, c. 1284, p. 5700, § 2, operative March 23, 1977.)*

§ 2988.5. Failure to comply with requirements of §§ 2985.8, 2988; liability; failure to disclose information required by chapter; multiple offenses; limitation of actions

(a) Except as otherwise provided by this section, any lessor who fails to comply with any requirement imposed under Section 2985.8 or 2988 for which no specific relief is provided with respect to any person shall be liable to such person in an amount equal to the sum of:

(1) Any actual damages sustained by such person as a result of the failure.

(2) In the case of an individual action, 25 percent of the total amount of monthly payments under the lease except that liability under this subparagraph shall not be less than one hundred dollars ($100) nor greater than one thousand dollars ($1,000); or in the case of a class action, such amount as the court may allow, except that as to each member of the class no minimum recovery shall be applicable, and the total recovery in such action shall not be more than the lesser of five hundred thousand dollars ($500,000) or 1 percent of the net worth of the lessor.

(3) The costs of the action, together with a reasonable attorney's fee as determined by the court.

(b) In determining the amount of award in any class action, the court shall consider, among other relevant factors, the amount of any actual damages sustained, the frequency and persistence of failure of compliance by the lessor, the resources of the lessor, the number of persons adversely affected, and the extent to which the lessor's failure of compliance was intentional.

(c) A lessor shall not be liable under this section if within 15 days after discovery of an error, and prior to the institution of an action under this section or the receipt of written notice of the error, the lessor notifies the person concerned of the error and makes whatever adjustments in the appropriate account are necessary to insure that the person will not be required to pay any amount in excess of the amount that should correctly have been disclosed.

(d) A lessor may not be held liable in any action brought under this section for a violation of this chapter if the lessor shows by a preponderance of evidence that the violation was not intentional and resulted from a bona fide error notwithstanding the maintenance of procedures reasonably adopted to avoid any such error.

(e) Except as otherwise specifically provided in this chapter, any civil action for a violation of this chapter which may be brought against the original lessor in any lease transaction may be maintained against any subsequent assignee of the original lessor where the violation from which the alleged liability arose is apparent on the face of the instrument assigned unless the assignment is involuntary.

(f) A person may not take any action to offset any amount for which a lessor is potentially liable to such person under paragraph (2) of subdivision (a) against any amount owing to such lessor by such person, unless the amount of the lessor's

§ 2988.5

liability to such person has been determined by judgment of a court of competent jurisdiction in an action to which such person was a party.

(g) No provision of this section imposing any liability shall apply to any act done or omitted in good faith conformity with any rule, regulation or interpretation of federal law, notwithstanding that after such act or omission has occurred, such rule, regulation or interpretation is amended, rescinded or determined by judicial or other authority to be invalid for any reason.

(h) The multiple failure to disclose any information required under this chapter to be disclosed in connection with a single lease transaction shall entitle the person to a single recovery under this section, but continued failure to disclose after a recovery has been granted shall give rise to rights to additional recoveries.

(i) Actions alleging a failure to disclose or otherwise comply with the requirements of this chapter shall be brought within one year of the termination of the lease contract. (Added by Stats.1976, c. 1284, p. 5700, § 2, operative March 23, 1977.)

§ 2988.7. Failure to comply with § 2985.8; rescission of contract

If the lessor fails to comply with Section 2985.8, as an alternative to an action under Section 2988.5, the lessee may rescind the contract if the failure to comply was willful, or if correction will increase the amount of the contract balance, unless the lessor waives the collection of the increased amount. (Added by Stats.1976, c. 1284, p. 5700, § 2, operative March 23, 1977.)

§ 2988.9. Award of reasonable attorney's fees and costs

Reasonable attorney's fees and costs shall be awarded to the prevailing party in any action on a lease contract subject to the provisions of this chapter regardless of whether the action is instituted by the lessor, assignee, or lessee. Where the defendant alleges in his or her answer that he or she tendered to the plaintiff the full amount to which he or she was entitled, and thereupon deposits in court, for the plaintiff, the amount so tendered, and the allegation is found to be true, then the defendant is deemed to be the prevailing party within the meaning of this section. (Added by Stats. 1976, c. 1284, p. 5700, § 2, operative March 23, 1977. Amended by Stats.2004, c. 183 (A.B.3082), § 42.)

§ 2989. Preemption of civil action; federal civil action on same facts

No civil action shall be filed against a lessor under the authority of this chapter if a federal civil action has previously been filed based on facts that give rise to a similar cause of action under this chapter. (Added by Stats.1976, c. 1284, p. 5700, § 2, operative March 23, 1977.)

§ 2989.2. Fair market value at expiration of lease; depreciation; method of establishment; notice of intent to sell motor vehicle; service on lessee; exception; contents

Where the lessee is to bear the risk of the motor vehicle's depreciation upon the scheduled expiration of the lease contract, the following applies:

(a) When disposing of a vehicle or obtaining cash bids for the purpose of setting the fair market value of a vehicle, the lessor shall act in a commercially reasonable manner in the customary market for such vehicle.

(b) Any provision in a lease contract to the contrary notwithstanding, at least 10 days written notice of intent to sell such motor vehicle shall be given by the holder of the contract to each lessee and guarantor, unless the lessor and lessee have agreed in writing to the amount of the lessee's liability under the lease contract after the lessee returns the motor vehicle to the lessor, or the lessee has satisfied the lease contract obligations by payment to the lessor. The notice shall be personally served or shall be sent by certified mail, return receipt requested, directed to the address of the lessee shown on the contract, unless the lessee has notified the holder in writing of a different address. The notice shall set forth separately any charges or sums due and state that the lessee will be liable for the difference between the amount of liability imposed on the lessee at the expiration of the lease term and the actual cash value of the motor vehicle when it is sold. The notice shall also state that the lessee has the right to submit a cash bid for the purchase of the vehicle. (Added by Stats.1976, c. 1284, p. 5700, § 2, operative March 23, 1977. Amended by Stats.1997, c. 800 (S.B.1291), § 13.)

§ 2989.4. Lessor; prohibited acts; nonliability for violations

(a) A lessor shall not:

(1) Fail to register the leased vehicle pursuant to the lease contract.

(2) Advertise any specific vehicle in the inventory of the lessor for lease without identifying such vehicle by either its vehicle identification number or license number.

(3) Refuse to lease a vehicle to any creditworthy person at the advertised total price, exclusive of sales tax, vehicle registration fees and finance charges.

(b) Notwithstanding Section 2988.5, a lessor shall not suffer civil liability for a violation of this section. (Added by Stats.1976, c. 1284, p. 5700, § 2, operative March 23, 1977.)

§ 2989.5. Records; availability to Department of Motor Vehicles; affidavit; court order; financial institution; report to supervising agency; report of action taken

(a) Except as provided in subdivision (c), a lessor shall make available to investigators of the Department of Motor Vehicles, upon presentation of an affidavit that the department has a consumer complaint within its jurisdiction, the records relevant to the transaction complained of. If the affidavit states that the department has reasonable cause to believe there is a pattern of conduct or common scheme in similar transactions, the records relevant to all such similar transactions shall be made available.

(b) Except as provided in subdivision (c), on petition of the department alleging the receipt of a consumer complaint within its jurisdiction and alleging that the lessor refuses to make available his records as required, the court shall order the lessor to make available such records or show cause why such records should not be produced. The department shall be awarded reasonable attorney's fees and costs if it prevails in such action.

(c) (1) In the case of a financial institution, or a subsidiary or affiliated corporation of such institution, the Director of Motor Vehicles shall report in writing an apparent violation, or failure to comply with this chapter, evidenced by a consumer complaint, to the agency or department of the state or federal government responsible for supervising the leasing activities of such institution.

(2) Within 20 days, such agency or department shall advise the director of the action taken with respect to such report.

(3) If such agency or department fails to so advise the director, the director may commence an action to compel the agency or department to cause the production of the records relevant to the consumer complaint. *(Added by Stats.1976, c. 1284, p. 5700, § 2, operative March 23, 1977.)*

§ 2989.6. Rules and regulations

The Director of Motor Vehicles may adopt and enforce rules and regulations as may be necessary to carry out or implement the provisions of this chapter.

Rules and regulations shall be adopted, amended or repealed in accordance with Chapter 4.5 (commencing with Section 11370) of Part 1 of Division 3 of Title 2 of the Government Code. *(Added by Stats.1976, c. 1284, p. 5700, § 2, operative March 23, 1977.)*

§ 2989.8. Violations; misdemeanor

Any person who shall knowingly and willfully violate any provision of this chapter shall be guilty of a misdemeanor. *(Added by Stats.1976, c. 1284, p. 5700, § 2, operative March 23, 1977.)*

§ 2990. Inapplicability of chapter to transaction regulated by Automobile Sales Finance Act

This chapter shall not apply to any transaction which is regulated by Chapter 2b (commencing with Section 2981) of this title. *(Added by Stats.1976, c. 1284, p. 5700, § 2, operative March 23, 1977.)*

§ 2991. Forms; Spanish language translations

Any prospective assignee that provides a lessor under a lease contract with any preprinted form for use as a lease contract shall, upon the request of a lessor, provide the lessor with a Spanish language translation of the preprinted form. *(Added by Stats.1999, c. 235 (A.B.713), § 1, operative Jan. 1, 2001.)*

§ 2992. Preprinted lease contract; design requirements and contents

A prospective assignee that provides a lessor under a lease contract with a preprinted form for use as a lease contract shall design the form in such a manner so as to provide on its face sufficient space for the lessor to include all disclosures and itemizations required pursuant to Section 2985.8 and shall also contain on its face a separate blank space no smaller than seven and one-half square inches for the lessor and lessee to memorialize trade-in, turn-in, and other individualized agreements. *(Added by Stats.2001, c. 287 (S.B.281), § 4.)*

Operative Effect

For operative effect of Stats.2001, c. 287 (S.B.281), see § 5 of that Act.

§ 2993. Repossession of vehicle connected with incident of violence notice; notice to subsequent assignee

A holder of a lease contract, or the agent of a holder, who has received a notice pursuant to Section 7507.6 of the Business and Professions Code, shall not make a subsequent assignment to skip trace, locate, or repossess the vehicle without simultaneously, and in the same manner by which the assignment is given, advising the assignee of the assignment of the information contained in the notice. As used in this section, "assignment" has the same meaning set forth in Section 7500.1 of the Business and Professions Code. *(Added by Stats.2007, c. 192 (S.B.659), § 5, eff. Sept. 7, 2007.)*

§ 2994. Repealed by Stats.1963, c. 819, § 2, eff. Jan. 1, 1965

CHAPTER 2E. CONTROLLED ESCROWS

Section
2995. Transfer of single-family residential dwelling; real estate developer; financial interest in escrow entity; damages; waiver.

§ 2995. Transfer of single-family residential dwelling; real estate developer; financial interest in escrow entity; damages; waiver

No real estate developer shall require as a condition precedent to the transfer of real property containing a single family residential dwelling that escrow services effectuating such transfer shall be provided by an escrow entity in which the real estate developer has a financial interest.

A real estate developer who violates the provisions of this section shall be liable to the purchaser of the real property in the amount of three times the amount charged for the escrow services, but in no event less than two hundred fifty dollars ($250), plus reasonable attorney's fees and costs.

For purposes of this section "financial interest" means ownership or control of 5 percent or more of an escrow entity.

For purposes of this section "real estate developer" means a person or entity having an ownership interest in real property which is improved by such person or entity with single family residential dwellings which are offered for sale to the public.

For purposes of this section "escrow entity" includes a person, firm or corporation.

Any waiver of the prohibition contained in this section shall be against public policy and void. *(Added by Stats.1978, c. 552, p. 1724, § 1, eff. Aug. 25, 1978.)*

CHAPTER 3. PLEDGE [REPEALED]

§§ 2996 to 3011. Repealed by Stats.1963, c. 819, § 2, eff. Jan. 1, 1965

CHAPTER 3A. TRUST RECEIPTS [REPEALED]

§§ 3012 to 3016.16. Repealed by Stats.1963, c. 819, p. 1997, § 2, eff. Jan. 1, 1965

CHAPTER 3B. ASSIGNMENT OF ACCOUNTS RECEIVABLE [REPEALED]

§§ 3017 to 3029. Repealed by Stats.1963, c. 819, p. 1997, § 2, eff. Jan. 1, 1965

CHAPTER 3C. INVENTORY LIENS [REPEALED]

§§ 3030 to 3039. Repealed by Stats.1963, c. 819, § 2, eff. Jan. 1, 1965

CHAPTER 3.5. HEALTH CARE LIENS

Section
3040. Lien for money paid or payable by insured or enrollee for health care services provided under health care service plan contract or disability insurance policy; limit on account.
3041 to 3043. Repealed.

§ 3040. Lien for money paid or payable by insured or enrollee for health care services provided under health care service plan contract or disability insurance policy; limit on account

(a) No lien asserted by a licensee of the Department of Managed Care or the Department of Insurance, and no lien of a medical group or an independent practice association, to the extent that it asserts or enforces a lien, for the recovery of money paid or payable to or on behalf of an enrollee or insured for health care services provided under a health care service plan contract or a disability insurance policy, when the right of the licensee, medical group, or independent practice association to assert that lien is granted in a plan contract subject to the Knox–Keene Health Care Service Plan Act of 1975 (Chapter 2.2 (commencing with Section 1340) of Division 2 of the Health and Safety Code) or a disability insurance policy subject to the Insurance Code, may exceed the sum of the reasonable costs actually paid by the licensee, medical group, or independent practice association to perfect the lien and one of the following:

(1) For health care services not provided on a capitated basis, the amount actually paid by the licensee, medical group, or independent practice association pursuant to that contract or policy to any treating medical provider.

(2) For health care services provided on a capitated basis, the amount equal to 80 percent of the usual and customary charge for the same services by medical providers that provide health care services on a noncapitated basis in the geographic region in which the services were rendered.

(b) If an enrollee or insured received health care services on a capitated basis and on a noncapitated basis, and the licensee, medical group, or independent practice association that provided the health care services on the capitated basis paid for the health care services the enrollee received on the noncapitated basis, then a lien that is subject to subdivision (a) may not exceed the sum of the reasonable costs actually paid to perfect the lien, and the amounts determined pursuant to both paragraphs (1) and (2) of subdivision (a).

(c) If the enrollee or insured engaged an attorney, then the lien subject to subdivision (a) may not exceed the lesser of the following amounts:

(1) The maximum amount determined pursuant to subdivision (a) or (b), whichever is applicable.

(2) One–third of the moneys due to the enrollee or insured under any final judgment, compromise, or settlement agreement.

(d) If the enrollee or insured did not engage an attorney, then the lien subject to subdivision (a) may not exceed the lesser of the following amounts:

(1) The maximum amount determined pursuant to subdivision (a) or (b), whichever is applicable.

(2) One–half of the moneys due to the enrollee or insured under any final judgment, compromise, or settlement agreement.

(e) Where a final judgment includes a special finding by a judge, jury, or arbitrator, that the enrollee or insured was partially at fault, the lien subject to subdivision (a) or (b) shall be reduced by the same comparative fault percentage by which the enrollee or insured's recovery was reduced.

(f) A lien subject to subdivision (a) or (b) is subject to pro rata reduction, commensurate with the enrollee's or insured's reasonable attorney's fees and costs, in accordance with the common fund doctrine.

(g) This section is not applicable to any of the following:

(1) A lien made against a workers' compensation claim.

(2) A lien for Medi–Cal benefits pursuant to Article 3.5 (commencing with Section 14124.70) of Chapter 7 of Part 3 of Division 9 of the Welfare and Institutions Code.

(3) A lien for hospital services pursuant to Chapter 4 (commencing with Section 3045.1).

(h) This section does not create any lien right that does not exist at law, and does not make a lien that arises out of an employee benefit plan or fund enforceable if preempted by federal law.

(i) The provisions of this section may not be admitted into evidence nor given in any instruction in any civil action or proceeding between an enrollee or insured and a third party. *(Added by Stats.2000, c. 848 (S.B.1471), § 1.)*

§§ 3041 to 3043. Repealed by Stats.1963, c. 819, § 2, eff. Jan. 1, 1965

CHAPTER 4. HOSPITAL LIENS

Section
3045.1. Lien for emergency and ongoing medical or other services upon damages recovered by person injured by accident or wrongful act.
3045.2. Applicability of lien whether damages recovered by judgment, settlement or compromise.
3045.3. Notice to injured person; contents; delivery of copy to insurance carrier.

Section	
3045.4.	Liability for payment to injured person after notice without satisfying lien.
3045.5.	Enforcement of lien by action; limitation.
3045.6.	Inapplicability of chapter to claims against common carriers.

Cross References

Liens in general, see Civil Code § 2872 et seq.

§ 3045.1. Lien for emergency and ongoing medical or other services upon damages recovered by person injured by accident or wrongful act

Every person, partnership, association, corporation, public entity, or other institution or body maintaining a hospital licensed under the laws of this state which furnishes emergency and ongoing medical or other services to any person injured by reason of an accident or negligent or other wrongful act not covered by Division 4 (commencing with Section 3201) or Division 4.5 (commencing with Section 6100) of the Labor Code, shall, if the person has a claim against another for damages on account of his or her injuries, have a lien upon the damages recovered, or to be recovered, by the person, or by his or her heirs or personal representative in case of his or her death to the extent of the amount of the reasonable and necessary charges of the hospital and any hospital affiliated health facility, as defined in Section 1250 of the Health and Safety Code, in which services are provided for the treatment, care, and maintenance of the person in the hospital or health facility affiliated with the hospital resulting from that accident or negligent or other wrongful act. *(Added by Stats.1961, c. 2080, p. 4340, § 1. Amended by Stats.1992, c. 302 (A.B.2733), § 1.)*

§ 3045.2. Applicability of lien whether damages recovered by judgment, settlement or compromise

The lien shall apply whether the damages are recovered, or are to be recovered, by judgment, settlement, or compromise. *(Added by Stats.1961, c. 2080, p. 4340, § 1.)*

§ 3045.3. Notice to injured person; contents; delivery of copy to insurance carrier

A lien shall not be effective, however, unless a written notice containing the name and address of the injured person, the date of the accident, the name and location of the hospital, the amount claimed as reasonable and necessary charges, and the name of each person, firm, or corporation known to the hospital and alleged to be liable to the injured person for the injuries received, is delivered or is mailed by registered mail, return receipt requested, postage prepaid, to each person, firm, or corporation known to the hospital and alleged to be liable to the injured person for the injuries sustained prior to the payment of any moneys to the injured person, his attorney, or legal representative as compensation for the injuries.

The hospital shall, also, deliver or mail by registered mail, return receipt requested, postage prepaid, a copy of the notice to any insurance carrier known to the hospital which has insured the person, firm, or corporation alleged to be liable to the injured person against the liability. The person, firm, or corporation alleged to be liable to the injured person shall, upon request of the hospital, disclose to the hospital the name of the insurance carrier which has insured it against the liability. *(Added by Stats.1961, c. 2080, p. 4340, § 1. Amended by Stats.1992, c. 302 (A.B.2733), § 2.)*

§ 3045.4. Liability for payment to injured person after notice without satisfying lien

Any person, firm, or corporation, including, but not limited to, an insurance carrier, making any payment to the injured person, or to his or her attorney, heirs, or legal representative, for the injuries he or she sustained, after the receipt of the notice as provided by Section 3045.3, without paying to the association, corporation, public entity, or other institution or body maintaining the hospital the amount of its lien claimed in the notice, or so much thereof as can be satisfied out of 50 percent of the moneys due under any final judgment, compromise, or settlement agreement after paying any prior liens shall be liable to the person, partnership, association, corporation, public entity, or other institution or body maintaining the hospital for the amount of its lien claimed in the notice which the hospital was entitled to receive as payment for the medical care and services rendered to the injured person. *(Added by Stats.1961, c. 2080, p. 4341, § 1. Amended by Stats.1992, c. 302 (A.B.2733), § 3.)*

§ 3045.5. Enforcement of lien by action; limitation

The person, partnership, association, corporation or other institution or body maintaining the hospital may, at any time within one year after the date of the payment to the injured person, or to his heirs, attorney, or legal representative, enforce its lien by filing an action at law against the person, firm, or corporation making the payment and to whom such notice was given as herein provided. *(Added by Stats.1961, c. 2080, p. 4341, § 1.)*

§ 3045.6. Inapplicability of chapter to claims against common carriers

The provisions of this chapter shall not apply to any claim or cause of action against a common carrier subject to the jurisdiction of the Public Utilities Commission or the Interstate Commerce Commission. *(Added by Stats.1961, c. 2080, p. 4341, § 1.)*

CHAPTER 5. RESPONDENTIA [REPEALED]

CHAPTER 6. OTHER LIENS

Section	
3046.	Vendor's lien.
3047.	Vendor's lien; waiver.
3048.	Vendor's lien; priority.
3049.	Repealed.
3050.	Purchaser's lien.
3051.	Possessory liens for services, repairs, etc.; exceptions.
3051a.	Possessory liens; services over $300 and safekeeping over $200 requested by nonowners; notice to holder of legal title.
3051.5.	Possessory lien; carriers; freightage; charges for services and advances; conditions; notice; sale; priority; application of sale proceeds; liability of shipper.
3051.6.	Carrier's lien for fines, penalties, costs, expenses, or interest incurred for false or erroneous certification of gross cargo weight.

OBLIGATIONS

Section
3052. Sale by lien holder at auction; notice of sale; redemption; application of proceeds.
3052a. Jeweler's lien; notice and sale.
3052b. Alternative lien-sale procedure; liens for charges under $150; conditions; notice of sale; redemption; disposition of proceeds.
3052.5. Service dealers registered with Bureau of Repair Services; lien; notice; disposition of products of nominal value; alternative methods.
3053. Factor's lien.
3054. Banker's or savings and loan association's lien; deposit accounts.
3055, 3056. Repealed.
3057, 3058. Repealed.
3059. Mechanic's lien.
3060. Mining liens.
3061. Threshermen's liens.
3061.5. Agricultural laborer's lien; liability of severed crops or farm products or proceeds from sale; limitations; exceptions; rights of buyer in ordinary course of business.
3061.6. Agricultural laborer's lien.
3062. Lien for service of stallion, jack, or bull.
3063. Lien for service of stallion, jack, or bull; verified claims; recording; contents; notice.
3064. Lien for service of stallion, jack, or bull; enforcement action; remedies.
3064.1. Forfeiture of right to pay for services of breeding animals.
3065. Loggers' and lumbermen's lien.
3065a. Loggers' and lumbermen's lien; duration; remedies.
3065b. Loggers' and lumbermen's lien; cessation of work defined.
3065c. Loggers' and lumbermen's lien; affidavit showing wages owed by contractor; filing; stop notice to mill operator; withholding funds due contractor.
3066. Cleaners' and launderers' liens; service and storage; sale; notice; proceeds; posted notices in receiving office.

Cross References

Apartment house keeper's lien, see Civil Code § 1861a.
Attachment lien, see Code of Civil Procedure § 488.500.
Bank's lien on articles held for safekeeping or storage, see Financial Code § 1641.
Bills of lading,
 Enforcement of lien, see Commercial Code § 7308.
 Lien of carrier, see Commercial Code § 7307.
Carrier's lien, freightage and services, see Civil Code § 2144.
Carrier's lien on luggage, see Civil Code § 2191.
Common interest developments, assessment liens, see Civil Code § 5740.
County aid and relief, lien, see Welfare and Institutions Code §§ 17108, 17109, 17400 et seq.
Debts of decedent, order of payment, see Probate Code § 11420.
Depositary's lien, see Civil Code §§ 1856, 1857.
Electronic and appliance repair, restriction on lien if excess charges levied, see Business and Professions Code § 9844.5.
Frozen food locker plants, lien for storage charges, see Health and Safety Code § 112590.
Hospitals, lien for emergency medical services, see Civil Code § 3045.1 et seq.
Innkeeper's lien, see Civil Code § 1861.
Liens on aircraft, see Code of Civil Procedure § 1208.61 et seq.
Marshaling liens, see Civil Code § 2899.
Restriction on liens for service by electronic repair or installation dealers, see Business and Professions Code § 9844.5.
Salary and wage liens, see Code of Civil Procedure § 1204 et seq.
Vehicles, liens, see Civil Code § 3067 et seq.
Warehouseman's lien, enforcement, see Commercial Code § 7210.

§ 3046. Vendor's lien

One who sells real property has a vendor's lien thereon, independent of possession, for so much of the price as remains unpaid and unsecured otherwise than by the personal obligation of the buyer. *(Enacted in 1872.)*

Cross References

Liens in general, see Civil Code § 2872 et seq.
Priority of mortgages and deeds of trust, see Civil Code § 2898.
Purchaser's lien on real property, see Civil Code § 3050.
Statute of frauds, see Civil Code § 1624.

§ 3047. Vendor's lien; waiver

Where a buyer of real property gives to the seller a written contract for payment of all or part of the price, an absolute transfer of such contract by the seller waives his lien to the extent of the sum payable under the contract, but a transfer of such contract in trust to pay debts, and return the surplus, is not a waiver of the lien. *(Enacted in 1872.)*

§ 3048. Vendor's lien; priority

The liens defined in sections 3046 and 3050 are valid against every one claiming under the debtor, except a purchaser or incumbrancer in good faith and for value. *(Enacted in 1872.)*

Cross References

Constructive notice, see Civil Code § 19.

§ 3049. Repealed by Stats.1931, c. 1070, p. 2258, § 2.

§ 3050. Purchaser's lien

One who pays to the owner any part of the price of real property, under an agreement for the sale thereof, has a special lien upon the property, independent of possession, for such part of the amount paid as he may be entitled to recover back, in case of a failure of consideration. *(Enacted in 1872.)*

Cross References

Extent of seller's lien, see Civil Code § 3048.
Vendor's lien on real property, see Civil Code § 3046 et seq.

§ 3051. Possessory liens for services, repairs, etc.; exceptions

Every person who, while lawfully in possession of an article of personal property, renders any service to the owner thereof, by labor or skill, employed for the protection, improvement, safekeeping, or carriage thereof, has a special lien thereon, dependent on possession, for the compensation, if any, which is due to him from the owner for such service; a person who makes, alters, or repairs any article of personal property, at the request of the owner, or legal possessor of the property, has a lien on the same for his reasonable charges for the balance due for such work done and materials furnished, and may retain possession of the same until the charges are paid; and foundry proprietors and persons conducting a foundry business, have a lien, dependent on possession, upon all patterns in their hands belonging to a customer, for the balance due them from such customers for foundry work; and plastic fabricators and persons conducting a plastic fabricating business, have a lien, dependent on possession, upon all patterns and molds in their hands belonging to a customer, for the balance due them from such customer for plastic fabrication work; and laundry proprietors and persons conducting a laundry business, and drycleaning establishment proprietors and persons conducting a drycleaning establishment, have a general lien, dependent on possession, upon all personal property in their hands belonging to a customer, for the balance due them from such customer for laundry work, and for the balance due them from such customers for drycleaning work, but nothing in this section shall be construed to confer a lien in favor of a wholesale drycleaner on materials received from a drycleaning establishment proprietor or a person conducting a drycleaning establishment; and veterinary proprietors and veterinary surgeons shall have a lien dependent on possession, for their compensation in caring for, boarding, feeding, and medical treatment of animals.

This section shall have no application to any vessel, as defined in Section 21 of the Harbors and Navigation Code, to any vehicle, as defined in Section 670 of the Vehicle Code, which is subject to registration pursuant to that code, to any manufactured home, as defined in Section 18007 of the Health and Safety Code, to any mobilehome, as defined in Section 18008 of the Health and Safety Code, or to any commercial coach, as defined in Section 18001.8 of the Health and Safety Code, whether or not the manufactured home, mobilehome, or commercial coach is subject to registration under the Health and Safety Code. *(Enacted in 1872. Amended by Code Am. 1877–78, c. 451, p. 89; Stats.1901, c. 108, p. 270, § 1; Stats.1907, c. 66, p. 85, § 1; Stats.1911, c. 435, p. 887, § 1; Stats.1929, c. 868, p. 1923, § 1; Stats.1935, c. 381, p. 1332, § 1; Stats.1945, c. 861, p. 1619, § 1; Stats.1949, c. 1436, p. 2499, § 4; Stats.1970, c. 1341, p. 2491, § 1; Stats.1976, c. 839, p. 1908, § 1; Stats.1978, c. 1005, p. 3083, § 1; Stats.1979, c. 600, p. 1863, § 1; Stats.1981, c. 202, p. 1125, § 1; Stats.1983, c. 1124, § 6, operative Jan. 1, 1984.)*

Cross References

Aircraft repair, special liens, see Business and Professions Code § 9798.1.
Carrier's lien,
  Freight, see Civil Code § 2144.
  Luggage, see Civil Code § 2191.
Cleaners' and launderers' liens, see Civil Code § 3066.
Electronic and appliance repair, restriction on lien if excess charges levied, see Business and Professions Code § 9844.5.
Lien for rental of parking space, see Civil Code § 3068.
Restoration of property as extinguishing lien, see Civil Code § 2913.

§ 3051a. Possessory liens; services over $300 and safekeeping over $200 requested by nonowners; notice to holder of legal title

That portion of any lien, as provided for in the next preceding section, in excess of three hundred dollars ($300) for any work, services, or care, or in excess of two hundred dollars ($200) for any safekeeping, rendered or performed at the request of any person other than the holder of the legal title, shall be invalid, unless prior to commencing any such work, service, care, or safekeeping, the person claiming such lien shall give actual notice in writing either by personal service or by registered letter addressed to the holder of the legal title to such property, if known. *(Added by Stats.1923, c. 338, p. 695, § 1. Amended by Stats.1931, c. 1048, p. 2202, § 1; Stats.1949, c. 1436, p. 2500, § 5; Stats.1959, c. 197, p. 2089, § 1; Stats.1968, c. 830, p. 1602, § 1; Stats.1978, c. 1005, p. 3084, § 2.)*

§ 3051.5. Possessory lien; carriers; freightage; charges for services and advances; conditions; notice; sale; priority; application of sale proceeds; liability of shipper

(a) A carrier has a lien on freight in its possession for the total amount owed the carrier by the shipper for freightage, charges for services and advances due on freight previously delivered upon the promise of the shipper to pay freightage, charges and advances, as provided in this section.

(b) The lien provided by this section shall not arise:

(1) Unless the carrier has notified the shipper, in writing, that failure to pay billed charges may result in a lien on future shipments, including the cost of storage and appropriate security for the subsequent shipment held pursuant to this section.

(2) As to any freight which consists of perishable goods.

(c) Except as otherwise provided in this section, the notice and sale provisions of Section 3052 shall apply to the sale of property subject to a lien provided by this section.

(d) No sale of property subject to a lien provided by this section may take place for at least 35 days from the date that possession of the property is delivered to the carrier but the notice period set forth in Section 3052 may run concurrently with the 35-day period provided by this subdivision. In addition to the notices required by Section 3052, the lienholder, at least 10 days prior to any sale of the property, shall notify the shipper and the consignee of the property, and each secured party having a perfected security interest in the property, of the date, time and place of the intended sale. This notice shall include the names of both the shipper and the consignee and shall describe the property to be sold.

(e) Any perfected security interest in the property is prior to the lien provided by this section. No sale of the property may be concluded if the amount bid at the sale is not at least equal to the total amount of all outstanding obligations secured by a perfected security interest in the property. If the minimum bid required for the sale of property pursuant to this subdivision is not received, the lienholder shall promptly release the property to the legal owner upon payment of the current amount for freightage, charges for services and advances due for shipment of that property, not including amounts due on freight previously delivered.

The proceeds of the sale shall be applied as follows:

(1) First, to secured parties having a perfected security interest, in the amounts to which they are respectively entitled.

(2) Second, to the discharge of the lien provided by this section and the costs of storage, appropriate security, and of the sale.

(3) The remainder, if any, to the legal owner of the property.

§ 3051.5

In the event of any violation by the lienholder of any provision of this subdivision the lienholder shall be liable to any secured party for all damages sustained by the secured party as a result thereof plus all expenses reasonably and necessarily incurred in the enforcement of the secured party's rights, including reasonable attorney's fees and costs of suit.

(f) The shipper shall be liable to the consignee for any damage which results from the failure of the property to reach the consignee as scheduled due to the carrier's proper exercise of its lien rights pursuant to this section. The measure of damages shall be determined as set forth in Section 2713 of the Commercial Code. (Added by Stats.1984, c. 1375, § 1.)

§ 3051.6. Carrier's lien for fines, penalties, costs, expenses, or interest incurred for false or erroneous certification of gross cargo weight

(a) Except as provided in subdivision (b), a carrier has a lien on freight in its possession for the total amount owed to the carrier by the owner or beneficial owner of the cargo being shipped for the aggregate amount of any fines, penalties, costs, expenses, or interest incurred by the carrier resulting from the inclusion of false or erroneous information as to gross cargo weight in a written or electronic certification provided by the owner, beneficial owner, or person responsible for making the certification pursuant to Section 508 of Title 49 of the United States Code.

(b) This section does not apply to any of the following freight:

(1) Perishable goods.

(2) Freight shipped by a means involving other than intermodal transportation, as that term is defined by Section 508 of Title 49 of the United States Code.

(3) Freight shipped by loaded containers or trailers having a gross projected cargo weight, including packing material and pallets, of less than 10,000 pounds.

(c) Any sale to foreclose a lien specified in this section shall be conducted in accordance with Section 3052, except that (1) the lien sale shall not take place for at least 35 days from the date that possession of the property is delivered to the carrier, but the notice period specified in Section 3052 may run concurrently with this 35-day period and (2), in addition to the notices required by Section 3052, at least 10 days prior to the sale of the property the lienholder shall notify the shipper and consignee of the property of the date, time, and place of the intended sale. This notice shall contain the names of the shipper and consignee and shall generally describe the property to be sold. (Added by Stats.1993, c. 757 (S.B.619), § 2.)

§ 3052. Sale by lien holder at auction; notice of sale; redemption; application of proceeds

If the person entitled to the lien provided in Section 3051 is not paid the amount due, and for which such lien is given, within 10 days after the same shall have become due, then such lienholder may proceed to sell such property, or so much thereof as may be necessary to satisfy such lien and costs of sale at public auction, and by giving at least 10 days' but not more than 20 days' previous notice of such sale by advertising in some newspaper published in the county in which such property is situated; or if there be no newspaper printed in such county, then by posting notice of sale in three of the most public places in the town and at the place where such property is to be sold, for 10 days previous to the date of the sale; provided, however, that within 20 days after such sale, the legal owner may redeem any such property so sold to satisfy such lien upon the payment of the amount thereof, all costs and expenses of such sale, together with interest on such sum at the rate of 12 percent per annum from the due date thereof or the date when the same were advanced until the repayment. The proceeds of the sale must be applied to the discharge of the lien and the cost of keeping and selling the property; the remainder, if any, must be paid over to the legal owner thereof. (Enacted in 1872. Amended by Stats. 1907, c. 66, § 2; Stats.1927, c. 368, p. 604, § 1; Stats.1949, c. 1436, p. 2500, § 6; Stats.1959, c. 781, p. 2775, § 1; Stats.1974, c. 1262, p. 2736, § 1, eff. Sept. 23, 1974, operative Nov. 1, 1974; Stats.1977, c. 579, p. 1840, § 34; Stats.1978, c. 1005, p. 3084, § 3.)

Cross References

Bovine brucellosis and tuberculosis, enforcement of lien, see Food and Agricultural Code §§ 10152, 10355, 10385.

Livestock, caring for after seizure, lien, see Food and Agricultural Code § 20439.

Wrongful conversion by lienor as extinguishing lien, see Civil Code § 2910.

§ 3052a. Jeweler's lien; notice and sale

Every person, firm, or corporation, engaged in performing work upon any watch, clock or jewelry, for a price, shall have a lien upon the watch, clock, or jewelry for the amount of any account that may be due for the work done thereon. The lien shall also include the value or agreed price, if any, of all materials furnished by the lienholder in connection with the work. If any account for work done or materials furnished shall remain unpaid for one year after completing the work, the lienholder may, upon 30 days notice in writing to the owner, specifying the amount due, and informing him that the payment of the amount due within 30 days will entitle him to redeem the property, sell any such article or articles at public or bona fide private sale to satisfy the account. The proceeds of the sale, after paying the expenses thereof, shall first be applied to liquidate the indebtedness secured by the lien and the balance, if any, shall be paid over to the owner.

The notice may be served by registered mail with return receipt demanded, directed to the owner's last known address, or, if the owner or his address be unknown, it may be posted in two public places in the town or city where the property is located. Nothing herein contained shall be construed as preventing the lienholder from waiving the lien herein provided for suing upon the amount if he elects to do so. (Added by Stats.1937, c. 279, p. 614, § 1.)

§ 3052b. Alternative lien-sale procedure; liens for charges under $150; conditions; notice of sale; redemption; disposition of proceeds

(a) The procedure in this section shall be an alternative to the lien-sale procedure provided in Section 3052, but applies only to liens under Section 3051 for charges not exceeding one hundred fifty dollars ($150), exclusive of additional charges and interest authorized by this section. As a condition precedent to using the procedure specified in this section, the lienholder shall have done all of the following:

(1) Provided the property owner with an accurate written summary of the lien provisions of this section.

(2) Obtained the property owner's address and telephone number, together with a written declaration signed by the property owner stating that the property owner has read and understands the summary provided pursuant to paragraph (1), at the time of entering into the transaction from which the lien arose.

(3) Posted, at the time of the transaction from which the lien arose, a notice which fully and fairly informs the public of the substance of this section. The notice shall be posted in a location clearly visible to the public in the lienholder's business premises.

(b) Any lienholder proceeding under this section shall notify the owner of the property subject to the lien upon completion of the work for which the lien is claimed. This notice shall be by first-class mail.

(c) If a property owner who has actually received notice pursuant to subdivision (b) fails to pay the charges for which the lien is claimed for 30 days following receipt of the notice, the lienholder may thereafter charge two dollars ($2) per day for storing the property subject to the lien and these charges shall also be secured by the lien.

(d) Not less than 30 days following the notice specified in subdivision (b), the lienholder shall notify the property owner by first-class mail that the property will be sold to satisfy the lien, unless the charges are paid within 30 days following the mailing of the notice.

(e) If the lienholder has complied with the notice requirements of subdivisions (b) and (d), not less than 30 days have elapsed since the mailing of the notice required by subdivision (d), and the property owner has not fully paid the original charges for which the lien is claimed plus any additional charges authorized by subdivision (c), the lienholder may sell the property subject to the lien at a public or bona fide private sale to satisfy the sum of those obligations, all costs and expenses of the sale, and interest at the rate of 12 percent per annum from 30 days following receipt of the notice specified in subdivision (b) or the date the same were advanced until repayment.

(f) However, the owner of the property sold pursuant to subdivision (e) may redeem the property sold to satisfy the lien, within 20 days following the sale, upon payment of all charges, costs and expenses, and interest specified in subdivision (e).

(g) The proceeds of the sale shall first be applied to the discharge of the lien, the costs of sale, and interest specified in subdivision (e). The remainder, if any, shall be paid to the former owner of the property so sold. *(Added by Stats.1991, c. 606 (A.B.1939), § 1.)*

§ 3052.5. Service dealers registered with Bureau of Repair Services; lien; notice; disposition of products of nominal value; alternative methods

(a) Sections 3052 and 3052b shall not apply to any service dealer registered with the Bureau of Repair Services pursuant to Chapter 20 (commencing with Section 9800) of Division 3 of the Business and Professions Code if the dealer reasonably believes that the serviced product is of nominal value. For purposes of this section, nominal value shall be ascertained as follows: the product is not readily salable for more than the legitimate charges against it, and either the original retail value of the product was under two hundred dollars ($200) and the product is over three years old, or the original retail value is over two hundred dollars ($200) and the product is over six years old.

Service dealers may use any available materials or information, including, but not limited to, industry publications, code dates, sales records, or receipts to assist in determining value and age of the serviced product.

(b) A service dealer may select one of the following alternative methods for the disposal of unclaimed serviced products determined to have a value as specified in subdivision (a):

(1) The service dealer may provide the owner of the product with the following written notice to be mailed following completion of work on the serviced product:

DATE BROUGHT IN _____
DATE MAILED _____
DATE PRODUCT TO BE SOLD IF NOT CLAIMED ___
NOTICE: YOUR PRODUCT HAS BEEN DETERMINED BY THIS SERVICE DEALER TO BE ONE WHICH WAS EITHER ORIGINALLY SOLD FOR LESS THAN $200 AND IS NOW OVER THREE YEARS OLD OR ONE WHICH WAS ORIGINALLY SOLD FOR MORE THAN $200 AND WHICH IS NOW OVER SIX YEARS OLD AND THE CHARGES FOR SERVICING YOUR PRODUCT WILL EXCEED ITS CURRENT VALUE. UNDER CALIFORNIA CIVIL CODE SECTION 3052.5(a) IF YOU OR YOUR AGENT FAIL TO CLAIM YOUR PRODUCT WITHIN 90 DAYS AFTER THE DEALER MAILS A COPY OF THIS NOTICE TO YOU IT MAY BE SOLD OR OTHERWISE DISPOSED OF BY HIM OR HER.

The notice shall be sent by certified mail, return receipt requested. A serviced product may be disposed of 90 days after the date of deliverance evidenced by the signature in the returned receipt.

(2) The service dealer may publish public notice of the intended sale in a newspaper of general circulation. The notice shall contain a description of the serviced product, the name of the serviced product owner, and the time by which and place where the product may be redeemed. The notice shall be published for a minimum of five times. A serviced product may be disposed of 90 days after the last date of publication.

(3) A service dealer may, upon receipt of any product to be serviced by him or her, provide the owner of the product with the following notice, written in at least 10–point boldface type:

DATE BROUGHT IN _____
DATE MAILED _____
DATE PRODUCT TO BE SOLD IF NOT CLAIMED ___
NOTICE: YOUR PRODUCT HAS BEEN DETERMINED BY THIS SERVICE DEALER TO BE ONE WHICH WAS EITHER ORIGINALLY SOLD FOR LESS THAN $200 AND IS NOW OVER THREE YEARS OLD OR ONE WHICH WAS ORIGINALLY SOLD FOR MORE THAN $200 AND WHICH IS NOW OVER SIX YEARS OLD AND THE CHARGES FOR

§ 3052.5

SERVICING YOUR PRODUCT WILL EXCEED ITS CURRENT VALUE. UNDER CALIFORNIA CIVIL CODE SECTION 3052.5(a) IF YOU OR YOUR AGENT FAIL TO CLAIM YOUR PRODUCT WITHIN 90 DAYS AFTER THE DEALER MAILS A COPY OF THIS NOTICE TO YOU IT MAY BE SOLD OR OTHERWISE DISPOSED OF BY HIM OR HER.

PRINT YOUR NAME AND MAILING ADDRESS WHERE NOTICE MAY BE SENT TO YOU IN THE SPACE PROVIDED BELOW AND SIGN WHERE INDICATED TO SHOW THAT YOU HAVE READ THIS NOTICE.

_____
(Print Name)

_____
(Street Address)

_____
(City, State and ZIP Code)

IF YOU DO NOT AGREE WITH THE ABOVE DETERMINED VALUE OF YOUR ITEM, DO NOT SIGN THIS DOCUMENT.

Signature: _____
(Owner or Agent)

This notice shall be signed, addressed, and dated by the owner, with a copy to be retained by both the owner and the service dealer. At the completion of service, the service dealer shall by first-class mail, mail a completed copy of the notice to the owner of the serviced product at the address given on the notice form. A serviced product may be disposed of 90 days after the date of mailing.

(c) For purposes of this section, an owner is the person or agent who authorizes the original service or repair, or delivers the product to the service dealer. *(Added by Stats.1977, c. 988, p. 2971, § 1. Amended by Stats.1991, c. 606 (A.B.1939), § 2; Stats.2006, c. 538 (S.B.1852), § 57.)*

§ 3053. Factor's lien

A factor has a general lien, dependent on possession, for all that is due to him as such, upon all articles of commercial value that are intrusted to him by the same principal. *(Enacted in 1872.)*

Cross References

Factor defined, see Civil Code § 2026.
Sale by commission merchant or warehouseman of property on consignment with advances made on it, see Civil Code § 2081.5.

§ 3054. Banker's or savings and loan association's lien; deposit accounts

(a) A banker, or a savings and loan association, has a general lien, dependent on possession, upon all property in their hands belonging to a customer, for the balance due to the banker or savings and loan association from the customer in the course of the business.

(b) The exercise of this lien with respect to deposit accounts shall be subject to the limitations and procedures set forth in Section 1411 or 6660 of the Financial Code. *(Enacted in 1872. Amended by Stats.1975, c. 948, p. 2121, § 1; Stats.1980, c. 1288, p. 4367, § 1; Stats.1987, c. 56, § 21; Stats.2019, c. 497 (A.B.991), § 30, eff. Jan. 1, 2020.)*

§§ 3055, 3056. Repealed by Stats.1937, c. 368, p. 1002, § 10001

§§ 3057, 3058. Repealed by Stats.1982, c. 497, p. 2139, §§ 11, 12, operative July 1, 1983

§ 3059. Mechanic's lien

The liens of mechanics, for materials and services upon real property, are regulated by Chapter 4 (commencing with Section 8400) of Title 2 of Part 6 of Division 4. *(Enacted in 1872. Amended by Stats.1975, c. 678, p. 1474, § 4; Stats.2010, c. 697 (S.B.189), § 13, operative July 1, 2012.)*

Cross References

Mechanics liens, see Civil Code § 8400 et seq.

§ 3060. Mining liens

(a) As used in this section, "mine" means a mining claim or real property worked on as a mine including, but not limited to, any quarry or pit, from which rock, gravel, sand, or any other mineral-containing property is extracted by any mining, or surface mining, operation.

(b) Any person who performs labor in a mine, either in its development or in working on it by the subtractive process, or furnishes materials to be used or consumed in it, has a lien upon the mine and the works owned and used by the owners for milling or reducing the ores from the mine, for the value of the work or labor done or materials furnished by each, whether done or furnished at the instance of the owner of the mine, or the owner's agent, and every contractor, subcontractor, superintendent, or other person having charge of any mining or work or labor performed in and about the mine, either as lessee or under a working bond or contract thereon, shall be held to be the agent of the owner for the purposes of this section. The liens provided for by this section shall be enforced in the same manner as those provided for by Part 6 (commencing with Section 8000) of Division 4.

(c) This section shall become operative on July 1, 2012. *(Added by Stats.1951, c. 1159, p. 2957, § 2. Amended by Stats.1969, c. 1362, p. 2752, § 1, operative Jan. 1, 1971; Stats.2010, c. 697 (S.B.189), § 14, operative July 1, 2012; Stats.2012, c. 263 (A.B.2654), § 2, eff. Sept. 7, 2012.)*

Cross References

Purchaser of interest of partner in mine, notice of liens, see Public Resources Code § 3947.
Work done at owner's instance in absence of notice of nonresponsibility, see Civil Code § 8442.

§ 3061. Threshermen's liens

Every person performing work or labor in, with, about, or upon any barley crusher, threshing machine or engine, horsepower, wagon, or other appliance thereof, while engaged in crushing or threshing, has a lien thereon to the extent of the value of his services. Such lien extends for ten days after any such person ceases such work or labor; provided, within that time, an action is brought to recover the amount of the claim. If judgment is given in favor of the plaintiff in any such action, and it is further found that he is entitled to a lien under the provisions of this section, property subject thereto, or so much thereof as may be necessary, may be sold to satisfy such judgment; but if several judgment[1] have been recovered against the same property for the enforcement of such liens, the proceeds of the sale must be divided pro rata among the judgment creditors. *(Added by Stats.1905, c. 461, p. 618, § 1.)*

¹ So in enrolled bill.

§ 3061.5. Agricultural laborer's lien; liability of severed crops or farm products or proceeds from sale; limitations; exceptions; rights of buyer in ordinary course of business

(a) Except as provided in subdivision (d), any person who as an employee shall, by his or her own labor, do or perform any work harvesting or transporting harvested crops or farm products as defined in Section 55403 of the Food and Agricultural Code which are owned and grown or produced by a limited partnership as defined in Section 15501 of the Corporations Code, has a lien upon any and all of the severed crops or severed farm products or proceeds from their sale for the value of the labor done up to a maximum of earnings for two weeks. The liens attach whether the work was done at the instance of the owner who is the grower or producer of severed crops or severed farm products or of any other person acting by or under the owner's authority, directly or indirectly, as contractor or otherwise; and every contractor, subcontractor, or other person having charge of the harvesting or transporting of the severed crops or severed farm products shall be held to be the agent of the owner for the purposes of this section.

(b) The liens provided for in this section attach from the date of the commencement of the work or labor, and are preferred liens, prior in dignity to all other liens, claims, or encumbrances. Except as provided in subdivisions (a) and (c) they shall not be limited as to amount by any contract price agreed upon between the owner who is the grower or producer of the severed crops or severed farm products and any contractor, but the several liens shall not in any case exceed in amount the reasonable value of the labor done, nor the price agreed upon for the labor between the claimant and his or her employer. In no event, where the claimant was employed by a contractor, or subcontractor, shall the lien extend to any labor not contemplated by, covered by, or reasonably necessary to the execution of, the original contract between the contractor and the owner who is the grower or producer of severed crops or severed farm products and of which contract, or modification thereof, the claimant had actual notice before the performance of the labor.

(c) The maximum liability of severed crops, severed farm products or the proceeds from their sale subject to liens under this section is limited to the lesser of actual proved claims or 25 percent of the fair market value of the severed crops, severed farm products, or 25 percent of the proceeds after their sale.

(d) No person has a lien if the owner who is the grower or producer of the severed crops, severed farm products, or their proceeds, who otherwise would be subject to a lien pursuant to subdivision (a), either gives directly, or requires a person or entity hired or used to furnish labor in connection with harvesting or transporting the severed crops, to give to the Labor Commissioner prior to the harvest and for 45 days after its completion, a bond executed by an admitted surety insurer in an amount and form acceptable to the Labor Commissioner, which is conditioned upon the payment of all wages found to be due and unpaid in connection with such operations under any provision of this code.

(e) A buyer in the ordinary course of business, as defined in paragraph (9) of subdivision (b) of Section 1201 of the Commercial Code, shall take free of any security interest created by this section, notwithstanding the fact that the lien is perfected and the buyer knows of its existence. *(Added by Stats.1976, c. 1059, p. 4688, § 1, operative July 1, 1977. Amended by Stats.1982, c. 517, p. 2327, § 76; Stats.2006, c. 254 (S.B.1481), § 3.)*

Application

For provision relating to application of Stats.2006, c. 254 (S.B.1481) to documents of title that are issued or bailments that arise before Jan. 1, 2007, see § 81 of that act.

Cross References

Bond and Undertaking Law, see Code of Civil Procedure § 995.010 et seq.

§ 3061.6. Agricultural laborer's lien

(a) The lien created by Section 3061.5 shall continue in force for a period of 45 days from the time the person claiming such lien shall have ceased to do or perform the work for which such lien is claimed, and such lien shall cease at the expiration of the 45 days unless the claimant, his or her assignee or successor in interest, files a claim with the Labor Commissioner or brings suit to foreclose the lien in which case the lien continues in force until the claim filed with the Labor Commissioner or the lien foreclosure suit is finally determined and closed. If a claim is filed with the Labor Commissioner, the Labor Commissioner shall act upon and finally determine such claim within 180 days after filing. In case such proceedings are not prosecuted to trial within two years after the commencement thereof, the court may in its discretion dismiss the same for want of prosecution.

(b) Upon filing a claim with the Labor Commissioner, the Labor Commissioner, if the owner who is the grower or producer has failed to satisfy the conditions of subdivision (d) of Section 3061.5, shall determine whether or not such owner of the severed crops, severed farm products, or their proceeds is capable financially of satisfying such claim. For purposes of this determination, it shall be proper for the Labor Commissioner after investigation to take into account the potential liability faced by such owner of such severed crops, severed farm products, or their proceeds. If the Labor Commissioner determines that a lien is necessary to protect the interest of claimants, the Labor Commissioner shall file such lien on the crop, the severed farm product, or their proceeds and notify, in writing, the owner and notify, in writing, all persons who have filed financing statements on the crop, the farm product, or their proceeds pursuant to the provisions of the Commercial Code.

(c) The plaintiff in any such lien foreclosure suit, at the time of issuing the summons or at any time afterwards, may have the severed crops or severed farm products or proceeds from their sale upon which such lien subsists attached, as provided in this code and Title 6.5 (commencing with Section 488.010) of Part 2 of the Code of Civil Procedure, upon

§ 3061.6

delivering to the clerk an affidavit, by or on behalf of the plaintiff, showing that: (1) the plaintiff, or his assignor or predecessor in interest, performed labor in harvesting or transporting the severed crops or severed farm products or both; (2) that such labor has not been paid for; (3) that the sum for which the attachment is asked does not exceed the lesser of the reasonable value of the services rendered or if earnings, does not exceed the lesser of two weeks unpaid earnings or reasonable value of actual services rendered, or 25 percent of the fair market value of the severed crop or severed farm product; and (4) that the attachment is not sought and the action is not brought to hinder, delay or defraud any creditor or creditors of any defendant.

(d) Any number of persons claiming liens under this section and Section 3061.5 may join in the same action and when separate actions are commenced, the court may consolidate them. If after sale of the property subject to the liens provided for in this section and Section 3061.5, under the judgment or decree of foreclosure of such lien or liens, there is a deficiency of proceeds, the proceeds shall be divided pro rata among the lien claimants whose liens are established, regardless of the order in which the liens were created or the order in which the suits to foreclose same were commenced. Judgment for the deficiency may be docketed against the party personally liable therefor and his sureties.

(e) Nothing contained in this section or Section 3061.5 shall be construed to impair or affect the right of any person to whom any debt may be due for work done, to maintain a personal action to recover such debt against the person liable therefor, or his sureties, either in connection with the lien suit or in a separate action. The person bringing such personal action may take out a separate attachment therefor, notwithstanding his or her lien, and in his or her affidavit to procure an attachment need not state that his or her demand is not secured by a lien, and the judgment, if any, obtained by the plaintiff in such personal action shall not be construed to impair or merge any lien held by the plaintiff under this section or Section 3061.5; provided that any money collected on the judgment shall be credited on the amount of such lien in any action brought to enforce the same, in accordance with the provisions of this section.

(f) If the lien has attached to perishable goods, the lienholder may, during the period for which the lien is in effect and prior to the filing of a foreclosure suit, obtain a court order for the sale of such perishable goods pursuant to the provisions of Section 488.530 of the Code of Civil Procedure; provided, however, that in the event that such perishable crop is subject in whole or in part to a valid marketing agreement which is in force between the owner who is the grower or producer and an agricultural marketing cooperative organized under the Food and Agricultural Code or similar laws of other states, the agricultural marketing cooperative may purchase or otherwise take possession or custody of such crop or portion thereof according to the terms of the marketing agreement. Any moneys due and payable to such owner who is the grower or producer in return for such crop shall be paid by the agricultural marketing cooperative to the court. *(Added by Stats.1976, c. 1059, p. 4689, § 2, operative July 1, 1977.)*

§ 3062. Lien for service of stallion, jack, or bull

Every owner or person having in charge any stallion, jack, or bull, used for propagating purposes, has a lien for the agreed price of its service upon any mare or cow and upon the offspring of such service, unless some willfully false representation concerning the breeding or pedigree of such stallion, jack, or bull has been made or published by the owner or person in charge thereof, or by some other person, at the request or instigation of such owner or person in charge. *(Added by Stats.1905, c. 461, p. 618, § 2.)*

§ 3063. Lien for service of stallion, jack, or bull; verified claims; recording; contents; notice

Every claimant of a lien provided for in the preceding section must, within 90 days after the service on account of which the lien is claimed, record in the office of the county recorder of the county where the mare or cow subject thereto is kept, a verified claim containing a particular description of the mare or cow, the date and place of service, the name of the owner or reputed owner of such mare or cow, a description by name, or otherwise, of the stallion, jack, or bull performing the service, the name of the owner or person in charge thereof, and the amount of the lien claimed. Such claim, so recorded, is notice to subsequent purchasers and encumbrancers of such mare or cow and of the offspring of such service for one year after such recording. *(Added by Stats.1905, c. 461, p. 618, § 3. Amended by Stats.1957, c. 815, p. 2031, § 1.)*

§ 3064. Lien for service of stallion, jack, or bull; enforcement action; remedies

An action to enforce any lien created under Section 3062 may be brought in any county wherein any of the property subject thereto may be found, and the plaintiff is entitled to the remedies provided in Section 3065 upon complying with such section, which is hereby made applicable to the proceedings in such action. *(Added by Stats.1905, c. 461, p. 619, § 4. Amended by Stats.1968 c. 48, p. 189, § 4.)*

§ 3064.1. Forfeiture of right to pay for services of breeding animals

Every person who wilfully advertises any cattle, horse, sheep, swine, or other domestic animal for purposes of copulation or profit as having a pedigree other than the true pedigree of such animal shall forfeit all right by law to collect pay for the services of such animal. *(Added by Stats.1955, c. 60, p. 501, § 1.)*

Cross References

False pedigree, see Food and Agricultural Code § 16501.

§ 3065. Loggers' and lumbermen's lien

Any person who shall, by his own labor, or by using his livestock, machinery or appliances, or both, do or perform any work or render any service in connection with felling, preparing or transporting any logs, or in manufacturing lumber or other timber products from such logs, including the production of tanbark, shall have a lien upon any and all of such logs and upon any and all of the lumber and other timber products manufactured therefrom, whether said work was done or service was rendered on the logs themselves, or any of them, or in manufacturing the lumber or other timber products from them, for the value of such labor done and for the value of the use of such livestock, machinery and appliances, or both, whether said work was done or service was rendered at the instance of the owner of such logs or timber products manufactured therefrom, or of any other person acting by his authority or under him, directly or indirectly, as contractor or otherwise; and every contractor, subcontractor or other person having charge of the felling, preparing or transporting of the said logs or of their manufacture into timber products shall be held to be the agent of the said owner for the purposes of this section.

The liens provided for in this section shall attach from the date of the commencement of such work or labor, or the date of the commencement of the use of such livestock, machinery or appliances, as the case may be, and shall be preferred liens, prior in dignity to all other liens, claims or encumbrances, except the landowner's claim for a reasonable stumpage in cases where the landowner himself is not the direct employer or contractor, as the case may be. They shall not be limited as to amount by any contract price agreed upon between the owner of said logs or timber products manufactured therefrom and any contractor, except as hereinafter provided, but said several liens shall not in any case exceed in amount the reasonable value of the labor done, or the reasonable value of the use of the livestock, machinery or appliances for which the lien is claimed, nor the price agreed upon for the same between the claimant and the person by whom he was employed or with whom the agreement to use livestock, machinery or appliances was made, nor in any case, where the claimant was employed by a contractor, or subcontractor, shall the lien extend to any labor or the use of any livestock, machinery or appliances not embraced within, contemplated by, covered by, or reasonably necessary to the execution of, the original contract between the contractor and the owner of such logs or timber products manufactured therefrom, or any modification thereof made by or with the consent of such owner, and of which said contract, or modification thereof, the claimant shall have had actual notice before the performance of such labor or the use of such livestock, machinery or appliances.

The recording of such original contract, or modification thereof, in the office of the county recorder of the county in which the timberland on which the work is to be done is situated or in which the logs are to be manufactured into timber products, as the case may be, before the commencement of the work, shall be equivalent to the giving of such actual notice by the owner to all persons performing work or using livestock, machinery or appliances thereunder. In case said original contract shall, before the work is commenced, be so recorded, together with a bond of the contractor with good and sufficient sureties in an amount not less than fifty (50) percent of the contract price named in said contract, which bond shall in addition to any conditions for the performance of the contract, be also conditioned for the payment in full of the claims of all persons performing labor, or using livestock, machinery or appliances, in the execution of such contract and shall also by its terms be made to inure to the benefit of any and all persons who perform labor or use livestock, machinery or appliances in the execution of the work to be done under the contract so as to give such persons, and their assigns or successors in interest, a right of action to recover upon said bond in any suit brought to enforce the liens provided for in this section, or in a separate suit brought on said bond, then the court must, where it would be equitable so to do, restrict the recovery under such liens to an aggregate amount equal to the amount found to be due from the owner of the said logs or timber products manufactured therefrom to the contractor, and render judgment against the contractor and his sureties on said bond for any deficiency or difference there may remain between said amount so found to be due to the claimants for such labor and for the use of such livestock, machinery and appliances. It is the intent and purpose of this section to limit the owner's liability, in all cases, to the measure of the contract price where he shall have filed or cause to be filed, in good faith, with his original contract a valid bond with good and sufficient sureties in the amount and upon the conditions herein provided. It shall be lawful for the owner of such logs and timber products to protect himself against any failure of the contractor to perform his contract and make full payment for all work done thereunder by exacting such bond or other security as he may deem satisfactory. *(Added by Stats.1905, c. 461, p. 619, § 5. Amended by Stats.1927, c. 505, p. 847, § 1; Stats.1973, c. 665, § 2.)*

Cross References

Salary and wage liens, see Code of Civil Procedure § 1204 et seq.

§ 3065a. Loggers' and lumbermen's lien; duration; remedies

The lien created by the last preceding section shall continue in force for a period of 30 days from the time the person claiming such lien shall have ceased to do or perform the work or render the service for which said lien is claimed, while such logs, lumber or other manufactured timber products are in the county in which such labor was performed or service rendered, and said lien shall cease at the expiration of the said 30 days unless the claimant thereof, or his assignee or successor in interest, brings suit to foreclose the same, in which case the lien continues in force until the said lien foreclosure suit is finally determined and closed, and in case such proceeding be not prosecuted to trial within two years after the commencement thereof, the court may in its discretion dismiss the same for want of prosecution. If any part of the property on which the lien existed is removed from the said county, the lien continues on the balance remaining in the county to the full extent of the claim.

The plaintiff in any such lien foreclosure suit may have the logs, lumber and other manufactured timber products upon which such lien subsists attached, as provided in this code and the Code of Civil Procedure.

Any number of persons claiming liens under this and the next preceding section may join in the same action and when separate actions are commenced, the court may consolidate them. Whenever upon the sale of the property subject to the liens provided for in this and the next preceding section, under the judgment or decree of foreclosure of such lien or liens, there is a deficiency of proceeds, the proceeds shall be divided pro rata among the lien claimants whose liens are established, regardless of the order in which the liens were created or the order in which the suits to foreclose same were commenced, and judgment for the deficiency may be docketed against the party personally liable therefor and his sureties, in like manner and with like effect as in actions for the foreclosure of mortgages.

Nothing contained in this or the next preceding section shall be construed to impair or affect the right of any person to whom any debt may be due for work done, or for the use of livestock, machinery or appliances, to maintain a personal action to recover said debt against the person liable therefor, or his sureties, either in connection with the lien suit or in a separate action, and the person bringing such personal action may take out a separate attachment therefor, notwithstanding his lien or the amount of his debt, and in his affidavit to procure an attachment he shall state that the attachment is made pursuant to this section, and the judgment, if any, obtained by the plaintiff in such personal action shall not be construed to impair or merge any lien held by said plaintiff under this or the next preceding section; provided, only, that any money collected on said judgment shall be credited on the amount of such lien in any action brought to enforce the same, in accordance with the provisions of this section. *(Added by Stats.1927, c. 505, p. 849, § 2. Amended by Stats.1974, c. 1516, p. 3335, § 4, operative Jan. 1, 1977.)*

§ 3065b. Loggers' and lumbermen's lien; cessation of work defined

As used in the next preceding section the words "the time the person claiming such lien shall have ceased to do or perform the work or render the service for which said lien is claimed" shall be construed to mean the final date work was done or services were rendered on any of the logs, lumber or other manufactured timber products on which the lien is claimed, so as to give the lien claimant, or his assignee or successor in interest, a full thirty days after final cessation of labor to bring suit to foreclose his lien on any or all of the logs, lumber or other manufactured timber products in question. *(Added by Stats.1929, c. 157, p. 301, § 1.)*

§ 3065c. Loggers' and lumbermen's lien; affidavit showing wages owed by contractor; filing; stop notice to mill operator; withholding funds due contractor

Whenever any faller, bucker, or millhand has a lien pursuant to Section 3065 and has not been paid for his labor by the contractor employing him, and money is owing to such contractor by a mill operator, any such faller, bucker, or millhand, or several of them acting jointly, may file with the Labor Commissioner an affidavit stating the amount of wages unpaid to him or them and describing the labor for which wages are owed and the period in which such labor was performed. If the Labor Commissioner finds the affidavit in order, he shall send to such mill operator a stop notice directing such mill operator to withhold funds in the amount of the unpaid wages from the contractor. The mill operator shall withhold such funds pursuant to the stop notice for 15 days from the date of service of the notice, subject to garnishment within that period by the faller, bucker, or millhand or any assignee thereof. *(Added by Stats.1957, c. 338, p. 977, § 1.)*

§ 3066. Cleaners' and launderers' liens; service and storage; sale; notice; proceeds; posted notices in receiving office

(a) Any garment, clothing, wearing apparel or household goods remaining in the possession of a person, firm, partnership or corporation, on which cleaning, pressing, glazing or washing has been done or upon which alterations or repairs have been made, or on which materials or supplies have been used or furnished, for a period of 90 days or more after the completion of such work may be sold to pay the reasonable or agreed charges and the costs of notifying the owner or owners. Provided, however, that the person, firm, partnership, or corporation to whom such charges are payable and owing shall first notify the owner or owners of the time and place of such sale. Provided further, that property that is to be placed in storage after any of the services or labors mentioned herein, shall not be affected by the provisions of this section.

(b) All garments, clothing, wearing apparel or household goods placed in storage, or on which any of the services or labors mentioned in the preceding section of this act have been performed and then placed in storage by agreement and remaining in the possession of a person, firm, partnership or corporation without the reasonable or agreed charges having been paid for a period of 12 months, may be sold to pay said charges. Provided that the person, firm, partnership or corporation to whom the charges are payable, shall first notify the owner or owners thereof of the time and place of sale. Provided, however, that the persons, firms, partnerships, or corporations operating as warehouses or warehousemen shall not be affected by this section.

(c) The posting or mailing of a registered letter, with a return address marked thereon, addressed to the owner or owners, at their address given at the time of delivery of the article or articles to a person, firm, partnership or corporation to render any of the services or labors set out in this act, stating the time and place of sale, shall constitute notice. Said notice shall be posted or mailed at least 30 days before the date of sale. The cost of posting or mailing said letter shall be added to the charges.

Where the address of an owner is unknown, a posting of notice, for a period of 30 days, at a prominent place in the receiving office of the person, firm, partnership or corporation required to give the notice is sufficient.

(d) The person, firm, partnership or corporation to whom the charges are payable, shall, from the proceeds of the sale, deduct the charges due plus the costs of notifying the owner and shall hold the overplus, if any, subject to the order of the owner and shall immediately thereafter mail to the owner thereof at his address, if known, a notice of the sale, the amount of the overplus, if any, due him, and at any time within 12 months, upon demand by the owner, pay to the owner said sums or overplus in his hands.

(e) All persons, firms, partnerships or corporations taking advantage of this act must keep posted in a prominent place in their receiving office or offices at all times one notice which shall read as follows:

"All articles cleaned, pressed, glazed, laundered, washed, altered or repaired and not called for in 90 days shall be sold to pay charges." "All articles stored by agreement and charges not having been paid for 12 months will be sold to pay charges." *(Added by Stats.1945, c. 910, p. 1695, § 1. Amended by Stats.1955, c. 665, p. 1158, § 1.)*

Cross References

Possessory lien of cleaners and launderers, see Civil Code § 3051.

CHAPTER 6.5. LIENS ON VEHICLES

Section
3067. Definitions.
3067.1. Forms.
3067.2. Manufactured homes, mobilehomes, or commercial coaches; application of chapter.
3068. Service lien.
3068.1. Towing, storage, or labor lien; storage charges; lien satisfaction; lienholder not liable.
3068.2. Tow truck operator; deficiency claim; towing and storage charges; lien sale processing fee; persons liable.
3069. Assignment of lien; notice to owner.
3070. Loss of lien through trick, fraud or device; revival of lien; improperly causing vehicle to be towed or removed to create or acquire lien; forfeiture of claims and liability to owner or lessee.
3071. Lien sale.
3071.3. Repealed.
3071.5. Vehicle in possession of lienor; release by registered or legal owner of interest.
3072. Lien sales; valuation of $4,000 or less.
3072.2. Repealed.
3073. Proceeds of sale; disposition; claims; limitation of actions.
3074. Lien sale preparations; fees.
3075. Repealed.
3076, 3077. Repealed.
3078, 3079. Repealed.

Cross References

Illegal dumping of harmful waste matter, impoundment and civil forfeiture, see Vehicle Code § 23112.7.
Lien on impounded vehicles, see Vehicle Code § 14602.
Liens for tolls and other charges, see Vehicle Code § 23303.
Perfecting liens or encumbrances on vehicles, see Vehicle Code § 6300 et seq.
Possessory liens for service, repairs, etc., see Civil Code § 3051 et seq.
Registration or transfer fee, lien, see Vehicle Code § 9800.
Removal of parked and abandoned vehicles, lien for towage and care, see Vehicle Code § 22851.

§ 3067. Definitions

Words used in this chapter which are defined in Division 1 of the Vehicle Code [1] shall have the same meaning as in the Vehicle Code. *(Added by Stats.1959, c. 3, p. 1791, § 3.)*

[1] Vehicle Code, § 100 et seq.

§ 3067.1. Forms

All forms required pursuant to the provisions of this chapter shall be prescribed by the Department of Motor Vehicles. The language used in the notices and declarations shall be simple and nontechnical. *(Added by Stats.1980, c. 1111, p. 3562, § 1.)*

§ 3067.2. Manufactured homes, mobilehomes, or commercial coaches; application of chapter

This chapter shall not apply to any manufactured home, as defined in Section 18007 of the Health and Safety Code, to any mobilehome, as defined in Section 18008 of the Health and Safety Code, or to any commercial coach, as defined in Section 18001.8 of the Health and Safety Code, whether or not the manufactured home, mobilehome, or commercial coach is subject to registration under the Health and Safety Code. *(Added by Stats.1983, c. 1124, § 7, operative Jan. 1, 1984.)*

§ 3068. Service lien

(a) Every person has a lien dependent upon possession for the compensation to which the person is legally entitled for making repairs or performing labor upon, and furnishing supplies or materials for, and for the storage, repair, or safekeeping of, and for the rental of parking space for, any vehicle of a type subject to registration under the Vehicle Code, subject to the limitations set forth in this chapter. The lien shall be deemed to arise at the time a written statement of charges for completed work or services is presented to the registered owner or 15 days after the work or services are completed, whichever occurs first. Upon completion of the work or services, the lienholder shall not dismantle, disengage, remove, or strip from the vehicle the parts used to complete the work or services.

(b)(1) Any lien under this section that arises because work or services have been performed on a vehicle with the consent of the registered owner shall be extinguished and no lien sale shall be conducted unless either of the following occurs:

(A) The lienholder applies for an authorization to conduct a lien sale within 30 days after the lien has arisen.

(B) An action in court is filed within 30 days after the lien has arisen.

(2) A person whose lien for work or services on a vehicle has been extinguished shall turn over possession of the vehicle, at the place where the work or services were performed, to the legal owner or the lessor upon demand of the legal owner or lessor, and upon tender by the legal owner or lessor, by cashier's check or in cash, of only the amount for storage, safekeeping, or parking space rental for the vehicle to which the person is entitled by subdivision (c).

(3) Any lien under this section that arises because work or services have been performed on a vehicle with the consent of the registered owner shall be extinguished, and no lien sale shall be conducted, if the lienholder, after written demand made by either personal service or certified mail with return receipt requested by the legal owner or the lessor to inspect the vehicle, fails to permit that inspection by the legal owner or lessor, or his or her agent, within a period of time not sooner than 24 hours nor later than 72 hours after the receipt of that written demand, during the normal business hours of the lienholder.

(4) Any lien under this section that arises because work or services have been performed on a vehicle with the consent of the registered owner shall be extinguished, and no lien sale shall be conducted, if the lienholder, after written demand made by either personal service or certified mail with return receipt requested by the legal owner or the lessor to receive a written copy of the work order or invoice reflecting the services or repairs performed on the vehicle and the authorization from the registered owner requesting the lienholder to perform the services or repairs, fails to provide that copy to

the legal owner or lessor, or his or her agent, within 10 days after the receipt of that written demand.

(c) The lienholder shall not charge the legal owner or lessor any amount for release of the vehicle in excess of the amounts authorized by this subdivision.

(1) That portion of the lien in excess of one thousand five hundred dollars ($1,500) for any work or services, or that amount, subject to the limitations contained in Section 10652.5 of the Vehicle Code, in excess of one thousand twenty-five dollars ($1,025) for any storage, safekeeping, or rental of parking space or, if an application for an authorization to conduct a lien sale has been filed pursuant to Section 3071 within 30 days after the commencement of the storage or safekeeping, in excess of one thousand two hundred fifty dollars ($1,250) for any storage or safekeeping, rendered or performed at the request of any person other than the legal owner or lessor, is invalid, unless prior to commencing any work, services, storage, safekeeping, or rental of parking space, the person claiming the lien gives actual notice in writing either by personal service or by registered letter addressed to the legal owner named in the registration certificate, and the written consent of that legal owner is obtained before any work, services, storage, safekeeping, or rental of parking space are performed.

(2) Subject to the limitations contained in Section 10652.5 of the Vehicle Code, if any portion of a lien includes charges for the care, storage, or safekeeping of, or for the rental of parking space for, a vehicle for a period in excess of 60 days, the portion of the lien that accrued after the expiration of that period is invalid unless Sections 10650 and 10652 of the Vehicle Code have been complied with by the holder of the lien.

(3) The charge for the care, storage, or safekeeping of a vehicle which may be charged to the legal owner or lessor shall not exceed that for one day of storage if, 24 hours or less after the vehicle is placed in storage, a request is made for the release of the vehicle. If the request is made more than 24 hours after the vehicle is placed in storage, charges may be imposed on a full, calendar-day basis for each day, or part thereof, that the vehicle is in storage.

(d) In any action brought by or on behalf of the legal owner or lessor to recover a vehicle alleged to be wrongfully withheld by the person claiming a lien pursuant to this section, the prevailing party shall be entitled to reasonable attorney's fees and costs, not to exceed one thousand seven hundred fifty dollars ($1,750). *(Added by Stats.1959, c. 3, p. 1791, § 3. Amended by Stats.1959, c. 197, p. 2089, § 2; Stats.1965, c. 1135, p. 2786, § 1; Stats.1968, c. 830, p. 1603, § 2; Stats.1974, c. 1262, p. 2736, § 2, eff. Sept. 23, 1974, operative Nov. 1, 1974; Stats.1978, c. 1005, p. 3084, § 4; Stats.1980, c. 1111, p. 3562, § 2; Stats.1983, c. 764, § 1; Stats.1988, c. 1092, § 4; Stats.1991, c. 727 (A.B.1882), § 1; Stats.1994, c. 799 (A.B.3164), § 1; Stats.2007, c. 121 (A.B. 1575), § 1.)*

Cross References

Legal owner defined, see Vehicle Code § 370.
Motor vehicles,
 Constructive notice of mortgage, see Vehicle Code § 6301.
Registered owner defined, see Vehicle Code § 505.

Removal of vessel from public waterways by peace officers, lifeguards, or marine safety officers, see Harbors and Navigation Code § 523.
Report of vehicles stored for 30 days, see Vehicle Code § 10652.
Revival of lost lien, see Civil Code § 3070.
Similar provision, see Civil Code § 3051.

§ 3068.1. Towing, storage, or labor lien; storage charges; lien satisfaction; lienholder not liable

(a)(1) Every person has a lien dependent upon possession for the compensation to which the person is legally entitled for towing, storage, or labor associated with recovery or load salvage of any vehicle subject to registration that has been authorized to be removed by a public agency, a private property owner pursuant to Section 22658 of the Vehicle Code, or a lessee, operator, or registered owner of the vehicle. The lien is deemed to arise on the date of possession of the vehicle. Possession is deemed to arise when the vehicle is removed and is in transit, or when vehicle recovery operations or load salvage operations have begun. A person seeking to enforce a lien for the storage and safekeeping of a vehicle shall impose no charge exceeding that for one day of storage if, 24 hours or less after the vehicle is placed in storage, the vehicle is released. If the release is made more than 24 hours after the vehicle is placed in storage, charges may be imposed on a full-calendar-day basis for each day, or part thereof, that the vehicle is in storage. If a request to release the vehicle is made and the appropriate fees are tendered and documentation establishing that the person requesting release is entitled to possession of the vehicle, or is the owner's insurance representative, is presented within the initial 24 hours of storage, and the storage facility fails to comply with the request to release the vehicle or is not open for business during normal business hours, then only one day's charge may be required to be paid until after the first business day. A "business day" is any day in which the lienholder is open for business to the public for at least eight hours. If the request is made more than 24 hours after the vehicle is placed in storage, charges may be imposed on a full-calendar-day basis for each day, or part thereof, that the vehicle is in storage.

(2) "Documentation" that would entitle a person to possession of the vehicle includes, but is not limited to, a certificate of ownership, vehicle registration, information in the possession of the lienholder including ownership information obtained from the Department of Motor Vehicles or a facially valid registration found within the vehicle, or a notarized letter or statement from the legal or registered owner providing authorization to release to a particular person with a government-issued photographic identification card. Documentation that establishes that a person is the owner's insurance representative includes, but is not limited to, a faxed letter or other letter from the owner's insurance company. A lienholder is not responsible for determining the authenticity of documentation specifically described in this subdivision that establishes either a person's entitlement to possession or that a person is the owner's insurance representative.

(b) If the vehicle has been determined to have a value not exceeding four thousand dollars ($4,000), the lien shall be satisfied pursuant to Section 3072. Lien sale proceedings pursuant to Section 3072 shall commence within 15 days of the date the lien arises. No storage shall accrue beyond the 15-day period unless lien sale proceedings pursuant to Section 3072 have commenced. The storage lien may be for a period not exceeding 60 days if a completed notice of a pending lien sale form has been filed pursuant to Section 3072 within 15 days after the lien arises. Notwithstanding this 60-day limitation, the storage lien may be for a period not exceeding 120 days if any one of the following occurs:

(1) A Declaration of Opposition form is filed with the department pursuant to Section 3072.

(2) The vehicle has an out-of-state registration.

(3) The vehicle identification number was altered or removed.

(4) A person who has an interest in the vehicle becomes known to the lienholder after the lienholder has complied with subdivision (b) of Section 3072.

(c) If the vehicle has been determined to have a value exceeding four thousand dollars ($4,000) pursuant to Section 22670 of the Vehicle Code, the lien shall be satisfied pursuant to Section 3071. The storage lien may be for a period not exceeding 120 days if an application for an authorization to conduct a lien sale has been filed pursuant to Section 3071.

(d)(1) Any lien under this section shall be extinguished, and a lien sale shall not be conducted, if any one of the following occurs:

(A) The lienholder, after written demand to inspect the vehicle made by either personal service or certified mail with return receipt requested by the legal owner or the lessor, fails to permit the inspection by the legal owner or lessor, or his or her agent, within a period of time of at least 24 hours, but not to exceed 72 hours, after the receipt of that written demand, during the normal business hours of the lienholder. The legal owner or lessor shall comply with inspection and vehicle release policies of the impounding public agency.

(B) The amount claimed for storage exceeds the posted rates.

(2) "Agent" includes, but is not limited to, any person designated to inspect the vehicle by the request of the legal owner or lessor, in writing or by telephone, to the lienholder. A lienholder is not responsible for determining the authenticity of documentation establishing a person's agency for the purposes of inspection of a vehicle.

(e) A lienholder shall not be liable for any claim or dispute directly arising out of the reliance on documentation specifically described in paragraph (2) of subdivision (a) for purposes of releasing a vehicle. (Added by Stats.1980, c. 1111, p. 3563, § 3. Amended by Stats.1984, c. 73, § 1; Stats.1987, c. 1091 § 1; Stats.1989, c. 457, § 1; Stats.1991, c. 727 (A.B.1882), § 2; Stats.1991, c. 1004 (S.B.887), § 1; Stats.1992, c. 1220 (A.B.3424), § 1; Stats.1994, c. 799 (A.B. 3164), § 2; Stats.1995, c. 404 (S.B.240), § 1; Stats.1996, c. 267 (S.B.223), § 1; Stats.1998, c. 203 (S.B.1650), § 1; Stats. 2010, c. 566 (A.B.519), § 1.)

§ 3068.2. Tow truck operator; deficiency claim; towing and storage charges; lien sale processing fee; persons liable

(a) A tow truck operator who has a lien on a vehicle pursuant to Section 3068.1 has a deficiency claim against the registered owner of the vehicle if the vehicle is not leased or leased with a driver for an amount equal to the towing and storage charges, not to exceed 120 days of storage, and the lien sale processing fee pursuant to Section 3074, less the amount received from the sale of the vehicle.

(b) A tow truck operator who has a lien on a vehicle pursuant to Section 3068.1 has a deficiency claim against the lessee of the vehicle if the vehicle is leased without a driver for an amount equal to the towing and storage charge, not to exceed 120 days of storage, and the lien sale processing fee described in Section 3074, less the amount received from the sale of the vehicle.

(c) Storage costs incurred after the sale shall not be included in calculating the amount received from the sale of the vehicle.

(d) A registered owner who has sold or transferred the owner's vehicle prior to the vehicle's removal and who was not responsible for creating the circumstances leading to the removal of the vehicle is not liable for any deficiency under this section if that registered owner has fulfilled the requirements of Section 5602 of the Vehicle Code. The person identified as the transferee in the notice submitted to the Department of Motor Vehicles shall be liable for the amount of any deficiency only if that person received notice of the transfer and is responsible for the event leading to abandonment of the vehicle or requested the removal.

(e) Except as provided in Section 22524.5 of the Vehicle Code, if the transferee is an insurer and the transferor is its insured or the transferor's agent or representative, the insurer shall not be liable for any deficiency, unless the insurer agrees at the time of the transfer, to assume liability for the deficiency. (Added by Stats.1994, c. 1220 (A.B.3132), § 2.5, eff. Sept. 30, 1994. Amended by Stats.2020, c. 50 (A.B.2319), § 1, eff. Jan. 1, 2021.)

§ 3069. Assignment of lien; notice to owner

Any lien provided for in this chapter for labor or materials, or for storage or safekeeping of a vehicle when abandoned on private property may be assigned by written instrument accompanied by delivery of possession of the vehicle, subject to the lien, and the assignee may exercise the rights of a lienholder as provided in this chapter. Any lienholder assigning a lien as authorized herein shall at the time of assigning the lien give written notice either by personal delivery or by registered or certified mail, to the registered and legal owner of the assignment, including the name and address of the person to whom the lien is assigned. (Added by Stats.1959, c. 3, p. 1791, § 3. Amended by Stats.1969, c. 125, p. 272, § 1.)

Cross References

Legal owner defined, see Vehicle Code § 370.
Registered owner defined, see Vehicle Code § 505.

§ 3070. Loss of lien through trick, fraud or device; revival of lien; improperly causing vehicle to be towed or removed to create or acquire lien; forfeiture of claims and liability to owner or lessee

(a) Whenever the possessory lien upon any vehicle is lost through trick, fraud, or device, the repossession of the vehicle by the lienholder revives the possessory lien but any lien so revived is subordinate to any right, title, or interest of any person under any sale, transfer, encumbrance, lien, or other interest acquired or secured in good faith and for value between the time of the loss of possession and the time of repossession.

(b) It is a misdemeanor for any person to obtain possession of any vehicle or any part thereof subject to a lien pursuant to this chapter by trick, fraud, or device.

(c) It is a misdemeanor for any person claiming a lien on a vehicle to knowingly violate this chapter.

(d)(1) Any person who improperly causes a vehicle to be towed or removed in order to create or acquire a lienhold interest enforceable under this chapter, or who violates subdivision (c), shall forfeit all claims for towing, removal, or storage, and shall be liable to the owner or lessee of the vehicle for the cost of removal, transportation, and storage, damages resulting from the towing, removal, transportation, or storage of the vehicle, attorneys' fees, and court costs.

(2) For purposes of this subdivision, "improperly causes a vehicle to be towed or removed" includes, but is not limited to, engaging in any of the following acts, the consequence of which is the towing or removal of a vehicle:

(A) Failure to comply with Section 10650, 10652.5, or 10655 of the Vehicle Code.

(B) Misrepresentation of information described in subdivision (b) of Section 10650 of the Vehicle Code.

(C) Failure to comply with Section 22658 of the Vehicle Code.

(D) Failure, when obtaining authorization for the removal of a vehicle from a vehicle owner or operator where a law enforcement officer is not present at the scene of an accident, to present a form for signature that plainly identifies all applicable towing and storage fees and charges by type and amount, and identifies the name and address of the storage facility unless a different storage facility is specified by the vehicle owner or operator, and to furnish a copy of the signed form to the owner or operator.

(E) Failure by the owner or operator of a facility used for the storage of towed vehicles to display, in plain view at all cashiers' stations, a sign not less than 17 by 22 inches in size with lettering not less than one inch in height, disclosing all storage fees and charges in force, including the maximum daily storage rate.

(F) Undertaking repairs or service on a vehicle which is being stored at a facility used for the storage of towed vehicles without first providing a written estimate to, and obtaining the express written consent of, the owner of the vehicle.

(G) The promise to pay or the payment of money or other valuable consideration by any owner or operator of a towing service to the owner or operator of the premises from which the vehicle is towed or removed, for the privilege of towing or removing the vehicle. (Added by Stats.1980, c. 1111, p. 3564, § 5. Amended by Stats.1991, c. 1004 (S.B.887), § 2; Stats. 1993, c. 479 (A.B.1113), § 1; Stats.1994, c. 799 (A.B.3164), § 3.)

Cross References

Fraud defined, see Civil Code §§ 1572, 1573.
Punishment for misdemeanor, see Penal Code §§ 19, 19.2.
Similar provisions, see Civil Code § 3051.

§ 3071. Lien sale

(a) A lienholder shall apply to the department for the issuance of an authorization to conduct a lien sale pursuant to this section for any vehicle with a value determined to be over four thousand dollars ($4,000). A filing fee shall be charged by the department and may be recovered by the lienholder if a lien sale is conducted or if the vehicle is redeemed. The application shall be executed under penalty of perjury and shall include all of the following information:

(1) A description of the vehicle, including make, year model, identification number, license number, and state of registration. For motorcycles, the engine number also shall be included. If the vehicle identification number is not available, the department shall request an inspection of the vehicle by a peace officer, licensed vehicle verifier, or departmental employee before accepting the application.

(2) The names and addresses of the registered and legal owners of the vehicle, if ascertainable from the registration certificates within the vehicle, and the name and address of any person whom the lienholder knows, or reasonably should know, claims an interest in the vehicle.

(3) A statement of the amount of the lien and the facts that give rise to the lien.

(b) Upon receipt of an application made pursuant to subdivision (a), the department shall do all of the following:

(1) Notify the vehicle registry agency of a foreign state of the pending lien sale, if the vehicle bears indicia of registration in that state.

(2) By certified mail, send a notice, a copy of the application, and a return envelope preaddressed to the department to the registered and legal owners at their addresses of record with the department, and to any other person whose name and address is listed in the application.

(c) The notice required pursuant to subdivision (b) shall include all of the following statements and information:

(1) An application has been made with the department for authorization to conduct a lien sale.

(2) The person has a right to a hearing in court.

(3) If a hearing in court is desired, a Declaration of Opposition form, signed under penalty of perjury, shall be signed and returned to the department within 10 days of the date that the notice required pursuant to subdivision (b) was mailed.

(4) If the Declaration of Opposition form is signed and returned to the department, the lienholder shall be allowed to sell the vehicle only if he or she obtains a court judgment, if he or she obtains a subsequent release from the declarant or if the declarant, cannot be served as described in subdivision (e).

(5) If a court action is filed, the declarant shall be notified of the lawsuit at the address shown on the Declaration of Opposition form and may appear to contest the claim.

(6) The person may be liable for court costs if a judgment is entered in favor of the lienholder.

(d) If the department receives the Declaration of Opposition form in the time specified, the department shall notify the lienholder within 16 days of the receipt of the form that a lien sale shall not be conducted unless the lienholder files an action in court within 30 days of the department's notice under this subdivision. A lien sale of the vehicle shall not be conducted unless judgment is subsequently entered in favor of the lienholder or the declarant subsequently releases his or her interest in the vehicle. If a money judgment is entered in favor of the lienholder and the judgment is not paid within five days after becoming final, then the judgment may be enforced by lien sale proceedings conducted pursuant to subdivision (f).

(e) Service on the declarant in person or by certified mail with return receipt requested, signed by the declarant or an authorized agent of the declarant at the address shown on the Declaration of Opposition form, shall be effective for the serving of process. If the lienholder has served the declarant by certified mail at the address shown on the Declaration of Opposition form and the mail has been returned unclaimed, or if the lienholder has attempted to effect service on the declarant in person with a marshal, sheriff, or licensed process server and the marshal, sheriff, or licensed process server has been unable to effect service on the declarant, the lienholder may proceed with the judicial proceeding or proceed with the lien sale without a judicial proceeding. The lienholder shall notify the department of the inability to effect service on the declarant and shall provide the department with a copy of the documents with which service on the declarant was attempted. Upon receipt of the notification of unsuccessful service, the department shall send authorization of the sale to the lienholder and send notification of the authorization to the declarant.

(f) Upon receipt of authorization to conduct the lien sale from the department, the lienholder shall immediately do all of the following:

(1) At least five days, but not more than 20 days, prior to the lien sale, not counting the day of the sale, give notice of the sale by advertising once in a newspaper of general circulation published in the county in which the vehicle is located. If there is no newspaper published in the county, notice shall be given by posting a Notice of Sale form in three of the most public places in the town in which the vehicle is located and at the place where the vehicle is to be sold for 10 consecutive days prior to and including the day of the sale.

(2) Send a Notice of Pending Lien Sale form 20 days prior to the sale but not counting the day of sale, by certified mail with return receipt requested, to each of the following:

(A) The registered and legal owners of the vehicle, if registered in this state.

(B) All persons known to have an interest in the vehicle.

(C) The department.

(g) All notices required by this section, including the notice forms prescribed by the department, shall specify the make, year model, vehicle identification number, license number, and state of registration, if available, and the specific date, exact time, and place of sale. For motorcycles, the engine number shall also be included.

(h) Following the sale of a vehicle, the person who conducts the sale shall do both of the following:

(1) Remove and destroy the vehicle's license plates.

(2) Within five days of the sale, submit a completed "Notice of Release of Liability" form to the Department of Motor Vehicles.

(i) The Department of Motor Vehicles shall retain all submitted forms described in paragraph (2) of subdivision (h) for two years.

(j) No lien sale shall be undertaken pursuant to this section unless the vehicle has been available for inspection at a location easily accessible to the public for at least one hour before the sale and is at the place of sale at the time and date specified on the notice of sale. Sealed bids shall not be accepted. The lienholder shall conduct the sale in a commercially reasonable manner.

(k) Within 10 days after the sale of any vehicle pursuant to this section, the legal or registered owner may redeem the vehicle upon the payment of the amount of the sale, all costs and expenses of the sale, together with interest on the sum at the rate of 12 percent per annum from the due date thereof or the date when that sum was advanced until the repayment. If the vehicle is not redeemed, all lien sale documents required by the department shall then be completed and delivered to the buyer.

(*l*) Any lien sale pursuant to this section shall be void if the lienholder does not comply with this chapter. Any lien for fees or storage charges for parking and storage of a motor vehicle shall be subject to Section 10652.5 of the Vehicle Code. (Added by Stats.1980, c. 1111, p. 3564, § 7. Amended by Stats.1984, c. 73, § 2; Stats.1987, c. 1091, § 2; Stats.1990, c. 1284 (A.B.3049), § 1; Stats.1992, c. 1220 (A.B.3424), § 2; Stats.1994, c. 799 (A.B.3164), § 4; Stats.1998, c. 203 (S.B. 1650), § 2; Stats.1999, c. 376 (A.B.327), § 1; Stats.2001, c. 127 (S.B.46), § 1, eff. July 30, 2001.)

Cross References

Abandoned vehicles, determination of value for lien sale purposes, see Vehicle Code § 22670.
Applicability of this section to enforcement of lien for towage and care of parked and abandoned vehicles after removal, see Vehicle Code § 22851.
Legal owner defined, see Vehicle Code § 370.
Motor vehicle fund, see Vehicle Code § 42270 et seq.
Publication, see Government Code § 6000 et seq.
Registered owner defined, see Vehicle Code § 505.
Self-storage facilities, liens and lien sales, see Business and Professions Code § 21702 et seq.
Similar provisions, see Civil Code § 3052.

§ 3071.3. Repealed by Stats.1980, c. 1111, p. 3566, § 8

§ 3071.5. Vehicle in possession of lienor; release by registered or legal owner of interest

(a) A registered or legal owner of a vehicle in the possession of a person holding a lien under this chapter may release any interest in the vehicle after the lien has arisen. The release shall be dated when signed and a copy shall be given at the time the release is signed to the person releasing the interest.

(b) The release shall be in at least 12-point type and shall contain all of the following information in simple, nontechnical language:

(1) A description of the vehicle, including the year and make, the engine or vehicle identification number, and the license number, if available.

(2) The names and addresses of the registered and legal owners of record with the Department of Motor Vehicles, if available.

(3) A statement of the amount of the lien and the facts concerning the claim which gives rise to the lien.

(4) A statement that the person releasing the interest understands that (i) he has a legal right to a hearing in court prior to any sale of the vehicle to satisfy the lien and (ii) he is giving up the right to appear to contest the claim of the lienholder.

(5) A statement that (i) the person releasing the interest gives up any interest he may have in the vehicle and (ii) he is giving the lienholder permission to sell the vehicle.

(c) The release required by this section shall not be filed with the department in connection with any transfer of interest in a vehicle. (Added by Stats.1974, c. 1262, p. 2739, § 4, eff. Sept. 23, 1974, operative Nov. 1, 1974. Amended by Stats.1978, c. 1005, p. 3089, § 7.)

§ 3072. Lien sales; valuation of $4,000 or less

(a) For vehicles with a value determined to be four thousand dollars ($4,000) or less, the lienholder shall apply to the department for the names and addresses of the registered and legal owners of record. The request shall include a description of the vehicle, including make, year, model, identification number, license number, and state of registration. If the vehicle identification number is not available, the Department of Motor Vehicles shall request an inspection of the vehicle by a peace officer, licensed vehicle verifier, or departmental employee before releasing the names and addresses of the registered and legal owners and interested parties.

(b) The lienholder shall, immediately upon receipt of the names and addresses, send, by certified mail with return receipt requested or by United States Postal Service Certificate of Mailing, a completed Notice of Pending Lien Sale form, a blank Declaration of Opposition form, and a return envelope preaddressed to the department, to the registered owner and legal owner at their addresses of record with the department, and to any other person known to have an interest in the vehicle. The lienholder shall additionally send a copy of the completed Notice of Pending Lien Sale form to the department by certified mail on the same day that the other notices are mailed pursuant to this subdivision.

(c) All notices to persons having an interest in the vehicle shall be signed under penalty of perjury and shall include all of the following information and statements:

(1) A description of the vehicle, including make, year model, identification number, license number, and state of registration. For motorcycles, the engine number shall also be included.

(2) The specific date, exact time, and place of sale, which shall be set not less than 31 days, but not more than 41 days, from the date of mailing.

(3) The names and addresses of the registered and legal owners of the vehicle and any other person known to have an interest in the vehicle.

(4) All of the following statements:

(A) The amount of the lien and the facts concerning the claim which gives rise to the lien.

(B) The person has a right to a hearing in court.

(C) If a court hearing is desired, a Declaration of Opposition form, signed under penalty of perjury, shall be signed and returned to the department within 10 days of the date the Notice of Pending Lien Sale form was mailed.

(D) If the Declaration of Opposition form is signed and returned, the lienholder shall be allowed to sell the vehicle only if he or she obtains a court judgment or if he or she obtains a subsequent release from the declarant or if the declarant cannot be served as described in subdivision (e).

(E) If a court action is filed, the declarant shall be notified of the lawsuit at the address shown on the Declaration of Opposition form and may appear to contest the claim.

(F) The person may be liable for court costs if a judgment is entered in favor of the lienholder.

(d) If the department receives the completed Declaration of Opposition form within the time specified, the department shall notify the lienholder within 16 days that a lien sale shall not be conducted unless the lienholder files an action in court within 30 days of the notice and judgment is subsequently entered in favor of the lienholder or the declarant subsequently releases his or her interest in the vehicle. If a money judgment is entered in favor of the lienholder and the judgment is not paid within five days after becoming final, then the judgment may be enforced by lien sale proceedings conducted pursuant to subdivision (f).

(e) Service on the declarant in person or by certified mail with return receipt requested, signed by the declarant or an authorized agent of the declarant at the address shown on the Declaration of Opposition form, shall be effective for the serving of process. If the lienholder has served the declarant by certified mail at the address shown on the Declaration of Opposition form and the mail has been returned unclaimed, or if the lienholder has attempted to effect service on the declarant in person with a marshal, sheriff, or licensed process server and the marshal, sheriff, or licensed process server has been unable to effect service on the declarant, the lienholder may proceed with the judicial proceeding or proceed with the lien sale without a judicial proceeding. The lienholder shall notify the Department of Motor Vehicles of the inability to effect service on the declarant and shall provide the Department of Motor Vehicles with a copy of the documents with which service on the declarant was attempted. Upon receipt of the notification of unsuccessful service, the Department of Motor Vehicles shall send authorization of the sale to the lienholder and shall send notification of the authorization to the declarant.

(f) At least 10 consecutive days prior to and including the day of the sale, the lienholder shall post a Notice of Pending

Lien Sale form in a conspicuous place on the premises of the business office of the lienholder and if the pending lien sale is scheduled to occur at a place other than the premises of the business office of the lienholder, at the site of the forthcoming sale. The Notice of Pending Lien Sale form shall state the specific date and exact time of the sale and description of the vehicle, including the make, year model, identification number, license number, and state of registration. For motorcycles, the engine number shall also be included. The notice of sale shall remain posted until the sale is completed.

(g) Following the sale of a vehicle, the person who conducts the sale shall do both of the following:

(1) Remove and destroy the vehicle's license plates.

(2) Within five days of the sale, submit a completed "Notice of Release of Liability" form with the Department of Motor Vehicles.

(h) The Department of Motor Vehicles shall retain all submitted forms described in paragraph (2) of subdivision (g) for two years.

(i) No lien sale shall be undertaken pursuant to this section unless the vehicle has been available for inspection at a location easily accessible to the public at least one hour before the sale and is at the place of sale at the time and date specified on the notice of sale. Sealed bids shall not be accepted. The lienholder shall conduct the sale in a commercially reasonable manner. All lien sale documents required by the department shall be completed and delivered to the buyer immediately following the sale.

(j) Any lien sale pursuant to this section shall be void if the lienholder does not comply with this chapter. Any lien for fees or storage charges for parking and storage of a motor vehicle shall be subject to Section 10652.5 of the Vehicle Code. *(Added by Stats.1980, c. 1111, p. 3566, § 10. Amended by Stats.1984, c. 73, § 3; Stats.1987, c. 1091, § 3; Stats. 1990, c. 1284 (A.B.3049), § 2; Stats.1992, c. 1220 (A.B.3424), § 3; Stats.1994, c. 799 (A.B.3164), § 5; Stats.1998, c. 203 (S.B.1650), § 3; Stats.1999, c. 376 (A.B.327), § 2; Stats.2001, c. 127 (S.B.46), § 2, eff. July 30, 2001.)*

Cross References

Abandoned vehicles, determination of value for lien sale purposes, see Vehicle Code § 22670.

Failure of registered owner of mobilehome, manufactured home, or recreational vehicle to pay costs of remediation, warehouseman's lien, see Health and Safety Code § 25400.47.

§ 3072.2. Repealed by Stats.1980, c. 1111, p. 3567, § 11

§ 3073. Proceeds of sale; disposition; claims; limitation of actions

The proceeds of a vehicle lien sale under this article shall be disposed of as follows:

(a) The amount necessary to discharge the lien and the cost of processing the vehicle shall be paid to the lienholder. The cost of processing shall not exceed seventy dollars ($70) for each vehicle valued at four thousand dollars ($4,000) or less, or one hundred dollars ($100) for each vehicle valued over four thousand dollars ($4,000).

(b) The balance, if any, shall be forwarded to the Department of Motor Vehicles within 15 days of any sale conducted pursuant to Section 3071 or within five days of any sale conducted pursuant to Section 3072 and deposited in the Motor Vehicle Account in the State Transportation Fund, unless federal law requires these funds to be disposed in a different manner.

(c) Any person claiming an interest in the vehicle may file a claim with the Department of Motor Vehicles for any portion of the funds from the lien sale that were forwarded to the department pursuant to subdivision (b). Upon a determination of the Department of Motor Vehicles that the claimant is entitled to an amount from the balance deposited with the department, the department shall pay that amount determined by the department, which amount shall not exceed the amount forwarded to the department pursuant to subdivision (b) in connection with the sale of the vehicle in which the claimant claims an interest. The department shall not honor any claim unless the claim has been filed within three years of the date the funds were deposited in the Motor Vehicle Account. *(Added by Stats.1980, c. 1111, p. 3567, § 13. Amended by Stats.1988, c. 511, § 1; Stats.1990, c. 1284 (A.B.3049), § 3; Stats.1992, c. 1220 (A.B.3424), § 4; Stats. 1994, c. 799 (A.B.3164), § 6; Stats.1998, c. 203 (S.B.1650), § 4.)*

§ 3074. Lien sale preparations; fees

The lienholder may charge a fee for lien sale preparations not to exceed seventy dollars ($70) in the case of a vehicle having a value determined to be four thousand dollars ($4,000) or less and not to exceed one hundred dollars ($100) in the case of a vehicle having a value determined to be greater than four thousand dollars ($4,000), from any person who redeems the vehicle prior to disposal or is paid through a lien sale pursuant to this chapter. These charges may commence and become part of the possessory lien when the lienholder requests the names and addresses of all persons having an interest in the vehicle from the Department of Motor Vehicles. Not more than 50 percent of the allowable fee may be charged until the lien sale notifications are mailed to all interested parties and the lienholder or registration service agent has possession of the required lien processing documents. This charge shall not be made in the case of any vehicle redeemed prior to 72 hours from the initial storage. *(Added by Stats.1995, c. 404 (S.B.240), § 3. Amended by Stats.1996, c. 676 (S.B.1111), § 1; Stats.1998, c. 203 (S.B. 1650), § 5.)*

§ 3075. Repealed by Stats.1983, c. 1124, § 8

§§ 3076, 3077. Repealed by Stats.1963, c. 819, §§ 18, 19, eff. Jan. 1, 1965

§§ 3078, 3079. Repealed by Stats.1931, c. 1070, § 2

CHAPTER 6.7. LIVESTOCK SERVICE LIEN

Section
3080. Definitions.
3080.01. Livestock services to which lien applicable; priority; amount.
3080.02. Additional rights and remedies of lienholder.
3080.03. Order for sale; application; contents; hearing; service on defendant.
3080.04. Notice of application and hearing.

Section

3080.05. Notice of opposition; contents; necessity of filing.
3080.06. Order authorizing sale; findings; contents; disposition of proceeds.
3080.07. Denial of order; grounds; return to defendant of livestock.
3080.08. Findings at hearing; basis; effect; waiver of defenses or of rights on admissibility of evidence.
3080.09. Application for order for substitution of undertaking for livestock.
3080.10. Order for release of livestock to owner; conditions.
3080.11. Undertaking; contents.
3080.12 to 3080.14. Repealed.
3080.15. Order authorizing sale or order for substitution of undertaking without noticed hearing.
3080.16. Sales of livestock; method; disposition of proceeds.
3080.17. Notice of sale.
3080.18. Public sale; defined; postponement; purchase by lienholder.
3080.19. Effect of sale; rights of purchaser.
3080.20. Release of interest by owner or other person.
3080.21. Retention of livestock to satisfy claim; proposal; notice; releases; sale after objection.
3080.22. Assignment of lien.

§ 3080. Definitions

As used in this chapter, the following definitions shall apply:

(a) "Livestock" means any cattle, sheep, swine, goat, or horse, mule, or other equine.

(b) "Livestock servicer" means any individual, corporation, partnership, joint venture, cooperative, association or any other organization or entity which provides livestock services.

(c) "Livestock services" means any and all grazing, feeding, boarding, general care, which includes animal health services, obtained or provided by the livestock servicer, or his employee, transportation or other services rendered by a person to livestock for the owner of livestock, or for any person acting by or under the owner's authority. (Added by Stats.1979, c. 600, p. 1863, § 2.)

§ 3080.01. Livestock services to which lien applicable; priority; amount

A livestock servicer shall have a general lien upon the livestock in its possession to secure the performance of all obligations of the owner of the livestock to the livestock servicer for both of the following:

(a) The provision of livestock services to the livestock in possession of the livestock servicer.

(b) The provision of livestock services to other livestock for which livestock services were provided in connection with or as part of the same livestock service transaction, if such livestock services were provided within the immediately preceding 12 months prior to the date upon which the lien arose. The lien shall have priority over all other liens upon and security interests in the livestock, shall arise as the charges for livestock services become due, and shall be dependent upon possession. The lien shall secure the owner's contractual obligations to the lienholder for the provision of livestock services, the lienholder's reasonable charges for the provision of livestock services after the lien has arisen as set forth in Section 3080.02, and the lienholder's costs of lien enforcement, including attorney's fees. (Added by Stats.1979, c. 600, p. 1863, § 2.)

§ 3080.02. Additional rights and remedies of lienholder

In addition to any other rights and remedies provided by law, a lienholder may:

(a) Retain possession of the livestock and charge the owner for the reasonable value of providing livestock services to the livestock until the owner's obligations secured by the lien have been satisfied.

(b) Proceed to sell all or any portion of the livestock pursuant to Section 3080.16 if:

(1) A judicial order authorizing sale has been entered pursuant to Section 3080.06;

(2) A judgment authorizing sale has been entered in favor of the lienholder on the claim which gives rise to the lien; or

(3) The owner of the livestock has released, after the lien has arisen, its interest in the livestock in the form prescribed by Section 3080.20.

(c) A lienholder may commence a legal action on its claim against the owner of the livestock or any other person indebted to the lienholder for services to the livestock and reduce the claim to judgment. When the lienholder has reduced the claim to judgment, any lien or levy or other form of enforcement which may be made upon the livestock by virtue of any execution based upon the judgment shall relate back to the attachment of and have the same priority as the livestock service lien. The lienholder may purchase at a judicial sale held pursuant to the execution on the judgment and thereafter hold the livestock free of any liens upon or security interests in the livestock. (Added by Stats.1979, c. 600, p. 1863, § 2.)

§ 3080.03. Order for sale; application; contents; hearing; service on defendant

Upon the filing of the complaint, or at any time thereafter prior to judgment, the lienholder may apply to the court in which the action was commenced for an order authorizing sale of livestock.

(a) The application shall include all of the following:

(1) A statement showing that the sale is sought pursuant to this chapter to enforce a livestock service lien;

(2) A statement of the amount the lienholder seeks to recover from the defendant and the date that amount became due;

(3) A statement setting forth the reasons why a sale should be held prior to judgment;

(4) A description of the livestock to be sold and an estimate of the fair market value thereof; and

(5) A statement of the manner in which the lienholder intends to sell the livestock. The statement shall include, but not be limited to, whether the sale will be public or private, the amount of proceeds expected from the sale, and, why the sale, if authorized, would conform to the standard of commercial reasonableness set forth in Section 3080.16.

(b) The application shall be supported by an affidavit or affidavits showing that on the facts presented therein the lienholder would be entitled to a judgment on the claim upon which the action is brought.

(c) A hearing shall be held in the court in which the lienholder has brought the action before an order authorizing sale is issued under this chapter. Except as provided in Section 3080.15, or as ordered by the court upon good cause shown, the defendant shall be served with a copy of all of the following at least 10 days prior to the date set for hearing:

(1) A summons and complaint;

(2) A notice of application and hearing; and

(3) An application and all affidavits filed in support thereof. *(Added by Stats.1979, c. 600, p. 1863, § 2.)*

§ 3080.04. Notice of application and hearing

The notice of application and hearing shall inform the defendant of all of the following:

(a) The date, time and place of the hearing on the application;

(b) That the order will issue if the court finds, after hearing, that the lienholder has established the probable validity of the claim and has satisfied the other requirements set forth in this chapter;

(c) The hearing is not held for the purpose of determining the actual validity of the claim which determination will be made in other proceedings in the action and will not be affected by the findings made at the hearing on the application for the order;

(d) If the order authorizing sale is issued, the lienholder may proceed to sell the livestock in the manner set forth in the order, and the sale proceeds will be deposited with the court pending judgment on the lienholder's claim;

(e) If the defendant desires to oppose the issuance of the order, the defendant must file with the court and serve on the lienholder a notice of opposition and supporting affidavit as required by Section 3080.05 no later than three days prior to the date set for hearing;

(f) At the hearing, the court may deny the lienholder's application if the defendant files an undertaking as set forth in Section 3080.11; and

(g) The notice shall contain the following statement: "You may seek the advice of an attorney as to any matters concerning the lienholder's complaint and application. If an attorney is to assist you, he or she should be consulted promptly. You or your attorney or both of you may be present at the hearing." *(Added by Stats.1979, c. 600, p. 1863, § 2.)*

§ 3080.05. Notice of opposition; contents; necessity of filing

(a) If a defendant desires to oppose the issuance of an order authorizing sale the defendant shall file and serve upon the lienholder a notice of opposition no later than three days prior to the date set for hearing. The notice shall:

(1) State the grounds upon which the defendant opposes the order;

(2) Be accompanied by an affidavit or affidavits supporting any factual issues raised;

(3) State whether the defendant is prepared to file an undertaking as provided in Section 3080.11; and

(4) If the defendant is prepared to file an undertaking, include an estimate of the amount of such undertaking as set forth in Section 3080.09 and the defendant's basis for the estimate.

(b) Except when the lienholder has made an ex parte application for an order as set forth in Section 3080.15, or for good cause shown, a defendant shall not be permitted to oppose the issuance of an order if it has failed to file a notice of opposition within the time prescribed. *(Added by Stats. 1979, c. 600, p. 1863, § 2.)*

§ 3080.06. Order authorizing sale; findings; contents; disposition of proceeds

(a) At the hearing, the court shall consider the showing made by the parties and shall issue an order authorizing the sale of the livestock if it finds all of the following:

(1) The claim upon which the lienholder's action is based is a claim giving rise to a lien upon which an order authorizing sale may be issued under this chapter;

(2) The lienholder has established the probable validity of the claim upon which the action is based;

(3) The lienholder has established the probable validity of the lien sought to be enforced by sale;

(4) The sale is necessary to prevent a possible decline in the value or condition of the livestock or that the sale should be held in the interest of equity;

(5) The sale is not sought for a purpose other than the recovery on the claim upon which the lien is based; and

(6) The sale, if conducted in the manner set forth in the application, would be conducted in a commercially reasonable manner.

(b) The order authorizing sale shall:

(1) Identify the livestock for which sale is authorized;

(2) Specify the manner of sale including the date, time, place, necessary publication or other notice; and

(3) Except as may be ordered pursuant to subdivision (c), direct the lienholder to deposit the proceeds of sale with the clerk of the court pending final judgment in the action.

(c) The court may in its discretion do either of the following:

(1) Authorize the lienholder to deduct and retain funds from the sale proceeds in an amount sufficient to compensate the lienholder for services provided to the livestock from the date that the lien arose until the date of sale.

(2) Determine the amount of sale proceeds reasonably necessary to satisfy the indebtedness secured by the livestock service lien and order any portion or all of the remaining sale proceeds distributed and applied as set forth in paragraph (3) of subdivision (c) of Section 3080.16.

The balance of sale proceeds, if any, remaining after any deductions authorized in this section shall be deposited with the clerk of the court pursuant to this section. *(Added by Stats.1979, c. 600, p. 1863, § 2.)*

§ 3080.07. Denial of order; grounds; return to defendant of livestock

(a) After hearing, the court may issue an order denying the lienholder's application if it finds that:

(1) A sale is not necessary prior to judgment; and

(2) The defendant has filed an undertaking pursuant to Section 3080.11.

(b) If the defendant has filed an undertaking pursuant to Section 3080.11, the order shall direct the lienholder to assemble and make the livestock available to defendant, or to defendant's agent, at a specified date, time and place. (Added by Stats.1979, c. 600, p. 1863, § 2.)

§ 3080.08. Findings at hearing; basis; effect; waiver of defenses or of rights on admissibility of evidence

(a) The court's findings at the hearing shall be made upon the basis of the pleadings and other papers in the record. Upon cause shown, the court may receive and consider additional oral or documentary evidence or points and authorities at the hearing, or it may continue the hearing to allow the production of such additional evidence or points and authorities.

(b) The court's findings at the hearing shall have no effect on the determination of any issues in the action other than issues relevant to the proceedings authorized by this chapter, nor shall they affect the rights of the defendant in any other action arising out of the same claim. The court's determinations at the hearing shall neither be admissible as evidence nor referred to at the trial of any such action.

(c) Neither the failure of the defendant to oppose the issuance of an order authorizing sale, nor the defendant's failure to rebut any evidence produced by the lienholder at the hearing held for the issuance of such order, shall constitute a waiver of any defense to the lienholder's claim in the action or in any other action or have any effect on the right of the defendant to produce or exclude evidence at the trial of such action. (Added by Stats.1979, c. 600, p. 1863, § 2.)

§ 3080.09. Application for order for substitution of undertaking for livestock

(a) At any time after the lienholder has filed a complaint and claimed a lien under this chapter, or at any time after the owner of the livestock has commenced an action to recover possession of the livestock, the owner of the livestock may apply to the court in which the action was brought for an order for substitution of an undertaking which meets the requirements of Section 3080.11 for the livestock held by the lienholder.

(b) The application for such order shall be executed under oath and, unless included within a notice of opposition to sale as set forth in Section 3080.05, or except for good cause shown, shall be made upon noticed motion. Unless the parties otherwise agree, a hearing shall be held on the motion not less than five nor more than 10 days after service of notice of motion. The application shall contain all of the following:

(1) A description of the livestock to be recovered;

(2) An estimate and the basis for the estimate of the fair market value of the livestock;

(3) A statement identifying and describing the sureties for the undertaking. (Added by Stats.1979, c. 600, p. 1863, § 2.)

§ 3080.10. Order for release of livestock to owner; conditions

After hearing, the court may enter an order directing the lienholder to release all or a portion of the livestock to the owner, or to the owner's agent. The order shall be conditioned upon the filing by the owner of an undertaking as set forth in Section 3080.11, and shall include all of the following:

(1) The amount of the undertaking required.

(2) The basis for the court's finding as to the fair market value of the livestock.

(3) A statement that the lienholder has the right to object to the undertaking pursuant to Section 995.910 of the Code of Civil Procedure.

(4) A description of the livestock to be substituted.

(5) A statement of the date, time, place and manner in which the lienholder is to turn over the livestock to the owner. (Added by Stats.1979, c. 600, p. 1863, § 2. Amended by Stats.1982, c. 517, p. 2328, § 77.)

§ 3080.11. Undertaking; contents

The undertaking to be substituted for livestock shall be by the owner to pay to the lienholder an amount equal to the sum of (1) the fair market value of the livestock sought to be recovered, and (2) the costs to be incurred by the lienholder in order to assemble and turn over the livestock. (Added by Stats.1979, c. 600, p. 1863, § 2. Amended by Stats.1982, c. 517, p. 2329, § 78.)

Cross References

Bond and Undertaking Law, see Code of Civil Procedure § 995.010 et seq.

§§ 3080.12 to 3080.14. Repealed by Stats.1982, c. 517, p. 2329, §§ 79 to 81

§ 3080.15. Order authorizing sale or order for substitution of undertaking without noticed hearing

(a) Except as otherwise provided by statute, or upon noticed hearing as provided in this chapter, no order authorizing sale or order for substitution of undertaking for livestock may issue unless it appears from facts shown by affidavit that great or irreparable injury would result to the party seeking the order if the issuance of the order were delayed until the matter could be heard upon noticed hearing.

(b) In addition to a specific statement of the facts showing great or irreparable injury, any application made under this section for either an order authorizing sale or an order substituting undertaking for livestock shall include the substantive requirements of an application made under Section 3080.03 or Section 3080.09, respectively.

(c) The court shall examine the ex parte application, supporting affidavits and other papers on record and may issue the order sought if it finds all of the following:

(1) The party seeking the order is entitled to the order under the substantive provisions of this chapter;

(2) The party seeking the order will suffer great and irreparable injury if the order is not issued; and

(3) If the ex parte application is made for an order authorizing sale, the court determines that the condition of the livestock will greatly deteriorate or the value of the livestock will greatly depreciate before an order authorizing sale could be obtained pursuant to noticed hearing.

(d) An order issued under this section shall contain such provisions as the court determines to be in the interests of justice and equity to the parties, taking into account the effects on all parties under the circumstances of the particular case. If an order authorizing sale issues under this section, the court may authorize the lienholder to take any action necessary to preserve the value of the livestock so long as the court has determined that such action would be commercially reasonable under the circumstances.

(e) Upon ex parte application of any party affected by an order issued under this section or, if the court so orders, after a noticed hearing, the court may modify or vacate the order if it determines that such action would be proper under the circumstances. *(Added by Stats.1979, c. 600, p. 1863, § 2.)*

§ 3080.16. Sales of livestock; method; disposition of proceeds

(a) Except as otherwise specified by the order authorizing sale or as agreed to by the parties after the lien has arisen, a sale of livestock under this chapter may be held in bulk or in parcels, at wholesale or retail, and at any time and place and on any terms, provided the lienholder acts in good faith and in a commercially reasonable manner. The livestock may be sold in its existing condition or following any commercially reasonable preparation or processing. The fact that a better price could have been obtained by a sale at a different time or in a different manner from that selected by the lienholder is not of itself sufficient to establish that the sale was not made in a commercially reasonable manner. If the lienholder either sells the livestock in the usual manner in any recognized market therefor or sells at the price current in such market at the time of the sale or, if it has otherwise sold in conformity with reasonable commercial sales practices for the type of livestock sold, it has sold in a commercially reasonable manner.

(b) Except as otherwise specified by order of the court, or as agreed to by all interested parties after the lien has arisen, the proceeds of sale shall be deposited with the clerk of the court in an interest-bearing account to abide the judgment in the action.

(c) Except as otherwise specified in the judgment in the action, the proceeds of sale shall be applied in the following order:

(1) For reasonable expenses incurred by the lienholder in enforcing the lien, including, but not limited to, the charges for livestock services from the date the lien arose to the date of sale; the costs of transporting and preparing the livestock for sale and of conducting the sale; and, the reasonable attorneys' fees and legal costs and expenses incurred by the lienholder;

(2) For satisfaction of the contractual indebtedness secured by the lien; and

(3) For satisfaction of indebtedness secured by any subordinate lien or security interest in the livestock if written notification or demand therefor is received by the court or the lienholder before the proceeds have been distributed. If requested by the lienholder, the holder of a subordinate lien or security interest must seasonably furnish reasonable proof to the court of its subordinate interest before the lienholder need comply with the demand.

(d) The lienholder must account to the owner of the livestock for any surplus and, unless otherwise provided in the judgment in the action, the owner shall be liable for any deficiency. *(Added by Stats.1979, c. 600, p. 1863, § 2.)*

§ 3080.17. Notice of sale

Except as otherwise agreed or specified by order of court, notice of sale shall be given as follows:

(a) A notice in writing of the date, time and place of sale shall be delivered personally or be deposited in the United States mail, postage prepaid, addressed to the owner of the livestock, at his last known address, and to any other person claiming a lien upon or security interest in the livestock, who had on file with the California Secretary of State on the date the lien arose a financing statement covering the livestock for which livestock services secured by the lien were provided at least five days before the date fixed for any public sale or before the day on or after which any private sale or other disposition is to be made.

(b) Notice of the time and place of a public sale shall also be given at least five days before the date of sale by publication once in a newspaper of general circulation published in the county in which the sale is to be held. If there is no such newspaper, notice shall be given by posting, for five days prior to sale, a notice of sale where the sale is to be conducted. *(Added by Stats.1979, c. 600, p. 1863, § 2.)*

§ 3080.18. Public sale; defined; postponement; purchase by lienholder

(a) Any sale of which notice is delivered or mailed and published as provided in this chapter and which is held as provided in this chapter is a public sale.

(b) Any public sale may be postponed from time to time by public announcement at the time and place last scheduled for sale.

(c) The lienholder may purchase the livestock at a public sale. *(Added by Stats.1979, c. 600, p. 1863, § 2.)*

§ 3080.19. Effect of sale; rights of purchaser

(a) A sale of livestock held pursuant to this chapter shall:

(1) Transfer to a purchaser for value all of the owner's rights in the livestock; and

(2) Discharge the lien under which the sale is made and any lien or security interest subordinate thereto.

(b) The purchaser shall take free of all such subordinate rights and interests even though the lienholder fails to comply with the requirements of this chapter or of any judicial proceeding if:

(1) In the case of a public sale, the purchaser has no knowledge of any defects in the sale and does not buy in

collusion with the lienholder, other bidders or the person conducting the sale; or

(2) In any other case, the purchaser acts in good faith. (Added by Stats.1979, c. 600, p. 1863, § 2.)

§ 3080.20. Release of interest by owner or other person

(a) The owner of livestock or any other person claiming an interest in livestock may release its interest in the livestock at any time after the lien has arisen. The release shall be in writing and dated when signed. A copy of the release shall be given to the person releasing the interest at the time the release is signed.

(b) The release shall contain all of the following information in simple, nontechnical language:

(1) A description of the livestock covered by the release and the releasing party's interest in the livestock;

(2) A statement of the amount of the lien to which the livestock is subject;

(3) A statement that the releasing party has a legal right to a hearing in court prior to any sale of the livestock to satisfy the lien;

(4) A statement by the releasing party that it is giving the lienholder permission to sell the livestock;

(5) A statement of the extent to which the releasing party gives up any interest it may have in the livestock or in the sale proceeds of the livestock; and,

(6) To the extent that the release is not given in full satisfaction of the lienholder's claim or claims against the releasing party, a statement by the releasing party that it is aware that the lienholder may still have a claim against it after the release has been executed. (Added by Stats.1979, c. 600, p. 1863, § 2.)

§ 3080.21. Retention of livestock to satisfy claim; proposal; notice; releases; sale after objection

At any time after a lien has arisen, the lienholder may propose to retain any portion or all of the livestock in satisfaction of any portion or all of the claim against the owner or other person indebted to the lienholder for livestock services. The proposal shall be made in writing to the owner and written notice thereof shall be given to any person entitled to receive notice under subdivision (a) of Section 3080.17. If, within 21 days after the notice was sent, the lienholder receives objection in writing from a person entitled to receive notification, the lienholder must proceed to sell the livestock and account for the proceeds pursuant to this chapter. In the absence of such written objection, the lienholder may retain the livestock, or so much thereof as proposed, in satisfaction of all or a portion of the claim against the owner and other person indebted to the lienholder for livestock services, upon the owner's and such other person's execution of a release conforming to Section 3080.20. (Added by Stats.1979, c. 600, p. 1863, § 2.)

§ 3080.22. Assignment of lien

Any lien provided for in this chapter may be assigned by written instrument accompanied by delivery of possession of the livestock, subject to the lien, and the assignee may exercise the rights of a lienholder as provided in this chapter.

Any lienholder assigning a lien as authorized herein shall at the time of assigning the lien give written notice of the assignment either by personal delivery or by registered or certified mail, to the legal owner and any other person entitled to receive notice under subdivision (a) of Section 3080.17, including the name and address of the person to whom the lien has been assigned. (Added by Stats.1979, c. 600, p. 1863, § 2.)

CHAPTER 7. STOPPAGE IN TRANSIT

Section
3081. Safe deposit corporations; disposal of unclaimed contents of boxes.

§ 3081. Safe deposit corporations; disposal of unclaimed contents of boxes

Any corporation engaged in the business of renting to the public safe deposit boxes may dispose of the unclaimed contents of the safe deposit boxes in the manner set forth in Sections 1660 to 1679, inclusive, of the Financial Code. (Added by Stats.1943, c. 846, p. 2659, § 19. Amended by Stats.1968, c. 48, p. 189, § 5.)

Cross References

Depositary's lien, sale, see Civil Code § 1857.
Liquidating bank, disposition of unclaimed property, see Financial Code § 689.
Remedies for nonpayment of safe deposit rental, see Financial Code § 1630 et seq.

CHAPTER 8. DESIGN PROFESSIONALS' LIENS [REPEALED]

§§ 3081.01 to 3081.096. Repealed by Stats.1961, c. 886, § 29, eff. June 28, 1991

§§ 3081.1 to 3081.8. Repealed by Stats.2010, c. 697 (S.B.189), § 15, operative July 1, 2012

§ 3081.81. Repealed by Stats.1961, c. 886, § 29, eff. June 28, 1961

§ 3081.9. Repealed by Stats.2010, c. 697 (S.B.189), § 15, operative July 1, 2012

§§ 3081.91 to 3081.93. Repealed by Stats.1961, c. 886, § 29 eff. June 28, 1961

§ 3081.10. Repealed by Stats.2010, c. 697 (S.B.189), § 15, operative July 1, 2012

Title 15

INTERNET NEUTRALITY

Section
3082 to 3090. Repealed.
3090.5. Repealed.
3091. Repealed.
3092 to 3099. Repealed.
3100. Definitions.

ARISING FROM PARTICULAR TRANSACTIONS

Section	
3101.	Prohibited activities for fixed broadband Internet access service providers; mobile broadband Internet access service providers.
3102.	Prohibition on services meant to evade the prohibitions in § 3101 or affect internet performance; mobile broadband Internet access service providers.
3103.	Applicability to emergency communication, public safety, or efforts to address unlawful activity.
3104.	Waiver of provisions.
3105, 3106.	Repealed.
3107, 3108.	Repealed.
3109.	Repealed.
3110 to 3111.	Repealed.
3111.5.	Repealed.
3112.	Repealed.
3113.	Repealed.
3114 to 3118.	Repealed.
3119 to 3122.	Repealed.
3123.	Repealed.
3124.	Repealed.
3125 to 3127.	Repealed.
3128 to 3131.	Repealed.
3132, 3133.	Repealed.
3134 to 3140.	Repealed.
3141, 3142.	Repealed.
3143 to 3154.	Repealed.
3155.	Repealed.
3156.	Repealed.
3157.	Repealed.
3158, 3159.	Repealed.
3160.	Repealed.
3161 to 3163.	Repealed.
3164, 3165.	Repealed.
3166.	Repealed.
3166.1.	Repealed.
3167, 3168.	Repealed.
3169, 3170.	Repealed.
3171.	Repealed.
3172 to 3176.5.	Repealed.
3177, 3178.	Repealed.
3179.	Repealed.
3180.	Repealed.
3181.	Repealed.
3182.	Repealed.
3183 to 3187.	Repealed.
3188, 3189.	Repealed.
3190 to 3193.	Repealed.
3194, 3195.	Repealed.
3196 to 3205.	Repealed.
3206 to 3209.	Repealed.
3210 to 3214.	Repealed.
3215 to 3224.	Repealed.
3225 to 3227.	Repealed.
3228.	Repealed.
3229 to 3234.	Repealed.
3235 to 3237.	Repealed.
3238.	Repealed.
3239, 3240.	Repealed.
3241.	Renumbered.
3242.	Repealed.
3243 to 3246.	Repealed.
3247.	Repealed.
3247.5.	Repealed.
3248 to 3251.	Repealed.
3251.5.	Repealed.
3252.	Repealed.
3253.	Repealed.
3254 to 3257.	Repealed.
3258 to 3265.	Repealed.
3265a to 3265e.	Repealed.
3265g.	Repealed.
3266.	Repealed.
3266a to 3266d.	Repealed.
3267.	Repealed.

Publisher's Note

The following table was provided by the California Law Revision Commission, to be published in "Report of the California Law Revision Commission on Chapter 697 of the Statutes of 2010" [40 Cal.L.Rev. Comm. Reports 49 [AR:apx5] (2010)].

DISPOSITION OF EXISTING LAW

The table below shows the disposition of former sections of existing law that were repealed by Chapter 697 of the Statutes of 2010 (Senate Bill 189 (Lowenthal)). All sections listed in the table are from the Civil Code. For further detail, see the Comment to the new provision in the enacted legislation.

Former Provision	New Provision(s)
3081.1	8014, 8300
3081.2	8302
3081.3	8304
3081.4	8306
3081.5	8308
3081.6	8310
3081.7	8312
3081.8	8314
3081.9	8316
3081.10	8318
3082	8000
3083	8506, 8532
3084	8416
3085	8004
3086 (except subd. (b))	8180, 9200
3086(b)	not continued
3087	8006
3088	8008, 8016
3089	8024
3090	8028
3092	8188, 9202
3093	8182, 8184, 9204, 9208
3094	8444
3095	8018
3096	8606, 9554
3097	8034, 8200
3097(a)	8200
3097(b)	8200
3097(c)	8102, 8202
3097(d)	8204
3097(e)	8212
3097(f)	8116
3097(g)	8206
3097(h)	8216
3097(i)	8172
3097(j)	8174
3097(k)	8104
3097(*l*)	8170, 8208
3097(m)	8170, 8208
3097(n)	8210

OBLIGATIONS

Former Provision	New Provision(s)
3097(o)	8214
3097(p)	not continued
3097.1	8118
3098	8034, 9300
3098(a)	9300, 9302, 9303, 9304
3098(b)	9306
3098(c)	9300
3098(d)	9304
3098(e)	not continued
3099	8036
3100	8038
3101	8040
3102	8042
3103	8044, 8502, 8506, 9352, 9354
3104	8046
3105	not continued
3106	8050
3109	8160
3110	8400, 8404, 8430, 9100
3110.5(a)(1)	8700
3110.5(a)(2)	8700
3110.5(b)	8710, 8720
3110.5(b)(1)	8722
3110.5(b)(2)	8724
3110.5(b)(3)	8726, 8728
3110.5(c)	8712, 8730
3110.5(d)	8716
3110.5(e)	8702
3110.5(f)	8704
3110.5(g)	8714
3111	8024, 9100
3112	8402, 8404, 8440, 9100
3114	8410
3115	8412
3116	8414
3117	8186
3118	8422
3123(a)	8430
3123(b)	8430
3123(c)	not continued
3124	8432
3128	8440, 8442
3129	8442
3130	8446
3131 (first paragraph)	8448
3131 (second paragraph)	not continued
3134	8450
3135	8454
3136	8456
3137	8458
3138	8452
3139	8458
3140	8434
3143	8424
3144	8460
3144.5	8424
3145	8460
3146	8461
3147	8462

Former Provision	New Provision(s)
3148	8490
3149	not continued
3150	8464
3151	8466
3152	8468
3153	8470
3154(a)	8480
3154(b)	8484, 8488
3154(c)	8486
3154(d)	8486
3154(e)	8486, 8488
3154(f)	8488, 8490
3154(g)	8488
3154(h)	8480
3154(i)	8480
3156	8160
3158	8520
3159	8508, 8530
3159(a)	8502, 8536, 8538
3159(b)	8542
3159(c)	8542
3160	8508
3161	8522
3162(a)	8536, 8538
3162(b)	8542
3162(c)	8542
3163	8534
3166	8544
3167	8540
3168	8504
3171	8510
3172	8550
3173	8554
3174	8556
3175	8552
3176	8558
3176.5	8560
3179	9000
3181	9100
3183	9500
3184	9356
3185	9362
3186	9358
3187	9360
3190	9450
3191	9452
3192	9454
3193	9456
3196	9364
3197	9400
3198	9402
3199	9404
3200	9406
3201	9408
3202	9410
3203	9412
3204	not continued
3205	9414
3210	9502
3211	9504
3212	9508

ARISING FROM PARTICULAR TRANSACTIONS § 3100

Former Provision	New Provision(s)
3213	9510
3214	9506
3225	8152
3226	8154
3227	8614, 9562
3235	8600
3236	8600, 8602
3237	8604
3239	8609
3240	8610
3242	8612
3247	9550
3248	9554
3249	9558
3250	9564
3251	9552
3252	9560
3258	8060
3259	8056
3259.5	8190
3260(a)	not continued
3260(b)	8810
3260(c)	8812
3260(c)(1)	not continued
3260(c)(2)	not continued
3260(d)	8814
3260(e)	8814
3260(f)	8816
3260(g)	8818
3260.1	8800
3260.2(a)	8830, 8832, 8834, 8836, 8840
3260.2(b)	8842
3260.2(c)	8838
3260.2(d)	8844
3260.2(e)	8846
3260.2(f)	8848
3260.2(g)	not continued
3261	8422
3262(a)	8122, 8124
3262(b)(1)	8126
3262(b)(2)	8128
3262(c)	8130
3262(d)(1)	8132
3262(d)(2)	8134
3262(d)(3)	8136
3262(d)(4)	8138
3262.5	8802
3263	8062
3264	8500, 9350
3265	9500
3266	8054
3267	8608, 9566

§§ 3082 to 3090. Repealed by Stats.2010, c. 697 (S.B.189), § 16, operative July 1, 2012

§ 3090.5. Repealed by Stats.1963, c. 819, p. 1997, § 2, eff. Jan. 1, 1965

§ 3091. Repealed by Stats.1994, c. 974 (A.B.3357), § 1

§§ 3092 to 3099. Repealed by Stats.2010, c. 697 (S.B.189), § 16, operative July 1, 2012

§ 3100. Definitions

For purposes of this title, the following definitions apply:

(a) "Application–agnostic" means not differentiating on the basis of source, destination, Internet content, application, service, or device, or class of Internet content, application, service, or device.

(b) "Broadband Internet access service" means a mass-market retail service by wire or radio provided to customers in California that provides the capability to transmit data to, and receive data from, all or substantially all Internet endpoints, including, but not limited to, any capabilities that are incidental to and enable the operation of the communications service, but excluding dial-up Internet access service. "Broadband Internet access service" also encompasses any service provided to customers in California that provides a functional equivalent of that service or that is used to evade the protections set forth in this title.

(c) "Class of Internet content, application, service, or device" means Internet content, or a group of Internet applications, services, or devices, sharing a common characteristic, including, but not limited to, sharing the same source or destination, belonging to the same type of content, application, service, or device, using the same application- or transport-layer protocol, or having similar technical characteristics, including, but not limited to, the size, sequencing, or timing of packets, or sensitivity to delay.

(d) "Content, applications, or services" means all Internet traffic transmitted to or from end users of a broadband Internet access service, including, but not limited to, traffic that may not fit clearly into any of these categories.

(e) "Edge provider" means any individual or entity that provides any content, application, or service over the Internet, and any individual or entity that provides a device used for accessing any content, application, or service over the Internet.

(f) "End user" means any individual or entity that uses a broadband Internet access service.

(g) "Enterprise service offering" means an offering to larger organizations through customized or individually negotiated arrangements or special access services.

(h) "Fixed broadband Internet access service" means a broadband Internet access service that serves end users primarily at fixed endpoints using stationary equipment. Fixed broadband Internet access service includes, but is not limited to, fixed wireless services including, but not limited to, fixed unlicensed wireless services, and fixed satellite services.

(i) "Fixed Internet service provider" means a business that provides fixed broadband Internet access service to an individual, corporation, government, or other customer in California.

(j) "Impairing or degrading lawful Internet traffic on the basis of Internet content, application, or service, or use of a nonharmful device" means impairing or degrading any of the following: (1) particular content, applications, or services; (2) particular classes of content, applications, or services; (3) lawful Internet traffic to particular nonharmful devices; or (4) lawful Internet traffic to particular classes of nonharmful devices. The term includes, without limitation, differentiating, positively or negatively, between any of the following: (1) particular content, applications, or services; (2) particular classes of content, applications, or services; (3) lawful Internet traffic to particular nonharmful devices; or (4) lawful Internet traffic to particular classes of nonharmful devices.

(k) "Internet service provider" means a business that provides broadband Internet access service to an individual, corporation, government, or other customer in California.

(l) "ISP traffic exchange" means the exchange of Internet traffic destined for, or originating from, an Internet service provider's end users between the Internet service provider's network and another individual or entity, including, but not limited to, an edge provider, content delivery network, or other network operator.

(m) "ISP traffic exchange agreement" means an agreement between an Internet service provider and another individual or entity, including, but not limited to, an edge provider, content delivery network, or other network operator, to exchange Internet traffic destined for, or originating from, an Internet service provider's end users between the Internet service provider's network and the other individual or entity.

(n) "Mass market" service means a service marketed and sold on a standardized basis to residential customers, small businesses, and other customers, including, but not limited to, schools, institutions of higher learning, and libraries. "Mass market" services also include broadband Internet access services purchased with support of the E-rate and Rural Health Care programs and similar programs at the federal and state level, regardless of whether they are customized or individually negotiated, as well as any broadband Internet access service offered using networks supported by the Connect America Fund or similar programs at the federal and state level. "Mass market" service does not include enterprise service offerings.

(o) "Mobile broadband Internet access service" means a broadband Internet access service that serves end users primarily using mobile stations. Mobile broadband Internet access service includes, but is not limited to, broadband Internet access services that use smartphones or mobile-network-enabled tablets as the primary endpoints for connection to the Internet, as well as mobile satellite broadband services.

(p) "Mobile Internet service provider" means a business that provides mobile broadband Internet access service to an individual, corporation, government, or other customer in California.

(q) "Mobile station" means a radio communication station capable of being moved and which ordinarily does move.

(r) "Paid prioritization" means the management of an Internet service provider's network to directly or indirectly favor some traffic over other traffic, including, but not limited to, through the use of techniques such as traffic shaping, prioritization, resource reservation, or other forms of preferential traffic management, either (1) in exchange for consideration, monetary or otherwise, from a third party, or (2) to benefit an affiliated entity.

(s) "Reasonable network management" means a network management practice that is reasonable. A network management practice is a practice that has a primarily technical network management justification, but does not include other business practices. A network management practice is reasonable if it is primarily used for, and tailored to, achieving a legitimate network management purpose, taking into account the particular network architecture and technology of the broadband Internet access service, and is as application-agnostic as possible.

(t) "Zero–rating" means exempting some Internet traffic from a customer's data usage allowance. *(Added by Stats. 2018, c. 976 (S.B.822), § 2, eff. Jan. 1, 2019.)*

§ 3101. Prohibited activities for fixed broadband Internet access service providers; mobile broadband Internet access service providers

(a) It shall be unlawful for a fixed Internet service provider, insofar as the provider is engaged in providing fixed broadband Internet access service, to engage in any of the following activities:

(1) Blocking lawful content, applications, services, or nonharmful devices, subject to reasonable network management.

(2) Impairing or degrading lawful Internet traffic on the basis of Internet content, application, or service, or use of a nonharmful device, subject to reasonable network management.

(3) Requiring consideration, monetary or otherwise, from an edge provider, including, but not limited to, in exchange for any of the following:

(A) Delivering Internet traffic to, and carrying Internet traffic from, the Internet service provider's end users.

(B) Avoiding having the edge provider's content, application, service, or nonharmful device blocked from reaching the Internet service provider's end users.

(C) Avoiding having the edge provider's content, application, service, or nonharmful device impaired or degraded.

(4) Engaging in paid prioritization.

(5) Engaging in zero-rating in exchange for consideration, monetary or otherwise, from a third party.

(6) Zero–rating some Internet content, applications, services, or devices in a category of Internet content, applications, services, or devices, but not the entire category.

(7)(A) Unreasonably interfering with, or unreasonably disadvantaging, either an end user's ability to select, access, and use broadband Internet access service or the lawful Internet content, applications, services, or devices of the end user's choice, or an edge provider's ability to make lawful content, applications, services, or devices available to end users. Reasonable network management shall not be a violation of this paragraph.

(B) Zero–rating Internet traffic in application-agnostic ways shall not be a violation of subparagraph (A) provided that no consideration, monetary or otherwise, is provided by any third party in exchange for the Internet service provider's decision whether to zero-rate traffic.

(8) Failing to publicly disclose accurate information regarding the network management practices, performance,

and commercial terms of its broadband Internet access services sufficient for consumers to make informed choices regarding use of those services and for content, application, service, and device providers to develop, market, and maintain Internet offerings.

(9) Engaging in practices, including, but not limited to, agreements, with respect to, related to, or in connection with, ISP traffic exchange that have the purpose or effect of evading the prohibitions contained in this section and Section 3102. Nothing in this paragraph shall be construed to prohibit Internet service providers from entering into ISP traffic exchange agreements that do not evade the prohibitions contained in this section and Section 3102.

(b) It shall be unlawful for a mobile Internet service provider, insofar as the provider is engaged in providing mobile broadband Internet access service, to engage in any of the activities described in paragraphs (1), (2), (3), (4), (5), (6), (7), (8), and (9) of subdivision (a). *(Added by Stats.2018, c. 976 (S.B.822), § 2, eff. Jan. 1, 2019.)*

§ 3102. Prohibition on services meant to evade the prohibitions in § 3101 or affect internet performance; mobile broadband Internet access service providers

(a) It shall be unlawful for a fixed Internet service provider to offer or provide services other than broadband Internet access service that are delivered over the same last-mile connection as the broadband Internet access service, if those services satisfy either of the following conditions:

(1) They have the purpose or effect of evading the prohibitions in Section 3101.

(2) They negatively affect the performance of broadband Internet access service.

(b) It shall be unlawful for a mobile Internet service provider to offer or provide services other than broadband Internet access service that are delivered over the same last-mile connection as the broadband Internet access service, if those services satisfy either of the conditions specified in paragraphs (1) and (2) of subdivision (a).

(c) Nothing in this section shall be construed to prohibit a fixed or mobile Internet service provider from offering or providing services other than broadband Internet access service that are delivered over the same last-mile connection as the broadband Internet access service and do not violate this section. *(Added by Stats.2018, c. 976 (S.B.822), § 2, eff. Jan. 1, 2019.)*

§ 3103. Applicability to emergency communication, public safety, or efforts to address unlawful activity

(a) Nothing in this title supersedes any obligation or authorization a fixed or mobile Internet service provider may have to address the needs of emergency communications or law enforcement, public safety, or national security authorities, consistent with or as permitted by applicable law, or limits the provider's ability to do so.

(b) Nothing in this title prohibits reasonable efforts by a fixed or mobile Internet service provider to address copyright infringement or other unlawful activity. *(Added by Stats. 2018, c. 976 (S.B.822), § 2, eff. Jan. 1, 2019.)*

§ 3104. Waiver of provisions

Notwithstanding Section 3268 or any other law, any waiver of the provisions of this title is contrary to public policy and shall be unenforceable and void. *(Added by Stats.2018, c. 976 (S.B.822), § 2, eff. Jan. 1, 2019.)*

§§ 3105, 3106. Repealed by Stats.2010, c. 697 (S.B.189), § 16, operative July 1, 2012

§§ 3107, 3108. Repealed by Stats.1963, c. 819, p. 1997, § 2, eff. Jan. 1, 1965

§ 3109. Repealed by Stats.2010, c. 697 (S.B.189), § 16, operative July 1, 2012

§§ 3110 to 3111. Repealed by Stats.2010, c. 697 (S.B.189), § 16, operative July 1, 2012

§ 3111.5. Repealed by Stats.1999, c. 795 (S.B.914), § 8

§ 3112. Repealed by Stats.2010, c. 697 (S.B.189), § 16, operative July 1, 2012

§ 3113. Repealed by Stats.1963, c. 819, p. 1997, § 2, eff. Jan. 1, 1965

§§ 3114 to 3118. Repealed by Stats.2010, c. 697 (S.B.189), § 16, operative July 1, 2012

§§ 3119 to 3122. Repealed by Stats.1963, c. 819, p. 1997, § 2, eff. Jan. 1, 1965

§ 3123. Repealed by Stats.2010, c. 697 (S.B.189), § 16, operative July 1, 2012

§ 3124. Repealed by Stats.2010, c. 697 (S.B.189), § 16, operative July 1, 2012

§§ 3125 to 3127. Repealed by Stats.1963, c. 819, p. 1997, § 2, eff. Jan. 1, 1965

§§ 3128 to 3131. Repealed by Stats.2010, c. 697 (S.B.189), § 16, operative July 1, 2012

§§ 3132, 3133. Repealed by Stats.1963, c. 819, p. 1997, § 2, eff. Jan. 1, 1965

§§ 3134 to 3140. Repealed by Stats.2010, c. 697 (S.B.189), § 16, operative July 1, 2012

§§ 3141, 3142. Repealed by Stats.1963, c. 819, p. 1997, § 2, eff. Jan. 1, 1965

§§ 3143 to 3154. Repealed by Stats.2010, c. 697 (S.B.189), § 16, operative July 1, 2012

§ 3155. Repealed by Stats.1963, c. 819, p. 1997, § 2, eff. Jan. 1, 1965

§ 3156. Repealed by Stats.2010, c. 697 (S.B.189), § 16, operative July 1, 2012

§ 3157. Repealed by Stats.1963, c. 819, p. 1997, § 2, eff. Jan. 1, 1965

§§ 3158, 3159 Repealed

OBLIGATIONS

§§ 3158, 3159. Repealed by Stats.2010, c. 697 (S.B.189), § 16, operative July 1, 2012

§ 3160. Repealed by Stats.2010, c. 697 (S.B.189), § 16, operative July 1, 2012

§§ 3161 to 3163. Repealed by Stats.2010, c. 697 (S.B.189), § 16, operative July 1, 2012

§§ 3164, 3165. Repealed by Stats.1963, c. 819, p. 1997, § 2, eff. Jan. 1, 1965

§ 3166. Repealed by Stats.2010, c. 697 (S.B.189), § 16, operative July 1, 2012

§ 3166.1. Repealed by Stats.1955, c. 198, p. 671, § 3; Stats.1955, c. 599, p. 1093, § 3

§§ 3167, 3168. Repealed by Stats.2010, c. 697 (S.B.189), § 16, operative July 1, 2012

§§ 3169, 3170. Repealed by Stats.1963, c. 819, p. 1997, § 2, eff. Jan. 1, 1965

§ 3171. Repealed by Stats.2010, c. 697 (S.B.189), § 16, operative July 1, 2012

§§ 3172 to 3176.5. Repealed by Stats.2010, c. 697 (S.B.189), § 16, operative July 1, 2012

§§ 3177, 3178. Repealed by Stats.1963, c. 819, p. 1997, § 2, eff. Jan. 1, 1965

§ 3179. Repealed by Stats.2010, c. 697 (S.B.189), § 16, operative July 1, 2012

§ 3180. Repealed by Stats.1963, c. 819, p. 1997, § 2, eff. Jan. 1, 1965

§ 3181. Repealed by Stats.2010, c. 697 (S.B.189), § 16, operative July 1, 2012

§ 3182. Repealed by Stats.1963, c. 819, p. 1997, § 2, eff. Jan. 1, 1965

§§ 3183 to 3187. Repealed by Stats.2010, c. 697 (S.B.189), § 16, operative July 1, 2012

§§ 3188, 3189. Repealed by Stats.1963, c. 819, p. 1997, § 2, eff. Jan. 1, 1965

§§ 3190 to 3193. Repealed by Stats.2010, c. 697 (S.B.189), § 16, operative July 1, 2012

§§ 3194, 3195. Repealed by Stats.1963, c. 819, p. 1997, § 2, eff. Jan. 1, 1965

§§ 3196 to 3205. Repealed by Stats.2010, c. 697 (S.B.189), § 16, operative July 1, 2012

§§ 3206 to 3209. Repealed by Stats.1963, c. 819, p. 1997, § 2, eff. Jan. 1, 1965

§§ 3210 to 3214. Repealed by Stats.2010, c. 697 (S.B.189), § 16, operative July 1, 2012

§§ 3215 to 3224. Repealed by Stats.1963, c. 819, p. 1997, § 2, eff. Jan. 1, 1965

§§ 3225 to 3227. Repealed by Stats.2010, c. 697 (S.B.189), § 16, operative July 1, 2012

§ 3228. Repealed by Stats.1982, c. 517, p. 2329, § 83

§§ 3229 to 3234. Repealed by Stats.1963, c. 819, p. 1997, § 2, eff. Jan. 1, 1965

§§ 3235 to 3237. Repealed by Stats.2010, c. 697 (S.B.189), § 16, operative July 1, 2012

§ 3238. Repealed by Stats.1963, c. 819, p. 1997, § 2, eff. Jan. 1, 1965

§§ 3239, 3240. Repealed by Stats.2010, c. 697 (S.B.189), § 16, operative July 1, 2012

§ 3241. Renumbered Civil Code § 3227 and amended by Stats.1995, c. 225 (A.B.901), § 4, eff. July 31, 1995

§ 3242. Repealed by Stats.2010, c. 697 (S.B.189), § 16, operative July 1, 2012

§§ 3243 to 3246. Repealed by Stats.1963, c. 819, p. 1997, § 2, eff. Jan. 1, 1965

§ 3247. Repealed by Stats.2010, c. 697 (S.B.189), § 16, operative July 1, 2012

§ 3247.5. Repealed by Stats.1985, c. 348, § 1, operative Jan. 1, 1987

§§ 3248 to 3251. Repealed by Stats.2010, c. 697 (S.B.189), § 16, operative July 1, 2012

§ 3251.5. Repealed by Stats.1972, c. 600, § 1, operative March 8, 1973

§ 3252. Repealed by Stats.2010, c. 697 (S.B.189), § 16, operative July 1, 2012

§ 3253. Repealed by Stats.1995, c. 225 (A.B.901), § 7, eff. July 31, 1995

§§ 3254 to 3257. Repealed by Stats.1963, c. 819, p. 1997, § 2, eff. Jan. 1, 1965

§§ 3258 to 3265. Repealed by Stats.2010, c. 697 (S.B.189), § 16, operative July 1, 2012

§§ 3265a to 3265e. Repealed by Stats.1963, c. 819, p. 1997, § 2, eff. Jan. 1, 1965

§ 3265g. Repealed by Stats.1953, c. 601, p. 1847, § 1

§ 3266. Repealed by Stats.2010, c. 697 (S.B.189), § 16, operative July 1, 2012

§§ 3266a to 3266d. Repealed by Stats.1963, c. 819, p. 1997, § 2, eff. Jan. 1, 1965

§ 3267. Repealed by Stats.2010, c. 697 (S.B.189), § 16, operative July 1, 2012

Title 16

GENERAL PROVISIONS

Section
3268. Waiver of code provisions.

§ 3268. Waiver of code provisions

Except where it is otherwise declared, the provisions of the foregoing titles of this part, in respect to the rights and obligations of parties to contracts, are subordinate to the intention of the parties, when ascertained in the manner prescribed by the chapter on the interpretation of contracts; and the benefit thereof may be waived by any party entitled thereto, unless such waiver would be against public policy. *(Enacted in 1872. Amended by Stats.1963, c. 819, p. 2001, § 20, eff. Jan. 1, 1965.)*

Cross References

Ascertainment of intention, see Civil Code § 1637 et seq.
Interpretation of contracts, see Civil Code § 1635 et seq.
Waiver of advantage, law established for public reason, see Civil Code § 3513.

Title 17

YEAR 2000 INFORMATION DISCLOSURES

Section
3269. Definitions.
3270. Disclosure of Year 2000 Problem or solutions thereto; liability in tort.
3271. Disclosure of Year 2000 Problem or solutions thereto; liability in tort; exclusion.
3272 to 3272.9. Repealed.

§ 3269. Definitions

For purposes of this title, the following definitions apply:

(a) "Year 2000 Problem" means any expected or actual computing, physical, enterprise, or distribution system complications that may occur in any computer system, computer program, software application, embedded systems, embedded chip calculations, or other computing application as a result of the year change from 1999 to 2000. These complications are often associated with the common programming practice of using a two-digit field to represent a year, resulting in erroneous date calculations, an ambiguous interpretation of the term "00," the failure to recognize the year 2000 as a leap year, the use of algorithms that use the year "99" or "00" as a flag for another function, or the use of applications, software, or hardware that are date sensitive.

(b) "Information" means any assessment, projection, estimate, planning document, objective, timetable, test plan, test date, or test result related to the implementation or verification of Year 2000 Problem processing capabilities of a computer system, computer program, software application, embedded systems, embedded chip calculations, or other computing application and intended to solve a Year 2000 Problem.

(c) "Disclosure" and "discloses" mean any dissemination or provision of information without any expectation or right to remuneration or fee therefor.

(d) "Person" means any individual, corporation, partnership, business entity, joint venture, association, the State of California or any of its subdivisions, or any other organization, or any combination thereof. *(Added by Stats.1998, c. 860 (S.B.1173), § 3, eff. Sept. 25, 1998. Amended by Stats. 1999, c. 83 (S.B.966), § 23.)*

§ 3270. Disclosure of Year 2000 Problem or solutions thereto; liability in tort

(a) Notwithstanding any other law, any person that discloses information regarding the Year 2000 Problem or any potential solutions to the problem, including, but not limited to, those persons described in subdivision (b), shall not be liable for damages in any tort action brought against that person regarding the Year 2000 Problem for any injury caused by, arising out of, or relating to, the use of the information disclosed, except as provided in Section 3271.

(b) This section shall apply to any person that, when making the disclosures described in subdivision (a), specifically disclaims the universal applicability of the potential solutions disclosed, and expresses a unique experience with any Year 2000 information.

(c) This section does not apply to prospective solutions sold or exchanged for profit or provided for profit by a person or entity holding itself out as a provider of Year 2000 solutions. *(Added by Stats.1998, c. 860 (S.B.1173), § 3, eff. Sept. 25, 1998.)*

§ 3271. Disclosure of Year 2000 Problem or solutions thereto; liability in tort; exclusion

(a) Section 3270 shall not apply if the claimant in an action described in that section establishes that the Year 2000 Problem information disclosure was all of the following:

(1) Material.

(2) False, inaccurate, or misleading.

(3) Either (A) made with the knowledge that the statement was false, inaccurate, or misleading, (B) if the information disclosed was a republication of or otherwise a repetition of information from another person, made without a disclosure that the information was based on information supplied by another person or made with the knowledge that the statement was false, inaccurate, or misleading, or (C) made with gross negligence in the determination of the truth or accuracy of the disclosure or in the determination of whether the disclosure was misleading.

(b) Nothing in this title shall be deemed to affect any other remedy available at law, including, but not limited to, temporary or permanent injunctive relief, against a public or private entity or individual with respect to Year 2000 Problem information disclosures. *(Added by Stats.1998, c. 860 (S.B. 1173), § 3, eff. Sept. 25, 1998.)*

§§ 3272 to 3272.9. Repealed by Stats.2015, c. 303 (A.B.731), § 32, eff. Jan. 1, 2016

Title 18

PROVIDERS OF HEALTH AND SAFETY LABOR OR SERVICES

Section
3273. Display of logo of public agency; contractors of public agency's; disclosure requirements; remedies.

§ 3273. Display of logo of public agency; contractors of public agency's; disclosure requirements; remedies

(a) It is unlawful for a person, firm, corporation, or association that is a nongovernmental entity and contracts to perform public health and safety labor or services for a public agency to display on a vehicle a logo of the public agency that reasonably could be interpreted or construed as implying that the labor or services are being provided by employees of the public agency, unless the vehicle conspicuously displays a statement indicating that the contractor is the service provider, contractor, or other appropriate descriptor, such as "SERVICE PROVIDED BY:" or "CONTRACTED BY:", immediately followed by all of the following:

(1) The logo and the name of the person, firm, corporation, or association that is the nongovernmental entity providing the public health and safety labor or services for the public agency.

(2) The state, or if outside of the United States, the country where the nongovernmental entity's controlling person, firm, corporation, or association is legally incorporated, organized, or formed.

(b) It is unlawful for a person or an employee of a person, firm, corporation, or association that is a nongovernmental entity and contracts to perform public health and safety labor or services for a public agency to wear a uniform bearing a logo of the public agency that reasonably could be interpreted or construed as implying that the labor or services are being provided by employees of the public agency, unless the uniform conspicuously displays the logo and the name of the person, firm, corporation, or association that is the nongovernmental entity providing the labor or services for the public agency.

(c) The disclosures required pursuant to subdivisions (a) and (b) shall apply to all labor or services provided pursuant to a contract entered into on or after January 1, 2015.

(d)(1) It is unlawful for a public agency to require, through a contract with a person, firm, corporation, or association that is a nongovernmental entity providing public health and safety labor or services, a person or employee of the nongovernmental entity to wear a badge containing the logo of the public agency.

(2) It is unlawful for a person, firm, corporation, or association that is a nongovernmental entity contracting to perform public health and safety labor or services for a public agency to require a person or its employee to wear a badge containing the logo of the public agency.

(e) For the purposes of subdivision (b), an identifying mark affixed to a uniform as required by state or federal law, and a local agency regulating the activity of the person, firm, corporation, or association shall not be construed as implying that the labor or services are being provided by employees of the public agency.

(f) If a vehicle or uniform displays more than one logo referring to the public agency, then the required disclosure shall be placed near the largest logo referring to the public agency.

(g) The disclosure requirements in subdivisions (a) and (b) of this section shall not apply to uniforms or vehicles if the person, firm, corporation, or association that is the nongovernmental entity is providing the labor or services for a public agency under Article 3.3 (commencing with Section 2430) of Chapter 2 of Division 2 of the Vehicle Code.

(h) The disclosure requirements in subdivisions (a) and (b) shall not apply to a public agency vehicle utilized by the nongovernmental entity during a declared state or federal disaster, mass-casualty incident, or other incident that requires the use of state or federal resources when the public agency requires the use of the public agency vehicle.

(i)(1) Violations of this section shall be subject to the remedies provided in the Consumers Legal Remedies Act (Title 1.5 (commencing with Section 1750)).

(2) The duties, rights, and remedies provided in this section are in addition to any other duties, rights, and remedies provided by state law.

(j) For the purposes of this section, the following terms have the following meanings:

(1) "Conspicuously displays" means to display a disclosure on the exterior of a vehicle or uniform in the same location as the logo of the public agency, placed prominently as compared with other words, statements, or designs displayed in connection with the logo of the public agency. With respect to a uniform, "in the same location" includes, but is not limited to, a location on the opposing shoulder, pocket, or similar opposing location relative to the location of the logo of the public agency.

(2) "Logo" means a symbol, graphic, seal, emblem, insignia, trade name, brand name, or picture identifying a person, firm, corporation, association, or public agency. "Logo" shall not mean the name of a public agency used alone.

(3) "Public agency" means a state entity, a city, county, city and county, special district, or other political subdivision of the state.

(4) "Public health and safety labor or services" means fire protection services, rescue services, prehospital emergency medical services, hazardous material emergency response services, and ambulance services. (Added by Stats.2014, c. 832 (S.B.556), § 1, eff. Jan. 1, 2015. Amended by Stats.2015, c. 25 (S.B.84), § 1, eff. June 24, 2015.)

Title 19

COVID-19 SMALL LANDLORD AND HOMEOWNER RELIEF ACT

Chapter		Section
1.	Title and Definitions	3273.01
2.	Mortgages	3273.10

CHAPTER 1. TITLE AND DEFINITIONS

Section
3273.01. Short title.
3273.1. Definitions.
3273.2. Applicability of provisions; mortgage or deed of trust that is secured by residential property containing no more than four dwelling units; depository institutions.

§ 3273.01. Short title

This title is known, and may be cited, as the "COVID–19 Small Landlord and Homeowner Relief Act of 2020." (Added by Stats.2020, c. 37 (A.B.3088), § 13, eff. Aug. 31, 2020.)

§ 3273.1. Definitions

For purposes of this title:

(a)(1) "Borrower" means any of the following:

(A) A natural person who is a mortgagor or trustor or a confirmed successor in interest, as defined in Section 1024.31 of Title 12 of the Code of Federal Regulations.

(B) An entity other than a natural person only if the secured property contains no more than four dwelling units and is currently occupied by one or more residential tenants.

(2) "Borrower" shall not include an individual who has surrendered the secured property as evidenced by either a letter confirming the surrender or delivery of the keys to the property to the mortgagee, trustee, beneficiary, or authorized agent.

(3) Unless the property securing the mortgage contains one or more deed-restricted affordable housing units or one or more affordable housing units subject to a regulatory restriction limiting rental rates that is contained in an agreement with a government agency, the following mortgagors shall not be considered a "borrower":

(A) A real estate investment trust, as defined in Section 856 of the Internal Revenue Code.[1]

(B) A corporation.

(C) A limited liability company in which at least one member is a corporation.

(4) "Borrower" shall also mean a person who holds a power of attorney for a borrower described in paragraph (1).

(b) "Effective time period" means the time period between the operational date of this title and December 1, 2021.

(c)(1) "Mortgage servicer" or "lienholder" means a person or entity who directly services a loan or who is responsible for interacting with the borrower, managing the loan account on a daily basis, including collecting and crediting periodic loan payments, managing any escrow account, or enforcing the note and security instrument, either as the current owner of the promissory note or as the current owner's authorized agent.

(2) "Mortgage servicer" or "lienholder" also means a subservicing agent to a master servicer by contract.

(3) "Mortgage servicer" shall not include a trustee, or a trustee's authorized agent, acting under a power of sale pursuant to a deed of trust. (Added by Stats.2020, c. 37 (A.B.3088), § 13, eff. Aug. 31, 2020. Amended by Stats.2021, c. 2 (S.B.91), § 8, eff. Jan. 29, 2021; Stats.2021, c. 27 (A.B.832), § 6, eff. June 28, 2021.)

[1] Internal Revenue Code sections are in Title 26 of the U.S.C.A.

§ 3273.2. Applicability of provisions; mortgage or deed of trust that is secured by residential property containing no more than four dwelling units; depository institutions

(a) The provisions of this title apply to a mortgage or deed of trust that is secured by residential property containing no more than four dwelling units, including individual units of condominiums or cooperatives, and that was outstanding as of the enactment date of this title.

(b) The provisions of this title shall apply to a depository institution chartered under federal or state law, a person covered by the licensing requirements of Division 9 (commencing with Section 22000) or Division 20 (commencing with Section 50000) of the Financial Code, or a person licensed pursuant to Part 1 (commencing with Section 10000) of Division 4 of the Business and Professions Code. (Added by Stats.2020, c. 37 (A.B.3088), § 13, eff. Aug. 31, 2020.)

CHAPTER 2. MORTGAGES

Section
3273.10. Written notice of forbearance request denial; identification of defects in request.
3273.11. Compliance with federal guidance regarding borrower options following a COVID–19 related forbearance.
3273.12. Offer of postforbearance loss mitigation option.
3273.14. Preferred language for communication about forbearance and postforbearance options.
3273.15. Remedies; attorney's fees and costs.
3273.16. Waivers.

§ 3273.10. Written notice of forbearance request denial; identification of defects in request

(a) If a mortgage servicer denies a forbearance request made during the effective time period, the mortgage servicer shall provide written notice to the borrower that sets forth the specific reason or reasons that forbearance was not provided, if both of the following conditions are met:

(1) The borrower was current on payment as of February 1, 2020.

(2) The borrower is experiencing a financial hardship that prevents the borrower from making timely payments on the mortgage obligation due, directly or indirectly, to the COVID–19 emergency.

(b) If the written notice in subdivision (a) cites any defect in the borrower's request, including an incomplete application or missing information, that is curable, the mortgage servicer shall do all of the following:

(1) Specifically identify any curable defect in the written notice.

(2) Provide 21 days from the mailing date of the written notice for the borrower to cure any identified defect.

(3) Accept receipt of the borrower's revised request for forbearance before the aforementioned 21–day period lapses.

(4) Respond to the borrower's revised request within five business days of receipt of the revised request.

(c) If a mortgage servicer denies a forbearance request, the declaration required by subdivision (b) of Section 2923.5 shall include the written notice together with a statement as to whether forbearance was or was not subsequently provided.

(d) A mortgage servicer, mortgagee, or beneficiary of the deed of trust, or an authorized agent thereof, who, with respect to a borrower of a federally backed mortgage, complies with the relevant provisions regarding forbearance in Section 4022 of the federal Coronavirus Aid, Relief, and Economic Security Act (the CARES Act) (Public Law 116–136), including any amendments or revisions to those provisions, shall be deemed to be in compliance with this section. A mortgage servicer of a nonfederally backed mortgage that provides forbearance that is consistent with the requirements of the CARES Act for federally backed mortgages shall be deemed to be in compliance with this section. *(Added by Stats.2020, c. 37 (A.B.3088), § 13, eff. Aug. 31, 2020.)*

§ 3273.11. Compliance with federal guidance regarding borrower options following a COVID–19 related forbearance

(a) A mortgage servicer shall comply with applicable federal guidance regarding borrower options following a COVID–19 related forbearance.

(b) Any mortgage servicer, mortgagee, or beneficiary of the deed of trust, or authorized agent thereof, who, with respect to a borrower of a federally backed loan, complies with the guidance to mortgagees regarding borrower options following a COVID–19–related forbearance provided by the Federal National Mortgage Association (Fannie Mae), the Federal Home Loan Mortgage Corporation (Freddie Mac), the Federal Housing Administration of the United States Department of Housing and Urban Development, the United States Department of Veterans Affairs, or the Rural Development division of the United States Department of Agriculture, including any amendments, updates, or revisions to that guidance, shall be deemed to be in compliance with this section.

(c) With respect to a nonfederally backed loan, any mortgage servicer, mortgagee, or beneficiary of the deed of trust, or authorized agent thereof, who, regarding borrower options following a COVID–19 related forbearance, reviews a customer for a solution that is consistent with the guidance to servicers, mortgagees, or beneficiaries provided by Fannie Mae, Freddie Mac, the Federal Housing Administration of the Department of Housing and Urban Development, the Department of Veterans Affairs, or the Rural Development division of the Department of Agriculture, including any amendments, updates or revisions to such guidance, shall be deemed to be in compliance with this section. *(Added by Stats.2020, c. 37 (A.B.3088), § 13, eff. Aug. 31, 2020.)*

§ 3273.12. Offer of postforbearance loss mitigation option

It is the intent of the Legislature that a mortgage servicer offer a borrower a postforbearance loss mitigation option that is consistent with the mortgage servicer's contractual or other authority. *(Added by Stats.2020, c. 37 (A.B.3088), § 13, eff. Aug. 31, 2020.)*

§ 3273.14. Preferred language for communication about forbearance and postforbearance options

A mortgage servicer shall communicate about forbearance and postforbearance options described in this article in the borrower's preferred language when the mortgage servicer regularly communicates with any borrower in that language. *(Added by Stats.2020, c. 37 (A.B.3088), § 13, eff. Aug. 31, 2020.)*

§ 3273.15. Remedies; attorney's fees and costs

(a) A borrower who is harmed by a material violation of this title may bring an action to obtain injunctive relief, damages, restitution, and any other remedy to redress the violation.

(b) A court may award a prevailing borrower reasonable attorney's fees and costs in any action based on any violation of this title in which injunctive relief against a sale, including a temporary restraining order, is granted. A court may award a prevailing borrower reasonable attorney's fees and costs in an action for a violation of this article in which relief is granted but injunctive relief against a sale is not granted.

(c) The rights, remedies, and procedures provided to borrowers by this section are in addition to and independent of any other rights, remedies, or procedures under any other law. This section shall not be construed to alter, limit, or negate any other rights, remedies, or procedures provided to borrowers by law. *(Added by Stats.2020, c. 37 (A.B.3088), § 13, eff. Aug. 31, 2020.)*

§ 3273.16. Waivers

Any waiver by a borrower of the provisions of this article is contrary to public policy and shall be void. *(Added by Stats.2020, c. 37 (A.B.3088), § 13, eff. Aug. 31, 2020.)*

Title 20

FIREARM INDUSTRY RESPONSIBILITY ACT

Section
3273.50. Definitions.
3273.51. Firearm industry standard of conduct; compliance; violations.
3273.52. Cause of action for violation; authorized party; remedies; rebuttable presumption of failure to implement reasonable controls; intervening acts.
3273.54. Construction and application of title.
3273.55. Operative date of title.

Operative Effect

For operative effect of Title 20, see Civil Code § 3273.55.

§ 3273.50. Definitions

Section operative July 1, 2023.

As used in this title, the following definitions apply:

(a) "Ammunition" has the same meaning as provided in subdivision (b) of Section 16150 of the Penal Code.

(b) "Firearm" has the same meaning as provided in subdivisions (a) and (b) of Section 16520 of the Penal Code.

(c) "Firearm accessory" means an attachment or device designed or adapted to be inserted into, affixed onto, or used in conjunction with a firearm that is designed, intended, or functions to alter or enhance the firing capabilities of a firearm, the lethality of the firearm, or a shooter's ability to hold and use a firearm.

(d) "Firearm-related product" means a firearm, ammunition, a firearm precursor part, a firearm component, and a firearm accessory that meets any of the following conditions:

(1) The item is sold, made, or distributed in California.

(2) The item is intended to be sold or distributed in California.

(3) The item is or was possessed in California and it was reasonably foreseeable that the item would be possessed in California.

(e) "Firearm precursor part" has the same meaning as provided in Section 16531 of the Penal Code.

(f) "Firearm industry member" shall mean a person, firm, corporation, company, partnership, society, joint stock company, or any other entity or association engaged in the manufacture, distribution, importation, marketing, wholesale, or retail sale of firearm-related products.

(g) "Reasonable controls" means reasonable procedures, acts, or practices that are designed, implemented, and enforced to do the following:

(1) Prevent the sale or distribution of a firearm-related product to a straw purchaser, a firearm trafficker, a person prohibited from possessing a firearm under state or federal law, or a person who the firearm industry member has reasonable cause to believe is at substantial risk of using a firearm-related product to harm themselves or another or of possessing or using a firearm-related product unlawfully.

(2) Prevent the loss or theft of a firearm-related product from the firearm industry member.

(3) Ensure that the firearm industry member complies with all provisions of California and federal law and does not otherwise promote the unlawful manufacture, sale, possession, marketing, or use of a firearm-related product. *(Added by Stats.2022, c. 98 (A.B.1594), § 3, eff. Jan. 1, 2023, operative July 1, 2023.)*

Operative Effect

For operative effect of this section, see Civil Code § 3273.55.

§ 3273.51. Firearm industry standard of conduct; compliance; violations

Section operative July 1, 2023.

(a) A firearm industry member shall comply with the firearm industry standard of conduct. It shall be a violation of the firearm industry standard of conduct for a firearm industry member to fail to comply with any requirement of this section.

(b) A firearm industry member shall do both of the following:

(1) Establish, implement, and enforce reasonable controls.

(2) Take reasonable precautions to ensure that the firearm industry member does not sell, distribute, or provide a firearm-related product to a downstream distributor or retailer of firearm-related products who fails to establish, implement, and enforce reasonable controls.

(c) A firearm industry member shall not manufacture, market, import, offer for wholesale sale, or offer for retail sale a firearm-related product that is abnormally dangerous and likely to create an unreasonable risk of harm to public health and safety in California. For the purposes of this subdivision, the following shall apply:

(1) A firearm-related product shall not be considered abnormally dangerous and likely to create an unreasonable risk of harm to public health and safety based on a firearm's inherent capacity to cause injury or lethal harm.

(2) There shall be a presumption that a firearm-related product is abnormally dangerous and likely to create an unreasonable risk of harm to public health and safety if any of the following is true:

(A) The firearm-related product's features render the product most suitable for assaultive purposes instead of lawful self-defense, hunting, or other legitimate sport and recreational activities.

(B) The firearm-related product is designed, sold, or marketed in a manner that foreseeably promotes conversion of legal firearm-related products into illegal firearm-related products.

(C) The firearm-related product is designed, sold, or marketed in a manner that is targeted at minors or other individuals who are legally prohibited from accessing firearms.

(d) A firearm industry member shall not engage in any conduct related to the sale or marketing of firearm-related products that is in violation of the following sections:

(1) Paragraph (1), (2), (3), (4), (5), (6), (7), (8), or (9) of subdivision (a) of Section 1770.

(2) Section 17200 of the Business and Professions Code.

(3) Section 17500 of the Business and Professions Code.

(4) Section 17508 of the Business and Professions Code.
(Added by Stats.2022, c. 98 (A.B.1594), § 3, eff. Jan. 1, 2023, operative July 1, 2023.)

Operative Effect

For operative effect of this section, see Civil Code § 3273.55.

§ 3273.52. Cause of action for violation; authorized party; remedies; rebuttable presumption of failure to implement reasonable controls; intervening acts

Section operative July 1, 2023.

(a) An act or omission by a firearm industry member in violation of the firearm industry standard of conduct set forth in Section 3273.51 shall be actionable under this section.

(b) A person who has suffered harm in California because of a firearm industry member's conduct described by subdivision (a) may bring an action in a court of competent jurisdiction.

(c)(1) The Attorney General may bring a civil action in a court of competent jurisdiction in the name of the people of the State of California to enforce this title and remedy harm caused by a violation of this title.

(2) A city attorney may bring a civil action in a court of competent jurisdiction in the name of the people of that city to enforce this title and remedy harm caused by a violation of this title.

(3) A county counsel may bring a civil action in a court of competent jurisdiction in the name of the people of that county to enforce this title and remedy harm caused by a violation of this title.

(d) If a court determines that a firearm industry member engaged in conduct described by subdivision (a), the court may award any or all of the following:

(1) Injunctive relief sufficient to prevent the firearm industry member and any other defendant from further violating the law.

(2) Damages.

(3) Attorney's fees and costs.

(4) Any other appropriate relief necessary to enforce this title and remedy the harm caused by the conduct.

(e)(1) In an action alleging that a firearm industry member failed to establish, implement, and enforce reasonable controls in violation of paragraph (1) of subdivision (b) of Section 3273.51, there shall be a rebuttable presumption that the firearm industry member failed to implement reasonable controls if both of the following conditions are satisfied:

(A) The firearm industry member's action or failure to act created a reasonably foreseeable risk that the harm alleged by the claimant would occur.

(B) The firearm industry member could have established, implemented, and enforced reasonable controls to prevent or substantially mitigate the risk that the harm would occur.

(2) If the rebuttable presumption described by paragraph (1) is established, the firearm industry member has the burden of proving by a preponderance of the evidence that the firearm industry member established, implemented, and enforced reasonable controls.

(f) An intervening act by a third party, including, but not limited to, criminal misuse of a firearm-related product, shall not preclude a firearm industry member from liability under this section. *(Added by Stats.2022, c. 98 (A.B.1594), § 3, eff. Jan. 1, 2023, operative July 1, 2023.)*

Operative Effect

For operative effect of this section, see Civil Code § 3273.55.

§ 3273.54. Construction and application of title

Section operative July 1, 2023.

(a) This title shall not be construed or implied to limit or impair in any way the right of a person or entity to pursue a legal action under any other authority.

(b) This title shall not be construed or implied to limit or impair in any way an obligation or requirement placed on a firearm industry member by any other authority.

(c) This title shall be construed and applied in a manner that is consistent with the requirements of the California and the United States Constitutions. *(Added by Stats.2022, c. 98 (A.B.1594), § 3, eff. Jan. 1, 2023, operative July 1, 2023.)*

Operative Effect

For operative effect of this section, see Civil Code § 3273.55.

§ 3273.55. Operative date of title

Section operative July 1, 2023.

This title shall become operative on July 1, 2023. *(Added by Stats.2022, c. 98 (A.B.1594), § 3, eff. Jan. 1, 2023, operative July 1, 2023.)*

Division 4
GENERAL PROVISIONS

Part	Section
1. Relief	3274
2. Special Relations of Debtor and Creditor	3429
3. Nuisance	3479
4. Maxims of Jurisprudence	3509
5. Common Interest Developments	4000
5.3. Commercial and Industrial Common Interest Developments	6500
5.5. Automatic Checkout System	7100
6. Works of Improvement	8000
7. Uniform Parentage Act [Repealed]	
8. Automatic Checkout System [Heading Renumbered]	

Part 1
RELIEF

Title	Section
1. Relief in General	3274
2. Compensatory Relief	3281
3. Specific and Preventive Relief	3366
4. Uniform Single Publication Act	3425.1
5. Uniform Trade Secrets Act	3426
6. Interference with Access to Health Care	3427
7. Duty of Health Care Service Plans and Managed Care Entities	3428

Title 1
RELIEF IN GENERAL

Section
3274. Species of relief.
3275. Relief in case of forfeiture.

§ 3274. Species of relief

As a general rule, compensation is the relief or remedy provided by the law of this State for the violation of private rights, and the means of securing their observance; and specific and preventive relief may be given in no other cases than those specified in this Part of the Civil Code. *(Enacted in 1872.)*

Cross References
Injunction, see Civil Code § 3420 et seq.
Preventive relief, see Civil Code §§ 3368, 3420 et seq.
Specific performance, see Civil Code § 3384 et seq.
Specific relief, see Civil Code §§ 3366, 3367, 3375 et seq.

§ 3275. Relief in case of forfeiture

Whenever, by the terms of an obligation, a party thereto incurs a forfeiture, or a loss in the nature of a forfeiture, by reason of his failure to comply with its provisions, he may be relieved therefrom, upon making full compensation to the other party, except in case of a grossly negligent, willful, or fraudulent breach of duty. *(Enacted in 1872.)*

Cross References
Damages for breach of contract, see Civil Code § 3300 et seq.
Damages for wrongs, see Civil Code § 3333 et seq.
Forfeitures, see Civil Code § 1442.
Lease, relief against forfeiture, see Code of Civil Procedure § 1179.
Medi–Cal reimbursement or prior authorization, non-application of this section, see Welfare and Institutions Code § 14018.5.
Performance, time for, see Civil Code §§ 1490 to 1492, 1657.
Relief not granted to enforce forfeiture, see Civil Code § 3369.

Title 2
COMPENSATORY RELIEF

Chapter	Section
1. Damages in General	3281
2. Measure of Damages	3300

CHAPTER 1. DAMAGES IN GENERAL

Article	Section
1. General Principles	3281
2. Interest as Damages	3287
3. Exemplary Damages	3294

ARTICLE 1. GENERAL PRINCIPLES

Section
3281. Damages; person suffering detriment.
3282. Detriment defined.
3283. Damages for detriment after commencement of action; future damages.

§ 3281. Damages; person suffering detriment

Every person who suffers detriment from the unlawful act or omission of another, may recover from the person in fault a compensation therefor in money, which is called damages. *(Enacted in 1872.)*

Cross References
Contracts, damages for breach, see Civil Code § 3300 et seq.
Exemplary damages, see Civil Code § 3294.
Exemplary damages and interest, damages exclusive of except where expressly mentioned, see Civil Code § 3357.
Limitation on amount of damages, see Civil Code § 3358.
Material violations of specified foreclosure provisions, action for injunctive relief by borrower prior to recording of trustee's deed upon sale, liability to borrower after recording of trustee's deed upon sale, effect of violation on validity of sale, third-party encumbrancer, attorney's fees and costs, application to entities described in subdivision (b) of Section 2924.18, see Civil Code § 2924.19.
Material violations of specified foreclosure provisions, action for injunctive relief by borrower prior to recording of trustee's deed upon sale, liability to borrower after recording of trustee's deed upon sale, effect of violation on validity of sale, third-party encumbrancer, signatory to specified consent judgment, attorney's fees and costs, see Civil Code § 2924.12.
New trial for excessive damages, see Code of Civil Procedure § 657.

§ 3281

Nominal damages, see Civil Code § 3360.
Reasonableness of damages, see Civil Code § 3359.
Remedy for wrong, see Civil Code § 3523.
Torts, damages for, see Civil Code § 3333 et seq.

§ 3282. Detriment defined

Detriment is a loss or harm suffered in person or property. *(Enacted in 1872.)*

§ 3283. Damages for detriment after commencement of action; future damages

Damages may be awarded, in a judicial proceeding, for detriment resulting after the commencement thereof, or certain to result in the future. *(Enacted in 1872.)*

ARTICLE 2. INTEREST AS DAMAGES

Section
3287. Interest on damages; right to recover; time from which interest runs; interest rate.
3288. Interest on damages; noncontractual obligation; discretion of jury.
3289. Rate of interest chargeable after breach of contract.
3289.5. Retail installment contract; finance charges; prejudgment interest.
3290. Waiver of interest by acceptance of principal.
3291. Actions to recover damages for personal injury; claim of interest in complaint; offers to compromise; public entities and public employees.

Cross References

Salary increases, formula, rate of interest on unpaid salary or judicial retiree benefits, see Government Code § 68203.

§ 3287. Interest on damages; right to recover; time from which interest runs; interest rate

(a) A person who is entitled to recover damages certain, or capable of being made certain by calculation, and the right to recover which is vested in the person upon a particular day, is entitled also to recover interest thereon from that day, except when the debtor is prevented by law, or by the act of the creditor from paying the debt. This section is applicable to recovery of damages and interest from any debtor, including the state or any county, city, city and county, municipal corporation, public district, public agency, or any political subdivision of the state.

(b) Every person who is entitled under any judgment to receive damages based upon a cause of action in contract where the claim was unliquidated, may also recover interest thereon from a date prior to the entry of judgment as the court may, in its discretion, fix, but in no event earlier than the date the action was filed.

(c) Unless another statute provides a different interest rate, in a tax or fee claim against a public entity that results in a judgment against the public entity, interest shall accrue at a rate equal to the weekly average one year constant maturity United States Treasury yield, but shall not exceed 7 percent per annum. That rate shall control until the judgment becomes enforceable under Section 965.5 or 970.1 of the Government Code, at which time interest shall accrue at an annual rate equal to the weekly average one year constant maturity United States Treasury yield at the time of the judgment plus 2 percent, but shall not exceed 7 percent per annum. *(Enacted in 1872. Amended by Stats.1955, c. 1477, p. 2689, § 1; Stats.1959, c. 1735, p. 4186, § 1; Stats.1967, c. 1230, p. 2997, § 1; Stats.2013, c. 424 (A.B.748), § 1.)*

Cross References

Breach of contract, interest as damages, see Civil Code § 3302.
Conversion, interest in actions for, see Civil Code § 3336.
Covenant against incumbrances, interest on breach, see Civil Code § 3305.
Covenants of seizin, right to convey, warranty and quiet enjoyment, interest on breach, see Civil Code § 3304.
Damages prescribed in Chapter as exclusive, etc., see Civil Code § 3357.
Interest included in judgment, see Code of Civil Procedure § 685.010 et seq.
Nonprofit corporations, award of prejudgment interest, see Corporations Code § 9243.
Salary increases, formula, rate of interest on unpaid salary or judicial retiree benefits, see Government Code § 68203.
Self dealing by director of nonprofit public benefit corporation, see Corporations Code § 5233.

§ 3288. Interest on damages; noncontractual obligation; discretion of jury

In an action for the breach of an obligation not arising from contract, and in every case of oppression, fraud, or malice, interest may be given, in the discretion of the jury. *(Enacted in 1872.)*

Cross References

Conversion, interest in, see Civil Code § 3336.
Eminent domain, interest on damages, see Code of Civil Procedure § 1263.015.
Nonprofit corporations, award of prejudgment interest, see Corporations Code § 9243.
Partition action, interest on disbursements, see Code of Civil Procedure § 874.030.
Self dealing by director of nonprofit public benefit corporation, see Corporations Code § 5233.

§ 3289. Rate of interest chargeable after breach of contract

(a) Any legal rate of interest stipulated by a contract remains chargeable after a breach thereof, as before, until the contract is superseded by a verdict or other new obligation.

(b) If a contract entered into after January 1, 1986, does not stipulate a legal rate of interest, the obligation shall bear interest at a rate of 10 percent per annum after a breach.

For the purposes of this subdivision, the term contract shall not include a note secured by a deed of trust on real property. *(Enacted in 1872. Amended by Stats.1985, c. 663, § 1; Stats.1986, c. 176, § 1, eff. June 23, 1986.)*

Cross References

Hospital and skilled nursing facility COVID–19 worker retention pay, disputes about employee status, retention payment amount, or covered entity's or covered service employer's failure to make retention payment, complaint and review procedure, see Labor Code § 1493.
Hospital and skilled nursing facility COVID–19 worker retention pay, disputes about physician status, retention payment amount, or physician entity's failure to make retention payment, complaint and review procedure, see Labor Code § 1493.

§ 3289.5. Retail installment contract; finance charges; prejudgment interest

For purposes of Section 3289, the rate of the contracted finance charge shall be the legal rate of interest stipulated by a retail installment contract subject to Chapter 1 (commencing with Section 1801) of Title 2 of Part 4 of Division 3. *(Added by Stats.1985, c. 224, § 1.)*

§ 3290. Waiver of interest by acceptance of principal

Accepting payment of the whole principal, as such, waives all claim to interest. *(Enacted in 1872.)*

§ 3291. Actions to recover damages for personal injury; claim of interest in complaint; offers to compromise; public entities and public employees

In any action brought to recover damages for personal injury sustained by any person resulting from or occasioned by the tort of any other person, corporation, association, or partnership, whether by negligence or by willful intent of the other person, corporation, association, or partnership, and whether the injury was fatal or otherwise, it is lawful for the plaintiff in the complaint to claim interest on the damages alleged as provided in this section.

If the plaintiff makes an offer pursuant to Section 998 of the Code of Civil Procedure which the defendant does not accept prior to trial or within 30 days, whichever occurs first, and the plaintiff obtains a more favorable judgment, the judgment shall bear interest at the legal rate of 10 percent per annum calculated from the date of the plaintiff's first offer pursuant to Section 998 of the Code of Civil Procedure which is exceeded by the judgment, and interest shall accrue until the satisfaction of judgment.

This section shall not apply to a public entity, or to a public employee for an act or omission within the scope of employment, and neither the public entity nor the public employee shall be liable, directly or indirectly, to any person for any interest imposed by this section. *(Added by Stats. 1982, c. 150, p. 493, § 1.)*

Cross References

Liability for natural gas, oil, drilling waste, discharges or exploration, see Harbors and Navigation Code § 294.

ARTICLE 3. EXEMPLARY DAMAGES

Section
3294. Exemplary damages; when allowable; definitions.
3294.5. Repealed.
3295. Protective order; prima facie case of liability prerequisite to certain evidence; discovery limitations; evidence of profits or financial condition.
3296. Insurers and health care service plans; punitive damage judgments; copies to commissioners; sanctions.

§ 3294. Exemplary damages; when allowable; definitions

(a) In an action for the breach of an obligation not arising from contract, where it is proven by clear and convincing evidence that the defendant has been guilty of oppression, fraud, or malice, the plaintiff, in addition to the actual damages, may recover damages for the sake of example and by way of punishing the defendant.

(b) An employer shall not be liable for damages pursuant to subdivision (a), based upon acts of an employee of the employer, unless the employer had advance knowledge of the unfitness of the employee and employed him or her with a conscious disregard of the rights or safety of others or authorized or ratified the wrongful conduct for which the damages are awarded or was personally guilty of oppression, fraud, or malice. With respect to a corporate employer, the advance knowledge and conscious disregard, authorization, ratification or act of oppression, fraud, or malice must be on the part of an officer, director, or managing agent of the corporation.

(c) As used in this section, the following definitions shall apply:

(1) "Malice" means conduct which is intended by the defendant to cause injury to the plaintiff or despicable conduct which is carried on by the defendant with a willful and conscious disregard of the rights or safety of others.

(2) "Oppression" means despicable conduct that subjects a person to cruel and unjust hardship in conscious disregard of that person's rights.

(3) "Fraud" means an intentional misrepresentation, deceit, or concealment of a material fact known to the defendant with the intention on the part of the defendant of thereby depriving a person of property or legal rights or otherwise causing injury.

(d) Damages may be recovered pursuant to this section in an action pursuant to Chapter 4 (commencing with Section 377.10) of Title 3 of Part 2 of the Code of Civil Procedure based upon a death which resulted from a homicide for which the defendant has been convicted of a felony, whether or not the decedent died instantly or survived the fatal injury for some period of time. The procedures for joinder and consolidation contained in Section 377.62 of the Code of Civil Procedure shall apply to prevent multiple recoveries of punitive or exemplary damages based upon the same wrongful act.

(e) The amendments to this section made by Chapter 1498 of the Statutes of 1987 apply to all actions in which the initial trial has not commenced prior to January 1, 1988. *(Enacted in 1872. Amended by Stats.1905, c. 463, p. 621, § 1; Stats.1980, c. 1242, p. 4217, § 1; Stats.1982, c. 174, § 1; Stats.1983, c. 408, § 1; Stats.1987, c. 1498, § 5; Stats.1988, c. 160, § 17; Stats.1992, c. 178 (S.B.1496), § 5.)*

Cross References

Animals, injuries to, see Civil Code § 3340.
Civil actions for abuse of elderly or dependent adults, liability for financial abuse, attorneys's fees and costs, limits on damages, and punitive damages awarded, see Welfare and Institutions Code § 15657.5.
Damages for torts in general, see Civil Code § 3333 et seq.
Damages prescribed by chapter 2 of this Title exclusive of exemplary damages, see Civil Code § 3357.
Forcible or unlawful entry, treble damages, see Code of Civil Procedure § 735.
Hospital and skilled nursing facility COVID–19 worker retention pay, liability for damages, see Labor Code § 1495.
Limitation of damages, exception under this Article, see Civil Code § 3358.
Liquidated damages, see Civil Code § 1671.

§ 3294

Mobilehome park tenancies, willful violations by park management, allowance for civil penalties or exemplary damages, see Civil Code § 798.86.

Personal representative, liability for double damages for fraud in sale, see Probate Code § 10381.

Persons of unsound mind, see Civil Code § 41.

Private Student Loan Collections Reform Act, violation of act, penalties, class actions, attorney's fees, exceptions, limitation of actions, see Civil Code § 1788.208.

Public entity not liable for damages awarded under this section, see Government Code § 818.

Public utilities, exemplary damages for wilful acts or omissions, see Public Utilities Code § 2106.

Reasonableness of damages, see Civil Code § 3359.

Stalking, liability for damages under this section, see Civil Code § 1708.7.

Treble damages, forcible or unlawful entry, see Code of Civil Procedure §§ 735, 1174.

Trespass, cutting, carrying off, or injuring trees, see Code of Civil Procedure § 733.

Unlawful detainer, treble damages, see Code of Civil Procedure § 1174.

Waste, see Code of Civil Procedure § 732.

Water service, double damages for failure of water company to furnish, see Public Utilities Code § 8203.

Wrongful taking from estate, see Probate Code §§ 859, 8870.

§ 3294.5. Repealed by Stats.2004, c. 227 (S.B.1102), § 8.5, operative July 1, 2006

§ 3295. Protective order; prima facie case of liability prerequisite to certain evidence; discovery limitations; evidence of profits or financial condition

(a) The court may, for good cause, grant any defendant a protective order requiring the plaintiff to produce evidence of a prima facie case of liability for damages pursuant to Section 3294, prior to the introduction of evidence of:

(1) The profits the defendant has gained by virtue of the wrongful course of conduct of the nature and type shown by the evidence.

(2) The financial condition of the defendant.

(b) Nothing in this section shall prohibit the introduction of prima facie evidence to establish a case for damages pursuant to Section 3294.

(c) No pretrial discovery by the plaintiff shall be permitted with respect to the evidence referred to in paragraphs (1) and (2) of subdivision (a) unless the court enters an order permitting such discovery pursuant to this subdivision. However, the plaintiff may subpoena documents or witnesses to be available at the trial for the purpose of establishing the profits or financial condition referred to in subdivision (a), and the defendant may be required to identify documents in the defendant's possession which are relevant and admissible for that purpose and the witnesses employed by or related to the defendant who would be most competent to testify to those facts. Upon motion by the plaintiff supported by appropriate affidavits and after a hearing, if the court deems a hearing to be necessary, the court may at any time enter an order permitting the discovery otherwise prohibited by this subdivision if the court finds, on the basis of the supporting and opposing affidavits presented, that the plaintiff has established that there is a substantial probability that the plaintiff will prevail on the claim pursuant to Section 3294.

Such order shall not be considered to be a determination on the merits of the claim or any defense thereto and shall not be given in evidence or referred to at the trial.

(d) The court shall, on application of any defendant, preclude the admission of evidence of that defendant's profits or financial condition until after the trier of fact returns a verdict for plaintiff awarding actual damages and finds that a defendant is guilty of malice, oppression, or fraud in accordance with Section 3294. Evidence of profit and financial condition shall be admissible only as to the defendant or defendants found to be liable to the plaintiff and to be guilty of malice, oppression, or fraud. Evidence of profit and financial condition shall be presented to the same trier of fact that found for the plaintiff and found one or more defendants guilty of malice, oppression, or fraud.

(e) No claim for exemplary damages shall state an amount or amounts.

(f) The amendments to this section made by Senate Bill No. 241 of the 1987–88 Regular Session apply to all actions in which the initial trial has not commenced prior to January 1, 1988. (Added by Stats.1979, c. 778, p. 2662, § 1. Amended by Stats.1980, c. 1242, p. 4218, § 2; Stats.1987, c. 1498, § 6.)

§ 3296. Insurers and health care service plans; punitive damage judgments; copies to commissioners; sanctions

(a) Whenever a judgment for punitive damages is entered against an insurer or health care service plan licensed pursuant to Chapter 2.2 (commencing with Section 1340) of Division 2 of the Health and Safety Code, the plaintiff in the action shall, within 10 days of entry of judgment, provide all of the following to the Commissioner of the Department of Insurance or the Director of the Department of Managed Health Care, whichever commissioner has regulatory jurisdiction over the insurer or health care service plan:

(1) A copy of the judgment.

(2) A brief recitation of the facts of the case.

(3) Copies of relevant pleadings, as determined by the plaintiff.

(b) The willful failure to comply with this section may, at the discretion of the trial court, result in the imposition of sanctions against the plaintiff or his or her attorney.

(c) This section shall apply to all judgments entered on or after January 1, 1995.

(d) "Insurer," for purposes of this section, means any person or entity transacting any of the classes of insurance described in Chapter 1 (commencing with Section 100) of Part 1 of Division 1 of the Insurance Code. (Added by Stats.1994, c. 1061 (A.B.3570), § 1. Amended by Stats.1999, c. 525 (A.B.78), § 7; Stats.2000, c. 857 (A.B.2903), § 5.)

CHAPTER 2. MEASURE OF DAMAGES

Article	Section
1. Damages for Breach of Contract	3300
2. Damages for Wrongs	3333
3. Penal Damages	3344
4. General Provisions	3353

ARTICLE 1. DAMAGES FOR BREACH OF CONTRACT

Section
3300. Measure.
3301. Certainty.
3302. Breach of obligation to pay money only.
3303. Repealed.
3304. Breach of covenant of seizin, of right to convey, of warranty, or of quiet enjoyment.
3305. Breach of covenant against incumbrances.
3306. Breach of agreement to convey real estate.
3306a. Breach of agreement to deliver quitclaim; minimum detriment.
3307. Breach of agreement to purchase real estate.
3308. Lease terminated for breach by lessee; measure of lessor's damages.
3309 to 3314. Repealed.
3315. Breach of carrier's obligation to receive goods, etc.
3316. Breach of carrier's obligation to deliver.
3317. Carrier's delay in delivery.
3318. Breach of warranty of agent's authority.
3319. Contract for private works of improvement; late payment penalty; terms; nature and application.
3320. Contracts for public works of improvement; progress and final retention payments to prime design professionals; dispute; penalty; nature and application.
3321. Contracts for public works of improvement; payment to subconsultant design professional; dispute; penalty; nature and application.
3322. Payment by broker of construction trucking services of transportation charges submitted by motor carrier of property in dump truck equipment; conditions; violations.

§ 3300. Measure

For the breach of an obligation arising from contract, the measure of damages, except where otherwise expressly provided by this Code, is the amount which will compensate the party aggrieved for all the detriment proximately caused thereby, or which, in the ordinary course of things, would be likely to result therefrom. *(Enacted in 1872. Amended by Code Am.1873–74, c. 612, p. 265, § 276.)*

Cross References

Breach of warranty, see Commercial Code § 2316.
Damages for,
  Specific wrongs, see Civil Code § 3334 et seq.
  Torts in general, see Civil Code § 3333.
Deceit, see Civil Code § 1709 et seq.
Detriment defined, see Civil Code § 3282.
Future damages, see Civil Code § 3283.
Instrument in writing, value in estimating damages, see Civil Code § 3356.
Interest on damages, see Civil Code § 3287 et seq.
Limitation of damages, see Civil Code § 3358.
Liquidated damages, see Civil Code § 1671.
Negligent operation of motor vehicle by minor, see Vehicle Code § 17707.
Peculiar value of property, see Civil Code § 3355.
Property value to seller or buyer, see Civil Code §§ 3353, 3354.
Reasonableness of damages, see Civil Code § 3359.
Species of relief, see Civil Code § 3274.
Trespass, cutting, carrying off, or injuring trees, see Code of Civil Procedure § 733.

Wrongful death, see Code of Civil Procedure § 377.60 et seq.

§ 3301. Certainty

No damages can be recovered for a breach of contract which are not clearly ascertainable in both their nature and origin. *(Enacted in 1872.)*

Cross References

Ascertainability of object, see Civil Code § 1596.
Ascertainment of amount of consideration, see Civil Code § 1611.
Liquidated damages, see Civil Code § 1671.
Reasonableness of damages, see Civil Code § 3359.
Statute of frauds, see Civil Code § 1624.

§ 3302. Breach of obligation to pay money only

The detriment caused by the breach of an obligation to pay money only, is deemed to be the amount due by the terms of the obligation, with interest thereon. *(Enacted in 1872.)*

Cross References

Damages not to exceed value of full performance, see Civil Code § 3358.
Detriment defined in general, see Civil Code § 3282.
Interest on damages, see Civil Code § 3287 et seq.
Liquidated damages, see Civil Code § 1671.

§ 3303. Repealed by Stats.1968, c. 113, p. 329, § 1

§ 3304. Breach of covenant of seizin, of right to convey, of warranty, or of quiet enjoyment

The detriment caused by the breach of a covenant of "seizin," of "right to convey," of "warranty," or of "quiet enjoyment," in a grant of an estate in real property, is deemed to be:

1. The price paid to the grantor; or, if the breach is partial only, such proportion of the price as the value of the property affected by the breach bore at the time of the grant to the value of the whole property;

2. Interest thereon for the time during which the grantee derived no benefit from the property, not exceeding five years;

3. Any expenses properly incurred by the covenantee in defending his possession. *(Enacted in 1872.)*

Cross References

Apportionment on termination of hiring, see Civil Code § 1935.
Quiet possession of hire, see Civil Code § 1927.
Unlawful detainer, see Code of Civil Procedure § 1161.

§ 3305. Breach of covenant against incumbrances

The detriment caused by the breach of a covenant against incumbrances in a grant of an estate in real property is deemed to be the amount which has been actually expended by the covenantee in extinguishing either the principal or interest thereof, not exceeding in the former case a proportion of the price paid to the grantor equivalent to the relative value at the time of the grant of the property affected by the breach, as compared with the whole, or, in the latter case, interest on a like amount. *(Enacted in 1872.)*

Cross References

Implied covenant free of incumbrances, see Civil Code § 1113.

Incumbrances defined, see Civil Code § 1114.

§ 3306. Breach of agreement to convey real estate

The detriment caused by the breach of an agreement to convey an estate in real property, is deemed to be the price paid, and the expenses properly incurred in examining the title and preparing the necessary papers, the difference between the price agreed to be paid and the value of the estate agreed to be conveyed at the time of the breach, the expenses properly incurred in preparing to enter upon the land, consequential damages according to proof, and interest. *(Enacted in 1872. Amended by Stats.1983, c. 262, § 1.)*

Cross References

Detriment defined, see Civil Code § 3282.
Fraudulent conveyances of realty, see Civil Code § 1227 et seq.
Grounds for recovery under contract for sale of realty, see Civil Code §§ 1689, 1691.
Statute of frauds, see Civil Code § 1624.
Wrongful occupation of real estate, see Civil Code § 3334.

§ 3306a. Breach of agreement to deliver quitclaim; minimum detriment

The minimum detriment caused by the breach of an agreement to execute and deliver a quitclaim deed to real property is deemed to be the expenses incurred by the promisee in quieting title to such property, and the expenses incidental to the entry upon such property. Such expenses which shall include reasonable attorneys' fees shall be fixed by the court in the quiet title action. *(Added by Stats.1935, c. 661, p. 1825, § 1.)*

Cross References

Actions to quiet title, see Code of Civil Procedure § 760.010 et seq.

§ 3307. Breach of agreement to purchase real estate

The detriment caused by the breach of an agreement to purchase an estate in real property is deemed to be the excess, if any, of the amount which would have been due to the seller under the contract over the value of the property to him or her, consequential damages according to proof, and interest. *(Enacted in 1872. Amended by Stats.1983, c. 262, § 2.)*

Cross References

Detriment defined, see Civil Code § 3282.
Enforcement of forfeiture, see Civil Code § 3369.
Grounds for recovery under contract for sale of realty, see Civil Code §§ 1689, 1691.
Relief in case of forfeiture, see Civil Code § 3275.

§ 3308. Lease terminated for breach by lessee; measure of lessor's damages

The parties to any lease of real or personal property may agree therein that if the lease shall be terminated by the lessor by reason of any breach thereof by the lessee, the lessor shall thereupon be entitled to recover from the lessee the worth at the time of the termination, of the excess, if any, of the amount of rent and charges equivalent to rent reserved in the lease for the balance of the stated term or any shorter period of time over the then reasonable rental value of the property for the same period.

The rights of the lessor under the agreement shall be cumulative to all other rights or remedies now or hereafter given to the lessor by law or by the terms of the lease; provided, however, that the election of the lessor to exercise the remedy hereinabove permitted shall be binding upon him or her and exclude recourse thereafter to any other remedy for rental or charges equivalent to rental or damages for breach of the covenant to pay the rent or charges accruing subsequent to the time of the termination. The parties to the lease may further agree therein that unless the remedy provided by this section is exercised by the lessor within a specified time the right thereto shall be barred.

This section does not apply to a lease of real property unless (a) the lease was executed before July 1, 1971, or (b) the terms of the lease were fixed by a lease, option, or other agreement executed before July 1, 1971.

This section does not apply to leases subject to Division 10 (commencing with Section 10101) of the Commercial Code. *(Added by Stats.1937, c. 504, p. 1494, § 1. Amended by Stats.1970, c. 89, p. 107, § 11, operative July 1, 1971; Stats. 1988, c. 1368, § 2, operative Jan. 1, 1990.)*

§§ 3309 to 3314. Repealed by Stats.1931, c. 1070, p. 2258, § 2

§ 3315. Breach of carrier's obligation to receive goods, etc.

The detriment caused by the breach of a carrier's obligation to accept freight, messages, or passengers, is deemed to be the difference between the amount which he had a right to charge for the carriage and the amount which it would be necessary to pay for the same service when it ought to be performed. *(Enacted in 1872.)*

Cross References

Carriage in general, see Civil Code § 2085 et seq.
Common carrier defined, see Civil Code § 2168.
Damages for refusing or postponing messages, see Civil Code § 2209.
Detriment defined in general, see Civil Code § 3282.
Messages other than by telephone or telegraph, see Civil Code § 2161.
Obligation of common carrier to,
  Accept freight, see Civil Code § 2169.
  Provide vehicles and seats for persons, see Civil Code §§ 2184, 2185.
Telegraphic messages, see Civil Code § 2207.

§ 3316. Breach of carrier's obligation to deliver

The detriment caused by the breach of a carrier's obligation to deliver freight, where he has not converted it to his own use, is deemed to be the value thereof at the place and on the day at which it should have been delivered, deducting the freightage to which he would have been entitled if he had completed the delivery. *(Enacted in 1872.)*

Cross References

Liability of issuer of through bill of lading, see Commercial Code § 7302.
Limitation of liability by contract, see Civil Code § 2176.
Obligations of carriers of property, see Civil Code § 2114 et seq.

Offense of selling property received, see Penal Code § 581.

§ 3317. Carrier's delay in delivery

The detriment caused by a carrier's delay in the delivery of freight, is deemed to be the depreciation in the intrinsic value of the freight during the delay, and also the depreciation, if any, in the market value thereof, otherwise than by reason of a depreciation in its intrinsic value, at the place where it ought to have been delivered, and between the day at which it ought to have been delivered, and the day of its actual delivery. *(Enacted in 1872.)*

Cross References

Liability for delay, see Civil Code § 2196.
Liability of issuer of through bill of lading, see Commercial Code § 7302.
Perishable property, see Civil Code § 2204.

§ 3318. Breach of warranty of agent's authority

The detriment caused by the breach of a warranty of an agent's authority, is deemed to be the amount which could have been recovered and collected from his principal if the warranty had been complied with, and the reasonable expenses of legal proceedings taken, in good faith, to enforce the act of the agent against his principal. *(Enacted in 1872.)*

Cross References

Agent defined, see Civil Code § 2295.
Authority of agents, see Civil Code § 2304 et seq.
Delegation of agency, see Civil Code § 2349 et seq.
Responsibility of agent to third persons, see Civil Code § 2343.
Warranty of agents' authority, see Civil Code § 2342.

§ 3319. Contract for private works of improvement; late payment penalty; terms; nature and application

(a) In each written contract for private works of improvement entered into on or after January 1, 1996, the contracting party and the design professional may agree to contractual provisions that include a late payment penalty, in lieu of any interest otherwise due. The terms of the late payment penalty shall be specifically set forth in the written contract.

(b) The penalty authorized pursuant to subdivision (a) shall be separate from, and in addition to, the design professionals liens provided by Chapter 3 (commencing with Section 8300) of Title 2 of Part 6 of Division 4, mechanics liens provided by Chapter 4 (commencing with Section 8400) of Title 2 of Part 6 of Division 4, and stop payment notices provided by Chapter 5 (commencing with Section 8500) of Title 2 of Part 6 of Division 4.

(c) None of the rights or obligations created or permitted by this section between design professionals and contracting parties shall apply to construction loan funds held by a lender pursuant to a construction loan agreement.

(d) For purposes of this section, the following definitions apply:

(1) "Contracting party" means any person or entity entering into a written contract with a design professional for professional design services for a private work of improvement.

(2) "Design professional" means a person licensed as an architect pursuant to Chapter 3 (commencing with Section 5500) of Division 3 of the Business and Professions Code, registered as a professional engineer pursuant to Chapter 7 (commencing with Section 6700) of Division 3 of the Business and Professions Code, or licensed as a land surveyor pursuant to Chapter 15 (commencing with Section 8700) of Division 3 of the Business and Professions Code. *(Added by Stats.1995, c. 429 (S.B.1286), § 1. Amended by Stats.1996, c. 124 (A.B.3470), § 10; Stats.2010, c. 697 (S.B.189), § 17, operative July 1, 2012.)*

§ 3320. Contracts for public works of improvement; progress and final retention payments to prime design professionals; dispute; penalty; nature and application

(a) In each contract for public works of improvement, entered into on or after January 1, 1996, the public agency shall pay to the prime design professional any progress payment within 30 days of receipt of a written demand for payment in accordance with the contract, and the final retention payment within 45 days of receipt of a written demand for payment in accordance with the contract. If the public agency disputes in good faith any portion of the amount due, it may withhold from the payment an amount not to exceed 150 percent of the disputed amount. The disputed amount withheld is not subject to any penalty authorized by this section.

(b) If any amount is wrongfully withheld or is not timely paid in violation of this section, the prime design professional shall be entitled to a penalty of 1½ percent for the improperly withheld amount, in lieu of any interest otherwise due, per month for every month that payment is not made. In any action for the collection of amounts withheld in violation of this section, the prevailing party is entitled to his or her reasonable attorney's fees and costs.

(c) The penalty described in subdivision (b) is separate from, and in addition to, the design professionals liens provided by Chapter 3 (commencing with Section 8300) of Title 2 of Part 6 of Division 4, mechanics liens provided by Chapter 4 (commencing with Section 8400) of Title 2 of Part 6 of Division 4, and stop payment notices on public works provided by Chapter 4 (commencing with Section 9350) of Title 3 of Part 6 of Division 4.

(d) This section does not apply to state agency contracts subject to Section 927.6 of the Government Code.

(e) None of the rights or obligations created by this section between prime design professionals and public agencies apply to construction loan funds held by a lender pursuant to a construction loan agreement.

(f) For purposes of this section:

(1) "Public agency" means the state, any county, any city, any city and county, any district, any public authority, any public agency, any municipal corporation, or other political subdivision or political corporation of the state.

(2) "Design professional" means a person licensed as an architect pursuant to Chapter 3 (commencing with Section 5500) of Division 3 of the Business and Professions Code, registered as a professional engineer pursuant to Chapter 7 (commencing with Section 6700) of Division 3 of the Business and Professions Code, or licensed as a land surveyor pursuant to Chapter 15 (commencing with Section 8700) of Division 3 of the Business and Professions Code.

§ 3320   GENERAL PROVISIONS

(3) "Prime design professional" means a design professional with a written contract directly with the public agency. *(Added by Stats.1995, c. 429 (S.B.1286), § 2. Amended by Stats.1996, c. 124 (A.B.3470), § 11; Stats.2000, c. 776 (A.B. 2890), § 1, eff. Sept. 27, 2000; Stats.2010, c. 697 (S.B.189), § 18, operative July 1, 2012.)*

§ 3321. Contracts for public works of improvement; payment to subconsultant design professional; dispute; penalty; nature and application

(a) In each contract for public works of improvement, a prime design professional shall pay to each subconsultant design professional the amount due him or her from the payment received, not later than 15 days after receipt of each progress payment or final retention payment. If the prime design professional disputes in good faith any portion of the amount due, he or she may withhold from the payment an amount not to exceed 150 percent of the disputed amount. The disputed amount withheld shall not be subject to any penalty authorized by this section.

(b) If any amount is wrongfully withheld or is not timely paid in violation of this section, the subconsultant design professional shall be entitled to a penalty of 1½ percent of the improperly withheld amount, in lieu of any interest otherwise due, per month, for each month that payment is not made. In any action for the collection of amounts withheld in violation of this section, the prevailing party shall be entitled to his or her reasonable attorney's fees and costs.

(c) The penalty described in subdivision (b) shall be separate from, and in addition to, the design professionals liens provided by Chapter 3 (commencing with Section 8300) of Title 2 of Part 6 of Division 4, mechanics liens provided by Chapter 4 (commencing with Section 8400) of Title 2 of Part 6 of Division 4, and stop payment notices on public works provided by Chapter 4 (commencing with Section 9350) of Title 3 of Part 6 of Division 4.

(d) None of the rights or obligations created by this section between prime design professionals and subconsultant design professionals shall apply to construction loan funds held by a lender pursuant to a construction loan agreement.

(e) For purposes of this section:

(1) "Public agency" means the state, any county, any city, any city and county, any district, any public authority, any public agency, any municipal corporation, or other political subdivision or political corporation of the state.

(2) "Design professional" means a person licensed as an architect pursuant to Chapter 3 (commencing with Section 5500) of Division 3 of the Business and Professions Code, registered as a professional engineer pursuant to Chapter 7 (commencing with Section 6700) of Division 3 of the Business and Professions Code, or licensed as a land surveyor pursuant to Chapter 15 (commencing with Section 8700) of Division 3 of the Business and Professions Code.

(3) "Prime design professional" means a design professional having a written contract directly with the public agency.

(4) "Subconsultant design professional" means a design professional having a written contract with a prime design professional. *(Added by Stats.1995, c. 429 (S.B.1286), § 3.*

Amended by Stats.1996, c. 124 (A.B.3470), § 12; Stats.2010, c. 697 (S.B.189), § 19, operative July 1, 2012.)

§ 3322. Payment by broker of construction trucking services of transportation charges submitted by motor carrier of property in dump truck equipment; conditions; violations

(a)(1) A broker of construction trucking services shall pay all transportation charges submitted by a motor carrier of property in dump truck equipment by the 25th day following the last day of the calendar month in which the transportation was performed, if the charges, including all necessary documentation, are submitted by the fifth day following the last day of the calendar month in which the transportation was performed. If there is a good faith dispute over a portion of the charges claimed, the broker may withhold payment of an amount not to exceed 150 percent of the estimated cost of the disputed amount.

(2) A broker who violates paragraph (1) shall pay to the motor carrier of property in dump truck equipment a penalty of 2 percent per month on the improperly withheld amount.

(3) In an action for the collection of moneys not paid in accordance with paragraph (1), the prevailing party shall be entitled to his or her attorney's fees and costs.

(b) For purposes of subdivision (a), the following definitions apply:

(1) A "broker of construction trucking services" means any person, excluding a licensed contractor, that, as a principal or agent, arranges for transportation services to be provided by an independent contractor motor carrier of property in dump truck equipment and who is responsible for paying the transportation charges of the motor carrier.

(2) A "motor carrier of property in dump truck equipment" means a motor carrier of property permitted by the Department of Motor Vehicles that hauls any type of construction commodity or material in dump truck equipment.

(c) Subdivision (a) only applies if a motor carrier of property is in compliance with Division 14.85 (commencing with Section 36000) of the Vehicle Code at the time the dump truck transportation work is performed. *(Added by Stats.2004, c. 518 (A.B.2201), § 1.)*

Cross References

Brokers of construction trucking services, surety bond required for furnishing construction transportation services, see Vehicle Code § 34510.5.

ARTICLE 2. DAMAGES FOR WRONGS

Section
3333.	Torts in general.
3333.1.	Negligence of health care provider; evidence of benefits and premiums paid; subrogation.
3333.2.	Negligence of health care provider or health care institution; noneconomic losses; limitations.
3333.3.	Negligence of plaintiff; injuries of plaintiff proximately caused by plaintiff's commission of any felony, or immediate flight therefrom; limitation.
3333.4.	Operation or use of motor vehicles; noneconomic losses; limitation.

Section	
3333.5.	Pipeline corporations; oil spills; liability; costs; attorneys' fees; clean-up responsibility; application of section; definitions.
3333.6.	Rejected.
3333.7.	Recovery of treble damages by injured person from employer of driver of commercial motor vehicle who was driving under the influence of alcohol or a controlled substance.
3333.8.	Legislative findings and declarations; fire suppression or other costs.
3334.	Real estate; wrongful occupation; value of the use of property.
3335.	Real estate; willful holding over.
3336.	Personal property; conversion; presumption.
3336.5.	Junk dealers or recyclers; possession of fire hydrants, fire department connections, manhole covers, or backflow devices; agency certification required; liability for wrongful possession; unknowing possession and notification after discovery; legislative intent regarding liability to third parties.
3337.	Personal property; conversion; subsequent application of property to benefit of owner.
3338.	Personal property; conversion; lienor's damages.
3339.	Legislative findings, declarations and intent; immigration status; severability.
3339.5.	Effect of immigration status on recovery sought by minor child; discovery; express application.
3339.10.	Immigration or citizenship status irrelevant to issues of liability or remedy in specified proceedings; discovery.
3340.	Injuries to animals; exemplary damages.
3341.	Liability of owner, possessor, or harborer of animal killing or injuring other animals; scienter; right to kill animal found committing injury; accidental killing or injury.
3342.	Dog bites; liability of owner; military or police work excluded; limitations.
3342.5.	Duty of owner; action; dogs trained to fight, attack, or kill; legislation by city and county.
3343.	Fraud in purchase, sale or exchange of property; additional damages.
3343.5.	Unlawful motor vehicle subleasing; persons entitled to bring action; relief granted by court; definitions.
3343.7.	Fraudulent inducement to join a nonprofit organization operated on cooperative basis by and for independent retailers; action for rescission of contract or damages.

§ 3333. Torts in general

For the breach of an obligation not arising from contract, the measure of damages, except where otherwise expressly provided by this Code, is the amount which will compensate for all the detriment proximately caused thereby, whether it could have been anticipated or not. *(Enacted in 1872.)*

Cross References

Abstinence from injuring others, see Civil Code § 1708.
Complaint for damages must state amount, see Code of Civil Procedure § 425.10 et seq.
Deceit, liability for, see Civil Code § 1709.
Exemplary damages for willful acts or omissions by public utilities, see Public Utilities Code § 2106.
Nominal damages, see Civil Code § 3360.
Obligations imposed by law, see Civil Code § 1708 et seq.
Public utilities, liability for damages, see Public Utilities Code § 2106.
Responsibility for willful acts and negligence, see Civil Code § 1714.
Tort claims act, see Government Code § 810 et seq.
Trespass for cutting trees, treble damages for, see Code of Civil Procedure § 733.
Usurpation of office, see Code of Civil Procedure § 807.
Waste, treble damages for, see Code of Civil Procedure § 732.
Wrongful death, damages for, see Code of Civil Procedure § 377.60 et seq.
Wrongful use of materials, damages, see Civil Code § 1033.

§ 3333.1. Negligence of health care provider; evidence of benefits and premiums paid; subrogation

(a) In the event the defendant so elects, in an action for personal injury against a health care provider based upon professional negligence, he may introduce evidence of any amount payable as a benefit to the plaintiff as a result of the personal injury pursuant to the United States Social Security Act,[1] any state or federal income disability or worker's compensation act, any health, sickness or income-disability insurance, accident insurance that provides health benefits or income-disability coverage, and any contract or agreement of any group, organization, partnership, or corporation to provide, pay for, or reimburse the cost of medical, hospital, dental, or other health care services. Where the defendant elects to introduce such evidence, the plaintiff may introduce evidence of any amount which the plaintiff has paid or contributed to secure his right to any insurance benefits concerning which the defendant has introduced evidence.

(b) No source of collateral benefits introduced pursuant to subdivision (a) shall recover any amount against the plaintiff nor shall it be subrogated to the rights of the plaintiff against a defendant.

(c) For the purposes of this section:

(1) "Health care provider" means any person licensed or certified pursuant to Division 2 (commencing with Section 500) of the Business and Professions Code, or licensed pursuant to the Osteopathic Initiative Act, or the Chiropractic Initiative Act, or licensed pursuant to Chapter 2.5 (commencing with Section 1440) of Division 2 of the Health and Safety Code; and any clinic, health dispensary, or health facility, licensed pursuant to Division 2 (commencing with Section 1200) of the Health and Safety Code. "Health care provider" includes the legal representatives of a health care provider;

(2) "Professional negligence" means a negligent act or omission to act by a health care provider in the rendering of professional services, which act or omission is the proximate cause of a personal injury or wrongful death, provided that such services are within the scope of services for which the provider is licensed and which are not within any restriction imposed by the licensing agency or licensed hospital. *(Added by Stats.1975, 2nd Ex.Sess., c. 1, p. 3968, § 24.5. Amended by Stats.1975, 2nd Ex.Sess., c. 2, p. 3990, § 1.19, eff. Sept. 24, 1975, operative Dec. 12, 1975; Stats.1976, c. 1079, p. 4852, § 4.)*

[1] 42 U.S.C.A. § 301 et seq.

§ 3333.2. Negligence of health care provider or health care institution; noneconomic losses; limitations

(a) In any action for injury against a health care provider or health care institution based on professional negligence, the injured plaintiff shall be entitled to recover noneconomic losses to compensate for pain, suffering, inconvenience, physical impairment, disfigurement and other nonpecuniary damage, subject to the limitations in this section.

(b) In any action for injury that does not involve wrongful death against one or more health care providers or health care institutions based on professional negligence, the following limitations shall apply:

(1) Civil liability for damages for noneconomic losses against one or more health care providers, collectively, shall not exceed three hundred fifty thousand dollars ($350,000), regardless of the number of health care providers, which does not include any unaffiliated health care providers that are responsible for noneconomic losses pursuant to paragraph (3).

(2) Civil liability for damages for noneconomic losses against one or more health care institutions, collectively, shall not exceed three hundred fifty thousand dollars ($350,000), regardless of the number of health care institutions, which does not include any unaffiliated health care institutions that are responsible for noneconomic losses pursuant to paragraph (3).

(3) Civil liability for damages for noneconomic losses against one or more health care providers or health care institutions that are unaffiliated with a defendant described in paragraph (1) or (2) based on acts of professional negligence separate and independent from the acts of professional negligence of a defendant described in paragraph (1) or (2) and that occurred at, or in relation to medical transport to, a health care institution unaffiliated with a health care institution described in paragraph (2), collectively, shall not exceed three hundred fifty thousand dollars ($350,000), regardless of the number of defendants described in this paragraph, which does not include any unaffiliated health care providers or unaffiliated health care institutions that are responsible for noneconomic losses pursuant to paragraph (1) or (2).

(c) In any action for wrongful death against one or more health care providers or health care institutions based on professional negligence, the following limitations shall apply:

(1) Civil liability for damages for noneconomic losses against one or more health care providers, collectively, shall not exceed five hundred thousand dollars ($500,000), regardless of the number of health care providers, which does not include any unaffiliated health care providers that are responsible for noneconomic losses pursuant to paragraph (3).

(2) Civil liability for damages for noneconomic losses against one or more health care institutions, collectively, shall not exceed five hundred thousand dollars ($500,000), regardless of the number of health care institutions, which does not include any unaffiliated health care institutions that are responsible for noneconomic losses pursuant to paragraph (3).

(3) Civil liability for damages for noneconomic losses against one or more health care providers or health care institutions that are unaffiliated with a defendant described in paragraph (1) or (2) based on acts of professional negligence separate and independent from the acts of professional negligence of a defendant described in paragraph (1) or (2) that occurred at, or in relation to medical transport to, a health care institution unaffiliated with a health care institution described in paragraph (2), collectively, shall not exceed five hundred thousand dollars ($500,000), regardless of the number of defendants described in this paragraph, which does not include any unaffiliated health care providers or unaffiliated health care institutions that are responsible for noneconomic losses pursuant to paragraph (1) or (2).

(d) No health care provider defendant shall be liable for damages for noneconomic losses in more than one of the categories set forth in this section, regardless of the application or combined application thereof.

(e) No health care institution defendant shall be liable for damages for noneconomic losses in more than one of the categories set forth in this section, regardless of the application or combined application thereof.

(f) The applicable dollar amounts set forth in this section apply regardless of the number of defendant health care providers or health care institutions against whom the claim is asserted or the number of separate causes of actions on which the claim is based. For a claim subject to subdivision (b), the applicable dollar amounts set forth in subdivisions (b), (g), and (h) provide three separate limits of liability that may apply. For a claim subject to subdivision (c), the applicable dollar amounts set forth in subdivisions (c), (g), and (h) provide three separate limits of liability that may apply.

(g) This section shall be deemed effective as of, and shall apply to all cases filed or arbitrations demanded on or after, January 1, 2023. Thereafter, the dollar amounts set forth in subdivision (b) shall increase by forty thousand dollars ($40,000) each January 1st for 10 years up to seven hundred fifty thousand dollars ($750,000), and the dollar amounts set forth in subdivision (c) shall increase each January 1st by fifty thousand dollars ($50,000) for 10 years up to one million dollars ($1,000,000). The dollar amount in effect at the time of judgment, arbitration award, or settlement shall apply to an action, subject to subdivision (h).

(h) The applicable amounts for noneconomic damages for personal injury of $750,000, and for wrongful death of $1,000,000, as set forth in subdivision (g), shall be adjusted for inflation on January 1 of each year by 2 percent beginning on January 1, 2034.

(i) In no action shall the amount of damages for noneconomic losses exceed * * * the applicable dollar amounts set forth in subdivisions (b), (c), (g), or (h).

(j) For the purposes of this section:

(1) "Health care provider" means any person licensed or certified pursuant to Division 2 (commencing with Section 500) of the Business and Professions Code, or licensed pursuant to the Osteopathic Initiative Act, or the Chiropractic Initiative Act, or licensed pursuant to Chapter 2.5 (commencing with Section 1440) of Division 2 of the Health and Safety Code; and any clinic, health dispensary, or health facility, licensed pursuant to * * * Chapter 1 (commencing with Section 1200) or Chapter 1.3 (commencing with Section 1248) of Division 2 of the Health and Safety Code, and does

not include health care institutions that are defined in paragraph (2). "Health care provider" includes the legal representatives of a health care provider * * * and the health care provider's employer, professional corporation, partnership, or other form of legally recognized professional practice organization.

(2) "Health care institution" means one or more health care facilities licensed pursuant to Chapter 2 (commencing with Section 1250) of Division 2 of the Health and Safety Code owned or operated by the same entity or its affiliates and includes all persons and entities for which vicarious liability theories, including, but not limited to, the doctrines of respondeat superior, actual agency, and ostensible agency, may apply.

(3) "Unaffiliated" means a specified health care provider, health care institution, or other entity not covered by the definition of affiliated, or affiliated with, as defined in Section 150 of the Corporations Code, or that is not employed by, performing under a contract with, an owner of, or in a joint venture with another specified entity, health care institution, health care provider, organized medical group, professional corporation, or partnership, or that is otherwise not in the same health system with that health care provider, health care institution, or other entity. Whether a health care provider, health care institution, or other entity is unaffiliated is determined at the time of the professional negligence.

(4) "Professional negligence" means a negligent act or omission to act by a health care provider in the rendering of professional services, which act or omission is the proximate cause of a personal injury or wrongful death, provided that such services are within the scope of services for which the provider is licensed and which are not within any restriction imposed by the licensing agency or licensed hospital. (Added by Stats.1975, 2nd Ex.Sess., c. 1, p. 3969, § 24.6. Amended by Stats.1975, 2nd Ex.Sess., c. 2, p. 3991, § 1.191, eff. Sept. 24, 1975, operative Dec. 12, 1975; Stats.2022, c. 17 (A.B.35), § 3, eff. Jan. 1, 2023.)

§ 3333.3. Negligence of plaintiff; injuries of plaintiff proximately caused by plaintiff's commission of any felony, or immediate flight therefrom; limitation

In any action for damages based on negligence, a person may not recover any damages if the plaintiff's injuries were in any way proximately caused by the plaintiff's commission of any felony, or immediate flight therefrom, and the plaintiff has been duly convicted of that felony. (Added by Initiative Measure (Prop. 213, § 3, approved Nov. 5, 1996, eff. Nov. 5, 1996).)

Cross References

Amendment or repeal of initiative statutes, see Cal. Const. Art. 2, § 10.

§ 3333.4. Operation or use of motor vehicles; noneconomic losses; limitation

(a) Except as provided in subdivision (c), in any action to recover damages arising out of the operation or use of a motor vehicle, a person shall not recover non-economic losses to compensate for pain, suffering, inconvenience, physical impairment, disfigurement, and other nonpecuniary damages if any of the following applies:

(1) The injured person was at the time of the accident operating the vehicle in violation of Section 23152 or 23153 of the Vehicle Code, and was convicted of that offense.

(2) The injured person was the owner of a vehicle involved in the accident and the vehicle was not insured as required by the financial responsibility laws of this state.

(3) The injured person was the operator of a vehicle involved in the accident and the operator can not establish his or her financial responsibility as required by the financial responsibility laws of this state.

(b) Except as provided in subdivision (c), an insurer shall not be liable, directly or indirectly, under a policy of liability or uninsured motorist insurance to indemnify for non-economic losses of a person injured as described in subdivision (a).

(c) In the event a person described in paragraph (2) of subdivision (a) was injured by a motorist who at the time of the accident was operating his or her vehicle in violation of Section 23152 or 23153 of the Vehicle Code, and was convicted of that offense, the injured person shall not be barred from recovering non-economic losses to compensate for pain, suffering, inconvenience, physical impairment, disfigurement, and other nonpecuniary damages. (Added by Initiative Measure (Prop. 213, § 3, approved Nov. 5, 1996, eff. Nov. 5, 1996).)

Cross References

Amendment or repeal of initiative statutes, see Cal. Const. Art. 2, § 10.

§ 3333.5. Pipeline corporations; oil spills; liability; costs; attorneys' fees; clean-up responsibility; application of section; definitions

(a) Each pipeline corporation that qualifies as a public utility within Section 216 of the Public Utilities Code that transports any crude oil or fraction thereof in a public utility oil pipeline system that meets the requirements of subdivision (h) shall be absolutely liable without regard to fault for any damages incurred by any injured party that arise out of, or are caused by, the discharge or leaking of crude oil or fraction thereof from the public utility pipeline.

(b) A pipeline corporation is not liable to an injured party under this section for any of the following:

(1) Damages, other than costs of removal incurred by the state or a local government caused solely by an act of war, hostilities, civil war, or insurrection or by an unanticipated grave natural disaster or other act of God of an exceptional, inevitable, and irresistible character, other than an earthquake, which damages could not have been prevented or avoided by the exercise of due care or foresight.

(2) Damages in the proportion caused by the negligence, intentional malfeasance, or criminal act of the landowner, or an agent, employee, or contractor of the landowner, upon whose property the pipeline system is located.

(3) Except as provided by paragraph (2), damages caused solely by the negligence or intentional malfeasance of the injured person.

(4) Except as provided by paragraph (2), damages caused solely by the criminal act of a third party other than the

pipeline corporation or an agent or employee of the pipeline corporation.

(5) Natural seepage from sources other than the public utility oil pipeline.

(6) Damages that arise out of, or are caused by, a discharge that is authorized by a state or federal permit.

(c) Damages for which a pipeline corporation is liable under this section are the following:

(1) All costs of response, containment, cleanup, removal, and treatment, including, but not limited to, monitoring and administration costs.

(2) Injury to, or economic losses resulting from destruction of or injury to, real or personal property.

(3) Injury to, destruction of, or loss of, natural resources, including, but not limited to, the reasonable cost of rehabilitating wildlife, habitat, and other resources and the reasonable cost of assessing that injury, destruction, or loss, in any action brought by the state, a county, city, or district.

(4) Loss of taxes, royalties, rents, use, or profit shares caused by the injury, destruction, loss, or impairment of use of real property, personal property, or natural resources.

(5) Loss of use and enjoyment of natural resources and other public resources or facilities in any action brought by the state, county, city, or district.

(d) The court may award reasonable costs of the suit, attorneys' fees, and the cost of any necessary expert witnesses to any prevailing plaintiff. The court may award reasonable costs of the suit, attorneys' fees, and the cost of any necessary expert witnesses to any prevailing defendant if the court finds that the plaintiff commenced or prosecuted the suit under this section in bad faith or solely for purposes of harassing the defendant.

(e)(1) A pipeline corporation shall immediately clean up all crude oil, or any fraction thereof, that leaks or is discharged from a pipeline subject to this section. Additionally, the pipeline corporation shall abate immediately, or as soon as practical, the effects of the leak or discharge and take all other necessary remedial action.

(2) A pipeline corporation may recover the costs of the activities specified in this section for which it is not at fault by means of any otherwise available cause of action, including, but not limited to, indemnification or subrogation.

(f) This section shall not apply to claims, or causes of action, for damages for personal injury or wrongful death.

(g) This section shall not prohibit any party from bringing any action for damages under any other provision or principle of law, including but not limited to, common law. However, damages shall not be awarded pursuant to this section to an injured party to the extent the same party is or has been awarded damages for the same injury under any other provision or principle of law.

(h) This section shall only apply to all of the following:

(1) The pipeline system proposed to be constructed by Pacific Pipeline System, Inc., identified in Public Utilities Commission Application No. 91–10–013, for which the maximum requirement of one hundred million dollars ($100,000,000) set forth in paragraph (1) of subdivision (j) shall apply.

(2) Any other public utility pipeline system for which construction is completed on or after January 1, 1996, other than a pipeline system the entire length of which is subject to the Lempert–Keene–Seastrand Oil Spill Prevention and Response Act, (Division 7.8 (commencing with Section 8750) of the Public Resources Code). If part, but not all, of a pipeline system is subject to the Lempert–Keene–Seastrand Oil Spill Prevention and Response Act, any evidence of financial responsibility that satisfies that act, and that meets the conditions of this section, shall be credited toward the requirements of this section.

(3) Any major relocation of three miles or greater of a portion of a pipeline system along substantially new alignments accomplished through the exercise of eminent domain. This section shall not apply to the portions of the pipeline not relocated.

(i) This section shall not apply to the following:

(1) A pipeline system in existence prior to January 1, 1996, that is converted to a public utility prior or subsequent to January 1, 1996.

(2) A public utility pipeline system not otherwise subject to this section, that is the object of repair, replacement or maintenance, unless that activity constitutes relocation as described in paragraph (3) of subdivision (h).

(j)(1) No pipeline system subject to this section shall be permitted to operate unless the State Fire Marshal certifies that the pipeline corporation demonstrates sufficient financial responsibility to respond to the liability imposed by this section. The minimum financial responsibility required by the State Fire Marshal shall be seven hundred fifty dollars ($750) times the maximum capacity of the pipeline in the number of barrels per day up to a maximum of one hundred million dollars ($100,000,000) per pipeline system, or a maximum of two hundred million dollars ($200,000,000) per multiple pipeline systems.

(2) For the purposes of this section, financial responsibility shall be demonstrated by evidence that is substantially equivalent to that required by regulations issued under Section 8670.37.54 of the Government Code, including insurance, surety bond, letter of credit, guaranty, qualification as a self-insurer, or combination thereof or any other evidence of financial responsibility. The State Fire Marshal shall require the documentation evidencing financial responsibility to be placed on file with that office, and shall administer the documentation in a manner substantially equivalent to that provided by regulations issued under Section 8670.37.54 of the Government Code. Financial responsibility shall be available for payment of claims for damages described in subdivision (c) of any party, including, but not limited to, the State of California, local governments, special districts, and private parties, that obtains a final judgment therefor against the pipeline corporation.

(k) The State Fire Marshal shall require evidence of financial responsibility to fund postclosure cleanup costs. The evidence of financial responsibility shall be 15 percent of the amount of financial responsibility required under subdivision (j) and shall be maintained by the pipeline corporation for four years from the date the pipeline is fully idled pursuant to a closure plan approved by the State Fire Marshal.

(*l*) "Fraction" of crude oil means a group of compounds collected by fractional distillation that condenses within the same temperature band, or a material that consists primarily of that group of compounds or of a mixture of those groups of compounds.

(m)(1) Notwithstanding Section 228 of the Public Utilities Code, for purposes of this section, "pipeline corporation" means every corporation or person directly operating, managing or owning any pipeline system that qualifies as a public utility within Section 216 of the Public Utilities Code and for compensation within this state.

(2) For purposes of this section, "owning" refers to the legal entity owning the pipeline system itself and does not include legal entities having an ownership interest, in whole or in part, in the entity owning the pipeline system or multiple pipeline systems.

(3) "Pipeline system" means a collective assemblage of intrastate line pipe, valves, and other appurtenances connected to line pipe, pumping units, fabricated assemblies associated with pumping units, metering and delivery station, and fabricated assemblies constructed for the same purpose at substantially the same time that form a facility through which crude oil or a fraction thereof moves in transportation. (Formerly § 3333.4, added by Stats.1995, c. 979, § 2. Renumbered § 3333.5 and amended by Stats.1998, c. 485 (A.B.2803), § 40.)

§ 3333.6. Rejected

§ 3333.7. Recovery of treble damages by injured person from employer of driver of commercial motor vehicle who was driving under the influence of alcohol or a controlled substance

(a) Notwithstanding any other provision of law, any person who suffers injury that is proximately caused by the driver of a commercial motor vehicle shall be entitled to recover treble damages from the driver's employer where it is shown both that the driver of a commercial motor vehicle was under the influence of alcohol or a controlled substance at the time that the injury was caused and that the driver's employer willfully failed at the time of the injury to comply with any of the requirements of federal law described in subdivision (a) of Section 34520 of the Vehicle Code in regard to the involved driver.

(b) For the purposes of subdivision (a), "willfully failed" has the same meaning as "willful failure" as defined in paragraph (3) of subdivision (c) of Section 34623 of the Vehicle Code.

(c) For purposes of subdivision (a), an "employer" is a person or entity who employs the driver or who contracts with an owner-operator, who meets the requirements set forth in subdivision (b) of Section 34624 of the Vehicle Code, to provide transportation services, and who is required to engage in mandatory substance abuse testing pursuant to subdivision (a) of Section 34520 of the Vehicle Code. This subdivision shall not be construed to change the definition of "employer," "employee," or "independent contractor" for any purpose.

(d) Nothing in this section is intended to preclude or affect existing rights. (Added by Stats.2001, c. 298 (S.B.871), § 1.)

Cross References

Employer responsibilities, commercial vehicle safety, self employment as driver, see Vehicle Code § 15242.
Safety regulations, compliance with federal drug and alcohol regulations, drug and alcohol testing, see Vehicle Code § 34520.
Suspension of motor carrier permit of motor carrier of property, grounds, see Vehicle Code § 34623.

§ 3333.8. Legislative findings and declarations; fire suppression or other costs

(a) The Legislature finds and declares that in order to meet fuel management goals, the state must rely on private entities to engage in prescribed burning for public benefit.

(b) Notwithstanding Sections 13009 and 13009.1 of the Health and Safety Code, no person shall be liable for any fire suppression or other costs otherwise recoverable pursuant to Section 13009 or 13009.1 of the Health and Safety Code resulting from a prescribed burn if all of the following conditions are met:

(1) The purpose of the burn is for wildland fire hazard reduction, ecological maintenance and restoration, cultural burning, silviculture, or agriculture.

(2) A person certified as a burn boss pursuant to Section 4477 of the Public Resources Code reviewed and approved a written prescription for the burn that includes adequate risk mitigation measures.

(3) The burn is conducted in compliance with the written prescription.

(4) The burn is authorized pursuant to Chapter 6 (commencing with Section 4411) or Chapter 7 (commencing with Section 4461) of Part 2 of Division 4 of the Public Resources Code.

(5) The burner has a landowner's written permission or the approval of the governing body of a Native American Tribe to burn.

(6) The burn is conducted in compliance with any air quality permit required pursuant to Article 3 (commencing with Section 41850) of Chapter 3 of Part 4 of Division 26 of the Health and Safety Code.

(7) Cultural burns conducted by a cultural fire practitioner are exempt from paragraphs (2) and (3).

(c) This section shall not be construed to grant immunity from fire suppression or other costs otherwise recoverable pursuant to Section 13009 or 13009.1 of the Health and Safety Code to any person whose conduct constitutes gross negligence.

(d) Nothing in this section affects the ability of a private or public entity plaintiff to bring a civil action against any defendant.

(e) "Cultural burn" means the intentional application of fire to land by Native American tribes, tribal organizations, or cultural fire practitioners to achieve cultural goals or objectives, including subsistence, ceremonial activities, biodiversity, or other benefits.

(f) "Cultural fire practitioner" means a person associated with a Native American tribe or tribal organization with experience in burning to meet cultural goals or objectives, including subsistence, ceremonial activities, biodiversity, or other benefits. *(Added by Stats.2021, c. 600 (S.B.332), § 1, eff. Jan. 1, 2022.)*

§ 3334. Real estate; wrongful occupation; value of the use of property

(a) The detriment caused by the wrongful occupation of real property, in cases not embraced in Section 3335 of this code, the Eminent Domain Law (Title 7 (commencing with Section 1230.010) of Part 3 of the Code of Civil Procedure), or Section 1174 of the Code of Civil Procedure, is deemed to include the value of the use of the property for the time of that wrongful occupation, not exceeding five years next preceding the commencement of the action or proceeding to enforce the right to damages, the reasonable cost of repair or restoration of the property to its original condition, and the costs, if any, of recovering the possession.

(b)(1) Except as provided in paragraph (2), for purposes of subdivision (a), the value of the use of the property shall be the greater of the reasonable rental value of that property or the benefits obtained by the person wrongfully occupying the property by reason of that wrongful occupation.

(2) If a wrongful occupation of real property subject to this section is the result of a mistake of fact of the wrongful occupier, the value of the use of the property, for purposes of subdivision (a), shall be the reasonable rental value of the property. *(Enacted in 1872. Amended by Stats.1979, c. 373, p. 1264, § 47; Stats.1992, c. 469 (A.B.2663), § 1.)*

Cross References

Failure of tenant to quit after notice, ground for unlawful detainer action, see Code of Civil Procedure § 1161.
Forcible or unlawful detainer, actual and statutory damages, see Code of Civil Procedure § 1174.
Forcible or unlawful entry, treble damages, see Code of Civil Procedure § 735.

§ 3335. Real estate; willful holding over

For willfully holding over real property, by a person who entered upon the same, as guardian or trustee for an infant, or by right of an estate terminable with any life or lives, after the termination of the trust or particular estate, without the consent of the party immediately entitled after such termination, the measure of damages is the value of the profits received during such holding over. *(Enacted in 1872.)*

Cross References

Forcible or unlawful entry, treble damages, see Code of Civil Procedure § 735.
Termination of trust, see Probate Code §§ 15407, 15409.
Wrongful occupation of real estate, see Code of Civil Procedure § 1174.

§ 3336. Personal property; conversion; presumption

The detriment caused by the wrongful conversion of personal property is presumed to be:

First—The value of the property at the time of the conversion, with the interest from that time, or, an amount sufficient to indemnify the party injured for the loss which is the natural, reasonable and proximate result of the wrongful act complained of and which a proper degree of prudence on his part would not have averted; and

Second—A fair compensation for the time and money properly expended in pursuit of the property. *(Enacted in 1872. Amended by Code Am.1873–74, c. 612, p. 266, § 277; Code Am.1877–78, c. 20, p. 89, § 1; Stats.1931, c. 633, p. 1358, § 1.)*

§ 3336.5. Junk dealers or recyclers; possession of fire hydrants, fire department connections, manhole covers, or backflow devices; agency certification required; liability for wrongful possession; unknowing possession and notification after discovery; legislative intent regarding liability to third parties

(a)(1) Any junk dealer or recycler who possesses a fire hydrant, fire department connection, including, but not limited to, brass fittings and parts, manhole cover or lid or part of that cover or lid, or backflow device or connection to that device or part of that device without a written certification from the agency or utility owning or previously owning the material shall be liable to the agency or utility for the wrongful possession of that material as provided in subdivision (b).

(2) A written certification under this subdivision shall be on the agency's or utility's letterhead and shall certify both that the agency or utility has sold the material described or is offering the material for sale, salvage, or recycling, and that the person possessing the certification or identified in the certification is authorized to negotiate the sale of that material.

(b) Except as provided in subdivision (c), a junk dealer or recycler in violation of this section shall be liable to the agency or utility owning or previously owning the prohibited material as described in subdivision (a) for the actual damages incurred by the agency or utility, including the value of the material, the cost of replacing the material, labor costs, and the costs of repairing any damage caused by the removal of the material. The court shall also award exemplary damages of three times the actual damages incurred by the agency or utility, unless the court decides that extenuating circumstances do not justify awarding these exemplary damages.

(c)(1) A junk dealer or recycler who unknowingly takes possession of one or more of the materials described in subdivision (a) as part of a load of otherwise nonprohibited materials without the written certification described in subdivision (a) shall notify the appropriate law enforcement agency by the end of the next business day upon discovery of the prohibited materials. Written confirmation of that notice shall relieve the junk dealer or recycler of liability to the agency or utility for the possession of those materials.

(2) The following definitions shall apply for purposes of this subdivision:

(A) "Appropriate law enforcement agency" means, in the case of any material described in subdivision (a) that is located within the territorial limits of an incorporated city, the police chief of the city or his or her designee, or, in the case of any material described in subdivision (a) that is located outside the territorial limits of an incorporated city, the sheriff of the county or his or her designee.

(B) "Written confirmation" means any confirmation received from the law enforcement agency as electronic mail, facsimile, or other written correspondence, including, but not limited to, a letter delivered in person or by certified mail.

(d) Nothing in this section is intended to create a basis for liability on the part of the junk dealers and recyclers to third parties for damages or injuries related to or arising from the theft of the materials described in this section. *(Added by Stats.2012, c. 393 (S.B.1045), § 2.)*

§ 3337. Personal property; conversion; subsequent application of property to benefit of owner

The presumption declared by the last section cannot be repelled, in favor of one whose possession was wrongful from the beginning, by his subsequent application of the property to the benefit of the owner, without his consent. *(Enacted in 1872.)*

§ 3338. Personal property; conversion; lienor's damages

One having a mere lien on personal property, cannot recover greater damages for its conversion, from one having a right thereto superior to his, after his lien is discharged, than the amount secured by the lien, and the compensation allowed by section three thousand three hundred and thirty-six for loss of time and expenses. *(Enacted in 1872.)*

§ 3339. Legislative findings, declarations and intent; immigration status; severability

The Legislature finds and declares the following:

(a) All protections, rights, and remedies available under state law, except any reinstatement remedy prohibited by federal law, are available to all individuals regardless of immigration status who have applied for employment, or who are or who have been employed, in this state.

(b) For purposes of enforcing state labor, employment, civil rights, consumer protection, and housing laws, a person's immigration status is irrelevant to the issue of liability, and in proceedings or discovery undertaken to enforce those state laws no inquiry shall be permitted into a person's immigration status unless the person seeking to make this inquiry has shown by clear and convincing evidence that this inquiry is necessary in order to comply with federal immigration law.

(c) The provisions of this section are declaratory of existing law.

(d) The provisions of this section are severable. If any provision of this section or its application is held invalid, that invalidity shall not affect other provisions or applications that can be given effect without the invalid provision or application. *(Added by Stats.2002, c. 1071 (S.B.1818), § 1. Amended by Stats.2017, c. 160 (A.B.1690), § 1, eff. Jan. 1, 2018.)*

Cross References

Evidence of immigration status, civil actions, see Evidence Code §§ 351.2, 351.3.

§ 3339.5. Effect of immigration status on recovery sought by minor child; discovery; express application

(a) The immigration status of a minor child seeking recovery under any applicable law is irrelevant to the issues of liability or remedy, except for employment-related prospective injunctive relief that would directly violate federal law.

(b) Discovery or other inquiry in a civil action or proceeding relating to a minor child's immigration status shall not be permitted except where the minor child's claims place the minor child's immigration status directly in contention or the person seeking to make this inquiry has shown by clear and convincing evidence that the inquiry is necessary in order to comply with federal immigration law.

(c) The provisions of this section are declaratory of existing law.

(d) The express application of this act to minors is not intended to imply that adults are not likewise protected by existing law in the same circumstances. *(Added by Stats.2015, c. 151 (A.B.560), § 1, eff. Jan. 1, 2016.)*

§ 3339.10. Immigration or citizenship status irrelevant to issues of liability or remedy in specified proceedings; discovery

(a) The immigration or citizenship status of any person is irrelevant to any issue of liability or remedy under Chapter 2 (commencing with Section 1940) of Title 5 of Part 4 of Division 3, Chapter 2 (commencing with Section 789) of Title 2 of Part 2 of Division 2 of this code, or under Chapter 4 (commencing with Section 1159) of Title 3 of Part 3 of the Code of Civil Procedure, or in any civil action involving a tenant's housing rights.

(b)(1) In proceedings or discovery undertaken in a civil action to enforce Chapter 2 (commencing with Section 1940) of Title 5 of Part 4 of Division 3, Chapter 2 (commencing with Section 789) of Title 2 of Part 2 of Division 2 of this code, or under Chapter 4 (commencing with Section 1159) of Title 3 of Part 3 of the Code of Civil Procedure, or in any civil action involving a tenant's housing rights, no inquiry shall be permitted into a person's immigration or citizenship status, except as follows:

(A) The tenant's claims or defenses raised place the person's immigration or citizenship status directly in contention.

(B) The person seeking to make this inquiry demonstrates by clear and convincing evidence that this inquiry is necessary in order to comply with federal immigration law.

(2) The assertion of an affirmative defense to an unlawful detainer action under Section 1161.4 of the Code of Civil Procedure does not constitute cause under this subdivision for discovery or other inquiry into that person's immigration or citizenship status. *(Added by Stats.2017, c. 489 (A.B.291), § 7, eff. Jan. 1, 2018.)*

§ 3340. Injuries to animals; exemplary damages

For wrongful injuries to animals being subjects of property, committed willfully or by gross negligence, in disregard of humanity, exemplary damages may be given. *(Enacted in 1872.)*

Cross References

Dogs as personalty, see Penal Code § 491.
Exemplary damages, see Civil Code § 3294.
Injury to animals, see Penal Code § 596 et seq.

§ 3340

Limitation of damages, exception under this section, see Civil Code § 3358.

§ 3341. Liability of owner, possessor, or harborer of animal killing or injuring other animals; scienter; right to kill animal found committing injury; accidental killing or injury

The owner, possessor, or harborer of any dog or other animal, that shall, on the premises of any person other than the owner, possessor, or harborer of such dog or other animal, kill, worry, or wound any bovine animal, swine, horse, mule, burro, sheep, angora goat, or cashmere goat, or poultry, shall be liable to the owner of the same for the damages and costs of suit, to be recovered in any court of competent jurisdiction:

1. In the prosecution of actions under the provisions of this chapter, it shall not be necessary for the plaintiff to show that the owner, possessor, or harborer of such dog or other animal, had knowledge of the fact that such dog or other animal would kill, wound or worry bovine animals, swine, horses, mules, burros, sheep, goats, or poultry.

2. Any person on finding any dog or dogs, or other animal, not on the premises of the owner or possessor of such dog or dogs, or other animal, worrying, wounding, or killing any bovine animals, swine, horses, mules, burros, sheep, angora or cashmere goats, may, at the time of finding such dog or dogs, or other animal, kill the same, and the owner or owners thereof shall sustain no action for damages against any person so killing such dog or dogs, or other animal.

Nothing in this section shall render an owner, possessor, or harborer of a dog liable for the accidental or unavoidable killing or injury of any bovine animal, swine, horse, mule, burro, sheep, angora goat, cashmere goat, or poultry which occurs in connection with or as an incident to the driving or herding the same from the premises of the owner, possessor, or harborer of the dog, whether such killing or injury occurs upon such premises or off of such premises. (Added by Stats.1883, c. 55, p. 283, § 1. Amended by Stats.1903, c. 51, p. 54, § 1; Stats.1945, c. 1327, p. 2500, § 1.)

Cross References

Damages to livestock or poultry, complaint, see Food and Agricultural Code § 31501 et seq.

§ 3342. Dog bites; liability of owner; military or police work excluded; limitations

(a) The owner of any dog is liable for the damages suffered by any person who is bitten by the dog while in a public place or lawfully in a private place, including the property of the owner of the dog, regardless of the former viciousness of the dog or the owner's knowledge of such viciousness. A person is lawfully upon the private property of such owner within the meaning of this section when he is on such property in the performance of any duty imposed upon him by the laws of this state or by the laws or postal regulations of the United States, or when he is on such property upon the invitation, express or implied, of the owner.

(b) Nothing in this section shall authorize the bringing of an action pursuant to subdivision (a) against any governmental agency using a dog in military or police work if the bite or bites occurred while the dog was defending itself from an annoying, harassing, or provoking act, or assisting an employee of the agency in any of the following:

(1) In the apprehension or holding of a suspect where the employee has a reasonable suspicion of the suspect's involvement in criminal activity.

(2) In the investigation of a crime or possible crime.

(3) In the execution of a warrant.

(4) In the defense of a peace officer or another person.

(c) Subdivision (b) shall not apply in any case where the victim of the bite or bites was not a party to, nor a participant in, nor suspected to be a party to or a participant in, the act or acts that prompted the use of the dog in the military or police work.

(d) Subdivision (b) shall apply only where a governmental agency using a dog in military or police work has adopted a written policy on the necessary and appropriate use of a dog for the police or military work enumerated in subdivision (b). (Added by Stats.1953, c. 37, p. 675, § 6. Amended by Stats.1988, c. 298, § 1.)

§ 3342.5. Duty of owner; action; dogs trained to fight, attack, or kill; legislation by city and county

(a) The owner of any dog that has bitten a human being shall have the duty to take such reasonable steps as are necessary to remove any danger presented to other persons from bites by the animal.

(b) Whenever a dog has bitten a human being on at least two separate occasions, any person, the district attorney, or city attorney may bring an action against the owner of the animal to determine whether conditions of the treatment or confinement of the dog or other circumstances existing at the time of the bites have been changed so as to remove the danger to other persons presented by the animal. This action shall be brought in the county where a bite occurred. The court, after hearing, may make any order it deems appropriate to prevent the recurrence of such an incident, including, but not limited to, the removal of the animal from the area or its destruction if necessary.

(c) Whenever a dog trained to fight, attack, or kill has bitten a human being, causing substantial physical injury, any person, including the district attorney, or city attorney may bring an action against the owner of the animal to determine whether conditions of the treatment or confinement of the dog or other circumstances existing at the time of the bites have been changed so as to remove the danger to other persons presented by the animal. This action shall be brought in the county where a bite occurred. The court, after hearing, may make any order it deems appropriate to prevent the recurrence of such an incident, including, but not limited to, the removal of the animal from the area or its destruction if necessary.

(d) Nothing in this section shall authorize the bringing of an action pursuant to subdivision (b) based on a bite or bites inflicted upon a trespasser, or by a dog used in military or police work if the bite or bites occurred while the dog was actually performing in that capacity.

(e) Nothing in this section shall be construed to prevent legislation in the field of dog control by any city, county, or city and county.

(f) Nothing in this section shall be construed to affect the liability of the owner of a dog under Section 3342 or any other provision of the law.

(g) A proceeding under this section is a limited civil case. (Added by Stats.1968, c. 1274, p. 2400, § 1. Amended by Stats.1976, c. 470, p. 1216, § 1; Stats.1984, c. 655, § 1; Stats.1998, c. 931 (S.B.2139), § 18, eff. Sept. 28, 1998.)

§ 3343. Fraud in purchase, sale or exchange of property; additional damages

(a) One defrauded in the purchase, sale or exchange of property is entitled to recover the difference between the actual value of that with which the defrauded person parted and the actual value of that which he received, together with any additional damage arising from the particular transaction, including any of the following:

(1) Amounts actually and reasonably expended in reliance upon the fraud.

(2) An amount which would compensate the defrauded party for loss of use and enjoyment of the property to the extent that any such loss was proximately caused by the fraud.

(3) Where the defrauded party has been induced by reason of the fraud to sell or otherwise part with the property in question, an amount which will compensate him for profits or other gains which might reasonably have been earned by use of the property had he retained it.

(4) Where the defrauded party has been induced by reason of the fraud to purchase or otherwise acquire the property in question, an amount which will compensate him for any loss of profits or other gains which were reasonably anticipated and would have been earned by him from the use or sale of the property had it possessed the characteristics fraudulently attributed to it by the party committing the fraud, provided that lost profits from the use or sale of the property shall be recoverable only if and only to the extent that all of the following apply:

(i) The defrauded party acquired the property for the purpose of using or reselling it for a profit.

(ii) The defrauded party reasonably relied on the fraud in entering into the transaction and in anticipating profits from the subsequent use or sale of the property.

(iii) Any loss of profits for which damages are sought under this paragraph have been proximately caused by the fraud and the defrauded party's reliance on it.

(b) Nothing in this section shall do either of the following:

(1) Permit the defrauded person to recover any amount measured by the difference between the value of property as represented and the actual value thereof.

(2) Deny to any person having a cause of action for fraud or deceit any legal or equitable remedies to which such person may be entitled. (Added by Stats.1935, c. 536, p. 1612, § 1. Amended by Stats.1971, c. 943, p. 1850, § 1.)

Cross References

Contracts,
   Breach of contract, damages, see Civil Code § 3300.
   Specific performance, see Civil Code § 3384.
Deceit,
   Damages, see Civil Code § 1709.
   Defined, see Civil Code § 1710.
Quiet title actions, see Code of Civil Procedure § 738 et seq.
Written instruments, cancellation, see Civil Code § 3412.

§ 3343.5. Unlawful motor vehicle subleasing; persons entitled to bring action; relief granted by court; definitions

(a) Any one or more of the following who suffers any damage proximately resulting from one or more acts of unlawful motor vehicle subleasing, as described in Chapter 12.7 (commencing with Section 570) of Title 13 of Part 1 of the Penal Code, may bring an action against the person who has engaged in those acts:

(1) A seller or other secured party under a conditional sale contract or a security agreement.

(2) A lender under a direct loan agreement.

(3) A lessor under a lease contract.

(4) A buyer under a conditional sale contract.

(5) A purchaser under a direct loan agreement, an agreement which provides for a security interest, or an agreement which is equivalent to these types of agreements.

(6) A lessee under a lease contract.

(7) An actual or purported transferee or assignee of any right or interest of a buyer, a purchaser, or a lessee.

(b) The court in an action under subdivision (a) may award actual damages; equitable relief, including, but not limited to, an injunction and restitution of money and property; punitive damages; reasonable attorney's fees and costs; and any other relief which the court deems proper.

(c) As used in this section, the following terms have the following meanings:

(1) "Buyer" has the meaning set forth in subdivision (c) of Section 2981.

(2) "Conditional sale contract" has the meaning set forth in subdivision (a) of Section 2981. Notwithstanding subdivision (k) of Section 2981, "conditional sale contract" includes any contract for the sale or bailment of a motor vehicle between a buyer and a seller primarily for business or commercial purposes.

(3) "Direct loan agreement" means an agreement between a lender and a purchaser whereby the lender has advanced funds pursuant to a loan secured by the motor vehicle which the purchaser has purchased.

(4) "Lease contract" means a lease contract between a lessor and lessee as this term and these parties are defined in Section 2985.7. Notwithstanding subdivision (d) of Section 2985.7, "lease contract" includes a lease for business or commercial purposes.

(5) "Motor vehicle" means any vehicle required to be registered under the Vehicle Code.

(6) "Person" means an individual, company, firm, association, partnership, trust, corporation, limited liability company, or other legal entity.

§ 3343.5 GENERAL PROVISIONS

(7) "Purchaser" has the meaning set forth in paragraph (30) of subdivision (b) of Section 1201 of the Commercial Code.

(8) "Security agreement" and "secured party" have the meanings set forth, respectively, in paragraphs (74) and (73) of subdivision (a) of Section 9102 of the Commercial Code. "Security interest" has the meaning set forth in paragraph (35) of subdivision (b) of Section 1201 of the Commercial Code.

(9) "Seller" has the meaning set forth in subdivision (b) of Section 2981, and includes the present holder of the conditional sale contract.

(d) The rights and remedies provided in this section are in addition to any other rights and remedies provided by law. (Added by Stats.1987, c. 1072, § 1. Amended by Stats.1994, c. 1010 (S.B.2053), § 52; Stats.1999, c. 991 (S.B.45), § 8.5, operative July 1, 2001; Stats.2006, c. 254 (S.B.1481), § 4; Stats.2013, c. 531 (A.B.502), § 1, operative July 1, 2014.)

Application

For provision relating to application of Stats.2006, c. 254 (S.B.1481) to documents of title that are issued or bailments that arise before Jan. 1, 2007, see § 81 of that act.

§ 3343.7. Fraudulent inducement to join a nonprofit organization operated on cooperative basis by and for independent retailers; action for rescission of contract or damages

An action may be brought against any nonprofit organization operated on a cooperative basis by and for independent retailers which wholesales goods and services primarily to its member retailers as described in paragraph (3) of subdivision (d) of Section 20001 of the Business and Professions Code or subdivision (c) of Section 31005 of the Corporations Code, for rescission of a membership contract entered into, or for any damages sustained, as a consequence of being fraudulently induced to join the organization. For purposes of this section, "fraudulently induced" means the misrepresentation of a material fact, or the omission of a material fact, including the failure of the organization to disclose all information required under subparagraph (H) of paragraph (3) of subdivision (d) of Section 20001 of the Business and Professions Code or paragraph (8) of subdivision (c) of Section 31005 of the Corporations Code, unless the defendant proves that the plaintiff knew the facts concerning the untruth or omission or that the defendant exercised reasonable care and did not know (or if the defendant had exercised reasonable care would not have known) of the untruth or omission. (Added by Stats.1989, c. 1380, § 2.)

ARTICLE 3. PENAL DAMAGES

Section
3344. Use of another's name, voice, signature, photograph, or likeness for advertising or selling or soliciting purposes.
3344.1. Deceased personality's name, voice, signature, photograph, or likeness; unauthorized use; damages and profits from use; protected uses; persons entitled to exercise rights; successors in interest or licensees; registration of claim.
3344.5. Campaign advertisement with unauthorized signature; cause of action.
3344.6. Campaign advertisement falsely representing official public documents; cause of action for damages.
3345. Unfair or deceptive practices against senior citizens, disabled persons, or veterans; treble damages.
3345.1. Commercial sexual exploitation against a minor or nonminor dependent; damages.
3346. Injuries to timber, trees, or underwood; treble damages; double damages; actual detriment.
3346a. Repealed.
3347, 3348. Repealed.

Cross References

Limitation of damages, exception under this Article, see Civil Code § 3358.

§ 3344. Use of another's name, voice, signature, photograph, or likeness for advertising or selling or soliciting purposes

(a) Any person who knowingly uses another's name, voice, signature, photograph, or likeness, in any manner, on or in products, merchandise, or goods, or for purposes of advertising or selling, or soliciting purchases of, products, merchandise, goods or services, without such person's prior consent, or, in the case of a minor, the prior consent of his parent or legal guardian, shall be liable for any damages sustained by the person or persons injured as a result thereof. In addition, in any action brought under this section, the person who violated the section shall be liable to the injured party or parties in an amount equal to the greater of seven hundred fifty dollars ($750) or the actual damages suffered by him or her as a result of the unauthorized use, and any profits from the unauthorized use that are attributable to the use and are not taken into account in computing the actual damages. In establishing such profits, the injured party or parties are required to present proof only of the gross revenue attributable to such use, and the person who violated this section is required to prove his or her deductible expenses. Punitive damages may also be awarded to the injured party or parties. The prevailing party in any action under this section shall also be entitled to attorney's fees and costs.

(b) As used in this section, "photograph" means any photograph or photographic reproduction, still or moving, or any videotape or live television transmission, of any person, such that the person is readily identifiable.

(1) A person shall be deemed to be readily identifiable from a photograph when one who views the photograph with the naked eye can reasonably determine that the person depicted in the photograph is the same person who is complaining of its unauthorized use.

(2) If the photograph includes more than one person so identifiable, then the person or persons complaining of the use shall be represented as individuals rather than solely as members of a definable group represented in the photograph. A definable group includes, but is not limited to, the following examples: a crowd at any sporting event, a crowd in any street or public building, the audience at any theatrical or stage production, a glee club, or a baseball team.

(3) A person or persons shall be considered to be represented as members of a definable group if they are represented in the photograph solely as a result of being present at the time the photograph was taken and have not been singled out as individuals in any manner.

(c) Where a photograph or likeness of an employee of the person using the photograph or likeness appearing in the advertisement or other publication prepared by or in behalf of the user is only incidental, and not essential, to the purpose of the publication in which it appears, there shall arise a rebuttable presumption affecting the burden of producing evidence that the failure to obtain the consent of the employee was not a knowing use of the employee's photograph or likeness.

(d) For purposes of this section, a use of a name, voice, signature, photograph, or likeness in connection with any news, public affairs, or sports broadcast or account, or any political campaign, shall not constitute a use for which consent is required under subdivision (a).

(e) The use of a name, voice, signature, photograph, or likeness in a commercial medium shall not constitute a use for which consent is required under subdivision (a) solely because the material containing such use is commercially sponsored or contains paid advertising. Rather it shall be a question of fact whether or not the use of the person's name, voice, signature, photograph, or likeness was so directly connected with the commercial sponsorship or with the paid advertising as to constitute a use for which consent is required under subdivision (a).

(f) Nothing in this section shall apply to the owners or employees of any medium used for advertising, including, but not limited to, newspapers, magazines, radio and television networks and stations, cable television systems, billboards, and transit ads, by whom any advertisement or solicitation in violation of this section is published or disseminated, unless it is established that such owners or employees had knowledge of the unauthorized use of the person's name, voice, signature, photograph, or likeness as prohibited by this section.

(g) The remedies provided for in this section are cumulative and shall be in addition to any others provided for by law. (Added by Stats.1971, c. 1595, p. 3426, § 1. Amended by Stats.1984, c. 1704, § 2.)

Validity

In the of case of Laws v. Sony Music Entertainment, Inc., C.A.9 (Cal.)2006, 448 F.3d 1134, 78 U.S.P.Q.2d 1910, certiorari denied 127 S.Ct. 1371, 549 U.S. 1252, 167 L.Ed.2d 159, federal copyright law preempted the plaintiff's claim under this section.

Cross References

Unauthorized use of deceased personality's name, voice, signature, photograph or likeness, damages and profits from use, see Civil Code § 3344.1.

§ 3344.1. Deceased personality's name, voice, signature, photograph, or likeness; unauthorized use; damages and profits from use; protected uses; persons entitled to exercise rights; successors in interest or licensees; registration of claim

(a)(1) Any person who uses a deceased personality's name, voice, signature, photograph, or likeness, in any manner, on or in products, merchandise, or goods, or for purposes of advertising or selling, or soliciting purchases of, products, merchandise, goods, or services, without prior consent from the person or persons specified in subdivision (c), shall be liable for any damages sustained by the person or persons injured as a result thereof. In addition, in any action brought under this section, the person who violated the section shall be liable to the injured party or parties in an amount equal to the greater of seven hundred fifty dollars ($750) or the actual damages suffered by the injured party or parties, as a result of the unauthorized use, and any profits from the unauthorized use that are attributable to the use and are not taken into account in computing the actual damages. In establishing these profits, the injured party or parties shall be required to present proof only of the gross revenue attributable to the use, and the person who violated the section is required to prove his or her deductible expenses. Punitive damages may also be awarded to the injured party or parties. The prevailing party or parties in any action under this section shall also be entitled to attorney's fees and costs.

(2) For purposes of this subdivision, a play, book, magazine, newspaper, musical composition, audiovisual work, radio or television program, single and original work of art, work of political or newsworthy value, or an advertisement or commercial announcement for any of these works, shall not be considered a product, article of merchandise, good, or service if it is fictional or nonfictional entertainment, or a dramatic, literary, or musical work.

(3) If a work that is protected under paragraph (2) includes within it a use in connection with a product, article of merchandise, good, or service, this use shall not be exempt under this subdivision, notwithstanding the unprotected use's inclusion in a work otherwise exempt under this subdivision, if the claimant proves that this use is so directly connected with a product, article of merchandise, good, or service as to constitute an act of advertising, selling, or soliciting purchases of that product, article of merchandise, good, or service by the deceased personality without prior consent from the person or persons specified in subdivision (c).

(b) The rights recognized under this section are property rights, freely transferable or descendible, in whole or in part, by contract or by means of any trust or any other testamentary instrument, executed before or after January 1, 1985. The rights recognized under this section shall be deemed to have existed at the time of death of any deceased personality who died prior to January 1, 1985, and, except as provided in subdivision (*o*), shall vest in the persons entitled to these property rights under the testamentary instrument of the deceased personality effective as of the date of his or her death. In the absence of an express transfer in a testamentary instrument of the deceased personality's rights in his or her name, voice, signature, photograph, or likeness, a provision in the testamentary instrument that provides for the disposition of the residue of the deceased personality's assets shall be effective to transfer the rights recognized under this section in accordance with the terms of that provision. The rights established by this section shall also be freely transferable or descendible by contract, trust, or any other testamentary instrument by any subsequent owner of the deceased personality's rights as recognized by this section. Nothing in this section shall be construed to render invalid or unenforceable

§ 3344.1

any contract entered into by a deceased personality during his or her lifetime by which the deceased personality assigned the rights, in whole or in part, to use his or her name, voice, signature, photograph, or likeness, regardless of whether the contract was entered into before or after January 1, 1985.

(c) The consent required by this section shall be exercisable by the person or persons to whom the right of consent, or portion thereof, has been transferred in accordance with subdivision (b), or if no transfer has occurred, then by the person or persons to whom the right of consent, or portion thereof, has passed in accordance with subdivision (d).

(d) Subject to subdivisions (b) and (c), after the death of any person, the rights under this section shall belong to the following person or persons and may be exercised, on behalf of and for the benefit of all of those persons, by those persons who, in the aggregate, are entitled to more than a one-half interest in the rights:

(1) The entire interest in those rights belongs to the surviving spouse of the deceased personality unless there are any surviving children or grandchildren of the deceased personality, in which case one-half of the entire interest in those rights belongs to the surviving spouse.

(2) The entire interest in those rights belongs to the surviving children of the deceased personality and to the surviving children of any dead child of the deceased personality unless the deceased personality has a surviving spouse, in which case the ownership of a one-half interest in rights is divided among the surviving children and grandchildren.

(3) If there is no surviving spouse, and no surviving children or grandchildren, then the entire interest in those rights belongs to the surviving parent or parents of the deceased personality.

(4) The rights of the deceased personality's children and grandchildren are in all cases divided among them and exercisable in the manner provided in Section 240 of the Probate Code according to the number of the deceased personality's children represented. The share of the children of a dead child of a deceased personality can be exercised only by the action of a majority of them.

(e) If any deceased personality does not transfer his or her rights under this section by contract, or by means of a trust or testamentary instrument, and there are no surviving persons as described in subdivision (d), then the rights set forth in subdivision (a) shall terminate.

(f)(1) A successor in interest to the rights of a deceased personality under this section or a licensee thereof shall not recover damages for a use prohibited by this section that occurs before the successor in interest or licensee registers a claim of the rights under paragraph (2).

(2) Any person claiming to be a successor in interest to the rights of a deceased personality under this section or a licensee thereof may register that claim with the Secretary of State on a form prescribed by the Secretary of State and upon payment of a fee as set forth in subdivision (d) of Section 12195 of the Government Code. The form shall be verified and shall include the name and date of death of the deceased personality, the name and address of the claimant, the basis of the claim, and the rights claimed.

(3) Upon receipt and after filing of any document under this section, the Secretary of State shall post the document along with the entire registry of persons claiming to be a successor in interest to the rights of a deceased personality or a registered licensee under this section upon the Secretary of State's Internet Web site. The Secretary of State may microfilm or reproduce by other techniques any of the filings or documents and destroy the original filing or document. The microfilm or other reproduction of any document under this section shall be admissible in any court of law. The microfilm or other reproduction of any document may be destroyed by the Secretary of State 70 years after the death of the personality named therein.

(4) Claims registered under this subdivision shall be public records.

(g) An action shall not be brought under this section by reason of any use of a deceased personality's name, voice, signature, photograph, or likeness occurring after the expiration of 70 years after the death of the deceased personality.

(h) As used in this section, "deceased personality" means any natural person whose name, voice, signature, photograph, or likeness has commercial value at the time of his or her death, or because of his or her death, whether or not during the lifetime of that natural person the person used his or her name, voice, signature, photograph, or likeness on or in products, merchandise, or goods, or for purposes of advertising or selling, or solicitation of purchase of, products, merchandise, goods, or services. A "deceased personality" shall include, without limitation, any such natural person who has died within 70 years prior to January 1, 1985.

(i) As used in this section, "photograph" means any photograph or photographic reproduction, still or moving, or any videotape or live television transmission, of any person, such that the deceased personality is readily identifiable. A deceased personality shall be deemed to be readily identifiable from a photograph if one who views the photograph with the naked eye can reasonably determine who the person depicted in the photograph is.

(j) For purposes of this section, the use of a name, voice, signature, photograph, or likeness in connection with any news, public affairs, or sports broadcast or account, or any political campaign, shall not constitute a use for which consent is required under subdivision (a).

(k) The use of a name, voice, signature, photograph, or likeness in a commercial medium shall not constitute a use for which consent is required under subdivision (a) solely because the material containing the use is commercially sponsored or contains paid advertising. Rather, it shall be a question of fact whether or not the use of the deceased personality's name, voice, signature, photograph, or likeness was so directly connected with the commercial sponsorship or with the paid advertising as to constitute a use for which consent is required under subdivision (a).

(*l*) Nothing in this section shall apply to the owners or employees of any medium used for advertising, including, but not limited to, newspapers, magazines, radio and television networks and stations, cable television systems, billboards, and transit advertisements, by whom any advertisement or solicitation in violation of this section is published or disseminated, unless it is established that the owners or employees had knowledge of the unauthorized use of the deceased personality's name, voice, signature, photograph, or likeness as prohibited by this section.

(m) The remedies provided for in this section are cumulative and shall be in addition to any others provided for by law.

(n) This section shall apply to the adjudication of liability and the imposition of any damages or other remedies in cases in which the liability, damages, and other remedies arise from acts occurring directly in this state. For purposes of this section, acts giving rise to liability shall be limited to the use, on or in products, merchandise, goods, or services, or the advertising or selling, or soliciting purchases of, products, merchandise, goods, or services prohibited by this section.

(o) Notwithstanding any provision of this section to the contrary, if an action was taken prior to May 1, 2007, to exercise rights recognized under this section relating to a deceased personality who died prior to January 1, 1985, by a person described in subdivision (d), other than a person who was disinherited by the deceased personality in a testamentary instrument, and the exercise of those rights was not challenged successfully in a court action by a person described in subdivision (b), that exercise shall not be affected by subdivision (b). In that case, the rights that would otherwise vest in one or more persons described in subdivision (b) shall vest solely in the person or persons described in subdivision (d), other than a person disinherited by the deceased personality in a testamentary instrument, for all future purposes.

(p) The rights recognized by this section are expressly made retroactive, including to those deceased personalities who died before January 1, 1985. *(Formerly § 990, added by Stats.1984, c. 1704, § 1. Amended by Stats.1988, c. 113, § 2, eff. May 25, 1988, operative July 1, 1988. Renumbered § 3344.1 and amended by Stats.1999, c. 998 (S.B.209), § 1. Amended by Stats.1999, c. 1000 (S.B.284), § 9.5; Stats.2007, c. 439 (S.B.771), § 1; Stats.2009, c. 88 (A.B.176), § 15; Stats. 2010, c. 20 (A.B.585), § 1; Stats.2011, c. 296 (A.B.1023), § 35.)*

Cross References

Penal damages, use of another's name, voice, signature, photograph, or likeness for advertising or selling or soliciting purposes, see Civil Code § 3344.

§ 3344.5. Campaign advertisement with unauthorized signature; cause of action

(a) Any person whose signature is used in violation of, and any candidate for elective office whose election or defeat is expressly advocated in any campaign advertisement that violates, subdivision (b) of Section 115.1 of the Penal Code, shall have a civil cause of action against any person committing the violation.

(b) If a mass mailing or other printed matter that violates subdivision (b) of Section 115.1 of the Penal Code expressly advocates the election or defeat of more than one candidate only a person whose signature is used and the candidate or candidates to whom the unauthorized signature directly relates shall have a civil cause of action pursuant to this section.

(c) Any person bringing a cause of action pursuant to this section may recover damages in an amount of two times the cost of the communication, but not to exceed fifty thousand dollars ($50,000), with regard to which the unauthorized signature was used.

(d) As used in this section, "signature" means either of the following:

(1) A handwritten or mechanical signature, or a copy thereof.

(2) Any representation of a person's name, including, but not limited to, a printed or typewritten representation, that serves the same purpose as a handwritten or mechanical signature. *(Added by Stats.1990, c. 1590 (S.B.1865), § 1, eff. Sept. 30, 1990. Amended by Stats.1993, c. 334 (A.B.1117), § 1.)*

§ 3344.6. Campaign advertisement falsely representing official public documents; cause of action for damages

(a) Any candidate for elective office whose election or defeat is expressly advocated in any campaign advertisement which violates subdivision (a) of Section 115.2 of the Penal Code shall have a civil cause of action against any person committing the violation.

(b) If a mass mailing or other printed matter which violates subdivision (a) of Section 115.2 of the Penal Code expressly advocates the election or defeat of more than one candidate, only the candidate or candidates to whom the misstatement or misrepresentation directly relates shall have a civil cause of action pursuant to this section.

(c) Any person bringing a cause of action pursuant to this section may recover damages in an amount of two times the cost of the communication, but not to exceed fifty thousand dollars ($50,000). *(Added by Stats.1991, c. 1051 (S.B.209), § 1.)*

§ 3345. Unfair or deceptive practices against senior citizens, disabled persons, or veterans; treble damages

(a) This section shall apply only in actions brought by, on behalf of, or for the benefit of * * * <u>those individuals specified in paragraphs (1) to (3), inclusive</u>, to redress unfair or deceptive acts or practices or unfair methods of competition.

(1) Senior citizens, as defined in subdivision (f) of Section 1761.

(2) Disabled persons, as defined in subdivision (g) of Section 1761.

(3) Veterans, as defined in Section 18540.4 of the Government Code.

(b) Whenever a trier of fact is authorized by a statute to impose either a fine, or a civil penalty or other penalty, or any other remedy the purpose or effect of which is to punish or deter, and the amount of the fine, penalty, or other remedy is subject to the trier of fact's discretion, the trier of fact shall consider the * * * factors <u>set forth in paragraphs (1) to (3), inclusive</u>, in addition to other appropriate factors, in determining the amount of fine, civil penalty or other penalty, or other remedy to impose. Whenever the trier of fact makes an affirmative finding in regard to one or more of the * * * factors <u>set forth in paragraphs (1) to (3), inclusive</u>, it may impose a fine, civil penalty or other penalty, or other remedy in an amount up to three times greater than authorized by the statute, or, where the statute does not authorize a specific amount, up to three times greater than the amount the trier of fact would impose in the absence of that affirmative finding.

(1) Whether the defendant knew or should have known that * * * their conduct was directed to one or more senior citizens * * *₂ disabled persons, or veterans.

(2) Whether the defendant's conduct caused one or more senior citizens * * *₂ disabled persons, or veterans to suffer: loss or encumbrance of a primary residence, principal employment, or source of income; substantial loss of property set aside for retirement, or for personal or family care and maintenance; or substantial loss of payments received under a pension or retirement plan or a government benefits program, or assets essential to the health or welfare of the senior citizen * * *₂ disabled person, or veteran.

(3) Whether one or more senior citizens * * *₂ disabled persons, or veterans are substantially more vulnerable than other members of the public to the defendant's conduct because of age, poor health or infirmity, impaired understanding, restricted mobility, or disability, and actually suffered substantial physical, emotional, or economic damage resulting from the defendant's conduct. (Added by Stats. 1988, c. 823, § 4. Amended by Stats.2022, c. 78 (A.B.1730), § 1, eff. Jan. 1, 2023.)

§ 3345.1. Commercial sexual exploitation against a minor or nonminor dependent; damages

(a) This section shall apply only in a civil action brought by, or on behalf of, or for the benefit of, a person who is a minor or nonminor dependent and is a victim of commercial sexual exploitation committed by a person who is over 18 years of age. For purposes of this section, the age of the victim, the status of the victim as a minor or nonminor dependent, and the age of the defendant is determined at the time of the defendant's act of commercial sexual exploitation of the victim.

(b) In a civil action brought by, on behalf of, or for the benefit of a minor, or nonminor dependent, against a person who engaged in any act of commercial sexual exploitation of a minor or nonminor dependent, whenever a trier of fact is authorized by a statute, other than subdivision (c), to impose either a fine, or a civil penalty or other penalty, or any other remedy the purpose or effect of which is to punish or deter, and the amount of the fine, penalty, or other remedy is subject to the trier of fact's discretion, the trier of fact shall consider all of the following factors, in addition to other appropriate factors, in determining the amount of fine, civil penalty, or other penalty, or other remedy to impose. If the trier of fact makes an affirmative finding in regard to one or more of the following factors, it may impose a fine, civil penalty, or other penalty, or other remedy in an amount up to three times greater than authorized by the statute, or, if the statute does not authorize a specific amount, up to three times greater than the amount the trier of fact would impose in the absence of that affirmative finding:

(1) Whether the defendant's conduct was directed to more than one minor or nonminor dependent.

(2) Whether one or more minors or nonminor dependents suffered substantial physical, emotional, or economic damage resulting from the defendant's conduct.

(3) Whether the defendant knew or reasonably should have known that the victim was a minor or nonminor dependent. It shall not be a defense to imposition of fines, penalties, or other remedies pursuant to this paragraph that the defendant was unaware of the victim's age or status as a nonminor dependent at the time of the act.

(c) If the trier of fact is not authorized by statute to impose a civil penalty in an action described in subdivision (b), the court may award a civil penalty not exceeding fifty thousand dollars ($50,000), and not less than ten thousand dollars ($10,000), for each act of commercial sexual exploitation committed by the defendant upon making an affirmative finding in regard to one or more of the factors set forth in paragraphs (1) to (3), inclusive, of subdivision (b). This penalty may be imposed in addition to any other remedy available in law or in equity.

(d) Any penalty imposed pursuant to this section shall be paid to the victim of the act of sexual exploitation.

(e) It shall not be a defense to the imposition of fines or penalties pursuant to this section that the victim consented to the act of commercial sexual exploitation.

(f) If the victim is under 18 years of age, the court, in its discretion, may order that any penalty imposed pursuant to this section be held in trust for the victim and used exclusively for the benefit and well-being of the victim. When the victim reaches 18 years of age or is emancipated, the trust shall expire and any unspent remainder shall be the sole property of the victim.

(g) As used in this section, the following terms have the following meanings:

(1) "Commercial sexual exploitation" means an act committed for the purpose of obtaining property, money, or anything else of value in exchange for, or as a result of, a sexual act of a minor or nonminor dependent, including, but not limited to, an act that would constitute a violation of any of the following:

(A) Sex trafficking of a minor in violation of subdivision (c) of Section 236.1 of the Penal Code.

(B) Pimping of a minor in violation of Section 266h of the Penal Code.

(C) Pandering of a minor in violation of subdivision (b) of Section 266i of the Penal Code.

(D) Procurement of a child under 16 years of age for lewd and lascivious acts in violation of Section 266j of the Penal Code.

(E) Solicitation of a child for a purpose that is either in violation of subparagraph (A) or pursuant to paragraph (3) of subdivision (b) of Section 647 of the Penal Code.

(F) An act of sexual exploitation described in subdivision (c) or (d) of Section 11165.1 of the Penal Code.

(2) "Nonminor dependent" has the same meaning as in subdivision (v) of Section 11400 of the Welfare and Institutions Code. (Added by Stats.2018, c. 166 (A.B.2105), § 1, eff. Jan. 1, 2019.)

§ 3346. Injuries to timber, trees, or underwood; treble damages; double damages; actual detriment

(a) For wrongful injuries to timber, trees, or underwood upon the land of another, or removal thereof, the measure of damages is three times such sum as would compensate for the actual detriment, except that where the trespass was casual or involuntary, or that the defendant in any action brought under this section had probable cause to believe that the land on which the trespass was committed was his own or the land of the person in whose service or by whose direction the act was done, the measure of damages shall be twice the sum as would compensate for the actual detriment, and excepting further that where the wood was taken by the authority of highway officers for the purpose of repairing a public highway or bridge upon the land or adjoining it, in which case judgment shall only be given in a sum equal to the actual detriment.

(b) The measure of damages to be assessed against a defendant for any trespass committed while acting in reliance upon a survey of boundary lines which improperly fixes the location of a boundary line, shall be the actual detriment incurred if both of the following conditions exist:

1. The trespass was committed by a defendant who either himself procured, or whose principal, lessor, or immediate predecessor in title procured the survey to be made; and

2. The survey was made by a person licensed under the laws of this State to practice land surveying.

(c) Any action for the damages specified by subdivisions (a) and (b) of this section must be commenced within five years from the date of the trespass. *(Added by Stats.1957, c. 2346, p. 4076, § 2.)*

Cross References

Civil action by public agency seeking damages caused by fire, pecuniary damages, ecological and environmental damages, reasonableness of damages, seeking to enhance damages prohibited, see Health and Safety Code § 13009.2.
Forest fires, see Public Resources Code § 4101 et seq.
Trespass for cutting, carrying off or injuring trees, damages, see Code of Civil Procedure §§ 733, 734.
Waste, treble damages, see Code of Civil Procedure § 732.

§ 3346a. Repealed by Stats.1931, c. 790, p. 1644, § 6; Stats.1939, c. 759, p. 2290, § 2

§§ 3347, 3348. Repealed by Stats.1994, c. 270 (A.B.3326), §§ 2, 3

ARTICLE 4. GENERAL PROVISIONS

Section
3353. Estimating damages; value to seller.
3354. Estimating damages; value to buyer.
3355. Property of peculiar value.
3356. Estimating damages; value of instrument in writing.
3357. Damages prescribed by chapter exclusive of exemplary damages and interest.
3358. Limitation of damages; exception.
3359. Reasonableness of damages.
3360. Nominal damages.
3361. Estimating damages; lost earnings; discrimination prohibited.

§ 3353. Estimating damages; value to seller

In estimating damages, the value of property to a seller thereof is deemed to be the price which he could have obtained therefor in the market nearest to the place at which it should have been accepted by the buyer, and at such time after the breach of the contract as would have sufficed, with reasonable diligence, for the seller to effect a resale. *(Enacted in 1872.)*

Cross References

Limitation of damages, see Civil Code § 3358.
Seller's damages for nonacceptance or repudiation, see Commercial Code § 2708.

§ 3354. Estimating damages; value to buyer

In estimating damages, except as provided by Sections 3355 and 3356, the value of property, to a buyer or owner thereof, deprived of its possession, is deemed to be the price at which he might have bought an equivalent thing in the market nearest to the place where the property ought to have been put into his possession, and at such time after the breach of duty upon which his right to damages is founded as would suffice, with reasonable diligence, for him to make such a purchase. *(Enacted in 1872.)*

Cross References

Buyer's damages for non-delivery or repudiation, see Commercial Code § 2713.

§ 3355. Property of peculiar value

Where certain property has a peculiar value to a person recovering damages for deprivation thereof, or injury thereto, that may be deemed to be its value against one who had notice thereof before incurring a liability to damages in respect thereof, or against a willful wrongdoer. *(Enacted in 1872.)*

§ 3356. Estimating damages; value of instrument in writing

For the purpose of estimating damages, the value of an instrument in writing is presumed to be equal to that of the property to which it entitles its owner. *(Enacted in 1872. Amended by Code Am.1873–74, c. 612, p. 266, § 278.)*

§ 3357. Damages prescribed by chapter exclusive of exemplary damages and interest

The damages prescribed by this Chapter are exclusive of exemplary damages and interest, except where those are expressly mentioned. *(Enacted in 1872.)*

Cross References

Exemplary damages, when allowable, see Civil Code § 3294.
Interest on damages, see Civil Code § 3287 et seq.

§ 3358. Limitation of damages; exception

Except as expressly provided by statute, no person can recover a greater amount in damages for the breach of an obligation, than he could have gained by the full performance thereof on both sides. *(Enacted in 1872. Amended by Stats.1977, c. 198, p. 720, § 9, operative July 1, 1978.)*

Cross References

Exemplary damages, when allowable, see Civil Code § 3294.
Liquidated damages, see Civil Code § 1671.
Penal damages, see Civil Code § 3346.

§ 3359. Reasonableness of damages

Damages must, in all cases, be reasonable, and where an obligation of any kind appears to create a right to unconscionable and grossly oppressive damages, contrary to substantial justice, no more than reasonable damages can be recovered. *(Enacted in 1872.)*

§ 3360. Nominal damages

When a breach of duty has caused no appreciable detriment to the party affected, he may yet recover nominal damages. *(Enacted in 1872.)*

§ 3361. Estimating damages; lost earnings; discrimination prohibited

Estimations, measures, or calculations of past, present, or future damages for lost earnings or impaired earning capacity resulting from personal injury or wrongful death shall not be reduced based on race, ethnicity, or gender. *(Added by Stats.2019, c. 136 (S.B.41), § 2, eff. Jan. 1, 2020.)*

Title 3

SPECIFIC AND PREVENTIVE RELIEF

Chapter	Section
1. General Principles	3366
1.5. Investment Advisers	3372
2. Specific Relief	3375
3. Preventive Relief	3420

CHAPTER 1. GENERAL PRINCIPLES

Section
3366. Allowance of specific or preventive relief.
3367. Specific relief; method of giving.
3368. Preventive relief; method of giving.
3369. Penalties or forfeitures; availability of specific or preventive relief.
3370. Repealed.
3370.1, 3370.2. Repealed.

§ 3366. Allowance of specific or preventive relief

Specific or preventive relief may be given as provided by the laws of this state. *(Enacted in 1872. Amended by Stats.1905, c. 465, p. 622, § 1.)*

Cross References

Cancellation of void or voidable instruments, see Civil Code § 3412.
Delivery of personalty, see Civil Code § 3380.
Limits to preventive relief, see Civil Code §§ 3274, 3423.
Mistake as barring specific relief, see Civil Code § 3391.
Penalty, specific performance not granted to enforce, see Civil Code § 3389.
Personal service contracts not specifically enforceable, see Civil Code § 3390.
Possession of personal property, see Civil Code § 3379 et seq.
Preventive relief by injunction, see Civil Code § 3420 et seq.
Realty transfer contracts, see Civil Code §§ 3375, 3387, 3395; Code of Civil Procedure §§ 1971, 1972.
Reformation of contracts, see Civil Code § 3399.
Restoration of destroyed or lost instruments, see Civil Code § 3415.
Specific performance of obligations, see Civil Code § 3384 et seq.
Unreasonable contracts, see Civil Code § 3391.

§ 3367. Specific relief; method of giving

Specific relief is given:

1. By taking possession of a thing, and delivering it to a claimant;

2. By compelling a party himself to do that which ought to be done; or,

3. By declaring and determining the rights of parties, otherwise than by an award of damages. *(Enacted in 1872.)*

Cross References

Delivery of personalty to true owner, see Civil Code § 3380.
Possession of realty, see Civil Code § 3375.
Realty transfer contracts, see Civil Code §§ 3375, 3387, 3395; Code of Civil Procedure §§ 1971, 1972.
Summary proceedings for obtaining possession of real property, see Code of Civil Procedure § 1159 et seq.
Writ of mandate, see Code of Civil Procedure § 1084 et seq.

§ 3368. Preventive relief; method of giving

Preventive relief is given by prohibiting a party from doing that which ought not to be done. *(Enacted in 1872.)*

Cross References

Certiorari, see Code of Civil Procedure § 1067 et seq.
Contempt, see Code of Civil Procedure § 1209 et seq.
Injunction, see Civil Code § 3420 et seq.; Code of Civil Procedure § 525 et seq.
Limited to specific cases, see Civil Code § 3274.
Prohibition, see Code of Civil Procedure § 1102 et seq.

§ 3369. Penalties or forfeitures; availability of specific or preventive relief

Neither specific nor preventive relief can be granted to enforce a penalty or forfeiture in any case, nor to enforce a penal law, except in a case of nuisance or as otherwise provided by law. *(Enacted in 1872. Amended by Stats. 1933, c. 953, p. 2482, § 1; Stats.1963, c. 1606, p. 3184, § 1; Stats.1972, c. 1084, p. 2020, § 1; Stats.1974, c. 746, p. 1654, § 1; Stats.1976, c. 1005, p. 2378, § 1; Stats.1977, c. 299, p. 1203, § 2.)*

Cross References

Injunctions, see Code of Civil Procedure § 525 et seq.

§ 3370. Repealed by Stats.1976, c. 837, p. 1906, § 1

§§ 3370.1, 3370.2. Repealed by Stats.1977, c. 299, p. 1204, §§ 3, 4

CHAPTER 1.5. INVESTMENT ADVISERS

Section
3372. Liability; exclusions.

§ 3372. Liability; exclusions

(a) Any person engaged in the business of advising others for compensation as to the advisability of purchasing, holding or selling property for investment and who represents himself or herself to be an expert with respect to investment decisions in such property, or any class of such property, shall be liable to any person to whom such advisory services are furnished for compensation and who is damaged by reason of such person's reliance upon such services, for the amount of such compensation and for such damages, unless the person rendering such services proves that such services were performed with the due care and skill reasonably to be expected of a person who is such an expert.

(b) For the purposes of this section, the following apply:

(1) A person represents that such person is an "expert" within the meaning of this section if such person represents that he or she is a "financial planner," "financial adviser," "financial counselor," "financial consultant" or an "investment adviser," "investment counselor" or "investment consultant" or that such person renders "financial planning services," "financial advisory services," "financial counseling services," "financial consulting services" or "investment advisory services," "investment counseling services" or "investment consulting services" or makes substantially equivalent representations with respect to such person's business or qualifications.

(2) "Person" includes an individual, corporation, partnership, limited liability company, joint venture, an association, joint stock company, a trust or unincorporated association.

(c) The following persons are not liable under the provisions of this section:

(1) Any person, when engaged in the purchase or sale of tangible personal property for his or her own account, and the agents and employees of such persons.

(2) Any person, and the agents and employees of such person, licensed under, exempted from licensing under, or not subject to licensing under by reason of an express exclusion from a definition contained in, the Commodity Exchange Act, the Investment Advisers Act of 1940, the California Commodity Law, the Corporate Securities Law of 1968, the Insurance Code, the Real Estate Law, or any state or federal law for the licensing and regulation of banks or savings and loan associations. *(Added by Stats.1978, c. 1380, p. 4573, § 1. Amended by Stats.1986, c. 698, § 1; Stats.1994, c. 1010 (S.B.2053), § 53.)*

CHAPTER 2. SPECIFIC RELIEF

Article	Section
1. Possession of Real Property	3375
2. Possession of Personal Property	3379
3. Specific Performance of Obligations	3384
4. Revision of Contracts	3399
5. Rescission of Contracts [Repealed]	
6. Cancellation of Instruments	3412

ARTICLE 1. POSSESSION OF REAL PROPERTY

Section
3375. Judgment for possession or requiring perfection of title.

§ 3375. Judgment for possession or requiring perfection of title

A person entitled to specific real property, by reason either of a perfected title, or of a claim to title which ought to be perfected, may recover the same in the manner prescribed by the Code of Civil Procedure, either by a judgment for its possession, to be executed by the sheriff, or by a judgment requiring the other party to perfect the title, and to deliver possession of the property. *(Enacted in 1872.)*

Cross References

Actions concerning interests in real estate, see Code of Civil Procedure § 760.010 et seq.
Description of property in pleading in action to recover real property, see Code of Civil Procedure § 455.
Forcible entry and detainer, see Code of Civil Procedure § 1159 et seq.
Place of trial of action for recovery of real property, see Code of Civil Procedure § 392.
Presumption of inadequacy of pecuniary compensation, see Civil Code § 3387.
Relief against person claiming under particular person, see Civil Code § 3395.
Restitution of property upon appellate court's reversal, see Code of Civil Procedure § 908.
Specific performance after part performance, see Code of Civil Procedure § 1972.
Specific performance of obligations, see Civil Code § 3384 et seq.
Summary judgment, see Code of Civil Procedure § 437c.

ARTICLE 2. POSSESSION OF PERSONAL PROPERTY

Section
3379. Recovery of possession.
3380. Specific delivery.

§ 3379. Recovery of possession

A person entitled to the immediate possession of specific personal property may recover the same in the manner provided by the Code of Civil Procedure. *(Enacted in 1872.)*

Cross References

Buyer's right to specific performance or replevin, see Commercial Code § 2716.
Claim and delivery, see Code of Civil Procedure § 511.010 et seq.

§ 3380. Specific delivery

Any person having the possession or control of a particular article of personal property, of which he is not the owner, may be compelled specifically to deliver it to the person entitled to its immediate possession. *(Enacted in 1872. Amended by Code Am.1873–74, c. 612, p. 266, § 279.)*

ARTICLE 3. SPECIFIC PERFORMANCE OF OBLIGATIONS

Section
3384. Compelling specific performance.
3385. Repealed.
3386. Mutuality of remedy.
3387. Breach of agreement to transfer real estate; presumption of inadequacy of damages.
3388. Enforcement of contract signed by one party only.
3389. Enforcement of contract imposing penalty or liquidated damages.
3390. Obligations not specifically enforceable.
3391. Parties who cannot be compelled to perform.
3392. Parties who cannot have specific performance.

GENERAL PROVISIONS

Section
3393. Repealed.
3394. Agreement for sale; seller without good title.
3395. Relief against parties claiming under person bound to perform.
3396. Unconstitutional.
3397. Repealed.

Cross References

Agricultural cooperative marketing agreements, specific enforcement, see Food and Agricultural Code §§ 54263, 54265.
Decedents' contracts, binding performance by personal representative, see Probate Code § 850 et seq.
Fish marketing agreements, specific performance, see Corporations Code § 13356.
Lien for liability on official bond, specific performance of agreement to sell realty affected, see Code of Civil Procedure § 996.510 et seq.
Negotiable document of title, compelling indorsement, see Commercial Code § 7506.
Oil and gas cooperative development agreements, specific performance, see Public Resources Code § 3301.
Revised contracts, specific enforcement, see Civil Code § 3402.
Sales contracts, buyer's right to specific performance or replevin, see Commercial Code § 2716.
Specific relief, compelling performance, see Civil Code § 3367.

§ 3384. Compelling specific performance

Except as otherwise provided in this Article, the specific performance of an obligation may be compelled. *(Enacted in 1872. Amended by Code Am.1873–74, c. 612, p. 266, § 280.)*

§ 3385. Repealed by Code Am.1873–74, c. 612, p. 267, § 281

§ 3386. Mutuality of remedy

Notwithstanding that the agreed counterperformance is not or would not have been specifically enforceable, specific performance may be compelled if:

(a) Specific performance would otherwise be an appropriate remedy; and

(b) The agreed counterperformance has been substantially performed or its concurrent or future performance is assured or, if the court deems necessary, can be secured to the satisfaction of the court. *(Enacted in 1872. Amended by Stats.1969, c. 156, p. 410, § 1.)*

Cross References

Parties who cannot have specific performance, see Civil Code § 3392.

§ 3387. Breach of agreement to transfer real estate; presumption of inadequacy of damages

It is to be presumed that the breach of an agreement to transfer real property cannot be adequately relieved by pecuniary compensation. In the case of a single-family dwelling which the party seeking performance intends to occupy, this presumption is conclusive. In all other cases, this presumption is a presumption affecting the burden of proof. *(Enacted in 1872. Amended by Stats.1931, c. 1070, p. 2261, § 11; Stats.1984, c. 937, § 1.)*

Cross References

Damages for conversion of personalty, see Civil Code § 3336.
Presumptions, see Evidence Code § 600 et seq.

§ 3388. Enforcement of contract signed by one party only

A party who has signed a written contract may be compelled specifically to perform it, though the other party has not signed it, if the latter has performed, or offers to perform it on his part, and the case is otherwise proper for enforcing specific performance. *(Enacted in 1872.)*

§ 3389. Enforcement of contract imposing penalty or liquidated damages

A contract otherwise proper to be specifically enforced, may be thus enforced, though a penalty is imposed, or the damages are liquidated for its breach, and the party in default is willing to pay the same. *(Enacted in 1872.)*

§ 3390. Obligations not specifically enforceable

The following obligations cannot be specifically enforced:

(a) An obligation to render personal service.

(b) An obligation to employ another in personal service.

(c) An agreement to perform an act which the party has not power lawfully to perform when required to do so.

(d) An agreement to procure the act or consent of the spouse of the contracting party, or of any other third person.

(e) An agreement, the terms of which are not sufficiently certain to make the precise act which is to be done clearly ascertainable. *(Enacted in 1872. Amended by Stats.1961, c. 461, p. 1551, § 5; Stats.2016, c. 50 (S.B.1005), § 12, eff. Jan. 1, 2017.)*

Cross References

Arbitration agreements, enforcement, see Code of Civil Procedure § 1281 et seq.
Personal service contracts,
 Enforcement, see Labor Code § 2855.
 Enforcement by injunction, see Code of Civil Procedure § 526.

§ 3391. Parties who cannot be compelled to perform

Specific performance cannot be enforced against a party to a contract in any of the following cases:

1. If he has not received an adequate consideration for the contract;

2. If it is not, as to him, just and reasonable;

3. If his assent was obtained by the misrepresentation, concealment, circumvention, or unfair practices of any party to whom performance would become due under the contract, or by any promise of such party which has not been substantially fulfilled; or;

4. If his assent was given under the influence of mistake, misapprehension, or surprise, except that where the contract provides for compensation in case of mistake, a mistake within the scope of such provision may be compensated for, and the contract specifically enforced in other respects, if proper to be so enforced. *(Enacted in 1872.)*

Cross References

Consideration,
 Generally, see Civil Code § 1605 et seq.
 Essential element of contract, see Civil Code § 1550.
Duress, see Civil Code § 1569.

Fraud, see Civil Code § 1571 et seq.
Menace, see Civil Code § 1570.
Mistake, see Civil Code § 1576 et seq.
Undue influence, see Civil Code § 1575.

§ 3392. Parties who cannot have specific performance

Specific performance cannot be enforced in favor of a party who has not fully and fairly performed all the conditions precedent on his part to the obligation of the other party, except where his failure to perform is only partial, and either entirely immaterial, or capable of being fully compensated, in which case specific performance may be compelled, upon full compensation being made for the default. *(Enacted in 1872.)*

Cross References

Condition precedent,
    Defined, see Civil Code §§ 708, 1436.
    Impossible or unlawful, see Civil Code § 1441.
    Offer of performance, see Civil Code § 1498.
    Performance, see Civil Code § 1439.
    Pleading performance, see Code of Civil Procedure §§ 457, 459.
    Proof of performance, see Code of Civil Procedure §§ 457, 459.
    Validity, see Civil Code § 709.

§ 3393. Repealed by Code Am.1873–74, c. 612, p. 267, § 281

§ 3394. Agreement for sale; seller without good title

An agreement for the sale of property cannot be specifically enforced in favor of a seller who cannot give to the buyer a title free from reasonable doubt. *(Enacted in 1872.)*

§ 3395. Relief against parties claiming under person bound to perform

Whenever an obligation in respect to real property would be specifically enforced against a particular person, it may be in like manner enforced against any other person claiming under him by a title created subsequently to the obligation, except a purchaser or encumbrancer in good faith and for value, and except, also, that any such person may exonerate himself by conveying all his estate to the person entitled to enforce the obligation. *(Enacted in 1872.)*

Cross References

Provision where person entitled to bring action dies before limitation expires, see Code of Civil Procedure § 366.1.

§ 3396. Unconstitutional

§ 3397. Repealed by Stats.1933, c. 25, p. 298, § 1301

ARTICLE 4. REVISION OF CONTRACTS

Section
3399. When contract may be revised.
3400. Presumption of intent to make an equitable and conscientious agreement.
3401. Principles of revision.
3402. Enforcement of revised contract.

§ 3399. When contract may be revised

When, through fraud or a mutual mistake of the parties, or a mistake of one party, which the other at the time knew or suspected, a written contract does not truly express the intention of the parties, it may be revised on the application of a party aggrieved, so as to express that intention, so far as it can be done without prejudice to rights acquired by third persons, in good faith and for value. *(Enacted in 1872.)*

Cross References

Erroneous parts of writing disregarded, see Civil Code § 1640.
Fraud defined, see Civil Code § 1571 et seq.
Mistake, see Civil Code § 1576 et seq.
Parol evidence to explain mistake, see Code of Civil Procedure § 1856.

§ 3400. Presumption of intent to make an equitable and conscientious agreement

For the purpose of revising a contract, it must be presumed that all the parties thereto intended to make an equitable and conscientious agreement. *(Enacted in 1872.)*

Cross References

Reasonable interpretation of contracts, see Civil Code § 1643.

§ 3401. Principles of revision

In revising a written instrument, the court may inquire what the instrument was intended to mean, and what were intended to be its legal consequences, and is not confined to the inquiry what the language of the instrument was intended to be. *(Enacted in 1872.)*

Cross References

Erroneous parts of writing disregarded, see Civil Code § 1640.
Reference to circumstances, see Civil Code § 1647.

§ 3402. Enforcement of revised contract

A contract may be first revised and then specifically enforced. *(Enacted in 1872.)*

ARTICLE 5. RESCISSION OF CONTRACTS [REPEALED]

§§ 3406 to 3408. Repealed by Stats.1961, c. 589, p. 1735, § 5

ARTICLE 6. CANCELLATION OF INSTRUMENTS

Section
3412. Grounds for cancellation.
3413. Instrument obviously void.
3414. Cancellation in part.
3415. Lost or destroyed documents; establishment; issuance of duplicate; security.

§ 3412. Grounds for cancellation

A written instrument, in respect to which there is a reasonable apprehension that if left outstanding it may cause serious injury to a person against whom it is void or voidable, may, upon his application, be so adjudged, and ordered to be delivered up or canceled. *(Enacted in 1872.)*

Cross References

Effect of cancellation, see Civil Code § 1699.
Quieting title to real and personal property, see Code of Civil Procedure § 760.010 et seq.

Rescission of contracts, see Civil Code § 1688 et seq.

§ 3413. Instrument obviously void

An instrument, the invalidity of which is apparent upon its face, or upon the face of another instrument which is necessary to the use of the former in evidence, is not to be deemed capable of causing injury, within the provisions of the last section. *(Enacted in 1872.)*

§ 3414. Cancellation in part

Where an instrument is evidence of different rights or obligations, it may be canceled in part, and allowed to stand for the residue. *(Enacted in 1872.)*

§ 3415. Lost or destroyed documents; establishment; issuance of duplicate; security

(a) An action may be maintained by any person interested in any private document or instrument in writing, which has been lost or destroyed, to prove or establish the document or instrument or to compel the issuance, execution, and acknowledgment of a duplicate of the document or instrument.

(b) If the document or instrument is a negotiable instrument, the court shall compel the owner of the negotiable instrument to give an indemnity bond to the person reissuing, reexecuting, or reacknowledging the same, against loss, damage, expense, or other liability that may be suffered by the person by reason of the issuance of the duplicate instrument or by the original instrument still remaining outstanding. *(Added by Stats.Ex.Sess.1906, c. 64, p. 86, § 1. Amended by Stats.1947, c. 313, p. 869, § 1; Stats.1982, c. 517, p. 2329, § 85; Stats.2006, c. 538 (S.B.1852), § 59.)*

Cross References

Bond and Undertaking Law, see Code of Civil Procedure § 995.010 et seq.
Lost, destroyed or stolen securities, action for new certificates, see Commercial Code § 8405; Corporations Code § 419.
Private records destroyed in disaster or calamity, see Code of Civil Procedure § 1953.10 et seq.
Public records destroyed in fire or calamity, see Code of Civil Procedure § 1953 et seq.
Re-establishment of destroyed land records, see Code of Civil Procedure § 751.01 et seq.
State bonds, reissuance upon loss or destruction, see Government Code § 16700 et seq.

CHAPTER 3. PREVENTIVE RELIEF

Section
3420. Preventive relief; injunction.
3421. Provisional injunctions.
3422. Final injunction; grounds.
3423. Injunction; circumstances requiring denial.
3424. Modification or dissolution of final injunction; notice and motion; service.

§ 3420. Preventive relief; injunction

Preventive relief is granted by injunction, provisional or final. *(Enacted in 1872.)*

Cross References

Injunction, see Code of Civil Procedure § 525 et seq.
Nuisance, action to enjoin or abate, see Code of Civil Procedure § 731 et seq.
Preventive relief, see Civil Code § 3368 et seq.
Restraint of injury to property during foreclosure, etc., see Code of Civil Procedure § 745.
Restricted to cases code specifies, see Civil Code § 3274.

§ 3421. Provisional injunctions

Provisional injunctions are regulated by the Code of Civil Procedure. *(Enacted in 1872.)*

Cross References

Preliminary injunctions, municipal courts, jurisdiction, see Code of Civil Procedure § 86.
Provisional injunction, see Code of Civil Procedure § 525 et seq.

§ 3422. Final injunction; grounds

Except where otherwise provided by this Title, a final injunction may be granted to prevent the breach of an obligation existing in favor of the applicant:

1. Where pecuniary compensation would not afford adequate relief;

2. Where it would be extremely difficult to ascertain the amount of compensation which would afford adequate relief;

3. Where the restraint is necessary to prevent a multiplicity of judicial proceedings; or,

4. Where the obligation arises from a trust. *(Enacted in 1872.)*

Cross References

Cooperative corporations, injunction against improper use of name or unauthorized business, see Corporations Code §§ 12311, 12678, 12679.
Corporate securities act violations, see Corporations Code § 25530.
Dissolution of corporation, involuntary proceedings, see Corporations Code § 1804.
Fish marketing contracts, enforcement, see Corporations Code § 13354.
Nuisances dangerous to health, see Health and Safety Code § 100170.
Prevention of injury to property during foreclosure, etc., see Code of Civil Procedure § 745.
Private nuisances, see Code of Civil Procedure § 731.
Similar provisions, see Code of Civil Procedure § 526.
Specific and preventive relief, restriction to cases specified in this Part, see Civil Code § 3274.

§ 3423. Injunction; circumstances requiring denial

An injunction may not be granted:

(a) To stay a judicial proceeding pending at the commencement of the action in which the injunction is demanded, unless this restraint is necessary to prevent a multiplicity of proceedings.

(b) To stay proceedings in a court of the United States.

(c) To stay proceedings in another state upon a judgment of a court of that state.

(d) To prevent the execution of a public statute, by officers of the law, for the public benefit.

(e) To prevent the breach of a contract the performance of which would not be specifically enforced, other than a contract in writing for the rendition of personal services from one to another where the promised service is of a special, unique, unusual, extraordinary, or intellectual character, which gives it peculiar value, the loss of which cannot be reasonably or adequately compensated in damages in an action at law, and where the compensation for the personal services is as follows:

(1) As to contracts entered into on or before December 31, 1993, the minimum compensation provided in the contract for the personal services shall be at the rate of six thousand dollars ($6,000) per annum.

(2) As to contracts entered into on or after January 1, 1994, the criteria of subparagraph (A) or (B), as follows, are satisfied:

(A) The compensation is as follows:

(i) The minimum compensation provided in the contract shall be at the rate of nine thousand dollars ($9,000) per annum for the first year of the contract, twelve thousand dollars ($12,000) per annum for the second year of the contract, and fifteen thousand dollars ($15,000) per annum for the third to seventh years, inclusive, of the contract.

(ii) In addition, after the third year of the contract, there shall actually have been paid for the services through and including the contract year during which the injunctive relief is sought, over and above the minimum contractual compensation specified in clause (i), the amount of fifteen thousand dollars ($15,000) per annum during the fourth and fifth years of the contract, and thirty thousand dollars ($30,000) per annum during the sixth and seventh years of the contract. As a condition to petitioning for an injunction, amounts payable under this clause may be paid at any time prior to seeking injunctive relief.

(B) The aggregate compensation actually received for the services provided under a contract that does not meet the criteria of subparagraph (A), is at least 10 times the applicable aggregate minimum amount specified in clauses (i) and (ii) of subparagraph (A) through and including the contract year during which the injunctive relief is sought. As a condition to petitioning for an injunction, amounts payable under this subparagraph may be paid at any time prior to seeking injunctive relief.

(3) Compensation paid in any contract year in excess of the minimums specified in subparagraphs (A) and (B) of paragraph (2) shall apply to reduce the compensation otherwise required to be paid under those provisions in any subsequent contract years.

However, an injunction may be granted to prevent the breach of a contract entered into between any nonprofit cooperative corporation or association and a member or stockholder thereof in respect to any provision regarding the sale or delivery to the corporation or association of the products produced or acquired by the member or stockholder.

(f) To prevent the exercise of a public or private office, in a lawful manner, by the person in possession.

(g) To prevent a legislative act by a municipal corporation. *(Enacted in 1872. Amended by Code Am.1873–74, c. 612, p. 267, § 282; Stats.1919, c. 226, p. 328; § 1; Stats.1925, c. 409, p. 829, § 1; Stats.1992, c. 177 (S.B.1459), § 1; Stats.1993, c. 5 (S.B.32), § 1, eff. April 3, 1993; Stats.1993, c. 836 (S.B.487), § 1.)*

Cross References

Franchise and income tax collections, injunction prohibited, see Revenue and Taxation Code § 19381.
Injunction, cases in which authorized, see Code of Civil Procedure § 526.
Motor vehicle fuel tax collections, injunction prohibited, see Revenue and Taxation Code § 8146.
Private railroad car tax collection, injunction prohibited, see Revenue and Taxation Code § 11571.
Sales or use tax collections, injunction prohibited, see Revenue and Taxation Code § 6931.
Specific and preventive relief, restriction to cases specified in this Part, see Civil Code § 3274.
Use fuel tax, injunction prohibited, see Revenue and Taxation Code § 9171.

§ 3424. Modification or dissolution of final injunction; notice and motion; service

(a) Upon notice and motion, the court may modify or dissolve a final injunction upon a showing that there has been a material change in the facts upon which the injunction was granted, that the law upon which the injunction was granted has changed, or that the ends of justice would be served by the modification or dissolution of the injunction.

(b) Service of this motion to modify or dissolve a final injunction shall be made upon the nonmoving party by one of the following methods:

(1) If the party has not appeared in the action, the motion shall be served in the same manner as a summons pursuant to Article 3 (commencing with Section 415.10) of Chapter 4 of Title 5 of Part 2 of the Code of Civil Procedure.

(2) If the party has appeared in the action, the motion shall be served either upon the party or his or her attorney, or upon the party if he or she has appeared without an attorney, either in the same manner as a summons pursuant to Article 3 (commencing with Section 415.10) of Chapter 4 of Title 5 of the Code of Civil Procedure or in the manner provided by Chapter 5 (commencing with Section 1010) of Title 14 of Part 2 of the Code of Civil Procedure.

(c) This section does not apply to a final injunction issued pursuant to the Family Code. *(Added by Stats.1995, c. 796 (S.B.45), § 1.5.)*

Title 4

UNIFORM SINGLE PUBLICATION ACT

Section
3425.1. Citation.
3425.2. Interpretation.
3425.3. One cause of action; recovery.
3425.4. Judgment as bar.
3425.5. Existing causes of action.

§ 3425.1. Citation

This title may be cited as the Uniform Single Publication Act. *(Added by Stats.1955, c. 867, p. 1481, § 1.)*

§ 3425.2. Interpretation

This act shall be so interpreted as to effectuate its purpose to make uniform the law of those states or jurisdictions which enact it. *(Added by Stats.1955, c. 867, p. 1481, § 1.)*

§ 3425.3. One cause of action; recovery

No person shall have more than one cause of action for damages for libel or slander or invasion of privacy or any other tort founded upon any single publication or exhibition or utterance, such as any one issue of a newspaper or book or magazine or any one presentation to an audience or any one broadcast over radio or television or any one exhibition of a motion picture. Recovery in any action shall include all damages for any such tort suffered by the plaintiff in all jurisdictions. (Added by Stats.1955, c. 867, p. 1481, § 1.)

Cross References

Responsibility for willful acts, see Civil Code § 1714.

§ 3425.4. Judgment as bar

A judgment in any jurisdiction for or against the plaintiff upon the substantive merits of any action for damages founded upon a single publication or exhibition or utterance as described in Section 3425.3 shall bar any other action for damages by the same plaintiff against the same defendant founded upon the same publication or exhibition or utterance. (Added by Stats.1955, c. 867, p. 1481, § 1.)

§ 3425.5. Existing causes of action

This title shall not be retroactive as to causes of action existing on its effective date. (Added by Stats.1955, c. 867, p. 1481, § 1.)

Title 5

UNIFORM TRADE SECRETS ACT

Section
3426. Short title.
3426.1. Definitions.
3426.2. Injunctions.
3426.3. Damages; royalties; exemplary damages.
3426.4. Awarding attorney's fees and costs.
3426.5. Preservation of secrecy in judicial proceeding.
3426.6. Time for bringing action.
3426.7. Construction with other statutes; other remedies; disclosure of public records.
3426.8. Application and construction of title.
3426.9. Severability of provisions.
3426.10. Misappropriations occurring prior to January 1, 1985; application of title.
3426.11. Privileged communications; trade secrets disclosed in official proceedings.

Cross References

Confidential business information, intentionally added ingredient, menstrual products, see Health and Safety Code § 111822.5.

Discovery relating to trade secrets, see Code of Civil Procedure § 2019.210.

Organic food producers, handlers, processors, and retailers, inspection of records, see Health and Safety Code § 110845.

Record keeping relating to products sold as organic, inspection by governmental agent or entity, exclusion from provisions governed by this title, see Food and Agricultural Code § 46029.

Well stimulation treatment fluid information claimed to contain trade secrets, provisions governing public disclosure, see Public Resources Code § 3160.

§ 3426. Short title

This title may be cited as the Uniform Trade Secrets Act. (Added by Stats.1984, c. 1724, § 1.)

Cross References

Agency request for disclosure of chemical compounds, protection of manufacturers' trade secrets, see Health and Safety Code § 57019.

Records maintained by auxiliary organizations, information related to fundraising plans, fundraising research, and solicitation strategies not subject to disclosure, see Education Code §§ 72696, 89916.

Records maintained by UC campus foundations, information related to fundraising plans, fundraising research, and solicitation strategies not subject to disclosure, see Education Code § 92956.

§ 3426.1. Definitions

As used in this title, unless the context requires otherwise:

(a) "Improper means" includes theft, bribery, misrepresentation, breach or inducement of a breach of a duty to maintain secrecy, or espionage through electronic or other means. Reverse engineering or independent derivation alone shall not be considered improper means.

(b) "Misappropriation" means:

(1) Acquisition of a trade secret of another by a person who knows or has reason to know that the trade secret was acquired by improper means; or

(2) Disclosure or use of a trade secret of another without express or implied consent by a person who:

(A) Used improper means to acquire knowledge of the trade secret; or

(B) At the time of disclosure or use, knew or had reason to know that his or her knowledge of the trade secret was:

(i) Derived from or through a person who had utilized improper means to acquire it;

(ii) Acquired under circumstances giving rise to a duty to maintain its secrecy or limit its use; or

(iii) Derived from or through a person who owed a duty to the person seeking relief to maintain its secrecy or limit its use; or

(C) Before a material change of his or her position, knew or had reason to know that it was a trade secret and that knowledge of it had been acquired by accident or mistake.

(c) "Person" means a natural person, corporation, business trust, estate, trust, partnership, limited liability company, association, joint venture, government, governmental subdivision or agency, or any other legal or commercial entity.

(d) "Trade secret" means information, including a formula, pattern, compilation, program, device, method, technique, or process, that:

(1) Derives independent economic value, actual or potential, from not being generally known to the public or to other persons who can obtain economic value from its disclosure or use; and

(2) Is the subject of efforts that are reasonable under the circumstances to maintain its secrecy. (Added by Stats.1984, c. 1724, § 1. Amended by Stats.1994, c. 1010 (S.B.2053), § 54.)

Cross References

Disclosure of sources of electrical generation, additional annual reporting by retail suppliers, see Public Utilities Code § 398.6.

District hospital board of directors meetings involving trade secrets, closed sessions, see Health and Safety Code § 32106.

Kern County Hospital Authority, meetings, see Health and Safety Code § 101855.

Plastic Pollution Prevention and Packaging Producer Responsibility Act, enforcement, trade secrets, see Public Resources Code § 42080.

Public employees' health benefits, disclosure of cost, utilization, actual claim payments, and contract allowance amounts for health care services rendered, see Government Code § 22854.5.

Records of certain health plans, meetings on health plan trade secrets, see Government Code § 54956.87.

Records maintained by auxiliary organizations; trade secrets not subject to disclosure, see Education Code §§ 72696.5, 89916.5.

§ 3426.2. Injunctions

(a) Actual or threatened misappropriation may be enjoined. Upon application to the court, an injunction shall be terminated when the trade secret has ceased to exist, but the injunction may be continued for an additional period of time in order to eliminate commercial advantage that otherwise would be derived from the misappropriation.

(b) If the court determines that it would be unreasonable to prohibit future use, an injunction may condition future use upon payment of a reasonable royalty for no longer than the period of time the use could have been prohibited.

(c) In appropriate circumstances, affirmative acts to protect a trade secret may be compelled by court order. *(Added by Stats.1984, c. 1724, § 1.)*

§ 3426.3. Damages; royalties; exemplary damages

(a) A complainant may recover damages for the actual loss caused by misappropriation. A complainant also may recover for the unjust enrichment caused by misappropriation that is not taken into account in computing damages for actual loss.

(b) If neither damages nor unjust enrichment caused by misappropriation are provable, the court may order payment of a reasonable royalty for no longer than the period of time the use could have been prohibited.

(c) If willful and malicious misappropriation exists, the court may award exemplary damages in an amount not exceeding twice any award made under subdivision (a) or (b). *(Added by Stats.1984, c. 1724, § 1.)*

§ 3426.4. Awarding attorney's fees and costs

If a claim of misappropriation is made in bad faith, a motion to terminate an injunction is made or resisted in bad faith, or willful and malicious misappropriation exists, the court may award reasonable attorney's fees and costs to the prevailing party. Recoverable costs hereunder shall include a reasonable sum to cover the services of expert witnesses, who are not regular employees of any party, actually incurred and reasonably necessary in either, or both, preparation for trial or arbitration, or during trial or arbitration, of the case by the prevailing party. *(Added by Stats.1984, c. 1724, § 1. Amended by Stats.2006, c. 62 (S.B.1636), § 1.)*

§ 3426.5. Preservation of secrecy in judicial proceeding

In an action under this title, a court shall preserve the secrecy of an alleged trade secret by reasonable means, which may include granting protective orders in connection with discovery proceedings, holding in-camera hearings, sealing the records of the action, and ordering any person involved in the litigation not to disclose an alleged trade secret without prior court approval. *(Added by Stats.1984, c. 1724, § 1.)*

§ 3426.6. Time for bringing action

An action for misappropriation must be brought within three years after the misappropriation is discovered or by the exercise of reasonable diligence should have been discovered. For the purposes of this section, a continuing misappropriation constitutes a single claim. *(Added by Stats.1984, c. 1724, § 1.)*

§ 3426.7. Construction with other statutes; other remedies; disclosure of public records

(a) Except as otherwise expressly provided, this title does not supersede any statute relating to misappropriation of a trade secret, or any statute otherwise regulating trade secrets.

(b) This title does not affect (1) contractual remedies, whether or not based upon misappropriation of a trade secret, (2) other civil remedies that are not based upon misappropriation of a trade secret, or (3) criminal remedies, whether or not based upon misappropriation of a trade secret.

(c) This title does not affect the disclosure of a record by a state or local agency under the California Public Records Act (Division 10 (commencing with Section 7920.000) of Title 1 of the Government Code). Any determination as to whether the disclosure of a record under the California Public Records Act constitutes a misappropriation of a trade secret and the rights and remedies with respect thereto shall be made pursuant to the law in effect before the operative date of this title. *(Added by Stats.1984, c. 1724, § 1. Amended by Stats.2021, c. 615 (A.B.474), § 52, eff. Jan. 1, 2022, operative Jan. 1, 2023.)*

§ 3426.8. Application and construction of title

This title shall be applied and construed to effectuate its general purpose to make uniform the law with respect to the subject of this title among states enacting it. *(Added by Stats.1984, c. 1724, § 1.)*

§ 3426.9. Severability of provisions

If any provision of this title or its application to any person or circumstances is held invalid, the invalidity does not affect other provisions or applications of the title which can be given effect without the invalid provision or application, and to this end the provisions of this title are severable. *(Added by Stats.1984, c. 1724, § 1.)*

§ 3426.10. Misappropriations occurring prior to January 1, 1985; application of title

This title does not apply to misappropriation occurring prior to January 1, 1985. If a continuing misappropriation otherwise covered by this title began before January 1, 1985, this title does not apply to the part of the misappropriation occurring before that date. This title does apply to the part of the misappropriation occurring on or after that date unless the appropriation was not a misappropriation under the law in effect before the operative date of this title. *(Added by Stats.1984, c. 1724, § 1.)*

§ 3426.11. Privileged communications; trade secrets disclosed in official proceedings

Notwithstanding subdivision (b) of Section 47, in any legislative or judicial proceeding, or in any other official proceeding authorized by law, or in the initiation or course of any other proceeding authorized by law and reviewable pursuant to Chapter 2 (commencing with Section 1084) of Title 1 of Part 3 of the Code of Civil Procedure, the voluntary, intentional disclosure of trade secret information, unauthorized by its owner, to a competitor or potential competitor of the owner of the trade secret information or the agent or representative of such a competitor or potential competitor is not privileged and is not a privileged communication for purposes of Part 2 (commencing with Section 43) of Division 1.

This section does not in any manner limit, restrict, impair, or otherwise modify either the application of the other subdivisions of Section 47 to the conduct to which this section applies or the court's authority to control, order, or permit access to evidence in any case before it.

Nothing in this section shall be construed to limit, restrict, or otherwise impair, the capacity of persons employed by public entities to report improper government activity, as defined in Section 10542 of the Government Code, or the capacity of private persons to report improper activities of a private business. *(Added by Stats.1992, c. 165 (A.B.1445), § 1.)*

Title 6

INTERFERENCE WITH ACCESS TO HEALTH CARE

Section
3427. Definitions.
3427.1. Commercial blockade.
3427.2. Civil damages; parties to action.
3427.3. Safeguarding individual privacy and prevention of harassment in civil proceeding.
3427.4. Construction.

§ 3427. Definitions

As used in this title:

(a) "Aggrieved" means and refers to any of the following persons or entities:

(1) A person physically present at a health care facility when a commercial blockade occurs whose access is obstructed or impeded.

(2) A person physically present at a health care facility when a commercial blockade occurs whose health care is disrupted.

(3) A health care facility where a commercial blockade occurs, its employees, contractors, or volunteers.

(4) The owner of a health care facility where a commercial blockade occurs or of the building or property upon which the health care facility is located.

(b) "Commercial blockade" means acts constituting the tort of commercial blockade, as defined in Section 3427.1.

(c) "Disrupting the normal functioning of a health care facility" means intentionally rendering or attempting to render a health care facility temporarily or permanently unavailable or unusable by a licensed health practitioner, the facility's staff, or patients. "Disrupting the normal functioning of a health care facility" does not include acts of the owner of the facility, an agent acting on behalf of the owner, or officers or employees of a governmental entity acting to protect the public health or safety.

(d) "Health care facility" means a facility that provides health care services directly to patients, including, but not limited to, a hospital, clinic, licensed health practitioner's office, health maintenance organization, diagnostic or treatment center, neuropsychiatric or mental health facility, hospice, or nursing home. *(Added by Stats.1994, c. 1193 (A.B.600), § 1.)*

§ 3427.1. Commercial blockade

It is unlawful, and constitutes the tort of commercial blockade for a person, alone or in concert with others, to intentionally prevent an individual from entering or exiting a health care facility by physically obstructing the individual's passage or by disrupting the normal functioning of a health care facility. *(Added by Stats.1994, c. 1193 (A.B.600), § 1.)*

§ 3427.2. Civil damages; parties to action

A person or health care facility aggrieved by the actions prohibited by this title may seek civil damages from those who committed the prohibited acts and those acting in concert with them. *(Added by Stats.1994, c. 1193 (A.B.600), § 1. Amended by Stats.1995, c. 91 (S.B.975), § 19.)*

§ 3427.3. Safeguarding individual privacy and prevention of harassment in civil proceeding

The court having jurisdiction over a civil proceeding under this title shall take all steps reasonably necessary to safeguard the individual privacy and prevent harassment of a health care patient, licensed health practitioner, or employee, client, or customer of a health care facility who is a party or witness in the proceeding, including granting protective orders. Health care patients, licensed health practitioners, and employees, clients, and customers of the health care facility may use pseudonyms to protect their privacy. *(Added by Stats. 1994, c. 1193 (A.B.600), § 1.)*

§ 3427.4. Construction

This title shall not be construed to impair any constitutionally protected activity or any activities protected by the labor laws of this state or the United States of America. *(Added by Stats.1994, c. 1193 (A.B.600), § 1.)*

Title 7

DUTY OF HEALTH CARE SERVICE PLANS AND MANAGED CARE ENTITIES

Section
3428. Duty of ordinary care; indemnity; liability; waiver; damages; exhaustion of procedures under medical review system.

§ 3428. Duty of ordinary care; indemnity; liability; waiver; damages; exhaustion of procedures under medical review system

(a) For services rendered on or after January 1, 2001, a health care service plan or managed care entity, as described in subdivision (f) of Section 1345 of the Health and Safety Code, shall have a duty of ordinary care to arrange for the provision of medically necessary health care service to its subscribers and enrollees, where the health care service is a benefit provided under the plan, and shall be liable for any and all harm legally caused by its failure to exercise that ordinary care when both of the following apply:

(1) The failure to exercise ordinary care resulted in the denial, delay, or modification of the health care service recommended for, or furnished to, a subscriber or enrollee.

(2) The subscriber or enrollee suffered substantial harm.

(b) For purposes of this section: (1) substantial harm means loss of life, loss or significant impairment of limb or bodily function, significant disfigurement, severe and chronic physical pain, or significant financial loss; (2) health care services need not be recommended or furnished by an in-plan provider, but may be recommended or furnished by any health care provider practicing within the scope of his or her practice; and (3) health care services shall be recommended or furnished at any time prior to the inception of the action, and the recommendation need not be made prior to the occurrence of substantial harm.

(c) Health care service plans and managed care entities are not health care providers under any provision of law, including, but not limited to, Section 6146 of the Business and Professions Code, Sections 3333.1 or 3333.2 of this code, or Sections 340.5, 364, 425.13, 667.7, or 1295 of the Code of Civil Procedure.

(d) A health care service plan or managed care entity shall not seek indemnity, whether contractual or equitable, from a provider for liability imposed under subdivision (a). Any provision to the contrary in a contract with providers is void and unenforceable.

(e) This section shall not create any liability on the part of an employer or an employer group purchasing organization that purchases coverage or assumes risk on behalf of its employees or on behalf of self-funded employee benefit plans.

(f) Any waiver by a subscriber or enrollee of the provisions of this section is contrary to public policy and shall be unenforceable and void.

(g) This section does not create any new or additional liability on the part of a health care service plan or managed care entity for harm caused that is attributable to the medical negligence of a treating physician or other treating health care provider.

(h) This section does not abrogate or limit any other theory of liability otherwise available at law.

(i) This section shall not apply in instances where subscribers or enrollees receive treatment by prayer, consistent with the provisions of subdivision (a) of Section 1270 of the Health and Safety Code, in lieu of medical treatment.

(j) Damages recoverable for a violation of this section include, but are not limited to, those set forth in Section 3333.

(k)(1) A person may not maintain a cause of action pursuant to this section against any entity required to comply with any independent medical review system or independent review system required by law unless the person or his or her representative has exhausted the procedures provided by the applicable independent review system.

(2) Compliance with paragraph (1) is not required in a case where either of the following applies:

(A) Substantial harm, as defined in subdivision (b), has occurred prior to the completion of the applicable review.

(B) Substantial harm, as defined, in subdivision (b), will imminently occur prior to the completion of the applicable review.

(3) This subdivision shall become operative only if Senate Bill 189 and Assembly Bill 55 of the 1999–2000 Regular Session are also enacted and enforceable.

(*l*) If any provision of this section or the application thereof to any person or circumstance is held to be unconstitutional or otherwise invalid or unenforceable, the remainder of the section and the application of those provisions to other persons or circumstances shall not be affected thereby.
(Added by Stats.1999, c. 536 (S.B.21), § 3.)

Cross References

Independent Medical Review System, see Health and Safety Code § 1374.30 et seq.; Insurance Code § 10169 et seq.

Part 2

SPECIAL RELATIONS OF DEBTOR AND CREDITOR

Title	Section
1. General Principles	3429
2. Void and Voidable Transfers and Undertakings	3439
3. Assignments for the Benefit of Creditors [Repealed]	

Title 1

GENERAL PRINCIPLES

Section	
3429.	Debtor defined.
3430.	Creditor defined.
3431.	Validity of debtor's contracts.
3432.	Payments or security in preference.
3433.	Marshaling assets.
3434.	Liability of lender financing design, manufacture, construction, repair, modification or improvement of real or personal property.

§ 3429. Debtor defined

A debtor, within the meaning of this Title, is one who, by reason of an existing obligation, is or may become liable to pay money to another, whether such liability is certain or contingent. *(Enacted in 1872.)*

§ 3430. Creditor defined

A creditor, within the meaning of this Title, is one in whose favor an obligation exists, by reason of which he is, or may become, entitled to the payment of money. *(Enacted in 1872.)*

§ 3431. Validity of debtor's contracts

In the absence of fraud, every contract of a debtor is valid against all his creditors, existing or subsequent, who have not acquired a lien on the property affected by such contract. *(Enacted in 1872.)*

§ 3432. Payments or security in preference

A debtor may pay one creditor in preference to another, or may give to one creditor security for the payment of his demand in preference to another. *(Enacted in 1872.)*

§ 3433. Marshaling assets

Where a creditor is entitled to resort to each of several funds for the satisfaction of his claim, and another person has an interest in, or is entitled as a creditor to resort to some, but not all of them, the latter may require the former to seek satisfaction from those funds to which the latter has no such claim, so far as it can be done without impairing the right of the former to complete satisfaction, and without doing injustice to third persons. *(Enacted in 1872.)*

Cross References

Marshaling liens, see Civil Code § 2899.

§ 3434. Liability of lender financing design, manufacture, construction, repair, modification or improvement of real or personal property

A lender who makes a loan of money, the proceeds of which are used or may be used by the borrower to finance the design, manufacture, construction, repair, modification or improvement of real or personal property for sale or lease to others, shall not be held liable to third persons for any loss or damage occasioned by any defect in the real or personal property so designed, manufactured, constructed, repaired, modified or improved or for any loss or damage resulting from the failure of the borrower to use due care in the design, manufacture, construction, repair, modification or improvement of such real or personal property, unless such loss or damage is a result of an act of the lender outside the scope of the activities of a lender of money or unless the lender has been a party to misrepresentations with respect to such real or personal property. *(Added by Stats.1969, c. 1584, p. 3222, § 1.)*

Title 2

VOID AND VOIDABLE TRANSFERS AND UNDERTAKINGS

Chapter	Section
1. Uniform Voidable Transactions Act	3439
2. Conveyance of Personal Property Without Delivery	3440
3. Undertaking in Voidable Transfer Action	3445

CHAPTER 1. UNIFORM VOIDABLE TRANSACTIONS ACT

Section	
3439.	Short title.
3439.01.	Definitions.
3439.02.	Insolvency.
3439.03.	Value.
3439.04.	Transfers voidable as to present and future creditors; factors to determining intent.
3439.05.	Transfers voidable as to present creditors.
3439.06.	When transfer is made or obligation is incurred.
3439.07.	Remedies of creditors.
3439.08.	Defenses, liability, and protection of transferee; burden of proof.
3439.09.	Extinguishment of cause of action.
3439.10.	Governing law.
3439.11.	Renumbered.
3439.12.	Supplementary provisions.
3439.13.	Uniformity of application and construction.
3439.14.	Application; prior provisions; construction.

§ 3439. Short title

This chapter may be cited as the Uniform Voidable Transactions Act. *(Added by Stats.1986, c. 383, § 2. Amended by Stats.2015, c. 44 (S.B.161), § 3, eff. Jan. 1, 2016.)*

Cross References

Actions for relief against transfer or obligation under this chapter, see Civil Code § 3446.
Attorney General, proceedings to set aside fraudulent conveyances, see Government Code § 12517.
Fraud as a question of fact, see Civil Code § 1574.
Penal provisions, see Penal Code §§ 154, 155.
Personal representative, recovery of property fraudulently conveyed by decedent, see Probate Code § 9653.
Retention of possession after sale of goods, rights of seller's creditors, see Commercial Code § 2402.
Security interests, filing required to perfect, see Commercial Code § 9302.
Unlawful transfers, see Civil Code § 1227 et seq.

§ 3439.01. Definitions

As used in this chapter the following definitions are applicable:

(a) "Asset" means property of a debtor, but the term does not include the following:

(1) Property to the extent it is encumbered by a valid lien.

(2) Property to the extent it is generally exempt under nonbankruptcy law.

(3) An interest in property held in tenancy by the entireties to the extent it is not subject to process by a creditor holding a claim against only one tenant.

(b) "Claim," except as used in "claim for relief," means a right to payment, whether or not the right is reduced to judgment, liquidated, unliquidated, fixed, contingent, matured, unmatured, disputed, undisputed, legal, equitable, secured, or unsecured.

(c) "Creditor" means a person that has a claim, and includes an assignee of a general assignment for the benefit of creditors, as defined in Section 493.010 of the Code of Civil Procedure, of a debtor.

(d) "Debt" means liability on a claim.

(e) "Debtor" means a person that is liable on a claim.

(f) "Electronic" means relating to technology having electrical, digital, magnetic, wireless, optical, electromagnetic, or similar capabilities.

(g) "Lien" means a charge against or an interest in property to secure payment of a debt or performance of an obligation, and includes a security interest created by agreement, a judicial lien obtained by legal or equitable process or proceedings, a common-law lien, or a statutory lien.

(h) "Organization" means a person other than an individual.

(i) "Person" means an individual, partnership, corporation, limited liability company, association, government or governmental subdivision, instrumentality or agency, business trust, estate, trust, business or nonprofit entity, or other legal entity.

(j) "Property" means anything that may be the subject of ownership.

(k) "Record" means information that is inscribed on a tangible medium or that is stored in an electronic or other medium and is retrievable in perceivable form.

(l) "Sign" means, with present intent to authenticate or adopt a record, to either (1) execute or adopt a tangible symbol, or (2) attach to or logically associate with the record an electronic symbol, sound, or process.

(m) "Transfer" means every mode, direct or indirect, absolute or conditional, voluntary or involuntary, of disposing of or parting with an asset or an interest in an asset, and includes payment of money, release, lease, license, and creation of a lien or other encumbrance.

(n) "Valid lien" means a lien that is effective against the holder of a judicial lien subsequently obtained by legal or equitable process or proceedings. (Added by Stats.1986, c. 383, § 2. Amended by Stats.1994, c. 1010 (S.B.2053), § 55; Stats.2015, c. 44 (S.B.161), § 4, eff. Jan. 1, 2016.)

§ 3439.02. Insolvency

(a) A debtor is insolvent if, at a fair valuation, the sum of the debtor's debts is greater than the sum of the debtor's assets.

(b) A debtor that is generally not paying the debtor's debts as they become due other than as a result of a bona fide dispute is presumed to be insolvent. The presumption imposes on the party against which the presumption is directed the burden of proving that the nonexistence of insolvency is more probable than its existence.

(c) Assets under this section do not include property that has been transferred, concealed, or removed with intent to hinder, delay, or defraud creditors or that has been transferred in a manner making the transfer voidable under this chapter.

(d) Debts under this section do not include an obligation to the extent it is secured by a valid lien on property of the debtor not included as an asset. (Added by Stats.1986, c. 383, § 2. Amended by Stats.2015, c. 44 (S.B.161), § 5, eff. Jan. 1, 2016.)

§ 3439.03. Value

Value is given for a transfer or an obligation if, in exchange for the transfer or obligation, property is transferred or an antecedent debt is secured or satisfied, but value does not include an unperformed promise made otherwise than in the ordinary course of the promisor's business to furnish support to the debtor or another person. (Added by Stats.1986, c. 383, § 2.)

§ 3439.04. Transfers voidable as to present and future creditors; factors to determining intent

(a) A transfer made or obligation incurred by a debtor is voidable as to a creditor, whether the creditor's claim arose before or after the transfer was made or the obligation was incurred, if the debtor made the transfer or incurred the obligation as follows:

(1) With actual intent to hinder, delay, or defraud any creditor of the debtor.

(2) Without receiving a reasonably equivalent value in exchange for the transfer or obligation, and the debtor either:

(A) Was engaged or was about to engage in a business or a transaction for which the remaining assets of the debtor were unreasonably small in relation to the business or transaction.

§ 3439.04

(B) Intended to incur, or believed or reasonably should have believed that the debtor would incur, debts beyond the debtor's ability to pay as they became due.

(b) In determining actual intent under paragraph (1) of subdivision (a), consideration may be given, among other factors, to any or all of the following:

(1) Whether the transfer or obligation was to an insider.

(2) Whether the debtor retained possession or control of the property transferred after the transfer.

(3) Whether the transfer or obligation was disclosed or concealed.

(4) Whether before the transfer was made or obligation was incurred, the debtor had been sued or threatened with suit.

(5) Whether the transfer was of substantially all the debtor's assets.

(6) Whether the debtor absconded.

(7) Whether the debtor removed or concealed assets.

(8) Whether the value of the consideration received by the debtor was reasonably equivalent to the value of the asset transferred or the amount of the obligation incurred.

(9) Whether the debtor was insolvent or became insolvent shortly after the transfer was made or the obligation was incurred.

(10) Whether the transfer occurred shortly before or shortly after a substantial debt was incurred.

(11) Whether the debtor transferred the essential assets of the business to a lienor that transferred the assets to an insider of the debtor.

(c) A creditor making a claim for relief under subdivision (a) has the burden of proving the elements of the claim for relief by a preponderance of the evidence. (Added by Stats.1986, c. 383, § 2. Amended by Stats.2004, c. 50 (S.B. 1408), § 1; Stats.2015, c. 44 (S.B.161), § 6, eff. Jan. 1, 2016.)

Cross References

Conveyances made with intent to defraud creditors or to hinder and delay creditors prohibited, see Penal Code § 531.

§ 3439.05. Transfers voidable as to present creditors

(a) A transfer made or obligation incurred by a debtor is voidable as to a creditor whose claim arose before the transfer was made or the obligation was incurred if the debtor made the transfer or incurred the obligation without receiving a reasonably equivalent value in exchange for the transfer or obligation and the debtor was insolvent at that time or the debtor became insolvent as a result of the transfer or obligation.

(b) A creditor making a claim for relief under subdivision (a) has the burden of proving the elements of the claim for relief by a preponderance of the evidence. (Added by Stats.1986, c. 383, § 2. Amended by Stats.2015, c. 44 (S.B. 161), § 7, eff. Jan. 1, 2016.)

§ 3439.06. When transfer is made or obligation is incurred

For the purposes of this chapter:

(a) A transfer is made:

(1) With respect to an asset that is real property other than a fixture, but including the interest of a seller or purchaser under a contract for the sale of the asset, when the transfer is so far perfected that a good faith purchaser of the asset from the debtor against which applicable law permits the transfer to be perfected cannot acquire an interest in the asset that is superior to the interest of the transferee; and

(2) With respect to an asset that is not real property or that is a fixture, when the transfer is so far perfected that a creditor on a simple contract cannot acquire a judicial lien otherwise than under this chapter that is superior to the interest of the transferee.

(b) If applicable law permits the transfer to be perfected as provided in subdivision (a) and the transfer is not so perfected before the commencement of an action for relief under this chapter, the transfer is deemed made immediately before the commencement of the action.

(c) If applicable law does not permit the transfer to be perfected as provided in subdivision (a), the transfer is made when it becomes effective between the debtor and the transferee.

(d) A transfer is not made until the debtor has acquired rights in the asset transferred.

(e) An obligation is incurred:

(1) If oral, when it becomes effective between the parties; or

(2) If evidenced by a record, when the record signed by the obligor is delivered to or for the benefit of the obligee. (Added by Stats.1986, c. 383, § 2. Amended by Stats.2015, c. 44 (S.B.161), § 8, eff. Jan. 1, 2016.)

§ 3439.07. Remedies of creditors

(a) In an action for relief against a transfer or obligation under this chapter, a creditor, subject to the limitations in Section 3439.08, may obtain:

(1) Avoidance of the transfer or obligation to the extent necessary to satisfy the creditor's claim.

(2) An attachment or other provisional remedy against the asset transferred or other property of the transferee in accordance with the procedures described in Title 6.5 (commencing with Section 481.010) of Part 2 of the Code of Civil Procedure, or as may otherwise be available under applicable law.

(3) Subject to applicable principles of equity and in accordance with applicable rules of civil procedure, the following:

(A) An injunction against further disposition by the debtor or a transferee, or both, of the asset transferred or other property of the transferee.

(B) Appointment of a receiver to take charge of the asset transferred or other property of the transferee.

(C) Any other relief the circumstances may require.

(b) If a creditor has commenced an action on a claim against the debtor, the creditor may attach the asset transferred or other property of the transferee if the remedy of attachment is available in the action under applicable law and the property is subject to attachment in the hands of the transferee under applicable law.

(c) If a creditor has obtained a judgment on a claim against the debtor, the creditor may levy execution on the asset transferred or its proceeds.

(d) A creditor who is an assignee of a general assignment for the benefit of creditors, as defined in Section 493.010 of the Code of Civil Procedure, may exercise any and all of the rights and remedies specified in this section if they are available to any one or more creditors of the assignor who are beneficiaries of the assignment, and, in that event (1) only to the extent the rights or remedies are so available and (2) only for the benefit of those creditors whose rights are asserted by the assignee. *(Added by Stats.1986, c. 383, § 2. Amended by Stats.2015, c. 44 (S.B.161), § 9, eff. Jan. 1, 2016.)*

§ 3439.08. Defenses, liability, and protection of transferee; burden of proof

(a) A transfer or obligation is not voidable under paragraph (1) of subdivision (a) of Section 3439.04, against a person that took in good faith and for a reasonably equivalent value given the debtor or against any subsequent transferee or obligee.

(b) To the extent a transfer is avoidable in an action by a creditor under paragraph (1) of subdivision (a) of Section 3439.07, the following rules apply:

(1) Except as otherwise provided in this section, the creditor may recover judgment for the value of the asset transferred, as adjusted under subdivision (c), or the amount necessary to satisfy the creditor's claim, whichever is less. The judgment may be entered against the following:

(A) The first transferee of the asset or the person for whose benefit the transfer was made.

(B) An immediate or mediate transferee of the first transferee, other than either of the following:

(i) A good faith transferee that took for value.

(ii) An immediate or mediate good faith transferee of a person described in clause (i).

(2) Recovery pursuant to paragraph (1) of subdivision (a), or subdivision (b), or subdivision (c) of Section 3439.07 of or from the asset transferred or its proceeds, or other property of the transferee, as applicable, by levy or otherwise, is available only against a person described in subparagraph (A) or (B) of paragraph (1).

(c) If the judgment under subdivision (b) is based upon the value of the asset transferred, the judgment shall be for an amount equal to the value of the asset at the time of the transfer, subject to adjustment as the equities may require.

(d) Notwithstanding voidability of a transfer or an obligation under this chapter, a good faith transferee or obligee is entitled, to the extent of the value given the debtor for the transfer or obligation, to the following:

(1) A lien on or a right to retain an interest in the asset transferred.

(2) Enforcement of an obligation incurred.

(3) A reduction in the amount of the liability on the judgment.

(e) A transfer is not voidable under paragraph (2) of subdivision (a) of Section 3439.04 or Section 3439.05 if the transfer results from either of the following:

(1) Termination of a lease upon default by the debtor when the termination is pursuant to the lease and applicable law.

(2) Enforcement of a lien in a noncollusive manner and in compliance with applicable law, including Division 9 (commencing with Section 9101) of the Commercial Code, other than a retention of collateral under Sections 9620 and 9621 of the Commercial Code and other than a voluntary transfer of the collateral by the debtor to the lienor in satisfaction of all or part of the secured obligation.

(f) The following rules determine the burden of proving matters referred to in this section:

(1) A party that seeks to invoke subdivision (a), (d), or (e) has the burden of proving the applicability of that subdivision.

(2) Except as otherwise provided in paragraph (3) or (4), the creditor has the burden of proving each applicable element of subdivision (b) or (c).

(3) The transferee has the burden of proving the applicability to the transferee of subparagraph (B) of paragraph (1) of subdivision (b).

(4) A party that seeks adjustment under subdivision (c) has the burden of proving the adjustment.

(g) The standard of proof required to establish matters referred to in this section is preponderance of the evidence. *(Added by Stats.1986, c. 383, § 2. Amended by Stats.1987, c. 40, § 1, eff. June 8, 1987; Stats.1999, c. 991 (S.B.45), § 9, operative July 1, 2001; Stats.2005, c. 34 (A.B.248), § 1, eff. July 7, 2005; Stats.2015, c. 44 (S.B.161), § 10, eff. Jan. 1, 2016.)*

§ 3439.09. Extinguishment of cause of action

A cause of action with respect to a transfer or obligation under this chapter is extinguished unless action is brought pursuant to subdivision (a) of Section 3439.07 or levy made as provided in subdivision (b) or (c) of Section 3439.07:

(a) Under paragraph (1) of subdivision (a) of Section 3439.04, not later than four years after the transfer was made or the obligation was incurred or, if later, not later than one year after the transfer or obligation was or could reasonably have been discovered by the claimant.

(b) Under paragraph (2) of subdivision (a) of Section 3439.04 or Section 3439.05, not later than four years after the transfer was made or the obligation was incurred.

(c) Notwithstanding any other provision of law, a cause of action under this chapter with respect to a transfer or obligation is extinguished if no action is brought or levy made within seven years after the transfer was made or the obligation was incurred. *(Added by Stats.1986, c. 383, § 2. Amended by Stats.2005, c. 34 (A.B.248), § 2, eff. July 7, 2005; Stats.2015, c. 44 (S.B.161), § 11, eff. Jan. 1, 2016.)*

§ 3439.10. Governing law

(a) In this section, the following rules determine a debtor's location:

(1) A debtor who is an individual is located at the individual's principal residence.

(2) A debtor that is an organization and has only one place of business is located at its place of business.

(3) A debtor that is an organization and has more than one place of business is located at its chief executive office.

(b) A claim in the nature of a claim under this chapter is governed by the local law of the jurisdiction in which the debtor is located when the transfer is made or the obligation is incurred. *(Added by Stats.2015, c. 44 (S.B.161), § 13, eff. Jan. 1, 2016.)*

§ 3439.11. Renumbered § 3439.13 and amended by Stats. 2015, c. 44 (S.B.161), § 14, eff. Jan. 1, 2016

§ 3439.12. Supplementary provisions

Unless displaced by the provisions of this chapter, the principles of law and equity, including the law merchant and the law relating to principal and agent, estoppel, laches, fraud, misrepresentation, duress, coercion, mistake, insolvency, or other validating or invalidating cause, supplement its provisions. *(Formerly § 3439.10, added by Stats.1986, c. 383, § 2. Renumbered § 3439.12 and amended by Stats.2015, c. 44 (S.B.161), § 12, eff. Jan. 1, 2016.)*

§ 3439.13. Uniformity of application and construction

This chapter shall be applied and construed to effectuate its general purpose to make uniform the law with respect to the subject of this chapter among states enacting it. *(Formerly § 3439.11, added by Stats.1986, c. 383, § 2. Renumbered § 3439.13 and amended by Stats.2015, c. 44 (S.B.161), § 14, eff. Jan. 1, 2016.)*

§ 3439.14. Application; prior provisions; construction

(a) The changes to this chapter made by the act adding this subdivision apply only to a right of action that accrued, transfer made, or obligation incurred, on or after the effective date of that act.

(b) This chapter, and the other changes in the law made by Chapter 383 of the Statutes of 1986, apply only to transfers made or obligations incurred before the effective date of the act that added subdivision (a) and on or after January 1, 1987. As to transfers made or obligations incurred prior to January 1, 1987, the law in effect at the time the transfer was made or the obligation was incurred shall apply.

(c) Section 3439.06 shall determine the date that a transfer was made or obligation incurred.

(d) The provisions of this chapter, insofar as they are substantially the same as the provisions of this chapter in effect on December 31, 2015, shall be construed as restatements and continuations, and not as new enactments. *(Formerly § 3439.12, added by Stats.1987, c. 40, § 2, eff. June 8, 1987. Renumbered § 3439.14 and amended by Stats.2015, c. 44 (S.B.161), § 15, eff. Jan. 1, 2016.)*

CHAPTER 2. CONVEYANCE OF PERSONAL PROPERTY WITHOUT DELIVERY

Section
3440. Transfers without delivery and actual and continued change of possession; invalidity; creditors.
3440.1. Exceptions; application of chapter.
3440.2. Invalidity of transfer; exception.
3440.3. Transfers satisfying specified provisions; invalidity.

Section
3440.4. Buyers purchasing transferred personal property from transferees or successors in interest; rights of buyers; effect of chapter.
3440.5. Rights of secured party acquiring security interest from transferee or successor.
3440.6. Actions; limitations.
3440.9. Application of chapter to Commercial Code provisions.
3441. Renumbered.
3442. Renumbered.
3443. Renumbered.

§ 3440. Transfers without delivery and actual and continued change of possession; invalidity; creditors

(a) Except as otherwise provided in this chapter, every transfer of personal property made by a person having at the time the possession of the property, and not accompanied by an immediate delivery followed by an actual and continued change of possession of the property, is void as against the transferor's creditors (secured or unsecured) at the time of the transfer and those who become creditors while the transferor remains in possession and the successors in interest of those creditors, and as against buyers from the transferor for value in good faith subsequent to the transfer.

(b) As used in this chapter, "creditor" means a person who has a claim, as defined in Section 3439.01, and includes an assignee of a general assignment for the benefit of creditors, as defined in Section 493.010 of the Code of Civil Procedure, of a debtor. "Creditor" also includes any person to whom the transferor's estate devolves in trust for the benefit of persons other than the transferor. Any such assignee or trustee may exercise any and all the rights and remedies specified in this chapter, if they are available to any one or more creditors of the assignor or transferor who are beneficiaries of the assignment or trust, and, in that event (1) only to the extent the rights or remedies are so available and (2) only for the benefit of those creditors whose rights are asserted by the assignee or trustee. *(Added by Stats.1951, c. 1687, p. 3884, § 2. Amended by Stats.1953, c. 1775, p. 3547, § 1; Stats.1959, c. 1794, p. 4274, § 1; Stats.1959, c. 1795, p. 4276, § 2; Stats.1963, c. 819, p. 2001, § 22, eff. Jan. 1, 1965; Stats.1967, c. 799, p. 2200, § 1; Stats.1982, c. 517, p. 2330, § 89; Stats.1985, c. 1368, § 1; Stats.1987, c. 40, § 3, eff. June 8, 1987.)*

Cross References

Action for relief against a fraudulent transfer or obligation, see Civil Code § 3446.
Conclusive presumptions, see Evidence Code § 620 et seq.
Personal representative, action by to recover fraudulently conveyed property, see Probate Code § 9653.
Tax liability of successors, see Revenue and Taxation Code §§ 6811, 6812; Unemployment Insurance Code § 1731 et seq.

§ 3440.1. Exceptions; application of chapter

This chapter does not apply to any of the following:

(a) Things in action.

(b) Ships or cargoes if either are at sea or in a foreign port.

(c) The sale of accounts, chattel paper, payment intangibles, or promissory notes governed by the Uniform Commercial Code, security interests, and contracts of bottomry or respondentia.

(d) Wines or brandies in the wineries, distilleries, or wine cellars of the makers or owners of the wines or brandies, or other persons having possession, care, and control of the wines or brandies, and the pipes, casks, and tanks in which the wines or brandies are contained, if the transfers are made in writing and executed and acknowledged, and if the transfers are recorded in the book of official records in the office of the county recorder of the county in which the wines, brandies, pipes, casks, and tanks are situated.

(e) A transfer or assignment made for the benefit of creditors generally or by an assignee acting under an assignment for the benefit of creditors generally.

(f) Property exempt from enforcement of a money judgment.

(g) Standing timber.

(h) Subject to the limitations in Section 3440.3, a transfer of personal property if all of the following conditions are satisfied:

(1) Before the date of the intended transfer, the transferor or the transferee files a financing statement, with respect to the property transferred, authorized in an authenticated record by the transferor. The financing statement shall be filed in the office of the Secretary of State in accordance with Chapter 5 (commencing with Section 9501) of Division 9 of the Commercial Code, but may use the terms "transferor" in lieu of "debtor" and "transferee" in lieu of "secured party." The provisions of Chapter 5 (commencing with Section 9501) of Division 9 of the Commercial Code shall apply as appropriate to the financing statement.

(2) The transferor or the transferee publishes a notice of the intended transfer one time in a newspaper of general circulation published in the public notice district in which the personal property is located, if there is one, and if there is none in the public notice district, then in a newspaper of general circulation in the county in which the personal property is located. The publication shall be completed not less than 10 days before the date the transfer occurs. The notice shall contain the name and address of the transferor and transferee and a general statement of the character of the personal property intended to be transferred, and shall indicate the place where the personal property is located and a date on or after which the transfer is to be made.

(i) Personal property not located within this state at the time of the transfer or attachment of the lien if the provisions of this subdivision are not used for the purpose of evading this chapter.

(j) A transfer of property that (1) is subject to a statute or treaty of the United States or a statute of this state that provides for the registration of transfers of title or issuance of certificates of title and (2) is so far perfected under that statute or treaty that a bona fide purchaser cannot acquire an interest in the property transferred that is superior to the interest of the transferee.

(k) A transfer of personal property in connection with a transaction in which the property is immediately thereafter leased by the transferor from the transferee provided the transferee purchased the property for value and in good faith pursuant to subdivision (c) of Section 10308 of the Commercial Code.

(*l*) Water supply property, as defined in Section 849 of the Public Utilities Code.

(m) A transfer of property by any governmental entity.

(n) For the purposes of this section, publication of notice in a public notice district is governed by Chapter 1.1 (commencing with Section 6080) of Division 7 of Title 1 of the Government Code. *(Formerly § 3441, added by Stats. 1982, c. 517, p. 2330, § 90. Renumbered § 3440.1 and amended by Stats.1985, c. 1368, § 6. Amended by Stats.1988, c. 1368, § 3, operative Jan. 1, 1990; Stats.1994, c. 668 (S.B.1405), § 3; Stats.1996, c. 854 (A.B.1890), § 3, eff. Sept. 24, 1996; Stats.1999, c. 991 (S.B.45), § 10, operative July 1, 2001; Stats.2004, c. 46 (S.B.772), § 3, eff. June 7, 2004; Stats.2005, c. 43 (A.B.238), § 1; Stats.2012, c. 60 (A.B.2667), § 1; Stats.2014, c. 482 (S.B.936), § 3, eff. Jan. 1, 2015; Stats.2016, c. 703 (A.B.2881), § 4, eff. Jan. 1, 2017.)*

Cross References

Bottomry, see Harbors and Navigation Code § 450 et seq.
Conflicting security interests in inventory, priorities, see Commercial Code § 9312.
Filing to perfect security interest, see Commercial Code § 9401 et seq.
Financing statement, necessity of filing, see Commercial Code §§ 9302, 9304, 9401, 9403.
Property exempt from enforcement of money judgment, see Code of Civil Procedure § 703.010 et seq.
Respondentia, see Harbors and Navigation Code § 470 et seq.
Secured transactions, see Commercial Code § 9101 et seq.
Security interest defined, see Commercial Code § 1201.
Things in action, transfer, see Civil Code § 953.

§ 3440.2. Invalidity of transfer; exception

Subject to Section 3440.3, a transfer of personal property shall not be void under Section 3440 as against a creditor of the transferor or as against a buyer from the transferor, if the creditor's or buyer's claim or right against the transferor arises after the date all of the requirements of subdivision (h) of Section 3440.1 have been met, other than the requirement that filing of the financing statement and publication of the notice referred to therein be completed prior to the transfer. *(Added by Stats.1985, c. 1368, § 2.)*

§ 3440.3. Transfers satisfying specified provisions; invalidity

A transfer of personal property, as to which the conditions set forth in subdivision (h) of Section 3440.1, Section 3440.2, or subdivision (b) of Section 3440.5 are satisfied, shall, nevertheless, be void under Section 3440 as against a person who has purchased the personal property from the transferor and who is a "buyer in the ordinary course of business," as defined in paragraph (9) of subdivision (b) of Section 1201 of the Commercial Code. *(Added by Stats.1985, c. 1368, § 3. Amended by Stats.2006, c. 254 (S.B.1481), § 5.)*

Application

For provision relating to application of Stats.2006, c. 254 (S.B.1481) to documents of title that are issued or bailments that arise before Jan. 1, 2007, see § 81 of that act.

§ 3440.4. Buyers purchasing transferred personal property from transferees or successors in interest; rights of buyers; effect of chapter

This chapter does not affect the rights of a buyer for value in good faith who purchases the transferred personal property from the transferee or from a successor in interest of the transferee, provided the transferor is no longer in possession of the personal property at the time of the purchase by that buyer. *(Added by Stats.1985, c. 1368, § 4.)*

§ 3440.5. Rights of secured party acquiring security interest from transferee or successor

(a) This chapter does not affect the rights of a secured party who, for value and in good faith, acquires a security interest in the transferred personal property from the transferee, or from the transferee's successor in interest, if the transferor is no longer in possession of the personal property at the time the security interest attaches.

(b) Additionally, except as provided in Section 3440.3, this chapter does not affect the rights of a secured party who acquires a security interest from the transferee, or from the transferee's successor in interest, in the personal property, if all of the following conditions are satisfied:

(1) On or before the date the security agreement is executed, the intended debtor or secured party files a financing statement with respect to the property transferred, signed by the intended debtor. The financing statement shall be filed in the office of the Secretary of State in accordance with Chapter 5 (commencing with Section 9501) of Division 9 of the Commercial Code, but shall use the terms "transferor" in lieu of "debtor," "transferee" in lieu of "secured party," and "secured party" in lieu of "assignee of secured party." The provisions of Chapter 5 (commencing with Section 9501) of Division 9 of the Commercial Code shall apply as appropriate to the financing statement. For the purpose of indexing, and in any certification of search, the Secretary of State may refer to any financing statement filed pursuant to this paragraph as a financing statement under the Commercial Code and may describe the transferor as a debtor and the transferee as a secured party.

(2) The intended debtor or secured party publishes a notice of the transfer one time in a newspaper of general circulation published in the public notice district in which the personal property is located, if there is one, and if there is none in the public notice district, then in a newspaper of general circulation in the county in which the personal property is located. The publication shall be completed not less than 10 days before the date of execution by the intended debtor of the intended security agreement. The notice shall contain the names and addresses of the transferor and transferee and of the intended debtor and secured party, a general statement of the character of the personal property transferred and intended to be subject to the security interest, the location of the personal property, and the date on or after which the security agreement is to be executed by the intended debtor.

(c) Compliance with paragraph (1) of subdivision (b) shall not perfect the security interest of the secured party. Perfection of that security interest shall be governed by Division 9 (commencing with Section 9101) of the Commercial Code.

(d) For the purposes of this section, publication of notice in a public notice district is governed by Chapter 1.1 (commencing with Section 6080) of Division 7 of Title 1 of the Government Code. *(Formerly § 3442, added by Stats. 1982, c. 517, p. 2331, § 91. Renumbered § 3440.5 and amended by Stats.1985, c. 1368, § 9. Amended by Stats.1999, c. 991 (S.B.45), § 11, operative July 1, 2001; Stats.2000, c. 1003 (S.B.2002), § 2, operative July 1, 2001; Stats.2016, c. 703 (A.B.2881), § 5, eff. Jan. 1, 2017.)*

§ 3440.6. Actions; limitations

No action shall be brought or levy made under this chapter more than one year after the earliest of the following dates:

(a) The date the person bringing the action or making the levy should have discovered the transfer in the exercise of reasonable diligence.

(b) The date the person bringing the action or making the levy obtained actual knowledge of the transfer.

(c) The date the delivery of, and actual and continued change of possession of, the property transferred occurred.

(d) If the financing statement filed pursuant to subdivision (h) of Section 3440.1 has not lapsed, the date the filing and publication requirements of subdivision (h) of Section 3440.1 were met, other than the requirement that the filing of the financing statement and publication of the notice referred to therein be completed prior to the transfer. *(Added by Stats.1985, c. 1368, § 5.)*

§ 3440.9. Application of chapter to Commercial Code provisions

Subdivision (2) of Section 2402 and subdivision (a) of Section 10308 of the Commercial Code are not restricted by the provisions of this chapter. *(Formerly § 3443, added by Stats.1982, c. 517, p. 2331, § 92. Renumbered § 3440.9 and amended by Stats.1985, c. 1368, § 10. Amended by Stats.1988, c. 1368, § 4, operative Jan. 1, 1990; Stats.1994, c. 668 (S.B.1405), § 4.)*

§ 3441. Renumbered § 3440.1 and amended by Stats.1985, c. 1368, § 6

§ 3442. Renumbered § 3440.5 and amended by Stats.1985, c. 1368, § 9

§ 3443. Renumbered § 3440.9 and amended by Stats.1985, c. 1368, § 10

CHAPTER 3. UNDERTAKING IN VOIDABLE TRANSFER ACTION

Section
3445. Definitions.
3446. Transferee; rights of disposition of property or obligation.
3447. Condition; payment to creditor.
3448. Amount.
3449. Effective date of undertaking.

Cross References

Bond and Undertaking Law, see Code of Civil Procedure § 995.010 et seq.

§ 3445. Definitions

As used in this chapter:

(a) "Transfer" means "transfer" as defined in Section 3439.01.

(b) "Creditor" means "creditor" as defined in Section 3439.01.

(c) "Transferee" means the person to whom property was transferred or an obligation was incurred, or the successors or assigns of the person. *(Added by Stats.1982, c. 517, p. 2332, § 93. Amended by Stats.1986, c. 383, § 4.)*

§ 3446. Transferee; rights of disposition of property or obligation

(a) In an action by a creditor for relief against a transfer or obligation under Chapter 1 (commencing with Section 3439) of Title 2 of Part 2 of Division 4 on the ground that the transfer or obligation is voidable as to the creditor, the transferee may give an undertaking as provided in this chapter.

(b) If an undertaking is given as provided in this chapter, the transferee may sell, encumber, transfer, convey, mortgage, pledge, or otherwise dispose of the property or obligation, or a part thereof, and the purchaser, encumbrancer, transferee, mortgagee, grantee, or pledgee of the property or obligation takes, owns, holds, and possesses the property or obligation unaffected by the action and any judgment that is rendered in the action. *(Added by Stats.1982, c. 517, p. 2332, § 93. Amended by Stats.1986, c. 383, § 5; Stats.2015, c. 44 (S.B.161), § 17, eff. Jan. 1, 2016.)*

§ 3447. Condition; payment to creditor

The undertaking shall be conditioned that, if it is determined in the action that the transfer or obligation was voidable as to the creditor, the transferee will pay to the creditor the lesser of the following amounts:

(a) The value of the property or obligation as estimated in the undertaking.

(b) The amount determined in the action to be due and owing to the creditor by the person who transferred the property or incurred the obligation. *(Added by Stats.1982, c. 517, p. 2332, § 93. Amended by Stats.1986, c. 383, § 6; Stats.2015, c. 44 (S.B.161), § 18, eff. Jan. 1, 2016.)*

§ 3448. Amount

The undertaking shall be in the lesser of the following amounts:

(a) Double the value of the property or obligation.

(b) Double the amount of the creditor's claim in the action. *(Added by Stats.1982, c. 517, p. 2332, § 93.)*

§ 3449. Effective date of undertaking

The undertaking becomes effective 10 days after service of the undertaking on the creditor. *(Added by Stats.1982, c. 517, p. 2332, § 93.)*

Title 3

ASSIGNMENTS FOR THE BENEFIT OF CREDITORS [REPEALED]

§§ 3450 to 3452. Repealed by Stats.1980, c. 135, p. 313, § 3

§§ 3453 to 3456. Repealed by Code Am.1873–74, c. 612, p. 267, § 281

§§ 3457 to 3473. Repealed by Stats.1980, c. 135, § 3

Part 3

NUISANCE

Title	Section
1. General Principles	3479
2. Public Nuisances	3490
3. Private Nuisances	3501
4. Motion Pictures	3504

Title 1

GENERAL PRINCIPLES

Section
3479. Nuisance; what constitutes.
3480. Public nuisance.
3481. Private nuisance.
3482. Acts under statutory authority not a nuisance.
3482.1. Operation or use of sport shooting ranges; civil liability or criminal prosecution; noise or noise pollution nuisance.
3482.5. Agricultural activity not a nuisance; exceptions; construction with other laws.
3482.6. Agricultural processing activity not a nuisance; increase in activity; construction with other laws.
3482.7. Repealed.
3482.8. Use of building or property for dogfighting or cockfighting; public nuisance.
3483. Continuing nuisance; liability of successive owners for failure to abate.
3484. Damages recoverable notwithstanding abatement.
3485. Illegal conduct involving unlawful weapons or ammunition purpose; unlawful detainer action by city prosecutor or city attorney to abate nuisance; notice; application; information provided to California Research Bureau.
3486. Illegal conduct involving controlled substance purpose; unlawful detainer action by city prosecutor or city attorney to abate nuisance in City of Los Angeles; notice; waiver of testimony costs; information provided to California Research Bureau.
3486.5. Application of Section 3486 to City of Long Beach, City of Sacramento, and City of Oakland; information provided to California Research Bureau.

Cross References

Abandoned excavations as public nuisances, see Government Code § 50230 et seq.
Actions to abate nuisances, see Code of Civil Procedure § 731 et seq.
Adjudication, stay on appeal, see Code of Civil Procedure § 917.8.
Advertising displays violating regulations, see Business and Professions Code § 5461.
Airport hazards as public nuisances, see Government Code § 50485.2.
Airport or airpark, presumption, see Code of Civil Procedure § 731b.
Alcoholic beverages,
  Place of unlawful sale as nuisance, see Penal Code § 11200.
  Unlicensed premises as nuisance, see Business and Professions Code § 25604.
California Land Reuse and Revitalization Act, definitions, applicable law, see Health and Safety Code § 25395.66.
Caprifig trees as nuisances, see Food and Agricultural Code § 6172.
Cesspools as public nuisances, see Water Code §§ 13950, 13951, 31103, 35503.
Commercial or industrial zone, permitted use, see Code of Civil Procedure § 731a.
Concealed weapon as nuisance, see Penal Code § 29300.
Controlled substances, place used for as a nuisance, see Health and Safety Code § 11570.
Cotton, nonconforming variety, nuisance, see Food and Agricultural Code § 52974 et seq.
County abatement procedure, special assessment, see Government Code § 25845.
County highways, encroachment as a nuisance, see Streets and Highways Code § 1484.
Department of Health Care Services, power to abate public nuisances, see Health and Safety Code § 100170.
Department of Public Health, power to abate public nuisances, see Health and Safety Code § 131075.
Destructive devices, possession as public nuisance, see Penal Code § 19000.
Diseased apiaries, nuisance, see Food and Agricultural Code § 29204.
Diseased fish, amphibia and aquatic plants, destruction as nuisance, see Fish and Game Code § 6302.
District attorney, abatement of nuisances, see Government Code § 26528.
Dourine infected animals as public nuisance, see Food and Agricultural Code § 9621.
Drinking water, noncompliance with standards as public nuisance, see Health and Safety Code § 116670.
Egg products and containers in violation of regulations as public nuisances, see Food and Agricultural Code § 27601.
Employee housing not conforming to regulations as public nuisance, see Health and Safety Code § 17060.
Encroachment on highways, public nuisance, see Streets and Highways Code §§ 723 et seq., 1484.
Fire hazard as public nuisance, see Public Resources Code § 4171 et seq.
Fire uncontrolled as public nuisance, abatement, see Public Resources Code § 4170.5.
Fish reduction plant as nuisance, see Fish and Game Code § 7707.
Fishing boats without permits, see Fish and Game Code § 7891.
Fishing nets illegally used as nuisance, see Fish and Game Code § 8630.
Food,
  Sanitation, violations as public nuisance, see Health and Safety Code § 112050.
  Unsafe, nuisance, see Health and Safety Code § 111890.
Forest insect pests and plant diseases as public nuisances, see Public Resources Code § 4713.
Gambling place as a nuisance, see Penal Code § 11225.
Gambling ship, means of conveyance to as public nuisance, see Penal Code § 11305 et seq.
Geothermal wells improperly located as public nuisances, see Public Resources Code §§ 3757, 3760.
Hive unoccupied, nuisance, see Food and Agricultural Code § 29177.
Illegal nets as public nuisance, see Fish and Game Code § 8630 et seq.
Junkyards, etc., as public nuisances, see Streets and Highways Code § 754.
Life insurance analyst, acting without license as public nuisance, see Insurance Code § 1845.
Lobster traps without buoys as public nuisance, see Fish and Game Code § 9007.
Machine gun, possession as public nuisance, see Penal Code § 32750.
Mobilehome parks, nuisance abatement, see Health and Safety Code §§ 18402, 18403.
Mosquito breeding place as public nuisance, abatement, see Health and Safety Code § 2053.

Motor vehicle operation, signs, devices or lights interfering with as public nuisances, see Vehicle Code § 21467.
Municipal abatement of weed and rubbish nuisances, see Government Code §§ 39501, 39502, 39560 et seq.
Municipal regulation and abatement of nuisances, see Government Code § 38771 et seq.
Nut, fruit and vegetable standards, nonconformance as nuisance, see Food and Agricultural Code § 43031 et seq.
Oil and gas, secondary recovery operations, see Code of Civil Procedure § 731c.
Oil and gas wells improperly spaced as public nuisance, see Public Resources Code §§ 3600, 3604.
Placer mine, unauthorized operation as public nuisance, see Public Resources Code § 3967.
Plant quarantine and pest control, abatement of nuisance, see Food and Agricultural Code §§ 5401 et seq., 5551 et seq., 5901 et seq., 6062, 7301 et seq., 7576 et seq.
Poultry meat in noncompliance with regulations as public nuisance, see Food and Agricultural Code § 25556.
Power of local governments to declare nuisances, see Water Code § 13002.
Produce carrying residue, see Food and Agricultural Code § 12641 et seq.
Prostitution, etc., building used for as a nuisance, see Penal Code § 11225.
Public and private property, unauthorized signs, etc., as public nuisances, see Penal Code § 556.3.
Public nuisance,
  Continuance after notice to abate, daily offenses, see Penal Code § 373a.
  Defined, see Penal Code § 370.
  Maintaining a misdemeanor, see Penal Code § 372.
Sanitary sewers discharging sewage in ocean, public nuisance, see Public Utilities Code § 10106.
Seed law nonconformance, abatement as nuisance, see Food and Agricultural Code § 52511 et seq.
Sewage disposal other than use of sewer system as public nuisance, see Government Code § 54352; Water Code §§ 31103, 35503.
Sewage or other waste discharge as nuisance, see Health and Safety Code § 5411.
State highways, encroachment as public nuisance, see Streets and Highways Code § 723 et seq.
State housing law, abatement of nuisances, see Health and Safety Code § 17980 et seq.
Swimming pool sanitation, violation of standards as public nuisance, see Health and Safety Code §§ 116060, 116063.
Tenant maintaining nuisance, unlawful detainer, see Code of Civil Procedure § 1161.
Uncapped artesian well as public nuisance, see Water Code §§ 305, 306.
Uncontrolled fire as public nuisance, see Public Resources Code § 4170.
Vegetation constituting a public nuisance, exemption from cutting permit, see Penal Code § 384a.
Vehicle or structure on highway for sale purposes, public nuisance, see Streets and Highways Code § 731.
Waste accumulation as public nuisance, see Public Resources Code § 4441.
Water quality, nuisance defined, see Water Code § 13050.
Weapon used in assault as nuisance, see Penal Code § 245.

§ 3479. Nuisance; what constitutes

Anything which is injurious to health, including, but not limited to, the illegal sale of controlled substances, or is indecent or offensive to the senses, or an obstruction to the free use of property, so as to interfere with the comfortable enjoyment of life or property, or unlawfully obstructs the free passage or use, in the customary manner, of any navigable lake, or river, bay, stream, canal, or basin, or any public park, square, street, or highway, is a nuisance. *(Enacted in 1872. Amended by Code Am.1873–74, c. 612, p. 268, § 284; Stats. 1996, c. 658 (A.B.2970), § 1.)*

Cross References

Abatement, right of action, see Code of Civil Procedure § 731.
Artesian wells, uncapped well as a public nuisance, see Water Code §§ 305, 306.
Blackjacks, etc., as nuisances, see Penal Code § 22290.
Cities, see Government Code § 38771 et seq.
City attorneys pursuing drug abatement actions, see Penal Code §§ 11105, 13300.
Concealed weapons, carrying as a nuisance, see Penal Code § 29300.
Criminal offender record information, local summary criminal history information provided to city attorneys pursuing drug abatement actions, see Penal Code § 13300.
Penal provisions, see Penal Code § 370 et seq.
Prostitution, building or place as nuisance, see Penal Code § 11225.
Weeds, rubbish and refuse as public nuisance, see Government Code § 39560 et seq.

§ 3480. Public nuisance

A public nuisance is one which affects at the same time an entire community or neighborhood, or any considerable number of persons, although the extent of the annoyance or damage inflicted upon individuals may be unequal. *(Enacted in 1872. Amended by Code Am.1873–74, c. 612, p. 268, § 285.)*

Cross References

Abatement, right of action, see Code of Civil Procedure § 731.
Artesian well, not capped, etc., to prevent waste, see Water Code §§ 305, 306.
Camelthorn, see Food and Agricultural Code § 7301 et seq.
Caprifig trees, see Food and Agricultural Code § 6172.
City attorneys pursuing drug abatement actions, see Penal Code §§ 11105, 13300.
Criminal offender record information, local summary criminal history information provided to city attorneys pursuing drug abatement actions, see Penal Code § 13300.
Diseased apiary, see Food and Agricultural Code § 29204 et seq.
Employee housing improperly maintained, see Health and Safety Code § 17060.
Honey unlawfully packed, etc., see Food and Agricultural Code § 29731 et seq.
Weeds as public nuisance, see Health and Safety Code §§ 14876, 14880.

§ 3481. Private nuisance

Every nuisance not included in the definition of the last section is private. *(Enacted in 1872.)*

Cross References

Remedies, etc., see Civil Code § 3501 et seq.
Spite fence as private nuisance, see Civil Code § 841.4.
Tree or shrub maintained in violation after installation of a solar collector, private nuisance, see Public Resources Code § 25983.

§ 3482. Acts under statutory authority not a nuisance

Nothing which is done or maintained under the express authority of a statute can be deemed a nuisance. *(Enacted in 1872.)*

Cross References

Issuance of state gambling license, construction, see Business and Professions Code § 19972.

§ 3482.1. Operation or use of sport shooting ranges; civil liability or criminal prosecution; noise or noise pollution nuisance

(a) As used in this section:

(1) "Person" means an individual, proprietorship, partnership, corporation, club, or other legal entity.

(2) "Sport shooting range" or "range" means an area designed and operated for the use of rifles, shotguns, pistols, silhouettes, skeet, trap, black powder, or any other similar sport or law enforcement training purpose.

(3) "Indoor shooting range" means a totally enclosed facility designed to offer a totally controlled shooting environment that includes impenetrable walls, floor and ceiling, adequate ventilation and lighting systems, and acoustical treatment for sound attenuation suitable for the range's approved use.

(4) "Nighttime" means between the hours of 10 p.m. and 7 a.m.

(b)(1) Except as provided in subdivision (f), a person who operates or uses a sport shooting range in this state shall not be subject to civil liability or criminal prosecution in any matter relating to noise or noise pollution resulting from the operation or use of the range if the range is in compliance with any noise control laws or ordinances that applied to the range and its operation at the time construction or operation of the range was approved by a local public entity having jurisdiction in the matter, or if there were no such laws or ordinances that applied to the range and its operation at that time.

(2) Except as provided in subdivision (f), a person who operates or uses a sport shooting range or law enforcement training range is not subject to an action for nuisance, and a court shall not enjoin the use or operation of a range, on the basis of noise or noise pollution if the range is in compliance with any noise control laws or ordinances that applied to the range and its operation at the time construction or operation of the range was approved by a local public entity having jurisdiction in the matter, or if there were no such laws or ordinances that applied to the range and its operation at that time.

(3) Rules or regulations adopted by any state department or agency for limiting levels of noise in terms of decibel level which may occur in the outdoor atmosphere shall not apply to a sport shooting range exempted from liability under this section.

(c) A person who acquires title to or who owns real property adversely affected by the use of property with a permanently located and improved sport shooting range may not maintain a nuisance action with respect to noise or noise pollution against the person who owns the range to restrain, enjoin, or impede the use of the range where there has been no substantial change in the nature or use of the range. This section does not prohibit actions for negligence or recklessness in the operation of the range or by a person using the range.

(d) A sport shooting range that is in operation and not in violation of existing law at the time of the enactment of an ordinance described in subdivision (b) shall be permitted to continue in operation even if the operation of the sport shooting range at a later date does not conform to a new ordinance or an amendment to an existing ordinance if there has been no substantial change in the nature or use of the range. Nothing in this section shall be construed to limit the authority of a local agency to enforce any term of a conditional use permit.

(e) Except as otherwise provided in this section, this section does not prohibit a local public entity having jurisdiction in the matter from regulating the location and construction of a sport shooting range after the effective date of this section.

(f) This section does not prohibit a local public entity having jurisdiction in the matter from requiring that noise levels at the nearest residential property line to a range not exceed the level of normal city street noise which shall not be more than 60 decibels for nighttime shooting. The subdivision does not abrogate any existing local standards for nighttime shooting. The operator of a sport shooting range shall not unreasonably refuse to use trees, shrubs, or barriers, when appropriate, to mitigate the noise generated by nighttime shooting. For the purpose of this section, a reasonable effort to mitigate is an action that can be accomplished in a manner and at a cost that does not impose an unreasonable financial burden upon the operator of the range.

(g) This section does not apply to indoor shooting ranges.

(h) This section does not apply to a range in existence prior to January 1, 1998, that is operated for law enforcement training purposes by a county of the sixth class if the range is located without the boundaries of that county and within the boundaries of another county. This subdivision shall become operative on July 1, 1999. *(Added by Stats.1997, c. 880 (S.B.517), § 1. Amended by Stats.1998, c. 141 (S.B.1620), § 1, eff. July 13, 1998.)*

§ 3482.5. Agricultural activity not a nuisance; exceptions; construction with other laws

(a)(1) No agricultural activity, operation, or facility, or appurtenances thereof, conducted or maintained for commercial purposes, and in a manner consistent with proper and accepted customs and standards, as established and followed by similar agricultural operations in the same locality, shall be or become a nuisance, private or public, due to any changed condition in or about the locality, after it has been in operation for more than three years if it was not a nuisance at the time it began.

(2) No activity of a district agricultural association that is operated in compliance with Division 3 (commencing with Section 3001) of the Food and Agricultural Code, shall be or become a private or public nuisance due to any changed condition in or about the locality, after it has been in operation for more than three years if it was not a nuisance at the time it began. This paragraph shall not apply to any activities of the 52nd District Agricultural Association that are conducted on the grounds of the California Exposition and State Fair, nor to any public nuisance action brought by a city, county, or city and county alleging that the activities,

operations, or conditions of a district agricultural association have substantially changed after more than three years from the time that the activities, operations, or conditions began.

(b) Paragraph (1) of subdivision (a) shall not apply if the agricultural activity, operation, or facility, or appurtenances thereof obstruct the free passage or use, in the customary manner, of any navigable lake, river, bay, stream, canal, or basin, or any public park, square, street, or highway.

(c) Paragraph (1) of subdivision (a) shall not invalidate any provision contained in the Health and Safety Code, Fish and Game Code, Food and Agricultural Code, or Division 7 (commencing with Section 13000) of the Water Code, if the agricultural activity, operation, or facility, or appurtenances thereof constitute a nuisance, public or private, as specifically defined or described in any of those provisions.

(d) This section shall prevail over any contrary provision of any ordinance or regulation of any city, county, city and county, or other political subdivision of the state. However, nothing in this section shall preclude a city, county, city and county, or other political subdivision of this state, acting within its constitutional or statutory authority and not in conflict with other provisions of state law, from adopting an ordinance that allows notification to a prospective homeowner that the dwelling is in close proximity to an agricultural activity, operation, facility, or appurtenances thereof and is subject to the provisions of this section consistent with Section 1102.6a.

(e) For purposes of this section, the term "agricultural activity, operation, or facility, or appurtenances thereof" shall include, but not be limited to, the cultivation and tillage of the soil, dairying, the production, cultivation, growing, and harvesting of any agricultural commodity including timber, viticulture, apiculture, or horticulture, the raising of livestock, fur bearing animals, fish, or poultry, and any practices performed by a farmer or on a farm as incident to or in conjunction with those farming operations, including preparation for market, delivery to storage or to market, or delivery to carriers for transportation to market. *(Added by Stats. 1981, c. 545, p. 2192, § 1. Amended by Stats.1991, c. 828 (S.B.1093), § 1; Stats.1992, c. 97 (A.B.1190), § 1.)*

§ 3482.6. Agricultural processing activity not a nuisance; increase in activity; construction with other laws

(a) No agricultural processing activity, operation, facility, or appurtenances thereof, conducted or maintained for commercial purposes, and in a manner consistent with proper and accepted customs and standards, shall be or become a nuisance, private or public, due to any changed condition in or about the locality, after it has been in continuous operation for more than three years if it was not a nuisance at the time it began.

(b) If an agricultural processing activity, operation, facility, or appurtenances thereof substantially increases its activities or operations after January 1, 1993, then a public or private nuisance action may be brought with respect to those increases in activities or operations that have a significant effect on the environment. For increases in activities or operations that have been in effect more than three years, there is a rebuttable presumption affecting the burden of producing evidence that the increase was not substantial.

(c) This section does not supersede any other provision of law, except other provisions of this part, if the agricultural processing activity, operation, facility, or appurtenances thereof, constitute a nuisance, public or private, as specifically defined or described in the provision.

(d) This section prevails over any contrary provision of any ordinance or regulation of any city, county, city and county, or other political subdivision of the state, except regulations adopted pursuant to Section 41700 of the Health and Safety Code as applied to agricultural processing activities, operations, facilities, or appurtenances thereof that are surrounded by housing or commercial development on January 1, 1993. However, nothing in this section precludes a city, county, city and county, or other political subdivision of this state, acting within its constitutional or statutory authority and not in conflict with other provisions of state law, from adopting an ordinance that allows notification to a prospective homeowner that the dwelling is in close proximity to an agricultural processing activity, operation, facility, or appurtenances thereof and is subject to provisions of this section consistent with Section 1102.6a.

(e) For the purposes of this section, the following definitions apply:

(1) "Agricultural processing activity, operation, facility, or appurtenances thereof" includes, but is not limited to, rendering plants licensed pursuant to Section 19300 of the Food and Agricultural Code and collection centers licensed pursuant to Section 19300.5 of the Food and Agricultural Code, the canning or freezing of agricultural products, the processing of dairy products, the production and bottling of beer and wine, the processing of meat and egg products, the drying of fruits and grains, the packing and cooling of fruits and vegetables, and the storage or warehousing of any agricultural products, and includes processing for wholesale or retail markets of agricultural products.

(2) "Continuous operation" means at least 30 days of agricultural processing operations per year.

(3) "Proper and accepted customs and standards" means the compliance with all applicable state and federal statutes and regulations governing the operation of the agricultural processing activity, operation, facility, or appurtenances thereof with respect to the condition or effect alleged to be a nuisance.

(f) This section does not apply to any litigation pending or cause of action accruing prior to January 1, 1993. *(Added by Stats.1992, c. 97 (A.B.1190), § 2. Amended by Stats.1993, c. 99 (A.B.258), § 1; Stats.1994, c. 146 (A.B.3601), § 17; Stats.1999, c. 329 (S.B.1274), § 1.)*

§ 3482.7. Repealed by Stats.1982, c. 1027, § 1.6, operative Jan. 1, 1985

§ 3482.8. Use of building or property for dogfighting or cockfighting; public nuisance

Any building or property used for the purpose of willfully conducting dogfighting in violation of Section 597.5 of the Penal Code or cockfighting in violation of subdivision (b) of Section 597b of the Penal Code is a public nuisance. *(Added by Stats.2011, c. 128 (S.B.426), § 1.)*

§ 3482.8

Cross References

Unlawful detainer for maintenance of public nuisance under this section by tenant or subtenant, restitution of possession of demised premises, see Code of Civil Procedure § 1161.

§ 3483. Continuing nuisance; liability of successive owners for failure to abate

Every successive owner of property who neglects to abate a continuing nuisance upon, or in the use of, such property, created by a former owner, is liable therefor in the same manner as the one who first created it. *(Enacted in 1872.)*

§ 3484. Damages recoverable notwithstanding abatement

The abatement of a nuisance does not prejudice the right of any person to recover damages for its past existence. *(Enacted in 1872.)*

Cross References

Nuisance, action to abate, damages, see Code of Civil Procedure § 731.

§ 3485. Illegal conduct involving unlawful weapons or ammunition purpose; unlawful detainer action by city prosecutor or city attorney to abate nuisance; notice; application; information provided to California Research Bureau

(a) To abate the nuisance caused by illegal conduct involving an unlawful weapons or ammunition on real property, the city prosecutor or city attorney may file, in the name of the people, an action for unlawful detainer against any person who is in violation of the nuisance or illegal purpose provisions of subdivision 4 of Section 1161 of the Code of Civil Procedure, with respect to that unlawful weapons or ammunition purpose. In filing this action, which shall be based upon an arrest or warrant by a law enforcement agency, reporting an offense committed on the property and documented by the observations of a law enforcement officer or agent, the city prosecutor or city attorney shall utilize the procedures set forth in Chapter 4 (commencing with Section 1159) of Title 3 of Part 3 of the Code of Civil Procedure, except that in cases filed under this section, the following also shall apply:

(1)(A) Prior to filing an action pursuant to this section, the city prosecutor or city attorney shall give 30 calendar days' written notice to the owner, requiring the owner to file an action for the removal of the person who is in violation of the nuisance or illegal purpose provisions of subdivision 4 of Section 1161 of the Code of Civil Procedure with respect to an unlawful weapons or ammunition purpose.

(B) This notice shall include sufficient documentation establishing a violation of the nuisance or illegal purpose provisions of subdivision 4 of Section 1161 of the Code of Civil Procedure and an advisement to the owner of the assignment provision contained in subparagraph (D). The notice shall be served upon the owner and the tenant in accordance with subdivision (e).

(C) The notice to the tenant shall, in at least 14–point bold type, meet the following requirements:

(i) The notice shall contain the following language:

"(Date)

(Name of tenant)

(Address of tenant)

Re: Civil Code Section 3485

Dear (name of tenant):

This letter is to inform you that an eviction action may soon be filed in court against you for suspected firearms activity. According to state law, Civil Code Section 3485 provides for eviction of persons engaging in such conduct, as described below.

(Name of police department) records indicate that you, (name of arrestee), were arrested on (date) for violations of (list violations) on (address of property).

A letter has been sent to the property owner(s) advising of your arrest and the requirements of state law, as well as the landlord's option to assign the unlawful detainer action to the (name of city attorney or prosecutor's office).

A list of legal assistance providers is provided below. Please note, this list is not exclusive and is provided for your information only; the (name of city attorney or prosecutor's office) does not endorse or recommend any of the listed agencies.

Sincerely,

(Name of deputy city attorney or city prosecutor)
Deputy City (Attorney or Prosecutor)

Notice to Tenant: This notice is not a notice of eviction. You should call (name of the city attorney or prosecutor pursuing the action) at (telephone number) or a legal assistance provider to stop the eviction action if any of the following is applicable:

(1) You are not the person named in this notice.

(2) The person named in the notice does not live with you.

(3) The person named in the notice has permanently moved.

(4) You do not know the person named in the notice.

(5) You want to request that only the person involved in the nuisance be evicted, allowing the other residents to stay.

(6) You have any other legal defense or legal reason to stop the eviction action. A list of legal assistance providers is attached to this notice. Some provide free legal assistance if you are eligible."

(ii) The notice shall be provided to the tenant in English and, as translated, in all of the languages identified in subdivision (b) of Section 1632 of the Civil Code.

(D) The owner shall, within 30 calendar days of the mailing of the written notice, either provide the city prosecutor or city attorney with all relevant information pertaining to the unlawful detainer case, or provide a written explanation setting forth any safety-related reasons for noncompliance, and an assignment to the city prosecutor or city attorney of the right to bring an unlawful detainer action against the tenant.

(E) The assignment shall be on a form provided by the city prosecutor or city attorney and may contain a provision for costs of investigation, discovery, and reasonable attorney's fees, in an amount not to exceed six hundred dollars ($600). An owner shall only be required to pay the costs or fees upon acceptance of the assignment and the filing of the action for unlawful detainer by the city prosecutor or the city attorney.

(F) If the city prosecutor or city attorney accepts the assignment of the right of the owner to bring the unlawful detainer action, the owner shall retain all other rights and duties, including the handling of the tenant's personal property, following issuance of the writ of possession and its delivery to and execution by the appropriate agency.

(2) Upon the failure of the owner to file an action pursuant to this section, or to respond to the city prosecutor or city attorney as provided in paragraph (1), or having filed an action, if the owner fails to prosecute it diligently and in good faith, the city prosecutor or city attorney may file and prosecute the action, and join the owner as a defendant in the action. This action shall have precedence over any similar proceeding thereafter brought by the owner, or to one previously brought by the owner and not prosecuted diligently and in good faith. Service of the summons and complaint upon the defendant owner shall be in accordance with Sections 415.10, 415.20, 415.30, 415.40, and 415.50 of the Code of Civil Procedure.

(3) If a jury or court finds the defendant tenant guilty of unlawful detainer in a case filed pursuant to paragraph (2), the city prosecutor or city attorney may be awarded costs, including the costs of investigation and discovery and reasonable attorney's fees. These costs shall be assessed against the defendant owner, to whom notice was directed pursuant to paragraph (1), and once an abstract of judgment is recorded, it shall constitute a lien on the subject real property.

(4) This section shall not prevent a local governing body from adopting and enforcing laws, consistent with this section, relating to weapons or ammunition abatement. If local laws duplicate or supplement this section, this section shall be construed as providing alternative remedies and not preempting the field.

(5) This section shall not prevent a tenant from receiving relief against a forfeiture of a lease pursuant to Section 1179 of the Code of Civil Procedure.

(6) In an unlawful detainer action filed pursuant to this section, the court shall make one of the following orders:

(A) If the grounds for an eviction have not been established pursuant to this section, the court shall dismiss, without prejudice, the unlawful detainer action.

(B) If the grounds for an eviction have been established pursuant to this section, the court shall do either of the following:

(i) Order that the tenant and all occupants be immediately evicted from the property.

(ii) Dismiss the unlawful detainer action with or without prejudice or stay execution of an eviction order for a reasonable length of time if the tenant establishes by clear and convincing evidence that the immediate eviction would pose an extreme hardship to the tenant and that the hardship outweighs the health, safety, or welfare of the neighbors or surrounding community. The court shall not find an extreme hardship solely on the basis of economic hardship or the financial inability of the tenant to pay for and secure other housing or lodging accommodations.

(C) If the grounds for a partial eviction have been established pursuant to subdivision (b), the court shall order that those persons be immediately removed and barred from the property, but the court shall not order the tenancy be terminated.

(b) In any proceeding brought under this section, the court may, upon a showing of good cause, issue a partial eviction ordering the removal of any person, including, but not limited to, members of the tenant's household if the court finds that the person has engaged in the activities described in subdivision (a). Persons removed pursuant to this section may be permanently barred from returning to or reentering any portion of the entire premises. The court may further order as an express condition of the tenancy that the remaining tenants shall not give permission to or invite any person who has been removed pursuant to this subdivision to return to or reenter any portion of the entire premises.

(c) For purposes of this section, "unlawful weapons or ammunition purpose" means the illegal use, manufacture, causing to be manufactured, importation, possession, possession for sale, sale, furnishing, or giving away of any of the following:

(1) A firearm, as defined in subdivision (a) of Section 16520 of the Penal Code.

(2) Any ammunition, as defined in subdivision (b) of Section 16150 of the Penal Code or in Section 16650 or 16660 of the Penal Code.

(3) Any assault weapon, as defined in Section 30510 or 30515 of the Penal Code.

(4) Any .50 BMG rifle, as defined in Section 30530 of the Penal Code.

(5) Any tear gas weapon, as defined in Section 17250 of the Penal Code.

(d) Notwithstanding subdivision (b) of Section 68097.2 of the Government Code, a public entity may waive all or part of the costs incurred in furnishing the testimony of a peace officer in an unlawful detainer action brought pursuant to this section.

(e) The notice and documentation described in paragraph (1) of subdivision (a) shall be given in writing and may be given either by personal delivery or by deposit in the United States mail in a sealed envelope, postage prepaid, addressed to the owner at the address known to the public entity giving the notice, or as shown on the last equalized assessment roll, if not known. Separate notice of not less than 30 calendar days and documentation shall be provided to the tenant in accordance with this subdivision. Service by mail shall be deemed to be completed at the time of deposit in the United States mail. Proof of giving the notice may be made by a declaration signed under penalty of perjury by any employee of the public entity which shows service in conformity with this section.

(f) This section shall apply only to the following courts:

(1) In the County of Los Angeles, any court having jurisdiction over unlawful detainer cases involving real property situated in the City of Los Angeles or the City of Long Beach.

(2) In the County of Sacramento, any court with jurisdiction over unlawful detainer cases involving real property situated in the City of Sacramento.

(3) In the County of Alameda, any court with jurisdiction over unlawful detainer cases involving real property situated in the City of Oakland.

(g)(1) In a template provided by the California Research Bureau, the city attorney and city prosecutor of each participating jurisdiction shall provide to the California Research Bureau the following information:

(A) The number of notices provided pursuant to paragraph (1) of subdivision (a).

(B) For each notice provided pursuant to paragraph (1) of subdivision (a), the following information:

(i) The name and age, as provided by the landlord, of each person residing at the noticed address.

(ii) The racial or ethnic identity of the tenant against whom the unlawful detainer is sought.

(C) Whether, upon notice, the case was filed by the owner, and if so, the filing date and number.

(D) Whether the assignment was executed by the owner to the city attorney or city prosecutor.

(E) Whether 3–day, 30–day, or 60–day notices were issued by the city attorney or city prosecutor, and if so, the date each was issued.

(F) Whether the case was filed by the city attorney or city prosecutor, and if so, the filing date and case number.

(G) For the cases filed by an owner, the city attorney, or the city prosecutor, the following information:

(i) If a judgment was entered, the date of the judgment, whether the judgment ordered an eviction or partial eviction, and whether the judgment was a default judgment, stipulated judgment, or judgment following trial.

(ii) Whether the case was withdrawn or in which the tenant prevailed.

(iii) Whether there was another disposition, and specifying the type of disposition.

(iv) Whether the defendant was represented by counsel.

(H) For the cases in which a notice was provided pursuant to subdivision (a), but no case was filed, the following information:

(i) Whether a tenant voluntarily vacated subsequent to receiving the notice.

(ii) Whether a tenant vacated a unit prior to the providing of the notice.

(iii) Whether there was another resolution, and specifying the type of resolution.

(2)(A) Information compiled pursuant to this section shall be reported annually to the California Research Bureau on or before January 20.

(B) The California Research Bureau shall thereafter submit a brief report to the Senate and Assembly Committees on Judiciary once on or before March 20, 2021, and once on or before March 20, 2023, summarizing the information collected pursuant to this section. The report shall be submitted in compliance with Section 9795 of the Government Code.

(3) Personally identifiable information submitted to the California Research Bureau pursuant to this section shall be confidential and shall not be publicly disclosed.

(h) A participating jurisdiction shall not be permitted to file, in the name of the people, an action for unlawful detainer pursuant to this section unless that jurisdiction has made a good faith effort to collect and timely report all information to the California Research Bureau required by subdivision (g).

(i) A defendant may raise as an affirmative defense, the failure of the participating jurisdiction to make a good faith effort to collect and timely report all information to the California Research Bureau required by subdivision (g) for the reporting period preceding the unlawful detainer action.

(j) This section shall remain in effect only until January 1, 2024, and as of that date is repealed. *(Added by Stats.2014, c. 339 (A.B.2310), § 1, eff. Sept. 15, 2014. Amended by Stats. 2018, c. 880 (A.B.2930), § 1, eff. Jan. 1, 2019.)*

Repeal

For repeal of this section, see its terms.

§ 3486. Illegal conduct involving controlled substance purpose; unlawful detainer action by city prosecutor or city attorney to abate nuisance in City of Los Angeles; notice; waiver of testimony costs; information provided to California Research Bureau

(a) To abate the nuisance caused by illegal conduct involving a controlled substance purpose on real property, the city prosecutor or city attorney may file, in the name of the people, an action for unlawful detainer against any person who is in violation of the nuisance or illegal purpose provisions of subdivision 4 of Section 1161 of the Code of Civil Procedure, with respect to that controlled substance purpose. In filing this action, which shall be based upon an arrest report by a law enforcement agency, reporting an offense committed on the property and documented by the observations of a police officer, the city prosecutor or city attorney shall use the procedures set forth in Chapter 4 (commencing with Section 1159) of Title 3 of Part 3 of the Code of Civil Procedure, except that in cases filed under this section, the following also shall apply:

(1)(A) Prior to filing an action pursuant to this section, the city prosecutor or city attorney shall give 30 calendar days' written notice to the owner, requiring the owner to file an action for the removal of the person who is in violation of the nuisance or illegal purpose provisions of subdivision 4 of Section 1161 of the Code of Civil Procedure with respect to a controlled substance purpose.

(B) This notice shall include sufficient documentation establishing a violation of the nuisance or illegal purpose provisions of subdivision 4 of Section 1161 of the Code of Civil Procedure and an advisement to the owner of the assignment provision contained in subparagraph (D). The notice shall be served upon the owner and the tenant in accordance with subdivision (e).

(C) The notice to the tenant shall, in at least 14–point bold type, meet the following requirements:

(i) The notice shall contain the following language:

"(Date)

(Name of tenant)
(Address of tenant)

Re: Civil Code Section 3486

Dear (name of tenant):

This letter is to inform you that an eviction action may soon be filed in court against you for suspected drug activity. According to state law, Civil Code Section 3486 provides for eviction of persons engaging in such conduct, as described below.

(Name of police department) records indicate that you, (name of arrestee), were arrested on (date) for violations of (list violations) on (address of property).

A letter has been sent to the property owner(s) advising of your arrest and the requirements of state law, as well as the landlord's option to assign the unlawful detainer action to the (name of city attorney or prosecutor's office).

A list of legal assistance providers is provided below. Please note, this list is not exclusive and is provided for your information only; the (name of city attorney or prosecutor's office) does not endorse or recommend any of the listed agencies.

Sincerely,

(Name of deputy city attorney or city prosecutor)

Deputy City (Attorney or Prosecutor)

Notice to Tenant: This notice is not a notice of eviction. You should call (name of the city attorney or prosecutor pursuing the action) at (telephone number) or a legal assistance provider to stop the eviction action if any of the following is applicable:

(1) You are not the person named in this notice.

(2) The person named in the notice does not live with you.

(3) The person named in the notice has permanently moved.

(4) You do not know the person named in the notice.

(5) You want to request that only the person involved in the nuisance be evicted, allowing the other residents to stay.

(6) You have any other legal defense or legal reason to stop the eviction action.

A list of legal assistance providers is attached to this notice. Some provide free legal assistance if you are eligible."

(ii) The notice shall be provided to the tenant in English and, as translated, in all of the languages identified in subdivision (a) of Section 1632 of the Civil Code.

(D) The owner shall, within 30 calendar days of the mailing of the written notice, either provide the city prosecutor or city attorney with all relevant information pertaining to the unlawful detainer case, or provide a written explanation setting forth any safety-related reasons for noncompliance, and an assignment to the city prosecutor or city attorney of the right to bring an unlawful detainer action against the tenant.

(E) The assignment shall be on a form provided by the city prosecutor or city attorney and may contain a provision for costs of investigation, discovery, and reasonable attorney's fees, in an amount not to exceed six hundred dollars ($600). An owner shall only be required to pay the costs or fees upon acceptance of the assignment and the filing of the action for unlawful detainer by the city prosecutor or city attorney.

(F) If the city prosecutor or city attorney accepts the assignment of the right of the owner to bring the unlawful detainer action, the owner shall retain all other rights and duties, including the handling of the tenant's personal property, following issuance of the writ of possession and its delivery to and execution by the appropriate agency.

(2) Upon the failure of the owner to file an action pursuant to this section, or to respond to the city prosecutor or city attorney as provided in paragraph (1), or having filed an action, if the owner fails to prosecute it diligently and in good faith, the city prosecutor or city attorney may file and prosecute the action, and join the owner as a defendant in the action. This action shall have precedence over any similar proceeding thereafter brought by the owner, or to one previously brought by the owner and not prosecuted diligently and in good faith. Service of the summons and complaint upon the defendant owner shall be in accordance with Sections 415.10, 415.20, 415.30, 415.40, and 415.50 of the Code of Civil Procedure.

(3) If a jury or court finds the defendant tenant guilty of unlawful detainer in a case filed pursuant to paragraph (2), the city prosecutor or city attorney may be awarded costs, including the costs of investigation and discovery and reasonable attorney's fees. These costs shall be assessed against the defendant owner, to whom notice was directed pursuant to paragraph (1), and once an abstract of judgment is recorded, it shall constitute a lien on the subject real property.

(4) This section does not prevent a local governing body from adopting and enforcing laws, consistent with this article, relating to drug abatement. If local laws duplicate or supplement this section, this section shall be construed as providing alternative remedies and not preempting the field.

(5) This section does not prevent a tenant from receiving relief against a forfeiture of a lease pursuant to Section 1179 of the Code of Civil Procedure.

(b) In any proceeding brought under this section, the court may, upon a showing of good cause, issue a partial eviction ordering the removal of any person, including, but not limited to, members of the tenant's household if the court finds that the person has engaged in the activities described in subdivision (a). Persons removed pursuant to this section may be permanently barred from returning to or reentering any portion of the entire premises. The court may further order as an express condition of the tenancy that the remaining tenants shall not give permission to or invite any person who has been removed pursuant to this subdivision to return to or reenter any portion of the entire premises.

(c) For the purposes of this section, "controlled substance purpose" means the manufacture, cultivation, importation into the state, transportation, possession, possession for sale, sale, furnishing, administering, or giving away, or providing a place to use or fortification of a place involving, cocaine, phencyclidine, heroin, methamphetamine, or any other controlled substance, in a violation of subdivision (a) of Section 11350, Section 11351, 11351.5, 11352, or 11359, subdivision (a) of Section 11360, or Section 11366, 11366.6, 11377, 11378, 11378.5, 11379, 11379.5, 11379.6, or 11383 of the Health and Safety Code.

(d) Notwithstanding subdivision (b) of Section 68097.2 of the Government Code, a public entity may waive all or part of the costs incurred in furnishing the testimony of a peace officer in an unlawful detainer action brought pursuant to this section.

(e) The notice and documentation described in paragraph (1) of subdivision (a) shall be given in writing and may be given either by personal delivery or by deposit in the United States mail in a sealed envelope, postage prepaid, addressed to the owner at the address known to the public entity giving the notice, or as shown on the last equalized assessment roll, if not known. Separate notice of not less than 30 calendar days and documentation shall be provided to the tenant in accordance with this subdivision. Service by mail shall be deemed to be completed at the time of deposit in the United States mail. Proof of giving the notice may be made by a declaration signed under penalty of perjury by any employee of the public entity which shows service in conformity with this section.

(f) In an unlawful detainer action filed pursuant to this section, the court shall make one of the following orders:

(1) If the grounds for an eviction have not been established pursuant to this section, the court shall dismiss, without prejudice, the unlawful detainer action.

(2) If the grounds for an eviction have been established pursuant to this section, the court shall do either of the following:

(A) Order that the tenant and all occupants be immediately evicted from the property.

(B) Dismiss the unlawful detainer action with or without prejudice or stay execution of an eviction order for a reasonable length of time if the tenant establishes by clear and convincing evidence that the immediate eviction would pose an extreme hardship to the tenant and that this hardship outweighs the health, safety, or welfare of the neighbors or surrounding community. However, the court shall not find an extreme hardship solely on the basis of an economic hardship or the financial inability of the tenant to pay for and secure other housing or lodging accommodations.

(3) If the grounds for a partial eviction have been established pursuant to subdivision (b), the court shall order that those persons be immediately removed and barred from the property, but the court shall not order the tenancy be terminated.

(g) This section applies only in the County of Los Angeles to a court having jurisdiction over unlawful detainer cases involving real property situated in the City of Los Angeles.

(h) This section shall become operative on January 1, 2014, only if the City of Los Angeles has regularly reported to the California Research Bureau as required by this section as it read during the period from January 1, 2010, to January 1, 2014, inclusive. For purposes of this section, the City of Los Angeles shall be deemed to have complied with this reporting requirement if the 2013 report to the Legislature by the California Research Bureau indicates that the City of Los Angeles has regularly reported to the bureau. (Added by Stats.2009, c. 244 (A.B.530), § 3, operative Jan. 1, 2014. Amended by Stats.2014, c. 341 (A.B.2485), § 1, eff. Sept. 15, 2014; Stats.2015, c. 303 (A.B.731), § 33, eff. Jan. 1, 2016.)

Cross References

Nuisance upon premises, landlord entitled to restitution of possession, service of notice to quit, see Code of Civil Procedure § 1161.

§ 3486.5. Application of Section 3486 to City of Long Beach, City of Sacramento, and City of Oakland; information provided to California Research Bureau

(a) Notwithstanding subdivision (g) of Section 3486, Section 3486 shall apply to the following courts:

(1) In the County of Los Angeles, in any court having jurisdiction over unlawful detainer cases involving real property situated in the City of Long Beach.

(2) In the County of Sacramento, in any court with jurisdiction over unlawful detainer cases involving real property situated in the City of Sacramento.

(3) In the County of Alameda, in any court having jurisdiction over unlawful detainer cases involving real property situated in the City of Oakland.

(b)(1) In a template provided by the California Research Bureau, the city attorney and city prosecutor of each authorized jurisdiction shall provide to the California Research Bureau the following information pertaining to cases filed pursuant to Section 3486:

(A) The number of notices provided pursuant to paragraph (1) of subdivision (a) of Section 3486.

(B) For each notice provided pursuant to paragraph (1) of subdivision (a) of Section 3486, the following information:

(i) The name and age, as provided by the landlord, of each person residing at the noticed address.

(ii) The racial or ethnic identity of the tenant against whom the unlawful detainer is sought.

(C) Whether, upon notice, the case was filed by the owner, and if so, the filing date and case number.

(D) Whether the assignment was executed by the owner to the city attorney or prosecutor.

(E) Whether 3–day, 30–day, or 60–day notices were issued by the city attorney or city prosecutor, and if so, the date each was issued.

(F) Whether the case was filed by the city attorney or city prosecutor, and if so, the filing date and case number.

(G) For the cases filed by an owner, the city attorney, or the city prosecutor, the following information:

(i) If a judgment was entered, the date of the judgment, whether the judgment ordered an eviction or partial eviction, and whether the judgment was a default judgment, stipulated judgment, or judgment following trial.

(ii) Whether the case was withdrawn or the tenant prevailed.

(iii) Whether there was another disposition, and the type of disposition.

(iv) Whether the defendant was represented by counsel.

(H) For cases in which a notice was provided pursuant to subdivision (a) of Section 3486, but no case was filed, the following information:

(i) Whether a tenant voluntarily vacated subsequent to receiving the notice.

(ii) Whether a tenant vacated a unit prior to the providing of the notice.

(iii) Whether there was another resolution and the type of resolution.

(2)(A) Information compiled pursuant to this section shall be reported annually to the California Research Bureau on or before January 20.

(B) The California Research Bureau shall thereafter submit a brief report to the Senate and Assembly Committees on Judiciary once on or before March 20, 2021, and once on or before March 20, 2023, summarizing the information collected pursuant to this section. The report for this section shall be submitted in compliance with Section 9795 of the Government Code and may be combined with the California Research Bureau report submitted for the pilot program established by Section 3485. Each report shall indicate whether the authorized jurisdictions have regularly reported to the bureau.

(3) Personally identifiable information submitted to the California Research Bureau pursuant to this section shall be confidential and shall not be publicly disclosed.

(c) A participating jurisdiction shall not be permitted to file, in the name of the people, an action for unlawful detainer pursuant to this section unless that jurisdiction has made a good faith effort to collect and timely report all information to the California Research Bureau required by subdivision (b).

(d) A defendant may raise as an affirmative defense the failure of the participating jurisdiction to make a good faith effort to collect and timely report all information to the California Research Bureau required by subdivision (g) of Section 3485 for the reporting period preceding the unlawful detainer action.

(e) This section shall remain in effect only until January 1, 2024, and as of that date is repealed. *(Added by Stats.2014, c. 341 (A.B.2485), § 2, eff. Sept. 15, 2014. Amended by Stats. 2018, c. 880 (A.B.2930), § 2, eff. Jan. 1, 2019.)*

Repeal

For repeal of this section, see its terms.

Title 2

PUBLIC NUISANCES

Section
3490. Lapse of time cannot legalize public nuisance.
3491. Remedies; public.
3492. Remedies; indictment or information; regulation.
3493. Remedies; private person.
3494. Abatement; parties authorized.
3494.5. Abatement; lead paint.
3495. Abatement; private person; method.
3496. Award of costs and attorney fees; cases where authorized.

Cross References

Action to abate, see Code of Civil Procedure § 731 et seq.
California Land Reuse and Revitalization Act, definitions, applicable law, see Health and Safety Code § 25395.66.
Cesspools and other means of sewage disposal, see Health and Safety Code § 4762.
Controlled substances, abatement of buildings, see Health and Safety Code § 11570 et seq.
Definition of public nuisance, see Civil Code § 3480.
Dourine, animal afflicted with, see Food and Agricultural Code § 9621.
Encroachment on,
 County highways, see Streets and Highways Code § 1484.
 State highways, see Streets and Highways Code § 723 et seq.
Health, abating or enjoining nuisances dangerous to, see Health and Safety Code §§ 100170, 131075.
Life insurance analyst, unlicensed, see Insurance Code § 1845.
Manufacture or commercial use in industrial zone, restrictions on right to abate, see Code of Civil Procedure § 731a.
Mausoleum or columbarium improperly constructed, see Health and Safety Code § 9676.
Mobilehome park, abatement, see Health and Safety Code § 18402.
Notice to abate, see Penal Code § 373a.
Nursery stock not in compliance with law, see Food and Agricultural Code § 53561.

Poultry meat not in compliance with regulations, see Food and Agricultural Code § 25556.

Swimming pools dangerous to health, see Health and Safety Code §§ 116060, 116063.

§ 3490. Lapse of time cannot legalize public nuisance

No lapse of time can legalize a public nuisance, amounting to an actual obstruction of public right. *(Enacted in 1872.)*

§ 3491. Remedies; public

The remedies against a public nuisance are:

1. Indictment or information;
2. A civil action; or,
3. Abatement. *(Enacted in 1872. Amended by Code Am.1880, c. 11, p. 1, § 1.)*

Cross References

Cities, abatement of nuisance, see Government Code § 38773.

§ 3492. Remedies; indictment or information; regulation

The remedy by indictment or information is regulated by the Penal Code. *(Enacted in 1872. Amended by Code Am.1880, c. 11, p. 1, § 2.)*

§ 3493. Remedies; private person

A private person may maintain an action for a public nuisance, if it is specially injurious to himself, but not otherwise. *(Enacted in 1872.)*

§ 3494. Abatement; parties authorized

A public nuisance may be abated by any public body or officer authorized thereto by law. *(Enacted in 1872.)*

Cross References

Awarding to Attorney General all costs of investigating and prosecuting the action relating to this section, see Code of Civil Procedure § 1021.8.

City attorney, action to abate by, see Code of Civil Procedure § 731.

District attorney,
  Civil action by to abate public nuisance, see Government Code § 26528.
  Duty to prosecute, see Code of Civil Procedure § 731; Penal Code § 373a.

§ 3494.5. Abatement; lead paint

(a)(1) A property owner who voluntarily participates in a lead paint abatement program, and all public entities, shall be immune from liability in any lawsuit where a responsible party seeks to recover any cost associated with a lead paint abatement program from a property owner or public entity.

(2) For purposes of this subdivision, participation in a lead paint abatement program may be as limited as submission of an application to a lead paint abatement program or as extensive as completion of all activities conducted pursuant to a lead paint abatement program.

(b)(1) A property owner's participation in a lead paint abatement program shall not be evidence that the participating property is any of the following:

(A) A nuisance.

(B) Substandard under Section 17920.3 of the Health and Safety Code or is in violation of Section 17920.10 of the Health and Safety Code, to the extent that those sections apply to lead-based paint or other substandard conditions controlled utilizing program funds.

(C) Untenantable under Section 1941.1 of the Civil Code, as that section applies to lead-based paint or other conditions controlled utilizing program funds.

(2) For the purposes of this subdivision, "participation in a lead paint abatement program" means that a property has been voluntarily enrolled in a lead paint abatement program, qualifies for inspection and services, is deemed to contain actionable lead-based paint, and has been satisfactorily abated, is in the process of being satisfactorily abated, or is awaiting abatement under the lead paint abatement program.

(c) For the purposes of this section:

(1) "Lead paint abatement program" means a program that satisfies both of the following:

(A) The program is created to abate lead-based paint.

(B) The program is created as a result of a judgment or settlement in any public nuisance or similar litigation.

(2) "Property owner" means the property owner as well as all agents or employees thereof acting within the course and scope of their agency or employment.

(3) "Public entities" includes the state, the Regents of the University of California, the Trustees of the California State University, a county, city, district, public authority, public agency, and any other political subdivision or public corporation in the state, including any employees or agents thereof acting within the course and scope of their employment or agency.

(4) "Responsible party" means a private party legally responsible for the inspection costs, abatement costs, or any other costs associated with a lead paint abatement program.

(d) This section shall not alter existing obligations on homeowners to maintain their property under applicable law or otherwise limit a tenant's legal remedies for addressing the presence of lead paint on a dwelling. *(Added by Stats.2019, c. 171 (A.B.206), § 1, eff. Jan. 1, 2020.)*

§ 3495. Abatement; private person; method

Any person may abate a public nuisance which is specially injurious to him by removing, or, if necessary, destroying the thing which constitutes the same, without committing a breach of the peace, or doing unnecessary injury. *(Enacted in 1872.)*

§ 3496. Award of costs and attorney fees; cases where authorized

In any of the following described cases, the court may award costs, including the costs of investigation and discovery, and reasonable attorney's fees, which are not compensated for pursuant to some other provision of law, to the prevailing party:

(a) In any case in which a governmental agency seeks to enjoin the sale, distribution, or public exhibition, for commercial consideration, of obscene matter, as defined in Section 311 of the Penal Code.

(b) In any case in which a governmental agency seeks to enjoin the use of a building or place for the purpose of illegal gambling, lewdness, assignation, human trafficking, or prostitution; or any case in which a governmental agency seeks to enjoin acts of illegal gambling, lewdness, assignation, human trafficking, or prostitution in or upon a building or place, as authorized in Article 2 (commencing with Section 11225) of Chapter 3 of Title 1 of Part 4 of the Penal Code.

(c) In any case in which a governmental agency seeks to enjoin the use of a building or place, or seeks to enjoin in or upon any building or place the unlawful sale, manufacture, service, storage, or keeping or giving away of any controlled substance, as authorized in Article 3 (commencing with Section 11570) of Chapter 10 of Division 10 of the Health and Safety Code.

(d) In any case in which a governmental agency seeks to enjoin the unlawful sale, service, storage, or keeping or giving away of alcoholic liquor, as authorized in Article 1 (commencing with Section 11200) of Chapter 3 of Title 1 of Part 4 of the Penal Code. *(Added by Stats.1982, c. 1267, p. 4671, § 1. Amended by Stats.1983, c. 1178, p. 4671, § 1; Stats.1987, c. 1076, § 1; Stats.2012, c. 254 (A.B.2212), § 1.)*

Title 3
PRIVATE NUISANCES

Section
3501. Remedies.
3502. Abatement; method.
3503. Abatement; notice.

Cross References

California Land Reuse and Revitalization Act, definitions, applicable law, see Health and Safety Code § 25395.66.

§ 3501. Remedies

The remedies against a private nuisance are:

1. A civil action; or,
2. Abatement. *(Enacted in 1872.)*

Cross References

Abatement, right of action, see Code of Civil Procedure § 731.
Agricultural processing, increased activities or operations, see Civil Code § 3482.6.
Building or place,
   Alcohol, unlawful sales, see Penal Code § 11200.
   Controlled substances, sales, see Health and Safety Code § 11570.
   Criminal street gangs, activities, see Penal Code § 186.22a.
   Gambling, prostitution or lewdness, see Penal Code § 11225.
Spite fence as private nuisance, see Civil Code § 841.4.

§ 3502. Abatement; method

A person injured by a private nuisance may abate it by removing, or, if necessary, destroying the thing which constitutes the nuisance, without committing a breach of the peace, or doing unnecessary injury. *(Enacted in 1872.)*

§ 3503. Abatement; notice

Where a private nuisance results from a mere omission of the wrongdoer, and cannot be abated without entering upon his land, reasonable notice must be given to him before entering to abate it. *(Enacted in 1872.)*

Title 4
MOTION PICTURES

Section
3504. Definitions.
3505. Exhibition of intentional killing or cruelty; nuisance.
3506. Commencement of actions; proper showing.
3507. Adversary trial; permanent injunctions; appeals; stay.
3507.1. Admissibility of evidence; burden of proof.
3507.2. Time for bringing actions; precedence over other actions; speedy and expeditious adjudication.
3507.3. Violations or disobedience of injunctions or orders; punishment.
3507.4. Distributors and producers; joint and several liability.
3508. Application of title; exceptions; federal supremacy.
3508.1. Misstatements by producers; misdemeanor.
3508.2. Severability.

§ 3504. Definitions

As used in this title:

(a) "Animal" means any amphibian, bird, mammal or reptile. It does not include any fish or insect.

(b) "Motion picture" means any motion picture, regardless of length or content, which is exhibited in a motion picture theater to paying customers, or is exhibited on television to paying customers or under the sponsorship of a paying advertiser. It shall not include motion pictures made for scientific, research, or educational purposes, or motion pictures exhibited as home movies, or amateur films, which are shown free or at cost to friends, neighbors or civic groups.

(c) "Person" means individuals, corporations, associations, partnerships, limited liability companies, trustees, lessees, agents and assignees. *(Added by Stats.1978, c. 1152, p. 3535, § 1. Amended by Stats.1994, c. 1010 (S.B.2053), § 56.)*

§ 3505. Exhibition of intentional killing or cruelty; nuisance

(a) The exhibition of any motion picture, if any intentional killing of, or cruelty to, a human being or an animal is shown in the motion picture and such intentional killing of, or cruelty to, a human being or an animal actually occurred in the production of the motion picture for the purpose of such production, is a nuisance, which shall be enjoined, abated, and prevented.

(b) As used in this section, "killing" and "cruelty" mean conduct which both (1) results in the death or the infliction of any physical injury or wound, including, but not limited to, any temporary or permanent physical harm resulting from the administration of any drug or chemical, and (2) is patently offensive to the average person, applying contemporary statewide community standards. It does not include conduct committed against a human being to which the human being has given his or her consent. In determining whether conduct is patently offensive, the trier of fact may consider any or all of the following: (i) the degree or extent of the physical injury inflicted, (ii) the manner in which the injury is inflicted, (iii) the extent to which the injuring or wounding or acts resulting therein are depicted on the screen, (iv) the number of instances of infliction of injury, wound or harm occurring in the making of the motion picture, and (v) whether such conduct is lawful or unlawful under any provision of law other than this title.

(c) For the purposes of this section, it shall not be a requirement that the entire motion picture and all of the conduct resulting therein be taken into account in determining whether a nuisance exists, and to this end, the Legislature finds and declares that any specific conduct which intentionally results in the killing of, or cruelty to, an animal or a human being in the making of a motion picture is unnecessary and is a nuisance, and that if a motion picture cannot be completed in the absence of such conduct, it is, therefore, a nuisance in its entirety. *(Added by Stats.1978, c. 1152, p. 3535, § 1.)*

§ 3506. Commencement of actions; proper showing

Whenever there is reasonable cause to believe that a nuisance as defined in this title is kept, maintained or is in existence in any county, the district attorney or the Attorney General, in the name of the people of the State of California, shall, on a proper showing, commence an action in equity to abate and prevent the nuisance and to perpetually enjoin the person conducting or maintaining it, and the owner, lessee or agent of the building, or place, in or upon which the nuisance exists, from maintaining or permitting it. As used herein, a proper showing to commence an action under this title must be based upon evidence independent of the motion picture itself that intentional killing of, or cruelty to, a human being or an animal actually occurred in the production of the motion picture for the purpose of such production. *(Added by Stats.1978, c. 1152, p. 3535, § 1.)*

§ 3507. Adversary trial; permanent injunctions; appeals; stay

Whenever an action is initiated under this title to abate an alleged nuisance, an adversary trial on the merits shall be held pursuant to Section 3507.2. If the court finds that the exhibition of the particular motion picture constitutes a nuisance, it shall issue a permanent injunction to abate and prevent the continuance or recurrence of such nuisance. No temporary restraining order or preliminary injunction shall be granted in such an action. An appeal may be taken from an order issuing a permanent injunction, and any injunction issued pursuant to this title by the trial court may be stayed by such court pending the outcome of such appeal. No appeal may be taken from a ruling by the trial court denying an injunction requested under this title. *(Added by Stats.1978, c. 1152, p. 3535, § 1.)*

§ 3507.1. Admissibility of evidence; burden of proof

In actions brought under this title, the motion picture shall be admissible into evidence. The burden of proof that the exhibition of the particular motion picture constitutes a nuisance shall be met by the district attorney or Attorney General only when clear and convincing evidence, independent of the motion picture itself, is provided that the acts alleged actually occurred in the production of the motion picture. *(Added by Stats.1978, c. 1152, p. 3535, § 1.)*

§ 3507.2. Time for bringing actions; precedence over other actions; speedy and expeditious adjudication

Actions brought under this title shall be brought as promptly as possible. Such actions shall have precedence over all actions, excepting criminal proceedings and election contests. It is also the intent of the Legislature that actions commenced under this title be adjudicated in the most speedy and expeditious manner. *(Added by Stats.1978, c. 1152, p. 3535, § 1.)*

§ 3507.3. Violations or disobedience of injunctions or orders; punishment

Any violation or disobedience of an injunction or order expressly provided for by this title is punishable as a contempt of court by a fine of not less than two hundred dollars ($200) nor more than one thousand dollars ($1,000). *(Added by Stats.1978, c. 1152, p. 3535, § 1.)*

§ 3507.4. Distributors and producers; joint and several liability

The distributor who furnished a motion picture to a person who is made a defendant in an action under this title, and the producer of a motion picture which is the subject of this title shall be jointly and severally liable, upon proof and after an opportunity to appear and interpose any appropriate defenses, to such person and the exhibitor for damages, including loss of profits, attorney's fees, and other costs of defending such action. Such distributor and such producer shall actively assist in such defense to the extent that such person possesses information necessary to such defense concerning the production of the motion picture which is not otherwise available to the defendant. The exhibitor shall not be liable upon any portion of any contract made on or after January 1, 1979, which requires the exhibition or advertisement of a motion picture subject to this title on or after the date of the filing of any action under this title, if the motion picture by final decision of a court is determined to be a nuisance under this title. *(Added by Stats.1978, c. 1152, p. 3535, § 1.)*

§ 3508. Application of title; exceptions; federal supremacy

(a) This title shall not apply to any of the following:

(1) The exhibition of any motion picture, such as a newsreel or documentary, involving acts of killing or cruelty which were not intentionally committed for the purpose of producing the motion picture.

(2) Any motion picture made, in whole or in part, prior to January 1, 1979.

(3) Any motion picture all or part of which has been edited or remade so that any previous conduct which constituted a nuisance under this title no longer appears.

(4) The taking of any animal as permitted by any provision of the Fish and Game Code or pursuant thereto in accordance with regulations adopted by the Fish and Game Commission unless the time, place, or manner of such taking violates any provision of law except this title. This title shall apply to any other animal whether or not the time, place, or manner of the taking is prohibited by any laws other than this title, however, this title shall not apply to the taking of any animal authorized by law in any other jurisdiction unless the

time, place or manner of such taking is prohibited by law or regulation.

(5) A motion picture which includes scenes of killing or cruelty to animals if the acts constituting the killing or cruelty were authorized by the laws governing such acts in the jurisdiction where the scenes were filmed.

(6) Any motion picture which bears within its contents a statement from the producer of the motion picture that all scenes depicting animals were filmed without the intentional killing of, or cruelty to an animal or that any killing or cruelty to an animal was authorized by the laws of the jurisdiction where the scenes were filmed or that the film is otherwise exempt under this title.

(7) Any motion picture if the exhibitor thereof has a written signed statement, or a copy thereof, from the producer of the motion picture that all scenes depicting animals were filmed without the intentional killing of, or cruelty to an animal or that any killing or cruelty to an animal was authorized by the laws of the jurisdiction where the scenes were filmed or that the film is otherwise exempt under this title.

(b) This title shall not apply in any case in which it would conflict with federal supremacy in the field of television broadcasting. *(Added by Stats.1978, c. 1152, p. 3535, § 1.)*

§ 3508.1. Misstatements by producers; misdemeanor

Any producer who willfully misstates or causes to be misstated any fact contained in a statement under paragraph (6) or (7) of Section 3508 is guilty of a misdemeanor. *(Added by Stats.1978, c. 1152, p. 3535, § 1.)*

§ 3508.2. Severability

If any provision of this title or the application thereof to any person or circumstances is held invalid, such invalidity shall not affect other provisions or applications of this title which can be given effect without the invalid provision or application, and to this end the provisions of this title are severable. *(Added by Stats.1978, c. 1152, p. 3535, § 1.)*

Part 4

MAXIMS OF JURISPRUDENCE

Section
3509. Intent and effect of maxims.
3510. Reason for rule ceasing.
3511. Reason same.
3512. Change of purpose.
3513. Waiver of advantage; law established for public reason.
3514. Use of rights.
3515. Consent; effect.
3516. Acquiescence in error.
3517. Advantage of own wrong.
3518. Fraudulent conveyances.
3519. Presumptive agency.
3520. Suffering from act of another.
3521. Benefit and burden.
3522. Essentials to use of thing granted.
3523. Remedy for wrong.
3524. Equally in right or in wrong.
3525. Preference of earliest right.
3526. Responsibility for unavoidable occurrences.
3527. Vigilance and delay.
3528. Form and substance.
3529. Presumption of performance.
3530. Nonexistence.
3531. Impossibilities.
3532. Idle acts.
3533. Trifles.
3534. Particular and general expressions.
3535. Contemporaneous exposition.
3536. Greater contains the less.
3537. Superfluity.
3538. Certainty.
3539. Time; void act.
3540. Incident follows principal.
3541. Interpretation; preference.
3542. Interpretation; reasonableness.
3543. Which of two innocent persons must suffer.
3545. Private transactions.
3546. Ordinary course of nature.
3547. Existence of things.
3548. Law obeyed.

§ 3509. Intent and effect of maxims

The maxims of jurisprudence hereinafter set forth are intended not to qualify any of the foregoing provisions of this code, but to aid in their just application. *(Enacted in 1872. Amended by Stats.2013, c. 76 (A.B.383), § 20.)*

§ 3510. Reason for rule ceasing

When the reason of a rule ceases, so should the rule itself. *(Enacted in 1872.)*

§ 3511. Reason same

Where the reason is the same, the rule should be the same. *(Enacted in 1872.)*

§ 3512. Change of purpose

One must not change his purpose to the injury of another. *(Enacted in 1872.)*

§ 3513. Waiver of advantage; law established for public reason

Any one may waive the advantage of a law intended solely for his benefit. But a law established for a public reason cannot be contravened by a private agreement. *(Enacted in 1872.)*

Cross References

Freedom from violence or intimidation, waiver of civil rights by contract, provisions of this section not abrogated, see Civil Code § 51.7.

§ 3514. Use of rights

One must so use his own rights as not to infringe upon the rights of another. *(Enacted in 1872.)*

Cross References

Abstinence from injuring others, see Civil Code § 1708.
Inalienable rights, see Cal. Const. Art. 1, § 1.
Responsibility for willful acts and negligence, see Civil Code § 1714.

§ 3515. Consent; effect

He who consents to an act is not wronged by it. *(Enacted in 1872.)*

Cross References

Ratification of contract voidable for want of consent, see Civil Code § 1588.

§ 3516. Acquiescence in error

Acquiescence in error takes away the right of objecting to it. *(Enacted in 1872.)*

§ 3517. Advantage of own wrong

No one can take advantage of his own wrong. *(Enacted in 1872.)*

§ 3518. Fraudulent conveyances

He who has fraudulently dispossessed himself of a thing may be treated as if he still had possession. *(Enacted in 1872.)*

Cross References

Action for relief against alleged fraudulent transfer, undertaking, see Civil Code § 3446.
Fraudulent transfers and instruments, see Civil Code § 3439 et seq.

§ 3519. Presumptive agency

He who can and does not forbid that which is done on his behalf, is deemed to have bidden it. *(Enacted in 1872.)*

§ 3520. Suffering from act of another

No one should suffer by the act of another. *(Enacted in 1872.)*

§ 3521. Benefit and burden

He who takes the benefit must bear the burden. *(Enacted in 1872.)*

Cross References

Assumption of obligation by acceptance of benefits, see Civil Code § 1589.

§ 3522. Essentials to use of thing granted

One who grants a thing is presumed to grant also whatever is essential to its use. *(Enacted in 1872.)*

§ 3523. Remedy for wrong

For every wrong there is a remedy. *(Enacted in 1872.)*

§ 3524. Equally in right or in wrong

Between those who are equally in the right, or equally in the wrong, the law does not interpose. *(Enacted in 1872.)*

§ 3525. Preference of earliest right

Between rights otherwise equal, the earliest is preferred. *(Enacted in 1872.)*

§ 3526. Responsibility for unavoidable occurrences

No man is responsible for that which no man can control. *(Enacted in 1872.)*

§ 3527. Vigilance and delay

The law helps the vigilant, before those who sleep on their rights. *(Enacted in 1872.)*

§ 3528. Form and substance

The law respects form less than substance. *(Enacted in 1872.)*

§ 3529. Presumption of performance

That which ought to have been done is to be regarded as done, in favor of him to whom, and against him from whom, performance is due. *(Enacted in 1872.)*

§ 3530. Nonexistence

That which does not appear to exist is to be regarded as if it did not exist. *(Enacted in 1872.)*

§ 3531. Impossibilities

The law never requires impossibilities. *(Enacted in 1872.)*

Cross References

Impossibility defined, see Civil Code § 1597.

§ 3532. Idle acts

The law neither does nor requires idle acts. *(Enacted in 1872.)*

§ 3533. Trifles

The law disregards trifles. *(Enacted in 1872.)*

§ 3534. Particular and general expressions

Particular expressions qualify those which are general. *(Enacted in 1872.)*

§ 3535. Contemporaneous exposition

Contemporaneous exposition is in general the best. *(Enacted in 1872.)*

§ 3536. Greater contains the less

The greater contains the less. *(Enacted in 1872.)*

§ 3537. Superfluity

Superfluity does not vitiate. *(Enacted in 1872.)*

§ 3538. Certainty

That is certain which can be made certain. *(Enacted in 1872.)*

§ 3539. Time; void act

Time does not confirm a void act. *(Enacted in 1872.)*

§ 3540. Incident follows principal

The incident follows the principal, and not the principal the incident. *(Enacted in 1872.)*

Cross References

Easements passing with property, see Civil Code § 1104.
Incidents, see Civil Code § 1084.

§ 3541. Interpretation; preference

An interpretation which gives effect is preferred to one which makes void. *(Enacted in 1872.)*

Cross References

Contracts, interpretation in favor of, see Civil Code § 1643.

§ 3542. Interpretation; reasonableness

Interpretation must be reasonable. *(Enacted in 1872.)*

§ 3543. Which of two innocent persons must suffer

Where one of two innocent persons must suffer by the act of a third, he, by whose negligence it happened, must be the sufferer. *(Enacted in 1872.)*

§ 3545. Private transactions

Private transactions are fair and regular. *(Added by Stats.1965, c. 299, p. 1357, § 11, operative Jan. 1, 1967.)*

§ 3546. Ordinary course of nature

Things happen according to the ordinary course of nature and the ordinary habits of life. *(Added by Stats.1965, c. 299, p. 1357, § 12, operative Jan. 1, 1967.)*

§ 3547. Existence of things

A thing continues to exist as long as is usual with things of that nature. *(Added by Stats.1965, c. 299, p. 1357, § 13, operative Jan. 1, 1967.)*

§ 3548. Law obeyed

The law has been obeyed. *(Added by Stats.1965, c. 299, p. 1357, § 14, operative Jan. 1, 1967.)*

Part 5
COMMON INTEREST DEVELOPMENTS

Chapter	Section
1. General Provisions	4000
2. Application of Act	4200
3. Governing Documents	4205
4. Ownership and Transfer of Interests	4500
5. Property Use and Maintenance	4700
6. Association Governance	4800
7. Finances	5500
8. Assessments and Assessment Collection	5600
9. Insurance and Liability	5800
10. Dispute Resolution and Enforcement	5850
11. Construction Defect Litigation	6000

Publisher's Note

The following table was provided by the California Law Revision Commission, and is reproduced with minor modifications. The original table was published in the California Law Revision Commission recommendation titled "Statutory Clarification and Simplification of CID Law" [40 Cal.L.Rev.Comm. Reports 235 (2010)].

DISPOSITION OF FORMER LAW

The table below shows the relationship between each provision of the former Davis–Stirling Common Interest Development Act and the corresponding provision of the new law.

Former Provision	New Provision(s)
1350	4000
1350.5	4005
1350.7	omitted, but see 4040, 4045, 4050
1351 (intro.)	4075
1351(a)	4080
1351(b)	4095
1351(c)	4100
1351(d)	4105
1351(e)(1)-(2)	4285
1351(e)(3) (except last ¶)	4285, 4290
1351(e)(last ¶)	4295
1351(f)	4125
1351(g)	4130
1351(h)	4135
1351(i)	4145
1351(j)	4150
1351(k)	4175
1351(*l*)	4185
1351(m)	4190
1352	4200
1352.5	4225(a)-(b), (d)
1353(a)(1) (1st & 2d sent.)	4250(a)
1353(a)(1)-(4) (except 1st & 2d sent.)	4255
1353(b)	4250(b)
1353.5	4705
1353.6	4710
1353.7	4720
1353.8	4735
1353.9	4745
1354	5975
1355(a)	4270(a)
1355(b) (1st sent.)	4260
1355(b)(1)	5115(e)
1355(b)(2)	4270(b)
1355(b)(3)	4270(a)(3)
1355.5	4230
1356	4275
1357(a)	4265(a)
1357(b) (except part of 1st sent.)	omitted
1357(b) (part of 1st sent.)	4265(b)
1357(c)	omitted
1357(d)	4265(c)
1357.100(a)	4340(a)
1357.100(b)	4340(b)
1357.110	4350
1357.120	4355
1357.130	4360
1357.140	4365
1357.150	4370
1358(a)	4625
1358(b)	4630
1358(c)	4635
1358(d)	4640
1358 (last ¶)	4650
1358 (next to last ¶)	4645
1359	4610
1360	4760
1360.2	4740
1360.5	4715
1361	4505
1361.5	4510
1362	4500
1363(a)	4800
1363(b)	omitted
1363(c)	4805
1363(d)	5000(a)
1363(e) (1st sent.)	5240(b)
1363(e) (2d sent.)	omitted
1363(f) (1st sent.)	5850(a)
1363(f) (2d sent.)	omitted
1363(g)	5855
1363(h)	4820
1363(i)	5865
1363.001	5400
1363.005	omitted
1363.03(a)	5105(a)
1363.03(b) (1st sent.)	5100(a)
1363.03(b) (2d & 3d sents.)	5115(b)
1363.03(b) (4th sent.)	5115(c)
1363.03(c)	5110
1363.03(d)	5130

COMMON INTEREST DEVELOPMENTS

Former Provision	New Provision(s)
1363.03(e)	5115(a)
1363.03(f)	5120(a)
1363.03(g)	5120(b)
1363.03(h)	5125(a)
1363.03(i)	5125(b)
1363.03(j)	5105(b)
1363.03(k)	5115(d)
1363.03(*l*)	5100(c)
1363.03(m)	5100(d)
1363.03(n)	5100(e)
1363.03(*o*)	omitted
1363.04	5135
1363.05(a)	4900
1363.05(b) (1st part of 1st sent.)	4925(a)
1363.05(b) (2d part of 1st sent.)	4935(a)
1363.05(b) (2d sent.)	4935(b)
1363.05(b) (3d sent.)	4925(a)
1363.05(c)	4935(e)
1363.05(d)	4950(a)
1363.05(e)	4950(b)
1363.05(f)	4920
1363.05(g)	4923
1363.05(h)	4925(b), 5000(b)
1363.05(i)	4930
1363.05(j)	4910
1363.05(k)(1)	4155
1363.05(k)(2)	4090
1363.07 (except (a)(3)(F))	4600
1363.07(a)(3)(F)	4202(a)(4)
1363.09 (re elections)	5145
1363.09(a)-(b) (re exclusive use grant)	4605
1363.09(a)-(b) (re open meetings)	4955
1363.1(a)	5375
1363.1(b) (except ¶ (1))	4158
1363.1(b)(1)	5385
1363.2(a)-(e)	5380(a)-(e)
1363.2(f) (except 1st cl. of 2d sent.)	4158
1363.2(f) (1st cl. of 2d sent.)	5385
1363.2(g)	5380(f)
1363.5	4280
1363.6	5405
1363.810	5900
1363.820	5905
1363.830	5910
1363.840	5915
1363.850	5920
1364(a)	4775(a)
1364(b)	4780
1364(c)	4775(b)
1364(d)-(e)	4785
1364(f)	4790
1365 (intro. cl.)	5300(b) (intro. cl.), 5305 (intro. cl.)
1365(a)(1)	5300(b)(1)
1365(a)(2) (intro. cl.)	5300(b)(2)
1365(a)(2)(A)-(D)	5565
1365(a)(3)(A)	5300(b)(4)
1365(a)(3)(B)	5300(b)(5)
1365(a)(3)(C)	5300(b)(6)
1365(a)(3)(D)	5300(b)(8)
1365(a)(4) (1st ¶)	5300(b)(7)
1365(a)(4) (2d ¶)	5300(d)
1365(a)(4) (3d ¶)	5300(a)
1365(b)	5300(b)(3)
1365(c)	5305
1365(d)	5320
1365(e)	5310(a)(7)
1365(f)(1) (except 2d cl. of 1st sent.)	5300(b)(9) (1st & 2d sent.)
1365(f)(1) (2d cl. of 1st sent.)	5300(a)
1365(f)(2)	5810
1365(f)(3)	5300(b)(9) (3d sent.)
1365(f)(4)	5300(b)(9) (4th sent. & 2d ¶)
1365.1	4040(b), 5730
1365.2(a)(1) (except (I)(ii)-(iii))	5200(a)
1365.2(a)(1)(I)(ii)	5225
1365.2(a)(1)(I)(iii)	5220
1365.2(a)(2) (except last cl.)	5200(b)
1365.2(a)(2) (last cl.)	5205(g) (2d sent.)
1365.2(b)	5205(a)-(b)
1365.2(c)(1)-(4)	5205(c)-(f)
1365.2(c)(5)	5205(g) (1st & 3d sents.)
1365.2(d)	5215
1365.2(e)	5230
1365.2(f)	5235
1365.2(g)	5240(c)
1365.2(h)	5205(h)
1365.2(i)-(j)	5210(a)-(b)
1365.2(k)	5210(c)
1365.2(*l*)	5240(a)
1365.2(m)	5240(d)
1365.2(n)	omitted
1365.2.5	5570
1365.2.5(b)(3)	5300(e)
1365.3	5580
1365.5(a)	5500
1365.5(b)	5510(a)
1365.5(c)(1)	5510(b)
1365.5(c)(2)	5515
1365.5(d)	5520
1365.5(e) (1)-(4), (5) (1st sent.)	5550
1365.5(e)(5) (except 1st sent.)	5560
1365.5(f)	4177
1365.5(g)	4178
1365.5(h)	omitted

GENERAL PROVISIONS

Former Provision	New Provision(s)
1365.6	5350(a)
1365.7	5800
1365.9	5805
1366(a) (1st sent.)	5600(a)
1366(a) (2d sent.)	5605(a)
1366(a) (3d sent.)	5605(c)
1366(b) (1st sent.)	5605(b)
1366(b) (2d sent.)	5605(c)
1366(b) (3d & 4th sent.)	5610 (intro.)
1366(b)(1)-(3)	5610(a)-(c)
1366(c)	5620
1366(d)	5615
1366(e)	5650(b)
1366(f)	5650(c)
1366.1	5600(b)
1366.2(a)	4210
1366.2(b)	omitted
1366.4	5625
1367	omitted, but see 5740
1367.1(a) (1st sent.)	5650(a)
1367.1(a) (2d sent.)	5660 (intro.)
1367.1(a)(1)-(6)	5660(a)-(f)
1367.1(b)	5655
1367.1(c)(1)(A)	5670
1367.1(c)(1)(B)	omitted, but see 5705(b)
1367.1(c)(2)	5673
1367.1(c)(3)	5665
1367.1(d) (1st - 5th sent.)	5675
1367.1(d) (6th sent.)	5685(a)
1367.1(d) (7th & 8th sent.)	5725(a)
1367.1(e)	5725(b)
1367.1(f)	5680
1367.1(g) (1st sent.)	5735
1367.1(g) (2d sent.)	5700(a)
1367.1(g) (3d sent.)	5710(a)
1367.1(g) (4th sent.)	5710(c) (intro.)
1367.1(g)(1)-(2)	5710(c)(1)-(2)
1367.1(h)	5700(b)
1367.1(i)	5685(b)
1367.1(j)	5710(b)
1367.1(k)	4040(b)
1367.1(*l*)	5690
1367.1(m)	omitted, but see 5740
1367.1(n)	omitted
1367.4(a)	5705(a), 5715(a), 5720(a)
1367.4(b)	5720(b)
1367.4(c) (intro.)	omitted, but see 5705, 5715
1367.4(c)(1)	5705(b)
1367.4(c)(2)	5705(c)
1367.4(c)(3)	5705(d)
1367.4(c)(4)	5715(b)
1367.4(d)	5720(c)(2)-(3)
1367.5	5685(c)
1367.6	5658
1368(a)	4525
1368(b)	4530
1368(c)(1)	4575
1368(c)(2)	4580
1368(c)(3)	4110
1368(d)	4540
1368(e)	4545
1368(f)	4535
1368(g)	omitted
1368.1	4730
1368.2	4528
1368.3	5980
1368.4	5985
1368.5	6150
1369	4615
1369.510	5925
1369.520	5930
1369.530	5935
1369.540	5940
1369.550	5945
1369.560	5950
1369.570	5955
1369.580	5960
1369.590	5965
1370	4215
1371	4220
1372	4020
1373	4202
1374	4201
1375	6000
1375.1	6100
1376	4725
1378	4765

CHAPTER 1. GENERAL PROVISIONS

Article	Section
1. Preliminary Provisions	4000
2. Definitions	4075

ARTICLE 1. PRELIMINARY PROVISIONS

Section
4000. Short title.
4001. Repealed.
4005. Effect of headings on scope, meaning, or intent of act.
4010. Continuation of prior law.
4020. Construction of zoning ordinances.
4035. Delivery of document to association.
4040. Individual delivery or individual notice.
4040. Individual delivery or individual notice.
4041. Member's preferred delivery method; annual notice to association.
4045. General delivery or general notice.
4050. Time of delivery.
4055. Electronic delivery; satisfaction of written information requirement.
4065. Approval by majority.
4070. Approval by majority of quorum.

§ 4000. Short title

This part shall be known and may be cited as the Davis–Stirling Common Interest Development Act. In a provision of this part, the part may be referred to as the act. *(Added by Stats.2012, c. 180 (A.B.805), § 2, operative Jan. 1, 2014.)*

Cross References

Right to display political campaign signs, see Civil Code § 799.10.

§ 4001. Repealed by Stats.1992, c. 162 (A.B.2650), § 3, operative Jan. 1, 1994

§ 4005. Effect of headings on scope, meaning, or intent of act

Division, part, title, chapter, article, and section headings do not in any manner affect the scope, meaning, or intent of this act. *(Added by Stats.2012, c. 180 (A.B.805), § 2, operative Jan. 1, 2014. Amended by Stats.2013, c. 183 (S.B.745), § 7.)*

§ 4010. Continuation of prior law

Nothing in the act that added this part shall be construed to invalidate a document prepared or action taken before January 1, 2014, if the document or action was proper under the law governing common interest developments at the time that the document was prepared or the action was taken. For the purposes of this section, "document" does not include a governing document. *(Added by Stats.2012, c. 180 (A.B.805), § 2, operative Jan. 1, 2014.)*

§ 4020. Construction of zoning ordinances

Unless a contrary intent is clearly expressed, a local zoning ordinance is construed to treat like structures, lots, parcels, areas, or spaces in like manner regardless of the form of the common interest development. *(Added by Stats.2012, c. 180 (A.B.805), § 2, operative Jan. 1, 2014.)*

§ 4035. Delivery of document to association

(a) If a provision of this act requires that a document be delivered to an association, the document shall be delivered to the person designated in the annual policy statement, prepared pursuant to Section 5310, to receive documents on behalf of the association. If no person has been designated to receive documents, the document shall be delivered to the president or secretary of the association.

(b) A document delivered pursuant to this section may be delivered by any of the following methods:

(1) By email, facsimile, or other electronic means, if the association has assented to that method of delivery.

(2) By personal delivery, if the association has assented to that method of delivery. If the association accepts a document by personal delivery it shall provide a written receipt acknowledging delivery of the document.

(3) By first-class mail, postage prepaid, registered or certified mail, express mail, or overnight delivery by an express service center. *(Added by Stats.2012, c. 180 (A.B.805), § 2, operative Jan. 1, 2014. Amended by Stats.2013, c. 183 (S.B.745), § 8.)*

Cross References

Association record inspection, requests to be delivered in writing, see Civil Code § 5260.

Common interest developments, restrictive covenants, deletion from declaration or other governing document, recording or filing of amended document, see Civil Code § 4225.

§ 4040. Individual delivery or individual notice

(a)(1) If a provision of this act requires an association to deliver a document by "individual delivery" or "individual notice," the association shall deliver that document in accordance with the preferred delivery method specified by the member pursuant to Section 4041.

(2) If the member has not provided a valid delivery method pursuant to Section 4041, the association shall deliver the document by first-class mail, registered or certified mail, express mail, or overnight delivery by an express service carrier addressed to the recipient at the address last shown on the books of the association.

(b) Upon receipt of a request by a member identifying a secondary email or mailing address for delivery of notices, pursuant to Section 5260, the association shall deliver an additional copy of both of the following to the secondary address identified in that request:

(1) The documents to be delivered to the member pursuant to Article 7 (commencing with Section 5300) of Chapter 6.

(2) The documents to be delivered to the member pursuant to Article 2 (commencing with Section 5650) of Chapter 8 and Section 5710.

(c) For the purposes of this section, an unrecorded provision of the governing documents providing for a particular method of delivery does not constitute agreement by a member to that method of delivery.

(d) This section shall become operative on January 1, 2023. *(Added by Stats.2021, c. 640 (S.B.392), § 2, eff. Jan. 1, 2022, operative Jan. 1, 2023.)*

Cross References

Amendment of declaration, petition, power of court to approve amendment, recording of amendment, individual delivery, see Civil Code § 4275.
Amendment of governing documents to delete construction or marketing provisions after completion by developer, requirements, see Civil Code § 4230.
Annual policy statement, contents, see Civil Code § 5310.
Assessments, individual notice of increases, see Civil Code § 5615.
Association records, availability to members, individual delivery, see Civil Code § 5205.
Board disciplinary proceedings, notice to member, see Civil Code § 5855.
Claim of lien, notice to members, see Civil Code § 4620.
Delivery of annual reports, see Civil Code § 5320.
Individual notice to members of changes in insurance coverage, see Civil Code § 5810.
Monetary penalties, provision of information to members, see Civil Code § 5850.
Sales of a separate interest in a common interest development, right of redemption, see Code of Civil Procedure § 729.035.
Standards for preparation of review of financial statement of association, delivery, see Civil Code § 5305.
Temporary removal of occupant for treatment of wood-destroying pests or organisms, notice, see Civil Code § 4785.

§ 4041. Member's preferred delivery method; annual notice to association

(a) A member shall, on an annual basis, provide written notice to the association of all of the following:

(1) The member's preferred delivery method for receiving notices from the association, which shall include the option of receiving notices at one or both of the following:

(A) A mailing address.

(B) A valid email address.

(2) An alternate or secondary delivery method for receiving notices from the association, which shall include the option to receive notices at one or both of the following:

(A) A mailing address.

(B) A valid email address.

(3) The name, mailing address, and, if available, valid email address of the owner's legal representative, if any, including any person with power of attorney or other person who can be contacted in the event of the member's extended absence from the separate interest.

(4) Whether the separate interest is owner-occupied, is rented out, if the parcel is developed but vacant, or if the parcel is undeveloped land.

(b)(1) The association shall solicit the annual notices described in subdivision (a) of each owner and, at least 30 days before making its own required disclosure under Sections 5300 and 5310, shall enter the data into its books and records.

(2) The association shall include in the solicitation required by paragraph (1) both of the following:

(A) Notification that the member does not have to provide an email address to the association.

(B) A simple method for the member to inform the association in writing that the member wishes to change their preferred delivery method for receiving notices from the association.

(c) If a member fails to provide the notices set forth in subdivision (a), the last mailing address provided in writing by the member or, if none, the property address shall be deemed to be the address to which notices are to be delivered.

(d)(1) To the extent that interests regulated in Chapter 2 (commencing with Section 11210) of Part 2 of Division 4 of the Business and Professions Code are part of a mixed-use project where those interests comprise a portion of a common interest development, the association, as defined in Section 4080, shall be deemed compliant with this section if, at least once annually, it obtains from the time-share plan association a copy of the list described in subdivision (e) of Section 11273 of the Business and Professions Code, and enters the data into its books and records.

(2) Notwithstanding subdivision (e) of Section 11273 of the Business and Professions Code, the time-share plan association shall provide the list required by paragraph (1) to the association at least annually for this purpose.

(e) For the purposes of this section, a valid email address is one that, after a notice is sent, does not result in a bounce or other error notification indicating failure of the message. If the association delivers a notice to a member's email address and finds that the email address provided is no longer valid, the association shall resend the notice to a mailing or email address identified by the member pursuant to Section 4040. *(Added by Stats.2016, c. 780 (S.B.918), § 1, eff. Jan. 1, 2017. Amended by Stats.2017, c. 278 (A.B.1412), § 1, eff. Jan. 1, 2018; Stats.2018, c. 91 (S.B.1173), § 1, eff. Jan. 1, 2019; Stats.2021, c. 640 (S.B.392), § 3, eff. Jan. 1, 2022; Stats.2022, c. 632 (S.B.1252), § 1, eff. Jan. 1, 2023.)*

§ 4045. General delivery or general notice

(a) If a provision of this act requires "general delivery" or "general notice," the document shall be provided by one or more of the following methods:

(1) Any method provided for delivery of an individual notice pursuant to Section 4040.

(2) Inclusion in a billing statement, newsletter, or other document that is delivered by one of the methods provided in this section.

(3) Posting the printed document in a prominent location that is accessible to all members, if the location has been designated for the posting of general notices by the association in the annual policy statement prepared pursuant to Section 5310.

(4) If the association broadcasts television programming for the purpose of distributing information on association business to its members, by inclusion in the programming.

(5) If the association maintains an internet website for the purpose of distributing information on association business to its members, by posting the notice on the association's internet website in a prominent location that is accessible to all members if designated as a location for posting general notices in the annual policy statement prepared pursuant to Section 5310.

(b) Notwithstanding subdivision (a), if a member requests to receive general notices by individual delivery, all general notices to that member, given under this section, shall be delivered pursuant to Section 4040. The option provided in this subdivision shall be described in the annual policy statement prepared pursuant to Section 5310. *(Added by Stats.2012, c. 180 (A.B.805), § 2, operative Jan. 1, 2014. Amended by Stats.2021, c. 640 (S.B.392), § 4, eff. Jan. 1, 2022.)*

Cross References

Association record inspection, requests to be delivered in writing, see Civil Code § 5260.
Board meetings, notice, see Civil Code § 4920.
Member elections, counting and tabulation of votes, reporting of tabulated results, see Civil Code § 5120.
Proposed rule change by board action, notice, meeting, see Civil Code § 4360.
Special meeting of members to reverse rule change, notice, voting requirements, effect of approved reversal, see Civil Code § 4365.

Use of reserve funds, notice of action, see Civil Code § 5520.

§ 4050. Time of delivery

(a) This section governs the delivery of a document pursuant to this act.

(b) If a document is delivered by mail, delivery is deemed to be complete on deposit into the United States mail.

(c) If a document is delivered by electronic means, delivery is complete at the time of transmission. *(Added by Stats. 2012, c. 180 (A.B.805), § 2, operative Jan. 1, 2014.)*

§ 4055. Electronic delivery; satisfaction of written information requirement

If the association or a member receives information by electronic delivery pursuant to Section 4040, and a provision of this act requires that the information be in writing, that requirement is satisfied if the information is provided in an electronic record capable of retention by the recipient at the time of receipt. An electronic record is not capable of retention by the recipient if the sender or its information processing system inhibits the ability of the recipient to print or store the electronic record. *(Added by Stats.2012, c. 180 (A.B.805), § 2, operative Jan. 1, 2014. Amended by Stats. 2021, c. 640 (S.B.392), § 5, eff. Jan. 1, 2022.)*

§ 4065. Approval by majority

If a provision of this act requires that an action be approved by a majority of all members, the action shall be approved or ratified by an affirmative vote of a majority of the votes entitled to be cast. *(Added by Stats.2012, c. 180 (A.B.805), § 2, operative Jan. 1, 2014.)*

Cross References

Damage by wood-destroying pests or organisms, delegation of responsibility for repair and maintenance, see Civil Code § 4780.
Extension of term of declaration, see Civil Code § 4265.

§ 4070. Approval by majority of quorum

If a provision of this act requires that an action be approved by a majority of a quorum of the members, the action shall be approved or ratified by an affirmative vote of a majority of the votes represented and voting in a duly held election in which a quorum is represented, which affirmative votes also constitute a majority of the required quorum. *(Added by Stats.2012, c. 180 (A.B.805), § 2, operative Jan. 1, 2014. Amended by Stats.2013, c. 183 (S.B.745), § 9.)*

Cross References

Amendment of governing documents to delete construction or marketing provisions after completion by developer, requirements, see Civil Code § 4230.
Assessments, exemption from execution by judgment creditor of association, see Civil Code § 5620.
Assessments, limitation on increases, see Civil Code § 5605.
Special meeting of members to reverse rule change, notice, voting requirements, effect of approved reversal, see Civil Code § 4365.

ARTICLE 2. DEFINITIONS

Section
4075. Construction of act.

GENERAL PROVISIONS

Section
4076. "Annual budget report" defined.
4078. "Annual policy statement" defined.
4080. "Association" defined.
4085. "Board" defined.
4090. "Board meeting" defined.
4095. "Common area" defined.
4100. "Common interest development" defined.
4101 to 4104. Repealed.
4105. "Community apartment project" defined.
4110. "Community service organization or similar entity" defined.
4120. "Condominium plan" defined.
4125. "Condominium project" defined.
4130. "Declarant" defined.
4135. "Declaration" defined.
4140. "Director" defined.
4145. "Exclusive use common area" defined.
4148. "General notice" defined.
4150. "Governing documents" defined.
4153. "Individual notice" defined.
4155. "Item of business" defined.
4158. "Managing agent" defined.
4160. "Member" defined.
4170. "Person" defined.
4175. "Planned development" defined.
4177. "Reserve accounts" defined.
4178. "Reserve account requirements" defined.
4185. "Separate interest" defined.
4190. "Stock cooperative" defined.

§ 4075. Construction of act

The definitions in this article govern the construction of this act. *(Added by Stats.2012, c. 180 (A.B.805), § 2, operative Jan. 1, 2014.)*

§ 4076. "Annual budget report" defined

"Annual budget report" means the report described in Section 5300. *(Added by Stats.2012, c. 180 (A.B.805), § 2, operative Jan. 1, 2014.)*

§ 4078. "Annual policy statement" defined

"Annual policy statement" means the statement described in Section 5310. *(Added by Stats.2012, c. 180 (A.B.805), § 2, operative Jan. 1, 2014.)*

§ 4080. "Association" defined

"Association" means a nonprofit corporation or unincorporated association created for the purpose of managing a common interest development. *(Added by Stats.2012, c. 180 (A.B.805), § 2, operative Jan. 1, 2014.)*

Cross References

Restrictive covenants based on discriminatory grounds, notice on copy of document, penalty for adding racially restrictive covenant, see Government Code § 12956.1.
Subdivided lands, application of provisions and regulations to interests or memberships in owners' associations, see Business and Professions Code § 11004.5.

§ 4085. "Board" defined

"Board" means the board of directors of the association. *(Added by Stats.2012, c. 180 (A.B.805), § 2, operative Jan. 1, 2014.)*

§ 4090. "Board meeting" defined

"Board meeting" means either of the following:

(a) A congregation, at the same time and place, of a sufficient number of directors to establish a quorum of the board, to hear, discuss, or deliberate upon any item of business that is within the authority of the board.

(b) A teleconference, where a sufficient number of directors to establish a quorum of the board, in different locations, are connected by electronic means, through audio or video, or both. A teleconference meeting shall be conducted in a manner that protects the rights of members of the association and otherwise complies with the requirements of this act. Except for a meeting that will be held solely in executive session or conducted under Section 5450, the notice of the teleconference meeting shall identify at least one physical location so that members of the association may attend, and at least one director or a person designated by the board shall be present at that location. Participation by directors in a teleconference meeting constitutes presence at that meeting as long as all directors participating are able to hear one another, as well as members of the association speaking on matters before the board. *(Added by Stats.2012, c. 180 (A.B.805), § 2, operative Jan. 1, 2014. Amended by Stats.2013, c. 183 (S.B.745), § 10; Stats.2021, c. 276 (S.B.391), § 1, eff. Sept. 23, 2021.)*

Cross References

Open meeting, executive session exception, see Civil Code § 4925.

§ 4095. "Common area" defined

(a) "Common area" means the entire common interest development except the separate interests therein. The estate in the common area may be a fee, a life estate, an estate for years, or any combination of the foregoing.

(b) Notwithstanding subdivision (a), in a planned development described in subdivision (b) of Section 4175, the common area may consist of mutual or reciprocal easement rights appurtenant to the separate interests. *(Added by Stats.2012, c. 180 (A.B.805), § 2, operative Jan. 1, 2014.)*

§ 4100. "Common interest development" defined

"Common interest development" means any of the following:

(a) A community apartment project.

(b) A condominium project.

(c) A planned development.

(d) A stock cooperative. *(Added by Stats.2012, c. 180 (A.B.805), § 2, operative Jan. 1, 2014.)*

Cross References

Action to enforce and foreclose an assessment lien on a common interest development as a limited civil case, see Code of Civil Procedure § 86.
Appearance by person other than plaintiff or defendant, parties created to manage a common interest development, see Code of Civil Procedure § 116.540.
Condominium projects, requirements of Subdivision Map Act, see Government Code § 66427.
Fire protection, fire retardant roof covering standards, see Health and Safety Code § 13132.7.

Incentives or concessions for lower income housing units and child care facilities, written findings relative to affordable housing, condominium projects, preliminary development proposals, judicial proceedings, development, density bonus, and parking ratios, see Government Code § 65915.

Local control of common interest developments and subdivision design and improvement, see Government Code § 66411.

Parked and abandoned vehicles, authority to remove vehicles, see Vehicle Code §§ 22651, 22651.05.

Public swimming pools in certain common interest developments, record-keeping requirement, see Health and Safety Code § 116048.

Real estate brokers, solicitation for transient occupancies, definition exemption, see Business and Professions Code § 10131.01.

Regulation of buildings used for human habitation, inspection of exterior elevated elements, section not applicable to common interest developments, see Health and Safety Code § 17973.

Restrictive covenants based on discriminatory grounds, recording of modification, submission to county counsel, filing, and public access, and unauthorized modifications, see Government Code § 12956.2.

Solicitation or acceptance of money for transient occupancy of dwelling unit in common interest development, see Civil Code § 1864.

Subdivided lands, common interest development general information statement, see Business and Professions Code § 11018.1.

§§ 4101 to 4104. Repealed by Stats.1992, c. 162 (A.B.2650), § 3, operative Jan. 1, 1994

§ 4105. "Community apartment project" defined

"Community apartment project" means a development in which an undivided interest in land is coupled with the right of exclusive occupancy of any apartment located thereon. *(Added by Stats.2012, c. 180 (A.B.805), § 2, operative Jan. 1, 2014.)*

§ 4110. "Community service organization or similar entity" defined

(a) "Community service organization or similar entity" means a nonprofit entity, other than an association, that is organized to provide services to residents of the common interest development or to the public in addition to the residents, to the extent community common area or facilities are available to the public.

(b) "Community service organization or similar entity" does not include an entity that has been organized solely to raise moneys and contribute to other nonprofit organizations that are qualified as tax exempt under Section 501(c)(3) of the Internal Revenue Code [1] and that provide housing or housing assistance. *(Added by Stats.2012, c. 180 (A.B.805), § 2, operative Jan. 1, 2014.)*

[1] Internal Revenue Code sections are in Title 26 of the U.S.C.A.

§ 4120. "Condominium plan" defined

"Condominium plan" means a plan described in Section 4285. *(Added by Stats.2012, c. 180 (A.B.805), § 2, operative Jan. 1, 2014.)*

§ 4125. "Condominium project" defined

(a) A "condominium project" means a real property development consisting of condominiums.

(b) A condominium consists of an undivided interest in common in a portion of real property coupled with a separate interest in space called a unit, the boundaries of which are described on a recorded final map, parcel map, or condominium plan in sufficient detail to locate all boundaries thereof. The area within these boundaries may be filled with air, earth, water, or fixtures, or any combination thereof, and need not be physically attached to land except by easements for access and, if necessary, support. The description of the unit may refer to (1) boundaries described in the recorded final map, parcel map, or condominium plan, (2) physical boundaries, either in existence, or to be constructed, such as walls, floors, and ceilings of a structure or any portion thereof, (3) an entire structure containing one or more units, or (4) any combination thereof.

(c) The portion or portions of the real property held in undivided interest may be all of the real property, except for the separate interests, or may include a particular three-dimensional portion thereof, the boundaries of which are described on a recorded final map, parcel map, or condominium plan. The area within these boundaries may be filled with air, earth, water, or fixtures, or any combination thereof, and need not be physically attached to land except by easements for access and, if necessary, support.

(d) An individual condominium within a condominium project may include, in addition, a separate interest in other portions of the real property. *(Added by Stats.2012, c. 180 (A.B.805), § 2, operative Jan. 1, 2014.)*

Cross References

Manufactured home, mobilehome and commercial modular foundation systems, installation requirements for fixture or improvement status, see Health and Safety Code § 18551.

Property tax, separate assessment of condominium units, see Revenue and Taxation Code § 2188.6.

Water reuse, use of recycled water for toilet and urinal flushing in condominium projects, see Water Code § 13553.

§ 4130. "Declarant" defined

"Declarant" means the person or group of persons designated in the declaration as declarant, or if no declarant is designated, the person or group of persons who sign the original declaration or who succeed to special rights, preferences, or privileges designated in the declaration as belonging to the signator of the original declaration. *(Added by Stats.2012, c. 180 (A.B.805), § 2, operative Jan. 1, 2014.)*

§ 4135. "Declaration" defined

"Declaration" means the document, however denominated, that contains the information required by Sections 4250 and 4255. *(Added by Stats.2012, c. 180 (A.B.805), § 2, operative Jan. 1, 2014.)*

Cross References

Property tax, separate assessment of condominium units, see Revenue and Taxation Code § 2188.6.

Restrictive covenants based on discriminatory grounds, notice on copy of document, penalty for adding racially restrictive covenant, see Government Code § 12956.1.

Water reuse, use of recycled water for toilet and urinal flushing in condominium projects, see Water Code § 13553.

§ 4140. "Director" defined

"Director" means a natural person who serves on the board. *(Added by Stats.2012, c. 180 (A.B.805), § 2, operative Jan. 1, 2014.)*

§ 4145. "Exclusive use common area" defined

(a) "Exclusive use common area" means a portion of the common area designated by the declaration for the exclusive use of one or more, but fewer than all, of the owners of the separate interests and which is or will be appurtenant to the separate interest or interests.

(b) Unless the declaration otherwise provides, any shutters, awnings, window boxes, doorsteps, stoops, porches, balconies, patios, exterior doors, doorframes, and hardware incident thereto, screens and windows or other fixtures designed to serve a single separate interest, but located outside the boundaries of the separate interest, are exclusive use common area allocated exclusively to that separate interest.

(c) Notwithstanding the provisions of the declaration, internal and external telephone wiring designed to serve a single separate interest, but located outside the boundaries of the separate interest, is exclusive use common area allocated exclusively to that separate interest. *(Added by Stats.2012, c. 180 (A.B.805), § 2, operative Jan. 1, 2014.)*

Cross References

Access for maintenance of telephone wiring, see Civil Code § 4790.

§ 4148. "General notice" defined

"General notice" means the delivery of a document pursuant to Section 4045. *(Added by Stats.2012, c. 180 (A.B.805), § 2, operative Jan. 1, 2014.)*

§ 4150. "Governing documents" defined

"Governing documents" means the declaration and any other documents, such as bylaws, operating rules, articles of incorporation, or articles of association, which govern the operation of the common interest development or association. *(Added by Stats.2012, c. 180 (A.B.805), § 2, operative Jan. 1, 2014.)*

Cross References

Fire protection, fire retardant roof covering standards, see Health and Safety Code § 13132.7.
Governing documents, restrictions, electric vehicle charging stations, see Civil Code § 4745.
Restrictive covenants based on discriminatory grounds, notice on copy of document, penalty for adding racially restrictive covenant, see Government Code § 12956.1.
Unenforceability of deeds, contracts or instruments prohibiting or restricting installation or use of solar energy system, see Civil Code § 714.

§ 4153. "Individual notice" defined

"Individual notice" means the delivery of a document pursuant to Section 4040. *(Added by Stats.2012, c. 180 (A.B.805), § 2, operative Jan. 1, 2014.)*

§ 4155. "Item of business" defined

"Item of business" means any action within the authority of the board, except those actions that the board has validly delegated to any other person or persons, managing agent, officer of the association, or committee of the board comprising less than a quorum of the board. *(Added by Stats.2012, c. 180 (A.B.805), § 2, operative Jan. 1, 2014.)*

§ 4158. "Managing agent" defined

(a) A "managing agent" is a person who, for compensation or in expectation of compensation, exercises control over the assets of a common interest development.

(b) A "managing agent" does not include any of the following:

(1) A regulated financial institution operating within the normal course of its regulated business practice.

(2) An attorney at law acting within the scope of the attorney's license. *(Added by Stats.2012, c. 180 (A.B.805), § 2, operative Jan. 1, 2014.)*

Cross References

Common interest development managers, management companies and parent companies, prohibited activities, see Business and Professions Code § 11505.

§ 4160. "Member" defined

"Member" means an owner of a separate interest. *(Added by Stats.2012, c. 180 (A.B.805), § 2, operative Jan. 1, 2014.)*

§ 4170. "Person" defined

"Person" means a natural person, corporation, government or governmental subdivision or agency, business trust, estate, trust, partnership, limited liability company, association, or other entity. *(Added by Stats.2012, c. 180 (A.B.805), § 2, operative Jan. 1, 2014.)*

§ 4175. "Planned development" defined

"Planned development" means a real property development other than a community apartment project, a condominium project, or a stock cooperative, having either or both of the following features:

(a) Common area that is owned either by an association or in common by the owners of the separate interests who possess appurtenant rights to the beneficial use and enjoyment of the common area.

(b) Common area and an association that maintains the common area with the power to levy assessments that may become a lien upon the separate interests in accordance with Article 2 (commencing with Section 5650) of Chapter 8. *(Added by Stats.2012, c. 180 (A.B.805), § 2, operative Jan. 1, 2014.)*

§ 4177. "Reserve accounts" defined

"Reserve accounts" means both of the following:

(a) Moneys that the board has identified for use to defray the future repair or replacement of, or additions to, those major components that the association is obligated to maintain.

(b) The funds received, and not yet expended or disposed of, from either a compensatory damage award or settlement to an association from any person for injuries to property, real or personal, arising from any construction or design defects. These funds shall be separately itemized from funds described in subdivision (a). *(Added by Stats.2012, c. 180 (A.B.805), § 2, operative Jan. 1, 2014.)*

§ 4178. "Reserve account requirements" defined

"Reserve account requirements" means the estimated funds that the board has determined are required to be available at a specified point in time to repair, replace, or restore those major components that the association is obligated to maintain. *(Added by Stats.2012, c. 180 (A.B. 805), § 2, operative Jan. 1, 2014.)*

§ 4185. "Separate interest" defined

(a) "Separate interest" has the following meanings:

(1) In a community apartment project, "separate interest" means the exclusive right to occupy an apartment, as specified in Section 4105.

(2) In a condominium project, "separate interest" means a separately owned unit, as specified in Section 4125.

(3) In a planned development, "separate interest" means a separately owned lot, parcel, area, or space.

(4) In a stock cooperative, "separate interest" means the exclusive right to occupy a portion of the real property, as specified in Section 4190.

(b) Unless the declaration or condominium plan, if any exists, otherwise provides, if walls, floors, or ceilings are designated as boundaries of a separate interest, the interior surfaces of the perimeter walls, floors, ceilings, windows, doors, and outlets located within the separate interest are part of the separate interest and any other portions of the walls, floors, or ceilings are part of the common area.

(c) The estate in a separate interest may be a fee, a life estate, an estate for years, or any combination of the foregoing. *(Added by Stats.2012, c. 180 (A.B.805), § 2, operative Jan. 1, 2014.)*

Cross References

Public swimming pools in certain common interest developments, record-keeping requirement, see Health and Safety Code § 116048.

§ 4190. "Stock cooperative" defined

(a) "Stock cooperative" means a development in which a corporation is formed or availed of, primarily for the purpose of holding title to, either in fee simple or for a term of years, improved real property, and all or substantially all of the shareholders of the corporation receive a right of exclusive occupancy in a portion of the real property, title to which is held by the corporation. The owners' interest in the corporation, whether evidenced by a share of stock, a certificate of membership, or otherwise, shall be deemed to be an interest in a common interest development and a real estate development for purposes of subdivision (f) of Section 25100 of the Corporations Code.

(b) A "stock cooperative" includes a limited equity housing cooperative which is a stock cooperative that meets the criteria of Section 817. *(Added by Stats.2012, c. 180 (A.B. 805), § 2, operative Jan. 1, 2014.)*

Cross References

Manufactured home, mobilehome and commercial modular foundation systems, installation requirements for fixture or improvement status, see Health and Safety Code § 18551.

Veterans' Farm and Home Purchase Act of 1974, cancellation of contract, stock cooperative to have opportunity to correct failure by purchaser, see Military and Veterans Code § 987.77.

CHAPTER 2. APPLICATION OF ACT

Section
4200. Creation of common interest development; application of act.
4201. Development not containing common area; application of act.
4201.5. Repealed.
4202. Commercial or industrial common interest developments.
4203, 4204. Repealed.

§ 4200. Creation of common interest development; application of act

This act applies and a common interest development is created whenever a separate interest coupled with an interest in the common area or membership in the association is, or has been, conveyed, provided all of the following are recorded:

(a) A declaration.

(b) A condominium plan, if any exists.

(c) A final map or parcel map, if Division 2 (commencing with Section 66410) of Title 7 of the Government Code requires the recording of either a final map or parcel map for the common interest development. *(Added by Stats.2012, c. 180 (A.B.805), § 2, operative Jan. 1, 2014.)*

Cross References

Water reuse, use of recycled water for toilet and urinal flushing in condominium projects, see Water Code § 13553.

§ 4201. Development not containing common area; application of act

Nothing in this act may be construed to apply to a real property development that does not contain common area. This section is declaratory of existing law. *(Added by Stats.2012, c. 180 (A.B.805), § 2, operative Jan. 1, 2014.)*

§ 4201.5. Repealed by Stats.1992, c. 162 (A.B.2650), § 3, operative Jan. 1, 1994

§ 4202. Commercial or industrial common interest developments

This part does not apply to a commercial or industrial common interest development, as defined in Section 6531. *(Added by Stats.2012, c. 180 (A.B.805), § 2, operative Jan. 1, 2014. Amended by Stats.2013, c. 605 (S.B.752), § 19.)*

Cross References

Pets within commercial and industrial common interest developments, see Civil Code § 6706.

§§ 4203, 4204. Repealed by Stats.1993, c. 219 (A.B.1500), §§ 32, 33

CHAPTER 3. GOVERNING DOCUMENTS

Article	Section
1. General Provisions	4205
2. Declaration	4250
3. Articles of Incorporation	4280
4. Condominium Plan	4285
5. Operating Rules	4340

ARTICLE 1. GENERAL PROVISIONS

Section
4205. Authority of documents.
4205.1, 4205.5. Repealed.
4206. Repealed.
4206.5, 4207. Repealed.
4208. Repealed.
4209. Repealed.
4210. Statements for collection of regular and special assessments, transfer fees, and other charges.
4211. Repealed.
4212. Repealed.
4213. Repealed.
4213.1 to 4214. Repealed.
4215. Liberal construction of instruments.
4216. Repealed.
4220. Boundaries of units; presumptions.
4225. Restrictive covenants; deletion from declaration or other governing document; recording or filing of amended document.
4230. Amendment of governing documents to delete construction or marketing provisions after completion by developer; requirements.
4235. Correction of statutory references in documents.

§ 4205. Authority of documents

(a) To the extent of any conflict between the governing documents and the law, the law shall prevail.

(b) To the extent of any conflict between the articles of incorporation and the declaration, the declaration shall prevail.

(c) To the extent of any conflict between the bylaws and the articles of incorporation or declaration, the articles of incorporation or declaration shall prevail.

(d) To the extent of any conflict between the operating rules and the bylaws, articles of incorporation, or declaration, the bylaws, articles of incorporation, or declaration shall prevail. (Added by Stats.2012, c. 180 (A.B.805), § 2, operative Jan. 1, 2014. Amended by Stats.2013, c. 183 (S.B.745), § 11.)

§§ 4205.1, 4205.5. Repealed by Stats.1992, c. 162 (A.B. 2650), § 3, operative Jan. 1, 1994

§ 4206. Repealed by Stats.1993, c. 219 (A.B.1500), § 34

§§ 4206.5, 4207. Repealed by Stats.1992, c. 162 (A.B.2650), § 3, operative Jan. 1, 1994

§ 4208. Repealed by Stats.1993, c. 219 (A.B.1500), § 35

§ 4209. Repealed by Stats.1992, c. 162 (A.B.2650), § 3, operative Jan. 1, 1994

§ 4210. Statements for collection of regular and special assessments, transfer fees, and other charges

In order to facilitate the collection of regular assessments, special assessments, transfer fees as authorized by Sections 4530, 4575, and 4580, and similar charges, the board is authorized to record a statement or amended statement identifying relevant information for the association. This statement may include any or all of the following information:

(a) The name of the association as shown in the declaration or the current name of the association, if different.

(b) The name and address of a managing agent or treasurer of the association or other individual or entity authorized to receive assessments and fees imposed by the association.

(c) A daytime telephone number of the authorized party identified in subdivision (b) if a telephone number is available.

(d) A list of separate interests subject to assessment by the association, showing the assessor's parcel number or legal description, or both, of the separate interests.

(e) The recording information identifying the declaration governing the association.

(f) If an amended statement is being recorded, the recording information identifying the prior statement or statements which the amendment is superseding. (Added by Stats.2012, c. 180 (A.B.805), § 2, operative Jan. 1, 2014.)

§ 4211. Repealed by Stats.1988, c. 228, § 4

§ 4212. Repealed by Stats.1992, c. 162 (A.B.2650), § 3, operative Jan. 1, 1994

§ 4213. Repealed by Stats.1993, c. 219 (A.B.1500), § 37

§§ 4213.1 to 4214. Repealed by Stats.1992, c. 162 (A.B. 2650), § 3, operative Jan. 1, 1994

§ 4215. Liberal construction of instruments

Any deed, declaration, or condominium plan for a common interest development shall be liberally construed to facilitate the operation of the common interest development, and its provisions shall be presumed to be independent and severable. Nothing in Article 3 (commencing with Section 715) of Chapter 2 of Title 2 of Part 1 of Division 2 shall operate to invalidate any provisions of the governing documents. (Added by Stats.2012, c. 180 (A.B.805), § 2, operative Jan. 1, 2014.)

§ 4216. Repealed by Stats.1993, c. 219 (A.B.1500), § 38

§ 4220. Boundaries of units; presumptions

In interpreting deeds and condominium plans, the existing physical boundaries of a unit in a condominium project, when the boundaries of the unit are contained within a building, or of a unit reconstructed in substantial accordance with the original plans thereof, shall be conclusively presumed to be its boundaries rather than the metes and bounds expressed in the deed or condominium plan, if any exists, regardless of settling or lateral movement of the building and regardless of minor variance between boundaries shown on the plan or in the deed and those of the building. *(Added by Stats.2012, c. 180 (A.B.805), § 2, operative Jan. 1, 2014.)*

§ 4225. Restrictive covenants; deletion from declaration or other governing document; recording or filing of amended document

(a) No declaration or other governing document shall include a restrictive covenant in violation of Section 12955 of the Government Code.

(b) Notwithstanding any other provision of law or provision of the governing documents, the board, without approval of the members, shall amend any declaration or other governing document that includes a restrictive covenant prohibited by this section to delete the restrictive covenant, and shall restate the declaration or other governing document without the restrictive covenant but with no other change to the declaration or governing document.

(c) If the declaration is amended under this section, the board shall record the restated declaration in each county in which the common interest development is located. If the articles of incorporation are amended under this section, the board shall file a certificate of amendment with the Secretary of State pursuant to Section 7814 of the Corporations Code.

(d) If after providing written notice to an association, pursuant to Section 4035, requesting that the association delete a restrictive covenant that violates subdivision (a), and the association fails to delete the restrictive covenant within 30 days of receiving the notice, the * * * Civil Rights Department, a city or county in which a common interest development is located, or any person may bring an action against the association for injunctive relief to enforce subdivision (a). The court may award attorney's fees to the prevailing party. *(Added by Stats.2012, c. 180 (A.B.805), § 2, operative Jan. 1, 2014. Amended by Stats.2022, c. 48 (S.B. 189), § 7, eff. June 30, 2022.)*

Cross References

Restrictive covenants based on discriminatory grounds,
   Notice on copy of document, penalty for adding racially restrictive covenant, see Government Code § 12956.1.
   Recording of modification, submission to county counsel, filing, and public access, and unauthorized modifications, see Government Code § 12956.2.

§ 4230. Amendment of governing documents to delete construction or marketing provisions after completion by developer; requirements

(a) Notwithstanding any provision of the governing documents to the contrary, the board may, after the developer has completed construction of the development, has terminated construction activities, and has terminated marketing activities for the sale, lease, or other disposition of separate interests within the development, adopt an amendment deleting from any of the governing documents any provision which is unequivocally designed and intended, or which by its nature can only have been designed or intended, to facilitate the developer in completing the construction or marketing of the development. However, provisions of the governing documents relative to a particular construction or marketing phase of the development may not be deleted under the authorization of this subdivision until that construction or marketing phase has been completed.

(b) The provisions which may be deleted by action of the board shall be limited to those which provide for access by the developer over or across the common area for the purposes of (1) completion of construction of the development, and (2) the erection, construction, or maintenance of structures or other facilities designed to facilitate the completion of construction or marketing of separate interests.

(c) At least 30 days prior to taking action pursuant to subdivision (a), the board shall deliver to all members, by individual delivery, pursuant to Section 4040, (1) a copy of all amendments to the governing documents proposed to be adopted under subdivision (a), and (2) a notice of the time, date, and place the board will consider adoption of the amendments. The board may consider adoption of amendments to the governing documents pursuant to subdivision (a) only at a meeting that is open to all members, who shall be given opportunity to make comments thereon. All deliberations of the board on any action proposed under subdivision (a) shall only be conducted in an open meeting.

(d) The board may not amend the governing documents pursuant to this section without the approval of a majority of a quorum of the members, pursuant to Section 4070. For the purposes of this section, "quorum" means more than 50 percent of the members who own no more than two separate interests in the development. *(Added by Stats.2012, c. 180 (A.B.805), § 2, operative Jan. 1, 2014.)*

§ 4235. Correction of statutory references in documents

(a) Notwithstanding any other provision of law or provision of the governing documents, if the governing documents include a reference to a provision of the Davis–Stirling Common Interest Development Act that was repealed and continued in a new provision by the act that added this section, the board may amend the governing documents, solely to correct the cross-reference, by adopting a board resolution that shows the correction. Member approval is not required in order to adopt a resolution pursuant to this section.

(b) A declaration that is corrected under this section may be restated in corrected form and recorded, provided that a copy of the board resolution authorizing the corrections is recorded along with the restated declaration. *(Added by Stats.2012, c. 180 (A.B.805), § 2, operative Jan. 1, 2014.)*

ARTICLE 2. DECLARATION

Section
4250. Contents of declaration.
4255. Notice of airport in vicinity; notice of San Francisco Bay Conservation and Development Commission jurisdiction.
4260. Amendment of declaration; authorization.
4265. Extension of term of declaration.
4270. Amendment of declaration; procedure.
4275. Amendment of declaration; petition; contents; filing; findings by court; power of court to approve amendment; recording amendment; delivery.

§ 4250. Contents of declaration

(a) A declaration, recorded on or after January 1, 1986, shall contain a legal description of the common interest development, and a statement that the common interest development is a community apartment project, condominium project, planned development, stock cooperative, or combination thereof. The declaration shall additionally set forth the name of the association and the restrictions on the use or enjoyment of any portion of the common interest development that are intended to be enforceable equitable servitudes.

(b) The declaration may contain any other matters the declarant or the members consider appropriate. *(Added by Stats.2012, c. 180 (A.B.805), § 2, operative Jan. 1, 2014.)*

§ 4255. Notice of airport in vicinity; notice of San Francisco Bay Conservation and Development Commission jurisdiction

(a) If a common interest development is located within an airport influence area, a declaration, recorded after January 1, 2004, shall contain the following statement:

"NOTICE OF AIRPORT IN VICINITY

This property is presently located in the vicinity of an airport, within what is known as an airport influence area. For that reason, the property may be subject to some of the annoyances or inconveniences associated with proximity to airport operations (for example: noise, vibration, or odors). Individual sensitivities to those annoyances can vary from person to person. You may wish to consider what airport annoyances, if any, are associated with the property before you complete your purchase and determine whether they are acceptable to you."

(b) For purposes of this section, an "airport influence area," also known as an "airport referral area," is the area in which current or future airport-related noise, overflight, safety, or airspace protection factors may significantly affect land uses or necessitate restrictions on those uses as determined by an airport land use commission.

(c) If a common interest development is within the San Francisco Bay Conservation and Development Commission jurisdiction, as described in Section 66610 of the Government Code, a declaration recorded on or after January 1, 2006, shall contain the following notice:

"NOTICE OF SAN FRANCISCO BAY CONSERVATION AND DEVELOPMENT COMMISSION JURISDICTION

This property is located within the jurisdiction of the San Francisco Bay Conservation and Development Commission. Use and development of property within the commission's jurisdiction may be subject to special regulations, restrictions, and permit requirements. You may wish to investigate and determine whether they are acceptable to you and your intended use of the property before you complete your transaction."

(d) The statement in a declaration acknowledging that a property is located in an airport influence area or within the jurisdiction of the San Francisco Bay Conservation and Development Commission does not constitute a title defect, lien, or encumbrance. *(Added by Stats.2012, c. 180 (A.B.805), § 2, operative Jan. 1, 2014.)*

§ 4260. Amendment of declaration; authorization

Except to the extent that a declaration provides by its express terms that it is not amendable, in whole or in part, a declaration that fails to include provisions permitting its amendment at all times during its existence may be amended at any time. *(Added by Stats.2012, c. 180 (A.B.805), § 2, operative Jan. 1, 2014.)*

§ 4265. Extension of term of declaration

(a) The Legislature finds that there are common interest developments that have been created with deed restrictions that do not provide a means for the members to extend the term of the declaration. The Legislature further finds that covenants and restrictions contained in the declaration, are an appropriate method for protecting the common plan of developments and to provide for a mechanism for financial support for the upkeep of common area including, but not limited to, roofs, roads, heating systems, and recreational facilities. If declarations terminate prematurely, common interest developments may deteriorate and the housing supply of affordable units could be impacted adversely. The Legislature further finds and declares that it is in the public interest to provide a vehicle for extending the term of the declaration if the extension is approved by a majority of all members, pursuant to Section 4065.

(b) A declaration that specifies a termination date, but that contains no provision for extension of the termination date, may be extended, before its termination date, by the approval of members pursuant to Section 4270.

(c) No single extension of the terms of the declaration made pursuant to this section shall exceed the initial term of the declaration or 20 years, whichever is less. However, more than one extension may occur pursuant to this section. *(Added by Stats.2012, c. 180 (A.B.805), § 2, operative Jan. 1, 2014.)*

§ 4270. Amendment of declaration; procedure

(a) A declaration may be amended pursuant to the declaration or this act. Except where an alternative process for approving, certifying, or recording an amendment is provided in Section 4225, 4230, 4235, or 4275, an amendment is effective after all of the following requirements have been met:

(1) The amendment has been approved by the percentage of members required by the declaration and any other person whose approval is required by the declaration.

(2) That fact has been certified in a writing executed and acknowledged by the officer designated in the declaration or by the association for that purpose, or if no one is designated, by the president of the association.

(3) The amendment has been recorded in each county in which a portion of the common interest development is located.

(b) If the declaration does not specify the percentage of members who must approve an amendment of the declaration, an amendment may be approved by a majority of all members, pursuant to Section 4065. *(Added by Stats.2012, c. 180 (A.B.805), § 2, operative Jan. 1, 2014. Amended by Stats.2016, c. 714 (S.B.944), § 6, eff. Jan. 1, 2017.)*

§ 4275. Amendment of declaration; petition; contents; filing; findings by court; power of court to approve amendment; recording amendment; delivery

(a) If in order to amend a declaration, the declaration requires members having more than 50 percent of the votes in the association, in a single class voting structure, or members having more than 50 percent of the votes in more than one class in a voting structure with more than one class, to vote in favor of the amendment, the association, or any member, may petition the superior court of the county in which the common interest development is located for an order reducing the percentage of the affirmative votes necessary for such an amendment. The petition shall describe the effort that has been made to solicit approval of the association members in the manner provided in the declaration, the number of affirmative and negative votes actually received, the number or percentage of affirmative votes required to effect the amendment in accordance with the existing declaration, and other matters the petitioner considers relevant to the court's determination. The petition shall also contain, as exhibits thereto, copies of all of the following:

(1) The governing documents.

(2) A complete text of the amendment.

(3) Copies of any notice and solicitation materials utilized in the solicitation of member approvals.

(4) A short explanation of the reason for the amendment.

(5) Any other documentation relevant to the court's determination.

(b) Upon filing the petition, the court shall set the matter for hearing and issue an ex parte order setting forth the manner in which notice shall be given.

(c) The court may, but shall not be required to, grant the petition if it finds all of the following:

(1) The petitioner has given not less than 15 days written notice of the court hearing to all members of the association, to any mortgagee of a mortgage or beneficiary of a deed of trust who is entitled to notice under the terms of the declaration, and to the city, county, or city and county in which the common interest development is located that is entitled to notice under the terms of the declaration.

(2) Balloting on the proposed amendment was conducted in accordance with the governing documents, this act, and any other applicable law.

(3) A reasonably diligent effort was made to permit all eligible members to vote on the proposed amendment.

(4) Members having more than 50 percent of the votes, in a single class voting structure, voted in favor of the amendment. In a voting structure with more than one class, where the declaration requires a majority of more than one class to vote in favor of the amendment, members having more than 50 percent of the votes of each class required by the declaration to vote in favor of the amendment voted in favor of the amendment.

(5) The amendment is reasonable.

(6) Granting the petition is not improper for any reason stated in subdivision (e).

(d) If the court makes the findings required by subdivision (c), any order issued pursuant to this section may confirm the amendment as being validly approved on the basis of the affirmative votes actually received during the balloting period or the order may dispense with any requirement relating to quorums or to the number or percentage of votes needed for approval of the amendment that would otherwise exist under the governing documents.

(e) Subdivisions (a) to (d), inclusive, notwithstanding, the court shall not be empowered by this section to approve any amendment to the declaration that:

(1) Would change provisions in the declaration requiring the approval of members having more than 50 percent of the votes in more than one class to vote in favor of an amendment, unless members having more than 50 percent of the votes in each affected class approved the amendment.

(2) Would eliminate any special rights, preferences, or privileges designated in the declaration as belonging to the declarant, without the consent of the declarant.

(3) Would impair the security interest of a mortgagee of a mortgage or the beneficiary of a deed of trust without the approval of the percentage of the mortgagees and beneficiaries specified in the declaration, if the declaration requires the approval of a specified percentage of the mortgagees and beneficiaries.

(f) An amendment is not effective pursuant to this section until the court order and amendment have been recorded in every county in which a portion of the common interest development is located. The amendment may be acknowledged by, and the court order and amendment may be recorded by, any person designated in the declaration or by the association for that purpose, or if no one is designated for that purpose, by the president of the association. Upon recordation of the amendment and court order, the declaration, as amended in accordance with this section, shall have the same force and effect as if the amendment were adopted in compliance with every requirement imposed by the governing documents.

(g) Within a reasonable time after the amendment is recorded the association shall deliver to each member, by individual delivery, pursuant to Section 4040, a copy of the amendment, together with a statement that the amendment has been recorded. *(Added by Stats.2012, c. 180 (A.B.805), § 2, operative Jan. 1, 2014.)*

ARTICLE 3. ARTICLES OF INCORPORATION

Section
4280. Association articles of incorporation; required statements.

§ 4280. Association articles of incorporation; required statements

(a) The articles of incorporation of an association filed with the Secretary of State shall include a statement, which shall be in addition to the statement of purposes of the corporation, that does all of the following:

(1) Identifies the corporation as an association formed to manage a common interest development under the Davis–Stirling Common Interest Development Act.

(2) States the business or corporate office of the association, if any, and, if the office is not on the site of the common interest development, states the front street and nearest cross street for the physical location of the common interest development.

(3) States the name and address of the association's managing agent, if any.

(b) The statement filed by an incorporated association with the Secretary of State pursuant to Section 8210 of the Corporations Code shall also contain a statement identifying the corporation as an association formed to manage a common interest development under the Davis–Stirling Common Interest Development Act.

(c) Documents filed prior to January 1, 2014, in compliance with former Section 1363.5, as it read on January 1, 2013, are deemed to be in compliance with this section. *(Added by Stats.2012, c. 180 (A.B.805), § 2, operative Jan. 1, 2014. Amended by Stats.2013, c. 605 (S.B.752), § 20.)*

Cross References

Real estate broker license renewal, course work in common interest development law, number of clock hours required, see Business and Professions Code § 10170.5.

Real estate broker licensure, proof of course completion in common interest development law, number of course equivalency hours required, see Business and Professions Code § 10153.2.

ARTICLE 4. CONDOMINIUM PLAN

Section
4285. Contents of condominium plan.
4290. Certificate consenting to recordation of condominium plan; signatures and acknowledgements.
4295. Amendment or revocation of condominium plan.
4300, 4301. Repealed.
4302. Repealed.
4303 to 4309. Repealed.

§ 4285. Contents of condominium plan

A condominium plan shall contain all of the following:

(a) A description or survey map of a condominium project, which shall refer to or show monumentation on the ground.

(b) A three-dimensional description of a condominium project, one or more dimensions of which may extend for an indefinite distance upwards or downwards, in sufficient detail to identify the common area and each separate interest.

(c) A certificate consenting to the recordation of the condominium plan pursuant to this act that is signed and acknowledged as provided in Section 4290. *(Added by Stats.2012, c. 180 (A.B.805), § 2, operative Jan. 1, 2014.)*

Cross References

Condominium projects, requirements of Subdivision Map Act, see Government Code § 66427.

Property tax, separate assessment of condominium units, see Revenue and Taxation Code § 2188.6.

Subdivided lands, conditional public report, recording of condominium plan and covenants, conditions and restrictions pursuant to this section, see Business and Professions Code § 11018.12.

§ 4290. Certificate consenting to recordation of condominium plan; signatures and acknowledgements

(a) The certificate consenting to the recordation of a condominium plan that is required by subdivision (c) of Section 4285 shall be signed and acknowledged by all of the following persons:

(1) The record owner of fee title to that property included in the condominium project.

(2) In the case of a condominium project that will terminate upon the termination of an estate for years, by all lessors and lessees of the estate for years.

(3) In the case of a condominium project subject to a life estate, by all life tenants and remainder interests.

(4) The trustee or the beneficiary of each recorded deed of trust, and the mortgagee of each recorded mortgage encumbering the property.

(b) Owners of mineral rights, easements, rights-of-way, and other nonpossessory interests do not need to sign the certificate.

(c) In the event a conversion to condominiums of a community apartment project or stock cooperative has been approved by the required number of owners, trustees, beneficiaries, and mortgagees pursuant to Section 66452.10 of the Government Code, the certificate need only be signed by those owners, trustees, beneficiaries, and mortgagees approving the conversion. *(Added by Stats.2012, c. 180 (A.B.805), § 2, operative Jan. 1, 2014. Amended by Stats.2013, c. 183 (S.B.745), § 12.)*

§ 4295. Amendment or revocation of condominium plan

A condominium plan may be amended or revoked by a recorded instrument that is acknowledged and signed by all the persons who, at the time of amendment or revocation, are persons whose signatures are required under Section 4290. *(Added by Stats.2012, c. 180 (A.B.805), § 2, operative Jan. 1, 2014.)*

Cross References

Stock cooperative or community apartment project, conversion to condominium, required number of favorable votes of owners, trustees or beneficiaries, see Government Code § 66452.10.

§§ 4300, 4301. Repealed by Stats.1992, c. 162 (A.B.2650), § 3, operative Jan. 1, 1994

§ 4302. Repealed by Stats.1980, c. 1191, p. 3996, § 2, eff. Sept. 29, 1980; Stats.1981, c. 714, § 466

§§ 4303 to 4309. Repealed by Stats.1992, c. 162 (A.B.2650), § 3, operative Jan. 1, 1994

ARTICLE 5. OPERATING RULES

Section
- 4340. Definitions.
- 4350. Requirements for validity and enforceability.
- 4350.5 to 4353. Repealed.
- 4355. Approved subject matters; board action to propose rule change; special meetings of members to reverse rule change.
- 4355.6 to 4357. Repealed.
- 4357.5. Repealed.
- 4358, 4358.5. Repealed.
- 4359. Repealed.
- 4360. Proposed rule change by board action; notice; meeting.
- 4361 to 4364. Repealed.
- 4365. Special meeting of members to reverse rule change; notice; voting requirements; effect of approved reversal.
- 4366. Repealed.
- 4370. Applicability of article to changes commenced before and after January 1, 2004.
- 4370.5. Repealed.
- 4370.6, 4371. Repealed.
- 4372, 4373. Repealed.
- 4380 to 4384. Repealed.
- 4384.5. Repealed.
- 4385. Repealed.
- 4390. Repealed.
- 4390.1, 4390.2. Repealed.
- 4390.3. Repealed.
- 4390.4 to 4390.9. Repealed.
- 4390.10. Repealed.
- 4390.11 to 4390.13. Repealed.
- 4390.14. Repealed.
- 4390.15 to 4390.19. Repealed.
- 4395. Repealed.
- 4400 to 4452. Repealed.
- 4453. Repealed.
- 4454 to 4458. Repealed.

Cross References

Member elections, adoption of rules in accordance with this Article, see Civil Code § 5105.

§ 4340. Definitions

For the purposes of this article:

(a) "Operating rule" means a regulation adopted by the board that applies generally to the management and operation of the common interest development or the conduct of the business and affairs of the association.

(b) "Rule change" means the adoption, amendment, or repeal of an operating rule by the board. *(Added by Stats.2012, c. 180 (A.B.805), § 2, operative Jan. 1, 2014.)*

§ 4350. Requirements for validity and enforceability

An operating rule is valid and enforceable only if all of the following requirements are satisfied:

(a) The rule is in writing.

(b) The rule is within the authority of the board conferred by law or by the declaration, articles of incorporation or association, or bylaws of the association.

(c) The rule is not in conflict with governing law and the declaration, articles of incorporation or association, or bylaws of the association.

(d) The rule is adopted, amended, or repealed in good faith and in substantial compliance with the requirements of this article.

(e) The rule is reasonable. *(Added by Stats.2012, c. 180 (A.B.805), § 2, operative Jan. 1, 2014. Amended by Stats. 2013, c. 183 (S.B.745), § 13.)*

§§ 4350.5 to 4353. Repealed by Stats.1992, c. 162 (A.B. 2650), § 3, operative Jan. 1, 1994

§ 4355. Approved subject matters; board action to propose rule change; special meetings of members to reverse rule change

(a) Sections 4360 and 4365 only apply to an operating rule that relates to one or more of the following subjects:

(1) Use of the common area or of an exclusive use common area.

(2) Use of a separate interest, including any aesthetic or architectural standards that govern alteration of a separate interest.

(3) Member discipline, including any schedule of monetary penalties for violation of the governing documents and any procedure for the imposition of penalties.

(4) Any standards for delinquent assessment payment plans.

(5) Any procedures adopted by the association for resolution of disputes.

(6) Any procedures for reviewing and approving or disapproving a proposed physical change to a member's separate interest or to the common area.

(7) Procedures for elections.

(b) Sections 4360 and 4365 do not apply to the following actions by the board:

(1) A decision regarding maintenance of the common area.

(2) A decision on a specific matter that is not intended to apply generally.

(3) A decision setting the amount of a regular or special assessment.

(4) A rule change that is required by law, if the board has no discretion as to the substantive effect of the rule change.

(5) Issuance of a document that merely repeats existing law or the governing documents. *(Added by Stats.2012, c. 180 (A.B.805), § 2, operative Jan. 1, 2014.)*

§§ 4355.6 to 4357. Repealed by Stats.1992, c. 162 (A.B. 2650), § 3, operative Jan. 1, 1994

§ 4357.5. Repealed by Stats.1993, c. 219 (A.B.1500), § 39

§§ 4358, 4358.5. Repealed by Stats.1992, c. 162 (A.B.2650), § 3, operative Jan. 1, 1994

§ 4359. Repealed by Stats.1993, c. 219 (A.B.1500), § 39.5

§ 4360. Proposed rule change by board action; notice; meeting

(a) The board shall provide general notice pursuant to Section 4045 of a proposed rule change at least 28 days before making the rule change. The notice shall include the text of the proposed rule change and a description of the purpose and effect of the proposed rule change. Notice is not required under this subdivision if the board determines that an immediate rule change is necessary to address an imminent threat to public health or safety or imminent risk of substantial economic loss to the association.

(b) A decision on a proposed rule change shall be made at a board meeting, after consideration of any comments made by association members.

(c) As soon as possible after making a rule change, but not more than 15 days after making the rule change, the board shall deliver general notice pursuant to Section 4045 of the rule change. If the rule change was an emergency rule change made under subdivision (d), the notice shall include the text of the rule change, a description of the purpose and effect of the rule change, and the date that the rule change expires.

(d) If the board determines that an immediate rule change is required to address an imminent threat to public health or safety, or an imminent risk of substantial economic loss to the association, it may make an emergency rule change, and no notice is required, as specified in subdivision (a). An emergency rule change is effective for 120 days, unless the rule change provides for a shorter effective period. A rule change made under this subdivision may not be readopted under this subdivision. *(Added by Stats.2012, c. 180 (A.B. 805), § 2, operative Jan. 1, 2014. Amended by Stats.2018, c. 836 (S.B.261), § 2, eff. Jan. 1, 2019.)*

§§ 4361 to 4364. Repealed by Stats.1992, c. 162 (A.B.2650), § 3, operative Jan. 1, 1994

§ 4365. Special meeting of members to reverse rule change; notice; voting requirements; effect of approved reversal

(a) Members of an association owning 5 percent or more of the separate interests may call a special vote of the members to reverse a rule change.

(b) A special vote of the members may be called by delivering a written request to the association. Not less than 35 days nor more than 90 days after receipt of a proper request, the association shall hold a vote of the members on whether to reverse the rule change, pursuant to Article 4 (commencing with Section 5100) of Chapter 6. The written request may not be delivered more than 30 days after the association gives general notice of the rule change, pursuant to Section 4045.

(c) For the purposes of Section 5225 of this code and Section 8330 of the Corporations Code, collection of signatures to call a special vote under this section is a purpose reasonably related to the interests of the members of the association. A member request to copy or inspect the membership list solely for that purpose may not be denied on the grounds that the purpose is not reasonably related to the member's interests as a member.

(d) The rule change may be reversed by the affirmative vote of a majority of a quorum of the members, pursuant to Section 4070, or if the declaration or bylaws require a greater percentage, by the affirmative vote of the percentage required.

(e) Unless otherwise provided in the declaration or bylaws, for the purposes of this section, a member may cast one vote per separate interest owned.

(f) A rule change reversed under this section may not be readopted for one year after the date of the vote reversing the rule change. Nothing in this section precludes the board from adopting a different rule on the same subject as the rule change that has been reversed.

(g) As soon as possible after the close of voting, but not more than 15 days after the close of voting, the board shall provide general notice pursuant to Section 4045 of the results of the member vote.

(h) This section does not apply to an emergency rule change made under subdivision (d) of Section 4360. *(Added by Stats.2012, c. 180 (A.B.805), § 2, operative Jan. 1, 2014.)*

§ 4366. Repealed by Stats.1992, c. 162 (A.B.2650), § 3, operative Jan. 1, 1994

§ 4370. Applicability of article to changes commenced before and after January 1, 2004

(a) This article applies to a rule change commenced on or after January 1, 2004.

(b) Nothing in this article affects the validity of a rule change commenced before January 1, 2004.

(c) For the purposes of this section, a rule change is commenced when the board takes its first official action leading to adoption of the rule change. *(Added by Stats.2012, c. 180 (A.B.805), § 2, operative Jan. 1, 2014.)*

§ 4370.5. Repealed by Stats.1993, c. 219 (A.B.1500), § 40

§§ 4370.6, 4371. Repealed by Stats.1992, c. 162 (A.B.2650), § 3, operative Jan. 1, 1994

§§ 4372, 4373. Repealed by Stats.1993, c. 219 (A.B.1500), §§ 41, 42

§§ 4380 to 4384. Repealed by Stats.1992, c. 162 (A.B.2650), § 3, operative Jan. 1, 1994

§ 4384.5. Repealed by Stats.1993, c. 876 (S.B.1068), § 1, operative Jan. 1, 1994

§ 4385. Repealed by Stats.1992, c. 162 (A.B.2650), § 3, operative Jan. 1, 1994

§ 4390. Repealed by Stats.1993, c. 219 (A.B.1500), § 44

§§ 4390.1, 4390.2. Repealed by Stats.1992, c. 162 (A.B.2650), § 3, operative Jan. 1, 1994

§ 4390.3. Repealed by Stats.1993, c. 876 (S.B.1068), § 2, operative Jan. 1, 1994

§§ 4390.4 to 4390.9. Repealed by Stats.1992, c. 162 (A.B. 2650), § 3, operative Jan. 1, 1994

§ 4390.10. Repealed by Stats.1992, c. 162 (A.B.2650), § 3, operative Jan. 1, 1994; Stats.1993, c. 876 (S.B.1068), § 3, operative Jan. 1, 1994

§§ 4390.11 to 4390.13. Repealed by Stats.1992, c. 162 (A.B.2650), § 3, operative Jan. 1, 1994

§ 4390.14. Repealed by Stats.1992, c. 162 (A.B.2650), § 3, operative Jan. 1, 1994; Stats.1993, c. 876 (S.B.1068), § 4, operative Jan. 1, 1994

§§ 4390.15 to 4390.19. Repealed by Stats.1992, c. 162 (A.B.2650), § 3, operative Jan. 1, 1994

§ 4395. Repealed by Stats.1993, c. 219 (A.B.1500), § 46

§§ 4400 to 4452. Repealed by Stats.1992, c. 162 (A.B.2650), § 3, operative Jan. 1, 1994

§ 4453. Repealed by Stats.1975, c. 1244, p. 3196, § 10

§§ 4454 to 4458. Repealed by Stats.1992, c. 162 (A.B.2650), § 3, operative Jan. 1, 1994

CHAPTER 4. OWNERSHIP AND TRANSFER OF INTERESTS

Article	Section
1. Ownership Rights and Interests	4500
2. Transfer Disclosure	4525
3. Transfer Fee	4575
4. Restrictions on Transfer	4600
5. Transfer of Separate Interest	4625

ARTICLE 1. OWNERSHIP RIGHTS AND INTERESTS

Section
4500. Ownership of common areas.
4501. Repealed.
4502. Repealed.
4503. Repealed.
4504. Repealed.
4505. Rights and easements of ingress, egress, and support.
4506 to 4509. Repealed.
4510. Physical access to owner or occupant's separate interest.
4511 to 4514. Repealed.
4515. Protection of members' and residents' rights to peacefully assemble and communicate; enumeration of protected activities; use of common areas for protected activities; civil remedies and penalty for infringement upon protected activities; retaliation for exercise of rights prohibited.
4516. Repealed.
4517 to 4521. Repealed.

§ 4500. Ownership of common areas

Unless the declaration otherwise provides, in a condominium project, or in a planned development in which the common area is owned by the owners of the separate interests, the common area is owned as tenants in common, in equal shares, one for each separate interest. *(Added by Stats.2012, c. 180 (A.B.805), § 2, operative Jan. 1, 2014.)*

§ 4501. Repealed by Stats.1992, c. 162 (A.B.2650), § 3, operative Jan. 1, 1994

§ 4502. Repealed by Stats.1970, c. 311, p. 706, § 3

§ 4503. Repealed by Stats.1992, c. 162 (A.B.2650), § 3, operative Jan. 1, 1994

§ 4504. Repealed by Stats.1970, c. 311, p. 706, § 4

§ 4505. Rights and easements of ingress, egress, and support

Unless the declaration otherwise provides:

(a) In a community apartment project and condominium project, and in those planned developments with common area owned in common by the owners of the separate interests, there are appurtenant to each separate interest nonexclusive rights of ingress, egress, and support, if necessary, through the common area. The common area is subject to these rights.

(b) In a stock cooperative, and in a planned development with common area owned by the association, there is an easement for ingress, egress, and support, if necessary, appurtenant to each separate interest. The common area is subject to these easements. *(Added by Stats.2012, c. 180 (A.B.805), § 2, operative Jan. 1, 2014.)*

§§ 4506 to 4509. Repealed by Stats.1992, c. 162 (A.B.2650), § 3, operative Jan. 1, 1994

§ 4510. Physical access to owner or occupant's separate interest

Except as otherwise provided in law, an order of the court, or an order pursuant to a final and binding arbitration decision, an association may not deny a member or occupant physical access to the member's or occupant's separate interest, either by restricting access through the common area to the separate interest, or by restricting access solely to the separate interest. *(Added by Stats.2012, c. 180 (A.B.805), § 2, operative Jan. 1, 2014.)*

§§ 4511 to 4514. Repealed by Stats.1992, c. 162 (A.B.2650), § 3, operative Jan. 1, 1994

§ 4515. Protection of members' and residents' rights to peacefully assemble and communicate; enumeration of protected activities; use of common areas for protected activities; civil remedies and penalty for infringement upon protected activities; retaliation for exercise of rights prohibited

(a) It is the intent of the Legislature to ensure that members and residents of common interest developments have the ability to exercise their rights under law to peacefully assemble and freely communicate with one another and with others with respect to common interest development living or for social, political, or educational purposes.

(b) The governing documents, including bylaws and operating rules, shall not prohibit a member or resident of a

§ 4515

common interest development from doing any of the following:

(1) Peacefully assembling or meeting with members, residents, and their invitees or guests during reasonable hours and in a reasonable manner for purposes relating to common interest development living, association elections, legislation, election to public office, or the initiative, referendum, or recall processes.

(2) Inviting public officials, candidates for public office, or representatives of homeowner organizations to meet with members, residents, and their invitees or guests and speak on matters of public interest.

(3) Using the common area, including the community or recreation hall or clubhouse, or, with the consent of the member, the area of a separate interest, for an assembly or meeting described in paragraph (1) or (2) when that facility or separate interest is not otherwise in use.

(4) Canvassing and petitioning the members, the association board, and residents for the activities described in paragraphs (1) and (2) at reasonable hours and in a reasonable manner.

(5) Distributing or circulating, without prior permission, information about common interest development living, association elections, legislation, election to public office, or the initiative, referendum, or recall processes, or other issues of concern to members and residents at reasonable hours and in a reasonable manner.

(6)(A) Using social media or other online resources to discuss any of the following, even if the content is critical of the association or its governance:

(i) Development living.

(ii) Association elections.

(iii) Legislation.

(iv) Election to public office.

(v) The initiative, referendum, or recall processes.

(vi) Any other issues of concern to members and residents.

(B) This paragraph does not require an association to provide social media or other online resources to members.

(C) This paragraph does not require an association to allow members to post content on the association's internet website.

(c) A member or resident of a common interest development shall not be required to pay a fee, make a deposit, obtain liability insurance, or pay the premium or deductible on the association's insurance policy, in order to use a common area for the activities described in paragraphs (1), (2), and (3) of subdivision (b).

(d) A member or resident of a common interest development who is prevented by the association or its agents from engaging in any of the activities described in this section may bring a civil or small claims court action to enjoin the enforcement of a governing document, including a bylaw and operating rule, that violates this section. The court may assess a civil penalty of not more than five hundred dollars ($500) for each violation.

(e) An association shall not retaliate against a member or a resident for exercising any of the rights contained in this section. (Added by Stats.2017, c. 236 (S.B.407), § 1, eff. Jan. 1, 2018. Amended by Stats.2022, c. 858 (A.B.1410), § 2, eff. Jan. 1, 2023.)

§ 4516. Repealed by Stats.1992, c. 162 (A.B.2650), § 3, operative Jan. 1, 1994

§§ 4517 to 4521. Repealed by Stats.1970, c. 311, p. 706, §§ 7 to 11

ARTICLE 2. TRANSFER DISCLOSURE

Section
4525. Sale or title transfer; provision of specified items to prospective purchasers.
4526. Repealed.
4528. Billing disclosures; form.
4530. Copies of requested documents; fees.
4531. Repealed.
4535. Additional requirements.
4540. Violations; penalties; attorney fees.
4545. Validity of title transferred in violation of article.
4550 to 4556. Repealed.

Cross References

Association records, time periods of required availability, see Civil Code § 5210.

§ 4525. Sale or title transfer; provision of specified items to prospective purchasers

(a) The owner of a separate interest shall provide the following documents to a prospective purchaser of the separate interest, as soon as practicable before the transfer of title or the execution of a real property sales contract, as defined in Section 2985:

(1) A copy of all governing documents. If the association is not incorporated, this shall include a statement in writing from an authorized representative of the association that the association is not incorporated.

(2) If there is a restriction in the governing documents limiting the occupancy, residency, or use of a separate interest on the basis of age in a manner different from that provided in Section 51.3, a statement that the restriction is only enforceable to the extent permitted by Section 51.3 and a statement specifying the applicable provisions of Section 51.3.

(3) A copy of the most recent documents distributed pursuant to Article 7 (commencing with Section 5300) of Chapter 6.

(4) A true statement in writing obtained from an authorized representative of the association as to the amount of the association's current regular and special assessments and fees, any assessments levied upon the owner's interest in the common interest development that are unpaid on the date of the statement, and any monetary fines or penalties levied upon the owner's interest and unpaid on the date of the statement. The statement obtained from an authorized representative shall also include true information on late charges, interest, and costs of collection which, as of the date of the statement, are or may be made a lien upon the owner's interest in a common interest development pursuant to Article 2 (commencing with Section 5650) of Chapter 8.

(5) A copy or a summary of any notice previously sent to the owner pursuant to Section 5855 that sets forth any alleged violation of the governing documents that remains unresolved at the time of the request. The notice shall not be deemed a waiver of the association's right to enforce the governing documents against the owner or the prospective purchaser of the separate interest with respect to any violation. This paragraph shall not be construed to require an association to inspect an owner's separate interest.

(6) A copy of the initial list of defects provided to each member pursuant to Section 6000, unless the association and the builder subsequently enter into a settlement agreement or otherwise resolve the matter and the association complies with Section 6100. Disclosure of the initial list of defects pursuant to this paragraph does not waive any privilege attached to the document. The initial list of defects shall also include a statement that a final determination as to whether the list of defects is accurate and complete has not been made.

(7) A copy of the latest information provided for in Section 6100.

(8) Any change in the association's current regular and special assessments and fees which have been approved by the board, but have not become due and payable as of the date disclosure is provided pursuant to this subdivision.

(9) If there is a provision in the governing documents that prohibits the rental or leasing of any of the separate interests in the common interest development to a renter, lessee, or tenant, a statement describing the prohibition.

(10) If requested by the prospective purchaser, a copy of the minutes of board meetings, excluding meetings held in executive session, conducted over the previous 12 months, that were approved by the board.

(b) This section does not apply to an owner that is subject to Section 11018.6 of the Business and Professions Code. *(Added by Stats.2012, c. 180 (A.B.805), § 2, operative Jan. 1, 2014. Amended by Stats.2013, c. 183 (S.B.745), § 14.)*

§ 4526. Repealed by Stats.1970, c. 311, p. 706, § 12

§ 4528. Billing disclosures; form

The form for billing disclosures required by Section 4530 shall be in at least 10–point type and substantially the following form:

CHARGES FOR DOCUMENTS PROVIDED AS REQUIRED BY SECTION 4525*

The seller may, in accordance with Section 4530 of the Civil Code, provide to the prospective purchaser, at no cost, current copies of any documents specified by Section 4525 that are in the possession of the seller.

A seller may request to purchase some or all of these documents, but shall not be required to purchase ALL of the documents listed on this form.

Property Address

Owner of Property

Owner's Mailing Address (If known or different from property address.)

Provider of the Section 4525 Items:

Print Name _____ Position or Title _____ Association or Agent

Date Form Completed

Check or Complete Applicable Column or Columns Below

Document	Civil Code Section Included	Fee for Document	Not Available (N/A), Not Applicable (N/App), or Directly Provided by Seller and confirmed in writing by Seller as a current document (DP)
Articles of Incorporation or statement that not incorporated	Section 4525(a)(1)		
CC&Rs	Section 4525(a)(1)		
Bylaws	Section 4525(a)(1)		
Operating Rules	Section 4525(a)(1)		
Age restrictions, if any	Section 4525(a)(2)		
Rental restrictions, if any	Section 4525(a)(9)		
Annual budget report or summary, including reserve study	Sections 5300 and 4525(a)(3)		
Assessment and reserve funding disclosure summary	Sections 5300 and 4525(a)(4)		
Financial statement review	Sections 5305 and 4525(a)(3)		
Assessment enforcement policy	Sections 5310 and 4525(a)(4)		
Insurance summary	Sections 5300 and 4525(a)(3)		
Regular assessment	Section 4525(a)(4)		
Special assessment	Section 4525(a)(4)		
Emergency assessment	Section 4525(a)(4)		
Other unpaid obligations of seller	Sections 5675 and 4525(a)(4)		
Approved changes to assessments	Sections 5300 and 4525(a)(4), (8)		
Settlement notice regarding common area defects	Sections 4525(a)(6), (7), and 6100		

§ 4528

Preliminary list of defects	Sections 4525(a)(6), 6000, and 6100
Notice(s) of violation	Sections 5855 and 4525(a)(5)
Required statement of fees	Section 4525
Minutes of regular board meetings conducted over the previous 12 months, if requested	Section 4525(a)(10)
Total fees for these documents:	

* The information provided by this form may not include all fees that may be imposed before the close of escrow. Additional fees that are not related to the requirements of Section 4525 shall be charged separately.

(Added by Stats.2012, c. 180 (A.B.805), § 2, operative Jan. 1, 2014. Amended by Stats.2013, c. 183 (S.B.745), § 15; Stats. 2014, c. 185 (A.B.2430), § 1, eff. Jan. 1, 2015; Stats.2017, c. 127 (A.B.690), § 2, eff. Jan. 1, 2018.)

Cross References

Certified common interest development managers, annual report to board of directors, contents, see Business and Professions Code § 11504.
Prospective managing agents, disclosures, see Civil Code § 5375.

§ 4530. Copies of requested documents; fees

(a)(1) Upon written request, the association shall, within 10 days of the mailing or delivery of the request, provide the owner of a separate interest, or any other recipient authorized by the owner, with a copy of all of the requested documents specified in Section 4525.

(2) The documents required to be made available pursuant to this section may be maintained in electronic form, and may be posted on the association's Internet Web site. Requesting parties shall have the option of receiving the documents by electronic transmission if the association maintains the documents in electronic form.

(3) Delivery of the documents required by this section shall not be withheld for any reason nor subject to any condition except the payment of the fee authorized pursuant to subdivision (b).

(b)(1) The association may collect a reasonable fee from the seller based upon the association's actual cost for the procurement, preparation, reproduction, and delivery of the documents requested pursuant to this section. An additional fee shall not be charged for the electronic delivery in lieu of a hard copy delivery of the documents requested.

(2) Upon receipt of a written request, the association shall provide, on the form described in Section 4528, a written or electronic estimate of the fees that will be assessed for providing the requested documents prior to processing the request in paragraph (1) of subdivision (a).

(3)(A) A cancellation fee for documents specified in subdivision (a) shall not be collected if either of the following applies:

(i) The request was canceled in writing by the same party that placed the order and work had not yet been performed on the order.

(ii) The request was canceled in writing and any work that had been performed on the order was compensated.

(B) The association shall refund all fees collected pursuant to paragraph (1) if the request was canceled in writing and work had not yet been performed on the order.

(C) If the request was canceled in writing, the association shall refund the share of fees collected pursuant to paragraph (1) that represents the portion of the work not performed on the order.

(4) Fees for any documents required by this section shall be distinguished from, separately stated, and separately billed from, all other fees, fines, or assessments billed as part of the transfer or sales transaction.

(5) Any documents not expressly required by Section 4525 to be provided to a prospective purchaser by the seller shall not be included in the document disclosure required by this section. Bundling of documents required to be provided pursuant to this section with other documents relating to the transaction is prohibited.

(6) A seller shall provide to the prospective purchaser, at no cost, current copies of any documents specified by Section 4525 that are in the possession of the seller.

(7) The fee for each document provided to the seller for the purpose of transmission to the prospective purchaser shall be individually itemized in the statement required to be provided by the seller to the prospective purchaser.

(8) It is the responsibility of the seller to compensate the association, person, or entity that provides the documents required to be provided by Section 4525 to the prospective purchaser.

(c) An association may contract with any person or entity to facilitate compliance with this section on behalf of the association.

(d) The association shall also provide a recipient authorized by the owner of a separate interest with a copy of the completed form specified in Section 4528 at the time the required documents are delivered. A seller may request to purchase some or all of these documents, but shall not be required to purchase all of the documents listed on the form specified in Section 4528. *(Added by Stats.2012, c. 180 (A.B.805), § 2, operative Jan. 1, 2014. Amended by Stats. 2013, c. 183 (S.B.745), § 16; Stats.2014, c. 185 (A.B.2430), § 2, eff. Jan. 1, 2015; Stats.2017, c. 127 (A.B.690), § 3, eff. Jan. 1, 2018.)*

Cross References

Managing agent, facilitation of delivery of disclosures, see Civil Code § 5376.
Prospective managing agents, disclosures, see Civil Code § 5375.
Statements for collection of regular and special assessments, transfer fees, and other charges, see Civil Code § 4210.
Transfer fees prohibited, exception for amount authorized by this section, see Civil Code § 4575.

§ 4531. Repealed by Stats.1992, c. 162 (A.B.2650), § 3, operative Jan. 1, 1994

§ 4535. Additional requirements

In addition to the requirements of this article, an owner transferring title to a separate interest shall comply with applicable requirements of Sections 1133 and 1134. *(Added by Stats.2012, c. 180 (A.B.805), § 2, operative Jan. 1, 2014.)*

§ 4540. Violations; penalties; attorney fees

Any person who willfully violates this article is liable to the purchaser of a separate interest that is subject to this section for actual damages occasioned thereby and, in addition, shall pay a civil penalty in an amount not to exceed five hundred dollars ($500). In an action to enforce this liability, the prevailing party shall be awarded reasonable attorney's fees. *(Added by Stats.2012, c. 180 (A.B.805), § 2, operative Jan. 1, 2014.)*

§ 4545. Validity of title transferred in violation of article

Nothing in this article affects the validity of title to real property transferred in violation of this article. *(Added by Stats.2012, c. 180 (A.B.805), § 2, operative Jan. 1, 2014.)*

§§ 4550 to 4556. Repealed by Stats.1992, c. 162 (A.B.2650), § 3, operative Jan. 1, 1994

ARTICLE 3. TRANSFER FEE

Section
4575. Transfer fees prohibited; exceptions.
4580. Application of transfer fee prohibition.

§ 4575. Transfer fees prohibited; exceptions

Except as provided in Section 4580, neither an association nor a community service organization or similar entity may impose or collect any assessment, penalty, or fee in connection with a transfer of title or any other interest except for the following:

(a) An amount not to exceed the association's actual costs to change its records.

(b) An amount authorized by Section 4530. *(Added by Stats.2012, c. 180 (A.B.805), § 2, operative Jan. 1, 2014.)*

Cross References

Statements for collection of regular and special assessments, transfer fees, and other charges, see Civil Code § 4210.

§ 4580. Application of transfer fee prohibition

The prohibition in Section 4575 does not apply to a community service organization or similar entity, or to a nonprofit entity that provides services to a common interest development under a declaration of trust, of either of the following types:

(a) An organization or entity that satisfies both of the following conditions:

(1) It was established before February 20, 2003.

(2) It exists and operates, in whole or in part, to fund or perform environmental mitigation or to restore or maintain wetlands or native habitat, as required by the state or local government as an express written condition of development.

(b) An organization or entity that satisfies all of the following conditions:

(1) It is not an organization or entity described by subdivision (a).

(2) It was established and received a transfer fee before January 1, 2004.

(3) On and after January 1, 2006, it offers a purchaser the following payment options for the fee or charge it collects at time of transfer:

(A) Paying the fee or charge at the time of transfer.

(B) Paying the fee or charge pursuant to an installment payment plan for a period of not less than seven years. If the purchaser elects to pay the fee or charge in installment payments, the organization or entity may also collect additional amounts that do not exceed the actual costs for billing and financing on the amount owed. If the purchaser sells the separate interest before the end of the installment payment plan period, the purchaser shall pay the remaining balance before the transfer. *(Added by Stats.2012, c. 180 (A.B.805), § 2, operative Jan. 1, 2014.)*

Cross References

Statements for collection of regular and special assessments, transfer fees, and other charges, see Civil Code § 4210.

ARTICLE 4. RESTRICTIONS ON TRANSFER

Section
4600. Exclusive use of common area; affirmative vote required; exceptions; contents of proposed measure.
4600.1 to 4601.5. Repealed.
4602. Repealed.
4603 to 4604.5. Repealed.
4605. Remedies.
4606 to 4609. Repealed.
4610. Restrictions on partition.
4611. Repealed.
4612. Repealed.
4615. Liens for labor and materials.
4620. Claim of lien; notice to members.

§ 4600. Exclusive use of common area; affirmative vote required; exceptions; contents of proposed measure

(a) Unless the governing documents specify a different percentage, the affirmative vote of members owning at least 67 percent of the separate interests in the common interest development shall be required before the board may grant exclusive use of any portion of the common area to a member.

(b) Subdivision (a) does not apply to the following actions:

(1) A reconveyance of all or any portion of that common area to the subdivider to enable the continuation of development that is in substantial conformance with a detailed plan of phased development submitted to the Real Estate Commissioner with the application for a public report.

(2) Any grant of exclusive use that is in substantial conformance with a detailed plan of phased development submitted to the Real Estate Commissioner with the application for a public report or in accordance with the governing documents approved by the Real Estate Commissioner.

(3) Any grant of exclusive use that is for any of the following reasons:

(A) To eliminate or correct engineering errors in documents recorded with the county recorder or on file with a public agency or utility company.

(B) To eliminate or correct encroachments due to errors in construction of any improvements.

(C) To permit changes in the plan of development submitted to the Real Estate Commissioner in circumstances where the changes are the result of topography, obstruction, hardship, aesthetic considerations, or environmental conditions.

(D) To fulfill the requirement of a public agency.

(E) To transfer the burden of management and maintenance of any common area that is generally inaccessible and not of general use to the membership at large of the association.

(F) To accommodate a disability.

(G) To assign a parking space, storage unit, or other amenity, that is designated in the declaration for assignment, but is not assigned by the declaration to a specific separate interest.

(H) To install and use an electric vehicle charging station in an owner's garage or a designated parking space that meets the requirements of Section 4745, where the installation or use of the charging station requires reasonable access through, or across, the common area for utility lines or meters.

(I) To install and use an electric vehicle charging station through a license granted by an association under Section 4745.

(J) To install and use a solar energy system on the common area roof of a residence that meets the requirements of Sections 714, 714.1, and, if applicable, Section 4746.

(K) To comply with governing law.

(c) Any measure placed before the members requesting that the board grant exclusive use of any portion of the common area shall specify whether the association will receive any monetary consideration for the grant and whether the association or the transferee will be responsible for providing any insurance coverage for exclusive use of the common area. *(Added by Stats.2012, c. 180 (A.B.805), § 2, operative Jan. 1, 2014. Amended by Stats.2017, c. 818 (A.B.634), § 2, eff. Jan. 1, 2018.)*

Cross References
Member election, procedures, see Civil Code § 5100.

§§ 4600.1 to 4601.5. Repealed by Stats.1992, c. 162 (A.B. 2650), § 3, operative Jan. 1, 1994

§ 4602. Repealed by Stats.1992, c. 162 (A.B.2650), § 3, operative Jan. 1, 1994; Stats.1993, c. 219 (A.B.1500), § 46.5

§§ 4603 to 4604.5. Repealed by Stats.1992, c. 162 (A.B. 2650), § 3, operative Jan. 1, 1994

§ 4605. Remedies

(a) A member of an association may bring a civil action for declaratory or equitable relief for a violation of Section 4600 by the association, including, but not limited to, injunctive relief, restitution, or a combination thereof, within one year of the date the cause of action accrues.

(b) A member who prevails in a civil action to enforce the member's rights pursuant to Section 4600 shall be entitled to reasonable attorney's fees and court costs, and the court may impose a civil penalty of up to five hundred dollars ($500) for each violation, except that each identical violation shall be subject to only one penalty if the violation affects each member equally. A prevailing association shall not recover any costs, unless the court finds the action to be frivolous, unreasonable, or without foundation. *(Added by Stats.2012, c. 180 (A.B.805), § 2, operative Jan. 1, 2014.)*

§§ 4606 to 4609. Repealed by Stats.1992, c. 162 (A.B.2650), § 3, operative Jan. 1, 1994

§ 4610. Restrictions on partition

(a) Except as provided in this section, the common area in a condominium project shall remain undivided, and there shall be no judicial partition thereof. Nothing in this section shall be deemed to prohibit partition of a cotenancy in a condominium.

(b) The owner of a separate interest in a condominium project may maintain a partition action as to the entire project as if the owners of all of the separate interests in the project were tenants in common in the entire project in the same proportion as their interests in the common area. The court shall order partition under this subdivision only by sale of the entire condominium project and only upon a showing of one of the following:

(1) More than three years before the filing of the action, the condominium project was damaged or destroyed, so that a material part was rendered unfit for its prior use, and the condominium project has not been rebuilt or repaired substantially to its state prior to the damage or destruction.

(2) Three-fourths or more of the project is destroyed or substantially damaged and owners of separate interests holding in the aggregate more than a 50–percent interest in the common area oppose repair or restoration of the project.

(3) The project has been in existence more than 50 years, is obsolete and uneconomic, and owners of separate interests holding in the aggregate more than a 50–percent interest in the common area oppose repair or restoration of the project.

(4) Any conditions in the declaration for sale under the circumstances described in this subdivision have been met. *(Added by Stats.2012, c. 180 (A.B.805), § 2, operative Jan. 1, 2014.)*

Cross References
Assignment of retail installment sale contract, effect on rights, equities or defenses, see Civil Code § 1804.2.
Condominium project, interests included in conveyance, judicial sale or transfer of separate interests, see Civil Code § 4630.
Restrictions upon severability of component interests, see Civil Code § 4650.

§ 4611. Repealed by Stats.1992, c. 162 (A.B.2650), § 3, operative Jan. 1, 1994

§ 4612. Repealed by Stats.1993, c. 219 (A.B.1500), § 46.7

§ 4615. Liens for labor and materials

(a) In a common interest development, no labor performed or services or materials furnished with the consent of, or at the request of, an owner in the common interest development or the owners' agent or contractor shall be the basis for the filing of a lien against any other property of another owner in the common interest development unless that other owner has expressly consented to or requested the performance of the labor or furnishing of the materials or services. However, express consent is deemed to have been given by the owner of any separate interest in the case of emergency repairs thereto.

(b) Labor performed or services or materials furnished for the common area, if duly authorized by the association, are deemed to be performed or furnished with the express consent of each separate interest owner.

(c) The owner of any separate interest may remove that owner's separate interest from a lien against two or more separate interests or any part thereof by doing either of the following:

(1) Pay to the holder of the lien the fraction of the total sum secured by the lien that is attributable to the owner's separate interest.

(2) Record a lien release bond, pursuant to Section 8424, in an amount equal to 125 percent of the sum secured by the lien that is attributable to the owner's separate interest. *(Added by Stats.2012, c. 180 (A.B.805), § 2, operative Jan. 1, 2014. Amended by Stats.2017, c. 44 (A.B.534), § 1, eff. Jan. 1, 2018; Stats.2018, c. 92 (S.B.1289), § 38, eff. Jan. 1, 2019.)*

§ 4620. Claim of lien; notice to members

If the association is served with a claim of lien pursuant to Part 6 (commencing with Section 8000) for a work of improvement on a common area, the association shall, within 60 days of service, give individual notice to the members, pursuant to Section 4040. *(Added by Stats.2017, c. 44 (A.B.534), § 2, eff. Jan. 1, 2018.)*

ARTICLE 5. TRANSFER OF SEPARATE INTEREST

Section
4625. Community apartment project; interests included in conveyance, judicial sale or transfer of separate interests.
4630. Condominium project; interests included in conveyance, judicial sale or transfer of separate interests.
4635. Planned development; interests included in conveyance, judicial sale or transfer of separate interests.
4640. Stock cooperative; interests included in conveyance, judicial sale or transfer of separate interests.
4645. Transfer of exclusive use areas.
4650. Restrictions upon severability of component interests.

§ 4625. Community apartment project; interests included in conveyance, judicial sale or transfer of separate interests

In a community apartment project, any conveyance, judicial sale, or other voluntary or involuntary transfer of the separate interest includes the undivided interest in the community apartment project. Any conveyance, judicial sale, or other voluntary or involuntary transfer of the owner's entire estate also includes the owner's membership interest in the association. *(Added by Stats.2012, c. 180 (A.B.805), § 2, operative Jan. 1, 2014.)*

§ 4630. Condominium project; interests included in conveyance, judicial sale or transfer of separate interests

In a condominium project the common area is not subject to partition, except as provided in Section 4610. Any conveyance, judicial sale, or other voluntary or involuntary transfer of the separate interest includes the undivided interest in the common area. Any conveyance, judicial sale, or other voluntary or involuntary transfer of the owner's entire estate also includes the owner's membership interest in the association. *(Added by Stats.2012, c. 180 (A.B.805), § 2, operative Jan. 1, 2014.)*

§ 4635. Planned development; interests included in conveyance, judicial sale or transfer of separate interests

In a planned development, any conveyance, judicial sale, or other voluntary or involuntary transfer of the separate interest includes the undivided interest in the common area, if any exists. Any conveyance, judicial sale, or other voluntary or involuntary transfer of the owner's entire estate also includes the owner's membership interest in the association. *(Added by Stats.2012, c. 180 (A.B.805), § 2, operative Jan. 1, 2014.)*

§ 4640. Stock cooperative; interests included in conveyance, judicial sale or transfer of separate interests

In a stock cooperative, any conveyance, judicial sale, or other voluntary or involuntary transfer of the separate interest includes the ownership interest in the corporation, however evidenced. Any conveyance, judicial sale, or other voluntary or involuntary transfer of the owner's entire estate also includes the owner's membership interest in the association. *(Added by Stats.2012, c. 180 (A.B.805), § 2, operative Jan. 1, 2014.)*

§ 4645. Transfer of exclusive use areas

Nothing in this article prohibits the transfer of exclusive use areas, independent of any other interest in a common interest subdivision, if authorization to separately transfer exclusive use areas is expressly stated in the declaration and the transfer occurs in accordance with the terms of the declaration. *(Added by Stats.2012, c. 180 (A.B.805), § 2, operative Jan. 1, 2014.)*

§ 4650. Restrictions upon severability of component interests

Any restrictions upon the severability of the component interests in real property which are contained in the declaration shall not be deemed conditions repugnant to the interest created within the meaning of Section 711. However, these restrictions shall not extend beyond the period in which the right to partition a project is suspended under Section 4610. *(Added by Stats.2012, c. 180 (A.B.805), § 2, operative Jan. 1, 2014.)*

CHAPTER 5. PROPERTY USE AND MAINTENANCE

Article	Section
1. Protected Uses	4700

GENERAL PROVISIONS

Article	Section
2. Modification of Separate Interest	4760
3. Maintenance	4775

ARTICLE 1. PROTECTED USES

Section
4700. Scope of article; related provisions.
4700.1 to 4700.3. Repealed.
4700.5 to 4700.10. Repealed.
4700.11. Repealed.
4701. Repealed.
4701.1. Repealed.
4701.2. Repealed.
4702. Repealed.
4703 to 4704.5. Repealed.
4705. Display of United States flag by owner on or in owner's separate interest or within exclusive use common area.
4706. Display of religious item on entry door or entry door frame of member's separate interest.
4707 to 4709. Repealed.
4710. Prohibition of posting or displaying noncommercial signs, posters, flags, or banners; permitted placement of posting or displaying; exceptions.
4715. Pets within common interest developments.
4720. Roof installation or repair; roofing materials.
4720.1, 4720.2. Repealed.
4721, 4722. Repealed.
4722.5. Repealed.
4723, 4724. Repealed.
4725. Restrictions on installation or use of video or television antenna; enforceability based on size; reasonable restrictions; application approval; attorney's fees.
4726. Repealed.
4726.1. Repealed.
4727 to 4728.5. Repealed.
4729. Repealed.
4730. Prohibition against association rule or regulation that arbitrarily or unreasonably restricts owner's ability to market his or her interest in common development; other enumerated restrictions.
4731, 4732. Repealed.
4735. Governing documents or architectural or landscaping guidelines or policies; void and unenforceable provisions; landscaping rules; certain fines or assessments prohibited; water-efficient landscaping measures in response to state of emergency.
4736. Governing documents; void and unenforceable provisions; pressure washing.
4739. Governing documents; prohibited provisions; rental or lease for periods of more than 30 days; parking restrictions and guest access to common facilities.
4740. Rental or leasing of separate interests; provisions in governing documents.
4741. Rental or leasing of separate interests, accessory dwelling units, or junior accessory dwelling units; provisions in governing documents; penalty for violations.
4745. Electric vehicle charging stations.
4745.1. EV-dedicated TOU meters.
4746. Request to install a solar energy system; requirements; additional provisions; definitions.
4747. Floor area ratio standards authorized for eligible housing development projects; applicability; legislative findings and declarations.

Section
4750. Backyard personal agriculture; scope of application; homeowners' association regulations.
4750.10. Renumbered.
4751. Accessory dwelling units or junior accessory dwelling units.
4752. Repealed.
4753. Use of clothesline or drying rack; conditions.

§ 4700. Scope of article; related provisions

This article includes provisions that limit the authority of an association or the governing documents to regulate the use of a member's separate interest. Nothing in this article is intended to affect the application of any other provision that limits the authority of an association to regulate the use of a member's separate interest, including, but not limited to, the following provisions:

(a) Sections 712 and 713, relating to the display of signs.

(b) Sections 714 and 714.1, relating to solar energy systems.

(c) Section 714.5, relating to structures that are constructed offsite and moved to the property in sections or modules.

(d) Sections 782, 782.5, and 6150 of this code and Section 12956.1 of the Government Code, relating to racial restrictions.

(e) Section 12927 of the Government Code, relating to the modification of property to accommodate a disability.

(f) Section 1597.40 of the Health and Safety Code, relating to the operation of a family day care home. *(Added by Stats.2012, c. 180 (A.B.805), § 2, operative Jan. 1, 2014.)*

§§ 4700.1 to 4700.3. Repealed by Stats.1992, c. 162 (A.B. 2650), § 3, operative Jan. 1, 1994

§§ 4700.5 to 4700.10. Repealed by Stats.1992, c. 162 (A.B. 2650), § 3, operative Jan. 1, 1994

§ 4700.11. Repealed by Stats.1993, c. 219 (A.B.1500), § 47

§ 4701. Repealed by Stats.1989, c. 1359, § 3.5, operative Jan. 1, 1991

§ 4701.1. Repealed by Stats.1992, c. 162 (A.B.2650), § 3, operative Jan. 1, 1994

§ 4701.2. Repealed by Stats.1988, c. 231, § 1, operative Jan. 1. 1994; Stats.1992, c. 162 (A.B.2650), § 3, operative Jan. 1, 1994

§ 4702. Repealed by Stats.1993, c. 219 (A.B.1500), § 48

§§ 4703 to 4704.5. Repealed by Stats.1992, c. 162 (A.B. 2650), § 3, operative Jan. 1, 1994

§ 4705. Display of United States flag by owner on or in owner's separate interest or within exclusive use common area

(a) Except as required for the protection of the public health or safety, no governing document shall limit or prohibit, or be construed to limit or prohibit, the display of the flag of the United States by a member on or in the member's separate interest or within the member's exclusive use common area.

(b) For purposes of this section, "display of the flag of the United States" means a flag of the United States made of fabric, cloth, or paper displayed from a staff or pole or in a window, and does not mean a depiction or emblem of the flag of the United States made of lights, paint, roofing, siding, paving materials, flora, or balloons, or any other similar building, landscaping, or decorative component.

(c) In any action to enforce this section, the prevailing party shall be awarded reasonable attorney's fees and costs. (Added by Stats.2012, c. 180 (A.B.805), § 2, operative Jan. 1, 2014.)

§ 4706. Display of religious item on entry door or entry door frame of member's separate interest

(a) Except as restricted in Section 1940.5,[1] no governing document shall limit or prohibit the display of one or more religious items on the entry door or entry door frame of the member's separate interest.

(b) If an association is performing maintenance, repair, or replacement of an entry door or door frame that serves a member's separate interest, the member may be required to remove a religious item during the time the work is being performed. After completion of the association's work, the member may again display or affix the religious item. The association shall provide individual notice to the member regarding the temporary removal of the religious item. (Added by Stats.2019, c. 154 (S.B.652), § 2, eff. Jan. 1, 2020.)

[1] So in enrolled bill. Probably should be Civil Code § 1940.45.

§§ 4707 to 4709. Repealed by Stats.1992, c. 162 (A.B.2650), § 3, operative Jan. 1, 1994

§ 4710. Prohibition of posting or displaying noncommercial signs, posters, flags, or banners; permitted placement of posting or displaying; exceptions

(a) The governing documents may not prohibit posting or displaying of noncommercial signs, posters, flags, or banners on or in a member's separate interest, except as required for the protection of public health or safety or if the posting or display would violate a local, state, or federal law.

(b) For purposes of this section, a noncommercial sign, poster, flag, or banner may be made of paper, cardboard, cloth, plastic, or fabric, and may be posted or displayed from the yard, window, door, balcony, or outside wall of the separate interest, but may not be made of lights, roofing, siding, paving materials, flora, or balloons, or any other similar building, landscaping, or decorative component, or include the painting of architectural surfaces.

(c) An association may prohibit noncommercial signs and posters that are more than nine square feet in size and noncommercial flags or banners that are more than 15 square feet in size. (Added by Stats.2012, c. 180 (A.B.805), § 2, operative Jan. 1, 2014.)

Cross References

Posting or displaying political signs by tenant, landlord not to prohibit, exception if posting violates terms of common interest development governing a document that satisfies criteria of this section, see Civil Code § 1940.4.

Right to display political campaign signs, see Civil Code § 799.10.

§ 4715. Pets within common interest developments

(a) No governing documents shall prohibit the owner of a separate interest within a common interest development from keeping at least one pet within the common interest development, subject to reasonable rules and regulations of the association. This section may not be construed to affect any other rights provided by law to an owner of a separate interest to keep a pet within the development.

(b) For purposes of this section, "pet" means any domesticated bird, cat, dog, aquatic animal kept within an aquarium, or other animal as agreed to between the association and the homeowner.

(c) If the association implements a rule or regulation restricting the number of pets an owner may keep, the new rule or regulation shall not apply to prohibit an owner from continuing to keep any pet that the owner currently keeps in the owner's separate interest if the pet otherwise conforms with the previous rules or regulations relating to pets.

(d) For the purposes of this section, "governing documents" shall include, but are not limited to, the conditions, covenants, and restrictions of the common interest development, and the bylaws, rules, and regulations of the association.

(e) This section shall become operative on January 1, 2001 [1], and shall only apply to governing documents entered into, amended, or otherwise modified on or after that date. (Added by Stats.2012, c. 180 (A.B.805), § 2, operative Jan. 1, 2014.)

[1] See former Civil Code § 1360.5, operative Jan. 1, 2001, from which this section is derived.

Cross References

Pets within commercial and industrial common interest developments, see Civil Code § 6706.

§ 4720. Roof installation or repair; roofing materials

(a) No association may require a homeowner to install or repair a roof in a manner that is in violation of Section 13132.7 of the Health and Safety Code.

(b) Governing documents of a common interest development located within a very high fire severity zone, as designated by the Director of Forestry and Fire Protection pursuant to Article 9 (commencing with Section 4201) of Chapter 1 of Part 2 of Division 4 of the Public Resources Code or by a local agency pursuant to Chapter 6.8 (commencing with Section 51175) of Part 1 of Division 1 of Title 5 of the Government Code, shall allow for at least one type of fire retardant roof covering material that meets the requirements of Section 13132.7 of the Health and Safety Code. (Added by Stats.2012, c. 180 (A.B.805), § 2, operative Jan. 1, 2014.)

§§ 4720.1, 4720.2. Repealed by Stats.1992, c. 46 (S.B.370), §§ 6, 7, eff. May 11, 1992, operative July 1, 1992

§§ 4721, 4722. Repealed by Stats.1993, c. 219 (A.B.1500), § 50, 51

§ 4722.5. Repealed by Stats.1994, c. 146 (A.B.3601), § 18; Stats.1994, c. 1269 (A.B.2208), § 1

§§ 4723, 4724. Repealed by Stats.1990, c. 1493 (A.B.3974), §§ 17, 19, operative March 1, 1991

§ 4725. Restrictions on installation or use of video or television antenna; enforceability based on size; reasonable restrictions; application approval; attorney's fees

(a) Any covenant, condition, or restriction contained in any deed, contract, security instrument, or other instrument affecting the transfer or sale of, or any interest in, a common interest development that effectively prohibits or restricts the installation or use of a video or television antenna, including a satellite dish, or that effectively prohibits or restricts the attachment of that antenna to a structure within that development where the antenna is not visible from any street or common area, except as otherwise prohibited or restricted by law, is void and unenforceable as to its application to the installation or use of a video or television antenna that has a diameter or diagonal measurement of 36 inches or less.

(b) This section shall not apply to any covenant, condition, or restriction, as described in subdivision (a), that imposes reasonable restrictions on the installation or use of a video or television antenna, including a satellite dish, that has a diameter or diagonal measurement of 36 inches or less. For purposes of this section, "reasonable restrictions" means those restrictions that do not significantly increase the cost of the video or television antenna system, including all related equipment, or significantly decrease its efficiency or performance and include all of the following:

(1) Requirements for application and notice to the association prior to the installation.

(2) Requirement of a member to obtain the approval of the association for the installation of a video or television antenna that has a diameter or diagonal measurement of 36 inches or less on a separate interest owned by another.

(3) Provision for the maintenance, repair, or replacement of roofs or other building components.

(4) Requirements for installers of a video or television antenna to indemnify or reimburse the association or its members for loss or damage caused by the installation, maintenance, or use of a video or television antenna that has a diameter or diagonal measurement of 36 inches or less.

(c) Whenever approval is required for the installation or use of a video or television antenna, including a satellite dish, the application for approval shall be processed by the appropriate approving entity for the common interest development in the same manner as an application for approval of an architectural modification to the property, and the issuance of a decision on the application shall not be willfully delayed.

(d) In any action to enforce compliance with this section, the prevailing party shall be awarded reasonable attorney's fees. *(Added by Stats.2012, c. 180 (A.B.805), § 2, operative Jan. 1, 2014.)*

§ 4726. Repealed by Stats.1992, c. 162 (A.B.2650), § 3, operative Jan. 1, 1994; Stats.1993, c. 876 (S.B.1068), § 7, operative Jan. 1, 1994

§ 4726.1. Repealed by Stats.1992, c. 162 (A.B.2650), § 3, operative Jan. 1, 1994

§§ 4727 to 4728.5. Repealed by Stats.1990, c. 1493 (A.B. 3974), §§ 23, 24 and 26, operative March 1, 1991

§ 4729. Repealed by Stats.1992, c. 46 (S.B.370), § 18, eff. May 11, 1992, operative July 1, 1992

§ 4730. Prohibition against association rule or regulation that arbitrarily or unreasonably restricts owner's ability to market his or her interest in common development; other enumerated restrictions

(a) Any provision of a governing document that arbitrarily or unreasonably restricts an owner's ability to market the owner's interest in a common interest development is void.

(b) No association may adopt, enforce, or otherwise impose any governing document that does either of the following:

(1) Imposes an assessment or fee in connection with the marketing of an owner's interest in an amount that exceeds the association's actual or direct costs. That assessment or fee shall be deemed to violate the limitation set forth in subdivision (b) of Section 5600.

(2) Establishes an exclusive relationship with a real estate broker through which the sale or marketing of interests in the development is required to occur. The limitation set forth in this paragraph does not apply to the sale or marketing of separate interests owned by the association or to the sale or marketing of common area by the association.

(c) For purposes of this section, "market" and "marketing" mean listing, advertising, or obtaining or providing access to show the owner's interest in the development.

(d) This section does not apply to rules or regulations made pursuant to Section 712 or 713 regarding real estate signs. *(Added by Stats.2012, c. 180 (A.B.805), § 2, operative Jan. 1, 2014.)*

§§ 4731, 4732. Repealed by Stats.1992, c. 162 (A.B.2650), § 3, operative Jan. 1, 1994

§ 4735. Governing documents or architectural or landscaping guidelines or policies; void and unenforceable provisions; landscaping rules; certain fines or assessments prohibited; water-efficient landscaping measures in response to state of emergency

(a) Notwithstanding any other law, a provision of the governing documents or architectural or landscaping guidelines or policies shall be void and unenforceable if it does any of the following:

(1) Prohibits, or includes conditions that have the effect of prohibiting, the use of low water-using plants as a group or as a replacement of existing turf.

(2) Prohibits, or includes conditions that have the effect of prohibiting, the use of artificial turf or any other synthetic surface that resembles grass.

(3) Has the effect of prohibiting or restricting compliance with either of the following:

(A) A water-efficient landscape ordinance adopted or in effect pursuant to subdivision (c) of Section 65595 of the Government Code.

(B) Any regulation or restriction on the use of water adopted pursuant to Section 353 or 375 of the Water Code.

(b) This section shall not prohibit an association from applying landscaping rules established in the governing documents, to the extent the rules fully conform with subdivision (a).

(c) Notwithstanding any other provision of this part, except as provided in subdivision (d), an association shall not impose a fine or assessment against an owner of a separate interest for reducing or eliminating the watering of vegetation or lawns during any period for which either of the following have occurred:

(1) The Governor has declared a state of emergency due to drought pursuant to subdivision (b) of Section 8558 of the Government Code.

(2) A local government has declared a local emergency due to drought pursuant to subdivision (c) of Section 8558 of the Government Code.

(d) Subdivision (c) shall not apply to an owner of a separate interest that, prior to the imposition of a fine or assessment described in subdivision (c), receives recycled water, as defined in Section 13050 of the Water Code, from a retail water supplier, as defined in Section 13575 of the Water Code, and fails to use that recycled water for landscaping irrigation.

(e) An owner of a separate interest upon which water-efficient landscaping measures have been installed in response to a declaration of a state of emergency described in subdivision (c) shall not be required to reverse or remove the water-efficient landscaping measures upon the conclusion of the state of emergency. *(Added by Stats.2012, c. 180 (A.B. 805), § 2, operative Jan. 1, 2014. Amended by Stats.2014, c. 164 (A.B.2100), § 1, eff. July 21, 2014; Stats.2014, c. 434 (S.B.992), § 1, eff. Sept. 18, 2014; Stats.2014, c. 421 (A.B. 2104), § 1, eff. Jan. 1, 2015; Stats.2014, c. 434 (S.B.992), § 1.5, eff. Sept. 18, 2014, operative Jan. 1, 2015; Stats.2015, c. 266 (A.B.349), § 2, eff. Sept. 4, 2015; Stats.2015, c. 780 (A.B.786), § 2.5, eff. Oct. 11, 2015.)*

Cross References

Water Conservation in Landscaping Act, see Government Code § 65591 et seq.

§ 4736. Governing documents; void and unenforceable provisions; pressure washing

(a) A provision of the governing documents shall be void and unenforceable if it requires pressure washing the exterior of a separate interest and any exclusive use common area appurtenant to the separate interest during a state or local government declared drought emergency.

(b) For purposes of this section, "pressure washing" means the use of a high-pressure sprayer or hose and potable water to remove loose paint, mold, grime, dust, mud, and dirt from surfaces and objects, including buildings, vehicles, and concrete surfaces. *(Added by Stats.2014, c. 434 (S.B.992), § 2, eff. Sept. 18, 2014.)*

§ 4739. Governing documents; prohibited provisions; rental or lease for periods of more than 30 days; parking restrictions and guest access to common facilities

(a) Notwithstanding Section 4740, an owner of a separate interest in a common interest development shall not be subject to a provision in a governing document, or amendments thereto, that prohibits the rental or leasing of a portion of the owner-occupied separate interest in that common interest development to a renter, lessee, or tenant for a period of more than 30 days.

(b) Nothing in this section shall permit an owner of a separate interest or a resident renting or leasing a portion of the owner-occupied separate interest to violate any provision of the association governing documents that govern conduct in the separate interest or common areas, or that govern membership rights or privileges, including, but not limited to, parking restrictions and guest access to common facilities. *(Added by Stats.2022, c. 858 (A.B.1410), § 3, eff. Jan. 1, 2023.)*

§ 4740. Rental or leasing of separate interests; provisions in governing documents

(a) An owner of a separate interest in a common interest development shall not be subject to a provision in a governing document or an amendment to a governing document that prohibits the rental or leasing of any of the separate interests in that common interest development to a renter, lessee, or tenant unless that governing document, or amendment thereto, was effective prior to the date the owner acquired title to their separate interest.

(b) For purposes of this section, the right to rent or lease the separate interest of an owner shall not be deemed to have terminated if the transfer by the owner of all or part of the separate interest meets at least one of the following conditions:

(1) Pursuant to Section 62 or 480.3 of the Revenue and Taxation Code, the transfer is exempt, for purposes of reassessment by the county tax assessor.

(2) Pursuant to subdivision (b) of, solely with respect to probate transfers, or subdivision (e), (f), or (g) of, Section 1102.2, the transfer is exempt from the requirements to prepare and deliver a Real Estate Transfer Disclosure Statement, as set forth in Section 1102.6.

(c) Prior to renting or leasing their separate interest as provided by this section, an owner shall provide the association verification of the date the owner acquired title to the separate interest and the name and contact information of the prospective tenant or lessee or the prospective tenant's or lessee's representative.

(d) Nothing in this section shall be deemed to revise, alter, or otherwise affect the voting process by which a common interest development adopts or amends its governing documents. *(Added by Stats.2012, c. 180 (A.B.805), § 2, operative Jan. 1, 2014. Amended by Stats.2020, c. 198 (A.B.3182), § 1, eff. Jan. 1, 2021.)*

§ 4741. Rental or leasing of separate interests, accessory dwelling units, or junior accessory dwelling units; provisions in governing documents; penalty for violations

(a) An owner of a separate interest in a common interest development shall not be subject to a provision in a governing document or an amendment to a governing document that prohibits, has the effect of prohibiting, or unreasonably restricts the rental or leasing of any of the separate interests, accessory dwelling units, or junior accessory dwelling units in that common interest development to a renter, lessee, or tenant.

(b) A common interest development shall not adopt or enforce a provision in a governing document or amendment to a governing document that restricts the rental or lease of separate interests within a common interest to less than 25 percent of the separate interests. Nothing in this subdivision prohibits a common interest development from adopting or enforcing a provision authorizing a higher percentage of separate interests to be rented or leased.

(c) This section does not prohibit a common interest development from adopting and enforcing a provision in a governing document that prohibits transient or short-term rental of a separate property interest for a period of 30 days or less.

(d) For purposes of this section, an accessory dwelling unit or junior accessory dwelling unit shall not be construed as a separate interest.

(e) For purposes of this section, a separate interest shall not be counted as occupied by a renter if the separate interest, or the accessory dwelling unit or junior accessory dwelling unit of the separate interest, is occupied by the owner.

(f) A common interest development shall comply with the prohibition on rental restrictions specified in this section on and after January 1, 2021, regardless of whether the common interest development has revised their governing documents to comply with this section. Notwithstanding any other provision of law or provision of the governing documents, the board, without approval of the members, shall amend any declaration or other governing document no later than July 1, 2022, that includes a restrictive covenant prohibited by this section by either deleting or restating the restrictive covenant to be compliant with this section, and shall restate the declaration or other governing document without the restrictive covenant but with no other change to the declaration or governing document. A board shall provide general notice pursuant to Section 4045 of the amendment at least 28 days before approving the amendment. The notice shall include the text of the amendment and a description of the purpose and effect of the amendment. The decision on the amendment shall be made at a board meeting, after consideration of any comments made by association members.

(g) A common interest development that willfully violates this section shall be liable to the applicant or other party for actual damages, and shall pay a civil penalty to the applicant or other party in an amount not to exceed one thousand dollars ($1,000).

(h) In accordance with Section 4740, this section does not change the right of an owner of a separate interest who acquired title to their separate interest before the effective date of this section to rent or lease their property. (Added by Stats.2020, c. 198 (A.B.3182), § 2, eff. Jan. 1, 2021. Amended by Stats.2021, c. 360 (A.B.1584), § 6, eff. Jan. 1, 2022.)

§ 4745. Electric vehicle charging stations

(a) Any covenant, restriction, or condition contained in any deed, contract, security instrument, or other instrument affecting the transfer or sale of any interest in a common interest development, and any provision of a governing document, as defined in Section 4150, that either effectively prohibits or unreasonably restricts the installation or use of an electric vehicle charging station within an owner's unit or in a designated parking space, including, but not limited to, a deeded parking space, a parking space in an owner's exclusive use common area, or a parking space that is specifically designated for use by a particular owner, or is in conflict with this section is void and unenforceable.

(b)(1) This section does not apply to provisions that impose reasonable restrictions on electric vehicle charging stations. However, it is the policy of the state to promote, encourage, and remove obstacles to the use of electric vehicle charging stations.

(2) For purposes of this section, "reasonable restrictions" are restrictions that do not significantly increase the cost of the station or significantly decrease its efficiency or specified performance.

(c) An electric vehicle charging station shall meet applicable health and safety standards and requirements imposed by state and local authorities, and all other applicable zoning, land use, or other ordinances, or land use permits.

(d) For purposes of this section, "electric vehicle charging station" means a station that is designed in compliance with the California Building Standards Code and delivers electricity from a source outside an electric vehicle into one or more electric vehicles. An electric vehicle charging station may include several charge points simultaneously connecting several electric vehicles to the station and any related equipment needed to facilitate charging plug-in electric vehicles.

(e) If approval is required for the installation or use of an electric vehicle charging station, the application for approval shall be processed and approved by the association in the same manner as an application for approval of an architectural modification to the property, and shall not be willfully avoided or delayed. The approval or denial of an application shall be in writing. If an application is not denied in writing within 60 days from the date of receipt of the application, the application shall be deemed approved, unless that delay is the result of a reasonable request for additional information.

(f) If the electric vehicle charging station is to be placed in a common area or an exclusive use common area, as designated in the common interest development's declaration, the following provisions apply:

(1) The owner first shall obtain approval from the association to install the electric vehicle charging station and the association shall approve the installation if the owner agrees in writing to do all of the following:

(A) Comply with the association's architectural standards for the installation of the charging station.

(B) Engage a licensed contractor to install the charging station.

(C) Within 14 days of approval, provide a certificate of insurance that names the association as an additional insured under the owner's insurance policy in the amount set forth in paragraph (3).

(D) Pay for both the costs associated with the installation of and the electricity usage associated with the charging station.

(2) The owner and each successive owner of the charging station shall be responsible for all of the following:

(A) Costs for damage to the charging station, common area, exclusive use common area, or separate interests resulting from the installation, maintenance, repair, removal, or replacement of the charging station.

(B) Costs for the maintenance, repair, and replacement of the charging station until it has been removed and for the restoration of the common area after removal.

(C) The cost of electricity associated with the charging station.

(D) Disclosing to prospective buyers the existence of any charging station of the owner and the related responsibilities of the owner under this section.

(3) The owner of the charging station, whether located within a separate unit or within the common area or exclusive use common area, shall, at all times, maintain a liability coverage policy. The owner that submitted the application to install the charging station shall provide the association with the corresponding certificate of insurance within 14 days of approval of the application. That owner and each successor owner shall provide the association with the certificate of insurance annually thereafter.

(4) A homeowner shall not be required to maintain a homeowner liability coverage policy for an existing National Electrical Manufacturers Association standard alternating current power plug.

(g) Except as provided in subdivision (h), installation of an electric vehicle charging station for the exclusive use of an owner in a common area, that is not an exclusive use common area, shall be authorized by the association only if installation in the owner's designated parking space is impossible or unreasonably expensive. In such cases, the association shall enter into a license agreement with the owner for the use of the space in a common area, and the owner shall comply with all of the requirements in subdivision (f).

(h) The association or owners may install an electric vehicle charging station in the common area for the use of all members of the association and, in that case, the association shall develop appropriate terms of use for the charging station.

(i) An association may create a new parking space where one did not previously exist to facilitate the installation of an electric vehicle charging station.

(j) An association that willfully violates this section shall be liable to the applicant or other party for actual damages, and shall pay a civil penalty to the applicant or other party in an amount not to exceed one thousand dollars ($1,000).

(k) In any action by a homeowner requesting to have an electric vehicle charging station installed and seeking to enforce compliance with this section, the prevailing plaintiff shall be awarded reasonable attorney's fees. *(Added by Stats.2012, c. 180 (A.B.805), § 2, operative Jan. 1, 2014. Amended by Stats.2018, c. 376 (S.B.1016), § 1, eff. Jan. 1, 2019.)*

Cross References

Exclusive use of common area, affirmative vote required, exception for electric vehicle charging station, see Civil Code § 4600.

Lease terms prohibiting or unreasonably restricting installation of electric vehicle charging station, exceptions, charging station requirements, see Civil Code § 1952.7.

§ 4745.1. EV-dedicated TOU meters

(a) Any covenant, restriction, or condition contained in any deed, contract, security instrument, or other instrument affecting the transfer or sale of any interest in a common interest development, and any provision of a governing document, as defined in Section 4150, that either effectively prohibits or unreasonably restricts the installation or use of an EV-dedicated TOU meter or is in conflict with this section is void and unenforceable.

(b)(1) This section does not apply to provisions that impose reasonable restrictions on the installation of an EV-dedicated TOU meter. However, it is the policy of the state to promote, encourage, and remove obstacles to the effective installation of EV-dedicated TOU meters.

(2) For purposes of this section, "reasonable restrictions" are restrictions based upon space, aesthetics, structural integrity, and equal access to these services for all homeowners, but an association shall attempt to find a reasonable way to accommodate the installation request, unless the association would need to incur an expense.

(c) An EV-dedicated TOU meter shall meet applicable health and safety standards and requirements imposed by state and local authorities, and all other applicable zoning, land use, or other ordinances, or land use permits.

(d) For purposes of this section, an "EV-dedicated TOU meter" means an electric meter supplied and installed by an electric utility, that is separate from, and in addition to, any other electric meter and is devoted exclusively to the charging of electric vehicles, and that tracks the time of use (TOU) when charging occurs. An "EV-dedicated TOU meter" includes any wiring or conduit necessary to connect the electric meter to an electric vehicle charging station, as defined in Section 4745, regardless of whether it is supplied or installed by an electric utility.

(e) If approval is required for the installation or use of an EV-dedicated TOU meter, the application for approval shall be processed and approved by the association in the same manner as an application for approval of an architectural modification to the property, and shall not be willfully avoided or delayed. The approval or denial of an application shall be in writing. If an application is not denied in writing within 60 days from the date of receipt of the application, the application shall be deemed approved, unless that delay is the result of a reasonable request for additional information.

§ 4745.1

(f) If the EV-dedicated TOU meter is to be placed in a common area or an exclusive use common area, as designated in the common interest development's declaration, the following provisions apply:

(1) The owner first shall obtain approval from the association to install the EV-dedicated TOU meter and the association shall approve the installation if the owner agrees in writing to do both of the following:

(A) Comply with the association's architectural standards for the installation of the EV-dedicated TOU meter.

(B) Engage the relevant electric utility to install the EV-dedicated TOU meter and, if necessary, a licensed contractor to install wiring or conduit necessary to connect the electric meter to an EV charging station.

(2) The owner and each successive owner of an EV-dedicated TOU meter shall be responsible for all of the following:

(A) Costs for damage to the EV-dedicated TOU meter, common area, exclusive use common area, or separate interests resulting from the installation, maintenance, repair, removal, or replacement of the EV-dedicated TOU meter.

(B) Costs for the maintenance, repair, and replacement of the EV-dedicated TOU meter until it has been removed and for the restoration of the common area after removal.

(C) Disclosing to prospective buyers the existence of any EV-dedicated TOU meter of the owner and the related responsibilities of the owner under this section.

(g) The association or owners may install an EV-dedicated TOU meter in the common area for the use of all members of the association and, in that case, the association shall develop appropriate terms of use for the EV-dedicated TOU meter.

(h) An association that willfully violates this section shall be liable to the applicant or other party for actual damages, and shall pay a civil penalty to the applicant or other party in an amount not to exceed one thousand dollars ($1,000).

(i) In any action by a homeowner requesting to have an EV-dedicated TOU meter installed and seeking to enforce compliance with this section, the prevailing plaintiff shall be awarded reasonable attorney's fees. *(Added by Stats.2018, c. 376 (S.B.1016), § 2, eff. Jan. 1, 2019.)*

§ 4746. Request to install a solar energy system; requirements; additional provisions; definitions

(a) When reviewing a request to install a solar energy system on a multifamily common area roof shared by more than one homeowner pursuant to Sections 714 and 714.1, an association shall require both of the following:

(1) An applicant to notify each owner of a unit in the building on which the installation will be located of the application to install a solar energy system.

(2) The owner and each successive owner to maintain a homeowner liability coverage policy at all times and provide the association with the corresponding certificate of insurance within 14 days of approval of the application and annually thereafter.

(b) When reviewing a request to install a solar energy system on a multifamily common area roof shared by more than one homeowner pursuant to Sections 714 and 714.1, an association may impose additional reasonable provisions that:

(1)(A) Require the applicant to submit a solar site survey showing the placement of the solar energy system prepared by a licensed contractor or the contractor's registered salesperson knowledgeable in the installation of solar energy systems to determine usable solar roof area. This survey or the costs to determine useable space shall not be deemed as part of the cost of the system as used in Section 714.

(B) The solar site survey shall also include a determination of an equitable allocation of the usable solar roof area among all owners sharing the same roof, garage, or carport.

(2) Require the owner and each successive owner of the solar energy system to be responsible for all of the following:

(A) Costs for damage to the common area, exclusive use common area, or separate interests resulting from the installation, maintenance, repair, removal, or replacement of the solar energy system.

(B) Costs for the maintenance, repair, and replacement of solar energy system until it has been removed and for the restoration of the common area, exclusive use common area, or separate interests after removal.

(C) Disclosing to prospective buyers the existence of any solar energy system of the owner and the related responsibilities of the owner under this section.

(c) For purposes of this section:

(1) "Association" has the same meaning as defined in Section 4080 or 6528.

(2) "Common area" has the same meaning as defined in Section 4095 or 6532.

(3) "Separate interest" has the same meaning as defined in Section 4185 or 6564.

(d) This section imposes additional requirements for any proposed installation of a solar energy system on a multifamily common area roof shared by more than one homeowner.

(e) This section does not diminish the authority of an association to impose reasonable provisions pursuant to Section 714.1. *(Added by Stats.2017, c. 818 (A.B.634), § 3, eff. Jan. 1, 2018.)*

§ 4747. Floor area ratio standards authorized for eligible housing development projects; applicability; legislative findings and declarations

(a) Any covenant, restriction, or condition contained in any deed, contract, security instrument, or other instrument affecting the transfer or sale of any interest in a planned development, and any provision of a governing document, is void and unenforceable if it effectively prohibits or unreasonably restricts an eligible housing development project from using the floor area ratio standards authorized under Section 65913.11 of the Government Code.

(b) This section does not apply to provisions that impose reasonable restrictions on an eligible housing development that do not make the implementation of the floor area standards authorized in Section 65913.11 of the Government Code infeasible.

(c) For purposes of this section:

(1) "Eligible housing development project" means a housing development project that meets the requirements of subdivision (b) of Section 65913.11 of the Government Code.

(2) "Reasonable restrictions" means restrictions that do not unreasonably increase the cost to construct, effectively prohibit the construction of, or extinguish the ability to otherwise construct an eligible housing development project using the floor area ratio standards in a manner authorized by Section 65913.11 of the Government Code.

(d) The Legislature finds and declares that the provision of adequate housing, in light of the severe shortage of housing at all income levels in this state, is a matter of statewide concern and that this section serves a significant and legitimate public purpose by eliminating potential restrictions that could inhibit the production of adequate housing. *(Added by Stats.2021, c. 363 (S.B.478), § 1, eff. Jan. 1, 2022.)*

§ 4750. Backyard personal agriculture; scope of application; homeowners' association regulations

(a) For the purposes of this section, "personal agriculture" has the same definition as in Section 1940.10.

(b) Any provision of a governing document, as defined in Section 4150, shall be void and unenforceable if it effectively prohibits or unreasonably restricts the use of a homeowner's backyard for personal agriculture.

(c)(1) This section does not apply to provisions that impose reasonable restrictions on the use of a homeowner's yard for personal agriculture.

(2) For purposes of this section, "reasonable restrictions" are restrictions that do not significantly increase the cost of engaging in personal agriculture or significantly decrease its efficiency.

(d) This section applies only to yards that are designated for the exclusive use of the homeowner.

(e) This section shall not prohibit a homeowners' association from applying rules and regulations requiring that dead plant material and weeds, with the exception of straw, mulch, compost, and other organic materials intended to encourage vegetation and retention of moisture in the soil, are regularly cleared from the backyard. *(Added by Stats.2014, c. 584 (A.B.2561), § 3, eff. Jan. 1, 2015.)*

§ 4750.10. Renumbered § 4753 and amended by Stats. 2016, c. 714 (S.B.944), § 7, eff. Jan. 1, 2017

§ 4751. Accessory dwelling units or junior accessory dwelling units

(a) Any covenant, restriction, or condition contained in any deed, contract, security instrument, or other instrument affecting the transfer or sale of any interest in a planned development, and any provision of a governing document, that either effectively prohibits or unreasonably restricts the construction or use of an accessory dwelling unit or junior accessory dwelling unit on a lot zoned for single-family residential use that meets the requirements of Section 65852.2 or 65852.22 of the Government Code, is void and unenforceable.

(b) This section does not apply to provisions that impose reasonable restrictions on accessory dwelling units or junior accessory dwelling units. For purposes of this subdivision, "reasonable restrictions" means restrictions that do not unreasonably increase the cost to construct, effectively prohibit the construction of, or extinguish the ability to otherwise construct, an accessory dwelling unit or junior accessory dwelling unit consistent with the provisions of Section 65852.2 or 65852.22 of the Government Code. *(Added by Stats.2019, c. 178 (A.B.670), § 2, eff. Jan. 1, 2020.)*

§ 4752. Repealed by Stats.1992, c. 162 (A.B.2650), § 3, operative Jan. 1, 1994

§ 4753. Use of clothesline or drying rack; conditions

(a) For the purposes of this section, "clothesline" includes a cord, rope, or wire from which laundered items may be hung to dry or air. A balcony, railing, awning, or other part of a structure or building shall not qualify as a clothesline.

(b) For the purposes of this section, "drying rack" means an apparatus from which laundered items may be hung to dry or air. A balcony, railing, awning, or other part of a structure or building shall not qualify as a drying rack.

(c) Any provision of a governing document, as defined in Section 4150, shall be void and unenforceable if it effectively prohibits or unreasonably restricts an owner's ability to use a clothesline or drying rack in the owner's backyard.

(d)(1) This section does not apply to provisions that impose reasonable restrictions on an owner's backyard for the use of a clothesline or drying rack.

(2) For purposes of this section, "reasonable restrictions" are restrictions that do not significantly increase the cost of using a clothesline or drying rack.

(3) This section applies only to backyards that are designated for the exclusive use of the owner.

(e) Nothing in this section shall prohibit an association from establishing and enforcing reasonable rules governing clotheslines or drying racks. *(Formerly § 4750.10, added by Stats.2015, c. 602 (A.B.1448), § 2, eff. Jan. 1, 2016. Renumbered § 4753 and amended by Stats.2016, c. 714 (S.B.944), § 7, eff. Jan. 1, 2017.)*

ARTICLE 2. MODIFICATION OF SEPARATE INTEREST

Section
4760. Modification of member's separate interest; facilitation of access for handicapped; approval by project association.
4761 to 4764. Repealed.
4765. Physical change to member's separate interest or common area; requirements to approve or disapprove proposed changes; notice of requirements.
4766 to 4774. Repealed.

§ 4760. Modification of member's separate interest; facilitation of access for handicapped; approval by project association

(a) Subject to the governing documents and applicable law, a member may do the following:

(1) Make any improvement or alteration within the boundaries of the member's separate interest that does not impair

§ 4760

the structural integrity or mechanical systems or lessen the support of any portions of the common interest development.

(2) Modify the member's separate interest, at the member's expense, to facilitate access for persons who are blind, visually handicapped, deaf, or physically disabled, or to alter conditions which could be hazardous to these persons. These modifications may also include modifications of the route from the public way to the door of the separate interest for the purposes of this paragraph if the separate interest is on the ground floor or already accessible by an existing ramp or elevator. The right granted by this paragraph is subject to the following conditions:

(A) The modifications shall be consistent with applicable building code requirements.

(B) The modifications shall be consistent with the intent of otherwise applicable provisions of the governing documents pertaining to safety or aesthetics.

(C) Modifications external to the dwelling shall not prevent reasonable passage by other residents, and shall be removed by the member when the separate interest is no longer occupied by persons requiring those modifications who are blind, visually handicapped, deaf, or physically disabled.

(D) Any member who intends to modify a separate interest pursuant to this paragraph shall submit plans and specifications to the association for review to determine whether the modifications will comply with the provisions of this paragraph. The association shall not deny approval of the proposed modifications under this paragraph without good cause.

(b) Any change in the exterior appearance of a separate interest shall be in accordance with the governing documents and applicable provisions of law. *(Added by Stats.2012, c. 180 (A.B.805), § 2, operative Jan. 1, 2014.)*

Cross References

Alcoholic beverages, club licenses for condominium homeowners' associations, license denied for discriminatory practices, see Business and Professions Code § 23428.20.

California housing finance agency, equal opportunity without discrimination, see Health and Safety Code § 50955.

Community development and housing, declaration of state antidiscrimination policy, discrimination prohibited, see Health and Safety Code § 33050.

Community development and housing, financial discrimination prohibited, see Health and Safety Code § 35811.

Community redevelopment, property disposition rehabilitation, nondiscrimination and nonsegregation, see Health and Safety Code §§ 33435 and 33436.

Floating home residency, private club membership not to be denied on discrimination basis, see Civil Code § 800.25.

Historical property rehabilitation, prohibited discrimination, see Health and Safety Code § 37630.

Inspections by real estate brokers or seller, scope, see Civil Code § 2079.3.

Mobilehome residency, private club membership not to be denied on discrimination basis, see Civil Code § 798.20.

Planning and zoning, prohibition against discrimination, exceptions, see Government Code § 65008.

Real estate licensees, grounds for disciplinary action, induced sale or listing due to adverse impact of persons in neighborhood with certain characteristics, see Business and Professions Code § 10177.

Real property, discriminatory restrictions in deeds, invalidity, see Civil Code §§ 782 and 782.5.

Redevelopment construction loans, nondiscrimination in construction and disposition of residences, see Health and Safety Code § 33769.

Residential property rehabilitation, open housing, equal opportunity in employment and contracts, see Health and Safety Code § 37923.

§§ 4761 to 4764. Repealed by Stats.1993, c. 219 (A.B.1500), § 52

§ 4765. Physical change to member's separate interest or common area; requirements to approve or disapprove proposed changes; notice of requirements

(a) This section applies if the governing documents require association approval before a member may make a physical change to the member's separate interest or to the common area. In reviewing and approving or disapproving a proposed change, the association shall satisfy the following requirements:

(1) The association shall provide a fair, reasonable, and expeditious procedure for making its decision. The procedure shall be included in the association's governing documents. The procedure shall provide for prompt deadlines. The procedure shall state the maximum time for response to an application or a request for reconsideration by the board.

(2) A decision on a proposed change shall be made in good faith and may not be unreasonable, arbitrary, or capricious.

(3) Notwithstanding a contrary provision of the governing documents, a decision on a proposed change may not violate any governing provision of law, including, but not limited to, the Fair Employment and Housing Act (Part 2.8 (commencing with Section 12900) of Division 3 of Title 2 of the Government Code), or a building code or other applicable law governing land use or public safety.

(4) A decision on a proposed change shall be in writing. If a proposed change is disapproved, the written decision shall include both an explanation of why the proposed change is disapproved and a description of the procedure for reconsideration of the decision by the board.

(5) If a proposed change is disapproved, the applicant is entitled to reconsideration by the board, at an open meeting of the board. This paragraph does not require reconsideration of a decision that is made by the board or a body that has the same membership as the board, at a meeting that satisfies the requirements of Article 2 (commencing with Section 4900) of Chapter 6. Reconsideration by the board does not constitute dispute resolution within the meaning of Section 5905.

(b) Nothing in this section authorizes a physical change to the common area in a manner that is inconsistent with an association's governing documents, unless the change is required by law.

(c) An association shall annually provide its members with notice of any requirements for association approval of physical changes to property. The notice shall describe the types of changes that require association approval and shall include a copy of the procedure used to review and approve or disapprove a proposed change. *(Added by Stats.2012, c. 180 (A.B.805), § 2, operative Jan. 1, 2014.)*

Cross References

Annual policy statement, contents, see Civil Code § 5310.

§§ 4766 to 4774. Repealed by Stats.1993, c. 219 (A.B.1500), § 52

ARTICLE 3. MAINTENANCE

Section
4775. Responsibility for repair, replacement, and maintenance.
4776. Repealed.
4777. Written notice of pesticide application; contents.
4778 to 4779. Repealed.
4780. Damage by wood-destroying pests or organisms.
4781 to 4784. Repealed.
4785. Temporary removal of occupant for treatment of wood-destroying pests or organisms.
4786 to 4789. Repealed.
4790. Access for maintenance of telephone wiring.
4791 to 4793. Repealed.

§ 4775. Responsibility for repair, replacement, and maintenance

(a)(1) Except as provided in paragraph (3), unless otherwise provided in the declaration of a common interest development, the association is responsible for repairing, replacing, and maintaining the common area.

(2) Unless otherwise provided in the declaration of a common interest development, the owner of each separate interest is responsible for repairing, replacing, and maintaining that separate interest.

(3) Unless otherwise provided in the declaration of a common interest development, the owner of each separate interest is responsible for maintaining the exclusive use common area appurtenant to that separate interest and the association is responsible for repairing and replacing the exclusive use common area.

(b) The costs of temporary relocation during the repair and maintenance of the areas within the responsibility of the association shall be borne by the owner of the separate interest affected.

(c) This section shall become operative on January 1, 2017. *(Added by Stats.2014, c. 405 (A.B.968), § 2, eff. Jan. 1, 2015, operative Jan. 1, 2017.)*

§ 4776. Repealed by Stats.1993, c. 219 (A.B.1500), § 52

§ 4777. Written notice of pesticide application; contents

(a) For the purposes of this section:

(1) "Adjacent separate interest" means a separate interest that is directly beside, above, or below a particular separate interest or the common area.

(2) "Authorized agent" means an individual, organization, or other entity that has entered into an agreement with the association to act on the association's behalf.

(3) "Broadcast application" means spreading pesticide over an area greater than two square feet.

(4) "Electronic delivery" means delivery of a document by electronic means to the electronic address at, or through which, an owner of a separate interest has authorized electronic delivery.

(5) "Licensed pest control operator" means anyone licensed by the state to apply pesticides.

(6) "Pest" means a living organism that causes damage to property or economic loss, or transmits or produces diseases.

(7) "Pesticide" means any substance, or mixture of substances, that is intended to be used for controlling, destroying, repelling, or mitigating any pest or organism, excluding antimicrobial pesticides as defined by the Federal Insecticide, Fungicide, and Rodenticide Act (7 U.S.C. Sec. 136(mm)).

(b)(1) An association or its authorized agent that applies any pesticide to a separate interest or to the common area without a licensed pest control operator shall provide the owner and, if applicable, the tenant of an affected separate interest and, if making broadcast applications, or using total release foggers or aerosol sprays, the owner and, if applicable, the tenant in an adjacent separate interest that could reasonably be impacted by the pesticide use with written notice that contains the following statements and information using words with common and everyday meaning:

(A) The pest or pests to be controlled.

(B) The name and brand of the pesticide product proposed to be used.

(C) "State law requires that you be given the following information:

CAUTION—PESTICIDES ARE TOXIC CHEMICALS. The California Department of Pesticide Regulation and the United States Environmental Protection Agency allow the unlicensed use of certain pesticides based on existing scientific evidence that there are no appreciable risks if proper use conditions are followed or that the risks are outweighed by the benefits. The degree of risk depends upon the degree of exposure, so exposure should be minimized.

If within 24 hours following application of a pesticide, a person experiences symptoms similar to common seasonal illness comparable to influenza, the person should contact a physician, appropriate licensed health care provider, or the California Poison Control System (1–800–222–1222).

For further information, contact any of the following: for Health Questions—the County Health Department (telephone number) and for Regulatory Information—the Department of Pesticide Regulation (916–324–4100)."

(D) The approximate date, time, and frequency with which the pesticide will be applied.

(E) The following notification:

"The approximate date, time, and frequency of this pesticide application is subject to change."

(2) At least 48 hours prior to application of the pesticide to a separate interest, the association or its authorized agent shall provide individual notice to the owner and, if applicable, the tenant of the separate interest and notice to an owner and, if applicable, the tenant occupying any adjacent separate

interest that is required to be notified pursuant to paragraph (1).

(3)(A) At least 48 hours prior to application of the pesticide to a common area, the association or its authorized agent shall, if practicable, post the written notice described in paragraph (1) in a conspicuous place in or around the common area in which the pesticide is to be applied. Otherwise, if not practicable, the association or its authorized agent shall provide individual notice to the owner and, if applicable, the tenant of the separate interest that is adjacent to the common area.

(B) If the pest poses an immediate threat to health and safety, thereby making compliance with notification prior to the pesticide application unreasonable, the association or its authorized agent shall post the written notice as soon as practicable, but not later than one hour after the pesticide is applied.

(4) Notice to tenants of separate interests shall be provided, in at least one of the following ways:

(A) First–class mail.

(B) Personal delivery to a tenant 18 years of age or older.

(C) Electronic delivery, if an electronic mailing address has been provided by the tenant.

(5)(A) Upon receipt of written notification, the owner of the separate interest or the tenant may agree in writing or, if notification was delivered electronically, the tenant may agree through electronic delivery, to allow the association or authorized agent to apply a pesticide immediately or at an agreed upon time.

(B)(i) Prior to receipt of written notification, the association or authorized agent may agree orally to an immediate pesticide application if the owner or, if applicable, the tenant requests that the pesticide be applied before the 48–hour notice of the pesticide product proposed to be used.

(ii) With respect to an owner or, if applicable, a tenant entering into an oral agreement for immediate pesticide application, the association or authorized agent, no later than the time of pesticide application, shall leave the written notice specified in paragraph (1) in a conspicuous place in the separate interest or at the entrance of the separate interest in a manner in which a reasonable person would discover the notice.

(iii) If any owner or, if applicable, any tenant of a separate interest or an owner or, if applicable, a tenant of an adjacent separate interest is also required to be notified pursuant to this subparagraph, the association or authorized agent shall provide that person with this notice as soon as practicable after the oral agreement is made authorizing immediate pesticide application, but in no case later than commencement of application of the pesticide.

(6) A copy of a written notice provided pursuant to paragraph (1) shall be attached to the minutes of the board meeting immediately subsequent the application of the pesticide. *(Added by Stats.2016, c. 330 (A.B.2362), § 2, eff. Jan. 1, 2017. Amended by Stats.2017, c. 561 (A.B.1516), § 19, eff. Jan. 1, 2018.)*

§§ 4778 to 4779. Repealed by Stats.1993, c. 219 (A.B.1500), § 52

§ 4780. Damage by wood-destroying pests or organisms

(a) In a community apartment project, condominium project, or stock cooperative, unless otherwise provided in the declaration, the association is responsible for the repair and maintenance of the common area occasioned by the presence of wood-destroying pests or organisms.

(b) In a planned development, unless a different maintenance scheme is provided in the declaration, each owner of a separate interest is responsible for the repair and maintenance of that separate interest as may be occasioned by the presence of wood-destroying pests or organisms. Upon approval of the majority of all members of the association, pursuant to Section 4065, that responsibility may be delegated to the association, which shall be entitled to recover the cost thereof as a special assessment. *(Added by Stats.2012, c. 180 (A.B.805), § 2, operative Jan. 1, 2014.)*

§§ 4781 to 4784. Repealed by Stats.1993, c. 219 (A.B.1500), § 52

§ 4785. Temporary removal of occupant for treatment of wood-destroying pests or organisms

(a) The association may cause the temporary, summary removal of any occupant of a common interest development for such periods and at such times as may be necessary for prompt, effective treatment of wood-destroying pests or organisms.

(b) The association shall give notice of the need to temporarily vacate a separate interest to the occupants and to the owners, not less than 15 days nor more than 30 days prior to the date of the temporary relocation. The notice shall state the reason for the temporary relocation, the date and time of the beginning of treatment, the anticipated date and time of termination of treatment, and that the occupants will be responsible for their own accommodations during the temporary relocation.

(c) Notice by the association shall be deemed complete upon either:

(1) Personal delivery of a copy of the notice to the occupants, and if an occupant is not the owner, individual delivery pursuant to Section 4040, of a copy of the notice to the owner.

(2) Individual delivery pursuant to Section 4040 to the occupant at the address of the separate interest, and if the occupant is not the owner, individual delivery pursuant to Section 4040, of a copy of the notice to the owner.

(d) For purposes of this section, "occupant" means an owner, resident, guest, invitee, tenant, lessee, sublessee, or other person in possession of the separate interest. *(Added by Stats.2012, c. 180 (A.B.805), § 2, operative Jan. 1, 2014.)*

§§ 4786 to 4789. Repealed by Stats.1993, c. 219 (A.B.1500), § 52

§ 4790. Access for maintenance of telephone wiring

Notwithstanding the provisions of the declaration, a member is entitled to reasonable access to the common area for the purpose of maintaining the internal and external telephone wiring made part of the exclusive use common area of the member's separate interest pursuant to subdivision (c) of

Section 4145. The access shall be subject to the consent of the association, whose approval shall not be unreasonably withheld, and which may include the association's approval of telephone wiring upon the exterior of the common area, and other conditions as the association determines reasonable. *(Added by Stats.2012, c. 180 (A.B.805), § 2, operative Jan. 1, 2014.)*

§§ 4791 to 4793. Repealed by Stats.1993, c. 219 (A.B.1500), § 52

CHAPTER 6. ASSOCIATION GOVERNANCE

Article	Section
1. Association Existence and Powers	4800
2. Board Meeting	4900
3. Member Meeting	5000
4. Member Election	5100
5. Record Inspection	5200
6. Recordkeeping	5260
7. Annual Reports	5300
8. Conflict of Interest	5350
9. Managing Agent	5375
10. Government Assistance	5400
11. Emergency Powers and Procedures	5450

ARTICLE 1. ASSOCIATION EXISTENCE AND POWERS

Section
4800. Management by association.
4800.1 to 4800.5. Repealed.
4800.6. Repealed.
4800.7. Repealed.
4800.8. Repealed.
4800.9. Repealed.
4800.10, 4800.11. Repealed.
4801. Repealed.
4801.1 to 4801.5. Repealed.
4801.6. Repealed.
4801.7 to 4804. Repealed.
4805. Powers of association.
4806, 4807. Repealed.
4808. Repealed.
4809 to 4813. Repealed.
4820. Consolidation of associations.

§ 4800. Management by association

A common interest development shall be managed by an association that may be incorporated or unincorporated. The association may be referred to as an owners' association or a community association. *(Added by Stats.2012, c. 180 (A.B.805), § 2, operative Jan. 1, 2014.)*

§§ 4800.1 to 4800.5. Repealed by Stats.1992, c. 162 (A.B. 2650), § 3, operative Jan. 1, 1994

§ 4800.6. Repealed by Stats.1993, c. 219 (A.B.1500), § 53

§ 4800.7. Repealed by Stats.1988, c. 729, § 2

§ 4800.8. Repealed by Stats.1993, c. 219 (A.B.1500), § 54

§ 4800.9. Repealed by Stats.1992, c. 162 (A.B.2650), § 3, operative Jan. 1, 1994

§§ 4800.10, 4800.11. Repealed by Stats.1993, c. 219 (A.B. 1500), §§ 55, 56; Stats.1993, c. 1101 (A.B.1469), §§ 1, 2, operative Jan. 1, 1994

§ 4801. Repealed by Stats.1992, c. 162 (A.B.2650), § 3, operative Jan. 1, 1994; Stats.1993, c. 219 (A.B.1500), § 57

§§ 4801.1 to 4801.5. Repealed by Stats.1992, c. 162 (A.B. 2650), § 3, operative Jan. 1, 1994

§ 4801.6. Repealed by Stats.1989, c. 1359, § 7, operative Jan. 1, 1991

§§ 4801.7 to 4804. Repealed by Stats.1992, c. 162 (A.B. 2650), § 3, operative Jan. 1, 1994

§ 4805. Powers of association

(a) Unless the governing documents provide otherwise, and regardless of whether the association is incorporated or unincorporated, the association may exercise the powers granted to a nonprofit mutual benefit corporation, as enumerated in Section 7140 of the Corporations Code, except that an unincorporated association may not adopt or use a corporate seal or issue membership certificates in accordance with Section 7313 of the Corporations Code.

(b) The association, whether incorporated or unincorporated, may exercise the powers granted to an association in this act. *(Added by Stats.2012, c. 180 (A.B.805), § 2, operative Jan. 1, 2014.)*

§§ 4806, 4807. Repealed by Stats.1992, c. 162 (A.B.2650), § 3, operative Jan. 1, 1994

§ 4808. Repealed by Stats.1970, c. 962, p. 1727, § 5

§§ 4809 to 4813. Repealed by Stats.1992, c. 162 (A.B.2650), § 3, operative Jan. 1, 1994

§ 4820. Consolidation of associations

Whenever two or more associations have consolidated any of their functions under a joint neighborhood association or similar organization, members of each participating association shall be (a) entitled to attend all meetings of the joint association other than executive sessions, (b) given reasonable opportunity for participation in those meetings, and (c) entitled to the same access to the joint association's records as they are to the participating association's records. *(Added by Stats.2012, c. 180 (A.B.805), § 2, operative Jan. 1, 2014.)*

ARTICLE 2. BOARD MEETING

Section
4900. Short title.
4910. Action on items outside of meeting prohibited; electronic transmissions as method of conducting meeting.
4920. Notice.
4923. Emergency board meeting.
4925. Open meeting; executive session exception.
4930. Subjects of meeting; issues not on agenda.
4935. Executive session.
4950. Meeting minutes.

Section
4955. Civil action for violation of article; costs and attorney's fees.

Cross References

Association record inspection, redaction, see Civil Code § 5215.
Proposed changes to governing documents, disapproval, board reconsideration not required, see Civil Code § 4765.
Reserve funding plan, inclusion of schedule of change in assessments, adoption by board, see Civil Code § 5560.

§ 4900. Short title

This article shall be known and may be cited as the Common Interest Development Open Meeting Act. *(Added by Stats.2012, c. 180 (A.B.805), § 2, operative Jan. 1, 2014.)*

§ 4910. Action on items outside of meeting prohibited; electronic transmissions as method of conducting meeting

(a) The board shall not take action on any item of business outside of a board meeting.

(b)(1) Notwithstanding Section 7211 of the Corporations Code, the board shall not conduct a meeting via a series of electronic transmissions, including, but not limited to, electronic mail, except as specified in paragraph (2).

(2) Electronic transmissions may be used as a method of conducting an emergency board meeting if all directors, individually or collectively, consent in writing to that action, and if the written consent or consents are filed with the minutes of the board meeting. These written consents may be transmitted electronically. *(Added by Stats.2012, c. 180 (A.B.805), § 2, operative Jan. 1, 2014.)*

§ 4920. Notice

(a) Except as provided in subdivision (b), the association shall give notice of the time and place of a board meeting at least four days before the meeting.

(b)(1) If a board meeting is an emergency meeting held pursuant to Section 4923, the association is not required to give notice of the time and place of the meeting.

(2) If a nonemergency board meeting is held solely in executive session, the association shall give notice of the time and place of the meeting at least two days prior to the meeting.

(3) If the association's governing documents require a longer period of notice than is required by this section, the association shall comply with the period stated in its governing documents. For the purposes of this paragraph, a governing document provision does not apply to a notice of an emergency meeting or a meeting held solely in executive session unless it specifically states that it applies to those types of meetings.

(c) Notice of a board meeting shall be given by general delivery pursuant to Section 4045.

(d) Notice of a board meeting shall contain the agenda for the meeting. *(Added by Stats.2012, c. 180 (A.B.805), § 2, operative Jan. 1, 2014. Amended by Stats.2013, c. 183 (S.B.745), § 17.)*

§ 4923. Emergency board meeting

An emergency board meeting may be called by the president of the association, or by any two directors other than the president, if there are circumstances that could not have been reasonably foreseen which require immediate attention and possible action by the board, and which of necessity make it impracticable to provide notice as required by Section 4920. *(Added by Stats.2012, c. 180 (A.B.805), § 2, operative Jan. 1, 2014.)*

§ 4925. Open meeting; executive session exception

(a) Any member may attend board meetings, except when the board adjourns to, or meets solely in, executive session. As specified in subdivision (b) of Section 4090, a member of the association shall be entitled to attend a teleconference meeting or the portion of a teleconference meeting that is open to members, and that meeting or portion of the meeting shall be audible to the members in a location specified in the notice of the meeting.

(b) The board shall permit any member to speak at any meeting of the association or the board, except for meetings of the board held in executive session. A reasonable time limit for all members of the association to speak to the board or before a meeting of the association shall be established by the board. *(Added by Stats.2012, c. 180 (A.B.805), § 2, operative Jan. 1, 2014.)*

Cross References

Actions for damages against common interest development builders, developers, or general contractors, see Civil Code § 6000.

§ 4930. Subjects of meeting; issues not on agenda

(a) Except as described in subdivisions (b) to (e), inclusive, the board may not discuss or take action on any item at a nonemergency meeting unless the item was placed on the agenda included in the notice that was distributed pursuant to subdivision (a) of Section 4920. This subdivision does not prohibit a member or resident who is not a director from speaking on issues not on the agenda.

(b) Notwithstanding subdivision (a), a director, a managing agent or other agent of the board, or a member of the staff of the board, may do any of the following:

(1) Briefly respond to statements made or questions posed by a person speaking at a meeting as described in subdivision (b) of Section 4925.

(2) Ask a question for clarification, make a brief announcement, or make a brief report on the person's own activities, whether in response to questions posed by a member or based upon the person's own initiative.

(c) Notwithstanding subdivision (a), the board or a director, subject to rules or procedures of the board, may do any of the following:

(1) Provide a reference to, or provide other resources for factual information to, its managing agent or other agents or staff.

(2) Request its managing agent or other agents or staff to report back to the board at a subsequent meeting concerning any matter, or take action to direct its managing agent or other agents or staff to place a matter of business on a future agenda.

(3) Direct its managing agent or other agents or staff to perform administrative tasks that are necessary to carry out this section.

(d) Notwithstanding subdivision (a), the board may take action on any item of business not appearing on the agenda distributed pursuant to subdivision (a) of Section 4920 under any of the following conditions:

(1) Upon a determination made by a majority of the board present at the meeting that an emergency situation exists. An emergency situation exists if there are circumstances that could not have been reasonably foreseen by the board, that require immediate attention and possible action by the board, and that, of necessity, make it impracticable to provide notice.

(2) Upon a determination made by the board by a vote of two-thirds of the directors present at the meeting, or, if less than two-thirds of total membership of the board is present at the meeting, by a unanimous vote of the directors present, that there is a need to take immediate action and that the need for action came to the attention of the board after the agenda was distributed pursuant to subdivision (a) of Section 4920.

(3) The item appeared on an agenda that was distributed pursuant to subdivision (a) of Section 4920 for a prior meeting of the board that occurred not more than 30 calendar days before the date that action is taken on the item and, at the prior meeting, action on the item was continued to the meeting at which the action is taken.

(e) Before discussing any item pursuant to subdivision (d), the board shall openly identify the item to the members in attendance at the meeting. *(Added by Stats.2012, c. 180 (A.B.805), § 2, operative Jan. 1, 2014.)*

§ 4935. Executive session

(a) The board may adjourn to, or meet solely in, executive session to consider litigation, matters relating to the formation of contracts with third parties, member discipline, personnel matters, or to meet with a member, upon the member's request, regarding the member's payment of assessments, as specified in Section 5665.

(b) The board shall adjourn to, or meet solely in, executive session to discuss member discipline, if requested by the member who is the subject of the discussion. That member shall be entitled to attend the executive session.

(c) The board shall adjourn to, or meet solely in, executive session to discuss a payment plan pursuant to Section 5665.

(d) The board shall adjourn to, or meet solely in, executive session to decide whether to foreclose on a lien pursuant to subdivision (b) of Section 5705.

(e) Any matter discussed in executive session shall be generally noted in the minutes of the immediately following meeting that is open to the entire membership. *(Added by Stats.2012, c. 180 (A.B.805), § 2, operative Jan. 1, 2014.)*

Cross References

Actions for damages against common interest development builders, developers, or general contractors, see Civil Code § 6000.

§ 4950. Meeting minutes

(a) The minutes, minutes proposed for adoption that are marked to indicate draft status, or a summary of the minutes, of any board meeting, other than an executive session, shall be available to members within 30 days of the meeting. The minutes, proposed minutes, or summary minutes shall be distributed to any member upon request and upon reimbursement of the association's costs for making that distribution.

(b) The annual policy statement, prepared pursuant to Section 5310, shall inform the members of their right to obtain copies of board meeting minutes and of how and where to do so. *(Added by Stats.2012, c. 180 (A.B.805), § 2, operative Jan. 1, 2014.)*

Cross References

Association records, time periods of required availability, see Civil Code § 5210.

§ 4955. Civil action for violation of article; costs and attorney's fees

(a) A member of an association may bring a civil action for declaratory or equitable relief for a violation of this article by the association, including, but not limited to, injunctive relief, restitution, or a combination thereof, within one year of the date the cause of action accrues.

(b) A member who prevails in a civil action to enforce the member's rights pursuant to this article shall be entitled to reasonable attorney's fees and court costs, and the court may impose a civil penalty of up to five hundred dollars ($500) for each violation, except that each identical violation shall be subject to only one penalty if the violation affects each member equally. A prevailing association shall not recover any costs, unless the court finds the action to be frivolous, unreasonable, or without foundation. *(Added by Stats.2012, c. 180 (A.B.805), § 2, operative Jan. 1, 2014.)*

ARTICLE 3. MEMBER MEETING

Section
5000. Use of parliamentary procedure.
5001 to 5004. Repealed.

§ 5000. Use of parliamentary procedure

(a) Meetings of the membership of the association shall be conducted in accordance with a recognized system of parliamentary procedure or any parliamentary procedures the association may adopt.

(b) The board shall permit any member to speak at any meeting of the membership of the association. A reasonable time limit for all members to speak at a meeting of the association shall be established by the board. *(Added by Stats.2012, c. 180 (A.B.805), § 2, operative Jan. 1, 2014.)*

§§ 5001 to 5004. Repealed by Stats.1992, c. 162 (A.B.2650), § 3, operative Jan. 1, 1994

ARTICLE 4. MEMBER ELECTION

Section
5100. Scope of article.
5101. Repealed.
5102. Repealed.
5103. Election by acclamation; conditions.
5104. Repealed.

Section
5105. Operating rules; disqualification from nomination as candidate.
5106 to 5108. Repealed.
5109. Repealed.
5110. Inspector of elections.
5110.150 to 5110.730. Repealed.
5110.740. Repealed.
5111 to 5113. Repealed.
5113.5. Repealed.
5114. Repealed.
5115. General notice of election; ballots; quorum; cumulative voting; election by mail; inclusion of text of proposed amendment of governing documents.
5116. Repealed.
5117. Repealed.
5118, 5119. Repealed.
5120. Counting and tabulation of votes; reporting of tabulated results.
5120.010 to 5120.330. Repealed.
5121. Repealed.
5122. Repealed.
5123. Repealed.
5124. Repealed.
5125. Custody of election materials.
5125.1, 5126. Repealed.
5127. Repealed.
5127.5. Repealed.
5127.6. Repealed.
5128. Repealed.
5129. Repealed.
5130. Proxies; definitions.
5131, 5132. Repealed.
5133, 5134. Repealed.
5135. Campaign funding.
5135.5 to 5137. Repealed.
5138. Repealed.
5145. Civil action for violation of article; attorney's fees and costs; superior court or small claims court.
5150, 5151. Repealed.
5152. Repealed.
5153 to 5156. Repealed.
5157, 5158. Repealed.
5159 to 5183. Repealed.

Cross References

Special meeting of members to reverse rule change, notice, voting requirements, effect of approved reversal, see Civil Code § 4365.

§ 5100. Scope of article

(a)(1) Notwithstanding any other law or provision of the governing documents, elections regarding assessments legally requiring a vote, election and removal of directors, amendments to the governing documents, or the grant of exclusive use of common area pursuant to Section 4600 shall be held by secret ballot in accordance with the procedures set forth in this article.

(2) An association shall hold an election for a seat on the board of directors in accordance with the procedures set forth in this article at the expiration of the corresponding director's term and at least once every four years.

(b) This article also governs an election on any topic that is expressly identified in the operating rules as being governed by this article.

(c) The provisions of this article apply to both incorporated and unincorporated associations, notwithstanding any contrary provision of the governing documents.

(d) The procedures set forth in this article shall apply to votes cast directly by the membership, but do not apply to votes cast by delegates or other elected representatives.

(e) In the event of a conflict between this article and the provisions of the Nonprofit Mutual Benefit Corporation Law (Part 3 (commencing with Section 7110) of Division 2 of Title 1 of the Corporations Code) relating to elections, the provisions of this article shall prevail.

(f) Directors shall not be required to be elected pursuant to this article if the governing documents provide that one member from each separate interest is a director. *(Added by Stats.2012, c. 180 (A.B.805), § 2, operative Jan. 1, 2014. Amended by Stats.2014, c. 661 (A.B.569), § 4, eff. Jan. 1, 2015; Stats.2019, c. 848 (S.B.323), § 1, eff. Jan. 1, 2020; Stats.2019, c. 858 (S.B.754), § 1.1, eff. Jan. 1, 2020; Stats.2021, c. 517 (A.B.502), § 1, eff. Jan. 1, 2022.)*

§ 5101. Repealed by Stats.1973, c. 987, p. 1898, § 2, operative Jan. 1, 1975

§ 5102. Repealed by Stats.1992, c. 162 (A.B.2650), § 3, operative Jan. 1, 1994

§ 5103. Election by acclamation; conditions

Notwithstanding the secret balloting requirement in Section 5100, or any contrary provision in the governing documents, when, as of the deadline for submitting nominations provided for in subdivision (a) of Section 5115, the number of qualified candidates is not more than the number of vacancies to be elected, as determined by the inspector or inspectors of the elections, the association may, but is not required to, consider the qualified candidates elected by acclamation if all of the following conditions have been met:

(a) The association has held a regular election for the directors in the last three years. The three-year time period shall be calculated from the date ballots were due in the last full election to the start of voting for the proposed election.

(b) The association provided individual notice of the election and the procedure for nominating candidates as follows:

(1) Initial notice at least 90 days before the deadline for submitting nominations provided for in subdivision (a) of Section 5115. The initial notice shall include all of the following:

(A) The number of board positions that will be filled at the election.

(B) The deadline for submitting nominations.

(C) The manner in which nominations can be submitted.

(D) A statement informing members that if, at the close of the time period for making nominations, there are the same number or fewer qualified candidates as there are board positions to be filled, then the board of directors may, after voting to do so, seat the qualified candidates by acclamation without balloting.

(2) A reminder notice between 7 and 30 days before the deadline for submitting nominations provided for in subdivi-

sion (a) of Section 5115. The reminder notice shall include all of the following:

(A) The number of board positions that will be filled at the election.

(B) The deadline for submitting nominations.

(C) The manner in which nominations can be submitted.

(D) A list of the names of all of the qualified candidates to fill the board positions as of the date of the reminder notice.

(E) A statement reminding members that if, at the close of the time period for making nominations, there are the same number or fewer qualified candidates as there are board positions to be filled, then the board of directors may, after voting to do so, seat the qualified candidates by acclamation without balloting. This statement is not required if, at the time the reminder notice will be delivered, the number of qualified candidates already exceeds the number of board positions to be filled.

(c)(1) The association provides, within seven business days of receiving a nomination, a written or electronic communication acknowledging the nomination to the member who submitted the nomination.

(2) The association provides, within seven business days of receiving a nomination, a written or electronic communication to the nominee, indicating either of the following:

(A) The nominee is a qualified candidate for the board of directors.

(B) The nominee is not a qualified candidate for the board of directors, the basis for the disqualification, and the procedure, which shall comply with Article 2 (commencing with Section 5900) of Chapter 10, by which the nominee may appeal the disqualification.

(3) The association may combine the written or electronic communication described in paragraphs (1) and (2) into a single written or electronic communication if the nominee and the nominator are the same person.

(d)(1) The association permits all candidates to run if nominated, except for nominees disqualified for running as allowed or required pursuant to subdivisions (b) to (e), inclusive, of Section 5105.

(2) Notwithstanding paragraph (1), an association may disqualify a nominee if the person has served the maximum number of terms or sequential terms allowed by the association.

(3) If an association disqualifies a nominee pursuant to this subdivision, an association in its election rules shall also require a director to comply with the same requirements.

(e) The association board votes to consider the qualified candidates elected by acclamation at a meeting pursuant to Article 2 (commencing with Section 4900) for which the agenda item reflects the name of each qualified candidate that will be seated by acclamation if the item is approved. (Added by Stats.2021, c. 517 (A.B.502), § 2.5, eff. Jan. 1, 2022.)

§ 5104. Repealed by Stats.1992, c. 162 (A.B.2650), § 3, operative Jan. 1, 1994

§ 5105. Operating rules; disqualification from nomination as candidate

(a) An association shall adopt operating rules in accordance with the procedures prescribed by Article 5 (commencing with Section 4340) of Chapter 3, that do all of the following:

(1) Ensure that if any candidate or member advocating a point of view is provided access to association media, newsletters, or internet websites during a campaign, for purposes that are reasonably related to that election, equal access shall be provided to all candidates and members advocating a point of view, including those not endorsed by the board, for purposes that are reasonably related to the election. The association shall not edit or redact any content from these communications, but may include a statement specifying that the candidate or member, and not the association, is responsible for that content.

(2) Ensure access to the common area meeting space, if any exists, during a campaign, at no cost, to all candidates, including those who are not incumbents, and to all members advocating a point of view, including those not endorsed by the board, for purposes reasonably related to the election.

(3) Specify the qualifications for candidates for the board and any other elected position, subject to subdivision (b), and procedures for the nomination of candidates, consistent with the governing documents. A nomination or election procedure shall not be deemed reasonable if it disallows any member from nominating themselves for election to the board.

(4) Specify the voting power of each membership, the authenticity, validity, and effect of proxies, and the voting period for elections, including the times at which polls will open and close, consistent with the governing documents.

(5) Specify a method of selecting one or three independent third parties as inspector or inspectors of elections utilizing one of the following methods:

(A) Appointment of the inspector or inspectors by the board.

(B) Election of the inspector or inspectors by the members of the association.

(C) Any other method for selecting the inspector or inspectors.

(6) Allow the inspector or inspectors to appoint and oversee additional persons to verify signatures and to count and tabulate votes as the inspector or inspectors deem appropriate, provided that the persons are independent third parties who meet the requirements in subdivision (b) of Section 5110.

(7) Require retention of, as association election materials, both a candidate registration list and a voter list. The candidate list shall include name and address of individuals nominated as a candidate for election to the board of directors. The voter list shall include name, voting power, and either the physical address of the voter's separate interest, the parcel number, or both. The mailing address for the ballot shall be listed on the voter list if it differs from the physical address of the voter's separate interest or if only the parcel number is used. The association shall permit members to verify the accuracy of their individual information on

both lists at least 30 days before the ballots are distributed. The association or member shall report any errors or omissions to either list to the inspector or inspectors who shall make the corrections within two business days.

(b) An association shall disqualify a person from a nomination as a candidate for not being a member of the association at the time of the nomination.

(1) This subdivision does not restrict a developer from making a nomination of a nonmember candidate consistent with the voting power of the developer as set forth in the regulations of the Department of Real Estate and the association's governing documents.

(2) If title to a separate interest parcel is held by a legal entity that is not a natural person, the governing authority of that legal entity shall have the power to appoint a natural person to be a member for purposes of this article.

(c) Through its bylaws or election operating rules adopted pursuant to subdivision (a) of Section 5105 only, an association may disqualify a person from nomination as a candidate pursuant to any of the following:

(1) Subject to paragraph (2) of subdivision (d), an association may require a nominee for a board seat, and a director during their board tenure, to be current in the payment of regular and special assessments, which are consumer debts subject to validation. If an association requires a nominee to be current in the payment of regular and special assessments, it shall also require a director to be current in the payment of regular and special assessments.

(2) An association may disqualify a person from nomination as a candidate if the person, if elected, would be serving on the board at the same time as another person who holds a joint ownership interest in the same separate interest parcel as the person and the other person is either properly nominated for the current election or an incumbent director.

(3) An association may disqualify a nominee if that person has been a member of the association for less than one year.

(4) An association may disqualify a nominee if that person discloses, or if the association is aware or becomes aware of, a past criminal conviction that would, if the person was elected, either prevent the association from purchasing the insurance required by Section 5806 or terminate the association's existing insurance coverage required by Section 5806 as to that person should the person be elected.

(d) An association may disqualify a person from nomination for nonpayment of regular and special assessments, but may not disqualify a nominee for nonpayment of fines, fines renamed as assessments, collection charges, late charges, or costs levied by a third party. The person shall not be disqualified for failure to be current in payment of regular and special assessments if either of the following circumstances is true:

(1) The person has paid the regular or special assessment under protest pursuant to Section 5658.

(2) The person has entered into and is in compliance with a payment plan pursuant to Section 5665.

(e) An association shall not disqualify a person from nomination if the person has not been provided the opportunity to engage in internal dispute resolution pursuant to Article 2 (commencing with Section 5900) of Chapter 10.

(f) Notwithstanding any other law, the rules adopted pursuant to this section may provide for the nomination of candidates from the floor of membership meetings or nomination by any other manner. Those rules may permit write-in candidates for ballots.

(g) Notwithstanding any other law, the rules adopted pursuant to this section shall do all of the following:

(1) Prohibit the denial of a ballot to a member for any reason other than not being a member at the time when ballots are distributed.

(2) Prohibit the denial of a ballot to a person with general power of attorney for a member.

(3) Require the ballot of a person with general power of attorney for a member to be counted if returned in a timely manner.

(4) Require the inspector or inspectors of elections to deliver, or cause to be delivered, at least 30 days before an election, to each member both of the following documents:

(A) The ballot or ballots.

(B) A copy of the election operating rules. Delivery of the election operating rules may be accomplished by either of the following methods:

(i) Posting the election operating rules to an internet website and including the corresponding internet website address on the ballot together with the phrase, in at least 12–point font: "The rules governing this election may be found here:"

(ii) Individual delivery.

(h) Election operating rules adopted pursuant to this section shall not be amended less than 90 days prior to an election. (Added by Stats.2012, c. 180 (A.B.805), § 2, operative Jan. 1, 2014. Amended by Stats.2019, c. 848 (S.B.323), § 2, eff. Jan. 1, 2020; Stats.2021, c. 642 (S.B.432), § 2, eff. Jan. 1, 2022.)

§§ 5106 to 5108. Repealed by Stats.1992, c. 162 (A.B.2650), § 3, operative Jan. 1, 1994

§ 5109. Repealed by Stats.1979, c. 638, p. 1971, § 2

§ 5110. Inspector of elections

(a) The association shall select an independent third party or parties as an inspector of elections. The number of inspectors of elections shall be one or three.

(b) For the purposes of this section, an independent third party includes, but is not limited to, a volunteer poll worker with the county registrar of voters, a licensee of the California Board of Accountancy, or a notary public. An independent third party may be a member, but may not be a director or a candidate for director or be related to a director or to a candidate for director. An independent third party may not be a person, business entity, or subdivision of a business entity who is currently employed or under contract to the association for any compensable services other than serving as an inspector of elections.

(c) The inspector or inspectors of elections shall do all of the following:

(1) Determine the number of memberships entitled to vote and the voting power of each.

(2) Determine the authenticity, validity, and effect of proxies, if any.

(3) Receive ballots.

(4) Hear and determine all challenges and questions in any way arising out of or in connection with the right to vote.

(5) Count and tabulate all votes.

(6) Determine when the polls shall close, consistent with the governing documents.

(7) Determine the tabulated results of the election.

(8) Perform any acts as may be proper to conduct the election with fairness to all members in accordance with this article, the Corporations Code, and all applicable rules of the association regarding the conduct of the election that are not in conflict with this article.

(d) An inspector of elections shall perform all duties impartially, in good faith, to the best of the inspector of election's ability, as expeditiously as is practical, and in a manner that protects the interest of all members of the association. If there are three inspectors of elections, the decision or act of a majority shall be effective in all respects as the decision or act of all. Any report made by the inspector or inspectors of elections is prima facie evidence of the facts stated in the report. *(Added by Stats.2012, c. 180 (A.B.805), § 2, operative Jan. 1, 2014. Amended by Stats. 2019, c. 848 (S.B.323), § 3, eff. Jan. 1, 2020.)*

§§ 5110.150 to 5110.730. Repealed by Stats.1992, c. 162 (A.B.2650), § 3, operative Jan. 1, 1994

§ 5110.740. Repealed by Stats.1993, c. 219 (A.B.1500), § 58

§§ 5111 to 5113. Repealed by Stats.1992, c. 162 (A.B.2650), § 3, operative Jan. 1, 1994

§ 5113.5. Repealed by Stats.1986, c. 820, § 15, operative July 1, 1987

§ 5114. Repealed by Stats.1992, c. 162 (A.B.2650), § 3, operative Jan. 1, 1994

§ 5115. General notice of election; ballots; quorum; cumulative voting; election by mail; inclusion of text of proposed amendment of governing documents

(a) An association shall provide general notice of the procedure and deadline for submitting a nomination at least 30 days before any deadline for submitting a nomination. Individual notice shall be delivered pursuant to Section 4040 if individual notice is requested by a member. This subdivision shall only apply to elections of directors and to recall elections.

(b) For elections of directors and for recall elections, an association shall provide general notice of all of the following at least 30 days before the ballots are distributed:

(1) The date and time by which, and the physical address where, ballots are to be returned by mail or handed to the inspector or inspectors of elections.

(2) The date, time, and location of the meeting at which ballots will be counted.

(3) The list of all candidates' names that will appear on the ballot.

(4) Individual notice of the above paragraphs shall be delivered pursuant to Section 4040 if individual notice is requested by a member.

(c) Ballots and two preaddressed envelopes with instructions on how to return ballots shall be mailed by first-class mail or delivered by the association to every member not less than 30 days prior to the deadline for voting. In order to preserve confidentiality, a voter may not be identified by name, address, or lot, parcel, or unit number on the ballot. The association shall use as a model those procedures used by California counties for ensuring confidentiality of vote by mail ballots, including all of the following:

(1) The ballot itself is not signed by the voter, but is inserted into an envelope that is sealed. This envelope is inserted into a second envelope that is sealed. In the upper left-hand corner of the second envelope, the voter shall sign the voter's name, indicate the voter's name, and indicate the address or separate interest identifier that entitles the voter to vote.

(2) The second envelope is addressed to the inspector or inspectors of elections, who will be tallying the votes. The envelope may be mailed or delivered by hand to a location specified by the inspector or inspectors of elections. The member may request a receipt for delivery.

(d) A quorum shall be required only if so stated in the governing documents or other provisions of law. If a quorum is required by the governing documents, each ballot received by the inspector of elections shall be treated as a member present at a meeting for purposes of establishing a quorum.

(e) An association shall allow for cumulative voting using the secret ballot procedures provided in this section, if cumulative voting is provided for in the governing documents.

(f) Except for the meeting to count the votes required in subdivision (a) of Section 5120, an election may be conducted entirely by mail unless otherwise specified in the governing documents.

(g) In an election to approve an amendment of the governing documents, the text of the proposed amendment shall be delivered to the members with the ballot. *(Added by Stats.2012, c. 180 (A.B.805), § 2, operative Jan. 1, 2014. Amended by Stats.2019, c. 848 (S.B.323), § 4, eff. Jan. 1, 2020; Stats.2021, c. 642 (S.B.432), § 3, eff. Jan. 1, 2022.)*

§ 5116. Repealed by Stats.1984, c. 1671, § 7

§ 5117. Repealed by Stats.1974, c. 1206, p. 2609, § 3

§§ 5118, 5119. Repealed by Stats.1992, c. 162 (A.B.2650), § 3, operative Jan. 1, 1994

§ 5120. Counting and tabulation of votes; reporting of tabulated results

(a) All votes shall be counted and tabulated by the inspector or inspectors of elections, or the designee of the inspector of elections, in public at a properly noticed open meeting of the board or members. Any candidate or other member of the association may witness the counting and tabulation of the votes. No person, including a member of the association or an employee of the management company, shall open or otherwise review any ballot prior to the time and place at which the ballots are counted and tabulated. The inspector of elections, or the designee of the inspector of elections, may verify the member's information and signature on the outer envelope prior to the meeting at which ballots are tabulated. Once a secret ballot is received by the inspector of elections, it shall be irrevocable.

(b) The tabulated results of the election shall be promptly reported to the board and shall be recorded in the minutes of the next meeting of the board and shall be available for review by members of the association. Within 15 days of the election, the board shall give general notice pursuant to Section 4045 of the tabulated results of the election. *(Added by Stats.2012, c. 180 (A.B.805), § 2, operative Jan. 1, 2014.)*

§§ 5120.010 to 5120.330. Repealed by Stats.1992, c. 162 (A.B.2650), § 3, operative Jan. 1, 1994

§ 5121. Repealed by Stats.1984, c. 1671, § 10

§ 5122. Repealed by Stats.1992, c. 162 (A.B.2650), § 3, operative Jan. 1, 1994

§ 5123. Repealed by Stats.1984, c. 1671, § 12

§ 5124. Repealed by Stats.1983, c. 775, § 1, operative Jan. 1, 1986

§ 5125. Custody of election materials

The sealed ballots, signed voter envelopes, voter list, proxies, and candidate registration list shall at all times be in the custody of the inspector or inspectors of elections or at a location designated by the inspector or inspectors until after the tabulation of the vote, and until the time allowed by Section 5145 for challenging the election has expired, at which time custody shall be transferred to the association. If there is a recount or other challenge to the election process, the inspector or inspectors of elections shall, upon written request, make the ballots available for inspection and review by an association member or the member's authorized representative. Any recount shall be conducted in a manner that preserves the confidentiality of the vote. *(Added by Stats.2012, c. 180 (A.B.805), § 2, operative Jan. 1, 2014. Amended by Stats.2019, c. 848 (S.B.323), § 5, eff. Jan. 1, 2020.)*

§§ 5125.1, 5126. Repealed by Stats.1992, c. 162 (A.B.2650), § 3, operative Jan. 1, 1994

§ 5127. Repealed by Stats.1993, c. 219 (A.B.1500), § 59

§ 5127.5. Repealed by Stats.1984, c. 1671, § 14

§ 5127.6. Repealed by Stats.1984, c. 1671, § 15

§ 5128. Repealed by Stats.1992, c. 162 (A.B.2650), § 3, operative Jan. 1, 1994

§ 5129. Repealed by Stats.1983, c. 842, § 9, operative Jan. 1, 1985

§ 5130. Proxies; definitions

(a) For purposes of this article, the following definitions shall apply:

(1) "Proxy" means a written authorization signed by a member or the authorized representative of the member that gives another member or members the power to vote on behalf of that member.

(2) "Signed" means the placing of the member's name on the proxy (whether by manual signature, typewriting, telegraphic transmission, or otherwise) by the member or authorized representative of the member.

(b) Proxies shall not be construed or used in lieu of a ballot. An association may use proxies if permitted or required by the bylaws of the association and if those proxies meet the requirements of this article, other laws, and the governing documents, but the association shall not be required to prepare or distribute proxies pursuant to this article.

(c) Any instruction given in a proxy issued for an election that directs the manner in which the proxyholder is to cast the vote shall be set forth on a separate page of the proxy that can be detached and given to the proxyholder to retain. The proxyholder shall cast the member's vote by secret ballot. The proxy may be revoked by the member prior to the receipt of the ballot by the inspector of elections as described in Section 7613 of the Corporations Code. *(Added by Stats. 2012, c. 180 (A.B.805), § 2, operative Jan. 1, 2014.)*

§§ 5131, 5132. Repealed by Stats.1992, c. 162 (A.B.2650), § 3, operative Jan. 1, 1994

§§ 5133, 5134. Repealed by Stats.1985, c. 1315, § 2

§ 5135. Campaign funding

(a) Association funds shall not be used for campaign purposes in connection with any association board election. Funds of the association shall not be used for campaign purposes in connection with any other association election except to the extent necessary to comply with duties of the association imposed by law.

(b) For the purposes of this section, "campaign purposes" includes, but is not limited to, the following:

(1) Expressly advocating the election or defeat of any candidate that is on the association election ballot.

(2) Including the photograph or prominently featuring the name of any candidate on a communication from the association or its board, excepting the ballot, ballot materials, or a communication that is legally required, within 30 days of an election. This is not a campaign purpose if the communication is one for which subdivision (a) of Section 5105 requires that equal access be provided to another candidate or advocate. *(Added by Stats.2012, c. 180 (A.B.805), § 2, operative Jan. 1, 2014.)*

§§ 5135.5 to 5137. Repealed by Stats.1985, c. 1315, § 2

§ 5138. Repealed by Stats.1992, c. 162 (A.B.2650), § 3, operative Jan. 1, 1994

§ 5145. Civil action for violation of article; attorney's fees and costs; superior court or small claims court

(a) A member of an association may bring a civil action for declaratory or equitable relief for a violation of this article by the association, including, but not limited to, injunctive relief, restitution, or a combination thereof, within one year of the date that the inspector or inspectors of elections notifies the board and membership of the election results or the cause of action accrues, whichever is later. If a member establishes, by a preponderance of the evidence, that the election procedures of this article, or the adoption of and adherence to rules provided by Article 5 (commencing with Section 4340) of Chapter 3, were not followed, a court shall void any results of the election unless the association establishes, by a preponderance of the evidence, that the association's noncompliance with this article or the election operating rules did not affect the results of the election. The findings of the court shall be stated in writing as part of the record.

(b) A member who prevails in a civil action to enforce the member's rights pursuant to this article shall be entitled to reasonable attorney's fees and court costs, and the court may impose a civil penalty of up to five hundred dollars ($500) for each violation, except that each identical violation shall be subject to only one penalty if the violation affects each member of the association equally. A prevailing association shall not recover any costs, unless the court finds the action to be frivolous, unreasonable, or without foundation. If a member prevails in a civil action brought in small claims court, the member shall be awarded court costs and reasonable attorney's fees incurred for consulting an attorney in connection with this civil action.

(c) A cause of action under subdivision (a) may be brought in either the superior court or, if the amount of the demand does not exceed the jurisdictional amount of the small claims court, in small claims court. *(Added by Stats.2012, c. 180 (A.B.805), § 2, operative Jan. 1, 2014. Amended by Stats. 2019, c. 848 (S.B.323), § 6, eff. Jan. 1, 2020.)*

§§ 5150, 5151. Repealed by Stats.1992, c. 162 (A.B.2650), § 3, operative Jan. 1, 1994

§ 5152. Repealed by Stats.1993, c. 219 (A.B.1500), § 60

§§ 5153 to 5156. Repealed by Stats.1992, c. 162 (A.B.2650), § 3, operative Jan. 1, 1994

§§ 5157, 5158. Repealed by Stats.1993, c. 219 (A.B.1500), § 61, 62

§§ 5159 to 5183. Repealed by Stats.1992, c. 162 (A.B.2650), § 3, operative Jan. 1, 1994

ARTICLE 5. RECORD INSPECTION

Section
5200. Definitions.
5201 to 5203. Repealed.
5205. Availability to members.
5210. Time periods of required availability.
5215. Redaction.
5216. Safe at Home member request; association duties.
5220. Information sharing; member opt out.
5225. Request for membership list.
5230. Prohibited use of list.
5235. Remedies.
5240. Construction with Corporations Code.

Cross References

Community service organization reports, information on components to complete disclosures or reserve reports, reliance upon and access to information, see Civil Code § 5580.

§ 5200. Definitions

For the purposes of this article, the following definitions shall apply:

(a) "Association records" means all of the following:

(1) Any financial document required to be provided to a member in Article 7 (commencing with Section 5300) or in Sections 5565 and 5810.

(2) Any financial document or statement required to be provided in Article 2 (commencing with Section 4525) of Chapter 4.

(3) Interim financial statements, periodic or as compiled, containing any of the following:

(A) Balance sheet.

(B) Income and expense statement.

(C) Budget comparison.

(D) General ledger. A "general ledger" is a report that shows all transactions that occurred in an association account over a specified period of time.

The records described in this paragraph shall be prepared in accordance with an accrual or modified accrual basis of accounting.

(4) Executed contracts not otherwise privileged under law.

(5) Written board approval of vendor or contractor proposals or invoices.

(6) State and federal tax returns.

(7) Reserve account balances and records of payments made from reserve accounts.

(8) Agendas and minutes of meetings of the members, the board, and any committees appointed by the board pursuant to Section 7212 of the Corporations Code; excluding, however, minutes and other information from executive sessions of the board as described in Article 2 (commencing with Section 4900).

(9) Membership lists, including name, property address, mailing address, email address, as collected by the association in accordance with Section 4041 where applicable, but not including information for members who have opted out pursuant to Section 5220.

(10) Check registers.

(11) The governing documents.

(12) An accounting prepared pursuant to subdivision (b) of Section 5520.

§ 5200

(13) An "enhanced association record" as defined in subdivision (b).

(14) "Association election materials" as defined in subdivision (c).

(b) "Enhanced association records" means invoices, receipts and canceled checks for payments made by the association, purchase orders approved by the association, bank account statements for bank accounts in which assessments are deposited or withdrawn, credit card statements for credit cards issued in the name of the association, statements for services rendered, and reimbursement requests submitted to the association.

(c) "Association election materials" means returned ballots, signed voter envelopes, the voter list of names, parcel numbers, and voters to whom ballots were to be sent, proxies, and the candidate registration list. Signed voter envelopes may be inspected but may not be copied. An association shall maintain association election materials for one year after the date of the election. *(Added by Stats.2012, c. 180 (A.B.805), § 2, operative Jan. 1, 2014. Amended by Stats. 2019, c. 848 (S.B.323), § 7, eff. Jan. 1, 2020; Stats.2021, c. 640 (S.B.392), § 6, eff. Jan. 1, 2022; Stats.2021, c. 642 (S.B.432), § 4, eff. Jan. 1, 2022.)*

Cross References

Attorney's fees and costs, generally, see Code of Civil Procedure § 1021.

Identity theft, see Civil Code § 1798.92 et seq.

Injunctions, provisional remedies and specific and preventive relief, generally, see Civil Code § 3420 et seq.; Code of Civil Procedure § 525 et seq.

§§ 5201 to 5203. Repealed by Stats.1992, c. 162 (A.B.2650), § 3, operative Jan. 1, 1994

§ 5205. Availability to members

(a) The association shall make available association records for the time periods and within the timeframes provided in Section 5210 for inspection and copying by a member of the association, or the member's designated representative.

(b) A member of the association may designate another person to inspect and copy the specified association records on the member's behalf. The member shall make this designation in writing.

(c) The association shall make the specified association records available for inspection and copying in the association's business office within the common interest development.

(d) If the association does not have a business office within the development, the association shall make the specified association records available for inspection and copying at a place agreed to by the requesting member and the association.

(e) If the association and the requesting member cannot agree upon a place for inspection and copying pursuant to subdivision (d) or if the requesting member submits a written request directly to the association for copies of specifically identified records, the association may satisfy the requirement to make the association records available for inspection and copying by delivering copies of the specifically identified records to the member by individual delivery pursuant to Section 4040 within the timeframes set forth in subdivision (b) of Section 5210.

(f) The association may bill the requesting member for the direct and actual cost of copying and mailing requested documents. The association shall inform the member of the amount of the copying and mailing costs, and the member shall agree to pay those costs, before copying and sending the requested documents.

(g) In addition to the direct and actual costs of copying and mailing, the association may bill the requesting member an amount not in excess of ten dollars ($10) per hour, and not to exceed two hundred dollars ($200) total per written request, for the time actually and reasonably involved in redacting an enhanced association record. If the enhanced association record includes a reimbursement request, the person submitting the reimbursement request shall be solely responsible for removing all personal identification information from the request. The association shall inform the member of the estimated costs, and the member shall agree to pay those costs, before retrieving the requested documents.

(h) Requesting parties shall have the option of receiving specifically identified records by electronic transmission or machine-readable storage media as long as those records can be transmitted in a redacted format that does not allow the records to be altered. The cost of duplication shall be limited to the direct cost of producing the copy of a record in that electronic format. The association may deliver specifically identified records by electronic transmission or machine-readable storage media as long as those records can be transmitted in a redacted format that prevents the records from being altered. *(Added by Stats.2012, c. 180 (A.B.805), § 2, operative Jan. 1, 2014.)*

Cross References

Assessment payment and delinquency, notice, contents, see Civil Code § 5660.

Attorney's fees and costs, generally, see Code of Civil Procedure § 1021.

Identity theft, see Civil Code § 1798.92 et seq.

Injunctions, provisional remedies and specific and preventive relief, generally, see Civil Code § 3420 et seq.; Code of Civil Procedure § 525 et seq.

§ 5210. Time periods of required availability

(a) Association records are subject to member inspection for the following time periods:

(1) For the current fiscal year and for each of the previous two fiscal years.

(2) Notwithstanding paragraph (1), minutes of member and board meetings are subject to inspection permanently. If a committee has decisionmaking authority, minutes of the meetings of that committee shall be made available commencing January 1, 2007, and shall thereafter be permanently subject to inspection.

(b) When a member properly requests access to association records, access to the requested records shall be granted within the following time periods:

(1) Association records prepared during the current fiscal year, within 10 business days following the association's receipt of the request.

(2) Association records prepared during the previous two fiscal years, within 30 calendar days following the association's receipt of the request.

(3) Any record or statement available pursuant to Article 2 (commencing with Section 4525) of Chapter 4, Article 7 (commencing with Section 5300), Section 5565, or Section 5810, within the timeframe specified therein.

(4) Minutes of member and board meetings, within the timeframe specified in subdivision (a) of Section 4950.

(5) Minutes of meetings of committees with decisionmaking authority for meetings commencing on or after January 1, 2007, within 15 calendar days following approval.

(6) Membership list, within the timeframe specified in Section 8330 of the Corporations Code.

(c) There shall be no liability pursuant to this article for an association that fails to retain records for the periods specified in subdivision (a) that were created prior to January 1, 2006. *(Added by Stats.2012, c. 180 (A.B.805), § 2, operative Jan. 1, 2014.)*

Cross References

Attorney's fees and costs, generally, see Code of Civil Procedure § 1021.

Identity theft, see Civil Code § 1798.92 et seq.

Injunctions, provisional remedies and specific and preventive relief, generally, see Civil Code § 3420 et seq.; Code of Civil Procedure § 525 et seq.

§ 5215. Redaction

(a) Except as provided in subdivision (b), the association may withhold or redact information from the association records if any of the following are true:

(1) The release of the information is reasonably likely to lead to identity theft. For the purposes of this section, "identity theft" means the unauthorized use of another person's personal identifying information to obtain credit, goods, services, money, or property. Examples of information that may be withheld or redacted pursuant to this paragraph include bank account numbers of members or vendors, social security or tax identification numbers, and check, stock, and credit card numbers.

(2) The release of the information is reasonably likely to lead to fraud in connection with the association.

(3) The information is privileged under law. Examples include documents subject to attorney-client privilege or relating to litigation in which the association is or may become involved, and confidential settlement agreements.

(4) The release of the information is reasonably likely to compromise the privacy of an individual member of the association.

(5) The information contains any of the following:

(A) Records of goods or services provided a la carte to individual members of the association for which the association received monetary consideration other than assessments.

(B) Records of disciplinary actions, collection activities, or payment plans of members other than the member requesting the records.

(C) Any person's personal identification information, including, without limitation, social security number, tax identification number, driver's license number, credit card account numbers, bank account number, and bank routing number.

(D) Minutes and other information from executive sessions of the board as described in Article 2 (commencing with Section 4900), except for executed contracts not otherwise privileged. Privileged contracts shall not include contracts for maintenance, management, or legal services.

(E) Personnel records other than the payroll records required to be provided under subdivision (b).

(F) Interior architectural plans, including security features, for individual homes.

(b) Except as provided by the attorney-client privilege, the association may not withhold or redact information concerning the compensation paid to employees, vendors, or contractors. Compensation information for individual employees shall be set forth by job classification or title, not by the employee's name, social security number, or other personal information.

(c) No association, officer, director, employee, agent, or volunteer of an association shall be liable for damages to a member of the association or any third party as the result of identity theft or other breach of privacy because of the failure to withhold or redact that member's information under this section unless the failure to withhold or redact the information was intentional, willful, or negligent.

(d) If requested by the requesting member, an association that denies or redacts records shall provide a written explanation specifying the legal basis for withholding or redacting the requested records. *(Added by Stats.2012, c. 180 (A.B.805), § 2, operative Jan. 1, 2014.)*

Cross References

Attorney's fees and costs, generally, see Code of Civil Procedure § 1021.

Identity theft, see Civil Code § 1798.92 et seq.

Injunctions, provisional remedies and specific and preventive relief, generally, see Civil Code § 3420 et seq.; Code of Civil Procedure § 525 et seq.

§ 5216. Safe at Home member request; association duties

(a) Notwithstanding any other law, upon request of a member of an association who is an active participant in the Safe at Home program, the association shall do both of the following:

(1) Accept and use the address designated by the Secretary of State as the Safe at Home participant's substitute address under the Safe at Home program for all association communications.

(2) Withhold or redact information that would reveal the name, community property address, or email address of the Safe at Home participant from both of the following:

(A) All resident community membership lists, including mailbox bank listings, resident directories, electronic keypads, unit property numbers, and internet web portal accounts.

(B) Any membership list that will be shared with other members of the association.

(b) An association shall keep member participation in the Safe at Home program confidential.

(c) For purposes of this section:

(1) "Community property address" means the address of the member's property within the community governed by the association.

(2) "Safe at Home participant" means a person certified as a program participant in the Safe at Home program.

(3) "Safe at Home program" means the address confidentiality program established pursuant to Chapter 3.1 (commencing with Section 6205) of Division 7 of Title 1 of the Government Code. *(Added by Stats.2021, c. 151 (A.B.611), § 2, eff. Jan. 1, 2022.)*

§ 5220. Information sharing; member opt out

A member of the association may opt out of the sharing of that member's name, property address, email address, and mailing address by notifying the association in writing that the member prefers to be contacted via the alternative process described in subdivision (c) of Section 8330 of the Corporations Code. This opt-out shall remain in effect until changed by the member. *(Added by Stats.2012, c. 180 (A.B.805), § 2, operative Jan. 1, 2014. Amended by Stats.2021, c. 640 (S.B.392), § 7, eff. Jan. 1, 2022.)*

Cross References

Association record inspection, requests to be delivered in writing, see Civil Code § 5260.
Attorney's fees and costs, generally, see Code of Civil Procedure § 1021.
Identity theft, see Civil Code § 1798.92 et seq.
Injunctions, provisional remedies and specific and preventive relief, generally, see Civil Code § 3420 et seq.; Code of Civil Procedure § 525 et seq.

§ 5225. Request for membership list

A member requesting the membership list shall state the purpose for which the list is requested which purpose shall be reasonably related to the requester's interest as a member. If the association reasonably believes that the information in the list will be used for another purpose, it may deny the member access to the list. If the request is denied, in any subsequent action brought by the member under Section 5235, the association shall have the burden to prove that the member would have allowed use of the information for purposes unrelated to the member's interest as a member. *(Added by Stats.2012, c. 180 (A.B.805), § 2, operative Jan. 1, 2014.)*

Cross References

Attorney's fees and costs, generally, see Code of Civil Procedure § 1021.
Identity theft, see Civil Code § 1798.92 et seq.
Injunctions, provisional remedies and specific and preventive relief, generally, see Civil Code § 3420 et seq.; Code of Civil Procedure § 525 et seq.
Special meeting of members to reverse rule change, notice, voting requirements, effect of approved reversal, see Civil Code § 4365.

§ 5230. Prohibited use of list

(a) The association records, and any information from them, may not be sold, used for a commercial purpose, or used for any other purpose not reasonably related to a member's interest as a member. An association may bring an action against any person who violates this article for injunctive relief and for actual damages to the association caused by the violation.

(b) This article may not be construed to limit the right of an association to damages for misuse of information obtained from the association records pursuant to this article or to limit the right of an association to injunctive relief to stop the misuse of this information.

(c)(1) An association or its managing agent shall not do either of the following:

(A) Sell a member's personal information for any purpose without the consent of the member.

(B) Transmit a member's personal information to a third party without the consent of the member unless required to do so by law, including, but not limited to, Article 5 (commencing with Section 5200).

(2) A member may bring an action against an association that violates this subdivision for injunctive relief and actual damages caused by the violation. A member shall be entitled to recover reasonable costs and expenses, including reasonable attorney's fees, in a successful action to enforce the member's rights under this subdivision.

(d) An association shall be entitled to recover reasonable costs and expenses, including reasonable attorney's fees, in a successful action to enforce its rights under this article. *(Added by Stats.2012, c. 180 (A.B.805), § 2, operative Jan. 1, 2014. Amended by Stats.2021, c. 640 (S.B.392), § 8, eff. Jan. 1, 2022.)*

Cross References

Attorney's fees and costs, generally, see Code of Civil Procedure § 1021.
Identity theft, see Civil Code § 1798.92 et seq.
Injunctions, provisional remedies and specific and preventive relief, generally, see Civil Code § 3420 et seq.; Code of Civil Procedure § 525 et seq.

§ 5235. Remedies

(a) A member may bring an action to enforce that member's right to inspect and copy the association records. If a court finds that the association unreasonably withheld access to the association records, the court shall award the member reasonable costs and expenses, including reasonable attorney's fees, and may assess a civil penalty of up to five hundred dollars ($500) for the denial of each separate written request.

(b) A cause of action under this section may be brought in small claims court if the amount of the demand does not exceed the jurisdiction of that court.

(c) A prevailing association may recover any costs if the court finds the action to be frivolous, unreasonable, or without foundation. *(Added by Stats.2012, c. 180 (A.B.805), § 2, operative Jan. 1, 2014.)*

Cross References

Attorney's fees and costs, generally, see Code of Civil Procedure § 1021.

Identity theft, see Civil Code § 1798.92 et seq.

Injunctions, provisional remedies and specific and preventive relief, generally, see Civil Code § 3420 et seq.; Code of Civil Procedure § 525 et seq.

§ 5240. Construction with Corporations Code

(a) As applied to an association and its members, the provisions of this article are intended to supersede the provisions of Sections 8330 and 8333 of the Corporations Code to the extent those sections are inconsistent.

(b) Except as provided in subdivision (a), members of the association shall have access to association records, including accounting books and records and membership lists, in accordance with Article 3 (commencing with Section 8330) of Chapter 13 of Part 3 of Division 2 of Title 1 of the Corporations Code.

(c) This article applies to any community service organization or similar entity that is related to the association, and to any nonprofit entity that provides services to a common interest development under a declaration of trust. This article shall operate to give a member of the organization or entity a right to inspect and copy the records of that organization or entity equivalent to that granted to association members by this article.

(d) This article shall not apply to any common interest development in which separate interests are being offered for sale by a subdivider under the authority of a public report issued by the Bureau of Real Estate so long as the subdivider or all subdividers offering those separate interests for sale, or any employees of those subdividers or any other person who receives direct or indirect compensation from any of those subdividers, comprise a majority of the directors. Notwithstanding the foregoing, this article shall apply to that common interest development no later than 10 years after the close of escrow for the first sale of a separate interest to a member of the general public pursuant to the public report issued for the first phase of the development. *(Added by Stats.2012, c. 180 (A.B.805), § 2, operative Jan. 1, 2014. Amended by Stats. 2013, c. 352 (A.B.1317), § 54, eff. Sept. 26, 2013, operative Jan. 1, 2014.)*

Cross References

Attorney's fees and costs, generally, see Code of Civil Procedure § 1021.

Identity theft, see Civil Code § 1798.92 et seq.

Injunctions, provisional remedies and specific and preventive relief, generally, see Civil Code § 3420 et seq.; Code of Civil Procedure § 525 et seq.

ARTICLE 6. RECORDKEEPING

Section
5260. Requests to be delivered in writing.

§ 5260. Requests to be delivered in writing

To be effective, any of the following requests shall be delivered in writing to the association, pursuant to Section 4035:

(a) A request to change the member's information in the association membership list.

(b) A request to add or remove a second email or mailing address for delivery of individual notices to the member, pursuant to Section 4040.

(c) A request for individual delivery of general notices to the member, pursuant to subdivision (b) of Section 4045, or a request to cancel a prior request for individual delivery of general notices.

(d) A request to opt out of the membership list pursuant to Section 5220, or a request to cancel a prior request to opt out of the membership list.

(e) A request to receive a full copy of a specified annual budget report or annual policy statement pursuant to Section 5320.

(f) A request to receive all reports in full, pursuant to subdivision (b) of Section 5320, or a request to cancel a prior request to receive all reports in full. *(Added by Stats.2012, c. 180 (A.B.805), § 2, operative Jan. 1, 2014. Amended by Stats.2021, c. 640 (S.B.392), § 9, eff. Jan. 1, 2022.)*

ARTICLE 7. ANNUAL REPORTS

Section
5300. Annual budget report.
5301, 5302. Repealed.
5305. Standards for preparation of review of financial statement of association.
5310. Annual policy statement; contents.
5311 to 5317. Repealed.
5320. Delivery of reports.

Cross References

Association records, time periods of required availability, see Civil Code § 5210.

Individual delivery or individual notice, see Civil Code § 4040.

Sale or title transfer, provision of specified items to prospective purchasers, see Civil Code § 4525.

§ 5300. Annual budget report

(a) Notwithstanding a contrary provision in the governing documents, an association shall distribute an annual budget report 30 to 90 days before the end of its fiscal year.

(b) Unless the governing documents impose more stringent standards, the annual budget report shall include all of the following information:

(1) A pro forma operating budget, showing the estimated revenue and expenses on an accrual basis.

(2) A summary of the association's reserves, prepared pursuant to Section 5565.

(3) A summary of the reserve funding plan adopted by the board, as specified in paragraph (5) of subdivision (b) of Section 5550. The summary shall include notice to members that the full reserve study plan is available upon request, and the association shall provide the full reserve plan to any member upon request.

(4) A statement as to whether the board has determined to defer or not undertake repairs or replacement of any major component with a remaining life of 30 years or less, including

a justification for the deferral or decision not to undertake the repairs or replacement.

(5) A statement as to whether the board, consistent with the reserve funding plan adopted pursuant to Section 5560, has determined or anticipates that the levy of one or more special assessments will be required to repair, replace, or restore any major component or to provide adequate reserves therefor. If so, the statement shall also set out the estimated amount, commencement date, and duration of the assessment.

(6) A statement as to the mechanism or mechanisms by which the board will fund reserves to repair or replace major components, including assessments, borrowing, use of other assets, deferral of selected replacements or repairs, or alternative mechanisms.

(7) A general statement addressing the procedures used for the calculation and establishment of those reserves to defray the future repair, replacement, or additions to those major components that the association is obligated to maintain. The statement shall include, but need not be limited to, reserve calculations made using the formula described in paragraph (4) of subdivision (b) of Section 5570, and may not assume a rate of return on cash reserves in excess of 2 percent above the discount rate published by the Federal Reserve Bank of San Francisco at the time the calculation was made.

(8) A statement as to whether the association has any outstanding loans with an original term of more than one year, including the payee, interest rate, amount outstanding, annual payment, and when the loan is scheduled to be retired.

(9) A summary of the association's property, general liability, earthquake, flood, and fidelity insurance policies. For each policy, the summary shall include the name of the insurer, the type of insurance, the policy limit, and the amount of the deductible, if any. To the extent that any of the required information is specified in the insurance policy declaration page, the association may meet its obligation to disclose that information by making copies of that page and distributing it with the annual budget report. The summary distributed pursuant to this paragraph shall contain, in at least 10–point boldface type, the following statement:

"This summary of the association's policies of insurance provides only certain information, as required by Section 5300 of the Civil Code, and should not be considered a substitute for the complete policy terms and conditions contained in the actual policies of insurance. Any association member may, upon request and provision of reasonable notice, review the association's insurance policies and, upon request and payment of reasonable duplication charges, obtain copies of those policies. Although the association maintains the policies of insurance specified in this summary, the association's policies of insurance may not cover your property, including personal property or real property improvements to or around your dwelling, or personal injuries or other losses that occur within or around your dwelling. Even if a loss is covered, you may nevertheless be responsible for paying all or a portion of any deductible that applies. Association members should consult with their individual insurance broker or agent for appropriate additional coverage."

(10) When the common interest development is a condominium project, a statement describing the status of the common interest development as a Federal Housing Administration (FHA)–approved condominium project pursuant to FHA guidelines, including whether the common interest development is an FHA-approved condominium project. The statement shall be in at least 10–point font on a separate piece of paper and in the following form:

"Certification by the Federal Housing Administration may provide benefits to members of an association, including an improvement in an owner's ability to refinance a mortgage or obtain secondary financing and an increase in the pool of potential buyers of the separate interest.

This common interest development [is/is not (circle one)] a condominium project. The association of this common interest development [is/is not (circle one)] certified by the Federal Housing Administration."

(11) When the common interest development is a condominium project, a statement describing the status of the common interest development as a federal Department of Veterans Affairs (VA)–approved condominium project pursuant to VA guidelines, including whether the common interest development is a VA-approved condominium project. The statement shall be in at least 10–point font on a separate piece of paper and in the following form:

"Certification by the federal Department of Veterans Affairs may provide benefits to members of an association, including an improvement in an owner's ability to refinance a mortgage or obtain secondary financing and an increase in the pool of potential buyers of the separate interest.

This common interest development [is/is not (circle one)] a condominium project. The association of this common interest development [is/is not (circle one)] certified by the federal Department of Veterans Affairs."

(12) A copy of the completed "Charges For Documents Provided" disclosure identified in Section 4528. For purposes of this section, "completed" means that the "Fee for Document" section of the form individually identifies the costs associated with providing each document listed on the form.

(c) The annual budget report shall be made available to the members pursuant to Section 5320.

(d) The summary of the association's reserves disclosed pursuant to paragraph (2) of subdivision (b) shall not be admissible in evidence to show improper financial management of an association, provided that other relevant and competent evidence of the financial condition of the association is not made inadmissible by this provision.

(e) The Assessment and Reserve Funding Disclosure Summary form, prepared pursuant to Section 5570, shall accompany each annual budget report or summary of the annual budget report that is delivered pursuant to this article. *(Added by Stats.2015, c. 184 (A.B.596), § 2, eff. Jan. 1, 2016, operative July 1, 2016. Amended by Stats.2017, c. 127 (A.B.690), § 4, eff. Jan. 1, 2018.)*

Cross References

Assessments, limitation on increases, see Civil Code § 5605.

Certified common interest development managers, annual report to board of directors, contents, see Business and Professions Code § 11504.

Community service organization reports, information on components to complete disclosures or reserve reports, reliance upon and access to information, see Civil Code § 5580.

Individual notice to members of changes in insurance coverage, see Civil Code § 5810.

Real estate broker license renewal, course work in common interest development law, number of clock hours required, see Business and Professions Code § 10170.5.

Real estate broker licensure, proof of course completion in common interest development law, number of course equivalency hours required, see Business and Professions Code § 10153.2.

Subdivided lands, sale or lease of any lot or parcel in subdivision, copies of specified documents for prospective purchasers or lessees, see Business and Professions Code § 11018.6.

§§ 5301, 5302. Repealed by Stats.1992, c. 162 (A.B.2650), § 3, operative Jan. 1, 1994

§ 5305. Standards for preparation of review of financial statement of association

Unless the governing documents impose more stringent standards, a review of the financial statement of the association shall be prepared in accordance with generally accepted accounting principles by a licensee of the California Board of Accountancy for any fiscal year in which the gross income to the association exceeds seventy-five thousand dollars ($75,000). A copy of the review of the financial statement shall be distributed to the members within 120 days after the close of each fiscal year, by individual delivery pursuant to Section 4040. *(Added by Stats.2012, c. 180 (A.B.805), § 2, operative Jan. 1, 2014.)*

Cross References

Real estate broker license renewal, course work in common interest development law, number of clock hours required, see Business and Professions Code § 10170.5.

Real estate broker licensure, proof of course completion in common interest development law, number of course equivalency hours required, see Business and Professions Code § 10153.2.

Subdivided lands, sale or lease of any lot or parcel in subdivision, copies of specified documents for prospective purchasers or lessees, see Business and Professions Code § 11018.6.

§ 5310. Annual policy statement; contents

(a) Within 30 to 90 days before the end of its fiscal year, the board shall distribute an annual policy statement that provides the members with information about association policies. The annual policy statement shall include all of the following information:

(1) The name and address of the person designated to receive official communications to the association, pursuant to Section 4035.

(2) A statement explaining that a member may submit a request to have notices sent to up to two different specified addresses, pursuant to Section 4040.

(3) The location, if any, designated for posting of a general notice, pursuant to subdivision (a) of Section 4045.

(4) Notice of a member's option to receive general notices by individual delivery, pursuant to subdivision (b) of Section 4045.

(5) Notice of a member's right to receive copies of meeting minutes, pursuant to subdivision (b) of Section 4950.

(6) The statement of assessment collection policies required by Section 5730.

(7) A statement describing the association's policies and practices in enforcing lien rights or other legal remedies for default in the payment of assessments.

(8) A statement describing the association's discipline policy, if any, including any schedule of penalties for violations of the governing documents pursuant to Section 5850.

(9) A summary of dispute resolution procedures, pursuant to Sections 5920 and 5965.

(10) A summary of any requirements for association approval of a physical change to property, pursuant to Section 4765.

(11) The mailing address for overnight payment of assessments, pursuant to Section 5655.

(12) Any other information that is required by law or the governing documents or that the board determines to be appropriate for inclusion.

(b) The annual policy statement shall be made available to the members pursuant to Section 5320. *(Added by Stats.2012, c. 180 (A.B.805), § 2, operative Jan. 1, 2014. Amended by Stats.2021, c. 640 (S.B.392), § 10, eff. Jan. 1, 2022.)*

Cross References

Real estate broker license renewal, course work in common interest development law, number of clock hours required, see Business and Professions Code § 10170.5.

Real estate broker licensure, proof of course completion in common interest development law, number of course equivalency hours required, see Business and Professions Code § 10153.2.

Subdivided lands, sale or lease of any lot or parcel in subdivision, copies of specified documents for prospective purchasers or lessees, see Business and Professions Code § 11018.6.

§§ 5311 to 5317. Repealed by Stats.1992, c. 162 (A.B.2650), § 3, operative Jan. 1, 1994

§ 5320. Delivery of reports

(a) When a report is prepared pursuant to Section 5300 or 5310, the association shall deliver one of the following documents to all members by individual delivery pursuant to Section 4040:

(1) The full report.

(2) A summary of the report that includes, on the first page, a general description of the content of the report and instructions, printed in at least 10–point boldface type, regarding how to request a complete copy of the report at no cost to the member.

§ 5320

(b) Notwithstanding subdivision (a), if a member has requested to receive all reports in full, the association shall deliver the full report to that member, rather than a summary of the report. *(Added by Stats.2012, c. 180 (A.B.805), § 2, operative Jan. 1, 2014. Amended by Stats.2021, c. 640 (S.B.392), § 11, eff. Jan. 1, 2022.)*

Cross References

Association record inspection, requests to be delivered in writing, see Civil Code § 5260.

Real estate broker license renewal, course work in common interest development law, number of clock hours required, see Business and Professions Code § 10170.5.

Real estate broker licensure, proof of course completion in common interest development law, number of course equivalency hours required, see Business and Professions Code § 10153.2.

Subdivided lands, sale or lease of any lot or parcel in subdivision, copies of specified documents for prospective purchasers or lessees, see Business and Professions Code § 11018.6.

ARTICLE 8. CONFLICT OF INTEREST

Section
5350. Applicability of Corporations Code provisions; prohibited actions.

§ 5350. Applicability of Corporations Code provisions; prohibited actions

(a) Notwithstanding any other law, and regardless of whether an association is incorporated or unincorporated, the provisions of Sections 7233 and 7234 of the Corporations Code shall apply to any contract or other transaction authorized, approved, or ratified by the board or a committee of the board.

(b) A director or member of a committee shall not vote on any of the following matters:

(1) Discipline of the director or committee member.

(2) An assessment against the director or committee member for damage to the common area or facilities.

(3) A request, by the director or committee member, for a payment plan for overdue assessments.

(4) A decision whether to foreclose on a lien on the separate interest of the director or committee member.

(5) Review of a proposed physical change to the separate interest of the director or committee member.

(6) A grant of exclusive use common area to the director or committee member.

(c) Nothing in this section limits any other provision of law or the governing documents that govern a decision in which a director may have an interest. *(Added by Stats.2012, c. 180 (A.B.805), § 2, operative Jan. 1, 2014.)*

ARTICLE 9. MANAGING AGENT

Section
5375. Prospective managing agent; written disclosures.
5375.5. Prospective manager or management firm; disclosure of potential conflict of interest.
5376. Facilitation of delivery of disclosures.
5380. Managing agent; deposit of funds received; requirements; separate record; commingling of funds.
5385. "Managing agent" does not include full-time employee of association.

§ 5375. Prospective managing agent; written disclosures

A prospective managing agent of a common interest development shall provide a written statement to the board as soon as practicable, but in no event more than 90 days, before entering into a management agreement which shall contain all of the following information concerning the managing agent:

(a) The names and business addresses of the owners or general partners of the managing agent. If the managing agent is a corporation, the written statement shall include the names and business addresses of the directors and officers and shareholders holding greater than 10 percent of the shares of the corporation.

(b) Whether or not any relevant licenses such as architectural design, construction, engineering, real estate, or accounting have been issued by this state and are currently held by the persons specified in subdivision (a). If a license is currently held by any of those persons, the statement shall contain the following information:

(1) What license is held.

(2) The dates the license is valid.

(3) The name of the licensee appearing on that license.

(c) Whether or not any relevant professional certifications or designations such as architectural design, construction, engineering, real property management, or accounting are currently held by any of the persons specified in subdivision (a), including, but not limited to, a professional common interest development manager. If any certification or designation is held, the statement shall include the following information:

(1) What the certification or designation is and what entity issued it.

(2) The dates the certification or designation is valid.

(3) The names in which the certification or designation is held.

(d) Disclose any business or company in which the common interest development manager or common interest development management firm has any ownership interests, profit-sharing arrangements, or other monetary incentives provided to the management firm or managing agent.

(e) Whether or not the common interest development manager or common interest development management firm receives a referral fee or other monetary benefit from a third-party provider distributing documents pursuant to Sections 4528 and 4530. *(Added by Stats.2012, c. 180 (A.B.805), § 2, operative Jan. 1, 2014. Amended by Stats.2017, c. 127 (A.B.690), § 5, eff. Jan. 1, 2018.)*

Cross References

Common interest development managers, management companies and parent companies, prohibited activities, see Business and Professions Code § 11505.

§ 5375.5. Prospective manager or management firm; disclosure of potential conflict of interest

A common interest development manager or common interest development management firm shall disclose, in writing, any potential conflict of interest when presenting a bid for service to an association's board of directors. "Conflict of interest," for purposes of this section, means:

(a) Any referral fee or other monetary benefit that could be derived from a business or company providing products or services to the association.

(b) Any ownership interests or profit-sharing arrangements with service providers recommended to, or used by, the association. *(Added by Stats.2017, c. 127 (A.B.690), § 6, eff. Jan. 1, 2018.)*

§ 5376. Facilitation of delivery of disclosures

The common interest development manager, common interest development management firm, or its contracted third-party agent shall facilitate the delivery of disclosures required pursuant to paragraph (1) of subdivision (a), paragraph (2) of subdivision (b), and subdivision (d), of Section 4530 if the common interest development manager, or common interest development management firm, is contractually responsible for delivering those documents. *(Added by Stats.2017, c. 127 (A.B.690), § 7, eff. Jan. 1, 2018.)*

§ 5380. Managing agent; deposit of funds received; requirements; separate record; commingling of funds

(a) A managing agent of a common interest development who accepts or receives funds belonging to the association shall deposit those funds that are not placed into an escrow account with a bank, savings association, or credit union or into an account under the control of the association, into a trust fund account maintained by the managing agent in a bank, savings association, or credit union in this state. All funds deposited by the managing agent in the trust fund account shall be kept in this state in a financial institution, as defined in Section 31041 of the Financial Code, which is insured by the federal government, or is a guaranty corporation subject to Section 14858 of the Financial Code, and shall be maintained there until disbursed in accordance with written instructions from the association entitled to the funds.

(b) At the written request of the board, the funds the managing agent accepts or receives on behalf of the association shall be deposited into an account in a bank, savings association, or credit union in this state that is insured by the Federal Deposit Insurance Corporation, National Credit Union Administration Insurance Fund, or a guaranty corporation subject to Section 14858 of the Financial Code, provided all of the following requirements are met:

(1) The account is in the name of the managing agent as trustee for the association or in the name of the association.

(2) All of the funds in the account are covered by insurance provided by an agency of the federal government or a guaranty corporation subject to Section 14858 of the Financial Code. Those funds may only be deposited in accounts that protect the principal. In no event may those funds be invested in stocks or high-risk investment options.

(3) The funds in the account are kept separate, distinct, and apart from the funds belonging to the managing agent or to any other person for whom the managing agent holds funds in trust.

(4) The managing agent discloses to the board the nature of the account, how interest will be calculated and paid, whether service charges will be paid to the depository and by whom, and any notice requirements or penalties for withdrawal of funds from the account.

(5) No interest earned on funds in the account shall inure directly or indirectly to the benefit of the managing agent or the managing agent's employees.

(6) Transfers of funds out of the association's reserve or operating accounts shall not be authorized without prior written approval from the board of the association unless the amount of the transfer is less than the following:

(A) The lesser of five thousand dollars ($5,000) or 5 percent of the estimated income in the annual operating budget, for associations with 50 or less separate interests.

(B) The lesser of ten thousand dollars ($10,000) or 5 percent of estimated income in the annual operating budget, for associations with 51 or more separate interests.

(c) The managing agent shall maintain a separate record of the receipt and disposition of all funds described in this section, including any interest earned on the funds.

(d) The managing agent shall not commingle the funds of the association with the managing agent's own money or with the money of others that the managing agent receives or accepts.

(e) The prevailing party in an action to enforce this section shall be entitled to recover reasonable legal fees and court costs.

(f) As used in this section, "completed payment" means funds received that clearly identify the account to which the funds are to be credited. *(Added by Stats.2012, c. 180 (A.B.805), § 2, operative Jan. 1, 2014. Amended by Stats. 2018, c. 396 (A.B.2912), § 2, eff. Jan. 1, 2019; Stats.2021, c. 270 (A.B.1101), § 1, eff. Jan. 1, 2022.)*

§ 5385. "Managing agent" does not include full-time employee of association

For the purposes of this article, "managing agent" does not include a full-time employee of the association. *(Added by Stats.2012, c. 180 (A.B.805), § 2, operative Jan. 1, 2014.)*

Cross References

Common interest development managers, management companies and parent companies, prohibited activities, see Business and Professions Code § 11505.

ARTICLE 10. GOVERNMENT ASSISTANCE

Section
5400. Online education course regarding role, duties, laws and responsibilities of board directors and prospective board directors and nonjudicial foreclosure process.
5405. Assistance with identification of common interest developments; submission of information by each association; time; notice of change of address; penalty for violation of filing requirements; availability of information.

§ 5400. Online education course regarding role, duties, laws and responsibilities of board directors and prospective board directors and nonjudicial foreclosure process

To the extent existing funds are available, the Department of Consumer Affairs and the Bureau of Real Estate shall develop an online education course for the board regarding the role, duties, laws, and responsibilities of directors and prospective directors, and the nonjudicial foreclosure process. *(Added by Stats.2012, c. 180 (A.B.805), § 2, operative Jan. 1, 2014. Amended by Stats.2013, c. 352 (A.B.1317), § 55, eff. Sept. 26, 2013, operative Jan. 1, 2014.)*

§ 5405. Assistance with identification of common interest developments; submission of information by each association; time; notice of change of address; penalty for violation of filing requirements; availability of information

(a) To assist with the identification of common interest developments, each association, whether incorporated or unincorporated, shall submit to the Secretary of State, on a form and for a fee not to exceed thirty dollars ($30) that the Secretary of State shall prescribe, the following information concerning the association and the development that it manages:

(1) A statement that the association is formed to manage a common interest development under the Davis-Stirling Common Interest Development Act.

(2) The name of the association.

(3) The street address of the business or corporate office of the association, if any.

(4) The street address of the association's onsite office, if different from the street address of the business or corporate office, or if there is no onsite office, the street address of the responsible officer or managing agent of the association.

(5) The name, address, and either the daytime telephone number or email address of the president of the association, other than the address, telephone number, or email address of the association's onsite office or managing agent.

(6) The name, street address, and daytime telephone number of the association's managing agent, if any.

(7) The county, and, if in an incorporated area, the city in which the development is physically located. If the boundaries of the development are physically located in more than one county, each of the counties in which it is located.

(8) If the development is in an unincorporated area, the city closest in proximity to the development.

(9) The front street and nearest cross street of the physical location of the development.

(10) The type of common interest development managed by the association.

(11) The number of separate interests in the development.

(b) The association shall submit the information required by this section as follows:

(1) By incorporated associations, within 90 days after the filing of its original articles of incorporation, and thereafter at the time the association files its statement of principal business activity with the Secretary of State pursuant to Section 8210 of the Corporations Code.

(2) By unincorporated associations, in July 2003, and in that same month biennially thereafter. Upon changing its status to that of a corporation, the association shall comply with the filing deadlines in paragraph (1).

(c) The association shall notify the Secretary of State of any change in the street address of the association's onsite office or of the responsible officer or managing agent of the association in the form and for a fee prescribed by the Secretary of State, within 60 days of the change.

(d) The penalty for an incorporated association's noncompliance with the initial or biennial filing requirements of this section shall be suspension of the association's rights, privileges, and powers as a corporation and monetary penalties, to the same extent and in the same manner as suspension and monetary penalties imposed pursuant to Section 8810 of the Corporations Code.

(e) The statement required by this section may be filed, notwithstanding suspension of the corporate powers, rights, and privileges under this section or under provisions of the Revenue and Taxation Code. Upon the filing of a statement under this section by a corporation that has suffered suspension under this section, the Secretary of State shall certify that fact to the Franchise Tax Board and the corporation may thereupon be relieved from suspension, unless the corporation is held in suspension by the Franchise Tax Board by reason of Section 23301, 23301.5, or 23775 of the Revenue and Taxation Code.

(f) The Secretary of State shall make the information submitted pursuant to paragraph (5) of subdivision (a) available only for governmental purposes and only to Members of the Legislature and the Business, Consumer Services, and Housing Agency, upon written request. All other information submitted pursuant to this section shall be subject to public inspection pursuant to the California Public Records Act (Division 10 (commencing with Section 7920.000) of Title 1 of the Government Code). The information submitted pursuant to this section shall be made available for governmental or public inspection.

(g) Whenever any form is filed pursuant to this section, it supersedes any previously filed form.

(h) The Secretary of State may destroy or otherwise dispose of any form filed pursuant to this section after it has been superseded by the filing of a new form. *(Added by Stats.2012, c. 180 (A.B.805), § 2, operative Jan. 1, 2014. Amended by Stats.2013, c. 353 (S.B.820), § 12, eff. Sept. 26, 2013, operative Jan. 1, 2014; Stats.2021, c. 615 (A.B.474), § 53, eff. Jan. 1, 2022, operative Jan. 1, 2023.)*

Cross References

Miscellaneous business entity filing fees, filing a statement pursuant to this section, see Government Code § 12191.

ARTICLE 11. EMERGENCY POWERS AND PROCEDURES

Section
5450. Application of section; alternative teleconference procedures; conditions.

§ 5450. Application of section; alternative teleconference procedures; conditions

(a) This section only applies to a common interest development if gathering in person is unsafe or impossible because the common interest development is in an area affected by one or more of the following conditions:

(1) A state of disaster or emergency declared by the federal government.

(2) A state of emergency proclaimed by the Governor under Section 8625 of the Government Code.

(3) A local emergency proclaimed by a local governing body or official under Section 8630 of the Government Code.

(b) Notwithstanding any other law or the association's governing documents, and except as provided in subdivision (d), a board meeting or meeting of the members may be conducted entirely by teleconference, without any physical location being held open for the attendance of any director or member, if all of the following conditions are satisfied:

(1) Notice of the first meeting that is conducted under this section for a particular disaster or emergency affecting the association is delivered to members by individual delivery.

(2) The notice for each meeting conducted under this section includes, in addition to other required content for meeting notices, all of the following:

(A) Clear technical instructions on how to participate by teleconference.

(B) The telephone number and electronic mail address of a person who can provide technical assistance with the teleconference process, both before and during the meeting.

(C) A reminder that a member may request individual delivery of meeting notices, with instructions on how to do so.

(3) Every director and member has the same ability to participate in the meeting that would exist if the meeting were held in person.

(4) Any vote of the directors shall be conducted by a roll call vote.

(5) Any person who is entitled to participate in the meeting shall be given the option of participating by telephone.

(c) If, as a result of the disaster or emergency, mail delivery or retrieval is not possible at any association onsite address and the address on file with the association for that member is the same association onsite address, then the association shall send the notice of the first meeting referenced in paragraph (1) of subdivision (b) to any email address provided to the association by that member, in writing, pursuant to paragraph (2) of subdivision (a) of Section 4040 or subdivision (b) of Section 4041.

(d) Subdivision (b) does not apply to a meeting at which ballots are counted and tabulated pursuant to Section 5120, unless both of the following conditions are met:

(1) The meeting at which ballots are to be counted and tabulated is conducted by video conference.

(2) The camera is placed in a location such that members can witness the inspector of elections counting and tabulating the votes.

(e) The remedies available pursuant to Section 4955 shall also be available to address violations of this section. *(Added by Stats.2021, c. 276 (S.B.391), § 2, eff. Sept. 23, 2021.)*

CHAPTER 7. FINANCES

Article	Section
1. Accounting	5500
2. Use of Reserve Funds	5510
3. Reserve Planning	5550

ARTICLE 1. ACCOUNTING

Section
5500. Duties of board.
5501. Board review requirements.
5502. Transfers shall not be authorized without board approval; exceptions.

§ 5500. Duties of board

Unless the governing documents impose more stringent standards, the board shall do all of the following:

(a) Review, on a monthly basis, a current reconciliation of the association's operating accounts.

(b) Review, on a monthly basis, a current reconciliation of the association's reserve accounts.

(c) Review, on a monthly basis, the current year's actual operating revenues and expenses compared to the current year's budget.

(d) Review, on a monthly basis, the latest account statements prepared by the financial institutions where the association has its operating and reserve accounts.

(e) Review, on a monthly basis, an income and expense statement for the association's operating and reserve accounts.

(f) Review, on a monthly basis, the check register, monthly general ledger, and delinquent assessment receivable reports. *(Added by Stats.2012, c. 180 (A.B.805), § 2, operative Jan. 1, 2014. Amended by Stats.2018, c. 396 (A.B.2912), § 3, eff. Jan. 1, 2019.)*

§ 5501. Board review requirements

The review requirements of Section 5500 may be met when every individual member of the board, or a subcommittee of the board consisting of the treasurer and at least one other board member, reviews the documents and statements described in Section 5500 independent of a board meeting, so long as the review is ratified at the board meeting subsequent to the review and that ratification is reflected in the minutes of that meeting. *(Added by Stats.2018, c. 396 (A.B.2912), § 4, eff. Jan. 1, 2019.)*

§ 5502. Transfers shall not be authorized without board approval; exceptions

(a) Notwithstanding any other law, transfers shall not be authorized from the association's reserve or operating accounts without prior written approval from the board of the association unless the amount of the transfer is less than the following:

(1) The lesser of five thousand dollars ($5,000) or 5 percent of the estimated income in the annual operating budget, for associations with 50 or less separate interests.

(2) The lesser of ten thousand dollars ($10,000) or 5 percent of the estimated income in the annual operating budget, for associations with 51 or more separate interests.

(b) This section applies in addition to any other applicable requirements of this part. *(Added by Stats.2018, c. 396 (A.B.2912), § 5, eff. Jan. 1, 2019. Amended by Stats.2019, c. 497 (A.B.991), § 31, eff. Jan. 1, 2020; Stats.2021, c. 270 (A.B.1101), § 2, eff. Jan. 1, 2022.)*

ARTICLE 2. USE OF RESERVE FUNDS

Section
5510. Signatures required for withdrawals; purpose of expenditure.
5515. Temporary transfers to general operating fund.
5520. Notice of action; accounting of expenses.

§ 5510. Signatures required for withdrawals; purpose of expenditure

(a) The signatures of at least two persons, who shall be directors, or one officer who is not a director and one who is a director, shall be required for the withdrawal of moneys from the association's reserve accounts.

(b) The board shall not expend funds designated as reserve funds for any purpose other than the repair, restoration, replacement, or maintenance of, or litigation involving the repair, restoration, replacement, or maintenance of, major components that the association is obligated to repair, restore, replace, or maintain and for which the reserve fund was established. *(Added by Stats.2012, c. 180 (A.B.805), § 2, operative Jan. 1, 2014.)*

§ 5515. Temporary transfers to general operating fund

(a) Notwithstanding Section 5510, the board may authorize the temporary transfer of moneys from a reserve fund to the association's general operating fund to meet short-term cashflow requirements or other expenses, if the board has provided notice of the intent to consider the transfer in a board meeting notice provided pursuant to Section 4920.

(b) The notice shall include the reasons the transfer is needed, some of the options for repayment, and whether a special assessment may be considered.

(c) If the board authorizes the transfer, the board shall issue a written finding, recorded in the board's minutes, explaining the reasons that the transfer is needed, and describing when and how the moneys will be repaid to the reserve fund.

(d) The transferred funds shall be restored to the reserve fund within one year of the date of the initial transfer, except that the board may, after giving the same notice required for considering a transfer, and, upon making a finding supported by documentation that a temporary delay would be in the best interests of the common interest development, temporarily delay the restoration.

(e) The board shall exercise prudent fiscal management in maintaining the integrity of the reserve account, and shall, if necessary, levy a special assessment to recover the full amount of the expended funds within the time limits required by this section. This special assessment is subject to the limitation imposed by Section 5605. The board may, at its discretion, extend the date the payment on the special assessment is due. Any extension shall not prevent the board from pursuing any legal remedy to enforce the collection of an unpaid special assessment. *(Added by Stats.2012, c. 180 (A.B.805), § 2, operative Jan. 1, 2014.)*

§ 5520. Notice of action; accounting of expenses

(a) When the decision is made to use reserve funds or to temporarily transfer moneys from the reserve fund to pay for litigation pursuant to subdivision (b) of Section 5510, the association shall provide general notice pursuant to Section 4045 of that decision, and of the availability of an accounting of those expenses.

(b) Unless the governing documents impose more stringent standards, the association shall make an accounting of expenses related to the litigation on at least a quarterly basis. The accounting shall be made available for inspection by members of the association at the association's office. *(Added by Stats.2012, c. 180 (A.B.805), § 2, operative Jan. 1, 2014.)*

ARTICLE 3. RESERVE PLANNING

Section
5550. Inspection of components; study minimum requirements.
5551. Definitions; inspection of exterior elevated elements; report to board; repair of elements; application of section.
5560. Reserve funding plan; inclusion of schedule of change in assessments; adoption by board; separate approval of assessment increase.
5565. Summary of association's reserves; contents.
5570. Form for disclosure of fiscal matters.
5580. Community service organization reports; information on components to complete disclosures or reserve reports; reliance upon and access to information.

§ 5550. Inspection of components; study minimum requirements

(a) At least once every three years, the board shall cause to be conducted a reasonably competent and diligent visual inspection of the accessible areas of the major components that the association is obligated to repair, replace, restore, or maintain as part of a study of the reserve account requirements of the common interest development, if the current replacement value of the major components is equal to or greater than one-half of the gross budget of the association, excluding the association's reserve account for that period. The board shall review this study, or cause it to be reviewed, annually and shall consider and implement necessary adjustments to the board's analysis of the reserve account requirements as a result of that review.

(b) The study required by this section shall at a minimum include:

(1) Identification of the major components that the association is obligated to repair, replace, restore, or maintain that, as of the date of the study, have a remaining useful life of less than 30 years.

(2) Identification of the probable remaining useful life of the components identified in paragraph (1) as of the date of the study.

(3) An estimate of the cost of repair, replacement, restoration, or maintenance of the components identified in paragraph (1).

(4) An estimate of the total annual contribution necessary to defray the cost to repair, replace, restore, or maintain the components identified in paragraph (1) during and at the end of their useful life, after subtracting total reserve funds as of the date of the study.

(5) A reserve funding plan that indicates how the association plans to fund the contribution identified in paragraph (4) to meet the association's obligation for the repair and replacement of all major components with an expected remaining life of 30 years or less, not including those components that the board has determined will not be replaced or repaired. *(Added by Stats.2012, c. 180 (A.B.805), § 2, operative Jan. 1, 2014.)*

Cross References

Annual budget report, contents, see Civil Code § 5300.

§ 5551. Definitions; inspection of exterior elevated elements; report to board; repair of elements; application of section

(a) For purposes of this section, the following definitions apply:

(1) "Associated waterproofing systems" include flashings, membranes, coatings, and sealants that protect the load-bearing components of exterior elevated elements from exposure to water.

(2) "Exterior elevated elements" mean the load-bearing components together with their associated waterproofing system.

(3) "Load–bearing components" means those components that extend beyond the exterior walls of the building to deliver structural loads to the building from decks, balconies, stairways, walkways, and their railings, that have a walking surface elevated more than six feet above ground level, that are designed for human occupancy or use, and that are supported in whole or in substantial part by wood or wood-based products.

(4) "Statistically significant sample" means a sufficient number of units inspected to provide 95 percent confidence that the results from the sample are reflective of the whole, with a margin of error of no greater than plus or minus 5 percent.

(5) "Visual inspection" means inspection through the least intrusive method necessary to inspect load-bearing components, including visual observation only or visual observation in conjunction with, for example, the use of moisture meters, borescopes, or infrared technology.

(b)(1) At least once every nine years, the board of an association of a condominium project shall cause a reasonably competent and diligent visual inspection to be conducted by a licensed structural engineer or architect of a random and statistically significant sample of exterior elevated elements for which the association has maintenance or repair responsibility.

(2) The inspection shall determine whether the exterior elevated elements are in a generally safe condition and performing in accordance with applicable standards.

(c) Prior to conducting the first visual inspection, the inspector shall generate a random list of the locations of each type of exterior elevated element. The list shall include all exterior elevated elements for which the association has maintenance or repair responsibility. The list shall be provided to the association for future use.

(d) The inspector shall perform the visual inspections in accordance with the random list generated pursuant to subdivision (c). If during the visual inspection the inspector observes building conditions indicating that unintended water or water vapor has passed into the associated waterproofing system, thereby creating the potential for damage to the load-bearing components, then the inspector may conduct a further inspection. The inspector shall exercise their best professional judgment in determining the necessity, scope, and breadth of any further inspection.

(e) Based upon the inspector's visual inspections, further inspection, and construction and materials expertise, the inspector shall issue a written report containing the following information:

(1) The identification of the building components comprising the load-bearing components and associated waterproofing system.

(2) The current physical condition of the load-bearing components and associated waterproofing system, including whether the condition presents an immediate threat to the health and safety of the residents.

(3) The expected future performance and remaining useful life of the load-bearing components and associated waterproofing system.

(4) Recommendations for any necessary repair or replacement of the load-bearing components and associated waterproofing system.

(f) The report issued pursuant to subdivision (e) shall be stamped or signed by the inspector, presented to the board, and incorporated into the study required by Section 5550.

(g)(1) If, after inspection of any exterior elevated element, the inspector advises that the exterior elevated element poses an immediate threat to the safety of the occupants, the inspector shall provide a copy of the inspection report to the association immediately upon completion of the report, and to the local code enforcement agency within 15 days of completion of the report. Upon receiving the report, the association shall take preventive measures immediately, including preventing occupant access to the exterior elevated element until repairs have been inspected and approved by the local enforcement agency.

(2) Local enforcement agencies shall have the ability to recover enforcement costs associated with the requirements of this section from the association.

(h) Each subsequent visual inspection conducted under this section shall commence with the next exterior elevated

§ 5551

element identified on the random list and shall proceed in order through the list.

(i) The first inspection shall be completed by January 1, 2025, and then every nine years thereafter in coordination with the reserve study inspection pursuant to Section 5550. All written reports shall be maintained for two inspection cycles as records of the association.

(j)(1) The association shall be responsible for complying with the requirements of this section.

(2) The continued and ongoing maintenance and repair of the load-bearing components and associated waterproofing systems in a safe, functional, and sanitary condition shall be the responsibility of the association as required by the association's governing documents.

(k) The inspection of buildings for which a building permit application has been submitted on or after January 1, 2020, shall occur no later than six years following the issuance of a certificate of occupancy. The inspection shall otherwise comply with the provisions of this section.

(*l*) This section shall only apply to buildings containing three or more multifamily dwelling units.

(m) The association board may enact rules or bylaws imposing requirements greater than those imposed by this section.

(n) A local government or local enforcement agency may enact an ordinance or other rule imposing requirements greater than those imposed by this section. *(Added by Stats.2019, c. 207 (S.B.326), § 1, eff. Jan. 1, 2020.)*

§ 5560. Reserve funding plan; inclusion of schedule of change in assessments; adoption by board; separate approval of assessment increase

(a) The reserve funding plan required by Section 5550 shall include a schedule of the date and amount of any change in regular or special assessments that would be needed to sufficiently fund the reserve funding plan.

(b) The plan shall be adopted by the board at an open meeting before the membership of the association as described in Article 2 (commencing with Section 4900) of Chapter 6.

(c) If the board determines that an assessment increase is necessary to fund the reserve funding plan, any increase shall be approved in a separate action of the board that is consistent with the procedure described in Section 5605. *(Added by Stats.2012, c. 180 (A.B.805), § 2, operative Jan. 1, 2014.)*

Cross References

Annual budget report, contents, see Civil Code § 5300.

§ 5565. Summary of association's reserves; contents

The summary of the association's reserves required by paragraph (2) of subdivision (b) of Section 5300 shall be based on the most recent review or study conducted pursuant to Section 5550, shall be based only on assets held in cash or cash equivalents, shall be printed in boldface type, and shall include all of the following:

(a) The current estimated replacement cost, estimated remaining life, and estimated useful life of each major component.

(b) As of the end of the fiscal year for which the study is prepared:

(1) The current estimate of the amount of cash reserves necessary to repair, replace, restore, or maintain the major components.

(2) The current amount of accumulated cash reserves actually set aside to repair, replace, restore, or maintain major components.

(3) If applicable, the amount of funds received from either a compensatory damage award or settlement to an association from any person for injuries to property, real or personal, arising out of any construction or design defects, and the expenditure or disposition of funds, including the amounts expended for the direct and indirect costs of repair of construction or design defects. These amounts shall be reported at the end of the fiscal year for which the study is prepared as separate line items under cash reserves pursuant to paragraph (2). Instead of complying with the requirements set forth in this paragraph, an association that is obligated to issue a review of its financial statement pursuant to Section 5305 may include in the review a statement containing all of the information required by this paragraph.

(c) The percentage that the amount determined for purposes of paragraph (2) of subdivision (b) equals the amount determined for purposes of paragraph (1) of subdivision (b).

(d) The current deficiency in reserve funding expressed on a per unit basis. The figure shall be calculated by subtracting the amount determined for purposes of paragraph (2) of subdivision (b) from the amount determined for purposes of paragraph (1) of subdivision (b) and then dividing the result by the number of separate interests within the association, except that if assessments vary by the size or type of ownership interest, then the association shall calculate the current deficiency in a manner that reflects the variation. *(Added by Stats.2012, c. 180 (A.B.805), § 2, operative Jan. 1, 2014.)*

Cross References

Association records, time periods of required availability, see Civil Code § 5210.

Real estate broker license renewal, course work in common interest development law, number of clock hours required, see Business and Professions Code § 10170.5.

Real estate broker licensure, proof of course completion in common interest development law, number of course equivalency hours required, see Business and Professions Code § 10153.2.

Subdivided lands, sale or lease of any lot or parcel in subdivision, copies of specified documents for prospective purchasers or lessees, see Business and Professions Code § 11018.6.

§ 5570. Form for disclosure of fiscal matters

(a) The disclosures required by this article with regard to an association or a property shall be summarized on the following form:

Assessment and Reserve Funding Disclosure Summary
For the Fiscal Year Ending ____

(1) The regular assessment per ownership interest is $____ per ____. Note: If assessments vary by the size or type of ownership interest, the assessment applicable to this ownership interest may be found on page ____ of the attached summary.

(2) Additional regular or special assessments that have already been scheduled to be imposed or charged, regardless of the purpose, if they have been approved by the board and/or members:

Date assessment will be due:	Amount per ownership interest per month or year (If assessments are variable, see note immediately below):	Purpose of the assessment:
	Total:	

Note: If assessments vary by the size or type of ownership interest, the assessment applicable to this ownership interest may be found on page ____ of the attached report.

(3) Based upon the most recent reserve study and other information available to the board of directors, will currently projected reserve account balances be sufficient at the end of each year to meet the association's obligation for repair and/or replacement of major components during the next 30 years?
Yes ____ No ____

(4) If the answer to (3) is no, what additional assessments or other contributions to reserves would be necessary to ensure that sufficient reserve funds will be available each year during the next 30 years that have not yet been approved by the board or the members?

Approximate date assessment will be due:	Amount per ownership interest per month or year:
	Total:

(5) All major components are included in the reserve study and are included in its calculations.

(6) Based on the method of calculation in paragraph (4) of subdivision (b) of Section 5570, the estimated amount required in the reserve fund at the end of the current fiscal year is $____, based in whole or in part on the last reserve study or update prepared by ____ as of ____ (month), ____ (year). The projected reserve fund cash balance at the end of the current fiscal year is $____, resulting in reserves being ____ percent funded at this date.

If an alternate, but generally accepted, method of calculation is also used, the required reserve amount is $____. (See attached explanation)

(7) Based on the method of calculation in paragraph (4) of subdivision (b) of Section 5570 of the Civil Code, the estimated amount required in the reserve fund at the end of each of the next five budget years is $____, and the projected reserve fund cash balance in each of those years, taking into account only assessments already approved and other known revenues, is $____, leaving the reserve at ____ percent funded. If the reserve funding plan approved by the association is implemented, the projected reserve fund cash balance in each of those years will be $____, leaving the reserve at ____ percent funded.

Note: The financial representations set forth in this summary are based on the best estimates of the preparer at that time. The estimates are subject to change. At the time this summary was prepared, the assumed long-term before-tax interest rate earned on reserve funds was ____ percent per year, and the assumed long-term inflation rate to be applied to major component repair and replacement costs was ____ percent per year.

(b) For the purposes of preparing a summary pursuant to this section:

(1) "Estimated remaining useful life" means the time reasonably calculated to remain before a major component will require replacement.

(2) "Major component" has the meaning used in Section 5550. Components with an estimated remaining useful life of more than 30 years may be included in a study as a capital asset or disregarded from the reserve calculation, so long as the decision is revealed in the reserve study report and reported in the Assessment and Reserve Funding Disclosure Summary.

(3) The form set out in subdivision (a) shall accompany each annual budget report or summary thereof that is delivered pursuant to Section 5300. The form may be supplemented or modified to clarify the information delivered, so long as the minimum information set out in subdivision (a) is provided.

(4) For the purpose of the report and summary, the amount of reserves needed to be accumulated for a component at a given time shall be computed as the current cost of replacement or repair multiplied by the number of years the component has been in service divided by the useful life of the component. This shall not be construed to require the board to fund reserves in accordance with this calculation. *(Added by Stats.2012, c. 180 (A.B.805), § 2, operative Jan. 1, 2014. Amended by Stats.2015, c. 349 (A.B.1516), § 1, eff. Jan. 1, 2016; Stats.2016, c. 714 (S.B.944), § 8, eff. Jan. 1, 2017.)*

Cross References

Annual budget report, contents, see Civil Code § 5300.

§ 5580. Community service organization reports; information on components to complete disclosures or reserve reports; reliance upon and access to information

(a) Unless the governing documents impose more stringent standards, any community service organization whose funding from the association or its members exceeds 10 percent of the organization's annual budget shall prepare and distribute to the association a report that meets the requirements of Section 5012 of the Corporations Code, and that describes in detail administrative costs and identifies the payees of those costs in a manner consistent with the provisions of Article 5 (commencing with Section 5200) of Chapter 6.

(b) If the community service organization does not comply with the standards, the report shall disclose the noncompliance in detail. If a community service organization is responsible for the maintenance of major components for which an association would otherwise be responsible, the community service organization shall supply to the association the information regarding those components that the association would use to complete disclosures and reserve reports required under this article and Section 5300. An association may rely upon information received from a community service organization, and shall provide access to the information pursuant to the provisions of Article 5 (commencing with Section 5200) of Chapter 6. *(Added by Stats.2012, c. 180 (A.B.805), § 2, operative Jan. 1, 2014.)*

CHAPTER 8. ASSESSMENTS AND ASSESSMENT COLLECTION

Article	Section
1. Establishment and Imposition of Assessments	5600
2. Assessment Payment and Delinquency	5650
3. Assessment Collection	5700

ARTICLE 1. ESTABLISHMENT AND IMPOSITION OF ASSESSMENTS

Section
5600. Levy of assessments; limit on amount.
5605. Limitation on increases.
5610. Increases for emergency situations.
5615. Individual notice of increases.
5620. Exemption from execution by judgment creditor of association.
5625. Levies on separate interests.

§ 5600. Levy of assessments; limit on amount

(a) Except as provided in Section 5605, the association shall levy regular and special assessments sufficient to perform its obligations under the governing documents and this act.

(b) An association shall not impose or collect an assessment or fee that exceeds the amount necessary to defray the costs for which it is levied. *(Added by Stats.2012, c. 180 (A.B.805), § 2, operative Jan. 1, 2014.)*

§ 5605. Limitation on increases

(a) Annual increases in regular assessments for any fiscal year shall not be imposed unless the board has complied with paragraphs (1), (2), (4), (5), (6), (7), and (8) of subdivision (b) of Section 5300 with respect to that fiscal year, or has obtained the approval of a majority of a quorum of members, pursuant to Section 4070, at a member meeting or election.

(b) Notwithstanding more restrictive limitations placed on the board by the governing documents, the board may not impose a regular assessment that is more than 20 percent greater than the regular assessment for the association's preceding fiscal year or impose special assessments which in the aggregate exceed 5 percent of the budgeted gross expenses of the association for that fiscal year without the approval of a majority of a quorum of members, pursuant to Section 4070, at a member meeting or election.

(c) For the purposes of this section, "quorum" means more than 50 percent of the members. *(Added by Stats.2012, c. 180 (A.B.805), § 2, operative Jan. 1, 2014.)*

Cross References

Reserve funding plan, inclusion of schedule of change in assessments, adoption by board, separate approval of assessment increase, see Civil Code § 5560.
Temporary transfers to general operating fund, see Civil Code § 5515.

§ 5610. Increases for emergency situations

Section 5605 does not limit assessment increases necessary for emergency situations. For purposes of this section, an emergency situation is any one of the following:

(a) An extraordinary expense required by an order of a court.

(b) An extraordinary expense necessary to repair or maintain the common interest development or any part of it for which the association is responsible where a threat to personal safety on the property is discovered.

(c) An extraordinary expense necessary to repair or maintain the common interest development or any part of it for which the association is responsible that could not have been reasonably foreseen by the board in preparing and distributing the annual budget report under Section 5300. However, prior to the imposition or collection of an assessment under this subdivision, the board shall pass a resolution containing written findings as to the necessity of the extraordinary expense involved and why the expense was not or could not have been reasonably foreseen in the budgeting process, and the resolution shall be distributed to the members with the notice of assessment. *(Added by Stats.2012, c. 180 (A.B.805), § 2, operative Jan. 1, 2014.)*

§ 5615. Individual notice of increases

The association shall provide individual notice pursuant to Section 4040 to the members of any increase in the regular or special assessments of the association, not less than 30 nor more than 60 days prior to the increased assessment becoming due. *(Added by Stats.2012, c. 180 (A.B.805), § 2, operative Jan. 1, 2014.)*

§ 5620. Exemption from execution by judgment creditor of association

(a) Regular assessments imposed or collected to perform the obligations of an association under the governing documents or this act shall be exempt from execution by a judgment creditor of the association only to the extent necessary for the association to perform essential services, such as paying for utilities and insurance. In determining the appropriateness of an exemption, a court shall ensure that only essential services are protected under this subdivision.

(b) This exemption shall not apply to any consensual pledges, liens, or encumbrances that have been approved by a majority of a quorum of members, pursuant to Section 4070, at a member meeting or election, or to any state tax lien, or to any lien for labor or materials supplied to the common area. *(Added by Stats.2012, c. 180 (A.B.805), § 2, operative Jan. 1, 2014.)*

§ 5625. Levies on separate interests

(a) Except as provided in subdivision (b), notwithstanding any provision of this act or the governing documents to the contrary, an association shall not levy assessments on separate interests within the common interest development based on the taxable value of the separate interests unless the association, on or before December 31, 2009, in accordance with its governing documents, levied assessments on those separate interests based on their taxable value, as determined by the tax assessor of the county in which the separate interests are located.

(b) An association that is responsible for paying taxes on the separate interests within the common interest development may levy that portion of assessments on separate interests that is related to the payment of taxes based on the taxable value of the separate interest, as determined by the tax assessor. *(Added by Stats.2012, c. 180 (A.B.805), § 2, operative Jan. 1, 2014.)*

ARTICLE 2. ASSESSMENT PAYMENT AND DELINQUENCY

Section
5650. Debt of owner of separate interest; time of delinquency; interest.
5655. Application of payment; receipt; mailing address for overnight payment.
5658. Disputed charge or sum levied by association; payment under protest; action in small claims court.
5660. Notice; contents.
5665. Payment plans; request; meeting; contents; default.
5670. Dispute resolution.
5673. Recording lien; decision made by board.
5675. Lien on separate interest; notice of delinquent assessment.
5680. Priority.
5685. Recording of lien.
5690. Recommencement of notice process for failure to comply with procedures.

Cross References

Assessment collection, enforcement of lien, see Civil Code § 5700.
Individual delivery or individual notice, see Civil Code § 4040.

Sale or title transfer, provision of specified items to prospective purchasers, see Civil Code § 4525.

§ 5650. Debt of owner of separate interest; time of delinquency; interest

(a) A regular or special assessment and any late charges, reasonable fees and costs of collection, reasonable attorney's fees, if any, and interest, if any, as determined in accordance with subdivision (b), shall be a debt of the owner of the separate interest at the time the assessment or other sums are levied.

(b) Regular and special assessments levied pursuant to the governing documents are delinquent 15 days after they become due, unless the declaration provides a longer time period, in which case the longer time period shall apply. If an assessment is delinquent, the association may recover all of the following:

(1) Reasonable costs incurred in collecting the delinquent assessment, including reasonable attorney's fees.

(2) A late charge not exceeding 10 percent of the delinquent assessment or ten dollars ($10), whichever is greater, unless the declaration specifies a late charge in a smaller amount, in which case any late charge imposed shall not exceed the amount specified in the declaration.

(3) Interest on all sums imposed in accordance with this section, including the delinquent assessments, reasonable fees and costs of collection, and reasonable attorney's fees, at an annual interest rate not to exceed 12 percent, commencing 30 days after the assessment becomes due, unless the declaration specifies the recovery of interest at a rate of a lesser amount, in which case the lesser rate of interest shall apply.

(c) Associations are hereby exempted from interest-rate limitations imposed by Article XV of the California Constitution, subject to the limitations of this section. *(Added by Stats.2012, c. 180 (A.B.805), § 2, operative Jan. 1, 2014.)*

Cross References

Sales of a separate interest in a common interest development, right of redemption, see Code of Civil Procedure § 729.035.

§ 5655. Application of payment; receipt; mailing address for overnight payment

(a) Any payments made by the owner of a separate interest toward a debt described in subdivision (a) of Section 5650 shall first be applied to the assessments owed, and, only after the assessments owed are paid in full shall the payments be applied to the fees and costs of collection, attorney's fees, late charges, or interest.

(b) When an owner makes a payment, the owner may request a receipt and the association shall provide it. The receipt shall indicate the date of payment and the person who received it.

(c) The association shall provide a mailing address for overnight payment of assessments. The address shall be provided in the annual policy statement. *(Added by Stats. 2012, c. 180 (A.B.805), § 2, operative Jan. 1, 2014.)*

Cross References

Annual policy statement, contents, see Civil Code § 5310.

§ 5658. Disputed charge or sum levied by association; payment under protest; action in small claims court

(a) If a dispute exists between the owner of a separate interest and the association regarding any disputed charge or sum levied by the association, including, but not limited to, an assessment, fine, penalty, late fee, collection cost, or monetary penalty imposed as a disciplinary measure, and the amount in dispute does not exceed the jurisdictional limits of the small claims court stated in Sections 116.220 and 116.221 of the Code of Civil Procedure, the owner of the separate interest may, in addition to pursuing dispute resolution pursuant to Article 3 (commencing with Section 5925) of Chapter 10, pay under protest the disputed amount and all other amounts levied, including any fees and reasonable costs of collection, reasonable attorney's fees, late charges, and interest, if any, pursuant to subdivision (b) of Section 5650, and commence an action in small claims court pursuant to Chapter 5.5 (commencing with Section 116.110) of Title 1 of the Code of Civil Procedure.

(b) Nothing in this section shall impede an association's ability to collect delinquent assessments as provided in this article or Article 3 (commencing with Section 5700). (Added by Stats.2012, c. 180 (A.B.805), § 2, operative Jan. 1, 2014.)

§ 5660. Notice; contents

At least 30 days prior to recording a lien upon the separate interest of the owner of record to collect a debt that is past due under Section 5650, the association shall notify the owner of record in writing by certified mail of the following:

(a) A general description of the collection and lien enforcement procedures of the association and the method of calculation of the amount, a statement that the owner of the separate interest has the right to inspect the association records pursuant to Section 5205, and the following statement in 14-point boldface type, if printed, or in capital letters, if typed:

"IMPORTANT NOTICE: IF YOUR SEPARATE INTEREST IS PLACED IN FORECLOSURE BECAUSE YOU ARE BEHIND IN YOUR ASSESSMENTS, IT MAY BE SOLD WITHOUT COURT ACTION."

(b) An itemized statement of the charges owed by the owner, including items on the statement which indicate the amount of any delinquent assessments, the fees and reasonable costs of collection, reasonable attorney's fees, any late charges, and interest, if any.

(c) A statement that the owner shall not be liable to pay the charges, interest, and costs of collection, if it is determined the assessment was paid on time to the association.

(d) The right to request a meeting with the board as provided in Section 5665.

(e) The right to dispute the assessment debt by submitting a written request for dispute resolution to the association pursuant to the association's "meet and confer" program required in Article 2 (commencing with Section 5900) of Chapter 10.

(f) The right to request alternative dispute resolution with a neutral third party pursuant to Article 3 (commencing with Section 5925) of Chapter 10 before the association may initiate foreclosure against the owner's separate interest, except that binding arbitration shall not be available if the association intends to initiate a judicial foreclosure. (Added by Stats.2012, c. 180 (A.B.805), § 2, operative Jan. 1, 2014.)

Cross References

Sales of a separate interest in a common interest development, right of redemption, see Code of Civil Procedure § 729.035.

§ 5665. Payment plans; request; meeting; contents; default

(a) An owner, other than an owner of any interest that is described in Section 11212 of the Business and Professions Code that is not otherwise exempt from this section pursuant to subdivision (a) of Section 11211.7 of the Business and Professions Code, may submit a written request to meet with the board to discuss a payment plan for the debt noticed pursuant to Section 5660. The association shall provide the owners the standards for payment plans, if any exists.

(b) The board shall meet with the owner in executive session within 45 days of the postmark of the request, if the request is mailed within 15 days of the date of the postmark of the notice, unless there is no regularly scheduled board meeting within that period, in which case the board may designate a committee of one or more directors to meet with the owner.

(c) Payment plans may incorporate any assessments that accrue during the payment plan period. Additional late fees shall not accrue during the payment plan period if the owner is in compliance with the terms of the payment plan.

(d) Payment plans shall not impede an association's ability to record a lien on the owner's separate interest to secure payment of delinquent assessments.

(e) In the event of a default on any payment plan, the association may resume its efforts to collect the delinquent assessments from the time prior to entering into the payment plan. (Added by Stats.2012, c. 180 (A.B.805), § 2, operative Jan. 1, 2014.)

Cross References

Board meetings, executive session, see Civil Code § 4935.
Sales of a separate interest in a common interest development, right of redemption, see Code of Civil Procedure § 729.035.

§ 5670. Dispute resolution

Prior to recording a lien for delinquent assessments, an association shall offer the owner and, if so requested by the owner, participate in dispute resolution pursuant to the association's "meet and confer" program required in Article 2 (commencing with Section 5900) of Chapter 10. (Added by Stats.2012, c. 180 (A.B.805), § 2, operative Jan. 1, 2014.)

Cross References

Sales of a separate interest in a common interest development, right of redemption, see Code of Civil Procedure § 729.035.

§ 5673. Recording lien; decision made by board

For liens recorded on or after January 1, 2006, the decision to record a lien for delinquent assessments shall be made only by the board and may not be delegated to an agent of the association. The board shall approve the decision by a majority vote of the directors in an open meeting. The board shall record the vote in the minutes of that meeting. (Added by Stats.2012, c. 180 (A.B.805), § 2, operative Jan. 1, 2014.)

Cross References

Sales of a separate interest in a common interest development, right of redemption, see Code of Civil Procedure § 729.035.

§ 5675. Lien on separate interest; notice of delinquent assessment

(a) The amount of the assessment, plus any costs of collection, late charges, and interest assessed in accordance with subdivision (b) of Section 5650, shall be a lien on the owner's separate interest in the common interest development from and after the time the association causes to be recorded with the county recorder of the county in which the separate interest is located, a notice of delinquent assessment, which shall state the amount of the assessment and other sums imposed in accordance with subdivision (b) of Section 5650, a legal description of the owner's separate interest in the common interest development against which the assessment and other sums are levied, and the name of the record owner of the separate interest in the common interest development against which the lien is imposed.

(b) The itemized statement of the charges owed by the owner described in subdivision (b) of Section 5660 shall be recorded together with the notice of delinquent assessment.

(c) In order for the lien to be enforced by nonjudicial foreclosure as provided in Sections 5700 to 5710, inclusive, the notice of delinquent assessment shall state the name and address of the trustee authorized by the association to enforce the lien by sale.

(d) The notice of delinquent assessment shall be signed by the person designated in the declaration or by the association for that purpose, or if no one is designated, by the president of the association.

(e) A copy of the recorded notice of delinquent assessment shall be mailed by certified mail to every person whose name is shown as an owner of the separate interest in the association's records, and the notice shall be mailed no later than 10 calendar days after recordation. (Added by Stats. 2012, c. 180 (A.B.805), § 2, operative Jan. 1, 2014.)

Cross References

Sales of a separate interest in a common interest development, right of redemption, see Code of Civil Procedure § 729.035.

§ 5680. Priority

A lien created pursuant to Section 5675 shall be prior to all other liens recorded subsequent to the notice of delinquent assessment, except that the declaration may provide for the subordination thereof to any other liens and encumbrances. (Added by Stats.2012, c. 180 (A.B.805), § 2, operative Jan. 1, 2014.)

Cross References

Sales of a separate interest in a common interest development, right of redemption, see Code of Civil Procedure § 729.035.

§ 5685. Recording of lien

(a) Within 21 days of the payment of the sums specified in the notice of delinquent assessment, the association shall record or cause to be recorded in the office of the county recorder in which the notice of delinquent assessment is recorded a lien release or notice of rescission and provide the owner of the separate interest a copy of the lien release or notice that the delinquent assessment has been satisfied.

(b) If it is determined that a lien previously recorded against the separate interest was recorded in error, the party who recorded the lien shall, within 21 calendar days, record or cause to be recorded in the office of the county recorder in which the notice of delinquent assessment is recorded a lien release or notice of rescission and provide the owner of the separate interest with a declaration that the lien filing or recording was in error and a copy of the lien release or notice of rescission.

(c) If it is determined that an association has recorded a lien for a delinquent assessment in error, the association shall promptly reverse all late charges, fees, interest, attorney's fees, costs of collection, costs imposed for the notice prescribed in Section 5660, and costs of recordation and release of the lien authorized under subdivision (b) of Section 5720, and pay all costs related to any related dispute resolution or alternative dispute resolution. (Added by Stats.2012, c. 180 (A.B.805), § 2, operative Jan. 1, 2014.)

Cross References

Sales of a separate interest in a common interest development, right of redemption, see Code of Civil Procedure § 729.035.

§ 5690. Recommencement of notice process for failure to comply with procedures

An association that fails to comply with the procedures set forth in this article shall, prior to recording a lien, recommence the required notice process. Any costs associated with recommencing the notice process shall be borne by the association and not by the owner of a separate interest. (Added by Stats.2012, c. 180 (A.B.805), § 2, operative Jan. 1, 2014.)

Cross References

Sales of a separate interest in a common interest development, right of redemption, see Code of Civil Procedure § 729.035.

ARTICLE 3. ASSESSMENT COLLECTION

Section
5700. Enforcement of lien.
5705. Debts for assessments that arise on and after Jan. 1, 2006; dispute resolution; board to make decision to initiate foreclosure of lien; notice.
5710. Trustee sale; procedure; notice; trustee fees.
5715. Debts for assessments that arise on and after Jan. 1, 2006; nonjudicial foreclosure.
5720. Debts for assessments that arise on and after Jan. 1, 2006; collection of delinquent assessments; application of limitation on foreclosure of assessment liens.
5725. Monetary charge for repair of damage to common area and facilities; monetary penalties.
5730. Inclusion of notice in annual policy statement.
5735. Assignment or pledge prohibited; exception.
5740. Application of article to liens.

GENERAL PROVISIONS

Cross References

Disputed charge or sum levied by association, payment under protest, action in small claims court, see Civil Code § 5658.

§ 5700. Enforcement of lien

(a) Except as otherwise provided in this article, after the expiration of 30 days following the recording of a lien created pursuant to Section 5675, the lien may be enforced in any manner permitted by law, including sale by the court, sale by the trustee designated in the notice of delinquent assessment, or sale by a trustee substituted pursuant to Section 2934a.

(b) Nothing in Article 2 (commencing with Section 5650) or in subdivision (a) of Section 726 of the Code of Civil Procedure prohibits actions against the owner of a separate interest to recover sums for which a lien is created pursuant to Article 2 (commencing with Section 5650) or prohibits an association from taking a deed in lieu of foreclosure. (Added by Stats.2012, c. 180 (A.B.805), § 2, operative Jan. 1, 2014.)

Cross References

Sales of a separate interest in a common interest development, right of redemption, see Code of Civil Procedure § 729.035.

§ 5705. Debts for assessments that arise on and after Jan. 1, 2006; dispute resolution; board to make decision to initiate foreclosure of lien; notice

(a) Notwithstanding any law or any provisions of the governing documents to the contrary, this section shall apply to debts for assessments that arise on and after January 1, 2006.

(b) Prior to initiating a foreclosure on an owner's separate interest, the association shall offer the owner and, if so requested by the owner, participate in dispute resolution pursuant to the association's "meet and confer" program required in Article 2 (commencing with Section 5900) of Chapter 10 or alternative dispute resolution as set forth in Article 3 (commencing with Section 5925) of Chapter 10. The decision to pursue dispute resolution or a particular type of alternative dispute resolution shall be the choice of the owner, except that binding arbitration shall not be available if the association intends to initiate a judicial foreclosure.

(c) The decision to initiate foreclosure of a lien for delinquent assessments that has been validly recorded shall be made only by the board and may not be delegated to an agent of the association. The board shall approve the decision by a majority vote of the directors in an executive session. The board shall record the vote in the minutes of the next meeting of the board open to all members. The board shall maintain the confidentiality of the owner or owners of the separate interest by identifying the matter in the minutes by the parcel number of the property, rather than by the name of the owner or owners. A board vote to approve foreclosure of a lien shall take place at least 30 days prior to any public sale.

(d) The board shall provide notice by personal service in accordance with the manner of service of summons in Article 3 (commencing with Section 415.10) of Chapter 4 of Title 5 of Part 2 of the Code of Civil Procedure to an owner of a separate interest who occupies the separate interest or to the owner's legal representative, if the board votes to foreclose upon the separate interest. The board shall provide written notice to an owner of a separate interest who does not occupy the separate interest by first-class mail, postage prepaid, at the most current address shown on the books of the association. In the absence of written notification by the owner to the association, the address of the owner's separate interest may be treated as the owner's mailing address. (Added by Stats.2012, c. 180 (A.B.805), § 2, operative Jan. 1, 2014.)

Cross References

Assessment payment and delinquency, lien on separate interest, see Civil Code § 5675.

Sales of a separate interest in a common interest development, right of redemption, see Code of Civil Procedure § 729.035.

§ 5710. Trustee sale; procedure; notice; trustee fees

(a) Any sale by the trustee shall be conducted in accordance with Sections 2924, 2924b, and 2924c applicable to the exercise of powers of sale in mortgages and deeds of trust.

(b) In addition to the requirements of Section 2924, the association shall serve a notice of default on the person named as the owner of the separate interest in the association's records or, if that person has designated a legal representative pursuant to this subdivision, on that legal representative. Service shall be in accordance with the manner of service of summons in Article 3 (commencing with Section 415.10) of Chapter 4 of Title 5 of Part 2 of the Code of Civil Procedure. An owner may designate a legal representative in a writing that is mailed to the association in a manner that indicates that the association has received it.

(c) The fees of a trustee may not exceed the amounts prescribed in Sections 2924c and 2924d, plus the cost of service for either of the following:

(1) The notice of default pursuant to subdivision (b).

(2) The decision of the board to foreclose upon the separate interest of an owner as described in subdivision (d) of Section 5705. (Added by Stats.2012, c. 180 (A.B.805), § 2, operative Jan. 1, 2014.)

Cross References

Assessment payment and delinquency, lien on separate interest, see Civil Code § 5675.

Individual delivery or individual notice, see Civil Code § 4040.

Sales of a separate interest in a common interest development, right of redemption, see Code of Civil Procedure § 729.035.

§ 5715. Debts for assessments that arise on and after Jan. 1, 2006; nonjudicial foreclosure

(a) Notwithstanding any law or any provisions of the governing documents to the contrary, this section shall apply to debts for assessments that arise on and after January 1, 2006.

(b) A nonjudicial foreclosure by an association to collect upon a debt for delinquent assessments shall be subject to a right of redemption. The redemption period within which the separate interest may be redeemed from a foreclosure sale under this paragraph ends 90 days after the sale. In addition to the requirements of Section 2924f, a notice of sale in connection with an association's foreclosure of a separate interest in a common interest development shall include a statement that the property is being sold subject to the right of redemption created in this section. *(Added by Stats.2012, c. 180 (A.B.805), § 2, operative Jan. 1, 2014.)*

Cross References

Sales of a separate interest in a common interest development, right of redemption, see Code of Civil Procedure § 729.035.

§ 5720. Debts for assessments that arise on and after Jan. 1, 2006; collection of delinquent assessments; application of limitation on foreclosure of assessment liens

(a) Notwithstanding any law or any provisions of the governing documents to the contrary, this section shall apply to debts for assessments that arise on and after January 1, 2006.

(b) An association that seeks to collect delinquent regular or special assessments of an amount less than one thousand eight hundred dollars ($1,800), not including any accelerated assessments, late charges, fees and costs of collection, attorney's fees, or interest, may not collect that debt through judicial or nonjudicial foreclosure, but may attempt to collect or secure that debt in any of the following ways:

(1) By a civil action in small claims court, pursuant to Chapter 5.5 (commencing with Section 116.110) of Title 1 of Part 1 of the Code of Civil Procedure. An association that chooses to proceed by an action in small claims court, and prevails, may enforce the judgment as permitted under Article 8 (commencing with Section 116.810) of Chapter 5.5 of Title 1 of Part 1 of the Code of Civil Procedure. The amount that may be recovered in small claims court to collect upon a debt for delinquent assessments may not exceed the jurisdictional limits of the small claims court and shall be the sum of the following:

(A) The amount owed as of the date of filing the complaint in the small claims court proceeding.

(B) In the discretion of the court, an additional amount to that described in subparagraph (A) equal to the amount owed for the period from the date the complaint is filed until satisfaction of the judgment, which total amount may include accruing unpaid assessments and any reasonable late charges, fees and costs of collection, attorney's fees, and interest, up to the jurisdictional limits of the small claims court.

(2) By recording a lien on the owner's separate interest upon which the association may not foreclose until the amount of the delinquent assessments secured by the lien, exclusive of any accelerated assessments, late charges, fees and costs of collection, attorney's fees, or interest, equals or exceeds one thousand eight hundred dollars ($1,800) or the assessments secured by the lien are more than 12 months delinquent. An association that chooses to record a lien under these provisions, prior to recording the lien, shall offer the owner and, if so requested by the owner, participate in dispute resolution as set forth in Article 2 (commencing with Section 5900) of Chapter 10.

(3) Any other manner provided by law, except for judicial or nonjudicial foreclosure.

(c) The limitation on foreclosure of assessment liens for amounts under the stated minimum in this section does not apply to any of the following:

(1) Assessments secured by a lien that are more than 12 months delinquent.

(2) Assessments owed by owners of separate interests in time-share estates, as defined in subdivision (x) of Section 11212 of the Business and Professions Code.

(3) Assessments owed by the developer. *(Added by Stats. 2012, c. 180 (A.B.805), § 2, operative Jan. 1, 2014.)*

Cross References

Assessment payment and delinquency, recording of lien, see Civil Code § 5685.

Sales of a separate interest in a common interest development, right of redemption, see Code of Civil Procedure § 729.035.

§ 5725. Monetary charge for repair of damage to common area and facilities; monetary penalties

(a) A monetary charge imposed by the association as a means of reimbursing the association for costs incurred by the association in the repair of damage to common area and facilities caused by a member or the member's guest or tenant may become a lien against the member's separate interest enforceable by the sale of the interest under Sections 2924, 2924b, and 2924c, provided the authority to impose a lien is set forth in the governing documents. It is the intent of the Legislature not to contravene Section 2792.26 of Title 10 of the California Code of Regulations, as that section appeared on January 1, 1996, for associations of subdivisions that are being sold under authority of a subdivision public report, pursuant to Part 2 (commencing with Section 11000) of Division 4 of the Business and Professions Code.

(b) A monetary penalty imposed by the association as a disciplinary measure for failure of a member to comply with the governing documents, except for the late payments, may not be characterized nor treated in the governing documents as an assessment that may become a lien against the member's separate interest enforceable by the sale of the interest under Sections 2924, 2924b, and 2924c. *(Added by Stats.2012, c. 180 (A.B.805), § 2, operative Jan. 1, 2014.)*

Cross References

Sales of a separate interest in a common interest development, right of redemption, see Code of Civil Procedure § 729.035.

§ 5730. Inclusion of notice in annual policy statement

(a) The annual policy statement, prepared pursuant to Section 5310, shall include the following notice, in at least 12-point type:

"NOTICE ASSESSMENTS AND FORECLOSURE

This notice outlines some of the rights and responsibilities of owners of property in common interest developments and the associations that manage them. Please refer to the sections of the Civil Code indicated for further information. A portion of the information in this notice applies only to liens recorded on or after January 1, 2003. You may wish to consult a lawyer if you dispute an assessment.

ASSESSMENTS AND FORECLOSURE

Assessments become delinquent 15 days after they are due, unless the governing documents provide for a longer time. The failure to pay association assessments may result in the loss of an owner's property through foreclosure. Foreclosure may occur either as a result of a court action, known as judicial foreclosure, or without court action, often referred to as nonjudicial foreclosure. For liens recorded on and after

January 1, 2006, an association may not use judicial or nonjudicial foreclosure to enforce that lien if the amount of the delinquent assessments or dues, exclusive of any accelerated assessments, late charges, fees, attorney's fees, interest, and costs of collection, is less than one thousand eight hundred dollars ($1,800). For delinquent assessments or dues in excess of one thousand eight hundred dollars ($1,800) or more than 12 months delinquent, an association may use judicial or nonjudicial foreclosure subject to the conditions set forth in Article 3 (commencing with Section 5700) of Chapter 8 of Part 5 of Division 4 of the Civil Code. When using judicial or nonjudicial foreclosure, the association records a lien on the owner's property. The owner's property may be sold to satisfy the lien if the amounts secured by the lien are not paid. (Sections 5700 through 5720 of the Civil Code, inclusive)

In a judicial or nonjudicial foreclosure, the association may recover assessments, reasonable costs of collection, reasonable attorney's fees, late charges, and interest. The association may not use nonjudicial foreclosure to collect fines or penalties, except for costs to repair common area damaged by a member or a member's guests, if the governing documents provide for this. (Section 5725 of the Civil Code)

The association must comply with the requirements of Article 2 (commencing with Section 5650) of Chapter 8 of Part 5 of Division 4 of the Civil Code when collecting delinquent assessments. If the association fails to follow these requirements, it may not record a lien on the owner's property until it has satisfied those requirements. Any additional costs that result from satisfying the requirements are the responsibility of the association. (Section 5675 of the Civil Code)

At least 30 days prior to recording a lien on an owner's separate interest, the association must provide the owner of record with certain documents by certified mail, including a description of its collection and lien enforcement procedures and the method of calculating the amount. It must also provide an itemized statement of the charges owed by the owner. An owner has a right to review the association's records to verify the debt. (Section 5660 of the Civil Code)

If a lien is recorded against an owner's property in error, the person who recorded the lien is required to record a lien release within 21 days, and to provide an owner certain documents in this regard. (Section 5685 of the Civil Code)

The collection practices of the association may be governed by state and federal laws regarding fair debt collection. Penalties can be imposed for debt collection practices that violate these laws.

PAYMENTS

When an owner makes a payment, the owner may request a receipt, and the association is required to provide it. On the receipt, the association must indicate the date of payment and the person who received it. The association must inform owners of a mailing address for overnight payments. (Section 5655 of the Civil Code)

An owner may, but is not obligated to, pay under protest any disputed charge or sum levied by the association, including, but not limited to, an assessment, fine, penalty, late fee, collection cost, or monetary penalty imposed as a disciplinary measure, and by so doing, specifically reserve the right to contest the disputed charge or sum in court or otherwise.

An owner may dispute an assessment debt by submitting a written request for dispute resolution to the association as set forth in Article 2 (commencing with Section 5900) of Chapter 10 of Part 5 of Division 4 of the Civil Code. In addition, an association may not initiate a foreclosure without participating in alternative dispute resolution with a neutral third party as set forth in Article 3 (commencing with Section 5925) of Chapter 10 of Part 5 of Division 4 of the Civil Code, if so requested by the owner. Binding arbitration shall not be available if the association intends to initiate a judicial foreclosure.

An owner is not liable for charges, interest, and costs of collection, if it is established that the assessment was paid properly on time. (Section 5685 of the Civil Code)

MEETINGS AND PAYMENT PLANS

An owner of a separate interest that is not a time-share interest may request the association to consider a payment plan to satisfy a delinquent assessment. The association must inform owners of the standards for payment plans, if any exists. (Section 5665 of the Civil Code)

The board must meet with an owner who makes a proper written request for a meeting to discuss a payment plan when the owner has received a notice of a delinquent assessment. These payment plans must conform with the payment plan standards of the association, if they exist. (Section 5665 of the Civil Code)"

(b) An association distributing the notice required by this section to an owner of an interest that is described in Section 11212 of the Business and Professions Code that is not otherwise exempt from this section pursuant to subdivision (a) of Section 11211.7 of the Business and Professions Code may delete from the notice described in subdivision (a) the portion regarding meetings and payment plans. *(Added by Stats.2012, c. 180 (A.B.805), § 2, operative Jan. 1, 2014.)*

§ 5735. Assignment or pledge prohibited; exception

(a) An association may not voluntarily assign or pledge the association's right to collect payments or assessments, or to enforce or foreclose a lien to a third party, except when the assignment or pledge is made to a financial institution or lender chartered or licensed under federal or state law, when acting within the scope of that charter or license, as security for a loan obtained by the association.

(b) Nothing in subdivision (a) restricts the right or ability of an association to assign any unpaid obligations of a former member to a third party for purposes of collection. *(Added by Stats.2012, c. 180 (A.B.805), § 2, operative Jan. 1, 2014.)*

Cross References

Sales of a separate interest in a common interest development, right of redemption, see Code of Civil Procedure § 729.035.

§ 5740. Application of article to liens

(a) Except as otherwise provided, this article applies to a lien created on or after January 1, 2003.

(b) A lien created before January 1, 2003, is governed by the law in existence at the time the lien was created. *(Added by Stats.2012, c. 180 (A.B.805), § 2, operative Jan. 1, 2014.)*

CHAPTER 9. INSURANCE AND LIABILITY

Section
5800. Tortious act or omission of volunteer officer or director of association managing residential development; liability; criteria; limitations.
5805. Tort actions against owner of separate interest; tenant-in-common in common area; association liability; insurance requirements.
5806. Maintenance of crime insurance, employee dishonesty coverage, fidelity bond coverage, or equivalent for directors, officers, and employees; amount; computer fraud; funds transfer fraud; dishonest acts by managing agent or management company.
5810. Individual notice to members of changes in insurance coverage.

§ 5800. Tortious act or omission of volunteer officer or director of association managing residential development; liability; criteria; limitations

(a) A volunteer officer or volunteer director described in subdivision (e) of an association that manages a common interest development that is residential or mixed use shall not be personally liable in excess of the coverage of insurance specified in paragraph (4) to any person who suffers injury, including, but not limited to, bodily injury, emotional distress, wrongful death, or property damage or loss as a result of the tortious act or omission of the volunteer officer or volunteer director if all of the following criteria are met:

(1) The act or omission was performed within the scope of the officer's or director's association duties.

(2) The act or omission was performed in good faith.

(3) The act or omission was not willful, wanton, or grossly negligent.

(4) The association maintained and had in effect at the time the act or omission occurred and at the time a claim is made one or more policies of insurance that shall include coverage for (A) general liability of the association and (B) individual liability of officers and directors of the association for negligent acts or omissions in that capacity; provided that both types of coverage are in the following minimum amounts:

(A) At least five hundred thousand dollars ($500,000) if the common interest development consists of 100 or fewer separate interests.

(B) At least one million dollars ($1,000,000) if the common interest development consists of more than 100 separate interests.

(b) The payment of actual expenses incurred by a director or officer in the execution of the duties of that position does not affect the director's or officer's status as a volunteer within the meaning of this section.

(c) An officer or director who at the time of the act or omission was a declarant, or who received either direct or indirect compensation as an employee from the declarant, or from a financial institution that purchased a separate interest at a judicial or nonjudicial foreclosure of a mortgage or deed of trust on real property, is not a volunteer for the purposes of this section.

(d) Nothing in this section shall be construed to limit the liability of the association for its negligent act or omission or for any negligent act or omission of an officer or director of the association.

(e) This section shall only apply to a volunteer officer or director who is a tenant of a residential separate interest in the common interest development or is an owner of no more than two separate interests and whose ownership in the common interest development consists exclusively of residential separate interests.

(f)(1) For purposes of paragraph (1) of subdivision (a), the scope of the officer's or director's association duties shall include, but shall not be limited to, both of the following decisions:

(A) Whether to conduct an investigation of the common interest development for latent deficiencies prior to the expiration of the applicable statute of limitations.

(B) Whether to commence a civil action against the builder for defects in design or construction.

(2) It is the intent of the Legislature that this section clarify the scope of association duties to which the protections against personal liability in this section apply. It is not the intent of the Legislature that these clarifications be construed to expand, or limit, the fiduciary duties owed by the directors or officers. *(Added by Stats.2012, c. 180 (A.B.805), § 2, operative Jan. 1, 2014. Amended by Stats.2017, c. 278 (A.B.1412), § 2, eff. Jan. 1, 2018.)*

§ 5805. Tort actions against owner of separate interest; tenant-in-common in common area; association liability; insurance requirements

(a) It is the intent of the Legislature to offer civil liability protection to owners of the separate interests in a common interest development that have common area owned in tenancy-in-common if the association carries a certain level of prescribed insurance that covers a cause of action in tort.

(b) Any cause of action in tort against any owner of a separate interest arising solely by reason of an ownership interest as a tenant-in-common in the common area of a common interest development shall be brought only against the association and not against the individual owners of the separate interests, if both of the insurance requirements in paragraphs (1) and (2) are met:

(1) The association maintained and has in effect for this cause of action, one or more policies of insurance that include coverage for general liability of the association.

(2) The coverage described in paragraph (1) is in the following minimum amounts:

(A) At least two million dollars ($2,000,000) if the common interest development consists of 100 or fewer separate interests.

(B) At least three million dollars ($3,000,000) if the common interest development consists of more than 100 separate interests. *(Added by Stats.2012, c. 180 (A.B.805), § 2, operative Jan. 1, 2014.)*

§ 5806. Maintenance of crime insurance, employee dishonesty coverage, fidelity bond coverage, or equivalent for directors, officers, and employees; amount; computer fraud; funds transfer fraud; dishonest acts by managing agent or management company

Unless the governing documents require greater coverage amounts, the association shall maintain crime insurance, employee dishonesty coverage, fidelity bond coverage, or their equivalent, for its directors, officers, and employees in an amount that is equal to or more than the combined amount of the reserves of the association and total assessments for three months. The coverage maintained by the association shall also include protection in an equal amount against computer fraud and funds transfer fraud. If the association uses a managing agent or management company, the association's crime insurance, employee dishonesty coverage, fidelity bond coverage, or their equivalent, shall additionally include coverage for, or otherwise be endorsed to provide coverage for, dishonest acts by that person or entity and its employees. Self-insurance does not meet the requirements of this section. (Added by Stats.2018, c. 396 (A.B. 2912), § 6, eff. Jan. 1, 2019. Amended by Stats.2021, c. 270 (A.B.1101), § 3, eff. Jan. 1, 2022.)

§ 5810. Individual notice to members of changes in insurance coverage

The association shall, as soon as reasonably practicable, provide individual notice pursuant to Section 4040 to all members if any of the policies described in the annual budget report pursuant to Section 5300 have lapsed, been canceled, and are not immediately renewed, restored, or replaced, or if there is a significant change, such as a reduction in coverage or limits or an increase in the deductible, as to any of those policies. If the association receives any notice of nonrenewal of a policy described in the annual budget report pursuant to Section 5300, the association shall immediately notify its members if replacement coverage will not be in effect by the date the existing coverage will lapse. (Added by Stats.2012, c. 180 (A.B.805), § 2, operative Jan. 1, 2014.)

Cross References

Association records, time periods of required availability, see Civil Code § 5210.

Real estate broker license renewal, course work in common interest development law, number of clock hours required, see Business and Professions Code § 10170.5.

Real estate broker licensure, proof of course completion in common interest development law, number of course equivalency hours required, see Business and Professions Code § 10153.2.

Subdivided lands, sale or lease of any lot or parcel in subdivision, copies of specified documents for prospective purchasers or lessees, see Business and Professions Code § 11018.6.

CHAPTER 10. DISPUTE RESOLUTION AND ENFORCEMENT

Article	Section
1. Discipline and Cost Reimbursement	5850
2. Internal Dispute Resolution	5900
3. Alternative Dispute Resolution Prerequisite to Civil Action	5925
4. Civil Action	5975

ARTICLE 1. DISCIPLINE AND COST REIMBURSEMENT

Section	
5850.	Monetary penalties; provision of information to members.
5855.	Board disciplinary proceedings; notice to member.
5865.	Authority of board to impose monetary penalties.
5875.	Enforcement actions for violation of governing documents during declared state or local emergency.

§ 5850. Monetary penalties; provision of information to members

(a) If an association adopts or has adopted a policy imposing any monetary penalty, including any fee, on any association member for a violation of the governing documents, including any monetary penalty relating to the activities of a guest or tenant of the member, the board shall adopt and distribute to each member, in the annual policy statement prepared pursuant to Section 5310, a schedule of the monetary penalties that may be assessed for those violations, which shall be in accordance with authorization for member discipline contained in the governing documents.

(b) Any new or revised monetary penalty that is adopted after complying with subdivision (a) may be included in a supplement that is delivered to the members individually, pursuant to Section 4040.

(c) A monetary penalty for a violation of the governing documents shall not exceed the monetary penalty stated in the schedule of monetary penalties or supplement that is in effect at the time of the violation.

(d) An association shall provide a copy of the most recently distributed schedule of monetary penalties, along with any applicable supplements to that schedule, to any member upon request. (Added by Stats.2012, c. 180 (A.B. 805), § 2, operative Jan. 1, 2014.)

§ 5855. Board disciplinary proceedings; notice to member

(a) When the board is to meet to consider or impose discipline upon a member, or to impose a monetary charge as a means of reimbursing the association for costs incurred by the association in the repair of damage to common area and facilities caused by a member or the member's guest or tenant, the board shall notify the member in writing, by either personal delivery or individual delivery pursuant to Section 4040, at least 10 days prior to the meeting.

(b) The notification shall contain, at a minimum, the date, time, and place of the meeting, the nature of the alleged violation for which a member may be disciplined or the nature of the damage to the common area and facilities for which a monetary charge may be imposed, and a statement that the member has a right to attend and may address the board at the meeting. The board shall meet in executive session if requested by the member.

(c) If the board imposes discipline on a member or imposes a monetary charge on the member for damage to the common area and facilities, the board shall provide the member a written notification of the decision, by either personal delivery or individual delivery pursuant to Section 4040, within 15 days following the action.

(d) A disciplinary action or the imposition of a monetary charge for damage to the common area shall not be effective against a member unless the board fulfills the requirements of this section. *(Added by Stats.2012, c. 180 (A.B.805), § 2, operative Jan. 1, 2014.)*

Cross References

Sale or title transfer, provision of specified items to prospective purchasers, see Civil Code § 4525.

§ 5865. Authority of board to impose monetary penalties

Nothing in Section 5850 or 5855 shall be construed to create, expand, or reduce the authority of the board to impose monetary penalties on a member for a violation of the governing documents. *(Added by Stats.2012, c. 180 (A.B. 805), § 2, operative Jan. 1, 2014.)*

§ 5875. Enforcement actions for violation of governing documents during declared state or local emergency

An association shall not pursue any enforcement actions for a violation of the governing documents, except those actions relating to the homeowner's nonpayment of assessments, during a declared state or local emergency if the nature of the emergency giving rise to the declaration makes it unsafe or impossible for the homeowner to either prevent or fix the violation. *(Added by Stats.2022, c. 858 (A.B.1410), § 4, eff. Jan. 1, 2023.)*

ARTICLE 2. INTERNAL DISPUTE RESOLUTION

Section
5900. Application of article.
5905. Fair, reasonable, and expeditious procedure to resolve disputes; use of local dispute resolution programs.
5910. Requirements of fair, reasonable, and expeditious dispute resolution program.
5910.1. Civil action; compliance with dispute resolution program.
5915. Application of section; use of procedures; dispute resolution agreements; conditions; fees.
5920. Annual policy statement; description of internal dispute resolution process.

Cross References

Assessment payment and delinquency,
  Dispute resolution, see Civil Code § 5670.
  Notice, contents, see Civil Code § 5660.
Debts for assessments that arise on and after Jan. 1, 2006,
  Collection of delinquent assessments, application of limitation on foreclosure of assessment liens, see Civil Code § 5720.
  Dispute resolution, board to make decision to initiate foreclosure of lien, see Civil Code § 5705.

§ 5900. Application of article

(a) This article applies to a dispute between an association and a member involving their rights, duties, or liabilities under this act, under the Nonprofit Mutual Benefit Corporation Law (Part 3 (commencing with Section 7110) of Division 2 of Title 1 of the Corporations Code), or under the governing documents of the common interest development or association.

(b) This article supplements, and does not replace, Article 3 (commencing with Section 5925), relating to alternative dispute resolution as a prerequisite to an enforcement action. *(Added by Stats.2012, c. 180 (A.B.805), § 2, operative Jan. 1, 2014.)*

§ 5905. Fair, reasonable, and expeditious procedure to resolve disputes; use of local dispute resolution programs

(a) An association shall provide a fair, reasonable, and expeditious procedure for resolving a dispute within the scope of this article.

(b) In developing a procedure pursuant to this article, an association shall make maximum, reasonable use of available local dispute resolution programs involving a neutral third party, including low-cost mediation programs such as those listed on the Internet Web sites of the Department of Consumer Affairs and the United States Department of Housing and Urban Development.

(c) If an association does not provide a fair, reasonable, and expeditious procedure for resolving a dispute within the scope of this article, the procedure provided in Section 5915 applies and satisfies the requirement of subdivision (a). *(Added by Stats.2012, c. 180 (A.B.805), § 2, operative Jan. 1, 2014.)*

Cross References

Proposed changes to governing documents, disapproval, board reconsideration not deemed dispute resolution under this section, see Civil Code § 4765.

§ 5910. Requirements of fair, reasonable, and expeditious dispute resolution program

A fair, reasonable, and expeditious dispute resolution procedure shall, at a minimum, satisfy all of the following requirements:

(a) The procedure may be invoked by either party to the dispute. A request invoking the procedure shall be in writing.

(b) The procedure shall provide for prompt deadlines. The procedure shall state the maximum time for the association to act on a request invoking the procedure.

(c) If the procedure is invoked by a member, the association shall participate in the procedure.

(d) If the procedure is invoked by the association, the member may elect not to participate in the procedure. If the member participates but the dispute is resolved other than by agreement of the member, the member shall have a right of appeal to the board.

(e) A written resolution, signed by both parties, of a dispute pursuant to the procedure that is not in conflict with the law or the governing documents binds the association and is judicially enforceable. A written agreement, signed by both parties, reached pursuant to the procedure that is not in conflict with the law or the governing documents binds the parties and is judicially enforceable.

(f) The procedure shall provide a means by which the member and the association may explain their positions. The member and association may be assisted by an attorney or another person in explaining their positions at their own cost.

§ 5910

(g) A member of the association shall not be charged a fee to participate in the process. *(Added by Stats.2012, c. 180 (A.B.805), § 2, operative Jan. 1, 2014. Amended by Stats. 2014, c. 411 (A.B.1738), § 1, eff. Jan. 1, 2015; Stats.2015, c. 303 (A.B.731), § 34, eff. Jan. 1, 2016.)*

§ 5910.1. Civil action; compliance with dispute resolution program

An association may not file a civil action regarding a dispute in which the member has requested dispute resolution unless the association has complied with Section 5910 by engaging in good faith in the internal dispute resolution procedures after a member invokes those procedures. *(Added by Stats.2019, c. 848 (S.B.323), § 8, eff. Jan. 1, 2020.)*

§ 5915. Application of section; use of procedures; dispute resolution agreements; conditions; fees

(a) This section applies to an association that does not otherwise provide a fair, reasonable, and expeditious dispute resolution procedure. The procedure provided in this section is fair, reasonable, and expeditious within the meaning of this article.

(b) Either party to a dispute within the scope of this article may invoke the following procedure:

(1) The party may request the other party to meet and confer in an effort to resolve the dispute. The request shall be in writing.

(2) A member of an association may refuse a request to meet and confer. The association shall not refuse a request to meet and confer.

(3) The board shall designate a director to meet and confer.

(4) The parties shall meet promptly at a mutually convenient time and place, explain their positions to each other, and confer in good faith in an effort to resolve the dispute. The parties may be assisted by an attorney or another person at their own cost when conferring.

(5) A resolution of the dispute agreed to by the parties shall be memorialized in writing and signed by the parties, including the board designee on behalf of the association.

(c) A written agreement reached under this section binds the parties and is judicially enforceable if it is signed by both parties and both of the following conditions are satisfied:

(1) The agreement is not in conflict with law or the governing documents of the common interest development or association.

(2) The agreement is either consistent with the authority granted by the board to its designee or the agreement is ratified by the board.

(d) A member shall not be charged a fee to participate in the process. *(Added by Stats.2012, c. 180 (A.B.805), § 2, operative Jan. 1, 2014. Amended by Stats.2014, c. 411 (A.B.1738), § 2, eff. Jan. 1, 2015; Stats.2015, c. 303 (A.B.731), § 35, eff. Jan. 1, 2016.)*

§ 5920. Annual policy statement; description of internal dispute resolution process

The annual policy statement prepared pursuant to Section 5310 shall include a description of the internal dispute resolution process provided pursuant to this article. *(Added by Stats.2012, c. 180 (A.B.805), § 2, operative Jan. 1, 2014.)*

ARTICLE 3. ALTERNATIVE DISPUTE RESOLUTION PREREQUISITE TO CIVIL ACTION

Section
5925. Definitions.
5930. Filing enforcement actions; application of section.
5935. Initiation of process; serving a Request for Resolution; personal delivery; acceptance or rejection of request.
5940. Timeline for completion of alternative dispute resolution; application of Evidence Code; costs.
5945. Tolling of statute of limitations.
5950. Certificates filed with initial pleading; grounds for demurrer or motion to strike.
5955. Referral of actions to alternative dispute resolution; stay of referred action; costs.
5960. Award of fees and costs.
5965. Annual summary of provisions of article; contents of summary; inclusion in annual policy statement.

Cross References

Assessment payment and delinquency, notice, contents, see Civil Code § 5660.
Common interest developments, application of internal dispute resolution provisions, see Civil Code § 5900.
Debts for assessments that arise on and after Jan. 1, 2006, dispute resolution, board to make decision to initiate foreclosure of lien, see Civil Code § 5705.

§ 5925. Definitions

As used in this article:

(a) "Alternative dispute resolution" means mediation, arbitration, conciliation, or other nonjudicial procedure that involves a neutral party in the decisionmaking process. The form of alternative dispute resolution chosen pursuant to this article may be binding or nonbinding, with the voluntary consent of the parties.

(b) "Enforcement action" means a civil action or proceeding, other than a cross-complaint, for any of the following purposes:

(1) Enforcement of this act.

(2) Enforcement of the Nonprofit Mutual Benefit Corporation Law (Part 3 (commencing with Section 7110) of Division 2 of Title 1 of the Corporations Code).

(3) Enforcement of the governing documents. *(Added by Stats.2012, c. 180 (A.B.805), § 2, operative Jan. 1, 2014.)*

§ 5930. Filing enforcement actions; application of section

(a) An association or a member may not file an enforcement action in the superior court unless the parties have endeavored to submit their dispute to alternative dispute resolution pursuant to this article.

(b) This section applies only to an enforcement action that is solely for declaratory, injunctive, or writ relief, or for that relief in conjunction with a claim for monetary damages not in excess of the jurisdictional limits stated in Sections 116.220 and 116.221 of the Code of Civil Procedure.

(c) This section does not apply to a small claims action.

(d) Except as otherwise provided by law, this section does not apply to an assessment dispute. *(Added by Stats.2012, c. 180 (A.B.805), § 2, operative Jan. 1, 2014.)*

§ 5935. Initiation of process; serving a Request for Resolution; personal delivery; acceptance or rejection of request

(a) Any party to a dispute may initiate the process required by Section 5930 by serving on all other parties to the dispute a Request for Resolution. The Request for Resolution shall include all of the following:

(1) A brief description of the dispute between the parties.

(2) A request for alternative dispute resolution.

(3) A notice that the party receiving the Request for Resolution is required to respond within 30 days of receipt or the request will be deemed rejected.

(4) If the party on whom the request is served is the member, a copy of this article.

(b) Service of the Request for Resolution shall be by personal delivery, first-class mail, express mail, facsimile transmission, or other means reasonably calculated to provide the party on whom the request is served actual notice of the request.

(c) A party on whom a Request for Resolution is served has 30 days following service to accept or reject the request. If a party does not accept the request within that period, the request is deemed rejected by the party. *(Added by Stats. 2012, c. 180 (A.B.805), § 2, operative Jan. 1, 2014.)*

§ 5940. Timeline for completion of alternative dispute resolution; application of Evidence Code; costs

(a) If the party on whom a Request for Resolution is served accepts the request, the parties shall complete the alternative dispute resolution within 90 days after the party initiating the request receives the acceptance, unless this period is extended by written stipulation signed by both parties.

(b) Chapter 2 (commencing with Section 1115) of Division 9 of the Evidence Code applies to any form of alternative dispute resolution initiated by a Request for Resolution under this article, other than arbitration.

(c) The costs of the alternative dispute resolution shall be borne by the parties. *(Added by Stats.2012, c. 180 (A.B.805), § 2, operative Jan. 1, 2014.)*

§ 5945. Tolling of statute of limitations

If a Request for Resolution is served before the end of the applicable time limitation for commencing an enforcement action, the time limitation is tolled during the following periods:

(a) The period provided in Section 5935 for response to a Request for Resolution.

(b) If the Request for Resolution is accepted, the period provided by Section 5940 for completion of alternative dispute resolution, including any extension of time stipulated to by the parties pursuant to Section 5940. *(Added by Stats.2012, c. 180 (A.B.805), § 2, operative Jan. 1, 2014.)*

§ 5950. Certificates filed with initial pleading; grounds for demurrer or motion to strike

(a) At the time of commencement of an enforcement action, the party commencing the action shall file with the initial pleading a certificate stating that one or more of the following conditions are satisfied:

(1) Alternative dispute resolution has been completed in compliance with this article.

(2) One of the other parties to the dispute did not accept the terms offered for alternative dispute resolution.

(3) Preliminary or temporary injunctive relief is necessary.

(b) Failure to file a certificate pursuant to subdivision (a) is grounds for a demurrer or a motion to strike unless the court finds that dismissal of the action for failure to comply with this article would result in substantial prejudice to one of the parties. *(Added by Stats.2012, c. 180 (A.B.805), § 2, operative Jan. 1, 2014.)*

§ 5955. Referral of actions to alternative dispute resolution; stay of referred action; costs

(a) After an enforcement action is commenced, on written stipulation of the parties, the matter may be referred to alternative dispute resolution. The referred action is stayed. During the stay, the action is not subject to the rules implementing subdivision (c) of Section 68603 of the Government Code.

(b) The costs of the alternative dispute resolution shall be borne by the parties. *(Added by Stats.2012, c. 180 (A.B.805), § 2, operative Jan. 1, 2014.)*

§ 5960. Award of fees and costs

In an enforcement action in which attorney's fees and costs may be awarded, the court, in determining the amount of the award, may consider whether a party's refusal to participate in alternative dispute resolution before commencement of the action was reasonable. *(Added by Stats.2012, c. 180 (A.B.805), § 2, operative Jan. 1, 2014.)*

§ 5965. Annual summary of provisions of article; contents of summary; inclusion in annual policy statement

(a) An association shall annually provide its members a summary of the provisions of this article that specifically references this article. The summary shall include the following language:

"Failure of a member of the association to comply with the alternative dispute resolution requirements of Section 5930 of the Civil Code may result in the loss of the member's right to sue the association or another member of the association regarding enforcement of the governing documents or the applicable law."

(b) The summary shall be included in the annual policy statement prepared pursuant to Section 5310. *(Added by Stats.2012, c. 180 (A.B.805), § 2, operative Jan. 1, 2014.)*

ARTICLE 4. CIVIL ACTION

Section
5975. Covenants and restrictions in declaration as equitable servitudes; enforcement; alternative dispute resolution.

Section
5980. Standing.
5985. Reduction of damages awarded; comparative fault of association.
5986. Authority of board to commence legal proceedings; application of section.

§ 5975. Covenants and restrictions in declaration as equitable servitudes; enforcement; alternative dispute resolution

(a) The covenants and restrictions in the declaration shall be enforceable equitable servitudes, unless unreasonable, and shall inure to the benefit of and bind all owners of separate interests in the development. Unless the declaration states otherwise, these servitudes may be enforced by any owner of a separate interest or by the association, or by both.

(b) A governing document other than the declaration may be enforced by the association against an owner of a separate interest or by an owner of a separate interest against the association.

(c) In an action to enforce the governing documents, the prevailing party shall be awarded reasonable attorney's fees and costs. (Added by Stats.2012, c. 180 (A.B.805), § 2, operative Jan. 1, 2014.)

§ 5980. Standing

An association has standing to institute, defend, settle, or intervene in litigation, arbitration, mediation, or administrative proceedings in its own name as the real party in interest and without joining with it the members, in matters pertaining to the following:

(a) Enforcement of the governing documents.

(b) Damage to the common area.

(c) Damage to a separate interest that the association is obligated to maintain or repair.

(d) Damage to a separate interest that arises out of, or is integrally related to, damage to the common area or a separate interest that the association is obligated to maintain or repair. (Added by Stats.2012, c. 180 (A.B.805), § 2, operative Jan. 1, 2014.)

Cross References

Construction defects, actions, binding effect upon original purchasers and successors-in-interest, see Civil Code § 945.

§ 5985. Reduction of damages awarded; comparative fault of association

(a) In an action maintained by an association pursuant to subdivision (b), (c), or (d) of Section 5980, the amount of damages recovered by the association shall be reduced by the amount of damages allocated to the association or its managing agents in direct proportion to their percentage of fault based upon principles of comparative fault. The comparative fault of the association or its managing agents may be raised by way of defense, but shall not be the basis for a cross-action or separate action against the association or its managing agents for contribution or implied indemnity, where the only damage was sustained by the association or its members. It is the intent of the Legislature in enacting this subdivision to require that comparative fault be pleaded as an affirmative defense, rather than a separate cause of action, where the only damage was sustained by the association or its members.

(b) In an action involving damages described in subdivision (b), (c), or (d) of Section 5980, the defendant or cross-defendant may allege and prove the comparative fault of the association or its managing agents as a setoff to the liability of the defendant or cross-defendant even if the association is not a party to the litigation or is no longer a party whether by reason of settlement, dismissal, or otherwise.

(c) Subdivisions (a) and (b) apply to actions commenced on or after January 1, 1993.

(d) Nothing in this section affects a person's liability under Section 1431, or the liability of the association or its managing agent for an act or omission that causes damages to another. (Added by Stats.2012, c. 180 (A.B.805), § 2, operative Jan. 1, 2014.)

Cross References

Construction defects, actions, binding effect upon original purchasers and successors-in-interest, see Civil Code § 945.

§ 5986. Authority of board to commence legal proceedings; application of section

(a) Subject to compliance with Section 6150, which requires the board to provide notice of a meeting with the members to discuss, among other things, problems that may lead to the filing of a civil action, before the board files a civil action against a declarant or other developer, or within 30 days after it files the action, if the association has reason to believe that the applicable statute of limitations will expire, and notwithstanding any provision to the contrary in the governing documents, the board shall have the authority to commence and pursue a claim, civil action, arbitration, prelitigation process pursuant to Section 6000 or Title 7 (commencing with Section 895) of Part 2 of Division 2, or other legal proceeding against a declarant, developer, or builder of a common interest development. If the board includes members appointed by, or affiliated with, the declarant, developer, or builder, the decision and authority to commence and pursue legal proceedings shall be vested solely in the nonaffiliated board members.

(b) The governing documents shall not impose any preconditions or limitations on the board's authority to commence and pursue any claim, civil action, arbitration, prelitigation process pursuant to Section 6000 or Title 7 (commencing with Section 895) of Part 2 of Division 2, or other legal proceeding against a declarant, developer, or builder of a common interest development. Any limitation or precondition, including, but not limited to, requiring a membership vote as a prerequisite to, or otherwise providing the declarant, developer, or builder with veto authority over, the board's commencement and pursuit of a claim, civil action, arbitration, prelitigation process, or legal proceeding against the declarant, developer, or builder, or any incidental decision of the board, including, but not limited to, retaining legal counsel or incurring costs or expenses, is unenforceable, null, and void. The failure to comply with those limitations or preconditions, if only, shall not be asserted as a defense to any claim or action described in this section.

(c) Notwithstanding subdivision (a) or (b), any provision in the governing documents imposing limitations or preconditions on the board's authority to commence and pursue claims shall be valid and enforceable if the provision is adopted solely by the nondeclarant affiliated members of the association and the provision is adopted in accordance with the requirements necessary to amend the governing documents of the association.

(d) This section applies to all governing documents, whether recorded before or after the effective date of this section, and applies retroactively to claims initiated before the effective date of this section, except if those claims have been resolved through an executed settlement, a final arbitration decision, or a final judicial decision on the merits.

(e) Nothing in this section extends any applicable statute of limitation or repose to file or initiate any claim, civil action, arbitration, prelitigation process, or other legal proceeding. Nothing in this section shall affect any other obligations of an association contained in Title 7 (commencing with Section 895) of Part 2 of Division 2, or any other provision in the covenants, conditions, and restrictions of the association related to arbitration or other alternative dispute resolution procedures. *(Added by Stats.2019, c. 207 (S.B.326), § 2, eff. Jan. 1, 2020.)*

CHAPTER 11. CONSTRUCTION DEFECT LITIGATION

Section
6000. Actions for damages against common interest development builders, developers, or general contractors.
6100. Settlement agreements regarding alleged defects; notice of resolution to members on record; disclosures.
6150. Written notice to members prior to filing civil action; contents.

§ 6000. Actions for damages against common interest development builders, developers, or general contractors

(a) Before an association files a complaint for damages against a builder, developer, or general contractor (respondent) of a common interest development based upon a claim for defects in the design or construction of the common interest development, all of the requirements of this section shall be satisfied with respect to the builder, developer, or general contractor.

(b) The association shall serve upon the respondent a "Notice of Commencement of Legal Proceedings." The notice shall be served by certified mail to the registered agent of the respondent, or if there is no registered agent, then to any officer of the respondent. If there are no current officers of the respondent, service shall be upon the person or entity otherwise authorized by law to receive service of process. Service upon the general contractor shall be sufficient to initiate the process set forth in this section with regard to any builder or developer, if the builder or developer is not amenable to service of process by the foregoing methods. This notice shall toll all applicable statutes of limitation and repose, whether contractual or statutory, by and against all potentially responsible parties, regardless of whether they were named in the notice, including claims for indemnity applicable to the claim for the period set forth in subdivision (c). The notice shall include all of the following:

(1) The name and location of the project.

(2) An initial list of defects sufficient to apprise the respondent of the general nature of the defects at issue.

(3) A description of the results of the defects, if known.

(4) A summary of the results of a survey or questionnaire distributed to homeowners to determine the nature and extent of defects, if a survey has been conducted or a questionnaire has been distributed.

(5) Either a summary of the results of testing conducted to determine the nature and extent of defects or the actual test results, if that testing has been conducted.

(c) Service of the notice shall commence a period, not to exceed 180 days, during which the association, the respondent, and all other participating parties shall try to resolve the dispute through the processes set forth in this section. This 180–day period may be extended for one additional period, not to exceed 180 days, only upon the mutual agreement of the association, the respondent, and any parties not deemed peripheral pursuant to paragraph (3) of subdivision (e). Any extensions beyond the first extension shall require the agreement of all participating parties. Unless extended, the dispute resolution process prescribed by this section shall be deemed completed. All extensions shall continue the tolling period described in subdivision (b).

(d) Within 25 days of the date the association serves the Notice of Commencement of Legal Proceedings, the respondent may request in writing to meet and confer with the board. Unless the respondent and the association otherwise agree, there shall be not more than one meeting, which shall take place no later than 10 days from the date of the respondent's written request, at a mutually agreeable time and place. The meeting shall be subject to subdivision (a) of Section 4925 and subdivisions (a) and (b) of Section 4935. The discussions at the meeting are privileged communications and are not admissible in evidence in any civil action, unless the association and the respondent consent in writing to their admission.

(e) Upon receipt of the notice, the respondent shall, within 60 days, comply with the following:

(1) The respondent shall provide the association with access to, for inspection and copying of, all plans and specifications, subcontracts, and other construction files for the project that are reasonably calculated to lead to the discovery of admissible evidence regarding the defects claimed. The association shall provide the respondent with access to, for inspection and copying of, all files reasonably calculated to lead to the discovery of admissible evidence regarding the defects claimed, including all reserve studies, maintenance records and any survey questionnaires, or results of testing to determine the nature and extent of defects. To the extent any of the above documents are withheld based on privilege, a privilege log shall be prepared and submitted to all other parties. All other potentially responsible parties shall have the same rights as the respondent regarding the production of documents upon receipt of written notice of the claim, and shall produce all relevant documents within 60 days of receipt of the notice of the claim.

(2) The respondent shall provide written notice by certified mail to all subcontractors, design professionals, their

insurers, and the insurers of any additional insured whose identities are known to the respondent or readily ascertainable by review of the project files or other similar sources and whose potential responsibility appears on the face of the notice. This notice to subcontractors, design professionals, and insurers shall include a copy of the Notice of Commencement of Legal Proceedings, and shall specify the date and manner by which the parties shall meet and confer to select a dispute resolution facilitator pursuant to paragraph (1) of subdivision (f), advise the recipient of its obligation to participate in the meet and confer or serve a written acknowledgment of receipt regarding this notice, advise the recipient that it will waive any challenge to selection of the dispute resolution facilitator if it elects not to participate in the meet and confer, advise the recipient that it may seek the assistance of an attorney, and advise the recipient that it should contact its insurer, if any. Any subcontractor or design professional, or insurer for that subcontractor, design professional, or additional insured, who receives written notice from the respondent regarding the meet and confer shall, prior to the meet and confer, serve on the respondent a written acknowledgment of receipt. That subcontractor or design professional shall, within 10 days of service of the written acknowledgment of receipt, provide to the association and the respondent a Statement of Insurance that includes both of the following:

(A) The names, addresses, and contact persons, if known, of all insurance carriers, whether primary or excess and regardless of whether a deductible or self-insured retention applies, whose policies were in effect from the commencement of construction of the subject project to the present and which potentially cover the subject claims.

(B) The applicable policy numbers for each policy of insurance provided.

(3) Any subcontractor or design professional, or insurer for that subcontractor, design professional, or additional insured, who so chooses, may, at any time, make a written request to the dispute resolution facilitator for designation as a peripheral party. That request shall be served contemporaneously on the association and the respondent. If no objection to that designation is received within 15 days, or upon rejection of that objection, the dispute resolution facilitator shall designate that subcontractor or design professional as a peripheral party, and shall thereafter seek to limit the attendance of that subcontractor or design professional only to those dispute resolution sessions deemed peripheral party sessions or to those sessions during which the dispute resolution facilitator believes settlement as to peripheral parties may be finalized. Nothing in this subdivision shall preclude a party who has been designated a peripheral party from being reclassified as a nonperipheral party, nor shall this subdivision preclude a party designated as a nonperipheral party from being reclassified as a peripheral party after notice to all parties and an opportunity to object. For purposes of this subdivision, a peripheral party is a party having total claimed exposure of less than twenty-five thousand dollars ($25,000).

(f)(1) Within 20 days of sending the notice set forth in paragraph (2) of subdivision (e), the association, respondent, subcontractors, design professionals, and their insurers who have been sent a notice as described in paragraph (2) of subdivision (e) shall meet and confer in an effort to select a dispute resolution facilitator to preside over the mandatory dispute resolution process prescribed by this section. Any subcontractor or design professional who has been given timely notice of this meeting but who does not participate, waives any challenge he or she may have as to the selection of the dispute resolution facilitator. The role of the dispute resolution facilitator is to attempt to resolve the conflict in a fair manner. The dispute resolution facilitator shall be sufficiently knowledgeable in the subject matter and be able to devote sufficient time to the case. The dispute resolution facilitator shall not be required to reside in or have an office in the county in which the project is located. The dispute resolution facilitator and the participating parties shall agree to a date, time, and location to hold a case management meeting of all parties and the dispute resolution facilitator, to discuss the claims being asserted and the scheduling of events under this section. The case management meeting with the dispute resolution facilitator shall be held within 100 days of service of the Notice of Commencement of Legal Proceedings at a location in the county where the project is located. Written notice of the case management meeting with the dispute resolution facilitator shall be sent by the respondent to the association, subcontractors and design professionals, and their insurers who are known to the respondent to be on notice of the claim, no later than 10 days prior to the case management meeting, and shall specify its date, time, and location. The dispute resolution facilitator in consultation with the respondent shall maintain a contact list of the participating parties.

(2) No later than 10 days prior to the case management meeting, the dispute resolution facilitator shall disclose to the parties all matters that could cause a person aware of the facts to reasonably entertain a doubt that the proposed dispute resolution facilitator would be able to resolve the conflict in a fair manner. The facilitator's disclosure shall include the existence of any ground specified in Section 170.1 of the Code of Civil Procedure for disqualification of a judge, any attorney-client relationship the facilitator has or had with any party or lawyer for a party to the dispute resolution process, and any professional or significant personal relationship the facilitator or his or her spouse or minor child living in the household has or had with any party to the dispute resolution process. The disclosure shall also be provided to any subsequently noticed subcontractor or design professional within 10 days of the notice.

(3) A dispute resolution facilitator shall be disqualified by the court if he or she fails to comply with this subdivision and any party to the dispute resolution process serves a notice of disqualification prior to the case management meeting. If the dispute resolution facilitator complies with this subdivision, he or she shall be disqualified by the court on the basis of the disclosure if any party to the dispute resolution process serves a notice of disqualification prior to the case management meeting.

(4) If the parties cannot mutually agree to a dispute resolution facilitator, then each party shall submit a list of three dispute resolution facilitators. Each party may then strike one nominee from the other parties' list, and petition the court, pursuant to the procedure described in subdivisions (n) and (o), for final selection of the dispute resolution

facilitator. The court may issue an order for final selection of the dispute resolution facilitator pursuant to this paragraph.

(5) Any subcontractor or design professional who receives notice of the association's claim without having previously received timely notice of the meet and confer to select the dispute resolution facilitator shall be notified by the respondent regarding the name, address, and telephone number of the dispute resolution facilitator. Any such subcontractor or design professional may serve upon the parties and the dispute resolution facilitator a written objection to the dispute resolution facilitator within 15 days of receiving notice of the claim. Within seven days after service of this objection, the subcontractor or design professional may petition the superior court to replace the dispute resolution facilitator. The court may replace the dispute resolution facilitator only upon a showing of good cause, liberally construed. Failure to satisfy the deadlines set forth in this subdivision shall constitute a waiver of the right to challenge the dispute resolution facilitator.

(6) The costs of the dispute resolution facilitator shall be apportioned in the following manner: one-third to be paid by the association; one-third to be paid by the respondent; and one-third to be paid by the subcontractors and design professionals, as allocated among them by the dispute resolution facilitator. The costs of the dispute resolution facilitator shall be recoverable by the prevailing party in any subsequent litigation pursuant to Section 1032 of the Code of Civil Procedure, provided however that any nonsettling party may, prior to the filing of the complaint, petition the facilitator to reallocate the costs of the dispute resolution facilitator as they apply to any nonsettling party. The determination of the dispute resolution facilitator with respect to the allocation of these costs shall be binding in any subsequent litigation. The dispute resolution facilitator shall take into account all relevant factors and equities between all parties in the dispute resolution process when reallocating costs.

(7) In the event the dispute resolution facilitator is replaced at any time, the case management statement created pursuant to subdivision (h) shall remain in full force and effect.

(8) The dispute resolution facilitator shall be empowered to enforce all provisions of this section.

(g)(1) No later than the case management meeting, the parties shall begin to generate a data compilation showing the following information regarding the alleged defects at issue:

(A) The scope of the work performed by each potentially responsible subcontractor.

(B) The tract or phase number in which each subcontractor provided goods or services, or both.

(C) The units, either by address, unit number, or lot number, at which each subcontractor provided goods or services, or both.

(2) This data compilation shall be updated as needed to reflect additional information. Each party attending the case management meeting, and any subsequent meeting pursuant to this section, shall provide all information available to that party relevant to this data compilation.

(h) At the case management meeting, the parties shall, with the assistance of the dispute resolution facilitator, reach agreement on a case management statement, which shall set forth all of the elements set forth in paragraphs (1) to (8), inclusive, except that the parties may dispense with one or more of these elements if they agree that it is appropriate to do so. The case management statement shall provide that the following elements shall take place in the following order:

(1) Establishment of a document depository, located in the county where the project is located, for deposit of documents, defect lists, demands, and other information provided for under this section. All documents exchanged by the parties and all documents created pursuant to this subdivision shall be deposited in the document depository, which shall be available to all parties throughout the prefiling dispute resolution process and in any subsequent litigation. When any document is deposited in the document depository, the party depositing the document shall provide written notice identifying the document to all other parties. The costs of maintaining the document depository shall be apportioned among the parties in the same manner as the costs of the dispute resolution facilitator.

(2) Provision of a more detailed list of defects by the association to the respondent after the association completes a visual inspection of the project. This list of defects shall provide sufficient detail for the respondent to ensure that all potentially responsible subcontractors and design professionals are provided with notice of the dispute resolution process. If not already completed prior to the case management meeting, the Notice of Commencement of Legal Proceedings shall be served by the respondent on all additional subcontractors and design professionals whose potential responsibility appears on the face of the more detailed list of defects within seven days of receipt of the more detailed list. The respondent shall serve a copy of the case management statement, including the name, address, and telephone number of the dispute resolution facilitator, to all the potentially responsible subcontractors and design professionals at the same time.

(3) Nonintrusive visual inspection of the project by the respondent, subcontractors, and design professionals.

(4) Invasive testing conducted by the association, if the association deems appropriate. All parties may observe and photograph any testing conducted by the association pursuant to this paragraph, but may not take samples or direct testing unless, by mutual agreement, costs of testing are shared by the parties.

(5) Provision by the association of a comprehensive demand which provides sufficient detail for the parties to engage in meaningful dispute resolution as contemplated under this section.

(6) Invasive testing conducted by the respondent, subcontractors, and design professionals, if they deem appropriate.

(7) Allowance for modification of the demand by the association if new issues arise during the testing conducted by the respondent, subcontractor, or design professionals.

(8) Facilitated dispute resolution of the claim, with all parties, including peripheral parties, as appropriate, and insurers, if any, present and having settlement authority.

The dispute resolution facilitators shall endeavor to set specific times for the attendance of specific parties at dispute resolution sessions. If the dispute resolution facilitator does not set specific times for the attendance of parties at dispute resolution sessions, the dispute resolution facilitator shall permit those parties to participate in dispute resolution sessions by telephone.

(i) In addition to the foregoing elements of the case management statement described in subdivision (h), upon mutual agreement of the parties, the dispute resolution facilitator may include any or all of the following elements in a case management statement: the exchange of consultant or expert photographs; expert presentations; expert meetings; or any other mechanism deemed appropriate by the parties in the interest of resolving the dispute.

(j) The dispute resolution facilitator, with the guidance of the parties, shall at the time the case management statement is established, set deadlines for the occurrence of each event set forth in the case management statement, taking into account such factors as the size and complexity of the case, and the requirement of this section that this dispute resolution process not exceed 180 days absent agreement of the parties to an extension of time.

(k)(1) At a time to be determined by the dispute resolution facilitator, the respondent may submit to the association all of the following:

(A) A request to meet with the board to discuss a written settlement offer.

(B) A written settlement offer, and a concise explanation of the reasons for the terms of the offer.

(C) A statement that the respondent has access to sufficient funds to satisfy the conditions of the settlement offer.

(D) A summary of the results of testing conducted for the purposes of determining the nature and extent of defects, if this testing has been conducted, unless the association provided the respondent with actual test results.

(2) If the respondent does not timely submit the items required by this subdivision, the association shall be relieved of any further obligation to satisfy the requirements of this subdivision only.

(3) No less than 10 days after the respondent submits the items required by this paragraph, the respondent and the board shall meet and confer about the respondent's settlement offer.

(4) If the board rejects a settlement offer presented at the meeting held pursuant to this subdivision, the board shall hold a meeting open to each member of the association. The meeting shall be held no less than 15 days before the association commences an action for damages against the respondent.

(5) No less than 15 days before this meeting is held, a written notice shall be sent to each member of the association specifying all of the following:

(A) That a meeting will take place to discuss problems that may lead to the filing of a civil action, and the time and place of this meeting.

(B) The options that are available to address the problems, including the filing of a civil action and a statement of the various alternatives that are reasonably foreseeable by the association to pay for those options and whether these payments are expected to be made from the use of reserve account funds or the imposition of regular or special assessments, or emergency assessment increases.

(C) The complete text of any written settlement offer, and a concise explanation of the specific reasons for the terms of the offer submitted to the board at the meeting held pursuant to subdivision (d) that was received from the respondent.

(6) The respondent shall pay all expenses attributable to sending the settlement offer to all members of the association. The respondent shall also pay the expense of holding the meeting, not to exceed three dollars ($3) per association member.

(7) The discussions at the meeting and the contents of the notice and the items required to be specified in the notice pursuant to paragraph (5) are privileged communications and are not admissible in evidence in any civil action, unless the association consents to their admission.

(8) No more than one request to meet and discuss a written settlement offer may be made by the respondent pursuant to this subdivision.

(*l*) All defect lists and demands, communications, negotiations, and settlement offers made in the course of the prelitigation dispute resolution process provided by this section shall be inadmissible pursuant to Sections 1119 to 1124, inclusive, of the Evidence Code and all applicable decisional law. This inadmissibility shall not be extended to any other documents or communications which would not otherwise be deemed inadmissible.

(m) Any subcontractor or design professional may, at any time, petition the dispute resolution facilitator to release that party from the dispute resolution process upon a showing that the subcontractor or design professional is not potentially responsible for the defect claims at issue. The petition shall be served contemporaneously on all other parties, who shall have 15 days from the date of service to object. If a subcontractor or design professional is released, and it later appears to the dispute resolution facilitator that it may be a responsible party in light of the current defect list or demand, the respondent shall renotice the party as provided by paragraph (2) of subdivision (e), provide a copy of the current defect list or demand, and direct the party to attend a dispute resolution session at a stated time and location. A party who subsequently appears after having been released by the dispute resolution facilitator shall not be prejudiced by its absence from the dispute resolution process as the result of having been previously released by the dispute resolution facilitator.

(n) Any party may, at any time, petition the superior court in the county where the project is located, upon a showing of good cause, and the court may issue an order, for any of the following, or for appointment of a referee to resolve a dispute regarding any of the following:

(1) To take a deposition of any party to the process, or subpoena a third party for deposition or production of documents, which is necessary to further prelitigation resolution of the dispute.

(2) To resolve any disputes concerning inspection, testing, production of documents, or exchange of information provided for under this section.

(3) To resolve any disagreements relative to the timing or contents of the case management statement.

(4) To authorize internal extensions of timeframes set forth in the case management statement.

(5) To seek a determination that a settlement is a good faith settlement pursuant to Section 877.6 of the Code of Civil Procedure and all related authorities. The page limitations and meet and confer requirements specified in this section shall not apply to these motions, which may be made on shortened notice. Instead, these motions shall be subject to other applicable state law, rules of court, and local rules. A determination made by the court pursuant to this motion shall have the same force and effect as the determination of a postfiling application or motion for good faith settlement.

(6) To ensure compliance, on shortened notice, with the obligation to provide a Statement of Insurance pursuant to paragraph (2) of subdivision (e).

(7) For any other relief appropriate to the enforcement of the provisions of this section, including the ordering of parties, and insurers, if any, to the dispute resolution process with settlement authority.

(o)(1) A petition filed pursuant to subdivision (n) shall be filed in the superior court in the county in which the project is located. The court shall hear and decide the petition within 10 days after filing. The petitioning party shall serve the petition on all parties, including the date, time, and location of the hearing no later than five business days prior to the hearing. Any responsive papers shall be filed and served no later than three business days prior to the hearing. Any petition or response filed under this section shall be no more than three pages in length.

(2) All parties shall meet with the dispute resolution facilitator, if one has been appointed and confer in person or by telephone prior to the filing of that petition to attempt to resolve the matter without requiring court intervention.

(p) As used in this section:

(1) "Association" shall have the same meaning as defined in Section 4080.

(2) "Builder" means the declarant, as defined in Section 4130.

(3) "Common interest development" shall have the same meaning as in Section 4100, except that it shall not include developments or projects with less than 20 units.

(q) The alternative dispute resolution process and procedures described in this section shall have no application or legal effect other than as described in this section.

(r) This section shall become operative on July 1, 2002, however it shall not apply to any pending suit or claim for which notice has previously been given.

(s) This section shall become inoperative on July 1, 2024, and, as of January 1, 2025, is repealed, unless a later enacted statute, that becomes operative on or before January 1, 2025, deletes or extends the dates on which it becomes inoperative and is repealed. *(Added by Stats.2012, c. 180 (A.B.805), § 2, operative Jan. 1, 2014. Amended by Stats.2016, c. 71 (A.B. 1963), § 1, eff. Jan. 1, 2017.)*

Inoperative Date and Repeal

For inoperative date and repeal of this section, see its terms.

Cross References

Common interest developments, dispute resolution and enforcement, civil action, authority of board to commence legal proceedings, see Civil Code § 5986.

Sale or title transfer, provision of specified items to prospective purchasers, see Civil Code § 4525.

§ 6100. Settlement agreements regarding alleged defects; notice of resolution to members on record; disclosures

(a) As soon as is reasonably practicable after the association and the builder have entered into a settlement agreement or the matter has otherwise been resolved regarding alleged defects in the common areas, alleged defects in the separate interests that the association is obligated to maintain or repair, or alleged defects in the separate interests that arise out of, or are integrally related to, defects in the common areas or separate interests that the association is obligated to maintain or repair, where the defects giving rise to the dispute have not been corrected, the association shall, in writing, inform only the members of the association whose names appear on the records of the association that the matter has been resolved, by settlement agreement or other means, and disclose all of the following:

(1) A general description of the defects that the association reasonably believes, as of the date of the disclosure, will be corrected or replaced.

(2) A good faith estimate, as of the date of the disclosure, of when the association believes that the defects identified in paragraph (1) will be corrected or replaced. The association may state that the estimate may be modified.

(3) The status of the claims for defects in the design or construction of the common interest development that were not identified in paragraph (1) whether expressed in a preliminary list of defects sent to each member of the association or otherwise claimed and disclosed to the members of the association.

(b) Nothing in this section shall preclude an association from amending the disclosures required pursuant to subdivision (a), and any amendments shall supersede any prior conflicting information disclosed to the members of the association and shall retain any privilege attached to the original disclosures.

(c) Disclosure of the information required pursuant to subdivision (a) or authorized by subdivision (b) shall not waive any privilege attached to the information.

(d) For the purposes of the disclosures required pursuant to this section, the term "defects" shall be defined to include any damage resulting from defects. *(Added by Stats.2012, c. 180 (A.B.805), § 2, operative Jan. 1, 2014.)*

Cross References

Sale or title transfer, provision of specified items to prospective purchasers, see Civil Code § 4525.

§ 6150. Written notice to members prior to filing civil action; contents

(a) Not later than 30 days before filing of any civil action by the association against the declarant or other developer of a common interest development for alleged damage to the common areas, alleged damage to the separate interests that the association is obligated to maintain or repair, or alleged damage to the separate interests that arises out of, or is integrally related to, damage to the common areas or separate interests that the association is obligated to maintain or repair, the board shall provide a written notice to each member of the association who appears on the records of the association when the notice is provided. This notice shall specify all of the following:

(1) That a meeting will take place to discuss problems that may lead to the filing of a civil action, in addition to the potential impacts thereof to the association and its members, including any financial impacts.

(2) The options, including civil actions, that are available to address the problems.

(3) The time and place of the meeting.

(b) Notwithstanding subdivision (a), if the association has reason to believe that the applicable statute of limitations will expire before the association files the civil action, the association may give the notice, as described above, within 30 days after the filing of the action. *(Added by Stats.2012, c. 180 (A.B.805), § 2, operative Jan. 1, 2014. Amended by Stats.2019, c. 207 (S.B.326), § 3, eff. Jan. 1, 2020.)*

Cross References

Commercial and industrial common interest developments, application of this section, see Civil Code § 6700.

Common interest developments, application of this section, see Civil Code § 4700.

Part 5.3

COMMERCIAL AND INDUSTRIAL COMMON INTEREST DEVELOPMENTS

Chapter	Section
1. General Provisions	6500
2. Application of Act	6580
3. Governing Documents	6600
4. Ownership and Transfer of Interests	6650
5. Property Use and Maintenance	6700
6. Association Governance	6750
7. Assessments and Assessment Collection	6800
8. Insurance and Liability	6840
9. Dispute Resolution and Enforcement	6850
10. Construction Defect Litigation	6870

Publisher's Note

The following table, showing the disposition of former Title 6 of Part 4 of Division 2 of the Civil Code (Civil Code § 1350 et seq.) into new Part 5.3 of Division 4 of the Civil Code (Civil Code § 6500 et seq.), was provided by the California Law Revision Commission, and is reproduced with minor modifications. The original table was published in the California Law Revision Commission recommendation titled "Commercial and Industrial Common Interest Developments" [42 Cal.L.Rev.Comm. Reports 1 (2012)], with revisions to the table, reflecting subsequent legislative action, published in a supplemental report titled "Report of the California Law Revision Commission on Chapter 605 of the Statutes of 2013 (Senate Bill 752)" [43 Cal.L.Rev.Comm. Reports 329 (Appendix 5) (2013)].

DISPOSITION OF FORMER LAW

The table below shows the disposition of each provision of the existing Davis–Stirling Common Interest Development Act in the proposed law. All references are to the Civil Code.

Former Provision	New Provision(s)
1350	not continued
1350.5	6502
1350.7	not continued
1351 (intro.)	6526
1351(a)	6528
1351(b)	6532
1351(c)	6534
1351(d)	not continued
1351(e)(1), (2)	6624
1351(e)(3)	6624, 6626(a)
1351(e) (next to last)	6626(b)-(c)
1351(e) (last)	6628
1351(f)	6542
1351(g)	6544
1351(h)	6546
1351(i)	6550
1351(j)	6552
1351(k)	6562
1351(*l*)	6564
1351(m)	6566
1352	6580
1352.5	6606(a)-(b), (d)
1353(a)(1) (1st & 2d sent.)	6614(a)
1353(a)(1) (except 1st & 2d sent.)-(a)(4)	not continued
1353(b)	6614(b)
1353.5	6702
1353.6	6704
1353.7	not continued (but see 6600(a))
1353.8	6712
1353.9	6713
1354(a)-(b)	6856
1354(c)	not continued
1355(a) (1st sent.)	6620(a) (1st sent.)
1355(a)(1)	6620(a)(2)
1355(a)(2)	6620(a)(3)
1355(a)(3)	6620(a)(4)
1355(b) (1st sent.)	6616
1355(b)(1)	6620(a)(1)
1355(b)(2)	6620(a)(2), 6620(b)
1355(b)(3)	6620(a)(3)
1355(b) (last sent.)	not continued
1355.5	6608
1356	not continued
1357(a)	6618(a)
1357(b) (1st sent.)	6618(b), 6620
1357(b) (2nd sent.)	not continued
1357(c)	not continued
1357(d)	6618(c)
1357.100(a)	6630
1357.100(b)	not continued
1357.110	6632
1357.120	not continued
1357.130	not continued
1357.140	not continued
1357.150	not continued
1358(a)	not continued
1358(b)	6662
1358(c)	6664
1358(d)	6666
1358 (next to last)	6668
1358 (last)	6670
1359	6656
1360	6714
1360.2	not continued
1360.5	not continued (but see 6706)
1361	6652
1361.5	6654
1362	6650
1363(a)	6750
1363(b)	not continued
1363(c)	6752
1363(d)	not continued
1363(e)	not continued
1363(f) (1st sent.)	6850
1363(f) (2nd sent.)	not continued
1363(g)	not continued
1363(h)	not continued
1363(i)	6854
1363.001	not continued
1363.005	not continued
1363.03	not continued
1363.04	not continued
1363.05	not continued
1363.07	not continued
1363.09	not continued
1363.1	not continued

GENERAL PROVISIONS

Former Provision	New Provision(s)
1363.2	not continued
1363.5	6622
1363.6	6760
1363.810	not continued
1363.820	not continued
1363.830	not continued
1363.840	not continued
1363.850	not continued
1364(a)	6716(a)
1364(b)	6718
1364(c)	6716(b)
1364(d)-(e)	6720
1364(f)	6722
1365	not continued
1365.1	not continued
1365.2	not continued
1365.2.5	not continued
1365.3	not continued
1365.5	not continued
1365.6	6758(a)
1365.7	not continued
1365.9	6840
1366(a) (1st sent.)	6800
1366(a) (except 1st sent.)	not continued
1366(b)	not continued
1366(c)	6804
1366(d)	not continued
1366(e)	not continued
1366(f)	not continued
1366.1	not continued
1366.2	not continued
1366.4	not continued
1367	not continued (but see 6828)
1367.1(a) (1st sent.)	6808(a)
1367.1(a) (2d sent.)	6812 (intro.)
1367.1(a)(1)-(3)	6812(a)-(c)
1367.1(a)(4)-(6)	not continued
1367.1(b) (1st sent.)	not continued
1367.1(b) (2nd - 4th sent.)	6810
1367.1(c)	not continued
1367.1(d) (1st - 5th sent.)	6814(a)-(e)
1367.1(d) (6th sent.)	6818(a)
1367.1(d) (7th sent.)	6824(a)
1367.1(d) (8th sent.)	not continued
1367.1(e)	6824(b)
1367.1(f)	6816
1367.1(g) (1st sent.)	6826
1367.1(g) (2d sent.)	6820(a)
1367.1(g) (3d sent.)	6822(a)
1367.1(g) (4th sent.)	6822(c) (intro.)
1367.1(g)(1)-(2)	6822(c)(1)-(2)
1367.1(h)	6820(b)
1367.1(i)	6818(b)
1367.1(j)	6822(b)
1367.1(k)	not continued
1367.1(*l*)	6819
1367.1(m)	not continued (but see 6828)
1367.1(n)	not continued
1367.4	not continued
1367.5	not continued
1367.6	not continued
1368	not continued
1368.1	6710
1368.2	not continued
1368.3	6858

Former Provision	New Provision(s)
1368.4	6860
1368.5	6876
1369	6658
1369.510	not continued
1369.520	not continued
1369.530	not continued
1369.540	not continued
1369.550	not continued
1369.560	not continued
1369.570	not continued
1369.580	not continued
1369.590	not continued
1370	6602
1371	6604
1372	6510
1373	6582(a), 6531
1374	6582(b)
1375	6870
1375.1	6874
1376	6708
1378	not continued

CHAPTER 1. GENERAL PROVISIONS

Article	Section
1. Preliminary Provisions	6500
2. Definitions	6526

ARTICLE 1. PRELIMINARY PROVISIONS

Section
6500. Short title.
6502. Effect of headings on scope, meaning, or intent of act.
6505. Continuation of prior law.
6510. Construction of zoning ordinances.
6512. Delivery of document to association.
6514. Individual delivery or individual notice.
6518. Time of delivery.
6520. Electronic delivery; satisfaction of written information requirement.
6522. Approval by majority.
6524. Approval by majority of quorum.

§ 6500. Short title

This part shall be known, and may be cited, as the Commercial and Industrial Common Interest Development Act. In a provision of this part, the part may be referred to as the act. *(Added by Stats.2013, c. 605 (S.B.752), § 21.)*

§ 6502. Effect of headings on scope, meaning, or intent of act

Division, part, title, chapter, article, and section headings do not in any manner affect the scope, meaning, or intent of this act. *(Added by Stats.2013, c. 605 (S.B.752), § 21.)*

§ 6505. Continuation of prior law

Nothing in the act that added this part shall be construed to invalidate a document prepared or action taken before January 1, 2014, if the document or action was proper under the law governing common interest developments at the time that the document was prepared or the action was taken. For the purposes of this section, "document" does not include a governing document. *(Added by Stats.2013, c. 605 (S.B.752), § 21.)*

§ 6510. Construction of zoning ordinances

Unless a contrary intent is clearly expressed, a local zoning ordinance is construed to treat like structures, lots, parcels, areas, or spaces in like manner regardless of the form of the common interest development. *(Added by Stats.2013, c. 605 (S.B.752), § 21.)*

§ 6512. Delivery of document to association

(a) If a provision of this act requires that a document be delivered to an association, the document shall be delivered to the person designated to receive documents on behalf of the association, in a written notice delivered by the association to members by individual delivery. If notice of this designation has not been given, the document shall be delivered to the president or secretary of the association.

(b) A document delivered pursuant to this section may be delivered by any of the following methods:

(1) First-class mail, postage prepaid, registered or certified mail, express mail, or overnight delivery by an express service carrier.

(2) By email, facsimile, or other electronic means, if the association has assented to that method of delivery.

(3) By personal delivery, if the association has assented to that method of delivery. If the association accepts a document by personal delivery it shall provide a written receipt acknowledging delivery of the document. *(Added by Stats.2013, c. 605 (S.B.752), § 21.)*

Cross References

Restrictive covenants, deletion from declaration or other governing document, recording or filing of amended document, see Civil Code § 6606.

§ 6514. Individual delivery or individual notice

(a) If a provision of this act requires that an association deliver a document by "individual delivery" or "individual notice," the document shall be delivered by one of the following methods:

(1) First-class mail, postage prepaid, registered or certified mail, express mail, or overnight delivery by an express service carrier. The document shall be addressed to the recipient at the address last shown on the books of the association.

(2) Email, facsimile, or other electronic means, if the recipient has consented, in writing, to that method of delivery. The consent may be revoked, in writing, by the recipient.

(b) For the purposes of this section, an unrecorded provision of the governing documents providing for a particular method of delivery does not constitute agreement by a member to that method of delivery. *(Added by Stats.2013, c. 605 (S.B.752), § 21.)*

Cross References

Amendment of governing documents to delete construction or marketing provisions after completion by developer, requirements, see Civil Code § 6608.
Claim of lien, notice to members, see Civil Code § 6660.
Service of process, generally, see Code of Civil Procedure § 410.10 et seq.
Temporary removal of occupant for treatment of wood-destroying pests or organisms, delivery of notice, see Civil Code § 6720.

§ 6518. Time of delivery

(a) This section governs the delivery of a document pursuant to this act.

(b) If a document is delivered by mail, delivery is deemed to be complete on deposit into the United States mail.

(c) If a document is delivered by electronic means, delivery is complete at the time of transmission. *(Added by Stats. 2013, c. 605 (S.B.752), § 21.)*

§ 6520. Electronic delivery; satisfaction of written information requirement

If the association or a member has consented to receive information by electronic delivery, and a provision of this act requires that the information be in writing, that requirement is satisfied if the information is provided in an electronic record capable of retention by the recipient at the time of receipt. An electronic record is not capable of retention by the recipient if the sender or its information processing system inhibits the ability of the recipient to print or store the electronic record. *(Added by Stats.2013, c. 605 (S.B.752), § 21.)*

§ 6522. Approval by majority

If a provision of this act requires that an action be approved by a majority of all members, the action shall be approved or ratified by an affirmative vote of a majority of the votes entitled to be cast. *(Added by Stats.2013, c. 605 (S.B.752), § 21.)*

Cross References

Amendment of declaration, procedure, see Civil Code § 6620.
Extension of term of declaration, see Civil Code § 6618.

§ 6524. Approval by majority of quorum

If a provision of this act requires that an action be approved by a majority of a quorum of the members, the action shall be approved or ratified by an affirmative vote of a majority of the votes represented and voting in a duly held election in which a quorum is represented, which affirmative votes also constitute a majority of the required quorum. *(Added by Stats.2013, c. 605 (S.B.752), § 21.)*

Cross References

Amendment of governing documents to delete construction or marketing provisions after completion by developer, requirements, see Civil Code § 6608.
Assessment and assessment collection, exemption from execution by judgment creditor of association, exception, see Civil Code § 6804.

ARTICLE 2. DEFINITIONS

Section
6526. Construction of act.
6528. "Association" defined.
6530. "Board" defined.
6531. "Commercial or industrial common interest development" defined.
6532. "Common area" defined.
6534. "Common interest development" defined.

GENERAL PROVISIONS

Section
6540. "Condominium plan" defined.
6542. "Condominium project" defined.
6544. "Declarant" defined.
6546. "Declaration" defined.
6548. "Director" defined.
6550. "Exclusive use common area" defined.
6552. "Governing documents" defined.
6553. "Individual notice" defined.
6554. "Member" defined.
6560. "Person" defined.
6562. "Planned development" defined.
6564. "Separate interest" defined.
6566. "Stock cooperative" defined.

§ 6526. Construction of act

The definitions in this article govern the construction of this act. *(Added by Stats.2013, c. 605 (S.B.752), § 21.)*

§ 6528. "Association" defined

"Association" means a nonprofit corporation or unincorporated association created for the purpose of managing a common interest development. *(Added by Stats.2013, c. 605 (S.B.752), § 21.)*

§ 6530. "Board" defined

"Board" means the board of directors of the association. *(Added by Stats.2013, c. 605 (S.B.752), § 21.)*

§ 6531. "Commercial or industrial common interest development" defined

A "commercial or industrial common interest development" means a common interest development that is limited to industrial or commercial uses by law or by a declaration of covenants, conditions, and restrictions that has been recorded in the official records of each county in which the common interest development is located. For the purposes of this section, "commercial use" includes, but is not limited to, the operation of a business that provides facilities for the overnight stay of its customers, employees, or agents. *(Added by Stats.2013, c. 605 (S.B.752), § 21.)*

§ 6532. "Common area" defined

(a) "Common area" means the entire common interest development except the separate interests therein. The estate in the common area may be a fee, a life estate, an estate for years, or any combination of the foregoing.

(b) Notwithstanding subdivision (a), in a planned development described in subdivision (b) of Section 6562, the common area may consist of mutual or reciprocal easement rights appurtenant to the separate interests. *(Added by Stats.2013, c. 605 (S.B.752), § 21.)*

§ 6534. "Common interest development" defined

"Common interest development" means any of the following:

(a) A condominium project.

(b) A planned development.

(c) A stock cooperative. *(Added by Stats.2013, c. 605 (S.B.752), § 21.)*

§ 6540. "Condominium plan" defined

"Condominium plan" means a plan described in Section 6624. *(Added by Stats.2013, c. 605 (S.B.752), § 21.)*

§ 6542. "Condominium project" defined

(a) A "condominium project" means a real property development consisting of condominiums.

(b) A condominium consists of an undivided interest in common in a portion of real property coupled with a separate interest in space called a unit, the boundaries of which are described on a recorded final map, parcel map, or condominium plan in sufficient detail to locate all boundaries thereof. The area within these boundaries may be filled with air, earth, water, or fixtures, or any combination thereof, and need not be physically attached to land except by easements for access and, if necessary, support. The description of the unit may refer to (1) boundaries described in the recorded final map, parcel map, or condominium plan, (2) physical boundaries, either in existence, or to be constructed, such as walls, floors, and ceilings of a structure or any portion thereof, (3) an entire structure containing one or more units, or (4) any combination thereof.

(c) The portion or portions of the real property held in undivided interest may be all of the real property, except for the separate interests, or may include a particular three-dimensional portion thereof, the boundaries of which are described on a recorded final map, parcel map, or condominium plan. The area within these boundaries may be filled with air, earth, water, or fixtures, or any combination thereof, and need not be physically attached to land except by easements for access and, if necessary, support.

(d) An individual condominium within a condominium project may include, in addition, a separate interest in other portions of the real property. *(Added by Stats.2013, c. 605 (S.B.752), § 21.)*

§ 6544. "Declarant" defined

"Declarant" means the person or group of persons designated in the declaration as declarant, or if no declarant is designated, the person or group of persons who sign the original declaration or who succeed to special rights, preferences, or privileges designated in the declaration as belonging to the signator of the original declaration. *(Added by Stats.2013, c. 605 (S.B.752), § 21.)*

§ 6546. "Declaration" defined

"Declaration" means the document, however denominated, that contains the information required by Section 6614. *(Added by Stats.2013, c. 605 (S.B.752), § 21.)*

§ 6548. "Director" defined

"Director" means a natural person who serves on the board. *(Added by Stats.2013, c. 605 (S.B.752), § 21.)*

§ 6550. "Exclusive use common area" defined

(a) "Exclusive use common area" means a portion of the common area designated by the declaration for the exclusive use of one or more, but fewer than all, of the owners of the separate interests and which is or will be appurtenant to the separate interest or interests.

(b) Unless the declaration otherwise provides, any shutters, awnings, window boxes, doorsteps, stoops, porches, balconies, patios, exterior doors, doorframes, and hardware incident thereto, screens and windows or other fixtures designed to serve a single separate interest, but located outside the boundaries of the separate interest, are exclusive use common area allocated exclusively to that separate interest.

(c) Notwithstanding the provisions of the declaration, internal and external telephone wiring designed to serve a single separate interest, but located outside the boundaries of the separate interest, is exclusive use common area allocated exclusively to that separate interest. *(Added by Stats.2013, c. 605 (S.B.752), § 21.)*

Cross References

Access for maintenance of telephone wiring, see Civil Code § 6722.

§ 6552. "Governing documents" defined

"Governing documents" means the declaration and any other documents, such as bylaws, operating rules, articles of incorporation, or articles of association, which govern the operation of the common interest development or association. *(Added by Stats.2013, c. 605 (S.B.752), § 21.)*

§ 6553. "Individual notice" defined

"Individual notice" means the delivery of a document pursuant to Section 6514. *(Added by Stats.2013, c. 605 (S.B.752), § 21.)*

Cross References

Monetary penalties, provision of information to members, see Civil Code § 6850.

§ 6554. "Member" defined

"Member" means an owner of a separate interest. *(Added by Stats.2013, c. 605 (S.B.752), § 21.)*

§ 6560. "Person" defined

"Person" means a natural person, corporation, government or governmental subdivision or agency, business trust, estate, trust, partnership, limited liability company, association, or other entity. *(Added by Stats.2013, c. 605 (S.B.752), § 21.)*

§ 6562. "Planned development" defined

"Planned development" means a real property development other than a condominium project, or a stock cooperative, having either or both of the following features:

(a) Common area that is owned either by an association or in common by the owners of the separate interests who possess appurtenant rights to the beneficial use and enjoyment of the common area.

(b) Common area and an association that maintains the common area with the power to levy assessments that may become a lien upon the separate interests in accordance with Article 2 (commencing with Section 6808) of Chapter 7. *(Added by Stats.2013, c. 605 (S.B.752), § 21.)*

§ 6564. "Separate interest" defined

(a) "Separate interest" has the following meanings:

(1) In a condominium project, "separate interest" means a separately owned unit, as specified in Section 6542.

(2) In a planned development, "separate interest" means a separately owned lot, parcel, area, or space.

(3) In a stock cooperative, "separate interest" means the exclusive right to occupy a portion of the real property, as specified in Section 6566.

(b) Unless the declaration or condominium plan, if any exists, otherwise provides, if walls, floors, or ceilings are designated as boundaries of a separate interest, the interior surfaces of the perimeter walls, floors, ceilings, windows, doors, and outlets located within the separate interest are part of the separate interest and any other portions of the walls, floors, or ceilings are part of the common area.

(c) The estate in a separate interest may be a fee, a life estate, an estate for years, or any combination of the foregoing. *(Added by Stats.2013, c. 605 (S.B.752), § 21.)*

§ 6566. "Stock cooperative" defined

"Stock cooperative" means a development in which a corporation is formed or availed of, primarily for the purpose of holding title to, either in fee simple or for a term of years, improved real property, and all or substantially all of the shareholders of the corporation receive a right of exclusive occupancy in a portion of the real property, title to which is held by the corporation. The owners' interest in the corporation, whether evidenced by a share of stock, a certificate of membership, or otherwise, shall be deemed to be an interest in a common interest development and a real estate development for purposes of subdivision (f) of Section 25100 of the Corporations Code. *(Added by Stats.2013, c. 605 (S.B.752), § 21.)*

CHAPTER 2. APPLICATION OF ACT

Section
6580. Creation of common interest development; application of act.
6582. Act applicable only to commercial or industrial common interest developments.

§ 6580. Creation of common interest development; application of act

Subject to Section 6582, this act applies and a common interest development is created whenever a separate interest coupled with an interest in the common area or membership in the association is, or has been, conveyed, provided all of the following are recorded:

(a) A declaration.

(b) A condominium plan, if any exists.

(c) A final map or parcel map, if Division 2 (commencing with Section 66410) of Title 7 of the Government Code requires the recording of either a final map or parcel map for the common interest development. *(Added by Stats.2013, c. 605 (S.B.752), § 21.)*

§ 6582. Act applicable only to commercial or industrial common interest developments

(a) This act applies only to a commercial or industrial common interest development.

§ 6582

(b) Nothing in this act may be construed to apply to a real property development that does not contain common area. This subdivision is declaratory of existing law. *(Added by Stats.2013, c. 605 (S.B.752), § 21.)*

CHAPTER 3. GOVERNING DOCUMENTS

Article	Section
1. General Provisions	6600
2. Declaration	6614
3. Articles of Incorporation	6622
4. Condominium Plan	6624
5. Operating Rules	6630

ARTICLE 1. GENERAL PROVISIONS

Section
6600. Authority of documents.
6602. Liberal construction of instruments.
6604. Boundaries of units; presumptions.
6606. Restrictive covenants; deletion from declaration or other governing document; recording or filing of amended document.
6608. Amendment of governing documents to delete construction or marketing provisions after completion by developer; requirements.
6610. References to provisions of Davis–Stirling Common Interest Development Act; corrections.

§ 6600. Authority of documents

(a) To the extent of any conflict between the governing documents and the law, the law shall prevail.

(b) To the extent of any conflict between the articles of incorporation and the declaration, the declaration shall prevail.

(c) To the extent of any conflict between the bylaws and the articles of incorporation or declaration, the articles of incorporation or declaration shall prevail.

(d) To the extent of any conflict between the operating rules and the bylaws, articles of incorporation, or declaration, the bylaws, articles of incorporation, or declaration shall prevail. *(Added by Stats.2013, c. 605 (S.B.752), § 21.)*

§ 6602. Liberal construction of instruments

Any deed, declaration, or condominium plan for a common interest development shall be liberally construed to facilitate the operation of the common interest development, and its provisions shall be presumed to be independent and severable. Nothing in Article 3 (commencing with Section 715) of Chapter 2 of Title 2 of Part 1 of Division 2 shall operate to invalidate any provisions of the governing documents. *(Added by Stats.2013, c. 605 (S.B.752), § 21.)*

§ 6604. Boundaries of units; presumptions

In interpreting deeds and condominium plans, the existing physical boundaries of a unit in a condominium project, when the boundaries of the unit are contained within a building, or of a unit reconstructed in substantial accordance with the original plans thereof, shall be conclusively presumed to be its boundaries rather than the metes and bounds expressed in the deed or condominium plan, if any exists, regardless of settling or lateral movement of the building and regardless of minor variance between boundaries shown on the plan or in the deed and those of the building. *(Added by Stats.2013, c. 605 (S.B.752), § 21.)*

§ 6606. Restrictive covenants; deletion from declaration or other governing document; recording or filing of amended document

(a) No declaration or other governing document shall include a restrictive covenant in violation of Section 12955 of the Government Code.

(b) Notwithstanding any other provision of law or provision of the governing documents, the board, without approval of the members, shall amend any declaration or other governing document that includes a restrictive covenant prohibited by this section to delete the restrictive covenant, and shall restate the declaration or other governing document without the restrictive covenant but with no other change to the declaration or governing document.

(c) If the declaration is amended under this section, the board shall record the restated declaration in each county in which the common interest development is located. If the articles of incorporation are amended under this section, the board shall file a certificate of amendment with the Secretary of State pursuant to Section 7814 of the Corporations Code.

(d) If after providing written notice to an association, pursuant to Section 6512, requesting that the association delete a restrictive covenant that violates subdivision (a), and the association fails to delete the restrictive covenant within 30 days of receiving the notice, * * * <u>Civil Rights Department</u>, a city or county in which a common interest development is located, or any person may bring an action against the association for injunctive relief to enforce subdivision (a). The court may award attorney's fees to the prevailing party. *(Added by Stats.2013, c. 605 (S.B.752), § 21. Amended by Stats.2022, c. 48 (S.B.189), § 8, eff. June 30, 2022.)*

§ 6608. Amendment of governing documents to delete construction or marketing provisions after completion by developer; requirements

(a) Notwithstanding any provision of the governing documents to the contrary, the board may, after the developer has completed construction of the development, has terminated construction activities, and has terminated marketing activities for the sale, lease, or other disposition of separate interests within the development, adopt an amendment deleting from any of the governing documents any provision which is unequivocally designed and intended, or which by its nature can only have been designed or intended, to facilitate the developer in completing the construction or marketing of the development. However, provisions of the governing documents relative to a particular construction or marketing phase of the development may not be deleted under the authorization of this subdivision until that construction or marketing phase has been completed.

(b) The provisions which may be deleted by action of the board shall be limited to those which provide for access by the developer over or across the common area for the purposes of (1) completion of construction of the development, and (2) the erection, construction, or maintenance of structures or other facilities designed to facilitate the completion of construction or marketing of separate interests.

(c) At least 30 days prior to taking action pursuant to subdivision (a), the board shall deliver to all members, by individual delivery pursuant to Section 6514, (1) a copy of all amendments to the governing documents proposed to be adopted under subdivision (a), and (2) a notice of the time, date, and place the board will consider adoption of the amendments.

The board may consider adoption of amendments to the governing documents pursuant to subdivision (a) only at a meeting that is open to all members, who shall be given opportunity to make comments thereon. All deliberations of the board on any action proposed under subdivision (a) shall only be conducted in an open meeting.

(d) The board may not amend the governing documents pursuant to this section without the approval of a majority of a quorum of the members, pursuant to Section 6524. For the purposes of this section, "quorum" means more than 50 percent of the members who own no more than two separate interests in the development. *(Added by Stats.2013, c. 605 (S.B.752), § 21.)*

§ 6610. References to provisions of Davis–Stirling Common Interest Development Act; corrections

(a) Notwithstanding any other law or provision of the governing documents, if the governing documents include a reference to a provision of the Davis–Stirling Common Interest Development Act that was continued in a new provision by the act that added this section, the board may amend the governing documents, solely to correct the cross-reference, by adopting a board resolution that shows the correction. Member approval is not required in order to adopt a resolution pursuant to this section.

(b) A declaration that is corrected under this section may be restated in corrected form and recorded, provided that a copy of the board resolution authorizing the corrections is recorded along with the restated declaration. *(Added by Stats.2013, c. 605 (S.B.752), § 21.)*

ARTICLE 2. DECLARATION

Section
6614. Contents of declaration.
6616. Amendment of declaration; authorization.
6618. Extension of term of declaration.
6620. Amendment of declaration; procedure.

§ 6614. Contents of declaration

(a) A declaration, recorded on or after January 1, 1986, shall contain a legal description of the common interest development, and a statement that the common interest development is a condominium project, planned development, stock cooperative, or combination thereof. The declaration shall additionally set forth the name of the association and the restrictions on the use or enjoyment of any portion of the common interest development that are intended to be enforceable equitable servitudes.

(b) The declaration may contain any other matters the declarant or the members consider appropriate. *(Added by Stats.2013, c. 605 (S.B.752), § 21.)*

§ 6616. Amendment of declaration; authorization

Except to the extent that a declaration provides by its express terms that it is not amendable, in whole or in part, a declaration that fails to include provisions permitting its amendment at all times during its existence may be amended at any time. *(Added by Stats.2013, c. 605 (S.B.752), § 21.)*

§ 6618. Extension of term of declaration

(a) The Legislature finds that there are common interest developments that have been created with deed restrictions that do not provide a means for the members to extend the term of the declaration. The Legislature further finds that covenants and restrictions, contained in the declaration, are an appropriate method for protecting the common plan of developments and to provide for a mechanism for financial support for the upkeep of common area including, but not limited to, roofs, roads, heating systems, and recreational facilities. If declarations terminate prematurely, common interest developments may deteriorate and the supply of affordable units could be impacted adversely. The Legislature further finds and declares that it is in the public interest to provide a vehicle for extending the term of the declaration if the extension is approved by a majority of all members, pursuant to Section 6522.

(b) A declaration that specifies a termination date, but that contains no provision for extension of the termination date, may be extended, before its termination date, by the approval of members pursuant to Section 6620.

(c) No single extension of the terms of the declaration made pursuant to this section shall exceed the initial term of the declaration or 20 years, whichever is less. However, more than one extension may occur pursuant to this section. *(Added by Stats.2013, c. 605 (S.B.752), § 21.)*

§ 6620. Amendment of declaration; procedure

(a) A declaration may be amended pursuant to the declaration or this act. An amendment is effective after all of the following requirements have been met:

(1) The proposed amendment has been delivered by individual notice to all members not less than 15 days and not more than 60 days prior to any approval being solicited.

(2) The amendment has been approved by the percentage of members required by the declaration and any other person whose approval is required by the declaration.

(3) That fact has been certified in a writing executed and acknowledged by the officer designated in the declaration or by the association for that purpose, or if no one is designated, by the president of the association.

(4) The amendment has been recorded in each county in which a portion of the common interest development is located.

(b) If the declaration does not specify the percentage of members who must approve an amendment of the declaration, an amendment may be approved by a majority of all members, pursuant to Section 6522. *(Added by Stats.2013, c. 605 (S.B.752), § 21.)*

ARTICLE 3. ARTICLES OF INCORPORATION

Section
6622. Association articles of incorporation; required statements.

§ 6622. Association articles of incorporation; required statements

(a) The articles of incorporation of an association filed with the Secretary of State shall include a statement, which shall be in addition to the statement of purposes of the corporation, that does all of the following:

(1) Identifies the corporation as an association formed to manage a common interest development under the Commercial and Industrial Common Interest Development Act.

(2) States the business or corporate office of the association, if any, and, if the office is not on the site of the common interest development, states the front street and nearest cross street for the physical location of the common interest development.

(3) States the name and address of the association's managing agent, if any.

(b) The statement filed by an incorporated association with the Secretary of State pursuant to Section 8210 of the Corporations Code shall also contain a statement identifying the corporation as an association formed to manage a common interest development under the Commercial and Industrial Common Interest Development Act.

(c) Documents filed prior to January 1, 2014, in compliance with former Section 1363.5, as it read on January 1, 2013, are deemed to be in compliance with this section. *(Added by Stats.2013, c. 605 (S.B.752), § 21.)*

ARTICLE 4. CONDOMINIUM PLAN

Section
6624. Contents of condominium plan.
6626. Certificate consenting to recordation of condominium plan; signatures and acknowledgements.
6628. Amendment or revocation of condominium plan.

§ 6624. Contents of condominium plan

A condominium plan shall contain all of the following:

(a) A description or survey map of a condominium project, which shall refer to or show monumentation on the ground.

(b) A three-dimensional description of a condominium project, one or more dimensions of which may extend for an indefinite distance upwards or downwards, in sufficient detail to identify the common area and each separate interest.

(c) A certificate consenting to the recordation of the condominium plan pursuant to this act that is signed and acknowledged as provided in Section 6626. *(Added by Stats.2013, c. 605 (S.B.752), § 21.)*

§ 6626. Certificate consenting to recordation of condominium plan; signatures and acknowledgements

(a) The certificate consenting to the recordation of a condominium plan that is required by subdivision (c) of Section 6624 shall be signed and acknowledged by all of the following persons:

(1) The record owner of fee title to that property included in the condominium project.

(2) In the case of a condominium project that will terminate upon the termination of an estate for years, by all lessors and lessees of the estate for years.

(3) In the case of a condominium project subject to a life estate, by all life tenants and remainder interests.

(4) The trustee or the beneficiary of each recorded deed of trust, and the mortgagee of each recorded mortgage encumbering the property.

(b) Owners of mineral rights, easements, rights-of-way, and other nonpossessory interests do not need to sign the certificate.

(c) In the event a conversion to condominiums of a stock cooperative has been approved by the required number of owners, trustees, beneficiaries, and mortgagees pursuant to Section 66452.10 of the Government Code, the certificate need only be signed by those owners, trustees, beneficiaries, and mortgagees approving the conversion. *(Added by Stats. 2013, c. 605 (S.B.752), § 21.)*

§ 6628. Amendment or revocation of condominium plan

A condominium plan may be amended or revoked by a recorded instrument that is acknowledged and signed by all the persons who, at the time of amendment or revocation, are persons whose signatures are required under Section 6626. *(Added by Stats.2013, c. 605 (S.B.752), § 21.)*

ARTICLE 5. OPERATING RULES

Section
6630. "Operating rule" defined.
6632. Requirements for validity and enforceability.

§ 6630. "Operating rule" defined

For the purposes of this article, "operating rule" means a regulation adopted by the board that applies generally to the management and operation of the common interest development or the conduct of the business and affairs of the association. *(Added by Stats.2013, c. 605 (S.B.752), § 21.)*

§ 6632. Requirements for validity and enforceability

An operating rule is valid and enforceable only if all of the following requirements are satisfied:

(a) The rule is in writing.

(b) The rule is within the authority of the board conferred by law or by the declaration, articles of incorporation or association, or bylaws of the association.

(c) The rule is not in conflict with governing law and the declaration, articles of incorporation or association, or bylaws of the association.

(d) The rule is reasonable, and is adopted, amended, or repealed in good faith. *(Added by Stats.2013, c. 605 (S.B. 752), § 21.)*

CHAPTER 4. OWNERSHIP AND TRANSFER OF INTERESTS

Article	Section
1. Ownership Rights and Interests	6650
2. Restrictions on Transfers	6656
3. Transfer of Separate Interest	6662

ARTICLE 1. OWNERSHIP RIGHTS AND INTERESTS

Section
6650. Ownership of common areas.
6652. Rights and easements of ingress, egress, and support.
6654. Physical access to owner or occupant's separate interest.

§ 6650. Ownership of common areas

Unless the declaration otherwise provides, in a condominium project, or in a planned development in which the common area is owned by the owners of the separate interests, the common area is owned as tenants in common, in equal shares, one for each separate interest. *(Added by Stats.2013, c. 605 (S.B.752), § 21.)*

§ 6652. Rights and easements of ingress, egress, and support

Unless the declaration otherwise provides:

(a) In a condominium project, and in those planned developments with common area owned in common by the owners of the separate interests, there are appurtenant to each separate interest nonexclusive rights of ingress, egress, and support, if necessary, through the common area. The common area is subject to these rights.

(b) In a stock cooperative, and in a planned development with common area owned by the association, there is an easement for ingress, egress, and support, if necessary, appurtenant to each separate interest. The common area is subject to these easements. *(Added by Stats.2013, c. 605 (S.B.752), § 21.)*

§ 6654. Physical access to owner or occupant's separate interest

Except as otherwise provided in law, an order of the court, or an order pursuant to a final and binding arbitration decision, an association may not deny a member or occupant physical access to the member's or occupant's separate interest, either by restricting access through the common area to the separate interest, or by restricting access solely to the separate interest. *(Added by Stats.2013, c. 605 (S.B.752), § 21.)*

ARTICLE 2. RESTRICTIONS ON TRANSFERS

Section
6656. Restrictions on partition.
6658. Liens for labor and materials.
6660. Claim of lien; notice to members.

§ 6656. Restrictions on partition

(a) Except as provided in this section, the common area in a condominium project shall remain undivided, and there shall be no judicial partition thereof. Nothing in this section shall be deemed to prohibit partition of a cotenancy in a condominium.

(b) The owner of a separate interest in a condominium project may maintain a partition action as to the entire project as if the owners of all of the separate interests in the project were tenants in common in the entire project in the same proportion as their interests in the common area. The court shall order partition under this subdivision only by sale of the entire condominium project and only upon a showing of one of the following:

(1) More than three years before the filing of the action, the condominium project was damaged or destroyed, so that a material part was rendered unfit for its prior use, and the condominium project has not been rebuilt or repaired substantially to its state prior to the damage or destruction.

(2) Three-fourths or more of the project is destroyed or substantially damaged and owners of separate interests holding in the aggregate more than a 50–percent interest in the common area oppose repair or restoration of the project.

(3) The project has been in existence more than 50 years, is obsolete and uneconomic, and owners of separate interests holding in the aggregate more than a 50–percent interest in the common area oppose repair or restoration of the project.

(4) Any conditions in the declaration for sale under the circumstances described in this subdivision have been met. *(Added by Stats.2013, c. 605 (S.B.752), § 21.)*

§ 6658. Liens for labor and materials

(a) In a common interest development, no labor performed or services or materials furnished with the consent of, or at the request of, an owner in the common interest development or the owners' agent or contractor shall be the basis for the filing of a lien against any other property of any other owner in the common interest development unless that other owner has expressly consented to or requested the performance of the labor or furnishing of the materials or services. However, express consent shall be deemed to have been given by the owner of any separate interest in the case of emergency repairs thereto.

(b) Labor performed or services or materials furnished for the common area, if duly authorized by the association, shall be deemed to be performed or furnished with the express consent of each separate interest owner.

(c) The owner of any separate interest may remove that owner's separate interest from a lien against two or more separate interests or any part thereof by doing either of the following:

(1) Pay to the holder of the lien the fraction of the total sum secured by the lien that is attributable to the owner's separate interest.

(2) Record a lien release bond, pursuant to Section 8424, in an amount equal to 125 percent of the sum secured by the lien that is attributable to the owner's separate interest. *(Added by Stats.2013, c. 605 (S.B.752), § 21. Amended by Stats.2017, c. 44 (A.B.534), § 3, eff. Jan. 1, 2018.)*

§ 6660. Claim of lien; notice to members

If the association is served with a claim of lien pursuant to Part 6 (commencing with Section 8000) for a work of

ARTICLE 3. TRANSFER OF SEPARATE INTEREST

Section
6662. Condominium project; interests included in conveyance, judicial sale or transfer of separate interests.
6664. Planned development; interests included in conveyance, judicial sale or transfer of separate interests.
6666. Stock cooperative; interests included in conveyance, judicial sale or transfer of separate interests.
6668. Transfer of exclusive use areas.
6670. Restrictions upon severability of component interests.

§ 6662. Condominium project; interests included in conveyance, judicial sale or transfer of separate interests

In a condominium project the common area is not subject to partition, except as provided in Section 6656. Any conveyance, judicial sale, or other voluntary or involuntary transfer of the separate interest includes the undivided interest in the common area. Any conveyance, judicial sale, or other voluntary or involuntary transfer of the owner's entire estate also includes the owner's membership interest in the association. *(Added by Stats.2013, c. 605 (S.B.752), § 21.)*

§ 6664. Planned development; interests included in conveyance, judicial sale or transfer of separate interests

In a planned development, any conveyance, judicial sale, or other voluntary or involuntary transfer of the separate interest includes the undivided interest in the common area, if any exists. Any conveyance, judicial sale, or other voluntary or involuntary transfer of the owner's entire estate also includes the owner's membership interest in the association. *(Added by Stats.2013, c. 605 (S.B.752), § 21.)*

§ 6666. Stock cooperative; interests included in conveyance, judicial sale or transfer of separate interests

In a stock cooperative, any conveyance, judicial sale, or other voluntary or involuntary transfer of the separate interest includes the ownership interest in the corporation, however evidenced. Any conveyance, judicial sale, or other voluntary or involuntary transfer of the owner's entire estate also includes the owner's membership interest in the association. *(Added by Stats.2013, c. 605 (S.B.752), § 21.)*

§ 6668. Transfer of exclusive use areas

Nothing in this article prohibits the transfer of exclusive use areas, independent of any other interest in a common interest subdivision, if authorization to separately transfer exclusive use areas is expressly stated in the declaration and the transfer occurs in accordance with the terms of the declaration. *(Added by Stats.2013, c. 605 (S.B.752), § 21.)*

§ 6670. Restrictions upon severability of component interests

Any restrictions upon the severability of the component interests in real property which are contained in the declaration shall not be deemed conditions repugnant to the interest created within the meaning of Section 711. However, these restrictions shall not extend beyond the period in which the right to partition a project is suspended under Section 6656. *(Added by Stats.2013, c. 605 (S.B.752), § 21.)*

CHAPTER 5. PROPERTY USE AND MAINTENANCE

Article	Section
1. Protected Uses	6700
2. Modification of Separate Interest	6714
3. Maintenance	6716

ARTICLE 1. PROTECTED USES

Section
6700. Scope of article; related provisions.
6702. Display of United States flag by owner on or in owner's separate interest or within exclusive use common area.
6704. Prohibition of posting or displaying noncommercial signs, posters, flags, or banners; permitted placement; exceptions.
6706. Pets within common interest developments.
6708. Restrictions on installation or use of video or television antenna; enforceability based on size; reasonable restrictions; application approval; attorney's fees.
6710. Prohibition against association rule or regulation that arbitrarily or unreasonably restricts owner's ability to market his or her interest in common development; other enumerated restrictions.
6712. Governing documents; void and unenforceable provisions.
6713. Restrictions on electric vehicle charging stations.

§ 6700. Scope of article; related provisions

This article includes provisions that limit the authority of an association or the governing documents to regulate the use of a member's separate interest. Nothing in this article is intended to affect the application of any other provision that limits the authority of an association to regulate the use of a member's separate interest, including, but not limited to, the following provisions:

(a) Sections 712 and 713, relating to the display of signs.

(b) Sections 714 and 714.1, relating to solar energy systems.

(c) Section 714.5, relating to structures that are constructed offsite and moved to the property in sections or modules.

(d) Sections 782, 782.5, and 6150 of this code and Section 12956.1 of the Government Code, relating to racial restrictions. *(Added by Stats.2013, c. 605 (S.B.752), § 21.)*

§ 6702. Display of United States flag by owner on or in owner's separate interest or within exclusive use common area

(a) Except as required for the protection of the public health or safety, no governing document shall limit or prohibit, or be construed to limit or prohibit, the display of the flag of the United States by a member on or in the member's separate interest or within the member's exclusive use common area.

(b) For purposes of this section, "display of the flag of the United States" means a flag of the United States made of fabric, cloth, or paper displayed from a staff or pole or in a window, and does not mean a depiction or emblem of the flag of the United States made of lights, paint, roofing, siding, paving materials, flora, or balloons, or any other similar building, landscaping, or decorative component.

(c) In any action to enforce this section, the prevailing party shall be awarded reasonable attorney's fees and costs. *(Added by Stats.2013, c. 605 (S.B.752), § 21.)*

§ 6704. Prohibition of posting or displaying noncommercial signs, posters, flags, or banners; permitted placement; exceptions

(a) The governing documents may not prohibit posting or displaying of noncommercial signs, posters, flags, or banners on or in a member's separate interest, except as required for the protection of public health or safety or if the posting or display would violate a local, state, or federal law.

(b) For purposes of this section, a noncommercial sign, poster, flag, or banner may be made of paper, cardboard, cloth, plastic, or fabric, and may be posted or displayed from the yard, window, door, balcony, or outside wall of the separate interest, but may not be made of lights, roofing, siding, paving materials, flora, or balloons, or any other similar building, landscaping, or decorative component, or include the painting of architectural surfaces.

(c) An association may prohibit noncommercial signs and posters that are more than nine square feet in size and noncommercial flags or banners that are more than 15 square feet in size. *(Added by Stats.2013, c. 605 (S.B.752), § 21.)*

§ 6706. Pets within common interest developments

Notwithstanding Section 4202, Section 4715 applies to an owner of a separate interest in a common interest development who kept a pet in that common interest development before January 1, 2014. *(Added by Stats.2013, c. 605 (S.B. 752), § 21.)*

§ 6708. Restrictions on installation or use of video or television antenna; enforceability based on size; reasonable restrictions; application approval; attorney's fees

(a) Any covenant, condition, or restriction contained in any deed, contract, security instrument, or other instrument affecting the transfer or sale of, or any interest in, a common interest development that effectively prohibits or restricts the installation or use of a video or television antenna, including a satellite dish, or that effectively prohibits or restricts the attachment of that antenna to a structure within that development where the antenna is not visible from any street or common area, except as otherwise prohibited or restricted by law, is void and unenforceable as to its application to the installation or use of a video or television antenna that has a diameter or diagonal measurement of 36 inches or less.

(b) This section shall not apply to any covenant, condition, or restriction, as described in subdivision (a), that imposes reasonable restrictions on the installation or use of a video or television antenna, including a satellite dish, that has a diameter or diagonal measurement of 36 inches or less. For purposes of this section, "reasonable restrictions" means those restrictions that do not significantly increase the cost of the video or television antenna system, including all related equipment, or significantly decrease its efficiency or performance and include all of the following:

(1) Requirements for application and notice to the association prior to the installation.

(2) Requirement of a member to obtain the approval of the association for the installation of a video or television antenna that has a diameter or diagonal measurement of 36 inches or less on a separate interest owned by another.

(3) Provision for the maintenance, repair, or replacement of roofs or other building components.

(4) Requirements for installers of a video or television antenna to indemnify or reimburse the association or its members for loss or damage caused by the installation, maintenance, or use of a video or television antenna that has a diameter or diagonal measurement of 36 inches or less.

(c) Whenever approval is required for the installation or use of a video or television antenna, including a satellite dish, the application for approval shall be processed by the appropriate approving entity for the common interest development in the same manner as an application for approval of an architectural modification to the property, and the issuance of a decision on the application shall not be willfully delayed.

(d) In any action to enforce compliance with this section, the prevailing party shall be awarded reasonable attorney's fees. *(Added by Stats.2013, c. 605 (S.B.752), § 21.)*

§ 6710. Prohibition against association rule or regulation that arbitrarily or unreasonably restricts owner's ability to market his or her interest in common development; other enumerated restrictions

(a) Any provision of a governing document that arbitrarily or unreasonably restricts an owner's ability to market the owner's interest in a common interest development is void.

(b) No association may adopt, enforce, or otherwise impose any governing document that does either of the following:

(1) Imposes an assessment or fee in connection with the marketing of an owner's interest in an amount that exceeds the association's actual or direct costs.

(2) Establishes an exclusive relationship with a real estate broker through which the sale or marketing of interests in the development is required to occur. The limitation set forth in this paragraph does not apply to the sale or marketing of separate interests owned by the association or to the sale or marketing of common area by the association.

(c) For purposes of this section, "market" and "marketing" mean listing, advertising, or obtaining or providing access to show the owner's interest in the development.

(d) This section does not apply to rules or regulations made pursuant to Section 712 or 713 regarding real estate signs. *(Added by Stats.2013, c. 605 (S.B.752), § 21.)*

§ 6712. Governing documents; void and unenforceable provisions

(a) Notwithstanding any other law, a provision of the governing documents shall be void and unenforceable if it does any of the following:

(1) Prohibits, or includes conditions that have the effect of prohibiting, the use of low water-using plants as a group.

(2) Has the effect of prohibiting or restricting compliance with either of the following:

(A) A water-efficient landscape ordinance adopted or in effect pursuant to subdivision (c) of Section 65595 of the Government Code.

(B) Any regulation or restriction on the use of water adopted pursuant to Section 353 or 375 of the Water Code.

(b) This section shall not prohibit an association from applying landscaping rules established in the governing documents, to the extent the rules fully conform with the requirements of subdivision (a). *(Added by Stats.2013, c. 605 (S.B.752), § 21.)*

§ 6713. Restrictions on electric vehicle charging stations

(a) Any covenant, restriction, or condition contained in any deed, contract, security instrument, or other instrument affecting the transfer or sale of any interest in a common interest development, and any provision of a governing document, as defined in Section 6552, that either effectively prohibits or unreasonably restricts the installation or use of an electric vehicle charging station in an owner's designated parking space, including, but not limited to, a deeded parking space, a parking space in an owner's exclusive use common area, or a parking space that is specifically designated for use by a particular owner, or is in conflict with the provisions of this section is void and unenforceable.

(b)(1) This section does not apply to provisions that impose reasonable restrictions on electric vehicle charging stations. However, it is the policy of the state to promote, encourage, and remove obstacles to the use of electric vehicle charging stations.

(2) For purposes of this section, "reasonable restrictions" are restrictions that do not significantly increase the cost of the station or significantly decrease its efficiency or specified performance.

(c) An electric vehicle charging station shall meet applicable health and safety standards and requirements imposed by state and local authorities, and all other applicable zoning, land use or other ordinances, or land use permits.

(d) For purposes of this section, "electric vehicle charging station" means a station that is designed in compliance with the California Building Standards Code and delivers electricity from a source outside an electric vehicle into one or more electric vehicles. An electric vehicle charging station may include several charge points simultaneously connecting several electric vehicles to the station and any related equipment needed to facilitate charging plug-in electric vehicles.

(e) If approval is required for the installation or use of an electric vehicle charging station, the application for approval shall be processed and approved by the association in the same manner as an application for approval of an architectural modification to the property, and shall not be willfully avoided or delayed. The approval or denial of an application shall be in writing. If an application is not denied in writing within 60 days from the date of receipt of the application, the application shall be deemed approved, unless that delay is the result of a reasonable request for additional information.

(f) If the electric vehicle charging station is to be placed in a common area or an exclusive use common area, as designated in the common interest development's declaration, the following provisions apply:

(1) The owner first shall obtain approval from the association to install the electric vehicle charging station and the association shall approve the installation if the owner agrees in writing to do all of the following:

(A) Comply with the association's architectural standards for the installation of the charging station.

(B) Engage a licensed contractor to install the charging station.

(C) Within 14 days of approval, provide a certificate of insurance that names the association as an additional insured under the owner's insurance policy in the amount set forth in paragraph (3).

(D) Pay for the electricity usage associated with the charging station.

(2) The owner and each successive owner of the charging station shall be responsible for all of the following:

(A) Costs for damage to the charging station, common area, exclusive use common area, or separate interests resulting from the installation, maintenance, repair, removal, or replacement of the charging station.

(B) Costs for the maintenance, repair, and replacement of the charging station until it has been removed and for the restoration of the common area after removal.

(C) The cost of electricity associated with the charging station.

(D) Disclosing to prospective buyers the existence of any charging station of the owner and the related responsibilities of the owner under this section.

(3) The owner and each successive owner of the charging station, at all times, shall maintain a liability coverage policy in the amount of one million dollars ($1,000,000), and shall name the association as a named additional insured under the policy with a right to notice of cancellation.

(4) An owner shall not be required to maintain a liability coverage policy for an existing National Electrical Manufacturers Association standard alternating current power plug.

(g) Except as provided in subdivision (h), installation of an electric vehicle charging station for the exclusive use of an owner in a common area, that is not an exclusive use common area, shall be authorized by the association only if installation in the owner's designated parking space is impossible or unreasonably expensive. In such cases, the association shall enter into a license agreement with the owner for the use of the space in a common area, and the owner shall comply with all of the requirements in subdivision (f).

(h) The association or owners may install an electric vehicle charging station in the common area for the use of all members of the association and, in that case, the association shall develop appropriate terms of use for the charging station.

(i) An association may create a new parking space where one did not previously exist to facilitate the installation of an electric vehicle charging station.

(j) An association that willfully violates this section shall be liable to the applicant or other party for actual damages, and shall pay a civil penalty to the applicant or other party in an amount not to exceed one thousand dollars ($1,000).

(k) In any action to enforce compliance with this section, the prevailing plaintiff shall be awarded reasonable attorney's fees. *(Added by Stats.2013, c. 605 (S.B.752), § 21.)*

ARTICLE 2. MODIFICATION OF SEPARATE INTEREST

Section
6714. Modification of member's separate interest; facilitation of access for handicapped; approval by association.

§ 6714. Modification of member's separate interest; facilitation of access for handicapped; approval by association

(a) Subject to the governing documents and applicable law, a member may do the following:

(1) Make any improvement or alteration within the boundaries of the member's separate interest that does not impair the structural integrity or mechanical systems or lessen the support of any portions of the common interest development.

(2) Modify the member's separate interest, at the member's expense, to facilitate access for persons who are blind, visually handicapped, deaf, or physically disabled, or to alter conditions which could be hazardous to these persons. These modifications may also include modifications of the route from the public way to the door of the separate interest for the purposes of this paragraph if the separate interest is on the ground floor or already accessible by an existing ramp or elevator. The right granted by this paragraph is subject to the following conditions:

(A) The modifications shall be consistent with applicable building code requirements.

(B) The modifications shall be consistent with the intent of otherwise applicable provisions of the governing documents pertaining to safety or aesthetics.

(C) Modifications external to the separate interest shall not prevent reasonable passage by other residents, and shall be removed by the member when the separate interest is no longer occupied by persons requiring those modifications who are blind, visually handicapped, deaf, or physically disabled.

(D) Any member who intends to modify a separate interest pursuant to this paragraph shall submit plans and specifications to the association for review to determine whether the modifications will comply with the provisions of this paragraph. The association shall not deny approval of the proposed modifications under this paragraph without good cause.

(b) Any change in the exterior appearance of a separate interest shall be in accordance with the governing documents and applicable provisions of law. *(Added by Stats.2013, c. 605 (S.B.752), § 21.)*

ARTICLE 3. MAINTENANCE

Section
6716. Responsibility for repair, replacement, or maintenance.
6718. Damage by wood-destroying pests or organisms.
6720. Temporary removal of occupant for treatment of wood-destroying pests or organisms.
6722. Access for maintenance of telephone wiring.

§ 6716. Responsibility for repair, replacement, or maintenance

(a) Unless otherwise provided in the declaration of a common interest development, the association is responsible for repairing, replacing, or maintaining the common area, other than exclusive use common area, and the owner of each separate interest is responsible for maintaining that separate interest and any exclusive use common area appurtenant to the separate interest.

(b) The costs of temporary relocation during the repair and maintenance of the areas within the responsibility of the association shall be borne by the owner of the separate interest affected. *(Added by Stats.2013, c. 605 (S.B.752), § 21.)*

§ 6718. Damage by wood-destroying pests or organisms

(a) In a condominium project or stock cooperative, unless otherwise provided in the declaration, the association is responsible for the repair and maintenance of the common area occasioned by the presence of wood-destroying pests or organisms.

(b) In a planned development, unless a different maintenance scheme is provided in the declaration, each owner of a separate interest is responsible for the repair and maintenance of that separate interest as may be occasioned by the presence of wood-destroying pests or organisms. Upon approval of the majority of all members of the association, pursuant to Section 6522, that responsibility may be delegated to the association, which shall be entitled to recover the cost thereof as a special assessment. *(Added by Stats.2013, c. 605 (S.B.752), § 21.)*

§ 6720. Temporary removal of occupant for treatment of wood-destroying pests or organisms

(a) The association may cause the temporary, summary removal of any occupant of a common interest development for such periods and at such times as may be necessary for prompt, effective treatment of wood-destroying pests or organisms.

(b) The association shall give notice of the need to temporarily vacate a separate interest to the occupants and to the owners, not less than 15 days nor more than 30 days prior to the date of the temporary relocation. The notice shall state the reason for the temporary relocation, the date and time of the beginning of treatment, the anticipated date and time of termination of treatment, and that the occupants will be responsible for their own accommodations during the temporary relocation.

(c) Notice by the association shall be deemed complete upon either:

(1) Personal delivery of a copy of the notice to the occupants, and, if an occupant is not the owner, individual

delivery pursuant to Section 6514 of a copy of the notice to the owner.

(2) Individual delivery pursuant to Section 6514 to the occupant at the address of the separate interest, and, if the occupant is not the owner, individual delivery pursuant to Section 6514 of a copy of the notice to the owner.

(d) For purposes of this section, "occupant" means an owner, resident, guest, invitee, tenant, lessee, sublessee, or other person in possession of the separate interest. *(Added by Stats.2013, c. 605 (S.B.752), § 21.)*

§ 6722. Access for maintenance of telephone wiring

Notwithstanding the provisions of the declaration, a member is entitled to reasonable access to the common area for the purpose of maintaining the internal and external telephone wiring made part of the exclusive use common area of the member's separate interest pursuant to subdivision (c) of Section 6550. The access shall be subject to the consent of the association, whose approval shall not be unreasonably withheld, and which may include the association's approval of telephone wiring upon the exterior of the common area, and other conditions as the association determines reasonable. *(Added by Stats.2013, c. 605 (S.B.752), § 21.)*

CHAPTER 6. ASSOCIATION GOVERNANCE

Article	Section
1. Association Existence and Powers	6750
2. Record Keeping	6756
3. Conflict of Interest	6758
4. Government Assistance	6760

ARTICLE 1. ASSOCIATION EXISTENCE AND POWERS

Section
6750. Management by association.
6752. Powers of association.

§ 6750. Management by association

A common interest development shall be managed by an association that may be incorporated or unincorporated. The association may be referred to as an owners' association or a community association. *(Added by Stats.2013, c. 605 (S.B.752), § 21.)*

§ 6752. Powers of association

(a) Unless the governing documents provide otherwise, and regardless of whether the association is incorporated or unincorporated, the association may exercise the powers granted to a nonprofit mutual benefit corporation, as enumerated in Section 7140 of the Corporations Code, except that an unincorporated association may not adopt or use a corporate seal or issue membership certificates in accordance with Section 7313 of the Corporations Code.

(b) The association, whether incorporated or unincorporated, may exercise the powers granted to an association in this act. *(Added by Stats.2013, c. 605 (S.B.752), § 21.)*

ARTICLE 2. RECORD KEEPING

Section
6756. Request to change member's information; delivery in writing.

§ 6756. Request to change member's information; delivery in writing

To be effective, a request to change the member's information in the association membership list shall be delivered in writing to the association, pursuant to Section 6512. *(Added by Stats.2013, c. 605 (S.B.752), § 21.)*

ARTICLE 3. CONFLICT OF INTEREST

Section
6758. Applicability of Corporations Code provisions; prohibited actions.

§ 6758. Applicability of Corporations Code provisions; prohibited actions

(a) Notwithstanding any other law, and regardless of whether an association is incorporated or unincorporated, the provisions of Sections 7233 and 7234 of the Corporations Code shall apply to any contract or other transaction authorized, approved, or ratified by the board or a committee of the board.

(b) A director or member of a committee shall not vote on any of the following matters:

(1) Discipline of the director or committee member.

(2) An assessment against the director or committee member for damage to the common area or facilities.

(3) A request, by the director or committee member, for a payment plan for overdue assessments.

(4) A decision whether to foreclose on a lien on the separate interest of the director or committee member.

(5) Review of a proposed physical change to the separate interest of the director or committee member.

(6) A grant of exclusive use common area to the director or committee member.

(c) Nothing in this section limits any other provision of law or the governing documents that govern a decision in which a director may have an interest. *(Added by Stats.2013, c. 605 (S.B.752), § 21.)*

ARTICLE 4. GOVERNMENT ASSISTANCE

Section
6760. Assistance with identification of commercial or industrial common interest developments; submission of information by each association; time; notice of change of address; penalty for violation of filing requirements.

§ 6760. Assistance with identification of commercial or industrial common interest developments; submission of information by each association; time; notice of change of address; penalty for violation of filing requirements

(a) To assist with the identification of commercial or industrial common interest developments, each association, whether incorporated or unincorporated, shall submit to the Secretary of State, on a form and for a fee, to cover the reasonable cost to the Secretary of State of processing the form, not to exceed thirty dollars ($30), that the Secretary of State shall prescribe, the following information concerning the association and the development that it manages:

(1) A statement that the association is formed to manage a common interest development under the Commercial and Industrial Common Interest Development Act.

(2) The name of the association.

(3) The street address of the business or corporate office of the association, if any.

(4) The street address of the association's onsite office, if different from the street address of the business or corporate office, or if there is no onsite office, the street address of the responsible officer or managing agent of the association.

(5) The name, address, and either the daytime telephone number or email address of the association's onsite office or managing agent.

(6) The name, street address, and daytime telephone number of the association's managing agent, if any.

(7) The county, and, if in an incorporated area, the city in which the development is physically located. If the boundaries of the development are physically located in more than one county, each of the counties in which it is located.

(8) If the development is in an unincorporated area, the city closest in proximity to the development.

(9) The front street and nearest cross street of the physical location of the development.

(10) The type of common interest development managed by the association.

(11) The number of separate interests in the development.

(b) The association shall submit the information required by this section as follows:

(1) By incorporated associations, within 90 days after the filing of its original articles of incorporation, and thereafter at the time the association files its statement of principal business activity with the Secretary of State pursuant to Section 8210 of the Corporations Code.

(2) By unincorporated associations, in July of 2003, and in that same month biennially thereafter. Upon changing its status to that of a corporation, the association shall comply with the filing deadlines in paragraph (1).

(c) The association shall notify the Secretary of State of any change in the street address of the association's onsite office or of the responsible officer or managing agent of the association in the form and for a fee, to cover the reasonable cost to the Secretary of State of processing the form, prescribed by the Secretary of State, within 60 days of the change.

(d) The penalty for an incorporated association's noncompliance with the initial or biennial filing requirements of this section shall be suspension of the association's rights, privileges, and powers as a corporation and monetary penalties, to the same extent and in the same manner as suspension and monetary penalties imposed pursuant to Section 8810 of the Corporations Code.

(e) The statement required by this section may be filed, notwithstanding suspension of the corporate powers, rights, and privileges under this section or under provisions of the Revenue and Taxation Code. Upon the filing of a statement under this section by a corporation that has suffered suspension under this section, the Secretary of State shall certify that fact to the Franchise Tax Board and the corporation may thereupon be relieved from suspension, unless the corporation is held in suspension by the Franchise Tax Board by reason of Section 23301, 23301.5, or 23775 of the Revenue and Taxation Code.

* * *

(f) Whenever any form is filed pursuant to this section, it supersedes any previously filed form.

(g) The Secretary of State may destroy or otherwise dispose of any form filed pursuant to this section after it has been superseded by the filing of a new form. *(Added by Stats.2013, c. 605 (S.B.752), § 21. Amended by Stats.2021, c. 615 (A.B.474), § 54, eff. Jan. 1, 2022, operative Jan. 1, 2023; Stats.2022, c. 617 (S.B.1202), § 2, eff. Jan. 1, 2023.)*

CHAPTER 7. ASSESSMENTS AND ASSESSMENT COLLECTION

Article	Section
1. Establishment and Imposition of Assessments	6800
2. Assessment Payment and Delinquency	6808
3. Assessment Collection	6820

ARTICLE 1. ESTABLISHMENT AND IMPOSITION OF ASSESSMENTS

Section
6800. Levy of assessments.
6804. Exemption from execution by judgment creditor of association.

§ 6800. Levy of assessments

The association shall levy regular and special assessments sufficient to perform its obligations under the governing documents and this act. *(Added by Stats.2013, c. 605 (S.B.752), § 21.)*

§ 6804. Exemption from execution by judgment creditor of association

(a) Regular assessments imposed or collected to perform the obligations of an association under the governing documents or this act shall be exempt from execution by a judgment creditor of the association only to the extent necessary for the association to perform essential services, such as paying for utilities and insurance. In determining the appropriateness of an exemption, a court shall ensure that only essential services are protected under this subdivision.

(b) This exemption shall not apply to any consensual pledges, liens, or encumbrances that have been approved by a majority of a quorum of members, pursuant to Section 6524, at a member meeting or election, or to any state tax lien, or to any lien for labor or materials supplied to the common area. *(Added by Stats.2013, c. 605 (S.B.752), § 21.)*

ARTICLE 2. ASSESSMENT PAYMENT AND DELINQUENCY

Section
6808. Debt of owner of separate interest.
6810. Payment toward assessment; receipt; mailing address for overnight payment.
6812. Notice prior to recording lien upon separate interest; contents.
6814. Lien on separate interest; notice of delinquent assessment.
6816. Priority of lien.
6818. Recording of lien.
6819. Recommencement of notice process for failure to comply with procedures.

§ 6808. Debt of owner of separate interest

A regular or special assessment and any late charges, reasonable fees and costs of collection, reasonable attorney's fees, if any, and interest, if any, shall be a debt of the owner of the separate interest at the time the assessment or other sums are levied. *(Added by Stats.2013, c. 605 (S.B.752), § 21.)*

§ 6810. Payment toward assessment; receipt; mailing address for overnight payment

(a) When an owner of a separate interest makes a payment toward an assessment, the owner may request a receipt and the association shall provide it. The receipt shall indicate the date of payment and the person who received it.

(b) The association shall provide a mailing address for overnight payment of assessments.

(c) An owner shall not be liable for any charges, interest, or costs of collection for an assessment payment that is asserted to be delinquent, if it is determined the assessment was paid on time to the association. *(Added by Stats.2013, c. 605 (S.B.752), § 21.)*

§ 6812. Notice prior to recording lien upon separate interest; contents

At least 30 days prior to recording a lien upon the separate interest of the owner of record to collect a debt that is past due under Section 6808, the association shall notify the owner of record in writing by certified mail of the following:

(a) A general description of the collection and lien enforcement procedures of the association and the method of calculation of the amount, a statement that the owner of the separate interest has the right to inspect the association records pursuant to Section 8333 of the Corporations Code, and the following statement in 14–point boldface type, if printed, or in capital letters, if typed:

"IMPORTANT NOTICE: IF YOUR SEPARATE INTEREST IS PLACED IN FORECLOSURE BECAUSE YOU ARE BEHIND IN YOUR ASSESSMENTS, IT MAY BE SOLD WITHOUT COURT ACTION."

(b) An itemized statement of the charges owed by the owner, including items on the statement which indicate the amount of any delinquent assessments, the fees and reasonable costs of collection, reasonable attorney's fees, any late charges, and interest, if any.

(c) A statement that the owner shall not be liable to pay the charges, interest, and costs of collection, if it is determined the assessment was paid on time to the association. *(Added by Stats.2013, c. 605 (S.B.752), § 21.)*

§ 6814. Lien on separate interest; notice of delinquent assessment

(a) The amount of the assessment, plus any costs of collection, late charges, and interest assessed in accordance with Section 6808, shall be a lien on the owner's separate interest in the common interest development from and after the time the association causes to be recorded with the county recorder of the county in which the separate interest is located, a notice of delinquent assessment, which shall state the amount of the assessment and other sums imposed in accordance with Section 6808, a legal description of the owner's separate interest in the common interest development against which the assessment and other sums are levied, and the name of the record owner of the separate interest in the common interest development against which the lien is imposed.

(b) The itemized statement of the charges owed by the owner described in subdivision (b) of Section 6812 shall be recorded together with the notice of delinquent assessment.

(c) In order for the lien to be enforced by nonjudicial foreclosure as provided in Sections 6820 and 6822, the notice of delinquent assessment shall state the name and address of the trustee authorized by the association to enforce the lien by sale.

(d) The notice of delinquent assessment shall be signed by the person designated in the declaration or by the association for that purpose, or if no one is designated, by the president of the association.

(e) A copy of the recorded notice of delinquent assessment shall be mailed by certified mail to every person whose name is shown as an owner of the separate interest in the association's records, and the notice shall be mailed no later than 10 calendar days after recordation. *(Added by Stats. 2013, c. 605 (S.B.752), § 21.)*

§ 6816. Priority of lien

A lien created pursuant to Section 6814 shall be prior to all other liens recorded subsequent to the notice of delinquent assessment, except that the declaration may provide for the subordination thereof to any other liens and encumbrances. *(Added by Stats.2013, c. 605 (S.B.752), § 21.)*

§ 6818. Recording of lien

(a) Within 21 days of the payment of the sums specified in the notice of delinquent assessment, the association shall record or cause to be recorded in the office of the county recorder in which the notice of delinquent assessment is recorded a lien release or notice of rescission and provide the owner of the separate interest a copy of the lien release or notice that the delinquent assessment has been satisfied.

(b) If it is determined that a lien previously recorded against the separate interest was recorded in error, the party who recorded the lien shall, within 21 calendar days, record or cause to be recorded in the office of the county recorder in which the notice of delinquent assessment is recorded a lien release or notice of rescission and provide the owner of the separate interest with a declaration that the lien filing or recording was in error and a copy of the lien release or notice of rescission. *(Added by Stats.2013, c. 605 (S.B.752), § 21.)*

§ 6819. Recommencement of notice process for failure to comply with procedures

An association that fails to comply with the procedures set forth in this section shall, prior to recording a lien, recommence the required notice process. Any costs associated with recommencing the notice process shall be borne by the association and not by the owner of a separate interest. *(Added by Stats.2013, c. 605 (S.B.752), § 21.)*

ARTICLE 3. ASSESSMENT COLLECTION

Section
6820. Enforcement of lien.
6822. Trustee sale; procedure; notice; trustee fees.
6824. Monetary charge for repair of damage to common area and facilities; monetary penalties.
6826. Assignment or pledge prohibited; exception.
6828. Application of article to liens.

§ 6820. Enforcement of lien

(a) Except as otherwise provided in this article, after the expiration of 30 days following the recording of a lien created pursuant to Section 6814, the lien may be enforced in any manner permitted by law, including sale by the court, sale by the trustee designated in the notice of delinquent assessment, or sale by a trustee substituted pursuant to Section 2934a.

(b) Nothing in Article 2 (commencing with Section 6808) or in subdivision (a) of Section 726 of the Code of Civil Procedure prohibits actions against the owner of a separate interest to recover sums for which a lien is created pursuant to Article 2 (commencing with Section 6808) or prohibits an association from taking a deed in lieu of foreclosure. *(Added by Stats.2013, c. 605 (S.B.752), § 21.)*

§ 6822. Trustee sale; procedure; notice; trustee fees

(a) Any sale by the trustee shall be conducted in accordance with Sections 2924, 2924b, and 2924c applicable to the exercise of powers of sale in mortgages and deeds of trust.

(b) In addition to the requirements of Section 2924, the association shall serve a notice of default on the person named as the owner of the separate interest in the association's records or, if that person has designated a legal representative pursuant to this subdivision, on that legal representative. Service shall be in accordance with the manner of service of summons in Article 3 (commencing with Section 415.10) of Chapter 4 of Title 5 of Part 2 of the Code of Civil Procedure. An owner may designate a legal representative in a writing that is mailed to the association in a manner that indicates that the association has received it.

(c) The fees of a trustee may not exceed the amounts prescribed in Sections 2924c and 2924d, plus the cost of service for the notice of default pursuant to subdivision (b). *(Added by Stats.2013, c. 605 (S.B.752), § 21.)*

§ 6824. Monetary charge for repair of damage to common area and facilities; monetary penalties

(a) A monetary charge imposed by the association as a means of reimbursing the association for costs incurred by the association in the repair of damage to common areas and facilities caused by a member or the member's guest or tenant may become a lien against the member's separate interest enforceable by the sale of the interest under Sections 2924, 2924b, and 2924c, provided the authority to impose a lien is set forth in the governing documents.

(b) A monetary penalty imposed by the association as a disciplinary measure for failure of a member to comply with the governing documents, except for the late payments, may not be characterized nor treated in the governing documents as an assessment that may become a lien against the member's separate interest enforceable by the sale of the interest under Sections 2924, 2924b, and 2924c. *(Added by Stats.2013, c. 605 (S.B.752), § 21.)*

§ 6826. Assignment or pledge prohibited; exception

(a) An association may not voluntarily assign or pledge the association's right to collect payments or assessments, or to enforce or foreclose a lien to a third party, except when the assignment or pledge is made to a financial institution or lender chartered or licensed under federal or state law, when acting within the scope of that charter or license, as security for a loan obtained by the association.

(b) Nothing in subdivision (a) restricts the right or ability of an association to assign any unpaid obligations of a former member to a third party for purposes of collection. *(Added by Stats.2013, c. 605 (S.B.752), § 21.)*

§ 6828. Application of article to liens

(a) Except as otherwise provided, this article applies to a lien created on or after January 1, 2014.

(b) A lien created before January 1, 2014, is governed by the law in existence at the time the lien was created. *(Added by Stats.2013, c. 605 (S.B.752), § 21.)*

CHAPTER 8. INSURANCE AND LIABILITY

Section
6840. Tort actions against owner of separate interest; tenant in common in common area; association liability; insurance requirements.

§ 6840. Tort actions against owner of separate interest; tenant in common in common area; association liability; insurance requirements

(a) It is the intent of the Legislature to offer civil liability protection to owners of the separate interests in a common interest development that have common area owned in tenancy in common if the association carries a certain level of prescribed insurance that covers a cause of action in tort.

(b) Any cause of action in tort against any owner of a separate interest arising solely by reason of an ownership interest as a tenant in common in the common area of a common interest development shall be brought only against the association and not against the individual owners of the separate interests, if both of the insurance requirements in paragraphs (1) and (2) are met:

(1) The association maintained and has in effect for this cause of action, one or more policies of insurance that include coverage for general liability of the association.

(2) The coverage described in paragraph (1) is in the following minimum amounts:

(A) At least two million dollars ($2,000,000) if the common interest development consists of 100 or fewer separate interests.

(B) At least three million dollars ($3,000,000) if the common interest development consists of more than 100 separate interests. *(Added by Stats.2013, c. 605 (S.B.752), § 21.)*

CHAPTER 9. DISPUTE RESOLUTION AND ENFORCEMENT

Article	Section
1. Disciplinary Action	6850
2. Civil Actions	6856

ARTICLE 1. DISCIPLINARY ACTION

Section
6850. Monetary penalties; provision of information to members.
6854. Authority of board to impose monetary penalties.

§ 6850. Monetary penalties; provision of information to members

(a) If an association adopts or has adopted a policy imposing any monetary penalty, including any fee, on any association member for a violation of the governing documents, including any monetary penalty relating to the activities of a guest or tenant of the member, the board shall adopt and distribute to each member, by individual notice, a schedule of the monetary penalties that may be assessed for those violations, which shall be in accordance with authorization for member discipline contained in the governing documents.

(b) Any new or revised monetary penalty that is adopted after complying with subdivision (a) may be included in a supplement that is delivered to the members individually, pursuant to Section 6553.

(c) A monetary penalty for a violation of the governing documents shall not exceed the monetary penalty stated in the schedule of monetary penalties or supplement that is in effect at the time of the violation.

(d) An association shall provide a copy of the most recently distributed schedule of monetary penalties, along with any applicable supplements to that schedule, to any member on request. *(Added by Stats.2013, c. 605 (S.B.752), § 21.)*

§ 6854. Authority of board to impose monetary penalties

Nothing in Section 6850 shall be construed to create, expand, or reduce the authority of the board to impose monetary penalties on a member for a violation of the governing documents. *(Added by Stats.2013, c. 605 (S.B.752), § 21.)*

ARTICLE 2. CIVIL ACTIONS

Section
6856. Covenants and restrictions in declaration as equitable servitudes; enforcement.
6858. Standing.
6860. Reduction of damages awarded; comparative fault of association.

§ 6856. Covenants and restrictions in declaration as equitable servitudes; enforcement

(a) The covenants and restrictions in the declaration shall be enforceable equitable servitudes, unless unreasonable, and shall inure to the benefit of and bind all owners of separate interests in the development. Unless the declaration states otherwise, these servitudes may be enforced by any owner of a separate interest or by the association, or by both.

(b) A governing document other than the declaration may be enforced by the association against an owner of a separate interest or by an owner of a separate interest against the association. *(Added by Stats.2013, c. 605 (S.B.752), § 21.)*

§ 6858. Standing

An association has standing to institute, defend, settle, or intervene in litigation, arbitration, mediation, or administrative proceedings in its own name as the real party in interest and without joining with it, the members, in matters pertaining to the following:

(a) Enforcement of the governing documents.

(b) Damage to the common area.

(c) Damage to a separate interest that the association is obligated to maintain or repair.

(d) Damage to a separate interest that arises out of, or is integrally related to, damage to the common area or a separate interest that the association is obligated to maintain or repair. *(Added by Stats.2013, c. 605 (S.B.752), § 21.)*

§ 6860. Reduction of damages awarded; comparative fault of association

(a) In an action maintained by an association pursuant to subdivision (b), (c), or (d) of Section 6858, the amount of damages recovered by the association shall be reduced by the amount of damages allocated to the association or its managing agents in direct proportion to their percentage of fault based upon principles of comparative fault. The comparative fault of the association or its managing agents may be raised by way of defense, but shall not be the basis for a cross-action or separate action against the association or its managing agents for contribution or implied indemnity, where the only damage was sustained by the association or its members. It is the intent of the Legislature in enacting this subdivision to require that comparative fault be pleaded as an affirmative defense, rather than a separate cause of action, where the only damage was sustained by the association or its members.

(b) In an action involving damages described in subdivision (b), (c), or (d) of Section 6858, the defendant or cross-defendant may allege and prove the comparative fault of the association or its managing agents as a setoff to the liability of the defendant or cross-defendant even if the association is not a party to the litigation or is no longer a party whether by reason of settlement, dismissal, or otherwise.

(c) Subdivisions (a) and (b) apply to actions commenced on or after January 1, 1993.

(d) Nothing in this section affects a person's liability under Section 1431, or the liability of the association or its managing agent for an act or omission that causes damages to another. *(Added by Stats.2013, c. 605 (S.B.752), § 21.)*

CHAPTER 10. CONSTRUCTION DEFECT LITIGATION

Section
6870.   Repealed.
6874.   Settlement agreements regarding alleged defects; notice of resolution to members on record; disclosures.
6876.   Written notice to members prior to filing civil action; contents.
7000 to 7003.   Repealed.
7004.   Repealed.
7004.5 to 7008.   Repealed.
7009.   Repealed.
7010 to 7018.   Repealed.
7020.   Repealed.
7021.   Repealed.

§ 6870. Repealed by Stats.2013, c. 605 (S.B.752), § 21, operative Jan. 1, 2018

§ 6874. Settlement agreements regarding alleged defects; notice of resolution to members on record; disclosures

(a) As soon as is reasonably practicable after the association and the builder have entered into a settlement agreement or the matter has otherwise been resolved regarding alleged defects in the common areas, alleged defects in the separate interests that the association is obligated to maintain or repair, or alleged defects in the separate interests that arise out of, or are integrally related to, defects in the common areas or separate interests that the association is obligated to maintain or repair, where the defects giving rise to the dispute have not been corrected, the association shall, in writing, inform only the members of the association whose names appear on the records of the association that the matter has been resolved, by settlement agreement or other means, and disclose all of the following:

(1) A general description of the defects that the association reasonably believes, as of the date of the disclosure, will be corrected or replaced.

(2) A good faith estimate, as of the date of the disclosure, of when the association believes that the defects identified in paragraph (1) will be corrected or replaced. The association may state that the estimate may be modified.

(3) The status of the claims for defects in the design or construction of the common interest development that were not identified in paragraph (1) whether expressed in a preliminary list of defects sent to each member of the association or otherwise claimed and disclosed to the members of the association.

(b) Nothing in this section shall preclude an association from amending the disclosures required pursuant to subdivision (a), and any amendments shall supersede any prior conflicting information disclosed to the members of the association and shall retain any privilege attached to the original disclosures.

(c) Disclosure of the information required pursuant to subdivision (a) or authorized by subdivision (b) shall not waive any privilege attached to the information.

(d) For the purposes of the disclosures required pursuant to this section, the term "defects" shall be defined to include any damage resulting from defects. *(Added by Stats.2013, c. 605 (S.B.752), § 21.)*

§ 6876. Written notice to members prior to filing civil action; contents

(a) Not later than 30 days prior to the filing of any civil action by the association against the declarant or other developer of a common interest development for alleged damage to the common areas, alleged damage to the separate interests that the association is obligated to maintain or repair, or alleged damage to the separate interests that arises out of, or is integrally related to, damage to the common areas or separate interests that the association is obligated to maintain or repair, the board shall provide a written notice to each member of the association who appears on the records of the association when the notice is provided. This notice shall specify all of the following:

(1) That a meeting will take place to discuss problems that may lead to the filing of a civil action.

(2) The options, including civil actions, that are available to address the problems.

(3) The time and place of this meeting.

(b) Notwithstanding subdivision (a), if the association has reason to believe that the applicable statute of limitations will expire before the association files the civil action, the association may give the notice, as described above, within 30 days after the filing of the action. *(Added by Stats.2013, c. 605 (S.B.752), § 21.)*

§§ 7000 to 7003. Repealed by Stats.1992, c. 162 (A.B.2650), § 4, operative Jan. 1, 1994

§ 7004. Repealed by Stats.1993, c. 219 (A.B.1500), § 63

§§ 7004.5 to 7008. Repealed by Stats.1992, c. 162 (A.B.2650), § 4, operative Jan. 1, 1994

§ 7009. Repealed by Stats.1993, c. 219 (A.B.1500), § 63.1

§§ 7010 to 7018. Repealed by Stats.1992, c. 162 (A.B.2650), § 4, operative Jan. 1, 1994

§ 7020. Repealed by Stats.1993, c. 219 (A.B.1500), § 63.2

§ 7021. Repealed by Stats.1992, c. 162 (A.B.2650), § 4, operative Jan. 1, 1994

Part 5.5

AUTOMATIC CHECKOUT SYSTEM

Section
7100. Readable prices on packaged consumer commodities; exemptions; listing and posting; definitions.
7101. Violations; civil fines; injunctions.
7102. Liability for losses and expenses; additional penalty; applicability.
7103. Unintentional error.
7104. Exclusive remedies.
7105. Short title.
7106. State preemption of item pricing.

§ 7100. Readable prices on packaged consumer commodities; exemptions; listing and posting; definitions

(a) Every retail grocery store or grocery department within a general retail merchandise store which uses a point-of-sale system shall cause to have a clearly readable price indicated on 85 percent of the total number of packaged consumer commodities offered for sale which are not exempt pursuant to subdivision (b).

The management of any such retail grocery store or grocery department shall determine the number of consumer commodities normally offered for sale on a daily basis, shall determine the consumer commodities to be exempted pursuant to this subdivision, and shall maintain a list of those consumer commodities exempt pursuant to this subdivision. The list shall be made available to a designated representative of the appropriate local union, the members of which are responsible for item pricing, in those stores or departments that have collective bargaining agreements, seven days prior to an item or items being exempted pursuant to this subdivision. In addition, the list shall be available and posted in a prominent place in the store seven days prior to an item or items being exempted pursuant to this subdivision.

(b) The provisions of this section shall not apply to any of the following:

(1) Any consumer commodity which was not generally item-priced on January 1, 1977, as determined by the Department of Food and Agriculture pursuant to subdivision (c) of Section 12604.5 of the Business and Professions Code, as in effect July 8, 1977.

(2) Any unpackaged fresh food produce, or to consumer commodities which are under three cubic inches in size, weigh less than three ounces, and are priced under forty cents ($0.40).

(3) Any consumer commodity offered as a sale item or as a special.

(4) Any business which has as its only regular employees the owner thereof, or the parent, spouse, or child of such owner, or, in addition thereto, not more than two other regular employees.

(5) Identical items within a multi-item package.

(6) Items sold through a vending machine.

(c) For the purposes of this section:

(1) "Point-of-sale system" means any computer or electronic system used by a retail establishment such as, but not limited to, Universal Product Code scanners, price lookup codes, or an electronic price lookup system as a means for determining the price of the item being purchased by a consumer.

(2) "Consumer commodity" includes:

(A) Food, including all material whether solid, liquid, or mixed, and whether simple or compound, which is used or intended for consumption by human beings or domestic animals normally kept as household pets, and all substances or ingredients added to any such material for any purpose. This definition shall not apply to individual packages of cigarettes or individual cigars.

(B) Napkins, facial tissues, toilet tissues, foil wrapping, plastic wrapping, paper toweling, and disposable plates and cups.

(C) Detergents, soaps, and other cleaning agents.

(D) Pharmaceuticals, including nonprescription drugs, bandages, female hygiene products, and toiletries.

(3) "Grocery department" means an area within a general retail merchandise store which is engaged primarily in the retail sale of packaged food, rather than food prepared for immediate consumption on or off the premises.

(4) "Grocery store" means a store engaged primarily in the retail sale of packaged food, rather than food prepared for consumption on the premises.

(5) "Sale item or special" means any consumer commodity offered in good faith for a period of 14 days or less, on sale at a price below the normal price that item is usually sold for in that store. The Department of Food and Agriculture shall determine the normal length of a sale held for consumer commodities generally item priced on January 1, 1977, in stores regulated pursuant to this chapter, and that period shall be used for the purposes of this subdivision. The department's determination as to the normal length of a sale shall be binding for the purposes of this section, but each such determination shall not exceed seven days. (Added by Stats.1981, c. 224, § 2. Amended by Stats.2006, c. 566 (A.B.2285), § 6.)

§ 7101. Violations; civil fines; injunctions

(a) The intentional violation of Section 7100 is punishable by a civil penalty of not less than twenty-five dollars ($25) nor more than five hundred dollars ($500).

(b) Failure to have a clearly readable price indicated on 12 units of the same item required to be item-priced of the same commodity shall constitute a presumption of intent to violate Section 7100.

(c) Every additional 12 units of the same item required to be item-priced that fail to have a price indicated on them shall constitute a presumption of intent to violate Section 7100.

(d) Each day that a violation continues shall also constitute a separate violation after notification thereof to the manager or assistant manager of the retail grocery store or the grocery department of the general retail merchandise store and shall constitute a presumption of intent to violate Section 7100.

(e) Notwithstanding any other provision of law, any person may bring an action to enjoin a violation of Section 7100. *(Added by Stats.1981, c. 224, § 2.)*

§ 7102. Liability for losses and expenses; additional penalty; applicability

Any person, firm, corporation, or association who violates Sections 7100 and 7101 shall be liable to any person injured for any losses and expenses thereby incurred, and for the sum of fifty dollars ($50) in addition thereto. The remedy set forth herein is applicable only to actions brought in the name of, and on behalf of, a single plaintiff and shall not be applicable in multiple plaintiff or class actions. *(Added by Stats.1981, c. 224, § 2.)*

§ 7103. Unintentional error

Improper pricing on the shelf or on the item due to unintentional error shall not constitute a violation of this division. *(Added by Stats.1981, c. 224, § 2.)*

§ 7104. Exclusive remedies

The remedies set forth in Sections 7101 and 7102 are the exclusive remedies available to any person, state or local agency or law enforcement official. *(Added by Stats.1981, c. 224, § 2.)*

§ 7105. Short title

This part shall be known and may be cited as the Rosenthal–Roberti Item Pricing Act. *(Added by Stats.1981, c. 224, § 2.)*

§ 7106. State preemption of item pricing

It is the intention of the Legislature that this part shall occupy the field with regard to item pricing and shall preempt all local ordinances, rules, or regulations concerning item pricing. *(Added by Stats.1981, c. 224, § 2.)*

Part 6

WORKS OF IMPROVEMENT

Title	Section
1. Works of Improvement Generally	8000
2. Private Works of Improvement	8160
3. Public Work of Improvement	9000

Operative Effect

For operative effect of Part 6, see Civil Code § 8052 and Stats.2010, c. 697 (S.B.189), § 105.

Cross References

Commercial and industrial common interest developments, claim of lien, notice to members, see Civil Code § 6660.
Common interest developments, claim of lien, notice to members, see Civil Code § 4620.

Title 1

WORKS OF IMPROVEMENT GENERALLY

Chapter	Section
1. General Provisions	8000
2. Notice	8100
3. Waiver and Release	8120
4. Bonds	8150

Operative Effect

For operative effect of Part 6, see Civil Code § 8052 and Stats.2010, c. 697 (S.B.189), § 105.

CHAPTER 1. GENERAL PROVISIONS

Article	Section
1. Definitions	8000
2. Miscellaneous Provisions	8052

Operative Effect

For operative effect of Part 6, see Civil Code § 8052 and Stats.2010, c. 697 (S.B.189), § 105.

ARTICLE 1. DEFINITIONS

Section
8000. Construction of part.
8002. "Admitted surety insurer" defined.
8004. "Claimant" defined.
8006. "Construction lender" defined.
8008. "Contract" defined.
8010. "Contract price" defined.
8012. "Contractor" defined.
8014. "Design professional" defined.
8016. "Direct contract" defined.
8018. "Direct contractor" defined.
8020. "Funds" defined.
8022. "Labor, service, equipment, or material" defined.
8024. "Laborer" defined.
8026. "Lien" defined.
8028. "Material supplier" defined.
8030. "Payment bond" defined.
8032. "Person" defined.
8034. "Preliminary notice" defined.

Section
8036. "Public entity" defined.
8038. "Public works contract" defined.
8040. "Site" defined.
8042. "Site improvement" defined.
8044. "Stop payment notice" defined.
8046. "Subcontractor" defined.
8048. "Work" defined.
8050. "Work of improvement" defined.

Operative Effect

For operative effect of Part 6, see Civil Code § 8052 and Stats.2010, c. 697 (S.B.189), § 105.

§ 8000. Construction of part

Unless the provision or context otherwise requires, the definitions in this article govern the construction of this part. *(Added by Stats.2010, c. 697 (S.B.189), § 20, operative July 1, 2012.)*

Operative Effect

For operative effect of Part 6, see Civil Code § 8052 and Stats.2010, c. 697 (S.B.189), § 105.

Cross References

Construction of and terms and conditions of bonds, see Civil Code § 8152 et seq.
Liberal construction, see Civil Code § 4.
Statutory construction,
   Duty of judge, see Code of Civil Procedure § 1858; Evidence Code §§ 310, 457.
   Intention of Legislature, see Code of Civil Procedure § 1859.

§ 8002. "Admitted surety insurer" defined

"Admitted surety insurer" has the meaning provided in Section 995.120 of the Code of Civil Procedure. *(Added by Stats.2010, c. 697 (S.B.189), § 20, operative July 1, 2012.)*

Operative Effect

For operative effect of Part 6, see Civil Code § 8052 and Stats.2010, c. 697 (S.B.189), § 105.

§ 8004. "Claimant" defined

"Claimant" means a person that has a right under this part to record a claim of lien, give a stop payment notice, or assert a claim against a payment bond, or do any combination of the foregoing. *(Added by Stats.2010, c. 697 (S.B.189), § 20, operative July 1, 2012.)*

Operative Effect

For operative effect of Part 6, see Civil Code § 8052 and Stats.2010, c. 697 (S.B.189), § 105.

Cross References

Lien, persons entitled to, see Civil Code § 8400.
Payment bond,
   Private works of improvement, see Civil Code § 8606.
   Public works of improvement, see Civil Code § 9554.
Stop payment notice,
   Contents, see Civil Code §§ 8502, 9352.
   Defined, see Civil Code § 8044.
   Notice, see Civil Code §§ 8506, 8508, 8530, 9354.

Private work, persons entitled, see Civil Code § 8520.
Public work, persons entitled, see Civil Code § 9100.
Withholding of funds, see Civil Code §§ 8536, 8538, 8542.

§ 8006. "Construction lender" defined

"Construction lender" means either of the following:

(a) A mortgagee or beneficiary under a deed of trust lending funds with which the cost of all or part of a work of improvement is to be paid, or the assignee or successor in interest of the mortgagee or beneficiary.

(b) An escrow holder or other person holding funds provided by an owner, lender, or another person as a fund for with which the cost of all or part of a work of improvement is to be paid. *(Added by Stats.2010, c. 697 (S.B.189), § 20, operative July 1, 2012.)*

Operative Effect

For operative effect of Part 6, see Civil Code § 8052 and Stats.2010, c. 697 (S.B.189), § 105.

Cross References

Work of improvement defined, see Civil Code § 8050.

§ 8008. "Contract" defined

"Contract" means an agreement that provides for all or part of a work of improvement. *(Added by Stats.2010, c. 697 (S.B.189), § 20, operative July 1, 2012.)*

Operative Effect

For operative effect of Part 6, see Civil Code § 8052 and Stats.2010, c. 697 (S.B.189), § 105.

Cross References

Contracts, generally, see Civil Code § 1549 et seq.
Ownership, see Civil Code § 669 et seq.
Work of improvement defined, see Civil Code § 8050.

§ 8010. "Contract price" defined

"Contract price" means the price agreed to in a direct contract for a work of improvement. *(Added by Stats.2010, c. 697 (S.B.189), § 20, operative July 1, 2012.)*

Operative Effect

For operative effect of Part 6, see Civil Code § 8052 and Stats.2010, c. 697 (S.B.189), § 105.

§ 8012. "Contractor" defined

"Contractor" includes a direct contractor, subcontractor, or both. This section does not apply to Sections 8018 and 8046. *(Added by Stats.2010, c. 697 (S.B.189), § 20, operative July 1, 2012.)*

Operative Effect

For operative effect of Part 6, see Civil Code § 8052 and Stats.2010, c. 697 (S.B.189), § 105.

§ 8014. "Design professional" defined

"Design professional" means a person licensed as an architect pursuant to Chapter 3 (commencing with Section 5500) of Division 3 of the Business and Professions Code, licensed as a landscape architect pursuant to Chapter 3.5 (commencing with Section 5615) of Division 3 of the Business and Professions Code, registered as a professional engineer pursuant to Chapter 7 (commencing with Section 6700) of Division 3 of the Business and Professions Code, or licensed as a land surveyor pursuant to Chapter 15 (commencing with Section 8700) of Division 3 of the Business and Professions Code. *(Added by Stats.2010, c. 697 (S.B.189), § 20, operative July 1, 2012.)*

Operative Effect

For operative effect of Part 6, see Civil Code § 8052 and Stats.2010, c. 697 (S.B.189), § 105.

§ 8016. "Direct contract" defined

"Direct contract" means a contract between an owner and a direct contractor that provides for all or part of a work of improvement. *(Added by Stats.2010, c. 697 (S.B.189), § 20, operative July 1, 2012.)*

Operative Effect

For operative effect of Part 6, see Civil Code § 8052 and Stats.2010, c. 697 (S.B.189), § 105.

Cross References

Contract defined, see Civil Code § 8008.
Contracts, generally, see Civil Code § 1549 et seq.
Direct contractor defined, see Civil Code § 8018.
Ownership, see Civil Code § 669 et seq.
Work of improvement defined, see Civil Code § 8050.

§ 8018. "Direct contractor" defined

"Direct contractor" means a contractor that has a direct contractual relationship with an owner. A reference in another statute to a "prime contractor" in connection with the provisions in this part means a "direct contractor." *(Added by Stats.2010, c. 697 (S.B.189), § 20, operative July 1, 2012.)*

Operative Effect

For operative effect of Part 6, see Civil Code § 8052 and Stats.2010, c. 697 (S.B.189), § 105.

Cross References

Owner, definition for purposes of notice of cessation, see Civil Code § 8188.
Ownership, see Civil Code § 669 et seq.
Recovery upon claim of lien by direct contractor or subcontractor, see Civil Code § 8434.

§ 8020. "Funds" defined

For the purposes of Title 3 (commencing with Section 9000), "funds" means warrant, check, money, or bonds (if bonds are to be issued in payment of the public works contract). *(Added by Stats.2010, c. 697 (S.B.189), § 20, operative July 1, 2012.)*

Operative Effect

For operative effect of Part 6, see Civil Code § 8052 and Stats.2010, c. 697 (S.B.189), § 105.

§ 8022. "Labor, service, equipment, or material" defined

"Labor, service, equipment, or material" includes, but is not limited to, labor, skills, services, material, supplies, equipment, appliances, power, and surveying, provided for a work of improvement. (Added by Stats.2010, c. 697 (S.B. 189), § 20, operative July 1, 2012.)

Operative Effect

For operative effect of Part 6, see Civil Code § 8052 and Stats.2010, c. 697 (S.B.189), § 105.

§ 8024. "Laborer" defined

(a) "Laborer" means a person who, acting as an employee, performs labor upon, or bestows skill or other necessary services on, a work of improvement.

(b) "Laborer" includes a person or entity to which a portion of a laborer's compensation for a work of improvement, including, but not limited to, employer payments described in Section 1773.1 of the Labor Code and implementing regulations, is paid by agreement with that laborer or the collective bargaining agent of that laborer.

(c) A person or entity described in subdivision (b) that has standing under applicable law to maintain a direct legal action, in its own name or as an assignee, to collect any portion of compensation owed for a laborer for a work of improvement, shall have standing to enforce any rights or claims of the laborer under this part, to the extent of the compensation agreed to be paid to the person or entity for labor on that improvement. This subdivision is intended to give effect to the longstanding public policy of this state to protect the entire compensation of a laborer on a work of improvement, regardless of the form in which that compensation is to be paid. (Added by Stats.2010, c. 697 (S.B.189), § 20, operative July 1, 2012.)

Operative Effect

For operative effect of Part 6, see Civil Code § 8052 and Stats.2010, c. 697 (S.B.189), § 105.

Cross References

Authority to serve stop payment notices, persons named in this section, see Civil Code §§ 8520, 8530, 9100.
Payment bond claims, preliminary notice required, exception for laborers defined pursuant to this section, see Civil Code §§ 8612, 9560.
Work of improvement defined, see Civil Code § 8050.

§ 8026. "Lien" defined

"Lien" means a lien under Title 2 (commencing with Section 8160) and includes a lien of a design professional under Section 8302, a lien for a work of improvement under Section 8400, and a lien for a site improvement under Section 8402. (Added by Stats.2010, c. 697 (S.B.189), § 20, operative July 1, 2012.)

Operative Effect

For operative effect of Part 6, see Civil Code § 8052 and Stats.2010, c. 697 (S.B.189), § 105.

§ 8028. "Material supplier" defined

"Material supplier" means a person that provides material or supplies to be used or consumed in a work of improvement. (Added by Stats.2010, c. 697 (S.B.189), § 20, operative July 1, 2012.)

Operative Effect

For operative effect of Part 6, see Civil Code § 8052 and Stats.2010, c. 697 (S.B.189), § 105.

Cross References

Work of improvement defined, see Civil Code § 8050.

§ 8030. "Payment bond" defined

(a) For the purposes of Title 2 (commencing with Section 8160), "payment bond" means a bond given under Section 8600.

(b) For the purposes of Title 3 (commencing with Section 9000), "payment bond" means a bond required by Section 9550. (Added by Stats.2010, c. 697 (S.B.189), § 20, operative July 1, 2012.)

Operative Effect

For operative effect of Part 6, see Civil Code § 8052 and Stats.2010, c. 697 (S.B.189), § 105.

Cross References

General provisions relating to bonds, see Civil Code § 8150 et seq.
Ownership, see Civil Code § 669 et seq.
Payment bond for private works, see Civil Code § 8600 et seq.
Payment bond for public works, see Civil Code § 9550 et seq.
Payment bond procured by landowner, mortgagee or trustee on site improvement, priority of liens, see Civil Code § 8458.
Payment bond procured by mortgagee or trustee, priority of liens, see Civil Code § 8452.
Suretyship, see Civil Code § 2787 et seq.

§ 8032. "Person" defined

"Person" means an individual, corporation, public entity, business trust, estate, trust, partnership, limited liability company, association, or other entity. (Added by Stats.2010, c. 697 (S.B.189), § 20, operative July 1, 2012.)

Operative Effect

For operative effect of Part 6, see Civil Code § 8052 and Stats.2010, c. 697 (S.B.189), § 105.

§ 8034. "Preliminary notice" defined

(a) For the purposes of Title 2 (commencing with Section 8160), "preliminary notice" means the notice provided for in Chapter 2 (commencing with Section 8200) of Title 2.

(b) For the purposes of Title 3 (commencing with Section 9000), "preliminary notice" means the notice provided for in Chapter 3 (commencing with Section 9300) of Title 3. (Added by Stats.2010, c. 697 (S.B.189), § 20, operative July 1, 2012.)

Operative Effect

For operative effect of Part 6, see Civil Code § 8052 and Stats.2010, c. 697 (S.B.189), § 105.

Cross References

Bonded stop notice, see Civil Code § 8532.
Claim of lien, see Civil Code § 8416.
County recorder, fees for filing notice, see Government Code § 27361.9.
Necessity of preliminary notice, see Civil Code §§ 8410, 9500.
Notice to surety and bond principal, see Civil Code §§ 8614, 9562.
Private works of improvement, recordation of notice of completion or cessation, notification requirements, see Civil Code § 8190.
Stop payment notice, contents, see Civil Code §§ 8502, 9352.
Validity of stop payment notice, see Civil Code § 8508.

§ 8036. "Public entity" defined

"Public entity" means the state, Regents of the University of California, a county, city, district, public authority, public agency, and any other political subdivision or public corporation in the state. *(Added by Stats.2010, c. 697 (S.B.189), § 20, operative July 1, 2012.)*

Operative Effect

For operative effect of Part 6, see Civil Code § 8052 and Stats.2010, c. 697 (S.B.189), § 105.

§ 8038. "Public works contract" defined

"Public works contract" has the meaning provided in Section 1101 of the Public Contract Code. *(Added by Stats.2010, c. 697 (S.B.189), § 20, operative July 1, 2012.)*

Operative Effect

For operative effect of Part 6, see Civil Code § 8052 and Stats.2010, c. 697 (S.B.189), § 105.

§ 8040. "Site" defined

"Site" means the real property on which a work of improvement is situated or planned. *(Added by Stats.2010, c. 697 (S.B.189), § 20, operative July 1, 2012.)*

Operative Effect

For operative effect of Part 6, see Civil Code § 8052 and Stats.2010, c. 697 (S.B.189), § 105.

§ 8042. "Site improvement" defined

"Site improvement" means any of the following work on real property:

(a) Demolition or removal of improvements, trees, or other vegetation.

(b) Drilling test holes.

(c) Grading, filling, or otherwise improving the real property or a street, highway, or sidewalk in front of or adjoining the real property.

(d) Construction or installation of sewers or other public utilities.

(e) Construction of areas, vaults, cellars, or rooms under sidewalks.

(f) Any other work or improvements in preparation of the site for a work of improvement. *(Added by Stats.2010, c. 697 (S.B.189), § 20, operative July 1, 2012.)*

Operative Effect

For operative effect of Part 6, see Civil Code § 8052 and Stats.2010, c. 697 (S.B.189), § 105.

Cross References

Lien of claimant making site improvement, see Civil Code § 8402.
Liens for site improvements, priority, see Civil Code § 8458.
Site improvement as separate direct contract, see Civil Code § 8454.

§ 8044. "Stop payment notice" defined

(a)(1) For the purposes of Title 2 (commencing with Section 8160), "stop payment notice" means the notice given by a claimant under Chapter 5 (commencing with Section 8500) of Title 2.

(2) A stop payment notice given under Title 2 (commencing with Section 8160) may be bonded or unbonded. A "bonded stop payment notice" is a notice given with a bond under Section 8532. An "unbonded stop payment notice" is a notice not given with a bond under Section 8532.

(3) Except to the extent Title 2 (commencing with Section 8160) distinguishes between a bonded and an unbonded stop payment notice, a reference in that title to a stop payment notice includes both a bonded and an unbonded notice.

(b) For the purposes of Title 3 (commencing with Section 9000), "stop payment notice" means the notice given by a claimant under Chapter 4 (commencing with Section 9350) of Title 3.

(c) A reference in another statute to a "stop notice" in connection with the remedies provided in this part means a stop payment notice. *(Added by Stats.2010, c. 697 (S.B.189), § 20, operative July 1, 2012.)*

Operative Effect

For operative effect of Part 6, see Civil Code § 8052 and Stats.2010, c. 697 (S.B.189), § 105.

Cross References

Notice to public entity of commencement of action to enforce payment of claim stated in stop payment notice, see Civil Code § 9504.
Preliminary notice (private work), necessity prior to stop payment notice, see Civil Code § 8200.
Preliminary notice (public work), stop payment notice, see Civil Code § 9300.
Private works of improvement, validity of stop payment notice, see Civil Code § 8508.
Stop payment notice,
  Private works, see Civil Code § 8500 et seq.
  Public works, see Civil Code § 9350 et seq.

§ 8046. "Subcontractor" defined

"Subcontractor" means a contractor that does not have a direct contractual relationship with an owner. The term includes a contractor that has a contractual relationship with a direct contractor or with another subcontractor. *(Added by Stats.2010, c. 697 (S.B.189), § 20, operative July 1, 2012.)*

Operative Effect

For operative effect of Part 6, see Civil Code § 8052 and Stats.2010, c. 697 (S.B.189), § 105.

§ 8046 GENERAL PROVISIONS

Cross References

Recovery upon claim of lien by direct contractor or subcontractor, see Civil Code § 8434.

§ 8048. "Work" defined

"Work" means labor, service, equipment, or material provided to a work of improvement. *(Added by Stats.2010, c. 697 (S.B.189), § 20, operative July 1, 2012.)*

Operative Effect

For operative effect of Part 6, see Civil Code § 8052 and Stats.2010, c. 697 (S.B.189), § 105.

§ 8050. "Work of improvement" defined

(a) "Work of improvement" includes, but is not limited to:

(1) Construction, alteration, repair, demolition, or removal, in whole or in part, of, or addition to, a building, wharf, bridge, ditch, flume, aqueduct, well, tunnel, fence, machinery, railroad, or road.

(2) Seeding, sodding, or planting of real property for landscaping purposes.

(3) Filling, leveling, or grading of real property.

(b) Except as otherwise provided in this part, "work of improvement" means the entire structure or scheme of improvement as a whole, and includes site improvement. *(Added by Stats.2010, c. 697 (S.B.189), § 20, operative July 1, 2012.)*

Operative Effect

For operative effect of Part 6, see Civil Code § 8052 and Stats.2010, c. 697 (S.B.189), § 105.

Cross References

Site improvement defined, see Civil Code § 8042.

ARTICLE 2. MISCELLANEOUS PROVISIONS

Section
8052. Operative date and effect.
8054. Transactions excluded from application of part.
8056. Application of Code of Civil Procedure.
8058. "Day" defined.
8060. Filing or recording with county recorder; satisfaction of provisions; procedure; charge and collection of fees.
8062. Construction of good faith and compliant acts.
8064. Acts on behalf of co-owner.
8066. Acts by agents.

Operative Effect

For operative effect of Part 6, see Civil Code § 8052 and Stats.2010, c. 697 (S.B.189), § 105.

§ 8052. Operative date and effect

(a) This part is operative on July 1, 2012.

(b) Notwithstanding subdivision (a), the effectiveness of a notice given or other action taken on a work of improvement before July 1, 2012, is governed by the applicable law in effect before July 1, 2012, and not by this part.

(c) A provision of this part, insofar as it is substantially the same as a previously existing provision relating to the same subject matter, shall be construed as a restatement and continuation thereof and not as a new enactment. *(Added by Stats.2010, c. 697 (S.B.189), § 20, operative July 1, 2012.)*

Operative Effect

For operative effect of Part 6, see the terms of this section and Stats.2010, c. 697 (S.B.189), § 105.

§ 8054. Transactions excluded from application of part

(a) This part does not apply to a transaction governed by the Oil and Gas Lien Act (Chapter 2.5 (commencing with Section 1203.50) of Title 4 of Part 3 of the Code of Civil Procedure).

(b) This part does not apply to or change improvement security under the Subdivision Map Act (Division 2 (commencing with Section 66410) of Title 7 of the Government Code).

(c) This part does not apply to a transaction governed by Sections 20457 to 20464, inclusive, of the Public Contract Code. *(Added by Stats.2010, c. 697 (S.B.189), § 20, operative July 1, 2012.)*

Operative Effect

For operative effect of Part 6, see Civil Code § 8052 and Stats.2010, c. 697 (S.B.189), § 105.

§ 8056. Application of Code of Civil Procedure

Except as otherwise provided in this part, Part 2 (commencing with Section 307) of the Code of Civil Procedure provides the rules of practice in proceedings under this part. *(Added by Stats.2010, c. 697 (S.B.189), § 20, operative July 1, 2012.)*

Operative Effect

For operative effect of Part 6, see Civil Code § 8052 and Stats.2010, c. 697 (S.B.189), § 105.

Cross References

Appeals, generally, see Code of Civil Procedure § 901 et seq.
New trials, generally, see Code of Civil Procedure § 656 et seq.
Verification of pleadings, see Code of Civil Procedure § 446.

§ 8058. "Day" defined

For purposes of this part, "day" means a calendar day. *(Added by Stats.2010, c. 697 (S.B.189), § 20, operative July 1, 2012.)*

Operative Effect

For operative effect of Part 6, see Civil Code § 8052 and Stats.2010, c. 697 (S.B.189), § 105.

§ 8060. Filing or recording with county recorder; satisfaction of provisions; procedure; charge and collection of fees

(a) If this part provides for filing a contract, plan, or other paper with the county recorder, the provision is satisfied by filing the paper in the office of the county recorder of the county in which the work of improvement or part of it is situated.

(b) If this part provides for recording a notice, claim of lien, release of lien, payment bond, or other paper, the provision is satisfied by filing the paper for record in the office of the county recorder of the county in which the work of improvement or part of it is situated.

(c) The county recorder shall number, index, and preserve a contract, plan, or other paper presented for filing under this part, and shall number, index, and transcribe into the official records, in the same manner as a conveyance of real property, a notice, claim of lien, payment bond, or other paper recorded under this part.

(d) The county recorder shall charge and collect the fees provided in Article 5 (commencing with Section 27360) of Chapter 6 of Part 3 of Division 2 of Title 3 of the Government Code for performing duties under this section. *(Added by Stats.2010, c. 697 (S.B.189), § 20, operative July 1, 2012.)*

Operative Effect

For operative effect of Part 6, see Civil Code § 8052 and Stats.2010, c. 697 (S.B.189), § 105.

Cross References

Authority to waive rights unless waiver contrary to public policy, see Civil Code § 3268.
County recorder,
  Books, see Government Code § 27230 et seq.
  Documents to be recorded, see Government Code § 27280 et seq.
  Duties, generally, see Government Code § 27201 et seq.
  Fees, see Government Code § 27360 et seq.
  Indexes, see Government Code § 27232 et seq.
  Recording, see Government Code § 27320 et seq.
Recording,
  Claim of lien, see Civil Code § 8412 et seq.
  Constructive notice, see Civil Code § 1213.
  Time instrument deemed recorded, see Civil Code § 1170.
Written notice to surety and bond principal, see Civil Code §§ 8614, 9562.

§ 8062. Construction of good faith and compliant acts

No act of an owner in good faith and in compliance with a provision of this part shall be construed to prevent a direct contractor's performance of the contract, or exonerate a surety on a performance or payment bond. *(Added by Stats.2010, c. 697 (S.B.189), § 20, operative July 1, 2012.)*

Operative Effect

For operative effect of Part 6, see Civil Code § 8052 and Stats.2010, c. 697 (S.B.189), § 105.

Cross References

Bond for release of funds held under stop payment notice, see Civil Code § 8510.
Contracts, interpretation, see Civil Code § 1635 et seq.
Owners, see Civil Code § 669.
Sureties,
  Payment bond for private works, see Civil Code § 8600 et seq.
  Payment bond for public works, see Code of Civil Procedure § 995.310 et seq.
  Release or exoneration prohibited in certain situations, see Civil Code § 8152.

§ 8064. Acts on behalf of co-owner

An owner may give a notice or execute or file a document under this part on behalf of a co-owner if the owner acts on the co-owner's behalf and includes in the notice or document the name and address of the co-owner on whose behalf the owner acts. *(Added by Stats.2010, c. 697 (S.B.189), § 20, operative July 1, 2012.)*

Operative Effect

For operative effect of Part 6, see Civil Code § 8052 and Stats.2010, c. 697 (S.B.189), § 105.

§ 8066. Acts by agents

An act that may be done by or to a person under this part may be done by or to the person's agent to the extent the act is within the scope of the agent's authority. *(Added by Stats.2010, c. 697 (S.B.189), § 20, operative July 1, 2012.)*

Operative Effect

For operative effect of Part 6, see Civil Code § 8052 and Stats.2010, c. 697 (S.B.189), § 105.

CHAPTER 2. NOTICE

Section
8100. Written notice.
8102. Information to be included in notice.
8104. Failure to pay laborer full compensation; additional information required.
8106. Manner of giving notice.
8108. Location for giving notice.
8110. Notice by mail.
8114. Posting of notice; conspicuous location.
8116. Completion of notice; time deemed given.
8118. Proof of notice; declaration.
8119. Work of improvement on common area; association deemed to be agent of owners; delivery or service of notices.

Operative Effect

For operative effect of Part 6, see Civil Code § 8052 and Stats.2010, c. 697 (S.B.189), § 105.

§ 8100. Written notice

Notice under this part shall be in writing. Writing includes printing and typewriting. *(Added by Stats.2010, c. 697 (S.B.189), § 20, operative July 1, 2012.)*

Operative Effect

For operative effect of Part 6, see Civil Code § 8052 and Stats.2010, c. 697 (S.B.189), § 105.

§ 8102. Information to be included in notice

(a) Notice under this part shall, in addition to any other information required by statute for that type of notice, include all of the following information to the extent known to the person giving the notice:

(1) The name and address of the owner or reputed owner.

(2) The name and address of the direct contractor.

(3) The name and address of the construction lender, if any.

§ 8102

(4) A description of the site sufficient for identification, including the street address of the site, if any. If a sufficient legal description of the site is given, the effectiveness of the notice is not affected by the fact that the street address is erroneous or is omitted.

(5) The name, address, and relationship to the parties of the person giving the notice.

(6) If the person giving the notice is a claimant:

(A) A general statement of the work provided.

(B) The name of the person to or for whom the work is provided.

(C) A statement or estimate of the claimant's demand, if any, after deducting all just credits and offsets.

(b) Notice is not invalid by reason of any variance from the requirements of this section if the notice is sufficient to substantially inform the person given notice of the information required by this section and other information required in the notice. *(Added by Stats.2010, c. 697 (S.B.189), § 20, operative July 1, 2012.)*

Operative Effect

For operative effect of Part 6, see Civil Code § 8052 and Stats.2010, c. 697 (S.B.189), § 105.

Cross References

Claim of lien, see Civil Code § 8416.
County recorder, fees for filing notice, see Government Code § 27361.9.
Necessity of preliminary notice, see Civil Code §§ 8410, 9500.
Notice to surety and bond principal, see Civil Code §§ 8614, 9562.
Private works of improvement, recordation of notice of completion or cessation, notification requirements, see Civil Code § 8190.
Validity of stop payment notice, see Civil Code § 8508.

§ 8104. Failure to pay laborer full compensation; additional information required

(a) A direct contractor or subcontractor on a work of improvement governed by this part that employs a laborer and fails to pay the full compensation due the laborer, including any employer payments described in Section 1773.1 of the Labor Code and implementing regulations, shall not later than the date the compensation became delinquent, give the laborer, the laborer's bargaining representative, if any, the construction lender or reputed construction lender, if any, and the owner or reputed owner, notice that includes all of the following information, in addition to the information required by Section 8102:

(1) The name and address of the laborer, and of any person or entity described in subdivision (b) of Section 8024 to which employer payments are due.

(2) The total number of straight time and overtime hours worked by the laborer on each job.

(3) The amount then past due and owing.

(b) Failure to give the notice required by subdivision (a) constitutes grounds for disciplinary action under the Contractors' State License Law, Chapter 9 (commencing with Section 7000) of Division 3 of the Business and Professions Code. *(Added by Stats.2010, c. 697 (S.B.189), § 20, operative July 1, 2012.)*

Operative Effect

For operative effect of Part 6, see Civil Code § 8052 and Stats.2010, c. 697 (S.B.189), § 105.

Cross References

Claim of lien, see Civil Code § 8416.
County recorder, fees for filing notice, see Government Code § 27361.9.
Necessity of preliminary notice, see Civil Code §§ 8410, 9500.
Notice to surety and bond principal, see Civil Code §§ 8614, 9562.
Private works of improvement, recordation of notice of completion or cessation, notification requirements, see Civil Code § 8190.
Validity of stop payment notice, see Civil Code § 8508.

§ 8106. Manner of giving notice

Except as otherwise provided by statute, notice under this part shall be given by any of the following means:

(a) Personal delivery.

(b) Mail in the manner provided in Section 8110.

(c) Leaving the notice and mailing a copy in the manner provided in Section 415.20 of the Code of Civil Procedure for service of summons and complaint in a civil action. *(Added by Stats.2010, c. 697 (S.B.189), § 20, operative July 1, 2012.)*

Operative Effect

For operative effect of Part 6, see Civil Code § 8052 and Stats.2010, c. 697 (S.B.189), § 105.

§ 8108. Location for giving notice

Except as otherwise provided by this part, notice under this part shall be given to the person to be notified at the person's residence, the person's place of business, or at any of the following addresses:

(a) If the person to be notified is an owner other than a public entity, the owner's address shown on the direct contract, the building permit, or a construction trust deed.

(b) If the person to be notified is a public entity, the office of the public entity or another address specified by the public entity in the contract or elsewhere for service of notices, papers, and other documents.

(c) If the person to be notified is a construction lender, the construction lender's address shown on the construction loan agreement or construction trust deed.

(d) If the person to be notified is a direct contractor or a subcontractor, the contractor's address shown on the building permit, on the contractor's contract, or on the records of the Contractors' State License Board.

(e) If the person to be notified is a claimant, the claimant's address shown on the claimant's contract, preliminary notice, claim of lien, stop payment notice, or claim against a payment bond, or on the records of the Contractors' State License Board.

(f) If the person to be notified is a surety on a bond, the surety's address shown on the bond for service of notices, papers, and other documents, or on the records of the Department of Insurance. *(Added by Stats.2010, c. 697 (S.B.189), § 20, operative July 1, 2012.)*

Operative Effect

For operative effect of Part 6, see Civil Code § 8052 and Stats.2010, c. 697 (S.B.189), § 105.

§ 8110. Notice by mail

Except as otherwise provided by this part, notice by mail under this part shall be given by registered or certified mail, express mail, or overnight delivery by an express service carrier. *(Added by Stats.2010, c. 697 (S.B.189), § 20, operative July 1, 2012.)*

Operative Effect

For operative effect of Part 6, see Civil Code § 8052 and Stats.2010, c. 697 (S.B.189), § 105.

§ 8114. Posting of notice; conspicuous location

A notice required by this part to be posted shall be displayed in a conspicuous location at the site. *(Added by Stats.2010, c. 697 (S.B.189), § 20, operative July 1, 2012.)*

Operative Effect

For operative effect of Part 6, see Civil Code § 8052 and Stats.2010, c. 697 (S.B.189), § 105.

§ 8116. Completion of notice; time deemed given

Notice under this part is complete and deemed to have been given at the following times:

(a) If given by personal delivery, when delivered.

(b) If given by mail, when deposited in the mail or with an express service carrier in the manner provided in Section 1013 of the Code of Civil Procedure.

(c) If given by leaving the notice and mailing a copy in the manner provided in Section 415.20 of the Code of Civil Procedure for service of summons in a civil action, five days after mailing.

(d) If given by posting, when displayed.

(e) If given by recording, when recorded in the office of the county recorder. *(Added by Stats.2010, c. 697 (S.B.189), § 20, operative July 1, 2012.)*

Operative Effect

For operative effect of Part 6, see Civil Code § 8052 and Stats.2010, c. 697 (S.B.189), § 105.

Cross References

Claim of lien, see Civil Code § 8416.
County recorder, fees for filing notice, see Government Code § 27361.9.
Necessity of preliminary notice, see Civil Code §§ 8410, 9500.
Notice to surety and bond principal, see Civil Code §§ 8614, 9562.
Private works of improvement, recordation of notice of completion or cessation, notification requirements, see Civil Code § 8190.
Validity of stop payment notice, see Civil Code § 8508.

§ 8118. Proof of notice; declaration

(a) Proof that notice was given to a person in the manner required by this part shall be made by a proof of notice declaration that states all of the following:

(1) The type or description of the notice given.

(2) The date, place, and manner of notice, and facts showing that notice was given in the manner required by statute.

(3) The name and address of the person to which notice was given, and, if appropriate, the title or capacity in which the person was given notice.

(b) If the notice is given by mail, the declaration shall be accompanied by one of the following:

(1) Documentation provided by the United States Postal Service showing that payment was made to mail the notice using registered or certified mail, or express mail.

(2) Documentation provided by an express service carrier showing that payment was made to send the notice using an overnight delivery service.

(3) A return receipt, delivery confirmation, signature confirmation, tracking record, or other proof of delivery or attempted delivery provided by the United States Postal Service, or a photocopy of the record of delivery and receipt maintained by the United States Postal Service, showing the date of delivery and to whom delivered, or in the event of nondelivery, by the returned envelope itself.

(4) A tracking record or other documentation provided by an express service carrier showing delivery or attempted delivery of the notice. *(Added by Stats.2010, c. 697 (S.B.189), § 20, operative July 1, 2012.)*

Operative Effect

For operative effect of Part 6, see Civil Code § 8052 and Stats.2010, c. 697 (S.B.189), § 105.

§ 8119. Work of improvement on common area; association deemed to be agent of owners; delivery or service of notices

(a) With respect to a work of improvement on a common area within a common interest development: (1) The association is deemed to be an agent of the owners of separate interests in the common interest development for all notices and claims required by this part. (2) If any provision of this part requires the delivery or service of a notice or claim to or on the owner of common area property, the notice or claim may be delivered to or served on the association.

(b) For the purposes of this section, the terms "association," "common area," "common interest development," and "separate interest" have the meanings provided in Article 2 (commencing with Section 4075) of Chapter 1 of Part 5 and Article 2 (commencing with Section 6526) of Chapter 1 of Part 5.3. *(Added by Stats.2017, c. 44 (A.B.534), § 5, eff. Jan. 1, 2018.)*

Operative Effect

For operative effect of Part 6, see Civil Code § 8052 and Stats.2010, c. 697 (S.B.189), § 105.

CHAPTER 3. WAIVER AND RELEASE

Section
8120. Application of chapter.
8122. Waiver or impairment of rights prohibited; exception.
8124. Release from lien or claim; conditions.

GENERAL PROVISIONS

Section
- 8126. Estoppel or impairment of lien or claim; conditions.
- 8128. Stop payment notice; reduction or release.
- 8130. Accord and satisfaction; effect of article.
- 8132. Conditional waiver and release on progress payment; form.
- 8134. Unconditional waiver and release on progress payment; form.
- 8136. Conditional waiver and release on final payment; form.
- 8138. Unconditional waiver and release on final payment; form.

Operative Effect

For operative effect of Part 6, see Civil Code § 8052 and Stats.2010, c. 697 (S.B.189), § 105.

§ 8120. Application of chapter

The provisions of this chapter apply to a work of improvement governed by this part. (Added by Stats.2010, c. 697 (S.B.189), § 20, operative July 1, 2012.)

Operative Effect

For operative effect of Part 6, see Civil Code § 8052 and Stats.2010, c. 697 (S.B.189), § 105.

§ 8122. Waiver or impairment of rights prohibited; exception

An owner, direct contractor, or subcontractor may not, by contract or otherwise, waive, affect, or impair any other claimant's rights under this part, whether with or without notice, and any term of a contract that purports to do so is void and unenforceable unless and until the claimant executes and delivers a waiver and release under this article. (Added by Stats.2010, c. 697 (S.B.189), § 20, operative July 1, 2012.)

Operative Effect

For operative effect of Part 6, see Civil Code § 8052 and Stats.2010, c. 697 (S.B.189), § 105.

Cross References

Contracts,
  Defined, see Civil Code § 8008.
  Direct contract defined, see Civil Code § 8016.
  Interpretation, see Civil Code § 1635 et seq.
Waiver of code provisions, see Civil Code § 3268.

§ 8124. Release from lien or claim; conditions

A claimant's waiver and release does not release the owner, construction lender, or surety on a payment bond from a lien or claim unless both of the following conditions are satisfied:

(a) The waiver and release is in substantially the form provided in this article and is signed by the claimant.

(b) If the release is a conditional release, there is evidence of payment to the claimant. Evidence of payment may be either of the following:

(1) The claimant's endorsement on a single or joint payee check that has been paid by the financial institution on which it was drawn.

(2) Written acknowledgment of payment by the claimant. (Added by Stats.2010, c. 697 (S.B.189), § 20, operative July 1, 2012.)

Operative Effect

For operative effect of Part 6, see Civil Code § 8052 and Stats.2010, c. 697 (S.B.189), § 105.

Cross References

Waiver of code provisions, see Civil Code § 3268.

§ 8126. Estoppel or impairment of lien or claim; conditions

An oral or written statement purporting to waive, release, impair or otherwise adversely affect a lien or claim is void and unenforceable and does not create an estoppel or impairment of the lien or claim unless either of the following conditions is satisfied:

(a) The statement is pursuant to a waiver and release under this article.

(b) The claimant has actually received payment in full for the claim. (Added by Stats.2010, c. 697 (S.B.189), § 20, operative July 1, 2012.)

Operative Effect

For operative effect of Part 6, see Civil Code § 8052 and Stats.2010, c. 697 (S.B.189), § 105.

Cross References

Waiver of code provisions, see Civil Code § 3268.

§ 8128. Stop payment notice; reduction or release

(a) A claimant may reduce the amount of, or release in its entirety, a stop payment notice. The reduction or release shall be in writing and may be given in a form other than a waiver and release form provided in this article.

(b) The writing shall identify whether it is a reduction of the amount of the stop payment notice, or a release of the notice in its entirety. If the writing is a reduction, it shall state the amount of the reduction, and the amount to remain withheld after the reduction.

(c) A claimant's reduction or release of a stop payment notice has the following effect:

(1) The reduction or release releases the claimant's right to enforce payment of the claim stated in the notice to the extent of the reduction or release.

(2) The reduction or release releases the person given the notice from the obligation to withhold funds pursuant to the notice to the extent of the reduction or release.

(3) The reduction or release does not preclude the claimant from giving a subsequent stop payment notice that is timely and proper.

(4) The reduction or release does not release any right of the claimant other than the right to enforce payment of the claim stated in the stop payment notice to the extent of the reduction or release. (Added by Stats.2010, c. 697 (S.B.189), § 20, operative July 1, 2012.)

Operative Effect

For operative effect of Part 6, see Civil Code § 8052 and Stats.2010, c. 697 (S.B.189), § 105.

Cross References

Waiver of code provisions, see Civil Code § 3268.

§ 8130. Accord and satisfaction; effect of article

This article does not affect the enforceability of either an accord and satisfaction concerning a good faith dispute or an agreement made in settlement of an action pending in court if the accord and satisfaction or agreement and settlement make specific reference to the lien or claim. *(Added by Stats.2010, c. 697 (S.B.189), § 20, operative July 1, 2012.)*

Operative Effect

For operative effect of Part 6, see Civil Code § 8052 and Stats.2010, c. 697 (S.B.189), § 105.

§ 8132. Conditional waiver and release on progress payment; form

If a claimant is required to execute a waiver and release in exchange for, or in order to induce payment of, a progress payment and the claimant is not, in fact, paid in exchange for the waiver and release or a single payee check or joint payee check is given in exchange for the waiver and release, the waiver and release shall be null, void, and unenforceable unless it is in substantially the following form:

CONDITIONAL WAIVER AND RELEASE ON PROGRESS PAYMENT

NOTICE: THIS DOCUMENT WAIVES THE CLAIMANT'S LIEN, STOP PAYMENT NOTICE, AND PAYMENT BOND RIGHTS EFFECTIVE ON RECEIPT OF PAYMENT. A PERSON SHOULD NOT RELY ON THIS DOCUMENT UNLESS SATISFIED THAT THE CLAIMANT HAS RECEIVED PAYMENT.

Identifying Information

Name of Claimant: _____
Name of Customer: _____
Job Location: _____
Owner: _____
Through Date: _____

Conditional Waiver and Release

This document waives and releases lien, stop payment notice, and payment bond rights the claimant has for labor and service provided, and equipment and material delivered, to the customer on this job through the Through Date of this document. Rights based upon labor or service provided, or equipment or material delivered, pursuant to a written change order that has been fully executed by the parties prior to the date that this document is signed by the claimant, are waived and released by this document, unless listed as an Exception below. This document is effective only on the claimant's receipt of payment from the financial institution on which the following check is drawn:

Maker of Check: _____
Amount of Check: $ _____
Check Payable to: _____

Exceptions

This document does not affect any of the following:
(1) Retentions.
(2) Extras for which the claimant has not received payment.
(3) The following progress payments for which the claimant has previously given a conditional waiver and release but has not received payment:
Date(s) of waiver and release: _____
Amount(s) of unpaid progress payment(s): $ _____
(4) Contract rights, including (A) a right based on rescission, abandonment, or breach of contract, and (B) the right to recover compensation for work not compensated by the payment.

Signature

Claimant's Signature: _____
Claimant's Title: _____
Date of Signature: _____

(Added by Stats.2010, c. 697 (S.B.189), § 20, operative July 1, 2012.)

Operative Effect

For operative effect of Part 6, see Civil Code § 8052 and Stats.2010, c. 697 (S.B.189), § 105.

Cross References

Contracts,
  Defined, see Civil Code § 8008.
  Direct contract defined, see Civil Code § 8016.
  Interpretation, see Civil Code § 1635 et seq.
Waiver of code provisions, see Civil Code § 3268.

§ 8134. Unconditional waiver and release on progress payment; form

If the claimant is required to execute a waiver and release in exchange for, or in order to induce payment of, a progress payment and the claimant asserts in the waiver that the claimant has, in fact, been paid the progress payment, the waiver and release shall be null, void, and unenforceable unless it is in substantially the following form, with the text of the "Notice to Claimant" in at least as large a type as the largest type otherwise in the form:

UNCONDITIONAL WAIVER AND RELEASE ON PROGRESS PAYMENT

NOTICE TO CLAIMANT: THIS DOCUMENT WAIVES AND RELEASES LIEN, STOP PAYMENT NOTICE, AND PAYMENT BOND RIGHTS UNCONDITIONALLY AND STATES THAT YOU HAVE BEEN PAID FOR GIVING UP THOSE RIGHTS. THIS DOCUMENT IS ENFORCEABLE AGAINST YOU IF YOU SIGN IT, EVEN IF YOU HAVE NOT BEEN PAID. IF YOU HAVE NOT BEEN PAID, USE A CONDITIONAL WAIVER AND RELEASE FORM.

Identifying Information

Name of Claimant: _____
Name of Customer: _____
Job Location: _____
Owner: _____
Through Date: _____

§ 8134   GENERAL PROVISIONS

Unconditional Waiver and Release

This document waives and releases lien, stop payment notice, and payment bond rights the claimant has for labor and service provided, and equipment and material delivered, to the customer on this job through the Through Date of this document. Rights based upon labor or service provided, or equipment or material delivered, pursuant to a written change order that has been fully executed by the parties prior to the date that this document is signed by the claimant, are waived and released by this document, unless listed as an Exception below. The claimant has received the following progress payment: $ _____

Exceptions

This document does not affect any of the following:
(1) Retentions.
(2) Extras for which the claimant has not received payment.
(3) Contract rights, including (A) a right based on rescission, abandonment, or breach of contract, and (B) the right to recover compensation for work not compensated by the payment.

Signature

Claimant's Signature: _____
Claimant's Title: _____
Date of Signature: _____

(Added by Stats.2010, c. 697 (S.B.189), § 20, operative July 1, 2012.)

Operative Effect

For operative effect of Part 6, see Civil Code § 8052 and Stats.2010, c. 697 (S.B.189), § 105.

Cross References

Contracts,
  Defined, see Civil Code § 8008.
  Direct contract defined, see Civil Code § 8016.
  Interpretation, see Civil Code § 1635 et seq.
Waiver of code provisions, see Civil Code § 3268.

§ 8136. Conditional waiver and release on final payment; form

If the claimant is required to execute a waiver and release in exchange for, or in order to induce payment of, a final payment and the claimant is not, in fact, paid in exchange for the waiver and release or a single payee check or joint payee check is given in exchange for the waiver and release, the waiver and release shall be null, void, and unenforceable unless it is in substantially the following form:

CONDITIONAL WAIVER AND RELEASE ON FINAL PAYMENT

NOTICE: THIS DOCUMENT WAIVES THE CLAIMANT'S LIEN, STOP PAYMENT NOTICE, AND PAYMENT BOND RIGHTS EFFECTIVE ON RECEIPT OF PAYMENT. A PERSON SHOULD NOT RELY ON THIS DOCUMENT UNLESS SATISFIED THAT THE CLAIMANT HAS RECEIVED PAYMENT.

Identifying Information

Name of Claimant: _____
Name of Customer: _____
Job Location: _____
Owner: _____

Conditional Waiver and Release

This document waives and releases lien, stop payment notice, and payment bond rights the claimant has for labor and service provided, and equipment and material delivered, to the customer on this job. Rights based upon labor or service provided, or equipment or material delivered, pursuant to a written change order that has been fully executed by the parties prior to the date that this document is signed by the claimant, are waived and released by this document, unless listed as an Exception below. This document is effective only on the claimant's receipt of payment from the financial institution on which the following check is drawn:

Maker of Check: _____
Amount of Check: $ _____
Check Payable to: _____

Exceptions

This document does not affect any of the following:
Disputed claims for extras in the amount of: $ _____

Signature

Claimant's Signature: _____
Claimant's Title: _____
Date of Signature: _____

(Added by Stats.2010, c. 697 (S.B.189), § 20, operative July 1, 2012.)

Operative Effect

For operative effect of Part 6, see Civil Code § 8052 and Stats.2010, c. 697 (S.B.189), § 105.

Cross References

Contracts,
  Defined, see Civil Code § 8008.
  Direct contract defined, see Civil Code § 8016.
  Interpretation, see Civil Code § 1635 et seq.
Waiver of code provisions, see Civil Code § 3268.

§ 8138. Unconditional waiver and release on final payment; form

If the claimant is required to execute a waiver and release in exchange for, or in order to induce payment of, a final payment and the claimant asserts in the waiver that the claimant has, in fact, been paid the final payment, the waiver and release shall be null, void, and unenforceable unless it is in substantially the following form, with the text of the "Notice to Claimant" in at least as large a type as the largest type otherwise in the form:

UNCONDITIONAL WAIVER AND RELEASE ON FINAL PAYMENT

NOTICE TO CLAIMANT: THIS DOCUMENT WAIVES AND RELEASES LIEN, STOP PAYMENT NOTICE, AND PAYMENT BOND RIGHTS UNCONDITIONALLY AND STATES THAT YOU HAVE BEEN PAID FOR GIVING UP THOSE RIGHTS. THIS DOCUMENT IS ENFORCE-

ABLE AGAINST YOU IF YOU SIGN IT, EVEN IF YOU HAVE NOT BEEN PAID. IF YOU HAVE NOT BEEN PAID, USE A CONDITIONAL WAIVER AND RELEASE FORM.

Identifying Information

Name of Claimant: _____
Name of Customer: _____
Job Location: _____
Owner: _____

Unconditional Waiver and Release

This document waives and releases lien, stop payment notice, and payment bond rights the claimant has for all labor and service provided, and equipment and material delivered, to the customer on this job. Rights based upon labor or service provided, or equipment or material delivered, pursuant to a written change order that has been fully executed by the parties prior to the date that this document is signed by the claimant, are waived and released by this document, unless listed as an Exception below. The claimant has been paid in full.

Exceptions

This document does not affect the following:
Disputed claims for extras in the amount of: $ _____

Signature

Claimant's Signature: _____
Claimant's Title: _____
Date of Signature: _____

(Added by Stats.2010, c. 697 (S.B.189), § 20, operative July 1, 2012.)

Operative Effect

For operative effect of Part 6, see Civil Code § 8052 and Stats.2010, c. 697 (S.B.189), § 105.

Cross References

Contracts,
  Defined, see Civil Code § 8008.
  Direct contract defined, see Civil Code § 8016.
  Interpretation, see Civil Code § 1635 et seq.
Waiver of code provisions, see Civil Code § 3268.

CHAPTER 4. BONDS

Section
8150. Application of Bond and Undertaking Law.
8152. Acts not releasing surety from liability on bond given under this part.
8154. Construction of bond; liability of surety; condition for recovery on bond.

Operative Effect

For operative effect of Part 6, see Civil Code § 8052 and Stats.2010, c. 697 (S.B.189), § 105.

§ 8150. Application of Bond and Undertaking Law

The Bond and Undertaking Law (Chapter 2 (commencing with Section 995.010) of Title 14 of Part 2 of the Code of Civil Procedure) applies to a bond given under this part, except to the extent this part prescribes a different rule or is inconsistent. (Added by Stats.2010, c. 697 (S.B.189), § 20, operative July 1, 2012.)

Operative Effect

For operative effect of Part 6, see Civil Code § 8052 and Stats.2010, c. 697 (S.B.189), § 105.

§ 8152. Acts not releasing surety from liability on bond given under this part

None of the following releases a surety from liability on a bond given under this part:

(a) A change, alteration, or modification to a contract, plan, specification, or agreement for a work of improvement or for work provided for a work of improvement.

(b) A change or modification to the terms of payment or an extension of the time for payment for a work of improvement.

(c) A rescission or attempted rescission of a contract, agreement, or bond.

(d) A condition precedent or subsequent in the bond purporting to limit the right of recovery of a claimant otherwise entitled to recover pursuant to a contract, agreement, or bond.

(e) In the case of a bond given for the benefit of claimants, the fraud of a person other than the claimant seeking to recover on the bond. (Added by Stats.2010, c. 697 (S.B.189), § 20, operative July 1, 2012.)

Operative Effect

For operative effect of Part 6, see Civil Code § 8052 and Stats.2010, c. 697 (S.B.189), § 105.

Cross References

Claimant defined, see Civil Code § 8004.
Sureties,
  Exoneration, see Civil Code § 2819 et seq.
  Notice of claim against payment bond, see Civil Code §§ 8614, 9562.
  Payment bond for public works, see Code of Civil Procedure § 995.010 et seq.
  Position, see Civil Code § 2832 et seq.
Surety insurers, list, see Insurance Code § 12070.
Suretyship created, see Civil Code § 2792 et seq.
Suretyship defined, see Civil Code §§ 2787, 2788.
Work of improvement defined, see Civil Code § 8050.

§ 8154. Construction of bond; liability of surety; condition for recovery on bond

(a) A bond given under this part shall be construed most strongly against the surety and in favor of all persons for whose benefit the bond is given.

(b) A surety is not released from liability to those for whose benefit the bond has been given by reason of a breach of the direct contract or on the part of any obligee named in the bond.

(c) Except as otherwise provided by statute, the sole conditions of recovery on the bond are that the claimant is a person described in Article 1 (commencing with Section 8400) of Chapter 4 of Title 2, or in Section 9100, and has not

§ 8154 GENERAL PROVISIONS

been paid the full amount of the claim. *(Added by Stats.2010, c. 697 (S.B.189), § 20, operative July 1, 2012.)*

Operative Effect

For operative effect of Part 6, see Civil Code § 8052 and Stats.2010, c. 697 (S.B.189), § 105.

Cross References

Construction of title, see Civil Code § 8000.
Interpretation of contracts, see Civil Code § 1635 et seq.
Material supplier defined, see Civil Code § 8028.
Sureties,
    Exoneration, see Civil Code § 2819 et seq.
    Liability, see Civil Code § 2806 et seq.
    Position, see Civil Code § 2832 et seq.
Suretyship,
    Generally, see Civil Code § 2787 et seq.
    Interpretation, see Civil Code § 2799 et seq.

Title 2
PRIVATE WORKS OF IMPROVEMENT

Chapter	Section
1. General Provisions	8160
2. Preliminary Notice	8200
3. Design Professionals Lien	8300
4. Mechanics Lien	8400
5. Stop Payment Notice	8500
6. Payment Bond	8600
7. Security for Large Project	8700
8. Prompt Payment	8800

Operative Effect

For operative effect of Part 6, see Civil Code § 8052 and Stats.2010, c. 697 (S.B.189), § 105.

CHAPTER 1. GENERAL PROVISIONS

Article	Section
1. Application of Title	8160
2. Construction Documents	8170
3. Completion	8180

Operative Effect

For operative effect of Part 6, see Civil Code § 8052 and Stats.2010, c. 697 (S.B.189), § 105.

ARTICLE 1. APPLICATION OF TITLE

Section
8160. Application of title.

Operative Effect

For operative effect of Part 6, see Civil Code § 8052 and Stats.2010, c. 697 (S.B.189), § 105.

§ 8160. Application of title

This title applies to a work of improvement that is not governed by Title 3 (commencing with Section 9000) of this part. *(Added by Stats.2010, c. 697 (S.B.189), § 20, operative July 1, 2012.)*

Operative Effect

For operative effect of Part 6, see Civil Code § 8052 and Stats.2010, c. 697 (S.B.189), § 105.

ARTICLE 2. CONSTRUCTION DOCUMENTS

Section
8170. Written direct contracts; contents.
8172. Building permits; application form; information regarding construction lenders.
8174. Construction trust deed; contents.

Operative Effect

For operative effect of Part 6, see Civil Code § 8052 and Stats.2010, c. 697 (S.B.189), § 105.

§ 8170. Written direct contracts; contents

(a) A written direct contract shall provide a space for the owner to enter the following information:

(1) The owner's name, address, and place of business, if any.

(2) The name and address of the construction lender, if any. This paragraph does not apply to a home improvement contract or swimming pool contract subject to Article 10 (commencing with Section 7150) of Chapter 9 of Division 3 of the Business and Professions Code.

(b) A written contract entered into between a direct contractor and subcontractor, or between subcontractors, shall provide a space for the name and address of the owner, direct contractor, and construction lender, if any. *(Added by Stats.2010, c. 697 (S.B.189), § 20, operative July 1, 2012.)*

Operative Effect

For operative effect of Part 6, see Civil Code § 8052 and Stats.2010, c. 697 (S.B.189), § 105.

Cross References

Claim of lien, see Civil Code § 8416.
County recorder, fees for filing notice, see Government Code § 27361.9.
Necessity of preliminary notice, see Civil Code §§ 8410, 9500.
Notice to surety and bond principal, see Civil Code §§ 8614, 9562.
Private works of improvement, recordation of notice of completion or cessation, notification requirements, see Civil Code § 8190.
Validity of stop payment notice, see Civil Code § 8508.

§ 8172. Building permits; application form; information regarding construction lenders

(a) A public entity that issues building permits shall, in its application form for a building permit, provide space and a designation for the applicant to enter the name, branch designation, if any, and address of the construction lender and shall keep the information on file open for public inspection during the regular business hours of the public entity.

(b) If there is no known construction lender, the applicant shall note that fact in the designated space.

(c) Failure of the applicant to indicate the name and address of the construction lender on the application does not relieve a person required to give the construction lender preliminary notice from that duty. *(Added by Stats.2010, c. 697 (S.B.189), § 20, operative July 1, 2012.)*

Operative Effect

For operative effect of Part 6, see Civil Code § 8052 and Stats.2010, c. 697 (S.B.189), § 105.

Cross References

Claim of lien, see Civil Code § 8416.
County recorder, fees for filing notice, see Government Code § 27361.9.
Necessity of preliminary notice, see Civil Code §§ 8410, 9500.
Notice to surety and bond principal, see Civil Code §§ 8614, 9562.
Private works of improvement, recordation of notice of completion or cessation, notification requirements, see Civil Code § 8190.
Validity of stop payment notice, see Civil Code § 8508.

§ 8174. Construction trust deed; contents

(a) A mortgage, deed of trust, or other instrument securing a loan, any of the proceeds of which may be used for a work of improvement, shall bear the designation "Construction Trust Deed" prominently on its face and shall state all of the following:

(1) The name and address of the construction lender.

(2) The name and address of the owner of the real property described in the instrument.

(3) A legal description of the real property that secures the loan and, if known, the street address of the property.

(b) Failure to comply with subdivision (a) does not affect the validity of the mortgage, deed of trust, or other instrument.

(c) Failure to comply with subdivision (a) does not relieve a person required to give preliminary notice from that duty.

(d) The county recorder of the county in which the instrument is recorded shall indicate in the general index of the official records of the county that the instrument secures a construction loan. *(Added by Stats.2010, c. 697 (S.B.189), § 20, operative July 1, 2012.)*

Operative Effect

For operative effect of Part 6, see Civil Code § 8052 and Stats.2010, c. 697 (S.B.189), § 105.

Cross References

Claim of lien, see Civil Code § 8416.
County recorder, fees for filing notice, see Government Code § 27361.9.
Necessity of preliminary notice, see Civil Code §§ 8410, 9500.
Notice to surety and bond principal, see Civil Code §§ 8614, 9562.
Private works of improvement, recordation of notice of completion or cessation, notification requirements, see Civil Code § 8190.
Validity of stop payment notice, see Civil Code § 8508.

ARTICLE 3. COMPLETION

Section
8180. Acts signifying completion.
8182. Notice of completion; recording; contents.
8184. Acceptance and recording of notice of completion.
8186. Multiple contracts; notice of completion for portion of work of improvement.
8188. Notice of cessation; recording; contents.

Section
8190. Notice of completion or cessation; copies to be provided.

Operative Effect

For operative effect of Part 6, see Civil Code § 8052 and Stats.2010, c. 697 (S.B.189), § 105.

§ 8180. Acts signifying completion

(a) For the purpose of this title, completion of a work of improvement occurs upon the occurrence of any of the following events:

(1) Actual completion of the work of improvement.

(2) Occupation or use by the owner accompanied by cessation of labor.

(3) Cessation of labor for a continuous period of 60 days.

(4) Recordation of a notice of cessation after cessation of labor for a continuous period of 30 days.

(b) Notwithstanding subdivision (a), if a work of improvement is subject to acceptance by a public entity, completion occurs on acceptance. *(Added by Stats.2010, c. 697 (S.B.189), § 20, operative July 1, 2012.)*

Operative Effect

For operative effect of Part 6, see Civil Code § 8052 and Stats.2010, c. 697 (S.B.189), § 105.

Cross References

Completion as commencement of running of limitation time, see Civil Code § 8609.
Notice of cessation, see Civil Code § 8188.
Notice of completion, contents, see Civil Code § 8182.
Time following completion for recording claim of lien, see Civil Code §§ 8412, 8414.
Work of improvement defined, see Civil Code § 8050.

§ 8182. Notice of completion; recording; contents

(a) An owner may record a notice of completion on or within 15 days after the date of completion of a work of improvement.

(b) The notice of completion shall be signed and verified by the owner.

(c) The notice shall comply with the requirements of Chapter 2 (commencing with Section 8100) of Title 1, and shall also include all of the following information:

(1) If the notice is given only of completion of a contract for a particular portion of the work of improvement as provided in Section 8186, the name of the direct contractor under that contract and a general statement of the work provided pursuant to the contract.

(2) If signed by the owner's successor in interest, the name and address of the successor's transferor.

(3) The nature of the interest or estate of the owner.

(4) The date of completion. An erroneous statement of the date of completion does not affect the effectiveness of the notice if the true date of completion is 15 days or less before the date of recordation of the notice.

(d) A notice of completion that does not comply with the provisions of this section is not effective.

(e) For the purpose of this section, "owner" means the owner who causes a building, improvement, or structure to be constructed, altered, or repaired, or that person's successor in interest at the date a notice of completion is recorded, whether the interest or estate of the owner be in fee, as vendee under a contract of purchase, as lessee, or other interest or estate less than the fee. Where the interest or estate is held by two or more persons as joint tenants or tenants in common, any one or more of the cotenants may be deemed to be the "owner" within the meaning of this section. *(Added by Stats.2010, c. 697 (S.B.189), § 20, operative July 1, 2012.)*

Operative Effect

For operative effect of Part 6, see Civil Code § 8052 and Stats.2010, c. 697 (S.B.189), § 105.

Cross References

Completion, equivalents, see Civil Code § 8180.
Direct contractor defined, see Civil Code § 8018.
Mode of recording, see Civil Code § 1169 et seq.
Multiple contracts, recording notice of completion for portion of work, see Civil Code § 8186.
Payment of wages, direct contractor liability, see Labor Code §§ 218.7, 218.8.

§ 8184. Acceptance and recording of notice of completion

A notice of completion in otherwise proper form, verified and containing the information required by this title, shall be accepted by the recorder for recording and is deemed duly recorded without acknowledgment. *(Added by Stats.2010, c. 697 (S.B.189), § 20, operative July 1, 2012.)*

Operative Effect

For operative effect of Part 6, see Civil Code § 8052 and Stats.2010, c. 697 (S.B.189), § 105.

Cross References

Completion, equivalents, see Civil Code § 8180.
Direct contractor defined, see Civil Code § 8018.
Mode of recording, see Civil Code § 1169 et seq.
Multiple contracts, recording notice of completion for portion of work, see Civil Code § 8186.

§ 8186. Multiple contracts; notice of completion for portion of work of improvement

If a work of improvement is made pursuant to two or more direct contracts, each covering a portion of the work of improvement:

(a) The owner may record a notice of completion of a direct contract for a portion of the work of improvement. On recordation of the notice of completion, for the purpose of Sections 8412 and 8414, a direct contractor is deemed to have completed the contract for which the notice of completion is recorded and a claimant other than a direct contractor is deemed to have ceased providing work.

(b) If the owner does not record a notice of completion under this section, the period for recording a claim of lien is that provided in Sections 8412 and 8414. *(Added by Stats. 2010, c. 697 (S.B.189), § 20, operative July 1, 2012.)*

Operative Effect

For operative effect of Part 6, see Civil Code § 8052 and Stats.2010, c. 697 (S.B.189), § 105.

Cross References

Duties of county recorder, see Civil Code § 8060.
Notice of completion, contents, see Civil Code § 8182.
Work of improvement defined, see Civil Code § 8050.

§ 8188. Notice of cessation; recording; contents

(a) An owner may record a notice of cessation if there has been a continuous cessation of labor on a work of improvement for at least 30 days prior to the recordation that continues through the date of the recordation.

(b) The notice shall be signed and verified by the owner.

(c) The notice shall comply with the requirements of Chapter 2 (commencing with Section 8100) of Title 1, and shall also include all of the following information:

(1) The date on or about which labor ceased.

(2) A statement that the cessation has continued until the recordation of the notice.

(d) For the purpose of this section, "owner" means the owner who causes a building, improvement, or structure to be constructed, altered, or repaired, or that person's successor in interest at the date a notice of cessation is recorded, whether the interest or estate of the owner be in fee, as vendee under a contract of purchase, as lessee, or other interest or estate less than the fee. Where the interest or estate is held by two or more persons as joint tenants or tenants in common, any one or more of the cotenants may be deemed to be the "owner" within the meaning of this section. *(Added by Stats.2010, c. 697 (S.B.189), § 20, operative July 1, 2012.)*

Operative Effect

For operative effect of Part 6, see Civil Code § 8052 and Stats.2010, c. 697 (S.B.189), § 105.

Cross References

Payment of wages, direct contractor liability, see Labor Code §§ 218.7, 218.8.

§ 8190. Notice of completion or cessation; copies to be provided

(a) An owner that records a notice of completion or cessation shall, within 10 days of the date the notice of completion or cessation is filed for record, give a copy of the notice to all of the following persons:

(1) A direct contractor.

(2) A claimant that has given the owner preliminary notice.

(b) The copy of the notice shall be given in compliance with the requirements of Chapter 2 (commencing with Section 8100) of Title 1.

(c) If the owner fails to give notice to a person as required by subdivision (a), the notice is ineffective to shorten the time within which that person may record a claim of lien under Sections 8412 and 8414. The ineffectiveness of the notice is the sole liability of the owner for failure to give notice to a person under subdivision (a).

(d) For the purpose of this section, "owner" means a person who has an interest in real property, or the person's successor in interest on the date a notice of completion or notice of cessation is recorded, who causes a building, improvement, or structure, to be constructed, altered, or repaired on the property. If the property is owned by two or more persons as joint tenants or tenants in common, any one or more of the cotenants may be deemed to be the "owner" within the meaning of this section. However, this section does not apply to any of the following owners:

(1) A person that occupies the real property as a personal residence, if the dwelling contains four or fewer residential units.

(2) A person that has a security interest in the property.

(3) A person that obtains an interest in the property pursuant to a transfer described in subdivision (b), (c), or (d) of Section 1102.2. *(Added by Stats.2010, c. 697 (S.B.189), § 20, operative July 1, 2012.)*

Operative Effect

For operative effect of Part 6, see Civil Code § 8052 and Stats.2010, c. 697 (S.B.189), § 105.

CHAPTER 2. PRELIMINARY NOTICE

Section
8200. Preliminary notice; persons to receive; necessity of compliance with this section; exceptions.
8202. Notice to property owner.
8204. Time for giving preliminary notice.
8206. Single or multiple preliminary notice.
8208. Information to be provided by direct contractor.
8210. Additional construction loans; information to be provided to persons giving preliminary notice.
8212. Waiver of rights void and unenforceable.
8214. Filing of preliminary notice; mailing of notification; destruction of documents; purpose of filing pursuant to this section.
8216. Subcontractors; failure to give notice as grounds for disciplinary action.

Operative Effect

For operative effect of Part 6, see Civil Code § 8052 and Stats.2010, c. 697 (S.B.189), § 105.

§ 8200. Preliminary notice; persons to receive; necessity of compliance with this section; exceptions

(a) Except as otherwise provided by statute, before recording a lien claim, giving a stop payment notice, or asserting a claim against a payment bond, a claimant shall give preliminary notice to the following persons:

(1) The owner or reputed owner.

(2) The direct contractor or reputed direct contractor to which the claimant provides work, either directly or through one or more subcontractors.

(3) The construction lender or reputed construction lender, if any.

(b) The notice shall comply with the requirements of Chapter 2 (commencing with Section 8100) of Title 1.

(c) Compliance with this section is a necessary prerequisite to the validity of a lien claim or stop payment notice under this title.

(d) Compliance with this section or with Section 8612 is a necessary prerequisite to the validity of a claim against a payment bond under this title.

(e) Notwithstanding the foregoing subdivisions:

(1) A laborer is not required to give preliminary notice.

(2) A claimant with a direct contractual relationship with an owner or reputed owner is required to give preliminary notice only to the construction lender or reputed construction lender, if any. *(Added by Stats.2010, c. 697 (S.B.189), § 20, operative July 1, 2012.)*

Operative Effect

For operative effect of Part 6, see Civil Code § 8052 and Stats.2010, c. 697 (S.B.189), § 105.

Cross References

Claim of lien, see Civil Code § 8416.
County recorder, fees for filing notice, see Government Code § 27361.9.
Necessity of preliminary notice, see Civil Code §§ 8410, 9500.
Notice to surety and bond principal, see Civil Code §§ 8614, 9562.
Private works of improvement, recordation of notice of completion or cessation, notification requirements, see Civil Code § 8190.
Validity of stop payment notice, see Civil Code § 8508.

§ 8202. Notice to property owner

(a) The preliminary notice shall comply with the requirements of Section 8102, and shall also include:

(1) A general description of the work to be provided.

(2) An estimate of the total price of the work provided and to be provided.

(3) The following statement in boldface type:

NOTICE TO PROPERTY OWNER

EVEN THOUGH YOU HAVE PAID YOUR CONTRACTOR IN FULL, if the person or firm that has given you this notice is not paid in full for labor, service, equipment, or material provided or to be provided to your construction project, a lien may be placed on your property. Foreclosure of the lien may lead to loss of all or part of your property. You may wish to protect yourself against this by (1) requiring your contractor to provide a signed release by the person or firm that has given you this notice before making payment to your contractor, or (2) any other method that is appropriate under the circumstances.

This notice is required by law to be served by the undersigned as a statement of your legal rights. This notice is not intended to reflect upon the financial condition of the contractor or the person employed by you on the construction project.

If you record a notice of cessation or completion of your construction project, you must within 10 days after recording, send a copy of the notice of completion to your contractor and the person or firm that has given you this notice. The notice must be sent by registered or certified mail. Failure to send the notice will extend the deadline to record a claim of lien. You are not required to send the notice if you are a residential homeowner of a dwelling containing four or fewer units.

§ 8202

(b) If preliminary notice is given by a subcontractor that has not paid all compensation due to a laborer, the notice shall include the name and address of the laborer and any person or entity described in subdivision (b) of Section 8024 to which payments are due.

(c) If an invoice for material or certified payroll contains the information required by this section and Section 8102, a copy of the invoice or payroll, given in compliance with the requirements of Chapter 2 (commencing with Section 8100) of Title 1, is sufficient. *(Added by Stats.2010, c. 697 (S.B.189), § 20, operative July 1, 2012.)*

Operative Effect

For operative effect of Part 6, see Civil Code § 8052 and Stats.2010, c. 697 (S.B.189), § 105.

Cross References

Claim of lien, see Civil Code § 8416.
County recorder, fees for filing notice, see Government Code § 27361.9.
Necessity of preliminary notice, see Civil Code §§ 8410, 9500.
Notice to surety and bond principal, see Civil Code §§ 8614, 9562.
Private works of improvement, recordation of notice of completion or cessation, notification requirements, see Civil Code § 8190.
Public work payment bond claims, preliminary bond notice, exception for laborers, see Civil Code § 9560.
Validity of stop payment notice, see Civil Code § 8508.

§ 8204. Time for giving preliminary notice

(a) A preliminary notice shall be given not later than 20 days after the claimant has first furnished work on the work of improvement. If work has been provided by a claimant who did not give a preliminary notice, that claimant shall not be precluded from giving a preliminary notice at any time thereafter. The claimant shall, however, be entitled to record a lien, give a stop payment notice, and assert a claim against a payment bond only for work performed within 20 days prior to the service of the preliminary notice, and at any time thereafter.

(b) A design professional who has furnished services for the design of the work of improvement and who gives a preliminary notice not later than 20 days after the work of improvement has commenced shall be deemed to have complied with Section 8200 with respect to the design services furnished, or to be furnished. *(Added by Stats.2010, c. 697 (S.B.189), § 20, operative July 1, 2012.)*

Operative Effect

For operative effect of Part 6, see Civil Code § 8052 and Stats.2010, c. 697 (S.B.189), § 105.

Cross References

Claim of lien, see Civil Code § 8416.
County recorder, fees for filing notice, see Government Code § 27361.9.
Necessity of preliminary notice, see Civil Code §§ 8410, 9500.
Notice to surety and bond principal, see Civil Code §§ 8614, 9562.
Private works of improvement, recordation of notice of completion or cessation, notification requirements, see Civil Code § 8190.
Validity of stop payment notice, see Civil Code § 8508.

§ 8206. Single or multiple preliminary notice

(a) Except as provided in subdivision (b), a claimant need give only one preliminary notice to each person to which notice must be given under this chapter with respect to all work provided by the claimant for a work of improvement.

(b) If a claimant provides work pursuant to contracts with more than one subcontractor, the claimant shall give a separate preliminary notice with respect to work provided pursuant to each contract.

(c) A preliminary notice that contains a general description of work provided by the claimant through the date of the notice also covers work provided by the claimant after the date of the notice whether or not they are within the scope of the general description contained in the notice. *(Added by Stats.2010, c. 697 (S.B.189), § 20, operative July 1, 2012.)*

Operative Effect

For operative effect of Part 6, see Civil Code § 8052 and Stats.2010, c. 697 (S.B.189), § 105.

Cross References

Claim of lien, see Civil Code § 8416.
County recorder, fees for filing notice, see Government Code § 27361.9.
Necessity of preliminary notice, see Civil Code §§ 8410, 9500.
Notice to surety and bond principal, see Civil Code §§ 8614, 9562.
Private works of improvement, recordation of notice of completion or cessation, notification requirements, see Civil Code § 8190.
Validity of stop payment notice, see Civil Code § 8508.

§ 8208. Information to be provided by direct contractor

A direct contractor shall make available to any person seeking to give preliminary notice the following information:

(a) The name and address of the owner.

(b) The name and address of the construction lender, if any. *(Added by Stats.2010, c. 697 (S.B.189), § 20, operative July 1, 2012.)*

Operative Effect

For operative effect of Part 6, see Civil Code § 8052 and Stats.2010, c. 697 (S.B.189), § 105.

Cross References

Claim of lien, see Civil Code § 8416.
County recorder, fees for filing notice, see Government Code § 27361.9.
Direct contractor defined, see Civil Code § 8018.
Necessity of preliminary notice, see Civil Code §§ 8410, 9500.
Notice to surety and bond principal, see Civil Code §§ 8614, 9562.
Private works of improvement, recordation of notice of completion or cessation, notification requirements, see Civil Code § 8190.
Validity of stop payment notice, see Civil Code § 8508.

§ 8210. Additional construction loans; information to be provided to persons giving preliminary notice

If one or more construction loans are obtained after commencement of a work of improvement, the owner shall give notice of the name and address of the construction lender or lenders to each person that has given the owner preliminary notice. *(Added by Stats.2010, c. 697 (S.B.189), § 20, operative July 1, 2012.)*

Operative Effect

For operative effect of Part 6, see Civil Code § 8052 and Stats.2010, c. 697 (S.B.189), § 105.

Cross References

Claim of lien, see Civil Code § 8416.
County recorder, fees for filing notice, see Government Code § 27361.9.
Necessity of preliminary notice, see Civil Code §§ 8410, 9500.
Notice to surety and bond principal, see Civil Code §§ 8614, 9562.
Private works of improvement, recordation of notice of completion or cessation, notification requirements, see Civil Code § 8190.
Validity of stop payment notice, see Civil Code § 8508.

§ 8212. Waiver of rights void and unenforceable

An agreement made or entered into by an owner whereby the owner agrees to waive the rights conferred on the owner by this chapter is void and unenforceable. *(Added by Stats.2010, c. 697 (S.B.189), § 20, operative July 1, 2012.)*

Operative Effect

For operative effect of Part 6, see Civil Code § 8052 and Stats.2010, c. 697 (S.B.189), § 105.

Cross References

Claim of lien, see Civil Code § 8416.
County recorder, fees for filing notice, see Government Code § 27361.9.
Necessity of preliminary notice, see Civil Code §§ 8410, 9500.
Notice to surety and bond principal, see Civil Code §§ 8614, 9562.
Private works of improvement, recordation of notice of completion or cessation, notification requirements, see Civil Code § 8190.
Validity of stop payment notice, see Civil Code § 8508.

§ 8214. Filing of preliminary notice; mailing of notification; destruction of documents; purpose of filing pursuant to this section

(a) Each person who has served a preliminary notice may file the preliminary notice with the county recorder. A preliminary notice filed pursuant to this section shall comply with the requirements of Section 8102.

(b) Upon the acceptance for recording of a notice of completion or notice of cessation the county recorder shall mail to those persons who have filed a preliminary notice, notification that a notice of completion or notice of cessation has been recorded on the property, and shall affix the date that the notice of completion or notice of cessation was recorded with the county recorder. The notification given by the county recorder under this section is not governed by the requirements of Chapter 2 (commencing with Section 8100) of Title 1.

(c) The failure of the county recorder to mail the notification to the person who filed a preliminary notice, or the failure of those persons to receive the notification or to receive complete notification, shall not affect the period within which a claim of lien is required to be recorded. However, the county recorder shall make a good faith effort to mail notification to those persons who have filed the preliminary notice under this section and to do so within five days after the recording of a notice of completion or notice of cessation.

(d) The county recorder may cause to be destroyed all documents filed pursuant to this section, two years after the date of filing.

(e) The preliminary notice that a person may file pursuant to this section is for the limited purpose of facilitating the mailing of notice by the county recorder of recorded notices of completion and notices of cessation. The notice that is filed is not a recordable document and shall not be entered into those official records of the county which by law impart constructive notice. Notwithstanding any other provision of law, the index maintained by the recorder of filed preliminary notices shall be separate and distinct from those indexes maintained by the county recorder of those official records of the county which by law impart constructive notice. The filing of a preliminary notice with the county recorder does not give rise to any actual or constructive notice with respect to any party of the existence or contents of a filed preliminary notice nor to any duty of inquiry on the part of any party as to the existence or contents of that notice. *(Added by Stats. 2010, c. 697 (S.B.189), § 20, operative July 1, 2012.)*

Operative Effect

For operative effect of Part 6, see Civil Code § 8052 and Stats.2010, c. 697 (S.B.189), § 105.

Cross References

Claim of lien, see Civil Code § 8416.
County recorder, fees for filing notice, see Government Code § 27361.9.
Necessity of preliminary notice, see Civil Code §§ 8410, 9500.
Notice to surety and bond principal, see Civil Code §§ 8614, 9562.
Private works of improvement, recordation of notice of completion or cessation, notification requirements, see Civil Code § 8190.
Validity of stop payment notice, see Civil Code § 8508.

§ 8216. Subcontractors; failure to give notice as grounds for disciplinary action

If the contract of any subcontractor on a particular work of improvement provides for payment to the subcontractor of more than four hundred dollars ($400), the failure of that subcontractor, licensed under the Contractors' State License Law (Chapter 9 (commencing with Section 7000) of Division 3 of the Business and Professions Code), to give the notice provided for in this chapter, constitutes grounds for disciplinary action under the Contractors' State License Law. *(Added by Stats.2010, c. 697 (S.B.189), § 20, operative July 1, 2012.)*

Operative Effect

For operative effect of Part 6, see Civil Code § 8052 and Stats.2010, c. 697 (S.B.189), § 105.

Cross References

Claim of lien, see Civil Code § 8416.
County recorder, fees for filing notice, see Government Code § 27361.9.
Necessity of preliminary notice, see Civil Code §§ 8410, 9500.
Notice to surety and bond principal, see Civil Code §§ 8614, 9562.
Private works of improvement, recordation of notice of completion or cessation, notification requirements, see Civil Code § 8190.

Validity of stop payment notice, see Civil Code § 8508.

CHAPTER 3. DESIGN PROFESSIONALS LIEN

Section
8300. "Design professional" defined.
8302. Circumstances giving rise to lien; amount.
8304. Entitlement to lien; conditions.
8306. Creation of lien; expiration; satisfaction.
8308. Application of part.
8310. Availability of mechanics lien.
8312. Time for recording claim of lien.
8314. Additional remedies.
8316. Priority of lien.
8318. Exemptions.
8319. Conversion of design professional lien to mechanics lien.

Operative Effect

For operative effect of Part 6, see Civil Code § 8052 and Stats.2010, c. 697 (S.B.189), § 105.

§ 8300. "Design professional" defined

For purposes of this chapter, a "design professional" is a person described in Section 8014 who provides services pursuant to a written contract with a landowner for the design, engineering, or planning of a work of improvement. (Added by Stats.2010, c. 697 (S.B.189), § 20, operative July 1, 2012.)

Operative Effect

For operative effect of Part 6, see Civil Code § 8052 and Stats.2010, c. 697 (S.B.189), § 105.

§ 8302. Circumstances giving rise to lien; amount

(a) A design professional has, from the date of recordation of a claim of lien under this chapter, a lien on the site notwithstanding the absence of commencement of the planned work of improvement, if the landowner who contracted for the design professional's services is also the owner of the site at the time of recordation of the claim of lien.

(b) The lien of the design professional is for the amount of the design professional's fee for services provided under the contract or the reasonable value of those services, whichever is less. The amount of the lien is reduced by the amount of any deposit or prior payment under the contract.

(c) A design professional may not record a claim of lien, and a lien may not be created, under this chapter unless a building permit or other governmental approval in furtherance of the work of improvement has been obtained in connection with or utilizing the services provided by the design professional. (Added by Stats.2010, c. 697 (S.B.189), § 20, operative July 1, 2012.)

Operative Effect

For operative effect of Part 6, see Civil Code § 8052 and Stats.2010, c. 697 (S.B.189), § 105.

§ 8304. Entitlement to lien; conditions

A design professional is not entitled to a lien under this chapter unless all of the following conditions are satisfied:

(a) The work of improvement for which the design professional provided services has not commenced.

(b) The landowner defaults in a payment required under the contract or refuses to pay the demand of the design professional made under the contract.

(c) Not less than 10 days before recording a claim of lien, the design professional gives the landowner notice making a demand for payment, and stating that a default has occurred under the contract and the amount of the default.

(d) The design professional records a claim of lien. The claim of lien shall include all of the following information:

(1) The name of the design professional.

(2) The amount of the claim.

(3) The current owner of record of the site.

(4) A legal description of the site.

(5) Identification of the building permit or other governmental approval for the work of improvement. (Added by Stats.2010, c. 697 (S.B.189), § 20, operative July 1, 2012.)

Operative Effect

For operative effect of Part 6, see Civil Code § 8052 and Stats.2010, c. 697 (S.B.189), § 105.

§ 8306. Creation of lien; expiration; satisfaction

(a) On recordation of the claim of lien, a lien is created in favor of the named design professional.

(b) The lien automatically expires and is null and void and of no further force or effect on the occurrence of either of the following events:

(1) The commencement of the work of improvement for which the design professional provided services.

(2) The expiration of 90 days after recording the claim of lien, unless the design professional commences an action to enforce the lien within that time.

(c) If the landowner partially or fully satisfies the lien, the design professional shall execute and record a document that evidences a partial or full satisfaction and release of the lien, as applicable. (Added by Stats.2010, c. 697 (S.B.189), § 20, operative July 1, 2012.)

Operative Effect

For operative effect of Part 6, see Civil Code § 8052 and Stats.2010, c. 697 (S.B.189), § 105.

§ 8308. Application of part

(a) Except as provided in subdivision (b), no provision of this part applies to a lien created under this chapter.

(b) The following provisions of this part apply to a lien created under this chapter:

(1) This chapter.

(2) Article 1 (commencing with Section 8000) of Chapter 1 of Title 1.

(3) Section 8424.

(4) Article 6 (commencing with Section 8460) of Chapter 4.

(5) Article 7 (commencing with Section 8480) of Chapter 4.

(6) Article 8 (commencing with Section 8490) of Chapter 4. *(Added by Stats.2010, c. 697 (S.B.189), § 20, operative July 1, 2012.)*

Operative Effect

For operative effect of Part 6, see Civil Code § 8052 and Stats.2010, c. 697 (S.B.189), § 105.

§ 8310. Availability of mechanics lien

This chapter does not affect the ability of a design professional to obtain a lien for a work of improvement under Section 8400. *(Added by Stats.2010, c. 697 (S.B.189), § 20, operative July 1, 2012.)*

Operative Effect

For operative effect of Part 6, see Civil Code § 8052 and Stats.2010, c. 697 (S.B.189), § 105.

§ 8312. Time for recording claim of lien

A design professional shall record a claim of lien under this chapter no later than 90 days after the design professional knows or has reason to know that the work of improvement will not be commenced. *(Added by Stats.2010, c. 697 (S.B.189), § 20, operative July 1, 2012.)*

Operative Effect

For operative effect of Part 6, see Civil Code § 8052 and Stats.2010, c. 697 (S.B.189), § 105.

§ 8314. Additional remedies

The creation of a lien under this chapter does not affect the ability of the design professional to pursue other remedies. *(Added by Stats.2010, c. 697 (S.B.189), § 20, operative July 1, 2012.)*

Operative Effect

For operative effect of Part 6, see Civil Code § 8052 and Stats.2010, c. 697 (S.B.189), § 105.

§ 8316. Priority of lien

(a) No lien created under this chapter affects or takes priority over the interest of record of a purchaser, lessee, or encumbrancer, if the interest of the purchaser, lessee, or encumbrancer in the real property was duly recorded before recordation of the claim of lien.

(b) No lien created under this chapter affects or takes priority over an encumbrance of a construction lender that funds the loan for the work of improvement for which the design professional provided services. *(Added by Stats.2010, c. 697 (S.B.189), § 20, operative July 1, 2012.)*

Operative Effect

For operative effect of Part 6, see Civil Code § 8052 and Stats.2010, c. 697 (S.B.189), § 105.

§ 8318. Exemptions

A design professional may not obtain a lien under this chapter for services provided for a work of improvement relating to a single-family, owner-occupied residence for which the expected construction cost is less than one hundred thousand dollars ($100,000). *(Added by Stats.2010, c. 697 (S.B.189), § 20, operative July 1, 2012.)*

Operative Effect

For operative effect of Part 6, see Civil Code § 8052 and Stats.2010, c. 697 (S.B.189), § 105.

§ 8319. Conversion of design professional lien to mechanics lien

(a) A design professional may convert a recorded design professional lien to a mechanics lien if all of the following requirements are met:

(1) The design professional lien expires pursuant to paragraph (1) of subdivision (b) of Section 8306.

(2) The design professional lien remains fully or partially unpaid.

(3) Within 30 days of the expiration of the design professional lien pursuant to paragraph (1) of subdivision (b) of Section 8306, the design professional records a mechanics lien for the amount of the unpaid design professional lien.

(4) The recorded mechanics lien states that it is a converted design professional lien but shall be recorded and enforced as a mechanics lien, except the design professional need not provide a preliminary notice to enforce this mechanics lien. This mechanics lien shall be effective as of the date of recordation of this mechanics lien and shall be given priority pursuant to the provisions of Section 8450.

(b) This section shall not apply if a design professional lien expires pursuant to paragraph (2) of subdivision (b) of Section 8306. *(Added by Stats.2011, c. 127 (S.B.424), § 1, operative July 1, 2012.)*

Operative Effect

For operative effect of Stats.2011, c. 127 (S.B.424), see § 2 of that Act.

CHAPTER 4. MECHANICS LIEN

Article	Section
1. Who is Entitled to Lien	8400
2. Conditions to Enforcing a Lien	8410
3. Amount of Lien	8430
4. Property Subject to Lien	8440
5. Priorities	8450
6. Enforcement of Lien	8460
7. Release Order	8480
8. Removal of Claim of Lien from Record	8490

Operative Effect

For operative effect of Part 6, see Civil Code § 8052 and Stats.2010, c. 697 (S.B.189), § 105.

ARTICLE 1. WHO IS ENTITLED TO LIEN

Section
8400. Persons providing work authorized for work of improvement.
8402. Persons providing work authorized for site improvement.

GENERAL PROVISIONS

Section
8404. Work authorized for work of improvement or site improvement.

Operative Effect

For operative effect of Part 6, see Civil Code § 8052 and Stats.2010, c. 697 (S.B.189), § 105.

§ 8400. Persons providing work authorized for work of improvement

A person that provides work authorized for a work of improvement, including, but not limited to, the following persons, has a lien right under this chapter:

(a) Direct contractor.

(b) Subcontractor.

(c) Material supplier.

(d) Equipment lessor.

(e) Laborer.

(f) Design professional. *(Added by Stats.2010, c. 697 (S.B.189), § 20, operative July 1, 2012.)*

Operative Effect

For operative effect of Part 6, see Civil Code § 8052 and Stats.2010, c. 697 (S.B.189), § 105.

Cross References

Assignment to Labor Commissioner of mechanics' liens of employees, see Labor Code § 96.
Authority to serve stop notice and bonded stop notices, see Civil Code §§ 8520, 8530, 9100.
Claim filed on two or more works of improvement, see Civil Code § 8446.
Forfeiture of right to lien or right to participate in distribution of funds for false notice, see Civil Code §§ 8504, 9454.
Home improvement contracts, statement of full and unconditional release from liens, see Business and Professions Code §§ 7159, 7159.5, 7159.14.
Improvements affixed to land of another by mistake, removal, see Civil Code § 1013.5.
Liens,
    Aircraft, repairmen, see Code of Civil Procedure § 1208.61 et seq.
    Cleaners' and launderers' liens, see Civil Code § 3066.
    Condominium project, see Civil Code §§ 4615, 6658.
    Contracts subject to general lien statutes, see Civil Code § 2877.
    Extinction, see Civil Code § 2909 et seq.
    Jeweler, see Civil Code § 3052a.
    Logger and sawmill, see Civil Code § 3065 et seq.
    Mining, see Civil Code § 3060.
    Oil and gas, see Code of Civil Procedure § 1203.50 et seq.
    Possessory liens for services, repairs, etc., see Civil Code § 3051.
    Salary and wages, preference, see Code of Civil Procedure § 1204 et seq.
    Seller of real property, see Civil Code § 3046 et seq.
    Sewer connection costs, see Health and Safety Code § 5463.
    Sewer districts, application of general lien laws, see Health and Safety Code § 5021.
    Storage, see Civil Code § 1856.
    Taxes, see Revenue and Taxation Code § 2187 et seq.
    Thresher's, see Civil Code § 3061.
    Vehicles, repairmen, see Civil Code § 3067 et seq.
Municipal courts, jurisdiction to enforce lien, see Code of Civil Procedure § 86.
Partition, costs as lien on share allotted to party, see Code of Civil Procedure §§ 873.260, 874.120.
Real property loans, failure to disclose lien, see Business and Professions Code § 10243.
Work of improvement defined, see Civil Code § 8050.
Written notice to surety and bond principal, see Civil Code §§ 8614, 9562.

§ 8402. Persons providing work authorized for site improvement

A person that provides work authorized for a site improvement has a lien right under this chapter. *(Added by Stats.2010, c. 697 (S.B.189), § 20, operative July 1, 2012.)*

Operative Effect

For operative effect of Part 6, see Civil Code § 8052 and Stats.2010, c. 697 (S.B.189), § 105.

Cross References

Authority to serve stop notice and bonded stop notices, see Civil Code §§ 8520, 8530, 9100.
Completion of separate residential units, effect on rights under this section, see Civil Code § 8448.
Liens for site improvements, priorities, see Civil Code § 8458.
Preliminary notice to property owner, see Civil Code § 8202.
Sidewalk construction, lien on adjoining property, see Streets and Highways Code § 5890.
Site improvement defined, see Civil Code § 8042.

§ 8404. Work authorized for work of improvement or site improvement

Work is authorized for a work of improvement or for a site improvement in any of the following circumstances:

(a) It is provided at the request of or agreed to by the owner.

(b) It is provided or authorized by a direct contractor, subcontractor, architect, project manager, or other person having charge of all or part of the work of improvement or site improvement. *(Added by Stats.2010, c. 697 (S.B.189), § 20, operative July 1, 2012.)*

Operative Effect

For operative effect of Part 6, see Civil Code § 8052 and Stats.2010, c. 697 (S.B.189), § 105.

Cross References

Assignment to Labor Commissioner of mechanics' liens of employees, see Labor Code § 96.
Authority to serve stop notice and bonded stop notices, see Civil Code §§ 8520, 8530, 9100.
Claim filed on two or more works of improvement, see Civil Code § 8446.
Forfeiture of right to lien or right to participate in distribution of funds for false notice, see Civil Code §§ 8504, 9454.
Home improvement contracts, statement of full and unconditional release from liens, see Business and Professions Code §§ 7159, 7159.5, 7159.14.
Improvements affixed to land of another by mistake, removal, see Civil Code § 1013.5.
Liens,
    Aircraft, repairmen, see Code of Civil Procedure § 1208.61 et seq.
    Cleaners' and launderers' liens, see Civil Code § 3066.
    Condominium project, see Civil Code §§ 4615, 6658.
    Contracts subject to general lien statutes, see Civil Code § 2877.

Extinction, see Civil Code § 2909 et seq.
Jeweler, see Civil Code § 3052a.
Logger and sawmill, see Civil Code § 3065 et seq.
Mining, see Civil Code § 3060.
Oil and gas, see Code of Civil Procedure § 1203.50 et seq.
Possessory liens for services, repairs, etc., see Civil Code § 3051.
Salary and wages, preference, see Code of Civil Procedure § 1204 et seq.
Seller of real property, see Civil Code § 3046 et seq.
Sewer connection costs, see Health and Safety Code § 5463.
Sewer districts, application of general lien laws, see Health and Safety Code § 5021.
Site improvements, priorities, see Civil Code § 8458.
Storage, see Civil Code § 1856.
Taxes, see Revenue and Taxation Code § 2187 et seq.
Thresher's, see Civil Code § 3061.
Vehicles, repairmen, see Civil Code § 3067 et seq.
Municipal courts, jurisdiction to enforce lien, see Code of Civil Procedure § 86.
Partition, costs as lien on share allotted to party, see Code of Civil Procedure §§ 873.260, 874.120.
Preliminary notice to property owner, see Civil Code § 8202.
Real property loans, failure to disclose lien, see Business and Professions Code § 10243.
Sidewalk construction, lien on adjoining property, see Streets and Highways Code § 5890.
Site improvement defined, see Civil Code § 8042.
Work of improvement defined, see Civil Code § 8050.
Written notice to surety and bond principal, see Civil Code §§ 8614, 9562.

ARTICLE 2. CONDITIONS TO ENFORCING A LIEN

Section
8410. Preliminary notice; proof of notice.
8412. Direct contractors; time for recording claim.
8414. Persons other than direct contractors; time for recording claim.
8416. Written statement; contents; form; recording; service.
8422. Erroneous information.
8424. Lien release bond.

Operative Effect

For operative effect of Part 6, see Civil Code § 8052 and Stats.2010, c. 697 (S.B.189), § 105.

§ 8410. Preliminary notice; proof of notice

A claimant may enforce a lien only if the claimant has given preliminary notice to the extent required by Chapter 2 (commencing with Section 8200) and made proof of notice. *(Added by Stats.2010, c. 697 (S.B.189), § 20, operative July 1, 2012.)*

Operative Effect

For operative effect of Part 6, see Civil Code § 8052 and Stats.2010, c. 697 (S.B.189), § 105.

Cross References

Registered pest control companies, full and unconditional release from liens, see Business and Professions Code § 8513.
Release of security furnished by subdivider, see Government Code § 66499.7.

Written notice to surety and bond principal, see Civil Code §§ 8614, 9562.

§ 8412. Direct contractors; time for recording claim

A direct contractor may not enforce a lien unless the contractor records a claim of lien after the contractor completes the direct contract, and before the earlier of the following times:

(a) Ninety days after completion of the work of improvement.

(b) Sixty days after the owner records a notice of completion or cessation. *(Added by Stats.2010, c. 697 (S.B.189), § 20, operative July 1, 2012.)*

Operative Effect

For operative effect of Part 6, see Civil Code § 8052 and Stats.2010, c. 697 (S.B.189), § 105.

Cross References

Completion of work, see Civil Code §§ 8180, 9200.
Direct contractor, see Civil Code § 8018.
Duties of county recorder, see Civil Code § 8060.
Limitation of time for commencement of action, see Civil Code § 8460.
Notice of cessation, contents, see Civil Code §§ 8188, 9202.
Notice of completion, contents, see Civil Code §§ 8182, 9204.
Work of improvement defined, see Civil Code § 8050.

§ 8414. Persons other than direct contractors; time for recording claim

A claimant other than a direct contractor may not enforce a lien unless the claimant records a claim of lien within the following times:

(a) After the claimant ceases to provide work.

(b) Before the earlier of the following times:

(1) Ninety days after completion of the work of improvement.

(2) Thirty days after the owner records a notice of completion or cessation. *(Added by Stats.2010, c. 697 (S.B.189), § 20, operative July 1, 2012.)*

Operative Effect

For operative effect of Part 6, see Civil Code § 8052 and Stats.2010, c. 697 (S.B.189), § 105.

Cross References

Completion of work, see Civil Code §§ 8180, 9200.
Duties of county recorder, see Civil Code § 8060.
Notice of cessation, contents, see Civil Code §§ 8188, 9202.
Notice of completion, contents, see Civil Code §§ 8182, 9204.
Work of improvement defined, see Civil Code § 8050.

§ 8416. Written statement; contents; form; recording; service

(a) A claim of mechanics lien shall be a written statement, signed and verified by the claimant, containing all of the following:

(1) A statement of the claimant's demand after deducting all just credits and offsets.

(2) The name of the owner or reputed owner, if known.

(3) A general statement of the kind of work furnished by the claimant.

(4) The name of the person by whom the claimant was employed or to whom the claimant furnished work.

(5) A description of the site sufficient for identification.

(6) The claimant's address.

(7) A proof of service affidavit completed and signed by the person serving a copy of the claim of mechanics lien pursuant to subdivision (c). The affidavit shall show the date, place, and manner of service, and facts showing that the service was made in accordance with this section. The affidavit shall show the name and address of the owner or reputed owner upon whom the copy of the claim of mechanics lien was served pursuant to paragraphs (1) or (2) of subdivision (c), and the title or capacity in which the person or entity was served.

(8) The following statement, printed in at least 10-point boldface type. The letters of the last sentence shall be printed in uppercase type, excepting the Internet Web site address of the Contractors' State License Board, which shall be printed in lowercase type:

"NOTICE OF MECHANICS LIEN
ATTENTION!
Upon the recording of the enclosed MECHANICS LIEN with the county recorder's office of the county where the property is located, your property is subject to the filing of a legal action seeking a court-ordered foreclosure sale of the real property on which the lien has been recorded. That legal action must be filed with the court no later than 90 days after the date the mechanics lien is recorded.

The party identified in the enclosed mechanics lien may have provided labor or materials for improvements to your property and may not have been paid for these items. You are receiving this notice because it is a required step in filing a mechanics lien foreclosure action against your property. The foreclosure action will seek a sale of your property in order to pay for unpaid labor, materials, or improvements provided to your property. This may affect your ability to borrow against, refinance, or sell the property until the mechanics lien is released.

BECAUSE THE LIEN AFFECTS YOUR PROPERTY, YOU MAY WISH TO SPEAK WITH YOUR CONTRACTOR IMMEDIATELY, OR CONTACT AN ATTORNEY, OR FOR MORE INFORMATION ON MECHANICS LIENS GO TO THE CONTRACTORS' STATE LICENSE BOARD WEB SITE AT www.cslb.ca.gov."

(b) A claim of mechanics lien in otherwise proper form, verified and containing the information required in subdivision (a), shall be accepted by the recorder for recording and shall be deemed duly recorded without acknowledgment.

(c) A copy of the claim of mechanics lien, which includes the Notice of Mechanics Lien required by paragraph (8) of subdivision (a), shall be served on the owner or reputed owner. Service shall be made as follows:

(1) For an owner or reputed owner to be notified who resides in or outside this state, by registered mail, certified mail, or first-class mail, evidenced by a certificate of mailing, postage prepaid, addressed to the owner or reputed owner at the owner's or reputed owner's residence or place of business address or at the address shown by the building permit on file with the authority issuing a building permit for the work, or as otherwise provided in Section 8174.

(2) If the owner or reputed owner cannot be served by this method, then the copy of the claim of mechanics lien may be given by registered mail, certified mail, or first-class mail, evidenced by a certificate of mailing, postage prepaid, addressed to the construction lender or to the original contractor.

(d) Service of the copy of the claim of mechanics lien by registered mail, certified mail, or first-class mail, evidenced by a certificate of mailing, postage prepaid, is complete at the time of the deposit of that first-class, certified, or registered mail.

(e) Failure to serve the copy of the claim of mechanics lien as prescribed by this section, including the Notice of Mechanics Lien required by paragraph (8) of subdivision (a), shall cause the claim of mechanics lien to be unenforceable as a matter of law. *(Added by Stats.2010, c. 697 (S.B.189), § 20, operative July 1, 2012. Amended by Stats.2011, c. 673 (A.B.456), § 2, operative July 1, 2012.)*

Operative Effect

For operative effect of Part 6, see Civil Code § 8052 and Stats.2010, c. 697 (S.B.189), § 105.

Cross References

Erroneous information in claim of lien, effect, see Civil Code § 8422.
Preliminary notice of mechanic's lien,
  Private work, see Civil Code § 8200.
  Public work, see Civil Code § 9300.

§ 8422. Erroneous information

(a) Except as provided in subdivisions (b) and (c), erroneous information contained in a claim of lien relating to the claimant's demand, credits and offsets deducted, the work provided, or the description of the site, does not invalidate the claim of lien.

(b) Erroneous information contained in a claim of lien relating to the claimant's demand, credits and offsets deducted, or the work provided, invalidates the claim of lien if the court determines either of the following:

(1) The claim of lien was made with intent to defraud.

(2) An innocent third party, without notice, actual or constructive, became the bona fide owner of the property after recordation of the claim of lien, and the claim of lien was so deficient that it did not put the party on further inquiry in any manner.

(c) Any person who shall willfully include in a claim of lien labor, services, equipment, or materials not furnished for the property described in the claim, shall thereby forfeit the person's lien. *(Added by Stats.2010, c. 697 (S.B.189), § 20, operative July 1, 2012. Amended by Stats.2011, c. 44 (S.B.190), § 5, operative July 1, 2012.)*

Operative Effect

For operative effect of Part 6, see Civil Code § 8052 and Stats.2010, c. 697 (S.B.189), § 105.

Cross References

Acquiescence in error, see Civil Code § 3516.

Claim of lien, see Civil Code § 8416.
Claimant defined, see Civil Code § 8004.
Construction lender, liability for misrepresentations, see Civil Code § 3434.
Demand required in a complaint, see Code of Civil Procedure § 425.10.
Demands which are compensated, see Code of Civil Procedure § 431.70.
Description in conveyance, rules for construing, see Code of Civil Procedure § 2077.
Description of real property in pleading, see Code of Civil Procedure § 455.
Forfeiture of right to lien for false stop payment notice, see Civil Code §§ 8504, 9454.
Fraud, actual or constructive, see Civil Code § 1571 et seq.
Instruments made with intent to defraud, see Civil Code §§ 1227, 1228.
Liens,
   Claim not due, see Civil Code § 2882.
   Creation, see Civil Code § 2881 et seq.
   Defined, see Code of Civil Procedure § 1180; Civil Code § 2872 et seq.
   Effect, see Civil Code § 2888 et seq.
   Extinction, see Civil Code § 2909 et seq.
   Judgment creditor, see Code of Civil Procedure § 708.410 et seq.
   Judgment debtor's death, see Code of Civil Procedure § 686.020.
   Mechanic's liens, regulated by, see Civil Code § 3059.
   Priority, see Civil Code § 2897 et seq.
   Redemption, see Civil Code § 2903 et seq.
Mistake,
   Generally, see Civil Code § 1576 et seq.
   Denial of specific performance, see Civil Code § 3391.
Notice, actual and constructive, see Civil Code §§ 18, 19.
Relief from judgment taken by mistake, etc., see Code of Civil Procedure § 473.
Reversal for error resulting in miscarriage of justice, see Cal. Const. Art. 6, § 13.
Set-off not prejudiced by assignment of thing in action, see Code of Civil Procedure § 368.
Sureties, situations not releasing, see Civil Code § 8152.
Undue influence, see Civil Code § 1575.

§ 8424. Lien release bond

(a) An owner of real property or an owner of any interest in real property subject to a recorded claim of lien, or a direct contractor or subcontractor affected by the claim of lien, that disputes the correctness or validity of the claim may obtain release of the real property from the claim of lien by recording a lien release bond. The principal on the bond may be the owner of the property, the direct contractor, or the subcontractor.

(b) The bond shall be conditioned on payment of any judgment and costs the claimant recovers on the lien. The bond shall be in an amount equal to 125 percent of the amount of the claim of lien or 125 percent of the amount allocated in the claim of lien to the real property to be released. The bond shall be executed by an admitted surety insurer.

(c) The bond may be recorded either before or after commencement of an action to enforce the lien. On recordation of the bond, the real property is released from the claim of lien and from any action to enforce the lien.

(d) A person that obtains and records a lien release bond shall give notice to the claimant. The notice shall comply with the requirements of Chapter 2 (commencing with Section 8100) of Title 1 and shall include a copy of the bond. Failure to give the notice required by this section does not affect the validity of the bond, but the statute of limitations for an action on the bond is tolled until notice is given. The claimant shall commence an action on the bond within six months after notice is given. *(Added by Stats.2010, c. 697 (S.B.189), § 20, operative July 1, 2012.)*

Operative Effect

For operative effect of Part 6, see Civil Code § 8052 and Stats.2010, c. 697 (S.B.189), § 105.

Cross References

Commencement of actions, see Civil Code § 8550.
Commercial and industrial common interest developments, liens for labor and materials, see Civil Code § 6658.
Common interest developments, liens for labor and materials, see Civil Code § 4615.
Direct contractor, see Civil Code § 8018.
General provisions relating to bonds, see Civil Code § 8150 et seq.
Ownership, see Civil Code § 669 et seq.
Subcontractor defined, see Civil Code § 8046.
Suretyship, see Civil Code § 2787 et seq.

ARTICLE 3. AMOUNT OF LIEN

Section
8430. Direct liens; amount.
8432. Work included in claim; filing of contract or modification as constructive notice.
8434. Recovery by direct contractor or subcontractor.

Operative Effect

For operative effect of Part 6, see Civil Code § 8052 and Stats.2010, c. 697 (S.B.189), § 105.

§ 8430. Direct liens; amount

(a) The lien is a direct lien for the lesser of the following amounts:

(1) The reasonable value of the work provided by the claimant.

(2) The price agreed to by the claimant and the person that contracted for the work.

(b) The lien is not limited in amount by the contract price for the work of improvement except as provided in Section 8600.

(c) This section does not preclude the claimant from including in a claim of lien work performed based on a written modification of the contract, or as a result of rescission, abandonment, or breach of the contract. If there is a rescission, abandonment, or breach of the contract, the amount of the lien may not exceed the reasonable value of the work provided by the claimant. *(Added by Stats.2010, c. 697 (S.B.189), § 20, operative July 1, 2012.)*

Operative Effect

For operative effect of Part 6, see Civil Code § 8052 and Stats.2010, c. 697 (S.B.189), § 105.

§ 8430

Cross References

Assignment to Labor Commissioner of mechanics' liens of employees, see Labor Code § 96.
Authority to serve stop notice and bonded stop notices, see Civil Code §§ 8520, 8530, 9100.
Claim filed on two or more works of improvement, see Civil Code § 8446.
Forfeiture of right to lien or right to participate in distribution of funds for false notice, see Civil Code §§ 8504, 9454.
Home improvement contracts, statement of full and unconditional release from liens, see Business and Professions Code §§ 7159, 7159.5, 7159.14.
Improvements affixed to land of another by mistake, removal, see Civil Code § 1013.5.
Liens,
    Aircraft, repairmen, see Code of Civil Procedure § 1208.61 et seq.
    Cleaners' and launderers' liens, see Civil Code § 3066.
    Condominium project, see Civil Code §§ 4615, 6658.
    Contracts subject to general lien statutes, see Civil Code § 2877.
    Duration of lien, see Civil Code § 8460.
    Extinction, see Civil Code § 2909 et seq.
    Jeweler, see Civil Code § 3052a.
    Logger and sawmill, see Civil Code § 3065 et seq.
    Mining, see Civil Code § 3060.
    Oil and gas, see Code of Civil Procedure § 1203.50 et seq.
    Possessory liens for services, repairs, etc., see Civil Code § 3051.
    Salary and wages, preference, see Code of Civil Procedure § 1204 et seq.
    Seller of real property, see Civil Code § 3046 et seq.
    Sewer connection costs, see Health and Safety Code § 5463.
    Sewer districts, application of general lien laws, see Health and Safety Code § 5021.
    Storage, see Civil Code § 1856.
    Taxes, see Revenue and Taxation Code § 2187 et seq.
    Thresher's, see Civil Code § 3061.
    Vehicles, repairmen, see Civil Code § 3067 et seq.
Municipal courts, jurisdiction to enforce lien, see Code of Civil Procedure § 86.
Partition, costs as lien on share allotted to party, see Code of Civil Procedure §§ 873.260, 874.120.
Real property loans, failure to disclose lien, see Business and Professions Code § 10243.
Work of improvement defined, see Civil Code § 8050.
Written notice to surety and bond principal, see Civil Code §§ 8614, 9562.

§ 8432. Work included in claim; filing of contract or modification as constructive notice

(a) A lien does not extend to work, whether or not the work is authorized by a direct contractor or subcontractor, if the work is not included in a direct contract or a modification of that contract, and the claimant had actual knowledge or constructive notice of the provisions of that contract or modification before providing the work.

(b) The filing of a contract or modification of that contract with the county recorder, before the commencement of a work of improvement, is constructive notice of the provisions of the contract or modification to a person providing work on that work of improvement. *(Added by Stats.2010, c. 697 (S.B.189), § 20, operative July 1, 2012.)*

Operative Effect

For operative effect of Part 6, see Civil Code § 8052 and Stats.2010, c. 697 (S.B.189), § 105.

Cross References

Contract defined, see Civil Code § 8008.
Direct contractor defined, see Civil Code § 8018.
Filing and recording, see Civil Code § 8060.
Public works generally, contractor's bond, see Civil Code § 9550.
Subcontractor defined, see Civil Code § 8046.
Work of improvement defined, see Civil Code § 8050.

§ 8434. Recovery by direct contractor or subcontractor

A direct contractor or a subcontractor may enforce a lien only for the amount due pursuant to that contractor's contract after deducting all lien claims of other claimants for work provided and embraced within that contract. *(Added by Stats.2010, c. 697 (S.B.189), § 20, operative July 1, 2012.)*

Operative Effect

For operative effect of Part 6, see Civil Code § 8052 and Stats.2010, c. 697 (S.B.189), § 105.

Cross References

Contract defined, see Civil Code § 8008.
Direct contractor defined, see Civil Code § 8018.
Subcontractor defined, see Civil Code § 8046.
Withholding and deduction of funds due contractor by owner on claim of lien against contractor, see Civil Code § 8470.

ARTICLE 4. PROPERTY SUBJECT TO LIEN

Section
8440. Attachment to work and real property.
8442. Interests in real property.
8444. Notice of nonresponsibility.
8446. One claim on two or more works of improvement; conditions.
8448. Separate residential units.

Operative Effect

For operative effect of Part 6, see Civil Code § 8052 and Stats.2010, c. 697 (S.B.189), § 105.

§ 8440. Attachment to work and real property

Subject to Section 8442, a lien attaches to the work of improvement and to the real property on which the work of improvement is situated, including as much space about the work of improvement as is required for the convenient use and occupation of the work of improvement. *(Added by Stats.2010, c. 697 (S.B.189), § 20, operative July 1, 2012.)*

Operative Effect

For operative effect of Part 6, see Civil Code § 8052 and Stats.2010, c. 697 (S.B.189), § 105.

Cross References

Duration of lien, see Civil Code § 8460.
Fee simple, see Civil Code § 762.
Liens for site improvements, priorities, see Civil Code § 8458.
Ownership in general, see Civil Code § 669 et seq.
Preliminary notice to property owner, see Civil Code § 8202.
Sidewalk construction, lien on adjoining property, see Streets and Highways Code § 5890.

Work of improvement defined, see Civil Code § 8050.

§ 8442. Interests in real property

The following interests in real property to which a lien attaches are subject to the lien:

(a) The interest of a person that contracted for the work of improvement.

(b) The interest of a person that did not contract for the work of improvement, if work for which the lien is claimed was provided with the knowledge of that person, unless that person gives notice of nonresponsibility under Section 8444. *(Added by Stats.2010, c. 697 (S.B.189), § 20, operative July 1, 2012.)*

Operative Effect

For operative effect of Part 6, see Civil Code § 8052 and Stats.2010, c. 697 (S.B.189), § 105.

Cross References

Duration of lien, see Civil Code § 8460.
Fee simple, see Civil Code § 762.
Ownership in general, see Civil Code § 669 et seq.
Work of improvement defined, see Civil Code § 8050.

§ 8444. Notice of nonresponsibility

(a) An owner of real property or a person claiming an interest in real property on which a work of improvement is situated that did not contract for the work of improvement may give notice of nonresponsibility.

(b) A notice of nonresponsibility shall be signed and verified by the owner.

(c) The notice shall comply with the requirements of Chapter 2 (commencing with Section 8100) of Title 1.

(d) The notice shall also include all of the following information:

(1) The nature of the owner's title or interest.

(2) The name of a purchaser under contract, if any, or lessee, if known.

(3) A statement that the person giving the notice is not responsible for claims arising from the work of improvement.

(e) A notice of nonresponsibility is not effective unless, within 10 days after the person giving notice has knowledge of the work of improvement, the person both posts and records the notice. *(Added by Stats.2010, c. 697 (S.B.189), § 20, operative July 1, 2012.)*

Operative Effect

For operative effect of Part 6, see Civil Code § 8052 and Stats.2010, c. 697 (S.B.189), § 105.

Cross References

Work of improvement defined, see Civil Code § 8050.

§ 8446. One claim on two or more works of improvement; conditions

A claimant may record one claim of lien on two or more works of improvement, subject to the following conditions:

(a) The works of improvement have or are reputed to have the same owner, or the work was contracted for by the same person for the works of improvement whether or not they have the same owner.

(b) The claimant in the claim of lien designates the amount due for each work of improvement. If the claimant contracted for a lump sum payment for work provided for the works of improvement and the contract does not segregate the amount due for each work of improvement separately, the claimant may estimate an equitable distribution of the amount due for each work of improvement based on the proportionate amount of work provided for each. If the claimant does not designate the amount due for each work of improvement, the lien is subordinate to other liens.

(c) If there is a single structure on real property of different owners, the claimant need not segregate the proportion of work provided for the portion of the structure situated on real property of each owner. In the lien enforcement action the court may, if it determines it equitable to do so, designate an equitable distribution of the lien among the real property of the owners.

(d) The lien does not extend beyond the amount designated as against other creditors having liens, by judgment, mortgage, or otherwise, on either the works of improvement or the real property on which the works of improvement are situated. *(Added by Stats.2010, c. 697 (S.B.189), § 20, operative July 1, 2012.)*

Operative Effect

For operative effect of Part 6, see Civil Code § 8052 and Stats.2010, c. 697 (S.B.189), § 105.

Cross References

Work of improvement defined, see Civil Code § 8050.

§ 8448. Separate residential units

(a) As used in this section, "separate residential unit" means one residential structure, including a residential structure containing multiple condominium units, together with any common area, garage, or other appurtenant improvements.

(b) If a work of improvement consists of the construction of two or more separate residential units:

(1) Each unit is deemed a separate work of improvement, and completion of each unit is determined separately for purposes of the time for recording a claim of lien on that unit. This paragraph does not affect any lien right under Section 8402 or 8446.

(2) Material provided for the work of improvement is deemed to be provided for use or consumption in each separate residential unit in which the material is actually used or consumed; but if the claimant is unable to segregate the amounts used or consumed in separate residential units, the claimant has the right to all the benefits of Section 8446. *(Added by Stats.2010, c. 697 (S.B.189), § 20, operative July 1, 2012.)*

Operative Effect

For operative effect of Part 6, see Civil Code § 8052 and Stats.2010, c. 697 (S.B.189), § 105.

§ 8448 GENERAL PROVISIONS

Cross References

Work of improvement defined, see Civil Code § 8050.

ARTICLE 5. PRIORITIES

Section
- 8450. Priority of lien under this chapter.
- 8452. Mortgage or deed of trust; recordation of payment bond; requirements.
- 8454. Site improvements as separate direct contract.
- 8456. Construction loan secured by mortgage or deed of trust; optional advance of funds.
- 8458. Liens for site improvements.

Operative Effect

For operative effect of Part 6, see Civil Code § 8052 and Stats.2010, c. 697 (S.B.189), § 105.

§ 8450. Priority of lien under this chapter

(a) A lien under this chapter, other than a lien provided for in Section 8402, has priority over a lien, mortgage, deed of trust, or other encumbrance on the work of improvement or the real property on which the work of improvement is situated, that (1) attaches after commencement of the work of improvement or (2) was unrecorded at the commencement of the work of improvement and of which the claimant had no notice.

(b) Subdivision (a) is subject to the exception provided for in Section 8452. *(Added by Stats.2010, c. 697 (S.B.189), § 20, operative July 1, 2012.)*

Operative Effect

For operative effect of Part 6, see Civil Code § 8052 and Stats.2010, c. 697 (S.B.189), § 105.

Cross References

Claim against two or more buildings or improvements, see Civil Code § 8446.
Effect of liens generally, see Civil Code § 2888 et seq.
Priority of liens generally, see Civil Code § 2897 et seq.
Sales taxes, priority of tax lien, see Revenue and Taxation Code § 6756.
Tax lien, see Revenue and Taxation Code § 19221.
Work of improvement defined, see Civil Code § 8050.

§ 8452. Mortgage or deed of trust; recordation of payment bond; requirements

A mortgage or deed of trust, otherwise subordinate to a lien under Section 8450, has priority over a lien for work provided after recordation of a payment bond that satisfies all of the following requirements:

(a) The bond refers to the mortgage or deed of trust.

(b) The bond is in an amount not less than 75 percent of the principal amount of the mortgage or deed of trust. *(Added by Stats.2010, c. 697 (S.B.189), § 20, operative July 1, 2012.)*

Operative Effect

For operative effect of Part 6, see Civil Code § 8052 and Stats.2010, c. 697 (S.B.189), § 105.

Cross References

General provisions relating to bonds, see Civil Code § 8150 et seq.
Payment bond for private works, see Civil Code § 9550 et seq.
Payment bond for public works, see Civil Code § 8600 et seq.

§ 8454. Site improvements as separate direct contract

If a site improvement is provided for in a direct contract separate from the direct contract for the remainder of the work of improvement, the site improvement is deemed a separate work of improvement and commencement of the site improvement is not commencement of the remainder of the work of improvement. *(Added by Stats.2010, c. 697 (S.B.189), § 20, operative July 1, 2012.)*

Operative Effect

For operative effect of Part 6, see Civil Code § 8052 and Stats.2010, c. 697 (S.B.189), § 105.

Cross References

Contract defined, see Civil Code § 8008.
Direct contract defined, see Civil Code § 8016.
Site improvement defined, see Civil Code § 8042.

§ 8456. Construction loan secured by mortgage or deed of trust; optional advance of funds

(a) This section applies to a construction loan secured by a mortgage or deed of trust that has priority over a lien under this chapter.

(b) An optional advance of funds by the construction lender that is used for construction costs has the same priority as a mandatory advance of funds by the construction lender, provided that the total of all advances does not exceed the amount of the original construction loan. *(Added by Stats. 2010, c. 697 (S.B.189), § 20, operative July 1, 2012.)*

Operative Effect

For operative effect of Part 6, see Civil Code § 8052 and Stats.2010, c. 697 (S.B.189), § 105.

§ 8458. Liens for site improvements

(a) Except as provided in subdivision (b), a lien provided for in Section 8402 has priority over:

(1) A mortgage, deed of trust, or other encumbrance that attaches after commencement of the site improvement.

(2) A mortgage, deed of trust, or other encumbrance that was unrecorded at the commencement of the site improvement and of which the claimant had no notice.

(3) A mortgage, deed of trust, or other encumbrance that was recorded before commencement of the site improvement, if given for the sole or primary purpose of financing the site improvement. This subdivision does not apply if the loan proceeds are, in good faith, placed in the control of the lender pursuant to a binding agreement with the borrower to the effect that (A) the proceeds are to be applied to the payment of claimants and (B) no portion of the proceeds will be paid to the borrower in the absence of satisfactory evidence that all claims have been paid or that the time for recording a claim of lien has expired and no claim of lien has been recorded.

(b) A mortgage or deed of trust, otherwise subordinate under subdivision (a), has priority over a lien provided for in Section 8402 if a payment bond in an amount not less than 50 percent of the principal amount of the mortgage or deed of trust is recorded before completion of the work of improvement. *(Added by Stats.2010, c. 697 (S.B.189), § 20, operative July 1, 2012.)*

Operative Effect

For operative effect of Part 6, see Civil Code § 8052 and Stats.2010, c. 697 (S.B.189), § 105.

Cross References

Claimant making site improvement, lien, see Civil Code § 8402.
General provisions relating to bonds, see Civil Code § 8150 et seq.
Payment bond for private works, see Civil Code § 8600 et seq.
Payment bond for public works, see Civil Code § 9550 et seq.
Site improvement defined, see Civil Code § 8042.
Work of improvement defined, see Civil Code § 8050.

ARTICLE 6. ENFORCEMENT OF LIEN

Section
8460. Time for commencement of action; exception for extension of credit.
8461. Recording of notice of pendency of action.
8462. Dismissal.
8464. Costs.
8466. Deficiency judgment.
8468. Personal actions; application for writ of attachment; judgment; credit for money collected.
8470. Defense by contractor at own expense; withholding and deducting funds due contractor; recovery of judgment and costs by owner.

Operative Effect

For operative effect of Part 6, see Civil Code § 8052 and Stats.2010, c. 697 (S.B.189), § 105.

§ 8460. Time for commencement of action; exception for extension of credit

(a) The claimant shall commence an action to enforce a lien within 90 days after recordation of the claim of lien. If the claimant does not commence an action to enforce the lien within that time, the claim of lien expires and is unenforceable.

(b) Subdivision (a) does not apply if the claimant and owner agree to extend credit, and notice of the fact and terms of the extension of credit is recorded (1) within 90 days after recordation of the claim of lien or (2) more than 90 days after recordation of the claim of lien but before a purchaser or encumbrancer for value and in good faith acquires rights in the property. In that event the claimant shall commence an action to enforce the lien within 90 days after the expiration of the credit, but in no case later than one year after completion of the work of improvement. If the claimant does not commence an action to enforce the lien within that time, the claim of lien expires and is unenforceable. *(Added by Stats.2010, c. 697 (S.B.189), § 20, operative July 1, 2012.)*

Operative Effect

For operative effect of Part 6, see Civil Code § 8052 and Stats.2010, c. 697 (S.B.189), § 105.

Cross References

Completion, see Civil Code §§ 8180, 9200.
County recorder,
 Duties in general, see Government Code § 27201 et seq.
 Recording of instruments affecting title and deeds for public purposes, see Government Code § 27280 et seq.
Jurisdiction, enforcement of mechanic's liens, justice and municipal courts, see Code of Civil Procedure § 86.
Right of claimant to personal action, see Civil Code § 8468.
Work of improvement defined, see Civil Code § 8050.

§ 8461. Recording of notice of pendency of action

After commencement of an action to enforce a lien, the plaintiff shall record in the office of the county recorder of the county, or of the several counties in which the property is situated, a notice of the pendency of the action, as provided in Title 4.5 (commencing with Section 405) of Part 2 of the Code of Civil Procedure, on or before 20 days after the commencement of the action. Only from the time of recording that notice shall a purchaser or encumbrancer of the property affected thereby be deemed to have constructive notice of the pendency of the action, and in that event only of its pendency against parties designated by their real names. *(Added by Stats.2010, c. 697 (S.B.189), § 20, operative July 1, 2012.)*

Operative Effect

For operative effect of Part 6, see Civil Code § 8052 and Stats.2010, c. 697 (S.B.189), § 105.

Cross References

Actions affecting real estate, lis pendens, see Code of Civil Procedure § 405.20 et seq.
Pending action defined, see Code of Civil Procedure § 1049.

§ 8462. Dismissal

Notwithstanding Section 583.420 of the Code of Civil Procedure, if an action to enforce a lien is not brought to trial within two years after commencement of the action, the court may in its discretion dismiss the action for want of prosecution. *(Added by Stats.2010, c. 697 (S.B.189), § 20, operative July 1, 2012.)*

Operative Effect

For operative effect of Part 6, see Civil Code § 8052 and Stats.2010, c. 697 (S.B.189), § 105.

Cross References

Private works of improvement, commencement of actions, see Civil Code § 8550.
Public works, commencement of actions, see Civil Code § 9502.

§ 8464. Costs

In addition to any other costs allowed by law, the court in an action to enforce a lien shall allow as costs to each claimant whose lien is established the amount paid to verify and record the claim of lien, whether the claimant is a plaintiff or defendant. *(Added by Stats.2010, c. 697 (S.B.189), § 20, operative July 1, 2012.)*

Operative Effect

For operative effect of Part 6, see Civil Code § 8052 and Stats.2010, c. 697 (S.B.189), § 105.

Cross References

Attorney's fees, enforcement of claim in bonded stop notice, see Civil Code § 8558.
Costs, see Code of Civil Procedure § 1021 et seq.
Deduction of costs on amount due contractor by owner for judgment on claim of lien against contractor, see Civil Code § 8470.

§ 8466. Deficiency judgment

If there is a deficiency of proceeds from the sale of property on a judgment for enforcement of a lien, a deficiency judgment may be entered against a party personally liable for the deficiency in the same manner and with the same effect as in an action to foreclose a mortgage. *(Added by Stats.2010, c. 697 (S.B.189), § 20, operative July 1, 2012.)*

Operative Effect

For operative effect of Part 6, see Civil Code § 8052 and Stats.2010, c. 697 (S.B.189), § 105.

Cross References

Deficiency judgment, enforcement and limitation of action, see Code of Civil Procedure § 580a.
Mortgage foreclosure actions, see Code of Civil Procedure § 725a et seq.
Secured transactions, procedure on default, see Commercial Code § 9501 et seq.

§ 8468. Personal actions; application for writ of attachment; judgment; credit for money collected

(a) This chapter does not affect any of the following rights of a claimant:

(1) The right to maintain a personal action to recover a debt against the person liable, either in a separate action or in an action to enforce a lien.

(2) The right to a writ of attachment. In an application for a writ of attachment, the claimant shall refer to this section. The claimant's recording of a claim of lien does not affect the right to a writ of attachment.

(3) The right to enforce a judgment.

(b) A judgment obtained by the claimant in a personal action described in subdivision (a) does not impair or merge the claim of lien, but any amount collected on the judgment shall be credited on the amount of the lien. *(Added by Stats.2010, c. 697 (S.B.189), § 20, operative July 1, 2012.)*

Operative Effect

For operative effect of Part 6, see Civil Code § 8052 and Stats.2010, c. 697 (S.B.189), § 105.

§ 8470. Defense by contractor at own expense; withholding and deducting funds due contractor; recovery of judgment and costs by owner

In an action to enforce a lien for work provided to a contractor:

(a) The contractor shall defend the action at the contractor's own expense. During the pendency of the action the owner may withhold from the direct contractor the amount of the lien claim.

(b) If the judgment in the action is against the owner or the owner's property, the owner may deduct the amount of the judgment and costs from any amount owed to the direct contractor. If the amount of the judgment and costs exceeds the amount owed to the direct contractor, or if the owner has settled with the direct contractor in full, the owner may recover from the direct contractor, or the sureties on a bond given by the direct contractor for faithful performance of the direct contract, the amount of the judgment and costs that exceed the contract price and for which the direct contractor was originally liable. *(Added by Stats.2010, c. 697 (S.B.189), § 20, operative July 1, 2012.)*

Operative Effect

For operative effect of Part 6, see Civil Code § 8052 and Stats.2010, c. 697 (S.B.189), § 105.

Cross References

Costs, see Civil Code § 8464.
Direct contract defined, see Civil Code § 8016.
Direct contractor defined, see Civil Code § 8018.

ARTICLE 7. RELEASE ORDER

Section
8480. Release order; other actions or claims; joinder of claims.
8482. Time for petition; notice.
8484. Verified petition; contents.
8486. Hearing date; service.
8488. Hearing; burden of production; burden of proof; effect of judgment; attorney fees.

Operative Effect

For operative effect of Part 6, see Civil Code § 8052 and Stats.2010, c. 697 (S.B.189), § 105.

§ 8480. Release order; other actions or claims; joinder of claims

(a) The owner of property or the owner of any interest in property subject to a claim of lien may petition the court for an order to release the property from the claim of lien if the claimant has not commenced an action to enforce the lien within the time provided in Section 8460.

(b) This article does not bar any other cause of action or claim for relief by the owner of the property. A release order does not bar any other cause of action or claim for relief by the claimant, other than an action to enforce the claim of lien that is the subject of the release order.

(c) A petition for a release order under this article may be joined with a pending action to enforce the claim of lien that is the subject of the petition. No other action or claim for relief may be joined with a petition under this article.

(d) Notwithstanding Section 8056, Chapter 2.5 (commencing with Section 1141.10) of Title 3 of Part 3 of the Code of Civil Procedure does not apply to a proceeding under this article. *(Added by Stats.2010, c. 697 (S.B.189), § 20, operative July 1, 2012.)*

Operative Effect

For operative effect of Part 6, see Civil Code § 8052 and Stats.2010, c. 697 (S.B.189), § 105.

§ 8482. Time for petition; notice

An owner of property may not petition the court for a release order under this article unless at least 10 days before filing the petition the owner gives the claimant notice demanding that the claimant execute and record a release of the claim of lien. The notice shall comply with the requirements of Chapter 2 (commencing with Section 8100) of Title 1, and shall state the grounds for the demand. *(Added by Stats.2010, c. 697 (S.B.189), § 20, operative July 1, 2012.)*

Operative Effect

For operative effect of Part 6, see Civil Code § 8052 and Stats.2010, c. 697 (S.B.189), § 105.

§ 8484. Verified petition; contents

A petition for a release order shall be verified and shall allege all of the following:

(a) The date of recordation of the claim of lien. A certified copy of the claim of lien shall be attached to the petition.

(b) The county in which the claim of lien is recorded.

(c) The book and page or series number of the place in the official records where the claim of lien is recorded.

(d) The legal description of the property subject to the claim of lien.

(e) Whether an extension of credit has been granted under Section 8460, if so to what date, and that the time for commencement of an action to enforce the lien has expired.

(f) That the owner has given the claimant notice under Section 8482 demanding that the claimant execute and record a release of the lien and that the claimant is unable or unwilling to do so or cannot with reasonable diligence be found.

(g) Whether an action to enforce the lien is pending.

(h) Whether the owner of the property or interest in the property has filed for relief in bankruptcy or there is another restraint that prevents the claimant from commencing an action to enforce the lien. *(Added by Stats.2010, c. 697 (S.B.189), § 20, operative July 1, 2012.)*

Operative Effect

For operative effect of Part 6, see Civil Code § 8052 and Stats.2010, c. 697 (S.B.189), § 105.

§ 8486. Hearing date; service

(a) On the filing of a petition for a release order, the clerk shall set a hearing date. The date shall be not more than 30 days after the filing of the petition. The court may continue the hearing only on a showing of good cause, but in any event the court shall rule and make any necessary orders on the petition not later than 60 days after the filing of the petition.

(b) The petitioner shall serve a copy of the petition and a notice of hearing on the claimant at least 15 days before the hearing. Service shall be made in the same manner as service of summons, or by certified or registered mail, postage prepaid, return receipt requested, addressed to the claimant as provided in Section 8108.

(c) Notwithstanding Section 8116, when service is made by mail, service is complete on the fifth day following deposit of the petition and notice in the mail. *(Added by Stats.2010, c. 697 (S.B.189), § 20, operative July 1, 2012.)*

Operative Effect

For operative effect of Part 6, see Civil Code § 8052 and Stats.2010, c. 697 (S.B.189), § 105.

§ 8488. Hearing; burden of production; burden of proof; effect of judgment; attorney fees

(a) At the hearing both (1) the petition and (2) the issue of compliance with the service and date for hearing requirements of this article are deemed controverted by the claimant. The petitioner has the initial burden of producing evidence on those matters. The petitioner has the burden of proof as to the issue of compliance with the service and date for hearing requirements of this article. The claimant has the burden of proof as to the validity of the lien.

(b) If judgment is in favor of the petitioner, the court shall order the property released from the claim of lien.

(c) The prevailing party is entitled to reasonable attorney's fees. *(Added by Stats.2010, c. 697 (S.B.189), § 20, operative July 1, 2012.)*

Operative Effect

For operative effect of Part 6, see Civil Code § 8052 and Stats.2010, c. 697 (S.B.189), § 105.

ARTICLE 8. REMOVAL OF CLAIM OF LIEN FROM RECORD

Section
8490. Order dismissing cause of action or judgment that no lien exists; contents; effect of order or judgment; recordable instrument; application.
8494. Expiration or recordation of order or judgment; actual or constructive notice.

Operative Effect

For operative effect of Part 6, see Civil Code § 8052 and Stats.2010, c. 697 (S.B.189), § 105.

§ 8490. Order dismissing cause of action or judgment that no lien exists; contents; effect of order or judgment; recordable instrument; application

(a) A court order dismissing a cause of action to enforce a lien or releasing property from a claim of lien, or a judgment that no lien exists, shall include all of the following information:

(1) The date of recordation of the claim of lien.

(2) The county in which the claim of lien is recorded.

(3) The book and page or series number of the place in the official records where the claim of lien is recorded.

§ 8490

(4) The legal description of the property.

(b) A court order or judgment under this section is equivalent to cancellation of the claim of lien and its removal from the record.

(c) A court order or judgment under this section is a recordable instrument. On recordation of a certified copy of the court order or judgment, the property described in the order or judgment is released from the claim of lien.

(d) This section does not apply to a court order dismissing an action to enforce a lien that is expressly stated to be without prejudice. *(Added by Stats.2010, c. 697 (S.B.189), § 20, operative July 1, 2012.)*

Operative Effect

For operative effect of Part 6, see Civil Code § 8052 and Stats.2010, c. 697 (S.B.189), § 105.

Cross References

Dismissal in general, see Code of Civil Procedure § 581.

§ 8494. Expiration or recordation of order or judgment; actual or constructive notice

If a claim of lien expires and is unenforceable under Section 8460, or if a court order or judgment is recorded under Section 8490, the claim of lien does not constitute actual or constructive notice of any of the matters contained, claimed, alleged, or contended in the claim of lien, or create a duty of inquiry in any person thereafter dealing with the affected property. *(Added by Stats.2010, c. 697 (S.B.189), § 20, operative July 1, 2012.)*

Operative Effect

For operative effect of Part 6, see Civil Code § 8052 and Stats.2010, c. 697 (S.B.189), § 105.

CHAPTER 5. STOP PAYMENT NOTICE

Article	Section
1. General Provisions	8500
2. Stop Payment Notice to Owner	8520
3. Stop Payment Notice to Construction Lender	8530
4. Priorities	8540
5. Enforcement of Claim Stated in Stop Payment Notice	8550

Operative Effect

For operative effect of Part 6, see Civil Code § 8052 and Stats.2010, c. 697 (S.B.189), § 105.

ARTICLE 1. GENERAL PROVISIONS

Section
8500. Exclusive remedy.
8502. Requirements; contents; amount claimed.
8504. False stop payment notice or willful inclusion of demand to withhold for work not provided.
8506. Notice.
8508. Validity of notice; conditions.
8510. Release bond.

Operative Effect

For operative effect of Part 6, see Civil Code § 8052 and Stats.2010, c. 697 (S.B.189), § 105.

§ 8500. Exclusive remedy

The rights of all persons furnishing work for any work of improvement, with respect to any fund for payment of construction costs, are governed exclusively by this chapter, and no person may assert any legal or equitable right with respect to the fund, other than a right created by a written contract between that person and the person holding the fund, except pursuant to the provisions of this chapter. *(Added by Stats.2010, c. 697 (S.B.189), § 20, operative July 1, 2012.)*

Operative Effect

For operative effect of Part 6, see Civil Code § 8052 and Stats.2010, c. 697 (S.B.189), § 105.

Cross References

Action against direct contractor or public entity, see Civil Code § 9502 et seq.
Action against sureties on payment bond, see Civil Code §§ 9558, 9564.
Action on bond for deficit after pro rata distribution, see Civil Code § 9452.
Action on payment bond for private works, see Civil Code § 8609 et seq.
Action on payment bond for public works, see Civil Code § 9558 et seq.
Bond for release of funds held under stop payment notice, see Civil Code § 8510.
Claim of lien, contents, see Civil Code § 8416.
Material supplier defined, see Civil Code § 8028.
Pro rata distribution of funds, see Civil Code §§ 8540, 9450.
Stop payment notices, limitation on enforcement of rights,
    Private works, see Civil Code § 8550.
    Public works, see Civil Code § 9502.
Transfer of obligations, see Civil Code § 1457 et seq.
Withholding of money on service of stop payment notice, see Civil Code §§ 8522, 8536, 9358.

§ 8502. Requirements; contents; amount claimed

(a) A stop payment notice shall comply with the requirements of Chapter 2 (commencing with Section 8100) of Title 1, and shall be signed and verified by the claimant.

(b) The notice shall include a general description of work to be provided, and an estimate of the total amount in value of the work to be provided.

(c) The amount claimed in the notice may include only the amount due the claimant for work provided through the date of the notice. *(Added by Stats.2010, c. 697 (S.B.189), § 20, operative July 1, 2012.)*

Operative Effect

For operative effect of Part 6, see Civil Code § 8052 and Stats.2010, c. 697 (S.B.189), § 105.

Cross References

Bond for release of funds held under stop payment notice, see Civil Code § 8510.
Bonded stop notice to construction lender, see Civil Code § 8532.
Claim of mechanics lien, contents, see Civil Code § 8416.

Notice to public entity of commencement of action to enforce payment of claim stated in stop payment notice, see Civil Code § 9504.
Payment bond, see Civil Code §§ 8606, 9554.
Preliminary 20-day notice (private work), necessity prior to stop payment notice, see Civil Code § 8200.
Preliminary 20-day notice (public work), stop payment notice, see Civil Code § 9300.
Private works of improvement, validity of stop payment notice, see Civil Code § 8508.
Recording, constructive notice, see Civil Code § 1213.
Stop payment notice,
    Private works, see Civil Code § 8500 et seq.
    Public works, see Civil Code § 9350 et seq.
Withholding by construction lender on receipt of stop payment notice, see Civil Code § 8536.

§ 8504. False stop payment notice or willful inclusion of demand to withhold for work not provided

A claimant that willfully gives a false stop payment notice or that willfully includes in the notice a demand to withhold for work that has not been provided forfeits all right to participate in the distribution of the funds withheld and all right to a lien under Chapter 4 (commencing with Section 8400). *(Added by Stats.2010, c. 697 (S.B.189), § 20, operative July 1, 2012.)*

Operative Effect

For operative effect of Part 6, see Civil Code § 8052 and Stats.2010, c. 697 (S.B.189), § 105.

Cross References

Bonded stop payment notice to construction lender, see Civil Code § 8532.
Public works, similar provision, see Civil Code § 9454.
Stop payment notice defined, see Civil Code § 8044.

§ 8506. Notice

(a) A stop payment notice to an owner shall be given to the owner or to the owner's architect, if any.

(b) A stop payment notice to a construction lender holding construction funds shall not be effective unless given to the manager or other responsible officer or person at the office or branch of the lender administering or holding the construction funds.

(c) A stop payment notice shall comply with the requirements of Chapter 2 (commencing with Section 8100) of Title 1. *(Added by Stats.2010, c. 697 (S.B.189), § 20, operative July 1, 2012.)*

Operative Effect

For operative effect of Part 6, see Civil Code § 8052 and Stats.2010, c. 697 (S.B.189), § 105.

Cross References

Construction lender defined, see Civil Code § 8006.
General provisions relating to bonds, see Civil Code § 8150 et seq.
Notice to public entity of commencement of action to enforce payment of claim stated in stop payment notice, see Civil Code § 9504.
Preliminary 20-day notice (private work), necessity prior to stop payment notice, see Civil Code § 8200.
Preliminary 20-day notice (public work), stop notice, see Civil Code § 9300.
Private works of improvement, validity of stop payment notice, see Civil Code § 8508.
Stop payment notice,
    Private works, see Civil Code § 8500 et seq.
    Public works, see Civil Code § 9350 et seq.

§ 8508. Validity of notice; conditions

A stop payment notice is not valid unless both of the following conditions are satisfied:

(a) The claimant gave preliminary notice to the extent required by Chapter 2 (commencing with Section 8200).

(b) The claimant gave the stop payment notice before expiration of the time within which a claim of lien must be recorded under Chapter 4 (commencing with Section 8400). *(Added by Stats.2010, c. 697 (S.B.189), § 20, operative July 1, 2012.)*

Operative Effect

For operative effect of Part 6, see Civil Code § 8052 and Stats.2010, c. 697 (S.B.189), § 105.

Cross References

Bond for release of funds held under stop notice, see Civil Code § 8510.
Bonded stop payment notice to construction lender, see Civil Code § 8532.
Claim of mechanics lien, contents, see Civil Code § 8416.
Payment bond, see Civil Code §§ 8606, 9554.
Recording, constructive notice, see Civil Code § 1213.
Stop payment notice, contents, see Civil Code § 8502.
Withholding by construction lender on receipt of stop payment notice, see Civil Code § 8536.

§ 8510. Release bond

(a) A person may obtain release of funds withheld pursuant to a stop payment notice by giving the person withholding the funds a release bond.

(b) A release bond shall be given by an admitted surety insurer and shall be conditioned for payment of any amount not exceeding the penal obligation of the bond that the claimant recovers on the claim, together with costs of suit awarded in the action. The bond shall be in an amount equal to 125 percent of the amount claimed in the stop payment notice.

(c) On receipt of a release bond, the person withholding funds pursuant to the stop payment notice shall release them. *(Added by Stats.2010, c. 697 (S.B.189), § 20, operative July 1, 2012.)*

Operative Effect

For operative effect of Part 6, see Civil Code § 8052 and Stats.2010, c. 697 (S.B.189), § 105.

Cross References

Bonded stop payment notice to construction lender, see Civil Code § 8532.
Ownership, see Civil Code § 669 et seq.
Stop payment notice defined, see Civil Code § 8044.

Withholding, see Civil Code §§ 8522, 8536, 8542.

ARTICLE 2. STOP PAYMENT NOTICE TO OWNER

Section
8520. Persons who may give notice.
8522. Withholding of sufficient amount to pay claim; exception.

Operative Effect

For operative effect of Part 6, see Civil Code § 8052 and Stats.2010, c. 697 (S.B.189), § 105.

§ 8520. Persons who may give notice

(a) A person that has a lien right under Chapter 4 (commencing with Section 8400), other than a direct contractor, may give the owner a stop payment notice.

(b) The owner may give notice, in compliance with the requirements of Chapter 2 (commencing with Section 8100) of Title 1, demanding that a person that has a lien right under Chapter 4 (commencing with Section 8400) give the owner a stop payment notice. If the person fails to give the owner a bonded or unbonded stop payment notice, the person forfeits the right to a lien under Chapter 4 (commencing with Section 8400). (Added by Stats.2010, c. 697 (S.B.189), § 20, operative July 1, 2012.)

Operative Effect

For operative effect of Part 6, see Civil Code § 8052 and Stats.2010, c. 697 (S.B.189), § 105.

Cross References

Bond for release of funds held under stop payment notice, see Civil Code § 8510.
Bonded stop payment notice to construction lender, see Civil Code § 8532.
Direct contractor defined, see Civil Code § 8018.
Mechanics' liens, see Civil Code § 8000 et seq.
Public work, persons authorized to serve stop payment notice, see Civil Code § 9100.

§ 8522. Withholding of sufficient amount to pay claim; exception

(a) Except as provided in subdivision (b), on receipt of a stop payment notice an owner shall withhold from the direct contractor or from any person acting under authority of a direct contractor a sufficient amount due or to become due to the direct contractor to pay the claim stated in the notice.

(b) The owner may, but is not required to, withhold funds if the owner has previously recorded a payment bond under Section 8600. If the owner does not withhold funds, the owner shall, within 30 days after receipt of the stop payment notice, give notice to the claimant that a payment bond has been recorded and provide the claimant a copy of the bond. The notice shall comply with the requirements of Chapter 2 (commencing with Section 8100) of Title 1. (Added by Stats.2010, c. 697 (S.B.189), § 20, operative July 1, 2012.)

Operative Effect

For operative effect of Part 6, see Civil Code § 8052 and Stats.2010, c. 697 (S.B.189), § 105.

Cross References

Bond for release of funds held under stop payment notice, see Civil Code § 8510.
Claim of mechanics lien, contents, see Civil Code § 8416.
Claimant defined, see Civil Code § 8004.
Duration of withholding, see Civil Code § 8550.
General provisions relating to bonds, see Civil Code § 8150 et seq.
Ownership, see Civil Code § 669 et seq.
Payment bond, see Civil Code §§ 8606, 9554.
Payment bond for private works, see Civil Code § 8600 et seq.
Pro rata distribution of funds, see Civil Code § 8540.

ARTICLE 3. STOP PAYMENT NOTICE TO CONSTRUCTION LENDER

Section
8530. Person who may give notice.
8532. Bond.
8534. Notice of objection to sufficiency of sureties; substitution.
8536. Withholding of sufficient funds; exception.
8538. Request for notice of election; requirements of notice; conditions for nonliability for failure to include copy of bond.

Operative Effect

For operative effect of Part 6, see Civil Code § 8052 and Stats.2010, c. 697 (S.B.189), § 105.

§ 8530. Person who may give notice

A person that has a lien right under Chapter 4 (commencing with Section 8400) may give a construction lender a stop payment notice. (Added by Stats.2010, c. 697 (S.B.189), § 20, operative July 1, 2012.)

Operative Effect

For operative effect of Part 6, see Civil Code § 8052 and Stats.2010, c. 697 (S.B.189), § 105.

Cross References

Bond for release of funds held under stop payment notice, see Civil Code § 8510.
Claim of mechanics lien, contents, see Civil Code § 8416.
Construction lender defined, see Civil Code § 8006.
Payment bond, see Civil Code §§ 8606, 9554.
Recording, constructive notice, see Civil Code § 1213.
Stop payment notice, contents, see Civil Code § 8502.
Withholding by construction lender on receipt of stop payment notice, see Civil Code § 8536.

§ 8532. Bond

A claimant may give a construction lender a stop payment notice accompanied by a bond in an amount equal to 125 percent of the amount of the claim. The bond shall be conditioned that if the defendant recovers judgment in an action to enforce payment of the claim stated in the stop payment notice or to enforce a claim of lien recorded by the claimant, the claimant will pay all costs that are awarded the owner, direct contractor, or construction lender, and all damages to the owner, direct contractor, or construction lender that result from the stop payment notice or recordation of the claim of lien, not exceeding the amount of the bond. (Added by Stats.2010, c. 697 (S.B.189), § 20, operative July 1, 2012.)

Operative Effect

For operative effect of Part 6, see Civil Code § 8052 and Stats.2010, c. 697 (S.B.189), § 105.

Cross References

Claimant defined, see Civil Code § 8004.
Construction lender defined, see Civil Code § 8006.
General provisions relating to bonds, see Civil Code § 8150 et seq.
Preliminary notice (public work), see Civil Code § 9300.
Stop payment notice,
   Contents, see Civil Code § 8502.
   Defined, see Civil Code § 8044.
   Private works of improvement, see Civil Code § 8500 et seq.
   Public works, see Civil Code § 9350 et seq.

§ 8534. Notice of objection to sufficiency of sureties; substitution

(a) A construction lender that objects to the sufficiency of sureties on the bond given with a bonded stop payment notice shall give notice to the claimant of the objection, within 20 days after the bonded stop payment notice is given. The notice shall comply with the requirements of Chapter 2 (commencing with Section 8100) of Title 1.

(b) The claimant may within 10 days after notice of the objection is given substitute for the initial bond a bond executed by an admitted surety insurer. If the claimant does not substitute a bond executed by an admitted surety insurer, the construction lender may disregard the bonded stop payment notice and release all funds withheld in response to that notice. *(Added by Stats.2010, c. 697 (S.B.189), § 20, operative July 1, 2012.)*

Operative Effect

For operative effect of Part 6, see Civil Code § 8052 and Stats.2010, c. 697 (S.B.189), § 105.

Cross References

Claimant defined, see Civil Code § 8004.
Construction lender defined, see Civil Code § 8006.
General provisions relating to bonds, see Civil Code § 8150 et seq.
Suretyship, see Civil Code § 2787 et seq.

§ 8536. Withholding of sufficient funds; exception

(a) Except as provided in subdivision (b), on receipt of a stop payment notice a construction lender shall withhold from the borrower or other person to whom the lender or the owner is obligated to make payments or advancement out of the construction fund sufficient funds to pay the claim stated in the notice.

(b) The construction lender may, at its option, elect not to withhold funds in any of the following circumstances:

(1) The stop payment notice is unbonded.

(2) The stop payment notice is given by a claimant other than a direct contractor, and a payment bond is recorded before the lender is given any stop payment notice. *(Added by Stats.2010, c. 697 (S.B.189), § 20, operative July 1, 2012.)*

Operative Effect

For operative effect of Part 6, see Civil Code § 8052 and Stats.2010, c. 697 (S.B.189), § 105.

Cross References

Bond for release of funds held under stop payment notice, see Civil Code § 8510.
Bonded stop payment notice to construction lender, see Civil Code § 8532.
Claim of mechanics lien, contents, see Civil Code § 8416.
Construction lender defined, see Civil Code § 8006.
Direct contractor defined, see Civil Code § 8018.
Duration of withholding, see Civil Code § 8550.
General provisions relating to bonds, see Civil Code § 8150 et seq.
Payment bond, see Civil Code §§ 8606, 9554.
Payment bond for private works, see Civil Code § 8600 et seq.
Pro rata distribution of funds, see Civil Code § 8554.
Public works, similar provision, see Civil Code § 9358.
Recording, constructive notice, see Civil Code § 1213.
Stop payment notice, contents, see Civil Code § 8502.

§ 8538. Request for notice of election; requirements of notice; conditions for nonliability for failure to include copy of bond

(a) The claimant may make a written request for notice of an election by the construction lender under Section 8536 not to withhold funds. The request shall be made at the time the claimant gives the construction lender the stop payment notice and shall be accompanied by a preaddressed, stamped envelope.

(b) If the construction lender elects not to withhold funds under Section 8536, the lender shall, within 30 days after making the election, give notice of that fact to a claimant who has requested notice of the election under subdivision (a). The notice shall comply with the requirements of Chapter 2 (commencing with Section 8100) of Title 1. If the basis of the election is the recordation of a payment bond under Section 8600, the construction lender shall include a copy of the bond with the notice.

(c) A construction lender is not liable for failure to include a copy of the bond with the notice under this section if all of the following conditions are satisfied:

(1) The failure was not intentional and resulted from a bona fide error.

(2) The lender maintains reasonable procedures to avoid an error of that type.

(3) The lender corrected the error not later than 20 days after the date the lender discovered the violation. *(Added by Stats.2010, c. 697 (S.B.189), § 20, operative July 1, 2012.)*

Operative Effect

For operative effect of Part 6, see Civil Code § 8052 and Stats.2010, c. 697 (S.B.189), § 105.

Cross References

Bond for release of funds held under stop payment notice, see Civil Code § 8510.
Bonded stop payment notice to construction lender, see Civil Code § 8532.
Claim of mechanics lien, contents, see Civil Code § 8416.
Construction lender defined, see Civil Code § 8006.
Direct contractor defined, see Civil Code § 8018.
Duration of withholding, see Civil Code § 8550.
General provisions relating to bonds, see Civil Code § 8150 et seq.
Payment bond, see Civil Code §§ 8606, 9554.
Payment bond for private works, see Civil Code § 8600 et seq.

§ 8538 GENERAL PROVISIONS

Pro rata distribution of funds, see Civil Code § 8554.
Public works, similar provision, see Civil Code § 9358.
Recording, constructive notice, see Civil Code § 1213.
Stop payment notice, contents, see Civil Code § 8502.

ARTICLE 4. PRIORITIES

Section
8540. Order of priority; pro rata distribution.
8542. Recovery of net amount due only; maximum amount required to be withheld.
8544. Assignment of construction loan funds; rights of claimant not affected.

Operative Effect

For operative effect of Part 6, see Civil Code § 8052 and Stats.2010, c. 697 (S.B.189), § 105.

§ 8540. Order of priority; pro rata distribution

(a) Funds withheld pursuant to a stop payment notice shall be distributed in the following order of priority:

(1) First, to pay claims of persons that have given a bonded stop payment notice. If funds are insufficient to pay the claims of those persons in full, the funds shall be distributed pro rata among the claimants in the ratio that the claim of each bears to the aggregate of all claims for which a bonded stop payment notice is given.

(2) Second, to pay claims of persons that have given an unbonded stop payment notice. If funds are insufficient to pay the claims of those persons in full, the funds shall be distributed among the claimants in the ratio that the claim of each bears to the aggregate of all claims for which an unbonded stop payment notice is given.

(b) Pro rata distribution under this section shall be made among the persons entitled to share in the distribution without regard to the order in which the person has given a stop payment notice or commenced an enforcement action. (Added by Stats.2010, c. 697 (S.B.189), § 20, operative July 1, 2012.)

Operative Effect

For operative effect of Part 6, see Civil Code § 8052 and Stats.2010, c. 697 (S.B.189), § 105.

Cross References

Bonded stop payment notice to construction lender, see Civil Code § 8532.
Public works, similar provision, see Civil Code § 9450.
Stop payment notice, contents, see Civil Code § 8502.
Withholding, see Civil Code §§ 8522, 8538, 8542.

§ 8542. Recovery of net amount due only; maximum amount required to be withheld

Notwithstanding Section 8540:

(a) If funds are withheld pursuant to a stop payment notice given to a construction lender by a direct contractor or subcontractor, the direct contractor or subcontractor may recover only the net amount due the direct contractor or subcontractor after deducting any funds that are withheld by the construction lender pursuant to the claims of subcontractors and material suppliers that have given a stop payment notice for work done on behalf of the direct contractor or subcontractor.

(b) In no event is the construction lender required to withhold, pursuant to a stop payment notice, more than the net amount provided in subdivision (a). Notwithstanding any other provision of this chapter, a construction lender is not liable for failure to withhold more than that net amount on receipt of a stop payment notice. (Added by Stats.2010, c. 697 (S.B.189), § 20, operative July 1, 2012.)

Operative Effect

For operative effect of Part 6, see Civil Code § 8052 and Stats.2010, c. 697 (S.B.189), § 105.

Cross References

Bond for release of funds held under stop payment notice, see Civil Code § 8510.
Bonded stop payment notice to construction lender, see Civil Code § 8532.
Claim of mechanics lien, contents, see Civil Code § 8416.
Construction lender defined, see Civil Code § 8006.
Direct contractor defined, see Civil Code § 8018.
Duration of withholding, see Civil Code § 8550.
General provisions relating to bonds, see Civil Code § 8150 et seq.
Payment bond, see Civil Code §§ 8606, 9554.
Payment bond for private works, see Civil Code § 8600 et seq.
Pro rata distribution of funds, see Civil Code § 8554.
Public works, similar provision, see Civil Code § 9358.
Recording, constructive notice, see Civil Code § 1213.
Stop payment notice, contents, see Civil Code § 8502.
Subcontractor defined, see Civil Code § 8046.

§ 8544. Assignment of construction loan funds; rights of claimant not affected

The rights of a claimant who gives a construction lender a stop payment notice are not affected by an assignment of construction loan funds made by the owner or direct contractor, and the stop payment notice has priority over the assignment, whether the assignment is made before or after the stop payment notice is given. (Added by Stats.2010, c. 697 (S.B.189), § 20, operative July 1, 2012.)

Operative Effect

For operative effect of Part 6, see Civil Code § 8052 and Stats.2010, c. 697 (S.B.189), § 105.

Cross References

Assignment of thing in action, effect on defense, see Code of Civil Procedure § 368.
Bonded stop notice to construction lender, see Civil Code § 8532.
Claimant defined, see Civil Code § 8004.
Construction lender defined, see Civil Code § 8006.
Stop notice, contents, see Civil Code § 8502.
Transfer of obligations, see Civil Code § 1457 et seq.
Transfer of things in action, see Civil Code § 954.

ARTICLE 5. ENFORCEMENT OF CLAIM STATED IN STOP PAYMENT NOTICE

Section
8550. Time for commencement of action; notice.
8552. Multiple claimants.
8554. Dismissal for want of prosecution.
8556. Dismissal or judgment; effect.

Section
8558. Attorney fees; prevailing party.
8560. Interest.

Operative Effect

For operative effect of Part 6, see Civil Code § 8052 and Stats.2010, c. 697 (S.B.189), § 105.

§ 8550. Time for commencement of action; notice

(a) A claimant shall commence an action to enforce payment of the claim stated in a stop payment notice at any time after 10 days from the date the claimant gives the stop payment notice.

(b) A claimant shall commence an action to enforce payment of the claim stated in a stop payment notice not later than 90 days after expiration of the time within which a stop payment notice must be given.

(c) An action under this section may not be brought to trial or judgment entered before expiration of the time provided in subdivision (b).

(d) If a claimant does not commence an action to enforce payment of the claim stated in a stop payment notice within the time prescribed in subdivision (b), the notice ceases to be effective and the person withholding funds pursuant to the notice shall release them.

(e) Within five days after commencement of an action to enforce payment of the claim stated in a stop payment notice, the claimant shall give notice of commencement of the action to the persons to whom the stop payment notice was given. The notice shall comply with the requirements of Chapter 2 (commencing with Section 8100) of Title 1. *(Added by Stats.2010, c. 697 (S.B.189), § 20, operative July 1, 2012.)*

Operative Effect

For operative effect of Part 6, see Civil Code § 8052 and Stats.2010, c. 697 (S.B.189), § 105.

Cross References

Bonded stop payment notice to construction lender, see Civil Code § 8532.
Claim of mechanics lien, contents, see Civil Code § 8416.
Limitation of actions, generally, see Code of Civil Procedure § 312 et seq.
Recording of claim of lien, see Civil Code § 8412.
Stop payment notice defined, see Civil Code § 8044.

§ 8552. Multiple claimants

If more than one claimant has given a stop payment notice:

(a) Any number of claimants may join in the same enforcement action.

(b) If claimants commence separate actions, the court first acquiring jurisdiction may order the actions consolidated.

(c) On motion of the owner or construction lender the court shall require all claimants to be impleaded in one action, to the end that the rights of all parties may be adjudicated in the action. *(Added by Stats.2010, c. 697 (S.B.189), § 20, operative July 1, 2012.)*

Operative Effect

For operative effect of Part 6, see Civil Code § 8052 and Stats.2010, c. 697 (S.B.189), § 105.

Cross References

Bonded stop payment notice to construction lender, see Civil Code § 8532.
Consolidation of actions, see Code of Civil Procedure § 1048.
Public works, consolidation of actions, see Civil Code § 9506.

§ 8554. Dismissal for want of prosecution

Notwithstanding Section 583.420 of the Code of Civil Procedure, if an action to enforce payment of the claim stated in a stop payment notice is not brought to trial within two years after commencement of the action, the court may in its discretion dismiss the action for want of prosecution. *(Added by Stats.2010, c. 697 (S.B.189), § 20, operative July 1, 2012.)*

Operative Effect

For operative effect of Part 6, see Civil Code § 8052 and Stats.2010, c. 697 (S.B.189), § 105.

Cross References

Dismissal for delay in prosecution, see Code of Civil Procedure § 583.110 et seq.
Mechanic's liens in general, dismissal, see Civil Code §§ 8462, 8490.
Public works, dismissal of actions, see Civil Code §§ 9508, 9510.

§ 8556. Dismissal or judgment; effect

A stop payment notice ceases to be effective, and a person withholding funds pursuant to the notice shall release them, in either of the following circumstances:

(a) An action to enforce payment of the claim stated in the stop payment notice is dismissed, unless expressly stated to be without prejudice.

(b) Judgment in an action to enforce payment of the claim stated in the stop payment notice is against the claimant. *(Added by Stats.2010, c. 697 (S.B.189), § 20, operative July 1, 2012.)*

Operative Effect

For operative effect of Part 6, see Civil Code § 8052 and Stats.2010, c. 697 (S.B.189), § 105.

Cross References

Bonded stop payment notice to construction lender, see Civil Code § 8532.
Claimant defined, see Civil Code § 8004.
Mechanic's liens in general, dismissal, see Civil Code §§ 8462, 8490.
Pro rata distribution of funds, see Civil Code § 8540.
Public works, dismissal of actions, see Civil Code §§ 9508, 9510.
Release of withheld funds, see Civil Code § 8510.
Withholding, see Civil Code §§ 8522, 8536, 8542.

§ 8558. Attorney fees; prevailing party

(a) In an action to enforce payment of the claim stated in a bonded stop payment notice, the prevailing party is entitled to a reasonable attorney's fee in addition to costs and damages.

(b) The court, on notice and motion by a party, shall determine who is the prevailing party or that there is no prevailing party for the purpose of this section, regardless of

§ 8558

whether the action proceeds to final judgment. The prevailing party is the party that recovers greater relief in the action, subject to the following limitations:

(1) If the action is voluntarily dismissed or dismissed pursuant to a settlement, there is no prevailing party.

(2) If the defendant tenders to the claimant the full amount to which the claimant is entitled, and deposits in court for the claimant the amount so tendered, and alleges those facts in the answer and the allegation is determined to be true, the defendant is deemed to be the prevailing party. *(Added by Stats.2010, c. 697 (S.B.189), § 20, operative July 1, 2012.)*

Operative Effect

For operative effect of Part 6, see Civil Code § 8052 and Stats.2010, c. 697 (S.B.189), § 105.

§ 8560. Interest

If the claimant is the prevailing party in an action to enforce payment of the claim stated in a bonded stop payment notice, any amount awarded on the claim shall include interest at the legal rate calculated from the date the stop payment notice is given. *(Added by Stats.2010, c. 697 (S.B.189), § 20, operative July 1, 2012.)*

Operative Effect

For operative effect of Part 6, see Civil Code § 8052 and Stats.2010, c. 697 (S.B.189), § 105.

CHAPTER 6. PAYMENT BOND

Section
- 8600. Application; restriction of lien enforcement.
- 8602. Bond or other security.
- 8604. Lending institutions; objections to bond.
- 8606. Nature of bond; principal; enforcement.
- 8608. Work done for direct contractor on bond; claim.
- 8609. Invalidity of provisions limiting actions.
- 8610. Bonds recorded before improvements completed; actions against sureties.
- 8612. Preliminary notice required; notice to surety and bond principal; extension; exceptions.
- 8614. Notice requirements.

Operative Effect

For operative effect of Part 6, see Civil Code § 8052 and Stats.2010, c. 697 (S.B.189), § 105.

§ 8600. Application; restriction of lien enforcement

(a) This section applies if, before the commencement of work, the owner in good faith files a direct contract with the county recorder, and records a payment bond of the direct contractor in an amount not less than 50 percent of the price stated in the direct contract.

(b) If the conditions of subdivision (a) are satisfied, the court shall, where equitable to do so, restrict lien enforcement under this title to the aggregate amount due from the owner to the direct contractor and shall enter judgment against the direct contractor and surety on the bond for any deficiency that remains between the amount due to the direct contractor and the whole amount due to claimants. *(Added by Stats.2010, c. 697 (S.B.189), § 20, operative July 1, 2012.)*

Operative Effect

For operative effect of Part 6, see Civil Code § 8052 and Stats.2010, c. 697 (S.B.189), § 105.

Cross References

Direct contract defined, see Civil Code § 8016.
Effect of bond on duty to withhold moneys pursuant to stop payment notice, see Civil Code § 8522.
Owners, see Civil Code § 669.
Payment bond, see Civil Code §§ 8606, 9554.
Public works, contractor's payment bond, see Civil Code § 9550 et seq.
Written notice to surety and bond principal, see Civil Code §§ 8614, 9562.

§ 8602. Bond or other security

Section 8600 does not preclude an owner from requiring a performance bond, payment bond, or other security as protection against a direct contractor's failure to perform the direct contract or to make full payment for all work provided pursuant to the contract. *(Added by Stats.2010, c. 697 (S.B.189), § 20, operative July 1, 2012.)*

Operative Effect

For operative effect of Part 6, see Civil Code § 8052 and Stats.2010, c. 697 (S.B.189), § 105.

Cross References

Direct contract defined, see Civil Code § 8016.
Owners, see Civil Code § 669.
Public works, contractor's payment bond, see Civil Code § 9550 et seq.

§ 8604. Lending institutions; objections to bond

(a) If a lending institution requires that a payment bond be given as a condition of lending money to finance a work of improvement, and accepts in writing as sufficient a bond given in fulfillment of the requirement, the lending institution may not thereafter object to the borrower as to the validity of the bond or refuse to make the loan based on an objection to the bond if the bond is given by an admitted surety insurer.

(b) For purposes of this section, a "lending institution" includes a commercial bank, savings and loan institution, credit union, or other organization or person engaged in the business of financing loans. *(Added by Stats.2010, c. 697 (S.B.189), § 20, operative July 1, 2012.)*

Operative Effect

For operative effect of Part 6, see Civil Code § 8052 and Stats.2010, c. 697 (S.B.189), § 105.

§ 8606. Nature of bond; principal; enforcement

(a) A payment bond under this title shall be conditioned for the payment in full of the claims of all claimants and shall by its terms inure to the benefit of all claimants so as to give a claimant a right of action to enforce the liability on the bond. The bond shall be given by an admitted surety insurer.

(b) An owner, direct contractor, or subcontractor may be the principal on the bond.

(c) A claimant may enforce the liability on the bond in an action to enforce a lien under this part or in a separate action on the bond. *(Added by Stats.2010, c. 697 (S.B.189), § 20, operative July 1, 2012.)*

Operative Effect

For operative effect of Part 6, see Civil Code § 8052 and Stats.2010, c. 697 (S.B.189), § 105.

Cross References

General provisions relating to bonds, see Civil Code § 8150 et seq.
Ownership, see Civil Code § 669 et seq.
Payment bond for private works, see Civil Code § 8600 et seq.
Payment bond for public works, see Civil Code § 9550 et seq.
Payment bond procured by landowner, mortgagee or trustee on site improvement, priority of liens, see Civil Code § 8458.
Payment bond procured by mortgagee or trustee, priority of liens, see Civil Code § 8452.
Suretyship, see Civil Code § 2787 et seq.

§ 8608. Work done for direct contractor on bond; claim

(a) This title does not give a claimant a right to recover on a direct contractor's payment bond given under this chapter unless the claimant provided work to the direct contractor either directly or through one or more subcontractors, pursuant to a direct contract.

(b) Nothing in this section affects the stop payment notice right of, and relative priorities among, design professionals and holders of secured interests in the real property. *(Added by Stats.2010, c. 697 (S.B.189), § 20, operative July 1, 2012.)*

Operative Effect

For operative effect of Part 6, see Civil Code § 8052 and Stats.2010, c. 697 (S.B.189), § 105.

Cross References

Claimant defined, see Civil Code § 8004.
Commencement of actions, see Civil Code § 8550.
Direct contractor defined, see Civil Code § 8018.
Payment bond, see Civil Code §§ 8606, 9554.

§ 8609. Invalidity of provisions limiting actions

Any provision in a payment bond attempting by contract to shorten the period prescribed in Section 337 of the Code of Civil Procedure for the commencement of an action on the bond shall not be valid under either of the following circumstances:

(a) If the provision attempts to limit the time for commencement of an action on the bond to a shorter period than six months from the completion of any work of improvement.

(b) As applied to any action brought by a claimant, unless the bond is recorded before the work of improvement is commenced. *(Added by Stats.2010, c. 697 (S.B.189), § 20, operative July 1, 2012.)*

Operative Effect

For operative effect of Part 6, see Civil Code § 8052 and Stats.2010, c. 697 (S.B.189), § 105.

Cross References

Action against direct contractor and public entity, see Civil Code § 9502 et seq.
Action on payment bond for public works, see Civil Code § 9558 et seq.
Claimant defined, see Civil Code § 8004.
Completion, see Civil Code §§ 8180, 9200.
Enforcement of lien, see Civil Code § 8410 et seq.
Limitation of actions, generally, see Code of Civil Procedure § 312 et seq.
Payment bond, see Civil Code §§ 8606, 9554.

§ 8610. Bonds recorded before improvements completed; actions against sureties

Notwithstanding Section 8609, if a payment bond under this title is recorded before completion of a work of improvement, an action to enforce the liability on the bond may not be commenced later than six months after completion of the work of improvement. *(Added by Stats.2010, c. 697 (S.B.189), § 20, operative July 1, 2012.)*

Operative Effect

For operative effect of Part 6, see Civil Code § 8052 and Stats.2010, c. 697 (S.B.189), § 105.

§ 8612. Preliminary notice required; notice to surety and bond principal; extension; exceptions

(a) In order to enforce a claim against a payment bond under this title, a claimant shall give the preliminary notice provided in Chapter 2 (commencing with Section 8200).

(b) If preliminary notice was not given as provided in Chapter 2 (commencing with Section 8200), a claimant may enforce a claim by giving written notice to the surety and the bond principal within 15 days after recordation of a notice of completion. If no notice of completion has been recorded, the time for giving written notice to the surety and the bond principal is extended to 75 days after completion of the work of improvement.

(c) Commencing July 1, 2012, and except as provided in subdivision (b), if the preliminary notice was required to be given by a person who has no direct contractual relationship with the contractor, and who has not given notice as provided in Chapter 2 (commencing with Section 8200), that person may enforce a claim by giving written notice to the surety and the bond principal, as provided in Section 8614, within 15 days after recordation of a notice of completion. If no notice of completion has been recorded, the time for giving written notice to the surety and the bond principal is extended to 75 days after completion of the work of improvement.

(d) Subdivision (c) shall not apply in either of the following circumstances:

(1) All progress payments, except for those disputed in good faith, have been made to a subcontractor who has a direct contractual relationship with the general contractor to whom the claimant has provided materials or services.

(2) The subcontractor who has a direct contractual relationship with the general contractor to whom the claimant has provided materials or services has been terminated from the project pursuant to the contract, and all progress payments, except those disputed in good faith, have been made as of the termination date.

(e) Pursuant to Section 8200, this section shall not apply to a laborer, as defined under Section 8024.

§ 8612

(f) This section shall become operative on July 1, 2012. *(Added by Stats.2010, c. 697 (S.B.189), § 20, operative July 1, 2012. Amended by Stats.2011, c. 700 (S.B.293), § 3, operative July 1, 2012.)*

Operative Effect

For operative effect of Part 6, see Civil Code § 8052 and Stats.2010, c. 697 (S.B.189), § 105.

§ 8614. Notice requirements

Notice to the principal and surety under Section 8612 shall comply with the requirements of Chapter 2 (commencing with Section 8100) of Title 1. *(Added by Stats.2010, c. 697 (S.B.189), § 20, operative July 1, 2012.)*

Operative Effect

For operative effect of Part 6, see Civil Code § 8052 and Stats.2010, c. 697 (S.B.189), § 105.

CHAPTER 7. SECURITY FOR LARGE PROJECT

Article	Section
1. Application of Chapter	8700
2. Security Requirement	8710
3. Form of Security	8720

Operative Effect

For operative effect of Part 6, see Civil Code § 8052 and Stats.2010, c. 697 (S.B.189), § 105.

ARTICLE 1. APPLICATION OF CHAPTER

Section
8700. Conditions for application of chapter.
8702. Chapter not applicable to specified works of improvement.
8704. Chapter not applicable to specified owners.

Operative Effect

For operative effect of Part 6, see Civil Code § 8052 and Stats.2010, c. 697 (S.B.189), § 105.

§ 8700. Conditions for application of chapter

(a) This chapter applies if any of the following conditions is satisfied:

(1) The owner of the fee interest in property contracts for a work of improvement on the property with a contract price greater than five million dollars ($5,000,000).

(2) The owner of a less than fee interest in property, including a leasehold interest, contracts for a work of improvement on the property with a contract price greater than one million dollars ($1,000,000).

(b) For the purpose of this section:

(1) The owner of the fee interest in property is not deemed to be the owner of a less than fee interest by reason of a mortgage, deed of trust, ground lease, or other lien or encumbrance or right of occupancy that encumbers the fee interest.

(2) A lessee of real property is deemed to be the owner of a fee interest in the real property if all of the following conditions are satisfied:

(A) The initial term of the lease is at least 35 years.

(B) The lease covers one or more lawful parcels under the Subdivision Map Act, Division 2 (commencing with Section 66410) of Title 7 of the Government Code, and any applicable local ordinance adopted under that act, in their entirety, including, but not limited to, a parcel approved pursuant to a certificate of compliance proceeding. *(Added by Stats.2010, c. 697 (S.B.189), § 20, operative July 1, 2012.)*

Operative Effect

For operative effect of Part 6, see Civil Code § 8052 and Stats.2010, c. 697 (S.B.189), § 105.

Cross References

Mechanics liens, generally, see Civil Code § 8400 et seq.

§ 8702. Chapter not applicable to specified works of improvement

This chapter does not apply to any of the following works of improvement:

(a) A single-family residence, including a single-family residence located within a subdivision, and any associated fixed work that requires the services of a general engineering contractor as defined in Section 7056 of the Business and Professions Code. As used in this subdivision, "single-family residence" means a real property improvement used or intended to be used as a dwelling unit for one family.

(b) A housing development eligible for a density bonus under Section 65915 of the Government Code. *(Added by Stats.2010, c. 697 (S.B.189), § 20, operative July 1, 2012.)*

Operative Effect

For operative effect of Part 6, see Civil Code § 8052 and Stats.2010, c. 697 (S.B.189), § 105.

Cross References

Mechanics liens, generally, see Civil Code § 8400 et seq.

§ 8704. Chapter not applicable to specified owners

This chapter does not apply to any of the following owners:

(a) A qualified publicly traded company or a wholly owned subsidiary of a qualified publicly traded company, if the obligations of the subsidiary pursuant to the contract for the work of improvement are guaranteed by the parent. As used in this subdivision, "qualified publicly traded company" means a company having a class of equity securities listed for trading on the New York Stock Exchange, the American Stock Exchange, or the NASDAQ stock market, and the nonsubordinated debt securities of which are rated as "investment grade" by either Fitch ICBA, Inc., Moody's Investor Services, Inc., Standard & Poor's Ratings Services, or a similar statistical rating organization that is nationally recognized for rating the creditworthiness of a publicly traded company. If at any time before final payment of all amounts due pursuant to the contract the nonsubordinated debt securities of the qualified publicly traded company are downgraded to below "investment grade" by any of those rating organizations, the owner is no longer exempt from this chapter.

(b) A qualified private company or a wholly owned subsidiary of a qualified private company, if the obligations of the subsidiary pursuant to the contract for the work of improvement are guaranteed by the parent. As used in this subdivision, "qualified private company" means a company that has no equity securities listed for trading on the New York Stock Exchange, the American Stock Exchange, or the NASDAQ stock market, and that has a net worth determined in accordance with generally accepted accounting principles in excess of fifty million dollars ($50,000,000). If at any time before final payment of all amounts due pursuant to the contract the net worth of the qualified private company is reduced below that level, the owner is no longer exempt from this chapter. *(Added by Stats.2010, c. 697 (S.B.189), § 20, operative July 1, 2012.)*

Operative Effect

For operative effect of Part 6, see Civil Code § 8052 and Stats.2010, c. 697 (S.B.189), § 105.

Cross References

Mechanics liens, generally, see Civil Code § 8400 et seq.

ARTICLE 2. SECURITY REQUIREMENT

Section
8710. Security and copy of recorded construction mortgage or deed of trust disclosing the amount of the construction loan to be provided to direct contractor.
8712. Failure to provide or maintain security.
8714. Waiver against public policy.
8716. Affect on rights of subcontractor.

Operative Effect

For operative effect of Part 6, see Civil Code § 8052 and Stats.2010, c. 697 (S.B.189), § 105.

§ 8710. Security and copy of recorded construction mortgage or deed of trust disclosing the amount of the construction loan to be provided to direct contractor

An owner described in subdivision (a) of Section 8700 shall provide the direct contractor all of the following:

(a) Security for the owner's payment obligation pursuant to the contract. The security shall be used only if the owner defaults on the payment obligation to the direct contractor. This subdivision does not apply to an owner that is the majority owner of the direct contractor.

(b) A copy, certified by the county recorder, of any recorded mortgage or deed of trust that secures the construction loan of a lending institution for the work of improvement, disclosing the amount of the loan. *(Added by Stats. 2010, c. 697 (S.B.189), § 20, operative July 1, 2012.)*

Operative Effect

For operative effect of Part 6, see Civil Code § 8052 and Stats.2010, c. 697 (S.B.189), § 105.

Cross References

Mechanics liens, generally, see Civil Code § 8400 et seq.

§ 8712. Failure to provide or maintain security

If an owner fails to provide or maintain the security required by this chapter, the direct contractor may give the owner notice demanding security. The notice shall comply with the requirements of Chapter 2 (commencing with Section 8100) of Title 1. If the owner does not provide or maintain the security within 10 days after notice demanding security is given, the direct contractor may suspend work until the owner provides or maintains the security. *(Added by Stats.2010, c. 697 (S.B.189), § 20, operative July 1, 2012.)*

Operative Effect

For operative effect of Part 6, see Civil Code § 8052 and Stats.2010, c. 697 (S.B.189), § 105.

Cross References

Mechanics liens, generally, see Civil Code § 8400 et seq.

§ 8714. Waiver against public policy

It is against public policy to waive the provisions of this chapter by contract. *(Added by Stats.2010, c. 697 (S.B.189), § 20, operative July 1, 2012.)*

Operative Effect

For operative effect of Part 6, see Civil Code § 8052 and Stats.2010, c. 697 (S.B.189), § 105.

Cross References

Mechanics liens, generally, see Civil Code § 8400 et seq.

§ 8716. Affect on rights of subcontractor

This chapter does not affect any statute providing for mechanics liens, stop payment notices, bond remedies, or prompt payment rights of a subcontractor, including the direct contractor's payment responsibilities under Section 7108.5 of the Business and Professions Code. *(Added by Stats.2010, c. 697 (S.B.189), § 20, operative July 1, 2012.)*

Operative Effect

For operative effect of Part 6, see Civil Code § 8052 and Stats.2010, c. 697 (S.B.189), § 105.

Cross References

Mechanics liens, generally, see Civil Code § 8400 et seq.

ARTICLE 3. FORM OF SECURITY

Section
8720. Means of providing security.
8722. Bond; requirements.
8724. Irrevocable letter of credit; requirements.
8726. Escrow account; requirements.
8728. Construction security escrow account; deposit or disbursement.
8730. Contract price not fixed price; amount of security.

Operative Effect

For operative effect of Part 6, see Civil Code § 8052 and Stats.2010, c. 697 (S.B.189), § 105.

§ 8720. Means of providing security

An owner shall provide security by any of the following means:

(a) A bond that satisfies Section 8722.

(b) An irrevocable letter of credit that satisfies Section 8724.

(c) An escrow account that satisfies Section 8726. *(Added by Stats.2010, c. 697 (S.B.189), § 20, operative July 1, 2012.)*

Operative Effect

For operative effect of Part 6, see Civil Code § 8052 and Stats.2010, c. 697 (S.B.189), § 105.

Cross References

Mechanics liens, generally, see Civil Code § 8400 et seq.

§ 8722. Bond; requirements

A bond under this chapter shall satisfy all of the following requirements:

(a) The bond shall be executed by an admitted surety insurer that is either listed in the Department of the Treasury's Listing of Approved Sureties (Department Circular 570) or that has an A.M. Best rating of A or better and has an underwriting limitation, under Section 12090 of the Insurance Code, greater than the amount of the bond.

(b) The bond shall be in an amount not less than 15 percent of the contract price for the work of improvement or, if the work of improvement is to be substantially completed within six months after the commencement of work, not less than 25 percent of the contract price.

(c) The bond shall be conditioned for payment on default by the owner of any undisputed amount pursuant to the contract that is due and payable for more than 30 days. *(Added by Stats.2010, c. 697 (S.B.189), § 20, operative July 1, 2012.)*

Operative Effect

For operative effect of Part 6, see Civil Code § 8052 and Stats.2010, c. 697 (S.B.189), § 105.

Cross References

Mechanics liens, generally, see Civil Code § 8400 et seq.

§ 8724. Irrevocable letter of credit; requirements

An irrevocable letter of credit under this chapter shall satisfy all of the following requirements:

(a) The letter of credit shall be issued by a financial institution, as defined in Section 5107 of the Financial Code, inuring to the benefit of the direct contractor.

(b) The letter of credit shall be in an amount not less than 15 percent of the contract price for the work of improvement or, if the work of improvement is to be substantially completed within six months after the commencement of work, not less than 25 percent of the contract price.

(c) The maturity date and other terms of the letter of credit shall be determined by agreement between the owner, the direct contractor, and the financial institution, except that the owner shall maintain the letter of credit in effect until the owner has satisfied its payment obligation to the direct contractor. *(Added by Stats.2010, c. 697 (S.B.189), § 20, operative July 1, 2012.)*

Operative Effect

For operative effect of Part 6, see Civil Code § 8052 and Stats.2010, c. 697 (S.B.189), § 105.

Cross References

Mechanics liens, generally, see Civil Code § 8400 et seq.

§ 8726. Escrow account; requirements

An escrow account under this chapter shall satisfy all of the following requirements:

(a) The account shall be designated as a "construction security escrow account."

(b) The account shall be located in this state and maintained with an escrow agent licensed under the Escrow Law, Division 6 (commencing with Section 17000) of the Financial Code, or with any person exempt from the Escrow Law under paragraph (1) or (3) of subdivision (a) of Section 17006 of the Financial Code.

(c) The owner shall deposit funds in the account in the amount provided in Section 8728. This chapter does not require a construction lender to agree to deposit proceeds of a construction loan in the account.

(d) The owner shall grant the direct contractor a perfected, first priority security interest in the account and in all funds deposited by the owner in the account and in their proceeds, established to the reasonable satisfaction of the direct contractor, which may be by a written opinion of legal counsel for the owner.

(e) The funds on deposit in the account shall be the sole property of the owner, subject to the security interest of the direct contractor. The owner and the direct contractor shall instruct the escrow holder to hold the funds on deposit in the account for the purpose of perfecting the direct contractor's security interest in the account and to disburse those funds only on joint authorization of the owner and the direct contractor, or pursuant to a court order that is binding on both of them. *(Added by Stats.2010, c. 697 (S.B.189), § 20, operative July 1, 2012.)*

Operative Effect

For operative effect of Part 6, see Civil Code § 8052 and Stats.2010, c. 697 (S.B.189), § 105.

Cross References

Mechanics liens, generally, see Civil Code § 8400 et seq.

§ 8728. Construction security escrow account; deposit or disbursement

The following provisions govern a deposit to or disbursement from a construction security escrow account under this chapter:

(a) Before the commencement of work the owner shall make an initial deposit to the account in an amount not less than 15 percent of the contract price for the work of improvement or, if the work of improvement is to be substantially completed within six months after the commencement of work, not less than 25 percent of the contract price.

(b) If the contract provides for a retention to be withheld from a periodic payment to the direct contractor, the owner shall deposit to the account the amount withheld as retention at the time the owner makes the corresponding payment to the direct contractor from which the retention is withheld.

(c) The amount required to be maintained on deposit shall not exceed the total amount remaining to be paid to the direct contractor pursuant to the contract or as adjusted by agreement between the owner and the direct contractor. If the amount on deposit equals or exceeds the total amount remaining to be paid to the direct contractor, the owner and the direct contractor shall authorize disbursement to the direct contractor for progress payments then due the direct contractor, but a party is not obligated to authorize disbursement that would cause the amount remaining on deposit following the disbursement to be less than the total amount remaining to be paid to the direct contractor.

(d) The owner and the direct contractor shall authorize the disbursement to the owner of any funds remaining on deposit after the direct contractor has been paid all amounts due pursuant to the contract. The owner and the direct contractor shall authorize the disbursement of funds on deposit pursuant to a court order that is binding on both of them. The owner and the direct contractor may agree in the contract to additional conditions for the disbursement of funds on deposit, except that the conditions may not cause the amount remaining on deposit to be less than the amount required under this section. *(Added by Stats.2010, c. 697 (S.B.189), § 20, operative July 1, 2012.)*

Operative Effect

For operative effect of Part 6, see Civil Code § 8052 and Stats.2010, c. 697 (S.B.189), § 105.

Cross References

Mechanics liens, generally, see Civil Code § 8400 et seq.

§ 8730. Contract price not fixed price; amount of security

If the contract price for a work of improvement is not a fixed price, the amount of security provided under this chapter shall be the guaranteed maximum price or, if there is no guaranteed maximum price, the owner's and direct contractor's good faith estimate of the reasonable value of the work to be provided pursuant to the contract. *(Added by Stats.2010, c. 697 (S.B.189), § 20, operative July 1, 2012.)*

Operative Effect

For operative effect of Part 6, see Civil Code § 8052 and Stats.2010, c. 697 (S.B.189), § 105.

Cross References

Mechanics liens, generally, see Civil Code § 8400 et seq.

CHAPTER 8. PROMPT PAYMENT

Article	Section
1. Progress Payment	8800
2. Retention Payment	8810
3. Stop Work Notice	8830

Operative Effect

For operative effect of Part 6, see Civil Code § 8052 and Stats.2010, c. 697 (S.B.189), § 105.

ARTICLE 1. PROGRESS PAYMENT

Section	
8800.	Progress payments; good faith disputes; liability of owner.
8802.	Payments to subcontractors; liability of direct contractor; additional remedies.

Operative Effect

For operative effect of Part 6, see Civil Code § 8052 and Stats.2010, c. 697 (S.B.189), § 105.

§ 8800. Progress payments; good faith disputes; liability of owner

(a) Except as otherwise agreed in writing by the owner and direct contractor, the owner shall pay the direct contractor, within 30 days after notice demanding payment pursuant to the contract is given, any progress payment due as to which there is no good faith dispute between them. The notice given shall comply with the requirements of Chapter 2 (commencing with Section 8100) of Title 1.

(b) If there is a good faith dispute between the owner and direct contractor as to a progress payment due, the owner may withhold from the progress payment an amount not in excess of 150 percent of the disputed amount.

(c) An owner that violates this section is liable to the direct contractor for a penalty of 2 percent per month on the amount wrongfully withheld, in place of any interest otherwise due. In an action for collection of the amount wrongfully withheld, the prevailing party is entitled to costs and a reasonable attorney's fee.

(d) This section does not supersede any requirement of Article 2 (commencing with Section 8810) relating to the withholding of a retention. *(Added by Stats.2010, c. 697 (S.B.189), § 20, operative July 1, 2012.)*

Operative Effect

For operative effect of Part 6, see Civil Code § 8052 and Stats.2010, c. 697 (S.B.189), § 105.

Cross References

Payment of wages, direct contractor liability, see Labor Code §§ 218.7, 218.8.

§ 8802. Payments to subcontractors; liability of direct contractor; additional remedies

(a) This section applies to a contract between a public utility and a direct contractor for all or part of a work of improvement.

(b) Unless the direct contractor and a subcontractor otherwise agree in writing, within 21 days after receipt of a progress payment from the public utility the direct contractor shall pay the subcontractor the amount allowed the direct contractor on account of the work performed by the subcontractor to the extent of the subcontractor's interest in the work. If there is a good faith dispute over all or part of the amount due on a progress payment from the direct contractor to a subcontractor, the direct contractor may withhold an amount not in excess of 150 percent of the disputed amount.

(c) A direct contractor that violates this section is liable to the subcontractor for a penalty of 2 percent of the disputed amount due per month for every month that payment is not made. In an action for collection of the amount wrongfully withheld, the prevailing party is entitled to costs and a reasonable attorney's fee.

(d) This section does not limit or impair a contractual, administrative, or judicial remedy otherwise available to a contractor or subcontractor in a dispute involving late payment or nonpayment by the contractor or deficient performance or nonperformance by the subcontractor. *(Added by Stats.2010, c. 697 (S.B.189), § 20, operative July 1, 2012.)*

Operative Effect

For operative effect of Part 6, see Civil Code § 8052 and Stats.2010, c. 697 (S.B.189), § 105.

ARTICLE 2. RETENTION PAYMENT

Section
8810. Scope of article.
8812. Time for payment of retention to direct contractor; conditional payment; good faith disputes.
8814. Time for payment of retention to subcontractor; specifically designated payments; good faith disputes.
8816. Notice that disputed work has been completed in accordance with contract; time for notice of acceptance or rejection; payment of retention relating to disputed work.
8818. Failure to make payment within required time; liability.
8820. Waiver against public policy.
8822. Retention payments withheld by lender pursuant to construction loan agreement.

Operative Effect

For operative effect of Part 6, see Civil Code § 8052 and Stats.2010, c. 697 (S.B.189), § 105.

§ 8810. Scope of article

This article governs a retention payment withheld by an owner from a direct contractor or by a direct contractor from a subcontractor. *(Added by Stats.2010, c. 697 (S.B.189), § 20, operative July 1, 2012.)*

Operative Effect

For operative effect of Part 6, see Civil Code § 8052 and Stats.2010, c. 697 (S.B.189), § 105.

Cross References

Construction contracts, indemnity agreements, see Civil Code § 2782 et seq.

§ 8812. Time for payment of retention to direct contractor; conditional payment; good faith disputes

(a) If an owner withholds a retention from a direct contractor, the owner shall, within 45 days after completion of the work of improvement, pay the retention to the contractor.

(b) If part of a work of improvement ultimately will become the property of a public entity, the owner may condition payment of a retention allocable to that part on acceptance of the part by the public entity.

(c) If there is a good faith dispute between the owner and direct contractor as to a retention payment due, the owner may withhold from final payment an amount not in excess of 150 percent of the disputed amount. *(Added by Stats.2010, c. 697 (S.B.189), § 20, operative July 1, 2012.)*

Operative Effect

For operative effect of Part 6, see Civil Code § 8052 and Stats.2010, c. 697 (S.B.189), § 105.

Cross References

Construction contracts, indemnity agreements, see Civil Code § 2782 et seq.
Payment of wages, direct contractor liability, see Labor Code §§ 218.7, 218.8.

§ 8814. Time for payment of retention to subcontractor; specifically designated payments; good faith disputes

(a) If a direct contractor has withheld a retention from one or more subcontractors, the direct contractor shall, within 10 days after receiving all or part of a retention payment, pay to each subcontractor from whom retention has been withheld that subcontractor's share of the payment.

(b) If a retention received by the direct contractor is specifically designated for a particular subcontractor, the direct contractor shall pay the retention payment to the designated subcontractor, if consistent with the terms of the subcontract.

(c) If a good faith dispute exists between the direct contractor and a subcontractor, the direct contractor may withhold from the retention to the subcontractor an amount not in excess of 150 percent of the estimated value of the disputed amount. *(Added by Stats.2010, c. 697 (S.B.189), § 20, operative July 1, 2012.)*

Operative Effect

For operative effect of Part 6, see Civil Code § 8052 and Stats.2010, c. 697 (S.B.189), § 105.

Cross References

Construction contracts, indemnity agreements, see Civil Code § 2782 et seq.
Payment of wages, direct contractor liability, see Labor Code §§ 218.7, 218.8.

§ 8816. Notice that disputed work has been completed in accordance with contract; time for notice of acceptance or rejection; payment of retention relating to disputed work

(a) If the direct contractor gives the owner, or a subcontractor gives the direct contractor, notice that work in dispute has been completed in accordance with the contract, the owner or direct contractor shall within 10 days give notice advising the notifying party of the acceptance or rejection of the disputed work. Both notices shall comply with the requirements of Chapter 2 (commencing with Section 8100) of Title 1.

(b) Within 10 days after acceptance of disputed work, the owner or direct contractor shall pay the portion of the retention relating to the disputed work. *(Added by Stats. 2010, c. 697 (S.B.189), § 20, operative July 1, 2012.)*

Operative Effect

For operative effect of Part 6, see Civil Code § 8052 and Stats.2010, c. 697 (S.B.189), § 105.

Cross References

Construction contracts, indemnity agreements, see Civil Code § 2782 et seq.

§ 8818. Failure to make payment within required time; liability

If an owner or direct contractor does not make a retention payment within the time required by this article:

(a) The owner or direct contractor is liable to the person to which payment is owed for a penalty of 2 percent per month on the amount wrongfully withheld, in place of any interest otherwise due.

(b) In an action for collection of the amount wrongfully withheld, the prevailing party is entitled to costs and reasonable attorney's fees. *(Added by Stats.2010, c. 697 (S.B.189), § 20, operative July 1, 2012.)*

Operative Effect

For operative effect of Part 6, see Civil Code § 8052 and Stats.2010, c. 697 (S.B.189), § 105.

Cross References

Construction contracts, indemnity agreements, see Civil Code § 2782 et seq.
Payment of wages, direct contractor liability, see Labor Code §§ 218.7, 218.8.

§ 8820. Waiver against public policy

It is against public policy to waive the provisions of this article by contract. *(Added by Stats.2010, c. 697 (S.B.189), § 20, operative July 1, 2012.)*

Operative Effect

For operative effect of Part 6, see Civil Code § 8052 and Stats.2010, c. 697 (S.B.189), § 105.

Cross References

Construction contracts, indemnity agreements, see Civil Code § 2782 et seq.

§ 8822. Retention payments withheld by lender pursuant to construction loan agreement

This article does not apply to a retention payment withheld by a lender pursuant to a construction loan agreement. *(Added by Stats.2010, c. 697 (S.B.189), § 20, operative July 1, 2012.)*

Operative Effect

For operative effect of Part 6, see Civil Code § 8052 and Stats.2010, c. 697 (S.B.189), § 105.

Cross References

Construction contracts, indemnity agreements, see Civil Code § 2782 et seq.

ARTICLE 3. STOP WORK NOTICE

Section
8830. "Stop work notice" defined.
8832. Conditions for stop work notice.
8834. Additional notice with stop work notice.
8836. Copy of notice to be given to construction lender.
8838. Liability for delay or damage; limitations on liability.
8840. Resolution of claim or cancellation of stop work notice; posting of notice.
8842. Other remedies.
8844. Expedited proceeding.
8846. Waiver against public policy.
8848. Application of article.

Operative Effect

For operative effect of Part 6, see Civil Code § 8052 and Stats.2010, c. 697 (S.B.189), § 105.

§ 8830. "Stop work notice" defined

"Stop work notice" means notice given under this article by a direct contractor to an owner that the contractor will stop work if the amount owed the contractor is not paid within 10 days after notice is given. *(Added by Stats.2010, c. 697 (S.B.189), § 20, operative July 1, 2012.)*

Operative Effect

For operative effect of Part 6, see Civil Code § 8052 and Stats.2010, c. 697 (S.B.189), § 105.

§ 8832. Conditions for stop work notice

If a direct contractor is not paid the amount due pursuant to a written contract within 35 days after the date payment is due under the contract, and there is no dispute as to the satisfactory performance of the contractor, the contractor may give the owner a stop work notice. The notice shall comply with the requirements of Chapter 2 (commencing with Section 8100) of Title 1. *(Added by Stats.2010, c. 697 (S.B.189), § 20, operative July 1, 2012.)*

Operative Effect

For operative effect of Part 6, see Civil Code § 8052 and Stats.2010, c. 697 (S.B.189), § 105.

§ 8834. Additional notice with stop work notice

A direct contractor that gives an owner a stop work notice shall give the following additional notice:

(a) At least five days before giving the stop work notice, the contractor shall post notice of intent to give a stop work notice. The notice shall comply with the requirements of Chapter 2 (commencing with Section 8100) of Title 1. In addition to posting the notice pursuant to Section 8114, the notice shall also be posted at the main office of the site, if one exists.

(b) At the same time the contractor gives the stop work notice, the contractor shall give a copy of the stop work notice to all subcontractors with whom the contractor has a direct contractual relationship on the work of improvement. *(Added by Stats.2010, c. 697 (S.B.189), § 20, operative July 1, 2012.)*

Operative Effect

For operative effect of Part 6, see Civil Code § 8052 and Stats.2010, c. 697 (S.B.189), § 105.

§ 8836. Copy of notice to be given to construction lender

Within five days after receipt of a stop work notice from a direct contractor, the owner shall give a copy of the notice to the construction lender, if any. The copy of the notice shall be given in compliance with the requirements of Chapter 2 (commencing with Section 8100) of Title 1. *(Added by Stats.2010, c. 697 (S.B.189), § 20, operative July 1, 2012.)*

Operative Effect

For operative effect of Part 6, see Civil Code § 8052 and Stats.2010, c. 697 (S.B.189), § 105.

§ 8838. Liability for delay or damage; limitations on liability

(a) The direct contractor or the direct contractor's surety, or a subcontractor or a subcontractor's surety, is not liable for delay or damage that the owner or a contractor of a subcontractor may suffer as a result of the direct contractor giving a stop work notice and subsequently stopping work for nonpayment, if the notice and posting requirements of this article are satisfied.

(b) A direct contractor's or original subcontractor's liability to a subcontractor or material supplier after the direct contractor stops work under this article is limited to the amount the subcontractor or material supplier could otherwise recover under this title for work provided up to the date the subcontractor or material supplier ceases work, subject to the following exceptions:

(1) The direct contractor's or original subcontractor's liability continues for work provided up to and including the 10-day notice period and not beyond.

(2) This subdivision does not limit liability for custom work, including materials that have been fabricated, manufactured, or ordered to specifications that are unique to the job. *(Added by Stats.2010, c. 697 (S.B.189), § 20, operative July 1, 2012.)*

Operative Effect

For operative effect of Part 6, see Civil Code § 8052 and Stats.2010, c. 697 (S.B.189), § 105.

§ 8840. Resolution of claim or cancellation of stop work notice; posting of notice

On resolution of the claim in the stop work notice or the direct contractor's cancellation of the stop work notice, the contractor shall post, and give subcontractors with whom the contractor has a direct contractual relationship on the work of improvement, notice of the resolution or cancellation. The notice shall comply with the requirements of Chapter 2 (commencing with Section 8100) of Title 1. In addition to posting the notice pursuant to Section 8114, the notice shall also be posted at the main office of the site, if one exists.

(Added by Stats.2010, c. 697 (S.B.189), § 20, operative July 1, 2012.)

Operative Effect

For operative effect of Part 6, see Civil Code § 8052 and Stats.2010, c. 697 (S.B.189), § 105.

§ 8842. Other remedies

A direct contractor's right to stop work under this article is in addition to other rights the direct contractor may have under the law. *(Added by Stats.2010, c. 697 (S.B.189), § 20, operative July 1, 2012.)*

Operative Effect

For operative effect of Part 6, see Civil Code § 8052 and Stats.2010, c. 697 (S.B.189), § 105.

§ 8844. Expedited proceeding

(a) If payment of the amount claimed is not made within 10 days after a stop work notice is given, the direct contractor, the direct contractor's surety, or an owner may in an expedited proceeding in the superior court in the county in which the private work of improvement is located, seek a judicial determination of liability for the amount due.

(b) The expedited proceeding shall be set for hearing or trial at the earliest possible date in order that it shall be quickly heard and determined, and shall take precedence over all other cases except older matter of the same character and other matters to which special precedence has been given. *(Added by Stats.2010, c. 697 (S.B.189), § 20, operative July 1, 2012.)*

Operative Effect

For operative effect of Part 6, see Civil Code § 8052 and Stats.2010, c. 697 (S.B.189), § 105.

§ 8846. Waiver against public policy

It is against public policy to waive the provisions of this article by contract. *(Added by Stats.2010, c. 697 (S.B.189), § 20, operative July 1, 2012.)*

Operative Effect

For operative effect of Part 6, see Civil Code § 8052 and Stats.2010, c. 697 (S.B.189), § 105.

§ 8848. Application of article

(a) This article applies to a contract entered into on or after January 1, 1999.

(b) This article does not apply to a retention withheld by a lender pursuant to a construction loan agreement. *(Added by Stats.2010, c. 697 (S.B.189), § 20, operative July 1, 2012.)*

Operative Effect

For operative effect of Part 6, see Civil Code § 8052 and Stats.2010, c. 697 (S.B.189), § 105.

Title 3
PUBLIC WORK OF IMPROVEMENT

Chapter	Section
1. General Provisions	9000
2. Completion	9200
3. Preliminary Notice	9300
4. Stop Payment Notice	9350
5. Payment Bond	9550

Operative Effect

For operative effect of Part 6, see Civil Code § 8052 and Stats.2010, c. 697 (S.B.189), § 105.

Cross References

Contractors, disciplinary proceedings, payment by prime contractors and subcontractors to subcontractors, violations, application to public works of improvement, see Business and Professions Code § 7108.5.

Contractors, disciplinary proceedings, payment of transportation charges submitted by dump truck carrier, application to public works of improvement, see Business and Professions Code § 7108.6.

Eminent domain, see Cal. Const. Art. 1, § 19.

Government contracts for architectural and engineering services, see Cal. Const. Art. 22, §§ 1, 2.

Professions and vocations generally, architecture, see Business and Professions Code § 5500 et seq.

CHAPTER 1. GENERAL PROVISIONS

Article	Section
1. Application of Title	9000
2. Claimants	9100

Operative Effect

For operative effect of Part 6, see Civil Code § 8052 and Stats.2010, c. 697 (S.B.189), § 105.

ARTICLE 1. APPLICATION OF TITLE

Section
9000. Application of title.

Operative Effect

For operative effect of Part 6, see Civil Code § 8052 and Stats.2010, c. 697 (S.B.189), § 105.

§ 9000. Application of title

This title applies to a work of improvement contracted for by a public entity. *(Added by Stats.2010, c. 697 (S.B.189), § 20, operative July 1, 2012.)*

Operative Effect

For operative effect of Part 6, see Civil Code § 8052 and Stats.2010, c. 697 (S.B.189), § 105.

Cross References

Work of improvement defined, see Civil Code § 8050.

ARTICLE 2. CLAIMANTS

Section
9100. Persons who may give stop payment notice or assert claim against payment bond.

Operative Effect

For operative effect of Part 6, see Civil Code § 8052 and Stats.2010, c. 697 (S.B.189), § 105.

§ 9100. Persons who may give stop payment notice or assert claim against payment bond

(a) Except as provided in subdivision (b), any of the following persons that have not been paid in full may give a stop payment notice to the public entity or assert a claim against a payment bond:

(1) A person that provides work for a public works contract, if the work is authorized by a direct contractor, subcontractor, architect, project manager, or other person having charge of all or part of the public works contract.

(2) A laborer.

(3) A person described in Section 4107.7 of the Public Contract Code.

(b) A direct contractor may not give a stop payment notice or assert a claim against a payment bond under this title. *(Added by Stats.2010, c. 697 (S.B.189), § 20, operative July 1, 2012.)*

Operative Effect

For operative effect of Part 6, see Civil Code § 8052 and Stats.2010, c. 697 (S.B.189), § 105.

Cross References

Assignment to Labor Commissioner of mechanics' liens of employees, see Labor Code § 96.

Authority to serve stop notice and bonded stop notices, see Civil Code §§ 8520, 8530, 9100.

Claim filed on two or more works of improvement, see Civil Code § 8446.

Commencement of action to enforce liability on payment bond, see Civil Code § 9558.

Forfeiture of right to lien or right to participate in distribution of funds for false notice, see Civil Code §§ 8504, 9454.

Home improvement contracts, statement of full and unconditional release from liens, see Business and Professions Code §§ 7159, 7159.5, 7159.14.

Improvements affixed to land of another by mistake, removal, see Civil Code § 1013.5.

Liens,
  Aircraft, repairmen, see Code of Civil Procedure § 1208.61 et seq.
  Cleaners' and launderers' liens, see Civil Code § 3066.
  Condominium project, see Civil Code §§ 4615, 6658.
  Contracts subject to general lien statutes, see Civil Code § 2877.
  Extinction, see Civil Code § 2909 et seq.
  Jeweler, see Civil Code § 3052a.
  Logger and sawmill, see Civil Code § 3065 et seq.
  Mining, see Civil Code § 3060.
  Oil and gas, see Code of Civil Procedure § 1203.50 et seq.
  Possessory liens for services, repairs, etc., see Civil Code § 3051.
  Salary and wages, preference, see Code of Civil Procedure § 1204 et seq.
  Seller of real property, see Civil Code § 3046 et seq.
  Sewer connection costs, see Health and Safety Code § 5463.
  Sewer districts, application of general lien laws, see Health and Safety Code § 5021.
  Site improvements, priorities, see Civil Code § 8458.
  Storage, see Civil Code § 1856.
  Taxes, see Revenue and Taxation Code § 2187 et seq.

§ 9100

Thresher's, see Civil Code § 3061.
Vehicles, repairmen, see Civil Code § 3067 et seq.
Municipal courts, jurisdiction to enforce lien, see Code of Civil Procedure § 86.
Partition, costs as lien on share allotted to party, see Code of Civil Procedure §§ 873.260, 874.120.
Payment of claims for work or materials furnished under public contract, see Civil Code § 9552.
Preliminary notice to property owner, see Civil Code § 8202.
Private works, persons authorized to serve stop notice, see Civil Code § 8520.
Procedure when judgment debtor contractor on public work, see Code of Civil Procedure § 708.760.
Real property loans, failure to disclose lien, see Business and Professions Code § 10243.
Sidewalk construction, lien on adjoining property, see Streets and Highways Code § 5890.
Site improvement defined, see Civil Code § 8042.
Stop payment notice, contents, service, see Civil Code §§ 8502, 8506, 9352, 9354.
Street work, claims and material suppliers, see Public Contract Code § 20459 et seq.
Work of improvement defined, see Civil Code § 8050.
Written notice to surety and bond principal, see Civil Code §§ 8614, 9562.

CHAPTER 2. COMPLETION

Section
9200. Time of completion.
9202. Notice of cessation; recording; requirements and contents.
9204. Notice of completion; recording; requirements and contents.
9208. Acceptance of notice of completion by recorder.

Operative Effect

For operative effect of Part 6, see Civil Code § 8052 and Stats.2010, c. 697 (S.B.189), § 105.

§ 9200. Time of completion

For the purpose of this title, completion of a work of improvement occurs at the earliest of the following times:

(a) Acceptance of the work of improvement by the public entity.

(b) Cessation of labor on the work of improvement for a continuous period of 60 days. This subdivision does not apply to a contract awarded under the State Contract Act, Part 2 (commencing with Section 10100) of Division 2 of the Public Contract Code. *(Added by Stats.2010, c. 697 (S.B. 189), § 20, operative July 1, 2012.)*

Operative Effect

For operative effect of Part 6, see Civil Code § 8052 and Stats.2010, c. 697 (S.B.189), § 105.

Cross References

Completion as commencement of running of limitation time, see Civil Code § 8609.
Notice of cessation, see Civil Code §§ 8188, 9202.
Notice of completion, contents, see Civil Code §§ 8182, 9204.
Time following completion for recording claim of lien, see Civil Code §§ 8412, 8414.

Work of improvement defined, see Civil Code § 8050.

§ 9202. Notice of cessation; recording; requirements and contents

(a) A public entity may record a notice of cessation if there has been a continuous cessation of labor for at least 30 days prior to the recordation that continues through the date of the recordation.

(b) The notice shall be signed and verified by the public entity or its agent.

(c) The notice shall comply with the requirements of Chapter 2 (commencing with Section 8100) of Title 1, and shall also include all of the following information:

(1) The date on or about which the labor ceased.

(2) A statement that the cessation has continued until the recordation of the notice. *(Added by Stats.2010, c. 697 (S.B.189), § 20, operative July 1, 2012.)*

Operative Effect

For operative effect of Part 6, see Civil Code § 8052 and Stats.2010, c. 697 (S.B.189), § 105.

§ 9204. Notice of completion; recording; requirements and contents

(a) A public entity may record a notice of completion on or within 15 days after the date of completion of a work of improvement.

(b) The notice shall be signed and verified by the public entity or its agent.

(c) The notice shall comply with the requirements of Chapter 2 (commencing with Section 8100) of Title 1, and shall also include the date of completion. An erroneous statement of the date of completion does not affect the effectiveness of the notice if the true date of completion is 15 days or less before the date of recordation of the notice. *(Added by Stats.2010, c. 697 (S.B.189), § 20, operative July 1, 2012.)*

Operative Effect

For operative effect of Part 6, see Civil Code § 8052 and Stats.2010, c. 697 (S.B.189), § 105.

Cross References

Completion, equivalents, see Civil Code §§ 8180, 9200.
Mode of recording, see Civil Code § 1169 et seq.
Multiple contracts, notice of completion by owner for portion of work of improvement, see Civil Code § 8186.

§ 9208. Acceptance of notice of completion by recorder

A notice of completion in otherwise proper form, verified and containing the information required by this title shall be accepted by the recorder for recording and is deemed duly recorded without acknowledgment. *(Added by Stats.2010, c. 697 (S.B.189), § 20, operative July 1, 2012.)*

Operative Effect

For operative effect of Part 6, see Civil Code § 8052 and Stats.2010, c. 697 (S.B.189), § 105.

WORKS OF IMPROVEMENT

Cross References

Completion, equivalents, see Civil Code §§ 8180, 9200.
Mode of recording, see Civil Code § 1169 et seq.
Multiple contracts, notice of completion by owner for portion of work of improvement, see Civil Code § 8186.

CHAPTER 3. PRELIMINARY NOTICE

Section
9300. Persons who should receive notice; persons not required to provide notice.
9302. Notice to be in compliance with Chapter 2 of Title 1; exception.
9303. Additional compliance requirements and contents.
9304. Stop payment notice or assertion of claim only for work provided within 20 days before giving preliminary notice.
9306. Failure of subcontractor to give notice; grounds for discipline.

Operative Effect

For operative effect of Part 6, see Civil Code § 8052 and Stats.2010, c. 697 (S.B.189), § 105.

§ 9300. Persons who should receive notice; persons not required to provide notice

(a) Except as otherwise provided by statute, before giving a stop payment notice or asserting a claim against a payment bond, a claimant shall give preliminary notice to the following persons:

(1) The public entity.

(2) The direct contractor to which the claimant provides work.

(b) Notwithstanding subdivision (a):

(1) A laborer is not required to give preliminary notice.

(2) A claimant that has a direct contractual relationship with a direct contractor is not required to give preliminary notice.

(c) Compliance with this section is a necessary prerequisite to the validity of a stop payment notice under this title.

(d) Compliance with this section or with Section 9562 is a necessary prerequisite to the validity of a claim against a payment bond under this title. *(Added by Stats.2010, c. 697 (S.B.189), § 20, operative July 1, 2012.)*

Operative Effect

For operative effect of Part 6, see Civil Code § 8052 and Stats.2010, c. 697 (S.B.189), § 105.

Cross References

Bonded stop payment notice to construction lender, see Civil Code § 8532.
Claim of mechanics lien, see Civil Code § 8416.
Claimant defined, see Civil Code § 8004.
Enforcement of stop payment notice, compliance with this chapter as prerequisite, see Civil Code § 9500.
Stop payment notice, contents, see Civil Code §§ 8502, 9352.
Stop payment notice for public work, see Civil Code § 9000 et seq.

§ 9302. Notice to be in compliance with Chapter 2 of Title 1; exception

(a) Except as provided in subdivision (b), preliminary notice shall be given in compliance with the requirements of Chapter 2 (commencing with Section 8100) of Title 1.

(b) If the public works contract is for work constructed by the Department of Public Works or the Department of General Services of the state, preliminary notice to the public entity shall be given to the disbursing officer of the department constructing the work. *(Added by Stats.2010, c. 697 (S.B.189), § 20, operative July 1, 2012.)*

Operative Effect

For operative effect of Part 6, see Civil Code § 8052 and Stats.2010, c. 697 (S.B.189), § 105.

Cross References

Bonded stop payment notice to construction lender, see Civil Code § 8532.
Claim of mechanics lien, see Civil Code § 8416.
Enforcement of stop payment notice, compliance with this chapter as prerequisite, see Civil Code § 9500.
Stop payment notice, contents, see Civil Code §§ 8502, 9352.
Stop payment notice for public work, see Civil Code § 9000 et seq.

§ 9303. Additional compliance requirements and contents

The preliminary notice shall comply with the requirements of Section 8102, and shall also include:

(a) A general description of the work to be provided.

(b) An estimate of the total price of the work provided and to be provided. *(Added by Stats.2010, c. 697 (S.B.189), § 20, operative July 1, 2012.)*

Operative Effect

For operative effect of Part 6, see Civil Code § 8052 and Stats.2010, c. 697 (S.B.189), § 105.

Cross References

Bonded stop payment notice to construction lender, see Civil Code § 8532.
Claim of mechanics lien, see Civil Code § 8416.
Enforcement of stop payment notice, compliance with this chapter as prerequisite, see Civil Code § 9500.
Stop payment notice, contents, see Civil Code §§ 8502, 9352.
Stop payment notice for public work, see Civil Code § 9000 et seq.

§ 9304. Stop payment notice or assertion of claim only for work provided within 20 days before giving preliminary notice

A claimant may give a stop payment notice or assert a claim against a payment bond only for work provided within 20 days before giving preliminary notice and at any time thereafter. *(Added by Stats.2010, c. 697 (S.B.189), § 20, operative July 1, 2012.)*

Operative Effect

For operative effect of Part 6, see Civil Code § 8052 and Stats.2010, c. 697 (S.B.189), § 105.

§ 9304 GENERAL PROVISIONS

Cross References

Bonded stop payment notice to construction lender, see Civil Code § 8532.
Claim of mechanics lien, see Civil Code § 8416.
Claimant defined, see Civil Code § 8004.
Enforcement of stop payment notice, compliance with this chapter as prerequisite, see Civil Code § 9500.
Stop payment notice, contents, see Civil Code §§ 8502, 9352.
Stop payment notice for public work, see Civil Code § 9000 et seq.

§ 9306. Failure of subcontractor to give notice; grounds for discipline

If the contract of any subcontractor on a particular work of improvement provides for payment to the subcontractor of more than four hundred dollars ($400), the failure of that subcontractor, licensed under the Contractors' State License Law (Chapter 9 (commencing with Section 7000) of Division 3 of the Business and Professions Code), to give the notice provided for in this chapter, constitutes grounds for disciplinary action under the Contractors' State License Law. *(Added by Stats.2010, c. 697 (S.B.189), § 20, operative July 1, 2012.)*

Operative Effect

For operative effect of Part 6, see Civil Code § 8052 and Stats.2010, c. 697 (S.B.189), § 105.

Cross References

Bonded stop payment notice to construction lender, see Civil Code § 8532.
Claim of mechanics lien, see Civil Code § 8416.
Enforcement of stop payment notice, compliance with this chapter as prerequisite, see Civil Code § 9500.
Stop payment notice, contents, see Civil Code §§ 8502, 9352.
Stop payment notice for public work, see Civil Code § 9000 et seq.
Subcontractor defined, see Civil Code § 8046.

CHAPTER 4. STOP PAYMENT NOTICE

Article	Section
1. General Provisions	9350
2. Summary Proceeding for Release of Funds	9400
3. Distribution of Funds Withheld	9450
4. Enforcement of Payment of Claim Stated in Stop Payment Notice	9500

Operative Effect

For operative effect of Part 6, see Civil Code § 8052 and Stats.2010, c. 697 (S.B.189), § 105.

ARTICLE 1. GENERAL PROVISIONS

Section
9350. Rights of persons furnishing work pursuant to public works contract.
9352. Stop payment notice; requirements; contents; amount claimed.
9354. Notice to public entity.
9356. Time for giving stop payment notice.
9358. Withholding of sufficient funds.
9360. Payment of funds before stop payment notice received; payment of amounts in excess of amount necessary to pay claims.
9362. Notice of time for commencing action to enforce payment of claim.
9364. Release bond; procedure.

Operative Effect

For operative effect of Part 6, see Civil Code § 8052 and Stats.2010, c. 697 (S.B.189), § 105.

§ 9350. Rights of persons furnishing work pursuant to public works contract

The rights of all persons furnishing work pursuant to a public works contract, with respect to any fund for payment of construction costs, are governed exclusively by this chapter, and no person may assert any legal or equitable right with respect to that fund, other than a right created by direct written contract between the person and the person holding the fund, except pursuant to the provisions of this chapter. *(Added by Stats.2010, c. 697 (S.B.189), § 20, operative July 1, 2012.)*

Operative Effect

For operative effect of Part 6, see Civil Code § 8052 and Stats.2010, c. 697 (S.B.189), § 105.

Cross References

Action against direct contractor or public entity, see Civil Code § 9502 et seq.
Action against sureties on payment bond, see Civil Code §§ 9558, 9564.
Action on bond for deficit after pro rata distribution, see Civil Code § 9452.
Action on payment bond for private works, see Civil Code § 8609 et seq.
Action on payment bond for public works, see Civil Code § 9558 et seq.
Bond for release of funds held under stop payment notice, see Civil Code § 8510.
Claim of mechanics lien, contents, see Civil Code § 8416.
Pro rata distribution of funds, see Civil Code §§ 8540, 9450.
Stop payment notices, limitation on enforcement of rights,
  Private works, see Civil Code § 8550.
  Public works, see Civil Code § 9502.
Transfer of obligations, see Civil Code § 1457 et seq.
Withholding of money on service of stop payment notice, see Civil Code §§ 8522, 8536, 9358.

§ 9352. Stop payment notice; requirements; contents; amount claimed

(a) A stop payment notice shall comply with the requirements of Chapter 2 (commencing with Section 8100) of Title 1, and shall be signed and verified by the claimant.

(b) The notice shall include a general description of work to be provided, and an estimate of the total amount in value of the work to be provided.

(c) The amount claimed in the notice may include only the amount due the claimant for work provided through the date of the notice. *(Added by Stats.2010, c. 697 (S.B.189), § 20, operative July 1, 2012.)*

Operative Effect

For operative effect of Part 6, see Civil Code § 8052 and Stats.2010, c. 697 (S.B.189), § 105.

Cross References

Notice to public entity of commencement of action to enforce payment of claim stated in stop payment notice, see Civil Code § 9504.
Preliminary notice (private work), necessity prior to stop payment notice, see Civil Code § 8200.
Preliminary notice (public work), stop payment notice, see Civil Code § 9300.
Private works of improvement, validity of stop payment notice, see Civil Code § 8508.
Stop payment notice,
    Private works, see Civil Code § 8500 et seq.
    Public works, see Civil Code § 9350 et seq.

§ 9354. Notice to public entity

(a) Except as provided in subdivision (b), a stop payment notice shall be given in compliance with the requirements of Chapter 2 (commencing with Section 8100) of Title 1.

(b) A stop payment notice shall be given to the public entity by giving the notice to the following person:

(1) In the case of a public works contract of the state, the director of the department that awarded the contract.

(2) In the case of a public works contract of a public entity other than the state, the office of the controller, auditor, or other public disbursing officer whose duty it is to make payment pursuant to the contract, or the commissioners, managers, trustees, officers, board of supervisors, board of trustees, common council, or other body by which the contract was awarded. *(Added by Stats.2010, c. 697 (S.B.189), § 20, operative July 1, 2012.)*

Operative Effect

For operative effect of Part 6, see Civil Code § 8052 and Stats.2010, c. 697 (S.B.189), § 105.

Cross References

Notice to public entity of commencement of action to enforce payment of claim stated in stop payment notice, see Civil Code § 9504.
Preliminary notice (private work), necessity prior to stop payment notice, see Civil Code § 8200.
Preliminary notice (public work), stop payment notice, see Civil Code § 9300.
Private works of improvement, validity of stop payment notice, see Civil Code § 8508.
Stop payment notice,
    Private works, see Civil Code § 8500 et seq.
    Public works, see Civil Code § 9350 et seq.

§ 9356. Time for giving stop payment notice

A stop payment notice is not effective unless given before the expiration of whichever of the following time periods is applicable:

(a) If a notice of completion, acceptance, or cessation is recorded, 30 days after that recordation.

(b) If a notice of completion, acceptance, or cessation is not recorded, 90 days after cessation or completion. *(Added by Stats.2010, c. 697 (S.B.189), § 20, operative July 1, 2012.)*

Operative Effect

For operative effect of Part 6, see Civil Code § 8052 and Stats.2010, c. 697 (S.B.189), § 105.

Cross References

Notice of cessation, see Civil Code §§ 8188, 9202.
Notice of completion, see Civil Code §§ 8182, 9204.
Service of stop payment notice, see Civil Code §§ 8506, 9354.
Commencement of action to enforce liability on bond, see Civil Code § 9558.

§ 9358. Withholding of sufficient funds

(a) The public entity shall, on receipt of a stop payment notice, withhold from the direct contractor sufficient funds due or to become due to the direct contractor to pay the claim stated in the stop payment notice and to provide for the public entity's reasonable cost of any litigation pursuant to the stop payment notice.

(b) The public entity may satisfy its duty under this section by refusing to release funds held in escrow under Section 10263 or 22300 of the Public Contract Code. *(Added by Stats.2010, c. 697 (S.B.189), § 20, operative July 1, 2012.)*

Operative Effect

For operative effect of Part 6, see Civil Code § 8052 and Stats.2010, c. 697 (S.B.189), § 105.

Cross References

Pro rata distribution of money, see Civil Code § 9450.
Public entity defined, see Civil Code § 8036.
Similar provision, private works, see Civil Code § 8536.

§ 9360. Payment of funds before stop payment notice received; payment of amounts in excess of amount necessary to pay claims

(a) This chapter does not prohibit payment of funds to a direct contractor or a direct contractor's assignee if a stop payment notice is not received before the disbursing officer actually surrenders possession of the funds.

(b) This chapter does not prohibit payment of any amount due to a direct contractor or a direct contractor's assignee in excess of the amount necessary to pay the total amount of all claims stated in stop payment notices received by the public entity at the time of payment plus any interest and court costs that might reasonably be anticipated in connection with the claims. *(Added by Stats.2010, c. 697 (S.B.189), § 20, operative July 1, 2012.)*

Operative Effect

For operative effect of Part 6, see Civil Code § 8052 and Stats.2010, c. 697 (S.B.189), § 105.

Cross References

Assignment of thing in action effect on defense, see Code of Civil Procedure § 368.
Contractors, classification, see Business and Professions Code § 7055 et seq.
Direct contractor defined, see Civil Code § 8018.
Payment of claims for work or materials furnished under public contract, see Civil Code § 9552.
Transfer of things in action, see Civil Code § 954.

§ 9362. Notice of time for commencing action to enforce payment of claim

(a) Not later than 10 days after each of the following events, the public entity shall give notice to a claimant that

§ 9362

has given a stop payment notice of the time within which an action to enforce payment of the claim stated in the stop payment notice must be commenced:

(1) Completion of a public works contract, whether by acceptance or cessation.

(2) Recordation of a notice of cessation or completion.

(b) The notice shall comply with the requirements of Chapter 2 (commencing with Section 8100) of Title 1.

(c) A public entity need not give notice under this section unless the claimant has paid the public entity ten dollars ($10) at the time of giving the stop payment notice. *(Added by Stats.2010, c. 697 (S.B.189), § 20, operative July 1, 2012.)*

Operative Effect

For operative effect of Part 6, see Civil Code § 8052 and Stats.2010, c. 697 (S.B.189), § 105.

Cross References

Certified mail as compliance with mailing requirements, see Civil Code § 17.
Claimant defined, see Civil Code § 8004.
Notice of completion, see Civil Code §§ 8182, 8184, 9204, 9208.
Public entity defined, see Civil Code § 8036.
Stop payment notice, see Civil Code §§ 8044, 8502, 8506, 9352, 9354.

§ 9364. Release bond; procedure

(a) A public entity may, in its discretion, permit the direct contractor to give the public entity a release bond. The bond shall be executed by an admitted surety insurer, in an amount equal to 125 percent of the claim stated in the stop payment notice, conditioned for the payment of any amount the claimant recovers in an action on the claim, together with court costs if the claimant prevails.

(b) On receipt of a release bond, the public entity shall not withhold funds from the direct contractor pursuant to the stop payment notice.

(c) The surety on a release bond is jointly and severally liable to the claimant with the sureties on any payment bond given under Chapter 5 (commencing with Section 9550). *(Added by Stats.2010, c. 697 (S.B.189), § 20, operative July 1, 2012.)*

Operative Effect

For operative effect of Part 6, see Civil Code § 8052 and Stats.2010, c. 697 (S.B.189), § 105.

Cross References

Direct contractor, see Civil Code § 8018.
General provisions relating to bonds, see Civil Code § 8150 et seq.
Payment bond, see Civil Code §§ 8606, 9554.
Payment bond for public works, see Civil Code § 9550 et seq.
Public entity defined, see Civil Code § 8036.
Stop payment notice, see Civil Code §§ 8044, 8502, 8506, 9352, 9354.

ARTICLE 2. SUMMARY PROCEEDING FOR RELEASE OF FUNDS

Section
9400. Release of funds; grounds.
9402. Affidavit; service on public entity; contents.
9404. Affidavit; service of copy on claimant.
9406. Counteraffidavit; service on public entity; release of funds if not served within time stated in public entity's notice.
9408. Action for declaration of rights of parties; commencement; notice of hearing; time for hearing.
9410. Affidavit and counteraffidavit to constitute pleadings; burden of proof.
9412. Findings not required; continuance of hearing; order at conclusion of hearing; service of copy of order on public entity.
9414. Determination not res judicata.

Operative Effect

For operative effect of Part 6, see Civil Code § 8052 and Stats.2010, c. 697 (S.B.189), § 105.

§ 9400. Release of funds; grounds

A direct contractor may obtain release of funds withheld pursuant to a stop payment notice under the summary proceeding provided in this article on any of the following grounds:

(a) The claim on which the notice is based is not a type for which a stop payment notice is authorized under this chapter.

(b) The claimant is not a person authorized under Section 9100 to give a stop payment notice.

(c) The amount of the claim stated in the stop payment notice is excessive.

(d) There is no basis for the claim stated in the stop payment notice. *(Added by Stats.2010, c. 697 (S.B.189), § 20, operative July 1, 2012.)*

Operative Effect

For operative effect of Part 6, see Civil Code § 8052 and Stats.2010, c. 697 (S.B.189), § 105.

§ 9402. Affidavit; service on public entity; contents

The direct contractor shall serve on the public entity an affidavit, together with a copy of the affidavit, in compliance with the requirements of Chapter 2 (commencing with Section 8100) of Title 1, that includes all of the following information:

(a) An allegation of the grounds for release of the funds and a statement of the facts supporting the allegation.

(b) A demand for the release of all or the portion of the funds that are alleged to be withheld improperly or in an excessive amount.

(c) A statement of the address of the contractor within the state for the purpose of permitting service by mail on the contractor of any notice or document. *(Added by Stats.2010, c. 697 (S.B.189), § 20, operative July 1, 2012.)*

Operative Effect

For operative effect of Part 6, see Civil Code § 8052 and Stats.2010, c. 697 (S.B.189), § 105.

Cross References

Contractors, classification, see Business and Professions Code § 7055 et seq.

Direct contractor defined, see Business and Professions Code § 8018.

§ 9404. Affidavit; service of copy on claimant

The public entity shall serve on the claimant a copy of the direct contractor's affidavit, together with a notice stating that the public entity will release the funds withheld, or the portion of the funds demanded, unless the claimant serves on the public entity a counteraffidavit on or before the time stated in the notice. The time stated in the notice shall be not less than 10 days nor more than 20 days after service on the claimant of the copy of the affidavit. The notice shall comply with the requirements of Chapter 2 (commencing with Section 8100) of Title 1. *(Added by Stats.2010, c. 697 (S.B.189), § 20, operative July 1, 2012.)*

Operative Effect

For operative effect of Part 6, see Civil Code § 8052 and Stats.2010, c. 697 (S.B.189), § 105.

Cross References

Certified mail as compliance with mailing requirements, see Civil Code § 17.
Claimant defined, see Civil Code § 8004.

§ 9406. Counteraffidavit; service on public entity; release of funds if not served within time stated in public entity's notice

(a) A claimant that contests the direct contractor's affidavit shall serve on the public entity a counteraffidavit alleging the details of the claim and describing the specific basis on which the claimant contests or rebuts the allegations of the contractor's affidavit. The counteraffidavit shall be served within the time stated in the public entity's notice, together with proof of service of a copy of the counteraffidavit on the direct contractor. The service of the counteraffidavit on the public entity and the copy of the affidavit on the direct contractor shall comply with the requirements of Chapter 2 (commencing with Section 8100) of Title 1.

(b) If no counteraffidavit with proof of service is served on the public entity within the time stated in the public entity's notice, the public entity shall immediately release the funds, or the portion of the funds demanded by the affidavit, without further notice to the claimant, and the public entity is not liable in any manner for their release.

(c) The public entity is not responsible for the validity of an affidavit or counteraffidavit under this article. *(Added by Stats.2010, c. 697 (S.B.189), § 20, operative July 1, 2012.)*

Operative Effect

For operative effect of Part 6, see Civil Code § 8052 and Stats.2010, c. 697 (S.B.189), § 105.

§ 9408. Action for declaration of rights of parties; commencement; notice of hearing; time for hearing

(a) If a counteraffidavit, together with proof of service, is served under Section 9406, either the direct contractor or the claimant may commence an action for a declaration of the rights of the parties.

(b) After commencement of the action, either the direct contractor or the claimant may move the court for a determination of rights under the affidavit and counteraffidavit. The party making the motion shall give not less than five days' notice of the hearing to the public entity and to the other party.

(c) The notice of hearing shall comply with the requirements of Chapter 2 (commencing with Section 8100) of Title 1. Notwithstanding Section 8116, when notice of the hearing is made by mail, the notice is complete on the fifth day following deposit of the notice in the mail.

(d) The court shall hear the motion within 15 days after the date of the motion, unless the court continues the hearing for good cause. *(Added by Stats.2010, c. 697 (S.B.189), § 20, operative July 1, 2012.)*

Operative Effect

For operative effect of Part 6, see Civil Code § 8052 and Stats.2010, c. 697 (S.B.189), § 105.

Cross References

Direct contractor defined, see Civil Code § 8018.
Declaratory relief, see Code of Civil Procedure § 1060 et seq.
Place of trial, generally, see Code of Civil Procedure § 392 et seq.
Superior court, see Cal. Const. Art. 6, §§ 4, 10, 11.

§ 9410. Affidavit and counteraffidavit to constitute pleadings; burden of proof

(a) The affidavit and counteraffidavit shall be filed with the court by the public entity and shall constitute the pleadings, subject to the power of the court to permit an amendment in the interest of justice. The affidavit of the direct contractor shall be deemed controverted by the counteraffidavit of the claimant, and both shall be received in evidence.

(b) At the hearing, the direct contractor has the burden of proof. *(Added by Stats.2010, c. 697 (S.B.189), § 20, operative July 1, 2012.)*

Operative Effect

For operative effect of Part 6, see Civil Code § 8052 and Stats.2010, c. 697 (S.B.189), § 105.

§ 9412. Findings not required; continuance of hearing; order at conclusion of hearing; service of copy of order on public entity

(a) No findings are required in a summary proceeding under this article.

(b) If at the hearing no evidence other than the affidavit and counteraffidavit is offered, the court may, if satisfied that sufficient facts are shown, make a determination on the basis of the affidavit and counteraffidavit. If the court is not satisfied that sufficient facts are shown, the court shall order the hearing continued for production of other evidence, oral or documentary, or the filing of other affidavits and counteraffidavits.

(c) At the conclusion of the hearing, the court shall make an order determining whether the demand for release is allowed. The court's order is determinative of the right of the claimant to have funds further withheld by the public entity.

§ 9412

(d) The direct contractor shall serve a copy of the court's order on the public entity in compliance with the requirements of Chapter 2 (commencing with Section 8100) of Title 1. *(Added by Stats.2010, c. 697 (S.B.189), § 20, operative July 1, 2012.)*

Operative Effect

For operative effect of Part 6, see Civil Code § 8052 and Stats.2010, c. 697 (S.B.189), § 105.

Cross References

Summary proceedings, see Code of Civil Procedure § 1132 et seq.

§ 9414. Determination not res judicata

A determination in a summary proceeding under this article is not res judicata with respect to a right of action by the claimant against either the principal or surety on a payment bond or with respect to a right of action against a party personally liable to the claimant. *(Added by Stats.2010, c. 697 (S.B.189), § 20, operative July 1, 2012.)*

Operative Effect

For operative effect of Part 6, see Civil Code § 8052 and Stats.2010, c. 697 (S.B.189), § 105.

Cross References

Judgments, effect of final order, see Code of Civil Procedure § 1908.

ARTICLE 3. DISTRIBUTION OF FUNDS WITHHELD

Section
9450. Insufficient funds to pay all claims; pro rata distribution.
9452. Unpaid deficit; recovery on payment bond.
9454. False stop payment notice or inclusion of work not provided for in contract.
9456. Priority of stop payment notice.

Operative Effect

For operative effect of Part 6, see Civil Code § 8052 and Stats.2010, c. 697 (S.B.189), § 105.

§ 9450. Insufficient funds to pay all claims; pro rata distribution

If funds withheld pursuant to a stop payment notice are insufficient to pay in full the claims of all persons who have given a stop payment notice, the funds shall be distributed among the claimants in the ratio that the claim of each bears to the aggregate of all claims for which a stop payment notice is given, without regard to the order in which the notices were given or enforcement actions were commenced. *(Added by Stats.2010, c. 697 (S.B.189), § 20, operative July 1, 2012.)*

Operative Effect

For operative effect of Part 6, see Civil Code § 8052 and Stats.2010, c. 697 (S.B.189), § 105.

Cross References

Claimant defined, see Civil Code § 8004.
Similar provision, private works, see Civil Code § 8540.

Withholding, see Civil Code § 9358.

§ 9452. Unpaid deficit; recovery on payment bond

Nothing in this chapter impairs the right of a claimant to recover from the direct contractor or the contractor's sureties in an action on a payment bond under Chapter 5 (commencing with Section 9550) any deficit that remains unpaid after the distribution under Section 9450. *(Added by Stats.2010, c. 697 (S.B.189), § 20, operative July 1, 2012.)*

Operative Effect

For operative effect of Part 6, see Civil Code § 8052 and Stats.2010, c. 697 (S.B.189), § 105.

Cross References

Payment bond for public works, see Civil Code § 9550 et seq.

§ 9454. False stop payment notice or inclusion of work not provided for in contract

A person that willfully gives a false stop payment notice to the public entity or that willfully includes in the notice work not provided for the public works contract for which the stop payment notice is given forfeits all right to participate in the distribution under Section 9450. *(Added by Stats.2010, c. 697 (S.B.189), § 20, operative July 1, 2012.)*

Operative Effect

For operative effect of Part 6, see Civil Code § 8052 and Stats.2010, c. 697 (S.B.189), § 105.

Cross References

Pro rata distribution of money, see Civil Code § 9450.
Similar provision, private works, see Civil Code § 8504.
Stop payment notice, see Civil Code §§ 8044, 8502, 8506, 9352, 9354.

§ 9456. Priority of stop payment notice

(a) A stop payment notice takes priority over an assignment by a direct contractor of any amount due or to become due pursuant to a public works contract, including contract changes, whether made before or after the giving of a stop payment notice, and the assignment has no effect on the rights of the claimant.

(b) Any garnishment of an amount due or to become due pursuant to a public works contract by a creditor of a direct contractor under Article 8 (commencing with Section 708.710) of Chapter 6 of Division 2 of Title 9 of Part 2 of the Code of Civil Procedure and any statutory lien on that amount is subordinate to the rights of a claimant. *(Added by Stats.2010, c. 697 (S.B.189), § 20, operative July 1, 2012.)*

Operative Effect

For operative effect of Part 6, see Civil Code § 8052 and Stats.2010, c. 697 (S.B.189), § 105.

Cross References

Assignment of thing in action effect on defense, see Code of Civil Procedure § 368.
Claimant defined, see Civil Code § 8004.
Contractors, classification, see Business and Professions Code § 7055 et seq.
Direct contractor, see Civil Code § 8018.
Transfer of obligations, see Civil Code § 1457 et seq.

Transfer of things in action, see Civil Code § 954.

ARTICLE 4. ENFORCEMENT OF PAYMENT OF CLAIM STATED IN STOP PAYMENT NOTICE

Section
9500. Claim filing procedures for actions against public entities.
9502. Commencement of action.
9504. Notice of commencement of action.
9506. Multiple claimants.
9508. Dismissal.
9510. Effect of dismissal or judgment.

Operative Effect

For operative effect of Part 6, see Civil Code § 8052 and Stats.2010, c. 697 (S.B.189), § 105.

§ 9500. Claim filing procedures for actions against public entities

(a) A claimant may not enforce payment of the claim stated in a stop payment notice unless the claimant has complied with all of the following conditions:

(1) The claimant has given preliminary notice to the extent required by Chapter 3 (commencing with Section 9300).

(2) The claimant has given the stop payment notice within the time provided in Section 9356.

(b) The claim filing procedures of Part 3 (commencing with Section 900) of Division 3.6 of Title 1 of the Government Code do not apply to an action under this article. *(Added by Stats.2010, c. 697 (S.B.189), § 20, operative July 1, 2012.)*

Operative Effect

For operative effect of Part 6, see Civil Code § 8052 and Stats.2010, c. 697 (S.B.189), § 105.

Cross References

Claimant defined, see Civil Code § 8004.
Stop notice, contents, see Civil Code §§ 8502, 9352.

§ 9502. Commencement of action

(a) The claimant shall commence an action against the public entity and the direct contractor to enforce payment of the claim stated in a stop payment notice at any time after 10 days from the date the claimant gives the stop payment notice.

(b) The claimant shall commence an action against the public entity and the direct contractor to enforce payment of the claim stated in a stop payment notice not later than 90 days after expiration of the time within which a stop payment notice must be given.

(c) An action under this section may not be brought to trial or judgment entered before expiration of the time provided in subdivision (b).

(d) If a claimant does not commence an action to enforce payment of the claim stated in a stop payment notice within the time provided in subdivision (b), the notice ceases to be effective and the public entity shall release funds withheld pursuant to the notice. *(Added by Stats.2010, c. 697 (S.B. 189), § 20, operative July 1, 2012.)*

Operative Effect

For operative effect of Part 6, see Civil Code § 8052 and Stats.2010, c. 697 (S.B.189), § 105.

Cross References

Action to enforce liability on payment bond, see Civil Code §§ 9559, 9564.
Direct contractor defined, see Civil Code § 8018.
Enforcement of lien, see Civil Code § 8410 et seq.
Place of trial, generally, see Code of Civil Procedure § 392 et seq.
Private works of improvement, enforcement of claim stated in stop payment notice, see Civil Code § 8550 et seq.
Public work contracts,
    Payment of direct contractor claims, see Civil Code § 9552.
    Procedure where judgment debtor contractor on public work, see Code of Civil Procedure § 708.760.
State, suits against, see Cal. Const. Art. 3, § 5.
Time of commencing actions, generally, see Code of Civil Procedure § 312 et seq.
Withholding, see Civil Code § 9358.

§ 9504. Notice of commencement of action

Within five days after commencement of an action to enforce payment of the claim stated in a stop payment notice, the claimant shall give notice of commencement of the action to the public entity in the same manner that a stop payment notice is given. *(Added by Stats.2010, c. 697 (S.B.189), § 20, operative July 1, 2012.)*

Operative Effect

For operative effect of Part 6, see Civil Code § 8052 and Stats.2010, c. 697 (S.B.189), § 105.

Cross References

Public entity defined, see Civil Code § 8036.

§ 9506. Multiple claimants

If more than one claimant has given a stop payment notice:

(a) Any number of claimants may join in the same enforcement action.

(b) If claimants commence separate actions, the court that first acquires jurisdiction may order the actions consolidated.

(c) On request of the public entity, the court shall require that all claimants be impleaded in one action and shall adjudicate the rights of all parties in the action. *(Added by Stats.2010, c. 697 (S.B.189), § 20, operative July 1, 2012.)*

Operative Effect

For operative effect of Part 6, see Civil Code § 8052 and Stats.2010, c. 697 (S.B.189), § 105.

Cross References

Consolidation of actions, see Code of Civil Procedure § 1048.
Private works of improvement, consolidation of actions, see Civil Code § 8552.

§ 9508. Dismissal

Notwithstanding Section 583.420 of the Code of Civil Procedure, if an action to enforce payment of the claim stated

§ 9508

in a stop payment notice is not brought to trial within two years after commencement of the action, the court may in its discretion dismiss the action for want of prosecution. *(Added by Stats.2010, c. 697 (S.B.189), § 20, operative July 1, 2012.)*

Operative Effect

For operative effect of Part 6, see Civil Code § 8052 and Stats.2010, c. 697 (S.B.189), § 105.

Cross References

Dismissal for delay in prosecution, see Code of Civil Procedure § 583.110 et seq.
Mechanics liens in general, dismissal of actions, see Civil Code §§ 8462, 8490.
Private works of improvement, dismissal of actions, see Civil Code §§ 8554, 8556.

§ 9510. Effect of dismissal or judgment

A stop payment notice ceases to be effective, and the public entity shall release funds withheld, in either of the following circumstances:

(a) An action to enforce payment of the claim stated in the stop payment notice is dismissed, unless expressly stated to be without prejudice.

(b) Judgment in an action to enforce payment of the claim stated in the stop payment notice is against the claimant. *(Added by Stats.2010, c. 697 (S.B.189), § 20, operative July 1, 2012.)*

Operative Effect

For operative effect of Part 6, see Civil Code § 8052 and Stats.2010, c. 697 (S.B.189), § 105.

Cross References

Claimant defined, see Civil Code § 8004.
Mechanics liens in general, dismissal of actions, see Civil Code §§ 8462, 8490.
Private works of improvement, dismissal of actions, see Civil Code §§ 8554, 8556.

CHAPTER 5. PAYMENT BOND

Section
9550. Necessity of bond; inclusion in call for bids; original and supplementary contracts.
9552. Payment bond not given and approved.
9554. Amount of bond; provisions regarding surety's obligation; conditioned for payment in full; subcontractor bond to indemnify contractor.
9558. Commencement of action to enforce liability on bond; limitations.
9560. Claim against payment bond; preliminary notice required; notice to surety and bond principal; extension; exceptions.
9562. Notice to principal and surety; requirements.
9564. Maintenance of action without filing stop notice or suing public entity or officer; attorney fees.
9566. Work done for direct contractor on bond; claim.

Operative Effect

For operative effect of Part 6, see Civil Code § 8052 and Stats.2010, c. 697 (S.B.189), § 105.

Cross References

Agreements between government and private entities, payment bonds for payment claims of laborers, mechanics, and materials suppliers, requirements, see Government Code § 5956.6.

§ 9550. Necessity of bond; inclusion in call for bids; original and supplementary contracts

(a) A direct contractor that is awarded a public works contract involving an expenditure in excess of twenty-five thousand dollars ($25,000) shall, before commencement of work, give a payment bond to and approved by the officer or public entity by whom the contract was awarded.

(b) A public entity shall state in its call for bids that a payment bond is required for a public works contract involving an expenditure in excess of twenty-five thousand dollars ($25,000).

(c) A payment bond given and approved under this section will permit performance of and provide coverage for work pursuant to a public works contract that supplements the contract for which the bond is given, if the requirement of a new bond is waived by the public entity.

(d) For the purpose of this section, a design professional is not deemed a direct contractor and is not required to give a payment bond.

(e) This section does not apply to a public works contract with a "state entity" as defined in subdivision (d) of Section 7103 of the Public Contract Code. *(Added by Stats.2010, c. 697 (S.B.189), § 20, operative July 1, 2012.)*

Operative Effect

For operative effect of Part 6, see Civil Code § 8052 and Stats.2010, c. 697 (S.B.189), § 105.

Cross References

Direct contractor defined, see Civil Code § 8018.
Payment bond, see Civil Code §§ 8606, 9554.
Public entity defined, see Civil Code § 8036.
Regulated public utility, contractor's bond, see Public Utilities Code § 773.

§ 9552. Payment bond not given and approved

If a payment bond is not given and approved as required by Section 9550:

(a) Neither the public entity awarding the public works contract nor any officer of the public entity shall audit, allow, or pay a claim of the direct contractor pursuant to the contract.

(b) A claimant shall receive payment of a claim pursuant to a stop payment notice in the manner provided by Chapter 4 (commencing with Section 9350). *(Added by Stats.2010, c. 697 (S.B.189), § 20, operative July 1, 2012.)*

Operative Effect

For operative effect of Part 6, see Civil Code § 8052 and Stats.2010, c. 697 (S.B.189), § 105.

§ 9554. Amount of bond; provisions regarding surety's obligation; conditioned for payment in full; subcontractor bond to indemnify contractor

(a) A payment bond shall be in an amount not less than 100 percent of the total amount payable pursuant to the public works contract. The bond shall be in the form of a bond and not a deposit in lieu of a bond. The bond shall be executed by an admitted surety insurer.

(b) The payment bond shall provide that if the direct contractor or a subcontractor fails to pay any of the following, the surety will pay the obligation and, if an action is brought to enforce the liability on the bond, a reasonable attorney's fee, to be fixed by the court:

(1) A person authorized under Section 9100 to assert a claim against a payment bond.

(2) Amounts due under the Unemployment Insurance Code with respect to work or labor performed pursuant to the public works contract.

(3) Amounts required to be deducted, withheld, and paid over to the Employment Development Department from the wages of employees of the contractor and subcontractors under Section 13020 of the Unemployment Insurance Code with respect to the work and labor.

(c) The payment bond shall be conditioned for the payment in full of the claims of all claimants and by its terms inure to the benefit of any person authorized under Section 9100 to assert a claim against a payment bond so as to give a right of action to that person or that person's assigns in an action to enforce the liability on the bond.

(d) The direct contractor may require that a subcontractor give a bond to indemnify the direct contractor for any loss sustained by the direct contractor because of any default of the subcontractor under this section. *(Added by Stats.2010, c. 697 (S.B.189), § 20, operative July 1, 2012.)*

Operative Effect

For operative effect of Part 6, see Civil Code § 8052 and Stats.2010, c. 697 (S.B.189), § 105.

Cross References

Bond and Undertaking Law, see Code of Civil Procedure § 995.010 et seq.
General provisions relating to bonds, see Civil Code § 8150 et seq.
Ownership, see Civil Code § 669 et seq.
Payment bond for private works, see Civil Code § 8600 et seq.
Payment bond for public works, see Civil Code § 9550 et seq.
Payment bond procured by landowner, mortgagee or trustee on site improvement, priority of liens, see Civil Code § 8458.
Payment bond procured by mortgagee or trustee, priority of liens, see Civil Code § 8452.
Stadium construction, joint powers agency, City of Santa Clara and Redevelopment Agency of the City of Santa Clara, see Government Code § 6532.
Sureties,
 Exoneration, see Civil Code § 2819 et seq.
 Liability, see Civil Code § 2806 et seq.
 Payment bond for private works, see Civil Code § 8612.
 Position, see Civil Code § 2832 et seq.
Surety insurers, list, see Insurance Code § 12070.

Suretyship, see Civil Code § 2787 et seq.

§ 9558. Commencement of action to enforce liability on bond; limitations

A claimant may commence an action to enforce the liability on the bond at any time after the claimant ceases to provide work, but not later than six months after the period in which a stop payment notice may be given under Section 9356. *(Added by Stats.2010, c. 697 (S.B.189), § 20, operative July 1, 2012.)*

Operative Effect

For operative effect of Part 6, see Civil Code § 8052 and Stats.2010, c. 697 (S.B.189), § 105.

Cross References

Action against direct contractor or public entity, see Civil Code § 9502 et seq.
Action on payment bond for private works, see Civil Code § 8609 et seq.
Claimant defined, see Civil Code § 8004.
Limitation of actions, generally, see Code of Civil Procedure § 312 et seq.
Private works, limitation of actions, see Civil Code § 8610.
Sureties,
 Exoneration, see Civil Code § 2819 et seq.
 Liability, see Civil Code § 2806 et seq.
Time of commencing civil actions, six months, see Code of Civil Procedure § 341.

§ 9560. Claim against payment bond; preliminary notice required; notice to surety and bond principal; extension; exceptions

(a) In order to enforce a claim against a payment bond, a claimant shall give the preliminary notice provided in Chapter 3 (commencing with Section 9300).

(b) If preliminary notice was not given as provided in Chapter 3 (commencing with Section 9300), a claimant may enforce a claim by giving written notice to the surety and the bond principal within 15 days after recordation of a notice of completion. If no notice of completion has been recorded, the time for giving written notice to the surety and the bond principal is extended to 75 days after completion of the work of improvement.

(c) Commencing July 1, 2012, and except as provided in subdivision (b), if the preliminary notice was required to be given by a person who has no direct contractual relationship with the contractor, and who has not given notice as provided in Chapter 3 (commencing with Section 9300), that person may enforce a claim by giving written notice to the surety and the bond principal, as provided in Section 9562, within 15 days after recordation of a notice of completion. If no notice of completion has been recorded, the time for giving written notice to the surety and the bond principal is extended to 75 days after completion of the work of improvement.

(d) Subdivision (c) shall not apply in either of the following circumstances:

(1) All progress payments, except for those disputed in good faith, have been made to a subcontractor who has a direct contractual relationship with the general contractor to whom the claimant has provided materials or services.

(2) The subcontractor who has a direct contractual relationship with the general contractor to whom the claimant has provided materials or services has been terminated from the project pursuant to the contract, and all progress payments, except those disputed in good faith, have been made as of the termination date.

(e) Pursuant to Section 9300, this section shall not apply to a laborer, as defined under Section 8024.

(f) This section shall become operative on July 1, 2012. *(Added by Stats.2010, c. 697 (S.B.189), § 20.1, operative July 1, 2012. Amended by Stats.2011, c. 700 (S.B.293), § 4, operative July 1, 2012.)*

Operative Effect

For operative effect of Part 6, see Civil Code § 8052 and Stats.2010, c. 697 (S.B.189), § 105.

Cross References

Claimant defined, see Civil Code § 8004.

§ 9562. Notice to principal and surety; requirements

Notice to the principal and surety under Section 9560 shall comply with the requirements of Chapter 2 (commencing with Section 8100) of Title 1. *(Added by Stats.2010, c. 697 (S.B.189), § 20, operative July 1, 2012.)*

Operative Effect

For operative effect of Part 6, see Civil Code § 8052 and Stats.2010, c. 697 (S.B.189), § 105.

Cross References

Private works of improvement, payment bond, notice requirements, see Civil Code § 8614.

§ 9564. Maintenance of action without filing stop notice or suing public entity or officer; attorney fees

(a) A claimant may maintain an action to enforce the liability of a surety on a payment bond whether or not the claimant has given the public entity a stop payment notice.

(b) A claimant may maintain an action to enforce the liability on the bond separately from and without commencement of an action against the public entity by whom the contract was awarded or against any officer of the public entity.

(c) In an action to enforce the liability on the bond, the court shall award the prevailing party a reasonable attorney's fee. *(Added by Stats.2010, c. 697 (S.B.189), § 20, operative July 1, 2012.)*

Operative Effect

For operative effect of Part 6, see Civil Code § 8052 and Stats.2010, c. 697 (S.B.189), § 105.

Cross References

Action against direct contractor or public entity, see Civil Code § 9502 et seq.
Action on payment bond for private works, see Civil Code § 8609 et seq.
Public entity defined, see Civil Code § 8036.
Stop notice, see Civil Code §§ 8044, 8502, 8506, 9352, 9354.
Sureties, situations not releasing, see Civil Code § 8152.

§ 9566. Work done for direct contractor on bond; claim

(a) A claimant does not have a right to recover on a payment bond unless the claimant provided work to the direct contractor either directly or through one or more subcontractors pursuant to a public works contract.

(b) Nothing in this section affects the stop payment notice rights of, and relative priorities among, design professionals. *(Added by Stats.2010, c. 697 (S.B.189), § 20, operative July 1, 2012.)*

Operative Effect

For operative effect of Part 6, see Civil Code § 8052 and Stats.2010, c. 697 (S.B.189), § 105.

Cross References

Claimant defined, see Civil Code § 8004.
Commencement of actions, see Civil Code § 8550.
Direct contractor defined, see Civil Code § 8018.
Payment bond, see Civil Code §§ 8606, 9554.
Subcontractor defined, see Civil Code § 8046.

Part 7

UNIFORM PARENTAGE ACT [REPEALED]

Part 8

AUTOMATIC CHECKOUT SYSTEM [HEADING RENUMBERED]

INDEX TO CIVIL CODE

ABANDONED EASEMENTS
Generally, **CC 887.010 et seq.**

ABANDONED OR UNCLAIMED PROPERTY
Generally, **CC 2081 et seq.**
Advances, sale of unclaimed property, **CC 2081.5**
Application of law,
  Carriers, **CC 2081.6**
  Lost property, **CC 2080.7**
Auctions and auctioneers,
  Carriers, notice, **CC 2081.1**
  Hospitals, **CC 1862.5**
  Notice, carriers, **CC 2081.1**
Bailment, **CC 2081 et seq.**
Bids and bidding, remaining on premises at termination of tenancy, **CC 1984, 1988**
California State University, **CC 2080.8**
Carriers, **CC 2081 et seq.**
Colleges and universities, **CC 2080.8**
Commission agents and merchants, **CC 2081 et seq.**
Confidential or privileged information, business records, disclosure, **CC 1799 et seq.**
Disposition. Sale, lease or other disposition, generally, post
Easements, **CC 887.010 et seq.**
Express companies, **CC 2081 et seq.**
Fees, officers, **CC 2082**
Hospitals, sale, **CC 1862.5**
Landlord and tenant, personal property, termination,
  Disposition, **CC 1980 et seq.**
  Notice, **CC 1946, 1946.1, 1950.5**
Leases. Sale, lease or other disposition, generally, post
Mobilehomes and mobilehome parks, declaration, **CC 798.61**
Museums, loans, long term or indefinite periods, **CC 1899 et seq.**
Notice,
  Disposition, personal property remaining at premises at termination of tenancy, **CC 1983 et seq.**
  Sale of property, carriers, **CC 2081.1**
Privileges and immunities, records and recordation, destruction, **CC 1798.84**
Railroads, **CC 2081 et seq.**
Records and recordation, destruction, privileges and immunities, **CC 1798.84**

ABANDONED OR UNCLAIMED PROPERTY—Cont'd
Safe deposit boxes, disposition, **CC 3081**
Sale, lease or other disposition,
  Advances, effect upon sale, **CC 2081.5**
  Carriers, **CC 2081.1 et seq.**
  Personal property, termination, **CC 1980 et seq., 1993 et seq.**
Servitude, **CC 811**
Storage costs, **CC 2081 et seq.**
  Personal property remaining on premises at termination of tenancy, **CC 1983, 1984**
Trust deeds, power of sale, surplus, **CC 2924j**
University of California, **CC 2080.8**
Warehouses, **CC 2081 et seq.**
  Storage liability, **CC 2081.4**

ABANDONMENT
Floating homes, **CC 800.36, 800.37**
Leases, this index
Mineral right lease, quitclaim deeds, **CC 883.140**
Servitude, **CC 811**

ABATEMENT
Adjoining landowners, spite fences, **CC 841.4**
Fences, spite fences, **CC 841.4**
Nuisance, this index
Spite fences, **CC 841.4**

ABATEMENT OF ACTIONS OR PROCEEDINGS
Choses in action, **CC 954**
Liens and incumbrances, motor vehicle liens, **CC 3070**
Motor vehicles, liens, **CC 3070**

ABETTORS
Accomplices and Accessories, generally, this index

ABODE
Domicile and Residence, generally, this index

ABORTION
Access, commercial blockade of facilities, **CC 3427 et seq.**
Actions and proceedings, **CC 43.6**
Blockade, commercial blockade of facilities, **CC 3427 et seq.**
Commercial blockade, facilities, **CC 3427 et seq.**
Confidential or privileged information, medical records, conflict of laws, **CC 56.108**

ABORTION—Cont'd
Conflict of laws, medical records, confidential or privileged information, **CC 56.108**
Consent, **CC 3427 et seq.**
Damages, commercial blockade, facilities, **CC 3427.2**
Genetic defects, action against parents for failure to abort, **CC 43.6**
Interference with access, **CC 3427 et seq.**
Medical records, confidential or privileged information, conflict of laws, **CC 56.108**
Orders of court, commercial blockade, facilities, **CC 3427.3**
Production of books and papers, medical records, conflict of laws, **CC 56.108**
Refusal, genetic defects, action against parents for failure to abort, **CC 43.6**
Subpoenas, medical records, conflict of laws, **CC 56.108**
Torts, commercial blockade of facilities, **CC 3427 et seq.**

ABSENCE AND ABSENTEES
Mobilehomes and mobilehome parks, medical care and treatment, subleases, **CC 798.23.5**
Power of attorney, termination, **CC 2357**

ABSOLUTE DELIVERY
Grant, **CC 1056**

ABSOLUTE OWNERSHIP
Interests in property, **CC 678, 679**

ABUSE
Child Abuse, generally, this index
Domestic Violence, generally, this index
Homeless persons, transitional housing, misconduct, **CC 1954.10 et seq.**
Psychiatric technicians, long term health care facilities, temporary employment, **CC 1812.543**
Spousal abuse. Domestic Violence, generally, this index
Vocational nursing, long term health care facilities, temporary employment, **CC 1812.543**

ABUTTING OWNERS
Adjoining Landowners, generally, this index

ACADEMIES
Private Schools, generally, this index

ACCELERATION
Mortgages, this index

ACCELERATION

ACCELERATION—Cont'd
Retail installment contracts, maturity in absence of default, CC 1804.1
Trust Deeds, this index

ACCESSION, ACCRETION AND AVULSION
Generally, CC 1000, 1013 et seq.
Bank of river or streams, sudden removal, CC 1015
Damages, wrongful use of materials, CC 1033
Election between thing and its value, CC 1032
Fixtures, this index
Formation of land by alluvion, CC 1014
Inseparable materials, title to property, CC 1029
Islands, CC 1016 et seq.
Materials of,
  Several owners, thing made from, title, CC 1030
  Wrongful use, damages, CC 1033
Nature and effect of alluvion, CC 1014, 1015
Owners and ownership,
  Thing made by uniting materials and workmanship, CC 1028
  Thing made by willful trespasser, CC 1031
  Thing made from materials of several owners, CC 1030
  Thing made of inseparable materials, CC 1029
Principal part,
  Determination by value or bulk, CC 1027
  Separation of lesser but more valuable part, CC 1026
Rights of owners of property, CC 732
Separation of lesser but more valuable part, CC 1026
Single thing formed from several things, owner of principal part, CC 1025
Uniting materials and workmanship, CC 1028
Uniting several things, CC 1025
Willful trespasser, ownership of thing made by, CC 1031
Workmanship and materials, uniting, CC 1028
Wrongful use of materials, damages, CC 1033

ACCESSORIES
Accomplices and Accessories, generally, this index

ACCESSORY OBLIGATION
Liens, extinction, CC 2909

ACCIDENT AND HEALTH INSURANCE
Health Insurance, generally, this index

ACCIDENTS
Animals, dog killing or injuring, CC 3341
Deposits, involuntary, CC 1815
Dog killing or injuring other animals, CC 3341
Health care facility liens, medical services rendered for injury caused by accident, CC 3045.1 et seq.

ACCIDENTS—Cont'd
Hospital liens, medical services rendered for injury caused by accident, CC 3045.1 et seq.
Insurance, generally, this index
Involuntary trusts, CC 2223 et seq.
Liens, hospital liens, medical services rendered, CC 3045.1 et seq.
Medical or surgical treatment, liens, emergencies, CC 3045.1 et seq.
Personal Injuries, generally, this index
Trusts and trustees, involuntary trusts, CC 2223 et seq.
Workers Compensation, generally, this index

ACCOMMODATIONS
Blind or visually impaired persons, civil rights, CC 54.1
Deaf or hard of hearing persons, civil rights, CC 54.1
Disabled persons, civil rights, CC 54.1
Nursing or convalescent homes contracts, termination on death, CC 1934.5
Speech impaired persons, civil rights, CC 54.1

ACCOMPLICES AND ACCESSORIES
Discrimination, CC 52
Support, arrearages, evasion, treble damages, CC 1714.4, 1714.41

ACCORD AND SATISFACTION
Generally, CC 1521 et seq.
Acceptance, consideration of accord, CC 1523
Checks, CC 1526
Commercial paper, checks or drafts, CC 1526
Conditions, part payment of disputed sum, CC 1525
Consideration,
  Acceptance, CC 1523
  Part performance agreement, CC 1524
Drafts, CC 1526
Execution, CC 1522
Mechanics liens, CC 8130
Obligations, this index
Part payment of disputed sum, CC 1525
Part performance, CC 1524

ACCOUNTANTS
Clients, sexual harassment, CC 51.9
Confidential or privileged information, business records, disclosure, CC 1799 et seq.
Damages, business records, disclosure, CC 1799.2
Disclosure, business records, bookkeeping services, CC 1799 et seq.
Harassment, sexual harassment, clients, CC 51.9
Privileges and immunities,
  Professional organization, CC 43.7, 43.8
  Referral services, CC 43.95
Referrals, limitation of liability, CC 43.95
Sexual harassment, clients, CC 51.9
Telephones, referral services, immunity, CC 43.95

ACCOUNTS AND ACCOUNTING
Business records, disclosure, bookkeeping services, CC 1799 et seq.
Damages, business records, disclosure, CC 1799.2
Debt settlement providers, fair debt settlement, CC 1788.302
Disclosure of business records, bookkeeping services, CC 1799 et seq.
Impound accounts, real estate transactions, CC 2954
  Retention and investment in state, CC 2955
Installment Sales, this index
Joint credit accounts, credit history, filing of information, CC 1812.30
Landlord and tenant, rent control system, apportionment or recovery of costs, CC 1947.15
Mobilehomes and mobilehome parks, disposal, abandonment, CC 798.61
Mortgages, this index
Payment processors, fair debt settlement, CC 1788.302

ACCRETION
Accession, Accretion and Avulsion, generally, this index

ACCUMULATIONS
Generally, CC 722 et seq.

ACCUSATION
Indictment and Information, generally, this index

ACIDS
Air Pollution, generally, this index

ACKNOWLEDGMENTS
Generally, CC 1180 et seq.
Actions and proceedings, identification of persons making acknowledgments, CC 1185
Assignment, instrument with power of sale of real property, CC 2932.5
Certificates and certification, CC 1188
  Action for correction, CC 1202
  Authentication, CC 1193
  Defective, CC 1202, 1207
  Forms, CC 1189
    Military officers, CC 1183.5
    Proof of execution, CC 1195
  Indorsement, CC 1188
  Proof of execution in lieu of, CC 1200
  Seals, affixation, CC 1193
Charge d'affaires of the United States, CC 1183
Chief clerk of assembly, CC 1181
City attorney, CC 1181
Clerk of board of supervisors, counties, powers, CC 1181
Commissioners, official,
  Authority to take, CC 1182
  Foreign countries, CC 1183

ACTIONS

ACKNOWLEDGMENTS—Cont'd
Consuls, CC 1183
County counsels, CC 1181
Court commissioners, CC 1181
Defective, validity, CC 1207
Discount buying services, attorney general, CC 1812.101
District attorneys, CC 1181
Foreign countries, CC 1183
Foreign states, CC 1182
    Forms, CC 1189
Forfeitures, perjury, CC 1185
Forms. Certificates and certification, ante
Identification of persons making, CC 1185
Indorsement of certificate, CC 1188
Installment sales,
    Buyer, delivery of copy of contract, CC 1803.7
    Payment by buyer, CC 1806.4
Lost or destroyed documents, action, CC 3415
Military officers, CC 1183.5
Ministers of United States, CC 1183
Motor Vehicles, this index
Municipal clerks, CC 1181
Notaries Public, generally, this index
Notice, certificates and certification, CC 1189
Officers authorized to take, CC 1180, 1181, 1184
Payment, installment sale, buyers payments, CC 1806.4
Proof of execution, CC 1195 et seq.
Requisites, CC 1185
Seals, affixing, CC 1193
Secretary of senate, CC 1181
Signatures, CC 1193
    Witnesses, CC 14
Trust Deeds, this index
Validity,
    Defectively executed instruments, CC 1207
    Law governing prior conveyances, CC 1205
Witnesses, CC 1185
    Proof of execution, CC 1195 et seq.

ACQUIRED IMMUNE DEFICIENCY SYNDROME (AIDS)
HIV, generally, this index

ACTIONS AND PROCEEDINGS
Abatement of Actions or Proceedings, generally, this index
Acknowledgments,
    Correction of certificates, CC 1202
    Identification of persons making, CC 1185
Administrative Law and Procedure, generally, this index
Adverse Possession, generally, this index
Animals, this index
Arbitration and Award, generally, this index
Art and Artists, this index
Assistive listening systems, deaf or hard of hearing persons, CC 54.8

ACTIONS AND PROCEEDINGS—Cont'd
Attachment, generally, this index
Autographed memorabilia, warranties, CC 1739.7
Automated license plate recognition, CC 1798.90.54
Blanket incumbrances on subdivisions, failure to notify buyers or lessees, CC 1133
Booking photographs, commercial use, CC 1798.91.1
Bookstores, personal information, disclosure, CC 1798.90
Breach of marriage promise, CC 43.4, 43.5
Building standards, construction defects, CC 896
Business and commerce, customer records, destruction, CC 1798.84
Business records, disclosures, CC 1799.2
Children and Minors, this index
Class Actions, generally, this index
Commencement of actions. Limitation of Actions, generally, this index
Complaints, generally, this index
Compromise and Settlement, generally, this index
Condominiums, this index
Confession of Judgment, generally, this index
Conflict of interest, insurance companies obligation to defend, appointment of independent counsel, CC 2860
Construction defects. Buildings, this index
Consumer Credit, this index
Consumer Credit Reporting Agencies, this index
Consumer Protection, this index
Consumers, privacy, disclosure, CC 1798.150
Contempt, generally, this index
Contractors, this index
Contracts, this index
Costs, generally, this index
Credit,
    Discrimination, marital status or sex, CC 1812.31 et seq.
    Identity and identification, theft, CC 1785.20.3
Credit Cards, this index
Credit services organizations, CC 1789.20, 1789.21
    Bonds (officers and fiduciaries), CC 1789.18
Criminal conversation, CC 43.5
Damages, generally, this index
Dating service contracts, CC 1694.4
Deaf or hard of hearing persons, assistive listening systems, CC 54.8
Debt settlement providers, fair debt settlement, CC 1788.305
Declaratory Judgments and Decrees, generally, this index
Decrees. Judgments and Decrees, generally, this index
Disclosure, business records, CC 1799.2

ACTIONS AND PROCEEDINGS—Cont'd
Discrimination, this index
Dissolution of marriage. Marriage, this index
Domestic partnership, negligence, emotional distress, CC 1714.01
Dormant mineral rights, termination, CC 883.210 et seq.
Easements, this index
Electronic commercial service violations, civil penalties, recovery, CC 1789.5
Embryos, crimes and offenses, CC 1708.5.6
Eminent Domain, generally, this index
Emotional distress, negligence, CC 1714.01
Equity, generally, this index
Evidence, generally, this index
Executions, generally, this index
False Imprisonment, generally, this index
Fine art multiples, CC 1745, 1745.5
Fixtures, removal, erroneously affixed to land, CC 1013.5
Floating home marinas, CC 800.200, 800.201
Forcible Entry and Detainer, generally, this index
Foreclosure. Mortgages, this index
Forfeitures, generally, this index
Freedom from violence, CC 52, 52.1
Garnishment, generally, this index
Gender violence, CC 52.4
Genetic defects, action for damages by child against parent, CC 43.6
Genetic testing, privacy, CC 56.182
Grocery stores, point of sale systems, CC 7102
Home equity sales contracts, CC 1695.7
Human trafficking, CC 52.5
Identity and Identification, this index
In vitro fertilization, crimes and offenses, CC 1708.5.6
Independent wholesale sales representatives, contracts, CC 1738.15
Injunction, generally, this index
Installment Sales, this index
Insurance, this index
Interest, usury, CC 1916–2
    Treble amount, limitations, CC 1916–3
Joinder of causes of action,
    Forcible entry and detainer, drugs and medicine, nuisance, CC 3486
    Identity and identification, theft, CC 1798.95
    Mechanics liens,
        Public buildings and works, stop notices, CC 9506
        Release, orders of court, CC 8480
Joinder of parties. Parties, this index
Judgments and Decrees, generally, this index
Labor disputes, freedom from violence, CC 52
Landlord and Tenant, this index
Leases, this index
Lewdness and obscenity, electronic transmissions, images, CC 1708.88
Libel and Slander, generally, this index

ACTIONS

ACTIONS AND PROCEEDINGS—Cont'd
Limitation of Actions, generally, this index
Loans,
    Construction or repair, real or personal property, lenders liability for defects, **CC 3434**
    Identity and identification, theft, **CC 1785.20.3**
Malicious destruction of property, treble damages, **CC 1721**
Marinas, floating homes, **CC 800.200, 800.201**
Marketing plans, seller assisted marketing plans, **CC 1812.218**
Marriage, this index
Mechanics Liens, this index
Mediation, generally, this index
Medical Malpractice, generally, this index
Medical Records, this index
Membership camping contracts, rescission or refund, **CC 1812.306**
Memorabilia, autographed, warranties, **CC 1739.7**
Minority groups, equal protection of laws, statutes, **CC 53.7**
Minors. Children and Minors, this index
Mobilehomes and Mobilehome Parks, this index
Mortgages, this index
Negligence, generally, this index
Nuisance, generally, this index
Ova, crimes and offenses, **CC 1708.5.6**
Parties, generally, this index
Partition, generally, this index
Payment processors, fair debt settlement, **CC 1788.305**
Point of sale systems, grocery stores, **CC 7102**
Political items, sale and manufacture, violations, **CC 1739.4**
Power of termination of fee simple, exercise, **CC 885.050**
Privileges and Immunities, generally, this index
Probate Proceedings, generally, this index
Process, generally, this index
Products Liability, generally, this index
Prophylactics, removal, **CC 1708.5**
Psychotherapists and psychotherapy, sexual exploitation, **CC 43.93**
Public policy, payment of amounts conceded to be due on contracts, **CC 1525**
Quieting Title, generally, this index
Reading, privacy, **CC 1798.90**
Real Estate, this index
Records and recordation, customer records, destruction, **CC 1798.84**
Recreational trails, entry on property, **CC 846.1**
Recreational vehicles, parks, attorney fees and costs, **CC 799.78**
Rent control, commercial property, public entities, **CC 1954.31**

ACTIONS AND PROCEEDINGS—Cont'd
Rent skimming, damages, **CC 891**
Revival. Abatement of Actions or Proceedings, generally, this index
Sales, this index
Security deposits, landlord and tenant, **CC 1950.5**
Seduction, **CC 43.5**
Seller assisted marketing plans, **CC 1812.218**
Service of process. Process, this index
Sex, force and violence, **CC 52.4**
Sexual battery, **CC 1708.5**
    Consent, children and minors, defense, **CC 1708.5.5**
Sexual exploitation, psychotherapists and psychotherapy, **CC 43.93**
Sexual orientation, **CC 52.45**
Slander. Libel and Slander, generally, this index
Slandering title, **CC 880.360**
Small Claims Courts, generally, this index
Social media, threats, **CC 1798.99.22**
Specific and preventive relief, **CC 3366 et seq.**
Specific Performance, generally, this index
Sperm, crimes and offenses, **CC 1708.5.6**
Stalking, **CC 1708.7**
Statute of limitations. Limitation of Actions, generally, this index
Stay of proceedings. Supersedeas or Stay, generally, this index
Stealthing, **CC 1708.5**
Subcutaneous implantation, identification devices, **CC 52.7**
Subpoenas, generally, this index
Subrogation, generally, this index
Supersedeas or Stay, generally, this index
Termination of dormant mineral rights, **CC 883.210 et seq.**
Third Parties, generally, this index
Time. Limitation of Actions, generally, this index
Torts, generally, this index
Trespass, generally, this index
Trust Deeds, this index
Vandalism, construction sites, **CC 1721**
Venue, generally, this index
Violence, freedom from, **CC 52.1**
Waste, generally, this index
Weight loss contracts, **CC 1694.9**
Wholesales, sales representatives, independents, contracts, **CC 1738.15**
Witnesses, generally, this index
Women, credit transactions, discrimination, **CC 1812.31 et seq.**

ACTS
Statutes, generally, this index

ACTS OF GOD
Carriers, liability for loss, **CC 2194**
Liability, **CC 3526**
Obligations, performance or offer of performance, excuse, **CC 1511**

ACTS OF LEGISLATURE
Statutes, generally, this index

ACUPUNCTURE
Privileges and immunities, peer review committees, liability, **CC 43.7, 43.8**

AD VALOREM TAXES
Taxation, generally, this index

ADDING MACHINES
Sale, identification number or mark altered or removed, **CC 1710.1**

ADDRESS
Automobile Sales Finance Act,
    Formalities of conditional sales contracts, **CC 2982**
    Repossessed motor vehicle, notice of intent to sell, **CC 2983.2**
Business addresses, mobilehome park owners, disclosure, **CC 798.28**
Change of address,
    Business and commerce, notice, **CC 1799.1b**
    Credit cards, notice, **CC 1799.1b**
    Telecommunications, notice, **CC 1799.1b**
Condominiums, notice, **CC 4041**
Consumer Credit Reporting Agencies, this index
Disclosure, grocery stores, club cards, **CC 1749.60 et seq.**
Electronic commercial service contracts, **CC 1789.3**
Employment agencies, contracts, employment agency and jobseeker, inclusion, **CC 1812.504**
Equalization state board, release, **CC 1798.69**
Grocery stores, club cards, disclosure, **CC 1749.60 et seq.**
Identity and identification, theft, **CC 1798.92 et seq.**
Landlord and tenant, multiunit dwellings, disclosures, **CC 1961 et seq.**
Mobilehomes and Mobilehome Parks, this index

ADJOINING LANDOWNERS
Adjacent support, **CC 801, 832**
Annoyance, height of structures, malicious intent, **CC 841.4**
Boundaries, maintenance, **CC 841**
Construction contracts, indemnity, **CC 2782.1**
Costs, fences, maintenance, **CC 841**
Covenants running with the land, **CC 1468 et seq.**
Damages, lateral support, **CC 832**
Division fences, right of maintenance, **CC 801**
Easements, lateral support, **CC 801**
Eminent domain, repair, reconstruction, temporary right of entry, **CC 1002**
Excavations on land, **CC 832**
Fences,
    Maintenance, **CC 801, 841**
    Spite fences, **CC 841.4**

ADJOINING LANDOWNERS—Cont'd
Height of structures, malicious intent, **CC 841.4**
Indemnity, construction contracts, entry on property, **CC 2782.1**
Lateral support, **CC 832**
Line trees, common ownership, **CC 834**
Maintenance of monuments and fences, **CC 841**
Monuments, maintenance, **CC 841**
Negligence, excavations, **CC 832**
Notice,
  Excavations, **CC 832**
  Fences, maintenance, **CC 841**
Nuisances, fence of excessive height, **CC 841.4**
Presumptions, fences, maintenance, costs, **CC 841**
Repairs, temporary right of entry, **CC 1002**
Support, right of lateral support,
  Easements, **CC 801**
  Excavations, **CC 832**
Trees, ownership, **CC 833, 834**

ADJOINING STATES
Foreign States, generally, this index

ADJUSTABLE RATE RESIDENTIAL MORTGAGE LOAN
Disclosures, prospective borrowers, **CC 1921**

ADMINISTRATIVE LAW AND PROCEDURE
Equal protection of laws, minority groups, **CC 53.7**
Expenses and expenditures, rent control, apportionment or recovery, **CC 1947.15**
Fees, rent control, apportionment or recovery, **CC 1947.15**
Fines and penalties. Auctions and Auctioneers, this index
Medical information, disclosure, **CC 56.10**
Minority groups, equal protection of laws, **CC 53.7**
Rent control, fees and expenses, apportionment or recovery, **CC 1947.15**

ADMINISTRATIVE PROCEDURE ACT
Administrative Law and Procedure, generally, this index

ADMISSIBILITY OF EVIDENCE
Evidence, generally, this index

ADMISSIONS
Hazardous substances and waste, commitment statements, responsibility acceptance, **CC 853**

ADOPTION
Agency adoption, disabled persons, discrimination, **CC 54.1**
Agents and agencies, medically necessary information, biological parents, disclosure, **CC 1798.24**
Birth parents, medically necessary information, disclosure, child or grandchild of adopted person, **CC 1798.24**

ADOPTION—Cont'd
Confidential or privileged information, governmental agencies, Information Practice Act, **CC 1798.24**
Information, medically necessary information, disclosure, child or grandchild of adopted person, **CC 1798.24**
Medically necessary information, disclosure, child or grandchild of adopted person, **CC 1798.24**
Personal information held by governmental agencies, disclosure, Information Practices Act, **CC 1798.24**

ADULT LOCAL CRIMINAL JUSTICE FACILITIES
Jails, generally, this index

ADULT OR SEXUALLY ORIENTED BUSINESSES
Lewdness and Obscenity, generally, this index

ADULTS
Abuse, indebtedness, duress or coercion, **CC 1798.97.1 et seq.**
Aged Persons, generally, this index
Domestic Partnership, generally, this index

ADVANCES AND ADVANCEMENTS
Abandoned or unclaimed property, sales, **CC 2081.5**
Depositary for hire, lien, **CC 1856**
Landlord and Tenant, this index
Leases, renewal, conditions, **CC 1950.8**
Lien of depositary for hire, **CC 1856**
Security deposits, landlord and tenant, **CC 1950.5**

ADVERSE OR PECUNIARY INTEREST
Conflict of Interest, generally, this index

ADVERSE POSSESSION
Generally, **CC 1006 et seq.**
Abandoned easements, **CC 887.010 et seq.**
Acquisition of title by adverse possession, **CC 1007**
Consent, permissive use, **CC 1008**
Damages, wrongful occupation, **CC 3334**
Deeds and conveyances, property adversely held, **CC 1047**
Easements,
  Abandoned easements, **CC 887.010 et seq.**
  Signs preventing prescription, **CC 1008**
Exemptions,
  Easements, signs preventing prescription, **CC 1008**
  Public property, **CC 1007**
  Public recreational use, restrictions, **CC 1009**
Mortgaging of property held adversely, **CC 2921**
Permissive use, **CC 1008**
Public lands, exemptions, **CC 1007**
Transfer of property, **CC 1047**

ADVERTISEMENTS

ADVERTISEMENTS
Agencies, Consumers Legal Remedies Act, application of law, **CC 1755**
Animals, breeding pedigree, **CC 3064.1**
Astaire Celebrity Image Protection Act, **CC 3344.1**
Bids and Bidding, generally, this index
Billboards. Outdoor Advertising, generally, this index
Celebrity image protection, **CC 3344.1**
Consumers Legal Remedies Act, **CC 1750 et seq.**
Costs, deceased celebrity image protection, **CC 3344.1**
Credit service organizations, fraud, **CC 1789.13**
Damages,
  Deceased celebrity image protection, **CC 3344.1**
  Names, photographs, voices, signatures, use without consent, **CC 3344**
  Unauthorized use, name, likeness, voice, signature, **CC 3344**
Dance studio services, **CC 1812.50 et seq.**
Deceased personality, celebrity image protection, **CC 3344.1**
Deceptive trade practices, **CC 1770**
Discount Buying Services, generally, this index
Elections, this index
Employment Agencies, this index
Employment counseling services, false advertisements, **CC 1812.513**
False advertisements. Fraud, generally, post
Famous persons, deceased celebrities, image protection, **CC 3344.1**
Floating homes, sale or rental by owner, **CC 800.80**
Fraud,
  Employment counseling services, **CC 1812.513**
  Job listing services, **CC 1812.520**
  Nurse registries, **CC 1812.533**
Furniture, unassembled furniture, consumer remedies, **CC 1770**
Genetic testing, privacy, **CC 56.181**
Good faith, Consumers Legal Remedies Act, **CC 1750 et seq.**
Grey market goods, disclosures, **CC 1797.8 et seq.**
Grey market products, disclosure, **CC 1770**
Health studio services, **CC 1812.92**
Highways and roads. Outdoor Advertising, generally, this index
Home health agencies, employment agencies distinguished, **CC 1812.508**
Job listing services, false advertisements, **CC 1812.520**
Landlord and tenant, animals, declawing, devocalizing, **CC 1942.7**
Leases, misrepresentation, Consumers Legal Remedies Act, **CC 1750 et seq.**
Likeness, deceased personality, celebrity image protection, **CC 3344.1**

I-5

ADVERTISEMENTS

ADVERTISEMENTS—Cont'd
Lost property, CC 2080.3
Misrepresentation. Fraud, generally, ante
Names,
  Deceased celebrity image protection, CC 3344.1
  Invasion of privacy, CC 3344
  Unauthorized use, CC 3344
  Use without consent, CC 3344
Nurses registries, CC 1812.533
Outdoor Advertising, generally, this index
Photography and Pictures, this index
Prices, unfair or deceptive trade practices, CC 1770
Probate proceedings, mobilehomes and mobilehome parks, CC 799.1.5
Rental purchase agreements, CC 1812.630
Sales,
  Lien on vehicle, CC 3072
  Mobilehomes and mobilehome parks, CC 799.1.5
Signatures,
  Deceased personality, celebrity image protection, CC 3344.1
  Unauthorized use, CC 3344
Television and radio, Consumers Legal Remedies Act, application of law, CC 1755
Trademarks, generally, this index
Unauthorized use of name or likeness, damages, CC 3344
Voice,
  Deceased personality, celebrity image protection, CC 3344.1
  Unauthorized use, CC 3344

AERONAUTICS
Aircraft, generally, this index

AEROPLANES
Aircraft, generally, this index

AFFIDAVITS
Conditional sales, motor vehicles, venue, CC 2984.4
Divorce action, privileged publication, CC 47
Finders of lost property, owner unknown, CC 2080.1
Homeless persons, transitional housing, misconduct, CC 1954.13
Innkeepers liens, writs of possession, CC 1861.5
Installment sales, venue, CC 1812.10
Liens and incumbrances, innkeepers liens, writs of possession, CC 1861.5
Livestock service liens, applications for court ordered sales, CC 3080.03
Lost or destroyed property, finders, police or sheriff, CC 2080.1
Timber and lumber, logger and lumbermen lien, compensation, CC 3065c
Trust deeds,
  Majority interest holders, beneficiaries, governing agreement, CC 2941.9

AFFIDAVITS—Cont'd
Trust deeds—Cont'd
  Substitution of trustees, CC 2934a

AFFILIATES
Discount buying services, CC 1812.117

AFFINITY
Relatives, generally, this index

AFFIRMATIONS
Oaths and Affirmations, generally, this index

AFFIRMATIVE DEFENSES
Medical records, release, CC 56.36
Video games, force and violence, CC 1746.1

AFFORDABLE HOUSING
Low and Moderate Income Housing, generally, this index

AFTERBORN CHILDREN
Future interests, CC 698
  Contingent interest, CC 739

AGE
Aged Persons, generally, this index
Condominiums, senior citizens, cohabitants, restrictions, CC 51.3
Discrimination, generally, this index
Housing, this index
Intergenerational housing developments, CC 51.3.5
Limited equity housing cooperatives, aged persons, cohabitants, restrictions, CC 51.3
Multiple family residential rental property, aged persons, cohabitants, restrictions, CC 51.3
Plan developments, cohabitants, restrictions, CC 51.3
Senior citizen housing, cohabitants, covenants, conditions, restrictions, CC 51.3
Stock cooperatives, senior citizens, cohabitants, restrictions, CC 51.3

AGE APPROPRIATE DESIGN CODE ACT
Generally, CC 1798.99.28 et seq.

AGED PERSONS
Abuse, indebtedness, duress or coercion, CC 1798.97.1 et seq.
Appreciation, shared appreciation loans for seniors, CC 1917.320 et seq.
Condominiums, cohabitants, age, covenants, conditions, restrictions, CC 51.3
Consumer credit reporting agencies, security freeze, fees, CC 1785.11.2
Consumer protection,
  Additional penalty, CC 3345
  Damages, CC 1780
Damages, consumer protection, unfair or deceptive practices, CC 3345
Disabled persons, housing, CC 51.3, 51.11
Disclosure, shared appreciation loans for seniors, CC 1917.710 et seq.

AGED PERSONS—Cont'd
Discrimination, generally, this index
Dwellings. Housing, generally, post
Fines and penalties, consumer protection, CC 1780, 3345
Fraud, fines and penalties, CC 1780, 3345
Guardian and Ward, generally, this index
Home solicitation, primary residence, improvements, CC 1770
Housing, CC 51.2 et seq.
  Age restrictions, CC 51.3
  Children and minors, dependent children, CC 51.3
  Cohabitants, covenants, conditions, restrictions, CC 51.3
  Construction, physical and social needs, CC 51.2
  Dependent children, CC 51.3
  Disabled persons, dependent children, CC 51.3
  Discrimination, housing sales or rentals, CC 51.2
  Exemptions, special design requirements, CC 51.4
  Guests, age restrictions, CC 51.3
  Intellectual and developmental disabilities, dependent children, CC 51.3
  Intergenerational housing developments, CC 51.3.5
  Permitted health care residents, CC 51.3
  Physical and social needs, CC 51.2
  Public reports, senior citizen housing developments, CC 51.3
  Sale or rental, discrimination, CC 51.2
  Senior citizen housing developments, CC 51.2 et seq.
  Shared appreciation loans, CC 1917.320 et seq.
  Special design requirements, exemptions, CC 51.4
  Terminal illness, dependent children, CC 51.3
Intergenerational housing developments, CC 51.3.5
Landlord and tenant,
  Abuse,
    Emergency services, law enforcement, CC 1946.8
    Termination, notice, CC 1946.7
  Cohabitants, restrictions, CC 51.3
  Discrimination, CC 51.2
  Limited equity housing cooperatives, cohabitants, age, covenants, conditions, restrictions, CC 51.3
Loans, shared appreciation loans, CC 1917.320 et seq.
Mobilehomes and Mobilehome Parks, this index
Multiple family residential rental property, cohabitants, age, covenants, conditions, restrictions, CC 51.3
Nursing Homes, generally, this index

AGRICULTURAL

AGED PERSONS—Cont'd
Personal attendants. Domestic Workers, generally, this index
Physical and social needs, housing, construction, CC 51.2
Planned unit development, cohabitants, age, covenants, conditions, restrictions, CC 51.3
Real estate, shared appreciation loans, CC 1917.320 et seq.
Rental housing, discrimination, CC 51.2
Shared appreciation loans, CC 1917.320 et seq.
Stock cooperative housing, cohabitants, age, covenants, conditions, restrictions, CC 51.3

AGENCY
Local Agencies, generally, this index
Public Agencies, generally, this index

AGENTS AND AGENCIES
Generally, CC 2019 et seq., 2295 et seq.
Absence and absentees, power of attorney, termination, CC 2357
Actual agency, classification, CC 2298
Application of law, CC 2345
Appointment, CC 2296
Art and artists,
  Commissions, sale, original works, CC 986
  Consignment, CC 1738 et seq.
Attorney in fact. Power of Attorney, generally, this index
Authority. Powers and duties, generally, post
Bona fide transactions, agency termination, CC 2356
Breach of warranty, damages, CC 3318
Capacity, CC 2296
Classification, CC 2298
Collecting agent, duties, CC 2021
Collection Agencies, generally, this index
Consideration, CC 2308
Construction of authority, CC 2321, 2322
Constructive notice, restrictions on authority, CC 2318
Creating agency, CC 2307
Credit ratings. Consumer Credit Reporting Agencies, generally, this index
Damages, breach of warranty, authority of agent, CC 3318
Death, termination of agency, CC 2355 et seq.
Delegation of authority, CC 2349 et seq.
Disobeying principals instructions, CC 2320
Duties. Powers and duties, generally, post
Employment Agencies, generally, this index
Escrows and Escrow Agents, generally, this index
Exceeding authority, CC 2333
Exclusive credit to agent, CC 2335
Execution of authority, incomplete, CC 2331
Exoneration of principals where exclusive credit given to agent, CC 2335

AGENTS AND AGENCIES—Cont'd
Expiration of term, CC 2355
Factors, generally, this index
Fraud, CC 2306
Frauds, statute of, real estate sales, CC 1624
Good faith, principal bound by acts under ostensible authority, CC 2334
Home equity sales contracts, equity purchasers, liability, CC 1695.15 et seq.
Incapacity, termination of agency, CC 2355, 2356
Indemnity and indemnification, CC 2775
Independent wholesale sales representatives, CC 1738.10 et seq.
Informing principal, CC 2020
Instructions by principal, disobedience, CC 2320
Instrument within scope of authority, binding principal, CC 2337
Insurance Agents, Solicitors or Brokers, generally, this index
Liability, CC 2342 et seq.
  Principals, CC 2330 et seq.
Limits of authority, CC 2019
Measure of authority, CC 2315
Mechanics liens, CC 8066
Mobilehomes and Mobilehome Parks, this index
Mortgages,
  Agent of mortgagee, collection, notice of default, CC 2924.3
  Trustees payments, CC 2924d
Mutual obligations of principals and third persons, CC 2330 et seq.
Negligence, responsibility of principals, CC 2338, 2339
Notice to agents or principals, CC 2332
  Restrictive authority, CC 2318
Oral authority, CC 2309
Ostensible agents, classification, CC 2298
Ostensible authority, principal bound by acts, CC 2334
Personal property, sales, CC 2323
Personal Property Brokers, generally, this index
Power of Attorney, generally, this index
Powers and duties, CC 2019, 2304 et seq.
  Absence of authority, fraud upon principal, CC 2306
  Actual authority, CC 2316
  Coupled with an interest, CC 2356
  Damages, breach of warranty, CC 3318
  Disobeying instructions, CC 2320
  Execution of authority, incomplete, CC 2331
  Instruments within scope of authority, binding principal, CC 2337
  Liability of principal, CC 2330 et seq.
  Necessary authority, CC 2319
  Oral and written authorizations, CC 2309
  Ostensible authority, CC 2317
    Liability of principal, CC 2334

AGENTS AND AGENCIES—Cont'd
Powers and duties—Cont'd
  Ratification, CC 2310 et seq.
  Rescission, CC 2314
  Restrictions on authority, notice, CC 2318
  Sales, CC 2323 et seq.
  Termination, CC 2355 et seq.
Presumptions, CC 3519
Proxies, application of law, CC 2356
Public Agencies, generally, this index
Qualifications, CC 2296
Ratification, authority of agents, CC 2310 et seq.
Real property. Real Estate Brokers and Salespersons, generally, this index
Relationship of parties, subagents, delegation of authority, CC 2350, 2351
Renunciation of agency, termination, CC 2355
Rescission, ratification of acts of agent, CC 2314
Responsibility, subagent, CC 2022
Restrictive authority, notice, CC 2318
Revocation, CC 2356
Scope of authority, CC 2304 et seq.
Security Agents and Broker Dealers, generally, this index
Setoff and counterclaim, third persons, rights, dealing with agent without knowledge of agency, CC 2336
State Agencies, generally, this index
Statute of Frauds, real estate sales, CC 1624
Statutory performance of acts required of principal, authority of agent, CC 2305
Subagents, CC 2349 et seq.
  Responsibility, CC 2022
Successors in interest, effect of termination upon, CC 2356
Surrender of property to third persons, time, CC 2344
Termination, CC 2355 et seq.
Third Parties, this index
Voidable transactions, application of law, CC 3439.12
Warranties, this index
Wholesalers, generally, this index
Written instruments, authority of agent, CC 2309

AGREEMENTS
Contracts, generally, this index

AGRICULTURAL ASSOCIATIONS AND SOCIETIES
District agricultural associations, nuisances, agricultural activities or facilities operations, CC 3482.5
Nuisances, agricultural activities or facilities operations, CC 3482.5

AGRICULTURAL COMMODITIES
Agricultural Products, generally, this index

AGRICULTURAL CONSERVATION EASEMENTS
Conservation Easements, generally, this index

I-7

AGRICULTURAL

AGRICULTURAL COOPERATIVE ASSOCIATIONS
Labor liens, **CC 3061.6**

AGRICULTURAL LABOR AND EMPLOYMENT
Actions and proceedings, debt for work, **CC 3061.6**
Attachment, foreclosure of lien, **CC 3061.6**
Bonds (officers and fiduciaries), compensation and salaries, **CC 3061.5**
Compensation and salaries, liens and incumbrances, **CC 3061.5, 3061.6**
Foreclosure of lien, **CC 3061.6**
Joinder of parties, liens, **CC 3061.6**
Liens and incumbrances, **CC 3061.5, 3061.6**
  Threshermen, **CC 3061**
Limited partnership, liens and incumbrances, **CC 3061.5, 3061.6**
Threshermen liens, **CC 3061**
Time, liens and incumbrances, **CC 3061.6**

AGRICULTURAL LAND
Charities, gleaning of agricultural products, immunity from damage actions, **CC 846.2**
Conservation Easements, generally, this index
Easements. Conservation Easements, generally, this index
Eminent domain, temporary entry, repairs, **CC 1002**
Gleaning, agricultural products, charitable purposes, immunity from damage actions, **CC 846.2**
Leases,
  Duration, **CC 717**
  Term of hiring, presumption, **CC 1943**
Privileges and immunities, damage actions, invitees, gleaning of farm products, **CC 846.2**
Transfers, notice, **CC 1103.4**

AGRICULTURAL MACHINERY AND EQUIPMENT
Crimes and offenses, farm machinery repair shops, **CC 1718**
Estimated price for labor and parts, repairs, **CC 1718**
Invoice, farm machinery repair shop, **CC 1718**
Labor cost, repairs, invoice, **CC 1718**
Repairs, farm machinery repair shop, **CC 1718**

AGRICULTURAL PEST CONTROL
Pest Control, generally, this index

AGRICULTURAL PRODUCTS
Air Pollution, generally, this index
Attachment, foreclosure of labor lien, **CC 3061.6**
Bulk grain storage, **CC 1880 et seq.**
  Private bulk grain storage, generally, post
Buyer in ordinary course of business, lien of labor, **CC 3061.5**
Conflict of laws, processing activities, nuisances, **CC 3482.6**

AGRICULTURAL PRODUCTS—Cont'd
Crimes and offenses, private bulk grain storage, **CC 1881.1**
Evidence, private bulk grain storage, bill of sale, **CC 1880.9**
Grocery stores, point of sale systems, **CC 7100 et seq.**
Harvesting, liens and incumbrances, **CC 3061.5, 3061.6**
Landlord and tenant, **CC 1940.10**
Liens and incumbrances, harvesting or transporting, **CC 3061.5, 3061.6**
Markets and marketing, labor liens, deposits in court, **CC 3061.6**
Nuisance, processing activities, **CC 3482.6**
Pest Control, generally, this index
Point of sale systems, grocery stores, **CC 7100 et seq.**
Presumptions, nuisances, processing activities, **CC 3482.6**
Private bulk grain storage, **CC 1880 et seq.**
  Bill of sale, **CC 1880.4 et seq.**
  Crimes and offenses, **CC 1881.1**
  Delivery, bill of sale, endorsement, **CC 1880.8**
  Depositary, status, **CC 1881.2**
  Endorsement, bill of sale, delivery, **CC 1880.8**
  Evidence, bill of sale, **CC 1880.9**
  Fines and penalties, **CC 1881.1**
  Forms,
    Bill of sale, **CC 1880.4, 1880.5**
    Notice of sale, **CC 1880.7**
  Marking, **CC 1880.2**
  Sale, **CC 1880.3**
    Notice, **CC 1880.7**
  Storage after delivery date, **CC 1881**
  Title to property, bill of sale, **CC 1880.6**
Processors,
  Nuisances, **CC 3482.6**
  Presumptions, nuisances, **CC 3482.6**
Sales, private bulk grain storage, **CC 1880.3**
Severance, growing crops, **CC 658, 660**
Storage. Private bulk grain storage, generally, ante
Zoning and planning, processing activities, nuisances, **CC 3482.6**

AGRICULTURAL VEHICLES
Agricultural Machinery and Equipment, generally, this index

AGRICULTURE
Animals, generally, this index
Easements, grazing and pasture rights, **CC 801, 802**
Employment. Agricultural Labor and Employment, generally, this index
Facilities, nuisances, **CC 3482.5**
Grazing rights, easements, **CC 801, 802**
Labor and employment. Agricultural Labor and Employment, generally, this index

AGRICULTURE—Cont'd
Land. Agricultural Land, generally, this index
Livestock. Animals, generally, this index
Machinery. Agricultural Machinery and Equipment, generally, this index
Notice,
  Homeowners, agricultural activities, **CC 3482.5**
  Private bulk grain storage, sale, **CC 1880.7**
Nuisance, activities, operations, facilities, **CC 3482.5**
Pasturage rights, easements, **CC 801, 802**
Pest Control, generally, this index
Products. Agricultural Products, generally, this index
Real estate. Agricultural Land, generally, this index
Zoning and Planning, generally, this index

AIDERS AND ABETTORS
Accomplices and Accessories, generally, this index

AIDS
HIV, generally, this index

AIR CONDITIONING
Community apartments, defects, disclosure, **CC 1134**
Consumer warranties, component parts, application of law, **CC 1795.1**
Stock cooperatives, defects, disclosure, **CC 1134**

AIR EASEMENTS
Generally, **CC 801**

AIR FORCE
Military Forces, generally, this index

AIR POLLUTION
Fees, certificate of compliance, conditional sales contracts, required information, **CC 2982**
Gasoline vapor control, service stations, marketing operations, **CC 1952.8**
Leases, service stations, gasoline vapor control systems, marketing operations, **CC 1952.8**
Motor vehicles,
  Gasoline, vapor control, **CC 1952.8**
  Service stations, gasoline vapor control systems, marketing operations, **CC 1952.8**
Service stations, gasoline vapor control systems, marketing operations, **CC 1952.8**

AIR RAID SHELTERS
Privileges and immunities, political subdivisions, **CC 1714.5**

AIRCRAFT
Airports and Landing Fields, generally, this index
Blind or visually impaired persons,
  Access to public conveyances, **CC 54 et seq.**

ANIMALS

AIRCRAFT—Cont'd
Blind or visually impaired persons—Cont'd
  Civil rights, CC 54.1
Damages, guide dogs accompanying blind person or trainer, CC 54.2
Deaf persons, public accommodations, CC 54.1 et seq.
Disabled persons,
  Access to public conveyances, CC 54 et seq.
  Civil rights, CC 54.1
Dogs, disabled persons, CC 54.1
Financial responsibility, private property, CC 846
Guide dogs, accompanying blind persons for training purposes, access, CC 54.1 et seq.
Installment sales, contracts, application of law, CC 1801.4
Landing fields. Airports and Landing Fields, generally, this index
Liability, personal injuries, private property, CC 846
Negligence, private property, CC 846
Personal injuries, liability, private property, CC 846
Unmanned aircraft, emergencies, interference, damages, CC 43.101
Warnings, liability, private property, CC 846

AIRPORTS AND LANDING FIELDS
Condominiums, declarations, disclosure, CC 4255
Deeds and conveyances, disclosure, CC 1103.4
Legal description, declarations, CC 4250
Real estate, transfers, disclosure, CC 1103.4

AIRSPACE
Invasion of privacy, CC 1708.8

ALCOHOLIC BEVERAGES
Attorney fees, injunctions, CC 3496
Beer manufacturers, nuisance status, CC 3482.6
Brandy, voidable transactions, application of law, CC 3440.1
Children and minors, social hosts, liability, CC 1714
Costs, injunction, CC 3496
Damages, liability of social hosts, CC 1714
Injunction, costs, CC 3496
Liability, social hosts, CC 1714
Nuisance, beer manufacturers and bottlers, nuisance status, CC 3482.6
Privileges and immunities, social hosts, CC 1714
Social hosts, liability, CC 1714
Wine,
  Nuisance, production, CC 3482.6
  Voidable transactions, application of law, CC 3440.1
Wine bottlers, nuisance, CC 3482.6

ALIENATION
Deeds and Conveyances, generally, this index

ALIENATION OF AFFECTIONS
Generally, CC 43.5
Foster children, CC 43.56

ALIENISTS
Psychiatrists and Psychiatry, generally, this index

ALIENS
Noncitizens, generally, this index

ALLERGIES
Epinephrine Auto Injectors, generally, this index

ALLEYS
Streets and Alleys, generally, this index

ALLUVION
Accession, Accretion and Avulsion, generally, this index

ALTERATION OF INSTRUMENTS
Contracts, this index

ALTERNATE RATES FOR ENERGY (CARE) PROGRAM
Generally, CC 798.43.1

ALTERNATIVE DISPUTE RESOLUTION
Arbitration and Award, generally, this index
Mediation, generally, this index

ALTERNATIVE OBLIGATIONS
Generally, CC 1448 et seq.

AMBASSADORS AND CONSULS
Acknowledgments, authorization to take, CC 1183
Agents and agencies, acknowledgments, CC 1183

AMBULANCES
Contractors, disclosure, CC 3273
Disclosure, contractors, CC 3273
Identity and identification, contractors, CC 3273

AMERICAN INDIANS
Indigenous Peoples, generally, this index

AMERICANS WITH DISABILITIES ACT
Unruh Civil Rights Act, violations, CC 51

AMMUNITION
Designs and designers, negligence, CC 1714
Distribution, negligence, CC 1714
Forcible entry and detainer, CC 3485
Markets and marketing, negligence, CC 1714
Negligence, designs and designers, distribution, markets and marketing, CC 1714

AMORTIZATION
Rent control expenses, landlords, CC 1947.15

AMUSEMENTS
Blind or visually impaired persons, civil rights, CC 54.1

AMUSEMENTS—Cont'd
Theaters and Shows, generally, this index

ANAPHYLACTIC REACTIONS
Epinephrine Auto Injectors, generally, this index

ANATOMICAL GIFTS
Registry, donate life California organ and tissue donor registry, drivers licenses, electronic devices and equipment, CC 1798.90.1
Tissue Banks, generally, this index

ANCESTRY
Deeds and conveyances, restrictions, CC 53
Discrimination, generally, this index

ANIMAL CONTROL OFFICERS
Landlord and tenant, termination, abandoned or unclaimed property, involuntary deposits, notice, CC 1816
Leases, termination, abandoned or unclaimed property, involuntary deposits, notice, CC 1816
Mortgages, foreclosure, abandoned or unclaimed property, involuntary deposits, notice, CC 1816

ANIMAL SHELTERS
Generally, CC 1815 et seq.
Notice, gratuitous depositaries, CC 1846

ANIMAL SLAUGHTERING
Prices, horses, notice, public auctions or sales, CC 1834.8

ANIMALS
Abandoned or unclaimed property,
  Care facility, CC 1834.5
  Involuntary deposits, CC 1815 et seq.
  Running at large, generally, post
Actions and proceedings,
  Dog bites, CC 3342.5
  Killing or injuring, CC 3341
  Tests, alternatives, CC 1834.9
Adoption,
  Euthanasia, running at large, CC 1834.4
  Running at large, euthanasia, CC 1834.4
Advertising, breeding, pedigree, CC 3064.1
Assignments, livestock service liens, CC 3080.22
Attorney fees,
  Injunction, tests, alternatives, CC 1834.9
  Service liens, CC 3080.01
Bailment, CC 1887
Blind or visually impaired persons. Service Animals, generally, this index
Breeding animals, liens for services, CC 3062 et seq.
Cats, generally, this index
Control officers. Animal Control Officers, generally, this index
Costs, injunction, tests, alternatives, CC 1834.9

I-9

ANIMALS

ANIMALS—Cont'd
Court orders, livestock service liens, **CC 3080.06 et seq.**
Cruelty, motion pictures, **CC 3504 et seq.**
Damages,
  Exemplary damages, **CC 3340**
  Injuries by, **CC 3341**
  Injuries to, **CC 3340**
Deaf or hard of hearing persons. Service Animals, generally, this index
Declawing, landlord and tenant, **CC 1942.7**
Depositories, involuntary deposits, running at large, **CC 1815 et seq.**
Deposits for hire of animals, **CC 1853**
Devocalizing, landlord and tenant, **CC 1942.7**
Disabled persons. Service Animals, generally, this index
Dogs, generally, this index
Estrays. Running at large, generally, post
Euthanasia, running at large, adoption, **CC 1834.4**
Exemplary damages for injuries, **CC 3340**
Exemptions, tests, alternatives, **CC 1834.9**
Fences, generally, this index
Fines and penalties, tests, alternatives, **CC 1834.9**
Fish and Game, generally, this index
Game. Fish and Game, generally, this index
Gratuitous depositaries, notice, **CC 1846**
Horses, generally, this index
Injunction, tests, alternatives, **CC 1834.9**
Injuring. Killing or injuring, generally, post
Involuntary deposits, running at large, **CC 1815 et seq.**
Judgments and decrees, service liens, reducing claim to judgment, **CC 3080.02**
Killing or injuring,
  Exemplary damages, **CC 3340**
  Motion pictures, **CC 3504 et seq.**
  Other animals, liability of owner, **CC 3341**
Leases, termination, abandoned or unclaimed property, involuntary deposits, **CC 1815 et seq.**
Legal Estates Principal and Income Law, **CC 731 et seq.**
Liens and incumbrances,
  Breeding animals, **CC 3062 et seq.**
  Service liens, generally, post
Loan for use, treatment, **CC 1887**
Lost or destroyed property, duties and compensation of finder, **CC 2080**
Manufacturers and manufacturing, tests, alternatives, **CC 1834.9**
Medical research, tests, alternatives, **CC 1834.9**
Mobilehomes and mobilehome parks, pets, fees, **CC 798.33**
Mortgages, foreclosure, abandoned or unclaimed property, involuntary deposits, **CC 1815 et seq.**
Motion pictures, killing of or cruelty to, **CC 3504 et seq.**

ANIMALS—Cont'd
Notice, gratuitous depositaries, **CC 1846**
Nuisance, agriculture, **CC 3482.5**
Orders of court, livestock service liens, **CC 3080.06 et seq.**
Ownership, **CC 655**
Pest Control, generally, this index
Pets, generally, this index
Proceedings. Actions and proceedings, generally, ante
Public policy, euthanasia, running at large, adoption, **CC 1834.4**
Rewards, running at large, **CC 1845**
Riding, private property owner, liability for injuries, **CC 846**
Running at large,
  Adoption, euthanasia, **CC 1834.4**
  Euthanasia, adoption, **CC 1834.4**
  Involuntary deposits, **CC 1815 et seq.**
Sales. Service liens, post
Service Animals, generally, this index
Service liens, **CC 3080 et seq.**
  Application,
    Sales, court ordered sales, **CC 3080.03**
    Substitution of an undertaking, **CC 3080.09**
  Assignment, **CC 3080.22**
  Attorney fees, **CC 3080.01**
  Burden of proof, court ordered sales or substitutions of undertaking for livestock, **CC 3080.15**
  Costs, actions to enforce liens, **CC 3080.01**
  Court orders, **CC 3080.06 et seq.**
  Evidence, **CC 3080.08**
    Burden of proof, court ordered sales or substitutions of undertaking for livestock, **CC 3080.15**
  Hearings, sales, court ordered sales, **CC 3080.06**
  Judgments and decrees, reducing claim to judgment, **CC 3080.02**
  Notice, sales, **CC 3080.04, 3080.17**
    Service of notice, **CC 3080.03**
  Objections, sales, notice of opposition, **CC 3080.05**
  Orders of court, **CC 3080.06 et seq.**
  Possession, retention of possession, **CC 3080.02, 3080.21**
  Priorities and preferences, **CC 3080.01**
    Sales, distribution of proceeds, **CC 3080.16**
  Publication, sales, notice of sale, **CC 3080.17**
  Release of interest by owner, **CC 3080.20**
  Release of livestock to owner, **CC 3080.10**
  Retaining possession, **CC 3080.21**
  Return of livestock to defendant, **CC 3080.07**
  Right to lien, **CC 3080.01**
  Rights and remedies, **CC 3080.02**
  Sales, **CC 3080.02 et seq., 3080.16**
    Application, **CC 3080.03**

ANIMALS—Cont'd
Service liens—Cont'd
  Sales—Cont'd
    Hearings, **CC 3080.06**
    Notice, **CC 3080.04, 3080.17**
    Objections, notice of opposition, **CC 3080.05**
    Proceeds, distribution, **CC 3080.16**
    Service of notice, sales, **CC 3080.03**
    Substitution of an undertaking, **CC 3080.09 et seq.**
    Sureties, substitution of an undertaking, **CC 3080.09 et seq.**
Strays. Running at large, generally, ante
Suits. Actions and proceedings, generally, ante
Tests, **CC 1834.9.3**
  Alternatives, **CC 1834.9**
  Venue, injunction, tests, alternatives, **CC 1834.9**
Veterinarians, generally, this index
Wild animals and birds. Fish and Game, generally, this index
Zoological Gardens, generally, this index

ANNUITIES
Mortgages, reverse mortgages, **CC 1923.2**
Shared appreciation loans, seniors, **CC 1917.320 et seq.**

ANONYMOUS WITNESS PROGRAM
Privileges and immunities, reports of crime, **CC 48.9**

ANSWER
Witnesses, generally, this index

ANTENNAS
Condominiums, **CC 4725**
  Business and commerce, **CC 6708**

ANTIDISCRIMINATION LAWS
Discrimination, generally, this index

ANTIHEART BALM STATUTE
Generally, **CC 43.5**

ANTITRUST ACT
Monopolies and Unfair Trade, generally, this index

APARTMENT HOUSES
See, also, Housing, generally, this index
Actions, lien of keepers, **CC 1861a**
Aged persons, discrimination, **CC 51.2**
Baggage, lien of keepers, **CC 1861a**
Bailment, **CC 1859 et seq.**
Building standards, water conservation, **CC 1101.1 et seq.**
Community apartments, **CC 4000 et seq.**
  Air conditioning, defects, disclosure, **CC 1134**
  Blanket incumbrances on subdivisions, notice, **CC 1133**
  Defects, disclosure, **CC 1134**
  Electrical defects, disclosure, **CC 1134**

APARTMENT HOUSES—Cont'd
Community apartments—Cont'd
Heating, defects, disclosure, **CC 1134**
Plumbing, defects, disclosure, **CC 1134**
Sale or lease, defect disclosure, **CC 1134**
Solar energy,
Applications, approval, **CC 714**
Restrictions, **CC 714.1**
Condominiums, generally, this index
Confidential or privileged information, rent control, **CC 1947.7**
Construction,
Aged persons, physical and social needs, **CC 51.2**
Lender, liability for defects, **CC 3434**
Cooperative Apartments, generally, this index
Deaf persons, public accommodations, **CC 54.1 et seq.**
Depository duties of keeper, baggage lien, **CC 1861a**
Discrimination, age discrimination, businesses selling or renting accommodations, **CC 51.2**
Elevators, posting notice, owner or agent for service of process or notice, **CC 1962.5**
Entry on property, water conservation, building standards, **CC 1101.5**
Eviction. Forcible Entry and Detainer, generally, this index
Excessive rent, refunds, **CC 1947.11**
Forcible Entry and Detainer, generally, this index
Foreign languages, leases, translations, **CC 1632**
Improvement and repair, loans, lenders liability for defects, **CC 3434**
Judgment, lien of keepers, enforcement, **CC 1861a**
Landlord and Tenant, generally, this index
Liens and incumbrances, **CC 1861a**
Loans,
Construction, lenders liability for defects, **CC 3434**
Repairs, lenders liability for defects, **CC 3434**
Low and Moderate Income Housing, generally, this index
Negligence, construction or repair, loans, lenders liability for defects, **CC 3434**
Notice, elevators, dumbwaiters and escalators, **CC 1962.5**
Order, lien of keepers, recovery of baggage or property, **CC 1861a**
Ordinances, rent control, **CC 1947.7 et seq.**
Party walls, easements, **CC 801**
Personal property, injury or loss, **CC 1859**
Pest Control, generally, this index
Property, injury or loss, **CC 1859**
Refunds, excessive rent, **CC 1947.11**
Rent, ordinances, **CC 1947.7 et seq.**
Senior citizen housing, establishment and preservation, **CC 51.2**

APARTMENT HOUSES—Cont'd
Solar energy, community apartments, applications, approval, **CC 714**
Spanish language, leases, translations, **CC 1632**
Translations, foreign languages, leases, **CC 1632**
Water conservation, building standards, **CC 1101.1 et seq.**

APOTHECARIES
Pharmacists, generally, this index

APPARATUS
Machinery and Equipment, generally, this index

APPEAL AND REVIEW
Civil Rights, this index
Condominiums, accounts and accounting, **CC 5500 et seq.**
Stay. Supersedeas or Stay, generally, this index
Supersedeas or Stay, generally, this index

APPEALS IN CRIMINAL PROSECUTIONS
Stories, felonies, sales, proceeds, **CC 2225**

APPLIANCES
Electronic Devices and Equipment, generally, this index
Mechanics Liens, generally, this index
Mobilehomes and mobilehome parks, warranties, **CC 1797 et seq.**
Service contracts, **CC 1790 et seq.**
Song Beverly Consumer Warranty Act, **CC 1790 et seq.**
Warranties, service contracts, **CC 1790 et seq.**

APPRAISAL AND APPRAISERS
Motor vehicles, leases, termination, disposition of vehicle, **CC 2987**
Real Estate, this index

APPROPRIATION OF WATER
Water Appropriation, generally, this index

AQUATIC ORGANISMS
Fish and Game, generally, this index

ARBITRATION AND AWARD
Computer aided transcription system, **CC 54.8**
Condominiums, this index
Construction contracts, public agencies, disputes, **CC 1670**
Consumer credit, purchases, limitation of actions, **CC 1788.56**
Deaf or hard of hearing persons, listening systems, **CC 54.8**
Easements, cost of maintenance and repair, **CC 845**
Hearing devices, **CC 54.8**
Home equity sales contracts, representatives, equity purchasers liability, **CC 1695.16**
Informal dispute settlement, nonconforming new motor vehicles, **CC 1793.22**

ARBITRATION AND AWARD—Cont'd
Judicial arbitration, easements, maintenance and repairs, **CC 845**
Listening systems, **CC 54.8**
Medical records, disclosure, **CC 56.10**
Mobilehomes and mobilehome parks, dispute resolution, rules, **CC 798.25.5**
Nonconforming new motor vehicles, qualified third party dispute resolution process, **CC 1793.22**
Public agencies, construction contracts, disputes, **CC 1670**
Qualified third party dispute resolution, nonconforming new motor vehicles, **CC 1793.22**
Suretyship and guaranty, arbitration awards against principal alone, conclusiveness against surety, **CC 2855**
Third party dispute resolution process, motor vehicle warranties, new motor vehicle warranties, **CC 1793.22**
Transcription system, computer aided, **CC 54.8**

ARCHITECTS
Consolidated cities and counties, contracts, indemnity, **CC 2782.8**
Districts, contracts, indemnity, **CC 2782.8**
Joint powers authorities, contracts, indemnity, **CC 2782.8**
Landscape Architects, generally, this index
Liens and incumbrances. Mechanics Liens, generally, this index
Mechanics Liens, generally, this index
Municipalities, contracts, indemnity, **CC 2782.8**
Privileges and immunities, referral services, **CC 43.95**
Public authorities, contracts, indemnity, **CC 2782.8**
Public corporations, contracts, indemnity, **CC 2782.8**
Referral services, limitation of liability, **CC 43.95**
Schools and school districts, contracts, indemnity, **CC 2782.8**
Telecommunications, referral services, immunity, **CC 43.95**

AREIAS CREDIT CARD FULL DISCLOSURE ACT
Generally, **CC 1748.10 et seq.**

AREIAS RETAIL INSTALLMENT ACCOUNT FULL DISCLOSURE ACT
Generally, **CC 1810.20 et seq.**

AREIAS ROBBINS CHARGE CARD FULL DISCLOSURE ACT
Generally, **CC 1748.20 et seq.**

ARMED FORCES
Military Forces, generally, this index

ARMS
Weapons, generally, this index

ARMY

ARMY
Military Forces, generally, this index

ARREARAGES
Support, this index

ARREST
Booking, photography and pictures, commercial use, CC 1798.91.1
Consumer credit reporting agencies, CC 1786.18
Contempt, generally, this index
Courts, CC 43.54
False Imprisonment, generally, this index
Good faith, privileges and immunities, peace officers, CC 43.55
Labor and employment, records and recordation, copies, CC 1786.53
Photography and pictures, booking, commercial use, CC 1798.91.1
Privileges and immunities, peace officers, CC 43.55
Searches and Seizures, generally, this index

ARSON
Damages, CC 1714.9
Injuries, liability, CC 1714.9

ART AND ARTISTS
Actions and proceedings,
  Commissions, sale, original works, **CC 986**
  Defacement or destruction of art objects, **CC 987**
  Fine art multiples, sales, **CC 1745, 1745.5**
Agents, consignments, **CC 1738 et seq.**
Alteration, physical alteration or destruction, **CC 987**
  Injunction, artistic integrity, preservation, **CC 989**
Application of law,
  Consignment, **CC 1738.9**
  Fine prints, sales, **CC 1741**
Attachment, commissions, sale, original work, exemptions, **CC 986**
Attorney fees,
  Defacement or destruction of art objects, actions for damages, **CC 987**
  Fine art multiples, sales, **CC 1745**
  Injunctions, preserving artistic integrity, **CC 989**
  Royalties, actions for payment, **CC 986**
  Sales, royalties, **CC 986**
Authenticity, certificate of authenticity, sale of fine prints, **CC 1740 et seq.**
Bonds (officers and fiduciaries), injunction, preserving artistic integrity, **CC 989**
Certificate of authenticity, sale of fine prints, **CC 1740**
Charities, sales, fine art multiples, disclosure exemption, **CC 1742.6**
Commissions, sale, original works of fine art, **CC 986**
Common law copyrights, reproduction rights, transfer, **CC 982**

ART AND ARTISTS—Cont'd
Compensation and salaries, commissions, original works, sales, **CC 986**
Compositions in letters or art, ownership, **CC 980 et seq.**
Consignments,
  Fine art multiples, **CC 1740 et seq.**
  Regulation, **CC 1738 et seq.**
Contracts,
  Commissions, waiver, sales, original works, **CC 986**
  Consignments, **CC 1738 et seq.**
Conveyance of rights, ownership, **CC 988**
Copies, fine art multiples, sales, **CC 1740 et seq.**
Costs,
  Fine art multiples, sales, **CC 1745**
  Removal, artistic integrity, **CC 989**
Damages,
  Defacement or destruction of art objects, **CC 987**
  Fine art multiples, sales, **CC 1745, 1745.5**
Death of artist, royalties, sales, **CC 986**
Defacement or destruction, **CC 987**
  Injunction, artistic integrity, preservation, **CC 989**
Defenses, fine prints, sales, **CC 1744.7**
Delivery, consignment, **CC 1738.5**
Derivative works, ownership rights, **CC 988**
Descent and distribution, defacement or destruction of art objects, damages, **CC 987**
Destruction, art objects, injunction, preservation of artistic integrity, **CC 989**
Disclosure, fine prints, sales, **CC 1740 et seq.**
Displays, conveyances, ownership, **CC 988**
Express warranties, fine art prints, sales, **CC 1744.7**
Films, common law copyrights, reproduction rights, transfer, **CC 982**
Fine art, multiples, sale, disclosure, **CC 1740 et seq.**
Fine prints, sale, disclosure, **CC 1740 et seq.**
Fines and penalties, multiples, sales, **CC 1745.5**
Framing, defacement or destruction, gross negligence, **CC 987**
Galleries, consignment, **CC 1738 et seq.**
Glass, original works in, sales, royalties, **CC 986**
Injunction,
  Artistic integrity preservation, **CC 989**
  Defacement or destruction of art objects, **CC 987**
  Fine art multiples, sales, **CC 1745.5**
Integrity of cultural, artistic creations, preservation, **CC 989**
Joint ownership, products, **CC 981**
Lawsuits. Actions and proceedings, generally, ante
Limitation of actions,
  Fine art multiples, sales, **CC 1745**

ART AND ARTISTS—Cont'd
Limitation of actions—Cont'd
  Injunctions, preserving artistic integrity, **CC 989**
Malicious mischief, defacement or destruction of fine art, **CC 987**
Multiples, sales, disclosure, **CC 1740 et seq.**
Mutilation, defacement or destruction, **CC 987**
  Injunction, artistic integrity, preservation, **CC 989**
Negligence, restoration or framing, defacement or destruction caused by gross negligence, **CC 987**
Notice, removal from real property, preserving artistic integrity, **CC 989**
Original work of authorship, ownership, **CC 980 et seq.**
Ownership, **CC 980 et seq.**
  Conveyance of rights, **CC 988**
Porcelain painting, **CC 997**
Preservation, **CC 987**
  Cultural and artistic creations, **CC 989**
Prints, sale, disclosure, **CC 1740 et seq.**
Privileges and immunities, fine prints, sales, **CC 1744.7**
Proceedings. Actions and proceedings, generally, ante
Property rights, conveyances, ownership, **CC 988**
Publication, **CC 983**
Religious artifacts, security interests for consumer credit contracts, **CC 1799.97**
Removal from real property, integrity preservation, **CC 989**
Reproductions,
  Multiples, fine prints, sales, **CC 1740 et seq.**
  Ownership rights, **CC 988**
  Right of reproduction, **CC 982**
Restoration, defacement or destruction, gross negligence, **CC 987**
Royalties, sales, **CC 986**
Sales,
  Commissions, original works of fine art, **CC 986**
  Common law copyrights, reproduction rights, **CC 982**
  Consignment, **CC 1738 et seq.**
  Multiples, fine prints, **CC 1740 et seq.**
Stained glass artistry, considered as fine art, **CC 997**
Subsequent or original producers, **CC 984**
Suits. Actions and proceedings, generally, ante
Transfer of ownership, **CC 982**
Waiver,
  Commissions, sale, original works, **CC 986**
  Consignment, **CC 1738.8**
  Defacement or destruction, damages, **CC 987**
Warranties, fine art prints, sales, **CC 1744.7**
Witness fees, experts, preserving artistic integrity, **CC 989**

ATTORNEY

ARTERY BANKS
Tissue Banks, generally, this index

ARTICHOKES
Agricultural Products, generally, this index

ARTISANS
Mechanics Liens, generally, this index

ARTISTS
Art and Artists, generally, this index

AS IS SALES
Mobilehomes and mobilehome parks, disclosure, waiver, CC 1102.1

ASBESTOS
See, also, Mines and Minerals, generally, this index
Consumer information, booklets, costs, CC 2079.11
Costs, consumer information booklets, CC 2079.11
Disclosure, real estate transfers, CC 2079.7
Notice, real estate transfers, CC 2079.7
Real estate brokers and salespersons, notice, CC 2079.7

ASEXUAL PERSONS
Sexual Orientation, generally, this index

ASSAULT AND BATTERY
Domestic Violence, generally, this index
Privacy, CC 1708.8
Protection, CC 43
Sexual Assault, generally, this index

ASSEMBLY
Actions and proceedings, condominiums, CC 4515
Condominiums, CC 4515
Stalking, CC 1708.7

ASSESSMENTS
Condominiums, this index
Consumer protection, Internet, children and minors, CC 1798.99.31
  Time, CC 1798.99.33
Supplemental tax assessments. Tax Assessments, this index
Tax Assessments, generally, this index

ASSIGNATION
Prostitution, generally, this index

ASSIGNMENT FOR BENEFIT OF CREDITORS
Change of possession, transfer of personal property, void as against creditors, CC 3440 et seq.
Transfer of personal property not accompanied by immediate delivery, CC 3440 et seq.

ASSIGNMENTS
Generally, CC 1039 et seq.
Animals, livestock service liens, CC 3080.22

ASSIGNMENTS—Cont'd
Business premises, lease, right to occupy, CC 1954.05
Campgrounds, membership camping contracts, CC 1812.308
Celebrity image protection, CC 3344.1
Change of possession, transfer of property, void as to creditors, CC 3440 et seq.
Compensation and Salaries, this index
Condominiums, assessments, collections, CC 5735
  Business and commerce, CC 6826
Contracts, CC 1457 et seq.
  Sale of land, CC 2985.1
Dance studio services contracts, CC 1812.56
Deceased celebrity image protection, CC 3344.1
Deeds and conveyances, contracts for sale of land, CC 2985.1
Defense to assigned instruments, CC 1459
Discount buying services, cutting off right of action, CC 1812.114
Forcible entry and detainer,
  Drugs and medicine, nuisance, CC 3486
  Weapons, CC 3485
Health studio services, contracts, CC 1812.88
Installment Sales, this index
Landlord and Tenant, this index
Leases, this index
Liens and incumbrances, vehicles, labor or materials, CC 3069
Livestock service liens, CC 3080.22
Motor Vehicles, this index
Nonnegotiable instruments, CC 1459
  Notice, sale of business, CC 955, 955.1
Power of sale of real property to secure payment, CC 2932.5
Profits, real estate, recordation, perfection of security interests, CC 2938
Records and recordation,
  Mortgages, CC 2938
  Power of sale, real estate, CC 2932.5
Rent, this index
Seller assisted marketing plans, CC 1812.211
Valuation of rent, leased business premises, holding over, CC 1954.05
Veterans, benefits, monopolies and unfair trade, CC 1770
Written instruments, CC 1459

ASSISTANCE
Social Services, generally, this index

ASSISTED HOUSING
Low and Moderate Income Housing, generally, this index

ASSISTED REPRODUCTION
Actions and proceedings, crimes and offenses, CC 1708.5.6
Damages, crimes and offenses, CC 1708.5.6

ASSOCIATIONS AND SOCIETIES
Charities, generally, this index

ASSOCIATIONS AND SOCIETIES—Cont'd
Corporation Taxes, generally, this index
Injunction, breach of contract with members, CC 3423
Interest, personal injury damages, CC 3291
Medical specialty societies, committee members, privileges and immunities, CC 43.7
Membership camping contracts, CC 1812.300 et seq.
Partnership, generally, this index
Personal injury damages, interest, CC 3291
Personal Property Brokers, generally, this index
Restaurants, generally, this index
Savings Associations, generally, this index
Small Businesses, generally, this index

ASTAIRE CELEBRITY IMAGE PROTECTION ACT
Generally, CC 3344.1

ASYLUMS
Mental Health, generally, this index

ATHLETICS
Astaire Celebrity Image Protection Act, CC 3344.1
Autographed memorabilia, warranties, CC 1739.7
Health Studios, generally, this index
Invasion of privacy, use of name, likeness, voice, signature, without consent, CC 3344
Memorabilia, autographed, warranties, CC 1739.7

ATOMIC WAR
War and Civil Defense, generally, this index

ATTACHMENT
See, also, Recorders, generally, this index
Art and artists, commissions, sale, original work, CC 986
Credit services organizations, deposits, CC 1789.24
Discount buying services, deposits in lieu of bonds, claims, CC 1812.105
Mechanics liens, CC 8468
Seller assisted marketing plans, deposits in lieu of bonds, claims, CC 1812.221
Voidable transactions, CC 3439.07

ATTORNEY FEES
See, also, Costs, generally, this index
Advertisements, deceased celebrity image protection, CC 3344.1
Alcoholic beverages, injunction, CC 3496
Art and Artists, this index
Assignation, injunction, CC 3496
Audio and video recordings, invasion of privacy, CC 1708.85
Autographed memorabilia, warranties, CC 1739.7
Automated license plate recognition, CC 1798.90.54

I-13

ATTORNEY

ATTORNEY FEES—Cont'd
Balloon payments, mortgages, trust deeds, notice, **CC 2924i**
Blanket incumbrances on subdivisions, action for failure to notify buyers or lessees, **CC 1133**
Blind or visually impaired persons,
    Civil rights, **CC 54.3**
    Injunction, public accommodations, **CC 55**
Booking photographs, commercial use, **CC 1798.91.1**
Buildings, construction defects, supersedeas or stay, prelitigation proceedings, noncompliance, **CC 930**
Business and commerce,
    Discrimination, **CC 52**
    Personal information, direct marketing, disclosure, **CC 1798.84**
Business records, disclosure, civil actions, **CC 1799.2**
Celebrity image protection, **CC 3344.1**
Civil rights, **CC 52, 52.1**
    Disabled persons, construction, accessibility, **CC 55.55**
Compromise and settlement, **CC 1717**
Condominiums, this index
Conservation easements, enforcement, **CC 815.7**
Consumer Credit, this index
Consumer Credit Reporting Agencies, this index
Consumer protection, **CC 1780, 3345**
Contracts,
    Actions and proceedings, **CC 1717**
    Book accounts, **CC 1717.5**
    Dating service contracts, **CC 1694.4**
    Endless chain schemes, **CC 1689.2**
    Foreign languages, translations, **CC 1632**
    Sale of land, Subdivision Map Act, noncompliance, **CC 2985.51**
    Spanish language, translations, **CC 1632**
    Weight loss contracts, **CC 1694.9**
Controlled escrows, real estate developers, **CC 2995**
Credit,
    Discrimination, marital status or sex, **CC 1812.34**
    Identity and identification, theft, **CC 1785.20.3**
Credit Cards, this index
Credit services organizations, actions and proceedings, **CC 1789.21**
Cruelty to or killing of human beings or animals, motion pictures, **CC 3507.4**
Dance studio contracts, **CC 1812.62**
Dating service contracts, violations, **CC 1694.4**
Deaf or hard of hearing persons, civil rights, **CC 54.3, 55**
Dealerships, **CC 86**
Debt settlement providers, fair debt settlement, **CC 1788.305**

ATTORNEY FEES—Cont'd
Deceased celebrity image protection, **CC 3344.1**
Defacement of property by minor, willful misconduct, imputed liability, **CC 1714.1**
Deposits, contracts, interest, **CC 1717**
Disclosure,
    Business records, civil actions, **CC 1799.2**
    Personal or confidential information, Information Practices Act, **CC 1798.46, 1798.48, 1798.53**
Discount buying services, damages, **CC 1812.123**
Discrimination, this index
Easements,
    Conservation easements, enforcement, **CC 815.7**
    Greenways, **CC 816.62**
Endless chain schemes, contracts, rescission, **CC 1689.2**
Entry on property, recreational trails, **CC 846.1**
Fine art multiples, sales, **CC 1745**
Fixtures erroneously affixed to land, removal, **CC 1013.5**
Floating homes, marinas, **CC 800.200**
Foreign languages, contracts, translations, **CC 1632**
Gambling, injunction, **CC 3496**
Gender violence, actions and proceedings, **CC 52.4**
Genetic testing, privacy, **CC 56.182**
Health services, contracts, violations, **CC 1812.94**
Home equity sales contracts, **CC 1695.7**
    Rescission, unconscionable advantage, **CC 1695.14**
Human trafficking, **CC 52.5**
    Injunction, **CC 3496**
Improvements, design professionals, **CC 3320**
    Subconsultants, **CC 3321**
Indebtedness, duress or coercion, **CC 1798.97.2, 1798.97.3**
Independent wholesale sales representatives, contracts, **CC 1738.16**
Information Practices Act, **CC 1798.46, 1798.48, 1798.53**
Installment Sales, this index
Internet, threats, orders of court, social media, **CC 1798.99.22**
Invasion of privacy, Information Practices Act, **CC 1798.53**
Job listing services, **CC 1812.523**
Landlord and Tenant, this index
Legal Estates Principal and Income Law, **CC 731.15**
Lewdness and obscenity, electronic transmissions, images, **CC 1708.88**
Libel and slander, abuse of children, dismissal of action, **CC 48.7**
Livestock service liens, enforcement, **CC 3080.01**

ATTORNEY FEES—Cont'd
Loans, identity and identification, theft, **CC 1785.20.3**
Malicious destruction of property, construction sites, treble damages, **CC 1721**
Marinas, floating homes, **CC 800.200**
Markets and marketing, Internet, disclosure, **CC 1749.8.4**
Mechanics Liens, this index
Medical Records, this index
Membership camping contracts, actions, **CC 1812.306**
Memorabilia, autographs, warranties, **CC 1739.7**
Mines and minerals,
    Lessees, liability, **CC 883.140**
    Termination actions, **CC 883.250**
Mobilehomes and Mobilehome Parks, this index
Mortgages, this index
Motion pictures,
    Invasion of privacy, **CC 1708.85**
    Killing of or cruelty to human beings or animals, **CC 3507.4**
Motor Vehicles, this index
Names, deceased celebrity image protection, **CC 3344.1**
Notice, intent to preserve interest in real property, slandering title, records and recordation, **CC 880.360**
Obscenity, injunction, **CC 3496**
Orders, crimes and offenses, stories by felons, sales, **CC 2225**
Payment processors, fair debt settlement, **CC 1788.305**
Prescription drug claims processor, reports, failure to file, **CC 2528**
Prevailing party, **CC 1717**
Privacy, invasion of privacy, altered depictions, lewdness and obscenity, **CC 1708.86**
Private schools, buildings and grounds, access, interference, obstructions, threats, **CC 1708.9**
Prostitution, injunction, **CC 3496**
Quieting title, slander, **CC 880.360**
Real Estate, this index
Records and recordation, slandering title, **CC 880.360**
Recreational vehicles, park tenants, occupants or residents, **CC 799.78**
Rent, skimming actions, **CC 891**
Rental purchase agreements, entitlement of consumers, **CC 1812.636**
Residential hotels, short term occupancies, **CC 1940.1**
School buildings and grounds, access, interference, obstructions, threats, **CC 1708.9**
Sex, force and violence, actions and proceedings, **CC 52.4**
Sexual assault, personal information, victim service providers, grants, injunction, **CC 1798.79.95**

AUDIO

ATTORNEY FEES—Cont'd
Sexual harassment, CC 52
Sexual orientation, CC 52.45
Slandering title, CC 880.360
Social media, threats, orders of court, CC 1798.99.22
Solar energy, CC 714
Spanish language, contracts, translations, CC 1632
Stalking, personal information, victim service providers, grants, injunction, CC 1798.79.95
State Agencies, this index
Student loans, private education lenders and loan collectors, actions and proceedings, CC 1788.208
Subcontractors, construction, reimbursement, defense fees and costs, CC 2782.05
Subcutaneous implantation, identification devices, CC 52.7
Title to property, slandering title, CC 880.360
Trade secrets, misappropriation, bad faith, CC 3426.4
Trust Deeds, this index
Vandalism, actions, treble damages, CC 1721
Warranties, breach of warranty, Song Beverly Consumer Warranty Act, CC 1794, 1794.1
Weight loss contracts, CC 1694.9
Wholesalers, sales representatives, contracts, CC 1738.16

ATTORNEY GENERAL
Actions and proceedings, consumers, privacy, CC 1798.155
Civil Rights, this index
Consumers, privacy, CC 1798.150, 1798.155, 1798.185
Dance studio contracts, actions for violations, CC 1812.63
Disabled persons, civil rights, injunction, CC 55.1
Discount buying services, acknowledgments, CC 1812.101
Medical records, negligence, release, CC 56.36
Opinions, consumers, privacy, CC 1798.155
Rules and regulations, consumers, privacy, CC 1798.185

ATTORNEY IN FACT
Power of Attorney, generally, this index

ATTORNEYS
Acknowledgments, instruments, county counsel or city attorney, CC 1181
Actions and proceedings, conspiracy with client, actions against, CC 1714.10
Affidavits, generally, this index
Appeal and review, client civil conspiracy, CC 1714.10
Arrangers of credit, real estate transactions, application of law, CC 2957
Attorney General, generally, this index
Civil rights, disabled persons, construction, accessibility, demand letters, CC 55.32

ATTORNEYS—Cont'd
Clients, sexual harassment, CC 51.9
Collection agencies,
  Consumer debts, communication with debtor instead of attorney, CC 1788.14
  Legal or judicial process, communications simulating, CC 1788.16
Compensation and salaries. Attorney Fees, generally, this index
Conspiracy with client, pleadings alleging, CC 1714.10
Contracts. Attorney Fees, this index
Debt settlement providers, fair debt settlement, application of law, CC 1788.304
Debtors and creditors, legal or judicial process, communication simulating, CC 1788.16
Defenses, attorney client civil conspiracy, CC 1714.10
Disabled persons, high frequency litigants, construction, accessibility, CC 55.54
Discovery, generally, this index
District Attorneys, generally, this index
Evidence, conspiracy, attorney client civil conspiracy, CC 1714.10
Fees. Attorney Fees, generally, this index
Harassment, sexual harassment, clients, CC 51.9
Health care service plans, punitive damages, failure to provide notice, CC 3296
Income. Attorney Fees, generally, this index
Insurance, this index
Judges, generally, this index
Limitation of actions, civil conspiracy, clients, tolling, CC 1714.10
Municipal Attorneys, generally, this index
Oil and gas pipelines, spills, CC 3333.5
Orders, conspiracy with client, pleading alleging, order allowing, CC 1714.10
Payment processors, fair debt settlement, application of law, CC 1788.304
Power of Attorney, generally, this index
Privileges and immunities,
  Referrals, CC 43.95
  State bar committee, CC 43.7, 43.8
Referrals,
  Limitation of liability, CC 43.95
  Nonprofit referral services, limitation of liability, CC 43.95
Sexual harassment, clients, CC 51.9
Waiver, conspiracy with client alleged, defense of failure to obtain order allowing pleading, CC 1714.10
Witnesses, generally, this index

ATTORNMENT
Grant of rents, reversions or remainders, CC 1111
Stranger, effect, CC 1948

ATTRACTIVE NUISANCE
Nuisance, generally, this index

AUCTIONS AND AUCTIONEERS
Generally, CC 1812.600 et seq.

AUCTIONS AND AUCTIONEERS—Cont'd
Abandoned or Unclaimed Property, this index
Actions and proceedings, CC 1812.600
Administrative fines. Fines and penalties, generally, post
Art and artists, commissions, sales, original works, CC 986
Attorney fees, CC 1812.600
Authority, CC 2362, 2363
Baggage and property of guests of apartment houses, CC 1861a
Bonds (officers and fiduciaries), CC 1812.600
Claims, CC 1812.600
Contracts, memoranda, binding on seller and bidder, CC 2363
Costs, actions and proceedings, CC 1812.600
Crimes and offenses, CC 1812.604, 1812.607, 1812.608
Deeds of trust, power of sale, exercise, CC 2924g
Deposits in lieu of bonds, CC 1812.600
Fines and penalties, CC 1812.600, 1812.604, 1812.607, 1812.608
Injunction, CC 1812.602
Internet, notice, CC 1812.610
Lost property, notice, publication expenses, payment prerequisite to vesting title in finder or successful bidder, CC 2080.3
Mobilehomes and mobilehome parks, personal property, removal, CC 798.36
Mortgages, power of sale, CC 2924g
Notice, CC 1812.610
  Bonds (officers and fiduciaries), CC 1812.600
Offenses. Crimes and offenses, generally, ante
Penalties. Fines and penalties, generally, ante
Power of sale in deed of trust or mortgage, exercise, CC 2924g
Powers and duties, CC 1812.605 et seq., 2362, 2363
Restitution, CC 1812.603
Rules and regulations, CC 2362
Trust deeds,
  Power of sale, exercise, CC 2924g
  Sales, attorneys authority to conduct for trustee, CC 2924a
Waiver, CC 1812.609

AUDIO AND VIDEO RECORDINGS
Attorney fees, invasion of privacy, CC 1708.85
Audits and auditors, royalties, CC 2500, 2501
Confidential or privileged information, invasion of privacy, CC 1708.85
Costs, invasion of privacy, CC 1708.85
Crimes and offenses, stories about felonies, sale proceeds, CC 2225
Fines and penalties, video recorder cassettes, sales and rental, disclosure of records, CC 1799.3
Invasion of privacy, CC 1708.8, 1708.85
Lewdness and Obscenity, generally, this index
Mobilehomes and mobilehome parks, collective meetings with homeowners, CC 798.53

I-15

AUDIO

AUDIO AND VIDEO RECORDINGS
—Cont'd
Music and musicians, royalties, audits and auditors, CC 2500, 2501
Obscenity. Lewdness and Obscenity, generally, this index
Original work of authorship, ownership, CC 980 et seq.
Pornography. Lewdness and Obscenity, generally, this index
Privacy,
   Invasion of privacy, CC 1708.8, 1708.85
   Rental or sales, disclosure records, fines, CC 1799.3
Rent, records and recordation, disclosure, CC 1799.3
Royalties, audits and auditors, CC 2500, 2501
Sales and rentals, disclosure of records, fines and penalties, CC 1799.3
Videoconferencing. Telecommunications, generally, this index

AUDITS AND AUDITORS
Audio and video recordings, royalties, CC 2500, 2501
Business records, bookkeeping services, disclosure, CC 1799 et seq.
Confidential or privileged information, tape recordings, royalties, CC 2501
Damages, business records, disclosure, CC 1799.2
Disclosure, business records, bookkeeping services, CC 1799 et seq.
Fees, tape recordings, royalties, CC 2501
Music and musicians, tape recordings, royalties, CC 2500, 2501
Royalties, tape recordings, CC 2500, 2501

AUNTS AND UNCLES
Relatives, generally, this index

AUTHORITIES
Architects, contracts, indemnity, CC 2782.8
Engineers, contracts, indemnity, CC 2782.8
Joint Powers Authorities, generally, this index
Landscape architects, contracts, indemnity, CC 2782.8
Surveys and surveyors, contracts, indemnity, CC 2782.8

AUTHORS
Ownership, original works, CC 980 et seq.

AUTO COURTS AND RESORTS
Hotels and Motels, generally, this index

AUTO INJECTORS
Epinephrine Auto Injectors, generally, this index

AUTOGRAPHED MEMORABILIA
Warranties, CC 1739.7

AUTOMATED LICENSE PLATE RECOGNITION
Generally, CC 1798.90.5 et seq.

AUTOMATED PEOPLE MOVERS
Elevators, Dumbwaiters and Escalators, generally, this index

AUTOMOBILE INSURANCE
Motor Vehicle Insurance, generally, this index

AUTOMOBILE SALES FINANCE ACT
Generally, CC 2981 et seq.

AUTOMOBILES
Motor Vehicles, generally, this index

AUTOMOTIVE CONSUMER NOTIFICATION ACT
Generally, CC 1793.23, 1793.24

AVENUES
Streets and Alleys, generally, this index

AVIATION
Aircraft, generally, this index

AVULSION
Accession, Accretion and Avulsion, generally, this index

AWARDS
Arbitration and Award, generally, this index

BABIES
Children and Minors, generally, this index

BACKGROUND CHECKS
Criminal History Information, generally, this index

BAD CHECKS
Negotiable Instruments, this index

BAD FAITH
Good Faith, generally, this index

BAGGAGE
Apartment house keepers, liens, CC 1861a
Buses, this index
Carriers, this index
Depositary for hire, liens, sale, CC 1857
Railroads, this index

BAILMENT
Generally, CC 1813 et seq., 1884 et seq., 1925 et seq., 1955 et seq.
Abandoned or unclaimed property, CC 2081 et seq.
Adverse claims, notice to beneficiary, CC 1825
Animals,
   Abandoned animals, care facilities, CC 1834.5
   Treatment, CC 1887
Apartment houses, CC 1859 et seq.
Apportionment, termination of hiring, CC 1935
Boarding and lodging houses, CC 1859 et seq.
Care required by bailee, CC 1886 et seq., 1928
   Gratuitous bailment, CC 1846

BAILMENT—Cont'd
Care required by bailee—Cont'd
   Storage, CC 1852
Charter party, ships and shipping, CC 1959
Claims, notice, CC 1825
Concealed defects, CC 1893
Consent, opening of fastened deposit, CC 1835
Coowners, delivery, CC 1827
Creation, CC 1813 et seq.
Damages,
   Indemnification, CC 1833
   Use of property for particular purpose, CC 1930
   Use of thing deposited, CC 1836
Death of party, termination of relationship, CC 1934
Debtors and creditors, deposits for exchange, CC 1878
Default, expenses, CC 1957
Defects, concealment, CC 1893
Delivery of property, CC 1955
   Demand, CC 1822 et seq.
   Joint tenants, CC 1827, 1828
   Place of delivery, CC 1824
Demand, return of article, CC 1822 et seq., 1895
Documents of Title, generally, this index
Duties, CC 1839
Expenses, CC 1956
   Default, CC 1957
   Freight and charges, storage until paid, CC 2081
   Indemnification, CC 1833
   Preservation, CC 1892
Fitness for use, CC 1955
Fraud, insurance coverage, CC 1858.2
Gratuitous, CC 1844 et seq.
Gross negligence, presumption, CC 1838
Hospitals, CC 1859 et seq.
Hotels and motels, CC 1859 et seq.
Indemnification for loss, CC 1833, 1894
Injury to property, liability, CC 1838
Insurance, customers' property left for alteration, repair, or sale, CC 1858 et seq.
Involuntary,
   Creation, CC 1815
   Duties, CC 1816
   Gratuitous, CC 1845
Joint tenants, delivery, CC 1827, 1828
Kinds, CC 1813
Liens and incumbrances, CC 1856, 1857
Limitation of liability, CC 1840
Loss of article,
   Indemnification, CC 1894
   Liability, CC 1838
Merger of interest, termination of relationship, CC 1933
Motels and motor courts, CC 1859 et seq.
Motor Vehicles, this index
Necessity of demand, return of article, CC 1823

I-16

BAILMENT—Cont'd
Negligence,
  Care required, **CC 1928**
  Limitation of liability, **CC 1840**
  Loss or injury to property, **CC 1838**
  Repairs, **CC 1889**
Notice,
  Adverse claim, **CC 1825**
  Detention of property from true owner, **CC 1826**
  Insurance coverage, **CC 1858 et seq.**
  Sale, **CC 1837**
  Wrongful detention, **CC 1826**
Obligations, **CC 1822 et seq.**
Parking lots and facilities, contracts, **CC 1630, 1630.5**
Perishable, sale, **CC 1837**
Place, return of article, **CC 1896, 1958**
Place of delivery, **CC 1824**
Presumptions, loss or injury to property, **CC 1838**
Purposes of use, **CC 1890**
Quiet enjoyment, **CC 1955**
Quiet possession, **CC 1927**
Relending, **CC 1891**
Repairs, **CC 1858 et seq., 1889, 1929, 1955**
  Receipts for goods, **CC 1858.1, 1858.2**
Rest homes, **CC 1859 et seq.**
Return of property, **CC 1894 et seq.**
  Time, **CC 1958**
Sanitariums, **CC 1859 et seq.**
Services, duties and liabilities, **CC 1839**
Ships and shipping, charter party, **CC 1959**
Storage, **CC 1851 et seq.**
  Care, degree required, **CC 1852**
  Freight and charges, payment, **CC 2081**
  Liens, **CC 1856, 1857**
  Motor vehicles, parking lots, contracts, **CC 1630, 1630.5**
  Termination, **CC 1854, 1855**
    Responsibility, **CC 2081.4**
Tenants in common, delivery, **CC 1827**
Termination of duties,
  Gratuitous bailment, **CC 1847**
  Storage, **CC 1854, 1855**
Termination of hiring, **CC 1931 et seq.**
Theft, parking lots and facilities, contracts, **CC 1630.5**
Time, return of property, **CC 1894, 1958**
Title to property, **CC 1885, 1926**
Unclaimed property, **CC 2081 et seq.**
Use of thing deposit, **CC 1835**
  Damages, **CC 1836**
Value of article, increase, **CC 1885**
Vehicle Leasing Act, **CC 2985.7 et seq.**
Wrongful detention, notice to true owner, **CC 1826**

BALLOON PAYMENTS
Installment sales, memorandum, subsequent purchases, **CC 1808.2, 1808.3**

BALLOON PAYMENTS—Cont'd
Notice, **CC 2924i**
Real estate, credit arrangers, disclosure, **CC 2956 et seq.**

BALLOT MEASURES
Initiative and Referendum, generally, this index

BANK AND CORPORATION TAXES
Corporation Taxes, generally, this index

BANK DEPOSITS AND COLLECTIONS
Abandoned or Unclaimed Property, generally, this index
Certificates of deposit, agricultural producers, satisfy wages, **CC 3061.5**
Checks, cashers, deferred deposits, **CC 1789.35**
  Licenses and permits, **CC 1789.37**
Crimes and offenses, stories of crime, proceeds, **CC 2225**
Debtors and creditors, offer of performance, notice, **CC 1500**
Deferred deposits, check cashers, **CC 1789.35**
  Licenses and permits, **CC 1789.37**
Electronic funds transfers. Funds Transfers, generally, this index
Funds Transfers, generally, this index
Garnishment, generally, this index
Joint account, **CC 683**
Liability, adverse claimants, customer property, limitations, **CC 3054**
Surety, agreement authorizing, **CC 2811**
Transfers. Funds Transfers, generally, this index
Unclaimed property. Abandoned or Unclaimed Property, generally, this index

BANKERS
Banks and Banking, generally, this index

BANKRUPTCY
Affirmation of debt, consumers, notice requirement, **CC 1788.14**
Consumer credit reports, contents of records, **CC 1785.13**
  Investigative reports, employment or insurance investigations, **CC 1786.18**
Debt collection, affirmation from bankrupt, **CC 1788.14**
Gift certificates, **CC 1749.6**
Seller assisted marketing plans, disclosure, **CC 1812.206**
Trusts and trustees,
  Recession, restoring record of title, **CC 1058.5**
  Restoring record title, **CC 1058.5**

BANKS AND BANKING
Abandoned or Unclaimed Property, generally, this index
Accounts and accounting,
  Condominiums, managers and management, **CC 5380**

BANKS AND BANKING—Cont'd
Accounts and accounting—Cont'd
  Funds Transfers, generally, this index
  Identity and identification, theft, **CC 1798.92 et seq.**
Agreements. Contracts, generally, post
Associations and societies. Savings Associations, generally, this index
Attorney fees, personal information, direct marketing, disclosure, **CC 1798.84**
Bills and notes. Negotiable Instruments, generally, this index
Borrowing. Loans, generally, post
Cards, debit cards, **CC 1748.30, 1748.31**
Clients, sexual harassment, **CC 51.9**
Collections. Bank Deposits and Collections, generally, this index
Construction loans, real or personal property, lenders liability for defects, **CC 3434**
Contracts,
  Bank holidays, performance, **CC 9**
  Foreign languages, translations, **CC 1632.5**
  Performance, Saturday or optional bank holiday, **CC 9**
Corporation Taxes, generally, this index
Costs, personal information, direct marketing, disclosure, **CC 1798.84**
Credit Cards, generally, this index
Credit Unions, generally, this index
Debit cards, **CC 1748.30, 1748.31**
Deposits. Bank Deposits and Collections, generally, this index
Direct marketing, personal information, disclosure, **CC 1798.83**
Disclosure,
  Home equity loan disclosure, **CC 2970, 2971**
  Personal information, direct marketing, **CC 1798.83**
Discount buying services, trust accounts, **CC 1812.116**
Electronic funds transfers. Funds Transfers, generally, this index
Filing, identity and identification, theft, **CC 1798.200 et seq.**
Fines and penalties,
  Contracts, foreign languages, translations, **CC 1632.5**
  Personal information, direct marketing, disclosure, **CC 1798.84**
Foreign languages, contracts, translations, **CC 1632.5**
Forms, contracts, foreign languages, translations, **CC 1632.5**
Funds Transfers, generally, this index
Harassment, sexual harassment, clients, **CC 51.9**
Holidays, optional bank holiday, transaction of business, **CC 7.1, 9**
Home equity loan disclosure, **CC 2970, 2971**
Housing loans, defects in property, lenders liability, **CC 3434**
Identity and identification, theft, filing, **CC 1798.200 et seq.**

BANKS

BANKS AND BANKING—Cont'd
Impound accounts, mortgages, interest, **CC 2954.8**
Improvement and repair of real or personal property, construction loans, lenders liability for defects in property, **CC 3434**
Interest,
  Impound accounts, **CC 2954.8**
  Variable rate, regulation, **CC 1916.6**
Letters of Credit, generally, this index
Liens and incumbrances, customer property, **CC 3054**
Loans,
  Extension of term, **CC 1916.5**
  Home equity loan disclosure, **CC 2970, 2971**
  Interest, variable rates, **CC 1916.5 et seq.**
  Mortgages, generally, post
  Motor vehicles, seller assisted financing, **CC 2982.5**
  Real estate, lenders liability for defective work, **CC 3434**
  Shared appreciation loans, **CC 1917 et seq.**
  Variable interest, **CC 1916.5 et seq.**
Markets and marketing, personal information, disclosure, **CC 1798.83**
Money Orders, generally, this index
Mortgages,
  Adjustable payment, adjustable rate loans, **CC 1916.7**
  Fiduciaries, **CC 2923.1**
  Foreign languages, translations, **CC 1632.5**
  Home equity loan disclosure, **CC 2970, 2971**
  Impound accounts, interest, **CC 2954.8**
  Rules and regulations, **CC 1916.12**
  Shared appreciation loans, **CC 1917 et seq.**
Motor vehicles, seller assisted financing, exemptions, **CC 2982.5**
Negotiable Instruments, generally, this index
Optional bank holiday, transaction of business, **CC 7.1, 9**
Personal information, direct marketing, disclosure, **CC 1798.83**
Real estate, repairs, bringing up to code, **CC 2932.6**
Records and recordation, customer records, destruction, **CC 1798.80 et seq.**
Renegotiable rate mortgages, **CC 1916.8, 1916.9**
Residential mortgage lenders. Mortgages, this index
Saturday, transaction of business, **CC 9**
Savings Associations, generally, this index
Sexual harassment, clients, **CC 51.9**
Shared appreciation loans, **CC 1917 et seq.**
Small Businesses, generally, this index
Social security, numbers and numbering, statements, **CC 1786.60**
Taxation. Corporation Taxes, generally, this index
Translations, foreign languages, contracts, **CC 1632.5**

BANKS AND BANKING—Cont'd
Unclaimed property. Abandoned or Unclaimed Property, generally, this index
Variable interest, **CC 1916.5 et seq.**

BARBERS
Discrimination,
  Prices, posting, **CC 51.6**
  Sex, **CC 55.61 et seq.**
Fines and penalties, prices, posting, discrimination, **CC 51.6**
Posting, prices, discrimination, **CC 51.6**
Prices, discrimination,
  Posting, **CC 51.6**
  Sex, **CC 55.61 et seq.**
Sex, discrimination, **CC 55.61 et seq.**

BASEBALL
Invasion of privacy, use of name, likeness, voice, signature, without consent, **CC 3344**

BEACHES
Zoning and Planning, generally, this index

BEAUTY CULTURE
Cosmetology, generally, this index

BED AND BREAKFAST INNS
Children and minors, **CC 1865**
Damages, children and minors, **CC 1865**
Eviction, guests, checkout time, **CC 1865**
Forcible entry and detainer, guests, checkout time, **CC 1865**
Guests, eviction, checkout time, **CC 1865**
Notice, guests, eviction, checkout time, **CC 1865**
Rates and charges, children and minors, **CC 1865**

BEHAVIORAL HEALTH
Mental Health, generally, this index

BENEFICIARIES
Accumulations, indigent persons, disposition, **CC 726**
Trust Deeds, this index

BENEVOLENT ASSOCIATIONS OR CORPORATIONS
Insurance, generally, this index

BEQUESTS
Gifts, Devises and Bequests, generally, this index

BEVERAGES
Alcoholic Beverages, generally, this index
Restaurants, generally, this index

BIAS AND PREJUDICE
Discrimination, generally, this index

BIAS CRIMES
Hate Crimes, generally, this index

BICYCLES
Manufacturers identification mark, removal, defacing, alteration or destruction, **CC 1710.1**
Motorized bicycles. Motorized Scooters, generally, this index
Motorized Scooters, generally, this index
Railroads, luggage, **CC 2181**
Sales, identification number or mark altered or removed, **CC 1710.1**

BIDS AND BIDDING
Actions relating to real estate, state, **CC 2931b**
Auctions and Auctioneers, generally, this index
Landlord and tenant, personal property remaining premises at termination of tenancy, **CC 1984, 1988**
Mobilehomes and mobilehome parks, abandonment, declaration, sale, **CC 798.61**
Mortgages, this index
Trust Deeds, this index

BILL OF RIGHTS
Homeowner Bill of Rights, **CC 2923.4 et seq.**

BILLBOARDS
Outdoor Advertising, generally, this index

BILLING ERRORS
Credit Cards, this index

BILLS
Negotiable Instruments, generally, this index

BILLS OF EXCHANGE
Negotiable Instruments, generally, this index

BILLS OF LADING
See, also, Documents of Title, generally, this index
Fines and penalties, false bills, invoices, or statements soliciting money, **CC 1716**

BILLS OF SALE
Constructive delivery, **CC 1059**
Delivery, **CC 1054 et seq.**
Escrow, delivery, **CC 1057**
Interpretation, **CC 1066 et seq.**
Irreconcilable parts, **CC 1070**
Mining machinery, **CC 1631**

BILLY
Weapons, generally, this index

BIRTH
Genetic diseases, actions against parent, **CC 43.6**

BIRTH DEFECTS
Genetic diseases. Diseases, this index

BISEXUAL PERSONS
Sexual Orientation, generally, this index

BLACK LIST
Business establishments, discrimination, **CC 51.5, 52**

BLACKJACKS
Weapons, generally, this index

BLANK FORMS
Forms, generally, this index

BLIGHTED AREAS
Community Development and Housing, generally, this index

BLIND OR VISUALLY IMPAIRED PERSONS
Animals. Service Animals, generally, this index
Attorneys fees, interference with civil rights, CC 54.3, 55
Charges, guide dog accompanying blind person or trainer, public places, CC 54.2
Civil rights, CC 51, 54 et seq.
Condominiums, accessibility, modification or change, CC 4760
Crimes and offenses, interference with civil rights, CC 54.2, 54.3
Damages,
  Guide dogs, CC 54.2
  Interference with civil rights, CC 54.3
Discrimination, generally, this index
Dogs. Service Animals, generally, this index
Fees, guide dog accompanying blind person or trainer, public places, CC 54.2
Guide dogs. Service Animals, generally, this index
Hotels and Motels, this index
Housing,
  Discrimination, CC 54.1
  Guide dogs, CC 54.2
  Injunction, CC 55
Identity and identification, guide dog trainers, public accommodations, CC 54.1, 54.2
Injunction, public accommodations, violation of access rights, CC 55, 55.1
Medical facilities, access, CC 54 et seq.
Negligence, failure to carry white canes or use guide dogs, CC 54.4
Pedestrians, white cane, failure to carry, CC 54.4
Public accommodations, access, CC 54 et seq.
Seeing eye dogs. Service Animals, generally, this index
Service Animals, generally, this index
Sidewalks, access to public facilities, CC 54 et seq.
Stations and depots, touch screen devices, CC 54.9
Touch screen devices, CC 54.9
Transportation, zoos or wild animal parks, CC 54.7
White Cane Safety Day, proclamation, CC 54.5
White canes, failure to carry, CC 54.4
Zoos or wild animal parks, admittance with guide dog, restriction, CC 54.7

BLOCKADE
Commercial blockade, health facilities, CC 3427 et seq.

BLOOD RELATIONSHIPS
Relatives, generally, this index

BLUE SKY LAW
Securities, generally, this index

BOARDING AND LODGING HOUSES
See, also, Housing, generally, this index
Baggage, liens, CC 1861 et seq.
Bailment, CC 1859 et seq.
Bed and Breakfast Inns, generally, this index
Blind or visually impaired persons, access to public accommodations, CC 54 et seq.
Children and minors, CC 1865
Damages,
  Children and minors, CC 1865
  Innkeepers liens, wrongful possession of property, CC 1861.15
Deaf persons, public accommodations, CC 54.1 et seq.
Disabled persons, access to public accommodations, CC 54 et seq.
Dogs, disabled persons, CC 54.1
Eviction,
  Guests, checkout time, CC 1865
  Owner occupied dwelling with single lodger, CC 1946.5
Forcible entry and detainer, guests, checkout time, CC 1865
Forfeitures, rates, failure to post, CC 1863
Guests, eviction, checkout time, CC 1865
Guide dogs, accompanying blind persons for training purposes, access, CC 54.1 et seq.
Injunctions, innkeepers liens, writs of possession, CC 1861.16, 1861.17
Liens and incumbrances, writs of possession, CC 1861 et seq.
Notice,
  Guests, eviction, checkout time, CC 1865
  Liens and incumbrances, writs of possession, CC 1861.8
  Single lodger in owner occupied dwelling eviction, CC 1946.5
Overcharges for use of facilities, notice, fines and penalties, CC 1863
Owner occupied dwellings, single lodger, eviction, CC 1946.5
Personal property,
  Fireproof safe, notice of nonliability, CC 1860
  Injury or loss, CC 1859
  Liens, CC 1861 et seq.
Pest Control, generally, this index
Privacy, CC 53.5
Property, liens, CC 1861 et seq.
Rates and charges,
  Children and minors, CC 1865
  Posting, CC 1863
Sales, innkeepers liens, CC 1861.24

BOARDS AND COMMISSIONS
Administrative Law and Procedure, generally, this index

BOARDS AND COMMISSIONS—Cont'd
Contracts. State Contracts, generally, this index
Crimes and offenses, information practices, CC 1798.55 et seq.
Disclosure, personal information, Information Practices Act, CC 1798 et seq.
Information Practices Act, CC 1798 et seq.
Medical information, disclosure, CC 56.10
Privacy, Information Practices Act, CC 1798 et seq.
Records and recordation,
  Disclosure, Information Practices Act, CC 1798 et seq.
  Information Practices Act, CC 1798 et seq.
Reports,
  Disclosure, Information Practices Act, CC 1798 et seq.
  Information Practices Act, CC 1798 et seq.
Right to privacy, Information Practices Act, CC 1798 et seq.

BOATS AND BOATING
Blind or visually impaired persons, access to public conveyances, CC 54 et seq.
Deaf persons, public accommodations, CC 54.1 et seq.
Disabled persons,
  Access to public conveyances, CC 54 et seq.
  Civil rights, CC 54.1
Dwellings. Floating Homes, generally, this index
Floating Homes, generally, this index
Guide dogs, accompanying blind persons for training purposes, access to public conveyances, CC 54.1 et seq.
Houseboats. Floating Homes, generally, this index
Pest Control, generally, this index
Residency on boat. Floating Homes, generally, this index
Ships and Shipping, generally, this index

BODILY INJURY
Personal Injuries, generally, this index

BODY SHAPING
Weight loss contracts, CC 1694.5 et seq.

BOILERS
Ships and Shipping, generally, this index

BOMB SHELTERS
Injuries sustained, exemption from liability, CC 1714.5

BONA FIDE PURCHASERS
Innocent Purchasers, generally, this index

BONDAGE
Human Trafficking, generally, this index

BONDS
Employees. Bonds (Officers and Fiduciaries), generally, this index

BONDS

BONDS—Cont'd
Fiduciaries. Bonds (Officers and Fiduciaries), generally, this index
Investments, generally, this index
Legal estates, Principal and Income Law, CC 731 et seq.
Legal investments. Investments, generally, this index
Official bonds. Bonds (Officers and Fiduciaries), generally, this index

BONDS (OFFICERS AND FIDUCIARIES)
Agricultural producers, satisfaction of wages, CC 3061.5
Art and artists, injunctions, preserving artistic integrity, CC 989
Autographed memorabilia, dealers, CC 1739.7
Condominiums, CC 5806
Credit services organizations, CC 1789.18
Dance studio, CC 1812.64, 1812.65
  Information, contract, CC 1812.54
Deposit in lieu of bond, contract for discount buying services, CC 1812.105
Discount buying services, CC 1812.103 et seq.
  Affiliates, CC 1812.117
Entry upon land, adjacent landowners, repair, reconstruction, CC 1002
Health studios, refunds, contracts, cancellation, new facilities, CC 1812.96
Job listing services, CC 1812.515
Mechanics Liens, this index
Memorabilia, dealers, CC 1739.7
Mortgage foreclosure consultants, registration, CC 2945.45
Nurses registries, CC 1812.525
Oil and gas pipelines, spills, CC 3333.5
Seller assisted marketing plans, filing, CC 1812.214

BONES
Tissue Banks, generally, this index

BOOK CLUBS
Members, sending goods to after notice of termination, CC 1584.6

BOOKS AND PAPERS
Acknowledgment of instruments, persons authorized, CC 1181
Business records, disclosure, bookkeeping services, CC 1799 et seq.
Crimes and offenses, stories, proceeds, CC 2225
Discovery, generally, this index
Employment Agencies, this index
Evidence, generally, this index
Letters and Other Correspondence, generally, this index
Lewdness and Obscenity, generally, this index
Libel and Slander, generally, this index
Libraries, generally, this index
Lost or Destroyed Documents, generally, this index

BOOKS AND PAPERS—Cont'd
Mortgages, separate sets, CC 1171
Obscenity. Lewdness and Obscenity, generally, this index
Recorders, generally, this index
Religious books, security interests for consumer credit contracts, CC 1799.97
Secretary of State, generally, this index
Uniform Single Publication Act, CC 3425.1 et seq.
Water appropriation, recording notices, CC 1421

BOOKSTORES
Personal information, disclosure, CC 1798.90, 1798.90.05

BORDERS
Boundaries, generally, this index

BORROWERS
Loans, generally, this index

BORROWING
Loans, generally, this index

BOTTOMRY
Mortgage provisions, exclusion, CC 2942
Priority, lien, exception, CC 2897
Provisions governing, CC 2877
Voidable transactions, application of law, CC 3440.1

BOUNDARIES
  Generally, CC 829 et seq.
Distributors, independent wholesale sales representatives, CC 1738.13
Independent wholesale sales representatives, CC 1738.13
Presumptions, roads or streets, CC 831
Sales, independent wholesale sales representatives, CC 1738.13
Trees, adjoining landowners, ownership, CC 833, 834
Wholesale sales representatives, independents, CC 1738.13

BOURBON
Alcoholic Beverages, generally, this index

BOXING AND WRESTLING
Gymnasiums, leases, notice, anabolic steroids, testosterone or human growth hormone, crimes and offenses, CC 1812.97

BOYCOTTS
Business establishments, discrimination, CC 51.5, 52

BOYS
Children and Minors, generally, this index

BRANDS, MARKS AND LABELS
Grey market goods, retail sellers, disclosures, CC 1797.81
Political items, sale and manufacture, CC 1739.3

BRANDS, MARKS AND LABELS—Cont'd
Service marks. Trademarks, generally, this index
Trademarks, generally, this index
Video games, force and violence, CC 1746.2

BRASS KNUCKLES
Weapons, generally, this index

BREACH OF CONTRACT
Contracts, this index

BRETT ALAN LAWS ACT
Firefighters rule, CC 1714.9

BRIBERY AND CORRUPTION
Real estate, appraisal and appraisers, CC 1090.5
Trade secrets, CC 3426 et seq.
Uniform Trade Secrets Act, CC 3426 et seq.

BRIEFS
Civil Rights, this index

BROADCASTS
Television and Radio, generally, this index

BROKERS
Art and artists, commissions, sales, original works, CC 986
Data, registration, CC 1798.99.80 et seq.
Insurance Agents, Solicitors or Brokers, generally, this index
Membership camping contracts, CC 1812.307
Mortgages, deceptive trade practices, CC 1770
Motor carriers, construction, rates and charges, CC 3322
Personal Property Brokers, generally, this index
Real Estate Brokers and Salespersons, generally, this index
Registration, data, CC 1798.99.80 et seq.
Security Agents and Broker Dealers, generally, this index

BROTHELS
Prostitution, generally, this index

BROTHERS AND SISTERS
Relatives, generally, this index

BUDGETS
Condominiums, homeowners associations, reports, CC 5300 et seq.

BUILDERS
Mechanics Liens, generally, this index

BUILDING AND LOAN ASSOCIATIONS
Savings Associations, generally, this index

BUILDING CODES
Building Standards, generally, this index

BUILDING PERMITS
Independent quality review, privileges and immunities, CC 43.99

BUILDINGS

BUILDING PERMITS—Cont'd
Mechanics liens, CC 8172, 8302
Zoning and Planning, generally, this index

BUILDING STANDARDS
Actions and proceedings, construction defects, CC 896
Condominiums, water conservation, CC 1101.1 et seq.
Construction defects, CC 896
  Buildings, this index
Contractors, generally, this index
Cooperative apartments, water conservation, CC 1101.1 et seq.
Defects, construction defects, CC 896
Defenses, construction defects, CC 945.5
General contractors. Contractors, this index
Landlord and tenant, water conservation, CC 1101.1 et seq.
Licenses and permits, water conservation, landlord and tenant, CC 1101.5
Negligence, general contractors, application of law, CC 936
Planned unit developments, water conservation, CC 1101.1 et seq.
Water conservation, CC 1101.1 et seq.

BUILDINGS
Access to buildings, disabled persons, injunction actions, violation of access rights, CC 55
Actions and proceedings. Construction defects, post
Advertisements. Outdoor Advertising, generally, this index
Apartment Houses, generally, this index
Application of law,
  Construction defects, CC 936, 938, 943, 945
  Enhanced protection agreements, CC 902
  Enhanced protection agreements, construction defects, CC 902
Architects, generally, this index
Attorney fees, construction defects, supersedeas or stay, prelitigation proceedings, noncompliance, CC 930
Attorneys, construction defects,
  Communications, CC 913
  Professions and occupations, commencement of actions, certificates, CC 937
Blind or visually impaired persons, civil rights, CC 54 et seq.
Building Permits, generally, this index
Burden of proof, construction defects, CC 942
Codes. Building Standards, generally, this index
Community Development and Housing, generally, this index
Construction,
  Building Permits, generally, this index
  Defects. Construction defects, generally, post
  Design defects, negligence,
    Indemnity, CC 2782 et seq.

BUILDINGS—Cont'd
Construction—Cont'd
  Design defects, negligence—Cont'd
    Liability limitation, CC 2782.5
Construction defects, CC 895 et seq.
  Actions and proceedings, CC 931 et seq.
    Burden of proof, CC 942
    Defenses, CC 945.5
    Enhanced protection agreements, CC 901 et seq.
    Evidence, CC 933, 934
    Burden of proof, CC 942
    Limitation of actions, CC 941
    Subsequently discovered claims, CC 932
  Application of law, CC 936, 938, 943, 945
  Attorney fees, supersedeas or stay, prelitigation proceedings, noncompliance, CC 930
  Attorneys,
    Communications, CC 913
    Professions and occupations, commencement of actions, certificates, CC 937
  Burden of proof, CC 942
  Claims, grounds, CC 931
  Communications, parties, CC 913
  Components, standards, CC 896
  Condominiums, application of law, CC 935
  Contractors, application of law, CC 936
  Contracts, enhanced protection agreements, CC 901 et seq.
  Damages, valuation, CC 944
  Deeds and conveyances, application of law, CC 945
  Defenses, CC 945.5
  Discovery, CC 912
  Dispute resolution, CC 914, 919, 928
  Effective date, CC 938
  Elections, enhanced protection agreements, other standards, CC 904, 905
  Enhanced protection agreements, CC 901 et seq.
  Evidence, actions and proceedings, CC 933, 934
  Exclusive remedies, CC 943
  Fit and finish items, warranties, CC 900
  Fraud, actions and proceedings, CC 931
  Independent quality review, building permits, privileges and immunities, CC 43.99
  Inspection and inspectors,
    Claims, CC 916
    Repairs, CC 922
  Limitation of actions, CC 941
    Extensions, CC 927
  Machinery and equipment, standards, CC 896
  Maintenance, enhanced protection agreements, obligations, CC 907
  Mediation, CC 914, 919, 928
  Notice,
    Claims, CC 910

BUILDINGS—Cont'd
Construction defects—Cont'd
  Notice—Cont'd
    Enhanced protection agreements, other standards, elections, CC 904
  Offers,
    Money, CC 929
    Repairs, CC 917 et seq.
  Original purchasers, application of law, CC 945
  Partial repairs, reasons, CC 924
  Plans and specifications, discovery, CC 912
  Prelitigation proceedings, CC 910 et seq.
  Records and recordation, repairs, CC 923
  Release,
    Dispute resolution, builders, noncompliance, CC 915, 920, 925
    Money, settlement, CC 929
    Repairs, CC 926
  Repairs, CC 921 et seq.
    Offers, CC 917 et seq.
  Standards, CC 896
  Subsequently discovered claims, CC 932
  Supersedeas or stay, prelitigation proceedings, noncompliance, CC 930
  Time, CC 930
    Effective date, CC 938
    Enhanced protection agreements, CC 903
    Limitation of actions, CC 941
    Repairs, offers, CC 918
  Unspecified standards, CC 897
  Waiver, repairs, CC 926
  Warranties, CC 896 et seq.
Construction permits. Building Permits, generally, this index
Contractors, generally, this index
Contracts, construction defects, enhanced protection agreements, CC 901 et seq.
Correctional Institutions, generally, this index
Damages, construction defects, CC 896 et seq.
  Valuation, CC 944
Defects. Construction defects, generally, ante
Defense shelters, injuries, exemption from liability, CC 1714.5
Defenses, construction defects, CC 945.5
Discovery, construction defects, CC 912
Dispute resolution, construction defects, CC 914, 919, 928
Dumbwaiters. Elevators, Dumbwaiters and Escalators, generally, this index
Elevators, Dumbwaiters and Escalators, generally, this index
Enhanced protection agreements, construction defects, CC 901 et seq.
Escalators. Elevators, Dumbwaiters and Escalators, generally, this index
Evidence, this index
Excavations, lateral land subjacent to support, CC 832
Fires and Fire Protection, generally, this index
First aid, trauma kits, privileges and immunities, CC 1714.29

BUILDINGS

BUILDINGS—Cont'd
Fit and finish items, construction defects, actions and proceedings, warranties, **CC 900**
Fixtures, generally, this index
Fraud, construction defects, actions and proceedings, **CC 931**
General contractors. Contractors, this index
Hospitals, generally, this index
Hotels and Motels, generally, this index
Housing, generally, this index
Inspection and inspectors, construction defects,
    Claims, **CC 916**
    Repairs, **CC 922**
Lateral and subjacent support, **CC 832**
Libraries, generally, this index
Licenses and permits. Building Permits, generally, this index
Life estates, repairs, **CC 840**
Limitation of actions,
    Construction defects, **CC 941**
        Extensions, **CC 927**
    Negligence liability, design defects, **CC 2782.5**
Maintenance and repairs, construction defects, **CC 921 et seq.**
    Enhanced protection agreements, **CC 907**
    Offers, **CC 917 et seq.**
Mechanics Liens, generally, this index
Mediation, construction defects, **CC 914, 919, 928**
Notice, construction defects,
    Claims, **CC 910**
    Enhanced protection agreements, other standards, elections, **CC 904**
Offers, construction defects,
    Money, **CC 929**
    Repairs, **CC 917 et seq.**
Outdoor Advertising, generally, this index
Party walls, easements, **CC 801**
Pest Control, generally, this index
Plans and specifications, construction defects, discovery, **CC 912**
Prisons. Correctional Institutions, generally, this index
Privileges and immunities,
    First aid, trauma kits, **CC 1714.29**
    Permits for construction, independent quality review, **CC 43.99**
Records and recordation, construction defects, repairs, **CC 923**
Release. Construction defects, ante
Repairs. Maintenance and repairs, generally, ante
School Buildings and Grounds, generally, this index
Standards. Building Standards, generally, this index
State Contracts, generally, this index
State standards. Building Standards, generally, this index

BUILDINGS—Cont'd
Statute of limitations. Limitation of actions, generally, ante
Supersedeas or stay, construction defects, prelitigation proceedings, noncompliance, **CC 930**
Supplemental tax assessments. Tax Assessments, this index
Time. Construction defects, ante
Trauma kits, first aid, privileges and immunities, **CC 1714.29**
Waiver, construction defects, repairs, **CC 926**
Warranties, construction defects, **CC 896 et seq.**
Zoning and Planning, generally, this index

BULLETS
Ammunition, generally, this index

BULLS
Animals, generally, this index

BURDEN OF PROOF
Evidence, this index

BUREAUS
Contracts. State Contracts, generally, this index

BURNED OR DESTROYED RECORDS AND DOCUMENTS
Lost or Destroyed Documents, generally, this index

BURNING
Fires and Fire Protection, generally, this index

BUSES
See, also, Motor Carriers, generally, this index
Baggage,
    Damage, liability limitation, **CC 2205**
    Delivery, **CC 2183**
    Liability, **CC 2182**
        Limitation of liability by agreement, **CC 2176**
    Liens, **CC 2191**
    Obligation to carry, **CC 2180**
Blind or visually impaired persons,
    Access to public conveyances, **CC 54 et seq.**
    Civil rights, **CC 54.1**
Care, degree required, **CC 2096 et seq.**
Charges. Rates and charges, generally, post
Charter buses, privacy, **CC 53.5**
Damages,
    Baggage, liability limitation, **CC 2205**
    Guide dogs accompanying blind person or trainer, **CC 54.2**
Deaf or hard of hearing persons, public accommodations, **CC 54.1 et seq.**
Delays, **CC 2104**
Deviation from proper route, **CC 2104**
Disabled persons,
    Access to public conveyances, **CC 54 et seq.**

BUSES—Cont'd
Disabled persons—Cont'd
    Civil rights, **CC 54.1**
Dogs, disabled persons, **CC 54.1**
Easements, stoppage rights, **CC 801**
Ejection of passenger, failure to pay fare, **CC 2188, 2190**
Guide dogs, accompanying blind person for training purposes, **CC 54.1 et seq.**
Injunction, disabled persons, denial of access to public conveyances, **CC 55**
Liens and incumbrances, luggage, **CC 2191**
Negligence, **CC 2096 et seq.**
Overloading, **CC 2102**
    Exception from requirement, **CC 2185**
Payment of fares, passengers, **CC 2187**
Rates and charges,
    Failure to pay, ejection of passengers, **CC 2188, 2190**
    Payment by passengers, **CC 2187**
Routes, deviation, **CC 2104**
Rules and regulations, passengers, rules of conduct, **CC 2186**
Safety, **CC 2100 et seq.**
Stagelines, damage to baggage, liability limitation, **CC 2205**
Stoppage rights, **CC 801**

BUSINESS AND COMMERCE
Accounts and accounting, sale of business, nonnegotiable instruments, **CC 955**
Actions and proceedings, customer records, destruction, **CC 1798.84**
Address, change of address, notice, **CC 1799.1b**
Attorney fees, personal information, direct marketing, disclosure, **CC 1798.84**
Automated license plate recognition, **CC 1798.90.5 et seq.**
Bookkeeping services, business records, disclosure, **CC 1799 et seq.**
Breach of security, personal information, disclosure, **CC 1798.82**
Change of address, notice, **CC 1799.1b**
Computers, breach of security, personal information, **CC 1798.82**
Condominiums, this index
Confidential or privileged information,
Customer records,
    Breach of security, disclosure, **CC 1798.82**
    Destruction, **CC 1798.80 et seq.**
    Drivers licenses, electronic devices and equipment, **CC 1798.90.1**
    Identification cards, electronic devices and equipment, **CC 1798.90.1**
    Personal information, security, **CC 1798.81.5**
Consumer Protection, generally, this index
Corporation Taxes, generally, this index
Corporations, generally, this index
Costs, personal information, direct marketing, disclosure, **CC 1798.84**

CAMPS

BUSINESS AND COMMERCE—Cont'd
Credit reporting agencies, CC 1785.41 et seq.
Crimes and offenses, drivers licenses, electronic devices and equipment, confidential or privileged information, CC 1798.90.1
Damages, customer records, destruction, CC 1798.84
Dealerships, Fair Dealership Law, CC 80 et seq.
Direct marketing, personal information, disclosure, CC 1798.83
Disclosure, personal information, direct marketing, CC 1798.83
Discrimination, CC 51 et seq.
   Consumers, discounts, unemployment, CC 51.13
   Franchises, CC 51.8
   Safety, recognition, CC 51.17
Drivers licenses, electronic devices and equipment, confidential or privileged information, CC 1798.90.1
Easements, right to transact upon land, CC 801
Electronic commerce, CC 1789 et seq.
Electronic mail,
   Breach of security, personal information, disclosure, CC 1798.29
   Customer records, breach of security, notice, CC 1798.82
Fair Dealership Law, CC 80 et seq.
Fines and penalties,
   Drivers licenses, electronic devices and equipment, confidential or privileged information, CC 1798.90.1
   Human trafficking, notice, CC 52.6
   Personal information, direct marketing, disclosure, CC 1798.84
Fixtures, removal by tenant, CC 1019
Franchise taxes. Corporation Taxes, generally, this index
Gift Certificates, generally, this index
Grocery stores, point of sale systems, CC 7100 et seq.
Human trafficking, notice, CC 52.6
Identification cards, electronic devices and equipment, confidential or privileged information, CC 1798.90.1
Injunction, customer records, destruction, CC 1798.84
Installment Sales, generally, this index
Invasion of privacy, use of name, likeness, voice, signature, without consent, CC 3344
Legal Estates Principal and Income Law, CC 731 et seq.
Licenses and permits, commercial property, rental controls, application of law, CC 1954.29
Markets and marketing, personal information, disclosure, CC 1798.83
Mental health digital services, confidential or privileged information, CC 56.06

BUSINESS AND COMMERCE—Cont'd
Monopolies and Unfair Trade, generally, this index
Notice,
   Breach of security, consumer protection, CC 1798.82
   Change of address, CC 1799.1b
Partnership, generally, this index
Penalties. Fines and penalties, generally, ante
Personal information,
   Direct marketing, disclosure, CC 1798.83
   Security, CC 1798.81.5
Point of sale systems, grocery stores, CC 7100 et seq.
Privacy, personal information, security, CC 1798.81.5
Privileged information. Confidential or privileged information, generally, ante
Privileges and immunities, records and recordation, abandoned or unclaimed property, destruction, CC 1798.84
Records and recordation. Business Records, generally, this index
Sales of business, nonnegotiable instruments, CC 955, 955.1
Secrets. Trade Secrets, generally, this index
Small Businesses, generally, this index
Trade Secrets, generally, this index
Trademarks, generally, this index
Transacting business, days, CC 9
Uniform Trade Secrets Act, CC 3426 et seq.
Waiver, electronic commerce, CC 1789.9

BUSINESS CORPORATIONS
Corporations, generally, this index

BUSINESS RECORDS
Bookkeeping services, disclosure, CC 1799 et seq.
Computers, breach of security, personal information, CC 1798.82
Corporation taxes, bookkeeping services, confidential or privileged information, CC 1799.1a
Customer records,
   Breach of security, disclosure, CC 1798.82
   Personal information, destruction, CC 1798.80 et seq.
Disclosure, bookkeeping services, CC 1799 et seq.
Income tax—federal, bookkeeping services, confidential or privileged information, CC 1799.1a
Income tax—state, bookkeeping services, confidential or privileged information, CC 1799.1a
Tax returns and reports, bookkeeping services, confidential or privileged information, CC 1799.1a

BUSINESS TAXES
Corporation Taxes, generally, this index
Income Tax—State, generally, this index

BUSINESS TAXES—Cont'd
Taxation, generally, this index

BUSINESS TRUSTS
Corporation Taxes, generally, this index

BUYERS CHOICE ACT
Generally, CC 1103.20 et seq.

CABLE TELEVISION
Connections, time period, service connection or repair, CC 1722
Damages, service connection or repair, time, violations, CC 1722
Notice, service connection or repair, CC 1722
Repairs, time, CC 1722
Time, service connection or repair, CC 1722

CABLES
Telecommunications, generally, this index

CAFETERIAS
Restaurants, generally, this index

CALAMITIES
Disasters, generally, this index

CALIFORNIA STATE UNIVERSITY
   See, also, Colleges and Universities, generally, this index
Abandoned or unclaimed property, CC 2080.8
Social security, numbers and numbering, encoding, CC 1798.85
Student loans. Colleges and Universities, this index

CAMERAS
Photography and Pictures, generally, this index

CAMP TRAILERS
Recreational Vehicles, generally, this index

CAMPAIGNS
Elections, this index

CAMPERS
Recreational Vehicles, generally, this index

CAMPS AND CAMPING
Actions and proceedings, membership camping contracts, rescission or refund, CC 1812.306
Assignments, membership camping contracts, CC 1812.308
Attorney fees, membership camping contracts, CC 1812.306
Brokers, membership camping contracts, CC 1812.307
Cabins,
   Eviction, CC 1866
   Forcible entry and detainer, CC 1866
Cancellation, membership camping contracts, CC 1812.303, 1812.304, 1812.307, 1812.314
Disclosures, membership camping contracts, CC 1812.302
Entry on land, hazardous conditions, warning, negligence, CC 846

CAMPS

CAMPS AND CAMPING—Cont'd
Eviction, CC 1866
Forcible entry and detainer, CC 1866
Invitees, warnings, hazardous conditions, negligence, CC 846
Leases, membership camping contracts, CC 1812.308
Membership camping contracts, CC 1812.300 et seq.
Mobilehomes and Mobilehome Parks, generally, this index
Negligence, hazardous conditions, warning, CC 846
Notice, membership camping contracts, CC 1812.302
  Cancellation, CC 1812.303, 1812.304, 1812.307, 1812.314
Personal injuries, negligence, hazardous conditions, CC 846
Private property,
  Entry on, negligence, hazardous conditions, warnings, CC 846
  Owner, liability for injuries, CC 846
Real property owners, duty to keep premises safe for taking of fish and game, CC 846
Rules and regulations, membership camping contracts, CC 1812.300 et seq.
Sales, membership camping contracts, CC 1812.307, 1812.308
Waiver, membership camping contracts, CC 1812.316

CANDIDATES
Elections, this index

CANNABIS
Drugs and Medicine, this index

CAPITAL IMPROVEMENTS
Improvements, generally, this index

CAPITAL STOCK
Shares and shareholders. Corporations, this index

CAR COMPANIES
Railroads, generally, this index

CAR INSURANCE
Motor Vehicle Insurance, generally, this index

CARBON
Air Pollution, generally, this index

CARBON MONOXIDE
Air Pollution, generally, this index

CARD KEYS
Oil and gas, automated dispensing outlets, liability after loss or theft, CC 1747.03

CARDIOPULMONARY RESUSCITATION
Emergency medical care, immunity from civil damages, CC 1714.2
Privileges and immunities, CC 1714.2

CARDS
Credit Cards, generally, this index

CARDS—Cont'd
Debit Cards, generally, this index
Identification Cards, generally, this index
Numbers and numbering, social security, CC 1798.85

CARRIERS
  See, also, Public Utilities, generally, this index
  Generally, CC 2085 et seq., 2168 et seq.
Abandoned or unclaimed property, CC 2081 et seq.
Acceptance of freight, duties, CC 2169
Accidents, starting on time, permissible delays, CC 2172
Accommodations for passengers, CC 2103
Act of God, damages to property, liability, CC 2194
Advances, freightage, liens and incumbrances, CC 3051.5
Apportionment, freight, CC 2140
  Bill of lading or contract, CC 2140
  Distance, according to, CC 2142
  Part not delivered, CC 2141
Arrival of freight, notice, CC 2120
Baggage,
  Delivery, CC 2183
  Injury or loss, limitation on liability, CC 2176, 2178
  Liability for, CC 2182
    Injury or loss, limitation, CC 2178, 2205
  Liens, CC 2191
  Loss or injury, liability, CC 2176, 2178
  Obligation to carry for passengers, CC 2180
  Tags, name and address of owner, CC 2205
Blind or visually impaired persons,
  Access to public conveyances, CC 54 et seq.
  Civil rights, CC 54.1
Boats and Boating, generally, this index
Breach of obligation to receive or deliver goods, CC 3315, 3316
Buses, generally, this index
Care, degree required,
  Freight, CC 2114
  Gratuitous carriage of persons, CC 2096
Charges. Rates and charges, generally, post
Chinaware, limitation of liability, CC 2200
City and county transportation systems, seating capacity, CC 2185
Clocks, limitation of liability, CC 2200
Commercial paper, loss, liability, CC 2177
Compensation and salaries, CC 2173
  Carrying freight further or more expeditiously, CC 2143
  Preferences, state or United States, CC 2171
Complaints against, neglect of carrier to operate in accordance with schedules of starting times, CC 2170
Consignee, liability for freight, CC 2138
Consignor, liability for freight, CC 2137
Contracts,
  Indemnity provision, CC 2784.5

CARRIERS—Cont'd
Contracts—Cont'd
  Limitation of liability, CC 2176
  Negligence, agreements of exoneration, CC 2175
  Special contracts, CC 2174
Costs, liens, fines, false certifications of gross cargo weight, CC 2144, 3051.6
Counties, transportation systems, seating capacity, CC 2185
Crimes and offenses. Fines and penalties, generally, post
Damages, CC 2194 et seq.
  Breach of obligation to receive or deliver goods, CC 3315, 3316
  Delay in delivery of freight, CC 3317
  Guide dogs accompanying blind person or trainer, CC 54.2
  Injury to property, liability, CC 2194, 2205
Deaf persons, public accommodations, CC 54.1 et seq.
Delays,
  Liability, CC 2196
  Passenger service, CC 2104
  Permissible, CC 2172
Delivery of freight,
  Baggage and luggage, CC 2182
  Breach of obligation to deliver, CC 3316
  Delay, damages, CC 3317
  Directions, CC 2115
  Manner and place, CC 2118, 2119
Disabled persons,
  Access to public conveyances, CC 54 et seq.
  Civil rights, CC 54.1
Discrimination, CC 2170
Dogs, disabled persons, CC 54.1
Easements, stoppage rights, CC 801
Ejection of passengers, fare, failure to pay, CC 2188, 2190
Encumbrances. Liens and incumbrances, generally, post
Exoneration, invalid agreements, CC 2175
Fares. Rates and charges, generally, post
Fines and penalties,
  False gross cargo weight certifications, liens, CC 2144, 3051.6
  Schedules of starting times, neglecting, CC 2170
  Starting time, failure to observe, CC 2170
Fraud,
  Agreements of exoneration, CC 2175
  Exoneration agreements, CC 2175
Freight, liens and incumbrances, CC 3051.5
Glass, limitation of liability, CC 2200
Gold, limitation of liability, CC 2200
Gratuitous,
  Obligations, CC 2089, 2090
  Persons, care, degree required, CC 2096
Guide dogs, accompanying blind person for training purposes, CC 54.1 et seq.
Highway carriers. Motor Carriers, generally, this index

I-24

CARRIERS—Cont'd
Hospitals, lien for medical services rendered, application of law, CC 3045.6
Indemnity provisions, contracts, CC 2784.5
Injunction actions, disabled persons, violation of access rights, CC 55
Interest, false certification of gross cargo weight, fines, liens, CC 2144, 3051.6
Kinds, CC 2086
Laces, limitation of liability, CC 2200
Letters, loss, liability, CC 2177
Liability,
  Consignee, CC 2138
    Prepaid shipments, delay, CC 2197.5
  Consignor, CC 2137
  Contracts, CC 2176
  Delays, CC 2196
  Luggage, CC 2182
  Storage or equipment rental charges, consignor and consignee causing delay, CC 2197
Liens and incumbrances,
  Advances, freight, CC 3051.5
  Fines, penalties and costs, false gross cargo weight certifications, CC 2144, 3051.6
  Freightage, CC 2144, 3051.5
  Luggage, CC 2191
  Perishable property, sale, CC 2204
Limitation of liability,
  Baggage, injury or loss of, CC 2205
  Contracts, CC 2176
Limitation of obligations, CC 2174
Luggage. Baggage, generally, ante
Mail, loss, liability, CC 2177
Marine carriers. Ships and Shipping, generally, this index
Messages,
  Care and diligence in transmission and delivery, CC 2162
  Compensation of messenger, CC 2161
  Delivery, CC 2161
    Care and diligence, CC 2162
  Other than by telegraph and telephone, CC 2161
  Transmission, care and diligence, CC 2162
Money,
  Advancement to discharge prior lien, freight, CC 2144
  Losing in mail, liability, CC 2177
Motor Carriers, generally, this index
Negligence, CC 2100, 2195
  Carriers of property, CC 2114
  Exoneration, agreements, CC 2175
  Gratuitous carriage, persons, CC 2096
Notice,
  Freight, arrival, CC 2120
  Liens and incumbrances, freightage, CC 3051.5
  Schedules of starting times, CC 2170
  Valuables, limitation of liability, CC 2200
Number of vehicles required, exception, CC 2184

CARRIERS—Cont'd
Obligations of carriers,
  Freight, CC 2114 et seq.
  Gratuitous carriers, CC 2089, 2090
Overcrowding or overloading,
  Carriers of persons, CC 2102
  Exceptions, CC 2185
Payment of fares, passengers, CC 2187
Payment of freightage, time, CC 2136
Penalties. Fines and penalties, generally, ante
Perishable property, sale for freightage, CC 2204
Pictures, limitation of liability, CC 2200
Plated ware, limitation of liability, CC 2200
Platinum, limitation of liability, CC 2200
Precious stones, limitation of liability, loss, CC 2200
Priorities and preferences,
  Freight, CC 2170, 2171
  Freightage liens, sales, CC 3051.5
Railroads, generally, this index
Rate of hire, manner of assent to, CC 2176
Rates and charges,
  Failure to pay, ejection of passengers, CC 2188, 2190
  Freightage, liens and incumbrances, CC 3051.5
  Natural increase of freight, CC 2139
  Payment by passengers, CC 2187
Routes, deviations from, carrier of persons, CC 2104
Rules and regulations, passenger service, CC 2186
Safety, passengers, CC 2100 et seq.
Salaries. Compensation and salaries, generally, ante
Sales,
  Freightage, time, CC 2204
  Liens and incumbrances, freightage, CC 3051.5
  Perishable property, liens for freightage, CC 2204
Schedules, starting times, establishing, CC 2170
Seating capacity, exception, CC 2185
Secured parties, freightage liens and incumbrances, sales, notice, CC 3051.5
Services other than carriage and delivery, CC 2203
Ships and Shipping, generally, this index
Silk, limitation of liability, CC 2200
Silver, limitation of liability, CC 2200
Speed, carriers of persons, CC 2104
Starting times,
  Permissible delays, CC 2172
  Schedules, CC 2170
State, preferences on time or price, CC 2171
Statuary, limitation of liability, CC 2200
Stoppage rights, easements, CC 801
Storage, freight, CC 2120
  Bond delivery, CC 2120

CARRIERS—Cont'd
Storage, freight—Cont'd
  Consignees failure to accept and remove, CC 2121
Street Railways, generally, this index
Tariffs. Rates and charges, generally, ante
Tickets, acceptance, CC 2176
Time,
  Payment, freightage, CC 2136
  Schedules,
    Establishment, CC 2170
    Permissible delays, CC 2172
Timepieces, limitation of liability, CC 2200
Tolls. Rates and charges, generally, ante
Treatment of passengers, accommodations, CC 2103
United States, preferences in time or price, CC 2171
Valuables, limitation of liability, CC 2200
Wages. Compensation and salaries, generally, ante
Watches, limitation of liability, CC 2200
Water carriers. Ships and Shipping, generally, this index
Writings, limitation of liability, CC 2200

CARS
Motor Vehicles, generally, this index

CASH
Money, generally, this index

CASH SALE PRICE
Installment Sales, this index

CASSETTES
Audio and Video Recordings, generally, this index

CASUALTY INSURANCE
Mortgages, exceeding replacement value, CC 2955.5

CATASTROPHES
Disasters, generally, this index

CATS
See, also,
  Animals, generally, this index
  Pets, generally, this index
Abandonment, care facility, CC 1834.5
Contracts, sales, CC 1670.10
Leases, CC 1670.10
Sales, contracts, CC 1670.10

CATTLE
Animals, generally, this index

CAUSES OF ACTION
Actions and Proceedings, generally, this index

CAVES
Exploration, CC 846
Private property owners, liability for injuries, CC 846

CELEBRITY

CELEBRITY IMAGE PROTECTION ACT
Generally, CC 3344.1

CEMETERIES AND DEAD BODIES
Easements, right of burial, CC 801, 802
Tissue Banks, generally, this index

CERTIFICATES AND CERTIFICATION
Acknowledgments, this index
Art and artists, fine prints, CC 1740 et seq.
Coerced debt, CC 1798.97.1
Collection agencies, identity and identification, theft, CC 1788.18
Condominiums, this index
Consumer credit, credit service organizations, registration, CC 1789.25
Contracts for sale of land, conditional certificate of compliance, CC 2985.51
Credit service organizations, registration, CC 1789.25
Debtors and creditors, identity and identification, theft, collection agencies, CC 1788.18
Executions, CC 1195
Fine prints, art, CC 1740 et seq.
Gift Certificates, generally, this index
Junk and junk dealers, fire hydrants, possession, CC 3336.5
Mortgage foreclosure consultants, registration, CC 2945.45
Rent control levels, housing, CC 1947.8

CERTIFICATES OF DISCHARGE
Mortgages, satisfaction, CC 2941

CERTIFICATES OF TITLE
Motor Vehicles, this index

CERTIFICATION
Certificates and Certification, generally, this index

CERTIFIED MAIL
Mail and Mailing, this index

CERTIFIED NURSE ASSISTANTS
Nurses, this index

CERTIFIED OR REGISTERED MAIL
Mail and Mailing, this index

CERTIFIED PUBLIC ACCOUNTANTS
Accountants, generally, this index

CHAIN SCHEMES
Rescission of contracts, CC 1689.2

CHAIR LIFTS
Elevators, Dumbwaiters and Escalators, generally, this index

CHANCERY
Equity, generally, this index

CHANGE OF ADDRESS
Address, this index

CHARACTER AND REPUTATION
Consumer Credit Reporting Agencies, generally, this index

CHARACTER AND REPUTATION—Cont'd
Libel and Slander, generally, this index
Slander. Libel and Slander, generally, this index

CHARGE CARDS
Credit Cards, generally, this index

CHARGE D'AFFAIRES OF THE UNITED STATES
Acknowledgments, CC 1183

CHARGES
Rates and Charges, generally, this index

CHARITIES
Conservators and Conservatorships, generally, this index
Eyes and eyesight, screenings, privileges and immunities, CC 1714.26
Fine art multiples, sales, disclosure, exemptions, CC 1742.6
Ophthalmologists, privileges and immunities, screenings, CC 1714.26
Optometrists, screenings, privileges and immunities, CC 1714.26

CHASTITY
Libel and slander, CC 46

CHATTEL MORTGAGES
Secured Transactions, generally, this index

CHATTELS
Personal Property, generally, this index

CHATTELS REAL
Tenancy for years, created on, CC 773

CHAUFFEURS LICENSES
Drivers licenses. Motor Vehicles, this index

CHECK CASHERS
Generally, CC 1789.30 et seq.

CHECKS
Negotiable Instruments, this index

CHEMICAL ENGINEERS
Engineers, generally, this index

CHEMICAL STORAGE TANKS
Consumer information, booklets, costs, CC 2079.11
Costs, consumer information booklets, CC 2079.11
Disclosure, real estate transfers, CC 2079.7
Notice, real estate transfers, CC 2079.7
Real estate brokers and salespersons, notice, CC 2079.7

CHEMICALS, CHEMISTRY AND CHEMISTS
Hazardous Substances and Waste, generally, this index
Pest Control, generally, this index

CHICO STATE COLLEGE
Colleges and Universities, generally, this index

CHILD ABUSE
Contracts, sex offense victims, CC 1669.5
Libel and slander, CC 48.7
Sexual abuse, contracts, victims, CC 1669.5

CHILD CARE AND DEVELOPMENT SERVICES
Employment agencies, referrals, trustline, CC 1812.5093

CHILD COUNSELORS
Marriage and Family Therapists, generally, this index

CHILD SUPPORT
Support, generally, this index

CHILDREN AND MINORS
Abuse. Child Abuse, generally, this index
Actions and proceedings,
  Damages, generally, post
  Genetic defects, action against parent for damages, CC 43.6
  Imputed liability of parents, willful misconduct, CC 1714.1
  Sex offense victims, contracts, enforcement, CC 1669.5
  Weapons, discharge, liability for injuries, CC 1714.3
Adoption, generally, this index
Agreements. Contracts, generally, post
Alienation of affections, foster children, CC 43.56
Attorney fees, defacement of property, imputed liability of parents, CC 1714.1
Bed and breakfast inns, CC 1865
Breastfeeding, public or private locations, CC 43.3
Camps and Camping, generally, this index
Child Abuse, generally, this index
Civil liability, firearms, discharge, CC 1714.3
Consent,
  Contracts, CC 1568.5
  Invasion of privacy, use of name, photograph, voice, signature, CC 3344
Consumer protection, Internet, CC 1798.99.28 et seq.
Contracts,
  Ability to make, CC 1556
  Capacity, CC 1557
  Consent, CC 1568.5
  Sex offense victims, CC 1669.5
Cost of living, damages, liability of parents, CC 1714.1
Counselors and counseling. Marriage and Family Therapists, generally, this index
Courts. Juvenile Courts, generally, this index
Credit cards, sales, identity and identification, CC 1798.99.1
Crimes and offenses,
  Contracts, sex offense victims, CC 1669.5
  Juvenile Delinquents and Dependents, generally, this index

I-26

CITY

CHILDREN AND MINORS—Cont'd
Cruelty. Child Abuse, generally, this index
Damages,
  Cost of living, liability of parents, CC 1714.1
  Genetic defects, action against parents, CC 43.6
  Insurance, liability of parents, CC 1714.1
  Liability of parents for acts of children, CC 1714.1
  Torts, liability of parent or guardian, CC 1714.1
  Weapons, discharge, liability, CC 1714.3
  Willful misconduct, liability of parent or guardian, CC 1714.1
Deaf or Hard of Hearing Persons, generally, this index
Defacement of property, willful misconduct, imputed liability of parents or guardian, CC 1714.1
Dependent children. Juvenile Delinquents and Dependents, generally, this index
Diseases, genetic diseases, action for damages against parent, CC 43.6
Enticement, CC 49
Existing person status, child conceived but not yet born, CC 43.1
Family Conciliation Court, generally, this index
Fines and penalties, sales, identity and identification, CC 1798.99.1
Force and violence, video games, CC 1746 et seq.
Foster homes. Social Services, this index
Gender neutrality, markets and marketing, retailers, CC 55.7, 55.8
Guardian and Ward, generally, this index
Identity and identification, sales, CC 1798.99.1
Imputation of willful misconduct, parent or guardian, CC 1714.1
Inflation, damages, liability of parents, CC 1714.1
Injunction, sex offense victims, contracts, CC 1669.5
Internet, consumer protection, CC 1798.99.28 et seq.
Invasion of privacy, names, photographs, voices, signature, use, CC 3344
Job listing services, child labor laws, CC 1812.521
Juvenile Courts, generally, this index
Juvenile Delinquents and Dependents, generally, this index
Kidnapping, CC 49
Liability, parents, willful misconduct, CC 1714.1
Malicious mischief, parental liability, CC 1714.1
Markets and marketing, retailers, gender neutrality, CC 55.7, 55.8
Marriage and Family Therapists, generally, this index
Medical records,
  Disclosure, employers, CC 56.21

CHILDREN AND MINORS—Cont'd
Medical records—Cont'd
  Release authorization, CC 56.10, 56.11
Misconduct, parent or guardian liability, willful misconduct, CC 1714.1
Names, use without consent, invasion of privacy, CC 3344
Neglected child. Juvenile Delinquents and Dependents, generally, this index
Personal attendants. Domestic Workers, generally, this index
Photography and pictures, use without consent, CC 3344
Privileges and immunities, rescue, motor vehicles, CC 43.102
Proceedings. Actions and proceedings, generally, ante
Protection, force, right to use, CC 50
Psychotherapists and psychotherapy, confidential or privileged information, records and recordation, noncustodial parents, CC 56.106
Rescue, motor vehicles, privileges and immunities, CC 43.102
Retailers, markets and marketing, gender neutrality, CC 55.7, 55.8
Sales, identity and identification, CC 1798.99.1
Schools and School Districts, generally, this index
Seduction, CC 49
Sex, gender neutrality, markets and marketing, retailers, CC 55.7, 55.8
Sexual assault, contracts, victims, CC 1669.5
Sexual battery, damages, consent, defense, CC 1708.5.5
Sexual exploitation,
  Contracts, victims, CC 1669.5
  Damages, treble damages, CC 3345.1
  Treble damages, CC 3345.1
Social Services, generally, this index
Special occupancy parks, CC 1866
Speech impaired persons. Deaf or Hard of Hearing Persons, generally, this index
Stores, markets and marketing, gender neutrality, CC 55.7, 55.8
Support, generally, this index
Torts, liability, parent or guardian, CC 1714.1
Vandalism, parental liability, CC 1714.1
Video games, force and violence, CC 1746 et seq.
Weapons, discharge, liability for injuries, CC 1714.3
Willful misconduct, liability of parents, CC 1714.1

CHINAWARE
Carriers, limitation of liability, CC 2200

CHIROPODY
Podiatrists, generally, this index

CHIROPRACTORS
Confidential or privileged information, CC 56 et seq.

CHIROPRACTORS—Cont'd
Immunities. Privileges and immunities, generally, post
Malpractice. Medical Malpractice, generally, this index
Medical information, confidentiality, CC 56 et seq.
Medical Malpractice, generally, this index
Negligence. Medical Malpractice, generally, this index
Privileges and immunities,
  Professional committee, CC 43.7, 43.8
  Referral services, CC 43.95
Professional negligence. Medical Malpractice, generally, this index
Referrals, services, limitation of liability, CC 43.95
Telephones and telegraphs, referral services, immunity, CC 43.95

CHOICE OF LAW
Conflict of Laws, generally, this index

CHOSE IN ACTION
Abatement of actions, CC 954
Transfer, CC 954

CIGARETTES AND CIGARS
  See, also,
    Smoking, generally, this index
    Tobacco and Tobacco Products, generally, this index
Grocery stores, point of sale systems, CC 7100 et seq.
Landlord and tenant, smoking, prohibiting, CC 1947.5
Leases, smoking, prohibiting, CC 1947.5
Notice, landlord and tenant, smoking, prohibiting, CC 1947.5
Products liability, CC 1714.45
  Public entities, civil actions, CC 1714.45
Rent, smoking, prohibiting, CC 1947.5

CINEMA
Motion Pictures, generally, this index

CIRCULARS
Advertisements, generally, this index

CITATIONS
Process, generally, this index

CITIES AND COUNTIES
Consolidated Cities and Counties, generally, this index

CITIES AND TOWNS
Municipalities, generally, this index

CITIZENS AND CITIZENSHIP
Landlord and tenant, information, CC 1940.3
Noncitizens, generally, this index

CITY
Municipalities, generally, this index

CITY ATTORNEYS
Municipal Attorneys, generally, this index

CITY

CITY JAILS
Jails, generally, this index

CIVIL ACTIONS
Actions and Proceedings, generally, this index

CIVIL CODE
Generally, **CC 1 et seq.**

CIVIL DEFENSE
War and Civil Defense, generally, this index

CIVIL ENGINEERS
Engineers, generally, this index

CIVIL MARRIAGE
Marriage, generally, this index

CIVIL PENALTIES
Fines and Penalties, generally, this index

CIVIL PROCESS
Process, generally, this index

CIVIL RIGHTS
Generally, **CC 51 et seq.**
Advisory, complaint, disabled persons, accessibility, **CC 55.3**
Appeal and review,
  Attorney general, briefs, service, **CC 51.1**
  Blind or visually impaired persons, attorney general, briefs, service, **CC 55.2**
  Disabled persons, attorney general, briefs, service, **CC 55.2**
Application of law, disabled persons, construction, accessibility, **CC 55.57**
Attorney fees, **CC 52, 52.1**
  Disabled persons, construction, accessibility, **CC 55.55**
Attorney general, **CC 52, 52.1**
  Appeal and review, briefs, service, **CC 51.1**
  Blind or visually impaired persons, appeal and review, briefs, service, **CC 55.2**
  Disabled persons, **CC 55.1**
    Appeal and review, briefs, service, **CC 55.2**
  Peace officers, **CC 52.3**
Attorneys, disabled persons, construction, accessibility, demand letters, **CC 55.32**
Blind or visually impaired persons, **CC 54 et seq.**
Briefs,
  Appeal and review, attorney general, service, **CC 51.1**
  Blind or visually impaired persons, appeal and review, attorney general, service, **CC 55.2**
  Disabled persons, appeal and review, attorney general, service, **CC 55.2**
Complaint, advisory, disabled persons, accessibility, **CC 55.3**
Conferences,
  Early evaluation conferences, disabled persons, construction, accessibility, **CC 55.54**
  Mandatory evaluation conferences, disabled persons, construction, accessibility, **CC 55.545**

CIVIL RIGHTS—Cont'd
Construction, disabled persons, standards, accessibility, **CC 55.3 et seq., 55.51 et seq.**
Contracts,
  Ability to make by persons deprived of, **CC 1556**
  Freedom from violence, waiver, **CC 51.7**
Costs, disabled persons, construction, accessibility, **CC 55.55**
Damages, disabled persons, construction, accessibility, **CC 55.56**
Demand letters, disabled persons, construction, accessibility, **CC 55.3 et seq.**
Disabled persons, **CC 54 et seq.**
  Construction, standards, accessibility, **CC 55.3 et seq., 55.51 et seq.**
Discrimination, generally, this index
Early evaluation conferences, disabled persons, construction, accessibility, **CC 55.54**
Evaluation conferences, disabled persons, construction, accessibility, **CC 55.54, 55.545**
Evidence, presumptions, damages, disabled persons, construction, accessibility, **CC 55.56**
Exemptions, advisory, complaint, disabled persons, accessibility, **CC 55.3**
Fines and penalties, **CC 52.1**
Force and violence, **CC 52**
  Freedom from, **CC 51.7**
    Actions and proceedings, **CC 52.1**
Forms, disabled persons, construction, accessibility, **CC 55.3**
Franchises, discrimination, **CC 51.8**
Freedom from violence, **CC 51.7**
  Actions and proceedings, **CC 52, 52.1**
High frequency litigants, disabled persons, construction, accessibility, **CC 55.54**
Identification devices, subcutaneous implantation, **CC 52.7**
Jurisdiction, actions and proceedings, **CC 52.2**
Limitation of actions, fines and penalties, **CC 52**
Mandatory evaluation conferences, disabled persons, construction, accessibility, **CC 55.545**
Marital status, **CC 51**
Noncitizens, **CC 51**
  Labor and employment, **CC 3339**
Notice, construction, disabled persons, accessibility, **CC 55.54**
  Mandatory evaluation conferences, **CC 55.545**
Peace officers, deprivation, actions and proceedings, **CC 52.3**
Presumptions, damages, disabled persons, construction, accessibility, **CC 55.56**
Protection, immigration, labor and employment, **CC 3339**
Review. Appeal and review, generally, ante
Sanctions, disabled persons, construction, accessibility, **CC 55.54**

CIVIL RIGHTS—Cont'd
Sexual orientation, **CC 51**
  Freedom from violence, intimidation, **CC 51.7**
Small claims courts, jurisdiction, **CC 52.2**
Solicitor general. Attorney general, generally, ante
Standards, disabled persons, construction, accessibility, **CC 55.3 et seq., 55.51 et seq.**
Statute of limitations, fines and penalties, **CC 52**
Subcutaneous implantation, identification devices, **CC 52.7**
Supersedeas or stay, disabled persons, construction, accessibility, **CC 55.54**
Unruh Civil Rights Act, **CC 51**

CIVIL SERVICE
Reports,
  Disclosure, Information Practices Act, **CC 1798 et seq.**
  Information Practices Act, **CC 1798 et seq.**

CLAIM AND DELIVERY
Generally, **CC 3379, 3380**

CLASS ACTIONS
Consumer credit, purchases, damages, **CC 1788.62**
Consumer credit reporting agencies, damages, **CC 1785.31 et seq.**
Consumers Legal Remedies Act, **CC 1750 et seq.**
Credit, discrimination, marital status or sex, **CC 1812.31**
Grocery stores, point of sale systems, **CC 7102**
Motor vehicle leasing contracts, damages, **CC 2988.5**
Notice, consumers, **CC 1781, 1782**
Student loans, private education lenders and loan collectors, damages, **CC 1788.208**

CLEANING, DYEING AND PRESSING
Discrimination,
  Prices, posting, **CC 51.6**
  Sex, **CC 55.61 et seq.**
Fines and penalties, prices, posting, discrimination, **CC 51.6**
Languages, posting, prices, discrimination, **CC 51.6**
Liens and incumbrances, **CC 3051 et seq.**
  Services and storage, sales to satisfy charges, procedure, **CC 3066**
Notice, sale of unclaimed clothing or goods, **CC 3066**
Posting, prices, discrimination, **CC 51.6**
Prices,
  Discrimination, sex, **CC 55.61 et seq.**
  Posting, discrimination, **CC 51.6**
Sex, discrimination, **CC 55.61 et seq.**
Unclaimed clothing or goods, sale, **CC 3066**

CLEMENCY
Executive clemency, Information Practices Act, **CC 1798 et seq.**

COLLECTION

CLERKS OF COURTS
Acknowledgments, CC 1181
Checks, dishonor, demand for payment, CC 1719
Drafts, dishonor, demand for payment, CC 1719
Negotiable instruments, dishonor, demand for payment, CC 1719
Stop payment orders, dishonored checks or drafts, demand for payment, CC 1719

CLINICAL LABORATORIES
Bioanalysts. Medical Malpractice, generally, this index
Medical Malpractice, generally, this index
Negligence. Medical Malpractice, generally, this index

CLINICAL SOCIAL WORKERS
Social Workers, this index

CLINICS
See, also, Health Facilities, generally, this index
Access, commercial blockade, CC 3427 et seq.
Blind or visually impaired persons, access, CC 54 et seq.
Blockade, commercial blockade, CC 3427 et seq.
Commercial blockade, CC 3427 et seq.
Medical Malpractice, generally, this index
Torts, commercial blockade, CC 3427 et seq.

CLOCKS
Carriers, limitation of liability, CC 2200

CLOTHESLINES
Condominiums, CC 4750.10
Landlord and tenant, CC 1940.20

CLOUD ON TITLE
Quieting Title, generally, this index

CLUBS
See, also, Associations and Societies, generally, this index
Mobilehomes and mobilehome parks, membership, discrimination, CC 798.20
Restaurants, generally, this index
Weapons, generally, this index

COACHES
Recreational Vehicles, generally, this index

COAST GUARD
See, also, Military Forces, generally, this index
Motor vehicles, warranties, CC 1795.8
Warranties, motor vehicles, CC 1795.8

COCKFIGHTING
Nuisance, CC 3482.8

COCKTAIL LOUNGES
Alcoholic Beverages, generally, this index

CODES
Grocery stores, point of sale systems, CC 7100 et seq.
Statutes, generally, this index

COERCION
Duress or Coercion, generally, this index

COFFEE SHOPS
Restaurants, generally, this index

COHABITATION
Fraudulent promise to cohabit, action for damages, CC 43.4

COLLAGES
Sale, CC 1740 et seq.

COLLATERAL
Consumer credit contracts, investment property, security interest, CC 1799.103
Repossessors and Repossession, generally, this index

COLLATERAL WARRANTIES
Heirs and devisees, abolition, CC 1115

COLLECTIBLES
Autographed memorabilia, warranties, CC 1739.7

COLLECTION AGENCIES
Abuse of process, CC 1788.15
Actions, civil liability, unfair practices, CC 1788.10 et seq.
Advertisements, claims for sale, CC 1788.12
Application of law, federal law, CC 1788.17
Attorney fees, unfair collection practices, CC 1788.30
Bankruptcy, affirmation of debt, consumer, notice requirement, CC 1788.14
Certificates and certification, identity and identification, theft, CC 1788.18
Civil liability, unfair practices, CC 1788.10 et seq.
Coerced debt, CC 1798.97.2
Communications,
  Debtor, attorney, CC 1788.14
  Legal or judicial process, simulating, deceptive practices, CC 1788.16
  Misrepresentations, unlawful practices, CC 1788.13
  Third parties, restrictions, CC 1788.12
Crimes and offenses,
  Identity and identification, theft, CC 1788.18
  Simulated judicial process, CC 1788.16
Damages, unlawful collection practices, CC 1788.30 et seq.
Deadbeat list, CC 1788.12
Debtor responsibilities, CC 1788.20 et seq.
Deceptive practices, legal or judicial process, communication simulating, CC 1788.16
Disclosure,
  Licenses and permits, communications, CC 1788.11

COLLECTION AGENCIES—Cont'd
Disclosure—Cont'd
  Unfair collection practices, CC 1788.12
Employers, communication with debtors employer, restrictions, CC 1788.12
Fair debt collection practices, CC 1788 et seq.
  Notice, CC 1812.700 et seq.
Federal law, CC 1788.17
Fees, collection from debtor, CC 1788.14
Fines and penalties, simulated judicial process, CC 1788.16
Fraud, CC 1788.13
Harassment, unfair collection practices, CC 1788.10 et seq.
Hospitals, this index
Identity and identification, theft, CC 1785.16.2, 1788.18
Information disclosure, unfair collection practices, CC 1788.12
Judgments and decrees, CC 1788.15
Judicial process, simulation, crimes and offenses, CC 1788.16
Legal process, communications simulating, deceptive practices, CC 1788.16
Legislative findings, CC 1788.1
Liability, unlawful collection practices, CC 1788.30 et seq.
Licenses and permits, disclosure, communications, CC 1788.11
Limitation of actions, notice, CC 1788.14
Notice,
  Fair debt collection practices, CC 1812.700 et seq.
  Identity and identification, theft, CC 1788.18
  Limitation of actions, CC 1788.14
Obscenity, collection of claims, use, CC 1788.11
Private education lenders and loan collectors, CC 1788.200 et seq.
Process, abuse of process, CC 1788.15
Profanity, collection of claims by use, CC 1788.11
Public policy, CC 1788.1
Publication, deadbeat list, CC 1788.12
Rosenthal Fair Debt Collection Practices Act, CC 1788 et seq.
Rules and regulations, CC 1788 et seq.
  Notice, CC 1812.700 et seq.
Service of process, defective service, CC 1788.15
Simulated judicial process, crimes and offenses, CC 1788.16
Statements, CC 1788.14.5
Student loans, private education lenders and loan collectors, CC 1788.200 et seq.
Telecommunications, use in collection, restrictions, CC 1788.11
Theft, identity and identification, CC 1785.16.2, 1788.18
Third parties, communications with, restrictions, CC 1788.12

COLLECTION

COLLECTION AGENCIES—Cont'd
Threats, unfair collection practices, CC 1788.10
Unfair practices, CC 1788.10 et seq.
Venue, CC 1788.15
Waiver, fair debt collection practices, CC 1788.33

COLLEGES AND UNIVERSITIES
Abandoned or unclaimed property, CC 2080.8
Attorney fees, student loans,
  Borrowers rights, CC 1788.103
  Private education lenders and loan collectors, actions and proceedings, CC 1788.208
Borrowers rights, student loans, CC 1788.100 et seq.
Class actions, student loans,
  Borrowers rights, CC 1788.103
  Private education lenders and loan collectors, damages, CC 1788.208
Collection agencies, student loans, private education lenders and loan collectors, CC 1788.200 et seq.
Consumer protection, student loans, borrowers rights, CC 1788.101 et seq.
Damages, student loans,
  Borrowers rights, CC 1788.103
  Private education lenders and loan collectors, CC 1788.208
Debtors and creditors. Student loans, generally, post
Default judgments, student loans, private education lenders and loan collectors, CC 1788.206
  Vacating or setting aside, CC 1788.207
Disabilities, accessibility, buildings, CC 54.27
Financial aid. Student loans, generally, post
Fraud, student loans, borrowers rights, CC 1788.101 et seq.
Identification cards, RFID (radio frequency identification), crimes and offenses, CC 1798.79, 1798.795
Indebtedness,
  Student loans, generally, post
  Transcripts, withholding, CC 1788.90 et seq.
Injunction, student loans, borrowers rights, CC 1788.103
Limitation of actions, student loans, private education lenders and loan collectors, CC 1788.204, 1788.208
Loans. Student loans, generally, post
Lost or destroyed property, CC 2080.8
Monopolies and unfair trade, student loans, borrowers rights, CC 1788.101 et seq.
Numbers and numbering, social security, encoding, CC 1798.85
Ombudspersons, student loans, borrowers rights, CC 1788.104
Restitution, student loans,
  Borrowers rights, CC 1788.103

COLLEGES AND UNIVERSITIES—Cont'd
Restitution, student loans—Cont'd
  Private education lenders and loan collectors, CC 1788.208
Sales, CC 1740 et seq.
Social security, numbers and numbering, encoding, CC 1798.85
Student aid commission, social security numbers, encoding, CC 1798.85
Student loans,
  Actions and proceedings,
    Borrowers rights, CC 1788.103
    Collections, CC 1788.200 et seq.
  Attorney fees,
    Borrowers rights, CC 1788.103
    Private education lenders and loan collectors, actions and proceedings, CC 1788.208
  Borrowers rights, CC 1788.100 et seq.
  Class actions,
    Borrowers rights, CC 1788.103
    Private education lenders and loan collectors, damages, CC 1788.208
  Collections, private education lenders and loan collectors, CC 1788.200 et seq.
  Complaints, private education lenders and loan collectors, CC 1788.205
  Compromise and settlement, private education lenders and loan collectors, CC 1788.203
  Consumer protection, borrowers rights, CC 1788.101 et seq.
  Costs,
    Borrowers rights, CC 1788.103
    Private education lenders and loan collectors, actions and proceedings, CC 1788.208
  Damages,
    Borrowers rights, CC 1788.103
    Private education lenders and loan collectors, CC 1788.208
  Default judgments, private education lenders and loan collectors, CC 1788.206
    Vacating or setting aside, CC 1788.207
  Documentation, private education lenders and loan collectors, CC 1788.202
  Fraud, borrowers rights, CC 1788.101 et seq.
  Information, private education lenders and loan collectors, CC 1788.202
  Injunction, borrowers rights, CC 1788.103
  Judgments and decrees, private education lenders and loan collectors, CC 1788.206
    Vacating or setting aside, CC 1788.207
  Monopolies and unfair trade, borrowers rights, CC 1788.101 et seq.
  Private education lenders, private education loan collectors, CC 1788.200 et seq.
  Restitution,
    Borrowers rights, CC 1788.103
    Private education lenders and loan collectors, CC 1788.208

COLLEGES AND UNIVERSITIES—Cont'd
Student loans—Cont'd
  Statute of limitations, private education lenders and loan collectors, CC 1788.204, 1788.208
  Writing, private education lenders and loan collectors, compromise and settlement, CC 1788.203
Transcripts, withholding, indebtedness, CC 1788.90 et seq.
Unclaimed property, CC 2080.8
University of California, generally, this index
Women, athletics, equal treatment, CC 1812.30 et seq.

COLLISIONS
Accidents, generally, this index

COLLUSION
Fraud, generally, this index

COLOR OF TITLE
Adverse Possession, generally, this index

COLORS AND COLORING
Cosmetics, generally, this index

COMBAT
War and Civil Defense, generally, this index

COMBINATIONS IN RESTRAINT OF TRADE
Monopolies and Unfair Trade, generally, this index

COMBUSTIBLES
Air Pollution, generally, this index

COMMERCE
Business and Commerce, generally, this index

COMMERCIAL AND INDUSTRIAL COMMON INTEREST DEVELOPMENT ACT
Generally, CC 6500 et seq.

COMMERCIAL BANKS
Banks and Banking, generally, this index

COMMERCIAL BLOCKADE
Health facilities, CC 3427 et seq.

COMMERCIAL BUILDINGS
Buildings, generally, this index

COMMERCIAL COACHES
Recreational Vehicles, generally, this index

COMMERCIAL CODE
Application of law,
  Electronic Transactions Act, CC 1633.3
  Uniform Electronic Transactions Act, CC 1633.3
Buyer in ordinary course of business, agricultural products, labor lien, CC 3061.5
Electronic funds transfers. Funds Transfers, generally, this index
Electronic Transactions Act, application of law, CC 1633.3

COMPENSATION

COMMERCIAL CODE—Cont'd
Funds Transfers, generally, this index
Letters of Credit, generally, this index
Uniform Electronic Transactions Act, application of law, **CC 1633.3**

COMMERCIAL CREDIT REPORTING AGENCIES
Generally, **CC 1785.41 et seq.**

COMMERCIAL FARMING ENTERPRISES
Agriculture, generally, this index

COMMERCIAL FINANCE LENDERS
Finance Lenders, generally, this index

COMMERCIAL MODULAR
Recreational Vehicles, generally, this index

COMMERCIAL PAPER
Negotiable Instruments, generally, this index

COMMERCIAL PROPERTY OWNERS GUIDE TO EARTHQUAKE SAFETY
Generally, **CC 2079.9**

COMMERCIAL VESSELS
Ships and Shipping, generally, this index

COMMERCIALS
Advertisements, generally, this index

COMMISSARIES
Stores, generally, this index

COMMISSION MERCHANTS
Abandoned or unclaimed property, **CC 2081 et seq.**

COMMISSIONS AND COMMISSIONERS
Boards and Commissions, generally, this index

COMMISSIONS (COMPENSATION)
Compensation and Salaries, this index

COMMISSIONS (OFFICIAL)
Acknowledgments, foreign countries, **CC 1183**

COMMITTEES
Privileges and immunities, professions, members, **CC 43.7**

COMMODITIES
Frauds, statute of, swaps or options, **CC 1624**

COMMON CARRIERS
Carriers, generally, this index
Marine carriers. Ships and Shipping, generally, this index
Motor Carriers, generally, this index
Railroads, generally, this index

COMMON INTEREST DEVELOPMENT OPEN MEETING ACT
Generally, **CC 4900 et seq.**

COMMON INTEREST DEVELOPMENTS
Generally, **CC 4000 et seq.**
Condominiums, generally, this index

COMMON KNOWLEDGE
Judicial Notice, generally, this index

COMMON LAW
Consumer Legal Remedies Act, class actions, **CC 1752**
Copyrights, reproduction rights, transfer, **CC 982**
Derogation of, civil code construction, **CC 4, 5**
Easements, abandonment, **CC 887.030**
Rule of decisions, **CC 22.2**

COMMON SCHOOL DISTRICTS
Schools and School Districts, generally, this index

COMMUNICABLE DISEASES
Diseases, generally, this index

COMMUNICATIONS
Collection Agencies, this index
Credit services organizations, **CC 1789.134**
    Confidential or privileged information, **CC 1789.135**
Debtors and creditors, legal or judicial process, communication simulating, **CC 1788.16**
Letters and Other Correspondence, generally, this index
Telecommunications, generally, this index
Television and Radio, generally, this index

COMMUNITY ANTENNA TELEVISION
Cable Television, generally, this index

COMMUNITY APARTMENTS
Apartment Houses, this index

COMMUNITY BASED ORGANIZATIONS
Nonprofit Organizations, generally, this index

COMMUNITY CARE FACILITIES
Foster homes. Social Services, this index

COMMUNITY COLLEGES AND DISTRICTS
Social security, numbers and numbering, encoding, **CC 1798.85**

COMMUNITY DEVELOPMENT AND HOUSING
Loans, shared appreciation loans, **CC 1917 et seq.**
Mortgages, shared appreciation loans, **CC 1917 et seq.**
Shared appreciation loans, **CC 1917 et seq.**

COMMUNITY FACILITIES DISTRICTS
Bonds,
    Liens and incumbrances, real estate, transfers, disclosure, **CC 1102.6b**
    Notice, liens and incumbrances, real estate, transfers, disclosure, **CC 1102.6b**
Contracts, assessments, real estate transfers, disclosure, **CC 1102.6b**
Liens and incumbrances, bonds, real estate, transfers, disclosure, **CC 1102.6b**

COMMUNITY FACILITIES DISTRICTS —Cont'd
Special taxes, real estate liens, transfers, disclosure, **CC 1102.6b**
Tax liens, real estate transfers, disclosure, **CC 1102.6b**

COMMUNITY PROPERTY
Documents, transfers, right of survivorship, **CC 682.1**
Nonprobate transfers, surviving spouses, rights, documents, **CC 682.1**
Ownership, **CC 682**
Sales, right of survivorship, documents, **CC 682.1**
Surviving spouses, transfers, documents, rights, **CC 682.1**

COMMUNITY REDEVELOPMENT
Community Development and Housing, generally, this index

COMPARATIVE NEGLIGENCE
Joint and several liability, noneconomic damages, **CC 1431.2**

COMPENSATION AND SALARIES
Assignments,
    Conditional sales, motor vehicles, **CC 2983.7**
    Installment contracts, provisions, **CC 1804.1**
    Mortgage foreclosure consultants, **CC 2945.4**
    Motor vehicle leasing contract, **CC 2986.3**
    Retail installment contracts, restriction on, **CC 1804.1**
Attachment, generally, this index
Attorney Fees, generally, this index
Carriers, this index
Commissions (compensation),
    Art and artists, original works, **CC 986**
    Escrow agents, fee splitting, **CC 1057.5**
    Garnishment, generally, this index
    Installment sales, seller and supervised financial organization, **CC 1801.6**
Debt settlement providers, fair debt settlement, **CC 1788.302**
Debtors and creditors, offer of performance, compensation for delay, **CC 1492**
Deposit for hire, **CC 1853**
Eminent Domain, generally, this index
Employment Agencies, this index
Fine arts, commissions, sale, original works, **CC 986**
Garnishment, generally, this index
Income Tax—State, generally, this index
Independent wholesale sales representatives, contracts, **CC 1738.13**
Lien holder, **CC 2892**
Royalties, generally, this index
Services, voluntary interference with property, **CC 2078**
Subrogation by employer, employees injuries under firemans rule, **CC 1714.9**
Wholesale sales representatives, independents, contracts, **CC 1738.13**

I-31

COMPENSATION

COMPENSATION AND SALARIES—Cont'd
Workers Compensation, generally, this index

COMPETITION
Deceptive business practices, consumers remedies, CC 1750 et seq.

COMPLAINTS
Consumer credit, purchases, CC 1788.58
Cross complaints, indebtedness, duress or coercion, CC 1798.97.5
Electronic commercial services, complaint resolution procedures, CC 1789.3
Homeless persons, shelters, occupancy, CC 1954.09
Student loans, private education lenders and loan collectors, CC 1788.205

COMPOSERS
Music and Musicians, generally, this index

COMPROMISE AND SETTLEMENT
Arbitration and Award, generally, this index
Consumer credit, purchases, CC 1788.54
Debt settlement providers, fair debt settlement, CC 1788.300 et seq.
Identification devices, subcutaneous implantation, CC 52.7
Interest, judgments above plaintiffs offer to settle, personal injury damages, CC 3291
Mechanics liens, CC 8130
Mediation, generally, this index
Payment processors, fair debt settlement, CC 1788.300 et seq.
Personal injury action, offered by plaintiff, refusal by defendant, interest, CC 3291
Refusal by defendant, judgment for plaintiff, interest, CC 3291
Subcutaneous implantation, identification devices, CC 52.7

COMPTOMETERS
Manufacturers identification mark, removal, defacing, alteration or destruction, CC 1710.1

COMPUTERS
Actions and proceedings,
  Transcripts, deaf or hard of hearing persons, CC 54.8
  Year 2000 information disclosure, immunity, CC 3269 et seq.
Automated license plate recognition, CC 1798.90.5 et seq.
Business and commerce, breach of security, personal information, CC 1798.82
Confidential or privileged information, Information Practices Act, CC 1798 et seq.
Consumer credit reporting agencies, security, CC 1798.81.6
Crimes and offenses, data, sales, CC 1724
Damages, year 2000 information disclosure, immunity, CC 3269 et seq.
Disclosure, year 2000 information disclosure, immunity, CC 3269 et seq.

COMPUTERS—Cont'd
Electronic funds transfers. Funds Transfers, generally, this index
Electronic Transactions Act, CC 1633.1 et seq.
Funds Transfers, generally, this index
Grocery stores, point of sale systems, CC 7100 et seq.
Information Practices Act, CC 1798 et seq.
Internet, generally, this index
Medical records, confidential or privileged information, business and commerce, CC 56.06
Monopolies and unfair trade, sales to private schools, CC 998
Privacy, rights, Information Practices Act, CC 1798 et seq.
Private schools, sales, monopolies and unfair trade, CC 998
Privileges and immunities, year 2000 problem, disclosure, CC 3269 et seq.
Rental purchase agreements, geophysical location tracking technology, notice, CC 1812.650
Sales,
  Data, crimes and offenses, CC 1724
  Private schools, monopolies and unfair trade, CC 998
Software, medical records, confidential or privileged information, business and commerce, CC 56.06
Two thousand, year 2000 information disclosure, immunity, CC 3269 et seq.
Uniform Electronic Transactions Act, CC 1633.1 et seq.

CONCEALMENT
Contract induced by, specific performance, CC 3391

CONCESSIONS
Criminal history information, disclosure, concessionaire application purposes, CC 1798.24a

CONCILIATION
Arbitration and Award, generally, this index

CONCILIATION COURTS
Family Conciliation Court, generally, this index

CONDEMNATION
Eminent Domain, generally, this index

CONDITIONAL ESTATES
Future Estates or Interests, generally, this index

CONDITIONAL OBLIGATIONS
Generally, CC 1434 et seq.

CONDITIONAL SALES
Consumers Legal Remedies Act, CC 1750 et seq.
Installment Sales, generally, this index
Motor Vehicle Insurance, this index

CONDITIONAL SALES—Cont'd
Motor Vehicles, this index
Secured Transactions, generally, this index

CONDITIONS PRECEDENT
Contracts, this index
Future Estates or Interests, generally, this index
Validity, CC 709

CONDITIONS SUBSEQUENT
Contracts, CC 1435
Future Estates or Interests, generally, this index

CONDOMINIUMS
Generally, CC 4000 et seq.
Access, separate interests, CC 4510
  Business and commerce, CC 6654
Accessory dwelling units,
  Covenants, CC 4751
  Leases, covenants, CC 4741
Accounts and accounting, CC 5500 et seq.
  Default, sales, CC 1675
Actions and proceedings, CC 5925 et seq., 5975 et seq.
Antennas, CC 4725
  Business and commerce, CC 6708
Arbitration and award, generally, post
Assembly, CC 4515
Business and commerce, post
Charging infrastructure, electric vehicles, meters, CC 4745.1
Common areas, exclusive use, homeowners associations, elections, CC 4605
Construction, defects, CC 5986, 6000 et seq.
  Business and commerce, CC 6870 et seq.
Designs and designers, defects, CC 6000, 6100
Electric vehicles, charging infrastructure, CC 4745
Flags, display, CC 4705
  Business and commerce, CC 6702
Homeowners associations, post
Mediation, generally, post
Meetings, CC 4955
Address, notice, CC 4041
Adverse or pecuniary interest. Conflict of interest, generally, post
Aged persons, cohabitants, age, covenants, conditions, restrictions, CC 51.3
Agendas, meetings, CC 4930
Air conditioning, defects, disclosure, CC 1134
Airports and landing fields, declarations, disclosure, CC 4255
Alterations, CC 4760, 4765
  Business and commerce, CC 6714
Alternative dispute resolution,
  Arbitration and award, generally, post
  Mediation, generally, post
Amendments,
  Declarations, CC 4225 et seq., 4260 et seq.
  Business and commerce, CC 6606 et seq., 6616, 6620

I-32

CONDOMINIUMS

CONDOMINIUMS—Cont'd
Amendments—Cont'd
  Plans and specifications, **CC 4295**
    Business and commerce, **CC 6628**
Annual reports, homeowners associations, **CC 5300 et seq.**
Antennas, **CC 4725**
  Business and commerce, **CC 6708**
Appeal and review, accounts and accounting, **CC 5500 et seq.**
Application of law, **CC 4010, 4200 et seq.**
  Business and commerce, **CC 6580, 6582**
Approval, electric vehicles, charging infrastructure, meters, **CC 4745.1**
Arbitration and award, **CC 5925 et seq.**
  Construction, defects, **CC 6000**
    Business and commerce, **CC 6870**
Articles of incorporation, **CC 4280**
  Business and commerce, **CC 6622**
Assembly, **CC 4515**
Assessments, **CC 5560 et seq., 5600 et seq.**
  Business and commerce, **CC 6800 et seq.**
  Liens and incumbrances, post
  Notice,
    Delinquency, **CC 5675, 5730**
      Foreclosure, **CC 5705, 5710**
      Liens and incumbrances, **CC 5660**
        Business and commerce, **CC 6812, 6814**
    Increase, **CC 5615**
Assignments, assessments, collections, **CC 5735**
  Business and commerce, **CC 6826**
Associations and societies,
  Business and commerce, **CC 6750 et seq.**
  Homeowners associations, generally, post
Attorney fees, **CC 5960**
  Antennas, **CC 4725**
    Business and commerce, **CC 6708**
  Assessments, delinquency, **CC 5650**
  Business and commerce, post
  Charging infrastructure, electric vehicles, meters, **CC 4745.1**
  Common areas, exclusive use, homeowners associations, elections, **CC 4605**
  Covenants, injunction, **CC 4225**
    Business and commerce, **CC 6606**
  Electric vehicles, charging infrastructure, **CC 4745**
  Flags, display, **CC 4705**
    Business and commerce, **CC 6702**
  Meetings, **CC 4955**
  Sales, disclosure, **CC 4540**
Audio and video recordings, meetings, emergencies, **CC 5450**
Award. Arbitration and award, generally, ante
Ballots, homeowners associations, **CC 5115, 5125**
Banks and banking, accounts and accounting, managers and management, **CC 5380**
Banners, display, **CC 4710**

CONDOMINIUMS—Cont'd
Blanket incumbrances on subdivisions, notice, **CC 1133**
Blind or visually impaired persons, accessibility, modification or change, **CC 4760**
Board of directors. Directors, generally, post
Bonds (officers and fiduciaries), **CC 5806**
Budgets, homeowners associations, reports, **CC 5300 et seq.**
Building standards, water conservation, **CC 1101.1 et seq.**
Business and commerce, **CC 6500 et seq.**
  Access, separate interests, **CC 6654**
  Actions and proceedings, **CC 6856 et seq.**
    Antennas, **CC 6708**
    Construction, defects, **CC 6870 et seq.**
    Electric vehicles, charging infrastructure, **CC 6713**
    Flags, display, **CC 6702**
  Alterations, **CC 6714**
  Amendments,
    Declarations, **CC 6606 et seq., 6616, 6620**
    Plans and specifications, **CC 6628**
  Antennas, **CC 6708**
  Application of law, **CC 6580, 6582**
  Arbitration and award, construction, defects, **CC 6870**
  Articles of incorporation, **CC 6622**
  Assessments, **CC 6800 et seq.**
  Assignments, assessments, collections, **CC 6826**
  Associations and societies, **CC 6750 et seq.**
  Attorney fees,
    Antennas, **CC 6708**
    Assessments, delinquency, **CC 6808**
    Covenants, injunction, **CC 6606**
    Electric vehicles, charging infrastructure, **CC 6713**
    Flags, display, **CC 6702**
  Certificates and certification, plans and specifications, records and recordation, **CC 6624, 6626**
  Collections, assessments, delinquency, **CC 6820 et seq.**
  Common areas, **CC 6650 et seq.**
    Maintenance and repairs, **CC 6716 et seq.**
  Comparative fault, damages, **CC 6860**
  Compromise and settlement, construction, defects, **CC 6870**
  Conflict of interest, associations and societies, **CC 6758**
  Construction, defects, **CC 6870 et seq.**
  Costs,
    Electric vehicles, charging infrastructure, **CC 6713**
    Flags, display, **CC 6702**
  Covenants, **CC 6606**
  Damages,
    Comparative fault, **CC 6860**
    Electric vehicles, charging infrastructure, **CC 6713**

CONDOMINIUMS—Cont'd
Business and commerce—Cont'd
  Declarations, **CC 6600 et seq., 6614 et seq.**
  Delinquency, assessments, **CC 6808 et seq.**
  Delivery, documents, **CC 6512 et seq.**
  Depositions, construction, defects, **CC 6870**
  Designs and designers, actions and proceedings, defects, **CC 6870 et seq.**
  Discipline, **CC 6850, 6854**
    Fines and penalties, **CC 6824**
  Disclosure, construction, defects, actions and proceedings, **CC 6874**
  Discovery, construction, defects, **CC 6870**
  Documents, delivery, **CC 6512 et seq.**
  Egress, common areas, **CC 6652**
  Electric vehicles, charging infrastructure, **CC 6713**
  Executions, assessments, **CC 6804**
  Extension of time, declarations, **CC 6618**
  Filing, secretary of state, **CC 6760**
  Fines and penalties, **CC 6850, 6854**
    Discipline, **CC 6824**
    Electric vehicles, charging infrastructure, **CC 6713**
  Flags, display, **CC 6702**
  Improvements, **CC 6714**
  Ingress, common areas, **CC 6652**
  Injunction, covenants, **CC 6606**
  Landscapes and landscaping, plants and plant products, water conservation, **CC 6712**
  Liability insurance, **CC 6840**
    Electric vehicles, charging infrastructure, **CC 6713**
  Liens and incumbrances, **CC 6658**
    Assessments, delinquency, **CC 6812 et seq.**
    Common areas, damages, **CC 6824**
    Notice, **CC 6660**
  Maintenance, **CC 6716 et seq.**
  Mediation, construction, defects, **CC 6870**
  Modification or change, **CC 6714**
  Motor vehicles, electric vehicles, charging infrastructure, **CC 6713**
  Notice,
    Assessments, delinquency, liens and incumbrances, **CC 6812, 6814**
    Construction, defects, actions and proceedings, **CC 6870 et seq.**
  Operating rules, **CC 6630, 6632**
  Partition, common areas, **CC 6656**
  Payment, assessments, **CC 6808 et seq.**
  Pest control, **CC 6718, 6720**
  Pets, **CC 6706**
  Plans and specifications, **CC 6624 et seq.**
  Plants and plant products, landscapes and landscaping, water conservation, **CC 6712**
  Pledges, assessments, collections, **CC 6826**
  Priorities and preferences, assessments, delinquency, liens and incumbrances, **CC 6816**

I-33

CONDOMINIUMS

CONDOMINIUMS—Cont'd
Business and commerce—Cont'd
  Privileges and immunities, CC 6840
  Protected uses, CC 6700 et seq.
  Records and recordation,
    Assessments, delinquency, liens and incumbrances, CC 6818
    Associations and societies, CC 6756
    Plans and specifications, certificates and certification, CC 6624, 6626
  Reference and referees, construction, defects, CC 6870
  Repairs, CC 6716 et seq.
  Restrictions, sales, CC 6710
  Revocation or suspension, plans and specifications, CC 6628
  Rules and regulations, CC 6630, 6632
  Sales,
    Assessments, delinquency, CC 6820, 6822
    Separate interests, CC 6662 et seq.
  Satellite dishes, CC 6708
  Secretary of state, filing, CC 6760
  Separate interests,
    Access, CC 6654
    Maintenance, CC 6716 et seq.
    Modification or change, CC 6714
    Protected uses, CC 6700 et seq.
    Sales, CC 6662 et seq.
  Service of process,
    Assessments, delinquency, foreclosure, CC 6822
    Construction, defects, CC 6870
  Signs and signals, display, CC 6704
  Subpoenas, construction, defects, CC 6870
  Telecommunications, common areas, wiring, maintenance, CC 6722
  Television and radio, antennas, CC 6708
  Tenancy in common, common areas, CC 6650
  Time, extension of time, declarations, CC 6618
  Title to property, CC 6650 et seq.
  Torts, privileges and immunities, CC 6840
  Water conservation, plants and plant products, landscapes and landscaping, CC 6712
Case management, construction, defects, actions and proceedings, CC 6000
Certificates and certification,
  Actions and proceedings, CC 5950
  Plans and specifications, records and recordation, CC 4285, 4290
    Business and commerce, CC 6624, 6626
Change. Modification or change, generally, post
Clotheslines, CC 4750.10
Collections, assessments, delinquency, CC 5700 et seq.
  Business and commerce, CC 6820 et seq.
Commerce. Business and commerce, generally, ante

CONDOMINIUMS—Cont'd
Common areas, CC 4500 et seq.
  Exclusive use, homeowners associations, elections, CC 4600
    Actions and proceedings, CC 4605
  Ingress, egress, CC 4505
  Liens and incumbrances,
    Damages, CC 5725
    Notice, CC 4620
  Maintenance and repairs, CC 4775 et seq.
    Business and commerce, CC 6716 et seq.
  Partition, CC 4610
  Tenancy in common, CC 4500
Comparative fault, damages,
  Business and commerce, CC 6860
  Homeowners associations, CC 5985
Compromise and settlement, defects, CC 6000
  Construction, business and commerce, CC 6870
Conditions,
  Aged persons, cohabitants, age, restrictions, CC 51.3
  Electric vehicles, charging infrastructure, meters, CC 4745.1
Confidential or privileged information, homeowners associations,
  Crime victims, CC 5216
  Records and recordation, inspection and inspectors, CC 5215
Conflict of interest,
  Business and commerce, associations and societies, CC 6758
  Directors, CC 5350
  Managers and management, disclosure, CC 5375.5
Construction, defects,
  Actions and proceedings, CC 935, 5986, 6000 et seq.
  Business and commerce, CC 6870 et seq.
Contracts, homeowners associations, inspection and inspectors, CC 5200 et seq.
Copies, homeowners associations, records and recordation, CC 5200 et seq.
Costs, CC 5960
  Charging infrastructure, electric vehicles, meters, CC 4745.1
  Common areas, exclusive use, homeowners associations, elections, CC 4605
  Electric vehicles, charging infrastructure, CC 4745
  Flags, display, CC 4705
    Business and commerce, CC 6702
  Meetings, CC 4955
Covenants, CC 4225
  Accessory dwelling units, junior dwelling units, CC 4751
  Leases, CC 4741
  Aged persons, cohabitants, age, restrictions, CC 51.3
  Business and commerce, CC 6606
  Electric vehicles, charging infrastructure, meters, CC 4745.1

CONDOMINIUMS—Cont'd
Covenants—Cont'd
  Leases, CC 4741
Crime victims, homeowners associations, confidential or privileged information, CC 5216
Damages,
  Default, sales, CC 1675
  Electric vehicles, charging infrastructure, CC 4745
    Business and commerce, CC 6713
  Homeowners associations,
    Comparative fault, CC 5985
    Records and recordation, CC 5230
  Meters, electric vehicles, charging infrastructure, CC 4745.1
  Sales, disclosure, CC 4540
Deaf or hard of hearing persons, accessibility, modification or change, CC 4760
Declarations, CC 4205 et seq., 4250 et seq.
  Actions and proceedings, CC 5975
  Business and commerce, CC 6600 et seq., 6614 et seq.
  Leases, CC 4739
Deeds and conveyances, CC 4525 et seq.
  Default, CC 1675
Default, sales, CC 1675
Defects, disclosure, CC 1134
Delinquency, assessments, CC 5650 et seq.
  Business and commerce, CC 6808 et seq.
Delivery,
  Documents, CC 4040 et seq.
    Business and commerce, CC 6512 et seq.
  Managers and management, disclosure, CC 5376
  Pesticides, notice, CC 4777
Depositions, construction, defects, CC 6000
  Business and commerce, CC 6870
Designs and designers, actions and proceedings, defects, CC 6000 et seq.
  Business and commerce, CC 6870 et seq.
Directors,
  Conflict of interest, CC 5350
  Education, CC 5400
  Meetings, generally, post
  Open meetings, CC 4900 et seq.
  Privileges and immunities, CC 5800
Discipline, CC 5850 et seq.
  Business and commerce, CC 6850, 6854
  Fines and penalties, CC 6824
  Fines and penalties, CC 5725
Disclosure,
  Airports and landing fields, declarations, CC 4255
  Construction, defects, actions and proceedings, CC 6100
    Business and commerce, CC 6874
  Defects, CC 1134
  Managers and management, conflict of interest, CC 5375.5
  Meters, electric vehicles, charging infrastructure, CC 4745.1

CONDOMINIUMS

CONDOMINIUMS—Cont'd
Disclosure—Cont'd
  Mortgages, earthquake insurance, institutional third party purchasers, **CC 2955.1**
  Reserves, **CC 5570**
  Sales, **CC 4525 et seq.**
Discovery, construction, defects, **CC 6000**
  Business and commerce, **CC 6870**
Display, religion, **CC 4706**
Dispute resolution, internal dispute resolution, **CC 5900 et seq.**
Documents, delivery, **CC 4040 et seq.**
  Business and commerce, **CC 6512 et seq.**
Drought, pressure washing, **CC 4736**
Drying racks, **CC 4750.10**
Education, directors, **CC 5400**
Egress, common areas, **CC 4505**
  Business and commerce, **CC 6652**
Elections. Homeowners associations, post
Electric vehicles. Motor vehicles, post
Electrical defects, disclosure, **CC 1134**
Electricity,
  Defects, disclosure, **CC 1134**
  Meters, electric vehicles, charging infrastructure, **CC 4745.1**
Electronic mail, pesticides, notice, **CC 4777**
Electronic transmissions, meetings, **CC 4910**
Emergencies, **CC 5450**
  Assessments, **CC 5610**
  Homeowners associations, actions and proceedings, **CC 5875**
  Meetings, **CC 4923**
Employees, privileges and immunities, **CC 5800**
Estates, **CC 783**
  Stock cooperatives, **CC 783.1**
Executions, assessments, **CC 5620**
  Business and commerce, **CC 6804**
Executive sessions, directors, **CC 4935**
Exemptions, rent controls, **CC 1954.52**
Expenses and expenditures, meters, electric vehicles, charging infrastructure, **CC 4745.1**
Extension of time, declarations, **CC 4265**
  Business and commerce, **CC 6618**
Fees, sales, **CC 4575, 4580**
Filing, secretary of state, **CC 5405**
  Business and commerce, **CC 6760**
Finance, **CC 5500 et seq.**
Financial statements and reports, homeowners associations, **CC 5300 et seq.**
  Inspection and inspectors, **CC 5200 et seq.**
Fines and penalties,
  Business and commerce, ante
  Common areas, exclusive use, homeowners associations, elections, **CC 4605**
  Discipline, **CC 5725**
  Electric vehicles, charging infrastructure, **CC 4745**
    Business and commerce, **CC 6713**

CONDOMINIUMS—Cont'd
Fines and penalties—Cont'd
  Homeowners associations, post
  Leases, **CC 4741**
  Meetings, **CC 4955**
  Meters, electric vehicles, charging infrastructure, **CC 4745.1**
  Sales, disclosure, **CC 4540**
Fires and fire protection, roofs, **CC 4720**
Flags, display, **CC 4705**
  Business and commerce, **CC 6702**
Floating homes, **CC 800.300 et seq.**
Foreclosure, assessments, delinquency, **CC 5705**
  Notice, **CC 5730**
Foreign languages, leases, translations, **CC 1632**
Forms, reserves, disclosure, **CC 5570**
Fraud, homeowners associations, records and recordation, inspection and inspectors, **CC 5215**
Funds, homeowners associations, elections, **CC 5135**
Governing documents. Declarations, generally, ante
Heating, defects, disclosure, **CC 1134**
Homeowners associations, **CC 4800 et seq.**
  Acclamation, elections, **CC 5103**
  Actions and proceedings, **CC 5980, 5985**
    Elections, **CC 5145**
    Emergencies, **CC 5875**
    Records and recordation, **CC 5230**
  Annual reports, **CC 5300 et seq.**
  Assessments, generally, ante
  Attorney fees,
    Elections, **CC 5145**
    Records and recordation, **CC 5230**
  Ballots, **CC 5115, 5125**
  Budgets, reports, **CC 5300 et seq.**
  Comparative fault, damages, **CC 5985**
  Confidential or privileged information,
    Crime victims, **CC 5216**
    Records and recordation, inspection and inspectors, **CC 5215**
  Contracts, inspection and inspectors, **CC 5200 et seq.**
  Copies, records and recordation, **CC 5200 et seq.**
  Costs,
    Elections, **CC 5145**
    Records and recordation, **CC 5230**
  Damages,
    Comparative fault, **CC 5985**
    Records and recordation, **CC 5230**
  Directors, generally, ante
  Discipline, **CC 5850 et seq.**
  Elections, **CC 5100 et seq.**
    Meetings, emergencies, **CC 5450**
    Operating rules, change, **CC 4365**
  Emergencies, actions and proceedings, **CC 5875**

CONDOMINIUMS—Cont'd
Homeowners associations—Cont'd
  Financial statements and reports, **CC 5300 et seq.**
    Inspection and inspectors, **CC 5200 et seq.**
  Fines and penalties, **CC 5850 et seq.**
    Elections, **CC 5145**
    Records and recordation, **CC 5230**
  Fraud, records and recordation, inspection and inspectors, **CC 5215**
  Funds, elections, **CC 5135**
  Identity and identification, theft, records and recordation, inspection and inspectors, **CC 5215**
  Injunction,
    Elections, **CC 5145**
    Records and recordation, **CC 5230**
  Inspection and inspectors,
    Elections, **CC 5110 et seq.**
    Records and recordation, **CC 5200 et seq.**
  Limitation of actions, elections, **CC 5145**
  Lists, inspection and inspectors, **CC 5225**
  Mail and mailing, ballots, **CC 5115**
  Meetings, **CC 5000**
  Mortgages, default, sales, notice, **CC 2924b**
  Privacy, records and recordation, inspection and inspectors, **CC 5215**
  Proxies, elections, **CC 5130**
  Records and recordation, **CC 5200 et seq.**
  Reports, **CC 5300 et seq.**
  Restitution, elections, **CC 5145**
  Sales, records and recordation, **CC 5230**
  Small claims courts, records and recordation, **CC 5230**
  Solar energy, applications, approval, **CC 714**
  Tax returns and reports, inspection and inspectors, **CC 5200 et seq.**
  Time, records and recordation, inspection and inspectors, **CC 5210**
  Trust deeds, default, sales, notice, **CC 2924b**
Identity and identification, theft, homeowners associations, records and recordation, inspection and inspectors, **CC 5215**
Improvements, **CC 4760, 4765**
  Business and commerce, **CC 6714**
Incumbrances. Liens and incumbrances, generally, post
Industry. Business and commerce, generally, ante
Ingress, common areas, **CC 4505**
  Business and commerce, **CC 6652**
Injunction,
  Common areas, exclusive use, homeowners associations, elections, **CC 4605**
  Covenants, **CC 4225**
    Business and commerce, **CC 6606**
  Homeowners associations,
    Elections, **CC 5145**
    Records and recordation, **CC 5230**
  Meetings, **CC 4955**

I-35

CONDOMINIUMS

CONDOMINIUMS—Cont'd
Innocent purchasers, rent controls, CC 1954.52
Inspection and inspectors,
  Exterior elevated elements, CC 5551
  Homeowners associations,
    Elections, CC 5110 et seq.
    Records and recordation, CC 5200 et seq.
Internal dispute resolution, CC 5900 et seq.
Junior accessory dwelling units, covenants, CC 4751
  Leases, CC 4741
Landscapes and landscaping, plants and plant products, water conservation, CC 4735
  Business and commerce, CC 6712
Leasehold, CC 783
Leases, CC 4740, 4741
  Declarations, CC 4739
  Foreign languages, translations, CC 1632
  Leasehold or subleaseholds, CC 783
  Spanish language, translations, CC 1632
Liability Insurance, this index
Liens and incumbrances, CC 4615
  Assessments, delinquency, CC 5660 et seq.
    Business and commerce, CC 6812 et seq.
    Collections, CC 5720
  Blanket incumbrances on subdivisions, CC 1133
  Business and commerce, ante
  Common areas,
    Damages, CC 5725
    Notice, CC 4620
Limitation of actions,
  Common areas, exclusive use, homeowners associations, elections, CC 4605
  Homeowners associations, elections, CC 5145
  Meetings, CC 4955
  Tolling, CC 5945
Liquidated damages, default, sales, CC 1675
Lists, homeowners associations, inspection and inspectors, CC 5225
Loans, shared appreciation loans, CC 1917 et seq.
Mail and mailing, pesticides, notice, CC 4777
Maintenance and repairs, CC 4775 et seq.
  Business and commerce, CC 6716 et seq.
  Meters, electric vehicles, charging infrastructure, CC 4745.1
  Religion, display, CC 4706
  Reserves, plans and specifications, CC 5550 et seq.
Managers and management, CC 5375 et seq.
Mechanics liens, CC 8448
Mediation, CC 5925 et seq.
  Construction, defects, CC 6000
    Business and commerce, CC 6870
Meet and confer, CC 5915
  Construction, defects, CC 6000
Meetings, CC 4900 et seq.
  Emergencies, CC 5450

CONDOMINIUMS—Cont'd
Meetings—Cont'd
  Homeowners associations, CC 5000
Members and membership. Homeowners associations, generally, ante
Minutes, meetings, CC 4950
Mobilehomes and Mobilehome Parks, this index
Modification or change, CC 4760, 4765
  Business and commerce, CC 6714
  Operating rules, CC 4360 et seq.
Monetary penalties. Fines and penalties, generally, ante
Mortgages,
  Default, sales, homeowners associations, notice, CC 2924b
  Earthquake insurance, institutional third party purchasers, disclosure, CC 2955.1
  Sales, records and recordation, CC 2924.1
  Shared appreciation loans, CC 1917 et seq.
Motor vehicles, electric vehicles, charging infrastructure, CC 4745
  Business and commerce, CC 6713
  Meters, CC 4745.1
Notice,
  Address, CC 4041
  Airports and landing fields, declarations, CC 4255
  Alternative dispute resolution, CC 5965
  Assessments, ante
  Blanket incumbrances on subdivisions, CC 1133
  Construction, defects, actions and proceedings, CC 6000 et seq.
    Business and commerce, CC 6870 et seq.
  Discipline, CC 5855
  Foreclosure, assessments, delinquency, CC 5730
  Liens and incumbrances, common areas, CC 4620
  Liquidated damages, default, sales, CC 1675
  Meetings, CC 4920
    Emergencies, CC 5450
  Operating rules, changes, CC 4360
  Pesticides, CC 4777
  Reserves, transfers, CC 5515, 5520
Officers and employees, privileges and immunities, CC 5800
Open meetings, directors, CC 4900 et seq.
Operating rules, CC 4340 et seq.
  Business and commerce, CC 6630, 6632
Orders of court,
  Construction, defects, CC 6000
  Declarations, amendments, reduction of votes, CC 4275
Partition, CC 4610
  Common areas, business and commerce, CC 6656
Payment, assessments, CC 5650 et seq.
  Business and commerce, CC 6808 et seq.
Penalties. Fines and penalties, generally, ante

CONDOMINIUMS—Cont'd
Peripheral parties, construction, defects, actions and proceedings, CC 6000
Personal information, homeowners associations, sales, transfers, CC 5230
Pest control, CC 4777, 4780, 4785
  Business and commerce, CC 6718, 6720
Petitions, declarations, amendments, reduction of votes, CC 4275
Pets, CC 4715
  Business and commerce, CC 6706
Plans and specifications, CC 4285 et seq.
  Business and commerce, CC 6624 et seq.
  Reserves, CC 5550 et seq.
Plants and plant products, landscapes and landscaping, water conservation, CC 4735
  Business and commerce, CC 6712
Pledges, assessments, collections, CC 5735
  Business and commerce, CC 6826
Plumbing, defects, disclosure, CC 1134
Posters, display, CC 4710
Powers and duties, emergencies, CC 5450
Pressure washing, drought, CC 4736
Priorities and preferences, assessments, delinquency, liens and incumbrances, CC 5680
  Business and commerce, CC 6816
Privacy, homeowners associations, records and recordation, inspection and inspectors, CC 5215
Privileges and immunities,
  Business and commerce, CC 6840
  Directors, CC 5800
Proceedings. Actions and proceedings, generally, ante
Process. Service of process, generally, post
Production of books and papers, construction, defects, CC 6000
Protected uses, CC 4700 et seq.
  Business and commerce, CC 6700 et seq.
Proxies, homeowners associations, elections, CC 5130
Reasonable restrictions, accessory dwelling units, junior accessory dwelling units, CC 4751
  Leases, CC 4741
Records and recordation,
  Assessments, delinquency, liens and incumbrances, CC 5673, 5685
  Business and commerce, ante
  Homeowners associations, inspection and inspectors, CC 5200 et seq.
  Mortgages, sales, CC 2924.1
  Plans and specifications, certificates and certification, CC 4285, 4290
    Business and commerce, CC 6624, 6626
Redemption, assessments, delinquency, foreclosure, CC 5715
Reference and referees, construction, defects, CC 6000
  Business and commerce, CC 6870

CONFISCATION

CONDOMINIUMS—Cont'd
Religion, display, **CC 4706**
Rent controls, **CC 1954.52**
Repairs. Maintenance and repairs, generally, ante
Reserves, **CC 5510 et seq.**
Restitution,
   Homeowners associations, elections, **CC 5145**
      Common areas, exclusive use, **CC 4605**
      Meetings, **CC 4955**
Restrictions,
   Aged persons, cohabitants, age, **CC 51.3**
   Covenants, generally, ante
   Meters, electric vehicles, charging infrastructure, **CC 4745.1**
   Sales, **CC 4600 et seq., 4730**
      Business and commerce, **CC 6710**
   Revocation or suspension, plans and specifications, **CC 4295**
      Business and commerce, **CC 6628**
Roofs, fires and fire protection, **CC 4720**
Rules and regulations, **CC 4340 et seq.**
   Business and commerce, **CC 6630, 6632**
Sales, **CC 4525 et seq.**
   Assessments, delinquency, **CC 5700, 5710**
      Business and commerce, **CC 6820**
   Business and commerce, ante
   Default, **CC 1675**
   Defects, disclosure, **CC 1134**
   Homeowners associations, records and recordation, **CC 5230**
San Francisco Bay conservation and development commission, declarations, disclosure, jurisdiction, **CC 4255**
Satellite dishes, **CC 4725**
   Business and commerce, **CC 6708**
Secretary of state, filing, **CC 5405**
   Business and commerce, **CC 6760**
Senior citizen housing, cohabitants, age, restrictions, **CC 51.3**
Separate interests,
   Access, **CC 4510**
      Business and commerce, **CC 6654**
   Business and commerce, ante
   Maintenance, **CC 4775 et seq.**
   Modification or change, **CC 4760, 4765**
   Pesticides, **CC 4777**
   Protected uses, **CC 4700 et seq.**
      Business and commerce, **CC 6700 et seq.**
   Sales, **CC 4625 et seq.**
      Business and commerce, **CC 6662 et seq.**
Service of process,
   Alternative dispute resolution, **CC 5935**
   Assessments, delinquency, foreclosure, **CC 5705, 5710**
      Business and commerce, **CC 6822**
   Construction, defects, **CC 6000**
      Business and commerce, **CC 6870**
Shared appreciation loans, **CC 1917 et seq.**

CONDOMINIUMS—Cont'd
Signs and signals, display, **CC 4710**
   Business and commerce, **CC 6704**
Small claims courts, assessments, delinquency, **CC 5658, 5720**
Solar energy,
   Homeowners associations, applications, approval, **CC 714**
   Restrictions, **CC 714.1**
Spanish language, contracts, translations, **CC 1632**
Statements, defects, disclosure, **CC 1134**
Statute of limitations. Limitation of actions, generally, ante
Stock cooperatives, estates, **CC 783.1**
Subcontractors, construction, defects, actions and proceedings, **CC 6000**
Subpoenas, construction, defects, **CC 6000**
   Business and commerce, **CC 6870**
Tax returns and reports, homeowners associations, inspection and inspectors, **CC 5200 et seq.**
Telecommunications,
   Common areas, wiring, maintenance, **CC 4790**
      Business and commerce, **CC 6722**
   Meetings, emergencies, **CC 5450**
Television and radio, antennas, **CC 4725**
   Business and commerce, **CC 6708**
Tenancy in common, common areas, **CC 4500**
   Business and commerce, **CC 6650**
Time,
   Alternative dispute resolution, **CC 5940**
   Extension of time, declarations, **CC 4265**
      Business and commerce, **CC 6618**
   Homeowners associations, records and recordation, inspection and inspectors, **CC 5210**
   Limitation of actions, generally, ante
Title to property, **CC 4500 et seq.**
   Business and commerce, **CC 6650 et seq.**
   Homeowners associations, generally, ante
   Separate interests, generally, ante
Torts, privileges and immunities,
   Business and commerce, **CC 6840**
   Directors, **CC 5800**
Trade and business. Business and commerce, generally, ante
Transfers, **CC 4525 et seq.**
   Reserves, **CC 5515, 5520**
Trust deeds,
   Default, sales, homeowners associations, notice, **CC 2924b**
   Sales, records and recordation, **CC 2924.1**
Water conservation,
   Building standards, **CC 1101.1 et seq.**
   Plants and plant products, landscapes and landscaping, **CC 4735**
      Business and commerce, **CC 6712**
Zoning and planning, local ordinances, **CC 4020**

CONDUCT
Weapons, standards, manufacturers and manufacturing, sales, **CC 3273.50 et seq.**

CONFESSION OF JUDGMENT
Conditional sales, motor vehicles, **CC 2983.7**
Contracts, home solicitation contracts, public policy, **CC 1689.12**
Home solicitation contracts, public policy, **CC 1689.12**
Retail installment contract provisions, **CC 1804.1**

CONFIDENTIAL OR PRIVILEGED INFORMATION
Audio and video recordings, invasion of privacy, **CC 1708.85**
Audits and auditors, tape recordings, royalties, **CC 2501**
Business and Commerce, this index
Condominiums, homeowners associations, records and recordation, inspection and inspectors, **CC 5215**
Consumer Credit Reporting Agencies, this index
Consumer Protection, this index
Corporations, drivers licenses, electronic devices and equipment, **CC 1798.90.1**
Credit services organizations, communications, **CC 1789.135**
Customers, destruction, **CC 1798.80 et seq.**
Disclosure, generally, this index
Genetic testing, privacy, **CC 56.18 et seq.**
Hospitals, this index
Information Practices Act, **CC 1798 et seq.**
Medical Records, this index
Motion pictures, invasion of privacy, **CC 1708.85**
Notice, consumer protection, breach of security, disclosure, **CC 1798.82**
Partnership, drivers licenses, electronic devices and equipment, **CC 1798.90.1**
Photography and pictures, invasion of privacy, **CC 1708.85**
Privacy, right to, Information Practices Act, **CC 1798 et seq.**
Psychiatric or psychological information, intentional disclosure, crimes and offenses, **CC 1798.57**
Public agencies, disclosure, district attorneys, **CC 1798.68**
Right to privacy, Information Practices Act, **CC 1798 et seq.**
Social security number, posting, **CC 1798.85**
State Agencies, this index
State Departments, this index
Trade Secrets, generally, this index

CONFIDENTIALITY OF MEDICAL INFORMATION ACT
Generally, **CC 56 et seq.**

CONFISCATION
Searches and Seizures, generally, this index

CONFLAGRATION

Fires and Fire Protection, generally, this index
Forest Fires, generally, this index

CONFLICT OF INTEREST

Condominiums, this index
Controlled escrows, real estate developers, **CC 2995**
Credit services organizations, **CC 1789.13**
Escrow agents, **CC 1057.5**

CONFLICT OF LAWS

Agricultural products, processing activities, nuisances, **CC 3482.6**
Construction, contracts, indemnity, **CC 2782.05**
Contracts,
    Construction, indemnity, **CC 2782.05**
    Law of place of performance, **CC 1646**
Indemnity, construction, contracts, **CC 2782.05**
Motor vehicles, service contracts, **CC 1794.41**
Personal property, law of domicile, **CC 946**
Real estate, law governing, **CC 755**
Water conservation, building standards, **CC 1101.8**

CONNECTED DEVICES

Internet, security, **CC 1798.91.04 et seq.**

CONSANGUINITY

Relatives, generally, this index

CONSERVATION

Easements. Conservation Easements, generally, this index
Fish and Game, generally, this index
Water Conservation, generally, this index
Zoning and Planning, generally, this index

CONSERVATION DEPARTMENT

Forest Fires, generally, this index

CONSERVATION EASEMENTS

Generally, **CC 815 et seq.**
Application of law, **CC 815.9**
    Marketable record title, **CC 880.240**
Attorney fees, **CC 815.7**
Characteristics, **CC 815.2**
Cities, acquisition, holding, **CC 815.3**
Damages, **CC 815.7**
Districts, acquisition, holding, **CC 815.3**
Duration, **CC 815.2**
Enforceable restriction, tax assessment purposes, **CC 815.10**
Enforcement, **CC 815.7**
Grantor, retention of all interests not conveyed, **CC 815.4**
Greenways, **CC 816.50 et seq.**
Indigenous peoples, **CC 815.3**
Injunction, **CC 815.7**
Marketable record title, application of law, **CC 880.240**
Native Americans, **CC 815.3**
Political subdivisions, **CC 815.9**
    Acquisition, holding, **CC 815.3**

CONSERVATION EASEMENTS—Cont'd

Records and recordation, **CC 815.5**
Restriction on acquisition, **CC 815.3**
Retention of all interests not conveyed, **CC 815.4**
State, acquiring, holding, **CC 815.3**
Statutory construction, **CC 816**
Tax assessments, enforceable restriction status, **CC 815.10**
Time, duration, **CC 815.2**

CONSERVATORS AND CONSERVATORSHIPS

See, also,
    Fiduciaries, generally, this index
    Guardian and Ward, generally, this index
Disclosure,
    Personal information held by public agencies, Information Practices Act, **CC 1798.24**
    Residential property transfers, **CC 1102.2**
Medical records, disclosure, **CC 56.10**

CONSERVATORS OF THE PEACE

Peace Officers, generally, this index

CONSIDERATION

Contracts, this index
Home equity sales contracts, **CC 1695.3, 1695.6**
Suretyship, **CC 2792, 2793**

CONSIGNMENT

Art and artists, fine prints, **CC 1744.9**
Fine art, regulation, **CC 1738 et seq.**
Nonconforming goods,
    Extension of warranty period during repairs or services, **CC 1795.7**
    Tolling period of warranties, **CC 1795.7**
Warranties,
    Extension, repair or services, **CC 1795.7**
    Tolling during period of repairs or services, **CC 1795.6**

CONSOLIDATED CITIES AND COUNTIES

See, also,
    Counties, generally, this index
    Municipalities, generally, this index
Adult local criminal justice facilities. Jails, generally, this index
Airports and Landing Fields, generally, this index
Architects, contracts, indemnity, **CC 2782.8**
Building Permits, generally, this index
Community Development and Housing, generally, this index
Community Facilities Districts, generally, this index
Conservation, easements, acquisition, holding, **CC 815.3**
Criminal history information, disclosure, concessionaire application purposes, **CC 1798.24a**

CONSOLIDATED CITIES AND COUNTIES —Cont'd

Development. Community Development and Housing, generally, this index
Easements, greenways, **CC 816.50 et seq.**
Engineers, contracts, indemnity, **CC 2782.8**
Firefighters and Fire Departments, generally, this index
Greenways, easements, **CC 816.50 et seq.**
Health Facilities, generally, this index
Housing, generally, this index
Jails, generally, this index
Landing fields. Airports and Landing Fields, generally, this index
Landscape architects, contracts, indemnity, **CC 2782.8**
Leases, lessor remedy for breach, **CC 1952.6**
Local criminal justice facilities. Jails, generally, this index
Low and Moderate Income Housing, generally, this index
Motor vehicles, shared mobility service providers, licenses and permits, contracts, **CC 2505**
Parks, generally, this index
Personal property, safekeeping, powers and duties, **CC 2080.10**
Planning and zoning. Zoning and Planning, generally, this index
Police, generally, this index
Property, safekeeping, powers and duties, **CC 2080.10**
Recreation and Recreational Facilities, generally, this index
Redevelopment. Community Development and Housing, generally, this index
Rescue, generally, this index
Sacramento City and County, generally, this index
Sheriffs, generally, this index
Social Services, generally, this index
Surveys and surveyors, contracts, indemnity, **CC 2782.8**
Zoning and Planning, generally, this index

CONSOLIDATION

Merger and Consolidation, generally, this index

CONSPIRACY

Attorneys and clients, conspiracy between, pleadings alleging, **CC 1714.10**
Pleadings, attorney conspiring with client, **CC 1714.10**

CONSTABLES

Arrest, generally, this index
Executions, generally, this index
Process, generally, this index
Service of process. Process, this index
Sheriffs, generally, this index

CONSTITUTION OF CALIFORNIA

Municipalities. Taxation, generally, this index

CONSUMER

CONSTITUTION OF CALIFORNIA—Cont'd
Will of supreme power expressed by civil code, **CC 22.1**

CONSTRUCTION
Actions and proceedings, lenders, real or personal property, liability for defects, **CC 3434**
Application of law, civil rights, disabled persons, accessibility, **CC 55.57**
Burden of proof, construction defects, **CC 942**
Certificates and certification, disabled persons, inspection and inspectors, accessibility, **CC 55.53**
Civil rights, disabled persons, standards, accessibility, **CC 55.3 et seq., 55.51 et seq.**
Condominiums, this index
Conflict of laws, contracts, indemnity, **CC 2782.05**
Contractors, generally, this index
Contracts, this index
Damages, defects, **CC 896 et seq.**
Defects. Buildings, this index
Defenses, construction defects, **CC 945.5**
Disabled persons, civil rights, standards, accessibility, **CC 55.3 et seq., 55.51 et seq.**
Evidence, construction defects, burden of proof, **CC 942**
General contractors. Contractors, this index
Housing, this index
Indemnity and indemnification, **CC 2782 et seq.**
Inspection and inspectors, disabled persons, accessibility, **CC 55.53**
Liens and incumbrances. Mechanics Liens, generally, this index
Loans, defects, damages, **CC 3434**
Malicious destruction of property actions, treble damages, **CC 1721**
Mechanics Liens, generally, this index
Notice, disabled persons,
  Civil rights, accessibility, **CC 55.54**
  Inspection and inspectors, accessibility, **CC 55.53**
Standards, civil rights, disabled persons, accessibility, **CC 55.3 et seq., 55.51 et seq.**
Statutes, this index
Supplemental tax assessments. Tax Assessments, this index
Tax Assessments, this index
Vandalism, actions, treble damages, **CC 1721**
Wrap up policies, insurance, contracts, indemnity, **CC 2782.9 et seq.**

CONSTRUCTION DEFECTS
Buildings, this index

CONSTRUCTION OF LAWS
Statutes, this index

CONSTRUCTION RELATED ACCESSIBILITY STANDARDS COMPLIANCE ACT
Generally, **CC 55.51 et seq.**

CONSTRUCTIVE INVASION OF PRIVACY LAW
Generally, **CC 1708.8**

CONSTRUCTIVE NOTICE
Notice, this index

CONSULTATION
Health care service plans, privileges and immunities, **CC 43.98**
Mortgage Foreclosure Consultants, generally, this index
Privileges and immunities, health care service plans, **CC 43.98**

CONSUMABLES
Sales, warranties, **CC 1793.35**

CONSUMER AFFAIRS DEPARTMENT
Collection Agencies, generally, this index
Medical quality review committees. Medical Malpractice, generally, this index
Registered nursing board. Medical Malpractice, generally, this index

CONSUMER CONTRACT AWARENESS ACT OF 1990
Generally, **CC 1799.200 et seq.**

CONSUMER COOPERATIVE CORPORATIONS
Cooperative Corporations, generally, this index

CONSUMER CREDIT
Generally, **CC 1789.10 et seq., 1799.90 et seq.**
Actions and proceedings,
  Credit denial, **CC 1787.3**
  Failure to give notice, **CC 1799.95**
  Purchases, **CC 1788.56 et seq.**
Application of law, credit services organizations, **CC 1789.22**
Applications for credit, fraud, **CC 1788.20**
Arbitration and award, purchases, limitation of actions, **CC 1788.56**
Attorney fees, **CC 1459.5**
  Cosigners, notice of adverse information, **CC 1799.102**
  Discrimination, marital status or sex, **CC 1812.34**
  Purchases, **CC 1788.62**
Bona fide purchasers for value, enforcement of security interest, **CC 1799.95**
Bonds (officers and fiduciaries), credit services organizations, **CC 1789.18**
Certificates and certification, credit services organizations, registration, **CC 1789.25**
Change of name, address or employment, notice, **CC 1788.21**
Class actions, purchases, damages, **CC 1788.62**

CONSUMER CREDIT—Cont'd
Collateral, investment property, security interest, **CC 1799.103**
Collection Agencies, generally, this index
Collection of debt, **CC 1788 et seq.**
  Notice, **CC 1812.700 et seq.**
Communications, credit services organizations, **CC 1789.134**
  Confidential or privileged information, **CC 1789.135**
Complaints, purchases, **CC 1788.58**
Compromise and settlement,
  Debt settlement providers, fair debt settlement, **CC 1788.300 et seq.**
  Purchases, **CC 1788.54**
Conditions precedent, actions, receipt of money, property or services, **CC 1799.95**
Cosigners, notice of adverse information, **CC 1799.101, 1799.102**
Costs, **CC 1459.5**
  Discrimination, marital status or sex, **CC 1812.34**
  Purchases, **CC 1788.62**
Credit Cards, generally, this index
Credit services, **CC 1789.10 et seq.**
Crimes and offenses,
  Credit services organizations, **CC 1789.20**
  Fraud, generally, post
Damages,
  Cosigners, notice of adverse information, **CC 1799.102**
  Credit services organizations, **CC 1789.21**
  Denial of credit, failure to give notice, **CC 1787.3**
  Purchases, **CC 1788.62**
  Reporting agencies, **CC 1785.31 et seq.**
  Unfair collection practices, **CC 1788.30 et seq.**
Debt settlement providers, fair debt settlement, **CC 1788.300 et seq.**
Decrees. Judgments and decrees, generally, post
Default judgments, purchases, **CC 1788.60**
Delinquency, cosigners, notice, **CC 1799.101, 1799.102**
Denial, **CC 1787.1 et seq.**
Disclosure,
  Credit services organizations, **CC 1789.13 et seq.**
  Denial of credit, **CC 1787.1 et seq.**
  Purchases, **CC 1788.52**
  Unfair collection practices, **CC 1788.12**
Discrimination, marital or sexual status, **CC 1812.30 et seq.**
English language, notice of responsibility, signers of contracts, **CC 1799.91 et seq.**
Extension of credit under an account, termination of account, **CC 1788.22**
Fair debt collection practices, **CC 1788 et seq.**
  Notice, **CC 1812.700 et seq.**
Fines and penalties, discrimination, marital status or sex, **CC 1812.33**

I-39

CONSUMER

CONSUMER CREDIT—Cont'd
Forms, notice, signers of contracts, responsibility, CC 1799.91
Fraud,
   Collection of debt, CC 1788.13
   Credit services organizations, CC 1789.13
   Debtor, application for credit, CC 1788.20
Holden Credit Denial Disclosure Act, CC 1787.1 et seq.
Household goods, security interest, CC 1799.100
Information statement, credit services organizations, CC 1789.14, 1789.15
Injunction,
   Credit services organizations, CC 1789.20
   Discrimination, marital or sexual status, CC 1812.32, 1812.33
Installment Sales, generally, this index
Interest, precomputed interest, CC 1799.5
Investment property, pledged as collateral, security interest, CC 1799.103
Judgments and decrees,
   Purchases, CC 1788.60
   Reporting agencies, CC 1786.18
   Reports, contents of records, CC 1785.13
Language, contracts, notice, CC 1799.91
Liability, unfair collection practices, CC 1788.30 et seq.
Limitation of actions,
   Denial, CC 1787.3
   Discrimination, marital status or sex, CC 1812.35
   Purchases, CC 1788.56, 1788.62
Mortgages, payoff demand statements, CC 2943.1
Notice,
   Application of law, CC 1799.99
   Change in name, address or employment, CC 1788.21
   Cosigners, notice of adverse information, CC 1799.101, 1799.102
   Credit services organizations, CC 1789.14 et seq.
   Denial, CC 1787.2
   Failure to give notice, CC 1799.95
   Fair debt collection practices, CC 1812.700 et seq.
   Federal notice requirements, substitution for state requirements, CC 1799.96
   Purchases, CC 1788.52
   Signers of contracts, responsibility, CC 1799.91 et seq.
   Waiver, CC 1799.98
Payment processors, fair debt settlement, CC 1788.300 et seq.
Precomputed interest, CC 1799.5
Purchases, CC 1788.50 et seq.
Receipts, purchases, CC 1788.54
Referral services, charges, CC 1789.13
Registration, credit service organizations, CC 1789.25

CONSUMER CREDIT—Cont'd
Religious books, artifacts or materials, security interests, CC 1799.97
Rental purchase agreements, application of law, CC 1812.622
Reports. Consumer Credit Reporting Agencies, generally, this index
Responsibilities, fair debt collection practices, CC 1788.20 et seq.
Retail installment sales. Installment Sales, generally, this index
Rosenthal Fair Debt Collection Practices Act, CC 1788 et seq.
Security interest, CC 1799.100
   Bona fide purchasers for value, CC 1799.95
   Investment property, pledged as collateral, CC 1799.103
   Religious books or materials, CC 1799.97
Service organizations, CC 1789.10 et seq.
Sex, discrimination, CC 1812.30 et seq.
Signatures,
   Contracts, notice of responsibility, CC 1799.91 et seq.
   Cosigners, notice, adverse information, CC 1799.101, 1799.102
Social security, numbers and numbering, posting, CC 1798.85
Spanish language, notice of responsibility, signers of contracts, CC 1799.91 et seq.
Statute of limitations. Limitation of actions, generally, ante
Trust deeds, payoff demand statements, CC 2943.1
Unlawful collection practices, CC 1788.10 et seq.
Void contracts, religious artifacts, books or materials as security interests, CC 1799.97
Waiver,
   Contracts, CC 1799.104
   Denial, disclosure, CC 1787.4
   Fair debt collection practices, CC 1788.33
   Precomputed interest, CC 1799.6
   Rights, credit services organizations, CC 1789.19
Women, discrimination, CC 1812.30 et seq.

CONSUMER CREDIT DENIAL ACT
Generally, CC 1787.1 et seq.

CONSUMER CREDIT REPORTING AGENCIES
Generally, CC 1785.1 et seq., 1786 et seq.
Access to files by consumer, CC 1785.10, 1785.15
Fees, CC 1785.17
Investigative consumer reporting agencies, CC 1786.10, 1786.11, 1786.22 et seq.
Accuracy of information,
   Dispute with consumer, CC 1785.16, 1785.21
   Furnishers, obligations, CC 1785.25
Actions and proceedings, CC 1786.18
   Federal actions pending, CC 1785.34

CONSUMER CREDIT REPORTING AGENCIES—Cont'd
Actions and proceedings—Cont'd
   Illegal access to files, fines, CC 1785.19
   Limitation of actions, CC 1785.33
Address,
   Change, security freeze, notice, CC 1785.11.3
   Disclosure, CC 1785.10
   Identity and identification, theft, CC 1785.20.3
   Investigative reporting agencies, notice, CC 1786.20
Adverse action based on report, CC 1785.20
Aged persons, security freeze, fees, CC 1785.11.2
Application of law, CC 1785.4, 1785.5
Arrest, CC 1786.18
Attorney fees,
   Actions for damages, CC 1785.19
   Cosigners, notice of adverse information, CC 1799.102
   Enforcement of liability, CC 1785.31 et seq.
   Investigations and investigators, CC 1786.50
   Investigative reporting agencies, privacy, CC 1786.20
   Security alerts, reports, CC 1785.11.1
Blocking information, police reports, CC 1785.16
Burden of proof, furnishers of information, disputes, compliance, CC 1785.25
Certificates and certification,
   Disclosure, CC 1786.16
   Resold reports, purposes, CC 1785.22
Check services company, security freeze, application of law, CC 1785.11.6
Class actions, damages, CC 1785.31 et seq.
Computers, security, CC 1798.81.6
Confidential or privileged information,
   Furnishing reports, authorization, CC 1785.11
   Procedures to restrict access, CC 1785.14
   Security freeze, reports, CC 1785.11.2
Contents of reports, CC 1785.13
   Investigative consumer credit reporting agencies, CC 1786.18
Copies, fines and penalties, CC 1785.10.1
Correction of reports, CC 1785.16, 1785.21, 1785.30
   Furnishers of information, obligations, CC 1785.25
   Investigative consumer credit reports, CC 1786.24
Cosigners, notice of adverse information, CC 1799.101, 1799.102
Costs, CC 1785.31 et seq.
   Illegal access, actions for damages, CC 1785.19
   Investigations and investigators, CC 1786.50

CONSUMER

CONSUMER CREDIT REPORTING AGENCIES—Cont'd
Costs—Cont'd
  Investigative reporting agencies, privacy, CC 1786.20
Credit scores, notice, CC 1785.15.1, 1785.15.2, 1785.20.2
Creditors, information providers, obligations, CC 1785.25, 1785.26
Criminal history information, CC 1786.18
Damages, CC 1785.31 et seq., 1789.21
  Cosigners, notice of adverse information, CC 1799.102
  Investigations and investigators, CC 1786.50 et seq.
  Investigative reporting agencies, privacy, CC 1786.20
Date of birth, change, security freeze, notice, CC 1785.11.3
Deeds and conveyances, records, application of law, CC 1785.35
Defamation, action for damages, CC 1785.32
Deletions,
  Disputes, reinserting, CC 1785.16
  Identity and identification, theft, CC 1785.16.1, 1788.18
  Reinvestigations, CC 1786.24
Delinquent claims, date of a delinquency, furnished information including, CC 1785.25
Demand deposit account information service company, security freeze, application of law, CC 1785.11.6
Denial of credit, statement of reasons, CC 1785.20
Disclosure, CC 1785.10 et seq., 1785.17, 1786.11
  Investigative consumer reporting agencies, CC 1786.10 et seq.
  Privacy, notice, CC 1786.20
  Procuring report for resale, CC 1785.22
  Required disclosures, scope, CC 1785.6
  Security freeze, CC 1785.11.11
Discrimination, marital or sexual status, CC 1812.30 et seq.
Disputed claims, hearing, CC 1785.16
Disputed information,
  Furnishers, obligations, CC 1785.25
  Reinvestigations, CC 1786.24
Dwelling houses, use of report in determining eligibility to hire, CC 1785.3, 1785.11, 1785.13, 1785.20
Evidence, information furnishers, compliance, CC 1785.25
Exemplary damages, CC 1785.31 et seq.
Exemptions, CC 1785.35
  Disclosure, cardholder information, CC 1748.12
Fair Credit Reporting Act, application of law, CC 1786.24
Fair employment and housing, CC 1786.20
Fees,
  Credit scores, notice, CC 1785.15.2

CONSUMER CREDIT REPORTING AGENCIES—Cont'd
Fees—Cont'd
  Disclosure of information, CC 1785.17, 1786.26
  Security freeze, CC 1785.11.11
  Reports, CC 1785.11.2
Fines and penalties,
  Actions for, illegal access to information, CC 1785.19
  Copies, CC 1785.10.1
  Security alerts, reports, CC 1785.11.1
Former jeopardy, CC 1785.34
Forms,
  Consumer notice, CC 1785.15
  Negative credit information reports, notice, CC 1785.26
Fraud,
  Damages, CC 1785.32
  Discovery, CC 1786.52
  Obtaining report under false pretenses, CC 1785.31
  Security alerts, reports, CC 1785.11.1
  Security freeze, reports, CC 1785.11.2
Fraud prevention services company, CC 1785.11.6
Furnishers of credit information, obligations, CC 1785.25, 1785.26
Furnishing report,
  Authorization, CC 1785.11
  Credit transaction not initiated by consumer, CC 1785.11
  Investigative consumer credit reporting agencies, CC 1786.12
Good faith, actions and proceedings, attorneys fees, CC 1785.31
Governmental agencies, furnishing information, CC 1785.12
  Investigative consumer credit reporting agencies, CC 1786.14
Housing, low and moderate income housing, CC 1954.06
Identity and identification, CC 1785.14
  Resold reports, users, CC 1785.22
  Security alerts, reports, CC 1785.11.1
  Security freeze, reports, CC 1785.11.2
  Theft, post
Illegal access, records, actions, fines, CC 1785.19
Indictment and information, CC 1786.18
Information contained in report, restrictions, CC 1785.13
Injunction, damages, CC 1785.31 et seq.
Inquiries, disclosure, CC 1785.10
Inspection of records, CC 1785.10, 1785.15
Internet,
  Notice,
    Labor and employment, investigative consumer reports, CC 1786.16
    Privacy, CC 1786.20
  Personal information, CC 1798.81.6

CONSUMER CREDIT REPORTING AGENCIES—Cont'd
Invasion of privacy, actions for damages, conditions precedent, CC 1785.32
Investigations and investigators,
  Accuracy of file, CC 1785.16, 1785.21
  Information furnishers, disputes, obligations, CC 1785.25
Joint credit accounts, credit history, filing of information, CC 1812.30
Judgments and decrees, CC 1786.18
Labor and employment, CC 1785.18
  Notice, CC 1785.20.5
Landlord and Tenant, this index
Libel and slander, conditions precedent, CC 1785.32
Liens and incumbrances, release, CC 1785.135
Limitation of actions, CC 1785.33
Malice, actions for damages, CC 1785.32
Marketing purposes, individual files, prevention from providing, CC 1785.19.5
Medical information, CC 1785.13
Motor vehicles, conditional sales, retention, CC 2984.5
Names,
  Change, security freeze, notice, CC 1785.11.3
  Identity and identification, theft, CC 1785.20.3
  Investigative reporting agencies, notice, CC 1786.20
Negative information, notice, CC 1785.26
Negligence,
  Exemplary damages, CC 1785.31 et seq.
  Investigative reporting agencies, privacy, CC 1786.20
Notice,
  Adverse action based on report, CC 1785.20
  Adverse information, cosigners, CC 1799.101, 1799.102
  Correction of report, CC 1785.16, 1785.21
  Cosigners, action for damages, failure to notify of adverse information, CC 1799.102
  Credit scores, CC 1785.15.1, 1785.15.2, 1785.20.2
  Denial, rates and rating organizations, CC 1786.40
  Forms, CC 1785.15
  Furnishers of information, inaccurate, CC 1785.25
  Identity and identification, theft, CC 1785.15, 1785.15.3, 1785.20.3
  Information suppliers, obligations, CC 1785.14
  Investigations and investigators, CC 1786.29
  Negative credit information, reports, CC 1785.26
  Police reports, blocking information, CC 1785.16
  Prequalifying reports, transactions not initiated by consumer, CC 1785.11

CONSUMER

CONSUMER CREDIT REPORTING AGENCIES—Cont'd
Notice—Cont'd
  Privacy, CC 1786.20
  Reinsertion, disputes, deleted information, CC 1785.16
  Reinvestigations, CC 1786.24
  Required notices, scope, CC 1785.6
  Risk scores, CC 1785.15.1, 1785.15.2, 1785.20.2
  Security alerts, reports, CC 1785.11.1, 1785.15
  Security freeze, CC 1785.11.2
    Reports, CC 1785.15
  Solicitation, lists, removal, CC 1785.11.8
  Transaction not initiated by consumer, CC 1785.20.1
    Exclusion from list, CC 1785.11
  Use of report to deny credit, CC 1785.20.5
Numbers and numbering. Telecommunications, post
Obligations, furnishers of credit information, CC 1785.25, 1785.26
Open end credit account, closed by consumer, notice, CC 1785.13
Password, security freeze, reports, CC 1785.11.2
Payment by cosigners, notice in record, CC 1799.101, 1799.102
Penalties. Fines and penalties, generally, ante
Personal information, Internet, CC 1798.81.6
Police reports, blocking information, CC 1785.16
Posting, privacy, notice, CC 1786.20
Powers and duties, CC 1785.10 et seq.
Prequalifying reports, transactions not initiated by consumer, notice, CC 1785.20.1
Privacy, notice, damages, CC 1786.20
Privileges and immunities, user disclosing to consumer, CC 1785.14
Procedures, CC 1785.14, 1786.20
Proceedings. Actions and proceedings, generally, ante
Public policy, CC 1785.1
Public records, disclosure of source, CC 1785.18
Rates and charges,
  Disclosure of information, CC 1785.17, 1786.26
  Reinvestigation, disputed information, CC 1785.16
Real estate, records, application of law, CC 1785.35
Records and recordation, CC 1785.14, 1785.18, 1786.20
  Inspection and inspectors, CC 1785.15
Reinvestigation, CC 1785.16, 1786.24
  Correction of reports, CC 1785.30
Remedies, investigations and investigators, CC 1786.50 et seq.
Renewal, security alerts, CC 1785.11.1
Rental purchase agreements, reports, CC 1812.640

CONSUMER CREDIT REPORTING AGENCIES—Cont'd
Resale,
  Identity and identification, theft, CC 1785.16.3
  Procuring report for, CC 1785.22
Restricting access to files, procedures, marketing purposes or offers of credit, CC 1785.19.5
Restrictions on information in report, CC 1785.13
Risk scores, notice, CC 1785.15.1, 1785.15.2, 1785.20.2
Security, computers, CC 1798.81.6
Security alerts, reports, CC 1785.11.1
  Notice, CC 1785.15
Security freeze, CC 1785.11.9 et seq.
  Reports, CC 1785.11.2
Social security, numbers and numbering,
  Change, security freeze, notice, CC 1785.11.3
  Identity and identification, theft, CC 1785.20.3
Solicitation, lists, removal, notice, CC 1785.11.8
State agencies,
  Furnishing information, investigative consumer credit reporting agencies, CC 1786.14
  Furnishing reports to, CC 1785.12
Subpoenas, inspection of records, CC 1785.11
Tax liens, CC 1786.18
Telecommunications,
  Applications, disclosure, CC 1785.3
  Numbers and numbering,
    Disclosure, CC 1785.10
    Notice,
      Investigative reporting agencies, CC 1786.20
      Labor and employment, CC 1786.16
  Security alerts, requesting, CC 1785.11.1
  Security freeze, reports, CC 1785.11.2
Theft, identity and identification, CC 1785.15, 1785.15.3, 1785.20.3
  Deletions, CC 1785.16.1, 1788.18
  Resale, CC 1785.16.3
  Security alerts, CC 1785.11.1
Time, information prohibited, CC 1785.13
Title of property, application of law, CC 1785.35
Transactions not initiated by consumer,
  Notice, CC 1785.20.1
  Reports, CC 1785.11
Use of reports, CC 1785.20 et seq.
Waiver, CC 1785.36
Warnings, investigations and investigators, CC 1786.29
Writing, consumer disputes in writing, requirement, CC 1785.16

CONSUMER FINANCE LENDERS
Finance Lenders, generally, this index

CONSUMER GOODS
Delivery, express warranties, time, CC 1793.01
Disclaimers, implied warranties, CC 1792.4
Express warranties, CC 1793
  Time, delivery, CC 1793.01
Fines and penalties, price discrimination, sex, CC 51.14
Fitness for particular purpose, implied warranties, CC 1792.1, 1792.2
Grocery stores, point of sale systems, CC 7100 et seq.
Implied warranty of fitness for particular purpose, CC 1792.1
Implied warranty of merchantability, CC 1792
Indemnity, implied warranty of merchantability, CC 1792
Installation, standards for warranty work, CC 1796, 1796.5
Layaway sales, regulation, CC 1749 et seq.
Legal Remedies Act, CC 1750 et seq.
Merchantability, implied warranties, CC 1792
Price discrimination, sex, CC 51.14
Refunds, debit cards, prepaid debit cards, CC 1748.40, 1748.41
Sales, this index
Service and repair facilities, warranties, CC 1793.1 et seq.
Service contracts, CC 1790 et seq.
Sex, price discrimination, CC 51.14
Song Beverly Consumer Warranty Act, CC 1790 et seq.
Time, express warranties, delivery, CC 1793.01
Used goods, warranties, CC 1795.5
Waiver, implied warranties, CC 1792.4
Warranties, CC 1790 et seq.

CONSUMER LEGAL REMEDIES ACT
Generally, CC 1750 et seq.

CONSUMER PRIVACY ACT
Generally, CC 1798.100 et seq.

CONSUMER PRODUCTS
Consumer Goods, generally, this index

CONSUMER PROTECTION
Actions and proceedings, CC 1780 et seq.
  Credit denial, CC 1787.3
  Customer records, destruction, CC 1798.84
  Legal Remedies Act, CC 1750 et seq.
Assessments, Internet, children and minors, CC 1798.99.31
  Time, CC 1798.99.33
Attorney fees, CC 1780, 3345
Automated license plate recognition, CC 1798.90.5 et seq.
Club cards, grocery stores, disclosure, CC 1749.60 et seq.
Colleges and universities, student loans, borrowers rights, CC 1788.101 et seq.
Confidential or privileged information,
  Customer records,
    Breach of security, disclosure, CC 1798.82

CONSUMER PROTECTION—Cont'd
Confidential or privileged information—Cont'd
  Customer records—Cont'd
    Destruction, **CC 1798.80 et seq.**
    Internet, children and minors, assessments, **CC 1798.99.31**
Contracts,
  Consumer contract awareness, **CC 1799.200 et seq.**
  Delivery of copy after signature, **CC 1799.202 et seq.**
  Seller assisted marketing plans, **CC 1812.200 et seq.**
  Service contracts, **CC 1790 et seq.**
Costs, actions, **CC 1780**
Credit. Consumer Credit, generally, this index
Credit services organizations, **CC 1789.13**
Damages, **CC 1780 et seq.**
  Consumer contracts, delivery, **CC 1799.205**
  Customer records, destruction, **CC 1798.84**
  Delivery, retail purchases, time, **CC 1722**
Debt settlement providers, fair debt settlement, **CC 1788.300 et seq.**
Deceptive trade practices. Monopolies and Unfair Trade, generally, this index
Delivery,
  Contracts, **CC 1799.202 et seq.**
  Retail purchases, time, **CC 1722**
Designs and designers, Internet, children and minors, **CC 1798.99.28 et seq.**
Disabled persons,
  Additional penalty, **CC 3345**
  Damages, **CC 1780**
Disclosure,
  Grocery stores, club cards, **CC 1749.60 et seq.**
  Internet, children and minors, assessments, **CC 1798.99.31**
Electronic mail,
  Breach of security, personal information, disclosure, **CC 1798.29**
  Customer records, breach of security, notice, **CC 1798.82**
Employment or insurance information, investigative consumer reporting agencies, **CC 1786 et seq.**
Escrows and escrow agents, deeds and conveyances, foreclosure, **CC 1103.20 et seq.**
Exemptions,
  Consumer contract awareness, **CC 1799.202**
  Internet, children and minors, **CC 1798.99.40**
Finance Lenders, generally, this index
Fines and penalties,
  Aged persons, disabled persons, **CC 1780**
  Veterans, **CC 3345**
  Internet, children and minors, **CC 1798.99.35**
Forms, customer records, breach of security, notice, **CC 1798.82**
Gray market goods, disclosure, **CC 1797.8 et seq.**

CONSUMER PROTECTION—Cont'd
Grocery stores,
  Club cards, disclosure, **CC 1749.60 et seq.**
  Point of sale systems, **CC 7100 et seq.**
Guarantors, delivery of copy of agreements, **CC 1799.206**
Immigration, **CC 3339**
Immunities, Internet, children and minors, **CC 1798.99.35**
Injunctions,
  Customer records, destruction, **CC 1798.84**
  Internet, children and minors, **CC 1798.99.35**
Installment Sales, generally, this index
Internet, children and minors, **CC 1798.99.28 et seq.**
Investigative consumer reporting agencies, **CC 1786 et seq.**
Language, warranties, plain language, **CC 1793.1**
Layaway sales, regulation, **CC 1749 et seq.**
Monopolies and Unfair Trade, generally, this index
Motor Vehicles, this index
Notice, breach of security, disclosure, **CC 1798.82**
Payment processors, fair debt settlement, **CC 1788.300 et seq.**
Penalties. Fines and penalties, generally, ante
Plain language, warranties, **CC 1793.1**
Privacy, Internet, children and minors, **CC 1798.99.28 et seq.**
Privileged information. Confidential or privileged information, generally, ante
Privileges and immunities, Internet, children and minors, **CC 1798.99.35**
Proceedings. Actions and proceedings, generally, ante
Public policy, Internet, children and minors, **CC 1798.99.29**
Records and recordation,
  Confidential or privileged information, generally, ante
  Personal information,
    Breach of security, disclosure, **CC 1798.82**
    Destruction, **CC 1798.80 et seq.**
Rental Purchase Agreements, generally, this index
Reports,
  Internet, children and minors, **CC 1798.99.32**
  Investigative consumer reporting agencies, **CC 1786 et seq.**
Restitution, **CC 1780 et seq.**
Retail installment sales. Installment Sales, generally, this index
Return of goods, refunds or exchanges, notice if not allowed, **CC 1723**
Seller assisted marketing plan, **CC 1812.200 et seq.**
Service connections, time, **CC 1722**
Service Contracts, generally, this index

CONSUMER PROTECTION—Cont'd
Simple language, warranties, **CC 1793.1**
Song Beverly Consumer Warranty Act, **CC 1790 et seq.**
Student loans, borrowers rights, **CC 1788.101 et seq.**
Supermarkets, club cards, disclosure, **CC 1749.60 et seq.**
Time,
  Delivery of retail purchases, **CC 1722**
  Internet, children and minors, assessments, **CC 1798.99.33**
Title insurance, deeds and conveyances, foreclosure, **CC 1103.20 et seq.**
Treble damages, aged persons, disabled persons, veterans, **CC 3345**
Unfair trade. Monopolies and Unfair Trade, generally, this index
Veterans, additional penalty, **CC 3345**
Waiver, consumer contract awareness, **CC 1799.207**
Warranties, **CC 1790 et seq.**

CONSUMERS
Deliveries, time, requirements, **CC 1722**
Discrimination, discounts, unemployment, **CC 51.13**
Electronic commerce, **CC 1789 et seq.**
Employment or insurance investigation, reporting agencies, **CC 1786 et seq.**
Medical records, privacy, sales, **CC 1798.130**
  Exemptions, **CC 1798.146, 1798.148**
Personal information, privacy, **CC 1798.100 et seq.**
Privacy, **CC 1798.100 et seq.**
Protection. Consumer Protection, generally, this index
Public utilities, service connection or repair, time, **CC 1722**
Waiver, electronic commerce, **CC 1789.9**

CONTAGIOUS DISEASES
Diseases, generally, this index

CONTAINERS
Brands, Marks and Labels, generally, this index
Labels. Brands, Marks and Labels, generally, this index
Landlord and tenant, agricultural products, **CC 1940.10**
Lost or abandoned, remaining on premises after termination of tenancy, liability of landlord, **CC 1983**

CONTAMINATION
Air Pollution, generally, this index

CONTEMPT
Homeless persons, transitional housing, misconduct, injunctions, **CC 1954.14**
Public officers and employees, authority to punish for contempt, **CC 1201**
Stories about felonies, sale proceeds, **CC 2225**

CONTINGENT

CONTINGENT ESTATES OR INTERESTS
Future Estates or Interests, generally, this index

CONTINGENT REMAINDERS
Future Estates or Interests, generally, this index

CONTRABAND
Weapons, generally, this index

CONTRACT ACT (PUBLIC WORKS)
State Contracts, generally, this index

CONTRACT OF ADHESION
Performance, time, CC 1657.1

CONTRACTORS
Actions and proceedings,
  Burden of proof, defects, **CC 942**
  Defects, **CC 896 et seq.**
    Burden of proof, **CC 942**
  Defenses, construction defects, **CC 945.5**
Adjacent landowners, entry on property, indemnity, **CC 2782.1**
Aged persons, home improvement business, installment sales, security interest, **CC 1804.1**
Ambulances, disclosure, **CC 3273**
Application of law, construction defects, **CC 936**
Attorney fees, construction, reimbursement, defense fees and costs, **CC 2782.05**
Bids and Bidding, generally, this index
Clients, sexual harassment, **CC 51.9**
Consumers, privacy, **CC 1798.100 et seq.**
Coterminous landowners, indemnity, construction contracts, **CC 2782.1**
Damages,
  Construction, reimbursement, defense fees and costs, **CC 2782.05**
  Defects, **CC 896 et seq.**
Defects. Buildings, this index
Defenses, construction defects, actions and proceedings, **CC 945.5**
Emergency medical technicians, disclosure, **CC 3273**
Entry on property, indemnity, construction contracts, **CC 2782.1**
Evidence,
  Burden of proof, defects, **CC 942**
  Construction defects, burden of proof, **CC 942**
Foreign languages, home improvement business, translations, **CC 1632**
General contractors, defects, **CC 936, 945.5**
  Damages, **CC 896 et seq.**
Harassment, sexual harassment, clients, **CC 51.9**
Home improvement business,
  Aged persons, installment sales, security interest, **CC 1804.1**
  Cancellation, **CC 1689.6**
    Notice, **CC 1689.7**

CONTRACTORS—Cont'd
Home improvement business—Cont'd
  Foreign languages, translations, **CC 1632**
  Installment sales, aged persons, security interest, **CC 1804.1**
  Language, **CC 1689.7**
  Notice, right to cancel, **CC 1689.7**
  Security interest, aged persons, installment sales, **CC 1804.1**
  Service and repair contract, right to cancel, **CC 1689.6**
  Spanish language, translations, **CC 1632**
Indemnity, adjacent owners, entry on property, **CC 2782.1 et seq.**
Installment sales, home improvement business, aged persons, security interest, **CC 1804.1**
Liens. Mechanics Liens, generally, this index
Logging, stop notice to withhold funds for lien, **CC 3065c**
Mechanics Liens, generally, this index
Medical records, confidential or privileged information, **CC 56 et seq.**
Mobilehomes and Mobilehome Parks, this index
Negligence, construction defects, application of law, **CC 936**
Personal information, consumers, privacy, **CC 1798.100 et seq.**
Privacy, consumers, **CC 1798.100 et seq.**
Proceedings. Actions and proceedings, generally, ante
Rescue, disclosure, **CC 3273**
Service contractors, home improvement business, right to cancel, **CC 1689.6**
Sexual harassment, clients, **CC 51.9**
Subcontractors, generally, this index
Suits. Actions and proceedings, generally, ante

CONTRACTS
  Generally, **CC 1549 et seq.**
Abolition, sealed and unsealed instruments, distinctions, **CC 1629**
Acceptance,
  Absolute, **CC 1585**
  Benefits, effect of acceptance, **CC 1589**
  Communication, **CC 1582**
  Conditions, performance, **CC 1584**
  Consideration, **CC 1584**
  Qualified, **CC 1585**
Accord and Satisfaction, generally, this index
Actions and proceedings, **CC 1717**
  Enforcement of obligations, **CC 1428**
  Evidence, generally, post
  Independent wholesale sales representatives, **CC 1738.15**
  Lost or destroyed documents, action to prove or establish, **CC 3415**
  Public policy, payment of amount conceded to be due on contracts, **CC 1525**
Rescission, relief based on, **CC 1692**
Unliquidated damages, interest, **CC 3287**
Adverse or pecuniary interest. Conflict of Interest, generally, this index

CONTRACTS—Cont'd
Alteration or cancellation, **CC 1697 et seq., 3412 et seq.**
  Credit services organizations, notice, **CC 1789.16**
  Dating service contracts, **CC 1694.1 et seq.**
  Destruction of contract, **CC 1699**
  Duplicate, **CC 1701**
  Home solicitation contracts, **CC 1689.5 et seq.**
  Oral contracts, **CC 1697**
  Partial cancellation, **CC 3414**
  Rescission, generally, post
  Seminar solicitation contracts or offers, **CC 1689.20 et seq.**
  Weight loss contracts, **CC 1694.6 et seq.**
Alternative obligations, **CC 1448 et seq.**
Ambiguities, **CC 1649**
Anticipatory breach, damages, **CC 1671**
Application of law, emergencies, repairs or services, home solicitation contract, **CC 1689.13**
Arbitration and Award, generally, this index
Ascertainment of consideration, **CC 1611 et seq.**
Assignments, **CC 1457 et seq.**
Athletic facilities, notice, anabolic steroids, testosterone, or human growth hormone, **CC 1812.97**
Attorney Fees, this index
Authorization, oral contracts, **CC 1622**
Avoidable, ratification, **CC 1588**
Banks and Banking, this index
Beneficiary,
  Material alteration by as cancellation, **CC 1700**
  Third party, enforcement, **CC 1559**
Benefits, acceptance as consent, **CC 1589**
Bids and Bidding, generally, this index
Book accounts, actions on, attorney fees and costs, **CC 1717.5**
Bottomry, generally, this index
Boxing and wrestling, gymnasiums, notice, anabolic steroids, testosterone, or human growth hormone, **CC 1812.97**
Breach of contract,
  Damages, **CC 3275, 3300 et seq.**
  Interest, **CC 3289, 3289.5**
  Limitations, amount, **CC 3358**
  Injunctions to prevent, **CC 3423**
  Liquidated damages, **CC 1671**
  Specific Performance, generally, this index
Burden of proof, consideration, **CC 1615**
Cancellation. Alteration or cancellation, generally, ante
Capacity, **CC 38 et seq., 1557**
Carriers, this index
Cats, sales, **CC 1670.10**
Certainty of contract, damages for breach, **CC 3301**
Children and Minors, this index

CONTRACTS

CONTRACTS—Cont'd

Choice of law, transaction without reasonable relation to state, **CC 1646.5**
Civil rights, freedom from violence, waiver, **CC 51.7**
Classification, **CC 1619**
Coercion. Duress or coercion, generally, post
Communication. Consent, post
Compensation and salaries, human trafficking, deductions, illegal contracts, **CC 1670.7**
Concurrent conditions, **CC 1435**
    Performance, **CC 1439**
Conditional obligations, **CC 1434 et seq.**
Conditional payments, amounts conceded to be due, **CC 1525**
Conditions, proposal, performance, **CC 1584**
Conditions precedent, **CC 1435**
    Performance, **CC 1439**
        Offer dependent, **CC 1498**
        Revocation of proposal, **CC 1587**
Conditions subsequent, **CC 1435**
Condominiums, homeowners associations, inspection and inspectors, **CC 5200 et seq.**
Confession of judgment, home solicitation contracts, public policy, **CC 1689.12**
Confinement, duress, **CC 1569**
Conflict of Interest, generally, this index
Conflict of laws, construction, indemnity, **CC 2782.05**
Consent, **CC 1565 et seq.**
    Acceptance benefits, effect, **CC 1589**
    Alteration, **CC 1697, 1700**
    Cancellation of instruments, **CC 1700**
    Communication, **CC 1581**
        Acceptance of proposal, mode of communicating, **CC 1582**
        Completion, **CC 1583**
    Destruction or cancellation, **CC 1700**
    Duress, **CC 1567, 1568**
    Freedom,
        Causes for defeating, **CC 1567, 1568**
        Lack of, **CC 1566**
    Mistake, **CC 1567, 1568**
    Modification, **CC 1697**
    Mutuality, **CC 1580**
    Necessity, **CC 1550**
    Ratification where void for want of, **CC 1588**
    Rescission, **CC 1689**
    Subsequent, ratification by, **CC 1588**
    Transfer of obligations, **CC 1457**
    Undue influence, **CC 1567, 1568**
Consideration, **CC 1605 et seq.**
    Acceptance when offered with proposal as acceptance of proposal, **CC 1584**
    Ascertainment, **CC 1611 et seq.**
    Burden of proof, **CC 1615**
    Executed or executory, **CC 1609, 1610**
    Failure, rescission, **CC 1689**
    Illegal, **CC 1608**
    Impossibility of ascertaining consideration, **CC 1612, 1613**

CONTRACTS—Cont'd

Consideration—Cont'd
    Joint and several, **CC 1659, 1660**
    Legal obligation, **CC 1606, 1607**
    Moral obligation, **CC 1606, 1607**
    Necessity, **CC 1550**
        Modification of instruments, **CC 1697**
    Oral agreements supported by new consideration, written contracts modification, **CC 1698**
    Presumption where instrument written, **CC 1614**
    Rescission of contract, failure of consideration, **CC 1689**
    Voluntary transfers, **CC 1040**
    Written instruments, presumption, **CC 1614**
Construction,
    Indemnity, **CC 2782 et seq.**
    Public agencies, disputes, **CC 1670**
    Wrap up policies, insurance, indemnity, **CC 2782.9 et seq.**
Consumer Contract Awareness Act of 1990, **CC 1799.200 et seq.**
Consumer Credit, generally, this index
Consumer Protection, this index
Contract of adhesion, performance, time, **CC 1657.1**
Contrary to policy of law, **CC 1668**
Contribution, joint obligations, **CC 1432**
Convalescent homes, hiring agreements, termination, patient death, **CC 1934.5**
Costs,
    Actions, **CC 1717**
    Book accounts, actions and proceedings, **CC 1717.5**
Creation,
    Manner, **CC 1619 et seq.**
    Obligation, **CC 1428**
Credit card issuers and retailers, contracts prohibiting price discounts for cash sales, **CC 1748**
Credit services organizations, **CC 1789.14 et seq.**
Crimes and offenses,
    Illegal contracts, generally, post
    Sale of land, subdivision maps, false statements, **CC 2985.51**
    Sex offense victims, children, **CC 1669.5**
    Witnesses, void, **CC 1670.11**
Custom and usage,
    Implied stipulations, **CC 1655**
    Interpretation, **CC 1644 et seq.**
Damages, **CC 1717**
    Breach of contract, ante
    Certainty of contract, damages for breach, **CC 3301**
    Dating service contracts, **CC 1694.4**
    Interest, **CC 3289**
        Retail installment contracts, finance charges, **CC 3289.5**
    Real property purchase contracts, default, **CC 1675 et seq.**

CONTRACTS—Cont'd

Damages—Cont'd
    Rescission, **CC 1692**
    Weight loss contracts, **CC 1694.9**
Dance studio services, state regulation, **CC 1812.50 et seq.**
Dating service contracts, **CC 1694 et seq.**
Deaf or Hard of Hearing Persons, this index
Dealerships, **CC 80 et seq.**
Death, this index
Debt settlement providers, fair debt settlement, **CC 1788.302**
Debtors, validity, **CC 3431**
Deeds and Conveyances, this index
Default, real property purchase contracts, liquidated damages, **CC 1675 et seq.**
Delay, notice of rescission, effect, **CC 1693**
Delivery, written contracts, **CC 1626**
Destruction. Lost or Destroyed Documents, generally, this index
Disabled Persons, this index
Discount Buying Services, generally, this index
Disputes,
    Public agencies, **CC 1670**
    Total money, payment of amount conceded, **CC 1525**
Distributors, independent wholesale sales representatives, **CC 1738.10 et seq.**
Dogs, sales, **CC 1670.10**
Duplicate, destruction or alteration, **CC 1701**
Duress or coercion, **CC 1567, 1568**
    Rescission, **CC 1689**
Easement maintenance obligations, snow removal, **CC 845**
Effective date, delivery of written instrument, **CC 1626**
Electronic commercial service, **CC 1789.3**
Electronic transmissions, Uniform Electronic Transactions Act, **CC 1633.1 et seq.**
Elements, **CC 1550**
Emergencies,
    Home solicitation, repairs or services, Application of law, **CC 1689.13**
        Cancellation, waiver, **CC 1689.15**
    Repairs or services, home solicitation contract,
        Application of law, **CC 1689.13**
        Cancellation, waiver, **CC 1689.15**
Employment Agencies, this index
Endless chain schemes, rescission, **CC 1689.2**
Equity. Home Equity Sales Contracts, generally, this index
Essential elements, **CC 1550**
Euro, medium of payment, **CC 1663**
Evidence,
    Consideration, burden of proof, **CC 1615**
    Crimes and offenses, void, **CC 1670.11**
    Financial contract (qualified), frauds, statute of, **CC 1624**
    Lost or destroyed documents, **CC 3415**
    Presumptions,
        Consideration, **CC 1614**

I-45

CONTRACTS

CONTRACTS—Cont'd
Evidence—Cont'd
  Presumptions—Cont'd
    Intent of parties, CC 3400
    Joint and several promises, CC 1659, 1660
    Joint contracts, CC 1431
    Uncertainties in language, CC 1654
    Qualified financial contract, frauds, statute of, CC 1624
    Sexual harassment, void, CC 1670.11
    Unconscionable contracts, CC 1670.5
Excuse,
  Failure to perform conditional obligations, CC 1440
  Nonperformance, CC 1511 et seq.
Executed contracts, CC 1661
Executory contracts, CC 1661
Exemption from responsibility, illegal contracts, CC 1668
Express contracts, CC 1619
Extinguishment, CC 1682
  Obligations, CC 1473
  Rescission, generally, post
Fair dealerships, CC 80 et seq.
Financial contract (qualified), frauds, statute of, CC 1624
Fine art, consignment, CC 1738 et seq.
Fines and penalties, sale of land, Subdivision Map Act, false statements, CC 2985.51
Forfeitures,
  Breach of contract, damages, CC 3275
  Conditions, construction, CC 1442
Fraud, generally, this index
Frauds, Statute of, generally, this index
Freedom of consent, CC 1565
General intent, particular causes subordinate to, CC 1650
Governing law, CC 1627
Harassment, duress, CC 1569
Health studios, CC 1812.80 et seq.
Holidays, performance on next business day, CC 11
Home Equity Sales Contracts, generally, this index
Home improvement goods or services, retail installment, sales, CC 1689.8
Home roof warranties, CC 1797.90 et seq.
Home Solicitation Contracts, generally, this index
Housing, this index
Human trafficking, compensation and salaries, deductions, illegal contracts, CC 1670.7
Identification of parties, CC 1558
Illegal contracts, CC 1667 et seq.
  Conditions void, CC 1441
  Rescission, CC 1689
Implied contracts, CC 1619
Implied incidents, CC 1656
Implied stipulations, CC 1655
Impossibility of object, CC 1597

CONTRACTS—Cont'd
Impossible condition, void, CC 1441
Imprisonment, duress, CC 1569
Inconsistent words, CC 1653
Indemnity,
  Construction, CC 2782 et seq.
  Public agencies, design professional, CC 2782.8
Independent wholesale sales representatives, CC 1738.10 et seq.
Industrial Loan Companies, this index
Injunction to prevent breach, CC 3423
Installment Sales, generally, this index
Intellectual and Developmental Disabilities, this index
Intent,
  Ambiguity or uncertainty, CC 1649
  Ascertainment, CC 1637 et seq.
    Language, effect, CC 1638
    Rules governing, CC 1637
    Written contracts, CC 1639
  Circumstances, consideration, CC 1647
  Inconsistent words, rejection, CC 1653
  Mutual giving effect, CC 1636
  Particular clauses subordinate to general intent, CC 1650
  Presumptions, equitable and conscientious agreement, CC 3400
  Revision of contracts, CC 3399 et seq.
  Whole contract, giving effect to, CC 1641
  Written contracts, disregard of writing where real intention not expressed, CC 1640
Interest,
  Damages, breach of contract, CC 3289
    Retail installment contracts, CC 3289.5
  Variable interest rate, CC 1916.5
Interpretation, CC 1429, 1635 et seq.
  Ambiguity, CC 1649
  Circumstances, reference to for explanation, CC 1647
  Definiteness, favoring, CC 1643
  Euro, medium of payment, CC 1663
  Favoring effectiveness in operation, CC 1643
  Foreign states, transactions without reasonable relation to state, CC 1646.5
  General intent, particular clauses subordinate to, CC 1650
  Implied incidents, CC 1656
  Implied stipulations, CC 1655
  Incidents, implied, CC 1656
  Inconsistent words, rejection, CC 1653
  Joint and several, promise, CC 1659, 1660
  Law of place of performance, CC 1646
  Lawfulness, favoring, CC 1643
  Object, restriction to, CC 1648
  Particular clauses, subordinate to general intent, CC 1650
  Partly written and partly printed, CC 1651
  Performance, time, CC 1657
    Contract of adhesion, CC 1657.1
  Presumptions, party causing uncertainty, CC 1654

CONTRACTS—Cont'd
Interpretation—Cont'd
  Printed forms, CC 1651
  Reasonableness, favoring, CC 1643
  Reconciliation of repugnancies, CC 1652
  Repugnancies, reconciliation, CC 1652
  Restriction to object, CC 1648
  Sense of words, CC 1644
    Technical words, CC 1645
  Several contracts as parts of one transaction, CC 1642
  Stipulations, implied, CC 1655
  Time of performance, CC 1657
    Contract of adhesion, CC 1657.1
  Transactions without reasonable relation to state, CC 1646.5
  Uncertainty, CC 1649
    Interpretation against party causing, CC 1654
  Uniformity, CC 1635
  Usage of place of performance, CC 1646
  Whole contracts, giving effect to, CC 1641
  Words, CC 1644
    Inconsistent, CC 1653
    Technical, CC 1645
Job listing services, written contracts, CC 1812.516
Joint contracts,
  Contribution, CC 1432
  Obligations imposed by, CC 1430
  Performance, CC 1474, 1475
  Presumptions, CC 1431, 1659, 1660
Joint debtors, release of one of two, effect, CC 1543
Joint obligations, CC 1430 et seq.
Labor disputes, freedom from violence, waiver, CC 51.7
Land contracts. Deeds and Conveyances, this index
Lapse of time, revocation of proposal, CC 1587
Lawful object, CC 1550
Lay away sales, CC 1749 et seq.
Leases, generally, this index
Legal obligations, consideration, CC 1606, 1607
Libel and slander, menace, CC 1570
Liquidated damages, CC 1671
  Real property purchase contracts, default, CC 1675 et seq.
Loans for exchange of property, CC 1902 et seq.
Lost or Destroyed Documents, generally, this index
Mailing unsolicited merchandise, contractual plans or arrangements, CC 1584.5
Manner of creating, CC 1619 et seq.
Marketing plans, seller assisted marketing plans, CC 1812.200 et seq.
Material alteration by beneficiary, destruction, CC 1700
Membership camping contracts, CC 1812.300 et seq.

CONTRACTS

CONTRACTS—Cont'd
Mental Health, this index
Mines and minerals, exploration or removal, lessors remedy for breach statutes, applicability, **CC 1952.4**
Minors. Children and Minors, this index
Mistake,
  Consent, **CC 1567, 1568**
    Rescission, **CC 1689**
  Fact, **CC 1577**
  Foreign law, **CC 1579**
  Intention of parties, written contracts failing to express, **CC 1640**
  Kinds, **CC 1576**
  Law, **CC 1578**
  Reformation, **CC 3399**
  Rescission, stipulations against right, **CC 1690**
  Specific performance, **CC 3391**
Mobilehomes and Mobilehome Parks, this index
Modification. Alteration or cancellation, generally, ante
Money conceded to be due, payment to reduce litigation, **CC 1525**
Moral obligation, consideration, **CC 1606, 1607**
Mortgages, generally, this index
Motor Vehicles, this index
Mutual intention of parties, giving effect, **CC 1636**
Mutuality, **CC 1565**
  Consent, **CC 1580**
Negligence, exemption from responsibility, illegal contracts, **CC 1668**
Negotiations, superseded, written instruments, **CC 1625**
Nonnegotiable, transfer, **CC 1459**
Notice,
  Alternative obligations, selection, **CC 1449**
  Cancellation,
    Home solicitation, contracts, **CC 1689.5 et seq.**
    Seminar sales solicitation contracts, **CC 1689.20 et seq.**
  Dating service contracts, cancellation, **CC 1694.1, 1694.2**
  Excuse for nonperformance, **CC 1511**
  Failure to perform conditional obligations, **CC 1440**
  Weight loss contracts, cancellation, **CC 1694.6, 1694.7**
Novation, generally, this index
Objects, **CC 1595 et seq.**
  Elements, **CC 1596**
  Impossibility, **CC 1597**
    Effect, **CC 1598**
  Necessity, **CC 1550**
  One of several unlawful, **CC 1599**
  Restrictions on interpretation, **CC 1648**
  Unlawful, **CC 1598**

CONTRACTS—Cont'd
Offenses. Crimes and offenses, generally, ante
Offer of performance, **CC 1485 et seq.**
Oppressive, duress, **CC 1569**
Oral contracts, **CC 1052, 1622**
  Modification of written contracts, **CC 1698**
Parol contracts. Oral contracts, generally, ante
Part payments, amounts concededly due, **CC 1525**
Partial cancellation, **CC 3414**
Partial performance, offer, **CC 1486**
Parties, **CC 1556 et seq.**
  Causing uncertainty, presumption, **CC 1654**
  Consent to modification, **CC 1697**
  Identification, **CC 1558**
  Mutual intention, giving effect, **CC 1636**
  Requirements, **CC 1550**
  Third party beneficiary, enforcement, **CC 1559**
Payment, amount conceded to be due in order to reduce litigated matters to lowest level of jurisdiction, **CC 1525**
Performance of,
  Obligation, **CC 1473 et seq.**
  Specific Performance, generally, this index
Personal injuries, exemption from responsibility, illegal contracts, **CC 1668**
Personal interest. Conflict of Interest, generally, this index
Personal Property Brokers, generally, this index
Pleadings,
  Rescission, **CC 1692**
  Service, notice of rescission, **CC 1691**
Precomputed finance charge contracts, **CC 1799.8**
Prejudice to public interest, rescission, **CC 1689**
Prescription drug claims processor, conditions precedent, **CC 2527, 2528**
Presumptions. Evidence, ante
Preventing performance, **CC 1511 et seq.**
Printed forms, controlled by written insertions, **CC 1651**
Proceedings. Actions and proceedings, generally, ante
Process, rescission, notice, **CC 1691**
Promises, good consideration, **CC 1605**
Proof. Evidence, generally, ante
Proposal, revocation,
  Method, **CC 1587**
  Time, **CC 1586**
Public interest prejudice, rescission, **CC 1689**
Public policy,
  Payment of amount conceded to be due, **CC 1525**
  Prejudice to public interest, **CC 1689**
  Real estate contracts, prepayment clauses, waiver, **CC 2985.6**
  Sex offense victims, children, **CC 1669.5**
Qualified acceptance, **CC 1585**

CONTRACTS—Cont'd
Qualified financial contract, frauds, statute of, **CC 1624**
Ratification where void for want of consent, **CC 1588**
Reasonable, contract of adhesion, performance, time, **CC 1657.1**
Reconciliation of repugnancies, **CC 1652**
Records and recordation, Uniform Electronic Transactions Act, **CC 1633.1 et seq.**
Reformation, **CC 3399 et seq.**
  Presumptions, intent to make equitable and conscientious agreement, **CC 3400**
  Principles of revision, **CC 3401**
  Specific performance, **CC 3402**
Refunds,
  Home solicitation contracts, cancellation, **CC 1689.10**
  Weight loss contracts, cancellation, **CC 1694.6**
Relatives, unlawful confinement, duress, **CC 1569**
Release, **CC 1541 et seq.**
Rent control, commercial property, application of law, **CC 1954.28**
Rental Purchase Agreements, generally, this index
Rescission, **CC 1688 et seq.**
  Actions and proceedings, **CC 1692**
  Consent not free, **CC 1566**
  Damages, **CC 1692**
  Defense or cross complaint, **CC 1692**
  Dental service contracts, **CC 1689.3**
  Endless chain schemes, **CC 1689.2**
  Grounds, **CC 1689**
  Home equity sales contracts, **CC 1695.14**
  Home solicitation contracts, **CC 1689.5 et seq.**
  Modification of contract, **CC 1698**
  Notice, **CC 1691**
    Delay, **CC 1693**
  Procedure, **CC 1691**
  Relief, **CC 1692**
  Restoration, **CC 1691**
    Delay in giving notice, **CC 1693**
  Stipulations, **CC 1690**
Respondentia, generally, this index
Restoration after rescission of contract, **CC 1691**
  Delay in giving notice, **CC 1693**
Retail installment contracts. Installment Sales, generally, this index
Retail sales, sales and use taxes, reimbursement, **CC 1656.1**
Retailers and credit card issuers, contracts prohibiting price discounts for cash sales, **CC 1748**
Revision, **CC 3399 et seq.**
Revocation, **CC 1587**
  Proposal, **CC 1586**
Sales, this index

CONTRACTS

CONTRACTS—Cont'd
Satisfaction. Accord and Satisfaction, generally, this index
Seals,
  Distinctions between sealed and unsealed instruments abolished, CC 1629
  Method of affixing, CC 1628
Security agents and broker dealers, electronic transmissions, CC 1633
Seller Assisted Marketing Plans, this index
Seminar sales solicitation contracts, cancellation rights, CC 1689.20 et seq.
Sense of words, technical words, CC 1645
Service Contracts, generally, this index
Several contracts as parts of one transaction, interpretation, CC 1642
Several obligations, CC 1430
Sex offense victims, children, CC 1669.5
Sexual harassment, witnesses, void, CC 1670.11
Sexual orientation, freedom from violence, waiver, CC 51.7
Signatures,
  Destruction, CC 1699
  One party only, specific performance, CC 3388
  Uniform Electronic Transactions Act, CC 1633.1 et seq.
Specific Performance, generally, this index
Sports, anabolic steroids, testosterone, or human growth hormone, CC 1812.97
State Contracts, generally, this index
Statute of Frauds. Frauds, Statute of, generally, this index
Stipulations, superseded, written instruments, CC 1625
Subcontractors, generally, this index
Subsequent conditions, CC 1435
Substitution. Novation, generally, this index
Suits. Actions and proceedings, generally, ante
Technical words, interpretation, CC 1645
Telecommunications, this index
Termination, nursing or convalescent homes, death of party, CC 1934.5
Third party beneficiary, enforcement, CC 1559
Time,
  Effective date, delivery, CC 1626
  Performance, CC 1657
    Contract of adhesion, CC 1657.1
  Revocation of proposal, CC 1586
    Lapse, CC 1587
Transfer of obligations, CC 1458
  Consent, CC 1457
Uncertainties in interpretation, CC 1654
Unconscionable contracts, CC 1670.5
Undue influence, consent, CC 1567, 1568
  Rescission, CC 1689
Uniform Electronic Transactions Act, CC 1633.1 et seq.
Uniformity of interpretation, CC 1635
Unlawful contracts. Illegal contracts, generally, ante

CONTRACTS—Cont'd
Unsolicited merchandise, mailing under contractual plans or arrangements, CC 1584.5
Validity, partial, CC 1599
Variable interest rate, CC 1916.5
Void, CC 1598, 3413
  Conditions, CC 1441
  Consideration, illegality, CC 1608
  Crimes and offenses, witnesses, CC 1670.11
  Partially, CC 1599
  Sex offense victims, children, CC 1669.5
  Sexual harassment, witnesses, CC 1670.11
Waiver,
  Attorneys fees, CC 1717
  Cancellation of home solicitation contract, CC 1689.12
  Consumer contract awareness, CC 1799.207
  Independent wholesale sales representatives, CC 1738.13
  Membership camping contracts, CC 1812.316
  Precomputed finance charge contract, CC 1799.85
  Provision of written contract, contract modification, CC 1698
Weight loss contracts, CC 1694.5 et seq.
Wholesale sales representatives, independents, CC 1738.10 et seq.
Willful injuries, exemption from responsibility, illegal contracts, CC 1668
Witnesses,
  Compensation, voidability, CC 1669.7
  Crimes and offenses, void, CC 1670.11
  Sexual harassment, void, CC 1670.11
Writing,
  Electronic Transactions Act, CC 1633.1 et seq.
  Uniform Electronic Transactions Act, CC 1633.1 et seq.

CONTRACTS FOR SALE OF LAND
Deeds and Conveyances, this index

CONTRIBUTIONS
Easements, maintenance and repairs, CC 845
Gifts, Devises and Bequests, generally, this index
Joint debtors, release, CC 1543
Joint or joint and several obligors, CC 1432

CONTROLLED ESCROW COMPANY
Real estate developers, CC 2995

CONTROLLED SUBSTANCES
Drugs and Medicine, generally, this index

CONVALESCENT NURSING HOMES
Nursing Homes, generally, this index

CONVERSION
Damages,
  Lienors, CC 3338
  Presumption, CC 3336

CONVERSION—Cont'd
Damages—Cont'd
  Subsequent application of property to benefit of owner, CC 3337
Demand, restoration of thing wrongfully acquired, CC 1713
Discount buying services, officers and employees, statement, CC 1812.106
Evidence, damages, presumptions, CC 3336
Liens and incumbrances, damages, CC 3338
Notice, restoration of thing wrongfully acquired, demand, CC 1713
Presumptions, damages, CC 3336
Restoration of property, CC 1712
  Demand for return, CC 1713

CONVEYANCES
Deeds and Conveyances, generally, this index

CONVICTS
Correctional Institutions, generally, this index
Jails, generally, this index

COOPERATIVE APARTMENTS
Building standards, water conservation, CC 1101.1 et seq.
Mobilehomes and Mobilehome Parks, this index
Mortgages, shared appreciation loans, CC 1917 et seq.
Shared appreciation loans, CC 1917 et seq.
Water conservation, building standards, CC 1101.1 et seq.

COOPERATIVE CORPORATIONS
Actions and proceedings, retailers, fraudulent inducement by wholesalers, CC 3343.7
Articles of incorporation,
  Limited equity housing cooperatives, CC 817
  Workforce housing cooperative trusts, CC 817.1
Attorney fees, limited equity housing cooperatives, CC 817.4
Bylaws,
  Limited equity housing cooperatives, CC 817
  Workforce housing cooperative trusts, CC 817.1
Costs, limited equity housing cooperatives, CC 817.4
Credit Unions, generally, this index
Directors,
  Limited equity housing cooperatives, CC 817
  Workforce housing cooperative trusts, CC 817.1
Dissolution,
  Limited equity housing cooperatives, CC 817.2
  Workforce housing cooperative trusts, CC 817.2
Floating homes, CC 800.300 et seq.
Fraud, retailers, actions against wholesalers, fraudulent inducement, CC 3343.7
Housing corporations,
  Limited equity housing cooperatives, CC 817 et seq.

CORRECTIONAL

COOPERATIVE CORPORATIONS—Cont'd
Housing corporations—Cont'd
Workforce housing cooperative trusts, **CC 817.1 et seq.**
Landlord and tenant, floating homes, **CC 800.300 et seq.**
Mobilehomes and mobilehome parks, **CC 799 et seq.**
Retailers, actions against wholesalers, fraudulent inducement, **CC 3343.7**
Sales, defect disclosure, **CC 1134**
Solar energy, stock cooperatives, applications, approval, **CC 714**
Sponsors, workforce housing cooperative trusts, **CC 817.3**
Stock cooperatives, **CC 4000 et seq.**
Aged persons, cohabitants, age, covenants, conditions, restrictions, **CC 51.3**
Air conditioning defects, disclosure, **CC 1134**
Blanket incumbrances on subdivisions, notice, **CC 1133**
Conditions, aged persons, cohabitants, age, restrictions, **CC 51.3**
Covenants, aged persons, cohabitants, age, restrictions, **CC 51.3**
Defects, disclosure, **CC 1134**
Electrical defects, disclosure, **CC 1134**
Heating defects, disclosure, **CC 1134**
Plumbing defects, disclosure, **CC 1134**
Restrictions, aged persons, cohabitants, age, **CC 51.3**
Senior citizen housing, cohabitants, age, restrictions, **CC 51.3**
Solar energy,
Applications, approval, **CC 714**
Restrictions, **CC 714.1**
Workforce housing cooperative trusts, **CC 817.1 et seq.**

COPARTNERSHIP
Partnership, generally, this index

COPYRIGHTS
Art works, conveyance of rights, ownership of physical work, **CC 988**
Legal Estates Principal and Income Law, **CC 731 et seq.**

CORN
Agricultural Products, generally, this index

CORNEAL EYE TISSUE
Tissue Banks, generally, this index

CORONERS
Medical records, disclosure, **CC 56.10**

CORPORATE SECURITIES LAW
Securities, generally, this index

CORPORATION TAXES
Bookkeeping services, confidential or privileged information, **CC 1799.1a**
Business records, bookkeeping services, confidential or privileged information, **CC 1799.1a**

CORPORATION TAXES—Cont'd
Confidential or privileged information, bookkeeping services, **CC 1799.1a**

CORPORATIONS
Acknowledgments, **CC 1185**
Certificates, forms, **CC 1190**
Bankruptcy, generally, this index
Banks and Banking, generally, this index
Capital stock. Shares and shareholders, generally, post
Carriers, generally, this index
Charities, generally, this index
Colleges and Universities, generally, this index
Commercial banks. Banks and Banking, generally, this index
Commercial credit reporting, **CC 1785.41 et seq.**
Confidential or privileged information, drivers licenses, electronic devices and equipment, **CC 1798.90.1**
Consumer cooperative corporations. Cooperative Corporations, generally, this index
Cooperative Corporations, generally, this index
Corporation Taxes, generally, this index
Credit reporting agencies, **CC 1785.41 et seq.**
Credit Unions, generally, this index
Crimes and offenses,
Drivers licenses, electronic devices and equipment, confidential or privileged information, **CC 1798.90.1**
Identification cards, electronic devices and equipment, confidential or privileged information, **CC 1798.90.1**
Dealerships, **CC 80 et seq.**
Dividends, legal estates, Principle and Income Law, **CC 731 et seq.**
Drivers licenses, electronic devices and equipment, confidential or privileged information, **CC 1798.90.1**
Fair dealerships, **CC 80 et seq.**
Filing, identity and identification, theft, **CC 1798.200 et seq.**
Fines and penalties,
Drivers licenses, electronic devices and equipment, confidential or privileged information, **CC 1798.90.1**
Identification cards, electronic devices and equipment, confidential or privileged information, **CC 1798.90.1**
Franchise taxes. Corporation Taxes, generally, this index
Identification cards, electronic devices and equipment, confidential or privileged information, **CC 1798.90.1**
Identity and identification, theft, filing, **CC 1798.200 et seq.**
Income tax. Corporation Taxes, generally, this index
Industrial Loan Companies, generally, this index
Insurance companies. Insurance, generally, this index

CORPORATIONS—Cont'd
Interest, personal injury damages, **CC 3291**
Legal Estates Principal and Income Law, **CC 731 et seq.**
Mechanics liens, security, large projects, application of law, **CC 8704**
Nonprofit Corporations, generally, this index
Personal injury damages, interest, **CC 3291**
Personal liability of officers, shareholders and others. Shares and shareholders, generally, post
Personal Property Brokers, generally, this index
Public Corporations, generally, this index
Public Utilities, generally, this index
Railroads, generally, this index
Reverse stock split. Shares and shareholders, generally, post
Seals, affixing to instruments, **CC 1628**
Securities, generally, this index
Shares and shareholders,
See, also, Securities, generally, this index
Income, Legal Estates Principal and Income Law, **CC 731 et seq.**
Legal Estates Principal and Income Law, **CC 731 et seq.**
Principal and income, **CC 731 et seq.**
Small Businesses, generally, this index
Stock and stockholders. Shares and shareholders, generally, ante
Suretyship and Guaranty, generally, this index
Taxation,
Corporation Taxes, generally, this index
Franchise taxes. Corporation Taxes, generally, this index
Theft, identity and identification, filing, **CC 1798.200 et seq.**
Torts, personal injury damages, interest, **CC 3291**
Trade Secrets, generally, this index
Trading Stamps, generally, this index
Universities. Colleges and Universities, generally, this index
Utilities. Public Utilities, generally, this index

CORRECTIONAL INSTITUTIONS
Acknowledgments, identity and identification, **CC 1185**
Attorney general, health care providers, defense, **CC 1542.1**
Disclosure, medical records, mental health, **CC 56.10**
Identity and identification, acknowledgments, **CC 1185**
Jails, generally, this index
Juvenile Delinquents and Dependents, generally, this index
Medical records, mental health, disclosure, **CC 56.10**
Mental health, medical records, disclosure, **CC 56.10**
Social security, numbers and numbering, veterans, disclosure, **CC 1798.85**

I-49

CORRESPONDENCE

CORRESPONDENCE
Letters and Other Correspondence, generally, this index

CORRUPTION
Bribery and Corruption, generally, this index

COSMETICIANS
Cosmetology, generally, this index

COSMETICS
Animals, tests, crimes and offenses, CC 1834.9.5
Crimes and offenses, animals, tests, CC 1834.9.5
Exports and imports, animals, tests, crimes and offenses, CC 1834.9.5
Fines and penalties, animals, tests, CC 1834.9.5
Tests, animals, crimes and offenses, CC 1834.9.5
Trade secrets, animals, tests, CC 1834.9.5

COSMETOLOGY
Barbers, generally, this index
Discrimination,
    Prices, posting, CC 51.6
    Sex, CC 55.61 et seq.
Fines and penalties, prices, posting, discrimination, CC 51.6
Languages, posting, prices, discrimination, CC 51.6
Posting, prices, discrimination, CC 51.6
Prices,
    Posting, discrimination, CC 51.6
    Sex, discrimination, CC 55.61 et seq.
Sex, discrimination, CC 55.61 et seq.

COST OF LIVING
Children and minors, damages, liability of parents, CC 1714.1
Guardian and ward, damages, liability of guardians, CC 1714.1
Juvenile delinquents and dependents, damages, liability of parents, CC 1714.1

COSTA HAWKINS RENTAL HOUSING ACT
Generally, CC 1954.50 et seq.

COSTA KEENE SEYMOUR COMMERCIAL PROPERTY INVESTMENT ACT
Generally, CC 1954.25 et seq.

COSTS
Adjoining landowners, fences, maintenance, CC 841
Alcoholic beverages, injunctions, CC 3496
Animals, injunction, tests, alternatives, CC 1834.9
Art and artists, fine art multiples, CC 1745
Assignation, place of, injunctions, awarding, CC 3496
Audio and video recordings, invasion of privacy, CC 1708.85

COSTS—Cont'd
Autographed memorabilia, warranties, CC 1739.7
Booking photographs, commercial use, CC 1798.91.1
Breach of warranty actions, Song Beverly Consumer Warranty Act, CC 1794
Business and commerce, personal information, direct marketing, disclosure, CC 1798.84
Business records, disclosures, civil actions, CC 1799.2
Celebrity image protection, CC 3344.1
Civil rights, disabled persons, construction, accessibility, CC 55.55
Condominiums, this index
Consumer Credit, this index
Consumer Credit Reporting Agencies, this index
Contracts, actions on, CC 1717
    Book accounts, CC 1717.5
Contracts for sale of land, Subdivision Map Act, noncompliance, CC 2985.51
Credit,
    Discrimination, marital status or sex, CC 1812.34
    Identity and identification, theft, CC 1785.20.3
Credit Cards, this index
Credit services organizations, CC 1789.21
Data,
    Brokers, registration, CC 1798.99.82
    Sales, crimes and offenses, CC 1724
Dealerships, CC 86
Debt settlement providers, fair debt settlement, CC 1788.305
Deceased celebrity image protection, CC 3344.1
Defacement of property, willful misconduct of minor, imputed liability of parents, CC 1714.1
Deposits, action on contract, interest bearing, CC 1717
Disclosure, business records, civil actions, CC 1799.2
Discount buying services, damages, CC 1812.123
Easements, greenways, CC 816.62
Fine art multiples, sales, CC 1745
Fixtures erroneously affixed to land, removal, CC 1013.5
Floating home marinas, CC 800.200
Gender violence, actions and proceedings, CC 52.4
Genetic testing, privacy, CC 56.182
Home equity sales contracts, rescission, unconscionable advantage, CC 1695.14
Human trafficking, CC 52.5
    Injunction, CC 3496
Identification devices, subcutaneous implantation, actions and proceedings, CC 52.7
Improvements,
    Design professionals, CC 3320

COSTS—Cont'd
Improvements—Cont'd
    Prime design professionals, disputes with subconsultants, CC 3321
Indebtedness, duress or coercion, CC 1798.97.2, 1798.97.3
Independent wholesale sales representatives, contracts, CC 1738.16
Installment Sales, this index
Internet, threats, orders of court, social media, CC 1798.99.22
Landlord and Tenant, this index
Leases, payment, renewal, conditions, CC 1950.8
Legal Estates Principal and Income Law, CC 731.15
Lewdness and obscenity, electronic transmissions, images, CC 1708.88
Libel and slander, abuse of children, dismissal of action, CC 48.7
Livestock service liens, actions to enforce liens, CC 3080.01
Loans, identity and identification, theft, CC 1785.20.3
Marinas, floating homes, CC 800.200
Markets and marketing, Internet, disclosure, CC 1749.8.4
Mechanics Liens, this index
Memorabilia, autographed, warranties, CC 1739.7
Mineral rights,
    Lessees, liability, CC 883.140
    Termination actions, rights owner liability, CC 883.250
Mobilehomes and Mobilehome Parks, this index
Mortgages, this index
Motion pictures, invasion of privacy, CC 1708.85
Motor Vehicles, this index
Names, deceased celebrity image protection, CC 3344.1
Obscenity, injunctions, awarding, CC 3496
Payment processors, fair debt settlement, CC 1788.305
Photography and pictures, invasion of privacy, CC 1708.85
Prescription drug claims processor, reports, failure to file, CC 2528
Privacy, invasion of privacy, altered depictions, lewdness and obscenity, CC 1708.86
Private schools, buildings and grounds, access, interference, obstructions, threats, CC 1708.9
Prostitution, injunctions, awarding, CC 3496
Real Estate, this index
Recreational vehicles, parks, actions affecting tenants, occupants or residents, CC 799.78
Rent skimming actions, residential real estate, CC 891
Rental purchase agreements, entitlement of consumers, CC 1812.636

I-50

COURT

COSTS—Cont'd
School buildings and grounds, access, interference, obstructions, threats, **CC 1708.9**
Sex, force and violence, actions and proceedings, **CC 52.4**
Sexual battery, **CC 1708.5**
Sexual orientation, **CC 52.45**
Slandering title, **CC 880.360**
Social media, threats, orders of court, **CC 1798.99.22**
State Agencies, this index
Student loans, private education lenders and loan collectors, actions and proceedings, **CC 1788.208**
Subcutaneous implantation, identification devices, actions and proceedings, **CC 52.7**
Title to property, slandering title, **CC 880.360**
Trade secrets, misappropriation, bad faith, **CC 3426.4**
Video recordings, invasion of privacy, **CC 1708.85**
Wholesale sales representatives, independents, contracts, **CC 1738.16**

COTENANTS
Joint Tenants, generally, this index

COTERMINOUS LANDOWNER
Adjoining Landowners, generally, this index

COUNSEL
Attorneys, generally, this index

COUNSELORS AND COUNSELING
Debt settlement providers, fair debt settlement, **CC 1788.300 et seq.**
Employment Counseling Services, generally, this index
Marriage and Family Therapists, generally, this index
Mental Health Counselors, generally, this index
Mortgages,
　Foreclosure, **CC 2923.5**
　Reverse mortgages, **CC 1923.2, 1923.5**
Payment processors, fair debt settlement, **CC 1788.300 et seq.**
Trust deeds, foreclosure, **CC 2923.5**

COUNTIES
Acknowledgments, **CC 1181**
Adult local criminal justice facilities. Jails, generally, this index
Adverse possession, acquisition of property by, exemptions, **CC 1007**
Architects, contracts, indemnity, **CC 2782.8**
Assessments. Tax Assessments, generally, this index
Attorneys,
　District Attorneys, generally, this index
　Medical records, negligence, release, **CC 56.36**
Building Permits, generally, this index
Building Standards, generally, this index

COUNTIES—Cont'd
Cable Television, generally, this index
Carriers, transportation system operated by county, seating capacity, **CC 2185**
Cities and counties. Consolidated Cities and Counties, generally, this index
Civil defense. War and Civil Defense, generally, this index
Community Development and Housing, generally, this index
Community Facilities Districts, generally, this index
Conservation easements, acquisition, holding, **CC 815.3**
Consolidated Cities and Counties, generally, this index
Contracts, shared mobility service providers, **CC 2505**
Convicts. Jails, generally, this index
Correctional institutions. Jails, generally, this index
Criminal history information, disclosure, concessionaire application purposes, **CC 1798.24a**
Damages, interest recoverable, **CC 3287**
Defense shelters, injuries, exemption from liability, **CC 1714.5**
Departments. Administrative Law and Procedure, generally, this index
Depositories, generally, this index
Development projects. Community Development and Housing, generally, this index
District Attorneys, generally, this index
Easements, greenways, **CC 816.50 et seq.**
Elections, generally, this index
Engineers, contracts, indemnity, **CC 2782.8**
Firefighters and Fire Departments, generally, this index
Greenways, easements, **CC 816.50 et seq.**
Health Facilities, generally, this index
Housing, generally, this index
Interest, damages, **CC 3287**
Jails, generally, this index
Landscape architects, contracts, indemnity, **CC 2782.8**
Leases, lessors remedy for breach statutes, applicability to invalidate lease, **CC 1952.6**
Licenses and permits, shared mobility service providers, **CC 2505**
Local criminal justice facilities. Jails, generally, this index
Lost or destroyed documents, regulating care, **CC 2080.4**
Motor vehicles, shared mobility service providers, licenses and permits, contracts, **CC 2505**
National defense. War and Civil Defense, generally, this index
Planning. Zoning and Planning, generally, this index
Prisoners. Jails, generally, this index

COUNTIES—Cont'd
Privileges and immunities, civil defense, **CC 1714.5**
Property, safekeeping, powers and duties, **CC 2080.10**
Public assistance. Social Services, generally, this index
Recorders, generally, this index
Redevelopment. Community Development and Housing, generally, this index
Rescue, generally, this index
Sacramento City and County, generally, this index
Shared mobility service providers, licenses and permits, contracts, **CC 2505**
Sheriffs, generally, this index
Surveys and surveyors, contracts, indemnity, **CC 2782.8**
Taxation, generally, this index
War and Civil Defense, generally, this index
Zoning and Planning, generally, this index

COUNTY AGENCIES
Comatose patients, medical information disclosure, **CC 56.10**
Medical records, disclosure, **CC 56.10**

COUNTY CLERKS
Acknowledgments, **CC 1181**

COUNTY COUNSELS
See, also, District Attorneys, generally, this index
Acknowledgment of instruments, **CC 1181**

COUNTY FIRE PROTECTION DISTRICTS
Fires and Fire Protection, generally, this index

COUNTY HEALTH FACILITIES
Health Facilities, generally, this index

COUNTY JAILS
Jails, generally, this index

COUNTY OFFICERS AND EMPLOYEES
Attorneys. District Attorneys, generally, this index
District Attorneys, generally, this index
Sheriffs, generally, this index

COUNTY RECORDERS
Recorders, generally, this index

COUNTY TREASURERS
Depositories, generally, this index
Interest, damages, recovery, **CC 3287**

COUNTY WARRANTS
Social Services, generally, this index

COURT CLERKS
Clerks of Courts, generally, this index

COURT COMMISSIONERS
Acknowledgments, **CC 1181**

COURT ORDERS
Orders of Court, generally, this index

COURTS

COURTS
Acknowledgments, foreign states, **CC 1182**
Arrest, **CC 43.54**
Clerks of Courts, generally, this index
Contempt, generally, this index
Costs, generally, this index
Deposits in Court, generally, this index
Disclosure, trade secrets, privileges and immunities, **CC 3426.11**
Fairness and equity, maxims of jurisprudence, **CC 3509 et seq.**
Family Conciliation Court, generally, this index
Fundamental rules, maxims of jurisprudence, **CC 3509 et seq.**
Guardian and Ward, generally, this index
Judges, generally, this index
Judgments and Decrees, generally, this index
Juvenile Courts, generally, this index
Maxims of jurisprudence, **CC 3509 et seq.**
Orders of Court, generally, this index
Rules of court, maxims of jurisprudence, **CC 3509 et seq.**
Small Claims Courts, generally, this index
Subpoenas, generally, this index
Trade secrets, disclosure in judicial proceedings, privilege, **CC 3426.11**
Venue, generally, this index
Witnesses, generally, this index

COURTS OF APPEAL
Acknowledgments, authority to take, **CC 1180**
Proof of instruments, authority to take, **CC 1180**

COURTS OF APPEAL CLERKS/EXECUTIVE OFFICERS
Acknowledgment of instruments, **CC 1180**

COURTS OF RECORD
Judges, generally, this index

COVENANTS
Aged persons, housing, cohabitants, age, **CC 51.3**
Apportionment, lessor of estate, **CC 1469, 1470**
Breach, damages, **CC 3304**
Condominiums, this index
Contiguous land, successive owners,
  Affirmative covenants, **CC 1469**
  Negative covenants, **CC 1470**
Deeds and Conveyances, this index
Discrimination, **CC 53**
Implied, **CC 1113**
Leases, contiguous land, **CC 1470**
Lessor of real estate, **CC 1469, 1470**
Liens and incumbrances, damages for breach, **CC 3305**
Mortgages, bids and bidding, low and moderate income housing, **CC 2924o**
Records and recordation, contiguous land, successive owners, **CC 1469, 1470**
Restrictions due to race, color, religion or national origin, **CC 53**

COVENANTS—Cont'd
Running with land. Covenants Running with Land, generally, this index
Sex discrimination, **CC 53**
Solar Energy Act, **CC 714**
Successive owners, contiguous land,
  Affirmative covenants, **CC 1469**
  Negative covenants, **CC 1470**
Trust deeds, bids and bidding, low and moderate income housing, **CC 2924o**

COVENANTS RUNNING WITH LAND
Generally, **CC 1460 et seq.**
Aged persons, housing, cohabitants, age, **CC 51.3**
Application of law, **CC 1461**
Apportionment, **CC 1467**
  Successive owners, **CC 1468**
Covenantors and covenantees land, **CC 1468**
Direct benefit of existing property, **CC 1462, 1463**
Environmental restrictions, **CC 1471**
Grantees covenants, **CC 1468**
Housing, low and moderate income housing, modification or change, **CC 714.6**
Landlord and tenant, rent payment, **CC 1462, 1463**
Modification or change, housing, low and moderate income housing, **CC 714.6**
Persons bound, **CC 1465**
Persons not bound, **CC 1466**
Quiet enjoyment, **CC 1462, 1463**
Records and recordation, successive owners, **CC 1468**
Rent, payment, **CC 1462, 1463**
Successive owners, interest in, **CC 1468**
Taxes, payment, **CC 1462, 1463**
Undivided interest in land, suspending right of partition or sale, **CC 1468**
Value, apportionment, **CC 1467**
  Successive owners, **CC 1468**
Warranties, **CC 1462, 1463**

COVID 19
Forbearance, mortgages, **CC 3273.1 et seq.**
Landlord and Tenant, this index
Mobilehomes and mobilehome parks,
  Exemptions, rental agreements, **CC 798.17**
  Termination, **CC 798.56**
Mortgages,
  First liens, foreclosure, modification or change, **CC 2924.15**
  Forbearance, **CC 3273.1 et seq.**
Rent, this index

COVID 19 SMALL LANDLORD AND HOMEOWNER RELIEF ACT
Generally, **CC 3273.1 et seq.**

COWS
Animals, generally, this index

CREAM
Cosmetology, generally, this index

CREDIT
Actions and proceedings, identity and identification, theft, **CC 1785.20.3**
Arrangers, real estate transactions, **CC 2956 et seq.**
Attorney fees, identity and identification, theft, **CC 1785.20.3**
Compromise and settlement, debt settlement providers, fair debt settlement, **CC 1788.300 et seq.**
Costs, identity and identification, theft, **CC 1785.20.3**
Credit ratings. Consumer Credit Reporting Agencies, generally, this index
Damages, identity and identification, theft, **CC 1785.20.3**
Debt settlement providers, fair debt settlement, **CC 1788.300 et seq.**
Discrimination, marital status or sex, **CC 1812.30 et seq.**
Factors, credit sales, **CC 2028**
Finance Lenders, generally, this index
Fines and penalties, discrimination, marital status or sex, **CC 1812.33**
Identity and identification, theft, **CC 1785.20.3, 1798.92 et seq.**
Installment Sales, this index
Letters of Credit, generally, this index
Married woman, obtaining credit in own name, **CC 1812.30 et seq.**
Notice, identity and identification, theft, **CC 1785.20.3**
Payment processors, fair debt settlement, **CC 1788.300 et seq.**
Public policy, **CC 1785.1**
Real estate transactions, arrangers, disclosure, **CC 2956 et seq.**
Theft, identity and identification, **CC 1785.20.3**
Unmarried persons, **CC 1812.30 et seq.**

CREDIT CARDS
Generally, **CC 1747 et seq.**
Accounts and accounting, numbers and numbering, receipts, printing, **CC 1747.09**
Actions and proceedings,
  Billing errors, failure to correct, **CC 1747.50, 1747.60**
  Cancelling or refusing to renew, **CC 1747.70**
  Identity and identification,
    Information, acceptance, **CC 1747.08**
    Theft, **CC 1785.20.3**
  Untrue credit information, recovery of damages, **CC 1747.70**
Activation, substitution, issuance, **CC 1747.05**
Address, change of address,
  Notice, **CC 1799.1b**
  Verification, **CC 1747.06**
Amount, payoff, notice, **CC 1748.13**
Ancestry, refusal to issue because of, **CC 1747.80**
Annual fee, disclosure, **CC 1748.22**

CREDIT

CREDIT CARDS—Cont'd
Application of law, secured credit card provisions, CC 1747.94
Applications,
   Disclosure, CC 1748.10, 1748.11, 1748.20 et seq.
      Installment sales, CC 1810.20, 1810.21
   Issuance, CC 1747.05
   Solicitation, address, change of address, verification, CC 1747.06
   Theft, identity and identification, disclosure, CC 1748.95
Areias Robbins Charge Card Full Disclosure Act, CC 1748.20 et seq.
Attorney fees,
   Billing errors, action for damages, CC 1747.50
   Failure to correct billing errors, CC 1747.50, 1747.60
   Identity and identification, theft, CC 1785.20.3
   Retailers, false charges, CC 1748.7
   Untrue credit information given by card issuer, damages, CC 1747.70
Billing errors,
   Correction, CC 1747.50
   Inquiry from cardholder regarding, issuer communicating unfavorable credit information, CC 1747.70
   Liability of card issuer or retailer, CC 1747.65
   Retailers, CC 1747.60
Cancellation,
   Damages for failure to correct billing error, CC 1747.70
   Notice to cardholder, CC 1747.85
Cash advance fees, disclosure, CC 1748.22
Cash payment discounts, CC 1748, 1748.1
Change of address, notice, CC 1799.1b
Charges,
   Billing errors, failure to correct, CC 1747.50
   Disclosure, CC 1748.10, 1748.11, 1748.20 et seq.
      Installment sales, CC 1810.20, 1810.21
   Finance charge, generally, post
   Issuers failure to respond to inquiry of cardholder, CC 1747.40
   Service charges, generally, post
   Surcharges, credit card sales, CC 1748.1
Checks,
   Condition of acceptance, CC 1725
   Finance charge, notice, CC 1748.9
Children and minors, sales, identity and identification, CC 1798.99.1
Commercial paper, condition of acceptance, CC 1725
Consolidation of actions, identity and identification, information, acceptance, CC 1747.08
Construction of laws, federal truth in lending, CC 1747.01
Consumer credit contracts, application of law, CC 1799.91

CREDIT CARDS—Cont'd
Consumer Credit Reporting Agencies, generally, this index
Contracts, retail price discounts for cash sales, CC 1748
Correction of billing errors, CC 1747.50
   Retailers, CC 1747.60
Costs,
   Failure to correct billing errors, CC 1747.50, 1747.60
   Identity and identification, theft, CC 1785.20.3
   Retailers, false charges, CC 1748.7
   Untrue credit information given by card issuer, action to recover damages, CC 1747.70
Crimes and offenses, retailers, processing charges for goods or services not received, CC 1748.7
Damages,
   Billing errors, failure to correct, CC 1747.50
   Cancellation or refusal to renew after action to recover damages, CC 1747.70
   Discrimination in issuing card, CC 1747.80
   Failure to correct billing errors, action to recover, CC 1747.50, 1747.60
   Identity and identification, theft, CC 1785.20.3
   Treble damages, generally, post
   Untrue credit information, CC 1747.70
Debit Cards, generally, this index
Deeds of trust, execution in connection with secured credit card, statements, CC 1747.94
Defenses, recovery of credit extended, right of card issuer, CC 1747.90
Disclosure, CC 1748.10 et seq., 1748.20 et seq.
   Finance charge, CC 1748.5
   Installment sales, CC 1810.20, 1810.21
   Marketing information, CC 1748.12
   Secured credit cards, CC 1747.94
   Waiver, CC 1748.14, 1748.23
Discounts for cash payment, CC 1748, 1748.1
Discrimination,
   Discounts for cash payments, CC 1748, 1748.1
   Refusal to issue card, CC 1747.80
Drivers licenses, identity and identification, acceptance, CC 1747.08
Electronic commercial services, application of law, CC 1789.7
Electronic fund transfer, CC 1747.03
Estimates, payoff, notice, CC 1748.13
Evidence, presumptions, disclosures, CC 1748.11, 1748.22
   Installment sales, CC 1810.21
False credit information, card issuer giving, CC 1747.70
Federal Truth in Lending Act, construction of laws, CC 1747.01
Fees, CC 1747.01
   Annual fee, disclosure, CC 1748.22

CREDIT CARDS—Cont'd
Fees—Cont'd
   Cash advance fees, disclosure, CC 1748.22
   Disclosure, CC 1748.10, 1748.11, 1748.20 et seq.
   Installment sales, membership fees, CC 1810.4
   Membership fees, disclosure, installment sales, CC 1810.21
   Participation fees, disclosure, installment sales, CC 1810.21
Finance charge,
   Billing error, failure to correct, CC 1747.50
   Checks, notice, CC 1748.9
   Disclosure, CC 1748.5, 1748.10, 1748.11, 1748.20 et seq.
      Installment sales, CC 1810.20, 1810.21
   Failure of issuer to respond to inquiry of cardholder, CC 1747.40
   Free period, disclosure, CC 1748.11
      Installment sales, CC 1810.21
   Installment sales, membership fee, CC 1810.4
   Request for information, CC 1748.5
   Retailer failing to correct billing errors, CC 1747.60
   Spread, disclosure, CC 1748.11
Fines and penalties,
   Discrimination, issuance, CC 1747.80
   Identity and identification, information, acceptance, CC 1747.08
Foreign states, disclosure, CC 1748.11
Free period, disclosure, installment sales, CC 1810.21
Identification cards, acceptance, CC 1747.08
Identity and identification,
   Information, acceptance, CC 1747.08
   Theft, CC 1785.20.3, 1798.92 et seq.
      Disclosure, CC 1748.95
Injunctions, identity and identification, information, acceptance, CC 1747.08
Inquiry, cardholder, failure of card issuer to give timely response, CC 1747.40
Installment Sales, this index
Interest,
   Billing error, failure to correct, CC 1747.50
   Checks, notice, CC 1748.9
   Disclosure, CC 1748.10, 1748.11, 1748.20 et seq.
   Failure of issuer to respond to inquiry of cardholder, CC 1747.40
   Finance charge, generally, ante
   Installment sales, membership fees, CC 1810.4
   Minimum payment warning, CC 1748.13
   Retailer failing to correct billing errors, CC 1747.60
Issuance, CC 1747.05
   Discrimination, CC 1747.80
   Married women, names, CC 1747.81
Liability,
   Billing errors, CC 1747.65

CREDIT

CREDIT CARDS—Cont'd
Liability—Cont'd
   Solicitation, applications, address, change of address, verification, CC 1747.06
   Ten or more cards issued, CC 1747.20
   Unauthorized use, CC 1747.10
   Limitation of liability, cardholder for unauthorized use, CC 1747.20
   Markets and marketing, disclosure, CC 1748.12
Married women, issuance, names, CC 1747.81
Membership fees, installment sales, CC 1810.4
   Disclosure, CC 1810.21
Minimum payment warning, CC 1748.13
Monopolies and unfair trade, CC 1747.94
Names, married women, CC 1747.81
Negotiable instruments, condition of acceptance, CC 1725
Notice,
   Applications, disclosures, CC 1748.10, 1748.11, 1748.20 et seq.
   Installment sales, CC 1810.21
Cancellation, notice to cardholder, CC 1747.85
Change of address, CC 1799.1b
Checks, finance charge, CC 1748.9
Defenses of cardholder against retailer, CC 1747.90
Disclosure, marketing information, CC 1748.12
Identity and identification, theft, CC 1785.20.3
Installment sales, membership fees, CC 1810.4
Marketing information, disclosure, CC 1748.12
Minimum payment warning, CC 1748.13
Numbers and numbering,
   Identity and identification, theft, CC 1798.92 et seq.
   Receipts, printing, CC 1747.09
Offers, applications, address, change of address, verification, CC 1747.06
Oral request, issuance, CC 1747.05
Participation fees, disclosure, installment sales, CC 1810.21
Payoff, amount, time, notice, CC 1748.13
Preprinted checks or drafts, notice, CC 1748.9
Presumptions, disclosures, CC 1748.11, 1748.22
   Installment sales, CC 1810.21
Proceedings. Actions and proceedings, generally, ante
Public policy, CC 1747.01
Punitive damages, discrimination in issuing card, CC 1747.80
Rates and charges. Charges, generally, ante
Receipts, numbers and numbering, printing, CC 1747.09
Recovery of credit extended, right of card issuer, CC 1747.90

CREDIT CARDS—Cont'd
Renewal, CC 1747.05
   Notice of refusal to renew, CC 1747.85
   Refusal following action for recovery of damages, CC 1747.70
Reports. Consumer Credit Reporting Agencies, generally, this index
Request, issuance, CC 1747.05
Retailers,
   Billing errors, CC 1747.60, 1747.65
   Contracts with card issuers prohibiting price discounts for cash sales, CC 1748
   Minimum payment warning, CC 1748.13
   Payments, goods or services not provided, crimes, CC 1748.7
   Receipts, numbers and numbering, printing, CC 1747.09
Sales, surcharges, CC 1748.1
Secured credit cards, disclosures, CC 1747.94
Service charges,
   Billing errors, failure to correct, CC 1747.50
   Issuers failure to respond to inquiry of cardholder, CC 1747.40
   Retailer failing to correct billing errors, CC 1747.60
Setoff and counterclaim, defenses of cardholder against retailer, CC 1747.90
Sex, refusal to issue because of, CC 1747.80
Solicitation,
   Applications, address, change of address, verification, CC 1747.06
   Disclosure, CC 1748.10, 1748.11, 1748.20 et seq., 1810.20 et seq.
   Lists, removal, notice, consumer credit reporting agencies, CC 1785.11.8
Statements,
   Deeds of trust, execution in connection with secured credit cards, CC 1747.94
   Finance charge, CC 1748.5
Substitution, issuance, CC 1747.05
Suits. Actions and proceedings, generally, ante
Surcharges, credit card sales, CC 1748.1
Ten or more cards, issuance, unauthorized use, liability, CC 1747.20
Theft, identity and identification, CC 1785.20.3
Disclosure, CC 1748.95
Time, payoff, notice, CC 1748.13
Timely response, card issuer to inquiry of cardholder, failure to give, CC 1747.40
Treble damages,
   Failure to correct billing errors, CC 1747.50, 1747.60
   Surcharges on credit card sales, CC 1748.1
   Untrue credit information given by card issuer, CC 1747.70
Unauthorized use,
   Liability of cardholder, CC 1747.10
   Ten or more cards issued, CC 1747.20
Unfair competition, CC 1747.94
Untrue credit information, card issuer giving,

CREDIT CARDS—Cont'd
Waiver, CC 1747.04
   Disclosure, CC 1748.14, 1748.23
Women, married women, issuance, names, CC 1747.81

CREDIT LIFE AND DISABILITY INSURANCE
Damages, debtor, CC 1812.402
Disclosure forms, claim procedure, creditors, CC 1812.402
Equitable relief, debtors, CC 1812.402
Foreclosure, liens, CC 1812.402
Forms, disclosure forms, claims procedure, CC 1812.402
Key persons, remedies of creditors, CC 1812.406
Liens and incumbrances, foreclosure, CC 1812.402
Motor vehicle conditional sales contracts, property subject to lien, CC 2984.2
Notice, disability claim, remedies of creditor, CC 1812.402
Open end credit program, remedies of creditor, CC 1812.405
Partial disability, remedies of creditors, CC 1812.402
Payment, claims paid within disability claim period, CC 1812.402
Remedies, CC 1812.400 et seq.
   Disclosure forms, claim procedure, CC 1812.402
   Foreclosure of liens, CC 1812.402
   Key persons, CC 1812.406
   Notice, disability claim, CC 1812.402
   Open end credit plans, CC 1812.405
   Partial disability, CC 1812.402
   Temporary disability, CC 1812.403
Temporary disability, CC 1812.403
Waiver, debtor rights, CC 1812.408

CREDIT RATINGS
Consumer Credit Reporting Agencies, generally, this index

CREDIT REPORTING AGENCIES
Consumer Credit Reporting Agencies, generally, this index

CREDIT SERVICES
Generally, CC 1789.10 et seq.

CREDIT UNIONS
Contracts, foreign languages, translations, CC 1632.5
Disclosure,
   Employers, CC 1788.3
   Home equity loan disclosure, CC 2970, 2971
Electronic funds transfers. Funds Transfers, generally, this index
Fines and penalties, contracts, foreign languages, translations, CC 1632.5
Foreign languages, contracts, translations, CC 1632.5

CRIMES

CREDIT UNIONS—Cont'd
Forms, contracts, foreign languages, translations, CC 1632.5
Funds Transfers, generally, this index
Home equity loan disclosure, CC 2970, 2971
Interest, impound accounts, mortgages, CC 2954.8
Loans, home equity loan disclosure, CC 2970, 2971
Money Orders, generally, this index
Mortgages,
   Fiduciaries, CC 2923.1
   Foreign languages, translations, CC 1632.5
   Home equity loan disclosure, CC 2970, 2971
   Impound accounts, interest, CC 2954.8
Officers and employees, disclosure, information, CC 1788.3
Records and recordation. Disclosure, generally, ante
Reports, disclosure, employers, CC 1788.3
Translations, foreign languages, contracts, CC 1632.5

CREDITORS
Debtors and Creditors, generally, this index

CREDITS
Credit, generally, this index

CREED
Discrimination, generally, this index

CREEKS
Rivers and Streams, generally, this index

CRIME VICTIMS
Compensation and salaries. Restitution, generally, this index
Dating, personal information, victim service providers, grants, CC 1798.79.8 et seq.
Indebtedness, duress or coercion, CC 1798.97.1 et seq.
Landlord and tenant, emergency services, law enforcement, CC 1946.8
Restitution, generally, this index
Stories, sale proceeds, CC 2225

CRIMES AND OFFENSES
Abettors. Accomplices and Accessories, generally, this index
Abuse. Child Abuse, generally, this index
Accomplices and Accessories, generally, this index
Actions and proceedings, stories, felonies, sales, proceeds, CC 2225
Aiders and abettors. Accomplices and Accessories, generally, this index
Anonymous witness program, immunity, CC 48.9
Arrest, generally, this index
Attorney fees, stories about felonies, sale proceeds, CC 2225
Auctions and Auctioneers, this index
Background checks. Criminal History Information, generally, this index

CRIMES AND OFFENSES—Cont'd
Bad checks. Negotiable Instruments, this index
Bias and prejudice. Hate Crimes, generally, this index
Bills, false bills, invoices, or statements soliciting money, CC 1716
Blanket incumbrances on subdivisions, failure to notify buyers or lessees, CC 1133
Booking, photography and pictures, commercial use, CC 1798.91.1
Bribery and Corruption, generally, this index
Child Abuse, generally, this index
Compensation and salaries, stories about felonies, sale proceeds, CC 2225
Computer aided transcription equipment, deaf or hard of hearing persons, CC 54.8
Conditional sales, motor vehicles, CC 2983.6
Confidential or privileged information, medical, psychiatric or psychological information, intentional disclosure, CC 1798.57
Consumer credit reports, contents of records, CC 1785.13
Contempt, generally, this index
Contracts, this index
Conviction of crime, check cashers, permits, CC 1789.37
Correctional Institutions, generally, this index
Corruption. Bribery and Corruption, generally, this index
Counsel for accused, stories about felonies, sale proceeds, CC 2225
Credit services organizations, CC 1789.20
Crime Victims, generally, this index
Damages,
   Criminals, injury or death, liability, CC 847
   Stories about felonies, sale proceeds, CC 2225
Dance studio contracts, CC 1812.63
Data, sales, CC 1724
Debtors and Creditors, this index
Deeds of trust, trustees sale, price fixing or default by bidder, CC 2924h
Defacing, generally, this index
Destruction or damaging of property. Malicious Mischief, generally, this index
Disclosure,
   Medical, psychiatric or psychological information, intentional disclosure, CC 1798.57
   Personal information held by governmental agencies, Information Practices Act, CC 1798.25
Discount buying services, CC 1812.125
District Attorneys, generally, this index
Domestic Violence, generally, this index
Drivers licenses. Motor Vehicles, this index
Duress or Coercion, generally, this index
Embryos, in vitro fertilization, actions and proceedings, CC 1708.5.6
Employment counseling, CC 1812.523
False charge of person with crime, CC 46
False Imprisonment, generally, this index

CRIMES AND OFFENSES—Cont'd
False representation. Fraud, generally, this index
Farm machinery repair shops, CC 1718
Fines and Penalties, generally, this index
Force and Violence, generally, this index
Forfeitures, generally, this index
Fraud, generally, this index
Gender violence, actions and proceedings, CC 52.4
Habitual criminals. Second and subsequent offenses, generally, post
Harassment, generally, this index
Hate Crimes, generally, this index
Home equity sales contracts, CC 1695.8
Homeless persons, transitional housing, misconduct, injunctions, CC 1954.14
Human Trafficking, generally, this index
In vitro fertilization, actions and proceedings, CC 1708.5.6
Indictment and Information, generally, this index
Information. Indictment and Information, generally, this index
Information Practices Act, CC 1798 et seq.
Installment sales, CC 1812.6
   Finance charge, advertisements, CC 1803.11
Intellectual property, stories about felonies, sale proceeds, CC 2225
Interest, usury, CC 1916–3
Interference, generally, this index
Interviews, stories about felonies, sale proceeds, CC 2225
Invoices, false invoices or statements soliciting money, CC 1716
Involuntary trusts, convicted felons, actions by beneficiaries, CC 2225
Jails, generally, this index
Job listing services, CC 1812.523
Judgments and decrees, stories, felonies, sales, proceeds, CC 2225
Juvenile Delinquents and Dependents, generally, this index
Larceny. Theft, generally, this index
Lewdness and Obscenity, generally, this index
Libel and Slander, generally, this index
Limitation of actions, stories, sales, CC 2225
Literary property, stories about felonies, sale proceeds, CC 2225
Loan sharking, CC 1916–3
Local detention facilities. Jails, generally, this index
Malicious Mischief, generally, this index
Markets and marketing, seller assisted marketing plans, CC 1812.217
Mobs. Riots and Mobs, generally, this index
Monopolies and Unfair Trade, generally, this index
Mortgage foreclosure consultants, registration, CC 2945.45
Mortgages, this index

I-55

CRIMES

CRIMES AND OFFENSES—Cont'd
Motor Vehicles, this index
Nuisance, generally, this index
Obscenity. Lewdness and Obscenity, generally, this index
Orders of court, stories about felonies, sale proceeds, CC 2225
Ova, in vitro fertilization, actions and proceedings, CC 1708.5.6
Penalties. Fines and Penalties, generally, this index
Periodicals, stories about felonies, sale proceeds, CC 2225
Perjury, generally, this index
Personal injuries,
    Criminal sustaining injury, exemption from liability, CC 847
    Stories about felonies, sale proceeds, CC 2225
Personal or confidential information, governmental agencies, disclosure, CC 1798.55 et seq.
Photography and pictures, booking, commercial use, CC 1798.91.1
Pornography. Lewdness and Obscenity, generally, this index
Principal and accessory. Accomplices and Accessories, generally, this index
Prisoners. Jails, generally, this index
Privileges and immunities,
    Anonymous witness program, CC 48.9
    Reports, anonymous witness program, CC 48.9
Profits, stories about felonies, sale proceeds, CC 2225
Prostitution, generally, this index
Publication, stories about felonies, sale proceeds, CC 2225
Radio frequency identification, CC 1798.79, 1798.795
Real property sales contracts, Subdivision Map Act, false statements, CC 2985.51
Receiving Stolen Goods, generally, this index
Recidivists. Second and subsequent offenses, generally, post
Records and recordation,
    Criminal History Information, generally, this index
    Information, CC 1798.55 et seq.
Rent skimming, CC 890 et seq.
Rental purchase agreements, CC 1812.647
Reports,
    Anonymous witness program, immunity, CC 48.9
    Fraud, libel and slander, privileges and immunities, CC 47
    Privileges and immunities, anonymous witness program, CC 48.9
Restitution, generally, this index
RFID (radio frequency identification), CC 1798.79, 1798.795
Riots and Mobs, generally, this index

CRIMES AND OFFENSES—Cont'd
Royalties, stories about felonies, sale proceeds, CC 2225
Searches and Seizures, generally, this index
Second and subsequent offenses,
    Grocery stores, point of sale systems, CC 7101
    Leases, cutting off public utilities to terminate lease, CC 789.3
    Sex discrimination, CC 52
Seller assisted marketing plans, CC 1812.217
Sex, force and violence, actions and proceedings, CC 52.4
Sex Offenses, generally, this index
Sexual Assault, generally, this index
Sexual Battery, generally, this index
Sexual orientation, actions and proceedings, CC 52.45
Skimming, radio frequency identification, CC 1798.79, 1798.795
Skimming of rent, residential real estate, CC 890 et seq.
Slander. Libel and Slander, generally, this index
Sperm, in vitro fertilization, actions and proceedings, CC 1708.5.6
Stalking, generally, this index
Statements soliciting money, false statements, CC 1716
Stories about felonies, sale proceeds, CC 2225
Supersedeas or Stay, generally, this index
Theft, generally, this index
Trafficking. Human Trafficking, generally, this index
Trespass, generally, this index
Trust deeds,
    Reconveyance, CC 2941.5
    Trustee sale, price fixing or default by bidder, CC 2924h
Usury Law violations, CC 1916-3
Vandalism, generally, this index
Venue, generally, this index
Victims of crime. Crime Victims, generally, this index
Witnesses, generally, this index

CRIMINAL CONVERSATION
Actions and proceedings, CC 43.5

CRIMINAL HISTORY INFORMATION
Concessionaire applications, information disclosure, CC 1798.24a
Consumer credit reporting agencies, CC 1786.18
Disclosure, concessionaire application purposes, CC 1798.24a
Long term health care facilities, nurses, temporary employment, CC 1812.542
Psychiatric technicians, long term health care facilities, temporary employment, CC 1812.542
Vocational nursing, long term health care facilities, temporary employment, CC 1812.542

CRIMINAL PROCEDURE
Crimes and Offenses, generally, this index

CROPS
Agricultural Products, generally, this index

CRUDE OIL
Oil and Gas, generally, this index

CUMULATIVE REMEDY
Invasion of privacy, name, photograph or other likeness, use without consent, CC 3344

CURE
Consumers, privacy, disclosure, CC 1798.150

CURRENCY
Euro, contracts, securities or instruments, medium of payment, CC 1663
Frauds, statute of, sales, CC 1624

CUSTOM AND USAGE
Words, giving special meaning by, CC 1644

CUSTOMERS
Consumer Protection, generally, this index
Personal information, security, CC 1798.81.5
Records and recordation, personal information, Breach of security, disclosure, CC 1798.82
    Destruction, CC 1798.80 et seq.

DAGGERS
Weapons, generally, this index

DAMAGES
    Generally, CC 3274 et seq.
Acceptance of principal, waiver of interest, CC 3290
Accession, wrongful use of materials, CC 1033
Adjoining landowners, excavations, CC 832
Adverse possession, wrongful possession, CC 3334
Advertisements, this index
Affidavits, evidence, pretrial discovery, CC 3295
Agents authority, breach of warranty, CC 3318
Amount of damages,
    Limitations, CC 3358
    Nominal damages, CC 3360
    Peculiar value of property, CC 3355
    Reasonableness, CC 3359
    Value, determining value, CC 3353 et seq.
Animals, this index
Anticipatory breach of contract, liquidated damages, CC 1671
Art and artists, defacement or destruction of art objects, CC 987
Ascertainment, breach of contract, CC 3301
Autographed memorabilia, CC 1739.7
Automated license plate recognition, CC 1798.90.54
Bailment, this index
Bed and breakfast inns, children and minors, CC 1865
Blind or visually impaired persons, guide dogs, CC 54.2

DAMAGES

DAMAGES—Cont'd
Booking photographs, commercial use, CC 1798.91.1
Breach of contract. Contracts, this index
Breach of covenants, CC 3304
    Liens and encumbrances, CC 3305
Breach of lease. Leases, this index
Breach of marriage promise, CC 43.4, 43.5
Breach of warranty, agents authority, CC 3318
Buildings, construction defects, valuation, CC 944
Business and commerce,
    Customer records, destruction, CC 1798.84
    Discrimination, treble damages, CC 52
Business records, disclosures, CC 1799.2
Cardiopulmonary resuscitation, emergencies, immunity, CC 1714.2
Carriers, this index
Celebrity image protection, CC 3344.1
Certainty of contract, damages for breach, CC 3301
Checks, cashers, CC 1789.35
Children and Minors, this index
Civil rights,
    Disabled persons, construction, accessibility, CC 55.56
    Violations, CC 52.1
Commercial blockade, health care facilities, CC 3427.2
Comparative fault, firemans rule, CC 1714.9
Compromise and settlement, personal injury actions, interest, CC 3291
Condominiums, this index
Conservation easements, CC 815.7
Construction, defects, CC 896
Consumer Credit, this index
Consumer Credit Reporting Agencies, this index
Consumer Protection, this index
Consumers, privacy, disclosure, CC 1798.150
Consumers Legal Remedies Act, CC 1750 et seq.
Contracts, this index
Controlled escrows, real estate developers, CC 2995
Conversion, this index
Covenants, breach, CC 3304
    Liens and encumbrances, CC 3305
Credit, identity and identification, theft, CC 1785.20.3
Credit Cards, this index
Credit life and disability insurance, debtors rights, CC 1812.402
Credit services organizations, CC 1789.21
    Bonds (officers and fiduciaries), CC 1789.18
Credit transactions, discrimination, marital status or sex, CC 1812.31
Cruelty to or killing of human beings or animals, motion pictures, CC 3507.4
Customer records, destruction, CC 1798.84
Dance studio contracts, CC 1812.62

DAMAGES—Cont'd
Dating service contracts, CC 1694.4
Deaf or hard of hearing persons, interfering with civil rights, CC 54.3
Debtors and Creditors, this index
Deeds and Conveyances, this index
Deep pocket rule, joint and several liability, CC 1431 et seq.
Defacement of property by minors, willful misconduct, imputed liability of parents, CC 1714.1
Depositories,
    Indemnification, CC 1833
    Use of thing deposited, CC 1836
Detriment,
    Future damages, CC 3283
    Recovery of damages, CC 3281
Disabled Persons, this index
Disclosures, business records, CC 1799.2
Discount buying services, actions for enforcement, CC 1812.123
Discretionary damages, interest, jury discretion, CC 3288
Discrimination, this index
Double damages, timber, injury to, CC 3346
Drones, emergencies, interference, CC 43.101
Easements,
    Conservation easements, CC 815.7
    Greenways, CC 816.62
Economic damages, joint and several liability, CC 1431.2
Electrical devices or appliances, sale with identification number or mark altered or removed, CC 1710.1
Embryos, crimes and offenses, CC 1708.5.6
Emergencies, cardiopulmonary resuscitation, immunity, CC 1714.2
Encumbrances. Liens and incumbrances, generally, post
Estimation, value, CC 3353, 3354
    Instrument in writing, CC 3356
Evidence,
    Exemplary damages, defendants wealth or profits, protective order requiring prima facie case of liability, CC 3295
    Presumptions,
        Inadequacy of breach of agreement to transfer real estate, CC 3387
        Written instruments, CC 3356
    Written instruments, information of value, presumptions, CC 3356
Excavations, adjoining landowners, CC 832
Exemplary damages, CC 3294
    Animals, injuries, CC 3340
    Art objects, defacement or destruction, CC 987
    Autographed memorabilia, CC 1739.7
    Blind or visually impaired persons, public accommodations, CC 54.3
    Celebrity image protection, CC 3344.1
    Consumer credit,
        Denial, CC 1787.3

DAMAGES—Cont'd
Exemplary damages—Cont'd
    Consumer credit—Cont'd
        Reporting agencies, CC 1785.31 et seq.
    Consumers Legal Remedies Act, CC 1750 et seq.
    Dance studio contracts, CC 1812.62
    Deaf or hard of hearing persons, public accommodations, CC 54.3
    Deceased celebrities, image protection, CC 3344.1
    Disabled persons, CC 54.3
    Domestic violence, torts, CC 1708.6
    Evidence, defendants wealth or profits, protective order requiring prima facie case of liability, CC 3295
    Exclusive of compensatory damages, CC 3357
    Gender violence, CC 52.4
    Health care service plans, notice, CC 3296
    Home equity sales contracts, CC 1695.7
    Homicide, CC 3294
    Identification devices, subcutaneous implantation, CC 52.7
    Insurance, notice, CC 3296
    Invasion of privacy, CC 1708.8
    Junk and junk dealers, fire hydrants, possession, CC 3336.5
    Lewdness and obscenity, electronic transmissions, images, CC 1708.88
    Memorabilia, autographed, CC 1739.7
    Mobilehomes and mobilehome parks, willful violations, CC 798.86
    Mortgage foreclosure consultants, CC 2945.6
    Privacy, invasion of privacy, CC 1708.8
        Altered depictions, lewdness and obscenity, CC 1708.86
    Protective orders, evidence of defendants wealth or profits, requirements to show prima facie case of liability, CC 3295
    Recycling, fire hydrants, possession, CC 3336.5
    Rent skimming, residential real estate, CC 891
    Rental purchase agreements, CC 1812.636
    Sex, force and violence, CC 52.4
    Sexual battery, CC 1708.5
    Sexual harassment, CC 52
    Sexual orientation, CC 52.45
    Stalking, CC 1708.7
    Subcutaneous implantation, identification devices, CC 52.7
    Trade secrets, misappropriation, CC 3426.3
    Treble damages, generally, post
Expenses, willful misconduct of children, imputed liability of parent or guardian, CC 1714.1
Famous persons, deceased celebrities, image protection, CC 3344.1
Fine art multiples, sales, CC 1745
Fraud, this index
Future damages, CC 3283

DAMAGES

DAMAGES—Cont'd
Gender violence, CC 52.4
Genetic defects, action against parent, CC 43.6
Genetic tests, disclosure, CC 56.17
Grocery stores, point of sale systems, CC 7101
Guardian and Ward, this index
Guide dogs, blind persons liability, CC 54.2
Hate crimes, CC 52, 52.1
Hazards, natural hazards, disclosure, residential property, CC 1103.13
Health Care Service Plans, this index
Health services, treble damages, CC 1812.94
Holden Credit Denial Closure Act, CC 1787.1 et seq.
Homicide, exemplary damages, CC 3294
Hotels and Motels, this index
Human trafficking, CC 52.5
Identification devices, subcutaneous implantation, CC 52.7
Identity and identification, theft, CC 1798.93
Immunity, emergencies, cardiopulmonary resuscitation, CC 1714.2
Imputed liability, willful misconduct of children, liability of parent or guardian, CC 1714.1
In vitro fertilization, crimes and offenses, CC 1708.5.6
Incumbrances. Liens and incumbrances, generally, post
Indebtedness, duress or coercion, CC 1798.97.2
Indemnity, generally, this index
Independent wholesale sales representatives, contracts, CC 1738.15
Information Practices Act, CC 1798.53, 1798.77
Innkeepers liens, wrongful possession of property, CC 1861.15
Installment Sales, this index
Interest, this index
Invasion of privacy, CC 1708.8
Investigative consumer reporting agencies, CC 1786.50 et seq.
Joint and Several Liability, generally, this index
Junk and junk dealers, fire hydrants, possession, CC 3336.5
Juvenile Delinquents and Dependents, this index
Land sales contracts, Subdivision Map Act, noncompliance, CC 2985.51
Landlord and Tenant, this index
Leases, this index
Lewdness and obscenity,
  Distribution, CC 52.8
  Electronic transmissions, images, CC 1708.88
Libel and Slander, this index
Liens and incumbrances,
  Blanket incumbrances, failure to notify buyers or lessees, CC 1133

DAMAGES—Cont'd
Liens and incumbrances—Cont'd
  Breach of covenant against, CC 3305
  Conversion of property, CC 3338
  Innkeepers liens, wrongful possession of property, CC 1861.15
Limitations, CC 3358
  Minor, discharge of weapon, CC 1714.3
  Weapons, minors discharge, CC 1714.3
Liquidated damages, CC 1671
  Condominiums, default, sales, CC 1675
  Default, real property purchase contracts, CC 1675 et seq.
  Enforcement of contract imposing, CC 3389
  Personal property, leases, CC 1671
  Real property purchase contracts, default, CC 1675 et seq.
  Specific performance of contract, CC 3389
Loans, identity and identification, theft, CC 1785.20.3
Malicious destruction of property actions, treble damages, CC 1721
Manufacturer identification marks, removal, defacing, alteration or destruction, CC 1710.1
Measure of damages, CC 3300 et seq.
  Breach of contract, CC 3300
  Torts, CC 3333
Mechanical devices or appliances, sale with identification number or mark altered or removed, CC 1710.1
Mechanics liens, stop notices, CC 8558
Medical Malpractice, this index
Medical Records, this index
Memorabilia, autographed, CC 1739.7
Mineral rights lessees, liability, CC 883.140
Mitigation, leases, breach, mitigation efforts of lessor, waiving right to damages, CC 1951.2
Mobilehomes and Mobilehome Parks, this index
Monopolies and Unfair Trade, this index
Mortgages, this index
Motels. Hotels and Motels, this index
Motion pictures, killing of or cruelty to human beings or animals, CC 3507.4
Motions, pretrial discovery, CC 3295
Natural hazards, disclosure, residential property, CC 1103.13
Nominal damages, CC 3360
  Medical records, negligence, release, CC 56.36
Noneconomic damages,
  Joint and several liability, CC 1431.2
  Lewdness and obscenity, electronic transmissions, images, CC 1708.88
Notice,
  Intent to preserve interest in real property, slandering title, recording, CC 880.360
  Peculiar value of property, CC 3355
  Punitive damages, insurers or health care service plans, CC 3296

DAMAGES—Cont'd
Nuisance, this index
Obligation to pay money only, breach of contract, CC 3302
Oil and gas pipelines, breaks, CC 3333.5
Ouster from possession action, cotenants, CC 843
Ova, crimes and offenses, CC 1708.5.6
Parents, action by child against parent for genetic defects, CC 43.6
Payment processors, fair debt settlement, CC 1788.305
Peculiar value of property, CC 3355
Penalties. Exemplary damages, generally, ante
Personal injury, interest, CC 3291
Personal Property, this index
Personal services, deceptive practices, Consumers Legal Remedies Act, CC 1750 et seq.
Point of sale systems, grocery stores, violations, CC 7101
Political items, sale and manufacture, CC 1739.4
Prescription drug claims processor, reports, failure to file, CC 2528
Preventive and specific relief, CC 3366 et seq.
Privacy, invasion of privacy, CC 1708.8
  Altered depictions, lewdness and obscenity, CC 1708.86
Private schools, buildings and grounds, access, interference, obstructions, threats, CC 1708.9
Privileges and Immunities, generally, this index
Protective orders, exemplary damages, evidence of defendants wealth or profits, CC 3295
Punitive damages. Exemplary damages, generally, ante
Quiet enjoyment, breach of covenant, CC 3304
Quitclaim deeds, breach of agreement to execute, CC 3306a
Railroads, this index
Real Estate, this index
Reasonableness, CC 3359
Records and recordation, customer records, destruction, CC 1798.84
Recreational trails, attorney fees, CC 846.1
Recreational vehicles, park tenants, violations, CC 799.79
Recycling, fire hydrants, possession, CC 3336.5
Rent skimming, residential real estate, CC 891
Rental purchase agreements,
  Entitlement of consumers, CC 1812.636
  Liability of consumers, CC 1812.627
Rescission of contract, claim for relief not inconsistent with claim for damages, CC 1692
Sales, this index
Seller assisted marketing plans, CC 1812.218
Serial numbers, removal, defacing, alteration or destruction, CC 1710.1

DAMAGES—Cont'd
Sex, force and violence, **CC 52.4**
Sex discrimination, **CC 52, 52.1**
Sexual harassment, **CC 51.9, 52**
Sexual orientation, **CC 52.45**
Shrubs, injuring or removing, **CC 3346**
Slander. Libel and Slander, this index
Social hosts, liability, alcoholic beverages, **CC 1714**
Solar energy, systems, **CC 714**
Solicitation, payment of money, false statement or invoice, **CC 1716**
Special damages,
    Domestic violence, torts, **CC 1708.6**
    Landlord and tenant, substandard conditions, rent, **CC 1942.4**
    Sexual battery, **CC 1708.5**
    Stalking, **CC 1708.7**
Special occupancy parks, eviction, notice, **CC 1866**
Specific and preventive relief, **CC 3366 et seq.**
Specific Performance, generally, this index
Sperm, crimes and offenses, **CC 1708.5.6**
Stalking, **CC 1708.7**
Student loans, private education lenders and loan collectors, **CC 1788.208**
Subcontractors, construction, reimbursement, defense fees and costs, **CC 2782.05**
Subcutaneous implantation, identification devices, **CC 52.7**
Subrogation, employers, firefighters, peace officers or emergency medical personnel, **CC 1714.9**
Surveys and surveyors, trespass, **CC 3346**
Title to property, slandering title, **CC 880.360**
Torts, generally, this index
Trade secrets, misappropriation, **CC 3426.3**
Treble damages,
    Business establishments, discrimination, **CC 52**
    Checks, dishonor, demand for payment, **CC 1719**
    Commercial vehicles, driving under the influence, **CC 3333.7**
    Consumer protection, aged persons, disabled persons, veterans, **CC 3345**
    Credit Cards, this index
    Dating service contracts, **CC 1694.4**
    Disabled persons, interfering with civil rights, **CC 54.3**
    Discount buying services, **CC 1812.123**
    Electrical device or appliance sold with identification mark or number altered or removed, **CC 1710.1**
    Health studio services, contracts, **CC 1812.94**
    Independent wholesale sales representatives, contracts, **CC 1738.15**
    Installment sales, wilful violations, **CC 1812.9**
    Interest payments, usury, **CC 1916–3**

DAMAGES—Cont'd
Treble damages—Cont'd
    Invasion of privacy, **CC 1708.8**
    Monopolies and unfair trade, social services, procurement, fees, **CC 1780**
    Motor carriers, driving under the influence, **CC 3333.7**
    Political items, sale and manufacture, violations, **CC 1739.4**
    Real estate developers, controlled escrows, **CC 2995**
    Sexual exploitation, children and minors, dependents, **CC 3345.1**
    Solicitation, false statements or invoices, **CC 1716**
    Support, arrearages, evasion, accomplices and accessories, **CC 1714.4, 1714.41**
    Timber, **CC 3346**
    Trees, cutting, carrying off or injuring, **CC 3346**
    Weight loss contracts, **CC 1694.9**
Trespass, this index
Trust Deeds, this index
Unconscionable damages, restrictions against, **CC 3359**
Unliquidated damages,
    Contracts, interest, **CC 3287**
    Interest, **CC 3287**
Unmanned aircraft, emergencies, interference, **CC 43.101**
Unsolicited goods, billing for, **CC 1584.5**
Usury, treble damages, **CC 1916–3**
Value, **CC 3353 et seq.**
Vandalism, actions, treble damages, **CC 1721**
Veterans, consumer protection, unfair or deceptive practices, **CC 3345**
Video games, force and violence, **CC 1746.3**
Violence, freedom from, **CC 52, 52.1**
Waiver of interest, acceptance of principal, **CC 3290**
Warranty, breach of covenant, **CC 3304**
Weight loss contracts, **CC 1694.9**
Wholesale sales representatives, independents, contracts, **CC 1738.15**
Wilful misconduct of minor, **CC 1714.1**
    Defacement of property, imputed liability of parents, **CC 1714.1**
Women, credit transactions, discrimination, **CC 1812.31**
Written instruments, estimation of value, **CC 3356**
Wrongful Death, generally, this index
Wrongful occupation, **CC 3334**

DAMS AND RESERVOIRS
Appropriation of waters, time, construction, **CC 1416**

DANCES AND DANCE HALLS
Contracts for dance studio services, state regulation, **CC 1812.50 et seq.**
Crimes and offenses, dance studio contracts, **CC 1812.63**

DANCES AND DANCE HALLS—Cont'd
Damages, dance studio contracts, **CC 1812.62**
Fraud, dance studio contracts, **CC 1812.60**
Studios, declarations, bonds (officers and fiduciaries), statement of gross income, **CC 1812.64**

DANGEROUS WEAPONS
Weapons, generally, this index

DATA
Brokers, registration, **CC 1798.99.80 et seq.**
Computers, generally, this index
Information, generally, this index
Motor vehicles, vehicle history reports, **CC 1784.1**
Sales, crimes and offenses, **CC 1724**

DATA PROCESSING
Computers, generally, this index

DATING
Crime victims, personal information, victim service providers, grants, **CC 1798.79.8 et seq.**
Service contracts, **CC 1694 et seq.**

DAVIS STIRLING COMMON INTEREST DEVELOPMENT ACT
Generally, **CC 4000 et seq.**

DAY CAMPS
Camps and Camping, generally, this index

DEAD BOLT LOCKS
Landlord and tenant, **CC 1941.3**

DEADLY WEAPONS
Weapons, generally, this index

DEAF OR HARD OF HEARING PERSONS
Actions and proceedings, assistive listening systems, **CC 54.8**
Animals. Service Animals, generally, this index
Assistive listening systems, civil or criminal proceedings, **CC 54.8**
Attorney fees, interference with civil rights, **CC 54.3, 55**
Computers, transcripts, civil or criminal proceedings, **CC 54.8**
Condominiums, accessibility, modification or change, **CC 4760**
Contracts,
    Health studio services, relief clause, **CC 1812.89**
    Revocation of proposal, **CC 1587**
    Termination, convalescent or nursing homes, **CC 1934.5**
Crimes and offenses,
    Interference with civil rights, **CC 54.3**
    Listening systems or computer aided transcriptions, **CC 54.8**
Damages, interfering with civil rights, **CC 54.3**
Dogs. Service Animals, generally, this index
Public accommodations, **CC 54.1 et seq.**

DEAF

DEAF OR HARD OF HEARING PERSONS —Cont'd

Signal dogs. Service Animals, generally, this index

Zoos or wild animal parks, admittance with signal dogs, restrictions, CC 54.7

DEATH

Advertisements, celebrity image protection, CC 3344.1

Agents, termination of agency, CC 2355 et seq.

Astaire Celebrity Image Protection Act, CC 3344.1

Bailment, termination of relationship, CC 1934

Celebrity image protection, CC 3344.1

Civil defense workers, liability, CC 1714.5

Contracts,
  Dating service contracts, CC 1694.3
  Revocation of proposal, CC 1587
  Termination, convalescent or nursing homes, CC 1934.5
  Weight loss contracts, cancellation, CC 1694.8

Convalescent homes, termination of contract, CC 1934.5

Crimes and offenses, criminal, injury or death caused by others negligence, liability, CC 847

Damages, homicide, exemplary damages, CC 3294

Dance studio services contract, relief clause, CC 1812.57

Dating service contracts, cancellation, CC 1694.3

Debit cards, liability, CC 1748.31

Disaster service worker, civil defense activities, liabilities, CC 1714.5

Disclosure, real estate, CC 1710.2

Exemplary damages, homicide, CC 3294

Health studios,
  Members, estate contract liability, CC 1812.89
  Services contract, relief clause, CC 1812.89

Indemnity, construction, contracts, CC 2782 et seq.

Insurance, generally, this index

Landlord and tenant, termination of relationship, CC 1934

Leases, termination, CC 1934

Legal Estates Principal and Income Law, CC 731.06

Limitation of actions, celebrity, image protection, CC 3344.1

Mortgages, residential property transfers, maturity date acceleration, CC 2924.6

Probate Proceedings, generally, this index

Real estate, disclosure, CC 1710.2

Residential property transfers, mortgages or trust deeds, maturity date acceleration, CC 2924.6

DEATH—Cont'd

Telecommunications, messages, priorities and preferences, CC 2207

Termination of contract, convalescent or nursing homes, CC 1934.5

Trust deeds, residential property transfers, maturity date acceleration, CC 2924.6

Weight loss contracts, cancellation, CC 1694.8

Wrongful Death, generally, this index

DEBIT CARDS

Generally, CC 1748.30, 1748.31

Accounts and accounting, numbers and numbering, receipts, printing, CC 1747.09

Numbers and numbering, accounts and accounting, receipts, printing, CC 1747.09

Prepaid debit cards, refunds, CC 1748.40, 1748.41

Receipts, accounts and accounting, numbers and numbering, printing, CC 1747.09

Refunds, prepaid debit cards, CC 1748.40, 1748.41

Retailers, receipts, numbers and numbering, printing, CC 1747.09

Waiver, CC 1748.32

DEBT SETTLEMENT PROVIDERS

Fair debt settlement, CC 1788.300 et seq.

DEBTORS AND CREDITORS

See, also, Indebtedness, generally, this index

Generally, CC 3429 et seq.

Ability, offer of performance, CC 1495

Abuse of process, debt collection practices, CC 1788.15

Accord and Satisfaction, generally, this index

Actions and proceedings,
  Credit services organizations, CC 1789.21
  Unfair debt collection practices, CC 1788.10 et seq.

Application of performance, CC 1479

Apportionment, performance, prevention, CC 1514

Art and artists, commissions, sale, original works, exemption from attachment or execution, CC 986

Assignments, leased business premises, CC 1954.05

Attachment, generally, this index

Attorney fees, discrimination, marital status or sex, CC 1812.34

Bank deposits and collections, offer of performance, notice, CC 1500

Bankruptcy, generally, this index

Bonds (officers and fiduciaries), credit services organizations, CC 1789.18

Breach of contract, damages, CC 3302

Business premises, lease, right of assignee to occupy, CC 1954.05

Certificates and certification, identity and identification, theft, collection agencies, CC 1788.18

DEBTORS AND CREDITORS—Cont'd

Change in name, address or employment, notice by debtor, CC 1788.21

Civil liability, unfair debt collection practices, CC 1788.10 et seq.

Collection Agencies, generally, this index

Commercial credit reporting agencies, CC 1785.41 et seq.

Communications, simulating legal or judicial process, deceptive practices, CC 1788.16

Compensation and salaries, performance, delay, CC 1492

Compromise and settlement, payment processors, fair debt settlement, CC 1788.300 et seq.

Conditions, offer of performance, CC 1494, 1498

Consideration,
  Performance, prevention, CC 1514
  Release, CC 1541

Construction or improvement loans, real or personal property, lenders liability for defects, CC 3434

Consumer Credit, generally, this index

Consumer Credit Reporting Agencies, generally, this index

Contracts,
  Credit services organizations, CC 1789.14 et seq.
  Debtors contracts, validity, CC 3431

Cosigners, delinquencies, notices, consumer credit contracts, CC 1799.101, 1799.102

Credit Cards, generally, this index

Credit Life and Disability Insurance, generally, this index

Credit services, CC 1789.10 et seq.

Crimes and offenses,
  Collection, simulated judicial process, CC 1788.16
  Credit services organizations, CC 1789.20
  Identity and identification, theft, collection agencies, CC 1788.18

Damages,
  Breach of obligation to pay, CC 3302
  Credit services organizations, CC 1789.21
  Debt settlement providers, fair debt settlement, CC 1788.305

Denial of credit, consumers, CC 1787.3

Deadbeat list, CC 1788.12

Debit Cards, generally, this index

Debt settlement providers, fair debt settlement, CC 1788.300 et seq.

Deceptive practices, legal or judicial process, communication simulating, CC 1788.16

Delay of performance, compensation, CC 1492

Delivery and change of possession, transfers of personal property without, void, CC 3440 et seq.

Denial of credit, consumers, CC 1787.1 et seq.

Deposit for exchange, relationship between parties, CC 1878

Deposit of funds, offer of performance, CC 1500, 1503

I-60

DEBTORS

DEBTORS AND CREDITORS—Cont'd
Directions for performance, extinguishment of obligation, CC 1476
Disagreement statement, commercial credit report, CC 1785.43
Disclosure,
    Credit services organizations, CC 1789.13 et seq.
    Debt settlement providers, fair debt settlement, contracts, CC 1788.302
    Denial of credit, consumers, CC 1787.1 et seq.
    Unfair debt collection practices, CC 1788.12
Discrimination, marital or sexual status, CC 1812.30 et seq.
Excuse for nonperformance, CC 1511
Extinguishment of obligations, performance in manner directed, CC 1476
Fair debt collection practices, CC 1788 et seq.
    Notice, CC 1812.700 et seq.
Financing statement, transfer of property, CC 3440.1, 3440.5
Fines and penalties,
    Discrimination, marital status or sex, CC 1812.33
    Simulated judicial process, collection, CC 1788.16
Forms, negative credit information, consumer credit reporting agencies, furnishing, CC 1785.26
Fraud,
    Application for credit, CC 1788.20
    Credit services organizations, CC 1789.13
    Debt collection practices, CC 1788.13
Frauds, statute of, promise to answer for debt of another, CC 1624
Garnishment, generally, this index
Good faith, offer to perform, CC 1493
Gratuitous depositary, refusal to accept offer of performance, CC 1505
Harassment, unfair debt collection practices, CC 1788.10 et seq.
Holden Credit Denial Disclosure Act, CC 1787.1 et seq.
Human Trafficking, generally, this index
Identity and identification, theft,
    Collection agencies, CC 1788.18
    Sales, CC 1785.16.2
Information disclosure, unfair debt collection practices, CC 1788.12
Injunction,
    Credit services organizations, CC 1789.20
    Discrimination, marital status or sex, CC 1812.32, 1812.33
Insolvency, generally, this index
Interest, obligation, offer of performance, CC 1504
Joint debtors and creditors,
    Credit history, filing of information, CC 1812.30
    Direction of performance of obligations, CC 1476

DEBTORS AND CREDITORS—Cont'd
Joint debtors and creditors—Cont'd
    Performance rendered to one, CC 1475
    Release, CC 1543
Judicial process, simulation, collection, crimes and offenses, CC 1788.16
Leased business premises, right of assignee to occupy, CC 1954.05
Legal process, communications simulating, deceptive practices, CC 1788.16
Limitation of actions,
    Discrimination, marital status or sex, CC 1812.35
    Notice, CC 1788.14
Marshaling assets, procedure, CC 3433
Notice,
    Denial of credit, consumers, CC 1787.2
    Fair debt collection practices, CC 1812.700 et seq.
    Identity and identification, theft, collection agencies, CC 1788.18
    Limitation of actions, CC 1788.14
    Negative credit information, consumer credit reporting agencies, furnishing, CC 1785.26
    Offer of performance, deposit of fund, CC 1500
    Refusal to accept performance before offer, CC 1515
Novation, generally, this index
Objections, offer of performance, CC 1501
Offenses. Crimes and offenses, generally, ante
Offer to perform obligation, CC 1485 et seq.
    Ability and willingness, CC 1495
    Condition, CC 1494
    Conditional, CC 1498
    Delay, compensation, CC 1492
    Deposit of bank offer, CC 1503
    Good faith, CC 1493
    Interest on obligation, CC 1504
    Objection to mode, CC 1501
    Payment, deposit of money, CC 1500
    Person required to make, CC 1487
    Place of offer, CC 1489
    Procedure, CC 1488
    Production of things to be delivered, CC 1496
    Receipts, delivery of property, CC 1499
    Refusal to accept, CC 1505
    Separation of thing offered, CC 1497
    Time, CC 1490, 1491
    Title to property, CC 1502
Options, place, offer of performance, CC 1489
Part performance, CC 1477
    Amounts, CC 1525
    Offer, CC 1486
Payment, preference, CC 3432
Payment processors, fair debt settlement, CC 1788.300 et seq.
Penalties,
    Discrimination, marital status or sex, CC 1812.33

DEBTORS AND CREDITORS—Cont'd
Penalties—Cont'd
    Simulated judicial process, collection, CC 1788.16
Performance, application, CC 1479
Possession, transfer of personal property without delivery, fraud, CC 3440 et seq.
Precomputed interest, CC 1799.5
Preferences, payments or security, CC 3432
Preventing performance of obligations, CC 1511 et seq.
    Creditor preventing performance, CC 1512
    Refusal to accept performance before offer, CC 1515
Priorities and preferences,
    Marshaling assets, CC 3433
    Payments or giving of security, CC 3432
    Voidable transactions, CC 3439 et seq.
Process, communication simulating, CC 1788.16
Production of things to be delivered, offer of performance, CC 1496
Profanity, collection of debt, use, CC 1788.12
Purchases, CC 1788.50 et seq.
Receipts,
    Delivery of property in performance, CC 1497
    Performance of obligation, CC 1499
Refusal to accept offer of performance, CC 1505, 1515
Release, CC 1541 et seq.
Reports. Consumer Credit Reporting Agencies, generally, this index
Repossessors and Repossession, generally, this index
Responsibilities, fair debt collection practices, CC 1788.20 et seq.
Rosenthal Fair Debt Collection Practices Act, CC 1788 et seq.
Sales, identity and identification, theft, CC 1785.16.2
Satisfaction. Accord and Satisfaction, generally, this index
Security, preference, CC 3432
Separation of thing offered, performance, offering, CC 1497
Services organizations, credit services organizations, CC 1789.10 et seq.
Share appreciation loans for seniors, nature of relationship, CC 1917.610
Simulated judicial process, collection, crimes and offenses, CC 1788.16
Statute of Frauds, promise to answer for debt of another, CC 1624
Telephones, use in collection of debt, unlawful practices, CC 1788.11
Theft, identity and identification,
    Collection agencies, CC 1788.18
    Sales, CC 1785.16.2
Third parties, actions and proceedings, satisfaction of debt, impairing rights of third party, CC 3433

DEBTORS

DEBTORS AND CREDITORS—Cont'd
Threats, unfair debt collection practices, **CC 1788.10**
Time, offer of performance, **CC 1490, 1491**
    Objection to mode, **CC 1501**
Title to property, offer of performance, **CC 1502**
Trafficking. Human Trafficking, generally, this index
Two or more obligations, performance, application, **CC 1479**
Unsecured creditors, transfer of personal property without change of possession, **CC 3440 et seq.**
Validity of debtors contracts, **CC 3431**
Void transfers, **CC 3440 et seq.**
Voidable Transactions, generally, this index
Waiver,
    Consumers rights, credit services organizations, **CC 1789.19**
    Fair debt collection practices, **CC 1788.33**
    Precomputed interest, **CC 1799.6**
Women, obtaining credit, discrimination, **CC 1812.30 et seq.**

DEBTS
Indebtedness, generally, this index

DECEDENTS ESTATES
Probate Proceedings, generally, this index

DECEIT
Fraud, generally, this index

DECEPTION
Fraud, generally, this index

DECEPTIVE TRADE PRACTICES
Monopolies and Unfair Trade, generally, this index

DECLARATORY JUDGMENTS AND DECREES
Consumers, privacy, disclosure, **CC 1798.150**
Indebtedness, duress or coercion, **CC 1798.97.3**
Landlord and tenant, animals, declawing, devocalizing, **CC 1942.7**
Prescription drug claims processor, reports, failure to file, **CC 2528**

DECREES
Declaratory Judgments and Decrees, generally, this index
Judgments and Decrees, generally, this index

DEDICATION
Private real property for public recreational use to supplement tax supported publicly owned facilities, **CC 1009**
State lands, ownership, **CC 670**

DEEDS AND CONVEYANCES
Generally, **CC 1039 et seq., 1091 et seq.**
Absolute, delivery, **CC 1056**

DEEDS AND CONVEYANCES—Cont'd
Acknowledgments,
    Prior to code, law governing, **CC 1205**
    Proof, conveyances prior to code, **CC 1206**
Adverse possession, transferability, **CC 1047**
Appurtenances, transfer of incidents, **CC 1084**
Asbestos, notice, **CC 2079.7**
Blind or visually impaired persons, discrimination, **CC 53**
Books, recordation, **CC 1171**
Breach of covenants, **CC 3304 et seq.**
Cancellation, **CC 1058**
Certified copy, recordation, **CC 1213**
Change of name, **CC 1096**
Chemical storage tanks, notice, **CC 2079.7**
Collateral warranties, abolition, **CC 1115**
Commercial property owners guide to earthquake safety, **CC 2079.9**
Conclusiveness, **CC 1107**
Condition precedent, performance, **CC 1110**
Condition subsequent,
    Defeat, reconveyance, **CC 1109**
    Limitation of actions, **CC 784**
Consolidated description, merger, **CC 1093**
Construction, **CC 1066 et seq.**
Constructive delivery, **CC 1059**
Constructive notice upon recording, **CC 1213**
Consumer credit reporting agencies, records, application of law, **CC 1785.35**
Contracts for sale of land, **CC 2985 et seq.**
    Appraisal and appraisers, discrimination, notice, **CC 1102.6g**
    Assignments, **CC 2985.1**
    Breach of agreement, damages, **CC 3306, 3307**
    Consequential damages, **CC 3306, 3307**
    Crimes and offenses, **CC 2985.2, 2985.3**
    Damages, breach of agreement, **CC 3306, 3307**
    Default, liquidated damages, **CC 1675 et seq.**
    Defective title, specific performance, **CC 3394**
    Disclosures upon transfer of residential property, **CC 1102 et seq.**
    Escrows and escrow agents, return, **CC 1057.3**
    Fines and penalties, **CC 2985.2, 2985.3**
    Form, **CC 2985.5**
    Impound accounts,
        Accounting, **CC 2954**
        Retention and investment in state, **CC 2955**
        Single family owner occupied dwellings, payment of taxes, **CC 2954**
    Installment payments,
        Insurance and taxes, **CC 2985.4**
        Misappropriation, **CC 2985.3**
    Insurance, pro rata payments, **CC 2985.4**
    Interests,
        Damages, breach of agreement, **CC 3306, 3307**

DEEDS AND CONVEYANCES—Cont'd
Contracts for sale of land—Cont'd
    Interests—Cont'd
        Variable rate, **CC 1916.5**
    Internet, sex offenses, registration, notice, **CC 2079.10a**
    Liens and incumbrances,
        Crimes and offenses, **CC 2985.2**
        Vendors lien, **CC 3046 et seq.**
    Liquidated damages, default, **CC 1675 et seq.**
    Merger of parcels, single instrument of conveyance or consolidated descriptions, **CC 1093**
    Mineral rights, **CC 883.110 et seq.**
    Misappropriation, installment payment, **CC 2985.3**
    Notice,
        Appraisal and appraisers, discrimination, **CC 1102.6g**
        Registered sex offenders, data base, **CC 2079.10a**
    Payment clauses, **CC 2985.6**
    Pledges, **CC 2985.1**
    Priorities and preferences, vendors lien, **CC 3048**
    Pro rata payments, insurance and taxes, **CC 2985.4**
    Public policy, prepayment clauses, waiver, **CC 2985.6**
    Purchasers lien, **CC 3050**
    Registered sex offenders, data base, notice, **CC 2079.10a**
    Security, assignments, **CC 2985.1**
    Sex offenses, registration, data base, notice, **CC 2079.10a**
    Single family residence,
        Options to purchase, documentary fees, **CC 1097**
        Owner occupied dwelling, impound account for payment of taxes, **CC 2954**
    Specific performance,
        Damages, **CC 3387**
        Defective title, **CC 3394**
    Statement of compliance, Subdivision Map Act, **CC 2985.51**
    Statement of years to complete payment, **CC 2985.5**
    Subdivision Map Act, statement of compliance, **CC 2985.51**
    Subordination agreements, **CC 2953.1 et seq.**
    Taxation,
        Estimate, **CC 2985.5**
        Impound accounts for payment,
            Accounting, **CC 2954**
            Retention and investment in state, **CC 2955**
        Pro rata payments, **CC 2985.4**
    Transfers, **CC 2985.1**
    Uniform Vendor and Purchaser Risk Act, **CC 1662**

DEEDS

DEEDS AND CONVEYANCES—Cont'd
Contracts for sale of land—Cont'd
    Variable interest rate, CC 1916.5
    Vendor and Purchaser Risk Act, CC 1662
    Waiver, prepayment clauses, CC 2985.6
Controlled escrows, developers, CC 2995
Copies, recording, CC 1213
Costs, home energy rating program, information, CC 2079.11
Covenants,
    Damages, breach of covenant, CC 3304
    Discrimination, CC 53, 782, 782.5
    Floor area ratio standards, housing development projects, restrictions, CC 4747
    Implied covenants, CC 1113
    Limitation of actions, CC 784
    Mobilehomes or manufactured homes, restrictions, CC 714.5
Covenants Running with Land, generally, this index
Crimes and offenses, contracts for sale of land, CC 2985.2, 2985.3
Damages,
    Breach of covenant, CC 3304
    Contracts for sale of land,
        Breach, CC 3306, 3307
        Specific performance, presumptions, CC 3387
    Natural hazards, disclosure, residential property, CC 1103.13
    Purchase, breach of agreement to purchase, CC 3307
    Quitclaim deeds, breach of agreement to execute, CC 3306a
Delivery,
    Absolute, CC 1056
    Constructive, CC 1059
    Date, presumption, CC 1055
    Escrow, CC 1057
    Natural hazard disclosure statement, residential property, CC 1103.10
    Necessity, CC 1054
    Presumptions, date, CC 1055
    Redelivery, CC 1058
Description of realty, rules for construing, consolidation of separate descriptions, merger, CC 1093
Disclosure,
    Environmental hazards, CC 2079.7
    Natural hazards, residential property, CC 1103 et seq.
    Residential property, CC 1102 et seq.
    Water conservation, building standards, CC 1101.4, 1101.5, 1102.155
Discrimination,
    Covenants, ante
    Restrictions, CC 782, 782.5
    Voiding deed, CC 782
Documentary fees, sale or lease of single family residence, CC 1097
Dwellings, single family, escrows, developer holding interest in required escrow entity, CC 2995

DEEDS AND CONVEYANCES—Cont'd
Earnest money, escrows, return, CC 1057.3
Easements, generally, this index
Environmental hazards, notice, CC 2079.7
Equity. Home Equity Sales Contracts, generally, this index
Escrows and escrow agents,
    Consumer protection, foreclosure, CC 1103.20 et seq.
    Delivery, CC 1057
    Return, CC 1057.3
    Single family dwellings, developer holding interest in required escrow entity, CC 2995
    Title insurance, notice, CC 1057.6
Essentials to use of thing is presumed granted, CC 3522
Estates for Years, this index
Estates of inheritance, implied covenants, CC 1113
Evidence,
    Contracts for sale of land, breach, damages, presumptions, CC 3387
    Conveyances prior to code, CC 1206
    Law governing, CC 1205
    Presumptions, generally, post
Executions,
    Power of attorney, form, CC 1095
    Prior to code, law governing, CC 1205
Exemptions,
    Fees, CC 1098.6
    Natural hazards, residential property, disclosure, CC 1103.1
Fees, CC 1098 et seq.
    Disclosure, CC 1102.6e
Floor area ratio standards, covenants, housing development projects, CC 4747
For sale signs, restraints on alienation, CC 712
Forest fires, fire hazard severity zones,
    Compliance, CC 1102.19
    Disclosure, CC 1102.6f
Formaldehyde, notice, CC 2079.7
Forms, CC 1092
    Disclosures upon transfers of residential property, CC 1102.6, 1102.6a
    Power of attorney, execution of instruments, CC 1095
    Prior to code, law governing, CC 1205
Fraud, natural hazards, disclosure, residential property, CC 1103.8
Fuel and chemical storage tanks, notice, CC 2079.7
Future interests, CC 699
    Attornment of tenants, CC 1111
Greater estate than owned, CC 1108
Hazards,
    Environmental hazards, notice, CC 2079.7
    Natural hazards, disclosure, residential property, CC 1103 et seq.
Home energy rating program, information, CC 2079.10
    Costs, CC 2079.11

DEEDS AND CONVEYANCES—Cont'd
Home Equity Sales Contracts, generally, this index
Implied covenants, CC 1113
Impound accounts. Contracts for sale of land, ante
Incidents of ownership, included in transfer, CC 1084
Instrument of defeasance affecting grant in absolute form, recording, necessity, CC 2950
Insurance, contracts for sale of land, pro rata payments, CC 2985.4
Interest, contracts for sale of land, damages, breach of agreement, CC 3306, 3307
Internet, contracts for sale of land, sex offenses, registration, notice, CC 2079.10a
Interpretation, CC 1066
    Favor of grantee, exception, CC 1069
    Irreconcilable parts, CC 1070
    Limitations, CC 1067
    Recitals, CC 1068
    Reservation of rights, CC 1069
    Words of inheritance or succession, CC 1072
Irreconcilable provisions, interpretation, CC 1070
Joint Tenants, generally, this index
Judicial notice, restrictive covenants, discrimination, CC 53
Land contracts. Contracts for sale of land, generally, ante
Lead base paint, notice, CC 2079.7
Liens and incumbrances, contracts for sale of land,
    Crimes and offenses, CC 2985.2
    Vendor lien, CC 3046 et seq.
Life estate, transfer of greater estate than owned, CC 1108
Limitations, interpretations, CC 1067
Lineal warranties, abolition, CC 1115
Marketable record title, CC 880.020 et seq.
Merger, single instrument of conveyance or consolidated description, CC 1093
Mineral rights, CC 883.110 et seq.
Mistake, natural hazards, disclosure, residential property, CC 1103.4, 1103.5
Modification or change, covenants, low and moderate income housing, CC 714.6
Names, change, CC 1096
Natural hazards, disclosure, residential property, CC 1103 et seq.
Nonacceptance of recorded deed, recording in county of location, CC 1058.5
Nonprofit organizations, conservation easements, CC 815 et seq.
Notice,
    Blanket incumbrances, subdivisions, CC 1133
    Constructive, recordation, CC 1213
    Environmental hazards, CC 2079.7
    Industrial use, residential property, CC 1102.17

I-63

DEEDS

DEEDS AND CONVEYANCES—Cont'd
Notice—Cont'd
  Names, change, **CC 1096**
  Nonacceptance, recording in county of location, **CC 1058.5**
  Registered sex offenders, data base, **CC 2079.10a**
Offers to purchase, disclosure statements, termination, **CC 1102.3**
Parties, acquisition of interest or benefit by stranger, **CC 1085**
Perpetuities. Rule Against Perpetuities, generally, this index
Personal property, transfer without change of possession, void as against creditors, **CC 3440 et seq.**
Pest control, structural pest control, inspection reports, certification, **CC 1099**
Power of attorney, execution of instruments, form, **CC 1095**
Prepayment clauses, real property sales contracts, **CC 2985.6**
Presumptions,
  Contracts for sale, damages, **CC 3387**
  Delivery date, **CC 1055**
  Fee simple title, **CC 1105**
Prior to code,
  Evidence, recording, **CC 1206**
  Law governing, **CC 1205**
Priority of recording subsequent conveyances, **CC 1214**
Privileges and immunities, natural hazards, disclosure, residential property, **CC 1103.4**
Public agency or officer, interpretation, **CC 1069**
Purchasers lien, **CC 3050**
Quiet enjoyment, breach of covenant, damages, **CC 3304**
Quieting Title, generally, this index
Quitclaim deeds,
  Breach of agreement to deliver, damages, **CC 3306a**
  Oil and gas, leases, **CC 883.140**
Race discrimination. Discrimination, generally, ante
Radon gas, notice, **CC 2079.7**
Recitals, interpretation, **CC 1068**
Reconveyance, conditions subsequent, defeat, **CC 1109**
Records and recordation, **CC 1171**
  Certified copies, **CC 1213**
  Constructive notice, **CC 1213**
    Change of name, **CC 1096**
  Copies, **CC 1213**
  Fees, **CC 1098.5**
  Innocent purchasers, rights under instrument first recorded, **CC 1107**
  Notice,
    Constructive, **CC 1213**
    Nonacceptance of deed, recording in county of location, **CC 1058.5**

DEEDS AND CONVEYANCES—Cont'd
Records and recordation—Cont'd
  Prior to code, law governing, **CC 1205**
  Priority, **CC 1214**
  Separate set of books, **CC 1171**
  Standing timber or trees, **CC 1220**
Redelivery, **CC 1058**
Registered sex offenders, data base, notice, **CC 2079.10a**
Release, unperformed contracts for sale of property, **CC 886.020 et seq.**
Rents, **CC 1111**
Reservation of rights, interpretation, **CC 1069**
Restraints on alienation, **CC 711**
  For sale signs, **CC 712**
Restrictions, limitation of actions, **CC 784**
Restrictive covenants. Covenants, generally, ante
Reversions, **CC 1111**
Revocation, **CC 1229, 1230**
Rights, mineral rights, **CC 883.110 et seq.**
Rule Against Perpetuities, generally, this index
Sex discrimination. Discrimination, generally, ante
Sex offenses, registration, data base, notice, **CC 2079.10a**
Shared appreciation loans for seniors, **CC 1917.320 et seq.**
Soil and water contamination, notice, **CC 2079.7**
Solar easements, minimum description, **CC 801.5**
Solar Rights Act, **CC 714**
Specific performance, **CC 3387**
  Defective title by seller, **CC 3394**
Statements, natural hazard disclosure statement, **CC 1103.2 et seq.**
Stranger, acquisition of interest or benefit, **CC 1085**
Structural pest control, inspection reports, certificates, **CC 1099**
Substituted disclosures, **CC 1102.6**
Supplemental tax assessments. Tax Assessments, this index
Surrendering or cancelling grant, **CC 1058**
Taxation. Contracts for sale of land, ante
Third parties, natural hazard disclosure statement, **CC 1103.2 et seq.**
Timber and lumber, recordation of instruments, **CC 1220**
Time,
  Creation of limitation or condition, **CC 749**
  Disclosure statements, **CC 1102.3**
  Presumptions, delivery date, **CC 1055**
  Revocation, power, **CC 1230**
  Unperformed contracts for sale, expiration, **CC 886.030, 886.040**
Title deeds, ownership, **CC 994**
Title insurance, consumer protection, foreclosure, **CC 1103.20 et seq.**
Trust Deeds, generally, this index

DEEDS AND CONVEYANCES—Cont'd
Uniform Vendor and Purchaser Risk Act, **CC 1662**
Unperformed contracts for sale of real property, marketable title, **CC 886.010 et seq.**
Unrecorded instrument, **CC 1217**
Vendor and Purchaser Risk Act, **CC 1662**
Voidable Transactions, generally, this index
Waiver, disclosure, transfers of residential property, **CC 1102**
Water and soil contamination, notice, **CC 2079.7**
Water conservation, building standards, **CC 1101.1 et seq.**
  Disclosure, **CC 1102.155**
Words of inheritance or succession, **CC 1072**

DEEDS OF TRUST
Trust Deeds, generally, this index

DEEP POCKET RULE
Joint and several liability, **CC 1431 et seq.**

DEEPFAKES
Lewdness and obscenity, **CC 1708.86**

DEFACING
Art objects, **CC 987**
Manufacturers identification marks, sale or disposal of merchandise, **CC 1710.1**
Willful misconduct of minors, imputed to parents, damages, **CC 1714.1**

DEFAMATION
Libel and Slander, generally, this index

DEFAULT
Condominiums, sales, **CC 1675**
Frauds, statute of, promise to answer for debt of another, **CC 1624**
Installment Sales, this index
Mortgages, this index
Recreational Vehicles, this index
Statute of Frauds, promise to answer for debt of another, **CC 1624**
Trust Deeds, this index

DEFAULT JUDGMENTS
Affidavits, vacating or setting aside, **CC 1788.61**
Application of law, vacating or setting aside, **CC 1788.61**
Consumer credit, purchases, **CC 1788.60**
Evidence, vacating or setting aside, **CC 1788.61**
Identity theft, vacating or setting aside, **CC 1788.61**
Mistake, identity and identification, vacating or setting aside, **CC 1788.61**
Motions,
  Notice, vacating or setting aside, **CC 1788.61**
  Vacating or setting aside, **CC 1788.61**
Notice, motions, vacating or setting aside, **CC 1788.61**

DEPOSITORIES

DEFAULT JUDGMENTS—Cont'd
Pleadings, vacating or setting aside, **CC 1788.61**
Student loans, private education lenders and loan collectors, **CC 1788.206**
 Vacating or setting aside, **CC 1788.207**
 Vacating or setting aside, motions, **CC 1788.61**

DEFENDANTS
Parties, generally, this index

DEFENSE SHELTERS
Injuries sustained in or upon, exemption from liability, exception, **CC 1714.5**

DEFERMENT
Installment Sales, this index

DEFERRED PAYMENT PRICE
Installment sales, memorandum, subsequent purchases, **CC 1808.3**

DEFIBRILLATORS
Privileges and immunities, **CC 1714.21**

DEFICIENCY JUDGMENTS
Mechanics liens, **CC 8466**
Mobilehomes, default, conditional sales contract, limitation, **CC 2983.8**

DEFINITIONS
Words and Phrases, generally, this index

DELINQUENT CHILDREN
Juvenile Delinquents and Dependents, generally, this index

DEMOLITION OF BUILDINGS
Water conservation, building standards, **CC 1101.6**

DENTAL HYGIENISTS
Privileges and immunities, professional committee, **CC 43.7, 43.8**

DENTISTS AND DENTISTRY
Children and minors, misconduct causing damage, imputed liability of parents for damages, **CC 1714.1**
Clients, sexual harassment, **CC 51.9**
Contracts,
 Patients, rescission, **CC 1689.3**
 Rescission, patients, **CC 1689.3**
Damages, imputed liability of parents for acts of children, **CC 1714.1**
Harassment, sexual harassment, clients, **CC 51.9**
Immunities. Privileges and immunities, generally, post
Malpractice. Medical Malpractice, generally, this index
Medical Malpractice, generally, this index
Negligence. Medical Malpractice, generally, this index
Plans and specifications, health programs, rescission, **CC 1689.3**

DENTISTS AND DENTISTRY—Cont'd
Privileges and immunities,
 Health care facilities, denial of staff privileges, **CC 43.97**
 Professional committee, **CC 43.7, 43.8**
 Referral services, **CC 43.95**
Referrals, limitation of liability, **CC 43.95**
Sexual harassment, clients, **CC 51.9**
Telecommunications, referral services, immunity, **CC 43.95**

DEPARTMENTAL BANKING
Banks and Banking, generally, this index

DEPARTMENTS
State Departments, generally, this index

DEPENDENT ADULTS
Abuse, landlord and tenant, termination, notice, **CC 1946.7**

DEPENDENT CHILDREN
Juvenile Delinquents and Dependents, generally, this index

DEPENDENTS
Juvenile Delinquents and Dependents, generally, this index
Sexual exploitation, treble damages, **CC 3345.1**

DEPOSITARIES
Depositories, generally, this index

DEPOSITIONS
Condominiums, construction, defects, **CC 6000**
 Business and commerce, **CC 6870**

DEPOSITORIES
 See, also, Bailment, generally, this index
 Generally, **CC 1813 et seq.**
Advances, liens, **CC 1856**
Adverse claims, notice to beneficiary, **CC 1825**
Alterations, customers leaving property, insurance, **CC 1858 et seq.**
Animals,
 Compensation, **CC 1853**
 Involuntary deposits, running at large, **CC 1815 et seq.**
Claims, notice, **CC 1825**
Compensation, deposit for hire, **CC 1853**
Consent, opening of fastened deposit, **CC 1835**
Coowners, delivery, **CC 1827**
Creation, **CC 1813 et seq.**
Damages,
 Indemnification, **CC 1833**
 Use of thing deposited, **CC 1836**
Debtors and creditors, gratuitous depositary, refusal to accept performance, **CC 1505**
Degree of care, deposits for hire, **CC 1852**
 Gratuitous depositary, **CC 1846**
Delivery,
 Demand, **CC 1822 et seq.**
 Joint tenants, **CC 1827, 1828**

DEPOSITORIES—Cont'd
Delivery—Cont'd
 Place of delivery, **CC 1824**
Demand, delivery, **CC 1822 et seq.**
Discount buying services, trust accounts, **CC 1812.116**
Duties, **CC 1839**
Evidence of deposit, loss or injury to thing deposited, **CC 1838**
Exchange, transfer of title, relationship between parties, **CC 1878**
Expenses and expenditures,
 Indemnification, **CC 1833**
 Liens and incumbrances, depositary for hire, **CC 1856**
Fastened deposit, opening, **CC 1835**
Gratuitous, **CC 1844 et seq.**
 Care, degree required, **CC 1846**
 Involuntary, **CC 1845**
 Termination of duties, **CC 1847**
Gross negligence, presumption, **CC 1838**
Hire, **CC 1851 et seq.**
 Care, degree required, **CC 1852**
 Termination, **CC 1854, 1855**
 Week or month, fraction, compensation, **CC 1853**
Indemnification, expenses, **CC 1833**
Injury to thing deposited, **CC 1838**
Involuntary,
 Creation, **CC 1815**
 Duties, **CC 1816**
 Gratuitous, **CC 1845**
Joint tenants, delivery, **CC 1827, 1828**
Kinds, **CC 1813**
Lien of deposit for hire, **CC 1856, 1857**
Limitation, liability, negligence, **CC 1840**
Loss of thing deposited, **CC 1838**
Negligence,
 Limitation of liability, **CC 1840**
 Loss or injury to thing deposited, **CC 1838**
Notice,
 Adverse claim, **CC 1825**
 Detention of property from true owner, **CC 1826**
 Sale, **CC 1837**
 Wrongful detention, **CC 1826**
Obligations, **CC 1822 et seq.**
Perishable, sale, **CC 1837, 1857**
Place of delivery, **CC 1824**
Presumptions, loss or injury, **CC 1838**
Repairs, customers property, insurance, **CC 1858 et seq.**
Sales, this index
Services, duties and liabilities, **CC 1839**
Storage. Hire, generally, ante
Tenants in common, delivery, **CC 1827**
Termination of deposit for hire, **CC 1854, 1855**
Termination of duties, gratuitous depositary, **CC 1847**
Title to property, deposit for exchange, **CC 1878**

DEPOSITORIES

DEPOSITORIES—Cont'd
Use of thing deposited, **CC 1835**
  Damages, **CC 1836**
Wrongful detention, notice to true owner, **CC 1826**
Wrongful use, damages, **CC 1836**

DEPOSITS
Bank Deposits and Collections, generally, this index
Credit services organizations, claims against deposits, **CC 1789.24**
Involuntary deposits, property, **CC 1815 et seq.**
Landlord and Tenant, this index
Obligation, performance to one of joint creditors, exception, **CC 1475**

DEPOSITS IN BANKS
Bank Deposits and Collections, generally, this index

DEPOSITS IN COURT
Agricultural marketing cooperatives, labor liens on crops, **CC 3061.6**
Conditional sales, motor vehicles, costs and fees in action, **CC 2983.4**
Motor vehicles, fees and costs, action on conditional sale contract, **CC 2983.4**

DESCENT AND DISTRIBUTION
Probate Proceedings, generally, this index
Succession, generally, this index

DESERTION
Juvenile Delinquents and Dependents, generally, this index
Support, generally, this index

DESIGNS AND DESIGNERS
Ammunition, negligence, **CC 1714**
Architects, generally, this index
Condominiums, actions and proceedings, defects, **CC 6000 et seq.**
  Business and commerce, **CC 6870 et seq.**
Consumer protection, Internet, children and minors, **CC 1798.99.28 et seq.**
Conversion, mechanics liens, **CC 8319**
Liens and incumbrances. Mechanics Liens, generally, this index
Mechanics Liens, generally, this index
Ownership, **CC 980 et seq.**
Publication, effect, **CC 983**
Weapons, negligence, **CC 1714**

DESTROYED DOCUMENTS
Lost or Destroyed Documents, generally, this index

DESTROYED PROPERTY
Lost or Destroyed Property, generally, this index

DETAINERS
Forcible Entry and Detainer, generally, this index

DETERIORATION OF GOODS
Deceptive practices, Consumers Legal Remedies Act, **CC 1750 et seq.**

DEVELOPMENT PROJECTS
Planned Unit Developments, generally, this index

DEVELOPMENTAL DISABILITIES
Intellectual and Developmental Disabilities, generally, this index

DEVICES
Touch screen devices, blind or visually impaired persons, **CC 54.9**

DEVISES AND DEVISEES
Gifts, Devises and Bequests, generally, this index

DICTAPHONES
Manufacturers identification mark, removal, defacing, alteration or destruction, **CC 1710.1**

DIES, TOOLS AND MOLDS
Destruction or disposition, transfer of customers rights and title, **CC 1140**

DIET
Weight loss contracts, **CC 1694.5 et seq.**

DIETITIANS
Immunities. Privileges and immunities, generally, post
Privileges and immunities,
  Committee members, **CC 43.7, 43.8**
  Referral services, **CC 43.95**
Referral services, limitation of liability, **CC 43.95**
Telephones, referral services, immunity, **CC 43.95**
Weight loss contracts, **CC 1694.5 et seq.**

DIRECT MARKETING
Business and commerce, personal information, disclosure, **CC 1798.83**

DIRECTORS
Condominiums, this index

DIRKS
Weapons, generally, this index

DISABILITY INSURANCE
Health Insurance, generally, this index

DISABLED PERSONS
Accessibility, standards, civil rights, construction, **CC 55.3 et seq., 55.51 et seq.**
Agreements. Contracts, generally, post
Amusements,
  Civil rights, **CC 54.1**
  Injunctions, violation of access rights, **CC 55**
Animals. Service Animals, generally, this index
Application of law, civil rights, construction, accessibility, **CC 55.57**

DISABLED PERSONS—Cont'd
Assistive devices, warranties, **CC 1790 et seq.**
Attorney fees, interference with civil rights, **CC 54.3, 55**
Attorney general, civil rights, injunction, **CC 55.1**
Blind or Visually Impaired Persons, generally, this index
Buildings,
  Access, public buildings, injunction, violation of access rights, **CC 55**
  Civil rights, **CC 54 et seq.**
Civil rights, **CC 51 et seq.**
  Construction, standards, accessibility, **CC 55.3 et seq., 55.51 et seq.**
Clinics, access, **CC 54 et seq.**
Condominiums, accessibility, modification or change, **CC 4760**
Construction, civil rights, standards, accessibility, **CC 55.3 et seq., 55.51 et seq.**
Consumer protection,
  Additional penalty, **CC 3345**
  Damages, **CC 1780**
Contracts,
  Dance studio services, relief clause, **CC 1812.57**
  Dating service contracts, cancellation, **CC 1694.3**
  Health studio services, relief clause, **CC 1812.89**
  Weight loss contracts, cancellation, **CC 1694.8**
Costs, accessibility, civil rights, construction, **CC 55.55**
Crimes and offenses, refusing access to public facilities, accommodations, **CC 54.3**
Damages,
  Civil rights, **CC 54.3**
    Construction, accessibility, **CC 55.55, 55.56**
  Consumer protection, unfair or deceptive practices, **CC 3345**
Dating service contracts, cancellation, **CC 1694.3**
Deaf or Hard of Hearing Persons, generally, this index
Deeds and conveyances,
  Discrimination, **CC 53**
  Restrictive covenants, discrimination, **CC 53**
Discrimination, **CC 51 et seq.**
  Adoption, **CC 54.1**
  Franchises, **CC 51.8**
  Housing, **CC 54.1**
    Injunctions, **CC 55**
  Private schools, **CC 54.1**
  Public conveyances, accommodations or housing, **CC 54 et seq.**
  Restrictive covenants, **CC 53**
  Service dogs, **CC 54.2**
District attorneys, civil rights, injunction, **CC 55.1**

I-66

DISABLED PERSONS—Cont'd
Dogs. Service Animals, generally, this index
Dwellings. Housing, generally, post
Eviction, aged persons, CC 51.3, 51.11
Evidence, presumptions, damages, construction, accessibility, CC 55.56
Fines and penalties, consumer protection, CC 1780, 3345
Forms, construction, accessibility, CC 55.3
Franchises, discrimination, CC 51.8
Fraud, CC 1780
    Fines and penalties, CC 1780, 3345
Guardian and Ward, generally, this index
Health studio members, contract liability, CC 1812.89
Hearings, aged persons, eviction, CC 51.3, 51.11
High frequency litigants, construction, accessibility, CC 55.54
Highways and roads, access, CC 54 et seq.
Hospitals, access, CC 54 et seq.
Hotels and motels,
    Access, CC 54 et seq.
    Civil rights, CC 54.1
Housing,
    Access, improvements or additions, rental housing, requirements, CC 51.5
    Aged persons, CC 51.3, 51.11
    Discrimination, CC 54.1
        Injunctions, CC 55, 55.1
    Modification, requirements, CC 51.5
Injunction, violation of access rights to public accommodations, CC 55, 55.1
Leases, accessibility, construction, standards, inspection and inspectors, CC 1938
Medical facilities, access, CC 54 et seq.
Mobilehomes and mobilehome parks,
    Accommodations, CC 798.29.6
    Subdivisions, cooperatives or condominiums, accommodations, CC 798.29.6
Mortgages, modification or change, forbearance, fines and penalties, CC 2944.8
Municipal attorneys, civil rights, injunction, CC 55.1
Notice,
    Aged persons, eviction, CC 51.3, 51.11
    Construction, civil rights, accessibility, CC 55.54
Personal attendants. Domestic Workers, generally, this index
Presumptions, damages, construction, accessibility, CC 55.56
Public accommodations, access, CC 54 et seq.
Recreational vehicles, removal from parks, CC 799.56
Roads and highways, access to public facilities, CC 54 et seq.
Sanctions, complaints, accessibility, construction, CC 55.54
Service Animals, generally, this index
Sidewalks,
    Access to public facilities, CC 54 et seq.

DISABLED PERSONS—Cont'd
Sidewalks—Cont'd
    Civil rights, CC 54 et seq.
    Injunction actions, violation of access rights, CC 55
Small Businesses, generally, this index
Speech impaired persons. Deaf or Hard of Hearing Persons, generally, this index
Standards, civil rights, construction, accessibility, CC 55.3 et seq., 55.51 et seq.
Streets and alleys, access for use, CC 54 et seq.
Transportation,
    Civil rights, CC 54.1
    Zoos or wild animal parks, CC 54.7
Weight loss contracts, CC 1694.5 et seq.
Wheelchairs, generally, this index
Zoos or wild animal parks, admittance with service dogs, restrictions, CC 54.7

DISASTER RELIEF
Medical records, disclosure, CC 56.10

DISASTERS
Civil defense activities, liability, CC 1714.5
Earthquakes, generally, this index
Floods and Flooding, generally, this index
Forest Fires, generally, this index
Home solicitation contracts, residential repair or restoration, cancellation, CC 1689.6, 1689.7, 1689.14
Hurricanes, generally, this index
Medical records, disaster relief organizations, disclosure, CC 56.10
Mortgages, prepayment penalties, CC 2954.9
Prepayment penalties, mortgages, CC 2954.9
Shelters, tort liability, CC 1714.5
Storms, generally, this index
Tidal Waves, generally, this index
Trust deeds, prepayment penalties, CC 2954.9
War and Civil Defense, generally, this index

DISCHARGE
Installment buyers obligations by payments, CC 1810.8
Mortgages, this index

DISCIPLINE
Condominiums, this index

DISCLAIMER
Fine art multiples,
    Charitable sales, disclosure, exemptions, CC 1742.6
    Sales, CC 1744.7, 1745
Fraud, solicitation, payment of money, written statement or invoice, CC 1716
Motor vehicles, leases, advertisements, CC 1939.19

DISCLOSURE
Generally, CC 1798 et seq.
Ambulances, contractors, CC 3273

DISCLOSURE—Cont'd
Attorney Fees, this index
Banks and Banking, this index
Bookkeeping services, business records, CC 1799 et seq.
Bookstores, personal information, CC 1798.90, 1798.90.05
Business records, bookkeeping services, CC 1799 et seq.
Club cards, grocery stores, CC 1749.60 et seq.
Community apartments, defects, sale, CC 1134
Condominiums, this index
Consent, Information Practices Act, CC 1798.24
Consumer Credit, this index
Consumer Credit Reporting Agencies, this index
Consumers, privacy, CC 1798.100 et seq.
Credit Cards, this index
Credit disability insurance, claims procedures forms, CC 1812.402
Credit services organizations, CC 1789.13 et seq.
Credit Unions, this index
Debtors and Creditors, this index
Deeds and Conveyances, this index
Environmental hazards, real estate transfers, CC 2079.7
Fine prints, sales, CC 1740 et seq.
Floating homes, names and addresses, CC 800.34
Floods and flooding, residential property, CC 1103 et seq.
Forest fires, residential property, CC 1103 et seq.
Genetic testing, privacy, CC 56.181
Grocery stores, club cards, CC 1749.60 et seq.
Hazards, natural hazards, residential property, CC 1103 et seq.
Health Care Service Plans, this index
Home equity loans, CC 2970, 2971
Home roof warranties, CC 1797.93
Installment Sales, this index
Insurance, this index
Internet, threats, reports, CC 1798.99.21
Invasion of privacy, Information Practices Act, CC 1798.53
Landlord and Tenant, this index
Leases, residential property, CC 1102 et seq.
Manufacturers and manufacturing, human trafficking, CC 1714.43
Markets and Marketing, this index
Medical Care and Treatment, this index
Medical Records, this index
Membership camping contracts, CC 1812.302
Mobilehomes and Mobilehome Parks, this index
Mortgages, this index
Motor Vehicles, this index
Natural hazards, residential property, CC 1103 et seq.

DISCLOSURE

DISCLOSURE—Cont'd
Prints, sales, CC 1740 et seq.
Real Estate, this index
Real Estate Brokers and Salespersons, this index
Rental Purchase Agreements, this index
Rescue, contractors, CC 3273
Retail installment sales contracts, CC 1801.5
Retailers, human trafficking, CC 1714.43
Reverse mortgages, CC 1923.5
Roof warranties, CC 1797.93
Seller assisted marketing plans, CC 1812.205, 1812.206
Shared appreciation loans, seniors, CC 1917.710 et seq.
Social media, threats, reports, CC 1798.99.21
Stock cooperative, defects, sale, CC 1134
Video cassette sales or rentals, records, fines, CC 1799.3
Water conservation, building standards, deeds and conveyances, CC 1101.4, 1101.5
Window security bars, residential property, CC 1102.16
Year 2000 computer problems, information disclosure, immunity, CC 3269 et seq.

DISCOUNT BUYING SERVICES

Generally, CC 1812.100 et seq.
Affiliates, CC 1812.117
Assignments, cutting off right of action, CC 1812.114
Attorney general, acknowledgments, CC 1812.101
Bonds (officers and fiduciaries), CC 1812.103 et seq.
    Affiliates, CC 1812.117
Cancellation, members and membership, fees, CC 1812.101
Cancellation of contract, CC 1812.118
Claims, deposits in lieu of bonds, CC 1812.105
Crimes and offenses, CC 1812.125
Damages, treble damages, CC 1812.123
Delivery date, CC 1812.116
Deposits in lieu of bonds, claims, CC 1812.105
Disclosures, CC 1812.106
Escrows and escrow agents, refunds, CC 1812.101
Fees, members and membership, CC 1812.101
Financing, CC 1812.109
Fraud, CC 1812.120
Letters of credit, affiliates, CC 1812.117
Officers and employees, crimes and offenses, CC 1812.106
Refunds, CC 1812.101
    Discontinuance of goods or services, CC 1812.121
Rescission, CC 1812.121
Restitution, CC 1812.123
Suretyship and guaranty, affiliates, CC 1812.117
Time, availability of services, CC 1812.110
Voidable contracts, CC 1812.119

DISCOUNT BUYING SERVICES—Cont'd
Waiver provisions, CC 1812.127
Written contracts, CC 1812.107

DISCOUNTS

Consumers Legal Remedies Act, CC 1750 et seq.
Contracts between credit card issuers and retailers prohibiting discounts for cash sales, CC 1748
Leases, lessor remedies for breach, computing worth at time of award, unpaid rent, CC 1951.2
Motor vehicle conditional sales, buyer inducements, referral of customers, CC 2982.1
Retail installment sales, unlawful inducement, buyer producing future sales, CC 1803.10

DISCOVERY

Buildings, construction defects, CC 912
Condominiums, construction, defects, CC 6000
    Business and commerce, CC 6870
Protective orders, negligence, release, CC 56.36

DISCRIMINATION

    See, also, Civil Rights, generally, this index
Generally, CC 51 et seq.
Accomplices and accessories, CC 52
Actions and proceedings, CC 52, 52.1
    Prices, business establishments, sex discrimination, CC 51.6
    Sex, small businesses, CC 55.61 et seq.
Aiders and abettors, CC 52
Attorney fees, CC 52, 52.1
    Dealerships, CC 86
    Fees, disabled persons, interference with civil rights, CC 54.3
Business and Commerce, this index
Cleaning, dyeing and pressing, prices, posting, CC 51.6
Consumers,
    Discounts, unemployment, CC 51.13
    Privacy, CC 1798.125
Covenants, deeds and conveyances, CC 53
Credit, marital status or sex, CC 1812.30 et seq.
Credit cards, refusal to issue, CC 1747.80
Damages, CC 52, 52.1
    Calculations, CC 3361
    Disabled persons, CC 54.3
Dealerships, CC 80 et seq.
Deeds and Conveyances, this index
Demand letters, sex, small businesses, CC 55.62
Disabled Persons, this index
Discount Buying Services, generally, this index
Dogs, disabled persons, public accommodations, CC 54.1
Fair dealerships, CC 80 et seq.
Fines and penalties, CC 52, 52.1

DISCRIMINATION—Cont'd
Force and violence,
    Fines and penalties, CC 52, 52.1
    Freedom from, CC 51.7
Foreign languages, CC 51
Franchises, CC 51.8
Gender tax, repeal, CC 51.6
Gender violence, actions and proceedings, CC 52.4
Highway patrol, dogs, public accommodations, emergencies, CC 54.25
Housing, this index
Immigration, CC 51
Injunction, violation of civil rights, CC 52.1
Jurisdiction, actions and proceedings, CC 52.2
Landlord and Tenant, this index
Language, CC 51
    Posting, prices, CC 51.6
Law enforcement, dogs, public accommodations, emergencies, CC 54.25
Leases, racial restrictions, CC 782, 782.5
Limitation of actions, fines and penalties, CC 52
Marital status, civil rights, CC 51
Noncitizens, CC 51
Notice, sex, small businesses, CC 55.62
Prices,
    Business establishments, sex discrimination, CC 51.6
    Sex, small businesses, CC 55.61 et seq.
Proceedings. Actions and proceedings, generally, ante
Public conveyances, blind or visually impaired persons, CC 54 et seq.
Real Estate, this index
Rental purchase agreements, CC 1812.642
Restrictive covenants, deeds and conveyances, CC 53
Safety, business and commerce, recognition, CC 51.17
Sex, small businesses, CC 55.61 et seq.
Sheriffs, dogs, public accommodations, emergencies, CC 54.25
Small businesses, sex, CC 55.61 et seq.
Small claims courts, jurisdiction, CC 52.2
Statute of limitations, fines and penalties, CC 52
Tailors, prices, posting, CC 51.6
Unruh Civil Rights Act, CC 51
Vendor and purchaser, racial restrictions, deeds, CC 782, 782.5

DISEASE MANAGEMENT ORGANIZATIONS

Medical records, disclosure, CC 56.10

DISEASES

Acquired immune deficiency syndrome (AIDS). HIV, generally, this index
Birth defects. Genetic diseases, generally, post
COVID 19, generally, this index
Genetic characteristics,
    Defects, action for damages against parent, CC 43.6

DOGS

DISEASES—Cont'd
Genetic characteristics—Cont'd
  Disclosure, insurance, **CC 56.265**
  Discrimination, **CC 51**
Genetic diseases,
  Action for damages against parent, **CC 43.6**
  Crimes and offenses, tests, disclosure, **CC 56.17**
  Tests, disclosure, **CC 56.17**
Hereditary disorders. Genetic diseases, generally, ante
HIV, generally, this index
Hospices, generally, this index
Libel and slander, imputation, **CC 46**
Managers and management, medical records, disclosure, **CC 56.10**
Medical records, disclosure,
  Application of law, **CC 56.30**
  Managers and management, **CC 56.10**
Occupational Diseases, generally, this index
Pest Control, generally, this index
Slander, **CC 46**
Vector control. Pest Control, generally, this index

DISMISSAL AND NONSUIT
Dormant mineral right termination action, **CC 883.250**
Indebtedness, duress or coercion, **CC 1798.97.3**
Mechanics Liens, this index

DISPENSARIES
Clinics, generally, this index

DISPOSAL
Mobilehomes and mobilehome parks,
  Abandonment, **CC 798.61**
  Notice, **CC 798.56a**

DISPUTE RESOLUTION
Arbitration and Award, generally, this index
Mediation, generally, this index

DISRUPTIVE BEHAVIOR
Health care facilities, commercial blockade, **CC 3427 et seq.**

DISSOLUTION
Marriage, this index

DISSOLUTION OF MARRIAGE
Marriage, this index

DISTILLED SPIRITS
Alcoholic Beverages, generally, this index

DISTRIBUTION OF DECEDENTS ESTATES
Succession, generally, this index

DISTRICT ATTORNEYS
Acknowledgments, instruments, **CC 1181**
Civil rights actions, **CC 52, 52.1**
  Disabled persons, **CC 55.1**

DISTRICT ATTORNEYS—Cont'd
Confidential or privileged information, public agencies, disclosure, **CC 1798.68**
Dance studio contracts, actions for violations, **CC 1812.63**
Disabled persons, civil rights, injunction, **CC 55.1**
Disclosure, public agencies, confidential or privileged information, **CC 1798.68**
Indictment and Information, generally, this index
Local agencies, confidential or privileged information, disclosure, **CC 1798.68**
Medical records, negligence, release, **CC 56.36**
Public agencies, disclosure, confidential or privileged information, **CC 1798.68**
State agencies, confidential or privileged information, disclosure, **CC 1798.68**

DISTRICTS
Architects, contracts, indemnity, **CC 2782.8**
Community Facilities Districts, generally, this index
Conservation, easements, acquisition, holding, **CC 815.3**
Damages, interest recoverable, **CC 3287**
Easements, greenways, **CC 816.50 et seq.**
Eminent Domain, generally, this index
Engineers, contracts, indemnity, **CC 2782.8**
Greenways, easements, **CC 816.50 et seq.**
Interest, damages, recovery, **CC 3287**
Landscape architects, contracts, indemnity, **CC 2782.8**
Leases, lessors remedy for breach, **CC 1952.6**
Officers and employees. Public Officers and Employees, generally, this index
Schools and School Districts, generally, this index
Surveys and surveyors, contracts, indemnity, **CC 2782.8**

DIVERSION OF WATERS
Water Appropriation, generally, this index

DIVISIONS
Contracts. State Contracts, generally, this index

DIVORCE
Dissolution of marriage. Marriage, this index

DNA
Genetic testing, privacy, **CC 56.18 et seq.**
Tests, genetic testing, privacy, **CC 56.18 et seq.**

DOCK RECEIPTS
Documents of Title, generally, this index

DOCK WARRANTS
Documents of Title, generally, this index

DOCTORS
Physicians and Surgeons, generally, this index

DOCUMENTS OF TITLE
Delivery, sale or lease of single family residence, **CC 1097**
Family residence, fees, delivery, **CC 1097**
Fees,
  Delivery, single family residence, **CC 1097**
  Sale or lease of single family residence, **CC 1097**
Residence, single family residence, delivery fees, **CC 1097**
Secured Transactions, generally, this index
Single family residence, fees, delivery, **CC 1097**

DOG BITE ACT
Generally, **CC 3342, 3342.5**

DOGS
See, also,
  Animals, generally, this index
  Pets, generally, this index
Abandoned or unclaimed property, care facility, **CC 1834.5**
Actions and proceedings, bites, **CC 3342.5**
Bites,
  Actions and proceedings, **CC 3342.5**
  Liability of owner, **CC 3342**
Contracts, sales, **CC 1670.10**
Damages,
  Biting, **CC 3342**
  Killing or injuring other animals, **CC 3341**
Deaf or hard of hearing persons. Service Animals, generally, this index
Disabled persons. Service Animals, generally, this index
Fighting,
  Biting, actions and proceedings, **CC 3342.5**
  Nuisance, **CC 3482.8**
Firefighters and fire departments, discrimination, public accommodations, emergencies, **CC 54.25**
Guide dogs. Service Animals, generally, this index
Harborer, liability, dogs killing or injuring other animals, **CC 3341**
Highway patrol, discrimination, public accommodations, emergencies, **CC 54.25**
Housing, disabled persons, discrimination, **CC 54.1**
Killer dogs, biting, actions and proceedings, **CC 3342.5**
Killing livestock or poultry, liability of owner, **CC 3341**
Law enforcement, discrimination, public accommodations, emergencies, **CC 54.25**
Leashes, Dog Bite Act, **CC 3342, 3342.5**
Liability of owner,
  Bites, **CC 3342, 3342.5**
  Killing or injuring other animals, **CC 3341**
Military forces, biting, exemptions, **CC 3342**
Public accommodations, disabled persons, discrimination, **CC 54.1**

I-69

DOGS

DOGS—Cont'd
Rescue, discrimination, public accommodations, emergencies, **CC 54.25**
Sales, contracts, **CC 1670.10**
Searches and seizures, public accommodations, discrimination, emergencies, **CC 54.25**
Service Animals, generally, this index
Sheriffs, discrimination, public accommodations, emergencies, **CC 54.25**
Signal dogs. Service Animals, generally, this index
Training, fighting or attacking, removal, **CC 3342.5**
Trespass, bites, actions and proceedings, **CC 3342.5**
Zoos and wild animal parks, disabled persons, restrictions, **CC 54.7**

DOMESTIC ABUSE
Domestic Violence, generally, this index

DOMESTIC ANIMALS
Animals, generally, this index

DOMESTIC CORPORATIONS
Corporations, generally, this index

DOMESTIC INSURERS
Insurance, generally, this index

DOMESTIC LABOR
Domestic Workers, generally, this index

DOMESTIC PARTNERSHIP
See, also, Marriage, generally, this index
Abuse. Domestic Violence, generally, this index
Actions and proceedings, negligence, emotional distress, **CC 1714.01**
Emotional distress, actions and proceedings, **CC 1714.01**
Health care providers, disclosure, **CC 56.1007**
Health care service plans, disclosure, **CC 56.1007**
Medical care and treatment, disclosure, **CC 56.1007**

DOMESTIC SERVICE OR WORK
Domestic Workers, generally, this index

DOMESTIC VIOLENCE
Actions and proceedings, torts, **CC 1708.6**
Attorney fees,
　Personal information, victim service providers, grants, injunction, **CC 1798.79.95**
　Torts, **CC 1708.6**
Costs,
　Personal information, victim service providers, grants, injunction, **CC 1798.79.95**
　Torts, **CC 1708.6**
Crime victims,
　Landlord and tenant, termination, notice, **CC 1946.7**
　Personal information, victim service providers, grants, **CC 1798.79.8 et seq.**
Damages, torts, **CC 1708.6**

DOMESTIC VIOLENCE—Cont'd
Emergency services, landlord and tenant, fines and penalties, **CC 1946.8**
Exemplary damages, torts, **CC 1708.6**
Financial assistance, victim service providers, personal information, **CC 1798.79.8 et seq.**
Grants, victim service providers, personal information, **CC 1798.79.8 et seq.**
Health care service plans, confidential or privileged information, **CC 56.107**
Indebtedness, duress or coercion, **CC 1798.97.1 et seq.**
Information, personal information, victim service providers, grants, **CC 1798.79.8 et seq.**
Injunction,
　Personal information, victim service providers, grants, **CC 1798.79.95**
　Torts, **CC 1708.6**
Landlord and tenant,
　Emergency services, fines and penalties, **CC 1946.8**
　Termination, notice, **CC 1946.7**
Limitation of actions, torts, **CC 1708.6**
Personal information, victim service providers, grants, **CC 1798.79.8 et seq.**
Punitive damages, torts, **CC 1708.6**
Shelters, personal information, grants, **CC 1798.79.8 et seq.**
Special damages, torts, **CC 1708.6**
Torts, **CC 1708.6**

DOMESTIC WORKERS
Employment agencies,
　Employer status, conditions, **CC 1812.5095**
　Personal interviews and verification of experience, **CC 1812.509**
　Registry, continuing contracts, **CC 1812.504**
Human Trafficking, generally, this index

DOMICILE AND RESIDENCE
See, also, Nonresidents, generally, this index
Contracts, independent wholesale sales representatives, **CC 1738.14**
Independent wholesale sales representatives, contracts, **CC 1738.14**
Installment Sales, this index
Mobilehome Residency Law, **CC 798 et seq.**
Personal property, law governing, **CC 946**
Sales, independent wholesale sales representatives, contracts, **CC 1738.14**
Wholesale sales representatives, independents, contracts, **CC 1738.14**

DONATE LIFE CALIFORNIA ORGAN AND TISSUE DONOR REGISTRY
Drivers licenses, electronic devices and equipment, **CC 1798.90.1**

DONATIONS
Gifts, Devises and Bequests, generally, this index

DONATIVE TRANSFERS
Gifts, Devises and Bequests, generally, this index

DOORS
Landlord and tenant, locks, **CC 1941.3**

DORMANT MINERAL RIGHTS
Termination, **CC 883.210 et seq.**

DRAFTS
Accord and satisfaction, **CC 1526**
Attorney fees, check cashers, **CC 1789.35**
Check cashers, **CC 1789.30 et seq.**
Clerks of courts, dishonor, demand for payment, **CC 1719**
Crimes and offenses, check cashers, **CC 1789.35**
Damages, check cashers, **CC 1789.35**
Demand for payment, dishonor, **CC 1719**
Dishonor, treble damages, **CC 1719**
Fees, check cashers, **CC 1789.30, 1789.35**
　Licenses and permits, **CC 1789.37**
Fines and penalties, check cashers, **CC 1789.35**
Identity and identification, check cashers, **CC 1789.30**
Injunction, check cashers, **CC 1789.35**
Licenses and permits, check cashers, **CC 1789.37**
Limitation of actions, check cashers, **CC 1789.35**
Monopolies and unfair trade, check cashers, **CC 1789.32**
Protests, accord and satisfaction, **CC 1526**
Statute of limitations, check cashers, **CC 1789.35**
Stop payment orders, dishonor, demand for payment, **CC 1719**
Treble damages, dishonor, **CC 1719**
Unfair business practices, check cashers, **CC 1789.32**
Waiver, cashers, **CC 1789.38**

DRAINS AND DRAINAGE
Community Facilities Districts, generally, this index
Landscape Architects, generally, this index
Zoning and Planning, generally, this index

DRAPERIES
Sales, warranties, **CC 1793.35**

DRAWINGS
Art and artists, commissions, sale, original works, **CC 986**

DRAYMEN
Mechanics Liens, generally, this index

DRINKS
Alcoholic Beverages, generally, this index

DRIVERS LICENSES
Motor Vehicles, this index

EASEMENTS

DRIVING RULES
Traffic Rules and Regulations, generally, this index

DROUGHT
Condominiums, pressure washing, CC 4736
Water Conservation, generally, this index

DRUGGISTS
Pharmacists, generally, this index

DRUGS AND MEDICINE
Attorney fees, injunctions, CC 3496
Cannabis,
   Confidential or privileged information, CC 56.06
   Contracts, CC 1550.5
   Medical records, confidential or privileged information, CC 56.06
   Public policy, CC 1550.5
Claims processor, prescription drugs, reports, CC 2527, 2528
Confidential or privileged information, medical records, CC 56 et seq.
Contracts, cannabis, CC 1550.5
Costs, injunctions, CC 3496
Crimes and offenses, recreational vehicles, parks, defaulting residents, CC 799.70
Dispensing,
   Opioid antagonists, overdose, CC 1714.22
   Privileges and immunities, opioid antagonists, overdose, CC 1714.22
Distribution,
   Confidential or privileged information, medical records, CC 56 et seq.
   Medical records, confidential or privileged information, CC 56 et seq.
   Records and recordation, confidential or privileged information, CC 56 et seq.
Emergencies, opioid antagonists, overdose, CC 1714.22
Epinephrine Auto Injectors, generally, this index
Forcible entry and detainer, nuisance, CC 3486, 3486.5
Hazardous Substances and Waste, generally, this index
Hemp. Cannabis, generally, ante
Human growth hormone, athletic facilities, leases, notice, crimes, CC 1812.97
Indian hemp. Cannabis, generally, ante
Injunction, costs, CC 3496
Los Angeles, forcible entry and detainer, nuisance, CC 3486
Manufacturers and manufacturing,
   Confidential or privileged information, medical records, CC 56 et seq.
   Medical records, confidential or privileged information, CC 56 et seq.
   Records and recordation, confidential or privileged information, CC 56 et seq.
Marijuana. Cannabis, generally, ante
Medical records,
   Confidential or privileged information, CC 56 et seq.

DRUGS AND MEDICINE—Cont'd
Medical records—Cont'd
   Disclosure, CC 56.30
Mobilehomes and mobilehome parks, grounds for termination of tenancy, CC 798.56
Oakland, forcible entry and detainer, nuisance, CC 3486.5
Opiates, overdose, opioid antagonists, CC 1714.22
Overdose, opioid antagonists, CC 1714.22
Pharmacists, generally, this index
Prescriptions,
   Claims, processors, powers and duties, CC 2527, 2528
   Opioid antagonists, overdose, CC 1714.22
   Privileges and immunities, opioid antagonists, overdose, CC 1714.22
Privileges and immunities, overdose, opioid antagonists, CC 1714.22
Production. Manufacturers and manufacturing, generally, ante
Public policy, cannabis, CC 1550.5
Recreational vehicles, parks, offenses, defaulting residents, CC 799.70
Reports, opioid antagonists, overdose, CC 1714.22
Sacramento City and County, forcible entry and detainer, nuisance, CC 3486.5
Sales,
   Confidential or privileged information, medical records, CC 56 et seq.
   Medical records, confidential or privileged information, CC 56 et seq.
   Records and recordation, confidential or privileged information, CC 56 et seq.
Testosterone, athletic facilities, leases, notice, crimes, CC 1812.97
Training, opioid antagonists, overdose, CC 1714.22

DRUGSTORES
Pharmacists, generally, this index

DRY CLEANERS AND LAUNDERERS
Cleaning, Dyeing and Pressing, generally, this index

DRYING RACKS
Condominiums, CC 4750.10
Landlord and tenant, CC 1940.20

DUE DATE
Acceleration clause, mortgages and trust deeds, incorporation in documents, CC 2924.5

DUMBWAITERS
Elevators, Dumbwaiters and Escalators, generally, this index

DUMPS AND DUMPING
Junk and Junk Dealers, generally, this index

DURESS OR COERCION
Contracts, this index

DURESS OR COERCION—Cont'd
Indebtedness, CC 1798.97.1 et seq.
Landlord and tenant, vacating premises, CC 1940.2
Real estate, appraisal and appraisers, CC 1090.5
Voidable transactions, application of law, CC 3439.12

DUST
Air Pollution, generally, this index

DWELLINGS
Housing, generally, this index

DYES
Cleaning, Dyeing and Pressing, generally, this index

EARNINGS
Compensation and Salaries, generally, this index

EARS
Deaf or Hard of Hearing Persons, generally, this index

EARTHQUAKE INSURANCE
Condominiums, mortgages, third party institutional purchasers, disclosure, CC 2955.1
Mortgages, condominiums, institutional third party purchasers, disclosure, CC 2955.1

EARTHQUAKES
   See, also, Disasters, generally, this index
Commercial property owners guide to earthquake safety, CC 2079.9
Costs, homeowners guide to earthquake safety, CC 2079.11
Deeds and conveyances,
   Commercial property owners guide to earthquake safety, CC 2079.9
   Disclosure, statements, CC 1103.2 et seq.
Disclosure, real estate, residential property, CC 1103 et seq.
Home solicitation contracts, residential repair or restoration, cancellation, CC 1689.6, 1689.7, 1689.14
Homeowners guide to earthquake safety,
   Costs, CC 2079.11
Real estate sales, CC 2079.8
Real Estate, this index

EASEMENTS
   Generally, CC 801 et seq.
Abandonment, CC 811, 887.010 et seq.
Actions and proceedings,
   Abandoned easements, CC 887.040 et seq.
   Enforcement of easement, CC 809
   Maintenance and repairs, CC 845
   Possessory action, CC 810
Adverse possession,
   Exemptions, CC 1007
   Signs preventing easements, CC 1008

I-71

EASEMENTS

EASEMENTS—Cont'd
Agreements,
    Costs of maintenance and repair, **CC 845**
    Maintenance obligations, snow removal, **CC 845**
Agriculture, grazing or pasture rights, **CC 801, 802**
Apportionment,
    Cost of maintenance and repair, **CC 845**
    Partition of dominant tenement, **CC 807**
Arbitration and award, maintenance and repair costs, **CC 845**
Attorney fees, conservation easements, enforcement, **CC 815.7**
Attorneys fees, greenways, **CC 816.62**
Burial, right of, **CC 801, 802**
Carriers, stoppage rights, **CC 801**
Cemeteries, right of burial, **CC 801, 802**
Churches, right of seat in, **CC 801, 802**
Classification, **CC 801, 802**
Common law, abandoned easements, **CC 887.030**
Consent to public use of land, notice, **CC 813**
Conservation Easements, generally, this index
Consolidation of interest, **CC 811**
Contracts, maintenance obligations, snow removal, **CC 845**
Contributions, maintenance and repairs, **CC 845**
Costs, greenways, **CC 816.62**
Creation, **CC 804**
Damages,
    Conservation easements, **CC 815.7**
    Greenways, **CC 816.62**
Destruction of property, extinguishment of servitude, **CC 811**
Enforcement, **CC 809**
Extent of servitude, determination, **CC 806**
Extinguishment, **CC 811**
Fish and Game, this index
Future estate, use by owner, **CC 808**
Grantors, conservation easements, retention of all interests not conveyed, **CC 815.4**
Grazing rights, **CC 801, 802**
Greenways, **CC 816.50 et seq.**
Injunction,
    Conservation easements, **CC 815.7**
    Enforcement, **CC 809**
    Greenways, **CC 816.62**
Intent of parties, **CC 806**
Judgments and decrees, maintenance and repair costs, **CC 845**
Judicial arbitration, maintenance and repairs, **CC 845**
Jurisdiction, maintenance and repairs, **CC 845**
Limitation, **CC 806**
    Holding, **CC 805**
Limitation of actions, negative easements, **CC 784**
Maintenance, costs, determination, **CC 845**
Merger and consolidation, extinguishment of easement, **CC 811**

EASEMENTS—Cont'd
Minerals, right of taking, **CC 801, 802**
Negative easements, limitation of actions, **CC 784**
Notice, preservation of abandoned easements, **CC 887.040 et seq.**
Obstruction to enjoyment, removal, future interests, **CC 808**
Orders, abandoned easements, **CC 887.080**
Parking, covenants for easement, cities or counties, preservation of easements, notice of intent, **CC 887.060**
Parties, action to enforce, **CC 809**
Partition, **CC 807**
Passing with conveyance, **CC 1104**
Pasture, right of, **CC 801, 802**
Permissive use, **CC 1008**
Persons who may create servitudes, **CC 804**
Possessory action, owner of servient tenements, **CC 810**
Prescription,
    Exemptions, **CC 1007**
    Signs preventing easements, **CC 1008**
Preservation of easement, notice of intent, recording, **CC 887.060, 887.070**
Proceedings. Actions and proceedings, generally, ante
Rates and charges, right of taking, **CC 802**
Records and recordation,
    Conservation easements, **CC 815.5**
    Greenways, **CC 816.60**
    Preservation of easement, notice of intent, recording, **CC 887.060, 887.070**
Rents, right of taking, **CC 802**
Rights of way, **CC 801, 802**
    Repair by owner, **CC 845**
Servient tenements,
    Creation, **CC 804**
    Holding, **CC 805**
    Possessory action, **CC 810**
Small claims courts, maintenance and repairs, **CC 845**
Snow removal, easement maintenance, **CC 845**
Solar Energy, this index
Specific performance, maintenance and repairs, **CC 845**
Statute of limitations, negative easements, **CC 784**
Stoppage rights conveyances, **CC 801**
Suits. Actions and proceedings, generally, ante
Tolls, right of taking, **CC 802**
Venue, maintenance and repairs, **CC 845**
Wood, right of taking, **CC 801, 802**
Zoning and Planning, generally, this index

EATING DISORDERS
Weight loss contracts, **CC 1694.5 et seq.**

EATING PLACES
Restaurants, generally, this index

EDUCATION
Colleges and Universities, generally, this index

EDUCATION—Cont'd
Schools and School Districts, generally, this index

EDUCATIONAL DEBT COLLECTION PRACTICES ACT
Generally, **CC 1788.90 et seq.**

EJECTION
Passengers, common carriers, **CC 2188, 2190**

EJECTMENT
Occupancy as color of title, **CC 1006**

ELDERLY PERSONS
Aged Persons, generally, this index

ELECTION OFFENSES
Advertisements, unauthorized signature use, **CC 3344.5**
Signatures, unauthorized signature use in advertisements, **CC 3344.5**

ELECTIONS
Actions and proceedings,
    Advertisements, false or forged campaign materials, **CC 3344.6**
    Unauthorized signature use in advertisements, **CC 3344.5**
Advertisements,
    Actions and proceedings, false or forged campaign materials, **CC 3344.6**
    False or forged campaign materials, **CC 1739 et seq.**
    Unauthorized signature use, **CC 3344.5**
Ballot measures. Initiative and Referendum, generally, this index
Buttons, fraudulent political items, sales, **CC 1739 et seq.**
Campaigns,
    Invasion of privacy, use of name, photograph, voice, signature, **CC 3344**
    Landlord and tenant, signs and signals, **CC 1940.4**
    Mobilehomes and mobilehome parks, signs and signals, **CC 798.51, 799.10**
    Political items, sale and manufacture, **CC 1739 et seq.**
    Signatures, unauthorized use in advertisements, **CC 3344.5**
    Signs and signals, mobilehomes and mobilehome parks, **CC 798.51, 799.10**
    Unauthorized signature use in advertisements, **CC 3344.5**
Candidates,
    Campaigns, generally, ante
    Libel and slander, broadcasting station, liability, **CC 48.5**
    Mobilehomes and mobilehome parks, signs and signals, **CC 798.51, 799.10**
    Signs and signals, mobilehomes and mobilehome parks, **CC 798.51, 799.10**
Canvass of votes. Recall, generally, this index
Damages,
    False or forged campaign materials, **CC 3344.6**

EMERGENCIES

ELECTIONS—Cont'd
Damages—Cont'd
Unauthorized signature use in advertisements, **CC 3344.5**
Fines and penalties, advertisements, false or forged campaign materials, **CC 3344.6**
Forged campaign materials, **CC 3344.6**
Sales, **CC 1739 et seq.**
Fraud, campaign materials, fraudulent or forged materials, **CC 3344.6**
Sales, **CC 1739 et seq.**
Initiative and Referendum, generally, this index
Invasion of privacy, use of name, photograph, voice, signature, **CC 3344**
Landlord and tenant, signs and signals, **CC 1940.4**
Libel and slander, radio station liability, **CC 48.5**
Measures submitted to voters. Initiative and Referendum, generally, this index
Political campaigns. Campaigns, generally, ante
Political items, sale and manufacture, **CC 1739 et seq.**
Posters, false or forged campaign materials, sales, **CC 1739 et seq.**
Recall, generally, this index
Referendum. Initiative and Referendum, generally, this index
Sales, political items, fraud, **CC 1739 et seq.**
Signatures, unauthorized use in advertisements, **CC 3344.5**
Signs and signals, campaigns, mobilehomes and mobilehome parks, **CC 798.51, 799.10**
Special elections. Recall, generally, this index
Stickers, false or forged campaign materials, sales, **CC 1739 et seq.**

ELECTORS
Elections, generally, this index

ELECTRIC APPLIANCES
Electronic Devices and Equipment, generally, this index

ELECTRIC VEHICLES
Motor Vehicles, this index

ELECTRICIANS
Electricity, generally, this index

ELECTRICITY
See, also, Public Utilities, generally, this index
Actions and proceedings, privacy, usage data, **CC 1798.99**
Community apartments, defects, disclosure, **CC 1134**
Confidential or privileged information, usage data, **CC 1798.98, 1798.99**
Customers, privacy, usage data, **CC 1798.98, 1798.99**
Damages, privacy, usage data, **CC 1798.99**

ELECTRICITY—Cont'd
Disclosure, privacy, usage data, **CC 1798.98, 1798.99**
Fences, security, **CC 835**
Grey market goods, incompatibility with United States electrical currents, disclosure, **CC 1797.81**
Landlord and tenant, unseparated meters, **CC 1940.9**
Leases, cutting off public utilities with intent to terminate lease, damages, **CC 789.3**
Liens and incumbrances. Mechanics Liens, generally, this index
Manufactured housing, warranties, **CC 1797 et seq.**
Mechanics Liens, generally, this index
Meters,
Condominiums, electric vehicles, charging infrastructure, **CC 4745.1**
Privacy, usage data, **CC 1798.98, 1798.99**
Mobilehomes and Mobilehome Parks, this index
Privacy, usage data, **CC 1798.98, 1798.99**
Renewable energy. Solar Energy, generally, this index
Solar Energy, generally, this index
Stock cooperatives, defects, disclosure, **CC 1134**
Weights and measures. Meters, generally, ante

ELECTRIFIED FENCES
Security, **CC 835**

ELECTRONIC COMMERCE
Generally, **CC 1789 et seq.**

ELECTRONIC COMMUNICATIONS
Telecommunications, generally, this index

ELECTRONIC DATA PROCESSING
Computers, generally, this index

ELECTRONIC DEVICES AND EQUIPMENT
Computers, generally, this index
Manufacturers identification mark, removal, defacing, alteration or destruction, **CC 1710.1**
Rental purchase agreements, geophysical location tracking technology, notice, **CC 1812.650**
Sales, identification number or mark altered or removed, **CC 1710.1**

ELECTRONIC FUNDS TRANSFERS
Funds Transfers, generally, this index

ELECTRONIC MAIL
See, also, Internet, generally, this index
Breach of security, personal information, disclosure, **CC 1798.29**

ELECTRONIC RECORDS
Audio and Video Recordings, generally, this index

ELECTRONIC TRACKING DEVICES
Motor vehicles, dealers, used vehicles, **CC 2983.37**

ELECTRONIC TRANSACTIONS ACT
Generally, **CC 1633.1 et seq.**

ELECTRONIC TRANSMISSIONS
See, also, Telecommunications, generally, this index
Condominiums, meetings, **CC 4910**
Contracts, Uniform Electronic Transactions Act, **CC 1633.1 et seq.**
Lewdness and obscenity, images, **CC 1708.88**
Medical records, confidential or privileged information, **CC 56.101**
Records and recordation, Uniform Electronic Transactions Act, **CC 1633.1 et seq.**
Security agents and broker dealers, contracts, **CC 1633**
Uniform Electronic Transactions Act, **CC 1633.1 et seq.**

ELEEMOSYNARY INSTITUTIONS
Charities, generally, this index

ELEMENTARY SCHOOLS
Schools and School Districts, generally, this index

ELEVATORS, DUMBWAITERS AND ESCALATORS
Apartment houses, owner or agent for service of process or notice, posting notice in elevator, **CC 1962.5**
Landlord and tenant, owner or agent for service of process or notice, posting notice in elevator, **CC 1962.5**
Leases, cutting off public utilities with intent to terminate lease, damages, **CC 789.3**
Notice, owner or agent for service of process or notice, posting in elevator, **CC 1962.5**

EMBEZZLEMENT
Discount buying services, officers and employees, statement, **CC 1812.106**

EMBLEMENTS
Agricultural Products, generally, this index

EMERGENCIES
Cardiopulmonary resuscitation, immunity from civil damages, **CC 1714.2**
Condominiums, this index
Contracts, this index
COVID 19, generally, this index
Defense shelters, liability for injuries, **CC 1714.5**
Disasters, generally, this index
Drones, interference, damages, **CC 43.101**
Entry on property, mobilehomes and mobilehome parks, **CC 799.2.5**
Epinephrine Auto Injectors, generally, this index
Floods and Flooding, generally, this index

EMERGENCIES

EMERGENCIES—Cont'd
Hazardous Substances and Waste, this index
Home Solicitation Contracts, this index
Mines and minerals, entry on property, notice, waiver, CC 848
Mobilehomes and Mobilehome Parks, this index
Mortgages, prepayment penalties, CC 2954.9
Personal emergency response unit, home solicitation contracts, cancellation, CC 1689.6, 1689.7
Prepayment penalties, mortgages, CC 2954.9
Privileges and immunities, cardiopulmonary resuscitation, CC 1714.2
Rescue, generally, this index
Shelters, damages, personal injuries, CC 1714.5
Storms, generally, this index
Trust deeds, prepayment penalties, CC 2954.9
Unmanned aircraft, interference, damages, CC 43.101
War, mitigating facilities, liability for injuries, CC 1714.5

EMERGENCY MEDICAL TECHNICIANS
Contractors, disclosure, CC 3273
Disclosure, contractors, CC 3273
Firefighters rule, CC 1714.9
Identity and identification, contractors, CC 3273
Personal injuries, liability, CC 1714.9

EMERGENCY SERVICES
Fines and penalties, landlord and tenant, CC 1946.8
Forcible entry and detainer, CC 1946.8
Landlord and tenant, fines and penalties, CC 1946.8
Leases, fines and penalties, CC 1946.8

EMERGENCY VEHICLES
Ambulances, generally, this index
Medical records, disclosure, radio transmissions, CC 56.10

EMINENT DOMAIN
Acquisition of, property, CC 1001
Easements, public utilities, private citizens, CC 1001
Legal Estates Principal and Income Law, CC 731 et seq.
Private citizens, utility easements, CC 1001
Reconstruction, adjacent lands, temporary right of entry, CC 1002
Rent,
　Control, commercial property, application of law, CC 1954.28
　Temporary entry on land, repair, CC 1002
Repair, adjacent lands, temporary right of entry, CC 1002
Temporary right of entry, repair, reconstruction, adjacent lands, CC 1002
Vendor and Purchaser Risk Act, CC 1662

EMOLUMENTS
Compensation and Salaries, generally, this index

EMOTIONAL DISTRESS
Negligence, actions and proceedings, CC 1714.01
Sexual harassment, CC 51.9

EMOTIONAL HEALTH
Mental Health, generally, this index

EMPLOYEE WELFARE BENEFIT PLANS
Medical records, disclosure, CC 56.10

EMPLOYEES
Labor and Employment, generally, this index

EMPLOYERS
Labor and Employment, generally, this index

EMPLOYMENT
Labor and Employment, generally, this index

EMPLOYMENT AGENCIES
　Generally, CC 1812.500 et seq.
Abandonment, job, lack of just cause, fees due, CC 1812.506
Actions and proceedings, CC 1812.523
Address, contracts, employment agency and jobseeker, inclusion, CC 1812.504
Advertisements, CC 1812.506 et seq.
　Bonds(officers and fiduciaries), licenses and permits, CC 1812.5095
　Job orders, CC 1812.507
　Misrepresentations,
　　Home health agencies, CC 1812.508
　　Job listing services, CC 1812.520
　Unfair competition, CC 1812.5095
Application of law, CC 1812.502
Attorney fees, CC 1812.523
Baby sitters, personal interview and verification of experience prior to placing, CC 1812.509
Bonds (officers and fiduciaries), CC 1812.503
　Advertising, CC 1812.5095
Books and papers. Records and recordation, generally, post
Business schools, application of law, CC 1812.502
Cessation of business, cancellation or termination of fiduciary bond, CC 1812.503
Child care and development services, referrals, trustline CC 1812.5093
Child care providers, referrals, trustline registry, CC 1812.5093
Children and minors, placement, child labor laws, application, CC 1812.509
Commissions (compensation), fees, calculation, CC 1812.505
Compensation and salaries,
　Advertised salary, starting salary, CC 1812.508
　Calculation of fees, CC 1812.505

EMPLOYMENT AGENCIES—Cont'd
Compensation and salaries—Cont'd
　Less than agreed upon, fees due upon termination of employment, CC 1812.506
　Written contract, inclusion in, CC 1812.504
Continuing contracts, domestic help, registry, CC 1812.504
Contracts,
　Domestic workers, CC 1812.5095
　Job listing services, written contracts, CC 1812.516
　Jobseekers, written contracts, CC 1812.504
Copies,
　Bonds (officers and fiduciaries), filing, CC 1812.503
　Fee schedules, job seekers, CC 1812.505
Costs, actions and proceedings, CC 1812.523
Crimes and offenses, CC 1812.523
　Conviction, discharge from job, fees due, CC 1812.506
　Fraud, generally, post
Daily hours of labor, written contract, inclusion, CC 1812.504
Death, jobseeker, refund of fees, CC 1812.506
Deposits,
　Bonds (officers and fiduciaries), in lieu of, CC 1812.503
　Fee deposits, failure to accept employment, return, CC 1812.506
Discharge for misconduct, fees due, CC 1812.506
Discharge for reasons other than misconduct, jobseekers, fees, CC 1812.506
Domestic Workers, this index
Employment Counseling Services, generally, this index
Enforcement, regulations, CC 1812.523
Exemptions, CC 1812.502
Expiration date, written contracts, inclusion, CC 1812.504
False advertisements or solicitations, CC 1812.506 et seq.
　Job listing services, CC 1812.520
Fees,
　Contracts, inclusion of fee and written contract, CC 1812.504
　Domestic workers, CC 1812.5095
　Failure to accept employment, refunds, CC 1812.506
　Job orders for employment, bona fide and in writing, prerequisite to acceptance of fees, CC 1812.507
　Schedules, copies to customers, CC 1812.505
　Splitting, prohibition, CC 1812.505
Fines and penalties, unfair competition, CC 1812.5095
Fraud, CC 1812.506 et seq.
　False advertising, CC 1812.507, 1812.508
　Job listing services, CC 1812.520
　Job seekers, qualifications to perform job, discharge, fees due, CC 1812.506

ENERGY

EMPLOYMENT AGENCIES—Cont'd
Fraud—Cont'd
   Unfair competition, misleading advertising, CC 1812.5095
Group job advertisements, CC 1812.508
Home health agencies, distinguished, advertisements, CC 1812.508
Illegal employment, CC 1812.509
Job listing services, CC 1812.521
Job listing services, CC 1812.515 et seq.
   Actions and proceedings, CC 1812.523
   Advertisements, false advertisements, CC 1812.520
   Application of law, CC 1812.502
   Attorney fees, CC 1812.523
   Bonds (officers and fiduciaries), CC 1812.515
   Cancellation, right to cancel contracts, notice, CC 1812.516
   Children and minors, child labor laws, CC 1812.521
   Compensation and salaries, advertisements, agreements, CC 1812.520
   Contracts, written contracts, CC 1812.516
   Costs, actions and proceedings, CC 1812.523
   Crimes and offenses, CC 1812.523
   Enforcement, regulations, CC 1812.523
   False advertisements, CC 1812.520
   Fees, CC 1812.517
      Schedules, customers, copies, CC 1812.505
   Illegal employment, CC 1812.521
   Job orders, prerequisite to collecting fee, CC 1812.519
   Labor organizations, strikes, notice to job seeker, CC 1812.521
   Notice, contracts, cancellation rights, CC 1812.516
   Records and recordation, CC 1812.522
   Refunds, CC 1812.518
      Fees, right to, CC 1812.516
   Remedies, violations, CC 1812.523
   Schedules, fee schedules, CC 1812.517
Job orders, job listing services, prerequisite to collecting fees, CC 1812.519
Jobseekers,
   Fee schedule, copy, CC 1812.505
   Written contracts, requirements, CC 1812.504
Labor disputes, notice to jobseekers, CC 1812.509
Labor organizations,
   Application of law, CC 1812.502
   Membership requirements, notice to jobseekers, CC 1812.509
Labor strikes or problems, discharge, fees due, CC 1812.506
Licenses and permits, advertisements, referring, CC 1812.5095
Long term health care facilities, nurses, temporary employment, CC 1812.509, 1812.540 et seq.

EMPLOYMENT AGENCIES—Cont'd
Monopolies and unfair trade, fines and penalties, CC 1812.5095
Names,
   Agency names, limitations, CC 1812.508
   Contracts, employment agency and jobseeker name, inclusion, CC 1812.504
Nonprofit corporations, application of law, CC 1812.502
Notice,
   Advertisements, special requirements, inclusion, CC 1812.508
   Domestic help, registry, continuing contracts, termination, CC 1812.504
   Fee schedules, failure to accept employment, right to return of fees, CC 1812.506
   Labor contracts, union membership requirements, CC 1812.509
   Nurses, long term health care facilities, temporary employment, CC 1812.509, 1812.540 et seq.
Nurses Registries, generally, this index
Nursing schools, application of law, CC 1812.502
Physical ability, inability to perform job, fees due after discharge, CC 1812.506
Professional associations, placement services, exemptions, CC 1812.502
Psychiatric technicians, long term health care facilities, temporary employment, CC 1812.540 et seq.
Records and recordation, CC 1812.522
   Advertised jobs, CC 1812.508, 1812.509
Referrals,
   Contracts, written contracts, CC 1812.504
   Domestic workers, CC 1812.5095
   Fraud, CC 1812.507
Refunds,
   Fees,
      Cessation of employment, CC 1812.506
      Failure to accept employment, CC 1812.506
   Right to, written contract, inclusion in, CC 1812.504
Registry, domestic help, continuing contracts, CC 1812.504
Remedies, violations, CC 1812.523
Right to refund, notice, inclusion in written contract, CC 1812.504
Salaries. Compensation and salaries, generally, ante
Special requirements, advertisements, notice, CC 1812.508
Sureties and suretyship, requirements, CC 1812.503
Temporary employment,
   Fees, CC 1812.505
   Losing job within 90 days, reduction of fee, CC 1812.504
Type of employment, inclusion in employment contract, CC 1812.504
Unfair competition, fines and penalties, CC 1812.5095

EMPLOYMENT AGENCIES—Cont'd
Vocational nursing, long term health care facilities, temporary employment, CC 1812.540 et seq.
Vocational schools, application of law, CC 1812.502

EMPLOYMENT AGENCY, EMPLOYMENT COUNSELING AND JOB LISTING SERVICES ACT
Generally, CC 1812.500 et seq.

EMPLOYMENT COUNSELING SERVICES
   See, also, Employment Agencies, generally, this index
   Generally, CC 1812.510 et seq.
   Actions and proceedings, CC 1812.523
   Advertisements, false advertisements, CC 1812.513
   Attorney fees, CC 1812.523
   Bonds (officers and fiduciaries), CC 1812.510
   Business, prohibition of conduct without bond, CC 1812.510
   Cancellation, contracts, right to cancel, notice, CC 1812.511
   Contracts, written contracts, CC 1812.511
   Costs, actions and proceedings, CC 1812.523
   Crimes and offenses, CC 1812.523
   Deposits, bonds (officers and fiduciaries), in lieu of, CC 1812.510
   Enforcement, regulations, CC 1812.523
   False advertisements, CC 1812.513
   Fees, CC 1812.512
   Notice, bonds (officers and fiduciaries), cancellation, CC 1812.510
   Records and recordation, CC 1812.522
      Advertisements, CC 1812.513
   Remedies, violations, CC 1812.523
   Right to cancel, contracts, CC 1812.511
   Schedules, fees schedules, CC 1812.512
   Sureties and suretyship, fiduciary bonds, CC 1812.510

ENCEPHALITIS
Pest Control, generally, this index

ENCLOSURES
Fences, generally, this index

ENCROACHMENTS
Fixtures erroneously affixed to land, removal, CC 1013.5

ENCUMBRANCES
Liens and Incumbrances, generally, this index

ENDLESS CHAIN SCHEMES
Rescission of contracts, CC 1689.2

ENDORSEMENT
Nonnegotiable instruments, transfer, CC 1459

ENEMY ATTACK
War and Civil Defense, generally, this index

ENERGY
Electricity, generally, this index

ENERGY

ENERGY—Cont'd
Heat and Heating Companies, generally, this index
Solar Energy, generally, this index

ENERGY CONSERVATION
Solar Energy, generally, this index

ENGINEERS
Disclosure, natural hazards, residential property, CC 1103.4
Districts, contracts, indemnity, CC 2782.8
Hazards, natural hazards, disclosure, residential property, CC 1103.4
Immunities. Privileges and immunities, generally, post
Indemnity, construction contracts, CC 2782.2
Joint powers authorities, contracts, indemnity, CC 2782.8
Land surveyors. Surveys and Surveyors, generally, this index
Liens and incumbrances. Mechanics Liens, generally, this index
Mechanics Liens, generally, this index
Natural hazards, disclosure, residential property, CC 1103.4
Privileges and immunities,
  Natural hazards, disclosure, residential property, CC 1103.4
  Professional organization, CC 43.7, 43.8
  Referral services, CC 43.95
Public authorities, contracts, indemnity, CC 2782.8
Public corporations, contracts, indemnity, CC 2782.8
Schools and school districts, contracts, indemnity, CC 2782.8
Surveys and Surveyors, generally, this index
Telecommunications, referral services, immunity, CC 43.95

ENGLISH LANGUAGE
See, also, Language, generally, this index
Consumer credit, contracts, signers, notice of responsibility, CC 1799.91 et seq.
Mortgage forms, notice of default cure, CC 2924c
Trust deeds, forms, notice of default cure, CC 2924c

ENGRAVERS AND ENGRAVING
Fine prints, sale, disclosure, CC 1740 et seq.

ENTICEMENT
Child from parent or guardian, CC 49

ENTRY ON PROPERTY
Apartment houses, water conservation, building standards, CC 1101.5
Attorney fees, recreational trails, CC 846.1
Construction contracts, indemnity, coterminous landowners, CC 2782.1
Emergencies, mobilehomes and mobilehome parks, CC 799.2.5

ENTRY ON PROPERTY—Cont'd
Floating homes, CC 800.32, 800.35
Forcible Entry and Detainer, generally, this index
Landlord and Tenant, this index
Mines and minerals, notice, mineral rights owners, CC 848
Notice, surveyors, CC 846.5
Recreational trails, attorney fees, CC 846.1
Trespass, generally, this index

ENVIRONMENT
Air Pollution, generally, this index
Covenants running with the land, CC 1471
Hazardous Substances and Waste, generally, this index
Notice, real estate transfers, CC 2079.7

ENVIRONMENTAL RESPONSIBILITY ACCEPTANCE ACT
Generally, CC 850 et seq.

EPINEPHRINE AUTO INJECTORS
Lay rescuers, CC 1714.23
Privileges and immunities, CC 1714.23
Rescue, lay rescuers, CC 1714.23

EQUAL OPPORTUNITY
Discrimination, generally, this index

EQUAL RIGHTS LAW
Generally, CC 51, 52, 52.1

EQUALIZATION OF TAXES
Taxation, this index

EQUIDAE
Horses, generally, this index

EQUINES
Horses, generally, this index

EQUIPMENT
Machinery and Equipment, generally, this index

EQUITABLE RELIEF
Credit life and disability insurance, debtors rights, CC 1812.402
Leases, this index
Stalking, CC 1708.7

EQUITABLE SERVITUDES
Fee simple estates, termination, powers, CC 885.060
Limitation of actions, CC 784

EQUITY
Generally, CC 3366 et seq.
Home Equity Sales Contracts, generally, this index
Leases, lessor right to equitable relief for breach, action for forcible entry and detainer, CC 1952, 1952.3
Marketable record title, application of principles, CC 880.030

EQUITY—Cont'd
Maxims, generally, this index
Motor vehicles, leases, CC 1939.25
  Business programs, CC 1939.21
Reverse mortgages, CC 1923 et seq.
  Translations, CC 1632
Sales. Home Equity Sales Contracts, generally, this index

EQUITY LOANS
Mortgages, this index

ERISA PENSION FUNDS
Mortgages shared appreciation loans, investments, CC 1917.210

EROSION
Landscape Architects, generally, this index

ESCALATORS
Elevators, Dumbwaiters and Escalators, generally, this index

ESCHEAT
See, also, Abandoned or Unclaimed Property, generally, this index
Installment sales, credit balances, CC 1810.3

ESCROWS AND ESCROW AGENTS
Actions and proceedings, rating service, CC 1785.28
Adverse or pecuniary interest, CC 1057.5
Attorney fees, real estate purchases and sales, return, CC 1057.3
Clients, sexual harassment, CC 51.9
Compensation and salaries, fee splitting, CC 1057.5
Conflict of interest, CC 1057.5
Consumer protection, deeds and conveyances, foreclosure, CC 1103.20 et seq.
Controlled escrows, developers, CC 2995
Damages,
  Rating service, CC 1785.28
  Real estate purchases and sales, return, CC 1057.3
Deeds and Conveyances, this index
Delivery, CC 1057
Disclosure,
  Natural hazards, residential property, CC 1103.11
  Title insurance, CC 1057.6
Discount buying services, refunds, CC 1812.101
Fees, splitting fees, CC 1057.5
Fines and penalties, failure to release escrow funds, CC 1057.3
Foreclosure, consumer protection, deeds and conveyances, CC 1103.20 et seq.
Harassment, sexual harassment, clients, CC 51.9
Hazards, natural hazards, disclosure, residential property, CC 1103.11
Instructions, preparation, statement, CC 1057.7

I-76

EVIDENCE

ESCROWS AND ESCROW AGENTS—Cont'd
Licenses and permits, instruction preparation, statement, CC 1057.7
Mortgages, this index
Natural hazards, disclosure, residential property, CC 1103.11
Notice, title insurance, CC 1057.6
Preparation of instructions, statement, CC 1057.7
Rating service, CC 1785.28, 1785.28.6
Real estate,
  Delivery, CC 1057
  Disclosure statements, residential property, CC 1102.11
  Dwellings, single family, developer having interest in required escrow agent, CC 2995
  Purchases and sales, return of escrow, CC 1057.3
Release, escrow funds, CC 1057.3
Residences, single family, transfers, developer having interest in required escrow entity, CC 2995
Seller assisted marketing plans, CC 1812.214
Sexual harassment, clients, CC 51.9
Splitting fees, CC 1057.5

ESPIONAGE
Trade secrets, CC 3426 et seq.

ESTATES
  Generally, CC 761 et seq.
Bids and bidding, actions relating to real estate, CC 2931b
Contingent estates. Future Estates or Interests, generally, this index
Enumeration, CC 761
Fee Simple, generally, this index
Fee tail, abolition, CC 763
Future Estates or Interests, generally, this index
Joint Tenants, generally, this index
Life Estates, generally, this index
Probate Proceedings, generally, this index
Termination, CC 789 et seq.
Time, creation of limitation or condition, CC 749

ESTATES FOR LIFE
Life Estates, generally, this index

ESTATES FOR YEARS
Bids and bidding, state as party, CC 2931b
Condominiums, CC 783
Deeds and conveyances,
  Notice, constructive, recordation, CC 1213
  Records and recordation,
    Certified copies, CC 1213
    Priority, CC 1214
    Subsequent purchaser, mortgagee, priority, CC 1214
  Transfer of greater estate than owned, CC 1108

ESTATES FOR YEARS—Cont'd
Deeds of trust. Trust deeds, generally, post
Eminent domain, parties, CC 2931a
Mortgages,
  Acceleration, CC 2954.10
  Default, notice, CC 2924c
    Agent of mortgagee, CC 2924.3
  Foreclosure, state as party, CC 2931a
  Priority, CC 2898
Notice, default, mortgages, deeds of trust, CC 2924b
Tax liens, foreclosure, state as party, CC 2931a
Tenant for years, deeds and conveyances, greater estate than that owned, CC 1108
Trust deeds,
  Acceleration, CC 2954.10
  Default, notice, agent of mortgagee, CC 2924.3
  Foreclosure, state as party, CC 2931a
  Priority, CC 2898
  Substitution of trustees, notice, CC 2934a

ESTATES OF DECEDENTS
Probate Proceedings, generally, this index

ESTOPPEL
Marketable record title, real estate, application of law, CC 880.030
Real estate, marketable record title, application of law, CC 880.030
Voidable transactions, application of law, CC 3439.12

ESTRAYS
Animals, this index

ETCHINGS
Common law copyrights, reproduction rights, transfer, CC 982

ETHNIC GROUPS
Discrimination, generally, this index

EURO
Contracts, securities or instruments, medium of payment, CC 1663

EVICTION
Forcible Entry and Detainer, generally, this index

EVIDENCE
Acknowledgments, generally, this index
Affidavits, generally, this index
Buildings, construction defects, actions and proceedings, CC 933, 934
  Burden of proof, CC 942
Burden of proof,
  Acknowledgments, identification of persons making, CC 1185
  Consideration, CC 1615
  Construction defects, CC 942
  Consumer credit reporting agencies, information furnishers, compliance, CC 1785.25

EVIDENCE—Cont'd
Burden of proof—Cont'd
  Contracts, want of consideration, CC 1615
  Credit services organizations, exemptions, CC 1789.19
  Defects, construction defects, CC 942
  Identification of persons making acknowledgments, CC 1185
  Indebtedness, duress or coercion, CC 1798.97.3
  Leases, abandonment of property, CC 1951.3
    Commercial property, CC 1951.35
  Livestock service liens, court ordered sales or substitutions of undertaking for livestock, CC 3080.15
  Rent skimming, affirmative defenses, CC 893
  Voidable transactions, CC 3439.04, 3439.05
Business Records, generally, this index
Certificates and certification, military officers, CC 1183.5
Construction, defects, burden of proof, CC 942
Contracts, this index
Conversion, damages, presumptions, CC 3336
Credit cards, presumptions, disclosures, CC 1748.11, 1748.22
  Installment sales, CC 1810.21
Cruelty to or killing of human beings or animals, motion pictures, CC 3507.1
Damages, this index
Deeds and Conveyances, this index
Depositary, loss of or injury to thing deposited, CC 1838
Discovery, generally, this index
Electronic Transactions Act, CC 1633.1 et seq.
Exemplary damages, defendants wealth or profits, protective order requiring prima facie case of liability, CC 3295
Expert testimony. Witnesses, this index
Fee simple title, presumptions, CC 1105
Homeless persons, transitional housing, misconduct, CC 1954.13
Hotels and motels, short term occupancy, presumptions, CC 1940.1
Inferences, consumers, privacy, CC 1798.140
Innocent purchasers, tax liens, extinction, CC 2911
Insolvency, presumptions, voidable transactions, CC 3439.02
Installment sales, contract, copy furnished buyer, CC 1803.7
Instruments, proof, CC 1203
Interest on loans, presumptions, CC 1914
Judicial Notice, generally, this index
Landlord and Tenant, this index
Leases, this index
Loans, interest, presumptions, CC 1914
Maxims, generally, this index
Mechanics liens, notice, CC 8118
Medical malpractice, benefits payable, CC 3333.1

I-77

EVIDENCE

EVIDENCE—Cont'd
Mobilehomes and mobilehome parks, abandonment, **CC 798.61**
Motion pictures, killing of or cruelty to human beings or animals, **CC 3507.1**
Noncitizens, status, **CC 3339**
Opinion and expert testimony. Witnesses, this index
Perjury, generally, this index
Presumptions,
    Acknowledgments, identification of persons making, **CC 1185**
    Adjoining landowners, fences, maintenance, costs, **CC 841**
    Agricultural products, processing activities, nuisances, **CC 3482.6**
    Agriculture, private bulk grain storage, bill of sale, **CC 1880.9**
    Boundaries, roads or streets, **CC 831**
    Consideration, written instrument, **CC 1614**
    Contracts, this index
    Contracts for sale of land, damages, **CC 3387**
    Conversion, damages, **CC 3336**
    Credit cards, disclosures, **CC 1748.11, 1748.22**
        Installment sales, **CC 1810.21**
    Damages, written instruments, information of value, **CC 3356**
    Deeds and Conveyances, this index
    Depositary, loss or injury to thing deposited, **CC 1838**
    Fee simple title passing, **CC 1105**
    Grocery stores, point of sale systems, **CC 7101**
    Hotels and motels, short term occupancy, **CC 1940.1**
    Identification of persons making acknowledgments, **CC 1185**
    Indebtedness, duress or coercion, **CC 1798.97.2**
    Innocent purchasers, tax liens, extinction, **CC 2911**
    Insolvency, voidable transactions, **CC 3439.02**
    Installment sales contract, copy furnished buyer, **CC 1803.7**
    Interest on loans, **CC 1914**
    Invasion of privacy, use of name, photograph, voice, signature, **CC 3344**
    Joint and several promises, **CC 1659, 1660**
    Joint obligations, **CC 1431**
    Landlord and Tenant, this index
    Leases,
        Holding over by tenant, **CC 1945**
        Term of hiring, **CC 1943**
    Loans, interest, **CC 1914**
    Maxims, generally, this index
    Military officers, acknowledgments, **CC 1183.5**
    Point of sale systems, grocery stores, **CC 7101**

EVIDENCE—Cont'd
Presumptions—Cont'd
    Public utilities, theft or diversion of services, **CC 1882.3**
    Tax assessments—special, extinction of lien, **CC 2911**
    Tax liens, extinction, **CC 2911**
    Writing, consideration, **CC 1614**
Privileges and Immunities, generally, this index
Psychotherapists and psychotherapy, sexual exploitation, **CC 43.93**
Questions of fact, invasion of privacy, use of name, photograph, signature, voice, **CC 3344**
Stalking, torts, **CC 1708.7**
Tax liens, extinction, presumptions, **CC 2911**
Telecommunications, this index
Unconscionable contracts, **CC 1670.5**
Uniform Electronic Transactions Act, **CC 1633.1 et seq.**
Video games, force and violence, **CC 1746.1**
Voidable Transactions, this index
Witnesses, generally, this index

EVIDENCES OF INDEBTEDNESS
Mortgage insurance, cancellation, conditions of extension of credit, **CC 2954.7**
Rent skimming, residential real estate, private actions, **CC 891**

EXCAVATIONS
Notice, owners of adjoining lands, **CC 832**

EXCHANGE, BILLS OF
Negotiable Instruments, generally, this index

EXCHANGE OF PROPERTY
Contracts, loan for exchange, **CC 1902 et seq.**
Loan for exchange, **CC 1902 et seq.**
Mobilehomes and mobilehome parks, **CC 798.70 et seq.**
Optional loan, application of law, **CC 1903**
Title to property, loan for exchange, **CC 1904**

EXECUTIONS
Art and artists, commissions, sale, original works, **CC 986**
Boarding and lodging house keepers, liens, **CC 1861a**
Certificates and certification, **CC 1195**
Credit services organizations, deposits, **CC 1789.24**
Discount buying services, deposits in lieu of bonds, claims, **CC 1812.105**
Innkeepers liens, writs of possession, **CC 1861 et seq.**
Liens and incumbrances,
    Boarding and lodging house keepers, **CC 1861a**
    Innkeepers liens, writs of possession, **CC 1861 et seq.**
Notice, certificates and certification, **CC 1195**
Seller assisted marketing plans, deposits in lieu of bonds, claims, **CC 1812.221**

EXECUTIONS—Cont'd
Voidable transactions, **CC 3439.07**
Writs, possession, innkeepers liens, **CC 1861 et seq.**

EXECUTIVE CLEMENCY
Information Practices Act, **CC 1798 et seq.**

EXECUTIVE DEPARTMENT
Attorney General, generally, this index
Communications, generally, this index
Governor, generally, this index
Secretary of State, generally, this index
State Agencies, generally, this index

EXECUTORS AND ADMINISTRATORS
Personal representatives. Probate Proceedings, this index

EXEMPLARY DAMAGES
Damages, this index

EXEMPTIONS
Art and artists, commissions, sale, original works, **CC 986**
Consumer credit denial, liability, **CC 1787.3**
Consumers Legal Remedies Act, **CC 1754, 1755**
Dance studios, bond or deposit with state, **CC 1812.67**
Electronic Transactions Act, **CC 1633.3**
Indebtedness, duress or coercion, **CC 1798.97.4**
Markets and marketing, Internet, disclosure, **CC 1749.8.5**
Medical Records, this index
Mobilehomes and Mobilehome Parks, this index
Natural hazards, residential property, disclosure, **CC 1103.1**
Rental purchase agreements, **CC 1812.622**
Uniform Electronic Transactions Act, **CC 1633.3**
Voidable transactions, application of law, **CC 3440.1**
Water conservation, building standards, **CC 1101.7**

EXERCISE
Health Studios, generally, this index

EXHIBITIONS AND EXHIBITORS
Art works, consignments, **CC 1738 et seq.**

EXONERATION
Suretyship and Guaranty, this index

EXPERT TESTIMONY
Witnesses, this index

EXPIRATION
Mineral right lease, quit claim deeds, **CC 883.140**

EXPLORATION
Natural resources, lessor remedy, lessee breach, **CC 1952.4**

FEAR

EXPLOSIVES
Ammunition, generally, this index
Residential real estate sales, disclosure statements, former federal or state ordnance locations, CC 1102.15

EXPORTS AND IMPORTS
Gray market goods, disclosure, CC 1797.8 et seq.
Television and radio, gray market goods, incompatibility with United States broadcast frequencies, CC 1797.81
Vector control. Pest Control, generally, this index
Warranties, gray market goods, disclosure, CC 1797.8 et seq.

EXPRESS COMPANIES
See, also, Public Utilities, generally, this index
Abandoned or unclaimed property, CC 2081 et seq.

EXPRESS WARRANTIES
Sales, this index
Warranties, generally, this index

EXPRESSWAYS
Freeways, generally, this index

EXPROPRIATION
Eminent Domain, generally, this index

EXTENDED CARE FACILITIES
Nursing Homes, generally, this index

EXTORTION
Real estate, appraisal and appraisers, CC 1090.5

EXTRADITION
Information Practices Act, CC 1798 et seq.

EYEGLASSES
Charities, privileges and immunities, CC 1714.26
Privileges and immunities, charities, CC 1714.26

EYES AND EYESIGHT
Blind or Visually Impaired Persons, generally, this index
Charities, screenings, privileges and immunities, CC 1714.26
Corneal eye tissue. Tissue Banks, generally, this index
Ophthalmologists, generally, this index
Optometrists, generally, this index
Privileges and immunities, screenings, charities, CC 1714.26
Screenings, charities, privileges and immunities, CC 1714.26
Tissue Banks, generally, this index

EYEWITNESSES
Witnesses, generally, this index

FABRIC CARE
Cleaning, Dyeing and Pressing, generally, this index

FACE
Cosmetology, generally, this index

FACSIMILES
Financial contract (qualified), frauds, statute of, evidence, CC 1624
Mortgages, transmittal of documents, CC 2943
Qualified financial contract, frauds, statute of, evidence, CC 1624

FACTORIES
Manufacturers and Manufacturing, generally, this index

FACTORS
Generally, CC 2026 et seq.
Authority, CC 2026
Actual authority, CC 2368
Credit sales, CC 2028
Authority, CC 2368
Delegation of authority, CC 2368
Guarantee of remittances, relief, CC 2030
Guaranty commission, CC 2029
Instructions, obedience, CC 2027
Insurance, authority to insure property consigned to factor, CC 2368
Obedience to instructions, CC 2027
Ostensible authority, CC 2369

FACTORS LIENS
Secured Transactions, generally, this index

FACTORY BUILT HOUSING
Housing, this index

FAIR DEALERSHIP LAW
Generally, CC 80 et seq.

FAIR DEBT SETTLEMENT PRACTICES ACT
Generally, CC 1788.300 et seq.

FAIR EMPLOYMENT AND HOUSING
Complaints, discrimination, CC 52
Consumer credit reporting agencies, CC 1786.20

FAIR MARKET VALUE
Shared appreciation loans, seniors, CC 1917.410 et seq.

FAIRNESS AND EQUITY
Maxims of jurisprudence, CC 3509 et seq.

FAITH HEALING
Health care service plans, medically necessary health care, application of law, CC 3428

FALSE ADVERTISING
Advertisements, generally, this index

FALSE ARREST
False Imprisonment, generally, this index

FALSE EVIDENCE
Perjury, generally, this index

FALSE IMPRISONMENT
Invasion of privacy, CC 1708.8
Privacy, invasion of privacy, CC 1708.8
Protection, CC 43

FALSE PRETENSES
Consumers Legal Remedies Act, CC 1750 et seq.

FALSE REPRESENTATIONS
Fraud, generally, this index

FALSE STATEMENTS
Fraud, generally, this index

FALSE SWEARING
Perjury, generally, this index

FAMILIES
Relatives, generally, this index

FAMILY CONCILIATION COURT
Computer aided transcription system, CC 54.8
Deaf or hard of hearing persons, listening systems, CC 54.8
Hearing devices, CC 54.8
Listening systems, CC 54.8
Transcription system, computer aided, CC 54.8

FAMILY COUNSELORS
Marriage and Family Therapists, generally, this index

FAMOUS PERSONS
Astaire Celebrity Image Protection Act, CC 3344.1

FARES
Rates and Charges, generally, this index

FARM LABOR
Agricultural Labor and Employment, generally, this index

FARM MACHINERY AND EQUIPMENT
Agricultural Machinery and Equipment, generally, this index

FARM PRODUCTS
Agricultural Products, generally, this index

FARM TRACTORS
Agricultural Machinery and Equipment, generally, this index

FARMLAND
Agricultural Land, generally, this index

FARMS AND FARMERS
Agriculture, generally, this index

FATHER AND CHILD
Children and Minors, generally, this index

FEAR
Duress or Coercion, generally, this index

FEAR

FEAR—Cont'd
Threats, generally, this index

FEDERAL GOVERNMENT
United States, generally, this index

FEDERAL HOME LOAN MORTGAGE CORPORATIONS
Adjustable payment, adjustable rate loans, CC 1916.7

FEDERAL NATIONAL MORTGAGE ASSOCIATION
Adjustable payment, adjustable rate loans, CC 1916.7

FEDERAL TRADE COMMISSION
Express warranties, conformity to regulations, CC 1793.1
New motor vehicles, informal dispute settlement, CC 1793.22

FEE SIMPLE
Generally, CC 761
Absolute, CC 763
Actions, injuries to inheritance, CC 826
Covenants, implied, CC 1113
Fee tail, CC 763
Implied covenants, CC 1113
Limitations, CC 773
Presumptions, CC 1105
Remainder in fee limited upon fee tail estate, CC 764
Rights of owner, CC 829
Subsequently acquired title, passage by operation of law, CC 1106
Words of inheritance or succession, CC 1072

FEE SIMPLE DETERMINABLE
Abolition, CC 885.020

FEE SPLITTING
Escrow agents, CC 1057.5

FEE TAIL
Abolished, CC 763
Contingent remainders, CC 764

FEET
Podiatrists, generally, this index

FELONIES
Crimes and Offenses, generally, this index

FEMALES
Women, generally, this index

FENCES
Adjoining landowners, maintenance, CC 801
Advertisements. Outdoor Advertising, generally, this index
Electrified, security, CC 835
Height,
 Electricity, security, CC 835
 Exceeding ten feet as nuisance, CC 841.4
Life estates, repairs, CC 840

FENCES—Cont'd
Maintenance,
 Coterminous owners, CC 841
 Division fence, coterminous owners, CC 801
Nuisance, excessive height, CC 841.4
Ordinances, electricity, security, CC 835
Outdoor Advertising, generally, this index
Repairs, life estates, CC 840
Security, electrified, CC 835
Signs and signals, electrified fences, security, CC 835
Spite, nuisance, CC 841.4
Warnings, electrified fences, security, CC 835

FERMENTED LIQUIDS
Alcoholic Beverages, generally, this index

FETUSES
Existing person status, CC 43.1

FIDELITY BONDS
Bonds (Officers and Fiduciaries), generally, this index

FIDELITY INSURANCE
Suretyship and Guaranty, generally, this index

FIDUCIARIES
Bonds (Officers and Fiduciaries), generally, this index
Conservators and Conservatorships, generally, this index
Guardian and Ward, generally, this index
Mortgages, residential mortgage lenders, CC 2923.1
Personal representatives. Probate Proceedings, this index
Real estate brokers and salespersons, CC 2079.24
Residential mortgage lenders, CC 2923.1
Trusts and Trustees, generally, this index

FIELD CROPS
Agricultural Products, generally, this index

FIERI FACIAS
Executions, generally, this index

FILLING STATIONS
Motor Vehicle Service Stations, generally, this index

FILMS
Motion Pictures, generally, this index

FINAL JUDGMENTS, DECREES AND ORDERS
Judgments and Decrees, generally, this index

FINANCE
Condominiums, CC 5500 et seq.

FINANCE CHARGE
Automobile Sales Finance Act, CC 2981.7, 2981.8, 2982
Contracts, precomputed finance charge contracts, CC 1799.8

FINANCE CHARGE—Cont'd
Credit Cards, this index
Dance studios, refund, CC 1812.57
Installment Sales, this index
Precomputed finance charge contract, CC 1799.8
Waiver, precomputed finance charge contract, CC 1799.85

FINANCE LENDERS
Advertisements, unsolicited advertising, unfair or deceptive trade practices, CC 1770
Contracts, foreign languages, translations, CC 1632.5
Disclosure, home equity loan disclosure, CC 2970, 2971
Fines and penalties, contracts, foreign languages, translations, CC 1632.5
Foreign languages, contracts, translations, CC 1632.5
Forms,
 Contracts, foreign languages, translations, CC 1632.5
 Unsolicited advertising, unfair or deceptive trade practices, CC 1770
Home equity loan disclosure, CC 2970, 2971
Mortgages,
 Fiduciaries, CC 2923.1
 Foreign languages, translations, CC 1632.5
 Home equity loan disclosure, CC 2970, 2971
Translations, foreign languages, contracts, CC 1632.5
Unfair or deceptive trade practices, unsolicited advertising, CC 1770

FINANCIAL ADVISORS
Financial Planners, generally, this index

FINANCIAL ADVISORY SERVICES
Investments, liability, CC 3372

FINANCIAL CONSULTANTS
Investments, liability, CC 3372

FINANCIAL CONTRACT (QUALIFIED)
Frauds, statute of, CC 1624

FINANCIAL COUNSELORS
Investments, liability, CC 3372

FINANCIAL INTEREST
Conflict of Interest, generally, this index

FINANCIAL PLANNERS
Credit services, CC 1789.10 et seq.
Harassment, sexual harassment, clients, CC 51.9
Investments, liability, CC 3372
Sexual harassment, clients, CC 51.9

FINANCIAL STATEMENTS AND REPORTS
Mobilehome managers collecting from prospective purchasers, disposition, CC 798.74

FINANCING STATEMENT
Secured Transactions, this index

I-80

FIRES

FINDER OF LOST PROPERTY
Generally, CC 2080 et seq.

FINE ART MULTIPLE
Sale, disclosure, CC 1740 et seq.

FINE ARTS
Art and Artists, generally, this index

FINE PRINTS
Art works, conveyance of rights, ownership of physical work, CC 988

FINES AND PENALTIES
See, also, Crimes and Offenses, generally, this index
Agriculture, private bulk grain storage, CC 1881.1
Auctions and Auctioneers, this index
Autographed memorabilia, CC 1739.7
Blanket incumbrances on subdivisions, failure to notify buyers or lessees, CC 1133
Boarding and lodging houses, excessive charges, CC 1863
Bookstores, personal information, disclosure, CC 1798.90
Bribery and Corruption, generally, this index
Business and Commerce, this index
Carriers, this index
Checks. Negotiable Instruments, this index
Civil rights, CC 52.1
Condominiums, this index
Consumer Credit Reporting Agencies, this index
Consumer Protection, this index
Consumers, privacy, CC 1798.155
Corruption. Bribery and Corruption, generally, this index
Cruelty to or killing of human beings or animals, motion pictures, CC 3507.3
Data, brokers, registration, CC 1798.99.82
Debtors and creditors, simulated judicial process, collection, CC 1788.16
Deeds and conveyances, contracts for sale of land, CC 2985.2, 2985.3
Deeds of trust, trustees sale, default by bidder, CC 2924h
Discrimination, CC 52, 52.1
Electronic commercial service violations, CC 1789.5
Exemplary damages. Damages, this index
Fine art multiples, sales, disclosures, CC 1745.5
Floating home marinas, CC 800.200
Force and violence, discrimination, CC 52, 52.1
Forfeitures, generally, this index
Fraud, this index
Freedom from violence, CC 52, 52.1
Genetic testing, privacy, CC 56.182
Genetic tests, disclosure, CC 56.17
Hate crimes, CC 52, 52.1
Highway patrol, dogs, discrimination, public accommodations, emergencies, CC 54.25

FINES AND PENALTIES—Cont'd
Home equity sales contracts, CC 1695.7, 1695.8
Hotels and Motels, this index
Installment Sales, this index
Interest, Usury Law violations, CC 1916-3
Invoices, false invoices, bills, or statements soliciting money, CC 1716
Jails, generally, this index
Killing of or cruelty to human beings or animals, motion pictures, CC 3507.3
Landlord and Tenant, this index
Law enforcement, dogs, discrimination, public accommodations, emergencies, CC 54.25
Leases, this index
Marinas, floating homes, CC 800.200
Mechanics Liens, this index
Memorabilia, autographed, warranties, CC 1739.7
Mortgage foreclosure consultants, CC 2945.7
Registration, CC 2945.45
Mortgages, this index
Motels. Hotels and Motels, this index
Motor Vehicles, this index
Point of sale systems, grocery stores, violations, CC 7101
Prepayment penalties, mortgages and trust deeds, CC 2954.9
Prescription drug claims processor, reports, failure to file, CC 2528
Privacy, invasion of privacy, CC 1708.8
Radio frequency identification, CC 1798.79
Reading, privacy, CC 1798.90
Real property sales contracts, Subdivision Map Act, false statements, CC 2985.51
Rent skimming, residential real estate, CC 892
Residential hotels, short term occupancies, CC 1940.1
Retailers, gender neutrality, markets and marketing, children and minors, CC 55.8
RFID (radio frequency identification), CC 1798.79
Second and subsequent offenses. Crimes and Offenses, this index
Security deposits, landlord and tenant, bad faith retention, CC 1950.5
Seller assisted marketing plans, CC 1812.217
Sex discrimination, CC 52, 52.1
Sexual harassment, CC 52
Skimming, radio frequency identification, CC 1798.79
Solar energy, systems, CC 714
Tailors, prices, posting, discrimination, CC 51.6
Trust Deeds, this index
Usury Law violations, CC 1916-3
Violence, freedom from, CC 52, 52.1
Warranties, breach of warranty, Song Beverly Consumer Warranty Act, CC 1794

FINGERPRINTS AND FINGERPRINTING
Check cashers, licenses and permits, CC 1789.37

FINGERPRINTS AND FINGERPRINTING —Cont'd
Criminal History Information, generally, this index

FIRE DEPARTMENTS
Firefighters and Fire Departments, generally, this index

FIRE HYDRANTS
Junk and junk dealers, possession, CC 3336.5
Recycling, possession, CC 3336.5

FIRE INSURANCE
Mortgages, exceeding replacement value, CC 2955.5
Personal property, deposited for repair, alteration, or sale, CC 1858 et seq.

FIRE NUISANCE
Fires and Fire Protection, generally, this index

FIREARM INDUSTRY RESPONSIBILITY ACT
Generally, CC 3273.50 et seq.

FIREARMS
Weapons, generally, this index

FIREFIGHTERS AND FIRE DEPARTMENTS
Arson, injuries, liability, CC 1714.9
Community Facilities Districts, generally, this index
Damages, injuries, liability, CC 1714.9
Discrimination, dogs, public accommodations, emergencies, CC 54.25
Dogs, discrimination, public accommodations, emergencies, CC 54.25
Fines and penalties, dogs, discrimination, public accommodations, emergencies, CC 54.25
Injuries, liability, CC 1714.9
Rescue, generally, this index
Volunteer firefighters and fire departments,
Gifts, devises and bequests, machinery and equipment, privileges and immunities, CC 1714.11
Liability, machinery and equipment, gifts, devises and bequests, privileges and immunities, CC 1714.11
Machinery and equipment, gifts, devises and bequests, privileges and immunities, CC 1714.11
Privileges and immunities, machinery and equipment, gifts, devises and bequests, CC 1714.11

FIREMAN'S RULE
Generally, CC 1714.9

FIRES AND FIRE PROTECTION
See, also,
Forest Fires, generally, this index
War and Civil Defense, generally, this index

FIRES

FIRES AND FIRE PROTECTION—Cont'd
Air Pollution, generally, this index
Brush fires. Forest Fires, generally, this index
Community Facilities Districts, generally, this index
Condominiums, roofs, **CC 4720**
Contractors, disclosure, **CC 3273**
Deposits, involuntary, **CC 1815**
Disclosure,
  Contractors, **CC 3273**
  Residential property, **CC 1103 et seq.**
Forest Fires, generally, this index
Gifts, devises and bequests, machinery and equipment, privileges and immunities, **CC 1714.11**
Home solicitation contracts, residential repair or restoration, cancellation, **CC 1689.6, 1689.7, 1689.14**
Identity and identification, contractors, **CC 3273**
Liability, machinery and equipment, gifts, devises and bequests, privileges and immunities, **CC 1714.11**
Machinery and equipment,
  Gifts, devises and bequests, privileges and immunities, **CC 1714.11**
  Liability, gifts, devises and bequests, privileges and immunities, **CC 1714.11**
  Privileges and immunities, gifts, devises and bequests, **CC 1714.11**
Prescribed burning, liability, **CC 3333.8**
Privileges and immunities,
  Machinery and equipment, gifts, devises and bequests, **CC 1714.11**
  Prescribed burning, **CC 3333.8**
Real estate, disclosure, residential property, **CC 1103 et seq.**
Roofs, condominiums, **CC 4720**
Zoning and Planning, generally, this index

FIRST AID
Buildings, trauma kits, privileges and immunities, **CC 1714.29**
Cardiopulmonary resuscitation, emergencies, immunity from civil damages, **CC 1714.2**
Civil defense activities, liabilities, **CC 1714.5**
Emergencies,
  Cardiopulmonary resuscitation, immunity from civil damages, **CC 1714.2**
  Tort liability, **CC 1714.5**

FISH AND GAME
Agriculture, nuisance, **CC 3482.5**
Captive animals, fur bearing animals raised in captivity, ownership, **CC 996**
Cats, generally, this index
Easements,
  Fishing, right of, **CC 801, 802**
  Right to take, **CC 801, 802**
Entry on property,
  Hazardous conditions, warning, negligence, **CC 846**

FISH AND GAME—Cont'd
Entry on property—Cont'd
  Safety, **CC 846**
Fur bearing mammals,
  Domestication, animals raised in captivity, **CC 996**
  Larceny, animals raised in captivity, **CC 996**
  Liens and incumbrances, animals raised in captivity, **CC 996**
  Ownership, raised in captivity, **CC 996**
  Trespass, animals raised in captivity, **CC 996**
Invitees, negligence, entry on land, hazardous conditions, **CC 846**
Larceny, fur bearing animals raised in captivity, **CC 996**
Membership camping contracts, **CC 1812.300 et seq.**
Mink. Fur bearing mammals, generally, ante
Negligence, entry on land, hazardous conditions, warning, **CC 846**
Oil and gas, spills, pipelines, damages, **CC 3333.5**
Owners and ownership. Title to property, generally, post
Permission, entry on property for purposes of taking, safety of premises, **CC 846**
Personal injuries,
  Entry on land, hazardous conditions, **CC 846**
  Private lands, entry, **CC 846**
Pine marten. Fur bearing mammals, generally, ante
Private lands, liability for injuries to hunters, **CC 846**
Safety, premises, entry on property for purposes of taking fish or game, **CC 846**
Title to property, **CC 656**
  Fur bearing animals raised in captivity, **CC 996**
  Safety, **CC 846**
Trespass, fur bearing animals raised in captivity, **CC 996**
Waiver, membership camping contracts, **CC 1812.316**
Warnings, hazardous conditions, entry on land, negligence, **CC 846**
Weasels. Fur bearing mammals, generally, ante

FISHING
Fish and Game, generally, this index

FITNESS FOR HUMAN OCCUPANCY
Generally, **CC 1941 et seq.**
Landlord and Tenant, this index

FIXTURES
Accession, accretion and avulsion, affixing without agreement to remove, **CC 1013**
  Removal of fixtures, **CC 1013.5**
  Tenant, **CC 1019**
Actions and proceedings, removal, **CC 1013.5**
Affixing without agreement to remove, **CC 1013**

FIXTURES—Cont'd
Attorney fees, actions for removal, **CC 1013.5**
Costs, removal, **CC 1013.5**
Damages, removal, **CC 1013.5**
Encroachments, removal, **CC 1013.5**
Good faith, erroneously affixed to land, removal, **CC 1013.5**
Home solicitation contracts, cancellation, **CC 1689.9**
Interlocutory judgments, removal of fixtures, **CC 1013.5**
Liens, erroneously affixed to land removal, **CC 1013.5**
Lis pendens, removal of improvements erroneously affixed to land, **CC 1013.5**
Mistake, affixing to land, removal, **CC 1013.5**
Options, removal, **CC 1013.5**
Parties, removal, **CC 1013.5**
Removal, **CC 1013.5**
  Tenants, **CC 1019**
Warranties, **CC 1793.2**
Water conservation, building standards, **CC 1101.1 et seq.**

FLAGS
Condominiums, display, **CC 4705**
  Business and commerce, **CC 6702**

FLIES
Pest Control, generally, this index

FLOATING HOME RESIDENCY LAW
Generally, **CC 800 et seq.**

FLOATING HOMES
Generally, **CC 800 et seq.**
Abandoned or unclaimed property, homes owned by marinas, **CC 800.37**
Abandonment, **CC 800.36**
Abatement, public nuisance, **CC 800.201**
Actions and proceedings,
  Common facilities or services, failure of management to maintain, **CC 800.91**
  Marinas, landlord tenant relations, **CC 800.200, 800.201**
Advertisements, sale or rental by owner, **CC 800.80**
Attorney fees, marinas, landlord tenant relations, **CC 800.200**
Common area facilities, **CC 800.30**
  Failure of management to maintain, actions, **CC 800.91**
Cooperatives and condominiums, **CC 800.300 et seq.**
Costs, marinas, landlord tenant relations, **CC 800.200**
Death, registered or legal owner, transfer of title, **CC 800.88**
Entry on premises,
  Forcible entry and detainer, **CC 800.75**
  Management, grounds, **CC 800.35**
  Right of entry, **CC 800.32**
Estates, ownership, **CC 800.88**

FORCIBLE

FLOATING HOMES—Cont'd
Fees and charges,
  Guests, **CC 800.44**
  Marinas, **CC 800.40 et seq.**
  Pets, **CC 800.43**
  Transfer or selling fees, **CC 800.83**
  Unlisted services, **CC 800.42**
Fines and penalties, marinas, landlord tenant relations, **CC 800.200**
Forcible entry and detainer, **CC 800.75**
Foreclosure, **CC 800.89**
Guests, fees, **CC 800.44**
Homeowners, meetings, **CC 800.60, 800.61**
Hookup, fees, **CC 800.47**
Installation and hookup, fees, **CC 800.47**
Joint tenants, sales to third parties, death of cotenant, **CC 800.88**
Landlord and tenant, **CC 800 et seq.**
Landscaping, fees, **CC 800.47**
Leases, **CC 800.20 et seq.**
  Termination of tenancy, **CC 800.70 et seq.**
Liens and incumbrances,
  Foreclosure, **CC 800.89**
  Management, **CC 800.50**
Managers and management,
  Actions against, **CC 800.200**
  Cooperatives and condominiums, **CC 800.300 et seq.**
  Entry on premises, **CC 800.32, 800.35**
  Liens, **CC 800.50**
  Prior approval of sale, requirement, **CC 800.85**
  Showing or listing for sale, restrictions, **CC 800.82**
Meetings, marinas, **CC 800.60, 800.61**
Notice,
  Abandoned or unclaimed property, **CC 800.36**
  Entry on premises, management, **CC 800.35**
  Management lease, duration, notice to homeowners, **CC 800.33**
  Rent increases, **CC 800.40, 800.40.5**
  Termination of tenancy, **CC 800.72**
  Unlisted services, fees, **CC 800.42**
  Vacation of tenancy, **CC 800.74**
Nuisance, **CC 800.201**
Pets, fees, **CC 800.43**
Possession, forcible entry and detainer, **CC 800.75**
Probate proceedings, sales to third parties, **CC 800.88**
Public nuisance, abatement, **CC 800.201**
Public utilities, separate billing, **CC 800.48**
Refunds, security deposits, **CC 800.49**
Removal of home, sale, requirement, **CC 800.84**
Rent, **CC 800.20 et seq.**
  Increases, **CC 800.40.5**
    Notice, **CC 800.40**
  Security deposits, **CC 800.49**
  Third party purchaser, requirement to sign, **CC 800.86**

FLOATING HOMES—Cont'd
Residency, marinas, **CC 800 et seq.**
Right of entry, management, **CC 800.32**
Rules and regulations, marinas, cooperatives or condominiums, **CC 800.30 et seq.**
Sales, **CC 800.30 et seq., 800.80 et seq.**
  Cooperatives and condominiums, sale by resident, **CC 800.300 et seq.**
  Fees, management, **CC 800.83**
  Ownership of marina, **CC 800.100**
  Prior approval by management, requirement, **CC 800.85**
  Removal of home, requirement, **CC 800.84**
Security deposits, rent, **CC 800.49**
Security interest, foreclosure, **CC 800.89**
Termination of tenancy, marinas, **CC 800.70 et seq.**
Transfer of title, **CC 800.80 et seq.**
  Marina, **CC 800.100**
Unlisted services, fees, **CC 800.42**
Utilities, separate billing, **CC 800.48**
Vacation of tenancy, **CC 800.74**
Zoning or use permits, notice, **CC 800.33**

FLOODS AND FLOODING
Community Facilities Districts, generally, this index
Disclosure, residential property, **CC 1103 et seq.**
Easements, **CC 801**
Home solicitation contracts, residential repair or restoration, cancellation, **CC 1689.6, 1689.7, 1689.14**

FOOD
Agricultural Products, generally, this index
Charities, privileges and immunities, **CC 1714.25**
Dietitians, generally, this index
Fish and Game, generally, this index
Grocery Stores, generally, this index
Privileges and immunities, gifts, devises and bequests, **CC 1714.25**
Restaurants, generally, this index
Support, generally, this index
Weight loss contracts, **CC 1694.5 et seq.**

FOOD BANKS
Food facility donations, **CC 1714.25**
Privileges and immunities, **CC 1714.25**

FOOD ESTABLISHMENTS
Food, generally, this index
Grocery Stores, generally, this index
Restaurants, generally, this index

FOOTBALL
Invasion of privacy, use of name, likeness, voice, signature, without consent, **CC 3344**

FORCE AND VIOLENCE
Actions and proceedings, **CC 52.1**
  Injunction, **CC 52**
Civil Rights, this index

FORCE AND VIOLENCE—Cont'd
Damages, civil rights, **CC 52, 52.1**
Discrimination, this index
Domestic Violence, generally, this index
Fines and penalties, discrimination, **CC 52, 52.1**
Freedom from force and violence, **CC 51.7**
Gender violence, actions and proceedings, **CC 52.4**
Hate crimes, **CC 51.7, 52**
Homeless persons, transitional housing, misconduct, **CC 1954.10 et seq.**
Injunction, **CC 52**
  Civil rights, **CC 52.1**
Intimidation, freedom from intimidation, **CC 51.7**
Landlord and tenant, vacating premises, **CC 1940.2**
Limitation of actions, fines and penalties, **CC 52**
Self defense, **CC 50**
Sex, actions and proceedings, **CC 52.4**
Social media, reports, **CC 1798.99.20 et seq.**
Statute of limitations, fines and penalties, **CC 52**
Video games, children and minors, **CC 1746 et seq.**

FORCIBLE ENTRY AND DETAINER
Generally, **CC 789 et seq.**
Affirmative defenses,
  Emergency services, law enforcement, **CC 1946.8**
  Inoperable locks, **CC 1941.3**
Amendment, complaint, damage action, **CC 1952, 1952.3**
Ammunition, **CC 3485**
Application of law, weapons, **CC 3485**
Assignments,
  Drugs and medicine, nuisance, **CC 3486**
  Weapons, **CC 3485**
Attorney fees,
  Drugs and medicine, nuisance, **CC 3486**
  Weapons, **CC 3485**
Bed and breakfast inns, guests, checkout time, **CC 1865**
Boarding and lodging houses, guests, checkout time, **CC 1865**
Breach of lease, lessors remedy, **CC 1952, 1952.3**
Camps and camping, **CC 1866**
Complaints, amendment, damage action, **CC 1952, 1952.3**
Consumer credit reporting agencies, use of information, **CC 1785.13**
Costs,
  Drugs and medicine, nuisance, **CC 3486**
  Weapons, **CC 3485**
Crimes and offenses, drugs and medicine, nuisance, **CC 3486**
Drugs and medicine, nuisance, **CC 3486, 3486.5**

FORCIBLE

FORCIBLE ENTRY AND DETAINER
—Cont'd
Emergency services, **CC 1946.8**
Evidence, habitability, breach presumption, **CC 1942.3**
Floating homes, marinas, **CC 800.75**
Forms, notice, weapons, **CC 3485**
Fraud, local rent stabilization and rent control programs, **CC 1947.10**
Habitability, breach, evidence, presumption, **CC 1942.3**
Hotels and motels, guests, checkout time, **CC 1865**
Incumbrances, drugs and medicine, nuisance, costs, **CC 3486**
Investigative consumer reporting agencies, use of information, **CC 1786.18**
Joinder of causes of action, drugs and medicine, nuisance, **CC 3486**
Law enforcement, **CC 1946.8**
Lessors right to damages or equitable relief for breach, effect of forcible entry and detainer action, **CC 1952, 1952.3**
Liens and incumbrances, drugs and medicine, nuisance, costs, **CC 3486**
Long Beach,
  Drugs and medicine, nuisance, **CC 3486.5**
  Weapons, **CC 3485**
Los Angeles,
  Drugs and medicine, nuisance, **CC 3486**
  Weapons, **CC 3485**
Mail and mailing, weapons, notice, **CC 3485**
Mortgages, **CC 2924n**
Motels and motor courts, guests, checkout time, **CC 1865**
Municipal attorneys, drugs and medicine, nuisance, assignments, **CC 3486**
Notice, **CC 790, 791**
  Drugs and medicine, nuisance, **CC 3486**
  Weapons, **CC 3485**
Nuisance, drugs and medicine, **CC 3486, 3486.5**
Oakland,
  Drugs and medicine, nuisance, **CC 3486.5**
  Weapons, **CC 3485**
Orders of court, weapons, **CC 3485**
Partial eviction,
  Drugs and medicine, nuisance, **CC 3486**
  Weapons, **CC 3485**
Parties, weapons, **CC 3485**
Personal property, return to tenant, **CC 1965**
Pleadings, damage action, **CC 1952, 1952.3**
Possessory action, **CC 793**
Presumptions,
  Emergency services, law enforcement, **CC 1946.8**
  Habitability, breach, **CC 1942.3**
Reentry, **CC 790, 791**
Rent, local rent stabilization and rent control programs, fraudulent eviction, **CC 1947.10**
Reports, drugs and medicine, nuisance, **CC 3486.5**

FORCIBLE ENTRY AND DETAINER
—Cont'd
Sacramento City and County,
  Drugs and medicine, nuisance, **CC 3486.5**
  Weapons, **CC 3485**
Service of process, drugs and medicine, nuisance, **CC 3486**
Special occupancy parks, **CC 1866**
Summary proceedings, **CC 792**
Time,
  Action for possession, **CC 793**
  Amendment, complaint, damage, action, **CC 1952, 1952.3**
Trust deeds, **CC 2924n**
Water supply, submeters, **CC 1954.213**
Weapons, **CC 3485**

FORECLOSURE
Disclosure, residential property transfers, **CC 1102.2**
Equity. Home Equity Sales Contracts, generally, this index
Escrows and escrow agents, consumer protection, deeds and conveyances, **CC 1103.20 et seq.**
Home Equity Sales Contracts, generally, this index
Liens and Incumbrances, this index
Mortgages, this index
Sales, home equity sales contracts, **CC 1695 et seq.**
Title insurance, consumer protection, deeds and conveyances, **CC 1103.20 et seq.**
Trust Deeds, this index

FOREIGN BORN PERSONS
Noncitizens, generally, this index

FOREIGN COUNTRIES
Acknowledgments, **CC 1183**
Choice of law. Conflict of Laws, generally, this index
Conflict of Laws, generally, this index
Euro, contracts, securities or instruments, medium of payment, **CC 1663**
Exports and Imports, generally, this index
Gray market goods, sales or leases, disclosure, **CC 1797.8 et seq.**
Language. Foreign Languages, generally, this index
Noncitizens, generally, this index

FOREIGN CURRENCY
Frauds, statute of, sales, **CC 1624**

FOREIGN LANGUAGES
Apartment houses, leases, translations, **CC 1632**
Attorney fees, contracts, translations, **CC 1632**
Banks and banking, contracts, translations, **CC 1632.5**
Civil rights, **CC 51**
Condominiums, leases, translations, **CC 1632**

FOREIGN LANGUAGES—Cont'd
Contractors, home improvement business, translations, **CC 1632**
Credit unions, contracts, translations, **CC 1632.5**
Discrimination, **CC 51**
Finance lenders, contracts, translations, **CC 1632.5**
Housing, contracts, translations, **CC 1632**
Industrial loan companies, contracts, translations, **CC 1632, 1632.5**
Installment sales, translations, **CC 1632**
Landlord and tenant, contracts, translations, **CC 1632**
Leases, translations, **CC 1632**
Loans, translations, **CC 1632**
Mobilehomes and mobilehome parks, leases, translations, **CC 1632**
Motor vehicles, contracts, translations, **CC 1632**
Personal property brokers, loans, translations, **CC 1632**
Real estate, loans, translations, **CC 1632**
Rent, contracts, translations, **CC 1632**
Residential mortgage lenders, contracts, translations, **CC 1632.5**
Reverse mortgages, translations, **CC 1632**
Savings associations, contracts, translations, **CC 1632.5**
Spanish Language, generally, this index

FOREIGN NATION
Foreign Countries, generally, this index

FOREIGN NATIONALS
Noncitizens, generally, this index

FOREIGN STATES
Acknowledgments, **CC 1182**
  Forms, **CC 1189**
Actions and proceedings, agreements, parties, transaction without reasonable relation to state, **CC 1646.5**
Choice of law. Conflict of Laws, generally, this index
Conflict of Laws, generally, this index
Contracts,
  Jurisdiction, agreement of parties, transaction without reasonable relation to state, **CC 1646.5**
  Mistake of laws, **CC 1579**
Credit cards, disclosures, **CC 1748.11**
Eminent Domain, generally, this index
Home roof warranties, standardized forms, **CC 1797.95**
Installment sales, transactions involving both local and out of state contacts, **CC 1802.19**
Notaries public, acknowledgments, **CC 1182**
Retirement and pensions, public systems, interest rates, **CC 1916.2**
Roof warranties, standardized forms, **CC 1797.95**
Warranties, roof warranties, standardized forms, **CC 1797.95**

FRAUD

FOREST FIRES
Deeds and conveyances, fire hazard severity zones,
    Compliance, **CC 1102.19**
    Disclosure, **CC 1102.6f**
Disclosure, residential property, **CC 1103 et seq.**
Hazardous fire areas, fire hazard severity zones, deeds and conveyances,
    Compliance, **CC 1102.19**
    Disclosure, **CC 1102.6f**
Privileges and immunities, prescribed burning, **CC 3333.8**
Real estate,
    Disclosure, residential property, **CC 1103 et seq.**
    Fire hazard severity zones,
        Compliance, **CC 1102.19**
        Disclosure, **CC 1102.6f**

FOREST PRODUCTS
Timber and Lumber, generally, this index

FORESTS AND FORESTRY
    See, also, Trees, generally, this index
Eminent domain, temporary entry, repairs, **CC 1002**
Fires. Forest Fires, generally, this index
Forest Fires, generally, this index
Lumber. Timber and Lumber, generally, this index
Reservations, appropriation of waters, time to commence works, **CC 1422**
Timber and Lumber, generally, this index
Zoning and Planning, generally, this index

FORFEITURES
    Generally, **CC 3275**
Acknowledgments, perjury, **CC 1185**
Boarding and lodging houses, rates, failure to post, **CC 1863**
Compensation and salaries, payment in lieu of forfeiture, **CC 3275**
Contracts,
    Breach of contract, damages, **CC 3275**
    Conditions, **CC 1442**
Future interests, forfeiture of precedent interest, **CC 741**
Grantees of rents and reversion, recovery, **CC 821**
Hotels and motels, rates of charges, failure to post, **CC 1863**
Liens and incumbrances, **CC 2889**
    Property deposited for repair, alteration, or sale, insurance, **CC 1858.2**
Mechanics liens, public buildings and works, stop notices, distribution, **CC 9454**
Mineral rights lessees, liability, **CC 883.140**
Mortgages, this index
Obligations, conditions involving forfeiture, construction, **CC 1442**
Personal Property Brokers, generally, this index

FORFEITURES—Cont'd
Precedent interest, effect on future interest, **CC 741**
Reimbursement, relief from forfeiture, **CC 3275**
Specific or preventive relief, **CC 3369**
Trust deeds, failure to deliver statements, **CC 2943**
Water appropriation, **CC 1419**

FORMALDEHYDE
Consumer information, booklets, costs, **CC 2079.11**
Costs, consumer information booklets, **CC 2079.11**
Disclosure, real estate transfers, **CC 2079.7**
Notice, real estate transfers, **CC 2079.7**
Real estate brokers and salespersons, notice, **CC 2079.7**

FORMER JEOPARDY
Consumer credit reporting agencies, **CC 1785.34**

FORMS
Banks and banking, contracts, foreign languages, translations, **CC 1632.5**
Consumer credit, notice, signers of contracts, responsibility, **CC 1799.91**
Credit life and disability insurance, claims procedure, **CC 1812.402**
Credit services organizations, contracts, cancellations, notice, **CC 1789.16**
Dating service contracts, **CC 1694.2**
Deeds and Conveyances, this index
Disclosure,
    Home roof warranties, **CC 1797.94**
    State agencies, Information Practices Act, **CC 1798.17**
Fine prints, sale, disclosure, **CC 1744**
Health studio contracts, cancellation form, **CC 1812.85**
Home equity sales contracts,
    Cancellation, notice, **CC 1695.5**
    Notice, **CC 1695.3**
Home roof warranties, **CC 1797.94**
Home solicitation contracts,
    Cancellation, **CC 1689.7**
    Notice of cancellation, **CC 1689.7**
Indebtedness, duress or coercion, certificates and certification, **CC 1798.97.1**
Installment sales, **CC 1803.2, 1803.3**
Instructions not to ship merchandise, seller consumer contractual plans or arrangements, **CC 1584.5**
Landlord and Tenant, this index
Membership camping contracts, **CC 1812.303, 1812.304, 1812.307, 1812.314**
Mobilehomes and Mobilehome Parks, this index
Mortgages, this index
Motor Vehicles, this index
Museums, notice of intent to preserve an interest in property on loan, **CC 1899.5**

FORMS—Cont'd
Prints, sale, disclosure, **CC 1744**
Private bulk grain storage,
    Bill of sale, **CC 1880.4, 1880.5**
    Notice of sale, **CC 1880.7**
Real Estate, this index
Rent, third parties, payment, **CC 1947.3**
Rental purchase agreements, **CC 1812.623**
Retail installment accounts, credit balance, refunds, **CC 1810.3**
Roof warranties, **CC 1797.94**
Savings associations, contracts, foreign languages, translations, **CC 1632.5**
Shared appreciation loans for seniors, disclosure, **CC 1917.711 et seq.**
Trust Deeds, this index
Warranties, roofs, **CC 1797.94**
Weight loss contracts, **CC 1694.7**

FOSTER HOMES
Social Services, this index

FOUNDATIONS
Charities, generally, this index

FOUNDRIES
Manufacturers and Manufacturing, generally, this index

FRANCHISE TAXES
Corporation Taxes, generally, this index

FRANCHISES
Blind or visually impaired persons, discrimination, **CC 51.8**
Civil rights, discrimination, **CC 51.8**
Disabled persons, discrimination, **CC 51.8**
Discrimination, **CC 51.8**
National origin, discrimination, **CC 51.8**
Race, discrimination, **CC 51.8**
Religion, discrimination, **CC 51.8**

FRAUD
Actual fraud, contracts, **CC 1571, 1572**
    Question of fact, **CC 1574**
Adding machines, sale with identification number or mark altered or removed, **CC 1710.1**
Advertisements, this index
Agents and agency, **CC 2306**
Bicycles, sale with identification number or mark altered or removed, **CC 1710.1**
Bills, written solicitation of money appearing as a bill, **CC 1716**
Buildings, construction defects, actions and proceedings, **CC 931**
Class of persons, intent to defraud, **CC 1711**
Classification, **CC 1571**
Comptometers, sale with identification number or mark altered or removed, **CC 1710.1**
Condominiums, homeowners associations, records and recordation, inspection and inspectors, **CC 5215**
Consent to contracts, **CC 1567, 1568**

FRAUD

FRAUD—Cont'd

Construction lender, liability for defects, real or personal property, CC 3434
Constructive fraud, contracts, CC 1571, 1573
Consumer affairs,
  Deceptive practices, CC 1770
  Grey market goods, disclosure, CC 1797.8 et seq.
Consumer Credit, this index
Consumer Credit Reporting Agencies, this index
Credit cards, issuer giving untrue credit information, CC 1747.70
Credit services organizations, CC 1789.13
Damages, CC 1709, 3343
  Aged persons, CC 3345
  Amount of damages, CC 3343
  Consumers Legal Remedies Act, CC 1750 et seq.
  Disabled persons, CC 3345
  Exemplary damages, CC 3294
  Interest, CC 3288
  Labor and employment, CC 3294
  Mechanical or electrical device or equipment, sale with identification number or mark altered or removed, CC 1710.1
  Promise to marry or to cohabit, CC 43.4
  Sale or exchange of property, CC 3343
  Solicitation of money, false invoices or statements, CC 1716
Dance studio services, state regulation, CC 1812.50 et seq.
Dating service contracts, CC 1694.4
Debit cards, CC 1748.30, 1748.31
Debt settlement providers, fair debt settlement, CC 1788.302
Debtors and Creditors, this index
Deeds and conveyances, natural hazards, disclosure, residential property, CC 1103.8
Dictaphones, sale with identification number or mark altered or removed, CC 1710.1
Disabled Persons, this index
Disclaimer, notice, solicitation, payment of money, written statement or invoice, CC 1716
Discount buying services, CC 1812.120
Disregard of contract not expressing real intention, CC 1640
Electrical device or equipment, sale with identification number or mark altered or removed, CC 1710.1
Employment counseling services, CC 1812.513
Endless chain schemes, CC 1689.2
Enforcement, oral contracts, CC 1623
Exchange of property, damages, CC 3343
Executions, manufacturers identification mark, removal, defacing, alteration or destruction, CC 1710.1
Exemplary damages, CC 3294
Exemption from responsibility, illegal contracts, CC 1668
False Imprisonment, generally, this index

FRAUD—Cont'd

Fines and penalties,
  Additional penalty, aged persons, disabled persons, veterans, CC 3345
  Aged persons, disabled persons, CC 1780
  Exemplary damages, CC 3294
Firearms, sale with identification number or mark altered or removed, CC 1710.1
Health studio services, contracts, CC 1812.80 et seq.
Home equity sales contracts, CC 1695.6, 1695.8
Illegal contracts, exemption from responsibility, CC 1668
Imprisonment (false). False Imprisonment, generally, this index
Improvements, construction loan, lender liability for defects, CC 3434
Injunction, unfair or fraudulent business practice, CC 3369
Intent to defraud, public, CC 1711
Interest, damages, CC 3288
Invoices, written statements soliciting money appearing as invoices, CC 1716
Involuntary trusts, CC 2223 et seq.
Job listing services, CC 1812.520
Landlord and tenant, owners and ownership, CC 890
Limitation of actions, Consumers Legal Remedies Act, CC 1783
Loans, construction or improvement, real or personal property, defects, lenders liability, CC 3434
Mechanical or electrical devices or equipment, sale with identification number or mark altered or removed, CC 1710.1
Notice, disclaimer, solicitation, payment of money, written statement or invoice, CC 1716
Nurse registries, CC 1812.533
Oral contracts, CC 1623
Particular class of persons, intent to defraud, CC 1711
Penalties. Fines and penalties, generally, ante
Phonograph, sale with identification number or mark altered or removed, CC 1710.1
Pianos, sale with identification number or mark altered or removed, CC 1710.1
Political items, sale and manufacture, CC 1739 et seq.
Radios, sale with identification number or mark altered or removed, CC 1710.1
Reformation, CC 3399
Rent, owners and ownership, CC 890
Reports, crimes and offenses, libel and slander, privileges and immunities, CC 47
Rescission of contract, CC 1689
Revision of contracts, CC 3399 et seq.
Safe, sale with identification number or mark altered or removed, CC 1710.1
Seller assisted marketing plans, CC 1812.200 et seq.

FRAUD—Cont'd

Serial numbers on merchandise, removal, defacing, alteration or destruction, CC 1710.1
Sewing machines, sale with identification number or mark altered or removed, CC 1710.1
Skimming (rent), CC 890
Solicitation, money, false statements or invoices, CC 1716
Specific performance, contracts induced by fraud, CC 3391
Statements, written solicitation of money appearing as statement, CC 1716
Statute of Frauds. Frauds, Statute of, generally, this index
Stipulations against right of rescinding contract, CC 1690
Suppression of fact, contracts, CC 1572
Trade secrets, CC 3426 et seq.
Treble damages, mechanical or electrical equipment sold with identification number or mark altered or removed, CC 1710.1
Typewriters, sale with identification number or mark altered or removed, CC 1710.1
Uniform Trade Secrets Act, CC 3426 et seq.
Unlawful contracts, exemption from responsibility, CC 1668
Vacuum cleaners, sale with identification number or mark altered or removed, CC 1710.1
Voidable Transactions, generally, this index
Washing machines, sale with identification number or mark altered or removed, CC 1710.1
Watches, sale with identification number or mark altered or removed, CC 1710.1
Weight loss contracts, CC 1694.9

FRAUDS, STATUTE OF

Generally, CC 1624
Brokers, real estate sales, CC 1624
Commodities, swaps or options, CC 1624
Currency, sales, CC 1624
Debts, special promise to answer for debt of another, CC 1624
Financial contract (qualified), CC 1624
Foreign currency, sales, CC 1624
Futures contracts, CC 1624
Leases for longer period than year, CC 1624
Loans, CC 1624
Memorandum of contract, necessity, CC 1624
Modification of contract, CC 1698
Mortgages, CC 1624
Oral contract,
  Enforcement, CC 1623
  Modification of written contracts, CC 1698
Qualified financial contract, CC 1624
Special promise to answer for debt, of another, CC 1624
Wills, CC 1624
Written contract, modification by oral contract, CC 1698

FRAUDULENT TRANSFERS
Voidable Transactions, generally, this index

FREEDOM OF SPEECH
Stalking, CC 1708.7

FREEHOLD ESTATES
Commencement in future, CC 773
Estate for life of third person, CC 766

FREEWAYS
Access, monuments, surveyors, CC 846.5
Billboards. Outdoor Advertising, generally, this index
Entry on property surveyors, CC 846.5
Monuments, surveyors access to, CC 846.5
Outdoor Advertising, generally, this index
Surveyors, access to monuments, CC 846.5
Traffic Rules and Regulations, generally, this index

FRIENDS
Medical care and treatment, disclosure, CC 56.1007

FRUIT TREES
Pest Control, generally, this index

FUEL AND CHEMICAL STORAGE TANKS
Consumer information, booklets, costs, CC 2079.11
Costs, consumer information booklets, CC 2079.11
Disclosure, real estate transfers, CC 2079.7
Notice, real estate transfers, CC 2079.7
Real estate brokers and salespersons, notice, CC 2079.7

FUMES
Air Pollution, generally, this index

FUMIGANTS
Pest Control, generally, this index

FUNDS
Arts and entertainment fund, CC 1708.8
Condominiums, homeowners associations, elections, CC 5135
Consumer privacy fund, CC 1798.160
Data brokers registry fund, CC 1798.99.82
Foreclosure consultant regulation fund, CC 2945.45
Investments, generally, this index

FUNDS TRANSFERS
Cards, debit cards, CC 1748.30, 1748.31
Credit cards, CC 1747.03
Debit Cards, generally, this index
Electronic Commerce Act of 1984, application of law, CC 1789.7
Landlord and tenant, CC 1962

FUNGICIDES
Pest Control, generally, this index

FUR BEARING MAMMALS
Fish and Game, this index

FURNITURE
Advertisements, unassembled furniture, consumer remedies, CC 1770
Landlord and tenant, removal by landlord without prior consent, intent to terminate lease, CC 789.3
Warranties, Song Beverly Consumer Warranty Act, CC 1790 et seq.

FUTURE ESTATES OR INTERESTS
Abridging preceding estate, CC 778
Accumulations, disposition, CC 722 et seq., 733
Actions and proceedings, injuries to inheritance, CC 826
After born children, CC 698
  Defeat of interest, CC 739
Alienation, CC 741
Alternative, CC 696
Attornments of tenants, reversions, conveyances, CC 1111
Commencement, CC 767
Condition precedent or subsequent, CC 708
  Nonperformance of condition, CC 1109
  Performance of condition, CC 1110
  Validity, CC 709
Contingent future interest, improbability of contingency, CC 697
Creation, time, CC 749
Deeds and conveyances, CC 699
Defeat of future interest,
  Birth, posthumous child, CC 739
  Condition provided, adjudication, CC 740
Dominant tenement, rights of owner, CC 808
Easements, use by owner, CC 808
Fee tails, CC 764
Forfeiture of precedent interest, CC 741
Improbability of contingency, CC 697
Income,
  Disposition, CC 722, 733
  Legal Estates Principal and Income Law, CC 731 et seq.
Injuries to inheritance, remedies, CC 826
Legal Estates Principal and Income Law, CC 731 et seq.
Liens and incumbrances, creation, CC 2883
Marketable title, powers of termination, CC 885.010 et seq.
Merger or consolidation of precedent interest, CC 741
Performance of condition precedent, passing of estate, CC 1110
Possibilities, CC 700
  Interest, transfers, CC 1045
Power of appointment, effect on vesting, CC 781
Powers of termination, marketable title, CC 885.010 et seq.
Premature determination of precedent interest, CC 742
Principal, Legal Estates Principal and Income Law, CC 731 et seq.

FUTURE ESTATES OR INTERESTS
—Cont'd
Recognition, CC 703
Reconveyances, conditions subsequent, failure to perform, CC 1109
Reentry, right of, transfer, conditions subsequent, failure to perform, CC 1046
Rents, grantees, actions, CC 821
Rule Against Perpetuities, CC 773
Termination, CC 739 et seq., 885.010 et seq.
Time of enjoyment, CC 688, 707
Title to property, transfer, CC 699
Transfer of title, CC 699

FUTURE PERFORMANCE
Specific performance, mutuality of remedy, CC 3386

FUTURES CONTRACTS
Frauds, statute of, CC 1624

GAMBLING
Costs, injunctions, awarding, CC 3496
Injunction, costs, awarding, CC 3496

GAME
Fish and Game, generally, this index

GAME BIRDS
Fish and Game, generally, this index

GAP WAIVERS
Motor vehicles, conditional sales, CC 2982.12
  Disclosure, CC 2982, 2982.2

GARAGES
Liens and incumbrances, CC 3067 et seq.

GARDENERS AND GARDENING
Landlord and tenant, CC 1940.10

GARNISHMENT
Credit services organizations, deposits, CC 1789.24
Discount buying services, deposits in lieu of bonds, claims, CC 1812.105
Executions, generally, this index
Mechanics liens, public buildings and works, stop notices, distribution, priorities and preferences, CC 9456
Seller assisted marketing plans, deposits in lieu of bonds, claims, CC 1812.221

GAS
Air Pollution, generally, this index
Oil and Gas, generally, this index

GAS COMPANIES
Oil and Gas, generally, this index

GAS STATIONS
Motor Vehicle Service Stations, generally, this index

GASOLINE STATIONS
Motor Vehicle Service Stations, generally, this index

GAY

GAY PERSONS
Sexual Orientation, generally, this index

GENDER
Sex, generally, this index

GENDER TAX REPEAL ACT
Generally, CC 51.6

GENERAL ASSEMBLY
Legislature, generally, this index

GENERAL CONTRACTORS
Contractors, this index

GENERAL CORPORATION LAW
Corporations, generally, this index

GENERAL ELECTIONS
Elections, generally, this index

GENERAL LAWS
Statutes, generally, this index

GENERAL NONPROFIT CORPORATION LAW
Nonprofit Corporations, generally, this index

GENERAL SALES TAX
Sales and Use Taxes, generally, this index

GENERAL SERVICES DEPARTMENT
Contracts. State Contracts, generally, this index
State Contracts, generally, this index

GENERAL SESSIONS
Legislature, generally, this index

GENERAL STORES
Stores, generally, this index

GENETIC CHARACTERISTICS
Diseases, this index

GENETIC DISEASES
Diseases, this index

GENETIC INFORMATION PRIVACY ACT
Generally, CC 56.18 et seq.

GENETIC TESTING
Privacy, CC 56.18 et seq.

GEOLOGISTS AND GEOPHYSICISTS
Disclosure, natural hazards, residential property, CC 1103.4
Hazards, natural hazards, disclosure, residential property, CC 1103.4
Natural hazards, disclosure, residential property, CC 1103.4
Privileges and immunities, natural hazards, disclosure, residential property, CC 1103.4

GEOLOGY
Mines and Minerals, generally, this index

GEOPHYSICISTS
Geologists and Geophysicists, generally, this index

GIFT CERTIFICATES
Generally, CC 1749.45 et seq.
Bankruptcy, CC 1749.6
Dormancy fees, CC 1749.5
Fees, CC 1749.5
Redemption, CC 1749.6
Refunds, CC 1749.5
Service fees, CC 1749.5
Trusts and trustees, CC 1749.6
Waiver, CC 1749.51

GIFTS, DEVISES AND BEQUESTS
Generally, CC 1146 et seq.
Causa mortis, revocability, CC 1148
Certificates and certification. Gift Certificates, generally, this index
Charities, generally, this index
Club members, sending goods to after notice of termination, CC 1584.6
Crimes and offenses, defendants, assistance in challenging criminal charges, CC 2225
Delivery, CC 1147
Fires and fire protection, machinery and equipment, privileges and immunities, CC 1714.11
Oral, delivery, CC 1147
Possession, verbal gifts, CC 1147
Probate Proceedings, generally, this index
Revocation, CC 1148
Sending unsolicited goods, CC 1584.5, 1584.6
Services, unsolicited services, CC 1584.5
Unsolicited goods, CC 1584.5
Verbal, delivery, CC 1147
Volunteer firefighters and fire departments, machinery and equipment, privileges and immunities, CC 1714.11
Wills, generally, this index

GIN
Alcoholic Beverages, generally, this index

GIRLS
Children and Minors, generally, this index

GLASS
Art works, originals, sales, royalties, CC 986
Carriers, limitation of liability, CC 2200
Stained glass artistry, fine arts, CC 997

GLEANERS
Donations, privileges and immunities, CC 1714.25

GNATS
Pest Control, generally, this index

GOATS
See, also, Animals, generally, this index
Dogs, killing or injuring, liability of owner, CC 3341

GOD
Acts of God, generally, this index

GOLD
See, also, Mines and Minerals, generally, this index

GOLD—Cont'd
Carriers, limitation of liability, CC 2200

GOOD FAITH
Arrest, peace officers, privileges and immunities, CC 43.55
Consumer credit denial, liability, CC 1787.3
Consumers Legal Remedies Act, damage actions, CC 1784
Debtors and creditors, offer to perform, CC 1493
Defibrillators, emergencies, privileges and immunities, CC 1714.21
Fixtures erroneously affixed to land, removal, CC 1013.5
Medical care and treatment, defibrillators, emergencies, privileges and immunities, CC 1714.21
Peace officers, arrest, privileges and immunities, CC 43.55
Police, arrest, privileges and immunities, CC 43.55
Sheriffs, arrest, privileges and immunities, CC 43.55
Voidable transactions, defenses, CC 3439.08

GOOD NEIGHBOR FENCE ACT
Generally, CC 841

GOOD SAMARITAN FOOD DONATION ACT
Generally, CC 1714.25

GOODS, WARES AND MERCHANDISE
Advertisements, deceased celebrity image protection, CC 3344.1
Bailment, generally, this index
Celebrity image protection, CC 3344.1
Clubs, termination of membership, receipt of unordered goods, CC 1584.6
Consumer Goods, generally, this index
Death, celebrity image protection, CC 3344.1
Deceptive practices, Consumers Legal Remedies Act, CC 1750 et seq.
Famous persons, celebrity image protection, CC 3344.1
Gray market goods, disclosure, CC 1797.8 et seq.
Grocery stores, point of sale systems, CC 7100 et seq.
Identity and identification, theft, CC 1798.92 et seq.
Installment Sales, generally, this index
Instructions not to ship merchandise, forms, seller consumer contractual plans, CC 1584.5
Layaway sales, regulation, CC 1749 et seq.
Mails and mailing, voluntary and unsolicited sending of goods, CC 1584.5
Manufacturers identification, removal, alteration or destruction, damages, CC 1710.1
Products Liability, generally, this index
Receiving Stolen Goods, generally, this index
Returns, refunds or exchanges, notice if not allowed, CC 1723

GOODS, WARES AND MERCHANDISE —Cont'd
Unauthorized use of name, likeness, voice, signature, **CC 3344**
Unsolicited, sending of, **CC 1584.5, 1584.6**

GOODWILL
Owners and ownership, **CC 655**

GOPHERS
Pest Control, generally, this index

GOVERNING LAW
Conflict of Laws, generally, this index

GOVERNMENT OWNERSHIP
Communications, generally, this index

GOVERNMENTAL AGENCIES
Public Agencies, generally, this index

GOVERNOR
Clemency, executive clemency, Information Practices Act, **CC 1798 et seq.**
Executive clemency, Information Practices Act, **CC 1798 et seq.**
White Cane Safety Day, proclamation, **CC 54.5**

GRADES AND GRADING
Consumers Legal Remedies Act, **CC 1750 et seq.**

GRAIN
Agricultural Products, generally, this index

GRAND JURY
Accusation. Indictment and Information, generally, this index
Indictment and Information, generally, this index

GRANDPARENTS AND GRANDCHILDREN
Adoption, medically necessary information, disclosure, **CC 1798.24**

GRANTS
See, also, Gifts, Devises and Bequests, generally, this index
Deeds and Conveyances, generally, this index
Stalking, victim service providers, personal information, **CC 1798.79.8 et seq.**

GRAPES AND GRAPEVINES
Pest Control, generally, this index

GRAPHIC ARTS
Common law copyrights, reproduction rights, transfer, **CC 982**

GRATUITIES
Gifts, Devises and Bequests, generally, this index

GRAZING AND GRAZING LANDS
Easements, **CC 801**
Servitude unattached, **CC 802**

GREENWAY DEVELOPMENT AND SUSTAINMENT ACT
Generally, **CC 816.50 et seq.**

GREY MARKET GOODS
Sales or leases, **CC 1797.8 et seq.**

GRIEVANCES
Complaints, generally, this index

GRIME
Air Pollution, generally, this index

GROCERIES
Food, generally, this index

GROCERY STORES
Club cards, disclosure, **CC 1749.60 et seq.**
Consumer protection, club cards, disclosure, **CC 1749.60 et seq.**
Disclosure, club cards, **CC 1749.60 et seq.**
Fines and penalties, point of sale systems, **CC 7101 et seq.**
Food donations, privileges and immunities, **CC 1714.25**
Monopolies and unfair trade, club cards, disclosure, **CC 1749.60 et seq.**
Point of sale systems, **CC 7100 et seq.**
Waiver, club cards, disclosure, **CC 1749.66**

GROSS NEGLIGENCE
Negligence, this index

GROWING CROPS
Agricultural Products, generally, this index

GUARANTEED ASSET PROTECTION WAIVERS
Motor vehicles, conditional sales, **CC 2982.12**
Disclosure, **CC 2982, 2982.2**

GUARANTOR
Consumer protection, delivery of agreement, **CC 1799.206**

GUARANTY
Suretyship and Guaranty, generally, this index

GUARDIAN AND WARD
See, also, Fiduciaries, generally, this index
Abduction, child, **CC 49**
Actions and proceedings, willful misconduct of minor, imputed liability of guardian, **CC 1714.1**
Conservators and Conservatorships, generally, this index
Cost of living, damages, liability of guardians, **CC 1714.1**
Damages,
  Cost of living, liability of guardians, **CC 1714.1**
  Holding over real property, **CC 3335**
  Inflation, liability of guardians, **CC 1714.1**
  Insurance, liability of guardians, **CC 1714.1**
  Willful misconduct of minor, imputed liability of guardian, **CC 1714.1**

GUARDIAN AND WARD—Cont'd
Defacement of property, willful misconduct of minor, imputed liability of guardian, **CC 1714.1**
Disclosure,
  Personal information maintained by governmental agencies, Information Practices Act, **CC 1798.24**
  Residential property transfers, **CC 1102.2**
Enticement of child, **CC 49**
Foreign mortgages, satisfaction, methods, **CC 2939.5**
Imputation of willful misconduct to guardian, **CC 1714.1**
Inflation, damages, liability of guardians, **CC 1714.1**
Insurance, damages, liability of guardians, **CC 1714.1**
Invasion of wards privacy, names, photographs, voice, signature, use without consent, **CC 3344**
Liability, willful misconduct of minor, **CC 1714.1**
Libel and slander, child abuse actions, **CC 48.7**
Medical records, disclosure to investigators, determination of need for guardianship, **CC 56.10**
Misconduct, willful misconduct of minor, imputed liability of guardian, **CC 1714.1**
Mortgages, satisfaction, **CC 2939.5**
Protection of ward, force, right to use, **CC 50**
Willful misconduct of minor, imputed liability of guardian, **CC 1714.1**

GUEST HOUSES
Restaurants, generally, this index

GUESTS
Floating homes, fees, **CC 800.41**
Mobilehome parks, occupancy fee, **CC 798.34**
Protection, force, right to use, **CC 50**

GUIDE DOGS
Service Animals, generally, this index

GUNS
Weapons, generally, this index

GYMNASIUMS
Boxing and wrestling, leases, notice, anabolic steroids, testosterone or human growth hormone, crimes and offenses, **CC 1812.97**
Health Studios, generally, this index

HABIT FORMING DRUGS
Drugs and Medicine, generally, this index

HABITUAL CRIMINALS
Second and subsequent offenses. Crimes and Offenses, this index

HAIR
Cosmetology, generally, this index

HAIRDRESSERS
Cosmetology, generally, this index

HANDGUNS

HANDGUNS
Weapons, generally, this index

HANDS
Cosmetology, generally, this index

HANDWRITING
Execution of instruments, proof by, CC 1198, 1199

HANG GLIDING
Private property, entry on, negligence, owner liability for injuries, CC 846

HARASSMENT
Contracts, duress, CC 1569
Debt collection, CC 1788.10 et seq.
Rental purchase agreements, collections, CC 1812.638
Sexual Harassment, generally, this index
Stalking, torts, CC 1708.7

HARBORS AND PORTS
Leases, municipalities, tide and submerged lands and uplands, CC 718
San Francisco Bay Area, generally, this index

HARRISON NARCOTIC ACT
Drugs and Medicine, generally, this index

HARVESTING
Equipment. Agricultural Machinery and Equipment, generally, this index

HARVESTING EQUIPMENT
Agricultural Machinery and Equipment, generally, this index

HATE CRIMES
Generally, CC 51.7, 52, 52.1
Limitation of actions, fines and penalties, CC 52
Statute of limitations, fines and penalties, CC 52

HAWKERS AND PEDDLERS
Sales and Use Taxes, generally, this index

HAZARDOUS MATERIALS
Hazardous Substances and Waste, generally, this index

HAZARDOUS SUBSTANCES AND WASTE
Actions and proceedings,
  Commitment statements, responsibility acceptance, CC 852
  Responsibility acceptance, commitment statements, CC 852
Admissions, commitment statements, responsibility acceptance, CC 853
Application of law, responsibility acceptance, releases, CC 851
Asbestos, generally, this index
Bins, secure drug take back bins, privileges and immunities, CC 1714.24
Books and papers, environmental hazards, costs, CC 2079.11

HAZARDOUS SUBSTANCES AND WASTE —Cont'd
Commitment statements, release, responsibility acceptance, CC 850 et seq.
Construction, subterranean contamination, indemnity, exception, CC 2782.6
Contractors, emergencies, disclosure, CC 3273
Costs, consumer information booklets, CC 2079.11
Damages, responsibility acceptance, commitment statements, CC 852
Discharge,
  Release, generally, post
  Responsibility acceptance, CC 850 et seq.
Disclosure, emergencies, contractors, CC 3273
Emergencies,
  Contractors, disclosure, CC 3273
  Disclosure, contractors, CC 3273
  Identity and identification, contractors, CC 3273
Entry on property, secured lenders, CC 2929.5
Forms, commitment statements, responsibility acceptance, CC 854
Housing, pipelines, sales, disclosure, CC 2079.10.5
Identity and identification, emergencies, contractors, CC 3273
Indemnity, construction contracts, subterranean contamination, exception, CC 2782.6
Liability, responsibility acceptance, CC 850 et seq.
Mediation, releases, responsibility acceptance, CC 852
Medical waste, secure drug take back bins, privileges and immunities, CC 1714.24
Mortgages, inspection of property, CC 2929.5
Notice, potential liability, releases, CC 850, 851
Pipes and pipelines, housing, sales, disclosure, CC 2079.10.5
Privileges and immunities, medical waste, secure drug take back bins, CC 1714.24
Real estate,
  Environmental hazards, notice, CC 2079.7
  Secured lenders, entry, inspection and inspectors, CC 2929.5
Release,
  Mediation, responsibility acceptance, CC 852
  Notice, potential liability, CC 850, 851
  Responsibility acceptance, CC 850 et seq.
Remedial actions,
  Commitment statements, responsibility acceptance, CC 850 et seq.
  Responsibility acceptance, CC 850 et seq.
Reports, responsibility acceptance, releases, CC 850, 851
Responsibility acceptance, releases, CC 850 et seq.
Secure drug take back bins, privileges and immunities, CC 1714.24
Spills,
  Mediation, responsibility acceptance, CC 852

HAZARDOUS SUBSTANCES AND WASTE —Cont'd
Spills—Cont'd
  Responsibility acceptance, CC 850 et seq.
Subterranean contamination, contracts, construction, CC 2782.6
Supersedeas or stay, responsibility acceptance, commitment statements, CC 852

HAZARDOUS WASTE
Hazardous Substances and Waste, generally, this index

HAZARDS
Disclosure, natural hazards, residential property, CC 1103 et seq.
Fishing, hunting, camping, entry on premises for, safety, CC 846
Natural hazards, disclosure, residential property, CC 1103 et seq.
Warnings, real property owner, CC 846

HEALTH AND SANITATION
Asbestos, generally, this index
Clinics, generally, this index
Cosmetics, generally, this index
Diseases, generally, this index
Drugs and Medicine, generally, this index
Genetic diseases. Diseases, this index
Hazardous Substances and Waste, generally, this index
Health Studios, generally, this index
Hereditary disorders. Diseases, this index
Hospitals, generally, this index
Medicine. Drugs and Medicine, generally, this index
Pest Control, generally, this index
Special occupancy parks, moving, CC 1867

HEALTH AND WELFARE BENEFITS
Social Services, generally, this index

HEALTH CARE FACILITIES
Health Facilities, generally, this index

HEALTH CARE LIENS
Generally, CC 3040

HEALTH CARE PROVIDERS
Access, commercial blockade, CC 3427 et seq.
Arson, emergency medical personnel, injuries, liability, CC 1714.9
Blockade, commercial blockade, CC 3427 et seq.
Business and commerce, medical information, confidential or privileged information, CC 56.06
Commercial blockade, CC 3427 et seq.
Confidential or privileged information, medical information, business and commerce, CC 56.06
Defibrillators, emergencies, privileges and immunities, CC 1714.21
Dentists and Dentistry, generally, this index

HEALTH

HEALTH CARE PROVIDERS—Cont'd
Domestic partnership, disclosure, **CC 56.1007**
Emergencies, privileges and immunities, defibrillators, **CC 1714.21**
Family, disclosure, **CC 56.1007**
Fines and penalties, medical information, business and commerce, confidential or privileged information, **CC 56.06**
Friends, disclosure, **CC 56.1007**
Health Care Service Plans, generally, this index
Health Insurance, generally, this index
Immunities. Privileges and immunities, generally, post
Malpractice. Medical Malpractice, generally, this index
Medical information, business and commerce, confidential or privileged information, **CC 56.06**
Medical Malpractice, generally, this index
Multiphasic screening units, unsolicited referrals, limitation of liability, **CC 43.9**
Negligence. Medical Malpractice, generally, this index
Nurses, generally, this index
Pharmacists, generally, this index
Physicians and Surgeons, generally, this index
Privileges and immunities,
    Defibrillators, emergencies, **CC 1714.21**
    Referrals, unsolicited, multiphasic screening units, **CC 43.9**
    State officers and employees, inmate care, **CC 1542.1**
Relatives, disclosure, **CC 56.1007**
Social security, numbers and numbering, posting, **CC 1798.85**
Torts, commercial blockade, **CC 3427 et seq.**

HEALTH CARE SERVICE PLANS
See, also, Insurance, generally, this index
Access, commercial blockade, **CC 3427 et seq.**
Actions and proceedings,
    Medical records, negligence, release, **CC 56.36**
    Medically necessary health care, powers and duties, **CC 3428**
Appeal and review, medically necessary health care, powers and duties, **CC 3428**
Attorneys, punitive damages, failure to provide notice, **CC 3296**
Authorizations, genetic tests, disclosure, **CC 56.17**
Blockade, commercial blockade, **CC 3427 et seq.**
Commercial blockade, **CC 3427 et seq.**
Confidential or privileged information, **CC 56 et seq.**
    Outpatient psychotherapy, records and recordation, **CC 56.104**
Consultants, privileges and immunities, **CC 43.98**
Crimes and offenses,
    Genetic tests, disclosure, **CC 56.17**

HEALTH CARE SERVICE PLANS—Cont'd
Crimes and offenses—Cont'd
    Medical records, negligence, release, **CC 56.36**
Damages,
    Genetic tests, disclosure, **CC 56.17**
    Medical records, negligence, release, **CC 56.36**
    Medically necessary health care, powers and duties, **CC 3428**
    Punitive damages, notice, **CC 3296**
Destruction, medical records, **CC 56.101**
Disclosure,
    Domestic partnership, **CC 56.1007**
    Family, **CC 56.1007**
    Friends, **CC 56.1007**
    Genetic tests, **CC 56.17**
    Medical records, **CC 56.10 et seq.**
    Relatives, **CC 56.1007**
Domestic partnership, disclosure, **CC 56.1007**
Domestic violence, confidential or privileged information, **CC 56.107**
Faith healing, medically necessary health care, application of law, **CC 3428**
Family, disclosure, **CC 56.1007**
Fines and penalties,
    Genetic characteristics, disclosure, **CC 56.17**
    Medical records, negligence, release, **CC 56.36**
Friends, disclosure, **CC 56.1007**
Gender identity or expression, confidential or privileged information, **CC 56.107**
Genetic characteristics, disclosure, **CC 56.17**
Health care liens, **CC 3040**
Indemnity, medically necessary health care, **CC 3428**
Judgments and decrees, punitive damages, notice, **CC 3296**
Liens and incumbrances, **CC 3040**
Medical information, confidentiality, **CC 56 et seq.**
Medical records, **CC 56 et seq.**
    Disclosure, **CC 56.10 et seq.**
    Outpatient psychotherapy, **CC 56.104**
Medically necessary health care, powers and duties, **CC 3428**
Negligence,
    Medical records, **CC 56.36, 56.101**
    Medically necessary health care, powers and duties, **CC 3428**
Nominal damages, medical records, negligence, release, **CC 56.36**
Notice, punitive damages, **CC 3296**
Ordinary care standard, medically necessary health care, powers and duties, **CC 3428**
Outpatients, psychotherapy, records and recordation, **CC 56.104**
Privileges and immunities,
    Consultants, **CC 43.98**
    Medical records, **CC 56.14**
Punitive damages, notice, **CC 3296**

HEALTH CARE SERVICE PLANS—Cont'd
Records and recordation,
    Genetic tests, disclosure, **CC 56.17**
    Medical records, generally, ante
    Mental health, outpatient psychotherapy, **CC 56.104**
    Outpatient psychotherapy, **CC 56.104**
Relatives, disclosure, **CC 56.1007**
Release, medical records, **CC 56.11**
    Negligence, **CC 56.36**
Reproductive health, confidential or privileged information, **CC 56.107**
Social security, numbers and numbering, posting, **CC 1798.85**
Substantial harm, medically necessary health care, powers and duties, **CC 3428**
Torts, commercial blockade, **CC 3427 et seq.**

HEALTH CARE SERVICES DEPARTMENT
Social Services, generally, this index

HEALTH CLUBS
Health Studios, generally, this index

HEALTH FACILITIES
Access, commercial blockade, **CC 3427 et seq.**
Blockade, commercial blockade, **CC 3427 et seq.**
Clinics, generally, this index
Commercial blockade, **CC 3427 et seq.**
Confidential or privileged information, **CC 56 et seq.**
Damages, commercial blockade, **CC 3427.2**
Hospitals, generally, this index
Liens and incumbrances, emergency and ongoing medical or other services, accidents or wrongful acts, **CC 3045.1 et seq.**
Malpractice. Medical Malpractice, generally, this index
Medical information, disclosure, **CC 56 et seq.**
Medical Malpractice, generally, this index
Medical Records, generally, this index
Nurses, generally, this index
Nursing Homes, generally, this index
Orders of court, commercial blockade, **CC 3427.3**
Privileges and immunities, denial of staff privileges, **CC 43.97**
Records and recordation,
    Emergency personnel, disclosure, **CC 56.10**
    Medical Records, generally, this index
Torts, commercial blockade, **CC 3427 et seq.**

HEALTH INSURANCE
Administrators, medical records, disclosure, **CC 56.26**
Credit Life and Disability Insurance, generally, this index
Damages, punitive damages, notice, **CC 3296**
Disclosure,
    Genetic characteristics, **CC 56.265**
    Medical records, **CC 56.265**

HEALTH

HEALTH INSURANCE—Cont'd
Genetic characteristics, disclosure, CC 56.265
Health care liens, CC 3040
Health Care Service Plans, generally, this index
Identification cards, RFID (radio frequency identification), crimes and offenses, CC 1798.79, 1798.795
Liens and incumbrances, CC 3040
Medical records, disclosure, CC 56.10, 56.15, 56.27, 56.265
Notice, punitive damages, CC 3296
Punitive damages, notice, CC 3296
Records and recordation. Medical records, generally, ante
Third parties, administrators, medical records, disclosure, CC 56.26

HEALTH MAINTENANCE ORGANIZATIONS
Health Care Service Plans, generally, this index

HEALTH STUDIOS
Generally, CC 1812.80 et seq.
Assignment, contracts, CC 1812.88
Attorney fees, contract violations, CC 1812.94
Bonds (officers and fiduciaries), refunds, contracts, cancellation, new facilities, CC 1812.96
Cancellation of contracts, CC 1812.85
Contracts, CC 1812.80 et seq.
Damages, CC 1812.94
Death of member, estate contract liabilities, CC 1812.89
Disability of member, contract liability, CC 1812.89
Fees for services, limitations, CC 1812.86
Fraud, CC 1812.92
Leases, notice, anabolic steroids, testosterone or human growth hormone, crimes, CC 1812.97
Refunds, contracts, cancellation, CC 1812.85
    New facilities, CC 1812.96
Time,
    Cancellation of contracts, CC 1812.85
    Contract duration, CC 1812.84
Transfer of contract from facility to facility, CC 1812.89
Trusts and trustees, accounts and accounting, new facilities, CC 1812.96
Void contracts, noncompliance with law, CC 1812.91
Waiver, buyers rights, CC 1812.93
Weight loss contracts, CC 1694.5 et seq.

HEARING AIDS
Warranties, CC 1793.02, 1795.6

HEARING IMPAIRMENT
Deaf or Hard of Hearing Persons, generally, this index

HEART BALM STATUTE
Generally, CC 43.5

HEAT AND HEATING COMPANIES
See, also, Public Utilities, generally, this index
Community apartments, defects, disclosure, CC 1134
Condominiums, defects, disclosure, CC 1134
Consumer warranties, component parts, application of law, CC 1795.1
Easements, CC 801
Leases, cutting off public utilities with intent to terminate lease, damages, CC 789.3
Manufactured housing, warranties, CC 1797 et seq.
Stock cooperatives, defects, disclosure, CC 1134

HEIRS
Life tenant taking as purchasers, CC 779
Succession, generally, this index
Warranties, conveyances, CC 1115
Wills, generally, this index

HEMP
Cannabis. Drugs and Medicine, this index

HEREDITARY DISORDERS
Genetic diseases. Diseases, this index

HIGH SCHOOLS OR SECONDARY SCHOOLS
See, also, Schools and School Districts, generally, this index
Buildings and grounds. School Buildings and Grounds, generally, this index
Disabled persons, accessibility, buildings, CC 54.27
Grounds. School Buildings and Grounds, generally, this index
School Buildings and Grounds, generally, this index

HIGH WATER MARK
Boundary, CC 830

HIGHER EDUCATION
Colleges and Universities, generally, this index

HIGHWAY CARRIERS
Motor Carriers, generally, this index

HIGHWAY PATROL
See, also, Peace Officers, generally, this index
Discrimination, dogs, public accommodations, emergencies, CC 54.25
Dogs, discrimination, public accommodations, emergencies, CC 54.25
Fines and penalties, dogs, discrimination, public accommodations, emergencies, CC 54.25
Penalties, dogs, discrimination, public accommodations, emergencies, CC 54.25
Traffic Rules and Regulations, generally, this index

HIGHWAYS AND ROADS
See, also, Streets and Alleys, generally, this index
Advertisements. Outdoor Advertising, generally, this index
Bicycles, generally, this index
Billboards. Outdoor Advertising, generally, this index
Blind or visually impaired persons, civil rights, CC 54 et seq.
Boundaries, presumptions, CC 831
Deeds and conveyances, land bounded by, CC 1112
Disabled persons, civil rights, CC 54 et seq.
Expressways. Freeways, generally, this index
Freeways, generally, this index
Interstate highways,
    Billboards. Outdoor Advertising, generally, this index
    Outdoor Advertising, generally, this index
Outdoor Advertising, generally, this index
Private roads, repair, CC 845
Railroads, generally, this index
Rules and regulations. Traffic Rules and Regulations, generally, this index
Signs and signals. Outdoor Advertising, generally, this index
State highways,
    Freeways, generally, this index
    Outdoor Advertising, generally, this index
    Railroads, generally, this index
Title to property, conveyance of land bounded by highway, CC 1112
Traffic Rules and Regulations, generally, this index

HIKING
Personal injuries, entry on private land, negligence, CC 846

HIRE
Depositories, this index

HIRING PROPERTY
Landlord and Tenant, generally, this index
Leases, generally, this index

HISTORICAL LANDMARKS, MARKERS AND MONUMENTS
Water conservation, building standards, exemptions, CC 1101.7

HISTORY
Motor vehicles, vehicle history reports, CC 1784.1

HIV
Actions and proceedings, real estate, disclosure, CC 1710.2
Disclosure, real estate, actions and proceedings, CC 1710.2
Landlord and tenant, disclosure, actions and proceedings, CC 1710.2
Real estate, disclosure, actions and proceedings, CC 1710.2

HOMELESS

HIV—Cont'd
Workers compensation, medical records, disclosure, CC 56.31

HMO
Health Care Service Plans, generally, this index

HOLDEN CREDIT DENIAL DISCLOSURE ACT
Generally, CC 1787.1 et seq.

HOLDER
Installment Sales, this index

HOLIDAYS
Generally, CC 7
Banks and banking, Saturdays or optional bank holidays, business transactions, CC 7.1, 9
Business performed on next business day, CC 11
Business transacted on, banks, Saturdays or optional bank holidays, CC 9
Computation of time, CC 10
Contracts, performance on next business day, CC 11
Optional bank holidays, business transacted, CC 9
Orders of court, applications, CC 1008
Time, computation, CC 10

HOME EQUITY LOAN DISCLOSURE ACT
Generally, CC 2970, 2971

HOME EQUITY SALES CONTRACTS
Generally, CC 1695 et seq.
Actions and proceedings, CC 1695.7
Agents, equity purchasers, liability, CC 1695.15 et seq.
Arbitration and award, representatives, equity purchasers liability, CC 1695.16
Attorneys fees, CC 1695.7
  Rescission, unconscionable advantage, CC 1695.14
Bona fide purchaser, CC 1695.12
  Rescission, unconscionable advantage, CC 1695.14
Cancellation, CC 1695.4, 1695.14
  Notice, CC 1695.3, 1695.5
  Unconscionable advantage, CC 1695.14
Consideration, CC 1695.6
  Terms, CC 1695.3
Constitutionality, CC 1695.11
Contents, CC 1695.3
Costs, CC 1695.7
  Rescission, unconscionable advantage, CC 1695.14
Crimes and offenses, CC 1695.8
Damages, CC 1695.7
  Representatives, equity purchasers, CC 1695.15 et seq.
Deceit, crimes and offenses, CC 1695.8
Documents, execution, CC 1695.6

HOME EQUITY SALES CONTRACTS —Cont'd
Equitable relief, CC 1695.7
Equity purchaser, liability, representatives, CC 1695.15 et seq.
Execution of conveyance, CC 1695.6
Exemplary damages, CC 1695.7
Fines and penalties, CC 1695.7, 1695.8
Fraud, CC 1695.6, 1695.8
Incumbrances, CC 1695.6
Legislative intent, CC 1695
Liability, equity purchasers, representatives, CC 1695.15 et seq.
Liens and incumbrances, CC 1695.6
Limitation of liability, equity purchasers, representatives, CC 1695.16
Loans, CC 1695.12
Misleading statements, CC 1695.6
Misrepresentation, crimes and offenses, CC 1695.8
Names, rescission, unconscionable advantage, CC 1695.14
Notice,
  Cancellation,
    Form, CC 1695.5
    Terms, CC 1695.3
  Rescission, unconscionable advantage, CC 1695.14
Offenses, CC 1695.8
Officers and employees, equity purchasers, liability, CC 1695.15 et seq.
Option to repurchase, CC 1695.12
Penalties, CC 1695.7, 1695.8
Proceedings, CC 1695.7
Real estate brokers and salespersons, equity purchasers, liability, CC 1695.15 et seq.
Records and recordation, CC 1695.6
  Rescission, unconscionable advantage, CC 1695.14
Rental agreement, terms, CC 1695.3
Representatives, equity purchasers, liability, CC 1695.15 et seq.
Repurchase, CC 1695.12
Rescission. Cancellation, generally, ante
Right of rescission, CC 1695.4
Signatures, CC 1695.2
Terms, CC 1695.3
Time, cancellation, CC 1695.4
Unconscionable advantage, CC 1695.13
  Rescission, CC 1695.14
Unenforceable waivers, CC 1695.10
Voidability, unconscionable advantage, CC 1695.14
Waiver, CC 1695.10
Writing, requirement, CC 1695.2

HOME HEALTH AGENCIES
Advertisements, employment agencies, CC 1812.508
Employment agencies, advertisements, CC 1812.508

HOME IMPROVEMENT BUSINESS
Contractors, this index

HOME ROOF WARRANTIES
Generally, CC 1797.90 et seq.

HOME SOLICITATION CONTRACTS
Aged persons, primary residence, improvements, CC 1770
Application of law,
  Emergency repairs or services, CC 1689.13
  Rental purchase agreements, CC 1812.628
Cancellation, CC 1689.5 et seq.
  Emergency repairs or services, waiver, CC 1689.15
  Forms, CC 1689.7
Confession of judgment, public policy, CC 1689.12
Courses of instruction, application of law, CC 1689.5 et seq.
Delivery and care of goods, cancellation of contract, CC 1689.11
Disasters, residential repair or restoration, cancellation, CC 1689.6, 1689.7, 1689.14
Emergencies,
  Application of law, CC 1689.13
  Cancellation, CC 1689.6, 1689.7, 1689.14
    Waiver, CC 1689.15
  Waiver, cancellation, CC 1689.15
Fixtures, cancellation, CC 1689.9
Forms, cancellation, CC 1689.7
Home improvement goods or services, liens, CC 1689.8
Leases, application of law, CC 1689.5 et seq.
Liens and incumbrances, CC 1689.8
Medical care and treatment, personal emergency response units, CC 1689.6, 1689.7
Notice of cancellation, CC 1689.6
  Forms, CC 1689.7
Personal emergency response units, CC 1689.6, 1689.7
Real estate, fixtures, cancellation, CC 1689.9
Refunds, cancellation, CC 1689.10
Rental purchase agreements, application of law, CC 1812.628
Repairs, disasters, cancellation, CC 1689.6, 1689.7, 1689.14
Rescission, CC 1689.5 et seq.
Restoration, disasters, cancellation, CC 1689.6, 1689.7, 1689.14
Returns, cancellation, CC 1689.7
Spanish language, CC 1689.7
Time, cancellation, CC 1689.6
Waiver, CC 1689.12

HOMELAND SECURITY
War and Civil Defense, generally, this index

HOMELESS PERSONS
Abuse, transitional housing, misconduct, CC 1954.10 et seq.
Affidavits, transitional housing, misconduct, CC 1954.13

I-93

HOMELESS

HOMELESS PERSONS—Cont'd
Complaints, shelters, occupancy, **CC 1954.09**
Construction of laws, shelters, occupancy, **CC 1954.091**
Crimes and offenses, transitional housing, misconduct, injunctions, **CC 1954.14**
Evidence, transitional housing, misconduct, **CC 1954.13**
Force and violence, transitional housing, misconduct, **CC 1954.10 et seq.**
Grievances, shelters, occupancy, **CC 1954.09**
Holding over, landlord and tenant, **CC 1942.8**
Hotels and motels, occupancy, **CC 1954.08 et seq.**
Injunctions, transitional housing, misconduct, **CC 1954.10 et seq.**
Labor and employment, transitional housing, misconduct, **CC 1954.10 et seq.**
Landlord and tenant,
   Holding over, **CC 1942.8**
   Occupancy, hotels and motels, shelters, **CC 1954.08 et seq.**
Misconduct, transitional housing, **CC 1954.10 et seq.**
Notice, transitional housing, misconduct, injunctions, **CC 1954.13**
Occupancy, hotels and motels, shelters, **CC 1954.08 et seq.**
Petitions, transitional housing, misconduct, injunctions, **CC 1954.13**
Possession, transitional housing, misconduct, injunctions, **CC 1954.17, 1954.18**
Rent, holding over, **CC 1942.8**
Shelters, occupancy, **CC 1954.08 et seq.**
Show cause orders, transitional housing, misconduct, **CC 1954.13**
Temporary restraining orders, transitional housing, misconduct, **CC 1954.10 et seq.**
Termination, occupancy,
   Hotels and motels, **CC 1954.092**
   Shelters, **CC 1954.09**
Time, shelters, occupancy, **CC 1954.091**
Transitional housing, misconduct, **CC 1954.10 et seq.**

HOMEOWNER BILL OF RIGHTS
Generally, **CC 2923.4 et seq.**

HOMEOWNERS ASSOCIATIONS
Condominiums, this index

HOMES
Housing, generally, this index

HOMESTEADS
Contracts. Home Equity Sales Contracts, generally, this index
Foreclosure. Home Equity Sales Contracts, generally, this index
Home Equity Sales Contracts, generally, this index
Sales. Home Equity Sales Contracts, generally, this index

HOMICIDE
Exemplary damages, wrongful death, **CC 3294**
Wrongful death, actions and proceedings, exemplary damages, **CC 3294**

HORSEBACK RIDING
Private property owner, liability for injuries, **CC 846**

HORSES
   See, also, Animals, generally, this index
Auctions and auctioneers, notice, purchase for slaughter, prices, **CC 1834.8**
Liens and incumbrances, stallions, **CC 3062 et seq.**
Notice, public auction or sale, purchase for slaughter, prices, **CC 1834.8**
Prices, purchase for slaughter, public auction or sale, notice, **CC 1834.8**
Public auction or sale, notice, purchase for slaughter, prices, **CC 1834.8**
Sales, purchase for slaughter, prices, **CC 1834.8**

HORTICULTURE
Leases of land, duration, **CC 717**

HOSPICES
Access, commercial blockade, **CC 3427 et seq.**
Blockade, commercial blockade, **CC 3427 et seq.**
Commercial blockade, **CC 3427 et seq.**
Torts, commercial blockade, **CC 3427 et seq.**

HOSPITAL SERVICE PLANS
Health Care Service Plans, generally, this index

HOSPITALS
   See, also, Health Facilities, generally, this index
Abandoned property, sale, **CC 1862.5**
Access, commercial blockade, **CC 3427 et seq.**
Accident and health insurance. Health Insurance, generally, this index
Actions and proceedings, lien, enforcing, **CC 3045.5**
Ambulances, generally, this index
Auction sale, unclaimed property, **CC 1862.5**
Bailment, **CC 1859 et seq.**
Blind or visually impaired persons, access, **CC 54 et seq.**
Blockade, commercial blockade, **CC 3427 et seq.**
Civil defense activities, temporary annexes, liability, **CC 1714.5**
Collection agencies,
   Complaints, **CC 1788.185**
   Notice, **CC 1788.14, 1788.52**
Collections,
   Complaints, **CC 1788.58, 1788.185**
   Notice, **CC 1788.14, 1788.52**
Commercial blockade, **CC 3427 et seq.**

HOSPITALS—Cont'd
Confidential or privileged information, **CC 56 et seq.**
   Collections, complaints, **CC 1788.58, 1788.185**
Damages,
   Children and minors, willful misconduct, **CC 1714.1**
   Staff privileges, denial, **CC 43.97**
Debtors and creditors,
   Complaints, **CC 1788.58, 1788.185**
   Notice, **CC 1788.14, 1788.52**
Drugs and Medicine, generally, this index
Emergencies,
   Liens, medical services rendered for injury caused by accident or wrongful act, **CC 3045.1 et seq.**
   Tort liability, **CC 1714.5**
Expenses and expenditures,
   Imputed liability of parents for acts of children, **CC 1714.1**
   Willful misconduct of children, imputed liability of parent or guardian, **CC 1714.1**
Health Insurance, generally, this index
Immunity. Privileges and immunities, generally, post
Liens and incumbrances, medical services rendered due to accident or wrongful act, **CC 3045.1 et seq.**
Limitation of actions, liens, enforcement, **CC 3045.5**
Medical information, disclosure, **CC 56 et seq.**
Medical Malpractice, generally, this index
Medical Records, generally, this index
Medicine. Drugs and Medicine, generally, this index
Negligence. Medical Malpractice, generally, this index
Notice, lien, emergency services rendered, **CC 3045.3**
Nurses, generally, this index
Officers and employees, privileges and immunities, denial, damages, **CC 43.97**
Personal property,
   Fireproof safe, notice of nonliability, **CC 1860**
   Injury or loss, **CC 1859**
   Unclaimed, sale, **CC 1862.5**
Privileged information. Confidential or privileged information, generally, ante
Privileges and immunities,
   Denial, staff privileges, **CC 43.97**
   Medical staff, committees, **CC 43.7, 43.8**
Professional negligence. Medical Malpractice, generally, this index
Records and recordation,
   Confidential or privileged information, generally, ante
   Medical Records, generally, this index
Sales, unclaimed personal property, **CC 1862.5**
Sanitariums, generally, this index

HOUSING

HOSPITALS—Cont'd
Torts, commercial blockade, **CC 3427 et seq.**
Unclaimed property, sale, **CC 1862.5**

HOTELS AND MOTELS
See, also, Housing, generally, this index
Attorney fees, short term occupancies, **CC 1940.1**
Baggage,
　Injury or loss, **CC 1859**
　Liens and incumbrances, writs of possession, **CC 1861 et seq.**
Bailment, **CC 1859 et seq.**
Bed and Breakfast Inns, generally, this index
Blind or visually impaired persons,
　Access to public accommodations, **CC 54 et seq.**
　Civil rights, **CC 54.1**
　Touch screen devices, **CC 54.9**
Boarding and Lodging Houses, generally, this index
Children and minors, **CC 1865**
Civil Rights Act, **CC 51 et seq.**
Damages,
　Children and minors, **CC 1865**
　Guide dogs accompanying blind person or trainer, **CC 54.2**
　Innkeepers liens, wrongful possession of property, **CC 1861.15**
Deaf or hard of hearing persons, public accommodations, **CC 54.1 et seq.**
Eviction, guests, checkout time, **CC 1865**
Evidence, presumptions, short term occupancy, **CC 1940.1**
Fines and penalties,
　Excessive charges, **CC 1863**
　Human trafficking, sex offenses, **CC 52.65**
　Short term occupancies, **CC 1940.1**
Forcible entry and detainer, guests, checkout time, **CC 1865**
Forfeitures, rates, failure to post, **CC 1863**
Guests, eviction, checkout time, **CC 1865**
Guide dogs, accompanying blind persons for training purposes, access to public accommodations, **CC 54.1 et seq.**
Homeless persons, occupancy, **CC 1954.08 et seq.**
Human trafficking, sex offenses, fines and penalties, **CC 52.65**
Injunction,
　Disabled persons, denial of access to public accommodations, **CC 55**
　Innkeepers liens, writs of possession, **CC 1861.16, 1861.17**
Inspections and inspectors, short term occupancy, **CC 1940.1**
Liens and incumbrances, **CC 1861 et seq.**
Moving or checking out, short term occupancies, **CC 1940.1**
Notice,
　Guests, eviction, checkout time, **CC 1865**
　Liens and incumbrances, writs of possession, **CC 1861.8**

HOTELS AND MOTELS—Cont'd
Overcharges for use of facilities, notice, fines and penalties, **CC 1863**
Penalties. Fines and penalties, generally, ante
Personal property,
　Fireproof safe, notice of nonliability, **CC 1860**
　Injury or loss, **CC 1859**
　Liens, **CC 1861 et seq.**
Pest Control, generally, this index
Possession, writs of possession, innkeepers liens, **CC 1861 et seq.**
Presumptions, short term occupancy, evidence, **CC 1940.1**
Privacy, **CC 53.5**
Process, service of process, innkeepers liens, writs of possession, **CC 1861.18**
Property,
　Injury or loss, **CC 1859**
　Liens and incumbrances, writs of possession, **CC 1861 et seq.**
Rates and charges,
　Children and minors, **CC 1865**
　Posting, **CC 1863**
Records and recordation, short term occupancy, **CC 1940.1**
Reports, short term occupancy, **CC 1940.1**
Sales, innkeepers liens, **CC 1861.24**
Service of process, innkeepers liens, writs of possession, **CC 1861.18**
Sex discrimination, **CC 51 et seq.**
Sex offenses, human trafficking, fines and penalties, **CC 52.65**
Short term occupancies, moving or checking out, **CC 1940.1**
Touch screen devices, blind or visually impaired persons, **CC 54.9**
Visually impaired persons. Blind or visually impaired persons, generally, ante
Waiver, innkeepers liens, writs of possession, **CC 1861.13**
Writs of possession, innkeepers liens, **CC 1861 et seq.**

HOUSE CATS
Cats, generally, this index

HOUSE TRAILERS
Mobilehomes and Mobilehome Parks, generally, this index

HOUSEBOATS
Floating Homes, generally, this index

HOUSEHOLD APPLIANCES
Song Beverly Consumer Warranty Act, **CC 1790 et seq.**

HOUSEHOLD GOODS
Furniture, generally, this index

HOUSEKEEPERS
Domestic Workers, generally, this index

HOUSING
See, also, Buildings, generally, this index

HOUSING—Cont'd
Accessory dwelling units, covenants, **CC 714.3**
Actions and proceedings, construction defects, **CC 895 et seq.**
Affordable housing. Low and Moderate Income Housing, generally, this index
Age,
　Discrimination, **CC 51.2**
　Intergenerational housing developments, **CC 51.3.5**
　Restrictions, **CC 51.3**
Aged Persons, this index
Ancestry. Discrimination, generally, post
Apartment Houses, generally, this index
Applications, COVID 19, indebtedness, **CC 1785.20.4**
Appreciation, shared appreciation loans for seniors, **CC 1917.320 et seq.**
Assignment or purchase, indebtedness, COVID 19, low and moderate income housing, **CC 1788.66**
Assistance. Low and Moderate Income Housing, generally, this index
Blind or Visually Impaired Persons, this index
Boarding and Lodging Houses, generally, this index
Boats and boating. Floating Homes, generally, this index
Community Development and Housing, generally, this index
Condominiums, generally, this index
Construction,
　Aged persons, physical and social needs, **CC 51.2**
　Contracts, indemnity, **CC 2782 et seq.**
　Indemnity, contracts, **CC 2782 et seq.**
　Lender, liability for defects, **CC 3434**
　Manufactured housing, generally, post
　Warranties, exemptions, **CC 1793.2**
　Wrap up policies, insurance, contracts, indemnity, **CC 2782.9 et seq.**
Construction defects. Buildings, this index
Contractors, generally, this index
Contracts,
　Construction, indemnity, **CC 2782 et seq.**
　Hazardous substances and waste, pipelines, disclosure, **CC 2079.10.5**
　Home roof warranties, **CC 1797.90 et seq.**
　Oil and gas pipelines, disclosure, **CC 2079.10.5**
Cooperative Apartments, generally, this index
County low rent housing. Discrimination, generally, post
Covenants, accessory dwelling units, **CC 714.3**
COVID 19, indebtedness, screening, **CC 1785.20.4**
Deaf persons, public accommodations, **CC 54.1 et seq.**
Deeds and conveyances,
　Covenants, low and moderate income housing, modification or change, **CC 714.6**

I-95

HOUSING

HOUSING—Cont'd
Deeds and conveyances—Cont'd
  Floor area ratio standards, covenants, housing development projects, **CC 4747**
Deeds of trust. Trust Deeds, generally, this index
Defects, construction defects, **CC 895 et seq.**
Development projects, floor area ratio standards, deeds and conveyances, restrictions, **CC 4747**
Disabled Persons, this index
Disclosure, oil and gas pipelines, sales, **CC 2079.10.5**
Discrimination, **CC 51.2 et seq.**
  Age, businesses selling or renting housing, **CC 51.2**
  Blind or visually impaired persons, **CC 54.1 et seq.**
  Disabled persons, **CC 54.1**
    Injunction, **CC 55**
  Injunction, disabled persons, **CC 55**
  Riverside County, aged persons, **CC 51.10 et seq.**
  Exemptions, **CC 51.2 et seq.**
Dogs, disabled persons, **CC 54.1**
Equity loans, reverse mortgages, **CC 1923 et seq.**
  Translations, **CC 1632**
Exemptions,
  Construction, warranties, **CC 1793.2**
  Warranties, construction, **CC 1793.2**
Factory built housing. Manufactured housing, generally, post
Familial status. Discrimination, generally, ante
Floating Homes, generally, this index
Floor area ratio standards, development projects, deeds and conveyances, restrictions, **CC 4747**
Forcible entry and detainer, owner occupied dwellings, lodgers, **CC 1946.5**
Foreign languages, contracts, translations, **CC 1632**
Fraud, construction or repair, defects, construction lenders, liability, **CC 3434**
General contractors. Contractors, this index
Hazardous substances and waste, pipelines, sales, disclosure, **CC 2079.10.5**
Home Equity Sales Contracts, generally, this index
Homeless Persons, generally, this index
Hotels and Motels, generally, this index
Indebtedness, COVID 19, screening, **CC 1785.20.4**
Indemnity, construction, contracts, **CC 2782 et seq.**
Indigent persons,
  Homeless Persons, generally, this index
  Low and Moderate Income Housing, generally, this index
Injunction, disabled persons, discrimination, **CC 55**
Installment sales, **CC 1801.4**

HOUSING—Cont'd
Intergenerational housing developments, **CC 51.3.5**
Loans,
  Assumption of loans, limitations, **CC 711.5**
  Construction or repair, lenders liability for defects, **CC 3434**
  Equity loans, reverse mortgages, **CC 1923 et seq.**
    Translations, **CC 1632**
  Interest, assumption of loans, **CC 711.5**
  Mortgages, generally, this index
  Reverse mortgages, **CC 1923 et seq.**
    Translations, **CC 1632**
  Shared appreciation loans, **CC 1917 et seq.**
Low and Moderate Income Housing, generally, this index
Manufactured housing,
  Conditions of ownership, real estate covenants, **CC 714.5**
  Contractors, warranties, **CC 1797.2**
  Costs, energy rating program, information, **CC 2079.11**
  Covenants restricting, **CC 714.5**
  Dealers, warranties, **CC 1797 et seq.**
  Defects, warranties, **CC 1797 et seq.**
  Disclosure, resale, **CC 1102 et seq.**
  Documents, written warranties, **CC 1797.3**
  Energy conservation, information, **CC 2079.10, 2079.11**
  Hazards, natural hazards, disclosure, **CC 1103 et seq.**
  Heat and heating, warranties, **CC 1797.3**
  Liens and incumbrances, application of law, **CC 3051, 3067.2**
  Mobilehomes and Mobilehome Parks, generally, this index
  Natural hazards, disclosure, **CC 1103 et seq.**
  Notice, buyers, substantial defects, notice, **CC 1797.3**
  Plumbers and plumbing, warranties, **CC 1797.3**
  Real estate brokers and salespersons, **CC 2079 et seq.**
  Records and recordation, warranties, **CC 1797.6**
  Recreational Vehicles, generally, this index
  Repair, warranties, sales, **CC 1797.3**
  Resale, disclosures, **CC 1102 et seq.**
  Restrictive covenants against, **CC 714.5**
  Roof warranties, **CC 1797.90 et seq.**
  Sales,
    Disclosure, **CC 1102 et seq.**
    Home energy rating program, information, **CC 2079.10**
    Warranties, **CC 1797 et seq.**
  School facilities fees, **CC 798.82, 799.8**
  Special Occupancy Parks, generally, this index
  Warranties, **CC 1797 et seq.**

HOUSING—Cont'd
Marinas, floating home residency, **CC 800 et seq.**
Marital status. Discrimination, generally, ante
Mobilehomes and Mobilehome Parks, generally, this index
Moderate income housing. Low and Moderate Income Housing, generally, this index
Modification or change, low and moderate income housing, covenants, **CC 714.6**
Modular housing. Manufactured housing, generally, ante
Mortgages, generally, this index
Motels. Hotels and Motels, generally, this index
Multifamily housing,
  Aged persons, cohabitants, age, covenants, conditions, restrictions, **CC 51.3**
  Mortgages, political subdivisions, sales, postponement, **CC 2924f**
  Trust deeds, political subdivisions, sales, postponement, **CC 2924f**
National origin. Discrimination, generally, ante
Negligence, construction or repair, loans, lenders liability defects, **CC 3434**
Notice,
  Hazardous substances and waste, pipelines, disclosure, **CC 2079.10.5**
  Oil and gas pipelines, disclosure, **CC 2079.10.5**
  Owner occupied dwellings, lodgers, eviction, **CC 1946.5**
  Transfer of mortgage or trust deed, **CC 2937**
Oil and gas pipelines, sales, disclosure, **CC 2079.10.5**
Ordinances, rent control, **CC 1947.7 et seq.**
Owner occupied single family dwellings, eviction, lodgers, **CC 1946.5**
Pest Control, generally, this index
Planned Unit Developments, generally, this index
Prefabricated housing. Manufactured housing, generally, ante
Public housing. Low and Moderate Income Housing, generally, this index
Race. Discrimination, generally, ante
Rehabilitation, loans, assumption of loans, limitations, **CC 711.5**
Religion. Discrimination, generally, ante
Rent, control,
  Confidential or privileged information, **CC 1947.7**
  Ordinances, **CC 1947.7 et seq.**
Rental housing. Apartment Houses, generally, this index
Repairs, loans, liability for defects, **CC 3434**
Reverse mortgages, **CC 1923 et seq.**
  Translations, **CC 1632**
Roof warranties, **CC 1797.90 et seq.**
Sale or lease, document fees, **CC 1097**
Sales,
  Age discrimination, **CC 51.2**

IDENTITY

HOUSING—Cont'd
Sales—Cont'd
Hazardous substances and waste, pipelines, disclosure, **CC 2079.10.5**
Home Equity Sales Contracts, generally, this index
Manufactured housing, ante
Oil and gas pipelines, disclosure, **CC 2079.10.5**
Screening, COVID 19, indebtedness, **CC 1785.20.4**
Service dogs, disabled persons, **CC 54.1**
Sex. Discrimination, generally, ante
Shared appreciation loans, **CC 1917 et seq.**
Seniors, **CC 1917.320 et seq.**
Signal dogs, deaf and hearing impaired persons, **CC 54.1**
Source of income. Discrimination, generally, ante
Spanish language, contracts, translations, **CC 1632**
Standards, floor area ratio standards, development projects, deeds and conveyances, **CC 4747**
State aid,
Loans, assumption of loans, limitations, **CC 711.5**
Low and Moderate Income Housing, generally, this index
Students. Discrimination, generally, ante
Subcontractors, construction, indemnity, **CC 2782 et seq.**
Wrap up policies, insurance, **CC 2782.9 et seq.**
Subdivided Lands, generally, this index
Supplemental tax assessments. Tax Assessments, this index
Supportive housing. Low and Moderate Income Housing, generally, this index
Transfers, mortgages, notice, **CC 2937**
Translations, foreign languages, contracts, **CC 1632**
Trust Deeds, generally, this index
Very low income housing. Low and Moderate Income Housing, generally, this index
Warranties,
Construction defects, **CC 896 et seq.**
Roofs, **CC 1797.90 et seq.**
Water conservation, information, **CC 2079.10**
Wrap up policies, insurance, construction, contracts, indemnity, **CC 2782.9 et seq.**

HOUSING AND COMMUNITY DEVELOPMENT DEPARTMENT
Mobilehomes and Mobilehome Parks, generally, this index

HOUSING FINANCE AGENCY
Low and Moderate Income Housing, generally, this index
Mortgages, insurance, cancellation, conditions of extension of credit, **CC 2954.7**

HUMAN CHORIONIC GONADOTROPIN
Drugs and Medicine, generally, this index

HUMAN GROWTH HORMONE
Athletic facilities, leases, notice, crimes, **CC 1812.97**

HUMAN IMMUNODEFICIENCY VIRUS
HIV, generally, this index

HUMAN RIGHTS
Civil Rights, generally, this index

HUMAN TRAFFICKING
Actions and proceedings, **CC 52.5**
Attorney fees, injunction, **CC 3496**
Business and commerce, notice, **CC 52.6**
Contracts, compensation and salaries, deductions, illegal contracts, **CC 1670.7**
Costs, injunction, **CC 3496**
Disclosure, retailers, **CC 1714.43**
Fines and penalties,
Business and commerce, notice, **CC 52.6**
Hotels and motels, sex offenses, **CC 52.65**
Hotels and motels, sex offenses, fines and penalties, **CC 52.65**
Injunction, **CC 52.5**
Attorney fees, **CC 3496**
Landlord and tenant,
Emergency services, law enforcement, **CC 1946.8**
Termination, notice, **CC 1946.7**
Limitation of actions, **CC 52.5**
Manufacturers and manufacturing, disclosure, **CC 1714.43**
Notice, business and commerce, **CC 52.6**
Posting, business and commerce, **CC 52.6**
Restitution, **CC 52.5**
Retailers, disclosure, **CC 1714.43**
Sex offenses, hotels and motels, fines and penalties, **CC 52.65**
Statute of limitations, **CC 52.5**
Training, business and commerce, **CC 52.6**

HUMBOLDT STATE COLLEGE
Colleges and Universities, generally, this index

HUNTERS AND HUNTING
Fish and Game, generally, this index

HURRICANES
Home solicitation contracts, residential repair or restoration, cancellation, **CC 1689.6, 1689.7, 1689.14**
Shelters, tort liability, **CC 1714.5**

HUSBANDS
Marriage, generally, this index

HYDROCARBON SUBSTANCES
Oil and Gas, generally, this index

HYPOTHECATION
Bottomry, generally, this index
Pledges, generally, this index
Respondentia, generally, this index

ICE AND SNOW
Easement maintenance, snow removal, **CC 845**

IDENTIFICATION CARDS
Check cashers, fees, issuance, **CC 1789.30**
Colleges and universities, RFID (radio frequency identification), crimes and offenses, **CC 1798.79, 1798.795**
Libraries, RFID (radio frequency identification), crimes and offenses, **CC 1798.79, 1798.795**
Motor Vehicles, this index
Numbers and numbering, social security, **CC 1798.85**
Radio frequency identification, crimes and offenses, **CC 1798.79, 1798.795**
RFID (radio frequency identification), crimes and offenses, **CC 1798.79, 1798.795**
Skimming, radio frequency identification, crimes and offenses, **CC 1798.79, 1798.795**
Social security, numbers and numbering, **CC 1798.85**

IDENTITY AND IDENTIFICATION
Actions and proceedings,
Acknowledgments, **CC 1185**
Subcutaneous implantation, **CC 52.7**
Theft, **CC 1798.93**
Ambulances, contractors, **CC 3273**
Attorney fees,
Subcutaneous implantation, **CC 52.7**
Theft, **CC 1798.93**
Cards. Identification Cards, generally, this index
Check cashers, **CC 1789.30, 1789.32**
Commercial credit reporting agencies, identity of sources, protection, **CC 1785.43**
Consumer Credit Reporting Agencies, this index
Contracts, parties, **CC 1558**
Corporations, theft, filing, **CC 1798.200 et seq.**
Credit Cards, this index
Crimes and offenses. Theft, generally, post
Devices, subcutaneous implantation, **CC 52.7**
Emergency medical technicians, contractors, **CC 3273**
Financial institutions, theft, filing, **CC 1798.200 et seq.**
Fines and penalties, subcutaneous identification devices, **CC 52.7**
Fires and fire protection, contractors, **CC 3273**
Guide dog trainers, public accommodations, **CC 54.1, 54.2**
Injunction,
Subcutaneous implantation, **CC 52.7**
Theft, **CC 1798.93**
Installment sales, goods and services, monthly statements, **CC 1810.3**
Jails, acknowledgments, **CC 1185**
Labor and Employment, this index
Landlord and tenant, multiunit dwellings, disclosures, **CC 1961 et seq.**
Mechanical or electrical devices or appliances, sale with mark or number altered or removed, **CC 1710.1**

I-97

IDENTITY

IDENTITY AND IDENTIFICATION—Cont'd

Mistake, default judgments, vacating or setting aside, **CC 1788.61**

Mortgages, unpaid balances, statements, **CC 2943**

Motor Vehicles, this index

Orders of court, theft, business entities, filing, **CC 1798.202**

Personal Information, generally, this index

Public accommodations, guide dog trainers, **CC 54.1, 54.2**

Public agencies, contractors, **CC 3273**

Radio frequency identification, theft, **CC 1798.79, 1798.795**

Rescue, contractors, **CC 3273**

RFID (radio frequency identification), theft, **CC 1798.79, 1798.795**

Show cause orders, theft, business entities, filing, **CC 1788.201**

Skimming, radio frequency identification, theft, **CC 1798.79, 1798.795**

Subcutaneous implantation, devices, **CC 52.7**

Theft, **CC 1798.92 et seq.**
  Collection agencies, **CC 1785.16.2, 1788.18**
  Condominiums, homeowners associations, records and recordation, inspection and inspectors, **CC 5215**
  Consumer Credit Reporting Agencies, this index
  Credit, **CC 1785.20.3**
  Credit cards, **CC 1785.20.3**
    Disclosure, **CC 1748.95**
  Debtors and creditors,
    Collection agencies, **CC 1788.18**
    Sales, **CC 1785.16.2**
  Default judgments, vacating or setting aside, **CC 1788.61**
  Financial institutions, filing, **CC 1798.200 et seq.**
  Fines and penalties, RFID (radio frequency identification), **CC 1798.79**
  Insurance, filing, **CC 1798.200 et seq.**
  Loans, **CC 1785.20.3**
  Orders of court, business entities, filing, **CC 1798.202**
  Radio frequency identification, **CC 1798.79, 1798.795**
  RFID (radio frequency identification), **CC 1798.79, 1798.795**
  Show cause orders, business entities, filing, **CC 1798.201**
  Skimming, radio frequency identification, **CC 1798.79, 1798.795**

Trainers, guide dog trainers and public accommodations, **CC 54.1, 54.2**

Trust deeds, unpaid balances, statements, **CC 2943**

ILLNESS
See, also,
  Diseases, generally, this index
  Health Facilities, generally, this index

ILLNESS—Cont'd

Debit cards, liability, **CC 1748.31**

Health Insurance, generally, this index

Telecommunications, emergency messages, priorities and preferences, **CC 2207**

IMMIGRATION

See, also, Noncitizens, generally, this index

Children and minors, evidence, **CC 3339.5**

Civil rights, **CC 51**
  Labor and employment, **CC 3339**

Consumer protection, **CC 3339**

Contracts, compensation and salaries, deductions, illegal contracts, **CC 1670.7**

Discovery, **CC 3339**
  Children and minors, **CC 3339.5**

Evidence,
  Children and minors, status, **CC 3339.5**
  Status, **CC 3339.5**

Labor and employment, **CC 3339**

Landlord and Tenant, this index

Liability, children and minors, status, evidence, **CC 3339.5**

Protection, labor and employment, **CC 3339**

Remedies,
  Children and minors, status, evidence, **CC 3339.5**
  Labor and employment, **CC 3339**

Rights, civil rights, labor and employment, **CC 3339**

Unauthorized immigration. Noncitizens, generally, this index

IMMORAL CONDUCT

Lewdness and Obscenity, generally, this index

IMMORALITY

Lewdness and Obscenity, generally, this index

IMMUNITIES

Privileges and Immunities, generally, this index

IMPLEMENTS

Machinery and Equipment, generally, this index

IMPLEMENTS OF HUSBANDRY

Agricultural Machinery and Equipment, generally, this index

IMPORTS

Exports and Imports, generally, this index

IMPOTENCY

Libel and slander, false imputation, **CC 46**

IMPOUND ACCOUNTS

Mortgages, this index

IMPRISONMENT

Correctional Institutions, generally, this index

Crimes and Offenses, generally, this index

Fines and Penalties, generally, this index

IMPROVEMENTS

Actions and proceedings,
  Design professionals, **CC 3320**
  Prime design professionals, disputes with subconsultants, **CC 3321**

Attorney fees,
  Design professionals, **CC 3320**
  Prime design professionals, disputes with subconsultants, **CC 3321**

Condominiums, this index

Contracts, design professionals,
  Private improvements, late payment penalty, **CC 3319**
  Public improvements, late payment penalty, **CC 3320**

Costs,
  Design professionals, **CC 3320**
  Prime design professionals, disputes with subconsultants, **CC 3321**

Design professionals,
  Private improvements, late payment penalty, **CC 3319**
  Public improvements, late payment penalty, **CC 3320**

Liens and incumbrances,
  Extinguishment by lapse of time, **CC 2911**
  Mechanics Liens, generally, this index

Malicious destruction of property, actions, construction sites, treble damages, **CC 1721**

Mechanics Liens, generally, this index

Prime design professionals, **CC 3320**
  Subconsultants, payment, **CC 3321**

Shared appreciation loans, seniors, **CC 1917.510, 1917.511**

Subconsultants, prime design professionals, payment, **CC 3321**

Vandalism, actions, treble damages, **CC 1721**

Visible improvements on or across private lands by governmental entity expending public funds, **CC 1009**

Water conservation, building standards, **CC 1101.1 et seq.**

IMPUTED LIABILITY

Parents, acts of children, **CC 1714.1**

IN CAMERA PROCEEDINGS

Trade secrets, misappropriation, **CC 3426.5**

INCENTIVES

Consumers, privacy, **CC 1798.125**

INCLOSURES

Fences, generally, this index

INCOME

Accumulations, **CC 722 et seq.**

Legal Estates Principal and Income Law, **CC 731 et seq.**

Principal, Legal Estates Principal and Income Law, **CC 731 et seq.**

INCOME TAX—FEDERAL

Bookkeeping services, confidential or privileged information, **CC 1799.1a**

INCOME TAX—FEDERAL—Cont'd

Business records, bookkeeping services, confidential or privileged information, **CC 1799.1a**

Confidential or privileged information, bookkeeping services, **CC 1799.1a**

Legal Estates Principal and Income Law, **CC 731 et seq.**

Mobilehomes and mobilehome parks, returns, credit rating, **CC 798.74**

Mortgages, interest paid, statement to mortgagor, **CC 2954.2**

INCOME TAX—STATE

Bookkeeping services, confidential or privileged information, **CC 1799.1a**

Business records, bookkeeping services, confidential or privileged information, **CC 1799.1a**

Confidential or privileged information, bookkeeping services, **CC 1799.1a**

Corporation Taxes, generally, this index

Information returns, check cashers, **CC 1789.30**

Mortgages, interest paid, statement to mortgagor, **CC 2954.2**

Returns, mobilehomes and mobilehome parks, credit rating, **CC 798.74**

INCORPORATED TOWNS

Municipalities, generally, this index

INCORRIGIBLE CHILDREN

Juvenile Delinquents and Dependents, generally, this index

INCUMBRANCES

Liens and Incumbrances, generally, this index

INDEBTEDNESS

See, also, Debtors and Creditors, generally, this index

Adults, abuse, duress or coercion, **CC 1798.97.1 et seq.**

Aged persons, abuse, duress or coercion, **CC 1798.97.1 et seq.**

Application of law, duress or coercion, **CC 1798.97.5**

Attorney fees, duress or coercion, **CC 1798.97.2, 1798.97.3**

Bankruptcy, generally, this index

Burden of proof, duress or coercion, **CC 1798.97.3**

Cards, debit cards, **CC 1748.30, 1748.31**

Certificates and certification, duress or coercion, **CC 1798.97.1**

Collection Agencies, generally, this index

Compromise and settlement, payment processors, fair debt settlement, **CC 1788.300 et seq.**

Construction of laws, duress or coercion, **CC 1798.97.4**

Costs, duress or coercion, **CC 1798.97.2, 1798.97.3**

INDEBTEDNESS—Cont'd

COVID 19, housing, screening, **CC 1785.20.4**

Crime victims, duress or coercion, **CC 1798.97.1 et seq.**

Cross complaints, duress or coercion, **CC 1798.97.5**

Damages, duress or coercion, **CC 1798.97.2**

Debit cards, **CC 1748.30, 1748.31**

Debt settlement providers, fair debt settlement, **CC 1788.300 et seq.**

Declaratory judgments and decrees, duress or coercion, **CC 1798.97.3**

Dismissal and nonsuit, duress or coercion, **CC 1798.97.3**

Domestic violence, duress or coercion, **CC 1798.97.1 et seq.**

Duress or coercion, **CC 1798.97.1 et seq.**

Exemptions, duress or coercion, **CC 1798.97.4**

Forms, duress or coercion, certificates and certification, **CC 1798.97.1**

Foster care, duress or coercion, **CC 1798.97.1 et seq.**

Housing, COVID 19, screening, **CC 1785.20.4**

Injunctions, duress or coercion, **CC 1798.97.3**

Insolvency, generally, this index

Limitation of actions, duress or coercion, **CC 1798.97.2, 1798.97.3**

Notice, duress or coercion, **CC 1798.97.2**

Payment processors, fair debt settlement, **CC 1788.300 et seq.**

Presumptions, duress or coercion, **CC 1798.97.2**

INDECENCY

Lewdness and Obscenity, generally, this index

INDEMNITY

See, also, Suretyship and Guaranty, generally, this index

Generally, **CC 2772 et seq.**

Agents, **CC 2775**

Carriers, public policy, **CC 2784.5**

Cartage contract, **CC 2784.5**

Conflict of laws, construction, contracts, **CC 2782.05**

Construction contracts, **CC 2782 et seq.**

Costs, **CC 2778**

Coterminous land owners, construction contracts, **CC 2782.1**

Defending actions, **CC 2778**

Engineers, construction contracts, **CC 2782.2**

Future Wrongful Act, validity, **CC 2773**

Housing, construction, contracts, **CC 2782 et seq.**

Interpretation of contract, **CC 2778**

Joint liability, **CC 2777**

Motor carriers, **CC 2784.5**

Notice, defense of actions, **CC 2778**

Oil and gas pipelines, spills, **CC 3333.5**

Past wrongful act, validity, **CC 2774**

Presumptions, **CC 2778**

Public policy,
Carriers, **CC 2784.5**

INDEMNITY—Cont'd

Public policy—Cont'd
Construction contracts, **CC 2782**

Real estate brokers and salespersons, agency contracts, modification or alteration, **CC 2079.23**

Reimbursement of person indemnifying, **CC 2779**

Retail seller against manufacturer, consumer sales, **CC 1792**

Rules of interpretation, **CC 2778**

Separate liability, **CC 2777**

Several persons, application, **CC 2776**

Solar energy, systems, **CC 714.1**

Subcontractors, housing, construction, **CC 2782 et seq.**

Subrogation, generally, this index

Sureties, **CC 2824**

Trucking contracts, indemnity provisions, **CC 2784.5**

Wrongful acts, **CC 2773, 2774**

INDEPENDENT WHOLESALE SALES REPRESENTATIVES CONTRACTUAL RELATIONS ACT OF 1990

Generally, **CC 1738.10 et seq.**

INDIAN HEMP

Cannabis. Drugs and Medicine, this index

INDIANS

Indigenous Peoples, generally, this index

INDICTMENT AND INFORMATION

Consumer credit reporting agencies, **CC 1786.18**

Contents of records, **CC 1785.13**

Labor and employment, records and recordation, copies, **CC 1786.53**

Nuisance, public, remedy against, **CC 3491, 3492**

INDIGENOUS PEOPLES

Conservation, easements, **CC 815.3**

Easements, greenways, **CC 816.50 et seq.**

Greenways, easements, **CC 816.50 et seq.**

INDIGENT PERSONS

Accumulations, disposition of funds, **CC 726**

Assistance. Social Services, generally, this index

County health facilities. Health Facilities, generally, this index

Health Facilities, generally, this index

Homeless Persons, generally, this index

Medi Cal Program, generally, this index

Social Services, generally, this index

INDUSTRIAL ACCIDENTS

Medical records, disclosure, application of law, **CC 56.30**

INDUSTRIAL BANKS

See, also, Industrial Loan Companies, generally, this index

INDUSTRIAL

INDUSTRIAL BANKS—Cont'd
Mortgages, fiduciaries, CC **2923.1**

INDUSTRIAL COMPENSATION LAW
Workers Compensation, generally, this index

INDUSTRIAL LOAN COMPANIES
Agreements. Contracts, generally, post
Conditional sales contracts, motor vehicles, insurance, CC **2982.8**
Contracts,
    Foreign languages, translations, CC **1632, 1632.5**
    Spanish language, translations, CC **1632**
Disclosure, home equity loan disclosure, CC **2970, 2971**
Fines and penalties, contracts, foreign languages, translations, CC **1632.5**
Foreign languages, contracts, translations, CC **1632, 1632.5**
Forms, contracts, foreign languages, translations, CC **1632.5**
Home equity loan disclosure, CC **2970, 2971**
Mortgages,
    Foreign languages, translations, CC **1632, 1632.5**
    Home equity loan disclosure, CC **2970, 2971**
    Spanish language, translations, CC **1632**
Motor vehicles, conditional sales, insurance, CC **2982.8**
Spanish language, contracts, translations, CC **1632**
Translations, foreign languages, contracts, CC **1632, 1632.5**

INDUSTRIAL PLANTS
Manufacturers and Manufacturing, generally, this index

INDUSTRIAL RELATIONS DEPARTMENT
Housing, generally, this index
Labor and Employment, generally, this index
Mobilehomes and Mobilehome Parks, generally, this index
Workers compensation division, medical records, disclosure, application of law, CC **56.30**

INDUSTRY
Manufacturers and Manufacturing, generally, this index

INEVITABLE ACCIDENTS
Acts of God, generally, this index

INFANTS
Children and Minors, generally, this index

INFECTIOUS DISEASES
Diseases, generally, this index

INFLATION
Cost of Living, generally, this index

INFORMATION
Computers, generally, this index

INFORMATION—Cont'd
Disclosure, generally, this index
Electronic commercial services, CC **1789.3**
Indictment and Information, generally, this index
Landlord and Tenant, this index
Mobilehomes and mobilehome parks, prospective homeowners, CC **798.74.5**
Rental purchase agreements, consumers, CC **1812.629**
Stalking, personal information, victim service providers, grants, CC **1798.79.8 et seq.**

INFORMATION PRACTICES ACT
Generally, CC **1798 et seq.**

INFORMATION TECHNOLOGY
Computers, generally, this index
Telecommunications, generally, this index

INFORMED CONSENT
Space flights, CC **2211, 2212**

INFORMERS
Personal information held by governmental agencies, exemption from access under Information Practices Act, CC **1798.41**

INHERITANCE
Succession, generally, this index

INITIATIVE AND REFERENDUM
Mobilehomes and mobilehome parks, signs and signals, CC **798.51, 799.10**
Signs and signals, mobilehomes and mobilehome parks, CC **798.51, 799.10**
Usury Law, CC **1916–1 et seq.**

INJECTORS
Epinephrine Auto Injectors, generally, this index

INJUNCTION
    Generally, CC **3366 et seq., 3420 et seq.**
Affidavits, homeless persons, transitional housing, misconduct, CC **1954.13**
Art and Artists, this index
Assignation, place of, injunctions, awarding, CC **3496**
Auctions and auctioneers, CC **1812.602**
Audio and video recordings, privacy, invasion of privacy, CC **1708.85**
Billing,
    Club members for goods sent after notice of termination, CC **1584.6**
    Unsolicited goods, CC **1584.5**
Civil rights, violations, CC **52, 52.1**
Condominiums, this index
Conservation easements, CC **815.7**
Consumer Credit, this index
Consumer credit reporting agencies, CC **1789.21**
Consumer transactions, CC **1780 et seq.**
Consumers, privacy, disclosure, CC **1798.150**
Consumers Legal Remedies Act, CC **1782**

INJUNCTION—Cont'd
Contracts, breach, injunction to prevent, CC **3423**
COVID 19, forbearance, mortgages, CC **3273.15**
Credit, discrimination, marital status or sex, CC **1812.32, 1812.33**
Credit cards, identity and identification, information, acceptance, CC **1747.08**
Credit services organizations, CC **1789.21**
    Violations, CC **1789.20**
Crimes and offenses, stories about felonies, sale proceeds, CC **2225**
Customer records, destruction, CC **1798.84**
Dance studio contracts, violations, CC **1812.63**
Data,
    Brokers, registration, CC **1798.99.82**
    Sales, crimes and offenses, CC **1724**
Debt settlement providers, fair debt settlement, CC **1788.305**
Debtors and Creditors, this index
Denial, circumstances requiring, CC **3423**
Disclosure, personal information held by governmental agencies, Information Practices Act, CC **1798.46, 1798.47**
Dissolution, material change in facts, CC **3424**
Easements, conservation easements, CC **815.7**
Final, grounds, CC **3422**
Fine art multiples, sales, disclosures, CC **1745.5**
Force and violence, freedom from, CC **52, 52.1**
Freedom from violence, CC **52, 52.1**
Gender violence, CC **52.4**
Goods, wares and merchandise, voluntary and unsolicited sending, CC **1584.5**
Grounds, CC **3422**
Homeless persons, transitional housing, misconduct, CC **1954.10 et seq.**
Hotels and Motels, this index
Impound accounts, mortgages, excess withholding, CC **2954.1**
Indebtedness, duress or coercion, CC **1798.97.3**
Innkeepers liens,
    Temporary restraining orders, CC **1861.16**
    Writs of possession, CC **1861.17**
Invasion of privacy, CC **1708.8, 1708.85**
    Invasion of privacy, altered depictions, lewdness and obscenity, CC **1708.86**
Landlord and Tenant, this index
Lewdness and obscenity, electronic transmissions, images, CC **1708.88**
Markets and marketing, Internet, disclosure, CC **1749.8.4**
Material change in facts, modification or dissolution, CC **3424**
Modification, material change in facts, CC **3424**
Mortgages, this index
Motion pictures,
    Invasion of privacy, CC **1708.85**

INSTALLMENT

INJUNCTION—Cont'd
Motion pictures—Cont'd
  Killing of or cruelty to animals or human beings, CC 3505 et seq.
Nonprofit corporations, breach of contract with members, CC 3423
Obscenity, costs, awarding, CC 3496
Payment processors, fair debt settlement, CC 1788.305
Petitions, homeless persons, transitional housing, misconduct, CC 1954.13
Photography and pictures, invasion of privacy, CC 1708.85
Preliminary injunctions, crimes and offenses, stories about felonies, sales, CC 2225
Prescription drug claims processor, reports, failure to file, CC 2528
Preventive relief, CC 3366 et seq.
Privacy. Invasion of privacy, generally, ante
Private schools, buildings and grounds, access, interference, obstructions, threats, CC 1708.9
Prostitution, costs, awarding, CC 3496
Provisional injunction, CC 3421
Public office, exercise of, CC 3423
Ranges, sport shooting ranges, CC 3482.1
Sales, goods or services, Consumers Legal Remedies Act, CC 1782
School buildings and grounds, access, interference, obstructions, threats, CC 1708.9
Service of process, modify or dissolve final injunction, CC 3424
Sex, force and violence, CC 52.4
Sexual assault, personal information, victim service providers, grants, CC 1798.79.95
Sexual battery, CC 1708.5
Sexual orientation, CC 52.45
Shooting ranges, CC 3482.1
Sport shooting ranges, CC 3482.1
Subcutaneous implantation, identification devices, CC 52.7
Supersedeas or stay, judicial proceeding, CC 3423
Temporary restraining orders,
  Homeless persons, transitional housing, misconduct, CC 1954.10 et seq.
  Mobilehomes and mobilehome parks, regulations, violations, CC 798.88
Threats, violation of civil rights, CC 52, 52.1
Trade secrets, misappropriation, CC 3426.2, 3426.4
Unsolicited goods, sending statement for, CC 1584.5
Violation, stalking, CC 1708.7
Voidable transactions, CC 3439.07
Witnesses, compensation and salaries, contracts, CC 1669.7

INJURIES
Personal Injuries, generally, this index

INMATES
Correctional Institutions, generally, this index

INMATES—Cont'd
Jails, generally, this index

INNKEEPERS
Bed and Breakfast Inns, generally, this index
Hotels and Motels, generally, this index

INNOCENT PURCHASERS
Condominiums, rent controls, CC 1954.52
Fine art, consignment sales, CC 1738 et seq.
Home equity sales contracts, CC 1695.12
Motor vehicles, conditional sale contract, CC 2983
Notice, CC 1227, 1228
Presumptions, public improvement liens, CC 2911
Prior recording of conveyances, CC 1214
Specific performance, real property obligations, relief against parties bound to perform, CC 3395
Voidable transactions, CC 3440 et seq.

INSANITY
Mental Health, generally, this index

INSECT PESTS AND PLANT DISEASES
Pest Control, generally, this index
Vector control. Pest Control, generally, this index

INSECTICIDES
Pest Control, generally, this index

INSOLVENCY
Assignments, leased business premises, right to occupy, CC 1954.05
Bankruptcy, generally, this index
Novation, insolvency of third person, rescission, CC 1533
Voidable transactions, CC 3439.02

INSPECTION AND INSPECTORS
Condominiums, this index
Dance studios, bonds (officers and fiduciaries), declaration of gross income, CC 1812.64
Entry on Property, generally, this index
Landlord and Tenant, this index
Motor Vehicles, this index
Personal information held by governmental agencies, Information Practices Act, CC 1798.34
Real Estate, this index
Real Estate Brokers and Salespersons, this index

INSTALLATION
Consumer goods, standards for warranty work, CC 1796, 1796.5
Roofs, warranties, CC 1797.90 et seq.

INSTALLMENT PAYMENTS
Motor vehicles, conditional sales, disclosure, CC 2982.2

INSTALLMENT SALES
Generally, CC 1801 et seq.

INSTALLMENT SALES—Cont'd
Acceleration of maturity by holder, CC 1804.1
Accounts and accounting, CC 1810 et seq.
  Credit balance, refunds, CC 1810.3
  Delinquency charges, CC 1810.12
Acknowledgment,
  Delivery of copy of contract to buyer, CC 1803.7
  Payment by buyer, CC 1806.4, 1810.8
Actions and proceedings,
  Notes in connection with installment account cutting off right of action, CC 1810.7
  Repossession, buyers default, CC 1812.2
  Venue, CC 1812.10
    Contract provisions, CC 1804.1
Add on sales, CC 1808.1 et seq.
Advances and advancements, CC 1803.2
Advertisements, finance charge, crimes and offenses, CC 1803.11
Affidavits, venue, CC 1812.10
Agreements,
  Refinancing, CC 1807.2
  Rescission, failure of buyer to obtain third party financing, CC 1803.9
  Retail installment account, CC 1810
Allocation of payments, CC 1810.6
Amount financed, memorandum, subsequent purchases, CC 1808.3
Annual fee, CC 1805.1
Annual statements, finance charges, CC 1810.11
Application of law, CC 1801.4
Assignments,
  Assignee, rights and liabilities, CC 1804.2
  Buyers agreement not to assert claim or defense against an assignee, CC 1804.1
  Buyers obligation as discharge by payment to last known holder in absence of notice of assignment, CC 1806.1
  Defense of buyer against sellers assignee, CC 1804.2
  Notice of equities and defenses, CC 1804.2
  Payments, last known holder of contract, CC 1806.1
  Restrictions on provisions in contract, CC 1804.1
  Sellers assignee subject to claims and defenses of buyer against seller, CC 1804.2
  Validity of assignment of contract or installment account as against creditors, subject to purchasers, CC 1809.1
  Wages, contract provisions, CC 1804.1
Attorney fees, CC 1811.1
  Agreement for payment, CC 1810.4
  Application of proceeds of resale, CC 1812.4
  Proceeds of resale, CC 1812.4
Avoidance of contract, charges against buyer, contract provisions, CC 1804.1
Balance,
  Monthly statement by seller or holder of installment account, CC 1810.3

INSTALLMENT

INSTALLMENT SALES—Cont'd
Balance—Cont'd
  Unpaid, finance charges, undelivered goods, CC 1810.10
Balloon payments, memorandum, subsequent purchases, CC 1808.2, 1808.3
Blanks,
  Filling in blank spaces by seller after contract is received, CC 1803.8
  Signature of buyer to contract containing blank spaces, CC 1803.4
Brokerage fee, seller and supervised financial organization, CC 1801.6
Cash sale price,
  Buyers obligation to pay until transmission of copy of contract, CC 1803.7
  Buyers obligation until memorandum on subsequent purchase is delivered, CC 1808.4
  Contents of statement to buyer by seller or holder of installment account, CC 1810.3
  Disclosure statement, failure of seller to deliver to buyer, CC 1810.1
  Provisions of contract, CC 1803.3
  Setting forth in memorandum when subsequent purchase is made, CC 1808.3
  Subsequent purchases, memorandum to set forth, CC 1808.2
Charges. Rates and charges, generally, post
Checks, dishonored, return fee, including in finance charges, CC 1805.4, 1810.4
Claims,
  Agreement by buyer not to assert against seller or assignee, CC 1804.1
  Deficiency claim, CC 1812.5
  Disposition of proceeds of resale after satisfaction of claims, CC 1812.4
Collection,
  Charges,
    Excluded from finance charge, CC 1810.4
    Seller or holder of retail installment account, CC 1810.4
  Costs, provisions of contract, CC 1803.6
  Delinquency charge, CC 1803.6
  Improperly collected amount credited against indebtedness, CC 1812.8
  Recovery,
    Charges, noncompliance with law, CC 1812.7
    Willful violations, CC 1812.9
  Restrictions on contracts, CC 1804.1
  Retail installment account, CC 1810.2
Commercial property, construction or sale, contracts, application of law, CC 1801.4
Commissions, inducement of sale, buyer producing future sales, CC 1803.10
Common ownership, seller and supervised financial organization, CC 1801.6
Complaint, venue, statement of facts, CC 1812.10

INSTALLMENT SALES—Cont'd
Computation, finance charges, maximum, CC 1805.1
Confession of judgment, restrictions, CC 1804.1
Consolidation, CC 1807.1 et seq.
Contingent commission, discount or rebate, inducement, buyer producing sales, CC 1803.10
Copies,
  Agreement, procurement of insurance, CC 1810.5
  Delivery contract to buyer, CC 1803.7, 1803.8
  Notice of resale of goods, CC 1812.3
  Seller or holder to transmit to buyer copy of insurance policies or certificates, CC 1803.5
  Transmission to buyer of copy of contract, CC 1803.7
Correction, failure to comply with provisions of law, CC 1812.8
Costs, CC 1811.1
  Agreement charging insurance to buyer, CC 1810.5
  Payment, CC 1810.4, 1811.1
Credit balance, refunds, CC 1810.3
Credit cards,
  Annual fee, finance charge, including in, CC 1810.4
  Disclosures, CC 1810.20, 1810.21
  Membership fees, CC 1810.4
Credits,
  Entry in passbook or payment book, CC 1806.2
  Improperly collected amount, CC 1812.8
  Refund credit, payment before maturity, CC 1806.3
Crimes and offenses, CC 1812.6
  Finance charge, advertisements, CC 1803.11
Damages,
  Breach of contract, finance charges, CC 3289.5
  Holders failure to render statement to buyer of sum due, CC 1812.2
  Treble damages, willful violation of law, CC 1812.9
Dance studio services, CC 1812.53
Date of retail installment contract, CC 1803.1
Dating service contracts, CC 1694.4
Debits and credits, monthly statement to buyer by seller or holder of installment account, CC 1810.3
Default,
  Acceleration by holder of maturity in absence of buyers default, CC 1804.1
  Collection costs from buyers failure to communicate with holder after default in payments, CC 1803.6
Repossession and resale, CC 1812.2 et seq.
Defenses,
  Agreement by buyer not to assert against seller or an assignee, CC 1804.1

INSTALLMENT SALES—Cont'd
Defenses—Cont'd
  Buyers claims and defenses against sellers assignee, CC 1804.2
  Notes in connection with installment account cutting off, CC 1810.7
Deferment,
  Buyers recovery on another persons willful violation of law, CC 1812.9
  Credit, deferred contract, payment anticipation, CC 1806.3
  Noncompliance with law as bar to recovery of deferral charge, CC 1812.7
  Scheduled payment, CC 1807.1
Deferred payment price, memorandum, subsequent purchases, CC 1808.3
Deficiency, proceeds of resale, CC 1812.5
Delinquency charge,
  Buyers recovery for willful violation of law, CC 1812.9
  Finance charge, CC 1810.4
  Noncompliance with law as bar to recovery, CC 1812.7
  Provisions of contract, CC 1803.6
  Retail installment accounts, CC 1810.12
  Seller or holder of retail installment account, CC 1810.4
Delivery,
  Copy,
    Contract to buyer, CC 1803.7, 1803.8
    Notice of resale of goods, CC 1812.3
  Instruments acknowledging payment, CC 1806.4, 1810.8
  Memorandum to buyer when subsequent purchase is made, CC 1808.2, 1808.3, 1808.4
  Notice,
    Buyers intention to resell goods or retain possession, CC 1812.3
    Insurance policies by seller or holder to buyer, CC 1803.5
  Statement, finance charges, CC 1810.1
Description of goods or services, statement to buyer by seller or holder of installment account, CC 1810.3
Discharge of buyers obligation by payment, CC 1806.1, 1810.8
Disclosure,
  Credit cards, CC 1810.20, 1810.21
  Determination of finance charge, CC 1810.1
  Retail installment account, CC 1810
  Retail sales agreements, terminology, CC 1801.5
Discount contingent upon buyer producing future sales, CC 1803.10
Dishonored checks, return fee, including in finance charge, CC 1805.4, 1810.4
Domicile and residence,
  Collection costs occasioned by buyers failure to notify holder of charge of, CC 1803.6
  Inclusion in contract, CC 1803.3
  Setting forth residence of buyer in memorandum when subsequent purchase is made, CC 1808.3

INSTALLMENT

INSTALLMENT SALES—Cont'd
Down payments,
  Allocation of payment, CC 1810.6
  Subsequent purchases, CC 1808.2
Dwellings, construction or sale, contracts, application of law, CC 1801.4
Election, rescission by buyer, failure to obtain third party financing, CC 1803.9
Escheat, credit balances, CC 1810.3
Exemptions, CC 1801.4
Expenses and expenditures,
  Agreement for charging cost of insurance to buyers, CC 1810.5
  Application of proceeds of resale, CC 1812.4
  Extension of credit, included in finance charge, CC 1805.4
  Finance charge, retail installment account, CC 1810.4
  Payment or tender by buyer to redeem goods, CC 1812.2
  Restrictions on taking, contracting for, CC 1805.4
  Seller or holder of retail installment account, CC 1810.4
Extension,
  Buyers recovery on another persons willful violation of law, CC 1812.9
  Credit,
    Deferred contract, anticipation of payment, CC 1806.3
    Expenses included in finance charge, CC 1805.4
  Noncompliance with law as bar to recovery, CC 1812.7
  Scheduled due date, CC 1807.1
Fees,
  Annual fee, CC 1805.1
  Attorney fees, generally, ante
  Brokerage or referral fees, supervised financial organization, CC 1801.6
  Contents of memorandum in case of subsequent purchase, CC 1808.3
  Credit card plans, membership fees, CC 1810.4
  Memorandum, subsequent purchases, CC 1808.2
  Provisions of contract, CC 1803.3
  Restriction on receiving, reserving, CC 1805.4
  Seller or holder of retail installment account, CC 1810.4
Finance charge, CC 1805.1 et seq.
  Add on transactions, CC 1808.1 et seq.
  Advertisements, crimes and offenses, CC 1803.11
  Annual statements, CC 1810.11
  Buyers recovery, willful violations, CC 1812.9
  Calculation, CC 1805.7
  Checks, dishonored, return fee, including, CC 1805.4, 1810.4
  Collection,
    Charges excluded from, CC 1810.4

INSTALLMENT SALES—Cont'd
Finance charge—Cont'd
  Collection—Cont'd
    Retail installment amount, CC 1810.2
  Contents, statement to buyer by seller or holder of installment accounts, CC 1810.3
  Credit card membership fee, CC 1810.4
  Crimes and offenses, advertisements, CC 1803.11
  Delinquency charges excluded from, CC 1810.4
  Expenses,
    Excluded from, CC 1810.4
    Extending credit, included in, CC 1805.4
  Fees, excluded from, CC 1810.4
  Inquiry, failure of creditor to respond to debtors inquiry, CC 1720
  Interest, CC 3289.5
  Limitation, CC 1805.1
  Maximum rates, CC 1805.8
    Computation, CC 1805.1
  Memorandum, subsequent purchases, CC 1808.2, 1808.3
  Noncompliance with law, recoveries, CC 1812.7
  Outstanding balance, undelivered goods, CC 1810.10
  Precomputed basis, CC 1805.9
  Prepayment, computation, unearned portion, CC 1803.3
  Provisions of contract, CC 1803.3
  Refinancing, CC 1807.2
  Refunds, CC 1803.2
    Prior to maturity, CC 1806.3
  Retail installment accounts, CC 1810.2
  Seller or holder of retail installment account, CC 1810.4
  Simple interest basis, CC 1805.9
  Statement,
    Method of computing, CC 1810.1
    Written statement, seller providing, CC 1810.11
  Undelivered goods, CC 1805.6
  Written statement, seller providing, CC 1810.11
Financing agency, terms and conditions of purchase of installment contract or installment account, CC 1809.1
Fines and penalties, CC 1812.6
  Disclosure statement, failure of seller to give buyer, CC 1810.1
  Financing, source, requirement, CC 1812.20
  Holders failure to render statement to buyer of sum due, CC 1812.2
Foreign languages, translations, CC 1632
Foreign states, transactions, local and out of state contacts, CC 1802.19
Forms, contract, CC 1803.2, 1803.3
Health studio services, CC 1812.89
Holder,
  Acceleration of maturity of amount owed in absence of buyers default, CC 1804.1

INSTALLMENT SALES—Cont'd
Holder—Cont'd
  Charges, retail installment account, CC 1810.4
  Collection,
    Cost taken by removal of goods without permission of holder, CC 1803.6
    Finance charge, retail installment accounts, CC 1810.2
  Discharge of buyers obligation by payment to last known holder, CC 1806.1, 1810.8
  Extension of scheduled due date or deferment of scheduled payment, CC 1807.1
  Monthly statements of installment account to buyer, CC 1810.3
  Procurement of insurance, CC 1803.5
  Repossession and resale, CC 1812.2 et seq.
  Transmission to buyer of instruments acknowledging payment, CC 1806.4, 1810.8
  Written statements to buyer of amount unpaid, CC 1806.2
Home improvement business,
  Aged persons, security interest, CC 1804.1
  Application of law, CC 1689.8
Home solicitation contracts, application of law, CC 1689.8
Identification, goods or services, monthly statements, CC 1810.3
Industrial property, construction or sale, contracts, application of law, CC 1801.4
Inquiry, failure of creditor to respond to debtors inquiry, CC 1720
Insurance,
  Additional cost of coverage due to extension or deferral, CC 1807.1
  Agreement concerning procurement of, CC 1810.5
  Contents of memorandum in case of subsequent purchase, CC 1808.3
  Memorandum, subsequent purchases, CC 1808.2
  Provisions of contract, CC 1803.3, 1803.5
  Separately charged to buyer, agreement, CC 1803.5, 1810.5
Interest, failure of creditor to respond to debtors inquiry, CC 1720
Investigations and investigators, finance charge inclusive of charges incident to, CC 1810.4
Judgment satisfying debt, finance charge refund credit, CC 1806.3
Liens and incumbrances,
  Provisions of retail installment contract, CC 1803.2
  Real estate, CC 1803.2, 1804.3
Loan commission, seller and supervised financial organization, CC 1801.6
Losses, sharing, seller and supervised financial organization, CC 1801.6
Lots or parcels of real property, contracts, application of law, CC 1801.4

INSTALLMENT

INSTALLMENT SALES—Cont'd
Mail and mailing,
  Change of terms, retail installment account, **CC 1810.3**
  Copy,
    Contract to buyer, **CC 1803.7**
    Insurance policies by seller or holder to buyer, **CC 1803.5**
  Instruments acknowledging payment, **CC 1806.4**
  Instruments to buyer, acknowledging payment, **CC 1810.8**
  Negotiation in making of sales without personal solicitation by sellers representative, **CC 1803.8**
  Notice,
    Holders intention to resell goods or retain possession, **CC 1812.3**
    Resale of goods, **CC 1812.3**
Marketing plans, seller assisted marketing plans, **CC 1812.200 et seq.**
Membership camping contracts, **CC 1812.300 et seq.**
Membership fees, credit card plans, **CC 1810.4**
Memorandum,
  Installment accounts, **CC 1810.3**
  Subsequent purchases, **CC 1808.2 et seq.**
Monthly installments, **CC 1805.2**
Monthly statements by seller or holder of installment account to buyer, **CC 1810.3**
Multiple purchases, allocation of payments, **CC 1810.6**
Names of seller and buyer, **CC 1803.3**
  Memorandum when subsequent purchase is made, **CC 1808.3**
New balance memorandum, subsequent purchases, **CC 1808.3**
Nonresidents, transactions involving both local and out of state contacts, **CC 1802.19**
Notice,
  Balloon payments, **CC 1807.3**
  Change in terms of open end account, **CC 1810.3**
  Collection costs taken by buyers failure to notify holder of change of residence, **CC 1803.6**
  Correction after notice of failure to comply with provisions of law, **CC 1812.8**
  Credit balance, notice of right to refund, **CC 1810.3**
  Credit cards, membership fees, **CC 1810.4**
  Discharge of buyers obligation by payment to last known holder in absence of notice, **CC 1806.1**
  Inclusion in retail installment contract of notice to buyer, **CC 1803.2**
  Membership fees, credit cards, **CC 1810.4**
  Repossession and resale, **CC 1812.2, 1812.3**
  Rescission by buyer, failure to obtain third party financing, **CC 1803.9**
  Retail installment account, agreements, changes, **CC 1810, 1810.4**

INSTALLMENT SALES—Cont'd
Notice—Cont'd
  Sellers or holders notice to buyer concerning insurance, **CC 1803.5**
  Time and place of resale of goods, **CC 1812.3**
  Unpaid balance, **CC 1806.2**
Number of installments, statement, memorandum on subsequent purchase, **CC 1808.3**
Official fees. Fees, generally, ante
Option of seller,
  Add subsequent purchases to contract, **CC 1808.1**
  Allocation of payments after subsequent purchase, **CC 1808.2**
Ownership, common ownership, seller and supervised financial organization, **CC 1801.6**
Pass book or payment book, **CC 1806.2**
Payment, **CC 1806.1 et seq.**
  Acknowledgments, **CC 1806.4**
  Agreement, attorney fees and costs, **CC 1810.4**
  Allocation of payments, **CC 1810.6**
    After subsequent purchases, **CC 1808.2 et seq.**
  Application,
    Previous payments when subsequent purchases made, **CC 1808.2 et seq.**
    Proceeds of resale, **CC 1812.4**
  Balloon payments, notice, **CC 1807.3**
  Buyers payment to redeem goods, **CC 1812.2**
  Cash sale price, failure to deliver statement, finance charges, **CC 1810.1**
  Contents,
    Memorandum in case of subsequent purchase, **CC 1808.3**
    Statement to buyer by seller or holder of installment account, **CC 1810.3**
  Deferment of scheduled payment, **CC 1807.1**
  Deferred payment price, add on transactions, **CC 1808.2**
  Down payments, subsequent purchases, **CC 1808.2**
  Extension of scheduled due date, **CC 1807.1**
  Increase, addition of subsequent purchases to contract, **CC 1808.1, 1808.2**
  Instruments acknowledging payment, **CC 1806.4**
  Obligation of buyer until memorandum or subsequent purchase is delivered, **CC 1808.4**
  Passbook, **CC 1806.2**
  Provisions of retail installment contract, **CC 1803.2, 1803.3, 1803.6**
  Refund credit for anticipation of payment, **CC 1806.3**
  Retail installment accounts, **CC 1810.8**
  Retention by seller of security interest in goods sold until full payment, **CC 1810.6**
  Series of transactions, **CC 1808.2**
  Statement as to minimum periodic payment required, **CC 1810.1**

INSTALLMENT SALES—Cont'd
Payment—Cont'd
  Time, **CC 1805.2**
Penalties. Fines and penalties, generally, ante
Place,
  Inclusion in contract of place of business of buyer and seller, **CC 1803.3**
  Notice of place of resale of goods, **CC 1812.3**
  Setting forth place of business of seller and buyer in memorandum when subsequent purchase is made, **CC 1808.3**
Place subsequent purchases, memorandum to set forth sellers place of business, **CC 1808.2**
Possession of buyer, finance charges, **CC 1810.10**
Power of attorney, restrictions on provisions in contract, **CC 1804.1**
Premiums, additional cost for insurance coverage due to extension or deferral, **CC 1807.1**
Prepayment, **CC 1803.2**
  Finance charge, computation, unearned portion, **CC 1803.3**
  Refund credit, **CC 1806.3**
Presumption, copy of contract furnished to buyer, **CC 1803.7**
Previous balance, memorandum, subsequent purchases, **CC 1808.3**
Printing,
  Acknowledgment by buyer of delivery of copy of contract, **CC 1803.7**
  Contract, printed portion, **CC 1803.1**
  Statement concerning service charges in application form used by seller, **CC 1810.1**
Proceedings. Actions and proceedings, generally, ante
Proceeds of resale, **CC 1812.4, 1812.5**
Procurement of insurance, **CC 1810.5**
Profits, sharing, seller and supervised financial organization, **CC 1801.6**
Promissory notes,
  Provisions of retail installment contract, **CC 1803.2**
  Retail installment accounts, **CC 1810.7**
Public policy, waiver by buyer of provisions of law, **CC 1801.1**
Rates and charges, **CC 1810.4**
  Finance charge, **CC 1805.1**
  Refinancing agreements, **CC 1807.2**
  Service charges, generally, post
Real estate security interests, contracts for goods,
  Limitations, **CC 1804.3**
  Warning to buyers, **CC 1803.2**
Rebates contingent upon buyer producing future sales, **CC 1803.10**
Redemption of goods, **CC 1812.2, 1812.3**
  Collateral after repossession, finance charge refund credit, **CC 1806.3**
Referral fee, seller and supervised financial organization, **CC 1801.6**

INSTRUMENTS

INSTALLMENT SALES—Cont'd
Refinancing, CC 1807.1 et seq.
    Noncompliance with law as bar to recovery of refinance charge, CC 1812.7
    Refund credit, payment before maturity, CC 1806.3
Refunds,
    Credit, payment before maturity, CC 1806.3
    Finance charge, payment before maturity, CC 1806.3
    Retail installment accounts, credit balance, CC 1810.3
    Service charge, CC 1803.2
Regulation Z, terminology, disclosures, CC 1801.5
Release of security, payment acknowledgment, CC 1806.4
Rental purchase agreements, application of law, CC 1812.622
Repossession and resale, CC 1812.2 et seq.
    Collateral, debt satisfaction, finance charge refund credit, CC 1806.3
    Restrictions, CC 1804.1
Rescission of contract,
    Charges against buyer, contract provisions, CC 1804.1
    Third party financing, buyers failure to obtain, CC 1803.9
Residence. Domicile and residence, generally, ante
Retail installment account, CC 1810 et seq.
    Acceptance, agreements, CC 1810
    Agreements, acceptance, CC 1810
    Change of terms, disclosure to buyer, CC 1810, 1810.3, 1810.4
    Credit balance, refunds, notice, CC 1810.3
    Delinquency charges, CC 1810.12
    Disclosure, CC 1810, 1810.12
        Fees, CC 1810.20, 1810.21
        Terminology, CC 1801.5
    Inquiry, failure of creditor to respond to debtors inquiry, CC 1720
    Insurance, separately charged to buyer, CC 1810.5
    Monthly statement to buyer, CC 1810.3
    Notice, agreements, changes, CC 1810, 1810.4
    Payments, application of law, CC 1810.8
    Penalties for noncompliance with provisions of law, CC 1812.7
    Provision for payment of attorneys fees and court costs, CC 1811.1
    Repossession and resale, default, CC 1812.2 et seq.
    Security interest, retention by seller, CC 1810.6
    Terms and conditions of purchase by financing agency, CC 1809.1
    Return fee, dishonored checks, CC 1805.4, 1810.4
Revolving accounts. Retail installment account, generally, ante

INSTALLMENT SALES—Cont'd
Security interest,
    Goods not subject to, CC 1804.3
    Multiple purchases, security interest release, CC 1810.6
    Retention by seller, CC 1810.6
Seller assisted marketing plans, CC 1812.200 et seq.
Semimonthly installments, CC 1805.2
Service charges,
    Add on transactions, CC 1808.3
    Annual fee, CC 1805.1
    Avoidance of contract, CC 1804.1
    Consolidated time balance, inclusion in, CC 1808.5
    Contents, memorandum on subsequent purchase, CC 1808.3
    Entry in passbook or payment book, CC 1806.2
    Extension of scheduled due date or deferment of scheduled payment, CC 1807.1
    Increase on addition of subsequent purchases to contract, CC 1808.1
    Inquiry, failure of creditor to respond to debtors inquiry, CC 1720
    Limitation, CC 1805.1
    Noncompliance with law as bar to recovery, CC 1812.7
    Penalty for wilful violation of law, CC 1812.9
    Printing statement concerning charges in application form use by seller, CC 1810.1
    Refund, CC 1803.2
        Credit, payment before maturity, CC 1806.3
    Rescission of contract, CC 1804.1
    Retail installment accounts, CC 1810.1
    Telephone statements concerning charges when negotiating installment accounts, CC 1810.1
    Wilful violation of law provisions effecting recovery of charges, CC 1812.9
Service of notice, resale, CC 1812.3
Services,
    Increase of total price by price of additional services, CC 1808.1
    Memorandum by seller to buyer when subsequent purchase is made, CC 1808.3
    Retail installment contract, CC 1803.3
Severability of Act, CC 1801.2
Sharing of profits and losses, seller and supervised financial organization, CC 1801.6
Signatures,
    Agreement,
        Extension or deferment, CC 1807.1
        Payment of attorney fees and costs, CC 1810.4
        Procurement of insurance, CC 1810.5, 1810.7

INSTALLMENT SALES—Cont'd
Signatures—Cont'd
    Buyer, CC 1803.3, 1803.4
Spanish language, translations, CC 1632
Statements,
    Annual, finance charges, CC 1810.11
    Credit balance, refunds, CC 1810.3
    Finance charges, CC 1810.1, 1810.11
    Holder to buyer of sum due and expenses in connection with repossession, CC 1812.2
    Identification, goods or services, CC 1810.3
    Monthly statements, seller or holder of retail installment account to buyer, CC 1810.3
    Printing statement concerning service charges on application form used by seller, CC 1810.1
    Written statement of finance charges, seller providing, CC 1810.11
Suits. Actions and proceedings, generally, ante
Surrender of collateral, debt satisfaction, finance charge refund credit, CC 1806.3
Telephone, negotiation in entering into sale without personal solicitation by sellers representative, CC 1803.8
Tender by buyer to redeem goods, CC 1812.2
Third party financing, rescission if buyer unable to obtain, CC 1803.9
Time, payments, CC 1805.2
Total of payments, memorandum, subsequent purchases, CC 1808.2
Translations, foreign languages, CC 1632
Treble damages, willful violations, CC 1812.9
Undelivered goods, finance charges, CC 1805.6, 1810.10
Unpaid balance,
    Contents of memorandum in case of subsequent purchase, CC 1808.3
    Entry in passbook or payment book, CC 1806.2
    Memorandum, subsequent purchases, CC 1808.2
    Service charge included in consolidated time balance, CC 1808.5
Venue, CC 1804.1, 1812.10
Verified complaint, statement of venue, CC 1812.10
Void character of prohibited provision in contract, CC 1804.4
Waiver,
    Buyer of provisions of law as contrary to public policy, CC 1801.1
    Restrictions on contracts, CC 1804.1
Weekly installments, CC 1805.2
Writing, retail installment contract, CC 1803.1

INSTALLMENTS
Contracts,
    Dance studio services, refund, CC 1812.57
    Health studio services, CC 1812.89

INSTRUMENTS
Books and Papers, generally, this index

INSTRUMENTS

INSTRUMENTS—Cont'd
Euro, medium of payment, **CC 1663**
Negotiable Instruments, generally, this index
Recorders, generally, this index

INSUFFICIENT FUNDS
Negotiable Instruments, this index

INSURANCE
Accident and health insurance. Health Insurance, generally, this index
Actions and proceedings,
  Concealing policy, privileged communications, **CC 47**
  Independent counsel, insurer obligation to provide, **CC 2860**
  Obligations to defend actions, conflict of interest, independent counsel, **CC 2860**
Agents. Insurance Agents, Solicitors or Brokers, generally, this index
Alteration, customers leaving personalty for alterations, **CC 1858 et seq.**
Annuities,
  Aged persons, shared appreciation loans, **CC 1917.320 et seq.**
  Life Insurance, generally, this index
Attorneys,
  Independent counsel, obligation to provide, **CC 2860**
  Obligation to defend actions, conflict of interest, independent counsel, **CC 2860**
  Professional liability insurance, underwriting committees, privileges and immunities, **CC 43.7**
  Punitive damages, failure to provide notice, **CC 3296**
Autographed memorabilia, dealers, **CC 1739.7**
Automobiles. Motor Vehicle Insurance, generally, this index
Bailment, personal property deposited for repair, alteration, or sale, **CC 1858 et seq.**
Brokers. Insurance Agents, Solicitors or Brokers, generally, this index
Cancellation. Mortgages, post
Children and minors, damages, liability of parents, **CC 1714.1**
Claims,
  Medical records, collection of information, **CC 56.27**
  Procedures forms, credit life and disability insurance, **CC 1812.402**
Condominiums,
  Construction, defects, actions and proceedings, **CC 6000**
  Liability Insurance, this index
Confidential or privileged information. Disclosure, generally, post
Conflict of interest,
  Actions, obligations to defend, independent counsel, **CC 2860**
  Independent counsel, insurer obligation to provide, **CC 2860**
Consumer credit reporting agencies, notice, denial, rates and rating organizations, **CC 1786.40**

INSURANCE—Cont'd
Consumer protection, notice, reports, **CC 1786 et seq.**
Contracts, real estate, contracts for sale of land, **CC 2954**
Counsel. Attorneys, generally, ante
Credit Life and Disability Insurance, generally, this index
Credit ratings. Consumer Credit Reporting Agencies, generally, this index
Customers leaving personal property for repairs, alterations or sale, **CC 1858 et seq.**
Damages, notice, punitive damages, **CC 3296**
Debtors and creditors. Credit Life and Disability Insurance, generally, this index
Deeds and conveyances, contracts for sale of land, pro rata payments, **CC 2985.4**
Denial,
  Consumer credit reporting agencies, notice, **CC 1786.40**
  Information, disclosure, **CC 1786.40**
Depositary for hire, lien, **CC 1856**
Disability insurance. Health Insurance, generally, this index
Disclosure,
  Claims, credit life and disability insurance, forms, **CC 1812.402**
  Contracts, shared mobility service providers, licenses and permits, **CC 2505**
  Credit life and disability insurance, claims procedure, **CC 1812.402**
  Information, denial, rates and rating organizations, **CC 1786.40**
  Medical records, post
  Shared mobility service providers, licenses and permits, contracts, **CC 2505**
Factors authority to insure property, **CC 2368**
Fidelity insurance. Suretyship and Guaranty, generally, this index
Filing, identity and identification, theft, **CC 1798.200 et seq.**
Forms, claims procedure, credit life and disability insurance, **CC 1812.402**
Genetic characteristics, disclosure, **CC 56.265**
Group insurance. Credit Life and Disability Insurance, generally, this index
Guarantee insurance. Suretyship and Guaranty, generally, this index
Health Care Service Plans, generally, this index
Health Insurance, generally, this index
Hospitals. Health Insurance, generally, this index
Identity and identification, theft, filing, **CC 1798.200 et seq.**
Indemnity, shared mobility service providers, licenses and permits, contracts, **CC 2505**
Information, disclosure, denial, rates and rating organizations, **CC 1786.40**
Inspection and inspectors, consumer reporting agencies, files, **CC 1786 et seq.**

INSURANCE—Cont'd
Installment Sales, this index
Interest, variable rate, **CC 1916.5**
Investigations and investigators, consumer investigations, **CC 1786 et seq.**
Judgments and decrees, punitive damages, notice, **CC 3296**
Kinds of insurance,
  Credit Life and Disability Insurance, generally, this index
  Health Insurance, generally, this index
  Liability Insurance, generally, this index
  Life Insurance, generally, this index
  Motor Vehicle Insurance, generally, this index
  Title Insurance, generally, this index
Lawyers. Attorneys, generally, ante
Legal Estates Principal and Income Law, **CC 731 et seq.**
Liability Insurance, generally, this index
Liens and incumbrances, depositary for hire for storage, **CC 1856**
Life Insurance, generally, this index
Loans, interest, variable rate, **CC 1916.5**
Medical care and treatment,
  Health Care Service Plans, generally, this index
  Health Insurance, generally, this index
Medical insurance. Health Insurance, generally, this index
Medical records,
  Disclosure, **CC 56.10, 56.15, 56.27, 56.265**
  Third party administrators, **CC 56.26**
  Health Insurance, this index
Memorabilia, dealers, **CC 1739.7**
Method of selecting independent counsel, contract provisions, **CC 2860**
Mortgages,
  Cancellation,
    Conditions, extensions of credit, **CC 2954.7**
    Notice, right of borrower, **CC 2954.6**
    Refunds, unused premiums, **CC 2954.65**
  Condominiums, earthquake insurance, institutional third party purchasers, disclosure, **CC 2955.1**
  Earthquake insurance, condominiums, institutional third party purchasers, disclosure, **CC 2955.1**
  Future payments, **CC 2954.12**
  Impound accounts for payment,
    Accounting, **CC 2954**
    Interest, **CC 2954.8**
    Retention and investment, **CC 2955**
  Notice,
    Right of cancellation, **CC 2954.6**
    Transfers, **CC 2937**
  Policies, period, **CC 2944.5**
  Refunds, unused premiums, **CC 2954.65**
  Transfers, notice, **CC 2937**
Motor Vehicle Insurance, generally, this index

INTEREST

INSURANCE—Cont'd
No fault vehicle insurance. Motor Vehicle Insurance, generally, this index
Notice,
   Consumer credit reporting agencies, denial, rates and rating organizations, **CC 1786.40**
   Customers depositing personalty for repair, alteration, or sale, **CC 1858 et seq.**
   Investigations, consumer reporting agencies, **CC 1786.16**
   Punitive damages, **CC 3296**
Oil and gas, pipelines, spills, **CC 3333.5**
Policies,
   Concealing existence, privileged communications, **CC 47**
   Period, third party interest, **CC 2944.5**
   Third party interest, period, **CC 2944.5**
Premiums,
   See, also, Rates and rating organizations, generally, post
   Installment sales, additional cost for insurance coverage due to extension or deferral, **CC 1807.1**
Privileges and immunities, concealing existence of policy, communications, **CC 47**
Proceedings. Actions and proceedings, generally, ante
Punitive damages, notice, **CC 3296**
Rates and rating organizations,
   Consumer credit reporting agencies, notice, **CC 1786.40**
   Disclosure, information, **CC 1786.40**
   Information, disclosure, **CC 1786.40**
   Notice, consumer credit reporting agencies, **CC 1786.40**
   Records and recordation, investigations, consumer reporting agencies, **CC 1786 et seq.**
Remedies. Credit Life and Disability Insurance, this index
Rental cars. Motor Vehicle Insurance, this index
Rental purchase agreements, prohibited provisions, **CC 1812.624**
Repairs, customers leaving personalty for repairs, **CC 1858 et seq.**
Reports, shared mobility service providers, licenses and permits, contracts, **CC 2505.5**
Sales, customers leaving personal property for purposes of sale, **CC 1858**
Service Contracts, generally, this index
Shared mobility devices, liability insurance, **CC 2505**
Signs and signals, shared mobility service providers, licenses and permits, contracts, **CC 2506**
Solar energy, **CC 4746**
Solicitors. Insurance Agents, Solicitors or Brokers, generally, this index
Subrogation, generally, this index
Suretyship and Guaranty, generally, this index

INSURANCE—Cont'd
Theft, identity and identification, filing, **CC 1798.200 et seq.**
Third parties, policy period, **CC 2944.5**
Title Insurance, generally, this index
Trust deeds,
   Cancellation, conditions of extension of credit, **CC 2954.7**
   Future payments, **CC 2954.12**
   Impound accounts for payment, retention and investment in state, **CC 2955**
   Notice,
     Right of cancellation, **CC 2954.6**
     Transfers, **CC 2937**
   Payment, event resulting in impairment of security, **CC 2924.7**
   Refunds, cancellation, **CC 2954.65**
   Transfers, notice, **CC 2937**
Variable interest rate, loans, **CC 1916.5**
Vehicles. Motor Vehicle Insurance, generally, this index
Waiver,
   Credit life and disability insurance provisions, **CC 1812.408**
   Independent counsel, insurance right, **CC 2860**
   Investigative consumer reporting agencies, **CC 1786.57**
Waterbeds, landlord and tenant, **CC 1940.5**

INSURANCE AGENTS, SOLICITORS OR BROKERS
Disclosure,
   Genetic characteristics, **CC 56.265**
   Medical records, **CC 56.265**
Genetic characteristics, disclosure, **CC 56.265**
Health insurance, disclosure, medical records, **CC 56.265**
Life insurance, disclosure, medical records, **CC 56.265**
Medical records, disclosure, **CC 56.265**
   Direct marketing, exemptions, **CC 1798.91**

INSURANCE COMMISSIONER
Medical records, disclosure, application of law, **CC 56.30**

INSURANCE COMPANIES
Insurance, generally, this index

INSURANCE DEPARTMENT
Insurance, generally, this index
Medical records, disclosure, application of law, **CC 56.30**

INSURERS
Insurance, generally, this index

INSURRECTION AND SEDITION
Deposits, involuntary, **CC 1815**

INTELLECTUAL AND DEVELOPMENTAL DISABILITIES
See, also, Mental Health, generally, this index

INTELLECTUAL AND DEVELOPMENTAL DISABILITIES—Cont'd
Abuse, disclosure, protection and advocacy agency, **CC 1798.24b**
Civil rights, **CC 54 et seq.**
Conservators and conservatorships, **CC 40**
Contracts,
   Capacity, **CC 38 et seq., 1556, 1557**
   Rescission, **CC 39**
   Revocation of proposal, **CC 1587**
Counselors in mental health. Mental Health Counselors, generally, this index
Damages, support, **CC 38**
Deeds and conveyances, rescission, **CC 39**
Discrimination, **CC 54 et seq.**
Evidence, presumptions, deeds and conveyances, rescission, **CC 39**
Guardian and Ward, generally, this index
Medical records, disclosure, application of law, **CC 56.30**
Mortgages, modification or change, forbearance, fines and penalties, **CC 2944.8**
Personal attendants. Domestic Workers, generally, this index
Protection and advocacy agency, disclosure, abuse or neglect, **CC 1798.24b**
Social Services, generally, this index
Support, liability, **CC 38**
Torts, **CC 41**

INTELLECTUAL DISABILITY
Intellectual and Developmental Disabilities, generally, this index

INTELLECTUAL PROPERTY
Generally, **CC 980 et seq.**
Crimes and offenses, stories about felonies, sale proceeds, **CC 2225**
Joint ownership, **CC 981**
Ownership, **CC 980 et seq.**
Publication, effect of making public, **CC 983**
Reproduction, right of reproduction, **CC 982**
Subsequent or original producers, **CC 984**
Transfer of ownership, **CC 892**

INTENTIONAL AND MALICIOUS DESTRUCTION OF PROPERTY
Vandalism, generally, this index

INTENTIONAL TORTS
Generally, **CC 3333 et seq.**
Torts, generally, this index

INTERCITY RAIL TRANSPORTATION
Railroads, generally, this index

INTEREST
Annual rate, unspecified time, **CC 1916**
Autographed memorabilia, warranties, **CC 1739.7**
Compound, **CC 1916–2**
Contracts, this index
Credit Cards, this index

INTEREST

INTEREST—Cont'd
Crimes and offenses,
  Stories about felonies, sale proceeds, CC 2225
  Usurious rate, CC 1916–3
Damages,
  Breach of covenant, CC 3304
  Discretion of jury, CC 3288
  Fraud, CC 3288
  Limit by contract, rate, CC 3289
  Obligation to pay money only, CC 3302
  Personal injuries, CC 3291
  Rate, limit by contract, CC 3289
  Right to recover, CC 3287
  Time from which interest runs, CC 3287
  Torts, personal injuries, CC 3291
  Treble amount, usury, CC 1916–3
  Unliquidated damages, CC 3287
  Waiver, acceptance of principal, CC 3290
Deeds of trust, variable rate, CC 1916.5
Fines and penalties, Usury Law violations, CC 1916–3
Installment sales, retail installment account, debtors inquiry, creditor not responding, CC 1720
Leases, lessor remedies for breach, computing worth at time of award, unpaid rent, CC 1951.2
Legal Estates Principal and Income Law, CC 731 et seq.
Limitation of actions, usury, CC 1916–3
Loan sharking, CC 1916–3
Loans, this index
Mechanics liens, stop notices, CC 8560
Memorabilia, autographed, warranties, CC 1739.7
Mortgages, this index
Offer to perform obligation, CC 1504
Precomputed interest, CC 1799.5
Presumption, CC 1914
Rates and charges,
  Usury, generally, post
  Variable rates, CC 1916.5 et seq.
Real Estate, this index
Renegotiable rate mortgages, CC 1916.8, 1916.9
Retail installment accounts, inquiry by debtor, creditor not responding, CC 1720
Retirement and pensions, public systems, foreign states, CC 1916.2
Reverse mortgages, CC 1923.2
Savings Associations, this index
Shared Appreciation Loans, this index
Statute of limitations, usury, CC 1916–3
Trust Deeds, this index
Truth in lending, shared appreciation loans for seniors, disclosure, CC 1917.712, 1917.713
Usury, CC 1916–1 et seq.
  Actions and proceedings, CC 1916–2, 1916–3
  Compound interest, CC 1916–2

INTEREST—Cont'd
Usury—Cont'd
  Crimes and offenses, CC 1916–3
  Damages, CC 1916–3
  Fines and penalties, CC 1916–3
  Limitation of actions, CC 1916–3
  Loan sharking, CC 1916–3
  Real estate brokers and dealers, real estate loan secured by liens, CC 1916.1
Variable rate, CC 1916.5 et seq.
Waiver, precomputed interest, CC 1799.6

INTEREST IN COMMON
Generally, CC 686

INTERFERENCE
Drones, emergencies, damages, CC 43.101
Private schools, buildings and grounds, access, obstructions, threats, CC 1708.9
Unmanned aircraft, emergencies, damages, CC 43.101
Voluntary interference with property, service without employment, CC 2078

INTERGENERATIONAL HOUSING DEVELOPMENTS
Generally, CC 51.3.5

INTERNAL REVENUE
Income Tax—Federal, generally, this index
Mortgages, default, sales, notice, CC 2924b
Trust deeds, default, sales, notice, CC 2924b

INTERNET
Actions and proceedings, threats, social media, CC 1798.99.22
Attorney fees, threats, orders of court, social media, CC 1798.99.22
Auctions and auctioneers, notice, CC 1812.610
Automated license plate recognition, privacy, CC 1798.90.5 et seq.
Broadband, neutrality, CC 3100 et seq.
Celebrity image protection, notice, CC 3344.1
Connected devices, security, CC 1798.91.04 et seq.
Consumer Credit Reporting Agencies, this index
Consumers, privacy, opt out rights, CC 1798.135
Costs, threats, orders of court, social media, CC 1798.99.22
Crimes and offenses, data, sales, CC 1724
Deceased celebrity, image protection, notice, CC 3344.1
Deeds and conveyances, contracts for sale of land, sex offenses, registration, notice, CC 2079.10a
Development, children and minors, consumer protection, CC 1798.99.28 et seq.
Disclosure, threats, reports, CC 1798.99.21
Force and violence, social media, reports, CC 1798.99.20 et seq.
Labor and employment, consumer credit reporting agencies, investigative consumer reports, notice, CC 1786.16

INTERNET—Cont'd
Manufacturers and manufacturing, connected devices, security, CC 1798.91.06
Markets and marketing, disclosure, CC 1749.8 et seq.
Mobilehomes and mobilehome parks, public utilities, fees, posting, CC 798.40
Neutrality, CC 3100 et seq.
Personal information, consumer credit reporting agencies, CC 1798.81.6
Privacy, children and minors, consumer protection, CC 1798.99.28 et seq.
Sales, data, crimes and offenses, CC 1724
Security, connected devices, CC 1798.91.04 et seq.
Service providers, neutrality, CC 3100 et seq.
Social security, numbers and numbering, posting, displaying, CC 1798.85
Threats, social media, reports, CC 1798.99.20 et seq.

INTERPLEADER
Mortgage foreclosure sales, CC 2924j

INTERPRETATION
Deeds and Conveyances, this index

INTERPRETERS AND TRANSLATORS
Proof of instruments, officer taking, authority to employ, CC 1201
Spanish language, trade or business contracts, CC 1632

INTERVENTION
Witnesses, compensation and salaries, contracts, CC 1669.7

INTERVIEWS
Crimes and offenses, stories about felonies, sale proceeds, CC 2225

INTESTATE SUCCESSION
Succession, generally, this index

INTIMATE PARTNER VIOLENCE
Domestic Violence, generally, this index

INTIMIDATION
Duress or Coercion, generally, this index
Threats, generally, this index

INTOXICATING LIQUORS
Alcoholic Beverages, generally, this index

INVASION
War and Civil Defense, generally, this index

INVASION OF PRIVACY
Privacy, this index

INVENTIONS
Joint ownership, CC 981
Ownership, CC 980 et seq.
Publication, effect, CC 983
Subsequent or original producers, CC 984

INVESTIGATIVE CONSUMER REPORTING AGENCIES
Consumer Credit Reporting Agencies, generally, this index

INVESTMENT SECURITIES
See, also, Securities, generally, this index
Frauds, statute of, **CC 1624**
Statute of Frauds, **CC 1624**

INVESTMENTS
Advisers, liability, **CC 3372**
Counselors liability, **CC 3372**
Impound accounts, real estate transactions, retention and investment in state, **CC 2955**
Retirement and Pensions, this index

INVITATIONS AND INVITEES
Recreation, hazardous conditions, warning, **CC 846**

INVOICES
False invoices, solicitation of payment of money, **CC 1716**
Farm machinery repair shop, **CC 1718**
Solicitation of payment of money, false invoices, **CC 1716**

INVOLUNTARY DEPOSITS
Property, **CC 1815 et seq.**

INVOLUNTARY TRUSTS
Generally, **CC 2223 et seq.**

ISLANDS
Accession, accretion and avulsion, **CC 1016 et seq.**
Formation by division of stream, ownership, **CC 1018**
Ownership,
  Navigable streams, **CC 1016**
  Nonnavigable streams, **CC 1017**
Title to property, **CC 1016 et seq.**

ISSUE
Children and Minors, generally, this index

ISSUES, PROOF AND VARIANCE
Evidence, generally, this index

ITEM PRICING
Grocery stores, point of sale systems, **CC 7100 et seq.**

JAILS
Acknowledgments, identity and identification, **CC 1185**
Identity and identification, acknowledgments, **CC 1185**
Social security, numbers and numbering, veterans, disclosure, **CC 1798.85**
Veterans, social security, numbers and numbering, disclosure, **CC 1798.85**

JEWELERS AND JEWELRY
Liens, notice and sale to satisfy, **CC 3052a**

JEWELERS AND JEWELRY—Cont'd
Notice, liens, sale to satisfy, **CC 3052a**

JOB LISTING SERVICES
Employment Agencies, this index

JOINDER OF CAUSES OF ACTION
Actions and Proceedings, this index

JOINDER OF PARTIES
Parties, this index

JOINT ADVENTURE
Joint Ventures, generally, this index

JOINT AND SEVERAL LIABILITY
Generally, **CC 1430 et seq.**
Contribution, **CC 1432**
Credit rating agencies, credit histories, filing of information, **CC 1812.30**
Deep pocket rule, **CC 1431 et seq.**
Immunity, law of, **CC 1431.3**
Indemnity, **CC 2777**
Manufactured housing, manufacturers, dealers, warranties, **CC 1797.3**
Mobilehome manufacturers and dealers, written warranties, **CC 1797.3**
Noneconomic damages, **CC 1431.2**
Parent or guardian, willful misconduct of children, **CC 1714.1**
Performance, **CC 1474, 1475**
Presumptions, **CC 1431**
Willful misconduct of children, imputed liability of parent or guardian, **CC 1714.1**

JOINT CONTRACTS
Contracts, this index

JOINT CREDIT ACCOUNTS
Credit reporting agencies, credit history, filing of information, **CC 1812.30**

JOINT DEBTORS AND CREDITORS
Debtors and Creditors, this index

JOINT OBLIGATIONS
Joint and Several Liability, generally, this index

JOINT POWERS AGREEMENTS
Authorities. Joint Powers Authorities, generally, this index

JOINT POWERS AUTHORITIES
Architects, contracts, indemnity, **CC 2782.8**
Engineers, contracts, indemnity, **CC 2782.8**
Landscape architects, contracts, indemnity, **CC 2782.8**
Surveys and surveyors, contracts, indemnity, **CC 2782.8**

JOINT TENANTS
Actions and proceedings, ouster from possession, **CC 843**
Application of law, **CC 683.2**
Bailment, delivery, **CC 1827, 1828**

JOINT TENANTS—Cont'd
Bank deposits, **CC 683, 1828**
Concurrent ownership, action for possession, **CC 843**
Consent, severance, real property, **CC 683.2**
Creation, method, **CC 683**
Depositories, delivery, **CC 1827, 1828**
Deposits,
  Bank account, **CC 683**
  Delivery to survivor, **CC 1828**
Floating homes, death of cotenant, sales to third parties, **CC 800.88**
Ouster from possession action, **CC 843**
Ownership of property, **CC 682**
Possession, ouster from possession, action, **CC 843**
Right of survivorship, **CC 683.2**
Safe deposit boxes, **CC 683.1**
Severance, **CC 683.2**
Simultaneous death, **CC 683.2**
Survivorship, right of survivorship, **CC 683.2**
Time, written demand for concurrent possession, **CC 843**

JOINT VENTURES
Dealerships, **CC 80 et seq.**
Fair dealership, **CC 80 et seq.**
Shared appreciation loans for seniors, **CC 1917.610**

JUDGES
Acknowledgments,
  Foreign countries, **CC 1183**
  United States courts, justices, judges or clerks, **CC 1182**
Foreign countries, acknowledgments, **CC 1183**
Judgments and Decrees, generally, this index
Orders of Court, generally, this index
Retirement and pensions, acknowledgements, retired court of appeal judges, **CC 1180**
Superior Court Judges, generally, this index

JUDGMENT CREDITORS
Executions, generally, this index
Garnishment, generally, this index

JUDGMENT DEBTORS
Executions, generally, this index
Garnishment, generally, this index

JUDGMENTS AND DECREES
See, also, Orders of Court, generally, this index
Accrual of interest, **CC 3287 et seq.**
Animals, service liens, reducing claims to judgment, **CC 3080.02**
Assignments, **CC 954.5**
Attachment, generally, this index
Certificates, acknowledgment, correction, **CC 1202**
Compromise and Settlement, generally, this index
Confession of Judgment, generally, this index

JUDGMENTS

JUDGMENTS AND DECREES—Cont'd
Consumer Credit, this index
Declaratory Judgments and Decrees, generally, this index
Default Judgments, generally, this index
Evidence, instruments, CC 1204
Executions, generally, this index
Fixtures erroneously affixed to land, removal, CC 1013.5
Garnishment, generally, this index
Health care service plans, punitive damages, notice, CC 3296
Identification devices, subcutaneous implantation, CC 52.7
Identity and identification, theft, CC 1798.93
Interest, CC 3287 et seq.
    Judgments above plaintiffs offer to settle, personal injury damages, CC 3291
Interlocutory judgments, fixtures erroneously affixed to land, removal, CC 1013.5
Libel and slander, bar, CC 3425.4
Livestock service liens, reducing claim to judgment, CC 3080.02
Mechanics liens, release, CC 8490
Mortgage foreclosure consultants, CC 2945.6
Offer of judgment. Compromise and Settlement, generally, this index
Personal injury damages, interest, judgments above plaintiffs offer to settle, CC 3291
Rate of interest, damages, CC 3289
Records and recordation, priority, CC 1214
Student loans, private education lenders and loan collectors, CC 1788.206
    Vacating or setting aside, CC 1788.207
Subcutaneous implantation, identification devices, CC 52.7
Supersedeas or Stay, generally, this index
Suretyship and Guaranty, this index
Time, interest on damages, accrual, CC 3287
Transfer of right, CC 954.5

JUDICIAL DISTRICTS
Judges, generally, this index

JUDICIAL NOTICE
Deeds and conveyances, restrictive covenants, discrimination, CC 53
Discrimination, real estate transactions, CC 53
Real estate transactions, discrimination, CC 53
Restrictive covenants, deeds and conveyances, discrimination, CC 53

JUDICIAL SALES
Executions, generally, this index
Trust deeds, foreclosure, priorities and preferences, bids and bidding, CC 2924p

JUNK AND JUNK DEALERS
Backflow devices, possession, CC 3336.5
Certificates and certification, fire hydrants, possession, CC 3336.5

JUNK AND JUNK DEALERS—Cont'd
Damages, fire hydrants, possession, CC 3336.5
Exemplary damages, fire hydrants, possession, CC 3336.5
Manholes, covers, possession, CC 3336.5

JURY
Contempt, generally, this index
Deaf or hard of hearing persons, listening devices, CC 54.8

JUSTICE COURTS
Claims courts. Small Claims Courts, generally, this index
Forcible Entry and Detainer, generally, this index
Small Claims Courts, generally, this index

JUSTICE DEPARTMENT
Attorney General, generally, this index
Juvenile Delinquents and Dependents, generally, this index
Rules and regulations, check cashers, permits, CC 1789.37

JUSTICES
Judges, generally, this index

JUVENILE COURTS
Computer aided transcription system, CC 54.8
Deaf or hard of hearing persons, listening systems, CC 54.8
Hearing devices, CC 54.8
Juvenile Delinquents and Dependents, generally, this index
Listening systems, CC 54.8
Transcription system, computer aided, CC 54.8

JUVENILE DELINQUENTS AND DEPENDENTS
Abuse. Child Abuse, generally, this index
Assistive listening system, deaf or hard of hearing persons, CC 54.8
Computers, transcripts, deaf or hard of hearing persons, CC 54
Cost of living, damages, liability of parents, CC 1714.1
Damages,
    Cost of living, CC 1714.1
    Insurance, CC 1714.1
    Willful misconduct, imputed liability of parents, CC 1714.1
Deaf or hard of hearing persons, listening systems, CC 54.8
Defacement of property, willful misconduct, imputed liability of parent or guardian, CC 1714.1
Foster homes. Social Services, this index
Guardian and Ward, generally, this index
Inflation, damages, liability of parents, CC 1714.1
Insurance, damages, liability of parents, CC 1714.1
Liability. Damages, generally, ante

JUVENILE DELINQUENTS AND DEPENDENTS—Cont'd
Small Businesses, generally, this index

JUVENILE FACILITIES DIVISION
Juvenile Delinquents and Dependents, generally, this index

KARNETTE RENTAL PURCHASE ACT
Generally, CC 1812.620 et seq.

KERN COUNTY STATE COLLEGE
Colleges and Universities, generally, this index

KEYS
Oil and gas, automated dispensing outlets, liability after loss or theft, CC 1747.03

KICKBACKS
Mortgages, CC 2924d
Trust deeds, CC 2924d

KIDNAPPING
Human Trafficking, generally, this index
Trafficking. Human Trafficking, generally, this index

KILLING
Animals, this index

KIN
Relatives, generally, this index

KNIVES
Weapons, generally, this index

KNOWLEDGE
Notice, generally, this index

KNUCKLES
Weapons, generally, this index

LABELS
Brands, Marks and Labels, generally, this index

LABOR AND EMPLOYMENT
Actions and proceedings, records and recordation, copies, CC 1786.53
Agencies. Employment Agencies, generally, this index
Agricultural Labor and Employment, generally, this index
Applications,
    Libel and slander, privileged communications, CC 47
    Notice, investigative consumer reports, CC 1786.16
Attorney fees, counseling services, CC 1812.523
Commercial blockade, health facilities, application of law, CC 3427.4
Compensation and Salaries, generally, this index
Counseling. Employment Counseling Services, generally, this index
Criminal history information, copies, CC 1786.53

LABOR AND EMPLOYMENT—Cont'd
Damages, fraud or malice, CC 3294
Discrimination, medical information, disclosure, use, CC 56.20 et seq.
Disputes. Labor Disputes, generally, this index
Domestic Workers, generally, this index
Elevators, Dumbwaiters and Escalators, generally, this index
Employment Agencies, generally, this index
Farm machinery repair shop, cost, CC 1718
Firefighters and Fire Departments, generally, this index
Fraud, damages, CC 3294
Garnishment, generally, this index
Identity and identification,
 RFID (radio frequency identification), crimes and offenses, CC 1798.79, 1798.795
 Theft, CC 1798.92 et seq.
Independent wholesale sales representatives, CC 1738.10 et seq.
Indictment and information, records and recordation, copies, CC 1786.53
Information, employment or insurance purposes, investigative consumer reporting agencies, CC 1786 et seq.
Injunction, breach of contract, CC 3423
Inspection and inspectors, employment investigations, consumer reporting agencies, files, CC 1786 et seq.
Internet, consumer credit reporting agencies, investigative consumer reports, notice, CC 1786.16
Invasion of privacy, use of name, photograph, voice, signature, CC 3344
Investigations and investigators, employment or insurance purposes, reporting agencies, CC 1786 et seq.
Judgments and decrees, records and recordation, copies, CC 1786.53
Letters of recommendation, personal information held by governmental agencies, Information Practices Act, CC 1798.38
Libel and slander,
 Employment references, privileged communications, CC 47
 Privileged communications, CC 47
Liens and incumbrances, CC 3051 et seq.
 Mechanics Liens, generally, this index
 Vehicle repair, CC 3067 et seq.
Mechanics Liens, generally, this index
Notice, applications for employment, investigative consumer reports, CC 1786.16
Occupational Diseases, generally, this index
Ownership of products, CC 655
Performance review, privileged communications, CC 47
Personal injuries, affecting ability to serve employer, CC 49
Personal Services, generally, this index
Physical examinations, medical records, release, CC 56.10
Preemployment physical examination, children and minors, release authorization of medical records, CC 56.10

LABOR AND EMPLOYMENT—Cont'd
Privileges and immunities,
 Employment references, communications, CC 47
 Libel and slander, CC 47
Protection, employees, force, right to use, CC 50
Records and recordation, employment investigations, consumer reporting agencies, CC 1786 et seq.
References, privileged communications, CC 47
Reports, employment investigations, consumer reporting agencies, CC 1786 et seq.
Retirement and Pensions, generally, this index
Salaries. Compensation and Salaries, generally, this index
Sales representatives, independent wholesale sales representatives, CC 1738.10 et seq.
Service without, CC 2078
Small Businesses, generally, this index
Specific performance, personal services, CC 3390
Subrogation, workers compensation benefits, employees injury under firemans rule, CC 1714.9
Tax liens, records and recordation, copies, CC 1786.53
Wages. Compensation and Salaries, generally, this index
Waiver, investigative consumer reporting agencies, CC 1786.57
Workers Compensation, generally, this index

LABOR DISPUTES
Contracts, freedom from violence, waiver, CC 51.7
Freedom from violence, CC 51.7
 Fines and penalties, CC 52
Lockouts, employment agencies, loss of job by customer, fees, CC 1812.506
Violence, freedom from, CC 51.7
 Fines and penalties, CC 52

LABOR ORGANIZATIONS
Employment agencies,
 Application of law, CC 1812.502
 Membership in union as requirement, notice, CC 1812.509

LABOR RELATIONS
Labor Disputes, generally, this index

LABORERS LIENS
Mechanics Liens, generally, this index

LACE
Carriers, limitation of liability, CC 2200

LACHES
Marketable record title, real estate, application of law, CC 880.030
Voidable transactions, application of law, CC 3439.12

LAGOONS
Lakes and Ponds, generally, this index

LAKES AND PONDS
Boundaries, CC 830
Fish and Game, generally, this index
Ownership, state, CC 670
State ownership, CC 670

LAND
Real Estate, generally, this index

LAND CONTRACTS
Contracts for sale of land. Deeds and Conveyances, this index

LAND SURVEYORS
Surveys and Surveyors, generally, this index

LAND USE PLANNING
Zoning and Planning, generally, this index

LANDING FIELDS
Airports and Landing Fields, generally, this index

LANDLORD AND TENANT
 Generally, CC 1925 et seq.
 Abandoned or unclaimed property, personal property, termination,
  Disposition, CC 1980 et seq.
  Notice, CC 1946, 1946.1, 1950.5
 Abandonment,
  Breach by lessee, CC 1951.2 et seq.
  Entry on property, CC 1954
 Abuse, termination, notice, CC 1946.7
 Access, preventing tenant reasonable access with intent to terminate lease, CC 789.3
 Actions and proceedings,
  Damages, generally, post
  Demolition, notice, CC 1940.6
  Evidence, generally, post
  Floating home marinas, CC 800.200, 800.201
  HIV, disclosure, CC 1710.2
  Immigration, disclosure, CC 1940.35
  Injunction, generally, post
  Locks, inoperable, CC 1941.3
  Personal property, return to tenant, termination of lease, CC 1965
  Quiet possession, interference, vacating premises, CC 1940.2
  Recovery of property or possession, notice, CC 1949
  Retaliatory actions by landlord, damages, CC 1942.5
  Security deposits, CC 1950.5
  Skimming of rent, damages, CC 891
  Substandard conditions, rent, CC 1942.4
  Waiver, lessees rights, CC 1953
 Address, multiunit dwellings, disclosures, CC 1961 et seq.
 Administrative expenses, rent control system, apportionment, CC 1947.15
 Advances and advancements, deposits,
  Nonresidential property, CC 1950.7

LANDLORD

LANDLORD AND TENANT—Cont'd
Advances and advancements, deposits—Cont'd
  Retention and return, CC 1950.5, 1953
Advertisements, animals, declawing, devocalizing, CC 1942.7
Aged Persons, this index
Agents and agencies,
  Demolition, notice, CC 1940.6
  Service of process, multiunit dwellings, disclosures, CC 1961 et seq.
Agricultural products, CC 1940.10
Agriculture, duration of tenancy, CC 717
Ambiguities, use restrictions, CC 1997.220
Amenities, reduction, COVID 19, CC 1942.9
Animal control officers, abandoned or unclaimed property, termination of tenancy, involuntary deposits, notice, CC 1816
Appeal and review, frivolous or delaying appeals, tenants recovery of cost, CC 1947.15
Application of law, optional procedure, disposition of personal property remaining on premises at termination of tenancy, CC 1981
Applications,
  COVID 19, indebtedness, CC 1785.20.4
  Screening, fees, CC 1950.6
Apportionment, termination of hiring, CC 1935
Arbitration, condition of premises, CC 1942.1
Assignments, CC 1995.010 et seq.
  Breach, remedies, CC 1995.300 et seq.
  Business premises, right to occupy, CC 1954.05
  Remedies,
    Assignee of lessee, CC 822
    Lessor, CC 823
  Rental rates, CC 1954.53
  Restrictions, consent required by landlord, CC 1995.010 et seq.
  Rights, CC 821
Associations and societies, tenants rights, trespass, CC 1942.6
At fault just cause, termination, CC 1946.2
Attorney fees,
  Demolition, notice, actions and proceedings, CC 1940.6
  Floating home marinas, CC 800.200
  Public utilities, termination of service, damages, CC 789.3
  Rent control, apportionment or recovery, CC 1947.15
  Retaliatory eviction, tenants complaint on tenantability, CC 1942.5
  Skimming of rent, CC 891
  Substandard conditions, rent, CC 1942.4
Attorneys fees, immigration, disclosure, CC 1940.35
Attornment, CC 1111
  Stranger, CC 1948

LANDLORD AND TENANT—Cont'd
Automatic renewal or extension of lease, CC 1945.5
Bad faith retention, security deposits, fines and penalties, CC 1950.5
Baggage, lien, CC 1861a
Bidding, tenants property, termination of tenancy, CC 1984, 1988
Blind or visually impaired persons, CC 54.1 et seq.
Breach of lease,
  Abandonment of property, CC 1951.2 et seq.
  Damages, CC 3308
  Forcible entry and detainer, CC 1952, 1952.3
Building standards, water conservation, CC 1101.1 et seq.
Cancellation, rent controls, CC 1954.535
  Owner established rental rates, CC 1954.53
Care required by tenant, CC 1928, 1941.2
Cash, rent, security deposits, CC 1947.3
Certificates of occupancy, owner established rental rates, CC 1954.52
Change in terms of lease, notice, effect, CC 827
Changing locks, preventing tenant reasonable access with intent to terminate lease, CC 789.3
Cigarettes and cigars, smoking, prohibiting, CC 1947.5
Citizens and citizenship, information, CC 1940.3
City lots, CC 718
Cleaning, security deposits, deductions, CC 1950.5
Clotheslines, CC 1940.20
Commercial property,
  Rent control, CC 1954.25 et seq.
  Termination, personal property, disposition, CC 1993 et seq.
Complaint on tenantability, retaliation by landlord, CC 1942.5
Confidential or privileged information, rent control, CC 1947.7
Consent,
  Assignment or sublease, CC 1995.010 et seq.
  Attornment, CC 1948
    Waiver, lessee rights, CC 1942.1
  Change in use, CC 1997.250, 1997.260
  Entry on property, CC 1954
Consumer credit reporting agencies, CC 1785.1 et seq., 1786 et seq., 1954.06
  Applicants, screening, fees, CC 1950.6
  Reusable tenant screening reports, CC 1950.1
  Unlawful detainer, CC 1785.13, 1786.18
Containers, agricultural products, CC 1940.10
Continuation of lease, abandonment and breach by lessee, CC 1951.4
Copies, CC 1962

LANDLORD AND TENANT—Cont'd
Costa Hawkins Rental Housing Act, CC 1954.50 et seq.
Costs,
  Floating home marinas, CC 800.200
  Immigration, disclosure, CC 1940.35
  Skimming of rent, CC 891
  Substandard conditions, rent, CC 1942.4
Covenants running with land, rent, payment, CC 1462, 1463
COVID 19,
  Actions and proceedings, retaliation, CC 1942.5
  Amenities, reduction, CC 1942.9
  Fees, indebtedness, CC 1942.9
  Indebtedness, screening, CC 1785.20.4
  Services, reduction, CC 1942.9
Credit checks, applicant screening, fees, CC 1950.6
Crime victims, emergency services, law enforcement, CC 1946.8
Crimes and offenses,
  Drugs and medicine, nuisance, forcible entry and detainer, CC 3486
  Rent skimming, residential real estate, CC 890 et seq.
Damages,
  Abandonment, breach by lessee, continuation of lease, CC 1951.4
  Access, preventing tenant reasonable access, intent to terminate lease, CC 789.3
  Assignments, breach of lease restrictions, CC 1995.300 et seq.
  Demolition, notice, CC 1940.6
  Force and violence, vacating premises, CC 1940.2
  Guide dog for blind person, CC 54.2
  Immigration, disclosure, CC 1940.35
  Innkeepers liens, wrongful possession of property, CC 1861.15
  Personal property or furnishings, termination of lease,
    Removal by landlord without prior consent, CC 789.3
    Return to tenant, CC 1965
  Punitive damages, retaliatory eviction, tenants complaint on tenantability, CC 1942.5
  Quiet possession, interference, vacating premises, CC 1940.2
  Rent control programs, fraudulent eviction of tenant, CC 1947.10
  Retaliatory eviction, tenants complaint of tenantability, CC 1942.5
  Skimming of rent, CC 891
  Substandard conditions, rent, CC 1942.4
  Threats, vacating premises, CC 1940.2
  Transfers, assignment or sublease, breach of lease restrictions, CC 1995.300 et seq.
  Use for particular purpose, CC 1930
Deaf persons, public accommodations, CC 54.1 et seq.

LANDLORD

LANDLORD AND TENANT—Cont'd

Death of party, termination of relationship, CC 1934
Declaratory judgments and decrees, animals, declawing, devocalizing, CC 1942.7
Deductions,
    Public utilities, rent, CC 1942.2
    Rent, repairs, CC 1942
    Security deposits, CC 1950.5
Deeds and conveyances, attornment, CC 1111
Delay by landlord, tenant recovery of cost, CC 1947.15
Demolition, notice, CC 1940.6
Dependent adults, abuse, termination, notice, CC 1946.7
Deposits. Security deposits, generally, post
Description of property remaining on premises at termination of tenancy, notice, CC 1983
Dilapidation, premises untenantable, CC 1941.1 et seq.
Disabled persons, CC 54.1 et seq.
Disclosure,
    Citizens and citizenship, CC 1940.3
    Demolition, CC 1940.6
    Immigration, threats, CC 1940.2
    Military ordinance locations, CC 1940.7
    Multiunit dwellings, process, CC 1961 et seq.
    Water supply, submeters, CC 1954.204
Discrimination,
    Age discrimination, CC 51.2
    Blind or visually impaired persons, CC 54 et seq.
    Disabled persons, availability of rental housing, CC 54.1 et seq.
Display, religion, CC 1940.45
Disposition, personal property, termination, CC 1980 et seq., 1993 et seq.
Documents, security deposits, deductions, CC 1950.5
Dogs, disabled persons, CC 54.1
Doors, locks, CC 1941.3
Double letting of rooms, CC 1950
Drugs and medicine, nuisance, forcible entry and detainer, CC 3486
Drying racks, CC 1940.20
Duress or coercion, vacating premises, CC 1940.2
Duties of tenant, CC 1941.2
Duty of due care by lessor, waiver, CC 1953
Elections, signs and signals, CC 1940.4
Electricity,
    Cutting off utilities to terminate lease, damages, CC 789.3
    Unseparated meters, CC 1940.9
Elevators,
    Cutting off utilities to terminate lease, damages, CC 789.3
    Multiunit dwellings, owner or agent for service of process or notice, disclosure, posting in elevator, CC 1962.5

LANDLORD AND TENANT—Cont'd

Emergencies, entry on property, CC 1954
Emergency services, fines and penalties, CC 1946.8
Entry on property, CC 1954
    Preventing tenants reasonable access, intent to terminate lease, CC 789.3
    Waiver, lessees rights, CC 1953
    Water conservation, building standards, CC 1101.5
    Water supply, submeters, CC 1954.211
Estimates, security deposits, deductions, CC 1950.5
Eviction,
    Forcible Entry and Detainer, generally, this index
    Retaliatory eviction, tenants complaint on tenantability, CC 1942.5
Evidence,
    Immigration, CC 3339.10
    Presumptions, generally, post
    Retaliation by landlord, tenants exercise of rights, CC 1942.5
    Security deposits, CC 1950.5
Exemptions,
    Locks, CC 1941.3
    Termination, just cause, CC 1946.2
Expenses and expenditures,
    Personal property, termination of lease,
        Disposition, CC 1984
        Return to tenant, CC 1965
    Rent control administrative and management expenses, apportionment or recovery, CC 1947.15
Extension of lease, automatic, CC 1945.5
Fair return, rent control system, calculation, CC 1947.15
Fees,
    Applicant screening, CC 1950.6
    COVID 19, indebtedness, CC 1942.9
    Rent control system, apportionment or recovery, CC 1947.15
    Water supply, submeters, CC 1954.213
Fines and penalties,
    Abuse, termination, notice, CC 1946.7
    Animals, declawing, devocalizing, CC 1942.7
    Demolition, notice, CC 1940.6
    Floating home marinas, CC 800.200
    Rent skimming, CC 892
    Security deposits, bad faith retention, CC 1950.5
    Water supply, submeters, CC 1954.208
Fitness for human occupancy, CC 1941 et seq.
    Repairs, rent deduction, CC 1942
    Untenantable dwellings, CC 1941.1
    Vacating premises, CC 1942
    Waiver, lessee rights, CC 1942.1
Fixtures, removal, CC 1019
Floating homes, marinas, CC 800 et seq.
Force and violence, vacating premises, CC 1940.2

LANDLORD AND TENANT—Cont'd

Forcible Entry and Detainer, generally, this index
Foreign languages, contracts, translations, CC 1632
Forms,
    Domestic violence, termination, CC 1946.7
    Notice, abandoned or unclaimed property, CC 1984, 1985
    Payment, CC 1962
Fraud, owners and ownership, CC 890
Frauds, statute of, leases longer than one year, CC 1624
Frivolous appeals by landlord, tenants recovery of cost, CC 1947.15
Funds transfers, CC 1962
Furniture, removal by landlord without prior written consent, intent to terminate lease, CC 789.3
Gas,
    Cutting off utilities to terminate lease, damages, CC 789.3
    Unseparated meters, CC 1940.9
Guide dogs, blind or visually impaired persons, access, training, CC 54.1, 54.2
Habitability, breach, evidence, presumption, CC 1942.3
Harassment, sexual harassment, CC 51.9
Heat, cutting off utilities to terminate lease, damages, CC 789.3
HIV, disclosure, actions and proceedings, CC 1710.2
Holding over,
    Continued possession and acceptance of rent, CC 1945
    Homeless persons, CC 1942.8
Homeless persons,
    Holding over, CC 1942.8
    Occupancy, hotels and motels, shelters, CC 1954.08 et seq.
Identity and identification, multiunit dwellings, disclosure, CC 1961 et seq.
Immigration,
    Disclosure, CC 1940.35
    Evidence, CC 3339.10
    Information, CC 1940.3
    Threats, CC 1940.2
Indebtedness, COVID 19, CC 1785.20.4
    Screening, CC 1785.20.4
Information,
    Citizens and citizenship, CC 1940.3
    Security deposits, deductions, CC 1950.5
    Tenants rights, trespass, CC 1942.6
Initial inspection, termination, CC 1950.5
Injunction,
    Animals, declawing, devocalizing, CC 1942.7
    Emergency services, law enforcement, CC 1946.8
    Immigration, disclosure, CC 1940.35
    Innkeepers liens, writs of possession, CC 1861.16, 1861.17

LANDLORD

LANDLORD AND TENANT—Cont'd
Injunction—Cont'd
  Unlawful actions to terminate lease, **CC 789.3**
Inside telephone wiring, landlord responsibility, **CC 1941.4**
Inspection and inspectors,
  Agricultural products, **CC 1940.10**
  Entry on property, **CC 1954**
  Termination, **CC 1950.5**
Insurance, waterbeds, **CC 1940.5**
Interest, security deposits, bad faith claim or retention by landlord, **CC 1950.5**
Interference, quiet possession, **CC 1940.2**
Internet, sex offenses, registration, notice, **CC 2079.10a**
Interruption of utilities with intent to terminate occupancy, damages, **CC 789.3**
Just cause, termination, **CC 1946.2**
Law enforcement, fines and penalties, **CC 1946.8**
Leases, generally, this index
Legal Estates Principal and Income Law, **CC 731 et seq.**
Licenses and permits, demolition, notice, **CC 1940.6**
Light, cutting off utilities to terminate lease, damages, **CC 789.3**
Limitation of liability, disposition of personal property remaining on premises at termination of tenancy, **CC 1983**
Locks and locking, **CC 1941.3**
  Changing locks, preventing tenant reasonable access with intent to terminate lease, **CC 789.3**
  Protective orders, **CC 1941.5, 1941.6**
Low and Moderate Income Housing, generally, this index
Mail and mailing,
  Notice,
    Entry on property, **CC 1954**
    Termination, **CC 1946, 1946.1**
  Security deposits, deductions, statements, **CC 1950.5**
Management expenses, rent control system, apportionment, **CC 1947.15**
Marinas, floating home residency, **CC 800 et seq.**
Materials, security deposits, deductions, **CC 1950.5**
Meetings, homeowners, floating home marinas, **CC 800.60, 800.61**
Merger of interest, termination of relationship, **CC 1933**
Meters, water supply, submeters, **CC 1954.201 et seq.**
Military forces, security deposits, **CC 1950.5**
Mold, dilapidation, **CC 1941.7**
Money, rent, security deposits, **CC 1947.3**
Municipal lots, **CC 718**
Names, **CC 1962**
Negligence, care required by tenant, **CC 1928**

LANDLORD AND TENANT—Cont'd
Net operating income, calculation, rent control system, **CC 1947.15**
No fault just cause, termination, **CC 1946.2**
Noncitizens,
  Disclosure, **CC 1940.35**
  Information, **CC 1940.3**
  Threats, **CC 1940.2**
Nonrefundable security deposits, **CC 1950.5**
Nonrenewal, rent controls, **CC 1954.535**
  Owner established rental rates, **CC 1954.53**
Notice,
  Actions and proceedings, recovery of property, **CC 1942.5, 1949**
  Cash, rent, security deposits, **CC 1947.3**
  Consumer credit reporting agencies, **CC 1786.16**
    Reports, **CC 1785.20**
  Demolition, **CC 1940.6**
  Disposition of personal property remaining on premises at termination of tenancy, **CC 1983 et seq.**
  Domestic violence, termination, **CC 1946.7**
  Elevators, dumbwaiters and escalators, **CC 1962.5**
  Entry on property, **CC 1954**
  Inspection and inspectors, termination, **CC 1950.5**
  Liens and incumbrances, innkeepers liens, writs of possession, **CC 1861.8**
  Locks and locking,
    Inoperable, **CC 1941.3**
    Protective orders, **CC 1941.5, 1941.6**
  Mail and mailing, ante
  Military ordinance locations, disclosure, **CC 1940.7**
  Money, rent, security deposits, **CC 1947.3**
  Month to month tenancy, **CC 827**
  Obligation to deliver to landlord, time, **CC 1949**
  Personal property,
    Remaining on premises at termination of tenancy, **CC 1983**
    Return to tenant, **CC 1965**
  Pest control, **CC 1940.8, 1940.8.5**
  Presumptions, **CC 1962**
  Process, multiunit dwellings, **CC 1961 et seq.**
  Protective orders, locks and locking, **CC 1941.5, 1941.6**
  Quit, holding over, homeless persons, **CC 1942.8**
  Reclaiming abandoned property, **CC 1984, 1985**
  Registered sex offenders, data base, **CC 2079.10a**
  Rent, increase, **CC 827**
  Repairs, rent, deductions, **CC 1942**
  Security deposits, transfer, **CC 1950.5**
  Smoking, prohibiting, **CC 1947.5**
  Tenancy not specified, renewal, **CC 1946.1**

LANDLORD AND TENANT—Cont'd
Notice—Cont'd
  Termination, post
  Terms of lease, effect, **CC 827**
  Waiver, lessees rights, **CC 1953**
Nuisance,
  Drugs and medicine, forcible entry and detainer, **CC 3486**
  Floating home marinas, **CC 800.201**
  Rent, **CC 1942.4**
Oil and gas,
  Cutting off utilities to terminate lease, damages, **CC 789.3**
  Unseparated meters, **CC 1940.9**
Orders of court,
  Entry on property, **CC 1954**
  Protective orders, locks and locking, **CC 1941.5, 1941.6**
  Repairs, **CC 1942.4**
Ordinances, rent stabilization and rent control, **CC 1947.7 et seq.**
Part of rooms, letting, **CC 1950**
Payment,
  Forms, **CC 1947.3, 1962**
  Time, **CC 1947**
Penalties. Fines and penalties, generally, ante
Permits, demolition, notice, **CC 1940.6**
Personal property,
  Disposition, termination, **CC 1980 et seq., 1993 et seq.**
  Removal by landlord without prior written consent, intent to terminate lease, **CC 789.3**
  Return, termination of lease, **CC 1965**
  Security deposits, future defaults, **CC 1950.5**
  Termination of lease, return to tenant, **CC 1965**
Pest control, notice, **CC 1940.8, 1940.8.5**
Pesticides, agricultural products, **CC 1940.10**
Pets,
  Abandoned or unclaimed property, termination of tenancy, **CC 1981**
    Involuntary deposits, **CC 1815 et seq.**
  Declawing, devocalizing, **CC 1942.7**
Possession, continued, **CC 1945**
Presumptions,
  Habitability, breach, **CC 1942.3**
  Holding over, **CC 1945**
  Notice, **CC 1962**
  Term of lease, **CC 1944**
Privileges and immunities, abandoned or unclaimed property, release, **CC 1989**
Privity of contract, sale of property, **CC 821**
Proceedings. Actions and proceedings, generally, ante
Process, service of process, multiunit dwellings, disclosure, **CC 1961 et seq.**
Protective orders, locks and locking, **CC 1941.5, 1941.6**
Public policy, assignment and sublease, **CC 1995.270**

LANDLORD AND TENANT—Cont'd
Public utilities,
  Actions and proceedings,
    Termination of service, damages, attorney fees, **CC 789.3**
    Unseparated gas and electric meters, **CC 1940.9**
  Damages, cutting off utilities with intent to terminate lease, **CC 789.3**
  Deductions, rent, **CC 1942.2**
  Unseparated gas and electric meters, **CC 1940.9**
Publication, sales, liens and incumbrances, **CC 1861a**
Punitive damages, retaliatory eviction, tenants complaint on tenantability, **CC 1942.5**
Quiet possession, **CC 1927**
  Interference, **CC 1940.2**
Rates and charges,
  Floating home marinas, **CC 800.40 et seq.**
  Water supply, submeters, **CC 1954.201 et seq.**
Records and recordation, water supply, submeters, **CC 1954.209**
Recovery proceedings for property, **CC 1942.5**
  Notice to landlord, **CC 1949**
Refrigeration, cutting off utilities to terminate lease, damages, **CC 789.3**
Refunds,
  Excessive rent, local rent control programs, **CC 1947.11**
  Security deposits, nonresidential property, **CC 1950.7**
Registered sex offenders, data base, notice, **CC 2079.10a**
Reimbursement, security deposits, **CC 1950.5**
Release of personal property remaining on premises at termination of tenancy, **CC 1987**
  Former tenants, liability of landlord, **CC 1989**
Religion, display, **CC 1940.45**
Relocation, termination, just cause, **CC 1946.2**
Removal,
  Fixtures, **CC 1019**
  Personal property or furnishings, **CC 789.3**
Renewal,
  Automatic, **CC 1945.5**
  Continued possession and acceptance of rent, **CC 1945**
  Notice, **CC 1946**
  Tenancy not specified, **CC 1946.1**
Rent, generally, this index
Rent Controls, generally, this index
Rent skimming, **CC 890 et seq.**
Repairs, **CC 1929, 1941**
  Entry on property, **CC 1954**
  Mold, dilapidation, **CC 1941.7**
  Notice, rent deduction, **CC 1942**
  Orders of court, **CC 1942.4**
  Rent deduction, limitations, **CC 1942**

LANDLORD AND TENANT—Cont'd
Repairs—Cont'd
  Security deposits, deductions, **CC 1950.5**
  Untenantable dwellings, **CC 1941.1**
  Waiver, lessee rights, **CC 1942.1**
  Water supply, submeters, **CC 1954.210**
Reports, reusable tenant screening reports, **CC 1950.1**
Restrictions,
  Aged persons, cohabitants, **CC 51.3**
  Use restrictions, **CC 1997.010 et seq.**
Restrictive covenants, religion, display, **CC 1940.45**
Retaliation,
  Complaint on tenantability, **CC 1942.5**
  Immigration, disclosure, **CC 1940.35**
Return of personal property, termination of lease, **CC 1965**
Reusable tenant screening reports, **CC 1950.1**
Rooms, double letting of rooms, **CC 1950**
Rules and regulations, floating home marinas, **CC 800.30 et seq.**
Sales,
  Entry on property, **CC 1954**
  Innkeepers liens, **CC 1861.24**
  Personal property, abandoned or unclaimed property, termination, **CC 1980 et seq.**
  Rights of new owner, **CC 821**
Screening,
  Applicants, fees, **CC 1950.6**
  Citizens and citizenship, **CC 1940.3**
  COVID 19, indebtedness, **CC 1785.20.4**
  Reusable tenant screening reports, **CC 1950.1**
Second and subsequent offenses, public utilities, cutting off to terminate lease, **CC 789.3**
Security deposits, **CC 1950.5**
  Cash, **CC 1947.3**
  Floating home marinas, **CC 800.49**
  Mobilehomes and mobilehome parks, **CC 798.39**
  Money, **CC 1947.3**
  Nonresidential property, **CC 1950.7**
  Waiver, lessees rights, **CC 1953**
Service of process, multiunit dwellings, disclosure, **CC 1961 et seq.**
Services, reduction, COVID 19, **CC 1942.9**
Sex offenses, registration, data base, notice, **CC 2079.10a**
Sexual harassment, **CC 51.9**
Signs and signals, elections, **CC 1940.4**
Skimming of rent, **CC 890 et seq.**
Smoking, prohibiting, **CC 1947.5**
Spanish language, contracts, translations, **CC 1632**
Special damages, substandard conditions, rent, **CC 1942.4**
Standards, submeters, water supply, **CC 1954.203**
Statements, security deposits, **CC 1950.5**

LANDLORD AND TENANT—Cont'd
Statute of Frauds, **CC 1624**
Storage, **CC 1965**
  Termination of tenancy, property remaining, **CC 1986 et seq.**
Subdivisions, owner established rental rates, **CC 1954.52**
Submeters, water supply, **CC 1954.201 et seq.**
Substandard conditions, rent, **CC 1942.4**
Subtenants, **CC 1995.010 et seq.**
  Breach, lease restrictions, remedies, **CC 1995.300 et seq.**
  Rent, **CC 1954.53**
Suits. Actions and proceedings, generally, ante
Supplies, security deposits, deductions, **CC 1950.5**
Telecommunications,
  Damages, cutoffs, **CC 789.3**
  Numbers and numbering, **CC 1962**
  Wires and wiring, **CC 1941.4**
Tenancy at will, **CC 761, 819**
  Chattel interests, **CC 765**
  Termination, **CC 789**
Tenancy for years, **CC 761, 819, 820**
  Chattels real, **CC 765, 773**
  Condominiums, **CC 783**
  Deeds and conveyances, **CC 1108**
  Foreign languages, contracts, translations, **CC 1632**
  Life estates, **CC 773**
  Remainders, **CC 773**
  Spanish language, contracts, translations, **CC 1632**
Tenancy from day to day, **CC 1947**
Tenancy from month to month,
  Foreign languages, contracts, translations, **CC 1632**
  Notice, **CC 827, 1946**
  Presumptions, **CC 1943, 1944**
  Spanish language, contracts, translations, **CC 1632**
  Termination, **CC 1946**
Tenancy from week to week, **CC 1947**
  Change of terms, notice, **CC 827**
Tenancy from year to year, **CC 1947**
  Foreign languages, contracts, translations, **CC 1632**
Tenancy in Common, generally, this index
Tenancy not specified, **CC 1946, 1946.1**
Tenancy of less than a month, **CC 827**
Termination, **CC 1931 et seq.**
  Abuse, notice, **CC 1946.7**
  Aged persons, abuse, notice, **CC 1946.7**
  Animals, abandoned or unclaimed property, involuntary deposits, **CC 1815 et seq.**
  Damages, **CC 3308**
    Just cause, **CC 1946.2**
  Dependent adults, abuse, notice, **CC 1946.7**
  Floating home marinas, **CC 800.70 et seq.**
  Homeless persons, holding over, **CC 1942.8**
  Human trafficking, notice, **CC 1946.7**

LANDLORD

LANDLORD AND TENANT—Cont'd
Termination—Cont'd
  Initial inspection, CC 1950.5
  Inspection and inspectors, CC 1950.5
  Just cause, CC 1946.2
  Notice, CC 1946
    Just cause, CC 1946.2
    Rent controls, CC 1954.535
    Tenancy at will, CC 789
    Tenancy not specified, CC 1946.1
  Personal property,
    Disposition, CC 1980 et seq., 1993 et seq.
    Return, CC 1965
  Rent controls, CC 1954.53, 1954.535
  Retaliatory eviction, tenants complaint on tenantability, CC 1942.5
  Tenancy at will, CC 789
  Tenancy not specified, CC 1946, 1946.1
Threats, vacating premises, CC 1940.2
Time,
  Entry on property, CC 1954
  Notice, rent, increase, CC 827
  Personal property, termination of lease,
    Remaining on premises, notice, CC 1983
    Return to tenant, CC 1965
  Rent,
    Deductions, repairs by lessee, CC 1942
    Payment, CC 1947
  Security deposits, refunds, CC 1950.7
  Title to property, CC 1926
    Fraud, CC 890
Tobacco and tobacco products, smoking, prohibiting, CC 1947.5
Town lots, CC 718
Transfers, CC 821, 1995.010 et seq.
  Abandonment, breach by lessee, CC 1951.4
  Breach, remedies, CC 1995.300 et seq.
Translations, foreign languages, contracts, CC 1632
Trespass, information, tenants rights, CC 1942.6
Unclaimed property, personal property, termination,
  Disposition, CC 1980 et seq.
  Notice, CC 1946, 1946.1, 1950.5
Unlawful detainer. Forcible Entry and Detainer, generally, this index
Untenantable buildings, CC 1941.1
Use restrictions, CC 1997.010 et seq.
Utilities. Public utilities, generally, ante
Vacancy Decontrol Law, CC 1954.50 et seq.
Vacating premises,
  Duress or coercion, CC 1940.2
  Untenantable buildings, CC 1942
Valuation, rent, assignment of leased business premises, CC 1954.05
Waiver,
  Automatic renewal or extension of lease, CC 1945.5
  Innkeepers liens, writs of possession, CC 1861.13

LANDLORD AND TENANT—Cont'd
Waiver—Cont'd
  Investigative consumer reporting agencies, CC 1786.57
  Lessees rights, CC 1942.1, 1953
  Security deposits, deductions, statements, CC 1950.5
  Water supply, submeters, CC 1954.215
Water conservation, building standards, CC 1101.1 et seq.
Water supply,
  Cutting off utilities to terminate lease, damages, CC 789.3
  Disclosure, submeters, CC 1954.204
  Entry on property, submeters, CC 1954.211
  Fees, submeters, CC 1954.213
  Fines and penalties, submeters, CC 1954.208
  Meters, submeters, CC 1954.201 et seq.
  Records and recordation, submeters, CC 1954.209
  Repairs, submeters, CC 1954.210
  Standards, submeters, CC 1954.203
  Waiver, submeters, CC 1954.215
Waterbeds, CC 1940.5
Windows, security devices, CC 1941.3
Written instruments. Leases, generally, this index

LANDSCAPE ARCHITECTS
Consolidated cities and counties, contracts, indemnity, CC 2782.8
Counties, contracts, indemnity, CC 2782.8
Districts, contracts, indemnity, CC 2782.8
Joint powers authorities, contracts, indemnity, CC 2782.8
Liens and incumbrances. Mechanics Liens, generally, this index
Mechanics Liens, generally, this index
Municipalities, contracts, indemnity, CC 2782.8
Public authorities, contracts, indemnity, CC 2782.8
Public corporations, contracts, indemnity, CC 2782.8
Schools and school districts, contracts, indemnity, CC 2782.8

LANDSCAPES AND LANDSCAPING
Architects. Landscape Architects, generally, this index
Condominiums, plants and plant products, water conservation, CC 4735
  Business and commerce, CC 6712
Mobilehomes and mobilehome parks, fees, CC 798.37
Zoning and Planning, generally, this index

LANES
Streets and Alleys, generally, this index

LANGUAGE
See, also, Foreign Languages, generally, this index

LANGUAGE—Cont'd
Civil rights, CC 51
Consumer credit, contracts, notice, CC 1799.91
Consumer warranties, plain language, CC 1793.1
English Language, generally, this index
Foreign Languages, generally, this index
Mortgage foreclosure consultants, contracts, CC 2945.3
Plain language,
  Consumer warranties, CC 1793.1
  Warranties, CC 1793.1
Spanish Language, generally, this index
Warranties, plain language, CC 1793.1

LANGUAGES
Language, generally, this index

LAPSE OF TIME
Contracts, revocation, CC 1587

LARCENY
Theft, generally, this index

LASCIVIOUSNESS
Lewdness and Obscenity, generally, this index

LATERAL SUPPORT
Adjoining landowners, CC 832
Easements, CC 801

LAUNDRIES
Cleaning, Dyeing and Pressing, generally, this index

LAW
Common Law, generally, this index
Legislature, generally, this index
Ordinances, generally, this index
Statutes, generally, this index
Uniform Laws, generally, this index

LAW ENFORCEMENT
Community Facilities Districts, generally, this index
Discrimination, dogs, public accommodations, emergencies, CC 54.25
Dogs, discrimination, public accommodations, emergencies, CC 54.25
Fines and penalties, dogs, discrimination, public accommodations, emergencies, CC 54.25
Forcible entry and detainer, CC 1946.8
Forms, disclosure notices, Information Practices Act, CC 1798.17
Invasion of privacy, investigations and investigators, CC 1708.8
Landlord and tenant, fines and penalties, CC 1946.8
Leases, fines and penalties, CC 1946.8
Medical records, disclosure, application of law, CC 56.30
Peace Officers, generally, this index
Penalties, dogs, discrimination, public accommodations, emergencies, CC 54.25

I-116

LEASES

LAW ENFORCEMENT—Cont'd
Personal or confidential information, disclosure by government agencies, Information Practices Act, **CC 1798.24**
Police, generally, this index
Sheriffs, generally, this index

LAW GOVERNING
Conflict of Laws, generally, this index

LAW OF THE ROAD
Traffic Rules and Regulations, generally, this index

LAWYERS
Attorneys, generally, this index

LAYAWAY SALES
Generally, **CC 1749 et seq.**

LEAD
Paint. Lead Base Paint, generally, this index

LEAD BASE PAINT
Abatement, **CC 3494.5**
Consumer information, booklets, costs, **CC 2079.11**
Costs, consumer information booklets, **CC 2079.11**
Disclosure, real estate transfers, **CC 2079.7**
Notice, real estate transfers, **CC 2079.7**
Privileges and immunities, abatement, **CC 3494.5**
Real estate brokers and salespersons, notice, **CC 2079.7**

LEASEBACKS
Voidable transactions, application of law, **CC 3440.1**

LEASES
Generally, **CC 1955 et seq.**
Abandoned or Unclaimed Property, this index
Abandonment,
  Breach by lessee,
    Combining notice of belief of abandonment with notice of right to reclaim abandoned property, **CC 1991**
    Continuation of lease in effect, **CC 1951.4**
    Termination of lease, **CC 1951.2**
    Establishment of abandonment, procedure, **CC 1951.3**
  Commercial property, **CC 1951.35**
Acceptance of rent, holding over, **CC 1945**
Access, preventing tenant reasonable access with intent to terminate lease, **CC 789.3**
Actions and proceedings,
  Consumer goods, statements, illegal contracts, **CC 1670.8**
  Consumers Legal Remedies Act, **CC 1750 et seq.**
  Damages, generally, post
  Evidence, generally, post
  Limitation of actions, generally, post
  Rent control, commercial property, public entities, **CC 1954.31**

LEASES—Cont'd
Advances and advancements, renewal, conditions, **CC 1950.8**
Aged persons, cohabitants, age restrictions, **CC 51.3**
Air pollution, gasoline vapor control system, service stations, marketing operations, **CC 1952.8**
Ambiguities, use restrictions, **CC 1997.220**
Animal control officers, termination, abandoned or unclaimed property, involuntary deposits, notice, **CC 1816**
Animals, termination, abandoned or unclaimed property, involuntary deposits, **CC 1815 et seq.**
Apportionment, termination of hiring, **CC 1935**
Assignments,
  Abandonment, breach by lessee, continuation of lease, **CC 1951.4**
  Breach, lease restrictions, damages, **CC 1995.300 et seq.**
  Business premises, right to occupy, **CC 1954.05**
  Consent, landlords consent required, **CC 1995.010 et seq.**
  Joint and several liability, assignees and tenants, **CC 1995.330**
  Remedies against,
    Assignee of lessee, **CC 822**
    Lessor, **CC 823**
  Restrictions, **CC 1995.010 et seq.**
  Rights, **CC 821**
Athletic facilities, notice, anabolic steroids, testosterone, or human growth hormone, crimes, **CC 1812.97**
Attorney fees,
  Payment, renewal, conditions, **CC 1950.8**
  Terminating lease, **CC 789.3**
Authorities, lessor remedy for breach statutes, applicability to invalidate lease, **CC 1952.6**
Automatic renewal or extension, **CC 1945.5**
Bailment, generally, this index
Belief of abandonment, notice by lessor, **CC 1951.3**
  Commercial property, **CC 1951.35**
Blind or visually impaired persons, discrimination, **CC 54.1**
  Guide dogs, **CC 54.2**
Boxers training gymnasiums, notice, anabolic steroids, testosterone, or human growth hormone, crimes, **CC 1812.97**
Breach of lease. Damages, generally, post
Burden of proof, abandonment, **CC 1951.3**
  Commercial property, **CC 1951.35**
Business premises, assignment, right to occupy, **CC 1954.05**
Campgrounds, membership camping contracts, **CC 1812.308**
Care required by lessee, **CC 1928**
Cats, **CC 1670.10**

LEASES—Cont'd
Changes,
  Notice, **CC 827**
  Use restrictions, **CC 1997.230, 1997.240**
Changing locks, preventing tenant reasonable access with intent to terminate lease, **CC 789.3**
Charging stations, electric vehicles, **CC 1952.7**
Cigarettes and cigars, smoking, prohibiting, **CC 1947.5**
Condominiums, this index
Consent,
  Assignment or sublease, landlords consent required, **CC 1995.010 et seq.**
  Change in use, use restrictions, **CC 1997.250, 1997.260**
Consumers, **CC 1750 et seq.**
  Statements, illegal contracts, **CC 1670.8**
Contiguous land, covenants with respect to, description, **CC 1469, 1470**
Continuation,
  Breach, **CC 1951.4**
  Payment, conditions, **CC 1950.8**
Costs, payment, renewal, conditions, **CC 1950.8**
Covenants with respect to contiguous real property, description of contiguous land, **CC 1470**
Crimes and offenses, stories about felonies, sale proceeds, **CC 2225**
Damages,
  Abandonment, breach by lessee, **CC 1951.4**
  Access, preventing tenant reasonable access, intent to terminate lease, **CC 789.3**
  Assignments, breach of lease restrictions, **CC 1995.300 et seq.**
  Consumers Legal Remedies Act, **CC 1750 et seq.**
  Forcible entry and detainer, effect on lessors right to damages for breach, **CC 1952, 1952.3**
  Guide dogs for blind persons, **CC 54.2**
  Lessee breach, **CC 3308**
  Personal property, disposition, termination, **CC 789.3, 1993.08**
  Public utilities, cutting off public utilities with intent to terminate lease, **CC 789.3**
  Termination, **CC 3308**
  Transfers, assignment or sublease, breach of restrictions, **CC 1995.300 et seq.**
  Use of property for particular purpose, **CC 1930**
  Use restrictions violations, **CC 1997.040**
Death of party, termination of relationship, **CC 1934**
Default,
  Expenses and expenditures, personal property leases, **CC 1957**
  Liquidated damages, **CC 1671**
Delivery, property, **CC 1955**
Disabled persons,
  Accessibility, construction, standards, inspection and inspectors, **CC 1938**

I-117

LEASES

LEASES—Cont'd

Disabled persons—Cont'd
  Discrimination, CC 54.1
Disclosure, residential property, CC 1102 et seq.
Discount, lessors remedies for breach, computing worth at time of award, unpaid rent, CC 1951.2
Discrimination, CC 53, 54.1
  Racial restrictions, CC 782, 782.5
Disposition, personal property, termination, CC 1993 et seq.
Dog Bite Act, CC 3342, 3342.5
Dogs, CC 1670.10
Electric vehicles, charging stations, CC 1952.7
Elevators, cutting off utilities with intent to terminate lease, damages, CC 789.3
Emergency services, fines and penalties, CC 1946.8
Entry, preventing tenants reasonable access, intent to terminate lease, CC 789.3
Equitable relief,
  Action for forcible entry and detainer, CC 1952.3
  Landlords right for breach, action for forcible entry and detainer, CC 1952
  Lessors right, lessees breach, CC 1951.8
Evidence,
  Abandonment, CC 1951.3
    Commercial property, CC 1951.35
  Holding over,
    Presumptions, CC 1945
    Tenant, CC 1945
  Presumptions,
    Holding over by lessee, CC 1945
    Term of hiring, CC 1943
  Term of hiring, presumptions, CC 1943
Exemptions, natural hazards, residential property, disclosure, CC 1103.1
Expenses and expenditures,
  Default, personal property leases, CC 1957
  Personal property, CC 1956
Exploration, natural resources, applicability, lessors remedy for breach, CC 1952.4
Express warranties, Song Beverly Consumer Warranty Act, CC 1795.4
Extension, automatic, CC 1945.5
Fines and penalties,
  Consumer goods, statements, illegal contracts, CC 1670.8
  Emergency services, law enforcement, CC 1946.8
  Payment, renewal, conditions, CC 1950.8
Fitness for human occupancy, CC 1941
Fitness for use, personal property, CC 1955
Floating home marinas, CC 800.20 et seq.
Forcible Entry and Detainer, generally, this index
Foreign languages, translations, CC 1632
Forms, notice of belief of abandonment, CC 1951.3
  Commercial property, CC 1951.35

LEASES—Cont'd

Fraud, Consumers Legal Remedies Act, CC 1750 et seq.
Frauds, statute of, leasing for period of more than one year, CC 1624
Furniture removal by landlord without prior written consent, intent to terminate lease, CC 789.3
Gas, cutting off utilities with intent to terminate lease, damages, CC 789.3
Gas leases. Oil and Gas Leases, generally, this index
Gasoline vapor control systems, service stations, marketing operations, CC 1952.8
Good faith, Consumers Legal Remedies Act, CC 1784
Grazing lands, term of hiring, presumption, CC 1943
Grey market goods, disclosures, CC 1797.8 et seq.
Grey market products, disclosure, CC 1770
Guide dogs, blind or visually impaired persons, training, CC 54.1, 54.2
Hazards, natural hazards, disclosure, residential property, CC 1103 et seq.
Health studios, notice, anabolic steroids, testosterone, or human growth hormone, crimes, CC 1812.97
Heat, cutting off utilities with intent to terminate lease, damages, CC 789.3
Home solicitation contracts, application of law, CC 1689.5 et seq.
Horticulture, land for purposes of, duration, CC 717
Incorporation by reference, unrecorded instruments, description, CC 1469
Indemnity,
  Liquidated damages, CC 1671
  Personal injuries, breach, CC 1951.2
Injunction,
  Consumers Legal Remedies Act, CC 1782
  Landlords unlawful actions to terminate lease, CC 789.3
Interest, lessor remedies for breach, computing worth at time of award, unpaid rent, CC 1951.2
Internet, sex offenses, registration, notice, CC 2079.10a
Interruption of utilities with intent to terminate lease, damages, CC 789.3
Invalidity, time limitations, CC 715
Key money, renewal, conditions, CC 1950.8
Law enforcement, fines and penalties, CC 1946.8
Legal Estates Principal and Income Law, CC 731 et seq.
Lights, cutting off utilities with intent to terminate lease, damages, CC 789.3
Limitation of actions,
  Consumers Legal Remedies Act, CC 1783
  Damages for termination, time for suit, agreement upon, CC 3308

LEASES—Cont'd

Limitation of actions—Cont'd
  Time limitations, lease validity, CC 715
Liquidated damages, CC 1671
  Breach of lease, CC 1951.5
Locks, changing locks, preventing tenant reasonable access with intent to terminate lease, CC 789.3
Mail and mailing, notice of reletting to lessee breaching after making advance payments, CC 1951.7
Marinas, floating homes, CC 800.20 et seq.
Merger of interest, termination of relationship, CC 1933
Mineral rights, CC 883.110 et seq.
Mines and Minerals, this index
Mitigation of damages for breach, efforts by lessor, waiver of damages, CC 1951.2
Mobilehomes and Mobilehome Parks, this index
Motor Vehicle Insurance, this index
Motor Vehicles, this index
Motorized wheelchairs, warranty, CC 1793.025
Municipalities, this index
Natural hazards, disclosure, residential property, CC 1103 et seq.
Natural resources, contracts to explore for or remove, lessors remedy for breach, CC 1952.4
Negligence, care required by lessee, CC 1928
Notice,
  Abandonment, belief of abandonment,
    Commercial property, CC 1951.35
    Lessor, CC 1951.3
  Anabolic steroids, testosterone or human growth hormone, crimes, CC 1812.97
  Blanket incumbrances on subdivisions, CC 1133
  Change in term, CC 827
  Personal property, disposition, termination, CC 1993.03 et seq.
  Public entities, rent control, commercial property, CC 1954.31
  Registered sex offenders, data base, CC 2079.10a
  Reletting, notice to lessee breaching, advances and advancements, CC 1951.7
  Smoking, prohibiting, CC 1947.5
Oil and Gas Leases, generally, this index
Option to buy,
  Disclosures, CC 1102 et seq.
  Time, disclosure statements, CC 1102.3
Ordinances, city property, CC 719
Payment, renewal, conditions, CC 1950.8
Personal injuries, lessor right under lease to indemnification, lessee breach, CC 1951.2
Personal property, CC 1925 et seq., 1955 et seq.
  Abandoned or unclaimed property, termination, disposition, CC 1993 et seq.
  Apportionment, termination of lease, CC 1935

LEASES

LEASES—Cont'd
Personal property—Cont'd
  Care required by lessee, CC 1928
  Death of party, termination of lease, CC 1934
  Default by lessor, expenses, CC 1957
  Expenses and expenditures, CC 1956
  Obligations of lessor, CC 1955
  Quiet possession, CC 1927
  Removal by landlord without prior written consent, intent to terminate lease, CC 789.3
  Rental Purchase Agreements, generally, this index
  Repairs, CC 1929
  Return, time and place, CC 1958
  Seller assisted marketing plans, CC 1812.200 et seq.
  Termination, CC 1932 et seq.
    Disposition, CC 1993 et seq.
  Title to property, CC 1926
  Use of property for a particular purpose, CC 1930
Place, return of personal property, CC 1958
Possession,
  Continued, renewal of leases, CC 1945
  Validity of lease, time limitations, CC 715
Proceedings. Actions and proceedings, generally, ante
Proof. Evidence, generally, ante
Public authorities, lessors remedy for breach statutes, CC 1952.6
Public entities,
  Lessor remedies for breach statutes, CC 1952.6
  Rent controls on commercial property, impasse notices, CC 1954.31
Public policy, assignment and sublease, CC 1995.270
Purchase of rented property. Rental Purchase Agreements, generally, this index
Quiet possession, CC 1927
Racial or ethnic group restrictions and deeds, effect, CC 782
Real estate brokers and salespersons, application of law, duty to prospective purchaser of residential property, CC 2079.1
Reasonable use of property, use restrictions, CC 1997.210
Receiver, lessor initiating appointment after breach, terminating lessees right to possess, CC 1951.4
Records and recordation, CC 1470
  Covenant, CC 1469
  Prior recording of subsequent interests and instruments, CC 1214
Refrigeration, cutting off utilities with intent to terminate lease, damages, CC 789.3
Registered sex offenders, data base, notice, CC 2079.10a
Reletting, notice to lessee breaching, advances and advancements, CC 1951.7

LEASES—Cont'd
Remedies, CC 1995.300 et seq.
  Use restrictions violations, CC 1997.040
Removal, personal property or furnishings, removal by landlord with intent to terminate lease, CC 789.3
Renewal, CC 1945.5
  Holding over, CC 1945
  Payment, conditions, CC 1950.8
Rent, generally, this index
Rent Controls, generally, this index
Rental Purchase Agreements, generally, this index
Repairs, CC 1941
  Lessee, CC 1929
  Personal property, CC 1955
Residual interest of lessor, liquidated damages, CC 1671
Restrictions,
  Race, color, religion or national origin, CC 53
  Use restrictions, CC 1997.010 et seq.
Returns, personal property, time, CC 1958
Sales,
  Personal property, abandoned or unclaimed property, termination, CC 1993.07
  Rights of new owner, CC 821
Second and subsequent offenses, landlords unlawful action to terminate lease, CC 789.3
Security deposits, CC 1950.5
Seller assisted marketing plans, CC 1812.200 et seq.
Service of process, notice of belief of abandonment, CC 1951.3
  Commercial property, CC 1951.35
Service stations, gasoline vapor control systems, marketing operations, CC 1952.8
Services, Consumers Legal Remedies Act, CC 1761
Sex offenses, registration, data base, notice, CC 2079.10a
Signs, display, CC 713
Single family residence, documents, fees, CC 1097
Smoking, prohibiting, CC 1947.5
Song Beverly Consumer Warranty Act, application of law, CC 1795.4
Spanish language, translations, CC 1632
Sports facilities, notice, anabolic steroids, testosterone, or human growth hormone, crimes, CC 1812.97
Stadiums, notice, testosterone, anabolic steroids or human growth hormones, crimes, CC 1812.97
Statements, consumer goods, illegal contracts, CC 1670.8
Statute of Frauds, leasing for longer period than one year, CC 1624
Statute of limitations. Limitation of actions, generally, ante
Subleases,
  Abandonment, breach by lessee, continuation of lease, CC 1951.4

LEASES—Cont'd
Subleases—Cont'd
  Damages, breach of restrictions, CC 1995.300 et seq.
  Motor vehicles, CC 3343.5
  Restrictions, CC 1995.010 et seq.
  Withholding consent to termination, continuing lease in effect, CC 1951.4
Suits. Actions and proceedings, generally, ante
Term of hiring, presumption, CC 1943
Termination, CC 1931 et seq.
  Abandoned or unclaimed property, disposition, CC 1993 et seq.
  Abandonment, CC 1951.3
    Commercial property, CC 1951.35
  Access, preventing reasonable access by tenant, damages, CC 789.3
  Animals, abandoned or unclaimed property, involuntary deposits, CC 1815 et seq.
  Breach by lessee and abandonment of property, CC 1951.2
    Continuing lease in effect, CC 1951.4
  Cutting off public utilities, damages, CC 789.3
  Personal property, disposition, CC 1993 et seq.
  Removal of personal property by landlord, without prior consent, damages, CC 789.3
  Withholding consent to termination, continuing lease in effect, CC 1951.4
Time,
  Abandonment, CC 1951.3
    Commercial property, CC 1951.35
  Change in terms, notice, CC 827
  Disclosure statements, CC 1102.3
  Limitation of actions, generally, ante
  Return of personal property, CC 1958
  Validity of lease, time limitations, CC 715
Title to property, CC 1926
Tobacco and tobacco products, smoking, prohibiting, CC 1947.5
Town or city lots, CC 718
Transfer of interest,
  Assignments, generally, ante
  Breach, restrictions, damages, CC 1995.300 et seq.
  Restrictions, CC 1995.010 et seq.
  Rights, CC 821
Translations, foreign languages, CC 1632
Unlawful detainer. Forcible Entry and Detainer, generally, this index
Use restrictions, CC 1997.010 et seq.
Validity, time limitations, CC 715
Vehicle Leasing Act, CC 2985.7 et seq.
Voidable, renewal or extension provision not set out, CC 1945.5
Waiver, lessor right to damages for breach, mitigation efforts, CC 1951.2
Warranties,
  Motorized wheelchairs, CC 1793.025

LEASES

LEASES—Cont'd
Warranties—Cont'd
  Song Beverly Consumer Warranty Act, application, CC 1795.4
  Wheelchairs, motorized wheelchairs, CC 1793.025
Wheelchairs, motorized wheelchairs, warranty, CC 1793.025
Withholding consent to subletting or assignment, continuing lease in effect, CC 1951.4

LEGACIES AND LEGATEES
Gifts, Devises and Bequests, generally, this index
Probate Proceedings, generally, this index
Wills, generally, this index

LEGAL ASSISTANCE
Attorneys, generally, this index

LEGAL ESTATES PRINCIPAL AND INCOME LAW
Generally, CC 731 et seq.

LEGAL HOLIDAYS
Holidays, generally, this index

LEGAL IMMIGRANTS
Noncitizens, generally, this index

LEGAL INVESTMENTS
Investments, generally, this index

LEGAL SEPARATION
Marriage, this index

LEGAL SERVICES
Attorney General, generally, this index
Attorneys, generally, this index
District Attorneys, generally, this index

LEGEND DRUGS
Drugs and Medicine, generally, this index

LEGISLATION
Statutes, generally, this index

LEGISLATIVE INTENT
Public Policy, generally, this index

LEGISLATURE
Assembly, chief clerk, acknowledgments, CC 1181
Committees,
  Disclosure, personal or confidential information held by governmental agencies, Information Practices Act, CC 1798.24
  Personal or confidential information held by governmental agencies, disclosure, Information Practices Act, CC 1798.24
Libel and slander, privileges and immunities, CC 47
Personal or confidential information held by governmental agencies, disclosure, Information Practices Act, CC 1798.24
Privileges and immunities, libel and slander, CC 47

LEGISLATURE—Cont'd
Senate, secretary, acknowledgments, CC 1181
Statutes, generally, this index
Trade secrets, disclosure in legislative proceedings, privilege, CC 3426.11
Witnesses, trade secret disclosure, privilege, CC 3426.11

LEMON LAW BUYBACK
Generally, CC 1793.23, 1793.24

LESBIANS
Sexual Orientation, generally, this index

LETTERS AND OTHER CORRESPONDENCE
Discovery, generally, this index
Joint ownership, CC 981
Ownership, authors, CC 980
Subsequent or original producers, CC 984
Transfer of ownership, CC 982

LETTERS OF ATTORNEY
Power of Attorney, generally, this index

LETTERS OF CREDIT
Discount buying services, affiliates, CC 1812.117
Distinguished from suretyship, CC 2787
Mechanics liens, large projects, CC 8724
Suretyship, distinguished, CC 2787

LEVERING REES MOTOR VEHICLE SALES AND FINANCE ACT
Generally, CC 2981 et seq.

LEWDNESS AND OBSCENITY
Actions and proceedings, electronic transmissions, images, CC 1708.88
Attorney fees,
  Electronic transmissions, images, CC 1708.88
  Injunction, awarding, CC 3496
Commercial exploitation, injunctions, cost awarding, CC 3496
Costs,
  Electronic transmissions, images, CC 1708.88
  Injunctions, awarding, CC 3496
Damages, distribution, CC 52.8
Distribution, damages, CC 52.8
Electronic transmissions, images, CC 1708.88
Injunction,
  Cost, awarding, CC 3496
  Electronic transmissions, images, CC 1708.88
Internet, images, CC 1708.88
Investigations and investigators, injunctions, awarding cost, CC 3496

LIABILITIES
Damages, generally, this index

LIABILITY INSURANCE
Charging stations, electric vehicles, CC 1947.6, 1952.7

LIABILITY INSURANCE—Cont'd
Condominiums, CC 5800 et seq.
  Business and commerce, CC 6840
  Electric vehicles, charging infrastructure, CC 4745
    Business and commerce, CC 6713
  Electric vehicles, charging stations, CC 1947.6, 1952.7
Mobilehomes and mobilehome parks, common area facilities, meetings, CC 798.51
Motor Vehicle Insurance, generally, this index
Motorized scooters, shared mobility devices, CC 2505
Shared mobility devices, CC 2505

LIBEL AND SLANDER
Generally, CC 44 et seq.
Abuse of children, CC 48.7
Actual malice, damages, CC 48a
Anonymous witness programs, immunity, CC 48.9
Attorney fees, child abuse, CC 48.7
Business qualifications, imputing disqualification, CC 46
Candidate for public office, liability, CC 48.5
Chastity, imputation of want of, CC 46
Children and minors, abuse of children, CC 48.7
Complaints, warrants issued upon, privileged publication, CC 47
Consumer credit reporting agencies,
  Conditions precedent, CC 1785.32
  Investigations and investigators, CC 1786.52
Correction, demand for, CC 48a
Costs, child abuse, CC 48.7
Damages, CC 48a
  Radio stations, liability, CC 48.5
  Single publication, cause of action, CC 3425.1 et seq.
  Special damages, CC 45a
  Title to property, CC 880.360
  Uniform Single Publication Act, CC 3425.1 et seq.
Destruction of evidence, privileged communications, exceptions, CC 47
Diseases, imputation, CC 46
Dissolution of marriage, privileges and immunities, pleadings, CC 47
Divorce actions, affidavits, CC 47
Employees of radio station, liability, CC 48.5
Evidence, destruction of evidence, privileged communications, exceptions, CC 47
False charge of crime, CC 46
Fraud, crimes and offenses, reports, privileges and immunities, CC 47
General damages, CC 48a
Immunities. Privileges and immunities, generally, post
Impotence, imputation, CC 46
Investigative consumer reporting agencies, CC 1786.52

LIBEL AND SLANDER—Cont'd
Job performance or qualifications, privileged communications, **CC 47**
Judgment as bar, **CC 3425.4**
Judicial proceedings, **CC 47**
Labor and employment,
Employment references, privileged communications, **CC 47**
Privileged communications, **CC 47**
Legal separation, pleadings, privileges and immunities, **CC 47**
Licensee of radio station, liability, **CC 48.5**
Limitation of actions, child abuse, **CC 48.7**
Malice, **CC 48**
Actual malice, damages, **CC 48a**
Meetings, public, privileged publications, **CC 47**
Notice, correction, demanding, **CC 48a**
Office, imputation of disqualification, **CC 46**
One cause of action, **CC 3425.3**
Operator of radio station, liability, **CC 48.5**
Parent and child, abuse of children, **CC 48.7**
Peace officers, misconduct, incompetency, allegations against, bringing action, **CC 47.5**
Per se, **CC 45a**
Privileges and immunities, **CC 47**
Anonymous witness program, **CC 48.9**
Employment references, **CC 47**
Malice, inference, **CC 48**
Publication or broadcast, **CC 47**
Profession, trade or business, injury in, **CC 46**
Protection from, **CC 43**
Public meetings, privileged publications, **CC 47**
Retraction, **CC 48a**
Sexual harassment, privileges and immunities, **CC 47**
Uniform single publication, **CC 3425.1 et seq.**
Construction, **CC 3425.2**
Interpretation of provisions, **CC 3425.2**
Judgment, **CC 3425.4**
One cause of action, **CC 3425.3**
Retroactiveness of law, **CC 3425.5**
Warrants, issuance upon complaint, privileged publication, **CC 47**
Weapons, schools and school districts, reports, damages, **CC 48.8**
Witnesses, anonymous witness programs, immunity, **CC 48.9**

LIBRARIES
Actions and proceedings, personal information, disclosure, **CC 1798.90**
Community Facilities Districts, generally, this index
Disclosure, personal information, **CC 1798.90, 1798.90.05**
Fines and penalties, personal information, disclosure, **CC 1798.90**
Identification cards, RFID (radio frequency identification), crimes and offenses, **CC 1798.79, 1798.795**

LIBRARIES—Cont'd
Invasion of privacy, **CC 1798.90, 1798.90.05**
Limitation of actions, personal information, disclosure, **CC 1798.90**
Personal information, disclosure, **CC 1798.90, 1798.90.05**
Privacy, **CC 1798.90, 1798.90.05**
Reports, personal information, disclosure, **CC 1798.90**
Searches and seizures, warrants, personal information, disclosure, **CC 1798.90.05**
Statute of limitations, personal information, disclosure, **CC 1798.90**

LICENSE PLATES
Motor Vehicles, this index

LICENSED VOCATIONAL NURSES
Vocational Nursing, generally, this index

LICENSES AND PERMITS
Addresses, release of licensees and applicants addresses, **CC 1798.61**
Building Permits, generally, this index
Building standards, water conservation, landlord and tenant, **CC 1101.5**
Check cashers, **CC 1789.37**
Drivers licenses. Motor Vehicles, this index
Entry on property,
Fishing, hunting, camping, safety, **CC 846**
Protective measures, excavations, **CC 832**
Equalization state board, names, release, **CC 1798.69**
Franchises, generally, this index
Landlord and tenant, demolition, notice, **CC 1940.6**
Letters of recommendation, personal information held by governmental agencies, Information Practices Act, **CC 1798.38**
Membership camping contracts, nondisturbance agreement, blanket incumbrance holder, **CC 1812.309**
Mobilehomes and Mobilehome Parks, this index
Names, release of licensees and applicants names, **CC 1798.61**
Radio frequency identification, crimes and offenses, **CC 1798.79, 1798.795**
RFID (radio frequency identification), crimes and offenses, **CC 1798.79, 1798.795**
Safety, entry on property for hunting, fishing, camping, **CC 846**
Skimming, radio frequency identification, crimes and offenses, **CC 1798.79, 1798.795**
Water conservation, building standards, landlord and tenant, **CC 1101.5**

LIENS AND INCUMBRANCES
Generally, **CC 2872 et seq.**
Accessory obligations, extinction, **CC 2909**
Agricultural Labor and Employment, this index
Alternative lien sale procedure, possessory liens, repairs or services, **CC 3052b**

LIENS AND INCUMBRANCES—Cont'd
Apartment house keepers, items exempt from, **CC 1861a**
Apartment houses, community apartments, blanket incumbrances on subdivisions, **CC 1133**
Auctions and auctioneers, sale of property, service dealers, **CC 3052.5**
Baggage, landlords, **CC 1861a**
Blanket incumbrances, subdivisions, **CC 1133**
Boarding and lodging house keepers, **CC 1861, 1861a**
Bottomry, generally, this index
Breach of covenant against, damages, **CC 3305**
Breeding animals, liens for services, **CC 3062 et seq.**
Bungalow court keepers, **CC 1861a**
Buses, luggage, **CC 2191**
Carriers, this index
Classification, **CC 2873**
Cleaners, service and storage, **CC 3066**
Compensation and salaries, **CC 2892**
Conclusiveness of grant, exception, **CC 1107**
Condominiums, this index
Consumer credit reporting agencies, release, **CC 1785.135**
Contracts, prepayment charges, **CC 2954.9**
Conversion of property, extinction, **CC 2910**
Cottages, keepers, **CC 1861a**
Creation, **CC 2881**
Credit disability insurance, foreclosure, **CC 1812.402**
Crimes and offenses, blanket incumbrances, failure to notify buyer or lessee, **CC 1133**
Damages, this index
Depositary for hire, **CC 1856, 1857**
Employment. Mechanics Liens, generally, this index
Extinction, **CC 2909 et seq.**
Factors, **CC 3053**
Farm labor, **CC 3061.5, 3061.6**
Fines and penalties,
Blanket incumbrances, failure to notify buyers or lessees, **CC 1133**
Prepayment penalties, **CC 2954.9**
Fixtures, removal, **CC 1013.5**
Forcible entry and detainer, nuisance, costs, drugs and medicine, **CC 3486**
Foreclosure,
Agricultural labor, **CC 3061.6**
Blanket incumbrances on subdivisions, **CC 1133**
Credit disability insurance, **CC 1812.402**
Forfeitures, **CC 2889**
Property deposited for repair, alteration, or sale, insurance, **CC 1858.2**
Foundries, **CC 3051 et seq.**
Fraudulent transfers, **CC 1227, 1228**
Fur bearing animals raised in captivity, **CC 996**
Future interests, **CC 2883**

LIENS

LIENS AND INCUMBRANCES—Cont'd

Harvesting crops, CC 3061.5, 3061.6
Health care facilities, medical services rendered due to accident or wrongful act, CC 3045.1 et seq.
Health care liens, CC 3040
Hearings, innkeepers liens, writs of possession, CC 1861.6
Home equity sales contracts, CC 1695.6
Home improvement contracts, retail installment sales, application of law, CC 1689.8
Home solicitation contracts, retail installment sales, CC 1689.8
Hospitals, medical services rendered due to accident or wrongful act, CC 3045.1 et seq.
Hotel keepers, CC 1861 et seq.
Innkeepers, CC 1861
Installment Sales, this index
Jack services, CC 3062 et seq.
Jewelers, CC 3052a
Labor liens, CC 3051 et seq.
    Motor vehicles, CC 3067 et seq.
Lapse of time, extinction, CC 2911
Laundries, CC 3051 et seq., 3066
Limitations, extinction of lien, lapse of time, CC 2911
Livestock service liens, CC 3080 et seq.
Lodging house keepers, CC 1861, 1861a
Loggers liens, CC 3065 et seq.
Luggage, common carriers of persons, CC 2191
Marshaling, CC 2899
Mechanics Liens, generally, this index
Mobilehomes and Mobilehome Parks, this index
Mortgages, generally, this index
Motel keepers, CC 1861 et seq.
Motor Vehicles, this index
Notice,
    Assignment of lien on vehicle for labor or materials, CC 3069
    Blanket incumbrances, subdivisions, CC 1133
    Innkeepers liens, writs of possession, CC 1861.8
    Sales,
        Possessory liens, repairs or services, CC 3052 et seq.
        Service dealers, CC 3052.5
    Stallions, jacks or bulls, breeding, CC 3063
Operation of law,
    Claim not due, CC 2882
    Creation by, CC 2881
Options, redemption, priority, CC 2906
Partial performance, extinction, CC 2912
Payment, prepayment, rates and charges, CC 2954.9
Personal obligation not implied by, CC 2890
Personal Property Brokers, generally, this index
Plastics, fabricators, CC 3051 et seq.

LIENS AND INCUMBRANCES—Cont'd

Possessory liens, services or repairs, CC 3051 et seq.
Prepayment, CC 2954.9
Priorities and preferences, CC 2897
    Contracts for sale of land, vendors lien, CC 3048
    Deeds and conveyances, contract for sale of land, vendors lien, CC 3048
    Loggers and lumbermen, CC 3065
    Marshaling assets, CC 2899
    Mechanics Liens, this index
    Redemption, option, real property, CC 2906
    Reverse mortgages, CC 1923.3
    Satisfaction by holder of special lien, CC 2876
    Shared appreciation loans, CC 1917.004
    Timber and lumber, loggers, CC 3065
Proprietors, CC 3051 et seq.
Public entities, medical services rendered due to accident or wrongful act, CC 3045.1 et seq.
Purchasers lien, real estate, CC 3050
Rates and charges, prepayment, contracts, CC 2954.9
Real estate sales, vendors lien, CC 3046 et seq.
Records and recordation, service of stallion, jack or bull, verified claims, CC 3063
Recreational Vehicles, this index
Redemption, CC 2903 et seq.
    Inferior holder, CC 2904
    Options, priority, CC 2906
    Possessory liens, repairs or services, CC 3052 et seq.
    Procedure, CC 2905
    Restraint of rights, CC 2889
    Subrogation, CC 2903
    Vehicles sold to satisfy lien, CC 3074
Rent skimming, reacquiring residential real estate, declaration of non incumbrance, CC 891
Repair services, CC 3051 et seq.
Respondentia, generally, this index
Restoration of property to owner, extinction of lien, CC 2913
Reverse mortgages, CC 1923.3
Sales,
    Alternative lien sale procedure, repairs and services, CC 3052b
    Extinction, CC 2910
    Innkeepers liens, CC 1861.24
    Jewelers, CC 3052a
    Possessory liens, repairs or services, CC 3051 et seq.
    Repairs of personal property, CC 3051 et seq.
    Service dealers, CC 3052.5
Satisfaction of prior lien, holder of special lien, CC 2876
Securities, exemptions, obligations, extent, CC 2891

LIENS AND INCUMBRANCES—Cont'd

Service dealers, registered with bureau of repair services, CC 3052.5
Services, CC 3051 et seq.
Sex discrimination, CC 53
Shared appreciation loans, CC 1917.003, 1917.004
    Aged persons, CC 1917.320 et seq., 1917.614, 1917.615
Special lien, prior liens, satisfaction by holder of special lien, CC 2876
Stallion services, CC 3062 et seq.
Storage, repairs of personal property, fees, CC 3052b
Subdivisions, blanket incumbrances, CC 1133
Subrogation, redemption rights, CC 2903
    Inferior lienholder, CC 2904
Suretyship and guaranty, innkeepers liens, injunction, CC 1861.21
Tax Liens, generally, this index
Threshing, CC 3061
Timber and lumber,
    Loggers, CC 3065 et seq.
    Recordation of instruments, CC 1220
Time, CC 2884
Title to property, CC 2888
Trespass, landlords, enforcement, CC 1861, 1861a
Trust Deeds, generally, this index
Vendor and purchaser, CC 3046 et seq.
Veterinarians, CC 3051 et seq.
Void, forfeitures and restraints upon redemption, CC 2889
Warehouses, mobilehomes and mobilehome parks, termination of tenancy, storage, CC 798.56a

LIFE ESTATES

Generally, CC 761
Condominiums, CC 783
Damages, holding over, CC 3335
Deeds and conveyances, greater estate than that owned, effect, CC 1108
Duties of tenant, CC 840
Freeholds, CC 765
Heirs, taking as purchasers, CC 779
Incidents of ownership, CC 818
Maintenance and repairs, CC 840
Ownership, rights, CC 818
Remainder,
    Injuries to inheritance, remedies, CC 826
    Limited as remainder on term of years, CC 773
    Time for taking effect, CC 780
Rent, recovery, CC 824, 825
Rights, CC 818
Term of years, limited as remainder on, CC 773
Termination, heirs, taking as purchaser, CC 779
Third person, freehold, CC 766

LOANS

LIFE ESTATES—Cont'd
Time, remainders, effective date, **CC 780**
Waste, **CC 840**

LIFE INSURANCE
Credit Life and Disability Insurance, generally, this index
Credit reports, application of law, **CC 1785.1 et seq.**
Disclosure,
   Genetic characteristics, **CC 56.265**
   Medical records, **CC 56.265**
Genetic characteristics, disclosure, **CC 56.265**
Medical records, disclosure, **CC 56.10, 56.15, 56.265**

LIGHT AND POWER COMPANIES
Electricity, generally, this index

LIGHTS AND LIGHTING
Easements, **CC 801**
Electricity, generally, this index
Leases, cutting off public utilities with intent to terminate lease, damages, **CC 789.3**

LIMITATION OF ACTIONS
Adverse Possession, generally, this index
Agriculture, facility operations, nuisance, **CC 3482.5**
Astaire Celebrity Image Protection Act, **CC 3344.1**
Bookstores, personal information, disclosure, **CC 1798.90**
Buildings, this index
Business records, disclosures, **CC 1799.2**
Celebrity image protection, **CC 3344.1**
Civil rights, fines and penalties, **CC 52**
Condition subsequent, deeds and conveyances, **CC 784**
Condominiums, this index
Consumer Credit, this index
Consumers Legal Remedies Act, **CC 1783**
Contracts for sale of land, Subdivision Map Act, noncompliance, **CC 2985.51**
Covenants, deeds and conveyances, **CC 784**
Debt settlement providers, fair debt settlement, **CC 1788.305**
Declarations, deeds and conveyances, **CC 784**
Disclosure, business records, **CC 1799.2**
Discrimination, fines and penalties, **CC 52**
Easements, negative easements, **CC 784**
Employment investigations, consumer reporting agencies, **CC 1786.52**
Equitable servitudes, **CC 784**
Famous persons, deceased celebrity image protection, **CC 3344.1**
Fine art multiples, sales, **CC 1745**
Five year statute of limitations, real estate, restrictions, **CC 784**
Force and violence, fines and penalties, **CC 52**
Gender violence, **CC 52.4**
Hate crimes, fines and penalties, **CC 52**
Human trafficking, **CC 52.5**

LIMITATION OF ACTIONS—Cont'd
Identity and identification,
   Subcutaneous implantation, **CC 52.7**
   Theft, **CC 1798.96**
Indebtedness, duress or coercion, **CC 1798.97.2, 1798.97.3**
Interest, usury, recovery of treble amount, **CC 1916-3**
Leases, this index
Libraries, personal information, disclosure, **CC 1798.90**
Marketable record title, **CC 880.250, 880.260**
Mechanics Liens, this index
Museums, injury or loss of property, indefinite or long term loans, **CC 1899.8, 1899.10**
Negative easements, **CC 784**
Payment processors, fair debt settlement, **CC 1788.305**
Political items, sale and manufacture, **CC 1739.4**
Power of termination, real estate, marketable title, **CC 885.050**
Privacy, invasion of privacy, altered depictions, lewdness and obscenity, **CC 1708.86**
Reading, privacy, **CC 1798.90**
Restrictions, real estate, **CC 784**
Sex, force and violence, **CC 52.4**
Sexual orientation, **CC 52.45**
Student loans, private education lenders and loan collectors, **CC 1788.204, 1788.208**
Subcutaneous implantation, identification devices, **CC 52.7**
Three year statute of limitations, Consumers Legal Remedies Act, **CC 1783**
Timber and lumber, injuries, **CC 3346**
Tolling, attorney client civil conspiracy, **CC 1714.10**
Trade secrets, misappropriation, **CC 3426.6**
Usury, treble damages, **CC 1916-3**
Voidable transactions, **CC 3439.09, 3440.6**

LIMITED EQUITY HOUSING COOPERATIVE
Aged persons, cohabitants, age, covenants, conditions, restrictions, **CC 51.3**

LINEAL WARRANTIES
Heirs and devises, abolition, **CC 1115**

LINES
Boundaries, generally, this index

LIQUEFIED PETROLEUM GAS
Mobilehomes and mobilehome parks, sales, **CC 798.44**
Sales, mobilehomes and mobilehome parks, **CC 798.44**

LIQUIDATED DAMAGES
Damages, this index

LIQUOR
Alcoholic Beverages, generally, this index

LIS PENDENS
Fixtures erroneously affixed to land, removal, **CC 1013.5**
Libel and slander, privileged publication, **CC 47**

LISTS
Consumers, privacy, **CC 1798.130**

LITERARY COMPOSITIONS
Crimes and offenses, stories about felonies, sale proceeds, **CC 2225**
Joint ownership, **CC 981**
Ownership, **CC 980**
Private writings, ownership, **CC 985**
Publication, **CC 983**
   Private writings, **CC 985**
Subsequent or original producers, **CC 984**
Transfers of ownership, **CC 982**

LITERATURE
Literary Compositions, generally, this index

LITHOGRAPHS AND LITHOGRAPHERS
Common law copyrights, reproduction rights, transfer, **CC 982**

LIVESTOCK
Animals, generally, this index

LIVESTOCK SERVICE LIENS
Generally, **CC 3080 et seq.**

LOAN SHARKING
Crimes and offenses, **CC 1916-3**

LOANS
See, also, Bailment, generally, this index
Actions and proceedings, identity and identification, theft, **CC 1785.20.3**
Appraisal, shared appreciation loans for seniors, fair market value, **CC 1917.412**
Attorney fees, identity and identification, theft, **CC 1785.20.3**
Banks and Banking, this index
Bottomry, generally, this index
Consumer Credit, generally, this index
Costs, identity and identification, theft, **CC 1785.20.3**
Credit Life and Disability Insurance, generally, this index
Credit services, **CC 1789.10 et seq.**
Damages, identity and identification, theft, **CC 1785.20.3**
Debt settlement providers, fair debt settlement, **CC 1788.300 et seq.**
Default, generally, this index
Disclosures, shared appreciation loans for seniors, **CC 1917.710 et seq.**
Employees of lender, variable interest rates, application of law, **CC 1916.5**
Equity loans, reverse mortgages, **CC 1923 et seq.**
   Translations, **CC 1632**
Estimates, fair market value, **CC 1917.410**

I-123

LOANS

LOANS—Cont'd
Exchange of property, **CC 1902 et seq.**
Extension of term, **CC 1916.5**
Fair market value, determination, shared appreciation loans for seniors, **CC 1917.410 et seq.**
Family loans, precomputed interest, application of law, **CC 1799.5**
Fees, shared appreciation loans for seniors, **CC 1917.331**
  Appraisal fees, **CC 1917.412**
Finance Lenders, generally, this index
Foreign languages, translations, **CC 1632**
Forms, shared appreciation loans for seniors, disclosure, **CC 1917.711 et seq.**
Frauds, statute of, **CC 1624**
Good faith, shared appreciation loans for seniors, fair market value estimates, **CC 1917.410**
Home equity loan disclosure, **CC 2970, 2971**
Household loans, precomputed interest, application of law, **CC 1799.5**
Housing, this index
Identity and identification, theft, **CC 1785.20.3**
Industrial Loan Companies, generally, this index
Installment sales, supervised financial organizations, **CC 1801.6**
Interest,
  Shared appreciation loans, seniors, **CC 1917.331, 1917.613, 1917.616**
  Variable rate, **CC 1916.5**
    Security documents, **CC 1916.6**
Maintenance and repair of property, lenders liability, **CC 3434**
Mechanics liens, stop notices, construction lenders, **CC 8530 et seq.**
Mortgages, generally, this index
Negligence, construction or repair of real or personal property, lenders liability, **CC 3434**
Notice,
  Identity and identification, theft, **CC 1785.20.3**
  Shared appreciation loans for seniors, **CC 1917.410, 1917.710**
  Variable interest rates, **CC 1916.5**
Payment, **CC 1913**
Payment processors, fair debt settlement, **CC 1788.300 et seq.**
Personal loans, precomputed interest, application of law, **CC 1799.5**
Personal property, loan for use, **CC 1884 et seq.**
Prepayment, shared appreciation loans for seniors, **CC 1917.333**
Presumptions, interest, **CC 1914**
Real Estate, this index
Refinancing, shared appreciation loans for seniors, **CC 1917.320 et seq.**
Renegotiable rate mortgages, **CC 1916.8, 1916.9**

LOANS—Cont'd
Repair of property, lenders liability for defects, **CC 3434**
Residential mortgage lenders. Mortgages, this index
Respondentia, generally, this index
Reverse mortgages, **CC 1923 et seq.**
  Translations, **CC 1632**
Savings Associations, this index
Shared Appreciation Loans, generally, this index
Spanish language, contracts, translations, **CC 1632**
Statute of Frauds, nonconsumer credit, **CC 1624**
Student loans. Colleges and Universities, this index
Theft, identity and identification, **CC 1785.20.3**
Translations, foreign languages, **CC 1632**
Truth in lending, shared appreciation loans for seniors, disclosure, **CC 1917.712, 1917.713**
Usury, civil and criminal liability, **CC 1916–3**
Variable interest rate, **CC 1916.5 et seq.**
  Security documents, **CC 1916.6**
Waiver,
  Precomputed interest, **CC 1799.6**
  Shared appreciation loans for seniors, borrowers rights, **CC 1917.611**

LOBBYING
Harassment, sexual harassment, **CC 51.9**
Sexual harassment, **CC 51.9**

LOCAL AGENCIES
See, also,
  Political Subdivisions, generally, this index
  Public Agencies, generally, this index
Cable Television, generally, this index
Cities and counties. Consolidated Cities and Counties, generally, this index
Community Facilities Districts, generally, this index
Confidential or privileged information, rent control, **CC 1947.7**
Consolidated Cities and Counties, generally, this index
Counties, generally, this index
Depositories, generally, this index
Disclosure, district attorneys, **CC 1798.68**
District attorneys, disclosure, confidential or privileged information, **CC 1798.68**
Districts, generally, this index
Eminent Domain, generally, this index
Mines and minerals, **CC 883.110 et seq.**
Municipalities, generally, this index
Records and recordation, district attorneys, **CC 1798.68**
Rent, control ordinances, **CC 1947.7 et seq.**
Subdivided Lands, generally, this index
Zoning and Planning, generally, this index

LOCAL CRIMINAL JUSTICE FACILITIES
Jails, generally, this index

LOCAL EDUCATIONAL AGENCIES
Schools and School Districts, generally, this index

LOCAL GOVERNMENT
Political Subdivisions, generally, this index

LOCAL PUBLIC ENTITIES
Public Entities, generally, this index

LOCAL ZONING AND PLANNING
Zoning and Planning, generally, this index

LOCKS AND LOCKING
Dead bolt locks, landlords, **CC 1941.3**
Landlord and Tenant, this index

LOCKUPS
Jails, generally, this index

LODGING
Blind or visually impaired persons, access to public accommodations, **CC 54 et seq.**
Disabled persons, access to public accommodations, **CC 54 et seq.**

LODGING HOUSES
Boarding and Lodging Houses, generally, this index

LOGGERS LIEN LAW
Generally, **CC 3065 et seq.**

LOGOS
Trademarks, generally, this index

LOGS AND LOGGING
Timber and Lumber, generally, this index

LONELY HEARTS CLUBS
Dating service contracts, **CC 1694 et seq.**

LONG BEACH
See, also, Municipalities, generally, this index
Forcible entry and detainer,
  Drugs and medicine, nuisance, **CC 3486.5**
  Weapons, **CC 3485**
Weapons, forcible entry and detainer, **CC 3485**

LONG BEACH STATE COLLEGE
Colleges and Universities, generally, this index

LONG TERM HEALTH CARE FACILITIES
Nursing Homes, generally, this index

LOS ANGELES
See, also, Municipalities, generally, this index
Drugs and medicine, forcible entry and detainer, nuisance, **CC 3486**
Forcible entry and detainer,
  Drugs and medicine, nuisance, **CC 3486**
  Weapons, **CC 3485**
Nuisance, forcible entry and detainer, drugs and medicine, **CC 3486**

MAIL

LOS ANGELES—Cont'd
Weapons, forcible entry and detainer, CC 3485

LOS ANGELES STATE COLLEGE OF APPLIED ARTS AND SCIENCES
Colleges and Universities, generally, this index

LOSSES
Installment sales, seller and supervised financial organization, sharing, CC 1801.6
Oil and gas, keys or card keys, automated dispensing outlets, liability after loss, CC 1747.03

LOST OR DESTROYED DOCUMENTS
Generally, CC 1699, 1700
Actions and proceedings, CC 3415
Copies, reissuance, action to compel, CC 3415
Establishment of loss or destruction, CC 3415
Evidence, action for, CC 3415

LOST OR DESTROYED PROPERTY
Generally, CC 2080 et seq.
Advertisements, CC 2080.3
Affidavits, finders, police or sheriff, CC 2080.1
Art works, consignment, CC 1738 et seq.
Auctions, publication of notice, expenses, payment, prerequisite to vesting title in successful bidder, CC 2080.3
California State University, CC 2080.8
Colleges and universities, CC 2080.8
Delivery, police or sheriff, CC 2080.1 et seq.
Documents. Lost or Destroyed Documents, generally, this index
Fees of officers, CC 2082
Finding lost property, CC 2080 et seq.
Municipal corporations, ordinances for care of lost property, CC 2080.4
Ordinances, care of lost property, CC 2080.4
Public agencies, disposition of, adoption of regulations, CC 2080.6
Publication, notice, expense payment, prerequisite to vesting title in finder or successful bidder, CC 2080.3
Restoration to owner, CC 2080.2
Sales, CC 2080.5
    Colleges and universities, CC 2080.8
    Notice, police departments, CC 2080.3 et seq.
Title to property, CC 2080.3
University of California, CC 2080.8

LOTIONS
Cosmetology, generally, this index

LOTS
Installment sales, contracts, application of law, CC 1801.4
Parking Lots and Facilities, generally, this index

LOTTERIES
Chain schemes, CC 1689.2

LOW AND MODERATE INCOME HOUSING
Attorney fees, covenants, modification or change, CC 714.6
Consumer credit reporting agencies, CC 1954.06
Costs, covenants, modification or change, CC 714.6
Covenants, modification or change, CC 714.6
COVID 19,
    Assignments, sales, indebtedness, CC 1788.66
    Indebtedness, assignments, sales, CC 1788.66
Development projects, floor area ratio standards, deeds and conveyances, CC 4747
Exemptions, covenants, modification or change, CC 714.6
Modification or change, covenants, CC 714.6
Shared appreciation loans, CC 1917 et seq.
Trust deeds, bids and bidding, covenants, CC 2924o

LOW INCOME HOUSING
Low and Moderate Income Housing, generally, this index

LUMBER
Timber and Lumber, generally, this index

LUMBERMEN'S LIEN LAW
Generally, CC 3065 et seq.

LUNCHEONETTES
Restaurants, generally, this index

LUNCHES
Food, generally, this index

LUNCHROOMS
Restaurants, generally, this index

LYRICISTS
Music and Musicians, generally, this index

MACHINERY AND EQUIPMENT
Agricultural Machinery and Equipment, generally, this index
Connected devices, Internet, security, CC 1798.91.04 et seq.
Electronic Devices and Equipment, generally, this index
Fires and Fire Protection, this index
Leases,
    Mechanics Liens, generally, this index
    Personal property taxation, reimbursement, CC 1656.5
Manufacturer identification mark, removal, defacing, alteration or destruction, CC 1710.1
Personal property taxation, leases, reimbursement, CC 1656.5
Reimbursement, personal property taxation, leases, CC 1656.5
Sales, identification number or mark altered or removed, CC 1710.1

MACHINERY AND EQUIPMENT—Cont'd
Volunteer firefighters and fire departments, gifts, devises and bequests, privileges and immunities, CC 1714.11
Warranties, Song Beverly Consumer Warranty Act, CC 1790 et seq.

MACHINISTS
Mechanics Liens, generally, this index

MAGAZINES
Advertisements, generally, this index
Art works, common law copyrights, reproduction rights, transfer, CC 982
Consumers Legal Remedies Act, application of law, CC 1755
Crimes and offenses, stories, sales, proceeds, CC 2225
Invasion of privacy, use of names, likeness, voice, signature, without consent, CC 3344
Lewdness and Obscenity, generally, this index
Publication, generally, this index
Uniform Single Publication Act, CC 3425.1 et seq.

MAGNETIC TAPE
Computers, generally, this index

MAGNUSON MOSS WARRANTY FEDERAL TRADE COMMISSION IMPROVEMENT ACT
Conformity requirements, CC 1793.1

MAIDS
Domestic Workers, generally, this index

MAIL AND MAILING
Carriers, loss, liability, CC 2177
Certified or registered mail,
    Certified mail as compliance with mailing requirements, CC 17
    Hospital lien, notice of emergency service rendered, CC 3045.3
    Mortgages, notices of default on sale, request for copies, CC 2924b
Notice, CC 17
    Assignment of lien on vehicle for labor and materials, CC 3069
    Emergency service rendered, hospital leave, CC 3045.3
    Mortgages, default, CC 2924b
    Real estate, consent to use of land, CC 813
    Trustees, default on sales, request for copies, CC 2924b
Real estate, notice of consent to use of land, CC 813
Requirements, CC 17
Trustees, notice of default on sales, requests for copies, CC 2924b
Condominiums, pesticides, notice, CC 4777
Goods, wares and merchandise, unsolicited goods, CC 1584.5
Installment Sales, this index

I-125

MAIL

MAIL AND MAILING—Cont'd
Landlord and Tenant, this index
Mechanics liens, notice, **CC 8110**
Mortgage foreclosure consultants, notice, **CC 2945.3**
Mortgages, foreclosure, notice, **CC 2924.8**
Motor Vehicles, this index
Notice, **CC 17**
    Assignment of contract, dance studio services, **CC 1812.56**
    Certified or registered mail, ante
    Health studio services, **CC 1812.88**
    Reletting, lessee committing breach after making advance payments, **CC 1951.7**
    Retail installment accounts, credit balance, refunds, **CC 1810.3**
Registered mail. Certified or registered mail, generally, ante
Requirements, **CC 17**
Retail installment accounts, credit balance, refunds, **CC 1810.3**
Social security, numbers and numbering, posting, **CC 1798.85**
Trust deeds, substitution of trustees, notice, **CC 2934a**
Unsolicited goods, **CC 1584.5**

MAINTENANCE AND REPAIRS
Buildings, this index
Condominiums, this index
Mobilehomes and Mobilehome Parks, this index
Mortgages, foreclosure, **CC 2929.3**
Motor Vehicles, this index
Trust deeds, foreclosure, **CC 2929.3**

MALARIA
Pest Control, generally, this index

MALICE
Damages, labor and employment, **CC 3294**
Labor and employment, damages, **CC 3294**

MALICIOUS DESTRUCTION OF PROPERTY
Vandalism, generally, this index

MALICIOUS MISCHIEF
Children and minors, parental liability, **CC 1714.1**
Customer's property deposited for repair, alteration or sale purposes, insurance, **CC 1858 et seq.**
Defacement, art objects, **CC 987**

MALPRACTICE
Medical Malpractice, generally, this index
Referral services, professional societies, limitation of liability, **CC 43.95**

MAMMALS
Fish and Game, generally, this index

MANAGED HEALTH CARE DEPARTMENT
Medical records, disclosure, **CC 56.30**

MANAGED HEALTH CARE PLANS
Health Care Service Plans, generally, this index

MANAGERS AND MANAGEMENT
Condominiums, **CC 5375 et seq.**
Diseases, medical records, disclosure, **CC 56.10**
Mobilehomes and Mobilehome Parks, this index

MANUFACTURED HOUSING
Housing, this index

MANUFACTURERS AND MANUFACTURING
Animals, tests, alternatives, **CC 1834.9**
Commercial credit reporting agencies, **CC 1785.41 et seq.**
Contracts, independent wholesale sales representatives, **CC 1738.10 et seq.**
Credit reporting agencies, **CC 1785.41 et seq.**
Defibrillators, **CC 1714.21**
Disclosure, human trafficking, **CC 1714.43**
Drugs and Medicine, this index
Fixtures, removal by tenants, **CC 1019**
Fraud, identification marks, removal, defacing, alteration or destruction, **CC 1710.1**
Gray market goods, disclosure, **CC 1797.8 et seq.**
Human trafficking, disclosure, **CC 1714.43**
Independent wholesale sales representatives, **CC 1738.10 et seq.**
Invoices, repair, Song Beverly Consumer Warranty Act, **CC 1793.1 et seq.**
Liens of proprietors, **CC 3051 et seq.**
Motor Vehicles, this index
Political items, **CC 1739 et seq.**
Products Liability, generally, this index
Repairs, warranties, **CC 1793.1 et seq.**
Sales, independent wholesale sales representatives, **CC 1738.10 et seq.**
Serial numbers, nameplates, defacing alteration or destruction, damages, **CC 1710.1**
Service and repair facilities, warranties, **CC 1793.1 et seq.**
Slavery, disclosure, **CC 1714.43**
Tests, animals, alternatives, **CC 1834.9**
Warranties, generally, this index
Wholesale sales representatives, independents, **CC 1738.10 et seq.**
Work orders, Song Beverly Consumer Warranty Act, **CC 1793.1 et seq.**

MANUFACTURING
Manufacturers and Manufacturing, generally, this index

MARINAS
Floating Homes, generally, this index

MARINE CARRIERS
Ships and Shipping, generally, this index

MARINE CORPS
Military Forces, generally, this index

MARINES
Military Forces, generally, this index

MARKET
Markets and Marketing, generally, this index

MARKETABLE RECORD TITLE
Real estate, **CC 880.020 et seq.**

MARKETING
Markets and Marketing, generally, this index

MARKETS AND MARKETING
Ammunition, negligence, **CC 1714**
Attorney fees, Internet, disclosure, **CC 1749.8.4**
Banks and banking, personal information, disclosure, **CC 1798.83**
Business and commerce,
    Consumer protection, **CC 1749.7**
    Personal information, disclosure, **CC 1798.83**
Club cards, grocery stores, disclosure, **CC 1749.60 et seq.**
Consumer protection, **CC 1749.7**
Costs, Internet, disclosure, **CC 1749.8.4**
Direct marketing, business and commerce, personal information, disclosure, **CC 1798.83**
Disclosure,
    Grocery stores, club cards, **CC 1749.60 et seq.**
    Internet, **CC 1749.8 et seq.**
    Medical records, direct marketing, **CC 1798.91**
Exemptions, Internet, disclosure, **CC 1749.8.5**
Fines and penalties,
    Internet, disclosure, **CC 1749.8.4**
    Seller assisted marketing plans, **CC 1812.217**
Fraud, seller assisted marketing plans, **CC 1812.200 et seq.**
Gender neutrality, children and minors, retailers, **CC 55.7, 55.8**
Grocery stores, club cards, disclosure, **CC 1749.60 et seq.**
Injunctions, Internet, disclosure, **CC 1749.8.4**
Internet, disclosure, **CC 1749.8 et seq.**
Medical records, direct marketing, disclosure, **CC 1798.91**
Notice, Internet, disclosure, **CC 1749.8.1**
Ranking, consumer protection, **CC 1749.7**
Retailers, children and minors, gender neutrality, **CC 55.7, 55.8**
Revocation or suspension, Internet, disclosure, **CC 1749.8.1, 1749.8.2**
Security, Internet, disclosure, **CC 1749.8.3**
Seller assisted marketing plans, **CC 1812.200 et seq.**
Sex, gender neutrality, children and minors, retailers, **CC 55.7, 55.8**
Stores, children and minors, gender neutrality, **CC 55.7, 55.8**

MAXIMS

MARKETS AND MARKETING—Cont'd
Suspension or revocation, Internet, disclosure, **CC 1749.8.1, 1749.8.2**
Verification, Internet, disclosure, **CC 1749.8.1**

MARKS
Brands, Marks and Labels, generally, this index
Trademarks, generally, this index

MARRIAGE
Abuse. Domestic Violence, generally, this index
Actions and proceedings,
  Alienation of affections, **CC 43.5**
  Breach of promise, **CC 43.4, 43.5**
  Fraud, breach of promise, **CC 43.4**
Annulment,
  Community Property, generally, this index
  Family Conciliation Court, generally, this index
  Support, generally, this index
Breach of promise to marry, action for damages, **CC 43.4**
Children and minors. Support, generally, this index
Community Property, generally, this index
Conditions, property transfers, **CC 710**
Contracts,
  Gift in contemplation, recovery, **CC 1590**
  Restraint of, **CC 1669**
Counseling. Marriage and Family Therapists, generally, this index
Credit, marital status, discrimination, **CC 1812.30 et seq.**
Credit cards, issuance in maiden name, **CC 1747.81**
Deeds and conveyances, conditions, **CC 710**
Dissolution of marriage,
  Community Property, generally, this index
  Disclosure, residential property transfers, **CC 1102.2**
  Family Conciliation Court, generally, this index
  Libel and slander, privileges and immunities, **CC 47**
  Mortgages, residential property transfers, maturity date acceleration, **CC 2924.6**
  Pleadings, libel and slander, privileges and immunities, **CC 47**
  Property. Community Property, generally, this index
  Residential property transfers, mortgages or trust deeds, maturity date acceleration, **CC 2924.6**
  Support, generally, this index
  Trust deeds, residential property transfers, maturity date acceleration, **CC 2924.6**
Divorce. Dissolution of marriage, generally, ante
Domestic Partnership, generally, this index
Domestic Violence, generally, this index
Family Conciliation Court, generally, this index

MARRIAGE—Cont'd
Fraud, breach of promise to marry, action for damages, **CC 43.4**
Gifts, devises and bequests, recovery, **CC 1590**
Joint Tenants, generally, this index
Legal separation,
  Community Property, generally, this index
  Family Conciliation Court, generally, this index
  Libel and slander, privileges and immunities, **CC 47**
  Mortgages, residential property transfers, maturity date acceleration, **CC 2924.6**
  Residential property transfers, mortgages or trust deeds, maturity date acceleration, **CC 2924.6**
  Support, generally, this index
  Trust deeds, residential property transfers, maturity date acceleration, **CC 2924.6**
Maiden name of wife, credit cards, issuance, **CC 1747.81**
Names, maiden or former name of wife, credit cards, issuance, **CC 1747.81**
Proceedings. Actions and proceedings, generally, ante
Property. Community Property, generally, this index
Protection, force, right to use, **CC 50**
Restraint of marriage,
  Conditions imposing, **CC 710**
  Contracts, **CC 1669**
Separate maintenance. Legal separation, generally, ante
Separation. Legal separation, generally, ante
Suits. Actions and proceedings, generally, ante
Support, generally, this index
Tenancy in Common, generally, this index

MARRIAGE AND FAMILY THERAPISTS
Actions and proceedings, sexual exploitation, **CC 43.93**
Evidence, sexual exploitation, **CC 43.93**
Immunities. Privileges and immunities, generally, post
Malpractice. Medical Malpractice, generally, this index
Medical Malpractice, generally, this index
Privileges and immunities,
  Professional organizations, **CC 43.8**
  Professional standards committees, **CC 43.7**
  Referral services, **CC 43.95**
  Threats, violent behavior, patients, protection, **CC 43.92**
Protection, threats, violent behavior, patients, privileges and immunities, **CC 43.92**
Referrals, limitation of liability, **CC 43.95**
Sexual exploitation, **CC 43.93**
Telecommunications, referral services, privileges and immunities, **CC 43.95**
Threats, violent behavior, patients, protection, privileges and immunities, **CC 43.92**

MARSHALLING ASSETS
Creditors, resort to several funds, **CC 3433**

MARSHALLING ASSETS—Cont'd
Liens, order of resort to property to satisfy, **CC 2899**

MASS TRANSIT
Buses, generally, this index
Passenger rail service. Railroads, this index
Railroads, generally, this index

MASTER AND SERVANT
Labor and Employment, generally, this index

MATERIALMEN
Mechanics Liens, generally, this index

MATERIALS
Landlord and tenant, security deposits, deductions, **CC 1950.5**
Mechanics Liens, generally, this index
Religious materials, security interests for consumer credit contracts, **CC 1799.97**

MATRIMONIAL REFERRAL SERVICES
Dating service contracts, **CC 1694 et seq.**

MAXIMS
  Generally, **CC 3509 et seq.**
Acquiescence in error as taking away right, **CC 3516**
Acts of God, **CC 3526**
Agency, presumptions, **CC 3519**
Benefit, taker must bear burden, **CC 3521**
Certainty, that which can be made, **CC 3538**
Consent to act, **CC 3515**
Contemporaneous exposition as best, **CC 3535**
Delay, enforcement of rights, **CC 3527**
Effect, **CC 3509**
Equal rights, **CC 3524**
Errors, acquiescence in, **CC 3516**
Existence of things, time, **CC 3547**
Exposition, contemporaneous as best, **CC 3535**
Fraudulent conveyances, effect on disposition, **CC 3518**
General expressions, qualification by particular, **CC 3534**
Greater contains less, **CC 3536**
Idle acts not required, **CC 3532**
Impossibilities not required, **CC 3531**
Incident follow principal, **CC 3540**
Infringing rights of others, **CC 3514**
Innocent persons, which must suffer, **CC 3543**
Intent and effect, **CC 3509**
Interpretation,
  Preference, **CC 3541**
  Reasonableness, **CC 3542**
Jurisprudence, **CC 3509 et seq.**
Less contained in greater, **CC 3536**
Nonexistence of things not appearing to exist, **CC 3530**
Obeyance of law, **CC 3548**
Objection, taking away by acquiescence in error, **CC 3516**
Particular expressions qualification of general, **CC 3534**

MAXIMS

MAXIMS—Cont'd
Performance, presumption, **CC 3529**
Preference, interpretation, **CC 3541**
Preference of earliest right, **CC 3525**
Principal, instance follows, **CC 3540**
Private transactions, fair and regular, **CC 3545**
Purpose, change to injure another, **CC 3512**
Remedy for wrong, **CC 3523**
Rules,
    Reason for ceasing, **CC 3510**
    Reason same, **CC 3511**
Substance, respect of law for, **CC 3528**
Suffering from another, **CC 3520**
Superfluity does not vitiate, **CC 3537**
Things happening, ordinary course of nature, **CC 3546**
Time,
    Existence of things, **CC 3547**
    Void act not confirmed by, **CC 3539**
Torts, taking advantage of own, **CC 3517**
Trifles disregarded, **CC 3533**
Unavoidable occurrences, responsibility, **CC 3526**
Vigilance, enforcement of rights, **CC 3527**
Waiver, advantage of law for own benefit, **CC 3513**

MDA
Drugs and Medicine, generally, this index

MEATS
Fish and Game, generally, this index
Game. Fish and Game, generally, this index

MECHANICAL DEVICES
Sale, identification number or mark altered or removed, **CC 1710.1**

MECHANICAL ENGINEERS
Engineers, generally, this index

MECHANICS
Liens. Mechanics Liens, generally, this index

MECHANICS LIENS
Generally, **CC 8000 et seq.**
Accord and satisfaction, **CC 8130**
Actions and proceedings, **CC 8460 et seq.**
    Public buildings and works,
        Payment bonds, **CC 9554 et seq.**
        Stop notices, **CC 9500 et seq.**
    Stop notices, **CC 8550 et seq.**
    Stop work notices, **CC 8844**
Agents, **CC 8066**
Amount of lien, **CC 8430 et seq.**
Application of law, **CC 3059, 8054, 8160, 8308**
    Public buildings and works, **CC 9000**
Assignments, stop notices, priorities and preferences, **CC 8544**
    Public buildings and works, distribution, **CC 9456**
Attachment, **CC 8468**

MECHANICS LIENS—Cont'd
Attorney fees,
    Progress payments, **CC 8800**
        Public utilities, **CC 8802**
    Public buildings and works, payment bonds, **CC 9554, 9564**
    Release, orders of court, **CC 8488**
    Retention payments, **CC 8818**
    Stop notices, **CC 8558**
Bonded stop payment notices. Stop notices, generally, post
Bonds (officers and fiduciaries), **CC 8150 et seq., 8532, 8534**
    Large projects, **CC 8722**
    Payment bonds, generally, post
    Public buildings and works, release, stop notices, **CC 9364**
    Release, post
Building permits, **CC 8302**
Cessation, notice, records and recordation, **CC 8188, 8190**
    Public buildings and works, **CC 9202**
Claims, **CC 8410 et seq.**
    Multiple improvements, **CC 8446**
    Notice, **CC 8416**
        Release, **CC 8494**
    Public buildings and works, **CC 9100**
    Records and recordation, **CC 8304, 8306**
        Time, **CC 8312**
Common areas, notice, **CC 8119**
Common interest developments, common areas, notice, **CC 8119**
Completion, **CC 8180 et seq.**
    Public buildings and works, **CC 9200 et seq.**
Compromise and settlement, **CC 8130**
Condominiums, **CC 8448**
    Common areas, notice, **CC 8119**
Contracts, **CC 8170**
    Amount of lien, **CC 8430 et seq.**
Conversion, designs and designers, **CC 8319**
Corporations, security, large projects, application of law, **CC 8704**
Costs, **CC 8464**
    Progress payments, **CC 8800**
        Public utilities, **CC 8802**
    Retention payments, **CC 8818**
    Stop notices, **CC 8558**
Damages, stop notices, **CC 8558**
Deficiency judgments, **CC 8466**
Dismissal and nonsuit, **CC 8462**
    Stop notices, **CC 8554**
        Public buildings and works, **CC 9508**
Distribution, public buildings and works, stop notices, **CC 9450 et seq.**
Enforcement, **CC 8410 et seq., 8460 et seq.**
    Stop notices, **CC 8550 et seq.**
        Public buildings and works, **CC 9500 et seq.**
Escrows and escrow agents, large projects, **CC 8726, 8728**
Evidence, notice, **CC 8118**

MECHANICS LIENS—Cont'd
Filing, preliminary notice, **CC 8214**
Fines and penalties,
    Progress payments, **CC 8800**
        Public utilities, **CC 8802**
    Retention payments, **CC 8818**
Forfeitures, public buildings and works, stop notices, distribution, **CC 9454**
Forms,
    Release, progress payments, **CC 8132**
    Waiver, progress payments, **CC 8132**
Garnishment, public buildings and works, stop notices, distribution, priorities and preferences, **CC 9456**
Hearings, release, orders of court, **CC 8486, 8488**
Interest, stop notices, **CC 8560**
Joinder of causes of action,
    Public buildings and works, stop notices, **CC 9506**
    Release, orders of court, **CC 8480**
Judgments and decrees, release, **CC 8490**
Large projects, security, **CC 8700 et seq.**
Letters of credit, large projects, **CC 8724**
Limitation of actions, **CC 8460**
    Bonds (officers and fiduciaries), release, **CC 8424**
    Payment bonds, **CC 8609, 8610**
    Public buildings and works,
        Payment bonds, **CC 9558**
        Stop notices, **CC 9362, 9502**
    Stop notices, **CC 8550**
Loans, stop notices, construction lenders, **CC 8530 et seq.**
Mail and mailing, notice, **CC 8110**
Multiple improvements, claims, **CC 8446**
Nonresponsibility, notice, **CC 8444**
Nonsuit. Dismissal and nonsuit, generally, ante
Notice, **CC 8052, 8100 et seq., 8304**
    Actions and proceedings, **CC 8461**
    Bonds (officers and fiduciaries), release, **CC 8424**
    Cessation, ante
    Completion, **CC 8182 et seq.**
    Coowners, **CC 8066**
    Nonresponsibility, **CC 8444**
    Payment bonds, **CC 8612, 8614**
    Preliminary notice, generally, post
    Public buildings and works, post
    Release, orders of court, **CC 8482**
    Retention payments, **CC 8816**
    Security, large projects, **CC 8712**
    Service of notice, **CC 8106 et seq.**
    Stop notices, generally, post
    Stop work notices, **CC 8830 et seq.**
Orders of court, release, **CC 8480 et seq.**
    Public buildings and works, summary proceedings, stop notices, **CC 9412**
Owners and ownership, stop notices, **CC 8520, 8522**
Payment, **CC 8800 et seq.**
    Progress payments, generally, post

MECHANICS LIENS—Cont'd
Payment—Cont'd
  Retention payments, **CC 8810 et seq.**
  Stop payment notices. Stop notices, generally, post
  Stop work notices, **CC 8830 et seq.**
Payment bonds, **CC 8600 et seq.**
  Notice, **CC 8612, 8614**
  Public buildings and works, **CC 9550 et seq.**
  Records and recordation, **CC 8600**
Penalties. Fines and penalties, generally, ante
Petitions, release, orders of court, **CC 8480 et seq.**
Posting,
  Notice, **CC 8114**
  Stop work notices, **CC 8834**
Preliminary notice, **CC 8200 et seq.**
  Enforcement, **CC 8410**
  Payment bonds, **CC 8612, 8614**
  Public buildings and works, **CC 9300 et seq.**
    Payment bonds, **CC 9560**
Priorities and preferences, **CC 8316, 8450 et seq.**
  Stop notices, **CC 8540 et seq.**
  Public buildings and works, **CC 9456**
Private works of improvement, **CC 8160 et seq.**
Proceedings. Actions and proceedings, generally, ante
Process, service of process,
  Claims, **CC 8416**
  Public buildings and works, stop notices, release, summary proceedings, **CC 9402 et seq.**
  Release, orders of court, **CC 8486**
Progress payments, **CC 8800, 8802**
  Waiver, release, forms, **CC 8132**
Proof of notice, **CC 8118**
  Enforcement, **CC 8410**
Public buildings and works, **CC 9000 et seq.**
  Actions and proceedings,
    Payment bonds, **CC 9554 et seq.**
    Stop notices, **CC 9500 et seq.**
  Application of law, **CC 9000**
  Assignments, stop notices, distribution, priorities and preferences, **CC 9456**
  Attorney fees, payment bonds, **CC 9554, 9564**
  Bonds (officers and fiduciaries), release, stop notices, **CC 9364**
  Cessation, notice, records and recordation, **CC 9202**
  Claims, **CC 9100**
  Completion, **CC 9200 et seq.**
  Dismissal and nonsuit, stop notices, **CC 9508**
  Distribution, stop notices, **CC 9450 et seq.**
  Enforcement, stop notices, **CC 9500 et seq.**
  Forfeitures, stop notices, distribution, **CC 9454**
  Garnishment, stop notices, distribution, priorities and preferences, **CC 9456**

MECHANICS LIENS—Cont'd
Public buildings and works—Cont'd
  Joinder of causes of action, stop notices, **CC 9506**
  Limitation of actions,
    Payment bonds, **CC 9558**
    Stop notices, **CC 9362, 9502**
  Notice,
    Preliminary notice, **CC 9300 et seq.**
      Payment bonds, **CC 9560**
    Records and recordation,
      Cessation, **CC 9202**
      Completion, **CC 9204, 9208**
  Orders of court, release, summary proceedings, stop notices, **CC 9412**
  Payment bonds, **CC 9550 et seq.**
    Preliminary notice, **CC 9300 et seq.**
    Payment bonds, **CC 9560**
  Priorities and preferences, stop notices, distribution, **CC 9456**
  Records and recordation, notice,
    Cessation, **CC 9202**
    Completion, **CC 9204, 9208**
  Release, stop notices,
    Bonds (officers and fiduciaries), **CC 9364**
    Summary proceedings, **CC 9400 et seq.**
  Res judicata, stop notices, release, summary proceedings, **CC 9414**
  Service of process, stop notices, release, summary proceedings, **CC 9402 et seq.**
  Stop notices, **CC 9350 et seq.**
  Summary proceedings, stop notices, release, **CC 9400 et seq.**
  Time, stop notices, **CC 9356, 9362**
Public utilities, progress payments, **CC 8802**
Recorders, **CC 8060**
Records and recordation,
  Bonds (officers and fiduciaries), release, **CC 8424**
  Cessation, notice, **CC 8188, 8190**
    Public buildings and works, **CC 9202**
  Claims, **CC 8304, 8306, 8412 et seq.**
    Time, **CC 8312**
  Completion, notice, **CC 8184 et seq.**
  Nonresponsibility, notice, **CC 8444**
  Payment bonds, **CC 8600**
  Preliminary notice, **CC 8214**
  Public buildings and works, ante
  Release, orders of court, **CC 8490**
Reduction, stop notices, **CC 8128**
Release, **CC 8120 et seq.**
  Bonds (officers and fiduciaries), **CC 8424**
  Stop notices, **CC 8510**
    Public buildings and works, **CC 9364**
  Orders of court, **CC 8480 et seq.**
Res judicata, public buildings and works, stop notices, release, summary proceedings, **CC 9414**
Retention payments, **CC 8810 et seq.**
Sales of property, possessory liens, repairs and services, **CC 3052 et seq.**

MECHANICS LIENS—Cont'd
Security, large projects, **CC 8700 et seq.**
Security interest, escrows and escrow agents, large projects, **CC 8726**
Service of notice, **CC 8106 et seq.**
Service of process. Process, ante
Settlement, **CC 8130**
Statute of limitations. Limitation of actions, generally, ante
Stop notices, **CC 8500 et seq.**
  Actions and proceedings, **CC 8550 et seq.**
  Assignments, priorities and preferences, **CC 8544**
  Attorney fees, **CC 8558**
  Costs, **CC 8558**
  Damages, **CC 8558**
  Dismissal and nonsuit, **CC 8554**
  Enforcement, **CC 8550 et seq.**
  Interest, **CC 8560**
  Limitation of actions, **CC 8550**
  Priorities and preferences, **CC 8540 et seq.**
  Public buildings and works, **CC 9350 et seq.**
  Reduction, **CC 8128**
  Release, **CC 8128**
    Bonds (officers and fiduciaries), **CC 8510**
Stop payment notices. Stop notices, generally, ante
Stop work notices, **CC 8830 et seq.**
Summary proceedings, public buildings and works, release, stop notices, **CC 9400 et seq.**
Sureties. Bonds (officers and fiduciaries), generally, ante
Time,
  Claims, records and recordation, **CC 8312, 8412, 8414**
  Notice, **CC 8116**
  Public buildings and works, stop notices, **CC 9356, 9362**
Unbonded stop payment notices. Stop notices, generally, ante
Waiver, **CC 8120 et seq.**
  Retention payments, **CC 8820**
  Security, large projects, **CC 8714**
  Stop work notices, **CC 8846**

MEDI CAL ACT
Medi Cal Program, generally, this index

MEDI CAL PROGRAM
See, also, Social Services, generally, this index
Disclosure, **CC 56.30**
  Information Practices Act, **CC 1798.24**
Health care liens, application of law, **CC 3040**
Liens and incumbrances, health care liens, application of law, **CC 3040**
Monopolies and unfair trade, procurement, fees, **CC 1770**
  Treble damages, **CC 1780**
Motorized wheelchairs, warranties, **CC 1793.025**

MEDI

MEDI CAL PROGRAM—Cont'd
Warranties, motorized wheelchairs, CC 1793.025

Wheelchairs, warranties, motorized wheelchairs, CC 1793.025

MEDIATION
Arbitration and Award, generally, this index

Buildings, construction defects, CC 914, 919, 928

Computer aided transcription system, CC 54.8

Condominiums, this index

Deaf or hard of hearing persons, listening systems, CC 54.8

Hazardous substances and waste, releases, responsibility acceptance, CC 852

Hearing devices, CC 54.8

Listening systems, CC 54.8

Transcription system, computer aided, CC 54.8

MEDICAID
Medi Cal Program, generally, this index

MEDICAL ASSISTANCE
Medi Cal Program, generally, this index

MEDICAL CARE AND TREATMENT
See, also, Health Facilities, generally, this index

Abortion, generally, this index

Access, commercial blockade, CC 3427 et seq.

Acquired immune deficiency syndrome. HIV, generally, this index

Aged persons, mobilehomes, support care services, CC 798.34

Allergies. Epinephrine Auto Injectors, generally, this index

Blockade, commercial blockade, CC 3427 et seq.

Civil damages, immunity, cardiopulmonary resuscitation, CC 1714.2

Clinics, generally, this index

Commercial blockade, CC 3427 et seq.

Confidential or privileged information. Medical Records, this index

Crimes and offenses, information, intentional disclosure, CC 1798.57

Damages,
  Commercial blockade, facilities, CC 3427.2
  Emergency cardiopulmonary resuscitation, privileges and immunities, CC 1714.2

Disclosure,
  Domestic partnership, CC 56.1007
  Friends, CC 56.1007
  Medical information, CC 56 et seq.
  Relatives, CC 56.1007

Diseases, generally, this index

Domestic partnership, disclosure, CC 56.1007

Drugs and Medicine, generally, this index

Emergencies,
  Epinephrine Auto Injectors, generally, this index
  Hospital liens, medical services rendered for injury caused by accident, CC 3045.1 et seq.

MEDICAL CARE AND TREATMENT—Cont'd
Emergencies—Cont'd
  Privileges and immunities, defibrillators, CC 1714.21

Epinephrine Auto Injectors, generally, this index

Examiners and examinations, multiphasic screening units, unsolicited referrals to health care providers, limitation of liability, CC 43.9

Family, disclosure, CC 56.1007

First Aid, generally, this index

Friends, disclosure, CC 56.1007

Good faith, defibrillators, emergencies, privileges and immunities, CC 1714.21

Health care liens, CC 3040

Health Care Providers, generally, this index

Health Care Service Plans, generally, this index

Health Facilities, generally, this index

Health Insurance, generally, this index

HIV, generally, this index

Home solicitation contracts, personal emergency response units, CC 1689.6, 1689.7

Hospices, generally, this index

Hospitals, generally, this index

Immunities. Privileges and immunities, generally, post

Immunity from civil damages, cardiopulmonary resuscitation, CC 1714.2

Imputed liability,
  Parents for acts of children, CC 1714.1
  Willful misconduct of children, liability of parent or guardian, CC 1714.1

Information,
  Adopted child or grandchild, medically necessary information, birth parents, disclosure, CC 1798.24
  Disclosure, CC 56 et seq.

Labor and employment, commercial blockade, application of law, CC 3427.4

Liens and incumbrances, health care liens, CC 3040

Malpractice. Medical Malpractice, generally, this index

Managed care. Health Care Service Plans, generally, this index

Mobilehomes and mobilehome parks, subleases, CC 798.23.5

Multiphasic screening units, unsolicited referrals to health care providers, limitation of liability, CC 43.9

Negligence. Medical Malpractice, generally, this index

Orders of court, commercial blockade, facilities, CC 3427.3

Personal emergency response units, home solicitation contracts, CC 1689.6, 1689.7

Physicians and Surgeons, generally, this index

Privileges and immunities,
  Defibrillators, CC 1714.21

MEDICAL CARE AND TREATMENT—Cont'd
Privileges and immunities—Cont'd
  Emergencies, defibrillators, CC 1714.21
  Limitation of liability, health care providers, unsolicited referrals, CC 43.9
  Referrals, CC 43.9

Professional negligence. Medical Malpractice, generally, this index

Records and recordation. Medical Records, generally, this index

Referrals, health care providers, limitation of liability, CC 43.9

Relatives, disclosure, CC 56.1007

Tests, referral to health care providers, limitation of liability, CC 43.9

Tissue Banks, generally, this index

Torts, commercial blockade, CC 3427 et seq.

MEDICAL INJURY COMPENSATION REFORM ACT
Medical Malpractice, generally, this index

MEDICAL INSURANCE
Health Insurance, generally, this index

MEDICAL MALPRACTICE
Generally, CC 3333.1

Collateral benefits, source, evidence, CC 3333.1

Compromise and settlement, authorization to disclose medical information, CC 56.105

Damages, CC 3333.2
  Collateral benefits, source, evidence, CC 3333.1
  Subrogation, CC 3333.1

Evidence, benefits payable, CC 3333.1

Exemptions, CC 1714.8

Immunities, CC 1714.8

Insurance,
  Compromise and settlement, authorization to disclose medical information, CC 56.105
  Medical records, authorization to disclose, compromise and settlement, CC 56.105

Limitation of actions, CC 1714.8

Limitations, damages, CC 3333.2

Medical records, release, CC 56.105

Noneconomic losses, CC 3333.2

Notice, request for medical information, compromise or settlement claims, CC 56.105

Privileges and immunities, CC 1714.8

Records and recordation, authorization to disclose medical information, CC 56.105

Sources, collateral benefits, evidence, CC 3333.1

Subrogation, CC 3333.1

MEDICAL PRACTICE ACT
Physicians and Surgeons, generally, this index

MEDICAL RECORDS
Generally, CC 56 et seq.

MEDICAL

MEDICAL RECORDS—Cont'd
Abortion, confidential or privileged information, conflict of laws, CC 56.108
Access, patients right to access, CC 56.28
  Corporations, CC 56.07
Actions and proceedings,
  Disclosure, CC 56.15
  Employers, CC 56.20
  Negligence, release, CC 56.36
Affirmative defenses, release, CC 56.36
Alcohol, disclosure, application of law, CC 56.30
Application of law, CC 56.27 et seq.
Arbitration, disclosure, CC 56.10
Attorney fees,
  Action for damages, CC 56.30
  Disclosure, violations, CC 56.35
  Negligence, release, CC 56.36
Attorney general, negligence, release, CC 56.36
Authorization,
  Patients right to access, CC 56.28
  Release, post
Cancelling authorization,
  Disclosure, CC 56.15
  Employers, CC 56.24
Children and Minors, this index
Comatose patients, information disclosure to government agencies, CC 56.10
Communicable diseases, application of law, disclosure, CC 56.30
Compensatory damages, disclosure violations, CC 56.35
Computers, confidential or privileged information, business and commerce, CC 56.06
Confidential or privileged information, CC 56 et seq.
  Business and commerce, CC 56.06
  Consumer credit reporting agencies, CC 1785.13
  Crimes and offenses, disclosure, CC 1798.57
  Disclosure, generally, post
  Electronic transmissions, CC 56.101
  Genetic testing, CC 56.18 et seq.
  Mental health, outpatient psychotherapy, CC 56.104
  Outpatient psychotherapy, CC 56.104
  Sales, CC 1798.130, 1798.146, 1798.148
Consent, direct marketing, disclosure, CC 1798.91
Contractors, confidential or privileged information, CC 56 et seq.
Copies, patient access, corporations, CC 56.07
Coroners, disclosure, CC 56.10
Corporations, release, CC 56.07
Costs,
  Disclosure, CC 56.35
  Negligence, release, CC 56.36
Counties, attorneys, negligence, release, CC 56.36
Crimes and offenses,
  Disclosure, CC 56.36

MEDICAL RECORDS—Cont'd
Crimes and offenses—Cont'd
  Negligence, release, CC 56.36
Damages,
  Disclosure, CC 56.35
    In violation of statute, CC 56.30
  Negligence, release, CC 56.36
Destruction, CC 56.101
Developmental disabilities, application of law, CC 56.30
Direct marketing, disclosure, CC 1798.91
Disaster relief organizations, disclosure, CC 56.10
Disclosure, CC 56.10 et seq.
  See, also, Release, generally, post
  Corporations, CC 56.07
  Damages, CC 56.30, 56.35
  Direct marketing, CC 1798.91
  Employers, CC 56.20 et seq.
  Exemptions, CC 56.25
  Insurance, CC 56.265
  Mental health, outpatient psychotherapy, CC 56.104
  Outpatient psychotherapy, CC 56.104
  Patients right to access, CC 56.28
  Third party administrators, health care insurance programs, CC 56.26
  Waiver of restrictions, CC 56.37
Discovery, negligence, release, CC 56.36
District attorneys, negligence, release, CC 56.36
Economic loss, disclosure, damages, CC 56.35
Electronic transmissions, confidential or privileged information, CC 56.101
Emergencies, disclosure, CC 56.10
Employee welfare benefit plans, disclosure, CC 56.10
Evidence, disclosure, CC 56.10
Exemptions,
  Confidentiality, CC 56.25
  Direct marketing, disclosure, CC 1798.91
  Disclosure, direct marketing, CC 1798.91
  Sales, consumers, privacy, CC 1798.146, 1798.148
Fines and penalties,
  Confidential or privileged information, business and commerce, CC 56.06
  Negligence, release, CC 56.36
Forms, release, CC 56.11
  Employers, CC 56.21
General information, disclosure, CC 56.16
Genetic testing, privacy, CC 56.18 et seq.
Good faith compliance, unauthorized use, CC 56.23
Government agencies, information disclosure, comatose patients, CC 56.10
Guardian and ward, determination of need for guardianship, disclosure of records, CC 56.10
Health care providers, officers and employees, CC 56.25

MEDICAL RECORDS—Cont'd
Health Care Service Plans, this index
Health Insurance, this index
Incompetent person, release, CC 56.11
Industrial accidents, disclosure, application of law, CC 56.30
Insurance, this index
Insurance agents, solicitors or brokers, disclosure, CC 56.265
  Direct marketing, exemptions, CC 1798.91
Labor and employment,
  Disclosure, CC 56.20 et seq.
  Use and disclosure of medical information, CC 56.20 et seq.
Law enforcement, disclosure, application of law, CC 56.30
Limitation, use, communication, CC 56.14
Managed care department, disclosure, CC 56.30
Markets and marketing, direct marketing, disclosure, CC 1798.91
Medical malpractice, compromise and settlement, authorization to disclose, CC 56.105
Medical survey, disclosure, application of law, CC 56.30
Mental Health, this index
Modification,
  Authorization, disclosure, CC 56.15
  Release authorization, CC 56.15
  Employers, CC 56.24
Municipal attorneys, negligence, release, CC 56.36
Negligence,
  Disposal, CC 56.101
  Release, CC 56.36
Nominal damages, negligence, release, CC 56.36
Notice,
  Authorization, cancellation, CC 56.15, 56.24
  Cancellation of authorization, CC 56.15
Orders of court, disclosure, CC 56.10
Outpatient psychotherapy, confidential or privileged information, CC 56.104
Patient discharge data, disclosure, application of law, CC 56.30
Patients, right to access, CC 56.28
Personal injury, disclosure, violations, CC 56.35
Pharmaceutical companies, confidential or privileged information, CC 56 et seq.
Preemployment physical examination, minors, release, CC 56.10
Preexisting release authorizations, CC 56.15
Privacy,
  Genetic testing, CC 56.18 et seq.
  Sales, CC 1798.130
    Exemptions, CC 1798.146, 1798.148
Privileged information. Confidential or privileged information, generally, ante
Privileges and immunities, release, CC 56.14, 56.36

MEDICAL

MEDICAL RECORDS—Cont'd
Production of books and papers, disclosure, **CC 56.10**
Professional use, disclosure, **CC 56.10**
Psychotherapists and Psychotherapy, this index
Public social services, disclosure, application of law, **CC 56.30**
Punitive damages, disclosure, **CC 56.35**
Release,
  Authorization, **CC 56.10, 56.11**
    Disclosure to other parties, **CC 56.13**
    Disclosure to other persons, employers, **CC 56.245**
  Cancelling, **CC 56.15**
    Employers, **CC 56.24**
  Children and minors, gender identity or expression, **CC 56.109**
  Corporations, **CC 56.07**
  Disclosure, generally, ante
  Employers, **CC 56.20 et seq.**
  Form, **CC 56.11**
    Employers, **CC 56.21**
  Gender identity or expression, children and minors, **CC 56.109**
  General information, **CC 56.16**
  Limitations, **CC 56.14**
  Mental health, outpatient psychotherapy, **CC 56.104**
  Negligence, **CC 56.36**
  Outpatient psychotherapy, **CC 56.104**
Sales,
  Consumers, privacy, **CC 1798.130**
    Exemptions, **CC 1798.146, 1798.148**
  Disclosure, **CC 1798.91**
Schools and school districts, disclosure, **CC 56.10**
Search warrant, disclosure, **CC 56.10**
Signatures, release authorization, **CC 56.11**
Software, confidential or privileged information, business and commerce, **CC 56.06**
Spouse, release, **CC 56.11**
State agencies, comatose patients, information disclosure to agency, **CC 56.10**
Statistics, disclosure, application of law, **CC 56.30**
Subpoenas, disclosure, **CC 56.10**
Summary, patient access, corporations, **CC 56.07**
Telecommunications, sales, disclosure, **CC 1798.91**
Third parties,
  Administrators, use, disclosure, **CC 56.26**
  Confidential or privileged information, **CC 56.10**
Tissue banks, disclosure **CC 56.10**
Violations, **CC 56.35 et seq.**
Waiver, disclosure, **CC 56.37**

MEDICINE
Drugs and Medicine, generally, this index

MEMBERSHIP CAMPING CONTRACTS
Generally, **CC 1812.300 et seq.**

MEMORABILIA
Autographed memorabilia, warranties, **CC 1739.7**

MEMORANDUM
Installment sales,
  Accounts, **CC 1810.3**
  Subsequent purchases, **CC 1808.2 et seq.**

MENACE
Duress or Coercion, generally, this index

MENTAL HEALTH
Abuse, disclosure, protection and advocacy agency, **CC 1798.24b**
Agreements. Contracts, generally, post
Business and commerce, mental health digital services, confidential or privileged information, **CC 56.06**
Children and minors, medical records, release, gender identity or expression, **CC 56.109**
Civil rights, **CC 54 et seq.**
Confidential or privileged information,
  Medical records, **CC 56.104**
  Mental health digital services, business and commerce, **CC 56.06**
Conservators and conservatorships, **CC 40**
Contracts,
  Capacity, **CC 38 et seq., 1556, 1557**
  Rescission, **CC 39**
  Revocation, **CC 1587**
Damages, support, **CC 38**
Deeds and conveyances, rescission, **CC 39**
Disclosure. Medical records, post
Discrimination, **CC 54 et seq.**
Guardian and Ward, generally, this index
Health care providers, digital services, business and commerce, confidential or privileged information, **CC 56.06**
Health care service plans, confidential or privileged information, **CC 56.107**
Records and recordation, **CC 56.104**
Hospitals,
  Access, commercial blockade, **CC 3427 et seq.**
  Commercial blockade, **CC 3427 et seq.**
Internet, mental health digital services,
  Business and commerce, confidential or privileged information, **CC 56.06**
  Data breaches, **CC 56.251**
Medical records,
  Application of law, **CC 56.30**
  Confidential or privileged information, **CC 56.104**
  Correctional institutions, disclosure, **CC 56.10**
  Disclosure, **CC 56.10**
    Application of law, **CC 56.30**
    Gender identity or expression, children and minors, **CC 56.109**

MENTAL HEALTH—Cont'd
Medical records—Cont'd
  Mental health digital services, business and commerce, confidential or privileged information, **CC 56.06**
Mental health digital services,
  Business and commerce, confidential or privileged information, **CC 56.06**
  Data breaches, **CC 56.251**
Mortgages, modification or change, forbearance, fines and penalties, **CC 2944.8**
Outpatients, psychotherapy, medical records, confidential or privileged information, **CC 56.104**
Personal attendants. Domestic Workers, generally, this index
Presumptions, deeds and conveyances, rescission, **CC 39**
Protection and advocacy agency, disclosure, abuse or neglect, **CC 1798.24b**
Psychotherapists and Psychotherapy, generally, this index
Records and recordation. Medical records, generally, ante
Social Services, generally, this index
Support, liability, **CC 38**
Torts, **CC 41**

MENTAL HEALTH COUNSELORS
Privileges and immunities,
  Professional committee, **CC 43.7, 43.8**
  Referral services, **CC 43.95**

MENTAL INSTITUTIONS
Intellectual and Developmental Disabilities, generally, this index
Mental Health, generally, this index

MERCHANDISE
Goods, Wares and Merchandise, generally, this index

MERCHANTS
Stores, generally, this index

MERGER AND CONSOLIDATION
Bailment, merger of interest, **CC 1933**
Consolidated Cities and Counties, generally, this index
Easements, extinguishment, **CC 811**
Landlord and tenant, **CC 1933**
Leases, merger of interest, **CC 1933**
Precedent interest, destruction, future interests, **CC 741**
Real estate, single instrument of conveyance or consolidated descriptions, **CC 1093**
Trusts and trustees, voluntary trusts, avoidance of merger, equitable and legal estate in same person, **CC 2225**

MESSAGES
Carriers, this index
Communications, generally, this index
Telecommunications, generally, this index

METAL KNUCKLES
Weapons, generally, this index

METERS
Electricity, this index

METHANE
Air Pollution, generally, this index

MICE
Pest Control, generally, this index

MICRA (MEDICAL INJURY COMPENSATION REFORM ACT)
Medical Malpractice, generally, this index

MIDWIVES
Malpractice. Medical Malpractice, generally, this index
Medical Malpractice, generally, this index
Negligence. Medical Malpractice, generally, this index
Privileges and immunities, peer review, CC 43.7, 43.8

MILITARY DEPARTMENT
Military Forces, generally, this index

MILITARY FORCES
Acknowledgments, CC 1183.5
Attestation, officers, CC 1183.5
Commissioned officers. Officers and employees, generally, post
Emergencies, orders or regulations, suspension of civil and criminal liability, CC 1714.6
Evidence, acknowledgments, presumptions, CC 1183.5
Landlord and tenant, security deposits, CC 1950.5
Motor vehicles, warranties, CC 1795.8
National guard,
  Motor vehicles, warranties, CC 1795.8
  Warranties, motor vehicles, CC 1795.8
Notaries public, authority, CC 1183.5
Oaths and affirmations, officers, administration, CC 1183.5
Officers and employees,
  Acknowledgments, CC 1183.5
  Attestation, CC 1183.5
  Oaths and affirmations, administration, CC 1183.5
Orders, emergencies, suspension of civil and criminal liability, CC 1714.6
Privileges and immunities, emergencies, orders or regulations, suspension of civil and criminal liability, CC 1714.6
Veterans, generally, this index
War and civil defense, orders or regulations, suspension of civil and criminal liability, CC 1714.6
Warranties, motor vehicles, CC 1795.8

MILLS
Manufacturers and Manufacturing, generally, this index

MINERAL RIGHTS
Generally, CC 883.110 et seq.

MINES AND MINERALS
Abandonment, mineral rights, CC 883.130
  Lease, CC 883.140
Actions and proceedings. Termination of mineral rights, post
Application of law, mineral rights, CC 883.120, 883.270
Asbestos, generally, this index
Attorney fees,
  Lessees, liability, CC 883.140
  Termination of mineral rights, CC 883.250
Contracts,
  Exploration or removal, applicability, lessors remedy for breach statutes, CC 1952.4
  Machinery sales, bill of sale, CC 1631
Deeds and conveyances, mineral rights, CC 883.110 et seq.
Disclosure, real estate, sales, CC 1103.4
Easements, CC 801, 802
Emergencies, entry on property, notice, waiver, CC 848
Entry on property, notice, mineral rights owners, CC 848
Exemptions, mineral rights reserved to United States, CC 883.120
Geologists and Geophysicists, generally, this index
Leases,
  Abandonment, quitclaim deed, CC 883.140
  Expiration or abandonment, quitclaim deed, CC 883.140
  Legal Estates Principal and Income Law, CC 731 et seq.
  Mineral rights, CC 883.110 et seq.
  Municipal corporations, CC 718, 718f
Legal Estates Principal and Income Law, CC 731 et seq.
Liens and incumbrances, CC 3060
Machinery and equipment, sales, bill of sale, CC 1631
Mineral rights, CC 883.110 et seq.
Municipal corporations, leases, CC 718f
Notice,
  Entry and excavation, owners of mineral rights, CC 848
  Preservation of mineral rights, notice of intent, CC 883.230, 883.250
Oil and Gas, generally, this index
Preservation of mineral rights, notice of intent, recording, CC 883.230, 883.250
Public utilities, notice, entry and excavation, mineral rights owners, CC 848
Quitclaim deed, mineral rights lease, expiration or abandonment, CC 883.140
Real estate, sales, disclosure, CC 1103.4
Records and recordation,
  Machinery sales, CC 1631
  Preservation of mineral rights, notice of intent, CC 883.230, 883.250

MINES AND MINERALS—Cont'd
Rights, mineral rights, CC 883.110 et seq.
  Notice, entry and excavation, CC 848
Royalties, generally, this index
Tenants for years or at will, CC 819
  Limitation of rights, CC 820
Termination of mineral rights, actions and proceedings, CC 883.240
  Dormant rights, CC 883.210, 883.220
  Effect of termination, CC 883.260
  Intent to preserve mineral rights, recording, CC 883.250
Time, dormant mineral rights, termination, CC 883.220
Zoning and Planning, generally, this index

MINORITIES
Minority Groups, generally, this index

MINORITY GROUPS
Actions and proceedings, equal protection of laws, statutes, CC 53.7
Administrative law and procedure, equal protection of laws, CC 53.7
Construction of laws, equal protection of laws, CC 53.7
Ordinances, equal protection of laws, CC 53.7
Statutes, equal protection of laws, CC 53.7

MINORS
Children and Minors, generally, this index

MISBRANDED
Brands, Marks and Labels, generally, this index

MISDEMEANORS
Crimes and Offenses, generally, this index

MISREPRESENTATION
Fraud, generally, this index

MISSING RECORDS
Lost or Destroyed Documents, generally, this index

MITES
Pest Control, generally, this index

MIXED MEDIA
Fine arts, common law copyrights, reproduction rights, transfer, CC 982

MOBILE DWELLINGS
Mobilehomes and Mobilehome Parks, generally, this index

MOBILEHOMES AND MOBILEHOME PARKS
  See, also, Recreational Vehicles, generally, this index
  Generally, CC 798 et seq.
Abandonment,
  Declaration, CC 798.61
  Right of entry, CC 799.2.5
Abatement, nuisance, common area facilities, CC 798.87

MOBILEHOMES

MOBILEHOMES AND MOBILEHOME PARKS—Cont'd

Absence and absentees, medical care and treatment, subleases, CC 798.23.5
Accessory buildings, entry on property, consent, CC 798.26
Accounts and accounting,
   Abandonment, declaration, sale, CC 798.61
   Disposal, abandonment, CC 798.61
Actions and proceedings, CC 798.84 et seq.
   Declaration of abandonment, CC 798.61
   Nuisance, common area facilities, CC 798.87
   Willful violations, damages, CC 798.86
Address,
   Business address, mobilehome park owner, disclosure, CC 798.28
   Disposal, CC 798.56a
      Abandonment, CC 798.61
Adults only regulations, CC 798.76
   Subdivisions, cooperatives or condominiums, third party purchasers, CC 799.5
Advertisements, sales, CC 798.70
   Subdivisions, cooperatives or condominiums, CC 799.1.5
Age,
   Live in health care, supportive care or supervision, CC 798.34, 799.9
   Requirements, older persons, CC 798.76, 799.5
Aged persons,
   Age, requirements, CC 798.76, 799.5
   Live in health care, supportive care or supervision, CC 798.34, 799.9
   Relatives, sharing mobilehomes, CC 798.34
   Resident owned mobilehome parks, sales, CC 799.5
Agents and agencies,
   Listings, transfers, CC 1086 et seq.
   Replacement, CC 798.71
   Sales, CC 798.70
Agreements. Contracts, generally, post
Alcoholic beverages, common area facilities, CC 798.51
Alternate rates for energy (CARE) program, master meter parks, CC 798.43.1
Amendments, park rules and regulations, procedures, CC 798.25
Appliances, warranties, CC 1797 et seq.
Application of law, CC 798.60
   Driveways, maintenance, CC 798.37.5
   Pets, CC 798.33
   Rent control, apportionment of expenses, CC 1947.15
   Sales, subdivisions, cooperatives or condominiums, CC 799.1
   State officers and employees, CC 798.13
   Trees, maintenance, CC 798.37.5
Arbitration and award, dispute resolution, rules, CC 798.25.5
As is sales, disclosure, waiver, CC 1102.1
Assistance center, signs and signals, CC 798.29

MOBILEHOMES AND MOBILEHOME PARKS—Cont'd

Attorney fees,
   Actions by tenants, CC 798.85
   Lien holders, foreclosure or termination of tenancy, CC 798.56a
   Management, CC 798.39.5
   Termination of tenancy proceedings, reimbursement, CC 798.56a
Auctions and auctioneers, personal property, removal, CC 798.36
Audio and video recordings, collective meetings with homeowners, CC 798.53
Bids and bidding, abandonment, declaration, CC 798.61
Billings,
   Services rendered but not in rental agreements, fees and charges, CC 798.32
   Utility service fees and charges, CC 798.41
Burden of proof, condition of mobilehome, removal from park, CC 798.73
Business addresses, mobilehome park owners, disclosure to homeowners, CC 798.28
Business operations, rules and regulations, owners and employees, CC 798.23
Campaigns, signs and signals, CC 798.51, 799.10
Candidates, signs and signals, CC 798.51, 799.10
Canvassing and petitioning homeowners and residents, noncommercial purposes, CC 798.51
Change of use, CC 798.10
Charges. Fees, generally, post
Children and minors, adults only regulations, compliance, CC 798.76
Cleaning deposits, common area facilities, meetings, CC 798.51
Clubs, discrimination, CC 798.20
Collective meetings, rules and regulations, CC 798.53
   Changes, CC 798.51
Common area facilities,
   Alcoholic beverages, CC 798.51
   Cleaning deposits, meetings, CC 798.51
   Collective meetings with homeowners, CC 798.53
   Gas, electricity and water, meters, CC 798.43
   Hours of operation, posting, CC 798.24
   Liability insurance, meetings, CC 798.51
   Managements failure to maintain, actions, notice, CC 798.84
   Parking, CC 798.51
   Public nuisances, CC 798.87
Condition of mobilehome, removal from park, CC 798.73
Conditional sales, default, deficiency judgments, limitation, CC 2983.8
Conditions of ownership,
   Covenants against mobilehomes, CC 714.5
   Management handling of resales, CC 798.71, 798.81

MOBILEHOMES AND MOBILEHOME PARKS—Cont'd

Condominiums. Subdivisions, cooperatives or condominiums, generally, post
Conflict of laws, CC 798.60
Consent,
   Entry on property, CC 798.26, 799.2.5
   Owner, sale or listing agreement, subdivision, cooperative or condominium, CC 799.2
   Park rules and regulations amendment, CC 798.25
   Showing or listing mobilehomes for sale, CC 798.71
   Trees, maintenance, CC 798.37.5
Construction of laws, CC 798.1
Constructive eviction, CC 798.55 et seq.
Consultation, park rules and regulations amendment, CC 798.25
Contractors,
   Display of warranties, CC 1797.5
   Warranties, CC 1797.2 et seq.
      Application of law, CC 1797.2
Contracts,
   Fee for lease for more than one year, CC 798.31
   Home roof warranties, CC 1797.90 et seq.
   Rentals, written rental agreements, CC 798.18
Controlled substances, grounds for termination of tenancy, CC 798.56
Cooperative apartments. Subdivisions, cooperatives or condominiums, generally, post
Copies, rental agreements, CC 798.16
Costs,
   Driveways, maintenance, CC 798.37.5
   Lien holders, foreclosure or termination of tenancy, CC 798.56a
   Management, CC 798.39.5
   Tenants actions, CC 798.85
   Termination of tenancy proceedings, reimbursement, CC 798.56a
   Trees, maintenance, CC 798.37.5
Covenants, CC 714.5
COVID 19,
   Exemptions, rental agreements, CC 798.17
   Termination, CC 798.56
Credit rating reports, management collecting fees from prospective purchasers, disposition, CC 798.74
Damages,
   Driveways, CC 798.37.5
   Public utilities, disruption, CC 798.42, 799.7
   Trees, CC 798.37.5
   Willful violations, CC 798.86
   Withholding of approval, purchaser, CC 798.74
Dealers,
   Agency listings, CC 1086 et seq.
   Warranties, CC 1797 et seq.
      Notice, display, CC 1797.5

MOBILEHOMES

MOBILEHOMES AND MOBILEHOME PARKS—Cont'd

Death, tenants, right of estate to sell, CC 798.70 et seq.
Declaration of abandonment, CC 798.61
Defect, warranties, CC 1797 et seq.
Deficiency judgments, sale of mobilehomes, limitation, CC 2983.8
Deposits,
    Cleaning deposits, common area facilities, meetings, CC 798.51
    Security deposits, CC 798.39
Descent and distribution, right to sell, CC 798.70 et seq.
Destruction, disasters, renewed tenancy, CC 798.62
Disasters, destruction, renewed tenancy, CC 798.62
Disclosure,
    As is sales, waiver, CC 1102.1
    Exemptions, CC 1102.2
    Gas, electric and water meters, common areas, CC 798.43
    Leases, CC 1102.3a
    Owners of parks, address and telephone number, CC 798.28
    Sales, post
    School facilities fees, CC 798.82, 799.8
    Time, sales, CC 798.75.5, 1102.3a
    Transfer of mobilehomes, CC 798.74.4
    Waiver, as is sales, CC 1102.1
Discrimination, club membership, CC 798.20
Disposal,
    Abandonment, CC 798.61
    Notice, CC 798.56a
Dispute resolution, regulations, CC 798.25.5
Disruption, public utilities, notice, CC 798.42, 799.7
Documents, dealer and manufacturer written warranty, forms, CC 1797.3
Driveways, maintenance, CC 798.37.5
    Entry on property, CC 798.26
Drugs and medicine, grounds for termination of tenancy, CC 798.56
Elections, campaigns, signs and signals, CC 798.51, 799.10
Electricity,
    Alternate rates for energy (CARE) program, master meter parks, CC 798.43.1
    Equipment, warranties, CC 1797 et seq.
    Meters, common areas and equipment, management compensation, CC 798.43
    Warranties, CC 1797 et seq.
Emergencies,
    Public utilities, disruption, CC 798.42, 799.7
    Right of entry, CC 798.26, 799.2.5
Encumbrances. Liens and incumbrances, generally, post
Enforcement of law, rules and regulations, CC 798.36
Entry on property, CC 799.2.5
    Consent, CC 798.26

MOBILEHOMES AND MOBILEHOME PARKS—Cont'd

Equipment, warranties, CC 1797 et seq.
Escrows and escrow agents,
    Agreements, purchases, CC 798.75
    Security deposits, CC 798.39
Eviction, CC 798.55 et seq.
    Unlawful occupants, CC 798.75
Evidence, abandonment, CC 798.61
Exchange of property, CC 798.70 et seq.
Exemplary damages, willful violations, CC 798.86
Exemptions,
    Disclosure, CC 1102.2
    Local rules and regulations, CC 798.17
    Natural hazards, residential property, disclosure, CC 1103.1
    Notice, sales, listing agreements, residents organizations, CC 798.80
    Ordinances, local ordinances, CC 798.17
    Rent controls, CC 798.21
    Rental agreements, CC 798.17
Fair Housing Act, domicile and residence, compliance, CC 798.76
Fees, CC 798.30 et seq.
    Agreement, maintenance of premises, CC 798.15
    Authorized fees, CC 798.31
    Disclosure, school facilities fees, CC 798.82, 799.8
    Financial reports or credit ratings, management collecting from prospective purchasers, disposition, CC 798.74
    Guests, CC 798.34
        Occupancy fee, CC 798.34
    Immediate family members, number of, CC 798.35
    Increase, fines and penalties, recovery of costs, CC 798.39.5
    Landscaping, CC 798.37
    Leases, fee for obtaining lease, CC 798.31
    Live in health care, supportive care or supervision, aged persons, CC 798.34, 799.9
    Local government ordinance, fees imposed by, CC 798.37
    Maintenance, land, premises, notice, CC 798.36
    Municipal fees assessments or charges, separate billings of homeowners, CC 798.49
    Personal property, removal, CC 798.36
    Pets, CC 798.33
    Public utilities, post
    Rent control, apportionment of costs, application of law, CC 1947.15
    Rules and regulations, amendments, CC 798.25
    Sales, CC 798.72
    School facilities fees, disclosure, CC 798.82, 799.8

MOBILEHOMES AND MOBILEHOME PARKS—Cont'd

Fees—Cont'd
    Security deposits, CC 798.39
    Separate designated charges, billing, CC 798.49
    Service fees, CC 798.37
        Unlisted services, CC 798.32
    Services not in rental agreements but rendered, notice, CC 798.32
    Transfer or selling fee, CC 798.72
    Unlisted services, CC 798.32
    Water supply, CC 798.40
Financing statements, management collection from prospective purchasers, disposition, CC 798.74
Fines and penalties,
    Increased rent or charges, recovery of costs, restriction, CC 798.39.5
    Willful violations, CC 798.86
Foreclosure, right to sell within park, CC 798.79
Foreign languages, leases, translations, CC 1632
Forms,
    Disclosure, sales, CC 1102.6d
    Notice, CC 798.15
    Written manufacturer and dealer warranties, CC 1797.3
Fraud, purchases, damages, CC 798.74
Guests, occupancy fee, CC 798.34
Hazards, natural hazards, disclosure, CC 1103 et seq.
Health and sanitation, motor vehicles, removal, CC 798.28.5
Health care workers, aged persons, CC 798.34
Hearings,
    Abandonment, declaration, CC 798.61
    Injunctions, regulation violation, CC 798.88
Heat and heating companies, warranties, CC 1797 et seq.
Home roof warranties, CC 1797.90 et seq.
Homeowner communications and meetings, CC 798.50 et seq.
Hookup fees, CC 798.37
Improvements, sales, CC 798.73.5
Income tax—state, returns, credit rating, CC 798.74
Increase, rent controls, CC 798.30.5
Incumbrances. Liens and incumbrances, generally, post
Information, prospective homeowners, CC 798.74.5
Initiative and referendum, signs and signals, CC 798.51, 799.10
Injunction,
    Homeowners or residents meetings, CC 798.52
    Violation of regulations, CC 798.88
Inspection and inspectors, rental agreements, notice, CC 798.17

MOBILEHOMES

MOBILEHOMES AND MOBILEHOME PARKS—Cont'd

Installation,
  Fees and charges, CC 798.37
  Roofs, warranties, CC 1797.90 et seq.
Interest, security deposits, CC 798.39
Internet, public utilities, fees, posting, CC 798.40
Inventory, abandonment, CC 798.61
Joint tenants, survivors right to sell, CC 798.70 et seq.
Junior lienholders, termination of tenancy, CC 798.56
Landlord and tenant,
  Rent controls, generally, post
  Rental agreements, written agreements, CC 798.18
  Termination, CC 1946.2
Landscaping fees, CC 798.37
Leases,
  Disclosure, CC 1102.3a
  Fees for obtaining lease, CC 798.31
  Foreign languages, translations, CC 1632
  Notice, CC 798.27
  Pets, CC 798.33
  Renewal, refusal to renew, CC 798.55 et seq.
  Rental agreements, CC 798.8, 798.15 et seq.
  Spanish language, translations, CC 1632
  Subleases, CC 798.23.5
    Managers and management, application of law, CC 798.23
  Termination, tenancy, CC 798.55 et seq.
Liability insurance, common area facilities, meetings, CC 798.51
Licenses and permits,
  Disposal, CC 798.56a
    Abandonment, CC 798.61
  Moving permit, waiver, rental agreements, CC 798.19
  Zoning permits, notice, CC 798.27
Liens and incumbrances, CC 798.38, 3051 et seq.
  Abandonment, declaration, sale, CC 798.61
  Application of law, CC 3051, 3067.2
  Termination of tenancy, junior lienholders, CC 798.56
  Warehouses, termination of tenancy, storage, CC 798.56a
Liquefied petroleum gas, sales, CC 798.44
Listing agreements, notice, residents organizations, CC 798.80
Live in health care, supportive care or supervision, aged persons, CC 799.9
Low and moderate income housing, alternate rates for energy (CARE) program, master meter parks, CC 798.43.1
Mail and mailing,
  Abandonment, declaration, notice, CC 798.61

MOBILEHOMES AND MOBILEHOME PARKS—Cont'd

Mail and mailing—Cont'd
  Service of notice, CC 798.14
Maintenance and repairs,
  Driveways, CC 798.37.5
    Entry on property, CC 798.26
  Entry on property, consent, CC 798.26
  Notice, CC 798.15
  Fees, CC 798.36
  Rules and regulations, owners and employees, CC 798.23
  Sales, CC 798.73.5
    Repossession, CC 798.79
  Survivors right to sell, CC 798.78
  Trees, CC 798.37.5
    Entry on property, CC 798.26
  Warranties, CC 1797 et seq.
Managers and management, CC 798.2
  Actions against, notice, CC 798.84
  Homeowners meetings with, CC 798.53
  Notice, sales, CC 798.71
  Resale of unit by owner, exclusive agency for management, CC 798.81
  Right of first refusal, sales, CC 798.19.5
  Rules and regulations, owners and employees, CC 798.23
  Sales, post
  Willful violations, fines and penalties, CC 798.86
Manufacturers and manufacturing, warranties, CC 1797 et seq.
Master meter parks, alternate rates for energy (CARE) program, CC 798.43.1
Maximum rental charge, local regulation, exemptions, CC 798.17
Medical care and treatment, subleases, CC 798.23.5
Meeting by tenants, residents or occupants, CC 798.50 et seq.
Warranty, display, CC 1797.5
Meetings, park rules and regulations amendment, CC 798.25
Mobilehome assistance center, signs and signals, CC 798.29
Motor vehicles, removal, unauthorized parking, CC 798.28.5
Moving permit, waiver, rental agreements, CC 798.19
Municipal assessments fees and charges, separate billing of homeowner, CC 798.49
Mutual benefit corporations, members and membership, application of law, CC 799.1
Names,
  Disposal, CC 798.56a
    Abandonment, CC 798.61
  Owner, disclosure to homeowner, CC 798.28
Natural hazards, disclosure, CC 1103 et seq.
Negligence, damage caused by, repairs, CC 798.73, 798.83
New construction, rent control, exemptions, CC 798.45

MOBILEHOMES AND MOBILEHOME PARKS—Cont'd

Nonresidents, rent controls, exemptions, CC 798.21
Notice,
  Abandonment, declaration, CC 798.61
  Acceptance as homeowner, CC 798.74
  Actions and proceedings, managements failure to maintain common facilities or reduction in services, CC 798.84
  Alternate rates for energy (CARE) program, master meter parks, CC 798.43.1
  Amendments, rules and regulations, CC 798.25
  Buyers, substantial defects in materials or workmanship, warranty notices, CC 1797.3
  Collective meetings,
    Changes, rules and regulations, improvements, CC 798.51
    Rules and regulations, CC 798.53
  Common area facilities, hours of operation, CC 798.24
  Disposal, CC 798.56a
  Fees, CC 798.30, 798.32
  Forms, CC 798.15
  Improvements, transfer of mobilehomes, CC 798.73.5
  Leases, CC 798.27
  Maintenance, land, premises, CC 798.15, 798.36
  Managers and management, sales, CC 798.71
  Modification, rent or terms of tenancy, CC 798.21
  Motor vehicles, removal, CC 798.28.5
  Nonpayment, CC 798.56
  Personal property, removal, CC 798.36
  Prospective homeowners, CC 798.74.5
  Public utilities, post
  Removal, CC 798.73
    Motor vehicles, CC 798.28.5
  Rent, CC 798.17
    Modification, CC 798.21
  Repairs, transfer of mobilehomes, CC 798.73.5
  Resident owned mobilehome parks, sales, CC 799.4
  Rules and regulations, amendments, CC 798.25
  Sales,
    Listing agreements, residents organizations, CC 798.80
    Managers and management, CC 798.71
    Repairs, CC 798.73.5
  Service of notice, personal delivery or by mail, CC 798.14
  State officers and employees, termination, CC 798.13
  Subdivisions, cooperatives or condominiums, sales, CC 799.4
  Termination of tenancy, CC 798.55 et seq.

MOBILEHOMES

MOBILEHOMES AND MOBILEHOME PARKS—Cont'd
Notice—Cont'd
  Terms of tenancy, modification, CC **798.21**
  Three or more violations, termination of tenancy, CC **798.56**
  Transfer of mobilehomes, repairs, CC **798.73.5**
  Trees, maintenance, CC **798.37.5**
  Vacation of tenancy, CC **798.59**
  Warranty, display, CC **1797.5**
  Zoning permits, leases, CC **798.27**
Nuisance,
  Common facilities, maintenance, CC **798.87**
  Grounds for termination of tenancy, CC **798.56**
Occupancy,
  Guests, occupancy fee, CC **798.34**
  Live in health, supportive care persons, CC **798.34**
Occupational licenses. Licenses and permits, generally, ante
Officers and employees, rules and regulations, compliance, CC **798.23**
Oil and gas,
  Alternate rates for energy (CARE) program, master meter parks, CC **798.43.1**
  Meters, common areas and equipment, management compensation, CC **798.43**
Open house signs, sales, advertising, CC **798.70**
Options, rental agreement rejection, homeowners, CC **798.17**
Outdoor advertising, CC **799.1.5**
Owners and ownership. Title to property, generally, post
Parking,
  Common area facilities, CC **798.51**
  Unauthorized vehicles, removal, CC **798.28.5**
Peaceful assembly, meetings in park, CC **798.50 et seq.**
Perjury, disposal, CC **798.56a**
  Abandonment, CC **798.61**
Permits. Licenses and permits, generally, ante
Personal property, removal, CC **798.36**
Petitions, injunctions, regulation violation, CC **798.88**
Pets, CC **798.33**
Photography and pictures, disposal, CC **798.56a**
  Abandonment, CC **798.61**
Plumbers and plumbing, warranties, CC **1797 et seq.**
Posting,
  Alternate rates for energy (CARE) program, master meter parks, CC **798.43.1**
  Common area facilities, hours of operation, CC **798.24**
  Liquefied petroleum gas, sales, CC **798.44**
  Motor vehicles, removal, notice, CC **798.28.5**

MOBILEHOMES AND MOBILEHOME PARKS—Cont'd
Proceedings. Actions and proceedings, generally, ante
Prostitution, grounds for termination of tenancy, CC **798.56**
Public nuisances, common facilities, physical maintenance, CC **798.87**
Public officials and others, meetings, homeowners and residents, CC **798.51**
Public policy, disclosure, sales, CC **1102.1**
Public utilities,
  Alternate rates for energy (CARE) program, master meter parks, CC **798.43.1**
  Collective meetings with homeowners, CC **798.53**
  Delinquency, termination of tenancy, sales, payment, CC **798.55**
  Fees, CC **798.41**
    Notice, CC **798.40**
    Separate billing, CC **798.41**
  Meters,
    Billing, CC **798.40**
    Common areas, CC **798.43**
  Notice,
    Disruption, CC **798.42, 799.7**
    Fees, CC **798.40, 798.41**
  Rental agreements, charges, CC **798.18**
  Right of entry, CC **798.26**
  Satisfaction of bills, survivors right to sell, CC **798.78**
  Separate meters, common area facilities or equipment, CC **798.43**
Purchases. Sales, generally, post
Rates and charges, water supply, CC **798.40**
Recall, signs and signals, CC **798.51, 799.10**
Records and recordation, warranties, CC **1797.6**
Recovery, abandoned mobilehome, CC **798.61**
Recreational Vehicle Parks, generally, this index
Refunds,
  Personal property, removal, sales, CC **798.36**
  Security deposits, CC **798.39**
Registration, guests, CC **798.34**
Rejection of rental agreements, homeowner option, CC **798.17**
Relatives,
  Fees and charges, CC **798.35**
  Senior homeowners, CC **798.34**
Removal, CC **798.73**
  Termination of tenancy, CC **798.55, 798.56a**
  Third party sales, CC **799.3**
  Unauthorized vehicles, parking, CC **798.28.5**
Renewals, automatic renewal of rental agreements, CC **798.17, 798.18**
Renewed tenancy, disasters, destruction, CC **798.62**
Rent,
  Advertisements, CC **799.1.5**
  Agreements, CC **798.15 et seq.**
  Waiver, CC **798.77**

MOBILEHOMES AND MOBILEHOME PARKS—Cont'd
Rent—Cont'd
  Collective meetings, rental agreements, CC **798.51, 798.53**
  Delinquency, termination of tenancy, sales, payment, CC **798.55**
  Guests, occupancy fee, CC **798.34**
  Increase,
    Fines and penalties, recovery of costs, CC **798.39.5**
    Notice, CC **798.30**
  Lien or security interest, CC **798.38**
  Local regulation, CC **798.17**
  Maintenance of land, premises, rent agreements, CC **798.15**
  Managers and management, application of law, CC **798.23**
  Medical care and treatment, absence and absentees, CC **798.23.5**
  Satisfaction, survivors right to sell premises, CC **798.78**
  Security interest or lien, CC **798.38**
  Written agreements, CC **798.18**
Rent controls, CC **798.21**
  Apportionment of expenses, application of law, CC **1947.15**
  Exemptions, CC **798.17, 798.21**
  Increase, CC **798.30.5**
  New construction, exemptions, CC **798.45**
  Nonresidents, exemptions, CC **798.21**
Repairs. Maintenance and repairs, generally, ante
Replacement, agents, CC **798.71**
Repossession, sale, payment of rent and utilities, CC **798.79**
Representatives, collective meetings with homeowners, CC **798.53**
Rescission, rental agreements, CC **798.17**
Residency Law, CC **798 et seq.**
Resident owned mobilehome parks, CC **799 et seq.**
Residents organizations, notice, sales, listing agreements, CC **798.80**
Restrictive covenants, CC **714.5**
Roof warranties, CC **1797.90 et seq.**
Rules and regulations, CC **798.23 et seq.**
  Adults only, CC **798.76**
  Subdivisions, cooperatives or condominiums, CC **799.5**
  Enforcement, fee, CC **798.36**
  Injunctions, enforcement, CC **798.88**
  Maintenance, land, premises, CC **798.15, 798.36**
  Meetings, CC **798.53**
    Changes, CC **798.51**
  Third party purchasers, compliance, CC **798.74, 798.75**
  Subdivisions, cooperatives or condominiums, CC **799.5**
Safety, motor vehicles, removal, CC **798.28.5**

MOBILEHOMES

MOBILEHOMES AND MOBILEHOME PARKS—Cont'd

Sales, CC 798.70 et seq.
  Abandonment, declaration, CC 798.61
  Agency listings, CC 1086 et seq.
  Agreements, CC 798.75
    Waiver, CC 798.77
  As is sales, disclosure, waiver, CC 1102.1
  Death of tenant, right of estate to sell, CC 798.70 et seq.
  Deficiency judgment, sale of mobilehomes, limitation, CC 2983.8
  Descent and distribution, right to sell, CC 798.70 et seq.
  Disclosure, CC 798.74.4, 798.75.5, 1102 et seq.
    Forms, CC 1102.6d
  Hazards, natural hazards, disclosure, CC 1103 et seq.
  Improvements, CC 798.73.5
  Joint tenants, survivors right to sell, CC 798.78
  Liquefied petroleum gas, CC 798.44
  Listing agreements, notice, residents organizations, CC 798.80
  Managers and management, CC 798.71
    Approval of sale to third party, CC 798.74, 798.75
    Right of first refusal, CC 798.19.5
    Subdivisions, cooperatives and condominiums, CC 799.4
  Natural hazards, disclosure, CC 1103 et seq.
  Negligence, damage caused by, repairs, CC 798.73, 798.83
  Notice, ante
  Open house signs, CC 798.70
  Park owner, termination of tenancy to make space for buyer, CC 798.58
  Payment of rent and utilities, CC 798.79
  Personal property, removal, CC 798.36
  Prior approval of purchaser by management, CC 798.74
  Removal of mobilehomes from park, CC 798.73
  Repairs, CC 798.73.5
  Repossession, payment of rent and utilities, CC 798.79
  Resale,
    Disclosures, CC 1102 et seq.
    Owner, CC 798.81
  Residents organizations, sale of park by owner, notice, CC 798.80
  Right of first refusal, owners and ownership, CC 798.19.5
  Rights, termination of tenancy, sale within park, CC 798.56a
  Subdivisions, cooperatives or condominiums, post
  Termination of tenancy, CC 798.55
    Sale of mobilehome within park, CC 798.56a

MOBILEHOMES AND MOBILEHOME PARKS—Cont'd

Sales—Cont'd
  Transfer or selling fee, CC 798.72
  Unlawful occupants, eviction, CC 798.75
  Warehousemens liens, termination of tenancy, storage, CC 798.56a
  Warranties, CC 1797 et seq.
Satisfaction of judgment, recovery of abandoned home before sale, CC 798.61
School facilities fees, disclosure, CC 798.82, 799.8
Secured transactions, CC 798.38
  Foreclosure, right to sell within park, CC 798.79
Security deposits, CC 798.39
Security interest, CC 798.38
  Abandonment, declaration, sale, CC 798.61
Senior homeowners. Aged persons, generally, ante
Service fees, CC 798.37
Service of notice, personal delivery or by mail, CC 798.14
Services not in rental agreements but rendered, charging, notice, CC 798.32
Sharing mobilehomes with relatives, senior homeowners, CC 798.34
Signs and signals,
  Advertisements, CC 798.70, 799.1.5
  Campaigns, CC 798.51, 799.10
  Mobilehome assistance center, CC 798.29
Small claims courts, willful violations, damages, CC 798.86
Spanish language, leases, translations, CC 1632
Special Occupancy Parks, generally, this index
State officers and employees, application of law, CC 798.13
Storage,
  Personal property, removal, CC 798.36
  Termination of tenancy, CC 798.56a
Subdivisions, cooperatives or condominiums, CC 799 et seq.
  Aged persons, live in health care, supportive care or supervision, CC 799.9
  Disabled persons, accommodations, CC 798.29.6
  Fees, live in health care, supportive care or supervision, aged persons, CC 799.9
  Live in health care, supportive care or supervision, aged persons, CC 799.9
  Removal, third party sales, CC 799.3
  Rules and regulations, third party purchasers, compliance, CC 799.5
  Sales,
    Advertisements, CC 799.1.5
    Application of law, CC 799.1
    Descent and distribution, right to sell, CC 798.70 et seq., 798.78
    Management, approval of sale to third party, CC 799.4
    Notice, CC 799.4

MOBILEHOMES AND MOBILEHOME PARKS—Cont'd

Subdivisions, cooperatives or condominiums—Cont'd
  Sales—Cont'd
    Prior approval, purchasers, CC 799.4
    Showing or listing agreement, consent of owner, CC 799.2
    Waiver of rights, CC 799.6
Subleases, CC 798.23.5
  Managers and management, application of law, CC 798.23
Submeter service, public utilities, rates and charges, CC 798.40
Succession, right to sell, CC 798.70 et seq.
Suits. Actions and proceedings, generally, ante
Supportive care persons, CC 798.34
Taxation, disposal, CC 798.56a, 798.61
Telephones, business telephone number, mobilehome park owner, disclosure, CC 798.28
Temporary restraining orders, regulations, violations, CC 798.88
Termination, CC 798.55 et seq.
  Grounds, CC 798.56
  State officers and employees, CC 798.13
Terms of rental agreements, CC 798.16
  Modification, notice, CC 798.21
Third parties, removal upon sale, CC 798.73
Time,
  Collective meetings with homeowners, CC 798.53
  Residents or occupants, CC 798.51
  Disclosure, sales, CC 798.75.5, 1102.3a
  Rental agreement, local regulation, CC 798.17
  Repairs covered by warranties, CC 1797.7
  Warranties, records, CC 1797.6
Title to property,
  Abandonment, sale, registration, CC 798.61
  Actions and proceedings, notice, CC 798.84
  Disclosure, CC 798.28
  Information, prospective homeowners, CC 798.74.5
  Notice, prospective homeowners, CC 798.74.5
  Prospective homeowners, information, CC 798.74.5
  Right of first refusal, sales, CC 798.19.5
  Rules and regulations, CC 798.23
  Sales, generally, ante
  Searches and seizures, termination, notice, costs, CC 798.55
Transfers, CC 798.70 et seq.
  Agents, managers and management, CC 798.71, 798.81
  Agreements, CC 798.75
    Waiver, CC 798.77
  Approval, CC 798.71, 798.81
    Purchaser, fees, CC 798.72
  Disclosure, CC 798.74.4

MORTGAGE

MOBILEHOMES AND MOBILEHOME PARKS—Cont'd
Transfers—Cont'd
  Fees, CC 798.72
  Improvements, CC 798.73.5
  Interview fee, prospective purchaser, CC 798.72
  Notice, repairs, CC 798.73.5
  Removal, CC 798.73
  Repairs, CC 798.73.5
  Sales by owner, prohibition, CC 798.71, 798.81
  Security deposits, CC 798.39
  Showing or listing, consent of owner, CC 798.71, 798.81
Translations, foreign languages, leases, CC 1632
Trees, maintenance, CC 798.37.5
  Entry on property, CC 798.26
Unenforceable regulations, CC 798.25.5
Unlawful occupants, eviction, CC 798.75
Unlisted services, charges, notice, CC 798.32
Utilities. Public utilities, generally, ante
Vacation of tenancy, notice, CC 798.59
Video recordings, collective meetings with homeowners, CC 798.53
Void regulations, CC 798.25.5
Waiver,
  Disclosure, as is sales, CC 1102.1
  Rental or sale agreements, CC 798.19, 798.77
  Rights, subdivisions, cooperatives or condominiums, CC 799.6
Warehouses, liens and incumbrances, termination of tenancy, storage, CC 798.56a
Warranties, CC 1797 et seq.
  Home roof warranties, CC 1797.90 et seq.
  Notice, display, CC 1797.5
Water supply,
  Billing, CC 798.40
  Meters, common areas and equipment, management compensation, CC 798.43
Written agreements, rent, CC 798.18
Written warranties, form, CC 1797.3
Zoning and planning, licenses and permits, notice, CC 798.27

MOBS
Riots and Mobs, generally, this index

MODERATE INCOME HOUSING
Low and Moderate Income Housing, generally, this index

MODULAR HOUSING
Manufactured housing. Housing, this index

MONEY
Carriers, losing in mail, CC 2177
Euro, contracts, securities or instruments, medium of payment, CC 1663
Finding lost property, CC 2080 et seq.
Identity and identification, theft, CC 1798.92 et seq.

MONEY—Cont'd
Landlord and tenant, rent, security deposits, CC 1947.3
Loss, CC 2080 et seq.
Rent, CC 1947.3
Solicitation of money, false statements or invoices, CC 1716
Tenant, rent, security deposits, CC 1947.3
Warrants for Payment of Money, generally, this index

MONEY ORDERS
Attorney fees, check cashers, CC 1789.35
Cashers, CC 1789.30 et seq.
Check cashers, CC 1789.30 et seq.
Crimes and offenses, check cashers, CC 1789.35
Damages, check cashers, CC 1789.35
Fees, check cashers, CC 1789.30, 1789.35
  Licenses and permits, CC 1789.37
Fines and penalties, check cashers, CC 1789.35
Identity and identification, check cashers, CC 1789.30
Injunction, check cashers, CC 1789.35
Licenses and permits, check cashers, CC 1789.37
Limitation of actions, check cashers, CC 1789.35
Monopolies and unfair trade, check cashers, CC 1789.32
Statute of limitations, check cashers, CC 1789.35
Unfair business practices, check cashers, CC 1789.32
Waiver, cashers, CC 1789.38

MONOPOLIES AND UNFAIR TRADE
Actions and proceedings, CC 1780 et seq.
  Damages, generally, post
Advertisements, price, CC 1770
Attorney fees, CC 1780
Check cashers, CC 1789.32
Colleges and universities, student loans, borrowers rights, CC 1788.101 et seq.
Consumers Legal Remedies Act, CC 1750 et seq.
Contracts, unconscionable contracts, CC 1770
Costs, actions and proceedings, CC 1780
Credit cards, CC 1747.94
Credit services, CC 1789.10 et seq.
Damages, CC 1780 et seq.
  Consumers Legal Remedies Act, CC 1750 et seq.
  Treble damages, social services, procurement, fees, CC 1780
Debt settlement providers, fair debt settlement, CC 1788.302
Discounts, Consumers Legal Remedies Act, CC 1750 et seq.
Drafts, check cashers, CC 1789.32
Electronic data processing, sales to private schools, CC 998

MONOPOLIES AND UNFAIR TRADE—Cont'd
Employment agencies, CC 1812.5095
Fines and penalties,
  Aged persons, CC 1780
  Disabled persons, CC 1780
Gray market goods,
  Disclosure, CC 1770
  Unfair competition, CC 1797.86
Grocery stores, club cards, disclosure, CC 1749.60 et seq.
Injunction, CC 1780, 3369
Money orders, check cashers, CC 1789.32
Negotiable instruments, check cashers, CC 1789.32
Payment processors, fair debt settlement, CC 1788.302
Price, advertisements, CC 1770
Private schools, electronic data processing, CC 998
Rebates, Consumers Legal Remedies Act, CC 1750 et seq.
Rental Purchase Agreements, generally, this index
Restitution, CC 1780
Schools, private schools, electronic data processing or telecommunications goods, CC 998
Social services, procurement, fees, CC 1770
  Treble damages, CC 1780
Student loans, borrowers rights, CC 1788.101 et seq.
Treble damages, social services, procurement, fees, CC 1780
Unconscionable contracts, CC 1770
Venue, CC 1780
Veterans, benefits, CC 1770
Warrants for payment of money, check cashers, CC 1789.32

MONUMENTS AND MEMORIALS
Maintenance, coterminous owners, CC 841

MOPEDS
Motorized Scooters, generally, this index

MORALS
Lewdness and Obscenity, generally, this index

MORTGAGE BROKERS AND LENDERS
Originators. Mortgages, this index
Residential mortgage lenders. Mortgages, this index

MORTGAGE FORECLOSURE CONSULTANTS
Generally, CC 2945 et seq.
Actions and proceedings, CC 2945.6
Agents, liability, CC 2945.9 et seq.
Assignments, wages, CC 2945.4
Attorney fees, CC 2945.6
Bonds (officers and fiduciaries), registration, CC 2945.45

I-139

MORTGAGE

MORTGAGE FORECLOSURE CONSULTANTS—Cont'd
Cancellation, notice, CC 2945.2, 2945.3
Certificates and certification, registration, CC 2945.45
Compensation, disclosure, CC 2945.3
Constitutionality, CC 2945.8
Contracts, CC 2945.3
Copy of the contract, CC 2945.3
Costs, CC 2945.6
Crimes and offenses, CC 2945.7
  Registration, CC 2945.45
Damages, CC 2945.6
Disclosure, consultants services and compensation, CC 2945.3
Encumbrances, CC 2945.4
Equitable relief, CC 2945.6
Exemplary damages, CC 2945.6
Fees, CC 2945.4
Fines and penalties, CC 2945.7
  Registration, CC 2945.45
Interest, CC 2945.4
Judgments, CC 2945.6
Liens and encumbrances, CC 2945.4
Limitation of liability, contract provisions, CC 2945.10
Mail and mailing, notice of cancellation, CC 2945.2
Notice, CC 2945.3
  Cancellation, CC 2945.2
Power of attorney, CC 2945.4
Public policy, CC 2945
Punitive damages, CC 2945.6
Registration, CC 2945.45
Representatives, liability, CC 2945.9 et seq.
Surplus funds, release, CC 2945.3, 2945.4
Third party transactions, CC 2945.4
Wage assignments, CC 2945.4
Waiver of rights, CC 2945.5
Writing, contract, CC 2945.3

MORTGAGE INSURANCE
Insurance, this index

MORTGAGES
Generally, CC 2920 et seq., 2947 et seq.
Abandoned or unclaimed property,
  Escheat to state, CC 2941.7
  Power of sale, surplus, CC 2924j
Absent mortgagee, release of mortgage, bonds (officers and fiduciaries), CC 2941.7
Acceleration, CC 2924c
  Enforceability, CC 2924.7
  Incorporation in documents, property with four or fewer residential units, CC 2924.5
  Junior mortgage, single family, owner occupied dwelling, CC 2949
  Prepayment penalty, prohibition, CC 2954.10
  Restrictions, CC 2924.6

MORTGAGES—Cont'd
Acceleration—Cont'd
  Second mortgages, CC 2949
Accounts and accounting,
  Accounting by mortgagee, CC 2954
  Annual report to mortgagor, CC 2954.2
  Impound accounts. Taxation, post
  Mortgagee, CC 2954
Acknowledgments, CC 2952
  Power of attorney, CC 2933
Actions and proceedings,
  COVID 19, forbearance, CC 3273.15
  Foreclosure, generally, post
  Foreclosure consultants, CC 2945.6
  Impound accounts, excess withholdings, CC 2954.1
  Modification or change, forbearance, fines and penalties, CC 2944.7
  Sales, rent, CC 2924m
  Satisfaction, discharge, CC 2941
  State as party, CC 2931a
Additional transfers, defeasance, CC 2925
Adjustable rates, CC 1916.7
  Disclosure, CC 1921
Advances and advancements,
  Certificate of discharge, CC 2941
  Reverse mortgages, CC 1923.2
Adverse possession of property, creation, CC 2921
Affidavits, bids and bidding, sales, CC 2924m
After acquired title, CC 2930
Aged persons,
  Modification or change, forbearance, fines and penalties, CC 2944.8
  Shared appreciation loans, CC 1917.320 et seq.
Agents,
  Notice, default, CC 2924.3
  Payments by trustees, CC 2924d
Ancient mortgages, marketable record title, CC 882.020 et seq.
Animal control officers, foreclosure, abandoned or unclaimed property, involuntary deposits, notice, CC 1816
Animals, foreclosure, abandoned or unclaimed property, involuntary deposits, CC 1815 et seq.
Annual report to mortgagor, CC 2954.2
Annuities,
  Reverse mortgages, CC 1923.2
  Shared appreciation loans for seniors, CC 1917.320 et seq.
Application of law, CC 2944
Appraisal and appraisers,
  Shared appreciation loans, seniors, fair market value, CC 1917.412
  Undue influence, CC 1090.5
Arrangers of credit, disclosure, CC 2956 et seq.
Arrearages, payment, cure of default, CC 2924c

MORTGAGES—Cont'd
As is condition sales, CC 2924h
Assignments,
  Power of sale, CC 2932.5
  Records and recordation, post
  Transfer of security, CC 2936
Assumption, Statute of Frauds, CC 1624
Attorney fees,
  Adjustable rate residential loans, descriptive information, prospective borrowers, failure to provide, CC 1921
  Balloon payments, notice, damages, CC 2924i
  Foreclosure, decrees, CC 2924d
  Insurance, exceeding replacement value, CC 2955.5
  Sales, CC 2924d
Auctions and auctioneers, power of sale, CC 2924g
Balloon payments, notice, CC 2924i
Banks and Banking, this index
Beneficiaries,
  Service of process, CC 2937.7
  Statements, CC 2943
Bids and bidding,
  Covenants, low and moderate income housing, CC 2924o
  Sales, CC 2924g, 2924h
  Rent, CC 2924m
Bonds (officers and fiduciaries), absent mortgagee, release of mortgage, CC 2941.7
Books and papers, records and recordation, CC 1171
Brokers,
  Originators, generally, post
  Residential mortgage lenders, generally, post
Casualty insurance, replacement value, CC 2955.5
Certificates and certification, CC 2952
  Discharge, post
  Reverse mortgages, counselors and counseling, CC 1923.2
Charges. Rates and charges, generally, post
Checks, default sales, payments, CC 2924h
Collections, agent of mortgagee, notice of default, CC 2924.3
Compensation and salaries, modification or change, forbearance, crimes and offenses, CC 2944.6 et seq.
Condominiums, this index
Confidential or privileged information, notice, CC 2924
Consent, delinquency notice, junior lien holders, CC 2924e
Constructive notice, assignments, recording, CC 2934
Consultants. Mortgage Foreclosure Consultants, generally, this index
Consumer credit, payoff demand statements, CC 2943.1

I-140

MORTGAGES

MORTGAGES—Cont'd
Consumer credit reporting agencies, records, application of law, **CC 1785.35**
Consumer handbook on adjustable rate mortgages, supplying to prospective borrowers, **CC 1921**
Contents, acceleration clause, incorporation in documents, **CC 2924.5**
Costs,
  Adjustable rate residential loans, descriptive information, prospective borrowers, failure to provide, **CC 1921**
  Disclosure, awarding, **CC 2924d**
  Payment, cure of default, **CC 2924c**
  Reverse mortgages, **CC 1923.2**
Counselors and counseling,
  Foreclosure, **CC 2923.5**
  Reverse mortgages, **CC 1923.2, 1923.5**
Covenant by lessor of real property, **CC 1469, 1470**
Covenants, bids and bidding, low and moderate income housing, **CC 2924o**
COVID 19,
  First liens, foreclosure, modification or change, **CC 2924.15**
  Forbearance, **CC 3273.1 et seq.**
Credit arrangers, disclosure, **CC 2956 et seq.**
Credit scores, notice, **CC 1785.15.1, 1785.15.2, 1785.20.2**
Credit services, **CC 1789.10 et seq.**
Credit Unions, this index
Crimes and offenses,
  Certificates of discharge, obligation to execute, **CC 2941.5**
  Foreclosure consultants, **CC 2945.7**
  Modification or change, forbearance, **CC 2944.6 et seq.**
  Trustees sale, default by bidder, **CC 2924h**
    Certificates of discharge, obligation to execute, **CC 2941.5**
Damages,
  Adjustable rate residential loans, descriptive information, prospective borrowers, **CC 1921**
  Balloon payments, final, notice, **CC 2924i**
  Certificate of discharge, recordings, **CC 2941**
  Delay in execution of certificate of discharge, **CC 2941**
  Failure to deliver statements, **CC 2943**
  Foreclosure, modification or change, **CC 2924.12, 2924.19**
  Foreclosure consultants, **CC 2945.6**
  Impound accounts, excess withholding, **CC 2954.1**
  Insurance, exceeding replacement value, **CC 2955.5**
  Reverse mortgages, **CC 1923.2**
  Trusts and trustees, default, **CC 2924**
Deceptive trade practices, brokers, **CC 1770**
Declarations, bids and bidding, sales, **CC 2924m**
Default,
  Agent of mortgagee, notice, **CC 2924.3**

MORTGAGES—Cont'd
Default—Cont'd
  Charges, notice, **CC 2954.5**
  Condominiums, sales, homeowners associations, notice, **CC 2924b**
  Cure, notice, form, **CC 2924c**
  Federal tax liens, notice, **CC 2924b**
  Notice, **CC 2923.55, 2924**
    Agent of mortgagee, collection, **CC 2924.3**
    Cure of default, form, **CC 2924c**
    Request for copies, **CC 2924b**
    Rescission, **CC 2924c**
    Transfer of mortgage, **CC 2937**
    Summaries, **CC 2923.3**
  Procedure, **CC 2924c**
  Summaries, notice, **CC 2923.3, 2924**
Defeasance on condition, transfer subject to proof, **CC 2925**
Delinquencies, notice, junior lien holders, **CC 2924e**
Delinquency charges, **CC 2954.4**
  Notice, **CC 2954.5**
Descriptive information, adjustable rate residential loans, supplying to prospective borrowers, **CC 1921**
Disabled persons, modification or change, forbearance, fines and penalties, **CC 2944.8**
Discharge,
  Ancient mortgages, **CC 882.030**
  Certificates and certification,
    Bonds (officers and fiduciaries), release of mortgage, absent mortgagee, **CC 2941.7**
    Damages for delay in execution, **CC 2941**
    Fees, **CC 2941**
    Foreign executors, administrators and guardians, **CC 2939.5**
    Obligation to execute, **CC 2941**
      Penalty for violation, **CC 2941.5**
    Payment, satisfaction or discharge, **CC 2939**
    Recording, **CC 2940**
Disclosure,
  Adjustable rate loans, descriptive information, **CC 1921**
  Arrangers of credit, **CC 2956 et seq.**
  Foreclosure, modification or change, servicers, **CC 2924.9**
  Foreclosure consultants, **CC 2945.3**
  Hazard insurance, improvements, replacement costs, **CC 2955.5**
  Home equity loans, **CC 2970, 2971**
  Prepayment penalties, **CC 2954.11**
  Reverse mortgages, **CC 1923.5**
  Servicers, foreclosure, modification or change, **CC 2924.9**
  Shared appreciation loans, seniors, **CC 1917.710 et seq.**
Discrimination, **CC 53**
Dual tracking, foreclosure, servicers, **CC 2923.4 et seq.**

MORTGAGES—Cont'd
Due date,
  Acceleration, generally, ante
  Balloon payments, notice, **CC 2924i**
  Statement to entitled person, **CC 2943**
Due diligence, foreclosure, meetings, financial condition, **CC 2923.5**
Due on sale clauses, acceleration, prepayment, **CC 2954.10**
Earthquake insurance, condominiums, institutional third party purchasers, disclosure, **CC 2955.1**
Election to sell, **CC 2924**
English language, forms, notice of default cure, **CC 2924c**
Equity line of credit, payoff demand statements, **CC 2943.1**
Equity loans,
  Disclosure, **CC 2970, 2971**
  Reverse mortgages, **CC 1923 et seq.**
  Translations, **CC 1632**
Equity purchasers, **CC 1695.15 et seq.**
Escheat to state, abandoned or unclaimed property, **CC 2941.7**
Escrows and escrow agents,
  Impound accounts. Taxation, post
  Interest, time for commencement of interest on a note, **CC 2948.5**
  Statement of unpaid balance, due date, **CC 2943**
  Taxes and insurance, accounts for payment, **CC 2954**
Estates for Years, this index
Estimates, fair market value, **CC 1917.410**
Evidence, balloon payments, notice, violations, **CC 2924i**
Exemptions, crimes and offenses, modification or change, forbearance, **CC 2944.7**
Facsimiles, transmittal of documents, **CC 2943**
Fair market value, determination, shared appreciation loans for seniors, **CC 1917.410 et seq.**
Federal tax liens, default, notice of sale, **CC 2924b**
Fees,
  Acceleration, conveyances, **CC 2954.10**
  Accounting for trust account moneys, **CC 2954**
  Certificate of discharge, **CC 2941**
  Crimes and offenses, modification or change, forbearance, **CC 2944.6 et seq.**
  Foreclosure consultants, **CC 2945.4**
  Junior lien holders, delinquency notice, **CC 2924e**
  Payment, cure of default, **CC 2924c**
  Reverse mortgages, **CC 1923.2**
  Shared appreciation loans, seniors, **CC 1917.331**
    Appraisal fees, **CC 1917.412**
Fictitious recording, **CC 2952**
Fiduciaries, residential mortgage lenders, **CC 2923.1**

MORTGAGES

MORTGAGES—Cont'd
Final payment, balloon, notice, **CC 2924i**
Finance Lenders, this index
Fines and penalties,
  Acceleration, conveyance, **CC 2954.10**
  Accounting for trust account moneys, **CC 2954**
  Certificate of discharge, recording, **CC 2941**
  Foreclosure, post
  Foreclosure consultants, **CC 2945.7**
  Foreign languages, translations, **CC 1632.5**
  Modification or change, forbearance, **CC 2944.6 et seq.**
  Prepayment, **CC 2954.9, 2954.11**
  Rebates and kickbacks, **CC 2924d**
  Servicers, foreclosure, **CC 2924.17**
  Trustee sale, price fixing or default by bidder, **CC 2924h**
Fire insurance, exceeding replacement value, **CC 2955.5**
First liens, foreclosure, modification or change, **CC 2923.6, 2924.9 et seq.**
Fixed rate loans, alternative offer to renegotiable rate loans, **CC 1916.9**
Forbearance,
  COVID 19, **CC 3273.1 et seq.**
  Crimes and offenses, **CC 2944.6 et seq.**
Forcible entry and detainer, **CC 2924n**
Foreclosure, **CC 2931**
  Animals, abandoned or unclaimed property, involuntary deposits, **CC 1815 et seq.**
  Attorney fees, **CC 2924d**
  Change of servicing agent, validity, **CC 2937**
  Consultants. Mortgage Foreclosure Consultants, generally, this index
  Costs, awarding, **CC 2924d**
  Counselors and counseling, **CC 2923.5**
  Damages, modification or change, **CC 2924.12, 2924.19**
  Disclosure, modification or change, servicers, **CC 2924.9**
  Dual tracking, servicers, **CC 2923.4 et seq.**
  Due diligence, meetings, financial condition, **CC 2923.5**
  Federal tax liens, notice of sale, **CC 2924b**
  Fines and penalties,
    Maintenance, **CC 2929.3, 2929.4**
    Servicers, **CC 2924.17**
  First liens, modification or change, **CC 2923.6, 2924.9 et seq.**
  Home Equity Sales Contracts, generally, this index
  Homeowner Bill of Rights, **CC 2923.4 et seq.**
  Injunction, modification or change, **CC 2924.12, 2924.19**
  Mail and mailing, notice, **CC 2924.8**
  Maintenance, **CC 2929.3**
  Meetings, financial condition, **CC 2923.5**
  Modification, servicers, **CC 2923.4 et seq.**
  Notice, **CC 2924, 2924f**
    Mail and mailing, **CC 2924.8**

MORTGAGES—Cont'd
Foreclosure—Cont'd
  Notice—Cont'd
    Maintenance, **CC 2929.3**
      Fines and penalties, **CC 2929.4**
    Request for copies, recording, contents, form, **CC 2924b**
    Surplus funds, consultants, **CC 2945.3**
    Transfer of obligation, notice, **CC 2937**
  Nuisance, abatement, assessments, **CC 2929.45**
  Priorities and preferences,
    Judicial sales, bids and bidding, **CC 2924p**
    Power of sale, **CC 2924j, 2924k**
  Repair of property acquired, **CC 2932.6**
  Servicers,
    Due diligence, meetings, financial condition, **CC 2923.5, 2923.55**
    Fines and penalties, **CC 2924.17**
    Modification, **CC 2923.4 et seq.**
    Single point of contact, **CC 2923.7**
  Single point of contact, servicers, **CC 2923.7**
  State as party, **CC 2931a, 2931b**
  Summaries, notice, **CC 2924f**
  Surplus funds, consultants, release, **CC 2945.3, 2945.4**
  Title insurance, records and recordation, liability, **CC 2924.26**
  Underwritten title company, records and recordation, liability, **CC 2924.26**
  Workout plans, **CC 2923.6**
Foreign executors and administrators, satisfaction of mortgages, **CC 2939.5**
Foreign languages, residential mortgage lenders, translations, **CC 1632.5**
Forfeitures,
  Accounting for trust moneys, **CC 2954**
  Delinquency notice, junior lien holders, **CC 2924e**
  Statements, failure to deliver, **CC 2943**
Forms, **CC 2922, 2948**
  Acceleration clause, incorporation in documents, **CC 2924.5**
  English language, notice of default cure, **CC 2924c**
  Equity line of credit, payoff demand statements, **CC 2943.1**
  Foreign languages, translations, **CC 1632.5**
  Notice, default, **CC 2924b**
    Cure, **CC 2924c**
  Shared appreciation loans, seniors, disclosure, **CC 1917.711 et seq.**
  Spanish language, notice of default cure, **CC 2924c**
  Subordination agreement, **CC 2953.3**
Frauds, statute of, **CC 1624**
Good faith, shared appreciation loans for seniors, fair market value estimate, **CC 1917.410**
Guaranty and suretyship, guarantors, waiver, **CC 2856**

MORTGAGES—Cont'd
Guides, reverse mortgages, **CC 1923.5**
Hazard insurance, exceeding replacement value, **CC 2955.5**
Home equity loans, disclosure requirements, **CC 2970, 2971**
Home Equity Sales Contracts, generally, this index
Homeowner Bill of Rights, **CC 2923.4 et seq.**
Impairment of security, acceleration of payment, **CC 2924.7**
Impound accounts. Taxation, post
Index, fictitious mortgage, **CC 2952**
Industrial banks, fiduciaries, **CC 2923.1**
Industrial Loan Companies, this index
Injunction,
  Adjustable rate residential loans, disclosures to prospective borrowers, **CC 1921**
  COVID 19, forbearance, **CC 3273.15**
  Foreclosure, modification or change, **CC 2924.12, 2924.19**
  Impound accounts, excess withholding, **CC 2954.1**
  Insurance, exceeding replacement value, **CC 2955.5**
Inspection and inspectors, hazardous substances and waste, **CC 2929.5**
Instrument of defeasance affecting grant in absolute form, recording, **CC 2950**
Insurance, this index
Intellectual and developmental disabilities, modification or change, forbearance, fines and penalties, **CC 2944.8**
Interest,
  Adjustable rates, **CC 1916.7**
    Disclosure, **CC 1921**
  Disclosure, **CC 1920**
  Impound accounts, **CC 2954.8**
  Notice, **CC 1920**
  Prepayment penalties, **CC 2954.11**
  Real estate brokers, real property loan secured by liens, **CC 1916.1**
  Renegotiable rates, **CC 1916.8, 1916.9**
  Reverse mortgages, **CC 1923.2**
  Shared appreciation loans, **CC 1917.005**
    Pension fund investments, **CC 1917.220**
    Seniors, **CC 1917.331, 1917.613, 1917.616, 1917.619**
    Truth in lending, disclosure, **CC 1917.712, 1917.713**
  Statements, **CC 2943**
  Time of commencement of interest on note, **CC 2948.5**
  Variable rate, **CC 1916.5 et seq.**
  Yearly payment, statement to mortgagor, **CC 2954.2**
Interest in property, mortgageable, **CC 2947**
Internal revenue, default, sales, notice, **CC 2924b**
Junior lien holders, delinquencies, notice, **CC 2924e**

MORTGAGES

MORTGAGES—Cont'd
Kickbacks, CC 2924d
Late payment, charges, CC 2954.4
  Notice, CC 2954.5
Legal Estates Principal and Income Law, CC 731 et seq.
Lenders. Residential mortgage lenders, generally, post
Limitation of actions,
  Modification or change, forbearance, fines and penalties, CC 2944.8
  Satisfaction, discharge, CC 2941
Line of credit, payoff demand statements, CC 2943.1
Low and moderate income housing, bids and bidding, covenants, CC 2924o
Mail and mailing, foreclosure, notice, CC 2924.8
Maintenance, foreclosure, CC 2929.3
Marketable record title, CC 880.020 et seq.
Mechanics liens, CC 8174
  Priorities and preferences, CC 8450 et seq.
Meetings, foreclosure, financial condition, CC 2923.5
Mental health, modification or change, forbearance, fines and penalties, CC 2944.8
Merger of parcels, single instrument of conveyance or consolidated description of parcels, CC 1093
Modification or change,
  Crimes and offenses, CC 2944.6 et seq.
  Foreclosure, CC 2923.4 et seq.
Mortgage Foreclosure Consultants, generally, this index
Multifamily housing, political subdivisions, sales, postponement, CC 2924f
Nature of obligation, CC 2928
Nonacceptance of deed, recording in county of location, CC 1058.5
Nonprofit corporations, sales, rent, CC 2924m
Notice,
  Balloon payments, CC 2924i
  Blanket incumbrances on subdivision, CC 1133
  Charges, default, delinquency, CC 2954.5
  Constructive notice, assignment, CC 2934
  Credit scores, CC 1785.15.1, 1785.15.2, 1785.20.2
  Default, ante
  Delinquencies, junior lien holders, CC 2924e
  Foreclosure, ante
  Forfeitures, junior lien holders, delinquencies, failure to give, CC 2924e
  Modification or change, forbearance, CC 2944.6
  Nonacceptance of deed, recording in county of location, CC 1058.5
  Privileged communications, CC 2924
  Renegotiable interest rates, loan renewal, CC 1916.8
  Request, junior lien holders, delinquency information, CC 2924e

MORTGAGES—Cont'd
Notice—Cont'd
  Rescission of default, CC 2924c
  Reverse mortgages, CC 1923.5
  Risk scores, CC 1785.15.1, 1785.15.2, 1785.20.2
  Sales, CC 2924, 2924f, 2924g, 2924j
  Shared appreciation loans, seniors, CC 1917.710 et seq.
    Fair market value, CC 1917.410
  Subordination agreement, CC 2953.2, 2953.3
  Transfer, CC 2937
Nuisance, foreclosure, abatement, assessments, CC 2929.45
Offenses. Crimes and offenses, generally, ante
Originators,
  Deceptive trade practices, CC 1770
  Disclosure, CC 2956 et seq.
  Fiduciaries, CC 2923.1
  Foreign languages, translations, CC 1632.5
Parties, foreclosure, state, CC 2931a
Payment,
  Acceleration, generally, ante
  Balloon payments, CC 2924i
  Prepayment, generally, post
Payoff demand statements, CC 2943
  Equity line of credit, CC 2943.1
  Reconveyance, fees, CC 2941.1
Penalties. Fines and penalties, generally, ante
Periodic payments, statement to entitled person, CC 2943
Personal obligation, CC 2928
Possession,
  Property adversely held, CC 2921
  Rights of mortgagee, CC 2927
  Special lien independent, CC 2923
Postponement, sales, CC 2924g
  Foreclosure, notice, CC 2924f
Power of attorney,
  Executions, CC 2933
  Foreclosure consultants, CC 2945.4
  Modification or change, forbearance, CC 2944.7
Power of sale, CC 2924f et seq.
  Abandoned or unclaimed property, surplus, CC 2924j
  Assignments, CC 2932.5
  Authority, CC 2932
  Notice, CC 2924j
  Priorities and preferences, CC 2924j, 2924k
  Restrictions on exercise, CC 2924
Preferences. Priorities and preferences, generally, post
Prepayment, CC 2954.9
  Acceleration, conveyance, fees, penalties, CC 2954.10
  Emergencies or natural disasters, prepayment penalties, CC 2954.9
  Fines and penalties, CC 2954.11
  Rates and charges, CC 2954.9

MORTGAGES—Cont'd
Prepayment—Cont'd
  Reverse mortgages, CC 1923.2
  Shared appreciation loans, seniors, CC 1917.333
Price fixing, bids, sale of property, CC 2924h
Priorities and preferences, CC 2898
  Bids and bidding, foreclosure, CC 2924p
  Power of sale, CC 2924j, 2924k
  Purchase money mortgage, CC 2898
  Recordation, CC 1214
  Shared appreciation loans, CC 1917.004
Proceedings. Actions and proceedings, generally, ante
Process,
  Beneficiaries, service, CC 2937.7
  State as party, CC 2931a
Proof, CC 2952
Prospective owner occupants, CC 2924m
Provisions governing, CC 2877
Public policy, CC 1916.12
Rates and charges,
  Acceleration, conveyance, CC 2954.10
  Default, delinquency, notice, CC 2954.5
  Late payment, CC 2954.4, 2954.5
  Prepayment, contracts, CC 2954.9
Real estate brokers and salespersons. Originators, generally, ante
Real property security instrument, CC 2953.1 et seq.
Sale of property, CC 2924f et seq.
Rebates, CC 2924d
Reconveyance,
  Fees, payoff demand statements, CC 2941.1
  Request, obligation to execute, CC 2941
Records and recordation,
  Assignments,
    Beneficial interest, CC 2934, 2935
    Power of sale, CC 2932.5
  Bonds (officers and fiduciaries) release of mortgage, absent mortgagee, CC 2941.7
  Certificate of discharge, CC 2940, 2941
  Discharge of mortgage, CC 2941
    Certificate, CC 2939
  Federal tax liens, default, notice of sale, CC 2924b
  Fictitious, CC 2952
  Instrument of defeasance, grant in absolute form, CC 2950
  Interest, time, CC 2948.5
  Liens, priority, waiver, CC 2934
  Location of recording, nonacceptance of prior deed, CC 1058.5
  Nonacceptance of record, recording in county of location, CC 1058.5
  Notice,
    Default, CC 2924, 2924b, 2937
    Nonacceptance of deed, CC 1058.5
  Power of attorney, CC 2933
  Prior recording, CC 1214
    Nonacceptance, CC 1058.5

I-143

MORTGAGES

MORTGAGES—Cont'd
Records and recordation—Cont'd
  Recorders, fictitious mortgage or deed of trust, liability, **CC 2952**
  Satisfaction, foreign executors, administrators and guardians, **CC 2939.5**
  Separate set of books, **CC 1171**
Reference, fictitious mortgages, **CC 2952**
Refinancing, shared appreciated loans, seniors, **CC 1917.330**
  Seniors, **CC 1917.320 et seq.**
Refunds, impound accounts, excess funds, **CC 2954.1**
Regulations. Rules and regulations, generally, post
Reinstatement, default, procedure, **CC 2924c**
Release,
  Absent mortgagee, bonds (officers and fiduciaries), **CC 2941.7**
  Ancient mortgages, **CC 882.030**
Renegotiable rates, **CC 1916.8, 1916.9**
Rent,
  Assignments, **CC 2938**
  Sales, **CC 2924m**
  Skimming, residential real estate, **CC 890 et seq.**
Repayment, reverse mortgages, **CC 1923.2**
Rescission, default,
  Notice, **CC 2924c**
  Sales, **CC 2924h**
Residential mortgage lenders,
  Fiduciaries, **CC 2923.1**
  Fines and penalties, foreign languages, translations, **CC 1632.5**
  Foreign languages, translations, **CC 1632.5**
  Forms, foreign languages, translations, **CC 1632.5**
  Originators, generally, ante
  Servicers, generally, post
  Translations, foreign languages, **CC 1632.5**
Residential property,
  Shared appreciation loans for seniors, **CC 1917.320 et seq.**
  Transfers, acceleration of maturity dates, **CC 2924.6**
Restrictions due to race, color, religion or national origin, **CC 53**
Reverse mortgages, **CC 1923 et seq.**
  Foreign languages, translations, **CC 1632**
  Translations, **CC 1632**
Risk scores, notice, **CC 1785.15.1, 1785.15.2, 1785.20.2**
Risks, foreclosure, bids and bidding, notice, **CC 2924f**
Rules and regulations,
  Reverse mortgages, **CC 1923 et seq.**
  Translations, **CC 1632**
  State and federal institutions, application of law, **CC 1916.12**
Sales,
  Foreclosure, generally, ante

MORTGAGES—Cont'd
Sales—Cont'd
  Power of sale, generally, ante
  Rent, **CC 2924m**
Satisfaction,
  Ancient mortgages, **CC 882.030**
  Foreign executors, administrators and guardians, **CC 2939.5**
  Obligation to execute certificate of discharge, **CC 2941**
    Penalty for violation, **CC 2941.5**
  Release of lien, absent mortgagee, **CC 2941.7**
Savings Associations, this index
Scope of lien, **CC 2926**
Second mortgages, default or acceleration based on obtaining second mortgage, **CC 2949**
Servicers,
  Damages, foreclosure, modification or change, **CC 2924.12, 2924.19**
  Disclosure, foreclosure, modification or change, **CC 2924.9**
  Fines and penalties, foreclosure, **CC 2924.17**
  First liens, foreclosure, modification or change, **CC 2923.6, 2924.9 et seq.**
  Foreclosure, ante
  Injunction, foreclosure, modification or change, **CC 2924.12, 2924.19**
Sex discrimination, **CC 53**
Shared Appreciation Loans, generally, this index
Short pay agreements, secured land transaction statements, **CC 2943**
Single point of contact, foreclosure, servicers, **CC 2923.7**
Skimming of rent, residential real estate, **CC 890 et seq.**
Solar Rights Act, **CC 714**
Spanish language, forms, notice of default cure, **CC 2924c**
Special lien, independent of possession, **CC 2923**
Specific performance, sales, rent, **CC 2924m**
Statements. Payoff demand statements, generally, ante
Statute of Frauds, **CC 1624**
Statutory rights, waiver, validity, **CC 2953**
Subagents, payment by trustees, **CC 2924d**
Subordination agreement,
  Exemptions, **CC 2953.5**
  Requirements, **CC 2953.3**
  Voidability, **CC 2953.4**
Subordination clause,
  Exemptions, **CC 2953.5**
  Requirements, **CC 2953.2**
  Voidability, **CC 2953.4**
Summaries, notice,
  Default, **CC 2923.3, 2924**
  Foreclosure, **CC 2924f**
Suretyship and guaranty, waiver, **CC 2856**

MORTGAGES—Cont'd
Surplus funds, foreclosure, consultants, release, **CC 2945.3, 2945.4**
Tax liens,
  Actions and proceedings, conflicting claims to title, **CC 2931a**
  Default, sales,
    Notice, **CC 2924, 2924b**
    Purchase by state, **CC 2931b**
Taxation,
  Impound accounts, **CC 2954 et seq.**
    Actions and proceedings, excess withholding, recovery of damages, **CC 2954.1**
    Amounts, required deposits, **CC 2954.1**
    Excess withholding, **CC 2954.1**
    Interest, **CC 2954.8**
    Restrictions, required deposits, **CC 2954.1**
    Retention and investment in state, **CC 2955**
    Single family, owner occupied dwellings, payment of taxes, **CC 2954**
  Nonpayment of taxes, acceleration of payments, **CC 2924.7**
Timber or lumber, recordation of instruments, **CC 1220**
Time,
  Acceleration, generally, ante
  Ancient mortgages, marketable record title, **CC 882.020**
  Interest, commencement of interest on note, **CC 2948.5**
  Notice of default and sale, request for copies, **CC 2924b**
  Satisfaction, discharge, **CC 2941**
Title subsequently acquired by mortgagor, **CC 2930**
Transfer,
  Notice, single family residence, **CC 2937**
  Subject to defeasance on condition, **CC 2925**
Translations, residential mortgage lenders, foreign languages, **CC 1632.5**
Trust Deeds, generally, this index
Trusts and Trustees, this index
Truth in lending, shared appreciation loans for seniors, disclosure, **CC 1917.712, 1917.713**
Undue influence, appraisal and appraisers, **CC 1090.5**
Unified sale, notice of sale, form, **CC 2924f**
Unpaid balance, statement to entitled person, **CC 2943**
Usury, real estate brokers loans, secured by liens, **CC 1916.1**
Variable interest rate, **CC 1916.5 et seq.**
Waiver,
  Avoidance of subordination clause, **CC 2953.4**
  Borrower, statutory rights, validity, exceptions, **CC 2953**
  Lien priority, recording, **CC 2934**
  Prepayment penalty, acceleration, **CC 2954.10**

MORTGAGES—Cont'd
Waiver—Cont'd
　Shared appreciation loans for seniors, borrowers rights, **CC 1917.611**
Waste, **CC 2929**
Workout plans, foreclosure, **CC 2923.6**
Worksheet guides, reverse mortgages, **CC 1923.5**
Writing, formalities, **CC 2922**

MOSAICS
Common law copyrights, reproduction rights, transfer, **CC 982**

MOSQUITOES
Pest Control, generally, this index

MOTELS
Hotels and Motels, generally, this index

MOTION PICTURES
Astaire Celebrity Image Protection Act, **CC 3344.1**
Attorney fees, invasion of privacy, **CC 1708.85**
Celebrity image protection, **CC 3344.1**
Confidential or privileged information, invasion of privacy, **CC 1708.85**
Costs, invasion of privacy, **CC 1708.85**
Crimes and offenses,
　Killing of or cruelty to human beings or animals, **CC 3505 et seq.**
　Stories about felonies, sale proceeds, **CC 2225**
Cruelty to human beings or animals, injunctions against, **CC 3505 et seq.**
Directors, sexual harassment, **CC 51.9**
Fines and penalties,
　Cruelty, **CC 3507.3**
　Death, **CC 3507.3**
Injunctions,
　Invasion of privacy, **CC 1708.85**
　Killing of or cruelty to animals or human beings, **CC 3505 et seq.**
Invasion of privacy, **CC 1708.85**
Killing of or cruelty to human beings or animals, **CC 3505 et seq.**
Lewdness and Obscenity, generally, this index
Obscenity. Lewdness and Obscenity, generally, this index
Pornography. Lewdness and Obscenity, generally, this index
Privacy, invasion of privacy, **CC 1708.85**
Producers, sexual harassment, **CC 51.9**
Sexual harassment, directors, producers, **CC 51.9**
Uniform Single Publication Act, **CC 3425.1 et seq.**

MOTOR CARRIERS
Arrival of freight, notice, **CC 2120**
Assessments, storage or equipment rental charges, assessment against motor carriers, liability for delay, **CC 2197, 2197.5**
Brokers, construction, rates and charges, **CC 3322**

MOTOR CARRIERS—Cont'd
Buses, generally, this index
Care, degree required, **CC 2114**
Construction, rates and charges, **CC 3322**
Damages, **CC 2194 et seq.**
　Driving under the influence, **CC 3333.7**
Delay,
　Liability, **CC 2196**
　Storage or equipment rental charges, liability, **CC 2197**
Equipment, rental charges, assessment against motor carriers, liability for delay, **CC 2197, 2197.5**
Fines and penalties, construction, **CC 3322**
Indemnity, exemptions, **CC 2784.5**
Insurance. Motor Vehicle Insurance, generally, this index
License plates. Motor Vehicles, this index
Negligence, **CC 2195**
　Degree of care required, **CC 2114**
Notice, freight, arrival, **CC 2120**
Perishable property, sale for freightage, **CC 2204**
Pest Control, generally, this index
Rates and charges, construction, **CC 3322**
Storage,
　Charges assessed against, liability for delay, **CC 2197, 2197.5**
　Consignees failure to accept and remove, **CC 2121**
Treble damages, driving under the influence, **CC 3333.7**

MOTOR COURTS
Hotels and Motels, generally, this index

MOTOR SCOOTERS
Motorized Scooters, generally, this index

MOTOR VEHICLE INSURANCE
Conditional sales, **CC 2982**
　Financing, **CC 2982.8**
　Form of contract, insurance notice, **CC 2984.1**
　Property subject to lien, **CC 2984.2**
　Statement, necessity, **CC 2984.1**
　Title to or lien upon property other than motor vehicle or accessories, **CC 2984.2**
Disclosure, personal information held by governmental agencies, Information Practices Act, **CC 1798.24**
Financing, conditional sales, **CC 2982.8**
Leases, **CC 1939.07, 2985.9**
　Contents, **CC 2985.8**
　Disclosure, damages, waiver, **CC 1939.09**
　Noncitizens, **CC 1939.33**
　Premiums, disclosure, **CC 2985.8**
　Waiver, damages, **CC 1939.09**
Noncitizens, leases, **CC 1939.33**
Notice, conditional sales contracts, warning, **CC 2984.1**
Premiums,
　Leases, disclosure, **CC 2985.8**

MOTOR VEHICLE INSURANCE—Cont'd
Premiums—Cont'd
　Sale of vehicle, title to or lien upon other property, **CC 2984.2**
Rental cars. Leases, generally, ante
Shared mobility devices, **CC 2505**
Traffic Rules and Regulations, generally, this index

MOTOR VEHICLE SERVICE STATIONS
Card keys, **CC 1747.02, 1747.03**
Liens and incumbrances, **CC 3067 et seq.**

MOTOR VEHICLES
Abandoned or unclaimed property, private property, lien for storage, assignment, **CC 3069**
Acknowledgments,
　Delivery, lease contracts, **CC 2986.4**
　Leases, damages, waiver, disclosure, **CC 1939.09**
　Motor vehicle purchase or proposal documents, **CC 2984.3**
Actions and proceedings,
　Crimes and offenses, generally, post
　Leases, post
　Subleasing, **CC 3343.5**
Address, liens and incumbrances, sale, application, **CC 3071, 3072**
Advertisements, leases, **CC 1939.19, 2989.4**
Affidavits,
　Actions, conditional sales, **CC 2984.4**
　Sale by lienholders, **CC 3073**
Agreements. Contracts, generally, post
Ambulances, generally, this index
Application of law, leases, **CC 1939.37**
Applications, liens and incumbrances, sale, **CC 3071, 3072**
Appraisal and appraisers, leases, termination, disposition of vehicle, **CC 2987**
Arbitration and award,
　Nonconforming new vehicles, **CC 1793.22**
　Reacquisition, problems with vehicle or nonfinancial terms, disclosure, **CC 1793.26**
Assignments,
　Conditional sales, post
　Lease contracts, **CC 2986.3, 2986.10**
　Leases, post
　Liens, **CC 3069**
　Security interest, force and violence, notice, repossessors and repossession, **CC 2984.6**
Attorney fees,
　Conditional sales, **CC 2983.4**
　Damages, action on lease contract, **CC 2988.9**
　Leases, post
　Liens, **CC 3068**
　Nonconforming new vehicles, **CC 1794**
Attorneys fees, leases, **CC 1939.25**
Automated license plate recognition, **CC 1798.90.5 et seq.**

MOTOR

MOTOR VEHICLES—Cont'd
Bad checks, conditional sales, fees, **CC 2982**
Bailment,
   Conditional sales, **CC 2981.5**
   Contracts,
      Form and construction, **CC 2981.5**
      Printing and requisites, **CC 1630, 1630.5**
   Leasing, **CC 2985.7 et seq.**
Blind or visually impaired persons, access to public conveyances, **CC 54 et seq.**
Buses, generally, this index
Business programs, leases, **CC 1939.21**
Buybacks, dealers and manufacturers, **CC 1793.23, 1793.24**
Cancellation,
   Conditional sales contracts, **CC 2982**
   Leases, **CC 2985.8, 2987**
   Service contracts, **CC 1794.41**
Carriers. Motor Carriers, generally, this index
Certificates and certification,
   Certificates of title, generally, post
   Sale by lienholders, value, **CC 3073**
Certificates of title,
   Lemon Law buyback, **CC 1793.23, 1793.24**
   Manufacturers, repurchased vehicles, **CC 1793.23, 1793.24**
   Repurchased vehicles, dealers or manufacturers, **CC 1793.23, 1793.24**
Charging infrastructure. Electric vehicles, post
Chattel mortgages. Security interest, generally, post
Chauffeurs licenses. Drivers licenses, generally, post
Children and minors,
   Privileges and immunities, rescue, **CC 43.102**
   Rescue, privileges and immunities, **CC 43.102**
Coast guard, warranties, **CC 1795.8**
Commercial vehicles,
   See, also, Motor Carriers, generally, this index
   Damages, driving under the influence, **CC 3333.7**
   Treble damages, driving under the influence, **CC 3333.7**
Common carriers. Motor Carriers, generally, this index
Compensation and salaries, assignments, leases, **CC 2986.3**
Complaints, venue, statement of facts, **CC 2984.4**
Compromise and settlement, reacquisition, problems with vehicle or nonfinancial terms, disclosure, **CC 1793.26**
Conditional sales, **CC 2981 et seq.**
   Acceleration of maturity, absence of default, **CC 2983.3**
   Acknowledgment, delivery of copy of contract to buyer, **CC 2984.3**
   Action on contract, **CC 2983.4**
      Venue, **CC 2984.4**

MOTOR VEHICLES—Cont'd
Conditional sales—Cont'd
   Affidavits, action on contract, **CC 2984.4**
   Air pollution, mandatory vehicle emission regulations, certificate of compliance with or waiver of, fees, **CC 2982**
   Assignments, **CC 2982.10**
      Assignee, rights and liabilities, **CC 2983.5**
      Corrections, time, **CC 2984**
      Documents, retention, **CC 2984.5**
      Enforcement of contract, assignee, **CC 2983**
      Equities and defenses of buyer against seller, **CC 2983.5**
         Buyer against seller, **CC 2983.5**
      Force and violence, notice, repossessors and repossession, **CC 2984.6**
      Third party, action or defense, **CC 2983.5**
      Wages, **CC 2983.7**
      Waiver of rights against assignee, **CC 2983.7**
   Attorneys fees and costs, **CC 2983.4**
   Bad check charge, **CC 2982**
   Bailment, **CC 2981.5**
   Bona fide purchaser, enforcement of contract, **CC 2983**
   Breach of contracts, used vehicle left as down payment, remedies, **CC 2982.7**
   Cancellation option agreements, used vehicles, disclosure, **CC 2982, 2982.2**
   Cancellation period, **CC 2982**
   Certified mail, notice of disposal of vehicle, **CC 2983.2**
   Charges, extension or deferral agreement, **CC 2982.3**
   Claims against seller, waiver, **CC 2983.7**
   Collection, costs and fees, **CC 2982**
      Illegal acts, waiver, **CC 2983.7**
   Commissions (compensation), buyer inducement, **CC 2982.1**
   Compensation for referral of customers, **CC 2982**
   Conditions of contract, **CC 2983.7**
   Confession of judgment, **CC 2983.7**
   Consideration, return, financing not obtained, **CC 2982.9**
   Consumer credit reporting agencies, retention, **CC 2984.5**
   Contents of contract, **CC 2982**
   Contingent compensation to buyer, referral of customers, **CC 2982.1**
   Cooling off period, **CC 2982**
   Copy, contract, delivery to buyers, **CC 2981.9, 2982**
   Corrections, compliance with law, **CC 2984**
   Cosigners, delinquency notice, **CC 2983.35**
   Credit statements, delivery to purchaser, **CC 2982**
   Crimes and offenses, **CC 2983.6**
   Debt cancellation agreements, disclosure, **CC 2982, 2982.2**

MOTOR VEHICLES—Cont'd
Conditional sales—Cont'd
   Default, **CC 2983.3**
      Deficiency judgment, limitation, **CC 2983.8**
   Defense, assignment of contract to third party, **CC 2983.5**
   Deferment or extension of due date, **CC 2982.3**
   Deferred cash down payment, reflecting item in contract, **CC 2982**
   Deficiency on sale of repossessed vehicle, liability, **CC 2983.8**
      Notice, **CC 2982**
   Delinquency charge, **CC 2982**
   Delinquency notice, cosigners, **CC 2983.35**
   Deposits in court, fees and costs, action on contract, **CC 2983.4**
   Disclosure, **CC 2982, 2982.2**
      Guaranteed asset protection waivers, **CC 2982.12**
   Discount, buyer inducements, referral of customers, **CC 2982.1**
   Dishonored checks, fees, **CC 2982**
   Documents,
      Fees, **CC 2982**
      Retention, **CC 2984.5**
   Down payments, **CC 2982**
      Finance charge, **CC 2982.5**
      Returned buyer, **CC 2982.7**
      Trade ins, **CC 2982.7, 2983**
   Due date, extension or deferment, **CC 2982.3**
   Electric vehicles, charging stations, **CC 2982, 2982.11**
   Enforcement of contract, **CC 2983, 2983.1**
   Errors, validity, **CC 2983**
   Exclusions, Retail Installment Sales Law, **CC 1802.1**
   Exemptions, **CC 2982.5**
   Extension or deferment of due date, **CC 2982.3**
   Failure to secure loan, rescission of sale contract, **CC 2982.5**
   Fees, document preparation, **CC 2982**
   Finance charge, **CC 2981.7 et seq.**
      Assignments, **CC 2982.10**
      Contracts, **CC 2982**
      Insurance, **CC 2982.8**
      Seller assisted loans, **CC 2982.5**
   Financing not obtained, rescission of contract or purchase order, **CC 2982.9**
   Fines and penalties, documents, retention, **CC 2984.5**
   Force and violence, notice, repossessors and repossession, assignments, **CC 2984.6**
   Foreign languages, translations, **CC 1632**
   Form of contract, **CC 2981.5, 2981.9, 2982**
   Guaranteed asset protection waivers, **CC 2982.12**
      Disclosure, **CC 2982, 2982.2**

MOTOR VEHICLES—Cont'd
Conditional sales—Cont'd
  Holder of contract, enforcement, **CC 2983.1**
  Inducement to buyer,
    Contingent compensation, buyer producing future sales, **CC 2982.1**
    Included in contract, **CC 2982**
  Installment payments, disclosure, **CC 2982.2**
  Insurance, **CC 2982**
    Disclosure, **CC 2982.2**
    Financing, **CC 2982.8**
    Notice, **CC 2982.8**
    Statement in contract, necessity, **CC 2984.1**
  Interest, unconscionable rates, **CC 2983.2**
  Irregular payments, maximum finance charge determination, **CC 2982**
  Jurisdiction, action on contract, **CC 2984.4**
  Leases, **CC 2981.5**
  Lien or title on other property, agreement unenforceable, **CC 2984.2**
  Mail, notice, disposal of repossessed or surrendered vehicle, **CC 2983.2**
  Maximum finance charges, irregular or unequal payments, **CC 2982**
  Notice, **CC 2982**
    Assignment of contract to third party, **CC 2983.5**
    Copy of contract, failure to deliver, **CC 2984.3**
    Corrections of contract, **CC 2984**
    Cosigners, delinquency, **CC 2983.35**
    Force and violence, repossessors and repossession, assignments, **CC 2984.6**
    Guaranteed asset protection waivers, **CC 2982.12**
    Insurance, **CC 2984.1**
      Responsibility, **CC 2982.8**
    Sale of repossessed vehicle, **CC 2983.2**
  Optional debt cancellation agreements, disclosure, **CC 2982**
  Optional DMV electronic filing fee, disclosure, **CC 2982**
  Payments, **CC 2982**
    Extension or deferment of due date, **CC 2982.3**
    Personal property, agreement for title or lien, **CC 2984.2**
    Pledge of contract, corrections, time, **CC 2984**
  Pledgee, enforcement of contract, **CC 2983**
  Pollution control certification fees, **CC 2982**
  Power of attorney to confess judgment, **CC 2983.7**
  Presumptions, delivery of copy of contract to buyer, **CC 2984.3**
  Proceeds of loan, seller assisted loans, **CC 2982.5**
  Property damage insurance, statement in contract, **CC 2984.1**
  Public liability insurance, statement in contract, **CC 2984.1**

MOTOR VEHICLES—Cont'd
Conditional sales—Cont'd
  Rates and charges, extension or deferral agreements, **CC 2982.3**
  Real property, agreement for title or lien, **CC 2984.2**
  Rebates, buyer inducements, referral of customers, **CC 2982.1**
  Redemption, sale of repossessed vehicle, **CC 2983.2**
  Referral of customer, compensation, **CC 2982**
    Buyers, unlawful inducement, **CC 2982.1**
  Refunds,
    Down payment, **CC 2982.7**
    Guaranteed asset protection waivers, **CC 2982.12**
    Unearned finance charge, **CC 2982**
  Reinstatement, contracts, **CC 2983.2, 2983.3**
  Remedies of buyer, breach by seller, **CC 2982.7**
  Repossessors and repossession,
    Absence of default, **CC 2983.3**
    Illegal acts, waiver, **CC 2983.7**
    Notice, sale, **CC 2983.2**
  Rescission of contract, **CC 2983.1**
    Failure to secure loan on conditions stated, **CC 2982.5**
  Security interest, generally, post
  Seller assisting buyer in obtaining loan, **CC 2982.5**
  Service contracts, disclosure, **CC 2982.2**
  Signature to contract, **CC 2981.9, 2982**
    Warning concerning insurance, **CC 2984.1**
  Signs and signals, new or used, disclosure, **CC 2982**
  Spanish language, contracts, translations, **CC 1632**
  Supervised financial organizations, **CC 2982.5**
    Loans, **CC 2982.5**
  Surface protection products, disclosure, **CC 2982, 2982.2**
  Surrender of vehicle, disposal, **CC 2983.2**
  Taxation, document preparation, **CC 2982**
  Termination, guaranteed asset protection waivers, **CC 2982.12**
  Theft, deterrent systems, disclosure, **CC 2982, 2982.2**
  Time, documents, retention, **CC 2984.5**
  Tires, fees, **CC 2982**
  Title to property, inclusion in contract, eligible property, **CC 2984.2**
  Total of payments, including in contract, **CC 2982**
  Trade ins, down payment, **CC 2982, 2982.7**
  Transfers, documents, retention, **CC 2984.5**
  Translations, foreign languages, **CC 1632**
  Treble damages, recovery by buyer, **CC 2983.1**
  Truth in lending, disclosures required in contract, **CC 2982**

MOTOR VEHICLES—Cont'd
Conditional sales—Cont'd
  Unconscionable interest rates, **CC 2983.2**
  Unearned portion of finance charge, method of computing, **CC 2982**
  Unequal payments, maximum finance charge determination, **CC 2982**
  Used vehicles, cancellation option agreements, disclosure, **CC 2982, 2982.2**
  Validity, **CC 2983, 2983.1**
  Venue, **CC 2983.7, 2984.4**
  Violence, notice, repossessors and repossession, assignments, **CC 2984.6**
  Waiver, rights of buyer, **CC 2983.7**
  Warning concerning insurance, **CC 2984.1**
  Writing, requirement, **CC 2981.9**
Condominiums, this index
Confidential or privileged information,
  Disclosure, generally, post
  Identification cards, business and commerce, electronic devices and equipment, **CC 1798.90.1**
  Reacquisition, problems with vehicle or nonfinancial terms, **CC 1793.26**
Conflict of laws, service contracts, **CC 1794.41**
Consumer credit reporting agencies, conditional sales, retention, **CC 2984.5**
Consumer protection,
  Repurchases, dealers or manufacturers, **CC 1793.23, 1793.24**
  Vehicle history reports, **CC 1784.1**
Contracts,
  Bailment or leasing of vehicle, **CC 2981.5**
  Conditional sales, generally, ante
  Parking or storage of vehicle, **CC 1630, 1630.5**
  Reacquisition, problems with vehicle or nonfinancial terms, disclosure, **CC 1793.26**
  Retention, **CC 2984.5**
  Shared mobility service providers, **CC 2505**
  Subleasing, actions and proceedings, **CC 3343.5**
  Time, retention, **CC 2984.5**
Cooling off period,
  Conditional sales contracts, **CC 2982**
  Lease or purchase contracts, **CC 2985.8**
Cosigners, delinquency notice, **CC 2983.35**
Costs,
  Disposition, liens and incumbrances, **CC 3073, 3074**
  Leases, post
  Liens and incumbrances, **CC 3068**
    Sales, **CC 3071 et seq.**
  Towing or removal, liens and incumbrances, **CC 3070**
Credit, conditional sales, statements, **CC 2982**
Credit cards, leases, **CC 1939.15**
Crimes and offenses,
  Conditional sales, **CC 2983.6**
  Drivers licenses, post

MOTOR

MOTOR VEHICLES—Cont'd
Crimes and offenses—Cont'd
  Fines and penalties, generally, post
  Larceny. Theft, generally, post
  Leases, post
  Liens and incumbrances, fraud, CC 3070
  Sales Finance Act, CC 2983.6
  Theft, generally, post
  Trick, fraud or device, liens and incumbrances, CC 3070
Customer facility charges, leases, CC 1939.17
Damages,
  Acceleration of sales contracts, presumptions, CC 2983.3
  Leases, post
  Towing, liens and incumbrances, CC 3070
Data, vehicle history reports, CC 1784.1
Dealers,
  Certificates of title, repurchased vehicles, CC 1793.23, 1793.24
  Contracts, service contracts, CC 1794.41
  Disclosure,
    Repurchase vehicles, CC 1793.23, 1793.24
    Warranty adjustment programs, CC 1795.91
  Foreign languages, translations, conditional sales, CC 1632
  Lemon Law buyback, CC 1793.23, 1793.24
  Notice,
    Repurchased vehicles, CC 1793.23, 1793.24
    Service bulletins, CC 1795.91
  Reacquisition, problems with vehicle or nonfinancial terms, disclosure, CC 1793.26
  Repurchased vehicles, notice, CC 1793.23, 1793.24
  Service contracts, CC 1794.41
  Spanish language, translations, conditional sales, CC 1632
  Used vehicles,
    Electronic tracking devices, CC 2983.37
    Warranties, CC 1795.51
  Warranties, adjustment programs, CC 1795.90 et seq.
Default, conditional sales contracts, CC 2983.3
Deficiency claims, tow truck operators, CC 3068.2
Delivery, leases, CC 1939.19
Disabled persons,
  Access to public conveyances, CC 54 et seq.
  Civil rights, CC 54.1
Disabled vehicles. Towing, generally, post
Discharge of lien, costs, CC 3073
Disclaimers, leases, advertisements, CC 1939.19
Disclosure,
  Conditional sales, CC 2982, 2982.2
    Guaranteed asset protection waivers, CC 2982.12
  Dealers, ante

MOTOR VEHICLES—Cont'd
Disclosure—Cont'd
  Leases, post
  Reacquisition, problems with vehicle or nonfinancial terms, CC 1793.26
  Repurchased vehicles, dealers or manufacturers, CC 1793.23, 1793.24
  Service contracts, CC 1794.41
Discounts, conditional sales contracts, CC 2982.1
Dispute resolution, nonconforming new vehicles, CC 1793.22
Distributors, reacquisition, problems with vehicle or nonfinancial terms, disclosure, CC 1793.26
Down payments. Conditional sales, ante
Drivers licenses,
  Business and commerce, electronic devices and equipment, confidential or privileged information, CC 1798.90.1
  Confidential or privileged information, business and commerce, electronic devices and equipment, CC 1798.90.1
  Corporations, electronic devices and equipment, confidential or privileged information, CC 1798.90.1
  Credit cards, identity and identification, acceptance, CC 1747.08
  Crimes and offenses,
    Business and commerce, electronic devices and equipment, confidential or privileged information, CC 1798.90.1
    Corporations, electronic devices and equipment, confidential or privileged information, CC 1798.90.1
    Partnership, electronic devices and equipment, confidential or privileged information, CC 1798.90.1
  Fines and penalties,
    Business and commerce, electronic devices and equipment, confidential or privileged information, CC 1798.90.1
    Corporations, electronic devices and equipment, confidential or privileged information, CC 1798.90.1
    Partnership, electronic devices and equipment, confidential or privileged information, CC 1798.90.1
  Identification cards, generally, post
  Identity and identification,
    Acknowledgments, CC 1185
    Theft, CC 1798.92 et seq.
  Information, sale, CC 1798.26
  Numbers and numbering,
    Grocery stores, club cards, disclosure, CC 1749.60 et seq.
    Identity and identification, theft, CC 1798.92 et seq.
  Partnership, electronic devices and equipment, confidential or privileged information, CC 1798.90.1
  Radio frequency identification, crimes and offenses, CC 1798.79, 1798.795

MOTOR VEHICLES—Cont'd
Drivers licenses—Cont'd
  Records and recordation, sale of information, CC 1798.26
  RFID (radio frequency identification), crimes and offenses, CC 1798.79, 1798.795
  Sales, information, CC 1798.26
  Skimming, radio frequency identification, crimes and offenses, CC 1798.79, 1798.795
Electric vehicles,
  Charging infrastructure,
    Condominiums, CC 4745
      Business and commerce, CC 6713
    Leases, CC 1947.6
  Conditional sales, charging stations, CC 2982, 2982.11
  Leases, charging stations, CC 1947.6
Electricity. Electric vehicles, generally, ante
Electronic surveillance, leases, CC 1939.23
Electronic tracking devices, dealers, used vehicles, CC 2983.37
Encumbrances. Liens and incumbrances, generally, post
Equity, leases, CC 1939.25
  Business programs, CC 1939.21
Estimates. Leases, post
Evidence, conditional sales contracts, presumptions, delivery, CC 2984.3
Farm vehicles. Agricultural Machinery and Equipment, generally, this index
Fees,
  Conditional sales contracts, document preparation, CC 2982
  Contracts, service contracts, cancellation, CC 1794.41
  Leases, CC 1939.19
  Service contracts, cancellation, CC 1794.41
Finance, Sales Finance Act, CC 2981 et seq.
Finance charge. Conditional sales, ante
Fines and penalties,
  Conditional sales, documents, retention, CC 2984.5
  Drivers licenses, ante
  Identification cards, business and commerce, electronic devices and equipment, confidential or privileged information, CC 1798.90.1
  Nonconforming new vehicles, CC 1794
Foreign languages, contracts, translations, CC 1632
Forfeitures, liens and incumbrances, towing or removal, CC 3070
Forms,
  Conditional sales contracts, CC 2981.9, 2982
  Leases, CC 2992
    Damages, notice, CC 1939.09
  Liens and incumbrances, CC 3067.1
Fraud, liens and incumbrances, CC 3070
Gag orders, reacquisition, problems with vehicle or nonfinancial terms, CC 1793.26

MOTOR VEHICLES—Cont'd
GAP waivers, conditional sales, **CC 2982.12**
  Disclosure, **CC 2982, 2982.2**
Gas stations. Motor Vehicle Service Stations, generally, this index
Gasoline stations. Motor Vehicle Service Stations, generally, this index
GPS based technology, leases, **CC 1939.23**
Guaranteed asset protection waivers, conditional sales, **CC 2982.12**
  Disclosure, **CC 2982, 2982.2**
Hangers, leases, disclosure, **CC 1939.31**
Hearings, liens and incumbrances, sale, application, **CC 3071, 3072**
History, vehicle history reports, **CC 1784.1**
House cars, warranties, **CC 1793.05**
Identification cards,
  Business and commerce, electronic devices and equipment, confidential or privileged information, **CC 1798.90.1**
  Confidential or privileged information, business and commerce, electronic devices and equipment, **CC 1798.90.1**
  Corporations, electronic devices and equipment, confidential or privileged information, **CC 1798.90.1**
  Credit cards, acceptance, **CC 1747.08**
  Crimes and offenses, business and commerce, electronic devices and equipment, confidential or privileged information, **CC 1798.90.1**
  Fines and penalties, business and commerce, electronic devices and equipment, confidential or privileged information, **CC 1798.90.1**
  Partnership, electronic devices and equipment, confidential or privileged information, **CC 1798.90.1**
  Radio frequency identification, crimes and offenses, **CC 1798.79, 1798.795**
  RFID (radio frequency identification), crimes and offenses, **CC 1798.79, 1798.795**
  Skimming, radio frequency identification, crimes and offenses, **CC 1798.79, 1798.795**
Identity and identification,
  Cards. Identification cards, generally, ante
  Lease contracts, contents, **CC 2985.8**
  Liens and incumbrances, sale, application, **CC 3071, 3072**
  Numbers and numbering, lien sales, missing numbers, inspection, **CC 3071, 3072**
Implements of husbandry. Agricultural Machinery and Equipment, generally, this index
Importers, reacquisition, problems with vehicle or nonfinancial terms, disclosure, **CC 1793.26**
Incumbrances. Liens and incumbrances, generally, post
Indebtedness, leases, cancellation, contracts, **CC 2985.8, 2985.9**

MOTOR VEHICLES—Cont'd
Informal dispute settlement, nonconforming new vehicles, **CC 1793.22**
Infrastructure, charging infrastructure. Electric vehicles, ante
Injunction, disabled persons, violation of rights of access to public accommodation, **CC 55**
Inspection and inspectors,
  Lien sales, lack of vehicle identification number, **CC 3071, 3072**
  Service contracts, **CC 1794.41**
Installment payments, conditional sales, disclosure, **CC 2982.2**
Insurance. Motor Vehicle Insurance, generally, this index
Judgments and decrees, reacquisition, problems with vehicle or nonfinancial terms, disclosure, **CC 1793.26**
Junk and Junk Dealers, generally, this index
Labor and employment. Liens and incumbrances, generally, post
Larceny. Theft, generally, post
Law of the road. Traffic Rules and Regulations, generally, this index
Leases, **CC 1939.01 et seq., 2985.7 et seq.**
  Acknowledgment of delivery, **CC 2986.4**
  Acknowledgments,
    Damages, waiver, disclosure, **CC 1939.09**
    Vans, safety, **CC 1939.35**
  Actions and proceedings, **CC 1939.25, 2988 et seq.**
    Business programs, **CC 1939.21**
  Advertisements, **CC 1939.19, 2989.4**
  Agent for service of process, **CC 1939.33**
  Application of law, **CC 1939.37**
  Appraisal and appraisers, disposition of vehicle, terminated leases, **CC 2987**
  Assignments,
    Force and violence, notice, repossessors and repossession, **CC 2993**
    Liabilities, equities and defenses, **CC 2986.10**
    Wages, **CC 2986.3**
  Attorney fees, **CC 1939.25, 2988.5, 2988.9**
    Business programs, **CC 1939.21**
  Business programs, **CC 1939.21**
  Cancellation period, **CC 2985.8, 2987**
  Class actions, **CC 2988.5**
  Complaints, investigation, **CC 2989.5**
  Conditional sales, **CC 2981.5**
  Confession of judgment, power of attorney, **CC 2986.3**
  Consumer credit contracts, **CC 1799.90 et seq.**
  Contents, **CC 2985.8, 2986.3**
  Contracts, **CC 2985.7 et seq.**
    Form and construction, **CC 2981.5**
  Cooling off period, **CC 2985.8**
  Costs, **CC 1939.25**
    Actions and proceedings, **CC 2988.9**
    Business programs, **CC 1939.21**

MOTOR VEHICLES—Cont'd
Leases—Cont'd
  Costs—Cont'd
    Licensing or transfer of title, refund, **CC 2986.5**
  Credit cards, **CC 1939.15**
  Crimes and offenses, **CC 2988.5, 2989.8**
    Subleases, damages, **CC 3343.5**
  Customer facility charges, **CC 1939.17**
  Damages, **CC 1939.03 et seq., 2988.5, 2988.9**
    Subleasing, **CC 3343.5**
  Deficiency claims, tow truck operators, **CC 3068.2**
  Depreciation, estimated residual value, liability of lessee, **CC 2988**
  Disclaimers, advertisements, **CC 1939.19**
  Disclosure, **CC 1939.19, 1939.31, 2985.8, 2985.71**
    Damages, waiver, **CC 1939.09**
  Electric vehicles, charging stations, **CC 1947.6**
  Electronic surveillance, **CC 1939.23**
  Equity, **CC 1939.25**
    Business programs, **CC 1939.21**
  Errors, discovery and adjustment, **CC 2988.5**
  Estimates, **CC 1939.19**
    Business programs, **CC 1939.21**
    Damages, **CC 1939.05**
    Depreciation, **CC 2988**
  Fair market value, termination, **CC 2989.2**
  Federal civil action, preemption, **CC 2989**
  Fees, **CC 1939.19**
  Force and violence, notice, repossessors and repossession, assignments, **CC 2993**
  Foreign languages, translations, **CC 1632**
  Forms, **CC 2992**
    Damages, notice, **CC 1939.09**
  Hangers, disclosure, **CC 1939.31**
  Identity and identification, **CC 2985.8**
  Impounding, **CC 1939.03**
  Indebtedness, cancellation, contracts, **CC 2985.8, 2985.9**
  Lessee bearing risk of depreciation, estimated residual value, **CC 2988**
  Lessors obligations, **CC 2989.4**
  Liability, **CC 2985.8**
  License plates, **CC 2985.8**
  Mileage, **CC 1939.19**
    Limitation, **CC 2985.8**
  Mitigation, damages, **CC 1939.07**
  Monopolies and unfair trade, credit cards, **CC 1939.15**
  Motor Vehicle Insurance, this index
  Noncitizens, **CC 1939.33**
  Notice,
    Consumer credit contracts, **CC 1799.91**
    Disposition of vehicle, terminated leases, **CC 2987**
    Electronic surveillance, **CC 1939.23**

MOTOR

MOTOR VEHICLES—Cont'd
Leases—Cont'd
  Notice—Cont'd
    Force and violence, repossessors and repossession, assignments, **CC 2993**
    Hangers, disclosure, **CC 1939.31**
    Sale, **CC 2989.2**
    Warning, **CC 2985.8**
  Optional DMV electronic filing fee, disclosure, **CC 2985.8**
  Payments, **CC 2985.8**
  Power of attorney, confession of judgment, **CC 2986.3**
  Preemption, federal civil actions, **CC 2989**
  Prepayments, **CC 2985.8**
  Presumptions, theft, **CC 1939.03**
  Process, service of process, noncitizens, **CC 1939.33**
  Quotes, **CC 1939.19**
    Business programs, **CC 1939.21**
  Rates and charges, **CC 1939.19**
  Rebates, discounts or commission, **CC 2986.12**
  Records and recordation,
    Electronic surveillance, **CC 1939.23**
    Inspection and inspectors, **CC 2989.5**
  Refunds, failure to execute lease contract, **CC 2986.13**
  Rescission of contract, **CC 2988.7**
  Rules and regulations, **CC 2989.6**
  Safety, vans, **CC 1939.35**
  Searches and seizures, warrants, electronic surveillance, **CC 1939.23**
  Security, **CC 2986.6**
  Service of process, noncitizens, **CC 1939.33**
  Spanish language, **CC 2991**
  Statute of limitations, action to recover damages, **CC 2988.5**
  Storage, **CC 1939.03**
  Subleasing, **CC 3343.5**
  Subpoenas, electronic surveillance, **CC 1939.23**
  Telecommunications, **CC 1939.22**
  Termination, setting fair market value, **CC 2989.2**
  Theft, **CC 1939.03**
  Title to property, documents, **CC 2985.9**
  Total loss, damages, **CC 1939.07**
  Tow truck operator liens, **CC 3068.2**
  Towing, **CC 1939.03**
  Trade ins, valuation, **CC 2985.8**
  Translations, foreign languages, **CC 1632**
  Used vehicles, **CC 2986.5**
  Valuation, **CC 2985.8**
  Vandalism, **CC 1939.03**
  Vans, safety, **CC 1939.35**
  Venue, **CC 1939.27, 2986.3**
  Violence, notice, repossessors and repossession, assignments, **CC 2993**
  Waiver, **CC 1939.29**
    Business programs, **CC 1939.21**

MOTOR VEHICLES—Cont'd
Leases—Cont'd
  Waiver—Cont'd
    Consumer credit contracts, **CC 1799.104**
    Damages, **CC 1939.09**
    Liability, **CC 2986.3**
  Warranties, **CC 2985.8, 2985.9**
    Adjustment programs, **CC 1795.90 et seq.**
Lemon Law buyback, **CC 1793.23, 1793.24**
Liability insurance. Motor Vehicle Insurance, generally, this index
License plates,
  Automated license plate recognition, **CC 1798.90.5 et seq.**
  Destruction, liens and incumbrances, sales, **CC 3071, 3072**
  Lease contracts, contents, **CC 2985.8**
  Liens and incumbrances, sales, destruction, **CC 3071, 3072**
  Sales, liens and incumbrances, destruction, **CC 3071, 3072**
Licenses and permits,
  Drivers licenses, generally, ante
  Plates. License plates, generally, ante
  Shared mobility service providers, **CC 2505**
Liens and incumbrances, **CC 3067 et seq.**
  Assignments, **CC 3069**
  Attorney fees, **CC 3068**
  Conditional sale contract, other personal or real property, **CC 2984.2**
  Costs, **CC 3068**
    Sales, **CC 3073, 3074**
  Crimes and offenses, fraud, **CC 3070**
  Extinguishment of lien, **CC 3068**
  Fees, sale, **CC 3071, 3072**
  Forms, **CC 3067.1**
  Fraud, **CC 3070**
  Leases, personal or real property, **CC 2986.6**
  Mobilehomes and mobilehome parks, application of law, **CC 3071**
  Possessory liens, **CC 3068, 3068.1**
  Proceeds of sale, disposition, **CC 3073**
  Reacquisition, problems with vehicle or nonfinancial terms, disclosure, **CC 1793.26**
  Redemption, **CC 3071, 3072**
  Release of interest by owner, **CC 3071.5**
  Repairs on vehicles, **CC 3067 et seq.**
  Sales, post
  Storage of vehicles, **CC 3067 et seq.**
  Time, storage, **CC 3068, 3068.1**
  Towing or removal, forfeiture of claims and liability for costs, **CC 3070**
  Limitation of actions, lease contracts, **CC 2988.5**
Loans,
  Conditional sales, generally, ante
  Seller assisting buyer, **CC 2982.5**
  Supervised financial organizations, **CC 2982.5**

MOTOR VEHICLES—Cont'd
Mail and mailing,
  Certified or registered mail, notice,
    Assignment of lien for labor or materials, **CC 3069**
    Sale to satisfy lien, **CC 3073**
  Conditional sales, notice, sale of vehicle, **CC 2982**
  Liens and incumbrances, sale, notice, **CC 3071, 3072**
Maintenance and repairs,
  Liens and incumbrances, generally, ante
  Motor Vehicle Service Stations, generally, this index
  Reimbursement, warranty adjustment programs, manufacturers, **CC 1795.92**
  Service contracts, **CC 1794.41**
  Warranty adjustment programs, **CC 1795.90 et seq.**
Manufacturers and manufacturing,
  Certificates of title, repurchased vehicles, **CC 1793.23, 1793.24**
  Contracts, service contracts, **CC 1794.41**
  Disclosure, repurchased vehicles, **CC 1793.23, 1793.24**
  Lemon Law, buybacks, **CC 1793.23, 1793.24**
  Notice,
    Repurchased vehicles, **CC 1793.23, 1793.24**
    Warranty adjustment programs, **CC 1795.92**
  Reacquisition, problems with vehicle or nonfinancial terms, disclosure, **CC 1793.26**
  Reimbursement, repairs, warranty adjustment programs, **CC 1795.92**
  Repurchased vehicles, notice, **CC 1793.23, 1793.24**
  Restitution, **CC 1793.2 et seq.**
  Sales and use taxes, reimbursement, restitution, **CC 1793.25**
  Service contracts, **CC 1794.41**
  Warranties,
    Adjustment programs, **CC 1795.90 et seq.**
    Housecars, **CC 1793.05**
Mechanics liens. Liens and incumbrances, generally, ante
Mileage,
  Leases, **CC 1939.19**
  Limitation, lease contract, **CC 2985.8**
Misdemeanors. Crimes and offenses, generally, ante
Mitigation, leases, damages, **CC 1939.07**
Mobilehomes and mobilehome parks, removal, **CC 798.28.5**
Modification or change, housecars, warranties, **CC 1793.05**
Monopolies and unfair trade, leases, **CC 1939.13**
  Credit cards, **CC 1939.15**
Motels. Hotels and Motels, generally, this index

MOTOR

MOTOR VEHICLES—Cont'd
Motor Vehicle Insurance, generally, this index
Motorized Scooters, generally, this index
Names, liens and incumbrances, sale, application, **CC 3071, 3072**
Negligence, passengers, degree of care required, **CC 2096**
New vehicles, nonconformities, consumer protection, **CC 1793.22**
Noncitizens, leases, **CC 1939.33**
Notice,
   Assignment of lien for labor or materials, **CC 3069**
   Conditional sales, ante
   Contracts, service contracts, cancellation, **CC 1794.41**
   Dealers, ante
   Leases, ante
   Liens and incumbrances, sale, **CC 3071, 3072**
   Manufacturers and manufacturing, warranty adjustment programs, **CC 1795.92**
   Mobilehomes and mobilehome parks, removal, **CC 798.28.5**
   Nonconforming new vehicles, consumer protection, **CC 1793.22**
   Repurchased vehicles, sales, dealers or manufacturers, **CC 1793.23, 1793.24**
   Sale to enforce lien, **CC 3071, 3072**
   Security interest, force and violence, repossessors and repossession, assignments, **CC 2984.6**
   Service bulletins, dealers, **CC 1795.91**
   Service contracts, cancellation, **CC 1794.41**
   Service of process, lien sales, inability to serve, **CC 3071, 3072**
Number plates. License plates, generally, ante
Numbers and numbering, missing vehicle identification number, lien sales, inspection, **CC 3071, 3072**
Off highway vehicles, private property owner, liability for riders injuries, **CC 846**
Offenses. Crimes and offenses, generally, ante
Operation rules. Traffic Rules and Regulations, generally, this index
Operators licenses. Drivers licenses, generally, ante
Option to purchase, lease contract, **CC 2985.8**
Optional debt cancellation agreements, conditional sales, disclosure, **CC 2982**
Optional DMV electronic filing fee,
   Conditional sales, disclosure, **CC 2982**
   Leases, disclosure, **CC 2985.8**
Ordinances,
   Parking, bailment contracts, **CC 1630**
   Storage, bailment contracts, **CC 1630**
Parking Lots and Facilities, generally, this index
Partnership, fees, conditional sales, disclosure, **CC 2982**
Passengers, degree of care required, **CC 2096**
Payment, leases, contract provisions, **CC 2985.8**

MOTOR VEHICLES—Cont'd
Penalties. Fines and penalties, generally, ante
Perjury, application for sale, liens and incumbrances, **CC 3071, 3072**
Plates. License plates, generally, ante
Plug in vehicles. Electric vehicles, generally, ante
Possessory liens, **CC 3068, 3068.1**
Prepayments, lease contracts, **CC 2985.8**
Private property, liability for riders injuries, **CC 846**
Privileges and immunities, children and minors, rescue, **CC 43.102**
Process,
   Leases, noncitizens, service of process, **CC 1939.33**
   Service of process, lien sales, inability to serve, **CC 3071, 3072**
Publication, liens and incumbrances, sale, notice, **CC 3071, 3072**
Purchase orders. Conditional sales, generally, ante
Purchases. Sales, generally, post
Qualified third party dispute resolution, nonconforming new vehicles, **CC 1793.22**
Quotes, leases, **CC 1939.19**
Rates and charges,
   Leases, **CC 1939.19**
   Storage, post
Reacquisition, problems with vehicle or nonfinancial terms, disclosure, **CC 1793.26**
Rebates,
   Conditional sales contracts, **CC 2982.1**
   Lease contracts, **CC 2986.12**
Records and recordation. Disclosure, generally, ante
Recreational Vehicles, generally, this index
Redemption, liens and incumbrances, sale, **CC 3071, 3072, 3074**
Refunds,
   Conditional sales, ante
   Lease contracts, failure to execute, **CC 2986.13**
   Service contracts, **CC 1794.41**
   Transfer of title, **CC 2986.5**
Registration,
   Information, sales, **CC 1798.26**
   Leases, **CC 2989.4**
      Documents, **CC 2985.9**
   Optional DMV electronic filing fee,
      Conditional sales, disclosure, **CC 2982**
      Leases, disclosure, **CC 2985.8**
   Records and recordation, sale of information, **CC 1798.26**
   Sale of information, **CC 1798.26**
Registration plates. License plates, generally, ante
Reimbursement, repairs, warranty adjustment programs, manufacturers, **CC 1795.92**
Release, interest in vehicle, garagemens lien, **CC 3071.5**

MOTOR VEHICLES—Cont'd
Removal,
   Disposition, liens and encumbrances, forfeiture, **CC 3070**
   Mobilehomes and mobilehome parks, unauthorized parking, **CC 798.28.5**
   Notice, mobilehomes and mobilehome parks, **CC 798.28.5**
   Unauthorized parking, mobilehomes and mobilehome parks, **CC 798.28.5**
Rental cars. Leases, generally, ante
Repairs. Maintenance and repairs, generally, ante
Replacement, conditional sales, title and liens, **CC 2984.2**
Reports, vehicle history reports, **CC 1784.1**
Repossessors and repossession. Conditional sales, ante
Repurchased vehicles, notice, dealers or manufacturers, **CC 1793.23, 1793.24**
Rescission,
   Conditional sales contract, failure to secure loan, **CC 2982.5**
   Financing not obtained, **CC 2982.9**
   Lease contract, **CC 2988.7**
Rescue, children and minors, privileges and immunities, **CC 43.102**
Restitution, manufacturers, **CC 1793.22, 1793.25**
Riders, private property owners liability for injuries, **CC 846**
Rules of the road. Traffic Rules and Regulations, generally, this index
Safety,
   Mobilehomes and mobilehome parks, removal, **CC 798.28.5**
   Removal, mobilehomes and mobilehome parks, **CC 798.28.5**
Sales,
   Conditional sales, generally, ante
   Costs, liens and incumbrances, **CC 3073, 3074**
   Dealers, generally, ante
   Financing, supervised organizations other than seller, **CC 2982.5**
   Lease contracts, termination, notice of sale, **CC 2989.2**
   Lemon Law buyback, **CC 1793.23, 1793.24**
   License plates, liens and incumbrances, destruction, **CC 3071, 3072**
   Liens and incumbrances, **CC 3071, 3072**
      Redemption, **CC 3074**
      Satisfaction, **CC 3072**
   Loans, supervised financial organizations other than seller, **CC 2982.5**
   New or used, disclosure, conditional sales, **CC 2982**
   New vehicles, nonconformities, **CC 1793.22**
   Redemption, **CC 3074**
   Repurchased vehicles, notice, dealers or manufacturers, **CC 1793.23, 1793.24**
   Satisfaction, **CC 3072**

MOTOR

MOTOR VEHICLES—Cont'd
Sales—Cont'd
  Supervised financial organizations, loans, **CC 2982.5**
  Warranties, adjustment programs, **CC 1795.90 et seq.**
Scooters. Motorized Scooters, generally, this index
Searches and seizures, warrants, leases, electronic surveillance, **CC 1939.23**
Secured transactions. Security interest, generally, post
Security deposits, lease contracts, **CC 2986.6**
Security interest,
  Assignments, force and violence, notice, repossessors and repossession, **CC 2984.6**
  Force and violence, notice, repossessors and repossession, assignments, **CC 2984.6**
  Leasing, **CC 2986.6**
  Notice, force and violence, repossessors and repossession, assignments, **CC 2984.6**
  Property subject to lien or inclusion of title, **CC 2984.2**
  Violence, notice, repossessors and repossession, assignments, **CC 2984.6**
Semitrailers. Motor Carriers, generally, this index
Service contracts, **CC 1794.41**
  Conditional sales contracts, property subject to lien or inclusion of title, **CC 2984.2**
Service stations. Motor Vehicle Service Stations, generally, this index
Shared mobility service providers, contracts, licenses and permits, **CC 2505**
Signatures, conditional sale contract, **CC 2981.9, 2982**
Song Beverly Consumer Warranty Act, **CC 1790 et seq.**
Spanish language, contracts, **CC 2991**
  Translations, conditional sales, **CC 1632**
Stolen vehicles. Theft, generally, post
Storage,
  Contracts, printing and requisites, **CC 1630.5**
  Leases, **CC 1939.03**
  Lien, **CC 3067 et seq.**
  Rates and charges, **CC 3068.1**
    Liens and incumbrances, **CC 3067 et seq.**
    Towing, **CC 3068.2**
  Tow truck operator liens, storage expenses, **CC 3068.2**
Subleasing, **CC 3343.5**
Subpoenas, leases, electronic surveillance, **CC 1939.23**
Supervised financial organizations, loans, **CC 2982.5**
Tanner Consumer Protection Act, **CC 1793.22**
Taxation, conditional sales, cash price including taxes, **CC 2981**
Telecommunications, leases, **CC 1939.22**
Termination, conditional sales, guaranteed asset protection waivers, **CC 2982.12**

MOTOR VEHICLES—Cont'd
Theft,
  Bailment contracts, parking lots and facilities, **CC 1630.5**
  Deterrent systems, conditional sales, disclosure, **CC 2982**
  Parking lots and facilities, bailment contracts, **CC 1630.5**
Time,
  Conditional sales, documents, retention, **CC 2984.5**
  Leases, **CC 1939.05**
  Liens and incumbrances, storage, **CC 3068, 3068.1**
  Service contracts, **CC 1794.41**
Tires,
  Conditional sales, fees, **CC 2982**
  Pest Control, generally, this index
  Vector control. Pest Control, generally, this index
Title to property,
  Certificates of title, generally, ante
  Leases, documents, **CC 2985.9**
  Transfer, leases, refunds, **CC 2986.5**
Towing,
  Claims, deficiency claims, **CC 3068.2**
  Deficiency claims, **CC 3068.2**
  Fees, lien sale processing fee, **CC 3068.2**
  Leases, **CC 1939.03**
  Liens and incumbrances, **CC 3068.2**
    Forfeiture of claims and liability for costs, **CC 3070**
  Storage liens, **CC 3068.2**
Tractors,
  Farm tractors. Agricultural Machinery and Equipment, generally, this index
  Truck tractors. Motor Carriers, generally, this index
Trade ins,
  Conditional sales, **CC 2982, 2982.7, 2983**
  Leases, valuation, **CC 2985.8**
Traffic Rules and Regulations, generally, this index
Transfer,
  Conditional sales, documents, retention, **CC 2984.5**
  Optional DMV electronic filing fee,
    Conditional sales, disclosure, **CC 2982**
    Leases, disclosure, **CC 2985.8**
  Warranty adjustment programs, **CC 1795.90 et seq.**
Trick, fraud or device, liens and incumbrances, **CC 3070**
Truth in lending, conditional sales, **CC 2982**
Unauthorized parking, mobilehomes and mobilehome parks, removal, **CC 798.28.5**
Used vehicles,
  Cancellation option agreements, conditional sales, disclosure, **CC 2982, 2982.2**
  Conditional sales, cancellation option agreements, disclosure, **CC 2982, 2982.2**

MOTOR VEHICLES—Cont'd
Used vehicles—Cont'd
  Leasing, **CC 2986.5**
  Sales, cancellation option agreements, disclosure, **CC 2982, 2982.2**
  Trade ins, generally, ante
Valuation, leases, **CC 2985.8**
Vandalism, leases, **CC 1939.03**
Venue, leases, **CC 1939.27, 2986.3**
Waiver, lease contracts, **CC 2986.3**
Warnings, lease agreements, **CC 2985.8**
Warranties,
  Adjustment programs, **CC 1795.90 et seq.**
  Arbitration and award, nonconformities, **CC 1793.22**
  Coast guard, **CC 1795.8**
  House cars, **CC 1793.05**
  Leases, **CC 2985.8, 2985.9**
  Lemon Law buyback, **CC 1793.23, 1793.24**
  Military forces, **CC 1795.8**
  National guard, **CC 1795.8**
  Nonconformities, arbitration and award, **CC 1793.22**
  Reacquisition, problems with vehicle or nonfinancial terms, disclosure, **CC 1793.26**
  Song Beverly Consumer Warranty Act, **CC 1790 et seq.**
Wrecks and wreckers. Towing, generally, ante

MOTOR VEHICLES DEPARTMENT
Motor Vehicles, generally, this index

MOTORBOATS
Boats and Boating, generally, this index

MOTORCYCLES
License plates. Motor Vehicles, this index
Motorized Scooters, generally, this index
Traffic Rules and Regulations, generally, this index

MOTORIZED SCOOTERS
Contracts, shared mobility service providers, **CC 2505**
Insurance, liability insurance, shared mobility service providers, **CC 2505**
Licenses and permits, shared mobility service providers, **CC 2505**
Shared mobility service providers, contracts, licenses and permits, **CC 2505**

MOTORIZED SKATEBOARDS
Shared mobility service providers, contracts, licenses and permits, **CC 2505**

MOTORIZED WHEELCHAIRS
Medi Cal program, warranties, **CC 1793.025**

MOVING PICTURES
Motion Pictures, generally, this index

MOVING WALKS
Elevators, Dumbwaiters and Escalators, generally, this index

MUSEUMS

MULTIFAMILY HOUSING
Housing, this index

MULTIPLE DWELLINGS
Apartment Houses, generally, this index
Condominiums, generally, this index
Cooperative Apartments, generally, this index
Planned Unit Developments, generally, this index

MULTIPLE LISTINGS
Real estate,
  Appraisers, CC 1087, 1088
  Brokers and salespersons, CC 1087, 1088

MULTIPLES
Fine art, sales, disclosure, CC 1740 et seq.

MUNICIPAL ATTORNEYS
Acknowledgment of instruments, CC 1181
Civil rights actions, CC 52, 52.1
  Disabled persons, CC 55.1
Dance studio contracts, actions for violations, CC 1812.63
Disabled persons, civil rights, injunction, CC 55.1
Forcible entry and detainer, nuisance, assignments, drugs and medicine, CC 3486
Medical records, negligence, release, CC 56.36

MUNICIPAL BONDS
Water appropriations, authorization, CC 1416

MUNICIPAL BUILDINGS AND GROUNDS
Eminent Domain, generally, this index

MUNICIPAL CLERKS
Acknowledgments, CC 1181

MUNICIPAL CORPORATIONS
Municipalities, generally, this index

MUNICIPAL COUNCIL
Ordinances, generally, this index

MUNICIPAL COURTS
Claims courts. Small Claims Courts, generally, this index
Small Claims Courts, generally, this index
Subpoenas, generally, this index

MUNICIPAL ELECTIONS
Interest, foreclosure consultants, CC 2945.4

MUNICIPAL LIBRARIES
Libraries, generally, this index

MUNICIPAL OFFICERS AND EMPLOYEES
Attorneys. Municipal Attorneys, generally, this index
Firefighters and Fire Departments, generally, this index
Legal advisor. Municipal Attorneys, generally, this index
Police, generally, this index

MUNICIPAL TREASURERS
Depositories, generally, this index

MUNICIPALITIES
Adverse possession against, CC 1007
Airports and Landing Fields, generally, this index
Alleys. Streets and Alleys, generally, this index
Architects, contracts, indemnity, CC 2782.8
Attorneys. Municipal Attorneys, generally, this index
Bids and bidding, leases, extended terms, CC 719
Building Permits, generally, this index
Building Standards, generally, this index
Cable Television, generally, this index
Chartered cities. Ordinances, generally, this index
Civil defense. War and Civil Defense, generally, this index
Community Development and Housing, generally, this index
Conservation easements, CC 815.3
Consolidated Cities and Counties, generally, this index
Criminal history information, disclosure, concessionaire, application purposes, CC 1798.24a
Damages, interest, CC 3287
Defense shelters, injuries, exemption from liability, CC 1714.5
Development. Community Development and Housing, generally, this index
Easements, greenways, CC 816.50 et seq.
Eminent Domain, generally, this index
Engineers, contracts, indemnity, CC 2782.8
Firefighters and Fire Departments, generally, this index
Fires and Fire Protection, generally, this index
Freeways, generally, this index
Greenways, easements, CC 816.50 et seq.
Health Facilities, generally, this index
Hearings, leases, extended term, CC 719
Housing, generally, this index
Improvements, generally, this index
Injunction, legislative acts, CC 3423
Interest, recoverable on damages, CC 3287
Jails, generally, this index
Landing fields. Airports and Landing Fields, generally, this index
Landscape architects, contracts, indemnity, CC 2782.8
Leases,
  City lots, CC 718
  Remedy for breach, CC 1952.6
  Term of lease, CC 719
Legislative acts, prevention by injunction, CC 3423
Libraries, generally, this index
Licenses and permits, shared mobility service providers, CC 2505
Los Angeles, generally, this index
Lost or destroyed property, ordinances regulating care, CC 2080.4

MUNICIPALITIES—Cont'd
Low and Moderate Income Housing, generally, this index
Manufacturers and manufacturing, tidelands, submerged lands and uplands, leases, CC 718
Motor vehicles, shared mobility service providers, licenses and permits, contracts, CC 2505
Museums, generally, this index
National defense. War and Civil Defense, generally, this index
Ordinances, generally, this index
Parking Lots and Facilities, generally, this index
Parks, generally, this index
Peace Officers, generally, this index
Personal property, safekeeping, powers and duties, CC 2080.10
Pest Control, generally, this index
Planning. Zoning and Planning, generally, this index
Police, generally, this index
Privileges and immunities, civil defense, CC 1714.5
Recreation and Recreational Facilities, generally, this index
Redevelopment. Community Development and Housing, generally, this index
Sacramento City and County, generally, this index
Schools and School Districts, generally, this index
Shared mobility service providers, licenses and permits, CC 2505
Social Services, generally, this index
Streets and Alleys, generally, this index
Subdivided Lands, generally, this index
Surveys and surveyors, contracts, indemnity, CC 2782.8
Tax Assessments, generally, this index
Taxation, generally, this index
War and Civil Defense, generally, this index
Water Appropriation, generally, this index
Waters and Watercourses, generally, this index
Zoning and Planning, generally, this index

MUNICIPALLY OWNED UTILITIES
Transportation, seating capacity, CC 2185

MUNITIONS
Real estate, residential, disclosure statements, CC 1102.15

MUSEUMS
Art and artists, commissions, sales, original works, CC 986
Conservation measures, long term or indefinite loans, CC 1899.6
Disposal of property, indefinite or long term loans, CC 1899.6
Donations, indefinite or long term loans, CC 1899.10

MUSEUMS

MUSEUMS—Cont'd

Forms, notice of intent to preserve an interest in property on loan, **CC 1899.5**

Intent to preserve an interest in property on loan, receipts, notices, **CC 1899.3**

Liens and incumbrances, conservation measures or disposal of property, long term or indefinite loans, **CC 1899.6**

Limitation of actions, injury or loss of property, indefinite or long term loans, **CC 1899.8, 1899.10**

Loans, indefinite or long term loans, **CC 1899 et seq.**

Notice,
    Forms, intent to preserve an interest in property on loan, **CC 1899.5**
    Injury or loss of property, indefinite or long term loans, **CC 1899.7**
    Loans, **CC 1899.2 et seq.**

Owners and ownership, loans of property to museum, **CC 1899 et seq.**

Privileges and immunities, long term or indefinite loans, disposal or conservation measures, **CC 1899.6**

Public policy, loans, **CC 1899**

Publication, notice, injury or loss of property, indefinite or long term loans, **CC 1899.7**

Receipts, loans, indefinite or long term loans, **CC 1899.3**

Specified term loans, **CC 1899.9**

Statute of limitations, injury or loss of property, indefinite or long term loans, **CC 1899.8, 1899.10**

Termination, loans of property to museum, **CC 1899.9**

Title to property, loans of property to museum, **CC 1899 et seq.**

MUSIC AND MUSICIANS

Audio and video recordings, royalties, audits and auditors, **CC 2500, 2501**

Audits and auditors, tape recordings, royalties, **CC 2500, 2501**

Phonographs, generally, this index

Royalties, generally, this index

MUTUAL BENEFIT CORPORATIONS

See, also, Nonprofit Corporations, generally, this index

Members and membership, mobilehomes and mobilehome parks, application of law, **CC 799.1**

Mobilehomes and mobilehome parks, members and membership, application of law, **CC 799.1**

NAMES

Advertisements, this index

Astaire Celebrity Image Protection Act, **CC 3344.1**

Attorney in fact, subscribing, **CC 1095**

Celebrity image protection, **CC 3344.1**

Change of name, deeds and conveyances, **CC 1096**

NAMES—Cont'd

Club cards, grocery stores, disclosure, **CC 1749.60 et seq.**

Consumer Credit Reporting Agencies, this index

Deeds and conveyances, change of name, **CC 1096**

Disclosure, grocery stores, club cards, **CC 1749.60 et seq.**

Electronic commercial service contracts, **CC 1789.3**

Equalization state board, release, **CC 1798.69**

Grocery stores, club cards, disclosure, **CC 1749.60 et seq.**

Home equity sales contracts, rescission, unconscionable advantage, **CC 1695.14**

Identity and identification, theft, **CC 1798.92 et seq.**

Installment sales, seller and buyer, **CC 1803.3**
    Memorandum when subsequent purchase is made, **CC 1808.3**

Invasion of privacy, advertisements and solicitations, use without consent, **CC 3344**

Landlord and tenant, **CC 1962**

Mobilehomes and Mobilehome Parks, this index

Power of attorney, execution of instruments, **CC 1095**

Privacy, invasion of privacy, pseudonyms, **CC 1708.85**

Signatures, generally, this index

Solicitation, use without consent, invasion of privacy, **CC 3344**

Taxation, equalization state board, release, **CC 1798.69**

Trademarks, generally, this index

NARCOTICS

Drugs and Medicine, generally, this index

NATIONAL DEFENSE

War and Civil Defense, generally, this index

NATIONAL EMERGENCY

Disasters, generally, this index

NATIONAL PARKS

Waters, appropriation, time to commence works, **CC 1422**

NATIONALITY

Discrimination, generally, this index

NATIVE AMERICANS

Indigenous Peoples, generally, this index

NATURAL DISASTERS

Disasters, generally, this index

NATURAL GAS

Oil and Gas, generally, this index

NATURAL HAZARDS

Disclosure, residential property, **CC 1103 et seq.**

NATURAL RESOURCES

Leases, lessors remedy for breach, contracts to explore or remove natural resources, **CC 1952.4**

NAVIGABLE WATERS

Waters and Watercourses, generally, this index

NAVIGATION

Ships and Shipping, generally, this index

Waters and Watercourses, generally, this index

NAVY

Military Forces, generally, this index

NEEDY CHILDREN

Social Services, generally, this index

NEGATIVE EASEMENTS

Limitation of actions, **CC 784**

NEGLECTED CHILDREN

Juvenile Delinquents and Dependents, generally, this index

NEGLIGENCE

Generally, **CC 1714**

Acknowledgments, identification of persons making, **CC 1185**

Adjoining landowners, excavations, **CC 832**

Agent, liability of principal, **CC 2338, 2339**

Air raid shelters, liability for injuries, **CC 1714.5**

Ammunition, designs and designers, distribution, markets and marketing, **CC 1714**

Art objects, restoring or framing, defacement or destruction, gross negligence, **CC 987**

Bailment, this index

Blind or visually impaired persons, failure to carry white canes or use guide dogs, **CC 54.4**

Building standards, general contractors, application of law, **CC 936**

Camping, entry on private land, personal injuries, hazardous conditions, warning, **CC 846**

Carriers, this index

Children and minors,
    Imputation to parent or guardian, willful misconduct, **CC 1714.1**
    Wilful misconduct, parental liability, **CC 1714.1**

Construction loans, real or personal property, defects, lenders liability, **CC 3434**

Consumer credit reporting agencies,
    Conditions precedent, **CC 1785.32**
    Damages, **CC 1785.31 et seq.**

Contracts, exemption from responsibility, illegal contracts, **CC 1668**

Contributory negligence, **CC 1714**

Crimes and offenses,
    Criminal act as proximate cause of injury, **CC 3333.3**
    Injury or death to criminal, liability, **CC 847**

NEGLIGENCE—Cont'd

Damages, **CC 3333 et seq.**
   Personal injury damages, interest, **CC 3291**
Death. Wrongful Death, generally, this index
Deposits and depositaries,
   Limitation of liability, **CC 1840**
   Loss or injury to thing deposited, **CC 1838**
Disasters, shelters, liability for death or injuries, **CC 1714.5**
Emotional distress, actions and proceedings, **CC 1714.01**
Excavations, adjoining landowners, **CC 832**
Felonies, proximate cause, damages, **CC 3333.3**
Firefighters, injury, liability, **CC 1714.9**
Firemans rule, **CC 1714.9**
Flight from felony, damages, **CC 3333.3**
General contractors, building standards, application of law, **CC 936**
Gross negligence,
   Art objects, restoration or framing, defacement or destruction, **CC 987**
   Defibrillators, **CC 1714.21**
   Emergency cardiopulmonary resuscitation, **CC 1714.2**
Health care service plans, medical records, **CC 56.36, 56.101**
Housing, construction and improvement loans, lenders liability for defects, **CC 3434**
Identification of persons making acknowledgments, **CC 1185**
Improvement and repair, real or personal property, lenders liability for defects, **CC 3434**
Indemnity, generally, this index
Innocent persons, which of two must suffer, **CC 3543**
Interest, personal injury damages, **CC 3291**
Landlord and tenant, care required by tenant, **CC 1928**
Leases, care required by lessee, **CC 1928**
Lenders liability for defects, real or personal property, construction loans, **CC 3434**
Medical Malpractice, generally, this index
Medical records,
   Disposal, **CC 56.101**
   Release, **CC 56.36**
Mobilehomes and mobilehome parks, damage caused by, repairs, **CC 798.73, 798.83**
Peace officers, injury, liability, **CC 1714.9**
Personal injury damages, interest, **CC 3291**
Personal property, management of property, **CC 1714**
Products Liability, generally, this index
Professional negligence. Medical Malpractice, generally, this index
Proximate cause, commission of felony, damages, **CC 3333.3**
Railroads, this index
Real estate, management of property, **CC 1714**
Recreational vehicle parks, removal, defaulting occupants, **CC 799.59**

NEGLIGENCE—Cont'd

Responsibility, **CC 1714**
School buses, **CC 2096**
War and civil defense, **CC 1714.5**
Weapons, designs and designers, distribution, markets and marketing, **CC 1714**
Wilful acts, **CC 1714**
   Children, imputed liability of parents, **CC 1714.1**
Wrongful Death, generally, this index

NEGOTIABLE INSTRUMENTS

Acceleration,
   Mortgages or trust deeds, incorporating acceleration clause in documents, **CC 2924.5**
   Motor vehicle conditional sales contract, **CC 2983.3**
Acceptance, credit cards as condition of acceptance, **CC 1725**
Accounts and accounting, notice, sale of business, nonnegotiable instruments, transfer, **CC 955**
Actions and proceedings, check cashers, **CC 1789.35**
Agents and agencies, collecting, duties, **CC 2021**
Applications, check cashers, licenses and permits, **CC 1789.37**
Assignments, nonnegotiable instruments, transfer, notice, sale of business, **CC 955, 955.1**
Attorney fees, check cashers, **CC 1789.35**
Bad checks,
   Check cashers, deferred deposits, **CC 1789.35**
   Clerks of courts, demand for payment, **CC 1719**
   Damages, **CC 1719**
   Deferred deposits, check cashers, **CC 1789.35**
   Dishonored checks, **CC 1719**
   Good faith dispute, stopping payment, **CC 1719**
   Return fee, installment sales, including in finance charge, **CC 1805.4, 1810.4**
   Treble damages, **CC 1719**
Carriers,
   Limitation of liability, **CC 2200**
   Loss, liability, **CC 2177**
Check cashers, **CC 1789.30 et seq.**
Checks,
   Acceptance, credit cards as condition of acceptance, **CC 1725**
   Accord and satisfaction, **CC 1526**
   Actions and proceedings, check cashers, **CC 1789.35**
   Attorney fees, cashers, **CC 1789.35**
   Bad checks, generally, ante
   Cashers, **CC 1789.30 et seq.**
   Clerks of courts, dishonor, demand for payment, **CC 1719**

NEGOTIABLE INSTRUMENTS—Cont'd

Checks—Cont'd
   Credit cards,
      Condition of acceptance, **CC 1725**
      Finance charge, notice, **CC 1748.9**
   Crimes and offenses,
      Bad checks, generally, ante
      Cashers, licenses and permits, **CC 1789.37**
   Damages, cashers, **CC 1789.35**
   Demand for payment, dishonor, treble damages, **CC 1719**
   Dishonor,
      Bad checks, generally, ante
      Clerks of courts, demand for payment, **CC 1719**
      Demand for payment, treble damages, **CC 1719**
      Return fee, installment sales, including in finance charge, **CC 1805.4, 1810.4**
   Fees,
      Cashers, **CC 1789.30, 1789.35, 1789.37**
      Deferred deposits, check cashers, **CC 1789.35**
   Fines and penalties,
      Cashers, licenses and permits, **CC 1789.37**
      Check cashers, **CC 1789.35**
      Credit cards, condition of acceptance, **CC 1725**
   Good faith dispute, stopping payment, **CC 1719**
   Guarantee cards, condition of acceptance, **CC 1725**
   Identity and identification, cashers, **CC 1789.30**
   Injunction,
      Check cashers, **CC 1789.35**
      Credit cards, condition of acceptance, **CC 1725**
   Installment sales, dishonor, return fee, including in finance charges, **CC 1805.4, 1810.4**
   Insufficient funds. Bad checks, generally, ante
   Jurisdiction, dishonor, demand for payment, **CC 1719**
   Licenses and permits, cashers, **CC 1789.37**
   Limitation of actions, check cashers, **CC 1789.35**
   Money Orders, generally, this index
   Monopolies and unfair trade, cashers, **CC 1789.32**
   Notice,
      Accord and satisfaction, protests, **CC 1526**
      Stop payment, **CC 1719**
   Protest, accord and satisfaction, **CC 1526**
   Satisfaction, accord and satisfaction, **CC 1526**
   Stop payment orders, dishonor, demand for payment, **CC 1719**
   Treble damages, demand for payment, **CC 1719**

NEGOTIABLE

NEGOTIABLE INSTRUMENTS—Cont'd
Checks—Cont'd
    Trust deeds, default sales, payments, **CC 2924h**
    Unfair business practices, check cashers, **CC 1789.30**
    Waiver, cashers, **CC 1789.38**
Clerks of courts, dishonor, demand for payment, **CC 1719**
Collection, agents, **CC 2021**
Contracts, dance studio services, **CC 1812.87**
Conviction of crime, check cashers business, permits, **CC 1789.37**
Credit cards,
    Checks, finance charge, notice, **CC 1748.9**
    Condition of acceptance, **CC 1725**
Crimes and offenses,
    Cashers, checks, licenses and permits, **CC 1789.37**
    Check cashers, fees, **CC 1789.35**
Damages, check cashers, **CC 1789.35**
Dance studio services, contracts, **CC 1812.55**
Dishonor, protests, accord and satisfaction, **CC 1526**
Documents of Title, generally, this index
Drafts, generally, this index
Electronic funds transfers. Funds Transfers, generally, this index
Fees,
    Checks, ante
    Deferred deposits, check cashers, **CC 1789.35**
Fines and penalties,
    Checks, ante
    Credit cards, condition of acceptance, **CC 1725**
Funds Transfers, generally, this index
Good faith, dispute, stop payment order, **CC 1719**
Government checks, check cashers, fees, **CC 1789.35**
Health studio services, contracts, **CC 1812.87**
Identity and identification, check cashers, **CC 1789.30**
Indorsements, assignment of nonnegotiable instruments, notice, sale of business, **CC 955**
Injunction, credit cards, condition of acceptance, **CC 1725**
Insufficient funds. Bad checks, generally, ante
Interest,
    Compound, **CC 1916–2**
    Variable rate, **CC 1916.5**
Jurisdiction, dishonor, drafts, checks, treble damages, **CC 1719**
Letters of Credit, generally, this index
Loans, extension of term, **CC 1916.5**
Lost or destroyed, security on bond, **CC 3415**
Money Orders, generally, this index
Monopolies and unfair trade, check cashers, **CC 1789.32**

NEGOTIABLE INSTRUMENTS—Cont'd
Mortgages, insurance, cancellation, conditions of extension of credit, **CC 2954.7**
Negotiable order of withdrawal, installment sales, dishonor, return fees, finance charges, **CC 1805.4, 1810.4**
Not sufficient funds checks. Bad checks, generally, ante
Notice,
    Accord and satisfaction, **CC 1526**
    Nonnegotiable instruments, transfer, sale of business, **CC 955, 955.1**
    Stop payment order, good faith dispute, **CC 1719**
NSF checks. Bad checks, generally, ante
Payroll checks, check cashers, fees, **CC 1789.35**
Receipts, check cashers, payroll and government checks, **CC 1789.35**
Return fee, dishonored checks, **CC 1805.4, 1810.4**
Returned checks. Bad checks, generally, ante
Rules and regulations, check cashers, permits, **CC 1789.37**
Share drafts, installment sales, return fee, including in finance charge, **CC 1805.4, 1810.4**
Stop payment order, good faith dispute, **CC 1719**
Transfer,
    Funds Transfers, generally, this index
    Nonnegotiable instruments, **CC 1459**
    Notice, sale of business, **CC 955, 955.1**
Treble damages, bad checks, **CC 1719**
Unfair business practices, check cashers, **CC 1789.32**
Variable interest rate, **CC 1916.5**
Worthless checks. Bad checks, generally, ante

NETWORKS
Internet, generally, this index
Telecommunications, generally, this index

NEUTRALITY
Internet, **CC 3100 et seq.**

NEWS EVENTS
Invasion of privacy, use of name, photograph, likeness, voice or signature without consent, **CC 3344**

NEWSPAPERS
Advertisements, generally, this index
Art works, common law copyrights, reproduction rights, transfer, **CC 982**
Consumers Legal Remedies Act, application of law, **CC 1755**
Crimes and offenses, stories, sale proceeds, **CC 2225**
Invasion of privacy, use of names, photograph, likeness, voice or signature without consent, **CC 3344**
Libel and Slander, generally, this index
Notice, generally, this index

NEWSPAPERS—Cont'd
Publication, generally, this index
Telecommunications, messages intended for publication, priorities and preferences, **CC 2207**
Uniform Single Publication Act, **CC 3425.1 et seq.**

NEXT OF KIN
Relatives, generally, this index

NITROGEN DIOXIDE
Air Pollution, generally, this index

NOISE POLLUTION
Freeways, generally, this index
Ranges, shooting ranges, **CC 3482.1**
Shooting ranges, **CC 3482.1**

NONCITIZENS
    See, also, Immigration, generally, this index
Civil rights, **CC 51**
Discrimination, **CC 51**
Landlord and Tenant, this index
Personal property, ownership, **CC 671**
Property, ownership, **CC 671**
Real estate, ownership, **CC 671**

NONCONFORMING GOODS
Sales, this index

NONECONOMIC DAMAGES
Joint and several liability, **CC 1431.2**

NONPROFIT CHARITABLE ORGANIZATIONS
Charities, generally, this index
Nonprofit Organizations, generally, this index

NONPROFIT CORPORATIONS
    See, also, Nonprofit Organizations, generally, this index
Bonds, leases, tax exempt bonds, remedy for breach of lease, **CC 1952.6**
Charities, generally, this index
Conservation Easements, generally, this index
Consumer cooperative corporations. Cooperative Corporations, generally, this index
Cooperative Corporations, generally, this index
Credit Unions, generally, this index
Employment agencies, application of law, **CC 1812.502**
Injunction to prevent breach of contract with members, **CC 3423**
Leases, public entities, lease subject to reversion to or vesting in, invalidation by lessors remedy for breach statutes, **CC 1952.6**
Mortgages, sales, rent, **CC 2924m**
Sales,
    Mortgages, rent, **CC 2924m**
    Trust deeds, rent, **CC 2924m**
Trust deeds, sales, rent, **CC 2924m**

NONPROFIT ORGANIZATIONS
    See, also, Nonprofit Corporations, generally, this index

NONPROFIT ORGANIZATIONS—Cont'd
Agricultural land, gleaning for farm products, privileges and immunities, **CC 846.2**
Charities, generally, this index
Conservation easements, **CC 815.3**
Easements. Conservation Easements, generally, this index
Greenways, easements, **CC 816.50 et seq.**

NONPUBLIC SCHOOLS
Private Schools, generally, this index

NONRESIDENTS
Contracts, independent wholesale sales representatives, **CC 1738.14**
Independent wholesale sales representatives, contracts, **CC 1738.14**
Installment sales, transactions involving both local and out of state contacts, **CC 1802.19**
Sales, independent wholesale sales representatives, contracts, **CC 1738.14**
Wholesale sales representatives, independents, contracts, **CC 1738.14**

NONSUFFICIENT FUNDS CHECKS
Bad checks. Negotiable Instruments, this index

NONSUPPORT
Support, generally, this index

NOTARIES PUBLIC
Actions and proceedings,
  Evidence, acknowledgments, **CC 1185**
  Perjury, certificates and certification, acknowledgments, **CC 1189**
Armed forces, **CC 1183.5**
Electronic Transactions Act, **CC 1633.11**
Evidence,
  Acknowledgments, **CC 1185**
  Identity and identification, **CC 1185**
Fines and penalties,
  Evidence, acknowledgments, **CC 1185**
  Perjury, certificates and certification, acknowledgments, **CC 1189**
Foreign countries, acknowledgments, **CC 1183**
Foreign states, acknowledgments, **CC 1182**
Identity and identification, evidence, **CC 1185**
Military forces, **CC 1183.5**
Perjury, certificates and certification, acknowledgments, **CC 1189**
Telecommunications, Electronic Transactions Act, **CC 1633.11**
Uniform Electronic Transactions Act, **CC 1633.11**
Witnesses, identity and identification, **CC 1185**

NOTES
Negotiable Instruments, generally, this index

NOTICE
Abatement of nuisance, **CC 3503**
Acknowledgments, certificates and certification, **CC 1189**
Adjoining landowners,
  Excavations, **CC 832**

NOTICE—Cont'd
Adjoining landowners—Cont'd
  Fences, maintenance, **CC 841**
Agents or principals, **CC 2332**
Assignment, health studio services contract, **CC 1812.88**
Autographed memorabilia, dealers, **CC 1739.7**
Boarding and Lodging Houses, this index
Camps and Camping, this index
Carriers, this index
Certified or registered mail. Mail and Mailing, this index
Civil rights, construction, disabled persons, accessibility, **CC 55.54**
Collection Agencies, this index
Commercial property, rent control, ordinances, **CC 1954.31**
Condominiums, this index
Constructive notice, **CC 18, 19**
  Agents, restrictions on authority, **CC 2318**
  Assignments, mortgages or trust deeds, records, **CC 2934**
  Consumer credit reporting agencies, real estate transactions, application of law, **CC 1785.35**
  Deeds and conveyances, record, **CC 1213**
  Leases, oil and gas leases, **CC 1219**
  Mortgages, assignments, recording, **CC 2934**
  Name, change, conveyance after, **CC 1096**
  Oil and gas lease, **CC 1219**
  Records and Recordation, this index
  Trust deeds, assignments, recording, **CC 2934**
Consumer Credit, this index
Consumer Credit Reporting Agencies, this index
Consumers, personal information, privacy, sales, **CC 1798.120**
Contracts, this index
Conversion, restoration of thing wrongfully acquired, demand, **CC 1713**
Credit Cards, this index
Credit services organizations,
  Contracts, cancellation, **CC 1789.16**
  Deposits, secretary of state, ceasing business, **CC 1789.24**
Creditors. Debtors and Creditors, this index
Damages, this index
Dating service contracts, cancellation, **CC 1694.1, 1694.2**
Debit cards, liability, **CC 1748.30, 1748.31**
Debtors and Creditors, this index
Deeds and Conveyances, this index
Defectively executed instruments, **CC 1207**
Depositories, this index
Disabled Persons, this index
Electronic Transactions Act, **CC 1633.3, 1633.10, 1633.16**
Employment Agencies, this index
Entry on property, surveyors, **CC 846.5**
Excavations, adjoining landowners, **CC 832**

NOTICE—Cont'd
Fair debt collection practices, **CC 1812.700 et seq.**
Floating Homes, this index
Forcible Entry and Detainer, this index
Fraud, solicitation, payment of money, written statement or invoice, disclaimer, **CC 1716**
Genetic testing, privacy, disclosure, **CC 56.181**
Home Equity Sales Contracts, this index
Home solicitation contracts, cancellation, **CC 1689.7**
Homeless persons, transitional housing, misconduct, injunctions, **CC 1954.13**
Horses, public auction or sale, purchase for slaughter, prices, **CC 1834.8**
Housing, this index
Indebtedness, duress or coercion, **CC 1798.97.2**
Indemnity, defense of actions, **CC 2778**
Installment Sales, this index
Insurance, this index
Invasion of privacy, use of name, photograph, likeness, voice or signature without consent, **CC 3344**
Judicial Notice, generally, this index
Landlord and Tenant, this index
Laundries, sale of unclaimed clothing or goods, **CC 3066**
Leases, this index
Libelous statements, demanding correction, **CC 48a**
Liens and Incumbrances, this index
Loans, this index
Mail and Mailing, this index
Markets and marketing, Internet, disclosure, **CC 1749.8.1**
Mechanics Liens, this index
Medical Records, this index
Membership camping contracts, **CC 1812.302**
  Cancellation, forms, **CC 1812.303, 1812.304**
Membership fees, installment sales, credit cards, **CC 1810.4**
Memorabilia, autographed, dealers, **CC 1739.7**
Mines and Minerals, this index
Mobilehomes and Mobilehome Parks, this index
Mortgages, this index
Motor Vehicles, this index
Museums, this index
Negotiable Instruments, this index
Nuisance, abatement, time required, **CC 3503**
Obligations, this index
Owner or mineral rights, intent to preserve right, recording of late notice, court permission, **CC 883.250**
Posting, generally, this index
Power of termination, exercise, **CC 885.050**
Publication, generally, this index
Real Estate, this index
Real property security instrument, subordination agreement, **CC 2953.2, 2953.3**

NOTICE

NOTICE—Cont'd
Records and Recordation, this index
Recreational Vehicles, this index
Rent, this index
Rent controls, commercial property, **CC 1954.31**
Rental Purchase Agreements, this index
Rescission of contract, **CC 1691**
Reverse mortgages, **CC 1923.5**
Sales, this index
San Francisco Bay area, real estate, sales, restrictions, **CC 1103.4**
Shared appreciation loans, seniors, disclosures, **CC 1917.710 et seq.**
Suretyship and Guaranty, this index
Surveys and surveyors, entry on property, **CC 846.5**
Telecommunications, this index
Trust Deeds, this index
Uniform Electronic Transactions Act, **CC 1633.3, 1633.10, 1633.16**
Unrecorded instruments, validity, **CC 1217**
Voidable Transactions, this index
Weight loss contracts, cancellation, **CC 1694.6, 1694.7**
Writs of possession, innkeepers liens, **CC 1861.8**

NOTIFICATION
Notice, generally, this index

NOVATION
Generally, **CC 1530 et seq.**
Forms of novation, **CC 1531**
Insolvency of third person, rescission, **CC 1541**
Methods, **CC 1531**
Modification of contract, application of law, **CC 1698**
Rescission, **CC 1533**
Rules applicable, **CC 1532**

NSF CHECKS
Bad checks. Negotiable Instruments, this index

NUISANCE
Generally, **CC 3479 et seq.**
Abatement, **CC 3491**
  Commercial property, rent controls, application of law, **CC 1954.28**
  Damages, generally, post
  Lead base paint, **CC 3494.5**
  Mortgages, foreclosure, assessments, **CC 2929.45**
  Motion pictures, killing of or cruelty to animals or human beings, **CC 3504 et seq.**
  Notice, private nuisance, **CC 3503**
  Private nuisance, **CC 3501 et seq.**
  Private persons, **CC 3493, 3495**
  Public officer or agency, **CC 3494**
  Successive property owners, liability for failure, **CC 3483**
  Trust deeds, foreclosure, assessments, **CC 2929.45**

NUISANCE—Cont'd
Acts under statutory authority, **CC 3482**
Adjoining landowners, spite fences, **CC 841.4**
Agricultural activity, operation of facility, **CC 3482.5**
Assignation, place of, injunctions, awarding, **CC 3496**
Attorney fees, injunctions, **CC 3496**
Cockfighting, **CC 3482.8**
Constitution, enjoining, costs, awarding, **CC 3496**
Continuing nuisance, liability of successive owners, **CC 3483**
Costs, injunctions, **CC 3496**
Damages,
  Abatement of nuisance, **CC 3484**
  Award of costs and attorney fees, **CC 3496**
  Recovery notwithstanding abatement of, **CC 3484**
Dogs, fighting, **CC 3482.8**
Drugs and medicine, costs, injunctions, **CC 3496**
Exceptions, acts under statutory authority, **CC 3482**
Exemptions, agricultural activities, **CC 3482.5, 3482.6**
Fences, excessive height, **CC 841.4**
Floating home marinas, **CC 800.201**
Forcible entry and detainer, drugs and medicine, **CC 3486, 3486.5**
Gambling, costs, injunction actions, **CC 3496**
Indictment or information, remedy against public nuisance, **CC 3491, 3492**
Landlord and Tenant, this index
Lapse of time, public nuisance, legalization, **CC 3490**
Lead base paint, abatement, **CC 3494.5**
Los Angeles, forcible entry and detainer, drugs and medicine, **CC 3486**
Marinas, floating homes, **CC 800.201**
Mortgages, foreclosure, abatement, assessments, **CC 2929.45**
Motion pictures, killing of or cruelty to human beings or animals, **CC 3505 et seq.**
Oakland, forcible entry and detainer, drugs and medicine, **CC 3486.5**
Obscenity, injunction, **CC 3496**
Preventive relief against, **CC 3369**
Private nuisances, **CC 3501 et seq.**
Private persons,
  Abatement of public nuisance, **CC 3495**
  Maintaining action against public nuisances, **CC 3493**
Public agencies, abatement, **CC 3494**
Ranges, sport shooting ranges, **CC 3482.1**
Recreational vehicles, parks, defaulting residents, **CC 799.70**
Remedies, **CC 3491 et seq.**
Sacramento City and County, forcible entry and detainer, drugs and medicine, **CC 3486.5**

NUISANCE—Cont'd
Shooting ranges, **CC 3482.1**
Specific relief against, **CC 3369**
Spite fences, **CC 841.4**
Sport shooting ranges, **CC 3482.1**
Statutory authority, acts under statutory authority, **CC 3482**
Successive property owners, failure to abate, **CC 3483**
Trust deeds, foreclosure, abatement, assessments, **CC 2929.45**

NUMBER PLATES
License plates. Motor Vehicles, this index

NURSERIES AND NURSERY STOCK
Pest Control, generally, this index
Trees, generally, this index

NURSES
Abuse, long term health care facilities, temporary employment, **CC 1812.543**
Assistants,
  Abuse, long term health care facilities, temporary employment, **CC 1812.543**
  Long term health care facilities, employment agencies, temporary employment, **CC 1812.509, 1812.540 et seq.**
Certified nurse assistants. Assistants, generally, ante
Contracts, registries, **CC 1812.526**
Criminal history information, long term health care facilities, temporary employment, **CC 1812.542**
Employment. Nurses Registries, generally, this index
Employment agencies, long term health care facilities, temporary employment, **CC 1812.509, 1812.540 et seq.**
Labor and employment. Nurses Registries, generally, this index
Licensed vocational nurses. Vocational Nursing, generally, this index
Malpractice. Medical Malpractice, generally, this index
Medical Malpractice, generally, this index
Negligence. Medical Malpractice, generally, this index
Psychiatric Technicians, generally, this index
Referrals. Nurses Registries, generally, this index
Registries. Nurses Registries, generally, this index
Vocational Nursing, generally, this index

NURSES REGISTRIES
Generally, **CC 1812.524 et seq.**
Advertisements, **CC 1812.533**
Bonds (officers and fiduciaries), **CC 1812.525**
Contracts, **CC 1812.526**
Deposits in lieu of bond, **CC 1812.525**
Experience and training, verification, **CC 1812.528**

NURSES REGISTRIES—Cont'd
Fees, **CC 1812.527**
  Prohibition,
    Registration fees, **CC 1812.530**
    Splitting, **CC 1812.531**
Fraud, **CC 1812.533**
Payment, assignments, **CC 1812.532**
Qualifications, verification, **CC 1812.528**
Records, **CC 1812.529**
Registration fees, prohibition, **CC 1812.530**
Schedules, fees schedules, **CC 1812.527**
Verification, claims as to experience and training, **CC 1812.528**

NURSING HOMES
See, also, Health Facilities, generally, this index
Abuse, nurses, temporary employment, **CC 1812.543**
Access, commercial blockade, **CC 3427 et seq.**
Accommodation contracts, termination, death of patient, **CC 1934.5**
Bailment, **CC 1859 et seq.**
Blockade, commercial blockade, **CC 3427 et seq.**
Commercial blockade, **CC 3427 et seq.**
Contracts, death, termination, **CC 1934.5**
Criminal history information, nurses, temporary employment, **CC 1812.542**
Death, termination of contract, **CC 1934.5**
Employment agencies, nurses, temporary employment, **CC 1812.509, 1812.540 et seq.**
Malpractice. Medical Malpractice, generally, this index
Medical Malpractice, generally, this index
Nurses, employment agencies, temporary employment, **CC 1812.509, 1812.540 et seq.**
Personal property,
  Fireproof safe, notice of nonliability, **CC 1860**
  Injury or loss, **CC 1859**
Psychiatric technicians, employment agencies, temporary employment, **CC 1812.540 et seq.**
Temporary employment, nurses, employment agencies, **CC 1812.509, 1812.540 et seq.**
Termination, contracts, death, **CC 1934.5**
Torts, commercial blockade, **CC 3427 et seq.**
Vocational nursing, employment agencies, temporary employment, **CC 1812.540 et seq.**

NUTRITION
See, also, Food, generally, this index
Dietitians, generally, this index
Weight loss contracts, **CC 1694.5 et seq.**

OAKLAND
See, also, Municipalities, generally, this index
Forcible entry and detainer,
  Drugs and medicine, nuisance, **CC 3486.5**

OAKLAND—Cont'd
Forcible entry and detainer—Cont'd
  Weapons, **CC 3485**
Weapons, forcible entry and detainer, **CC 3485**

OATHS AND AFFIRMATIONS
Acknowledgments of instruments, **CC 1185**
Affidavits, generally, this index
Electronic Transactions Act, **CC 1633.11**
Identification of persons making acknowledgments, **CC 1185**
Instruments, proof, authority of officers taking to administer, **CC 1201**
Perjury, generally, this index
Proof of instruments, officer taking authority to administer, **CC 1201**
Telecommunications, Electronic Transactions Act, **CC 1633.11**
Uniform Electronic Transactions Act, **CC 1633.11**

OATS
Agricultural Products, generally, this index

OBJECTS
Contracts, this index

OBLIGATIONS
  Generally, **CC 1427 et seq.**
Accord and satisfaction, **CC 1521 et seq.**
  Execution, effect, **CC 1522**
  Part performance, **CC 1524**
Actions to enforce, **CC 1428**
Alternative obligations, **CC 1448 et seq.**
Assignment, nonnegotiable instruments, **CC 1459**
Benefits, assumption of obligation by acceptance of benefits, **CC 1589**
Breach, interest on damages, jury question, **CC 3288**
Burden of obligation, transfer, **CC 1457**
Classifications, **CC 1430**
Concurrent conditions, performance, **CC 1439**
Conditional obligations, **CC 1434 et seq.**
  Part payment of disputed fund, **CC 1525**
Conditions,
  Offer of performance, **CC 1494, 1498**
  Part payment, disputed fund, **CC 1525**
Conditions precedent, performance, **CC 1439**
Conditions subsequent, **CC 1435**
Consent, transfer of obligations, **CC 1457**
Consideration, moral or legal obligation as consideration for contract, **CC 1606**
Contributions among joint obligors, **CC 1432**
Covenants Running with Land, generally, this index
Creation, **CC 1428**
Enforcement, **CC 1428**
Extinction, **CC 1473 et seq.**
  General release, **CC 1542**
  Joint obligees, one of, **CC 1475**
  Performance,
    Act applicable to two or more obligations, **CC 1479**

OBLIGATIONS—Cont'd
Extinction—Cont'd
Performance—Cont'd
  Causes excusing, **CC 1511**
    Preventing by, **CC 1514**
  Creditors,
    Direction by, **CC 1476**
    Prevention by, **CC 1512**
  Joint creditors directing manner of performance, **CC 1476**
  Joint debtors, one of several, **CC 1474**
  Joint obligees, performance to one of, **CC 1475**
  Offer, **CC 1485 et seq.**
    Ability to perform, **CC 1495**
    Additional offer, **CC 1494**
    Compensation for delay, **CC 1492**
    Conditions, dependent upon performance, **CC 1498**
    Custody of thing offered, **CC 1503**
    Deposit of thing offered, **CC 1503**
    Effect upon interest and incidents of obligation, **CC 1504**
    Good faith, **CC 1493**
    Interest on obligation, effect of offer, **CC 1504**
    Objections to mode of offer, time, **CC 1501**
    Partial, **CC 1486**
    Payment, deposit and notice, **CC 1500**
    Person required to make, **CC 1487**
    Place of offer, **CC 1489**
    Prevention of performance or offer, **CC 1511 et seq.**
    Procedure in making, **CC 1488**
    Production of things to be delivered, **CC 1496**
    Receipt for property delivered, **CC 1499**
    Refusal of thing offered, **CC 1505**
    Refusal to accept performance before offer, **CC 1515**
    Rules, **CC 1485**
    Separation of thing offered, **CC 1497**
    Time, **CC 1490, 1491**
    Title to thing offered, **CC 1502**
    Willingness to perform, **CC 1495**
  One of joint creditors, **CC 1475**
  One of several joint obligors, **CC 1474**
  Order of performance, several obligations, **CC 1479**
  Partial performance, **CC 1477**
  Prevention of performance, **CC 1511 et seq.**
  Refusal to accept before offer, **CC 1515**
Release, **CC 1541 et seq.**
Forfeiture, conditions involving, **CC 1442**
Good faith, offer of performance, **CC 1493**
Illegal conditions, void, **CC 1441**
Imposed by law, **CC 1708 et seq.**
Impossible or unlawful conditions, void, **CC 1441**

OBLIGATIONS

OBLIGATIONS—Cont'd
Interpretation, CC 1429
   Conditions involving forfeiture, CC 1442
Joint creditors directing manner of performance, CC 1476
Joint or several, CC 1430 et seq.
   Presumption, CC 1431
Moral or legal obligation as consideration for contract, CC 1606
Nonnegotiable instructions, transfer by indorsement, CC 1459
Notice,
   Nonperformance, conditional obligations, CC 1440
   Offer of performance, deposit of funds, CC 1500
   Selection between alternative acts, CC 1449
Offer of performance, CC 1485 et seq.
Operation of law, arising from, enforcement, CC 1428
Owners of realty, CC 840 et seq.
Ownership, subject to, CC 655
Partial payment, amounts concededly due, CC 1525
Partial performance, CC 1477
   Accord and satisfaction, CC 1524
   Offer of, CC 1486
Payment, CC 1478
   Disputed sum, partial payment, CC 1525
Performance, CC 1473
   Act applicable to two or more obligations, CC 1479
   Excused, CC 1440
      Conditional obligation, CC 1440
   Extinction, ante
   Joint debtors, one of several, CC 1474
   Necessity, CC 1439
   Offer of performance, CC 1485 et seq.
   Partial performance, CC 1477
   Prevention of performance, CC 1511 et seq.
   Specific performance, CC 3384 et seq.
Precedent condition, CC 1435, 1436
   Performance, CC 1439
Presumption, joint obligations, CC 1431
Prevention of performance, CC 1511 et seq.
Real estate, owners obligations, CC 840 et seq.
Receipts, delivery of property in performance, CC 1497
Release, CC 1541 et seq.
Satisfaction. Accord and satisfaction, generally, ante
Several or joint, CC 1430 et seq.
   Presumption, CC 1431
Specific performance, CC 3384 et seq.
Subsequent condition, CC 1435
Time, offer of performance, CC 1490, 1491
Transfer of obligations, CC 1457 et seq.
Two or more obligations, application of performance, CC 1479
Void for impossible or unlawful conditions, CC 1441

OBLIGATIONS—Cont'd
Waiver of code provisions, CC 3268

OBLITERATION
Records. Lost or Destroyed Documents, generally, this index

OBSCENITY
Lewdness and Obscenity, generally, this index

OBSTRUCTION OF JUSTICE
Interference, generally, this index

OBSTRUCTIONS
Commercial blockade, health care facilities, CC 3427 et seq.
Health care facilities, commercial blockade, CC 3427 et seq.
Private schools, buildings and grounds, access, threats, interference, CC 1708.9

OCCUPANCY
Acquisition of property by, CC 1000
Adverse Possession, generally, this index
Homeless persons, hotels and motels, shelters, CC 1954.08 et seq.

OCCUPATIONAL DISEASES
Disclosure, insurance, CC 56.265
Insurance, disclosure, CC 56.265
Insurance agents, solicitors or brokers, disclosure, CC 56.265
Investigations and investigators, disclosure of medical information, CC 56.26
Medical information, investigations, disclosure, CC 56.26

OCCUPATIONAL ILLNESS
Occupational Diseases, generally, this index

OCCUPATIONS
Professions and Occupations, generally, this index

ODORS
Air Pollution, generally, this index

OFF STREET PARKING
Parking Lots and Facilities, generally, this index

OFFENSES
Crimes and Offenses, generally, this index

OFFERS
Bids and Bidding, generally, this index
Buildings, construction defects,
   Money, CC 929
   Repairs, CC 917 et seq.

OFFICIAL ADVERTISEMENTS
Advertisements, generally, this index

OFFICIAL BONDS
Bonds (Officers and Fiduciaries), generally, this index

OIL AND GAS
See, also, Motor Vehicle Service Stations, generally, this index
Actions and proceedings, privacy, usage data, CC 1798.99
Automated dispensing outlet, keys or card keys, credit cards, CC 1747.03
Confidential or privileged information, usage data, CC 1798.98, 1798.99
Contracts, exploration or removal, applicability, lessors remedy for breach statutes, CC 1952.4
Customers, privacy, usage data, CC 1798.98, 1798.99
Damages, privacy, usage data, CC 1798.99
Disclosure, privacy, usage data, CC 1798.98, 1798.99
Distribution. Oil and Gas Pipelines, generally, this index
Keys and key cards, automated dispensing outlet, petroleum products, credit card, CC 1747.03
Landlord and tenant, unseparated meters, CC 1940.9
Leases. Oil and Gas Leases, generally, this index
Legal Estates Principal and Income Law, CC 731 et seq.
Letters of credit, pipelines, spills, CC 3333.5
Liability, key or card key holders, automated dispensing outlets, losses after notice of loss or theft, CC 1747.03
Loss, key or card key, automated dispensing outlets, liability after notice of loss, CC 1747.03
Meters, privacy, usage data, CC 1798.98, 1798.99
Mineral rights, CC 883.110 et seq.
Pipelines. Oil and Gas Pipelines, generally, this index
Powers of termination, reversionary interests, application of law, CC 885.015
Privacy, usage data, CC 1798.98, 1798.99
Real estate, powers of termination, marketable title, application of law, CC 885.015
Records and recordation, leases, CC 1219
Rights, mineral rights, CC 883.110 et seq.
Spills, damages, CC 3333.5
Theft, keys or key cards, automated dispensing outlets, liability after notice of loss or theft, CC 1747.03
Transmission. Oil and Gas Pipelines, generally, this index

OIL AND GAS LEASES
Generally, CC 718f
Constructive notice, CC 1219
Determinable by future event, CC 718f
Legal Estates Principal and Income Law, CC 731 et seq.
Mineral rights, CC 883.110 et seq.
Municipalities, CC 718, 718f

ORDINANCES

OIL AND GAS LEASES—Cont'd
Notice, constructive notice, CC 1219
Records and recordation, CC 1219
Rights, mineral rights, CC 883.110 et seq.
Rule Against Perpetuities, CC 718, 718f
Tidelands, municipalities, CC 718
Town lots, CC 718, 718f

OIL AND GAS PIPELINES
Attorney fees, spills, CC 3333.5
Bonds (officers and fiduciaries), spills, CC 3333.5
Breaks, damages, CC 3333.5
Damages, breaks, CC 3333.5
Housing, sales, disclosure, CC 2079.10.5
Indemnification, spills, CC 3333.5
Insurance, spills, CC 3333.5
Letters of credit, spills, CC 3333.5
Subrogations, spills, CC 3333.5

OIL PIPELINE ENVIRONMENTAL RESPONSIBILITY ACT
Generally, CC 3333.5

OIL STATIONS
Motor Vehicle Service Stations, generally, this index

OLD AGE
Aged Persons, generally, this index

OLD PERSONS
Aged Persons, generally, this index

OMBUDSPERSONS
Colleges and universities, student loans, borrowers rights, CC 1788.104

ONLINE INFORMATION SYSTEMS
Internet, generally, this index

ONLINE VIOLENCE PROTECTION ACT
Generally, CC 1798.99.20 et seq.

OPEN END CREDIT
Shared appreciation loans for seniors, CC 1917.320 et seq.

OPEN MEETINGS
Condominiums, directors, CC 4900 et seq.

OPEN SPACE LANDS
Nonprofit organizations, conservation easements, CC 815 et seq.

OPERATORS LICENSES
Drivers licenses. Motor Vehicles, this index

OPHTHALMOLOGISTS
Charities, privileges and immunities, screenings, CC 1714.26
Privileges and immunities, charities, screenings, CC 1714.26
Screenings, charities, privileges and immunities, CC 1714.26

OPINION AND EXPERT TESTIMONY
Witnesses, this index

OPPRESSION
Duress or Coercion, generally, this index

OPTICIANS
Malpractice. Medical Malpractice, generally, this index
Medical Malpractice, generally, this index
Negligence. Medical Malpractice, generally, this index
Professional negligence. Medical Malpractice, generally, this index

OPTIONS
Accession, material, use without knowledge thing or value, CC 1032
Debtors and creditors, offer of performance, place, CC 1489
Fixtures erroneously affixed to land, removal, CC 1013.5
Home equity sales contracts, CC 1695.12
Installments sales, sellers option to add subsequent purchases to contract, CC 1808.1
Liens and incumbrances, redemption, priority, CC 2906
Mobilehomes and mobilehome parks, rental agreement rejection, homeowners, CC 798.17
Real Estate, this index

OPTOMETRISTS
See, also, Eyes and Eyesight, generally, this index
Charities, screenings, privileges and immunities, CC 1714.26
Immunities. Privileges and immunities, generally, post
Malpractice. Medical Malpractice, generally, this index
Medical Malpractice, generally, this index
Negligence. Medical Malpractice, generally, this index
Privileges and immunities,
  Charities, screenings, CC 1714.26
  Professional organization, CC 43.7, 43.8
  Referral services, CC 43.95
Professional negligence. Medical Malpractice, generally, this index
Referrals, limitation of liability, CC 43.95
Screenings, charities, privileges and immunities, CC 1714.26
Telephones, referral services, immunity, CC 43.95

ORAL CONTRACTS
Generally, CC 1052
Contracts, this index

ORANGE COUNTY STATE COLLEGE
Colleges and Universities, generally, this index

ORDERS
Garnishment, generally, this index
Military forces, emergencies, suspension of civil and criminal liability, CC 1714.6

ORDERS FOR PAYMENT OF MONEY
Warrants for Payment of Money, generally, this index

ORDERS OF COURT
Abortion, commercial blockade, facilities, CC 3427.3
Animals, livestock service liens, CC 3080.06 et seq.
Condominiums,
  Construction, defects, CC 6000
  Declarations, amendments, reduction of votes, CC 4275
Contempt, generally, this index
Crime victims, stories by felons, actions for proceeds, CC 2225
Disclosure, personal information held by governmental agencies, Information Practices Act, CC 1798.24
Easements, abandoned easements, CC 887.080
Forcible entry and detainer, weapons, CC 3485
Health facilities, commercial blockade, CC 3427.3
Holidays, applications, CC 1008
Identity and identification, theft, business entities, filing, CC 1798.202
Injunction, generally, this index
Internet, threats, social media, CC 1798.99.22
Landlord and Tenant, this index
Livestock service liens, CC 3080.06 et seq.
Locks and locking, landlord and tenant, protective orders, CC 1941.5, 1941.6
Mechanics liens, release, CC 8480 et seq.
Public buildings and works, summary proceedings, stop notices, CC 9412
Nuisances, motion pictures, cruelty to or killing of human beings or animals, CC 3507
Protective orders,
  Internet, threats, social media, CC 1798.99.22
  Landlord and tenant, locks and locking, CC 1941.5, 1941.6
  Social media, threats, CC 1798.99.22
Service of process. Process, this index
Social media, threats, CC 1798.99.22
Threats, social media, CC 1798.99.22

ORDINANCES
Apartment houses, rent control, CC 1947.7 et seq.
Counties, unclaimed property, care, CC 2080.4
Equal protection of laws, minority groups, CC 53.7
Fences, electricity, security, CC 835
Leases, extended term, CC 719
Lost or destroyed property, care, CC 2080.4
Minority groups, equal protection of laws, CC 53.7
Rent control, housing, CC 1947.7 et seq.
Rosenthal Roberti Item Pricing Act, preemption of local ordinances, CC 7106

ORDINANCES

ORDINANCES—Cont'd
Signs, real estate, sale or lease, **CC 713**
Storage contracts, printing and requisites, **CC 1630**
Unclaimed property, care, **CC 2080.4**

ORDNANCE
Real estate, residential, disclosure statements, **CC 1102.15**

ORGANIZATIONS
Associations and Societies, generally, this index

ORGANIZED CAMPS
Camps and Camping, generally, this index

ORNAMENTAL TREES
Trees, generally, this index

ORPHANS AND ORPHANAGES
Foster homes. Social Services, this index

OSTEOPATHS
Confidential or privileged information, medical records, **CC 56 et seq.**
Malpractice. Medical Malpractice, generally, this index
Medical information, confidentiality, **CC 56 et seq.**
Medical Malpractice, generally, this index
Negligence. Medical Malpractice, generally, this index
Professional negligence. Medical Malpractice, generally, this index

OTHER STATES
Foreign States, generally, this index

OUTDOOR ADVERTISING
Consumers Legal Remedies Act, application of law, **CC 1755**
Easements, prescriptive rights, **CC 1008**
Exemptions, Consumers Legal Remedies Act, **CC 1755**
Fraud, Consumers Legal Remedies Act, application of law, **CC 1755**
Invasion of privacy, use of names, photograph, voice or signature, **CC 3334**
Mobilehomes and mobilehome parks, **CC 799.1.5**
Real property, sales, restraints on alienation, **CC 712**

OVERWEIGHT PERSONS
Weight loss contracts, **CC 1694.5 et seq.**

OWNERS AND OWNERSHIP
Title to Property, generally, this index

PACIFIC OCEAN
Tidal Waves, generally, this index

PAINTS AND PAINTING
Art and Artists, generally, this index
Children and minors, defacing property of another, imputed liability of parents, **CC 1714.1**

PAINTS AND PAINTING—Cont'd
Defacing, children and minors, imputed liability of parents, **CC 1714.1**
Lead Base Paint, generally, this index
Malicious destruction of property actions, construction sites, treble damages, **CC 1721**

PANDEMICS
COVID 19, generally, this index

PAPERS
Books and Papers, generally, this index
Negotiable Instruments, generally, this index
Newspapers, generally, this index

PARACHUTE JUMP
Sport parachuting, personal injuries, entry on private land, negligence, **CC 846**

PARAMEDICS
Emergency Medical Technicians, generally, this index

PARENTAL LIABILITY ACT
Generally, **CC 1714.1**

PARENTS ACCOUNTABILITY AND CHILD PROTECTION ACT
Generally, **CC 1798.99.1**

PARK AND PLAYGROUND ACT OF 1909
Parks, generally, this index

PARK TRAILERS
Recreational Vehicles, generally, this index

PARKING
Lots. Parking Lots and Facilities, generally, this index

PARKING LOTS AND FACILITIES
Bailments, contracts, printing and requisites, **CC 1630, 1630.5**
Contracts, printing and requisites, **CC 1630, 1630.5**
Mobilehomes and Mobilehome Parks, generally, this index
Ordinances, bailment contracts, **CC 1630**
Theft, bailment contracts, **CC 1630.5**
Zoning and Planning, generally, this index

PARKS
See, also, Recreation and Recreational Facilities, generally, this index
Community Facilities Districts, generally, this index
Membership camping contracts, **CC 1812.300 et seq.**
Mobilehomes and Mobilehome Parks, generally, this index
Recreational Vehicle Park Occupancy Law, **CC 799.20 et seq.**
Special Occupancy Parks, generally, this index
Waiver, membership camping contracts, **CC 1812.316**

PARKS—Cont'd
Zoning and Planning, generally, this index

PARKS AND RECREATION DEPARTMENT
Parks, generally, this index
Recreation and Recreational Facilities, generally, this index

PAROCHIAL SCHOOLS
Private Schools, generally, this index

PAROL CONTRACTS
Oral contracts. Contracts, this index

PAROLE AND PROBATION
Consumer credit reports, contents of records, **CC 1785.13**
Medical records, disclosure, **CC 56.10**
Probation officers. Mental Health Counselors, generally, this index

PART PERFORMANCE
Debtors and Creditors, this index

PARTIES
Compulsory joinder. Joinder of parties, generally, post
Contempt, generally, this index
Contracts, this index
Deeds and conveyances, acquisition of interest or benefit by stranger, **CC 1085**
Easements, enforcement, **CC 809**
Estate, partition of real estate, **CC 2931a**
Fixtures erroneously affixed to land, removal, **CC 1013.5**
Joinder of parties,
  Agricultural labor liens, **CC 3061.6**
  Identity and identification, theft, **CC 1798.94, 1798.95**
Mortgage foreclosure, state, **CC 2931a**
Permissive joinder. Joinder of parties, generally, ante
State, action to determine conflicting claims of real property, **CC 2931a**
Third Parties, generally, this index
Witnesses, generally, this index

PARTITION
Apportionment, easements, **CC 807**
Condominiums, **CC 4610**
Covenants running with land, undivided interest, **CC 1468**
Easements, **CC 807**
Parties, state, **CC 2931a**
State as party, **CC 2931a**

PARTNER ABUSE
Domestic Violence, generally, this index

PARTNERSHIP
Collection Agencies, generally, this index
Commercial credit reporting agencies, **CC 1785.41 et seq.**
Confidential or privileged information, drivers licenses, electronic devices and equipment, **CC 1798.90.1**

PERSONAL

PARTNERSHIP—Cont'd
Crimes and offenses, drivers licenses, electronic devices and equipment, confidential or privileged information, **CC 1798.90.1**
Dealerships, **CC 80 et seq.**
Domestic Partnership, generally, this index
Drivers licenses, electronic devices and equipment, confidential or privileged information, **CC 1798.90.1**
Fair dealerships, **CC 80 et seq.**
Fines and penalties, drivers licenses, electronic devices and equipment, confidential or privileged information, **CC 1798.90.1**
Identification cards, electronic devices and equipment, confidential or privileged information, **CC 1798.90.1**
Interest, personal injury damages, **CC 3291**
Joint Ventures, generally, this index
Limited partnership, liens and incumbrances, agricultural labor and employment, **CC 3061.5, 3061.6**
Motor vehicles, fees, conditional sales, disclosure, **CC 2982**
Ownership of property, **CC 682**
Personal injury damages, interest, **CC 3291**
Personal Property Brokers, generally, this index
Shared appreciation loans for seniors, **CC 1917.610**

PARTY
Parties, generally, this index

PARTY WALLS
Easements, **CC 801**

PASSENGER RAIL SERVICE
Railroads, this index

PASSENGER SERVICE
Railroads, this index

PASSENGERS
Blind or visually impaired persons, civil rights, **CC 54.1**
Disabled persons, civil rights, **CC 54.1**

PASSING OFF
Fraud, generally, this index

PASSPORTS
Identification, acknowledgments, **CC 1185**

PASTURES
Easements, **CC 801, 802**

PATENTS
Legal Estates Principal and Income Law, **CC 731 et seq.**

PATROL
Highway Patrol, generally, this index
Police, generally, this index

PAY
Compensation and Salaries, generally, this index

PAYMENT
Advances and Advancements, generally, this index
Carriers,
  Fares, passengers, **CC 2187**
  Freightage, time, **CC 2136**
Deeds and conveyances, land sale contracts, prepayment privileges, **CC 2985.6**
Installment Sales, this index
Landlord and Tenant, this index
Mechanics Liens, this index
Money Orders, generally, this index
Prepayment,
  Land sale contracts, **CC 2985.6**
  Mortgages, this index
Receipts, generally, this index
Rental Purchase Agreements, this index
Royalties, generally, this index
Warrants for Payment of Money, generally, this index

PAYMENT PROCESSORS
Fair debt settlement, **CC 1788.300 et seq.**

PAYOFF DEMAND STATEMENTS
Mortgages, this index
Trust Deeds, this index

PAYROLL
Check cashers, fees, **CC 1789.35**

PAYROLL DEDUCTIONS
Compensation and Salaries, generally, this index

PEACE OFFICERS
See, also, Law Enforcement, generally, this index
Actions and proceedings,
  Civil rights, deprivation, **CC 52.3**
  Libel and slander, **CC 47.5**
Arrest, generally, this index
Civil rights, deprivation, actions and proceedings, **CC 52.3**
Complaints, libel and slander, false accusations, **CC 47.5**
Constitutional rights, deprivation, **CC 52.3**
Criminal conduct, allegations against, defamation, action for, **CC 47.5**
Damages, firemans rule, **CC 1714.9**
Discrimination, dogs, public accommodations, emergencies, **CC 54.25**
Dogs, discrimination, public accommodations, emergencies, **CC 54.25**
Duress or coercion, civil rights, privileges and immunities, application of law, **CC 52.1**
Fines and penalties, dogs, discrimination, public accommodations, emergencies, **CC 54.25**
Good faith, arrest, privileges and immunities, **CC 43.55**
Highway Patrol, generally, this index
Injunction, civil rights, deprivation, **CC 52.3**

PEACE OFFICERS—Cont'd
Intimidation, civil rights, privileges and immunities, application of law, **CC 52.1**
Libel and slander, **CC 47.5**
Misconduct, defamation, **CC 47.5**
Police, generally, this index
Privileges and immunities, arrest, **CC 43.55**
Searches and Seizures, generally, this index
Sheriffs, generally, this index
State police. Highway Patrol, generally, this index
Traffic Rules and Regulations, generally, this index

PECUNIARY INTEREST
Conflict of Interest, generally, this index

PEN GUNS
Weapons, generally, this index

PENAL INSTITUTIONS
Correctional Institutions, generally, this index

PENALTIES
Fines and Penalties, generally, this index

PENDING ACTIONS
Generally, **CC 6**
Repeal of statutes, **CC 20**

PENITENTIARIES
Correctional Institutions, generally, this index

PENSIONS
Retirement and Pensions, generally, this index

PERFORMANCE BONDS
Bonds (Officers and Fiduciaries), generally, this index

PERIODICALS
Magazines, generally, this index

PERISHABLE PROPERTY
Agricultural labor liens, **CC 3061.6**
Common carriers, sale for freightage, **CC 2204**
Depositories, sale, goods in danger of perishing, **CC 1837**

PERJURY
Dance studios, bonds (officers and fiduciaries), declaration of gross income, **CC 1812.64**
Electronic Transactions Act, **CC 1633.11**
Mobilehomes and mobilehome parks, disposal, **CC 798.56a**
  Abandonment, **CC 798.61**
Notaries public, certificates and certification, acknowledgments, **CC 1189**
Uniform Electronic Transactions Act, **CC 1633.11**

PERMITS
Licenses and Permits, generally, this index

PERPETUITIES
Rule Against Perpetuities, generally, this index

PERSONAL ATTENDANTS
Domestic Workers, generally, this index

PERSONAL

PERSONAL EMERGENCY RESPONSE UNITS
Home solicitation contracts, **CC 1689.6, 1689.7**

PERSONAL IDENTIFYING INFORMATION
Personal Information, generally, this index

PERSONAL INCOME TAX
Income Tax—State, generally, this index

PERSONAL INFORMATION
Condominiums, homeowners associations, sales, transfers, **CC 5230**
Consumers, privacy, **CC 1798.100 et seq.**
Disclosure, **CC 1798 et seq.**
    Consumers, **CC 1798.100 et seq.**

PERSONAL INJURIES
Abstinence from injuring others, obligation, **CC 1708**
Aircraft, private property, liability, **CC 846**
Children and minors,
    Weapons, discharge, liability for injuries, **CC 1714.3**
    Willful misconduct, parental liability, **CC 1714.1**
Civil defense workers, liability, **CC 1714.5**
Comparative fault, several liability, noneconomic damages, **CC 1431.2**
Contracts, exemption from responsibility, illegal contracts, **CC 1668**
Damages, generally, this index
Defense shelters, exemption from liability, exception, **CC 1714.5**
Disaster service worker, civil defense activities, liabilities, **CC 1714.5**
Emergencies, cardiopulmonary resuscitation, immunity from civil damages, **CC 1714.2**
Emergency medical technicians, liability, **CC 1714.9**
Force to protect from, right to use, **CC 50**
Health Insurance, generally, this index
Hospitals, liens and incumbrances, emergency medical services, **CC 3045.1 et seq.**
Immunity from civil damages, emergency cardiopulmonary resuscitation, **CC 1714.2**
Indemnity,
    Construction, contracts, **CC 2782 et seq.**
    Lessors right under lease, liability for injuries, lessees breach, **CC 1951.2**
Leases, right of lessor to indemnity under, lessees breach, **CC 1951.2**
Liens and incumbrances, hospitals, emergency services, **CC 3045.1 et seq.**
Medical Malpractice, generally, this index
Negligence, generally, this index
Noneconomic damages, several liability, **CC 1431.2**
Paramedics, liability, **CC 1714.9**
Protection from injury, **CC 43**
Punitive damages. Damages, this index
Recreation, entry on private land, negligence, **CC 846**

PERSONAL INJURIES—Cont'd
Sexual harassment, **CC 51.9**
Workers Compensation, generally, this index

PERSONAL PROPERTY
    Generally, **CC 654 et seq., 946 et seq.**
Abandoned or Unclaimed Property, generally, this index
Abstinence from injuring, **CC 1708**
Acquisition, methods, **CC 1000**
Actions and proceedings, conflict of law, **CC 946**
Agents, sale, **CC 2323**
Attachment, generally, this index
Auctions and Auctioneers, generally, this index
Bailment, generally, this index
Borrowing, loan of personal property for use, **CC 1884 et seq.**
Brokers. Personal Property Brokers, generally, this index
Classification, **CC 657, 702**
Community Property, generally, this index
Conflict of laws, **CC 946**
Consolidated cities and counties, safekeeping, powers and duties, **CC 2080.10**
Contracts,
    Exemption from responsibility, illegal contracts, **CC 1668**
    Sales, records and recordation, **CC 1624.5**
Damages,
    Exemption from responsibility, illegal contracts, **CC 1668**
    Illegal contracts, exemption from responsibility, **CC 1668**
    Liquidated damages, leases, **CC 1671**
    Wrongful use of materials, **CC 1033**
Delivery, wrongful possession, **CC 3380**
Diseases, generally, this index
Disposition, personal property remaining on premises at termination of tenancy, **CC 1980 et seq.**
Domicile, conflict of laws, **CC 946**
Elections, between thing and its value, **CC 1032**
Executions, generally, this index
Fixtures, generally, this index
Forcible entry and detainer, return to tenant, **CC 1965**
Foreign states, conflict of law, **CC 946**
Forfeitures, generally, this index
Gifts, Devises and Bequests, generally, this index
Goods, Wares and Merchandise, generally, this index
Hiring of personal property, **CC 1925 et seq., 1955 et seq.**
Hospitals, this index
Hotels and Motels, this index
Improvement or repair,
    Defects, lender liability, **CC 3434**
    Voluntary interference with property, compensation, **CC 2078**

PERSONAL PROPERTY—Cont'd
Increased value, loan for use, **CC 1885**
Innkeepers, injury or loss, **CC 1859**
Inseparable materials, title to property, **CC 1029**
Jurisdiction, conflict of laws, **CC 946**
Landlord and Tenant, this index
Leases, this index
Liens and Incumbrances, generally, this index
Liquidated damages, leases, **CC 1671**
Loans,
    For use of property, **CC 1884 et seq.**
    Improvement or repairs, lenders liability for defective work, **CC 3434**
Materials,
    Several owners, ownership of things made from, **CC 1030**
    Wrongful use, damages, **CC 1033**
Mobilehomes and mobilehome parks, removal, **CC 798.36**
Municipalities, safekeeping, powers and duties, **CC 2080.10**
Negligence, management of property, **CC 1714**
Repair or improvement, lenders liability, **CC 3434**
Nonnegotiable written contract, transfer, **CC 1459**
Oral contracts, **CC 1052**
Partition, generally, this index
Persons authorized to own, **CC 671**
Political subdivisions, safekeeping, powers and duties, **CC 2080.10**
Possession, action to recover, **CC 3379, 3380**
Possibility, interest, transfer, **CC 1045**
Principal part,
    Determination by value or bulk, **CC 1027**
    Separation of lesser but more valuable part, **CC 1026**
Public agencies, safekeeping, powers and duties, **CC 2080.10**
Recorders, generally, this index
Recovery of possession, **CC 3379, 3380**
Rental Purchase Agreements, generally, this index
Repossessors and Repossession, generally, this index
Restoration of thing wrongfully acquired, **CC 1712, 1713**
Rule Against Perpetuities, generally, this index
Sales, generally, this index
Secured Transactions, generally, this index
Seller assisted marketing plans, **CC 1812.200 et seq.**
Separation of lesser but more valuable part, accession, **CC 1026**
Single thing formed from several things, owner of principal part, **CC 1025**
Specific performance, recovery of possession, **CC 3379**
Storage, tenants property remaining on premises at termination of tenancy, disposition, **CC 1965, 1980 et seq.**

PHOTOGRAPHY

PERSONAL PROPERTY—Cont'd
Theft, generally, this index
Title to Property, generally, this index
Transfer of Property, generally, this index
Unclaimed property. Abandoned or Unclaimed Property, generally, this index
Uniting materials and workmanship, accession, CC 1028
Uniting several things, accession by, CC 1025
Use, loan for use, CC 1884 et seq.
Void transfers as against creditors, CC 3440 et seq.
Voluntary interference with property, compensation, CC 2078
Willful trespasser, ownership of thing made, CC 1031
Wills, generally, this index
Workmanship and materials, uniting, CC 1028
Wrongful use of materials, damages, CC 1033

PERSONAL PROPERTY ACCESSION ACT
Generally, CC 1025 et seq.

PERSONAL PROPERTY BROKERS
Finance Lenders, generally, this index
Foreign languages, loans, translations, CC 1632
Loans, foreign languages, translations, CC 1632
Spanish language, contracts, translations, CC 1632

PERSONAL PROPERTY TAXATION
Machinery and equipment, leases, reimbursement, CC 1656.5
Sales and Use Taxes, generally, this index
Use taxes. Sales and Use Taxes, generally, this index

PERSONAL REPRESENTATIVES
Probate Proceedings, this index

PERSONAL RIGHTS
Generally, CC 43 et seq.

PERSONAL SERVICE
Service of process. Process, this index

PERSONAL SERVICES
Consumers Legal Remedies Act, CC 1750 et seq.
Contracts,
  Injunctions to prevent breach, CC 3423
  Specific performance, restrictions against, CC 3390
Injunction, breach of contract, CC 3423
Specific performance, restrictions against, CC 3390

PERSONS WITH DISABILITIES
Disabled Persons, generally, this index

PEST CONTROL
Condominiums, CC 4780, 4785
  Business and commerce, CC 6718, 6720

PEST CONTROL—Cont'd
Landlord and tenant, notice, CC 1940.8, 1940.8.5
Structural pest control,
  Certificates and certification, inspection reports, real estate transfers, CC 1099
  Certified copy, inspection reports, real estate transfers, CC 1099
  Deeds and conveyances, certified copy of inspection report, CC 1099
  Husband and wife, real estate transfers, delivery of certified copy of inspection report, CC 1099
  Inspection and inspectors, reports, real estate transfers, certified copy, CC 1099
  Landlord and tenant, notice, CC 1940.8, 1940.8.5
  Real estate transfers, certified copy of inspection report, CC 1099
  Reports, inspection, certified copy, real estate transfers, CC 1099
  Title to property, transfer, certified copy of inspection report, CC 1099

PESTICIDE REGULATION DEPARTMENT
Pest Control, generally, this index

PESTICIDES
See, also, Pest Control, generally, this index
Landlord and tenant, agricultural products, CC 1940.10

PESTILENCE
Diseases, generally, this index

PESTS
Control. Pest Control, generally, this index

PETIT LARCENY
Theft, generally, this index

PETROLEUM
Oil and Gas, generally, this index

PETROLEUM ENGINEERS
Engineers, generally, this index

PETROLEUM PRODUCTS
Oil and Gas, generally, this index

PETS
Cats, generally, this index
Condominiums, CC 4715
  Business and commerce, CC 6706
Declawing, landlord and tenant, CC 1942.7
Devocalizing, landlord and tenant, CC 1942.7
Dogs, generally, this index
Floating homes, CC 800.43
Landlord and Tenant, this index
Mobilehome parks, fees, CC 798.33

PHARMACEUTICAL COMPANIES
Medical records, confidential or privileged information, CC 56 et seq.

PHARMACISTS
Immunity. Privileges and immunities, generally, post

PHARMACISTS—Cont'd
Malpractice. Medical Malpractice, generally, this index
Medical Malpractice, generally, this index
Negligence. Medical Malpractice, generally, this index
Prescriptions. Drugs and Medicine, this index
Privileges and immunities,
  Professional committee, CC 43.7, 43.8
  Referral services, CC 43.95
Referrals, limitation of liability, CC 43.95
Social security, numbers and numbering, posting, CC 1798.85
Telecommunications, referral services, immunity, CC 43.95

PHIALS
Drugs and Medicine, generally, this index

PHILANTHROPY
Charities, generally, this index

PHONOGRAPHS
Club members, sending after notice of termination, CC 1584.6
Identification number or mark altered or removed, sales, CC 1710.1
Manufacturers identification mark, removal, defacing, alteration or destruction, CC 1710.1

PHOTOGRAPHY AND PICTURES
Advertisements,
  Deceased celebrity image protection, CC 3344.1
  Unauthorized use of photographs, CC 3344
  Use without consent, CC 3344
Arrest, booking, commercial use, CC 1798.91.1
Astaire Celebrity Image Protection Act, CC 3344.1
Attorney fees, invasion of privacy, CC 1708.85
Automated license plate recognition, CC 1798.90.5 et seq.
Booking photographs, commercial use, CC 1798.91.1
Carriers, limitation of liability, CC 2200
Celebrity image protection, CC 3344.1
Confidential or privileged information, invasion of privacy, CC 1708.85
Costs, invasion of privacy, CC 1708.85
Fine prints, sales, CC 1740 et seq.
Injunctions, invasion of privacy, CC 1708.85
Internet, lewdness and obscenity, images, CC 1708.88
Invasion of privacy. Privacy, post
Lewdness and Obscenity, generally, this index
Mobilehomes and mobilehome parks, disposal, CC 798.56a
Motion Pictures, generally, this index
Obscenity. Lewdness and Obscenity, generally, this index
Ownership, works of art, conveyances, CC 988
Pornography. Lewdness and Obscenity, generally, this index

PHOTOGRAPHY

PHOTOGRAPHY AND PICTURES—Cont'd
Privacy, invasion of privacy, **CC 1708.8, 1708.85**
  Advertisements and solicitations, use without consent, **CC 3344**
Sales, fine prints, **CC 1740 et seq.**
Solicitation, use without consent, invasion of privacy, **CC 3344**
Works of art, conveyance of rights, ownership, **CC 988**

PHYSICAL INVASION OF PRIVACY LAW
Generally, **CC 1708.8**

PHYSICAL THERAPISTS
Malpractice. Medical Malpractice, generally, this index
Professional negligence. Medical Malpractice, generally, this index

PHYSICALLY DISABLED PERSONS
Disabled Persons, generally, this index

PHYSICIAN ASSISTANTS
Medical Malpractice, generally, this index

PHYSICIANS AND SURGEONS
  See, also, Medical Care and Treatment, generally, this index
Access, commercial blockade, **CC 3427 et seq.**
Actions and proceedings,
  Medical Malpractice, generally, this index
  Sexual exploitation, **CC 43.93**
Blockade, commercial blockade, **CC 3427 et seq.**
Cannabis. Drugs and Medicine, this index
Chiropractors, generally, this index
Clients, sexual harassment, **CC 51.9**
Clinics, generally, this index
Commercial blockade, **CC 3427 et seq.**
Controlled substances. Drugs and Medicine, generally, this index
Disabled persons, physicians offices, access, **CC 54 et seq.**
Discipline, notice, complaints, **CC 43.96**
Drugs and Medicine, generally, this index
Education, defibrillators, **CC 1714.21**
Evidence, sexual exploitation, **CC 43.93**
Harassment, sexual harassment, clients, **CC 51.9**
Health care liens, **CC 3040**
Health Insurance, generally, this index
Hospitals, privileges and immunities, denial, damages, **CC 43.97**
Immunities. Privileges and immunities, generally, post
Liens and incumbrances, health care liens, **CC 3040**
Malpractice. Medical Malpractice, generally, this index
Medical Malpractice, generally, this index
Medical Records, generally, this index
Medicine. Drugs and Medicine, generally, this index

PHYSICIANS AND SURGEONS—Cont'd
Narcotics. Drugs and Medicine, generally, this index
Negligence. Medical Malpractice, generally, this index
Offices, disabled persons, access, **CC 54 et seq.**
Ophthalmologists, generally, this index
Peer review, medical records,
  Disclosure, **CC 56.10**
  Obtaining, **CC 56.15**
Prescriptions. Drugs and Medicine, this index
Privilege of physician patient, **CC 56 et seq.**
  Malpractice claim, compromise or settlement, authorization to disclose medical information, **CC 56.105**
Privileges and immunities,
  Defibrillators, **CC 1714.21**
  Discipline, complainants, **CC 43.96**
  Health care facilities, denial of staff privileges, **CC 43.97**
  Professional committee, **CC 43.7, 43.8**
  Referral services, **CC 43.95**
  Threats, violent behavior, patients, protection, **CC 43.92**
Protection, threats, violent behavior, patients, privileges and immunities, **CC 43.92**
Psychiatric Technicians, generally, this index
Psychiatrists and Psychiatry, generally, this index
Psychologists and Psychology, generally, this index
Psychotherapists and Psychotherapy, generally, this index
Records and recordation,
  Confidential or privileged information, **CC 56 et seq.**
  Medical Records, generally, this index
Referrals, limitation of liability, **CC 43.95**
Sexual exploitation, **CC 43.93**
Sexual harassment, clients, **CC 51.9**
Telecommunications, referral services, privileges and immunities, **CC 43.95**
Threats, violent behavior, patients, protection, privileges and immunities, **CC 43.92**
Torts, commercial blockade, **CC 3427 et seq.**

PIANOS
Sale, identification number or mark altered or removed, **CC 1710.1**

PICNICS
Private property, entry on, negligence, owner liability for injuries, **CC 846**

PICTURES
Photography and Pictures, generally, this index

PILOT PROGRAMS
Discrimination, business and commerce, safety, recognition, **CC 51.17**

PILOTS
Aircraft, generally, this index

PIPES AND PIPELINES
Oil and Gas Pipelines, generally, this index
Plumbers and Plumbing, generally, this index

PISTOLS
Weapons, generally, this index

PLACE OF TRIAL
Venue, generally, this index

PLAINTIFF
Parties, generally, this index

PLANES
Aircraft, generally, this index

PLANNED UNIT DEVELOPMENTS
  Generally, **CC 4000 et seq.**
Aged persons, cohabitants, **CC 51.3**
Floor area ratio standards, deeds and conveyances, covenants, **CC 4747**
Solar energy, **CC 714.1**
Water conservation, building standards, **CC 1101.1 et seq.**

PLANNING
Zoning and Planning, generally, this index

PLANS AND SPECIFICATIONS
Condominiums, this index
Health Care Service Plans, generally, this index
Land use planning. Zoning and Planning, generally, this index
Zoning and Planning, generally, this index

PLANTS AND PLANT PRODUCTS
Condominiums, landscapes and landscaping, water conservation, **CC 4735**
  Business and commerce, **CC 6712**
Pest Control, generally, this index

PLASTICS
Liens and incumbrances, fabricators, **CC 3051 et seq.**

PLATED WARE
Carriers, limitation of liability, **CC 2200**

PLATES
License plates. Motor Vehicles, this index

PLATFORM LIFTS
Elevators, Dumbwaiters and Escalators, generally, this index

PLATINUM
Carriers, limitation of liability, **CC 2200**

PLAYGROUNDS AND RECREATION CENTERS
Parks, generally, this index

PLEADINGS
Complaints, generally, this index
Conspiracy, attorney and client, **CC 1714.10**
Injunction, generally, this index

POPULAR

PLEDGES
Condominiums, assessments, collections, **CC 5735**
  Business and commerce, **CC 6826**
Motor vehicles, conditional sale contract,
  Corrections, time, **CC 2984**
  Enforcement by pledgee, **CC 2983**
Provisions governing, **CC 2877**
Secured Transactions, generally, this index

PLUG IN VEHICLES
Electric vehicles. Motor Vehicles, this index

PLUMBERS AND PLUMBING
Building standards, water conservation, **CC 1101.1 et seq.**
Community apartments, defects, disclosure, **CC 1134**
Condominiums, defects, disclosure, **CC 1134**
Manufactured housing, warranties, **CC 1797 et seq.**
Stock cooperatives, defects, disclosure, **CC 1134**
Water conservation, building standards, **CC 1101.1 et seq.**

PLURAL NUMBER
Statutory construction, **CC 14**

PODIATRISTS
Discipline, notice, complainants, **CC 43.96**
Immunities. Privileges and immunities, generally, post
Malpractice. Medical Malpractice, generally, this index
Medical Malpractice, generally, this index
Negligence. Medical Malpractice, generally, this index
Notice, discipline, complainants, **CC 43.96**
Privileges and immunities,
  Discipline, complainants, **CC 43.96**
  Health care facilities, denial of staff privileges, **CC 43.97**
  Professional committee, **CC 43.7, 43.8**
  Referral services, **CC 43.95**
Referrals, limitation of liability, **CC 43.95**
Telecommunications, referral services, immunity, **CC 43.95**

POINT OF SALE SYSTEMS
Grocery stores, **CC 7100 et seq.**

POISONS
Pest Control, generally, this index

POLICE
See, also,
  Law Enforcement, generally, this index
  Peace Officers, generally, this index
Actions and proceedings, libel and slander, **CC 47.5**
Arrest, generally, this index
Arson, injuries, liability, **CC 1714.9**
Community Facilities Districts, generally, this index

POLICE—Cont'd
Complaints, libel and slander, false accusations, **CC 47.5**
Consumer credit reporting agencies, reports, blocking information, **CC 1785.16**
Crimes and offenses, false accusations against, defamation, **CC 47.5**
Discrimination, dogs, public accommodations, emergencies, **CC 54.25**
Dogs,
  Biting, exemptions, **CC 3342**
  Discrimination, public accommodations, emergencies, **CC 54.25**
Duress or coercion, civil rights, privileges and immunities, application of law, **CC 52.1**
Fines and penalties, dogs, discrimination, public accommodations, emergencies, **CC 54.25**
Firemans rule, **CC 1714.9**
Good faith, arrest, privileges and immunities, **CC 43.55**
Highway Patrol, generally, this index
Injuries, policemen, liability, **CC 1714.9**
Intimidation, civil rights, privileges and immunities, application of law, **CC 52.1**
Invasion of privacy, **CC 1708.8**
Libel and slander, **CC 47.5**
Lost property, delivery, **CC 2080.1**
Misconduct, false complaints, action for defamation, **CC 47.5**
Personal or confidential information, disclosure by government agencies, Information Practices Act, **CC 1798.24**
Privileges and immunities, arrest, **CC 43.55**
Recreational vehicles, removal of persons from vehicles, **CC 799.58**
Rescue, generally, this index
Searches and Seizures, generally, this index
Threats, civil rights, privileges and immunities, application of law, **CC 52.1**
Traffic Rules and Regulations, generally, this index

POLICIES
Insurance, this index

POLITICAL CAMPAIGNS
Campaigns. Elections, this index

POLITICAL CODE
Construction, 1872 Code, **CC 23 et seq.**

POLITICAL SUBDIVISIONS
Airports and Landing Fields, generally, this index
Cable Television, generally, this index
Civil defense shelters, injuries, liability, **CC 1714.5**
Community Facilities Districts, generally, this index
Conflict of interest, easements, **CC 815.9**
Consolidated Cities and Counties, generally, this index

POLITICAL SUBDIVISIONS—Cont'd
Counties, generally, this index
Defense shelters, injuries, exemption from liability, **CC 1714.5**
Districts, generally, this index
Eminent Domain, generally, this index
Health Facilities, generally, this index
Landing fields. Airports and Landing Fields, generally, this index
Leases, lessors remedy for breach statutes, applicability to invalidate lease, **CC 1952.6**
Local Agencies, generally, this index
Municipalities, generally, this index
Parking Lots and Facilities, generally, this index
Personal property, safekeeping, powers and duties, **CC 2080.10**
Privileges and immunities, defense shelters or other emergency facilities, **CC 1714.5**
Property, safekeeping, powers and duties, **CC 2080.10**
Public Entities, generally, this index
Schools and School Districts, generally, this index
Taxation, generally, this index
War and civil defense, shelters, injuries, liability, **CC 1714.5**

POLITICS
Limitation of actions, political items, sale and manufacture, **CC 1739.4**
Sale and manufacture, political items, **CC 1739 et seq.**
Statute of limitations, political items, sale and manufacture, **CC 1739.4**

POLLUTION
Air Pollution, generally, this index
Hazardous Substances and Waste, generally, this index

PONDS
Lakes and Ponds, generally, this index

POPULAR NAME LAWS
Accession Act,
  Personal property, **CC 1025 et seq.**
  Real property, **CC 1013 et seq.**
Accord and Satisfaction Law, **CC 1521 et seq.**
Add on Act, installment sales, **CC 1801.1 et seq.**
Age Appropriate Design Code Act, **CC 1798. 99.28 et seq.**
Antiheart Balm Statute, **CC 43.5**
Areias Retail Installment Account Full Disclosure Act, **CC 1810.20, 1810.21**
Areias Robbins Charge Card Full Disclosure Act, **CC 1748.10, 1748.11, 1748.20 et seq.**
Astaire Celebrity Image Protection Act, **CC 3344.1**
Automobile Sales Finance Act, **CC 2981 et seq.**

I-167

POPULAR

POPULAR NAME LAWS—Cont'd

Automotive Consumer Notification Act, CC 1793.23, 1793.24
Bankers Lien Statute, CC 3054
Brett Alan Laws Act, firefighters rule, CC 1714.9
Bulk Grain Storage Law, private, CC 1880 et seq.
Business Establishments Act, equal rights, CC 51, 52
Buyers Choice Act, CC 1103.20 et seq.
Celebrity Image Protection Act, CC 3344.1
Civil Code, CC 1 et seq.
Civil Rights Act, CC 51 et seq.
Commercial and Industrial Common Interest Development Act, CC 6500 et seq.
Common Interest Development Open Meeting Act, CC 4900 et seq.
Confidentiality of Medical Information Act, CC 56 et seq.
Construction Related Accessibility Standards Compliance Act, CC 55.51 et seq.
Constructive Invasion of Privacy Law, CC 1708.8
Consumer Contract Awareness Act, CC 1799.200 et seq.
Consumer Credit Reporting Agencies Act, CC 1785.1 et seq.
Consumer Privacy Act, CC 1798.100 et seq.
Consumer Warranty Act, CC 1790 et seq.
Consumers Legal Remedies Act, CC 1750 et seq.
Conveyance Law (real estate), CC 1091 et seq.
Costa Hawkins Rental Housing Act, CC 1954.50 et seq.
Costa Keene Seymour Commercial Property Investment Act, CC 1954.25 et seq.
COVID 19 Small Landlord and Homeowner Relief Act, CC 3273.1 et seq.
Credit Sales Act (Unruh), CC 1801 et seq.
Credit Services Act, CC 1789.10 et seq.
Damage Act, CC 3281 et seq.
Davis Stirling Common Interest Development Act, CC 4000 et seq.
Deep pocket rule, joint and several liability, CC 1431 et seq.
Dog Bite Act, CC 3342, 3342.5
Educational Debt Collection Practices Act, CC 1788.90 et seq.
Electronic Commerce Act, CC 1789 et seq.
Electronic Transactions Act (Uniform Law), CC 1633.1 et seq.
Employment Agency, Employment Counseling and Job Listing Services Act, CC 1812.500 et seq.
Environmental Responsibility Acceptance Act, CC 850 et seq.
Equal Rights Law, CC 51, 52
Fair Dealership Law, CC 80
Fair debt collection practices, CC 1788 et seq.
Fair Debt Settlement Practices Act, CC 1788.300 et seq.

POPULAR NAME LAWS—Cont'd

Firearm Industry Responsibility Act, CC 3273.50 et seq.
Floating Home Residency Law, CC 800 et seq.
Gender Tax Repeal Act, CC 51.6
Genetic Information Privacy Act, CC 56.18 et seq.
Good Neighbor Fence Act, CC 841
Good Samaritan Food Donation Act, CC 1714.25
Greenway Development and Sustainment Act, CC 816.50 et seq.
Heart Balm Statute, CC 43.5
Holden Credit Denial Disclosure Act, CC 1787.1 et seq.
Home Equity Loan Disclosure Act, CC 2970, 2971
Homeowner Bill of Rights, CC 2923.4 et seq.
Identity Theft Resolution Act, CC 1785.16.2, 1788.18
Independent Wholesale Sales Representatives Contractual Relations Act, CC 1738.10 et seq.
Information Practices Act, CC 1798 et seq.
Innkeepers Act, CC 1859 et seq.
Investigative Consumer Reporting Agencies Act, consumer employment or insurance investigation, CC 1786 et seq.
Item Pricing Act, CC 7100 et seq.
Karnette Rental Purchase Act, CC 1812.620 et seq.
Legal Estates Principal and Income Law, CC 731 et seq.
Lemon Law buyback, CC 1793.23, 1793.24
Levering Rees Motor Vehicle Sales and Finance Act, CC 2981 et seq.
Libel and Slander Act, CC 44 et seq.
Lien Law (loggers and lumbermen), CC 3065 et seq.
Loggers Lien Law, CC 3065 et seq.
Lost Money and Goods Law, CC 2080 et seq.
Lumbermen's Lien Law, CC 3065 et seq.
Mobilehome Residency Law, CC 798 et seq.
Online Violence Protection Act, CC 1798.99.20 et seq.
Parental Liability Act, CC 1714.1
Parents Accountability and Child Protection Act, CC 1798.99.1
Personal Property Accession Act, CC 1025 et seq.
Physical Invasion of Privacy Law, CC 1708.8
Privacy Rights Act, CC 1798.100 et seq.
Private Bulk Grain Storage Law, CC 1880 et seq.
Private Student Loan Collections Reform Act, CC 1788.200 et seq.
Protection of Dogs and Cats from Unnecessary Testing Act, CC 1834.9.3
Public Accommodations Act, CC 52
Purchaser and Vendor Risk Act, CC 1662
Ralph Civil Rights Act, CC 51.7, 52
Reader Privacy Act, CC 1798.90, 1798.90.05

POPULAR NAME LAWS—Cont'd

Recordation Law, CC 1213 et seq.
Recreational Vehicle Park Occupancy Law, CC 799.20 et seq.
Rees Levering Motor Vehicle Sales and Finance Act, CC 2981 et seq.
Rental Purchase Act, CC 1812.620 et seq.
Repair and Deduct Act (real estate), CC 1941, 1942
Retail Installment Sales Act, CC 1801 et seq.
Reverse Mortgage Elder Protection Act, CC 1923.2, 1923.5
Rosenthal Fair Debt Collection Practices Act, CC 1788 et seq.
Rosenthal Roberti Item Pricing Act, CC 7100 et seq.
Sales Finance Act (motor vehicles), CC 2981 et seq.
Satisfaction and Accord Act, CC 1521 et seq.
Shared Appreciation Loan Law, CC 1917 et seq.
Single Publication Act, CC 3425.1 et seq.
Slander, CC 44 et seq.
Small Business Gender Discrimination in Services Compliance Act, CC 55.61 et seq.
Solar Rights Act, CC 714
Song Beverly Consumer Warranty Act, CC 1790 et seq.
Song Beverly Credit Card Act, CC 1747 et seq.
Space Flight Liability and Immunity Act, CC 2210 et seq.
Statute of Frauds, CC 1624
Supermarket Club Card Disclosure Act, CC 1749.60 et seq.
Tactical Response to Traumatic Injuries Act, CC 1714.29
Tanner Consumer Protection Act, CC 1793.22
Tenant, Homeowner and Small Landlord Relief and Stabilization Act, CC 798.56, 1942.5, 1946.2, 2924.15, 3273.1 et seq.
Tenant Protection Act, CC 1946.2, 1947.12, 1947.13
Tom Bane Civil Rights Act, CC 52.1
Trade Secrets Act, CC 3426 et seq.
Transitional Housing Participant Misconduct Act, CC 1954.10 et seq.
Transparency in Supply Chains Act, CC 1714.43
Treble Damage Act (timber), CC 3346
Uniform Electronic Transactions Act, CC 1633.1 et seq.
Uniform Single Publication Act, CC 3425.1 et seq.
Uniform Trade Secrets Act, CC 3426 et seq.
Uniform Vendor and Purchaser Risk Act, CC 1662
Uniform Voidable Transactions Act, CC 3439 et seq.
Unruh Act (credit sales), CC 1801 et seq.
Unruh Civil Rights Act, CC 51, 52
Usury Law, CC 1916–1 et seq.

PRIORITIES

POPULAR NAME LAWS—Cont'd
Vacancy Decontrol Law, **CC 1954.50 et seq.**
Vandalism Act, **CC 1714.1**
Vehicle Leasing Act, **CC 2985.7 et seq.**
Vendor and Purchaser Risk Act, **CC 1662**
Voidable Transactions Act, **CC 3439 et seq.**
Willie L. Brown, Jr. Bill Lockyer Civil Liability Reform Act, **CC 1714.45, 2860, 3294, 3295**
Year 2000 Information Disclosure Law, **CC 3269 et seq.**

PORCELAIN
Painting, fine art, **CC 997**

PORNOGRAPHY
Lewdness and Obscenity, generally, this index

POSSESSION
Adverse Possession, generally, this index
Forcible Entry and Detainer, generally, this index
Gifts, devises and bequests, verbal gifts, **CC 1147**
Homeless persons, transitional housing, misconduct, injunctions, **CC 1954.18**
Marketable record title, application of law, **CC 880.240**
Mortgages, this index
Quieting Title, generally, this index
Real Estate, this index

POSSIBILITIES OF REVERTER
Abolition, **CC 885.020**

POSTAL SERVICE
Mail and Mailing, generally, this index

POSTING
Advertisements. Outdoor Advertising, generally, this index
Barbers, prices, discrimination, **CC 51.6**
Cleaning, dyeing and pressing, prices, discrimination, **CC 51.6**
Cosmetology, prices, discrimination, **CC 51.6**
Human trafficking, business and commerce, **CC 52.6**
Languages, discrimination, prices, **CC 51.6**
Mobilehomes and Mobilehome Parks, this index
Outdoor Advertising, generally, this index
Sale to satisfy lien on vehicle, notice, **CC 3072, 3073**
Social security, numbers and numbering, **CC 1798.85**
Tailors, prices, discrimination, **CC 51.6**
Water appropriation, notice, **CC 1415**

POSTSECONDARY EDUCATION
Colleges and Universities, generally, this index

POULTRY AND POULTRY PRODUCTS
Nuisance, activity, operation, facility, **CC 3482.5**

POWER BOATS
Boats and Boating, generally, this index

POWER COMPANIES
Electricity, generally, this index

POWER OF ATTORNEY
See, also, Fiduciaries, generally, this index
Generally, **CC 2400**
Acknowledgments,
Mortgages, **CC 2933**
Revocation, instruments affecting real property, **CC 1216**
Application of law, **CC 2400**
Conditional sales, motor vehicles, **CC 2983.7**
Forms, execution of instruments, **CC 1095**
Mortgages, this index
Personal Property Brokers, generally, this index
Records and recordation, revocation or suspension, instruments affecting real property, **CC 1216**
Retail installment contract, restrictions on provisions, **CC 1804.1**
Revocation or suspension, instruments affecting real property, **CC 1216**
Signatures, execution of instruments, **CC 1095**
Termination, **CC 2357**

POWER OF SALE
Mortgages, this index

POWERS OF TERMINATION
Real estate, marketable title, **CC 885.010 et seq.**

PRACTICE OF LAW
Attorneys, generally, this index

PRECOMPUTED INTEREST
Generally, **CC 1799.5**

PREFABRICATED HOUSING
Manufactured housing. Housing, this index

PREFERENCES
Priorities and Preferences, generally, this index

PREGNANCY
Abortion, generally, this index
Termination. Abortion, generally, this index

PREPAID HEALTH PLANS
Health Care Service Plans, generally, this index

PRESCRIPTIONS
Drugs and Medicine, this index

PRESS
Newspapers, generally, this index

PRESSERS AND PRESSING
Cleaning, Dyeing and Pressing, generally, this index

PRESUMPTIONS
Evidence, this index

PRICE FIXING
Monopolies and Unfair Trade, generally, this index

PRICES
Barbers, posting, discrimination, **CC 51.6**
Cleaning, dyeing and pressing, posting, discrimination, **CC 51.6**
Contracts between credit card issuers and retailers prohibiting lower prices for cash sales, **CC 1748**
Cosmetology, posting, discrimination, **CC 51.6**
Gender tax, repeal, **CC 51.6**
Grocery stores, point of sale systems, **CC 7100 et seq.**
Horses, public auction or sale, purchase for slaughter, notice, **CC 1834.8**
Installment Sales, generally, this index
Sex, discrimination,
Business establishments, services, **CC 51.6**
Small businesses, **CC 55.61 et seq.**
Small businesses, sex, discrimination, **CC 55.61 et seq.**
Tailors, posting, discrimination, **CC 51.6**
Valuation, generally, this index

PRINCIPAL AND ACCESSORY
Accomplices and Accessories, generally, this index

PRINCIPAL AND AGENT
Agents and Agencies, generally, this index

PRINCIPAL AND SURETY
Suretyship and Guaranty, generally, this index

PRINTING
Contracts, interpretation, **CC 1651**
Crimes and offenses, stories about felonies, sale proceeds, **CC 2225**
Installment Sales, this index
Lewdness and Obscenity, generally, this index
Libel and Slander, generally, this index
Obscenity. Lewdness and Obscenity, generally, this index
Outdoor Advertising, generally, this index
Ownership, art works, conveyance of rights, **CC 988**
Pornography. Lewdness and Obscenity, generally, this index

PRINTS
Fine prints, sale, disclosure, **CC 1740 et seq.**
Sale, disclosure, **CC 1740 et seq.**
Works of art, conveyance of rights, ownership, **CC 988**

PRIORITIES AND PREFERENCES
Carriers, acceptance of freight, **CC 2170, 2171**
Debtors and Creditors, this index
Earliest right preferred, **CC 3525**
Innkeepers liens, sales, disposition of proceeds, **CC 1861.24**
Judicial sales, bids and bidding, foreclosure, **CC 2924p**
Landlord and tenant, security deposits, **CC 1950.5**
Liens and Incumbrances, this index

PRIORITIES

PRIORITIES AND PREFERENCES—Cont'd
Livestock service liens, CC 3080.01
Mechanics Liens, this index
Mortgages, this index
Real estate, lien redemption, options, priority, CC 2906
Reverse mortgages, liens, CC 1923.3
Security deposits, rental agreements, CC 1950.5
Telecommunications, messages, order of transmission, CC 2207, 2208
Time, earliest right preferred, CC 3525
Trust Deeds, this index

PRISONS AND PRISONERS
Correctional Institutions, generally, this index
Jails, generally, this index

PRIVACY
Airspace, invasion of privacy, CC 1708.8
Altered depictions, invasion of privacy, lewdness and obscenity, CC 1708.86
Assault and battery, CC 1708.8
Attorney fees, invasion of privacy, altered depictions, lewdness and obscenity, CC 1708.86
Audio and Video Recordings, this index
Automated license plate recognition, CC 1798.90.5 et seq.
Boarding and lodging houses, CC 53.5
Bookstores, CC 1798.90, 1798.90.05
Business and commerce,
  Personal information, security, CC 1798.81.5
  Records, disclosure, bookkeeping services, CC 1799 et seq.
Charter buses, CC 53.5
Condominiums, homeowners associations, records and recordation, inspection and inspectors, CC 5215
Consumer credit reporting agencies, notice, damages, CC 1786.20
Consumers, CC 1798.100 et seq.
Corrections, consumers, personal information, CC 1798.106
Costs, invasion of privacy, altered depictions, lewdness and obscenity, CC 1708.86
Damages, invasion of privacy, CC 1708.8
  Altered depictions, lewdness and obscenity, CC 1708.86
Electricity, usage data, CC 1798.98, 1798.99
Exemplary damages, invasion of privacy, CC 1708.8
Exemptions, medical records, sales, CC 1798.146, 1798.148
False imprisonment, invasion of privacy, CC 1708.8
Fines and penalties, invasion of privacy, CC 1708.8
Genetic testing, CC 56.18 et seq.
Hotels and motels, CC 53.5
Identification devices, subcutaneous implantation, CC 52.7

PRIVACY—Cont'd
Information Practices Act, CC 1798 et seq.
Injunction, invasion of privacy, CC 1708.8, 1708.85
  Altered depictions, lewdness and obscenity, CC 1708.86
Invasion of privacy, CC 1708.8
  Advertisements and solicitations, CC 3344
  Altered depictions, lewdness and obscenity, CC 1708.86
  Bookstores, CC 1798.90, 1798.90.05
  Consumer credit reporting agencies, conditions precedent, CC 1785.32
  Information Practices Act, CC 1798 et seq.
  Investigative consumer reporting agencies, action for damages, CC 1786.52
  Libraries, CC 1798.90, 1798.90.05
  Motion pictures, CC 1708.85
  Photography and Pictures, this index
  Pseudonyms, CC 1708.85
  Reading, CC 1798.90, 1798.90.05
  Uniform Single Publication Act, CC 3425.1 et seq.
Investigative consumer reporting agencies, action for damages, CC 1786.52
Lewdness and obscenity, invasion of privacy, altered depictions, CC 1708.86
Libraries, CC 1798.90, 1798.90.05
Limitation of actions, invasion of privacy, altered depictions, lewdness and obscenity, CC 1708.86
Medical Records, this index
Motels and motor courts, CC 53.5
Motion pictures, invasion of privacy, CC 1708.85
Names, pseudonyms, invasion of privacy, CC 1708.85
Oil and gas, usage data, CC 1798.98, 1798.99
Penalties, invasion of privacy, CC 1708.8
Personal information, consumers, CC 1798.100 et seq.
Photography and Pictures, this index
Police, invasion of privacy, CC 1708.8
Probable cause, consumers, CC 1798.199.50, 1798.199.55
Pseudonyms, invasion of privacy, CC 1708.85
Public officers and employees, invasion of privacy, CC 1708.8
Punitive damages, invasion of privacy, altered depictions, lewdness and obscenity, CC 1708.86
Reading, CC 1798.90, 1798.90.05
Social security, numbers and numbering, posting, CC 1798.85
Subcutaneous implantation, identification devices, CC 52.7
Subpoenas, consumers, CC 1798.199.70

PRIVACY PROTECTION AGENCY
Generally, CC 1798.199.10 et seq.

PRIVACY RIGHTS ACT
Generally, CC 1798.100 et seq.

PRIVATE BULK GRAIN STORAGE
Generally, CC 1880 et seq.
Agricultural Products, this index

PRIVATE COLLEGES AND UNIVERSITIES
Loans, student loans. Colleges and Universities, this index
Student loans. Colleges and Universities, this index

PRIVATE CORPORATIONS
Corporations, generally, this index

PRIVATE SCHOOLS
See, also, Schools and School Districts, generally, this index
Access, buildings and grounds, interference, obstructions, threats, CC 1708.9
Actions and proceedings, buildings and grounds, access, interference, obstructions, threats, CC 1708.9
Attorney fees, buildings and grounds, access, interference, obstructions, threats, CC 1708.9
Buildings and grounds, access, interference, obstructions, threats, CC 1708.9
Computers, purchases, CC 998
Costs, buildings and grounds, access, interference, obstructions, threats, CC 1708.9
Damages, buildings and grounds, access, interference, obstructions, threats, CC 1708.9
Electronic data processing, monopolies and unfair trade, CC 998
Entry, buildings and grounds, interference, obstructions, threats, CC 1708.9
Exceptional children, discrimination, CC 54.1
Exit, buildings and grounds, interference, obstructions, threats, CC 1708.9
Injunction, buildings and grounds, access, interference, obstructions, threats, CC 1708.9
Interference, buildings and grounds, access, obstructions, threats, CC 1708.9
Monopolies and unfair trade, electronic data processing or telecommunications goods, CC 998
Obstructions, buildings and grounds, access, interference, threats, CC 1708.9
Opinion and expert testimony, buildings and grounds, interference, obstructions, threats, CC 1708.9
Purchases, computers or telecommunications equipment, CC 998
Telecommunications goods, monopolies and unfair trade, CC 998

PRIVATE STUDENT LOAN COLLECTIONS REFORM ACT
Generally, CC 1788.200 et seq.

PRIVILEGED COMMUNICATIONS
Confidential or Privileged Information, generally, this index

PROCESS

PRIVILEGES AND IMMUNITIES
Abandoned or unclaimed property, records and recordation, destruction, **CC 1798.84**
Accountants, this index
Agents, anonymous witness program, reports of crime, **CC 48.9**
Agricultural land, charities, gleaning for farm products, damage actions, **CC 846.2**
Alienation of affection, foster homes, **CC 43.56**
Anonymous witness program, **CC 48.9**
Application of law, joint and several liability, **CC 1431.3**
Arrest, peace officers, **CC 43.55**
Art and artists, fine prints, sales, **CC 1744.9**
Attorneys, this index
Cardiopulmonary resuscitation, emergencies, civil damages, **CC 1714.2**
Chiropractors, this index
Computers, year 2000 problem, disclosure, **CC 3269 et seq.**
Consultants, health care service plans, **CC 43.98**
Consumer protection, Internet, children and minors, **CC 1798.99.35**
Consumers, privacy, disclosure, **CC 1798.145**
Debit cards, **CC 1748.31**
Defibrillators, **CC 1714.21**
Dental hygienists, professional committee, **CC 43.7, 43.8**
Dentists and Dentistry, this index
Dietitians, this index
Electronic commercial service providers, **CC 1789.6**
Employees, anonymous witness program, reports of crime, **CC 48.9**
Engineers, this index
Epinephrine auto injectors, **CC 1714.23**
Eyes and eyesight, screenings, charities, **CC 1714.26**
Fine prints, sales, **CC 1744.9**
Food banks, **CC 1714.25**
Geologists and geophysicists, natural hazards, disclosure, residential property, **CC 1103.4**
Hazards, natural hazards, disclosure, residential property, **CC 1103.4**
Health Care Providers, this index
Hospitals, this index
Joint and several liability, **CC 1431.3**
Judicial proceedings, libel and slander, **CC 47**
Land sales contracts, prepayment privileges, **CC 2985.6**
Landlord and tenant, abandoned or unclaimed property, release, **CC 1989**
Lead base paint, abatement, **CC 3494.5**
Libel and Slander, this index
Marriage and Family Therapists, this index
Medical Care and Treatment, this index
Medical records, release, **CC 56.14, 56.36**
Mental health counselors,
    Professional committee, **CC 43.7, 43.8**
    Referral services, **CC 43.95**

PRIVILEGES AND IMMUNITIES—Cont'd
Museums, long term or indefinite loans, disposal or conservation measures, **CC 1899.6**
Natural hazards, disclosure, residential property, **CC 1103.4**
Ophthalmologists, charities, screenings, **CC 1714.26**
Optometrists, this index
Peer review committees, **CC 43.91**
Pharmacists, this index
Physicians and Surgeons, this index
Podiatrists, this index
Prepayment privileges, land sale contracts, **CC 2985.6**
Products liability, consumer products known by consumers to be inherently unsafe, **CC 1714.45**
Professional societies, referral services, **CC 43.95**
Professions and occupations, committee members, **CC 43.7**
Psychologists and Psychology, this index
Railroads, trespassers, **CC 1714.7**
Ranges, shooting ranges, **CC 3482.1**
Real estate, natural hazards, disclosure, residential property, **CC 1103.4**
Real Estate Brokers and Salespersons, this index
Referral services, professional societies, **CC 43.95**
Reports, crime, anonymous witness program, **CC 48.9**
Sexual harassment, libel and slander, **CC 47**
Shooting ranges, **CC 3482.1**
Space flights, **CC 2210 et seq.**
Sport shooting ranges, **CC 3482.1**
Surveys and surveyors, natural hazards, disclosure, residential property, **CC 1103.4**
Trauma kits, first aid, buildings, **CC 1714.29**
Veterinarians, this index
Volunteer firefighters and fire departments, machinery and equipment, gifts, devises and bequests, **CC 1714.11**

PROBABLE CAUSE
Privacy, consumers, **CC 1798.199.50, 1798.199.55**

PROBATE OF WILLS
Probate Proceedings, generally, this index

PROBATE PROCEEDINGS
See, also, Wills, generally, this index
Administrators. Personal representatives, generally, post
Advertisements, mobilehomes and mobilehome parks, **CC 799.1.5**
Art and artists, defacement or destruction of art objects, **CC 987**
Astaire Celebrity Image Protection Act, **CC 3344.1**
Celebrity image protection, **CC 3344.1**

PROBATE PROCEEDINGS—Cont'd
Children and minors, celebrity image protection, **CC 3344.1**
Conservators and Conservatorships, generally, this index
Disclosure, residential property transfers, **CC 1102.2**
Executors and administrators. Personal representatives, generally, post
Fiduciaries. Personal representatives, generally, post
Floating homes, sales to third parties, **CC 800.88**
Freehold, **CC 765**
Guardian and Ward, generally, this index
Medical records, disclosure, conservators and conservatorships, **CC 56.10**
Mobilehomes and mobilehome parks,
    Advertisements, **CC 799.1.5**
    Sales, rights, **CC 798.70 et seq.**
Personal representatives,
    Art works, consignments, **CC 1738 et seq.**
    Foreign mortgages, satisfaction, **CC 2939.5**
    Fraud, **CC 2939.5**
    Harassment, sexual harassment, **CC 51.9**
    Mortgages, satisfaction, foreign executors and administrators, **CC 2939.5**
    Sexual harassment, **CC 51.9**
Property, acquisition, **CC 1000**
Sales, mobilehomes and mobilehome parks, **CC 799.1.5**
Surviving spouse, celebrity image protection, **CC 3344.1**
Undue influence, involuntary trusts, **CC 2223 et seq.**

PROCEEDINGS
Actions and Proceedings, generally, this index

PROCESS
Agent for service of process,
    Credit service organizations, nonresidents, **CC 1789.25**
    Landlord and tenant, multiunit dwellings, disclosure, **CC 1961 et seq.**
Attachment, generally, this index
Collection agencies, communication simulating, **CC 1788.16**
Garnishment, generally, this index
Injunction, generally, this index
Landlord and tenant, disclosure, multiunit dwellings, **CC 1961 et seq.**
Mechanics Liens, this index
Mortgage foreclosure, state as party, **CC 2931a**
Mortgages, beneficiary, service, **CC 2937.7**
Motor Vehicles, this index
Quieting Title, generally, this index
Rescission of contract, notice, **CC 1691**
Service of process,
    Condominiums, this index
    Credit service organizations, nonresidents, **CC 1789.25**

PROCESS

PROCESS—Cont'd
Service of process—Cont'd
  Injunction, modify or dissolve, **CC 3424**
  Innkeepers liens, writs of possession, **CC 1861.18**
  Landlord and tenant, multiunit dwellings, disclosure, **CC 1961 et seq.**
  Mechanics Liens, this index
  Rescission of contract, notice, **CC 1691**
  Writs of possession, innkeepers liens, **CC 1861.18**
Subpoenas, generally, this index
Trust deeds,
  Foreclosure, state as party, **CC 2931a**
  Trustors, service on trustees, **CC 2937.7**

PRODUCE
Agricultural Products, generally, this index

PRODUCERS
Agricultural Products, generally, this index

PRODUCTION OF BOOKS AND PAPERS
Abortion, medical records, conflict of laws, **CC 56.108**
Condominiums, construction, defects, **CC 6000**

PRODUCTS LIABILITY
Cigarettes and cigars, **CC 1714.45**
Common consumer products, application of law, **CC 1714.45**
Inherently unsafe products, application of law, **CC 1714.45**
Privileges and immunities, consumer products known by consumers to be inherently unsafe, **CC 1714.45**
Tobacco and tobacco products, **CC 1714.45**

PROFANITY AND OFFENSIVE LANGUAGE
Collection agencies, use, **CC 1788.11**
Debt collection, use, **CC 1788.11**

PROFESSIONAL ENGINEERS
Engineers, generally, this index

PROFESSIONAL SPORTS
Athletics, generally, this index

PROFESSIONS AND OCCUPATIONS
Accountants, generally, this index
Architects, generally, this index
Attorneys, generally, this index
Automated license plate recognition, **CC 1798.90.5 et seq.**
Barbers, generally, this index
Chiropody. Podiatrists, generally, this index
Chiropractors, generally, this index
Committees, standards, members, privileges and immunities, **CC 43.7**
Contractors, generally, this index
Cosmetology, generally, this index
Debt settlement providers, fair debt settlement, **CC 1788.300 et seq.**
Dentists and Dentistry, generally, this index

PROFESSIONS AND OCCUPATIONS —Cont'd
Electricians. Electricity, generally, this index
Emergency Medical Technicians, generally, this index
Engineers, generally, this index
Harassment, sexual harassment, **CC 51.9**
Health Care Providers, generally, this index
Insurance Agents, Solicitors or Brokers, generally, this index
Investment advisers, liability, **CC 3372**
Landscape Architects, generally, this index
Libel and slander, imputing general disqualification, **CC 46**
Notaries Public, generally, this index
Nurses, generally, this index
Ophthalmologists, generally, this index
Optometrists, generally, this index
Payments, payment processors, fair debt settlement, **CC 1788.300 et seq.**
Pharmacists, generally, this index
Physicians and Surgeons, generally, this index
Plumbers and Plumbing, generally, this index
Podiatrists, generally, this index
Privileges and immunities, standards committee members, **CC 43.7**
Psychiatric Technicians, generally, this index
Psychiatrists and Psychiatry, generally, this index
Psychologists and Psychology, generally, this index
Psychotherapists and Psychotherapy, generally, this index
Referrals, professional societies, limitation of liability, **CC 43.95**
Repossessors and Repossession, generally, this index
Sexual harassment, **CC 51.9**
Social Workers, generally, this index
Veterinarians, generally, this index
Vocational Nursing, generally, this index

PROFIT SHARING PLANS
Accumulation of income, **CC 724**
Income accumulation, **CC 724**

PROFITS
Assignments, real estate, recordation, perfection of security interests, **CC 2938**
Crimes and offenses, stories about felonies, sale proceeds, **CC 2225**
Installment sales, seller and supervised financial organization, sharing, **CC 1801.6**
Records and recordation, real estate, assignments, perfection of security interests, **CC 2938**
Security interests, perfection, real estate, recordation of assignment, **CC 2938**

PROGRESS PAYMENTS
Mechanics Liens, this index

PROMISES
Good consideration, contracts, **CC 1605**

PROMISSORY NOTES
Negotiable Instruments, generally, this index

PROOF
Evidence, generally, this index

PROPERTY
Generally, **CC 654 et seq.**
Art works, conveyance of rights, ownership, **CC 988**
Astaire Celebrity Image Protection Act, **CC 3344.1**
Boundaries, generally, this index
Celebrity image protection, **CC 3344.1**
Classification, **CC 657**
Community Property, generally, this index
Conditions, ownership, **CC 707 et seq.**
Deeds and Conveyances, generally, this index
Exchange of Property, generally, this index
Future Estates or Interests, generally, this index
Identity and identification, theft, **CC 1798.92 et seq.**
Income, generally, this index
Interests in property, **CC 678 et seq.**
Investment advisers, liability, **CC 3372**
Involuntary deposits, **CC 1815 et seq.**
Joint Tenants, generally, this index
Leases, generally, this index
Loan for use, **CC 1884 et seq.**
Lost or Destroyed Property, generally, this index
Partition, generally, this index
Perishable Property, generally, this index
Personal Property, generally, this index
Protection, force, right to use, **CC 50**
Real Estate, generally, this index
Rental Purchase Agreements, generally, this index
Tenancy in Common, generally, this index
Time,
  Creation of limitation, condition or interest, **CC 749**
  Interest as to time, **CC 688**
Title to Property, generally, this index
Transfer of Property, generally, this index
Use, loan for use, **CC 1884 et seq.**

PROPERTY ACQUISITION LAW
Eminent domain, temporary right of entry, repair, reconstruction, **CC 1002**

PROPERTY DAMAGE
Damages, generally, this index

PROPERTY TAXES
Taxation, generally, this index

PROPHYLACTICS
Actions and proceedings, removal, **CC 1708.5**
Removal, actions and proceedings, **CC 1708.5**

PROSECUTING ATTORNEYS
District Attorneys, generally, this index

PUBLIC

PROSECUTORS
District Attorneys, generally, this index

PROSTITUTION
Attorneys fees, injunctions, awarding, CC 3496
Costs, injunctions, awarding, CC 3496
Human Trafficking, generally, this index
Injunction, costs, attorneys fees, awarding, CC 3496
Mobilehomes and mobilehome parks, grounds for termination of tenancy, CC 798.56
Recreational vehicles, parks, defaulting residents, CC 799.70
Trafficking. Human Trafficking, generally, this index

PROTECTION OF DOGS AND CATS FROM UNNECESSARY TESTING ACT
Generally, CC 1834.9.3

PROTECTIVE ORDERS
Orders of Court, this index

PROTESTS
Stalking, CC 1708.7

PROVISIONAL INJUNCTIONS
Generally, CC 3421

PROXIES
Condominiums, homeowners associations, elections, CC 5130

PSYCHIATRIC DISABILITIES
Mental Health, generally, this index

PSYCHIATRIC TECHNICIANS
Abuse, long term health care facilities, temporary employment, CC 1812.543
Criminal history information, long term health care facilities, temporary employment, CC 1812.542
Employment agencies, long term health care facilities, temporary employment, CC 1812.540 et seq.
Long term health care facilities, employment agencies, temporary employment, CC 1812.540 et seq.
Malpractice. Medical Malpractice, generally, this index
Negligence. Medical Malpractice, generally, this index

PSYCHIATRISTS AND PSYCHIATRY
Actions and proceedings, sexual exploitation, CC 43.93
Crimes and offenses, information, intentional disclosure, CC 1798.57
Evidence, sexual exploitation, CC 43.93
Privileges and immunities, threats, violent behavior, patients, protection, CC 43.92
Protection, threats, violent behavior, patients, privileges and immunities, CC 43.92
Sexual exploitation, CC 43.93
Technicians. Psychiatric Technicians, generally, this index

PSYCHIATRISTS AND PSYCHIATRY—Cont'd
Threats, violence, patients, protection, privileges and immunities, CC 43.92

PSYCHOLOGISTS AND PSYCHOLOGY
Actions and proceedings, sexual exploitation, CC 43.93
Evidence, sexual exploitation, CC 43.93
Malpractice. Medical Malpractice, generally, this index
Medical Malpractice, generally, this index
Negligence. Medical Malpractice, generally, this index
Privileges and immunities,
Health care facilities, denial of staff privileges, CC 43.97
Professional organization, CC 43.7, 43.8
Referral services, CC 43.95
Threats, violent behavior, patients, protection, CC 43.92
Professional negligence. Medical Malpractice, generally, this index
Protection, threats, violent behavior, patients, privileges and immunities, CC 43.92
Referrals, services, limitation of liability, CC 43.95
Sexual exploitation, CC 43.93
Telecommunications, referral services, immunity, CC 43.95
Threats, violence, patients, protection, privileges and immunities, CC 43.92

PSYCHOTHERAPISTS AND PSYCHOTHERAPY
Actions and proceedings, sexual exploitation, CC 43.93
Clients, sexual harassment, CC 51.9
Confidential or privileged information, medical records, CC 56.104
Children and minors, noncustodial parents, CC 56.106
Evidence, sexual exploitation, CC 43.93
Harassment, sexual harassment, clients, CC 51.9
Medical records,
Confidential or privileged information, CC 56.104
Children and minors, noncustodial parents, CC 56.106
Disclosure, CC 56.10
Peer review, privileges and immunities, CC 43.7
Privileges and immunities,
Peer review, CC 43.7
Threats, violent behavior, patients, protection, CC 43.92
Protection, threats, violent behavior, patients, privileges and immunities, CC 43.92
Records and recordation. Medical records, generally, ante
Sexual exploitation, CC 43.93
Sexual harassment, clients, CC 51.9

PSYCHOTHERAPISTS AND PSYCHOTHERAPY—Cont'd
Threats, violence, patients, protection, privileges and immunities, CC 43.92

PUBLIC ACCOMMODATIONS
Discrimination, CC 51 et seq.

PUBLIC ACCOUNTANTS
Accountants, generally, this index

PUBLIC AFFAIRS
Invasion of privacy, use of name, photograph, likeness, voice or signature, without consent, CC 3344

PUBLIC AGENCIES
Adverse possession, exemption from claims, CC 1007
Civil defense shelters, injuries sustained in or upon, liability, CC 1714.5
Confidential or privileged information, disclosure, district attorneys, CC 1798.68
Construction, contracts,
Disputes, CC 1670
Indemnity, CC 2782 et seq.
Contractors, disclosure, CC 3273
Contracts, indemnity, design professionals, CC 2782.8
Deeds and conveyances, interpretation, CC 1069
Defense shelters, injuries, exemption from liability, CC 1714.5
Depositories, generally, this index
Disclosure,
Contractors, CC 3273
District attorneys, CC 1798.68
District attorneys, confidential or privileged information, disclosure, CC 1798.68
Employees. Public Officers and Employees, generally, this index
Identity and identification, contractors, CC 3273
Indemnity,
Construction contracts, CC 2782 et seq.
Contracts, design professionals, CC 2782.8
Information Practices Act, disclosure, district attorneys, CC 1798.68
Leases, lessors remedy for breach, CC 1952.6
Local Agencies, generally, this index
Lost or destroyed property, disposition, adoption of regulations, CC 2080.6
Nuisances, abatement authorized, CC 3494
Officers and employees. Public Officers and Employees, generally, this index
Personal property, safekeeping, powers and duties, CC 2080.10
Property, safekeeping, powers and duties, CC 2080.10
State Agencies, generally, this index
Subdivided Lands, generally, this index
War and national defense, shelters, injuries sustained in or upon, liability, CC 1714.5

PUBLIC

PUBLIC ASSISTANCE
Social Services, generally, this index

PUBLIC AUCTIONS
Auctions and Auctioneers, generally, this index

PUBLIC AUTHORITIES
Authorities, generally, this index

PUBLIC BODIES
Political Subdivisions, generally, this index
Public Agencies, generally, this index

PUBLIC BUILDINGS AND WORKS
Community Facilities Districts, generally, this index
Contracts. State Contracts, generally, this index
Improvements, generally, this index
Mechanics Liens, this index
State Contracts, generally, this index

PUBLIC CALAMITIES
Disasters, generally, this index

PUBLIC CONTRACTS
State Contracts, generally, this index

PUBLIC CORPORATIONS
Architects, contracts, indemnity, CC 2782.8
Engineers, contracts, indemnity, CC 2782.8
Landscape architects, contracts, indemnity, CC 2782.8
Leases, breach statutes, CC 1952.6
Surveys and surveyors, contracts, indemnity, CC 2782.8

PUBLIC EATING PLACES
Restaurants, generally, this index

PUBLIC ENEMIES
Obligations, excuse for prevention of performance, CC 1511

PUBLIC ENTITIES
Commercial property, rent control, CC 1954.25 et seq.
Eminent Domain, generally, this index
Hospitals, liens, medical services rendered due to accident or wrongful act, CC 3045.1 et seq.
Liens and incumbrances, hospital liens, medical services rendered due to accident or wrongful act, CC 3045.1 et seq.
Officers and employees. Public Officers and Employees, generally, this index
Rent control, commercial property, CC 1954.25 et seq.

PUBLIC FUNDS
Funds, generally, this index

PUBLIC HIGHWAYS
Highways and Roads, generally, this index

PUBLIC HOSPITALS
Hospitals, generally, this index

PUBLIC HOUSING
Low and Moderate Income Housing, generally, this index

PUBLIC IMPROVEMENTS
Improvements, generally, this index

PUBLIC INSTRUCTION
Schools and School Districts, generally, this index

PUBLIC LANDS
Adverse possession, exemptions, CC 1007
Easements, greenways, CC 816.50 et seq.
Exemptions, adverse possession, CC 1007
Greenways, easements, CC 816.50 et seq.
Marketable record title, application of law, CC 880.240
Ownership, CC 669, 670
Title to property, marketable record title, application of law, CC 880.240
Water bottoms, state ownership, CC 670

PUBLIC LIBRARIES
Libraries, generally, this index

PUBLIC NOTICE
Advertisements, generally, this index
Notice, generally, this index

PUBLIC NUISANCES
Nuisance, generally, this index

PUBLIC OFFICERS AND EMPLOYEES
Bonds (Officers and Fiduciaries), generally, this index
Bribery and Corruption, generally, this index
Confidential or privileged information, privileged broadcasts and publications, defamation, CC 47
Corruption. Bribery and Corruption, generally, this index
Crimes and offenses. Bribery and Corruption, generally, this index
Deeds and conveyances, interpretation, CC 1069
Drones, emergencies, interference, damages, CC 43.101
Elections, generally, this index
Injunction, prevent exercise of office, CC 3423
Interest, personal injury damages, CC 3291
Invasion of privacy, investigations and investigators, CC 1708.8
Official bonds. Bonds (Officers and Fiduciaries), generally, this index
Privacy, invasion of privacy, investigations and investigators, CC 1708.8
Privileges and immunities,
  Publication and broadcasts, CC 47
  Unmanned aircraft, emergencies, interference, CC 43.101
Recall, generally, this index
State Officers and Employees, generally, this index

PUBLIC PERSONALITIES
Astaire Celebrity Image Protection Act, CC 3344.1

PUBLIC POLICY
Animals, euthanasia, running at large, adoption, CC 1834.4
Collection agencies, CC 1788.1
Conservation easements, CC 815
Consumer credit reporting agencies, CC 1785.1
Contracts, this index
Credit, CC 1785.1
Credit cards, CC 1747.01
Credit services, CC 1789.11
Dance studio contracts, CC 1812.50 et seq.
Deeds and conveyances, contracts for sale of land, prepayment clauses, waiver, CC 2985.6
Discount buying services, CC 1812.100
Easements, conservation easements, CC 815
Electronic commerce, CC 1789
Home solicitation contracts, confession of judgment, CC 1689.12
Indemnity,
  Carriers, CC 2784.5
  Construction contracts, CC 2782
Installment sales, waiver by buyer of law, CC 1801.1
Investigative consumer reporting agencies, CC 1786
Landlord and tenant, assignment and sublease, CC 1995.270
Leases, assignment and sublease, CC 1995.270
Marketable record title, real estate, CC 880.020
Mortgages, CC 1916.12
  Foreclosure consultants, CC 2945
Museums, loans, CC 1899
Real Estate, this index
Rental purchase agreements, CC 1812.621
Song Beverly Consumer Warranty Act, CC 1790.1
Warranties, Song Beverly Consumer Warranty Act, CC 1790.1
Water conservation, building standards, CC 1101.1

PUBLIC PROPERTY
Public Lands, generally, this index

PUBLIC PROSECUTORS
District Attorneys, generally, this index

PUBLIC RECORDS
Records and Recordation, generally, this index

PUBLIC ROADS
Highways and Roads, generally, this index

PUBLIC SAFETY
Safety, generally, this index

PUBLIC SAFETY OFFICERS
Peace Officers, generally, this index

RAILROADS

PUBLIC SCHOOLS
Schools and School Districts, generally, this index

PUBLIC SEALS
Seals, generally, this index

PUBLIC SERVICE CORPORATIONS
Public Utilities, generally, this index

PUBLIC SOCIAL SERVICES
Social Services, generally, this index

PUBLIC STATUTES
Statutes, generally, this index

PUBLIC USE
Eminent Domain, generally, this index

PUBLIC UTILITIES
Adverse possession, exemption from claims, CC 1007
Attorney fees, theft or diversion of services, CC 1882.2
Carriers, generally, this index
Costs, theft or diversion of services, CC 1882.2
Customers, service connection or repairs, time, CC 1722
Damages,
   Service connections or repairs, time, violations, CC 1722
   Theft of services, CC 1882 et seq.
Diversion of services, CC 1882 et seq.
Easements, private citizens, eminent domain, CC 1001
Electricity, generally, this index
Eminent domain, private citizens, easements, CC 1001
Floating homes, separate billing, CC 800.48
Gas. Oil and Gas, generally, this index
Heat and Heating Companies, generally, this index
Injunction, theft or diversion of services, CC 1882.4
Landlord and Tenant, this index
Leases, cutting off public utilities with intent to terminate lease, damages, CC 789.3
Mechanics liens, progress payments, CC 8802
Meters,
   Actions for damages, tampering, CC 1882 et seq.
   Tampering, action for damages, CC 1882 et seq.
Mines and minerals, notice, entry and excavation, mineral rights owners, CC 848
Mobilehomes and Mobilehome Parks, this index
Natural gas. Oil and Gas, generally, this index
Notice, service connections or repairs, time, CC 1722
Oil and Gas, generally, this index
Oil and Gas Pipelines, generally, this index
Pipelines. Oil and Gas Pipelines, generally, this index

PUBLIC UTILITIES—Cont'd
Presumptions, theft or diversion of services, CC 1882.3
Property, adverse possession, exemptions, CC 1007
Railroads, generally, this index
Repairs, time period, CC 1722
Service connection or repairs, time, CC 1722
Solar Energy, generally, this index
Street Railways, generally, this index
Tampering, actions for damages, CC 1882 et seq.
Telecommunications, generally, this index
Theft, services, CC 1882 et seq.
Time,
   Repairs or service connections, CC 1722
   Service connection or repairs, CC 1722
Zoning and Planning, generally, this index

PUBLIC WAYS
Highways and Roads, generally, this index
Streets and Alleys, generally, this index

PUBLIC WELFARE
Social Services, generally, this index

PUBLICATION
Artistic products, CC 983
Inventions or designs, CC 983
Letters and other correspondence, CC 983, 985
Lewdness and Obscenity, generally, this index
Libel and Slander, generally, this index
Museums, notice, injury or loss of property, indefinite or long term loans, CC 1899.7
Obscenity. Lewdness and Obscenity, generally, this index
Pornography. Lewdness and Obscenity, generally, this index
Private writings, CC 985
Voidable transactions, transfer of property, CC 3440.1, 3440.5
   Claim made after date of publication, CC 3440.2
Writings, private, CC 985

PUNISHMENT
Crimes and Offenses, generally, this index
Fines and Penalties, generally, this index

PUNITIVE DAMAGES
Exemplary damages. Damages, this index

PUPILS
Schools and School Districts, generally, this index

PURCHASER
Vendor and Purchaser, generally, this index

PURCHASER AND VENDOR RISK ACT
Generally, CC 1662

PURCHASES
See, also, Sales, generally, this index

PURCHASES—Cont'd
Consumer credit, CC 1788.50 et seq.
Debtors and creditors, CC 1788.50 et seq.
Taxation. Sales and Use Taxes, generally, this index

PURE FOOD AND DRUG LAWS
Drugs and Medicine, generally, this index
Food, generally, this index

QUARRIES
Tenants for years or at will, CC 819
   Limitation of rights, CC 820

QUIET ENJOYMENT
Breach of covenant, damages, CC 3304

QUIETING TITLE
Adverse Possession, generally, this index
Attorney fees, slandering title, CC 880.360
Costs, slandering title, CC 880.360
Damages,
   Breach of agreement to deliver quit claim deed, CC 3306a
   Slandering title, CC 880.360
Occupancy, title by, right to commence or maintain action, CC 1006
Records and recordation, slandering title, CC 880.360
Slandering title, CC 880.360

RACE
Discrimination, generally, this index

RADIO
Television and Radio, generally, this index

RADON GAS
Consumer information, booklets, costs, CC 2079.11
Costs, consumer information booklets, CC 2079.11
Disclosure, real estate transfers, CC 2079.7
Notice, real estate transfers, CC 2079.7
Real estate brokers and salespersons, notice, CC 2079.7

RAIL TRANSIT SYSTEMS
Railroads, generally, this index

RAILROADS
See, also,
   Carriers, generally, this index
   Public Utilities, generally, this index
Abandoned or unclaimed property, storage until freight and charges paid, CC 2081 et seq.
Acceptance of freight, obligation, CC 2169
Actions and proceedings, trespass, trains, recovery for injuries, CC 1714.7
Arrival of freight, notice, CC 2120
Baggage,
   Bicycles carried as luggage, CC 2181
   Delivery, CC 2183
   Injury or loss, limitation on liability, CC 2176, 2178

RAILROADS

RAILROADS—Cont'd
Baggage—Cont'd
  Liability, **CC 2182**
  Liens, **CC 2191**
  Obligation to carry for passengers, **CC 2180**
Bicycles, luggage, **CC 2181**
Blind or visually impaired persons,
  Access to public conveyances, **CC 54 et seq.**
  Civil rights, **CC 54.1**
Care, degree required, freight, **CC 2114**
Charges. Rates and charges, generally, post
Contracts,
  Limitation of liability, **CC 2176**
  Negligence, agreements of exoneration, **CC 2175**
Corporation Taxes, generally, this index
Damages, **CC 2194 et seq.**
  Guide dogs accompanying blind person or trainer, **CC 54.2**
  Limitation on liability, **CC 2176**
  Trespass, recovery for injuries, **CC 1714.7**
Deaf persons, public accommodations, **CC 54.1 et seq.**
Delay, liability, **CC 2196**
Disabled persons,
  Access, **CC 54 et seq.**
  Civil rights, **CC 54.1**
Discrimination in charges or facilities, **CC 2170**
Dogs, disabled persons, **CC 54.1**
Exoneration, invalid agreements, **CC 2175**
Fares. Rates and charges, generally, post
Fraud, exoneration agreements, **CC 2175**
Injunction, disabled persons, denial of access to public conveyances, **CC 55**
Liens and incumbrances, luggage, **CC 2191**
Locomotives, trespassing upon, recovery for injuries, **CC 1714.7**
Luggage. Baggage, generally, ante
Necessary works, right of way, extent, **CC 801.7**
Negligence, **CC 2195**
  Exoneration, agreements, **CC 2175**
  Freight, **CC 2114**
Notice, freight, arrival, **CC 2120**
Overcrowding or overloading, passengers, **CC 2102**
Passenger service,
  Accommodations, **CC 2103**
  Baggage, generally, ante
  Care required, **CC 2100 et seq.**
  Delays, **CC 2104**
  Ejection, failure to pay, **CC 2188, 2190**
  Failure to pay fare, ejection, **CC 2188, 2190**
  Negligence, **CC 2100 et seq.**
  Overcrowding, **CC 2102**
    Exceptions, **CC 2185**
  Payment of fares, **CC 2187**
  Right of way, necessary works, **CC 801.7**
  Rules of conduct, **CC 2186**

RAILROADS—Cont'd
Passenger service—Cont'd
  Seating capacity, **CC 2185**
  Tickets, limitation of liability, **CC 2176**
  Treatment, **CC 2103**
Perishable property, sale for freightage, **CC 2204**
Pest Control, generally, this index
Priorities and preferences, freight, **CC 2170 et seq.**
Rates and charges,
  Failure to pay, ejection of passengers, **CC 2188, 2190**
  Payment by passengers, **CC 2187**
Right of way, necessary works, extent of grant, **CC 801.7**
Safety, passenger service, **CC 2100 et seq.**
Sales, perishable property, freightage, **CC 2204**
Storage, freight, **CC 2120**
  Consignees failure to accept and remove, **CC 2121**
Street Railways, generally, this index
Tariffs. Rates and charges, generally, ante
Taxation. Corporation Taxes, generally, this index
Tolls. Rates and charges, generally, ante
Trespass, personal injuries, **CC 1714.7**
Zoning and Planning, generally, this index

RALPH CIVIL RIGHTS ACT
Generally, **CC 51.7**

RANCHES
Real estate, transfers, notice, **CC 1103.4**

RANGES
Sport shooting ranges, **CC 3482.1**

RATES AND CHARGES
Buses, this index
Carriers, this index
Dance studio lessons, statement in contract, **CC 1812.54**
Delinquency charges, retail installment accounts, **CC 1810.12**
Easements, right of taking, **CC 802**
Electronic commercial service, contracts, **CC 1789.3**
Finance Charge, generally, this index
Floating home marinas, **CC 800.40 et seq.**
Installment accounts, delinquency charges, **CC 1810.12**
Installment Sales, this index
Marinas, floating homes, **CC 800.40 et seq.**
Mortgages, this index
Railroads, this index
Rebates, generally, this index
Trust Deeds, this index
Valuation, generally, this index

RATES AND RATING ORGANIZATIONS
Insurance, this index

RATS
Pest Control, generally, this index

RAZORS
Weapons, generally, this index

READER PRIVACY ACT
Generally, **CC 1798.90, 1798.90.05**

READING
Privacy, **CC 1798.90, 1798.90.05**

REAL ESTATE
Generally, **CC 654 et seq., 755 et seq.**
Abandoned or Unclaimed Property, generally, this index
Abstinence from injuring, **CC 1708**
Access, monuments, surveyors, **CC 846.5**
Accession, Accretion and Avulsion, generally, this index
Accretion. Accession, Accretion and Avulsion, generally, this index
Acquisition, methods, **CC 1000**
Actions and proceedings,
  Damages, generally, post
  HIV, disclosure, **CC 1710.2**
  Slandering title, **CC 880.360**
  Unperformed contracts for sale of land, release, **CC 886.020 et seq.**
Adjoining Landowners, generally, this index
Adverse Possession, generally, this index
Advertisements, restraining right to display sign advertising property for sale, **CC 712, 713**
Agents. Real Estate Brokers and Salespersons, generally, this index
Agricultural Land, generally, this index
Airports and landing fields, transfers, disclosure, **CC 1103.4**
Amendment of disclosures, residential property, sales, **CC 1102.9**
Ancient mortgages, deeds of trust, marketable record title, **CC 882.020 et seq.**
Application of law, **CC 755, 1089, 1102.2**
  Disclosure, **CC 1103.15**
Appraisal and appraisers,
  Bribery and corruption, **CC 1090.5**
  Discrimination, contracts for sale of land, notice, **CC 1102.6g**
  Duress or coercion, **CC 1090.5**
  Extortion, **CC 1090.5**
  Management companies, undue influence, **CC 1090.5**
  Multiple listing service, **CC 1087, 1088**
  Notice, discrimination, contracts for sale of land, **CC 1102.6g**
  Sexual harassment, **CC 51.9**
  Threats, **CC 1090.5**
  Undue influence, **CC 1090.5**
Appraisers. Appraisal and appraisers, generally, ante
Arrangers of credit, disclosures, **CC 2956 et seq.**

REAL

REAL ESTATE—Cont'd
Asbestos, notice, **CC 2079.7**
Assignments,
  Power of sale, mortgages, **CC 2932.5**
  Rents or profits, perfection of security interests, recordation, **CC 2938**
Attorney fees,
  Developers, controlled escrows, **CC 2995**
  Escrows and escrow agents, sales, return of escrow, **CC 1057.3**
  Sales contracts, Subdivision Map Act, noncompliance, **CC 2985.51**
  Slandering title, **CC 880.360**
Auctions and Auctioneers, generally, this index
Avulsion. Accession, Accretion and Avulsion, generally, this index
Blind or visually impaired persons, discrimination, **CC 53**
Boundaries, generally, this index
Bribery and corruption, appraisal and appraisers, **CC 1090.5**
Brokers. Real Estate Brokers and Salespersons, generally, this index
Burden of proof, notice of intent to preserve interest, presumption, **CC 880.310**
Business and commerce,
  Earthquakes, safety, owners guide, **CC 2079.9**
  Rent control, **CC 1954.25 et seq.**
Buyers or prospective buyers, residential property, reasonable care, **CC 2079.5**
Certificates and certification, sales contracts, conditional certificate of compliance, **CC 2985.51**
Chemical storage tanks, notice, **CC 2079.7**
Classification, **CC 657**
  Interests, **CC 701**
Closings, home roof warranties, disclosure, **CC 1797.96**
Coercion, appraisal and appraisers, **CC 1090.5**
Community Development and Housing, generally, this index
Community Property, generally, this index
Conflict of interest, developers, controlled escrows, **CC 2995**
Conflict of laws, laws governing, **CC 755**
Consent to use, notice, **CC 813**
Construction loans, defects in property, lenders liability, **CC 3434**
Consumer credit reporting agencies, records, application of law, **CC 1785.35**
Contracts, fraud or willful injury, exemption from responsibility, illegal contracts, **CC 1668**
Contracts for sale of land. Deeds and Conveyances, this index
Conveyances. Deeds and Conveyances, generally, this index
Corruption, appraisal and appraisers, **CC 1090.5**
Costs,
  Developers, controlled escrows, **CC 2995**

REAL ESTATE—Cont'd
Costs—Cont'd
  Sales contracts, Subdivision Map Act, noncompliance, **CC 2985.51**
  Slandering title, **CC 880.360**
Covenants. Deeds and Conveyances, this index
Covenants Running with Land, generally, this index
Credit arrangers, disclosure, **CC 2956 et seq.**
Crimes and offenses, injury or death, criminals, liability, **CC 847**
Damages,
  Contracts, breach, **CC 3306, 3307**
  Developers, controlled escrows, **CC 2995**
  Disclosures upon transfers of residential property, liability for transferring without, **CC 1102.13**
  Escrows and escrow agents, purchases and sales, return, **CC 1057.3**
  Exemption from responsibility, illegal contracts, **CC 1668**
  Holding over, **CC 3335**
  Liquidated damages, default on purchase contracts, **CC 1675 et seq.**
  Natural hazards, disclosure, residential property, **CC 1103.13**
  Purchases, breach of agreement to purchase, **CC 3307**
  Slandering title, **CC 880.360**
  Subdivision Map Act, noncompliance, sales contracts, **CC 2985.51**
  Wrongful occupation, **CC 3334**
Death, disclosure, **CC 1710.2**
Declarations, restrictions, limitation of actions, **CC 784**
Deeds and Conveyances, generally, this index
Default, purchase contracts, liquidated damages, **CC 1675 et seq.**
Delivery,
  Disclosures, residential property sales, **CC 1102.10**
  Natural hazard disclosure statement, residential property, **CC 1103.10**
Description, consolidated description, single instrument of conveyance, **CC 1093**
Developments,
  Commercial property, rent control, **CC 1954.25 et seq.**
  Controlled escrows, **CC 2995**
Disabled persons, discrimination, **CC 53**
Disclosure,
  Arrangers of credit, **CC 2956 et seq.**
  Credit analysis, **CC 2956 et seq.**
  Death, **CC 1710.2**
  Environmental hazards, **CC 2079.7**
  Residential property transfer, **CC 1102 et seq.**
  Transfers, residential property, **CC 1102 et seq.**
Discrimination, **CC 53, 782, 782.5**
  Racial restrictions, deeds, **CC 782, 782.5**

REAL ESTATE—Cont'd
Duress or coercion, appraisal and appraisers, **CC 1090.5**
Earnest money, escrows, return, **CC 1057.3**
Earthquakes,
  Commercial property owners guide to earthquake safety, **CC 2079.9**
Disclosure,
  Residential property, **CC 1103 et seq.**
  Statements, **CC 1103.2 et seq.**
Easements, generally, this index
Eminent Domain, generally, this index
Entry on Property, generally, this index
Environmental hazards, notice, **CC 2079.7**
Equity. Home Equity Sales Contracts, generally, this index
Errors, inaccuracies, or omissions, disclosure statements, residential property, **CC 1102.4**
Escrows and Escrow Agents, this index
Estates, generally, this index
Executions, generally, this index
Exemptions, natural hazards, residential property, disclosure, **CC 1103.1**
Explosives, former federal or state ordnance locations, residential property, disclosure statements, **CC 1102.15**
Extortion, appraisal and appraisers, **CC 1090.5**
Fee Simple, generally, this index
Fences, generally, this index
Fines and penalties, sales, contracts, **CC 2985.2, 2985.3**
Fires and fire protection, disclosure, residential property, **CC 1103 et seq.**
Fixtures, generally, this index
Floods and flooding, disclosure, residential property, **CC 1103 et seq.**
For sale signs, restraints on alienation, **CC 712**
Forcible Entry and Detainer, generally, this index
Foreclosure, generally, this index
Foreign languages, loans, translations, **CC 1632**
Forest Fires, this index
Formaldehyde, notice, **CC 2079.7**
Former federal or state ordnance locations, residential property sales, disclosures, **CC 1102.15**
Forms,
  Contracts, **CC 2985.5**
  Disclosures upon transfer of residential property, **CC 1102.6, 1102.6a**
  Notice of intent to preserve interest in real property, marketable record title, **CC 880.340**
Fraud, natural hazards, disclosure, residential property, **CC 1103.8**
Frauds, statute of, **CC 1624**
Fuel and chemical storage tanks, notice, **CC 2079.7**

REAL

REAL ESTATE—Cont'd
Future Estates or Interests, generally, this index
Hazards, natural hazards, disclosure, residential property, CC 1103 et seq.
HIV, disclosure, actions and proceedings, CC 1710.2
Home Equity Sales Contracts, generally, this index
Home roof warranties, CC 1797.90 et seq.
Home solicitation contracts, fixtures, cancellation, CC 1689.9
Housing, generally, this index
Husband and wife. Community Property, generally, this index
Improvements, generally, this index
Information subsequently rendered inaccurate, disclosure statements, residential property, CC 1102.5
Inspection and inspectors,
  Residential property transfers, disclosure, CC 1102.6, 1102.6a
  Secured lenders, environmentally impaired property, CC 2929.5
Instruments of title, ownership, CC 994
Insurance, sales, contracts, impound accounts, CC 2954, 2955
Interest,
  Breach of contract to convey, damages, CC 3306, 3307
  Sales, variable rates, CC 1916.5
  Undivided interest, right to partition or sell, CC 1468
Internet, sales, sex offenses, registration, notice, CC 2079.10a
Joint Tenants, generally, this index
Landlord and Tenant, generally, this index
Law governing, CC 755
Lead based paint, notice, CC 2079.7
Leases, generally, this index
Legal Estates Principal and Income Law, CC 731 et seq.
Liability, residential property transfer disclosures, willful or negligent violations, CC 1102.13
Liens and Incumbrances, generally, this index
Life Estates, generally, this index
Liquidated damages, default on purchase contracts, CC 1675 et seq.
Loans,
  Construction or repairs, lenders liability for defects, CC 3434
  Credit scores, notice, CC 1785.15.1, 1785.15.2, 1785.20.2
  Foreign languages, translations, CC 1632
  Notice, credit scores, CC 1785.15.1, 1785.15.2, 1785.20.2
  Risk scores, notice, CC 1785.15.1, 1785.15.2, 1785.20.2
  Shared Appreciation Loans, generally, this index
  Spanish language, contracts, translations, CC 1632

REAL ESTATE—Cont'd
Mail and mailing,
  Disclosures, residential property sales, CC 1102.10
  Registered mail, notice of consent to use of land, CC 813
Management companies, appraisal and appraisers, undue influence, CC 1090.5
Marketable record title, CC 880.020 et seq.
Mechanics Liens, generally, this index
Merger, separate parcels, single instrument of conveyance or consolidated description, CC 1093
Mines and minerals, sales, disclosure, CC 1103.4
Monuments and memorials, surveyors access to, CC 846.5
Mortgages, generally, this index
Motor vehicles, conditional sale contract, title to or lien on real estate, CC 2984.2
Natural hazards, disclosure, residential property, CC 1103 et seq.
Negligence, management of property, CC 1714
Noncitizens, ownership, CC 671
Notice,
  Consent to use of land, CC 813
  Environmental hazards, CC 2079.7
  Mineral rights, entry and excavation, CC 848
  Preservation of interest, recording, CC 880.310 et seq.
  Title insurance, escrow transactions, CC 1057.6
  Unexercised purchase options, expiration, marketable title, CC 884.020
Occupancy, title by, extent, CC 1006
Offers to purchase, disclosure statements, termination, CC 1102.3
Options to purchase,
  Disclosure, CC 1102 et seq.
  Purchase, unexercised, marketable title, CC 884.010 et seq.
  Secured parties, redemption, priority, CC 2906
  Unexercised, marketable record title, CC 884.010 et seq.
Ordinances, signs, sale or lease, CC 713
Ordnance locations, federal or state, former sites, residential property sales, CC 1102.15
Outdoor advertising, sales, restraints on alienation, CC 712
Partition, generally, this index
Permission for public use, recorded notice, CC 813
Persons authorized to own, CC 671
Pest Control, generally, this index
Portable signs, sales, right of way, CC 713
Possession,
  Forcible Entry and Detainer, generally, this index
  Marketable record title, application of law, CC 880.240

REAL ESTATE—Cont'd
Possession—Cont'd
  Willful holding over, damages, CC 3335
  Wrongful occupation, damages, CC 3334
Power of sale, assignment, CC 2932.5
Powers of termination, marketable title, CC 885.010 et seq.
Preservation of interest, notice, recording, CC 880.310 et seq.
Presumptions, fee simple title, CC 1105
Privileges and immunities, natural hazards, disclosure, residential property, CC 1103.4
Proceedings. Actions and proceedings, generally, ante
Profits, assignments, recordation, perfection of security interests, CC 2938
Public improvements. Improvements, generally, this index
Public Lands, generally, this index
Public policy,
  Commercial property, rent control, CC 1954.25
  Conservation easements, CC 815
  Disclosure statements, residential property, CC 1102.1
  Marketable record title, CC 880.020
Public recreational use of private property, supplementing tax supported publicly owned facilities, CC 1009
Purchases. Sales, generally, post
Quieting Title, generally, this index
Radon gas, notice, CC 2079.7
Ranches, transfers, notice, CC 1103.4
Recorders, generally, this index
Records and Recordation, generally, this index
Redemption, generally, this index
Registered mail, notice of consent to use of land, CC 813
Release, unperformed contracts for sale of property, CC 886.020 et seq.
Rent, generally, this index
Reports, inspection reports, disclosures, CC 1102.6
Rescission rights of buyers, CC 1102.6
Residential property, disclosures upon transfer, CC 1102 et seq.
Restraints on alienation, for sale signs, CC 712
Restrictions,
  Limitation of actions, CC 784
  Race, color, religion or national origin, CC 53
Reverse mortgages, CC 1923 et seq.
  Translations, CC 1632
Right of Way, generally, this index
Roof warranties, CC 1797.90 et seq.
Rule Against Perpetuities, generally, this index
Safety of premises, entry for fishing, hunting, camping, CC 846
Sales,
  Agreements subject to statute of frauds, CC 1624

REAL

REAL ESTATE—Cont'd
Sales—Cont'd
  Airports and landing fields, disclosure, **CC 1103.4**
  Assessments, contracts, community facilities, disclosure, **CC 1102.6b**
  Assignment of power, **CC 2932.5**
  Breach of contract,
    Purchase, **CC 3307**
    Quitclaim deed, failure to execute and deliver, **CC 3306a**
  Commercial property owners guide to earthquake safety, **CC 2079.9**
  Community facilities, special tax liens, disclosure, **CC 1102.6b**
  Contracts, default, **CC 3307**
    Liquidated damages, **CC 1675 et seq.**
  Contracts for sale of land. Deeds and Conveyances, this index
  Costs, home energy rating program, information, **CC 2079.11**
  Credit arrangers, disclosure, **CC 2956 et seq.**
  Death of occupant, disclosure, **CC 1710.2**
  Disclosure, transfer of residential property, **CC 1102 et seq.**
  Earthquakes, disclosure, statements, **CC 1103.2 et seq.**
  Escrows and escrow agents, return, **CC 1057.3**
  HIV, disclosure, **CC 1710.2**
  Home energy rating program, information, **CC 2079.10**
    Costs, **CC 2079.11**
  Home Equity Sales Contracts, generally, this index
  Internet, sex offenses, registration, notice, **CC 2079.10a**
  Marketable record title, **CC 880.020 et seq.**
  Mines and minerals, disclosure, **CC 1103.4**
  Notice,
    Intention, **CC 1103.4**
    Registered sex offenders, data base, **CC 2079.10a**
  Options to purchase, unexercised, marketable record title, **CC 884.010 et seq.**
  Portable signs, right of way, **CC 713**
  Power in instrument to secure payment, assignment, effect, **CC 2932.5**
  Public policy, marketable record title, **CC 880.020**
  Registered sex offenders, data base, notice, **CC 2079.10a**
  San Francisco Bay area, restrictions, notice, **CC 1103.4**
  Sex offenses, registration, data base, notice, **CC 2079.10a**
  Signs, **CC 713**
    Restraints on alienation, **CC 712**
  Supplemental tax assessments, disclosure, **CC 1102.6c**
  Temporary signs, right of way, **CC 713**

REAL ESTATE—Cont'd
Sales—Cont'd
  Unperformed contracts for, marketable title, **CC 886.010 et seq.**
Salespersons. Real Estate Brokers and Salespersons, generally, this index
San Francisco Bay area, sales, restrictions, notice, **CC 1103.4**
School Buildings and Grounds, generally, this index
Secured Transactions, this index
Securities, **CC 2953.1 et seq.**
Security, window bars, disclosure, **CC 1102.16**
Security interest, assignment of profits or rent, recordation, perfection of security interest, **CC 2938**
Sex discrimination, **CC 53**
Shared Appreciation Loans, generally, this index
Signs, sale or lease, display, **CC 712, 713**
Skimming of rent, residential property, **CC 890 et seq.**
Slandering title, **CC 880.360**
Soil and water contamination, notice, **CC 2079.7**
Solar Energy Act, **CC 714**
Specific Performance, this index
State lands. Public Lands, generally, this index
Statements, natural hazard disclosure statement, **CC 1103.2 et seq.**
Statute of Frauds, **CC 1624**
Structural pest control, inspection reports, certificates, **CC 1099**
Subdivided Lands, generally, this index
Substituted disclosures, **CC 1102.6**
Suits. Actions and proceedings, generally, ante
Supplemental tax assessments. Tax Assessments, this index
Surveys and Surveyors, generally, this index
Taxation, generally, this index
Temporary signs, sales, right of way, **CC 713**
Tenancy at will, **CC 761, 819**
Tenancy for years, **CC 761, 819**
Tenancy in Common, generally, this index
Third parties, natural hazard disclosure statement, **CC 1103.2 et seq.**
Threats, appraisal and appraisers, **CC 1090.5**
Time,
  Ancient mortgages, marketable record title, **CC 882.020 et seq.**
  Disclosure statements, transfers, **CC 1102.3**
  Future Estates or Interests, generally, this index
Title Insurance, generally, this index
Title to Property, generally, this index
Transfers. Deeds and Conveyances, generally, this index
Trust Deeds, generally, this index
Unclaimed property. Abandoned or Unclaimed Property, generally, this index
Undivided interests, right to partition or sell, **CC 1468**

REAL ESTATE—Cont'd
Undue influence, appraisal and appraisers, **CC 1090.5**
Unexercised options, purchase, marketable record title, **CC 884.010 et seq.**
Uniform Vendor and Purchaser Risk Act, **CC 1662**
Unperformed contracts for sale of, marketable title, **CC 886.010**
Valuation. Appraisal and appraisers, generally, ante
Vendor and Purchaser Risk Act, **CC 1662**
Waiver, transfers, disclosure requirements, **CC 1102**
Warranties, home roof warranties, **CC 1797.90 et seq.**
Water and soil contamination, notice, **CC 2079.7**
Water conservation, building standards, disclosure, **CC 1102.155**
Window security bars, residential property, disclosure, **CC 1102.16**
Written instruments. Deeds and Conveyances, generally, this index
Wrongful occupation, damages, **CC 3334**
Zoning and Planning, generally, this index

REAL ESTATE APPRAISERS
Appraisal and appraisers. Real Estate, this index

REAL ESTATE BROKERS AND SALESPERSONS
Actions and proceedings,
  HIV, disclosure, **CC 1710.2**
  Peer review committees, privileges and immunities, **CC 43.91**
Agency,
  Listings, **CC 1086 et seq.**
  Residential property, **CC 2079.12 et seq.**
Application of law, **CC 1089, 2079.25**
Appraisal and appraisers. Real Estate, this index
Arrangements, transient occupancies, records and account books, **CC 1864**
Arrangers of credit, disclosure, **CC 2956 et seq.**
Asbestos, notice, **CC 2079.7**
Books and papers, transient occupancies, **CC 1864**
Care, standard of care, duty to prospective purchasers of residential property, **CC 2079.2**
Chemical storage tanks, notice, **CC 2079.7**
Clients, sexual harassment, **CC 51.9**
Commercial property, disclosure, agency, **CC 2079.12 et seq.**
Committees, peer review committees, privileges and immunities, **CC 43.91**
Compensation and salaries, agency, residential property, **CC 2079.19**
Conflict of interest, agency, residential property, **CC 2079.12 et seq.**

REAL

REAL ESTATE BROKERS AND SALESPERSONS—Cont'd
Contracts,
  Agency contracts, modification or alteration, **CC 2079.23**
  Employment contract, Statute of Frauds, **CC 1624**
Credit arrangers, disclosure, **CC 2956 et seq.**
Damages,
  Disclosure requirements, willful or negligent violations, **CC 1102.13**
  Peer review committees, privileges and immunities, **CC 43.91**
Death, disclosure, **CC 1710.2**
Disclosure,
  Agency, residential property, **CC 2079.12 et seq.**
  Arrangers of credit, **CC 2956 et seq.**
  Commercial property, agency, **CC 2079.12 et seq.**
  Death, **CC 1710.2**
  Dual agents, residential property, **CC 2079.12 et seq.**
  Duty to prospective purchasers of residential property, **CC 2079 et seq.**
  Environmental hazards, **CC 2079.7**
  Residential property transfers, **CC 1102 et seq.**
Dual agency, **CC 2079.21**
  Residential property, **CC 2079.12 et seq.**
Duty to prospective purchaser of residential property, **CC 2079 et seq.**
Environmental hazards, notice, **CC 2079.7**
Escrows and escrow agents, return, **CC 1057.3**
Exemptions, natural hazards, residential property, disclosure, **CC 1103.1**
Fiduciaries, duties, **CC 2079.24**
Formaldehyde, notice, **CC 2079.7**
Forms, agency, disclosure, residential property, **CC 2079.14, 2079.16**
Frauds, statute of, employment contracts, **CC 1624**
Fuel and chemical storage tanks, notice, **CC 2079.7**
Harassment, sexual harassment, clients, **CC 51.9**
Hazards,
  Environmental hazards, notice, **CC 2079.7**
  Natural hazards, disclosure, residential property, **CC 1103 et seq.**
HIV, actions and proceedings, disclosure, **CC 1710.2**
Home equity sales contracts, equity purchasers, liability, **CC 1695.15 et seq.**
Indemnity, agency contracts, modification or alteration, **CC 2079.23**
Inspection and inspectors,
  Duty to prospective purchaser of residential property, **CC 2079 et seq.**
  Residential property, disclosures upon transfer, **CC 1102.6, 1102.6a**
Lead base paint, notice, **CC 2079.7**

REAL ESTATE BROKERS AND SALESPERSONS—Cont'd
Leases, application of law, duty to prospective purchasers of residential property, **CC 2079.1**
Liability, residential property transfer disclosures, willful or negligent violations, **CC 1102.13**
Licenses and permits,
  Inspection, title or use of property, **CC 2079.3**
  Qualifications, peer review committees, privileges and immunities, **CC 43.91**
Limitation of actions, duty to prospective purchaser of residential property, **CC 2079.4**
Listings, agency, **CC 1086 et seq.**
  Residential property, **CC 2079.12 et seq.**
Loans, usury, **CC 1916.1**
Manufactured housing, **CC 2079 et seq.**
Multiple listing service, **CC 1087, 1088**
Natural hazards, disclosure, residential property, **CC 1103 et seq.**
Notice, environmental hazards, **CC 2079.7**
Peer review committees, privileges and immunities, **CC 43.91**
Privileges and immunities,
  Death, occupants, disclosure, **CC 1710.2**
  Disclosure statements, residential property, errors, inaccuracies, or omissions, **CC 1102.4**
  Natural hazards, disclosure, residential property, **CC 1103.4**
  Peer review committees, **CC 43.91**
Professional conduct standards, **CC 2079**
Radon gas, notice, **CC 2079.7**
Records and recordation,
  Inspection and inspectors, **CC 2079.3**
  Natural hazards, disclosure, residential property, **CC 1103.12**
  Residential property transfer disclosures, **CC 1102.12**
  Transient occupancies, **CC 1864**
Residential property, agency, **CC 2079.12 et seq.**
Selling agents, residential property, **CC 2079.12 et seq.**
Sexual harassment, clients, **CC 51.9**
Signs, sale or lease, display, **CC 712, 713**
Soil and water contamination, notice, **CC 2079.7**
Solicitation, transient occupancies, records and account books, **CC 1864**
Standard of care, residential property, prospective purchasers, **CC 2079.2**
Standards,
  Peer review committees, privileges and immunities, **CC 43.91**
  Professional conduct, **CC 2079**
Statute of Frauds, employment contracts, **CC 1624**
Transient occupancies, records and account books, **CC 1864**

REAL ESTATE BROKERS AND SALESPERSONS—Cont'd
Usury, loans, **CC 1916.1**
Water and soil contamination, notice, **CC 2079.7**

REAL ESTATE INVESTMENT TRUSTS
Corporation Taxes, generally, this index

REAL PROPERTY
Real Estate, generally, this index

REAL PROPERTY SECURITY INSTRUMENT
Generally, **CC 2953.1 et seq.**

REBATES
Consumers Legal Remedies Act, **CC 1750 et seq.**
Installment sales, unlawful inducement, **CC 1803.10**
Mortgages, **CC 2924d**
Trust deeds, **CC 2924d**
Unfair trade practices, Consumers Legal Remedies Act, **CC 1750 et seq.**

RECALL
Mobilehomes and mobilehome parks, signs and signals, **CC 798.51, 799.10**
Signs and signals, mobilehomes and mobilehome parks, **CC 798.51, 799.10**

RECEIPTS
Consumer credit, purchases, **CC 1788.54**
Debit cards, accounts and accounting, numbers and numbering, printing, **CC 1747.09**
Debtor right to for property delivered in performance of obligation, **CC 1499**

RECEIVERS AND RECEIVERSHIP
Leases, lessor initiating appointment, terminating breaching lessees right to possess, **CC 1951.4**
Voidable transactions, **CC 3439.07**

RECEIVING STOLEN GOODS
Exemptions, **CC 1712**
Notice, restoration of property, **CC 1713**
Restoration of property, **CC 1712**

RECIDIVISTS
Second and subsequent offenses. Crimes and Offenses, this index

RECLAIMED GOODS
Misrepresentation, Consumers Legal Remedies Act, **CC 1750 et seq.**

RECORDATION LAW
Generally, **CC 1213 et seq.**

RECORDERS
Conveyances. Deeds and Conveyances, generally, this index
Deeds and Conveyances, generally, this index
Duties, **CC 1172**
Mechanics liens, **CC 8060**

I-180

RECORDERS—Cont'd
Social security, numbers and numbering, truncation, **CC 1798.89**

RECORDING DEVICES
Audio and Video Recordings, generally, this index

RECORDS AND RECORDATION
Generally, **CC 1169 et seq.**
Access, information practices, **CC 1798 et seq.**
Ancient mortgages, deeds of trust, marketable record title, **CC 882.020 et seq.**
Audio and Video Recordings, generally, this index
Bona fide purchasers, prior recording, effect, **CC 1214**
Bookkeeping services, disclosure, **CC 1799 et seq.**
Burned or destroyed records and documents. Lost or Destroyed Documents, generally, this index
Business Records, generally, this index
Certified copies,
　Defectively executed instruments, effect, **CC 1207**
　Recording in other counties, **CC 1218**
Condominiums, this index
Confidential or Privileged Information, generally, this index
Constructive notice,
　Change of name, deeds and conveyances, **CC 1096**
　Conveyances, **CC 1213**
　Oil and gas leases, **CC 1219**
Consumer Credit Reporting Agencies, this index
Copies,
　Admissibility in evidence, **CC 1207**
　Recording in other counties, **CC 1218**
Covenants running with land, successive owners, **CC 1468**
Criminal History Information, generally, this index
Customers, personal information,
　Breach of security, disclosure, **CC 1798.82**
　Destruction, **CC 1798.80 et seq.**
Damages, customer records, destruction, **CC 1798.84**
Deeds and Conveyances, this index
Defectively executed instruments, effect, **CC 1207**
Destroyed or lost records. Lost or Destroyed Documents, generally, this index
Disclosure, generally, this index
Discount buying services, escrows and escrow agents, refunds, **CC 1812.101**
Easements, this index
Electronic transmissions, Uniform Electronic Transactions Act, **CC 1633.1 et seq.**
Employment Agencies, this index
Exemptions, access, information practices, **CC 1798.40, 1798.41**

RECORDS AND RECORDATION—Cont'd
Forms, preservation of interest in real estate, notice of intent, **CC 880.340**
Guest records, privacy, **CC 53.5**
Health Care Service Plans, this index
Health records. Medical Records, generally, this index
Home equity sales contracts, **CC 1695.6**
　Rescission, unconscionable advantage, **CC 1695.14**
Indexes, preserving interest in real estate, notice of intent, **CC 880.350**
Information Practices Act, personal information, disclosure, **CC 1798 et seq.**
Injunction, customer records, destruction, **CC 1798.84**
Investigative consumer reporting agencies, **CC 1786 et seq.**
Job listing services, **CC 1812.522**
Leases, this index
Limitation of actions, marketable record title, **CC 880.250, 880.260**
Lost records. Lost or Destroyed Documents, generally, this index
Marketable record title, **CC 880.020 et seq.**
Mechanics Liens, this index
Medical Records, generally, this index
Mines and Minerals, this index
Mortgages, this index
Notice,
　Consent to use of land, **CC 813**
　Constructive notice, generally, ante
　Marketable record title, **CC 880.310 et seq.**
　Preservation of interest in real estate, **CC 880.310 et seq.**
Nurses registries, **CC 1812.529**
Passenger manifest records, privacy, **CC 53.5**
Personal information, disclosure, Information Practices Act, **CC 1798 et seq.**
Place of recording, **CC 1169**
Preservation of interest, real estate, notice, **CC 880.310 et seq.**
Privacy, generally, this index
Real Estate Brokers and Salespersons, this index
Rent, assignment,
　Mortgages, present transfer of assignors interest, **CC 2938**
　Perfection of security interests, **CC 2938**
Rental purchase agreements, prices, **CC 1812.644**
Right to privacy, Information Practices Act, **CC 1798 et seq.**
Seller assisted marketing plans, **CC 1812.213**
Signatures, Electronic Transactions Act, **CC 1633.1 et seq.**
Slandering title, **CC 880.360**
Standing timber or trees, contracts for purchase or sale, **CC 1220**
State, this index
State Agencies, this index

RECORDS AND RECORDATION—Cont'd
State Departments, this index
Time,
　Instrument deemed recorded, **CC 1170**
　Prior recording of subsequent interests or instruments, **CC 1214**
Title deeds, real property, effect of not keeping, **CC 994**
Trees, standing, contracts, purchase or sale, **CC 1220**
Trust Deeds, this index
Uniform Electronic Transactions Act, **CC 1633.1 et seq.**
Unrecorded instruments, validity, **CC 1217**
Writing,
　Electronic Transactions Act, **CC 1633.1 et seq.**
　Uniform Electronic Transactions Act, **CC 1633.1 et seq.**

RECREATION AND RECREATIONAL FACILITIES
See, also, Parks, generally, this index
Boats and Boating, generally, this index
Camps and Camping, generally, this index
Community Facilities Districts, generally, this index
Hazardous conditions, warning, negligence, **CC 846**
Invitees, hazardous conditions, warnings, **CC 846**
Membership camping contracts, **CC 1812.300 et seq.**
Negligence, hazardous conditions, warning, **CC 846**
Personal injuries, entry on private land, negligence, **CC 846, 846.1**
Private property,
　Liability for injuries, **CC 846, 846.1**
　Public recreational use to supplement tax supported publicly owned facilities, **CC 1009**
Recreational Trails, generally, this index
Trails. Recreational Trails, generally, this index
Vehicle parks, eminent domain, **CC 799.70**
Waiver, membership camping contracts, **CC 1812.316**
Zoning and Planning, generally, this index

RECREATIONAL TRAILER PARKS
Mobilehomes and Mobilehome Parks, generally, this index

RECREATIONAL TRAILS
Actions and proceedings, entry on property, **CC 846.1**
Attorney fees, entry on property, **CC 846.1**
Damages, entry on property, attorney fees, **CC 846.1**
Entry on property, actions and proceedings, **CC 846.1**
Private lands, entry on property, damages, **CC 846.1**

RECREATIONAL

RECREATIONAL VEHICLE PARK OCCUPANCY LAW
Generally, CC 799.20 et seq.

RECREATIONAL VEHICLE PARKS
Generally, CC 799.20 et seq.
Application of law, CC 799.41
Eviction, CC 799.55 et seq.
Renting space for accommodation, CC 798.22
Special Occupancy Parks, generally, this index

RECREATIONAL VEHICLES
Actions and proceedings, parks, attorney fees and costs, CC 799.78
Agreements, registration agreements, CC 799.43
Annoyance, parks, defaulting residents, CC 799.70
Attorney fees, parks, CC 799.78
Construction of laws, CC 799.21
Contracts, registration agreement, parks, CC 799.43
Controlled substances, offenses, parks, defaulting residents, CC 799.70
Costs, park tenants, CC 799.78
Cumulative rights, CC 799.40
Damages, park tenants, violations, CC 799.79
Default,
  Parks, CC 799.55 et seq.
  Removal, CC 799.46
Removal, parks, CC 799.46
Disabled persons, removal from parks, CC 799.56
Eminent domain, parks, defaulting residents, CC 799.70
Fees, recreational vehicle parks,
  Defaulting residents nonpayment, termination, CC 799.70
  Nonpayment, termination of tenancy, CC 799.65
Fines and penalties, management, actions against, CC 799.79
Incumbrances. Liens and incumbrances, generally, post
Liens and incumbrances,
  Application of law, CC 3051, 3067.2
  Defaulting occupants, tenants or residents, CC 799.75
Mobilehomes and Mobilehome Parks, generally, this index
Negligence, removal, recreational vehicle parks, CC 799.59
Notice,
  Defaulting occupants, removal, parks, CC 799.55 et seq.
  Defaulting residents, termination of occupancy, CC 799.70, 799.71
  Defaulting tenants, termination of tenancy, CC 799.65, 799.66
Nuisance, parks, defaulting residents, CC 799.70
Occupant registration agreements,
  Requirements, CC 799.43

RECREATIONAL VEHICLES—Cont'd
Occupant registration agreements—Cont'd
  Waiver of rights, CC 799.42
Park Occupancy Law, CC 799.20 et seq.
Parks. Recreational Vehicle Parks, generally, this index
Police, notice, removal, recreational vehicle parks, CC 799.58
Prostitution, parks, defaulting residents, CC 799.70
Reasonable and ordinary care, removal, recreational vehicle parks, CC 799.59
Recreational Vehicle Park Occupancy Law, CC 799.20 et seq.
Registration, parks, CC 799.43
Removal, vehicle parks, CC 799.46
Rent, parks,
  Defaulting residents, nonpayment, termination, CC 799.70
  Nonpayment, termination of tenancy, CC 799.65 et seq.
  Time, CC 799.45
  Waiver of rights, CC 799.42
Rules and regulations,
  Parks, occupants copy, CC 799.44
  Recreational vehicle parks, defaulting residents, CC 799.70
Secured storage facility, removal, recreational vehicle parks, CC 799.57 et seq.
Service of process, removal, recreational vehicle parks, CC 799.56
Sheriffs, removal of persons from vehicles, CC 799.58
Special Occupancy Parks, generally, this index
Tenants, vehicle parks, CC 799.20 et seq.
Termination, parks, CC 799.55 et seq.
Terms, registration agreements, parks, CC 799.43
Towing,
  Parks, defaulting occupants, CC 799.57
  Removal from occupancy parks, defaulting occupants, CC 799.57 et seq.
Utilities, parks, nonpayment,
  Defaulting residence, CC 799.70
  Termination of tenancy, CC 799.65 et seq.
Vehicle Park Occupancy Law, CC 799.20 et seq.
Waiver, rental agreement, CC 799.42
Warnings, removal of vehicles from premises, signs and signals, CC 799.46

RECREATIONAL VESSELS
Boats and Boating, generally, this index

RECYCLING
Backflow devices, possession, CC 3336.5
Certificates and certification, fire hydrants, possession, CC 3336.5
Damages, fire hydrants, possession, CC 3336.5
Exemplary damages, fire hydrants, possession, CC 3336.5
Manholes, covers, possession, CC 3336.5

RED WOLF
Fish and Game, generally, this index

REDEMPTION
Condominiums, assessments, delinquency, foreclosure, CC 5715
Gift certificates, CC 1749.6
Installment sales,
  Buyer or persons redemption of goods, CC 1812.2
  Contract collateral after repossession, finance charge refund credit, CC 1806.3
Liens and Incumbrances, this index
Motor vehicles, sale of repossessed vehicle, CC 2983.2

REENTRY
Transferability of right, CC 1046

REES LEVERING MOTOR VEHICLE SALES AND FINANCE ACT
Generally, CC 2981 et seq.

REFERENCE AND REFEREES
Condominiums, construction, defects, CC 6000
Business and commerce, CC 6870

REFERENDUM
Initiative and Referendum, generally, this index

REFINANCING
Installment Sales, this index

REFORMATION
Contracts, this index

REFORMATORIES
Correctional Institutions, generally, this index

REFRIGERATION AND REFRIGERATORS
Leases, cutting off public utilities with intent to terminate lease, damages, CC 789.3

REFUNDS
Consumer goods, debit cards, prepaid debit cards, CC 1748.40, 1748.41
Dance studios, lessons, CC 1812.54
Debit cards, prepaid debit cards, CC 1748.40, 1748.41
Finance charge, dance studios, CC 1812.57
Floating homes, security deposits, CC 800.49
Gift certificates, CC 1749.5
Health studios, contracts, cancellation, CC 1812.85
  New facilities, CC 1812.96
Impound accounts, mortgages, excess funds, CC 2954.1
Installment Sales, this index
Mobilehomes and mobilehome parks, personal property, removal, sales, CC 798.36
Motor Vehicles, this index
Service charge, installment sales, CC 1803.2
Weight loss contracts, cancellation, CC 1694.6

REGISTERED DIETITIANS
Dietitians, generally, this index

RENT

REGISTERED MAIL
Certified or registered mail. Mail and Mailing, this index

REGISTERED NURSES
Nurses, generally, this index

REGISTERS AND REGISTRIES
Anatomical gifts, donate life California organ and tissue donor registry, drivers licenses, electronic devices and equipment, **CC 1798.90.1**
Donate life California organ and tissue donor registry, drivers licenses, electronic devices and equipment, **CC 1798.90.1**
Nurses Registries, generally, this index
Tissue banks, donate life California organ and tissue donor registry, drivers licenses, electronic devices and equipment, **CC 1798.90.1**

REGISTRATION
Consumer credit, credit service organizations, **CC 1789.25**
Credit service organizations, **CC 1789.25**
Data, brokers, **CC 1798.99.80 et seq.**
Equalization state board, names, release, **CC 1798.69**
Mortgages, foreclosure consultants, **CC 2945.45**
Motor Vehicles, this index
Sex Offenses, this index
Taxation, equalization state board, names, release, **CC 1798.69**

REGISTRATION PLATES
License plates. Motor Vehicles, this index

REGISTRIES
Registers and Registries, generally, this index

REGULATED INVESTMENT COMPANIES
Corporation Taxes, generally, this index

REIMBURSEMENT
Landlord and tenant, security deposits, **CC 1950.5**
Motor vehicles, warranty adjustment programs, repairs, manufacturers, **CC 1795.92**

RELATIVES
Children and Minors, generally, this index
Community Property, generally, this index
Contracts, unlawful confinement, duress, **CC 1569**
Descent and distribution. Succession, generally, this index
Domestic Partnership, generally, this index
Domestic Violence, generally, this index
Health care providers, disclosure, **CC 56.1007**
Health care service plans, disclosure, **CC 56.1007**
Marriage, generally, this index
Protection, force, right to use, **CC 50**

RELATIVES—Cont'd
Succession, generally, this index
Support, generally, this index

RELEASE
Extinction of obligations, **CC 1541**
Garagemen liens, interest in vehicle, **CC 3071.5**
Hazardous Substances and Waste, this index
Health care service plans, medical records, **CC 56.11**
Negligence, **CC 56.36**
Mechanics Liens, this index
Medical Records, this index
Obligations, **CC 1541 et seq.**
Trust Deeds, this index

RELIGION
Condominiums, display, **CC 4706**
Deeds and conveyances, restrictive covenants, **CC 53**
Discrimination, generally, this index
Display,
Condominiums, **CC 4706**
Landlord and tenant, **CC 1940.45**
Franchises, discrimination, **CC 51.8**
Landlord and tenant, display, **CC 1940.45**
Mobilehomes and mobilehome parks, club membership, discrimination, **CC 798.20**
Security interests, consumer credit contracts, artifacts, books or materials, **CC 1799.97**

RELIGIOUS ORGANIZATIONS AND SOCIETIES
Easements, church seats, **CC 801, 802**

REMAINDERS AND REMAINDERMEN
Future Estates or Interests, generally, this index

REMEDIES
Children and minors, immigration, status, evidence, **CC 3339.5**
Immigration, children and minors, status, evidence, **CC 3339.5**
Noncitizens, labor and employment, **CC 3339**
Voidable transactions, **CC 3439.07**

REMUNERATION
Compensation and Salaries, generally, this index

RENEGOTIABLE RATE MORTGAGE LOANS
Generally, **CC 1916.8, 1916.9**

RENEWABLE ENERGY
Solar Energy, generally, this index

RENT
Acceptance, **CC 1945**
Adjoining landowners, temporary entry, repairs, **CC 1002**
Age discrimination, businesses renting housing, **CC 51.2**

RENT—Cont'd
Assignments, **CC 1954.53**
Business premises, **CC 1954.05**
Indebtedness, COVID 19, **CC 1788.66**
Mortgages, present transfer of assignors interest, **CC 2938**
Records and recordation, perfection of security interests, **CC 2938**
Cash, **CC 1947.3**
Certificates of occupancy, owner established rates, **CC 1954.52**
Charging stations, electric vehicles, **CC 1947.6**
Cigarettes and cigars, smoking, prohibiting, **CC 1947.5**
Commercial property, **CC 1954.25 et seq.**
Confidential or privileged information, control, **CC 1947.7**
Controls. Rent Controls, generally, this index
Conveyance, **CC 1111**
COVID 19,
Assignments,
Indebtedness, **CC 1788.66**
Sales, indebtedness, **CC 1788.66**
Indebtedness, **CC 1785.20.4**
Assignments, sales, **CC 1788.66**
Crimes and offenses, skimming, residential real estate, **CC 890 et seq.**
Deductions, repairs by lessees, limit, **CC 1942**
Double letting of rooms, **CC 1950**
Easements, right of taking, **CC 802**
Electric vehicles, charging stations, **CC 1947.6**
Excessive rent, local rent control programs, **CC 1947.11**
Fines and penalties, skimming of rent, **CC 892**
Floating Homes, this index
Foreign languages, contracts, translations, **CC 1632**
Forms, third parties, payment, **CC 1947.3**
Fraud, owners and ownership, **CC 890**
Future interests, actions, **CC 821**
Holding over, homeless persons, **CC 1942.8**
Home equity sales contracts, **CC 1695.3**
Homeless persons, holding over, **CC 1942.8**
Hotels and motels, rental controls, uniform system, **CC 1954.25 et seq.**
Increase,
Notice, residential dwellings, **CC 827**
Retaliation against tenant for exercise of rights, **CC 1942.5**
Initial rental rate, establishment by owner, **CC 1954.52, 1954.53**
Legal Estates Principal and Income Law, **CC 731 et seq.**
Life estates, recovery, **CC 824, 825**
Local rent stabilization and rent control, **CC 1947.7 et seq.**
Marinas, floating homes, **CC 800.20 et seq.**
Mobilehomes and Mobilehome Parks, this index
Money, **CC 1947.3**
Mortgages, this index

I-183

RENT

RENT—Cont'd
Motels and motor courts, rent control, uniform system, CC 1954.25 et seq.
Nonprofit corporations,
  Mortgages, CC 2924m
  Trust deeds, CC 2924m
Notice,
  Cash, CC 1947.3
  Increase, residential dwellings, CC 827
  Smoking, prohibiting, CC 1947.5
Owners and ownership,
  Fraud, CC 890
  Rates, CC 1954.52, 1954.53
Payment,
  Form, CC 1947.3
  Time, CC 1947
Purchase of rented property. Rental Purchase Agreements, generally, this index
Rates and charges, controls. Rent Controls, generally, this index
Records and recordation, assignments, CC 2938
Recreational Vehicles, this index
Reduction, rent control, landlords petition without merit, CC 1947.15
Refunds, excessive rent, local rent control programs, CC 1947.11
Residential dwellings, increase, notice, CC 827
Reversions, CC 1111
Sales, indebtedness, COVID 19, CC 1788.66
Sales and Use Taxes, generally, this index
Security interest, perfection, recordation of assignments, CC 2938
Skimming, residential property, CC 890 et seq.
Smoking, prohibiting, CC 1947.5
Spanish language, contracts, translations, CC 1632
Stabilization, local rent stabilization and rent control, CC 1947.7 et seq.
Subtenants, CC 1954.53
Third parties, payment, CC 1947.3
Time,
  Notice, increase, CC 827
  Payment, CC 1947
Tobacco and tobacco products, smoking, prohibiting, CC 1947.5

RENT CONTROLS
Generally, CC 1947.7 et seq., 1954.25 et seq., 1954.50 et seq.
Cancellation, CC 1954.535
  Owner established rental rates, CC 1954.53
Certificates of occupancy, owner established rates, CC 1954.52
Commercial property, CC 1954.25 et seq.
Condominiums, CC 1954.52
Exemptions, newly constructed units, owner established rental rates, CC 1954.52
Mobilehomes and Mobilehome Parks, this index
Nonrenewal, CC 1954.535
  Owner established rental rates, CC 1954.53

RENT CONTROLS—Cont'd
Notice, termination, CC 1954.535
  Owner established rental rates, CC 1954.535
Owner established rental rates, CC 1954.52, 1954.53
San Francisco City and County, temporary displacement, compensation and salaries, CC 1947.9
Subdivisions, owner established rental rates, CC 1954.52
Termination, CC 1954.535
  Owner established rental rates, CC 1954.53
Zoning and planning, commercial property, application of law, CC 1954.29

RENTAL CARS
Generally, CC 2985.7 et seq.
Leases. Motor Vehicles, this index

RENTAL HOUSING
Apartment Houses, generally, this index

RENTAL PURCHASE ACT
Generally, CC 1812.620 et seq.

RENTAL PURCHASE AGREEMENTS
Generally, CC 1812.620 et seq.
Adjustments, income interruption or reduction, payments, CC 1812.632
Advertisements, CC 1812.630
Application of law,
  Cumulative effect, CC 1812.648
  Home solicitation contracts, CC 1812.628
Attorney fees, entitlement of consumers, CC 1812.636
Balloon payments, CC 1812.624
Bona fide errors, liability, CC 1812.637
Cancellation, before taking possession, CC 1812.628
Collections,
  Cosigners, notice, CC 1812.643
  Deceptive or unfair practices, CC 1812.638, 1812.639
  Prohibited provisions, CC 1812.624
Communications, deceptive or unfair practices, collections, CC 1812.638, 1812.639
Computers, geophysical location tracking technology, notice, CC 1812.650
Consent, electronic devices and equipment, geophysical location tracking technology, CC 1812.650
Consumer credit,
  Application of law, CC 1812.622
  Reporting agencies, reports, CC 1812.640
Copies, CC 1812.629
Cosigners, notice, CC 1812.643
Costs, entitlement of consumers, CC 1812.636
Credit checks, CC 1812.630
Crimes and offenses, CC 1812.647
Cumulative effect of law, CC 1812.648
Damages,
  Entitlement of consumers, CC 1812.636

RENTAL PURCHASE AGREEMENTS—Cont'd
Damages—Cont'd
  Liability of consumers, CC 1812.627
Deceptive rental practices, CC 1812.638, 1812.639
Default, CC 1812.631
Deposits, security deposits, CC 1812.625
Disclosure,
  Advertisements, CC 1812.630
  Cosigners, CC 1812.643
  Documents, CC 1812.623
  Electronic devices and equipment, geophysical location tracking technology, CC 1812.650
Discrimination, CC 1812.642
Down payments, CC 1812.624
Electronic devices and equipment, geophysical location tracking technology, notice, CC 1812.650
Errors, liability, CC 1812.637
Exemplary damages, entitlement of consumers, CC 1812.636
Exemptions, CC 1812.622
Fees,
  Disclosure on document, CC 1812.623
  Late payment fees, CC 1812.626
  Prohibited fees, CC 1812.624
  Repair or replacement of property, CC 1812.633
Forms, CC 1812.623
Geophysical location tracking technology, electronic devices and equipment, notice, CC 1812.650
Harassment, collections, CC 1812.638
Home solicitation contracts, application of law, CC 1812.628
Information, providing to consumers, CC 1812.629
Installment sales, application of law, CC 1812.622
Insurance, prohibited provisions, CC 1812.624
Interruption of income, payment adjustment, CC 1812.632
Late payment fees, CC 1812.626
Liability, consumers, damages or losses, CC 1812.627
Maintenance of property, CC 1812.633
  Service contracts, following transfer of property, CC 1812.635
Misrepresentation, collections, CC 1812.638, 1812.639
Modification of law, CC 1812.646
Notice,
  Acquiring ownership, CC 1812.632
  Cosigners, CC 1812.643
  Disclosure on document, CC 1812.623
  Electronic devices and equipment, geophysical location tracking technology, CC 1812.650
  Errors, CC 1812.637

RESTRICTIVE

RENTAL PURCHASE AGREEMENTS
—Cont'd
Ownership of property, acquisitions, payment, CC 1812.632
Payment,
 Acquiring ownership, CC 1812.632
 Advertisements, disclosure, CC 1812.630
 Damages, entitlement of consumers, CC 1812.636
 Deceptive or unfair practices, collections, CC 1812.638, 1812.639
 Default, CC 1812.631
 Income interruption or reduction, CC 1812.632
 Late payment fees, CC 1812.626
 Prohibited provisions, CC 1812.624
 Schedule on document, CC 1812.623
Prices,
 Records, CC 1812.644
 Total amount of payments, CC 1812.632
Prohibited provisions, CC 1812.624
Promotional materials, consumer references, CC 1812.641
Public policy, CC 1812.621
Records and recordation, prices, CC 1812.644
Reduction of income, payment adjustment, CC 1812.632
References, consumer credit, solicitation, CC 1812.641
Reinstatement, following default, CC 1812.631
Repair or replacement of property, CC 1812.633
 Service contracts, following transfer of ownership, CC 1812.635
Reports, consumer credit reporting agencies, CC 1812.640
Repossession, prohibited provisions, CC 1812.624
Secured transactions, application of law, CC 1812.622
Security deposits, CC 1812.625
Security interest, prohibited provisions, CC 1812.624
Service contracts, following transfer of ownership, CC 1812.634
Severability of law, CC 1812.649
Smartphones, geophysical location tracking technology, notice, CC 1812.650
Solicitation, consumer references, CC 1812.641
Transfer of warranties, consumers, CC 1812.634
Unfair or deceptive practices, CC 1812.638, 1812.639
Venue, CC 1812.645
 Collection actions, CC 1812.624
Waiver of law, CC 1812.646
Waiver of rights, prohibited provisions, CC 1812.624
Warranties, transfer to consumers, CC 1812.634
Written documents, form, CC 1812.623

REPORTS
Bookstores, personal information, disclosure, CC 1798.90
Commercial credit reports, CC 1785.41 et seq.
Consumer Credit Reporting Agencies, generally, this index
Credit ratings. Consumer Credit Reporting Agencies, generally, this index
Crimes and Offenses, this index
Debit cards, liability, CC 1748.31
Forcible entry and detainer, drugs and medicine, nuisance, CC 3486.5
Landlord and tenant, reusable tenant screening reports, CC 1950.1
Printing, generally, this index
Reading, privacy, CC 1798.90
Rental purchase agreements, consumer credit reporting agencies, CC 1812.640
Social media, threats, CC 1798.99.20 et seq.
Tax Returns and Reports, generally, this index
Threats, social media, CC 1798.99.20 et seq.

REPOSSESSORS AND REPOSSESSION
Conditions subsequent, breach, transferability of right of reentry, CC 1046
Installment sales, debt satisfaction, finance charge refund credit, CC 1806.3
Rental purchase agreements, provisions, CC 1812.624

REPRESENTATION
Legislature, generally, this index

REPRESENTATIVE ACTIONS
Class Actions, generally, this index

REPRODUCTIONS
Art and Artists, this index
Fine art multiples, sale, disclosure, CC 1740 et seq.
Political items, labeling, CC 1739.3
Prints, sale, disclosure, CC 1740 et seq.

REPRODUCTIVE HEALTH
Abortion, generally, this index

RES JUDICATA
Mechanics liens, public buildings and works, release, summary proceedings, stop notices, CC 9414

RESCUE
Contractors, disclosure, CC 3273
Disclosure, contractors, CC 3273
Epinephrine auto injectors, lay rescuers, CC 1714.23
Identity and identification, contractors, CC 3273

RESEARCH
Statistics, personal information maintained by governmental agencies, Information Practices Act, CC 1798.24

RESERVATION OF RIGHTS
Deeds and conveyances, interpretation, CC 1069

RESERVES
Condominiums, CC 5510 et seq.

RESIDENCE
Domicile and Residence, generally, this index

RESIDENTIAL BUILDINGS
Housing, generally, this index

RESIDENTIAL MORTGAGE LENDERS
Mortgages, this index

RESIDENTIAL STOCK COOPERATIVES
Disclosure, transfers, CC 1102 et seq.

RESIDENTS
Domicile and Residence, generally, this index

RESOURCE RECOVERY
Recycling, generally, this index

RESPONDENTIA
Mortgage provisions, exclusion, CC 2942
Priority of lien, exception, CC 2897
Provisions governing, CC 2877
Voidable transactions, application of law, CC 3440.1

REST HOMES
Nursing Homes, generally, this index

RESTAURANTS
Blind or visually impaired persons, access to public accommodations, CC 54 et seq.
Civil Rights Act, CC 51 et seq.
Disabled persons, access, public accommodations, CC 54 et seq.
Gifts, devises and bequests, privileges and immunities, CC 1714.25
Sex discrimination, CC 51 et seq.

RESTITUTION
Auctions and auctioneers, CC 1812.603
Condominiums, this index
Discount buying services, damages, CC 1812.123
Human trafficking, CC 52.5
Identification devices, subcutaneous implantation, CC 52.7
Monopolies and unfair trade, CC 1780
Motor vehicles, manufacturers, CC 1793.2, 1793.25
Stories about felonies, sale proceeds, CC 2225
Student loans, private education lenders and loan collectors, CC 1788.208
Subcutaneous implantation, identification devices, CC 52.7
Unfair trade, CC 1780

RESTRAINING ORDERS
Injunction, generally, this index

RESTRAINT OF TRADE
Monopolies and Unfair Trade, generally, this index

RESTRICTIVE COVENANTS
Covenants. Deeds and Conveyances, this index

RETAIL

RETAIL
Retailers, generally, this index

RETAIL FOOD FACILITIES
Grocery Stores, generally, this index

RETAIL INSTALLMENT SALES
Generally, CC 1801 et seq.
Installment Sales, generally, this index

RETAIL SALES
Installment Sales, generally, this index
Sales, generally, this index

RETAIL SELLER
Retailers, generally, this index

RETAILERS
See, also, Stores, generally, this index
Children and minors, markets and marketing, gender neutrality, CC 55.7, 55.8
Credit Cards, this index
Defenses, service or repair transactions, delivery, CC 1722
Disclosure, human trafficking, CC 1714.43
Fines and penalties, gender neutrality, markets and marketing, children and minors, CC 55.8
Gender neutrality, children and minors, markets and marketing, CC 55.7, 55.8
Grocery Stores, generally, this index
Human trafficking, disclosure, CC 1714.43
Markets and marketing, children and minors, gender neutrality, CC 55.7, 55.8
Return of goods, refunds or exchanges, notice if not allowed, CC 1723
Sales and Use Taxes, generally, this index
Service Contracts, generally, this index
Sex, gender neutrality, children and minors, markets and marketing, CC 55.7, 55.8
Slavery, disclosure, CC 1714.43
Time, service or repair transactions, delivery, CC 1722

RETALIATION
Anonymous witness programs, privileges and immunities, CC 48.9
Landlord and tenant, immigration, disclosure, CC 1940.35

RETIREMENT AND PENSIONS
ERISA pension funds, shared appreciation loans, investments, CC 1917.210, 1917.220
Exemptions, foreign public retirement systems, interest rates, CC 1916.2
Investments,
    ERISA pension funds, shared appreciation loans, CC 1917.210
    Shared appreciation loans, CC 1917.210, 1917.220
Loans, investments, shared appreciation loans, CC 1917.210, 1917.220

RETRACTION
Libel, CC 48a

RETURNS
Tax Returns and Reports, generally, this index

REVENUE
Taxation, generally, this index

REVERSE MORTGAGE ELDER PROTECTION ACT
Generally, CC 1923.2, 1923.5

REVERSE MORTGAGES
Generally, CC 1923 et seq.
Mortgages, this index

REVERSION
Future Estates or Interests, generally, this index

REVIVAL
Abatement of Actions or Proceedings, generally, this index

REVOLVERS
Weapons, generally, this index

REVOLVING ACCOUNTS
Retail installment account. Installment Sales, this index

REWARDS
Animals, running at large, CC 1845

RFID
Radio frequency identification, crimes and offenses, CC 1798.79

RIFLES
Weapons, generally, this index

RIGHT OF ENTRY
Entry on Property, generally, this index

RIGHT OF WAY
Easements, CC 801, 802
Repair and maintenance, costs, determination, CC 845
Zoning and Planning, generally, this index

RIGHT TO PRIVACY
Privacy, generally, this index

RIOT GUNS
Weapons, generally, this index

RIOTS AND MOBS
See, also, War and Civil Defense, generally, this index
Deposits, involuntary, CC 1815
Home solicitation contracts, residential repair or restoration, cancellation, CC 1689.6, 1689.7, 1689.14

RIVERS AND STREAMS
Accession, Accretion and Avulsion, generally, this index
Avulsion. Accession, Accretion and Avulsion, generally, this index
Boundaries, CC 830

RIVERS AND STREAMS—Cont'd
Fish and Game, generally, this index
Floods and Flooding, generally, this index
Islands, generally, this index
Ownership, state, CC 670
State ownership, CC 670

RIVERSIDE COUNTY
See, also, Counties, generally, this index
Housing, aged persons,
    Discrimination, CC 51.10 et seq.
    Exemptions, CC 51.2 et seq.

RNA
Genetic testing, privacy, CC 56.18 et seq.

ROADS
Highways and Roads, generally, this index

ROCK COLLECTING
Private property owner, liability for injuries, CC 846

ROCKS
Outdoor Advertising, generally, this index

RODENTS
Pest Control, generally, this index

ROOFS
Warranties, home roofs, CC 1797.90 et seq.

ROOMING HOUSES
Boarding and Lodging Houses, generally, this index

ROSENTHAL FAIR DEBT COLLECTION PRACTICES ACT
Generally, CC 1788 et seq.

ROSENTHAL ROBERTI ITEM PRICING ACT
Generally, CC 7100 et seq.

ROYALTIES
Audio and video recordings, audits and auditors, CC 2500, 2501
Audits and auditors, tape recordings, CC 2500, 2501
Crimes and offenses, stories about felonies, proceeds, CC 2225
Legal Estates Principal and Income Law, CC 731 et seq.

RULE AGAINST PERPETUITIES
Future estates, authorization and limitations, CC 773
Minerals, oil and gas, lease, CC 718, 718f
Restraints on alienation, CC 711

RULE IN SHELLEY'S CASE
Abolition, CC 779

RULES OF EVIDENCE
Evidence, generally, this index

RULES OF NAVIGATION
Ships and Shipping, generally, this index

SALES

RULES OF THE ROAD
Traffic Rules and Regulations, generally, this index

RUM
Alcoholic Beverages, generally, this index

RUNNING AT LARGE
Animals, this index

RYE
Agricultural Products, generally, this index

SACRAMENTO CITY AND COUNTY
See, also, Consolidated Cities and Counties, generally, this index
Drugs and medicine, forcible entry and detainer, nuisance, **CC 3486.5**
Forcible entry and detainer,
   Drugs and medicine, nuisance, **CC 3486.5**
   Weapons, **CC 3485**
Nuisance, forcible entry and detainer, drugs and medicine, **CC 3486.5**
Weapons, forcible entry and detainer, **CC 3485**

SACRAMENTO COUNTY
Sacramento City and County, generally, this index

SAFES
Hotels and motels, personal property, guests, notice of nonliability, **CC 1860**
Manufacturers identification mark, removal, defacing, alteration or destruction, **CC 1710.1**
Sale, identification number or mark altered or removed, **CC 1710.1**

SAFETY
Carriers, passengers, **CC 2100 et seq.**
Discrimination, business and commerce, recognition, **CC 51.17**
Fires and Fire Protection, generally, this index
Special occupancy parks, moving, **CC 1867**

SAILBOATS
Boats and Boating, generally, this index

SAILORS
Military Forces, generally, this index

SALARIES
Compensation and Salaries, generally, this index

SALES
Abandoned or Unclaimed Property, this index
Actions and proceedings,
   Breach of warranty, Song Beverly Consumer Warranty Act, **CC 1790 et seq.**
   Consumers Legal Remedies Act, **CC 1750 et seq.**
   Contracts, consumer goods, statements, illegal contracts, **CC 1670.8**
   Independent wholesale sales representatives, contracts, **CC 1738.15**

SALES—Cont'd
Agents and agencies, **CC 2323 et seq.**
Agriculture, private bulk grain storage, **CC 1880.3**
Art and Artists, this index
As is sales, mobilehomes and mobilehome parks, disclosure, waiver, **CC 1102.1**
Assistive devices, disabled persons, warranties, **CC 1793.02**
Attorney fees, breach of warranty, Song Beverly Consumer Warranty Act, **CC 1794, 1794.1**
Auctions and Auctioneers, generally, this index
Autographed memorabilia, warranties, **CC 1739.7**
Bailment,
   Customers leaving personalty for sale, insurance, **CC 1858 et seq.**
   Perishable goods, **CC 1837**
Bids and Bidding, generally, this index
Bills of Sale, generally, this index
Bona fide purchasers. Innocent Purchasers, generally, this index
Boundaries, independent wholesale sales representatives, **CC 1738.13**
Breach of contract, liquidated damages, **CC 1671**
Breach of warranty, Song Beverly Consumer Warranty Act, **CC 1790 et seq.**
Campgrounds, membership camping contracts, **CC 1812.308**
Carriers, this index
Cash discounts, **CC 1748.1**
Clothing, warranties, **CC 1793.35**
Club members, after notice of termination, **CC 1584.6**
Condominiums, this index
Conforming. Nonconforming goods, generally, post
Consignment, generally, this index
Consumables, warranties, **CC 1793.35**
Consumer goods,
   Consumers Legal Remedies Act, **CC 1750 et seq.**
   Delivery, time, **CC 1722**
   Legal Remedies Act, **CC 1750 et seq.**
   Nonconforming goods, **CC 1793.3**
   Registration cards, disclosure, **CC 1793.1**
   Repair and service facilities, warranties, **CC 1793.1 et seq.**
   Service and repair facilities, warranties, **CC 1793.1 et seq.**
   Statements, contracts, illegal contracts, **CC 1670.8**
   Warranties, **CC 1790 et seq.**
Consumers, personal information, privacy, **CC 1798.100 et seq.**
Contracts,
   Consumer goods, statements, illegal contracts, **CC 1670.8**
   Consumers Legal Remedies Act, **CC 1750 et seq.**

SALES—Cont'd
Contracts—Cont'd
   Independent wholesale sales representatives, **CC 1738.10 et seq.**
   Liquidated damages, breach of contract, **CC 1671**
   Records and recordation, **CC 1624.5**
   Statements, consumer goods, illegal contracts, **CC 1670.8**
Cosmetics, generally, this index
Credit, returned goods, grey market goods, **CC 1797.85**
Credit cards, issuers and retailers, contracts prohibiting price discounts for cash sales, **CC 1748**
Credit sales. Installment Sales, generally, this index
Credit services organizations, **CC 1789.10 et seq.**
Crimes and offenses, stories about felonies, sale proceeds, **CC 2225**
Damages,
   Breach of warranty, Song Beverly Consumer Warranty Act, **CC 1794**
   Consumers Legal Remedies Act, **CC 1750 et seq.**
   Delivery, consumer purchases, violations, **CC 1722**
   Fraud, **CC 3343**
   Indemnity, retail seller against manufacturer, consumer sales, **CC 1792**
   Liquidated damages, **CC 1671**
Dance studio services, **CC 1812.50 et seq.**
Data, crimes and offenses, **CC 1724**
Dealerships, **CC 80 et seq.**
Deceptive practices, **CC 1770**
Delivery,
   Consumer purchases, time, **CC 1722**
   Express warranties, time, **CC 1793.01**
   Nonconforming goods, Song Beverly Consumer Warranty Act, **CC 1793.2 et seq.**
   Notice, **CC 1722**
   Retail sales, time, **CC 1722**
   Time, consumer purchases, **CC 1722**
Depositories,
   Customers property, insurance, **CC 1858 et seq.**
   Liens and incumbrances, **CC 1857**
   Perishables, **CC 1837**
Disabled persons, assistive devices, warranties, **CC 1793.02**
Disclaimers,
   Implied warranties, **CC 1792.4**
   Warranties, Song Beverly Consumer Warranty Act, **CC 1791.3**
Disclosure,
   Medical records, **CC 1798.91**
   Service and repair facilities accompanying warranty, Song Beverly Consumer Warranty Act, **CC 1793.1**
Discount Buying Services, generally, this index

SALES

SALES—Cont'd
Distributors, independent wholesale sales representatives, **CC 1738.10 et seq.**
Documents of Title, generally, this index
Draperies, warranties, **CC 1793.35**
Drugs and Medicine, this index
Electrical device or appliance with identification number or mark altered or removed, **CC 1710.1**
Exemptions,
    Medical records, disclosure, **CC 1798.91**
    Unsolicited sending of goods, **CC 1584.5**
Express warranties, **CC 1793**
    Song Beverly Consumer Warranty Act, **CC 1790 et seq.**
    Time, delivery, **CC 1793.01**
    Used goods, **CC 1795.5**
Factors, generally, this index
Fair dealerships, **CC 80 et seq.**
False invoices or statements, solicitation of money, **CC 1716**
Financial contract (qualified), frauds, statute of, **CC 1624**
Fine art, consignments, **CC 1738 et seq.**
Fine print, disclosure, **CC 1740 et seq.**
Fines and penalties,
    Breach of warranty, Song Beverly Consumer Warranty Act, **CC 1794**
    Consumer goods, statements, contracts, illegal contracts, **CC 1670.8**
Floating Homes, this index
Fraud,
    Consumers Legal Remedies Act, **CC 1750 et seq.**
    Damages, **CC 3343**
Gift Certificates, generally, this index
Gifts, devises and bequests, unsolicited sending of goods, **CC 1584.5**
Good faith, Consumers Legal Remedies Act, **CC 1784**
Goods. Nonconforming goods, generally, post
Grey market goods, disclosures, **CC 1770, 1797.8**
Grocery stores, point of sale systems, **CC 7100 et seq.**
Guaranty. Warranties, generally, post
Health studio services, **CC 1812.80 et seq.**
Home Equity Sales Contracts, generally, this index
Home Solicitation Contracts, generally, this index
Hotels and motels, innkeepers liens, **CC 1861.24**
Housing, this index
Identity and identification, Consumers Legal Remedies Act, **CC 1750 et seq.**
Implied warranties,
    Disclaimers, **CC 1792.4**
    Fitness for particular purpose, **CC 1792.1, 1792.2**
    Merchantability, **CC 1792**

SALES—Cont'd
Implied warranties—Cont'd
    Song Beverly Consumer Warranty Act, **CC 1790 et seq.**
    Waiver, **CC 1792.3, 1792.4**
Indemnity, retail seller against manufacturer, consumer sales, **CC 1792**
Independent wholesale sales representatives, **CC 1738.10 et seq.**
Innkeepers liens, **CC 1861.24**
Innocent Purchasers, generally, this index
Installment Sales, generally, this index
Invoices, repair, Song Beverly Consumer Warranty Act, **CC 1793.1 et seq.**
Landlord and Tenant, this index
Lay away practices, regulation, **CC 1749 et seq.**
Letters of Credit, generally, this index
Lewd or obscene material. Lewdness and Obscenity, generally, this index
Liens and Incumbrances, this index
Limitation of actions, Consumers Legal Remedies Act, **CC 1783**
Liquefied petroleum gas, mobilehomes and mobilehome parks, **CC 798.44**
Lost or Destroyed Property, this index
Magnuson Moss Warranty Federal Trade Commission Improvement Act, warranty standards, **CC 1793.1**
Mail order businesses, autographed memorabilia, warranties, **CC 1739.7**
Manufactured housing. Housing, this index
Markets and Marketing, generally, this index
Mechanical device or appliance with identification number or mark altered or removed, **CC 1710.1**
Medical Records, this index
Members of organization, termination, **CC 1584.6**
Membership camping contracts, **CC 1812.307, 1812.308**
Memorabilia, autographed, warranties, **CC 1739.7**
Merchantability, implied warranties, **CC 1792**
Mining machinery, bill of sale, **CC 1631**
Mobilehomes and Mobilehome Parks, this index
Monopolies and Unfair Trade, generally, this index
Motels and motor courts, innkeepers liens, **CC 1861.24**
Motor Vehicles, this index
Motorized wheelchairs, warranty, **CC 1793.025**
Nonconforming goods,
    Consumer goods, **CC 1793.3**
    Consumers Legal Remedies Act, **CC 1750 et seq.**
    Extension of warranty period during repairs or services, **CC 1795.7**
    Song Beverly Consumer Warranty Act, **CC 1793.2 et seq.**

SALES—Cont'd
Nonconforming goods—Cont'd
    Tolling period of warranties, **CC 1795.7**
Nonprofit corporations, mortgages, trust deeds, rent, **CC 2924m**
Notice,
    Baggage and property of apartment house, guests, **CC 1861a**
    Breach of security, consumer protection, **CC 1798.82**
    Delivery, **CC 1722**
    Landlord and tenant, disposition of personal property remaining on premises at termination of tenancy, **CC 1984**
    Nonconforming goods, buyers duty, Song Beverly Consumer Warranty Act, **CC 1793.3**
    Service and repair facilities available to buyer, Song Beverly Consumer Warranty Act, **CC 1793.1**
Offers, mails, return of forms to prevent shipment, **CC 1584.5**
Options, subsequent purchases or retail installment contract, **CC 1808.1**
Payment, solicitation, false statements or invoices, **CC 1716**
Point of sale systems, grocery stores, **CC 7100 et seq.**
Political items, **CC 1739 et seq.**
Prices, unfair or deceptive trade practices, **CC 1770**
Prints, disclosure, **CC 1740 et seq.**
Proceedings. Actions and proceedings, generally, ante
Purchase of rented property. Rental Purchase Agreements, generally, this index
Qualified financial contract, frauds, statute of, **CC 1624**
Real Estate, this index
Refunds, grey market goods, **CC 1797.85**
Remedies, Consumers Legal Remedies Act, **CC 1750 et seq.**
Rent, indebtedness, COVID 19, **CC 1788.66**
Rental Purchase Agreements, generally, this index
Repair and service facilities, Song Beverly Consumer Warranty Act, **CC 1793.1 et seq.**
Replacement of nonconforming goods, **CC 1793.35**
Retail installment sales. Installment Sales, generally, this index
Retailers, generally, this index
Return of goods, refund or exchange, notice if not allowed, **CC 1723**
San Francisco Bay area, real estate, restrictions, notice, **CC 1103.4**
Sculpture costs, **CC 1740 et seq.**
Securities, generally, this index
Seller Assisted Marketing Plans, generally, this index
Seminar solicitation contracts, cancellation rights, **CC 1689.20 et seq.**

I-188

SAVINGS

SALES—Cont'd
Service and repair facilities, Song Beverly Consumer Warranty Act, **CC 1793.1 et seq.**
Service Contracts, generally, this index
Services, unsolicited services, **CC 1584.5**
Social security, numbers and numbering, **CC 1798.85**
Solicitation, generally, this index
Song Beverly Consumer Warranty Act, **CC 1790 et seq.**
Specifications, inconsistent sample or model, Consumers Legal Remedies Act, **CC 1750 et seq.**
Statements, consumer goods, contracts, illegal contracts, **CC 1670.8**
Surcharges, credit card sales, **CC 1748.1**
Tax on sales. Sales and Use Taxes, generally, this index
Telecommunications, this index
Time,
    Delivery, consumer purchases, **CC 1722**
    Express warranties, delivery, **CC 1793.01**
    Repair and servicing, Song Beverly Consumer Warranty Act, **CC 1793.2**
    Warranties, duration, Song Beverly Consumer Warranty Act, **CC 1791.1**
Title to property, unperformed contracts for, marketable title, **CC 886.010 et seq.**
Trading Stamps, generally, this index
Treble damages, breach of warranty, Song Beverly Consumer Warranty Act, **CC 1794 et seq.**
Trust Deeds, this index
Uniform Vendor and Purchaser Risk Act, **CC 1662**
Unsolicited sending of goods, **CC 1584.5**
Used goods, warranties, **CC 1795.5**
Valuation, generally, this index
Video games, force and violence, **CC 1746 et seq.**
Waiver, implied warranties, **CC 1792.4**
Warranties, **CC 1790 et seq.**
    Consumers Legal Remedies Act, **CC 1750 et seq.**
    Expiration, repairs or service, **CC 1795.6**
    Express warranties, generally, ante
    Extension, repairs or services, **CC 1795.7**
    Fitness for particular purpose, implied warranties, **CC 1792.1, 1792.2**
    Implied warranties, generally, ante
    Merchantability, **CC 1792**
    Mobilehomes, **CC 1797 et seq.**
    Motorized wheelchairs, **CC 1793.025**
    Registration cards, disclosure, **CC 1793.1**
    Service and repair facilities, **CC 1793.1 et seq.**
    Song Beverly Consumer Warranty Act, **CC 1790 et seq.**
    Standards for warranty work, **CC 1796, 1796.5**
    Tolling, repairs or service, **CC 1795.6**

SALES—Cont'd
Warranties—Cont'd
    Used goods, **CC 1795.5**
    Waiver, implied warranties, **CC 1792.3**
    Wheelchairs, motorized wheelchairs, **CC 1793.025**
    Wheelchairs, motorized wheelchairs, warranty, **CC 1793.025**
    Wholesalers, generally, this index
    Work orders, Song Beverly Consumer Warranty Act, **CC 1793.1 et seq.**

SALES AND USE TAXES
Collection, **CC 1656.1**
Contracts, retail sales, reimbursement, **CC 1656.1**
Motor vehicles,
    Manufacturers and manufacturing, reimbursement, restitution to buyer, **CC 1793.25**
    Reimbursement, manufacturer, restitution to buyer, **CC 1793.25**
Reimbursement, retail sales, **CC 1656.1**

SALES FINANCE ACT
Automobiles, **CC 2981 et seq.**

SALES TAXES
Sales and Use Taxes, generally, this index

SALESPERSONS
Independent wholesale sales representatives, **CC 1738.10 et seq.**
Insurance Agents, Solicitors or Brokers, generally, this index
Real Estate Brokers and Salespersons, generally, this index
Wholesalers, generally, this index

SAME SEX RELATIONSHIPS
Sexual Orientation, generally, this index

SAN BERNARDINO RIVERSIDE STATE COLLEGE
Colleges and Universities, generally, this index

SAN DIEGO STATE COLLEGE
Colleges and Universities, generally, this index

SAN FERNANDO VALLEY STATE COLLEGE
Colleges and Universities, generally, this index

SAN FRANCISCO BAY AREA
Notice, real estate, sales, restrictions, **CC 1103.4**
Real estate, sales, restrictions, notice, **CC 1103.4**
Sales, real estate, restrictions, notice, **CC 1103.4**

SAN FRANCISCO BAY CONSERVATION AND DEVELOPMENT COMMISSION
Condominiums, declarations, disclosure, jurisdiction, **CC 4255**

SAN FRANCISCO CITY AND COUNTY
See, also,
    Consolidated Cities and Counties, generally, this index
    Municipalities, generally, this index
Rent controls, temporary displacement, compensation and salaries, **CC 1947.9**

SAN FRANCISCO STATE COLLEGE
Colleges and Universities, generally, this index

SAN MATEO COUNTY STATE COLLEGE
Colleges and Universities, generally, this index

SAN MATEO SANTA CLARA COUNTY STATE COLLEGE
Colleges and Universities, generally, this index

SANDWICH STANDS
Restaurants, generally, this index

SANITARIUMS
Bailment, **CC 1859 et seq.**
Intellectual and Developmental Disabilities, generally, this index
Personal property,
    Fireproof safe, notice of nonliability, **CC 1860**
    Injury or loss, **CC 1859**

SATISFACTION
Accord and Satisfaction, generally, this index
Mortgages, this index
Trust Deeds, this index

SAVINGS AND LOAN ASSOCIATIONS
Savings Associations, generally, this index

SAVINGS ASSOCIATIONS
Adjustable payment, adjustable rate loan, **CC 1916.7**
Construction loans, defects in property, lenders liability, **CC 3434**
Contracts, foreign languages, translations, **CC 1632.5**
Debtors and creditors, offer of performance, notice, **CC 1500**
Disclosure, home equity loan disclosure, **CC 2970, 2971**
Discount buying services, trust account, **CC 1812.116**
Electronic funds transfers. Funds Transfers, generally, this index
Fines and penalties, contracts, foreign languages, translations, **CC 1632.5**
Foreign languages, contracts, translations, **CC 1632.5**
Forms, contracts, foreign languages, translations, **CC 1632.5**
Funds Transfers, generally, this index
Home equity loan disclosure, **CC 2970, 2971**
Impound accounts,
    Interest, **CC 2954.8**
    Mortgages, interest, **CC 2954.8**
Interest,
    Impound accounts, mortgages, **CC 2954.8**

I-189

SAVINGS

SAVINGS ASSOCIATIONS—Cont'd
Interest—Cont'd
    Variable rate, **CC 1916.5, 1916.8, 1916.9**
Liens and incumbrances,
    Customer property, **CC 3054**
    Mortgages, generally, post
Loans,
    Defects in property, lenders liability, **CC 3434**
    Extension of term, **CC 1916.5**
    Home equity loans, disclosure, **CC 2970, 2971**
    Interest, variable rate, **CC 1916.5, 1916.8, 1916.9**
    Mortgages, generally, post
    Motor vehicles, seller assisted financing, **CC 2982.5**
    Shared appreciation loans, **CC 1917 et seq.**
    Variable interest, **CC 1916.5, 1916.8, 1916.9**
Mortgages,
    Adjustable payment, adjustable rate loan, **CC 1916.7**
    Fiduciaries, **CC 2923.1**
    Foreign languages, translations, **CC 1632.5**
    Home equity loan disclosure, **CC 2970, 2971**
    Impound accounts, interest, **CC 2954.8**
    Rules and regulations, **CC 1916.12**
    Shared appreciation loans, **CC 1917 et seq.**
Motor vehicles, seller assisted financing, exemptions, **CC 2982.5**
Real estate,
    Mortgages, generally, ante
    Repair and maintenance, bringing up to code, **CC 2932.6**
Renegotiable rate mortgages, **CC 1916.8, 1916.9**
Shared appreciation loans, **CC 1917 et seq.**
Social security, numbers and numbering, statements, **CC 1786.60**
Translations, foreign languages, contracts, **CC 1632.5**
Variable interest rate, **CC 1916.5, 1916.9**

SAVINGS BANKS
Savings Associations, generally, this index

SAWED OFF SHOTGUNS
Weapons, generally, this index

SCHOOL BONDS
Community Facilities Districts, generally, this index

SCHOOL BUILDINGS AND GROUNDS
Access, interference, obstructions, threats, **CC 1708.9**
Actions and proceedings, access, interference, obstructions, threats, **CC 1708.9**
Attorney fees, access, interference, obstructions, threats, **CC 1708.9**
Community Facilities Districts, generally, this index
Costs, access, interference, obstructions, threats, **CC 1708.9**

SCHOOL BUILDINGS AND GROUNDS—Cont'd
Entry, interference, obstructions, threats, **CC 1708.9**
Exit, interference, obstructions, threats, **CC 1708.9**
Fines and penalties, access, interference, obstructions, threats, **CC 1708.9**
Injunctions, access, interference, obstructions, threats, **CC 1708.9**
Interference, obstructions, threats, access, **CC 1708.9**
Obstructions, interference, threats, access, **CC 1708.9**
Opinion and expert testimony, fees, access, interference, obstructions, threats, **CC 1708.9**
Threats, obstructions, interference, access, **CC 1708.9**

SCHOOL BUSES
Negligence, **CC 2096**

SCHOOL DISTRICTS
Schools and School Districts, generally, this index

SCHOOLS AND SCHOOL DISTRICTS
Architects, contracts, indemnity, **CC 2782.8**
Buildings and grounds. School Buildings and Grounds, generally, this index
Colleges and Universities, generally, this index
Community Facilities Districts, generally, this index
Disabled persons, accessibility, **CC 54.27**
Engineers, contracts, indemnity, **CC 2782.8**
Facilities. School Buildings and Grounds, generally, this index
Grounds. School Buildings and Grounds, generally, this index
Indebtedness, transcripts, withholding, **CC 1788.90 et seq.**
Landscape architects, contracts, indemnity, **CC 2782.8**
Libel and slander, violence, reports, damages, **CC 48.8**
Medical records, disclosure, **CC 56.10**
Mobilehomes and mobilehome parks, school facilities fees, written disclosure, **CC 799.8**
Nonpublic schools. Private Schools, generally, this index
Parochial schools. Private Schools, generally, this index
Private Schools, generally, this index
Recreation and Recreational Facilities, generally, this index
Reports, violence, libel and slander, damages, **CC 48.8**
School Buildings and Grounds, generally, this index
Surveys and surveyors, contracts, indemnity, **CC 2782.8**
Threats, libel and slander, reports, damages, **CC 48.8**

SCHOOLS AND SCHOOL DISTRICTS—Cont'd
Transcript of record, withholding, indebtedness, **CC 1788.90 et seq.**
Violence,
    Libel and slander, reports, damages, **CC 48.8**
    Reports, libel and slander, damages, **CC 48.8**

SCHOOLTEACHERS
Harassment, sexual harassment, **CC 51.9**
Sexual harassment, **CC 51.9**

SCOOTERS
Motorized Scooters, generally, this index

SCOWS
Ships and Shipping, generally, this index

SCULPTURE
Art and artists, commissions, sale, original works, **CC 986**
Common law copyrights, reproduction rights, transfer, **CC 982**
Costs, sales, **CC 1740 et seq.**

SEALS
Abolition of distinction between sealed and unsealed instrument, **CC 1629**
Acknowledgments, affixing, **CC 1193**
Affixing to instruments, **CC 1628**
Distinction between sealed and unsealed instruments abolished, **CC 1629**

SEARCH AND RESCUE
Rescue, generally, this index

SEARCHES AND SEIZURES
Repossessors and Repossession, generally, this index
Warrants,
    Bookstores, personal information, disclosure, **CC 1798.90.05**
    Libraries, personal information, disclosure, **CC 1798.90.05**
    Medical records, **CC 56.10**
    Personal information, governmental agencies, disclosure, Information Practices Act, **CC 1798.24**
    Reading, privacy, **CC 1798.90.05**

SECONDHAND GOODS AND DEALERS
Consumers Legal Remedies Act, **CC 1750 et seq.**
Junk and Junk Dealers, generally, this index

SECRETARY OF STATE
Condominiums, filing, **CC 5405**
Business and commerce, **CC 6760**
Credit services organizations, deposits, **CC 1789.24, 1789.26**
Dance studios, filing fees, **CC 1812.69**
Discount buying services, contracts, deposits in lieu of bonds, **CC 1812.105, 1812.129**
Elections, generally, this index

SECRETARY OF STATE—Cont'd
Fees, dance studios, **CC 1812.69**
Notice, credit services organizations, deposits, ceasing business, **CC 1789.24**

SECRETS AND SECRECY
Confidential or Privileged Information, generally, this index
Trade Secrets, generally, this index

SECTARIAN SCHOOLS
Private Schools, generally, this index

SECURED TRANSACTIONS
Acceleration clause, mortgages or trust deeds, incorporation of clause in documents, **CC 2924.5**
Assignments, execution and delivery, **CC 954.5**
Consumer credit contracts, household goods, **CC 1799.100**
Consumer goods, household goods, restrictions, **CC 1799.100**
Enforcement, security interest, personal property, consumer credit, **CC 1799.100**
Financing statement,
   Agricultural labor lien, notice, **CC 3061.6**
   Filing, agricultural labor lien, notice, **CC 3061.6**
   Variable interest, **CC 1916.6**
Household goods, restrictions, **CC 1799.100**
Interest, variable interest, security documents, **CC 1916.6**
Liens and incumbrances, factors, **CC 3053**
Perfection, assignments, execution and delivery, **CC 954.5**
Real estate,
   Environmentally impaired property, entry and inspection, **CC 2929.5**
   Options, lien redemption, priority, **CC 2906**
   Solar energy, **CC 714**
Rental purchase agreements, application of law, **CC 1812.622**
Security agreements, variable interest, **CC 1916.6**
Solar energy, real property, **CC 714**
Variable interest, security document, **CC 1916.6**

SECURITIES
Agents. Security Agents and Broker Dealers, generally, this index
Brokers. Security Agents and Broker Dealers, generally, this index
Dealers. Security Agents and Broker Dealers, generally, this index
Euro, medium of payment, **CC 1663**
Investment advisors, liability, **CC 3372**
Lost or destroyed negotiable instruments, **CC 3415**
Pensions. Retirement and Pensions, generally, this index
Retirement and Pensions, generally, this index

SECURITIES AGENTS AND BROKER DEALERS
Security Agents and Broker Dealers, generally, this index

SECURITY
See, also, Bonds (Officers and Fiduciaries), generally, this index
Automated license plate recognition, **CC 1798.90.5 et seq.**
Electricity, fences, **CC 835**
Eminent domain, temporary entry on land, repairs, **CC 1002**
Fences, electricity, **CC 835**
Genetic testing, privacy, **CC 56.18 et seq.**
Markets and marketing, Internet, disclosure, **CC 1749.8.3**
Mechanics liens, large projects, **CC 8700 et seq.**
Window bars, residential property, disclosure, **CC 1102.16**

SECURITY AGENTS AND BROKER DEALERS
Applications, contracts, electronic transmissions, **CC 1633**
Contracts, electronic transmissions, **CC 1633**
Digital signatures, contracts, **CC 1633**
Disclosure, contracts, electronic transmissions, **CC 1633**
Electronic transmissions, contracts, **CC 1633**
Signatures, contracts, digital signatures, **CC 1633**
Verification, contracts, electronic transmissions, **CC 1633**

SECURITY DEPOSITS
Floating homes, **CC 800.49**
Landlord and Tenant, this index
Rental purchase agreements, **CC 1812.625**

SECURITY INTEREST
Assignments, rents or profits from real estate, recordation, **CC 2938**
Collateral, investment property, consumer credit contracts, **CC 1799.103**
Consumer Credit, this index
Installment Sales, this index
Investment property, collateral, consumer credit contracts, **CC 1799.103**
Mechanics liens, escrows and escrow agents, large projects, **CC 8726**
Motor Vehicles, this index
Religious books, artifacts or materials, consumer credit contracts, **CC 1799.97**
Rental purchase agreements, prohibited provisions, **CC 1812.624**
Secured Transactions, generally, this index

SEDUCTION
Actions and proceedings, **CC 43.5**
Children and minors, **CC 49**

SEEING EYE DOGS
Service Animals, generally, this index

SEGREGATION
Discrimination, generally, this index

SEISMIC SAFETY
Earthquakes, generally, this index

SEISMOLOGICAL DISTURBANCES
Earthquakes, generally, this index

SEIZURES
Searches and Seizures, generally, this index

SELF DEFENSE
Force, right to use, **CC 50**
Protection from bodily harm, **CC 43**

SELF INSURANCE
Customer depositing personalty for repair, alteration or sale, **CC 1858.3**

SELLER ASSISTED MARKETING PLANS
Generally, **CC 1812.200 et seq.**
Actions and proceedings, **CC 1812.218**
Assignments, **CC 1812.211**
Bankruptcy, disclosure, **CC 1812.206**
Bond (officers and fiduciaries), filing, **CC 1812.214**
Books and records, **CC 1812.213**
Burden of proof, exemptions, **CC 1812.216**
Claims, deposits in lieu of bonds, **CC 1812.221**
Contracts, **CC 1812.200 et seq.**
   Cancellation, **CC 1812.208**
   Provisions, **CC 1812.209**
   Voidability, **CC 1812.215**
Crimes and offenses, **CC 1812.217**
Damages, **CC 1812.218**
Deposits in lieu of bond, claims, **CC 1812.221**
Disclosures, **CC 1812.205, 1812.206**
Down payments, **CC 1812.210**
Escrow and escrow accounts, **CC 1812.214**
Exemptions, burden of proof, **CC 1812.216**
Fees, **CC 1812.203**
Filing,
   Agent for service of process, foreign corporation, **CC 1812.214**
   Disclosure statements, **CC 1812.203**
Fines and penalties, **CC 1812.217**
Fraud, voidable contract, **CC 1812.215**
Information sheet, **CC 1812.206**
Records, **CC 1812.213**
Remedies, **CC 1812.219**
Representations, **CC 1812.204**
Restrictions, activities and representations, **CC 1812.204**
Revocation or suspension, registration, for cause, **CC 1812.203**
Service of process, **CC 1812.214**
Waiver, **CC 1812.216**

SEMINARIES
Colleges and Universities, generally, this index

SEMINARS
Sales solicitation contracts, cancellation rights, **CC 1689.20 et seq.**

SEMITRAILERS

SEMITRAILERS
Motor Carriers, generally, this index

SENIOR CITIZENS
Aged Persons, generally, this index

SENTENCE AND PUNISHMENT
Crimes and Offenses, generally, this index
Fines and Penalties, generally, this index

SEPARATE MAINTENANCE
Legal separation. Marriage, this index

SEPARATION
Legal separation. Marriage, this index

SERIAL NUMBERS
Alteration, destruction, sale or possession of merchandise, CC 1710.1

SERVANTS
Domestic Workers, generally, this index

SERVICE ANIMALS
Accompaniment, CC 54.1, 54.2
Damages caused by, CC 54.2
Failure to use, CC 54.4
Fees, public accommodations, accompanying blind person or trainer, CC 54.2
Licenses and permits, training licenses, public accommodations, CC 54.1, 54.2
Public accommodations, CC 54.1 et seq.
Rental units, acceptance of dog, CC 54.1
Trainers, public accommodations, CC 54.1, 54.2
Zoos or wild animal parks, CC 54.7

SERVICE CHARGES
Credit Cards, this index
Installment Sales, this index

SERVICE CONTRACTS
Generally, CC 1790 et seq.
Home protection contracts, cancellation, CC 1689.5 et seq.
Rental purchase agreements, following transfer of ownership, CC 1812.635
Song Beverly Consumer Warranty Act, CC 1790 et seq.

SERVICE MARKS
Trademarks, generally, this index

SERVICE OF PROCESS
Process, this index

SERVICE STATIONS
Motor Vehicle Service Stations, generally, this index

SERVIENT TENEMENTS
Easements, this index

SERVITUDES
Generally, CC 801 et seq.
Easements, generally, this index

SETBACK LINES
Zoning and Planning, generally, this index

SETOFF AND COUNTERCLAIM
Agents, rights of third persons dealing with agent without knowledge of agency, CC 2336
Credit cards, defenses of cardholder against retailer, setoff against care issuer, CC 1747.90

SETTLEMENT
Compromise and Settlement, generally, this index

SEVERAL LIABILITY
Joint and Several Liability, generally, this index

SEVERANCE
Joint tenancy, real property, CC 683.2

SEWERS AND SEWER SYSTEMS
Zoning and Planning, generally, this index

SEWING MACHINES
Manufacturers identification mark, removal, defacing, alteration or destruction, CC 1710.1

SEX
Actions and proceedings, force and violence, CC 52.4
Attorney fees, force and violence, actions and proceedings, CC 52.4
Children and minors, markets and marketing, retailers, gender neutrality, CC 55.7, 55.8
Construction of laws, CC 14
Consumer goods, price discrimination, CC 51.14
Costs, force and violence, actions and proceedings, CC 52.4
Crimes and offenses, force and violence, actions and proceedings, CC 52.4
Damages, force and violence, CC 52.4
Discrimination, generally, this index
Exemplary damages, force and violence, CC 52.4
Force and violence, actions and proceedings, CC 52.4
Injunction, force and violence, CC 52.4
Limitation of actions, force and violence, CC 52.4
Markets and marketing, retailers, children and minors, gender neutrality, CC 55.7, 55.8
Mobilehomes and mobilehome parks, club membership, discrimination, CC 798.20
Price discrimination, consumer goods, CC 51.14
Retailers, markets and marketing, children and minors, gender neutrality, CC 55.7, 55.8
Statute of limitations, force and violence, CC 52.4
Stores, markets and marketing, children and minors, gender neutrality, CC 55.7, 55.8
Violence, actions and proceedings, CC 52.4
Women, generally, this index

SEX DISCRIMINATION
Discrimination, generally, this index

SEX OFFENSES
Children and minors, CC 1669.5
Contracts, victims, CC 1669.5
Deeds and conveyances, registered sex offenders, data base, notice, CC 2079.10a
Human Trafficking, generally, this index
Leases, registered sex offenders, data base, notice, CC 2079.10a
Lewdness and Obscenity, generally, this index
Notice, real estate, lease or sale, data base, CC 2079.10a
Real estate, lease or sale, registered sex offenders, data base, notice, CC 2079.10a
Registration,
  Deeds and conveyances, data base, notice, CC 2079.10a
  Leases, data base, notice, CC 2079.10a
  Notice, real estate, lease or sale, data base, CC 2079.10a
  Real estate, lease or sale, data base, notice, CC 2079.10a
Sexual Assault, generally, this index
Sexual Battery, generally, this index
Trafficking. Human Trafficking, generally, this index

SEXUAL ASSAULT
Attorney fees, personal information, victim service providers, grants, injunction, CC 1798.79.95
Contracts, children and minors, victims, CC 1669.5
Costs, personal information, victim service providers, grants, injunction, CC 1798.79.95
Crime victims,
  Landlord and tenant, termination, notice, CC 1946.7
  Personal information, victim service providers, grants, CC 1798.79.8 et seq.
Damages, CC 1708.5
Equitable relief, CC 1708.5
Financial assistance, victim service providers, personal information, CC 1798.79.8 et seq.
Grants, victim service providers, personal information, CC 1798.79.8 et seq.
Information, personal information, victim service providers, grants, CC 1798.79.8 et seq.
Injunction, personal information, victim service providers, grants, CC 1798.79.95
Landlord and tenant,
  Emergency services, law enforcement, CC 1946.8
  Termination, notice, CC 1946.7
Personal information, victim service providers, grants, CC 1798.79.8 et seq.
Prophylactics, removal, CC 1708.5
Sexual Battery, generally, this index

SHORT

SEXUAL ASSAULT—Cont'd
Shelters, personal information, grants, CC 1798.79.8 et seq.
Stealthing, CC 1708.5

SEXUAL BATTERY
See, also, Sexual Assault, generally, this index
Damages, CC 1708.5
Consent, children and minors, defense, CC 1708.5.5
Prophylactics, removal, CC 1708.5
Stealthing, CC 1708.5

SEXUAL EXPLOITATION
Children and Minors, this index

SEXUAL HARASSMENT
Attorney fees, CC 52
Business relationship, CC 51.9
Contracts, witnesses, void, CC 1670.11
Damages, CC 51.9, 52
Emotional distress, CC 51.9
Evidence, contracts, void, CC 1670.11
Fines and penalties, CC 52
Labor and employment, business relationship, CC 51.9
Libel and slander, privileges and immunities, CC 47
Personal injuries, CC 51.9
Privileges and immunities, libel and slander, CC 47
Professional relationship, CC 51.9
Punitive damages, CC 52
Verification, complaints and answers, CC 51.9
Witnesses, contracts, void, CC 1670.11

SEXUAL ORIENTATION
Actions and proceedings, CC 52.45
Attorney fees, CC 52.45
Civil rights, CC 51.7
Contracts, freedom from violence, waiver, CC 51.7
Costs, CC 52.45
Crimes and offenses, actions and proceedings, CC 52.45
Damages, CC 52.45
Discrimination, CC 51.7
Civil rights, CC 51
Domestic Partnership, generally, this index
Freedom from violence or intimidation, CC 51.7
Injunction, CC 52.45
Limitation of actions, CC 52.45
Marriage, generally, this index
Punitive damages, damages, CC 52.45
Statute of limitations, CC 52.45

SEXUAL RELATIONS
Prostitution, generally, this index
Sex Offenses, generally, this index

SHARED APPRECIATION LOANS
Generally, CC 1917 et seq.

SHARED APPRECIATION LOANS—Cont'd
Aged persons, CC 1917.320 et seq.
Application of law, CC 1917.002, 1917.005
Seniors, CC 1917.334, 1917.612
Appraisal and appraisers, seniors, CC 1917.410 et seq.
Contingent interests,
Deferred interests, CC 1917
Seniors, CC 1917.616
Disclosure, seniors, CC 1917.710 et seq.
ERISA pension fund, investments, CC 1917.210, 1917.220
Fair market value, seniors, CC 1917.410 et seq.
Forms, seniors, disclosure, CC 1917.711 et seq.
Improvements, seniors, CC 1917.510, 1917.511
Interest, CC 1917.002
Pension funds, usury exemption, CC 1917.220
Seniors, CC 1917.331, 1917.613, 1917.619
Contingent interest, usury, CC 1917.616
Truth in lending, disclosure, CC 1917.712, 1917.713
Usury, exemptions, CC 1917.005
Investments, pension funds, CC 1917.210, 1917.220
Liens and incumbrances, CC 1917.003, 1917.004
Seniors, CC 1917.614, 1917.615
Notice, seniors, CC 1917.710 et seq.
Pension funds, investments, CC 1917.210, 1917.220
Prepayment, seniors, CC 1917.333
Refinancing, seniors, CC 1917.330
Seniors, CC 1917.320 et seq.
Status of borrowers and lenders, CC 1917.001
Seniors, CC 1917.610
Terms and conditions, seniors, CC 1917.330
Trust Deeds, this index
Truth in lending, loans for seniors, disclosure, CC 1917.712, 1917.713
Usury exemption, CC 1917.005
Pension fund investments, CC 1917.220
Seniors, CC 1917.613, 1917.619
Contingent interest, CC 1917.616
Valuation of property, seniors, CC 1917.410 et seq.
Waiver, borrowers rights, seniors, CC 1917.611

SHARES AND SHAREHOLDERS
Corporations, this index

SHEEP
See, also, Animals, generally, this index
Dogs, killing or injuring, liability of owner, CC 3341

SHELLEY'S CASE
Rule abolished, CC 779

SHELTERS
Designation, emergencies, liability, CC 1714.5

SHELTERS—Cont'd
Sexual assault, personal information, grants, CC 1798.79.8 et seq.
Stalking, personal information, grants, CC 1798.79.8 et seq.

SHERIFFS
Arrest, generally, this index
Arson, injuries, liability, CC 1714.9
Attachment, generally, this index
Discrimination, dogs, public accommodations, emergencies, CC 54.25
Dogs, discrimination, public accommodations, emergencies, CC 54.25
Executions, generally, this index
Fines and penalties, dogs, discrimination, public accommodations, emergencies, CC 54.25
Firemans rule, CC 1714.9
Good faith, arrest, privileges and immunities, CC 43.55
Injury to sheriffs, liability, CC 1714.9
Jails, generally, this index
Lost property, delivery, CC 2080.1
Prisons and prisoners. Jails, generally, this index
Privileges and immunities, arrest, CC 43.55
Process, generally, this index
Recreational vehicle parks, notice, removal, CC 799.58
Searches and Seizures, generally, this index

SHIPS AND SHIPPING
See, also, Carriers, generally, this index
Bailment, charter party, CC 1959
Bottomry, generally, this index
Cargo. Respondentia, generally, this index
Charter party, bailment, CC 1959
Deaf persons, public accommodations, CC 54.1 et seq.
Duties, CC 2088
Federal law, CC 2088
Leases, charter party, CC 1959
Pest Control, generally, this index
Records and recordation, transfers, CC 1173
Sales, recording of transfers, CC 1173
Transfer of title or interest,
Recording, CC 1173
Sales, written instruments, CC 1135
Voidable transactions, at sea or in foreign port, application of law, CC 3440.1
Wrecks and wrecked property, deposits, involuntary, CC 1815
Written instruments, sales, CC 1135

SHOOTING RANGES
Generally, CC 3482.1

SHOPS
Stores, generally, this index

SHORT ORDER CAFES
Restaurants, generally, this index

SHORT

SHORT TITLES
Popular Name Laws, generally, this index

SHOTGUNS
Weapons, generally, this index

SHOW CAUSE ORDERS
Homeless persons, transitional housing, misconduct, CC 1954.13
Identity and identification, theft, business entities, filing, CC 1798.201

SHOWS
Motion Pictures, generally, this index
Theaters and Shows, generally, this index

SIBLINGS
Relatives, generally, this index

SIDEWALKS
Blind or visually impaired persons, civil rights, CC 54 et seq.
Disabled Persons, this index

SIGHT
Eyes and Eyesight, generally, this index

SIGNAL DOGS
Service Animals, generally, this index

SIGNALS
Signs and Signals, generally, this index

SIGNATURES
Acknowledgments, officers taking, CC 1193
Advertisements,
  Deceased celebrity image protection, CC 3344.1
  Unauthorized use, CC 3344
Astaire Celebrity Image Protection Act, CC 3344.1
Celebrity image protection, CC 3344.1
Consumer credit contracts, notice of responsibility, CC 1799.91 et seq.
Contracts, this index
Electronic signatures,
  Security agents and broker dealers, contracts, CC 1633
  Uniform Electronic Transactions Act, CC 1633.1 et seq.
Home equity sales contracts, CC 1695.2
In vitro fertilization, crimes and offenses, actions and proceedings, CC 1708.5.6
Installment Sales, this index
Medical records, release, authorization, CC 56.11
Mortgages, request for order of default and of sale, CC 2924b
Security agents and broker dealers, contracts, digital signatures, CC 1633
Suretyship, CC 2793
Telecommunications, Uniform Electronic Transactions Act, CC 1633.1 et seq.
Trust deeds, request for order of default and of sale, CC 2924b

SIGNATURES—Cont'd
Uniform Electronic Transactions Act, CC 1633.1 et seq.

SIGNS AND SIGNALS
Autographed memorabilia, warranties, CC 1739.7
Condominiums, display, CC 4710
  Business and commerce, CC 6704
Electricity, fences, security, CC 835
Fences, electrified fences, security, CC 835
Grey market goods, retail sellers, disclosures, CC 1797.81
Initiative and referendum, mobilehomes and mobilehome parks, CC 798.51, 799.10
Landlord and tenant, elections, CC 1940.4
Mobilehomes and Mobilehome Parks, this index
Outdoor Advertising, generally, this index
Prescriptive rights, easements, CC 1008
Real estate, sale or lease, display, CC 712, 713
Recall, mobilehomes and mobilehome parks, CC 798.51, 799.10

SILK
Carriers, limitation of liability, CC 2200

SILK SCREENS
Common law copyrights, reproduction rights, transfer, CC 982

SILVER
See, also, Mines and Minerals, generally, this index
Carriers, limitation of liability, CC 2200

SINGLE FAMILY DWELLINGS
Housing, generally, this index

SINGLE FAMILY RESIDENTIAL HOUSING
Housing, generally, this index

SINGLE PUBLICATION ACT
Generally, CC 3425.1 et seq.

SINGULAR
Construction of laws, CC 14

SISTER STATES
Foreign States, generally, this index

SISTERS
Relatives, generally, this index

SKIMMING (RENT)
Generally, CC 890

SKUNKS
Fur bearing mammals. Fish and Game, this index

SLANDER
Libel and Slander, generally, this index

SLANDERING TITLE
Real estate, CC 880.360

SLAVERY
Human Trafficking, generally, this index
Retailers, manufacturers and manufacturing, disclosure, CC 1714.43

SLIDES
Photography and Pictures, generally, this index

SLINGSHOTS
Weapons, generally, this index

SMALL BUSINESS GENDER DISCRIMINATION IN SERVICES COMPLIANCE ACT
Generally, CC 55.61 et seq.

SMALL BUSINESSES
Actions and proceedings, discrimination, sex, CC 55.61 et seq.
Discrimination, sex, CC 55.61 et seq.
Sex, discrimination, CC 55.61 et seq.

SMALL CLAIMS COURTS
Checks, wrongful dishonor, treble damages, jurisdiction, CC 1719
Civil rights, jurisdiction, CC 52.2
Computer aided transcription system, CC 54.8
Condominiums, assessments, delinquency, CC 5658, 5720
Deaf or hard of hearing persons, listening systems, CC 54.8
Discrimination, jurisdiction, CC 52.2
Easements, maintenance and repairs, CC 845
Hearing devices, CC 54.8
Jurisdiction, civil rights, CC 52.2
Listening systems, CC 54.8
Mobilehomes and mobilehome parks, willful violations, damages, CC 798.86
Transcription system, computer aided, CC 54.8

SMALL EMPLOYERS
Small Businesses, generally, this index

SMELLS
Air Pollution, generally, this index

SMOG
Air Pollution, generally, this index

SMOKE
Air Pollution, generally, this index

SMOKING
Cigarettes and Cigars, generally, this index
Landlord and tenant, prohibiting, CC 1947.5
Leases, prohibiting, CC 1947.5
Notice, landlord and tenant, prohibiting, CC 1947.5
Products liability, CC 1714.45
Rent, prohibiting, CC 1947.5
Tobacco and Tobacco Products, generally, this index

SOCIAL ACTIVITIES
Dating service contracts, CC 1694 et seq.

SOCIAL HOSTS
Alcoholic beverages, liability, CC 1714

SOCIAL MEDIA

Force and violence, reports, CC 1798.99.20 et seq.

Threats, reports, CC 1798.99.20 et seq.

SOCIAL SECURITY

Numbers and numbering. Social Security Numbers, generally, this index

SOCIAL SECURITY NUMBERS

Banks and banking, statements, CC 1786.60

Cards, CC 1798.85

Club cards, grocery stores, disclosure, CC 1749.60 et seq.

Confidential or privileged information, CC 1798.85

Consumer credit reporting agencies,
    Identity and identification, theft, CC 1785.20.3
    Security freeze, change, CC 1785.11.3

Correctional institutions, veterans, disclosure, CC 1798.85

Disclosure, CC 1798.85
    Grocery stores, club cards, CC 1749.60 et seq.

Financial institutions, statements, CC 1786.60

Grocery stores, club cards, disclosure, CC 1749.60 et seq.

Health care providers, posting, CC 1798.85

Health care service plans, posting, CC 1798.85

Identity and identification, theft, CC 1798.92 et seq.

Internet, posting, CC 1798.85

Jails, veterans, disclosure, CC 1798.85

Mail and mailing, posting, CC 1798.85

Pharmacists, posting, CC 1798.85

Posting, CC 1798.85

Records and recordation, truncation, CC 1798.89

Sales, CC 1798.85

Savings and loan associations, statements, CC 1786.60

Savings banks, statements, CC 1786.60

Waiver, confidential or privileged information, CC 1798.86

SOCIAL SERVICES

CalWORKs. Medi Cal Program, generally, this index

Certified homes of foster family agencies. Foster homes, generally, post

Disclosure, personal information held by governmental subdivisions, Information Practices Act, CC 1798.24

Family homes. Foster homes, generally, post

Foster homes,
    Alienation of affection, CC 43.56
    Indebtedness, duress or coercion, CC 1798.97.1 et seq.
    Privileges and immunities, alienation of affection, CC 43.56

Health care and services. Medi Cal Program, generally, this index

SOCIAL SERVICES—Cont'd

Homeless persons, transitional housing, misconduct, CC 1954.10 et seq.

Identification cards, RFID (radio frequency identification), crimes and offenses, CC 1798.79, 1798.795

Medi Cal Program, generally, this index

Medical assistance. Medi Cal Program, generally, this index

Misconduct, transitional housing, homeless persons, CC 1954.10 et seq.

Monopolies and unfair trade, procurement, fees, CC 1770
    Treble damages, CC 1780

Personal information, disclosure, CC 1798.24

Social Workers, generally, this index

Transitional housing, homeless persons, misconduct, CC 1954.10 et seq.

Unfair trade, procurement, fees, CC 1770
    Treble damages, CC 1780

SOCIAL WORKERS

Actions and proceedings, sexual exploitation, CC 43.93

Clinical social workers,
    Medical Malpractice, generally, this index
    Privileges and immunities,
        Professional societies, CC 43.7, 43.8
        Referral services, CC 43.95
    Referrals, limitation of liability, CC 43.95
    Telecommunications, referral services, privileges and immunities, CC 43.95

Evidence, sexual exploitation, CC 43.93

Marriage and Family Therapists, generally, this index

Privileges and immunities,
    Clinical social workers, ante
    Threats, violent behavior, patients, protection, CC 43.92

Protection, threats, violent behavior, patients, privileges and immunities, CC 43.92

Sexual exploitation, CC 43.93

Threats, violent behavior, patients, protection, privileges and immunities, CC 43.92

SOCIETIES

Associations and Societies, generally, this index

SOLAR ENERGY

Generally, CC 714, 714.1

Attorney fees, CC 714

Building standards, electricity, CC 714

Certificates and certification,
    System and installation, CC 714
    Water supply, CC 714

Common areas, CC 4746

Community apartments,
    Applications, approval, CC 714
    Restrictions, CC 714.1

Condominiums,
    Homeowners associations, applications, approval, CC 714

SOLAR ENERGY—Cont'd

Condominiums—Cont'd
    Restrictions, CC 714.1

Damages, systems, CC 714

Deeds and conveyances, CC 714
    Easements, CC 801.5

Easements, CC 801, 801.5
    Solar Energy Act, CC 714

Fines and penalties, solar rights, CC 714

Grants, certificates and certification, public entities, compliance, CC 714

Indemnity and indemnification, systems, CC 714.1

Installation, notice, CC 4746

Insurance, CC 4746

Loans, certificates and certification, public entities, compliance, CC 714

Notice, installation, CC 4746

Planned developments, restrictions, CC 714.1

Restrictions, systems, CC 714.1

Stock cooperatives,
    Applications, approval, CC 714
    Restrictions, CC 714.1

Surveys and surveyors, CC 4746

SOLAR RIGHTS ACT

Generally, CC 714

SOLDIERS, SAILORS AND MARINES

Military Forces, generally, this index

Veterans, generally, this index

SOLICITATION

Credit Cards, this index

False statements or invoices, damages, CC 1716

Names, use without consent, invasion of privacy, CC 3344

Payment of money, soliciting by false statement or invoice, CC 1716

Photographs or other likeness, use without consent, invasion of privacy, CC 3344

Purchases of products, unauthorized use of name, photograph, voice, signature, CC 3344

Rental purchase agreements, consumer references, CC 1812.641

Sales. Telecommunications, this index

Signatures, use without consent, invasion of privacy, CC 3344

Voice, use without consent, invasion of privacy, CC 3344

SOLICITOR GENERAL

Attorney General, generally, this index

SOLID WASTE

Diversion. Recycling, generally, this index

Hazardous Substances and Waste, generally, this index

Junk and Junk Dealers, generally, this index

Recycling, generally, this index

Zoning and Planning, generally, this index

SOLVENCY

SOLVENCY
Insolvency, generally, this index

SONG BEVERLY CONSUMER WARRANTY ACT
Generally, CC 1790 et seq.

SONG BEVERLY CREDIT CARD ACT
Generally, CC 1747 et seq.

SONGS
Music and Musicians, generally, this index

SOOT
Air Pollution, generally, this index

SOUND RECORDINGS
Audio and Video Recordings, generally, this index

SPACE
Flights, CC 2210 et seq.
Private space activities, flights, CC 2210 et seq.

SPACE FLIGHT LIABILITY AND IMMUNITY ACT
Generally, CC 2210 et seq.

SPACE FORCE
Military Forces, generally, this index

SPANISH LANGUAGE
See, also, Language, generally, this index
Attorney fees, contracts, translations, CC 1632
Business or trade contracts, translations, CC 1632
Consumer credit contracts, signers, notice or responsibility, CC 1799.91 et seq.
Contracts, business or trade contracts, translations, CC 1632
Home solicitation contracts, CC 1689.7
Mortgage forms, notice of default cure, CC 2924c
Motor vehicles, leases, contracts, CC 2991
Trust deeds, forms, notice of default cure, CC 2924c

SPECIAL DAMAGES
Damages, this index

SPECIAL DISTRICTS
Personal property, safekeeping, powers and duties, CC 2080.10
Property, safekeeping, powers and duties, CC 2080.10

SPECIAL EDUCATION
Intellectual and Developmental Disabilities, generally, this index

SPECIAL FIRE PROTECTION ZONES
Fires and Fire Protection, generally, this index

SPECIAL OCCUPANCY PARKS
Children and minors, CC 1866
Damages, eviction, notice, CC 1866

SPECIAL OCCUPANCY PARKS—Cont'd
Dangers, moving, CC 1867
Eviction, CC 1866
Fines and penalties, eviction, notice, CC 1866
Forcible entry and detainer, CC 1866
Health and sanitation, moving, CC 1867
Imminent danger, moving, CC 1867
Minors, CC 1866
Notice, eviction, CC 1866
Safety, moving, CC 1867

SPECIAL PRORATERS
Debtors and Creditors, generally, this index

SPECIFIC PERFORMANCE
Generally, CC 3384 et seq.
Appropriate remedy, CC 3386
Concurrent performance, assurance, CC 3386
Condition precedent, CC 3392
Counterperformance, substantial performance, CC 3386
Deeds and conveyances, CC 3387
  Defective title, CC 3394
Defective title by seller, CC 3394
Easements, maintenance and repairs, CC 845
Evidence, presumptions, contracts for sale of land, inadequacy of damages, CC 3387
Fines and penalties, enforcement of contract imposing penalty, CC 3389
Fraud, contracts entered into by, CC 3391
Future performance, assurance, CC 3386
Good faith purchasers, relief against, CC 3395
Inadequacy of damages, presumption, contracts for sale of land, CC 3387
Innocent purchasers, CC 3395
Labor contracts, personal service, CC 3390
Liquidated damages, enforcement, CC 3389
Mistakes, contracts entered into by, CC 3391
Mortgages, sales, rent, CC 2924m
Mutuality of remedy, CC 3386
Obligations not specifically enforceable, CC 3390
Parties who cannot be compelled to perform, CC 3391
Penalties, enforcement of contract imposing penalty, CC 3389
Personal property, possession, CC 3379, 3380
Personal service obligations, CC 3390
Presumptions, real estate, contracts for sale of land, CC 3387
Real estate,
  Defective title by seller, CC 3394
  Perfecting title, possession of real estate, CC 3375
  Presumption of inadequacy damages, CC 3387
  Relief against parties claiming under person bound to perform, CC 3395
Reformed contracts, enforcement, CC 3402
Revised contract, CC 3402
Signature of contract by one party only, CC 3388

SPECIFIC PERFORMANCE—Cont'd
Title to property,
  Defective, CC 3394
  Perfecting, possession of real estate, CC 3375
Trust deeds, sales, rent, CC 2924m

SPEECH IMPAIRED PERSONS
Deaf or Hard of Hearing Persons, generally, this index

SPELUNKING
Generally, CC 846

SPERM
Tissue Banks, generally, this index

SPIRITUOUS LIQUORS
Alcoholic Beverages, generally, this index

SPITE FENCES
Malicious erection or maintenance, CC 841.4

SPONSORS
Goods or services, sale or lease, Consumers Legal Remedies Act, CC 1750 et seq.
Workforce housing cooperative trusts, CC 817.3

SPORT SHOOTING RANGES
Generally, CC 3482.1

SPORTING EVENTS
Athletics, generally, this index

SPORTS
Athletics, generally, this index

SPORTS ARENAS OR PAVILIONS
Leases, notice, anabolic steroids, crimes, CC 1812.97

SPOUSAL ABUSE
Domestic Violence, generally, this index

SPOUSES
Marriage, generally, this index

SPRAYING
Pest Control, generally, this index

SQUIRRELS
Pest Control, generally, this index

STAINED GLASS ARTISTRY
Fine arts, CC 997

STAIRWAY CHAIR LIFTS
Elevators, Dumbwaiters and Escalators, generally, this index

STAKEHOLDERS
Escrows and Escrow Agents, generally, this index

STALKING
Attorney fees, personal information, victim service providers, grants, injunction, CC 1798.79.95

STALKING—Cont'd
Costs, personal information, victim service providers, grants, injunction, **CC 1798.79.95**
Crime victims,
  Landlord and tenant, termination, notice, **CC 1946.7**
  Personal information, victim service providers, grants, **CC 1798.79.8 et seq.**
Financial assistance, victim service providers, personal information, **CC 1798.79.8 et seq.**
Grants, victim service providers, personal information, **CC 1798.79.8 et seq.**
Information, personal information, victim service providers, grants, **CC 1798.79.8 et seq.**
Injunction,
  Personal information, victim service providers, grants, **CC 1798.79.95**
  Violation of restraining orders, **CC 1708.7**
Landlord and tenant,
  Emergency services, law enforcement, **CC 1946.8**
  Termination, notice, **CC 1946.7**
Personal information, victim service providers, grants, **CC 1798.79.8 et seq.**
Shelters, personal information, grants, **CC 1798.79.8 et seq.**
Torts, **CC 1708.7**

STALLIONS AND JACKS
Horses, generally, this index

STAMPS
Trading Stamps, generally, this index

STANDARD OF CARE
Real estate brokers and salespersons, residential property, prospective purchasers, **CC 2079.2**

STANDARDS
Building Standards, generally, this index
Civil rights, disabled persons, construction, accessibility, **CC 55.51 et seq.**
Construction, civil rights, disabled persons, accessibility, **CC 55.51 et seq.**
Consumers Legal Remedies Act, **CC 1750 et seq.**
Disabled persons, civil rights, construction, accessibility, **CC 55.51 et seq.**
Fraud, goods or services, Consumers Legal Remedies Act, **CC 1750 et seq.**

STATE
Access, records, personal information, **CC 1798.30 et seq.**
Actions and proceedings, tax lien enforcement, **CC 2931c**
Boards and Commissions, generally, this index
Carriers, preferences, **CC 2171**
Civil defense. War and Civil Defense, generally, this index

STATE—Cont'd
Claims,
  Actions and proceedings, personal information, maintenance and disclosure, violations, **CC 1798.45 et seq.**
  Information, personal information, maintenance and disclosure, **CC 1798.45 et seq.**
Commissions and commissioners. Boards and Commissions, generally, this index
Confidential or privileged information, personal information, requirements to maintain or disclosure, **CC 1798 et seq.**
Conservation easements, acquisition, holding, **CC 815.3**
Contracts. State Contracts, generally, this index
Crimes and offenses, personal information in state records, disclosure, **CC 1798.55 et seq.**
Damages,
  Interest recoverable, **CC 3287**
  Personal information in agency records, disclosure, **CC 1798.45 et seq.**
Departments. State Departments, generally, this index
Elections, generally, this index
Electronic Transactions Act, signatures, **CC 1633.17**
Eminent Domain, generally, this index
Employees. State Officers and Employees, generally, this index
Foreign States, generally, this index
Holidays, generally, this index
Improvements, generally, this index
Income Tax—State, generally, this index
Information Practices Act, **CC 1798 et seq.**
Initiative and Referendum, generally, this index
Injunction, records, personal information, disclosure, **CC 1798.46, 1798.47**
Interest, damages interest on, **CC 3287**
Islands, ownership, navigable streams, **CC 1016**
Lands. Public Lands, generally, this index
Legislature, generally, this index
Liens and incumbrances,
  Action to enforce, **CC 2931c**
  Records, disclosure, **CC 1798.67**
  Tax Liens, generally, this index
Mineral rights, **CC 883.110 et seq.**
Mortgage foreclosure, parties, **CC 2931a, 2931b**
National defense. War and Civil Defense, generally, this index
Officers and employees. State Officers and Employees, generally, this index
Ownership of property, **CC 669, 670**
Personal information, requirements to maintain or disclosure, **CC 1798 et seq.**
Personnel. State Officers and Employees, generally, this index

STATE—Cont'd
Privacy, Information Practices Act, **CC 1798 et seq.**
Process, mortgage foreclosure, **CC 2931a**
Property. Public Lands, generally, this index
Public Lands, generally, this index
Public Policy, generally, this index
Real estate. Public Lands, generally, this index
Records and recordation,
  Access, personal information, **CC 1798.30 et seq.**
  Disclosure, Information Practices Act, **CC 1798 et seq.**
  Information Practices Act, **CC 1798 et seq.**
  Personal information, disclosure, **CC 1798 et seq.**
Right of Way, generally, this index
Secretary of State, generally, this index
Signatures, Electronic Transactions Act, **CC 1633.17**
Tax Liens, generally, this index
Taxation, generally, this index
Telecommunications, priorities and preferences, **CC 2207, 2208**
Trust deeds, foreclosure, party, **CC 2931a**
Uniform Electronic Transactions Act, signatures, **CC 1633.17**
War and Civil Defense, generally, this index

STATE AGENCIES
See, also, Public Agencies, generally, this index
Access, records, personal information, **CC 1798.30 et seq.**
Actions and proceedings, personal information, maintenance and disclosure, violations, **CC 1798.45 et seq.**
Administrative Law and Procedure, generally, this index
Attorney fees, personal information in agency records, disclosure, **CC 1798.46, 1798.48, 1798.53**
Attorneys, fees. Attorney fees, generally, ante
Breach of security, personal information, disclosure, **CC 1798.29**
Claims, personal information, maintenance and disclosure, violations, **CC 1798.45 et seq.**
Comatose patients, medical information disclosure, **CC 56.10**
Computers, breach of security, personal information, **CC 1798.29**
Confidential or privileged information,
  Breach of security, personal information, disclosure, **CC 1798.29**
  Conflict of laws, personal information, **CC 1798.70 et seq.**
Disclosure,
  Breach of security, **CC 1798.29**
  District attorneys, **CC 1798.68**
  Information Practices Act, **CC 1798 et seq.**
  Personal information, disclosure, **CC 1798 et seq.**

STATE

STATE AGENCIES—Cont'd
Confidential or privileged information—Cont'd
  Safeguards, disclosure of personal information, **CC 1798.21**
Contracts. State Contracts, generally, this index
Costs, personal information in agency records, disclosure, **CC 1798.46, 1798.48, 1798.53**
Crimes and offenses, personal information in agency records, disclosure, **CC 1798.55 et seq.**
Damages, personal information in agency records, disclosure, **CC 1798.45 et seq.**
Disclosure,
  Confidential or privileged information, district attorneys, **CC 1798.68**
  Personal information, Information Practices Act, **CC 1798 et seq.**
District attorneys, confidential or privileged information, disclosure, **CC 1798.68**
Electronic mail, breach of security, notice, **CC 1798.29**
Eminent Domain, generally, this index
Employees. State Officers and Employees, generally, this index
Fees, records and recordation, personal information, copies, **CC 1798.33**
Fines and penalties, personal information in agency records, disclosure, **CC 1798.55 et seq.**
Forms, breach of security, **CC 1798.29**
  Personal information, notice, **CC 1798.82**
Information Practices Act, **CC 1798 et seq.**
Injunction, records, personal information, disclosure, **CC 1798.46, 1798.47**
Judgments and decrees, personal information in agency records, disclosure, **CC 1798.47**
Liens and incumbrances, records, disclosure, **CC 1798.67**
Limitation of actions, personal information in agency records, disclosure, **CC 1798.49**
Mail and mailing, lists, removal of names and addresses, **CC 1798.62**
Notice,
  Information Practices Act, contents, **CC 1798.17**
  Personal information, breach of security, **CC 1798.29**
Officers and employees. State Officers and Employees, generally, this index
Personal information on individuals, requirements to maintain, **CC 1798 et seq.**
Personal property, safekeeping, powers and duties, **CC 2080.10**
Privacy, Information Practices Act, **CC 1798 et seq.**
Privacy protection agency, **CC 1798.199.10 et seq.**
Privileged information. Confidential or privileged information, generally, ante
Property, safekeeping, powers and duties, **CC 2080.10**

STATE AGENCIES—Cont'd
Records and recordation,
  Access, personal information, **CC 1798.30 et seq.**
  Actions and proceedings, personal information, maintenance and disclosure, **CC 1798.45 et seq.**
  Amendment or correction, personal information, **CC 1798.35 et seq.**
  Application of law, personal or confidential information, **CC 1798.70 et seq.**
  Conflict of laws, personal or confidential information, **CC 1798.70 et seq.**
  Constitutional right to privacy, individual personal information, **CC 1798.73**
  Contracts, operation or maintenance, Information Practices Act, **CC 1798.19**
  Copies, personal information, fees, **CC 1798.33**
  Crimes and offenses, personal information, disclosure, **CC 1798.55 et seq.**
  Disclosure,
    District attorneys, **CC 1798.68**
    Information Practices Act, **CC 1798 et seq.**
  Discovery, criminal or civil litigation, **CC 1798.76**
  District attorneys, disclosure of personal or confidential information, **CC 1798.68**
  Fees, personal information, copies, **CC 1798.33**
  Fines and penalties, personal information in agency records, disclosure, **CC 1798.55 et seq.**
  Information Practices Act, **CC 1798 et seq.**
  Injunction, personal information, disclosure, **CC 1798.46, 1798.47**
  Inspection and inspectors, personal information, **CC 1798.34**
  Liens and incumbrances, disclosure, **CC 1798.67**
  Names and addresses, sale or rental for commercial purposes, **CC 1798.60**
  Personal information, requirements, **CC 1798 et seq.**
  Processing and servicing of records, **CC 1798.64**
  Rules of conduct, Information Practices Act, **CC 1798.20**
  Safeguards, disclosure of personal information, **CC 1798.21**
  Storage, **CC 1798.64**
  Student records, **CC 1798.74**
Reports,
  Disclosure, Information Practices Act, **CC 1798 et seq.**
  Information Practices Act, **CC 1798 et seq.**
State Contracts, generally, this index
State Officers and Employees, generally, this index
Storage, records, **CC 1798.64**

STATE BANKS
Banks and Banking, generally, this index

STATE BOARDS AND COMMISSIONS
Boards and Commissions, generally, this index

STATE CANDIDATES
Elections, generally, this index

STATE COLLEGES
Colleges and Universities, generally, this index

STATE COMMISSIONS AND COMMISSIONERS
Boards and Commissions, generally, this index

STATE CONTRACTS
Letters of recommendation, personal information held by governmental agencies, Information Practices Act, **CC 1798.38**
Operation or maintenance of records, Information Practices Act, **CC 1798.19**
Records and recordation, operation or maintenance, Information Practices Act, **CC 1798.19**

STATE DEPARTMENTS
Administrative Law and Procedure, generally, this index
Confidential or privileged information,
  Information Practices Act, **CC 1798 et seq.**
  Personal information, disclosure, **CC 1798 et seq.**
  Safeguards, disclosure of personal information, **CC 1798.21**
Contracts. State Contracts, generally, this index
Crimes and offenses, personal information in departmental records, disclosure, **CC 1798.55 et seq.**
Disclosure, personal information, Information Practices Act, **CC 1798 et seq.**
Employees. State Officers and Employees, generally, this index
Fines and penalties, personal information in departmental records, disclosure, **CC 1798.55 et seq.**
Highway patrol department. Highway Patrol, generally, this index
Information Practices Act, **CC 1798 et seq.**
Officers and employees. State Officers and Employees, generally, this index
Personal information on individuals, requirements to maintain, **CC 1798 et seq.**
Privacy, Information Practices Act, **CC 1798 et seq.**
Privileged information. Confidential or privileged information, generally, ante
Records and recordation,
  Access, personal records, **CC 1798.30 et seq.**
  Information Practices Act, **CC 1798 et seq.**
  Personal information, requirements, **CC 1798 et seq.**
State Contracts, generally, this index

STATE EMPLOYEES
State Officers and Employees, generally, this index

STOCK

STATE HEALTH FACILITIES
Health Facilities, generally, this index

STATE HIGHWAY PATROL
Highway Patrol, generally, this index

STATE HOUSING LAW
Housing, generally, this index

STATE INSTITUTIONS
Officers and employees. State Officers and Employees, generally, this index

STATE LANDS
Public Lands, generally, this index

STATE OFFICERS AND EMPLOYEES
See, also, Public Officers and Employees, generally, this index
Attorney General, generally, this index
Bribery and Corruption, generally, this index
Corruption. Bribery and Corruption, generally, this index
Crimes and offenses,
  Bribery and Corruption, generally, this index
  Personal information contained in state records, disclosure, CC 1798.55 et seq.
Disclosure, Information Practices Act, CC 1798 et seq.
Governor, generally, this index
Highway Patrol, generally, this index
Information Practices Act, CC 1798 et seq.
Privileges and immunities, inmate health care, CC 1542.1
Records and recordation,
  Disclosure, Information Practices Act, CC 1798 et seq.
  Information Practices Act, CC 1798 et seq.
  Right to privacy, Information Practices Act, CC 1798 et seq.

STATE PATROL
Highway Patrol, generally, this index

STATE POLICE
Highway Patrol, generally, this index

STATE POLICY
Public Policy, generally, this index

STATE PRISONS
Correctional Institutions, generally, this index

STATE PROPERTY
Public Lands, generally, this index

STATE TREASURER
Unclaimed property. Abandoned or Unclaimed Property, generally, this index

STATE TREASURY
See, also, Funds, generally, this index
Arts and entertainment fund, CC 1708.8
Foreclosure consultant regulation fund, CC 2945.45

STATEMENTS
Collection agencies, CC 1788.14.5

STATEMENTS—Cont'd
Contracts for sale of land, compliance with Subdivision Map Act, CC 2985.51
Credit cards, deeds of trust, execution in connection with secured credit cards, CC 1747.94
Deeds and conveyances, natural hazard disclosure statement, CC 1103.2 et seq.
Deeds of trust, execution in connection with secured credit cards, CC 1747.94
Disclosure statements, deeds of trust executed in connection with secured credit cards, CC 1747.94
Installment Sales, this index
Landlord and tenant, security deposits, CC 1950.5
Motor vehicle conditional sales, credit statements, CC 2982
Precomputed finance charge contracts, CC 1799.8
Precomputed interest, loans, CC 1799.5
Real estate, natural hazard disclosure statement, CC 1103.2 et seq.
Secured credit cards, deeds of trust executed in connection with, CC 1747.94
Security deposits, landlord and tenant, CC 1950.5

STATEWIDE REGISTRY
Registers and Registries, generally, this index

STATIONS AND DEPOTS
Blind or visually impaired persons, touch screen devices, CC 54.9
Touch screen devices, blind or visually impaired persons, CC 54.9

STATISTICS
Disclosure, personal information maintained by governmental agencies, Information Practices Act, CC 1798.24
Medical records, disclosure, application of law, CC 56.30

STATUARY
Carriers, limitation of liability, CC 2200
Consignments, CC 1738 et seq.
  Art works, CC 1738 et seq.

STATUTE OF FRAUDS
Frauds, Statute of, generally, this index

STATUTE OF LIMITATIONS
Limitation of Actions, generally, this index

STATUTES
Choice of law. Conflict of Laws, generally, this index
Commercial Code, generally, this index
Common law, derogation, CC 4
Conflict of Laws, generally, this index
Construction of laws, CC 4, 13
  Consumers, privacy, CC 1798.198
  Easements, conservation easements, CC 816
  1872 Code, CC 23 et seq.

STATUTES—Cont'd
Construction of laws—Cont'd
  Homeless persons, shelters, occupancy, CC 1954.091
  Indebtedness, duress or coercion, CC 1798.97.4
  Minority groups, equal protection of laws, CC 53.7
  Stalking, CC 1708.7
  Weapons, manufacturers and manufacturing, sales, conduct, standards, CC 3273.54
Equal protection of laws, minority groups, CC 53.7
Frauds, Statute of, generally, this index
Initiative and Referendum, generally, this index
Maxims, generally, this index
Minority groups, equal protection of laws, CC 53.7
Popular Name Laws, generally, this index
Referendum. Initiative and Referendum, generally, this index
Repeals, CC 20
School elections, indebtedness, duress or coercion, CC 1798.97.6
Uniform Laws, generally, this index
Will of supreme power, CC 22.1

STAY OF PROCEEDINGS
Supersedeas or Stay, generally, this index

STEALING
Theft, generally, this index

STEALTHING
Actions and proceedings, CC 1708.5

STEAM HEAT
Heat and Heating Companies, generally, this index

STEAMBOATS AND STEAMSHIPS
Ships and Shipping, generally, this index

STIPENDS
Compensation and Salaries, generally, this index

STIPULATIONS
Fines and penalties, CC 52

STOCK
Animals, generally, this index

STOCK AND STOCKHOLDERS
Shares and shareholders. Corporations, this index

STOCK BROKERS AND DEALERS
Security Agents and Broker Dealers, generally, this index

STOCK COOPERATIVES
Cooperative Corporations, this index

STOCK CORPORATIONS
Corporations, generally, this index

I-199

STOCKHOLDERS

STOCKHOLDERS
Shares and shareholders. Corporations, this index

STOLEN PROPERTY
Theft, generally, this index

STOLEN VEHICLES
Theft. Motor Vehicles, this index

STOP NOTICES
Mechanics Liens, this index

STORAGE
Abandoned or unclaimed property, carriers, CC 2081
Automated license plate recognition, CC 1798.90.52
Bailment, this index
Gasoline vapor control systems, service stations, marketing operations, CC 1952.8
Liens and encumbrances, cleaners and launderers, CC 3066
Motor Vehicles, this index
Personal property of tenants, termination of lease, return, CC 1965
Private bulk grain storage. Agricultural Products, this index
Service stations, gasoline vapor control systems, marketing operations, CC 1952.8
Tissue Banks, generally, this index

STORES
Children and minors, markets and marketing, gender neutrality, CC 55.7, 55.8
Defenses, service or repair transactions, delivery, CC 1722
Delivery, time, CC 1722
Fines and penalties, gender neutrality, markets and marketing, children and minors, CC 55.8
Gender neutrality, markets and marketing, children and minors, CC 55.7, 55.8
Grocery Stores, generally, this index
Markets and marketing, children and minors, gender neutrality, CC 55.7, 55.8
Retailers, generally, this index
Return of goods, refunds or exchanges, notice if not allowed, CC 1723
Sex, gender neutrality, markets and marketing, children and minors, CC 55.7, 55.8
Time, service or repair transactions, delivery, CC 1722

STORIES
Crimes and offenses, stories about felonies, sale proceeds, CC 2225

STORMS
Community Facilities Districts, generally, this index
Home solicitation contracts, residential repair or restoration, cancellation, CC 1689.6, 1689.7, 1689.14
Hurricanes, generally, this index

STORMS—Cont'd
Shelters, tort liability, CC 1714.5

STP
Drugs and Medicine, generally, this index

STRAYS
Running at large. Animals, this index

STREAMS
Rivers and Streams, generally, this index

STREET RAILWAYS
See, also,
   Carriers, generally, this index
   Public Utilities, generally, this index
Blind or visually impaired persons,
   Access to public conveyances, CC 54 et seq.
   Civil rights, CC 54.1
Damages, guide dogs accompanying blind person or trainer, CC 54.2
Deaf persons, public accommodations, CC 54.1 et seq.
Disabled persons, access to public conveyances, CC 54 et seq.
Guide dogs, accompanying blind persons for training purposes, access, CC 54.1 et seq.
Overloading, exception, CC 2185
Seats, exception, CC 2185
Zoning and Planning, generally, this index

STREETCARS
Street Railways, generally, this index

STREETS AND ALLEYS
See, also, Highways and Roads, generally, this index
Blind or visually impaired persons, civil rights, CC 54 et seq.
Boundaries, presumptions, CC 831
Disabled persons, civil rights, CC 54 et seq.
Freeways, generally, this index
Traffic Rules and Regulations, generally, this index
Zoning and Planning, generally, this index

STRIKES
Labor Disputes, generally, this index

STRUCTURAL ENGINEERS
Engineers, generally, this index

STRUCTURAL PEST CONTROL
Pest Control, this index

STRUCTURES
Buildings, generally, this index

STUDENT LOANS
Colleges and Universities, this index

STUDENTS
Colleges and Universities, this index
Schools and School Districts, generally, this index

STUDIOS
Dance studios, contracts, CC 1812.50 et seq.

SUBCONTRACTORS
Attorney fees, construction, reimbursement, defense fees and costs, CC 2782.05
Damages, construction, reimbursement, defense fees and costs, CC 2782.05
Housing, construction, indemnity, CC 2782 et seq.
Wrap up policies, insurance, CC 2782.9 et seq.
Indemnity, housing, construction, CC 2782 et seq.
Mechanics Liens, generally, this index

SUBDIVIDED LANDS
Actions and proceedings, sales contracts, Subdivision Map Act, noncompliance, CC 2985.51
Attorney fees, blanket incumbrance, failure to give notice, CC 1133
Damages,
   Blanket incumbrance, failure to give notice, CC 1133
   Sales contracts, Subdivision Map Act, noncompliance, CC 2985.51
Fines and penalties, blanket incumbrance, failure to give notice, CC 1133
Intergenerational housing developments, CC 51.3.5
Landlord and tenant, owner established rental rates, CC 1954.52
Leases, blanket incumbrance, notice, CC 1133
Liens and incumbrances, blanket incumbrance, notice, CC 1133
Notice,
   Blanket incumbrance, CC 1133
   Buyers or lessees, blanket incumbrances, CC 1133
Rent controls, owner established rental rates, CC 1954.52
Sales, contracts,
   Prepayment, CC 2985.6
   Statement of compliance, Subdivision Map Act, CC 2985.51

SUBDIVISION MAPS
Contracts, sale of land, statement of compliance, Subdivision Map Act, CC 2985.51

SUBLEASES
Leases, this index

SUBMERGED OR OVERFLOWED LANDS
Boundaries, CC 830
Leases, municipality, CC 718

SUBPOENAS
Abortion, medical records, conflict of laws, CC 56.108
Condominiums, construction, defects, CC 6000
Business and commerce, CC 6870
Consumer credit reporting agencies, inspection of records, CC 1785.11
Contempt, generally, this index
Evidence, proof of instrument, officers taking, authority to issue, CC 1201

SURETYSHIP

SUBPOENAS—Cont'd
Oil and gas pipelines, spills, **CC 3333.5**
Personal information held by governmental agencies, disclosure, Information Practices Act, **CC 1798.24**
Privacy, consumers, **CC 1798.199.70**
Proof of instruments, officers taking, authority to issue, **CC 1201**

SUBROGATION
Firefighters, injury to, willful acts or want of ordinary care, **CC 1714.9**
Liens, redemption, right, **CC 2903**
  Inferior lien holder, **CC 2904**
Medical malpractice, collateral benefits sources, **CC 3333.1**
Peace officers, injury to, willful acts or want of ordinary care, **CC 1714.9**
Sureties, creditors rights against principal, **CC 2848**

SUBSTANCE USE DISORDERS
See, also, Drugs and Medicine, generally, this index
Homeless persons, transitional housing, misconduct, **CC 1954.10 et seq.**
Medical records, disclosure, **CC 56.30**

SUBSTITUTION
Credit cards, issuance, **CC 1747.05**

SUBTENANTS
  Generally, **CC 1995.010 et seq.**
Landlord and Tenant, this index

SUCCESSION
Art and artists, defacement or destruction of art objects, **CC 987**
Freehold, **CC 765**
Mobilehomes and mobilehome parks, right to sell, **CC 798.70 et seq.**
Property, acquisition, **CC 1000**

SUFFRAGE
Elections, generally, this index

SUITS
Actions and Proceedings, generally, this index
Equity, generally, this index

SULPHUR DIOXIDE
Air Pollution, generally, this index

SUMMARY JUDGMENT
Confession of Judgment, generally, this index

SUMMARY PROCEEDINGS
Forcible entry and detainer, **CC 792**
Mechanics liens, stop notices, public buildings and works, release, **CC 9400 et seq.**

SUN
Solar Energy, generally, this index

SUNDAY
Holiday, **CC 7**

SUPERHIGHWAYS
Freeways, generally, this index

SUPERIOR COURT JUDGES
Acknowledgments, **CC 1180**
Proof of instruments, **CC 1180**
Retired judges, acknowledgments, authority to take, **CC 1180**

SUPERIOR COURTS
Acknowledgments, **CC 1180**
Adoption, generally, this index
Contempt, generally, this index
Eminent Domain, generally, this index
Judges. Superior Court Judges, generally, this index
Judgments and Decrees, generally, this index
Jurisdiction, mineral right termination actions, **CC 883.240**
Juvenile Courts, generally, this index
Probate Proceedings, generally, this index
Small Claims Courts, generally, this index
Subpoenas, generally, this index

SUPERMARKET CLUB CARD DISCLOSURE ACT
Generally, **CC 1749.60 et seq.**

SUPERMARKETS
Grocery Stores, generally, this index

SUPERSEDEAS OR STAY
Buildings, construction defects, prelitigation proceedings, noncompliance, **CC 930**
Civil rights, disabled persons, construction, accessibility, **CC 55.54**
Hazardous substances and waste, responsibility acceptance, commitment statements, **CC 852**
Human trafficking, **CC 52.5**

SUPPLEMENTAL TAX ASSESSMENTS
Tax Assessments, this index

SUPPORT
Accomplices and accessories, arrearages, evasion, treble damages, **CC 1714.4, 1714.41**
Arrearages,
  Accomplices and accessories, evasion, treble damages, **CC 1714.4, 1714.41**
  Assets, transfers, accomplices and accessories, treble damages, **CC 1714.4, 1714.41**
  Avoidance, accomplices and accessories, treble damages, **CC 1714.4, 1714.41**
  Damages, evasion, accomplices and accessories, **CC 1714.4, 1714.41**
  Escape, accomplices and accessories, treble damages, **CC 1714.4, 1714.41**
  Evasion, accomplices and accessories, treble damages, **CC 1714.4, 1714.41**
  Treble damages, evasion, accomplices and accessories, **CC 1714.4, 1714.41**
Assets, transfers, arrearages, accomplices and accessories, treble damages, **CC 1714.4, 1714.41**

SUPPORT—Cont'd
Beneficiaries, destitute, direction of sum for from accumulations of income from property, **CC 726**
Damages, arrearages, evasion, accomplices and accessories, **CC 1714.4, 1714.41**
Delinquency. Arrearages, generally, ante
Payment. Arrearages, generally, ante
Treble damages, arrearages, evasion, accomplices and accessories, **CC 1714.4, 1714.41**

SUPPORTIVE HOUSING
Low and Moderate Income Housing, generally, this index

SUPREME COURT
Acknowledgments, instruments, **CC 1180**
Proof of instruments, **CC 1180**

SUPREME COURT CLERK/EXECUTIVE OFFICER
Acknowledgment of instruments, **CC 1180**

SUPREME COURT JUSTICES
Retired justices, acknowledgments, **CC 1180**

SURETY BONDS
Bonds (Officers and Fiduciaries), generally, this index

SURETYSHIP AND GUARANTY
See, also, Bonds (Officers and Fiduciaries), generally, this index
Generally, **CC 2787 et seq.**
Acceptance, offer to become surety, **CC 2795**
Actions and proceedings, creditors, failure to proceed against principal, exoneration of surety, **CC 2845**
Agreement to accept less, creditor and debtor, effect on surety, **CC 2822**
Alteration of obligation, **CC 2821**
  Exoneration, **CC 2819**
Apparent principal as surety, **CC 2832**
Arbitration awards, against principal alone, conclusiveness against surety, **CC 2855**
Benefits of securities for performance, **CC 2849**
  Creditor entitled to, **CC 2854**
Bonds (Officers and Fiduciaries), generally, this index
Compelling principal to perform obligations, **CC 2846**
Conditional obligations, **CC 2806**
  Notice of default, **CC 2808**
Consent of principal, necessity, **CC 2788**
Consideration, necessity, **CC 2792, 2793**
Construction, rules, **CC 2837**
Continuing guaranty, revocation, **CC 2815**
Contribution, cosureties, **CC 2848**
Cosureties, contributions, **CC 2848**
Creation, **CC 2792 et seq.**
Decrees. Judgments and decrees, generally, post

SURETYSHIP

SURETYSHIP AND GUARANTY—Cont'd
Default, conditional obligation, notice, CC 2808
Delay in proceeding by creditor, exoneration, CC 2823
Demand, payment or performance, liability without, CC 2807
Deposits, money and assets, agreement authorizing, CC 2811
Disability of principal, liability of surety, CC 2810
Discharge,
   Obligation, property of principal first applied to, CC 2850
   Principal, CC 2825
Discount buying services, affiliates, CC 1812.117
Distinction between sureties and guarantors abolished, CC 2787
Distinction between sureties and letter of credit, CC 2787
Exoneration, CC 2819 et seq.
   Alteration of original obligation, CC 2819
   Creditors neglect to proceed against principal, CC 2845
   Delay in proceeding by creditor, CC 2823
   Discharge of principal, CC 2825
   Impairment of remedies or rights,
     Against principal, CC 2819
     Rescission of agreement, CC 2821
   Indemnified surety, liability notwithstanding modification or release, CC 2824
   Offer of performance, CC 2839
   Partial satisfaction of obligation, CC 2822
   Performance, CC 2839
   Suspension or impairment of remedies, CC 2819
     Creditors void promise, CC 2820
Impairment of remedy, CC 2819 et seq.
Implied terms of contract, CC 2799
Incomplete contracts, CC 2799
Indemnification, CC 2824
Injunction, innkeepers liens, writs of possession, CC 1861.21 et seq.
Innkeepers liens, injunction, writs of possession, CC 1861.21
Interpretation,
   Contracts creating, CC 2799 et seq.
   Rules, CC 2837
Judgments and decrees, CC 2838
   Against surety, relationship of parties, CC 2838
   Arbitration awards, against principal alone, conclusiveness against surety, CC 2855
Knowledge of principal, necessity, CC 2788
Lesser debt agreed upon, effect on surety liability, CC 2822
Letter of credit, distinguished, CC 2787
Liability, CC 2788, 2806 et seq.
   Arbitration awards against principal alone, conclusiveness against surety, CC 2855

SURETYSHIP AND GUARANTY—Cont'd
Liability—Cont'd
   Disability of principal, CC 2810
   Money and assets deposited, CC 2811
Liens and incumbrances, innkeepers liens, injunction, writs of possession, CC 1861.21
Limitations, liabilities, CC 2809
Lost or destroyed documents, CC 3415
Mortgages, guarantors, waiver, CC 2856
Notice,
   Acceptance of offer, CC 2795
   Default upon conditional obligation, CC 2808
   Payment or performance, liability without, CC 2807
Obligations, CC 2800 et seq.
Offer of performance, exoneration, CC 2839
Original obligation, writing, necessity, CC 2794
Partial satisfaction of obligation, effect, CC 2822
Payment, liability without demand or notice, CC 2807
Performance,
   Benefits of securities for, CC 2849
     Creditor entitled to, CC 2854
   Compelling principal, CC 2846
   Exoneration, CC 2839
Property of principal first applied to discharge of obligation, CC 2850
Reimbursement, surety by principal, CC 2847
Relationship of parties, CC 2832 et seq.
Rescission of agreement, CC 2821
Revocation, continuing guaranty, CC 2815
Rules of interpretation, CC 2837
Securities for performance, benefits of, CC 2849
   Creditor entitled to, CC 2854
Signature, creating suretyship, CC 2793
Subrogation, creditors rights against principal, CC 2848
Suspension of remedy,
   Creditors void promise, CC 2820
   Exoneration of surety, CC 2819
Trust deeds, guarantors, waiver, CC 2856
Waiver, CC 2856
Written instrument, CC 2793, 2794

SURFACE WATERS
Waters and Watercourses, generally, this index

SURGEONS
Physicians and Surgeons, generally, this index

SURVEYS AND SURVEYORS
Access, monuments, CC 846.5
Consolidated cities and counties, contracts, indemnity, CC 2782.8
Damages, trespass, CC 3346
Disclosure, natural hazards, residential property, CC 1103.4

SURVEYS AND SURVEYORS—Cont'd
Districts, contracts, indemnity, CC 2782.8
Entry on property, access to monuments, CC 846.5
Hazards, natural hazards, disclosure, residential property, CC 1103.4
Joint powers authorities, contracts, indemnity, CC 2782.8
Liens and incumbrances. Mechanics Liens, generally, this index
Limitation of actions, trespass, CC 3346
Mechanics Liens, generally, this index
Monuments and memorials, access to, CC 846.5
Natural hazards, disclosure, residential property, CC 1103.4
Notice, entry on property, CC 846.5
Privileges and immunities, natural hazards, disclosure, residential property, CC 1103.4
Public authorities, contracts, indemnity, CC 2782.8
Public corporations, contracts, indemnity, CC 2782.8
Solar energy, CC 4746

SWEATSHOPS
Human Trafficking, generally, this index

TACTICAL RESPONSE TO TRAUMATIC INJURIES ACT
Generally, CC 1714.29

TAGS
Licenses and Permits, generally, this index

TAILORS
Prices,
   Discrimination, sex, CC 55.61 et seq.
   Posting, discrimination, CC 51.6

TAKING
Eminent Domain, generally, this index
Fish and Game, generally, this index

TANGIBLE PERSONAL PROPERTY
Personal Property, generally, this index

TANNER CONSUMER PROTECTION ACT
New motor vehicles, CC 1793.22

TAPE RECORDINGS
Audio and Video Recordings, generally, this index

TARIFFS
Rates and Charges, generally, this index

TAVERNS AND SALOONS
Restaurants, generally, this index

TAX AND FEE ADMINISTRATION DEPARTMENT
Equalization of taxes. Taxation, this index

TAX ASSESSMENTS
Appraisal and appraisers. Supplemental tax assessments, generally, post

TAX ASSESSMENTS—Cont'd

Base year value. Supplemental tax assessments, generally, post

Change in ownership. Supplemental tax assessments, generally, post

Conservation easements, enforceable restriction status, **CC 815.10**

Construction. Supplemental tax assessments, generally, post

Covenants running with land, payment of assessments, **CC 1462, 1463**

Disclosure, supplemental tax assessments, transfers, **CC 1102.6c**

Equalization of taxes. Taxation, this index

Incumbrance as including, **CC 1114**

Legal Estates Principal and Income Law, **CC 731.15**

Life tenants, payment, **CC 840**

New construction. Supplemental tax assessments, generally, post

Supplemental tax assessments,
   Disclosure, transfers, **CC 1102.6c**
   Notice, transfers, **CC 1102.6c**
   Transfers, disclosure, **CC 1102.6c**

Title to property. Supplemental tax assessments, generally, ante

Valuation. Supplemental tax assessments, generally, ante

TAX ASSESSMENTS—SPECIAL

Extinction of lien, presumptions, **CC 2911**

Presumptions, extinction of lien, **CC 2911**

TAX EQUALIZATION

Equalization of taxes. Taxation, this index

TAX LIENS

Actions and proceedings, state, enforcement of lien, **CC 2931c**

Community facilities districts, real estate transfers, disclosure, **CC 1102.6b**

Consumer credit reporting agencies, **CC 1786.18**
   Contents of records, **CC 1785.13**

Default sale, purchase by state, **CC 2931b**

Eminent domain, **CC 2931a**

Extinguishment, presumptions, **CC 2911**

Federal tax liens, mortgages, notice of default and sale, **CC 2924b**

Incumbrance as including, **CC 1114**

Innocent purchasers, presumptions against extinction, **CC 2911**

Jurisdiction,
   Priorities, **CC 2931a**
   State enforcement, **CC 2931c**

Labor and employment, records and recordation, copies, **CC 1786.53**

Mortgages, this index

Presumptions, extinction of lien, **CC 2911**

Priorities and preferences, **CC 2931a**

Purchase of property by public entities, state, **CC 2931b**

Records and recordation, notice, **CC 2885**

TAX RETURNS AND REPORTS

Bookkeeping services, confidential or privileged information, **CC 1799.1a**

Business records, bookkeeping services, confidential or privileged information, **CC 1799.1a**

Condominiums, homeowners associations, inspection and inspectors, **CC 5200 et seq.**

TAXATION

Address, equalization state board, release, **CC 1798.69**

Assessments. Tax Assessments, generally, this index

Autographed memorabilia, resale certificate numbers, **CC 1739.7**

Corporation Taxes, generally, this index

Covenants running with land, payment, **CC 1462, 1463**

Equalization of taxes,
   Address, release, **CC 1798.69**
   Licenses and permits, names, release, **CC 1798.69**
   Names, release, **CC 1798.69**
   Registration, names, release, **CC 1798.69**

Fines and penalties. Motor Vehicles, this index

Franchise taxes. Corporation Taxes, generally, this index

Income Tax—Federal, generally, this index

Income Tax—State, generally, this index

Incumbrances. Tax Liens, generally, this index

Levy of tax. Tax Assessments, generally, this index

Licenses and permits, equalization state board, names, release, **CC 1798.69**

Liens. Tax Liens, generally, this index

Life tenants, payment, **CC 840**

Mortgages, this index

Names, equalization state board, release, **CC 1798.69**

Registration, equalization state board, names, release, **CC 1798.69**

Reports. Tax Returns and Reports, generally, this index

Returns. Tax Returns and Reports, generally, this index

Sales and Use Taxes, generally, this index

Supplemental tax assessments. Tax Assessments, this index

Tax equalization. Equalization of taxes, generally, ante

Use taxes. Sales and Use Taxes, generally, this index

Valuation. Equalization of taxes, generally, ante

TAXING AGENCIES

Taxation, generally, this index

TEAMSTERS

Mechanics Liens, generally, this index

TECHNICIANS

Emergency Medical Technicians, generally, this index

TECHNOLOGY

Information technologies. Telecommunications, generally, this index

TELECOMMUNICATIONS

See, also, Public Utilities, generally, this index

Address, change of address, notice, **CC 1799.1b**

Advertisements, unsolicited advertising, prerecorded messages, notice requirements, **CC 1770**

Application of law, Uniform Electronic Transactions Act, **CC 1633.3**

Business and commerce, numbers and numbering, mobilehome park owners, disclosure, **CC 798.28**

Cancellation,
   Electronic Transactions Act, **CC 1633.16**
   Uniform Electronic Transactions Act, **CC 1633.16**

Change of address, notice, **CC 1799.1b**

Collections, agencies, use in collection of debt, restrictions, **CC 1788.11**

Computers, generally, this index

Condominiums, this index

Consumer Credit Reporting Agencies, this index

Consumer goods, sales, private schools, monopolies and unfair trade, **CC 998**

Contracts,
   Illegal contracts, solicitation, **CC 1670.6**
   Qualified financial contract, frauds, statute of, evidence, **CC 1624**
   Sales, illegal contracts, **CC 1670.6**
   Solicitation, illegal contracts, **CC 1670.6**
   Uniform Electronic Transactions Act, **CC 1633.1 et seq.**

Credit cards, payoff, amount, time, **CC 1748.13**

Damages,
   Nine one one (911), privileges and immunities, providers, **CC 1714.55**
   Refusing or postponing messages, **CC 2209**

Databases. Computers, generally, this index

Death, messages, priorities and preferences, **CC 2207**

Debt collection practices, **CC 1788.11**

Disabled persons, telephone facilities, access, **CC 54.1**

Disclosure,
   Medical records, sales, **CC 1798.91**
   Mobilehome park owners, business telephone numbers, **CC 798.28**

Dissemination, unsolicited prerecorded messages, notice requirements, **CC 1770**

Electronic commercial service contracts, **CC 1789.3**

Electronic funds transfers. Funds Transfers, generally, this index

TELECOMMUNICATIONS

TELECOMMUNICATIONS—Cont'd
Emergencies, messages, priorities and preferences, CC 2207
Errors, Electronic Transactions Act, CC 1633.10
Evidence,
   Electronic Transactions Act, CC 1633.1 et seq.
   Qualified financial contract, frauds, statute of, CC 1624
   Uniform Electronic Transactions Act, CC 1633.1 et seq.
Exemptions, Uniform Electronic Transactions Act, CC 1633.3
Financial contract (qualified), frauds, statute of, evidence, CC 1624
Fines and penalties, messages, refusing or postponing, CC 2209
Funds Transfers, generally, this index
Illnesses, emergency messages, priorities and preferences, CC 2207
Installment sales, negotiations by telephone, CC 1803.8
Internet, generally, this index
Labor and employment, consumer credit reporting agencies, investigative consumer reports, notice, CC 1786.16
Landlord and Tenant, this index
Leases, cutting off public utilities with intent to terminate lease, damages, CC 789.3
Medical records, sales, disclosure, CC 1798.91
Mobilehomes and mobilehome parks, business telephone numbers, mobilehome park owners, disclosure, CC 798.28
Monopolies and unfair trade, sales to private schools, CC 998
Newspapers, messages intended for publication in priorities and preferences, CC 2207
Nine one one (911),
   Damages, privileges and immunities, providers, CC 1714.55
   Privileges and immunities, providers, CC 1714.55
Notaries public, Electronic Transactions Act, CC 1633.11
Notice,
   Change of address, CC 1799.1b
   Electronic Transactions Act, CC 1633.3, 1633.10, 1633.16
   Uniform Electronic Transactions Act, CC 1633.3, 1633.10, 1633.16
Numbers and numbering,
   Consumer Credit Reporting Agencies, this index
   Identity and identification, theft, CC 1798.92 et seq.
   Labor and employment, notice, investigative consumer reports, CC 1786.16
Oaths and affirmations, Electronic Transactions Act, CC 1633.11
Orders, records and recordation, transmission, CC 2207, 2208

TELECOMMUNICATIONS—Cont'd
Postponing messages, damages, CC 2209
Prerecorded messages, unsolicited, disseminating, notice requirements, CC 1770
Priorities and preferences, messages, order of transmission, CC 2207, 2208
Private schools, sales, monopolies and unfair trade, CC 998
Privileges and immunities, nine one one (911), providers, CC 1714.55
Qualified financial contract, frauds, statute of, evidence, CC 1624
Records and recordation, Uniform Electronic Transactions Act, CC 1633.1 et seq.
Refusing messages, damages, CC 2209
Registration, CC 2209
Sales,
   Autographed memorabilia, warranties, CC 1739.7
   Contracts, illegal contracts, CC 1670.6
   Medical records, disclosure, CC 1798.91
   Private schools, monopolies and unfair trade, CC 998
Signatures, Uniform Electronic Transactions Act, CC 1633.1 et seq.
Solicitation. Sales, generally, ante
Stalking, CC 1708.7
Telemarketing. Sales, generally, ante
Transmissions. Electronic Transmissions, generally, this index
Uniform Electronic Transactions Act, CC 1633.1 et seq.
United States, priorities and preferences, CC 2207, 2208
Wireless telecommunications,
   Rental purchase agreements, smartphones, geophysical location tracking technology, notice, CC 1812.650
   Smartphones, rental purchase agreements, geophysical location tracking technology, notice, CC 1812.650

TELEGRAMS
Telecommunications, generally, this index

TELEMARKETING
Sales. Telecommunications, this index

TELEPHONES
Telecommunications, generally, this index

TELEVISION AND RADIO
See, also, Public Utilities, generally, this index
Art works, common law copyrights, reproduction rights, CC 982
Astaire Celebrity Image Protection Act, CC 3344.1
Audio and Video Recordings, generally, this index
Cable Television, generally, this index
Celebrity image protection, CC 3344.1
Condominiums, antennas, CC 4725
   Business and commerce, CC 6708

TELEVISION AND RADIO—Cont'd
Consumers Legal Remedies Act, application of law, CC 1755
Crimes and offenses, stories about felonies, sale proceeds, CC 2225
Exemptions, Consumers Legal Remedies Act, CC 1755
Exports and imports, incompatibility with United States broadcast frequencies, CC 1797.81
Grey market goods, incompatibility with United States broadcast frequencies, CC 1797.81
Invasion of privacy, use of name, photograph, voice, signature, CC 3344
Libel and Slander, generally, this index
Manufacturers identification mark, removal, defacing, alteration or destruction, CC 1710.1
Radio frequency identification, crimes and offenses, CC 1798.79
RFID (radio frequency identification), crimes and offenses, CC 1798.79
Sales, identification number or mark altered or removed, CC 1710.1
Skimming, radio frequency identification, crimes and offenses, CC 1798.79
Uniform single publication, CC 3425.1 et seq.

TENANCY AT WILL
Landlord and Tenant, this index

TENANCY FOR YEARS
Landlord and Tenant, this index

TENANCY FROM MONTH TO MONTH
Landlord and Tenant, this index

TENANCY IN COMMON
Condominiums, common areas, CC 4500
   Business and commerce, CC 6650
Depositories, delivery, CC 1827
Ownership of property, CC 682
Partition, generally, this index

TENANT, HOMEOWNER AND SMALL LANDLORD RELIEF AND STABILIZATION ACT
Generally, CC 798.56, 1942.5, 1946.2, 2924.15, 3273.1 et seq.

TENANT PROTECTION ACT
Generally, CC 1946.2, 1947.12, 1947.13

TENANTS
Generally, CC 1925 et seq.
Landlord and Tenant, generally, this index

TENT CAMPS
Mobilehomes and Mobilehome Parks, generally, this index

TESTAMENTS
Wills, generally, this index

TESTIMONY
Evidence, generally, this index

TISSUE

TESTIMONY—Cont'd
Witnesses, generally, this index

TESTS
Animals, **CC 1834.9.3**
  Alternatives, **CC 1834.9**
DNA, genetic testing, privacy, **CC 56.18 et seq.**
Genetic testing, privacy, **CC 56.18 et seq.**

TEXTILES
Fires and Fire Protection, generally, this index

THEATERS AND SHOWS
Blind or visually impaired persons, access to public accommodations, **CC 54 et seq.**
Dances and Dance Halls, generally, this index
Deaf persons, public accommodations, **CC 54.1 et seq.**
Disabled persons, access, **CC 54 et seq.**
Discrimination, **CC 51 et seq.**
Motion Pictures, generally, this index

THEFT
Bailment, parking lots and facilities, contracts, **CC 1630.5**
Collection agencies, identity and identification, **CC 1785.16.2, 1788.18**
Consumer Credit Reporting Agencies, this index
Credit, identity and identification, **CC 1785.20.3**
Data, sales, **CC 1724**
Debit cards, liability, **CC 1748.31**
Debtors and creditors, identity and identification,
  Collection agencies, **CC 1788.18**
  Sales, **CC 1785.16.2**
Fur bearing animals raised in captivity, **CC 996**
Identity and Identification, this index
Keys or card keys, automated dispensing outlets, petroleum products, liability after theft, **CC 1747.03**
Loans, identity and identification, **CC 1785.20.3**
Motor Vehicles, this index
Oil and gas, keys or card keys, automated dispensing outlets, liability after theft, **CC 1747.03**
Parking lots and facilities, bailment contracts, **CC 1630.5**
Receiving Stolen Goods, generally, this index
Restoration of property, **CC 1712**
  Demand for return, **CC 1713**
Uniform Trade Secrets Act, **CC 3426 et seq.**

THEFT INSURANCE
Repair, alteration or sale, **CC 1858 et seq.**

THERAPISTS AND THERAPY
Marriage and Family Therapists, generally, this index
Psychotherapists and Psychotherapy, generally, this index

THIRD PARTIES
Agents and agencies,
  Ratification of authority, rights of third persons, **CC 2313**
  Responsibility of agents, **CC 2342 et seq.**
  Rights when dealing with agent without knowledge of agency, **CC 2336**
Beneficiaries contract, enforcement, **CC 1559**
Consumers, privacy, **CC 1798.100 et seq.**
Deeds and conveyances, natural hazard disclosure statement, **CC 1103.2 et seq.**
Estate for life of third person, freehold, **CC 766**
Genetic defects, **CC 43.6**
Home solicitation, aged persons, improvements, **CC 1770**
Medical records, confidential or privileged information, **CC 56.10**
Mortgage foreclosure consultants, **CC 2945.4**
Privacy, consumers, **CC 1798.100 et seq.**
Real estate, natural hazard disclosure statement, **CC 1103.2 et seq.**
Rent, payment, **CC 1947.3**

THREATS
Civil rights, violation, injunction, **CC 52, 52.1**
Duress or Coercion, generally, this index
Injunctions, violation of civil rights, **CC 52, 52.1**
Landlord and tenant, vacating premises, **CC 1940.2**
Marriage and family therapists, violent behavior, patients, protection, privileges and immunities, **CC 43.92**
Peace officers, civil rights, privileges and immunities, application of law, **CC 52.1**
Physicians and surgeons, violent behavior, patients, protection, privileges and immunities, **CC 43.92**
Private schools, buildings and grounds, access, obstructions, interference, **CC 1708.9**
Psychiatrists and psychiatry, violent behavior, patients, protection, privileges and immunities, **CC 43.92**
Psychologists and psychology, violent behavior, patients, protection, privileges and immunities, **CC 43.92**
Psychotherapists and psychotherapy, violent behavior, patients, protection, privileges and immunities, **CC 43.92**
Real estate, appraisal and appraisers, **CC 1090.5**
Reports, social media, **CC 1798.99.20 et seq.**
Social media, reports, **CC 1798.99.20 et seq.**
Social workers, violent behavior, patients, protection, privileges and immunities, **CC 43.92**
Stalking, **CC 1708.7**

THRESHING LIENS
Generally, **CC 3061**

THROUGH HIGHWAYS
Highways and Roads, generally, this index

TICKETS
Rates and Charges, generally, this index

TICKS
Pest Control, generally, this index

TIDAL WAVES
Home solicitation contracts, residential repair or restoration, cancellation, **CC 1689.6, 1689.7, 1689.14**

TIMBER AND LUMBER
Acknowledgments, contracts for sale, **CC 1220**
Contracts, acknowledgments, **CC 1220**
Damages, cutting, carrying off or injuring, **CC 3346**
Easements, right to take, **CC 801, 802**
Highways and roads, taking for highway purposes, damages, **CC 3346**
Injuries, treble damages, **CC 3346**
Legal Estates Principal and Income Law, **CC 731 et seq.**
Liens and encumbrances,
  Loggers, **CC 3065 et seq.**
  Recordation of instruments, **CC 1220**
Limitation of actions, injuries, **CC 3346**
Mortgages,
  Acknowledgment of instruments, **CC 1220**
  Contracts or writings, recording, **CC 1220**
Nuisances, activity, operation, facility, **CC 3482.5**
Records and recordation, contracts, purchase or sale, standing timber or trees, **CC 1220**
Sales, contracts, acknowledgments, **CC 1220**
Statute of limitations, injuries, **CC 3346**
Voidable transactions, application of law, **CC 3440.1**

TIMBER WOLF
Fish and Game, generally, this index

TIMEPIECES
Carriers, limitation of liability, **CC 2200**

TIRES
Pest Control, generally, this index
Vector control. Pest Control, generally, this index

TISSUE BANKS
Actions and proceedings, in vitro fertilization, crimes and offenses, **CC 1708.5.6**
Consent, in vitro fertilization, crimes and offenses, actions and proceedings, **CC 1708.5.6**
Crimes and offenses, in vitro fertilization, consent, actions and proceedings, **CC 1708.5.6**
Damages, in vitro fertilization, crimes and offenses, **CC 1708.5.6**
Disclosure, medical records, **CC 56.10**
Donate life California organ and tissue donor registry, drivers licenses, electronic devices and equipment, **CC 1798.90.1**

TISSUE

TISSUE BANKS—Cont'd
Medical records, disclosure, **CC 56.10**
Records and recordation, medical records, disclosure, **CC 56.10**
Registry, donate life California organ and tissue donor registry, drivers licenses, electronic devices and equipment, **CC 1798.90.1**

TITLE INSURANCE
Consumer protection, deeds and conveyances, foreclosure, **CC 1103.20 et seq.**
Deeds and conveyances, consumer protection, foreclosure, **CC 1103.20 et seq.**
Escrows and escrow agents, notice, **CC 1057.6**
Foreclosure, consumer protection, deeds and conveyances, **CC 1103.20 et seq.**
Mortgages, foreclosure, records and recordation, liability, **CC 2924.26**
Notice, escrows and escrow agents, **CC 1057.6**
Underwritten title company, mortgages, foreclosure, records and recordation, liability, **CC 2924.26**

TITLE TO PROPERTY
Generally, **CC 669 et seq.**
Abandoned or Unclaimed Property, generally, this index
Absolute or qualified ownership, **CC 678 et seq.**
Accession, Accretion and Avulsion, generally, this index
Actions and proceedings,
    Slandering title, **CC 880.360**
    Unperformed contracts for sale, action to clear title, **CC 886.020 et seq.**
Adverse Possession, generally, this index
Agriculture, private bulk grain storage, bill of sale, **CC 1880.6**
Ancient interest, marketable record title, **CC 880.020 et seq.**
Ancient mortgages, deeds of trust, marketable record title, **CC 882.020 et seq.**
Art works, conveyance of rights, ownership of physical work, **CC 988**
Attorney fees, slandering title, **CC 880.360**
Bailment, **CC 1885, 1926**
Boundaries, generally, this index
Color of title, occupancy, **CC 1006**
Conditions subsequent, powers of termination, marketable title, **CC 885.010 et seq.**
Conservation easements, marketable record title, application of law, **CC 880.240**
Consumer credit reporting agencies, records, application of law, **CC 1785.35**
Contracts for sale of land. Deeds and Conveyances, this index
Costs, slandering title, notice of intent to preserve interest in real property, recording, **CC 880.360**
Damages, slandering title, **CC 880.360**
Debtors and creditors, offer to perform obligations, **CC 1502**

TITLE TO PROPERTY—Cont'd
Defective title, specific performance, **CC 3394**
Deposits for exchange, **CC 1878**
Destroyed land records, **CC 2080.3**
Dies, tools and molds, transfer of customers rights and title, **CC 1140**
Discrimination, **CC 53**
Documents of Title, generally, this index
Exchange, loan, **CC 1904**
Fee Simple, generally, this index
Fee tail,
    Abolished, **CC 763**
    Contingent remainders, **CC 764**
Finders of lost property, **CC 2080.3**
Fish and Game, this index
Forms, notice of intent to preserve interest in real property, **CC 880.340**
Future estates or interests, transfer of title, **CC 699**
Instruments essential to ownership, **CC 994**
Intellectual property, **CC 980 et seq.**
Interest in common, excluded interests, **CC 686**
Joint Tenants, generally, this index
Leases, **CC 1926**
Legal Estates Principal and Income Law, **CC 731 et seq.**
Liens and incumbrances, **CC 2888**
Life Estates, generally, this index
Limitation of actions, marketable record title, **CC 880.250, 880.260**
Loan for exchange of property, **CC 1904**
Marketable record title, **CC 880.020 et seq.**
    Time, post
Mobilehomes and Mobilehome Parks, this index
Molds, dies and tools, transfer of customers rights and title, **CC 1140**
Mortgages, title subsequently acquired, **CC 2930**
Occupancy, color of title, **CC 1006**
Options to purchase, unexercised, marketable title, **CC 884.010 et seq.**
Pest control inspection reports, delivery of certified copy of transcript title, **CC 1099**
Possession, marketable record title, application of law, **CC 880.240**
Powers of termination, marketable title, **CC 885.010 et seq.**
Preservation of interest, marketable record title, **CC 880.310 et seq.**
Presumptions, notice of intent to preserve interest, recording, **CC 880.310**
Public policy, marketable record title, **CC 880.020**
Public recreational use of private property to supplement tax supported publicly owned facilities, **CC 1009**
Qualified ownership, **CC 680**
Quieting Title, generally, this index
Record title, marketability, **CC 880.020 et seq.**

TITLE TO PROPERTY—Cont'd
Records and recordation,
    Marketable record title, real estate, **CC 880.020 et seq.**
    Slandering title, **CC 880.360**
Rights, **CC 829**
Several ownership, **CC 681**
Slandering title, **CC 880.360**
Specific performance,
    Defective title, **CC 3394**
    Perfecting title, judgment for possession, **CC 3375**
Statute of limitations, marketable record title, **CC 880.250, 880.260**
Structural pest control, inspection reports, delivery of certificate, transfer of title, **CC 1099**
Time, marketable record title,
    Ancient mortgages, **CC 882.020 et seq.**
    Application of law, **CC 880.250**
    Expiration of records, interest, **CC 880.260**
    Unperformed contracts for sale, expiration, **CC 886.030, 886.040**
Tools, dies and molds, transfer of customers rights and title, **CC 1140**
Unclaimed property. Abandoned or Unclaimed Property, generally, this index
United States, marketable record title, application of law, **CC 880.240**
Unperformed contracts for sale,
    Action to release, **CC 886.020 et seq.**
    Real property, marketable title, **CC 886.010 et seq.**

TITLES OF ACTS
Popular Name Laws, generally, this index

TOBACCO AND TOBACCO PRODUCTS
See, also, Smoking, generally, this index
Cigarettes and Cigars, generally, this index
Landlord and tenant, smoking, prohibiting, **CC 1947.5**
Leases, smoking, prohibiting, **CC 1947.5**
Notice, landlord and tenant, smoking, prohibiting, **CC 1947.5**
Products liability, **CC 1714.45**
Rent, smoking, prohibiting, **CC 1947.5**

TOLLS
Rates and Charges, generally, this index

TOM BANE CIVIL RIGHTS ACT
Generally, **CC 52.1**

TONICS
Cosmetology, generally, this index

TORTS
Generally, **CC 3333 et seq.**
Air raid shelters, liability for injuries, **CC 1714.5**
Blockade, health facilities, commercial blockade, **CC 3427 et seq.**
Disasters, shelters, liability for death or injuries, **CC 1714.5**

TRANSACTIONS

TORTS—Cont'd
Domestic violence, CC 1708.6
Emergency cardiopulmonary resuscitation, immunity from civil damages, CC 1714.2
Firemans rule, CC 1714.9
Immunity from civil damages, emergency cardiopulmonary resuscitation, CC 1714.2
Injury, firefighters, peace officers or emergency medical personnel, CC 1714.9
Invasion of privacy. Privacy, this index
Medical Malpractice, generally, this index
Negligence, generally, this index
Personal Injuries, generally, this index
Products Liability, generally, this index
Stalking, CC 1708.7
Wrongful Death, generally, this index

TOUCH SCREEN DEVICES
Blind or visually impaired persons, CC 54.9

TOWING
Motor Vehicles, this index

TOWNS
See, also, Municipalities, generally, this index
Eminent Domain, generally, this index
Fire companies. Firefighters and Fire Departments, generally, this index
Health Facilities, generally, this index
Lease of lots reserving rent, duration, CC 718
Water supply, appropriations, construction of works, time, CC 1416

TOWNSHIPS
Health Facilities, generally, this index

TOXIC MATERIALS
Hazardous Substances and Waste, generally, this index

TOXIC SUBSTANCES
Hazardous Substances and Waste, generally, this index

TOXIC SUBSTANCES CONTROL DEPARTMENT
Hazardous Substances and Waste, generally, this index

TOXIC WASTE
Hazardous Substances and Waste, generally, this index

TOYS
Bicycles, generally, this index

TRACKS
Railroads, generally, this index
Street Railways, generally, this index

TRACTORS
Farm tractors. Agricultural Machinery and Equipment, generally, this index
Motor Carriers, generally, this index

TRADE AND BUSINESS
Business and Commerce, generally, this index

TRADE SECRETS
Generally, CC 3426 et seq.
Actions and proceedings, misappropriation, CC 3426 et seq.
Application of law, Uniform Act, CC 3426.7 et seq.
Attorney fees, bad faith, CC 3426.4
Bad faith claims, misappropriation, attorneys fees, CC 3426.4
Bribery, CC 3426 et seq.
Costs, misappropriation, bad faith, CC 3426.4
Damages, misappropriation, CC 3426.3
Disclosure, legislative or judicial proceedings, privileges and immunities, CC 3426.11
Discovery,
  Inspection and inspectors, protective orders, CC 3426.5
  Misappropriations, protective orders, CC 3426.5
Espionage, CC 3426 et seq.
Exemplary damages, misappropriation, CC 3426.3
Injunctions, misappropriation, CC 3426.2, 3426.4
Judicial proceedings, disclosure, privilege, CC 3426.11
Legislative proceedings, disclosure, privilege, CC 3426.11
Limitation of actions, misappropriation, CC 3426.6
Misappropriation, CC 3426 et seq.
Misrepresentation, CC 3426 et seq.
Privileges and immunities, disclosure in legislative or judicial proceedings, CC 3426.11
Records and recordation, sealing, misappropriation actions, CC 3426.5
Statute of limitations, misappropriation, CC 3426.6
Theft, CC 3426 et seq.
Uniform Trade Secrets Act, CC 3426 et seq.
Unjust enrichment, misappropriation, CC 3426.3
Willful malicious misappropriation, exemplary damages, CC 3426.3

TRADEMARKS
Dealerships, CC 80 et seq.
Fair dealerships, CC 80 et seq.
Ownership of trademarks, CC 655

TRADING STAMPS
Consumers Legal Remedies Act, CC 1750 et seq.
Damages, Consumers Legal Remedies Act, CC 1750 et seq.
Merchandise value, advertising or display statement, Consumers Legal Remedies Act, CC 1750 et seq.

TRAFFIC RULES AND REGULATIONS
Accidents, reports, disclosure, information practices, CC 1798 et seq.

TRAFFIC RULES AND REGULATIONS —Cont'd
Agricultural Machinery and Equipment, generally, this index
Ambulances, generally, this index
Carriers, speed, CC 2104
Driving under the influence,
  Damages, commercial vehicles, CC 3333.7
  Treble damages, commercial vehicles, CC 3333.7
Farm vehicles. Agricultural Machinery and Equipment, generally, this index
Hitchhiking, railroads, injuries, recovery, CC 1714.7
Implements of husbandry. Agricultural Machinery and Equipment, generally, this index
Pedestrians, blind or visually impaired persons, failure to carry white cane or use guide dog, CC 54.4
Speed,
  Buses, CC 2104
  Carrier of persons, CC 2104
Towing. Motor Vehicles, this index
Tractors, farm tractors. Agricultural Machinery and Equipment, generally, this index

TRAFFIC SIGNS AND SIGNALS
Conditional sales, new or used, CC 2982

TRAFFICKING
Human Trafficking, generally, this index

TRAILER PARKS
Mobilehomes and Mobilehome Parks, generally, this index

TRAILERS
Mobilehomes and Mobilehome Parks, generally, this index
Motor Carriers, generally, this index
Recreational Vehicles, generally, this index

TRAILS
Recreational Trails, generally, this index

TRAINED NURSES
Nurses, generally, this index

TRAINERS
Guide dogs, public accommodations, CC 54.1, 54.2

TRAINING
Defibrillators, CC 1714.21
Medicine, opioid antagonists, overdose, CC 1714.22

TRAINS
Railroads, generally, this index

TRAMWAYS
Street Railways, generally, this index

TRANSACTIONS AND USE TAXES
Sales and Use Taxes, generally, this index

TRANSCRIPT

TRANSCRIPT OF RECORD

Administrative Law and Procedure, generally, this index

TRANSFER OF PROPERTY

Generally, CC 1039 et seq.

Adverse possession, CC 1047

Breach of condition subsequent, right of reentry or repossession, CC 1046

Change of possession, creditors, CC 3440 et seq.

Deeds and Conveyances, generally, this index

Delivery, grant, CC 1054 et seq.

Escrows and Escrow Agents, generally, this index

Floating homes, CC 800.80 et seq.

Home roof warranties, CC 1797.92

Incidents of ownership, included in transfer, CC 1084

Oral transfers, CC 1052

Parties, acquisition of interest or benefit by stranger, CC 1085

Possibility, transfer, CC 1045

Right of reentry, CC 1046

Voidable transactions, CC 3439 et seq.

TRANSITIONAL HOUSING PARTICIPANT MISCONDUCT ACT

Generally, CC 1954.10 et seq.

TRANSMISSIONS

Electronic Transmissions, generally, this index

TRANSPARENCY IN SUPPLY CHAINS ACT

Generally, CC 1714.43

TRANSPLANTS

Tissue Banks, generally, this index

TRANSPORTATION

Blind or visually impaired persons, civil rights, CC 54.1

Buses, generally, this index

Deaf persons, public accommodations, CC 54.1 et seq.

Highways and Roads, generally, this index

Railroads, generally, this index

Service stations, gasoline vapor control systems, marketing operations, CC 1952.8

TRAPS AND TRAPPING

Pest Control, generally, this index

TRAUMA

Buildings, first aid, trauma kits, privileges and immunities, CC 1714.29

TRAVEL TRAILERS

Mobilehomes and Mobilehome Parks, generally, this index

Recreational Vehicles, generally, this index

TREBLE DAMAGES

Damages, this index

TREES

See, also, Timber and Lumber, generally, this index

Adjoining landowners, boundaries, ownership, CC 833, 834

Advertisements. Outdoor Advertising, generally, this index

Boundaries, ownership, CC 833, 834

Damages,
Cutting, carrying off or injuring, CC 3346
Treble, injury to or removal, CC 3346

Injuries to, treble damages, CC 3346

Outdoor Advertising, generally, this index

Owners and ownership,
Line trees, common, CC 834
Trunks wholly on land of one owner, CC 833

Products. Timber and Lumber, generally, this index

Recording contracts for purchase or sale, CC 1220

TRESPASS

Accession to property, ownership of product made, CC 1031

Animals, fur bearing animals raised in captivity, CC 996

Apartments, house keepers, enforcement of lien, CC 1861a

Damages,
Injuries to trees and lumber, CC 3346
Timber and lumber, cutting, carrying off or injuring trees, CC 3346
Trees, cutting, carrying off or injuring, CC 3346

Landlord and tenant, CC 1942.6

Limitation of actions, surveying, CC 3346

Trees and timber, injuries to, damages, CC 3346

TRIAL

Consolidation of actions, credit cards, identity and identification, information, acceptance, CC 1747.08

Costs, generally, this index

Deaf or hard of hearing persons, assistive listening devices or computer aided transcription, CC 54.8

Process, generally, this index

Venue, generally, this index

Witnesses, generally, this index

TRIAL COURTS

Courts, generally, this index

TROLLEY COACHES

Street Railways, generally, this index

TROVER

Conversion, generally, this index

TRUCK TRACTORS

Motor Carriers, generally, this index

TRUCKS

Motor Carriers, generally, this index

TRUST COMPANIES

Corporation Taxes, generally, this index

Electronic funds transfers. Funds Transfers, generally, this index

Funds Transfers, generally, this index

Money Orders, generally, this index

TRUST DEEDS

See, also, Mortgages, generally, this index

Abandoned or unclaimed property, power of sale, surplus, CC 2924j

Absentees, mortgage release, bonds (officers and fiduciaries), CC 2941.7

Acceleration, CC 2924c
Enforceability, CC 2924.7
Incorporation of acceleration clause in documents, CC 2924.5
Junior deed of trust, single family, owner occupied dwelling, CC 2949
Maturity deeds, residential property transfers, CC 2924.6
Prepayment penalty, prohibition, CC 2954.10
Second mortgage, CC 2949

Accounts and accounting, beneficiary, accounting by, CC 2954

Acknowledgments, CC 2952
Majority interest holders, beneficiaries, governing agreement, CC 2941.9
Substitution of trustees, CC 2934a

Actions and proceedings,
Declarations of nonmonetary status, trustees, CC 2924l
Foreclosure, generally, post
Sales, rent, CC 2924m
Satisfaction, reconveyance, CC 2941

Advance fee, reconveyance, CC 2941

Agents, payments by trustees, CC 2924d

Ancient trust deeds, marketable record title, CC 882.020 et seq.

Application of law, trusts and trustees, CC 2934b

Arrangers of credit, disclosure, CC 2956 et seq.

Arrearages, payment, cure of default, CC 2924c

As is condition sales, CC 2924h

Assignments, beneficial interest, recording, CC 2934, 2935

Assumption, Statute of Frauds, CC 1624

Attorney fees,
Balloon payments, notice, damages, CC 2924i
Release of obligation, damages, CC 2941
Sales, CC 2924d

Auctions and auctioneers, power of sale, CC 2924g

Authentication, optically imaged reproductions, reconveyance, CC 2941

Balloon payments, notice, CC 2924i

Beneficiaries,
Majority interest holders, governing agreement, CC 2941.9

TRUST

TRUST DEEDS—Cont'd
Beneficiaries—Cont'd
  Process, service on trustees, CC 2937.7
  Statements, CC 2943
  Substitution of trustees, execution, CC 2934a
Bids and bidding,
  Covenants, low and moderate income housing, CC 2924o
  Sales, CC 2924g, 2924h
    Rent, CC 2924m
Bonds (officers and fiduciaries), absentee mortgagees, release, CC 2941.7
Certificates and certification, CC 2952
Confidential or privileged information, notice, CC 2924
Consent, delinquency notice, junior lien holders, CC 2924e
Constructive notice, assignments, recording, CC 2934
Contracts for prepayment charges, CC 2954.9
Costs,
  Mortgages, payment to cure default, CC 2924c
  Payment, care of default, CC 2924c
Counselors and counseling, foreclosure, CC 2923.5
Covenant by lessor of real property, CC 1469, 1470
Covenants, bids and bidding, low and moderate income housing, CC 2924o
Credit arrangers, disclosure, CC 2956 et seq.
Credit cards, secured credit cards, statements, CC 1747.94
Crimes and offenses,
  Reconveyance, CC 2941.5
  Trustees sale, default by bidder, CC 2924h
Damages,
  Balloon payments, final notice, CC 2924i
  Declarations of nonmonetary status, trustees, CC 2924l
  Failure to deliver statements, CC 2943
  Reconveyance, recording, CC 2941
  Release of obligation, failure to execute reconveyance, CC 2941
  Trusts and trustees, default, CC 2924
Declarations of nonmonetary status, trustees as defendants, CC 2924l
Default,
  Condominiums, sales, homeowners associations, notice, CC 2924b
  Cure, CC 2924c
  Notice, CC 2924
    Request for copies, CC 2924b
    Rescission, CC 2924c, 2937
    Summaries, CC 2923.3
  Sales, payments, CC 2924h
  Summaries, notice, CC 2923.3, 2924
Delinquencies, notice, junior lien holders, CC 2924e
Delinquency charges, CC 2954.4
  Notice, CC 2954.5

TRUST DEEDS—Cont'd
Deposits, impound accounts, CC 2955
Discharge,
  Ancient deeds, CC 882.030
  Reconveyance, generally, post
Disclosure,
  Arrangers of credit, CC 2956 et seq.
  Prepayment penalties, CC 2954.11
Due date,
  Acceleration, incorporation of acceleration clause in documents, CC 2924.5
  Balloon payments, notice, CC 2924i
Due diligence, foreclosure, meetings, financial condition, CC 2923.5
Due on sale clauses, acceleration, prepayment penalties, CC 2954.10
Election to sell, CC 2924
English language, forms, notice of default cure, CC 2924c
Equity line of credit, payoff demand statements, CC 2943.1
Escrows and escrow agents,
  Impound accounts, generally, post
  Interest, time, CC 2948.5
  Statement of unpaid balance, due date, CC 2943
Estates for Years, this index
Evidence,
  Balloon payments, notice of violations, CC 2924i
  Substitution of trustees, CC 2934a
Fees,
  Acceleration, conveyances, CC 2954.10
  Accounting for trust account moneys, CC 2954
  Attorney fees, generally, ante
  Junior lien holders, delinquency notice, CC 2924e
  Payment, cure of default, CC 2924c
  Reconveyance, CC 2941
Fictitious, recording, CC 2952
Final payment, balloon, notice, CC 2924i
Fines and penalties,
  Acceleration, conveyance, CC 2954.10
  Accounting for trust account moneys, CC 2954
  Certificates of discharge, obligations to execute, CC 2941.5
  Foreclosure, maintenance, CC 2929.3, 2929.4
  Prepayment, CC 2954.9, 2954.11
  Rebates and kickbacks, CC 2924d
  Reconveyance, CC 2941, 2941.5
  Trustees sale, default by bidder, CC 2924h
Forcible entry and detainer, CC 2924n
Foreclosure,
  Change of servicing agent, validity, CC 2937
  Counselors and counseling, CC 2923.5
  Due diligence, meetings, financial condition, CC 2923.5
  Fines and penalties, maintenance, CC 2929.3, 2929.4

TRUST DEEDS—Cont'd
Foreclosure—Cont'd
  Maintenance, CC 2929.3
  Meetings, financial condition, CC 2923.5
  Notice, CC 2924f
    Maintenance, CC 2929.3
    Fines and penalties, CC 2929.4
  Sale, transfer of obligation, CC 2937
  Nuisance, abatement, assessments, CC 2929.45
  Priorities and preferences,
    Judicial sales, bids and bidding, CC 2924p
    Power of sale, CC 2924j, 2924k
  State as party, requirements, CC 2931a
  Summaries, notice, CC 2924f
Forfeitures,
  Delinquency notice, junior lien holders, CC 2924e
  Failure to prepare and deliver statements, CC 2943
Forms,
  Acceleration clause, incorporation in documents, CC 2924.5
  English language, notice of default cure, CC 2924c
  Equity line of credit, payoff demand statements, CC 2943.1
  Notice of default cure possibility, CC 2924c
  Spanish language, notice of default cure, CC 2924c
  Subordination agreement, CC 2953.3
Frauds, statute of, CC 1624
Guaranty and suretyship, guarantors, waiver, CC 2856
Impairment of security, acceleration of payments, enforceability, CC 2924.7
Impound accounts,
  Accounting, CC 2954
  Retention and investment in state, CC 2955
  Single family owner occupied dwellings, payment of taxes, CC 2954
Indexes, fictitious deeds, CC 2952
Injunction, impound accounts, investments, CC 2955
Insurance, this index
Interest,
  Prepayment penalties, CC 2954.11
  Rate, statement to entitled persons, CC 2943
  Time, CC 2948.5
  Variable rate, CC 1916.5
Internal revenue, default, sales, notice, CC 2924b
Junior lien holders, delinquencies, notice, CC 2924e
Kickbacks, CC 2924d
Late payment, charges, CC 2954.4
  Notice, CC 2954.5
Limitation of actions,
  Ancient deeds of trust, marketable record title, CC 882.020 et seq.

TRUST

TRUST DEEDS—Cont'd
Limitation of actions—Cont'd
   Satisfaction, reconveyance, **CC 2941**
Line of credit, payoff demand statements, **CC 2943.1**
Loans, shared appreciation loans, **CC 1917 et seq.**
Low and moderate income housing, bids and bidding, covenants, **CC 2924o**
Mail and mailing, substitution of trustees, notice, **CC 2934a**
Maintenance, foreclosure, **CC 2929.3**
Majority interest holders, beneficiaries, governing agreement, **CC 2941.9**
Marketable record title, **CC 880.020 et seq.**
   Ancient deeds, **CC 882.020 et seq.**
Mechanics liens, **CC 8174**
   Priorities and preferences, **CC 8450 et seq.**
Meetings, foreclosure, financial condition, **CC 2923.5**
Merger of parcels, single instrument of conveyance or consolidated description of parcels, **CC 1093**
Multifamily housing, political subdivisions, sales, postponement, **CC 2924f**
Nonmonetary status, declarations of, trustees as defendants, **CC 2941**
Nonprofit corporations, sales, rent, **CC 2924m**
Notice,
   Balloon payments, **CC 2924i**
   Blanket incumbrances on subdivisions, **CC 1133**
   Constructive notice, assignments, records, **CC 2934**
   Default, ante
   Delinquencies, junior lien holders, **CC 2924e**
   Foreclosure, ante
   Forfeitures, junior lien holders, delinquencies, failure to give, **CC 2924e**
   Majority interest holders, beneficiaries, governing agreement, **CC 2941.9**
   Privileged communications, **CC 2924**
   Request, junior lien holders, delinquency information, **CC 2924e**
   Sales, post
   Shared appreciation loans, seniors, **CC 1917.714**
   Subordination agreements, **CC 2953.2, 2953.3**
   Substitution of trustees, **CC 2934a**
   Transfer, single family residence, **CC 2937**
Nuisance, abatement, foreclosure, assessments, **CC 2929.45**
Optically imaged reproductions, reconveyance, **CC 2941**
Parties, foreclosure, state, **CC 2931a**
Payment,
   Acceleration, conveyance, fees, penalties, **CC 2954.10**
   Prepayment, rates and charges, **CC 2954.9**
Payoff demand statements, **CC 2943**
   Equity line of credit, **CC 2943.1**

TRUST DEEDS—Cont'd
Payoff demand statements—Cont'd
   Reconveyance, fees, **CC 2941.1**
Penalties. Fines and penalties, generally, ante
Postponement, sales, **CC 2924g**
   Foreclosure, notice, **CC 2924f**
Power of sale, **CC 2924f et seq.**
   Abandoned or unclaimed property, surplus, **CC 2924j**
   Attorney authority to conduct, **CC 2924a**
   Notice, **CC 2924j**
   Priorities and preferences, **CC 2924j, 2924k**
Prepayment, **CC 2954.9**
   Emergencies and natural disasters, prepayment penalty, **CC 2954.9**
Prepayment penalties, **CC 2954.11**
Price fixing, bids, sale of property, **CC 2924h**
Priorities and preferences,
   Estate for years, **CC 2898**
   Foreclosure, judicial sales, bids and bidding, **CC 2924p**
   Power of sale, **CC 2924j, 2924k**
   Purchase money mortgage, **CC 2898**
   Shared appreciation loans, **CC 1917.004**
Privileged communications, notice, **CC 2924**
Process,
   State as party, **CC 2931a**
   Trustors, service on trustees, **CC 2937.7**
Proof, **CC 2952**
Prospective owner occupants, **CC 2924m**
Purchase money, priority, **CC 2898**
Rates and charges,
   Acceleration, conveyance, **CC 2954.10**
   Late payment, **CC 2954.4, 2954.5**
   Prepayment, contracts, **CC 2954.9**
   Real property security instrument, **CC 2953.1 et seq.**
   Sale of property, **CC 2924f et seq.**
Rebates, **CC 2924d**
Reconveyance,
   Fees, **CC 2941**
      Payoff demand statements, **CC 2941.1**
   Obligation to execute, **CC 2941**
      Penalty for violation, **CC 2941.5**
   Optically imaged reproductions, **CC 2941**
   Recording, **CC 2941**
   Reproductions, optical imaging, **CC 2941**
Records and recordation,
   Fictitious, **CC 2952**
   Interest, time, **CC 2948.5**
   Lien priority, waiver, **CC 2934**
   Majority interest holders, beneficiaries, governing agreement, **CC 2941.9**
   Notice of default and sale, **CC 2924**
      Requests for copies, **CC 2934a**
      Transfer of obligation, notice, **CC 2937**
   Reconveyance, **CC 2941**
   Release of obligation, **CC 2941**
   Substitution of trustees, **CC 2934a**
Reference, fictitious deeds, **CC 2952**

TRUST DEEDS—Cont'd
Reinstatement, after default, procedure, **CC 2924c**
Release,
   Absentee mortgagees, bonds (officers and fiduciaries), **CC 2941.7**
   Ancient deeds, **CC 882.030**
   Failure of trustees to execute reconveyance, **CC 2941**
Rent,
   Sales, **CC 2924m**
   Skimming, residential real estate, **CC 890 et seq.**
Reproductions, optical imaging, reconveyance, **CC 2941**
Rescission, default,
   Notice, **CC 2924c**
   Sales, **CC 2924h**
Resignation, trusts and trustees, substitution of trustees, **CC 2934a**
Risks, foreclosure, bids and bidding, notice, **CC 2924f**
Sales,
   Foreclosure, generally, ante
   Notice, **CC 2924, 2924f, 2924g, 2924j**
      Request for copies, **CC 2924b**
   Power of sale, generally, ante
   Rent, **CC 2924m**
Satisfaction,
   Ancient deeds, **CC 882.030**
   Obligation to execute certificate of discharge, **CC 2941**
   Penalty for violation, **CC 2941.5**
Secured credit cards, statements, **CC 1747.94**
Secured Transactions, generally, this index
Shared appreciation loans, **CC 1917 et seq.**
   Seniors, lien securing total obligation, **CC 1917.614**
   Notice, **CC 1917.714**
Short pay agreements, secured land transaction statements, **CC 2943**
Skimming of rent, residential real estate, **CC 890 et seq.**
Spanish language, forms, notice of default cure, **CC 2924c**
Specific performance, sales, rent, **CC 2924m**
Statements. Payoff demand statements, generally, ante
Statute of Frauds, **CC 1624**
Statutory rights, waiver, validity, **CC 2953**
Subagents, payments by trustees, **CC 2924d**
Subordination clause or agreement, **CC 2953.1 et seq.**
Substitution of trustees, **CC 2934a**
   Reconveyances, **CC 2941.7**
Summaries, notice,
   Default, **CC 2923.3, 2924**
   Foreclosure, **CC 2924f**
Suretyship and guaranty, guarantors, waiver, **CC 2856**
Taxation, impound accounts for payment,
   Accounting, **CC 2954**

TUMULTS

TRUST DEEDS—Cont'd
Taxation, impound accounts for payment
—Cont'd
  Retention and investment in state, **CC 2955**
Time,
  Ancient deeds, marketable record title, **CC 882.020**
  Interest, **CC 2948.5**
  Maturity date acceleration, residential property transfers, **CC 2924.6**
  Satisfaction, reconveyance, **CC 2941**
Transfers, notice, single family residence, **CC 2937**
Trusts and trustees,
  Application of law, **CC 2934b**
  Damages, default, **CC 2924**
  Declarations of nonmonetary status, **CC 2924l**
  Fees,
    Cure of default, **CC 2924c**
    Sales, **CC 2924d**
  Power of sale, attorney, **CC 2924a**
  Residential property transfers, maturity date acceleration, **CC 2924.6**
  Service of process, on trustees, **CC 2937.7**
  Substitution, **CC 2934a**
    Reconveyances, **CC 2941.7**
Unified sales, notice of sale, form, **CC 2924f**
Variable interest rate, **CC 1916.5**
Waiver,
  Borrower, statutory rights, validity, exceptions, **CC 2953**
  Lien priority, recording, **CC 2934**
  Prepayment penalty, acceleration, **CC 2954.10**
  Rights of subordination clause, **CC 2953.4**
  Single family, owner occupied dwelling, acceleration or default, junior trust deed, **CC 2949**
Written authentication, optically imaged reproductions, reconveyance, **CC 2941**

TRUST RECEIPTS
Secured Transactions, generally, this index

TRUSTS AND TRUSTEES
See, also, Fiduciaries, generally, this index
Accidents, involuntary trusts, **CC 2223 et seq.**
Accounts and accounting, health studios, new facilities, **CC 1812.96**
Accumulations, income from property, direction by, **CC 724**
Acknowledgments, substitution of trustees, **CC 2934a**
Actions and proceedings,
  Convicted felons, beneficiaries, recovery of interest in involuntary trusts, **CC 2225**
  Stories, sales, convicted felons, involuntary trusts, **CC 2225**
Affidavits, substitution of trustees, **CC 2934a**
Agents and agencies,
  Construction of authority, **CC 2322**

TRUSTS AND TRUSTEES—Cont'd
Agents and agencies—Cont'd
  Payment by trustee, **CC 2924d**
Application of law, trust deeds, **CC 2934b**
Art works, consignment, **CC 1738 et seq.**
Attorney fees, cure of default, **CC 2924c**
Beneficiaries,
  Convicted felons, recovery of interest in involuntary trusts, **CC 2225**
  Voluntary trusts, avoidance of merger, legal and equitable estates in same person, **CC 2225**
Celebrity image protection, **CC 3344.1**
Clients, sexual harassment, **CC 51.9**
Contempt, involuntary trusts, sale of convicted felon stories, **CC 2225**
Covenant by lessor of real property, **CC 1469, 1470**
Crimes and offenses,
  Involuntary trusts, criminal gains, **CC 2223 et seq.**
  Stories about felonies, sale proceeds, **CC 2225**
Damages, holding over real property, **CC 3335**
Deceased celebrity image protection, **CC 3344.1**
Deeds and conveyances, contracts for sale of land, installment payments, **CC 2985.4**
Deposits, **CC 1586**
Disclosure, residential property transfers, **CC 1102.2**
Discount buying services, accounts, **CC 1812.116**
Electronic Transactions Act, testamentary trusts, application of law, **CC 1633.3**
Express trusts, stories by felons, sale proceeds, **CC 2225**
Forms,
  Default on sale, request for copies, **CC 2924b**
  Sales, notice of default, **CC 2924b**
Fraud, involuntary trustee, **CC 2223 et seq.**
Gift certificates, **CC 1749.6**
Harassment, sexual harassment, clients, **CC 51.9**
Health studios, accounts and accounting, new facilities, **CC 1812.96**
Injunction,
  Involuntary trusts, convicted felons, sale of stories, **CC 2225**
  Obligation arising from, **CC 3422**
Involuntary trusts, **CC 2223 et seq.**
  Stories by felons, sale proceeds, **CC 2225**
Lienholders, restoration of priority, **CC 1058.5**
Limitation of actions, involuntary trusts, **CC 2224.5**
Convicted felon stories, sales, **CC 2225**
Merger and consolidation, equitable and legal estates in same person, avoidance or termination, **CC 2225**
Mistake, involuntary trusts, **CC 2223 et seq.**
Mortgages, **CC 2954**
  Damages, default, **CC 2924**

TRUSTS AND TRUSTEES—Cont'd
Mortgages—Cont'd
  Default, cure, **CC 2924c**
  Investments, state, retention, **CC 2955**
  Power of sale, **CC 2924**
  Residential property transfers, maturity date acceleration, **CC 2924.6**
  Sales, **CC 2924d**
Notice, rescission, restoring record title, **CC 1058.5**
Priorities and preferences, restoration, **CC 1058.5**
Publication, substitution of trustee, **CC 2934a**
Records and recordation, assignments, beneficial interest, **CC 2934, 2935**
Rescission, restoring record title, **CC 1058.5**
Residential property transfers, trust deeds, maturity date acceleration, **CC 2924.6**
Resignation, substitution of trustees, **CC 2934a**
Restoring record title, rescission of deeds, **CC 1058.5**
Sales, stories, convicted felons, involuntary trusts, **CC 2225**
Secured Transactions, generally, this index
Sexual harassment, clients, **CC 51.9**
Stories, convicted felons, sales, involuntary trusts, **CC 2225**
Substitution,
  Acknowledgments, **CC 2934a**
  Method, **CC 2934a**
Termination, voluntary trusts, avoidance of merger, equitable and legal estate in same person, **CC 2225**
Testamentary trusts,
  Electronic Transactions Act, application of law, **CC 1633.3**
  Uniform Electronic Transactions Act, application of law, **CC 1633.3**
Trust Deeds, this index
Undue influence, involuntary trusts, **CC 2223 et seq.**
Uniform Electronic Transactions Act, testamentary trusts, application of law, **CC 1633.3**
Validity, voluntary trusts, merger, equitable and legal estates, **CC 2225**
Venue, involuntary trusts, actions to recover interest in, **CC 2225**
Voluntary trusts, avoidance of merger, equitable and legal estates, **CC 2225**
Workforce housing cooperative trusts, **CC 817.1 et seq.**
Wrongful detention, involuntary trustee, **CC 2223**

TRUTH IN LENDING
Motor vehicle conditional sales contract, **CC 2982**
Shared appreciation loans for seniors, disclosure, **CC 1917.712, 1917.713**

TUMULTS
Riots and Mobs, generally, this index

TYPEWRITERS

TYPEWRITERS
Sale, identification number of mark altered or removed, CC 1710.1

TYPHOID FEVER
Diseases, generally, this index

UNAUTHORIZED IMMIGRATION
Noncitizens, generally, this index

UNCLAIMED PROPERTY
Abandoned or Unclaimed Property, generally, this index

UNDERTAKINGS
Bonds (Officers and Fiduciaries), generally, this index

UNDOCUMENTED IMMIGRANTS
Noncitizens, generally, this index

UNDUE INFLUENCE
Contracts, this index
Mortgages, appraisal and appraisers, CC 1090.5
Real estate, appraisal and appraisers, CC 1090.5

UNEMPLOYMENT
Small Businesses, generally, this index

UNEMPLOYMENT COMPENSATION
Actions and proceedings, lien of state, enforcing, CC 2931c
Liens and incumbrances, action to enforce, CC 2931c

UNFAIR BUSINESS PRACTICES
Monopolies and Unfair Trade, generally, this index

UNFAIR DISCRIMINATION
Discrimination, generally, this index

UNFAIR TRADE
Monopolies and Unfair Trade, generally, this index

UNIFORM COMMERCIAL CODE
Commercial Code, generally, this index

UNIFORM LAWS
Electronic Transactions Act, CC 1633.1 et seq.
Single Publication Act, CC 3425.1 et seq.
Trade Secrets Act, CC 3426 et seq.
Vendor and Purchaser Risk Act, CC 1662
Voidable Transactions Act, CC 3439 et seq.

UNIFORM SINGLE PUBLICATION
Libel and Slander, this index

UNIFORM VOIDABLE TRANSACTIONS ACT
Generally, CC 3439 et seq.

UNINCORPORATED ASSOCIATIONS
Associations and Societies, generally, this index

UNITED STATES
Alien insurers admitted in other states, trusts, acknowledgments, authorization to take, CC 1183
Carriers, preferences, CC 2171
Income Tax—Federal, generally, this index
Military Forces, generally, this index
Mines and minerals, CC 883.110 et seq.
Real estate,
  Marketable record title, application of law, CC 880.240
  Title to property, CC 755
Ships and shipping, registered under laws, recording, CC 1173
Telecommunications, messages, priorities and preferences, CC 2207, 2208

UNITED STATES AGENCIES AND INSTITUTIONS
Comatose patients, medical information disclosure, CC 56.10
Medical records, comatose patients, information disclosure, CC 56.10

UNITED STATES COURTS
Acknowledgments, CC 1182

UNITED STATES POSTAL SERVICE
Mail and Mailing, generally, this index

UNIVERSITIES
Colleges and Universities, generally, this index

UNIVERSITY OF CALIFORNIA
  See, also, Colleges and Universities, generally, this index
Abandoned or unclaimed property, CC 2080.8
Confidential or privileged information, research, disclosure, CC 1798.24
Lost or destroyed property, CC 2080.8
Numbers and numbering, social security, posting, CC 1798.85
Personal information, research, disclosure, CC 1798.24
Police, unclaimed property, care and disposition, CC 2080.8
Posting, social security, numbers and numbering, CC 1798.85
Research, personal or confidential information, disclosures, Information Practices Act, CC 1798.24
Restitution, unclaimed property, CC 2080.8
Sales, unclaimed property, CC 2080.8
Social security, numbers and numbering, posting, CC 1798.85
Student loans. Colleges and Universities, this index

UNLAWFUL DETAINER
Forcible Entry and Detainer, generally, this index

UNMANNED AIRCRAFT
Emergencies, interference, damages, CC 43.101

UNPAID BALANCE
Installment Sales, this index

UNRUH CIVIL RIGHTS ACT
Generally, CC 51

UNRUH CREDIT SALES ACT
Generally, CC 1801 et seq.

URBAN RENEWAL
Community Development and Housing, generally, this index

USE TAXES
Sales and Use Taxes, generally, this index

USED PROPERTY
Misrepresentation, Consumers Legal Remedies Act, CC 1750 et seq.

USED VEHICLES
Motor Vehicles, this index

USES AND TRUSTS
Trusts and Trustees, generally, this index

USURY
Interest, this index

UTILITIES
Public Utilities, generally, this index

VACANCY DECONTROL
Generally, CC 1954.50 et seq.

VACUUM CLEANERS
Manufacturer identification mark, removal, defacing, alteration or destruction, CC 1710.1

VALUATION
Accession of personal property, election between thing made and value, CC 1032
Covenants running with land,
  Apportionment, CC 1467
  Successive owners, CC 1468
Exchange of property, loan, CC 1904

VANDALISM
  See, also, Defacing, generally, this index
Actions and proceedings, construction sites, treble damages, CC 1721
Attorney fees, construction sites, CC 1721
Construction sites, actions, treble damages, CC 1721
Damages, treble damages, actions, CC 1721
Malicious Mischief, generally, this index
Motor vehicles, leases, CC 1939.03

VANS
Leases, safety, CC 1939.35

VARIABLE INTEREST RATES
Generally, CC 1916.5 et seq.

VAUDEVILLE
Theaters and Shows, generally, this index

VECTOR
Pest Control, generally, this index

VOIDABLE

VEHICLE LEASING ACT
Generally, **CC 2985.7 et seq.**

VEHICLES
Motor Vehicles, generally, this index

VENDING MACHINES
Grocery stores, point of sale systems, application of law, **CC 7100**

VENDOR AND PURCHASER
Conclusiveness of grant, **CC 1107**
Credit arrangers, real estate, disclosure, **CC 2956 et seq.**
Disclosure,
    Real estate, credit arrangers, **CC 2956 et seq.**
    Residential property transfers, **CC 1102 et seq.**
Discrimination, housing, racial restrictions, deeds, **CC 782, 782.5**
Liens and incumbrances, **CC 3046 et seq.**
Life tenant, heirs, **CC 779**
Risk Act, **CC 1662**
Single family residence, document of title, fees, **CC 1097**
Statute of Frauds, agreement authorizing purchase or sale of real estate, **CC 1624**
Uniform Risk Act, **CC 1662**

VENDOR AND PURCHASER RISK ACT
Generally, **CC 1662**

VENTURA COUNTY STATE COLLEGE
Colleges and Universities, generally, this index

VENUE
Affidavits,
    Conditional sales, motor vehicles, **CC 2984.4**
    Installment sales, **CC 1812.10**
Animals, injunction, tests, alternatives, **CC 1834.9**
Conditional sales, motor vehicles, **CC 2983.7, 2984.4**
Consumers Legal Remedies Act, **CC 1780**
Crime victims, stories about felonies, actions for proceeds, **CC 2225**
Dog bites, **CC 3342.5**
Easements, maintenance and repairs, **CC 845**
Installment sales,
    Affidavits, **CC 1812.10**
    Contract provisions, **CC 1804.1**
Mineral right termination action, **CC 883.240**
Monopolies and unfair trade, **CC 1780**
Rental purchase agreements, **CC 1812.645**
    Collection actions, **CC 1812.624**
Statement of facts,
    Conditional sales, motor vehicles, **CC 2984.4**
    Installment sales, **CC 1812.10**
Unfair trade, **CC 1780**
Witnesses, compensation and salaries, contracts, **CC 1669.7**

VERMIN
Pest Control, generally, this index

VESSELS
Boats and Boating, generally, this index
Ships and Shipping, generally, this index

VESTED REMAINDERS
Future Estates or Interests, generally, this index

VESTED RIGHTS
Generally, **CC 6**
Statutes, repeal, **CC 20**

VETERANS
Assignments, benefits, monopolies and unfair trade, **CC 1770**
Benefits, monopolies and unfair trade, **CC 1770**
Consumer protection, additional penalty, **CC 3345**
Correctional institutions, social security, numbers and numbering, disclosure, **CC 1798.85**
Damages, consumer protection, unfair or deceptive practices, **CC 3345**
Entitlements, monopolies and unfair trade, **CC 1770**
Fines and penalties, consumer protection, **CC 3345**
Fraud, consumer protection, **CC 3345**
Jails, social security, numbers and numbering, disclosure, **CC 1798.85**
Monopolies and unfair trade, benefits, **CC 1770**
Unfair trade, benefits, **CC 1770**

VETERINARIANS
Abandoned animals, **CC 1834.5**
Drugs and Medicine, generally, this index
Immunities. Privileges and immunities, generally, post
Liens and incumbrances, **CC 3051 et seq.**
Malpractice. Medical Malpractice, generally, this index
Medical Malpractice, generally, this index
Medicine. Drugs and Medicine, generally, this index
Negligence. Medical Malpractice, generally, this index
Privileges and immunities,
    Referral services, **CC 43.95**
    Standards, committee members, **CC 43.7, 43.8**
Referral services, limitation of liability, **CC 43.95**
Telecommunications, referral services, privileges and immunities, **CC 43.95**

VICTIMS OF CRIME
Crime Victims, generally, this index

VIDEO GAMES
Children and minors, force and violence, **CC 1746 et seq.**
Force and violence, children and minors, **CC 1746 et seq.**

VIDEO RECORDINGS
Audio and Video Recordings, generally, this index

VIDEOCONFERENCING
Telecommunications, generally, this index

VILLAGES
Health Facilities, generally, this index

VIOLENCE
Force and Violence, generally, this index

VISION
Eyes and Eyesight, generally, this index

VISUAL ARTS
Art and Artists, generally, this index

VISUALLY IMPAIRED PERSONS
Blind or Visually Impaired Persons, generally, this index

VOCATIONAL NURSING
Abuse, long term health care facilities, temporary employment, **CC 1812.543**
Criminal history information, long term health care facilities, temporary employment, **CC 1812.542**
Employment agencies, long term health care facilities, temporary employment, **CC 1812.540 et seq.**
Long term health care facilities, employment agencies, temporary employment, **CC 1812.540 et seq.**
Psychiatric Technicians, generally, this index

VODKA
Alcoholic Beverages, generally, this index

VOICE
Advertisements, unauthorized use, **CC 3344**
Astaire Celebrity Image Protection Act, **CC 3344.1**

VOICE RECORDING
Audio and Video Recordings, generally, this index

VOIDABLE TRANSACTIONS
    Generally, **CC 1227 et seq., 3439 et seq., 3518**
Accounts, sale of, application of law, **CC 3440.1**
Actions and proceedings, **CC 3439.07 et seq.**
Actions to set aside, **CC 3440.1**
Application of law, **CC 3439.12 et seq., 3440.1**
    Commercial Code, **CC 3440.9**
Assignment for benefit of creditors, **CC 3440 et seq.**
    Application of law, **CC 3440.1**
Assignments, remedies, **CC 3439.07**
Attachment, **CC 3439.07**
Bottomry, application of law, **CC 3440.1**
Brandy, application of law, **CC 3440.1**
Burden of proof, **CC 3439.04, 3439.05**
    Good faith, **CC 3439.08**

I-213

VOIDABLE

VOIDABLE TRANSACTIONS—Cont'd
Buyer for value in good faith, transfer of property when transferor no longer in possession, **CC 3440.4**
Buyer in ordinary course of business, filing of financing statement, **CC 3440.3**
Chattel paper, sale of, application of law, **CC 3440.1**
Claims, **CC 3439.04**
Consideration, **CC 3439.03**
Defenses, **CC 3439.08**
Delivery, **CC 3440 et seq.**
Evidence,
  Burden of proof, **CC 3439.04, 3439.05**
  Good faith, **CC 3439.08**
  Presumptions, insolvency, **CC 3439.02**
Exceptions, **CC 3440.1**
Executions, **CC 3439.07**
Exempt property, application of law, **CC 3440.1**
Financing statement, **CC 3440.1, 3440.5**
  Buyer in ordinary course of business, **CC 3440.3**
  Filing,
    Creditors claim arising after date of filing, **CC 3440.2**
    Limitation of actions, **CC 3440.6**
Good faith, defenses, **CC 3439.08**
Good faith purchasers, transfer of property when transferor no longer in possession, **CC 3440.4**
Government entities, application of law, **CC 3440.1**
Injunction, **CC 3439.07**
Insolvency, **CC 3439.02**
Intent, **CC 3439.04**
Leaseback transactions, exemptions, **CC 3440.1**
Liens and incumbrances, **CC 1227, 1228**
Limitation of actions, **CC 3439.09, 3440.6**
Maxim of jurisprudence, **CC 3518**
Monterey Peninsula water management district, application of law, **CC 3440.1**
Mortgages, undertaking, **CC 3445 et seq.**
Notice,
  Claim arising after notice of transfer, **CC 3440.2**
  Intent to transfer, **CC 3440.1, 3440.5**
  Security agreements, financing statement filed, **CC 3440.1, 3440.5**
Pledges, undertakings, **CC 3445 et seq.**
Possession, **CC 3440 et seq.**
Presumptions, insolvency, **CC 3439.02**
Publication of notice, transfer of property, **CC 3440.1, 3440.5**
  Claims arising after publication, **CC 3440.2**
Receivers and receivership, **CC 3439.07**
Remedies, **CC 3439.07**
Respondentia, application of law, **CC 3440.1**
Sales, undertaking, **CC 3445 et seq.**
Secured transactions,
  Application of law, **CC 3440.1, 3440.5**

VOIDABLE TRANSACTIONS—Cont'd
Secured transactions—Cont'd
  Financing statement, generally, ante
Ships and shipping, at sea or in foreign port, application of law, **CC 3440.1**
Statute of limitations, **CC 3439.09, 3440.6**
Things in action, application of law, **CC 3440.1**
Timber, application of law, **CC 3440.1**
Transfers, **CC 3439.06**
Treatment as if possession retained, **CC 3518**
Undertakings, **CC 3445 et seq.**
Value given, **CC 3439.03**
Wines, application of law, **CC 3440.1**

VOIDABLE TRANSACTIONS ACT
Generally, **CC 3439 et seq.**

VOLUNTARY INTERFERENCE WITH PROPERTY
Service without employment, **CC 2078**

VOLUNTEER FIREFIGHTERS AND FIRE DEPARTMENTS
Firefighters and Fire Departments, this index

VOTERS AND VOTING
Elections, generally, this index

WAGES
Compensation and Salaries, generally, this index

WALKOUTS
Labor Disputes, generally, this index

WALLET GUN
Weapons, generally, this index

WALLS
Advertisements. Outdoor Advertising, generally, this index
Easements, right of using as party wall, **CC 801**
Excavations, protection, **CC 832**
Outdoor Advertising, generally, this index
Party wall, easements, **CC 801**

WAR AND CIVIL DEFENSE
  See, also, Veterans, generally, this index
Air raids, defense shelters, tort liability, governmental subdivision, **CC 1714.5**
Defense shelters, liability for damages, **CC 1714.5**
Disaster council, sheltered designation, liability, **CC 1714.5**
Disaster service workers,
  Emergencies, liability for injuries during, **CC 1714.5**
  Liability, **CC 1714.5**
Fallout shelters, liability for damages, **CC 1714.5**
Injuries, liability, defense shelters, **CC 1714.5**
Labor and employment,
  Injuries, liability, **CC 1714.5**
  Liability, injuries, **CC 1714.5**

WAR AND CIVIL DEFENSE—Cont'd
Mass care centers, liability, **CC 1714.5**
Military orders or regulations, suspension of civil and criminal liability, **CC 1714.6**
Negligence, **CC 1714.5**
Shelters, injuries, municipal liability, **CC 1714.5**
Torts, **CC 1714.5**
Veterans, generally, this index

WARDS
Guardian and Ward, generally, this index

WAREHOUSES
Abandoned or unclaimed property, storage until freight and charges paid, **CC 2081 et seq.**
Liens and incumbrances, mobilehomes and mobilehome parks, termination of tenancy, storage, **CC 798.56a**

WARNINGS
Aircraft, liability, private property, **CC 846**
Electricity, fences, security, **CC 835**
Fences, electrified fences, security, **CC 835**
Fishing, hunting, camping, entry on property, safety, **CC 846**
Real property owners, hazardous conditions, **CC 846**
Recreational vehicle parks, removal from premises, **CC 799.46**
Space flights, **CC 2211, 2212**

WARRANTIES
Generally, **CC 1790 et seq.**
Actions and proceedings, breach, **CC 1794, 1794.1**
Agents and agencies,
  Authority, **CC 2342**
    Breach, damages, **CC 3318**
  Sale, authority,
    Personal property, **CC 2323**
    Real property, **CC 2324**
Appliance and electronic products, service and repair facilities, **CC 1793.03**
Art and artists, fine art multiples, sales, **CC 1744.7**
Attorney fees, breach, **CC 1794, 1794.1**
Auctioneers, authority, **CC 2362**
Breach of warranty, covenant, damages, **CC 3304**
Buildings, construction defects, **CC 896 et seq.**
Coast guard, motor vehicles, **CC 1795.8**
Collateral, abolished, **CC 1115**
Consumer warranties, plain language, **CC 1793.1**
Costs, breach, **CC 1794**
Covenants running with land, **CC 1462, 1463**
Damages, breach, **CC 1794, 1794.1**
Electronic or appliance products, service and repair facilities, **CC 1793.03**
Expiration, repairs or service, **CC 1795.6**

WATER

WARRANTIES—Cont'd
Factory built housing, CC 1797 et seq.
Farm machinery repair shop, CC 1718
Fine art multiples, sales, disclosure, CC 1744.7
Fines and penalties, breach, CC 1794
Fixtures, CC 1793.2
Grey market goods, CC 1797.8 et seq.
  Disclosure, CC 1770
Hearing aids, CC 1793.02, 1795.6
Home roof warranties, CC 1797.90 et seq.
Housing,
  Construction defects, CC 896 et seq.
  Factory built, CC 1797 et seq.
Implied warranties. Sales, this index
Independent repair services, contracts of manufacturer, CC 1790 et seq.
Leases, this index
Lineal, abolished, CC 1115
Manufactured housing, CC 1797 et seq.
  Home roof warranties, CC 1797.90 et seq.
Military forces, motor vehicles, CC 1795.8
Mobilehomes and Mobilehome Parks, this index
Motor Vehicles, this index
Motorized wheelchairs, CC 1793.025
National guard, motor vehicles, CC 1795.8
Plain language, consumer warranties, CC 1793.1
Rental purchase agreements, transfer to consumers, CC 1812.634
Repair and service facilities, CC 1793.1 et seq.
Roofs, homes, CC 1797.90 et seq.
Sales, this index
Service and repair facilities, CC 1793.1 et seq.
Service Contracts, generally, this index
Song Beverly Consumer Warranty Act, CC 1790 et seq.
Standards for warranty work, CC 1796, 1796.5
Tolling, repairs or service, CC 1795.6
Transferability, home roof warranties, CC 1797.92
Used goods, CC 1795.5
Wheelchairs, motorized wheelchairs, CC 1793.025

WARRANTS
Searches and Seizures, this index

WARRANTS FOR PAYMENT OF MONEY
Attorney fees, check cashers, CC 1789.35
Cashers, CC 1789.30 et seq.
Check cashers, CC 1789.30 et seq.
Crimes and offenses, check cashers, CC 1789.35
Damages, check cashers, CC 1789.35
Fees, check cashers, CC 1789.30, 1789.35
  Licenses and permits, CC 1789.37
Fines and penalties, check cashers, CC 1789.35

WARRANTS FOR PAYMENT OF MONEY—Cont'd
Identity and identification, check cashers, CC 1789.30
Injunction, check cashers, CC 1789.35
Licenses and permits, check cashers, CC 1789.37
Limitation of actions, check cashers, CC 1789.35
Monopolies and unfair trade, check cashers, CC 1789.32
Statute of limitations, check cashers, CC 1789.35
Unfair business practices, check cashers, CC 1789.32
Waiver, cashers, CC 1789.38

WASHING MACHINES
Manufacturer identification mark, removal, defacing, alteration or destruction, CC 1710.1
Sale, identification number or mark altered or removed, CC 1710.1

WASTE
Future estate in dominant tenement, CC 808
Future interests, grantees, actions, CC 821
Hazardous Substances and Waste, generally, this index
Life estates, CC 840

WATCHES
Carriers, limitation of liability, CC 2200
Sale, identification number or mark altered or removed, CC 1710.1

WATER
Waters and Watercourses, generally, this index

WATER APPROPRIATION
Applications, notice, CC 1415
Books and papers, recording notices, CC 1421
Change, diversion or use, relation back to time of notice, CC 1418
Claimants, previously acquired rights, CC 1420
Construction of works, time for commencement, CC 1416
  Public reservations, CC 1422
Counties,
  Bonds, authorization, CC 1416
  Construction of works, time, CC 1416
Dams and reservoirs, time, construction, CC 1416
Existing claimants, CC 1420
Forest reservations, commencement of works in, time, CC 1422
Forfeitures, CC 1419
Municipal bonds, authorization, CC 1416
National parks, commencement of work in national parks, time, CC 1422
Notice, CC 1415
  Recording, CC 1421
Point of diversion, notice, posting, CC 1415

WATER APPROPRIATION—Cont'd
Posting, notice, CC 1415
Priorities and preferences, CC 1414
Public reservations, time to commence works, CC 1422
Records and recordation, notice, CC 1415, 1421
Relation back of use to time of notice, CC 1418
Time,
  Commencement of works on public reservations, CC 1422
  Construction of works, CC 1416
  Use, relation back to time of notice, CC 1418
Towns, construction of works, time, CC 1416

WATER CARRIERS
Ships and Shipping, generally, this index

WATER CONSERVATION
Apartment houses, building standards, CC 1101.1 et seq.
Application of law, building standards, CC 1101.2
Building standards, CC 1101.1 et seq.
Condominiums, this index
Conflict of laws, building standards, CC 1101.8
Cooperative apartments, building standards, CC 1101.1 et seq.
Deeds and conveyances, building standards, CC 1101.1 et seq.
  Disclosure, CC 1102.155
Demolition of buildings, building standards, CC 1101.6
Disclosure, building standards, deeds and conveyances, CC 1101.4, 1101.5
Exemptions, building standards, CC 1101.7
Fixtures, building standards, CC 1101.1 et seq.
Historical landmarks, markers and monuments, building standards, exemptions, CC 1101.7
Housing, information, CC 2079.10
Improvements, building standards, CC 1101.1 et seq.
Landlord and tenant, building standards, CC 1101.1 et seq.
Licenses and permits, building standards, CC 1101.4
  Landlord and tenant, CC 1101.5
Ordinances, building standards, CC 1101.8
Planned unit developments, building standards, CC 1101.1 et seq.
Plumbers and plumbing, building standards, CC 1101.1 et seq.
Public policy, building standards, CC 1101.1
Real estate, building standards, disclosure, CC 1102.155

WATER CONSERVATION DISTRICTS
Appropriation of water. Water Appropriation, generally, this index

I-215

WATER

WATER CONSERVATION DISTRICTS —Cont'd
Water Appropriation, generally, this index

WATER RIGHTS
Appropriation. Water Appropriation, generally, this index
Flow without diminution or disturbance, easements, CC 801
Receiving from or discharging upon land, easements, CC 801

WATER SPORTS
Private property owners, liability for injuries, CC 846
Real property owners, duty to keep premises safe for taking of fish and game, CC 846

WATER SUPPLY
Conservation. Water Conservation, generally, this index
Landlord and Tenant, this index
Leases, cutting off public utilities with intent to terminate lease, damages, CC 789.3
Plumbers and Plumbing, generally, this index
Towns, appropriations, construction of works, time, CC 1416

WATERBEDS
Landlord and tenant, CC 1940.5

WATERCRAFT
Boats and Boating, generally, this index
Ships and Shipping, generally, this index

WATERFOWL
Fish and Game, generally, this index

WATERS AND WATERCOURSES
Adverse possession, acquisition by, exemptions, CC 1007
Appropriation. Water Appropriation, generally, this index
Boats and Boating, generally, this index
Boundaries, CC 830
Conservation. Water Conservation, generally, this index
Discharges, upon land, easements, CC 801
Easements, CC 801
Fish and Game, generally, this index
Floods and Flooding, generally, this index
Lakes and Ponds, generally, this index
Ownership, state, CC 670
Rivers and Streams, generally, this index
State, CC 670
Zoning and Planning, generally, this index

WAYS
Highways and Roads, generally, this index

WEAPONS
Actions and proceedings, manufacturers and manufacturing, sales, conduct, standards, CC 3273.52
Ammunition, generally, this index

WEAPONS—Cont'd
Attorney fees, manufacturers and manufacturing, sales, conduct, standards, CC 3273.52
Bullets. Ammunition, generally, this index
Conduct, standards, manufacturers and manufacturing, sales, CC 3273.50 et seq.
Construction of laws, manufacturers and manufacturing, sales, conduct, standards, CC 3273.54
Damages,
  Discharge by minors, liability, CC 1714.3
  Manufacturers and manufacturing, sales, conduct, standards, CC 3273.52
Designs and designers, negligence, CC 1714
Distribution, negligence, CC 1714
Forcible entry and detainer, CC 3485
Injunction,
  Manufacturers and manufacturing, sales, conduct, standards, CC 3273.52
  Shooting ranges, CC 3482.1
Libel and slander, schools and school districts, reports, damages, CC 48.8
Long Beach, forcible entry and detainer, CC 3485
Los Angeles, forcible entry and detainer, CC 3485
Manufacturers and manufacturing,
  Conduct, standards, CC 3273.50 et seq.
  Identification marks, removal, defacing, alteration or destruction, CC 1710.1
Markets and marketing, negligence, CC 1714
Negligence, designs and designers, distribution, markets and marketing, CC 1714
Nuisance, shooting ranges, CC 3482.1
Oakland, forcible entry and detainer, CC 3485
Privileges and immunities, shooting ranges, CC 3482.1
Ranges, sport shooting ranges, CC 3482.1
Reports, schools and school districts, libel and slander, damages, CC 48.8
Sacramento City and County, forcible entry and detainer, CC 3485
Sales,
  Conduct, standards, CC 3273.50 et seq.
  Identification marks, altered or removed, CC 1710.1
Schools and school districts,
  Libel and slander, reports, damages, CC 48.8
  Reports, libel and slander, damages, CC 48.8
Sports, shooting ranges, CC 3482.1
Standards, manufacturers and manufacturing, conduct, sales, CC 3273.50 et seq.
Target ranges, CC 3482.1

WEARING APPAREL
Cleaning, Dyeing and Pressing, generally, this index
Dyeing. Cleaning, Dyeing and Pressing, generally, this index
Pressing. Cleaning, Dyeing and Pressing, generally, this index

WEARING APPAREL—Cont'd
Sales, warranties, CC 1793.35

WEATHER
Storms, generally, this index

WEBSITES
Internet, generally, this index

WEIGHT LOSS CONTRACTS
Generally, CC 1694.5 et seq.

WELFARE
Social Services, generally, this index

WHARVES, DOCKS AND PIERS
Leases, municipalities, tidelands and submerged lands, CC 718
Pest Control, generally, this index

WHEELCHAIRS
Disclosure, reasons for return of motorized wheelchair, CC 1793.025
Motorized wheelchairs, warranties, CC 1793.025
Warranties, CC 1793.025

WHISKEY
Alcoholic Beverages, generally, this index

WHITE CANE SAFETY DAY
Proclamation, CC 54.5

WHOLESALERS
Contracts, sales representatives, CC 1738.10 et seq.
Independent sales representatives, CC 1738.10 et seq.
Labor and employment, nonemployee sales representatives, CC 1738.10 et seq.
Sales representatives, CC 1738.10 et seq.

WILD ANIMALS AND BIRDS
Fish and Game, generally, this index

WILDFIRES
Forest Fires, generally, this index

WILDLIFE
Fish and Game, generally, this index

WILLFUL AND WANTON ACTS
Children, imputed liability of parents, CC 1714.1
Defibrillators, CC 1714.21
Design professionals, public agencies, CC 2782.6

WILLIE L. BROWN, JR. BILL LOCKYER CIVIL LIABILITY REFORM ACT
Generally, CC 1714.45, 3294, 3295

WILLS
Accumulation, income of property, direction by, CC 724
Acquisition of property by, CC 1000
Administrators, personal representatives. Probate Proceedings, this index

WORDS

WILLS—Cont'd
Advertisements, deceased celebrity image protection, CC 3344.1
Application of law,
  Electronic Transactions Act, CC 1633.3
  Uniform Electronic Transactions Act, CC 1633.3
Celebrity image protection, CC 3344.1
Crimes and offenses, stories about felonies, sale proceeds, CC 2225
Deceased celebrity image protection, CC 3344.1
Electronic Transactions Act, application of law, CC 1633.3
Famous persons, deceased celebrity image protection, CC 3344.1
Frauds, statute of, CC 1624
Probate Proceedings, generally, this index
Recorders, generally, this index
Statute of Frauds, CC 1624
Uniform Electronic Transactions Act, application of law, CC 1633.3

WINDOWS
Landlord and tenant, security devices, CC 1941.3
Security bars, residential property, disclosure, CC 1102.16

WITHHOLDING ORDERS
Garnishment, generally, this index

WITNESSES
Acknowledgments,
  Proof of execution, CC 1195 et seq.
  Requisites, CC 1185
Anonymous witness program, reports of crime, privileges and immunities, CC 48.9
Contracts, this index
Expert testimony. Opinion and expert testimony, generally, post
Fees, contracts, voidability, CC 1669.7
Handwriting, proof, CC 1198, 1199
Injunction, compensation and salaries, contracts, CC 1669.7
Intervention, compensation and salaries, contracts, CC 1669.7
Libel and slander, anonymous witness program, privileges and immunities, CC 48.9
Notaries public, identity and identification, CC 1185
Opinion and expert testimony,
  Autographed memorabilia, warranties, CC 1739.7
  Fees, fine art multiples, sales, CC 1745
  Fine art multiples, sales, CC 1745
  Memorabilia, autographed, warranties, CC 1739.7
  Private schools, buildings and grounds, interference, obstructions, threats, CC 1708.9
  School buildings and grounds, access, interference, obstructions, threats, CC 1708.9

WITNESSES—Cont'd
Perjury, generally, this index
Privileges and Immunities, generally, this index
Retaliatory actions, anonymous witness program, privileges and immunities, CC 48.9
Signature, mark, CC 14
Subpoenas, generally, this index
Venue, compensation and salaries, contracts, CC 1669.7

WIVES
Marriage, generally, this index

WOMEN
Abortion, generally, this index
Civil rights. Discrimination, generally, this index
Credit, obtaining, discrimination, CC 1812.30 et seq.
Credit cards, issuance to married women, names, CC 1747.81
Discrimination, generally, this index
Domestic Violence, generally, this index
Mobilehomes and mobilehome parks, club membership, discrimination, CC 798.20
Support, generally, this index

WOOD
Pest Control, generally, this index
Timber and Lumber, generally, this index

WORDS AND PHRASES
Abandoned mobilehome, CC 798.61
Absolute ownership, CC 679
Abuse, homeless persons, transitional housing, misconduct, CC 1954.12
Abusive practices, colleges and universities, student loans, borrowers rights, CC 1788.101
Accepted credit card, CC 1747.02
Accepted debit cards, CC 1748.30
  Consumer goods, refunds, CC 1748.40
Accord, CC 1521
Accounts, debit cards, CC 1748.30
Acknowledged personal delivery, mineral rights, entry and excavation, notice, CC 848
Actual agency, CC 2299
Actual authority, CC 2316
Actual awareness, hazardous substances and waste, releases, CC 850
Actual contingent interest, shared appreciation loans for seniors, CC 1917.320
Actual damages, hate crimes, CC 52
Actual fraud, contracts, CC 1572
Actual knowledge, invasion of privacy, CC 1708.8
Actual life expectancy, shared appreciation loans for seniors, CC 1917.320
Actual malice, libel and slander, CC 48a
Actual moisture barrier, construction defects, CC 895

WORDS AND PHRASES—Cont'd
Actual notice, CC 18, 19
Additional charges, motor vehicles, leases, business programs, CC 1939.21
Additional financial information, mobilehomes and mobilehome parks, sales, approval, CC 798.74
Additional mandatory charges, motor vehicles, leases, CC 1939.01
Adequate documentation, indebtedness, duress or coercion, CC 1798.97.1
Adequate notice,
  Credit cards, CC 1747.02
  Debit cards, CC 1748.30
Adjacent,
  Greenways, easements, CC 816.52
  Landowners, CC 1002
Adjacent dwelling units, landlord and tenant, pest control, CC 1940.8.5
Adjacent separate interest, condominiums, pest control, CC 4777
Adjoining, boundaries, maintenance, CC 841
Adjustable rate residential mortgage loan, disclosures, CC 1921
Adjustment program, motor vehicle warranties, CC 1795.90
Administrator, service contracts, warranties, CC 1791
Adopted by a federal agency, animals, tests, alternatives, CC 1834.9
Advance payments, leases, notice to breaching lessee of reletting, CC 1951.7
Adverse actions,
  Consumer credit reporting, CC 1785.3
  Labor and employment, records and recordation, copies, CC 1786.53
Adverse information, consumer credit reporting agencies, CC 1799.101
Advertisement,
  Auctions and auctioneers, CC 1812.601
  Rental purchase agreements, CC 1812.622
Advertising and marketing, consumers, privacy, CC 1798.140
AED, automatic external defibrillators, emergencies, CC 1714.21
Affiliate of the licensed real estate broker, trust deeds, CC 2934a
  Majority interest holders, beneficiaries, governing agreements, CC 2941.9
Affiliates,
  Bookkeeping services, tax returns and reports, confidential or privileged information, CC 1799.1a
  Discount buying services, CC 1812.117
  Floating home marinas, transfers, CC 800.100
  Mobilehomes and mobilehome parks, transfers, notice, CC 798.80
  Motor vehicles, vehicle history reports, CC 1784.1
  Warranties, CC 1791.1
Affirmative authorizations, genetic testing, privacy, CC 56.18

I-217

WORDS

WORDS AND PHRASES—Cont'd

Affirmative consent, warranties, CC 1791.1
Affordable housing developments, covenants, modification or change, CC 714.6
Agencies,
   Breach of security, personal information, CC 1798.29
   Employment agency, CC 1812.501
   Information Practices Act, CC 1798.3
   Real estate brokers and salespersons, CC 2079.13
Agents, CC 2295
   HIV, real estate actions, CC 1710.2
   Motor vehicles, storage, liens and incumbrances, CC 3068.1
   Property listings, CC 1086
Aggregate consumer information, privacy, CC 1798.140
Aggrieved, commercial blockade, health facilities, CC 3427
Agreements,
   Electronic Transactions Act, CC 1633.2
   Foreign languages, translations, CC 1632
Agricultural activities, operation or facility, or appurtenances thereof, nuisances, CC 3482.5
Agricultural processing activity, operation, facility, or appurtenances thereof, CC 3482.6
Airport concession fees, motor vehicles, leases, CC 1939.01
Airport influence area, condominiums, declarations, disclosure, CC 4255
Airport referral area, condominiums, declarations, disclosure, CC 4255
All inclusive trust deed, housing credit arrangers, CC 2957
ALPR end user, automated license plate recognition end user, CC 1798.90.5
ALPR information, automated license plate recognition information, CC 1798.90.5
ALPR operators, automated license plate recognition operators, CC 1798.90.5
ALPR system, automated license plate recognition system, CC 1798.90.5
Altered depictions, privacy, invasion of privacy, lewdness and obscenity, CC 1708.86
Alternative dispute resolution, condominiums, CC 5925
Alternative test methods, animals, CC 1834.9.3
Amount financed,
   Installment sales, CC 1802.11
   Motor vehicles, conditional sales, CC 2981
Anabolic steroids, athletic facilities, CC 1812.97
Anaphylaxis, epinephrine auto injectors, privileges and immunities, CC 1714.23
Animal tests, cosmetics, crimes and offenses, CC 1834.9.5
Animals,
   Landlord and tenant, declawing, devocalizing, CC 1942.7

WORDS AND PHRASES—Cont'd

Animals—Cont'd
   Motion pictures, killing of or cruelty to, CC 3504
   Tests, alternatives, CC 1834.9
Annual budget reports, condominiums, CC 4076
Annual policy statements, condominiums, CC 4078
Annuity base amount, shared appreciation loans for seniors, CC 1917.320
Anonymous witness program, immunity, CC 48.9
Antique, secured transactions, CC 1799.100
Appliances, rental purchase agreements, CC 1812.622
Applicable leases, mortgages, foreclosure, first liens, CC 2924.15
Applicants,
   Consumer credit denial, CC 1787.2
   Landlord and tenant, screening fees, CC 1950.6
Application agnostic, Internet, neutrality, CC 3100
Application for occupancy, landlord and tenant, animals, declawing, devocalizing, CC 1942.7
Application for stay and early evaluation conferences, disabled persons, civil rights, accessibility, CC 55.52
Application screening fee, landlord and tenant, CC 1950.6
Appropriate law enforcement agencies, junk and junk dealers, fire hydrants, possession, CC 3336.5
Appropriate trade premises, home solicitation contracts or offers, CC 1689.5
Appurtenances, CC 662
Arms length transactions, mortgages, foreclosure, first liens, CC 2924.15
Arranger of credit, housing disclosures, CC 2957
Art dealer, CC 1738
   Commissions, sales, original works, CC 986
   Fine prints, CC 1740
Artists, CC 1738
   Commissions, sale, original works, CC 986
   Defacement or destruction of fine art, CC 987
   Ownership of works, CC 988
As is, consumer warranties, CC 1791.3
Assisted housing development, landlord and tenant, consumer credit reporting agencies, CC 1954.06
Assistive device, Song Beverly Consumer Warranty Act, CC 1791
Associated waterproofing systems, condominiums, CC 5551
Association election materials, condominiums, inspection and inspectors, CC 5200
Association records, condominiums, inspection and inspectors, CC 5200

WORDS AND PHRASES—Cont'd

Associations, condominiums, CC 4080
   Business and commerce, CC 6528
Athletic facilities, anabolic steroids, testosterone or human growth hormone, CC 1812.97
Auction, CC 1812.601
Auction company, CC 1812.601
Auctioneers, CC 1812.601, 1812.610
Authentication, Internet, connected devices, security, CC 1798.91.05
Authorization, medical records, confidential or privileged information, CC 56.05
Authorized agents,
   Condominiums, pest control, CC 4777
   Landlord and tenant, pest control, CC 1940.8.5
Authorized driver, motor vehicles, leases, CC 1939.01
Authorized persons, data, sales, crimes and offenses, CC 1724
Authorized recipient, medical records, confidential or privileged information, CC 56.05
Authorized representatives, privacy, invasion of privacy, altered depictions, lewdness and obscenity, CC 1708.86
Autographed collectibles, memorabilia, CC 1739.7
Automated license plate recognition end user, CC 1798.90.5
Automated license plate recognition information, CC 1798.90.5
Automated license plate recognition operators, CC 1798.90.5
Automated license plate recognition system, CC 1798.90.5
Automated transaction, Electronic Transactions Act, CC 1633.2
Balloon payment loan, CC 2924i
Balloon payment note, housing credit arrangers, CC 2957
Balloon payments, rental purchase agreements, CC 1812.624
Beneficiaries,
   Involuntary trusts, CC 2225
   Secured land transactions statements, CC 2943
   Stories about felonies, CC 2225
Beneficiary interest, involuntary trusts, CC 2225
Beneficiary statement, secured land transaction statements, CC 2943
Best financial interest of a student loan borrower, colleges and universities, student loans, borrowers rights, CC 1788.101
Bicycles, contracts, licenses and permits,
   Shared mobility devices, CC 2505
   Shared mobility service providers, CC 2505.5
Bids and services, electronic commerce, CC 1789.2

WORDS AND PHRASES—Cont'd

Bill of sale, private bulk grain storage, **CC 1880.1**
Billing agent,
  Landlord and tenant, water supply, submeters, **CC 1954.202**
  Mobilehomes and mobilehome parks, water supply, **CC 798.40**
Billing cycle, installment sales, **CC 1802.17**
Billing error, credit cards, **CC 1747.02**
Biological samples, genetic testing, privacy, **CC 56.18**
Biometric information, consumers, privacy, **CC 1798.140**
Blanket encumbrance, membership camping contracts, **CC 1812.300**
Board meetings, condominiums, **CC 4090**
Boardinghouse, liens and incumbrances, **CC 1861.1**
Boards, condominiums, **CC 4085**
  Business and commerce, **CC 6530**
Bona fide error,
  Motor vehicles, terminated leases, disposition of vehicle, **CC 2987**
  Rental purchase agreements, **CC 1812.637**
Bonded stop payment notice, mechanics liens, **CC 8044**
Book service, personal information, disclosure, **CC 1798.90**
Booking photographs, commercial use, **CC 1798.91.1**
Bookkeeping services, disclosure of business records, **CC 1799**
Books, personal information, disclosure, **CC 1798.90**
Borrowers,
  Colleges and universities, student loans, **CC 1788.100**
  Landlord and tenant, mortgages, COVID 19, **CC 3273.2**
  Mortgages, foreclosure, meetings, financial condition, **CC 2923.5**
  Secured lenders, environmentally impaired property, **CC 2929.5**
  Shared appreciation loans, senior citizens, **CC 1917.320**
  Student loans, collections, **CC 1788.201**
Borrowers instruction to suspend and close equity line of credit, mortgages, payoff demand statements, **CC 2943.1**
Borrowers life expectancy, shared appreciation loans for seniors, **CC 1917.320**
Borrowers with disabilities, colleges and universities, student loans, **CC 1788.100**
Borrowers working in public service, colleges and universities, student loans, **CC 1788.100**
Breach of the security of the system,
  Customer records, personal information, disclosure, **CC 1798.82**
  State agencies, personal information, disclosure, **CC 1798.29**

WORDS AND PHRASES—Cont'd

Broadband Internet access services, neutrality, **CC 3100**
Broadcast, libel and slander, **CC 48.5**
Broadcast application,
  Condominiums, pest control, **CC 4777**
  Landlord and tenant, pest control, **CC 1940.8.5**
Broker dealer, securities, contracts, electronic transmissions, **CC 1633**
Brokers of construction trucking services, motor carriers, **CC 3322**
Builders, construction, defects,
  Condominiums, **CC 6000**
  Business and commerce, **CC 6870**
  Prelitigation proceedings, **CC 911**
Bundled sales, foreclosure, bids and bidding, priorities and preferences, **CC 2924p**
Business,
  Consumer goods,
    Refunds, **CC 1748.40**
    Sex, price discrimination, **CC 51.14**
  Consumers, privacy, **CC 1798.140**
  Customer records, destruction, **CC 1798.80**
  Drivers licenses, electronic devices and equipment, confidential or privileged information, **CC 1798.90.1**
  Electricity, privacy, usage data, **CC 1798.98**
Business controller information, consumers, privacy, **CC 1798.145**
Business days,
  Home equity sales contracts, **CC 1695.1**
  Home solicitation sales, **CC 1689.5**
  Membership camping contracts, **CC 1812.303**
  Mortgages, **CC 2924b**
    Default notices, **CC 2924c**
  Motor vehicles, storage liens, **CC 3068.1**
  Qualified financial contract, frauds, statute of, **CC 1624**
  Seminar sales solicitation contracts, **CC 1689.24**
Business entities, disclosure of business records, bookkeeping services, **CC 1799**
Business entity filing, identity and identification, theft, **CC 1798.200**
Business program sponsors, motor vehicles, leases, **CC 1939.21**
Business programs, motor vehicles, leases, **CC 1939.21**
Business purpose, consumers, privacy, **CC 1798.140**
Business renters, motor vehicles, **CC 1939.21**
Buy back, seller assisted marketing plan, **CC 1812.201**
Buyer's agents, real estate, **CC 2079.13**
Buyers,
  Automobile Sales Finance Act, **CC 2981**
  Installment sales, **CC 1802.4**
  Motor vehicles, subleasing, **CC 3343.5**
  Private bulk grain storage, **CC 1880.1**

WORDS AND PHRASES—Cont'd

Buyers—Cont'd
  Real estate brokers and salespersons, agency, **CC 2079.13**
  Song Beverly Consumer Warranty Act, **CC 1791**
Calendar week, mortgages and trust deeds, sales, **CC 2924f**
Call provision,
  Balloon payments, **CC 2924i**
  Housing credit arrangers, **CC 2957**
Campaign purposes, condominiums, homeowners associations, funds, **CC 5135**
Campground, membership camping contracts, **CC 1812.300**
Camping sites, membership camping contracts, **CC 1812.300**
Canine or feline toxicological experiments, tests, **CC 1834.9.3**
Capital lease, landlord and tenant, breach remedies, **CC 1952.6**
Card issuer, credit cards, **CC 1747.02**
Cardholder,
  Consumer goods, refunds, **CC 1748.40**
  Credit cards, **CC 1747.02**
  Disclosures, **CC 1748.12**
  Grocery stores, club cards, disclosure, **CC 1749.61**
Caregivers, intergenerational housing developments, **CC 51.3.5**
Cash, gift certificates, redemption, **CC 1749.5**
Cash price,
  Automobile Sales Finance Act, **CC 2981**
  Installment sales, **CC 1802.8**
  Rental purchase agreements, **CC 1812.622**
Cash proceeds, real estate, assignments, **CC 2938**
Catalog or similar sale, Song Beverly Consumer Warranty Act, **CC 1791**
Cats, tests, **CC 1834.9.3**
Cause it to be recorded, mortgages, **CC 2941**
Cause to be recorded, mortgages, **CC 2941**
Certificate of authenticity, sale of fine arts, **CC 1740**
Certified access specialists, disabled persons, civil rights, accessibility, **CC 55.52**
Cessation of occupancy, shared appreciation loan, senior citizens, **CC 1917.320**
Change of use,
  Floating home marinas, **CC 800.7**
  Mobilehome Residency Law, **CC 798.10**
Charge card, disclosures, **CC 1748.21**
Charge card issuer, disclosures, **CC 1748.21**
Charge cardholder, **CC 1748.21**
Chargeback, independent wholesale sales representatives, **CC 1738.12**
Charged off consumer debit, purchases, **CC 1788.50**
Charging stations, electric vehicles, leases, **CC 1947.6, 1952.7**
Charter party, bailment, **CC 1959**

WORDS

WORDS AND PHRASES—Cont'd

Chattel interests, CC 765
Chattels real, CC 765
Check casher, CC 1789.31
Check guarantee card, CC 1725
Chemical substances, animals, tests, CC 1834.9.3
Children,
    Consumer protection, Internet, CC 1798.99.30
    Rescue, motor vehicles, privileges and immunities, CC 43.102
Claim period, credit disability insurance, CC 1812.401
Claimants,
    Construction defects, CC 895
    Identity and identification, theft, CC 1798.92
    Indebtedness, duress or coercion, CC 1798.97.1
    Mechanics liens, CC 8004
Claims,
    Education, disabled persons, accessibility, buildings, CC 54.27
    Indebtedness, duress or coercion, CC 1798.97.1
    Voidable transactions, CC 3439.01
Class of Internet content, application, service, or device, neutrality, CC 3100
Claws, landlord and tenant, animals, CC 1942.7
Clear and conspicuous,
    Medical records, markets and marketing, CC 1798.91
    Warranties, CC 1791
Clear and prominent notice, rental purchase agreements, electronic devices and equipment, geophysical location tracking technology, CC 1812.650
Clearly and conspicuously, warranties, CC 1791
Close of escrow,
    Construction defects, CC 895
    Real estate sales, return, CC 1057.3
Clotheslines,
    Condominiums, CC 4750.10
    Landlord and tenant, CC 1940.20
Clothing, Song Beverly Consumer Warranty Act, CC 1791
Club card issuer, grocery stores, disclosure, CC 1749.61
Coerced debt, CC 1798.97.1
Cohabitants,
    Riverside County, aged persons, housing, discrimination, CC 51.11
    Senior citizen housing, CC 51.3
Collected, consumers, privacy, CC 1798.140
Collection, consumers, privacy, CC 1798.140
Collection action, consumer credit reporting agencies, CC 1799.101
Collectors, medical waste, privileges and immunities, secure drug take back bins, CC 1714.24

WORDS AND PHRASES—Cont'd

Collects, consumers, privacy, CC 1798.140
Color, fraud, solicitation, payment of money, written statement or invoice, CC 1716
Color prominently contrasting, solicitation, payment of money, written statement or invoice, CC 1716
Commercial blockade, health facilities, CC 3427
Commercial credit report, CC 1785.42
Commercial credit reporting agency, CC 1785.42
Commercial or industrial common interest developments, CC 6531
Commercial property, leases, disabled persons, accessibility, construction, standards, inspection and inspectors, CC 1938
Commercial purposes,
    Consumers, privacy, CC 1798.140
    Information Practices Act, CC 1798.3
Commercial real property,
    Leases, termination, personal property, disposition, CC 1993
    Real estate brokers and salespersons, disclosure, agency, CC 2079.13
    Rent control, CC 1954.26
    Water conservation, building standards, CC 1101.3
Commercial rental control, rent controls, commercial property, CC 1954.26
Commercial uses,
    Condominiums, business and commerce, CC 6531
    Defacement or destruction of art objects, CC 987
Commissioners, colleges and universities, student loans, borrowers rights, CC 1788.100
Commitment statement, hazardous substances and waste, releases, CC 850
Common areas, condominiums, CC 4095
    Business and commerce, CC 6532
Common carriers, CC 2168
    Sleeping car companies, baggage, limitation of liability, CC 2178
Common interest developments, CC 4100
    Business and commerce, CC 6534
    Construction, defects, CC 6000
    Business and commerce, CC 6870
Communications, credit services, CC 1789.12
Community apartment projects, CC 4105
Community of interest, dealerships, CC 81
Community property, CC 687
Community property addresses, condominiums, homeowners associations, confidential or privileged information, crime victims, CC 5216
Community service organization or similar entity, condominiums, CC 4110
Comparable units, rent control, CC 1954.51
Compensating controls, consumer credit reporting agencies, computers, security, CC 1798.81.6

WORDS AND PHRASES—Cont'd

Compensation, medical waste, privileges and immunities, secure drug take back bins, CC 1714.24
Complaint,
    Civil rights, disabled persons, accessibility, CC 55.3
    Education, disabled persons, accessibility, buildings, CC 54.27
Completed payments, condominiums, managers and management, CC 5380
Completion, water appropriation, CC 1417
Computer program, Electronic Transactions Act, CC 1633.2
Computer system, rental purchase agreements, CC 1812.622
Condition concurrent, contracts, CC 1437
Condition precedent, CC 1436
    Property ownership, CC 708
Condition subsequent,
    Contracts, CC 1438
    Property ownership, CC 708
Conditional limitation, future estates or interests, CC 778
Conditional obligation, CC 1434
Conditional sale contract,
    Automobile Sales Finance Act, CC 2981
    Motor vehicles, subleasing, CC 3343.5
Condominium plans, CC 4120
    Business and commerce, CC 6540
Condominium projects, CC 4125
    Business and commerce, CC 6542
Condominiums, CC 783
Confidential communications requests, medical records, CC 56.05
Confidential information, real estate brokers and salespersons, CC 2079.13
Connected devices, Internet, security, CC 1798.91.05
Consent,
    Consumers, privacy, CC 1798.140
    Privacy, invasion of privacy, altered depictions, lewdness and obscenity, CC 1708.86
Conservation easements, CC 815.1
Conserve, art defacement or destruction, CC 987
Consignees, carriers, CC 2110
Consignments, CC 1738
Consignors, carriers, CC 2110
Conspicuous posting,
    Breach of security, personal information, disclosure, CC 1798.29
    State agencies, breach of security, personal information, CC 1798.82
Conspicuously displays, public agencies, contractors, disclosure, CC 3273
Constant yield, vehicle leasing, CC 2985.7
Construction contract, indemnity, CC 2783
Construction defects, indemnity, CC 2782
Construction lenders, mechanics liens, CC 8006

WORDS

WORDS AND PHRASES—Cont'd
Construction managers, subcontractors, damages, reimbursement, defense fees and costs, **CC 2782.05**
Construction related accessibility claims,
 Civil rights, **CC 55.3**
  Disabled persons, **CC 55.52**
 Education, disabled persons, accessibility, buildings, **CC 54.27**
Construction related accessibility standards, disabled persons, civil rights, **CC 55.52**
Constructive fraud, contracts, **CC 1573**
Constructive notice, **CC 18, 19**
Consumable, Song Beverly Consumer Warranty Act, **CC 1791**
Consumer commodity, Rosenthal Roberti Item Pricing Act, **CC 7100**
Consumer contract, **CC 1799.201**
Consumer contract guaranty, consumer protection, **CC 1799.201**
Consumer credit, fair debt collection practices, **CC 1788.2**
Consumer credit contract, **CC 1799.90**
Consumer credit report, **CC 1785.3**
 Debt collection, **CC 1788.2**
Consumer credit reporting agencies, credit cards, disclosures, **CC 1748.12**
Consumer credit transactions, debt collection, **CC 1788.2**
Consumer debt, fair debt collection practices, **CC 1788.2**
Consumer goods, **CC 1749.1**
 Song Beverly Consumer Warranty Act, **CC 1791**
Consumer price index for all urban consumers for all items,
 CPI U, rent control, **CC 1947.12**
 Floating homes, rent increases, **CC 800.40.5**
 Mobilehomes and mobilehome parks, rent controls, **CC 798.30.5**
Consumer products, markets and marketing, Internet, disclosure, **CC 1749.8**
Consumer reporting agencies,
 Debt collection, **CC 1788.2**
 Landlord and tenant, reusable tenant screening reports, **CC 1950.1**
 Student loans, collections, **CC 1788.201**
Consumer reports,
 Landlord and tenant, reusable tenant screening reports, **CC 1950.1**
 Student loans, collections, **CC 1788.201**
Consumers,
 Autographed memorabilia, **CC 1739.7**
 Bookkeeping services, tax returns and reports, confidential or privileged information, **CC 1799.1a**
 Consumers Legal Remedies Act, **CC 1761**
 Contract awareness, **CC 1799.201**
 Credit reporting, **CC 1785.3**
 Credit services, **CC 1789.12**
 Discount buying services, **CC 1812.117**

WORDS AND PHRASES—Cont'd
Consumers—Cont'd
 Electronic commerce, **CC 1789.2**
 Escrows and escrow agents, rating service, **CC 1785.28**
 Fair debt settlement, **CC 1788.301**
 Genetic testing, privacy, **CC 56.18**
 Investigative Consumer Reporting Agencies Act, **CC 1786.2**
 Motor vehicles, warranty adjustment programs, **CC 1795.90**
 Privacy, **CC 1798.140**
 Rental purchase agreements, **CC 1812.622**
Contactless identification document systems, RFID (radio frequency identification), crimes and offenses, **CC 1798.795**
Content, social media, threats, **CC 1798.99.20**
Content, applications, or services, Internet, neutrality, **CC 3100**
Contingent deferred interest, shared appreciation loans, **CC 1917**
Continuing guaranty, **CC 2814**
Continuous operation, agricultural processing activities, nuisances, **CC 3482.6**
Contract for dance studio lessons and other services, **CC 1812.51**
Contract for discount buying services, **CC 1812.101**
Contract for health studio services, **CC 1812.81**
Contract for sale of real property, marketable title, **CC 886.010**
Contract of carriage, **CC 2085**
Contract or sale,
 Home solicitation contracts, **CC 1689.7**
 Seminar sales solicitation contracts, cancellation rights, **CC 1689.21**
Contract price, mechanics liens, **CC 8010**
Contract testing facility, animals, tests, alternatives, **CC 1834.9**
Contracting party, private improvements, design professionals, **CC 3319**
Contractors,
 Consumer warranties, **CC 1797.1**
 Consumers, privacy, **CC 1798.140, 1798.145**
 Mechanics liens, **CC 8012**
 Medical records, confidential or privileged information, **CC 56.05**
Contracts, **CC 1549**
 Damages, **CC 3289**
 Electronic Transactions Act, **CC 1633.2**
 Foreign languages, translations, **CC 1632**
 Home equity sales contracts, **CC 1695.1**
 Installment sales, **CC 1802.6**
 Mechanics liens, **CC 8008**
 Mortgage foreclosure consultants, **CC 2945.1**
 Precomputed finance charge contracts, **CC 1799.8**
Control, trust deeds, **CC 2934a**
 Majority interest holders, beneficiaries, governing agreements, **CC 2941.9**

WORDS AND PHRASES—Cont'd
Controlled substance purpose, forcible entry and detainer, nuisance, **CC 3486**
Conveyances, **CC 1215**
Convicted felon,
 Involuntary trusts, **CC 2225**
 Stories about felonies, **CC 2225**
Copy, consumer contract awareness, **CC 1799.201**
Cosigners,
 Consumer credit reporting agencies, **CC 1799.101**
 Motor vehicles, conditional sales, **CC 2983.35**
 Student loans, collections, **CC 1788.201**
Cosmetics, animals, tests, crimes and offenses, **CC 1834.9.5**
Cost of removal, artistic integrity, preservation, **CC 989**
Cost of rental, rental purchase agreements, **CC 1812.622**
Counties, **CC 14**
Court issued subpoena, warrant, or order, hotels and motels, charter buses, records and recordation, privacy, **CC 53.5**
Court of competent jurisdiction, civil rights, jurisdiction, **CC 52.2**
Court order, landlord and tenant, locks and locking, **CC 1941.5, 1941.6**
Covenants running with the land, **CC 1460**
Covered persons, finance lenders, unsolicited advertising, unfair or deceptive trade practices, **CC 1770**
CPI U, consumer price index for all urban consumers for all items, rent control, **CC 1947.12**
CPR, automatic external defibrillators, emergencies, **CC 1714.21**
Credible threat, stalking, **CC 1708.7**
Credit,
 Credit transactions regarding women, **CC 1812.30**
 Housing purchases, **CC 2957**
Credit account, change of address, notice, **CC 1799.1b**
Credit card, **CC 1747.02**
 Commercial paper, condition of acceptance, **CC 1725**
 Payoff, notice, **CC 1748.13**
Credit denial, consumers, **CC 1787.2**
Credit disability insurance, creditors remedies, **CC 1812.401**
Credit documents, housing purchases, **CC 2957**
Credit score, consumer credit reporting agencies, notice, **CC 1785.15.1**
Credit services organization, **CC 1789.12**
Credit transaction that is not initiated by the consumer, consumer credit reporting, **CC 1785.3**
Creditors, **CC 3430**
 Consumer credit contract, **CC 1799.90**

WORDS

WORDS AND PHRASES—Cont'd
Creditors—Cont'd
  Consumer credit denial, CC 1787.2
  Consumer credit reporting agencies, CC 1785.26
  Credit disability insurance, CC 1812.401
  Fair debt settlement, CC 1788.301
  Motor vehicles, conditional sales, cosigners, CC 2983.35
  Student loans, collections, CC 1788.201
  Transfers of personal property, void against creditors, CC 3440
  Voidable transactions, CC 3439.01, 3445
Creditors remedies, credit disability insurance, CC 1812.401
Criminal actions, human trafficking, CC 52.5
Cross context behavioral advertising, consumers, privacy, CC 1798.140
Cruelty, motion pictures, human beings or animals, CC 3505
Cultural burn, prescribed burning, liability, CC 3333.8
Cultural fire practitioners, prescribed burning, liability, CC 3333.8
Customer facility charges, motor vehicles, leases, CC 1939.01
Customers,
  Deposits for repair, alteration, or sale, insurance, CC 1858
  Dies, tools and molds, ownership, CC 1140
  Electricity, privacy, usage data, CC 1798.98
  Personal information, direct marketing, disclosure, CC 1798.83
  Records and recordation, destruction, CC 1798.80
  Utility services, theft or diversion, CC 1882
Daily or weekly news publication, libel and slander, CC 48a
Damage waiver, motor vehicles, leases, CC 1939.01
Damages, CC 3281
  Deeds and conveyances, Subdivision Map Act, CC 2985.51
Dark patterns,
  Consumers, privacy, CC 1798.140
  Genetic testing, privacy, CC 56.18
Data,
  Electricity, privacy, usage data, CC 1798.98
  RFID (radio frequency identification), crimes and offenses, CC 1798.795
Data brokers, registration, CC 1798.99.80
Data furnishers, credit services, CC 1789.12
Data protection impact assessments, consumer protection, Internet, children and minors, CC 1798.99.30
Dating service contract, CC 1694
Days,
  Consumer contract awareness, CC 1799.201
  Mechanics liens, CC 8058
Dealers,
  Autographed memorabilia, CC 1739.7

WORDS AND PHRASES—Cont'd
Dealers—Cont'd
  Mobilehomes and mobilehome parks, consumer warranties, CC 1797.1
  Motor vehicles,
    Repurchases, notice, CC 1793.23
    Warranty adjustment programs, CC 1795.90
Dealership, CC 81
Debit card, CC 1748.30
  Consumer goods, refunds, CC 1748.40
Debit card issuer, CC 1748.30
Debit cardholder, CC 1748.30
Debt,
  Colleges and universities, schools and school districts, transcripts, withholding, CC 1788.92
  Fair collection practices, CC 1788.2
  Fair debt settlement, CC 1788.301
  Voidable transactions, CC 3439.01
Debt buyers, consumer credit, CC 1788.50
Debt collection, CC 1788.2
Debt collectors, fair debt collection practices, CC 1788.2
Debt settlement providers, fair debt settlement, CC 1788.301
Debt settlement services, fair debt settlement, CC 1788.301
Debtors, CC 3429
  Collection, CC 1788.2
  Credit disability insurance, CC 1812.401
  Duress or coercion, CC 1798.97.1
  Identity and identification, theft, collection agencies, CC 1788.18
  Student loans, collections, CC 1788.201
  Voidable transactions, CC 3439.01
Deceased personality, celebrity image protection, CC 3344.1
Deceit, CC 1710
Declarant, condominiums, CC 4130
  Business and commerce, CC 6544
Declaration, condominiums, CC 4135
  Business and commerce, CC 6546
Declared emergencies, peace officers, dogs, discrimination, public accommodations, CC 54.25
Declawing, landlord and tenant, animals, CC 1942.7
Defamation, CC 44
Default, consumer protection, Internet, children and minors, CC 1798.99.30
Defaulting occupant, recreational vehicle park, CC 799.22
Defaulting resident, recreational vehicle parks, CC 799.23
Defaulting tenant, recreational vehicle parks, CC 799.24
Defects, condominiums, construction, disclosure, CC 6100
  Business and commerce, CC 6874
Deferred deposit, check cashers, CC 1789.31

WORDS AND PHRASES—Cont'd
Defibrillator, emergencies, CC 1714.21
Deidentified, consumers, privacy, CC 1798.140
Delinquency, consumer credit reporting agencies, CC 1799.101
Delinquent debts, collection agencies, CC 1788.14.5
Deliver, rent controls, commercial property, CC 1954.26
Delivery, secured land transaction statements, CC 2943
Demand for money, civil rights, disabled persons, accessibility, CC 55.3
Demand letters,
  Civil rights, disabled persons, construction, accessibility, CC 55.3
  Sex, discrimination, small businesses, CC 55.62
Departments,
  Colleges and universities, student loans, borrowers rights, CC 1788.100
  Discrimination, business and commerce, safety, recognition, CC 51.17
Depicted individuals, privacy, invasion of privacy, lewdness and obscenity, CC 1708.86
Depose, CC 14
Deposit for exchange, CC 1818
Deposit for keeping, CC 1817
Depositaries, CC 1814
  Customer deposit of personal property for repair, alteration or sale, insurance, CC 1858
Depositary for hire, CC 1851
Depositor, CC 1814
Deposits, employment agencies, CC 1812.501
Depraved, video games, force and violence, CC 1746
Design defect, indemnity, CC 2784
Design professional,
  Contracts, indemnity, public agencies, CC 2782.8
  Mechanics liens, CC 8014, 8300
  Prime design professionals, CC 3321
  Private improvements, CC 3319
  Public improvements, CC 3320
Designated methods for submitting requests, consumers, privacy, CC 1798.140
Designed moisture barrier, construction defects, CC 895
Despicable conduct, privacy, invasion of privacy, altered depictions, lewdness and obscenity, CC 1708.86
Detriment, damages, CC 3282
Developer, rent controls, commercial property, CC 1954.26
Devices, consumers, privacy, CC 1798.140
Devocalizing, landlord and tenant, animals, CC 1942.7
Digital signature, security agents and broker dealers, contracts, CC 1633
Digitization, privacy, invasion of privacy, altered depictions, lewdness and obscenity, CC 1708.86

WORDS

WORDS AND PHRASES—Cont'd

Diligent search, mortgages, release of mortgage, absent mortgagee, **CC 2941.7**

Direct care service, long term health care facilities, employment agencies, nurses, temporary employment, **CC 1812.540**

Direct contractors, mechanics liens, **CC 8018**

Direct contracts, mechanics liens, **CC 8016**

Direct loan agreement, motor vehicles, subleasing, **CC 3343.5**

Direct marketing purposes,
  Business and commerce, personal information, disclosure, **CC 1798.83**
  Medical records, **CC 1798.91**

Direct to consumer genetic testing companies, privacy, **CC 56.18**

Directors,
  Condominiums, **CC 4140**
    Business and commerce, **CC 6548**
  Consumers, privacy, **CC 1798.145**

Disabilities,
  Civil rights, **CC 54**
  Dating service contracts, **CC 1694.3**
  Discrimination, **CC 51, 51.5**
  Health studio contracts, **CC 1812.89**
  Weight loss contracts, **CC 1694.8**

Disability claim period, credit disability insurance, **CC 1812.401**

Disabled, aged persons, housing, **CC 51.3, 51.11**

Disabled persons,
  Consumers Legal Remedies Act, **CC 1761**
  Mortgages, modification or change, forbearance, fines and penalties, **CC 2944.8**

Disabling injury or illness, aged persons, housing, **CC 51.3, 51.11**

Disasters, home solicitation contracts, **CC 1689.14**

Disclose,
  Business and commerce, personal information, direct marketing, **CC 1798.83**
  Information practices, **CC 1798.3**
  Privacy, invasion of privacy, altered depictions, lewdness and obscenity, **CC 1708.86**

Disclosure, year 2000 computer problem, dissemination of information, **CC 3269**

Discount buying organization, **CC 1812.101**

Discount prices, **CC 1812.101**

Display of the flag of the United States,
  condominiums, **CC 4705**
  Business and commerce, **CC 6702**

Disposal, mobilehomes and mobilehome parks, **CC 798.56a**
  Abandonment, **CC 798.61**

Dispose, mobilehomes and mobilehome parks, **CC 798.56a**
  Abandonment, **CC 798.61**

Disrupting the normal functioning of a health care facility, commercial blockade, **CC 3427**

Distributors,
  Independent wholesale sales representatives, **CC 1738.12**

WORDS AND PHRASES—Cont'd

Distributors—Cont'd
  Song Beverly Consumer Warranty Act, **CC 1791**

Divert, utility services, **CC 1882**

Documentation, motor vehicles, storage, liens and incumbrances, **CC 3068.1**

Dogs, tests, **CC 1834.9.3**

Domestic agency, employment, **CC 1812.501**

Domestic agency operating as a registry, employment agencies, **CC 1812.504**

Dominant tenements, **CC 803**

Downpayment,
  Automobile Sales Finance Act, **CC 2981**
  Seller assisted marketing plan, **CC 1812.201**

Drying racks,
  Condominiums, **CC 4750.10**
  Landlord and tenant, **CC 1940.20**

Dual agent, real estate brokers and salespersons, agency, **CC 2079.13**

Due diligence, mortgages, foreclosure,
  Meetings, financial condition, **CC 2923.5**
  Sales, **CC 2924j**
  Servicers, **CC 2923.55**

Duress, contracts, **CC 1569**

Dwelling unit,
  Landlord and tenant, **CC 1940**
  Riverside County, aged persons, housing, discrimination, **CC 51.11**
  Senior citizen housing, **CC 51.3**

Easements, **CC 801**
  Abandoned easements, **CC 887.010**

Economic damages, joint and several liability, **CC 1431.2**

Edge providers, Internet, neutrality, **CC 3100**

Education entity, disabled persons, accessibility, buildings, **CC 54.27**

Educational standardized assessments or educational assessments, consumers, privacy, **CC 1798.145**

Effective time period, landlord and tenant, mortgages, COVID 19, **CC 3273.2**

Electric utility, solar energy, easements, **CC 801.5**

Electric vehicle charging stations,
  Condominiums, **CC 4745**
    Business and commerce, **CC 6713**
  Leases, **CC 1947.6, 1952.7**

Electrified security fences, **CC 835**

Electronic,
  Security agents and broker dealers, contracts, **CC 1633**
  Uniform Electronic Transactions Act, **CC 1633.2**
  Voidable transactions, **CC 3439.01**

Electronic agent, Uniform Electronic Transactions Act, **CC 1633.2**

Electronic commercial service, electronic commerce, **CC 1789.2**

Electronic communication device, stalking, **CC 1708.7**

WORDS AND PHRASES—Cont'd

Electronic delivery,
  Condominiums, pest control, **CC 4777**
  Landlord and tenant, pest control, notice, **CC 1940.8.5**

Electronic devices, rental purchase agreements, **CC 1812.622**

Electronic funds transfer, rent, **CC 1947.3**

Electronic record,
  Security agents and broker dealers, contracts, **CC 1633**
  Uniform Electronic Transactions Act, **CC 1633.2**

Electronic sets, rental purchase agreements, **CC 1812.622**

Electronic signatures,
  Security agents and broker dealers, contracts, **CC 1633**
  Uniform Electronic Transactions Act, **CC 1633.2**

Electronic surveillance technology, motor vehicles, leases, **CC 1939.01**

Eligible bidders,
  Foreclosure, priorities and preferences, **CC 2924p**
  Trust deeds, sales, rent, **CC 2924m**

Eligible housing projects, floor area ratio standards, deeds and conveyances, restrictions, **CC 4747**

Eligible tenant buyers, trust deeds, **CC 2924m**

Emergencies,
  Mines and minerals, entry on property, notice, waiver, **CC 848**
  Mobilehomes and mobilehome parks, utility services, disruption, **CC 798.42, 799.7**

Employees, auctions and auctioneers, **CC 1812.601**

Employees who regularly have contact with customers, personal information, direct marketing, disclosure, **CC 1798.83**

Employers,
  Auctions and auctioneers, **CC 1812.601**
  Commercial vehicles, driving under the influence, treble damages, **CC 3333.7**
  Employment agencies, **CC 1812.501**

Employment agency,
  Domestic service, **CC 1812.5095**
  Regulation, **CC 1812.501**

Employment counseling service, regulation, **CC 1812.501**

Employment purposes,
  Consumer credit reporting, **CC 1785.3**
  Investigative Consumer Reporting Agencies Act, **CC 1786.2**

Encrypted,
  Customer records, breach of security, disclosure, **CC 1798.82**
  State agencies, breach of security, Disclosure, **CC 1798.29**
  Personal information, **CC 1798.82**

Encryption key, security, breach, **CC 1798.29, 1798.82**

I-223

WORDS

WORDS AND PHRASES—Cont'd

End users, Internet, neutrality, **CC 3100**
Enforcement actions, condominiums, **CC 5925**
Engage in business, colleges and universities, student loans, borrowers rights, **CC 1788.100**
Enhanced association records, condominiums, inspection and inspectors, **CC 5200**
Enhanced protection agreements, buildings, construction defects, **CC 901**
Enrollees, medical records, confidential or privileged information, **CC 56.05**
Enterprise service offerings, Internet, neutrality, **CC 3100**
Entitled person, secured land transaction statements, **CC 2943**
Epinephrine auto injectors, privileges and immunities, **CC 1714.23**
Equipment, seller assisted marketing plan, **CC 1812.201**
Equity line of credit, mortgages, payoff demand statements, **CC 2943.1**
Equity purchaser, home equity sales contracts, **CC 1695.1**
Equity seller, home equity sales contracts, **CC 1695.1**
Escrow, **CC 1057**
    Rating service, **CC 1785.28**
Escrow entity, controlled escrows of real estate developers, **CC 2995**
Escrow service, consumer protection, deeds and conveyances, foreclosure, **CC 1103.22**
Established business relationship, personal information, direct marketing, disclosure, **CC 1798.83**
Estimated remaining useful life, condominiums, disclosure, reserves, **CC 5570**
Estimated time for repair, motor vehicles, leases, **CC 1939.01**
Estimated time for replacement, motor vehicles, leases, **CC 1939.01**
Euro, contracts, securities or instruments, **CC 1663**
European currency unit, contracts, securities or instruments, **CC 1663**
EV dedicated TOU meters, condominiums, electric vehicles, charging infrastructure, **CC 4745.1**
Evidence demonstrating the existence of the tenancy, trust deeds, **CC 2924m**
Evidence of debt,
    Loans, variable interest rates, **CC 1916.5**
    Mortgages, **CC 1918.5**
Exclusive use common areas, condominiums, **CC 4145**
    Business and commerce, **CC 6550**
Executed contracts, **CC 1661**
Execution,
    Natural hazard disclosure statement, residential property, **CC 1103.3**
    Real estate, disclosure statements, **CC 1102.3**

WORDS AND PHRASES—Cont'd

Executory contracts, **CC 1661**
Exemplary damages, libel and slander, **CC 48a**
Exempt entities, student loans, collections, **CC 1788.201**
Existing, applicable California law, real estate, disclosure, **CC 1102.1**
Existing statutory law, real estate, disclosure, **CC 1102.1**
Express consent,
    Genetic testing, privacy, **CC 56.18**
    Rental purchase agreements, **CC 1812.622**
Express contract, **CC 1620**
Express warranty, Song Beverly Consumer Warranty Act, **CC 1791.2**
Extension of credit,
    Credit services, **CC 1789.12**
    Identity and identification, theft, **CC 1785.20.3**
Extenuating circumstances, debit cards, liability, **CC 1748.31**
Exterior elevated elements, condominiums, **CC 5551**
Facilities, obstructions, school buildings and grounds, health facilities, **CC 1708.9**
Factor, **CC 2026, 2367**
Failure to maintain, mortgages, foreclosure, **CC 2929.3**
Fair market value, motor vehicles, leases, **CC 2988**
Farm machinery, repair shops, **CC 1718**
Farm machinery repair shop, **CC 1718**
Fee simple, **CC 762**
Fees,
    Art and artists, injunctions, preserving artistic integrity, **CC 989**
    Employment agencies, **CC 1812.501**
    Rental purchase agreements, **CC 1812.622**
Felonies,
    Involuntary trusts, **CC 2225**
    Stories about felonies, **CC 2225**
15 passenger vans, leases, **CC 1939.35**
File,
    Consumer credit reporting, **CC 1785.3**
    Investigative Consumer Reporting Agencies Act, **CC 1786.2**
Filing a police report, rental purchase agreements, electronic devices and equipment, geophysical location tracking technology, **CC 1812.650**
Finance charge,
    Automobile Sales Finance Act, **CC 2981**
    Credit sales, **CC 1802.10**
Financial institutions,
    Consumer contract awareness, **CC 1799.201**
    Mobilehomes and mobilehome parks, termination of tenancy, **CC 798.56**
    Mortgage impound accounts, **CC 2954.8**
Financial interest, controlled escrows developers, **CC 2995**

WORDS AND PHRASES—Cont'd

Financing agency, installment sales, **CC 1802.16**
Fine art multiple, prints, **CC 1740**
Fine arts, **CC 982, 1738**
    Commissions, sale, original works, **CC 986**
    Defacement or destruction, **CC 987**
    Integrity preservation, **CC 989**
Fine prints, sale, **CC 1740**
Firearm accessories, manufacturers and manufacturing, sales, conduct, standards, **CC 3273.50**
Firearm industry members, conduct, standards, **CC 3273.50**
Firearm related products, manufacturers and manufacturing, sales, conduct, standards, **CC 3273.50**
Firm offer of credit, consumer credit reporting, **CC 1785.3**
First written communication, collection agencies, notice, limitation of actions, **CC 1788.14**
Fixed broadband Internet access services, neutrality, **CC 3100**
Fixed Internet service providers, neutrality, **CC 3100**
Fixtures, **CC 660**
Floating home marina, **CC 800.4**
Follows, stalking, torts, **CC 1708.7**
Food bank, food donations, **CC 1714.25**
For a commercial purpose, invasion of privacy, **CC 1708.8**
For compensation, aged persons, housing, permitted health care residents, **CC 51.3**
Foreclosure consultant, mortgage foreclosure consultants, **CC 2945.1**
Former district, community colleges, reorganization, landlord and tenant explosives, **CC 1940.7**
Former federal or state ordnance locations, residential property, disclosure statements, **CC 1102.15**
Fraction, oil spills, damages, **CC 3333.5**
Frame, art defacement or destruction, **CC 987**
Franchisees, credit card crimes, **CC 1748.7**
Franchises, discount buying services, **CC 1812.117**
Franchisors, credit card crimes, **CC 1748.7**
Fraud,
    Damages, **CC 3294**
    Indebtedness, duress or coercion, **CC 1798.97.1**
Fraudulent concealment, privacy, consumers, **CC 1798.199.70**
Fraudulently induced, cooperatives, retailers, actions, **CC 3343.7**
Free period, credit cards, disclosure, **CC 1810.21**
Free ride period, credit cards, disclosure, **CC 1810.21**
Freehold estates, **CC 765**
Freight, carriers, **CC 2110**

WORDS

WORDS AND PHRASES—Cont'd

Full and equal access, disabled persons, **CC 54.1**
Funds, mechanics liens, **CC 8020**
Future interests, **CC 690**
Gender, **CC 14**
   Discrimination, **CC 51**
Gender discrimination in pricing services claims, small businesses, **CC 55.62**
Gender expression, discrimination, **CC 51**
Gender violence, actions and proceedings, **CC 52.4**
General agent, **CC 2297**
General contractors, damages, construction, reimbursement, defense fees and costs, **CC 2782.05**
General damages, libel and slander, **CC 48a**
General ledgers, condominiums, inspection and inspectors, **CC 5200**
General lien, **CC 2874**
General merchandise retailer, credit card crimes, **CC 1748.7**
General notice, condominiums, **CC 4148**
Genetic characteristic, health care service plans, disclosure, **CC 56.17**
Genetic data,
   Business and commerce, personal information, security, **CC 1798.81.5, 1798.82**
   Privacy, **CC 56.18**
   State agencies, breach of security, disclosure, **CC 1798.29**
Genetic information, discrimination, **CC 51**
Genetic testing, privacy, **CC 56.18**
Geophysical location tracking technology, rental purchase agreements, **CC 1812.622**
Gift certificates, **CC 1749.45**
Gifts, **CC 1146**
Gleaners, donations, privileges and immunities, **CC 1714.25**
Good consideration, contracts, **CC 1605**
Good faith,
   Natural hazards, disclosure, residential property, **CC 1103.7**
   Real estate,
      Credit disclosures, **CC 2961**
      Residential property transfer disclosures, **CC 1102.7**
Good faith dispute,
   Checks, stopping payment, **CC 1719**
   Real estate purchases and sales, escrow return, **CC 1057.3**
Goods,
   Auctions and auctioneers, **CC 1812.601**
   Consumer contract awareness, **CC 1799.201**
   Consumer goods, sex, price discrimination, **CC 51.14**
   Consumers Legal Remedies Act, **CC 1761**
   Home solicitation contracts, **CC 1689.5**
   Retail installment sales, **CC 1802.1**
   Seminar sales solicitation contracts, **CC 1689.24**

WORDS AND PHRASES—Cont'd

Governing documents, condominiums, **CC 4150**
   Business and commerce, **CC 6552**
   Pets, **CC 4715**
Government entities, reading, privacy, **CC 1798.90**
Governmental agency, Uniform Electronic Transactions Act, **CC 1633.2**
Governmental emergency organization, personal injuries, liability, **CC 1714.5**
Governmental entity, Information Practices Act, **CC 1798.3**
Grain, private bulk grain storage, **CC 1880.1**
Grantor, dealerships, **CC 81**
Grants, **CC 1053**
   Dealerships, **CC 81**
Gratuitous deposit, **CC 1844**
Greenway easements, **CC 816.52**
Greenways, easements, **CC 816.52**
Grey market goods, consumer protection, **CC 1797.8**
Grocery department, Rosenthal Roberti Item Pricing Act, **CC 7100**
Grocery store, Rosenthal Roberti Item Pricing Act, **CC 7100**
Gross negligence, art defacement or destruction, **CC 987**
Guaranteed asset protection waivers, motor vehicles, conditional sales, **CC 2981**
Guarantor, **CC 2787**
   Consumer contract awareness, **CC 1799.201**
Guardians, foreign mortgages, **CC 2939.5**
Guest records, privacy, **CC 53.5**
Guests,
   Hotels and motels, eviction, checkout time, **CC 1865**
   Recreational vehicle parks, **CC 799.25**
Guide dogs, **CC 54.1**
Handler of a search and rescue dog, discrimination, public accommodations, emergencies, **CC 54.25**
Harasses, stalking, **CC 1708.7**
Harm reduction, homeless persons, occupancy, hotels and motels, shelters, **CC 1954.08**
Hazard insurance coverage, mortgages, **CC 2955.5**
Hazardous substances, secured lenders, environmentally impaired property, **CC 2929.5**
Health care facilities, commercial blockade, **CC 3427**
Health care institutions, medical malpractice, damages, **CC 3333.2**
Health care providers,
   Limitation of liability, **CC 43.9**
   Medical malpractice, **CC 3333.1**
      Damages, **CC 3333.2**
      Limitation of liability, **CC 1714.8**
Health care service plans, medical records, confidential or privileged information, **CC 56.05**

WORDS AND PHRASES—Cont'd

Health insurance information,
   Business and commerce, security, **CC 1798.81.5**
   Customer records, breach of security, disclosure, **CC 1798.82**
   State agencies, breach of security, disclosure, **CC 1798.29**
Health practitioners, landlord and tenant, domestic violence, termination, notice, **CC 1946.7**
Heinous, video games, force and violence, **CC 1746**
High volume third party sellers, markets and marketing, Internet, disclosure, **CC 1749.8**
Hiring, **CC 1925**
Holders,
   Dance studio contracts, **CC 1812.62**
   Health studio services, contracts, **CC 1812.94**
   Installment sales, **CC 1802.13**
   Motor vehicles, conditional sales, **CC 2981**
      Cosigners, **CC 2983.35**
Holidays, **CC 7**
Home appliance, Song Beverly Consumer Warranty Act, **CC 1791**
Home electronic product, Song Beverly Consumer Warranty Act, **CC 1791**
Home equity loan, disclosure, **CC 2970**
Home generated pharmaceutical waste, privileges and immunities, secure drug take back bins, **CC 1714.24**
Home improvement goods or services, retail installment sales, **CC 1689.8**
Home solicitation, consumers, legal remedies, **CC 1761**
Home solicitation contract or offer, **CC 1689.5**
Homeless persons, transitional housing, misconduct, **CC 1954.12**
Homeowners,
   Floating home marinas, **CC 800.6**
   Mobilehomes and mobilehome parks, **CC 798.9**
Homeowners responsibilities and liabilities, mobilehomes, **CC 798.56a**
Homepage, consumers, privacy, **CC 1798.140**
Hotels,
   Guests, eviction, checkout time, **CC 1865**
   Human trafficking, sex offenses, fines and penalties, **CC 52.65**
   Touch screen devices, blind or visually impaired persons, **CC 54.9**
Household, consumers, privacy, **CC 1798.140**
Household goods, secured transactions, **CC 1799.100**
Household members, landlord and tenant, domestic violence, termination, notice, **CC 1946.7**
Housing,
   Riverside County, aged persons, discrimination, **CC 51.11**
   Senior citizens, **CC 51.3**

WORDS

WORDS AND PHRASES—Cont'd

Housing accommodation, disabled persons, CC 54.1
ICCVAM, animals, tests, alternatives, CC 1834.9
Identification device, subcutaneous implantation, CC 52.7
Identification documents, RFID (radio frequency identification), crimes and offenses, CC 1798.795
Identifying characteristics, invasion of privacy, CC 1708.85
Identity theft, CC 1798.92
   Condominiums, homeowners associations, records and recordation, inspection and inspectors, CC 5215
Immediate family,
   Floating home marinas, CC 800.45
   Mobilehome Residency Law, CC 798.35
   Stalking, CC 1708.7
Immediate family members, landlord and tenant, domestic violence, termination, notice, CC 1946.7
Immigration or citizenship status, landlord and tenant, CC 1940.05
Imminent danger, special occupancy parks, moving, CC 1867
Impairing or degrading lawful Internet traffic on the basis of Internet content, application, or service, or use of a nonharmful device, neutrality, CC 3100
Impasse notice, rent controls, commercial property, CC 1954.26
Implied contract, CC 1621
Implied warranty of fitness, CC 1791.1
Implied warranty of merchantability, Song Beverly Consumer Warranty Act, CC 1791.1
Impossibility, contracts, CC 1597
Impound account, mortgages, statements, interest paid, CC 2954.2
Impression, fine prints, sale, CC 1740
Improper means, Uniform Trade Secrets Act, CC 3426.1
Improperly causes a vehicle to be towed or removed, liens and incumbrances, CC 3070
Improvements, mortgages, CC 2955.5
In place transfers, floating homes, rent increases, CC 800.40.5
In this state, colleges and universities, student loans, borrowers rights, CC 1788.100
In writing, medical records, markets and marketing, CC 1798.91
Income, Legal Estates Principal and Income Law, CC 731.03
Income of property, CC 748
Incumbrances, CC 1114
Indemnity, CC 2772
Independent contractors, consumers, privacy, CC 1798.145
Independent repair or service facility, Song Beverly Consumer Warranty Act, CC 1791

WORDS AND PHRASES—Cont'd

Individual,
   Customer records, destruction, CC 1798.80
   Disclosure of business records, bookkeeping services, CC 1799
   Information Practices Act, CC 1798.3
   Privacy, invasion of privacy, altered depictions, lewdness and obscenity, CC 1708.86
Individual in an emergency, landlord and tenant, CC 1946.8
Individual notice, condominiums, CC 4153
   Business and commerce, CC 6553
Individually identifiable, medical records, markets and marketing, CC 1798.91
Individuals who are deaf or hard of hearing, listening systems, judicial proceedings, CC 54.8
Indoor shooting range, CC 3482.1
Infer, consumers, privacy, CC 1798.140
Inferences, consumers, privacy, CC 1798.140
Information,
   Uniform Electronic Transactions Act, CC 1633.2
   Year 2000 computer problem, disclosure of information, CC 3269
Information processing system, Uniform Electronic Transactions Act, CC 1633.2
Initial cash payment, seller assisted marketing plan, CC 1812.201
Initial payment, seller assisted marketing plan, CC 1812.201
Inland carriers, CC 2087
Inn, liens and incumbrances, CC 1861.1
Inquiry,
   Credit cards, CC 1747.02, 1747.60
   Retail installment accounts, debtor, CC 1720
Inside telephone wiring, landlord and tenant, CC 1941.4
Inspected by a CASp (certified access specialist), disabled persons, civil rights, accessibility, CC 55.52
Installment account, CC 1802.7
Installment loan, prepayment penalties, CC 2954.11
Installment loan feature, prepayment penalties, CC 2954.11
Institutional third party,
   Cancellation for credit purposes, CC 2954.7
   Condominiums, mortgages, earthquake insurance, disclosure, CC 2955.1
   Mortgage insurance, future payments, CC 2954.12
Institutions, foreclosure, bids and bidding, priorities and preferences, CC 2924p
Insurers,
   Loans, variable interest rates, CC 1916.5
   Punitive damages, notice, CC 3296
Intentionally interacts, consumers, privacy, CC 1798.140
Interest, CC 1915

WORDS AND PHRASES—Cont'd

Interest in common, CC 685
Interfere, obstructions, school buildings and grounds, health facilities, CC 1708.9
Internet service providers, neutrality, CC 3100
Intimate body parts, invasion of privacy, CC 1708.85
Intimate parts, sexual battery, damages, CC 1708.5
Intimidate, obstructions, school buildings and grounds, health facilities, CC 1708.9
Intimidation by threat of violence, CC 51.7
Introduction of the euro, contracts, securities or instruments, CC 1663
Inventory, Song Beverly Consumer Warranty Act, CC 1795.4
Investigative consumer reporting agency, CC 1786.2
Involuntary, deposits, CC 1815
Involuntary deposit, property, CC 1815
ISP traffic exchange, Internet, neutrality, CC 3100
ISP traffic exchange agreements, Internet, neutrality, CC 3100
Item of business, condominiums, CC 4155
Item of information, consumer credit reporting, CC 1785.3
Jeopardize the validity and reliability of that educational standardized assessment or educational assessment, consumers, privacy, CC 1798.145
Job listing service, regulation, CC 1812.501
Job orders, employment agencies, CC 1812.501
Jobber, independent wholesale sales representatives, CC 1738.12
Jobseeker, employment agencies, CC 1812.501
Joint authority, CC 12
Joint interest, property, CC 683
Just cause, landlord and tenant, termination, CC 1946.2
Key factors, consumer credit reporting agencies, credit score, notice, CC 1785.15.1
Key person, credit life and disability insurance, CC 1812.406
Keys, RFID (radio frequency identification), crimes and offenses, CC 1798.795
Killing, motion pictures, human beings or animals, CC 3505
Labor, service, equipment or material, mechanics liens, CC 8022
Laborer, mechanics liens, CC 8024
Land, CC 659
   Condominiums, CC 659
Landlords,
   Abandoned or unclaimed property, disposition, tenancy termination, CC 1980
   Applicant screening, CC 1950.6
   Assignment or sublease, CC 1995.020
   Consumer credit reporting agencies, CC 1954.06
   Leases,
      Restrictions, CC 1997.020

WORDS

WORDS AND PHRASES—Cont'd
Landlords—Cont'd
  Leases—Cont'd
    Termination, personal property, disposition, CC 1993
    Pest control, notice, CC 1940.8.5
    Reusable tenant screening reports, CC 1950.1
    Water supply, submeters, CC 1954.202
Landowners, boundaries, maintenance, CC 841
Last known address, mortgages, CC 2924b
  Notices of default and of sale, CC 2924b
Law enforcement entities, reading, privacy, CC 1798.90
Law enforcement officers, credit cards, theft, identity and identification, disclosure, CC 1748.95
Laws, CC 22
Layaway, CC 1749.1
Lead paint abatement program, CC 3494.5
Lease contract,
  Motor vehicles, subleasing, CC 3343.5
  Vehicle leasing, CC 2985.7
Leases,
  Assignment or sublease, CC 1995.020
  Breach, remedies of lessor, CC 1951
  Rents, issues, and profits of real property, CC 2938
  Song Beverly Consumer Warranty Act, CC 1791
  Use restrictions, CC 1997.020
Lender,
  Adjustable rate residential mortgage loans, disclosures, CC 1921
  Shared appreciation loans, senior citizens, CC 1917.320
Lenders address, museums, indefinite or long term loans, CC 1899.1
Lenders appreciation share, shared appreciation loans for seniors, CC 1917.320
Lending institutions, mechanics liens, payment bonds, CC 8610
Lessee,
  Mineral rights, CC 883.140
  Motor vehicle warranty adjustment programs, CC 1795.90
  Song Beverly Consumer Warranty Act, CC 1791
  Vehicle leasing, CC 2985.7
Lessor,
  Mineral rights, CC 883.140
  Rental purchase agreements, CC 1812.622
  Song Beverly Consumer Warranty Act, CC 1791
  Vehicle leasing, CC 2985.7
Lessors costs, rental purchase agreements, CC 1812.622
Levying officer, innkeepers lien, CC 1861.1
Libel, CC 45
  On its face, CC 45a

WORDS AND PHRASES—Cont'd
Licensed health care professionals, medical records, confidential or privileged information, CC 56.05
Licensed nursing staff, long term health care facilities, employment agencies, temporary employment, CC 1812.540
Licensed persons,
  Appraisal and appraisers, contracts for sale of land, discrimination, CC 1102.6g
  Residential mortgage lenders, fiduciaries, CC 2923.1
Licensed pest control operators,
  Landlord and tenant, notice, CC 1940.8.5
  Pest control, condominiums, CC 4777
Licensees, colleges and universities, student loans, borrowers rights, CC 1788.100
Licenses, business and commerce, personal information, security, CC 1798.81.5
Lien, CC 2872
  Mechanics liens, CC 8026
  Voidable transactions, CC 3439.01
Likely to be accessed by children, consumer protection, Internet, CC 1798.99.30
Limited edition,
  Autographed memorabilia, CC 1739.7
  Fine prints, CC 1740
Limited equity housing cooperatives, CC 817
Limited interest, CC 692
Listing, mobilehomes and mobilehome parks, sales, CC 798.71
Listing agent, real estate brokers and salespersons, CC 2079.13
Listing agreements, real estate brokers and salespersons, agency, CC 2079.13
Listing price, real estate brokers and salespersons, agency, CC 2079.13
Litigation expenses, mineral rights termination actions, CC 883.250
Livestock, liens and incumbrances, CC 3080
Livestock servicer, liens and incumbrances, CC 3080
Livestock services, liens, CC 3080
Load bearing components, condominiums, CC 5551
Loan for use, personal property, CC 1884
Loan to value ratio, motor vehicles, conditional sales, guaranteed asset protection waivers, CC 2982.12
Loans,
  Money, CC 1912
  Museums, indefinite or long term loans, CC 1899.1
  Precomputed interest, CC 1799.5
Loans for exchange, CC 1902
Local agencies,
  Greenways, easements, CC 816.52
  Rent control ordinances, CC 1947.7, 1947.8
Local child support enforcement agency, consumer credit reporting, CC 1785.3
Local public entities, shared appreciation loans, CC 1917.006

WORDS AND PHRASES—Cont'd
Located, museums, loans, indefinite or long term, CC 1899.2
Locks, landlord and tenant, protective orders, CC 1941.5, 1941.6
Lodger, eviction and owner occupied dwelling, CC 1946.5
Logos, public agencies, contractors, disclosure, CC 3273
Long term health care facilities, employment agencies, nurses, temporary employment, CC 1812.540
Luggage, carriers, CC 2181
Made or arranged, real estate brokers loans, CC 1916.1
Maintain,
  Business and commerce, personal information, security, CC 1798.81.5
  Information Practices Act, CC 1798.3
Major components, condominiums, reserves, disclosure, CC 5570
Major life activities, Consumers Legal Remedies Act, CC 1761
Major systems, residential property disclosure, CC 1134
Malice,
  Damages, CC 3294
  Privacy, invasion of privacy, altered depictions, lewdness and obscenity, CC 1708.86
Management,
  Floating home residency, CC 800.2
  Mobilehome Residency Law, CC 798.2
  Recreational vehicle parks, CC 799.26
Management employees, consumers, privacy, CC 1798.145
Managing agents, condominiums, CC 4158, 5385
Manufactured homes, consumer warranties, CC 1797.1
Manufactured product, buildings, construction defects, CC 896
Manufacturers,
  Animals, tests, alternatives, CC 1834.9
  Cosmetics, animals, tests, crimes and offenses, CC 1834.9.5
  Human trafficking, CC 1714.43
  Independent wholesale sales representatives, CC 1738.12
  Internet, connected devices, security, CC 1798.91.05
  Motor vehicles, warranties, CC 1795.90
  Song Beverly Consumer Warranty Act, CC 1791
Marine carriers, CC 2087
Marketing,
  Condominiums, sales, restrictions, CC 4730
  Business and commerce, CC 6710
  Medical records, confidential or privileged information, CC 56.05
Marketing information,
  Credit cards, disclosures, CC 1748.12

WORDS

WORDS AND PHRASES—Cont'd

Marketing information—Cont'd
 Grocery stores, club cards, disclosure, **CC 1749.61**
Marketplace sellers, consumer protection, **CC 1749.7**
Marketplaces, consumer protection, **CC 1749.7**
Markets, condominiums, sales, restrictions, **CC 4730**
 Business and commerce, **CC 6710**
Mass market services, Internet, neutrality, **CC 3100**
Master, fine prints, **CC 1740**
Material,
 Involuntary trusts, **CC 2225**
 Stories about felonies, **CC 2225**
Material suppliers, mechanics liens, **CC 8028**
Mediation, hazardous substances and waste, releases, **CC 850**
Medical condition, discrimination, **CC 51, 51.5, 54**
Medical examiner, forensic pathologist, or coroner, mental hospitals, **CC 56.10**
Medical identity theft, medical records, release, **CC 56.36**
Medical information,
 Business and commerce, security, **CC 1798.81.5**
 Confidentiality, **CC 56.05**
 Customer records, breach of security, disclosure, **CC 1798.82**
 Investigative Consumer Reporting Agencies Act, **CC 1786.2**
 Markets and marketing, **CC 1798.91**
 State agencies, breach of security, disclosure, **CC 1798.29**
Medical research, animals, tests, **CC 1834.9.3**
 Alternatives, **CC 1834.9**
Medical specialty societies, peer review, liability, **CC 43.7**
Medical staff members, consumers, privacy, **CC 1798.145**
Meets applicable standards, disabled persons, civil rights, accessibility, **CC 55.52**
Member of the armed forces, warranties, **CC 1791**
Members, condominiums, **CC 4160**
 Business and commerce, **CC 6554**
Membership camping contract broker, membership camping contracts, **CC 1812.300**
Membership camping contracts, **CC 1812.300**
Membership camping operator, **CC 1812.300**
Membership program, motor vehicles, leases, **CC 1939.01**
Menace, contracts, **CC 1570**
Mental health application information, medical records, confidential or privileged information, **CC 56.05**
Mental health digital services, medical records, confidential or privileged information, **CC 56.05**
Military borrowers, colleges and universities, student loans, borrowers rights, **CC 1788.100**

WORDS AND PHRASES—Cont'd

Mineral rights, **CC 883.110**
Mines, liens and incumbrances, **CC 3060**
Minimum late fees, colleges and universities, student loans, borrowers rights, **CC 1788.101**
Minority groups, equal protection of laws, statutes, **CC 53.7**
Minors, video games, force and violence, **CC 1746**
Misappropriation, Uniform Trade Secrets Act, **CC 3426.1**
Misrepresent or omit material information, colleges and universities, student loans, borrowers rights, **CC 1788.101**
Mistake of fact, contracts, **CC 1577**
Mobile broadband Internet access services, neutrality, **CC 3100**
Mobile Internet service providers, neutrality, **CC 3100**
Mobile stations, Internet, neutrality, **CC 3100**
Mobilehome park, **CC 798.4**
Mobilehomes, **CC 798.3**
 Abandonment, **CC 798.61**
 Consumer warranties, **CC 1797.1**
Modification documents, covenants, low and moderate income housing, **CC 714.6**
Molder, dies, molds and forms, ownership, **CC 1140**
Monitoring technology, rental purchase agreements, **CC 1812.622**
Monthly annuity, shared appreciation loans for seniors, **CC 1917.320**
Months, **CC 14**
Mortgage broker or lender, deceptive practices, **CC 1770**
Mortgage brokerage services, fiduciaries, **CC 2923.1**
Mortgage brokers, fiduciaries, **CC 2923.1**
Mortgage servicers, landlord and tenant, COVID 19, **CC 3273.2**
Mortgagee, statements, interest paid, **CC 2954.2**
Mortgages,
 Default sales, **CC 2920**
 Statements, interest paid, **CC 2954.2**
Motel or hotel, homeless persons, occupancy, **CC 1954.08**
Motels, innkeepers lien, **CC 1861.1**
Motion pictures, killing of or cruelty to human beings or animals, **CC 3504**
Motor carrier of property in dump truck equipment, **CC 3322**
Motor home, warranties, consumer protection, **CC 1793.22**
Motor vehicle credit agreement, cosigners, delinquency, notice, **CC 2983.35**
Motor vehicles,
 Conditional sales, **CC 2981**
 Leases, **CC 1939.01, 2985.7**
 Subleasing, **CC 3343.5**
 Warranty adjustment programs, **CC 1795.90**

WORDS AND PHRASES—Cont'd

Multifamily residential real property, water conservation, building standards, **CC 1101.3**
Multiphasic screening unit, medical care and treatment, **CC 43.9**
Multiple, fine prints, **CC 1740**
Multiple acts of rent skimming, residential real estate, **CC 890**
Multiple listing service, property listings, **CC 1087**
Museum, indefinite or long term loans, **CC 1899.1**
Mutuality of consent, contracts, **CC 1580**
Nearby, landowners, **CC 1002**
Necessary information, colleges and universities, student loans, borrowers rights, **CC 1788.102**
Necessary technology, touch screen devices, blind or visually impaired persons, **CC 54.9**
Negative credit information, consumer credit reporting agencies, **CC 1785.26**
Negative response, hazardous substances and waste, releases, **CC 850**
Negotiable instrument, credit card as condition of acceptance, **CC 1725**
Negotiation notice, rent controls, commercial property, **CC 1954.26**
Neighborhood area, military ordinance locations, **CC 1102.15, 1940.7**
Net advance, shared appreciation loans for seniors, **CC 1917.320**
Net appreciated value, shared appreciation loans, senior citizens, **CC 1917.320**
Neutral third party, hazardous substances and waste, releases, **CC 850**
New construction, mobilehomes and mobilehome parks, **CC 798.7**
New mobilehome park construction, **CC 798.7**
New motor vehicles, breach of warranty, **CC 1793.22**
New qualified buyer, condominiums, sales, default, **CC 1675**
Nighttime, shooting ranges, **CC 3482.1**
Nine one one (911) service, privileges and immunities, providers, **CC 1714.55**
Noncompliant plumbing fixtures, water conservation, building standards, **CC 1101.3**
Nonconformity, new motor vehicles, consumer protection, **CC 1793.22**
Nondisturbance agreement, membership camping contracts, **CC 1812.300**
Noneconomic damages, joint and several liability, **CC 1431.2**
Nonprofit charitable organizations, eyes and eyesight, privileges and immunities, screenings, **CC 1714.26**
Nonviolent, obstructions, school buildings and grounds, health facilities, **CC 1708.9**
Notice, **CC 18, 19**
 Auctions and auctioneers, **CC 1812.610**

WORDS

WORDS AND PHRASES—Cont'd

Notice—Cont'd
   Consumer credit reporting agency, CC 1799.101
   Credit disability insurance, CC 1812.401

Notice of potential liability, hazardous substances and waste, releases, CC 850

Notice recipient, hazardous substances and waste, releases, CC 850

Notification threshold, hazardous substances and waste, releases, CC 850

Novation, CC 1530

Nude, privacy, invasion of privacy, altered depictions, lewdness and obscenity, CC 1708.86

Nuisance, CC 3479, 3480

Nurses registry, employment agencies, CC 1812.501, 1812.524

Nursing service,
   Long term health care facilities, employment agencies, temporary employment, CC 1812.540
   Nurses registries, CC 1812.524

Oaths, CC 14

Object of a contract, CC 1595

Obligations, CC 1427
   Consumer credit reporting agency, CC 1799.101

Obligor, service contracts, warranties, CC 1791

Obscene materials,
   Distribution, damages, CC 52.8
   Lewdness and obscenity, electronic transmissions, images, CC 1708.88

Occupancy, recreational vehicle parks, CC 799.27

Occupants,
   Condominiums, pest control, CC 4785
      Business and commerce, CC 6720
   Landlord and tenant, emergency services, law enforcement, CC 1946.8
   Recreational vehicle parks, CC 799.28

Occupied by a tenant, mortgages, foreclosure, first liens, CC 2924.15

Occupy, recreational vehicle parks, CC 799.27

Offensive contact, sexual battery, damages, CC 1708.5

Offer to purchase, real estate brokers and salespersons, agency, CC 2079.13

Offering price, real estate brokers and salespersons, agency, CC 2079.13

Offers, membership camping contracts, CC 1812.300

Officers, consumers, privacy, CC 1798.145

Official fees, installment sales, CC 1802.14

Older borrowers, colleges and universities, student loans, borrowers rights, CC 1788.100

On loan, museums, indefinite or long term loans, CC 1899.1

Online dating service, contracts, CC 1694

Online identifiers, invasion of privacy, CC 1708.85

WORDS AND PHRASES—Cont'd

Online marketplaces, disclosure, CC 1749.8

Online service, product, or feature, consumer protection, children and minors, CC 1798.99.30

Open end credit card account, payoff, notice, CC 1748.13

Open end credit plan, credit disability insurance, CC 1812.405

Operating rules, condominiums, CC 4340
   Business and commerce, CC 6630

Operation and maintenance, hazardous substances and waste, releases, CC 850

Operative date, powers of termination, CC 885.070

Opioid antagonists, drugs and medicine, overdose, CC 1714.22

Opioid overdose prevention and treatment program, drugs and medicine, CC 1714.22

Oppression, damages, CC 3294

Organ procurement organizations, drivers licenses, electronic devices and equipment, CC 1798.90.1

Organizations,
   Artistic integrity preservation, CC 989
   Voidable transactions, CC 3439.01

Original, trust deeds, reconveyance, CC 2941

Original creditors, student loans, collections, CC 1788.201

Original political item, sale and manufacture, CC 1739.2

Ostensible,
   Agency, CC 2300
   Authority, CC 2317

Overpayments, colleges and universities, student loans, borrowers rights, CC 1788.100

Oversight agency, hazardous substances and waste, releases, CC 850

Owner occupied, mortgages, foreclosure,
   First liens, modification or change, CC 2924.15
   Meetings, financial condition, CC 2923.5

Owner occupied residences, shared appreciation loans, CC 1917.006

Owners,
   Consumers, privacy, CC 1798.145
   Landlord and tenant,
      Abandoned or unclaimed property, disposition, CC 1980
      Animals, declawing, devocalizing, CC 1942.7
      Termination, CC 1946.2
   Leases, termination, personal property, disposition, CC 1993
   Mechanics liens,
      Cessation, notice, CC 8188, 8190
      Completion, notice, CC 8182
   Mortgage foreclosure consultant, CC 2945.1
   Rent controls, CC 1947.12, 1954.51
      Commercial property, CC 1954.26

Ownership, CC 654

WORDS AND PHRASES—Cont'd

Ownership information, consumers, privacy, CC 1798.145

Ownership or management,
   Floating home cooperatives and condominiums, CC 800.300
   Subdivisions, cooperatives or condominiums for mobilehomes, CC 799

Owning, oil and gas pipelines, damages, CC 3333.5

Owns, business and commerce, personal information, security, CC 1798.81.5

Paid prioritization, Internet, neutrality, CC 3100

Parents, discount buying services, CC 1812.117

Parks,
   Mobilehome Residency Law, CC 798.6
   Recreational vehicle park, CC 799.30

Partial payment, colleges and universities, student loans, borrowers rights, CC 1788.100

Participant injury, space flight, CC 2210

Participants,
   Homeless persons, transitional housing, misconduct, CC 1954.12
   Space flight, CC 2210

Participation in a lead paint abatement program, CC 3494.5

Partnerships, interest, CC 684

Party's own interpreter, contracts, foreign languages, CC 1632

Pass a check on insufficient funds, commercial paper, CC 1719

Passenger manifest records, privacy, CC 53.5

Patients, medical records, confidential or privileged information, CC 56.05

Pattern of conduct, stalking, CC 1708.7

Payment bonds, mechanics liens, CC 8030

Payment processing services, fair debt settlement, CC 1788.301

Payment processors, fair debt settlement, CC 1788.301

Payments, performance of obligation for delivery of money, CC 1478

Payoff demand statement, secured land transaction statements, CC 2943

Peace officers or firefighters dogs, public accommodations, emergencies, CC 54.25

Penalties, landlord and tenant, emergency services, law enforcement, CC 1946.8

Per job basis, farm machinery repair shop, CC 1718

Percentage change in the cost of living,
   Floating homes, rent increases, CC 800.40.5
   Mobilehomes and mobilehome parks, rent controls, CC 798.30.5
   Rent controls, CC 1947.12

Permitted health care resident,
   Riverside County, aged persons, housing, discrimination, CC 51.11
   Senior citizen housing, CC 51.3

WORDS

WORDS AND PHRASES—Cont'd
Perpetual interest, **CC 691**
Person authorized to record the notice of default or the notice of sale, mortgages, **CC 2924b**
Person or entity, domestic violence, personal information, victim service providers, grants, **CC 1798.79.8**
Personal agriculture, landlord and tenant, **CC 1940.10**
Personal emergency response unit, health care, **CC 1689.6**
Personal identification information, credit cards, acceptance, **CC 1747.08**
Personal identifying information, theft, **CC 1798.92**
Personal information,
  Business and commerce,
    Direct marketing, disclosure, **CC 1798.83**
    Security, **CC 1798.81.5**
  Consumers, privacy, **CC 1798.140**
  Customer records,
    Breach of security, disclosure, **CC 1798.82**
    Destruction, **CC 1798.80**
  Identification devices, subcutaneous implantation, **CC 52.7**
  Information Practices Act, **CC 1798.3**
  Reading, disclosure, **CC 1798.90**
  State agencies, breach of security, disclosure, **CC 1798.29**
Personal property, **CC 14, 663**
Personally identifying information, domestic violence, victim service providers, grants, **CC 1798.79.8**
Persons, **CC 14**
  Animals, tests, alternatives, **CC 1834.9**
  Art defacement or destruction, **CC 987**
  Auctions and auctioneers, **CC 1812.601**
  Autographed memorabilia, **CC 1739.7**
  Automated license plate recognition, **CC 1798.90.5**
  Automobile Sales Finance Act, **CC 2981**
  Booking photographs, commercial use, **CC 1798.91.1**
  Business entities, filing, identity and identification, theft, **CC 1798.200**
  Business establishment discrimination, **CC 51.5**
  Children and minors, medical records, release, gender identity or expression, **CC 56.109**
  Colleges and universities, student loans, borrowers rights, **CC 1788.100**
  Condominiums, **CC 4170**
    Business and commerce, **CC 6560**
  Consumer credit reporting, **CC 1785.3**
  Consumer credit reporting agency, **CC 1799.101**
  Consumers, privacy, **CC 1798.140**
  Consumers Legal Remedies Act, **CC 1761**
  Credit services, **CC 1789.12**
  Dealerships, **CC 81**

WORDS AND PHRASES—Cont'd
Persons—Cont'd
  Debt collection, **CC 1788.2**
  Disclosure of business records, bookkeeping services, **CC 1799**
  Employment agencies, **CC 1812.501**
  Fair debt settlement, **CC 1788.301**
  Fine arts, consignments, **CC 1738**
  Fine prints, **CC 1740**
  Food, donations, privileges and immunities, **CC 1714.25**
  Genetic testing, privacy, **CC 56.18**
  Identification devices, subcutaneous implantation, **CC 52.7**
  Indebtedness, duress or coercion, **CC 1798.97.1**
  Information Practices Act, **CC 1798.3**
  Installment sales, **CC 1802.15**
  Investigative Consumer Reporting Agencies Act, **CC 1786.2**
  Investment advisers liability, **CC 3372**
  Mechanics liens, **CC 8032**
  Membership camping contracts, **CC 1812.300**
  Mortgage foreclosure consultants, **CC 2945.1**
  Motion pictures, killing of or cruelty to human beings or animals, **CC 3505**
  Motor vehicles, subleasing, **CC 3343.5**
  Privacy, invasion of privacy, altered depictions, lewdness and obscenity, **CC 1708.86**
  Rent skimming, residential real estate, **CC 890**
  Seller assisted marketing plan, **CC 1812.201**
  Sport shooting ranges, **CC 3482.1**
  Uniform Electronic Transactions Act, **CC 1633.2**
  Uniform Trade Secrets Act, **CC 3426.1**
  Utilities services, theft or diversion, **CC 1882**
  Vehicle leasing, **CC 2985.7**
  Video games, force and violence, **CC 1746**
  Voidable transactions, **CC 3439.01**
  Year 2000 information disclosure, **CC 3269**
Persons who hire, landlord and tenant, **CC 1940**
Pesticides,
  Condominiums, **CC 4777**
  Landlord and tenant, notice, **CC 1940.8.5**
Pests, condominiums, **CC 4777**
Pets,
  Condominiums, **CC 4715**
  Mobilehomes and mobilehome parks, **CC 798.33**
Pharmaceutical company, medical records, confidential or privileged information, **CC 56.05**
Photographs,
  Celebrity image protection, **CC 3344.1**
  Invasion of privacy, use without consent, **CC 3344**

WORDS AND PHRASES—Cont'd
Photographs—Cont'd
  Unauthorized use in advertising, **CC 3344**
Physical barrier, guide dogs admitted to zoos, **CC 54.7**
Physical evidence, destruction of evidence, privileged communications, exceptions, **CC 47**
Physical obstructions, school buildings and grounds, health facilities, **CC 1708.9**
Physical or mental impairment, Consumers Legal Remedies Act, **CC 1761**
Pipeline corporations, oil and gas pipelines, damages, **CC 3333.5**
Pipeline system, oil and gas pipelines, damages, **CC 3333.5**
Place of business, Song Beverly Consumer Warranty Act, **CC 1791**
Place of public accommodation, disabled persons, civil rights, accessibility, **CC 55.52**
Place under surveillance, stalking, torts, **CC 1708.7**
Plaintiffs,
  Innkeepers liens, **CC 1861.1**
  Privacy, invasion of privacy, altered depictions, lewdness and obscenity, **CC 1708.86**
Planned developments, **CC 4175**
  Condominiums, business and commerce, **CC 6562**
Plant crop, landlord and tenant, **CC 1940.10**
Plural number, **CC 14**
Point of sale system, prices, **CC 7100**
Police reports, landlord and tenant, locks and locking, **CC 1941.5, 1941.6**
Political item, sale and manufacture, **CC 1739.1**
Porcelain painting, fine art, **CC 997**
Position of authority, sexual battery, damages, consent, defense, children and minors, **CC 1708.5.5**
Posthumous multiple, fine prints, **CC 1744**
Power of sale, ancient mortgages, deeds of trust, **CC 882.020**
Power of termination, marketable title, **CC 885.010**
Precise geolocation, consumers, privacy, **CC 1798.140**
Precomputed basis,
  Automobile Sales Finance Act, **CC 2981**
  Retail installment sales, **CC 1802.21**
Precomputed finance charge, contracts, **CC 1799.8**
Precomputed interest, loans, **CC 1799.5**
Preliminary notice, mechanics liens, **CC 8034**
Prelitigation letters, education, disabled persons, accessibility, buildings, **CC 54.27**
Premises, leases, termination, personal property, disposition, **CC 1993**
Prepaid debit cards, consumer goods, refunds, **CC 1748.40**

WORDS AND PHRASES—Cont'd

Prequalifying report, consumer credit reporting, CC 1785.3
Prescription drug claims processor, pharmacists, contracts, CC 2527
Present interest, CC 689
Prevailing market rent, residential rent control, CC 1954.51
Prevailing party, contracts, actions, CC 1717
Prevailing rates, shared appreciation loans, senior citizens, CC 1917.320
Previous homeowners, mobilehomes and mobilehome parks, disasters, destruction, renewed tenancy, CC 798.62
Prices, rent controls, commercial property, CC 1954.26
Primary obligor, consumer credit reporting agency, CC 1799.101
Prime design professional, public improvements, CC 3320, 3321
Principal, Legal Estates Principal and Income Law, CC 731.03
Private, personal, and familial activity, invasion of privacy, CC 1708.8
Private areas, landlord and tenant,
  Agricultural products, CC 1940.10
  Clotheslines, drying racks, CC 1940.20
Private bulk storage, CC 1880.1
Private duty nurses, nurses registries, CC 1812.524
Private education lenders, student loans, collections, CC 1788.201
Private education loan collection actions, student loans, collections, CC 1788.201
Private education loan collectors, student loans, collections, CC 1788.201
Private education loans, student loans, collections, CC 1788.201
Private nuisance, CC 3481
Privileged publication, libel and slander, CC 47
Probabilistic identifiers, consumers, privacy, CC 1798.140
Probable validity, innkeepers liens, CC 1861.1
Proceeds,
  Involuntary trusts, CC 2225
  Stories about felonies, CC 2225
Processing, consumers, privacy, CC 1798.140
Product, seller assisted marketing plan, CC 1812.201
Product liability action, consumer products known by consumers to be inherently unsafe, CC 1714.45
Professional negligence,
  Health care providers, CC 43.9
  Medical malpractice, CC 3333.1
    Damages, CC 3333.2
Professional society,
  Committee members, immunity from liability, CC 43.7
  Referral services, CC 43.95
Profiling,
  Consumer protection, Internet, children and minors, CC 1798.99.30

WORDS AND PHRASES—Cont'd

Profiling—Cont'd
  Consumers, privacy, CC 1798.140
Profit, crimes and offenses, stories about felonies, proceeds, CC 2225
Profiteer of the felony, trusts and trustees, CC 2225
Program misconduct, homeless persons, transitional housing, CC 1954.12
Program operators, transitional housing, homeless persons, misconduct, CC 1954.12
Program sites, transitional housing, homeless persons, misconduct, CC 1954.12
Programs, opioid overdose prevention and treatment program, drugs and medicine, CC 1714.22
Projected contingent interest, shared appreciation loans for seniors, CC 1917.320
Projected loan amount, shared appreciation loans for seniors, CC 1917.320
Promises, landlord and tenant, abandoned or unclaimed property, disposition, CC 1980
Proof, fine prints, CC 1740
Proper and accepted customs and standards, agricultural processing activities, nuisances, CC 3482.6
Proper identification,
  Consumer credit reporting, CC 1785.15
  Employment or insurance investigations, consumer reporting agencies, CC 1786.22
Property, CC 14, 654
  Deposits for repair, alteration, or sale, insurance, CC 1858
  Escrow, real estate purchases and sales, return, CC 1057.3
  Estate tax, CC 1057.3
  Landlord and tenant, water supply, submeters, CC 1954.202
  Mortgages and trust deeds, sales, CC 2924f
  Museums, loans, indefinite or long term, CC 1899.1
  Voidable transactions, CC 3439.01
Property owners,
  Home equity sales contracts, CC 1695.1
  Landlord and tenant, religion, display, CC 1940.45
  Lead base paint, abatement, CC 3494.5
Prospective buyer, residential real property disclosures, CC 1134
Prospective owner occupants,
  Foreclosure, bids and bidding, priorities and preferences, CC 2924p
  Trust deeds, CC 2924m
Protected consumers, consumer credit reporting agencies, security freeze, CC 1785.11.9
Protected individuals, medical records, confidential or privileged information, CC 56.05
Protected tenants, locks and locking, CC 1941.5, 1941.6

WORDS AND PHRASES—Cont'd

Provider of health care, medical records, confidential or privileged information, CC 56.05
Provider of service, electronic commerce, CC 1789.2
Providers,
  Reading, privacy, CC 1798.90
  Shared mobility devices, contracts, licenses and permits, CC 2505
Proxy, condominiums, homeowners associations, elections, CC 5130
Pseudonymization, consumers, privacy, CC 1798.140
Pseudonymize, consumers, privacy, CC 1798.140
Psychotherapists,
  Children and minors, records and recordation, confidential or privileged information, noncustodial parents, CC 56.106
  Medical records, confidential or privileged information, CC 56.104
  Sexual exploitation, CC 43.93
  Sexual harassment, CC 51.9
Psychotherapy, sexual exploitation, CC 43.93
Public agencies,
  Abandoned or unclaimed property, CC 2080.6
  Automated license plate recognition, CC 1798.90.5
  Contractors, disclosure, CC 3273
  Contracts, indemnity, design professional, CC 2782.8
  Improvements, design professionals, CC 3320
  Personal property, safekeeping, powers and duties, CC 2080.10
  Public improvements, prime design professionals, CC 3321
Public entities,
  Booking photographs, commercial use, CC 1798.91.1
  Landlord and tenant, immigration,
    Disclosure, CC 1940.3
    Information, CC 1940.3
  Lead base paint, abatement, CC 3494.5
  Lessor remedies for lease breach, CC 1952.6
  Mechanics liens, CC 8036
  Mortgages, multifamily housing, sales, postponement, CC 2924f
  Rent controls, CC 1954.51
    Commercial property, CC 1954.26
Public health and safety labor or services, contractors, disclosure, CC 3273
Public nuisance, CC 3480
Public or semipublic internet based service or application, social media, threats, CC 1798.99.20
Public records, labor and employment, copies, CC 1786.53
Public safety agencies, nine one one (911), privileges and immunities, providers, CC 1714.55

WORDS

WORDS AND PHRASES—Cont'd

Public sale, livestock service liens, **CC 3080.18**
Public social services, monopolies and unfair trade, procurement, fees, **CC 1770**
Publicly display, social security, numbers and numbering, disclosure, **CC 1798.85**
Publicly post, social security, numbers and numbering, disclosure, **CC 1798.85**
Purchase order, Automobile Sales Finance Act, **CC 2981**
Purchasers,
  Membership camping contracts, **CC 1812.300**
  Motor vehicles, subleasing, **CC 3343.5**
  Seller assisted marketing plan, **CC 1812.201**
Purchases, housing credit arrangers, **CC 2957**
Qualified business rentals, motor vehicles, **CC 1939.21**
Qualified defendants, disabled persons, civil rights, accessibility, **CC 55.52**
Qualified financial contract, frauds, statute of, **CC 1624**
Qualified mobilehome parks, rent controls, **CC 798.30.5**
Qualified ownership, **CC 680**
Qualified permanent resident,
  Aged persons, housing, **CC 51.3**
  Riverside County, aged persons, housing, discrimination, **CC 51.11**
  Senior citizen housing, **CC 51.3**
Qualified persons, buildings, permits for construction, independent quality review, privileges and immunities, **CC 43.99**
Qualified private companies, mechanics liens, security, large projects, **CC 8704**
Qualified publicly traded companies, mechanics liens, security, large projects, **CC 8704**
Qualified requests, colleges and universities, student loans, borrowers rights, **CC 1788.100**
Qualified third parties, landlord and tenant, domestic violence, termination, **CC 1946.7**
  Notice, **CC 1946.7**
Qualified third party professionals, indebtedness, duress or coercion, **CC 1798.97.1**
Qualified written requests, colleges and universities, student loans, borrowers rights, **CC 1788.100**
Qualifying resident,
  Riverside County, aged persons, housing, discrimination, **CC 51.11**
  Senior citizens housing, **CC 51.3**
Quorum, condominiums,
  Assessments, **CC 5605**
  Business and commerce, declarations, amendments, **CC 6608**
  Declarations, amendments, **CC 4230**
Quotes, motor vehicles, leases, **CC 1939.01**
  Business programs, **CC 1939.21**
Radio, libel and slander, **CC 48.5**
Radio broadcast, libel and slander, **CC 48.5**
Radio frequency identification, crimes and offenses, **CC 1798.795**

WORDS AND PHRASES—Cont'd

Railroad corporation, easements, **CC 801.7**
Range, sport shooting, **CC 3482.1**
Ranking, consumer protection, **CC 1749.7**
Ratio utility billing system, landlord and tenant, water supply, submeters, **CC 1954.202**
Readers, RFID (radio frequency identification), crimes and offenses, **CC 1798.795**
Readily identifiable, invasion of privacy, use of names, photographs and other likenesses without consent, **CC 3344**
Real estate developer, controlled escrows, **CC 2995**
Real property, **CC 14, 658**
  Assignments, **CC 2938**
  Brokers and salespersons, agency, **CC 2079.13**
Real property sales contract, **CC 2985**
  Statement of compliance, Subdivision Map Act, **CC 2985.51**
Real property security, environmentally impaired property, **CC 2929.5**
Real property security instrument, **CC 2953.1**
Real property transaction, brokers and salespersons, agency, **CC 2079.13**
Reasonable belief,
  Landlord and tenant, abandoned or unclaimed property, disposition, **CC 1980**
  Leases, termination, personal property, disposition, **CC 1993**
Reasonable controls, weapons, manufacturers and manufacturing, sales, conduct, standards, **CC 3273.50**
Reasonable costs, charging stations, electric vehicles, leases, **CC 1952.7**
Reasonable costs associated with the landlords removal and storage of the personal property, **CC 1965**
Reasonable network management, Internet, neutrality, **CC 3100**
Reasonable restrictions,
  Charging stations, electric vehicles, leases, **CC 1952.7**
  Condominiums,
    Accessory dwelling units, junior dwelling units, **CC 4751**
    Antennas, **CC 4725**
      Business and commerce, **CC 6708**
    Clotheslines, drying racks, **CC 4750.10**
    Electric vehicles, charging infrastructure, **CC 4745**
      Business and commerce, **CC 6713**
      Meters, **CC 4745.1**
    Covenants, accessory dwelling units, **CC 714.3**
    Housing development projects, floor area ratio standards, deeds and conveyances, **CC 4747**
Reasonable standards, charging stations, electric vehicles, leases, **CC 1952.7**

WORDS AND PHRASES—Cont'd

Reasonable steps, hazardous substances and waste, releases, **CC 850**
Reconnection, utility services, theft or diversion, **CC 1882**
Recorded contract for sale of real property, marketable title, **CC 886.010**
Recorded deed restrictions, mortgages, multifamily housing, political subdivisions, sales, postponement, **CC 2924f**
Records,
  Abandoned or unclaimed property, landlord and tenant, **CC 1980, 1993**
  Consumer credit reporting agencies, security freeze, **CC 1785.11.9**
  Customer records, destruction, **CC 1798.80**
  Disclosure of business records, bookkeeping services, **CC 1799**
  Information practices, **CC 1798.3**
  Uniform Electronic Transactions Act, **CC 1633.2**
  Voidable transactions, **CC 3439.01**
Recreational purpose, private property owners, liability for personal injuries, **CC 846**
Recreational vehicle, parks, **CC 799.29**
Recreational vehicle park, **CC 799.30**
Recurring obligation, mortgages, default notices, **CC 2924c**
Refunds, consumer goods, debit cards, **CC 1748.40**
Registration fee, employment agencies, **CC 1812.501**
Regulation M,
  Foreign languages, contracts, translations, **CC 1632**
  Vehicle leasing, **CC 2985.7**
Regulation Z,
  Automobile Sales Finance Act, **CC 2981**
  Balloon payments, **CC 2924i**
  Credit cards, **CC 1810.21**
  Foreign languages, contracts, translations, **CC 1632**
  Installment sales, **CC 1802.18**
Regulations, impound accounts, real estate transactions, **CC 2954**
Regulatory agencies, Information Practices Act, **CC 1798.3**
Regulatory agreements, mortgages, multifamily housing, political subdivisions, sales, postponement, **CC 2924f**
Release,
  Hazardous substances and waste, responsibility acceptance, **CC 850**
  Secured lenders, environmentally impaired property, **CC 2929.5**
Release report, hazardous substances and waste, **CC 850**
Religion, discrimination, **CC 51**
Religious items, landlord and tenant, display, **CC 1940.45**
Remainder, **CC 769**
Remainderman, legal estates, Principal and Income Law, **CC 731.03**

WORDS

WORDS AND PHRASES—Cont'd
Remedial actions, hazardous substances and waste, responsibility acceptance, **CC 850**
Remote technical assistance, rental purchase agreements, **CC 1812.622**
Remotely, RFID (radio frequency identification), crimes and offenses, **CC 1798.795**
Removal action, hazardous substances and waste, releases, **CC 850**
Renegotiable rate mortgage loans, **CC 1916.8**
Rent,
    Breach of lease, remedies of lessor, **CC 1951**
    Rent controls, commercial property, **CC 1954.26**
Rent skimming, residential real estate, **CC 890**
Rental agreement,
    Floating home marinas, **CC 800.5**
    Mobilehome Residency Law, **CC 798.8**
    Water supply, submeters, **CC 1954.202**
Rental companies, motor vehicles, **CC 1939.01**
Rental price, machinery and equipment, personal property taxation, reimbursement, **CC 1656.5**
Rental purchase agreements, **CC 1812.622**
Rentals, waterbeds, **CC 1940.5**
Renters, motor vehicles, **CC 1939.01**
Renting, water supply, submeters, **CC 1954.202**
Replaced in kind, mobilehome warranties, **CC 1797.3**
Representation, autographed memorabilia, **CC 1739.7**
Representative of the felon, involuntary trusts, **CC 2225**
Representatives,
    Consumer credit reporting agencies, security freeze, **CC 1785.11.9**
    Home equity sales contracts, equity purchasers, **CC 1695.15**
    Mortgage foreclosure consultants, **CC 2945.9**
Require, coerce or compel, identification devices, subcutaneous implantation, **CC 52.7**
Research, consumers, privacy, **CC 1798.140**
Reserve account requirements, condominiums, **CC 4178**
Reserve accounts, condominiums, **CC 4177**
Residence in foreclosure,
    Home equity sales contracts, **CC 1695.1**
    Mortgage foreclosure consultants, **CC 2945.1**
Resident owned mobilehome parks, **CC 799**
Residential mortgage loans, brokers, fiduciaries, **CC 2923.1**
Residential property, purchase contracts, **CC 1675**
Residential real property, **CC 2924.6**
    Landlord and tenant, termination, **CC 1946.2**
    Rent control, **CC 1947.12, 1954.51**
Residential real property in foreclosure, home equity sales contracts, **CC 1695.1**

WORDS AND PHRASES—Cont'd
Residents,
    Floating home cooperatives and condominiums, **CC 800.300**
    Floating home marinas, **CC 800.8**
    Intergenerational housing developments, **CC 51.3.5**
    Landlord and tenant, emergency services, law enforcement, **CC 1946.8**
    Mobilehomes and mobilehome parks, **CC 798.11**
    Recreational vehicle parks, **CC 799.31**
    Subdivisions, cooperatives or condominiums for mobilehomes, **CC 799**
Resides, military forces, landlord and tenant, security deposits, **CC 1950.5**
Response action, hazardous substances and waste, releases, **CC 850**
Responses,
    Credit cards, **CC 1747.02**
    Inquiry by debtor, retail installment accounts, **CC 1720**
Responsible party,
    Hazardous substances and waste, responsibility acceptance, **CC 850**
    Lead base paint, abatement, **CC 3494.5**
Restore, art defacement or destruction, **CC 987**
Restriction, real estate, limitation of actions, **CC 784**
Restriction on transfer, leases, **CC 1995.020**
Restriction on use, lease use restrictions, **CC 1997.020**
Restrictive covenants, low and moderate income housing, modification or change, **CC 714.6**
Retail, commercial paper, credit card as condition of acceptance, **CC 1725**
Retail buyer,
    Installment sales, **CC 1802.4**
    Song Beverly Consumer Warranty Act, **CC 1791**
Retail credit card, payoff, notice, **CC 1748.13**
Retail installment account, **CC 1802.7**
Retail installment contract, **CC 1802.6**
Retail installment sale, **CC 1802.5**
Retail motor fuel dispenser, credit cards, **CC 1747.02**
Retail motor fuel payment island automated cashiers, credit cards, **CC 1747.02**
Retail seller, **CC 1749.1**
    Human trafficking, **CC 1714.43**
    Installment sales, **CC 1802.3**
    Song Beverly Consumer Warranty Act, **CC 1791**
Retailers, credit cards, **CC 1747.02**
Return to the retail seller, Song Beverly Consumer Warranty Act, **CC 1791**
Reusable tenant screening reports, **CC 1950.1**
Reverse mortgage, **CC 1923**
Reversion, **CC 768**
Reviewing the account, consumer credit reporting agencies, security freeze, **CC 1785.11.2**

WORDS AND PHRASES—Cont'd
Revolving account, installment sales, **CC 1802.7**
RFID (radio frequency identification), crimes and offenses, **CC 1798.795**
Right of reentry, powers of termination, **CC 885.010**
Right of repossession for breach of condition subsequent, powers of termination, **CC 885.010**
Right of reproduction, intellectual property, **CC 982**
Royalty recipient, tape recordings, audits and auditors, **CC 2500**
Royalty reporting party, tape recordings, audits and auditors, **CC 2500**
Rule changes, condominiums, **CC 4340**
Safe at home participants, condominiums, homeowners associations, confidential or privileged information, crime victims, **CC 5216**
Safe at home program, condominiums, homeowners associations, confidential or privileged information, crime victims, **CC 5216**
Sale item or special, Rosenthal Roberti Item Pricing Act, **CC 7100**
Sale or transfer, water conservation, building standards, **CC 1101.3**
Sales,
    Consumers, privacy, **CC 1798.140**
    Grey market goods, consumer protection, **CC 1797.8**
    Installment sales, **CC 1802.5**
    Involuntary trusts, **CC 2225**
    Membership camping contracts, **CC 1812.300**
    Real estate brokers and salespersons, agency, **CC 2079.13**
    Shared appreciation loans, senior citizens, **CC 1917.320**
    Song Beverly Consumer Warranty Act, **CC 1791**
    Stories about felonies, **CC 2225**
Satisfaction, **CC 1523**
Satisfactory evidence, identification of persons making acknowledgments, **CC 1185**
School linked services coordinators, medical records, disclosure, **CC 56.10**
Schools,
    Indebtedness, transcripts, withholding, **CC 1788.92**
    Violence, libel and slander, reports, damages, **CC 48.8**
Search and rescue dogs, discrimination, public accommodations, emergencies, **CC 54.25**
Secretaries, mortgages, **CC 1918.5**
Secretary designee, mortgages, **CC 1918.5**
Sections, **CC 14**
Secure drug take back bins, medical waste, privileges and immunities, **CC 1714.24**
Secured credit card, credit cards, **CC 1747.02**

WORDS

WORDS AND PHRASES—Cont'd

Secured investment, seller assisted marketing plan, **CC 1812.201**
Secured lenders, environmentally impaired property, **CC 2929.5**
Secured party, motor vehicles, subleasing, **CC 3343.5**
Security, rental agreements, **CC 1950.5**
Security agreements, motor vehicles, subleasing, **CC 3343.5**
Security alert, consumer credit reporting agencies, **CC 1785.11.1**
Security and integrity, consumers, privacy, **CC 1798.140**
Security credential, breach, **CC 1798.29, 1798.82**
Security documents,
   Housing credit arrangers, **CC 2957**
   Loans, variable interest rates, **CC 1916.5**
   Mortgages, **CC 1918.5**
Security features, Internet, connected devices, **CC 1798.91.05**
Security freeze, consumer credit reporting agencies, **CC 1785.11.2, 1785.11.9**
Security interest, installment credit, **CC 1803.2**
Security procedure, Uniform Electronic Transactions Act, **CC 1633.2**
Sell,
   Consumers, privacy, **CC 1798.140**
   Membership camping contracts, **CC 1812.300**
   Real estate brokers and salespersons, **CC 2079.13**
   Social security, numbers and numbering, **CC 1798.85**
Seller assisted marketing plan, **CC 1812.201**
Seller's agents, real estate, **CC 2079.13**
Sellers,
   Automobile Sales Finance Act, **CC 2981**
   Consumer contract awareness, **CC 1799.201**
   Consumer protection, deeds and conveyances, foreclosure, title insurance, escrows and escrow agents, **CC 1103.22**
   Installment sales, **CC 1802.3**
   Installment sales finance charges, **CC 1810.11**
   Membership camping contracts, **CC 1812.300**
   Motor vehicles, subleasing, **CC 3343.5**
   Private bulk grain storage, **CC 1880.1**
   Real estate brokers and salespersons, agency, **CC 2079.13**
   Seller assisted marketing plan, **CC 1812.201**
   Song Beverly Consumer Warranty Act, **CC 1791**
Selling, consumers, privacy, **CC 1798.140**
Semiannual period, loans, variable interest rates, **CC 1916.5**
Seminar sales solicitation contract or offer, **CC 1689.24**
Seminar setting, sales solicitation contracts, **CC 1689.24**

WORDS AND PHRASES—Cont'd

Senior citizen housing development, **CC 51.3**
   Riverside County, housing, discrimination, **CC 51.11**
Senior citizens,
   Aged person housing, **CC 51.3**
   Consumers Legal Remedies Act, **CC 1761**
   Home solicitation contracts, **CC 1689.5**
   Intergenerational housing developments, **CC 51.3.5**
   Mortgages, modification or change, forbearance, fines and penalties, **CC 2944.8**
   Riverside County, housing, discrimination, **CC 51.11**
   Seminar solicitation contracts, **CC 1689.24**
Senior homeowner,
   Mobilehome parks, live in health care, supportive care or supervision, **CC 799.9**
   Mobilehomes and mobilehome parks, **CC 798.34**
Sensitive personal information, consumers, privacy, **CC 1798.140**
Sensitive services, confidential or privileged information, medical records, **CC 56.05**
Separate interest, condominiums, **CC 4185**
   Business and commerce, **CC 6564**
Separate residential units, mechanics liens, **CC 8448**
Serious physical abuse, video games, force and violence, **CC 1746**
Service bulletin, motor vehicle warranty adjustment programs, **CC 1795.90**
Service contract,
   Automobile sales finance, **CC 2981**
   Rental purchase agreements, **CC 1812.635**
   Song Beverly Consumer Warranty Act, **CC 1791**
Service contract administrators, warranties, **CC 1791**
Service contract sellers, warranties, **CC 1791**
Service contractors, warranties, **CC 1791**
Service dog, disabled persons, **CC 54.1**
Service providers,
   Consumers, privacy, **CC 1798.140**
   Genetic testing, privacy, **CC 56.18**
Services,
   Consumer contract awareness, **CC 1799.201**
   Consumers, privacy, **CC 1798.140**
   Consumers Legal Remedies Act, **CC 1761**
   Home solicitation contracts, **CC 1689.5**
   Installment sales, **CC 1802.2**
   Mortgage foreclosure consultants, **CC 2945.1**
   Seller assisted marketing plan, **CC 1812.201**
   Seminar sales solicitation contracts, **CC 1689.24**
Servicing, colleges and universities, student loans, borrowers rights, **CC 1788.100**
Servient tenements, **CC 803**
Settlement accounts, fair debt settlement, **CC 1788.301**

WORDS AND PHRASES—Cont'd

Several ownership, **CC 681**
Sex, discrimination, **CC 51**
Sex, race, color, religion, ancestry, national origin, disability, medical condition, genetic information, marital status, sexual orientation, citizenship, primary language or immigration status, discrimination, **CC 51**
Sex trafficking, hotels and motels, fines and penalties, **CC 52.65**
Sexual battery, **CC 1708.5**
Sexual conduct, privacy, invasion of privacy, altered depictions, **CC 1708.86**
Sexual contact, psychotherapists, **CC 43.93**
Sexual orientation,
   Civil rights, **CC 51.7**
   Discrimination, **CC 51**
Sexual orientation violence, **CC 52.45**
Sexually explicit material, privacy, invasion of privacy, altered depictions, **CC 1708.86**
Shared, consumers, privacy, **CC 1798.140**
Shared appreciation loan for seniors, **CC 1917.320**
Shared appreciation loans, **CC 1917, 1917.006**
Shared mobility devices, contracts, licenses and permits, **CC 2505**
Shared mobility service providers, contracts, licenses and permits, **CC 2505**
Shares, consumers, privacy, **CC 1798.140**
Sharing, consumers, privacy, **CC 1798.140**
Shelter program administrators, homeless persons, occupancy, **CC 1954.08**
Shelter program operators, homeless persons, occupancy, **CC 1954.08**
Shelter program participants, homeless persons, occupancy, **CC 1954.08**
Short pay agreement, secured land transaction statements, **CC 2943**
Short pay demand statement, secured land transaction statements, **CC 2943**
Short pay request, secured land transaction statements, **CC 2943**
Signal dog, deaf and hearing impaired persons, **CC 54.1**
Signatures, **CC 14**
   Election offenses, **CC 3344.5**
Signed,
   Condominiums, homeowners associations, elections, **CC 5130**
   Fine prints, sale, **CC 1740**
Significant facilities, membership camping contracts, **CC 1812.302**
Significant risks, consumer credit reporting agencies, computers, security, **CC 1798.81.6**
Significantly, solar energy, **CC 714**
Signs, voidable transactions, **CC 3439.01**
Simple interest basis,
   Automobile Sales Finance Act, **CC 2981**
   Retail installment sales, **CC 1802.20**
Single family owner occupied dwellings, **CC 2954.4**
   Impound accounts, **CC 2954**

WORDS

WORDS AND PHRASES—Cont'd

Single family owner occupied dwellings —Cont'd
    Mortgage or trust deed, acceleration or default, junior encumbrances, CC **2949**

Single family residences, mechanics liens, security, large projects, CC **8702**

Single family residential property, real estate brokers and salespersons, CC **2079.13**

Single family residential real property,
    Real estate brokers and salespersons, CC **2079.13**
    Water conservation, building standards, CC **1101.3**

Single point of contact, mortgages, foreclosure, servicers, CC **2923.7**

Site improvements, mechanics liens, CC **8042**

Sites,
    Disabled persons, civil rights, accessibility, CC **55.52**
    Hazardous substances and waste, responsibility acceptance, CC **850**
    Mechanics liens, CC **8040**
    Special occupancy parks, eviction, CC **1866**

Slander, CC **46**

Social media platforms, threats, CC **1798.99.20**

Solar energy systems, CC **714, 801**
    Easements, CC **801.5**

Sold,
    Consumers, privacy, CC **1798.140**
    Real estate brokers and salespersons, agency, CC **2079.13**

Solicitations, finance lenders, unsolicited advertising, unfair or deceptive trade practices, CC **1770**

Space, special occupancy parks, imminent danger, moving, CC **1867**

Space flight activities, CC **2210**

Space flight entity, CC **2210**

Special agent, CC **2297**

Special circumstances, aged persons, housing, dependent children, CC **51.3**

Special damages, libel and slander, CC **48a**

Special lien, CC **2875**

Sport shooting range, CC **3482.1**

Spouses, CC **14**

Standard service, prices, posting, discrimination, CC **51.6**

State, landlord and tenant, immigration,
    Disclosure, CC **1940.3**
    Information, CC **1940.3**

State or local child support enforcement agency, consumer credit reporting, CC **1785.3**

Stated interest rate, shared appreciation loans for seniors, CC **1917.320**

Statistically significant sample, condominiums, inspections and inspectors, CC **5551**

Stock cooperatives, CC **4190**
    Condominiums, CC **783.1**
        Business and commerce, CC **6566**

WORDS AND PHRASES—Cont'd

Stop notices, mechanics liens, CC **8044**

Stop payment notices, mechanics liens, CC **8044**

Stop work notices, mechanics liens, CC **8830**

Storage, deposits for hire, CC **1851**

Storage facilities, private bulk grain storage, CC **1880.1**

Story, involuntary trusts, CC **2225**

Structure,
    Condominiums, sales, default, CC **1675**
    Construction defects, CC **895**

Structure or area inspected, disabled persons, construction, accessibility, CC **55.56**

Student credit card, CC **1747.02**

Student loan accounts, colleges and universities, borrowers rights, CC **1788.100**

Student loan borrowers, collections, CC **1788.201**

Student loan servicers, colleges and universities, borrowers rights, CC **1788.100**

Student loan services, colleges and universities, borrowers rights, CC **1788.104**

Student loans, colleges and universities, borrowers rights, CC **1788.100**

Subconsultant design professional, public improvements, CC **3321**

Subcontractors,
    Damages, construction, reimbursement, defense fees and costs, CC **2782.05**
    Mechanics liens, CC **8046**

Subcutaneous, identification devices, implantation, CC **52.7**

Subdivisions, blanket incumbrance, notice, CC **1133**

Subject, commercial credit reporting agency, CC **1785.42**

Subject individuals, booking photographs, commercial use, CC **1798.91.1**

Submeters,
    Mobilehomes and mobilehome parks, water supply, CC **798.40**
    Water supply, landlord and tenant, CC **1954.202**

Subordinate judicial duties, innkeepers liens, CC **1861.28**

Subordination agreements, secured land transactions, CC **2953.1**

Subordination clause, secured land transactions, CC **2953.1**

Substantial compliance, rent control ordinances, CC **1947.7**

Substantial defects in materials and workmanship, consumer warranties, CC **1797.1**

Substantial emotional distress, stalking, torts, CC **1708.7**

Substantial harm, health care service plans, medically necessary health care, powers and duties, CC **3428**

Substantially equivalent disclosure notice, community facilities districts, real estate, bonds, CC **1102.6b**

WORDS AND PHRASES—Cont'd

Substantially remodel, landlord and tenant, termination, just cause, CC **1946.2**

Substantially similar, consumer goods, sex, price discrimination, CC **51.14**

Sufficient proof of authority, consumer credit reporting agencies, security freeze, CC **1785.11.9**

Sufficient proof of identification, consumer credit reporting agencies, security freeze, CC **1785.11.9**

Supermarket club card, disclosure, CC **1749.61**

Supermarkets, club cards, disclosure, CC **1749.61**

Supervised financial organization,
    Foreign languages, contracts, translations, CC **1632, 1632.5**
    Installment sales, CC **1801.6**
    Motor vehicle conditional sales, CC **2982.5**
    Variable interest rates, CC **1916.5**

Supervisory employees, human trafficking, sex offenses, hotels and motels, fines and penalties, CC **52.65**

Suppliers, cosmetics, animals, tests, crimes and offenses, CC **1834.9.5**

Supplies, seller assisted marketing plan, CC **1812.201**

Surety, CC **2787**

Surface protection product, motor vehicles, finance, CC **2981**

Suspend, mortgages, equity line of credit, payoff demand statements, CC **2943.1**

Sworn written certifications, indebtedness, duress or coercion, CC **1798.97.1**

System of records, information practices, CC **1798.3**

Tamper, utility services, CC **1882**

Tax return, bookkeeping services, confidential or privileged information, CC **1799.1a**

Telephone account, change of address, notice, CC **1799.1b**

Telephone facilities, disabled persons, CC **54.1**

Tenancy,
    Floating home marinas, CC **800.9**
    Mobilehome Residency Law, CC **798.12**
    Rent control, CC **1947.12, 1954.51**
    Termination, just cause, CC **1946.2**

Tenants,
    Abandoned or unclaimed property, disposition, tenancy termination, CC **1980**
    Leases,
        Restrictions, CC **1997.020**
        Termination, personal property, disposition, CC **1993**
    Legal Estates Principal and Income Law, CC **731.03**
    Locks and locking, CC **1941.5, 1941.6**
    Recreational vehicle parks, CC **799.32**
    Rent controls, commercial property, CC **1954.26**
    Subtenant or assignee, CC **1995.020**

WORDS

WORDS AND PHRASES—Cont'd

Tenants—Cont'd
   Waterbeds, CC 1940.5
Terms, rent controls, commercial property, CC 1954.26
Testify, CC 14
Testing facilities, animals, CC 1834.9.3
The party's own interpreter, contracts, translations, financial institutions, CC 1632.5
The purpose of housing onsite employees, mobilehomes and mobilehome parks, rent, managers and management, CC 798.23
Theft deterrent device, motor vehicles, finance, CC 2981
Therapeutic deception, sexual exploitation, psychotherapists, CC 43.93
Therapeutic relationship, sexual exploitation, psychotherapists, CC 43.93
Thing in action, CC 953
Third parties,
   Business and commerce, personal information, direct marketing, disclosure, CC 1798.83
   Consumer credit reporting agencies, privacy, CC 1786.20
   Consumers, privacy, CC 1798.140
   Genetic testing, advertisements, CC 56.181
Third party sellers, markets and marketing, Internet, disclosure, CC 1749.8
Third party service providers, hotels and motels, charter buses, records and recordation, privacy, CC 53.5
Threshold amount, leases, personal property, abandoned or unclaimed property, termination, sales, CC 1993.07
Timely, debtors inquiry failure of creditor to response, retail installment accounts, CC 1720
Timely response, credit cards, CC 1747.02
Title insurance, consumer protection, deeds and conveyances, foreclosure, CC 1103.22
Torture, video games, force and violence, CC 1746
Total loan obligation, share appreciation loans for seniors, CC 1917.320
Total of payments,
   Automobile Sales Finance Act, CC 2981
   Installment sales, CC 1802.12
   Rental purchase agreements, CC 1812.622
Total sale price, installment sales, CC 1802.9
Tourism commission assessments, motor vehicles, leases, CC 1939.01
Trade secrets, Uniform Act, CC 3426.1
Traditional animal test method, alternatives, CC 1834.9
Trailer, retail installment sales, CC 1802.1
Transaction,
   Consumers Legal Remedies Act, CC 1761
   Uniform Electronic Transactions Act, CC 1633.2
Transfer fees, deeds and conveyances, CC 1098

WORDS AND PHRASES—Cont'd

Transferees,
   Estate taxes, CC 1710.2
   HIV, real estate actions, CC 1710.2
   Voidable transactions, CC 3445
Transfers,
   Leases, CC 1995.020
   Property, CC 1039
   Voidable transactions, CC 3439.01, 3445
Transition age youth, intergenerational housing developments, CC 51.3.5
Transitional housing program, homeless persons, misconduct, CC 1954.12
Trauma informed, homeless persons, occupancy, hotels and motels, shelters, CC 1954.08
Trauma kits, buildings, first aid, privileges and immunities, CC 1714.29
Truck stops, human trafficking, posting, CC 52.6
Trustees, trust deeds, nonmonetary status, declarations, CC 2924l
Unaffiliated, medical malpractice, damages, CC 3333.2
Unauthorized, lewdness and obscenity, distribution, damages, CC 52.8
Unauthorized access, destruction, use, modification, or disclosure, Internet, connected devices, security, CC 1798.91.05
Unauthorized use,
   Credit cards, CC 1747.02
   Debit cards, CC 1748.30
Unbonded stop payment notice, mechanics liens, CC 8044
Undue influence, contracts, CC 1575
Unimproved real property, real property sales contracts, CC 2985.51
Unintended water, construction defects, CC 895
Unique identifiers, consumers, privacy, CC 1798.140
Unique personal identifiers, consumers, privacy, CC 1798.140
Unlawful, contracts, CC 1667
Unlawful Sex Act, children and minors, contracts, CC 1669.5
Unlawful weapons or ammunition purpose, forcible entry and detainer, CC 3485
Unpaid balance,
   Automobile Sales Finance Act, CC 2981
   Installment sales, CC 1802.11
Unreasonable fees, social services, monopolies and unfair trade, procurement, CC 1770
Unrelated use, bookkeeping services, tax returns and reports, confidential or privileged information, CC 1799.1a
Unsolicited, lewdness and obscenity, electronic transmissions, images, CC 1708.88
Unsolicited referrals, health care providers, CC 43.9
Urban waterways, greenways, easements, CC 816.52

WORDS AND PHRASES—Cont'd

Useful life, buildings, construction defects, CC 896
Users,
   Reading, privacy, CC 1798.90
   Social media, threats, CC 1798.99.20
Utilities, theft or diversion of services, CC 1882
Utility service,
   Eminent domain, CC 1001
   Theft or diversion, CC 1882
Vacancy decontrol, rent control, CC 1947.15
Valid lien, voidable transactions, CC 3439.01
Validated alternative test method, animals, CC 1834.9
Valuation, real estate, appraisal and appraisers, undue influence, CC 1090.5
Vehicle history databases, CC 1784.1
Vehicle history information, CC 1784.1
Vehicle history report providers, CC 1784.1
Vehicle history reports, CC 1784.1
Vehicle information, consumers, privacy, CC 1798.145
Vehicle license fees, motor vehicles, leases, CC 1939.01
Vehicle license recovery fees, motor vehicles, leases, CC 1939.01
Vehicle registration fees, motor vehicles, leases, CC 1939.01
Verifiable consumer request, privacy, CC 1798.140
Verify, markets and marketing, Internet, disclosure, CC 1749.8
Vessel dealers, consumers, privacy, CC 1798.145
Vessel information, consumers, privacy, CC 1798.145
Victim of identity theft, CC 1798.92
Victim of violent crime advocates, landlord and tenant, domestic violence, termination, CC 1946.7
Victim service providers, domestic violence, personal information, grants, CC 1798.79.8
Victims of abuse, landlord and tenant, emergency services, law enforcement, CC 1946.8
Victims of crime, landlord and tenant, emergency services, law enforcement, CC 1946.8
Video game, force and violence, CC 1746
Violent posts, social media, CC 1798.99.20
Violent video games, force and violence, CC 1746
Vision screenings, charities, privileges and immunities, CC 1714.26
Visual inspections, condominiums, CC 5551
Visually impaired, CC 54.6
Voluntary deposit, CC 1814
Voluntary transfer, property, CC 1040
Warrant of arrest regular upon its face, privileges and immunities, CC 43.55

ZOOS

WORDS AND PHRASES—Cont'd
Water conserving plumbing fixture, building standards, CC 1101.3
Water purveyors,
  Landlord and tenant, submeters, CC 1954.202
  Mobilehomes and mobilehome parks, CC 798.40
Water service, landlord and tenant, submeters, CC 1954.202
Wholesale sales representative, independents, contracts, CC 1738.12
Wild animal park, guide dogs, CC 54.7
Willfully,
  Mortgages and trust deeds, discharge, CC 2941.5
  Secured land transaction statements, CC 2943
Wills, CC 14
With all faults, consumer warranties, CC 1791.3
Within three years following the last prior use, molds, dies, forms, ownership, CC 1140
Work of art, ownership, CC 988
Work of improvement, mechanics liens, CC 8050
Workforce housing cooperative trusts, CC 817.1
Works, mechanics liens, CC 8048
Worth at the time of award, lessor remedies for breach of lease, CC 1951.2
Writings, CC 14
Written action, hazardous substances and waste, releases, CC 850
Written authorization, health care service plans, genetic tests, CC 56.17
Written confirmation, junk and junk dealers, fire hydrants, possession, CC 3336.5
Written consent, medical records, markets and marketing, CC 1798.91
Year 2000 problem, computers, disclosure of information, CC 3269
Zero rating, Internet, neutrality, CC 3100

WORKERS COMPENSATION
Appeals boards, medical records, disclosure, application of law, CC 56.30
Disclosure, HIV, medical records, CC 56.31
Health care liens, application of law, CC 3040
HIV, medical records, disclosure, CC 56.31
Insurance, wrap up policies, construction, contracts, indemnity, CC 2782.9 et seq.
Liens and incumbrances, health care liens, application of law, CC 3040

WORKERS COMPENSATION—Cont'd
Medical records,
  Disclosure, application of law, CC 56.30
  HIV, disclosure, CC 56.31
Wrap up policies, insurance, construction, contracts, indemnity, CC 2782.9 et seq.

WORKFORCE HOUSING COOPERATIVE TRUSTS
Generally, CC 817.1 et seq.

WORKSHOPS
Manufacturers and Manufacturing, generally, this index

WORLD LANGUAGES
Foreign Languages, generally, this index

WORLD WAR II
Veterans, generally, this index

WORLD WAR VETERANS
Veterans, generally, this index

WORLD WIDE WEB
Internet, generally, this index

WORSHIP
Religion, generally, this index

WORTHLESS CHECKS
Bad checks. Negotiable Instruments, this index

WRITING
Carriers, limitation of liability, CC 2200

WRITS
Attachment, generally, this index
Injunction, generally, this index
Possession, innkeepers liens, CC 1861 et seq.

WRITTEN INSTRUMENTS
Abolition, sealed and unsealed instruments, distinctions, CC 1629
Assignment, nonnegotiable instrument, CC 1459
Cancellation, CC 3412 et seq.
  Partial cancellation, CC 3414
  Void instruments, CC 3413
Consideration, presumption, CC 1614
Damages, estimation of value, CC 3356
Frauds, Statute of, generally, this index
Handwriting, proof on execution of instruments, CC 1198, 1199
Mortgages, requirement, CC 2922
Nonnegotiable, transfer, CC 1459
Presumptions, consideration, CC 1614

WRITTEN INSTRUMENTS—Cont'd
Sealed and unsealed, distinctions abolished, CC 1629
Seals, method of affixing, CC 1628
Ship transfer, CC 1135
Suretyship, creation, CC 2793
  Original obligations, CC 2794
Unrecorded, validity, CC 1217

WRONGFUL DEATH
Children and minors, willful misconduct, imputed parental liability, CC 1714.1
Comparative fault, several liability, noneconomic damages, CC 1431.2
Exemplary damages, homicide, CC 3294
Homicide, exemplary damages, CC 3294
Imputed liability of parents, willful misconduct of children, CC 1714.1
Joint and several liability, noneconomic damages, CC 1431.2
Noneconomic damages, several liability, CC 1431.2

YEAR 2000 PROBLEM
Disclosure, privileges and immunities, CC 3269 et seq.

YEARS
Estates for Years, generally, this index

YOUTHFUL OFFENDERS
Juvenile Delinquents and Dependents, generally, this index

ZONING AND PLANNING
Agricultural products, processing activities, nuisances, CC 3482.6
Condominiums, local ordinances, CC 4020
Floating homes, permits, notice, CC 800.33
Notice, industrial use, residential property, deeds and conveyances, CC 1102.17
Outdoor Advertising, generally, this index
Ranges, sport shooting ranges, CC 3482.1
Rent control, commercial property, application of law, CC 1954.29
Shooting ranges, CC 3482.1
Sport shooting ranges, CC 3482.1
Subdivided Lands, generally, this index

ZOOLOGICAL GARDENS
Blind or visually impaired persons, guide dogs, admittance, CC 54.7
Dogs, disabled persons, restrictions, CC 54.7
Transportation, disabled persons, CC 54.7

ZOOS
Zoological Gardens, generally, this index